Peterson's® Four-Year Colleges 2016

PETERSON'S®

PETERSON'S®

About Peterson's®

Peterson's® is excited to be celebrating 50 years of trusted educational publishing. It's a milestone we're quite proud of, as we continue to provide the most accurate, dependable, high-quality education content in the field, providing you with everything you need to succeed. No matter where you are on your academic or professional path, you can rely on Peterson's® publications and its online information at **www.petersons.com** for the most up-to-date education exploration data, expert test-prep tools, and the highest-quality career success resources—everything you need to achieve your educational goals.

For more information, contact Peterson's, 3 Columbia Circle, Suite 205, Albany, NY 12203-5158;
800-338-3282 Ext. 54229; or visit us online at **www.petersons.com**.

Previous editions published as *Peterson's Annual Guide to Undergraduate Study* © 1970, 1971, 1972, 1973, 1974, 1975, 1976, 1977, 1978, 1979, 1980, 1981, 1982 and as *Peterson's Four-Year Colleges* © 1983, 1984, 1985, 1986, 1987, 1988, 1989, 1990, 1991, 1992, 1993, 1994, 1995, 1996, 1997, 1998, 1999, 2000, 2001, 2002, 2003, 2004, 2005, 2006, 2007, 2008, 2009, 2010, 2011, 2012, 2013, 2014

Cover photo of Seton Hall University credit: Milan Stanic Photography.

ISSN 1544-2330
ISBN 978-0-7689-3956-9

Printed in the United States of America

10 9 8 7 6 5 4 3 2 1 17 16 15

Forty-sixth Edition

Contents

A Note from the Peterson's® Editors

For nearly fifty years, Peterson's® has given students and parents the most comprehensive, up-to-date information on undergraduate institutions in the United States and Canada. *Peterson's® Four-Year Colleges 2016* features advice and tips on the college search and selection process, such as how to consider the factors that truly make a difference during your search, how to understand the application process, and how to get financial aid. Each year, Peterson's® researches the data published in *Peterson's® Four-Year Colleges*. The information is furnished by the colleges and is accurate at the time of publishing.

Opportunities abound for students, and this guide can help you find what you want in a number of ways:

- For application and admissions advice and guidance, just head to **THE ADVICE CENTER.** The "College Admissions Countdown Calendar" outlines pertinent month-by-month milestones. "Choosing Your Top Ten Colleges" gets you started on putting together the most important Top Ten list you have ever made. You'll find some excellent advice in the article, "Planning is Essential on the Road to College," by Sarah E. Gibbs, Director of Admissions at Grove City College. Next, "Surviving Standardized Tests" describes frequently used tests and what you need to know to succeed on them. Of course, part of the college selection process involves visiting the schools themselves, and "The Whys and Whats of College Visits" is the planner you need to make those trips well worth your while. Be sure to check out the articles on specific institutions and programs that may be just right for you, including "Honors Programs and Colleges: Smart Choices for an Undergraduate Education," "Public and Private Colleges and Universities—How to Choose," "Distance Education—It's Closer than You Think," and "Why Not Women's Colleges?" Next, "Applying 101" provides advice on how best to approach the application phase of the process. If you can't make sense out of the early decision/early action conundrum, "The 'Early Decision' Decision" may help clarify it for you. The article "Coming to America: Tips for International Students Considering Study in the U.S." offers helpful information and expert tips from professionals who work with international students at colleges and universities throughout the United States. For essential information on how to meet your education expenses, you'll find the "Financial Aid Countdown Calendar" followed by the articles "Who's Paying for This? Financial Aid Basics" and "Middle Income Families: Making the Financial Aid Process Work." Finally, you'll want to read through the "How to Use This Guide" section, which explains the information presented for each individual college, how Peterson's collects its data, and how Peterson's determines eligibility for inclusion in this guide.
- Next up is the **PROFILES** section. Here you'll find our unparalleled college profiles, arranged alphabetically by state, U.S. territories, and by country. They provide need-to-know information about accredited four-year colleges—including entrance difficulty, campus setting, total enrollment, student-faculty ratio, application deadlines, expenses, most frequently chosen baccalaureate fields, and academic programs. The contact information appears at the conclusion of each college profile. Display ads, which appear near some of the institutions' profiles, have been provided and paid for by those colleges or universities that wished to supplement their profile data with additional information about their institution. A star ★ next to the name of a school signifies that, in addition to having a display ad and Close-Up (or in-depth description) in this book, the school also has an expanded profile on Peterson's website at www.petersons.com. In "Other Colleges to Consider," you'll find helpful contact information for those schools that have not submitted current, detailed information to Peterson's in the last two years.
- More than 200 two-page narrative descriptions appear as **COLLEGE CLOSE-UPS**—descriptions written by admissions or college officials that provide great detail about each school. They are edited to provide a consistent format across entries for your ease of comparison.
- If you already have specifics in mind, such as a particular major or institution, turn to the **INDEXES** section. Here you can search for a school based on major, entrance difficulty, cost ranges, and geography. If you already have colleges in mind that pique your interest, you can use the "Alphabetical Listing of Colleges and Universities" to search for these schools. Page numbers referring to all information presented about a college are conveniently referenced.

Peterson's® publishes a full line of books—college and grad guides, education exploration, test preparation, financial aid, and career preparation. Peterson's® publications can be found at high school guidance offices, college libraries and career centers, and your local bookstore and library. Peterson's® books are also available as ebooks and online at www.petersonsbooks.com.

We welcome any comments or suggestions you may have about this publication. Your feedback will help us make educational dreams possible for you—and others like you.

Colleges will be pleased to know that Peterson's® helped you in your selection. Admissions staff members are more than happy to answer questions, address specific problems, and help in any way they can. The editors at Peterson's® wish you great success in your college search!

NOTICE: Certain portions of or information contained in this book have been submitted and paid for by the educational institution identified, and such institutions take full responsibility for the accuracy, timeliness, completeness and functionality of such content. Such portions or information include (i) each display ad in the "Profiles" section from pages 55 through 1334 that comprises a half or full page of information covering a single educational institution, and (ii) each two-page description in the "College Close-Up" section from pages 1336 through 1745.

The Advice Center

College Admissions Countdown Calendar

This practical month-by-month calendar is designed to help you stay on top of the process of applying to college. For most students, the process begins in September of the junior year of high school and ends in June of the senior year. You may want to begin considering financial aid options, reviewing your academic schedule, and attending college fairs before your junior year.

JUNIOR YEAR

September

- Check with your counselor to make sure your course credits will meet college requirements.
- Be sure you are involved in one or two extracurricular activities.
- Begin building your personal list of colleges.

October

- Register for and take the PSAT/NMSQT®.

November

- Strive to get the best grades you can. A serious effort will provide you with the most options during the application process.

December

- Get involved in a community service activity.
- Begin to read newspapers and a weekly news magazine.
- Buy *Peterson's® Master the SAT®,* or *The Real ACT®* and begin to study for the tests.

January

- With your school counselor, decide when to take the ACT®, SAT®, and SAT Subject Tests™ (and which Subject Tests to take). If English is not your primary language and you are planning on attending a college in North America, decide when to take the TOEFL®.
- Keep your grades up!

February

- Plan a challenging schedule of classes for your senior year.
- Think about which teachers you will ask to write recommendations.
- Check http://www.nacacnet.org/ and click on "College Fairs" for up-to-date schedules and locations of college fairs.

March

- Register for the tests you will take in the spring (ACT®, SAT®, SAT Subject Tests™, or the TOEFL®).
- Meet with your school counselor to discuss college choices.
- Review your transcript and test scores with your counselor to determine how competitive your range of choices should be.
- Develop a preliminary list of fifteen to twenty colleges and universities.
- Start scheduling campus visits. The best time is when school is in session (but never during final exams). Summers are OK but will not show you what the college is really like. If possible, save your top college choices for the fall. Be aware, however, that fall is the busiest visit season, and you will need advance planning. Don't forget to write thank you letters to your interviewers.

April

- Take any standardized tests for which you have registered.
- Create a list of your potential college choices and begin to record personal and academic information that can be transferred later to your college applications.

May

- Plan college visits and make appointments.
- Structure your summer plans to include advanced academic work, travel, volunteer work, or a job.
- Confirm your academic schedule for the fall.

Summer

- Write to any colleges on your list that do not accept the Common Application to request application forms.
- Begin working on your application essays

SENIOR YEAR

September

- Register for the ACT®, SAT®, SAT Subject Tests™, or the TOEFL®, as necessary.
- Check with your school counselor for the fall visiting schedule of college reps.
- Ask appropriate teachers if they would write recommendations for you. Don't forget to write thank you letters when they accept.
- Meet with your counselor to compile your final list of colleges.

October

- Mail or send early applications electronically after carefully checking them to be sure they are completely filled out.
- Photocopy or print extra copies of your applications to use as a backup.
- Take the tests for which you have registered.
- Don't be late! Keep track of all deadlines for transcripts, recommendations, financial aid, etc.

November

- Be sure that you have requested your ACT® and SAT® scores be sent to your colleges of choice.
- Complete and submit all applications. Print or photocopy an extra copy for your records.

December

- Take any necessary tests: ACT®, SAT®, SAT Subject Tests™, or the TOEFL®.
- Meet with your counselor to verify that all is in order and that transcripts are out to colleges.

January

- Prepare the Free Application for Federal Student Aid (FAFSA), available at www.fafsa.ed.gov or through your school counseling office. An estimated income tax statement (which can be corrected later) can be used. The sooner you apply for financial aid, the better your chances.

February

- Submit your FAFSA either online or via U.S. mail.
- Be sure your midyear report has gone out to the colleges to which you've applied.
- Let colleges know of any new honors or accomplishments that were not in your original application.

March

- Register for any Advanced Placement (AP) tests you might take.
- Be sure you have received a FAFSA acknowledgment.

April

- Review the acceptances and financial aid offers you receive.
- Go back to visit one or two of your top-choice colleges.
- Notify your college of choice that you have accepted its offer (and send in a deposit by May 1).
- Notify the colleges you have chosen not to attend of your decision.

May

- Take AP tests.

June

- Graduate! Congratulations and best of luck.

Choosing Your Top Ten Colleges

By using all the information in the various sections of this guide, you will find colleges worthy of the most important top-ten list on the planet—yours.

The first thing you will need to do is decide what type of institution of higher learning you want to attend. Each of the thousands of four-year colleges and universities in the United States is as unique as the people applying to it. Although listening to the voices and media hype around you can make it sound as though there are only a few elite schools worth attending, this simply is not true. By considering some of the following criteria, you will soon find that the large pool of interesting colleges can be narrowed down to a more reasonable number.

SIZE AND CATEGORY

Schools come in all shapes and sizes, from tiny rural colleges of 400 students to massive state university systems serving 100,000 students or more. If you are coming from a small high school, a college with 3,500 students may seem large to you. If you are currently attending a high school with 3,000 students, selecting a college of a similar size may not feel like a new enough experience. Some students coming from very large impersonal high schools are looking for a place where they will be recognized from the beginning and offered a more personal approach. If you don't have a clue about what size might feel right to you, try visiting a couple of nearby colleges of varying sizes. You do not have to be seriously interested in them; just feel what impact the number of students on campus has on you.

Large Universities

Large universities offer a wide range of educational, athletic, and social experiences. Universities offer a full scope of undergraduate majors and award master's and doctoral degrees as well. Universities are usually composed of several smaller colleges. Depending on your interest in a major field or area of study, you would likely apply to a specific college within the university. Each college has the flexibility to set its own standards for admission, which may differ from the overall average of the university. The colleges within a university system also set their own course requirements for earning a degree.

Universities may be public or private. Some large private universities, such as Harvard, Yale, Princeton, University of Pennsylvania, New York University, Northwestern, and Stanford, are well-known for their high entrance standards, the excellence of their education, and the success rates of their graduates. These institutions place a great deal of emphasis on research and compete aggressively for grants from the federal government to fund these projects. Large public universities, such as the State University of New York (SUNY) System, University of Michigan, University of Texas, University of Illinois, University of Washington, and University of North Carolina, also support excellent educational programs, compete for and win research funding, and have successful graduates. Public universities usually offer substantially lower tuition rates to in-state students, although their tuition rates for out-of-state residents are often comparable to those of private institutions.

At many large universities, sports play a major role on campus. Athletics can dominate the calendar and set the tone year-round at some schools. Alumni travel from far and wide to attend their alma mater's football or basketball games, and the campus—and frequently the entire town—grinds to a halt when there is a home game. Athletes are heroes and dominate campus social life.

What are some other features of life on a university campus? Every kind of club imaginable, from literature to bioengineering and chorus to politics, can be found on most college campuses. You will be able to play the intramural version of almost every sport in which the university fields interscholastic teams and join fraternities, sororities, and groups dedicated to social action. You can become a member of a band, an orchestra, or perhaps a chamber music group or work on the newspaper, the literary magazine, or the website. The list can go on and on. You may want to try out a new interest or two or pursue what you have always been interested in and make like-minded friends along the way.

Take a look at the size of the classrooms in the larger universities and envision yourself sitting in that atmosphere. Would this offer a learning environment that would benefit you?

Liberal Arts Colleges

If you have considered large universities and come to the conclusion that all that action could be a distraction, a small liberal arts college might be right for you. Ideally tucked away on a picture-perfect campus, a liberal arts college generally has fewer than 5,000 students. The mission of most liberal arts schools is learning for the sake of learning, with a strong emphasis on creating lifelong learners who will be able to apply their education to any number of careers. This contrasts with objectives of the profession-based preparation of specialized colleges.

Liberal arts colleges cannot offer the breadth of courses provided by the large universities. As a result, liberal arts colleges try to create a niche for themselves. For instance, a college may place its emphasis on its humanities departments, whose professors are all well-known published authors and international presenters in their areas of expertise. A college may highlight its science departments by providing state-of-the-art-facilities where undergraduates conduct research side by side with top-notch professors and copublish their findings in the most prestigious scientific journals in the country. The personal approach is very important at liberal arts colleges. Whether in advisement, course selection, athletic programs tailored to students' interests, or dinner with the department head at her home, liberal arts colleges emphasize that they get to know their students.

If they are so perfect, why doesn't everyone choose a liberal arts college? Well, the small size limits options. Fewer people may mean less diversity. The fact that many of these colleges encourage a study-abroad option (a student elects to spend a semester or a year studying in another country) reduces the number of students on campus even further. Some liberal arts colleges have a certain reputation that does not appeal to some students. You should ask yourself questions about the campus life that most appeals to you. Will you fit in with the campus culture? Will the small size mean that you go through your social options quickly? Check out the activities listed on the Student Center bulletin board. Does the student body look diverse enough for you? Will what is happening keep you busy and interested? Do the students have input into decision making? Do they create the social climate of the school?

Small Universities

Smaller universities often combine stringent admissions policies, handpicked faculty members, and attractive scholarship packages. These institutions generally have undergraduate enrollments of about 4,000 students. Some are more famous for their graduate and professional schools but have also established strong undergraduate colleges. Smaller universities balance the great majors options of large universities with a smaller campus community. They offer choices but not to the same extent as large universities. On the other hand, by limiting admissions and enrollment, they manage to cultivate some of the characteristics of a liberal arts college. Like a liberal arts college, a small university may emphasize a particular program and go out of its way to draw strong candidates in a specific area, such as premed, to its campus. Universities such as The Johns Hopkins University, University of Notre Dame, Vanderbilt University, Washington University in St. Louis, and Wesleyan University in Connecticut are a few examples of this category.

Technical or Specialized Colleges

Another alternative to the liberal arts college or large university is the technical or otherwise specialized college. Its goal is to offer a specialized and saturated experience in a particular field of study. Such an institution might limit its course offerings to engineering and science, the performing or fine arts, or business. Schools such as California Institute of Technology, Carnegie Mellon University, Massachusetts Institute of Technology, and Rensselaer Polytechnic Institute concentrate on attracting the finest math and science students in the country. At other schools, like Bentley College in Massachusetts or Bryant College in Rhode Island, students eat, sleep, and breathe business. These institutions are purists at heart and strong believers in the necessity of focused, specialized study to produce excellence in their graduates' achievements. If you are certain about your chosen path in life and want to immerse yourself in subjects such as math, music, or business, you will fit right in.

Religious Colleges

Many private colleges have religious origins, and many of these have become secular institutions with virtually no trace of their religious roots. Others remain dedicated to a religious way of education. What sets religious colleges apart is the way they combine faith, learning, and student life. Faculty members and administrators are hired with faith as a criterion as much as their academic credentials.

Single-Gender Colleges

There are strong arguments that being able to pursue one's education without the distraction, competition, and stress caused by the presence of the opposite sex helps a student evolve a stronger sense of her or his self-worth; achieve more academically; have a more fulfilling, less pressured social schedule; and achieve more later in life. For various historic, social, and psychological reasons, there are many more all-women than all-men colleges. A strict single-sex environment is rare. Even though the undergraduate day college adheres to an all-female or all-male admissions policy, coeducational evening classes or graduate programs and coordinate facilities and classes shared with nearby coed or opposite-sex institutions can result in a good number of students of the opposite sex being found on campus. If you want to concentrate on your studies and hone your leadership qualities, a single-gender school is an option.

LOCATION

Location and distance from home are two other important considerations. If you have always lived in the suburbs, choosing an urban campus can be an adventure, but after a week of the urban experience, will you long for a grassy campus and open space? On the other hand, if you choose a college in a rural area, will you run screaming into the Student Center some night looking for noise, lights, and people? The location—urban, rural, or suburban—can directly affect how easy or how difficult adjusting to college life will be for you.

Don't forget to factor in distance from home. Everyone going off to college wants to think he or she won't be homesick, but sometimes it's nice to get a home-cooked meal or to do the laundry in a place that does not require quarters. Even your kid sister may seem like less of a nuisance after a couple of months away.

Here are some questions you might ask yourself as you go through the selection process: In what part of the country do I want to be? How far away from home do I want to be? What is the cost of returning home? Do I need to be close to a city? How close? How large of a city? Would city life distract me? Would I concentrate better in a setting that is more rural or more suburban?

ENTRANCE DIFFICULTY

Many students will look at a college's entrance difficulty as an indicator of whether or not they will be admitted. For instance, if you have an excellent academic record, you might wish to primarily consider those colleges that are highly competitive. Although entrance difficulty does not translate directly to quality of education, it indicates which colleges are attracting large numbers of high-achieving students. A high-achieving student body usually translates into prestige for the college and its graduates. Prestige has some advantages but should definitely be viewed as a secondary factor that might tip the scales when all the other important factors are equal. Never base your decision on prestige alone!

The other principle to keep in mind when considering this factor is to not sell yourself short. If everything else tells you that a college might be right for you, but your numbers just miss that college's average range, apply there anyway. Your numbers—grades and test scores—are undeniably important in the admissions decision, but there are other considerations. First, lower grades in honors or AP courses will impress colleges more than top grades in regular-track courses because they demonstrate that you are the kind of student willing to accept challenges. Second, admissions directors are looking for different qualities in students that can be combined to create a multifaceted class. For example, if you did poorly in your freshman and sophomore years but made a great improvement in your grades in later years, this usually will impress a college. If you are likely to contribute to your class because of your special personal qualities, a strong sense of commitment and purpose, unusual and valuable experiences, or special interests and talents, these factors can outweigh numbers that are weaker than average. Nevertheless, be practical. Overreach yourself in a few applications, but put the bulk of your effort into gaining admission to colleges where you have a realistic chance for admission.

THE PRICE OF AN EDUCATION

The price tag for higher education continues to rise, and it has become an increasingly important factor for people. While it is necessary to consider your family's resources when choosing a list of colleges to which you might apply, never eliminate a college solely because of cost. There are many ways to pay for college, including loans, and a college education will never depreciate in value, unlike other purchases. It is an investment in yourself and will pay back the expense many times over in your lifetime.

Surviving Standardized Tests

WHAT ARE STANDARDIZED TESTS?

Colleges and universities in the United States use tests to help evaluate applicants' readiness for admission or to place them in appropriate courses. The tests that are most frequently used by colleges are the ACT® of American College Testing, Inc., and the College Board's SAT®. In addition, the Educational Testing Service (ETS) offers the TOEFL® test, which evaluates the English-language proficiency of nonnative speakers. The tests are offered at designated testing centers located at high schools and colleges throughout the United States and U.S. territories and at testing centers in various countries throughout the world.

Upon request, special accommodations for students with documented visual, hearing, physical, or learning disabilities are available. Examples of special accommodations include tests in Braille or large print and such aids as a reader, recorder, magnifying glass, or sign language interpreter. Additional testing time may be allowed in some instances. Contact the appropriate testing program or your guidance counselor for details on how to request special accommodations.

THE ACT®

The ACT® is a standardized college entrance examination that measures knowledge and skills in English, mathematics, reading, and science reasoning and the application of these skills to future academic tasks. The ACT® consists of four multiple-choice tests.

Test 1: English

- 75 questions, 45 minutes
- Usage and mechanics
- Rhetorical skills

Test 2: Mathematics

- 60 questions, 60 minutes
- Pre-algebra
- Elementary algebra
- Intermediate algebra
- Coordinate geometry
- Plane geometry
- Trigonometry

Test 3: Reading

- 40 questions, 35 minutes
- Prose fiction
- Humanities
- Social studies
- Natural sciences

Test 4: Science

- 40 questions, 35 minutes
- Data representation
- Research summary
- Conflicting viewpoints

Each section is scored from 1 to 36 and is scaled for slight variations in difficulty. Students are not penalized for incorrect responses. The composite score is the average of the four scaled scores. The ACT® Plus Writing includes the four multiple-choice tests and a writing test, which measures writing skills emphasized in high school English classes and in entry-level college composition courses.

- To prepare for the ACT®, ask your guidance counselor for a free guidebook, "Preparing for the ACT®," or download it at www.act.org/aap/pdf/Preparing-for-the-ACT.pdf. Besides providing general test-preparation information and additional test-taking strategies, this guidebook provides full-length practice tests, including a Writing test, information about the optional Writing Test, strategies to prepare for the tests, and what to expect on test day.

DON'T FORGET TO . . .

- ❑ Take the SAT® or ACT® before application deadlines.
- ❑ Note that test registration deadlines precede test dates by about six weeks.
- ❑ Register to take the TOEFL® test if English is not your native language and you are planning on studying at a North American college.
- ❑ Contact the College Board or American College Testing, Inc., in advance if you need special accommodations when taking tests.

THE SAT®

The SAT® measures developed critical reading and mathematical reasoning abilities as they relate to successful performance in college. It is intended to supplement the secondary school record and other information about the student in assessing readiness for college. There is one unscored, experimental section on the exam, which is used for equating and/or pretesting purposes and can cover either the mathematics or critical reading area.

Critical Reading

- 67 questions, 70 minutes
- Sentence completion
- Passage-based reading

Mathematics

- 54 questions, 70 minutes
- Multiple-choice
- Student-produced response (grid-ins)

Writing

- 49 questions plus essay, 60 minutes
- Identifying sentence errors
- Improving paragraphs

- Improving sentences
- Essay

Students receive one point for each correct response and lose a fraction of a point for each incorrect response (except for student-produced responses). These points are totaled to produce the raw scores, which are then scaled to equalize the scores for slight variations in difficulty for various editions of the test. The critical reading, writing, and mathematics scaled scores range from 200–800 per section. The total scaled score range is from 600–2400.

Changes to the SAT

The SAT® is changing in the spring of 2016! According to the College Board, the redesigned SAT® will have these sections: Evidence-Based Reading and Writing, Math, and the Essay. It will be based on 1600 points—the top scores for the Math section and the Evidence-Based Reading and Writing section will be 800, and the Essay score will be reported separately.

According to the College Board's website, the "Eight Key Changes" are the following:

- **Relevant Words in Context:** Students will need to interpret the meaning of words based on the context of the passage in which they appear. The focus will be on "relevant" words—not obscure ones.
- **Command of Evidence:** In addition to demonstrating writing skills, students will need to show that they're able to interpret, synthesize, and use evidence found in a wide range of sources.
- **Essay Analyzing a Source:** Students will read a passage and explain how the author builds an argument, supporting support their claims with actual data from the passage.
- **Math Focused on Three Key Areas:** Problem Solving and Data Analysis (using ratios, percentages, and proportional reasoning to solve problems in science, social science, and career contexts), the Heart of Algebra (mastery of linear equations and systems), and Passport to Advanced Math (more complex equations and the manipulation they require).
- **Problems Grounded in Real-World Contexts:** All of the questions will be grounded in the real world, directly related to work performed in college.
- **Analysis in Science and in Social Studies:** Students will need to apply reading, writing, language, and math skills to answer questions in contexts of science, history, and social studies.
- **Founding Documents and Great Global Conversation:** Students will find an excerpt from one of the Founding Documents—such as the Declaration of Independence, the Constitution, and the Bill of Rights—or a text from the "Great Global Conversation" about freedom, justice, and human dignity.
- **No Penalty for Wrong Answers:** Students will earn points for the questions they answer correctly.

If you'll be taking the test after March 2016, you should check out the College Board's website at https://www.collegeboard.org/delivering-opportunity/sat/redesign for the most up-to-date information.

Top 10 Ways Not to Take the Test

10. Cramming the night before the test.
9. Not becoming familiar with the directions before you take the test.
8. Not becoming familiar with the format of the test before you take it.
7. Not knowing how the test is graded.
6. Spending too much time on any one question.
5. Second-guessing yourself.
4. Not checking spelling, grammar, and sentence structure in essays.
3. Writing a one-paragraph essay.
2. Forgetting to take a deep breath to keep from—
1. Losing It!

SAT SUBJECT TESTS™

Subject Tests are required by some institutions for admission and/or placement in freshman-level courses. Each Subject Test measures one's knowledge of a specific subject and the ability to apply that knowledge. Students should check with each institution for its specific requirements. In general, students are required to take three Subject Tests (one English, one mathematics, and one of their choice).

Subject Tests are given in the following areas: biology, chemistry, Chinese, French, German, Italian, Japanese, Korean, Latin, literature, mathematics, modern Hebrew, physics, Spanish, U.S. history, and world history. These tests are 1 hour long and are primarily multiple-choice tests. Three Subject Tests may be taken on one test date.

Scored like the current SAT®, students gain a point for each correct answer and lose a fraction of a point for each incorrect answer. The raw scores are then converted to scaled scores that range from 200 to 800.

THE TOEFL® INTERNET-BASED TEST (IBT)

The Test of English as a Foreign Language Internet-Based Test (TOEFL® iBT) is designed to help assess a student's grasp of English if it is not the student's first language. Performance on the TOEFL® test may help interpret scores on the critical reading sections of the SAT®. The test consists of four integrated sections: speaking, listening, reading, and writing. The TOEFL® iBT emphasizes integrated skills. The paper-based versions of the TOEFL® will continue to be administered in certain countries where the Internet-based version has not yet been introduced. For further information, visit www.toefl.org.

WHAT OTHER TESTS SHOULD I KNOW ABOUT?

The AP Program

This program allows high school students to try college-level work and build valuable skills and study habits in the process. Subject matter is explored in more depth in AP courses than in other high school classes. A qualifying score on an AP test—which varies from school to school—can earn you college credit or advanced placement. Getting qualifying grades on enough exams can even earn you a full year's credit and sophomore standing at more than 1,500 higher-education institutions. There are more than thirty AP courses across multiple subject areas, including art history, biology, and computer science. Speak to your guidance counselor for information about your school's offerings.

College-Level Examination Program (CLEP)

The CLEP enables students to earn college credit for what they already know, whether it was learned in school, through independent study, or through other experiences outside of the classroom. More than 2,900 colleges and universities now award credit for qualifying scores on one or more of the 33 CLEP exams. The exams, which are 90 minutes in length and are primarily multiple choice, are administered at participating colleges and universities. For more information, check out the website at www.collegeboard.com/clep.

WHAT CAN I DO TO PREPARE FOR THESE TESTS?

Know what to expect. Get familiar with how the tests are structured, how much time is allowed, and the directions for each type of question. Get plenty of rest the night before the test and eat breakfast that morning.

There are a variety of products, from books to software to videos, available to help you prepare for most standardized tests. Find the learning style that suits you best. As for which products to buy, there are two major categories— those created by the test-makers and those created by private companies. The best approach is to talk to someone who has been through the process and find out which product or products he or she recommends.

Some students report significant increases in scores after participating in coaching programs. Longer-term programs (40 hours) seem to raise scores more than short-term programs (20 hours), but beyond 40 hours, score gains are minor. Math scores appear to benefit more from coaching than critical reading scores.

Resources

There is a variety of ways to prepare for standardized tests—find a method that fits your schedule and your budget. But you should definitely prepare. Far too many students walk into these tests cold, either because they find standardized tests frightening or annoying or they just haven't found the time to study. The key is that these exams are standardized. That means these tests are largely the same from administration to administration; they always test the same concepts. They have to, or else you couldn't compare the scores of people who took the tests on different dates. The numbers or words may change, but the underlying content doesn't.

So how do you prepare? At the very least, you should review relevant material, such as math formulas and commonly used vocabulary words, and know the directions for each question type or test section. You should take at least one practice test and review your mistakes so you don't make them again on the test day. Beyond that, you know best how much preparation you need. You'll also find lots of material in libraries or bookstores to help you: books and software from the test-makers and from other publishers (including Peterson's) or live courses that range from national test-preparation companies to teachers at your high school who offer classes.

Planning is Essential on the Road to College

Sarah E. Gibbs, Director of Admissions
Grove City College

The road to college is much like a journey. It can appear overwhelming, exciting, and at times too far away to be tangible. However, much like planning a road trip there is preparation involved, and it is always best to start that planning early. You must first figure out where you want to go, how you want to get there, and what you want to do once you arrive. Each decision will require a different path—a path that may or may not look the same as that of your friends.

The same is true when considering college planning. If you start earlier making short-term and long-term goals, it will help you determine what the next steps are and should be. For instance, if you start your freshman year determining you want to graduate with a certain GPA, that decision will dictate your next steps, such as studying, choosing to take a harder curriculum, and prioritizing your involvement in activities.

Once you establish your short-term and long-term goals, you need to make wise decisions about those goals. For instance, if you do not do well in a class, do not make a rash decision to withdraw from any rigorous curriculum in that subject. Continue to take challenging classes, but realize you may need to seek out help or tutors to help you achieve your goal.

In addition to thinking through your goals for academics, you must also consider your personal interests and activities. These interests may determine your focus for the type of college you would like to attend. Decide early on what your passion(s) are, and invest your time wisely in those pursuits. If you know those pursuits may not be what you want to pursue in college, you may need to spend some time on college campuses determining what you do like and what you may want to pursue at that campus.

Ask yourself the question that most students do not: Am I ready for college? If the answer is no, then ask yourself what you need to do to be ready? What decisions will get you there?

When looking at applicants, most private colleges will look holistically at the student, taking into consideration their commitment, dedication, and character. These attributes, along with their academic performance and specific major pursuit, indicate whether a student should succeed at our campuses. Having a holistic review process also helps the student if they take advantage of the interview process. Allowing admission counselors to become your advocate as they get to know you is essential.

Ultimately, the sooner you start planning, the better prepared you will be for the journey you are about to take. Not only will you be prepared for the college planning process, you will be well equipped for attending college—and then achieving your goals and dreams for beyond college.

Sarah E Gibbs has spent seventeen years serving families in higher education. She is currently the Director of Admission at Grove City College (PA).

The Whys and Whats of College Visits

Dawn B. Sova, Ph.D.

The campus visit should not be a passive activity for you and your parents. Take the initiative and gather information beyond that provided in the official tour. You will see many important indicators during your visit that will tell you more about the true character of a college and its students than the tour guide will reveal. Know what to look for and how to assess the importance of such indicators.

WHAT SHOULD YOU ASK AND WHAT SHOULD YOU LOOK FOR?

Your first stop on a campus visit is the visitor center or admissions office, where you will probably have to wait to meet with a counselor. Colleges usually plan to greet visitors later than the appointed time in order to give them the opportunity to review some of the campus information that is liberally scattered throughout the visitor waiting room. Take advantage of the time to become even more familiar with the college by arriving 15 to 30 minutes before your appointment to observe the behavior of staff members and to browse through the yearbooks and student newspapers that will be available.

If you prepare in advance, you will have already reviewed the college catalog and map of the campus. These materials familiarize you with the academic offerings and the physical layout of the campus, but the true character of the college and its students emerges in other ways.

Begin your investigation with the visitor center staff members. As a student's first official contact with the college, they should make every effort to welcome prospective students and project a friendly image.

- How do they treat you and other prospective students who are waiting? Are they friendly and willing to speak with you, or do they try their hardest to avoid eye contact and conversation?
- Are they friendly with each other and with students who enter the office, or are they curt and unwilling to help?
- Does the waiting room have a friendly feeling or is it cold and sterile?

If the visitor center staff members seem indifferent to prospective students, there is little reason to believe that they will be warm and welcoming to current students. View such behavior as a warning to watch very carefully the interaction of others with you during the tour. An indifferent or unfriendly reception in the admissions office may be simply the first of many signs that attending this college will not be a pleasant experience.

Look through several yearbooks and see the types of activities that are actually photographed, as opposed to the activities that colleges promise in their promotional literature. Some questions are impossible to answer if the college is very large, but for small and moderately sized colleges the yearbook is a good indicator of campus activity.

- Has the number of clubs and organizations increased or decreased in the past five years?
- Do the same students appear repeatedly in activities?
- Do sororities and fraternities dominate campus activities?
- Are participants limited to one sex or one ethnic group, or is there diversity?
- Are all activities limited to the campus, or are students involved in activities in the community?

Use what you observe in the yearbooks as a means of forming a more complete understanding of the college, but don't base your entire impression on just one facet. If time permits, look through several copies of the school newspaper, which should reflect the major concerns and interests of the students. The paper is also a good way to learn about the campus social life.

- Does the paper contain a mix of national and local news?
- What products or services are advertised?
- How assertive are the editorials?
- With what topics are the columnists concerned?
- Are movies and concerts that meet your tastes advertised or reviewed?
- What types of ads appear in the classified section?

The newspaper should be a public forum for students, and, as such, should reflect the character of the campus and of the student body. A paper that deals only with seemingly safe and well-edited topics on the editorial page and in regular feature columns might indicate administrative censorship. A lack of ads for restaurants might indicate either a lack of good places to eat or that area restaurants do not welcome student business. A limited mention of movies, concerts, or other entertainment might reveal a severely limited campus social life. Even if ads and reviews are included, you should still balance how such activities reflect your tastes.

You will have only a limited amount of time to ask questions during your initial meeting with the admissions counselor, for very few schools include a formal interview in the initial campus visit or tour. Instead, this brief meeting is often just a nicety that allows the admissions office to begin a file for the student and to record some initial impressions. Save your questions for the tour guide and for students on campus you meet along the way.

HOW CAN YOU ASSESS THE TRUE CHARACTER OF A COLLEGE AND ITS STUDENTS?

Colleges do not train their tour guides to deceive prospective students, but they do caution guides to avoid unflattering topics and campus sites. Does this mean that you will see only a sugarcoated version of life on a particular college campus? Not at all, especially not if you are observant.

Most organized campus visits include such campus facilities as dormitories, dining halls, libraries, student activity and recreation centers, and the health and student services centers. Some may only be pointed out, while you will walk through others. Either way, you will find that many signs of the true character of the college emerge if you keep your eyes open.

Bulletin boards in dormitories and student centers contain a wealth of information about campus activities, student concerns, and campus groups. Read the posters, notices, and messages to learn what *really* interests students. Unlike ads in the school newspaper, posters put up by students advertise both on-and off-campus events, so they will give you an idea of what is also available in the surrounding community.

Review the notices, which may cover either campuswide events or events that concern only small groups of students. The catalog may not mention a performance group, but an individual dormitory with its own small theater may offer regular productions. Poetry readings, jam sessions, writers' groups, and other activities may be announced and show diversity of student interests.

Even the brief bulletin board messages offering objects for sale and noting objects that people want to purchase reveal a lot about a campus. Are most of the items computer related? Or do the messages specify audio equipment or musical instruments? Are offers to trade goods or services posted? Don't ignore the "ride wanted" messages. Students who want to share rides home during a break may specify widely diverse geographical locations. If so, then you know that the student body is not limited to only the immediate area or one locale. Other messages can also enhance your knowledge of the true character of the campus and its students.

As you walk through various buildings, examine their condition carefully.

- Is the paint peeling, and do the exteriors look worn?
- Are the exteriors and interiors of the building clean?
- Is the equipment in the classrooms up-to-date or outdated?

Pay particular attention to the dormitories, especially to factors that might affect your safety. Observe the appearance of the structure, and ask about the security measures in and around the dormitories.

- Are the dormitories noisy or quiet?
- Do they seem crowded?
- How good is the lighting around each dormitory?
- Are the dormitories spread throughout the campus or are they clustered in one main area?
- Who has access to the dormitories in addition to students?
- How secure are the means by which students enter and leave the dormitory?

While you are on the subject of dormitory safety, you should also ask about campus safety. Don't expect that the guide will rattle off a list of crimes that have been committed in the past year. To obtain that information, access the recent year of issues of *The Chronicle of Higher Education* and locate its yearly report on campus crime. Also ask the guide about safety measures that the campus police take and those that students have initiated.

- Can students request escorts to their residences late at night?
- Do campus shuttle buses run at frequent intervals all night?
- Are "blue-light" telephones liberally placed throughout the campus for students to use to call for help?
- Do the campus police patrol the campus regularly?

If the guide does not answer your questions satisfactorily, wait until after the tour to contact the campus police or traffic office for answers.

Campus tours usually just point out the health services center without taking the time to walk through. Even if you don't see the inside of the building, you should take a close look at the location of the health services center and ask the guide questions about services.

- How far is the health center from the dormitories?
- Is a doctor always on call?
- Does the campus transport sick students from their dormitories or must they walk?
- What are the operating hours of the health center?
- Does the health center refer students to a nearby hospital?

If the guide can't answer your questions, visit the health center later and ask someone there.

Most campus tours take pride in showing students their activities centers, which may contain snack bars, game rooms, workout facilities, and other means of entertainment. Should you scrutinize this building as carefully as the rest? Of course. Outdated and poorly maintained activity equipment contributes to your total impression of the college. You should also ask about the hours, availability, and cost (no, the activities are usually not free) of using the bowling alleys, pool tables, air hockey tables, and other amenities.

As you walk through campus with the tour, also look carefully at the appearance of the students who pass. The way in which both men and women groom themselves, the way they dress, and even their physical bearing communicate a lot more than any guidebook can. If everyone seems to conform to the same look, you might feel that you would be uncomfortable at the college, however nonconformist that look might be. On the other hand, you might not feel comfortable on a campus that stresses diversity of dress and behavior, and your observations now can save you discomfort later.

- Does every student seem to wear a sorority or fraternity t-shirt or jacket?
- Is everyone of your sex sporting the latest fad haircut?
- Do all of the men or the women seem to be wearing expensive name-brand clothes?
- Do most of the students seem to be working hard to look outrageous with regards to clothing, hair color, and body art?
- Would you feel uncomfortable in a room full of these students?

Is appearance important to you? If it is, then you should consider very seriously if you answer yes to any of the above questions. You don't have to be the same as everyone else on campus, but standing out too much may make you unhappy.

As you observe the physical appearance of the students, also listen to their conversations as you pass them. What are they talking about? How are they speaking? Are their voices and accents all the same, or do you hear diversity in their speech? Are you offended by their language? Think how you will feel if surrounded by the same speech habits and patterns for four years.

WHERE SHOULD YOU VISIT ON YOUR OWN?

Your campus visit is not over when the tour ends because you will probably have many questions yet to be answered and many places to still be seen. Where you go depends upon the extent to which the organized tour covers the campus. Your tour should take you to view residential halls, health and student services centers, the gymnasium or field house, dining halls, the library, and recreational centers. If any of the facilities on this list have been omitted, visit them on your own and ask questions of the students and staff members you meet. In addition, you should step off campus and gain an impression of the surrounding community. You will probably become bored with life on campus and spend at least some time off campus. Make certain that you know what the surrounding area is like.

The campus tour leaves little time to ask impromptu questions of current students, but you can do so after the tour. Eat lunch in one of the dining halls. Most will allow visitors to pay cash to experience a typical student meal. Food may not be important to you now while you are living at home and can simply take anything you want from the refrigerator at any time, but it will be when you are away at college with only a meal ticket to feed you.

- How clean is the dining hall? Consider serving tables, floors, and seating.
- What is the quality of the food?
- How big are the portions?
- How much variety do students have at each meal?
- How healthy are the food choices?

While you are eating, try to strike up a conversation with students and tell them that you are considering attending their college. Their reactions and advice can be eye-opening. Ask them questions about the academic atmosphere and the professors.

- Are the classes large or small?
- Do the majority of the professors only lecture or are tutorials and seminars common?
- Is the emphasis of the faculty career-oriented or abstract?
- Are the teaching methods innovative and stimulating or boring and dull?
- Is the academic atmosphere pressured, lax, or somewhere in between?
- Which are the strong majors? The weak majors?
- Is the emphasis on grades or social life or a mix of both at the college?
- How hard do students have to work to receive high grades?

Current students can also give you the inside line on the true nature of the college social life. You may gain some idea through looking in the yearbook, in the newspaper, and on the bulletin boards, but students will reveal the true highs and lows of campus life. Ask them about drug use, partying, dating, drinking, and anything else that may affect your life as a student.

- Which are the most popular club activities?
- What do students do on weekends? Do most go home?
- How frequently do concerts occur on campus? Who has recently performed?
- How can you become involved in specific activities (name them)?
- How strictly are campus rules enforced and how severe are penalties?
- What counseling services are available?
- Are academic tutoring services available?
- Do they feel that the faculty really cares about students, especially freshmen?

You will receive the most valuable information from current students, but you will only be able to speak with them after the tour is over. And you might have to risk rejection as you try to initiate conversations with students who might not want to reveal how they feel about the campus. Still, the value of this information is worth the chance.

If you have the time, you should also visit the library to see just how accessible research materials are and to observe the physical layout. The catalog usually specifies the days and hours of operation, as well as the number of volumes contained in the library and the number of periodicals to which it subscribes. A library also requires accessibility, good lighting, an adequate number of study carrels, and lounge areas for students. Many colleges have created 24-hour study lounges for students who find the residence halls too noisy for studying, although most colleges claim that they designate areas of the residences as "quiet study" areas. You may not be interested in any of this information, but when you are a student you will have to make frequent use of the campus library so you should know what is available. You should at least ask how extensive their holdings are in your proposed major area. If they have virtually nothing, you will have to spend a lot of time ordering items via interlibrary loan or making copies, which can become expensive. The ready answer of students that they will obtain their information from the Internet is unpleasantly countered by professors who demand journal articles with documentation.

Make a point of at least driving through the community surrounding the college because you will be spending time there shopping, dining, working in a part-time job, or attending events. Even the largest and best-stocked campus will not meet all of your social and personal needs. If you can spare the time, stop in several stores to see if they welcome college students.

- Is the surrounding community suburban, urban, or rural?
- Does the community offer stores of interest, such as bookstores, craft shops, and boutiques?
- Do the businesses employ college students?
- Does the community have a movie or stage theater?
- Are there several types of interesting restaurants?
- Do there seem to be any clubs that court a college clientele?
- Is the center of activity easy to walk to, or do you need other transportation?

You might feel that a day is not enough to answer all of your questions, but even answering some questions will provide you with a stronger basis for choosing a college. Many students visit a college campus several times before making their decision. Keep in mind that for the rest of your life you will be associated with the college that you attend. You will spend four years of your life at this college. The effort of spending several days to obtain the information to make your decision is worthwhile.

Dawn B. Sova, Ph.D., is a former newspaper reporter and columnist, as well as the author of more than eight books and numerous magazine articles. She teaches creative and research writing, as well as scientific and technical writing, newswriting, and journalism.

Honors Programs and Colleges: Smart Choices for an Undergraduate Education

Dr. Joan Digby

In general, students and their parents are guided toward a narrow selection of colleges and universities based on reputation, conversations with friends, or promotional material. Few people think to approach the college search focused on honors opportunities. As a result, students with extraordinary talents and interests miss out on a rich variety of untapped financial resources and exciting college experiences.

The smarter approach is to seek out a distinctive education that caters to students' great diversity of intellectual and creative strengths. If you are a strong student filled with ideas, longing for creative expression and ready to take on career-shaping challenges, then an honors education is just for you. Honors programs and colleges offer some of the finest undergraduate degrees available at U.S. colleges and do it with students in mind. The essence of honors is personal attention, top faculty, enlightening seminars, illuminating study-travel experiences, research options, and career-building internships—all designed to enhance a classic education and prepare you for life achievements. And here is an eye-opening bonus: Honors programs and colleges may reward your past academic performance by giving you scholarships that will help you pay for your higher education!

Take your choice of institutions: community college, state or private, two- or four-year, college or large research university. There are honors opportunities in each. What they share is an unqualified commitment to academic excellence. Honors education teaches students to think and write clearly, be excited by ideas, and become independent, creative, self-confident learners. It prepares exceptional students for professional choices in every imaginable sphere of life: arts and sciences, engineering, business, health, education, medicine, theater, music, film, journalism, media, law, politics—invent your own professional goal and honors will guide you to it! Whichever honors program or college you choose, you can be sure to enjoy an extraordinarily fulfilling undergraduate education.

WHO ARE HONORS STUDENTS?

Who are you? Perhaps a high school junior filling out your first college application, a community college student seeking to transfer to a four-year college, or possibly a four-year college student doing better than you had expected. You might be an international student, a varsity athlete, captain of the debate team, or second violin in the orchestra. Whether you are the first person in your family to attend college or an adult with a grown family seeking a new career, honors might well be right for you. Honors programs admit students with every imaginable background and educational goal.

How does honors satisfy students and give them something special? Read what students in some honors programs and colleges say. Although they refer to particular honors colleges or programs, their experiences are typical of what students find exciting about honors education on hundreds of campuses around the country.

> "Being an honors program student has been a life-changing experience for me. I have gained tremendously in knowledge, experience, and self-esteem. I have learned so much more in the program than any textbook could teach about the value of encouraging support and positive thinking."
>
> *—Cheri, Mount Wachusett Community College*

> "I've been in a healing ceremony in Ecuador and have performed music on stage. I've guided my peers and Navajo children, hiked the Grand Canyon, and so much more. Sometimes, experience speaks for itself; always, it creates paths, opens eyes, and helps us find our places. Thanks to my honors program, I've experienced these wonders and accomplishments. Now I know that there are no greater lessons than how to learn and love discovery."
>
> *—April, University of North Florida*

> "The Honors College has been my home away from home. In the midst of a diverse, fairly large university, it has provided me with the intimacy that I needed... My freshman-year living situation on the honors floor... allowed me to find like-minded students early in my college career."
>
> *—Brian, Davidson Honors College, University of Montana*

> "I was able to transition from an honors program at a two-year institution into an honors program at a four-

year institution without any reservations or tribulations."

—*Rachel, Harrisburg Area Community College*

"Every single professor is in love with what they do and it shows in their research, their amazing teaching, and their interaction with students outside of the classroom. The undergraduate journey can be very difficult at times, but as an Honors College student, you're sure to have plenty of support every step of the way."

—*Walteria, Wilkes Honors College, Florida Atlantic University*

"The class size is perfect and I've been able to make some of my closest relationships with students and teachers through the program. The majority of honors faculty I have encountered have been overwhelmingly helpful... and my favorite courses have been honors classes."

—*Ellen, Eastern Illinois University*

"Our professor met us at a local restaurant the last evening of class, and we shared a wonderful dinner. It had such a familiar feel to it because these are students I have known throughout my four years in the program."

—*Betsy, University of La Verne*

"For the last two years, I have investigated new synthetic methods under the direction of a professor emeritus. Through the University Honors College, I am able to pursue this interest in chemistry and other academic endeavors... that have allowed me to develop my academic potential and contribute to the scientific body of knowledge."

—*Justin, University of Pittsburgh*

"The most rewarding part of being a member of the honors program is the joy of doing creative, meaningful projects with faculty I love."

—*Meleia, Hartwick College*

"I would... like to add a word of praise for the way the curriculum is structured. It has deepened and enriched my thinking and helped me develop tools to negotiate the complex world we live in."

—*Monideepa, Southeastern Louisiana University*

"We have a better time... our discussions get rather heated. In a lot of classes, only one or two students will speak up, but in the honors classes, it's a free-for-all."

—*Jonathan, Reinhardt College*

"My internship at a major international bank gave me an in-depth look into the world of investment and accounting. Funded by the Honors College, I was able to study business and culture in Shanghai, China, for a month. These valuable experiences are helping me to develop professionally, academically, and personally."

—*Jenny, Honors College, The College of Staten Island, CUNY*

"The honors thesis was the key factor during the selection process at my future employer.... It helped me to get the job and have an advantage over others. It is a lot of work but, in the end, it is worth it."

—*Olgierd, Lee Honors College, Western Michigan University*

These portraits don't tell the whole story, but they should give you a sense of what it means to be part of an honors program or college. One of the great strengths of honors programs and colleges is that they are nurturing environments that encourage students to be well-rounded and help students make life choices.

WHAT IS AN HONORS PROGRAM?

An honors program is a sequence of courses designed specifically to encourage independent and creative learning. For more than half a century, honors education—given definition by the National Collegiate Honors Council—has been an institution on U.S. campuses. Although honors programs have many different designs, there are typical components. At two-year colleges, the programs often concentrate on special versions of general education courses and may have individual capstone projects that come out of students' special interests. At four-year colleges and universities, honors programs are generally designed for students of almost every major in every college on campus. In growing numbers, they are given additional prominence as honors colleges. Whether a program or a college, honors often includes a general education or "core" component followed by advanced courses (often called colloquia or seminars). Some programs have honors contracts that shape existing courses into honors components to suit the needs of individual students. Many have interdisciplinary or collaborative seminars that bring students of different majors together to discuss a complex topic with faculty members from different disciplines. A good number have final thesis, capstone, or creative projects, which may or may not be in the departmental major. Almost always, honors curriculum is incorporated within whatever number of credits is required of every student for graduation. Honors very rarely requires students to take additional credits. Students who complete an honors program or honors college curriculum frequently receive transcript and diploma notations as well as certificates, medallions, or other citations at graduation ceremonies.

In every case, catering to the student as an individual plays a central role in honors course design. Most honors classes are small (fewer than 20 students); most are discussion-oriented, giving students a chance to present their own interpretations of ideas and even teach a part of the course. Many classes are interdisciplinary, which means they are taught by faculty members from two or more departments, providing different perspectives on a subject. All honors classes help students develop and articulate their own perspectives by cultivating both verbal and written style. They help students mature intellectually, preparing them to engage in their own explorations and research. Some programs even extend the options for self-growth to study abroad and internships in science, government, the arts, or business related to the major. Other programs encourage or require community service as part of the honors experience. In every case, honors is an experiential education that deepens classroom learning and extends far beyond.

Despite their individual differences, all honors programs and honors colleges rely on faculty members who enjoy working with bright, independent students. The ideal honors faculty members are open-minded, encouraging master teachers. They want to see their students achieve at their highest capacity and are glad to spend time with students in discussions and laboratories, on field trips and at conferences, or online in e-mail. They often influence career decisions, are inspiring role models, and remain friends long after they have served as thesis advisers.

WHERE ARE HONORS PROGRAMS AND HONORS COLLEGES LOCATED?

Because honors programs and honors colleges include students from many different departments or colleges, they usually have their own offices and space on campus. Some have their own buildings. Most programs have honors centers or lounges, where students gather together for informal conversations, luncheons, discussions, lectures, and special projects.

Many honors students have cultivated strong personal interests that have nothing to do with classes. They may be multilingual; they may be fine artists or poets, musicians or racing car enthusiasts, mothers or fathers. Some volunteer in hospitals or do landscape gardening to pay for college. Many work in retail stores and catering. Some are avid sports enthusiasts, while others collect antiques. When they get together in honors lounges, there is always an interesting mixture of ideas!

In the honors center, you will also find the honors director or dean. The honors director often serves as a personal adviser to all of the students in the program. Many programs also have peer counselors and mentors who are upperclass honors students and know the ropes from a student's perspective and experience. Some have specially assigned honors advisers who guide honors students through their degrees, assist in registration, and answer every imaginable question. The honors office area usually is a good place to meet people, ask questions, and solve problems.

In general, honors provides an environment in which students feel free to talk about their passionate interests and ideas knowing that they will find good listeners and, sometimes, even arguers. There is no end to conversations among honors students. Like many students in honors, you may feel a great relief in finding a sympathetic group that respects your intelligence and creativity. In honors, you can be eccentric; you can be yourself! Some lifelong friendships, even marriages, are the result of social relationships developed in honors programs.

ARE YOU READY FOR HONORS?

Admission to honors programs and honors colleges is generally based on a combination of several factors: high school or previous college grades, experience taking AP or IB courses, SAT or ACT scores, personal essay, and extracurricular achievements. To stay in honors, students need to maintain a certain grade point average (GPA) and show progress toward the completion of the specific honors program or college requirements. Since you have probably exceeded admissions standards all along, maintaining your GPA will not be as big a problem as it sounds. Your professors and your honors director are there to help you succeed in the program. Most honors programs have very low attrition rates because students enjoy classes and do well.

Of course, you must be careful about how you budget your time for studying. Honors encourages well-rounded, diversified students, so you should play a sport, work at the radio station, join clubs of interest, or pledge a sorority or fraternity. You might find a job in the student center or library that will help you pay for your car expenses and that also is reasonable. But remember, each activity takes time, and you must strike the balance that leaves you enough time to do your homework, write papers, prepare for seminar discussions, do your research, and do well on exams. Choose the jobs and activities that attract you, but never let them overshadow your primary purpose—which is to be a student.

Sometimes even the very best students who apply for admission into an honors program or college are frightened by the thought of speaking in front of a group, giving seminar papers, or writing a thesis. But if you understand how the programs work, you will see that there is nothing to fear. The basis of honors is confidence in the student and building the student's self-confidence. Admittance to an honors program means you have already demonstrated your academic achievement in high school or college classes. Once in the honors environment, you learn how to formulate and structure ideas so that you can apply critical judgment to sets of facts and opinions. In small seminar classes, you practice discussion and arguments, so by the time you come to the senior thesis or project, the method is second nature. For most honors students, the senior thesis, performance, or portfolio presentation is the project that gives them the greatest fulfillment and pride. In many honors programs and colleges, students present their work either to other students or to faculty members in their major departments. Students often present their work at regional and national honors conferences. Some students even publish their work jointly with their faculty mentors. These are great achievements, and they come naturally with the training. There is nothing to fear. Honors will prepare you for life.

Dr. Joan Digby is Director of the Honors Program and Professor of English at Long Island University, C.W. Post Campus. She was also President of the National Collegiate Honors Council from 1999 to 2000.

Public and Private Colleges and Universities—How to Choose

Debra Humphreys

As you survey the thousands of four-year colleges in the country and weigh the options before you, it is important to be aware of how colleges differ and what kind of educational experience each college offers you. In every state in the country, you will find both public and private colleges and universities. What are the differences between public and private colleges, and how should you approach the decision to attend one or the other? What are some common misconceptions regarding both public and private colleges that you should know about before you eliminate an entire category of institution from your list of prospective schools?

WHAT ARE THE BASIC CHARACTERISTICS OF PUBLIC AND PRIVATE INSTITUTIONS?

Over the course of the nation's history, what began as a small group of mostly church-affiliated colleges has grown in both size and complexity. Over the years, education in the United States became increasingly democratized, and more and more state-sponsored institutions and state systems of higher education emerged. These included small colleges, sometimes called "normal schools," designed to train school teachers for the expanding public school system; land-grant colleges and universities brought into existence with federal support in the mid-nineteenth century in order to prepare workers to expand the nation's agricultural and technological capacity; and large state systems that evolved in the twentieth century and now include two-year colleges, basic four-year institutions, and large research universities, all supported at least in part by state revenues.

While there are some clear distinctions to be made, even some of the core characteristics of public and private colleges vary from state to state. In general, a public institution receives at least part of its operating budget from state tax revenues, operates with a mandate and mission from the state where it is located, and is accountable to the elected officials of that state. Most private colleges and universities are independent, not-for-profit institutions. They operate with revenues from tuition; income from endowments; private gifts and bequests; and federal, private, or corporate foundation grants. These institutions are primarily accountable to a board of trustees, usually made up of local or national business and community leaders and esteemed alumni.

There are also a small but growing number of for-profit colleges whose operating revenues include tuition dollars but also might include investor financing. Some of these colleges are owned and operated by publicly traded corporations. Most of the following generalizations about private institutions however refer to the more familiar not-for-profit independent college previously described.

While the distinction between public and private institutions might seem clear at first, these two kinds of colleges and universities actually share many characteristics. All accredited colleges and universities in the country—whether public or private, for profit or not—are entitled to receive public funds from the federal government in the form of direct grants and loans for eligible students, support for student work-study programs, and competitive grants to support research or campus programs. In exchange for this federal support, all schools undergo a peer-reviewed accreditation process by a regional accreditor authorized by the federal government's Department of Education.

Whether a college is public or private, you should know if it is accredited and therefore an institution whose students are eligible for all available federal financial aid. Accreditation status also provides you with assurance that the school operates in a fiscally responsible manner and that its academic programs have been deemed sound by an outside group of educators from its peer institutions.

HOW ARE PUBLIC AND PRIVATE COLLEGES AND UNIVERSITIES RUN?

In many ways, your experience as a student will not differ significantly based on what type of governance system a college or university uses. However, some knowledge of this might be useful in making choices among the various options. Private colleges and universities tend to have more independence and autonomy in how they are run, with boards of trustees that oversee financial and other program and life on campus at these schools. Public colleges and universities often have more complex governing structures with boards of regents or other types of oversight committees made up of politically appointed or elected officials exercising more or less oversight and intrusion into their day-to-day operations. New York, for instance, has a board of regents that oversees the system's campuses and is more actively involved in reviewing and revising curricular requirements that apply to institutions throughout the system. Other states have multiple public colleges, each with its own board overseeing each campus' operations with more or less intrusion into day-to-day operations.

Whether an institution is public or private, you will want to ask lots of questions about campus climate and academic programs in order to help you determine if a school is right for you. Being aware of some facts about public and private institutions will help you frame these questions to get truly useful answers.

ARE ALL PUBLIC COLLEGES AND UNIVERSITIES BIG AND IMPERSONAL?

Like private institutions, public colleges come in all shapes and sizes. Some are large institutions offering multiple degrees and majors to both undergraduate and graduate students alike. These institutions offer students many curricular options as well as access to leading scholars and an environment where cutting-edge academic research is conducted. While an institution of this size and scope might seem intimidating at first, remember that there are large institutions that do take very seriously their undergraduate programs. While you may receive less customized attention at a larger institution, many large public and private research universities offer options such as smaller honors programs, academic learning communities with smaller cohorts of students, or theme residence halls that can minimize the potential that you will get lost in the crowd.

If you are considering a large research institution— whether it is public or private—you should ask questions about the undergraduate program. What is the student-faculty ratio for undergraduates? What is the average class size, especially for introductory first-year courses? How many courses are taught by graduate students, and what sort of teacher training do those students receive? Are there opportunities for undergraduate students to participate in research projects with university faculty members?

In addition to the large, public research universities, there are many other smaller, state-funded regional institutions that still offer a wide range of both liberal arts and sciences fields as well as professional fields of study. Many states also offer small, public liberal arts colleges that share many of the defining characteristics of traditional, private liberal arts colleges. In 1987, some of these institutions formed the Council of Public Liberal Arts Colleges (COPLAC). COPLAC schools pride themselves on providing students of high ability and from all backgrounds access to a quality liberal education. These colleges and universities have been nationally recognized as outstanding in many ways. They offer small classes, innovations in teaching, personal interactions with faculty members, opportunities for faculty-supervised research, and supportive atmospheres. Most of them are located on campuses in rural or small-town settings. In addition to offering rigorous and well-integrated undergraduate programs, these institutions often charge far less tuition than many private colleges do. More information can be found at http://www.coplac.org.

These public liberal arts colleges, along with more traditional private liberal arts institutions, do offer unique learning environments that research suggests often lead to higher levels of student achievement. Liberal arts colleges tend to offer a high degree of student-faculty interaction, high levels of student engagement with both in-class and out-of-class experiences, and lots of opportunities for collaborative and innovative learning practices. Businesses are also increasingly asking for exactly the set of skills and capacities that a liberal education provides, whether offered in a traditional liberal arts college setting or within a larger university that grants degrees in both liberal arts and other fields. Many public liberal arts and more comprehensive colleges and universities also now offer students a rigorous liberal education while integrating liberal learning into professional degree programs, for instance in health sciences, engineering, or education.

ARE PUBLIC COLLEGES CHEAPER THAN PRIVATE COLLEGES?

The cost of college is not easy to calculate and is not limited simply to the advertised price of tuition. It is absolutely not the case that attending a public college will always cost a student less money than attending a private institution. It is true that the basic tuition for in-state or out-of-state students attending public colleges is on average less expensive than the advertised tuition rate at private institutions. It is very important, however, to note that many private colleges and universities offer significant amounts of financial aid—often beyond the basic federal loans and grants available to all students. Many, but not all, private colleges have large endowments that allow them to effectively discount the standard, published tuition rates for a great number of their students. The National Association of College and University Business Officers sampled a small group of private colleges and discovered that only 10 percent of entering students were paying the full, advertised tuition. Ninety percent of their students received price discounts in the form of scholarships or financial aid. In other words, don't write off a college simply because its tuition looks extremely high relative to other institutions.

Both private and public institutions, however, have been fiscally stressed in recent years because of declining values of stock portfolios in endowments or because of declining state revenues resulting from the deteriorating economy. It is safe to say that for many students in the coming years, it will become increasingly difficult to get large amounts of financial aid. Many institutions, however, remain committed to widening access to more students from less economically privileged backgrounds. In addition, students demonstrating high levels of academic achievement are being rewarded at both private and public institutions—both in terms of admission and financial aid.

It is important to look carefully at the tuition and the financial aid requirements and availability at each school you are considering, private or public. In-state and out-of-state tuitions and the difference between them varies substantially from state to state. Out-of-state tuition also varies from state to state but still tends to be lower than average private tuition levels.

Policies vary as well for determining state residency status. In many states, the policy for dependent students requires that their parents must have lived in the state for at least twelve months prior to attendance in order to qualify for in-state tuition. For independent students, the requirement of twelve months residence prior to enrollment applies to the student. Independent status must be verified and generally entails proof that a student receives no support from parents or other relatives living in or out of the state in question. As budgets have increasingly tightened, states have over the past several years made it increasingly difficult to establish in-state residence after matriculating at a school. Exceptions are sometimes made, however, for students from migrant, refugee, or military families.

IS IT EASIER TO GAIN ADMISSION TO A PUBLIC INSTITUTION ESPECIALLY AS A STATE RESIDENT?

Few public colleges and universities automatically admit students who graduate from a public high school in their state. Many, however, give preference in admissions and financial assistance to in-state residents. Moreover, some states have implemented policies that guarantee admission to at least one of the state's public institutions for all students graduating in a top percentage of their high school classes.

There are, indeed, more highly selective private than public institutions. Many public colleges and universities, however, do admit very few applicants. These highly selective institutions might draw their students from a national pool of applicants and can be among the most selective in the country. However, the national universities and liberal arts colleges with the lowest acceptance rates in the country are mostly all private institutions.

While some public institutions offer virtually open admissions to state residents, it is important for all prospective students to realize that even an open-admission institution will require incoming students to meet certain academic standards before being admitted to credit-bearing courses. In most cases, public and private institutions give incoming students a series of placement exams that determines at what level the student can begin his or her course work. Depending on the results of these exams, a student may be required to take and pass one or more remedial courses before being admitted to courses that will actually count towards a degree.

Since each state's requirements are different and shift often, you should not assume that, regardless of your academic background, admission is automatic to your local state college. In the current climate—with costs rising and competition across systems tightening—admission rates are dropping at many public institutions.

IS THE CLIMATE ON A PUBLIC COLLEGE CAMPUS SIGNIFICANTLY DIFFERENT THAN THAT ON A PRIVATE COLLEGE CAMPUS?

The social and academic climate at colleges and universities varies substantially, and public institutions do not necessarily offer a distinctively different climate than private institutions do. You can find, at some public institutions, the small, residential environment traditionally associated with private liberal arts colleges. You will also find the presence of fraternities and sororities at both public and private institutions. You should look carefully at whether a school in which you are interested has fraternities and sororities and how much influence the Greek system has on college life. At some institutions, fraternities and sororities dominate the entire social life of the campus.

One campus environment that can only be found at a private institution is a highly religious environment. Many early colleges and universities were founded by churches or religious orders. Some of these institutions no longer retain a strong affiliation with one church or denomination. Others do retain a strong affiliation, and church traditions can heavily influence the climate of these institutions. Usually, these campuses will admit a student from any religious background, but they may require students to attend chapel services and/or take religion or theology courses to graduate. In addition, some college missions and curricula are influenced by their religious affiliations. For instance, many Catholic institutions have a strong commitment to community service and social justice. Students may find, at these institutions, curricula related to social justice issues and requirements that they complete a community-service learning activity or course to graduate. Institutions with a strong mission are also often able to develop more coherent, cohesive, and innovative curricula for their students.

Finally, other important climate factors to consider include whether a college or university is in an urban or rural setting; what the diversity of the student body is in terms of geographic, religious, or racial/ethnic background; if most students live on campus or commute from home; and finally if the college dominates the life of the community in which it is located. Each of these options has advantages and disadvantages you will want to weigh in making your decisions.

ARE PRIVATE COLLEGES MORE ACADEMICALLY RIGOROUS THAN PUBLIC COLLEGES?

Private colleges and universities are not necessarily more academically rigorous than public institutions. You will find rigorous, intellectually challenging, and innovative academic programs at both private and public institutions. There is also a common misconception that schools that are more highly selective have the most effective or engaging academic programs. Research suggests that there is no connection between the selectivity of an institution and the presence of effective or innovative teaching and learning practices. There is, however, preliminary research that suggests that the academic quality of

Questions to Ask as You Evaluate Prospective Colleges and Universities

- Does the college offer a distinctive first-year experience?
- Does the college offer a small-size freshman seminar for all students?
- Are all students required to complete a senior project or assignment that allows them to integrate all that they have learned and demonstrate acquired skills and knowledge?
- Are students encouraged or required to complete internships and/or service learning courses?
- Are students encouraged to study abroad? Is support for study abroad provided to all students and are study abroad experiences integrated into a student's overall curricula?
- Does the college offer learning communities, especially in the student's early years?
- Are students required to complete rigorous writing courses not only in the freshman year but also across the curriculum in whatever major he or she chooses to pursue?
- Are there opportunities for students to pursue independent research or creative projects under the supervision of a senior faculty member?

one's peers does seem to have an impact on the grade point averages of fellow students.

Nothing could be more important in your decision-making process than evaluating the nature of academic programs at prospective colleges or universities. Across both public and private institutions, there have been exciting and important changes in how colleges and universities are organizing undergraduate curricula. Many promising programs have been proven to result in higher levels of student retention, graduation, satisfaction, and academic achievement.

Many colleges and universities also now participate in the National Survey of Student Engagement. This survey asks students in both their first and last years about a series of effective educational practices and the degree to which they are engaged in the academic life of their school. Issues that are examined in the survey include the level of academic challenge, active and collaborative learning opportunities, the nature of student-faculty interactions, the number of enriching educational experiences available, and the supportive nature of the campus environment. Ask if the school you are considering participates in this survey and if you can see the results from recent classes of students.

THE PRIVATE/PUBLIC CHOICE

While there are distinct differences between public and private colleges and universities you should not limit your choice—whatever your background—to only one type of institution. There are wonderful opportunities at many different kinds of schools. The availability of many kinds of financial aid may bring private institutions with high-tuition levels within reach for you, whatever your financial background. Whether a school is highly selective or has open admissions, you should also be able to find a college or university that will challenge you academically and provide you with a supportive environment in which to live, learn, and pursue a college degree of lasting value.

Debra Humphreys is Vice President for Policy and Public Engagement for the Association of American Colleges and Universities.

Distance Education—It's Closer Than You Think

You may not realize it, but as an incoming college student, you are joining a revolution that is radically changing education. It's called distance learning. From kindergarten up to postgraduate degrees, distance learning is fast becoming an essential teaching tool. Most of the colleges and universities you are considering for a bachelor's degree offer distance learning in one form or another. Most likely you will be a distance learner at some point, whether during college or graduate school or throughout your career.

In case you're not familiar with distance learning—or asynchronous learning, online learning, or distance education—it means you don't sit in a classroom facing a teacher. You can be hundreds of miles or minutes from the teacher and other students. Most often you connect through the Internet to the teacher, fellow students, and study materials. However, increasingly sophisticated technologies, such as virtual laboratories, simulations, and interactive multimedia, are also used. You may run across the term "blended learning." Many institutions incorporate online learning into their face-to-face classes. In fact, a number of colleges require that a part of all classes is online.

FROM SNAIL-MAIL COURSES TO LEADING-EDGE TECHNOLOGY

Talk about change. Distance education began in the late 1800s, when schools mailed correspondence courses to farmers who wanted to learn how to grow better crops. Since technology came along, distance learning has become accessible and widespread. At first educators were skeptical, but as name-plate universities began to incorporate it into their teaching methodology, distance education became accepted.

When brick-and-mortar colleges and universities first considered distance education, the goal was to make it as good as face-to-face education. Now, says Ray Schroeder, Professor Emeritus of Communication and Director of the Center for Online Learning, Research, and Service (COLRS), at the University of Illinois at Springfield, "Field research shows that online learning technologies are better than face-to-face learning in a number of ways." Having taught online, he has seen firsthand how students participate more in discussions and learn from one another. Peg Miller, Ph.D., former Coordinator of Academic Support for Distributed Learning, University of Central Florida, cites a survey she conducted every other semester that compares face-to-face and distance learners at her institution. She has found that students from face-to-face and online classes were almost identical in the grades they earned and in their satisfaction with the classes.

ON THE UPSWING

Many reasons have caused the phenomenal growth of distance education. It's convenient and user-friendly, plus the scope of classes is stunning. Not that you'll likely begin your college years with classes in forensics or grading diamonds, but they are offered and indicate the enormous variety of courses. Along with many others in education, Michael P. Lambert, former executive director of the Distance Education Training Council, feels that online learning has transformed how people learn. "You no longer sit in a box with 35 other people where you might never raise your hand," he says. Adds Gerald Heeger, former President of the University of Maryland University College (UMUC), "Online learning gets rid of the limitations of geography and time. And as bandwidth increases, we will do more and more."

PROCEED WITH CAUTION

Now that you're convinced that distance education sounds great, sign me up, it's only fair to warn you that perhaps you shouldn't start your bachelor's degree totally online. Distance learning changes how you study, respond to your teachers, participate in class discussions, and take exams. If you're not prepared for the differences, you can easily fall behind and even fail. Though the age of online students continues to drop, most are older, have had some life experience since graduating from high school, and have the self-discipline, maturity, and self-motivation, that distance education demands. The average age of distance students is in the mid-30s, and 95 percent of them work full-time. They know what they want from college and are willing to meet the rigors of online learning, which are considerable.

Of course, some students straight from high school do successfully start college as distance learners because they've already had some online learning experience. Some take online classes in high school or advanced-placement and college courses. At Stevens Institute of Technology's Web Campus, incoming freshmen brush up on math and precalculus online before their first fall semester. At first, Nathan Kahl, former instructor for the Euclid Program at Stevens Institute of Technology Web Campus, was skeptical that high school graduates could succeed in the online courses he taught, but he saw that "everyone quickly got into the swing of things." He admits that he underestimated the students' ability to learn online. Heeger agrees "There's no reason why a bright junior in high school who is ready to take college freshmen courses can't do it."

The University of Phoenix Online (parent company: Apollo Group, Inc.) has developed a bachelor's degree program specifically for incoming freshmen of any age—including those just out of high school. In today's job market, a college education is a necessity, yet many students have life situations that prevent them from attending. Notes former president of Apollo Group, Inc., Brian Mueller about the accommodations their program makes for students who are new to higher education, "It is our experience that if you create an online classroom, it must have all the features that incoming students need, which are small, highly interactive, and collaborative classes." Their freshman classes average 15 and require that the instructor has consistent contact with the students. New freshmen also get a tremendous amount of support in writing, math, and online research skills and have the help of an academic counselor who closely tracks them for ten weeks into their first semester. "We think there are more students coming out of high school who must have jobs, so we took the model for working adults and created an environment for traditional students that combines education and work," says Mueller.

However, not all educators have the same experience with incoming freshmen. Jimmy Reeves, Ph.D., Professor of Chemistry and Coordinator of the Tablet PC Initiative at the University of North Carolina at Wilmington, teaches both online and face-to-face classes and knows how students can react. Freshmen who fail his face-to-face class sometimes ask to take his class online. He says no because the discipline required is rare among 19-year-old students. "Junior and senior college students do well, but it has more to do with their level of maturity and the reasons why they're in college," he says, referring to the fact that many incoming college students want to experiment or come because their parents demand it. "Without any real desire to learn or sense of why they're in college, it's easy to get distracted in online classes," he notes. You can't hide in the back of a lecture hall half asleep on Monday morning and hope for the best on multiple-choice questions. In online classes, your active participation is noticed and taken into account for final grades.

Attending college isn't just about acquiring knowledge in a particular field in order to get a job. It's also about learning social skills and meeting people with different ideas from diverse backgrounds. "If you want to live in a dorm and have bull sessions on the meaning of life with the kids down the hall, then being a fully online freshman student isn't for you," advises Cynthia Davis, Acting Vice Provost and Dean of the Undergraduate School at the University of Maryland University College (UMUC). She adds that sometimes students mistakenly think getting a bachelor's degree online will take less time than physically attending classes or won't require as much work. But as she points out, online classes demand the same amount of effort, if not more, than face-to-face classes.

WHAT'S IT GOING TO BE LIKE?

Blended learning or mixed-mode classes, combining face-to-face and online instruction, are becoming a permanent fixture in higher education. Students might sit in a classroom on Monday but take the remaining two classes for that week online. Professors routinely post the syllabus, class calendar, or PowerPoint lectures. Reeves says that it's rare to see college classes without some Web-based materials. Davis comments that UMUC routinely Web-enhances all of its face-to-face classes with companion Web classrooms. Students can have optional online discussions or print copies of class materials.

"We find more students use online technology to enhance their studies and get better grades," comments Schroeder. Educators see a trend of students enrolling in one university and taking courses from other institutions. For instance, say you're in an art class but want to study German cathedral architecture, which your university doesn't have but another one offers online. It's only a matter of time before this will be a standard option for college students.

LOTS TO LOOK FOR, LOTS TO AVOID, LOTS TO ASK

Though much of distance education depends on the Internet, you can't just type in "distance education" and see what comes up in a search for a college. You must seriously research and do background checks to make sure a diploma mill doesn't hand you a bachelor's degree that isn't credible. There are plenty of places to get information. Petersons.com offers a database of colleges and universities that have online courses, as well as totally online distance education providers. "You have to be a good consumer," recommends Heeger. "It's no different from getting a loan. You don't borrow money from people you never heard of. You shouldn't get degrees from people you never heard of." Schroeder suggests checking the course completion of online programs, their enrollment, and growth of programs. "Just as one checks with friends and colleagues about the quality of consumer services, such as computers and cars, one should check with students who are enrolled in online programs," he advises.

Is the Institution Accredited by a Valid Accrediting Body?

There are several kinds of accrediting organizations:

- The six regional accrediting agencies recognized by the U.S. Department of Education
- The Council for Higher Education Accreditation (www.chea.org)
- Other institutional accrediting agencies, such as the Accrediting Council for Independent Colleges and Schools and the Distance Education and Training Council
- Specialized accrediting agencies that cover schools offering everything from acupuncture to veterinary medicine
- Other discipline-based accrediting organizations, such as those for law and business schools

Can You Transfer Credits Received Online from One Institution to Another?

Policies vary greatly among universities and colleges. Though distance education is widely accepted, there are so many places where students can take bogus online courses that institutions are justifiably cautious. If students do decide they want to get a bachelor's degree completely online, they need to be sure the campus-based program and distance education program offer the same degree. At most institutions, both on-campus and online degrees are the same, but others do differ-

Test-Drive an Online Class

Just like face-to-face instruction, online classes are different, depending on the course material and how each teacher chooses to structure the course, but here's a typical scenario of what it's like to be a distance learner.

Getting started. First you'll want to get to the general information page for the class, which you'll visit often. The professor's contact information, the class calendar, the syllabus, and announcements on quizzes and tests or links to other pages on which you'll find posted discussion questions may be found here. Some teachers will ask you to tell something about yourself to the other students in the class. Be sure to read the syllabus, which will outline the course and tell you when assignments are due and how grades are determined.

Responding to discussion questions. Those students who never raised their hands will get a shock in online courses. Responding with thoughtful answers to online discussion groups is mandatory. Usually the teacher will assign reading material and then post a discussion question. The material might be from your textbook or websites. You must respond to the question and possibly to the postings of other students in the class. Teachers will gauge your participation in the class and how well you learn the material.

Interacting with fellow students and your teacher. Ray Schroeder, Professor Emeritus of Communication and Director of the Center for Online Learning, Research, and Service (COLRS) at the University of Illinois at Springfield, gives talks about distance education. Often he'll ask his audience to recall their favorite class from elementary school up to college and what made it so memorable. Was it the textbook? The actual classroom? The view out the window? When he asks if it was the interaction among students and with the teacher, the audience realizes that's what made the class good. "Both in person and online, learning takes place in the interaction," says Schroeder. "Otherwise, we would do just as well to read a book or watch a video to learn." In online classes, interaction between you and the professor and other students is an enormous part of your success.

Nathan Kahl, former instructor for the Euclid Program at Stevens Institute of Technology Web Campus, explains, "Distance students expect that their teachers will be online at least as much as they are." The level of interaction expected from you will vary by school and course, but you should know that in online courses, you must be an active participant. On the flip side, teachers carefully monitor discussions to make sure the more talkative students don't dominate. Keith W. Miller, Professor of Computer Science at the University of Illinois at Springfield, interacts with his students in a variety of ways. "I make announcements to the whole class on the homepage. I send e-mails to the whole class. I enter into the electronic discussions on the bulletin board forums, and post daily reminders and assignments to the course calendar. The students interact with me using e-mail, notes in their assignments, and via the bulletin boards. Now and then someone calls me at my office on the phone, but that's rare." He likes to answer his e-mails at least once a day, which means that his students get much more feedback than they would if he were physically in a classroom with them.

As do most online teachers, Cynthia Davis, Associate Dean of Academic Affairs in the School of Undergraduate Studies at the University of Maryland University College, gets students to participate with a weekly discussion topic. "If we're reading a novel," she says, "I ask them to discuss the role of the narrator or analyze a passage. The students respond individually and then respond to other students' comments."

Attending virtual lectures. Some online courses allow you to hear and see the professor or other guest speakers who are also online. If you want to ask a question, there's a button to indicate you want to speak. Everyone else can hear you as if you all were in the same room. Other professors add voice to PowerPoint lectures, which you can view when you want to, not at some prearranged time.

Taking quizzes and tests. No more waiting weeks to get your tests back. Online technology in some courses instantly zaps back the corrected test and notes that you missed question six and need to study page 54 of the textbook. Just like in face-to-face classes, you have an allotted amount of time to take the quiz. Some online courses may have automated components, such as instant quizzes and animated and interactive practice sessions. Others have mandatory proctored exams at a nearby community college or learning center for students who are off campus.

entiate in the degrees conferred, and it will show up on your diploma.

What Kind of Refund Policy Does the University Have for Distance Learners?

It might become painfully apparent for students that online learning is not for them, and they want to drop out. Find out ahead of time about the refund policy for online classes. What happens if you're ill during an online class? How can you make up the work? Even before taking any classes, you should find out if you're suited for online learning. Many institutions offer self-assessment tests on their websites.

What Online Services Does the College Provide?

Is the dorm wired? Can you get an e-mail address from the university? What about browsers and computer compatibility? Ask how the Internet is part of face-to-face classes. To what extent is the library online, and is it available 24/7 for research? Ask about writing and math labs and help-desk support. Look for online tutorials that show students how to use the school's specific software. Is there a tech fee?

IF YOU'RE LEARNING ONLINE, YOU BETTER HAVE THESE

Since online learning is part of college, it's helpful to know what to expect ahead of time, rather than three weeks into the class, when you feel like throwing your laptop out the window and would happily settle for sitting in the back row of the nearest classroom. Here are the five skills and abilities that successful online students must have:

1. You must have the self-discipline to do things you don't want to do when you don't want to do them.

If you're a procrastinator, you'll find the catch-up tactics that served you well in face-to-face classes won't work online. "Students get the idea they can whiz by without studying, or they came from high schools where they weren't pushed," cautions Heeger. "Maybe they never got Fs in high school, but they do here." That's because they don't realize they're responsible for learning the material on their own. The burden is on you to keep up with the homework. It doesn't take long to fall far behind in online classes.

Typically, students in face-to-face and online classes need 2 hours for work outside of class for every hour in class. But online students often forget to add that hour. For every hour they would have to sit in a traditional classroom, they should be listening, studying, thinking, writing, responding to discussions, and getting ready for tests, plus the 2 hours outside of class. Three classes a week—that's 9 to 10 hours for one class. Online teachers keep students on track with weekly quizzes and homework assignments. If students start lagging, they're likely to get an e-mail from the professor asking what's going on. Claudine SchWeber, Ph.D., Chair of the Doctor of Management Program at the University of Maryland University College, has taught online for years and states, "My classes are structured by weekly readings, activities, and discussions. Students can't decide to get around to doing the work when they feel like it. It must be done at the instructor's pace. The first shot of online can be a shock to their system."

2. You must have the ability to manage your time without anyone telling you do your homework NOW.

In high school, students usually can put off studying until the weekend. "That doesn't work in college. You can't write complex papers the night before," says Karen L. Kirkendall, Ph.D., Associate Professor of Liberal and Integrative Studies and Director of the Capitol Scholars Honors Program at the University of Illinois at Springfield. She teaches both online and face-to-face classes and has seen first-time online students who have never failed before start to slip and suddenly realize they are in big trouble. "My online classes are extraordinarily structured so I pretty much know when students aren't engaged, which I monitor by seeing how much they participate in online discussions," she notes.

Distance Learning Myths

As distance education becomes more accepted, people will readily discard some of the myths on this list. But for now, they persist.

Distance learning is for people on ranches 200 miles from the nearest freeway. Geography is not a factor. Many distance learners who are located across the campus or a few miles away just don't want to deal with the commute or have a work schedule that conflicts with being in a class at a certain time. They appreciate the flexibility that distance education gives them.

Distance learning is easier than face-to-face classes. Once you start an online class, you'll knock that myth off the list. Still, some students think it will be easier. When they realize they must not only respond to discussion questions but also comment on the responses from other students, they wonder why they ever thought distance education was going to be easy. Online teachers normally keep track of how their students progress with frequent monitoring and quizzes.

I'll get a better education in face-to-face classes. Much research has been conducted comparing the two and consistently, online learning is equivalent or better. Teachers of online courses now have plenty of precedents to follow, training and research to help them teach better, and technology to prepare for classes and keep up with their students' progress.

I'll talk to a computer all day. Yes, you are in front of a computer as a distance learner, but you also interact with professors and other students much more than you ever would in a core freshman class of 200. Teachers have sophisticated software to facilitate interaction. Even though you don't physically see your teachers, they put a great deal of effort into class preparation and reading e-mails. Some get as many as 3,000 e-mails in a ten-week class. Distance learners often get to know fellow students much more easily online than they would walking in and out of a class.

I need to be a computer geek. If you can handle the simplest maneuvers around a computer, such as attaching documents to e-mails or going to a specified Web address, you can be a distance learner. And you'll have tech support to help out if you run into problems.

Distance education is cheaper than face-to-face. Too bad this is a myth. It costs the same as a traditional college if you attend a recognized institution. Most students pay for distance education through student loans.

3. You must have the skills to communicate your thoughts in writing.

"Online participation in class discussions isn't instant messaging. You are what you write in online classes," advises SchWeber. Most of the work in online classes is written, whether it's participation in discussions, homework, quizzes, papers, or tests.

Since you'll communicate by e-mail and post your thoughts, netiquette is essential. You need to think differently online than when speaking on the phone or face-to-face. "You can't write a report that sounds like you are hanging out with friends," advises SchWeber. "When you are totally online, the only image people (including your professor) have of you is how you write." Kirkendall has reprimanded students who sent e-mails showing disrespect to the teacher because they were upset about something. Probably they would never respond that way if face-to-face. "Never hit the submit button when you're angry," Kirkendall cautions.

4. You must have the ability to research worthwhile information on the Web.

You need to know what's junk and what's reliable. In addition, professors take plagiarism very seriously, especially because it's so easy to do.

5. You must have some computer skills and know some computer-speak.

Those who design the software and set up how a distance learning class is taught are careful to make sure the technology doesn't get in the way of learning; however, you should know the basics. "In some classes, certain downloads are required, such as Adobe Acrobat, but in general, the skills are not beyond the abilities used daily by most elementary school children," says Schroeder, pointing out that if distance programs use expensive or exotic technology, they defeat the purpose. He reports that most computers that are five years old have the speed, memory, and capability to support online learning. Some classes might require a microphone. You should be familiar with some of the computer jargon so that if you're asked to post something or use a drop box, add an attachment, or take part in a threaded discussion, you'll know what you need to do. Just about every distance learning provider has online tutorials to familiarize you with their particular online software. If you run into technical problems, help-desk support is available.

Why Not Women's Colleges?

Before we start talking about the many advantages that women's colleges offer, let's get some myths out of the way. It is almost certain that the minute you hear "women's colleges" in the same sentence with "choosing colleges" you immediately think: no boys, no fun, no way!

Maybe that is why some girls who visit Joan Jaffe's office at Mills College in San Francisco, California, rush in to tell her that they just saw some guys on the campus of this women's college. Jaffe, Associate Dean of Admission, frequently gets this reaction from the young women who visit the campus. That's because many think that if they go to a women's college they are never going to see a guy within 2 miles of the campus gates, which, by the way, will clang shut behind them, leaving them secluded inside a heavily guarded male-free zone.

KISS MYTH NUMBER ONE GOOD-BYE

Forget iron gates. The first myth to get rid of is the one that assumes attending a women's college means kissing your social life good-bye. In fact, as Patricia Gibbs, Vice President for Student Affairs, Dean of Students at Wesleyan College in Macon, Georgia, points out, "If you were a guy looking for a date, where would you go?" Not only that, the majority of women's colleges are near, if not next to, coed campuses. Most share activities with other colleges and universities, and many have reciprocal agreements so that guys can take classes at the women's college and vice versa.

When it comes to dating, women's colleges offer the best of both worlds. You can hang out with guys when you want to and then retreat to your own lovely environment (women's dorms usually are beautiful) and hang out with the girls. Julie Binder, who transferred from the University of Wisconsin to all-women's Barnard College in New York City, notes that there is open registration with Columbia University, which just happens to be right next door. "Campus life is shared. Sports are shared," she says.

As you dig deeper into this myth, you will find that attending a women's college is not about isolation, it's about options. You get to choose if you want to be in classes, clubs, and organizations only with women or mingle with the men.

SCRATCH MYTH NUMBER TWO

Myth Number Two: Women's colleges are just a bunch of catty, competitive females waiting for the right moment to scratch each other's eyes out. Scratch that myth, too. Instead, women's colleges cultivate an environment of sisterhood—women who look out for one another. Most women's colleges encourage women in the upper-level classes to help their younger classmates. Talking to their "big sisters," newcomers can find out what classes to take and which professors are best, and they find a sympathetic ear for the problems that most first-year college students face.

The Rich Traditions in Women's Colleges

Tradition plays an important part of the experience women have in women's colleges. They run the gamut from solemn ceremonies of passing along the bond of sisterhood to the fun of secret surprises. "Women's colleges have a strong sense of tradition," says Amy Shaver, former Academic Dean at Stephens College in Columbia, Missouri. It's also a wonderful way to help women from all social, economic, religious, and ethnic backgrounds to share a common experience and pass it on to the next generation of students. "Traditions bond women over the generations," says Jennifer Rickard, former Dean of Admissions and Financial Aid at Bryn Mawr College, who notes that it's not unusual at all to have students today singing songs and participating in ceremonies that the class of 1945 did and which will be the same when today's students have their twenty-year reunion.

Here's a sampling of the many traditions you'll find on women's college campuses:

Lantern Night At Bryn Mawr's Lantern Night, women gather around a fountain on campus. Each woman is given a lantern as a symbol of knowledge and learning. Each class has a color, and as the lanterns are passed from the sophomores to the first-year students, songs are sung in Greek that are the same as the ones sung 100 years ago around the same fountain.

Senior Paint Night Mills College seniors get the okay to paint the campus in their class color. Along with brushes and cans of paint, they are given a few guidelines as to what can and cannot be painted, but the rest is up to them.

The Crossing of the Bridge As women students come to Stephens to begin their college education, they cross over a bridge on campus in a ceremony symbolizing their entrance into the world of academia. At graduation, they cross over another bridge on campus and are welcomed into the alumnae society.

Candlelight Induction Ceremony Spelman students dressed in white dresses and black shoes light candles and hear the charge to be the best they can be. While the candles are still lit, they sing the Spelman hymn.

Midnight Breakfast At Barnard, the night before finals, the president of the college, deans, and professors make breakfast for the students.

"The sense of community is very strong at women's colleges," observes Fran Samuels, former Director of College Counseling at The Master's School in Dobbs Ferry, New York. "The myth is that a women's college will be cliquish. In truth, the women are supportive of each other." The strong bonds of sisterhood that naturally develop connect students to their college, its history, and its students—past, present, and future. Many women's colleges designate a rotating color for each incoming class. For example, if the freshman class you enter is dubbed the golden hearts, by the time you graduate, you are connected to all the golden hearts who graduated ahead of you and all the golden hearts who will graduate after you.

TOSS MYTH NUMBER THREE

Another myth that should be tossed out is that women's colleges don't prepare you for the "real world." Well, try saying that to the 12 women members of Congress who graduated from women's colleges. Or to the 15 women on *Business Week*'s list of the rising stars in corporate America. Although you are not in a totally coed situation, on the other hand you are in an environment in which you can gain skills to think critically and learn to meet challenges. Becky Marsh, Director of Communications and Marketing at Whitfield School, in St. Louis, Missouri, points out that when you first ride a bike, training wheels allow you to learn how to balance. Once you are ready to race down the street, you take them off. Same with women's colleges. The focus is on your education and your strengths, and who you are. You graduate ready to take on the obstacles of the real world. "In high school, I had the feeling that boys were given more opportunities to share their knowledge. It was harder and more intimidating for me to share my opinions in a coed class," says Brittany Johnson, from Spelman College in Atlanta, Georgia. "Now I feel like I can do anything."

Graduates of women's colleges feel empowered and willing to confront any limits to their abilities. While in college, they have many opportunities to assume leadership roles and see women in leadership positions as professors and deans. "They don't doubt whether they can do anything. Instead, they ask, 'Why can't I do it now?'" reports Amy Shaver, former Academic Dean at Stephens College in Columbia, Missouri. Women can find their own voices and establish their own ways of approaching things that will ultimately make them successful in a male-dominated world. They learn from seeing other women students and professors engaged in the intellectual process.

THE ADVANTAGES

As more young women find out about the advantages that women's colleges offer them, they like what they see. Maybe that is why attendance at women's colleges is growing. Learning leadership skills tops the list of advantages. Says Shaver, "Women in a same-sex environment are more likely to take risks and speak up in class. They are more willing to stand up and voice an opinion." If you think about it, students get plenty of practice at a women's college because all the leadership roles go to women. From day one on a women's campus, you will see women leading the entire college or involved in interesting and significant research. You get more exposure to what leadership is and what to expect as a leader. "Leadership becomes ingrained," notes Jennifer Fondiller, Dean of Admissions and Financial Aid at Barnard College in New York City.

You might not realize it, but women react differently in classrooms with all women. They tend to speak up with confidence and test their ideas more readily when they are not competing with men. Researchers find that even as early as the fifth grade, girls are taught differently than boys. Teachers call on boys more frequently and don't ask girls the more thought-provoking questions or to critically analyze problems. In coed situations, the more aggressive and competitive guys take over, whereas in all-female classes, research indicates there is much more give-and-take and exchange of ideas.

Coming from a coed public school, Johnson realized that more attention was given to the guys in her classes, but at Spelman, she says, "Everyone is on the same path." Arlene Cash, Vice President for Enrollment Management at Spelman, notes that women don't have to vie for attention or retreat into the intellectual background in all-women classes. In a coed class, the environment becomes more adversarial. "Women feel they have to perform. In women's colleges they become more academically involved and interact with faculty members more frequently," says Debbie Greenberg, former College Counselor at Whitfield School. Speaking of the rich interaction that occurs in her classes at Barnard, Binder says, "The diversity of experience around the discussion table is unparalleled."

YOU CAN SUCCEED

Shaver characterizes the environment in women's colleges as one in which there is no fear of failing when the social pressures and dynamics of men and women are removed from the classroom. Women's colleges give women the opportunity to explore different avenues without the fear of failing. "We challenge them to become what they want to become," says Gibbs from Wesleyan. "No one says, 'You can't do that because you are a woman.'" At the same time, you are interacting with other women who have the same goals as you, which reinforces who you are. Or, as Jennifer Rickard, former Dean of Admissions and Financial Aid at Bryn Mawr College, in Bryn Mawr, Pennsylvania, points out, women are not just sitting in classes to do well on exams and get good grades. They also are figuring out what they want to do with their education. "There's less expectation to conform to an external measure," she says.

Many women's colleges foster self-government and give their students responsibilities they might not find in a coed institution. At Bryn Mawr, for instance, students pay a self-government association fee as part of their tuition. This is put into a fund that is controlled by a student government that takes ownership of how the students want to govern themselves. "This isn't student government making only recommendations to the administration as to how to allocate the budget to the different student groups vying for funds," notes Rickard. "You have students dealing with real-world management issues, such as resource allocation."

Since women's colleges are smaller than big coed universities, women receive all the benefits that students get from a small liberal arts college in addition to the advantages that only a women's college offers. A big plus is interaction with professors and staff, which is hard to achieve when you are one of 200 students in a lecture hall taught by a graduate student.

What Made You Choose a Women's College?

When she got to the point of choosing which college to attend, Wisambi Loundu had plenty of options. Coming from San Diego, the California universities were a logical choice. Women's colleges were not on her list. In fact, she hardly knew they existed. Her first thought when someone suggested a women's college to her was, "I'm not going to a school full of girls minus boys." Her second thought was just as negative. "If it's all girls, they will always be fighting." The third and fourth thoughts assumed that a women's college wouldn't prepare her for the real world, plus she would be isolated.

But then her math teacher's daughter told her about Bryn Mawr, and as Wisambi started exploring the possibility, the advantages of a women's college started lining up. However, it wasn't until she visited Bryn Mawr that she really began to see herself there. "I fell in love with the campus," says Wisambi. "It was like nothing I'd ever seen before." Her stay in the dorm added to her steadily growing thoughts that Bryn Mawr might be it. "The girls I stayed with in the dorm were so friendly. At first I was suspicious, but I saw it was not a front. Plus, there were girls from all over the world."

But Wisambi didn't make her final decision just yet. She decided to look at other schools, like Wellesley and the University of California schools, as well as Stanford. Meanwhile, her friend told her more about Bryn Mawr. "She said I'd make lasting friends and she talked about how the academics would train me for the outside world even if there were no men on campus. Bryn Mawr would build my identity as a woman."

She still wasn't convinced and made a second visit, along with visits to Wellesley and Stanford, which she says were nice, but too big. It would be too hard to make friends there, she thought. When the time came to make her final selection, she chose Bryn Mawr.

Now at Bryn Mawr, how does Wisambi feel about her choice? The academics are more challenging than she anticipated but doable, and she is excited about the internships she will be able to access. She also finds that the staff and teachers at Bryn Mawr go out of their way to make her feel at home. "They match us up with a mentor and professor," she says.

How about dating? Since Bryn Mawr is part of a tri-college community, guys are around, though Wisambi says you have to make an effort to meet people on other campuses.

Talking to seniors who are getting ready to head out to the "real world," Wisambi can see that they are full of confidence and don't think for a minute that they won't do well. "And that's a positive," she says.

Women's colleges tend to foster seminar-style classes taught by full professors, many of them women. "You have an expert teaching you," says Gibbs. Faculty members get to know their students and can challenge them intellectually on an individual basis. "Within two days, all my teachers knew my name," recalls Johnson, who says she was given each professor's e-mail address, home phone number, and all the contact information she needed and was encouraged to reach out to them.

Women are encouraged to achieve their intellectual goals. Professors often will point out specific programs that they know suit the student's interests. Add to this the opportunities to conduct research with a professor, and in many cases actually present research findings to a professional society, and you can see why women graduate with a terrific resume before they even start their careers. Rickard mentions the opportunity that Bryn Mawr students have to work on funded projects with professors during the summer and then present the results along with them at conferences. "It's a window into the academic world and the world of the intellectual," she notes. It's no surprise that women in women's colleges major in math and science at a higher national average than women in coed institutions.

Paid and unpaid internships, too, are more available for women at women's colleges, mainly because of the network of women graduates in business and industry who want to help their "sisters" at their alma maters. "I'm getting my professional edge now," says Binder, who is interested in TV production and had a paid internship as a production assistant while a sophomore at Barnard. "You will have an amazing resume by the time you graduate," she says.

Peggy Hock, Ph.D., former College Counselor at Notre Dame High School in San Jose, California, points out that colleges naturally rely on their alumni to come forward with networking opportunities for students; however, the alumnae of women's colleges tend to be more loyal and willing to give of their time. This translates into many more opportunities for internships, mentoring, and job possibilities. At Barnard, for example, the career office has an alumna mentor network. Students can call, ask questions, and get advice about career choices. At alumnae events, current students mix with the graduates. Binder takes full advantage of the Web log of women who are working all over the world and willing to spend time online with Barnard students. She applied for a job at a public relations firm in New York after contacting a fellow Barnard graduate working there. She met with her and subsequently got a letter of recommendation.

HOW TO CHOOSE

Choosing a women's college isn't any different from choosing a coed college. You should definitely visit the campus and don't be afraid to ask lots of questions—even the ones that might make you uncomfortable. Because women's colleges are similar to small coed liberal arts colleges, make sure that you don't compare a women's campus to a big university.

Janet Ashley, former Interim Director for Admissions at Spelman College, advises high school women to ask what a women's college can give them academically. "Their choice depends on what their goals are," she says.

If you're worried about the dating scene, ask about the levels of interaction with guys and how close the relationships are with neighboring institutions.

"Look at the individuality of each women's college," suggests Rickard, "because each has its own personality."

Look at the school before looking at the fact that it's a women's college, and on the flip side, don't rule out a school just because it is a women's college. "So many students make quick decisions about where to apply," warns Fondiller, noting that sometimes the decision hinges on what schools a friend is applying to rather than if that institution really fits the student. Many women's colleges specialize in certain fields like science, math, or theater.

Famous Firsts from Women's Colleges

Quick, from which college did the first woman to be named Secretary of State graduate? Or the woman scientist who identified the Hong Kong flu? Or the first woman executive vice president of the American Stock Exchange? Here's a big clue. They were all graduates of women's colleges.

SENATOR

- Barbara Mikulski (MD)—Mount Saint Agnes College

REPRESENTATIVES (Current and Former)

- Tammy Baldwin (WI)—Smith College
- Donna Christian-Christensen (VI)—St. Mary's College
- Rosa DeLauro (CT)—Marymount College
- Jane Harman (CA)—Smith College
- Gabrielle Giffords (AZ, 2007–12)—Scripps College
- Eddie Bernice Johnson (TX)—Saint Mary's College
- Barbara Lee (CA)—Mills College
- Nita Lowey (NY)—Mount Holyoke College
- Betty McCollum (MN)—College of Saint Catherine
- Nancy Pelosi (CA), first woman elected as Speaker of the House of Representatives—Trinity College
- Allyson Schwartz (PA)—Simmons College

FORMER SECRETARY OF STATE

- Hillary Rodham Clinton (NY)—Wellesley College

OTHER FAMOUS WOMEN FIRSTS

- Madeleine Albright, first woman to be named Secretary of State in the United States, appointed in 1997—Wellesley College
- Jane Amsterdam, first woman editor, the New York Post—Cedar Crest College
- Emily Green Balch, first woman to receive the Nobel Peace Prize in 1946—Bryn Mawr College
- Catherine Brewer Benson, first woman to receive a college bachelor's degree—Wesleyan College
- Earla Biekert, first scientist to identify the Hong Kong flu virus—Wesleyan College
- Cathleen Black, first woman leader of the American Newspaper Publishers Association—Trinity Washington University
- Sarah Porter Boehmler, first woman executive vice president of American Stock Exchange—Sweet Briar College
- Jane Matilda Bolin, first African American woman judge in the United States—Wellesley College
- Dorothy L. Brown, first African American woman general surgeon in the South—Bennett College for Women
- Pearl S. Buck, first American woman to win the Nobel Prize in Literature—Randolph-Macon Woman's College
- Ila Burdett, Georgia's first female Rhodes Scholar—Agnes Scott College
- Dorothy Vredenburgh Bush, first woman secretary of the Democratic National Party—Mississippi University for Women
- Hon. Audrey J. S. Carrion, first Hispanic woman judge Circuit Court for Baltimore City—College of Notre Dame of Maryland
- Rachel Carson, first environmentalist who awakened public consciousness through her book, *Silent Spring*—Chatham University
- Barbara Cassani, first woman CEO of a commercial airline—Mount Holyoke College
- Elaine L. Chao, U.S. Secretary of Labor, 2001; First Asian American woman appointed to a President's cabinet—Mount Holyoke College

Adapted from the website of the Women's College Coalition at http://www.womenscolleges.org.

Applying 101

The words "applying yourself" have several important meanings in the college application process. One meaning refers to the fact that you need to keep focused during this important time in your life, keep your priorities straight, and know the dates that your applications are due so you can apply on time. The phrase might also refer to the person who is really responsible for your application—you.

You are the only person who should compile your college application. You need to take ownership of this process. The guidance counselor is not responsible for completing your applications, and neither are your parents. College applications must be completed in addition to your normal workload at school, college visits, and SAT, ACT, or TOEFL testing.

THE APPLICATION

The application is your way of introducing yourself to a college admissions office. As with any introduction, you want to make a good first impression. The first thing you should do in presenting your application is to find out what the college or university needs from you. Read the application carefully to find out the application fee and deadline, required standardized tests, number of essays, interview requirements, and anything else you can do or submit to help improve your chances for acceptance.

FOLLOW THESE TIPS WHEN FILLING OUT YOUR APPLICATIONS

- **Follow the directions to the letter.** You don't want to be in a position to ask an admissions officer for exceptions due to your inattentiveness.
- **Proofread all parts of your application,** including your essay. Again, the final product indicates to the admissions staff how meticulous and careful you are in your work.
- **Submit your application as early as possible,** provided all of the pieces are available. If there is a problem with your application, this will allow you to work through it with the admissions staff in plenty of time. If you wait until the last minute, it not only takes away that cushion but also reflects poorly on your sense of priorities.
- **Keep a copy of the completed application,** whether it is a photocopy or a copy saved on your computer.

Completing college applications yourself helps you learn more about the schools to which you are applying. The information a college asks for in its application can tell you much about the school. State university applications often tell you how they are going to view their applicants. Usually, they select students based on GPAs and test scores. Colleges that request an interview, ask you to respond to a few open-ended questions, or require an essay are interested in a more personal approach to the application process and may be looking for different types of students than those sought by a state school.

In addition to submitting the actual application, there are several other items that are commonly required. You will be responsible for ensuring that your standardized test scores and your high school transcript arrive at the colleges to which you apply. Most colleges will ask that you submit teacher recommendations as well. Select teachers who know you and your abilities well and allow them plenty of time to complete the recommendations. When all portions of the application have been completed and sent in, whether electronically or by mail, make sure you follow up with the college to ensure their receipt.

THE APPLICATION ESSAY

Whereas the other portions of your application—your transcript, test scores, and involvement in extracurricular activities—are a reflection of what you've accomplished up to this point, your application essay is an opportunity to present yourself in the here and now. The essay shows your originality and verbal skills and how you approach a topic or problem and express your opinion.

Some colleges may request one essay or a combination of essays and short-answer topics to learn more about who you are and how well you can communicate your thoughts. Common essay topics cover such simple themes as writing about yourself and your experiences or why you want to attend that particular school. Other colleges will ask that you show your imaginative or creative side by writing about a favorite author, for instance, or commenting on a hypothetical situation. In such cases, they will be looking at your thought processes and level of creativity.

Admissions officers, particularly those at small or mid-size colleges, use the essay to determine how you, as a student, will fit into life at that college. The essay, therefore, is a critical component of the application process. Here are some tips for writing a winning essay:

- Colleges are looking for an honest representation of who you are and what you think. Make sure that the tone of the essay reflects enthusiasm, maturity, creativity, the ability to communicate, talent, and your leadership skills.
- Be sure you set aside enough time to write the essay, revise it, and revise it *again.* Running "spell check" will only detect a fraction of the errors you probably made on your first pass at writing it. Take a break and then come back to it and reread it. You will probably notice other style, content, and grammar problems—and ways that you can improve the essay overall.

- Always answer the question that is being asked, making sure that you are specific, clear, and true to your personality.
- Enlist the help of reviewers who know you well— friends, parents, teachers—since they are likely to be the most honest and will keep you on track in the presentation of your true self.

THE PERSONAL INTERVIEW

Although it is relatively rare that a personal interview is required, many colleges recommend that you take this opportunity for a face-to-face discussion with a member of the admissions staff. Read through the application materials to determine whether or not a college places great emphasis on the interview. If they strongly recommend that you have one, it may work against you to forego it.

In contrast to a group interview and some alumni interviews, which are intended to provide information about a college, the personal interview is viewed both as an information session and as further evaluation of your skills and strengths. You will meet with a member of the admissions staff who will be assessing your personal qualities, high school preparation, and your capacity to contribute to undergraduate life at the institution. On average, these meetings last about 45 minutes—a relatively short amount of time in which to gather information and leave the desired impression—so here are some suggestions on how to make the most of it.

Scheduling Your Visit

Generally, students choose to visit campuses in the summer or fall of their senior year. Both times have their advantages. A summer visit, when the campus is not in session, generally allows for a less hectic visit and interview. Visiting in the fall, on the other hand, provides the opportunity to see what campus life is like in full swing. If you choose the fall, consider arranging an overnight trip so that you can stay in one of the college dormitories. At the very least, you should make your way around campus to take part in classes, athletic events, and social activities. Always make an appointment and avoid scheduling more than two college interviews on any given day. Multiple interviews in a single day hinder your chances of making a good impression, and your impressions of the colleges will blur into each other as you hurriedly make your way from place to place.

Preparation

Know the basics about the college before going for your interview. Read the college catalog and website in addition to this guide. You will be better prepared to ask questions that are not answered in the literature and that will give you a better understanding of what the college has to offer. You should also spend some time thinking about your strengths and weaknesses and, in particular, what you are looking for in a college education. You will find that as you get a few interviews under your belt, they will get easier. You might consider starting with a college that is not a top contender on your list, so that the stakes are not as high.

Asking Questions

Inevitably, your interviewer will ask you, "Do you have any questions?" Not having one may suggest that you're unprepared or, even worse, not interested. When you do ask questions, make sure that they are ones that matter to you and that have a bearing on your decision about whether or not to attend that college. The questions that you ask will give the interviewer some insight into your personality and priorities. Avoid asking questions that are answered in the college literature—again, a sign of unpreparedness. Although the interviewer will undoubtedly pose questions to you, the interview should not be viewed merely as a question-and-answer session. If a conversation evolves out of a particular question, so much the better. Your interviewer can learn a great deal about you from how you sustain a conversation. Similarly, you will be able to learn a great deal about the college in a conversational format.

Separate the Interview from the Interviewer

Many students base their feelings about a college solely on their impressions of the interviewer. Try not to characterize a college based only on your personal reaction, however, since your impressions can be skewed by whether you and your interviewer hit it off. Pay lots of attention to everything else that you see, hear, and learn about a college. Once on campus, you may never see your interviewer again.

In the end, remember to relax and be yourself. Your interviewer will expect you to be somewhat nervous, which will relieve some of the pressure. Don't drink jitters-producing caffeinated beverages prior to the interview, and suppress nervous fidgets like leg-wagging, finger-drumming, or bracelet jangling. Consider your interview an opportunity to put forth your best effort and to enhance everything that the college knows about you up to this point.

THE FINAL DECISION

Once you have received your acceptance letters, it is time to go back and look at the whole picture. Provided you received more than one acceptance, you are now in a position to compare your options. The best way to do this is to compare your original list of important college-ranking criteria with what you've discovered about each college along the way. In addition, you and your family will need to factor in the financial aid component. You will need to look beyond these cost issues and the quantifiable pros and cons of each college, however, and know that you have a good feeling about your final choice. Before sending off your acceptance letter, you need to feel confident that the college will feel like home for the next four years. Once the choice is made, the only hard part will be waiting for an entire summer before heading off to college!

The "Early Decision" Decision

Maybe a senior you knew last year didn't get into the college he wanted. He said it was because he didn't apply early decision. Maybe your friend's mom told your mom that unless students apply early decision, their chances of getting into top schools are slim to none, even though they have great grades and spectacular essays. Maybe you figure you'd better get in on the early decision action.

All of the above are true—well, sort of—because many students applying to college get the term "early decision" backwards. High school guidance and college counselors run into this kind of thinking all the time and suggest putting "decision" before "early"—as in making a wise decision about committing to a college before applying early. For some students, early decision is a great option. For others, early decision is loaded with pitfalls and dangers.

"When students come back in the fall of their senior year, I often hear 'I know I want to apply early. Can you help me choose the school?'" says Kathy Cleaver, Co-Director of College Counseling at Durham Academy in Durham, North Carolina. She compares that to saying, "I know I want to get married, please help me pick the man." Continues Cleaver, "First you have to fall in love with the school and know it's your first choice and then join the circus for early decision." She's referring to the media hype flying around high school halls about early decision—it's easy to fall prey to the early decision madness. Hot competition to get into "top" schools creates early decision anxiety. Michael "Mickey" Gilbert, Guidance Counselor at Passaic High School in Passaic, New Jersey, throws out some scary numbers that confirm that, yes, the competition for admittance to top schools is white-hot. There are about 30,000 high schools in the United States, and although the majority of high school seniors apply to institutions in their own states, there are still limited spaces in the "top" schools and the eight Ivy League schools. "No wonder kids think that early decision is the way to go," speculates Gilbert. Early decision panic sets in because students are convinced that if they get their applications in early, they have an edge. Sometimes early decision might make the difference, but there are many issues to consider before taking the early decision leap.

EARLY THIS, EARLY THAT

With all the buzz about early decision, do you really know what it means along with all the other early options, such as early action and early notification? And what about the variations of early decision? Each institution can have its own version of early decision, meaning that deadlines and criteria are different. There's the early decision that notifies students by December, there's the early decision round two, and then there is the early action/single choice.

Seeing the confusion, the National Association for College Admission Counseling (NACAC) developed a standard set of definitions. NACAC is an education association of secondary school counselors, college and university admissions and financial aid officers, counselors, and other individuals who work with students as they transition from high school to college. While each institution has its own variations of each early option, an understanding of the basic differences can help. The list that follows was adapted from the definitions found on the NACAC website (www.nacacnet.org).

Early Decision

- Early decision is the application process in which students make a commitment to a first-choice institution where, if admitted, they definitely will enroll. Should a student who applies for financial aid not be offered an award that makes attendance possible, the student may decline the offer of admission and be released from the early decision commitment.
- While pursuing admission under an early decision plan, students may apply to other institutions, but may have only one early decision application pending at any time.
- The institution must notify the applicant of the decision within a reasonable and clearly stated period of time after the early decision deadline. Usually, a nonrefundable deposit must be made well in advance of May 1.
- A student applying for financial aid must adhere to institutional early decision aid application deadlines.
- The institution will respond to an application for financial aid at or near the time of an offer of admission.
- The early decision application supercedes all other applications. Immediately upon acceptance of an offer of admission, a student must withdraw all other applications and make no subsequent applications.
- The application form will include a request for a parent and a counselor signature, in addition to the student's signature, indicating an understanding of the early decision commitment and agreement to abide by its terms.

Early Action

- Early action is the application process in which students make application to an institution of preference and receive a decision well in advance of the institution's regular response date. Students who are admitted under early action are not obligated to accept the institution's offer of admission or to submit a deposit until the regular reply date (not prior to May 1).

- A student may apply to other colleges without restriction.
- The institution must notify the applicant of the decision within a reasonable and clearly stated period of time after the early action deadline.
- A student applying for financial aid must adhere to institutional aid application deadlines.
- A student admitted under an early action plan may not be required to make a commitment prior to May 1, but may be encouraged to do so as soon as a final college choice is made. Colleges that solicit commitments to offers of early action admission and/or financial assistance prior to May 1 may do so provided those offers include a clear statement that written requests for extensions until May 1 will be granted, and that such requests will not jeopardize a student's status for admission or financial aid.

Regular Decision

- Regular decision is the application process in which a student submits an application to an institution by a specified date and receives a decision within a reasonable and clearly stated period of time, but not later than April 15.
- A student may apply to other colleges without restriction.
- The institution will state a deadline for completion of applications and will respond to completed applications by a specified date.
- A student applying for financial aid must adhere to institutional aid application deadlines.
- A student admitted under a regular decision plan may not be required to make a commitment prior to May 1, but may be encouraged to do so as soon as a final college choice is made. Colleges that solicit commitments to offers of admission and/or financial assistance prior to May 1 may do so provided those offers include a clear statement that written requests for extensions until May 1 will be granted, and that such requests will not jeopardize a student's status for admission or financial aid.

Rolling Admission

- Rolling admission is the application process in which an institution reviews applications as they are completed and renders admission decisions to students throughout the admission cycle.
- A student may apply to other colleges without restriction.
- The institution will respond to completed applications in a timely manner.
- A student applying for financial aid must adhere to institutional aid application deadlines.
- A student admitted under a rolling admission plan may not be required to make a commitment prior to May 1, but may be encouraged to do so as soon as a final college choice is made. Colleges that solicit commitments to offers of admission and/or financial assistance prior to May 1 may do so provided those offers include a clear statement that written requests for extensions until May 1 will be granted, and that such requests will not jeopardize a student's status for admission or financial aid.

Wait List

- Wait list is an admission decision option utilized by institutions to protect against shortfalls in enrollment. Wait lists are sometimes made necessary because of the uncertainty of the admission process, as students submit applications for admission to multiple institutions and may receive several offers of admission. By placing a student on the wait list, an institution does not initially offer or deny admission, but extends to a candidate the possibility of admission in the future before the institution's admission cycle is concluded.
- The institution will ensure that a wait list, if necessary, is of reasonable length and is maintained for a reasonable period of time, but never later than August 1.
- In the letter offering a wait list position, the institution should provide a past wait list history, which describes the number of students placed on the wait list(s), the number offered admission from the wait list, and the availability of financial aid. Students should be given an indication of when they can expect to be notified of a final admission decision.
- An institution must resolve final status and notify wait list candidates as soon after May 1 as possible.
- The institution will not require students to submit deposits to remain on a wait list or pressure students for a commitment to enroll prior to sending an official offer of admission in writing.

There is one more option, called early action/single choice (EASC), that some highly selective schools such as Harvard, Yale, Princeton, and Stanford have begun using. Early action/single choice is a nonbinding early admission option for freshman applicants that replaces early decision. With this change, students learn about their admission decision in December without being required to reply until May 1. This option allows students to apply to as many colleges as they want under a regular admission time frame. The difference is that the early action/single choice option does not allow a candidate to apply to other schools under any type of early action, early decision, or early notification program. Students are asked to sign a statement in their application agreeing to file only one early application.

Each of these options has variations, depending on the institution using them. Some schools have a November 1 deadline for early decision round one. Smaller schools have a deadline of November 15, while others have a December 1 deadline. Then there's an early decision round two. To make matters even more complicated, some schools with early decision say that students can't apply to other institutions if they've sent in an early decision application to their admissions office. Others say it's okay to apply to other schools at the same time you're applying early decision to them, but if they send you an acceptance, you must withdraw the other applications.

PARENTS, SOME ADVICE FOR YOU

Though guidance counselors stress that high school students should make the final decision about which college to attend, they also say that parents are a very important part of the decision equation. Parents can help as organizers of all the information and provide the support needed to make a good choice. "Little things like setting up file folders and keeping track of deadlines can keep a student on track," advises David Gibson, College Advisor at St. Mary's Parish in Annapolis, Maryland.

Along with their children, parents also need to understand the basics of early option terminology as it applies to each institution being considered. Five different colleges might have five different early decision criteria. Read the fine print, and make note of deadlines.

What really will help—you, your child, and your wallet—is to understand the basics about financial aid. Says Shawn Leftwich, Director of Undergraduate Admissions at Wheaton College in Illinois, "Have an in-depth discussion with the financial aid officer so that you are aware of the ramifications, restrictions, and implications of the financial aid offer."

If possible, make an appointment to visit with a financial aid officer at the college while your child is visiting the campus. Bring your tax forms and discuss the prospects of financial aid. "Financial aid people are straight shooters. It's not in their best interest to tell you one thing to get your foot in the door and then turn around and pull the rug out from under you," says Bill McClintick, Dean of College Relations and Outreach at Mercerburg Academy. "Parents might not like the answer they get from the financial aid officer, but they will get a candid assessment of their eligibility for financial aid."

Leftwich suggests having an honest discussion with your child early in the college selection process. Talk about what you can realistically afford, what colleges will appropriately challenge him or her, if location is a factor, and what kind of environment best suits your child. Whichever option your child uses to apply, you both will know the decision is an informed one.

Just because two institutions have an application process called early decision or early action doesn't mean that their policies are identical. "There is no common terminology, even among the colleges that have early decision," says Christoph Guttentag, Dean of Undergraduate Admissions at Duke University in Durham, North Carolina. He also points out that just when you think you've got the definitions figured out, institutions change them. "Colleges are always balancing the needs of their institution and the needs of students," he comments.

EARLY DECISION: A MATCHMAKING TOOL OR A CLEVER STRATEGY?

Despite the differences in what actually constitutes early decision, it has become more of a strategy than a matchmaking tool, according to Bill McClintick, Director of College Counseling at Mercersburg Academy in Mercersburg, Pennsylvania. He also chairs the national steering committee on admissions standards for NACAC. The focus of early decision used to be on matching the student with the college and letting the admissions office know that that institution is where the student wants to be above all others. Today, early decision is misunderstood and misused. High school seniors think that they must use the early decision tactic to get an edge. The result, says McClintick is "at many of the top places, early decision applications have gone through the roof."

Though high school students may have exaggerated ideas of how much early decision can really help them, it is true that it does give a small segment of students applying at highly selective schools an advantage. Generally, the more selective the institution, the more small differences matter. "Even if it's a small increase, you need everything you can get," states John Latting, Ph.D., Emory University's Assistant Vice Provost for Undergraduate Enrollment and Dean of Admission.

"Remember," cautions McClintick, "we're only talking about a small slice of kids in the grand scheme of things." He mentions 5 percent of high school seniors nationally who aspire to the "top" institutions. State colleges and universities fill a much lower percentage of their freshman class with early decision applications. "I don't believe that more kids are chasing the same number of spots," says Jon Reider, Director of College Counseling at San Francisco University High School in San Francisco, California. "Students are applying to more and more schools, even with the early decision option on the side. This is inflating the selectivity of some colleges beyond what it used to be." In reality, 90 percent of students apply regular admission. Interest in early decision comes from a relatively small segment of the college applicant pool.

THE BENEFITS OF EARLY DECISION

There are clear benefits for students who apply for early decision. Aside from the fact that early decision does play a role in acceptance rates for a relatively small percentage of students at a small number of schools, early decision is a good option. The caveat is that students must know, without a shred of doubt, that one institution, above all others, is the best match for their goals and their likes and dislikes, and that based on grades and test scores, they solidly match the institution's criteria for admission. The option to go early decision should be taken after extensive research, multiple visits to the campus, and talking to a lot of people. "Early decision is for those who can put their hearts and souls into one application," advises Cleaver.

There are other advantages. You have to make only one choice, and you will know by December if you've been accepted. You have to fill out only one application. You are not chewing your nails over your list of possibilities during the Christmas holiday. Instead, you know where you're going and can sit back and enjoy the rest of your senior year, while others in your class are madly filling out applications, writing essays, and agonizing over the thin envelopes that arrive in the mail. Says Guttentag, "The advantage of having that challenging process over with is not insignificant."

The "Early Decision" Decision

Early decision is helpful for admissions officers at selective colleges because it allows them to make decisions between well-qualified students and select those who really want to be at their institution. As Shawn Leftwich, Director of Undergraduate Admissions at Wheaton College in Illinois, points out, early decision is for the students who are strongly committed. "We like you. You like us. We know you're coming, and we can fill our freshman class." However, on the flip side, she adds that some students aren't so sure about which college they want to attend, and early decision only makes the process more stressful.

Before you decide to go with early decision, consider early action. Many high school counselors lean toward early action, which is another good option. With early action you're able to apply later in the process. This means you will be able to take the SATs again. Your first-semester grades and AP classes taken in the first semester of your senior year can be used to evaluate your eligibility. You have September and October to visit several campuses while they are in session and plenty of time to do the research to put more than one school on your list.

THE PITFALLS OF EARLY DECISION

Though early decision has benefits, before you jump into it, look at the ramifications of that option. Advises Gilbert, "Early decision might give you an edge, but the tradeoff is not so great."

Perhaps the most compelling reason why students should seriously examine early decision before jumping at it is because they are bound by an agreement to attend that school if accepted. Students sign a pledge to attend that institution and are required to withdraw applications from all other schools. They also are obligated to accept the financial aid award that the institution gives them. An early decision is a binding decision. "Regardless," advises David Gibson, of David Gibson College Advising, LLC, in Annapolis, Maryland, "students don't learn about their financial aid awards until March or April, and if the award funding is not at all acceptable because the family's financial need was not met, they need to decline the offer and begin searching for a new college. March or April is not a good time to start applying to new colleges."

How binding is binding? Though no school can force a student to attend if they've signed an early decision agreement, students who decide not to attend that school hurt others with that decision. High school counselors have to sign the binding agreement, along with parents, and must state that they will not send out transcripts to other institutions. Many institutions will not accept the application of a student who applied early decision elsewhere and backed out of the agreement. Admissions officers may find out in May that an early decision student is not coming, so they'll call the counselor and ask if the student applied to another school. If so, often a phone call to the other institution is made and acceptance denied. Sometimes the counselor loses a good reputation with that institution, putting applicants who follow in subsequent years at a disadvantage.

QUESTIONS TO ASK YOURSELF BEFORE APPLYING EARLY DECISION

What if you don't get accepted early decision—then what? Speaking from the experience of seeing students deal with early decision rejection letters, Reider says, "Some of your friends are getting acceptance letters, and you get one thin envelope and the pain of rejection. You've given the early decision institution your best shot and you lost." Cleaver has seen kids in her high school end up thinking they won't get in anywhere. "This is the first time they've faced a big rejection and news they don't want to hear," she says, noting that because of the timetable of early decision, letters often come right around exam time in December.

When students apply regular decision, meaning they wait until well into their senior year and apply to several different institutions, it's "all or some," quips Latting. "With early decision, it's all or nothing." Many application deadlines for regular decision are in January. If you get that rejection letter from the school you were counting on, that doesn't give you much time to apply to other schools, much less visit them.

Are you ready to make such a drastic decision so early in your senior year? A lot can change in how you think about your future between the beginning of your senior year and graduation. With six or seven months behind you as a senior, you might be in a better position to compare colleges in April than you were back in September. Think about it—you're making the decision about where you want to spend the next four years of your life in early October of your senior year!

Have you given yourself enough time to pick one college above all others? If you want to apply early decision, you should start making plans to do so in your junior year. In order to apply early decision, you must have your ACTs or SATs taken, campus visits done, a final choice made, a dynamite essay written, a stellar application filled out, and teacher recommendation letters collected. That's a lot to cram into the end of your junior year and a few months into your senior year.

Have you given an admissions office enough information to make a decision about you? The more information the admissions office has about grades and classes you took and activities and leadership positions you held, the better they can decide if you're a good match for them. Do you really want decisions being made about you based on sophomore and junior grades and activities? What happens to that AP English class you finally felt ready to take the beginning of your senior year? What about that calculus class you aced in the first semester of your senior year? Admissions won't be able to assess that on an early decision application.

After the consequences of signing a binding agreement, the financial aspect of early decision is the next biggest pitfall. "You can't compare financial aid offers," says Latting. "You have only one offer." Students won't know if they're eligible for Pell grants or merit scholarships. Government FAFSA forms are not submitted until January, and students might not find out how much aid they can get until March or April, long after the early decision agreement was signed and sealed. "This means that if they are accepted, they are then obligated to a college that might not fund them to the level of their financial need," says Gibson. Students who apply early action or regular decision are in a better position to negotiate financial aid packages.

EARLY DECISION REJECTION

In case you haven't heard, fat is good, thin is bad. Thin envelopes from college admissions offices usually mean a single-page letter saying good luck, we wish you the best, but you're not going to be attending our school next fall. However stated, it's hard to be rejected, especially when you've applied early decision, which states to the college and to yourself that this is the college you've decided is the only one you really, really want to attend above all others.

But thin envelopes don't mean the end of the world. Cleaver advises to not let early decision get control of you. "There are too many choices of colleges for you not to get into college. You might not get into Princeton, but there are many other wonderful schools if you do the research to look for a good match. Early decision is a tool to use to apply, but it is not always the best tool."

Objecting to the term "perfect match," Reider asks, "Does it really matter what kind of car you drive? There are twenty different colleges that can get you where you want to go. You'll be successful in most places."

HOW TO DO EARLY DECISION THE RIGHT WAY

Taking the early decision option requires more than gathering information, filling out an application, writing an essay, and waiting for an envelope to come in the mail or an e-mail to hit your Inbox. If you're going to be serious about early decision, the time to start is in your junior year.

Research the institutions at the top of your list. Think through what you want out of college—not just in terms of a future career, but also factors such as location, size, distance from home, sports, and other activities. Think about who you want to be. "It has to be a love connection," says Cleaver. Tune out all the early decision talk and do your homework about each college. Then ask yourself if one stands out above all the others you've researched. Is this the one to which you can commit to a binding agreement? Are you in the competition to be admitted? Will you have the funds to attend this college?

"Admissions can tell if your application is from the heart," Cleaver cautions. Students ask her how to make their applications "look like they want to go there." She replies that what they put on an application and in an essay has to pour out of their hearts. Students who visit the campus and sit in on a class or a campus organization have the edge if something really clicked with them. They will write a convincing application. Perhaps they'll tell about how exciting the professor they heard was or how wonderful it is that the college has a chess club. Cleaver observes that kids usually write about an institution's sports team or about the ivy-covered walls of the campus on their application essay instead of writing about some interesting aspect of the university that spoke to them, which takes research, time, and reflection. "Don't make the mistake of chasing a name and not being a good consumer," cautions McClintick. Part of being a good consumer is to make sure you are a reasonably competitive applicant. This means looking at the school's admission criteria and statistics. What percentage of the freshman class is filled with early decision and early action students? If it's a high percentage, then you might want to reconsider where that school falls on your wish list. How many students return for their sophomore year? If more than 10 percent leave after their freshman year, that should tell you something about student satisfaction—and ultimately yours.

One of the most important ways to choose the right school is to visit the campus, perhaps multiple times and preferably with students on campus. "Campus visits are a critical time to talk with undergraduates and to find out what the academic, social, and physical climate is like," advises Guttentag. If you're staying in a dorm on Tuesday night during a visit, you can tell how serious kids are about their work. What kinds of conversations are they having? "Are these the kind of kids you want to spend four years of your life with?" asks McClintick.

After you've thoroughly investigated all the aspects of a college and decided it's at the absolute top of your list, after you are familiar with the early decision requirements at that institution, and after you've determined that you have a good chance of getting into that institution, then you can say early decision is for you. For those who are not so sure, fortunately, colleges and universities have plenty of other options for admission.

Coming to America: Tips for International Students Considering Study in the U.S.

Introduction: Why Study in the United States?

Are you thinking about going to a college or university in the United States? If you're looking at this book, you probably are! All around the world, students like you, pursuing higher education, are considering that possibility. They envision themselves on modern, high-tech campuses in well-known cities, surrounded by American students, taking classes and having fun. A degree from a U.S. school would certainly lead to success and fortune, either back in your home country or perhaps even in the United States, wouldn't it?

It can be done—but becoming a student at a college or university in the U.S. requires academic talent, planning, time, effort, and money. While there may be only a small number of institutions of higher learning in your country, there are more than 2,800 four-year colleges and universities in the United States. Choosing one, being accepted, and then traveling and becoming a student in America is a big undertaking.

If this is your dream, here is some helpful information and expert tips from professionals who work with international students at colleges and universities throughout the United States.

Timing and Planning

The journey to a college or university in the U.S. often starts years in advance. Most international students choose to study in the U.S. because of the high quality of academics. Your family may also have a lot of input on this decision, too.

"We always tell students they should be looking in the sophomore year, visiting in the junior year, and applying in the senior year," says Father Francis E. Chambers, OSA, D.Min., Associate Director of International Admission at Villanova University. He stresses that prospective students need to be taking challenging courses in the years leading up to college. "We want to see academic rigor. Most admission decisions are based on the first six semesters—senior year is too late."

Heidi Gregori-Gahan, Assistant Provost for International Programs at the University of Southern Indiana agrees that it's important to start early. "Plan ahead and do your homework. There is so much to choose from—so many schools, programs, degrees, and experiences. It can be overwhelming."

While students in some countries may pay an agent to help them get into a school in the United States, Gregori-Gahan often directs potential international students to EducationUSA (http://educationusa.state.gov), a U.S. State Department network of over 400 international student advising centers in more than 170 countries. "They are there to provide unbiased information about studying in the United States and help you understand the process and what you need to do."

Two to three years of advance planning is also recommended by Daphne Durham, who has been an international student adviser at Harvard, Suffolk University, Valdosta State University, and the University of Georgia. She points out that the academic schedule in other countries is often different than that of the United States, so you need to synchronize your calendar accordingly.

You will have to take several tests in order to gain admission to a U.S. school, so it's important to know when those tests are given in your country, then register and take them so your scores will be available when you apply. Even if you have taken English in school, you will probably have to take The Test of English as a Foreign Language (TOEFL®), but some schools also accept the International English Language Testing Sytem (IELTS). You will probably also have to take the SAT® or ACT® tests, which are achievement or aptitude tests, and are usually required of all students applying for admission, not just international students.

"Make sure you understand how the international admissions process works at the school or schools you want to attend," says Durham. "What test scores are needed and when? Does the school have a fixed calendar or rolling admissions?" Those are just some of the many factors that can impact your application and could make a difference in when you are able to start school.

"Every university is unique in what's required and what they need to do. Even navigating each school's different website can be challenging," explains Gregori-Gahan.

Searching for Schools

This book contains information on thousands of four-year colleges and universities, and it will be a valuable resource for you in your search and application process. But with so many options, how do you decide which school you should attend?

"Where I find a big difference with international students is if their parents don't recognize the school, they don't apply to the school," says Fr. Chambers. "They could be overlooking a lot of great schools. They have to look outside the box."

The school Gregori-Gahan represents is in Evansville, Indiana, and it probably isn't familiar to students abroad. "Not many people have heard of anything beyond New York and California and maybe Florida. I like to tell students that this is 'real America.' But happy international students on our campus have recruited others to come here."

She points out that Internet technology has made a huge difference in the search process for international students. Websites full of information, live chat, webinars, virtual tours, and admission interviews via Skype have made it easier for potential students to connect with U.S. institutions, get more information, and be better able to visualize the campus.

One thing than will help narrow your search for a school is knowing specifically what you want to study. You need to know what the course of study is called in the United States, what it means, and what is required in order to study that subject. You also need to consider your future plans. What are your goals and objectives? What do you plan to do after earning your degree?

"If you're going to overcome the hurdles and get to a U.S. school, you have to have a directed path chosen," says Durham.

The other thing that could help your search process is finding a school that is a good fit.

Fit Is Important

You want your clothing and shoes to fit you properly and be comfortable, so a place where you will spend four or more years of your life studying should also be comfortable and appropriate for you. So how can you determine if a particular school is a good fit?

"We really recommend international students visit first. Yes, there are websites and virtual tours, but there's still nothing that beats an in-person visit," says Fr. Chambers. He estimates that 50 to 60 percent of Villanova's international students visited the campus before enrolling.

"It can be hard to get a sense of a place—you're so far away and you're probably not going to set foot on campus until you arrive," says Gregori-Gahan. "There is a high potential for culture shock."

You need to ask yourself what is important to you in a campus environment, then do some homework to ensure that the schools you are considering meet those needs. Here are some things to consider when it comes to fit:

- **Location:** Is it important for you to be in a well-known city or is a part of the United States that is unfamiliar a possibility? "Look at geographic areas, but also cost of living," recommends Durham. "Be sure to factor in transportation costs also, especially if you plan to return to your home country regularly."
- **Student population:** Some small schools have just 1,000 students while larger ones may have 30,000 students or more.
- **Familiar faces:** Is it important for you to be at a school with others from your home nation or region?
- **Climate:** Some students want a climate similar to where they live now, but others are open and curious about seasons and weather conditions they may not have ever experienced. "We do have four seasons here," says Gregori-Gahan. "Sometimes students who come here from tropical regions are concerned about the winters. The first snow is so exciting, but after that, students may not be aware of how cold it really is."
- **Amenities:** Do you want to find your own housing or choose a school where the majority of students live on campus? Is there public transportation available or is it necessary to walk or have a bicycle or car? Does the school or community have access to things that are important to you culturally and meet the traditions you want to follow?
- **Campus size:** Some campuses are tightly compacted into a few city blocks but others cover hundreds of acres of land. "International students are amazed by how green and spacious our campus is, with blooming flowers, trees, and lots of grass," says Gregori-Gahan.
- **Academic offerings:** Does this school offer the program you want to study? Can you complete it in four years or perhaps sooner? What sort of internship and career services are available?
- **Finances:** Can you afford to attend this school? Is there any sort of financial assistance available for international students?
- **Support services:** Durham suggests students look carefully at each school's offerings for international students. "Does the school have online guidance for getting your visa? Is ESL tutoring available? Does the school offer host family or community friend programs?" She also suggests you look for campus support groups for students from your country or region.

Looking at the listings and reading the in-depth descriptions in this book can help you search for a school that is a good fit for you.

Government Requirements

The one thing that every international student must have in order to study in the United States is a student visa. Having accurate advice and following all the necessary steps regarding the visa process is essential to being able to enter this country and start school.

As you schedule your tests and application deadlines, you must also consider how long it will take to get your visa. This varies depending on where you live; in some countries, extensive background checks are required. The subject you plan to study can also impact your visa status; it does help to have a major rather than be undeclared. The U.S. State Department website, http://travel.state.gov/content/visas/english/study-exchange.html, can give you an idea of how long it will take.

In addition to the visa, you will also need a Form I-20, which is a U.S. government immigration form. You must have that form when you get to the United States.

"It's very different from being a tourist. You need to be prepared to meet with an immigration officer and be interviewed about your college," explains Durham. "Where you are going, why you are going, where the school is located, what you are studying and so on."

You also need to keep in mind that there are reporting requirements once you are a student in the U.S. Every semester, your adviser has to report to the government to confirm that you are enrolled in and attending school in order for you to stay in the United States.

Finances

Part of the visa process includes having the funds to pay for the cost of your schooling and support yourself. Finances are a huge hurdle in the process of becoming a college student in the United States.

"It's crucial. So many foreign systems offer 'free' higher education to students. How is your family going to handle the ongoing expense of attending college for four years or longer in the United States?" Durham reiterates that planning ahead is key because there are so many details. Student loans require a U.S.-based cosigner. Each school has its own financial aid deadlines. You have to factor in your own government's requirements, such currency exchange and fund transfers.

The notion that abundant funds are available to assist international students is not true. Sometimes state schools may offer diversity waivers or there may be special scholarship opportunities for international students. But attending school in the U.S. is still a costly venture.

"We do offer financial aid to international students, but they still have to be able to handle a large portion of the costs. Full-need scholarships are not likely," explained Fr. Chambers. "Sometimes students think that once they get here, it will all work out and the funds will be there. But the scenario for the first year has to be repeated each year they are on campus.

Once You Arrive...

You've taken your tests, researched schools, found a good fit, applied, got accepted, arranged the financing, gotten your visa and I-20, and made it to the campus in the United States. Now what?

You can expect the school where you have enrolled to be welcoming and helpful, but within reason. If you arrive on a weekend, or at a time outside of the time when international students are scheduled to arrive, the assistance you need may not be available to you.

Every school offers different levels of assistance to international students. For instance, Villanova offers a full-service office that can assist students with everything from visas, to employment, to finding a place for students to stay over breaks.

Fr. Chambers attends the international student orientation session to greet the students he's worked with through the recruitment and application process. "But I rarely see an international student after that. I think that bodes well for them being integrated into the entire university."

"Those of us who work with international students are really working to help them adjust," says Gregori-Gahan. "International students get here well before school starts so they can get over jet lag. We have orientation sessions and pair them with peer advisers who help them navigate the first few days, and we assure them that we are there for them."

Students should be open to their new setting, but they should be prepared that things may not be at all how they had envisioned during their planning and searching process. "While you may think you'll meet lots of Americans, don't underestimate the importance of community with your traditional home culture and people," says Durham.

Don't Make These Mistakes

The journey to college attendance in the United States is a long one, with many steps. The experts warn about mistakes to avoid along the way.

"Not reading through everything thoroughly and not understanding what the program of study really is and what will it cost. You have to be really clear on the important details," says Gregori-Gahan.

"Every school does things differently," cautions Fr. Chambers. "International students must be aware of that as they are applying."

Durham stresses that going to school in the United States is too big a decision to leave to someone else. "Students need to know about their school—they have to be in charge of their application."

"It involves a lot of work to be successful and happy and not surprised by too many things," Gregori-Gahan says.

Hopefully now, you are more informed and better prepared to pursue your dream of studying at a college or university in the United States.

Financial Aid Countdown Calendar

JUNIOR YEAR

Fall

Now is the time to get serious about the colleges in which you are interested. Meet with your guidance counselor to help you narrow down your choices. Hopefully by the spring, your list will have five to ten solid choices. College visits are always a great idea—remember this will be the place you will call home for four years, so start your campus visits soon!

- ❑ Register for the PSAT/NMSQT®.
- ❑ Check out local financial aid nights in the area. Be sure to attend these valuable sessions, especially if this is the first time your family is sending someone off to college. Try to become familiar with common financial aid terms. Start reviewing the literature available and begin to familiarize yourself with the various programs. A good booklet is published by the U.S. Department of Education, "Funding Your Education: The Guide to Federal Student Aid" and is available at any financial aid office or on the web at https://studentaid.ed.gov/sites/default/files/funding-your-education.pdf.
- ❑ In October, take the PSAT/NMSQT®.
- ❑ Do some web browsing! There are many free scholarship search engines, such as Petersons.com. Also, head to the bookstore or library and pick up a copy of *Peterson's® Scholarships, Grants & Prizes,* which features details on billions of dollars of aid from private sources, or *Best Scholarships for the Best Students,* which offers great info on scholarships, fellowships, and experiential learning programs for top students.
- ❑ Ask your parents to contact their employers, unions, and any religious and fraternal organizations with which they have a connection to learn about possible scholarship opportunities.
- ❑ Check with your high school guidance counselor for the qualifications and deadlines of local scholarship awards. Many guidance counselors report that there are few applicants for these awards.

Winter

- ❑ Keep checking for scholarships! Remember that this is the one area over which you have control. The harder you work, the better your chances for success!
- ❑ Register and study for the ACT® or SAT® and SAT Subject Tests™.

Spring

- ❑ Spring Break—a great time to visit colleges. Remember your top ten list? Time to start narrowing it down.
- ❑ Review the requirements for local scholarships. What can you do now and over the summer to improve your chances?
- ❑ Take the ACT® or SAT®. Good luck!
- ❑ Look for a summer job, especially one that ties in with your college plans. For example, if you want to major in premed, why not try to get a job at a hospital or with a laboratory?

Summer

- ❑ College visit time! Ask: Is this where I see myself getting my undergraduate degree? Can I adjust to the seasons, the town surrounding the campus, the distance from home, the college size? Does this school feel right for me?
- ❑ Why not get a jump on college (and maybe save some money!) and enroll for a college course at the local community college? Or, better yet, do some extra prep work for the ACT® or SAT®!

SENIOR YEAR

Fall

How's the college list coming? Can you get your list down to five or six choices? Your guidance counselor can help with this process. Once you have your top choices, make a list of what each college requires for admission and financial aid. Be sure your list includes all deadlines. Attend a financial aid night presentation with your parents. Some of these sessions offer help in completing forms; others offer a broader view of the process. Contact the presenter (usually a local college financial aid professional) to be sure you are getting the information you need.

- ❑ Do any of these colleges require the CSS/Financial Aid PROFILE® financial aid application? Many private colleges use this form for institutional aid. You need to file this comprehensive form in late September or early October. For more information or to find out which colleges use this supplemental form, go to http://profileonline.collegeboard.com/index.jsp. (Website registration is free; however, PROFILE® is a fee-based application).
- ❑ Don't falter now in your scholarship search. Get the applications filed by the published deadlines.
- ❑ Register now if you are planning to retake the SAT®.
- ❑ Most important, start completing your college applications—the earlier, the better! If you are interested in early decision or early action, now is the time! Remember, accuracy and completeness are a must!

Winter

- ❑ Ensure all college applications are completed.
- ❑ Get the Free Application for Federal Student Aid (FAFSA). This is the key form for financial aid for every school across the country. Remember, watch your deadlines, but do not file until after January 1. Be sure to keep a copy of the form, whether you file electronically or with the paper application. Do you have some questions? Call the local financial aid office. Many states have special toll-free call-in programs in January and February, Financial Aid Awareness Month. Be sure that you have completed each school's required forms.
- ❑ As the letters of admission start to arrive, the financial aid award letters should be right behind them. Important question for parents: What is the bottom line? Remember, aid at a lower-cost state school will be less than a higher-cost private college. But what will you be required to pay? This can be confusing, so consider gift aid (scholarships and grants), student loans, and parent loans. The school with the lowest sticker price (tuition, fees, and room and board) might not be the best bargain when you look at the overall financial aid package.

Spring

- ❑ Still not sure where to go? The financial aid package at your top choice just not enough? Call the financial aid office and the admissions office. Talk it over. While schools don't like to bargain, they are usually willing to take a second look. Is there something unusual about your family's financial situation that might impact your parents' ability to pay?
- ❑ By May 1, you must make your final decision. Notify your chosen college and find out what you need to do next. Tell the other colleges you are not accepting their offers of admission and financial aid.

Summer

- ❑ Time to crunch the numbers. Parents, get information from the college on the total charges for the coming fall term. Deduct the aid package and then plan for how the balance will be paid. Contact the college financial aid office for the best parental loan program. If you want to arrange for a payment plan, contact the business office for further information. Most schools have deferred payment plans available for a nominal fee.

Congratulations! Remember that you need to reapply for aid every year!

Who's Paying for This? Financial Aid Basics

A college education can be expensive—costing more than $150,000 for four years at some of the higher priced private colleges and universities. Even at the lower-cost state colleges and universities, the cost of a four-year education can approach $60,000. Determining how you and your family will come up with the necessary funds to pay for your education requires planning, perseverance, and learning as much as you can about the options that are available to you. But before you get discouraged, College Board statistics show that 53 percent of full-time students attend four-year public and private colleges with tuition and fees less than $9,000, while 20 percent attend colleges that have tuition and fees more than $36,000. College costs tend to be less in the western states and higher in New England.

Paying for college should not be looked at as a four-year financial commitment. For many families, paying the total cost of a student's college education out of current income and savings is usually not realistic. For families that have planned ahead and have financial savings established for higher education, the burden is a lot easier. But for most, meeting the cost of college requires the pooling of current income and assets and investing in longer-term loan options. These family resources, together with financial assistance from state, federal, and institutional sources, enable millions of students each year to attend the institution of their choice.

FINANCIAL AID PROGRAMS

There are three types of financial aid:

1. Gift-aid—Scholarships and grants are funds that do not have to be repaid.
2. Loans—Loans must be repaid, usually after graduation; the amount you have to pay back is the total you've borrowed plus any accrued interest. This is considered a source of self-help aid.
3. Student employment—Student employment is a job arranged for you by the financial aid office. This is another source of self-help aid.

The federal government has four major grant programs—the Federal Pell Grant, the Federal Supplemental Educational Opportunity Grant, Academic Competitiveness Grants (ACG), and National SMART (Science and Mathematics Access to Retain Talent) grants. ACG and SMART grants are limited to students who qualify for a Pell Grant and are awarded to a select group of students. Overall, these grants are targeted to low-to-moderate income families with significant financial need. The federal government also sponsors a student employment program called the Federal Work-Study Program, which offers jobs both on and off campus, and several loan programs, including those for students and for parents of undergraduate students.

There are two types of student loan programs: subsidized and unsubsidized. The subsidized Federal Direct Loan and the Federal Perkins Loan are need-based, government-subsidized loans. Students who borrow through these programs do not have to pay interest on the loan until after they graduate or leave school. The unsubsidized Federal Direct Loan and the Federal Direct PLUS Loan Program are not based on need, and borrowers are responsible for the interest while the student is in school. These loans are administered by different methods. Once you choose your college, the financial aid office will guide you through this process.

After you've submitted your financial aid application and you've been accepted for admission, each college will send you a letter describing your financial aid award. Most award letters show estimated college costs, how much you and your family are expected to contribute, and the amount and types of aid you have been awarded. Most students are awarded aid from a combination of sources and programs. Hence, your award is often called a financial aid "package."

SOURCES OF FINANCIAL AID

Millions of students and families apply for financial aid each year. Financial aid from all sources exceeds $143 billion per year. The largest single source of aid is the federal government, which will award more than $100 billion this year.

The next largest source of financial aid is found in the college and university community. Most of this aid is awarded to students who have a demonstrated need based on the Federal Methodology. Some institutions use a different formula, the Institutional Methodology (IM), to award their own funds in conjunction with other forms of aid. Institutional aid may be either need-based or non-need based. Aid that is not based on need is usually awarded for a student's academic performance (merit awards), specific talents or abilities, or to attract the type of students a college seeks to enroll.

Another source of financial aid is from state government. All states offer grant and/or scholarship aid, most of which is need-based. However, more and more states are offering substantial merit-based aid programs. Most state programs award aid only to students attending college in their home state.

Other sources of financial aid include:

- Private agencies
- Foundations
- Corporations
- Clubs

- Fraternal and service organizations
- Civic associations
- Unions
- Religious groups that award grants, scholarships, and low-interest loans
- Employers that provide tuition reimbursement benefits for employees and their children

More information about these different sources of aid is available from high school guidance offices, public libraries, college financial aid offices, directly from the sponsoring organizations, and online at www.petersons.com/college-search/scholarship-search.aspx.

HOW NEED-BASED FINANCIAL AID IS AWARDED

When you apply for aid, your family's financial situation is analyzed using a government-approved formula called the Federal Methodology. This formula looks at five items:

1. Demographic information of the family
2. Income of the parents
3. Assets of the parents
4. Income of the student
5. Assets of the student

This analysis determines the amount you and your family are expected to contribute toward your college expenses, called your Expected Family Contribution, or EFC. If the EFC is equal to or more than the cost of attendance at a particular college, then you do not demonstrate financial need. However, even if you don't have financial need, you may still qualify for aid, as there are grants, scholarships, and loan programs that are not need-based.

If the cost of your education is greater than your EFC, then you do demonstrate financial need and qualify for assistance. The amount of your financial need that can be met varies from school to school. Some are able to meet your full need, while others can only cover a certain percentage of need. Here's the formula:

Cost of Attendance
− Expected Family Contribution
= Financial Need

The EFC remains constant, but your need will vary according to the costs of attendance at a particular college. In general, the higher the tuition and fees at a particular college, the higher the cost of attendance will be. Expenses for books and supplies, room and board, transportation, and other miscellaneous items are included in the overall cost of attendance. It is important to remember that you do not have to be low-income to qualify for financial aid. Many middle and upper-middle income families qualify for need-based financial aid.

APPLYING FOR FINANCIAL AID

Every student must complete the Free Application for Federal Student Aid (FAFSA) to be considered for financial aid. The FAFSA is available from your high school guidance office, many public libraries, colleges in your area, or directly from the U.S. Department of Education.

Students are encouraged to apply for federal student aid on the Web. The electronic version of the FAFSA can be accessed at http://www.fafsa.ed.gov. Both the student and at least one parent must apply for a federal PIN at http:// www.pin.ed.gov. The PIN serves as your electronic signature when applying for aid on the Web.

To award their own funds, some colleges require an additional application, the CSS/Financial Aid PROFILE® form. The PROFILE asks supplemental questions that some colleges and awarding agencies feel provide a more accurate assessment of the family's ability to pay for college. It is up to the college to decide whether it will use only the FAFSA or both the FAFSA and the PROFILE. PROFILE applications are available from the high school guidance office and on the Web. Both the paper application and the website list those colleges and programs that require the PROFILE application.

If Every College You're Applying to for Fall 2016 Requires the FAFSA

. . . then it's pretty simple: Complete the FAFSA after January 1, 2016, being certain to send it in before any college-imposed deadlines. (You are not permitted to send in the 2016–17 FAFSA before January 1, 2016.) Most college FAFSA application deadlines are in February or early March. It is easier if you have all your financial records for the previous year available, but if that is not possible, you are strongly encouraged to use estimated figures.

After you send in your FAFSA, either with the paper application or electronically, you'll receive a Student Aid Report (SAR) that includes all of the information you reported and shows your EFC. If you provided an e-mail address, the SAR is sent to you electronically; otherwise, you will receive a SAR or SAR Acknowledgment in the mail, which lists your FAFSA information but may require you to make any corrections on the FAFSA website. Be sure to review the SAR, checking to see if the information you reported is accurately represented. If you used estimated numbers to complete the FAFSA, you may have to resubmit the SAR with any corrections to the data. The college(s) you have designated on the FAFSA will receive the information you reported and will use that data to make their decision. In many instances, the colleges to which you've applied will ask you to send copies of your and your parents' federal income tax returns for 2015, plus any other documents needed to verify the information you reported.

If a College Requires the PROFILE

Step 1: Register for the CSS/Financial Aid PROFILE in the fall of your senior year in high school. You can apply for the PROFILE online at http://profileonline.collegeboard.com/prf/index.jsp. Registration information with a list of the colleges that require the PROFILE is available in most high school guidance offices. There is a fee for using the Financial Aid PROFILE application ($25 for the first college, which includes the $9 application fee, and $16 for each additional college). You must pay for the service by credit card when you register. If you do not have a credit card, you will be billed. A limited number of fee waivers are automatically granted to first-time applicants based on the financial information provided on the PROFILE.

Step 2: Fill out your customized CSS/Financial Aid PROFILE. Once you register, your application will be immediately available online and will have questions that all students must complete, questions which must be completed by the student's parents (unless the student is independent and the colleges or programs selected do not require parental information), and *may* have supplemental questions needed by one or more of your schools or programs. If required, those will be found in Section Q of the application.

In addition to the PROFILE application you complete online, you may also be required to complete a Business/ Farm Supplement via traditional paper format. Completion of this form is not a part of the online process. If this form is required, instructions on how to download and print the supplemental form are provided. If your biological or adoptive parents are separated or divorced and your colleges and programs require it, your noncustodial parent may be asked to complete the Noncustodial PROFILE.

Once you complete and submit your PROFILE application, it will be processed and sent directly to your requested colleges and programs.

IF YOU DON'T QUALIFY FOR NEED-BASED AID

If you are not eligible for need-based aid, you can still find ways to lessen your burden.

Here are some suggestions:

- Search for merit scholarships. You can start at the initial stages of your application process. College merit awards are increasingly important as more and more colleges award these to students they especially want to attract. As a result, applying to a college at which your qualifications put you at the top of the entering class may give you a larger merit award. Another source of aid to look for is private scholarships that are given for special skills and talents. Additional information can be found at www.finaid.org.
- Seek employment during the summer and the academic year. The student employment office at your college can help you locate a school-year job. Many colleges and local businesses have vacancies remaining after they have hired students who are receiving Federal Work-Study Program financial aid.
- Borrow through the unsubsidized Federal Direct Loan program. This is generally available to all students. The terms and conditions are similar to the subsidized loans. The biggest difference is that the borrower is responsible for the interest while still in college, although the government permits students to delay paying the interest right away and add the accrued interest to the total amount owed. You must file the FAFSA to be considered.
- After you've secured what you can through scholarships, working, and borrowing, you and your parents will be expected to meet your share of the college bill (the Expected Family Contribution). Many colleges offer monthly payment plans that spread the cost over the academic year. If the monthly payments are too high, parents can borrow through the Federal Direct PLUS Loan Program, through one of the many private education loan programs available, or through home equity loans and lines of credit. Families seeking assistance in financing college expenses should inquire at the financial aid office about what programs are available at the college. Some families seek the advice of professional financial advisers and tax consultants.

How to Use This Guide

PROFILES

The **PROFILES** section contains basic data in capsule form for quick review and comparison. Organized by state, more than 2,000 colleges and universities are listed alphabetically, followed by their city and state and website URL. Those schools that offer a special, detailed listing at www.petersons.com, as well as a two-page description in this guide, will also have a ★ next to their name.

The following outline of the format shows the section headings and the items that each section covers. Any item that does not apply to a particular college or for which no information was supplied is omitted from that college's listing. Display ads, which appear near some of the institutions' profiles, have been provided and paid for by those colleges and universities that chose to supplement their profile with additional information.

Category Overviews

Type of Institution

Private institutions are designated as *independent* (nonprofit), *proprietary* (profit-making), or *independent with a specific religious denomination or affiliation*. Nondenominational or interdenominational religious orientation is possible and would be indicated. Public institutions are designated by the source of funding. Designations include *federal, state, province, commonwealth* (Puerto Rico), *territory* (U.S. territories), *county, district* (an educational administrative unit often having boundaries different from units of local government), *city, state and local* (local may refer to county, district, or city), or *state-related* (funded primarily by the state but administratively autonomous). *Religious affiliation* may follow, along with year founded. Each institution is classified as one of the following:

- Primarily two-year: Awards baccalaureate degrees but majority of students are enrolled in two-year programs.
- Four-year: Awards baccalaureate degrees; may also award associate degrees; does not award graduate (postbaccalaureate) degrees.
- Five-year: Awards a five-year baccalaureate in a professional field such as architecture or pharmacy; does not award graduate degrees.
- Upper-level: Awards baccalaureate degrees, but entering students must have at least two years of previous college-level credit; may also offer graduate degrees.
- Comprehensive: Awards baccalaureate degrees; may also award associate degrees; offers graduate degree programs, primarily at the master's, specialist's, or professional level, although one or two doctoral programs may be offered.
- University: Offers four years of undergraduate work, plus graduate degrees through the doctorate in more than two academic or professional fields.

Setting

Designated as *urban* (located within a major city), *suburban* (a residential area within commuting distance of a major city), *small town* (a small but compactly settled area not within commuting distance of a major city), or *rural* (a remote and sparsely populated area).

Endowment

The total dollar value of funds and/or property donated to the institution or the multicampus educational system of which the institution is a part.

Student body

An institution is *coed* (coeducational—admits men and women), *primarily* (80 percent or more) *women, primarily men, women only,* or *men only.* A few schools are designated as *undergraduate: women only; graduate: coed* or *undergraduate: men only; graduate: coed.*

Entrance

The five levels of entrance difficulty *(most difficult, very difficult, moderately difficult, minimally difficult,* and *noncompetitive)* are based on the percentage of applicants who were accepted for fall 2014 freshman admission (or, in the case of upper-level schools, for entering-class admission) and on the high school class rank and standardized test scores of the accepted freshmen who actually enrolled in fall 2014. The colleges were asked to select the level that most closely corresponds to their entrance difficulty, according to these guidelines.

UNDERGRAD STUDENTS

Number of full-time or part-time undergraduates. Number of states and territories that students come from; percentages of undergraduates who are out-of state; live on campus; Black or African American, non-Hispanic/Latino; Hispanic/Latino; Asian, non-Hispanic/Latino; Native Hawaiian or other Pacific Islander, non-Hispanic/Latino; American Indian or Alaska Native, non-Hispanic/Latino American Indian or Alaska Native, non-Hispanic/Latino; two or more races, non-Hispanic/Latino; race/ethnicity unknown; international; and percentage of students who transferred in are given.

Freshmen

Admission: Figures are given for the number of students who applied for fall 2014 admission, the number of those who were admitted, and the number who enrolled. *Average high school GPA:* Freshman statistics include the average high school GPA. *Test scores:* Percentage of freshmen who took the SAT and received critical reading, math, and writing scores above 500, above 600, and above 700; as well as percentage of freshmen taking the ACT who received a composite score of 18 or higher, 24 or higher, and 30 or higher.

Retention: The percentage of full-time freshmen who returned the following year for the fall semester/term.

FACULTY

Total: The total number of faculty members; percentage of full-time faculty members as of fall 2014; and percentage of total faculty members who hold terminal degrees. *Student/faculty ratio:* School's estimate of the ratio of matriculated undergraduate students to faculty members teaching undergraduate courses.

ACADEMICS

Calendar: Most colleges indicate one of the following: 4-1-4, 4-4-1, or a similar arrangement (two terms of equal length plus an abbreviated winter or spring term, with the numbers referring to months); semesters; trimesters; quarters; 3-3 (three courses for each of three terms); modular (the academic year is divided into small blocks of time; courses of varying lengths are assembled according to individual programs); or standard year (for most Canadian institutions). *Degrees:* This names the full range of levels of certificates, diplomas, and degrees, including prebaccalaureate, baccalaureate, graduate, and professional, that are offered by this institution.

Special study options: Details on study options available at each college, such as accelerated degree program, academic remediation for entering students, Advanced Placement credit, cooperative education programs, distance learning, double majors, English as a second language (ESL), and external degree programs. *ROTC:* Army, Naval, or Air Force Reserve Officers' Training Corps programs offered either on campus, at a branch campus [designated by a (b)], or at a cooperating host institution [designated by (c)].

Unusual degree programs: Information is offered here on any unique programs at the institution, such as 3-2 engineering, computer science, or business administration programs.

Computers: Information is provided on the numbers of computers/terminals available on campus for general student use, what computer technology is accessible to students, and availability of a campuswide network and wireless campus network.

STUDENT LIFE

Housing options: Institution's policy about whether students are permitted to live off-campus or are required to live on campus for a specified period; whether freshmen only, coed, single-sex, cooperative, and disabled student housing options are available; whether campus housing is leased by the school and/or provided by a third party; whether freshman applicants are given priority for college housing. "College housing not available" indicates that no college-owned or -operated housing facilities are provided for undergraduates and that noncommuting students must arrange for their own accommodations.

Activities and organizations: Information on clubs and organizations, including sororities and fraternities.

Athletics: Membership in one or more of the following athletic associations is indicated by initials: NCAA: National Collegiate Athletic Association; NAIA: National Association of Intercollegiate Athletics; NCCAA: National Christian College Athletic Association; USCAA: United States Collegiate Athletic Association; and CIS: Canadian Interuniversity Sport. The overall NCAA division in which all or most intercollegiate teams compete is designated by I, II, or III. All teams that do not compete in this division are listed as exceptions.

Sports offered by the college are divided into two groups: *Intercollegiate* ("M" or "W" following the name of each sport indicates that it is offered for men or women) and *Intramural.* An "s" in parentheses following an "M" or "W" for an intercollegiate sport indicates that athletic scholarships (or grants-in-aid) are offered for men or women in that sport, and a "c" indicates a club team as opposed to a varsity team.

Campus security: Campus safety measures including 24-hour emergency response devices (phones and alarms) and patrols by trained security personnel, student patrols, late-night transport-escort service, and controlled dormitory access (key, security card, etc.).

Student services: Information indicates services offered to students by the college, such as legal services, health clinics, personal-psychological counseling, and women's centers.

COSTS & FINANCIAL AID

Costs: Costs are given for the 2015–16 academic year or for the 2014–15 academic year if 2015–16 figures were not yet available. *Tuition:* Annual expenses may be expressed as a comprehensive fee (including full-time tuition, mandatory fees, and college room and board) or as separate figures for full-time tuition, fees, room and board, or room only. For public institutions where tuition differs according to residence, separate figures are given for area or state residents and for nonresidents. Part-time tuition is expressed in terms of a per-unit rate (per credit, per semester hour, etc.).

The tuition structure at some institutions is complex in that freshmen and sophomores may be charged a different rate from that for juniors and seniors, a professional or vocational division may have a different fee structure from the liberal arts division of the same institution, or part-time tuition may be prorated on a sliding scale according to the number of credit hours taken. Tuition and fees may vary according to academic program, campus/location, class time (day, evening, weekend), course/credit load, course level, degree level, reciprocity agreements, and student level. *Room and board* charges are reported as an average for one academic year and may vary according to the board plan selected, campus/location, type of housing facility, or student level. *Payment plans* may include tuition prepayment, installment payments, and deferred payment. A tuition prepayment plan gives a student the option of locking in the current tuition rate for the entire term of enrollment by paying the full amount in advance rather than year by year. *Waivers:* availability of full or partial undergraduate tuition waivers to minority students, children of alumni, employees or their children, adult students, and senior citizens may be listed.

Financial Aid: This information represents aid awarded to undergraduates for the available academic year. Figures are given for the number of undergraduates who applied for aid, the number who were judged to have need, and the number who had their need met. The number of Federal Work-Study Programs and/or part-time jobs and average earnings are listed, as well as the number of non-need-based awards. The *Average percent of need met* for those determined to have need, *Average financial aid package* awarded to undergraduates (the amount of scholarships, grants, work-study payments, or loans in the institutionally administered financial aid package divided by the number of students who received any financial aid-amounts used to pay the officially designated Expected Family Contribution (EFC), *Average need-based loan, Average need-based gift aid,* and *Average non-need-based aid* are given. *Average indebtedness upon graduation,* which is the average per-borrower indebtedness of the last graduating undergraduate class from amounts borrowed at this institution through any loan programs, excluding parent loans, is listed last.

APPLYING

Standardized Tests

The most commonly required standardized tests are the ACT®, SAT®, and SAT Subject Tests™. These and other standardized tests may be used for selective admission, as a basis for counseling or course placement, or for both purposes. This section notes if a test is used for admission or placement and whether it is required, required for some, or recommended. In addition to the ACT and SAT, the following standardized entrance and placement examinations are referred to by their initials: ABLE (Adult Basic Learning Examination); ACT ASSET (ACT Assessment of Skills for Successful Entry and Transfer); ACT PEP (ACT Proficiency Examination Program); CAT (California Achievement Tests); CELT (Comprehensive English Language Test); CPAt (Career Programs Assessment); CPT (Computerized Placement Test); DAT (Differential Aptitude Test); LSAT (Law School Admission Test); MAPS (Multiple Assessment Program Service); MCAT (Medical College Admission Test); MMPI (Minnesota Multiphasic Personality Inventory); OAT (Optometry Admission Test); PAA (Prueba de Aptitud Académica—Spanish-language version of SAT); PCAT (Pharmacy College Admission Test); PSAT/NMSQT® (Preliminary SAT/National Merit Scholarship Qualifying Test); SCAT (Scholastic College Aptitude Test); TABE (Test of Adult Basic Education); TASP (Texas Academic Skills Program); TOEFL® (Test of English as a Foreign Language); WPCT (Washington Pre-College Test).

Options: This includes the following: Early admission—(highly qualified students may matriculate before graduating from high school); Early action—admission plan that allows students to apply and be notified of an admission decision well in advance of the regular notification dates (if accepted, the candidate is not committed to enroll; students may reply to the offer under the college's regular reply policy); Deferred entrance—practice of permitting accepted students to postpone enrollment, usually for a period of one academic term or year; Early decision deadline—plan that permits students to apply and be notified of an admission decision (and financial aid offer, if applicable) well in advance of the regular notification date, and applicants agree to accept an offer of admission and to withdraw their applications from other colleges.

Application fee: The fee required with an application is noted.

Required, Required for some, and Recommended: Other application requirements are grouped into three categories and may include an essay, standardized test scores, a high school transcript, a minimum high school grade point average (expressed as a number on a scale of 0 to 4.0, where 4.0 equals A, 3.0 equals B, etc.), letters of recommendation, an interview on campus or with local alumni, and, for certain types of schools or programs, special requirements such as a musical audition or an art portfolio.

Application deadlines and notification: Admission application deadlines and dates for notification of acceptance or rejection are given either as specific dates or as rolling and continuous. Rolling means that applications are processed as they are received, and qualified students are accepted as long as there are openings. Continuous means that applicants are notified of acceptance or rejection as applications are processed up until the date indicated or the actual beginning of classes. The application deadline and the notification date for transfers are given if they differ from the dates for freshmen. Early decision and early action application deadlines and notification dates are also indicated when relevant.

CONTACT

The name, title, mailing address, and phone number of the person to contact for further information are given at the end of the profile. The fax number and e-mail address may also be provided.

Additional Information

Each school that has a College Close-Up and a half-page display in this guide will have a cross-reference with the page numbers of the half-page display and Close-Up.

Other Colleges To Consider

Here you'll find a list of additional four-year institutions and their contact information. These schools did not provide information in Peterson's Annual Survey of Undergraduate Institutions in recent years, but we've provided their contact information to help you find the additional information you may be seeking.

COLLEGE CLOSE-UPS

The over 200 two-page descriptions provide an inside look at colleges and universities. The descriptions provide a wealth of information that is crucial in the college decision-making process—components such as tuition, financial aid, and major fields of study. Prepared exclusively by college officials, the descriptions are designed to help give students a better sense of the individuality of each institution, in terms that include campus environment, student activities, and lifestyle. The absence of any college or university does not constitute an editorial decision on the part of Peterson's. In essence, these descriptions are an open forum for colleges and universities, on a voluntary basis, to communicate their particular message to prospective college students. The colleges included have paid a fee to Peterson's to provide this information. The College Close-Ups are edited to provide a consistent format across entries for your ease of comparison.

INDEXES

Here you'll find easy-to-use breakdowns of schools' majors, entrance difficulty, and cost ranges. In addition, you'll find an "Advertisers Index," a "Geographical Listing of College Close-Ups," and an "Alphabetical Listing of Colleges and Universities."

Majors

This listing presents hundreds of undergraduate fields of study that are currently offered, according to the colleges' responses on *Peterson's® Annual Survey of Undergraduate Institutions*. The majors appear in alphabetical order, each followed by an alphabetical list of the schools that offer a bachelor's-level program in that particular field. Liberal Arts and Studies indicates a general program with no specified major.

The terms used are those of the U.S. Department of Education Classification of Instructional Programs (CIP). Many institutions, however, use different terms. Although the term major is used in this guide, some colleges may use other terms, such as concentration, program of study, or field.

Entrance Difficulty

This listing groups colleges by their own assessment of their entrance difficulty level. The colleges were asked to select the level that most closely corresponds to their entrance difficulty. Institutions for which high school class rank and/or standardized test scores do not apply as admission criteria were asked to select the level that best indicates their entrance difficulty as compared to other institutions.

Cost Ranges

Colleges are grouped into thirteen price ranges, from under $2000 to $30,000 and over.

DATA COLLECTION PROCEDURES

The data contained in the **PROFILES** and **INDEXES** sections were researched between winter 2014 and spring 2015 through *Peterson's® Annual Survey of Undergraduate Institutions*. Questionnaires were sent to the more than 4,600 colleges and universities that met the outlined inclusion criteria. All data included in this edition have been submitted by officials (usually admissions and financial aid officers, registrars, or institutional research personnel) at the colleges. Some of the institutions that submitted data were contacted directly by the Peterson's research staff to verify unusual figures, resolve discrepancies, or obtain additional data. All usable information received in time for publication has been included. The omission of any particular item from the **PROFILES** and **INDEXES** sections signifies that the information is either not applicable to that institution or not available. Because of Peterson's comprehensive editorial review and because all material comes directly from college officials, we believe that the information presented is accurate. You should check with a specific college or university at the time of application to verify such figures as tuition and fees, which may have changed since this guide's publication.

CRITERIA FOR INCLUSION IN THIS BOOK

The term "four-year college" is the commonly used designation for institutions that grant the baccalaureate degree. Four years is the expected amount of time required to earn this degree, although some bachelor's degree programs may be completed in three years, others require five years, and part-time programs may take considerably longer. Upper-level institutions offer only the junior and senior years and accept only students with two years of college-level credit. Therefore, "four-year college" is a conventional term that accurately describes most of the institutions included in this guide, but should not be taken literally in all cases.

To be included in this guide, an institution must have full accreditation or be a candidate for accreditation (preaccreditation) status by an institutional or specialized accrediting body recognized by the U.S. Department of Education or the Council for Higher Education Accreditation (CHEA). Institutional accrediting bodies, which review each institution as a whole, include the six regional associations of schools and colleges (Middle States, New England, North Central, Northwest, Southern, and Western), each of which is responsible for a specified portion of the United States and its territories. Other institutional accrediting bodies are national in scope and accredit specific kinds of institutions (e.g., Bible colleges, independent colleges, and rabbinical and Talmudic schools). Program registration by the New York State Board of Regents is considered to be the equivalent of institutional accreditation, since the board requires that all programs offered by an institution meet its standards before recognition is granted. A Canadian institution must be chartered and authorized to grant degrees by the provincial government, affiliated with a chartered institution, or accredited by a recognized U.S. accrediting body. This guide also includes institutions outside the United States that are accredited by these U.S. accrediting bodies. There are recognized specialized or professional accrediting bodies in more than forty different fields, each of which is authorized to accredit institutions or specific programs in its particular field. For specialized institutions that offer programs in one field only, we designate this to be the equivalent of institutional accreditation. A full explanation of the accrediting process and complete information on recognized, institutional (regional and national) and specialized accrediting bodies can be found online at www.chea.org or at www2.ed.gov/admins/finaid/accred/index.html.

NOTICE: Certain portions of or information contained in this book have been submitted and paid for by the educational institution identified, and such institutions take full responsibility for the accuracy, timeliness, completeness and functionality of such content. Such portions or information include (i) each display ad in the "Profiles" section from pages 55 through 1334 that comprises a half or full page of information covering a single educational institution, and (ii) each two-page description in the "College Close-Up" section from pages 1336 through 1745.

Institutional Changes Since *Peterson's*® *Four-Year Colleges* 2015

The following is an alphabetical listing of institutions that have closed, merged with other institutions, or changed their names or status since *Peterson's*® *Four-Year Colleges* 2015.

AIB College of Business (Des Moines, IA): *closed.*

Alberta Bible College (Calgary, AB, Canada): *not accredited by an agency recognized by USDE or CHEA at the time of publication.*

Alliant International University (San Diego, CA): *name changed to Alliant International University–San Diego.*

American Institute (Celebration, FL): *name changed to American College for Medical Careers.*

American InterContinental University South Florida (Weston, FL): *closed.*

Armstrong Atlantic State University (Savannah, GA): *name changed to Armstrong State University.*

Ave Maria University–Latin American Campus (San Marcos, Nicaragua): *closed.*

Baker College of Allen Park (Allen Park, MI): *merged into a single entry for Baker College (Flint, MI) by request from the institution.*

Baker College of Auburn Hills (Auburn Hills, MI): *merged into a single entry for Baker College (Flint, MI) by request from the institution.*

Baker College of Cadillac (Cadillac, MI): *merged into a single entry for Baker College (Flint, MI) by request from the institution.*

Baker College of Clinton Township (Clinton Township, MI): *merged into a single entry for Baker College (Flint, MI) by request from the institution.*

Baker College of Flint (Flint, MI): *profile includes entire Baker College system by request from the institution.*

Baker College of Jackson (Jackson, MI): *merged into a single entry for Baker College (Flint, MI) by request from the institution.*

Baker College of Muskegon (Muskegon, MI): *merged into a single entry for Baker College (Flint, MI) by request from the institution.*

Baker College of Owosso (Owosso, MI): *merged into a single entry for Baker College (Flint, MI) by request from the institution.*

Baker College of Port Huron (Port Huron, MI): *merged into a single entry for Baker College (Flint, MI) by request from the institution.*

Baptist Bible College of Pennsylvania (Clarks Summit, PA): *name changed to Summit University.*

Bauder College (Atlanta, GA): *closed.*

Bay Path College (Longmeadow, MA): *name changed to Bay Path University.*

Bethesda University of California (Anaheim, CA): *name changed to Bethesda University.*

Brown College (Brooklyn Center, MN): *name changed to Sanford-Brown College.*

Caldwell College (Caldwell, NJ): *name changed to Caldwell University.*

California College (San Diego, CA): *name changed to California College San Diego.*

Capitol College (Laurel, MD): *name changed to Capitol Technology University.*

College of Mount St. Joseph (Cincinnati, OH): *name changed to Mount St. Joseph University.*

College of Saint Mary Magdalen (Warner, NH): *name changed to Northeast Catholic College.*

The College of Saints John Fisher & Thomas More (Fort Worth, TX): *closed.*

Colorado Mountain College, Alpine Campus (Steamboat Springs, CO): *name changed to Colorado Mountain College.*

Colorado Mountain College, Timberline Campus (Leadville, CO): *name changed to Colorado Mountain College.*

Corcoran College of Art and Design (Washington, DC): *merged as a unit into The George Washington University (Washington, DC).*

Delaware Valley College (Doylestown, PA): *name changed to Delaware Valley University.*

DeVry University (Daly City, CA): *closed.*

DeVry University (Elk Grove, CA): *closed.*

DeVry University (Miami, FL): *closed.*

DeVry University (Columbus, OH): *closed.*

DeVry University (Richardson, TX): *closed.*

DeVry University (Bellevue, WA): *closed.*

DeVry University (Waukesha, WI): *closed.*

Harrington College of Design (Chicago, IL): *closed.*

Heritage Baptist College and Heritage Theological Seminary (Cambridge, ON, Canada): *name changed to Heritage College and Seminary.*

International Academy of Design & Technology (Orlando, FL): *closed.*

International Academy of Design & Technology (Tampa, FL): *closed.*

International Academy of Design & Technology (Chicago, IL): *closed.*

International Academy of Design & Technology (Henderson, NV): *closed.*

International Academy of Design & Technology (San Antonio, TX): *closed.*

International Academy of Design & Technology (Seattle, WA): *name changed to Sanford-Brown College.*

International Baptist College (Chandler, AZ): *name changed to International Baptist College and Seminary.*

ITT Technical Institute (Grand Rapids, MI): *closed.*

ITT Technical Institute (Germantown, WI): *closed.*

John Hancock University (Oakbrook Terrace, IL): *name changed to Ellis University.*

Jones International University (Centennial, CO): *closed.*

Lexington College (Chicago, IL): *closed.*

Institutional Changes Since Peterson's® Four-Year Colleges 2015

Lindenwood University–Belleville (Belleville, IL): *merged into a single entry for Lindenwood University (St. Charles, MO) by request from the institution.*

Luther Rice University (Lithonia, GA): *name changed to Luther Rice College & Seminary.*

Maranatha Baptist Bible College (Watertown, WI): *name changed to Maranatha Baptist University.*

Minnesota School of Business–Moorhead (Moorhead, MN): *name changed to Globe University–Moorhead.*

Minnesota School of Business–Shakopee (Shakopee, MN): *closed.*

Morrison University (Reno, NV): *closed.*

Mount St. Mary's College (Los Angeles, CA): *name changed to Mount Saint Mary's University.*

New England School of Communications (Bangor, ME): *merged as a unit into Husson University (Bangor, ME).*

New Life Theological Seminary (Charlotte, NC): *name changed to Charlotte Christian College and Theological Seminary.*

Northland International University (Dunbar, WI): *will become a campus of Southern Baptist Theological Seminary (Louisville, KY).*

Northwood University, Florida Campus (West Palm Beach, FL): *is now Keiser University.*

Ohio Mid-Western College (Sharonville, OH): *not accredited by an agency recognized by USDE or CHEA at the time of publication.*

The Richard Stockton College of New Jersey (Galloway, NJ): *name changed to Stockton University.*

Sanford College of Nursing (Bismarck, ND): *merged as a unit into North Dakota State University (Fargo, ND).*

Sojourner-Douglass College (Baltimore, MD): *closed.*

Southern Methodist College (Orangeburg, SC): *not accredited by an agency recognized by USDE or CHEA at the time of publication.*

Southwest Florida College (Fort Myers, FL): *name changed to Southern Technical College.*

State University of New York Institute of Technology (Utica, NY): *name changed to State University of New York Polytechnic Institute.*

Sweet Briar College (Sweet Briar, VA): *closed.*

Tennessee Temple University (Chattanooga, TN): *closed.*

Texas A&M Health Science Center (College Station, TX): *merged into a single entry for Texas A&M University (College Station, TX) by request from the institution.*

Texas A&M University at Galveston (Galveston, TX): *merged into a single entry for Texas A&M University (College Station, TX) by request from the institution.*

Texas State University–San Marcos (San Marcos, TX): *name changed to Texas State University.*

The University of British Columbia–Okanagan (Kelowna, BC, Canada): *name changed to The University of British Columbia–Okanagan Campus.*

University of Phoenix–Central Massachusetts Campus (Westborough, MA): *closed.*

University of Phoenix–Chattanooga Campus (Chattanooga, TN): *now a Learning Center, not a Campus.*

University of Phoenix–Cheyenne Campus (Cheyenne, WY): *closed.*

University of Phoenix–Cincinnati Campus (West Chester, OH): *closed.*

University of Phoenix–Columbus Ohio Campus (Columbus, OH): *closed.*

University of Phoenix–Denver Campus (Lone Tree, CO): *name changed to University of Phoenix–Colorado Campus.*

University of Phoenix–Eastern Washington Campus (Spokane, WA): *closed.*

University of Phoenix–Louisiana Campus (Metairie, LA): *now a Learning Center, not a Campus.*

University of Phoenix–Madison Campus (Madison, WI): *closed.*

University of Phoenix–Metro Detroit Campus (Troy, MI): *closed.*

University of Phoenix–Minneapolis/St. Louis Park Campus (St. Louis Park, MN): *name changed to University of Phoenix–Minneapolis/St. Paul Campus.*

University of Phoenix–Northwest Arkansas Campus (Rogers, AR): *closed.*

University of Phoenix–Omaha Campus (Omaha, NE): *closed.*

University of Phoenix–Pittsburgh Campus (Pittsburgh, PA): *closed.*

University of Phoenix–Southern Colorado Campus (Colorado Springs, CO): *name changed to University of Phoenix–Colorado Springs Downtown Campus.*

University of Phoenix–Springfield Campus (Springfield, MO): *closed.*

University of Phoenix–Tulsa Campus (Tulsa, OK): *now a Learning Center, not a Campus.*

University of Phoenix–West Florida Campus (Temple Terrace, FL): *now a Learning Center, not a Campus.*

University of Phoenix–Wichita Campus (Wichita, KS): *closed.*

University of South Florida–St. Petersburg Campus (St. Petersburg, FL): *name changed to University of South Florida, St. Petersburg.*

Valley Forge Christian College (Phoenixville, PA): *name changed to University of Valley Forge.*

Valley Forge Christian College Woodbridge Campus (Woodbridge, VA): *name changed to University of Valley Forge Virginia Campus.*

Virginia Intermont College (Bristol, VA): *closed.*

World College (Virginia Beach, VA): *closed.*

Profiles

NOTICE: Certain portions of or information contained in this book have been submitted and paid for by the educational institution identified, and such institutions take full responsibility for the accuracy, timeliness, completeness and functionality of such content. Such portions or information include (i) each display ad in the "Profiles" section from pages 55 through 1334 that comprises a half or full page of information covering a single educational institution, and (ii) each two-page description in the "College Close-Up" section from pages 1336 through 1745.

A ★ indicates that the school has detailed information with a Premium Profile on Petersons.com.

UNITED STATES AND U.S. TERRITORIES

ALABAMA

Alabama State University

Montgomery, Alabama

http://www.alasu.edu/

- **State-supported** comprehensive, founded 1867, part of Alabama Commission on Higher Education
- **Urban** 172-acre campus
- **Coed** 4,803 undergraduate students, 91% full-time, 61% women, 39% men
- **Minimally difficult** entrance level, 53% of applicants were admitted

UNDERGRAD STUDENTS

4,374 full-time, 429 part-time. 33% are from out of state; 92% Black or African American, non-Hispanic/Latino; 1% Hispanic/Latino; 0.2% Asian, non-Hispanic/Latino; 0.1% Native Hawaiian or other Pacific Islander, non-Hispanic/Latino; 0.1% American Indian or Alaska Native, non-Hispanic/Latino; 1% Two or more races, non-Hispanic/Latino; 1% Race/ethnicity unknown; 2% international; 3% transferred in; 34% live on campus.

Freshmen

Admission: 7,673 applied, 4,087 admitted, 1,081 enrolled. ***Average high school GPA:*** 2.8. ***Test scores:*** SAT critical reading scores over 500: 18%; SAT math scores over 500: 19%; ACT scores over 18: 41%; SAT critical reading scores over 600: 1%; SAT math scores over 600: 1%; ACT scores over 24: 5%.

Retention: 57% of full-time freshmen returned.

ACADEMICS

Calendar: semesters. *Degrees:* bachelor's, master's, doctoral, post-master's, and postbachelor's certificates.

Special study options: academic remediation for entering students, advanced placement credit, cooperative education, distance learning, double majors, freshman honors college, honors programs, independent study, internships, part-time degree program, student-designed majors, summer session for credit. ***ROTC:*** Army (c), Air Force (b).

Computers: 541 computers/terminals and 1,082 ports are available on campus for general student use. Students can access the following: computer help desk, free student e-mail accounts, online (class) grades, online (class) registration, online (class) schedules. Campuswide network is available. Wireless service is available via entire campus.

STUDENT LIFE

Housing options: men-only, women-only, special housing for students with disabilities. Campus housing is university owned.

Activities and organizations: drama/theater group, student-run newspaper, radio station, choral group, marching band, Alpha Kappa Alpha Sorority Inc, Empower Ministry, Nu Alpha Nu Service Fraternity Inc, Gamma Sigma Sigma National Service Sorority Inc, Delta Sigma Theta Sorority Inc, national fraternities, national sororities.

Athletics Member NCAA. All Division I. ***Intercollegiate sports:*** baseball M(s), basketball M(s)/W(s), bowling W(s), cheerleading M(s)/W(s), cross-country running M(s)/W(s), football M(s), golf M(s)/W(s), soccer W(s), softball W(s), tennis M(s)/W(s), track and field M(s)/W(s), volleyball W(s). ***Intramural sports:*** basketball M, football M.

Campus security: 24-hour emergency response devices and patrols, late-night transport/escort service, self-defense education, well-lit campus.

Student services: health clinic, personal/psychological counseling.

COSTS & FINANCIAL AID

Costs (2014–15) ***One-time required fee:*** $150. ***Tuition:*** state resident $6936 full-time, $289 per credit hour part-time; nonresident $13,872 full-time, $578 per credit hour part-time. Full-time tuition and fees vary according to course load and degree level. Part-time tuition and fees vary according to course load and degree level. ***Required fees:*** $446 per term part-time. ***Room and board:*** $5422. Room and board charges vary according to board plan and housing facility. ***Payment plan:*** deferred payment. ***Waivers:*** employees or children of employees.

Financial Aid Of all full-time matriculated undergraduates who enrolled in 2014, 4,320 applied for aid, 4,201 were judged to have need, 1,714 had their need fully met. 651 Federal Work-Study jobs (averaging $1800). In 2014, 86 non-need-based awards were made. ***Average percent of need met:*** 83. ***Average financial aid package:*** $18,385. ***Average need-based loan:*** $3297. ***Average need-based gift aid:*** $4642. ***Average non-need-based aid:*** $9669. ***Average indebtedness upon graduation:*** $32,629.

APPLYING

Standardized Tests *Required:* SAT or ACT (for admission).

Options: electronic application, early admission, deferred entrance.

Application fee: $25.

Required: high school transcript, minimum 2.0 GPA. ***Recommended:*** essay or personal statement, interview.

Application deadlines: 7/31 (freshmen), 7/31 (transfers).

Notification: continuous (freshmen), continuous (transfers).

CONTACT

Mr. John Dow, Director of Admissions and Recruitment, Alabama State University, 915 South Jackson Street, Montgomery, AL 36101-0271. *Phone:* 334-229-4291. *Toll-free phone:* 800-253-5037. *Fax:* 334-229-4984. *E-mail:* admissions@alasu.edu.

★ Amridge University

Montgomery, Alabama

http://www.amridgeuniversity.edu/

- **Independent** university, founded 1967, affiliated with Church of Christ
- **Urban** 10-acre campus
- **Endowment** $7.1 million
- **Coed** 278 undergraduate students, 60% full-time, 56% women, 44% men
- **Minimally difficult** entrance level

UNDERGRAD STUDENTS

167 full-time, 111 part-time. Students come from 48 states and territories; 75% are from out of state; 44% Black or African American, non-Hispanic/Latino; 1% Hispanic/Latino; 0.4% Asian, non-Hispanic/Latino; 29% Race/ethnicity unknown; 96% transferred in.

Freshmen

Admission: 10 enrolled.

Retention: 75% of full-time freshmen returned.

FACULTY

Total: 64, 56% full-time, 70% with terminal degrees.

Student/faculty ratio: 10:1.

ACADEMICS

Calendar: semesters. *Degrees:* associate, bachelor's, master's, and doctoral.

Special study options: academic remediation for entering students, accelerated degree program, adult/continuing education programs, advanced placement credit, distance learning, double majors, external degree program, independent study, internships, part-time degree program, services for LD students, summer session for credit.

Computers: 5 computers/terminals are available on campus for general student use. Students can access the following: computer help desk, free student e-mail accounts, online (class) grades, online (class) registration, online (class) schedules, access to over 20 million monographs and journals online. Campuswide network is available. Wireless service is available via entire campus.

STUDENT LIFE

Housing options: college housing not available.

Activities and organizations: Amridge University Student Advisory Committee.

Campus security: 24-hour emergency response devices, security guards.

COSTS & FINANCIAL AID

Costs (2014–15) ***Tuition:*** $6000 full-time, $400 per semester hour part-time. Full-time tuition and fees vary according to course load and student level. Part-time tuition and fees vary according to course load and student level. No tuition increase for student's term of enrollment. ***Required fees:*** $900 full-time, $450 per term part-time. ***Payment plan:*** installment. ***Waivers:*** employees or children of employees.

Financial Aid Of all full-time matriculated undergraduates who enrolled in 2013, 322 applied for aid, 266 were judged to have need, 102 had their need fully met. In 2013, 168 non-need-based awards were made. ***Average percent of need met:*** 52. ***Average financial aid package:*** $8735. ***Average need-based gift aid:*** $3065. ***Average non-need-based aid:*** $2980. ***Average indebtedness upon graduation:*** $10,500.

APPLYING

Standardized Tests *Required for some:* SAT or ACT (for admission).

Options: electronic application, early admission.

Application fee: $50.

Required: high school transcript, minimum 2.0 GPA.

Application deadlines: rolling (freshmen), rolling (out-of-state freshmen), rolling (transfers).

CONTACT

Mrs. Sheridan Wiggins, Admissions Officer, Amridge University, 1200 Taylor Road, Montgomery, AL 36117. *Phone:* 334-387-3877 Ext. 7532. *Toll-free phone:* 888-790-8080. *Fax:* 334-387-3878. *E-mail:* admissions@amridgeuniversity.edu.

See this page for display ad and page 1340 for the College Close-Up.

Athens State University

Athens, Alabama

http://www.athens.edu/

- **State-supported** upper-level, founded 1822
- **Small-town** 45-acre campus
- **Coed** 3,129 undergraduate students, 43% full-time, 65% women, 35% men
- **Noncompetitive** entrance level

UNDERGRAD STUDENTS

1,342 full-time, 1,787 part-time. Students come from 18 states and territories; 1 other country; 4% are from out of state; 12% Black or African American, non-Hispanic/Latino; 2% Hispanic/Latino; 0.5% Asian, non-Hispanic/Latino; 0.1% Native Hawaiian or other Pacific Islander, non-Hispanic/Latino; 2% American Indian or Alaska Native, non-Hispanic/Latino; 2% Two or more races, non-Hispanic/Latino; 3% Race/ethnicity unknown; 0.6% international; 25% transferred in.

FACULTY

Total: 207, 41% full-time, 38% with terminal degrees.

Student/faculty ratio: 17:1.

ACADEMICS

Calendar: semesters. *Degree:* certificates and bachelor's.

Special study options: adult/continuing education programs, advanced placement credit, cooperative education, distance learning, double majors, independent study, internships, off-campus study, part-time degree program, study abroad, summer session for credit.

Computers: 210 computers/terminals are available on campus for general student use. Students can access the following: online (class) registration, grades, transcripts, schedules, e-mail. Campuswide network is available.

STUDENT LIFE

Housing options: college housing not available.

Activities and organizations: drama/theater group, student-run newspaper, national sororities.

Athletics ***Intramural sports:*** table tennis M/W, volleyball M/W.

Student services: personal/psychological counseling.

COSTS & FINANCIAL AID

Costs (2014–15) ***Tuition:*** state resident $5370 full-time; nonresident $10,740 full-time. ***Required fees:*** $750 full-time. ***Payment plan:*** installment. ***Waivers:*** senior citizens and employees or children of employees.

Financial Aid Of all full-time matriculated undergraduates who enrolled in 2012, 918 applied for aid, 2 were judged to have need. ***Average financial aid package:*** $12,024.

APPLYING
Options: electronic application, deferred entrance.
Application fee: $30.
Notification: continuous (transfers).

CONTACT
Athens State University, 300 North Beaty Street, Athens, AL 35611. *Phone:* 256-233-8151. *Toll-free phone:* 800-522-0272.

Auburn University
Auburn University, Alabama
http://www.auburn.edu/

- **State-supported** university, founded 1856
- **Small-town** 1875-acre campus with easy access to Atlanta, Birmingham
- **Endowment** $640.7 million
- **Coed** 20,629 undergraduate students, 91% full-time, 49% women, 51% men
- **Moderately difficult** entrance level, 83% of applicants were admitted

UNDERGRAD STUDENTS
18,853 full-time, 1,776 part-time. Students come from 54 states and territories; 48 other countries; 38% are from out of state; 7% Black or African American, non-Hispanic/Latino; 2% Hispanic/Latino; 2% Asian, non-Hispanic/Latino; 0.7% American Indian or Alaska Native, non-Hispanic/Latino; 1% Race/ethnicity unknown; 2% international; 6% transferred in; 22% live on campus.

Freshmen
Admission: 16,958 applied, 14,154 admitted, 4,592 enrolled. ***Average high school GPA:*** 3.77. ***Test scores:*** SAT critical reading scores over 500: 87%; SAT math scores over 500: 90%; SAT writing scores over 500: 83%; ACT scores over 18: 100%; SAT critical reading scores over 600: 36%; SAT math scores over 600: 46%; SAT writing scores over 600: 33%; ACT scores over 24: 80%; SAT critical reading scores over 700: 8%; SAT math scores over 700: 11%; SAT writing scores over 700: 7%; ACT scores over 30: 31%.
Retention: 90% of full-time freshmen returned.

FACULTY
Total: 1,384, 87% full-time, 89% with terminal degrees.
Student/faculty ratio: 18:1.

ACADEMICS
Calendar: semesters. *Degrees:* bachelor's, master's, doctoral, post-master's, and postbachelor's certificates.
Special study options: accelerated degree program, adult/continuing education programs, advanced placement credit, cooperative education, distance learning, double majors, English as a second language, freshman honors college, honors programs, independent study, internships, off-campus study, part-time degree program, services for LD students, study abroad, summer session for credit. ***ROTC:*** Army (b), Navy (b), Air Force (b).
Unusual degree programs: 3-2 engineering.
Computers: 1,722 computers/terminals are available on campus for general student use. Students can access the following: computer help desk, free student e-mail accounts, online (class) grades, online (class) registration, pay Bursar online, course materials available online. Campuswide network is available. 100% of college-owned or -operated housing units are wired for high-speed Internet access. Wireless service is available via entire campus.

STUDENT LIFE
Housing options: coed, men-only, women-only, special housing for students with disabilities. Campus housing is university owned.
Activities and organizations: drama/theater group, student-run newspaper, radio and television station, choral group, marching band, Student Government Association, University Program Council, IMPACT (volunteer opportunities), International Student Organization, student media (AU Plainsman newspaper, WEGL radio, Glomerata yearbook, Eagle Eye television, AU Circle literary journal), national fraternities, national sororities.
Athletics Member NCAA. All Division I except football (Division I-A). ***Intercollegiate sports:*** baseball M(s), basketball M(s)/W(s), cross-country running M(s)/W(s), equestrian sports W(s), golf M(s)/W(s), gymnastics W(s), soccer W(s), softball W(s), swimming and diving M(s)/W(s), tennis M(s)/W(s), track and field M(s)/W(s), volleyball W(s). ***Intramural sports:*** badminton M/W, basketball M/W, bowling M/W, crew M(c)/W(c), football M/W, golf M/W, ice hockey M(c), lacrosse M(c)/W(c), racquetball M/W, rugby M(c)/W(c), sailing M(c)/W(c), skiing (downhill) M(c)/W(c), soccer M/W, softball M/W, swimming and diving M/W, table tennis M/W, tennis M/W, track and field M/W, ultimate Frisbee M/W, volleyball M/W, water polo M(c)/W(c), wrestling M(c)/W(c).
Campus security: 24-hour emergency response devices and patrols, late-night transport/escort service, controlled dormitory access.
Student services: health clinic, personal/psychological counseling.

COSTS & FINANCIAL AID
Costs (2014–15) ***Tuition:*** state resident $8592 full-time, $358 per semester hour part-time; nonresident $25,776 full-time, $1074 per semester hour part-time. Full-time tuition and fees vary according to program and reciprocity agreements. Part-time tuition and fees vary according to course load, program, and reciprocity agreements. ***Required fees:*** $1608 full-time, $804 per term part-time. ***Room and board:*** $12,178; room only: $6892. Room and board charges vary according to board plan and housing facility. ***Payment plan:*** installment. ***Waivers:*** employees or children of employees.
Financial Aid Of all full-time matriculated undergraduates who enrolled in 2013, 11,762 applied for aid, 6,831 were judged to have need, 979 had their need fully met. 211 Federal Work-Study jobs (averaging $3902). In 2013, 2796 non-need-based awards were made. ***Average percent of need met:*** 45. ***Average financial aid package:*** $10,804. ***Average need-based loan:*** $4553. ***Average need-based gift aid:*** $7109. ***Average non-need-based aid:*** $5265. ***Average indebtedness upon graduation:*** $27,146.

APPLYING
Standardized Tests *Required:* SAT or ACT (for admission).
Options: electronic application, early admission, early action, deferred entrance.
Application fee: $50.
Required: essay or personal statement, high school transcript, minimum 2.0 GPA. ***Required for some:*** minimum 3.0 GPA. ***Recommended:*** minimum 3.0 GPA.
Application deadlines: 2/1 (freshmen), 2/1 (out-of-state freshmen), rolling (transfers), 10/1 (early action).
Notification: 2/15 (freshmen), 2/15 (out-of-state freshmen), continuous (transfers), 10/15 (early action).

CONTACT
Ms. Cindy Singley, Director, University Recruitment, Auburn University, Auburn University, AL 36849. *Phone:* 334-844-4080. *Toll-free phone:* 800-AUBURN9. *E-mail:* admissions@auburn.edu.

Auburn University at Montgomery
Montgomery, Alabama
http://www.aum.edu/

- **State-supported** comprehensive, founded 1967, part of Auburn University
- **Suburban** 500-acre campus
- **Coed** 4,377 undergraduate students, 70% full-time, 63% women, 37% men
- **Moderately difficult** entrance level, 80% of applicants were admitted

UNDERGRAD STUDENTS
3,081 full-time, 1,296 part-time. Students come from 41 states and territories; 37 other countries; 4% are from out of state; 33% Black or African American, non-Hispanic/Latino; 0.8% Hispanic/Latino; 2% Asian, non-Hispanic/Latino; 0.2% Native Hawaiian or other Pacific Islander, non-Hispanic/Latino; 0.4% American Indian or Alaska Native, non-Hispanic/Latino; 3% Two or more races, non-Hispanic/Latino; 2% Race/ethnicity unknown; 4% international; 11% transferred in; 20% live on campus.

Freshmen

Admission: 2,123 applied, 1,702 admitted, 613 enrolled. ***Average high school GPA:*** 3.3. ***Test scores:*** SAT critical reading scores over 500: 42%; ACT scores over 18: 98%; SAT critical reading scores over 600: 13%; ACT scores over 24: 25%; SAT critical reading scores over 700: 4%; ACT scores over 30: 1%.

Retention: 65% of full-time freshmen returned.

FACULTY

Total: 360, 60% full-time.

Student/faculty ratio: 15:1.

ACADEMICS

Calendar: semesters. *Degrees:* certificates, bachelor's, master's, doctoral, and post-master's certificates.

Special study options: academic remediation for entering students, advanced placement credit, cooperative education, distance learning, double majors, English as a second language, honors programs, independent study, internships, off-campus study, part-time degree program, services for LD students, study abroad, summer session for credit. ***ROTC:*** Army (b), Air Force (c).

Computers: 760 computers/terminals are available on campus for general student use. Students can access the following: campus intranet, computer help desk, free student e-mail accounts, online (class) grades, online (class) registration, online (class) schedules, apply online, check financial aid status, make a payment, apply for student housing, make an appointment with an advisor, access the bookstore. Campuswide network is available. 100% of college-owned or -operated housing units are wired for high-speed Internet access. Wireless service is available via entire campus.

STUDENT LIFE

Housing options: coed. Campus housing is university owned.

Activities and organizations: drama/theater group, student-run newspaper, television station, choral group, Student Government Association, Baptist Campus Ministries, Campus Activities Board, Greek Life, Residence Hall Association, national fraternities, national sororities.

Athletics Member NAIA. ***Intercollegiate sports:*** baseball M(s), basketball M(s)/W(s), cheerleading M(s)/W(s), cross-country running M(s)/W(s), soccer M(s)/W(s), softball W(s), tennis M(s)/W(s). ***Intramural sports:*** archery M(c)/W(c), basketball M/W, football M/W, golf M(c)/W(c), soccer M(c)/W(c), softball M/W, table tennis M(c)/W(c), tennis M/W, ultimate Frisbee M(c)/W(c), volleyball M/W.

Campus security: 24-hour emergency response devices and patrols, student patrols, late-night transport/escort service, controlled dormitory access, personal safety seminars, and emergency preparedness seminars.

Student services: health clinic, personal/psychological counseling.

COSTS & FINANCIAL AID

Costs (2014–15) ***Tuition:*** state resident $8430 full-time, $281 per credit hour part-time; nonresident $18,990 full-time, $633 per credit hour part-time. Full-time tuition and fees vary according to course load and degree level. Part-time tuition and fees vary according to course load and degree level. ***Required fees:*** $650 full-time. ***Room and board:*** $5390; room only: $4190. Room and board charges vary according to housing facility. ***Payment plan:*** installment. ***Waivers:*** senior citizens and employees or children of employees.

Financial Aid Of all full-time matriculated undergraduates who enrolled in 2014, 2,310 applied for aid, 2,022 were judged to have need, 402 had their need fully met. In 2014, 70 non-need-based awards were made. ***Average financial aid package:*** $7236. ***Average need-based loan:*** $4071. ***Average need-based gift aid:*** $4730. ***Average non-need-based aid:*** $3966.

APPLYING

Standardized Tests *Required:* SAT or ACT (for admission).

Options: electronic application, deferred entrance.

Required: high school transcript.

Application deadlines: rolling (freshmen), rolling (transfers).

Notification: continuous (freshmen), continuous (out-of-state freshmen), continuous (transfers).

CONTACT

Miss Sumer Swaim, Senior Recruitment Associate, Auburn University at Montgomery, PO Box 244023, Montgomery, AL 36124. *Phone:* 334-244-3615. *Toll-free phone:* 800-227-2649. *Fax:* 334-244-3795. *E-mail:* admissions@aum.edu.

★ Birmingham-Southern College

Birmingham, Alabama

http://www.bsc.edu/

- **Independent Methodist** 4-year, founded 1856
- **Urban** 196-acre campus with easy access to Birmingham
- **Endowment** $51.7 million
- **Coed** 1,231 undergraduate students, 98% full-time, 47% women, 53% men
- **Moderately difficult** entrance level, 65% of applicants were admitted

UNDERGRAD STUDENTS

1,208 full-time, 23 part-time. Students come from 33 states and territories; 18 other countries; 41% are from out of state; 8% Black or African American, non-Hispanic/Latino; 3% Hispanic/Latino; 4% Asian, non-Hispanic/Latino; 0.9% American Indian or Alaska Native, non-Hispanic/Latino; 0.6% Two or more races, non-Hispanic/Latino; 0.9% Race/ethnicity unknown; 2% transferred in; 85% live on campus.

Freshmen

Admission: 1,846 applied, 1,202 admitted, 327 enrolled. ***Average high school GPA:*** 3.48. ***Test scores:*** SAT critical reading scores over 500: 78%; SAT math scores over 500: 81%; SAT writing scores over 500: 72%; ACT scores over 18: 100%; SAT critical reading scores over 600: 32%; SAT math scores over 600: 35%; SAT writing scores over 600: 21%; ACT scores over 24: 73%; SAT critical reading scores over 700: 7%; SAT math scores over 700: 7%; SAT writing scores over 700: 7%; ACT scores over 30: 20%.

Retention: 81% of full-time freshmen returned.

FACULTY

Total: 114, 75% full-time, 76% with terminal degrees.

Student/faculty ratio: 13:1.

ACADEMICS

Calendar: 4-1-4. *Degree:* bachelor's.

Special study options: advanced placement credit, cooperative education, double majors, honors programs, independent study, internships, off-campus study, part-time degree program, student-designed majors, study abroad, summer session for credit. ***ROTC:*** Army (c), Air Force (c).

Unusual degree programs: 3-2 engineering with Auburn University, Columbia University, Washington University in St. Louis, University of Alabama at Birmingham; nursing with Vanderbilt University; environmental studies with Duke University.

Computers: 306 computers/terminals and 306 ports are available on campus for general student use. Students can access the following: campus intranet, computer help desk, free student e-mail accounts, online (class) grades, online (class) registration, online (class) schedules. Campuswide network is available. 100% of college-owned or -operated housing units are wired for high-speed Internet access. Wireless service is available via entire campus.

STUDENT LIFE

Housing options: on-campus residence required through sophomore year; coed, men-only, women-only, special housing for students with disabilities. Campus housing is university owned. Freshman campus housing is guaranteed.

Activities and organizations: drama/theater group, student-run newspaper, choral group, marching band, Black Student Union, Southern Bouldering Club, Student Government Association, Multi- Cultural Awareness Organization, BSC Chapter of Habitat for Humanity, national fraternities, national sororities.

Athletics Member NCAA. All Division III. ***Intercollegiate sports:*** baseball M, basketball M/W, cheerleading M/W, cross-country running M/W, football M, golf M/W, lacrosse M/W, soccer M/W, softball W, swimming and diving M/W, tennis M/W, track and field M/W, volleyball W. ***Intramural sports:*** basketball M/W, football M/W, racquetball M/W, soccer M/W, softball M, table tennis M/W, tennis M/W, ultimate Frisbee M/W, volleyball M/W, water polo M/W.

Campus security: 24-hour emergency response devices and patrols, late-night transport/escort service, controlled dormitory access, vehicle safety inspections for students, emergency phone stations throughout campus.

Student services: health clinic, personal/psychological counseling.

COSTS & FINANCIAL AID

Costs (2015–16) ***One-time required fee:*** $200. ***Comprehensive fee:*** $44,478 includes full-time tuition ($31,954), mandatory fees ($1174), and room and board ($11,350). Full-time tuition and fees vary according to program and reciprocity agreements. Part-time tuition and fees vary according to course load, program, and reciprocity agreements. ***College room only:*** $6600. Room and board charges vary according to board plan and housing facility. ***Payment plan:*** installment. ***Waivers:*** employees or children of employees.

Financial Aid Of all full-time matriculated undergraduates who enrolled in 2013, 796 applied for aid, 654 were judged to have need, 180 had their need fully met. In 2013, 478 non-need-based awards were made. ***Average percent of need met:*** 84. ***Average financial aid package:*** $26,237. ***Average need-based loan:*** $4876. ***Average need-based gift aid:*** $9327. ***Average non-need-based aid:*** $17,309. ***Average indebtedness upon graduation:*** $32,250.

APPLYING

Standardized Tests *Required:* SAT or ACT (for admission).

Options: electronic application, early action, deferred entrance.

Application fee: $40.

Required: essay or personal statement, high school transcript, minimum 2.0 GPA, 1 letter of recommendation. ***Required for some:*** interview. ***Recommended:*** interview.

Notification: 3/1 (freshmen), 12/15 (early action).

CONTACT

Ms. Jennifer Waters, Director of Admission, Birmingham-Southern College, Box 549008, Birmingham, AL 35254. *Phone:* 205-226-4696. *Toll-free phone:* 800-523-5793. *Fax:* 205-226-3074. *E-mail:* jwaters@bsc.edu.

Brown Mackie College–Birmingham

Birmingham, Alabama

http://www.brownmackie.edu/birmingham

- **Proprietary** 4-year, part of Education Management Corporation
- **Coed**

ACADEMICS

Degrees: diplomas, associate, and bachelor's.

CONTACT

Brown Mackie College–Birmingham, 105 Vulcan Road, Suite 100, Birmingham, AL 35209. *Phone:* 205-909-1500. *Toll-free phone:* 888-299-4699.

Columbia Southern University

Orange Beach, Alabama

http://www.columbiasouthern.edu/

- **Proprietary** comprehensive, founded 1993
- **Small-town** campus
- **Coed** 14,973 undergraduate students, 47% full-time, 37% women, 63% men
- **Noncompetitive** entrance level, 100% of applicants were admitted

UNDERGRAD STUDENTS

7,005 full-time, 7,968 part-time. Students come from 54 states and territories; 50 other countries; 91% are from out of state; 23% Black or African American, non-Hispanic/Latino; 6% Hispanic/Latino; 2% Asian, non-Hispanic/Latino; 0.2% Native Hawaiian or other Pacific Islander, non-Hispanic/Latino; 0.8% American Indian or Alaska Native, non-Hispanic/Latino; 3% Two or more races, non-Hispanic/Latino; 6% Race/ethnicity unknown; 15% transferred in.

Freshmen

Admission: 1,654 applied, 1,654 admitted, 663 enrolled.

FACULTY

Total: 548, 23% full-time, 53% with terminal degrees.

Student/faculty ratio: 60:1.

ACADEMICS

Calendar: 9 weeks of instruction, LifePace Learning: 10-week courses that are self-paced. *Degrees:* certificates, associate, bachelor's, master's, and postbachelor's certificates (offers only distance learning degree programs).

Special study options: academic remediation for entering students, adult/continuing education programs, distance learning, off-campus study, part-time degree program, services for LD students.

Computers: Students can access the following: computer help desk, online (class) grades, online (class) registration, online (class) schedules, Student portals for learning modules, policy updates, and other institutional information.

STUDENT LIFE

Activities and organizations: Student Veteran Association, American Criminal Justice Association, Delta Epsilon Tou (DET) - Alumni Honor Society.

COSTS

Costs (2015–16) ***One-time required fee:*** $95. ***Tuition:*** $5040 full-time, $210 per credit hour part-time. Full-time tuition and fees vary according to course load. Part-time tuition and fees vary according to course load. ***Waivers:*** employees or children of employees.

APPLYING

Options: electronic application.

Required for some: high school transcript.

Application deadlines: rolling (freshmen), rolling (transfers).

CONTACT

Director of Admissions, Columbia Southern University, 21982 University Lane, Orange Beach, AL 36561. *Phone:* 251-981-3771. *Toll-free phone:* 800-977-8449. *Fax:* 251-224-0540. *E-mail:* admissions@columbiasouthern.edu.

Faulkner University

Montgomery, Alabama

http://www.faulkner.edu/

- **Independent** university, founded 1942, affiliated with Church of Christ
- **Urban** 75-acre campus with easy access to Montgomery
- **Endowment** $21.0 million
- **Coed** 2,668 undergraduate students, 68% full-time, 60% women, 40% men
- **Minimally difficult** entrance level, 50% of applicants were admitted

UNDERGRAD STUDENTS

1,821 full-time, 847 part-time. Students come from 28 states and territories; 27 other countries; 14% are from out of state; 46% Black or African American, non-Hispanic/Latino; 2% Hispanic/Latino; 0.5% Asian, non-Hispanic/Latino; 0.1% Native Hawaiian or other Pacific Islander, non-Hispanic/Latino; 0.6% American Indian or Alaska Native, non-Hispanic/Latino; 2% Two or more races, non-Hispanic/Latino; 3% Race/ethnicity unknown; 2% international; 19% transferred in; 19% live on campus.

Freshmen

Admission: 2,319 applied, 1,153 admitted, 407 enrolled. ***Average high school GPA:*** 3.18. ***Test scores:*** SAT critical reading scores over 500: 37%; SAT math scores over 500: 42%; SAT writing scores over 500: 34%; ACT scores over 18: 91%; SAT critical reading scores over 600: 3%; SAT math scores over 600: 7%; SAT writing scores over 600: 3%; ACT scores over 24: 18%; SAT critical reading scores over 700: 2%; SAT writing scores over 700: 2%; ACT scores over 30: 1%.

Retention: 60% of full-time freshmen returned.

FACULTY

Total: 247, 42% full-time, 49% with terminal degrees.

Student/faculty ratio: 18:1.

ACADEMICS
Calendar: semesters. *Degrees:* associate, bachelor's, master's, and doctoral.

Special study options: academic remediation for entering students, accelerated degree program, adult/continuing education programs, advanced placement credit, distance learning, double majors, English as a second language, freshman honors college, honors programs, independent study, internships, off-campus study, part-time degree program, services for LD students, study abroad, summer session for credit. ***ROTC:*** Army (c), Air Force (c).

Computers: 445 computers/terminals and 790 ports are available on campus for general student use. Students can access the following: campus intranet, computer help desk, free student e-mail accounts, online (class) grades, online (class) registration, online (class) schedules, student account access. Campuswide network is available. 100% of college-owned or -operated housing units are wired for high-speed Internet access. Wireless service is available via entire campus.

STUDENT LIFE
Housing options: on-campus residence required through junior year; men-only, women-only, special housing for students with disabilities. Campus housing is university owned. Freshman campus housing is guaranteed.

Activities and organizations: drama/theater group, student-run newspaper, choral group, marching band, student government, Marching Band, Dinner Theatre, Acappella Chorus, Phi Lambda/Kappa Social Clubs.

Athletics Member NAIA. ***Intercollegiate sports:*** baseball M(s), basketball M(s)/W(s), cheerleading M(s)(c)/W(s)(c), football M(s), golf M(s)/W(s), soccer M(s)/W(s), softball W(s), volleyball W(s). ***Intramural sports:*** basketball M/W, bowling M/W, golf M/W, racquetball M/W, soccer M/W, softball M/W, table tennis M/W, ultimate Frisbee M/W, volleyball M/W.

Campus security: 24-hour emergency response devices and patrols, late-night transport/escort service, controlled dormitory access.

Student services: health clinic, personal/psychological counseling.

COSTS & FINANCIAL AID
Costs (2014–15) ***One-time required fee:*** $575. ***Comprehensive fee:*** $25,720 includes full-time tuition ($17,020), mandatory fees ($1730), and room and board ($6970). Full-time tuition and fees vary according to class time, location, and program. Part-time tuition: $500 per semester hour. Part-time tuition and fees vary according to class time, location, and program. ***Required fees:*** $288 per term part-time. ***College room only:*** $3330. Room and board charges vary according to board plan and housing facility. ***Payment plans:*** installment, deferred payment. ***Waivers:*** adult students and employees or children of employees.

Financial Aid Of all full-time matriculated undergraduates who enrolled in 2013, 1,521 applied for aid, 1,201 were judged to have need, 33 had their need fully met. In 2013, 72 non-need-based awards were made. ***Average percent of need met:*** 59. ***Average financial aid package:*** $5950. ***Average need-based loan:*** $5300. ***Average need-based gift aid:*** $5700. ***Average non-need-based aid:*** $2200. ***Average indebtedness upon graduation:*** $29,000. ***Financial aid deadline:*** 8/1.

APPLYING
Standardized Tests *Required:* SAT or ACT (for admission).

Options: electronic application, early admission, deferred entrance.

Application fee: $25.

Required: high school transcript, minimum 2.0 GPA. ***Recommended:*** essay or personal statement, 2 letters of recommendation, interview.

Application deadlines: rolling (freshmen), rolling (out-of-state freshmen), rolling (transfers).

Notification: continuous (freshmen), continuous (out-of-state freshmen), continuous (transfers).

CONTACT
Mr. Neil Scott, Director of Admissions, Faulkner University, 5345 Atlanta Highway, Montgomery, AL 36109-3398. *Phone:* 334-386-7200. *Toll-free phone:* 800-879-9816. *Fax:* 334-386-7137. *E-mail:* nscott@faulkner.edu.

Huntingdon College

Montgomery, Alabama

http://www.huntingdon.edu/

- **Independent United Methodist** 4-year, founded 1854
- **Suburban** 71-acre campus with easy access to Birmingham
- **Coed** 1,160 undergraduate students, 79% full-time, 49% women, 51% men

UNDERGRAD STUDENTS
912 full-time, 248 part-time. Students come from 30 states and territories; 8 other countries; 18% are from out of state; 20% Black or African American, non-Hispanic/Latino; 3% Hispanic/Latino; 0.8% Asian, non-Hispanic/Latino; 0.2% Native Hawaiian or other Pacific Islander, non-Hispanic/Latino; 1% American Indian or Alaska Native, non-Hispanic/Latino; 3% Two or more races, non-Hispanic/Latino; 9% Race/ethnicity unknown; 0.7% international; 11% transferred in; 62% live on campus.

Freshmen
Admission: 227 enrolled. ***Average high school GPA:*** 3.44. ***Test scores:*** SAT critical reading scores over 500: 45%; SAT math scores over 500: 42%; ACT scores over 18: 96%; SAT critical reading scores over 600: 9%; SAT math scores over 600: 15%; ACT scores over 24: 29%; SAT critical reading scores over 700: 3%; ACT scores over 30: 2%.

Retention: 71% of full-time freshmen returned.

FACULTY
Total: 109, 38% full-time, 54% with terminal degrees.

Student/faculty ratio: 15:1.

ACADEMICS
Calendar: semesters. *Degree:* bachelor's.

Special study options: adult/continuing education programs, advanced placement credit, distance learning, double majors, freshman honors college, honors programs, independent study, internships, off-campus study, part-time degree program, services for LD students, student-designed majors, study abroad, summer session for credit. ***ROTC:*** Army (c), Air Force (c).

Computers: 8 computers/terminals are available on campus for general student use. Students can access the following: campus intranet, free student e-mail accounts, online (class) grades, online (class) registration, online (class) schedules, online library, student web hosting. Campuswide network is available. 100% of college-owned or -operated housing units are wired for high-speed Internet access. Wireless service is available via classrooms, dorm rooms, learning centers, libraries, student centers.

STUDENT LIFE
Housing options: on-campus residence required through junior year; coed, men-only, women-only, special housing for students with disabilities. Campus housing is university owned. Freshman campus housing is guaranteed.

Activities and organizations: drama/theater group, student-run newspaper, choral group, marching band, Student Government Association, Campus Activities Board, Voice of Justice, Freshman Forum, Exchange Club, national fraternities, national sororities.

Athletics Member NCAA. All Division III. ***Intercollegiate sports:*** baseball M, basketball M/W, football M, golf M/W, lacrosse M/W, soccer M/W, softball W, tennis M/W, volleyball W, wrestling M. ***Intramural sports:*** baseball W(c), basketball M/W, cheerleading M(c)/W(c), football M/W, soccer M/W, softball M/W.

Campus security: 24-hour emergency response devices and patrols, late-night transport/escort service, controlled dormitory access, electronic video surveillance, weather alert broadcasts.

Student services: health clinic.

COSTS & FINANCIAL AID
Costs (2014–15) ***Comprehensive fee:*** $33,100 includes full-time tuition ($23,500), mandatory fees ($1050), and room and board ($8550). Full-time tuition and fees vary according to course load, program, and student level. Part-time tuition: $980 per credit hour. Part-time tuition and fees vary according to course load and program. No tuition increase for student's term of enrollment. ***Room and board:*** Room and board charges vary according to housing facility. ***Payment plans:*** installment, deferred

payment. ***Waivers:*** children of alumni and employees or children of employees.

Financial Aid Of all full-time matriculated undergraduates who enrolled in 2014, 766 applied for aid, 681 were judged to have need, 111 had their need fully met. 147 Federal Work-Study jobs (averaging $974). In 2014, 218 non-need-based awards were made. ***Average percent of need met:*** 68. ***Average financial aid package:*** $17,249. ***Average need-based loan:*** $4401. ***Average need-based gift aid:*** $6956. ***Average non-need-based aid:*** $10,489. ***Average indebtedness upon graduation:*** $25,714.

APPLYING
Standardized Tests *Required:* SAT or ACT (for admission).

Required: high school transcript. ***Required for some:*** essay or personal statement, 3 letters of recommendation, interview, auditions for music students; portfolios for art.

CONTACT
Office of Admission, Huntingdon College, 1500 East Fairview Avenue, Montgomery, AL 36106-2148. *Phone:* 334-833-4497. *Toll-free phone:* 800-763-0313. *Fax:* 334-833-4347. *E-mail:* admiss@huntingdon.edu.

ITT Technical Institute

Bessemer, Alabama

http://www.itt-tech.edu/

- **Proprietary** primarily 2-year, founded 1994, part of ITT Educational Services, Inc.
- **Suburban** campus
- **Coed**
- **Minimally difficult** entrance level

ACADEMICS
Calendar: quarters. *Degrees:* associate and bachelor's.

STUDENT LIFE
Housing options: college housing not available.

Campus security: 24-hour emergency response devices.

CONTACT
Director of Recruitment, ITT Technical Institute, 6270 Park South Drive, Bessemer, AL 35022. *Phone:* 205-497-5700. *Toll-free phone:* 800-488-7033.

ITT Technical Institute

Madison, Alabama

http://www.itt-tech.edu/

- **Proprietary** primarily 2-year, part of ITT Educational Services, Inc.
- **Coed**
- **Minimally difficult** entrance level

ACADEMICS
Degrees: associate and bachelor's.

STUDENT LIFE
Housing options: college housing not available.

CONTACT
Director of Recruitment, ITT Technical Institute, 9238 Madison Boulevard, Suite 500, Madison, AL 35758. *Phone:* 256-542-2900. *Toll-free phone:* 877-628-5960.

ITT Technical Institute

Mobile, Alabama

http://www.itt-tech.edu/

- **Proprietary** primarily 2-year, part of ITT Educational Services, Inc.
- **Coed**
- **Minimally difficult** entrance level

ACADEMICS
Degrees: associate and bachelor's.

STUDENT LIFE
Housing options: college housing not available.

CONTACT
Director of Recruitment, ITT Technical Institute, Office Mall South, 3100 Cottage Hill Road, Building 3, Mobile, AL 36606. *Phone:* 251-472-4760. *Toll-free phone:* 877-327-1013.

Jacksonville State University

Jacksonville, Alabama

http://www.jsu.edu/

- **State-supported** comprehensive, founded 1883
- **Small-town** 459-acre campus with easy access to Birmingham
- **Coed** 7,647 undergraduate students, 75% full-time, 57% women, 43% men
- **Minimally difficult** entrance level, 83% of applicants were admitted

UNDERGRAD STUDENTS
5,733 full-time, 1,914 part-time. 18% are from out of state; 23% Black or African American, non-Hispanic/Latino; 1% Hispanic/Latino; 0.6% Asian, non-Hispanic/Latino; 0.1% Native Hawaiian or other Pacific Islander, non-Hispanic/Latino; 0.7% American Indian or Alaska Native, non-Hispanic/Latino; 3% Race/ethnicity unknown; 2% international; 9% transferred in; 25% live on campus.

Freshmen
Admission: 2,969 applied, 2,472 admitted, 1,185 enrolled. ***Average high school GPA:*** 3.25. ***Test scores:*** SAT critical reading scores over 500: 46%; SAT math scores over 500: 40%; ACT scores over 18: 89%; SAT critical reading scores over 600: 14%; SAT math scores over 600: 8%; ACT scores over 24: 41%; SAT critical reading scores over 700: 3%; SAT math scores over 700: 1%; ACT scores over 30: 5%.

Retention: 72% of full-time freshmen returned.

FACULTY
Total: 466, 69% full-time.

Student/faculty ratio: 19:1.

ACADEMICS
Calendar: semesters. *Degrees:* bachelor's, master's, doctoral, post-master's, and postbachelor's certificates.

Special study options: academic remediation for entering students, accelerated degree program, adult/continuing education programs, advanced placement credit, cooperative education, distance learning, double majors, honors programs, independent study, internships, part-time degree program, services for LD students, summer session for credit. ***ROTC:*** Army (b).

Computers: 350 computers/terminals are available on campus for general student use. Students can access the following: computer help desk, free student e-mail accounts, online (class) grades, online (class) registration, online (class) schedules. Campuswide network is available.

STUDENT LIFE
Housing options: coed, men-only, women-only, special housing for students with disabilities. Campus housing is university owned.

Activities and organizations: drama/theater group, student-run newspaper, radio and television station, choral group, marching band, Student Government Association, Archaeology Club, Campus Fellowship Clubs, Computer Science Club, Biology Club, national fraternities, national sororities.

Athletics Member NCAA. All Division I except football (Division I-AA). ***Intercollegiate sports:*** baseball M(s), basketball M(s)/W(s), cross-country running M(s)/W(s), golf M(s)/W(s), riflery M(s)/W(s), soccer W(s), softball W(s), tennis M(s)/W(s), volleyball W(s). ***Intramural sports:*** badminton M(c)/W(c), basketball M(c)/W(c), bowling M(c)/W(c), football M(c), golf M(c)/W(c), racquetball M(c)/W(c), soccer M(c)/W(c), softball M(c)/W(c), table tennis M(c)/W(c), tennis M(c)/W(c), volleyball M(c)/W(c).

Campus security: 24-hour emergency response devices and patrols, student patrols, late-night transport/escort service, controlled dormitory access, night security officer in female residence halls.

Student services: health clinic, personal/psychological counseling.

COSTS & FINANCIAL AID
Costs (2015–16) ***Tuition:*** state resident $8490 full-time, $283 per credit hour part-time; nonresident $16,980 full-time, $566 per credit hour part-time. ***Required fees:*** $300 full-time, $150 per term part-time. ***Room and***

board: $6985. Room and board charges vary according to board plan and housing facility. ***Payment plan:*** installment. ***Waivers:*** employees or children of employees.

Financial Aid Of all full-time matriculated undergraduates who enrolled in 2013, 5,040 applied for aid, 4,972 were judged to have need. ***Average financial aid package:*** $9254. ***Average need-based loan:*** $984. ***Average need-based gift aid:*** $4464.

APPLYING

Standardized Tests *Required:* SAT or ACT (for admission).

Options: electronic application, early admission, deferred entrance.

Application fee: $35.

Required: high school transcript.

Application deadlines: rolling (freshmen), rolling (out-of-state freshmen), rolling (transfers).

Notification: continuous (freshmen), continuous (out-of-state freshmen), continuous (transfers).

CONTACT

Mr. Andrew Green, Director of Admission, Jacksonville State University, 700 Pelham Road North, Jacksonville, AL 36265. *Phone:* 256-782-5363. *Toll-free phone:* 800-231-5291. *Fax:* 256-782-5291. *E-mail:* info@jsu.edu.

Judson College

Marion, Alabama

http://www.judson.edu/

- **Independent Baptist** 4-year, founded 1838
- **Rural** 118-acre campus with easy access to Birmingham
- **Coed, primarily women** 376 undergraduate students, 71% full-time, 97% women, 3% men
- **Moderately difficult** entrance level, 63% of applicants were admitted

UNDERGRAD STUDENTS

266 full-time, 110 part-time. 24% are from out of state; 15% Black or African American, non-Hispanic/Latino; 1% Hispanic/Latino; 0.9% Asian, non-Hispanic/Latino; 0.6% American Indian or Alaska Native, non-Hispanic/Latino; 0.6% Two or more races, non-Hispanic/Latino; 4% Race/ethnicity unknown; 1% international; 19% transferred in; 71% live on campus.

Freshmen

Admission: 322 applied, 203 admitted, 83 enrolled. ***Average high school GPA:*** 3.47. ***Test scores:*** SAT critical reading scores over 500: 100%; SAT math scores over 500: 80%; SAT writing scores over 500: 100%; ACT scores over 18: 93%; SAT critical reading scores over 600: 60%; SAT math scores over 600: 20%; SAT writing scores over 600: 60%; ACT scores over 24: 35%; SAT critical reading scores over 700: 40%; ACT scores over 30: 10%.

Retention: 55% of full-time freshmen returned.

FACULTY

Total: 39, 64% full-time, 72% with terminal degrees.

Student/faculty ratio: 10:1.

ACADEMICS

Calendar: semesters plus 2-month term. *Degrees:* associate and bachelor's.

Special study options: academic remediation for entering students, accelerated degree program, adult/continuing education programs, advanced placement credit, distance learning, double majors, external degree program, honors programs, independent study, internships, off-campus study, part-time degree program, services for LD students, student-designed majors, study abroad, summer session for credit. ***ROTC:*** Army (c).

Computers: Students can access the following: computer help desk, free student e-mail accounts, online (class) grades, online (class) registration, online (class) schedules. Campuswide network is available. 100% of college-owned or -operated housing units are wired for high-speed Internet access. Wireless service is available via computer labs, dorm rooms, libraries, student centers.

STUDENT LIFE

Housing options: on-campus residence required through senior year; women-only. Campus housing is university owned. Freshman campus housing is guaranteed.

Activities and organizations: drama/theater group, student-run newspaper, choral group, marching band, Student Government Association, Campus Ministries, Faith-Based Service Learning Activities, Ambassadors, Science Club.

Athletics Member NCCAA, USCAA. ***Intercollegiate sports:*** basketball W(s), equestrian sports W, soccer W(s), softball W(s), tennis W(s)(c), volleyball W(s). ***Intramural sports:*** basketball W, field hockey W, softball W, swimming and diving W, tennis W, volleyball W.

Campus security: 24-hour emergency response devices and patrols, late-night transport/escort service, controlled dormitory access.

Student services: personal/psychological counseling.

APPLYING

Standardized Tests *Required:* SAT or ACT (for admission).

Options: electronic application, early admission, deferred entrance.

Application fee: $40.

Required: high school transcript, minimum 2.0 GPA.

Application deadlines: rolling (freshmen), rolling (out-of-state freshmen), rolling (transfers).

Notification: continuous (freshmen), continuous (out-of-state freshmen), continuous (transfers).

CONTACT

Ms. Layne Calhoun, Executive Director of Enrollment Services, Judson College, 302 Bibb Street, Marion, AL 36756. *Phone:* 334-683-5110. *Toll-free phone:* 800-447-9472. *Fax:* 334-683-5282. *E-mail:* admissions@judson.edu.

★ Samford University

Birmingham, Alabama

http://www.samford.edu/

- **Independent Baptist** university, founded 1841
- **Suburban** 318-acre campus
- **Endowment** $277.5 million
- **Coed** 3,051 undergraduate students, 96% full-time, 65% women, 35% men
- **Moderately difficult** entrance level, 60% of applicants were admitted

UNDERGRAD STUDENTS

2,915 full-time, 136 part-time. Students come from 39 states and territories; 17 other countries; 65% are from out of state; 7% Black or African American, non-Hispanic/Latino; 6% Hispanic/Latino; 0.9% Asian, non-Hispanic/Latino; 0.2% American Indian or Alaska Native, non-Hispanic/Latino; 1% Two or more races, non-Hispanic/Latino; 0.4% Race/ethnicity unknown; 3% international; 4% transferred in; 72% live on campus.

Freshmen

Admission: 4,577 applied, 2,725 admitted, 730 enrolled. ***Average high school GPA:*** 3.6. ***Test scores:*** SAT critical reading scores over 500: 82%; SAT math scores over 500: 79%; SAT writing scores over 500: 78%; ACT scores over 18: 99%; SAT critical reading scores over 600: 35%; SAT math scores over 600: 32%; SAT writing scores over 600: 32%; ACT scores over 24: 72%; SAT critical reading scores over 700: 6%; SAT math scores over 700: 6%; SAT writing scores over 700: 5%; ACT scores over 30: 17%.

Retention: 88% of full-time freshmen returned.

FACULTY

Total: 485, 63% full-time, 71% with terminal degrees.

Student/faculty ratio: 13:1.

ACADEMICS

Calendar: 4-1-4. *Degrees:* certificates, bachelor's, master's, doctoral, and post-master's certificates.

Special study options: accelerated degree program, adult/continuing education programs, distance learning, double majors, English as a second language, honors programs, independent study, internships, off-campus study, part-time degree program, services for LD students, study abroad, summer session for credit. ***ROTC:*** Army (c), Air Force (c).

Unusual degree programs: 3-2 engineering with The University of Alabama at Birmingham, Auburn University, and Mercer University (Georgia).

Computers: 330 computers/terminals and 400 ports are available on campus for general student use. Students can access the following: campus intranet, computer help desk, free student e-mail accounts, online (class) grades, online (class) registration, online (class) schedules, free online storage and tech support. Campuswide network is available. 100% of college-owned or -operated housing units are wired for high-speed Internet access. Wireless service is available via entire campus.

STUDENT LIFE

Housing options: on-campus residence required through sophomore year; men-only, women-only. Campus housing is university owned. Freshman campus housing is guaranteed.

Activities and organizations: drama/theater group, student-run newspaper, radio station, choral group, marching band, Zeta Tau Alpha Sorority, Chi Omega Sorority, Alpha Delta Pi Sorority, Phi Mu Sorority, Alpha Omicron Pi Sorority, national fraternities, national sororities.

Athletics Member NCAA. All Division I except football (Division I-AA). ***Intercollegiate sports:*** baseball M(s), basketball M(s)/W(s), cross-country running M(s)/W(s), golf M(s)/W(s), soccer W(s), softball W(s), tennis M(s)/W(s), track and field M(s)/W(s), volleyball W(s). ***Intramural sports:*** basketball M/W, golf M/W, racquetball M/W, soccer M/W, softball M/W, table tennis M/W, ultimate Frisbee M/W, volleyball M/W.

Campus security: 24-hour emergency response devices and patrols, late-night transport/escort service, Nighttime Campus Access Control Gate, and lighted pathways/sidewalks.

Student services: health clinic, personal/psychological counseling, legal services.

COSTS & FINANCIAL AID

Costs (2015–16) ***Comprehensive fee:*** $38,604 includes full-time tuition ($27,520), mandatory fees ($850), and room and board ($10,234). Full-time tuition and fees vary according to course load and program. Part-time tuition: $920 per credit hour. Part-time tuition and fees vary according to course load and program. ***Required fees:*** $320 per credit hour part-time. ***College room only:*** $5694. Room and board charges vary according to board plan, housing facility, and student level. ***Payment plan:*** installment. ***Waivers:*** employees or children of employees.

Financial Aid Of all full-time matriculated undergraduates who enrolled in 2013, 1,681 applied for aid, 1,232 were judged to have need, 272 had their need fully met. 356 Federal Work-Study jobs (averaging $1744). 602 state and other part-time jobs (averaging $1523). In 2013, 1224 non-need-based awards were made. ***Average percent of need met:*** 66. ***Average financial aid package:*** $17,866. ***Average need-based loan:*** $3687. ***Average need-based gift aid:*** $14,046. ***Average non-need-based aid:*** $9636. ***Average indebtedness upon graduation:*** $26,543.

APPLYING

Standardized Tests *Required:* SAT or ACT (for admission).

Options: electronic application, early admission, deferred entrance.

Application fee: $40.

Required: essay or personal statement, high school transcript, 1 letter of recommendation, official scores on ACT or SAT. ***Required for some:*** interview.

Application deadlines: 7/31 (freshmen), 7/31 (out-of-state freshmen), rolling (transfers).

Notification: continuous until 11/1 (freshmen), continuous until 11/1 (out-of-state freshmen).

CONTACT

Mr. Brian L. Kennedy, Director of Recruitment, Samford University, 800 Lakeshore Drive, Samford Hall, Birmingham, AL 35229-0002. *Phone:* 205-726-4176. *Toll-free phone:* 800-888-7218. *Fax:* 205-726-2171. *E-mail:* blkenned@samford.edu.

Selma University

Selma, Alabama

http://www.selmauniversity.edu/

- **Independent Baptist** comprehensive, founded 1878
- **Small-town** 50-acre campus
- **Endowment** $2.5 million
- **Coed** 398 undergraduate students, 84% full-time, 68% women, 32% men

UNDERGRAD STUDENTS

333 full-time, 65 part-time. Students come from 7 states and territories; 4% are from out of state; 96% Black or African American, non-Hispanic/Latino; 0.5% Hispanic/Latino; 3% Two or more races, non-Hispanic/Latino; 39% transferred in; 85% live on campus.

Freshmen

Admission: 135 enrolled. ***Average high school GPA:*** 2.15.

Retention: 37% of full-time freshmen returned.

FACULTY

Total: 36, 42% full-time, 17% with terminal degrees.

Student/faculty ratio: 12:1.

ACADEMICS

Calendar: semesters. *Degrees:* bachelor's and master's.

Special study options: academic remediation for entering students, double majors, independent study, off-campus study, summer session for credit.

Computers: Campuswide network is available. Wireless service is available via entire campus.

STUDENT LIFE

Housing options: on-campus residence required for freshman year; coed. Campus housing is university owned.

Activities and organizations: choral group, Ministers Union, Student Government.

Athletics Member NCCAA. ***Intercollegiate sports:*** baseball M, basketball M/W.

Campus security: 24-hour patrols.

COSTS

Costs (2015–16) ***Comprehensive fee:*** $9125 includes full-time tuition ($6480), mandatory fees ($145), and room and board ($2500). Full-time tuition and fees vary according to program. Part-time tuition: $250 per credit hour. Part-time tuition and fees vary according to program. ***Payment plan:*** installment. ***Waivers:*** employees or children of employees.

APPLYING

Standardized Tests *Required for some:* SAT or ACT (for admission). *Recommended:* SAT or ACT (for admission).

Required: essay or personal statement, high school transcript, 3 letters of recommendation.

CONTACT

Selma University, 1501 Lapsley Street, Selma, AL 36701-5299. *Phone:* 334-872-2533 Ext. 116.

Southeastern Bible College

Birmingham, Alabama

http://www.sebc.edu/

- **Independent nondenominational** 4-year, founded 1935
- **Suburban** 22-acre campus
- **Coed** 173 undergraduate students, 76% full-time, 45% women, 55% men
- **Noncompetitive** entrance level, 100% of applicants were admitted

UNDERGRAD STUDENTS

131 full-time, 42 part-time. Students come from 10 states and territories; 7% are from out of state; 31% Black or African American, non-Hispanic/Latino; 2% Hispanic/Latino; 0.6% Asian, non-Hispanic/Latino; 0.6% American Indian or Alaska Native, non-Hispanic/Latino; 0.6% Two or more races, non-Hispanic/Latino; 3% Race/ethnicity unknown; 29% live on campus.

Freshmen
Admission: 27 applied, 27 admitted. ***Test scores:*** ACT scores over 18: 75%.
Retention: 69% of full-time freshmen returned.

FACULTY
Total: 22, 32% full-time, 45% with terminal degrees.
Student/faculty ratio: 12:1.

ACADEMICS
Calendar: semesters. *Degrees:* diplomas, associate, and bachelor's.
Special study options: academic remediation for entering students, adult/continuing education programs, advanced placement credit, double majors, internships, part-time degree program, services for LD students, summer session for credit.
Computers: 25 computers/terminals are available on campus for general student use. Students can access the following: free student e-mail accounts. 100% of college-owned or -operated housing units are wired for high-speed Internet access. Wireless service is available via entire campus.

STUDENT LIFE
Housing options: men-only, women-only. Campus housing is university owned.
Activities and organizations: choral group, Student Council, Student Missions Fellowship, chorale.
Campus security: student patrols, controlled dormitory access.

COSTS & FINANCIAL AID
Costs (2014–15) ***Tuition:*** $10,920 full-time, $390 per semester hour part-time. Full-time tuition and fees vary according to program. Part-time tuition and fees vary according to program. ***Required fees:*** $450 full-time, $225 per term part-time. ***Room only:*** $2550. ***Payment plan:*** installment. ***Waivers:*** employees or children of employees.
Financial Aid Of all full-time matriculated undergraduates who enrolled in 2013, 128 applied for aid, 116 were judged to have need, 1 had their need fully met. In 2013, 6 non-need-based awards were made. ***Average percent of need met:*** 72. ***Average financial aid package:*** $12,000. ***Average need-based loan:*** $4500. ***Average need-based gift aid:*** $6500. ***Average non-need-based aid:*** $3800.

APPLYING
Standardized Tests *Required:* SAT or ACT (for admission).
Options: electronic application, deferred entrance.
Application fee: $30.
Required: essay or personal statement, high school transcript, minimum 1.5 GPA, 2 letters of recommendation. ***Required for some:*** interview.

CONTACT
Ms. Deidra Whitfield, Admissions Counselor, Southeastern Bible College, 2545 Valleydale Road, Birmingham, AL 35244. *Phone:* 205-970-9210. *Toll-free phone:* 800-749-8878. *Fax:* 205-970-9207. *E-mail:* deidra.whitfield@sebc.edu.

South University

Montgomery, Alabama

http://www.southuniversity.edu/montgomery/

- **Proprietary** comprehensive, founded 1887, part of Education Management Corporation
- **Coed**

ACADEMICS
Calendar: quarters. *Degrees:* associate, bachelor's, master's, and post-master's certificates.

CONTACT
South University, 5355 Vaughn Road, Montgomery, AL 36116-1120. *Phone:* 334-395-8800. *Toll-free phone:* 866-629-2962.

Spring Hill College

Mobile, Alabama

http://www.shc.edu/

- **Independent Roman Catholic (Jesuit)** comprehensive, founded 1830
- **Suburban** 450-acre campus
- **Coed** 1,274 undergraduate students, 95% full-time, 60% women, 40% men
- **Moderately difficult** entrance level, 52% of applicants were admitted

UNDERGRAD STUDENTS
1,215 full-time, 59 part-time. Students come from 35 states and territories; 18 other countries; 60% are from out of state; 15% Black or African American, non-Hispanic/Latino; 6% Hispanic/Latino; 1% Asian, non-Hispanic/Latino; 0.1% Native Hawaiian or other Pacific Islander, non-Hispanic/Latino; 0.7% American Indian or Alaska Native, non-Hispanic/Latino; 4% Two or more races, non-Hispanic/Latino; 4% Race/ethnicity unknown; 2% international; 3% transferred in; 80% live on campus.

Freshmen
Admission: 6,245 applied, 3,233 admitted, 360 enrolled. ***Average high school GPA:*** 3.53. ***Test scores:*** SAT critical reading scores over 500: 65%; SAT math scores over 500: 73%; ACT scores over 18: 99%; SAT critical reading scores over 600: 26%; SAT math scores over 600: 25%; ACT scores over 24: 55%; SAT critical reading scores over 700: 6%; ACT scores over 30: 9%.
Retention: 73% of full-time freshmen returned.

FACULTY
Total: 126, 65% full-time, 69% with terminal degrees.
Student/faculty ratio: 13:1.

ACADEMICS
Calendar: semesters. *Degrees:* certificates, bachelor's, master's, post-master's, and postbachelor's certificates.
Special study options: academic remediation for entering students, accelerated degree program, adult/continuing education programs, advanced placement credit, distance learning, double majors, honors programs, independent study, internships, off-campus study, part-time degree program, services for LD students, student-designed majors, study abroad, summer session for credit. ***ROTC:*** Army (c), Air Force (c).
Unusual degree programs: 3-2 engineering with Marquette University, University of Alabama at Birmingham, University of Florida, Auburn University, Texas A&M University, University of South Alabama.
Computers: Students can access the following: campus intranet, computer help desk, free student e-mail accounts, online (class) grades, online (class) registration, online (class) schedules. Campuswide network is available. 100% of college-owned or -operated housing units are wired for high-speed Internet access. Wireless service is available via computer centers, computer labs, dorm rooms, libraries, student centers.

STUDENT LIFE
Housing options: on-campus residence required through senior year; coed. Campus housing is university owned. Freshman campus housing is guaranteed.
Activities and organizations: drama/theater group, student-run newspaper, choral group, Fraternities and sororities, SHAPe, National Society of Leadership and Success, Peer One Project, Chemistry Club, national fraternities, national sororities.
Athletics Member NAIA. ***Intercollegiate sports:*** baseball M(s), basketball M(s)/W(s), cross-country running M(s)/W(s), golf M(s)/W(s), soccer M(s)/W(s), softball W(s), tennis M(s)/W(s), track and field M(s)/W(s), volleyball W(s). ***Intramural sports:*** basketball M/W, bowling M/W, football M/W, racquetball M/W, rugby M(c), soccer M/W, ultimate Frisbee M/W, volleyball M/W.
Campus security: 24-hour emergency response devices and patrols, late-night transport/escort service, controlled dormitory access.
Student services: health clinic, personal/psychological counseling.

COSTS & FINANCIAL AID
Costs (2014–15) ***Comprehensive fee:*** $44,164 includes full-time tuition ($30,506), mandatory fees ($1962), and room and board ($11,696). Part-time tuition: $975 per credit hour. ***Required fees:*** $50 per credit hour part-time. ***College room only:*** $6300. Room and board charges vary according

to board plan and housing facility. ***Payment plan:*** installment. ***Waivers:*** employees or children of employees.

Financial Aid Of all full-time matriculated undergraduates who enrolled in 2014, 963 applied for aid, 843 were judged to have need, 114 had their need fully met. In 2014, 311 non-need-based awards were made. ***Average percent of need met:*** 88. ***Average financial aid package:*** $26,574. ***Average need-based loan:*** $2124. ***Average need-based gift aid:*** $23,568. ***Average non-need-based aid:*** $18,148. ***Average indebtedness upon graduation:*** $31,855.

APPLYING

Standardized Tests *Required:* SAT or ACT (for admission).

Options: electronic application, early admission, deferred entrance.

Application fee: $25.

Required: essay or personal statement, high school transcript, 1 letter of recommendation. ***Recommended:*** minimum 2.5 GPA, interview.

Application deadlines: 7/15 (freshmen), 7/15 (out-of-state freshmen), rolling (transfers).

Notification: continuous (freshmen), continuous (out-of-state freshmen), continuous (transfers).

CONTACT

Mrs. Allison Miller, Admissions, Campus Visit Coordinator, Spring Hill College, 4000 Dauphin Street, Mobile, AL 36608-1791. *Phone:* 251-380-3032. *Toll-free phone:* 800-SHC-6704. *Fax:* 251-460-2186. *E-mail:* amiller@shc.edu.

Troy University

Troy, Alabama

http://www.troy.edu/

- **State-supported** comprehensive, founded 1887, part of Troy University System
- **Small-town** 906-acre campus
- **Endowment** $56.6 million
- **Coed** 15,115 undergraduate students, 60% full-time, 61% women, 39% men
- **Moderately difficult** entrance level, 44% of applicants were admitted

UNDERGRAD STUDENTS

9,018 full-time, 6,097 part-time. Students come from 52 states and territories; 52 other countries; 32% are from out of state; 34% Black or African American, non-Hispanic/Latino; 3% Hispanic/Latino; 0.8% Asian, non-Hispanic/Latino; 0.1% Native Hawaiian or other Pacific Islander, non-Hispanic/Latino; 0.8% American Indian or Alaska Native, non-Hispanic/Latino; 2% Two or more races, non-Hispanic/Latino; 4% Race/ethnicity unknown; 3% international; 9% transferred in; 35% live on campus.

Freshmen

Admission: 6,336 applied, 2,797 admitted, 1,900 enrolled. ***Test scores:*** SAT math scores over 500: 57%; SAT writing scores over 500: 25%; ACT scores over 18: 88%; SAT math scores over 600: 19%; ACT scores over 24: 37%; SAT math scores over 700: 5%; ACT scores over 30: 4%.

Retention: 76% of full-time freshmen returned.

FACULTY

Total: 1,110, 48% full-time, 57% with terminal degrees.

Student/faculty ratio: 18:1.

ACADEMICS

Calendar: semesters. *Degrees:* associate, bachelor's, master's, doctoral, and post-master's certificates.

Special study options: academic remediation for entering students, accelerated degree program, advanced placement credit, distance learning, double majors, English as a second language, honors programs, independent study, internships, part-time degree program, services for LD students, summer session for credit. ***ROTC:*** Army (b), Air Force (b).

Computers: 12,792 computers/terminals and 18,117 ports are available on campus for general student use. Students can access the following: campus intranet, computer help desk, free student e-mail accounts, online (class) grades, online (class) registration, online (class) schedules. Campuswide network is available. Wireless service is available via classrooms, dorm rooms, libraries.

STUDENT LIFE

Housing options: on-campus residence required for freshman year; coed, men-only, women-only. Campus housing is university owned. Freshman campus housing is guaranteed.

Activities and organizations: drama/theater group, student-run newspaper, television station, choral group, marching band, T-Day/Athletic Events (Homecoming), Activities Council, Pep Rallies, national fraternities, national sororities.

Athletics Member NCAA. All Division I except football (Division I-A). ***Intercollegiate sports:*** baseball M(s), basketball M(s)/W(s), cross-country running M(s)/W(s), golf M(s)/W(s), soccer W(s), softball W(s), tennis M(s)/W(s), track and field M(s)/W(s), volleyball W(s). ***Intramural sports:*** basketball M/W, bowling M/W, cross-country running M/W, football M, golf M/W, soccer W, softball W, tennis M/W, track and field M/W, volleyball W.

Campus security: 24-hour emergency response devices and patrols, student patrols, late-night transport/escort service, controlled dormitory access.

Student services: health clinic, personal/psychological counseling.

COSTS & FINANCIAL AID

Costs (2014–15) ***Tuition:*** state resident $6528 full-time, $264 per credit hour part-time; nonresident $13,056 full-time, $528 per credit hour part-time. Full-time tuition and fees vary according to location and program. Part-time tuition and fees vary according to location and program. ***Required fees:*** $1036 full-time, $35 per credit hour part-time, $50 per term part-time. ***Room and board:*** $6498; room only: $3724. Room and board charges vary according to board plan and housing facility. ***Payment plan:*** installment. ***Waivers:*** employees or children of employees.

Financial Aid Of all full-time matriculated undergraduates who enrolled in 2014, 6,342 applied for aid, 6,316 were judged to have need. In 2014, 2226 non-need-based awards were made. ***Average financial aid package:*** $4497. ***Average need-based loan:*** $4470. ***Average need-based gift aid:*** $4659. ***Average non-need-based aid:*** $5844.

APPLYING

Standardized Tests *Required:* SAT or ACT (for admission).

Options: electronic application, deferred entrance.

Application fee: $30.

Required: high school transcript. ***Recommended:*** interview.

Application deadlines: rolling (freshmen), rolling (transfers).

CONTACT

Mr. Buddy Starling, Dean of Enrollment Management, Troy University, University Avenue, Troy, AL 36082. *Phone:* 334-670-3243. *Toll-free phone:* 800-551-9716. *Fax:* 334-670-3733. *E-mail:* bstar@troy.edu.

Tuskegee University

Tuskegee, Alabama

http://www.tuskegee.edu/

- **Independent** comprehensive, founded 1881
- **Small-town** 5000-acre campus
- **Endowment** $113.7 million
- **Coed**
- **Moderately difficult** entrance level

FACULTY

Student/faculty ratio: 14:1.

ACADEMICS

Calendar: semesters. *Degrees:* bachelor's, master's, and doctoral.

STUDENT LIFE

Housing options: on-campus residence required through sophomore year; coed, men-only, women-only. Campus housing is university owned. Freshman applicants given priority for college housing.

Activities and organizations: drama/theater group, student-run newspaper, television station, choral group, marching band, student government, Marching Band, State Clubs, Fraternities, Sororities, national fraternities, national sororities.

Athletics Member NCAA. All Division II.

Campus security: 24-hour emergency response devices and patrols, late-night transport/escort service.

Student services: health clinic, personal/psychological counseling.

COSTS & FINANCIAL AID

Costs (2014–15) ***Comprehensive fee:*** $28,224 includes full-time tuition ($18,560), mandatory fees ($560), and room and board ($9104). Full-time tuition and fees vary according to course level, course load, degree level, and program. Part-time tuition and fees vary according to course level, course load, degree level, and program. ***College room only:*** $4300. Room and board charges vary according to board plan and housing facility.

Financial Aid Of all full-time matriculated undergraduates who enrolled in 2013, 2,519 applied for aid, 2,147 were judged to have need, 1,379 had their need fully met. 620 Federal Work-Study jobs (averaging $2014). 416 state and other part-time jobs (averaging $4755). In 2013, 597 non-need-based awards were made. ***Average percent of need met:*** 85. ***Average financial aid package:*** $19,250. ***Average need-based loan:*** $6006. ***Average need-based gift aid:*** $800. ***Average non-need-based aid:*** $6000. ***Average indebtedness upon graduation:*** $26,500.

APPLYING

Standardized Tests *Required:* SAT or ACT (for admission).

Options: electronic application, early admission.

Application fee: $25.

Required: high school transcript, minimum 3.0 GPA, ACT or SAT (prefer SAT).

CONTACT

Mrs. Elizabeth Dadzie, Associate Vice President, Enrollment Management, Tuskegee University, 1200 Old Montgomery Road, Margaret Murray Hall - Admissions, Tuskegee, AL 36088. *Phone:* 800-622-6531. *Toll-free phone:* 800-622-6531. *Fax:* 334-727-5750. *E-mail:* admissions@mytu.tuskegee.edu.

United States Sports Academy

Daphne, Alabama

http://www.ussa.edu/

- **Independent** upper-level, founded 1972
- **Suburban** 10-acre campus
- **Endowment** $1.0 million
- **Coed** 99 undergraduate students, 17% full-time, 19% women, 81% men
- 37% of applicants were admitted

UNDERGRAD STUDENTS

17 full-time, 82 part-time. 13% Black or African American, non-Hispanic/Latino; 6% Hispanic/Latino; 2% Asian, non-Hispanic/Latino; 4% Two or more races, non-Hispanic/Latino; 32% Race/ethnicity unknown.

Freshmen

Admission: 125 applied, 46 admitted.

FACULTY

Total: 34, 21% full-time, 79% with terminal degrees.

Student/faculty ratio: 12:1.

ACADEMICS

Calendar: continuous. *Degrees:* certificates, diplomas, bachelor's, master's, doctoral, and post-master's certificates.

Special study options: distance learning.

Computers: 1 computer/terminal is available on campus for general student use. Students can access the following: computer help desk, free student e-mail accounts, online (class) grades, online (class) registration, online (class) schedules. Campuswide network is available.

STUDENT LIFE

Activities and organizations: Alumni Association.

Campus security: electronically operated building entrances.

COSTS

Costs (2015–16) ***Tuition:*** $360 per credit hour part-time. ***Waivers:*** employees or children of employees.

APPLYING

Options: electronic application.

Application fee: $50.

Notification: continuous (transfers).

CONTACT

United States Sports Academy, One Academy Drive, Daphne, AL 36526-7055. *Phone:* 251-626-3303 Ext. 7127. *Toll-free phone:* 800-223-2668.

The University of Alabama

Tuscaloosa, Alabama

http://www.ua.edu/

- **State-supported** university, founded 1831, part of University of Alabama System
- **Suburban** 1000-acre campus with easy access to Birmingham
- **Endowment** $673.6 million
- **Coed** 30,752 undergraduate students, 90% full-time, 54% women, 46% men
- **Moderately difficult** entrance level, 51% of applicants were admitted

UNDERGRAD STUDENTS

27,737 full-time, 3,015 part-time. Students come from 52 states and territories; 56 other countries; 50% are from out of state; 11% Black or African American, non-Hispanic/Latino; 3% Hispanic/Latino; 1% Asian, non-Hispanic/Latino; 0.1% Native Hawaiian or other Pacific Islander, non-Hispanic/Latino; 0.4% American Indian or Alaska Native, non-Hispanic/Latino; 3% Two or more races, non-Hispanic/Latino; 0.3% Race/ethnicity unknown; 3% international; 5% transferred in; 27% live on campus.

Freshmen

Admission: 33,736 applied, 17,221 admitted, 6,824 enrolled. ***Average high school GPA:*** 3.65. ***Test scores:*** SAT critical reading scores over 500: 75%; SAT math scores over 500: 77%; SAT writing scores over 500: 70%; ACT scores over 18: 100%; SAT critical reading scores over 600: 32%; SAT math scores over 600: 34%; SAT writing scores over 600: 27%; ACT scores over 24: 69%; SAT critical reading scores over 700: 9%; SAT math scores over 700: 13%; SAT writing scores over 700: 6%; ACT scores over 30: 36%.

Retention: 87% of full-time freshmen returned.

FACULTY

Total: 1,776, 70% full-time, 74% with terminal degrees.

ACADEMICS

Calendar: semesters. *Degrees:* bachelor's, master's, doctoral, and post-master's certificates.

Special study options: academic remediation for entering students, accelerated degree program, adult/continuing education programs, advanced placement credit, cooperative education, distance learning, double majors, English as a second language, external degree program, freshman honors college, honors programs, independent study, internships, off-campus study, part-time degree program, services for LD students, student-designed majors, study abroad, summer session for credit. ***ROTC:*** Army (b), Air Force (b).

Computers: 2,500 computers/terminals and 9,000 ports are available on campus for general student use. Students can access the following: campus intranet, computer help desk, free student e-mail accounts, online (class) grades, online (class) registration, online (class) schedules. Campuswide network is available. 100% of college-owned or -operated housing units are wired for high-speed Internet access. Wireless service is available via entire campus.

STUDENT LIFE

Housing options: on-campus residence required for freshman year; coed, men-only, women-only, special housing for students with disabilities. Campus housing is university owned and leased by the school. Freshman campus housing is guaranteed.

Activities and organizations: drama/theater group, student-run newspaper, radio station, choral group, marching band, ABXY Gaming Network, Association of Residence Communities, International Student Association, Student Government Association, Black Student Union, national fraternities, national sororities.

Athletics Member NCAA. All Division I except football (Division I-A). ***Intercollegiate sports:*** badminton M(c)/W(c), baseball M(s), basketball M(s)/W(s), bowling M(c), cheerleading M(s)/W(s), crew M(c)/W(s), cross-country running M(s)/W(s), equestrian sports M(c)/W(c), golf M(s)/W(s), gymnastics W(s), ice hockey M(c), lacrosse M(c)/W(c), racquetball M(c)/W(c), rugby M(c)/W(c), soccer M(c)/W(s), softball

advanced placement credit, double majors, honors programs, independent study, internships, part-time degree program, services for LD students, summer session for credit. ***ROTC:*** Army (c), Air Force (c).

Unusual degree programs: 3-2 engineering with University of South Alabama.

Computers: 120 computers/terminals are available on campus for general student use. Students can access the following: campus intranet, computer help desk, free student e-mail accounts, online (class) grades, online (class) registration, online (class) schedules. Campuswide network is available. 100% of college-owned or -operated housing units are wired for high-speed Internet access. Wireless service is available via classrooms, computer centers, computer labs, dorm rooms, learning centers, libraries, student centers.

STUDENT LIFE

Housing options: on-campus residence required through sophomore year; men-only, women-only. Campus housing is university owned. Freshman campus housing is guaranteed.

Activities and organizations: drama/theater group, choral group, Campus Activity Board, Baptist Campus Ministry, Student Government Association, Fellowship of Christian Athletes.

Athletics Member NAIA. ***Intercollegiate sports:*** baseball M(s), basketball M(s)/W(s), cheerleading W(s), cross-country running M(s)/W(s), golf M(s)/W(s), soccer M(s)/W(s), softball W(s), tennis M(s)/W(s), track and field M(s)/W(s), volleyball W(s). ***Intramural sports:*** basketball M/W, golf M/W, soccer M/W, softball M/W, tennis M/W, track and field M/W, volleyball M/W.

Campus security: 24-hour emergency response devices and patrols, controlled dormitory access, text alerts.

Student services: health clinic, personal/psychological counseling.

COSTS & FINANCIAL AID

Costs (2014–15) ***Comprehensive fee:*** $29,250 includes full-time tuition ($18,720), mandatory fees ($980), and room and board ($9550). Full-time tuition and fees vary according to course load. Part-time tuition: $667 per credit hour. Part-time tuition and fees vary according to course load. ***Required fees:*** $356 per year part-time. ***College room only:*** $5710. Room and board charges vary according to housing facility. ***Payment plan:*** installment. ***Waivers:*** employees or children of employees.

Financial Aid Of all full-time matriculated undergraduates who enrolled in 2014, 919 applied for aid, 867 were judged to have need, 866 had their need fully met. 63 Federal Work-Study jobs (averaging $2175). In 2014, 123 non-need-based awards were made. ***Average percent of need met:*** 68. ***Average financial aid package:*** $17,569. ***Average need-based loan:*** $4571. ***Average need-based gift aid:*** $5219. ***Average non-need-based aid:*** $9728. ***Average indebtedness upon graduation:*** $28,250.

APPLYING

Standardized Tests *Required:* SAT or ACT (for admission).

Options: electronic application, deferred entrance.

Application fee: $25.

Required: high school transcript, minimum 2.8 GPA.

Application deadlines: rolling (freshmen), rolling (out-of-state freshmen), rolling (transfers).

Notification: continuous (freshmen), continuous (out-of-state freshmen), continuous (transfers).

CONTACT

Mrs. Charity Wittner, Director of Enrollment Services, University of Mobile, 5735 College Parkway, Mobile, AL 36613-2842. *Phone:* 251-442-2507. *Toll-free phone:* 800-946-7267. *Fax:* 251-442-2498. *E-mail:* cwittner@umobile.edu.

University of Montevallo

Montevallo, Alabama

http://www.montevallo.edu/

- **State-supported** comprehensive, founded 1896
- **Small-town** 160-acre campus with easy access to Birmingham
- **Endowment** $16.6 million
- **Coed** 2,620 undergraduate students, 90% full-time, 66% women, 34% men
- **Moderately difficult** entrance level, 74% of applicants were admitted

UNDERGRAD STUDENTS

2,350 full-time, 270 part-time. Students come from 17 other countries; 5% are from out of state; 14% Black or African American, non-Hispanic/Latino; 2% Hispanic/Latino; 0.6% Asian, non-Hispanic/Latino; 0.1% Native Hawaiian or other Pacific Islander, non-Hispanic/Latino; 0.7% American Indian or Alaska Native, non-Hispanic/Latino; 2% Two or more races, non-Hispanic/Latino; 6% Race/ethnicity unknown; 1% international; 6% transferred in; 47% live on campus.

Freshmen

Admission: 1,821 applied, 1,353 admitted, 531 enrolled. ***Average high school GPA:*** 3.35. ***Test scores:*** ACT scores over 18: 96%; ACT scores over 24: 46%; ACT scores over 30: 8%.

Retention: 74% of full-time freshmen returned.

FACULTY

Total: 223, 65% full-time, 70% with terminal degrees.

Student/faculty ratio: 16:1.

ACADEMICS

Calendar: semesters. *Degrees:* bachelor's, master's, and post-master's certificates.

Special study options: academic remediation for entering students, accelerated degree program, advanced placement credit, distance learning, double majors, honors programs, independent study, internships, part-time degree program, services for LD students, study abroad, summer session for credit. ***ROTC:*** Army (c), Air Force (c).

Unusual degree programs: 3-2 engineering with Auburn University, University of Alabama at Birmingham.

Computers: 340 computers/terminals are available on campus for general student use. Students can access the following: campus intranet, computer help desk, free student e-mail accounts, online (class) grades, online (class) registration, online (class) schedules. Campuswide network is available. 100% of college-owned or -operated housing units are wired for high-speed Internet access. Wireless service is available via classrooms, computer centers, computer labs, dorm rooms, libraries, student centers.

STUDENT LIFE

Housing options: on-campus residence required for freshman year; coed, men-only, women-only. Campus housing is university owned. Freshman campus housing is guaranteed.

Activities and organizations: drama/theater group, student-run newspaper, television station, choral group, Student Government Association, University Programming Council, Campus Ministries, Greek Life, Environmental Club, national fraternities, national sororities.

Athletics Member NCAA. All Division II. ***Intercollegiate sports:*** baseball M(s), basketball M(s)/W(s), cheerleading W, cross-country running M/W, golf M(s)/W(s), lacrosse W, soccer M(s)/W(s), softball W, tennis W(s), track and field M/W, volleyball W(s). ***Intramural sports:*** basketball M/W, bowling M, football M, golf M, tennis M/W, volleyball M/W.

Campus security: 24-hour emergency response devices and patrols, late-night transport/escort service, controlled dormitory access.

Student services: health clinic, personal/psychological counseling.

COSTS & FINANCIAL AID

Costs (2014–15) ***Tuition:*** state resident $9990 full-time, $333 per credit hour part-time; nonresident $20,550 full-time, $685 per credit hour part-time. ***Required fees:*** $670 full-time. ***Room and board:*** $6400; room only: $4000. Room and board charges vary according to housing facility. ***Waivers:*** employees or children of employees.

Financial Aid Of all full-time matriculated undergraduates who enrolled in 2014, 1,735 applied for aid, 1,531 were judged to have need, 173 had their need fully met. 102 Federal Work-Study jobs (averaging $1800). In 2014, 509 non-need-based awards were made. ***Average percent of need met:*** 53. ***Average financial aid package:*** $10,076. ***Average need-based loan:*** $4132. ***Average need-based gift aid:*** $6475. ***Average non-need-based aid:*** $9307. ***Average indebtedness upon graduation:*** $27,090.

APPLYING

Standardized Tests *Required:* SAT or ACT (for admission). *Recommended:* ACT (for admission).

Options: electronic application, early admission, deferred entrance.

Application fee: $30.

Required: high school transcript, minimum 2.0 GPA. ***Recommended:*** interview.

Application deadlines: 8/1 (freshmen), rolling (transfers).

Notification: 9/1 (freshmen).

CONTACT
Mr. Greg Embry, Director of Admissions, University of Montevallo, University of Montevallo, Office of Admissions, Station 6030, Montevallo, AL 35115-6030. *Phone:* 205-665-6030. *Toll-free phone:* 800-292-4349. *Fax:* 205-665-6032. *E-mail:* admissions@montevallo.edu.

University of North Alabama

Florence, Alabama

http://www.una.edu/

- **State-supported** comprehensive, founded 1830
- **Urban** 200-acre campus with easy access to Huntsville
- **Endowment** $27.8 million
- **Coed** 5,885 undergraduate students, 79% full-time, 57% women, 43% men
- **Minimally difficult** entrance level, 68% of applicants were admitted

UNDERGRAD STUDENTS
4,648 full-time, 1,237 part-time. Students come from 41 states and territories; 41 other countries; 16% are from out of state; 13% Black or African American, non-Hispanic/Latino; 3% Hispanic/Latino; 0.8% Asian, non-Hispanic/Latino; 0.1% Native Hawaiian or other Pacific Islander, non-Hispanic/Latino; 0.9% American Indian or Alaska Native, non-Hispanic/Latino; 2% Two or more races, non-Hispanic/Latino; 5% Race/ethnicity unknown; 4% international; 10% transferred in; 22% live on campus.

Freshmen
Admission: 2,765 applied, 1,877 admitted, 944 enrolled. ***Average high school GPA:*** 3.13. ***Test scores:*** SAT critical reading scores over 500: 46%; SAT math scores over 500: 50%; ACT scores over 18: 91%; SAT critical reading scores over 600: 25%; SAT math scores over 600: 11%; ACT scores over 24: 37%; SAT critical reading scores over 700: 4%; ACT scores over 30: 3%.

Retention: 72% of full-time freshmen returned.

FACULTY
Total: 365, 69% full-time, 59% with terminal degrees.

Student/faculty ratio: 17:1.

ACADEMICS
Calendar: semesters. *Degrees:* bachelor's, master's, post-master's, and postbachelor's certificates.

Special study options: academic remediation for entering students, accelerated degree program, advanced placement credit, cooperative education, distance learning, double majors, English as a second language, freshman honors college, honors programs, independent study, internships, off-campus study, part-time degree program, services for LD students, student-designed majors, study abroad, summer session for credit. ***ROTC:*** Army (b).

Computers: 929 computers/terminals are available on campus for general student use. Students can access the following: campus intranet, computer help desk, free student e-mail accounts, online (class) grades, online (class) registration, online (class) schedules. Campuswide network is available. 100% of college-owned or -operated housing units are wired for high-speed Internet access. Wireless service is available via entire campus.

STUDENT LIFE
Housing options: coed, men-only, women-only. Campus housing is university owned and is provided by a third party.

Activities and organizations: drama/theater group, student-run newspaper, radio station, choral group, marching band, Student Government Association, University Program Council, Baptist campus ministries, Physical Education Majors Club, Residence Hall Association, national fraternities, national sororities.

Athletics Member NCAA. All Division II. ***Intercollegiate sports:*** baseball M(s), basketball M(s)/W(s), cheerleading M(s)/W(s), cross-country running M(s)/W(s), football M(s), golf M(s), soccer W(s), softball W(s), tennis M(s)/W(s), volleyball W(s). ***Intramural sports:*** badminton M/W, baseball M, basketball M/W, bowling M/W, cross-country running M/W, football M/W, golf M, racquetball M/W, rugby M, softball W, swimming and diving M/W, table tennis M/W, tennis M/W, volleyball M/W, weight lifting M/W.

Campus security: 24-hour emergency response devices and patrols, student patrols, late-night transport/escort service, controlled dormitory access.

Student services: health clinic, personal/psychological counseling, women's center.

COSTS & FINANCIAL AID
Costs (2014–15) ***Tuition:*** state resident $7320 full-time, $244 per credit hour part-time; nonresident $14,640 full-time, $488 per credit hour part-time. Full-time tuition and fees vary according to course load and program. Part-time tuition and fees vary according to course load and program. ***Required fees:*** $1753 full-time. ***Room and board:*** $6327. Room and board charges vary according to board plan and housing facility. ***Payment plan:*** installment. ***Waivers:*** senior citizens and employees or children of employees.

Financial Aid Of all full-time matriculated undergraduates who enrolled in 2013, 2,796 applied for aid, 2,460 were judged to have need, 411 had their need fully met. 171 Federal Work-Study jobs (averaging $1603). 476 state and other part-time jobs (averaging $1621). In 2013, 636 non-need-based awards were made. ***Average percent of need met:*** 63. ***Average financial aid package:*** $7409. ***Average need-based loan:*** $3603. ***Average need-based gift aid:*** $4096. ***Average non-need-based aid:*** $3970. ***Average indebtedness upon graduation:*** $29,839.

APPLYING
Standardized Tests *Required:* SAT or ACT (for admission).

Options: electronic application, early admission, deferred entrance.

Application fee: $25.

Required: high school transcript, minimum 2.0 GPA, 13 approved units from high school academic core.

Application deadlines: rolling (freshmen), rolling (out-of-state freshmen), rolling (transfers).

CONTACT
Mrs. Kim O. Mauldin, Director of Admissions, University of North Alabama, One Harrison Plaza, Florence, AL 35632-0001. *Phone:* 256-765-4680. *Toll-free phone:* 800-TALK-UNA. *Fax:* 256-765-4329. *E-mail:* admissions@una.edu.

University of South Alabama

Mobile, Alabama

http://www.southalabama.edu/

- **State-supported** university, founded 1963
- **Suburban** 1225-acre campus
- **Endowment** $157.1 million
- **Coed** 11,479 undergraduate students, 79% full-time, 56% women, 44% men
- **Moderately difficult** entrance level, 84% of applicants were admitted

UNDERGRAD STUDENTS
9,090 full-time, 2,389 part-time. Students come from 52 states and territories; 76 other countries; 18% are from out of state; 24% Black or African American, non-Hispanic/Latino; 3% Hispanic/Latino; 3% Asian, non-Hispanic/Latino; 0.1% Native Hawaiian or other Pacific Islander, non-Hispanic/Latino; 0.6% American Indian or Alaska Native, non-Hispanic/Latino; 2% Two or more races, non-Hispanic/Latino; 1% Race/ethnicity unknown; 4% international; 8% transferred in; 29% live on campus.

Freshmen
Admission: 5,614 applied, 4,688 admitted, 2,073 enrolled. ***Average high school GPA:*** 3.41. ***Test scores:*** SAT critical reading scores over 500: 57%; SAT math scores over 500: 55%; SAT writing scores over 500: 43%; ACT scores over 18: 93%; SAT critical reading scores over 600: 17%; SAT math scores over 600: 20%; SAT writing scores over 600: 12%; ACT scores over 24: 41%; SAT critical reading scores over 700: 3%; SAT math

CONTACT
Mr. Kirk Kluver, Director of Undergraduate Admissions, The University of Alabama at Birmingham, 1701 11th Avenue South, Birmingham, AL 35294-4412. *Phone:* 205-934-8221. *Toll-free phone:* 800-421-8743. *Fax:* 205-975-7114. *E-mail:* chooseuab@uab.edu.

The University of Alabama in Huntsville

Huntsville, Alabama

http://www.uah.edu/

- **State-supported** university, founded 1950, part of University of Alabama System
- **Suburban** 400-acre campus
- **Endowment** $73.9 million
- **Coed** 5,618 undergraduate students, 77% full-time, 43% women, 57% men
- **Moderately difficult** entrance level, 82% of applicants were admitted

UNDERGRAD STUDENTS
4,304 full-time, 1,314 part-time. 10% are from out of state; 12% Black or African American, non-Hispanic/Latino; 4% Hispanic/Latino; 4% Asian, non-Hispanic/Latino; 1% American Indian or Alaska Native, non-Hispanic/Latino; 2% Two or more races, non-Hispanic/Latino; 4% Race/ethnicity unknown; 4% international; 12% transferred in; 21% live on campus.

Freshmen
Admission: 2,104 applied, 1,726 admitted, 724 enrolled. ***Average high school GPA:*** 3.69. ***Test scores:*** SAT critical reading scores over 500: 83%; SAT math scores over 500: 88%; ACT scores over 18: 99%; SAT critical reading scores over 600: 46%; SAT math scores over 600: 48%; ACT scores over 24: 78%; SAT critical reading scores over 700: 14%; SAT math scores over 700: 17%; ACT scores over 30: 30%.
Retention: 77% of full-time freshmen returned.

FACULTY
Total: 484, 62% full-time, 68% with terminal degrees.
Student/faculty ratio: 16:1.

ACADEMICS
Calendar: semesters. *Degrees:* certificates, bachelor's, master's, doctoral, post-master's, and postbachelor's certificates.
Special study options: academic remediation for entering students, advanced placement credit, cooperative education, distance learning, double majors, English as a second language, honors programs, independent study, internships, off-campus study, part-time degree program, services for LD students, student-designed majors, study abroad, summer session for credit. ***ROTC:*** Army (c).
Unusual degree programs: 3-2 engineering with Oakwood College, Morehouse College, Clark Atlanta University, Spelman College.
Computers: 1,227 computers/terminals and 5,330 ports are available on campus for general student use. Students can access the following: campus intranet, computer help desk, free student e-mail accounts, online (class) grades, online (class) registration, online (class) schedules. Campuswide network is available. 100% of college-owned or -operated housing units are wired for high-speed Internet access. Wireless service is available via classrooms, computer centers, computer labs, dorm rooms, learning centers, libraries, student centers.

STUDENT LIFE
Housing options: on-campus residence required through sophomore year; coed, cooperative, special housing for students with disabilities. Campus housing is university owned. Freshman campus housing is guaranteed.
Activities and organizations: drama/theater group, student-run newspaper, choral group, Student Government Association, Student Run Sports, International Student Association, CRU, Blue Crew, national fraternities, national sororities.
Athletics Member NCAA. All Division II except ice hockey (Division I). ***Intercollegiate sports:*** baseball M(s), basketball M(s)/W(s), cheerleading M(s)/W(s), crew M(c)/W(c), cross-country running M(s)/W(s), ice hockey M(s), lacrosse M(c)/W(c), soccer M(s)/W(s), softball W(s), tennis M(s)/W(s), track and field M(s)/W(s), volleyball W(s). ***Intramural sports:*** basketball M/W, football M/W, racquetball M/W, soccer M/W, softball M/W, tennis M/W, ultimate Frisbee M/W, volleyball M/W.
Campus security: 24-hour emergency response devices and patrols, late-night transport/escort service, controlled dormitory access, Sworn Police Department with state certified police officers; 24/7 dispatch center; community policing efforts.
Student services: health clinic, personal/psychological counseling.

COSTS & FINANCIAL AID
Costs (2014–15) ***Tuition:*** state resident $9158 full-time, $355 per credit hour part-time; nonresident $21,232 full-time, $815 per credit hour part-time. Full-time tuition and fees vary according to course load and program. Part-time tuition and fees vary according to course load and program. ***Room and board:*** $8433; room only: $5753. Room and board charges vary according to board plan and housing facility. ***Payment plan:*** installment. ***Waivers:*** employees or children of employees.
Financial Aid Of all full-time matriculated undergraduates who enrolled in 2014, 3,616 applied for aid, 2,327 were judged to have need, 267 had their need fully met. In 2014, 824 non-need-based awards were made. ***Average percent of need met:*** 56. ***Average financial aid package:*** $9868. ***Average need-based loan:*** $7858. ***Average need-based gift aid:*** $6814. ***Average non-need-based aid:*** $8291. ***Average indebtedness upon graduation:*** $29,421. ***Financial aid deadline:*** 7/31.

APPLYING
Standardized Tests *Required:* SAT or ACT (for admission).
Options: electronic application, deferred entrance.
Application fee: $30.
Required: high school transcript.
Application deadlines: 8/20 (freshmen), 8/20 (out-of-state freshmen), 8/20 (transfers).
Notification: continuous (freshmen), continuous (transfers).

CONTACT
Ms. Sally Badoud, Interim Director of Admissions, The University of Alabama in Huntsville, Enrollment Services, 301 Sparkman Drive, Huntsville, AL 35899. *Phone:* 256-824-2771. *Toll-free phone:* 800-UAH-CALL. *Fax:* 256-824-4539. *E-mail:* uahadmissions@uah.edu.

University of Mobile

Mobile, Alabama

http://www.umobile.edu/

- **Independent Southern Baptist** comprehensive, founded 1961
- **Suburban** 880-acre campus
- **Endowment** $23.6 million
- **Coed** 1,466 undergraduate students, 87% full-time, 65% women, 35% men
- **Moderately difficult** entrance level, 58% of applicants were admitted

UNDERGRAD STUDENTS
1,282 full-time, 184 part-time. Students come from 39 states and territories; 23 other countries; 22% are from out of state; 21% Black or African American, non-Hispanic/Latino; 2% Hispanic/Latino; 0.5% Asian, non-Hispanic/Latino; 2% American Indian or Alaska Native, non-Hispanic/Latino; 2% Two or more races, non-Hispanic/Latino; 4% Race/ethnicity unknown; 4% international; 8% transferred in; 49% live on campus.

Freshmen
Admission: 1,009 applied, 590 admitted, 275 enrolled. ***Average high school GPA:*** 3.3. ***Test scores:*** SAT critical reading scores over 500: 33%; SAT math scores over 500: 35%; ACT scores over 18: 94%; SAT critical reading scores over 600: 9%; SAT math scores over 600: 2%; ACT scores over 24: 35%; ACT scores over 30: 4%.
Retention: 77% of full-time freshmen returned.

FACULTY
Total: 172, 49% full-time, 42% with terminal degrees.
Student/faculty ratio: 12:1.

ACADEMICS
Calendar: semesters. *Degrees:* associate, bachelor's, and master's.
Special study options: academic remediation for entering students, accelerated degree program, adult/continuing education programs,

W(s), swimming and diving M(s)/W(s), table tennis M(c)/W(c), tennis M(s)/W(s), track and field M(s)/W(s), ultimate Frisbee M(c)/W(c), volleyball M(c)/W(s), water polo M(c), weight lifting M(c)/W(c), wrestling M(c). ***Intramural sports:*** badminton M/W, basketball M/W, bowling M/W, golf M/W, racquetball M/W, soccer M/W, swimming and diving M/W, table tennis M/W, tennis M/W, ultimate Frisbee M/W, volleyball M/W.

Campus security: 24-hour emergency response devices and patrols, late-night transport/escort service, controlled dormitory access, 24-hour patrols by University of Alabama Police (UAPD), certified law enforcement personnel.

Student services: health clinic, personal/psychological counseling, women's center, legal services.

COSTS & FINANCIAL AID

Costs (2014–15) ***Tuition:*** state resident $9826 full-time; nonresident $24,950 full-time. Full-time tuition and fees vary according to course load. Part-time tuition and fees vary according to course load. ***Room and board:*** $8866; room only: $5600. Room and board charges vary according to board plan and housing facility. ***Payment plans:*** installment, deferred payment. ***Waivers:*** employees or children of employees.

Financial Aid Of all full-time matriculated undergraduates who enrolled in 2013, 14,389 applied for aid, 11,355 were judged to have need, 1,709 had their need fully met. In 2013, 5878 non-need-based awards were made. ***Average percent of need met:*** 50. ***Average financial aid package:*** $11,617. ***Average need-based loan:*** $4328. ***Average need-based gift aid:*** $9178. ***Average non-need-based aid:*** $12,209. ***Average indebtedness upon graduation:*** $29,320.

APPLYING

Standardized Tests *Required:* SAT or ACT (for admission).

Options: electronic application, early admission.

Application fee: $40.

Required: high school transcript, minimum 3.0 GPA. ***Required for some:*** essay or personal statement, 2 letters of recommendation, interview.

Application deadlines: 5/1 (freshmen), 5/1 (out-of-state freshmen), 3/1 (transfers).

Notification: continuous (freshmen), continuous (out-of-state freshmen), continuous (transfers).

CONTACT

Ms. Mary K. Spiegel, Executive Director of Undergraduate Admissions, The University of Alabama, Box 870132, Tuscaloosa, AL 35487. *Phone:* 205-348-5666. *Toll-free phone:* 800-933-BAMA. *Fax:* 205-348-9046. *E-mail:* admissions@ua.edu.

The University of Alabama at Birmingham

Birmingham, Alabama

http://www.uab.edu/

- **State-supported** university, founded 1969, part of University of Alabama System
- **Urban** 323-acre campus with easy access to Birmingham
- **Endowment** $432.5 million
- **Coed** 11,679 undergraduate students, 73% full-time, 58% women, 42% men
- **Moderately difficult** entrance level, 86% of applicants were admitted

UNDERGRAD STUDENTS

8,472 full-time, 3,207 part-time. Students come from 45 states and territories; 53 other countries; 9% are from out of state; 26% Black or African American, non-Hispanic/Latino; 3% Hispanic/Latino; 5% Asian, non-Hispanic/Latino; 0.1% Native Hawaiian or other Pacific Islander, non-Hispanic/Latino; 0.2% American Indian or Alaska Native, non-Hispanic/Latino; 4% Two or more races, non-Hispanic/Latino; 1% Race/ethnicity unknown; 2% international; 12% transferred in; 21% live on campus.

Freshmen

Admission: 5,710 applied, 4,893 admitted, 1,748 enrolled. ***Average high school GPA:*** 3.59. ***Test scores:*** ACT scores over 18: 99%; ACT scores over 24: 55%; ACT scores over 30: 15%.

Retention: 83% of full-time freshmen returned.

FACULTY

Total: 948, 91% full-time, 85% with terminal degrees.

Student/faculty ratio: 18:1.

ACADEMICS

Calendar: semesters. *Degrees:* certificates, bachelor's, master's, doctoral, post-master's, and postbachelor's certificates.

Special study options: academic remediation for entering students, accelerated degree program, adult/continuing education programs, advanced placement credit, cooperative education, distance learning, double majors, English as a second language, freshman honors college, honors programs, independent study, internships, off-campus study, part-time degree program, services for LD students, student-designed majors, study abroad, summer session for credit. ***ROTC:*** Army (b), Air Force (c).

Unusual degree programs: 3-2 engineering with Biomedical Engineering 5th Year Master's Program; Fast-Track Program - Civil Engineering, Electrical Engineering, Materials Engineering, and Mechanical Engineering; BS/MS in biology; BS/MS in computer science; Public Health Fifth Year Master's Program.

Computers: Students can access the following: campus intranet, computer help desk, free student e-mail accounts, online (class) grades, online (class) registration, online (class) schedules, transcript requests. Campuswide network is available. 100% of college-owned or -operated housing units are wired for high-speed Internet access. Wireless service is available via classrooms, computer centers, computer labs, dorm rooms, learning centers, libraries, student centers.

STUDENT LIFE

Housing options: coed, special housing for students with disabilities. Campus housing is university owned and is provided by a third party. Freshman applicants given priority for college housing.

Activities and organizations: drama/theater group, student-run newspaper, radio station, choral group, marching band, campus ministries, service-oriented groups, sports-affiliated groups, national fraternities, national sororities.

Athletics Member NCAA. All Division I. ***Intercollegiate sports:*** baseball M(s), basketball M(s)/W(s), cross-country running W(s), golf M(s)/W(s), soccer M(s)/W(s), softball W(s), tennis M(s)/W(s), track and field W(s), volleyball W(s). ***Intramural sports:*** badminton M(c)/W(c), basketball M/W, football M/W, lacrosse M(c)/W(c), rugby M(c), soccer M/W, softball M/W, table tennis M(c)/W(c), tennis M(c)/W(c), ultimate Frisbee M/W, wrestling M(c).

Campus security: 24-hour emergency response devices and patrols, late-night transport/escort service, controlled dormitory access.

Student services: health clinic, personal/psychological counseling, women's center.

COSTS & FINANCIAL AID

Costs (2014–15) ***Tuition:*** state resident $9280 full-time, $295 per credit hour part-time; nonresident $21,220 full-time, $693 per credit hour part-time. Full-time tuition and fees vary according to course load, program, and reciprocity agreements. Part-time tuition and fees vary according to course load, program, and reciprocity agreements. ***Room only:*** $5720. Room and board charges vary according to board plan and housing facility. ***Payment plan:*** installment. ***Waivers:*** employees or children of employees.

Financial Aid Of all full-time matriculated undergraduates who enrolled in 2013, 6,055 applied for aid, 5,080 were judged to have need, 248 had their need fully met. In 2013, 1328 non-need-based awards were made. ***Average percent of need met:*** 48. ***Average financial aid package:*** $8941. ***Average need-based loan:*** $4161. ***Average need-based gift aid:*** $4602. ***Average non-need-based aid:*** $6850. ***Average indebtedness upon graduation:*** $28,164.

APPLYING

Standardized Tests *Required:* SAT or ACT (for admission).

Options: electronic application, early admission, deferred entrance.

Application fee: $30.

Required: high school transcript, ACT or SAT.

Application deadlines: 6/1 (freshmen), 6/1 (transfers).

Notification: continuous (freshmen), continuous (transfers).

Student services: health clinic, personal/psychological counseling.

COSTS & FINANCIAL AID

Costs (2014–15) ***Comprehensive fee:*** $28,224 includes full-time tuition ($18,560), mandatory fees ($560), and room and board ($9104). Full-time tuition and fees vary according to course level, course load, degree level, and program. Part-time tuition and fees vary according to course level, course load, degree level, and program. ***College room only:*** $4300. Room and board charges vary according to board plan and housing facility.

Financial Aid Of all full-time matriculated undergraduates who enrolled in 2013, 2,519 applied for aid, 2,147 were judged to have need, 1,379 had their need fully met. 620 Federal Work-Study jobs (averaging $2014). 416 state and other part-time jobs (averaging $4755). In 2013, 597 non-need-based awards were made. ***Average percent of need met:*** 85. ***Average financial aid package:*** $19,250. ***Average need-based loan:*** $6006. ***Average need-based gift aid:*** $800. ***Average non-need-based aid:*** $6000. ***Average indebtedness upon graduation:*** $26,500.

APPLYING

Standardized Tests *Required:* SAT or ACT (for admission).

Options: electronic application, early admission.

Application fee: $25.

Required: high school transcript, minimum 3.0 GPA, ACT or SAT (prefer SAT).

CONTACT

Mrs. Elizabeth Dadzie, Associate Vice President, Enrollment Management, Tuskegee University, 1200 Old Montgomery Road, Margaret Murray Hall - Admissions, Tuskegee, AL 36088. *Phone:* 800-622-6531. *Toll-free phone:* 800-622-6531. *Fax:* 334-727-5750. *E-mail:* admissions@mytu.tuskegee.edu.

United States Sports Academy

Daphne, Alabama

http://www.ussa.edu/

- **Independent** upper-level, founded 1972
- **Suburban** 10-acre campus
- **Endowment** $1.0 million
- **Coed** 99 undergraduate students, 17% full-time, 19% women, 81% men
- 37% of applicants were admitted

UNDERGRAD STUDENTS

17 full-time, 82 part-time. 13% Black or African American, non-Hispanic/Latino; 6% Hispanic/Latino; 2% Asian, non-Hispanic/Latino; 4% Two or more races, non-Hispanic/Latino; 32% Race/ethnicity unknown.

Freshmen

Admission: 125 applied, 46 admitted.

FACULTY

Total: 34, 21% full-time, 79% with terminal degrees.

Student/faculty ratio: 12:1.

ACADEMICS

Calendar: continuous. *Degrees:* certificates, diplomas, bachelor's, master's, doctoral, and post-master's certificates.

Special study options: distance learning.

Computers: 1 computer/terminal is available on campus for general student use. Students can access the following: computer help desk, free student e-mail accounts, online (class) grades, online (class) registration, online (class) schedules. Campuswide network is available.

STUDENT LIFE

Activities and organizations: Alumni Association.

Campus security: electronically operated building entrances.

COSTS

Costs (2015–16) ***Tuition:*** $360 per credit hour part-time. ***Waivers:*** employees or children of employees.

APPLYING

Options: electronic application.

Application fee: $50.

Notification: continuous (transfers).

CONTACT

United States Sports Academy, One Academy Drive, Daphne, AL 36526-7055. *Phone:* 251-626-3303 Ext. 7127. *Toll-free phone:* 800-223-2668.

The University of Alabama

Tuscaloosa, Alabama

http://www.ua.edu/

- **State-supported** university, founded 1831, part of University of Alabama System
- **Suburban** 1000-acre campus with easy access to Birmingham
- **Endowment** $673.6 million
- **Coed** 30,752 undergraduate students, 90% full-time, 54% women, 46% men
- **Moderately difficult** entrance level, 51% of applicants were admitted

UNDERGRAD STUDENTS

27,737 full-time, 3,015 part-time. Students come from 52 states and territories; 56 other countries; 50% are from out of state; 11% Black or African American, non-Hispanic/Latino; 3% Hispanic/Latino; 1% Asian, non-Hispanic/Latino; 0.1% Native Hawaiian or other Pacific Islander, non-Hispanic/Latino; 0.4% American Indian or Alaska Native, non-Hispanic/Latino; 3% Two or more races, non-Hispanic/Latino; 0.3% Race/ethnicity unknown; 3% international; 5% transferred in; 27% live on campus.

Freshmen

Admission: 33,736 applied, 17,221 admitted, 6,824 enrolled. ***Average high school GPA:*** 3.65. ***Test scores:*** SAT critical reading scores over 500: 75%; SAT math scores over 500: 77%; SAT writing scores over 500: 70%; ACT scores over 18: 100%; SAT critical reading scores over 600: 32%; SAT math scores over 600: 34%; SAT writing scores over 600: 27%; ACT scores over 24: 69%; SAT critical reading scores over 700: 9%; SAT math scores over 700: 13%; SAT writing scores over 700: 6%; ACT scores over 30: 36%.

Retention: 87% of full-time freshmen returned.

FACULTY

Total: 1,776, 70% full-time, 74% with terminal degrees.

ACADEMICS

Calendar: semesters. *Degrees:* bachelor's, master's, doctoral, and post-master's certificates.

Special study options: academic remediation for entering students, accelerated degree program, adult/continuing education programs, advanced placement credit, cooperative education, distance learning, double majors, English as a second language, external degree program, freshman honors college, honors programs, independent study, internships, off-campus study, part-time degree program, services for LD students, student-designed majors, study abroad, summer session for credit. ***ROTC:*** Army (b), Air Force (b).

Computers: 2,500 computers/terminals and 9,000 ports are available on campus for general student use. Students can access the following: campus intranet, computer help desk, free student e-mail accounts, online (class) grades, online (class) registration, online (class) schedules. Campuswide network is available. 100% of college-owned or -operated housing units are wired for high-speed Internet access. Wireless service is available via entire campus.

STUDENT LIFE

Housing options: on-campus residence required for freshman year; coed, men-only, women-only, special housing for students with disabilities. Campus housing is university owned and leased by the school. Freshman campus housing is guaranteed.

Activities and organizations: drama/theater group, student-run newspaper, radio station, choral group, marching band, ABXY Gaming Network, Association of Residence Communities, International Student Association, Student Government Association, Black Student Union, national fraternities, national sororities.

Athletics Member NCAA. All Division I except football (Division I-A). ***Intercollegiate sports:*** badminton M(c)/W(c), baseball M(s), basketball M(s)/W(s), bowling M(c), cheerleading M(s)/W(s), crew M(c)/W(s), cross-country running M(s)/W(s), equestrian sports M(c)/W(c), golf M(s)/W(s), gymnastics W(s), ice hockey M(c), lacrosse M(c)/W(c), racquetball M(c)/W(c), rugby M(c)/W(c), soccer M(c)/W(s), softball

to board plan and housing facility. ***Payment plan:*** installment. ***Waivers:*** employees or children of employees.

Financial Aid Of all full-time matriculated undergraduates who enrolled in 2014, 963 applied for aid, 843 were judged to have need, 114 had their need fully met. In 2014, 311 non-need-based awards were made. ***Average percent of need met:*** 88. ***Average financial aid package:*** $26,574. ***Average need-based loan:*** $2124. ***Average need-based gift aid:*** $23,568. ***Average non-need-based aid:*** $18,148. ***Average indebtedness upon graduation:*** $31,855.

APPLYING

Standardized Tests *Required:* SAT or ACT (for admission).

Options: electronic application, early admission, deferred entrance.

Application fee: $25.

Required: essay or personal statement, high school transcript, 1 letter of recommendation. ***Recommended:*** minimum 2.5 GPA, interview.

Application deadlines: 7/15 (freshmen), 7/15 (out-of-state freshmen), rolling (transfers).

Notification: continuous (freshmen), continuous (out-of-state freshmen), continuous (transfers).

CONTACT

Mrs. Allison Miller, Admissions, Campus Visit Coordinator, Spring Hill College, 4000 Dauphin Street, Mobile, AL 36608-1791. *Phone:* 251-380-3032. *Toll-free phone:* 800-SHC-6704. *Fax:* 251-460-2186. *E-mail:* amiller@shc.edu.

Troy University

Troy, Alabama

http://www.troy.edu/

- **State-supported** comprehensive, founded 1887, part of Troy University System
- **Small-town** 906-acre campus
- **Endowment** $56.6 million
- **Coed** 15,115 undergraduate students, 60% full-time, 61% women, 39% men
- **Moderately difficult** entrance level, 44% of applicants were admitted

UNDERGRAD STUDENTS

9,018 full-time, 6,097 part-time. Students come from 52 states and territories; 52 other countries; 32% are from out of state; 34% Black or African American, non-Hispanic/Latino; 3% Hispanic/Latino; 0.8% Asian, non-Hispanic/Latino; 0.1% Native Hawaiian or other Pacific Islander, non-Hispanic/Latino; 0.8% American Indian or Alaska Native, non-Hispanic/Latino; 2% Two or more races, non-Hispanic/Latino; 4% Race/ethnicity unknown; 3% international; 9% transferred in; 35% live on campus.

Freshmen

Admission: 6,336 applied, 2,797 admitted, 1,900 enrolled. ***Test scores:*** SAT math scores over 500: 57%; SAT writing scores over 500: 25%; ACT scores over 18: 88%; SAT math scores over 600: 19%; ACT scores over 24: 37%; SAT math scores over 700: 5%; ACT scores over 30: 4%.

Retention: 76% of full-time freshmen returned.

FACULTY

Total: 1,110, 48% full-time, 57% with terminal degrees.

Student/faculty ratio: 18:1.

ACADEMICS

Calendar: semesters. *Degrees:* associate, bachelor's, master's, doctoral, and post-master's certificates.

Special study options: academic remediation for entering students, accelerated degree program, advanced placement credit, distance learning, double majors, English as a second language, honors programs, independent study, internships, part-time degree program, services for LD students, summer session for credit. ***ROTC:*** Army (b), Air Force (b).

Computers: 12,792 computers/terminals and 18,117 ports are available on campus for general student use. Students can access the following: campus intranet, computer help desk, free student e-mail accounts, online (class) grades, online (class) registration, online (class) schedules. Campuswide network is available. Wireless service is available via classrooms, dorm rooms, libraries.

STUDENT LIFE

Housing options: on-campus residence required for freshman year; coed, men-only, women-only. Campus housing is university owned. Freshman campus housing is guaranteed.

Activities and organizations: drama/theater group, student-run newspaper, television station, choral group, marching band, T-Day/Athletic Events (Homecoming), Activities Council, Pep Rallies, national fraternities, national sororities.

Athletics Member NCAA. All Division I except football (Division I-A). ***Intercollegiate sports:*** baseball M(s), basketball M(s)/W(s), cross-country running M(s)/W(s), golf M(s)/W(s), soccer W(s), softball W(s), tennis M(s)/W(s), track and field M(s)/W(s), volleyball W(s). ***Intramural sports:*** basketball M/W, bowling M/W, cross-country running M/W, football M, golf M/W, soccer W, softball W, tennis M/W, track and field M/W, volleyball W.

Campus security: 24-hour emergency response devices and patrols, student patrols, late-night transport/escort service, controlled dormitory access.

Student services: health clinic, personal/psychological counseling.

COSTS & FINANCIAL AID

Costs (2014–15) ***Tuition:*** state resident $6528 full-time, $264 per credit hour part-time; nonresident $13,056 full-time, $528 per credit hour part-time. Full-time tuition and fees vary according to location and program. Part-time tuition and fees vary according to location and program. ***Required fees:*** $1036 full-time, $35 per credit hour part-time, $50 per term part-time. ***Room and board:*** $6498; room only: $3724. Room and board charges vary according to board plan and housing facility. ***Payment plan:*** installment. ***Waivers:*** employees or children of employees.

Financial Aid Of all full-time matriculated undergraduates who enrolled in 2014, 6,342 applied for aid, 6,316 were judged to have need. In 2014, 2226 non-need-based awards were made. ***Average financial aid package:*** $4497. ***Average need-based loan:*** $4470. ***Average need-based gift aid:*** $4659. ***Average non-need-based aid:*** $5844.

APPLYING

Standardized Tests *Required:* SAT or ACT (for admission).

Options: electronic application, deferred entrance.

Application fee: $30.

Required: high school transcript. ***Recommended:*** interview.

Application deadlines: rolling (freshmen), rolling (transfers).

CONTACT

Mr. Buddy Starling, Dean of Enrollment Management, Troy University, University Avenue, Troy, AL 36082. *Phone:* 334-670-3243. *Toll-free phone:* 800-551-9716. *Fax:* 334-670-3733. *E-mail:* bstar@troy.edu.

Tuskegee University

Tuskegee, Alabama

http://www.tuskegee.edu/

- **Independent** comprehensive, founded 1881
- **Small-town** 5000-acre campus
- **Endowment** $113.7 million
- **Coed**
- **Moderately difficult** entrance level

FACULTY

Student/faculty ratio: 14:1.

ACADEMICS

Calendar: semesters. *Degrees:* bachelor's, master's, and doctoral.

STUDENT LIFE

Housing options: on-campus residence required through sophomore year; coed, men-only, women-only. Campus housing is university owned. Freshman applicants given priority for college housing.

Activities and organizations: drama/theater group, student-run newspaper, television station, choral group, marching band, student government, Marching Band, State Clubs, Fraternities, Sororities, national fraternities, national sororities.

Athletics Member NCAA. All Division II.

Campus security: 24-hour emergency response devices and patrols, late-night transport/escort service.

scores over 700: 4%; SAT writing scores over 700: 1%; ACT scores over 30: 8%.
Retention: 71% of full-time freshmen returned.

FACULTY
Total: 991, 55% full-time.
Student/faculty ratio: 20:1.

ACADEMICS
Calendar: semesters. *Degrees:* certificates, bachelor's, master's, doctoral, post-master's, and postbachelor's certificates.
Special study options: academic remediation for entering students, accelerated degree program, adult/continuing education programs, advanced placement credit, cooperative education, distance learning, double majors, English as a second language, freshman honors college, honors programs, independent study, internships, part-time degree program, services for LD students, student-designed majors, study abroad, summer session for credit. ***ROTC:*** Army (b), Air Force (b).
Computers: Students can access the following: campus intranet, computer help desk, free student e-mail accounts, online (class) grades, online (class) registration, online (class) schedules. Campuswide network is available. 100% of college-owned or -operated housing units are wired for high-speed Internet access. Wireless service is available via entire campus.

STUDENT LIFE
Housing options: coed, special housing for students with disabilities. Campus housing is university owned and is provided by a third party.
Activities and organizations: drama/theater group, student-run newspaper, radio and television station, choral group, marching band, Student Government Association, African American Student Association, Council of International Student Organizations, Alpha Epsilon Delta Pre-Health Professions, Panhellenic Council, national fraternities, national sororities.
Athletics Member NCAA. All Division I. ***Intercollegiate sports:*** baseball M(s), basketball M(s)/W(s), cross-country running M(s)/W(s), football M(s), golf M(s)/W(s), soccer W(s), softball W(s), tennis M(s)/W(s), track and field M(s)/W(s), volleyball W(s). ***Intramural sports:*** badminton M/W, basketball M/W, bowling M/W, cheerleading M(c)/W(c), golf M/W, racquetball M/W, sailing M(c)/W(c), soccer M/W, softball M/W, table tennis M/W, tennis M/W, ultimate Frisbee M/W, volleyball M/W, water polo M/W.
Campus security: 24-hour emergency response devices and patrols, late-night transport/escort service.
Student services: health clinic, personal/psychological counseling, women's center, legal services.

COSTS & FINANCIAL AID
Costs (2014–15) ***Tuition:*** state resident $8610 full-time, $287 per credit hour part-time; nonresident $17,220 full-time, $554 per credit hour part-time. Full-time tuition and fees vary according to course load and program. Part-time tuition and fees vary according to course load and program. ***Room and board:*** $7100; room only: $3800. Room and board charges vary according to board plan and housing facility. ***Payment plan:*** installment. ***Waivers:*** employees or children of employees.
Financial Aid Of all full-time matriculated undergraduates who enrolled in 2012, 6,361 applied for aid, 5,293 were judged to have need, 559 had their need fully met. In 2012, 889 non-need-based awards were made. ***Average percent of need met:*** 56. ***Average financial aid package:*** $9343. ***Average need-based loan:*** $4281. ***Average need-based gift aid:*** $6447. ***Average non-need-based aid:*** $4813.

APPLYING
Standardized Tests *Required for some:* SAT or ACT (for admission).
Options: electronic application, early admission.
Application fee: $35.
Required: high school transcript. ***Required for some:*** essay or personal statement, minimum 3.0 GPA, 1 letter of recommendation, Accelerated College Enrollment Program students are required to have a minimum high school GPA of 3.0. The Early Admission students are required to have a minimum high school GPA of 3.5. ***Recommended:*** minimum 2.5 GPA.
Application deadlines: 7/15 (freshmen), 7/15 (out-of-state freshmen), 7/15 (transfers).
Notification: continuous (freshmen), continuous (out-of-state freshmen), continuous (transfers).

CONTACT
Mr. Christopher A. Lynch, Director, New Student Recruitment, University of South Alabama, Mobile, AL 36688-0002. *Phone:* 251-460-6141. *Toll-free phone:* 800-872-5247. *Fax:* 251-460-7876. *E-mail:* recruitment@southalabama.edu.

The University of West Alabama
Livingston, Alabama
http://www.uwa.edu/

- **State-supported** comprehensive, founded 1835
- **Small-town** 514-acre campus
- **Endowment** $26,500
- **Coed** 1,922 undergraduate students, 88% full-time, 56% women, 44% men
- **Minimally difficult** entrance level, 72% of applicants were admitted

UNDERGRAD STUDENTS
1,694 full-time, 228 part-time. Students come from 26 states and territories; 17 other countries; 21% are from out of state; 41% Black or African American, non-Hispanic/Latino; 2% Hispanic/Latino; 0.2% Asian, non-Hispanic/Latino; 0.1% Native Hawaiian or other Pacific Islander, non-Hispanic/Latino; 0.2% American Indian or Alaska Native, non-Hispanic/Latino; 1% Two or more races, non-Hispanic/Latino; 5% Race/ethnicity unknown; 6% international; 11% transferred in; 47% live on campus.

Freshmen
Admission: 1,014 applied, 730 admitted, 350 enrolled. ***Test scores:*** ACT scores over 18: 90%; ACT scores over 24: 22%; ACT scores over 30: 2%.
Retention: 64% of full-time freshmen returned.

FACULTY
Total: 251, 49% full-time, 73% with terminal degrees.
Student/faculty ratio: 14:1.

ACADEMICS
Calendar: semesters. *Degrees:* certificates, associate, bachelor's, master's, and post-master's certificates.
Special study options: academic remediation for entering students, accelerated degree program, advanced placement credit, cooperative education, distance learning, double majors, English as a second language, honors programs, independent study, internships, off-campus study, part-time degree program, services for LD students, summer session for credit. ***ROTC:*** Air Force (c).
Unusual degree programs: 3-2 engineering with Auburn University, The University of Alabama at Birmingham, Mississippi State University, The University of Alabama; forestry with Auburn University; nursing with University of Alabama; social work with University of Alabama; Wildlife: Auburn University.
Computers: 400 computers/terminals are available on campus for general student use. Students can access the following: computer help desk, free student e-mail accounts, online (class) grades, online (class) registration, online (class) schedules, Wireless intranet is available campuswide for all students. Campuswide network is available. 100% of college-owned or -operated housing units are wired for high-speed Internet access. Wireless service is available via entire campus.

STUDENT LIFE
Housing options: on-campus residence required for freshman year; coed. Campus housing is university owned. Freshman campus housing is guaranteed.
Activities and organizations: drama/theater group, student-run newspaper, television station, choral group, marching band, The UWA Band, The Student Government Association, The UWA Choir, Fellowship of Christian Athletes (FCA), UWA Ambassadors, national fraternities, national sororities.
Athletics Member NCAA. All Division II. ***Intercollegiate sports:*** baseball M(s), basketball M(s)/W(s), cross-country running M(s)/W(s), football M(s), golf M(s)/W(s), soccer M(s)/W(s), softball W(s), tennis M(s)/W(s), track and field M(s)/W(s), volleyball W(s). ***Intramural sports:*** archery M/W, basketball M/W, bowling M/W, cheerleading

M(c)/W(c), football M/W, golf M/W, soccer M/W, softball M/W, table tennis M/W, tennis M/W, ultimate Frisbee M/W, volleyball M/W.

Campus security: 24-hour emergency response devices and patrols, student patrols, late-night transport/escort service, controlled dormitory access.

Student services: health clinic, personal/psychological counseling.

COSTS & FINANCIAL AID
Costs (2014–15) ***Tuition:*** state resident $6868 full-time, $292 per credit hour part-time; nonresident $13,736 full-time, $584 per credit hour part-time. Full-time tuition and fees vary according to course load, degree level, and program. Part-time tuition and fees vary according to course load, degree level, and program. ***Required fees:*** $1150 full-time. ***Room and board:*** $6256; room only: $3800. Room and board charges vary according to board plan and housing facility. ***Payment plan:*** installment. ***Waivers:*** employees or children of employees.

Financial Aid Of all full-time matriculated undergraduates who enrolled in 2013, 1,434 applied for aid, 1,342 were judged to have need, 9 had their need fully met. 157 Federal Work-Study jobs (averaging $2475). 34 state and other part-time jobs (averaging $1920). In 2013, 4 non-need-based awards were made. ***Average percent of need met:*** 21. ***Average financial aid package:*** $10,803. ***Average need-based gift aid:*** $4965. ***Average non-need-based aid:*** $2588. ***Average indebtedness upon graduation:*** $31,901.

APPLYING
Standardized Tests *Required:* SAT or ACT (for admission).

Options: electronic application.

Application fee: $35.

Required: high school transcript, minimum 2.0 GPA.

Application deadlines: rolling (freshmen), rolling (transfers).

Notification: continuous (freshmen), continuous (transfers).

CONTACT
Mrs. Brenda Edwards, Admissions Technical Coordinator, The University of West Alabama, Station 4, Livingston, AL 35470. *Phone:* 205-652-3699. *Toll-free phone:* 888-636-8800. *Fax:* 205-652-3881. *E-mail:* belliott@uwa.edu.

ALASKA

Alaska Bible College
Glennallen, Alaska
http://www.akbible.edu/

- **Independent nondenominational** 4-year, founded 1966
- **Small-town** 2-acre campus
- **Coed**
- **Minimally difficult** entrance level

FACULTY
Student/faculty ratio: 3:1.

ACADEMICS
Calendar: semesters. *Degrees:* certificates, associate, and bachelor's.

STUDENT LIFE
Housing options: on-campus residence required through sophomore year; men-only, women-only. Campus housing is university owned. Freshman campus housing is guaranteed.

Activities and organizations: student-run radio station.

Campus security: 24-hour emergency response devices.

FINANCIAL AID
Financial Aid ***Financial aid deadline:*** 7/1.

APPLYING
Standardized Tests *Required:* SAT or ACT (for admission).

Options: electronic application, deferred entrance.

Application fee: $35.

Required: essay or personal statement, high school transcript, minimum 2.0 GPA, interview, 3 reference forms.

CONTACT
Nikki Palmer, Director of Admissions, Alaska Bible College, PO Box 289, Glennallen, AK 99588. *Phone:* 907-822-3201 Ext. 224. *Toll-free phone:* 800-478-7884. *Fax:* 907-822-5027. *E-mail:* npalmer@akbible.edu.

Alaska Pacific University
Anchorage, Alaska
http://www.alaskapacific.edu/

- **Independent** comprehensive, founded 1959
- **Urban** 170-acre campus
- **Endowment** $42.0 million
- **Coed** 326 undergraduate students, 66% full-time, 63% women, 37% men
- **Minimally difficult** entrance level, 42% of applicants were admitted

UNDERGRAD STUDENTS
215 full-time, 111 part-time. Students come from 30 states and territories; 32% are from out of state; 3% Black or African American, non-Hispanic/Latino; 4% Hispanic/Latino; 3% Asian, non-Hispanic/Latino; 1% Native Hawaiian or other Pacific Islander, non-Hispanic/Latino; 18% American Indian or Alaska Native, non-Hispanic/Latino; 9% Two or more races, non-Hispanic/Latino; 9% Race/ethnicity unknown; 19% transferred in; 26% live on campus.

Freshmen
Admission: 328 applied, 138 admitted, 19 enrolled. ***Average high school GPA:*** 3.41. ***Test scores:*** SAT critical reading scores over 500: 82%; SAT math scores over 500: 18%; ACT scores over 18: 90%; SAT critical reading scores over 600: 37%; SAT math scores over 600: 18%; ACT scores over 24: 30%; SAT critical reading scores over 700: 10%.

Retention: 77% of full-time freshmen returned.

FACULTY
Total: 91, 52% full-time, 51% with terminal degrees.

Student/faculty ratio: 7:1.

ACADEMICS
Calendar: semesters. *Degrees:* certificates, associate, bachelor's, master's, doctoral, and postbachelor's certificates.

Special study options: academic remediation for entering students, accelerated degree program, adult/continuing education programs, advanced placement credit, distance learning, double majors, independent study, internships, part-time degree program, services for LD students, student-designed majors, study abroad, summer session for credit. ***ROTC:*** Army (c), Air Force (c).

Unusual degree programs: 3-2 Environmental Science.

Computers: 105 computers/terminals and 480 ports are available on campus for general student use. Students can access the following: campus intranet, computer help desk, free student e-mail accounts, online (class) grades, online (class) registration, online (class) schedules. Campuswide network is available. 100% of college-owned or -operated housing units are wired for high-speed Internet access. Wireless service is available via entire campus.

STUDENT LIFE
Housing options: on-campus residence required through sophomore year; coed. Campus housing is university owned. Freshman campus housing is guaranteed.

Activities and organizations: drama/theater group, student-run newspaper, choral group, ASAPU (Associated Students of Alaska Pacific University), Photography Club, Dive Club, Basketball club, Spectrum Club.

Athletics ***Intramural sports:*** basketball M/W, skiing (cross-country) M/W, soccer M/W, volleyball M/W.

Campus security: 24-hour emergency response devices, student patrols, late-night transport/escort service, controlled dormitory access.

Student services: personal/psychological counseling.

COSTS & FINANCIAL AID
Costs (2015–16) ***Comprehensive fee:*** $26,680 includes full-time tuition ($19,500), mandatory fees ($180), and room and board ($7000). Full-time tuition and fees vary according to course load, degree level, program, and reciprocity agreements. Part-time tuition: $812 per semester hour. Part-time tuition and fees vary according to course load, degree level, and

program. ***Room and board:*** Room and board charges vary according to board plan and housing facility. ***Payment plans:*** installment, deferred payment. ***Waivers:*** employees or children of employees.

Financial Aid Of all full-time matriculated undergraduates who enrolled in 2014, 181 applied for aid, 160 were judged to have need. 20 Federal Work-Study jobs (averaging $748). In 2014, 21 non-need-based awards were made. ***Average percent of need met:*** 30. ***Average financial aid package:*** $9714. ***Average need-based loan:*** $4347. ***Average need-based gift aid:*** $4406. ***Average non-need-based aid:*** $6627. ***Average indebtedness upon graduation:*** $8922.

APPLYING

Standardized Tests *Required:* SAT or ACT (for admission).

Options: electronic application, deferred entrance.

Application fee: $25.

Required: high school transcript, minimum 2.5 GPA.

Application deadlines: 8/1 (freshmen), 8/1 (out-of-state freshmen), 8/1 (transfers).

Notification: continuous (freshmen), continuous (out-of-state freshmen), continuous (transfers).

CONTACT

Mr. Carter Caywood, Director of Admissions, Alaska Pacific University, 4101 University Drive, Anchorage, AK 99508. *Phone:* 907-564-8248. *Toll-free phone:* 800-252-7528. *Fax:* 907-564-8317. *E-mail:* admissions@alaskapacific.edu.

★ University of Alaska Fairbanks

Fairbanks, Alaska

http://www.uaf.edu/

- **State-supported** university, founded 1917, part of University of Alaska System
- **Small-town** 2250-acre campus
- **Endowment** $90.6 million
- **Coed** 7,563 undergraduate students, 46% full-time, 58% women, 42% men
- **Minimally difficult** entrance level, 74% of applicants were admitted

UNDERGRAD STUDENTS

3,491 full-time, 4,072 part-time. Students come from 51 states and territories; 36 other countries; 14% are from out of state; 2% Black or African American, non-Hispanic/Latino; 5% Hispanic/Latino; 1% Asian, non-Hispanic/Latino; 0.3% Native Hawaiian or other Pacific Islander, non-Hispanic/Latino; 13% American Indian or Alaska Native, non-Hispanic/Latino; 4% Two or more races, non-Hispanic/Latino; 31% Race/ethnicity unknown; 1% international; 6% transferred in; 29% live on campus.

Freshmen

Admission: 1,575 applied, 1,164 admitted, 942 enrolled. ***Average high school GPA:*** 3.21. ***Test scores:*** SAT critical reading scores over 500: 70%; SAT math scores over 500: 68%; SAT writing scores over 500: 52%; ACT scores over 18: 82%; SAT critical reading scores over 600: 33%; SAT math scores over 600: 30%; SAT writing scores over 600: 18%; ACT scores over 24: 40%; SAT critical reading scores over 700: 5%; SAT math scores over 700: 5%; SAT writing scores over 700: 1%; ACT scores over 30: 7%.

Retention: 78% of full-time freshmen returned.

FACULTY

Total: 993, 38% full-time, 60% with terminal degrees.

Student/faculty ratio: 11:1.

ACADEMICS

Calendar: semesters. *Degrees:* certificates, associate, bachelor's, master's, doctoral, and postbachelor's certificates.

Special study options: academic remediation for entering students, accelerated degree program, advanced placement credit, cooperative education, distance learning, double majors, English as a second language, external degree program, honors programs, independent study, internships, off-campus study, part-time degree program, services for LD students, student-designed majors, study abroad, summer session for credit. ***ROTC:*** Army (b).

Unusual degree programs: 3-2 engineering; Computer Science.

Computers: 125 computers/terminals and 22 ports are available on campus for general student use. Students can access the following:

campus intranet, computer help desk, free student e-mail accounts, online (class) grades, online (class) registration, online (class) schedules, university portal, campus wireless access. Campuswide network is available. 100% of college-owned or -operated housing units are wired for high-speed Internet access. Wireless service is available via entire campus.

STUDENT LIFE

Housing options: coed, special housing for students with disabilities. Campus housing is university owned. Freshman applicants given priority for college housing.

Activities and organizations: drama/theater group, student-run newspaper, radio and television station, choral group, Alpha Phi Omega, Festival of Native Arts, Aurora Aerial Arts, Parkour and Free Running Club, Gender and Sexuality Alliance, national fraternities, national sororities.

Athletics Member NCAA. All Division II except ice hockey (Division I). ***Intercollegiate sports:*** basketball M(s)/W(s), cross-country running M(s)/W(s), ice hockey M(s), riflery M(s)/W(s), skiing (cross-country) M(s)/W(s), swimming and diving W(s), volleyball W(s). ***Intramural sports:*** archery M(c)/W(c), badminton M(c)/W(c), basketball M/W, bowling M(c)/W(c), cross-country running M(c)/W(c), fencing M(c)/W(c), football M/W, ice hockey M/W, skiing (downhill) M(c)/W(c), soccer M/W, softball M(c)/W(c), tennis M(c)/W(c), ultimate Frisbee M/W, volleyball M/W.

Campus security: 24-hour emergency response devices and patrols, student patrols, late-night transport/escort service, controlled dormitory access, ID check at door of residence halls, crime prevention and safety workshops.

Student services: health clinic, personal/psychological counseling, women's center, legal services.

COSTS & FINANCIAL AID

Costs (2015–16) ***Tuition:*** state resident $6060 full-time, $183 per credit part-time; nonresident $20,040 full-time, $649 per credit part-time. Full-time tuition and fees vary according to course level, course load, location, and reciprocity agreements. Part-time tuition and fees vary according to course level, course load, location, and reciprocity agreements. ***Required fees:*** $1310 full-time. ***Room and board:*** $8242; room only: $3922. Room and board charges vary according to board plan, housing facility, and location. ***Payment plans:*** installment, deferred payment. ***Waivers:*** children of alumni, senior citizens, and employees or children of employees.

Financial Aid Of all full-time matriculated undergraduates who enrolled in 2013, 2,873 applied for aid, 1,956 were judged to have need, 230 had their need fully met. 50 Federal Work-Study jobs (averaging $5332). In 2013, 496 non-need-based awards were made. ***Average percent of need met:*** 53. ***Average financial aid package:*** $7745. ***Average need-based loan:*** $3833. ***Average need-based gift aid:*** $6262. ***Average non-need-based aid:*** $3519. ***Average indebtedness upon graduation:*** $29,906. ***Financial aid deadline:*** 7/1.

APPLYING

Standardized Tests *Required:* SAT or ACT (for admission).

Options: electronic application, deferred entrance.

Application fee: $50.

Required: high school transcript, minimum 2.5 GPA.

Application deadlines: 6/15 (freshmen), 6/15 (out-of-state freshmen), 6/15 (transfers).

Notification: continuous (freshmen), continuous (out-of-state freshmen), continuous (transfers).

CONTACT

Ms. Libby Eddy, Registrar and Director of Admissions, University of Alaska Fairbanks, PO Box 757480, Fairbanks, AK 99775-7480. *Phone:* 907-474-7500. *Toll-free phone:* 800-478-1823. *Fax:* 907-474-7097. *E-mail:* admissions@uaf.edu.

See previous page for display ad and page 1656 for the College Close-Up.

University of Alaska Southeast, Sitka Campus

Sitka, Alaska

http://www.uas.alaska.edu/

- **State-supported** primarily 2-year, founded 1962, part of University of Alaska System
- **Small-town** campus
- **Coed** 1,552 undergraduate students
- **Noncompetitive** entrance level

UNDERGRAD STUDENTS

Students come from 10 states and territories; 2 other countries.

FACULTY

Total: 59, 32% full-time.

Student/faculty ratio: 13:1.

ACADEMICS

Calendar: semesters. *Degrees:* certificates, diplomas, associate, bachelor's, and master's.

Special study options: academic remediation for entering students, adult/continuing education programs, advanced placement credit, cooperative education, distance learning, double majors, English as a second language, independent study, internships, off-campus study, part-time degree program, services for LD students, study abroad, summer session for credit.

Computers: 13 computers/terminals are available on campus for general student use. Students can access the following: campus intranet, computer help desk, free student e-mail accounts, online (class) grades, online (class) registration, online (class) schedules, online student financial accounts and payment capability. Campuswide network is available. Wireless service is available via entire campus.

STUDENT LIFE

Housing options: college housing not available; coed. Campus housing is provided by a third party.

Activities and organizations: Student Government Association, Phi Theta Kappa Honor Society.

Campus security: 24-hour emergency response devices.

Student services: personal/psychological counseling.

COSTS

Costs (2015–16) ***One-time required fee:*** $50. ***Tuition:*** state resident $4224 full-time, $176 per credit part-time; nonresident $4224 full-time, $176 per credit part-time. Full-time tuition and fees vary according to degree level, location, and program. Part-time tuition and fees vary according to degree level, location, and program. UAS Sitka campus programs have no non-resident tuition rates. ***Required fees:*** $856 full-time, $36 per credit part-time. ***Room only:*** $4800. Room and board charges vary according to housing facility. ***Payment plan:*** installment. ***Waivers:*** senior citizens and employees or children of employees.

APPLYING

Options: electronic application, early admission, deferred entrance.

Application fee: $35.

Required: high school transcript, minimum 2.0 GPA. ***Required for some:*** essay or personal statement.

Application deadlines: rolling (freshmen), rolling (out-of-state freshmen), rolling (transfers).

Notification: continuous (freshmen), continuous (out-of-state freshmen), continuous (transfers).

CONTACT

Ms. Teal Gordon, Admissions Representative, University of Alaska Southeast, Sitka Campus, UAS Sitka, 1332 Seward Ave., Sitka, AK 99835. *Phone:* 907-747-7726. *Toll-free phone:* 800-478-6653. *Fax:* 907-747-7731. *E-mail:* ktgordon@uas.alaska.edu.

ARIZONA

Argosy University, Phoenix

Phoenix, Arizona

http://www.argosy.edu/phoenix-arizona/default.aspx

- **Proprietary** university, founded 1997
- **Urban** campus
- **Coed**

ACADEMICS
Calendar: semesters. *Degrees:* associate, bachelor's, master's, and doctoral.

CONTACT
Argosy University, Phoenix, 2233 West Dunlap Avenue, Phoenix, AZ 85021. *Phone:* 602-216-2600. *Toll-free phone:* 866-216-2777.

Arizona Christian University

Phoenix, Arizona

http://arizonachristian.edu/

- **Independent Conservative Baptist** 4-year, founded 1960
- **Urban** 19-acre campus with easy access to Phoenix
- **Endowment** $1.9 million
- **Coed** 737 undergraduate students, 81% full-time, 45% women, 55% men

UNDERGRAD STUDENTS
596 full-time, 141 part-time. Students come from 27 states and territories; 9 other countries; 23% are from out of state; 7% Black or African American, non-Hispanic/Latino; 15% Hispanic/Latino; 2% Asian, non-Hispanic/Latino; 0.7% Native Hawaiian or other Pacific Islander, non-Hispanic/Latino; 0.9% American Indian or Alaska Native, non-Hispanic/Latino; 5% Two or more races, non-Hispanic/Latino; 6% Race/ethnicity unknown; 2% international; 16% transferred in; 33% live on campus.

Freshmen
Admission: 154 enrolled. ***Test scores:*** SAT critical reading scores over 500: 45%; SAT math scores over 500: 41%; ACT scores over 18: 91%; SAT critical reading scores over 600: 11%; SAT math scores over 600: 10%; ACT scores over 24: 34%; SAT critical reading scores over 700: 3%; SAT math scores over 700: 3%; ACT scores over 30: 4%.
Retention: 69% of full-time freshmen returned.

FACULTY
Total: 98, 14% full-time.
Student/faculty ratio: 15:1.

ACADEMICS
Calendar: 4-4-1. *Degrees:* associate and bachelor's.
Special study options: academic remediation for entering students, adult/continuing education programs, advanced placement credit, cooperative education, distance learning, double majors, independent study, internships, part-time degree program, services for LD students, study abroad, summer session for credit. ***ROTC:*** Air Force (c).
Computers: 37 computers/terminals are available on campus for general student use. Students can access the following: free student e-mail accounts, online (class) grades, online (class) registration, online (class) schedules. Campuswide network is available. 100% of college-owned or -operated housing units are wired for high-speed Internet access. Wireless service is available via entire campus.

STUDENT LIFE
Housing options: on-campus residence required through sophomore year; men-only, women-only, special housing for students with disabilities. Campus housing is university owned. Freshman campus housing is guaranteed.
Activities and organizations: drama/theater group, student-run newspaper, choral group, Student Leadership Council, Vitality, Pre-Law Society, Ultimate Frisbee Club, English Club.
Athletics Member NAIA, NCCAA. ***Intercollegiate sports:*** baseball M(s), basketball M(s)/W(s), cross-country running M(s)/W(s), football M(s), golf M(s)/W(s), soccer M(s)/W(s), softball W(s), tennis M(s)/W(s), track and field M(s)/W(s), volleyball W(s). ***Intramural sports:*** basketball M/W, bowling M/W, football M/W, soccer M/W, table tennis M/W, ultimate Frisbee M/W, volleyball M/W.
Campus security: 24-hour emergency response devices, student patrols, late-night transport/escort service, controlled dormitory access, Weekend - 24-hour patrol by trained security personnel; Weekday - 20-hour patrol with a guard on call.
Student services: personal/psychological counseling.

COSTS & FINANCIAL AID
Costs (2015–16) ***Comprehensive fee:*** $33,110 includes full-time tuition ($22,230), mandatory fees ($990), and room and board ($9890). Full-time tuition and fees vary according to class time, course load, and program. Part-time tuition: $930 per credit hour. Part-time tuition and fees vary according to class time, course load, and program. ***Required fees:*** $495 per term part-time. ***Room and board:*** Room and board charges vary according to board plan. ***Payment plan:*** installment. ***Waivers:*** employees or children of employees.
Financial Aid Of all full-time matriculated undergraduates who enrolled in 2014, 503 applied for aid, 446 were judged to have need. In 2014, 52 non-need-based awards were made. ***Average financial aid package:*** $15,811. ***Average need-based loan:*** $3705. ***Average need-based gift aid:*** $13,195. ***Average non-need-based aid:*** $5414. ***Average indebtedness upon graduation:*** $26,228. ***Financial aid deadline:*** 6/5.

APPLYING
Standardized Tests *Required:* SAT or ACT (for admission).
Required: essay or personal statement, high school transcript, minimum 2.0 GPA, 1 letter of recommendation. ***Required for some:*** interview.

CONTACT
Tiffany Swartz, Assistant Director of Admissions, Arizona Christian University, 2625 E Cactus Rd, Phoenix, AZ 85032. *Phone:* 602-3864144. *Toll-free phone:* 800-247-2697. *Fax:* 602-4042159. *E-mail:* tiffany.swartz@arizonachristian.edu.

Arizona State University at the Downtown Phoenix campus

Phoenix, Arizona

https://campus.asu.edu/downtown/

- **State-supported** comprehensive, founded 2006
- **Urban** 17-acre campus with easy access to Phoenix
- **Coed** 9,150 undergraduate students, 88% full-time, 66% women, 34% men
- **Moderately difficult** entrance level, 79% of applicants were admitted

UNDERGRAD STUDENTS
8,067 full-time, 1,083 part-time. Students come from 51 states and territories; 26 other countries; 25% are from out of state; 6% Black or African American, non-Hispanic/Latino; 27% Hispanic/Latino; 4% Asian, non-Hispanic/Latino; 0.3% Native Hawaiian or other Pacific Islander, non-Hispanic/Latino; 2% American Indian or Alaska Native, non-Hispanic/Latino; 4% Two or more races, non-Hispanic/Latino; 0.8% Race/ethnicity unknown; 1% international; 16% live on campus.

Freshmen
Admission: 4,835 applied, 3,813 admitted. ***Average high school GPA:*** 3.49. ***Test scores:*** SAT critical reading scores over 500: 70%; SAT math scores over 500: 71%; ACT scores over 18: 95%; SAT critical reading scores over 600: 23%; SAT math scores over 600: 23%; ACT scores over 24: 49%; SAT critical reading scores over 700: 4%; SAT math scores over 700: 2%; ACT scores over 30: 8%.
Retention: 84% of full-time freshmen returned.

FACULTY
Total: 479, 79% full-time, 66% with terminal degrees.
Student/faculty ratio: 25:1.

ACADEMICS
Degrees: certificates, bachelor's, master's, doctoral, and postbachelor's certificates.
Special study options: accelerated degree program, advanced placement credit, cooperative education, distance learning, double majors, freshman honors college, honors programs, independent study, internships, off-campus study, part-time degree program, services for LD students,

student-designed majors, study abroad, summer session for credit. ***ROTC:*** Army (c), Navy (c), Air Force (c).

Computers: 486 computers/terminals are available on campus for general student use. Students can access the following: campus intranet, computer help desk, free student e-mail accounts, online (class) grades, online (class) registration, online (class) schedules, My Apps offers enrolled students, faculty and staff access to software applications for use online, in the classroom, by download, or for purchase. My Apps is free of charge and is accessible from any computer using your ASURITE UserID and password. Campuswide network is available. 100% of college-owned or -operated housing units are wired for high-speed Internet access. Wireless service is available via classrooms, computer centers, computer labs, dorm rooms, learning centers, libraries, student centers.

STUDENT LIFE

Housing options: on-campus residence required for freshman year; coed, special housing for students with disabilities. Campus housing is provided by a third party. Freshman applicants given priority for college housing.

Activities and organizations: drama/theater group, student-run newspaper, radio and television station, Non-Profit Leadership and Management, Exercise and Wellness Organization, Parks and Recreation Student Organization, Barrett Leadership and Service Team at Downtown, DPC Aware.

Athletics Member NCAA. All Division I. ***Intercollegiate sports:*** baseball M(s), basketball M(s)/W(s), cross-country running M(s)/W(s), football M(s), golf M(s)/W(s), gymnastics W(s), ice hockey M(s), soccer W(s), softball W(s), swimming and diving M(s)/W(s), tennis W(s), track and field M(s)/W(s), volleyball W(s), water polo W(s), wrestling M(s). ***Intramural sports:*** basketball M/W, football M/W, racquetball M/W, soccer M/W, softball M/W, table tennis M/W, ultimate Frisbee M/W, volleyball M/W.

Campus security: 24-hour emergency response devices and patrols, late-night transport/escort service.

Student services: health clinic, personal/psychological counseling.

COSTS & FINANCIAL AID

Costs (2014–15) ***Tuition:*** state resident $9454 full-time, $677 per credit hour part-time; nonresident $23,830 full-time, $993 per credit hour part-time. Full-time tuition and fees vary according to program. Part-time tuition and fees vary according to program. ***Required fees:*** $673 full-time. ***Room and board:*** $11,974; room only: $8334. Room and board charges vary according to board plan and housing facility. ***Payment plan:*** installment. ***Waivers:*** employees or children of employees.

Financial Aid Of all full-time matriculated undergraduates who enrolled in 2013, 6,131 applied for aid, 5,358 were judged to have need, 901 had their need fully met. 343 Federal Work-Study jobs (averaging $2669). 1,083 state and other part-time jobs (averaging $3714). In 2013, 933 non-need-based awards were made. ***Average percent of need met:*** 58. ***Average financial aid package:*** $13,166. ***Average need-based loan:*** $4191. ***Average need-based gift aid:*** $8705. ***Average non-need-based aid:*** $7349. ***Average indebtedness upon graduation:*** $22,498.

APPLYING

Standardized Tests *Required for some:* SAT or ACT (for admission), SAT Subject Tests (for admission). *Recommended:* SAT or ACT (for admission).

Options: electronic application.

Application fee: $50.

Required: high school transcript, minimum 3.0 GPA, application fee is $65 for nonresidents; additional requirements for Honors College and certain majors. ***Required for some:*** essay or personal statement, letters of recommendation, application fee is $65 for nonresidents; additional requirements for Honors College and certain majors.

Application deadlines: rolling (freshmen), rolling (transfers).

Notification: continuous (freshmen), continuous (transfers).

CONTACT

Admission Services, Arizona State University, Arizona State University at the Downtown Phoenix campus, PO Box 870112, Tempe, AZ 85287-0112. *Phone:* 480-965-7788. *Fax:* 480-965-3610. *E-mail:* admissions@asu.edu.

Arizona State University at the Polytechnic campus

Mesa, Arizona

https://campus.asu.edu/polytechnic

- **State-supported** comprehensive, founded 1995
- **Suburban** 581-acre campus with easy access to Phoenix
- **Coed** 3,750 undergraduate students, 86% full-time, 27% women, 73% men
- **Moderately difficult** entrance level, 77% of applicants were admitted

UNDERGRAD STUDENTS

3,230 full-time, 520 part-time. Students come from 45 states and territories; 39 other countries; 20% are from out of state; 4% Black or African American, non-Hispanic/Latino; 19% Hispanic/Latino; 5% Asian, non-Hispanic/Latino; 0.4% Native Hawaiian or other Pacific Islander, non-Hispanic/Latino; 2% American Indian or Alaska Native, non-Hispanic/Latino; 3% Two or more races, non-Hispanic/Latino; 0.8% Race/ethnicity unknown; 8% international; 24% live on campus.

Freshmen

Admission: 2,136 applied, 1,639 admitted. ***Average high school GPA:*** 3.4. ***Test scores:*** SAT critical reading scores over 500: 74%; SAT math scores over 500: 81%; ACT scores over 18: 97%; SAT critical reading scores over 600: 31%; SAT math scores over 600: 42%; ACT scores over 24: 58%; SAT critical reading scores over 700: 7%; SAT math scores over 700: 9%; ACT scores over 30: 12%.

Retention: 82% of full-time freshmen returned.

FACULTY

Total: 202, 94% full-time, 74% with terminal degrees.

Student/faculty ratio: 19:1.

ACADEMICS

Calendar: semesters. *Degrees:* certificates, bachelor's, master's, and doctoral.

Special study options: accelerated degree program, advanced placement credit, cooperative education, distance learning, double majors, freshman honors college, honors programs, independent study, internships, off-campus study, part-time degree program, services for LD students, student-designed majors, study abroad, summer session for credit. ***ROTC:*** Army (c), Navy (c), Air Force (c).

Computers: 535 computers/terminals are available on campus for general student use. Students can access the following: campus intranet, computer help desk, free student e-mail accounts, online (class) grades, online (class) registration, online (class) schedules, My Apps offers enrolled students, faculty and staff access to software applications for use online, in the classroom, by download, or for purchase. My Apps is free of charge and is accessible from any computer using your ASURITE UserID and password. Campuswide network is available. 100% of college-owned or -operated housing units are wired for high-speed Internet access. Wireless service is available via classrooms, computer centers, computer labs, dorm rooms, learning centers, libraries, student centers.

STUDENT LIFE

Housing options: on-campus residence required for freshman year; coed, special housing for students with disabilities. Campus housing is university owned and is provided by a third party. Freshman applicants given priority for college housing.

Activities and organizations: student-run newspaper, VIDA at ASU, Environmental Technology Management Club ASU Polytechnic, Women in Science & Engineering, Wildlife Restoration Student Association, Pre Veterinary Medical Association of ASU.

Athletics Member NCAA. All Division I. ***Intercollegiate sports:*** baseball M(s), basketball M(s)/W(s), cross-country running M(s)/W(s), football M(s), golf M(s)/W(s), gymnastics W(s), ice hockey M(s), soccer W(s), softball W(s), swimming and diving M(s)/W(s), tennis W(s), track and field M(s)/W(s), volleyball W(s), water polo W(s), wrestling M(s). ***Intramural sports:*** badminton M/W, basketball M/W, football M/W, racquetball M/W, soccer M(c)/W(c), softball M(c)/W(c), table tennis M/W, tennis M/W, ultimate Frisbee M/W, volleyball M/W.

Campus security: 24-hour emergency response devices and patrols, late-night transport/escort service.

Student services: health clinic, personal/psychological counseling.

COSTS & FINANCIAL AID
Costs (2014–15) ***Tuition:*** state resident $9138 full-time, $677 per credit hour part-time; nonresident $22,639 full-time, $993 per credit hour part-time. Full-time tuition and fees vary according to program. Part-time tuition and fees vary according to program. ***Required fees:*** $673 full-time. ***Room and board:*** $10,720; room only: $7080. Room and board charges vary according to board plan and housing facility. ***Payment plan:*** installment. ***Waivers:*** employees or children of employees.

Financial Aid Of all full-time matriculated undergraduates who enrolled in 2013, 2,123 applied for aid, 1,860 were judged to have need, 368 had their need fully met. 110 Federal Work-Study jobs (averaging $2916). 584 state and other part-time jobs (averaging $4246). In 2013, 264 non-need-based awards were made. ***Average percent of need met:*** 57. ***Average financial aid package:*** $13,733. ***Average need-based loan:*** $4338. ***Average need-based gift aid:*** $8454. ***Average non-need-based aid:*** $6263. ***Average indebtedness upon graduation:*** $26,463.

APPLYING
Standardized Tests *Required for some:* SAT or ACT (for admission), SAT Subject Tests (for admission). *Recommended:* SAT or ACT (for admission).

Options: electronic application.

Application fee: $50.

Required: high school transcript, minimum 3.0 GPA, application fee is $65 for nonresidents; additional requirements for Honors College and certain majors. ***Required for some:*** essay or personal statement, letters of recommendation, application fee is $65 for nonresidents; additional requirements for Honors College and certain majors.

Application deadlines: rolling (freshmen), rolling (transfers).

Notification: continuous (freshmen), continuous (transfers).

CONTACT
Admission Services, Arizona State University, Arizona State University at the Polytechnic campus, PO Box 870112, Tempe, AZ 85287-0112.
Phone: 480-965-7788. *Fax:* 480-965-3610. *E-mail:* admissions@asu.edu.

Arizona State University at the Tempe campus

Tempe, Arizona

http://www.asu.edu/

- **State-supported** university, founded 1885
- **Urban** 592-acre campus with easy access to Phoenix
- **Coed** 39,968 undergraduate students, 91% full-time, 44% women, 56% men
- **Moderately difficult** entrance level, 84% of applicants were admitted

UNDERGRAD STUDENTS
36,265 full-time, 3,703 part-time. Students come from 54 states and territories; 97 other countries; 24% are from out of state; 4% Black or African American, non-Hispanic/Latino; 19% Hispanic/Latino; 7% Asian, non-Hispanic/Latino; 0.2% Native Hawaiian or other Pacific Islander, non-Hispanic/Latino; 1% American Indian or Alaska Native, non-Hispanic/Latino; 4% Two or more races, non-Hispanic/Latino; 0.8% Race/ethnicity unknown; 11% international; 9% transferred in; 23% live on campus.

Freshmen
Admission: 22,581 applied, 19,042 admitted, 7,647 enrolled. ***Average high school GPA:*** 3.46. ***Test scores:*** SAT critical reading scores over 500: 77%; SAT math scores over 500: 84%; ACT scores over 18: 98%; SAT critical reading scores over 600: 36%; SAT math scores over 600: 44%; ACT scores over 24: 65%; SAT critical reading scores over 700: 8%; SAT math scores over 700: 10%; ACT scores over 30: 16%.

Retention: 86% of full-time freshmen returned.

FACULTY
Total: 2,277, 89% full-time, 83% with terminal degrees.

Student/faculty ratio: 22:1.

ACADEMICS
Calendar: semesters. *Degrees:* certificates, bachelor's, master's, doctoral, post-master's, and postbachelor's certificates (profile includes data for the West, Polytechnic and Downtown Phoenix campuses).

Special study options: accelerated degree program, advanced placement credit, cooperative education, distance learning, double majors, English as a second language, freshman honors college, honors programs, independent study, internships, off-campus study, part-time degree program, services for LD students, student-designed majors, study abroad, summer session for credit. ***ROTC:*** Army (b), Navy (b), Air Force (b).

Computers: 2,421 computers/terminals are available on campus for general student use. Students can access the following: campus intranet, computer help desk, free student e-mail accounts, online (class) grades, online (class) registration, online (class) schedules, My Apps offers enrolled students, faculty and staff access to software applications for use online, in the classroom, by download, or for purchase. My Apps is free of charge and is accessible from any computer using your ASURITE UserID and password. Campuswide network is available. 100% of college-owned or -operated housing units are wired for high-speed Internet access. Wireless service is available via classrooms, computer centers, computer labs, dorm rooms, learning centers, libraries, student centers.

STUDENT LIFE
Housing options: on-campus residence required for freshman year; coed, special housing for students with disabilities. Campus housing is university owned and is provided by a third party. Freshman applicants given priority for college housing.

Activities and organizations: drama/theater group, student-run newspaper, choral group, marching band, Sigma Kappa, Pi Beta Phi, Kappa Alpha Theta, Alpha Phi, Delta Zeta, national fraternities, national sororities.

Athletics Member NCAA. All Division I except football (Division I-A). ***Intercollegiate sports:*** baseball M(s), basketball M(s)/W(s), cross-country running M(s)/W(s), golf M(s)/W(s), gymnastics M(s)(c)/W(s), ice hockey M(s), soccer W(s), softball W(s), swimming and diving M(s)/W(s), tennis W(s), track and field M(s)/W(s), volleyball W(s), water polo W(s), wrestling M(s). ***Intramural sports:*** badminton M/W, baseball M(c), basketball M/W, bowling M/W, cheerleading M(c)/W(c), crew M(c)/W(c), equestrian sports M(c)/W(c), fencing M(c)/W(c), field hockey M(c)/W(c), golf M(c)/W(c), lacrosse M(c)/W(c), racquetball M(c)/W(c), rugby M(c)/W(c), sailing M(c)/W(c), soccer M(c)/W(c), softball M/W, table tennis M/W, tennis M(c)/W(c), ultimate Frisbee M(c)/W(c), volleyball M(c)/W(c), water polo M(c)/W(c), weight lifting M(c)/W(c).

Campus security: 24-hour emergency response devices and patrols, late-night transport/escort service.

Student services: health clinic, personal/psychological counseling.

COSTS & FINANCIAL AID
Costs (2014–15) ***Tuition:*** state resident $9454 full-time, $677 per credit hour part-time; nonresident $23,830 full-time, $993 per credit hour part-time. Full-time tuition and fees vary according to program. Part-time tuition and fees vary according to program. ***Required fees:*** $673 full-time. ***Room and board:*** $10,010; room only: $6370. Room and board charges vary according to board plan and housing facility. ***Payment plan:*** installment. ***Waivers:*** employees or children of employees.

Financial Aid Of all full-time matriculated undergraduates who enrolled in 2013, 24,421 applied for aid, 20,199 were judged to have need, 3,848 had their need fully met. 1,077 Federal Work-Study jobs (averaging $2406). 5,551 state and other part-time jobs (averaging $3324). In 2013, 6734 non-need-based awards were made. ***Average percent of need met:*** 61. ***Average financial aid package:*** $13,362. ***Average need-based loan:*** $4150. ***Average need-based gift aid:*** $9007. ***Average non-need-based aid:*** $7688. ***Average indebtedness upon graduation:*** $21,920.

APPLYING
Standardized Tests *Required for some:* SAT or ACT (for admission), SAT Subject Tests (for admission). *Recommended:* SAT or ACT (for admission).

Options: electronic application.

Application fee: $50.

Required: high school transcript, minimum 3.0 GPA, application fee is $65 for nonresidents; additional requirements for Honors College and certain majors. ***Required for some:*** essay or personal statement, letters of recommendation, application fee is $65 for nonresidents; additional requirements for Honors College and certain majors.

Application deadlines: rolling (freshmen), rolling (transfers).

Notification: continuous (freshmen), continuous (transfers).

COLLEGES AT-A-GLANCE

CONTACT
Admission Services, Arizona State University, Arizona State University at the Tempe campus, PO Box 870112, Tempe, AZ 85287-0112. *Phone:* 480-965-7788. *Fax:* 480-965-3610. *E-mail:* admissions@asu.edu.

Arizona State University at the West campus

Glendale, Arizona

https://campus.asu.edu/west

- **State-supported** comprehensive, founded 1984
- **Urban** 278-acre campus with easy access to Phoenix
- **Coed** 3,296 undergraduate students, 84% full-time, 61% women, 39% men
- **Moderately difficult** entrance level, 78% of applicants were admitted

UNDERGRAD STUDENTS
2,768 full-time, 528 part-time. Students come from 41 states and territories; 17 other countries; 13% are from out of state; 5% Black or African American, non-Hispanic/Latino; 28% Hispanic/Latino; 5% Asian, non-Hispanic/Latino; 0.3% Native Hawaiian or other Pacific Islander, non-Hispanic/Latino; 2% American Indian or Alaska Native, non-Hispanic/Latino; 3% Two or more races, non-Hispanic/Latino; 1% Race/ethnicity unknown; 2% international; 11% live on campus.

Freshmen
Admission: 1,288 applied, 1,002 admitted. ***Average high school GPA:*** 3.53. ***Test scores:*** SAT critical reading scores over 500: 70%; SAT math scores over 500: 71%; ACT scores over 18: 94%; SAT critical reading scores over 600: 25%; SAT math scores over 600: 24%; ACT scores over 24: 47%; SAT critical reading scores over 700: 2%; SAT math scores over 700: 2%; ACT scores over 30: 6%.
Retention: 86% of full-time freshmen returned.

FACULTY
Total: 260, 87% full-time, 78% with terminal degrees.
Student/faculty ratio: 14:1.

ACADEMICS
Calendar: semesters. *Degrees:* certificates, bachelor's, master's, doctoral, and postbachelor's certificates.
Special study options: accelerated degree program, advanced placement credit, cooperative education, distance learning, double majors, freshman honors college, honors programs, independent study, internships, off-campus study, part-time degree program, services for LD students, student-designed majors, study abroad, summer session for credit. ***ROTC:*** Army (c), Navy (c), Air Force (c).
Computers: 612 computers/terminals are available on campus for general student use. Students can access the following: campus intranet, computer help desk, free student e-mail accounts, online (class) grades, online (class) registration, online (class) schedules, My Apps offers enrolled students, faculty and staff access to software applications for use online, in the classroom, by download, or for purchase. My Apps is free of charge and is accessible from any computer using your ASURITE UserID and password. Campuswide network is available. 100% of college-owned or -operated housing units are wired for high-speed Internet access. Wireless service is available via classrooms, computer centers, computer labs, dorm rooms, learning centers, libraries, student centers.

STUDENT LIFE
Housing options: on-campus residence required for freshman year; coed, special housing for students with disabilities. Campus housing is university owned and is provided by a third party. Freshman applicants given priority for college housing.
Activities and organizations: student-run newspaper, Teachers of the Future, American Medical Student Association, Psi Chi-Psychology Club, Filmmaking Club at ASU West campus, Native American Student Organization.
Athletics Member NCAA. All Division I. ***Intercollegiate sports:*** baseball M(s), basketball M(s)/W(s), cross-country running M(s)/W(s), football M(s), golf M(s)/W(s), gymnastics W(s), ice hockey M(s), soccer W(s), softball W(s), swimming and diving M(s)/W(s), tennis W(s), track and field M(s)/W(s), volleyball W(s), water polo W(s), wrestling M(s). ***Intramural sports:*** basketball M/W, bowling M/W, racquetball M/W, soccer M/W, softball M/W, table tennis M/W, ultimate Frisbee M/W, volleyball M/W.
Campus security: 24-hour emergency response devices and patrols, late-night transport/escort service.
Student services: health clinic, personal/psychological counseling.

COSTS & FINANCIAL AID
Costs (2014–15) ***Tuition:*** state resident $9138 full-time, $677 per credit hour part-time; nonresident $22,639 full-time, $993 per credit hour part-time. Full-time tuition and fees vary according to program. Part-time tuition and fees vary according to program. ***Required fees:*** $673 full-time. ***Room and board:*** $9440; room only: $5800. Room and board charges vary according to board plan and housing facility. ***Payment plan:*** installment. ***Waivers:*** employees or children of employees.
Financial Aid Of all full-time matriculated undergraduates who enrolled in 2013, 2,288 applied for aid, 2,102 were judged to have need, 299 had their need fully met. 120 Federal Work-Study jobs (averaging $2509). 435 state and other part-time jobs (averaging $3339). In 2013, 174 non-need-based awards were made. ***Average percent of need met:*** 59. ***Average financial aid package:*** $11,817. ***Average need-based loan:*** $4328. ***Average need-based gift aid:*** $8077. ***Average non-need-based aid:*** $6575. ***Average indebtedness upon graduation:*** $18,585.

APPLYING
Standardized Tests *Required for some:* SAT or ACT (for admission), SAT Subject Tests (for admission). *Recommended:* SAT or ACT (for admission).
Options: electronic application.
Application fee: $50.
Required: high school transcript, minimum 3.0 GPA, application fee is $65 for nonresidents; additional requirements for Honors College and certain majors. ***Required for some:*** essay or personal statement, letters of recommendation, application fee is $65 for nonresidents; additional requirements for Honors College and certain majors.
Application deadlines: rolling (freshmen), rolling (transfers).
Notification: continuous (freshmen), continuous (transfers).

CONTACT
Admission Services, Arizona State University, Arizona State University at the West campus, PO Box 870112, Tempe, AZ 85287-7011. *Phone:* 480-965-7788. *Fax:* 480-965-3610. *E-mail:* admissions@asu.edu.

The Art Institute of Phoenix

Phoenix, Arizona

http://www.artinstitutes.edu/phoenix/

- **Proprietary** 4-year, founded 1995, part of Education Management Corporation
- **Suburban** campus
- **Coed**

ACADEMICS
Calendar: quarters. *Degrees:* diplomas, associate, and bachelor's.

CONTACT
The Art Institute of Phoenix, 2233 West Dunlap Avenue, Phoenix, AZ 85021-2859. *Phone:* 602-331-7500. *Toll-free phone:* 800-474-2479.

The Art Institute of Tucson

Tucson, Arizona

http://www.artinstitutes.edu/tucson/

- **Proprietary** 4-year, founded 2007
- **Coed**

ACADEMICS
Degrees: diplomas, associate, and bachelor's.

CONTACT
The Art Institute of Tucson, 5099 East Grant Road, Suite 100, Tucson, AZ 85712. *Phone:* 520-318-2700. *Toll-free phone:* 866-690-8850.

Brown Mackie College–Phoenix

Phoenix, Arizona

http://www.brownmackie.edu/phoenix/

- **Proprietary** primarily 2-year, part of Education Management Corporation
- **Coed**

ACADEMICS
Degrees: diplomas, associate, and bachelor's.

CONTACT
Brown Mackie College–Phoenix, 13430 North Black Canyon Highway, Suite 190, Phoenix, AZ 85029. *Phone:* 602-337-3044. *Toll-free phone:* 866-824-4793.

Brown Mackie College–Tucson

Tucson, Arizona

http://www.brownmackie.edu/tucson/

- **Proprietary** primarily 2-year, founded 1972, part of Education Management Corporation
- **Suburban** campus
- **Coed**

ACADEMICS
Degrees: diplomas, associate, and bachelor's.

CONTACT
Brown Mackie College–Tucson, 4585 East Speedway, Suite 204, Tucson, AZ 85712. *Phone:* 520-319-3300.

CollegeAmerica–Flagstaff

Flagstaff, Arizona

http://www.collegeamerica.edu/

- **Private** primarily 2-year, part of Center for Excellence in Higher Education, Stevens-Henager College, CollegeAmerica, California College San Diego, Independence University
- **Small-town** campus
- **Coed** 205 undergraduate students, 100% full-time, 75% women, 25% men
- **Noncompetitive** entrance level

UNDERGRAD STUDENTS
205 full-time. 1% Black or African American, non-Hispanic/Latino; 11% Hispanic/Latino; 60% American Indian or Alaska Native, non-Hispanic/Latino; 0.5% Two or more races, non-Hispanic/Latino.

Freshmen
Admission: 121 enrolled.

FACULTY
Total: 14, 64% full-time.
Student/faculty ratio: 15:1.

ACADEMICS
Degrees: associate and bachelor's.
Special study options: academic remediation for entering students, internships.
Computers: Students can access the following: campus intranet, computer help desk, online (class) grades, online (class) schedules. Wireless service is available via entire campus.

STUDENT LIFE
Housing options: college housing not available.

COSTS
Costs (2014–15) ***Tuition:*** $42,411 per degree program part-time. Full-time tuition and fees vary according to course load, degree level, program, and reciprocity agreements. No tuition increase for student's term of enrollment. Tuition cost varies by program. Prospective students should contact the school for current tuition costs. ***Payment plan:*** installment. ***Waivers:*** minority students, adult students, and employees or children of employees.

APPLYING
Required: essay or personal statement, high school transcript, interview, references.

CONTACT
CollegeAmerica–Flagstaff, 399 South Malpais, Flagstaff, AZ 86001. *Phone:* 928-213-6060 Ext. 1402. *Toll-free phone:* 800-622-2894.

DeVry University

Mesa, Arizona

http://www.devry.edu/

- **Proprietary** comprehensive
- **Coed**

ACADEMICS
Calendar: semesters. *Degrees:* associate, bachelor's, and master's.

COSTS
Costs (2014–15) ***Tuition:*** $17,052 full-time, $609 per credit hour part-time. ***Required fees:*** $80 full-time.

CONTACT
Admissions Office, DeVry University, 1201 South Alma Road, Suite 5450, Mesa, AZ 85210-2011. *Phone:* 480-827-1511. *Toll-free phone:* 866-338-7941.

DeVry University

Phoenix, Arizona

http://www.devry.edu/

- **Proprietary** comprehensive, founded 1967, part of DeVry University
- **Urban** campus
- **Coed** 730 undergraduate students, 51% full-time, 28% women, 72% men
- **Minimally difficult** entrance level

UNDERGRAD STUDENTS
375 full-time, 355 part-time. 9% are from out of state; 7% Black or African American, non-Hispanic/Latino; 27% Hispanic/Latino; 5% Asian, non-Hispanic/Latino; 0.5% Native Hawaiian or other Pacific Islander, non-Hispanic/Latino; 5% American Indian or Alaska Native, non-Hispanic/Latino; 1% Two or more races, non-Hispanic/Latino; 0.8% international; 25% transferred in.

Freshmen
Admission: 61 enrolled.

FACULTY
Total: 123, 21% full-time.
Student/faculty ratio: 9:1.

ACADEMICS
Calendar: semesters. *Degrees:* associate, bachelor's, master's, and postbachelor's certificates.
Special study options: adult/continuing education programs, part-time degree program.
Computers: Students can access the following: online (class) registration.

STUDENT LIFE
Housing options: college housing not available.

COSTS
Costs (2014–15) ***Tuition:*** $17,052 full-time, $609 per credit hour part-time. ***Required fees:*** $80 full-time.

APPLYING
Application fee: $40.
Required: high school transcript, interview.

CONTACT
DeVry University, 2149 West Dunlap Avenue, Phoenix, AZ 85021-2995. *Phone:* 602-870-9222. *Toll-free phone:* 866-338-7941.

Dunlap-Stone University

Phoenix, Arizona

http://www.dunlap-stone.edu/

- **Proprietary** 4-year, founded 1995
- **Urban** campus with easy access to Phoenix
- **Coed** 500 undergraduate students

UNDERGRAD STUDENTS
Students come from 25 states and territories.

FACULTY
Total: 100.
Student/faculty ratio: 15:1.

ACADEMICS
Calendar: semesters 3 semesters per year (fall, spring, summer). *Degrees:* certificates, associate, and bachelor's.

Special study options: academic remediation for entering students, accelerated degree program, advanced placement credit, distance learning, independent study, internships.

APPLYING
Options: electronic application, deferred entrance.

Application deadlines: rolling (freshmen), rolling (out-of-state freshmen), rolling (transfers).

Notification: continuous (freshmen), continuous (out-of-state freshmen), continuous (transfers).

CONTACT
Dunlap-Stone University, 19820 North 7th Street, Suite #100, Phoenix, AZ 85024. *Phone:* 602-648-5750. *Toll-free phone:* 800-474-8013.

★ Embry-Riddle Aeronautical University–Prescott

Prescott, Arizona

http://www.embryriddle.edu/

- **Independent** comprehensive, founded 1978
- **Small-town** 547-acre campus with easy access to Phoenix
- **Coed** 1,984 undergraduate students, 94% full-time, 23% women, 77% men
- **Moderately difficult** entrance level, 80% of applicants were admitted

UNDERGRAD STUDENTS
1,869 full-time, 115 part-time. Students come from 47 states and territories; 97 other countries; 78% are from out of state; 2% Black or African American, non-Hispanic/Latino; 6% Hispanic/Latino; 6% Asian, non-Hispanic/Latino; 0.6% Native Hawaiian or other Pacific Islander, non-Hispanic/Latino; 0.4% American Indian or Alaska Native, non-Hispanic/Latino; 9% Two or more races, non-Hispanic/Latino; 10% Race/ethnicity unknown; 10% international; 5% transferred in; 45% live on campus.

Freshmen
Admission: 1,779 applied, 1,426 admitted, 505 enrolled. ***Average high school GPA:*** 3.62. ***Test scores:*** SAT critical reading scores over 500: 78%; SAT math scores over 500: 88%; SAT writing scores over 500: 114%; ACT scores over 18: 97%; SAT critical reading scores over 600: 36%; SAT math scores over 600: 50%; SAT writing scores over 600: 74%; ACT scores over 24: 74%; SAT critical reading scores over 700: 7%; SAT math scores over 700: 11%; SAT writing scores over 700: 21%; ACT scores over 30: 21%.

Retention: 82% of full-time freshmen returned.

ACADEMICS
Calendar: semesters. *Degrees:* bachelor's and master's.

Special study options: academic remediation for entering students, accelerated degree program, adult/continuing education programs, advanced placement credit, cooperative education, distance learning, double majors, honors programs, independent study, internships, part-time degree program, services for LD students, student-designed majors, study abroad, summer session for credit. ***ROTC:*** Army (b), Air Force (b).

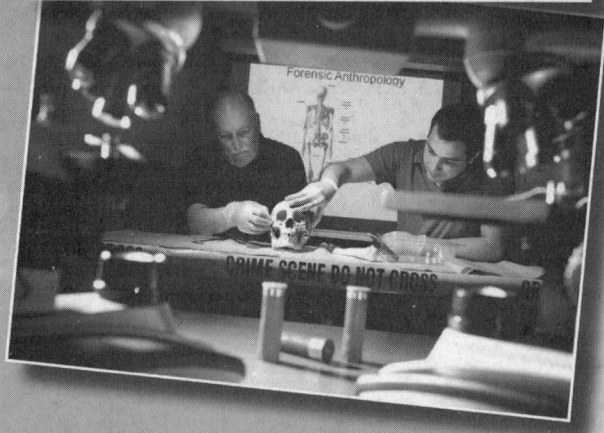

Computers: 730 computers/terminals are available on campus for general student use. Students can access the following: campus intranet, computer help desk, free student e-mail accounts, online (class) grades, online (class) registration, online (class) schedules. Campuswide network is available. 100% of college-owned or -operated housing units are wired for high-speed Internet access. Wireless service is available via entire campus.

STUDENT LIFE
Housing options: on-campus residence required for freshman year; coed. Campus housing is university owned. Freshman campus housing is guaranteed.

Activities and organizations: student-run newspaper, radio station, Hawaii Club, Strike Eagles, Theta XI, American Institute of Aeronautics and Astronautics (AIAA), Arnold Air Society, national fraternities, national sororities.

Athletics Member NAIA. ***Intercollegiate sports:*** cross-country running M(s)/W(s), golf M(s)/W(s), soccer M(s)/W(s), softball W(s), volleyball W(s), wrestling M(s). ***Intramural sports:*** basketball M/W, bowling M(c)/W(c), football M/W, racquetball M/W, rock climbing M/W, soccer M/W, softball M/W, table tennis M/W, tennis M/W, ultimate Frisbee M(c)/W(c), volleyball M/W.

Campus security: 24-hour emergency response devices and patrols, student patrols, late-night transport/escort service.

Student services: health clinic, personal/psychological counseling.

COSTS & FINANCIAL AID
Costs (2015–16) ***Comprehensive fee:*** $43,044 includes full-time tuition ($31,944), mandatory fees ($1200), and room and board ($9900). Part-time tuition: $1331 per credit hour. ***College room only:*** $5600. Room and board charges vary according to board plan, housing facility, and location. ***Payment plan:*** installment. ***Waivers:*** employees or children of employees.

Financial Aid Of all full-time matriculated undergraduates who enrolled in 2014, 1,613 applied for aid, 1,284 were judged to have need. 28 Federal Work-Study jobs (averaging $1147). 537 state and other part-time jobs (averaging $2311). ***Average financial aid package:*** $16,608. ***Average need-based loan:*** $4232. ***Average need-based gift aid:*** $14,191.

APPLYING
Standardized Tests *Recommended:* SAT or ACT (for admission).

Options: electronic application, deferred entrance.

Application fee: $50.

Required: high school transcript, minimum 2.0 GPA, 2 letters of recommendation, medical examination for flight students. ***Recommended:*** essay or personal statement, minimum 3.0 GPA, interview.

Application deadlines: rolling (freshmen), rolling (out-of-state freshmen), rolling (transfers).

Notification: continuous (freshmen), continuous (out-of-state freshmen), continuous (transfers).

CONTACT
Embry-Riddle Aeronautical University–Prescott, 3700 Willow Creek Road, Prescott, AZ 863013720. *Phone:* 800-888-3728. *Toll-free phone:* 800-888-3728. *Fax:* 928-777-6606. *E-mail:* pradmit@erau.edu.

See next page for display ad and page 1434 for the College Close-Up.

Harrison Middleton University
Tempe, Arizona
http://www.hmu.edu/

- **Independent** comprehensive, founded 1998
- **Suburban** campus with easy access to Phoenix
- **Coed** 79 undergraduate students, 100% full-time, 47% women, 53% men

UNDERGRAD STUDENTS
79 full-time. 98% are from out of state.

FACULTY
Total: 23, 74% full-time, 43% with terminal degrees.

Student/faculty ratio: 1:1.

ACADEMICS
Calendar: continuous. *Degrees:* diplomas, associate, bachelor's, master's, and doctoral.

Special study options: advanced placement credit, distance learning, double majors, independent study, student-designed majors, summer session for credit.

COSTS
Costs (2015–16) ***One-time required fee:*** $400. ***Tuition:*** $5400 full-time. ***Payment plan:*** installment.

APPLYING
Options: electronic application.

Application fee: $50.

Required: high school transcript, interview. ***Required for some:*** essay or personal statement, 2 letters of recommendation.

Application deadlines: rolling (freshmen), rolling (out-of-state freshmen), rolling (transfers).

Notification: continuous (freshmen), continuous (out-of-state freshmen), continuous (transfers).

CONTACT
Harrison Middleton University, 1105 East Broadway, Tempe, AZ 85282. *Phone:* 877-248.6724. *Toll-free phone:* 877-248-6724.

ITT Technical Institute
Phoenix, Arizona
http://www.itt-tech.edu/

- **Proprietary** primarily 2-year, founded 1972, part of ITT Educational Services, Inc.
- **Urban** campus
- **Coed**
- **Minimally difficult** entrance level

ACADEMICS
Calendar: quarters. *Degrees:* associate and bachelor's.

STUDENT LIFE
Housing options: college housing not available.

FINANCIAL AID
Financial Aid Of all full-time matriculated undergraduates who enrolled in 2013, 10 Federal Work-Study jobs (averaging $4000).

CONTACT
Director of Recruitment, ITT Technical Institute, 10220 North 25th Avenue, Suite 100, Phoenix, AZ 85021. *Phone:* 602-749-7900. *Toll-free phone:* 877-221-1132.

ITT Technical Institute
Phoenix, Arizona
http://www.itt-tech.edu/

- **Proprietary** primarily 2-year, part of ITT Educational Services, Inc.
- **Coed**

ACADEMICS
Calendar: quarters. *Degrees:* associate and bachelor's.

CONTACT
Director of Recruitment, ITT Technical Institute, 1840 N. 95th Avenue, Suite 132, Phoenix, AZ 85037. *Phone:* 623-474-7900. *Toll-free phone:* 800-210-1178.

ITT Technical Institute
Tempe, Arizona
http://www.itt-tech.edu/

- **Proprietary** 4-year, founded 1963, part of ITT Educational Services, Inc.
- **Coed**
- **Minimally difficult** entrance level

ACADEMICS
Degrees: associate and bachelor's.

STUDENT LIFE
Housing options: college housing not available.

CONTACT
Director of Recruitment, ITT Technical Institute, 5005 S. Wendler Drive, Tempe, AZ 85282. *Phone:* 602-437-7500. *Toll-free phone:* 800-879-4881.

ITT Technical Institute
Tucson, Arizona
http://www.itt-tech.edu/

- **Proprietary** primarily 2-year, founded 1984, part of ITT Educational Services, Inc.
- **Urban** campus
- **Coed**
- **Minimally difficult** entrance level

ACADEMICS
Calendar: quarters. *Degrees:* associate and bachelor's.

STUDENT LIFE
Housing options: college housing not available.

CONTACT
Director of Recruitment, ITT Technical Institute, 1455 West River Road, Tucson, AZ 85704. *Phone:* 520-408-7488. *Toll-free phone:* 800-870-9730.

National Paralegal College
Phoenix, Arizona
http://nationalparalegal.edu/

- **Proprietary** comprehensive
- **Coed** 1,095 undergraduate students

UNDERGRAD STUDENTS
Students come from 56 states and territories; 2 other countries.

Freshmen
Admission: 1,582 admitted.

FACULTY
Total: 33, 15% full-time, 97% with terminal degrees.

ACADEMICS
Degrees: certificates, associate, bachelor's, and master's.

Special study options: academic remediation for entering students, accelerated degree program, distance learning, part-time degree program, summer session for credit.

Unusual degree programs: Legal and Paralegal Studies, Taxation studies.

COSTS
Costs (2014–15) ***One-time required fee:*** $195. ***Tuition:*** $6600 full-time, $275 per credit part-time. ***Required fees:*** $275 per credit part-time. ***Payment plans:*** tuition prepayment, installment.

APPLYING
Options: electronic application.

Required for some: high school transcript. ***Recommended:*** essay or personal statement, interview.

Application deadlines: rolling (freshmen), rolling (out-of-state freshmen), rolling (transfers).

Notification: continuous (freshmen), continuous (out-of-state freshmen), continuous (transfers).

CONTACT
Admissions Office, National Paralegal College, 717 East Maryland Avenue, Suite 115, Phoenix, AZ 85014. *Phone:* 845-371-9101. *Toll-free phone:* 800-371-6105. *Fax:* 866-347-2744. *E-mail:* info@nationalparalegal.edu.

Northcentral University
Prescott Valley, Arizona
http://www.ncu.edu/

- **Proprietary** upper-level
- **Coed**
- **Minimally difficult** entrance level

FACULTY
Student/faculty ratio: 7:1.

ACADEMICS
Calendar: continuous. *Degrees:* bachelor's, master's, doctoral, post-master's, and postbachelor's certificates (offers only distance learning programs).

COSTS
Costs (2014–15) ***One-time required fee:*** $250. ***Tuition:*** $10,000 full-time, $1250 per course part-time. ***Payment plans:*** tuition prepayment, installment.

APPLYING
Options: electronic application.

CONTACT
Northcentral University, 10000 East University Drive, Prescott Valley, AZ 86314. *Phone:* 480-253-3535. *Toll-free phone:* 866-776-0331.

★ Northern Arizona University
Flagstaff, Arizona
http://www.nau.edu/

- **State-supported** university, founded 1899, part of Arizona University System, under the Arizona Board of Regents
- **Small-town** 740-acre campus
- **Coed** 23,845 undergraduate students, 81% full-time, 58% women, 42% men
- **Moderately difficult** entrance level, 91% of applicants were admitted

UNDERGRAD STUDENTS
19,361 full-time, 4,484 part-time. Students come from 51 states and territories; 72 other countries; 28% are from out of state; 3% Black or African American, non-Hispanic/Latino; 20% Hispanic/Latino; 2% Asian, non-Hispanic/Latino; 0.2% Native Hawaiian or other Pacific Islander, non-Hispanic/Latino; 3% American Indian or Alaska Native, non-Hispanic/Latino; 5% Two or more races, non-Hispanic/Latino; 0.6% Race/ethnicity unknown; 5% international; 12% transferred in; 29% live on campus.

Freshmen
Admission: 27,780 applied, 25,153 admitted, 5,035 enrolled. ***Average high school GPA:*** 3.49. ***Test scores:*** SAT critical reading scores over 500: 64%; SAT math scores over 500: 64%; SAT writing scores over 500: 52%; ACT scores over 18: 91%; SAT critical reading scores over 600: 19%; SAT math scores over 600: 19%; SAT writing scores over 600: 13%; ACT scores over 24: 42%; SAT critical reading scores over 700: 2%; SAT math scores over 700: 2%; SAT writing scores over 700: 1%; ACT scores over 30: 4%.

Retention: 74% of full-time freshmen returned.

FACULTY
Total: 1,644, 64% full-time.

Student/faculty ratio: 19:1.

ACADEMICS
Calendar: semesters. *Degrees:* certificates, bachelor's, master's, doctoral, post-master's, and postbachelor's certificates.

Special study options: accelerated degree program, advanced placement credit, cooperative education, distance learning, double majors, English as a second language, freshman honors college, honors programs, independent study, internships, off-campus study, part-time degree program, services for LD students, study abroad, summer session for credit. ***ROTC:*** Army (b), Air Force (b).

Unusual degree programs: 3-2 business administration; engineering; forestry; Criminology and Criminal Justice, Educational Specialties, Geography, Planning and Recreation, Psychology.

Computers: Students can access the following: campus intranet, computer help desk, free student e-mail accounts, online (class) grades, online (class) registration, online (class) schedules. Campuswide network is available. 100% of college-owned or -operated housing units are wired for high-speed Internet access. Wireless service is available via entire campus.

STUDENT LIFE

Housing options: coed, men-only, women-only, special housing for students with disabilities. Campus housing is university owned. Freshman campus housing is guaranteed.

Activities and organizations: drama/theater group, student-run newspaper, radio and television station, choral group, marching band, national fraternities, national sororities.

Athletics Member NCAA. All Division I. ***Intercollegiate sports:*** basketball M(s)/W(s), cross-country running M(s)/W(s), football M(s), golf W(s), soccer W(s), swimming and diving W(s), tennis M(s)/W(s), track and field M(s)/W(s), volleyball W(s). ***Intramural sports:*** archery M(c)/W(c), badminton M/W, baseball M(c)/W(c), basketball M/W, cheerleading M(c)/W(c), fencing M(c)/W(c), football M(c)/W(c), gymnastics M(c)/W(c), ice hockey M(c)/W(c), lacrosse M(c)/W(c), racquetball M/W, rugby M(c)/W(c), soccer M/W, softball M(c)/W(c), tennis M(c)/W(c), ultimate Frisbee M(c)/W(c), volleyball M/W, water polo M(c)/W(c), wrestling M(c)/W(c).

Campus security: 24-hour emergency response devices and patrols, late-night transport/escort service, controlled dormitory access.

Student services: health clinic, personal/psychological counseling, legal services.

COSTS & FINANCIAL AID

Costs (2014–15) ***Tuition:*** state resident $9120 full-time; nonresident $21,640 full-time. Full-time tuition and fees vary according to course load, location, and reciprocity agreements. Part-time tuition and fees vary according to course load, location, and reciprocity agreements. No tuition increase for student's term of enrollment. ***Required fees:*** $870 full-time. ***Room and board:*** $9020; room only: $4990. Room and board charges vary according to board plan and housing facility. ***Payment plan:*** installment. ***Waivers:*** employees or children of employees.

Financial Aid Of all full-time matriculated undergraduates who enrolled in 2013, 14,219 applied for aid, 11,638 were judged to have need, 1,286 had their need fully met. In 2013, 2271 non-need-based awards were made. ***Average percent of need met:*** 63. ***Average financial aid package:*** $10,622. ***Average need-based loan:*** $4239. ***Average need-based gift aid:*** $6226. ***Average non-need-based aid:*** $5658. ***Average indebtedness upon graduation:*** $23,602.

APPLYING

Standardized Tests *Required for some:* SAT (for admission), ACT (for admission), SAT or ACT (for admission), SAT and SAT Subject Tests or ACT (for admission), SAT Subject Tests (for admission), ACT/SAT test scores required for home-schooled students.

Options: electronic application, deferred entrance.

Application fee: $25.

Required: high school transcript, minimum 3.0 GPA, Completion of 16 required college preparatory courses with minimum 2.0 in each subject area.

Application deadlines: rolling (freshmen), rolling (out-of-state freshmen), rolling (transfers).

Notification: continuous (freshmen), continuous (out-of-state freshmen), continuous (transfers).

CONTACT

Undergraduate Admissions, Northern Arizona University, Box 4084, Flagstaff, AZ 86011. *Phone:* 928-523-5511. *Toll-free phone:* 888-MORE-NAU. *Fax:* 928-523-6023. *E-mail:* Admissions@nau.edu.

Penn Foster College

Scottsdale, Arizona

http://www.pennfostercollege.edu/

- **Proprietary** primarily 2-year
- **Coed** 28,900 undergraduate students, 60% women, 40% men

UNDERGRAD STUDENTS

28,900 part-time. Students come from 50 states and territories; 5 other countries.

FACULTY

Total: 164, 26% full-time, 7% with terminal degrees.

ACADEMICS

Degrees: certificates, associate, and bachelor's.

Special study options: academic remediation for entering students, accelerated degree program, cooperative education, distance learning, external degree program, independent study, internships, off-campus study, part-time degree program, services for LD students.

Computers: Students can access the following: online (class) grades, online (class) registration, Most course materials are online.

STUDENT LIFE

Housing options: college housing not available.

Activities and organizations: Online Community hosts academic interest groups, clubs, etc. that are open to students around the world.

COSTS

Costs (2015–16) ***Tuition:*** $79 per credit part-time. Part-time tuition and fees vary according to course load and program. ***Payment plan:*** installment.

APPLYING

Options: electronic application.

Application fee: $75.

Required: high school transcript.

Application deadlines: rolling (freshmen), rolling (out-of-state freshmen).

CONTACT

Admissions, Penn Foster College, 14300 North Northsight Boulevard, Suite 120, Scottsdale, AZ 85260. *Phone:* 480-315-4950. *Toll-free phone:* 800-471-3232.

Prescott College

Prescott, Arizona

http://www.prescott.edu/

- **Independent** comprehensive, founded 1966
- **Small-town** 13-acre campus
- **Endowment** $1.5 million
- **Coed** 464 undergraduate students, 80% full-time, 59% women, 41% men
- **Moderately difficult** entrance level, 68% of applicants were admitted

UNDERGRAD STUDENTS

371 full-time, 93 part-time. Students come from 47 states and territories; 10 other countries; 90% are from out of state; 2% Black or African American, non-Hispanic/Latino; 6% Hispanic/Latino; 2% Asian, non-Hispanic/Latino; 3% American Indian or Alaska Native, non-Hispanic/Latino; 4% Two or more races, non-Hispanic/Latino; 13% Race/ethnicity unknown; 0.9% international; 22% transferred in; 16% live on campus.

Freshmen

Admission: 573 applied, 388 admitted, 41 enrolled. ***Average high school GPA:*** 3.17. ***Test scores:*** SAT critical reading scores over 500: 62%; SAT writing scores over 500: 52%; ACT scores over 18: 82%; SAT critical reading scores over 600: 33%; SAT writing scores over 600: 19%; ACT scores over 24: 47%; SAT critical reading scores over 700: 5%; SAT writing scores over 700: 5%; ACT scores over 30: 12%.

Retention: 79% of full-time freshmen returned.

FACULTY

Total: 109, 58% full-time, 45% with terminal degrees.

Student/faculty ratio: 9:1.

ACADEMICS

Calendar: quarters (4-week blocks followed by 10-week terms for each quarter). *Degrees:* bachelor's, master's, doctoral, post-master's, and postbachelor's certificates.

Special study options: adult/continuing education programs, advanced placement credit, distance learning, double majors, external degree program, independent study, internships, off-campus study, services for LD students, student-designed majors, study abroad, summer session for credit.

Computers: 100 computers/terminals and 20 ports are available on campus for general student use. Students can access the following: campus intranet, computer help desk, free student e-mail accounts, online (class) grades, online (class) schedules, Learning Management System (Moodle), free E-portfolios. Campuswide network is available. 100% of college-owned or -operated housing units are wired for high-speed Internet access. Wireless service is available via entire campus.

STUDENT LIFE

Housing options: on-campus residence required for freshman year; coed. Campus housing is university owned. Freshman campus housing is guaranteed.

Activities and organizations: drama/theater group, choral group, Student Union, Catalyst, WEB (Women's Empowerment Breakthrough), HUB (Helping Understand Bikes), Aztlan Center.

Campus security: 24-hour emergency response devices, late-night transport/escort service, controlled dormitory access.

Student services: personal/psychological counseling.

FINANCIAL AID

Financial Aid Of all full-time matriculated undergraduates who enrolled in 2013, 325 applied for aid, 298 were judged to have need, 18 had their need fully met. In 2013, 87 non-need-based awards were made. ***Average percent of need met:*** 60. ***Average financial aid package:*** $19,706. ***Average need-based loan:*** $4821. ***Average need-based gift aid:*** $14,569. ***Average non-need-based aid:*** $8642. ***Average indebtedness upon graduation:*** $27,213.

APPLYING

Standardized Tests *Required:* SAT or ACT (for admission).

Options: electronic application, early decision, deferred entrance.

Required: essay or personal statement, high school transcript, 1 letter of recommendation. ***Required for some:*** interview.

Application deadlines: 8/15 (freshmen), 8/15 (out-of-state freshmen), 8/15 (transfers).

Early decision deadline: 12/1.

Notification: continuous (freshmen), continuous (out-of-state freshmen), continuous (transfers), 12/15 (early decision).

CONTACT

Nancy Simmons, Admissions Coordinator, Prescott College, 220 Grove Avenue, Prescott, AZ 86301. *Phone:* 928-350-2100. *Toll-free phone:* 877-350-2100. *Fax:* 928-776-5242. *E-mail:* admissions@prescott.edu.

The University of Arizona

Tucson, Arizona

http://www.arizona.edu/

- **State-supported** university, founded 1885, part of Arizona Board of Regents
- **Urban** 392-acre campus
- **Endowment** $683.6 million
- **Coed** 32,987 undergraduate students, 90% full-time, 52% women, 48% men
- **Moderately difficult** entrance level, 75% of applicants were admitted

UNDERGRAD STUDENTS

29,529 full-time, 3,458 part-time. Students come from 112 other countries; 28% are from out of state; 4% Black or African American, non-Hispanic/Latino; 25% Hispanic/Latino; 6% Asian, non-Hispanic/Latino; 0.3% Native Hawaiian or other Pacific Islander, non-Hispanic/Latino; 1% American Indian or Alaska Native, non-Hispanic/Latino; 4% Two or more races, non-Hispanic/Latino; 1% Race/ethnicity unknown; 6% international; 6% transferred in; 20% live on campus.

Freshmen

Admission: 32,723 applied, 24,417 admitted, 7,744 enrolled. ***Average high school GPA:*** 3.37. ***Test scores:*** SAT critical reading scores over 500: 69%; SAT math scores over 500: 73%; SAT writing scores over 500: 66%; ACT scores over 18: 92%; SAT critical reading scores over 600: 28%; SAT math scores over 600: 36%; SAT writing scores over 600: 24%; ACT scores over 24: 53%; SAT critical reading scores over 700: 5%; SAT math scores over 700: 8%; SAT writing scores over 700: 4%; ACT scores over 30: 12%.

Retention: 82% of full-time freshmen returned.

FACULTY

Total: 1,834, 86% full-time.

Student/faculty ratio: 22:1.

ACADEMICS

Calendar: semesters. *Degrees:* bachelor's, master's, doctoral, post-master's, and postbachelor's certificates.

Special study options: accelerated degree program, adult/continuing education programs, advanced placement credit, cooperative education, distance learning, double majors, English as a second language, external degree program, freshman honors college, honors programs, independent study, internships, off-campus study, part-time degree program, services for LD students, student-designed majors, study abroad, summer session for credit. ***ROTC:*** Army (b), Navy (b), Air Force (b).

Computers: Students can access the following: campus intranet, computer help desk, free student e-mail accounts, online (class) grades, online (class) registration, online (class) schedules. Campuswide network is available. Wireless service is available via classrooms, computer centers, computer labs, dorm rooms, learning centers, libraries, student centers.

STUDENT LIFE

Housing options: coed, women-only, special housing for students with disabilities. Campus housing is university owned and leased by the school. Freshman applicants given priority for college housing.

Activities and organizations: drama/theater group, student-run newspaper, radio and television station, choral group, marching band, national fraternities, national sororities.

Athletics Member NCAA. All Division I except football (Division I-A). ***Intercollegiate sports:*** badminton M(c)/W(c), baseball M(s), basketball M(s)/W(s), cheerleading M(c)/W(c), cross-country running M(s)/W(s), golf M(s)/W(s), gymnastics W(s), ice hockey M(c), lacrosse M(c)/W(c), racquetball M(c)/W(c), rugby M(c)/W(c), soccer M(c)/W(s), softball W(s), swimming and diving M(s)/W(s), tennis M(s)/W(s), track and field M(s)/W(s), ultimate Frisbee M(c)/W(c), volleyball M(c)/W(s), water polo M(c)/W(c). ***Intramural sports:*** basketball M/W, football M/W, racquetball M/W, soccer M/W, table tennis M/W, tennis M/W, ultimate Frisbee M/W, volleyball M/W, water polo M/W.

Campus security: 24-hour patrols, student patrols, late-night transport/escort service, emergency telephones.

Student services: health clinic, personal/psychological counseling, women's center, legal services.

COSTS & FINANCIAL AID

Costs (2015–16) ***Tuition:*** state resident $9576 full-time, $684 per credit hour part-time; nonresident $27,374 full-time, $1141 per credit hour part-time. Full-time tuition and fees vary according to course level, course load, degree level, location, program, reciprocity agreements, and student level. Part-time tuition and fees vary according to course level, course load, degree level, location, program, reciprocity agreements, and student level. No tuition increase for student's term of enrollment. ***Required fees:*** $1005 full-time, $87 per credit hour part-time. ***Room and board:*** $9700; room only: $7000. Room and board charges vary according to board plan and housing facility. ***Payment plan:*** installment. ***Waivers:*** employees or children of employees.

Financial Aid Of all full-time matriculated undergraduates who enrolled in 2014, 18,554 applied for aid, 15,580 were judged to have need, 1,371 had their need fully met. In 2014, 5372 non-need-based awards were made. ***Average percent of need met:*** 60. ***Average financial aid package:*** $12,790. ***Average need-based loan:*** $4293. ***Average need-based gift aid:*** $10,726. ***Average non-need-based aid:*** $8099. ***Average indebtedness upon graduation:*** $22,761.

APPLYING

Standardized Tests *Recommended:* SAT or ACT (for admission).

Options: electronic application, early admission.

Application fee: $50.

Required: essay or personal statement, high school transcript. ***Required for some:*** minimum 3.0 GPA, interview.

Application deadlines: 5/1 (freshmen), rolling (transfers).

Notification: continuous (freshmen).

CONTACT

The University of Arizona, Tucson, AZ 85721. *Phone:* 520-621-3705.

ARKANSAS

Arkansas State University

Jonesboro, Arkansas

http://www.astate.edu/

- **State-supported** comprehensive, founded 1909, part of Arkansas State University System
- **Small-town** 1376-acre campus with easy access to Memphis
- **Endowment** $51.9 million
- **Coed** 9,857 undergraduate students, 76% full-time, 57% women, 43% men
- **Moderately difficult** entrance level, 72% of applicants were admitted

UNDERGRAD STUDENTS

7,465 full-time, 2,392 part-time. Students come from 40 states and territories; 46 other countries; 10% are from out of state; 14% Black or African American, non-Hispanic/Latino; 2% Hispanic/Latino; 0.8% Asian, non-Hispanic/Latino; 0.1% Native Hawaiian or other Pacific Islander, non-Hispanic/Latino; 0.4% American Indian or Alaska Native, non-Hispanic/Latino; 2% Two or more races, non-Hispanic/Latino; 0.9% Race/ethnicity unknown; 5% international; 9% transferred in; 30% live on campus.

Freshmen

Admission: 5,086 applied, 3,682 admitted, 1,698 enrolled. ***Average high school GPA:*** 3.47. ***Test scores:*** SAT critical reading scores over 500: 32%; SAT math scores over 500: 62%; SAT writing scores over 500: 18%; ACT scores over 18: 98%; SAT critical reading scores over 600: 3%; SAT math scores over 600: 21%; ACT scores over 24: 51%; ACT scores over 30: 8%.

Retention: 75% of full-time freshmen returned.

FACULTY

Total: 700, 72% full-time, 50% with terminal degrees.

Student/faculty ratio: 17:1.

ACADEMICS

Calendar: semesters. *Degrees:* certificates, associate, bachelor's, master's, doctoral, post-master's, and postbachelor's certificates.

Special study options: academic remediation for entering students, accelerated degree program, advanced placement credit, distance learning, double majors, English as a second language, honors programs, independent study, internships, off-campus study, part-time degree program, services for LD students, study abroad, summer session for credit. ***ROTC:*** Army (b).

Computers: 800 computers/terminals and 5,304 ports are available on campus for general student use. Students can access the following: campus intranet, computer help desk, free student e-mail accounts, online (class) grades, online (class) registration, online (class) schedules. Campuswide network is available. 95% of college-owned or -operated housing units are wired for high-speed Internet access. Wireless service is available via entire campus.

STUDENT LIFE

Housing options: on-campus residence required for freshman year; coed, men-only, women-only. Campus housing is university owned.

Activities and organizations: drama/theater group, student-run newspaper, radio and television station, choral group, marching band, ASU Rugby, Black Student Association, Student Activities Board, Honors College Association, Student Government Association, national fraternities, national sororities.

Athletics Member NCAA. All Division I except football (Division I-A). ***Intercollegiate sports:*** baseball M(s), basketball M(s)/W(s), bowling W(s), cross-country running M(s)/W(s), golf M(s)/W(s), soccer W(s), tennis W(s), track and field M(s)/W(s), volleyball W(s). ***Intramural sports:*** badminton M/W, basketball M/W, bowling M/W, football M/W, golf M/W, rugby M(c), soccer M/W, softball M/W, table tennis M/W, tennis M/W, ultimate Frisbee M/W, volleyball M/W.

Campus security: 24-hour emergency response devices and patrols, student patrols, late-night transport/escort service, controlled dormitory access, check-in desk; video surveillance cameras.

Student services: health clinic, personal/psychological counseling.

COSTS & FINANCIAL AID

Costs (2014–15) ***Tuition:*** state resident $5760 full-time, $192 per credit hour part-time; nonresident $11,520 full-time, $384 per credit hour part-time. Full-time tuition and fees vary according to course load, location, and program. Part-time tuition and fees vary according to course load, location, and program. ***Required fees:*** $1960 full-time, $63 per credit hour part-time, $35 per term part-time. ***Room and board:*** $7750. Room and board charges vary according to board plan, housing facility, and student level. ***Payment plan:*** installment. ***Waivers:*** senior citizens and employees or children of employees.

Financial Aid Of all full-time matriculated undergraduates who enrolled in 2014, 6,567 applied for aid, 6,301 were judged to have need, 3,460 had their need fully met. 180 Federal Work-Study jobs (averaging $3400). 350 state and other part-time jobs (averaging $3800). In 2014, 749 non-need-based awards were made. ***Average percent of need met:*** 51. ***Average financial aid package:*** $10,500. ***Average need-based loan:*** $8100. ***Average need-based gift aid:*** $10,000. ***Average non-need-based aid:*** $5575. ***Average indebtedness upon graduation:*** $25,000. ***Financial aid deadline:*** 7/1.

APPLYING

Standardized Tests *Required:* SAT or ACT (for admission). *Required for some:* ACT ASSET; ACT Compass; TOEFL, IELTS, PTE or Proof of English Proficiency for international students. *Recommended:* ACT (for admission).

Options: electronic application, early admission.

Application fee: $15.

Required: high school transcript, minimum 2.8 GPA, ACT composite score of 21 plus a 2.75 high school GPA, immunization, selective service.

Application deadlines: rolling (freshmen), rolling (transfers).

Notification: continuous (freshmen), continuous (transfers).

CONTACT

Ms. Tracy Finch, Director of Admissions, Records, and Registration, Arkansas State University, PO Box 1570, State University, AR 72467. *Phone:* 870-972-2031. *Toll-free phone:* 800-382-3030. *Fax:* 870-972-3406. *E-mail:* admissions@astate.edu.

Arkansas Tech University

Russellville, Arkansas

http://www.atu.edu/

- **State-supported** comprehensive, founded 1909
- **Small-town** 559-acre campus
- **Endowment** $22.7 million
- **Coed** 11,099 undergraduate students, 63% full-time, 55% women, 45% men
- **Moderately difficult** entrance level, 86% of applicants were admitted

UNDERGRAD STUDENTS

7,028 full-time, 4,071 part-time. Students come from 40 states and territories; 36 other countries; 5% are from out of state; 8% Black or African American, non-Hispanic/Latino; 6% Hispanic/Latino; 1% Asian, non-Hispanic/Latino; 0.1% Native Hawaiian or other Pacific Islander, non-Hispanic/Latino; 1% American Indian or Alaska Native, non-Hispanic/Latino; 3% Two or more races, non-Hispanic/Latino; 3% international; 5% transferred in; 31% live on campus.

Freshmen

Admission: 4,162 applied, 3,590 admitted, 1,946 enrolled. ***Average high school GPA:*** 3.18. ***Test scores:*** SAT critical reading scores over 500: 53%; SAT math scores over 500: 60%; ACT scores over 18: 82%; SAT critical reading scores over 600: 27%; SAT math scores over 600: 33%; ACT scores over 24: 36%; SAT math scores over 700: 13%; ACT scores over 30: 4%.

Retention: 67% of full-time freshmen returned.

FACULTY
Total: 561, 62% full-time, 41% with terminal degrees.

Student/faculty ratio: 20:1.

ACADEMICS
Calendar: semesters. *Degrees:* certificates, associate, bachelor's, master's, and post-master's certificates.

Special study options: academic remediation for entering students, accelerated degree program, adult/continuing education programs, advanced placement credit, distance learning, double majors, English as a second language, honors programs, independent study, internships, off-campus study, part-time degree program, services for LD students, study abroad, summer session for credit. ***ROTC:*** Army (c).

Computers: 1,124 computers/terminals are available on campus for general student use. Students can access the following: campus intranet, computer help desk, free student e-mail accounts, online (class) grades, online (class) registration, online (class) schedules. Campuswide network is available. 100% of college-owned or -operated housing units are wired for high-speed Internet access. Wireless service is available via classrooms, computer centers, computer labs, dorm rooms, learning centers, libraries, student centers.

STUDENT LIFE
Housing options: on-campus residence required through sophomore year; coed, men-only, women-only, special housing for students with disabilities. Campus housing is university owned. Freshman campus housing is guaranteed.

Activities and organizations: drama/theater group, student-run newspaper, radio and television station, choral group, marching band, national fraternities, national sororities.

Athletics Member NCAA. All Division II. ***Intercollegiate sports:*** baseball M(s), basketball M(s)/W(s), cheerleading M(s)/W(s), cross-country running W(s), football M(s), golf M(s)/W(s), softball W(s), tennis W(s), volleyball W(s). ***Intramural sports:*** basketball M/W, bowling M/W, racquetball M/W, soccer M/W, softball M/W, table tennis M/W, ultimate Frisbee M/W, volleyball M/W.

Campus security: 24-hour emergency response devices and patrols, student patrols, late-night transport/escort service, controlled dormitory access.

Student services: health clinic, personal/psychological counseling.

COSTS & FINANCIAL AID
Costs (2014–15) ***Tuition:*** state resident $6270 full-time, $209 per credit hour part-time; nonresident $12,540 full-time, $418 per credit hour part-time. Full-time tuition and fees vary according to course load and location. Part-time tuition and fees vary according to course load and location. ***Required fees:*** $978 full-time, $22 per credit hour part-time, $159 per term part-time. ***Room and board:*** $6734; room only: $3972. Room and board charges vary according to board plan, housing facility, and location. ***Payment plans:*** installment, deferred payment. ***Waivers:*** senior citizens and employees or children of employees.

Financial Aid Of all full-time matriculated undergraduates who enrolled in 2013, 6,331 applied for aid, 4,807 were judged to have need, 447 had their need fully met. In 2013, 816 non-need-based awards were made. ***Average percent of need met:*** 62. ***Average financial aid package:*** $8760. ***Average need-based loan:*** $3694. ***Average need-based gift aid:*** $4411. ***Average non-need-based aid:*** $6450. ***Average indebtedness upon graduation:*** $29,865.

APPLYING
Standardized Tests *Required:* SAT or ACT (for admission).

Options: electronic application, early action, deferred entrance.

Required: high school transcript, minimum 2.0 GPA.

Notification: continuous (freshmen), continuous (transfers).

CONTACT
Ms. Shauna Donnell, Director of Enrollment Management, Arkansas Tech University, Doc Bryan Student Services Building, Suite 141, Russellville, AR 72801. *Phone:* 479-968-0343. *Toll-free phone:* 800-582-6953. *Fax:* 479-964-0522. *E-mail:* tech.enroll@atu.edu.

★ Harding University
Searcy, Arkansas

http://www.harding.edu/

- **Independent** university, founded 1924, affiliated with Church of Christ
- **Small-town** 350-acre campus with easy access to Little Rock
- **Endowment** $105.2 million
- **Coed** 4,428 undergraduate students, 93% full-time, 54% women, 46% men
- **Moderately difficult** entrance level, 76% of applicants were admitted

UNDERGRAD STUDENTS
4,105 full-time, 323 part-time. Students come from 50 states and territories; 49 other countries; 74% are from out of state; 4% Black or African American, non-Hispanic/Latino; 3% Hispanic/Latino; 0.7% Asian, non-Hispanic/Latino; 0.1% Native Hawaiian or other Pacific Islander, non-Hispanic/Latino; 0.8% American Indian or Alaska Native, non-Hispanic/Latino; 1% Two or more races, non-Hispanic/Latino; 0.4% Race/ethnicity unknown; 7% international; 5% transferred in; 72% live on campus.

Freshmen

Admission: 2,180 applied, 1,663 admitted, 1,041 enrolled. ***Average high school GPA:*** 3.58. ***Test scores:*** SAT critical reading scores over 500: 73%; SAT math scores over 500: 76%; ACT scores over 18: 97%; SAT critical reading scores over 600: 37%; SAT math scores over 600: 38%; ACT scores over 24: 61%; SAT critical reading scores over 700: 12%; SAT math scores over 700: 8%; ACT scores over 30: 18%.

Retention: 82% of full-time freshmen returned.

FACULTY
Total: 499, 57% full-time, 51% with terminal degrees.

Student/faculty ratio: 15:1.

ACADEMICS
Calendar: semesters. *Degrees:* bachelor's, master's, doctoral, and post-master's certificates.

Special study options: academic remediation for entering students, accelerated degree program, adult/continuing education programs, advanced placement credit, cooperative education, distance learning, double majors, English as a second language, freshman honors college, honors programs, independent study, internships, part-time degree program, services for LD students, student-designed majors, study abroad, summer session for credit.

Computers: 512 computers/terminals and 3,200 ports are available on campus for general student use. Students can access the following: campus intranet, computer help desk, free student e-mail accounts, online (class) grades, online (class) registration, online (class) schedules. Campuswide network is available. 100% of college-owned or -operated housing units are wired for high-speed Internet access. Wireless service is available via entire campus.

STUDENT LIFE
Housing options: on-campus residence required through senior year; men-only, women-only, special housing for students with disabilities. Campus housing is university owned. Freshman campus housing is guaranteed.

Activities and organizations: drama/theater group, student-run newspaper, radio and television station, choral group, marching band, Bisons for Christ, Harding in Action, Spring Break Campaigns, HUmanity.

Athletics Member NCAA. All Division II. ***Intercollegiate sports:*** baseball M(s), basketball M(s)/W(s), cheerleading W, cross-country running M(s)/W(s), football M(s), golf M(s)/W(s), lacrosse M(c), rugby M(c), soccer M(s)/W(s), tennis M(s)/W(s), track and field M(s)/W(s), ultimate Frisbee M(c)/W(c), volleyball W(s). ***Intramural sports:*** basketball M/W, cross-country running M/W, football M/W, golf M/W, racquetball M/W, soccer M/W, softball M/W, swimming and diving M/W, table tennis M/W, tennis M/W, track and field M/W, ultimate Frisbee M/W, volleyball M/W, weight lifting M/W.

Campus security: 24-hour emergency response devices and patrols, student patrols, late-night transport/escort service, controlled dormitory access.

Student services: health clinic, personal/psychological counseling.

COSTS & FINANCIAL AID
Costs (2014–15) ***Comprehensive fee:*** $23,556 includes full-time tuition ($16,560), mandatory fees ($480), and room and board ($6516). Full-time tuition and fees vary according to course load. Part-time tuition: $552 per credit hour. Part-time tuition and fees vary according to course load. ***Required fees:*** $25 per credit hour part-time. ***College room only:*** $3290. Room and board charges vary according to board plan and housing facility. ***Payment plans:*** tuition prepayment, installment. ***Waivers:*** senior citizens and employees or children of employees.

Financial Aid Of all full-time matriculated undergraduates who enrolled in 2013, 3,185 applied for aid, 2,535 were judged to have need, 865 had their need fully met. 522 Federal Work-Study jobs (averaging $780). 1,581 state and other part-time jobs (averaging $1666). In 2013, 551 non-need-based awards were made. ***Average percent of need met:*** 72. ***Average financial aid package:*** $15,108. ***Average need-based loan:*** $6547. ***Average need-based gift aid:*** $8837. ***Average non-need-based aid:*** $6157. ***Average indebtedness upon graduation:*** $24,120.

APPLYING
Standardized Tests *Required:* SAT or ACT (for admission).

Options: electronic application, early admission, early action, deferred entrance.

Application fee: $50.

Required: essay or personal statement, high school transcript, 3 letters of recommendation.

Application deadlines: rolling (freshmen), rolling (out-of-state freshmen), rolling (transfers).

Notification: continuous (freshmen), continuous (out-of-state freshmen), continuous (transfers).

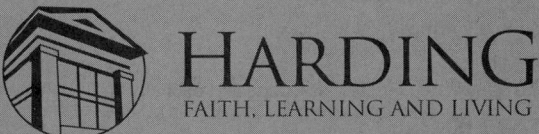

CONTACT
Mr. Glenn Dillard, Assistant Vice President for Enrollment Management, Harding University, Box 12255, Searcy, AR 72149-2255. *Phone:* 501-279-4407. *Toll-free phone:* 800-477-4407. *Fax:* 501-279-4129. *E-mail:* admissions@harding.edu.

See this page for display ad and page 1468 for the College Close-Up.

Henderson State University

Arkadelphia, Arkansas

http://www.hsu.edu/

- **State-supported** comprehensive, founded 1890
- **Small-town** 151-acre campus with easy access to Little Rock
- **Endowment** $12.3 million
- **Coed**
- **Moderately difficult** entrance level

FACULTY
Student/faculty ratio: 15:1.

ACADEMICS
Calendar: semesters. *Degrees:* certificates, bachelor's, master's, post-master's, and postbachelor's certificates.

STUDENT LIFE
Housing options: on-campus residence required through sophomore year; coed, men-only, women-only, cooperative. Campus housing is university owned and is provided by a third party. Freshman applicants given priority for college housing.

Activities and organizations: drama/theater group, student-run newspaper, radio and television station, choral group, marching band, Heart and Key, Student Government Association, Residence Hall Association, national fraternities, national sororities.

Athletics Member NCAA. All Division II.

Campus security: 24-hour emergency response devices and patrols, late-night transport/escort service, controlled dormitory access, We offer "Reddie Rides" to those students/employees who need rides to their cars or dorms at night.

Student services: health clinic, personal/psychological counseling.

COSTS & FINANCIAL AID
Costs (2014–15) *Tuition:* state resident $5970 full-time, $191 per credit hour part-time; nonresident $12,330 full-time, $395 per credit hour part-

time. Full-time tuition and fees vary according to course load and location. Part-time tuition and fees vary according to course load and location. ***Required fees:*** $1591 full-time. ***Room and board:*** $6350. Room and board charges vary according to board plan and housing facility.

Financial Aid Of all full-time matriculated undergraduates who enrolled in 2013, 2,621 applied for aid, 2,355 were judged to have need, 793 had their need fully met. In 2013, 149 non-need-based awards were made. ***Average percent of need met:*** 84. ***Average financial aid package:*** $12,619. ***Average need-based loan:*** $3877. ***Average need-based gift aid:*** $4700. ***Average non-need-based aid:*** $5798.

APPLYING

Standardized Tests *Required:* SAT or ACT (for admission). *Recommended:* ACT (for admission).

Options: electronic application, deferred entrance.

Required: high school transcript. ***Required for some:*** essay or personal statement, 3 letters of recommendation. ***Recommended:*** minimum 2.5 GPA.

CONTACT

Ms. Vikita Hardwrick, Director of University Relations/Admissions, Henderson State University, 1100 Henderson Street, PO Box 7560, Arkadelphia, AR 71999-0001. *Phone:* 870-230-5028. *Toll-free phone:* 800-228-7333. *Fax:* 870-230-5066. *E-mail:* hardwrv@hsu.edu.

Hendrix College

Conway, Arkansas

http://www.hendrix.edu/

- **Independent United Methodist** comprehensive, founded 1876
- **Suburban** 180-acre campus with easy access to Little Rock
- **Endowment** $179.7 million
- **Coed** 1,348 undergraduate students, 99% full-time, 55% women, 45% men
- **Very difficult** entrance level, 83% of applicants were admitted

UNDERGRAD STUDENTS

1,339 full-time, 9 part-time. Students come from 35 states and territories; 25 other countries; 56% are from out of state; 5% Black or African American, non-Hispanic/Latino; 5% Hispanic/Latino; 6% Asian, non-Hispanic/Latino; 0.1% Native Hawaiian or other Pacific Islander, non-Hispanic/Latino; 2% American Indian or Alaska Native, non-Hispanic/Latino; 0.7% Two or more races, non-Hispanic/Latino; 0.5% Race/ethnicity unknown; 4% international; 2% transferred in; 90% live on campus.

Freshmen

Admission: 1,665 applied, 1,379 admitted, 314 enrolled. ***Average high school GPA:*** 3.9. ***Test scores:*** SAT critical reading scores over 500: 85%; SAT math scores over 500: 88%; ACT scores over 18: 100%; SAT critical reading scores over 600: 47%; SAT math scores over 600: 54%; ACT scores over 24: 85%; SAT critical reading scores over 700: 13%; SAT math scores over 700: 9%; ACT scores over 30: 38%.

Retention: 87% of full-time freshmen returned.

FACULTY

Total: 147, 73% full-time, 83% with terminal degrees.

Student/faculty ratio: 11:1.

ACADEMICS

Calendar: semesters. *Degrees:* bachelor's and master's.

Special study options: advanced placement credit, cooperative education, double majors, English as a second language, external degree program, independent study, internships, off-campus study, services for LD students, student-designed majors, study abroad. ***ROTC:*** Army (c).

Unusual degree programs: 3-2 engineering with Columbia University, Vanderbilt University, Washington University in St. Louis; public health BA/MPH with University of Arkansas Medical School.

Computers: 75 computers/terminals are available on campus for general student use. Students can access the following: campus intranet, computer help desk, free student e-mail accounts, online (class) grades, online (class) registration, online (class) schedules. Campuswide network is available. 100% of college-owned or -operated housing units are wired for high-speed Internet access. Wireless service is available via entire campus.

STUDENT LIFE

Housing options: on-campus residence required through senior year; coed, men-only, women-only. Campus housing is university owned. Freshman campus housing is guaranteed.

Activities and organizations: drama/theater group, student-run newspaper, radio station, choral group, Volunteer Action Center, student government, Music ensembles, Unity, Social Committee.

Athletics Member NCAA. All Division III. ***Intercollegiate sports:*** baseball M, basketball M/W, cross-country running M/W, field hockey W, football M, golf M/W, lacrosse M/W, soccer M/W, softball W, swimming and diving M/W, tennis M/W, track and field M/W, volleyball W. ***Intramural sports:*** basketball M/W, cheerleading M/W, football M/W, racquetball M/W, soccer M/W, softball M/W, table tennis M/W, tennis M/W, ultimate Frisbee M/W.

Campus security: 24-hour emergency response devices and patrols, late-night transport/escort service, controlled dormitory access.

Student services: health clinic, personal/psychological counseling.

COSTS & FINANCIAL AID

Costs (2014–15) ***Comprehensive fee:*** $52,114 includes full-time tuition ($40,520), mandatory fees ($350), and room and board ($11,244). Full-time tuition and fees vary according to course load and student level. Part-time tuition: $4874 per course. Part-time tuition and fees vary according to course load and student level. ***College room only:*** $5790. Room and board charges vary according to board plan and housing facility. ***Payment plan:*** installment. ***Waivers:*** employees or children of employees.

Financial Aid Of all full-time matriculated undergraduates who enrolled in 2014, 1,036 applied for aid, 812 were judged to have need, 304 had their need fully met. 524 Federal Work-Study jobs (averaging $1884). 264 state and other part-time jobs (averaging $1537). In 2014, 499 non-need-based awards were made. ***Average percent of need met:*** 81. ***Average financial aid package:*** $30,702. ***Average need-based loan:*** $4175. ***Average need-based gift aid:*** $26,759. ***Average non-need-based aid:*** $25,014. ***Average indebtedness upon graduation:*** $26,203.

APPLYING

Standardized Tests *Required:* SAT or ACT (for admission).

Options: electronic application, early action.

Application fee: $40.

Required: essay or personal statement, high school transcript. ***Required for some:*** interview. ***Recommended:*** 1 letter of recommendation.

Application deadlines: 6/1 (freshmen), 7/1 (transfers), 11/15 (early action).

Notification: continuous (freshmen), continuous (transfers), 12/15 (early action).

CONTACT

Mr. Fred Baker, Associate Vice President for Enrollment and Director of Admission, Hendrix College, 1600 Washington Avenue, Conway, AR 72032. *Phone:* 501-450-1362. *Toll-free phone:* 800-277-9017. *Fax:* 501-450-3843. *E-mail:* baker@hendrix.edu.

ITT Technical Institute

Little Rock, Arkansas

http://www.itt-tech.edu/

- **Proprietary** primarily 2-year, founded 1993, part of ITT Educational Services, Inc.
- **Urban** campus
- **Coed**
- **Minimally difficult** entrance level

ACADEMICS

Calendar: quarters. *Degrees:* associate and bachelor's.

STUDENT LIFE

Housing options: college housing not available.

CONTACT

Director of Recruitment, ITT Technical Institute, 12200 Westhaven Drive, Little Rock, AR 72211. *Phone:* 501-565-5550. *Toll-free phone:* 800-359-4429.

John Brown University

Siloam Springs, Arkansas

http://www.jbu.edu/

- **Independent interdenominational** comprehensive, founded 1919
- **Small-town** 200-acre campus
- **Endowment** $98.0 million
- **Coed** 1,781 undergraduate students, 88% full-time, 57% women, 43% men
- **Moderately difficult** entrance level, 69% of applicants were admitted

UNDERGRAD STUDENTS
1,565 full-time, 216 part-time. Students come from 42 states and territories; 40 other countries; 47% are from out of state; 3% Black or African American, non-Hispanic/Latino; 6% Hispanic/Latino; 1% Asian, non-Hispanic/Latino; 0.1% Native Hawaiian or other Pacific Islander, non-Hispanic/Latino; 2% American Indian or Alaska Native, non-Hispanic/Latino; 3% Two or more races, non-Hispanic/Latino; 3% Race/ethnicity unknown; 6% international; 3% transferred in; 77% live on campus.

Freshmen
Admission: 1,201 applied, 828 admitted, 300 enrolled. ***Average high school GPA:*** 3.7. ***Test scores:*** SAT critical reading scores over 500: 82%; SAT math scores over 500: 83%; SAT writing scores over 500: 70%; ACT scores over 18: 99%; SAT critical reading scores over 600: 43%; SAT math scores over 600: 36%; SAT writing scores over 600: 28%; ACT scores over 24: 70%; SAT critical reading scores over 700: 7%; SAT math scores over 700: 4%; ACT scores over 30: 17%.

Retention: 84% of full-time freshmen returned.

FACULTY
Total: 200, 39% full-time, 52% with terminal degrees.

Student/faculty ratio: 14:1.

ACADEMICS
Calendar: semesters. *Degrees:* associate, bachelor's, and master's.

Special study options: accelerated degree program, adult/continuing education programs, distance learning, double majors, English as a second language, external degree program, honors programs, independent study, internships, services for LD students, study abroad. ***ROTC:*** Army (c), Air Force (c).

Computers: 100 computers/terminals are available on campus for general student use. Students can access the following: campus intranet, computer help desk, free student e-mail accounts, online (class) grades, online (class) registration, online (class) schedules. Campuswide network is available. 100% of college-owned or -operated housing units are wired for high-speed Internet access. Wireless service is available via classrooms, dorm rooms, learning centers, libraries, student centers.

STUDENT LIFE
Housing options: on-campus residence required through junior year; coed, men-only, women-only, special housing for students with disabilities. Campus housing is university owned. Freshman campus housing is guaranteed.

Activities and organizations: drama/theater group, student-run newspaper, radio station, choral group, Student Government Association, Student Ministries Organization, Student Activities Club, Student Missionary Fellowship.

Athletics Member NAIA. ***Intercollegiate sports:*** basketball M(s)/W(s), cheerleading M(s)/W(s), cross-country running M(s)/W(s), golf M(s), soccer M(s)/W(s), tennis M(s)/W(s), volleyball W(s). ***Intramural sports:*** baseball M, basketball M/W, football M/W, golf M, racquetball M/W, rugby M, soccer M/W, softball M/W, table tennis M/W, tennis M/W, ultimate Frisbee M/W, volleyball M/W.

Campus security: 24-hour emergency response devices and patrols, late-night transport/escort service, controlled dormitory access.

Student services: health clinic, personal/psychological counseling.

COSTS & FINANCIAL AID
Costs (2015–16) ***Comprehensive fee:*** $33,132 includes full-time tuition ($23,398), mandatory fees ($1070), and room and board ($8664). Full-time tuition and fees vary according to course load. Part-time tuition: $752 per credit hour. Part-time tuition and fees vary according to course load. ***Room and board:*** Room and board charges vary according to board plan and housing facility. ***Payment plan:*** installment. ***Waivers:*** employees or children of employees.

Financial Aid Of all full-time matriculated undergraduates who enrolled in 2013, 1,042 applied for aid, 906 were judged to have need, 107 had their need fully met. In 2013, 372 non-need-based awards were made. ***Average percent of need met:*** 71. ***Average financial aid package:*** $18,043. ***Average need-based loan:*** $3217. ***Average need-based gift aid:*** $14,447. ***Average non-need-based aid:*** $14,329. ***Average indebtedness upon graduation:*** $24,525.

APPLYING
Standardized Tests *Required:* SAT or ACT (for admission).

Options: electronic application, deferred entrance.

Application fee: $25.

Required: essay or personal statement, high school transcript, minimum 2.5 GPA, 2 letters of recommendation. ***Recommended:*** interview.

Application deadlines: rolling (freshmen), rolling (transfers).

Notification: continuous (freshmen), continuous (transfers).

CONTACT
Mr. Jared Burgess, Director of Visitation Program, John Brown University, 2000 West University, Siloam Springs, AR 72761. *Phone:* 479-524-7190. *Toll-free phone:* 877-JBU-INFO. *Fax:* 479-524-4196. *E-mail:* JBurgess@jbu.edu.

Lyon College

Batesville, Arkansas

http://www.lyon.edu/

- **Independent Presbyterian** 4-year, founded 1872
- **Small-town** 136-acre campus
- **Endowment** $38.4 million
- **Coed** 711 undergraduate students, 97% full-time, 47% women, 53% men
- **Moderately difficult** entrance level, 61% of applicants were admitted

UNDERGRAD STUDENTS
689 full-time, 22 part-time. Students come from 21 states and territories; 10 other countries; 7% Black or African American, non-Hispanic/Latino; 6% Hispanic/Latino; 2% Asian, non-Hispanic/Latino; 1% American Indian or Alaska Native, non-Hispanic/Latino; 6% Race/ethnicity unknown; 3% international; 78% live on campus.

Freshmen
Admission: 1,952 applied, 1,199 admitted, 254 enrolled. ***Average high school GPA:*** 3.59. ***Test scores:*** SAT critical reading scores over 500: 60%; SAT math scores over 500: 67%; SAT writing scores over 500: 40%; ACT scores over 18: 99%; SAT critical reading scores over 600: 17%; SAT math scores over 600: 21%; SAT writing scores over 600: 4%; ACT scores over 24: 54%; SAT critical reading scores over 700: 10%; SAT math scores over 700: 3%; SAT writing scores over 700: 2%; ACT scores over 30: 12%.

Retention: 74% of full-time freshmen returned.

FACULTY
Total: 73, 56% full-time, 56% with terminal degrees.

Student/faculty ratio: 14:1.

ACADEMICS
Calendar: semesters. *Degree:* bachelor's.

Special study options: accelerated degree program, advanced placement credit, double majors, independent study, internships, off-campus study, part-time degree program, student-designed majors, study abroad, summer session for credit.

Unusual degree programs: 3-2 engineering with University of Missouri-Rolla, University of Arkansas, University of Minnesota.

Computers: 101 computers/terminals are available on campus for general student use. Students can access the following: campus intranet, computer help desk, free student e-mail accounts, online (class) grades, online (class) registration, online (class) schedules. Campuswide network is available. 100% of college-owned or -operated housing units are wired for high-speed Internet access. Wireless service is available via entire campus.

STUDENT LIFE
Housing options: on-campus residence required through junior year; coed, men-only, women-only. Campus housing is university owned. Freshman campus housing is guaranteed.

Activities and organizations: drama/theater group, student-run newspaper, choral group, Wesley Fellowship, Gay-Straight Alliance, Alpha Xi Delta Sorority, Fellowship of Christian Athletes, Young Democrats/Japanese Culture Club, national fraternities, national sororities.

Athletics Member NAIA. ***Intercollegiate sports:*** baseball M(s), basketball M(s)/W(s), cross-country running M(s)/W(s), football M(s), golf M(s)/W(s), soccer M(s)/W(s), softball W(s), volleyball W(s), wrestling M(s)/W(s). ***Intramural sports:*** badminton M/W, basketball M/W, football M/W, softball M/W, table tennis M/W, tennis M/W, ultimate Frisbee M/W, volleyball M/W.

Campus security: 24-hour patrols, late-night transport/escort service, controlled dormitory access.

Student services: health clinic, personal/psychological counseling.

COSTS & FINANCIAL AID
Costs (2015–16) ***Comprehensive fee:*** $33,390 includes full-time tuition ($25,040), mandatory fees ($240), and room and board ($8110). Full-time tuition and fees vary according to course load. Part-time tuition: $835 per credit hour. ***Room and board:*** Room and board charges vary according to board plan and housing facility. ***Payment plan:*** installment. ***Waivers:*** employees or children of employees.

Financial Aid Of all full-time matriculated undergraduates who enrolled in 2013, 509 applied for aid, 448 were judged to have need, 107 had their need fully met. 152 Federal Work-Study jobs (averaging $997). 3 state and other part-time jobs (averaging $1000). In 2013, 80 non-need-based awards were made. ***Average percent of need met:*** 82. ***Average financial aid package:*** $21,722. ***Average need-based loan:*** $4297. ***Average need-based gift aid:*** $18,274. ***Average non-need-based aid:*** $13,550. ***Average indebtedness upon graduation:*** $27,603.

APPLYING
Standardized Tests *Required:* SAT or ACT (for admission).

Options: electronic application, early admission, early action, deferred entrance.

Application fee: $25.

Required: high school transcript, minimum 2.5 GPA. ***Required for some:*** essay or personal statement, 2 letters of recommendation.

Application deadlines: rolling (freshmen), rolling (transfers).

Notification: continuous (freshmen), continuous (transfers).

CONTACT
Office of Enrollment Services, Lyon College, 2300 Highland Road, Batesville, AR 72501. *Phone:* 870-307-7250. *Toll-free phone:* 800-423-2542. *Fax:* 870-307-7542. *E-mail:* admissions@lyon.edu.

Ouachita Baptist University

Arkadelphia, Arkansas

http://www.obu.edu/

- **Independent Baptist** 4-year, founded 1886
- **Small-town** 200-acre campus with easy access to Little Rock
- **Endowment** $93.3 million
- **Coed**
- **Moderately difficult** entrance level

FACULTY
Student/faculty ratio: 12:1.

ACADEMICS
Calendar: semesters. *Degrees:* associate and bachelor's.

STUDENT LIFE
Housing options: on-campus residence required through senior year; men-only, women-only, special housing for students with disabilities. Campus housing is university owned and leased by the school. Freshman campus housing is guaranteed.

Activities and organizations: drama/theater group, student-run newspaper, television station, choral group, marching band, Phi Beta Lambda, Campus Activities Board, Student Education Association, Student Foundation, International Club.

Athletics Member NCAA. All Division II.

Campus security: 24-hour emergency response devices and patrols, controlled dormitory access.

Student services: health clinic, personal/psychological counseling.

COSTS & FINANCIAL AID
Costs (2014–15) ***Comprehensive fee:*** $30,220 includes full-time tuition ($22,800), mandatory fees ($520), and room and board ($6900). Full-time tuition and fees vary according to degree level. Part-time tuition: $630 per semester hour. Part-time tuition and fees vary according to degree level. ***Room and board:*** Room and board charges vary according to housing facility. ***Payment plans:*** installment, deferred payment.

Financial Aid Of all full-time matriculated undergraduates who enrolled in 2014, 1,116 applied for aid, 900 were judged to have need, 321 had their need fully met. 325 Federal Work-Study jobs (averaging $1681). 141 state and other part-time jobs (averaging $1648). In 2014, 500 non-need-based awards were made. ***Average percent of need met:*** 84. ***Average financial aid package:*** $21,016. ***Average need-based loan:*** $3855. ***Average need-based gift aid:*** $14,241. ***Average non-need-based aid:*** $9937. ***Average indebtedness upon graduation:*** $24,252. ***Financial aid deadline:*** 6/1.

APPLYING
Standardized Tests *Required:* SAT or ACT (for admission).

Options: deferred entrance.

Required: high school transcript, minimum 2.8 GPA. ***Recommended:*** interview.

CONTACT
Mrs. Lori Motl, Director of Admissions Counseling, Ouachita Baptist University, OBU Box 3776, Arkadelphia, AR 71998-0001. *Phone:* 870-245-5110. *Toll-free phone:* 800-342-5628. *Fax:* 870-245-5500. *E-mail:* motll@obu.edu.

Philander Smith College

Little Rock, Arkansas

http://www.philander.edu/

- **Independent United Methodist** 4-year, founded 1877
- **Urban** 25-acre campus
- **Coed** 567 undergraduate students, 92% full-time, 64% women, 36% men
- **Minimally difficult** entrance level, 52% of applicants were admitted

UNDERGRAD STUDENTS
521 full-time, 46 part-time. 50% are from out of state; 90% Black or African American, non-Hispanic/Latino; 0.4% Hispanic/Latino; 0.5% Asian, non-Hispanic/Latino; 0.2% Native Hawaiian or other Pacific Islander, non-Hispanic/Latino; 0.2% American Indian or Alaska Native, non-Hispanic/Latino; 2% Two or more races, non-Hispanic/Latino; 6% international; 9% transferred in; 40% live on campus.

Freshmen
Admission: 3,330 applied, 1,730 admitted, 112 enrolled. ***Average high school GPA:*** 2.88. ***Test scores:*** SAT critical reading scores over 500: 33%; SAT math scores over 500: 38%; ACT scores over 18: 65%; SAT critical reading scores over 600: 10%; SAT math scores over 600: 24%; ACT scores over 24: 14%; ACT scores over 30: 1%.

FACULTY
Total: 56, 82% full-time, 54% with terminal degrees.

Student/faculty ratio: 11:1.

ACADEMICS
Calendar: semesters. *Degree:* bachelor's.

Special study options: academic remediation for entering students, accelerated degree program, adult/continuing education programs, advanced placement credit, cooperative education, double majors, independent study, internships, part-time degree program, services for LD students, study abroad, summer session for credit. ***ROTC:*** Army (c).

Unusual degree programs: 3-2 engineering.

Computers: Students can access the following: campus intranet, computer help desk, free student e-mail accounts, online (class) grades, online (class) registration, online (class) schedules. Campuswide network

is available. 100% of college-owned or -operated housing units are wired for high-speed Internet access. Wireless service is available via entire campus.

STUDENT LIFE

Housing options: on-campus residence required for freshman year; coed. Campus housing is university owned.

Activities and organizations: drama/theater group, choral group, Student Government Association, Panther Programming Council, Panther Dolls, Panther Newscast, Religious Life Council, national fraternities, national sororities.

Athletics Member NAIA. ***Intercollegiate sports:*** basketball M(s)/W(s), track and field M(s)/W(s), volleyball W(s).

Campus security: 24-hour emergency response devices and patrols, student patrols, controlled dormitory access.

Student services: health clinic, personal/psychological counseling.

COSTS & FINANCIAL AID

Costs (2014–15) ***One-time required fee:*** $150. ***Comprehensive fee:*** $21,478 includes full-time tuition ($11,804), mandatory fees ($610), and room and board ($9064). Full-time tuition and fees vary according to course load, program, and student level. Part-time tuition: $495 per credit hour. Part-time tuition and fees vary according to course load, program, and student level. ***College room only:*** $5908. ***Payment plans:*** installment, deferred payment. ***Waivers:*** employees or children of employees.

Financial Aid Of all full-time matriculated undergraduates who enrolled in 2013, 477 applied for aid, 460 were judged to have need, 31 had their need fully met. 82 Federal Work-Study jobs (averaging $2600). In 2013, 46 non-need-based awards were made. ***Average percent of need met:*** 54. ***Average financial aid package:*** $13,369. ***Average need-based loan:*** $4009. ***Average need-based gift aid:*** $9858. ***Average non-need-based aid:*** $15,490. ***Average indebtedness upon graduation:*** $35,968.

APPLYING

Standardized Tests *Required:* SAT or ACT (for admission).

Options: electronic application, deferred entrance.

Application fee: $25.

Required: high school transcript.

CONTACT

Ms. Bertha Owens, Recruitment Admissions and Registrar, Philander Smith College, 900 West Daisy Bates Drive, Little Rock, AR 72202. *Phone:* 501-370-5303. *Toll-free phone:* 800-446-6772. *Fax:* 501-370-5385.

Southern Arkansas University–Magnolia

Magnolia, Arkansas

http://www.saumag.edu/

- **State-supported** comprehensive, founded 1909, part of Southern Arkansas University System
- **Small-town** 1491-acre campus
- **Endowment** $30.4 million
- **Coed** 3,036 undergraduate students, 83% full-time, 57% women, 43% men
- **Moderately difficult** entrance level, 71% of applicants were admitted

UNDERGRAD STUDENTS

2,531 full-time, 505 part-time. Students come from 28 states and territories; 29 other countries; 22% are from out of state; 28% Black or African American, non-Hispanic/Latino; 3% Hispanic/Latino; 0.7% Asian, non-Hispanic/Latino; 0.4% American Indian or Alaska Native, non-Hispanic/Latino; 1% Race/ethnicity unknown; 3% international; 8% transferred in; 45% live on campus.

Freshmen

Admission: 2,502 applied, 1,787 admitted, 724 enrolled. ***Average high school GPA:*** 3.27. ***Test scores:*** SAT critical reading scores over 500: 34%; SAT math scores over 500: 40%; ACT scores over 18: 82%; SAT critical reading scores over 600: 11%; SAT math scores over 600: 11%; ACT scores over 24: 31%; ACT scores over 30: 3%.

Retention: 63% of full-time freshmen returned.

FACULTY

Total: 274, 58% full-time, 43% with terminal degrees.

Student/faculty ratio: 15:1.

ACADEMICS

Calendar: semesters. *Degrees:* certificates, associate, bachelor's, and master's.

Special study options: academic remediation for entering students, accelerated degree program, adult/continuing education programs, advanced placement credit, distance learning, double majors, English as a second language, freshman honors college, honors programs, independent study, internships, part-time degree program, services for LD students, study abroad, summer session for credit.

Computers: 199 computers/terminals and 199 ports are available on campus for general student use. Students can access the following: campus intranet, computer help desk, free student e-mail accounts, online (class) grades, online (class) registration, online (class) schedules. Campuswide network is available. 100% of college-owned or -operated housing units are wired for high-speed Internet access. Wireless service is available via computer centers, computer labs, dorm rooms, libraries, student centers.

STUDENT LIFE

Housing options: on-campus residence required through sophomore year; coed, men-only, women-only. Campus housing is university owned and is provided by a third party. Freshman campus housing is guaranteed.

Activities and organizations: drama/theater group, student-run newspaper, radio station, choral group, marching band, Student Government Association, Student Activities Board, Resident Hall Association, Residential College, International Student Association, national fraternities, national sororities.

Athletics Member NCAA. All Division II. ***Intercollegiate sports:*** baseball M(s), basketball M(s)/W(s), cheerleading M(s)(c)/W(s)(c), cross-country running M(s)/W(s), football M(s), golf M/W, softball W(s), tennis W(s), track and field M(s)/W(s), volleyball W(s). ***Intramural sports:*** badminton M/W, basketball M/W, football M, golf M/W, soccer M/W, softball M/W, swimming and diving M/W, table tennis M/W, tennis M/W, ultimate Frisbee M/W, volleyball M/W.

Campus security: 24-hour emergency response devices, student patrols, late-night transport/escort service, controlled dormitory access.

Student services: health clinic, personal/psychological counseling.

COSTS & FINANCIAL AID

Costs (2014–15) ***Tuition:*** state resident $6300 full-time, $210 per hour part-time; nonresident $9750 full-time, $325 per hour part-time. Full-time tuition and fees vary according to course load. Part-time tuition and fees vary according to course load. ***Required fees:*** $1268 full-time, $44 per hour part-time, $18 per term part-time. ***Room and board:*** $5422; room only: $2700. Room and board charges vary according to board plan and housing facility. ***Waivers:*** children of alumni, senior citizens, and employees or children of employees.

Financial Aid Of all full-time matriculated undergraduates who enrolled in 2012, 2,093 applied for aid, 1,883 were judged to have need, 560 had their need fully met. 482 Federal Work-Study jobs (averaging $1240). 123 state and other part-time jobs (averaging $1432). In 2012, 264 non-need-based awards were made. ***Average percent of need met:*** 73. ***Average financial aid package:*** $12,717. ***Average need-based loan:*** $2614. ***Average need-based gift aid:*** $4426. ***Average non-need-based aid:*** $5973. ***Average indebtedness upon graduation:*** $13,120.

APPLYING

Standardized Tests *Required:* SAT or ACT (for admission). *Recommended:* ACT (for admission).

Options: electronic application, early admission, deferred entrance.

Required: high school transcript. ***Required for some:*** interview.

Application deadlines: 8/27 (freshmen), 8/27 (transfers).

CONTACT

Southern Arkansas University–Magnolia, 100 East University, Magnolia, AR 71753. *Phone:* 870-235-4040. *Toll-free phone:* 800-332-7286.

University of Arkansas

Fayetteville, Arkansas

http://www.uark.edu/

- **State-supported** university, founded 1871, part of University of Arkansas System
- **Suburban** 410-acre campus
- **Coed** 21,836 undergraduate students, 88% full-time, 52% women, 48% men
- **Moderately difficult** entrance level, 62% of applicants were admitted

UNDERGRAD STUDENTS

19,243 full-time, 2,593 part-time. Students come from 52 states and territories; 117 other countries; 39% are from out of state; 5% Black or African American, non-Hispanic/Latino; 7% Hispanic/Latino; 3% Asian, non-Hispanic/Latino; 0.1% Native Hawaiian or other Pacific Islander, non-Hispanic/Latino; 1% American Indian or Alaska Native, non-Hispanic/Latino; 3% Two or more races, non-Hispanic/Latino; 0.4% Race/ethnicity unknown; 3% international; 6% transferred in; 25% live on campus.

Freshmen

Admission: 18,984 applied, 11,777 admitted, 4,571 enrolled. ***Average high school GPA:*** 3.63. ***Test scores:*** SAT critical reading scores over 500: 77%; SAT math scores over 500: 82%; ACT scores over 18: 100%; SAT critical reading scores over 600: 30%; SAT math scores over 600: 37%; ACT scores over 24: 74%; SAT critical reading scores over 700: 5%; SAT math scores over 700: 6%; ACT scores over 30: 19%.

Retention: 83% of full-time freshmen returned.

FACULTY

Total: 1,288, 86% full-time, 77% with terminal degrees.

Student/faculty ratio: 19:1.

ACADEMICS

Calendar: semesters. *Degrees:* certificates, bachelor's, master's, doctoral, post-master's, and postbachelor's certificates.

Special study options: academic remediation for entering students, accelerated degree program, advanced placement credit, cooperative education, distance learning, double majors, English as a second language, external degree program, freshman honors college, honors programs, independent study, internships, off-campus study, part-time degree program, services for LD students, study abroad, summer session for credit. ***ROTC:*** Army (b), Air Force (b).

Unusual degree programs: business administration; law, engineering.

Computers: 3,669 computers/terminals and 24 ports are available on campus for general student use. Students can access the following: computer help desk, free student e-mail accounts, online (class) grades, online (class) registration, online (class) schedules. Campuswide network is available. 100% of college-owned or -operated housing units are wired for high-speed Internet access. Wireless service is available via entire campus.

STUDENT LIFE

Housing options: on-campus residence required for freshman year; coed, women-only, special housing for students with disabilities. Campus housing is university owned. Freshman campus housing is guaranteed.

Activities and organizations: drama/theater group, student-run newspaper, radio and television station, choral group, marching band, Associated Student Government, Catholic Campus Ministry, Chinese Students and Scholars, Alpha Lambda Delta, Student Alumni Association, national fraternities, national sororities.

Athletics Member NCAA. All Division I except football (Division I-A). ***Intercollegiate sports:*** baseball M(s), basketball M(s)/W(s), cross-country running M(s)/W(s), golf M(s)/W(s), gymnastics W(s), soccer W(s), softball W(s), swimming and diving W(s), tennis M(s)/W(s), track and field M(s)/W(s), volleyball W(s). ***Intramural sports:*** badminton M/W, baseball M(c), basketball M/W, bowling M/W, crew M(c)/W(c), fencing M(c)/W(c), golf M/W, ice hockey M(c), lacrosse M(c)/W(c), racquetball M/W, riflery M(c)/W(c), rugby M(c)/W(c), skiing (downhill) M(c)/W(c), soccer M/W, softball M/W, swimming and diving M(c)/W(c), table tennis M/W, tennis M/W, ultimate Frisbee M/W, volleyball M(c)/W.

Campus security: 24-hour emergency response devices and patrols, student patrols, late-night transport/escort service, controlled dormitory access, RAD (Rape Aggression Defense program).

Student services: health clinic, personal/psychological counseling, women's center, legal services.

COSTS & FINANCIAL AID

Costs (2014–15) ***Tuition:*** state resident $6824 full-time, $227 per credit hour part-time; nonresident $18,914 full-time, $630 per credit hour part-time. Full-time tuition and fees vary according to course load, location, and program. Part-time tuition and fees vary according to course load, location, and program. ***Required fees:*** $1386 full-time. ***Room and board:*** $9454; room only: $6014. Room and board charges vary according to board plan, housing facility, and location. ***Payment plan:*** installment. ***Waivers:*** senior citizens and employees or children of employees.

Financial Aid Of all full-time matriculated undergraduates who enrolled in 2014, 12,335 applied for aid, 8,586 were judged to have need, 1,120 had their need fully met. 1,092 Federal Work-Study jobs (averaging $2797). In 2014, 2620 non-need-based awards were made. ***Average percent of need met:*** 57. ***Average financial aid package:*** $9264. ***Average need-based loan:*** $4362. ***Average need-based gift aid:*** $6706. ***Average non-need-based aid:*** $4895. ***Average indebtedness upon graduation:*** $24,120.

APPLYING

Standardized Tests *Required:* SAT or ACT (for admission).

Options: electronic application, early admission, early action.

Application fee: $40.

Required: high school transcript, minimum 3.0 GPA, 20 ACT composite score or 930 SAT total (math and critical reading only), completion of 17 core academic units. ***Required for some:*** essay or personal statement.

Application deadlines: 8/1 (freshmen), 8/1 (transfers), 11/1 (early action).

Notification: continuous until 9/1 (freshmen), continuous (transfers), 12/15 (early action).

CONTACT

Cliff Murphy, Associate Director of Admissions, University of Arkansas, 232 Silas H. Hunt Hall, Office of Admissions, Fayetteville, AR 72701-1201. *Phone:* 479-575-5346. *Toll-free phone:* 800-377-8632. *Fax:* 479-575-7515. *E-mail:* uofa@uark.edu.

University of Arkansas at Little Rock

Little Rock, Arkansas

http://www.ualr.edu/

- **State-supported** university, founded 1927, part of University of Arkansas System
- **Urban** 229-acre campus
- **Coed** 9,384 undergraduate students, 52% full-time, 59% women, 41% men
- **Minimally difficult** entrance level, 59% of applicants were admitted

UNDERGRAD STUDENTS

4,921 full-time, 4,463 part-time. 2% are from out of state; 27% Black or African American, non-Hispanic/Latino; 7% Hispanic/Latino; 2% Asian, non-Hispanic/Latino; 0.3% American Indian or Alaska Native, non-Hispanic/Latino; 8% Two or more races, non-Hispanic/Latino; 3% international; 12% transferred in; 2% live on campus.

Freshmen

Admission: 1,751 applied, 1,038 admitted, 726 enrolled. ***Average high school GPA:*** 3.21. ***Test scores:*** SAT critical reading scores over 500: 40%; SAT math scores over 500: 71%; SAT writing scores over 500: 25%; ACT scores over 18: 91%; SAT math scores over 600: 14%; SAT writing scores over 600: 6%; ACT scores over 24: 40%; ACT scores over 30: 6%.

Retention: 71% of full-time freshmen returned.

FACULTY

Total: 740, 61% full-time, 44% with terminal degrees.

Student/faculty ratio: 13:1.

ACADEMICS

Calendar: semesters. *Degrees:* certificates, associate, bachelor's, master's, doctoral, post-master's, and postbachelor's certificates.

Special study options: academic remediation for entering students, accelerated degree program, adult/continuing education programs, advanced placement credit, cooperative education, distance learning,

double majors, English as a second language, freshman honors college, honors programs, independent study, internships, part-time degree program, student-designed majors, study abroad, summer session for credit. ***ROTC:*** Army (b).

Computers: Students can access the following: campus intranet, computer help desk, free student e-mail accounts, online (class) grades, online (class) registration, online (class) schedules. Campuswide network is available. Wireless service is available via entire campus.

STUDENT LIFE
Housing options: on-campus residence required for freshman year; coed, special housing for students with disabilities. Freshman applicants given priority for college housing.

Activities and organizations: drama/theater group, student-run newspaper, radio and television station, student government, University Program Council, Housing Activities Council, International Student Organization, Panhellenic Council, national fraternities, national sororities.

Athletics Member NCAA. All Division I. ***Intercollegiate sports:*** baseball M(s), basketball M(s)/W, cross-country running M(s)/W(s), golf M(s)/W(s), soccer M/W(s), swimming and diving W, track and field M/W(s), volleyball W(s). ***Intramural sports:*** archery M/W, badminton M/W, basketball M, bowling M/W, football M/W, golf M/W, swimming and diving M/W, table tennis M/W, tennis M/W, volleyball M/W.

Campus security: 24-hour emergency response devices and patrols, student patrols, late-night transport/escort service, controlled dormitory access.

Student services: health clinic.

COSTS
Costs (2014–15) ***One-time required fee:*** $40. ***Tuition:*** state resident $6180 full-time, $206 per credit hour part-time; nonresident $17,250 full-time, $575 per credit hour part-time. Full-time tuition and fees vary according to course load, degree level, and program. Part-time tuition and fees vary according to course load, degree level, and program. ***Required fees:*** $1754 full-time, $877 per year part-time. ***Room and board:*** $5530. Room and board charges vary according to board plan and housing facility. ***Payment plan:*** deferred payment. ***Waivers:*** senior citizens and employees or children of employees.

APPLYING
Standardized Tests *Required:* SAT or ACT (for admission).

Options: electronic application, early admission, deferred entrance.

Application fee: $40.

Required: high school transcript, minimum 2.5 GPA, proof of immunization.

CONTACT
Ms. Tammy Harrison, Director of Admissions, University of Arkansas at Little Rock, 2801 South University Avenue, Little Rock, AR 72204-1099. *Phone:* 501-569-3127. *Toll-free phone:* 800-482-8892. *Fax:* 501-569-8956. *E-mail:* twharrison@ualn.edu.

University of Arkansas at Pine Bluff
Pine Bluff, Arkansas
http://www.uapb.edu/

- **State-supported** comprehensive, founded 1873, part of University of Arkansas System
- **Urban** 327-acre campus
- **Endowment** $3.4 million
- **Coed** 2,401 undergraduate students, 91% full-time, 54% women, 46% men
- 39% of applicants were admitted

UNDERGRAD STUDENTS
2,188 full-time, 213 part-time. Students come from 38 states and territories; 12 other countries; 37% are from out of state; 93% Black or African American, non-Hispanic/Latino; 1% Hispanic/Latino; 0.4% Asian, non-Hispanic/Latino; 0.1% American Indian or Alaska Native, non-Hispanic/Latino; 0.2% Race/ethnicity unknown; 0.7% international; 7% transferred in; 41% live on campus.

Freshmen

Admission: 3,508 applied, 1,357 admitted, 496 enrolled. ***Average high school GPA:*** 2.83. ***Test scores:*** SAT critical reading scores over 500: 10%; SAT math scores over 500: 20%; ACT scores over 18: 50%; ACT scores over 24: 6%.

Retention: 62% of full-time freshmen returned.

FACULTY
Total: 196, 80% full-time, 56% with terminal degrees.

Student/faculty ratio: 15:1.

ACADEMICS
Calendar: semesters. *Degrees:* certificates, associate, bachelor's, master's, and doctoral.

Special study options: academic remediation for entering students, accelerated degree program, adult/continuing education programs, advanced placement credit, cooperative education, distance learning, double majors, English as a second language, external degree program, honors programs, independent study, internships, off-campus study, part-time degree program, services for LD students, summer session for credit. ***ROTC:*** Army (b).

Unusual degree programs: 3-2 engineering with University of Arkansas at Fayetteville.

Computers: 175 computers/terminals and 1,400 ports are available on campus for general student use. Students can access the following: campus intranet, computer help desk, free student e-mail accounts, online (class) grades, online (class) registration, online (class) schedules. Campuswide network is available. Wireless service is available via classrooms, computer centers, computer labs, dorm rooms, learning centers, libraries.

STUDENT LIFE
Housing options: men-only, women-only. Campus housing is university owned.

Activities and organizations: drama/theater group, student-run newspaper, choral group, marching band, Union Programming Board, Student Government Association, Pan Hellenic Council, Lion Year Book, Arkansawyer Newspaper, national fraternities, national sororities.

Athletics Member NCAA, NAIA. All NCAA Division I except football (Division I-AA). ***Intercollegiate sports:*** baseball M, basketball M(s)/W(s), cross-country running M/W, golf M(s), track and field M/W, volleyball W(s). ***Intramural sports:*** baseball M, basketball M, bowling M/W, cross-country running M, football M/W, golf M/W, gymnastics M/W, racquetball M/W, softball M/W, swimming and diving M/W, table tennis M/W, tennis M/W, track and field M/W, volleyball M/W, weight lifting M/W.

Campus security: 24-hour emergency response devices and patrols.

Student services: health clinic, personal/psychological counseling.

COSTS & FINANCIAL AID
Costs (2014–15) ***Tuition:*** state resident $6178 full-time, $148 per credit hour part-time; nonresident $11,908 full-time, $337 per credit hour part-time. Full-time tuition and fees vary according to course level, degree level, and location. Part-time tuition and fees vary according to course level, degree level, and location. ***Room and board:*** $7200. Room and board charges vary according to board plan and housing facility. ***Payment plan:*** installment. ***Waivers:*** senior citizens and employees or children of employees.

Financial Aid Of all full-time matriculated undergraduates who enrolled in 2005, 2,825 applied for aid, 2,825 were judged to have need, 1,200 had their need fully met. 328 Federal Work-Study jobs (averaging $1000). ***Average percent of need met:*** 70. ***Average financial aid package:*** $8121. ***Average need-based loan:*** $4500. ***Average need-based gift aid:*** $1000.

APPLYING
Standardized Tests *Required:* SAT or ACT (for admission).

Options: electronic application, early admission, deferred entrance.

Required: high school transcript, minimum 2.0 GPA.

Notification: continuous (freshmen), continuous (transfers).

CONTACT
University of Arkansas at Pine Bluff, 1200 North University Drive, Pine Bluff, AR 71601-2799. *Phone:* 870-575-8492. *Toll-free phone:* 800-621-7440.

University of Arkansas–Fort Smith

Fort Smith, Arkansas

http://uafs.edu/

- **State and locally supported** 4-year, founded 1928, part of University of Arkansas System
- **Suburban** 170-acre campus
- **Endowment** $79.4 million
- **Coed** 6,823 undergraduate students, 67% full-time, 56% women, 44% men
- **Minimally difficult** entrance level, 56% of applicants were admitted

UNDERGRAD STUDENTS

4,581 full-time, 2,242 part-time. Students come from 33 states and territories; 23 other countries; 14% are from out of state; 5% Black or African American, non-Hispanic/Latino; 9% Hispanic/Latino; 5% Asian, non-Hispanic/Latino; 0.1% Native Hawaiian or other Pacific Islander, non-Hispanic/Latino; 3% American Indian or Alaska Native, non-Hispanic/Latino; 5% Two or more races, non-Hispanic/Latino; 0.1% Race/ethnicity unknown; 2% international; 6% transferred in; 13% live on campus.

Freshmen

Admission: 4,001 applied, 2,252 admitted, 1,187 enrolled. ***Average high school GPA:*** 3.23. ***Test scores:*** ACT scores over 18: 86%; ACT scores over 24: 35%; ACT scores over 30: 2%.

Retention: 66% of full-time freshmen returned.

FACULTY

Total: 412, 57% full-time.

Student/faculty ratio: 18:1.

ACADEMICS

Calendar: semesters. *Degrees:* certificates, associate, and bachelor's.

Special study options: academic remediation for entering students, accelerated degree program, adult/continuing education programs, advanced placement credit, cooperative education, distance learning, double majors, English as a second language, external degree program, honors programs, independent study, internships, off-campus study, part-time degree program, services for LD students, study abroad, summer session for credit. ***ROTC:*** Army (b), Air Force (c).

Computers: 1,553 computers/terminals and 2,000 ports are available on campus for general student use. Students can access the following: campus intranet, computer help desk, free student e-mail accounts, online (class) grades, online (class) registration, online (class) schedules, online subscription databases, information portal, online course management system and online courses. Campuswide network is available. 100% of college-owned or -operated housing units are wired for high-speed Internet access. Wireless service is available via entire campus.

STUDENT LIFE

Housing options: coed, special housing for students with disabilities. Campus housing is university owned.

Activities and organizations: drama/theater group, student-run newspaper, choral group, Campus Activities Board, Phi Beta Lambda, Student Alumni Association, Non-Traditional Students, Grand Avenue Baptist College Ministry (Reach), national fraternities, national sororities.

Athletics Member NCAA. All Division II. ***Intercollegiate sports:*** baseball M(s), basketball M(s)/W(s), cross-country running M(s)/W(s), golf M(s)/W(s), tennis M(s)/W(s), volleyball W(s). ***Intramural sports:*** basketball M/W, cheerleading M/W, football M/W, golf M/W, soccer M/W, softball M/W, ultimate Frisbee M/W, volleyball M/W.

Campus security: 24-hour emergency response devices and patrols, student patrols, late-night transport/escort service, controlled dormitory access.

Student services: health clinic, personal/psychological counseling.

COSTS & FINANCIAL AID

Costs (2014–15) ***Tuition:*** state resident $4170 full-time, $139 per credit hour part-time; nonresident $11,400 full-time, $380 per credit hour part-time. Full-time tuition and fees vary according to course load and program. Part-time tuition and fees vary according to course load and program. ***Required fees:*** $1721 full-time, $50 per credit hour part-time, $71 per credit hour part-time. ***Room and board:*** $8077; room only: $5472. Room and board charges vary according to board plan and housing facility. ***Payment plan:*** installment. ***Waivers:*** senior citizens and employees or children of employees.

Financial Aid Of all full-time matriculated undergraduates who enrolled in 2004, 2,564 applied for aid, 2,232 were judged to have need, 215 had their need fully met. 110 Federal Work-Study jobs (averaging $3000). 94 state and other part-time jobs (averaging $3000). In 2004, 350 non-need-based awards were made. ***Average percent of need met:*** 62. ***Average financial aid package:*** $5568. ***Average need-based loan:*** $3183. ***Average need-based gift aid:*** $3504. ***Average non-need-based aid:*** $2643. ***Average indebtedness upon graduation:*** $7339.

APPLYING

Standardized Tests *Required:* SAT or ACT (for admission), ACT Compass (in lieu of SAT or ACT) (for admission).

Options: electronic application, deferred entrance.

Required: high school transcript, minimum 2.0 GPA.

Application deadlines: rolling (freshmen), rolling (transfers).

CONTACT

Ms. Kelly Westeen, Director of Admissions, University of Arkansas–Fort Smith, 5210 Grand Avenue, PO Box 3649, Fort Smith, AR 72913-3649. *Phone:* 479-788-7106. *Toll-free phone:* 888-512-5466. *Fax:* 479-424-6106. *E-mail:* kelly.westeen@uafortsmith.edu.

University of Central Arkansas

Conway, Arkansas

http://www.uca.edu/

- **State-supported** university, founded 1907
- **Small-town** 365-acre campus
- **Coed** 9,842 undergraduate students, 83% full-time, 58% women, 42% men
- **Moderately difficult** entrance level, 94% of applicants were admitted

UNDERGRAD STUDENTS

8,172 full-time, 1,670 part-time. Students come from 43 states and territories; 59 other countries; 9% are from out of state; 20% Black or African American, non-Hispanic/Latino; 4% Hispanic/Latino; 2% Asian, non-Hispanic/Latino; 0.2% Native Hawaiian or other Pacific Islander, non-Hispanic/Latino; 0.5% American Indian or Alaska Native, non-Hispanic/Latino; 3% Two or more races, non-Hispanic/Latino; 1% Race/ethnicity unknown; 4% international; 6% transferred in; 38% live on campus.

Freshmen

Admission: 5,160 applied, 4,864 admitted, 2,232 enrolled. ***Average high school GPA:*** 3.36. ***Test scores:*** SAT critical reading scores over 500: 44%; SAT math scores over 500: 65%; SAT writing scores over 500: 45%; ACT scores over 18: 92%; SAT critical reading scores over 600: 14%; SAT math scores over 600: 26%; SAT writing scores over 600: 15%; ACT scores over 24: 45%; SAT critical reading scores over 700: 2%; SAT math scores over 700: 6%; ACT scores over 30: 10%.

Retention: 70% of full-time freshmen returned.

FACULTY

Total: 727, 74% full-time.

ACADEMICS

Calendar: semesters. *Degrees:* associate, bachelor's, master's, doctoral, post-master's, and postbachelor's certificates.

Special study options: academic remediation for entering students, accelerated degree program, advanced placement credit, cooperative education, distance learning, double majors, English as a second language, freshman honors college, honors programs, independent study, internships, part-time degree program, services for LD students, summer session for credit. ***ROTC:*** Army (b).

Unusual degree programs: 3-2 engineering with Arkansas Tech University in Russellville.

Computers: 660 computers/terminals are available on campus for general student use. Students can access the following: campus intranet, computer help desk, free student e-mail accounts, online (class) grades, online (class) registration, online (class) schedules. Campuswide network is available. Wireless service is available via entire campus.

STUDENT LIFE
Housing options: on-campus residence required for freshman year; coed, men-only, women-only, special housing for students with disabilities. Campus housing is university owned and leased by the school. Freshman campus housing is guaranteed.

Activities and organizations: drama/theater group, student-run newspaper, radio and television station, choral group, marching band, Bears Den, Greek Organizations, national fraternities, national sororities.

Athletics Member NCAA. All Division I. ***Intercollegiate sports:*** baseball M(s), basketball M(s)/W(s), cheerleading M(s)(c)/W(s)(c), cross-country running M(s)/W(s), football M(s), golf M(s)/W(s), soccer M(s)/W(s), softball W(s), tennis W(s), track and field M(s)/W(s), volleyball W(s). ***Intramural sports:*** basketball M/W, soccer M/W, softball M/W, tennis W, track and field M/W, volleyball M/W.

Campus security: 24-hour emergency response devices and patrols, student patrols, late-night transport/escort service, controlled dormitory access.

Student services: health clinic, personal/psychological counseling, women's center.

COSTS & FINANCIAL AID
Costs (2014–15) ***Tuition:*** state resident $5918 full-time, $197 per credit hour part-time; nonresident $11,835 full-time, $395 per credit hour part-time. Full-time tuition and fees vary according to course load. Part-time tuition and fees vary according to course load. ***Required fees:*** $1971 full-time. ***Room and board:*** $5778. Room and board charges vary according to board plan and housing facility. ***Payment plan:*** installment. ***Waivers:*** senior citizens and employees or children of employees.

Financial Aid ***Financial aid deadline:*** 7/1.

APPLYING
Standardized Tests *Required:* SAT or ACT (for admission).

Options: electronic application, early admission, deferred entrance.

Application fee: $25.

Required: high school transcript.

Application deadlines: rolling (freshmen), rolling (transfers).

Notification: continuous (freshmen), continuous (transfers).

CONTACT
Admissions Office, University of Central Arkansas, 201 Donaghey Avenue, Bernard 100, Conway, AR 72035. *Phone:* 501-450-3120. *Toll-free phone:* 800-243-8245. *Fax:* 501-450-5228. *E-mail:* admissions@uca.edu.

University of the Ozarks

Clarksville, Arkansas

http://www.ozarks.edu/

- **Independent Presbyterian** 4-year, founded 1834
- **Small-town** campus
- **Coed**
- **Moderately difficult** entrance level

FACULTY
Student/faculty ratio: 10:1.

ACADEMICS
Calendar: semesters. *Degree:* bachelor's.

STUDENT LIFE
Housing options: on-campus residence required through sophomore year; coed, men-only, women-only. Campus housing is university owned. Freshman campus housing is guaranteed.

Athletics Member NCAA. All Division III.

Campus security: 24-hour emergency response devices and patrols, late-night transport/escort service.

COSTS
Costs (2014–15) ***Comprehensive fee:*** $31,725 includes full-time tuition ($24,350), mandatory fees ($600), and room and board ($6775). Part-time tuition: $996 per credit hour. ***College room only:*** $3200. Room and board charges vary according to board plan and housing facility.

APPLYING
Standardized Tests *Required:* SAT or ACT (for admission).

Options: deferred entrance.

Application fee: $30.

Required: minimum 2.0 GPA. ***Required for some:*** essay or personal statement, high school transcript, interview.

CONTACT
Ms. Kim Myrick, Vice President for Enrollment Management, University of the Ozarks, 415 North College Avenue, Clarksville, AR 72830-2880. *Phone:* 479-979-1227. *Toll-free phone:* 800-264-8636. *Fax:* 479-979-1417. *E-mail:* admiss@ozarks.edu.

Williams Baptist College

Walnut Ridge, Arkansas

http://www.wbcoll.edu/

- **Independent Southern Baptist** 4-year, founded 1941
- **Rural** 180-acre campus
- **Coed** 560 undergraduate students, 88% full-time, 54% women, 46% men
- **Minimally difficult** entrance level, 67% of applicants were admitted

UNDERGRAD STUDENTS
495 full-time, 65 part-time. Students come from 23 states and territories; 6 other countries; 31% are from out of state; 8% Black or African American, non-Hispanic/Latino; 2% Hispanic/Latino; 0.2% Asian, non-Hispanic/Latino; 0.9% American Indian or Alaska Native, non-Hispanic/Latino; 0.7% Race/ethnicity unknown; 2% international; 10% transferred in; 65% live on campus.

Freshmen
Admission: 622 applied, 415 admitted, 164 enrolled. ***Average high school GPA:*** 3.2. ***Test scores:*** ACT scores over 18: 88%; ACT scores over 24: 22%; ACT scores over 30: 3%.

FACULTY
Total: 54, 46% full-time, 41% with terminal degrees.

Student/faculty ratio: 13:1.

ACADEMICS
Calendar: semesters. *Degrees:* associate and bachelor's.

Special study options: adult/continuing education programs, advanced placement credit, double majors, independent study, internships, off-campus study, part-time degree program, services for LD students, student-designed majors, study abroad, summer session for credit. ***ROTC:*** Army (c).

Computers: 70 computers/terminals are available on campus for general student use. Students can access the following: campus intranet, computer help desk, free student e-mail accounts, online (class) grades, online (class) registration, online (class) schedules. Campuswide network is available.

STUDENT LIFE
Housing options: on-campus residence required through sophomore year; men-only, women-only. Campus housing is university owned. Freshman campus housing is guaranteed.

Activities and organizations: drama/theater group, choral group.

Athletics Member NAIA, NCCAA. ***Intercollegiate sports:*** baseball M(s), basketball M(s)/W(s), cross-country running M(s)/W(s), golf M(s), soccer M(s)/W(s), softball W(s), volleyball W(s), wrestling M(s). ***Intramural sports:*** basketball M/W, cheerleading W(c), football M, golf M/W, racquetball M/W, softball M/W, table tennis M/W, tennis M/W, ultimate Frisbee M(c)/W(c), volleyball M/W.

Campus security: 24-hour emergency response devices, student patrols, controlled dormitory access.

Student services: health clinic, personal/psychological counseling.

COSTS & FINANCIAL AID
Costs (2015–16) ***Comprehensive fee:*** $23,430 includes full-time tuition ($15,400), mandatory fees ($1030), and room and board ($7000). Part-time tuition: $640 per credit hour. Part-time tuition and fees vary according to course load. ***Room and board:*** Room and board charges vary according to board plan. ***Payment plan:*** installment. ***Waivers:*** senior citizens and employees or children of employees.

Financial Aid Of all full-time matriculated undergraduates who enrolled in 2013, 392 applied for aid, 330 were judged to have need. 191 Federal Work-Study jobs (averaging $1320). 20 state and other part-time jobs (averaging $1400). ***Average financial aid package:*** $17,732. ***Average need-based loan:*** $3650. ***Average need-based gift aid:*** $4447. ***Average indebtedness upon graduation:*** $20,077.

APPLYING

Standardized Tests *Required:* SAT or ACT (for admission).

Options: electronic application.

Required: high school transcript, minimum 2.5 GPA. ***Required for some:*** essay or personal statement, 2 letters of recommendation, interview.

Application deadlines: rolling (freshmen), rolling (out-of-state freshmen), rolling (transfers).

CONTACT

Mr. Andrew Watson, Director of Admissions, Williams Baptist College, PO Box 3737, Walnut Ridge, AR 72476. *Phone:* 870-759-4118. *Toll-free phone:* 800-722-4434. *Fax:* 870-759-4163. *E-mail:* awatson@wbcoll.edu.

CALIFORNIA

★ Academy of Art University

San Francisco, California

http://www.academyart.edu/

- **Proprietary** comprehensive, founded 1929
- **Urban** 3-acre campus
- **Coed** 10,044 undergraduate students, 56% full-time, 57% women, 43% men
- **Noncompetitive** entrance level, 100% of applicants were admitted

UNDERGRAD STUDENTS

5,622 full-time, 4,422 part-time. Students come from 55 states and territories; 98 other countries; 40% are from out of state; 7% Black or African American, non-Hispanic/Latino; 11% Hispanic/Latino; 8% Asian, non-Hispanic/Latino; 0.6% Native Hawaiian or other Pacific Islander, non-Hispanic/Latino; 0.5% American Indian or Alaska Native, non-Hispanic/Latino; 2% Two or more races, non-Hispanic/Latino; 21% Race/ethnicity unknown; 25% international; 11% transferred in; 14% live on campus.

Freshmen

Admission: 2,852 applied, 2,852 admitted, 1,159 enrolled.

Retention: 75% of full-time freshmen returned.

FACULTY

Total: 1,484, 19% full-time, 19% with terminal degrees.

Student/faculty ratio: 16:1.

ACADEMICS

Calendar: semesters. *Degrees:* certificates, associate, bachelor's, and master's.

Special study options: academic remediation for entering students, adult/continuing education programs, distance learning, English as a second language, independent study, internships, part-time degree program, services for LD students, summer session for credit.

Computers: 1,720 computers/terminals are available on campus for general student use. Students can access the following: free student e-mail accounts, online (class) grades, online (class) registration, online (class) schedules, provide support for students taking online courses. Campuswide network is available. 100% of college-owned or -operated housing units are wired for high-speed Internet access. Wireless service is available via classrooms, computer labs, dorm rooms, libraries.

STUDENT LIFE

Housing options: coed, men-only, women-only, special housing for students with disabilities. Campus housing is university owned and leased by the school. Freshman campus housing is guaranteed.

Activities and organizations: drama/theater group, student-run newspaper, radio and television station, Tea Time Animation, Beyond the Front Row, Children's Book Club, Comic Book Club, Empower, national fraternities, national sororities.

Athletics Member NCAA. All Division II. ***Intercollegiate sports:*** baseball M(s), basketball M(s)/W(s), cross-country running M(s)/W(s), golf M(s)/W(s), soccer M(s)/W(s), softball W(s), tennis W(s), track and field M(s)/W(s), volleyball W(s).

Campus security: 24-hour emergency response devices and patrols, late-night transport/escort service, controlled dormitory access, ID check at all buildings.

COSTS & FINANCIAL AID

Costs (2015–16) ***Comprehensive fee:*** $39,510 includes full-time tuition ($25,050), mandatory fees ($300), and room and board ($14,160). Full-time tuition and fees vary according to course load. Part-time tuition: $835 per unit. Part-time tuition and fees vary according to course load. ***Room and board:*** Room and board charges vary according to board plan and housing facility. ***Payment plan:*** installment.

Financial Aid Of all full-time matriculated undergraduates who enrolled in 2013, 2,924 applied for aid, 2,690 were judged to have need, 43 had their need fully met. 117 Federal Work-Study jobs (averaging $3604). In 2013, 61 non-need-based awards were made. ***Average percent of need met:*** 33. ***Average financial aid package:*** $10,229. ***Average need-based loan:*** $3970. ***Average need-based gift aid:*** $9020. ***Average non-need-based aid:*** $6936. ***Average indebtedness upon graduation:*** $25,575.

APPLYING

Options: electronic application, early admission, deferred entrance.

Application fee: $100.

Required: high school transcript. ***Recommended:*** minimum 2.0 GPA, interview, Undergraduate applicants are not required to submit a portfolio, but may do so for possible waiver of foundation or major classes for graduate admissions.

Application deadlines: rolling (freshmen), rolling (transfers).

Notification: continuous (freshmen), continuous (transfers).

CONTACT

Admissions, Academy of Art University, 79 New Montgomery Street, San Francisco, CA 94105. *Phone:* 800-544-2787. *Toll-free phone:* 800-544-ARTS. *Fax:* 415-618-6287. *E-mail:* info@academyart.edu.

See previous page for display ad and page 1336 for the College Close-Up.

Academy of Couture Art

Beverly Hills, California

http://www.academyofcoutureart.edu/

- **Proprietary** primarily 2-year
- **Urban** campus with easy access to Los Angeles
- **Coed**

ACADEMICS

Degrees: associate and bachelor's.

STUDENT LIFE

Housing options: college housing not available.

Campus security: 24-hour emergency response devices and patrols.

CONTACT

Academy of Couture Art, 8484 Wilshire Boulevard, Suite 730, Beverly Hills, CA 90211. *Phone:* 310-360-8888.

Alliant International University–San Diego

San Diego, California

http://www.alliant.edu/

- **Independent** university, founded 1952, part of Alliant International University
- **Suburban** 60-acre campus with easy access to San Diego
- **Coed**

FACULTY

Student/faculty ratio: 9:1.

ACADEMICS

Calendar: semesters. *Degrees:* certificates, bachelor's, master's, doctoral, and postbachelor's certificates.

STUDENT LIFE

Housing options: coed. Campus housing is university owned.

Activities and organizations: student-run newspaper, Residence Hall Association, Latino Students Association, Finance Club, student government, Sigma Iota Epsilon.

Campus security: 24-hour emergency response devices and patrols, student patrols, late-night transport/escort service.

Student services: health clinic, personal/psychological counseling.

COSTS & FINANCIAL AID

Costs (2014–15) ***Comprehensive fee:*** $27,080 includes full-time tuition ($15,336), mandatory fees ($476), and room and board ($11,268). Part-time tuition: $639 per credit. ***Required fees:*** $130 per term part-time. ***College room only:*** $7560.

Financial Aid Of all full-time matriculated undergraduates who enrolled in 2014, 146 applied for aid, 144 were judged to have need, 3 had their need fully met. 37 Federal Work-Study jobs (averaging $2500). In 2014, 23 non-need-based awards were made. ***Average percent of need met:*** 67. ***Average financial aid package:*** $17,285. ***Average need-based loan:*** $5500. ***Average need-based gift aid:*** $13,925. ***Average non-need-based aid:*** $4000. ***Average indebtedness upon graduation:*** $15,000.

APPLYING

Options: electronic application, deferred entrance.

Application fee: $65.

Required: high school transcript, minimum 2.0 GPA.

CONTACT

Alliant International University–San Diego, 10455 Pomerado Road, San Diego, CA 92131-1799. *Phone:* 858-635-4772. *Toll-free phone:* 866-825-5426.

American Jewish University

Bel Air, California

http://www.aju.edu/

- **Independent Jewish** comprehensive, founded 1947
- **Suburban** 28-acre campus with easy access to Los Angeles
- **Endowment** $21.6 million
- **Coed**
- **Minimally difficult** entrance level

FACULTY

Student/faculty ratio: 3:1.

ACADEMICS

Calendar: semesters. *Degrees:* bachelor's and master's.

STUDENT LIFE

Housing options: coed. Campus housing is university owned. Freshman campus housing is guaranteed.

Activities and organizations: Wellness Club, Political Science Club, Israel Club, Comedy Club, LGBT Alliance.

Campus security: 24-hour emergency response devices, controlled dormitory access.

Student services: health clinic, personal/psychological counseling.

COSTS & FINANCIAL AID

Costs (2014–15) ***Comprehensive fee:*** $44,234 includes full-time tuition ($27,312), mandatory fees ($1820), and room and board ($15,102). Full-time tuition and fees vary according to course load and degree level. Part-time tuition: $1138 per unit. Part-time tuition and fees vary according to course load and degree level. ***College room only:*** $7098. Room and board charges vary according to board plan and housing facility.

Financial Aid Of all full-time matriculated undergraduates who enrolled in 2014, 58 applied for aid, 58 were judged to have need. 33 Federal Work-Study jobs (averaging $834). In 2014, 10 non-need-based awards were made. ***Average percent of need met:*** 95. ***Average financial aid package:*** $29,132. ***Average need-based loan:*** $5500. ***Average need-based gift aid:*** $8229. ***Average non-need-based aid:*** $3000. ***Average indebtedness upon graduation:*** $30,000.

APPLYING

Standardized Tests *Recommended:* SAT or ACT (for admission).

Options: electronic application, deferred entrance.

Application fee: $35.

Required: essay or personal statement, high school transcript, 2 letters of recommendation.

CONTACT
Mr. Yosef Funke, Director of Undergraduate Admissions, American Jewish University, Familian Campus, 15600 Mulholland Drive, Los Angeles, CA 90077-1599. *Phone:* 310-440-1250. *Toll-free phone:* 888-853-6763. *Fax:* 310-471-3657. *E-mail:* admissions@aju.edu.

Antioch University Santa Barbara

Santa Barbara, California

http://www.antiochsb.edu/

- **Independent** upper-level, founded 1977, part of Antioch University
- **Urban** campus
- **Coed** 192 undergraduate students, 52% full-time, 63% women, 37% men
- **Moderately difficult** entrance level

UNDERGRAD STUDENTS
99 full-time, 93 part-time. Students come from 12 other countries; 2% Black or African American, non-Hispanic/Latino; 18% Hispanic/Latino; 3% Asian, non-Hispanic/Latino; 0.5% Native Hawaiian or other Pacific Islander, non-Hispanic/Latino; 1% American Indian or Alaska Native, non-Hispanic/Latino; 1% Race/ethnicity unknown; 22% international.

ACADEMICS
Calendar: quarters. *Degrees:* certificates, bachelor's, master's, and doctoral.
Special study options: academic remediation for entering students, accelerated degree program, cooperative education, distance learning, external degree program, independent study, internships, off-campus study, part-time degree program, services for LD students, student-designed majors, summer session for credit.
Computers: 16 computers/terminals are available on campus for general student use. Students can access the following: computer help desk, free student e-mail accounts, online (class) grades, online (class) registration, online (class) schedules. Campuswide network is available. Wireless service is available via entire campus.

STUDENT LIFE
Housing options: college housing not available.
Activities and organizations: student-run newspaper.
Campus security: late-night transport/escort service.

COSTS & FINANCIAL AID
Costs (2014–15) ***Tuition:*** $17,316 full-time, $481 per unit part-time. Full-time tuition and fees vary according to course load and degree level. Part-time tuition and fees vary according to course load and degree level. ***Required fees:*** $300 full-time, $100 per term part-time. ***Payment plan:*** installment. ***Waivers:*** employees or children of employees.
Financial Aid Of all full-time matriculated undergraduates who enrolled in 2003, 23 Federal Work-Study jobs (averaging $2120).

APPLYING
Standardized Tests *Required for some:* TOEFL required for international students.
Options: electronic application, deferred entrance.
Application fee: $60.
Notification: continuous (transfers).

CONTACT
Mrs. Sharisse Estomo, Assistant Director of Admissions, Antioch University Santa Barbara, 602 Anacapa Street, Santa Barbara, CA 93101. *Phone:* 805-962-8179 Ext. 5113. *Toll-free phone:* 866-526-8462. *Fax:* 805-962-4786. *E-mail:* sestomo@antioch.edu.

Argosy University, Inland Empire

Ontario, California

http://www.argosy.edu/locations/inland-empire/

- **Proprietary** university, founded 2006
- **Coed**

ACADEMICS
Degrees: certificates, associate, bachelor's, master's, and doctoral.

CONTACT
Argosy University, Inland Empire, 3401 Centre Lake Drive, Suite 200, Ontario, CA 91761. *Phone:* 909-472-0800. *Toll-free phone:* 866-217-9075.

Argosy University, Los Angeles

Santa Monica, California

http://www.argosy.edu/locations/los-angeles/

- **Proprietary** university
- **Coed**

ACADEMICS
Degrees: certificates, associate, bachelor's, master's, and doctoral.

CONTACT
Argosy University, Los Angeles, 5230 Pacific Concourse, Suite 200, Santa Monica, CA 90045. *Phone:* 310-531-9700. *Toll-free phone:* 866-505-0332.

Argosy University, Orange County

Orange, California

http://www.argosy.edu/locations/los-angeles-orange-county/

- **Proprietary** university
- **Urban** campus
- **Coed**

ACADEMICS
Calendar: semesters. *Degrees:* certificates, associate, bachelor's, master's, and doctoral.

CONTACT
Argosy University, Orange County, 601 South Lewis Street, Orange, CA 92868. *Phone:* 714-620-3700. *Toll-free phone:* 800-716-9598.

Argosy University, San Diego

San Diego, California

http://www.argosy.edu/locations/san-diego/

- **Proprietary** university
- **Coed**

ACADEMICS
Degrees: associate, bachelor's, master's, and doctoral.

CONTACT
Argosy University, San Diego, 1615 Murray Canyon Road, Suite 100, San Diego, CA 92108. *Phone:* 619-321-3000. *Toll-free phone:* 866-505-0333.

Argosy University, San Francisco Bay Area

Alameda, California

http://www.argosy.edu/locations/san-francisco/

- **Proprietary** university, founded 1998, part of Education Management Corporation
- **Coed**

ACADEMICS
Calendar: semesters. *Degrees:* associate, bachelor's, master's, and doctoral.

CONTACT
Argosy University, San Francisco Bay Area, 1005 Atlantic Avenue, Alameda, CA 94501. *Phone:* 510-217-4700. *Toll-free phone:* 866-215-2777.

Art Center College of Design

Pasadena, California

http://www.artcenter.edu/

- **Independent** comprehensive, founded 1930
- **Suburban** 175-acre campus with easy access to Los Angeles
- **Coed** 1,824 undergraduate students, 87% full-time, 50% women, 50% men
- **Very difficult** entrance level, 81% of applicants were admitted

UNDERGRAD STUDENTS

1,578 full-time, 246 part-time. 21% are from out of state; 1% Black or African American, non-Hispanic/Latino; 11% Hispanic/Latino; 35% Asian, non-Hispanic/Latino; 0.3% Native Hawaiian or other Pacific Islander, non-Hispanic/Latino; 0.2% American Indian or Alaska Native, non-Hispanic/Latino; 4% Two or more races, non-Hispanic/Latino; 1% Race/ethnicity unknown; 27% international; 10% transferred in.

Freshmen

Admission: 534 applied, 432 admitted, 174 enrolled.

ACADEMICS

Calendar: semesters. *Degrees:* bachelor's and master's.

Special study options: advanced placement credit, independent study, internships, study abroad, summer session for credit.

Computers: 470 computers/terminals and 502 ports are available on campus for general student use. Students can access the following: campus intranet, computer help desk, free student e-mail accounts, online (class) grades, online (class) registration, online (class) schedules. Campuswide network is available. Wireless service is available via entire campus.

STUDENT LIFE

Housing options: college housing not available.

Activities and organizations: student-run radio station, ACSG, Christian Fellowship, INT International Club, Art Center Business Club, Story Club.

Campus security: 24-hour emergency response devices and patrols.

Student services: personal/psychological counseling.

FINANCIAL AID

Financial Aid ***Average financial aid package:*** $17,803. ***Average need-based loan:*** $10,169. ***Average need-based gift aid:*** $14,627.

APPLYING

Standardized Tests *Required for some:* SAT (for admission), ACT (for admission), SAT or ACT (for admission).

Options: electronic application, deferred entrance.

Application fee: $50.

Required: essay or personal statement, high school transcript, portfolio.

CONTACT

Ms. Kit Baron, Vice President, Admissions and Enrollment Management, Art Center College of Design, 1700 Lida Street, Pasadena, CA 91103. *Phone:* 626-396-2322. *Fax:* 626-795-0578. *E-mail:* kit.baron@artcenter.edu.

The Art Institute of California–Hollywood, a campus of Argosy University

North Hollywood, California

http://www.artinstitutes.edu/hollywood/

- **Proprietary** 4-year, founded 1992, part of Education Management Corporation
- **Urban** campus
- **Coed**

ACADEMICS

Calendar: quarters. *Degrees:* diplomas, associate, and bachelor's.

CONTACT

The Art Institute of California–Hollywood, a campus of Argosy University, 5250 Lankershim Boulevard, North Hollywood, CA 91601. *Phone:* 818-299-5100. *Toll-free phone:* 877-468-6232.

The Art Institute of California–Inland Empire, a campus of Argosy University

San Bernardino, California

http://www.artinstitutes.edu/inlandempire/

- **Proprietary** 4-year, part of Education Management Corporation
- **Suburban** campus
- **Coed**

ACADEMICS

Degrees: diplomas, associate, and bachelor's.

CONTACT

The Art Institute of California–Inland Empire, a campus of Argosy University, 674 East Brier Drive, San Bernardino, CA 92408. *Phone:* 909-915-2100. *Toll-free phone:* 800-353-0812.

The Art Institute of California–Los Angeles, a campus of Argosy University

Santa Monica, California

http://www.artinstitutes.edu/losangeles/

- **Proprietary** 4-year, part of Education Management Corporation
- **Urban** campus
- **Coed**

ACADEMICS

Calendar: quarters. *Degrees:* diplomas, associate, and bachelor's.

CONTACT

The Art Institute of California–Los Angeles, a campus of Argosy University, 2900 31st Street, Santa Monica, CA 90405-3035. *Phone:* 310-752-4700. *Toll-free phone:* 888-646-4610.

The Art Institute of California–Orange County, a campus of Argosy University

Santa Ana, California

http://www.artinstitutes.edu/orangecounty/

- **Proprietary** 4-year, founded 2000, part of Education Management Corporation
- **Urban** campus with easy access to Orange County
- **Coed**

ACADEMICS

Calendar: quarters. *Degrees:* diplomas, associate, and bachelor's.

CONTACT

The Art Institute of California–Orange County, a campus of Argosy University, 3601 West Sunflower Avenue, Santa Ana, CA 92704. *Phone:* 714-830-0200. *Toll-free phone:* 888-549-3055.

The Art Institute of California–Sacramento, a campus of Argosy University

Sacramento, California

http://www.artinstitutes.edu/sacramento/

- **Proprietary** 4-year
- **Coed**

ACADEMICS

Degrees: diplomas, associate, and bachelor's.

CONTACT

The Art Institute of California–Sacramento, a campus of Argosy University, 2850 Gateway Oaks Drive, Suite 100, Sacramento, CA 95833. *Phone:* 916-830-6320. *Toll-free phone:* 800-477-1957.

The Art Institute of California–San Diego, a campus of Argosy University

San Diego, California

http://www.artinstitutes.edu/sandiego/

- **Proprietary** 4-year, founded 1981, part of Education Management Corporation
- **Urban** campus
- **Coed**

ACADEMICS
Calendar: quarters. *Degrees:* diplomas, associate, and bachelor's.

CONTACT
The Art Institute of California–San Diego, a campus of Argosy University, 7650 Mission Valley Road, San Diego, CA 92108. *Phone:* 858-598-1200. *Toll-free phone:* 866-275-2422.

The Art Institute of California–San Francisco, a campus of Argosy University

San Francisco, California

http://www.artinstitutes.edu/sanfrancisco/

- **Proprietary** comprehensive, founded 1939, part of Education Management Corporation
- **Urban** campus
- **Coed**

ACADEMICS
Calendar: quarters. *Degrees:* diplomas, associate, bachelor's, and master's.

CONTACT
The Art Institute of California–San Francisco, a campus of Argosy University, 1170 Market Street, San Francisco, CA 94102. *Phone:* 415-865-0198. *Toll-free phone:* 888-493-3261.

The Art Institute of California–Silicon Valley, a campus of Argosy University

Sunnyvale, California

http://www.artinstitutes.edu/siliconvalley/

- **Proprietary** 4-year
- **Coed**

ACADEMICS
Degrees: diplomas, associate, and bachelor's.

CONTACT
The Art Institute of California–Silicon Valley, a campus of Argosy University, 1120 Kifer Road, Sunnyvale, CA 94086. *Phone:* 408-962-6400. *Toll-free phone:* 866-583-7961.

Azusa Pacific University

Azusa, California

http://www.apu.edu/

- **Independent nondenominational** university, founded 1899
- **Suburban** 60-acre campus with easy access to Los Angeles
- **Endowment** $58.9 million
- **Coed** 6,160 undergraduate students, 88% full-time, 64% women, 36% men
- **Moderately difficult** entrance level, 82% of applicants were admitted

UNDERGRAD STUDENTS
5,400 full-time, 760 part-time. 18% are from out of state; 5% Black or African American, non-Hispanic/Latino; 26% Hispanic/Latino; 9% Asian, non-Hispanic/Latino; 0.9% Native Hawaiian or other Pacific Islander, non-Hispanic/Latino; 0.2% American Indian or Alaska Native, non-Hispanic/Latino; 7% Two or more races, non-Hispanic/Latino; 3% Race/ethnicity unknown; 2% international; 9% transferred in; 57% live on campus.

Freshmen
Admission: 5,202 applied, 4,257 admitted, 1,046 enrolled. ***Average high school GPA:*** 3.64. ***Test scores:*** SAT critical reading scores over 500: 72%; SAT math scores over 500: 72%; SAT writing scores over 500: 69%; ACT scores over 18: 94%; SAT critical reading scores over 600: 27%; SAT math scores over 600: 28%; SAT writing scores over 600: 23%; ACT scores over 24: 53%; SAT critical reading scores over 700: 5%; SAT math scores over 700: 5%; SAT writing scores over 700: 3%; ACT scores over 30: 10%.
Retention: 85% of full-time freshmen returned.

FACULTY
Total: 1,219, 37% full-time, 26% with terminal degrees.
Student/faculty ratio: 12:1.

ACADEMICS
Calendar: semesters. *Degrees:* certificates, bachelor's, master's, doctoral, post-master's, and postbachelor's certificates.
Special study options: academic remediation for entering students, accelerated degree program, adult/continuing education programs, advanced placement credit, cooperative education, distance learning, double majors, English as a second language, freshman honors college, honors programs, independent study, internships, off-campus study, part-time degree program, services for LD students, study abroad, summer session for credit. ***ROTC:*** Army (b), Air Force (c).
Computers: Students can access the following: campus intranet, computer help desk, free student e-mail accounts, online (class) grades, online (class) registration, online (class) schedules. Campuswide network is available. Wireless service is available via entire campus.

STUDENT LIFE
Housing options: on-campus residence required through sophomore year; coed, men-only, women-only. Campus housing is university owned and leased by the school. Freshman applicants given priority for college housing.
Activities and organizations: drama/theater group, student-run newspaper, radio and television station, choral group, marching band, community service groups, choir, outreach ministries groups, Habitat for Humanity, Multi-Ethnic Student Alliance (MESA).
Athletics Member NCAA, NAIA. All NCAA Division II. ***Intercollegiate sports:*** baseball M(s), basketball M(s)/W(s), cross-country running M(s)/W(s), football M(s), gymnastics W(s), soccer M(s)/W(s), softball W(s), swimming and diving W(s), tennis M(s)/W(s), track and field M(s)/W(s), volleyball W(s). ***Intramural sports:*** basketball M/W, cheerleading W(c), football M/W, rugby M(c), skiing (downhill) M/W, soccer M/W, softball M/W, tennis M/W, volleyball M/W.
Campus security: 24-hour emergency response devices and patrols, student patrols, late-night transport/escort service, controlled dormitory access.
Student services: health clinic, personal/psychological counseling, women's center.

COSTS & FINANCIAL AID
Costs (2014–15) ***Tuition:*** $32,516 full-time. ***Required fees:*** $580 full-time. ***Room only:*** $5290. Room and board charges vary according to board plan and housing facility. ***Payment plan:*** installment.
Financial Aid Of all full-time matriculated undergraduates who enrolled in 2013, 5,292 applied for aid, 4,252 were judged to have need, 378 had their need fully met. In 2013, 934 non-need-based awards were made. ***Average percent of need met:*** 35. ***Average financial aid package:*** $18,522. ***Average need-based loan:*** $4303. ***Average need-based gift aid:*** $10,107. ***Average non-need-based aid:*** $7704. ***Average indebtedness upon graduation:*** $20,612.

APPLYING
Standardized Tests *Required:* SAT or ACT (for admission).
Options: electronic application, early admission, early action.
Application fee: $45.
Required: essay or personal statement, high school transcript, 1 letter of recommendation. ***Required for some:*** interview.
Application deadlines: 6/1 (freshmen), 6/1 (transfers), 10/15 (early action).
Notification: continuous until 10/1 (freshmen), continuous (transfers), 2/15 (early action).

CONTACT
Ms. Lynnette Barnes, Processing Coordinator, Azusa Pacific University, 901 East Alosta Avenue, PO Box 7000, Undergraduate Admissions, 7221, Azusa, CA 91702-7000. *Phone:* 626-815-6000 Ext. 3419. *Toll-free phone:* 800-TALK-APU. *E-mail:* admissions@apu.edu.

Biola University

La Mirada, California

http://www.biola.edu/

- **Independent interdenominational** university, founded 1908
- **Suburban** 95-acre campus with easy access to Los Angeles
- **Coed** 4,373 undergraduate students, 98% full-time, 63% women, 37% men
- **Moderately difficult** entrance level, 75% of applicants were admitted

UNDERGRAD STUDENTS
4,268 full-time, 105 part-time. 22% are from out of state; 2% Black or African American, non-Hispanic/Latino; 18% Hispanic/Latino; 16% Asian, non-Hispanic/Latino; 0.3% Native Hawaiian or other Pacific Islander, non-Hispanic/Latino; 0.1% American Indian or Alaska Native, non-Hispanic/Latino; 6% Two or more races, non-Hispanic/Latino; 2% Race/ethnicity unknown; 3% international; 7% transferred in; 61% live on campus.

Freshmen
Admission: 3,874 applied, 2,921 admitted, 944 enrolled. ***Average high school GPA:*** 3.51. ***Test scores:*** SAT critical reading scores over 500: 75%; SAT math scores over 500: 74%; SAT writing scores over 500: 74%; ACT scores over 18: 96%; SAT critical reading scores over 600: 34%; SAT math scores over 600: 33%; SAT writing scores over 600: 30%; ACT scores over 24: 59%; SAT critical reading scores over 700: 7%; SAT math scores over 700: 6%; SAT writing scores over 700: 4%; ACT scores over 30: 11%.

Retention: 87% of full-time freshmen returned.

FACULTY
Total: 527, 49% full-time.

Student/faculty ratio: 16:1.

ACADEMICS
Calendar: 4-1-4. *Degrees:* certificates, bachelor's, master's, doctoral, post-master's, and postbachelor's certificates.

Special study options: advanced placement credit, cooperative education, distance learning, double majors, English as a second language, honors programs, independent study, internships, off-campus study, part-time degree program, services for LD students, study abroad, summer session for credit. ***ROTC:*** Army (c), Air Force (c).

Unusual degree programs: 3-2 engineering.

Computers: 200 computers/terminals are available on campus for general student use. Students can access the following: campus intranet, computer help desk, free student e-mail accounts, online (class) grades, online (class) registration, online (class) schedules. Campuswide network is available. 100% of college-owned or -operated housing units are wired for high-speed Internet access. Wireless service is available via entire campus.

STUDENT LIFE
Housing options: on-campus residence required for freshman year; coed, men-only, women-only, special housing for students with disabilities. Campus housing is university owned. Freshman campus housing is guaranteed.

Activities and organizations: drama/theater group, student-run newspaper, radio and television station, choral group, Adventure Club, Guerilla Film Society, Biola Cross-Fit, Xopoc Dance Team, Lacrosse Club.

Athletics Member NAIA. ***Intercollegiate sports:*** baseball M(s), basketball M(s)/W(s), cross-country running M(s)/W(s), golf M(s)/W(s), soccer M(s)/W(s), softball W(s), swimming and diving M(s)/W(s), tennis M(s)/W(s), track and field M(s)/W(s), volleyball W(s). ***Intramural sports:*** archery M(c)/W(c), basketball M/W, bowling M/W, cheerleading W(c), football M/W, lacrosse M(c)/W(c), rugby M(c), soccer M/W, softball M/W, tennis M/W, ultimate Frisbee M/W, volleyball M(c)/W, water polo M(c)/W(c).

Campus security: 24-hour emergency response devices and patrols, late-night transport/escort service, controlled dormitory access.

Student services: health clinic, personal/psychological counseling.

COSTS & FINANCIAL AID
Costs (2015–16) ***Tuition:*** $34,498 full-time, $1438 per unit part-time. ***Room only:*** Room and board charges vary according to board plan, housing facility, and location. ***Payment plan:*** installment.

Financial Aid Of all full-time matriculated undergraduates who enrolled in 2013, 3,246 applied for aid, 2,847 were judged to have need, 178 had their need fully met. 324 Federal Work-Study jobs (averaging $1475). In 2013, 918 non-need-based awards were made. ***Average percent of need met:*** 49. ***Average financial aid package:*** $18,515. ***Average need-based loan:*** $3751. ***Average need-based gift aid:*** $13,164. ***Average non-need-based aid:*** $7028. ***Average indebtedness upon graduation:*** $34,107.

APPLYING
Standardized Tests *Required:* SAT or ACT (for admission).

Options: electronic application, early decision, early action, deferred entrance.

Application fee: $55.

Required: essay or personal statement, high school transcript. ***Required for some:*** interview. ***Recommended:*** minimum 3.0 GPA.

Application deadlines: 3/1 (freshmen), 3/1 (out-of-state freshmen), 3/1 (transfers), 11/15 (early action).

Notification: 4/1 (freshmen), 4/1 (out-of-state freshmen), 4/1 (transfers), 1/15 (early action).

CONTACT
Mrs. Michelle Reider, Associate Director of Undergraduate Admissions, Biola University, 13800 Biola Avenue, La Mirada, CA 90639. *Phone:* 562-903-4752. *Toll-free phone:* 800-652-4652. *E-mail:* admissions@biola.edu.

California Baptist University

Riverside, California

http://www.calbaptist.edu/

- **Independent Southern Baptist** comprehensive, founded 1950
- **Suburban** 160-acre campus with easy access to Los Angeles
- **Endowment** $14.0 million
- **Coed** 6,435 undergraduate students, 87% full-time, 63% women, 37% men
- **Moderately difficult** entrance level, 80% of applicants were admitted

UNDERGRAD STUDENTS
5,571 full-time, 864 part-time. Students come from 43 states and territories; 22 other countries; 5% are from out of state; 8% Black or African American, non-Hispanic/Latino; 32% Hispanic/Latino; 5% Asian, non-Hispanic/Latino; 1% Native Hawaiian or other Pacific Islander, non-Hispanic/Latino; 0.7% American Indian or Alaska Native, non-Hispanic/Latino; 5% Two or more races, non-Hispanic/Latino; 6% Race/ethnicity unknown; 2% international; 12% transferred in; 39% live on campus.

Freshmen
Admission: 4,211 applied, 3,355 admitted, 1,099 enrolled. ***Average high school GPA:*** 3.35. ***Test scores:*** SAT critical reading scores over 500: 45%; SAT math scores over 500: 45%; SAT writing scores over 500: 42%; ACT scores over 18: 79%; SAT critical reading scores over 600: 11%; SAT math scores over 600: 13%; SAT writing scores over 600: 9%; ACT scores over 24: 31%; SAT critical reading scores over 700: 1%; SAT math scores over 700: 1%; SAT writing scores over 700: 1%; ACT scores over 30: 2%.

Retention: 83% of full-time freshmen returned.

FACULTY
Total: 623, 45% full-time, 39% with terminal degrees.

Student/faculty ratio: 18:1.

ACADEMICS
Calendar: 2-4-4-2. *Degrees:* bachelor's, master's, and postbachelor's certificates.

Special study options: academic remediation for entering students, accelerated degree program, adult/continuing education programs,

advanced placement credit, distance learning, double majors, English as a second language, honors programs, internships, off-campus study, part-time degree program, services for LD students, study abroad, summer session for credit. ***ROTC:*** Army (b), Air Force (c).

Computers: 279 computers/terminals are available on campus for general student use. Students can access the following: campus intranet, computer help desk, free student e-mail accounts, online (class) grades, online (class) registration, online (class) schedules. Campuswide network is available. 70% of college-owned or -operated housing units are wired for high-speed Internet access. Wireless service is available via entire campus.

STUDENT LIFE

Housing options: on-campus residence required for freshman year; men-only, women-only, cooperative. Campus housing is university owned. Freshman applicants given priority for college housing.

Activities and organizations: drama/theater group, student-run newspaper, choral group, International Service Projects, United States Service Projects, CBU Crazies (Campus Spirit), Summer of Service, Associated Students of California Baptist University (government and leadership).

Athletics Member NCAA. All Division II. ***Intercollegiate sports:*** baseball M(s), basketball M(s)/W(s), cheerleading W(s), cross-country running M(s)/W(s), golf M(s)/W(s), soccer M(s)/W(s), softball W(s), swimming and diving M(s)/W(s), track and field M(s)/W(s), volleyball M(s)/W(s), water polo M(s)/W(s), wrestling M(s). ***Intramural sports:*** basketball M/W, bowling M/W, football M/W, golf M/W, rock climbing M/W, soccer M/W, softball W, table tennis M/W, ultimate Frisbee M/W, volleyball M/W.

Campus security: 24-hour emergency response devices and patrols, late-night transport/escort service, controlled dormitory access.

Student services: health clinic, personal/psychological counseling.

COSTS & FINANCIAL AID

Costs (2014–15) ***One-time required fee:*** $310. ***Comprehensive fee:*** $38,792 includes full-time tuition ($27,612), mandatory fees ($1810), and room and board ($9370). Full-time tuition and fees vary according to course load and location. Part-time tuition: $1062 per unit. Part-time tuition and fees vary according to course load and location. ***Required fees:*** $175 per term part-time. ***College room only:*** $4940. Room and board charges vary according to board plan and housing facility. ***Payment plan:*** installment. ***Waivers:*** employees or children of employees.

Financial Aid Of all full-time matriculated undergraduates who enrolled in 2014, 5,075 applied for aid, 4,708 were judged to have need, 321 had their need fully met. 294 Federal Work-Study jobs (averaging $949). In 2014, 264 non-need-based awards were made. ***Average percent of need met:*** 51. ***Average financial aid package:*** $16,344. ***Average need-based loan:*** $4495. ***Average need-based gift aid:*** $12,329. ***Average non-need-based aid:*** $6959. ***Average indebtedness upon graduation:*** $33,409.

APPLYING

Standardized Tests *Required:* SAT or ACT (for admission). *Recommended:* SAT and SAT Subject Tests or ACT (for admission).

Options: electronic application, early action, deferred entrance.

Application fee: $45.

Required: essay or personal statement, minimum 2.0 GPA, 2 letters of recommendation. ***Required for some:*** high school transcript.

Application deadlines: rolling (freshmen), rolling (out-of-state freshmen), rolling (transfers), 12/15 (early action).

Notification: continuous (freshmen), continuous (out-of-state freshmen), continuous (transfers), 1/31 (early action).

CONTACT

Mr. Allen Johnson, Dean of Admissions, California Baptist University, 8432 Magnolia Avenue, Riverside, CA 92504-3297. *Phone:* 951-343-4212. *Toll-free phone:* 877-228-8866. *Fax:* 951-343-4525. *E-mail:* admissions@calbaptist.edu.

California Christian College

Fresno, California

http://www.calchristiancollege.edu/

- **Independent Free Will Baptist** 4-year
- **Urban** 5-acre campus
- **Endowment** $103,645
- **Coed** 20 undergraduate students, 65% full-time, 20% women, 80% men
- **Noncompetitive** entrance level

UNDERGRAD STUDENTS

13 full-time, 7 part-time. Students come from 2 states and territories; 5% are from out of state; 10% Black or African American, non-Hispanic/Latino; 30% Hispanic/Latino; 10% Two or more races, non-Hispanic/Latino; 20% transferred in; 25% live on campus.

FACULTY

Total: 9, 44% with terminal degrees.

Student/faculty ratio: 3:1.

ACADEMICS

Calendar: semesters. *Degrees:* associate and bachelor's.

Special study options: academic remediation for entering students, cooperative education, distance learning, independent study, part-time degree program.

Computers: 5 computers/terminals are available on campus for general student use. Students can access the following: wireless Internet access. Campuswide network is available. 100% of college-owned or -operated housing units are wired for high-speed Internet access. Wireless service is available via entire campus.

STUDENT LIFE

Housing options: on-campus residence required through sophomore year; men-only, women-only. Campus housing is university owned.

Student services: personal/psychological counseling.

COSTS & FINANCIAL AID

Costs (2014–15) ***Comprehensive fee:*** $13,340 includes full-time tuition ($7920), mandatory fees ($620), and room and board ($4800). Part-time tuition: $330 per unit. ***Payment plan:*** installment.

Financial Aid Of all full-time matriculated undergraduates who enrolled in 2013, 14 applied for aid, 13 were judged to have need. 5 Federal Work-Study jobs (averaging $1824). ***Average percent of need met:*** 70. ***Average financial aid package:*** $13,547. ***Average need-based loan:*** $4063. ***Average need-based gift aid:*** $4965.

APPLYING

Standardized Tests *Required:* standardized Bible content tests (for admission). *Recommended:* SAT or ACT (for admission).

Options: electronic application.

Application fee: $40.

Required: essay or personal statement, high school transcript, minimum 2.0 GPA, 2 letters of recommendation, statement of faith, moral/ethical statement. ***Recommended:*** interview.

Application deadlines: rolling (freshmen), rolling (transfers).

Notification: continuous (freshmen), continuous (transfers).

CONTACT

California Christian College, 4881 East University Avenue, Fresno, CA 93703-3533. *Phone:* 559-251-4215.

California College of the Arts

San Francisco, California

http://www.cca.edu/

- **Independent** comprehensive, founded 1907
- **Urban** 4-acre campus with easy access to San Francisco, Oakland
- **Endowment** $30.3 million
- **Coed** 1,572 undergraduate students, 96% full-time, 63% women, 37% men

UNDERGRAD STUDENTS

1,509 full-time, 63 part-time. Students come from 47 states and territories; 52 other countries; 34% are from out of state; 4% Black or African American, non-Hispanic/Latino; 13% Hispanic/Latino; 16% Asian, non-

Hispanic/Latino; 1% Native Hawaiian or other Pacific Islander, non-Hispanic/Latino; 0.3% American Indian or Alaska Native, non-Hispanic/Latino; 8% Race/ethnicity unknown; 27% international; 12% transferred in; 22% live on campus.

Freshmen
Admission: 273 enrolled. ***Average high school GPA:*** 3.27. ***Test scores:*** SAT critical reading scores over 500: 68%; SAT math scores over 500: 72%; SAT writing scores over 500: 64%; ACT scores over 18: 84%; SAT critical reading scores over 600: 28%; SAT math scores over 600: 36%; SAT writing scores over 600: 27%; ACT scores over 24: 45%; SAT critical reading scores over 700: 5%; SAT math scores over 700: 9%; SAT writing scores over 700: 3%; ACT scores over 30: 12%.

Retention: 81% of full-time freshmen returned.

FACULTY
Total: 484, 19% full-time, 63% with terminal degrees.

Student/faculty ratio: 8:1.

ACADEMICS
Calendar: semesters. *Degrees:* bachelor's and master's.

Special study options: academic remediation for entering students, advanced placement credit, cooperative education, double majors, English as a second language, independent study, internships, off-campus study, part-time degree program, services for LD students, student-designed majors, study abroad, summer session for credit.

Computers: 400 computers/terminals and 80 ports are available on campus for general student use. Students can access the following: computer help desk, free student e-mail accounts, online (class) grades, online (class) registration, online (class) schedules, online course evaluations, Learning Management System, VoiceThread, Lynda.com,print payments. Campuswide network is available. 100% of college-owned or -operated housing units are wired for high-speed Internet access. Wireless service is available via classrooms, computer centers, computer labs, dorm rooms, learning centers, libraries, student centers.

STUDENT LIFE
Housing options: coed, special housing for students with disabilities. Campus housing is university owned and leased by the school. Freshman applicants given priority for college housing.

Activities and organizations: Anime Night, International Student Alliance, FARM, Queer Straight Alliance, Student of Color Coalition, national fraternities, national sororities.

Campus security: 24-hour emergency response devices and patrols, late-night transport/escort service, controlled dormitory access, Student Taxi voucher for emergencies.

Student services: personal/psychological counseling.

COSTS & FINANCIAL AID
Costs (2015–16) ***Tuition:*** $1733 per credit part-time. Full-time tuition and fees vary according to degree level. Part-time tuition and fees vary according to degree level. ***Room only:*** Room and board charges vary according to housing facility. ***Payment plan:*** installment. ***Waivers:*** employees or children of employees.

Financial Aid Of all full-time matriculated undergraduates who enrolled in 2014, 918 applied for aid, 872 were judged to have need, 37 had their need fully met. 798 Federal Work-Study jobs (averaging $2922). 74 state and other part-time jobs (averaging $3672). In 2014, 272 non-need-based awards were made. ***Average percent of need met:*** 59. ***Average financial aid package:*** $27,460. ***Average need-based loan:*** $4848. ***Average need-based gift aid:*** $22,574. ***Average non-need-based aid:*** $9292. ***Average indebtedness upon graduation:*** $34,237.

APPLYING
Standardized Tests *Recommended:* SAT or ACT (for admission).

Required: essay or personal statement, minimum 2.0 GPA, 2 letters of recommendation, portfolio of creative work required for all. ***Required for some:*** high school transcript, interview.

CONTACT
Ms. Robynne Royster, Director of Admissions, California College of the Arts, 1111 Eighth Street, San Francisco, CA 94107. *Phone:* 415-703-9523 Ext. 9532. *Toll-free phone:* 800-447-1ART. *Fax:* 415-703-9539. *E-mail:* enroll@cca.edu.

California Institute of Integral Studies

San Francisco, California

http://www.ciis.edu/

- **Independent** upper-level, founded 1968
- **Urban** campus with easy access to San Francisco
- **Endowment** $1.4 million
- **Coed** 104 undergraduate students, 92% full-time, 65% women, 35% men
- 96% of applicants were admitted

UNDERGRAD STUDENTS
96 full-time, 8 part-time. 14% Black or African American, non-Hispanic/Latino; 22% Hispanic/Latino; 4% Asian, non-Hispanic/Latino; 1% Native Hawaiian or other Pacific Islander, non-Hispanic/Latino; 1% American Indian or Alaska Native, non-Hispanic/Latino; 8% Two or more races, non-Hispanic/Latino; 6% Race/ethnicity unknown; 1% international; 53% transferred in.

Freshmen
Admission: 74 applied, 71 admitted.

FACULTY
Total: 179, 31% full-time.

Student/faculty ratio: 11:1.

ACADEMICS
Calendar: semesters. *Degrees:* bachelor's, master's, doctoral, and postbachelor's certificates.

Special study options: adult/continuing education programs, external degree program.

Computers: 25 computers/terminals are available on campus for general student use. Students can access the following: campus intranet, free student e-mail accounts, online (class) grades, online (class) registration, online (class) schedules. Campuswide network is available. 100% of college-owned or -operated housing units are wired for high-speed Internet access. Wireless service is available via classrooms, libraries, student centers.

STUDENT LIFE
Housing options: college housing not available.

Activities and organizations: drama/theater group, Student Alliance, People of Color, Queer@CIIS, International Students and Friends, AWARE - Awaking to Whiteness and Racism Everywhere.

Student services: personal/psychological counseling.

COSTS & FINANCIAL AID
Costs (2014–15) ***Tuition:*** $24,840 full-time, $690 per credit part-time. ***Required fees:*** $255 full-time, $255 per year part-time, $85 per term part-time. ***Payment plan:*** installment.

Financial Aid Of all full-time matriculated undergraduates who enrolled in 2013, 62 applied for aid, 60 were judged to have need. 6 Federal Work-Study jobs (averaging $3275). ***Average percent of need met:*** 32. ***Average financial aid package:*** $10,954. ***Average need-based loan:*** $6009. ***Average need-based gift aid:*** $5819.

APPLYING
Options: electronic application.

Application fee: $65.

CONTACT
Veronica Palafox, Admissions Counselor, California Institute of Integral Studies, 1453 Mission Street, San Francisco, CA 94103. *Phone:* 415-575-6156. *Fax:* 415-575-1268. *E-mail:* admissions@ciis.edu.

California Institute of Technology

Pasadena, California

http://www.caltech.edu/

- **Independent** university, founded 1891
- **Suburban** 124-acre campus with easy access to Los Angeles
- **Endowment** $2.2 billion
- **Coed** 983 undergraduate students, 100% full-time, 36% women, 64% men
- **Most difficult** entrance level, 9% of applicants were admitted

UNDERGRAD STUDENTS
983 full-time. 63% are from out of state; 2% Black or African American, non-Hispanic/Latino; 12% Hispanic/Latino; 44% Asian, non-Hispanic/Latino; 0.1% American Indian or Alaska Native, non-Hispanic/Latino; 6% Two or more races, non-Hispanic/Latino; 9% international; 0.3% transferred in; 85% live on campus.

Freshmen
Admission: 6,525 applied, 576 admitted, 226 enrolled. ***Test scores:*** SAT critical reading scores over 500: 100%; SAT math scores over 500: 100%; SAT writing scores over 500: 100%; ACT scores over 18: 100%; SAT critical reading scores over 600: 100%; SAT math scores over 600: 100%; SAT writing scores over 600: 100%; ACT scores over 24: 100%; SAT critical reading scores over 700: 92%; SAT math scores over 700: 100%; SAT writing scores over 700: 91%; ACT scores over 30: 99%.
Retention: 97% of full-time freshmen returned.

FACULTY
Total: 354, 93% full-time, 95% with terminal degrees.
Student/faculty ratio: 3:1.

ACADEMICS
Calendar: 3 ten-week terms. *Degrees:* bachelor's, master's, doctoral, and post-master's certificates.
Special study options: cooperative education, double majors, English as a second language, independent study, off-campus study, services for LD students, student-designed majors, study abroad. ***ROTC:*** Army (c), Air Force (c).
Unusual degree programs: 3-2 engineering with Bowdoin College, Bryn Mawr College, Grinnell College, Haverford College, Mt. Holyoke College, Oberlin College, Occidental College, Ohio Wesleyan University, Pomona College, Reed College, Spelman College, Wesleyan University, Whitman College.
Computers: 120 computers/terminals and 1,250 ports are available on campus for general student use. Students can access the following: campus intranet, computer help desk, free student e-mail accounts, online (class) grades, online (class) registration, online (class) schedules. Campuswide network is available. 100% of college-owned or -operated housing units are wired for high-speed Internet access. Wireless service is available via entire campus.

STUDENT LIFE
Housing options: on-campus residence required for freshman year; coed, special housing for students with disabilities. Campus housing is university owned. Freshman campus housing is guaranteed.
Activities and organizations: drama/theater group, student-run newspaper, choral group, Instrumental music groups, Entrepreneur's Club, Glee Club, Theater arts, Ultimate Disc Club.
Athletics Member NCAA. All Division III. ***Intercollegiate sports:*** baseball M, basketball M/W, cross-country running M/W, fencing M/W, soccer M/W(c), swimming and diving M/W, tennis M/W, track and field M/W, volleyball M(c)/W, water polo M/W. ***Intramural sports:*** badminton M(c)/W(c), basketball M/W, football M/W, soccer M/W, softball M/W, ultimate Frisbee M/W, volleyball M/W.
Campus security: 24-hour emergency response devices and patrols, late-night transport/escort service, controlled dormitory access.
Student services: health clinic, personal/psychological counseling, women's center.

COSTS & FINANCIAL AID
Costs (2014–15) ***One-time required fee:*** $500. ***Comprehensive fee:*** $56,280 includes full-time tuition ($41,790), mandatory fees ($1572), and room and board ($12,918). Part-time tuition: $387 per credit. ***College room only:*** $7281. Room and board charges vary according to housing facility. ***Payment plans:*** installment, deferred payment. ***Waivers:*** employees or children of employees.
Financial Aid Of all full-time matriculated undergraduates who enrolled in 2014, 596 applied for aid, 495 were judged to have need, 495 had their need fully met. 278 Federal Work-Study jobs (averaging $3193). 31 state and other part-time jobs (averaging $2609). ***Average percent of need met:*** 100. ***Average financial aid package:*** $41,669. ***Average need-based loan:*** $4624. ***Average need-based gift aid:*** $37,557. ***Average indebtedness upon graduation:*** $12,104.

APPLYING
Standardized Tests *Required:* SAT or ACT (for admission), SAT and SAT Subject Tests or ACT (for admission).
Options: electronic application, early admission, early action, deferred entrance.
Application fee: $75.
Required: essay or personal statement, high school transcript, 2 letters of recommendation.
Application deadlines: 1/3 (freshmen), 2/15 (transfers), 11/1 (early action).
Notification: 4/1 (freshmen), 5/1 (transfers), 12/15 (early action).

CONTACT
Mr. Jarrid James Whitney, Director of Admissions, California Institute of Technology, 383 South Hill Avenue, Mail Code 10-90, Pasadena, CA 91125. *Phone:* 626-395-6341. *Fax:* 626-683-3026.

California Institute of the Arts

Valencia, California

http://www.calarts.edu/

- **Independent** comprehensive, founded 1961
- **Suburban** 60-acre campus with easy access to Los Angeles
- **Endowment** $101.6 million
- **Coed** 895 undergraduate students, 99% full-time, 49% women, 51% men
- **Very difficult** entrance level, 31% of applicants were admitted

UNDERGRAD STUDENTS
887 full-time, 8 part-time. Students come from 42 states and territories; 23 other countries; 51% are from out of state; 8% Black or African American, non-Hispanic/Latino; 12% Hispanic/Latino; 11% Asian, non-Hispanic/Latino; 0.1% Native Hawaiian or other Pacific Islander, non-Hispanic/Latino; 0.7% American Indian or Alaska Native, non-Hispanic/Latino; 4% Two or more races, non-Hispanic/Latino; 1% Race/ethnicity unknown; 7% international; 16% transferred in; 40% live on campus.

Freshmen
Admission: 1,237 applied, 378 admitted, 151 enrolled.
Retention: 79% of full-time freshmen returned.

FACULTY
Total: 314, 51% full-time, 54% with terminal degrees.
Student/faculty ratio: 7:1.

ACADEMICS
Calendar: semesters. *Degrees:* bachelor's, master's, doctoral, and postbachelor's certificates.
Special study options: advanced placement credit, cooperative education, double majors, independent study, internships, services for LD students, student-designed majors, study abroad.
Computers: 42 computers/terminals and 1,000 ports are available on campus for general student use. Students can access the following: campus intranet, computer help desk, free student e-mail accounts, online (class) grades, online (class) registration, online (class) schedules. Campuswide network is available. 100% of college-owned or -operated housing units are wired for high-speed Internet access. Wireless service is available via libraries, student centers.

STUDENT LIFE
Housing options: coed, special housing for students with disabilities. Campus housing is university owned. Freshman applicants given priority for college housing.
Activities and organizations: drama/theater group, student-run radio and television station, choral group, Student Council, FISK - Graphic Arts Club, Soccer Club, Korean Bible Study, Black Student Union.
Campus security: 24-hour emergency response devices and patrols, late-night transport/escort service, controlled dormitory access.
Student services: health clinic, personal/psychological counseling.

COSTS & FINANCIAL AID
Costs (2015–16) ***Tuition:*** $43,400 full-time. ***Required fees:*** $576 full-time. ***Room only:*** $6100. ***Payment plan:*** installment.

Financial Aid Of all full-time matriculated undergraduates who enrolled in 2010, 734 applied for aid, 655 were judged to have need, 36 had their need fully met. 236 Federal Work-Study jobs (averaging $2515). 4 state and other part-time jobs (averaging $1500). In 2010, 59 non-need-based awards were made. ***Average percent of need met:*** 74. ***Average financial aid package:*** $30,448. ***Average need-based loan:*** $9445. ***Average need-based gift aid:*** $16,573. ***Average non-need-based aid:*** $7043. ***Average indebtedness upon graduation:*** $49,928.

APPLYING

Options: electronic application.

Application fee: $70.

Required: essay or personal statement, high school transcript, 2 letters of recommendation, portfolio or audition. ***Required for some:*** interview.

Application deadlines: 1/5 (freshmen), 1/5 (transfers).

Notification: continuous until 4/1 (freshmen), continuous until 4/1 (transfers).

CONTACT

Molly Ryan, Director of Admissions, California Institute of the Arts, 24700 McBean Parkway, Valencia, CA 91355-2340. *Phone:* 661-255-1050. *Toll-free phone:* 800-545-2787. *Fax:* 661-253-7710. *E-mail:* admiss@calarts.edu.

See below for display ad and page 1378 for the College Close-Up.

California Lutheran University

Thousand Oaks, California

http://www.callutheran.edu/

- **Independent Lutheran** comprehensive, founded 1959
- **Suburban** 290-acre campus with easy access to Los Angeles
- **Endowment** $86.2 million
- **Coed** 2,808 undergraduate students, 94% full-time, 56% women, 44% men
- **Moderately difficult** entrance level, 61% of applicants were admitted

UNDERGRAD STUDENTS

2,648 full-time, 160 part-time. Students come from 33 states and territories; 52 other countries; 19% are from out of state; 4% Black or African American, non-Hispanic/Latino; 25% Hispanic/Latino; 7% Asian, non-Hispanic/Latino; 0.6% Native Hawaiian or other Pacific Islander, non-Hispanic/Latino; 1% American Indian or Alaska Native, non-Hispanic/Latino; 3% Two or more races, non-Hispanic/Latino; 4% Race/ethnicity unknown; 4% international; 9% transferred in; 51% live on campus.

Freshmen

Admission: 6,490 applied, 3,957 admitted, 556 enrolled. ***Average high school GPA:*** 3.7. ***Test scores:*** SAT critical reading scores over 500: 77%; SAT math scores over 500: 79%; SAT writing scores over 500: 75%; ACT scores over 18: 99%; SAT critical reading scores over 600: 26%; SAT math scores over 600: 29%; SAT writing scores over 600: 23%; ACT scores over 24: 62%; SAT critical reading scores over 700: 3%; SAT math scores over 700: 4%; SAT writing scores over 700: 3%; ACT scores over 30: 7%.

Retention: 83% of full-time freshmen returned.

FACULTY

Total: 443, 43% full-time, 54% with terminal degrees.

Student/faculty ratio: 16:1.

ACADEMICS

Calendar: semesters. *Degrees:* certificates, bachelor's, master's, doctoral, post-master's, and postbachelor's certificates.

Special study options: accelerated degree program, adult/continuing education programs, advanced placement credit, cooperative education, double majors, honors programs, independent study, internships, off-campus study, part-time degree program, services for LD students, student-designed majors, study abroad, summer session for credit. ***ROTC:*** Army (c), Air Force (c).

Unusual degree programs: 3-2 computer science, political public policy and administration.

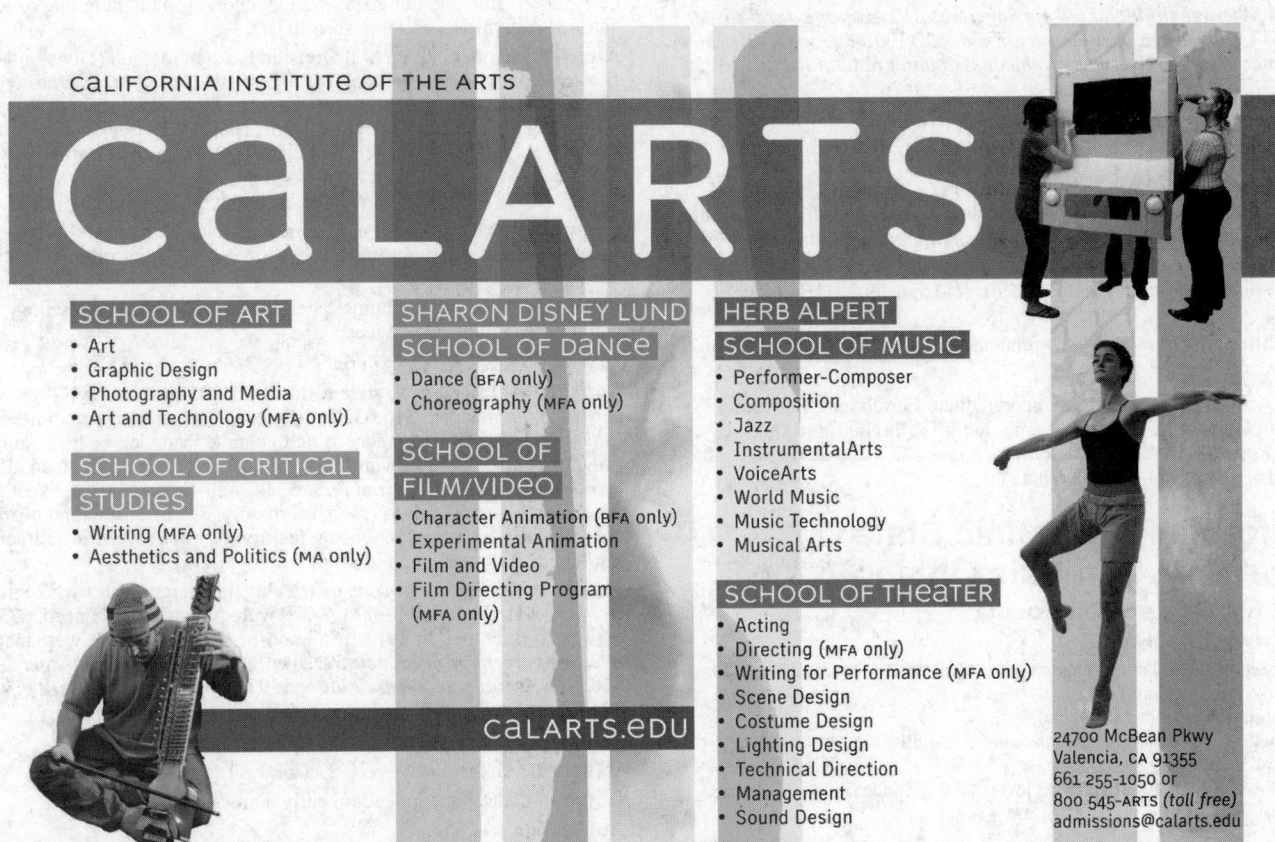

Computers: 334 computers/terminals are available on campus for general student use. Students can access the following: campus intranet, computer help desk, free student e-mail accounts, online (class) grades, online (class) registration, online (class) schedules. Campuswide network is available. 100% of college-owned or -operated housing units are wired for high-speed Internet access. Wireless service is available via entire campus.

STUDENT LIFE

Housing options: on-campus residence required through junior year; coed, special housing for students with disabilities. Campus housing is university owned. Freshman campus housing is guaranteed.

Activities and organizations: drama/theater group, student-run newspaper, radio and television station, choral group, student government, recreation, sports fan, or club sports related, service organizations, campus ministry or other religiously affiliated organization, multicultural organizations.

Athletics Member NCAA. All Division III. ***Intercollegiate sports:*** baseball M, basketball M/W, cheerleading M/W, cross-country running M/W, football M, golf M/W, soccer M/W, softball W, swimming and diving M/W, tennis M/W, track and field M/W, volleyball M/W, water polo M/W. ***Intramural sports:*** basketball M(c)/W(c), football M(c)/W(c), lacrosse M(c)/W(c), rugby M(c)/W(c), soccer M(c)/W(c), softball M(c)/W(c), tennis M(c)/W(c), volleyball M(c)/W(c), water polo M(c)/W(c).

Campus security: 24-hour emergency response devices and patrols, late-night transport/escort service, controlled dormitory access, escort service; shuttle service.

Student services: health clinic, personal/psychological counseling, women's center.

COSTS & FINANCIAL AID

Costs (2014–15) ***Comprehensive fee:*** $49,990 includes full-time tuition ($37,140), mandatory fees ($450), and room and board ($12,400). Part-time tuition: $1180 per credit hour. ***College room only:*** $6730. Room and board charges vary according to board plan and housing facility. ***Payment plan:*** installment.

Financial Aid Of all full-time matriculated undergraduates who enrolled in 2014, 2,502 applied for aid, 1,791 were judged to have need, 215 had their need fully met. 360 Federal Work-Study jobs (averaging $2500). In 2014, 718 non-need-based awards were made. ***Average percent of need met:*** 64. ***Average financial aid package:*** $25,730. ***Average need-based loan:*** $4720. ***Average need-based gift aid:*** $22,100. ***Average non-need-based aid:*** $15,150. ***Average indebtedness upon graduation:*** $24,230.

APPLYING

Standardized Tests *Required:* SAT or ACT (for admission).

Options: electronic application, early action, deferred entrance.

Application fee: $25.

Required: essay or personal statement, high school transcript, minimum 2.8 GPA, 1 letter of recommendation. ***Recommended:*** minimum 3.0 GPA, interview.

Application deadlines: 1/1 (freshmen), 6/1 (transfers), 11/1 (early action).

Notification: 4/1 (freshmen), continuous (transfers), 1/15 (early action).

CONTACT

Dr. Michael Elgarico, Dean of Undergraduate Enrollment, California Lutheran University, Office of Admission, #1350, Thousand Oaks, CA 91360. *Phone:* 805-493-3135. *Toll-free phone:* 877-258-3678. *Fax:* 805-493-3114. *E-mail:* cluadm@clunet.edu.

California Polytechnic State University, San Luis Obispo

San Luis Obispo, California

http://www.calpoly.edu/

- **State-supported** comprehensive, founded 1901, part of California State University System
- **Suburban** 6000-acre campus
- **Coed** 19,246 undergraduate students, 97% full-time, 46% women, 54% men
- **Moderately difficult** entrance level, 31% of applicants were admitted

UNDERGRAD STUDENTS

18,578 full-time, 668 part-time. 12% are from out of state; 0.7% Black or African American, non-Hispanic/Latino; 15% Hispanic/Latino; 12% Asian, non-Hispanic/Latino; 0.2% Native Hawaiian or other Pacific Islander, non-Hispanic/Latino; 0.2% American Indian or Alaska Native, non-Hispanic/Latino; 7% Two or more races, non-Hispanic/Latino; 5% Race/ethnicity unknown; 1% international; 4% transferred in; 37% live on campus.

Freshmen

Admission: 43,812 applied, 13,533 admitted, 4,662 enrolled. ***Average high school GPA:*** 3.88. ***Test scores:*** SAT critical reading scores over 500: 93%; SAT math scores over 500: 98%; ACT scores over 18: 100%; SAT critical reading scores over 600: 53%; SAT math scores over 600: 70%; ACT scores over 24: 87%; SAT critical reading scores over 700: 9%; SAT math scores over 700: 20%; ACT scores over 30: 30%.

Retention: 93% of full-time freshmen returned.

FACULTY

Total: 1,345, 61% full-time, 57% with terminal degrees.

Student/faculty ratio: 20:1.

ACADEMICS

Calendar: quarters. *Degrees:* bachelor's and master's.

Special study options: academic remediation for entering students, advanced placement credit, cooperative education, distance learning, double majors, English as a second language, honors programs, internships, off-campus study, part-time degree program, services for LD students, study abroad, summer session for credit. ***ROTC:*** Army (b).

Computers: Students can access the following: campus intranet, free student e-mail accounts, online (class) grades, online (class) registration, online (class) schedules. Campuswide network is available. Wireless service is available via classrooms, computer centers, computer labs, dorm rooms, learning centers, libraries, student centers.

STUDENT LIFE

Housing options: coed, special housing for students with disabilities. Campus housing is university owned.

Activities and organizations: drama/theater group, student-run newspaper, radio and television station, choral group, marching band, national fraternities, national sororities.

Athletics Member NCAA. All Division I except football (Division I-AA). ***Intercollegiate sports:*** baseball M(s), basketball M(s)/W(s), cross-country running M(s)/W(s), golf M(s)/W(s), soccer M(s)/W(s), softball W(s), swimming and diving M(s)/W(s), tennis M(s)/W(s), track and field M(s)/W(s), volleyball W(s), wrestling M(s). ***Intramural sports:*** badminton M/W, basketball M/W, football M/W, racquetball M/W, soccer M/W, softball M/W, table tennis M/W, tennis M/W, volleyball M/W.

Campus security: 24-hour emergency response devices and patrols, student patrols, late-night transport/escort service, controlled dormitory access.

Student services: health clinic, personal/psychological counseling, women's center, legal services.

COSTS & FINANCIAL AID

Costs (2014–15) ***Tuition:*** state resident $5472 full-time, $3174 per year part-time; nonresident $16,632 full-time, $7638 per year part-time. Full-time tuition and fees vary according to course load, degree level, and program. Part-time tuition and fees vary according to course load, degree level, and program. ***Required fees:*** $3447 full-time, $3003 per year part-time. ***Room and board:*** $11,447; room only: $6754. Room and board charges vary according to housing facility. ***Payment plan:*** installment. ***Waivers:*** employees or children of employees.

Financial Aid Of all full-time matriculated undergraduates who enrolled in 2013, 11,184 applied for aid, 7,729 were judged to have need, 573 had their need fully met. In 2013, 1562 non-need-based awards were made. ***Average percent of need met:*** 59. ***Average financial aid package:*** $10,279. ***Average need-based loan:*** $3977. ***Average need-based gift aid:*** $3488. ***Average non-need-based aid:*** $1978.

APPLYING

Standardized Tests *Required:* SAT or ACT (for admission).

Options: electronic application, early admission, early decision.

Application fee: $55.

Required: high school transcript.

Application deadlines: 11/30 (freshmen), 11/30 (transfers).

Early decision deadline: 10/31.

Notification: 4/1 (freshmen), 4/1 (transfers), 12/15 (early decision).

CONTACT

Mr. James Maraviglia, Associate Vice Provost for Marketing and Enrollment Development, California Polytechnic State University, San Luis Obispo, Admissions Office, 1 Grand Avenue, San Luis Obispo, CA 93407-0031. *Phone:* 805-756-2311. *Fax:* 805-756-5911. *E-mail:* admissions@calpoly.edu.

California State Polytechnic University, Pomona

Pomona, California

http://www.cpp.edu/

- **State-supported** comprehensive, founded 1938, part of California State University System
- **Urban** 1400-acre campus with easy access to Los Angeles
- **Endowment** $86.7 million
- **Coed** 22,395 undergraduate students, 88% full-time, 44% women, 56% men
- **Moderately difficult** entrance level, 52% of applicants were admitted

UNDERGRAD STUDENTS

19,717 full-time, 2,678 part-time. Students come from 33 states and territories; 51 other countries; 1% are from out of state; 3% Black or African American, non-Hispanic/Latino; 38% Hispanic/Latino; 24% Asian, non-Hispanic/Latino; 0.2% Native Hawaiian or other Pacific Islander, non-Hispanic/Latino; 0.2% American Indian or Alaska Native, non-Hispanic/Latino; 4% Two or more races, non-Hispanic/Latino; 5% Race/ethnicity unknown; 5% international; 12% transferred in; 11% live on campus.

Freshmen

Admission: 32,801 applied, 17,014 admitted, 3,658 enrolled. ***Average high school GPA:*** 3.42. ***Test scores:*** SAT critical reading scores over 500: 58%; SAT math scores over 500: 71%; ACT scores over 18: 89%; SAT critical reading scores over 600: 19%; SAT math scores over 600: 35%; ACT scores over 24: 49%; SAT critical reading scores over 700: 2%; SAT math scores over 700: 7%; ACT scores over 30: 10%.

Retention: 88% of full-time freshmen returned.

FACULTY

Total: 1,155, 49% full-time, 55% with terminal degrees.

Student/faculty ratio: 25:1.

ACADEMICS

Calendar: quarters. *Degrees:* bachelor's, master's, and doctoral.

Special study options: academic remediation for entering students, adult/continuing education programs, advanced placement credit, cooperative education, distance learning, double majors, English as a second language, honors programs, internships, off-campus study, part-time degree program, services for LD students, study abroad, summer session for credit. ***ROTC:*** Army (b).

Computers: 1,875 computers/terminals are available on campus for general student use. Students can access the following: campus intranet, computer help desk, free student e-mail accounts, online (class) grades, online (class) registration, online (class) schedules. Campuswide network is available. 100% of college-owned or -operated housing units are wired for high-speed Internet access. Wireless service is available via entire campus.

STUDENT LIFE

Housing options: on-campus residence required for freshman year; coed, special housing for students with disabilities. Campus housing is university owned and is provided by a third party. Freshman applicants given priority for college housing.

Activities and organizations: drama/theater group, student-run newspaper, choral group, Rose Float Club, Ridge Runners Ski Club, Barkada (Asian club), American Marketing Association, Cal Poly Society of Accountants, national fraternities, national sororities.

Athletics Member NCAA. All Division II. ***Intercollegiate sports:*** baseball M(s), basketball M(s)/W(s), cross-country running M(s)/W(s), soccer M(s)/W(s), track and field M(s)/W(s), volleyball W(s). ***Intramural sports:*** basketball M/W, bowling M/W, football M/W, softball M/W, volleyball M/W.

Campus security: 24-hour emergency response devices and patrols, student patrols, late-night transport/escort service, controlled dormitory access, video camera surveillance.

Student services: health clinic, personal/psychological counseling, women's center.

COSTS & FINANCIAL AID

Costs (2014–15) ***Tuition:*** state resident $5472 full-time; nonresident $16,632 full-time. Full-time tuition and fees vary according to course load, degree level, and program. Part-time tuition and fees vary according to course load, degree level, and program. ***Required fees:*** $1400 full-time, $248 per credit part-time. ***Room and board:*** $13,284; room only: $8112. Room and board charges vary according to board plan and housing facility. ***Payment plans:*** installment, deferred payment. ***Waivers:*** employees or children of employees.

Financial Aid Of all full-time matriculated undergraduates who enrolled in 2014, 15,319 applied for aid, 13,400 were judged to have need, 497 had their need fully met. 239 Federal Work-Study jobs (averaging $2585). In 2014, 7 non-need-based awards were made. ***Average percent of need met:*** 55. ***Average financial aid package:*** $10,915. ***Average need-based loan:*** $4486. ***Average need-based gift aid:*** $9708. ***Average non-need-based aid:*** $1159. ***Average indebtedness upon graduation:*** $22,245.

APPLYING

Standardized Tests *Required:* SAT or ACT (for admission).

Options: electronic application.

Application fee: $55.

Required: high school transcript, minimum 2.0 GPA.

Application deadlines: 11/30 (freshmen), 11/30 (transfers).

Notification: continuous (freshmen), 5/1 (transfers).

CONTACT

Mr. Andrew M. Wright, Director of Admissions, California State Polytechnic University, Pomona, 3801 West Temple Ave, Bldg. 98-T2, Room 6, Pomona, CA 91768-2557. *Phone:* 909-869-3130. *Fax:* 909-869-4529. *E-mail:* awright@cpp.edu.

California State University, Bakersfield

Bakersfield, California

http://www.csub.edu/

- **State-supported** comprehensive, founded 1970, part of California State University System
- **Urban** 575-acre campus
- **Coed**
- **Moderately difficult** entrance level

ACADEMICS

Calendar: quarters. *Degrees:* bachelor's and master's.

STUDENT LIFE

Housing options: coed, special housing for students with disabilities.

Athletics Member NCAA. All Division II except wrestling (Division I).

Campus security: 24-hour emergency response devices and patrols, late-night transport/escort service.

COSTS & FINANCIAL AID

Costs (2014–15) ***Tuition:*** state resident $5473 full-time; nonresident $16,632 full-time, $248 per credit hour part-time. ***Room and board:*** $10,926; room only: $6369.

Financial Aid Of all full-time matriculated undergraduates who enrolled in 2013, 4,904 applied for aid, 4,042 were judged to have need, 148 had their need fully met. ***Average percent of need met:*** 69. ***Average financial aid package:*** $4300. ***Average need-based loan:*** $1437. ***Average need-based gift aid:*** $3503. ***Average indebtedness upon graduation:*** $10,871.

APPLYING

Standardized Tests *Required for some:* SAT or ACT (for admission).

Options: electronic application, deferred entrance.

Application fee: $55.

Required: high school transcript.

CONTACT

Debra Blowers, Assistant Director, Admissions and Evaluations, California State University, Bakersfield, 9001 Stockdale Highway, Balersfield, CA 93311-1099. *Phone:* 661-664-3036. *Toll-free phone:* 800-788-2782. *E-mail:* admissions@csub.edu.

California State University, Chico

Chico, California

http://www.csuchico.edu/

- **State-supported** comprehensive, founded 1887, part of California State University System
- **Small-town** 119-acre campus
- **Endowment** $52.6 million
- **Coed** 16,255 undergraduate students, 90% full-time, 52% women, 48% men
- **Moderately difficult** entrance level, 75% of applicants were admitted

UNDERGRAD STUDENTS

14,605 full-time, 1,650 part-time. 1% are from out of state; 2% Black or African American, non-Hispanic/Latino; 26% Hispanic/Latino; 6% Asian, non-Hispanic/Latino; 0.1% Native Hawaiian or other Pacific Islander, non-Hispanic/Latino; 0.6% American Indian or Alaska Native, non-Hispanic/Latino; 5% Two or more races, non-Hispanic/Latino; 8% Race/ethnicity unknown; 4% international; 9% transferred in; 13% live on campus.

Freshmen

Admission: 20,360 applied, 15,250 admitted, 2,945 enrolled. ***Test scores:*** SAT critical reading scores over 500: 50%; SAT math scores over 500: 52%; ACT scores over 18: 83%; SAT critical reading scores over 600: 10%; SAT math scores over 600: 12%; ACT scores over 24: 27%; SAT critical reading scores over 700: 1%; ACT scores over 30: 1%.

Retention: 87% of full-time freshmen returned.

FACULTY

Total: 968, 47% full-time, 54% with terminal degrees.

Student/faculty ratio: 24:1.

ACADEMICS

Calendar: semesters. *Degrees:* certificates, bachelor's, master's, post-master's, and postbachelor's certificates.

Special study options: academic remediation for entering students, adult/continuing education programs, advanced placement credit, cooperative education, distance learning, double majors, English as a second language, external degree program, honors programs, independent study, internships, off-campus study, part-time degree program, services for LD students, student-designed majors, study abroad, summer session for credit.

Computers: 1,212 computers/terminals and 1,205 ports are available on campus for general student use. Students can access the following: campus intranet, computer help desk, free student e-mail accounts, online (class) grades, online (class) registration, online (class) schedules, student account information, calendar, transcripts. Campuswide network is available. 100% of college-owned or -operated housing units are wired for high-speed Internet access. Wireless service is available via entire campus.

STUDENT LIFE

Housing options: coed, women-only, special housing for students with disabilities. Campus housing is university owned. Freshman applicants given priority for college housing.

Activities and organizations: drama/theater group, student-run newspaper, radio station, choral group, Pre-Medical Association, Health Professionals Association (HPA), Audio Engineering Society, Student Association Of Social Work SASW (Undergraduate), Recreation Hospitality and Parks Society (RHAPS), national fraternities, national sororities.

Athletics Member NCAA. All Division II. ***Intercollegiate sports:*** baseball M(s), basketball M(s)/W(s), cross-country running M(s)/W(s), field hockey W(c), golf M(s)/W(s), soccer M(s)/W(s), softball W(s), track and field M(s)/W(s), volleyball W(s). ***Intramural sports:*** basketball M/W, softball M/W, table tennis M/W, volleyball M/W.

Campus security: 24-hour emergency response devices and patrols, student patrols, late-night transport/escort service, controlled dormitory access, crime prevention workshops, RAD self-defense program, Chico Safe Rides, blue light emergency phones, freshmen safety orientation.

Student services: health clinic, personal/psychological counseling, women's center, legal services.

COSTS & FINANCIAL AID

Costs (2014–15) ***Tuition:*** state resident $7002 full-time; nonresident $18,162 full-time. Full-time tuition and fees vary according to degree level. Part-time tuition and fees vary according to course load and degree level. ***Required fees:*** $1530 full-time. ***Room and board:*** $11,626. Room and board charges vary according to board plan and housing facility. ***Payment plans:*** installment, deferred payment. ***Waivers:*** senior citizens and employees or children of employees.

Financial Aid Of all full-time matriculated undergraduates who enrolled in 2013, 10,838 applied for aid, 9,158 were judged to have need, 1,393 had their need fully met. In 2013, 90 non-need-based awards were made. ***Average percent of need met:*** 63. ***Average financial aid package:*** $16,090. ***Average need-based loan:*** $4598. ***Average need-based gift aid:*** $9865. ***Average non-need-based aid:*** $1868.

APPLYING

Standardized Tests *Required:* SAT or ACT (for admission).

Options: electronic application, deferred entrance.

Application fee: $55.

Required: high school transcript, GPA determined buy using 10th /11th grade college preparatory courses only (excluding PE).

Application deadlines: 11/30 (freshmen), 11/30 (transfers).

Notification: 3/1 (freshmen), 3/1 (transfers).

CONTACT

Admissions Counselor, California State University, Chico, 400 West First Street, Chico, CA 95929-0722. *Phone:* 530-898-6322. *Toll-free phone:* 800-542-4426. *Fax:* 530-898-6456. *E-mail:* info@csuchico.edu.

California State University, Dominguez Hills

Carson, California

http://www.csudh.edu/

- **State-supported** comprehensive, founded 1960, part of California State University System
- **Urban** 350-acre campus with easy access to Los Angeles
- **Endowment** $11.8 million
- **Coed** 12,617 undergraduate students, 70% full-time, 63% women, 37% men
- **Moderately difficult** entrance level, 81% of applicants were admitted

UNDERGRAD STUDENTS

8,790 full-time, 3,827 part-time. Students come from 17 states and territories; 37 other countries; 15% Black or African American, non-Hispanic/Latino; 58% Hispanic/Latino; 9% Asian, non-Hispanic/Latino; 0.3% Native Hawaiian or other Pacific Islander, non-Hispanic/Latino; 0.2% American Indian or Alaska Native, non-Hispanic/Latino; 3% Two or more races, non-Hispanic/Latino; 4% Race/ethnicity unknown; 3% international; 21% transferred in; 5% live on campus.

Freshmen

Admission: 8,257 applied, 6,691 admitted, 1,342 enrolled. ***Average high school GPA:*** 3.12. ***Test scores:*** SAT critical reading scores over 500: 14%; SAT math scores over 500: 18%; SAT writing scores over 500: 16%; ACT scores over 18: 49%; SAT critical reading scores over 600: 1%; SAT math scores over 600: 2%; SAT writing scores over 600: 1%; ACT scores over 24: 3%.

Retention: 80% of full-time freshmen returned.

FACULTY

Total: 793, 32% full-time, 51% with terminal degrees.

Student/faculty ratio: 26:1.

ACADEMICS
Calendar: semesters. *Degrees:* bachelor's, master's, post-master's, and postbachelor's certificates.

Special study options: academic remediation for entering students, accelerated degree program, advanced placement credit, cooperative education, distance learning, double majors, external degree program, honors programs, independent study, internships, off-campus study, part-time degree program, services for LD students, student-designed majors, study abroad, summer session for credit. ***ROTC:*** Army (b), Air Force (c).

Computers: 1,100 computers/terminals and 1,100 ports are available on campus for general student use. Students can access the following: campus intranet, computer help desk, free student e-mail accounts, online (class) grades, online (class) registration, online (class) schedules. Campuswide network is available. 100% of college-owned or -operated housing units are wired for high-speed Internet access. Wireless service is available via entire campus.

STUDENT LIFE
Housing options: coed, special housing for students with disabilities. Campus housing is university owned.

Activities and organizations: drama/theater group, student-run newspaper, radio station, choral group, American Marketing Association, Phi Sigma Sigma, Organization of African Studies, Latino Student Business Association, Circle K, national fraternities, national sororities.

Athletics Member NCAA. All Division II. ***Intercollegiate sports:*** baseball M(s), basketball M(s)/W(s), golf M(s), soccer M(s)/W(s), softball W(s), track and field W(s), volleyball W(s). ***Intramural sports:*** basketball M/W, football M/W, soccer M/W, softball M/W, swimming and diving M/W, tennis M/W, volleyball M/W, weight lifting M/W.

Campus security: 24-hour emergency response devices, student patrols, late-night transport/escort service, Campus Police Patrol Division is staffed 24 hours a day, 7 days a week. Officers are vested with full police powers.

Student services: health clinic, personal/psychological counseling, women's center.

COSTS & FINANCIAL AID
Costs (2014–15) ***Tuition:*** state resident $5472 full-time; nonresident $16,632 full-time, $372 per credit part-time. ***Required fees:*** $662 full-time. ***Room and board:*** $10,956. Room and board charges vary according to housing facility. ***Payment plan:*** installment. ***Waivers:*** senior citizens and employees or children of employees.

Financial Aid Of all full-time matriculated undergraduates who enrolled in 2014, 6,931 applied for aid, 6,660 were judged to have need, 120 had their need fully met. 233 Federal Work-Study jobs (averaging $1571). In 2014, 180 non-need-based awards were made. ***Average percent of need met:*** 35. ***Average financial aid package:*** $6278. ***Average need-based loan:*** $2211. ***Average need-based gift aid:*** $5134. ***Average non-need-based aid:*** $4025. ***Average indebtedness upon graduation:*** $16,768. ***Financial aid deadline:*** 5/15.

APPLYING
Standardized Tests *Required for some:* SAT or ACT (for admission).

Options: electronic application.

Application fee: $55.

Required: high school transcript.

Application deadlines: rolling (freshmen), rolling (transfers).

Notification: continuous (freshmen), continuous (transfers).

CONTACT
Information Center, California State University, Dominguez Hills, 1000 East Victoria Street, Carson, CA 90747-0001. *Phone:* 310-243-3696. *E-mail:* info@csudh.edu.

California State University, East Bay

Hayward, California

http://www.csueastbay.edu/

- **State-supported** comprehensive, founded 1957, part of California State University System
- **Suburban** 343-acre campus with easy access to San Francisco Bay Area
- **Endowment** $9.2 million
- **Coed**
- **Moderately difficult** entrance level

FACULTY
Student/faculty ratio: 24:1.

ACADEMICS
Calendar: quarters. *Degrees:* certificates, bachelor's, master's, doctoral, and postbachelor's certificates.

STUDENT LIFE
Housing options: coed, special housing for students with disabilities. Campus housing is university owned.

Activities and organizations: drama/theater group, student-run newspaper, radio and television station, choral group, Vietnamese Student Association, Accounting Association, Filipino-American Students Association, Movimiento Estudiantil Chicano, Hayward Orientation Team, national fraternities, national sororities.

Athletics Member NCAA, NAIA. All NCAA Division III.

Campus security: 24-hour emergency response devices and patrols, late-night transport/escort service.

Student services: health clinic, personal/psychological counseling, legal services.

COSTS & FINANCIAL AID
Costs (2014–15) ***Tuition:*** state resident $6564 full-time, $1058 per term part-time; nonresident $15,492 full-time, $2546 per term part-time. Full-time tuition and fees vary according to course load and reciprocity agreements. Part-time tuition and fees vary according to course load and reciprocity agreements. ***Required fees:*** $364 per term part-time. ***Room and board:*** $12,246. Room and board charges vary according to board plan.

Financial Aid Of all full-time matriculated undergraduates who enrolled in 2014, 7,378 applied for aid, 7,130 were judged to have need, 216 had their need fully met. ***Average percent of need met:*** 59. ***Average financial aid package:*** $11,016. ***Average need-based loan:*** $6751. ***Average need-based gift aid:*** $8564. ***Average indebtedness upon graduation:*** $18,684.

APPLYING
Standardized Tests *Required for some:* SAT or ACT (for admission).

Options: electronic application.

Application fee: $55.

Required: high school transcript, minimum 2.0 GPA, California State University eligibility index.

CONTACT
Greg Smith, Enrollment Development and Management, California State University, East Bay, 25800 Carlos Bee Boulevard, Hayward, CA 94542-3000. *Phone:* 510-885-3249. *E-mail:* admissions@csueeastbay.edu.

California State University, Fresno

Fresno, California

http://www.csufresno.edu/

- **State-supported** comprehensive, founded 1911, part of California State University System
- **Urban** 1399-acre campus
- **Coed** 20,510 undergraduate students, 87% full-time, 57% women, 43% men
- **Minimally difficult** entrance level, 59% of applicants were admitted

UNDERGRAD STUDENTS
17,752 full-time, 2,758 part-time. 1% are from out of state; 4% Black or African American, non-Hispanic/Latino; 45% Hispanic/Latino; 15% Asian, non-Hispanic/Latino; 0.2% Native Hawaiian or other Pacific Islander, non-Hispanic/Latino; 0.3% American Indian or Alaska Native, non-Hispanic/Latino; 3% Two or more races, non-Hispanic/Latino; 5%

Race/ethnicity unknown; 4% international; 9% transferred in; 5% live on campus.

Freshmen

Admission: 18,953 applied, 11,256 admitted, 3,422 enrolled. ***Test scores:*** SAT critical reading scores over 500: 27%; SAT math scores over 500: 31%; SAT writing scores over 500: 26%; ACT scores over 18: 58%; SAT critical reading scores over 600: 5%; SAT math scores over 600: 6%; SAT writing scores over 600: 4%; ACT scores over 24: 12%; SAT critical reading scores over 700: 1%; ACT scores over 30: 1%.

Retention: 83% of full-time freshmen returned.

FACULTY

Total: 1,291, 50% full-time.

Student/faculty ratio: 22:1.

ACADEMICS

Calendar: semesters. *Degrees:* bachelor's, master's, doctoral, post-master's, and postbachelor's certificates.

Special study options: academic remediation for entering students, accelerated degree program, adult/continuing education programs, advanced placement credit, cooperative education, distance learning, double majors, English as a second language, freshman honors college, honors programs, independent study, internships, off-campus study, part-time degree program, services for LD students, student-designed majors, study abroad, summer session for credit. ***ROTC:*** Army (b), Air Force (b).

Computers: Students can access the following: campus intranet, computer help desk, free student e-mail accounts, online (class) grades, online (class) registration, online (class) schedules. Campuswide network is available. Wireless service is available via classrooms, computer centers, computer labs, learning centers, libraries, student centers.

STUDENT LIFE

Housing options: coed, men-only, women-only. Campus housing is university owned.

Activities and organizations: drama/theater group, student-run newspaper, radio station, choral group, marching band, national fraternities, national sororities.

Athletics Member NCAA. All Division I except football (Division I-A). ***Intercollegiate sports:*** baseball M(s), basketball M(s)/W(s), cross-country running M(s)/W(s), equestrian sports W(s), golf M(s)/W(s), lacrosse W(s), soccer W(s), softball W(s), swimming and diving W(s), tennis M(s)/W(s), track and field M(s)/W(s), volleyball W(s). ***Intramural sports:*** archery M/W, badminton M/W, baseball M, basketball M/W, bowling M/W, cross-country running M/W, equestrian sports W, fencing M/W, golf M/W, gymnastics M/W, racquetball M/W, tennis M/W, volleyball M/W.

Campus security: 24-hour emergency response devices and patrols, late-night transport/escort service, controlled dormitory access.

Student services: health clinic, personal/psychological counseling, women's center.

COSTS & FINANCIAL AID

Costs (2014–15) ***Tuition:*** state resident $6298 full-time; nonresident $17,446 full-time, $372 per credit hour part-time. ***Room and board:*** $10,604. Room and board charges vary according to board plan. ***Payment plan:*** installment.

Financial Aid Of all full-time matriculated undergraduates who enrolled in 2014, 14,478 applied for aid, 13,399 were judged to have need, 2,310 had their need fully met. 224 Federal Work-Study jobs (averaging $4261). In 2014, 666 non-need-based awards were made. ***Average percent of need met:*** 73. ***Average financial aid package:*** $12,478. ***Average need-based loan:*** $3999. ***Average need-based gift aid:*** $10,319. ***Average non-need-based aid:*** $1269. ***Average indebtedness upon graduation:*** $12,851.

APPLYING

Standardized Tests *Required:* SAT or ACT (for admission).

Options: electronic application.

Application fee: $55.

Required: high school transcript, minimum 2.0 GPA.

CONTACT

Mr. Andy Hernandez, Admissions Officer, California State University, Fresno, 5150 North Maple Avenue, M/S JA 57, Fresno, CA 93740-8026. *Phone:* 559-278-6115. *Fax:* 559-278-4812. *E-mail:* andyhe@csufresno.edu.

California State University, Fullerton

Fullerton, California

http://www.fullerton.edu/

- **State-supported** comprehensive, founded 1957, part of California State University System
- **Suburban** 236-acre campus with easy access to Los Angeles
- **Endowment** $34.4 million
- **Coed** 32,726 undergraduate students, 82% full-time, 55% women, 45% men
- **Moderately difficult** entrance level, 44% of applicants were admitted

UNDERGRAD STUDENTS

26,762 full-time, 5,964 part-time. Students come from 38 states and territories; 62 other countries; 1% are from out of state; 2% Black or African American, non-Hispanic/Latino; 38% Hispanic/Latino; 21% Asian, non-Hispanic/Latino; 0.2% Native Hawaiian or other Pacific Islander, non-Hispanic/Latino; 0.2% American Indian or Alaska Native, non-Hispanic/Latino; 4% Two or more races, non-Hispanic/Latino; 4% Race/ethnicity unknown; 6% international; 12% transferred in; 6% live on campus.

Freshmen

Admission: 40,955 applied, 18,212 admitted, 4,357 enrolled. ***Average high school GPA:*** 3.53. ***Test scores:*** SAT critical reading scores over 500: 53%; SAT math scores over 500: 64%; ACT scores over 18: 85%; SAT critical reading scores over 600: 12%; SAT math scores over 600: 20%; ACT scores over 24: 30%; SAT critical reading scores over 700: 1%; SAT math scores over 700: 3%; ACT scores over 30: 3%.

Retention: 89% of full-time freshmen returned.

FACULTY

Total: 2,044, 46% full-time, 53% with terminal degrees.

Student/faculty ratio: 25:1.

ACADEMICS

Calendar: semesters. *Degrees:* bachelor's, master's, doctoral, post-master's, and postbachelor's certificates.

Special study options: academic remediation for entering students, adult/continuing education programs, advanced placement credit, cooperative education, distance learning, double majors, honors programs, independent study, internships, off-campus study, part-time degree program, services for LD students, student-designed majors, study abroad, summer session for credit. ***ROTC:*** Army (b).

Computers: 2,000 computers/terminals are available on campus for general student use. Students can access the following: campus intranet, computer help desk, free student e-mail accounts, online (class) grades, online (class) registration, online (class) schedules. Campuswide network is available. Wireless service is available via entire campus.

STUDENT LIFE

Housing options: coed. Campus housing is university owned. Freshman applicants given priority for college housing.

Activities and organizations: drama/theater group, student-run newspaper, radio station, choral group, Pan-Hellenic Council, American Marketing Association, Lacrosse Club, Samaritans (volunteer service club), Human Services Student Association, national fraternities, national sororities.

Athletics Member NCAA. All Division I. ***Intercollegiate sports:*** archery M(c)/W(c), baseball M(s), basketball M(s)/W(s), bowling M(c)/W(c), cross-country running M(s)/W(s), equestrian sports M(c)/W(c), golf M(s)/W(s), ice hockey M(c)/W(c), lacrosse M(c)/W(c), rugby M(c)/W(c), sailing M(c)/W(c), skiing (downhill) M(c)/W(c), soccer M(s)/W(s), softball W(s), tennis W(s), track and field M(s)/W(s), ultimate Frisbee M(c)/W(c), volleyball M(c)/W(s), water polo M(c)/W(c). ***Intramural sports:*** badminton M/W, basketball M/W, bowling M/W, football M/W, racquetball M/W, rugby M, skiing (downhill) M/W, soccer M, softball M/W, swimming and diving M/W, table tennis M/W, tennis M(c)/W(c), volleyball M/W.

Campus security: 24-hour emergency response devices and patrols, student patrols, late-night transport/escort service, controlled dormitory access.

Student services: health clinic, personal/psychological counseling, women's center, legal services.

COSTS & FINANCIAL AID

Costs (2014–15) ***Tuition:*** state resident $5472 full-time, $4016 per year part-time; nonresident $16,632 full-time, $6249 per year part-time. Full-time tuition and fees vary according to course load. Part-time tuition and fees vary according to course load. ***Required fees:*** $844 full-time, $844 per year part-time. ***Room and board:*** $13,510. Room and board charges vary according to board plan and housing facility. ***Payment plans:*** installment, deferred payment. ***Waivers:*** senior citizens and employees or children of employees.

Financial Aid Of all full-time matriculated undergraduates who enrolled in 2013, 24,175 applied for aid, 19,582 were judged to have need, 9,540 had their need fully met. 227 Federal Work-Study jobs (averaging $3805). In 2013, 1498 non-need-based awards were made. ***Average percent of need met:*** 56. ***Average financial aid package:*** $13,546. ***Average need-based loan:*** $5765. ***Average need-based gift aid:*** $10,010. ***Average non-need-based aid:*** $7989. ***Average indebtedness upon graduation:*** $14,965.

APPLYING

Standardized Tests *Required:* SAT (for admission), SAT or ACT (for admission).

Options: electronic application.

Application fee: $55.

Required: high school transcript, minimum 2.0 GPA.

Application deadlines: 11/30 (freshmen), 11/30 (transfers).

Notification: continuous (freshmen), continuous (transfers).

CONTACT

Ms. Nancy J. Dority, Assistant Vice President of Enrollment Services, California State University, Fullerton, Office of Admissions and Records, PO Box 34080, Fullerton, CA 92834-9480. *Phone:* 657-278-2370. *Fax:* 657-278-2356. *E-mail:* admissions@fullerton.edu.

California State University, Long Beach

Long Beach, California

http://www.csulb.edu/

- **State-supported** comprehensive, founded 1949, part of California State University System
- **Suburban** 320-acre campus with easy access to Los Angeles
- **Endowment** $57.0 million
- **Coed** 31,523 undergraduate students, 86% full-time, 56% women, 44% men
- **Moderately difficult** entrance level, 36% of applicants were admitted

UNDERGRAD STUDENTS

27,174 full-time, 4,349 part-time. Students come from 39 states and territories; 90 other countries; 1% are from out of state; 4% Black or African American, non-Hispanic/Latino; 38% Hispanic/Latino; 23% Asian, non-Hispanic/Latino; 0.5% Native Hawaiian or other Pacific Islander, non-Hispanic/Latino; 0.5% American Indian or Alaska Native, non-Hispanic/Latino; 5% Two or more races, non-Hispanic/Latino; 4% Race/ethnicity unknown; 6% international; 12% transferred in; 30% live on campus.

Freshmen

Admission: 56,357 applied, 20,326 admitted, 4,335 enrolled. ***Average high school GPA:*** 3.52. ***Test scores:*** SAT critical reading scores over 500: 59%; SAT math scores over 500: 69%; ACT scores over 18: 86%; SAT critical reading scores over 600: 16%; SAT math scores over 600: 27%; ACT scores over 24: 42%; SAT critical reading scores over 700: 1%; SAT math scores over 700: 3%; ACT scores over 30: 4%.

Retention: 90% of full-time freshmen returned.

FACULTY

Total: 2,149, 44% full-time, 58% with terminal degrees.

Student/faculty ratio: 24:1.

ACADEMICS

Calendar: semesters. *Degrees:* bachelor's, master's, doctoral, and postbachelor's certificates.

Special study options: academic remediation for entering students, accelerated degree program, adult/continuing education programs, advanced placement credit, distance learning, double majors, English as a second language, honors programs, independent study, internships, off-campus study, part-time degree program, services for LD students, student-designed majors, study abroad, summer session for credit. ***ROTC:*** Army (b).

Computers: 2,000 computers/terminals are available on campus for general student use. Campuswide network is available.

STUDENT LIFE

Housing options: coed.

Activities and organizations: drama/theater group, student-run newspaper, radio and television station, choral group, national fraternities, national sororities.

Athletics Member NCAA. All Division I. ***Intercollegiate sports:*** archery M(c)/W(c), badminton M(c)/W(c), basketball M(s)/W(s), bowling M(c)/W(c), crew M(c)/W(c), cross-country running M(s)/W(s), fencing M(c)/W(c), golf M/W, rugby M(c), sailing M(c)/W(c), skiing (downhill) M(c)/W(c), soccer M(c)/W(s), softball W(s), table tennis M(c), tennis W(s), track and field M(s)/W(s), volleyball M(s)/W(s), water polo M(s)/W(s). ***Intramural sports:*** basketball M/W, gymnastics M/W, racquetball M/W, softball W, swimming and diving M/W, table tennis W(c), tennis W, track and field M(c)/W(c), volleyball M/W.

Campus security: 24-hour emergency response devices and patrols, student patrols, late-night transport/escort service.

Student services: health clinic, personal/psychological counseling, women's center, legal services.

COSTS & FINANCIAL AID

Costs (2014–15) ***Tuition:*** state resident $5440 full-time; nonresident $14,368 full-time, $372 per unit part-time. Full-time tuition and fees vary according to degree level and program. Part-time tuition and fees vary according to course load, degree level, and program. ***Required fees:*** $980 full-time. ***Room and board:*** $11,688. Room and board charges vary according to board plan. ***Payment plan:*** installment. ***Waivers:*** senior citizens and employees or children of employees.

Financial Aid Of all full-time matriculated undergraduates who enrolled in 2014, 22,097 applied for aid, 20,042 were judged to have need, 9,087 had their need fully met. In 2014, 2113 non-need-based awards were made. ***Average percent of need met:*** 83. ***Average financial aid package:*** $13,662. ***Average need-based loan:*** $3811. ***Average need-based gift aid:*** $6538. ***Average non-need-based aid:*** $2356. ***Average indebtedness upon graduation:*** $16,579.

APPLYING

Standardized Tests *Required:* SAT or ACT (for admission).

Options: electronic application.

Application fee: $55.

Required: high school transcript. ***Required for some:*** minimum 2.0 GPA.

Application deadlines: 11/30 (freshmen), 11/30 (transfers).

Notification: continuous (freshmen), continuous (transfers).

CONTACT

Mr. Thomas Enders, Director of Enrollment Services, California State University, Long Beach, Brotman Hall, 1250 Bellflower Boulevard, Long Beach, CA 90840. *Phone:* 562-985-4641.

California State University, Los Angeles

Los Angeles, California

http://www.calstatela.edu/

- **State-supported** comprehensive, founded 1947, part of California State University System
- **Urban** 173-acre campus with easy access to Los Angeles
- **Endowment** $23.6 million
- **Coed** 20,668 undergraduate students, 86% full-time, 58% women, 42% men
- **Moderately difficult** entrance level, 61% of applicants were admitted

UNDERGRAD STUDENTS
17,741 full-time, 2,927 part-time. 0.3% are from out of state; 4% Black or African American, non-Hispanic/Latino; 61% Hispanic/Latino; 16% Asian, non-Hispanic/Latino; 0.2% Native Hawaiian or other Pacific Islander, non-Hispanic/Latino; 0.1% American Indian or Alaska Native, non-Hispanic/Latino; 2% Two or more races, non-Hispanic/Latino; 4% Race/ethnicity unknown; 6% international; 14% transferred in; 4% live on campus.

Freshmen
Admission: 31,011 applied, 18,939 admitted, 3,230 enrolled. ***Average high school GPA:*** 3.21. ***Test scores:*** SAT critical reading scores over 500: 20%; SAT math scores over 500: 27%; SAT writing scores over 500: 20%; ACT scores over 18: 48%; SAT critical reading scores over 600: 3%; SAT math scores over 600: 6%; SAT writing scores over 600: 10%; ACT scores over 24: 7%.

Retention: 84% of full-time freshmen returned.

FACULTY
Total: 1,120, 40% full-time, 48% with terminal degrees.

Student/faculty ratio: 31:1.

ACADEMICS
Calendar: quarters. *Degrees:* certificates, bachelor's, master's, doctoral, and postbachelor's certificates.

Special study options: academic remediation for entering students, accelerated degree program, adult/continuing education programs, advanced placement credit, cooperative education, distance learning, double majors, English as a second language, freshman honors college, honors programs, independent study, internships, off-campus study, part-time degree program, services for LD students, student-designed majors, study abroad, summer session for credit. ***ROTC:*** Army (c), Air Force (c).

Unusual degree programs: 3-2 nursing.

Computers: 1,500 computers/terminals are available on campus for general student use. Students can access the following: campus intranet, computer help desk, free student e-mail accounts, online (class) grades, online (class) registration, online (class) schedules. Campuswide network is available. 100% of college-owned or -operated housing units are wired for high-speed Internet access. Wireless service is available via classrooms, computer centers, computer labs, dorm rooms, learning centers, libraries, student centers.

STUDENT LIFE
Housing options: coed. Campus housing is university owned.

Activities and organizations: drama/theater group, student-run newspaper, radio and television station, choral group, Society of Hispanic Engineering and Science Students, Institute of Electrical and Electronics Engineer, Sigma Delta PI, Asian Unified, Society of Automotive Engineers, national fraternities, national sororities.

Athletics Member NCAA. All Division II. ***Intercollegiate sports:*** baseball M(s), basketball M(s)/W(s), cross-country running W(s), soccer M(s)/W(s), tennis W(s), track and field M(s)/W(s), volleyball W(s). ***Intramural sports:*** basketball M/W, bowling M/W, gymnastics M/W, racquetball M/W, skiing (cross-country) M/W, soccer M/W, softball M/W, swimming and diving M/W, tennis M/W, track and field M/W, volleyball M/W, water polo M/W, wrestling M.

Campus security: 24-hour emergency response devices, student patrols, late-night transport/escort service.

Student services: health clinic, personal/psychological counseling, women's center, legal services.

COSTS & FINANCIAL AID
Costs (2015–16) ***Tuition:*** state resident $5472 full-time; nonresident $14,400 full-time. Full-time tuition and fees vary according to course level and course load. Part-time tuition and fees vary according to course level and course load. ***Required fees:*** $868 full-time. ***Room and board:*** $12,833. Room and board charges vary according to board plan and housing facility. ***Payment plan:*** installment. ***Waivers:*** employees or children of employees.

Financial Aid Of all full-time matriculated undergraduates who enrolled in 2013, 14,477 applied for aid, 13,248 were judged to have need, 1,197 had their need fully met. In 2013, 35 non-need-based awards were made. ***Average percent of need met:*** 77. ***Average financial aid package:*** $12,724. ***Average need-based loan:*** $4094. ***Average need-based gift aid:*** $9932. ***Average non-need-based aid:*** $3736. ***Average indebtedness upon graduation:*** $18,099.

APPLYING
Standardized Tests *Required for some:* SAT or ACT (for admission).

Options: electronic application, early admission.

Application fee: $55.

Required: high school transcript.

Application deadlines: 11/30 (freshmen), 11/30 (transfers).

Notification: 8/30 (freshmen), 8/30 (transfers).

CONTACT
Vince Lopez, Director of Outreach and Recruitment, California State University, Los Angeles, 5151 State University Drive, Los Angeles, CA 90032-8530. *Phone:* 323-343-3839. *E-mail:* admission@calstatela.edu.

California State University, Monterey Bay

Seaside, California

http://www.csumb.edu/

- **State-supported** comprehensive, founded 1994, part of California State University System
- **Small-town** 1387-acre campus with easy access to San Jose
- **Coed** 6,234 undergraduate students, 93% full-time, 62% women, 38% men
- **Moderately difficult** entrance level, 69% of applicants were admitted

UNDERGRAD STUDENTS
5,783 full-time, 451 part-time. 2% are from out of state; 7% Black or African American, non-Hispanic/Latino; 35% Hispanic/Latino; 6% Asian, non-Hispanic/Latino; 0.9% Native Hawaiian or other Pacific Islander, non-Hispanic/Latino; 1% American Indian or Alaska Native, non-Hispanic/Latino; 7% Two or more races, non-Hispanic/Latino; 4% Race/ethnicity unknown; 5% international; 14% transferred in; 43% live on campus.

Freshmen
Admission: 14,684 applied, 10,185 admitted, 1,305 enrolled. ***Average high school GPA:*** 3.23. ***Test scores:*** SAT critical reading scores over 500: 46%; SAT math scores over 500: 46%; SAT writing scores over 500: 41%; ACT scores over 18: 75%; SAT critical reading scores over 600: 9%; SAT math scores over 600: 9%; SAT writing scores over 600: 6%; ACT scores over 24: 25%; SAT critical reading scores over 700: 1%; SAT math scores over 700: 1%; ACT scores over 30: 1%.

Retention: 84% of full-time freshmen returned.

FACULTY
Total: 422, 29% full-time, 45% with terminal degrees.

Student/faculty ratio: 29:1.

ACADEMICS
Calendar: semesters. *Degrees:* bachelor's and master's.

Special study options: academic remediation for entering students, accelerated degree program, advanced placement credit, cooperative education, distance learning, double majors, independent study, internships, off-campus study, part-time degree program, services for LD students, student-designed majors, study abroad, summer session for credit.

Computers: Students can access the following: campus intranet, computer help desk, free student e-mail accounts, online (class) grades, online (class) registration, online (class) schedules. Campuswide network is available. 100% of college-owned or -operated housing units are wired for high-speed Internet access. Wireless service is available via entire campus.

STUDENT LIFE
Housing options: on-campus residence required through sophomore year; coed, special housing for students with disabilities. Campus housing is university owned. Freshman applicants given priority for college housing.

Activities and organizations: drama/theater group, student-run newspaper, radio station, choral group, Asian Pacific Islander Association, Black Students United, MEChA, Rugby Sports Club, Psi Chi/Psychology Society, national fraternities, national sororities.

Athletics Member NCAA. All Division II. ***Intercollegiate sports:*** baseball M(s), basketball M(s)/W(s), cross-country running M(s)/W(s), golf M(s)/W(s), sailing M/W, soccer M(s)/W(s), softball W(s), volleyball W(s), water polo W(s). ***Intramural sports:*** basketball M/W, football M, soccer M/W, softball M/W, ultimate Frisbee M/W, volleyball M/W.

Campus security: 24-hour emergency response devices and patrols, student patrols, late-night transport/escort service, controlled dormitory access.

Student services: health clinic, personal/psychological counseling, women's center.

COSTS & FINANCIAL AID

Costs (2014–15) ***Tuition:*** state resident $0 full-time; nonresident $11,160 full-time, $372 per credit hour part-time. Full-time tuition and fees vary according to course load and degree level. Part-time tuition and fees vary according to course load and degree level. ***Required fees:*** $5963 full-time, $1833 per term part-time. ***Room and board:*** $10,112. Room and board charges vary according to board plan and housing facility. ***Payment plan:*** installment. ***Waivers:*** senior citizens and employees or children of employees.

Financial Aid Of all full-time matriculated undergraduates who enrolled in 2013, 3,882 applied for aid, 3,339 were judged to have need, 484 had their need fully met. In 2013, 59 non-need-based awards were made. ***Average percent of need met:*** 75. ***Average financial aid package:*** $10,686. ***Average need-based loan:*** $4241. ***Average need-based gift aid:*** $9282. ***Average non-need-based aid:*** $2937. ***Average indebtedness upon graduation:*** $21,745. ***Financial aid deadline:*** 6/1.

APPLYING

Standardized Tests *Required:* SAT or ACT (for admission).

Options: electronic application, deferred entrance.

Application fee: $55.

Required: high school transcript, minimum 2.0 GPA.

CONTACT

Mr. John Larsen, Assistant Director of Recruitment, California State University, Monterey Bay, 100 Campus Center, Seaside, CA 93955. *Phone:* 831-582-3738. *Fax:* 831-582-3783. *E-mail:* admissions@csumb.edu.

California State University, Northridge

Northridge, California

http://www.csun.edu/

- **State-supported** comprehensive, founded 1958, part of California State University System
- **Urban** 356-acre campus with easy access to Los Angeles
- **Coed**
- **Moderately difficult** entrance level

FACULTY

Student/faculty ratio: 27:1.

ACADEMICS

Calendar: semesters. *Degrees:* bachelor's and master's.

STUDENT LIFE

Activities and organizations: drama/theater group, student-run newspaper, radio station, choral group, national fraternities, national sororities.

Athletics Member NCAA. All Division I except football (Division II).

Campus security: 24-hour emergency response devices, late-night transport/escort service.

Student services: health clinic, personal/psychological counseling, women's center.

COSTS & FINANCIAL AID

Costs (2014–15) ***Tuition:*** state resident $0 full-time; nonresident $11,160 full-time. ***Required fees:*** $6544 full-time. ***Room and board:*** $10,980. Room and board charges vary according to board plan and housing facility.

Financial Aid Of all full-time matriculated undergraduates who enrolled in 2012, 19,395 applied for aid, 18,341 were judged to have need. In 2012, 1031 non-need-based awards were made. ***Average financial aid package:*** $19,329. ***Average need-based loan:*** $6400. ***Average need-based gift aid:*** $15,946. ***Average non-need-based aid:*** $1855. ***Average indebtedness upon graduation:*** $17,534.

APPLYING

Standardized Tests *Required:* SAT or ACT (for admission).

Options: electronic application.

Application fee: $55.

Required: high school transcript.

CONTACT

Ms. Mary Baxton, Associate Director of Admissions and Records, California State University, Northridge, 18111 Nordhoff Street, Northridge, CA 91330-8207. *Phone:* 818-677-3777. *Fax:* 818-677-3766. *E-mail:* admissions.records@csun.edu.

California State University, Sacramento

Sacramento, California

http://www.csus.edu/

- **State-supported** comprehensive, founded 1947, part of California State University System
- **Urban** 300-acre campus
- **Coed** 26,648 undergraduate students, 74% full-time, 56% women, 44% men
- **Moderately difficult** entrance level, 100% of applicants were admitted

UNDERGRAD STUDENTS

19,812 full-time, 6,836 part-time. 1% are from out of state; 6% Black or African American, non-Hispanic/Latino; 23% Hispanic/Latino; 21% Asian, non-Hispanic/Latino; 1% Native Hawaiian or other Pacific Islander, non-Hispanic/Latino; 0.8% American Indian or Alaska Native, non-Hispanic/Latino; 6% Two or more races, non-Hispanic/Latino; 5% Race/ethnicity unknown; 2% international; 13% transferred in; 4% live on campus.

Freshmen

Admission: 3,694 applied, 3,694 admitted, 3,695 enrolled. ***Average high school GPA:*** 3.27. ***Test scores:*** SAT math scores over 500: 41%; SAT writing scores over 500: 34%; ACT scores over 18: 69%; SAT math scores over 600: 10%; SAT writing scores over 600: 7%; ACT scores over 24: 17%; SAT math scores over 700: 1%; SAT writing scores over 700: 1%; ACT scores over 30: 1%.

Retention: 82% of full-time freshmen returned.

FACULTY

Total: 1,491, 44% full-time.

Student/faculty ratio: 26:1.

ACADEMICS

Calendar: semesters. *Degrees:* bachelor's, master's, and doctoral.

Special study options: off-campus study, part-time degree program. ***ROTC:*** Army (c), Air Force (b).

Computers: Students can access the following: computer help desk, free student e-mail accounts, online (class) grades, online (class) registration, online (class) schedules, online transcripts. Campuswide network is available. Wireless service is available via entire campus.

STUDENT LIFE

Housing options: coed, special housing for students with disabilities. Campus housing is university owned.

Athletics Member NCAA. All Division I except football (Division I-AA). ***Intercollegiate sports:*** baseball M(s), basketball M(s)/W(s), bowling M(c)/W(c), cheerleading M/W, crew M(s)/W(s), cross-country running M(s)/W(s), golf M(s)/W, gymnastics W(s), ice hockey M(c), lacrosse M(c)/W(c), racquetball M(c)/W(c), rugby M(c), skiing (downhill) M(c)/W(c), soccer M(s)/W(s), softball W(s), tennis M(s)/W(s), track and field M(s)/W(s), volleyball M(c)/W(s). ***Intramural sports:*** basketball M/W, crew M/W, football M/W, golf M/W, ice hockey M, skiing (downhill) M/W, soccer M/W, softball M/W, table tennis M/W, tennis M/W, volleyball M/W, water polo M/W, weight lifting M/W.

Campus security: 24-hour emergency response devices and patrols, student patrols, late-night transport/escort service, controlled dormitory access.

COSTS & FINANCIAL AID
Costs (2014–15) ***Tuition:*** state resident $5472 full-time; nonresident $16,632 full-time, $372 per credit hour part-time. ***Required fees:*** $1130 full-time. ***Room only:*** $6538. Room and board charges vary according to board plan and housing facility.

Financial Aid Of all full-time matriculated undergraduates who enrolled in 2013, 17,289 applied for aid, 15,802 were judged to have need, 850 had their need fully met. In 2013, 20 non-need-based awards were made. ***Average percent of need met:*** 60. ***Average financial aid package:*** $10,808. ***Average need-based loan:*** $4350. ***Average need-based gift aid:*** $9625. ***Average non-need-based aid:*** $1047. ***Average indebtedness upon graduation:*** $4402.

APPLYING
Standardized Tests *Required for some:* SAT or ACT (for admission).

Options: electronic application, early decision, early action, deferred entrance.

Application fee: $55.

Required: minimum 2.0 GPA. ***Required for some:*** high school transcript.

CONTACT
Mr. Emiliano Diaz, Director of University Outreach Services, California State University, Sacramento, 6000 J Street, Lassen Hall, Sacramento, CA 95819-6048. *Phone:* 916-278-3901. *Fax:* 916-278-5603. *E-mail:* admissions@csus.edu.

California State University, San Bernardino

San Bernardino, California

http://www.csusb.edu/

- **State-supported** comprehensive, founded 1965, part of California State University System
- **Suburban** 430-acre campus with easy access to Los Angeles
- **Coed** 16,676 undergraduate students, 89% full-time, 61% women, 39% men
- **Moderately difficult** entrance level, 65% of applicants were admitted

UNDERGRAD STUDENTS
14,769 full-time, 1,907 part-time. 1% are from out of state; 6% Black or African American, non-Hispanic/Latino; 58% Hispanic/Latino; 6% Asian, non-Hispanic/Latino; 0.2% Native Hawaiian or other Pacific Islander, non-Hispanic/Latino; 0.2% American Indian or Alaska Native, non-Hispanic/Latino; 3% Two or more races, non-Hispanic/Latino; 5% Race/ethnicity unknown; 7% international; 14% transferred in; 8% live on campus.

Freshmen
Admission: 12,951 applied, 8,372 admitted, 2,724 enrolled. ***Average high school GPA:*** 3.23. ***Test scores:*** SAT critical reading scores over 500: 24%; SAT math scores over 500: 27%; SAT writing scores over 500: 21%; ACT scores over 18: 56%; SAT critical reading scores over 600: 3%; SAT math scores over 600: 4%; SAT writing scores over 600: 2%; ACT scores over 24: 8%; ACT scores over 30: 1%.

Retention: 88% of full-time freshmen returned.

FACULTY
Total: 923, 47% full-time, 47% with terminal degrees.

Student/faculty ratio: 30:1.

ACADEMICS
Calendar: quarters. *Degrees:* certificates, bachelor's, master's, doctoral, and postbachelor's certificates.

Special study options: academic remediation for entering students, accelerated degree program, advanced placement credit, cooperative education, distance learning, double majors, honors programs, independent study, internships, off-campus study, part-time degree program, services for LD students, student-designed majors, study abroad, summer session for credit. ***ROTC:*** Army (b), Air Force (b).

Computers: Students can access the following: computer help desk, free student e-mail accounts, online (class) grades, online (class) registration, online (class) schedules. Campuswide network is available. Wireless service is available via entire campus.

STUDENT LIFE
Housing options: coed, women-only, special housing for students with disabilities. Campus housing is university owned and is provided by a third party. Freshman applicants given priority for college housing.

Activities and organizations: drama/theater group, student-run newspaper, radio and television station, choral group, national fraternities, national sororities.

Athletics Member NCAA. All Division II. ***Intercollegiate sports:*** baseball M(s), basketball M(s)/W(s), cross-country running W, golf M(s), soccer M(s)/W(s), softball W(s), track and field W, volleyball W(s).

Campus security: 24-hour emergency response devices and patrols, student patrols, late-night transport/escort service, residence staff on call 24 hours.

Student services: health clinic, personal/psychological counseling, women's center, legal services.

COSTS & FINANCIAL AID
Costs (2014–15) ***Tuition:*** state resident $5472 full-time, $3174 per year part-time; nonresident $16,632 full-time, $248 per unit part-time. Part-time tuition and fees vary according to course load. ***Required fees:*** $1086 full-time, $1086 per year part-time. ***Room and board:*** $9933. Room and board charges vary according to board plan and housing facility. ***Payment plan:*** installment. ***Waivers:*** senior citizens and employees or children of employees.

Financial Aid Of all full-time matriculated undergraduates who enrolled in 2013, 12,424 applied for aid, 11,712 were judged to have need, 1,431 had their need fully met. 291 Federal Work-Study jobs (averaging $3936). In 2013, 43 non-need-based awards were made. ***Average percent of need met:*** 74. ***Average financial aid package:*** $8834. ***Average need-based loan:*** $4097. ***Average need-based gift aid:*** $9397. ***Average non-need-based aid:*** $3848. ***Average indebtedness upon graduation:*** $18,950.

APPLYING
Standardized Tests *Recommended:* SAT or ACT (for admission).

Options: electronic application, early admission, early action.

Application fee: $55.

Required: high school transcript, minimum 2.0 GPA.

Application deadlines: rolling (freshmen), rolling (transfers).

Notification: continuous (freshmen), continuous (transfers).

CONTACT
Julie Rogers, Assistant Director of Admissions and Evaluations, California State University, San Bernardino, 5500 University Parkway, University Hall, Room 115, San Bernardino, CA 92407-2397. *Phone:* 909-537-5211. *Fax:* 909-537-7034. *E-mail:* moreinfo@mail.csusb.edu.

California State University, San Marcos

San Marcos, California

http://www.csusm.edu/

- **State-supported** comprehensive, founded 1990, part of California State University System
- **Suburban** 304-acre campus with easy access to San Diego
- **Coed** 11,555 undergraduate students, 79% full-time, 60% women, 40% men
- **Moderately difficult** entrance level, 85% of applicants were admitted

UNDERGRAD STUDENTS
9,099 full-time, 2,456 part-time. 2% are from out of state; 3% Black or African American, non-Hispanic/Latino; 39% Hispanic/Latino; 10% Asian, non-Hispanic/Latino; 0.4% Native Hawaiian or other Pacific Islander, non-Hispanic/Latino; 0.4% American Indian or Alaska Native, non-Hispanic/Latino; 5% Two or more races, non-Hispanic/Latino; 6% Race/ethnicity unknown; 3% international; 14% transferred in; 99% live on campus.

Freshmen
Admission: 10,728 applied, 9,102 admitted, 2,167 enrolled. ***Average high school GPA:*** 3.19. ***Test scores:*** SAT math scores over 500: 43%; SAT writing scores over 500: 38%; ACT scores over 18: 73%; SAT math

scores over 600: 7%; SAT writing scores over 600: 6%; ACT scores over 24: 15%.

Retention: 83% of full-time freshmen returned.

FACULTY
Total: 687, 34% full-time.

Student/faculty ratio: 27:1.

ACADEMICS
Calendar: semesters. *Degrees:* bachelor's, master's, and doctoral.

Special study options: academic remediation for entering students, adult/continuing education programs, advanced placement credit, distance learning, double majors, English as a second language, independent study, internships, off-campus study, part-time degree program, services for LD students, student-designed majors, study abroad, summer session for credit. ***ROTC:*** Army (c), Navy (c), Air Force (c).

Computers: Students can access the following: computer help desk, free student e-mail accounts, online (class) registration, online (class) schedules. Campuswide network is available.

STUDENT LIFE
Housing options: special housing for students with disabilities. Campus housing is provided by a third party.

Activities and organizations: drama/theater group, student-run newspaper, choral group, national fraternities, national sororities.

Athletics Member NAIA. ***Intercollegiate sports:*** baseball M, basketball M/W, cross-country running M/W, golf M/W, soccer M/W, softball W, track and field M/W.

Campus security: 24-hour emergency response devices and patrols, student patrols, late-night transport/escort service.

Student services: health clinic, personal/psychological counseling, women's center.

COSTS & FINANCIAL AID
Costs (2014–15) ***Tuition:*** state resident $0 full-time; nonresident $16,092 full-time, $372 per unit part-time. Part-time tuition and fees vary according to course load. ***Required fees:*** $7164 full-time, $2433 per term part-time. ***Room and board:*** Room and board charges vary according to housing facility. ***Waivers:*** senior citizens and employees or children of employees.

Financial Aid Of all full-time matriculated undergraduates who enrolled in 2012, 5,899 applied for aid, 5,156 were judged to have need, 12 had their need fully met. In 2012, 2 non-need-based awards were made. ***Average percent of need met:*** 61. ***Average financial aid package:*** $5307. ***Average need-based loan:*** $1289. ***Average need-based gift aid:*** $4867. ***Average non-need-based aid:*** $375.

APPLYING
Standardized Tests *Required for some:* SAT or ACT (for admission).

Options: electronic application.

Application fee: $55.

Required: high school transcript.

Application deadlines: 11/30 (freshmen), 11/30 (transfers).

Notification: continuous (freshmen), continuous (transfers).

CONTACT
Scott Hagg, Director of Admissions, California State University, San Marcos, 333 South Twin Oaks Valley Road, San Marcos, CA 92096-0001. *Phone:* 760-750-4848. *Fax:* 760-750-3248. *E-mail:* apply@csusm.edu.

California State University, Stanislaus

Turlock, California

http://www.csustan.edu/

- **State-supported** comprehensive, founded 1957, part of California State University System
- **Suburban** 228-acre campus
- **Endowment** $12.0 million
- **Coed** 7,847 undergraduate students, 85% full-time, 64% women, 36% men
- **Moderately difficult** entrance level, 73% of applicants were admitted

UNDERGRAD STUDENTS
6,698 full-time, 1,149 part-time. Students come from 31 states and territories; 45 other countries; 1% are from out of state; 2% Black or African American, non-Hispanic/Latino; 47% Hispanic/Latino; 11% Asian, non-Hispanic/Latino; 0.7% Native Hawaiian or other Pacific Islander, non-Hispanic/Latino; 0.4% American Indian or Alaska Native, non-Hispanic/Latino; 4% Two or more races, non-Hispanic/Latino; 6% Race/ethnicity unknown; 3% international; 12% transferred in; 8% live on campus.

Freshmen
Admission: 6,265 applied, 4,555 admitted, 1,232 enrolled. ***Average high school GPA:*** 3.26. ***Test scores:*** SAT critical reading scores over 500: 29%; SAT math scores over 500: 33%; SAT writing scores over 500: 27%; ACT scores over 18: 55%; SAT critical reading scores over 600: 5%; SAT math scores over 600: 4%; SAT writing scores over 600: 4%; ACT scores over 24: 13%; ACT scores over 30: 1%.

Retention: 85% of full-time freshmen returned.

FACULTY
Total: 521, 50% full-time, 59% with terminal degrees.

Student/faculty ratio: 22:1.

ACADEMICS
Calendar: semesters. *Degrees:* bachelor's, master's, doctoral, and post-master's certificates.

Special study options: academic remediation for entering students, advanced placement credit, cooperative education, distance learning, double majors, English as a second language, honors programs, independent study, internships, off-campus study, part-time degree program, services for LD students, student-designed majors, study abroad, summer session for credit.

Computers: 258 computers/terminals are available on campus for general student use. Students can access the following: computer help desk, free student e-mail accounts, online (class) grades, online (class) registration, online (class) schedules. Campuswide network is available. 100% of college-owned or -operated housing units are wired for high-speed Internet access. Wireless service is available via entire campus.

STUDENT LIFE
Housing options: coed. Campus housing is university owned and leased by the school.

Activities and organizations: drama/theater group, student-run newspaper, radio station, choral group, Alpha Xi Delta, Phi Sigma Sigma, Kappa Sigma, Tau Kappa Epsilon, Theta Chi, national fraternities, national sororities.

Athletics Member NCAA. All Division II. ***Intercollegiate sports:*** baseball M(s), basketball M(s)/W(s), cross-country running M(s)/W(s), golf M(s), soccer M(s)/W(s), softball W(s), tennis W(s), track and field M(s)/W(s), volleyball W(s). ***Intramural sports:*** basketball M/W, cheerleading M(c)/W(c), football M/W, soccer M/W, ultimate Frisbee M/W, volleyball M/W.

Campus security: 24-hour emergency response devices and patrols, student patrols, late-night transport/escort service, controlled dormitory access.

Student services: health clinic, personal/psychological counseling, women's center.

COSTS & FINANCIAL AID
Costs (2014–15) ***Tuition:*** state resident $5472 full-time; nonresident $16,632 full-time. Full-time tuition and fees vary according to course load, degree level, and reciprocity agreements. Part-time tuition and fees vary according to course load, degree level, and reciprocity agreements. ***Required fees:*** $1019 full-time, $1019 per term part-time. ***Room and board:*** $11,900. Room and board charges vary according to board plan and housing facility. ***Payment plan:*** installment. ***Waivers:*** employees or children of employees.

Financial Aid Of all full-time matriculated undergraduates who enrolled in 2012, 5,235 applied for aid, 4,964 were judged to have need, 945 had their need fully met. 148 Federal Work-Study jobs (averaging $3433). In 2012, 21 non-need-based awards were made. ***Average percent of need met:*** 70. ***Average financial aid package:*** $14,722. ***Average need-based loan:*** $5135. ***Average need-based gift aid:*** $9343. ***Average non-need-based aid:*** $1976.

APPLYING

Standardized Tests *Required for some:* SAT or ACT (for admission).

Options: electronic application.

Application fee: $55.

Required for some: high school transcript. ***Recommended:*** minimum 3.0 GPA.

Application deadlines: 11/30 (freshmen), 11/30 (transfers).

Notification: continuous (freshmen), continuous (transfers).

CONTACT

Student Outreach, California State University, Stanislaus, One University Circle, Turlock, CA 95382. *Phone:* 209-667-3122. *Toll-free phone:* 800-300-7420. *Fax:* 209-667-6536. *E-mail:* outreach_help_desk@csustan.edu.

★ Chapman University

Orange, California

http://www.chapman.edu/

- **Independent** comprehensive, founded 1861, affiliated with Christian Church (Disciples of Christ)
- **Suburban** 78-acre campus with easy access to Los Angeles
- **Endowment** $273.8 million
- **Coed** 6,281 undergraduate students, 96% full-time, 60% women, 40% men
- **Very difficult** entrance level, 47% of applicants were admitted

UNDERGRAD STUDENTS

6,004 full-time, 277 part-time. Students come from 47 states and territories; 85 other countries; 26% are from out of state; 1% Black or African American, non-Hispanic/Latino; 14% Hispanic/Latino; 10% Asian, non-Hispanic/Latino; 0.3% Native Hawaiian or other Pacific Islander, non-Hispanic/Latino; 0.3% American Indian or Alaska Native, non-Hispanic/Latino; 6% Two or more races, non-Hispanic/Latino; 3% Race/ethnicity unknown; 4% international; 7% transferred in; 32% live on campus.

Freshmen

Admission: 12,507 applied, 5,883 admitted, 1,422 enrolled. ***Average high school GPA:*** 3.69. ***Test scores:*** SAT critical reading scores over 500: 93%; SAT math scores over 500: 95%; SAT writing scores over 500: 96%; ACT scores over 18: 100%; SAT critical reading scores over 600: 52%; SAT math scores over 600: 55%; SAT writing scores over 600: 58%; ACT scores over 24: 86%; SAT critical reading scores over 700: 8%; SAT math scores over 700: 10%; SAT writing scores over 700: 12%; ACT scores over 30: 23%.

Retention: 91% of full-time freshmen returned.

FACULTY

Total: 914, 46% full-time.

Student/faculty ratio: 14:1.

ACADEMICS

Calendar: 4-1-4. *Degrees:* bachelor's, master's, and doctoral.

Special study options: academic remediation for entering students, adult/continuing education programs, advanced placement credit, distance learning, double majors, honors programs, independent study, internships, off-campus study, part-time degree program, services for LD students, student-designed majors, study abroad, summer session for credit. ***ROTC:*** Army (c), Air Force (c).

Unusual degree programs: 3-2 business administration; engineering with University of California, Irvine.

Computers: Students can access the following: campus intranet, computer help desk, free student e-mail accounts, online (class) grades, online (class) registration, online (class) schedules. Campuswide network is available. 100% of college-owned or -operated housing units are wired for high-speed Internet access. Wireless service is available via entire campus.

STUDENT LIFE

Housing options: coed, special housing for students with disabilities. Campus housing is university owned. Freshman campus housing is guaranteed.

Activities and organizations: drama/theater group, student-run newspaper, radio station, choral group, Gamma Beta Phi, Alpha Kappa

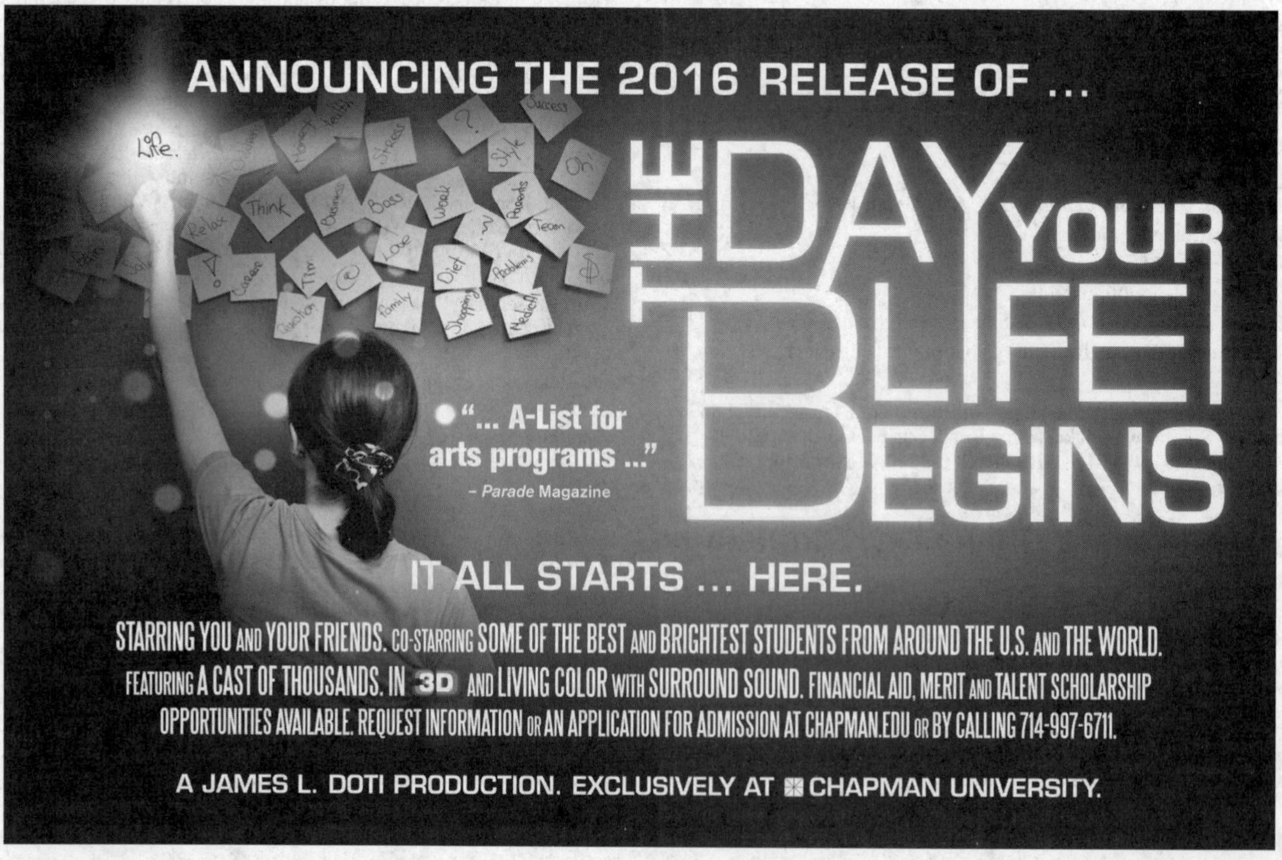

Psi Professional Business Fraternity, Public Relations Student Society of America, Black Student Union, Disciples on Campus, national fraternities, national sororities.

Athletics Member NCAA. All Division III. ***Intercollegiate sports:*** baseball M, basketball M/W, cheerleading W(c), crew M(c)/W(c), cross-country running M/W, football M, golf M, ice hockey M(c), lacrosse M(c)/W, soccer M/W, softball W, swimming and diving M/W, tennis M/W, track and field M/W, volleyball M(c)/W, water polo M/W. ***Intramural sports:*** basketball M/W, soccer M/W, ultimate Frisbee M/W, volleyball M/W.

Campus security: 24-hour emergency response devices and patrols, late-night transport/escort service, controlled dormitory access, full safety education program.

Student services: health clinic, personal/psychological counseling.

COSTS & FINANCIAL AID

Costs (2015–16) ***Comprehensive fee:*** $61,090 includes full-time tuition ($46,500), mandatory fees ($760), and room and board ($13,830). Part-time tuition: $1445 per credit. ***College room only:*** $9444. Room and board charges vary according to board plan and housing facility. ***Payment plans:*** tuition prepayment, installment, deferred payment. ***Waivers:*** employees or children of employees.

Financial Aid Of all full-time matriculated undergraduates who enrolled in 2014, 4,038 applied for aid, 3,513 were judged to have need, 402 had their need fully met. 3,018 Federal Work-Study jobs (averaging $2942). In 2014, 1366 non-need-based awards were made. ***Average percent of need met:*** 72. ***Average financial aid package:*** $32,247. ***Average need-based loan:*** $4825. ***Average need-based gift aid:*** $15,855. ***Average non-need-based aid:*** $16,618. ***Average indebtedness upon graduation:*** $27,979.

APPLYING

Standardized Tests *Required:* SAT or ACT (for admission). *Recommended:* SAT Subject Tests (for admission).

Options: electronic application, early action.

Application fee: $65.

Required: essay or personal statement, high school transcript, 1 letter of recommendation. ***Required for some:*** Audition required for music, dance, and theatre majors. Portfolio required for art and film majors. Supplemental application required for all talent-based majors.

Application deadlines: 1/15 (freshmen), 3/15 (transfers), 11/1 (early action).

Notification: 3/15 (freshmen), 4/15 (transfers), 1/10 (early action).

CONTACT

Ms. Marcela Mejia-Martinez, Director of Admission, Chapman University, One University Drive, Orange, CA 92866. *Phone:* 714-997-6711. *Toll-free phone:* 888-CUAPPLY. *Fax:* 714-997-6713. *E-mail:* admit@chapman.edu.

See previous page for display ad and page 1394 for the College Close-Up.

Claremont McKenna College

Claremont, California

http://www.claremontmckenna.edu/

- **Independent** comprehensive, founded 1946
- **Suburban** 69-acre campus with easy access to Los Angeles
- **Endowment** $699.5 million
- **Coed** 1,301 undergraduate students, 100% full-time, 48% women, 52% men
- **Most difficult** entrance level, 11% of applicants were admitted

UNDERGRAD STUDENTS

1,298 full-time, 3 part-time. Students come from 46 states and territories; 31 other countries; 56% are from out of state; 4% Black or African American, non-Hispanic/Latino; 12% Hispanic/Latino; 10% Asian, non-Hispanic/Latino; 0.1% Native Hawaiian or other Pacific Islander, non-Hispanic/Latino; 0.1% American Indian or Alaska Native, non-Hispanic/Latino; 7% Two or more races, non-Hispanic/Latino; 6% Race/ethnicity unknown; 17% international; 2% transferred in; 97% live on campus.

Freshmen

Admission: 6,043 applied, 651 admitted, 327 enrolled. ***Test scores:*** SAT critical reading scores over 500: 100%; SAT math scores over 500: 100%; SAT writing scores over 500: 100%; ACT scores over 18: 100%; SAT critical reading scores over 600: 98%; SAT math scores over 600: 97%; SAT writing scores over 600: 99%; ACT scores over 24: 100%; SAT critical reading scores over 700: 57%; SAT math scores over 700: 71%; SAT writing scores over 700: 61%; ACT scores over 30: 80%.

Retention: 96% of full-time freshmen returned.

FACULTY

Total: 165, 88% full-time, 98% with terminal degrees.

Student/faculty ratio: 8:1.

ACADEMICS

Calendar: semesters. *Degrees:* bachelor's and master's.

Special study options: advanced placement credit, double majors, honors programs, independent study, internships, off-campus study, services for LD students, student-designed majors, study abroad. ***ROTC:*** Army (b), Air Force (c).

Unusual degree programs: 3-2 engineering with Accredited Engineering School.

Computers: 220 computers/terminals are available on campus for general student use. Students can access the following: campus intranet, computer help desk, free student e-mail accounts, online (class) grades, online (class) registration, online (class) schedules. Campuswide network is available. 100% of college-owned or -operated housing units are wired for high-speed Internet access. Wireless service is available via entire campus.

STUDENT LIFE

Housing options: on-campus residence required for freshman year; coed, special housing for students with disabilities. Campus housing is university owned. Freshman campus housing is guaranteed.

Activities and organizations: drama/theater group, student-run newspaper, radio station, choral group, The Forum - student newspaper, ASCMC - student government, Debate/Forensics Club, SOURCE, Rotaract.

Athletics Member NCAA. All Division III. ***Intercollegiate sports:*** archery M(c)/W(c), baseball M, basketball M/W, cheerleading M(c)/W(c), cross-country running M/W, equestrian sports M(c)/W(c), fencing M(c)/W(c), field hockey M(c)/W(c), football M, golf M/W, lacrosse M(c)/W, rugby M(c)/W(c), sailing M(c)/W(c), skiing (downhill) M(c)/W(c), soccer M/W, softball W, swimming and diving M/W, tennis M/W, track and field M/W, volleyball M(c)/W, water polo M/W. ***Intramural sports:*** basketball M/W, bowling M/W, crew M/W, football M, soccer M/W, squash M/W, table tennis M/W, tennis M/W, ultimate Frisbee M/W, volleyball M/W, water polo M/W, weight lifting M/W.

Campus security: 24-hour emergency response devices and patrols, student patrols, late-night transport/escort service, controlled dormitory access.

Student services: health clinic, personal/psychological counseling.

COSTS & FINANCIAL AID

Costs (2014–15) ***Comprehensive fee:*** $62,215 includes full-time tuition ($47,150), mandatory fees ($245), and room and board ($14,820). Part-time tuition: $7858 per course. Part-time tuition and fees vary according to course load. ***College room only:*** $7900. Room and board charges vary according to board plan and housing facility. ***Payment plan:*** installment. ***Waivers:*** employees or children of employees.

Financial Aid Of all full-time matriculated undergraduates who enrolled in 2013, 604 applied for aid, 526 were judged to have need, 526 had their need fully met. In 2013, 59 non-need-based awards were made. ***Average percent of need met:*** 100. ***Average financial aid package:*** $40,677. ***Average need-based gift aid:*** $39,099. ***Average non-need-based aid:*** $20,635. ***Average indebtedness upon graduation:*** $23,273. ***Financial aid deadline:*** 2/1.

APPLYING

Standardized Tests *Required:* SAT or ACT (for admission). *Required for some:* SAT Subject Tests (for admission), TOEFL or IELTS scores are required of students for whom English is not their first language and the primary language of instruction in high school was not English.

Options: electronic application, early decision, deferred entrance.

Application fee: $60.

Required: essay or personal statement, high school transcript, 3 letters of recommendation. ***Required for some:*** interview.

Application deadlines: 1/1 (freshmen), 4/1 (transfers).

Early decision deadline: 11/1 (for plan 1), 1/1 (for plan 2).

Notification: 4/1 (freshmen), 5/15 (transfers), 12/15 (early decision plan 1), 2/15 (early decision plan 2).

CONTACT

Ms. Jennifer Sandoval-Dancs, Director of Admission, Claremont McKenna College, Office of Admission and Financial Aid, 888 Columbia Avenue, Claremont, CA 91711. *Phone:* 909-621-8088. *Fax:* 909-621-8516. *E-mail:* jennifer.sandoval@cmc.edu.

Cogswell Polytechnical College

Sunnyvale, California

http://www.cogswell.edu/

- **Independent** comprehensive, founded 1887
- **Suburban** 2-acre campus with easy access to San Francisco, San Jose
- **Coed** 612 undergraduate students, 79% full-time, 25% women, 75% men
- **Moderately difficult** entrance level, 44% of applicants were admitted

UNDERGRAD STUDENTS

483 full-time, 129 part-time. Students come from 13 states and territories; 2 other countries; 10% are from out of state; 4% Black or African American, non-Hispanic/Latino; 17% Hispanic/Latino; 15% Asian, non-Hispanic/Latino; 2% Native Hawaiian or other Pacific Islander, non-Hispanic/Latino; 0.2% American Indian or Alaska Native, non-Hispanic/Latino; 11% Two or more races, non-Hispanic/Latino; 8% Race/ethnicity unknown; 0.7% international; 9% transferred in; 30% live on campus.

Freshmen

Admission: 605 applied, 265 admitted, 140 enrolled. ***Average high school GPA:*** 2.95. ***Test scores:*** SAT critical reading scores over 500: 74%; SAT math scores over 500: 67%; SAT writing scores over 500: 54%; ACT scores over 18: 50%; SAT critical reading scores over 600: 7%; SAT math scores over 600: 20%; SAT writing scores over 600: 14%.

Retention: 86% of full-time freshmen returned.

FACULTY

Total: 70, 24% full-time, 17% with terminal degrees.

Student/faculty ratio: 15:1.

ACADEMICS

Calendar: semesters. *Degrees:* bachelor's and master's.

Special study options: academic remediation for entering students, advanced placement credit, cooperative education, double majors, internships, part-time degree program, student-designed majors, summer session for credit.

Computers: 224 computers/terminals are available on campus for general student use. Students can access the following: computer help desk, free student e-mail accounts, online (class) grades, online (class) registration, online (class) schedules. Campuswide network is available. Wireless service is available via entire campus.

STUDENT LIFE

Housing options: coed. Campus housing is provided by a third party. Freshman campus housing is guaranteed.

Activities and organizations: choral group, ASB, Game Development club, Audio Production and Engineering club, Comic Club, Women's club.

Campus security: 24-hour emergency response devices.

Student services: personal/psychological counseling.

COSTS & FINANCIAL AID

Costs (2015–16) ***Tuition:*** $16,460 full-time, $644 per credit part-time. Full-time tuition and fees vary according to course load, degree level, and program. Part-time tuition and fees vary according to course load, degree level, and program. ***Required fees:*** $180 full-time. ***Room only:*** $8000. Room and board charges vary according to housing facility. ***Payment plan:*** deferred payment. ***Waivers:*** employees or children of employees.

Financial Aid Of all full-time matriculated undergraduates who enrolled in 2011, 14 Federal Work-Study jobs (averaging $1900).

APPLYING

Standardized Tests *Recommended:* SAT or ACT (for admission).

Options: electronic application, deferred entrance.

Required: essay or personal statement, high school transcript, minimum 2.0 GPA, . ***Required for some:*** portfolio for Digital Art and Animation, Digital Audio Technology and Digital Media Management majors. ***Recommended:*** minimum 2.7 GPA, interview.

Application deadlines: rolling (freshmen), rolling (out-of-state freshmen), rolling (transfers).

Notification: continuous (freshmen), continuous (out-of-state freshmen), continuous (transfers).

CONTACT

Aaron Kark, Director of Admissions, Cogswell Polytechnical College, 1175 Bordeaux Drive, Sunnyvale, CA 94089-1299. *Phone:* 408-498-5156. *Toll-free phone:* 800-264-7955. *Fax:* 408-747-0764. *E-mail:* akark@cogswell.edu.

The Colburn School Conservatory of Music

Los Angeles, California

http://www.colburnschool.edu/

- **Independent** comprehensive, founded 1980
- **Urban** campus with easy access to Los Angeles
- **Coed** 59 undergraduate students, 100% full-time, 53% women, 47% men
- **Most difficult** entrance level, 5% of applicants were admitted

UNDERGRAD STUDENTS

59 full-time. Students come from 20 states and territories; 10 other countries; 86% are from out of state; 2% Black or African American, non-Hispanic/Latino; 2% Hispanic/Latino; 22% Asian, non-Hispanic/Latino; 6% Two or more races, non-Hispanic/Latino; 20% international; 7% transferred in; 100% live on campus.

Freshmen

Admission: 500 applied, 26 admitted, 12 enrolled.

FACULTY

Total: 43, 23% full-time, 30% with terminal degrees.

Student/faculty ratio: 11:1.

ACADEMICS

Calendar: semesters. *Degrees:* certificates, diplomas, bachelor's, master's, and postbachelor's certificates.

Special study options: academic remediation for entering students, advanced placement credit, double majors, English as a second language.

Computers: 12 computers/terminals are available on campus for general student use. Students can access the following: campus intranet, computer help desk, free student e-mail accounts. Campuswide network is available. 100% of college-owned or -operated housing units are wired for high-speed Internet access. Wireless service is available via classrooms, computer centers, computer labs, dorm rooms, libraries.

STUDENT LIFE

Housing options: on-campus residence required through junior year; coed. Campus housing is university owned. Freshman campus housing is guaranteed.

Athletics ***Intramural sports:*** table tennis M/W.

Campus security: 24-hour emergency response devices and patrols, controlled dormitory access.

Student services: personal/psychological counseling.

COSTS

Costs (2015–16) ***Comprehensive fee:*** includes mandatory fees ($3000).

APPLYING

Standardized Tests *Recommended:* SAT or ACT (for admission).

Options: electronic application, deferred entrance.

Application fee: $120.

Required: essay or personal statement, high school transcript, 2 letters of recommendation, interview, pre-screening DVD, in-person audition by invitation.

Application deadlines: 12/1 (freshmen), 12/1 (transfers).

Notification: 4/1 (freshmen), 4/1 (transfers).

CONTACT

Ms. Jessica Cameron, Interim Manager of Admissions, The Colburn School Conservatory of Music, 200 South Grand Avenue, Los Angeles, CA 90012. *Phone:* 213-621-4534. *Fax:* 213-625-0371. *E-mail:* admissions@colburnschool.edu.

★ Coleman University

San Diego, California

http://www.coleman.edu/

CONTACT

Admissions Department, Coleman University, 7380 Parkway Drive, La Mesa, CA 91942-1532. *Phone:* 619-465-3990. *Toll-free phone:* 800-430-2030. *E-mail:* jschafer@cts.com.

Concordia University

Irvine, California

http://www.cui.edu/

- **Independent** comprehensive, founded 1972, affiliated with Lutheran Church–Missouri Synod, part of The Concordia University System
- **Suburban** 70-acre campus with easy access to Los Angeles
- **Endowment** $23.0 million
- **Coed** 1,918 undergraduate students, 92% full-time, 64% women, 36% men
- **Moderately difficult** entrance level, 86% of applicants were admitted

UNDERGRAD STUDENTS

1,760 full-time, 158 part-time. Students come from 35 states and territories; 25 other countries; 11% are from out of state; 3% Black or African American, non-Hispanic/Latino; 18% Hispanic/Latino; 6% Asian, non-Hispanic/Latino; 0.5% Native Hawaiian or other Pacific Islander, non-Hispanic/Latino; 0.4% American Indian or Alaska Native, non-Hispanic/Latino; 4% Two or more races, non-Hispanic/Latino; 17% Race/ethnicity unknown; 4% international; 10% transferred in; 48% live on campus.

Freshmen

Admission: 2,220 applied, 1,911 admitted, 352 enrolled. ***Average high school GPA:*** 3.43. ***Test scores:*** SAT critical reading scores over 500: 56%; SAT math scores over 500: 56%; SAT writing scores over 500: 50%; ACT scores over 18: 90%; SAT critical reading scores over 600: 16%; SAT math scores over 600: 22%; SAT writing scores over 600: 12%; ACT scores over 24: 42%; SAT critical reading scores over 700: 2%; SAT math scores over 700: 3%; SAT writing scores over 700: 3%; ACT scores over 30: 7%.

Retention: 79% of full-time freshmen returned.

FACULTY

Total: 409, 24% full-time, 38% with terminal degrees.

Student/faculty ratio: 18:1.

ACADEMICS

Calendar: semesters. *Degrees:* associate, bachelor's, master's, and doctoral (associate's degree for international students only).

Special study options: academic remediation for entering students, accelerated degree program, adult/continuing education programs, advanced placement credit, distance learning, double majors, honors programs, independent study, internships, off-campus study, part-time degree program, services for LD students, study abroad, summer session for credit.

Computers: 64 computers/terminals are available on campus for general student use. Students can access the following: computer help desk, free student e-mail accounts, online (class) grades, online (class) registration, online (class) schedules. Campuswide network is available. 100% of college-owned or -operated housing units are wired for high-speed Internet access. Wireless service is available via entire campus.

STUDENT LIFE

Housing options: coed, women-only, special housing for students with disabilities. Campus housing is university owned. Freshman campus housing is guaranteed.

Activities and organizations: drama/theater group, student-run newspaper, choral group, intramurals, Screaming Eagles, Lacrosse, Abbey West, LEAD Student Activities.

Athletics Member NAIA. ***Intercollegiate sports:*** baseball M(s), basketball M(s)/W(s), cross-country running M(s)/W(s), lacrosse M(s)(c)/W(s)(c), soccer M(s)/W(s), softball W(s), swimming and diving M(s)/W(s), tennis M(s)/W(s), track and field M(s)/W(s), volleyball M(s)/W(s), water polo M(s)/W(s). ***Intramural sports:*** basketball M/W, bowling M/W, cheerleading M(c)/W(c), football M/W, soccer M/W, softball M/W, track and field M/W, ultimate Frisbee M/W, volleyball M/W.

Campus security: 24-hour emergency response devices and patrols, student patrols, late-night transport/escort service, lighted walkways, 24-hour dispatch.

Student services: health clinic, personal/psychological counseling.

COSTS & FINANCIAL AID

Costs (2015–16) ***Comprehensive fee:*** $41,580 includes full-time tuition ($31,040), mandatory fees ($650), and room and board ($9890). Full-time tuition and fees vary according to course load. Part-time tuition: $925 per unit. Part-time tuition and fees vary according to course load. ***Required fees:*** $325 per term part-time. ***College room only:*** $5700. Room and board charges vary according to board plan and housing facility. ***Payment plan:*** installment. ***Waivers:*** employees or children of employees.

Financial Aid Of all full-time matriculated undergraduates who enrolled in 2014, 1,418 applied for aid, 1,210 were judged to have need, 157 had their need fully met. 60 Federal Work-Study jobs (averaging $2145). In 2014, 280 non-need-based awards were made. ***Average percent of need met:*** 60. ***Average financial aid package:*** $18,883. ***Average need-based loan:*** $4445. ***Average need-based gift aid:*** $15,811. ***Average non-need-based aid:*** $8409. ***Average indebtedness upon graduation:*** $28,072. ***Financial aid deadline:*** 3/2.

APPLYING

Standardized Tests *Required:* SAT or ACT (for admission).

Options: electronic application, early action, deferred entrance.

Application fee: $50.

Required: essay or personal statement, high school transcript, 1 letter of recommendation. ***Recommended:*** minimum 2.8 GPA, interview.

Application deadlines: rolling (freshmen), rolling (transfers), 12/1 (early action).

Notification: continuous (freshmen), continuous (transfers), 12/15 (early action).

CONTACT

Mr. Doug Wible, Director of Undergraduate Admissions, Concordia University, 1530 Concordia West, Irvine, CA 92612-3299. *Phone:* 800-229-1200. *Toll-free phone:* 800-229-1200. *Fax:* 949-214-3520. *E-mail:* admission@cui.edu.

Design Institute of San Diego

San Diego, California

http://www.disd.edu/

- **Proprietary** 4-year, founded 1977
- **Urban** campus with easy access to San Diego
- **Coed** 171 undergraduate students, 62% full-time, 91% women, 9% men

UNDERGRAD STUDENTS

106 full-time, 65 part-time. Students come from 30 states and territories; 7 other countries; 9% are from out of state; 5% Black or African American, non-Hispanic/Latino; 18% Hispanic/Latino; 7% Asian, non-Hispanic/Latino; 0.6% Race/ethnicity unknown; 8% international; 15% transferred in.

Freshmen

Admission: 9 enrolled.

Retention: 58% of full-time freshmen returned.

FACULTY
Total: 31, 13% full-time.
Student/faculty ratio: 12:1.

ACADEMICS
Calendar: semesters. *Degree:* bachelor's.
Special study options: internships, part-time degree program, services for LD students, study abroad, summer session for credit.
Computers: 61 computers/terminals are available on campus for general student use. Students can access the following: campus intranet, free student e-mail accounts, computer lab tutors and support from the IT Department. Campuswide network is available. Wireless service is available via classrooms, computer centers, computer labs.

STUDENT LIFE
Housing options: college housing not available.
Activities and organizations: ASID Student Chapter, IIDA Student Chapter, A Bridge for Kids non-profit organization Community Service Event, Student Mentor Program.
Campus security: Security Guard patrols during the semester from 5:30 - 10:30 pm Monday - Thursday. No classes on Friday past 5:00 pm.

COSTS
Costs (2014–15) ***Tuition:*** $20,400 full-time, $850 per credit part-time. Full-time tuition and fees vary according to course load. Part-time tuition and fees vary according to course load. ***Required fees:*** $5 per term part-time. ***Payment plans:*** installment, deferred payment.

APPLYING
Required: essay or personal statement, high school transcript, 2 letters of recommendation. ***Required for some:*** All previously attended College official transcripts must be submitted. ***Recommended:*** minimum 2.0 GPA, interview.

CONTACT
Mrs. Kairyn Haines, Director of Admission, Design Institute of San Diego, 8555 Commerce Avenue, San Diego, CA 92121. *Phone:* 858-566-1200 Ext. 1011. *Toll-free phone:* 800-619-4337. *Fax:* 858-566-2711. *E-mail:* admissions@disd.edu.

DeVry University
Alhambra, California
http://www.devry.edu/
- **Proprietary** comprehensive
- **Coed**

ACADEMICS
Degrees: associate, bachelor's, and master's.

COSTS
Costs (2014–15) ***Tuition:*** $17,052 full-time, $609 per credit hour part-time. ***Required fees:*** $80 full-time.

CONTACT
Admissions Office, DeVry University, 1000 S. Fremont Ave., Building A-11, Alhambra, CA 91803. *Phone:* 626-293-4300. *Toll-free phone:* 866-338-7941.

DeVry University
Anaheim, California
http://www.devry.edu/
- **Proprietary** comprehensive
- **Coed**

ACADEMICS
Degrees: associate, bachelor's, and master's.

COSTS
Costs (2014–15) ***Tuition:*** $17,052 full-time, $609 per credit hour part-time. ***Required fees:*** $80 full-time.

CONTACT
Admissions Office, DeVry University, 1900 South State College Boulevard, Suite 150, Anaheim, CA 92806-6136. *Phone:* 714-935-3200. *Toll-free phone:* 866-338-7941.

DeVry University
Bakersfield, California
http://www.devry.edu/
- **Proprietary** 4-year
- **Coed**

ACADEMICS
Degrees: associate and bachelor's.

COSTS
Costs (2014–15) ***Tuition:*** $17,052 full-time, $609 per credit hour part-time. ***Required fees:*** $80 full-time.

CONTACT
Admissions Office, DeVry University, 3000 Ming Avenue, Bakersfield, CA 93304-4136. *Phone:* 661-833-7120. *Toll-free phone:* 866-338-7941.

DeVry University
Fremont, California
http://www.devry.edu/
- **Proprietary** comprehensive, founded 1998
- **Suburban** campus with easy access to San Francisco
- **Coed**

ACADEMICS
Calendar: semesters. *Degrees:* associate, bachelor's, and master's.

COSTS & FINANCIAL AID
Costs (2014–15) ***Tuition:*** $17,052 full-time, $609 per credit hour part-time. ***Required fees:*** $80 full-time.
Financial Aid Of all full-time matriculated undergraduates who enrolled in 2007, 505 applied for aid, 483 were judged to have need, 6 had their need fully met. In 2007, 34 non-need-based awards were made. ***Average percent of need met:*** 37. ***Average financial aid package:*** $12,445. ***Average need-based loan:*** $7034. ***Average need-based gift aid:*** $7847. ***Average non-need-based aid:*** $17,920. ***Average indebtedness upon graduation:*** $70,191.

CONTACT
Admissions Office, DeVry University, 6600 Dumbarton Circle, Fremont, CA 94555. *Phone:* 510-574-1200. *Toll-free phone:* 866-338-7941.

DeVry University
Long Beach, California
http://www.devry.edu/
- **Proprietary** comprehensive, founded 1984, part of DeVry University
- **Urban** campus
- **Coed**

ACADEMICS
Calendar: semesters. *Degrees:* associate, bachelor's, and master's.

COSTS & FINANCIAL AID
Costs (2014–15) ***Tuition:*** $17,052 full-time, $609 per credit hour part-time. ***Required fees:*** $80 full-time.
Financial Aid Of all full-time matriculated undergraduates who enrolled in 2007, 221 applied for aid, 213 were judged to have need, 5 had their need fully met. In 2007, 14 non-need-based awards were made. ***Average percent of need met:*** 44. ***Average financial aid package:*** $14,244. ***Average need-based loan:*** $8555. ***Average need-based gift aid:*** $8196. ***Average non-need-based aid:*** $16,538. ***Average indebtedness upon graduation:*** $36,961.

CONTACT
Admissions Office, DeVry University, 3880 Kilroy Airport Way, Long Beach, CA 90806. *Phone:* 562-427-0861. *Toll-free phone:* 866-338-7941.

DeVry University
Oakland, California
http://www.devry.edu/
- **Proprietary** comprehensive
- **Coed**

ACADEMICS
Degrees: associate, bachelor's, and master's.

COSTS
Costs (2014–15) ***Tuition:*** $17,052 full-time, $609 per credit hour part-time. ***Required fees:*** $80 full-time.

CONTACT
Admissions Office, DeVry University, 505 14th Street, Suite 100, Oakland, CA 94612. *Phone:* 510-267-1340. *Toll-free phone:* 866-338-7941.

DeVry University
Oxnard, California
http://www.devry.edu/

- **Proprietary** comprehensive
- **Coed**

ACADEMICS
Calendar: semesters. *Degrees:* associate, bachelor's, and master's.

COSTS
Costs (2014–15) ***Tuition:*** $17,052 full-time, $609 per credit hour part-time. ***Required fees:*** $80 full-time.

CONTACT
Admissions Office, DeVry University, 300 E. Esplanade Drive, Suite 100, Oxnard, CA 93036. *Phone:* 805-604-3350. *Toll-free phone:* 866-338-7941.

DeVry University
Palmdale, California
http://www.devry.edu/

- **Proprietary** comprehensive, founded 1999, part of DeVry University
- **Suburban** campus
- **Coed**

ACADEMICS
Calendar: semesters. *Degrees:* associate, bachelor's, and master's.

COSTS & FINANCIAL AID
Costs (2014–15) ***Tuition:*** $17,052 full-time, $609 per credit hour part-time. ***Required fees:*** $80 full-time.

Financial Aid Of all full-time matriculated undergraduates who enrolled in 2002, 759 applied for aid, 711 were judged to have need, 20 had their need fully met. In 2002, 57 non-need-based awards were made. ***Average percent of need met:*** 42. ***Average financial aid package:*** $9557. ***Average need-based loan:*** $5887. ***Average need-based gift aid:*** $6070. ***Average non-need-based aid:*** $11,795.

CONTACT
Admissions Office, DeVry University, 39115 Trade Center Drive Suite 100, Palmdale, CA 93551. *Phone:* 661-224-2920. *Toll-free phone:* 866-338-7941.

DeVry University
Pomona, California
http://www.devry.edu/

- **Proprietary** comprehensive, founded 1983, part of DeVry University
- **Urban** campus
- **Coed** 1,501 undergraduate students, 38% full-time, 43% women, 57% men
- **Minimally difficult** entrance level

UNDERGRAD STUDENTS
574 full-time, 927 part-time. 4% are from out of state; 9% Black or African American, non-Hispanic/Latino; 40% Hispanic/Latino; 8% Asian, non-Hispanic/Latino; 2% Native Hawaiian or other Pacific Islander, non-Hispanic/Latino; 0.7% American Indian or Alaska Native, non-Hispanic/Latino; 2% Two or more races, non-Hispanic/Latino; 9% Race/ethnicity unknown; 1% international; 26% transferred in.

Freshmen
Admission: 79 enrolled.

FACULTY
Total: 96, 21% full-time.
Student/faculty ratio: 22:1.

ACADEMICS
Calendar: semesters. *Degrees:* associate, bachelor's, master's, and postbachelor's certificates.
Special study options: adult/continuing education programs, part-time degree program.
Computers: Students can access the following: online (class) registration.

STUDENT LIFE
Housing options: college housing not available.

COSTS
Costs (2014–15) ***Tuition:*** $17,052 full-time, $609 per credit hour part-time. ***Required fees:*** $80 full-time.

APPLYING
Application fee: $40.
Required: high school transcript, interview.

CONTACT
DeVry University, 901 Corporate Center Drive, Pomona, CA 91768-2642. *Phone:* 909-622-8866. *Toll-free phone:* 866-338-7941.

DeVry University
San Diego, California
http://www.devry.edu/

- **Proprietary** comprehensive
- **Coed**

ACADEMICS
Calendar: semesters. *Degrees:* associate, bachelor's, and master's.

COSTS
Costs (2014–15) ***Tuition:*** $17,052 full-time, $609 per credit hour part-time. ***Required fees:*** $80 full-time.

CONTACT
Admissions Office, DeVry University, 2655 Camino Del Rio North, Suite 350, San Diego, CA 92108-1633. *Phone:* 619-683-2446. *Toll-free phone:* 866-338-7941.

DeVry University
Sherman Oaks, California
http://www.devry.edu/

- **Proprietary** comprehensive
- **Coed**

ACADEMICS
Degrees: associate, bachelor's, and master's.

COSTS & FINANCIAL AID
Costs (2014–15) ***Tuition:*** $17,052 full-time, $609 per credit hour part-time. ***Required fees:*** $80 full-time.

Financial Aid Of all full-time matriculated undergraduates who enrolled in 2007, 120 applied for aid, 108 were judged to have need, 4 had their need fully met. In 2007, 19 non-need-based awards were made. ***Average percent of need met:*** 39. ***Average financial aid package:*** $11,834. ***Average need-based loan:*** $8480. ***Average need-based gift aid:*** $6691. ***Average non-need-based aid:*** $17,847. ***Average indebtedness upon graduation:*** $31,200.

CONTACT
Admissions Office, DeVry University, 15301 Ventura Boulevard, D-100, Sherman Oaks, CA 91403. *Phone:* 818-713-8111. *Toll-free phone:* 866-338-7941.

★ Dominican University of California

San Rafael, California

http://www.dominican.edu/

- **Independent** comprehensive, founded 1890, affiliated with Roman Catholic Church
- **Suburban** 85-acre campus with easy access to San Francisco
- **Endowment** $34.8 million
- **Coed** 1,478 undergraduate students, 82% full-time, 74% women, 26% men
- **Moderately difficult** entrance level, 81% of applicants were admitted

UNDERGRAD STUDENTS

1,213 full-time, 265 part-time. Students come from 31 states and territories; 11 other countries; 2% are from out of state; 4% Black or African American, non-Hispanic/Latino; 21% Hispanic/Latino; 20% Asian, non-Hispanic/Latino; 1% Native Hawaiian or other Pacific Islander, non-Hispanic/Latino; 0.4% American Indian or Alaska Native, non-Hispanic/Latino; 4% Two or more races, non-Hispanic/Latino; 16% Race/ethnicity unknown; 1% international; 6% transferred in; 35% live on campus.

Freshmen

Admission: 2,076 applied, 1,680 admitted, 262 enrolled. ***Average high school GPA:*** 3.25. ***Test scores:*** SAT critical reading scores over 500: 65%; SAT math scores over 500: 66%; SAT writing scores over 500: 67%; ACT scores over 18: 93%; SAT critical reading scores over 600: 13%; SAT math scores over 600: 18%; SAT writing scores over 600: 16%; ACT scores over 24: 38%; SAT critical reading scores over 700: 1%; SAT writing scores over 700: 1%; ACT scores over 30: 2%.

Retention: 82% of full-time freshmen returned.

FACULTY

Total: 326, 31% full-time, 36% with terminal degrees.

Student/faculty ratio: 9:1.

ACADEMICS

Calendar: semesters. *Degrees:* bachelor's and master's.

Special study options: accelerated degree program, adult/continuing education programs, distance learning, double majors, external degree program, honors programs, independent study, internships, part-time degree program, student-designed majors, study abroad.

Unusual degree programs: 3-2 occupational therapy.

Computers: 195 computers/terminals and 700 ports are available on campus for general student use. Students can access the following: computer help desk, free student e-mail accounts, online (class) grades, online (class) registration, online (class) schedules, Microsoft Office Applications (Word, Excel, PowerPoint). Campuswide network is available. 100% of college-owned or -operated housing units are wired for high-speed Internet access. Wireless service is available via entire campus.

STUDENT LIFE

Housing options: coed, special housing for students with disabilities. Campus housing is university owned. Freshman applicants given priority for college housing.

Activities and organizations: drama/theater group, student-run newspaper, radio station, choral group, Filipino Cultural Club, BSU, Perceptions, Global Ambassadors, Intramural Club/Programming.

Athletics Member NCAA. All Division II. ***Intercollegiate sports:*** basketball M(s)/W(s), cross-country running M(s)/W(s), golf M(s)/W(s), lacrosse M(s), soccer M(s)/W(s), softball W(s), tennis W(s), volleyball W(s). ***Intramural sports:*** badminton M/W, bowling M/W, cheerleading W, sailing M/W, skiing (downhill) M/W, soccer M/W, softball M/W, table tennis M/W, tennis M/W, ultimate Frisbee M/W, volleyball M/W, weight lifting M/W.

Campus security: 24-hour patrols, late-night transport/escort service, controlled dormitory access, 24-hour security on campus accessible by phone.

Student services: health clinic, personal/psychological counseling.

COSTS & FINANCIAL AID

Costs (2015–16) ***Comprehensive fee:*** $55,930 includes full-time tuition ($42,100), mandatory fees ($450), and room and board ($13,380). Full-time tuition and fees vary according to course load. Part-time tuition: $1760 per credit. Part-time tuition and fees vary according to course load.

Required fees: $150 per term part-time. ***College room only:*** $7880. Room and board charges vary according to board plan. ***Payment plan:*** installment. ***Waivers:*** employees or children of employees.

Financial Aid Of all full-time matriculated undergraduates who enrolled in 2012, 1,260 applied for aid, 1,152 were judged to have need, 90 had their need fully met. In 2012, 220 non-need-based awards were made. ***Average percent of need met:*** 62. ***Average financial aid package:*** $25,404. ***Average need-based loan:*** $4263. ***Average need-based gift aid:*** $20,883. ***Average non-need-based aid:*** $11,575.

APPLYING

Standardized Tests *Required:* SAT or ACT (for admission).

Options: electronic application, deferred entrance.

Required: essay or personal statement, high school transcript, 1 letter of recommendation. ***Recommended:*** interview.

Application deadlines: 2/1 (freshmen), 2/1 (transfers).

Notification: continuous (freshmen), continuous (transfers).

CONTACT

Ms. Nichelle Passanisi, Director of Undergraduate Admissions, Dominican University of California, 50 Acacia Avenue, San Rafael, CA 94901-2298. *Phone:* 415-485-3206. *Toll-free phone:* 888-323-6763. *Fax:* 415-485-3214. *E-mail:* nichelle.passanisi@dominican.edu.

See previous page for display ad and page 1420 for the College Close-Up.

★ FIDM/Fashion Institute of Design & Merchandising, Los Angeles Campus

Los Angeles, California

http://www.fidm.edu/

- **Proprietary** primarily 2-year, founded 1969, part of The Fashion Institute of Design and Merchandising/FIDM
- **Urban** campus
- **Coed** 3,142 undergraduate students, 88% full-time, 90% women, 10% men
- **Moderately difficult** entrance level, 52% of applicants were admitted

UNDERGRAD STUDENTS

2,773 full-time, 369 part-time. Students come from 65 other countries; 32% are from out of state; 6% Black or African American, non-Hispanic/Latino; 23% Hispanic/Latino; 12% Asian, non-Hispanic/Latino; 0.7% Native Hawaiian or other Pacific Islander, non-Hispanic/Latino; 0.4% American Indian or Alaska Native, non-Hispanic/Latino; 3% Two or more races, non-Hispanic/Latino; 7% Race/ethnicity unknown; 14% international; 16% transferred in; 10% live on campus.

Freshmen

Admission: 1,348 applied, 698 admitted, 446 enrolled.

Retention: 96% of full-time freshmen returned.

FACULTY

Total: 275, 27% full-time.

Student/faculty ratio: 21:1.

ACADEMICS

Calendar: quarters. *Degrees:* associate and bachelor's (also includes Orange County Campus).

Special study options: academic remediation for entering students, adult/continuing education programs, advanced placement credit, cooperative education, distance learning, English as a second language, independent study, internships, part-time degree program, services for LD students, study abroad, summer session for credit.

Computers: Students can access the following: campus intranet, online (class) grades, online (class) registration, online (class) schedules. Campuswide network is available. Wireless service is available via computer centers, learning centers, libraries, student centers.

STUDENT LIFE
Housing options: coed, men-only, women-only. Campus housing is leased by the school.

Activities and organizations: Cross-Cultural Student Alliance, Fashion Industry Club, Phi Theta Kappa Honor Society, Student Council, MODE.

Campus security: 24-hour emergency response devices and patrols, late-night transport/escort service.

Student services: personal/psychological counseling.

COSTS & FINANCIAL AID
Costs (2014–15) ***Tuition:*** $28,965 full-time. Full-time tuition and fees vary according to course load and program. Part-time tuition and fees vary according to course load and program. ***Required fees:*** $965 full-time. ***Payment plan:*** installment. ***Waivers:*** employees or children of employees.

Financial Aid Of all full-time matriculated undergraduates who enrolled in 2013, 88 Federal Work-Study jobs (averaging $2935).

APPLYING
Standardized Tests *Recommended:* SAT or ACT (for admission).

Options: electronic application, deferred entrance.

Application fee: $225.

Required: essay or personal statement, high school transcript, minimum 2.0 GPA, 3 letters of recommendation, interview, major-determined project.

Application deadlines: rolling (freshmen), rolling (out-of-state freshmen), rolling (transfers).

CONTACT
Ms. Susan Aronson, Director of Admissions, FIDM/Fashion Institute of Design & Merchandising, Los Angeles Campus, Los Angeles, CA 90015. *Phone:* 213-624-1201. *Toll-free phone:* 800-624-1200. *Fax:* 213-624-4799. *E-mail:* saronson@fidm.com.

See previous page for display ad and page 1442 for the College Close-Up.

FIDM/Fashion Institute of Design & Merchandising, San Francisco Campus

San Francisco, California

http://www.fidm.edu/

- **Proprietary** primarily 2-year, founded 1973, part of The Fashion Institute of Design and Merchandising/FIDM
- **Urban** campus
- **Coed** 527 undergraduate students, 88% full-time, 92% women, 8% men
- **Moderately difficult** entrance level, 54% of applicants were admitted

UNDERGRAD STUDENTS
463 full-time, 64 part-time. Students come from 14 other countries; 7% are from out of state; 3% Black or African American, non-Hispanic/Latino; 24% Hispanic/Latino; 19% Asian, non-Hispanic/Latino; 2% Native Hawaiian or other Pacific Islander, non-Hispanic/Latino; 0.8% American Indian or Alaska Native, non-Hispanic/Latino; 4% Two or more races, non-Hispanic/Latino; 6% Race/ethnicity unknown; 6% international; 19% transferred in.

Freshmen
Admission: 258 applied, 139 admitted, 99 enrolled. ***Test scores:*** ACT scores over 18: 100%; ACT scores over 24: 40%; ACT scores over 30: 10%.

Retention: 89% of full-time freshmen returned.

FACULTY
Total: 62, 19% full-time.

Student/faculty ratio: 17:1.

ACADEMICS
Calendar: quarters. *Degrees:* associate and bachelor's.

Special study options: academic remediation for entering students, adult/continuing education programs, advanced placement credit, cooperative education, distance learning, English as a second language, honors programs, independent study, internships, off-campus study, part-time degree program, services for LD students, study abroad, summer session for credit.

Computers: Students can access the following: campus intranet, online (class) grades, online (class) registration, online (class) schedules. Campuswide network is available. Wireless service is available via computer centers, libraries, student centers.

STUDENT LIFE
Housing options: college housing not available.

Activities and organizations: MODE, Student Council, Phi Theta Kappa- National Honor Society, Fashion Industry Club, Cross-Cultural Student Alliance.

Campus security: 24-hour emergency response devices and patrols.

Student services: personal/psychological counseling.

COSTS
Costs (2014–15) ***Tuition:*** $28,965 full-time. Full-time tuition and fees vary according to course load and program. Part-time tuition and fees vary according to course load and program. ***Required fees:*** $965 full-time. ***Payment plan:*** installment. ***Waivers:*** employees or children of employees.

APPLYING
Standardized Tests *Recommended:* SAT or ACT (for admission).

Options: electronic application, deferred entrance.

Application fee: $225.

Required: essay or personal statement, high school transcript, 3 letters of recommendation, interview, major-determined project.

Application deadlines: rolling (freshmen), rolling (out-of-state freshmen), rolling (transfers).

CONTACT
Ms. Susan Aronson, Director of Admissions, FIDM/Fashion Institute of Design & Merchandising, San Francisco Campus, San Francisco, CA 94108. *Phone:* 213-624-1201. *Toll-free phone:* 800-422-3436. *Fax:* 415-296-7299. *E-mail:* info@fidm.com.

Fresno Pacific University

Fresno, California

http://www.fresno.edu/

- **Independent** comprehensive, founded 1944, affiliated with Mennonite Brethren Church
- **Suburban** 50-acre campus with easy access to Fresno
- **Coed**
- **Moderately difficult** entrance level

FACULTY
Student/faculty ratio: 13:1.

ACADEMICS
Calendar: semesters. *Degrees:* certificates, associate, bachelor's, master's, and postbachelor's certificates.

STUDENT LIFE
Housing options: on-campus residence required through junior year; men-only, women-only, special housing for students with disabilities. Campus housing is university owned and leased by the school. Freshman campus housing is guaranteed.

Activities and organizations: drama/theater group, student-run newspaper, choral group.

Athletics Member NCAA. All Division II.

Campus security: 24-hour emergency response devices and patrols, student patrols, late-night transport/escort service, controlled dormitory access, 24-hour monitored closed-circuit security cameras.

Student services: health clinic, personal/psychological counseling.

COSTS & FINANCIAL AID
Costs (2014–15) ***Comprehensive fee:*** $33,998 includes full-time tuition ($26,250), mandatory fees ($388), and room and board ($7360). Full-time tuition and fees vary according to course level, degree level, and program.

Part-time tuition: $938 per unit. Part-time tuition and fees vary according to course level, degree level, and program. ***Required fees:*** $194 per term part-time. ***College room only:*** $2700. Room and board charges vary according to board plan and housing facility.

Financial Aid Of all full-time matriculated undergraduates who enrolled in 2012, 1,968 applied for aid, 1,875 were judged to have need, 112 had their need fully met. In 2012, 167 non-need-based awards were made. ***Average percent of need met:*** 55. ***Average financial aid package:*** $14,778. ***Average need-based loan:*** $4460. ***Average need-based gift aid:*** $8002. ***Average non-need-based aid:*** $9329. ***Average indebtedness upon graduation:*** $21,992.

APPLYING

Standardized Tests *Required:* SAT or ACT (for admission).

Options: electronic application, early admission, deferred entrance.

Application fee: $40.

Required: essay or personal statement, high school transcript, 1 letter of recommendation. ***Required for some:*** interview. ***Recommended:*** minimum 3.1 GPA.

CONTACT

Andy Johnson, Director of Undergraduate Admissions, Fresno Pacific University, 1717 South Chestnut Avenue, Fresno, CA 93727. *Phone:* 559-453-2000. *Toll-free phone:* 800-660-6089. *Fax:* 559-453-2007. *E-mail:* andy.johnson@fresno.edu.

Harvey Mudd College

Claremont, California

http://www.hmc.edu/

- **Independent** 4-year, founded 1955, part of The Claremont Colleges Consortium
- **Suburban** 33-acre campus with easy access to Los Angeles
- **Endowment** $283.7 million
- **Coed** 804 undergraduate students, 100% full-time, 46% women, 54% men
- **Most difficult** entrance level, 14% of applicants were admitted

UNDERGRAD STUDENTS

802 full-time, 2 part-time. Students come from 41 states and territories; 24 other countries; 50% are from out of state; 2% Black or African American, non-Hispanic/Latino; 10% Hispanic/Latino; 21% Asian, non-Hispanic/Latino; 0.4% American Indian or Alaska Native, non-Hispanic/Latino; 6% Two or more races, non-Hispanic/Latino; 5% Race/ethnicity unknown; 12% international; 0.1% transferred in; 99% live on campus.

Freshmen

Admission: 3,678 applied, 524 admitted, 194 enrolled. ***Test scores:*** SAT critical reading scores over 500: 100%; SAT math scores over 500: 100%; SAT writing scores over 500: 89%; ACT scores over 18: 100%; SAT critical reading scores over 600: 98%; SAT math scores over 600: 100%; SAT writing scores over 600: 86%; ACT scores over 24: 100%; SAT critical reading scores over 700: 68%; SAT math scores over 700: 93%; SAT writing scores over 700: 57%; ACT scores over 30: 94%.

FACULTY

Total: 107, 87% full-time, 100% with terminal degrees.

Student/faculty ratio: 8:1.

ACADEMICS

Calendar: semesters. *Degree:* bachelor's.

Special study options: double majors, internships, off-campus study, services for LD students, student-designed majors, study abroad. ***ROTC:*** Army (c), Air Force (b).

Unusual degree programs: 3-2 engineering; economics/engineering with Claremont McKenna College and /engineering with Scripps College.

Computers: 120 computers/terminals and 860 ports are available on campus for general student use. Students can access the following: campus intranet, computer help desk, free student e-mail accounts, online (class) grades, online (class) registration, online (class) schedules. Campuswide network is available. 100% of college-owned or -operated housing units are wired for high-speed Internet access. Wireless service is available via entire campus.

STUDENT LIFE

Housing options: on-campus residence required for freshman year; coed. Campus housing is university owned. Freshman campus housing is guaranteed.

Activities and organizations: drama/theater group, student-run newspaper, radio station, choral group, Claremont Colleges Ballroom Dance Company, Science Bus, Society of Women Engineers (SWE), Intervarsity Christian Fellowship, Gonzo Unicycle Madness (Unicycle Club).

Athletics Member NCAA. All Division III. ***Intercollegiate sports:*** baseball M, basketball M/W, cross-country running M/W, football M, golf M/W, lacrosse W, soccer M/W, softball W, swimming and diving M/W, tennis M/W, track and field M/W, volleyball W, water polo M/W. ***Intramural sports:*** basketball M/W, bowling M/W, equestrian sports M(c)/W(c), fencing M(c)/W(c), football M/W, lacrosse M(c), rugby M(c)/W(c), soccer M/W, tennis M/W, ultimate Frisbee M(c)/W(c), volleyball M(c)/W, water polo M/W.

Campus security: 24-hour emergency response devices and patrols, late-night transport/escort service, controlled dormitory access.

Student services: health clinic, personal/psychological counseling, women's center.

COSTS & FINANCIAL AID

Costs (2014–15) ***One-time required fee:*** $100. ***Comprehensive fee:*** $64,427 includes full-time tuition ($48,315), mandatory fees ($279), and room and board ($15,833). Part-time tuition: $1510 per unit. Part-time tuition and fees vary according to course load. ***College room only:*** $8494. Room and board charges vary according to board plan. ***Payment plan:*** installment. ***Waivers:*** employees or children of employees.

Financial Aid Of all full-time matriculated undergraduates who enrolled in 2013, 495 applied for aid, 422 were judged to have need, 422 had their need fully met. 157 Federal Work-Study jobs (averaging $574). 28 state and other part-time jobs (averaging $5785). In 2013, 178 non-need-based awards were made. ***Average percent of need met:*** 100. ***Average financial aid package:*** $38,557. ***Average need-based loan:*** $5039. ***Average need-based gift aid:*** $35,558. ***Average non-need-based aid:*** $10,546. ***Average indebtedness upon graduation:*** $24,503. ***Financial aid deadline:*** 2/1.

APPLYING

Standardized Tests *Required:* SAT or ACT (for admission), SAT Subject Tests (for admission), SAT or ACT and the SAT Subject Test in Math 2 and a second SAT Subject exam (for admission).

Options: electronic application, early admission, early decision, deferred entrance.

Application fee: $70.

Required: essay or personal statement, high school transcript, 3 letters of recommendation. ***Recommended:*** interview.

Application deadlines: 1/1 (freshmen), 4/1 (transfers).

Early decision deadline: 11/15 (for plan 1), 1/1 (for plan 2).

Notification: 4/1 (freshmen), 5/15 (transfers), 12/15 (early decision plan 1), 2/15 (early decision plan 2).

CONTACT

Peter Osgood, Director of Admission, Harvey Mudd College, 301 Platt Boulevard, Claremont, CA 91711. *Phone:* 909-621-8011. *Fax:* 909-607-7046. *E-mail:* admission@hmc.edu.

Henley-Putnam University

Santa Clara, California

http://www.henley-putnam.edu/

- **Proprietary** comprehensive, founded 1991
- **Coed**

ACADEMICS

Degrees: certificates, bachelor's, master's, and doctoral (offers only online degree programs).

Special study options: adult/continuing education programs, external degree program, part-time degree program.

Computers: Students can access the following: campus intranet, computer help desk, free student e-mail accounts, online courses. Campuswide network is available.

APPLYING
Options: electronic application.
Required for some: essay or personal statement, high school transcript, interview, official transcripts from all colleges and universities attended; background checks.
Application deadlines: rolling (freshmen), rolling (out-of-state freshmen), rolling (transfers).

CONTACT
Henley-Putnam University, 2804 Mission College Boulevard, Suite 240, Santa Clara, CA 95054. *Phone:* 408-453-9900 Ext. 9928. *Toll-free phone:* 88-852-8746 (in-state); 888-852-8746 (out-of-state).

Holy Names University
Oakland, California
http://www.hnu.edu/

- **Independent Roman Catholic** comprehensive, founded 1868
- **Urban** 60-acre campus with easy access to San Francisco
- **Coed**
- **Moderately difficult** entrance level

FACULTY
Student/faculty ratio: 10:1.

ACADEMICS
Calendar: semesters. *Degrees:* certificates, bachelor's, master's, post-master's, and postbachelor's certificates.

STUDENT LIFE
Housing options: coed. Campus housing is university owned. Freshman campus housing is guaranteed.
Activities and organizations: drama/theater group, choral group, Drama Club, Latinos Unidos, Black Student Union, Biology Club, Hiking Club.
Athletics Member NCAA. All Division II.
Campus security: 24-hour emergency response devices, late-night transport/escort service, controlled dormitory access, 24-hour security main gate.
Student services: personal/psychological counseling.

COSTS & FINANCIAL AID
Costs (2014–15) ***Comprehensive fee:*** $45,402 includes full-time tuition ($34,058), mandatory fees ($430), and room and board ($10,914). Full-time tuition and fees vary according to course level, course load, degree level, program, and reciprocity agreements. Part-time tuition: $1160 per unit. Part-time tuition and fees vary according to course level, course load, degree level, program, and reciprocity agreements. ***Required fees:*** $215 per term part-time. ***College room only:*** $5736. Room and board charges vary according to board plan and housing facility.
Financial Aid Of all full-time matriculated undergraduates who enrolled in 2006, 373 applied for aid, 247 were judged to have need, 58 had their need fully met. 50 Federal Work-Study jobs (averaging $1699). 53 state and other part-time jobs (averaging $1750). In 2006, 77 non-need-based awards were made. ***Average percent of need met:*** 43. ***Average financial aid package:*** $15,554. ***Average need-based loan:*** $4154. ***Average need-based gift aid:*** $13,258. ***Average non-need-based aid:*** $10,557. ***Average indebtedness upon graduation:*** $10,500. ***Financial aid deadline:*** 6/30.

APPLYING
Standardized Tests *Required:* SAT or ACT (for admission).
Options: electronic application, deferred entrance.
Application fee: $20.
Required: essay or personal statement, high school transcript, 1 letter of recommendation, 1 recommendation minimum, 3 maximum. Letters must be in English. ***Required for some:*** interview.

CONTACT
Holy Names University, 3500 Mountain Boulevard, Oakland, CA 94619-1699. *Phone:* 510-436-1124. *Toll-free phone:* 800-430-1321.

Hope International University
Fullerton, California
http://www.hiu.edu/

- **Independent** comprehensive, founded 1928, affiliated with Christian Churches and Churches of Christ
- **Suburban** 16-acre campus with easy access to Los Angeles
- **Endowment** $6.3 million
- **Coed** 819 undergraduate students, 79% full-time, 55% women, 45% men
- **Moderately difficult** entrance level, 31% of applicants were admitted

UNDERGRAD STUDENTS
648 full-time, 171 part-time. Students come from 44 states and territories; 7 other countries; 8% are from out of state; 6% Black or African American, non-Hispanic/Latino; 20% Hispanic/Latino; 3% Asian, non-Hispanic/Latino; 1% Native Hawaiian or other Pacific Islander, non-Hispanic/Latino; 0.5% American Indian or Alaska Native, non-Hispanic/Latino; 11% Two or more races, non-Hispanic/Latino; 21% Race/ethnicity unknown; 0.4% international; 7% transferred in; 46% live on campus.

Freshmen
Admission: 635 applied, 196 admitted, 94 enrolled. ***Average high school GPA:*** 3.04. ***Test scores:*** SAT critical reading scores over 500: 26%; SAT math scores over 500: 22%; ACT scores over 18: 52%; SAT critical reading scores over 600: 1%; SAT math scores over 600: 3%; ACT scores over 24: 4%.
Retention: 80% of full-time freshmen returned.

FACULTY
Total: 254, 17% full-time, 33% with terminal degrees.
Student/faculty ratio: 10:1.

ACADEMICS
Calendar: 4-1-4. *Degrees:* certificates, associate, bachelor's, master's, and postbachelor's certificates.
Special study options: academic remediation for entering students, adult/continuing education programs, advanced placement credit, distance learning, double majors, English as a second language, independent study, internships, off-campus study, part-time degree program, services for LD students, study abroad. ***ROTC:*** Army (c).
Computers: 30 computers/terminals are available on campus for general student use. Students can access the following: computer help desk, free student e-mail accounts, online (class) grades, online (class) registration, online (class) schedules, 30 Internet hotspots on campus. Campuswide network is available. 100% of college-owned or -operated housing units are wired for high-speed Internet access. Wireless service is available via entire campus.

STUDENT LIFE
Housing options: on-campus residence required through sophomore year; men-only, women-only. Campus housing is university owned. Freshman campus housing is guaranteed.
Activities and organizations: drama/theater group, student-run newspaper, choral group, Campus Ministries, International Student Organization, Musical Theater, Student Government, Student Publications.
Athletics Member NAIA, NCCAA. ***Intercollegiate sports:*** basketball M(s)/W(s), cheerleading M/W, cross-country running M(s)/W(s), golf M(s)/W(s), soccer M(s)/W(s), softball W(s), tennis M(s)/W(s), track and field M(s)/W(s), volleyball M(s)/W(s). ***Intramural sports:*** table tennis M/W, ultimate Frisbee M/W, volleyball M/W.
Campus security: 24-hour emergency response devices and patrols, late-night transport/escort service, controlled dormitory access.
Student services: personal/psychological counseling.

COSTS & FINANCIAL AID
Costs (2015–16) ***Comprehensive fee:*** $37,600 includes full-time tuition ($27,900), mandatory fees ($650), and room and board ($9050). Full-time tuition and fees vary according to course level, course load, degree level, location, program, and reciprocity agreements. Part-time tuition: $1230 per unit. Part-time tuition and fees vary according to course level, course load, degree level, location, program, and reciprocity agreements. ***College room only:*** $4800. Room and board charges vary according to board plan.

Payment plan: installment. ***Waivers:*** employees or children of employees.

Financial Aid Of all full-time matriculated undergraduates who enrolled in 2013, 619 applied for aid, 589 were judged to have need, 49 had their need fully met. 53 Federal Work-Study jobs (averaging $2000). 87 state and other part-time jobs (averaging $2000). In 2013, 16 non-need-based awards were made. ***Average percent of need met:*** 52. ***Average financial aid package:*** $15,340. ***Average need-based loan:*** $4256. ***Average need-based gift aid:*** $8366. ***Average non-need-based aid:*** $10,875. ***Average indebtedness upon graduation:*** $24,091.

APPLYING

Standardized Tests *Required:* SAT or ACT (for admission).

Options: electronic application.

Application fee: $40.

Required: essay or personal statement, high school transcript, minimum 2.5 GPA, 2 letters of recommendation, rank in upper 50% of high school class. ***Required for some:*** interview.

Application deadlines: rolling (freshmen), rolling (out-of-state freshmen), rolling (transfers).

Notification: continuous (freshmen), continuous (out-of-state freshmen), continuous (transfers).

CONTACT

Ms. Midge Madden, Office Manager, Hope International University, 2500 East Nutwood Avenue, Fullerton, CA 92831-3138. *Phone:* 714-879-3901 Ext. 2240. *Toll-free phone:* 866-722-HOPE. *Fax:* 714-681-7423. *E-mail:* mfmadden@hiu.edu.

Humboldt State University

Arcata, California

http://www.humboldt.edu/

- **State-supported** comprehensive, founded 1913, part of California State University System
- **Rural** 161-acre campus
- **Endowment** $33.0 million
- **Coed** 7,962 undergraduate students, 94% full-time, 54% women, 46% men
- **Moderately difficult** entrance level, 77% of applicants were admitted

UNDERGRAD STUDENTS

7,446 full-time, 516 part-time. Students come from 49 states and territories; 21 other countries; 6% are from out of state; 4% Black or African American, non-Hispanic/Latino; 30% Hispanic/Latino; 3% Asian, non-Hispanic/Latino; 0.3% Native Hawaiian or other Pacific Islander, non-Hispanic/Latino; 1% American Indian or Alaska Native, non-Hispanic/Latino; 6% Two or more races, non-Hispanic/Latino; 7% Race/ethnicity unknown; 1% international; 12% transferred in; 26% live on campus.

Freshmen

Admission: 11,912 applied, 9,119 admitted, 1,386 enrolled. ***Average high school GPA:*** 3.2. ***Test scores:*** SAT critical reading scores over 500: 53%; SAT math scores over 500: 48%; SAT writing scores over 500: 46%; ACT scores over 18: 78%; SAT critical reading scores over 600: 16%; SAT math scores over 600: 11%; SAT writing scores over 600: 10%; ACT scores over 24: 28%; SAT critical reading scores over 700: 2%; SAT math scores over 700: 1%; SAT writing scores over 700: 1%; ACT scores over 30: 2%.

Retention: 74% of full-time freshmen returned.

FACULTY

Total: 570, 38% full-time, 47% with terminal degrees.

Student/faculty ratio: 24:1.

ACADEMICS

Calendar: semesters. *Degrees:* bachelor's, master's, post-master's, and postbachelor's certificates.

Special study options: academic remediation for entering students, adult/continuing education programs, advanced placement credit, cooperative education, distance learning, double majors, English as a second language, honors programs, independent study, internships, off-campus study, part-time degree program, services for LD students, student-designed majors, study abroad, summer session for credit.

Computers: 1,098 computers/terminals are available on campus for general student use. Students can access the following: computer help desk, free student e-mail accounts, online (class) grades, online (class) registration, online (class) schedules. Campuswide network is available. 100% of college-owned or -operated housing units are wired for high-speed Internet access. Wireless service is available via entire campus.

STUDENT LIFE

Housing options: coed. Campus housing is university owned. Freshman applicants given priority for college housing.

Activities and organizations: drama/theater group, student-run newspaper, radio station, choral group, marching band, Bicycle Learning Center, Campus Center for Appropriate Technology (CCAT), Youth Educational Services, HOLA, MECHA, national fraternities, national sororities.

Athletics Member NCAA. All Division II. ***Intercollegiate sports:*** basketball M(s)/W(s), cheerleading W(c), crew M(c)/W, cross-country running M(s)/W(s), football M(s), lacrosse M(c), soccer M(s)/W(s), softball W(s), track and field M(s)/W(s), volleyball W(s). ***Intramural sports:*** baseball M(c), basketball M/W, fencing M(c)/W(c), rugby M(c)/W(c), soccer M/W, ultimate Frisbee M(c)/W(c), volleyball M(c), water polo M(c).

Campus security: 24-hour emergency response devices and patrols, late-night transport/escort service, controlled dormitory access.

Student services: health clinic, personal/psychological counseling, women's center.

COSTS & FINANCIAL AID

Costs (2015–16) ***Tuition:*** state resident $7190 full-time, $372 per credit part-time; nonresident $18,350 full-time, $372 per credit part-time. Full-time tuition and fees vary according to degree level. Part-time tuition and fees vary according to course load and degree level. ***Required fees:*** $1266 per term part-time. ***Room and board:*** $12,114; room only: $7434. Room and board charges vary according to board plan and housing facility. ***Payment plan:*** installment. ***Waivers:*** employees or children of employees.

Financial Aid Of all full-time matriculated undergraduates who enrolled in 2013, 6,231 applied for aid, 5,529 were judged to have need, 409 had their need fully met. In 2013, 126 non-need-based awards were made. ***Average percent of need met:*** 70. ***Average financial aid package:*** $13,368. ***Average need-based loan:*** $6978. ***Average need-based gift aid:*** $7992. ***Average non-need-based aid:*** $357. ***Average indebtedness upon graduation:*** $19,351.

APPLYING

Standardized Tests *Required for some:* SAT or ACT (for admission).

Options: electronic application.

Application fee: $55.

Required: high school transcript, minimum 2.0 GPA.

Application deadlines: 11/30 (freshmen), 11/30 (out-of-state freshmen), 11/30 (transfers).

Notification: continuous (freshmen), continuous (out-of-state freshmen), continuous (transfers).

CONTACT

Mr. Steven Ladwig, Interim Director of Admissions, Humboldt State University, 1 Harpst Street, Arcata, CA 95521. *Phone:* 707-826-4402. *Toll-free phone:* 866-850-9556. *Fax:* 707-826-6190. *E-mail:* hsuinfo@humboldt.edu.

Interior Designers Institute

Newport Beach, California

http://www.idi.edu/

- **Proprietary** comprehensive, founded 1984
- **Suburban** 1-acre campus with easy access to Los Angeles, San Diego
- **Coed**

ACADEMICS

Degrees: certificates, associate, bachelor's, and master's.

APPLYING

Application fee: $95.

Required: high school transcript.

CONTACT
Interior Designers Institute, 1061 Camelback Road, Newport Beach, CA 92660.

ITT Technical Institute
Clovis, California
http://www.itt-tech.edu/

- **Proprietary** 4-year, founded 2005, part of ITT Educational Services, Inc.
- **Coed**
- **Minimally difficult** entrance level

ACADEMICS
Calendar: quarters. *Degrees:* associate and bachelor's.

STUDENT LIFE
Housing options: college housing not available.

CONTACT
Director of Recruitment, ITT Technical Institute, 362 N. Clovis Avenue, Clovis, CA 93612. *Phone:* 559-325-5400. *Toll-free phone:* 800-564-9771.

ITT Technical Institute
Concord, California
http://www.itt-tech.edu/

- **Proprietary** 4-year, part of ITT Educational Services, Inc.
- **Coed**
- **Minimally difficult** entrance level

ACADEMICS
Calendar: quarters. *Degrees:* associate and bachelor's.

CONTACT
Director of Recruitment, ITT Technical Institute, 1140 Galaxy Way, Suite 400, Concord, CA 94520. *Phone:* 925-674-8200. *Toll-free phone:* 800-211-7062.

ITT Technical Institute
Corona, California
http://www.itt-tech.edu/

- **Proprietary** 4-year
- **Coed**
- **Minimally difficult** entrance level

ACADEMICS
Degrees: associate and bachelor's.

CONTACT
Director of Recruitment, ITT Technical Institute, 4160 Temescal Canyon Road, Suite 100, Corona, CA 92883. *Phone:* 951-277-5400. *Toll-free phone:* 877-764-9661.

ITT Technical Institute
Culver City, California
http://www.itt-tech.edu/

- **Proprietary** primarily 2-year, part of ITT Educational Services, Inc.
- **Coed**

ACADEMICS
Calendar: quarters. *Degrees:* associate and bachelor's.

CONTACT
Director of Recruitment, ITT Technical Institute, 6101 W. Centinela Avenue, Suite 180, Culver City, CA 90230. *Phone:* 310-417-5800. *Toll-free phone:* 800-215-6151.

ITT Technical Institute
Lathrop, California
http://www.itt-tech.edu/

- **Proprietary** primarily 2-year, founded 1997, part of ITT Educational Services, Inc.
- **Coed**
- **Minimally difficult** entrance level

ACADEMICS
Calendar: quarters. *Degrees:* associate and bachelor's.

STUDENT LIFE
Housing options: college housing not available.

CONTACT
Director of Recruitment, ITT Technical Institute, 16916 South Harlan Road, Lathrop, CA 95330. *Phone:* 209-858-0077. *Toll-free phone:* 800-346-1786.

ITT Technical Institute
National City, California
http://www.itt-tech.edu/

- **Proprietary** primarily 2-year, founded 1981, part of ITT Educational Services, Inc.
- **Suburban** campus
- **Coed**
- **Minimally difficult** entrance level

ACADEMICS
Calendar: quarters. *Degrees:* associate and bachelor's.

STUDENT LIFE
Housing options: college housing not available.

CONTACT
Director of Recruitment, ITT Technical Institute, 401 Mile of Cars Way, National City, CA 91950. *Phone:* 619-327-1800. *Toll-free phone:* 800-883-0380.

ITT Technical Institute
Oakland, California
http://www.itt-tech.edu/

- **Proprietary** primarily 2-year, part of ITT Educational Services, Inc.
- **Coed**

ACADEMICS
Calendar: quarters. *Degrees:* associate and bachelor's.

CONTACT
Director of Recruitment, ITT Technical Institute, 7901 Oakport Street, Suite 3000, Oakland, CA 94621. *Phone:* 510-553-2800. *Toll-free phone:* 877-442-5833.

ITT Technical Institute
Orange, California
http://www.itt-tech.edu/

- **Proprietary** primarily 2-year, founded 1982, part of ITT Educational Services, Inc.
- **Suburban** campus
- **Coed**
- **Minimally difficult** entrance level

ACADEMICS
Calendar: quarters. *Degrees:* associate and bachelor's.

STUDENT LIFE
Housing options: college housing not available.

FINANCIAL AID
Financial Aid Of all full-time matriculated undergraduates who enrolled in 2013, 20 Federal Work-Study jobs (averaging $5000).

CONTACT
Director of Recruitment, ITT Technical Institute, 4000 West Metropolitan Drive, Suite 100, Orange, CA 92868. *Phone:* 714-941-2400.

ITT Technical Institute
Oxnard, California
http://www.itt-tech.edu/

- **Proprietary** primarily 2-year, founded 1993, part of ITT Educational Services, Inc.
- **Urban** campus
- **Coed**
- **Minimally difficult** entrance level

ACADEMICS
Calendar: quarters. *Degrees:* associate and bachelor's.

STUDENT LIFE
Housing options: college housing not available.

CONTACT
Director of Recruitment, ITT Technical Institute, 2051 Solar Drive, Suite 150, Oxnard, CA 93036. *Phone:* 805-988-0143. *Toll-free phone:* 800-530-1582.

ITT Technical Institute
Rancho Cordova, California
http://www.itt-tech.edu/

- **Proprietary** primarily 2-year, founded 1954, part of ITT Educational Services, Inc.
- **Urban** campus
- **Coed**
- **Minimally difficult** entrance level

ACADEMICS
Calendar: quarters. *Degrees:* associate and bachelor's.

STUDENT LIFE
Housing options: college housing not available.

CONTACT
Director of Recruitment, ITT Technical Institute, 10863 Gold Center Drive, Rancho Cordova, CA 95670-6034. *Phone:* 916-851-3900. *Toll-free phone:* 800-488-8466.

ITT Technical Institute
San Bernardino, California
http://www.itt-tech.edu/

- **Proprietary** primarily 2-year, founded 1987, part of ITT Educational Services, Inc.
- **Urban** campus
- **Coed**
- **Minimally difficult** entrance level

ACADEMICS
Calendar: quarters. *Degrees:* associate and bachelor's.

STUDENT LIFE
Housing options: college housing not available.

CONTACT
Director of Recruitment, ITT Technical Institute, 670 East Carnegie Drive, San Bernardino, CA 92408. *Phone:* 909-806-4600. *Toll-free phone:* 800-888-3801.

ITT Technical Institute
San Dimas, California
http://www.itt-tech.edu/

- **Proprietary** primarily 2-year, founded 1982, part of ITT Educational Services, Inc.
- **Suburban** campus
- **Coed**
- **Minimally difficult** entrance level

ACADEMICS
Calendar: quarters. *Degrees:* associate and bachelor's.

STUDENT LIFE
Housing options: college housing not available.

FINANCIAL AID
Financial Aid Of all full-time matriculated undergraduates who enrolled in 2013, 20 Federal Work-Study jobs (averaging $4500).

CONTACT
Director of Recruitment, ITT Technical Institute, 650 West Cienega Avenue, San Dimas, CA 91773. *Phone:* 909-971-2300. *Toll-free phone:* 800-414-6522.

ITT Technical Institute
Sylmar, California
http://www.itt-tech.edu/

- **Proprietary** primarily 2-year, founded 1982, part of ITT Educational Services, Inc.
- **Urban** campus
- **Coed**
- **Minimally difficult** entrance level

ACADEMICS
Calendar: quarters. *Degrees:* associate and bachelor's.

STUDENT LIFE
Housing options: college housing not available.

CONTACT
Director of Recruitment, ITT Technical Institute, 12669 Encinitas Avenue, Sylmar, CA 91342-3664. *Phone:* 818-364-5151. *Toll-free phone:* 800-363-2086 (in-state); 800-636-2086 (out-of-state).

ITT Technical Institute
Torrance, California
http://www.itt-tech.edu/

- **Proprietary** primarily 2-year, founded 1987, part of ITT Educational Services, Inc.
- **Urban** campus
- **Coed**
- **Minimally difficult** entrance level

ACADEMICS
Calendar: quarters. *Degrees:* associate and bachelor's.

STUDENT LIFE
Housing options: college housing not available.

FINANCIAL AID
Financial Aid Of all full-time matriculated undergraduates who enrolled in 2013, 6 Federal Work-Study jobs (averaging $4000).

CONTACT
Director of Recruitment, ITT Technical Institute, 2555 West 190th Street, Suite 125, Torrance, CA 90504. *Phone:* 310-965-5900.

John Paul the Great Catholic University
Escondido, California
http://www.jpcatholic.com/

- **Independent religious** comprehensive, founded 2006
- **Urban** campus with easy access to San Diego
- **Coed** 196 undergraduate students, 76% full-time, 42% women, 58% men
- **Moderately difficult** entrance level, 88% of applicants were admitted

UNDERGRAD STUDENTS
148 full-time, 48 part-time. Students come from 35 states and territories; 51% are from out of state; 20% Hispanic/Latino; 6% Asian, non-Hispanic/Latino; 0.6% Native Hawaiian or other Pacific Islander, non-Hispanic/Latino; 1% American Indian or Alaska Native, non-Hispanic/Latino; 3% Two or more races, non-Hispanic/Latino; 11% Race/ethnicity unknown; 10% transferred in; 78% live on campus.

Freshmen
Admission: 120 applied, 105 admitted, 59 enrolled. ***Average high school GPA:*** 3.4. ***Test scores:*** SAT critical reading scores over 500: 66%; SAT math scores over 500: 54%; SAT writing scores over 500: 69%; ACT scores over 18: 89%; SAT critical reading scores over 600: 40%; SAT

math scores over 600: 20%; SAT writing scores over 600: 29%; ACT scores over 24: 68%; SAT critical reading scores over 700: 9%; SAT math scores over 700: 3%; SAT writing scores over 700: 3%; ACT scores over 30: 16%.

Retention: 76% of full-time freshmen returned.

FACULTY

Total: 24, 25% full-time, 21% with terminal degrees.

Student/faculty ratio: 18:1.

ACADEMICS

Calendar: quarters. *Degrees:* certificates, bachelor's, master's, and postbachelor's certificates.

Special study options: advanced placement credit, distance learning, independent study, internships, part-time degree program, services for LD students, study abroad, summer session for credit.

Computers: 23 computers/terminals are available on campus for general student use. Students can access the following: online (class) schedules. Campuswide network is available. 100% of college-owned or -operated housing units are wired for high-speed Internet access. Wireless service is available via entire campus.

STUDENT LIFE

Housing options: on-campus residence required through senior year; men-only, women-only. Campus housing is leased by the school. Freshman campus housing is guaranteed.

Activities and organizations: choral group, Student government, Swing dance club, Artist affiliation, Gaming club.

Campus security: student patrols, controlled dormitory access, Leased campus housing provides own security.

Student services: personal/psychological counseling.

COSTS & FINANCIAL AID

Costs (2015–16) ***Tuition:*** $24,000 full-time, $667 per credit part-time. No tuition increase for student's term of enrollment. ***Required fees:*** $900 full-time. ***Room only:*** $8100.

Financial Aid Of all full-time matriculated undergraduates who enrolled in 2013, 104 applied for aid, 104 were judged to have need. ***Average percent of need met:*** 53. ***Average financial aid package:*** $16,928. ***Average need-based loan:*** $3921. ***Average need-based gift aid:*** $11,816. ***Financial aid deadline:*** 4/15.

APPLYING

Standardized Tests *Required for some:* SAT or ACT (for admission).

Options: electronic application, deferred entrance.

Application fee: $20.

Required: essay or personal statement, high school transcript, minimum 2.6 GPA, 2 letters of recommendation. ***Required for some:*** interview.

Application deadlines: rolling (freshmen), rolling (out-of-state freshmen), rolling (transfers).

Notification: continuous (freshmen), continuous (out-of-state freshmen), continuous (transfers).

CONTACT

Mr. Martin Harold, Vice President of Admissions, John Paul the Great Catholic University, 220 W. Grand Ave, Escondido, CA 92025. *Phone:* 858-653-6740 Ext. 1101. *Fax:* 858-653-3791. *E-mail:* mharold@jpcatholic.com.

Laguna College of Art & Design

Laguna Beach, California

http://www.lcad.edu/

- **Independent** comprehensive, founded 1962
- **Small-town** 9-acre campus with easy access to Los Angeles
- **Endowment** $1.7 million
- **Coed** 514 undergraduate students, 91% full-time, 60% women, 40% men
- **Very difficult** entrance level, 88% of applicants were admitted

UNDERGRAD STUDENTS

466 full-time, 48 part-time. Students come from 32 states and territories; 13 other countries; 42% are from out of state; 2% Black or African American, non-Hispanic/Latino; 15% Hispanic/Latino; 17% Asian, non-Hispanic/Latino; 15% Race/ethnicity unknown; 3% international; 14% transferred in; 11% live on campus.

Freshmen

Admission: 245 applied, 215 admitted, 68 enrolled. ***Average high school GPA:*** 3.25. ***Test scores:*** SAT critical reading scores over 500: 88%; SAT math scores over 500: 80%; ACT scores over 18: 100%; SAT critical reading scores over 600: 66%; SAT math scores over 600: 32%; ACT scores over 24: 80%; SAT critical reading scores over 700: 16%; SAT math scores over 700: 10%; ACT scores over 30: 10%.

Retention: 84% of full-time freshmen returned.

FACULTY

Total: 105, 13% full-time, 3% with terminal degrees.

Student/faculty ratio: 12:1.

ACADEMICS

Calendar: semesters. *Degrees:* certificates, bachelor's, master's, and postbachelor's certificates.

Special study options: double majors, independent study, internships, part-time degree program, services for LD students.

Computers: 85 computers/terminals are available on campus for general student use. Students can access the following: campus intranet, computer help desk, free student e-mail accounts, online (class) grades, online (class) registration, online (class) schedules. Campuswide network is available. 100% of college-owned or -operated housing units are wired for high-speed Internet access. Wireless service is available via entire campus.

STUDENT LIFE

Housing options: coed. Campus housing is leased by the school. Freshman applicants given priority for college housing.

Campus security: late-night transport/escort service.

Student services: personal/psychological counseling.

COSTS & FINANCIAL AID

Costs (2015–16) ***Tuition:*** $28,100 full-time, $1170 per credit part-time. Full-time tuition and fees vary according to degree level. Part-time tuition and fees vary according to course load and degree level. ***Room only:*** $9100. ***Payment plan:*** installment.

Financial Aid Of all full-time matriculated undergraduates who enrolled in 2012, 434 applied for aid, 395 were judged to have need, 2 had their need fully met. 21 Federal Work-Study jobs (averaging $2000). In 2012, 10 non-need-based awards were made. ***Average percent of need met:*** 72. ***Average financial aid package:*** $16,101. ***Average need-based loan:*** $5500. ***Average need-based gift aid:*** $5500. ***Average non-need-based aid:*** $4500. ***Average indebtedness upon graduation:*** $38,000.

APPLYING

Standardized Tests *Recommended:* SAT or ACT (for admission).

Options: early admission, early decision, deferred entrance.

Application fee: $45.

Required: essay or personal statement, high school transcript, minimum 2.5 GPA, portfolio. ***Required for some:*** 2 letters of recommendation, interview.

Application deadlines: rolling (freshmen), rolling (out-of-state freshmen), rolling (transfers), rolling (early action).

Early decision deadline: rolling (for plan 1), rolling (for plan 2).

Notification: continuous (freshmen), continuous (out-of-state freshmen), continuous (transfers), rolling (early decision plan 1), rolling (early decision plan 2), rolling (early action).

CONTACT

Madison Keyes, Admissions Coordinator, Laguna College of Art & Design, 2222 Laguna Canyon Road, Laguna Beach, CA 92651. *Phone:* 949-376-6000 Ext. 248. *Toll-free phone:* 800-255-0762. *E-mail:* mkeyes@lcad.edu.

La Sierra University
Riverside, California
http://www.lasierra.edu/

- **Independent Seventh-day Adventist** comprehensive, founded 1922, part of Seventh-Day Adventist Education System
- **Suburban** 100-acre campus with easy access to Los Angeles
- **Coed** 2,119 undergraduate students, 90% full-time, 58% women, 42% men
- **Minimally difficult** entrance level, 41% of applicants were admitted

UNDERGRAD STUDENTS
1,899 full-time, 220 part-time. Students come from 30 states and territories; 41 other countries; 6% are from out of state; 7% Black or African American, non-Hispanic/Latino; 43% Hispanic/Latino; 15% Asian, non-Hispanic/Latino; 2% Native Hawaiian or other Pacific Islander, non-Hispanic/Latino; 0.3% American Indian or Alaska Native, non-Hispanic/Latino; 4% Two or more races, non-Hispanic/Latino; 0.2% Race/ethnicity unknown; 13% international; 10% transferred in; 31% live on campus.

Freshmen
Admission: 4,707 applied, 1,913 admitted, 467 enrolled. ***Average high school GPA:*** 3.36. ***Test scores:*** SAT critical reading scores over 500: 36%; SAT math scores over 500: 38%; SAT writing scores over 500: 35%; ACT scores over 18: 61%; SAT critical reading scores over 600: 8%; SAT math scores over 600: 16%; SAT writing scores over 600: 10%; ACT scores over 24: 21%; SAT critical reading scores over 700: 1%; SAT math scores over 700: 2%; SAT writing scores over 700: 1%; ACT scores over 30: 4%.

Retention: 77% of full-time freshmen returned.

FACULTY
Total: 240, 41% full-time, 49% with terminal degrees.

Student/faculty ratio: 15:1.

ACADEMICS
Calendar: quarters. *Degrees:* certificates, bachelor's, master's, doctoral, post-master's, and postbachelor's certificates.

Special study options: academic remediation for entering students, accelerated degree program, adult/continuing education programs, advanced placement credit, distance learning, double majors, English as a second language, honors programs, independent study, internships, off-campus study, part-time degree program, services for LD students, student-designed majors, study abroad, summer session for credit.

Unusual degree programs: business administration with White memorial branch (CA), Riverside branch (CA), Glendale branch (CA), Chino Branch (CA); criminal justice at Corona Branch.

Computers: 300 computers/terminals are available on campus for general student use. Students can access the following: computer help desk, free student e-mail accounts, online (class) grades, online (class) registration, online (class) schedules. Campuswide network is available. Wireless service is available via entire campus.

STUDENT LIFE
Housing options: on-campus residence required for freshman year; men-only, women-only, cooperative. Campus housing is university owned. Freshman campus housing is guaranteed.

Activities and organizations: drama/theater group, student-run newspaper, choral group, Student Association of LSU, Korean Student Association, Students In Free Enterprise (SIFE), Ol Club, Black Student Association.

Athletics Member NAIA. ***Intercollegiate sports:*** basketball M/W, golf M, soccer M, softball W, volleyball W. ***Intramural sports:*** baseball M, basketball M/W, soccer M, softball W, volleyball W.

Campus security: 24-hour emergency response devices and patrols, student patrols, late-night transport/escort service.

Student services: health clinic, personal/psychological counseling, women's center.

COSTS & FINANCIAL AID
Costs (2015–16) ***Comprehensive fee:*** $38,270 includes full-time tuition ($29,340), mandatory fees ($1130), and room and board ($7800). Full-time tuition and fees vary according to course load, degree level, and location. Part-time tuition: $815 per quarter hour. Part-time tuition and fees vary according to course load, degree level, and location. ***Room and board:*** Room and board charges vary according to board plan and housing facility. ***Payment plan:*** installment. ***Waivers:*** employees or children of employees.

Financial Aid Of all full-time matriculated undergraduates who enrolled in 2013, 1,604 applied for aid, 1,482 were judged to have need, 110 had their need fully met. 222 Federal Work-Study jobs (averaging $1677). In 2013, 346 non-need-based awards were made. ***Average percent of need met:*** 69. ***Average financial aid package:*** $22,673. ***Average need-based loan:*** $5189. ***Average need-based gift aid:*** $18,288. ***Average non-need-based aid:*** $7869. ***Average indebtedness upon graduation:*** $25,171. ***Financial aid deadline:*** 8/15.

APPLYING
Standardized Tests *Required:* SAT or ACT (for admission).

Options: electronic application, deferred entrance.

Required: essay or personal statement, high school transcript, minimum 2.0 GPA, 2 letters of recommendation, Eligibility Index Table (combination of GPA and test scores). ***Required for some:*** interview.

Application deadlines: 2/1 (freshmen), 2/1 (out-of-state freshmen), 7/1 (transfers).

Notification: continuous (freshmen), continuous (out-of-state freshmen), continuous (transfers).

CONTACT
Ms. Ivy Teheda, Assistant Director of Admissions, La Sierra University, 4500 Riverwalk Parkway, Riverside, CA 92515. *Phone:* 951-7852957. *Toll-free phone:* 800-874-5587. *Fax:* 951-7852447. *E-mail:* iteheda@lasierra.edu.

Lincoln University
Oakland, California
http://www.lincolnuca.edu/

- **Independent** comprehensive, founded 1919
- **Urban** campus
- **Coed** 91 undergraduate students, 81% full-time, 57% women, 43% men
- **Minimally difficult** entrance level, 82% of applicants were admitted

UNDERGRAD STUDENTS
74 full-time, 17 part-time. Students come from 44 other countries; 4% Black or African American, non-Hispanic/Latino; 7% Hispanic/Latino; 30% Asian, non-Hispanic/Latino; 37% international.

Freshmen
Admission: 130 applied, 106 admitted. ***Average high school GPA:*** 2.5.

FACULTY
Total: 37, 30% full-time, 78% with terminal degrees.
Student/faculty ratio: 20:1.

ACADEMICS
Calendar: semesters. *Degrees:* certificates, bachelor's, master's, and doctoral.

Special study options: advanced placement credit, double majors, English as a second language, summer session for credit.

Computers: 32 computers/terminals are available on campus for general student use. Students can access the following: computer help desk, free student e-mail accounts, online (class) schedules. Campuswide network is available. Wireless service is available via entire campus.

STUDENT LIFE
Housing options: college housing not available.

Campus security: 24-hour emergency response devices.

Student services: personal/psychological counseling.

COSTS
Costs (2014–15) ***Tuition:*** $9600 full-time, $400 per unit part-time. Full-time tuition and fees vary according to course level, course load, degree level, and program. Part-time tuition and fees vary according to course level, course load, degree level, and program. ***Required fees:*** $400 full-time, $400 per year part-time. ***Payment plan:*** installment. ***Waivers:*** employees or children of employees.

APPLYING
Options: electronic application, deferred entrance.

Application fee: $75.

Required: high school transcript, minimum 2.0 GPA. ***Required for some:*** essay or personal statement, letters of recommendation, interview.

Application deadlines: 7/19 (freshmen), 7/19 (transfers).

CONTACT

Ms. Vanessa Juwono, Admissions Officer, Lincoln University, 401 15th Street, Oakland, CA 94612. *Phone:* 510-628-8010 Ext. 8030. *Toll-free phone:* 888-810-9998. *Fax:* 510-628-8012. *E-mail:* admissions@lincolnuca.edu.

★ Los Angeles Film School

Hollywood, California

http://www.lafilm.edu/

- **Proprietary** 4-year
- **Urban** Easy access to Hollywood
- **Coed**
- 85% of applicants were admitted

Freshmen

Admission: 1,505 applied, 1,272 admitted.

ACADEMICS

Degrees: associate and bachelor's.

APPLYING

Options: electronic application.

Application fee: $75.

Required: essay or personal statement, high school transcript, interview.

CONTACT

Los Angeles Film School, 6363 Sunset Boulevard, Hollywood, CA 90028. *Toll-free phone:* 877-952-3456.

Loyola Marymount University

Los Angeles, California

http://www.lmu.edu/

- **Independent Roman Catholic** comprehensive, founded 1911
- **Suburban** 142-acre campus with easy access to Los Angeles
- **Endowment** $458.0 million
- **Coed** 6,184 undergraduate students, 96% full-time, 57% women, 43% men
- **Very difficult** entrance level, 53% of applicants were admitted

UNDERGRAD STUDENTS

5,925 full-time, 259 part-time. Students come from 52 states and territories; 71 other countries; 22% are from out of state; 6% Black or African American, non-Hispanic/Latino; 22% Hispanic/Latino; 11% Asian, non-Hispanic/Latino; 0.1% Native Hawaiian or other Pacific Islander, non-Hispanic/Latino; 0.2% American Indian or Alaska Native, non-Hispanic/Latino; 8% Two or more races, non-Hispanic/Latino; 7% international; 6% transferred in; 52% live on campus.

Freshmen

Admission: 12,117 applied, 6,387 admitted, 1,348 enrolled. ***Average high school GPA:*** 3.75. ***Test scores:*** SAT critical reading scores over 500: 92%; SAT math scores over 500: 92%; SAT writing scores over 500: 92%; ACT scores over 18: 100%; SAT critical reading scores over 600: 48%; SAT math scores over 600: 60%; SAT writing scores over 600: 51%; ACT scores over 24: 88%; SAT critical reading scores over 700: 7%; SAT math scores over 700: 11%; SAT writing scores over 700: 10%; ACT scores over 30: 27%.

Retention: 91% of full-time freshmen returned.

ACADEMICS

Calendar: semesters. *Degrees:* bachelor's, master's, doctoral, post-master's, and postbachelor's certificates.

Special study options: academic remediation for entering students, accelerated degree program, advanced placement credit, cooperative education, double majors, English as a second language, honors programs, independent study, internships, part-time degree program, services for LD students, student-designed majors, study abroad, summer session for credit. ***ROTC:*** Army (c), Navy (c), Air Force (b).

Unusual degree programs: 3-2 engineering.

Computers: 780 computers/terminals and 2,000 ports are available on campus for general student use. Students can access the following: campus intranet, computer help desk, free student e-mail accounts, online (class) grades, online (class) registration, online (class) schedules. Campuswide network is available. 100% of college-owned or -operated housing units are wired for high-speed Internet access. Wireless service is available via entire campus.

STUDENT LIFE

Housing options: coed, men-only, women-only, special housing for students with disabilities. Campus housing is university owned. Freshman applicants given priority for college housing.

Activities and organizations: drama/theater group, student-run newspaper, radio and television station, choral group, Greek, Honors Program, Sursum Corda, Ignatians, Belles, national fraternities, national sororities.

Athletics Member NCAA. All Division I. ***Intercollegiate sports:*** baseball M(s), basketball M(s)/W(s), cheerleading M/W, crew M/W(s), cross-country running M(s)/W(s), golf M(s), soccer M(s)/W(s), softball W(s), swimming and diving W(s), tennis M(s)/W(s), track and field M/W, volleyball W(s), water polo M(s)/W(s). ***Intramural sports:*** baseball M(c), basketball M/W(c), football M/W, ice hockey M(c), lacrosse M(c)/W(c), rugby M(c), skiing (downhill) M(c)/W(c), soccer M(c)/W(c), table tennis M/W, tennis M(c)/W(c), volleyball M(c)/W(c).

Campus security: 24-hour emergency response devices and patrols, late-night transport/escort service, controlled dormitory access.

Student services: health clinic, personal/psychological counseling.

COSTS & FINANCIAL AID

Costs (2014–15) ***One-time required fee:*** $225. ***Comprehensive fee:*** $55,767 includes full-time tuition ($40,680), mandatory fees ($692), and room and board ($14,395). Full-time tuition and fees vary according to reciprocity agreements. Part-time tuition: $1697 per credit hour. Part-time tuition and fees vary according to course load. ***College room only:*** $9995. Room and board charges vary according to board plan and housing facility. ***Payment plans:*** installment, deferred payment. ***Waivers:*** employees or children of employees.

Financial Aid Of all full-time matriculated undergraduates who enrolled in 2013, 4,510 applied for aid, 3,489 were judged to have need, 651 had their need fully met. 1,525 Federal Work-Study jobs (averaging $1876). 2,127 state and other part-time jobs (averaging $1972). In 2013, 1322 non-need-based awards were made. ***Average percent of need met:*** 65. ***Average financial aid package:*** $26,949. ***Average need-based loan:*** $5704. ***Average need-based gift aid:*** $19,402. ***Average non-need-based aid:*** $9432. ***Average indebtedness upon graduation:*** $30,243. ***Financial aid deadline:*** 7/30.

APPLYING

Standardized Tests *Required:* SAT or ACT (for admission).

Options: electronic application, early admission, early action, deferred entrance.

Application fee: $60.

Required: essay or personal statement, high school transcript, 1 letter of recommendation. ***Required for some:*** portfolios or auditions for animation, dance, music, or theatre arts majors. ***Recommended:*** interview.

Application deadlines: 1/15 (freshmen), 3/15 (transfers), 11/1 (early action).

Notification: continuous (freshmen), continuous (transfers), 12/20 (early action).

CONTACT

Loyola Marymount University, One LMU Drive, Los Angeles, CA 90045-2659. *Phone:* 310-338-2750. *Toll-free phone:* 800-LMU-INFO.

Marymount California University

Rancho Palos Verdes, California

http://www.marymountcalifornia.edu/

- **Independent Roman Catholic** comprehensive, founded 1932
- **Suburban** 26-acre campus with easy access to Los Angeles
- **Endowment** $9.9 million
- **Coed** 1,086 undergraduate students, 95% full-time, 54% women, 46% men
- **Minimally difficult** entrance level, 62% of applicants were admitted

UNDERGRAD STUDENTS

1,033 full-time, 53 part-time. Students come from 24 states and territories; 34 other countries; 6% are from out of state; 8% Black or African American, non-Hispanic/Latino; 35% Hispanic/Latino; 4% Asian, non-Hispanic/Latino; 0.8% Native Hawaiian or other Pacific Islander, non-Hispanic/Latino; 0.3% American Indian or Alaska Native, non-Hispanic/Latino; 3% Two or more races, non-Hispanic/Latino; 8% Race/ethnicity unknown; 21% international; 9% transferred in; 40% live on campus.

Freshmen

Admission: 1,586 applied, 987 admitted, 314 enrolled. ***Average high school GPA:*** 2.88. ***Test scores:*** SAT critical reading scores over 500: 30%; SAT math scores over 500: 29%; SAT writing scores over 500: 31%; ACT scores over 18: 50%; SAT critical reading scores over 600: 4%; SAT math scores over 600: 7%; SAT writing scores over 600: 4%; ACT scores over 24: 9%; SAT math scores over 700: 2%; SAT writing scores over 700: 1%.

Retention: 72% of full-time freshmen returned.

FACULTY

Total: 114, 29% full-time, 43% with terminal degrees.

Student/faculty ratio: 18:1.

ACADEMICS

Calendar: semesters. *Degrees:* certificates, associate, bachelor's, and master's.

Special study options: academic remediation for entering students, accelerated degree program, adult/continuing education programs, advanced placement credit, distance learning, English as a second language, honors programs, independent study, internships, off-campus study, part-time degree program, services for LD students, study abroad, summer session for credit.

Unusual degree programs: 3-2 business administration with MBA.

Computers: 200 computers/terminals are available on campus for general student use. Students can access the following: campus intranet, computer help desk, free student e-mail accounts, online (class) grades, online (class) registration, online (class) schedules. Campuswide network is available. 100% of college-owned or -operated housing units are wired for high-speed Internet access. Wireless service is available via entire campus.

STUDENT LIFE

Housing options: on-campus residence required for freshman year; coed. Campus housing is university owned. Freshman applicants given priority for college housing.

Activities and organizations: drama/theater group, student-run radio station, choral group.

Athletics Member NAIA. ***Intercollegiate sports:*** golf M/W, lacrosse M/W, soccer M(s). ***Intramural sports:*** basketball M/W, golf M/W, lacrosse M/W, soccer M/W, softball M/W, swimming and diving M/W, track and field M/W, volleyball M/W.

Campus security: 24-hour emergency response devices and patrols, late-night transport/escort service, controlled dormitory access.

Student services: health clinic, personal/psychological counseling.

COSTS & FINANCIAL AID

Costs (2014–15) ***One-time required fee:*** $275. ***Comprehensive fee:*** $44,655 includes full-time tuition ($31,112), mandatory fees ($545), and room and board ($12,998). Full-time tuition and fees vary according to degree level and location. Part-time tuition: $1350 per credit hour. Part-time tuition and fees vary according to degree level and location. ***Required fees:*** $250 per year part-time. ***College room only:*** $8200. Room and board charges vary according to board plan and housing facility. ***Payment plan:*** installment. ***Waivers:*** senior citizens and employees or children of employees.

Financial Aid Of all full-time matriculated undergraduates who enrolled in 2014, 587 applied for aid, 561 were judged to have need, 26 had their need fully met. In 2014, 51 non-need-based awards were made. ***Average percent of need met:*** 75. ***Average financial aid package:*** $23,671. ***Average need-based loan:*** $5500. ***Average need-based gift aid:*** $22,417. ***Average indebtedness upon graduation:*** $9421. ***Financial aid deadline:*** 2/15.

APPLYING

Standardized Tests *Recommended:* SAT or ACT (for admission).

Options: electronic application, early admission, deferred entrance.

Application fee: $50.

Required: high school transcript. ***Required for some:*** essay or personal statement, interview. ***Recommended:*** minimum 2.0 GPA.

Application deadlines: 7/1 (freshmen), 8/15 (transfers).

Notification: continuous until 9/1 (freshmen), continuous until 9/1 (transfers).

CONTACT

Mr. Jeremy Smotherman, Director of Admissions, Marymount California University, 30800 Palos Verdes Drive East, Rancho Palos Verdes, CA 90275-6299. *Phone:* 310-377-5501 Ext. 7211. *Fax:* 310-265-0962. *E-mail:* admissions@marymountcalifornia.edu.

The Master's College and Seminary

Santa Clarita, California

http://www.masters.edu/

- **Independent nondenominational** comprehensive, founded 1927
- **Suburban** 110-acre campus with easy access to Los Angeles
- **Endowment** $17.2 million
- **Coed** 1,137 undergraduate students, 87% full-time, 48% women, 52% men
- **Moderately difficult** entrance level, 76% of applicants were admitted

UNDERGRAD STUDENTS

992 full-time, 145 part-time. Students come from 41 states and territories; 20 other countries; 27% are from out of state; 4% Black or African American, non-Hispanic/Latino; 10% Hispanic/Latino; 7% Asian, non-Hispanic/Latino; 0.6% Native Hawaiian or other Pacific Islander, non-Hispanic/Latino; 0.3% American Indian or Alaska Native, non-Hispanic/Latino; 7% Two or more races, non-Hispanic/Latino; 5% Race/ethnicity unknown; 5% international; 10% transferred in; 82% live on campus.

Freshmen

Admission: 485 applied, 368 admitted, 195 enrolled. ***Average high school GPA:*** 3.62. ***Test scores:*** SAT critical reading scores over 500: 74%; SAT math scores over 500: 63%; SAT writing scores over 500: 65%; ACT scores over 18: 94%; SAT critical reading scores over 600: 38%; SAT math scores over 600: 22%; SAT writing scores over 600: 26%; ACT scores over 24: 55%; SAT critical reading scores over 700: 10%; SAT math scores over 700: 4%; SAT writing scores over 700: 2%; ACT scores over 30: 7%.

Retention: 86% of full-time freshmen returned.

FACULTY

Total: 186, 31% full-time, 28% with terminal degrees.

Student/faculty ratio: 10:1.

ACADEMICS

Calendar: semesters. *Degrees:* bachelor's, master's, and doctoral.

Special study options: academic remediation for entering students, accelerated degree program, adult/continuing education programs, advanced placement credit, cooperative education, distance learning, double majors, English as a second language, external degree program, independent study, internships, part-time degree program, services for LD students, study abroad, summer session for credit. ***ROTC:*** Army (c), Air Force (c).

Computers: 57 computers/terminals are available on campus for general student use. Students can access the following: computer help desk, free student e-mail accounts, online (class) grades, online (class) registration, online (class) schedules. Campuswide network is available. Wireless service is available via entire campus.

STUDENT LIFE
Housing options: on-campus residence required through junior year; men-only, women-only. Campus housing is university owned. Freshman campus housing is guaranteed.

Activities and organizations: drama/theater group, choral group, Collegiate Singers Chorus, Summer Missions, intramural Sports, Church Ministries, Theatre Arts Group.

Athletics Member NAIA, NCCAA. ***Intercollegiate sports:*** baseball M(s), basketball M(s)/W(s), cross-country running M(s)/W(s), golf M(s), soccer M(s)/W(s), track and field M(s)/W(s), volleyball W(s). ***Intramural sports:*** basketball M/W, soccer M/W, volleyball M/W.

Campus security: 24-hour patrols.

Student services: health clinic, personal/psychological counseling.

COSTS & FINANCIAL AID
Costs (2014–15) ***Comprehensive fee:*** $39,580 includes full-time tuition ($29,440), mandatory fees ($420), and room and board ($9720). Full-time tuition and fees vary according to course load, degree level, and program. Part-time tuition: $1235 per credit hour. Part-time tuition and fees vary according to course load, degree level, and program. ***Room and board:*** Room and board charges vary according to board plan. ***Payment plan:*** installment. ***Waivers:*** employees or children of employees.

Financial Aid Of all full-time matriculated undergraduates who enrolled in 2013, 908 applied for aid, 804 were judged to have need, 111 had their need fully met. 62 Federal Work-Study jobs (averaging $2602). 183 state and other part-time jobs (averaging $2359). In 2013, 160 non-need-based awards were made. ***Average percent of need met:*** 66. ***Average financial aid package:*** $21,043. ***Average need-based loan:*** $4327. ***Average need-based gift aid:*** $16,745. ***Average non-need-based aid:*** $9106. ***Average indebtedness upon graduation:*** $26,442.

APPLYING
Standardized Tests *Required:* SAT or ACT (for admission).

Options: electronic application, early admission, early action, deferred entrance.

Application fee: $40.

Required: essay or personal statement, high school transcript, minimum 2.8 GPA, 2 letters of recommendation. ***Recommended:*** interview.

Application deadlines: 9/1 (freshmen), 9/1 (out-of-state freshmen), 9/1 (transfers), 11/15 (early action).

Notification: 3/15 (freshmen), 3/15 (transfers), 12/22 (early action).

CONTACT
Mr. John Melcon, Director of Admissions, The Master's College and Seminary, 21726 Placerita Canyon Road, Santa Clarita, CA 91321. *Phone:* 661-362-2601. *Toll-free phone:* 800-568-6248. *Fax:* 661-362-2718. *E-mail:* admissions@masters.edu.

★ Menlo College
Atherton, California
http://www.menlo.edu/

- **Independent** 4-year, founded 1927
- **Small-town** 45-acre campus with easy access to San Francisco
- **Endowment** $30.0 million
- **Coed** 772 undergraduate students, 98% full-time, 40% women, 60% men
- **Moderately difficult** entrance level, 45% of applicants were admitted

UNDERGRAD STUDENTS
760 full-time, 12 part-time. Students come from 20 states and territories; 33 other countries; 17% are from out of state; 7% Black or African American, non-Hispanic/Latino; 21% Hispanic/Latino; 7% Asian, non-Hispanic/Latino; 2% Native Hawaiian or other Pacific Islander, non-Hispanic/Latino; 0.8% American Indian or Alaska Native, non-Hispanic/Latino; 8% Two or more races, non-Hispanic/Latino; 7% Race/ethnicity unknown; 13% international; 11% transferred in; 60% live on campus.

Freshmen
Admission: 3,935 applied, 1,773 admitted, 194 enrolled. ***Average high school GPA:*** 3.2. ***Test scores:*** SAT critical reading scores over 500: 49%; SAT math scores over 500: 50%; SAT writing scores over 500: 41%; ACT scores over 18: 83%; SAT critical reading scores over 600: 9%; SAT math scores over 600: 14%; SAT writing scores over 600: 9%; ACT scores over 24: 17%; SAT critical reading scores over 700: 1%; SAT math scores over 700: 2%; SAT writing scores over 700: 3%; ACT scores over 30: 3%.
Retention: 80% of full-time freshmen returned.

FACULTY
Total: 101, 28% full-time, 52% with terminal degrees.

Student/faculty ratio: 15:1.

ACADEMICS
Calendar: semesters. *Degree:* bachelor's.

Special study options: academic remediation for entering students, accelerated degree program, adult/continuing education programs, advanced placement credit, double majors, English as a second language, independent study, internships, part-time degree program, services for LD students, student-designed majors, study abroad, summer session for credit.

Computers: 220 computers/terminals are available on campus for general student use. Students can access the following: campus intranet, computer help desk, free student e-mail accounts, online (class) grades, online (class) registration, online (class) schedules. Campuswide network is available. 100% of college-owned or -operated housing units are wired for high-speed Internet access. Wireless service is available via classrooms, computer centers, computer labs, dorm rooms, learning centers, libraries, student centers.

STUDENT LIFE
Housing options: on-campus residence required through sophomore year; coed, men-only, women-only. Campus housing is university owned.

Activities and organizations: International Club, Student Government, SERV, Finance Club, Hawaiian Club.

Athletics Member NAIA. ***Intercollegiate sports:*** basketball M(s)/W(s), cheerleading M(s)/W(s), golf M(s)/W(s), soccer M(s)/W(s), softball W(s), volleyball W(s), wrestling M(s)/W(s). ***Intramural sports:*** basketball M(c)/W(c).

Campus security: 24-hour emergency response devices and patrols, controlled dormitory access.

Student services: personal/psychological counseling, women's center.

COSTS & FINANCIAL AID
Costs (2015–16) ***Comprehensive fee:*** $51,380 includes full-time tuition ($38,100), mandatory fees ($650), and room and board ($12,630). Part-time tuition: $1588 per credit. ***Room and board:*** Room and board charges vary according to housing facility. ***Payment plan:*** installment. ***Waivers:*** employees or children of employees.

Financial Aid Of all full-time matriculated undergraduates who enrolled in 2014, 522 applied for aid, 478 were judged to have need, 54 had their need fully met. 345 Federal Work-Study jobs (averaging $1024). In 2014, 168 non-need-based awards were made. ***Average percent of need met:*** 66. ***Average financial aid package:*** $28,874. ***Average need-based loan:*** $3741. ***Average need-based gift aid:*** $25,073. ***Average non-need-based aid:*** $12,737. ***Average indebtedness upon graduation:*** $29,943.

APPLYING
Standardized Tests *Required:* SAT or ACT (for admission).

Options: electronic application, early admission, early action, deferred entrance.

Application fee: $40.

Required: essay or personal statement, high school transcript, 1 letter of recommendation. ***Recommended:*** minimum 2.5 GPA, interview.

Application deadlines: 4/1 (freshmen), 4/1 (out-of-state freshmen), 6/1 (transfers), 11/15 (early action).

Notification: continuous (freshmen), continuous (out-of-state freshmen), continuous (transfers), 1/15 (early action).

CONTACT
Priscila Priscila, Associate Dean of Enrollment Management, Menlo College, 1000 El Camino Real, Atherton, CA 94027. *Phone:* 650-543-3786. *Toll-free phone:* 800-556-3656. *Fax:* 650-543-4496. *E-mail:* admissions@menlo.edu.

★ Mills College
Oakland, California
http://www.mills.edu/

- **Independent** comprehensive, founded 1852
- **Urban** 135-acre campus with easy access to San Francisco
- **Endowment** $189.0 million
- **Undergraduate: women only; graduate: coed** 917 undergraduate students, 95% full-time, 100% women
- **Moderately difficult** entrance level, 76% of applicants were admitted

UNDERGRAD STUDENTS
875 full-time, 42 part-time. Students come from 37 states and territories; 5 other countries; 24% are from out of state; 7% Black or African American, non-Hispanic/Latino; 23% Hispanic/Latino; 11% Asian, non-Hispanic/Latino; 0.5% Native Hawaiian or other Pacific Islander, non-Hispanic/Latino; 0.5% American Indian or Alaska Native, non-Hispanic/Latino; 10% Two or more races, non-Hispanic/Latino; 2% Race/ethnicity unknown; 2% international; 12% transferred in; 58% live on campus.

Freshmen
Admission: 1,869 applied, 1,423 admitted, 188 enrolled. ***Average high school GPA:*** 3.66. ***Test scores:*** SAT critical reading scores over 500: 88%; SAT math scores over 500: 73%; SAT writing scores over 500: 84%; ACT scores over 18: 100%; SAT critical reading scores over 600: 49%; SAT math scores over 600: 28%; SAT writing scores over 600: 33%; ACT scores over 24: 70%; SAT critical reading scores over 700: 9%; SAT math scores over 700: 4%; SAT writing scores over 700: 6%; ACT scores over 30: 20%.
Retention: 71% of full-time freshmen returned.

FACULTY
Total: 197, 54% full-time, 79% with terminal degrees.
Student/faculty ratio: 11:1.

ACADEMICS
Calendar: semesters. *Degrees:* certificates, bachelor's, master's, doctoral, and postbachelor's certificates.

Special study options: accelerated degree program, adult/continuing education programs, advanced placement credit, double majors, English as a second language, independent study, internships, off-campus study, part-time degree program, services for LD students, student-designed majors, study abroad, summer session for credit. ***ROTC:*** Army (c).

Unusual degree programs: 3-2 business administration; engineering with University of Southern California; Education; Public Policy; Infant Mental Health.

Computers: 299 computers/terminals are available on campus for general student use. Students can access the following: campus intranet, computer help desk, free student e-mail accounts, online (class) grades, online (class) registration, online (class) schedules, online degree audit. Campuswide network is available. 100% of college-owned or -operated housing units are wired for high-speed Internet access. Wireless service is available via entire campus.

STUDENT LIFE
Housing options: coed, women-only, cooperative, special housing for students with disabilities. Campus housing is university owned. Freshman campus housing is guaranteed.

Activities and organizations: student-run newspaper, choral group, Mouthing Off, The Campanil, Workers of Faith, Mujeres Unidas, Earth CORPS.

Athletics Member NCAA. All Division III. ***Intercollegiate sports:*** crew W, cross-country running W, soccer W, swimming and diving W, tennis W, volleyball W. ***Intramural sports:*** badminton W, cheerleading W(c), softball W, tennis M/W.

Campus security: 24-hour emergency response devices and patrols, late-night transport/escort service, controlled dormitory access.

Student services: health clinic, personal/psychological counseling, women's center.

COSTS & FINANCIAL AID
Costs (2014–15) ***Comprehensive fee:*** $55,832 includes full-time tuition ($41,618), mandatory fees ($1300), and room and board ($12,914). Full-time tuition and fees vary according to course load. Part-time tuition: $6936 per course. Part-time tuition and fees vary according to course load. ***Room and board:*** Room and board charges vary according to board plan

and housing facility. ***Payment plan:*** installment. ***Waivers:*** employees or children of employees.

Financial Aid Of all full-time matriculated undergraduates who enrolled in 2013, 813 applied for aid, 786 were judged to have need, 115 had their need fully met. 303 Federal Work-Study jobs (averaging $3031). 266 state and other part-time jobs (averaging $2526). In 2013, 111 non-need-based awards were made. ***Average percent of need met:*** 79. ***Average financial aid package:*** $37,766. ***Average need-based loan:*** $7725. ***Average need-based gift aid:*** $20,275. ***Average non-need-based aid:*** $15,279. ***Average indebtedness upon graduation:*** $24,861.

APPLYING

Standardized Tests *Required:* SAT or ACT (for admission). *Recommended:* SAT Subject Tests (for admission).

Options: electronic application, early action, deferred entrance.

Application fee: $50.

Required: high school transcript, 2 letters of recommendation, Essay or graded paper. ***Required for some:*** high school transcript. ***Recommended:*** interview.

Application deadlines: 1/15 (freshmen), 3/1 (transfers), 11/15 (early action).

Notification: 3/30 (freshmen), 4/1 (transfers), 12/1 (early action).

CONTACT

Ms. Belinda Zazueta, Director of Undergraduate Admissions, Mills College, 5000 MacArthur Boulevard, Oakland, CA 94613-1301. *Phone:* 510-430-2135. *Toll-free phone:* 800-87-MILLS. *Fax:* 510-430-3314. *E-mail:* admission@mills.edu.

See previous page for display ad and page 1526 for the College Close-Up.

★ Mount Saint Mary's University

Los Angeles, California

http://www.msmu.edu/

- **Independent Roman Catholic** comprehensive, founded 1925
- **Urban** 56-acre campus with easy access to Los Angeles
- **Endowment** $127.6 million
- **Coed, primarily women** 2,667 undergraduate students, 77% full-time, 93% women, 7% men

UNDERGRAD STUDENTS

2,047 full-time, 620 part-time. Students come from 18 states and territories; 7 other countries; 1% are from out of state; 7% Black or African American, non-Hispanic/Latino; 60% Hispanic/Latino; 17% Asian, non-Hispanic/Latino; 0.6% Native Hawaiian or other Pacific Islander, non-Hispanic/Latino; 0.4% American Indian or Alaska Native, non-Hispanic/Latino; 2% Two or more races, non-Hispanic/Latino; 3% Race/ethnicity unknown; 0.5% international; 3% transferred in; 20% live on campus.

Freshmen

Admission: 494 enrolled. ***Average high school GPA:*** 3.4. ***Test scores:*** SAT critical reading scores over 500: 30%; SAT math scores over 500: 26%; SAT writing scores over 500: 32%; SAT critical reading scores over 600: 5%; SAT math scores over 600: 4%; SAT writing scores over 600: 5%; SAT writing scores over 700: 1%.

Retention: 77% of full-time freshmen returned.

FACULTY

Total: 459, 25% full-time, 34% with terminal degrees.

Student/faculty ratio: 12:1.

ACADEMICS

Calendar: semesters. *Degrees:* associate, bachelor's, master's, doctoral, and post-master's certificates.

Special study options: academic remediation for entering students, accelerated degree program, advanced placement credit, cooperative education, distance learning, double majors, English as a second language, honors programs, independent study, internships, off-campus study, part-time degree program, services for LD students, student-designed majors, study abroad, summer session for credit.

Computers: 170 computers/terminals are available on campus for general student use. Students can access the following: campus intranet, computer help desk, free student e-mail accounts, online (class) grades, online (class) registration, online (class) schedules. Campuswide network is available. 100% of college-owned or -operated housing units are wired for high-speed Internet access. Wireless service is available via entire campus.

STUDENT LIFE

Housing options: men-only, women-only. Campus housing is university owned. Freshman applicants given priority for college housing.

Activities and organizations: drama/theater group, student-run newspaper, choral group, Na Pua O Ka Aina, Pangkat Pilipino, Alpha Tau Delta, California Nursing Student Association, Mount Movement.

Athletics ***Intramural sports:*** basketball M/W, soccer M/W, softball M/W, swimming and diving M/W, tennis M/W, volleyball M/W.

Campus security: 24-hour emergency response devices and patrols, late-night transport/escort service, controlled dormitory access.

Student services: health clinic, personal/psychological counseling, women's center.

COSTS & FINANCIAL AID

Costs (2015–16) ***Comprehensive fee:*** $47,061 includes full-time tuition ($34,934), mandatory fees ($1010), and room and board ($11,117). Full-time tuition and fees vary according to course load, degree level, and program. Part-time tuition: $1456 per unit. Part-time tuition and fees vary according to course load, degree level, and program. ***Room and board:*** Room and board charges vary according to board plan and housing facility. ***Payment plan:*** installment. ***Waivers:*** employees or children of employees.

Financial Aid Of all full-time matriculated undergraduates who enrolled in 2013, 1,965 applied for aid, 1,912 were judged to have need, 4 had their need fully met. In 2013, 115 non-need-based awards were made. ***Average percent of need met:*** 72. ***Average financial aid package:*** $28,423. ***Average need-based loan:*** $3688. ***Average need-based gift aid:*** $12,379. ***Average non-need-based aid:*** $13,386. ***Average indebtedness upon graduation:*** $37,494.

APPLYING

Standardized Tests *Required:* SAT or ACT (for admission).

Required: essay or personal statement, high school transcript, minimum 2.5 GPA, 1 letter of recommendation. ***Recommended:*** 2 letters of recommendation, interview.

CONTACT

Renee Rouzan-Kay, Director of Admissions, Mount Saint Mary's University, 12001 Chalon Road, Los Angeles, CA 90049-1599. *Phone:* 310-954-4250. *Toll-free phone:* 800-999-9893. *Fax:* 310-954-4259. *E-mail:* admissions@msmu.edu.

National University

La Jolla, California

http://www.nu.edu/

- **Independent** comprehensive, founded 1971, part of National University System
- **Urban** campus with easy access to San Diego - Carlsbad
- **Endowment** $581.3 million
- **Coed** 9,721 undergraduate students, 39% full-time, 57% women, 43% men
- **Minimally difficult** entrance level

UNDERGRAD STUDENTS

3,798 full-time, 5,923 part-time. Students come from 51 states and territories; 38 other countries; 9% are from out of state; 10% Black or African American, non-Hispanic/Latino; 26% Hispanic/Latino; 11% Asian, non-Hispanic/Latino; 2% Native Hawaiian or other Pacific Islander, non-Hispanic/Latino; 0.7% American Indian or Alaska Native, non-Hispanic/Latino; 5% Two or more races, non-Hispanic/Latino; 5% Race/ethnicity unknown; 1% international; 42% transferred in.

Freshmen

Admission: 170 enrolled.

Retention: 60% of full-time freshmen returned.

FACULTY

Total: 1,092, 29% full-time, 38% with terminal degrees.

Student/faculty ratio: 20:1.

ACADEMICS
Calendar: continuous. *Degrees:* certificates, associate, bachelor's, master's, post-master's, and postbachelor's certificates.

Special study options: academic remediation for entering students, accelerated degree program, adult/continuing education programs, advanced placement credit, cooperative education, distance learning, double majors, English as a second language, independent study, internships, off-campus study, part-time degree program, services for LD students, study abroad, summer session for credit. ***ROTC:*** Army (c), Air Force (c).

Computers: 2,800 computers/terminals are available on campus for general student use. Students can access the following: computer help desk, online (class) grades, online (class) registration, online (class) schedules. Campuswide network is available. Wireless service is available via entire campus.

STUDENT LIFE
Housing options: college housing not available.

Activities and organizations: student-run television station.

Campus security: 24-hour emergency response devices and patrols, late-night transport/escort service.

FINANCIAL AID
Financial Aid Of all full-time matriculated undergraduates who enrolled in 2013, 3,076 applied for aid, 2,293 were judged to have need, 75 had their need fully met. ***Average percent of need met:*** 78. ***Average financial aid package:*** $8518. ***Average need-based loan:*** $10,480. ***Average need-based gift aid:*** $8284. ***Average indebtedness upon graduation:*** $12,076.

APPLYING
Options: electronic application, deferred entrance.

Application fee: $60.

Required: high school transcript, minimum 2.0 GPA, interview. ***Required for some:*** essay or personal statement, TEAS Exam for BSN Students.

Application deadlines: rolling (freshmen), rolling (transfers).

Notification: continuous (freshmen), continuous (transfers).

CONTACT
National University, 11255 North Torrey Pines Road, La Jolla, CA 92037-1011. *Phone:* 800-628-8648 Ext. 7205. *Toll-free phone:* 800-NAT-UNIV.

★ NewSchool of Architecture and Design

San Diego, California

http://www.newschoolarch.edu/

- **Proprietary** comprehensive, founded 1980
- **Urban** 1-acre campus
- **Coed, primarily men**
- **Moderately difficult** entrance level

FACULTY
Student/faculty ratio: 9:1.

ACADEMICS
Calendar: quarters. *Degrees:* bachelor's and master's.

STUDENT LIFE
Housing options: college housing not availableCampus housing is provided by a third party.

Activities and organizations: student-run newspaper, American Institute of Architects student chapter, Student Council, Night Owls, Alpha Rho Chi - Numisius Chapter, CMSA.

Campus security: 24-hour emergency response devices.

Student services: personal/psychological counseling.

COSTS & FINANCIAL AID
Costs (2014–15) ***Tuition:*** $24,450 full-time. ***Required fees:*** $450 full-time.

Financial Aid Of all full-time matriculated undergraduates who enrolled in 2000, 71 applied for aid. 6 Federal Work-Study jobs (averaging $1544). In 2000, 6 non-need-based awards were made. ***Average percent of need met:*** 90. ***Average financial aid package:*** $9700. ***Average non-need-based aid:*** $5000. ***Average indebtedness upon graduation:*** $40,000.

APPLYING
Standardized Tests *Required:* SAT or ACT (for admission).

Options: electronic application, early decision.

Application fee: $75.

Required: essay or personal statement, minimum 2.5 GPA. ***Required for some:*** high school transcript, portfolio.

CONTACT
John Kim, Director of Enrollment Management, NewSchool of Architecture and Design, 1249 F Street, San Diego, CA 92101. *Phone:* 619-684-8841. *Toll-free phone:* 800-490-7081. *E-mail:* jkim@newschoolarch.edu.

Notre Dame de Namur University

Belmont, California

http://www.ndnu.edu/

- **Independent Roman Catholic** comprehensive, founded 1851
- **Suburban** 50-acre campus with easy access to San Francisco
- **Endowment** $16.3 million
- **Coed**
- **Moderately difficult** entrance level

FACULTY
Student/faculty ratio: 11:1.

ACADEMICS
Calendar: semesters. *Degrees:* bachelor's, master's, doctoral, and postbachelor's certificates.

STUDENT LIFE
Housing options: on-campus residence required through sophomore year; coed. Campus housing is university owned. Freshman campus housing is guaranteed.

Activities and organizations: drama/theater group, student-run newspaper, choral group, Associated Students of Notre Dame de Namur University, BizCom, Rotaract, Students for Sustainability, International Club.

Athletics Member NCAA. All Division II.

Campus security: 24-hour emergency response devices and patrols, late-night transport/escort service, controlled dormitory access.

Student services: health clinic, personal/psychological counseling.

COSTS & FINANCIAL AID
Costs (2014–15) ***Comprehensive fee:*** $44,316 includes full-time tuition ($31,422), mandatory fees ($400), and room and board ($12,494). Full-time tuition and fees vary according to degree level and program. Part-time tuition: $1014 per unit. Part-time tuition and fees vary according to degree level and program. ***College room only:*** $8114. Room and board charges vary according to board plan and housing facility.

Financial Aid Of all full-time matriculated undergraduates who enrolled in 2012, 761 applied for aid, 723 were judged to have need, 29 had their need fully met. 167 Federal Work-Study jobs (averaging $1991). In 2012, 35 non-need-based awards were made. ***Average percent of need met:*** 53. ***Average financial aid package:*** $22,173. ***Average need-based loan:*** $4767. ***Average need-based gift aid:*** $18,050. ***Average non-need-based aid:*** $7189. ***Average indebtedness upon graduation:*** $31,915.

APPLYING
Standardized Tests *Required:* SAT or ACT (for admission).

Options: electronic application, early admission, early action, deferred entrance.

Application fee: $50.

Required: essay or personal statement, high school transcript. ***Required for some:*** interview, audition for music programs.

CONTACT
Notre Dame de Namur University, 1500 Ralston Avenue, Belmont, CA 94002-1908. *Phone:* 650-508-3600. *Toll-free phone:* 800-263-0545.

Occidental College
Los Angeles, California
http://www.oxy.edu/

- **Independent** comprehensive, founded 1887
- **Urban** 120-acre campus with easy access to Los Angeles
- **Endowment** $406.1 million
- **Coed** 2,132 undergraduate students, 99% full-time, 56% women, 44% men
- **Very difficult** entrance level, 42% of applicants were admitted

UNDERGRAD STUDENTS
2,101 full-time, 31 part-time. Students come from 46 states and territories; 34 other countries; 48% are from out of state; 4% Black or African American, non-Hispanic/Latino; 15% Hispanic/Latino; 12% Asian, non-Hispanic/Latino; 0.2% Native Hawaiian or other Pacific Islander, non-Hispanic/Latino; 0.1% American Indian or Alaska Native, non-Hispanic/Latino; 10% Two or more races, non-Hispanic/Latino; 2% Race/ethnicity unknown; 6% international; 2% transferred in; 79% live on campus.

Freshmen
Admission: 6,071 applied, 2,552 admitted, 546 enrolled. ***Average high school GPA:*** 3.65. ***Test scores:*** SAT critical reading scores over 500: 99%; SAT math scores over 500: 99%; SAT writing scores over 500: 99%; ACT scores over 18: 100%; SAT critical reading scores over 600: 79%; SAT math scores over 600: 80%; SAT writing scores over 600: 81%; ACT scores over 24: 98%; SAT critical reading scores over 700: 22%; SAT math scores over 700: 28%; SAT writing scores over 700: 26%; ACT scores over 30: 49%.

Retention: 93% of full-time freshmen returned.

FACULTY
Total: 266, 64% full-time, 61% with terminal degrees.

Student/faculty ratio: 10:1.

ACADEMICS
Calendar: semesters. *Degrees:* bachelor's and master's.

Special study options: advanced placement credit, double majors, honors programs, independent study, internships, off-campus study, services for LD students, student-designed majors, study abroad. ***ROTC:*** Army (c), Air Force (c).

Unusual degree programs: 3-2 engineering with California Institute of Technology.

Computers: Students can access the following: campus intranet, computer help desk, free student e-mail accounts, online (class) grades, online (class) registration, online (class) schedules. Campuswide network is available. Wireless service is available via classrooms, computer centers, computer labs, dorm rooms, learning centers, libraries, student centers.

STUDENT LIFE
Housing options: on-campus residence required through junior year; coed, women-only. Campus housing is university owned. Freshman campus housing is guaranteed.

Activities and organizations: drama/theater group, student-run newspaper, radio station, choral group, Dance Production, FEAST (gardening), Oxypreneurship, Vagina Monologues, national sororities.

Athletics Member NCAA. All Division III. ***Intercollegiate sports:*** baseball M, basketball M/W, cross-country running M/W, football M, golf M/W, lacrosse M(c)/W, rugby M(c)/W(c), soccer M/W, softball W, swimming and diving M/W, tennis M/W, track and field M/W, ultimate Frisbee M(c)/W(c), volleyball W, water polo M/W. ***Intramural sports:*** basketball M/W, soccer M/W.

Campus security: 24-hour emergency response devices and patrols, late-night transport/escort service, controlled dormitory access.

Student services: health clinic, personal/psychological counseling, women's center.

FINANCIAL AID
Financial Aid Of all full-time matriculated undergraduates who enrolled in 2013, 1,348 applied for aid, 1,185 were judged to have need, 1,179 had their need fully met. 825 Federal Work-Study jobs (averaging $2653). 273 state and other part-time jobs (averaging $1494). In 2013, 279 non-need-based awards were made. ***Average percent of need met:*** 100. ***Average financial aid package:*** $43,195. ***Average need-based loan:*** $6282. ***Average need-based gift aid:*** $35,661. ***Average non-need-based aid:*** $9928. ***Average indebtedness upon graduation:*** $29,962. ***Financial aid deadline:*** 2/1.

APPLYING
Standardized Tests *Required:* SAT or ACT (for admission). *Recommended:* SAT Subject Tests (for admission).

Options: electronic application, early admission, early decision, deferred entrance.

Application fee: $60.

Required: essay or personal statement, high school transcript, 2 letters of recommendation.

Application deadlines: 1/10 (freshmen), 4/1 (transfers).

Early decision deadline: 11/15 (for plan 1), 1/1 (for plan 2).

CONTACT
Ms. Sally Stone Richmond, Dean of Admission, Occidental College, 1600 Campus Road, Los Angeles, CA 90041. *Phone:* 323-259-2700. *Toll-free phone:* 800-825-5262. *Fax:* 323-341-4875. *E-mail:* admission@oxy.edu.

Otis College of Art and Design
Los Angeles, California
http://www.otis.edu/

- **Independent** comprehensive, founded 1918
- **Urban** 5-acre campus
- **Coed** 1,032 undergraduate students, 99% full-time, 65% women, 35% men
- **Moderately difficult** entrance level, 46% of applicants were admitted

UNDERGRAD STUDENTS
1,018 full-time, 14 part-time. Students come from 26 states and territories; 15 other countries; 13% are from out of state; 3% Black or African American, non-Hispanic/Latino; 13% Hispanic/Latino; 32% Asian, non-Hispanic/Latino; 0.3% Native Hawaiian or other Pacific Islander, non-Hispanic/Latino; 0.6% American Indian or Alaska Native, non-Hispanic/Latino; 6% Two or more races, non-Hispanic/Latino; 3% Race/ethnicity unknown; 19% international; 11% transferred in; 9% live on campus.

Freshmen
Admission: 1,584 applied, 733 admitted, 160 enrolled. ***Average high school GPA:*** 3.17. ***Test scores:*** SAT critical reading scores over 500: 51%; SAT math scores over 500: 56%; ACT scores over 18: 83%; SAT critical reading scores over 600: 12%; SAT math scores over 600: 22%; ACT scores over 24: 35%; SAT critical reading scores over 700: 1%; SAT math scores over 700: 5%; ACT scores over 30: 5%.

Retention: 81% of full-time freshmen returned.

FACULTY
Total: 272, 20% full-time, 42% with terminal degrees.

Student/faculty ratio: 4:1.

ACADEMICS
Calendar: semesters. *Degrees:* bachelor's and master's.

Special study options: academic remediation for entering students, adult/continuing education programs, advanced placement credit, cooperative education, double majors, freshman honors college, honors programs, independent study, internships, off-campus study, services for LD students, student-designed majors, study abroad, summer session for credit.

Computers: 400 computers/terminals are available on campus for general student use. Students can access the following: campus intranet, computer help desk, free student e-mail accounts, online (class) grades, online (class) registration, online (class) schedules. Campuswide network is available. Wireless service is available via entire campus.

STUDENT LIFE
Housing options: Campus housing is provided by a third party. Freshman applicants given priority for college housing.

Activities and organizations: Student Government Association, international students organization, Otis Students in Service (OASIS), Literary Magazine Club, Campus Crusade.

Athletics ***Intramural sports:*** skiing (downhill) W, soccer M.

Campus security: 24-hour patrols.

Student services: personal/psychological counseling.

COSTS & FINANCIAL AID

Costs (2014–15) ***Comprehensive fee:*** $38,330 includes full-time tuition ($37,380) and room and board ($950).

Financial Aid Of all full-time matriculated undergraduates who enrolled in 2014, 733 applied for aid, 701 were judged to have need, 47 had their need fully met. In 2014, 180 non-need-based awards were made. ***Average percent of need met:*** 60. ***Average financial aid package:*** $26,104. ***Average need-based loan:*** $4696. ***Average need-based gift aid:*** $20,241. ***Average non-need-based aid:*** $9919. ***Average indebtedness upon graduation:*** $33,694.

APPLYING

Standardized Tests *Required:* SAT or ACT (for admission).

Options: electronic application, early admission.

Application fee: $50.

Required: essay or personal statement, high school transcript, minimum 2.5 GPA, portfolio. ***Recommended:*** interview.

Application deadlines: rolling (freshmen), rolling (transfers).

Notification: continuous (freshmen), continuous (transfers).

CONTACT

Otis College of Art and Design, 9045 Lincoln Boulevard, Los Angeles, CA 90045-9785. *Phone:* 310-665-2577. *Toll-free phone:* 800-527-OTIS.

Pacific Union College

Angwin, California

http://www.puc.edu/

- **Independent Seventh-day Adventist** comprehensive, founded 1882
- **Rural** 200-acre campus with easy access to San Francisco Bay Area
- **Coed**
- **Moderately difficult** entrance level

FACULTY

Student/faculty ratio: 14:1.

ACADEMICS

Calendar: quarters. *Degrees:* certificates, associate, bachelor's, and master's.

STUDENT LIFE

Housing options: on-campus residence required through senior year; men-only, women-only. Campus housing is university owned.

Activities and organizations: drama/theater group, student-run newspaper, choral group, Student Association, Business Club, Asian Student Association, Korean Adventist Student Association, Student Organization of Latinos.

Athletics Member NAIA.

Campus security: 24-hour emergency response devices and patrols, late-night transport/escort service.

Student services: health clinic, personal/psychological counseling, women's center.

COSTS & FINANCIAL AID

Costs (2014–15) ***Comprehensive fee:*** $35,616 includes full-time tuition ($27,081), mandatory fees ($1050), and room and board ($7485). Full-time tuition and fees vary according to course load. Part-time tuition and fees vary according to course load. No tuition increase for student's term of enrollment.

Financial Aid Of all full-time matriculated undergraduates who enrolled in 2013, 1,441 applied for aid, 1,150 were judged to have need, 11 had their need fully met. 225 Federal Work-Study jobs (averaging $2916). In 2013, 295 non-need-based awards were made. ***Average percent of need met:*** 12. ***Average financial aid package:*** $22,489. ***Average need-based loan:*** $4778. ***Average need-based gift aid:*** $16,283. ***Average non-need-based aid:*** $8264. ***Average indebtedness upon graduation:*** $42,153.

APPLYING

Standardized Tests *Required:* SAT or ACT (for admission).

Options: electronic application, deferred entrance.

Application fee: $30.

Required: high school transcript, minimum 2.3 GPA, 3 letters of recommendation.

CONTACT

Mr. Craig Philpott, Associate Director, Admissions, Pacific Union College, Enrollment Services, One Angwin Avenue, Angwin, CA 94508. *Phone:* 800-862-7080. *Toll-free phone:* 800-862-7080. *Fax:* 707-965-6671. *E-mail:* enroll@puc.edu.

Palo Alto University

Palo Alto, California

http://www.paloaltou.edu/

- **Independent** upper-level
- **Rural** campus with easy access to San Francisco Bay Area/Silicon Valley
- **Coed** 194 undergraduate students, 97% full-time, 70% women, 30% men

UNDERGRAD STUDENTS

189 full-time, 5 part-time. Students come from 1 other state; 4 other countries; 3% Black or African American, non-Hispanic/Latino; 23% Hispanic/Latino; 27% Asian, non-Hispanic/Latino; 1% Native Hawaiian or other Pacific Islander, non-Hispanic/Latino; 8% Two or more races, non-Hispanic/Latino; 5% Race/ethnicity unknown; 3% international; 45% transferred in.

ACADEMICS

Degrees: bachelor's, master's, and doctoral.

COSTS

Costs (2014–15) ***Tuition:*** $15,671 full-time. Full-time tuition and fees vary according to class time and program. No tuition increase for student's term of enrollment. ***Required fees:*** $4757 full-time.

CONTACT

Mr. Michael Teodosio, Assistant Director of Undergraduate Admissions, Palo Alto University, 935 East Meadow Drive, Palo Alto, CA 94303-4232. *Phone:* 650-417-2050. *Toll-free phone:* 800-818-6136. *E-mail:* undergrad@paloaltou.edu.

Pepperdine University

Malibu, California

http://www.pepperdine.edu/

- **Independent** university, founded 1937, affiliated with Church of Christ
- **Suburban** 830-acre campus with easy access to Los Angeles
- **Endowment** $790.5 million
- **Coed** 3,451 undergraduate students, 91% full-time, 59% women, 41% men
- **Very difficult** entrance level, 35% of applicants were admitted

UNDERGRAD STUDENTS

3,129 full-time, 322 part-time. Students come from 52 states and territories; 71 other countries; 41% are from out of state; 6% Black or African American, non-Hispanic/Latino; 13% Hispanic/Latino; 13% Asian, non-Hispanic/Latino; 0.3% Native Hawaiian or other Pacific Islander, non-Hispanic/Latino; 0.4% American Indian or Alaska Native, non-Hispanic/Latino; 9% Two or more races, non-Hispanic/Latino; 4% Race/ethnicity unknown; 9% international; 3% transferred in; 54% live on campus.

Freshmen

Admission: 8,914 applied, 3,161 admitted, 656 enrolled. ***Average high school GPA:*** 3.61. ***Test scores:*** SAT critical reading scores over 500: 94%; SAT math scores over 500: 96%; SAT writing scores over 500: 94%; ACT scores over 18: 100%; SAT critical reading scores over 600: 58%; SAT math scores over 600: 65%; SAT writing scores over 600: 60%; ACT scores over 24: 91%; SAT critical reading scores over 700: 12%; SAT math scores over 700: 20%; SAT writing scores over 700: 14%; ACT scores over 30: 27%.

Retention: 93% of full-time freshmen returned.

FACULTY

Total: 709, 54% full-time, 74% with terminal degrees.

Student/faculty ratio: 13:1.

ACADEMICS

Calendar: semesters. *Degrees:* bachelor's, master's, and doctoral.

Special study options: adult/continuing education programs, advanced placement credit, double majors, honors programs, independent study, internships, part-time degree program, student-designed majors, study abroad, summer session for credit. ***ROTC:*** Army (c), Air Force (c).

Unusual degree programs: 3-2 engineering with University of Southern California School of Engineering, or Washington University School of Engineering in St. Louis; 5-year BS/MBA program -Pepperdine's Graziadio School of Business and Management offers a program that allows Seaver College business majors to earn their bachelor's and MBA or International MBA degrees in just five years.

Computers: 218 computers/terminals and 139 ports are available on campus for general student use. Students can access the following: campus intranet, computer help desk, free student e-mail accounts, online (class) grades, online (class) registration, online (class) schedules. Campuswide network is available. 100% of college-owned or -operated housing units are wired for high-speed Internet access. Wireless service is available via entire campus.

STUDENT LIFE

Housing options: on-campus residence required through sophomore year; men-only, women-only, special housing for students with disabilities. Campus housing is university owned. Freshman campus housing is guaranteed.

Activities and organizations: drama/theater group, student-run newspaper, radio and television station, choral group, Latino Student Association, Black Student Union, Panhellenic Council, Interfraternity Council, International Justice Mission, national fraternities, national sororities.

Athletics Member NCAA. All Division I. ***Intercollegiate sports:*** baseball M(s), basketball M(s)/W(s), cheerleading M/W, crew M(c)/W(c), cross-country running M(s)/W(s), field hockey W(c), golf M(s)/W(s), lacrosse M(c), rugby M(c), sailing M(c)/W(c), soccer M(c)/W(s), swimming and diving W(s), tennis M(s)/W(s), volleyball M(s)/W(s), water polo M(s)/W(c). ***Intramural sports:*** badminton M/W, basketball M/W, cross-country running M/W, football M/W, golf M/W, lacrosse M, soccer M/W, softball M/W, swimming and diving M/W, tennis M/W, volleyball M/W.

Campus security: 24-hour emergency response devices and patrols, student patrols, late-night transport/escort service, controlled dormitory access, front gate security, 24-hour security in residence halls, controlled access, crime prevention programs.

Student services: health clinic, personal/psychological counseling.

COSTS & FINANCIAL AID

Costs (2014–15) ***Comprehensive fee:*** $60,082 includes full-time tuition ($46,440), mandatory fees ($252), and room and board ($13,390). Part-time tuition: $1455 per credit hour. ***Room and board:*** Room and board charges vary according to board plan and housing facility. ***Payment plan:*** installment. ***Waivers:*** employees or children of employees.

Financial Aid Of all full-time matriculated undergraduates who enrolled in 2014, 2,627 applied for aid, 1,753 were judged to have need, 361 had their need fully met. In 2014, 501 non-need-based awards were made. ***Average percent of need met:*** 79. ***Average financial aid package:*** $40,131. ***Average need-based loan:*** $5460. ***Average need-based gift aid:*** $37,394. ***Average non-need-based aid:*** $18,784. ***Average indebtedness upon graduation:*** $31,884.

APPLYING

Standardized Tests *Required:* SAT or ACT (for admission).

Options: electronic application.

Application fee: $65.

Required: essay or personal statement, high school transcript, 2 letters of recommendation.

Application deadlines: 1/5 (freshmen), 1/5 (out-of-state freshmen), 1/5 (transfers).

Notification: 4/1 (freshmen), 4/1 (out-of-state freshmen), 4/1 (transfers).

CONTACT

Mrs. Laura Kalinkewicz, Director of Admission, Enrollment Management, Seaver College, Pepperdine University, 24255 Pacific Coast Highway, Malibu, CA 90263. *Phone:* 310-506-4392. *E-mail:* laura.reisert@pepperdine.edu.

See below for display ad and page 1566 for the College Close-Up.

Pitzer College

Claremont, California

http://www.pitzer.edu/

- **Independent** 4-year, founded 1963, part of The Claremont Colleges Consortium
- **Suburban** 35-acre campus with easy access to Los Angeles
- **Endowment** $118.4 million
- **Coed**
- **Very difficult** entrance level

FACULTY
Student/faculty ratio: 10:1.

ACADEMICS
Calendar: semesters. *Degree:* bachelor's.

STUDENT LIFE
Housing options: on-campus residence required for freshman year; coed, women-only, cooperative, special housing for students with disabilities. Campus housing is university owned. Freshman campus housing is guaranteed.

Activities and organizations: drama/theater group, student-run newspaper, radio station, choral group, Student Senate, The Other Side, Without A Box, Residence Hall Association.

Athletics Member NCAA. All Division III.

Campus security: 24-hour emergency response devices and patrols, late-night transport/escort service, controlled dormitory access.

Student services: health clinic, personal/psychological counseling, women's center.

COSTS & FINANCIAL AID
Costs (2014–15) ***Comprehensive fee:*** $61,750 includes full-time tuition ($46,720), mandatory fees ($272), and room and board ($14,758). Part-time tuition: $5840 per course. Part-time tuition and fees vary according to course load. ***College room only:*** $8538. Room and board charges vary according to board plan. ***Payment plans:*** installment, deferred payment.

Financial Aid Of all full-time matriculated undergraduates who enrolled in 2013, 408 applied for aid, 345 were judged to have need, 345 had their need fully met. In 2013, 8 non-need-based awards were made. ***Average percent of need met:*** 100. ***Average financial aid package:*** $40,635. ***Average need-based loan:*** $3421. ***Average need-based gift aid:*** $35,107. ***Average non-need-based aid:*** $5000. ***Average indebtedness upon graduation:*** $18,030. ***Financial aid deadline:*** 2/1.

APPLYING
Standardized Tests *Required for some:* SAT or ACT (for admission).

Options: electronic application, early decision, deferred entrance.

Application fee: $60.

Required: essay or personal statement, high school transcript, minimum 2.0 GPA, 3 letters of recommendation. ***Recommended:*** interview.

CONTACT
Mr. Angel Perez, Vice President for Admission and Financial Aid, Pitzer College, 1050 North Mills Avenue, Claremont, CA 91711-6101. *Phone:* 909-621-8129. *Toll-free phone:* 800-748-9371. *Fax:* 909-621-8770. *E-mail:* admission@pitzer.edu.

Platt College San Diego

San Diego, California

http://www.platt.edu/

- **Proprietary** 4-year, founded 1879
- **Suburban** 1-acre campus
- **Coed**

FACULTY
Student/faculty ratio: 21:1.

ACADEMICS
Calendar: continuous. *Degree:* certificates, diplomas, and bachelor's.

STUDENT LIFE
Housing options: college housing not available.

Campus security: 24-hour emergency response devices, surveillance cameras, security guard for evening session.

Student services: personal/psychological counseling.

APPLYING
Standardized Tests *Required:* Wonderlic aptitude test (for admission). *Recommended:* SAT or ACT (for admission), SAT and SAT Subject Tests or ACT (for admission), SAT Subject Tests (for admission).

Options: early admission, deferred entrance.

Application fee: $110.

Required: essay or personal statement, high school transcript, interview.

CONTACT
Ms. Kimberly Harbert, Director of Admissions, Platt College San Diego, 6250 El Cajon Boulevard, San Diego, CA 92115-3919. *Phone:* 619-265-0107. *Toll-free phone:* 866-752-8826. *Fax:* 619-265-8655. *E-mail:* kharbert@platt.edu.

Point Loma Nazarene University

San Diego, California

http://www.pointloma.edu/

- **Independent Nazarene** comprehensive, founded 1902
- **Suburban** 93-acre campus with easy access to San Diego
- **Endowment** $25.7 million
- **Coed** 2,568 undergraduate students, 97% full-time, 64% women, 36% men
- **Moderately difficult** entrance level, 70% of applicants were admitted

UNDERGRAD STUDENTS
2,493 full-time, 75 part-time. 17% are from out of state; 2% Black or African American, non-Hispanic/Latino; 22% Hispanic/Latino; 5% Asian, non-Hispanic/Latino; 0.9% Native Hawaiian or other Pacific Islander, non-Hispanic/Latino; 0.9% American Indian or Alaska Native, non-Hispanic/Latino; 6% Two or more races, non-Hispanic/Latino; 0.9% Race/ethnicity unknown; 0.5% international; 8% transferred in; 67% live on campus.

Freshmen
Admission: 3,036 applied, 2,111 admitted, 588 enrolled. ***Average high school GPA:*** 3.76. ***Test scores:*** SAT critical reading scores over 500: 82%; SAT math scores over 500: 82%; SAT writing scores over 500: 79%; ACT scores over 18: 100%; SAT critical reading scores over 600: 30%; SAT math scores over 600: 36%; SAT writing scores over 600: 26%; ACT scores over 24: 71%; SAT critical reading scores over 700: 4%; SAT math scores over 700: 5%; SAT writing scores over 700: 4%; ACT scores over 30: 13%.

Retention: 85% of full-time freshmen returned.

FACULTY
Total: 351, 39% full-time, 49% with terminal degrees.

Student/faculty ratio: 14:1.

ACADEMICS
Calendar: semesters. *Degrees:* certificates, bachelor's, master's, and post-master's certificates.

Special study options: academic remediation for entering students, adult/continuing education programs, advanced placement credit, distance learning, double majors, honors programs, independent study, internships, off-campus study, part-time degree program, services for LD students, study abroad, summer session for credit. ***ROTC:*** Army (c), Navy (c), Air Force (c).

Computers: 346 computers/terminals and 5,320 ports are available on campus for general student use. Students can access the following: campus intranet, computer help desk, free student e-mail accounts, online (class) grades, online (class) registration, online (class) schedules. Campuswide network is available. 100% of college-owned or -operated housing units are wired for high-speed Internet access. Wireless service is available via entire campus.

STUDENT LIFE
Housing options: on-campus residence required for freshman year; men-only, women-only, special housing for students with disabilities. Campus housing is university owned. Freshman campus housing is guaranteed.

Activities and organizations: drama/theater group, student-run newspaper, radio and television station, choral group.

Athletics Member NCAA. All Division II. ***Intercollegiate sports:*** baseball M(s), basketball M(s)/W(s), cross-country running W(s), golf W(s), soccer M(s)/W(s), tennis M(s)/W(s), track and field W(s), volleyball W(s). ***Intramural sports:*** basketball M/W, cheerleading M(c)/W(c), football M/W, rugby M(c)/W(c), soccer M/W, softball M/W, tennis M/W, volleyball M/W.

Campus security: 24-hour patrols, student patrols, late-night transport/escort service.

Student services: health clinic, personal/psychological counseling, women's center.

COSTS & FINANCIAL AID

Costs (2014–15) ***Comprehensive fee:*** $41,006 includes full-time tuition ($30,800), mandatory fees ($606), and room and board ($9600). Full-time tuition and fees vary according to course load. Part-time tuition: $1285 per credit hour. Part-time tuition and fees vary according to course load. ***Room and board:*** Room and board charges vary according to board plan. ***Payment plan:*** installment. ***Waivers:*** senior citizens and employees or children of employees.

Financial Aid Of all full-time matriculated undergraduates who enrolled in 2013, 2,023 applied for aid, 1,723 were judged to have need, 261 had their need fully met. In 2013, 399 non-need-based awards were made. ***Average percent of need met:*** 63. ***Average financial aid package:*** $21,589. ***Average need-based loan:*** $4802. ***Average need-based gift aid:*** $15,892. ***Average non-need-based aid:*** $8656. ***Average indebtedness upon graduation:*** $32,649.

APPLYING

Standardized Tests *Required:* SAT or ACT (for admission). *Recommended:* SAT (for admission), ACT (for admission).

Options: electronic application, early action.

Application fee: $50.

Required: essay or personal statement, high school transcript, minimum 2.8 GPA, 2 letters of recommendation.

Application deadlines: 2/15 (freshmen), 11/15 (early action).

Notification: 4/1 (freshmen), 12/21 (early action).

CONTACT

Shannon Hutchison, Director of Undergraduate Admissions, Point Loma Nazarene University, 3900 Lomaland Drive, San Diego, CA 92106. *Phone:* 619-849-2541. *Toll-free phone:* 800-733-7770. *Fax:* 619-849-2601. *E-mail:* admissions@pointloma.edu.

Pomona College

Claremont, California

http://www.pomona.edu/

- **Independent** 4-year, founded 1887
- **Suburban** 140-acre campus with easy access to Los Angeles
- **Endowment** $2.1 million
- **Coed** 1,650 undergraduate students, 99% full-time, 51% women, 49% men
- **Most difficult** entrance level, 12% of applicants were admitted

UNDERGRAD STUDENTS

1,634 full-time, 16 part-time. Students come from 47 states and territories; 26 other countries; 72% are from out of state; 7% Black or African American, non-Hispanic/Latino; 14% Hispanic/Latino; 13% Asian, non-Hispanic/Latino; 0.1% Native Hawaiian or other Pacific Islander, non-Hispanic/Latino; 0.2% American Indian or Alaska Native, non-Hispanic/Latino; 7% Two or more races, non-Hispanic/Latino; 7% Race/ethnicity unknown; 9% international; 0.3% transferred in; 99% live on campus.

Freshmen

Admission: 7,727 applied, 942 admitted, 450 enrolled. ***Test scores:*** SAT critical reading scores over 500: 100%; SAT math scores over 500: 100%; SAT writing scores over 500: 100%; ACT scores over 18: 100%; SAT critical reading scores over 600: 98%; SAT math scores over 600: 98%; SAT writing scores over 600: 97%; ACT scores over 24: 100%; SAT critical reading scores over 700: 73%; SAT math scores over 700: 75%; SAT writing scores over 700: 75%; ACT scores over 30: 83%.

Retention: 99% of full-time freshmen returned.

FACULTY

Total: 232, 81% full-time, 91% with terminal degrees.

Student/faculty ratio: 8:1.

ACADEMICS

Calendar: semesters. *Degree:* bachelor's.

Special study options: advanced placement credit, double majors, independent study, internships, off-campus study, services for LD students, student-designed majors, study abroad. ***ROTC:*** Army (c), Air Force (c).

Unusual degree programs: 3-2 engineering with California Institute of Technology, Washington University in St. Louis, Dartmouth College.

Computers: 180 computers/terminals are available on campus for general student use. Students can access the following: computer help desk, free student e-mail accounts, online (class) grades, online (class) registration, online (class) schedules. Campuswide network is available. 100% of college-owned or -operated housing units are wired for high-speed Internet access. Wireless service is available via entire campus.

STUDENT LIFE

Housing options: on-campus residence required for freshman year; coed. Campus housing is university owned. Freshman campus housing is guaranteed.

Activities and organizations: drama/theater group, student-run newspaper, radio station, choral group, student government, music/choral organizations, service organizations, intramural sports, outdoor activities club.

Athletics Member NCAA. All Division III. ***Intercollegiate sports:*** baseball M, basketball M/W, cross-country running M/W, football M, golf M/W, lacrosse W, soccer M/W, softball W, swimming and diving M/W, tennis M/W, track and field M/W, ultimate Frisbee M(c)/W(c), volleyball M(c)/W, water polo M/W. ***Intramural sports:*** badminton M(c)/W(c), basketball M/W, crew W(c), cross-country running M/W, equestrian sports M(c)/W(c), fencing M/W, field hockey M(c)/W(c), football M, golf M/W, lacrosse M(c), racquetball M/W, rock climbing M/W, skiing (cross-country) M(c)/W(c), skiing (downhill) M(c)/W(c), soccer M/W, softball M/W, squash M/W, swimming and diving M/W, tennis M/W, track and field M/W, ultimate Frisbee M, volleyball M/W, water polo M/W.

Campus security: 24-hour emergency response devices and patrols, late-night transport/escort service, controlled dormitory access.

Student services: health clinic, personal/psychological counseling, women's center.

COSTS & FINANCIAL AID

Costs (2014–15) ***Comprehensive fee:*** $60,532 includes full-time tuition ($45,500), mandatory fees ($332), and room and board ($14,700). ***Room and board:*** Room and board charges vary according to board plan. ***Payment plan:*** installment. ***Waivers:*** employees or children of employees.

Financial Aid Of all full-time matriculated undergraduates who enrolled in 2013, 1,135 applied for aid, 894 were judged to have need, 894 had their need fully met. 150 Federal Work-Study jobs (averaging $1598). 836 state and other part-time jobs (averaging $1857). ***Average percent of need met:*** 100. ***Average financial aid package:*** $43,395. ***Average need-based gift aid:*** $41,443. ***Average indebtedness upon graduation:*** $16,273. ***Financial aid deadline:*** 3/1.

APPLYING

Standardized Tests *Required:* SAT and SAT Subject Tests or ACT (for admission).

Options: electronic application, early admission, early decision, deferred entrance.

Application fee: $70.

Required: essay or personal statement, high school transcript, 2 letters of recommendation. ***Recommended:*** interview, Supplemental forms for visual and performing arts and science research are available.

Application deadlines: 1/1 (freshmen), 3/15 (transfers).

Early decision deadline: 11/1 (for plan 1), 1/1 (for plan 2).

Notification: 4/1 (freshmen), 5/15 (transfers), 12/15 (early decision plan 1), 2/15 (early decision plan 2).

CONTACT
Mr. C. Seth Allen, Vice President for Enrollment and Dean of Admissions and Financial Aid, Pomona College, 333 North College Way, Claremont, CA 91711. *Phone:* 909-621-8134. *Fax:* 909-621-8952. *E-mail:* admissions@pomona.edu.

Saint Mary's College of California

Moraga, California

http://www.stmarys-ca.edu/

- **Independent Roman Catholic** upper-level, founded 1863
- **Suburban** 420-acre campus with easy access to San Francisco
- **Endowment** $143.9 million
- **Coed**
- **Moderately difficult** entrance level

FACULTY
Student/faculty ratio: 12:1.

ACADEMICS
Calendar: 4-1-4. *Degrees:* bachelor's, master's, and doctoral.

STUDENT LIFE
Housing options: coed, men-only, women-only, special housing for students with disabilities. Campus housing is university owned. Freshman campus housing is guaranteed.

Activities and organizations: drama/theater group, student-run newspaper, radio and television station, choral group, Gael Force, Campus Activities Board, LASA-Latin American Student Association-Black Student Union, La Hermandad, Asian Pacific America Student Association.

Athletics Member NCAA. All Division I.

Campus security: 24-hour emergency response devices and patrols, late-night transport/escort service.

Student services: health clinic, personal/psychological counseling, women's center.

COSTS & FINANCIAL AID
Costs (2014–15) ***Comprehensive fee:*** $55,520 includes full-time tuition ($41,230), mandatory fees ($150), and room and board ($14,140). Part-time tuition: $5160 per credit hour. Part-time tuition and fees vary according to course load and program. ***College room only:*** $7710. Room and board charges vary according to board plan and housing facility. ***Payment plans:*** tuition prepayment, installment.

Financial Aid Of all full-time matriculated undergraduates who enrolled in 2013, 2,317 applied for aid, 2,139 were judged to have need, 152 had their need fully met. 328 Federal Work-Study jobs (averaging $2014). In 2013, 255 non-need-based awards were made. ***Average percent of need met:*** 61. ***Average financial aid package:*** $26,434. ***Average need-based loan:*** $4367. ***Average need-based gift aid:*** $21,270. ***Average non-need-based aid:*** $13,387. ***Average indebtedness upon graduation:*** $33,000.

APPLYING
Standardized Tests *Required:* SAT or ACT (for admission).

Options: electronic application, early action, deferred entrance.

Application fee: $55.

CONTACT
Mr. Michael McKeon, Dean of Admissions, Saint Mary's College of California, PO Box 4800, Moraga, CA 94575-4800. *Phone:* 925-631-4224. *Toll-free phone:* 800-800-4SMC. *Fax:* 925-376-7193. *E-mail:* smcadmit@stmarys-ca.edu.

Samuel Merritt University

Oakland, California

http://www.samuelmerritt.edu/

- **Independent** upper-level, founded 1909
- **Urban** 1-acre campus with easy access to San Francisco
- **Coed, primarily women** 601 undergraduate students, 86% full-time, 83% women, 17% men
- **Moderately difficult** entrance level

UNDERGRAD STUDENTS
515 full-time, 86 part-time. Students come from 3 states and territories; 1 other country; 0.3% are from out of state; 3% Black or African American, non-Hispanic/Latino; 14% Hispanic/Latino; 25% Asian, non-Hispanic/Latino; 1% Native Hawaiian or other Pacific Islander, non-Hispanic/Latino; 0.2% American Indian or Alaska Native, non-Hispanic/Latino; 9% Two or more races, non-Hispanic/Latino; 5% Race/ethnicity unknown; 0.2% international; 40% transferred in.

FACULTY
Total: 278, 32% full-time, 35% with terminal degrees.

Student/faculty ratio: 8:1.

ACADEMICS
Calendar: trimesters. *Degrees:* bachelor's, master's, and doctoral (bachelor's degree offered jointly with Saint Mary's College of California).

Special study options: academic remediation for entering students, accelerated degree program, advanced placement credit, cooperative education, distance learning, independent study, internships, off-campus study, services for LD students. ***ROTC:*** Army (c), Air Force (c).

Computers: 152 computers/terminals are available on campus for general student use. Students can access the following: campus intranet, computer help desk, free student e-mail accounts, online (class) grades, online (class) registration, online (class) schedules. Campuswide network is available. Wireless service is available via entire campus.

STUDENT LIFE
Housing options: college housing not available.

Activities and organizations: Student Body Association, California Podiatric Medical Students' Association (CPMSA), International Healthcare Club, Community Service Honor Society, Scholars in Service.

Campus security: 24-hour emergency response devices and patrols, late-night transport/escort service, 24-hour controlled access.

Student services: health clinic, personal/psychological counseling.

COSTS & FINANCIAL AID
Costs (2015–16) ***Tuition:*** $42,880 full-time, $1807 per credit part-time. Full-time tuition and fees vary according to program. Part-time tuition and fees vary according to program. ***Required fees:*** $1234 full-time. ***Payment plan:*** installment.

Financial Aid Of all full-time matriculated undergraduates who enrolled in 2009, 495 applied for aid, 448 were judged to have need, 20 had their need fully met. 120 Federal Work-Study jobs (averaging $1583). ***Average percent of need met:*** 69. ***Average financial aid package:*** $32,000. ***Average need-based loan:*** $10,457. ***Average need-based gift aid:*** $20,000.

APPLYING
Options: electronic application, deferred entrance.

Application fee: $50.

Notification: continuous (transfers).

CONTACT
Samuel Merritt University, 3100 Telegraph Avenue, Oakland, CA 94609-3108. *Phone:* 510-869-1508. *Toll-free phone:* 800-607-6377.

San Diego Christian College

Santee, California

http://www.sdcc.edu/

- **Independent nondenominational** 4-year, founded 1970
- **Suburban** 10-acre campus with easy access to San Diego
- **Coed** 939 undergraduate students, 90% full-time, 50% women, 50% men
- **Moderately difficult** entrance level, 56% of applicants were admitted

UNDERGRAD STUDENTS
842 full-time, 97 part-time. Students come from 49 states and territories; 16 other countries; 27% are from out of state; 13% Black or African American, non-Hispanic/Latino; 20% Hispanic/Latino; 2% Asian, non-Hispanic/Latino; 1% Native Hawaiian or other Pacific Islander, non-Hispanic/Latino; 0.3% American Indian or Alaska Native, non-Hispanic/Latino; 3% Two or more races, non-Hispanic/Latino; 15% Race/ethnicity unknown; 2% international; 15% transferred in; 36% live on campus.

Freshmen
Admission: 409 applied, 227 admitted, 129 enrolled. ***Average high school GPA:*** 3.4. ***Test scores:*** SAT critical reading scores over 500: 39%; SAT math scores over 500: 46%; SAT writing scores over 500: 48%; ACT scores over 18: 81%; SAT critical reading scores over 600: 19%; SAT math scores over 600: 11%; SAT writing scores over 600: 14%; ACT scores over 24: 42%; SAT critical reading scores over 700: 5%; SAT math scores over 700: 1%; ACT scores over 30: 13%.

Retention: 76% of full-time freshmen returned.

FACULTY
Total: 101, 18% full-time, 17% with terminal degrees.

Student/faculty ratio: 19:1.

ACADEMICS
Calendar: semesters. *Degrees:* associate, bachelor's, and postbachelor's certificates.

Special study options: academic remediation for entering students, accelerated degree program, adult/continuing education programs, advanced placement credit, distance learning, double majors, honors programs, independent study, internships, off-campus study, part-time degree program, services for LD students, student-designed majors, study abroad, summer session for credit. ***ROTC:*** Army (c), Air Force (c).

Computers: 35 computers/terminals are available on campus for general student use. Students can access the following: computer help desk, free student e-mail accounts, online (class) grades, online (class) schedules, All wireless campus. Students have access to online storage, web-based programs. Campuswide network is available. 100% of college-owned or -operated housing units are wired for high-speed Internet access. Wireless service is available via entire campus.

STUDENT LIFE
Housing options: on-campus residence required through sophomore year; men-only, women-only. Campus housing is leased by the school. Freshman campus housing is guaranteed.

Activities and organizations: drama/theater group, choral group, ASB - Student Government, Service & Community Engagement, Ministry Teams, Flight team, SALSA.

Athletics Member NAIA. ***Intercollegiate sports:*** baseball M(s), basketball M(s)/W(s), cross-country running M(s)/W(s), soccer M(s)/W(s), softball W, tennis M(s)/W(s), volleyball W(s). ***Intramural sports:*** basketball M/W, soccer M/W, softball M/W, ultimate Frisbee M/W, volleyball M/W.

Campus security: 24-hour emergency response devices and patrols, late-night transport/escort service.

Student services: health clinic, personal/psychological counseling.

COSTS & FINANCIAL AID
Costs (2015–16) ***Comprehensive fee:*** $38,970 includes full-time tuition ($26,850), mandatory fees ($1620), and room and board ($10,500). Full-time tuition and fees vary according to class time, course load, location, and program. Part-time tuition: $1150 per credit. Part-time tuition and fees vary according to class time, course load, and program. ***Required fees:*** $250 per term part-time. ***Room and board:*** Room and board charges vary according to board plan and location. ***Payment plan:*** installment. ***Waivers:*** employees or children of employees.

Financial Aid Of all full-time matriculated undergraduates who enrolled in 2013, 831 applied for aid, 706 were judged to have need, 58 had their need fully met. 20 Federal Work-Study jobs (averaging $2458). 9 state and other part-time jobs (averaging $2200). In 2013, 11 non-need-based awards were made. ***Average percent of need met:*** 81. ***Average financial aid package:*** $14,556. ***Average need-based loan:*** $4256. ***Average need-based gift aid:*** $5926. ***Average non-need-based aid:*** $3541. ***Average indebtedness upon graduation:*** $19,212. ***Financial aid deadline:*** 7/15.

APPLYING
Standardized Tests *Required for some:* SAT or ACT (for admission).

Options: electronic application, deferred entrance.

Application fee: $25.

Required: essay or personal statement, high school transcript, 2 letters of recommendation. ***Required for some:*** interview. ***Recommended:*** minimum 2.8 GPA.

Application deadlines: rolling (freshmen), rolling (out-of-state freshmen), rolling (transfers).

Notification: continuous (freshmen), continuous (out-of-state freshmen), continuous (transfers).

CONTACT
Christine Roberts, Admissions Manager, San Diego Christian College, 200 Riverview Parkway, Santee, CA 92017. *Phone:* 619-201-8760. *Toll-free phone:* 800-676-2242. *Fax:* 619-201-8749. *E-mail:* christine.roberts@sdcc.edu.

San Diego State University
San Diego, California
http://www.sdsu.edu/

- **State-supported** university, founded 1897, part of California State University System
- **Urban** 283-acre campus with easy access to San Diego
- **Endowment** $201.1 million
- **Coed** 28,362 undergraduate students, 88% full-time, 55% women, 45% men
- **Moderately difficult** entrance level, 34% of applicants were admitted

UNDERGRAD STUDENTS
25,088 full-time, 3,274 part-time. Students come from 54 states and territories; 114 other countries; 7% are from out of state; 4% Black or African American, non-Hispanic/Latino; 31% Hispanic/Latino; 13% Asian, non-Hispanic/Latino; 0.3% Native Hawaiian or other Pacific Islander, non-Hispanic/Latino; 0.3% American Indian or Alaska Native, non-Hispanic/Latino; 6% Two or more races, non-Hispanic/Latino; 5% Race/ethnicity unknown; 6% international; 11% transferred in; 14% live on campus.

Freshmen
Admission: 56,921 applied, 19,625 admitted, 5,054 enrolled. ***Average high school GPA:*** 3.69. ***Test scores:*** SAT critical reading scores over 500: 74%; SAT math scores over 500: 82%; SAT writing scores over 500: 72%; ACT scores over 18: 97%; SAT critical reading scores over 600: 26%; SAT math scores over 600: 38%; SAT writing scores over 600: 24%; ACT scores over 24: 60%; SAT critical reading scores over 700: 2%; SAT math scores over 700: 5%; SAT writing scores over 700: 2%; ACT scores over 30: 9%.

Retention: 88% of full-time freshmen returned.

FACULTY
Total: 1,714, 44% full-time, 61% with terminal degrees.

Student/faculty ratio: 28:1.

ACADEMICS
Calendar: semesters. *Degrees:* bachelor's, master's, doctoral, and postbachelor's certificates.

Special study options: academic remediation for entering students, advanced placement credit, distance learning, double majors, English as a second language, external degree program, freshman honors college, honors programs, internships, off-campus study, services for LD students, study abroad, summer session for credit. ***ROTC:*** Army (b), Navy (b), Air Force (b).

Computers: 1,200 computers/terminals are available on campus for general student use. Students can access the following: computer help desk, free student e-mail accounts, online (class) grades, online (class) registration, online (class) schedules, Blackboard. Campuswide network is available. 100% of college-owned or -operated housing units are wired for high-speed Internet access. Wireless service is available via entire campus.

STUDENT LIFE
Housing options: on-campus residence required for freshman year; coed, special housing for students with disabilities. Campus housing is university owned. Freshman applicants given priority for college housing.

Activities and organizations: drama/theater group, student-run newspaper, radio and television station, choral group, marching band, AB Samahan, Asian Pacific Student Alliance, Enviro-Business Society, M.E.Ch.A de SDSU, Social fraternities and sororities, including both general and culturally based organizations, national fraternities, national sororities.

Athletics Member NCAA. All Division I. ***Intercollegiate sports:*** baseball M(s), basketball M(s)/W(s), crew W(s), cross-country running W(s), football M(s), golf M(s)/W(s), lacrosse W(s), soccer M(s)/W(s), softball W(s), swimming and diving W(s), tennis M(s)/W(s), track and field W(s), volleyball W(s), water polo W(s). ***Intramural sports:*** basketball M/W, bowling M/W, cheerleading W(c), crew M(c), football M/W, ice hockey M(c), lacrosse M(c)/W(c), racquetball M/W, rugby M(c), skiing (downhill) M(c)/W(c), soccer M(c)/W(c), softball M/W, tennis M(c)/W(c), ultimate Frisbee M(c)/W(c), volleyball M(c)/W(c), water polo M(c)/W(c).

Campus security: 24-hour emergency response devices and patrols, student patrols, late-night transport/escort service.

Student services: health clinic, personal/psychological counseling, women's center.

COSTS & FINANCIAL AID

Costs (2014–15) ***Tuition:*** state resident $5472 full-time; nonresident $16,632 full-time. Full-time tuition and fees vary according to course load, degree level, location, and program. Part-time tuition and fees vary according to course load, degree level, location, and program. ***Required fees:*** $1394 full-time. ***Room and board:*** $14,745. Room and board charges vary according to board plan and housing facility. ***Payment plan:*** installment. ***Waivers:*** employees or children of employees.

Financial Aid Of all full-time matriculated undergraduates who enrolled in 2014, 17,300 applied for aid, 14,500 were judged to have need, 1,600 had their need fully met. 650 Federal Work-Study jobs (averaging $1900). In 2014, 1100 non-need-based awards were made. ***Average percent of need met:*** 70. ***Average financial aid package:*** $10,800. ***Average need-based loan:*** $4100. ***Average need-based gift aid:*** $9900. ***Average non-need-based aid:*** $2300. ***Average indebtedness upon graduation:*** $18,400. ***Financial aid deadline:*** 3/2.

APPLYING

Standardized Tests *Required:* SAT or ACT (for admission).

Options: electronic application.

Application fee: $55.

Required: high school transcript.

Application deadlines: 11/30 (freshmen), 11/30 (out-of-state freshmen), 11/30 (transfers).

Notification: 3/1 (freshmen), 3/1 (out-of-state freshmen), 3/1 (transfers).

CONTACT

Office of Admissions, San Diego State University, 5500 Campanile Drive, San Diego, CA 92182-7455. *Phone:* 619-594-6336. *Toll-free phone:* 855-594-6336 (in-state); 855-594-3983 (out-of-state). *E-mail:* admissions@sdsu.edu.

San Francisco Art Institute

San Francisco, California

http://www.sfai.edu/

- **Independent** comprehensive, founded 1871
- **Urban** 4-acre campus with easy access to San Francisco
- **Endowment** $9.3 million
- **Coed** 467 undergraduate students, 92% full-time, 57% women, 43% men
- **Moderately difficult** entrance level, 95% of applicants were admitted

UNDERGRAD STUDENTS

430 full-time, 37 part-time. Students come from 26 other countries; 46% are from out of state; 2% Black or African American, non-Hispanic/Latino; 17% Hispanic/Latino; 4% Asian, non-Hispanic/Latino; 0.4% Native Hawaiian or other Pacific Islander, non-Hispanic/Latino; 0.4% American Indian or Alaska Native, non-Hispanic/Latino; 8% Two or more races, non-Hispanic/Latino; 2% Race/ethnicity unknown; 18% international; 13% transferred in; 27% live on campus.

Freshmen

Admission: 427 applied, 406 admitted, 81 enrolled. ***Average high school GPA:*** 3.09. ***Test scores:*** SAT critical reading scores over 500: 53%; SAT math scores over 500: 63%; SAT writing scores over 500: 52%; ACT scores over 18: 80%; SAT critical reading scores over 600: 21%; SAT math scores over 600: 21%; SAT writing scores over 600: 5%; ACT scores over 24: 60%; ACT scores over 30: 20%.

Retention: 69% of full-time freshmen returned.

FACULTY

Total: 142, 13% full-time, 82% with terminal degrees.

Student/faculty ratio: 11:1.

ACADEMICS

Calendar: semesters. *Degrees:* bachelor's, master's, and postbachelor's certificates.

Special study options: academic remediation for entering students, adult/continuing education programs, advanced placement credit, double majors, English as a second language, external degree program, honors programs, independent study, internships, off-campus study, part-time degree program, services for LD students, study abroad, summer session for credit.

Computers: 150 computers/terminals are available on campus for general student use. Students can access the following: computer help desk, free student e-mail accounts, online (class) grades, online (class) registration, online (class) schedules. Campuswide network is available. 100% of college-owned or -operated housing units are wired for high-speed Internet access. Wireless service is available via entire campus.

STUDENT LIFE

Housing options: on-campus residence required for freshman year; coed. Campus housing is leased by the school and is provided by a third party. Freshman applicants given priority for college housing.

Activities and organizations: student-run newspaper, radio station, DocuPhoto, Junior Varsity Players, People's Union of Collaborative Arts, SFAI Music Factory, Shield Club.

Campus security: 24-hour patrols, security cameras.

Student services: personal/psychological counseling.

COSTS & FINANCIAL AID

Costs (2014–15) ***Comprehensive fee:*** $55,762 includes full-time tuition ($39,226), mandatory fees ($870), and room and board ($15,666). Full-time tuition and fees vary according to degree level. Part-time tuition: $1718 per unit. Part-time tuition and fees vary according to degree level. ***College room only:*** $11,500. Room and board charges vary according to housing facility. ***Payment plan:*** installment. ***Waivers:*** employees or children of employees.

Financial Aid Of all full-time matriculated undergraduates who enrolled in 2013, 278 applied for aid, 255 were judged to have need, 36 had their need fully met. In 2013, 155 non-need-based awards were made. ***Average percent of need met:*** 47. ***Average financial aid package:*** $36,909. ***Average need-based loan:*** $4598. ***Average need-based gift aid:*** $16,370. ***Average non-need-based aid:*** $9084. ***Average indebtedness upon graduation:*** $25,931. ***Financial aid deadline:*** 5/31.

APPLYING

Standardized Tests *Recommended:* SAT or ACT (for admission).

Options: electronic application, deferred entrance.

Application fee: $75.

Required: essay or personal statement, high school transcript, 1 letter of recommendation, portfolio for BFA applicants, critical essay for BA applicants. ***Recommended:*** minimum 2.0 GPA, interview.

Application deadlines: rolling (freshmen), rolling (out-of-state freshmen), rolling (transfers).

Notification: continuous (freshmen), continuous (out-of-state freshmen), continuous (transfers).

CONTACT

Office of Admissions, San Francisco Art Institute, 800 Chestnut Street, San Francisco, CA 94133. *Phone:* 415-749-4500. *Toll-free phone:* 800-345-SFAI. *Fax:* 415-749-4592. *E-mail:* admissions@sfai.edu.

San Francisco Conservatory of Music

San Francisco, California

http://www.sfcm.edu/

- **Independent** comprehensive, founded 1917
- **Urban** 2-acre campus with easy access to San Francisco Bay Area
- **Endowment** $37.3 million
- **Coed** 171 undergraduate students, 99% full-time, 44% women, 56% men

UNDERGRAD STUDENTS
170 full-time, 1 part-time. Students come from 19 states and territories; 17 other countries; 35% are from out of state; 2% Black or African American, non-Hispanic/Latino; 8% Hispanic/Latino; 11% Asian, non-Hispanic/Latino; 0.6% Native Hawaiian or other Pacific Islander, non-Hispanic/Latino; 9% Two or more races, non-Hispanic/Latino; 9% Race/ethnicity unknown; 28% international; 7% transferred in; 46% live on campus.

Freshmen
Admission: 41 enrolled.
Retention: 82% of full-time freshmen returned.

FACULTY
Total: 108, 27% full-time, 26% with terminal degrees.
Student/faculty ratio: 7:1.

ACADEMICS
Calendar: semesters. *Degrees:* diplomas, bachelor's, master's, post-master's, and postbachelor's certificates.

Special study options: academic remediation for entering students, advanced placement credit, English as a second language, independent study, internships, services for LD students.

Computers: 13 computers/terminals and 350 ports are available on campus for general student use. Students can access the following: campus intranet, computer help desk, free student e-mail accounts, online (class) grades, online (class) registration, online (class) schedules. Campuswide network is available. Wireless service is available via entire campus.

STUDENT LIFE
Housing options: coed. Campus housing is leased by the school and is provided by a third party. Freshman campus housing is guaranteed.

Activities and organizations: drama/theater group, choral group, Yoga Group, Meditation Group.

Campus security: 24-hour emergency response devices and patrols, controlled dormitory access, resident assistant on-call for residential hall residents.

Student services: personal/psychological counseling.

COSTS & FINANCIAL AID
Costs (2014–15) ***Tuition:*** $40,000 full-time, $1764 per credit part-time. Part-time tuition and fees vary according to course load. ***Required fees:*** $992 full-time, $992 per year part-time. ***Room only:*** $7000. Room and board charges vary according to housing facility. ***Payment plan:*** installment. ***Waivers:*** employees or children of employees.

Financial Aid Of all full-time matriculated undergraduates who enrolled in 2014, 157 applied for aid, 157 were judged to have need, 20 had their need fully met. 24 Federal Work-Study jobs (averaging $2500). 5 state and other part-time jobs (averaging $1500). In 2014, 12 non-need-based awards were made. ***Average percent of need met:*** 59. ***Average financial aid package:*** $30,600. ***Average need-based loan:*** $12,970. ***Average need-based gift aid:*** $22,360. ***Average non-need-based aid:*** $12,450. ***Average indebtedness upon graduation:*** $24,500.

APPLYING
Standardized Tests *Recommended:* SAT or ACT (for admission).
Required: essay or personal statement, high school transcript, minimum 2.5 GPA, 2 letters of recommendation, audition, pre-screen recording in select areas. ***Required for some:*** interview.

CONTACT
Ms. Melissa Cocco-Mitten, Director of Admissions, San Francisco Conservatory of Music, 50 Oak Street, San Francisco, CA 94102. *Phone:* 800-899-7326. *Fax:* 415-503-6299. *E-mail:* admit@sfcm.edu.

San Francisco State University
San Francisco, California
http://www.sfsu.edu/

- **State-supported** university, founded 1899, part of California State University System
- **Urban** 142-acre campus
- **Endowment** $65.4 million
- **Coed** 25,938 undergraduate students, 84% full-time, 57% women, 43% men
- **Moderately difficult** entrance level, 66% of applicants were admitted

UNDERGRAD STUDENTS
21,713 full-time, 4,225 part-time. 1% are from out of state; 5% Black or African American, non-Hispanic/Latino; 22% Hispanic/Latino; 28% Asian, non-Hispanic/Latino; 1% Native Hawaiian or other Pacific Islander, non-Hispanic/Latino; 0.3% American Indian or Alaska Native, non-Hispanic/Latino; 6% Two or more races, non-Hispanic/Latino; 8% Race/ethnicity unknown; 7% international; 12% transferred in; 13% live on campus.

Freshmen
Admission: 31,963 applied, 21,087 admitted, 3,754 enrolled. ***Average high school GPA:*** 3.22. ***Test scores:*** SAT critical reading scores over 500: 47%; SAT math scores over 500: 51%; ACT scores over 18: 81%; SAT critical reading scores over 600: 11%; SAT math scores over 600: 14%; ACT scores over 24: 26%; SAT critical reading scores over 700: 1%; SAT math scores over 700: 1%; ACT scores over 30: 2%.
Retention: 84% of full-time freshmen returned.

ACADEMICS
Calendar: semesters. *Degrees:* certificates, bachelor's, master's, doctoral, post-master's, and postbachelor's certificates.

Special study options: academic remediation for entering students, adult/continuing education programs, advanced placement credit, cooperative education, distance learning, double majors, English as a second language, honors programs, independent study, internships, off-campus study, part-time degree program, services for LD students, student-designed majors, study abroad, summer session for credit. ***ROTC:*** Army (c), Air Force (c).

Computers: 1,700 computers/terminals and 1,400 ports are available on campus for general student use. Students can access the following: campus intranet, computer help desk, free student e-mail accounts, online (class) grades, online (class) registration, online (class) schedules. Campuswide network is available. 100% of college-owned or -operated housing units are wired for high-speed Internet access. Wireless service is available via entire campus.

STUDENT LIFE
Housing options: coed, women-only, special housing for students with disabilities. Campus housing is university owned. Freshman applicants given priority for college housing.

Activities and organizations: drama/theater group, student-run newspaper, radio and television station, choral group, national fraternities, national sororities.

Athletics Member NCAA. All Division II. ***Intercollegiate sports:*** baseball M(s), basketball M(s)/W(s), cross-country running M(s)/W(s), soccer M(s)/W(s), softball W(s), track and field W(s), volleyball W(s), wrestling M(s). ***Intramural sports:*** basketball M/W, cheerleading M(c)/W(c), rugby M(c)/W(c), soccer M/W, tennis M/W, volleyball M/W, water polo M(c)/W(c).

Campus security: 24-hour emergency response devices and patrols, student patrols, late-night transport/escort service, controlled dormitory access.

Student services: health clinic, personal/psychological counseling, women's center, legal services.

COSTS & FINANCIAL AID
Costs (2014–15) ***Tuition:*** state resident $5472 full-time; nonresident $16,632 full-time. Full-time tuition and fees vary according to course load. Part-time tuition and fees vary according to course load. ***Required fees:*** $996 full-time. ***Room and board:*** Room and board charges vary according to board plan and housing facility. ***Payment plan:*** installment. ***Waivers:*** senior citizens and employees or children of employees.

Financial Aid Of all full-time matriculated undergraduates who enrolled in 2014, 16,688 applied for aid, 15,007 were judged to have need, 3,784 had their need fully met. In 2014, 261 non-need-based awards were made. ***Average percent of need met:*** 72. ***Average financial aid package:*** $11,297. ***Average need-based loan:*** $4530. ***Average need-based gift aid:*** $8236. ***Average non-need-based aid:*** $1738. ***Average indebtedness upon graduation:*** $22,741.

APPLYING

Standardized Tests *Required:* SAT or ACT (for admission).

Options: electronic application.

Application fee: $55.

Required: high school transcript.

Application deadlines: 11/30 (freshmen), 11/30 (transfers).

Notification: 10/1 (freshmen), 12/1 (transfers).

CONTACT

Admissions Officer, San Francisco State University, 1600 Holloway Avenue, San Francisco, CA 94132-1722. *Phone:* 415-338-1113. *Fax:* 415-338-7196. *E-mail:* ugadmit@sfsu.edu.

San Jose State University

San Jose, California

http://www.sjsu.edu/

- **State-supported** comprehensive, founded 1857, part of California State University System
- **Urban** 152-acre campus
- **Coed** 26,664 undergraduate students, 80% full-time, 48% women, 52% men
- **Very difficult** entrance level, 60% of applicants were admitted

UNDERGRAD STUDENTS

21,341 full-time, 5,323 part-time. 0.4% are from out of state; 3% Black or African American, non-Hispanic/Latino; 25% Hispanic/Latino; 35% Asian, non-Hispanic/Latino; 0.8% Native Hawaiian or other Pacific Islander, non-Hispanic/Latino; 0.1% American Indian or Alaska Native, non-Hispanic/Latino; 5% Two or more races, non-Hispanic/Latino; 4% Race/ethnicity unknown; 5% international; 15% transferred in; 14% live on campus.

Freshmen

Admission: 29,734 applied, 17,793 admitted, 3,486 enrolled. ***Average high school GPA:*** 3.38. ***Test scores:*** SAT critical reading scores over 500: 53%; SAT math scores over 500: 68%; SAT writing scores over 500: 50%; ACT scores over 18: 87%; SAT critical reading scores over 600: 14%; SAT math scores over 600: 28%; SAT writing scores over 600: 13%; ACT scores over 24: 35%; SAT critical reading scores over 700: 1%; SAT math scores over 700: 5%; SAT writing scores over 700: 2%; ACT scores over 30: 5%.

Retention: 83% of full-time freshmen returned.

FACULTY

Total: 1,694, 37% full-time.

Student/faculty ratio: 28:1.

ACADEMICS

Calendar: semesters. *Degrees:* bachelor's and master's.

Special study options: academic remediation for entering students, adult/continuing education programs, advanced placement credit, distance learning, double majors, honors programs, independent study, internships, off-campus study, part-time degree program, services for LD students, student-designed majors, study abroad, summer session for credit. ***ROTC:*** Army (c), Air Force (b).

Computers: Students can access the following: computer help desk, online (class) registration. Campuswide network is available. Wireless service is available via entire campus.

STUDENT LIFE

Housing options: on-campus residence required for freshman year; coed, men-only, women-only, cooperative, special housing for students with disabilities. Freshman applicants given priority for college housing.

Activities and organizations: drama/theater group, student-run newspaper, radio and television station, choral group, marching band, national fraternities, national sororities.

Athletics Member NCAA. All Division I except football (Division I-A). ***Intercollegiate sports:*** baseball M(s), basketball M(s)/W(s), cross-country running M(s)/W(s), golf M(s)/W(s), gymnastics W(s), soccer M(s)/W(s), softball W(s), swimming and diving W(s), tennis W(s), track and field W(s), volleyball W(s), water polo W(s). ***Intramural sports:*** badminton M(c)/W(c), bowling M(c)/W(c), ice hockey M(c)/W(c), lacrosse M(c)/W(c), rugby M(c), soccer M(c)/W(c), softball M/W, swimming and diving M(c)/W(c), track and field M(c)/W(c), ultimate Frisbee M(c)/W(c), volleyball M(c)/W(c), water polo M/W, wrestling M(c)/W(c).

Campus security: 24-hour emergency response devices and patrols, student patrols, late-night transport/escort service.

Student services: health clinic, personal/psychological counseling, women's center.

COSTS & FINANCIAL AID

Costs (2015–16) ***Tuition:*** state resident $0 full-time; nonresident $11,600 full-time. ***Required fees:*** $7323 full-time. ***Room and board:*** $11,810; room only: $7150.

Financial Aid Of all full-time matriculated undergraduates who enrolled in 2013, 16,248 applied for aid, 14,865 were judged to have need, 3,465 had their need fully met. In 2013, 46 non-need-based awards were made. ***Average percent of need met:*** 75. ***Average financial aid package:*** $14,235. ***Average need-based loan:*** $7271. ***Average need-based gift aid:*** $7500. ***Average non-need-based aid:*** $1863. ***Average indebtedness upon graduation:*** $23,467. ***Financial aid deadline:*** 6/15.

APPLYING

Standardized Tests *Required:* SAT or ACT (for admission).

Options: electronic application.

Application fee: $55.

Required: high school transcript.

Application deadlines: 11/30 (freshmen), 11/30 (transfers).

Notification: continuous (freshmen), continuous (transfers).

CONTACT

Admissions Office, San Jose State University, One Washington Square, San Jose, CA 95192-0001. *Phone:* 408-283-7500. *Fax:* 408-924-2050. *E-mail:* admissions@sjsu.edu.

Santa Clara University

Santa Clara, California

http://www.scu.edu/

- **Independent Roman Catholic (Jesuit)** university, founded 1851
- **Suburban** 106-acre campus with easy access to San Francisco, San Jose
- **Coed** 5,486 undergraduate students, 98% full-time, 50% women, 50% men
- **Moderately difficult** entrance level, 49% of applicants were admitted

UNDERGRAD STUDENTS

5,389 full-time, 97 part-time. 26% are from out of state; 3% Black or African American, non-Hispanic/Latino; 17% Hispanic/Latino; 15% Asian, non-Hispanic/Latino; 0.2% Native Hawaiian or other Pacific Islander, non-Hispanic/Latino; 0.1% American Indian or Alaska Native, non-Hispanic/Latino; 7% Two or more races, non-Hispanic/Latino; 6% Race/ethnicity unknown; 3% international; 3% transferred in; 52% live on campus.

Freshmen

Admission: 14,985 applied, 7,395 admitted, 1,319 enrolled. ***Average high school GPA:*** 3.67. ***Test scores:*** SAT critical reading scores over 500: 97%; SAT math scores over 500: 99%; ACT scores over 18: 100%; SAT critical reading scores over 600: 72%; SAT math scores over 600: 85%; ACT scores over 24: 97%; SAT critical reading scores over 700: 17%; SAT math scores over 700: 34%; ACT scores over 30: 53%.

Retention: 96% of full-time freshmen returned.

FACULTY

Total: 917, 56% full-time, 79% with terminal degrees.

Student/faculty ratio: 12:1.

ACADEMICS

Calendar: quarters. *Degrees:* bachelor's, master's, doctoral, post-master's, and postbachelor's certificates.

Special study options: advanced placement credit, cooperative education, double majors, honors programs, independent study, internships, off-campus study, services for LD students, student-designed majors, study abroad, summer session for credit. ***ROTC:*** Army (b), Air Force (c).

Computers: 824 computers/terminals are available on campus for general student use. Students can access the following: campus intranet, computer help desk, free student e-mail accounts, online (class) grades, online (class) registration, online (class) schedules. Campuswide network is available. 100% of college-owned or -operated housing units are wired for high-speed Internet access. Wireless service is available via entire campus.

STUDENT LIFE

Housing options: coed, special housing for students with disabilities. Campus housing is university owned. Freshman applicants given priority for college housing.

Activities and organizations: drama/theater group, student-run newspaper, radio station, choral group, Santa Clara Community Action Program (SCCAP), Ruff Riders (Spirit Group), Multicultural Center (MCC), Into the Wild (Outdoor Wilderness Organization), Alpha Kappa Psi (Business Fraternity).

Athletics Member NCAA. All Division I. ***Intercollegiate sports:*** baseball M(s), basketball M(s)/W(s), crew M/W, cross-country running M(s)/W(s), golf M(s)/W(s), soccer M(s)/W(s), softball W(s), tennis M(s)/W(s), track and field M(s)/W(s), volleyball W(s), water polo M(s)/W(s). ***Intramural sports:*** badminton M/W, basketball M/W, cheerleading W(c), equestrian sports M(c)/W(c), field hockey W(c), football M/W, ice hockey M(c), lacrosse M(c)/W(c), rugby M(c)/W(c), sailing M(c)/W(c), soccer M/W, softball M/W, swimming and diving M(c)/W(c), table tennis M/W, tennis M/W, volleyball M/W.

Campus security: 24-hour emergency response devices and patrols, late-night transport/escort service, controlled dormitory access.

Student services: health clinic, personal/psychological counseling.

COSTS & FINANCIAL AID

Costs (2014–15) ***Comprehensive fee:*** $56,733 includes full-time tuition ($43,812) and room and board ($12,921). Part-time tuition: $1217 per unit. Part-time tuition and fees vary according to course load. ***Room and board:*** Room and board charges vary according to board plan, housing facility, location, and student level. ***Payment plan:*** installment. ***Waivers:*** employees or children of employees.

Financial Aid Of all full-time matriculated undergraduates who enrolled in 2014, 3,421 applied for aid, 2,652 were judged to have need, 804 had their need fully met. 258 Federal Work-Study jobs (averaging $2961). In 2014, 1442 non-need-based awards were made. ***Average percent of need met:*** 72. ***Average financial aid package:*** $30,016. ***Average need-based loan:*** $5003. ***Average need-based gift aid:*** $23,155. ***Average non-need-based aid:*** $13,120. ***Average indebtedness upon graduation:*** $26,759.

APPLYING

Standardized Tests *Required:* SAT or ACT (for admission).

Options: electronic application, early decision, early action, deferred entrance.

Application fee: $55.

Required: essay or personal statement, high school transcript, 1 letter of recommendation.

Application deadlines: 1/7 (freshmen), 4/1 (transfers), 11/1 (early action).

Early decision deadline: 11/1.

Notification: continuous until 4/1 (freshmen), continuous (transfers), 12/15 (early decision), 12/23 (early action).

CONTACT

Ms. Sandra Hayes, Dean of Undergraduate Admissions, Santa Clara University, 500 El Camino Real, Santa Clara, CA 95053. *Phone:* 408-554-4700. *Fax:* 408-554-5255. *E-mail:* Admission@scu.edu.

Scripps College

Claremont, California

http://www.scrippscollege.edu/

- **Independent** 4-year, founded 1926
- **Suburban** 37-acre campus with easy access to Los Angeles
- **Endowment** $310.5 million
- **Women only** 972 undergraduate students, 100% full-time
- **Very difficult** entrance level, 27% of applicants were admitted

UNDERGRAD STUDENTS

968 full-time, 4 part-time. Students come from 44 states and territories; 17 other countries; 50% are from out of state; 3% Black or African American, non-Hispanic/Latino; 9% Hispanic/Latino; 19% Asian, non-Hispanic/Latino; 0.1% Native Hawaiian or other Pacific Islander, non-Hispanic/Latino; 0.1% American Indian or Alaska Native, non-Hispanic/Latino; 6% Two or more races, non-Hispanic/Latino; 9% Race/ethnicity unknown; 4% international; 97% live on campus.

Freshmen

Admission: 2,782 applied, 758 admitted, 250 enrolled. ***Average high school GPA:*** 4.12. ***Test scores:*** SAT critical reading scores over 500: 100%; SAT math scores over 500: 100%; SAT writing scores over 500: 100%; ACT scores over 18: 100%; SAT critical reading scores over 600: 93%; SAT math scores over 600: 86%; SAT writing scores over 600: 95%; ACT scores over 24: 99%; SAT critical reading scores over 700: 43%; SAT math scores over 700: 32%; SAT writing scores over 700: 45%; ACT scores over 30: 62%.

Retention: 95% of full-time freshmen returned.

FACULTY

Total: 121, 74% full-time, 97% with terminal degrees.

Student/faculty ratio: 10:1.

ACADEMICS

Calendar: semesters. *Degrees:* bachelor's and postbachelor's certificates.

Special study options: accelerated degree program, advanced placement credit, double majors, independent study, internships, off-campus study, services for LD students, student-designed majors, study abroad. ***ROTC:*** Army (c), Air Force (c).

Unusual degree programs: 3-2 business administration with Claremont Graduate University; engineering with Stanford University, University of Southern California, Harvey Mudd College, University of California, Berkeley, Washington University in St. Louis, Columbia University, Rensselaer and Boston University; American politics, economics, philosophy, public policy, international studies, or religion with Claremont Graduate University.

Computers: 151 computers/terminals and 320 ports are available on campus for general student use. Students can access the following: campus intranet, computer help desk, free student e-mail accounts, online (class) grades, online (class) registration, online (class) schedules, 2 ports per dorm room. Campuswide network is available. 100% of college-owned or -operated housing units are wired for high-speed Internet access. Wireless service is available via entire campus.

STUDENT LIFE

Housing options: on-campus residence required for freshman year; women-only, special housing for students with disabilities. Campus housing is university owned. Freshman campus housing is guaranteed.

Activities and organizations: drama/theater group, student-run newspaper, radio station, choral group, Scripps Associated Students.

Athletics Member NCAA. All Division III. ***Intercollegiate sports:*** basketball W, cross-country running W, fencing W(c), golf W, lacrosse W, rugby W(c), skiing (downhill) W(c), soccer W, softball W, swimming and diving W, tennis W, track and field W, ultimate Frisbee W(c), volleyball W, water polo W. ***Intramural sports:*** basketball W, soccer W, softball W, volleyball W, water polo W.

Campus security: 24-hour emergency response devices and patrols, late-night transport/escort service, controlled dormitory access.

Student services: health clinic, personal/psychological counseling, women's center.

COSTS & FINANCIAL AID

Costs (2014–15) ***Comprehensive fee:*** $61,940 includes full-time tuition ($47,164), mandatory fees ($214), and room and board ($14,562). Full-

time tuition and fees vary according to course load and degree level. Part-time tuition: $5896 per course. Part-time tuition and fees vary according to course load and degree level. ***College room only:*** $7934. Room and board charges vary according to board plan. ***Payment plans:*** tuition prepayment, installment. ***Waivers:*** employees or children of employees.

Financial Aid Of all full-time matriculated undergraduates who enrolled in 2013, 511 applied for aid, 417 were judged to have need, 417 had their need fully met. In 2013, 128 non-need-based awards were made. ***Average percent of need met:*** 100. ***Average financial aid package:*** $40,179. ***Average need-based loan:*** $3541. ***Average need-based gift aid:*** $34,792. ***Average non-need-based aid:*** $19,712. ***Average indebtedness upon graduation:*** $20,060. ***Financial aid deadline:*** 2/1.

APPLYING
Standardized Tests *Required:* SAT or ACT (for admission).

Options: electronic application, early admission, early decision, deferred entrance.

Application fee: $60.

Required: essay or personal statement, high school transcript, 2 letters of recommendation, School report, completed by the student's secondary school counselor. ***Recommended:*** minimum 3.0 GPA.

Application deadlines: 1/1 (freshmen), 1/1 (out-of-state freshmen), 4/1 (transfers).

Early decision deadline: 11/15 (for plan 1), 1/1 (for plan 2).

Notification: 4/1 (freshmen), 4/1 (out-of-state freshmen), 5/15 (transfers), 12/15 (early decision plan 1), 2/15 (early decision plan 2).

CONTACT
Laura Stratton, Director of Admission, Scripps College, 1030 Columbia Avenue, Claremont, CA 91711. *Phone:* 909-621-8149. *Toll-free phone:* 800-770-1333. *Fax:* 909-607-7508. *E-mail:* admission@scrippscollege.edu.

Shasta Bible College
Redding, California
http://www.shasta.edu/

- **Independent nondenominational** comprehensive, founded 1971
- **Small-town** 55-acre campus
- **Coed** 44 undergraduate students, 66% full-time, 36% women, 64% men
- **Noncompetitive** entrance level, 83% of applicants were admitted

UNDERGRAD STUDENTS
29 full-time, 15 part-time. Students come from 6 states and territories; 3 other countries; 25% are from out of state; 4% Black or African American, non-Hispanic/Latino; 10% Hispanic/Latino; 8% Asian, non-Hispanic/Latino; 2% Native Hawaiian or other Pacific Islander, non-Hispanic/Latino; 15% Race/ethnicity unknown; 30% transferred in; 77% live on campus.

Freshmen
Admission: 18 applied, 15 admitted, 8 enrolled.
Retention: 63% of full-time freshmen returned.

FACULTY
Total: 37, 24% full-time, 38% with terminal degrees.
Student/faculty ratio: 3:1.

ACADEMICS
Calendar: semesters. *Degrees:* certificates, diplomas, associate, bachelor's, and master's.

Special study options: academic remediation for entering students, accelerated degree program, adult/continuing education programs, cooperative education, distance learning, double majors, independent study, part-time degree program, summer session for credit.

Computers: 7 computers/terminals are available on campus for general student use. Students can access the following: campus intranet, free student e-mail accounts, online (class) schedules. Campuswide network is available. Wireless service is available via classrooms, computer centers, computer labs, learning centers, libraries, student centers.

STUDENT LIFE
Housing options: on-campus residence required through senior year; men-only, women-only. Campus housing is university owned. Freshman applicants given priority for college housing.

Activities and organizations: student-run newspaper, choral group, Associated Student Body.

Campus security: 24-hour emergency response devices, student patrols.

Student services: personal/psychological counseling.

FINANCIAL AID
Financial Aid Of all full-time matriculated undergraduates who enrolled in 2010, 59 applied for aid, 44 were judged to have need. 19 Federal Work-Study jobs (averaging $800). 3 state and other part-time jobs (averaging $824). In 2010, 8 non-need-based awards were made. ***Average percent of need met:*** 50. ***Average financial aid package:*** $2500. ***Average need-based loan:*** $4000. ***Average need-based gift aid:*** $2500.

APPLYING
Options: electronic application, early admission.

Application fee: $50.

Required: essay or personal statement, high school transcript, 4 letters of recommendation. ***Required for some:*** interview.

Application deadlines: rolling (freshmen), rolling (out-of-state freshmen).

Notification: continuous (freshmen), continuous (out-of-state freshmen).

CONTACT
Connie Barton, Registrar, Shasta Bible College, 2951 Goodwater Avenue, Redding, CA 96002. *Phone:* 530-221-4275 Ext. 26. *Toll-free phone:* 800-800-4SBC. *Fax:* 530-221-6929. *E-mail:* registrar@shasta.edu.

Silicon Valley University
San Jose, California
http://www.svuca.edu/

- **Proprietary** comprehensive
- **Urban** 1-acre campus with easy access to San Jose
- **Coed**
- **Noncompetitive** entrance level

FACULTY
Student/faculty ratio: 13:1.

ACADEMICS
Calendar: trimesters. *Degrees:* certificates, diplomas, bachelor's, master's, and doctoral.

STUDENT LIFE
Housing options: college housing not available.

Activities and organizations: SVU Student Association, Chinese Students Association.

Campus security: 24-hour emergency response devices and patrols.

COSTS
Costs (2014–15) ***Tuition:*** $10,400 full-time, $325 per credit hour part-time. Full-time tuition and fees vary according to course level, course load, and program. Part-time tuition and fees vary according to course level, course load, and program. ***Required fees:*** $975 full-time, $325 per credit hour part-time, $325 per term part-time.

APPLYING
Standardized Tests *Recommended:* SAT and SAT Subject Tests or ACT (for admission).

Options: electronic application, deferred entrance.

Application fee: $75.

Required: high school transcript, minimum 1.8 GPA, copy of diploma. ***Required for some:*** interview. ***Recommended:*** essay or personal statement.

CONTACT
Luna Liu, Admissions Office, Silicon Valley University, 2160 Lundy Ave Ste# 110, San Jose, CA 95131. *Phone:* 408-435-8989 Ext. 111. *E-mail:* admission-office@svuca.edu.

Simpson University
Redding, California
http://www.simpsonu.edu/

- **Independent** comprehensive, founded 1921, affiliated with The Christian and Missionary Alliance
- **Suburban** 100-acre campus
- **Endowment** $5.8 million
- **Coed** 1,068 undergraduate students, 95% full-time, 66% women, 34% men
- **Moderately difficult** entrance level, 57% of applicants were admitted

UNDERGRAD STUDENTS
1,019 full-time, 49 part-time. Students come from 23 states and territories; 13 other countries; 11% are from out of state; 3% Black or African American, non-Hispanic/Latino; 12% Hispanic/Latino; 3% Asian, non-Hispanic/Latino; 0.1% Native Hawaiian or other Pacific Islander, non-Hispanic/Latino; 3% American Indian or Alaska Native, non-Hispanic/Latino; 3% Two or more races, non-Hispanic/Latino; 12% Race/ethnicity unknown; 2% international; 12% transferred in; 40% live on campus.

Freshmen

Admission: 598 applied, 343 admitted, 127 enrolled. ***Average high school GPA:*** 3.44. ***Test scores:*** SAT critical reading scores over 500: 61%; SAT math scores over 500: 67%; SAT writing scores over 500: 51%; ACT scores over 18: 89%; SAT critical reading scores over 600: 13%; SAT math scores over 600: 16%; SAT writing scores over 600: 13%; ACT scores over 24: 36%; SAT critical reading scores over 700: 2%; SAT math scores over 700: 1%; SAT writing scores over 700: 3%; ACT scores over 30: 2%.

Retention: 73% of full-time freshmen returned.

FACULTY
Total: 220, 23% full-time, 34% with terminal degrees.

Student/faculty ratio: 11:1.

ACADEMICS
Calendar: semesters. *Degrees:* certificates, associate, bachelor's, master's, and postbachelor's certificates.

Special study options: academic remediation for entering students, accelerated degree program, adult/continuing education programs, advanced placement credit, distance learning, double majors, honors programs, independent study, internships, off-campus study, part-time degree program, services for LD students, student-designed majors, study abroad, summer session for credit.

Computers: 50 computers/terminals are available on campus for general student use. Students can access the following: campus intranet, computer help desk, free student e-mail accounts, online (class) grades, online (class) registration, online (class) schedules. Campuswide network is available. 100% of college-owned or -operated housing units are wired for high-speed Internet access. Wireless service is available via entire campus.

STUDENT LIFE
Housing options: on-campus residence required through junior year; men-only, women-only, special housing for students with disabilities. Campus housing is university owned. Freshman campus housing is guaranteed.

Activities and organizations: drama/theater group, student-run newspaper, choral group, Summer Missions Trips, Asian Fellowship, Vida, Psychology Club.

Athletics Member NAIA, NCCAA. ***Intercollegiate sports:*** baseball M(s), basketball M(s)/W(s), cross-country running M(s)/W(s), golf M(s)/W(s), soccer M(s)/W(s), softball W(s), volleyball W(s), wrestling M(s). ***Intramural sports:*** basketball M/W, volleyball M(c).

Campus security: 24-hour emergency response devices and patrols, student patrols, late-night transport/escort service, controlled dormitory access, emergency whistle program and monthly campus safety meetings.

Student services: health clinic, personal/psychological counseling.

COSTS & FINANCIAL AID
Costs (2014–15) ***Comprehensive fee:*** $32,200 includes full-time tuition ($24,300) and room and board ($7900). Full-time tuition and fees vary according to course load. Part-time tuition and fees vary according to course load. ***Room and board:*** Room and board charges vary according to board plan. ***Payment plan:*** deferred payment. ***Waivers:*** employees or children of employees.

Financial Aid Of all full-time matriculated undergraduates who enrolled in 2014, 731 applied for aid, 675 were judged to have need, 59 had their need fully met. 65 Federal Work-Study jobs (averaging $1490). In 2014, 46 non-need-based awards were made. ***Average percent of need met:*** 55. ***Average financial aid package:*** $19,571. ***Average need-based loan:*** $8281. ***Average need-based gift aid:*** $14,678. ***Average non-need-based aid:*** $9673. ***Average indebtedness upon graduation:*** $28,161.

APPLYING
Standardized Tests *Required:* SAT or ACT (for admission). *Recommended:* SAT Subject Tests (for admission).

Options: electronic application, early action, deferred entrance.

Application fee: $25.

Required: essay or personal statement, high school transcript, minimum 3.0 GPA, 2 letters of recommendation, Christian commitment. ***Required for some:*** interview.

Application deadlines: rolling (freshmen), rolling (transfers).

Notification: continuous (freshmen), continuous (transfers).

CONTACT
Mrs. Kendell Kluttz, Director of Undergraduate Admissions, Simpson University, 2211 College View Drive, Redding, CA 96003-8606. *Phone:* 530-226-5600. *Toll-free phone:* 888-9-SIMPSON. *Fax:* 530-226-4861. *E-mail:* admissions@simpsonu.edu.

Soka University of America
Aliso Viejo, California
http://www.soka.edu/

- **Independent** comprehensive, founded 2001
- **Suburban** 103-acre campus with easy access to Los Angeles, San Diego
- **Endowment** $1.1 billion
- **Coed** 412 undergraduate students, 100% full-time, 60% women, 40% men
- **Most difficult** entrance level, 43% of applicants were admitted

UNDERGRAD STUDENTS
411 full-time, 1 part-time. Students come from 35 states and territories; 45 other countries; 20% are from out of state; 5% Black or African American, non-Hispanic/Latino; 10% Hispanic/Latino; 19% Asian, non-Hispanic/Latino; 0.2% Native Hawaiian or other Pacific Islander, non-Hispanic/Latino; 1% American Indian or Alaska Native, non-Hispanic/Latino; 2% Two or more races, non-Hispanic/Latino; 7% Race/ethnicity unknown; 38% international; 99% live on campus.

Freshmen

Admission: 405 applied, 176 admitted, 100 enrolled. ***Average high school GPA:*** 3.82. ***Test scores:*** SAT critical reading scores over 500: 76%; SAT math scores over 500: 100%; SAT writing scores over 500: 95%; ACT scores over 18: 100%; SAT critical reading scores over 600: 41%; SAT math scores over 600: 73%; SAT writing scores over 600: 44%; ACT scores over 24: 84%; SAT critical reading scores over 700: 13%; SAT math scores over 700: 29%; SAT writing scores over 700: 17%; ACT scores over 30: 25%.

Retention: 95% of full-time freshmen returned.

FACULTY
Total: 70, 66% full-time, 84% with terminal degrees.

Student/faculty ratio: 8:1.

ACADEMICS
Calendar: semesters. *Degrees:* bachelor's and master's.

Special study options: cooperative education, independent study, internships, off-campus study, services for LD students, study abroad.

Computers: 100 computers/terminals and 100 ports are available on campus for general student use. Students can access the following: campus intranet, computer help desk, free student e-mail accounts, online (class) grades, online (class) registration, online (class) schedules, Angel courseware/PeopleSoft Portal. Campuswide network is available. 100% of college-owned or -operated housing units are wired for high-speed Internet access. Wireless service is available via entire campus.

STUDENT LIFE

Housing options: on-campus residence required through senior year; coed, cooperative, special housing for students with disabilities. Campus housing is university owned. Freshman campus housing is guaranteed.

Activities and organizations: choral group, Josho Daiko (Japanese Drum Club), Rhythmission (Hip Hop Dance Club), Sualseros (Salsa Dance Club), Ka Pilina Ho'olokahi (Hawaiian Dance Club), Soul Wings (Choir).

Athletics Member NAIA. ***Intercollegiate sports:*** cross-country running M(s)/W(s), soccer M(s)/W(s), swimming and diving M(s)/W(s), track and field M(s)/W(s). ***Intramural sports:*** badminton M/W, baseball M(c), basketball M/W, cheerleading M(c)/W(c), football M/W, golf M(c), racquetball M(c)/W(c), soccer M(c)/W(c), softball M/W, tennis M/W, volleyball M(c)/W(c), water polo M/W, weight lifting M/W.

Campus security: 24-hour emergency response devices and patrols, student patrols, late-night transport/escort service, controlled dormitory access.

Student services: health clinic, personal/psychological counseling.

COSTS & FINANCIAL AID

Costs (2015–16) ***Comprehensive fee:*** $42,110 includes full-time tuition ($28,938), mandatory fees ($1704), and room and board ($11,468). Full-time tuition and fees vary according to class time, course load, and program. Part-time tuition: $1206 per credit. Part-time tuition and fees vary according to class time, course load, and program. ***Room and board:*** Room and board charges vary according to board plan. ***Payment plans:*** installment, deferred payment. ***Waivers:*** employees or children of employees.

Financial Aid Of all full-time matriculated undergraduates who enrolled in 2013, 393 applied for aid, 380 were judged to have need, 180 had their need fully met. 28 Federal Work-Study jobs (averaging $1579). In 2013, 13 non-need-based awards were made. ***Average percent of need met:*** 92. ***Average financial aid package:*** $30,691. ***Average need-based loan:*** $5724. ***Average need-based gift aid:*** $23,474. ***Average non-need-based aid:*** $12,158. ***Average indebtedness upon graduation:*** $17,439. ***Financial aid deadline:*** 3/2.

APPLYING

Standardized Tests *Required:* SAT or ACT (for admission), The associated ACT writing test is required for students who choose to take the ACT only (for admission).

Options: electronic application, early admission, early action, deferred entrance.

Application fee: $45.

Required: essay or personal statement, high school transcript, 2 letters of recommendation, Applications will be evaluated only when all required materials have been received. It is the students responsibility to ensure that all of the required documents have been requested of the school they are attending and submitted. ***Recommended:*** interview.

Application deadlines: 1/15 (freshmen), 1/15 (out-of-state freshmen), 11/1 (early action).

Notification: 3/1 (freshmen), 3/1 (out-of-state freshmen), 12/1 (early action).

CONTACT

Maura Grainger, Admission Operations Coordinator, Soka University of America, Enrollment Services, 1 University Drive, Aliso Viejo, CA 92656. *Phone:* 949-480-4151 Ext. 4151. *Toll-free phone:* 888-600-SOKA. *Fax:* 949-480-4151. *E-mail:* mgrainger@soka.edu.

Sonoma State University

Rohnert Park, California

http://www.sonoma.edu/

- **State-supported** comprehensive, founded 1960, part of California State University System
- **Small-town** 280-acre campus with easy access to San Francisco
- **Endowment** $28.0 million
- **Coed**
- **Moderately difficult** entrance level

FACULTY

Student/faculty ratio: 25:1.

ACADEMICS

Calendar: semesters. *Degrees:* bachelor's and master's.

STUDENT LIFE

Housing options: coed, women-only, special housing for students with disabilities. Campus housing is university owned. Freshman applicants given priority for college housing.

Activities and organizations: drama/theater group, student-run newspaper, radio station, choral group, Accounting Forum, Sonoma Earth Action, Re-Entry Student Association, Lacrosse Club, Inter-Varsity Christian Fellowship, national fraternities, national sororities.

Athletics Member NCAA. All Division II.

Campus security: 24-hour emergency response devices and patrols, student patrols, late-night transport/escort service, controlled dormitory access.

Student services: health clinic, personal/psychological counseling, women's center, legal services.

COSTS & FINANCIAL AID

Costs (2014–15) ***Tuition:*** state resident $5472 full-time; nonresident $16,632 full-time. Full-time tuition and fees vary according to course load and degree level. Part-time tuition and fees vary according to course load and degree level. ***Required fees:*** $1804 full-time. ***Room and board:*** $11,799. Room and board charges vary according to housing facility.

Financial Aid Of all full-time matriculated undergraduates who enrolled in 2013, 5,077 applied for aid, 4,022 were judged to have need, 134 had their need fully met. 224 Federal Work-Study jobs (averaging $2882). 592 state and other part-time jobs (averaging $2700). In 2013, 211 non-need-based awards were made. ***Average percent of need met:*** 66. ***Average financial aid package:*** $10,349. ***Average need-based loan:*** $4034. ***Average need-based gift aid:*** $9541. ***Average non-need-based aid:*** $1280. ***Average indebtedness upon graduation:*** $20,744.

APPLYING

Standardized Tests *Required:* SAT or ACT (for admission).

Options: electronic application, early admission.

Application fee: $55.

Required: high school transcript.

CONTACT

Mr. Gustavo Flores, Director of Admissions, Sonoma State University, 1801 East Cotati Avenue, Rohnert Park, CA 94928-3609. *Phone:* 707-664-2778. *E-mail:* gustavo.flores@sonoma.edu.

Southern California Institute of Architecture

Los Angeles, California

http://www.sciarc.edu/

- **Independent** comprehensive, founded 1972
- **Urban** campus with easy access to Los Angeles
- **Coed** 263 undergraduate students, 97% full-time, 36% women, 64% men
- **Moderately difficult** entrance level, 81% of applicants were admitted

UNDERGRAD STUDENTS

254 full-time, 9 part-time. Students come from 12 states and territories; 28 other countries; 8% are from out of state; 2% Black or African American, non-Hispanic/Latino; 10% Hispanic/Latino; 19% Asian, non-Hispanic/Latino; 1% Native Hawaiian or other Pacific Islander, non-Hispanic/Latino; 2% Two or more races, non-Hispanic/Latino; 0.4% Race/ethnicity unknown; 44% international; 3% transferred in.

Freshmen

Admission: 203 applied, 164 admitted, 33 enrolled. ***Average high school GPA:*** 3.3. ***Test scores:*** SAT critical reading scores over 500: 64%; SAT math scores over 500: 86%; SAT writing scores over 500: 67%; SAT critical reading scores over 600: 18%; SAT math scores over 600: 68%; SAT writing scores over 600: 28%; SAT critical reading scores over 700: 4%; SAT math scores over 700: 29%; SAT writing scores over 700: 7%.

Retention: 92% of full-time freshmen returned.

FACULTY

Total: 74, 45% full-time, 69% with terminal degrees.

Student/faculty ratio: 15:1.

ACADEMICS
Calendar: semesters. *Degrees:* bachelor's and master's.

Special study options: academic remediation for entering students, advanced placement credit, cooperative education, English as a second language, internships, study abroad, summer session for credit.

Computers: 85 computers/terminals and 600 ports are available on campus for general student use. Students can access the following: campus intranet, computer help desk, free student e-mail accounts, online (class) grades, online (class) registration, online (class) schedules. Campuswide network is available. Wireless service is available via entire campus.

STUDENT LIFE
Housing options: college housing not available.

Activities and organizations: Student Union.

Campus security: 24-hour emergency response devices and patrols, electronically operated school entrances (e.g., access only with key/security card available to students 24/7).

Student services: personal/psychological counseling.

COSTS & FINANCIAL AID
Costs (2015–16) ***Tuition:*** $0 full-time. Full-time tuition and fees vary according to course load. ***Required fees:*** $2450 full-time.

Financial Aid Of all full-time matriculated undergraduates who enrolled in 2014, 110 applied for aid, 105 were judged to have need. In 2014, 17 non-need-based awards were made. ***Average percent of need met:*** 29. ***Average financial aid package:*** $18,567. ***Average need-based loan:*** $4527. ***Average need-based gift aid:*** $16,237. ***Average non-need-based aid:*** $8705. ***Average indebtedness upon graduation:*** $39,287.

APPLYING
Standardized Tests *Required:* SAT or ACT (for admission).

Options: electronic application, deferred entrance.

Application fee: $85.

Required: essay or personal statement, high school transcript, 3 letters of recommendation, portfolio of creative visual work, resume, statement of purpose, application, application fee, test score (SAT/ACT and TOEFL/IELTS for international students). ***Required for some:*** interview. ***Recommended:*** minimum 3.0 GPA.

Application deadlines: 1/15 (freshmen), 5/1 (transfers).

Notification: continuous until 4/1 (freshmen), continuous until 6/1 (transfers).

CONTACT
Jamie Black, Admissions Assistant, Southern California Institute of Architecture, 960 East Third Street, Los Angeles, CA 90013. *Phone:* 213-356-5373. *Fax:* 213-613-2260. *E-mail:* admissions@sciarc.edu.

Southern California Institute of Technology

Anaheim, California

http://www.scitech.edu/

- **Proprietary** 4-year, founded 1987
- **Urban** campus with easy access to Anaheim, Los Angeles, San Diego
- **Coed** 538 undergraduate students, 100% full-time, 7% women, 93% men

UNDERGRAD STUDENTS
538 full-time. 8% Black or African American, non-Hispanic/Latino; 46% Hispanic/Latino; 15% Asian, non-Hispanic/Latino; 1% Native Hawaiian or other Pacific Islander, non-Hispanic/Latino; 0.2% American Indian or Alaska Native, non-Hispanic/Latino; 4% Two or more races, non-Hispanic/Latino; 0.7% Race/ethnicity unknown.

Freshmen
Admission: 538 enrolled.

Retention: 86% of full-time freshmen returned.

FACULTY
Student/faculty ratio: 21:1.

ACADEMICS
Degrees: certificates, diplomas, associate, and bachelor's.

Special study options: accelerated degree program, adult/continuing education programs, double majors, English as a second language.

Computers: 300 computers/terminals are available on campus for general student use. Students can access the following: campus intranet. Campuswide network is available. Wireless service is available via entire campus.

STUDENT LIFE
Housing options: college housing not available.

Campus security: late-night transport/escort service.

COSTS & FINANCIAL AID
Costs (2014–15) ***Tuition:*** $15,500 full-time. Full-time tuition and fees vary according to program. Part-time tuition and fees vary according to program. No tuition increase for student's term of enrollment. ***Required fees:*** $660 full-time. ***Payment plans:*** tuition prepayment, installment.

Financial Aid Of all full-time matriculated undergraduates who enrolled in 2013, 8 Federal Work-Study jobs (averaging $2800).

APPLYING
Standardized Tests *Required:* entrance exam (for admission).

Required: interview. ***Required for some:*** high school transcript.

CONTACT
Mrs. Sam Rokni, Southern California Institute of Technology, 525 N Muller St, Anaheim, CA 92801. *Phone:* 714-300-0300 Ext. 227. *Fax:* 714-300-0311. *E-mail:* admissions@scitech.edu.

Southern California Seminary

El Cajon, California

http://www.socalsem.edu/

- **Independent interdenominational** comprehensive, founded 1946
- **Suburban** 15-acre campus with easy access to San Diego
- **Endowment** $114,070
- **Coed** 62 undergraduate students, 26% full-time, 24% women, 76% men
- **Moderately difficult** entrance level, 88% of applicants were admitted

UNDERGRAD STUDENTS
16 full-time, 46 part-time. Students come from 5 states and territories; 2 other countries; 5% are from out of state; 19% Black or African American, non-Hispanic/Latino; 16% Hispanic/Latino; 16% Asian, non-Hispanic/Latino; 3% Two or more races, non-Hispanic/Latino; 6% Race/ethnicity unknown; 5% international; 10% transferred in.

Freshmen
Admission: 25 applied, 22 admitted, 5 enrolled.

FACULTY
Total: 55, 20% full-time, 42% with terminal degrees.

Student/faculty ratio: 10:1.

ACADEMICS
Degrees: associate, bachelor's, master's, and doctoral.

Special study options: academic remediation for entering students, accelerated degree program, adult/continuing education programs, cooperative education, distance learning, independent study, internships, off-campus study, part-time degree program, services for LD students, student-designed majors, summer session for credit.

Computers: 5 computers/terminals are available on campus for general student use. Students can access the following: computer help desk, free student e-mail accounts, online (class) grades, online (class) registration, online (class) schedules. Campuswide network is available.

STUDENT LIFE
Housing options: college housing not available.

Campus security: 24-hour emergency response devices and patrols.

COSTS
Costs (2015–16) ***Tuition:*** $13,860 full-time. Full-time tuition and fees vary according to course level, course load, degree level, program, reciprocity agreements, and student level. Part-time tuition and fees vary according to course level, course load, degree level, program, reciprocity agreements, and student level. ***Required fees:*** $384 full-time. ***Payment plan:*** installment.

APPLYING

Options: electronic application, early admission, deferred entrance.

Required: essay or personal statement, high school transcript, minimum 2.5 GPA, .

Notification: 8/28 (freshmen).

CONTACT

Southern California Seminary, 2075 East Madison Avenue, El Cajon, CA 92019. *Phone:* 619-201-8959.

Stanford University

Stanford, California

http://www.stanford.edu/

- **Independent** university, founded 1891
- **Suburban** 8180-acre campus with easy access to San Francisco, San Jose
- **Endowment** $21.4 billion
- **Coed** 7,089 undergraduate students, 99% full-time, 47% women, 53% men
- **Most difficult** entrance level, 5% of applicants were admitted

UNDERGRAD STUDENTS

7,019 full-time, 70 part-time. Students come from 52 states and territories; 90 other countries; 54% are from out of state; 6% Black or African American, non-Hispanic/Latino; 16% Hispanic/Latino; 20% Asian, non-Hispanic/Latino; 0.4% Native Hawaiian or other Pacific Islander, non-Hispanic/Latino; 1% American Indian or Alaska Native, non-Hispanic/Latino; 11% Two or more races, non-Hispanic/Latino; 0.5% Race/ethnicity unknown; 8% international; 0.4% transferred in; 92% live on campus.

Freshmen

Admission: 42,167 applied, 2,145 admitted, 1,677 enrolled. ***Average high school GPA:*** 4.16. ***Test scores:*** SAT critical reading scores over 500: 100%; SAT math scores over 500: 100%; SAT writing scores over 500: 100%; ACT scores over 18: 100%; SAT critical reading scores over 600: 94%; SAT math scores over 600: 97%; SAT writing scores over 600: 96%; ACT scores over 24: 99%; SAT critical reading scores over 700: 69%; SAT math scores over 700: 78%; SAT writing scores over 700: 74%; ACT scores over 30: 88%.

Retention: 98% of full-time freshmen returned.

FACULTY

Total: 1,583, 98% full-time, 99% with terminal degrees.

Student/faculty ratio: 4:1.

ACADEMICS

Calendar: quarters. *Degrees:* bachelor's, master's, and doctoral.

Special study options: advanced placement credit, distance learning, double majors, English as a second language, honors programs, independent study, internships, off-campus study, services for LD students, student-designed majors, study abroad, summer session for credit. ***ROTC:*** Army (c), Navy (c), Air Force (c).

Computers: 1,000 computers/terminals and 22,000 ports are available on campus for general student use. Students can access the following: campus intranet, computer help desk, free student e-mail accounts, online (class) grades, online (class) registration, online (class) schedules. Campuswide network is available. 100% of college-owned or -operated housing units are wired for high-speed Internet access. Wireless service is available via entire campus.

STUDENT LIFE

Housing options: on-campus residence required for freshman year; coed, women-only, cooperative, special housing for students with disabilities. Campus housing is university owned. Freshman campus housing is guaranteed.

Activities and organizations: drama/theater group, student-run newspaper, radio and television station, choral group, marching band, Ram's Head (theatre club), Axe Committee (athletic support), Business Association of Stanford Entrepreneurial Students, Asian-American Student Association, Stanford Daily, national fraternities, national sororities.

Athletics Member NCAA, NAIA. All NCAA Division I. ***Intercollegiate sports:*** archery M(c)/W(c), badminton M(c)/W(c), baseball M(s), basketball M(s)/W(s), cheerleading M(c)/W(c), crew M(s)/W(s), cross-country running M(s)/W(s), equestrian sports M(c)/W(c), fencing M(s)/W(s), field hockey W(s), football M(s), golf M(s)/W(s), gymnastics M(s)/W(s), ice hockey M(c), lacrosse M(c)/W(s), racquetball M(c)/W(c), rock climbing M(c)/W(c), rugby M(c)/W(c), sailing M/W, skiing (downhill) M(c)/W(c), soccer M(s)/W(s), softball W(s), squash M(c)/W, swimming and diving M(s)/W(s), tennis M(s)/W(s), track and field M(s)/W(s), ultimate Frisbee M(c)/W(c), volleyball M(s)/W(s), water polo M(s)/W(s), wrestling M(s). ***Intramural sports:*** badminton M/W, baseball M(c), basketball M(c)/W(c), bowling M/W, cross-country running M(c)/W(c), football M/W, lacrosse W(c), racquetball M/W, rock climbing M/W, soccer M(c)/W(c), softball M/W, swimming and diving M(c)/W(c), table tennis M(c)/W(c), tennis M(c)/W(c), track and field M/W, ultimate Frisbee M/W, volleyball M/W, water polo M/W.

Campus security: 24-hour emergency response devices and patrols, late-night transport/escort service, controlled dormitory access.

Student services: health clinic, personal/psychological counseling, women's center, legal services.

COSTS & FINANCIAL AID

Costs (2015–16) ***One-time required fee:*** $591. ***Comprehensive fee:*** $59,836 includes full-time tuition ($45,729) and room and board ($14,107). ***Room and board:*** Room and board charges vary according to board plan. ***Payment plan:*** installment. ***Waivers:*** employees or children of employees.

Financial Aid Of all full-time matriculated undergraduates who enrolled in 2013, 3,814 applied for aid, 3,414 were judged to have need, 2,997 had their need fully met. 588 Federal Work-Study jobs (averaging $2316). 1,785 state and other part-time jobs (averaging $2219). In 2013, 18 non-need-based awards were made. ***Average percent of need met:*** 100. ***Average financial aid package:*** $44,043. ***Average need-based loan:*** $3026. ***Average need-based gift aid:*** $41,620. ***Average non-need-based aid:*** $8980. ***Average indebtedness upon graduation:*** $19,230.

APPLYING

Standardized Tests *Required:* SAT or ACT (for admission). *Recommended:* SAT Subject Tests (for admission).

Options: electronic application, early action, deferred entrance.

Application fee: $90.

Required: essay or personal statement, high school transcript, 2 letters of recommendation.

Application deadlines: 1/3 (freshmen), 3/15 (transfers), 11/1 (early action).

Notification: 4/1 (freshmen), 5/15 (transfers), 12/15 (early action).

CONTACT

Rick Shaw, Dean of Undergraduate Admission and Financial Aid, Stanford University, Montag Hall, 355 Galvez Street, Stanford, CA 94305-3020. *Phone:* 650-723-2091. *Fax:* 650-725-2846. *E-mail:* admission@stanford.edu.

Thomas Aquinas College

Santa Paula, California

http://www.thomasaquinas.edu/

- **Independent Roman Catholic** 4-year, founded 1971
- **Rural** 131-acre campus with easy access to Los Angeles
- **Endowment** $16.9 million
- **Coed** 378 undergraduate students, 100% full-time, 49% women, 51% men
- **Very difficult** entrance level, 83% of applicants were admitted

UNDERGRAD STUDENTS

378 full-time. Students come from 37 states and territories; 10 other countries; 57% are from out of state; 15% Hispanic/Latino; 1% Asian, non-Hispanic/Latino; 0.5% American Indian or Alaska Native, non-Hispanic/Latino; 6% Two or more races, non-Hispanic/Latino; 2% Race/ethnicity unknown; 4% international; 99% live on campus.

Freshmen

Admission: 185 applied, 153 admitted, 89 enrolled. ***Average high school GPA:*** 3.75. ***Test scores:*** SAT critical reading scores over 500: 99%; SAT math scores over 500: 98%; SAT writing scores over 500: 97%; ACT scores over 18: 100%; SAT critical reading scores over 600: 85%; SAT math scores over 600: 51%; SAT writing scores over 600: 67%; ACT

scores over 24: 76%; SAT critical reading scores over 700: 33%; SAT math scores over 700: 8%; SAT writing scores over 700: 22%; ACT scores over 30: 43%.

Retention: 97% of full-time freshmen returned.

FACULTY

Total: 37, 86% full-time, 81% with terminal degrees.

Student/faculty ratio: 11:1.

ACADEMICS

Calendar: semesters. *Degree:* bachelor's.

Special study options: cooperative education.

Computers: 20 computers/terminals and 24 ports are available on campus for general student use. Students can access the following: free student e-mail accounts. Campuswide network is available.

STUDENT LIFE

Housing options: on-campus residence required through senior year; men-only, women-only. Campus housing is university owned. Freshman campus housing is guaranteed.

Activities and organizations: drama/theater group, choral group, Musical Groups (Choir, Chamber Orchestra), Theatre Groups, Language Clubs, Pro-Life Ministry, religious groups.

Athletics ***Intramural sports:*** basketball M/W, football M, soccer M/W, softball M/W, table tennis M/W, tennis M/W, ultimate Frisbee M/W, volleyball M/W.

Campus security: daily security patrol.

Student services: personal/psychological counseling.

COSTS & FINANCIAL AID

Costs (2015–16) ***Comprehensive fee:*** $32,450 includes full-time tuition ($24,500) and room and board ($7950). ***Payment plan:*** installment.

Financial Aid Of all full-time matriculated undergraduates who enrolled in 2014, 293 applied for aid, 288 were judged to have need, 288 had their need fully met. 256 state and other part-time jobs (averaging $3982). ***Average percent of need met:*** 100. ***Average financial aid package:*** $22,171. ***Average need-based loan:*** $5753. ***Average need-based gift aid:*** $15,755. ***Average indebtedness upon graduation:*** $16,263. ***Financial aid deadline:*** 3/2.

APPLYING

Standardized Tests *Required:* SAT or ACT (for admission).

Options: electronic application.

Required: essay or personal statement, high school transcript, 3 letters of recommendation. ***Required for some:*** interview. ***Recommended:*** minimum 3.0 GPA.

Application deadlines: rolling (freshmen), rolling (out-of-state freshmen).

Notification: continuous (freshmen), continuous (out-of-state freshmen).

CONTACT

Mr. Jonathan P. Daly, Director of Admissions, Thomas Aquinas College, 10000 Ojai Road, Santa Paula, CA 93060-9621. *Phone:* 805-525-4417 Ext. 5901. *Toll-free phone:* 800-634-9797. *Fax:* 805-421-5905. *E-mail:* admissions@thomasaquinas.edu.

Trident University International

Cypress, California

http://www.trident.edu/

- **Independent** university
- **Urban** campus
- **Coed**
- **Minimally difficult** entrance level

FACULTY

Student/faculty ratio: 25:1.

ACADEMICS

Calendar: four 12 week sessions per year. *Degrees:* certificates, diplomas, bachelor's, master's, doctoral, post-master's, and postbachelor's certificates (offers only online degree programs).

STUDENT LIFE

Housing options: college housing not available.

COSTS & FINANCIAL AID

Costs (2014–15) ***Tuition:*** $8400 full-time, $350 per credit hour part-time. ***Payment plans:*** installment, deferred payment.

Financial Aid Of all full-time matriculated undergraduates who enrolled in 2009, 650 applied for aid, 650 were judged to have need, 552 had their need fully met. In 2009, 55 non-need-based awards were made. ***Average percent of need met:*** 98. ***Average financial aid package:*** $4415. ***Average need-based gift aid:*** $3293. ***Average non-need-based aid:*** $5898. ***Average indebtedness upon graduation:*** $38,298.

APPLYING

Options: electronic application.

Required: high school transcript. ***Required for some:*** essay or personal statement. ***Recommended:*** interview.

CONTACT

Trident University International, 5757 Plaza Drive, Suite 100, Cypress, CA 90630. *Phone:* 800-579-3197.

University of California, Berkeley

Berkeley, California

http://www.berkeley.edu/

- **State-supported** university, founded 1868, part of University of California System
- **Urban** 1232-acre campus with easy access to San Francisco
- **Coed** 27,126 undergraduate students, 97% full-time, 52% women, 48% men
- 16% of applicants were admitted

UNDERGRAD STUDENTS

26,320 full-time, 806 part-time. 15% are from out of state; 2% Black or African American, non-Hispanic/Latino; 14% Hispanic/Latino; 35% Asian, non-Hispanic/Latino; 0.3% Native Hawaiian or other Pacific Islander, non-Hispanic/Latino; 0.2% American Indian or Alaska Native, non-Hispanic/Latino; 5% Two or more races, non-Hispanic/Latino; 3% Race/ethnicity unknown; 14% international; 8% transferred in; 26% live on campus.

Freshmen

Admission: 73,779 applied, 11,816 admitted, 5,466 enrolled. ***Average high school GPA:*** 3.85. ***Test scores:*** SAT critical reading scores over 500: 94%; SAT math scores over 500: 96%; SAT writing scores over 500: 95%; ACT scores over 18: 100%; SAT critical reading scores over 600: 75%; SAT math scores over 600: 83%; SAT writing scores over 600: 79%; ACT scores over 24: 91%; SAT critical reading scores over 700: 37%; SAT math scores over 700: 54%; SAT writing scores over 700: 45%; ACT scores over 30: 63%.

Retention: 97% of full-time freshmen returned.

FACULTY

Total: 2,272, 72% full-time, 99% with terminal degrees.

Student/faculty ratio: 17:1.

ACADEMICS

Calendar: semesters. *Degrees:* bachelor's, master's, doctoral, and postbachelor's certificates.

Special study options: accelerated degree program, adult/continuing education programs, advanced placement credit, double majors, English as a second language, honors programs, independent study, internships, off-campus study, services for LD students, student-designed majors, study abroad, summer session for credit. ***ROTC:*** Army (b), Navy (b), Air Force (b).

Computers: Students can access the following: computer help desk, free student e-mail accounts, online (class) grades, online (class) registration, online (class) schedules. Campuswide network is available. Wireless service is available via classrooms, computer centers, computer labs, dorm rooms, learning centers, libraries, student centers.

STUDENT LIFE

Housing options: coed, men-only, women-only, cooperative, special housing for students with disabilities. Campus housing is university owned and is provided by a third party. Freshman campus housing is guaranteed.

Activities and organizations: drama/theater group, student-run newspaper, radio and television station, choral group, marching band, national fraternities, national sororities.

Athletics Member NCAA. All Division I. ***Intercollegiate sports:*** baseball M, basketball M/W, crew M/W, cross-country running M/W, field hockey W, football M, golf M/W, gymnastics M/W, lacrosse M/W, rugby M, soccer M/W, softball W, swimming and diving M/W, tennis M/W, track and field M/W, volleyball W, water polo M/W. ***Intramural sports:*** basketball M/W, soccer M/W, softball M/W, tennis M/W, ultimate Frisbee M/W, volleyball M/W.

Campus security: 24-hour emergency response devices and patrols, late-night transport/escort service, controlled dormitory access, Office of Emergency Preparedness.

Student services: health clinic, personal/psychological counseling, women's center, legal services.

COSTS & FINANCIAL AID

Costs (2014–15) ***Tuition:*** state resident $11,220 full-time; nonresident $35,850 full-time. ***Required fees:*** $1752 full-time. ***Room and board:*** $15,438. Room and board charges vary according to board plan and housing facility. ***Payment plan:*** installment.

Financial Aid Of all full-time matriculated undergraduates who enrolled in 2013, 15,501 applied for aid, 12,077 were judged to have need, 11,641 had their need fully met. In 2013, 1612 non-need-based awards were made. ***Average percent of need met:*** 98. ***Average financial aid package:*** $23,517. ***Average need-based loan:*** $4672. ***Average need-based gift aid:*** $23,099. ***Average non-need-based aid:*** $5053. ***Average indebtedness upon graduation:*** $17,468. ***Financial aid deadline:*** 3/2.

APPLYING

Standardized Tests *Required:* SAT or ACT (for admission). *Recommended:* SAT Subject Tests (for admission).

Options: electronic application.

Application fee: $70.

Required: essay or personal statement.

CONTACT

University of California, Berkeley, Berkeley, CA 94720-1500.

University of California, Davis

Davis, California

http://www.ucdavis.edu/

- **State-supported** university, founded 1905, part of University of California System
- **Suburban** 5300-acre campus with easy access to San Francisco
- **Coed** 27,728 undergraduate students, 99% full-time, 58% women, 42% men
- **Very difficult** entrance level, 41% of applicants were admitted

UNDERGRAD STUDENTS

27,314 full-time, 414 part-time. 4% are from out of state; 2% Black or African American, non-Hispanic/Latino; 18% Hispanic/Latino; 34% Asian, non-Hispanic/Latino; 0.5% Native Hawaiian or other Pacific Islander, non-Hispanic/Latino; 0.2% American Indian or Alaska Native, non-Hispanic/Latino; 5% Two or more races, non-Hispanic/Latino; 3% Race/ethnicity unknown; 8% international; 11% transferred in; 25% live on campus.

Freshmen

Admission: 60,506 applied, 24,541 admitted, 5,398 enrolled. ***Average high school GPA:*** 4. ***Test scores:*** SAT critical reading scores over 500: 82%; SAT math scores over 500: 89%; SAT writing scores over 500: 86%; ACT scores over 18: 98%; SAT critical reading scores over 600: 47%; SAT math scores over 600: 64%; SAT writing scores over 600: 54%; ACT scores over 24: 81%; SAT critical reading scores over 700: 11%; SAT math scores over 700: 28%; SAT writing scores over 700: 14%; ACT scores over 30: 36%.

Retention: 93% of full-time freshmen returned.

FACULTY

Total: 1,792, 90% full-time, 98% with terminal degrees.

Student/faculty ratio: 17:1.

ACADEMICS

Calendar: quarters. *Degrees:* bachelor's, master's, doctoral, post-master's, and postbachelor's certificates.

Special study options: academic remediation for entering students, adult/continuing education programs, advanced placement credit, double majors, English as a second language, freshman honors college, honors programs, independent study, internships, part-time degree program, services for LD students, student-designed majors, study abroad, summer session for credit. ***ROTC:*** Army (b), Navy (c), Air Force (c).

Computers: Students can access the following: campus intranet, computer help desk, free student e-mail accounts, online (class) grades, online (class) registration, online (class) schedules, software packages. Campuswide network is available. 100% of college-owned or -operated housing units are wired for high-speed Internet access. Wireless service is available via classrooms, libraries.

STUDENT LIFE

Housing options: coed, women-only, cooperative, special housing for students with disabilities. Campus housing is university owned, leased by the school and is provided by a third party. Freshman campus housing is guaranteed.

Activities and organizations: drama/theater group, student-run newspaper, radio and television station, choral group, marching band, national fraternities, national sororities.

Athletics Member NCAA. All Division I except football (Division I-AA). ***Intercollegiate sports:*** baseball M(s), basketball M(s)/W(s), cross-country running M(s)/W(s), field hockey W(s), golf M(s)/W(s), gymnastics W(s), lacrosse W(s), soccer M(s)/W(s), softball W(s), swimming and diving W(s), tennis M(s)/W(s), track and field M(s)/W(s), volleyball W(s), water polo M(s)/W(s). ***Intramural sports:*** archery M(c)/W(c), badminton M(c)/W(c), basketball M/W, crew M(c)/W(c), equestrian sports M(c)/W(c), fencing M(c)/W(c), football M/W, golf M/W, gymnastics M(c), ice hockey M(c)/W, lacrosse M(c)/W(c), racquetball M(c)/W(c), riflery M(c)/W(c), rugby M(c), sailing M(c)/W(c), skiing (cross-country) M(c)/W(c), skiing (downhill) M(c)/W(c), soccer M/W, softball M/W, swimming and diving W(c), table tennis M/W, tennis M/W, volleyball M(c)/W, water polo W(c).

Campus security: 24-hour emergency response devices and patrols, student patrols, late-night transport/escort service, controlled dormitory access, Campus Violence Prevention Program (CVPP).

Student services: health clinic, personal/psychological counseling, women's center, legal services.

COSTS & FINANCIAL AID

Costs (2014–15) ***Tuition:*** state resident $11,220 full-time; nonresident $34,098 full-time. ***Required fees:*** $2676 full-time. ***Room and board:*** $14,218. Room and board charges vary according to board plan. ***Payment plan:*** deferred payment.

Financial Aid Of all full-time matriculated undergraduates who enrolled in 2013, 19,485 applied for aid, 17,000 were judged to have need, 2,445 had their need fully met. In 2013, 894 non-need-based awards were made. ***Average percent of need met:*** 78. ***Average financial aid package:*** $19,685. ***Average need-based loan:*** $5638. ***Average need-based gift aid:*** $16,619. ***Average non-need-based aid:*** $5690. ***Average indebtedness upon graduation:*** $19,970.

APPLYING

Standardized Tests *Required:* SAT or ACT (for admission).

Options: electronic application.

Application fee: $70.

Required: essay or personal statement, high school transcript, minimum 2.8 GPA, high school subject requirements.

Application deadlines: 11/30 (freshmen), 11/30 (transfers).

Notification: 3/15 (freshmen), continuous until 3/15 (transfers).

CONTACT

University of California, Davis, CA. *E-mail:* undergraduateadmissions@ucdavis.edu.

University of California, Irvine

Irvine, California

http://www.uci.edu/

- **State-supported** university, founded 1965, part of University of California System
- **Suburban** 1477-acre campus with easy access to Los Angeles
- **Coed** 24,489 undergraduate students, 99% full-time, 54% women, 46% men
- **Very difficult** entrance level, 37% of applicants were admitted

UNDERGRAD STUDENTS
24,139 full-time, 350 part-time. Students come from 46 states and territories; 72 other countries; 2% are from out of state; 2% Black or African American, non-Hispanic/Latino; 24% Hispanic/Latino; 41% Asian, non-Hispanic/Latino; 0.1% Native Hawaiian or other Pacific Islander, non-Hispanic/Latino; 4% Two or more races, non-Hispanic/Latino; 3% Race/ethnicity unknown; 12% international; 8% transferred in; 41% live on campus.

Freshmen
Admission: 66,505 applied, 24,890 admitted, 5,435 enrolled. ***Average high school GPA:*** 3.94. ***Test scores:*** SAT critical reading scores over 500: 73%; SAT math scores over 500: 90%; SAT writing scores over 500: 82%; SAT critical reading scores over 600: 33%; SAT math scores over 600: 58%; SAT writing scores over 600: 36%; SAT critical reading scores over 700: 8%; SAT math scores over 700: 22%; SAT writing scores over 700: 7%.
Retention: 92% of full-time freshmen returned.

FACULTY
Total: 1,458, 80% full-time, 98% with terminal degrees.
Student/faculty ratio: 19:1.

ACADEMICS
Calendar: quarters. *Degrees:* bachelor's, master's, doctoral, and postbachelor's certificates.
Special study options: accelerated degree program, advanced placement credit, distance learning, double majors, English as a second language, honors programs, independent study, internships, off-campus study, services for LD students, study abroad, summer session for credit. ***ROTC:*** Army (b), Air Force (c).
Computers: 1,500 computers/terminals are available on campus for general student use. Students can access the following: campus intranet, computer help desk, free student e-mail accounts, online (class) grades, online (class) registration, online (class) schedules. Campuswide network is available. Wireless service is available via entire campus.

STUDENT LIFE
Housing options: coed, men-only, women-only, special housing for students with disabilities. Campus housing is university owned and is provided by a third party. Freshman campus housing is guaranteed.
Activities and organizations: drama/theater group, student-run newspaper, radio station, choral group, marching band, national fraternities, national sororities.
Athletics Member NCAA. All Division I. ***Intercollegiate sports:*** archery M(c)/W(c), badminton M(c)/W(c), baseball M(s), basketball M(s)/W(s), crew M(c)/W(c), cross-country running M(s)/W(s), fencing M(c)/W(c), golf M(s)/W(s), lacrosse M(c)/W(c), rugby M(c)/W(c), sailing M(c)/W(c), soccer M(s)/W(s), table tennis M(c)/W(c), tennis M(s)/W(s), track and field M(s)/W(s), ultimate Frisbee M(c)/W(c), volleyball M(s)/W(s), water polo M(s)/W(s), wrestling M(c)/W(c). ***Intramural sports:*** basketball M/W, bowling M/W, football M/W, racquetball M/W, soccer M/W, softball M/W, swimming and diving M/W, table tennis M/W, tennis M/W, track and field M/W, ultimate Frisbee M/W, volleyball M/W, water polo M/W, wrestling M/W.
Campus security: 24-hour emergency response devices and patrols, student patrols, late-night transport/escort service, controlled dormitory access.
Student services: health clinic, personal/psychological counseling.

COSTS & FINANCIAL AID
Costs (2014–15) ***Tuition:*** state resident $11,220 full-time; nonresident $34,098 full-time. ***Required fees:*** $3537 full-time. ***Room and board:*** $12,638. Room and board charges vary according to board plan and housing facility. ***Payment plan:*** installment. ***Waivers:*** employees or children of employees.
Financial Aid Of all full-time matriculated undergraduates who enrolled in 2014, 18,687 applied for aid, 16,641 were judged to have need, 3,449 had their need fully met. 3,053 Federal Work-Study jobs (averaging $1628). 2,503 state and other part-time jobs (averaging $1840). In 2014, 470 non-need-based awards were made. ***Average percent of need met:*** 81. ***Average financial aid package:*** $21,475. ***Average need-based loan:*** $6741. ***Average need-based gift aid:*** $17,317. ***Average non-need-based aid:*** $8541. ***Average indebtedness upon graduation:*** $20,319. ***Financial aid deadline:*** 6/20.

APPLYING
Standardized Tests *Required:* SAT or ACT (for admission). *Recommended:* SAT Subject Tests (for admission).
Options: electronic application.
Application fee: $70.
Required: essay or personal statement, high school transcript.
Application deadlines: 11/30 (freshmen), 11/30 (transfers).
Notification: 3/31 (freshmen), 4/30 (transfers).

CONTACT
University of California, Irvine, UC IRVINE Office of Admissions and Relations with Schools, 260 Aldrich Hall, Irvine, CA 92697-1075. *Phone:* 949-824-6703. *Fax:* 949-824-2951. *E-mail:* admissions@uci.edu.

University of California, Los Angeles

Los Angeles, California

http://www.ucla.edu/

- **State-supported** university, founded 1919, part of University of California System
- **Urban** 419-acre campus with easy access to Los Angeles
- **Endowment** $2.6 billion
- **Coed** 29,633 undergraduate students, 98% full-time, 56% women, 44% men
- **Very difficult** entrance level, 19% of applicants were admitted

UNDERGRAD STUDENTS
29,033 full-time, 600 part-time. Students come from 53 states and territories; 99 other countries; 10% are from out of state; 3% Black or African American, non-Hispanic/Latino; 20% Hispanic/Latino; 30% Asian, non-Hispanic/Latino; 0.3% Native Hawaiian or other Pacific Islander, non-Hispanic/Latino; 0.1% American Indian or Alaska Native, non-Hispanic/Latino; 5% Two or more races, non-Hispanic/Latino; 2% Race/ethnicity unknown; 13% international; 11% transferred in; 45% live on campus.

Freshmen
Admission: 86,548 applied, 16,059 admitted, 5,764 enrolled. ***Average high school GPA:*** 4.31. ***Test scores:*** SAT critical reading scores over 500: 92%; SAT math scores over 500: 94%; SAT writing scores over 500: 93%; ACT scores over 18: 100%; SAT critical reading scores over 600: 69%; SAT math scores over 600: 76%; SAT writing scores over 600: 74%; ACT scores over 24: 86%; SAT critical reading scores over 700: 28%; SAT math scores over 700: 46%; SAT writing scores over 700: 37%; ACT scores over 30: 53%.
Retention: 97% of full-time freshmen returned.

FACULTY
Total: 2,657, 76% full-time, 98% with terminal degrees.
Student/faculty ratio: 17:1.

ACADEMICS
Calendar: quarters. *Degrees:* bachelor's, master's, and doctoral.
Special study options: accelerated degree program, advanced placement credit, double majors, freshman honors college, honors programs, independent study, internships, off-campus study, services for LD students, student-designed majors, study abroad, summer session for credit. ***ROTC:*** Army (b), Navy (b), Air Force (b).
Computers: 4,000 computers/terminals are available on campus for general student use. Students can access the following: campus intranet, computer help desk, free student e-mail accounts, online (class) grades, online (class) registration, online (class) schedules. Campuswide network

is available. 100% of college-owned or -operated housing units are wired for high-speed Internet access. Wireless service is available via entire campus.

STUDENT LIFE

Housing options: coed, special housing for students with disabilities. Campus housing is university owned. Freshman campus housing is guaranteed.

Activities and organizations: drama/theater group, student-run newspaper, radio and television station, choral group, marching band, national fraternities, national sororities.

Athletics Member NCAA. All Division I except football (Division I-A). ***Intercollegiate sports:*** baseball M(s), basketball M(s)/W(s), crew W(s), cross-country running M(s)/W(s), golf M(s)/W(s), gymnastics W(s), soccer M(s)/W(s), softball W(s), swimming and diving W(s), tennis M(s)/W(s), track and field M(s)/W(s), volleyball M(s)/W(s), water polo M(s)/W(s). ***Intramural sports:*** archery M/W, badminton M/W, basketball M/W, bowling M/W, crew M/W, cross-country running M/W, fencing M/W, field hockey W, football M/W, golf M/W, gymnastics M/W, ice hockey M/W, lacrosse M/W, racquetball M/W, riflery M/W, rugby M/W, sailing M/W, skiing (cross-country) M/W, skiing (downhill) M/W, soccer M/W, softball M/W, squash M/W, swimming and diving M/W, table tennis M/W, tennis M/W, track and field M/W, ultimate Frisbee M/W, volleyball M/W, water polo M/W.

Campus security: 24-hour emergency response devices and patrols, student patrols, late-night transport/escort service, controlled dormitory access.

Student services: health clinic, personal/psychological counseling, women's center, legal services.

COSTS & FINANCIAL AID

Costs (2014–15) ***One-time required fee:*** $165. ***Tuition:*** state resident $11,220 full-time; nonresident $34,098 full-time. ***Required fees:*** $1809 full-time. ***Room and board:*** $13,135. Room and board charges vary according to board plan and housing facility.

Financial Aid Of all full-time matriculated undergraduates who enrolled in 2014, 17,699 applied for aid, 16,057 were judged to have need, 4,027 had their need fully met. 2,463 Federal Work-Study jobs (averaging $1818). 743 state and other part-time jobs (averaging $1113). In 2014, 807 non-need-based awards were made. ***Average percent of need met:*** 83. ***Average financial aid package:*** $22,405. ***Average need-based loan:*** $6771. ***Average need-based gift aid:*** $18,806. ***Average non-need-based aid:*** $4539. ***Average indebtedness upon graduation:*** $20,759.

APPLYING

Standardized Tests *Required:* SAT or ACT (for admission).

Options: electronic application.

Application fee: $70.

Required: essay or personal statement, high school transcript.

Application deadlines: 11/30 (freshmen), 11/30 (out-of-state freshmen), 11/30 (transfers).

Notification: 3/31 (freshmen), 3/31 (out-of-state freshmen), 4/30 (transfers).

CONTACT

University of California, Los Angeles, 405 Hilgard Avenue, Los Angeles, CA 90095. *Phone:* 310-825-3101.

University of California, Merced

Merced, California

http://www.ucmerced.edu/

- **State-supported** university, part of University of California System
- **Small-town** 815-acre campus with easy access to Fresno
- **Endowment** $35.3 million
- **Coed** 5,884 undergraduate students, 99% full-time, 52% women, 48% men
- **Moderately difficult** entrance level, 67% of applicants were admitted

UNDERGRAD STUDENTS

5,811 full-time, 73 part-time. Students come from 12 states and territories; 19 other countries; 6% Black or African American, non-Hispanic/Latino; 46% Hispanic/Latino; 25% Asian, non-Hispanic/Latino; 0.6% Native Hawaiian or other Pacific Islander, non-Hispanic/Latino; 0.2% American Indian or Alaska Native, non-Hispanic/Latino; 4% Two or more races, non-Hispanic/Latino; 0.9% Race/ethnicity unknown; 4% international; 2% transferred in; 36% live on campus.

Freshmen

Admission: 16,261 applied, 10,925 admitted, 1,551 enrolled. ***Average high school GPA:*** 3.53. ***Test scores:*** SAT critical reading scores over 500: 51%; SAT math scores over 500: 60%; SAT writing scores over 500: 49%; ACT scores over 18: 88%; SAT critical reading scores over 600: 13%; SAT math scores over 600: 21%; SAT writing scores over 600: 12%; ACT scores over 24: 32%; SAT critical reading scores over 700: 2%; SAT math scores over 700: 4%; SAT writing scores over 700: 1%; ACT scores over 30: 4%.

Retention: 84% of full-time freshmen returned.

FACULTY

Total: 347, 87% full-time, 82% with terminal degrees.

Student/faculty ratio: 20:1.

ACADEMICS

Degrees: bachelor's, master's, and doctoral.

Special study options: academic remediation for entering students, advanced placement credit, double majors, independent study, internships, off-campus study, part-time degree program, services for LD students, study abroad, summer session for credit.

Computers: 230 computers/terminals are available on campus for general student use. Students can access the following: campus intranet, computer help desk, free student e-mail accounts, online (class) grades, online (class) registration, online (class) schedules, Free student calendar, free 10Gb online cloud storage, free MS Office for registered students. Campuswide network is available. 100% of college-owned or -operated housing units are wired for high-speed Internet access. Wireless service is available via entire campus.

STUDENT LIFE

Housing options: coed, special housing for students with disabilities. Campus housing is university owned. Freshman campus housing is guaranteed.

Activities and organizations: drama/theater group, student-run newspaper, radio station, choral group, marching band, Philipino American Alliance, Vietnamese Student Association, Intervarsity Christian Fellowship, Latino Associated Students, Hip Hop Movement, national fraternities, national sororities.

Athletics Member NAIA. ***Intercollegiate sports:*** basketball M(s)/W(s), cross-country running M(s)/W(s), golf M(c)/W(c), soccer M(s)/W(s), volleyball M(s)/W(s). ***Intramural sports:*** archery M/W, baseball M(c), basketball M/W, cheerleading M(c)/W(c), football M/W, lacrosse M(c)/W(c), soccer M/W, softball M(c)/W(c), table tennis M(c)/W(c), ultimate Frisbee M/W, volleyball M/W, weight lifting M(c)/W(c), wrestling M(c)/W(c).

Campus security: 24-hour emergency response devices and patrols, student patrols, late-night transport/escort service, controlled dormitory access.

Student services: health clinic, personal/psychological counseling, women's center, legal services.

COSTS & FINANCIAL AID

Costs (2014–15) ***Tuition:*** state resident $13,070 full-time; nonresident $35,948 full-time. ***Required fees:*** $1743 full-time. ***Room and board:*** $14,718. Room and board charges vary according to board plan. ***Waivers:*** employees or children of employees.

Financial Aid Of all full-time matriculated undergraduates who enrolled in 2013, 5,325 applied for aid, 4,986 were judged to have need, 1,727 had their need fully met. In 2013, 50 non-need-based awards were made. ***Average percent of need met:*** 86. ***Average financial aid package:*** $22,672. ***Average need-based loan:*** $5206. ***Average need-based gift aid:*** $18,557. ***Average non-need-based aid:*** $9634. ***Average indebtedness upon graduation:*** $21,314.

APPLYING

Standardized Tests *Required:* SAT or ACT (for admission).

Options: electronic application.

Application fee: $70.

Required: essay or personal statement, high school transcript, minimum 3.0 high school GPA for California residents.

Application deadlines: 11/30 (freshmen), 11/30 (transfers).

Notification: 3/1 (freshmen), 3/1 (transfers).

CONTACT

Ms. Susan Fauroat, Associate Director, Admissions and Outreach, University of California, Merced, 5200 North Lake Road, Merced, CA 95343. *Phone:* 209-228-4779. *E-mail:* admissions@ucmerced.edu.

University of California, Riverside

Riverside, California

http://www.ucr.edu/

- **State-supported** university, founded 1954, part of University of California System
- **Urban** 1200-acre campus with easy access to Los Angeles
- **Endowment** $138.8 million
- **Coed** 18,782 undergraduate students, 98% full-time, 52% women, 48% men
- **Very difficult** entrance level, 58% of applicants were admitted

UNDERGRAD STUDENTS

18,445 full-time, 337 part-time. Students come from 41 states and territories; 52 other countries; 0.7% are from out of state; 5% Black or African American, non-Hispanic/Latino; 37% Hispanic/Latino; 36% Asian, non-Hispanic/Latino; 0.4% Native Hawaiian or other Pacific Islander, non-Hispanic/Latino; 0.2% American Indian or Alaska Native, non-Hispanic/Latino; 4% Two or more races, non-Hispanic/Latino; 1% Race/ethnicity unknown; 3% international; 7% transferred in; 34% live on campus.

Freshmen

Admission: 36,101 applied, 21,044 admitted, 4,279 enrolled. ***Average high school GPA:*** 3.68. ***Test scores:*** SAT critical reading scores over 500: 74%; SAT math scores over 500: 83%; SAT writing scores over 500: 77%; ACT scores over 18: 97%; SAT critical reading scores over 600: 28%; SAT math scores over 600: 45%; SAT writing scores over 600: 32%; ACT scores over 24: 57%; SAT critical reading scores over 700: 3%; SAT math scores over 700: 11%; SAT writing scores over 700: 5%; ACT scores over 30: 11%.

Retention: 90% of full-time freshmen returned.

FACULTY

Total: 974, 84% full-time, 98% with terminal degrees.

Student/faculty ratio: 19:1.

ACADEMICS

Calendar: quarters. *Degrees:* bachelor's, master's, doctoral, and postbachelor's certificates.

Special study options: accelerated degree program, adult/continuing education programs, advanced placement credit, distance learning, double majors, honors programs, independent study, internships, off-campus study, services for LD students, study abroad, summer session for credit. ***ROTC:*** Army (c), Air Force (c).

Unusual degree programs: 3-2 engineering with five-year joint BS/MS programs in chemical and environmental engineering, computer science and engineering, electrical engineering, mechanical engineering.

Computers: 556 computers/terminals are available on campus for general student use. Students can access the following: campus intranet, computer help desk, free student e-mail accounts, online (class) grades, online (class) registration, online (class) schedules, online viewing of financial information. Campuswide network is available. 100% of college-owned or -operated housing units are wired for high-speed Internet access. Wireless service is available via entire campus.

STUDENT LIFE

Housing options: coed, special housing for students with disabilities. Campus housing is university owned and is provided by a third party. Freshman campus housing is guaranteed.

Activities and organizations: drama/theater group, student-run newspaper, radio station, choral group, American Red Cross at University of California Riverside, Student Alumni Association, American Medical Student Association, Running Club at UCR, Circle K International, national fraternities, national sororities.

Athletics Member NCAA. All Division I. ***Intercollegiate sports:*** baseball M(s), basketball M(s)/W(s), cross-country running M(s)/W(s), golf M(s), soccer M(s)/W(s), softball W(s), tennis M/W, volleyball W(s). ***Intramural sports:*** badminton M/W, basketball M/W, racquetball M/W, rugby M(c)/W(c), soccer M/W, softball M/W, table tennis M(c)/W(c), tennis M/W, volleyball M/W, wrestling M(c).

Campus security: 24-hour emergency response devices and patrols, student patrols, late-night transport/escort service, controlled dormitory access.

Student services: health clinic, personal/psychological counseling, women's center, legal services.

COSTS & FINANCIAL AID

Costs (2015–16) ***Tuition:*** state resident $11,220 full-time, $5610 per year part-time; nonresident $34,098 full-time, $17,049 per year part-time. Full-time tuition and fees vary according to course load. Part-time tuition and fees vary according to course load. ***Required fees:*** $2087 full-time. ***Room and board:*** $15,000. Room and board charges vary according to board plan and housing facility. ***Payment plan:*** deferred payment.

Financial Aid Of all full-time matriculated undergraduates who enrolled in 2014, 16,039 applied for aid, 14,448 were judged to have need, 3,276 had their need fully met. 2,929 Federal Work-Study jobs (averaging $1508). In 2014, 620 non-need-based awards were made. ***Average percent of need met:*** 82. ***Average financial aid package:*** $21,068. ***Average need-based loan:*** $6345. ***Average need-based gift aid:*** $16,766. ***Average non-need-based aid:*** $12,155. ***Average indebtedness upon graduation:*** $21,166. ***Financial aid deadline:*** 3/2.

APPLYING

Standardized Tests *Required:* SAT or ACT (for admission). *Recommended:* SAT Subject Tests (for admission).

Options: electronic application.

Application fee: $70.

Required: essay or personal statement, high school transcript, minimum 3.0 GPA.

Application deadlines: 11/30 (freshmen), 11/30 (transfers).

Notification: continuous until 2/1 (freshmen), continuous until 3/1 (transfers).

CONTACT

Ms. Emily D Engelschall, Director, Undergraduate Recruitment, University of California, Riverside, 3221 Student Services, 900 University Avenue, Riverside, CA 92521. *Phone:* 951-827-3986. *Fax:* 951-827-6346. *E-mail:* discover@ucr.edu.

University of California, Santa Barbara

Santa Barbara, California

http://www.ucsb.edu/

- **State-supported** university, founded 1909, part of University of California System
- **Suburban** 989-acre campus
- **Endowment** $137.6 million
- **Coed** 20,238 undergraduate students, 98% full-time, 53% women, 47% men
- **Very difficult** entrance level, 36% of applicants were admitted

UNDERGRAD STUDENTS

19,913 full-time, 325 part-time. Students come from 48 states and territories; 79 other countries; 4% are from out of state; 2% Black or African American, non-Hispanic/Latino; 25% Hispanic/Latino; 21% Asian, non-Hispanic/Latino; 0.4% Native Hawaiian or other Pacific Islander, non-Hispanic/Latino; 0.2% American Indian or Alaska Native, non-Hispanic/Latino; 6% Two or more races, non-Hispanic/Latino; 1% Race/ethnicity unknown; 6% international; 8% transferred in; 38% live on campus.

Freshmen

Admission: 66,813 applied, 24,283 admitted, 4,738 enrolled. ***Average high school GPA:*** 3.98. ***Test scores:*** SAT critical reading scores over 500: 90%; SAT math scores over 500: 94%; SAT writing scores over 500: 94%; ACT scores over 18: 99%; SAT critical reading scores over 600: 58%; SAT math scores over 600: 71%; SAT writing scores over 600: 64%; ACT

scores over 24: 78%; SAT critical reading scores over 700: 15%; SAT math scores over 700: 28%; SAT writing scores over 700: 21%; ACT scores over 30: 31%.

Retention: 92% of full-time freshmen returned.

FACULTY
Total: 1,079, 83% full-time, 100% with terminal degrees.

Student/faculty ratio: 17:1.

ACADEMICS
Calendar: quarters plus 6-week summer term. *Degrees:* bachelor's, master's, doctoral, post-master's, and postbachelor's certificates.

Special study options: accelerated degree program, advanced placement credit, cooperative education, double majors, English as a second language, honors programs, independent study, internships, off-campus study, services for LD students, student-designed majors, study abroad, summer session for credit. ***ROTC:*** Army (b), Air Force (c).

Computers: 700 computers/terminals are available on campus for general student use. Students can access the following: computer help desk, free student e-mail accounts, online (class) grades, online (class) registration, online (class) schedules. Campuswide network is available. 100% of college-owned or -operated housing units are wired for high-speed Internet access. Wireless service is available via classrooms, computer labs, dorm rooms, libraries, student centers.

STUDENT LIFE
Housing options: on-campus residence required for freshman year; coed, cooperative. Campus housing is university owned and is provided by a third party. Freshman applicants given priority for college housing.

Activities and organizations: drama/theater group, student-run newspaper, radio and television station, choral group, national fraternities, national sororities.

Athletics Member NCAA. All Division I. ***Intercollegiate sports:*** baseball M(s), basketball M(s)/W(s), bowling M(c)/W(c), crew M(c)/W(c), cross-country running M(s)/W(s), equestrian sports M(c)/W(c), fencing M(c)/W(c), field hockey W(c), golf M(s), gymnastics M(s)/W(s), lacrosse M(c)/W(c), rugby M(c), sailing M(c)/W(c), skiing (downhill) M(c)/W(c), soccer M(s)/W(s), softball W(s), swimming and diving M(s)/W(s), tennis M(s)/W(s), track and field M(s)/W(s), ultimate Frisbee M(c)/W(c), volleyball M(s)/W(s), water polo M(s)/W(s). ***Intramural sports:*** badminton M/W, basketball M/W, bowling M/W, cross-country running M/W, football M/W, golf M/W, gymnastics M/W, racquetball M/W, soccer M/W, softball M/W, squash M/W, tennis M/W, ultimate Frisbee M/W, volleyball M/W, water polo M/W.

Campus security: 24-hour emergency response devices and patrols, student patrols, late-night transport/escort service, controlled dormitory access.

Student services: health clinic, personal/psychological counseling, women's center, legal services.

COSTS & FINANCIAL AID
Costs (2014–15) ***Tuition:*** state resident $11,220 full-time; nonresident $34,098 full-time. ***Required fees:*** $2640 full-time. ***Room and board:*** $14,128. Room and board charges vary according to board plan and housing facility. ***Payment plan:*** installment.

Financial Aid Of all full-time matriculated undergraduates who enrolled in 2014, 14,437 applied for aid, 12,285 were judged to have need, 3,051 had their need fully met. In 2014, 369 non-need-based awards were made. ***Average percent of need met:*** 82. ***Average financial aid package:*** $22,572. ***Average need-based loan:*** $6250. ***Average need-based gift aid:*** $17,948. ***Average non-need-based aid:*** $12,066. ***Average indebtedness upon graduation:*** $21,045.

APPLYING
Standardized Tests *Required:* SAT or ACT (for admission). *Recommended:* SAT Subject Tests (for admission).

Options: electronic application.

Application fee: $70.

Required: essay or personal statement, high school transcript. ***Required for some:*** interview.

Application deadlines: 11/30 (freshmen), 11/30 (out-of-state freshmen), 11/30 (transfers).

Notification: 3/15 (freshmen), 3/15 (out-of-state freshmen), 5/1 (transfers).

CONTACT
Office of Admissions, University of California, Santa Barbara, 1210 Cheadle Hall, Santa Barbara, CA 93106-2014. *Phone:* 805-893-2881. *Fax:* 805-893-2676. *E-mail:* admissions@sa.ucsb.edu.

University of California, Santa Cruz

Santa Cruz, California

http://www.ucsc.edu/

- **State-supported** university, founded 1965, part of University of California System
- **Small-town** 2000-acre campus with easy access to San Francisco, San Jose
- **Endowment** $150.8 million
- **Coed** 16,277 undergraduate students, 97% full-time, 53% women, 47% men
- **Very difficult** entrance level, 57% of applicants were admitted

UNDERGRAD STUDENTS
15,825 full-time, 452 part-time. Students come from 44 states and territories; 50 other countries; 2% are from out of state; 2% Black or African American, non-Hispanic/Latino; 32% Hispanic/Latino; 20% Asian, non-Hispanic/Latino; 0.2% Native Hawaiian or other Pacific Islander, non-Hispanic/Latino; 0.2% American Indian or Alaska Native, non-Hispanic/Latino; 7% Two or more races, non-Hispanic/Latino; 2% Race/ethnicity unknown; 2% international; 7% transferred in; 98% live on campus.

Freshmen
Admission: 40,193 applied, 22,914 admitted, 4,035 enrolled. ***Average high school GPA:*** 3.45. ***Test scores:*** SAT critical reading scores over 500: 73%; SAT math scores over 500: 81%; SAT writing scores over 500: 75%; ACT scores over 18: 92%; SAT critical reading scores over 600: 37%; SAT math scores over 600: 48%; SAT writing scores over 600: 37%; ACT scores over 24: 62%; SAT critical reading scores over 700: 7%; SAT math scores over 700: 11%; SAT writing scores over 700: 6%; ACT scores over 30: 14%.

Retention: 89% of full-time freshmen returned.

FACULTY
Total: 831, 64% full-time, 80% with terminal degrees.

ACADEMICS
Calendar: quarters. *Degrees:* bachelor's, master's, doctoral, and postbachelor's certificates.

Special study options: accelerated degree program, advanced placement credit, cooperative education, double majors, freshman honors college, honors programs, independent study, internships, off-campus study, services for LD students, student-designed majors, study abroad, summer session for credit. ***ROTC:*** Army (c), Navy (c), Air Force (c).

Computers: Students can access the following: campus intranet, computer help desk, free student e-mail accounts, online (class) grades, online (class) registration, online (class) schedules. Campuswide network is available. 100% of college-owned or -operated housing units are wired for high-speed Internet access. Wireless service is available via entire campus.

STUDENT LIFE
Housing options: coed, men-only, women-only, cooperative. Campus housing is university owned. Freshman campus housing is guaranteed.

Activities and organizations: drama/theater group, student-run newspaper, radio and television station, choral group, Filipino Student Association, Movimiento Estudiantil Chicano de Aztlan, CSA (Chinese Student Association), A/BSA (African/Black Student Alliance), SEC (Student Environmental Center), national fraternities, national sororities.

Athletics Member NCAA. All Division III. ***Intercollegiate sports:*** badminton M(c)/W(c), baseball M(c)/W(c), basketball M/W, cheerleading M(c)/W(c), cross-country running M(c)/W, equestrian sports M(c)/W(c), fencing M(c)/W(c), golf W, lacrosse M(c), racquetball M(c)/W(c), rugby M(c)/W(c), soccer M/W, swimming and diving M/W, table tennis M(c)/W(c), tennis M/W, track and field M(c)/W(c), ultimate Frisbee M(c)/W(c), volleyball M/W, water polo M(c)/W(c). ***Intramural sports:*** basketball M/W, soccer M/W, softball M/W, ultimate Frisbee M/W, volleyball M/W, water polo M/W.

Campus security: 24-hour emergency response devices and patrols, late-night transport/escort service, controlled dormitory access, evening main gate security, campus police force and fire station.

Student services: health clinic, personal/psychological counseling, women's center.

COSTS & FINANCIAL AID

Costs (2014–15) ***Tuition:*** state resident $12,192 full-time; nonresident $35,070 full-time. Part-time tuition and fees vary according to course load. ***Required fees:*** $1206 full-time. ***Room and board:*** $14,730. Room and board charges vary according to board plan and housing facility. ***Payment plan:*** installment.

Financial Aid Of all full-time matriculated undergraduates who enrolled in 2013, 12,434 applied for aid, 10,829 were judged to have need, 2,853 had their need fully met. 4,561 Federal Work-Study jobs (averaging $1956). In 2013, 427 non-need-based awards were made. ***Average percent of need met:*** 86. ***Average financial aid package:*** $22,938. ***Average need-based loan:*** $6332. ***Average need-based gift aid:*** $18,489. ***Average non-need-based aid:*** $6639. ***Average indebtedness upon graduation:*** $22,523. ***Financial aid deadline:*** 6/3.

APPLYING

Standardized Tests *Required:* SAT or ACT (for admission).

Options: electronic application.

Application fee: $70.

Required: essay or personal statement, high school transcript, minimum high school GPA of 3.0 for California residents, 3.4 for non-residents.

Application deadlines: 11/30 (freshmen), 11/30 (transfers).

Notification: 3/31 (freshmen), 4/30 (transfers).

CONTACT

Michael McCawley, Director, Admissions, University of California, Santa Cruz, 1156 High Street, Santa Cruz, CA 95064. *Phone:* 831-459-2374. *Fax:* 831-459-4163. *E-mail:* admissions@ucsc.edu.

University of La Verne

La Verne, California

http://www.laverne.edu/

- **Independent** university, founded 1891
- **Suburban** 66-acre campus with easy access to Los Angeles
- **Endowment** $63.2 million
- **Coed** 2,713 undergraduate students, 97% full-time, 59% women, 41% men
- **Moderately difficult** entrance level, 47% of applicants were admitted

UNDERGRAD STUDENTS

2,626 full-time, 87 part-time. Students come from 19 states and territories; 10 other countries; 4% are from out of state; 5% Black or African American, non-Hispanic/Latino; 51% Hispanic/Latino; 6% Asian, non-Hispanic/Latino; 0.5% Native Hawaiian or other Pacific Islander, non-Hispanic/Latino; 0.1% American Indian or Alaska Native, non-Hispanic/Latino; 5% Two or more races, non-Hispanic/Latino; 2% Race/ethnicity unknown; 5% international; 7% transferred in; 31% live on campus.

Freshmen

Admission: 8,233 applied, 3,833 admitted, 563 enrolled. ***Average high school GPA:*** 3.43. ***Test scores:*** SAT critical reading scores over 500: 57%; SAT math scores over 500: 56%; SAT writing scores over 500: 54%; ACT scores over 18: 92%; SAT critical reading scores over 600: 9%; SAT math scores over 600: 14%; SAT writing scores over 600: 7%; ACT scores over 24: 24%; SAT critical reading scores over 700: 1%; SAT math scores over 700: 2%; ACT scores over 30: 2%.

Retention: 86% of full-time freshmen returned.

FACULTY

Total: 459, 47% full-time, 38% with terminal degrees.

Student/faculty ratio: 14:1.

ACADEMICS

Calendar: 4-1-4. *Degrees:* certificates, bachelor's, master's, doctoral, and postbachelor's certificates (also offers continuing education program with significant enrollment not reflected in profile).

Special study options: academic remediation for entering students, accelerated degree program, adult/continuing education programs, advanced placement credit, distance learning, double majors, English as a second language, freshman honors college, honors programs, independent study, internships, off-campus study, part-time degree program, services for LD students, student-designed majors, study abroad, summer session for credit. ***ROTC:*** Army (c).

Computers: 520 computers/terminals and 410 ports are available on campus for general student use. Students can access the following: computer help desk, free student e-mail accounts, online (class) grades, online (class) registration, online (class) schedules, MyLaVerne (online). Campuswide network is available. 100% of college-owned or -operated housing units are wired for high-speed Internet access. Wireless service is available via entire campus.

STUDENT LIFE

Housing options: coed, men-only, women-only. Campus housing is university owned. Freshman campus housing is guaranteed.

Activities and organizations: drama/theater group, student-run newspaper, radio and television station, choral group, Associated Students of La Verne, Latino Student Forum, Black Student Union, Psi Chi, Voices in Action, national fraternities, national sororities.

Athletics Member NCAA. All Division III. ***Intercollegiate sports:*** baseball M, basketball M/W, cross-country running M/W, football M, golf M, soccer M/W, softball W, swimming and diving M/W, tennis M/W, track and field M/W, volleyball W, water polo M/W.

Campus security: 24-hour emergency response devices and patrols, late-night transport/escort service, controlled dormitory access.

Student services: health clinic, personal/psychological counseling.

COSTS & FINANCIAL AID

Costs (2015–16) ***Comprehensive fee:*** $51,070 includes full-time tuition ($37,100), mandatory fees ($1460), and room and board ($12,510). Full-time tuition and fees vary according to location. Part-time tuition: $1083 per semester hour. Part-time tuition and fees vary according to location. ***College room only:*** $6580. Room and board charges vary according to board plan and housing facility. ***Payment plans:*** installment, deferred payment. ***Waivers:*** employees or children of employees.

Financial Aid Of all full-time matriculated undergraduates who enrolled in 2014, 2,297 applied for aid, 2,166 were judged to have need, 186 had their need fully met. 311 Federal Work-Study jobs (averaging $2246). 1,070 state and other part-time jobs (averaging $8857). In 2014, 378 non-need-based awards were made. ***Average percent of need met:*** 43. ***Average financial aid package:*** $29,286. ***Average need-based loan:*** $4974. ***Average need-based gift aid:*** $10,923. ***Average non-need-based aid:*** $20,664. ***Average indebtedness upon graduation:*** $28,215.

APPLYING

Standardized Tests *Required:* SAT or ACT (for admission).

Options: electronic application, deferred entrance.

Application fee: $50.

Required: essay or personal statement, high school transcript, 2 letters of recommendation.

Application deadlines: 2/1 (freshmen), 4/1 (transfers).

Notification: continuous (freshmen), continuous (transfers).

CONTACT

Ms. Ana Liza V. Zell, Associate Dean of Undergraduate Admission, University of La Verne, 1950 Third Street, La Verne, CA 91750. *Phone:* 800-876-4858. *Toll-free phone:* 800-876-4858. *Fax:* 909-392-2714. *E-mail:* admissions@ulv.edu.

★ University of Redlands

Redlands, California

http://www.redlands.edu/

- **Independent** comprehensive, founded 1907
- **Small-town** 140-acre campus with easy access to Los Angeles
- **Endowment** $110.8 million
- **Coed**
- **Moderately difficult** entrance level

FACULTY

Student/faculty ratio: 14:1.

ACADEMICS
Calendar: 4-4-1. *Degrees:* bachelor's, master's, doctoral, post-master's, and postbachelor's certificates.

STUDENT LIFE
Housing options: on-campus residence required through senior year; coed, men-only, women-only, cooperative, special housing for students with disabilities. Campus housing is university owned. Freshman campus housing is guaranteed.

Activities and organizations: drama/theater group, student-run newspaper, radio station, choral group, Associated Students, service organizations, cultural organizations, social awareness groups.

Athletics Member NCAA. All Division III.

Campus security: 24-hour emergency response devices and patrols, student patrols, late-night transport/escort service, controlled dormitory access.

Student services: health clinic, personal/psychological counseling, women's center.

COSTS & FINANCIAL AID
Costs (2014–15) ***One-time required fee:*** $150. ***Comprehensive fee:*** $55,896 includes full-time tuition ($42,836), mandatory fees ($350), and room and board ($12,710). Full-time tuition and fees vary according to program. Part-time tuition: $1339 per credit hour. Part-time tuition and fees vary according to course load and program. ***Required fees:*** $116 per year part-time. ***Room and board:*** Room and board charges vary according to board plan and housing facility.

Financial Aid Of all full-time matriculated undergraduates who enrolled in 2013, 2,479 applied for aid, 2,067 were judged to have need, 520 had their need fully met. In 2013, 396 non-need-based awards were made. ***Average percent of need met:*** 85. ***Average financial aid package:*** $31,679. ***Average need-based loan:*** $5171. ***Average need-based gift aid:*** $28,780. ***Average non-need-based aid:*** $15,455. ***Average indebtedness upon graduation:*** $32,231.

APPLYING
Standardized Tests *Required:* SAT or ACT (for admission).

Options: electronic application, early admission, early action, deferred entrance.

Application fee: $30.

Required: essay or personal statement, high school transcript, 2 letters of recommendation. ***Recommended:*** interview.

CONTACT
University of Redlands, 1200 East Colton Avenue, PO Box 3080, Redlands, CA 92373-0999. *Phone:* 909-748-8159. *Toll-free phone:* 800-455-5064.

See this page for display ad and page 1698 for the College Close-Up.

University of San Diego
San Diego, California
http://www.sandiego.edu/

- **Independent Roman Catholic** university, founded 1949
- **Urban** 180-acre campus with easy access to San Diego
- **Endowment** $368.8 million
- **Coed** 5,741 undergraduate students, 97% full-time, 55% women, 45% men
- **Very difficult** entrance level, 46% of applicants were admitted

UNDERGRAD STUDENTS
5,541 full-time, 200 part-time. Students come from 52 states and territories; 61 other countries; 37% are from out of state; 3% Black or African American, non-Hispanic/Latino; 19% Hispanic/Latino; 6% Asian, non-Hispanic/Latino; 0.3% Native Hawaiian or other Pacific Islander, non-Hispanic/Latino; 0.5% American Indian or Alaska Native, non-Hispanic/Latino; 6% Two or more races, non-Hispanic/Latino; 4% Race/ethnicity unknown; 7% international; 6% transferred in; 40% live on campus.

Freshmen
Admission: 14,247 applied, 6,589 admitted, 1,129 enrolled. ***Average high school GPA:*** 3.9. ***Test scores:*** SAT critical reading scores over 500: 93%; SAT math scores over 500: 96%; SAT writing scores over 500: 93%; ACT scores over 18: 100%; SAT critical reading scores over 600: 57%; SAT

math scores over 600: 65%; SAT writing scores over 600: 59%; ACT scores over 24: 90%; SAT critical reading scores over 700: 9%; SAT math scores over 700: 15%; SAT writing scores over 700: 12%; ACT scores over 30: 35%.

Retention: 90% of full-time freshmen returned.

FACULTY
Total: 897, 45% full-time, 76% with terminal degrees.

Student/faculty ratio: 15:1.

ACADEMICS
Calendar: 4-1-4. *Degrees:* bachelor's, master's, doctoral, post-master's, and postbachelor's certificates.

Special study options: advanced placement credit, double majors, English as a second language, honors programs, independent study, internships, part-time degree program, services for LD students, study abroad, summer session for credit. ***ROTC:*** Army (c), Navy (b), Air Force (c).

Computers: 946 computers/terminals and 4,250 ports are available on campus for general student use. Students can access the following: campus intranet, computer help desk, free student e-mail accounts, online (class) grades, online (class) registration, online (class) schedules. Campuswide network is available. 100% of college-owned or -operated housing units are wired for high-speed Internet access. Wireless service is available via entire campus.

STUDENT LIFE
Housing options: on-campus residence required through sophomore year; coed, men-only, women-only, special housing for students with disabilities. Campus housing is university owned. Freshman campus housing is guaranteed.

Activities and organizations: drama/theater group, student-run newspaper, radio and television station, choral group, Panhellenic Council, Interfraternity Council, Habitat for Humanity, PRIDE, Outdoor Adventures, national fraternities, national sororities.

Athletics Member NCAA. All Division I except football (Division I-AA). ***Intercollegiate sports:*** baseball M(s), basketball M(s)/W(s), crew M/W(s), cross-country running M(s)/W(s), equestrian sports M(c)/W(c), golf M(s), lacrosse M(c)/W(c), rock climbing M(c)/W(c), rugby M(c), soccer M(s)/W(s), softball W(s), swimming and diving W(s), tennis M(s)/W(s), track and field W(s), ultimate Frisbee M(c)/W(c), volleyball M(c)/W(s). ***Intramural sports:*** baseball M(c), basketball M/W, football M/W, golf M(c)/W(c), soccer M(c)/W(c), softball M/W, tennis M/W, ultimate Frisbee M/W, volleyball M/W(c), water polo M(c)/W(c).

Campus security: 24-hour emergency response devices and patrols, late-night transport/escort service, controlled dormitory access.

Student services: health clinic, personal/psychological counseling, women's center, legal services.

COSTS & FINANCIAL AID
Costs (2014–15) ***Comprehensive fee:*** $54,818 includes full-time tuition ($42,330), mandatory fees ($578), and room and board ($11,910). Part-time tuition: $1460 per unit. Part-time tuition and fees vary according to course load. ***Room and board:*** Room and board charges vary according to board plan and housing facility. ***Payment plan:*** installment. ***Waivers:*** employees or children of employees.

Financial Aid Of all full-time matriculated undergraduates who enrolled in 2013, 3,432 applied for aid, 3,015 were judged to have need, 417 had their need fully met. 505 Federal Work-Study jobs (averaging $1973). In 2013, 744 non-need-based awards were made. ***Average percent of need met:*** 70. ***Average financial aid package:*** $31,056. ***Average need-based loan:*** $7862. ***Average need-based gift aid:*** $24,438. ***Average non-need-based aid:*** $14,025. ***Average indebtedness upon graduation:*** $30,225.

APPLYING
Standardized Tests *Required:* SAT or ACT (for admission).

Options: electronic application, deferred entrance.

Application fee: $55.

Required: essay or personal statement, high school transcript, 1 letter of recommendation.

Application deadlines: 12/15 (freshmen), 3/1 (transfers).

Notification: 4/1 (freshmen), continuous until 6/30 (transfers).

CONTACT
Ms. Minh-Ha Hoang, Director of Admission, University of San Diego, 5998 Alcala Park, San Diego, CA 92110. *Phone:* 619-260-4506. *Toll-free phone:* 800-248-4873. *Fax:* 619-260-6836. *E-mail:* admissions@sandiego.edu.

★ University of San Francisco
San Francisco, California
http://www.usfca.edu/

- **Independent Roman Catholic (Jesuit)** university, founded 1855
- **Urban** 55-acre campus
- **Endowment** $274.2 million
- **Coed** 6,845 undergraduate students, 95% full-time, 62% women, 38% men
- **Moderately difficult** entrance level, 60% of applicants were admitted

UNDERGRAD STUDENTS
6,529 full-time, 316 part-time. Students come from 53 states and territories; 63 other countries; 21% are from out of state; 3% Black or African American, non-Hispanic/Latino; 20% Hispanic/Latino; 20% Asian, non-Hispanic/Latino; 0.6% Native Hawaiian or other Pacific Islander, non-Hispanic/Latino; 0.3% American Indian or Alaska Native, non-Hispanic/Latino; 7% Two or more races, non-Hispanic/Latino; 2% Race/ethnicity unknown; 19% international; 7% transferred in; 35% live on campus.

Freshmen
Admission: 17,448 applied, 10,478 admitted, 1,502 enrolled. ***Average high school GPA:*** 3.6. ***Test scores:*** SAT critical reading scores over 500: 81%; SAT math scores over 500: 88%; SAT writing scores over 500: 37%; ACT scores over 18: 99%; SAT critical reading scores over 600: 34%; SAT math scores over 600: 42%; SAT writing scores over 600: 6%; ACT scores over 24: 65%; SAT critical reading scores over 700: 4%; SAT math scores over 700: 6%; ACT scores over 30: 12%.

Retention: 87% of full-time freshmen returned.

FACULTY
Student/faculty ratio: 12:1.

ACADEMICS
Calendar: 4-1-4. *Degrees:* bachelor's, master's, doctoral, post-master's, and postbachelor's certificates.

Special study options: adult/continuing education programs, advanced placement credit, cooperative education, distance learning, double majors, English as a second language, external degree program, honors programs, independent study, internships, off-campus study, part-time degree program, services for LD students, student-designed majors, study abroad, summer session for credit. ***ROTC:*** Army (b), Air Force (c).

Unusual degree programs: 3-2 engineering with University of Southern California; physics.

Computers: 261 computers/terminals are available on campus for general student use. Students can access the following: campus intranet, computer help desk, free student e-mail accounts, online (class) grades, online (class) registration, online (class) schedules. Campuswide network is available. Wireless service is available via classrooms, computer centers, computer labs, dorm rooms, learning centers, libraries, student centers.

STUDENT LIFE
Housing options: on-campus residence required for freshman year; coed, women-only. Campus housing is university owned and leased by the school. Freshman campus housing is guaranteed.

Activities and organizations: drama/theater group, student-run newspaper, radio and television station, choral group, marching band, national fraternities, national sororities.

Athletics Member NCAA. All Division I. ***Intercollegiate sports:*** baseball M(s), basketball M(s)/W(s), cross-country running M(s)/W(s), golf M(s)/W(s), soccer M(s)/W(s), softball M(c)/W(c), tennis M(s)/W(s), track and field M/W(s), volleyball M(c)/W(s). ***Intramural sports:*** basketball M/W, bowling M/W, fencing M(c)/W(c), football M/W, golf M(c)/W(c), lacrosse M(c), racquetball M/W, rugby M(c)/W(c), skiing (cross-country) M(c)/W(c), soccer M/W, softball M/W, swimming and diving M/W, table tennis M/W, tennis M/W, volleyball M/W.

Campus security: 24-hour emergency response devices and patrols, student patrols, late-night transport/escort service, controlled dormitory access.

Student services: health clinic, personal/psychological counseling, women's center.

COSTS & FINANCIAL AID

Costs (2015–16) ***Comprehensive fee:*** $56,284 includes full-time tuition ($42,180), mandatory fees ($454), and room and board ($13,650). Full-time tuition and fees vary according to course load, degree level, location, program, and reciprocity agreements. Part-time tuition: $1500 per credit. Part-time tuition and fees vary according to course load, degree level, location, program, and reciprocity agreements. ***Required fees:*** $454 per year part-time. ***College room only:*** $9170. Room and board charges vary according to board plan and housing facility. ***Payment plan:*** installment. ***Waivers:*** employees or children of employees.

Financial Aid Of all full-time matriculated undergraduates who enrolled in 2014, 4,596 applied for aid, 3,583 were judged to have need, 385 had their need fully met. 580 Federal Work-Study jobs (averaging $3402). 1,063 state and other part-time jobs (averaging $4053). In 2014, 643 non-need-based awards were made. ***Average percent of need met:*** 59. ***Average financial aid package:*** $37,283. ***Average need-based loan:*** $4955. ***Average need-based gift aid:*** $22,199. ***Average non-need-based aid:*** $11,198. ***Average indebtedness upon graduation:*** $31,098.

APPLYING

Standardized Tests *Required:* SAT or ACT (for admission), SAT Writing and Reading are used for Core Curriculum placement in the Foundation of Communication Core requirements. If English is not the student's native language, they are required to submit official results of the TOEFL, IELTS or PTE Academic (for admission).

Options: electronic application, early admission, early decision, early action, deferred entrance.

Application fee: $55.

Required: essay or personal statement, high school transcript, 1 letter of recommendation, test scores for first-year applicants. ***Recommended:*** minimum 3.0 GPA.

Application deadlines: 1/15 (freshmen), 1/15 (transfers), 11/15 (early action).

Early decision deadline: 11/15.

Notification: continuous until 4/1 (freshmen), continuous until 8/15 (transfers), 1/1 (early decision), 1/1 (early action).

CONTACT

Mr. Michael Hughes, Associate Dean and Director, Admission, University of San Francisco, 2130 Fulton Street, San Francisco, CA 94117-1080. *Phone:* 415-422-6563. *Toll-free phone:* 800-CALL-USF. *E-mail:* admissions@usfca.edu.

See below for display ad and page 1700 for the College Close-Up.

University of Southern California

Los Angeles, California

http://www.usc.edu/

- **Independent** university, founded 1880
- **Urban** 229-acre campus with easy access to Los Angeles
- **Endowment** $4.6 billion
- **Coed** 18,740 undergraduate students, 96% full-time, 50% women, 50% men
- **Most difficult** entrance level, 18% of applicants were admitted

UNDERGRAD STUDENTS

18,058 full-time, 682 part-time. Students come from 56 states and territories; 111 other countries; 32% are from out of state; 4% Black or African American, non-Hispanic/Latino; 14% Hispanic/Latino; 22% Asian, non-Hispanic/Latino; 0.2% Native Hawaiian or other Pacific Islander, non-Hispanic/Latino; 0.1% American Indian or Alaska Native, non-Hispanic/Latino; 5% Two or more races, non-Hispanic/Latino; 5% Race/ethnicity unknown; 13% international; 8% transferred in; 33% live on campus.

Freshmen

Admission: 51,920 applied, 9,358 admitted, 3,098 enrolled. ***Average high school GPA:*** 3.73. ***Test scores:*** SAT critical reading scores over 500: 98%; SAT math scores over 500: 99%; SAT writing scores over 500: 98%;

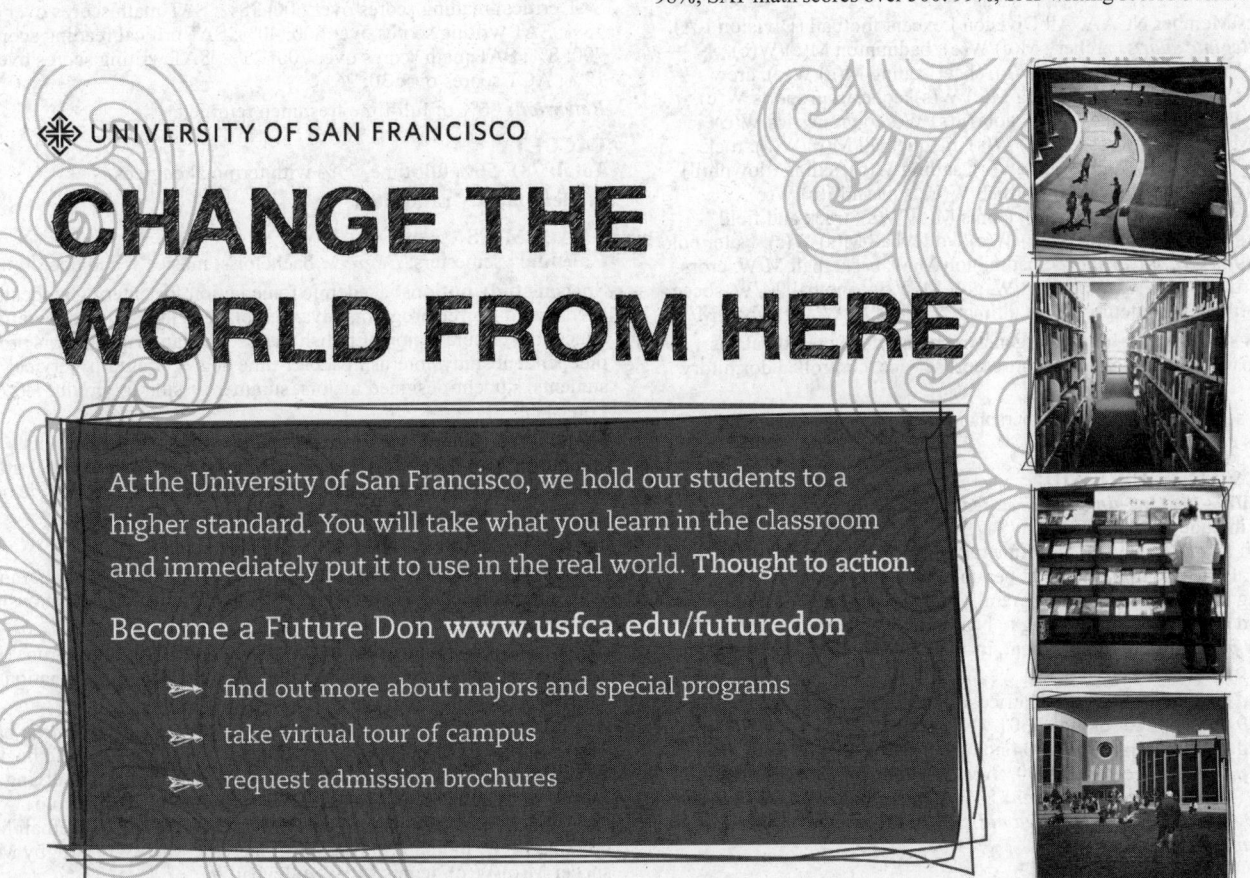

ACT scores over 18: 100%; SAT critical reading scores over 600: 84%; SAT math scores over 600: 90%; SAT writing scores over 600: 89%; ACT scores over 24: 97%; SAT critical reading scores over 700: 36%; SAT math scores over 700: 58%; SAT writing scores over 700: 50%; ACT scores over 30: 73%.

Retention: 97% of full-time freshmen returned.

FACULTY

Total: 3,268, 57% full-time, 80% with terminal degrees.

Student/faculty ratio: 9:1.

ACADEMICS

Calendar: semesters. *Degrees:* bachelor's, master's, doctoral, post-master's, and postbachelor's certificates.

Special study options: accelerated degree program, advanced placement credit, cooperative education, distance learning, double majors, English as a second language, freshman honors college, honors programs, independent study, internships, off-campus study, part-time degree program, services for LD students, student-designed majors, study abroad, summer session for credit. ***ROTC:*** Army (b), Navy (b), Air Force (b).

Unusual degree programs: 3-2 engineering with more than 20 liberal art colleges nationwide.

Computers: Students can access the following: campus intranet, computer help desk, free student e-mail accounts, online (class) grades, online (class) registration, online (class) schedules, online degree progress, financial aid applications, document sharing, calendars, personal Web space, customizable Web portal, course management systems (including data and video). Campuswide network is available. 100% of college-owned or -operated housing units are wired for high-speed Internet access. Wireless service is available via entire campus.

STUDENT LIFE

Housing options: coed, special housing for students with disabilities. Campus housing is university owned and is provided by a third party. Freshman campus housing is guaranteed.

Activities and organizations: drama/theater group, student-run newspaper, radio and television station, choral group, marching band, national fraternities, national sororities.

Athletics Member NCAA. All Division I except football (Division I-A). ***Intercollegiate sports:*** archery M(c)/W(c), badminton M(c)/W(c), baseball M(s), basketball M(s)/W(s), cheerleading M(c)/W(c), crew M(c)/W(s), cross-country running M(c)/W(s), equestrian sports W(c), fencing W(c), field hockey W(c), golf M(s)/W(s), gymnastics W(c), ice hockey M(c)/W(c), lacrosse M(c)/W(s), racquetball M(c)/W(c), rock climbing M(c)/W(c), rugby M(c)/W(c), sailing W(c), skiing (downhill) M(c)/W(c), soccer M(c)/W(s), softball W(c), squash M(c)/W(c), swimming and diving M(s)/W(s), tennis M(s)/W(s), track and field M(s)/W(s), ultimate Frisbee M(c)/W(c), volleyball M(s)/W(s), water polo M(s)/W(s). ***Intramural sports:*** badminton M/W, basketball M/W, cross-country running M/W, football M/W, golf M/W, racquetball M/W, soccer M/W, softball M/W, tennis M/W, ultimate Frisbee M/W, volleyball M/W.

Campus security: 24-hour emergency response devices and patrols, student patrols, late-night transport/escort service, controlled dormitory access.

Student services: health clinic, personal/psychological counseling, women's center, legal services.

COSTS & FINANCIAL AID

Costs (2014–15) ***One-time required fee:*** $350. ***Comprehensive fee:*** $61,614 includes full-time tuition ($47,562), mandatory fees ($718), and room and board ($13,334). Full-time tuition and fees vary according to program. Part-time tuition: $1602 per unit. Part-time tuition and fees vary according to course load and program. ***College room only:*** $8034. Room and board charges vary according to board plan and housing facility. ***Payment plans:*** tuition prepayment, installment. ***Waivers:*** employees or children of employees.

Financial Aid Of all full-time matriculated undergraduates who enrolled in 2013, 9,559 applied for aid, 7,301 were judged to have need, 6,732 had their need fully met. In 2013, 3134 non-need-based awards were made. ***Average percent of need met:*** 100. ***Average financial aid package:*** $43,170. ***Average need-based loan:*** $6606. ***Average need-based gift aid:*** $30,656. ***Average non-need-based aid:*** $19,014. ***Average indebtedness upon graduation:*** $28,541.

APPLYING

Standardized Tests *Required:* SAT or ACT (for admission).

Options: electronic application, deferred entrance.

Application fee: $80.

Required: essay or personal statement, high school transcript.

Application deadlines: 1/15 (freshmen), 1/15 (out-of-state freshmen), 2/1 (transfers).

Notification: 4/1 (freshmen), 4/1 (out-of-state freshmen), 6/1 (transfers).

CONTACT

Timothy Brunold, Dean of Admission, University of Southern California, University Park Campus, Los Angeles, CA 90089. *Phone:* 213-740-1111. *Fax:* 213-821-0200. *E-mail:* admitusc@usc.edu.

University of the Pacific

Stockton, California

http://www.pacific.edu/

- **Independent** university, founded 1851
- **Suburban** 175-acre campus with easy access to Sacramento
- **Coed** 3,810 undergraduate students, 97% full-time, 52% women, 48% men
- **Moderately difficult** entrance level, 55% of applicants were admitted

UNDERGRAD STUDENTS

3,713 full-time, 97 part-time. 7% are from out of state; 3% Black or African American, non-Hispanic/Latino; 18% Hispanic/Latino; 33% Asian, non-Hispanic/Latino; 0.6% Native Hawaiian or other Pacific Islander, non-Hispanic/Latino; 0.6% American Indian or Alaska Native, non-Hispanic/Latino; 5% Two or more races, non-Hispanic/Latino; 4% Race/ethnicity unknown; 7% international; 6% transferred in; 46% live on campus.

Freshmen

Admission: 15,183 applied, 8,335 admitted, 924 enrolled. ***Average high school GPA:*** 3.49. ***Test scores:*** SAT critical reading scores over 500: 78%; SAT math scores over 500: 84%; SAT writing scores over 500: 78%; SAT critical reading scores over 600: 38%; SAT math scores over 600: 53%; SAT writing scores over 600: 40%; SAT critical reading scores over 700: 8%; SAT math scores over 700: 22%; SAT writing scores over 700: 12%; ACT scores over 30: 26%.

Retention: 86% of full-time freshmen returned.

FACULTY

Total: 781, 56% full-time, 77% with terminal degrees.

Student/faculty ratio: 14:1.

ACADEMICS

Calendar: semesters. *Degrees:* bachelor's, master's, and doctoral.

Special study options: academic remediation for entering students, accelerated degree program, advanced placement credit, cooperative education, double majors, English as a second language, honors programs, independent study, internships, part-time degree program, services for LD students, student-designed majors, summer session for credit. ***ROTC:*** Air Force (c).

Computers: Students can access the following: campus intranet, computer help desk, free student e-mail accounts, online (class) grades, online (class) registration, online (class) schedules. Campuswide network is available. Wireless service is available via entire campus.

STUDENT LIFE

Housing options: on-campus residence required through sophomore yearCampus housing is university owned. Freshman campus housing is guaranteed.

Activities and organizations: drama/theater group, student-run newspaper, radio station, choral group, national fraternities, national sororities.

Athletics Member NCAA. All Division I. ***Intercollegiate sports:*** baseball M(s), basketball M(s)/W(s), cross-country running W(s), field hockey W(s), golf M(s), soccer W(s), softball W(s), swimming and diving M(s)/W(s), tennis M(s)/W(s), volleyball M(s)/W(s), water polo M(s)/W(s). ***Intramural sports:*** badminton M(c)/W(c), basketball M/W, bowling M/W, football M/W, golf M, lacrosse M(c)/W(c), rugby M(c), soccer M(c)/W(c), tennis M/W, volleyball W.

Campus security: 24-hour emergency response devices and patrols, late-night transport/escort service, controlled dormitory access.

Student services: health clinic, personal/psychological counseling, legal services.

COSTS & FINANCIAL AID

Costs (2014–15) ***Comprehensive fee:*** $53,924 includes full-time tuition ($40,822), mandatory fees ($520), and room and board ($12,582). Part-time tuition: $1408 per credit hour. Part-time tuition and fees vary according to course load. ***Room and board:*** Room and board charges vary according to board plan and housing facility. ***Payment plan:*** deferred payment. ***Waivers:*** employees or children of employees.

Financial Aid Of all full-time matriculated undergraduates who enrolled in 2014, 2,844 applied for aid, 2,621 were judged to have need, 295 had their need fully met. In 2014, 551 non-need-based awards were made. ***Average financial aid package:*** $31,221. ***Average need-based loan:*** $8451. ***Average need-based gift aid:*** $22,930. ***Average non-need-based aid:*** $10,364.

APPLYING

Standardized Tests *Required:* SAT or ACT (for admission). *Recommended:* SAT and SAT Subject Tests or ACT (for admission), SAT Subject Tests (for admission).

Options: electronic application, early decision, early action.

Application fee: $35.

Required: essay or personal statement, high school transcript.

Application deadlines: 1/15 (freshmen), 6/1 (transfers), 11/15 (early action).

Notification: continuous (freshmen), continuous (transfers), 1/15 (early action).

CONTACT

Mr. Rich Toledo, Director of Admissions, University of the Pacific, 3601 Pacific Avenue, Stockton, CA 95211-0197. *Phone:* 209-946-2211. *Fax:* 209-946-2413. *E-mail:* admissions@pacific.edu.

University of the West

Rosemead, California

http://www.uwest.edu/

- **Independent** comprehensive, founded 1991
- **Suburban** 10-acre campus
- **Coed** 142 undergraduate students, 89% full-time, 56% women, 44% men
- **Moderately difficult** entrance level, 85% of applicants were admitted

UNDERGRAD STUDENTS

127 full-time, 15 part-time. Students come from 2 states and territories; 12 other countries; 1% Black or African American, non-Hispanic/Latino; 45% Hispanic/Latino; 13% Asian, non-Hispanic/Latino; 2% Two or more races, non-Hispanic/Latino; 1% Race/ethnicity unknown; 34% international; 9% transferred in; 35% live on campus.

Freshmen

Admission: 235 applied, 200 admitted, 21 enrolled. ***Average high school GPA:*** 2.43.

Retention: 80% of full-time freshmen returned.

FACULTY

Total: 59, 31% full-time, 54% with terminal degrees.

Student/faculty ratio: 10:1.

ACADEMICS

Calendar: semesters. *Degrees:* certificates, diplomas, bachelor's, master's, doctoral, post-master's, and postbachelor's certificates.

Special study options: academic remediation for entering students, accelerated degree program, adult/continuing education programs, cooperative education, double majors, English as a second language, independent study, internships, part-time degree program, summer session for credit.

Computers: 501 computers/terminals are available on campus for general student use. Students can access the following: computer help desk, free student e-mail accounts, online (class) grades, online (class) registration. Campuswide network is available. 100% of college-owned or -operated housing units are wired for high-speed Internet access. Wireless service is available via entire campus.

STUDENT LIFE

Housing options: coed, special housing for students with disabilities. Campus housing is university owned. Freshman campus housing is guaranteed.

Activities and organizations: Buddhawest Club, Music Club, Explorer Club, Badminton Club, Chaplaincy Club.

Campus security: 24-hour patrols.

Student services: personal/psychological counseling.

FINANCIAL AID

Financial Aid Of all full-time matriculated undergraduates who enrolled in 2003, 30 applied for aid, 18 were judged to have need. 20 state and other part-time jobs.

APPLYING

Options: electronic application, deferred entrance.

Application fee: $50.

Required: essay or personal statement, high school transcript, minimum 2.0 GPA, 3 letters of recommendation. ***Required for some:*** interview.

Application deadlines: 6/15 (freshmen), 6/15 (out-of-state freshmen), 6/15 (transfers).

Notification: 7/15 (freshmen), 7/15 (out-of-state freshmen), 7/15 (transfers).

CONTACT

University of the West, 1409 North Walnut Grove Avenue, Rosemead, CA 91770. *Phone:* 626-571-8811 Ext. 120.

Vanguard University of Southern California

Costa Mesa, California

http://www.vanguard.edu/

- **Independent** comprehensive, founded 1920, affiliated with Assemblies of God
- **Suburban** 38-acre campus with easy access to Los Angeles
- **Coed** 1,987 undergraduate students, 76% full-time, 67% women, 33% men
- **Moderately difficult** entrance level, 58% of applicants were admitted

UNDERGRAD STUDENTS

1,504 full-time, 483 part-time. Students come from 34 states and territories; 13 other countries; 10% are from out of state; 4% Black or African American, non-Hispanic/Latino; 36% Hispanic/Latino; 4% Asian, non-Hispanic/Latino; 0.8% Native Hawaiian or other Pacific Islander, non-Hispanic/Latino; 0.3% American Indian or Alaska Native, non-Hispanic/Latino; 5% Two or more races, non-Hispanic/Latino; 3% Race/ethnicity unknown; 0.7% international; 5% transferred in; 47% live on campus.

Freshmen

Admission: 1,352 applied, 787 admitted, 318 enrolled. ***Average high school GPA:*** 3.21. ***Test scores:*** SAT critical reading scores over 500: 47%; SAT math scores over 500: 39%; ACT scores over 18: 73%; SAT critical reading scores over 600: 14%; SAT math scores over 600: 8%; ACT scores over 24: 26%; SAT critical reading scores over 700: 1%; SAT math scores over 700: 2%; ACT scores over 30: 5%.

Retention: 75% of full-time freshmen returned.

FACULTY

Total: 243, 25% full-time, 48% with terminal degrees.

Student/faculty ratio: 15:1.

ACADEMICS

Calendar: semesters. *Degrees:* certificates, associate, bachelor's, and master's.

Special study options: accelerated degree program, adult/continuing education programs, advanced placement credit, distance learning, double majors, independent study, internships, off-campus study, part-time degree program, services for LD students, study abroad, summer session for credit. ***ROTC:*** Air Force (c).

Computers: 100 computers/terminals and 50 ports are available on campus for general student use. Students can access the following: computer help desk, free student e-mail accounts, online (class) grades, online (class) registration, online (class) schedules. Campuswide network is available. 100% of college-owned or -operated housing units are wired for high-speed Internet access. Wireless service is available via entire campus.

STUDENT LIFE
Housing options: on-campus residence required through sophomore year; coed, men-only, women-only, special housing for students with disabilities. Campus housing is university owned. Freshman campus housing is guaranteed.

Activities and organizations: drama/theater group, student-run newspaper, choral group, local outreach, Global Missions, student organizations/clubs, choral groups.

Athletics Member NAIA. ***Intercollegiate sports:*** baseball M(s), basketball M(s)/W(s), cross-country running M(s)/W(s), soccer M(s)/W(s), softball W(s), track and field M(s)/W(s), volleyball W(s). ***Intramural sports:*** basketball M/W, football M/W, soccer M/W, softball M/W, volleyball M/W.

Campus security: 24-hour emergency response devices and patrols, student patrols, late-night transport/escort service, controlled dormitory access.

Student services: health clinic, personal/psychological counseling, women's center.

COSTS & FINANCIAL AID
Costs (2014–15) ***Comprehensive fee:*** $39,470 includes full-time tuition ($29,980), mandatory fees ($70), and room and board ($9420). Full-time tuition and fees vary according to course load. Part-time tuition: $1250 per credit hour. Part-time tuition and fees vary according to course load. ***College room only:*** $4870. Room and board charges vary according to board plan and housing facility. ***Payment plan:*** installment. ***Waivers:*** employees or children of employees.

Financial Aid Of all full-time matriculated undergraduates who enrolled in 2014, 1,397 applied for aid, 1,275 were judged to have need, 156 had their need fully met. In 2014, 105 non-need-based awards were made. ***Average percent of need met:*** 33. ***Average financial aid package:*** $13,017. ***Average need-based gift aid:*** $6070. ***Average non-need-based aid:*** $6850. ***Financial aid deadline:*** 3/2.

APPLYING
Standardized Tests *Required:* SAT or ACT (for admission).

Options: electronic application, early admission, early action, deferred entrance.

Application fee: $45.

Required: essay or personal statement, high school transcript, minimum 2.8 GPA, 2 letters of recommendation. ***Required for some:*** interview.

Application deadlines: 8/1 (freshmen), 12/1 (early action).

Notification: 5/1 (freshmen), continuous (transfers).

CONTACT
Kristi Pruett, Undergraduate Admissions, Vanguard University of Southern California, 55 Fair Drive, Costa Mesa, CA 92626. *Phone:* 800-722-6279 Ext. 4107. *Toll-free phone:* 800-722-6279. *Fax:* 714-966-5471. *E-mail:* admissions@vanguard.edu.

Westmont College
Santa Barbara, California
http://www.westmont.edu/

CONTACT
Mrs. Joyce Luy, Dean of Admission, Westmont College, 955 La Paz Road, Santa Barbara, CA 93108. *Phone:* 805-565-6200. *Toll-free phone:* 800-777-9011. *Fax:* 805-565-6234. *E-mail:* admissions@westmont.edu.

See below for display ad and page 1732 for the College Close-Up.

★ Whittier College
Whittier, California
http://www.whittier.edu/

- **Independent** comprehensive, founded 1887
- **Suburban** 95-acre campus with easy access to Los Angeles
- **Coed** 1,665 undergraduate students, 98% full-time, 55% women, 45% men
- **Moderately difficult** entrance level, 62% of applicants were admitted

UNDERGRAD STUDENTS
1,640 full-time, 25 part-time. Students come from 36 states and territories; 27 other countries; 16% are from out of state; 6% Black or African American, non-Hispanic/Latino; 44% Hispanic/Latino; 10% Asian, non-Hispanic/Latino; 0.1% Native Hawaiian or other Pacific Islander, non-Hispanic/Latino; 0.7% American Indian or Alaska Native, non-Hispanic/Latino; 4% Two or more races, non-Hispanic/Latino; 0.4% Race/ethnicity unknown; 4% international; 6% transferred in; 50% live on campus.

Freshmen
Admission: 4,850 applied, 3,001 admitted, 388 enrolled. ***Average high school GPA:*** 3.51. ***Test scores:*** SAT critical reading scores over 500: 64%; SAT math scores over 500: 69%; SAT writing scores over 500: 62%; ACT scores over 18: 95%; SAT critical reading scores over 600: 21%; SAT math scores over 600: 24%; SAT writing scores over 600: 22%; ACT scores over 24: 47%; SAT critical reading scores over 700: 3%; SAT math scores over 700: 3%; SAT writing scores over 700: 2%; ACT scores over 30: 5%.

Retention: 86% of full-time freshmen returned.

FACULTY
Total: 170, 66% full-time, 81% with terminal degrees.

Student/faculty ratio: 13:1.

ACADEMICS
Calendar: 4-1-4. *Degrees:* bachelor's, master's, and doctoral.

Special study options: academic remediation for entering students, accelerated degree program, adult/continuing education programs, advanced placement credit, distance learning, double majors, independent study, internships, off-campus study, services for LD students, student-designed majors, study abroad, summer session for credit. ***ROTC:*** Army (c).

Unusual degree programs: 3-2 engineering with University of Southern California, University of Minnesota.

Computers: 175 computers/terminals are available on campus for general student use. Students can access the following: campus intranet, computer help desk, free student e-mail accounts, online (class) grades, online (class) registration, online (class) schedules. Campuswide network is available. 100% of college-owned or -operated housing units are wired for high-speed Internet access. Wireless service is available via entire campus.

STUDENT LIFE
Housing options: on-campus residence required through junior year; coed, special housing for students with disabilities. Campus housing is university owned. Freshman campus housing is guaranteed.

Activities and organizations: drama/theater group, student-run newspaper, radio and television station, choral group, Hispanic Students Association, Hawaiian Islander Club, Black Student Union, Asian Students Association, Environment & Sustainability - Raising Awareness for the Environment / Urban Agriculture / Food Recovery Network.

Athletics Member NCAA. All Division III. ***Intercollegiate sports:*** baseball M, basketball M/W, cross-country running M/W, football M, golf M/W, lacrosse M/W, soccer M/W, softball W, swimming and diving M/W, tennis M/W, track and field M/W, volleyball W, water polo M/W. ***Intramural sports:*** basketball M/W, softball M/W, volleyball M/W.

Campus security: 24-hour emergency response devices and patrols, late-night transport/escort service, controlled dormitory access.

Student services: health clinic, personal/psychological counseling.

COSTS & FINANCIAL AID
Costs (2014–15) ***One-time required fee:*** $200. ***Comprehensive fee:*** $53,881 includes full-time tuition ($41,246), mandatory fees ($390), and room and board ($12,245). Part-time tuition: $1720 per unit. Part-time tuition and fees vary according to course load. ***College room only:*** $6720. Room and board charges vary according to board plan. ***Payment plan:*** installment. ***Waivers:*** children of alumni and employees or children of employees.

Financial Aid Of all full-time matriculated undergraduates who enrolled in 2014, 1,384 applied for aid, 1,268 were judged to have need, 203 had their need fully met. 411 Federal Work-Study jobs (averaging $2260). 464 state and other part-time jobs (averaging $1931). In 2014, 282 non-need-based awards were made. ***Average percent of need met:*** 77. ***Average financial aid package:*** $33,071. ***Average need-based loan:*** $5614. ***Average need-based gift aid:*** $29,397. ***Average non-need-based aid:*** $19,946. ***Average indebtedness upon graduation:*** $37,379. ***Financial aid deadline:*** 6/30.

APPLYING
Standardized Tests *Required:* SAT or ACT (for admission). *Recommended:* SAT Subject Tests (for admission).

Options: electronic application, early action, deferred entrance.

Application fee: $50.

Required: essay or personal statement, high school transcript, minimum 2.0 GPA, 2 letters of recommendation. ***Required for some:*** minimum 3.5 GPA. ***Recommended:*** minimum 2.5 GPA, interview.

Application deadlines: rolling (freshmen), rolling (transfers), 11/15 (early action).

Notification: continuous (freshmen), 3/1 (transfers), 12/31 (early action).

CONTACT
Mr. Kieron Miller, Director of Admission, Whittier College, Office of Admission, 13406 East Philadelphia Street, Whittier, CA 90608-0634. *Phone:* 562-907-4238. *Fax:* 562-907-4870. *E-mail:* admission@whittier.edu.

William Jessup University
Rocklin, California
http://www.jessup.edu/

- **Independent nondenominational** comprehensive, founded 1939
- **Suburban** 126-acre campus with easy access to Sacramento
- **Coed** 1,146 undergraduate students, 83% full-time, 58% women, 42% men
- **Moderately difficult** entrance level, 76% of applicants were admitted

UNDERGRAD STUDENTS
952 full-time, 194 part-time. Students come from 15 states and territories; 3 other countries; 5% are from out of state; 5% Black or African American, non-Hispanic/Latino; 16% Hispanic/Latino; 3% Asian, non-Hispanic/Latino; 0.5% Native Hawaiian or other Pacific Islander, non-Hispanic/Latino; 1% American Indian or Alaska Native, non-Hispanic/Latino; 3% Two or more races, non-Hispanic/Latino; 3% Race/ethnicity unknown; 0.3% international; 12% transferred in; 49% live on campus.

Freshmen
Admission: 558 applied, 423 admitted, 212 enrolled. ***Average high school GPA:*** 3.3. ***Test scores:*** SAT critical reading scores over 500: 56%; SAT math scores over 500: 47%; SAT writing scores over 500: 45%; ACT scores over 18: 78%; SAT critical reading scores over 600: 17%; SAT math scores over 600: 9%; SAT writing scores over 600: 13%; ACT scores over 24: 39%; SAT critical reading scores over 700: 1%; SAT math scores over 700: 1%; SAT writing scores over 700: 1%; ACT scores over 30: 7%.

Retention: 79% of full-time freshmen returned.

FACULTY
Total: 187, 18% full-time, 35% with terminal degrees.

Student/faculty ratio: 12:1.

ACADEMICS
Calendar: semesters. *Degrees:* certificates, associate, bachelor's, master's, and postbachelor's certificates.

Special study options: accelerated degree program, adult/continuing education programs, advanced placement credit, distance learning, double majors, independent study, internships, off-campus study, part-time degree program, services for LD students, study abroad, summer session for credit. ***ROTC:*** Air Force (c).

Computers: 55 computers/terminals are available on campus for general student use. Students can access the following: campus intranet, computer help desk, free student e-mail accounts, online (class) grades, online (class) registration, online (class) schedules, Ports are by request. Campuswide network is available. 100% of college-owned or -operated housing units are wired for high-speed Internet access. Wireless service is available via entire campus.

STUDENT LIFE
Housing options: on-campus residence required through junior year; men-only, women-only. Campus housing is university owned and is provided by a third party. Freshman campus housing is guaranteed.

Activities and organizations: drama/theater group, choral group.

Athletics Member NAIA. ***Intercollegiate sports:*** baseball M(s), basketball M(s)/W(s), cross-country running M(s)/W(s), golf M(s), soccer M(s)/W(s), softball W(s), track and field M(s)/W(s), volleyball W(s). ***Intramural sports:*** basketball M/W, softball M/W, table tennis M/W, volleyball M/W.

Campus security: student patrols, late-night transport/escort service, controlled dormitory access, day and evening patrols by trained security personnel.

Student services: personal/psychological counseling.

COSTS & FINANCIAL AID
Costs (2015–16) ***Comprehensive fee:*** $36,758 includes full-time tuition ($26,480) and room and board ($10,278). Full-time tuition and fees vary according to course load. Part-time tuition: $1120 per credit. Part-time tuition and fees vary according to course load. ***Room and board:*** Room and board charges vary according to board plan and housing facility. ***Payment plan:*** deferred payment. ***Waivers:*** employees or children of employees.

Financial Aid Of all full-time matriculated undergraduates who enrolled in 2014, 857 applied for aid, 772 were judged to have need, 89 had their need fully met. 123 Federal Work-Study jobs (averaging $1551). 87 state and other part-time jobs (averaging $1206). In 2014, 149 non-need-based awards were made. ***Average percent of need met:*** 65. ***Average financial aid package:*** $20,123. ***Average need-based loan:*** $4465. ***Average need-based gift aid:*** $16,497. ***Average non-need-based aid:*** $7249. ***Average indebtedness upon graduation:*** $23,636.

APPLYING
Standardized Tests *Required:* SAT or ACT (for admission).

Options: electronic application.

Application fee: $45.

Required: essay or personal statement, high school transcript, minimum 2.0 GPA. ***Required for some:*** 1 letter of recommendation, interview. ***Recommended:*** 1 letter of recommendation, interview.

Application deadlines: 8/15 (freshmen), 8/15 (transfers).

Notification: continuous (freshmen), continuous (transfers).

CONTACT
Admissions Office, Traditional Undergraduate Admission, William Jessup University, 333 Sunset Boulevard, Rocklin, CA 95765. *Phone:* 916-577-2222. *Fax:* 916-577-2220. *E-mail:* admissions@jessup.edu.

Woodbury University
Burbank, California
http://www.woodbury.edu/

- **Independent** comprehensive, founded 1884
- **Suburban** 22-acre campus with easy access to Los Angeles
- **Endowment** $19.4 million
- **Coed**
- **Moderately difficult** entrance level

FACULTY
Student/faculty ratio: 10:1.

ACADEMICS
Calendar: semesters. *Degrees:* bachelor's and master's.

STUDENT LIFE
Housing options: coed. Campus housing is university owned and is provided by a third party. Freshman applicants given priority for college housing.

Activities and organizations: Associated Student Government, American Institute of Architecture Students, Armenian Student Association, La Voz Unida, Collegiate Entrepreneurs' Organization (CEO), national fraternities, national sororities.

Campus security: 24-hour patrols, late-night transport/escort service, controlled dormitory access.

Student services: health clinic, personal/psychological counseling.

FINANCIAL AID
Financial Aid Of all full-time matriculated undergraduates who enrolled in 2013, 885 applied for aid, 848 were judged to have need, 15 had their need fully met. 106 Federal Work-Study jobs (averaging $904). In 2013, 109 non-need-based awards were made. ***Average percent of need met:*** 53. ***Average financial aid package:*** $21,758. ***Average need-based loan:*** $4796. ***Average need-based gift aid:*** $17,297. ***Average non-need-based aid:*** $9503. ***Average indebtedness upon graduation:*** $35,216.

APPLYING
Standardized Tests *Required:* SAT or ACT (for admission).

Options: electronic application, deferred entrance.

Application fee: $50.

Required: minimum 2.0 GPA. ***Required for some:*** high school transcript. ***Recommended:*** essay or personal statement, minimum 3.0 GPA, 2 letters of recommendation.

CONTACT
Ruth Lorenzana, Director of Admissions, Woodbury University, 7500 Glenoaks Boulevard, Burbank, CA 91510-7846. *Phone:* 800-784-9663. *Toll-free phone:* 800-784-WOOD. *Fax:* 818-767-0032. *E-mail:* admissions@woodbury.edu.

COLORADO

★ Adams State University
Alamosa, Colorado
http://www.adams.edu/

- **State-supported** comprehensive, founded 1921
- **Small-town** 90-acre campus with easy access to Pueblo
- **Endowment** $67,762
- **Coed** 2,138 undergraduate students, 85% full-time, 48% women, 52% men
- **Moderately difficult** entrance level, 65% of applicants were admitted

UNDERGRAD STUDENTS
1,810 full-time, 328 part-time. Students come from 44 states and territories; 12 other countries; 23% are from out of state; 7% Black or African American, non-Hispanic/Latino; 32% Hispanic/Latino; 1% Asian, non-Hispanic/Latino; 0.4% Native Hawaiian or other Pacific Islander, non-Hispanic/Latino; 1% American Indian or Alaska Native, non-Hispanic/Latino; 4% Two or more races, non-Hispanic/Latino; 3% Race/ethnicity unknown; 9% transferred in; 47% live on campus.

Freshmen
Admission: 2,826 applied, 1,847 admitted, 493 enrolled. ***Average high school GPA:*** 3.07. ***Test scores:*** SAT critical reading scores over 500: 41%; SAT math scores over 500: 54%; ACT scores over 18: 74%; SAT critical reading scores over 600: 11%; SAT math scores over 600: 16%; ACT scores over 24: 20%; SAT critical reading scores over 700: 1%; ACT scores over 30: 1%.

Retention: 58% of full-time freshmen returned.

FACULTY
Total: 182, 60% full-time, 46% with terminal degrees.

Student/faculty ratio: 17:1.

ACADEMICS
Calendar: semesters. *Degrees:* associate, bachelor's, master's, and doctoral.

Special study options: academic remediation for entering students, accelerated degree program, adult/continuing education programs, advanced placement credit, distance learning, double majors, independent study, internships, off-campus study, part-time degree program, services for LD students, student-designed majors, study abroad, summer session for credit.

Computers: 322 computers/terminals are available on campus for general student use. Students can access the following: campus intranet, computer help desk, free student e-mail accounts, online (class) grades, online (class) registration, online (class) schedules. Campuswide network is available. 100% of college-owned or -operated housing units are wired for high-speed Internet access. Wireless service is available via classrooms, computer centers, computer labs, dorm rooms, learning centers, libraries, student centers.

STUDENT LIFE

Housing options: on-campus residence required through sophomore year; coed, men-only, women-only. Campus housing is university owned. Freshman campus housing is guaranteed.

Activities and organizations: drama/theater group, student-run newspaper, radio station, choral group, marching band, Student Programming Board, student government, Semillas de la Tierra, Newman Club, Fellowship of Christian Athletes.

Athletics Member NCAA. All Division II. ***Intercollegiate sports:*** baseball M(s), basketball M(s)/W(s), cross-country running M(s)/W(s), football M(s), golf M(s)/W(s), lacrosse M(s)/W(s), soccer M(s)/W(s), softball W(s), swimming and diving M(s)/W(s), track and field M(s)/W(s), volleyball W(s), wrestling M(s). ***Intramural sports:*** basketball M/W, bowling M/W, cheerleading M(c)/W(c), football M/W, golf M(c)/W(c), racquetball M/W, rock climbing M/W, rugby M(c)/W(c), skiing (cross-country) M/W, skiing (downhill) M/W, soccer M/W, softball M/W, swimming and diving M/W, volleyball M/W, water polo M/W.

Campus security: 24-hour emergency response devices and patrols, student patrols, late-night transport/escort service, controlled dormitory access.

Student services: personal/psychological counseling.

COSTS & FINANCIAL AID

Costs (2014–15) ***Tuition:*** state resident $5160 full-time, $215 per credit hour part-time; nonresident $15,960 full-time, $665 per credit hour part-time. Full-time tuition and fees vary according to course load. Part-time tuition and fees vary according to course load. ***Required fees:*** $2791 full-time, $115 per credit hour part-time. ***Room and board:*** $8400; room only: $4000. Room and board charges vary according to board plan and housing facility. ***Payment plans:*** installment, deferred payment. ***Waivers:*** senior citizens and employees or children of employees.

Financial Aid Of all full-time matriculated undergraduates who enrolled in 2013, 1,765 applied for aid, 1,526 were judged to have need, 11 had their need fully met. 295 Federal Work-Study jobs (averaging $952). 328 state and other part-time jobs (averaging $1155). ***Average percent of need met:*** 58. ***Average financial aid package:*** $12,058. ***Average need-based loan:*** $3785. ***Average need-based gift aid:*** $7099. ***Average indebtedness upon graduation:*** $28,584.

APPLYING

Standardized Tests *Required:* SAT or ACT (for admission).

Options: electronic application, early admission, deferred entrance.

Application fee: $30.

Required: high school transcript, minimum 2.0 GPA. ***Required for some:*** essay or personal statement, interview, audition for music majors, portfolio for art majors.

Application deadlines: rolling (freshmen), rolling (out-of-state freshmen), rolling (transfers).

Notification: continuous (freshmen), continuous (out-of-state freshmen), continuous (transfers).

CONTACT

Miss Michelle Romero, Associate Director of Admissions, Adams State University, 208 Edgemont Boulevard, Alamosa, CO 81101. *Phone:* 719-587-7712. *Toll-free phone:* 800-824-6494. *Fax:* 719-587-7522. *E-mail:* admissions@adams.edu.

Argosy University, Denver

Denver, Colorado

http://www.argosy.edu/locations/denver/

- **Proprietary** university
- **Coed**

ACADEMICS

Degrees: associate, bachelor's, master's, and doctoral.

CONTACT

Argosy University, Denver, 7600 East Eastman Avenue, Denver, CO 80231. *Phone:* 303-923-4110. *Toll-free phone:* 866-431-5981.

The Art Institute of Colorado

Denver, Colorado

http://www.artinstitutes.edu/denver/

- **Proprietary** 4-year, founded 1952, part of Education Management Corporation
- **Urban** campus
- **Coed**

ACADEMICS

Calendar: quarters. *Degrees:* diplomas, associate, and bachelor's.

CONTACT

The Art Institute of Colorado, 1200 Lincoln Street, Denver, CO 80203. *Phone:* 303-837-0825. *Toll-free phone:* 800-275-2420.

Aspen University

Denver, Colorado

http://www.aspen.edu/

- **Independent** comprehensive, founded 1987
- **Coed**
- **Moderately difficult** entrance level

ACADEMICS

Calendar: 5 terms per year. *Degrees:* certificates, bachelor's, master's, and doctoral.

APPLYING

Options: electronic application.

Application fee: $50.

CONTACT

Aspen University, 720 South Colorado Boulevard, Suite 1150N, Denver, CO 80246-1930. *Phone:* 303-333-4224. *Toll-free phone:* 800-441-4746.

The Colorado College

Colorado Springs, Colorado

http://www.coloradocollege.edu/

- **Independent** comprehensive, founded 1874
- **Urban** 90-acre campus with easy access to Denver
- **Endowment** $680.4 million
- **Coed** 2,050 undergraduate students, 99% full-time, 53% women, 47% men
- **Very difficult** entrance level, 18% of applicants were admitted

UNDERGRAD STUDENTS

2,036 full-time, 14 part-time. Students come from 51 states and territories; 57 other countries; 82% are from out of state; 2% Black or African American, non-Hispanic/Latino; 9% Hispanic/Latino; 5% Asian, non-Hispanic/Latino; 0.4% American Indian or Alaska Native, non-Hispanic/Latino; 8% Two or more races, non-Hispanic/Latino; 3% Race/ethnicity unknown; 6% international; 2% transferred in; 76% live on campus.

Freshmen

Admission: 7,602 applied, 1,361 admitted, 549 enrolled. ***Test scores:*** SAT critical reading scores over 500: 99%; SAT math scores over 500: 100%; SAT writing scores over 500: 99%; ACT scores over 18: 100%; SAT critical reading scores over 600: 85%; SAT math scores over 600: 90%; SAT writing scores over 600: 86%; ACT scores over 24: 96%; SAT critical reading scores over 700: 34%; SAT math scores over 700: 39%; SAT writing scores over 700: 33%; ACT scores over 30: 58%.

Retention: 94% of full-time freshmen returned.

FACULTY

Total: 202, 84% full-time.

Student/faculty ratio: 10:1.

ACADEMICS

Calendar: modular. *Degrees:* bachelor's and master's (master's degree in education only).

Special study options: advanced placement credit, double majors, English as a second language, independent study, internships, off-campus study, services for LD students, student-designed majors, study abroad, summer session for credit. ***ROTC:*** Army (c).

Unusual degree programs: 3-2 engineering with Rensselaer Polytechnic Institute, Washington University in St. Louis, University of Southern California, Columbia University.

Computers: 396 computers/terminals are available on campus for general student use. Students can access the following: campus intranet, computer help desk, free student e-mail accounts, online (class) grades, online (class) registration, online (class) schedules. Campuswide network is available. 100% of college-owned or -operated housing units are wired for high-speed Internet access. Wireless service is available via entire campus.

STUDENT LIFE

Housing options: on-campus residence required through junior year; coed, men-only, women-only. Campus housing is university owned. Freshman campus housing is guaranteed.

Activities and organizations: drama/theater group, student-run newspaper, choral group, national fraternities, national sororities.

Athletics Member NCAA. All Division III except ice hockey (Division I), soccer (Division I). ***Intercollegiate sports:*** baseball M(c), basketball M/W, cross-country running M/W, equestrian sports M(c)/W(c), ice hockey M(s)/W(c), lacrosse M/W, rugby M(c)/W(c), skiing (downhill) M(c)/W(c), soccer M/W(s), softball W(c), swimming and diving M/W, tennis M/W, track and field M/W, ultimate Frisbee M(c)/W(c), volleyball W, water polo W(c). ***Intramural sports:*** basketball M/W, football M, ice hockey M/W, racquetball M/W, soccer M/W, softball M/W, table tennis M/W, ultimate Frisbee M/W, volleyball M/W.

Campus security: 24-hour emergency response devices and patrols, late-night transport/escort service, controlled dormitory access, whistle program, student escort service, good campus lighting.

Student services: health clinic, personal/psychological counseling.

COSTS & FINANCIAL AID

Costs (2014–15) ***One-time required fee:*** $150. ***Comprehensive fee:*** $57,162 includes full-time tuition ($46,000), mandatory fees ($410), and room and board ($10,752). Part-time tuition: $7667 per course. Part-time tuition and fees vary according to course load. ***College room only:*** $6176. Room and board charges vary according to board plan and housing facility. ***Payment plan:*** installment. ***Waivers:*** employees or children of employees.

Financial Aid Of all full-time matriculated undergraduates who enrolled in 2012, 872 applied for aid, 756 were judged to have need, 751 had their need fully met. 324 Federal Work-Study jobs (averaging $1892). 121 state and other part-time jobs (averaging $1903). In 2012, 178 non-need-based awards were made. ***Average percent of need met:*** 99. ***Average financial aid package:*** $37,780. ***Average need-based loan:*** $5261. ***Average need-based gift aid:*** $30,508. ***Average non-need-based aid:*** $8729. ***Average indebtedness upon graduation:*** $20,566. ***Financial aid deadline:*** 2/15.

APPLYING

Standardized Tests *Required for some:* SAT or ACT (for admission), SAT Subject Tests (for admission).

Options: electronic application, early decision, early action, deferred entrance.

Application fee: $60.

Required: essay or personal statement, high school transcript, 2 letters of recommendation. ***Recommended:*** interview.

Application deadlines: 1/15 (freshmen), 3/1 (transfers), 11/10 (early action).

Early decision deadline: 11/10 (for plan 1), 1/1 (for plan 2).

Notification: 4/1 (freshmen), 5/1 (transfers), 12/15 (early decision plan 1), 2/6 (early decision plan 2), 12/18 (early action).

CONTACT

Mr. Carlos Jiminez, Director of Admission - Outreach and Recruitment, The Colorado College, 14 East Cache La Poudre Street, Colorado Springs, CO 80903-3294. *Phone:* 719-389-6344. *Toll-free phone:* 800-542-7214. *Fax:* 719-389-6816. *E-mail:* admission@coloradocollege.edu.

Colorado Heights University

Denver, Colorado

http://www.chu.edu/

- **Independent** comprehensive, founded 1989, part of Teikyo University Group
- **Urban** 76-acre campus with easy access to Denver
- **Coed**

FACULTY

Student/faculty ratio: 12:1.

ACADEMICS

Degrees: certificates, bachelor's, and master's.

STUDENT LIFE

Housing options: coed. Campus housing is university owned.

Activities and organizations: student-run newspaper, Art Club, Marketing Club, Technology Club, Spirituality Matters, Magazine Club.

Campus security: 24-hour emergency response devices and patrols, student patrols, late-night transport/escort service, controlled dormitory access.

Student services: personal/psychological counseling.

COSTS & FINANCIAL AID

Costs (2014–15) ***Tuition:*** $9000 full-time, $250 per credit hour part-time. Full-time tuition and fees vary according to course load. Part-time tuition and fees vary according to course load. ***Required fees:*** $273 per term part-time. ***Room only:*** $3600.

Financial Aid Of all full-time matriculated undergraduates who enrolled in 2012, 25 applied for aid, 25 were judged to have need. 35 state and other part-time jobs (averaging $2400). ***Average percent of need met:*** 25. ***Average financial aid package:*** $11,000. ***Average need-based gift aid:*** $923.

APPLYING

Options: electronic application, deferred entrance.

Application fee: $50.

Required: high school transcript.

CONTACT

Marina Nochevnaya, Assistant Director of Admissions, Colorado Heights University, 3001 South Federal Boulevard, Denver, CO 80236-2711. *Phone:* 303-937-4257. *E-mail:* mnochevnaya@chu.edu.

Colorado Mesa University

Grand Junction, Colorado

http://www.coloradomesa.edu/

- **State-supported** comprehensive, founded 1925
- **Small-town** 86-acre campus
- **Coed** 9,003 undergraduate students, 77% full-time, 54% women, 46% men
- **Minimally difficult** entrance level, 82% of applicants were admitted

UNDERGRAD STUDENTS

6,969 full-time, 2,034 part-time. 13% are from out of state; 3% Black or African American, non-Hispanic/Latino; 16% Hispanic/Latino; 1% Asian, non-Hispanic/Latino; 0.6% Native Hawaiian or other Pacific Islander, non-Hispanic/Latino; 0.8% American Indian or Alaska Native, non-Hispanic/Latino; 4% Two or more races, non-Hispanic/Latino; 3% Race/ethnicity unknown; 0.6% international; 7% transferred in; 23% live on campus.

Freshmen

Admission: 5,881 applied, 4,842 admitted, 1,872 enrolled. ***Average high school GPA:*** 3.08. ***Test scores:*** SAT critical reading scores over 500: 40%; SAT math scores over 500: 46%; ACT scores over 18: 77%; SAT critical reading scores over 600: 8%; SAT math scores over 600: 11%; ACT scores over 24: 25%; SAT critical reading scores over 700: 1%; SAT math scores over 700: 2%; ACT scores over 30: 3%.

Retention: 66% of full-time freshmen returned.

ACADEMICS

Calendar: semesters. *Degrees:* certificates, associate, bachelor's, master's, doctoral, and postbachelor's certificates.

Special study options: academic remediation for entering students, accelerated degree program, adult/continuing education programs, advanced placement credit, distance learning, double majors, honors programs, internships, off-campus study, part-time degree program, services for LD students, study abroad, summer session for credit.

Computers: 525 computers/terminals are available on campus for general student use. Students can access the following: campus intranet, computer help desk, free student e-mail accounts, online (class) grades, online (class) registration, online (class) schedules. Campuswide network is available. 100% of college-owned or -operated housing units are wired for high-speed Internet access. Wireless service is available via entire campus.

STUDENT LIFE

Housing options: on-campus residence required through sophomore year; coed, women-only, special housing for students with disabilities. Campus housing is university owned. Freshman applicants given priority for college housing.

Activities and organizations: drama/theater group, student-run newspaper, radio and television station, choral group, marching band, Environmental Club, Student Body Association, KMSA radio station, Rodeo Club, Campus Residents Association, national fraternities.

Athletics Member NCAA. All Division II. ***Intercollegiate sports:*** baseball M(s), basketball M(s)/W(s), cross-country running M(s)/W(s), football M(s), golf M(s)/W(s), lacrosse M(s)/W(s), rugby M(c)/W(c), skiing (cross-country) M(c)/W(c), skiing (downhill) M(c)/W(c), soccer M(s)/W(s), softball W(s), swimming and diving M(s)/W(s), tennis M(s)/W(s), track and field M(s)/W(s), volleyball W(s), wrestling M(s). ***Intramural sports:*** badminton M/W, basketball M/W, bowling M(c)/W(c), equestrian sports M/W, football M/W, lacrosse W(c), racquetball M/W, soccer M/W, softball M/W, tennis M/W, ultimate Frisbee M/W, volleyball M/W, water polo M/W.

Campus security: 24-hour emergency response devices and patrols, late-night transport/escort service, controlled dormitory access.

Student services: health clinic, personal/psychological counseling, legal services.

COSTS & FINANCIAL AID

Costs (2014–15) ***Tuition:*** state resident $6357 full-time, $227 per credit hour part-time; nonresident $16,961 full-time, $606 per credit hour part-time. Full-time tuition and fees vary according to course load. Part-time tuition and fees vary according to course load. ***Required fees:*** $758 full-time, $27 per credit hour part-time. ***Room and board:*** $8706; room only: $4616. Room and board charges vary according to board plan and housing facility. ***Payment plan:*** installment. ***Waivers:*** employees or children of employees.

Financial Aid Of all full-time matriculated undergraduates who enrolled in 2013, 6,044 applied for aid, 4,944 were judged to have need, 708 had their need fully met. In 2013, 368 non-need-based awards were made. ***Average percent of need met:*** 59. ***Average financial aid package:*** $8317. ***Average need-based loan:*** $3676. ***Average need-based gift aid:*** $5853. ***Average non-need-based aid:*** $2939. ***Average indebtedness upon graduation:*** $26,740.

APPLYING

Standardized Tests *Required:* SAT or ACT (for admission).

Options: electronic application, deferred entrance.

Application fee: $30.

Required: high school transcript. ***Recommended:*** 2 letters of recommendation.

Application deadlines: rolling (freshmen), rolling (out-of-state freshmen), rolling (transfers).

Notification: continuous (freshmen), continuous (out-of-state freshmen), continuous (transfers).

CONTACT

Admissions, Colorado Mesa University, 1100 North Avenue, Grand Junction, CO 81501. *Phone:* 970-248-1875. *Toll-free phone:* 800-982-MESA. *Fax:* 970-248-1973. *E-mail:* admissions@coloradomeas.edu.

Colorado School of Mines

Golden, Colorado

http://www.mines.edu/

- **State-supported** university, founded 1874
- **Small-town** 503-acre campus with easy access to Denver, Boulder, Colorado Springs
- **Endowment** $271.0 million
- **Coed** 4,456 undergraduate students, 95% full-time, 26% women, 74% men
- **Very difficult** entrance level, 36% of applicants were admitted

UNDERGRAD STUDENTS

4,241 full-time, 215 part-time. Students come from 51 states and territories; 48 other countries; 40% are from out of state; 1% Black or African American, non-Hispanic/Latino; 8% Hispanic/Latino; 4% Asian, non-Hispanic/Latino; 0.2% American Indian or Alaska Native, non-Hispanic/Latino; 5% Two or more races, non-Hispanic/Latino; 2% Race/ethnicity unknown; 6% international; 4% transferred in; 35% live on campus.

Freshmen

Admission: 12,340 applied, 4,501 admitted, 1,000 enrolled. ***Average high school GPA:*** 3.8. ***Test scores:*** SAT critical reading scores over 500: 99%; SAT math scores over 500: 100%; SAT writing scores over 500: 93%; ACT scores over 18: 100%; SAT critical reading scores over 600: 73%; SAT math scores over 600: 95%; SAT writing scores over 600: 58%; ACT scores over 24: 100%; SAT critical reading scores over 700: 15%; SAT math scores over 700: 42%; SAT writing scores over 700: 11%; ACT scores over 30: 59%.

Retention: 94% of full-time freshmen returned.

FACULTY

Total: 504, 53% full-time, 62% with terminal degrees.

Student/faculty ratio: 16:1.

ACADEMICS

Calendar: semesters. *Degrees:* bachelor's, master's, doctoral, and post-master's certificates.

Special study options: accelerated degree program, advanced placement credit, cooperative education, double majors, honors programs, independent study, internships, off-campus study, services for LD students, study abroad, summer session for credit. ***ROTC:*** Army (b), Air Force (b).

Computers: 448 computers/terminals are available on campus for general student use. Students can access the following: campus intranet, computer help desk, free student e-mail accounts, online (class) grades, online (class) registration, online (class) schedules. Campuswide network is available. 100% of college-owned or -operated housing units are wired for high-speed Internet access. Wireless service is available via entire campus.

STUDENT LIFE

Housing options: on-campus residence required for freshman year; coed. Campus housing is university owned and is provided by a third party. Freshman campus housing is guaranteed.

Activities and organizations: drama/theater group, student-run newspaper, radio station, choral group, marching band, Society of Women Engineers, Residence Hall Association, Associated Students of Colorado School of Mines, Student Professional Societies/ and/ Religious Organizations, Multicultural Engineering Program, national fraternities, national sororities.

Athletics Member NCAA. All Division II. ***Intercollegiate sports:*** baseball M(s), basketball M(s)/W(s), bowling M(c)/W(c), cross-country running M(s)/W(s), football M(s), golf M, ice hockey M(c)/W(c), lacrosse M(c)/W(c), rugby M(c)/W(c), soccer M(s)/W(s), softball W(s), swimming and diving M/W, track and field M(s)/W(s), volleyball W(s), wrestling M(s). ***Intramural sports:*** badminton M/W, basketball M/W, bowling M/W, cross-country running M/W, equestrian sports M/W, field hockey M/W, football M/W, golf M/W, lacrosse M, racquetball M/W, skiing (downhill) M/W, soccer M/W, softball M/W, swimming and diving M/W, table tennis M/W, tennis M/W, track and field M/W, ultimate Frisbee M/W, volleyball M/W, wrestling M.

Campus security: 24-hour emergency response devices and patrols, late-night transport/escort service, controlled dormitory access, full service, community oriented law enforcement agency employing fully trained police officers.

Student services: health clinic, personal/psychological counseling, women's center.

COSTS & FINANCIAL AID

Costs (2014–15) ***Tuition:*** state resident $14,790 full-time, $493 per credit hour part-time; nonresident $31,470 full-time, $1049 per credit hour part-time. Full-time tuition and fees vary according to course load. ***Required fees:*** $2128 full-time. ***Room and board:*** $10,484. Room and board charges vary according to board plan and housing facility. ***Payment plan:*** installment. ***Waivers:*** employees or children of employees.

Financial Aid Of all full-time matriculated undergraduates who enrolled in 2013, 2,788 applied for aid, 2,103 were judged to have need, 425 had their need fully met. 303 Federal Work-Study jobs (averaging $1572). 1,530 state and other part-time jobs (averaging $2242). In 2013, 1009 non-need-based awards were made. ***Average percent of need met:*** 55. ***Average financial aid package:*** $12,191. ***Average need-based loan:*** $4764. ***Average need-based gift aid:*** $4835. ***Average non-need-based aid:*** $7666. ***Average indebtedness upon graduation:*** $23,667.

APPLYING

Standardized Tests *Required:* SAT or ACT (for admission).

Options: electronic application, deferred entrance.

Application fee: $45.

Required: high school transcript. ***Required for some:*** essay or personal statement, interview. ***Recommended:*** minimum 3.8 GPA, rank in upper quartile of high school class.

Application deadlines: 5/1 (freshmen), 5/1 (transfers).

Notification: continuous until 10/1 (freshmen), continuous until 10/1 (transfers).

CONTACT

Mrs. Joanne Lambert, Assistant Director of Enrollment Management, Colorado School of Mines, Student Center, 1600 Maple Street, Golden, CO 80401. *Phone:* 303-273-3220. *Toll-free phone:* 800-446-9488 Ext. 3220. *Fax:* 303-273-3509. *E-mail:* admit@mines.edu.

Colorado State University

Fort Collins, Colorado

http://www.colostate.edu/

- **State-supported** university, founded 1870, part of Colorado State University System
- **Urban** 582-acre campus with easy access to Denver
- **Endowment** $284.5 million
- **Coed** 23,858 undergraduate students, 89% full-time, 51% women, 49% men
- **Moderately difficult** entrance level, 80% of applicants were admitted

UNDERGRAD STUDENTS

21,253 full-time, 2,605 part-time. Students come from 56 states and territories; 72 other countries; 20% are from out of state; 2% Black or African American, non-Hispanic/Latino; 10% Hispanic/Latino; 2% Asian, non-Hispanic/Latino; 0.1% Native Hawaiian or other Pacific Islander, non-Hispanic/Latino; 0.5% American Indian or Alaska Native, non-Hispanic/Latino; 3% Two or more races, non-Hispanic/Latino; 4% Race/ethnicity unknown; 4% international; 6% transferred in; 25% live on campus.

Freshmen

Admission: 16,667 applied, 13,416 admitted, 4,353 enrolled. ***Average high school GPA:*** 3.61. ***Test scores:*** SAT critical reading scores over 500: 82%; SAT math scores over 500: 85%; ACT scores over 18: 99%; SAT critical reading scores over 600: 38%; SAT math scores over 600: 40%; ACT scores over 24: 63%; SAT critical reading scores over 700: 5%; SAT math scores over 700: 6%; ACT scores over 30: 12%.

Retention: 86% of full-time freshmen returned.

FACULTY

Total: 1,029, 98% full-time, 99% with terminal degrees.

Student/faculty ratio: 16:1.

ACADEMICS

Calendar: semesters. *Degrees:* certificates, bachelor's, master's, and doctoral.

Special study options: accelerated degree program, advanced placement credit, cooperative education, distance learning, double majors, English as a second language, honors programs, independent study, internships, off-campus study, part-time degree program, services for LD students, study abroad, summer session for credit. ***ROTC:*** Army (b), Air Force (b).

Unusual degree programs: 3-2 engineering.

Computers: 2,700 computers/terminals and 3,000 ports are available on campus for general student use. Students can access the following: campus intranet, computer help desk, free student e-mail accounts, online (class) grades, online (class) registration, online (class) schedules, personalized portal services including transcripts and financials (billing, financial aid). Campuswide network is available. 100% of college-owned or -operated housing units are wired for high-speed Internet access. Wireless service is available via classrooms, computer centers, computer labs, dorm rooms, learning centers, libraries, student centers.

STUDENT LIFE

Housing options: on-campus residence required for freshman year; coed, special housing for students with disabilities. Campus housing is university owned. Freshman campus housing is guaranteed.

Activities and organizations: drama/theater group, student-run newspaper, radio and television station, choral group, marching band, Golden Key International Honor Society, Council of International Student Affairs, Campus Crusade for Christ, Associated Students of CSU (ASCSU Student Government), Snowriders, national fraternities, national sororities.

Athletics Member NCAA. All Division I except football (Division I-A). ***Intercollegiate sports:*** baseball M(c), basketball M(s)/W(s), crew M(c)/W(c), cross-country running M(s)/W(s), field hockey M(c)/W(c), golf M(s)/W(s), ice hockey M(c)/W(c), lacrosse M(c)/W(c), rugby M(c)/W(c), skiing (downhill) M(c)/W(c), soccer M(c)/W(s), softball W(s), swimming and diving M(c)/W(s), tennis M(c)/W(s), track and field M(s)/W(s), ultimate Frisbee M(c)/W(c), volleyball W(s), water polo M(c)/W(c), wrestling M(c)/W(c). ***Intramural sports:*** basketball M/W, bowling M/W, golf M/W, racquetball M/W, soccer M/W, softball M/W, ultimate Frisbee M/W, volleyball M/W.

Campus security: 24-hour emergency response devices and patrols, student patrols, late-night transport/escort service, controlled dormitory access.

Student services: health clinic, personal/psychological counseling, women's center, legal services.

COSTS & FINANCIAL AID

Costs (2014–15) ***Tuition:*** state resident $7868 full-time, $357 per credit hour part-time; nonresident $24,048 full-time, $1202 per credit hour part-time. Full-time tuition and fees vary according to course level, course load, program, and student level. Part-time tuition and fees vary according to course level, course load, program, and student level. ***Required fees:*** $2029 full-time, $46 per credit hour part-time, $229 per term part-time. ***Room and board:*** $10,488; room only: $5104. Room and board charges vary according to board plan, housing facility, and location. ***Waivers:*** employees or children of employees.

Financial Aid Of all full-time matriculated undergraduates who enrolled in 2012, 16,060 applied for aid, 11,854 were judged to have need, 935 had their need fully met. In 2012, 2196 non-need-based awards were made. ***Average percent of need met:*** 67. ***Average financial aid package:*** $11,806. ***Average need-based loan:*** $6629. ***Average need-based gift aid:*** $8274. ***Average non-need-based aid:*** $4245. ***Average indebtedness upon graduation:*** $23,726.

APPLYING

Standardized Tests *Required:* SAT or ACT (for admission).

Options: electronic application, early action, deferred entrance.

Application fee: $50.

Required: essay or personal statement, high school transcript, 1 letter of recommendation.

Application deadlines: 2/1 (freshmen), 6/1 (transfers), 12/1 (early action).

Notification: continuous until 10/1 (freshmen), continuous (transfers), 2/1 (early action).

CONTACT
Mr. Bryan Whish, Director, Colorado State University, Ammons Hall, Fort Collins, CO 80523-1062. *Phone:* 970-491-6909. *Fax:* 970-491-7799. *E-mail:* admissions@colostate.edu.

Colorado State University–Pueblo

Pueblo, Colorado

http://www.colostate-pueblo.edu/

- **State-supported** comprehensive, founded 1933, part of Colorado State University System
- **Small-town** 275-acre campus with easy access to Colorado Springs
- **Coed** 5,192 undergraduate students, 70% full-time, 54% women, 46% men
- **Moderately difficult** entrance level, 93% of applicants were admitted

UNDERGRAD STUDENTS
3,644 full-time, 1,548 part-time. 8% Black or African American, non-Hispanic/Latino; 32% Hispanic/Latino; 1% Asian, non-Hispanic/Latino; 0.1% Native Hawaiian or other Pacific Islander, non-Hispanic/Latino; 0.6% American Indian or Alaska Native, non-Hispanic/Latino; 4% Two or more races, non-Hispanic/Latino; 2% Race/ethnicity unknown; 2% international; 3% transferred in.

Freshmen
Admission: 4,236 applied, 3,930 admitted, 910 enrolled. ***Average high school GPA:*** 3.18. ***Test scores:*** SAT critical reading scores over 500: 42%; SAT math scores over 500: 51%; ACT scores over 18: 81%; SAT critical reading scores over 600: 7%; SAT math scores over 600: 12%; ACT scores over 24: 24%; ACT scores over 30: 2%.

Retention: 63% of full-time freshmen returned.

FACULTY
Total: 372, 46% full-time.

Student/faculty ratio: 16:1.

ACADEMICS
Calendar: semesters. *Degrees:* bachelor's and master's.

Special study options: academic remediation for entering students, accelerated degree program, advanced placement credit, cooperative education, distance learning, double majors, English as a second language, external degree program, honors programs, independent study, internships, off-campus study, part-time degree program, services for LD students, study abroad, summer session for credit. ***ROTC:*** Army (b).

Unusual degree programs: 3-2 business administration; biology, chemistry, biochemistry, MBA with concentration in computer information systems.

Computers: Students can access the following: free student e-mail accounts, online (class) grades, online (class) registration, online (class) schedules. Campuswide network is available. 100% of college-owned or -operated housing units are wired for high-speed Internet access.

STUDENT LIFE
Housing options: on-campus residence required for freshman year; coed, special housing for students with disabilities. Campus housing is university owned, leased by the school and is provided by a third party. Freshman campus housing is guaranteed.

Activities and organizations: student-run newspaper, radio and television station, choral group, marching band, national fraternities, national sororities.

Athletics Member NCAA. All Division II. ***Intercollegiate sports:*** baseball M(s), basketball M(s)/W(s), bowling M(c)/W(c), cheerleading M(c)/W(c), cross-country running W(s), football M(s), golf M(s)/W(s), ice hockey M(c), soccer M(s)/W(s), softball W(s), tennis M(s)/W(s), track and field W(s), volleyball W(s), wrestling M(s). ***Intramural sports:*** basketball M/W, golf M/W, lacrosse M/W(c), racquetball M(c)/W(c), rugby M(c)/W(c), soccer M/W, softball W, squash M/W, table tennis M/W, ultimate Frisbee M/W, volleyball M/W.

Campus security: 24-hour emergency response devices and patrols, late-night transport/escort service, controlled dormitory access.

Student services: health clinic, personal/psychological counseling.

COSTS & FINANCIAL AID
Costs (2014–15) ***Tuition:*** state resident $5824 full-time, $216 per credit hour part-time; nonresident $16,765 full-time, $650 per credit hour part-time. Full-time tuition and fees vary according to course load and reciprocity agreements. Part-time tuition and fees vary according to course load and reciprocity agreements. ***Required fees:*** $2010 full-time, $67 per credit hour part-time. ***Room and board:*** $9016; room only: $5410. Room and board charges vary according to board plan. ***Payment plans:*** installment, deferred payment. ***Waivers:*** senior citizens and employees or children of employees.

Financial Aid Of all full-time matriculated undergraduates who enrolled in 2013, 3,297 applied for aid, 2,827 were judged to have need, 163 had their need fully met. In 2013, 212 non-need-based awards were made. ***Average percent of need met:*** 57. ***Average financial aid package:*** $9327. ***Average need-based loan:*** $3849. ***Average need-based gift aid:*** $6542. ***Average non-need-based aid:*** $3408. ***Average indebtedness upon graduation:*** $28,457.

APPLYING
Standardized Tests *Required:* SAT or ACT (for admission).

Options: electronic application, deferred entrance.

Application fee: $25.

Required: minimum 2.0 GPA. ***Required for some:*** high school transcript.

CONTACT
Mrs. Dana Trujillo, Director of Admissions, Colorado State University–Pueblo, 2200 Bonforte Boulevard, Pueblo, CO 81001-4901. *Phone:* 719-549-2391. *Fax:* 719-549-2419. *E-mail:* dana.trujillo@colostate-pueblo.edu.

DeVry University

Colorado Springs, Colorado

http://www.devry.edu/

- **Proprietary** comprehensive, founded 2001, part of DeVry University
- **Urban** campus
- **Coed**

ACADEMICS
Calendar: semesters. *Degrees:* associate, bachelor's, and master's.

COSTS & FINANCIAL AID
Costs (2014–15) ***Tuition:*** $17,052 full-time, $609 per credit hour part-time. ***Required fees:*** $80 full-time.

Financial Aid Of all full-time matriculated undergraduates who enrolled in 2003, 114 applied for aid, 109 were judged to have need. In 2003, 6 non-need-based awards were made. ***Average percent of need met:*** 36. ***Average financial aid package:*** $8534. ***Average need-based loan:*** $5145. ***Average need-based gift aid:*** $4919. ***Average non-need-based aid:*** $8253.

CONTACT
Admissions Office, DeVry University, 1175 Kelly Johnson Boulevard, Colorado Springs, CO 80920. *Phone:* 719-632-3000. *Toll-free phone:* 866-338-7941.

DeVry University

Westminster, Colorado

http://www.devry.edu/

- **Proprietary** comprehensive, founded 1945
- **Urban** campus
- **Coed** 409 undergraduate students, 33% full-time, 40% women, 60% men

UNDERGRAD STUDENTS
136 full-time, 273 part-time. 7% are from out of state; 6% Black or African American, non-Hispanic/Latino; 14% Hispanic/Latino; 1% Asian, non-Hispanic/Latino; 0.7% Native Hawaiian or other Pacific Islander, non-Hispanic/Latino; 1% American Indian or Alaska Native, non-Hispanic/Latino; 1% Two or more races, non-Hispanic/Latino; 7% Race/ethnicity unknown; 0.5% international; 24% transferred in.

Freshmen
Admission: 20 enrolled.

FACULTY
Total: 44, 16% full-time.

Student/faculty ratio: 13:1.

ACADEMICS
Calendar: semesters. *Degrees:* associate, bachelor's, master's, and postbachelor's certificates.

COSTS & FINANCIAL AID
Costs (2014–15) ***Tuition:*** $17,052 full-time, $609 per credit hour part-time. ***Required fees:*** $80 full-time.

Financial Aid Of all full-time matriculated undergraduates who enrolled in 2007, 148 applied for aid, 136 were judged to have need, 6 had their need fully met. In 2007, 17 non-need-based awards were made. ***Average percent of need met:*** 37. ***Average financial aid package:*** $11,971. ***Average need-based loan:*** $8024. ***Average need-based gift aid:*** $6094. ***Average non-need-based aid:*** $13,350. ***Average indebtedness upon graduation:*** $11,071.

APPLYING
Application fee: $40.

Application deadlines: rolling (freshmen), rolling (transfers).

Notification: continuous (freshmen), continuous (transfers).

CONTACT
Admissions Office, DeVry University, 1870 West 122nd Avenue, Westminster, CO 80234-2010. *Phone:* 303-280-7400. *Toll-free phone:* 866-338-7941.

Fort Lewis College

Durango, Colorado

http://www.fortlewis.edu/

- **State-supported** comprehensive, founded 1911
- **Small-town** 350-acre campus
- **Endowment** $5.8 million
- **Coed** 3,751 undergraduate students, 93% full-time, 48% women, 52% men
- **Moderately difficult** entrance level, 88% of applicants were admitted

UNDERGRAD STUDENTS
3,479 full-time, 272 part-time. Students come from 50 states and territories; 17 other countries; 47% are from out of state; 0.9% Black or African American, non-Hispanic/Latino; 10% Hispanic/Latino; 0.6% Asian, non-Hispanic/Latino; 0.2% Native Hawaiian or other Pacific Islander, non-Hispanic/Latino; 24% American Indian or Alaska Native, non-Hispanic/Latino; 6% Two or more races, non-Hispanic/Latino; 2% Race/ethnicity unknown; 0.7% international; 10% transferred in; 38% live on campus.

Freshmen
Admission: 2,560 applied, 2,240 admitted, 779 enrolled. ***Average high school GPA:*** 3.21. ***Test scores:*** SAT critical reading scores over 500: 60%; SAT math scores over 500: 56%; SAT writing scores over 500: 88%; ACT scores over 18: 90%; SAT critical reading scores over 600: 24%; SAT math scores over 600: 17%; SAT writing scores over 600: 45%; ACT scores over 24: 33%; SAT critical reading scores over 700: 3%; SAT math scores over 700: 1%; SAT writing scores over 700: 12%; ACT scores over 30: 3%.

Retention: 60% of full-time freshmen returned.

FACULTY
Total: 239, 70% full-time, 65% with terminal degrees.

Student/faculty ratio: 19:1.

ACADEMICS
Calendar: modified trimesters. *Degrees:* bachelor's, master's, and postbachelor's certificates.

Special study options: academic remediation for entering students, advanced placement credit, double majors, honors programs, independent study, internships, services for LD students, student-designed majors, study abroad, summer session for credit.

Unusual degree programs: 3-2 social work with Psychology or Sociology majors may be able to complete both their Bachelor's degree and their Master of Social Work degrees in a total of five years through the Fort Lewis College and University of Denver Graduate Degree Program.

Computers: 825 computers/terminals are available on campus for general student use. Students can access the following: campus intranet, computer help desk, free student e-mail accounts, online (class) grades, online (class) registration, online (class) schedules. Campuswide network is available. 100% of college-owned or -operated housing units are wired for high-speed Internet access. Wireless service is available via entire campus.

STUDENT LIFE
Housing options: on-campus residence required for freshman year; coed, special housing for students with disabilities. Campus housing is university owned. Freshman applicants given priority for college housing.

Activities and organizations: drama/theater group, student-run newspaper, radio station, KDUR - Campus/community radio, Environmental Center, Student Union Productions, Dance Co-Motion, Engineers without Borders.

Athletics Member NCAA. All Division II. ***Intercollegiate sports:*** baseball M(c), basketball M(s)/W(s), cheerleading M(c)/W(c), cross-country running M(s)/W(s), fencing M(c)/W(c), football M(s), golf M(s), ice hockey M(c)/W(c), lacrosse M(c)/W(s), rock climbing M(c)/W(c), rugby M(c)/W(c), skiing (cross-country) M(c)/W(c), skiing (downhill) M(c)/W(c), soccer M(s)/W(s), softball W(s), ultimate Frisbee M(c)/W(c), volleyball W(s), wrestling M(c)/W(c). ***Intramural sports:*** badminton M/W, basketball M/W, football M/W, golf M/W, racquetball M/W, soccer M/W, softball M/W, ultimate Frisbee M/W, volleyball M/W.

Campus security: 24-hour emergency response devices and patrols, late-night transport/escort service, controlled dormitory access.

Student services: health clinic, personal/psychological counseling.

COSTS & FINANCIAL AID
Costs (2015–16) ***Tuition:*** state resident $5856 full-time, $244 per credit hour part-time; nonresident $16,072 full-time, $670 per credit hour part-time. Full-time tuition and fees vary according to course load and reciprocity agreements. Part-time tuition and fees vary according to course load and reciprocity agreements. ***Required fees:*** $1745 full-time. ***Room and board:*** $9130; room only: $4530. Room and board charges vary according to board plan and housing facility. ***Payment plan:*** installment. ***Waivers:*** minority students and employees or children of employees.

Financial Aid Of all full-time matriculated undergraduates who enrolled in 2013, 2,779 applied for aid, 2,342 were judged to have need, 392 had their need fully met. In 2013, 264 non-need-based awards were made. ***Average percent of need met:*** 92. ***Average financial aid package:*** $13,918. ***Average need-based loan:*** $3748. ***Average need-based gift aid:*** $4808. ***Average non-need-based aid:*** $3748. ***Average indebtedness upon graduation:*** $19,507.

APPLYING
Standardized Tests *Required:* SAT or ACT (for admission).

Options: electronic application, early action, deferred entrance.

Application fee: $40.

Required: high school transcript. ***Required for some:*** interview. ***Recommended:*** essay or personal statement, 2 letters of recommendation.

CONTACT
Fort Lewis College, 1000 Rim Drive, Durango, CO 81301-3999. *Phone:* 970-247-7184. *Toll-free phone:* 877-FLC-COLO.

ITT Technical Institute

Aurora, Colorado

http://www.itt-tech.edu/

- **Proprietary** primarily 2-year
- **Coed**
- **Minimally difficult** entrance level

ACADEMICS
Degrees: associate and bachelor's.

CONTACT
Director of Recruitment, ITT Technical Institute, 12500 East Iliff Avenue, Suite 100, Aurora, CO 80014. *Phone:* 303-695-6317. *Toll-free phone:* 877-832-8460.

ITT Technical Institute
Westminster, Colorado
http://www.itt-tech.edu/

- **Proprietary** primarily 2-year, founded 1984, part of ITT Educational Services, Inc.
- **Suburban** campus
- **Coed**
- **Minimally difficult** entrance level

ACADEMICS
Calendar: quarters. *Degrees:* associate and bachelor's.

STUDENT LIFE
Housing options: college housing not available.

CONTACT
Director of Recruitment, ITT Technical Institute, 8620 Wolff Court, Suite 100, Westminster, CO 80031. *Phone:* 303-288-4488. *Toll-free phone:* 800-395-4488.

Johnson & Wales University
Denver, Colorado
http://www.jwu.edu/denver/

- **Independent** 4-year, founded 1993
- **Small-town** campus
- **Coed** 1,363 undergraduate students, 92% full-time, 60% women, 40% men
- **Moderately difficult** entrance level, 82% of applicants were admitted

UNDERGRAD STUDENTS
1,255 full-time, 108 part-time. 61% are from out of state; 8% Black or African American, non-Hispanic/Latino; 16% Hispanic/Latino; 2% Asian, non-Hispanic/Latino; 0.1% Native Hawaiian or other Pacific Islander, non-Hispanic/Latino; 0.8% American Indian or Alaska Native, non-Hispanic/Latino; 6% Two or more races, non-Hispanic/Latino; 10% Race/ethnicity unknown; 0.8% international; 7% transferred in; 39% live on campus.

Freshmen
Admission: 1,990 applied, 1,636 admitted, 310 enrolled. ***Average high school GPA:*** 3.18. ***Test scores:*** SAT critical reading scores over 500: 50%; SAT math scores over 500: 46%; SAT writing scores over 500: 55%; SAT critical reading scores over 600: 12%; SAT math scores over 600: 10%; SAT writing scores over 600: 10%.
Retention: 81% of full-time freshmen returned.

FACULTY
Total: 114, 47% full-time.
Student/faculty ratio: 17:1.

ACADEMICS
Calendar: quarters. *Degrees:* associate, bachelor's, and master's.
Special study options: academic remediation for entering students, accelerated degree program, adult/continuing education programs, advanced placement credit, cooperative education, English as a second language, honors programs, independent study, internships, part-time degree program, services for LD students, study abroad, summer session for credit. ***ROTC:*** Army (b).
Computers: Students can access the following: campus intranet, computer help desk, free student e-mail accounts, online (class) grades, online (class) registration, online (class) schedules. Campuswide network is available. Wireless service is available via entire campus.

STUDENT LIFE
Housing options: on-campus residence required for freshman year; coed, special housing for students with disabilities. Campus housing is university owned. Freshman campus housing is guaranteed.
Activities and organizations: drama/theater group, student-run newspaper.
Athletics Member NAIA. ***Intercollegiate sports:*** baseball M, basketball M/W, cheerleading M/W, golf M, soccer M, tennis M/W. ***Intramural sports:*** basketball M/W, football M/W, volleyball M/W.
Campus security: 24-hour emergency response devices and patrols, student patrols, late-night transport/escort service.

COSTS & FINANCIAL AID
Costs (2015–16) ***Tuition:*** $29,226 full-time, $196 per credit hour part-time. ***Required fees:*** $350 full-time.
Financial Aid Of all full-time matriculated undergraduates who enrolled in 2010, 1,279 applied for aid, 1,106 were judged to have need, 153 had their need fully met. In 2010, 265 non-need-based awards were made. ***Average percent of need met:*** 67. ***Average financial aid package:*** $16,423. ***Average need-based loan:*** $5006. ***Average need-based gift aid:*** $6325. ***Average non-need-based aid:*** $6332.

APPLYING
Standardized Tests *Required for some:* SAT or ACT (for admission).
Options: electronic application, early admission, deferred entrance.
Required: high school transcript. ***Required for some:*** essay or personal statement, minimum 2.8 GPA, interview. ***Recommended:*** minimum 2.0 GPA.

CONTACT
Kim Medina, Director of Admissions, Johnson & Wales University, 7150 Montview Boulevard, Denver, CO 80220. *Phone:* 303-256-9300. *Toll-free phone:* 877-598-3368. *Fax:* 303-598-3368. *E-mail:* den@admissions.jwu.edu.

Naropa University
Boulder, Colorado
http://www.naropa.edu/

- **Independent** comprehensive, founded 1974
- **Urban** 12-acre campus with easy access to Denver
- **Endowment** $6.8 million
- **Coed** 386 undergraduate students, 95% full-time, 67% women, 33% men
- **Moderately difficult** entrance level, 70% of applicants were admitted

UNDERGRAD STUDENTS
366 full-time, 20 part-time. Students come from 41 states and territories; 10 other countries; 60% are from out of state; 2% Black or African American, non-Hispanic/Latino; 11% Hispanic/Latino; 1% Asian, non-Hispanic/Latino; 0.3% American Indian or Alaska Native, non-Hispanic/Latino; 11% Two or more races, non-Hispanic/Latino; 10% Race/ethnicity unknown; 3% international; 25% transferred in; 20% live on campus.

Freshmen
Admission: 157 applied, 110 admitted, 40 enrolled.
Retention: 70% of full-time freshmen returned.

FACULTY
Total: 182, 24% full-time, 54% with terminal degrees.
Student/faculty ratio: 9:1.

ACADEMICS
Calendar: semesters. *Degrees:* bachelor's and master's.
Special study options: advanced placement credit, cooperative education, double majors, independent study, internships, off-campus study, part-time degree program, services for LD students, student-designed majors, study abroad, summer session for credit.
Computers: 48 computers/terminals are available on campus for general student use. Students can access the following: campus intranet, computer help desk, free student e-mail accounts, online (class) grades, online (class) registration, online (class) schedules. Campuswide network is available. 100% of college-owned or -operated housing units are wired for high-speed Internet access. Wireless service is available via entire campus.

STUDENT LIFE
Housing options: on-campus residence required for freshman year; coed. Campus housing is university owned. Freshman campus housing is guaranteed.
Activities and organizations: drama/theater group, choral group, Student Union of Naropa, ROOT: Reconnecting on Outdoor Terrain, Team Asana (yoga club), Pagans at Naropa (pagan spirituality club), Semicolon (writing and publications club).

Campus security: late-night transport/escort service, controlled dormitory access, foot and vehicle patrol 4:30 pm to midnight, 24 hour on-call Safety and Security Manager.

Student services: personal/psychological counseling.

COSTS & FINANCIAL AID

Costs (2015–16) ***Comprehensive fee:*** $40,184 includes full-time tuition ($30,400), mandatory fees ($180), and room and board ($9604). Full-time tuition and fees vary according to course load. Part-time tuition: $995 per credit. Part-time tuition and fees vary according to course load. ***Required fees:*** $340 per term part-time. ***Payment plan:*** installment. ***Waivers:*** employees or children of employees.

Financial Aid Of all full-time matriculated undergraduates who enrolled in 2014, 286 applied for aid, 272 were judged to have need, 2 had their need fully met. 160 Federal Work-Study jobs (averaging $3013). 12 state and other part-time jobs (averaging $2590). In 2014, 14 non-need-based awards were made. ***Average percent of need met:*** 90. ***Average financial aid package:*** $35,101. ***Average need-based loan:*** $11,070. ***Average need-based gift aid:*** $24,236. ***Average non-need-based aid:*** $6738. ***Average indebtedness upon graduation:*** $23,755.

APPLYING

Options: electronic application, deferred entrance.

Application fee: $50.

Required: essay or personal statement, high school transcript, 1 letter of recommendation.

Application deadlines: rolling (freshmen), rolling (out-of-state freshmen), rolling (transfers).

Notification: continuous (freshmen), continuous (out-of-state freshmen), continuous (transfers).

CONTACT

Karen Wills, Assistant Dean of Undergraduate Admissions, Naropa University, 2130 Arapahoe Avenue, Boulder, CO 80302. *Phone:* 303-245-4693. *Toll-free phone:* 800-772-6951. *Fax:* 303-546-3536. *E-mail:* kwills@naropa.edu.

Nazarene Bible College

Colorado Springs, Colorado

http://www.nbc.edu/

- **Independent** 4-year, founded 1967, affiliated with Church of the Nazarene
- **Urban** 64-acre campus with easy access to Colorado Springs
- **Endowment** $2.2 million
- **Coed** 762 undergraduate students, 16% full-time, 37% women, 63% men
- **Noncompetitive** entrance level, 38% of applicants were admitted

UNDERGRAD STUDENTS

124 full-time, 638 part-time. Students come from 48 states and territories; 5 other countries; 55% are from out of state; 6% Black or African American, non-Hispanic/Latino; 7% Hispanic/Latino; 0.8% Asian, non-Hispanic/Latino; 0.4% Native Hawaiian or other Pacific Islander, non-Hispanic/Latino; 1% American Indian or Alaska Native, non-Hispanic/Latino; 3% Two or more races, non-Hispanic/Latino; 11% transferred in.

Freshmen

Admission: 452 applied, 172 admitted, 28 enrolled.

Retention: 50% of full-time freshmen returned.

FACULTY

Total: 100, 9% full-time, 52% with terminal degrees.

Student/faculty ratio: 10:1.

ACADEMICS

Calendar: quarters. *Degrees:* certificates, diplomas, associate, and bachelor's.

Special study options: academic remediation for entering students, accelerated degree program, advanced placement credit, distance learning, double majors, independent study, internships, part-time degree program, summer session for credit.

Computers: 10 computers/terminals are available on campus for general student use. Campuswide network is available. Wireless service is available via entire campus.

STUDENT LIFE

Housing options: college housing not available.

Campus security: student patrols.

Student services: personal/psychological counseling.

COSTS & FINANCIAL AID

Costs (2015–16) ***Tuition:*** $10,800 full-time, $450 per credit hour part-time. Full-time tuition and fees vary according to program. Part-time tuition and fees vary according to program. ***Required fees:*** $600 full-time, $25 part-time. ***Payment plan:*** installment. ***Waivers:*** employees or children of employees.

Financial Aid Of all full-time matriculated undergraduates who enrolled in 2012, 91 applied for aid, 88 were judged to have need. 9 Federal Work-Study jobs (averaging $2031). ***Average percent of need met:*** 48. ***Average financial aid package:*** $4500. ***Average need-based loan:*** $4500. ***Average need-based gift aid:*** $2500. ***Average indebtedness upon graduation:*** $31,242.

APPLYING

Options: electronic application, deferred entrance.

Required: high school transcript.

Application deadlines: 7/11 (freshmen), 7/11 (transfers).

Notification: continuous (freshmen), continuous (transfers).

CONTACT

Scott McConnaughey, Director of Admissions/Admissions Counselor, Nazarene Bible College, 1111 Academy Park Loop, Colorado Springs, CO 80910-3704. *Phone:* 719-884-5062. *Toll-free phone:* 800-873-3873. *Fax:* 719-884-5199. *E-mail:* SEMcConnaughey@nbc.edu.

Regis University

Denver, Colorado

http://www.regis.edu/

- **Independent Roman Catholic (Jesuit)** comprehensive, founded 1877
- **Suburban** 90-acre campus with easy access to Denver
- **Endowment** $54.8 million
- **Coed** 5,009 undergraduate students, 50% full-time, 61% women, 39% men
- **Moderately difficult** entrance level, 96% of applicants were admitted

UNDERGRAD STUDENTS

2,501 full-time, 2,508 part-time. Students come from 51 states and territories; 15 other countries; 33% are from out of state; 5% Black or African American, non-Hispanic/Latino; 19% Hispanic/Latino; 4% Asian, non-Hispanic/Latino; 0.2% Native Hawaiian or other Pacific Islander, non-Hispanic/Latino; 0.6% American Indian or Alaska Native, non-Hispanic/Latino; 3% Two or more races, non-Hispanic/Latino; 6% Race/ethnicity unknown; 1% international; 10% transferred in; 48% live on campus.

Freshmen

Admission: 2,422 applied, 2,326 admitted, 481 enrolled. ***Average high school GPA:*** 3.48. ***Test scores:*** SAT critical reading scores over 500: 63%; SAT math scores over 500: 66%; SAT writing scores over 500: 65%; ACT scores over 18: 97%; SAT critical reading scores over 600: 27%; SAT math scores over 600: 25%; SAT writing scores over 600: 24%; ACT scores over 24: 57%; SAT critical reading scores over 700: 3%; SAT math scores over 700: 1%; SAT writing scores over 700: 1%; ACT scores over 30: 13%.

Retention: 78% of full-time freshmen returned.

FACULTY

Total: 855, 35% full-time, 48% with terminal degrees.

Student/faculty ratio: 14:1.

ACADEMICS

Calendar: semesters. *Degrees:* certificates, bachelor's, master's, doctoral, post-master's, and postbachelor's certificates.

Special study options: academic remediation for entering students, accelerated degree program, adult/continuing education programs, advanced placement credit, cooperative education, distance learning, double majors, freshman honors college, honors programs, independent study, internships, off-campus study, part-time degree program, services for LD students, student-designed majors, study abroad, summer session for credit. ***ROTC:*** Army (c), Navy (c), Air Force (c).

Unusual degree programs: 3-2 engineering with Washington University in St. Louis.

Computers: 547 computers/terminals and 1,000 ports are available on campus for general student use. Students can access the following: campus intranet, computer help desk, free student e-mail accounts, online (class) grades, online (class) registration, online (class) schedules, Wireless access available throughout the campus. Campuswide network is available. 100% of college-owned or -operated housing units are wired for high-speed Internet access. Wireless service is available via entire campus.

STUDENT LIFE

Housing options: on-campus residence required through sophomore year; coed, special housing for students with disabilities. Campus housing is university owned. Freshman applicants given priority for college housing.

Activities and organizations: drama/theater group, student-run newspaper, radio station, choral group, Musical Theater Club, student government, Club Sports, Outdoor Adventure, Black Student Association.

Athletics Member NCAA. All Division II. ***Intercollegiate sports:*** baseball M(s), basketball M(s)/W(s), cross-country running M(s)/W(s), golf M(s)/W(s), lacrosse W(s), soccer M(s)/W(s), softball W(s), volleyball W(s). ***Intramural sports:*** basketball M/W, cheerleading M/W, ice hockey M, lacrosse M, rugby M, soccer M/W, ultimate Frisbee M/W, volleyball M/W.

Campus security: 24-hour emergency response devices and patrols, student patrols, late-night transport/escort service, controlled dormitory access.

Student services: health clinic, personal/psychological counseling.

COSTS & FINANCIAL AID

Costs (2015–16) ***Comprehensive fee:*** $43,540 includes full-time tuition ($33,110), mandatory fees ($600), and room and board ($9830). Full-time tuition and fees vary according to course load, location, program, and reciprocity agreements. Part-time tuition: $1035 per credit hour. Part-time tuition and fees vary according to course load, location, program, and reciprocity agreements. ***Required fees:*** $150 per term part-time. ***College room only:*** $5400. Room and board charges vary according to board plan and housing facility. ***Payment plans:*** installment, deferred payment. ***Waivers:*** employees or children of employees.

Financial Aid Of all full-time matriculated undergraduates who enrolled in 2013, 1,992 applied for aid, 1,724 were judged to have need, 197 had their need fully met. 410 Federal Work-Study jobs (averaging $1635). 422 state and other part-time jobs (averaging $1829). In 2013, 469 non-need-based awards were made. ***Average percent of need met:*** 77. ***Average financial aid package:*** $26,920. ***Average need-based loan:*** $4504. ***Average need-based gift aid:*** $16,998. ***Average non-need-based aid:*** $11,479. ***Average indebtedness upon graduation:*** $28,461.

APPLYING

Standardized Tests *Required:* SAT or ACT (for admission).

Options: electronic application, deferred entrance.

Application fee: $50.

Required: essay or personal statement, high school transcript. ***Required for some:*** minimum 2.5 GPA, 1 letter of recommendation, interview.

Application deadlines: rolling (freshmen), rolling (out-of-state freshmen), rolling (transfers).

Notification: continuous until 9/15 (freshmen), continuous (out-of-state freshmen), continuous (transfers).

CONTACT

Ms. Sarah Engel, Director of Admissions, Regis University, 3333 Regis Boulevard, Mail Code A-12, Denver, CO 80221. *Phone:* 303-458-4900. *Toll-free phone:* 800-388-2366 Ext. 4900. *Fax:* 303-964-5534. *E-mail:* regisadm@regis.edu.

Rocky Mountain College of Art + Design

Lakewood, Colorado

http://www.rmcad.edu/

- **Proprietary** comprehensive, founded 1963
- **Urban** 23-acre campus with easy access to Denver
- **Coed** 1,019 undergraduate students, 58% full-time, 66% women, 34% men
- **Moderately difficult** entrance level

UNDERGRAD STUDENTS

588 full-time, 431 part-time. Students come from 47 states and territories; 1 other country; 47% are from out of state; 9% Black or African American, non-Hispanic/Latino; 9% Hispanic/Latino; 2% Asian, non-Hispanic/Latino; 4% American Indian or Alaska Native, non-Hispanic/Latino; 1% Two or more races, non-Hispanic/Latino; 15% Race/ethnicity unknown; 0.2% international; 28% transferred in.

Freshmen

Admission: 53 enrolled.

Retention: 53% of full-time freshmen returned.

FACULTY

Total: 159, 24% full-time, 8% with terminal degrees.

Student/faculty ratio: 15:1.

ACADEMICS

Calendar: trimesters. *Degrees:* certificates, bachelor's, and master's.

Special study options: academic remediation for entering students, accelerated degree program, advanced placement credit, cooperative education, distance learning, independent study, internships, off-campus study, part-time degree program, services for LD students, study abroad, summer session for credit.

Computers: 320 computers/terminals and 320 ports are available on campus for general student use. Students can access the following: campus intranet, computer help desk, free student e-mail accounts, online (class) grades, online (class) registration, online (class) schedules, wireless network, discounted software/hardware, RTD/public transit, printers, scanners, equipment check-out (i.e. cameras, laptops, etc). Campuswide network is available. Wireless service is available via entire campus.

STUDENT LIFE

Housing options: college housing not available.

Activities and organizations: The American Institute of Graphic Arts (AIGA), The American Society of Interior Designers (ASID), Gay Straight Alliance, Game Art + Design Club, Animation Club.

Campus security: 24-hour emergency response devices, late-night transport/escort service, Campus is patrolled by trained security personnel during campus hours.

Student services: personal/psychological counseling.

COSTS & FINANCIAL AID

Costs (2015–16) ***Tuition:*** $15,870 full-time, $594 per credit part-time. Full-time tuition and fees vary according to course load, degree level, and location. Part-time tuition and fees vary according to course load, degree level, and location. ***Required fees:*** $525 full-time. ***Payment plan:*** installment. ***Waivers:*** employees or children of employees.

Financial Aid Of all full-time matriculated undergraduates who enrolled in 2013, 453 applied for aid, 406 were judged to have need, 29 had their need fully met. 20 Federal Work-Study jobs (averaging $2984). 30 state and other part-time jobs (averaging $3606). In 2013, 91 non-need-based awards were made. ***Average percent of need met:*** 71. ***Average financial aid package:*** $19,249. ***Average need-based loan:*** $4419. ***Average need-based gift aid:*** $4760. ***Average non-need-based aid:*** $5591. ***Average indebtedness upon graduation:*** $29,156.

APPLYING

Options: electronic application.

Application fee: $50.

Required: essay or personal statement, high school transcript, minimum 2.0 GPA, interview, portfolio.

Application deadlines: rolling (freshmen), rolling (transfers).
Notification: continuous (freshmen), continuous (transfers).

CONTACT

Mr. Marc Abraham, Director of Admissions, Rocky Mountain College of Art + Design, 1600 Pierce Street, Lakewood, CO 80214. *Phone:* 321-256-9223. *Toll-free phone:* 800-888-ARTS. *E-mail:* mabraham@rmcad.edu.

★ United States Air Force Academy

Colorado Springs, Colorado

http://www.usafa.edu/

- **Federally supported** 4-year, founded 1954
- **Suburban** 18,000-acre campus with easy access to Colorado Springs, Denver
- **Endowment** $56.0 million
- **Coed** 3,952 undergraduate students, 100% full-time, 22% women, 78% men
- **Most difficult** entrance level, 13% of applicants were admitted

UNDERGRAD STUDENTS

3,952 full-time. Students come from 35 other countries; 87% are from out of state; 6% Black or African American, non-Hispanic/Latino; 10% Hispanic/Latino; 4% Asian, non-Hispanic/Latino; 0.6% Native Hawaiian or other Pacific Islander, non-Hispanic/Latino; 0.4% American Indian or Alaska Native, non-Hispanic/Latino; 6% Two or more races, non-Hispanic/Latino; 6% Race/ethnicity unknown; 1% international; 100% live on campus.

Freshmen

Admission: 9,050 applied, 1,206 admitted, 1,138 enrolled. ***Average high school GPA:*** 3.85. ***Test scores:*** SAT critical reading scores over 500: 98%; SAT math scores over 500: 100%; ACT scores over 18: 100%; SAT critical reading scores over 600: 74%; SAT math scores over 600: 87%; ACT scores over 24: 100%; SAT critical reading scores over 700: 17%; SAT math scores over 700: 29%; ACT scores over 30: 56%.

Retention: 93% of full-time freshmen returned.

FACULTY

Total: 510, 99% full-time, 57% with terminal degrees.

Student/faculty ratio: 8:1.

ACADEMICS

Calendar: semesters. *Degree:* bachelor's.

Special study options: academic remediation for entering students, advanced placement credit, English as a second language, honors programs, independent study, internships, off-campus study, study abroad, summer session for credit.

Computers: 160 computers/terminals and 5,000 ports are available on campus for general student use. Students can access the following: campus intranet, computer help desk, free student e-mail accounts, online (class) grades, online (class) registration, online (class) schedules. Campuswide network is available. 100% of college-owned or -operated housing units are wired for high-speed Internet access. Wireless service is available via entire campus.

STUDENT LIFE

Housing options: on-campus residence required through senior year; coed. Campus housing is university owned. Freshman campus housing is guaranteed.

Activities and organizations: drama/theater group, student-run radio station, choral group, marching band, Recreational Ski Club, Men's and Women's Rugby Club, Cycling Club, Aviation Club, Drum and Bugle Corps.

Athletics Member NCAA. All Division I. ***Intercollegiate sports:*** archery M(c)/W(c), baseball M, basketball M/W, cheerleading M/W, cross-country running M/W, equestrian sports M(c)/W(c), fencing M/W, football M, golf M/W(c), gymnastics M/W, ice hockey M, lacrosse M/W(c), racquetball M(c)/W(c), riflery M/W, rock climbing M(c)/W(c), skiing (cross-country) M(c)/W(c), skiing (downhill) M(c)/W(c), soccer M/W, softball W(c), swimming and diving M/W, tennis M/W, track and field M/W, ultimate Frisbee M(c)/W(c), volleyball M(c)/W, water polo M/W(c), weight lifting M(c)/W(c), wrestling M. ***Intramural sports:*** basketball M/W, cross-country running M/W, racquetball M/W, rugby M(c)/W(c), soccer M/W, softball M/W, ultimate Frisbee M/W, volleyball M/W, wrestling M.

Campus security: 24-hour emergency response devices and patrols, late-night transport/escort service, controlled dormitory access, self-defense education, well-lit campus.

Student services: health clinic, personal/psychological counseling, women's center, legal services.

COSTS

Costs (2014–15) ***Comprehensive fee:*** Tuition, room and board, and medical and dental care are provided by the US government. Each cadet receives a salary from which to pay for uniforms, supplies, and personal expenses.

APPLYING

Standardized Tests *Required:* SAT or ACT (for admission).

Options: electronic application.

Required: essay or personal statement, high school transcript, letters of recommendation, interview, authorized nomination, Candidate Fitness Assessment, Medical Examination.

Application deadlines: 12/31 (freshmen), 12/31 (transfers).

Notification: continuous until 10/15 (freshmen), continuous until 10/15 (transfers).

CONTACT

Selections Division Admission Counselor, United States Air Force Academy, HQ USAFA/RR, 2304 Cadet Drive, Suite 2400, USAF Academy, CO 80840-5025. *Phone:* 800-443-9266. *Toll-free phone:* 800-443-9266. *Fax:* 719-333-3012.

★ University of Colorado Boulder

Boulder, Colorado

http://www.colorado.edu/

- **State-supported** university, founded 1876, part of University of Colorado System
- **Suburban** 600-acre campus with easy access to Denver
- **Endowment** $511.0 million
- **Coed** 26,426 undergraduate students, 92% full-time, 44% women, 56% men
- **Moderately difficult** entrance level, 84% of applicants were admitted

UNDERGRAD STUDENTS

24,245 full-time, 2,181 part-time. Students come from 52 states and territories; 107 other countries; 38% are from out of state; 2% Black or African American, non-Hispanic/Latino; 10% Hispanic/Latino; 5% Asian, non-Hispanic/Latino; 0.1% Native Hawaiian or other Pacific Islander, non-Hispanic/Latino; 0.3% American Indian or Alaska Native, non-Hispanic/Latino; 4% Two or more races, non-Hispanic/Latino; 1% Race/ethnicity unknown; 5% international; 5% transferred in; 29% live on campus.

Freshmen

Admission: 28,768 applied, 24,230 admitted, 5,869 enrolled. ***Average high school GPA:*** 3.58. ***Test scores:*** SAT critical reading scores over 500: 85%; SAT math scores over 500: 90%; ACT scores over 18: 99%; SAT critical reading scores over 600: 42%; SAT math scores over 600: 53%; ACT scores over 24: 79%; SAT critical reading scores over 700: 8%; SAT math scores over 700: 13%; ACT scores over 30: 26%.

Retention: 84% of full-time freshmen returned.

FACULTY

Total: 1,927, 74% full-time, 78% with terminal degrees.

Student/faculty ratio: 18:1.

ACADEMICS

Calendar: semesters. *Degrees:* bachelor's, master's, doctoral, and post-master's certificates.

Special study options: accelerated degree program, adult/continuing education programs, advanced placement credit, cooperative education, distance learning, double majors, English as a second language, freshman honors college, honors programs, independent study, internships, off-campus study, part-time degree program, services for LD students, student-designed majors, study abroad, summer session for credit. ***ROTC:*** Army (b), Navy (b), Air Force (b).

Computers: 1,804 computers/terminals are available on campus for general student use. Students can access the following: campus intranet, computer help desk, free student e-mail accounts, online (class) grades, online (class) registration, online (class) schedules, training, tutorials, workshops, and seminars; standard and academic software; student government voting. Campuswide network is available. 100% of college-owned or -operated housing units are wired for high-speed Internet access. Wireless service is available via entire campus.

STUDENT LIFE

Housing options: on-campus residence required for freshman year; coed, special housing for students with disabilities. Campus housing is university owned and is provided by a third party. Freshman campus housing is guaranteed.

Activities and organizations: drama/theater group, student-run newspaper, radio station, choral group, marching band, student government, Environmental Center, Ski and Snowboard Club, AIESEC (international leadership organization), Program Council, national fraternities, national sororities.

Athletics Member NCAA. All Division I except football (Division I-A). ***Intercollegiate sports:*** baseball M(c), basketball M(s)/W(s), cheerleading M/W, crew M(c)/W(c), cross-country running M(s)/W(s), equestrian sports M(c)/W(c), fencing M(c)/W(c), field hockey M(c)/W(c), golf M(s)/W(s), ice hockey M(c)/W(c), lacrosse M(c)/W(s), racquetball M(c)/W(c), rugby M(c)/W(c), skiing (cross-country) M(s)/W(s), skiing (downhill) M(s)/W(s), soccer M(c)/W(s), softball W(c), swimming and diving M(c)/W(c), tennis M(c)/W(s), track and field M(s)/W(s), ultimate Frisbee M(c)/W(c), volleyball M(c)/W(s), water polo M(c)/W(c), wrestling M(c). ***Intramural sports:*** basketball M/W, ice hockey M/W, soccer M/W, tennis M/W, ultimate Frisbee M/W, volleyball M/W, water polo M/W.

Campus security: 24-hour emergency response devices and patrols, student patrols, late-night transport/escort service, controlled dormitory access, University police department.

Student services: health clinic, personal/psychological counseling, women's center, legal services.

COSTS & FINANCIAL AID

Costs (2014–15) ***One-time required fee:*** $182. ***Tuition:*** state resident $9048 full-time; nonresident $31,410 full-time. Full-time tuition and fees vary according to program. Part-time tuition and fees vary according to course load and program. ***Required fees:*** $1741 full-time. ***Room and board:*** $12,810. Room and board charges vary according to board plan, housing facility, and location. ***Payment plan:*** deferred payment. ***Waivers:*** senior citizens and employees or children of employees.

Financial Aid Of all full-time matriculated undergraduates who enrolled in 2014, 12,446 applied for aid, 9,171 were judged to have need, 3,559 had their need fully met. 1,127 Federal Work-Study jobs (averaging $1743). 708 state and other part-time jobs (averaging $2600). In 2014, 5724 non-need-based awards were made. ***Average percent of need met:*** 80. ***Average financial aid package:*** $16,269. ***Average need-based loan:*** $6418. ***Average need-based gift aid:*** $10,380. ***Average non-need-based aid:*** $10,019. ***Average indebtedness upon graduation:*** $25,126.

APPLYING

Standardized Tests *Required:* SAT or ACT (for admission).

Options: electronic application, early action, deferred entrance.

Application fee: $50.

Required: essay or personal statement, high school transcript, 1 letter of recommendation. ***Required for some:*** audition for music program. ***Recommended:*** minimum 3.0 GPA.

Application deadlines: 1/15 (freshmen), 3/1 (transfers), 11/15 (early action).

Notification: 4/1 (freshmen), continuous until 3/1 (transfers), 2/1 (early action).

CONTACT

Admissions Office, University of Colorado Boulder, Regent Administrative Center 125, 552 UCB, Boulder, CO 80309. *Phone:* 303-492-6301. *Fax:* 303-735-2501. *E-mail:* apply@colorado.edu.

University of Colorado Colorado Springs

Colorado Springs, Colorado

http://www.uccs.edu/

- **State-supported** university, founded 1965, part of University of Colorado System
- **Urban** 532-acre campus with easy access to Colorado Springs
- **Coed** 9,489 undergraduate students, 78% full-time, 52% women, 48% men
- **Moderately difficult** entrance level, 92% of applicants were admitted

UNDERGRAD STUDENTS

7,365 full-time, 2,124 part-time. Students come from 49 states and territories; 40 other countries; 12% are from out of state; 4% Black or African American, non-Hispanic/Latino; 15% Hispanic/Latino; 3% Asian, non-Hispanic/Latino; 0.3% Native Hawaiian or other Pacific Islander, non-Hispanic/Latino; 0.5% American Indian or Alaska Native, non-Hispanic/Latino; 7% Two or more races, non-Hispanic/Latino; 2% Race/ethnicity unknown; 1% international; 11% transferred in; 13% live on campus.

Freshmen

Admission: 7,619 applied, 7,036 admitted, 1,722 enrolled. ***Average high school GPA:*** 3.27. ***Test scores:*** SAT critical reading scores over 500: 73%; SAT math scores over 500: 73%; SAT writing scores over 500: 58%; ACT scores over 18: 94%; SAT critical reading scores over 600: 22%; SAT math scores over 600: 27%; SAT writing scores over 600: 16%; ACT scores over 24: 46%; SAT critical reading scores over 700: 2%; SAT math scores over 700: 4%; SAT writing scores over 700: 2%; ACT scores over 30: 6%.

Retention: 66% of full-time freshmen returned.

FACULTY

Total: 745, 60% full-time, 42% with terminal degrees.

Student/faculty ratio: 17:1.

ACADEMICS

Calendar: semesters. *Degrees:* bachelor's, master's, doctoral, and postbachelor's certificates.

Special study options: accelerated degree program, adult/continuing education programs, advanced placement credit, cooperative education, distance learning, double majors, English as a second language, honors programs, independent study, internships, off-campus study, part-time degree program, services for LD students, student-designed majors, study abroad, summer session for credit. ***ROTC:*** Army (b).

Unusual degree programs: 3-2 business administration; engineering; nursing; chemistry, criminal justice.

Computers: 959 computers/terminals and 2,586 ports are available on campus for general student use. Students can access the following: campus intranet, computer help desk, free student e-mail accounts, online (class) grades, online (class) registration, online (class) schedules, wireless network, student portal, learning management system. Campuswide network is available. 100% of college-owned or -operated housing units are wired for high-speed Internet access. Wireless service is available via entire campus.

STUDENT LIFE

Housing options: on-campus residence required for freshman year; coed, men-only, women-only, special housing for students with disabilities. Campus housing is university owned. Freshman applicants given priority for college housing.

Activities and organizations: drama/theater group, student-run newspaper, radio and television station, choral group, Fans Initiating Growth Honor and Tradition (spirit club), Pi Beta Phi, Sustainability Club, Gamers (computing), El Circulo, national fraternities, national sororities.

Athletics Member NCAA. All Division II. ***Intercollegiate sports:*** basketball M(s)/W(s), cross-country running M(s)/W(s), golf M(s)/W(s), soccer M(s)/W(s), softball W(s), track and field M(s)/W(s), volleyball W(s).

Campus security: 24-hour emergency response devices and patrols, student patrols, late-night transport/escort service, controlled dormitory access, emergency text messaging.

Student services: health clinic, personal/psychological counseling.

COSTS & FINANCIAL AID

Costs (2014–15) ***One-time required fee:*** $100. ***Tuition:*** state resident $7710 full-time, $332 per credit hour part-time; nonresident $20,250 full-time, $675 per credit hour part-time. Full-time tuition and fees vary according to course level, course load, degree level, location, program, reciprocity agreements, and student level. Part-time tuition and fees vary according to course level, course load, degree level, location, program, reciprocity agreements, and student level. ***Required fees:*** $1433 full-time, $388 per term part-time, $388 per term part-time. ***Room and board:*** $9150. Room and board charges vary according to board plan and housing facility. ***Payment plan:*** installment. ***Waivers:*** employees or children of employees.

Financial Aid Of all full-time matriculated undergraduates who enrolled in 2013, 5,536 applied for aid, 4,167 were judged to have need, 163 had their need fully met. 190 Federal Work-Study jobs (averaging $2385). 237 state and other part-time jobs (averaging $3004). In 2013, 248 non-need-based awards were made. ***Average percent of need met:*** 46. ***Average financial aid package:*** $7805. ***Average need-based loan:*** $4203. ***Average need-based gift aid:*** $5481. ***Average non-need-based aid:*** $3750. ***Average indebtedness upon graduation:*** $19,780.

APPLYING

Standardized Tests *Required:* SAT or ACT (for admission).

Options: electronic application, deferred entrance.

Application fee: $50.

Required: high school transcript. ***Required for some:*** minimum 2.0 GPA, GED certificate in lieu of high school transcript; SAT or ACT test scores are required for most new students.

Application deadlines: rolling (freshmen), rolling (out-of-state freshmen), rolling (transfers).

Notification: continuous (freshmen), continuous (out-of-state freshmen), continuous (transfers).

CONTACT

Mr. Chris Beiswanger, Director of Student Recruitment and Admissions Counseling, University of Colorado Colorado Springs, 1420 Austin Bluffs Parkway, Colorado Springs, CO 80918. *Phone:* 719-255-3088. *Toll-free phone:* 800-990-8227 Ext. 3383. *E-mail:* cbeiswan@uccs.edu.

University of Colorado Denver

Denver, Colorado

http://www.ucdenver.edu/

- **State-supported** university, founded 1912, part of University of Colorado System
- **Urban** 171-acre campus with easy access to Denver
- **Endowment** $419.8 million
- **Coed** 13,509 undergraduate students, 59% full-time, 54% women, 46% men
- **Moderately difficult** entrance level, 73% of applicants were admitted

UNDERGRAD STUDENTS

7,996 full-time, 5,513 part-time. Students come from 50 states and territories; 42 other countries; 8% are from out of state; 5% Black or African American, non-Hispanic/Latino; 17% Hispanic/Latino; 10% Asian, non-Hispanic/Latino; 0.1% Native Hawaiian or other Pacific Islander, non-Hispanic/Latino; 0.4% American Indian or Alaska Native, non-Hispanic/Latino; 4% Two or more races, non-Hispanic/Latino; 3% Race/ethnicity unknown; 10% international; 12% transferred in; 5% live on campus.

Freshmen

Admission: 7,220 applied, 5,270 admitted, 1,367 enrolled. ***Average high school GPA:*** 3.37. ***Test scores:*** SAT critical reading scores over 500: 72%; SAT math scores over 500: 71%; ACT scores over 18: 94%; SAT critical reading scores over 600: 28%; SAT math scores over 600: 27%; ACT scores over 24: 43%; SAT critical reading scores over 700: 4%; SAT math scores over 700: 6%; ACT scores over 30: 5%.

Retention: 72% of full-time freshmen returned.

FACULTY

Total: 3,816, 86% full-time, 69% with terminal degrees.

Student/faculty ratio: 16:1.

ACADEMICS

Calendar: semesters. *Degrees:* bachelor's, master's, doctoral, and post-master's certificates.

Special study options: accelerated degree program, advanced placement credit, cooperative education, distance learning, double majors, English as a second language, honors programs, independent study, internships, off-campus study, part-time degree program, services for LD students, student-designed majors, study abroad, summer session for credit. ***ROTC:*** Army (c), Air Force (c).

Unusual degree programs: 3-2 criminal justice (BACJ/MCJ).

Computers: 750 computers/terminals are available on campus for general student use. Students can access the following: campus intranet, computer help desk, free student e-mail accounts, online (class) grades, online (class) registration, online (class) schedules. Campuswide network is available. 100% of college-owned or -operated housing units are wired for high-speed Internet access. Wireless service is available via entire campus.

STUDENT LIFE

Housing options: on-campus residence required for freshman year; coed. Campus housing is provided by a third party. Freshman applicants given priority for college housing.

Activities and organizations: drama/theater group, student-run newspaper, choral group, Veterans Student Organization (Service), Golden Key Honor Society (Academic), Minority Association for Pre-Health Students (Health), Future Doctors of Denver, Intercultural Club Beijing (Cultural and Social).

Athletics ***Intercollegiate sports:*** basketball M(c)/W(c), ice hockey M(c), lacrosse M(c)/W(c), soccer M(c)/W(c), volleyball M(c)/W(c). ***Intramural sports:*** badminton M(c)/W(c), baseball M(c)/W(c), cheerleading W(c), cross-country running M(c)/W(c), golf M(c)/W(c), tennis M(c)/W(c), ultimate Frisbee M(c)/W(c).

Campus security: 24-hour emergency response devices and patrols, student patrols, late-night transport/escort service.

Student services: health clinic, personal/psychological counseling.

COSTS & FINANCIAL AID

Costs (2014–15) ***Tuition:*** state resident $8760 full-time, $292 per credit hour part-time; nonresident $27,030 full-time, $901 per credit hour part-time. Full-time tuition and fees vary according to course level, course load, degree level, location, program, reciprocity agreements, and student level. Part-time tuition and fees vary according to course level, course load, degree level, location, program, reciprocity agreements, and student level. ***Required fees:*** $1225 full-time, $1225 per year part-time. ***Room and board:*** $11,140; room only: $7640. Room and board charges vary according to board plan. ***Payment plans:*** installment, deferred payment. ***Waivers:*** employees or children of employees.

Financial Aid Of all full-time matriculated undergraduates who enrolled in 2013, 5,489 applied for aid, 4,692 were judged to have need, 177 had their need fully met. 266 Federal Work-Study jobs (averaging $3140). 200 state and other part-time jobs (averaging $3758). In 2013, 444 non-need-based awards were made. ***Average percent of need met:*** 51. ***Average financial aid package:*** $9059. ***Average need-based loan:*** $4333. ***Average need-based gift aid:*** $6907. ***Average non-need-based aid:*** $3114. ***Average indebtedness upon graduation:*** $21,502.

APPLYING

Standardized Tests *Required:* SAT or ACT (for admission).

Options: electronic application, deferred entrance.

Application fee: $50.

Required: high school transcript, minimum 2.5 GPA. ***Required for some:*** essay or personal statement, minimum 3.0 GPA, audition, portfolio, entrance exam for some programs. ***Recommended:*** essay or personal statement.

Application deadlines: 7/22 (freshmen), 7/22 (out-of-state freshmen), 7/22 (transfers).

Notification: continuous (freshmen), continuous (out-of-state freshmen), continuous (transfers).

CONTACT

Office of Admissions, University of Colorado Denver, PO Box 173364, Campus Box 167, Denver, CO 80217. *Phone:* 303-556-2704. *E-mail:* admissions@ucdenver.edu.

University of Denver

Denver, Colorado

http://www.du.edu/

- **Independent** university, founded 1864
- **Urban** 125-acre campus with easy access to Denver
- **Endowment** $467.3 million
- **Coed** 5,643 undergraduate students, 94% full-time, 54% women, 46% men
- **Moderately difficult** entrance level, 76% of applicants were admitted

UNDERGRAD STUDENTS
5,304 full-time, 339 part-time. Students come from 52 states and territories; 57 other countries; 54% are from out of state; 3% Black or African American, non-Hispanic/Latino; 9% Hispanic/Latino; 4% Asian, non-Hispanic/Latino; 0.1% Native Hawaiian or other Pacific Islander, non-Hispanic/Latino; 0.4% American Indian or Alaska Native, non-Hispanic/Latino; 3% Two or more races, non-Hispanic/Latino; 3% Race/ethnicity unknown; 10% international; 3% transferred in; 47% live on campus.

Freshmen
Admission: 13,670 applied, 10,456 admitted, 1,424 enrolled. ***Average high school GPA:*** 3.68. ***Test scores:*** SAT critical reading scores over 500: 90%; SAT math scores over 500: 95%; SAT writing scores over 500: 81%; ACT scores over 18: 100%; SAT critical reading scores over 600: 53%; SAT math scores over 600: 58%; SAT writing scores over 600: 35%; ACT scores over 24: 86%; SAT critical reading scores over 700: 9%; SAT math scores over 700: 12%; SAT writing scores over 700: 4%; ACT scores over 30: 32%.
Retention: 86% of full-time freshmen returned.

FACULTY
Total: 1,282, 54% full-time, 63% with terminal degrees.
Student/faculty ratio: 11:1.

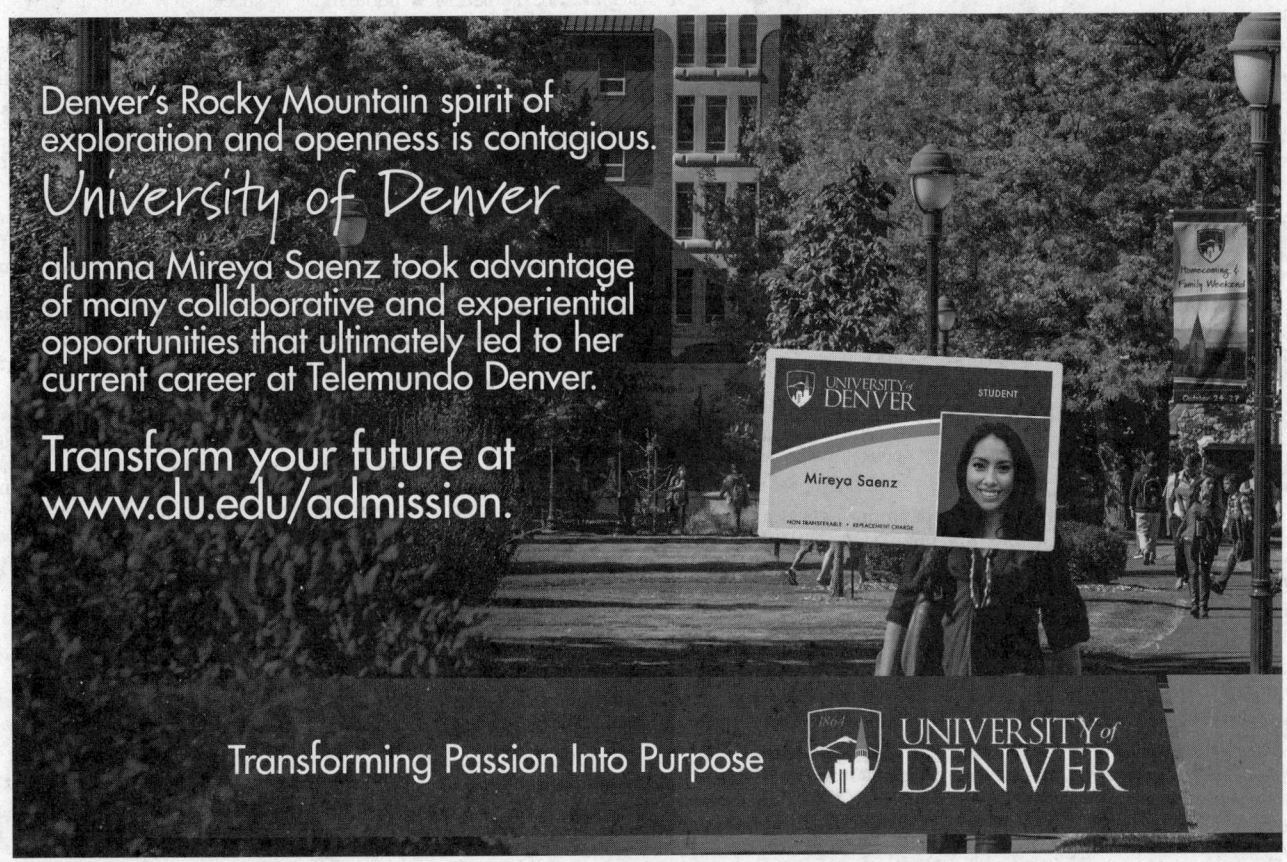

ACADEMICS
Calendar: quarters; semesters for law school. *Degrees:* certificates, bachelor's, master's, doctoral, post-master's, and postbachelor's certificates.
Special study options: accelerated degree program, adult/continuing education programs, advanced placement credit, cooperative education, distance learning, double majors, English as a second language, freshman honors college, honors programs, independent study, internships, off-campus study, part-time degree program, services for LD students, student-designed majors, study abroad, summer session for credit. ***ROTC:*** Army (c), Air Force (c).
Unusual degree programs: 3-2 business administration; engineering; social work; art history; public policy; accounting; international studies; education; environmental science; and geography.
Computers: 150 computers/terminals and 35,000 ports are available on campus for general student use. Students can access the following: campus intranet, computer help desk, free student e-mail accounts, online (class) grades, online (class) registration, online (class) schedules. Campuswide network is available. 95% of college-owned or -operated housing units are wired for high-speed Internet access. Wireless service is available via entire campus.

STUDENT LIFE
Housing options: on-campus residence required through sophomore year; coed, men-only, women-only, cooperative. Campus housing is university owned. Freshman campus housing is guaranteed.
Activities and organizations: drama/theater group, student-run newspaper, radio station, choral group, Club Sports Council, Alpine Club, DU Programs Board, Greek Life Council, Residence Hall Association, national fraternities, national sororities.
Athletics Member NCAA. All Division I. ***Intercollegiate sports:*** baseball M(c), basketball M(s)/W(s), cross-country running M(c)/W(c), equestrian sports M(c)/W(c), golf M(s)/W(s), gymnastics W(s), ice hockey M(s)/W(c), lacrosse M(s)/W(s), racquetball M(c)/W(c), skiing (cross-country) M(s)/W(s), skiing (downhill) M(s)/W(s), soccer M(s)/W(s), softball W(c), swimming and diving M(s)/W(s), tennis M(s)/W(s), volleyball W(s), water polo M(c)/W(c). ***Intramural sports:*** basketball M/W, field hockey M(c)/W(c), football M/W, golf M(c)/W(c), ice hockey

M(c), lacrosse M(c)/W(c), racquetball M(c)/W(c), rock climbing M(c)/W(c), rugby M(c), skiing (downhill) M(c)/W(c), soccer M(c)/W(c), softball M/W, tennis M(c)/W(c), ultimate Frisbee M(c)/W(c), volleyball M(c)/W(c).

Campus security: 24-hour emergency response devices and patrols, late-night transport/escort service, controlled dormitory access, 24-hour locked residence hall entrances.

Student services: health clinic, personal/psychological counseling, women's center.

COSTS & FINANCIAL AID

Costs (2014–15) ***Comprehensive fee:*** $53,199 includes full-time tuition ($41,112), mandatory fees ($978), and room and board ($11,109). Full-time tuition and fees vary according to course load and program. Part-time tuition: $1142 per credit hour. Part-time tuition and fees vary according to course load and program. ***College room only:*** $6723. Room and board charges vary according to board plan and housing facility. ***Payment plans:*** installment, deferred payment. ***Waivers:*** senior citizens and employees or children of employees.

Financial Aid Of all full-time matriculated undergraduates who enrolled in 2014, 2,826 applied for aid, 2,202 were judged to have need, 846 had their need fully met. 380 Federal Work-Study jobs (averaging $2993). 197 state and other part-time jobs (averaging $3119). In 2014, 2003 non-need-based awards were made. ***Average percent of need met:*** 86. ***Average financial aid package:*** $34,455. ***Average need-based loan:*** $4181. ***Average need-based gift aid:*** $28,597. ***Average non-need-based aid:*** $14,724. ***Average indebtedness upon graduation:*** $29,050. ***Financial aid deadline:*** 5/1.

APPLYING

Standardized Tests *Required:* SAT or ACT (for admission).

Options: electronic application, early admission, early action, deferred entrance.

Application fee: $60.

Required: essay or personal statement, high school transcript, 2 letters of recommendation. ***Required for some:*** minimum 2.0 GPA. ***Recommended:*** interview.

Application deadlines: 1/15 (freshmen), rolling (transfers), 11/1 (early action).

Notification: 3/15 (freshmen), continuous (transfers), 1/15 (early action).

CONTACT

Mr. Todd R. Rinehart, Associate Vice Chancellor for Enrollment, University of Denver, 2197 South University Boulevard, Denver, CO 80208. *Phone:* 303-871-3125. *Toll-free phone:* 800-525-9495. *Fax:* 303-871-3301. *E-mail:* admission@du.edu.

See previous page for display ad and page 1662 for the College Close-Up.

University of Northern Colorado

Greeley, Colorado

http://www.unco.edu/

- **State-supported** university, founded 1890
- **Suburban** 260-acre campus with easy access to Denver
- **Endowment** $82.4 million
- **Coed** 9,424 undergraduate students, 88% full-time, 63% women, 37% men
- **Moderately difficult** entrance level, 71% of applicants were admitted

UNDERGRAD STUDENTS

8,324 full-time, 1,100 part-time. Students come from 47 states and territories; 34 other countries; 13% are from out of state; 4% Black or African American, non-Hispanic/Latino; 17% Hispanic/Latino; 2% Asian, non-Hispanic/Latino; 0.2% Native Hawaiian or other Pacific Islander, non-Hispanic/Latino; 0.3% American Indian or Alaska Native, non-Hispanic/Latino; 3% Two or more races, non-Hispanic/Latino; 16% Race/ethnicity unknown; 2% international; 7% transferred in; 37% live on campus.

Freshmen

Admission: 7,831 applied, 5,551 admitted, 1,905 enrolled. ***Average high school GPA:*** 3.3. ***Test scores:*** SAT critical reading scores over 500: 62%; SAT math scores over 500: 63%; ACT scores over 18: 88%; SAT critical reading scores over 600: 15%; SAT math scores over 600: 23%; ACT scores over 24: 34%; SAT critical reading scores over 700: 3%; SAT math scores over 700: 3%; ACT scores over 30: 3%.

Retention: 68% of full-time freshmen returned.

FACULTY

Total: 770, 64% full-time.

Student/faculty ratio: 17:1.

ACADEMICS

Calendar: semesters. *Degrees:* bachelor's, master's, and doctoral.

Special study options: academic remediation for entering students, accelerated degree program, adult/continuing education programs, advanced placement credit, cooperative education, distance learning, double majors, English as a second language, external degree program, honors programs, independent study, internships, off-campus study, part-time degree program, services for LD students, student-designed majors, study abroad, summer session for credit. ***ROTC:*** Army (b), Air Force (b).

Computers: 1,719 computers/terminals and 825 ports are available on campus for general student use. Students can access the following: computer help desk, free student e-mail accounts, online (class) grades, online (class) registration, online (class) schedules. Campuswide network is available. 100% of college-owned or -operated housing units are wired for high-speed Internet access. Wireless service is available via entire campus.

STUDENT LIFE

Housing options: on-campus residence required for freshman year; coed, women-only, special housing for students with disabilities. Campus housing is university owned. Freshman campus housing is guaranteed.

Activities and organizations: drama/theater group, student-run newspaper, radio and television station, choral group, marching band, Fraternities and Sororities, Club Sports, Campus Religious/Spiritual Organizations, Academic Clubs, Services Clubs, national fraternities, national sororities.

Athletics Member NCAA. All Division I. ***Intercollegiate sports:*** baseball M(s), basketball M(s)/W(s), cross-country running W(s), football M(s), golf M(s)/W(s), ice hockey M(c), lacrosse M(c), rugby M(c)/W(c), soccer M(c)/W(s), softball W(s), swimming and diving W(s), tennis M(s)/W(s), track and field M(s)/W(s), volleyball W(s), wrestling M(s). ***Intramural sports:*** basketball M/W, football M/W, soccer M/W, softball M/W, volleyball M/W, water polo M/W.

Campus security: 24-hour emergency response devices and patrols, student patrols, late-night transport/escort service, controlled dormitory access.

Student services: health clinic, personal/psychological counseling, women's center, legal services.

COSTS & FINANCIAL AID

Costs (2014–15) ***Tuition:*** state resident $6024 full-time, $239 per credit hour part-time; nonresident $17,568 full-time, $707 per credit hour part-time. Full-time tuition and fees vary according to location and program. Part-time tuition and fees vary according to location and program. ***Required fees:*** $1709 full-time, $78 per credit hour part-time. ***Room and board:*** $10,360; room only: $4800. Room and board charges vary according to board plan and housing facility. ***Payment plan:*** installment. ***Waivers:*** employees or children of employees.

Financial Aid Of all full-time matriculated undergraduates who enrolled in 2013, 6,582 applied for aid, 5,647 were judged to have need, 1,896 had their need fully met. 185 Federal Work-Study jobs (averaging $2967). 493 state and other part-time jobs (averaging $2842). In 2013, 994 non-need-based awards were made. ***Average percent of need met:*** 75. ***Average financial aid package:*** $6601. ***Average need-based loan:*** $3827. ***Average need-based gift aid:*** $3996. ***Average non-need-based aid:*** $230. ***Average indebtedness upon graduation:*** $25,446.

APPLYING

Standardized Tests *Recommended:* SAT or ACT (for admission).

Options: electronic application, deferred entrance.

Application fee: $45.

Required for some: essay or personal statement, high school transcript.

Application deadlines: 8/1 (freshmen), 8/1 (out-of-state freshmen), rolling (transfers).

Notification: continuous (freshmen), continuous (transfers).

CONTACT

Sean Broghammer, Director of Admissions, University of Northern Colorado, Campus Box 10, Carter Hall 3006, Greeley, CO 80639. *Phone:* 970-351-2881. *Toll-free phone:* 888-700-4UNC. *Fax:* 970-351-2984. *E-mail:* admissions@unco.edu.

Western State Colorado University

Gunnison, Colorado

http://www.western.edu/

- **State-supported** comprehensive, founded 1901
- **Rural** 381-acre campus
- **Coed** 2,338 undergraduate students, 79% full-time, 42% women, 58% men
- **Moderately difficult** entrance level, 97% of applicants were admitted

UNDERGRAD STUDENTS

1,855 full-time, 483 part-time. Students come from 50 states and territories; 8 other countries; 27% are from out of state; 3% Black or African American, non-Hispanic/Latino; 9% Hispanic/Latino; 1% Asian, non-Hispanic/Latino; 0.5% Native Hawaiian or other Pacific Islander, non-Hispanic/Latino; 0.3% American Indian or Alaska Native, non-Hispanic/Latino; 4% Two or more races, non-Hispanic/Latino; 6% Race/ethnicity unknown; 0.5% international; 7% transferred in; 45% live on campus.

Freshmen

Admission: 1,199 applied, 1,168 admitted, 454 enrolled. ***Average high school GPA:*** 3.13. ***Test scores:*** SAT critical reading scores over 500: 49%; SAT math scores over 500: 57%; ACT scores over 18: 86%; SAT critical reading scores over 600: 13%; SAT math scores over 600: 15%; ACT scores over 24: 30%; SAT critical reading scores over 700: 1%; SAT math scores over 700: 2%; ACT scores over 30: 3%.

Retention: 70% of full-time freshmen returned.

FACULTY

Total: 141, 82% full-time, 77% with terminal degrees.

Student/faculty ratio: 17:1.

ACADEMICS

Calendar: semesters. *Degrees:* bachelor's, master's, and postbachelor's certificates.

Special study options: academic remediation for entering students, adult/continuing education programs, advanced placement credit, double majors, honors programs, independent study, internships, off-campus study, part-time degree program, services for LD students, study abroad, summer session for credit.

Computers: 181 computers/terminals and 600 ports are available on campus for general student use. Students can access the following: computer help desk, free student e-mail accounts, online (class) grades, online (class) registration, online (class) schedules. Campuswide network is available. 100% of college-owned or -operated housing units are wired for high-speed Internet access. Wireless service is available via entire campus.

STUDENT LIFE

Housing options: on-campus residence required through sophomore year; coed, men-only, women-only. Campus housing is university owned. Freshman campus housing is guaranteed.

Activities and organizations: drama/theater group, student-run newspaper, radio and television station, choral group, Mountain Search and Rescue Team, Student Government Association, Rodeo Club, wilderness pursuits, Peak Productions.

Athletics Member NCAA. All Division II. ***Intercollegiate sports:*** baseball M(c), basketball M(s)/W(s), cheerleading M(c)/W(c), cross-country running M(s)/W(s), football M(s), ice hockey M(c), lacrosse M(c)/W(c), rock climbing M(c)/W(c), rugby M(c)/W(c), skiing (cross-country) M(c)/W(c), skiing (downhill) M(c)/W(c), soccer M(c)/W(s), swimming and diving W(s), track and field M(s)/W(s), volleyball M(c)/W(s), wrestling M(s)/W(c). ***Intramural sports:*** basketball M/W, football M/W, golf M/W, soccer M/W, softball M/W, table tennis M/W, tennis M/W, ultimate Frisbee M/W, volleyball M/W.

Campus security: 24-hour emergency response devices and patrols, student patrols, late-night transport/escort service, controlled dormitory access.

Student services: health clinic, personal/psychological counseling.

COSTS & FINANCIAL AID

Costs (2014–15) ***Tuition:*** state resident $5539 full-time, $231 per credit hour part-time; nonresident $15,984 full-time, $666 per credit hour part-time. Full-time tuition and fees vary according to course load and reciprocity agreements. Part-time tuition and fees vary according to course load and reciprocity agreements. ***Required fees:*** $2335 full-time. ***Room and board:*** $9050; room only: $4794. Room and board charges vary according to board plan and housing facility. ***Payment plans:*** installment, deferred payment. ***Waivers:*** senior citizens and employees or children of employees.

Financial Aid Of all full-time matriculated undergraduates who enrolled in 2014, 1,372 applied for aid, 1,056 were judged to have need, 184 had their need fully met. 173 Federal Work-Study jobs (averaging $1443). 176 state and other part-time jobs (averaging $1679). In 2014, 316 non-need-based awards were made. ***Average percent of need met:*** 56. ***Average financial aid package:*** $12,202. ***Average need-based loan:*** $3578. ***Average need-based gift aid:*** $5748. ***Average non-need-based aid:*** $4104. ***Average indebtedness upon graduation:*** $21,251.

APPLYING

Standardized Tests *Required:* SAT or ACT (for admission).

Options: electronic application, deferred entrance.

Application fee: $30.

Required: essay or personal statement, high school transcript, interview. ***Recommended:*** minimum 2.5 GPA.

Notification: continuous until 11/15 (freshmen), continuous until 11/15 (out-of-state freshmen), continuous (transfers).

CONTACT

Mr. Paul Fitzgerald, Director of Admissions, Western State Colorado University, 600 North Adams Street, Gunnison, CO 81231. *Phone:* 970-943-2211. *Toll-free phone:* 800-876-5309. *E-mail:* admissions@western.edu.

CONNECTICUT

★ Albertus Magnus College

New Haven, Connecticut

http://www.albertus.edu/

- **Independent Roman Catholic** comprehensive, founded 1925
- **Suburban** 50-acre campus
- **Coed** 1,256 undergraduate students, 91% full-time, 65% women, 35% men
- **Moderately difficult** entrance level, 67% of applicants were admitted

UNDERGRAD STUDENTS

1,146 full-time, 110 part-time. Students come from 10 states and territories; 3 other countries; 5% are from out of state; 34% Black or African American, non-Hispanic/Latino; 15% Hispanic/Latino; 0.5% Asian, non-Hispanic/Latino; 0.2% Native Hawaiian or other Pacific Islander, non-Hispanic/Latino; 0.2% American Indian or Alaska Native, non-Hispanic/Latino; 1% Two or more races, non-Hispanic/Latino; 6% Race/ethnicity unknown; 0.9% international; 9% transferred in; 40% live on campus.

Freshmen

Admission: 780 applied, 519 admitted, 159 enrolled. ***Average high school GPA:*** 2.6. ***Test scores:*** SAT critical reading scores over 500: 38%; SAT math scores over 500: 37%; SAT writing scores over 500: 47%; ACT scores over 18: 91%; SAT critical reading scores over 600: 13%; SAT math scores over 600: 9%; SAT writing scores over 600: 12%; ACT scores over 24: 53%; SAT critical reading scores over 700: 2%; SAT writing scores over 700: 2%; ACT scores over 30: 5%.

Retention: 84% of full-time freshmen returned.

FACULTY

Total: 134, 39% full-time, 51% with terminal degrees.

Student/faculty ratio: 14:1.

ACADEMICS

Calendar: semesters. *Degrees:* certificates, diplomas, associate, bachelor's, master's, post-master's, and postbachelor's certificates.

Special study options: academic remediation for entering students, accelerated degree program, adult/continuing education programs, advanced placement credit, distance learning, double majors, English as a second language, freshman honors college, honors programs, independent study, internships, part-time degree program, services for LD students, student-designed majors, study abroad, summer session for credit.

Unusual degree programs: 3-2 business administration; social work.

Computers: 117 computers/terminals are available on campus for general student use. Students can access the following: campus intranet, computer help desk, free student e-mail accounts, online (class) grades, online (class) registration, online (class) schedules, online class sessions - Moodle. Campuswide network is available. 100% of college-owned or -operated housing units are wired for high-speed Internet access. Wireless service is available via entire campus.

STUDENT LIFE

Housing options: coed, women-only. Campus housing is university owned. Freshman applicants given priority for college housing.

Activities and organizations: drama/theater group, choral group, Student Government Association, College Drama, Campus ministry.

Athletics Member NCAA. All Division III. ***Intercollegiate sports:*** baseball M, basketball M/W, golf M/W, lacrosse M/W, soccer M/W, softball W, tennis M/W, volleyball M/W. ***Intramural sports:*** basketball M/W, soccer M/W.

Campus security: 24-hour emergency response devices and patrols, late-night transport/escort service, controlled dormitory access.

Student services: health clinic, personal/psychological counseling.

COSTS & FINANCIAL AID

Costs (2014–15) ***Comprehensive fee:*** $41,890 includes full-time tuition ($28,440), mandatory fees ($490), and room and board ($12,960). Full-time tuition and fees vary according to program. Part-time tuition: $1185 per credit. Part-time tuition and fees vary according to program. ***Room and board:*** Room and board charges vary according to board plan. ***Payment plan:*** installment. ***Waivers:*** senior citizens and employees or children of employees.

Financial Aid Of all full-time matriculated undergraduates who enrolled in 2014, 1,119 applied for aid, 1,086 were judged to have need, 45 had their need fully met. 97 Federal Work-Study jobs (averaging $1633). In 2014, 6 non-need-based awards were made. ***Average percent of need met:*** 44. ***Average financial aid package:*** $15,366. ***Average need-based loan:*** $4228. ***Average need-based gift aid:*** $11,176. ***Average non-need-based aid:*** $15,445. ***Average indebtedness upon graduation:*** $33,975.

APPLYING

Standardized Tests *Required:* SAT or ACT (for admission). *Recommended:* SAT Subject Tests (for admission).

Options: electronic application, deferred entrance.

Application fee: $35.

Required: high school transcript, minimum 2.0 GPA, 1 letter of recommendation. ***Required for some:*** essay or personal statement, interview.

Application deadlines: rolling (freshmen), rolling (transfers).

Notification: continuous (freshmen), continuous (transfers).

CONTACT

Mr. Nilvio Perez, Director of Admission, Albertus Magnus College, 700 Prospect Street, New Haven, CT 06511-1189. *Phone:* 203-773-8501 Ext. 8501. *Toll-free phone:* 800-578-9160. *Fax:* 203-773-5248. *E-mail:* admissions@albertus.edu.

Central Connecticut State University

New Britain, Connecticut

http://www.ccsu.edu/

- **State-supported** comprehensive, founded 1849, part of Connecticut State Colleges & Universities (ConnSCU)
- **Suburban** 314-acre campus
- **Endowment** $60.8 million
- **Coed** 9,911 undergraduate students, 78% full-time, 47% women, 53% men
- **Moderately difficult** entrance level, 60% of applicants were admitted

UNDERGRAD STUDENTS

7,702 full-time, 2,209 part-time. Students come from 29 states and territories; 41 other countries; 3% are from out of state; 11% Black or African American, non-Hispanic/Latino; 13% Hispanic/Latino; 4% Asian, non-Hispanic/Latino; 0.1% Native Hawaiian or other Pacific Islander, non-Hispanic/Latino; 0.2% American Indian or Alaska Native, non-Hispanic/Latino; 3% Two or more races, non-Hispanic/Latino; 3% Race/ethnicity unknown; 1% international; 11% transferred in; 22% live on campus.

Freshmen

Admission: 8,173 applied, 4,940 admitted, 1,369 enrolled. ***Average high school GPA:*** 3. ***Test scores:*** SAT critical reading scores over 500: 53%; SAT math scores over 500: 55%; SAT writing scores over 500: 52%; ACT scores over 18: 97%; SAT critical reading scores over 600: 10%; SAT math scores over 600: 11%; SAT writing scores over 600: 10%; ACT scores over 24: 22%; SAT critical reading scores over 700: 1%; SAT math scores over 700: 1%; SAT writing scores over 700: 1%.

Retention: 80% of full-time freshmen returned.

FACULTY

Total: 952, 47% full-time, 53% with terminal degrees.

Student/faculty ratio: 15:1.

ACADEMICS

Calendar: semesters. *Degrees:* bachelor's, master's, doctoral, post-master's, and postbachelor's certificates.

Special study options: academic remediation for entering students, adult/continuing education programs, advanced placement credit, cooperative education, distance learning, double majors, English as a second language, honors programs, independent study, internships, off-campus study, part-time degree program, services for LD students, student-designed majors, study abroad, summer session for credit. ***ROTC:*** Army (c), Air Force (c).

Computers: 750 computers/terminals are available on campus for general student use. Students can access the following: campus intranet, computer help desk, free student e-mail accounts, online (class) grades, online (class) registration, online (class) schedules. Campuswide network is available. 100% of college-owned or -operated housing units are wired for high-speed Internet access. Wireless service is available via entire campus.

STUDENT LIFE

Housing options: coed, women-only, special housing for students with disabilities. Campus housing is university owned.

Activities and organizations: drama/theater group, student-run newspaper, radio and television station, choral group, Inter-Residence Council, student radio station, Program Council, Outing Club, NAACP, national fraternities, national sororities.

Athletics Member NCAA. All Division I except football (Division I-AA). ***Intercollegiate sports:*** baseball M(s), basketball M(s)/W(s), cross-country running M(s)/W(s), fencing M(c)/W(c), golf M(s)/W(s), lacrosse M(c)/W(s), soccer M(s)/W(s), softball W(s), swimming and diving W(s), track and field M(s)/W(s), volleyball W(s). ***Intramural sports:*** basketball M/W, field hockey W(c), football M, rugby M(c)/W(c), soccer M/W, softball M/W, volleyball M/W.

Campus security: 24-hour emergency response devices and patrols, student patrols, late-night transport/escort service, controlled dormitory access.

Student services: health clinic, personal/psychological counseling, women's center.

COSTS & FINANCIAL AID

Costs (2014–15) ***Tuition:*** state resident $4600 full-time, $193 per credit hour part-time; nonresident $14,886 full-time, $197 per credit hour part-time. Full-time tuition and fees vary according to course level, course load, and program. Part-time tuition and fees vary according to course level, course load, and program. ***Required fees:*** $4277 full-time, $232 per credit hour part-time. ***Room and board:*** $10,872; room only: $6322. Room and board charges vary according to board plan. ***Payment plan:*** installment. ***Waivers:*** senior citizens and employees or children of employees.

Financial Aid Of all full-time matriculated undergraduates who enrolled in 2014, 7,030 applied for aid, 6,045 were judged to have need, 287 had their need fully met. 286 Federal Work-Study jobs (averaging $1426). In 2014, 201 non-need-based awards were made. ***Average percent of need met:*** 61. ***Average financial aid package:*** $8672. ***Average need-based loan:*** $4272. ***Average need-based gift aid:*** $5880. ***Average non-need-based aid:*** $4008. ***Average indebtedness upon graduation:*** $24,000. ***Financial aid deadline:*** 9/15.

APPLYING

Standardized Tests *Required:* SAT or ACT (for admission).

Options: electronic application.

Application fee: $50.

Required: essay or personal statement, high school transcript, minimum 2.0 GPA. ***Required for some:*** interview. ***Recommended:*** minimum 3.0 GPA, 1 letter of recommendation.

Application deadlines: 6/1 (freshmen), 6/1 (transfers).

Notification: continuous until 10/15 (freshmen), continuous until 10/15 (transfers).

CONTACT

Central Connecticut State University, 1615 Stanley Street, New Britain, CT 06050. *Phone:* 860-832-2285. *Toll-free phone:* 860-832-2278 (in-state); 860-733-2278 (out-of-state). *Fax:* 860-832-2522. *E-mail:* admissions@ccsu.edu.

Charter Oak State College

New Britain, Connecticut

http://www.charteroak.edu/

- **State-supported** 4-year, founded 1973, part of Connecticut State Colleges & Universities (ConnSCU)
- **Suburban** campus
- **Coed** 1,929 undergraduate students, 20% full-time, 67% women, 33% men
- **Noncompetitive** entrance level

UNDERGRAD STUDENTS

386 full-time, 1,543 part-time. 22% are from out of state; 18% Black or African American, non-Hispanic/Latino; 13% Hispanic/Latino; 1% Asian, non-Hispanic/Latino; 0.1% Native Hawaiian or other Pacific Islander, non-Hispanic/Latino; 0.3% American Indian or Alaska Native, non-Hispanic/Latino; 3% Two or more races, non-Hispanic/Latino; 3% Race/ethnicity unknown; 0.6% international; 36% transferred in.

FACULTY

Total: 173, 50% with terminal degrees.

Student/faculty ratio: 16:1.

ACADEMICS

Calendar: continuous. *Degrees:* certificates, associate, and bachelor's (offers only external degree programs).

Special study options: accelerated degree program, adult/continuing education programs, advanced placement credit, distance learning, double majors, external degree program, independent study, off-campus study, part-time degree program, services for LD students, student-designed majors, summer session for credit.

STUDENT LIFE

Housing options: college housing not available.

COSTS & FINANCIAL AID

Costs (2014–15) ***Tuition:*** state resident $7890 full-time, $263 per credit part-time; nonresident $10,380 full-time, $346 per credit part-time. Full-time tuition and fees vary according to course load. Part-time tuition and fees vary according to course load. ***Required fees:*** $702 full-time, $234 per term part-time. ***Payment plan:*** installment.

Financial Aid Of all full-time matriculated undergraduates who enrolled in 2003, 355 applied for aid, 226 were judged to have need, 25 had their need fully met. ***Average percent of need met:*** 75. ***Average financial aid package:*** $4464. ***Average need-based loan:*** $1800.

APPLYING

Options: electronic application, deferred entrance.

Application fee: $75.

Required: Applicants must have earned at least 9 college credits and be at least 16 years of age. A high school diploma or GED is required to qualify for federal financial aid. Charter Oak accepts transfer students only.

Notification: continuous (transfers).

CONTACT

Charter Oak State College, CT. *Phone:* 860-515-3858.

Connecticut College

New London, Connecticut

http://www.connecticutcollege.edu/

- **Independent** comprehensive, founded 1911
- **Small-town** 702-acre campus
- **Endowment** $237.0 million
- **Coed** 1,893 undergraduate students, 99% full-time, 62% women, 38% men
- **Very difficult** entrance level, 38% of applicants were admitted

UNDERGRAD STUDENTS

1,873 full-time, 20 part-time. Students come from 42 states and territories; 74 other countries; 83% are from out of state; 3% Black or African American, non-Hispanic/Latino; 9% Hispanic/Latino; 4% Asian, non-Hispanic/Latino; 3% Two or more races, non-Hispanic/Latino; 5% Race/ethnicity unknown; 5% international; 1% transferred in; 99% live on campus.

Freshmen

Admission: 5,394 applied, 2,028 admitted, 498 enrolled. ***Test scores:*** SAT critical reading scores over 500: 100%; SAT math scores over 500: 99%; SAT writing scores over 500: 100%; SAT critical reading scores over 600: 90%; SAT math scores over 600: 90%; SAT writing scores over 600: 92%; SAT critical reading scores over 700: 29%; SAT math scores over 700: 29%; SAT writing scores over 700: 37%.

Retention: 91% of full-time freshmen returned.

FACULTY

Total: 254, 70% full-time, 80% with terminal degrees.

Student/faculty ratio: 9:1.

ACADEMICS

Calendar: semesters. *Degrees:* bachelor's and master's.

Special study options: accelerated degree program, adult/continuing education programs, advanced placement credit, double majors, independent study, internships, off-campus study, part-time degree program, services for LD students, student-designed majors, study abroad.

Unusual degree programs: 3-2 engineering with Washington University in St. Louis.

Computers: Students can access the following: campus intranet, computer help desk, free student e-mail accounts, online (class) grades, online (class) registration, online (class) schedules, Moodle course web pages. Campuswide network is available. 100% of college-owned or -operated housing units are wired for high-speed Internet access. Wireless service is available via classrooms, computer centers, computer labs, dorm rooms, learning centers, libraries, student centers.

STUDENT LIFE

Housing options: on-campus residence required through sophomore year; coed. Campus housing is university owned. Freshman campus housing is guaranteed.

Activities and organizations: drama/theater group, student-run newspaper, radio station, choral group, Student Government Association, Student Activity Council, Unity House organizations, sports clubs, student radio station.

Athletics Member NCAA. All Division III. ***Intercollegiate sports:*** baseball M(c), basketball M/W, crew M/W, cross-country running M/W, equestrian sports M(c)/W(c), field hockey W, ice hockey M/W, lacrosse M/W, rugby W(c), sailing M/W, skiing (cross-country) M(c)/W(c), skiing (downhill) M(c)/W(c), soccer M/W, squash M/W, swimming and diving M/W, tennis M/W, track and field M/W, ultimate Frisbee M(c)/W(c), volleyball M/W, water polo M/W. ***Intramural sports:*** basketball M/W, football M, golf M/W, ice hockey M/W, lacrosse M, soccer M/W, softball M/W, tennis M/W, volleyball M/W.

Campus security: 24-hour emergency response devices and patrols, late-night transport/escort service, controlled dormitory access.

Student services: health clinic, personal/psychological counseling, women's center.

COSTS & FINANCIAL AID

Costs (2014–15) ***Comprehensive fee:*** $60,895 includes full-time tuition ($47,420), mandatory fees ($320), and room and board ($13,155). Part-time tuition: $1413 per credit hour. ***College room only:*** $7590. Room and board charges vary according to board plan. ***Payment plan:*** installment. ***Waivers:*** senior citizens and employees or children of employees.

Financial Aid Of all full-time matriculated undergraduates who enrolled in 2014, 1,077 applied for aid, 968 were judged to have need, 968 had their need fully met. ***Average percent of need met:*** 100. ***Average financial aid package:*** $39,458. ***Average need-based loan:*** $4621. ***Average need-based gift aid:*** $35,885. ***Average indebtedness upon graduation:*** $28,321.

APPLYING

Options: electronic application, early decision, deferred entrance.

Application fee: $60.

Required: essay or personal statement, high school transcript, minimum 2.0 GPA, 1 letter of recommendation, Supplement to Common Application. ***Recommended:*** interview.

Application deadlines: 1/1 (freshmen), 4/1 (transfers).

Early decision deadline: 11/15 (for plan 1), 1/1 (for plan 2).

Notification: 3/31 (freshmen), 5/15 (transfers), 12/15 (early decision plan 1), 2/15 (early decision plan 2).

CONTACT

Ms. Martha C. Merrill, Dean of Admissions and Financial Aid, Connecticut College, 270 Mohegan Avenue, New London, CT 06320-4196. *Phone:* 860-439-2200. *Fax:* 860-439-4301. *E-mail:* admission@conncoll.edu.

Eastern Connecticut State University

Willimantic, Connecticut

http://www.easternct.edu/

- **State-supported** comprehensive, founded 1889, part of Connecticut State Colleges & Universities (ConnSCU)
- **Small-town** 182-acre campus with easy access to Hartford
- **Coed** 5,139 undergraduate students, 83% full-time, 53% women, 47% men
- **Moderately difficult** entrance level, 63% of applicants were admitted

UNDERGRAD STUDENTS

4,288 full-time, 851 part-time. Students come from 23 states and territories; 52 other countries; 4% are from out of state; 7% Black or African American, non-Hispanic/Latino; 9% Hispanic/Latino; 2% Asian, non-Hispanic/Latino; 0.1% Native Hawaiian or other Pacific Islander, non-Hispanic/Latino; 0.2% American Indian or Alaska Native, non-Hispanic/Latino; 3% Two or more races, non-Hispanic/Latino; 9% Race/ethnicity unknown; 1% international; 9% transferred in; 53% live on campus.

Freshmen

Admission: 4,756 applied, 3,001 admitted, 883 enrolled. ***Average high school GPA:*** 3.07.

Retention: 77% of full-time freshmen returned.

FACULTY

Total: 470, 43% full-time.

Student/faculty ratio: 16:1.

ACADEMICS

Calendar: semesters. *Degrees:* associate, bachelor's, and master's.

Special study options: accelerated degree program, advanced placement credit, cooperative education, distance learning, double majors, external degree program, honors programs, independent study, internships, off-campus study, part-time degree program, services for LD students, student-designed majors, study abroad, summer session for credit. ***ROTC:*** Army (c), Air Force (c).

Computers: 2,500 computers/terminals are available on campus for general student use. Students can access the following: computer help desk, free student e-mail accounts, online (class) grades, online (class) registration, online (class) schedules. Campuswide network is available. 100% of college-owned or -operated housing units are wired for high-speed Internet access. Wireless service is available via classrooms, dorm rooms, libraries, student centers.

STUDENT LIFE

Housing options: coed. Campus housing is university owned. Freshman campus housing is guaranteed.

Activities and organizations: drama/theater group, student-run newspaper, radio and television station, choral group, Repertory Dance Troupe, Rugby Club, Biology Club, Education Club, Psychology Club.

Athletics Member NCAA. All Division III. ***Intercollegiate sports:*** baseball M, basketball M/W, cheerleading M(c)/W(c), cross-country running M/W, field hockey W, football M(c), ice hockey M(c)/W(c), lacrosse M/W, rugby M(c), soccer M/W, softball W, swimming and diving W, track and field M/W, volleyball W. ***Intramural sports:*** basketball M/W, fencing M(c)/W(c), field hockey M/W, football M/W, golf M/W, soccer M/W, softball M/W, tennis M/W, ultimate Frisbee M/W, volleyball M/W.

Campus security: 24-hour emergency response devices and patrols, student patrols, late-night transport/escort service, controlled dormitory access.

Student services: health clinic, personal/psychological counseling, women's center.

COSTS & FINANCIAL AID

Costs (2014–15) ***Tuition:*** state resident $4600 full-time, $433 per credit hour part-time; nonresident $14,886 full-time, $437 per credit hour part-time. Part-time tuition and fees vary according to course load. ***Required fees:*** $4960 full-time. ***Room and board:*** $11,650; room only: $6682. Room and board charges vary according to board plan and housing facility. ***Payment plan:*** installment. ***Waivers:*** employees or children of employees.

Financial Aid Of all full-time matriculated undergraduates who enrolled in 2013, 3,574 applied for aid, 2,901 were judged to have need, 254 had their need fully met. In 2013, 142 non-need-based awards were made. ***Average percent of need met:*** 56. ***Average financial aid package:*** $8659. ***Average need-based loan:*** $4403. ***Average need-based gift aid:*** $6010. ***Average non-need-based aid:*** $2927. ***Average indebtedness upon graduation:*** $26,921.

APPLYING

Options: electronic application, deferred entrance.

Application fee: $50.

Required: high school transcript. ***Required for some:*** interview. ***Recommended:*** essay or personal statement, rank in upper 50% of high school class.

Application deadlines: rolling (freshmen), rolling (out-of-state freshmen), rolling (transfers).

Notification: continuous (freshmen), continuous (out-of-state freshmen), continuous (transfers).

CONTACT

Christopher Dorsey, Associate Director of Admissions, Eastern Connecticut State University, 83 Windham Street, Willimantic, CT 06226. *Phone:* 860-465-5286. *Fax:* 860-465-5544. *E-mail:* admissions@easternct.edu.

Fairfield University

Fairfield, Connecticut

http://www.fairfield.edu/

- **Independent Roman Catholic (Jesuit)** comprehensive, founded 1942
- **Suburban** 200-acre campus with easy access to New York City
- **Endowment** $313.1 million
- **Coed** 3,982 undergraduate students, 93% full-time, 59% women, 41% men
- **Moderately difficult** entrance level, 72% of applicants were admitted

UNDERGRAD STUDENTS

3,688 full-time, 294 part-time. Students come from 35 states and territories; 34 other countries; 71% are from out of state; 2% Black or African American, non-Hispanic/Latino; 7% Hispanic/Latino; 2% Asian, non-Hispanic/Latino; 0.1% Native Hawaiian or other Pacific Islander, non-Hispanic/Latino; 0.1% American Indian or Alaska Native, non-Hispanic/Latino; 1% Two or more races, non-Hispanic/Latino; 9% Race/ethnicity unknown; 2% international; 1% transferred in; 76% live on campus.

Freshmen

Admission: 9,978 applied, 7,137 admitted, 1,056 enrolled. *Average high school GPA:* 3.45. *Test scores:* SAT critical reading scores over 500: 93%; SAT math scores over 500: 94%; SAT writing scores over 500: 93%; ACT scores over 18: 100%; SAT critical reading scores over 600: 41%; SAT math scores over 600: 54%; SAT writing scores over 600: 51%; ACT scores over 24: 84%; SAT critical reading scores over 700: 4%; SAT math scores over 700: 5%; SAT writing scores over 700: 8%; ACT scores over 30: 12%.

Retention: 89% of full-time freshmen returned.

FACULTY

Total: 611, 42% full-time, 67% with terminal degrees.

Student/faculty ratio: 11:1.

ACADEMICS

Calendar: semesters. *Degrees:* bachelor's, master's, doctoral, post-master's, and postbachelor's certificates.

Special study options: accelerated degree program, adult/continuing education programs, advanced placement credit, distance learning, double majors, honors programs, independent study, internships, off-campus study, part-time degree program, services for LD students, student-designed majors, study abroad, summer session for credit. ***ROTC:*** Army (c), Air Force (c).

Computers: 131 computers/terminals are available on campus for general student use. Students can access the following: campus intranet, computer help desk, free student e-mail accounts, online (class) grades, online (class) registration, online (class) schedules. Campuswide network is available. 100% of college-owned or -operated housing units are wired for high-speed Internet access. Wireless service is available via entire campus.

STUDENT LIFE

Housing options: coed, special housing for students with disabilities. Campus housing is university owned. Freshman campus housing is guaranteed.

Activities and organizations: drama/theater group, student-run newspaper, radio and television station, choral group, Glee Club, Fairfield University Student Association, Intramural/Club Sports, Campus Ministry, Colleges Against Cancer/Relay for Life.

Athletics Member NCAA. All Division I. ***Intercollegiate sports:*** baseball M(s), basketball M(s)/W(s), crew M(s)/W(s), cross-country running M(s)/W(s), field hockey W(s), golf M(s)/W(s), lacrosse M(s)/W(s), soccer M(s)/W(s), softball W(s), swimming and diving M(s)/W(s), tennis M(s)(c)/W(s), volleyball W(s). ***Intramural sports:*** baseball M(c), basketball M/W, cheerleading M(c)/W(c), cross-country running M(c)/W(c), equestrian sports M(c)/W(c), field hockey W(c), golf M/W, ice hockey M(c), lacrosse M(c)/W(c), rugby M(c)/W(c), sailing M(c)/W(c), skiing (downhill) M(c)/W(c), soccer M/W, softball M/W, table tennis M/W, tennis M/W, ultimate Frisbee M(c)/W(c), volleyball M/W.

Campus security: 24-hour emergency response devices and patrols, late-night transport/escort service, controlled dormitory access, bicycle patrols.

Student services: health clinic, personal/psychological counseling.

COSTS & FINANCIAL AID

Costs (2014–15) ***One-time required fee:*** $230. ***Comprehensive fee:*** $56,960 includes full-time tuition ($43,170), mandatory fees ($600), and room and board ($13,190). Full-time tuition and fees vary according to class time, course level, course load, degree level, and program. Part-time tuition: $725 per credit hour. Part-time tuition and fees vary according to class time, course level, course load, degree level, and program. ***Required fees:*** $60 per term part-time. ***College room only:*** $8080. Room and board charges vary according to board plan and housing facility. ***Payment plan:*** installment. ***Waivers:*** employees or children of employees.

Financial Aid Of all full-time matriculated undergraduates who enrolled in 2014, 2,467 applied for aid, 1,793 were judged to have need, 285 had their need fully met. 277 Federal Work-Study jobs (averaging $1012). In 2014, 1202 non-need-based awards were made. ***Average percent of need met:*** 87. ***Average financial aid package:*** $30,054. ***Average need-based loan:*** $4938. ***Average need-based gift aid:*** $15,682. ***Average non-need-based aid:*** $15,452. ***Average indebtedness upon graduation:*** $27,918. ***Financial aid deadline:*** 2/15.

APPLYING

Options: electronic application, early admission, early decision, early action, deferred entrance.

Application fee: $60.

Required: essay or personal statement, high school transcript, 1 letter of recommendation. ***Recommended:*** interview.

Application deadlines: 1/15 (freshmen), 5/1 (transfers), 11/1 (early action).

Early decision deadline: 11/15 (for plan 1), 1/15 (for plan 2).

Notification: 4/1 (freshmen), 12/15 (early decision plan 1), 2/15 (early decision plan 2), 12/20 (early action).

CONTACT

Alison Hildenbrand, Director of Admission, Fairfield University, 1073 North Benson Road, Fairfield, CT 06824. *Phone:* 203-254-4100. *Fax:* 203-254-4199. *E-mail:* admis@fairfield.edu.

Goodwin College

East Hartford, Connecticut

http://www.goodwin.edu/

- **Independent** primarily 2-year, founded 1999
- **Suburban** 660-acre campus with easy access to Hartford
- **Coed** 3,440 undergraduate students, 18% full-time, 82% women, 18% men
- **Minimally difficult** entrance level

UNDERGRAD STUDENTS

612 full-time, 2,828 part-time. 3% are from out of state; 22% Black or African American, non-Hispanic/Latino; 17% Hispanic/Latino; 2% Asian, non-Hispanic/Latino; 0.1% Native Hawaiian or other Pacific Islander, non-Hispanic/Latino; 0.3% American Indian or Alaska Native, non-Hispanic/Latino; 2% Two or more races, non-Hispanic/Latino; 0.2% Race/ethnicity unknown; 0.1% international; 14% transferred in.

Freshmen

Admission: 480 applied, 318 enrolled.

Retention: 62% of full-time freshmen returned.

FACULTY

Total: 312, 29% full-time, 21% with terminal degrees.

Student/faculty ratio: 10:1.

ACADEMICS

Calendar: semesters. *Degrees:* certificates, associate, and bachelor's.

Special study options: academic remediation for entering students, adult/continuing education programs, advanced placement credit, distance learning, double majors, English as a second language, internships, off-campus study, part-time degree program, services for LD students, summer session for credit.

Computers: Students can access the following: campus intranet, computer help desk, free student e-mail accounts, online (class) grades, online (class) registration, online (class) schedules. Campuswide network is available. Wireless service is available via entire campus.

STUDENT LIFE
Housing options: college housing not available.
Activities and organizations: choral group.
Athletics ***Intramural sports:*** basketball M, football M/W, soccer M/W, softball M/W.
Campus security: 24-hour emergency response devices, late-night transport/escort service, evening security patrolman.
Student services: personal/psychological counseling.

COSTS & FINANCIAL AID
Costs (2014–15) ***Tuition:*** $18,900 full-time, $590 per credit hour part-time. Full-time tuition and fees vary according to course load and program. Part-time tuition and fees vary according to course load and program. ***Required fees:*** $500 full-time. ***Payment plan:*** installment. ***Waivers:*** employees or children of employees.
Financial Aid Of all full-time matriculated undergraduates who enrolled in 2011, 76 Federal Work-Study jobs (averaging $2878). ***Average percent of need met:*** 47. ***Average financial aid package:*** $16,041. ***Average need-based gift aid:*** $12,269. ***Average non-need-based aid:*** $11,687.

APPLYING
Options: electronic application, early admission, deferred entrance.
Application fee: $50.
Required: essay or personal statement, high school transcript, minimum 2.0 GPA, medical exam. ***Recommended:*** 2 letters of recommendation, interview.

CONTACT
Mr. Nicholas Lentino, Assistant Vice President for Admissions, Goodwin College, One Riverside Drive, East Hartford, CT 06118. *Phone:* 860-727-6765. *Toll-free phone:* 800-889-3282. *Fax:* 860-291-9550. *E-mail:* nlentino@goodwin.edu.

Holy Apostles College and Seminary
Cromwell, Connecticut
http://www.holyapostles.edu/

- **Independent Roman Catholic** comprehensive, founded 1956
- **Suburban** 17-acre campus with easy access to Hartford, New Haven
- **Endowment** $674,168
- **Coed**
- **Noncompetitive** entrance level

FACULTY
Student/faculty ratio: 2:1.

ACADEMICS
Calendar: semesters. *Degrees:* certificates, associate, bachelor's, master's, post-master's, and postbachelor's certificates.

STUDENT LIFE
Housing options: college housing not available.
Activities and organizations: Pro-Life Organization.

COSTS
Costs (2014–15) ***One-time required fee:*** $50. ***Tuition:*** $10,800 full-time, $1335 per course part-time. ***Required fees:*** $70 full-time, $445 per credit hour part-time, $35 per term part-time.

APPLYING
Standardized Tests *Recommended:* SAT (for admission).
Options: deferred entrance.
Application fee: $50.
Required: high school transcript. ***Required for some:*** interview.

CONTACT
Fr. Peter Samuel Kucer, Academic Dean, Holy Apostles College and Seminary, 33 Prospect Hill Road, Cromwell, CT 06416. *Phone:* 860-632-3063. *Fax:* 860-632-3030. *E-mail:* pkucer@holyapostles.edu.

Lincoln College of New England
Southington, Connecticut
http://www.lincolncollegene.edu/

- **Proprietary** 4-year, founded 1966
- **Small-town** 32-acre campus with easy access to Hartford
- **Coed** 715 undergraduate students, 63% full-time, 73% women, 27% men
- **Minimally difficult** entrance level

UNDERGRAD STUDENTS
451 full-time, 264 part-time. Students come from 22 states and territories; 14% are from out of state; 21% Black or African American, non-Hispanic/Latino; 19% Hispanic/Latino; 1% Asian, non-Hispanic/Latino; 0.1% Native Hawaiian or other Pacific Islander, non-Hispanic/Latino; 0.4% American Indian or Alaska Native, non-Hispanic/Latino; 8% Two or more races, non-Hispanic/Latino; 6% Race/ethnicity unknown.

Freshmen
Admission: 161 enrolled.
Retention: 42% of full-time freshmen returned.

FACULTY
Total: 125, 28% full-time.
Student/faculty ratio: 11:1.

ACADEMICS
Calendar: semesters. *Degrees:* certificates, associate, and bachelor's.
Special study options: academic remediation for entering students, adult/continuing education programs, advanced placement credit, distance learning, independent study, internships, part-time degree program, services for LD students, summer session for credit.
Computers: 54 computers/terminals are available on campus for general student use. Students can access the following: free student e-mail accounts, online (class) grades, online (class) schedules.

STUDENT LIFE
Housing options: coed, special housing for students with disabilities. Campus housing is university owned. Freshman applicants given priority for college housing.
Activities and organizations: student-run radio station, Student Government Association, Student Ambassador Club, Criminal Justice Club, Mortuary Science, Dental.
Athletics Member NJCAA. ***Intercollegiate sports:*** basketball M/W. ***Intramural sports:*** basketball M/W.
Campus security: 24-hour patrols, late-night transport/escort service.
Student services: personal/psychological counseling.

COSTS & FINANCIAL AID
Costs (2014–15) ***Comprehensive fee:*** $25,940 includes full-time tuition ($18,780), mandatory fees ($1160), and room and board ($6000). Part-time tuition: $710 per credit. ***Required fees:*** $580 per term part-time. ***College room only:*** $4400.
Financial Aid Of all full-time matriculated undergraduates who enrolled in 2013, 92 Federal Work-Study jobs (averaging $2000). 30 state and other part-time jobs.

APPLYING
Options: electronic application.
Application fee: $25.
Required: high school transcript. ***Required for some:*** essay or personal statement, interview. ***Recommended:*** essay or personal statement.
Application deadlines: rolling (freshmen), rolling (out-of-state freshmen), rolling (transfers).
Notification: continuous (freshmen), continuous (out-of-state freshmen), continuous (transfers).

CONTACT
Mr. John Alonso, Director of Admissions, Lincoln College of New England, 2279 Mount Vernon Road, Southington, CT 06489. *Phone:* 860-628-4751 Ext. 40904. *Toll-free phone:* 800-825-0087. *Fax:* 860-628-6444. *E-mail:* jalonso@lincolncollegene.edu.

Mitchell College

New London, Connecticut

http://www.mitchell.edu/

- **Independent** 4-year, founded 1938
- **Suburban** 67-acre campus with easy access to Hartford, CT and Providence RI
- **Endowment** $8.5 million
- **Coed** 778 undergraduate students, 85% full-time, 48% women, 52% men
- **Minimally difficult** entrance level, 70% of applicants were admitted

UNDERGRAD STUDENTS
661 full-time, 117 part-time. 45% are from out of state; 14% Black or African American, non-Hispanic/Latino; 12% Hispanic/Latino; 2% Asian, non-Hispanic/Latino; 0.1% Native Hawaiian or other Pacific Islander, non-Hispanic/Latino; 2% American Indian or Alaska Native, non-Hispanic/Latino; 3% Two or more races, non-Hispanic/Latino; 2% Race/ethnicity unknown; 1% international; 6% transferred in; 55% live on campus.

Freshmen
Admission: 1,028 applied, 720 admitted, 146 enrolled.

Retention: 59% of full-time freshmen returned.

FACULTY
Total: 68, 31% full-time.

Student/faculty ratio: 16:1.

ACADEMICS
Calendar: semesters. *Degrees:* associate and bachelor's.

Special study options: advanced placement credit, cooperative education, double majors, independent study, internships, part-time degree program, services for LD students, student-designed majors, summer session for credit.

Computers: 176 computers/terminals are available on campus for general student use. Students can access the following: campus intranet, computer help desk, free student e-mail accounts, online (class) grades, online (class) schedules, online student portfolios, online course requests. Campuswide network is available. 100% of college-owned or -operated housing units are wired for high-speed Internet access. Wireless service is available via entire campus.

STUDENT LIFE
Housing options: coed, men-only, women-only. Campus housing is university owned. Freshman applicants given priority for college housing.

Activities and organizations: drama/theater group, student-run radio station, choral group, Mitchell College Drama Society, Sigma Alpha Pi Leadership Society, Behavioral Science, Early Childhood, Gaming Club.

Athletics Member NCAA. All Division III. ***Intercollegiate sports:*** baseball M, basketball M/W, cross-country running M/W, golf M, lacrosse M, sailing M/W, soccer M/W, softball W, tennis M/W, volleyball W. ***Intramural sports:*** basketball M/W, cheerleading M/W, rugby M/W, sailing M/W, soccer M/W, softball M/W, tennis M/W, volleyball M/W.

Campus security: 24-hour emergency response devices and patrols, student patrols, late-night transport/escort service, controlled dormitory access.

Student services: health clinic, personal/psychological counseling.

COSTS & FINANCIAL AID
Costs (2014–15) ***Comprehensive fee:*** $43,500 includes full-time tuition ($29,160), mandatory fees ($1840), and room and board ($12,500). Part-time tuition: $295 per credit hour. Part-time tuition and fees vary according to course load. ***College room only:*** $6500. Room and board charges vary according to housing facility. ***Payment plan:*** installment. ***Waivers:*** employees or children of employees.

Financial Aid Of all full-time matriculated undergraduates who enrolled in 2004, 491 applied for aid, 414 were judged to have need. 44 Federal Work-Study jobs (averaging $1000). In 2004, 70 non-need-based awards were made. ***Average percent of need met:*** 89. ***Average financial aid package:*** $16,357. ***Average need-based loan:*** $2904. ***Average need-based gift aid:*** $8058. ***Average non-need-based aid:*** $2890.

APPLYING
Options: electronic application, early admission, early decision, deferred entrance.

Application fee: $30.

Required: essay or personal statement, high school transcript, minimum 2.0 GPA, 1 letter of recommendation. ***Recommended:*** interview.

Application deadlines: rolling (freshmen), rolling (out-of-state freshmen), rolling (transfers).

Early decision deadline: 11/15.

Notification: continuous (freshmen), continuous (out-of-state freshmen), continuous (transfers), 12/1 (early decision).

CONTACT
Mr. Bob Martin, Director of Admissions, Mitchell College, 437 Pequot Avenue, New London, CT 06320. *Phone:* 860-701-5178. *Toll-free phone:* 800-443-2811. *Fax:* 860-444-1209. *E-mail:* admissions@mitchell.edu.

Paier College of Art, Inc.

Hamden, Connecticut

http://www.paiercollegeofart.edu/

- **Proprietary** 4-year, founded 1946
- **Suburban** 3-acre campus with easy access to New York City
- **Coed** 129 undergraduate students, 71% full-time, 62% women, 38% men

UNDERGRAD STUDENTS
91 full-time, 38 part-time. Students come from 2 states and territories; 5% Black or African American, non-Hispanic/Latino; 11% Hispanic/Latino; 4% Asian, non-Hispanic/Latino; 2% Two or more races, non-Hispanic/Latino; 8% Race/ethnicity unknown; 5% transferred in.

Freshmen
Admission: 22 enrolled. ***Average high school GPA:*** 3.5. ***Test scores:*** SAT critical reading scores over 500: 55%; SAT math scores over 500: 28%.

Retention: 92% of full-time freshmen returned.

FACULTY
Total: 36, 22% full-time, 67% with terminal degrees.

Student/faculty ratio: 4:1.

ACADEMICS
Calendar: semesters plus 1 summer session. *Degree:* certificates, diplomas, and bachelor's.

Special study options: academic remediation for entering students, advanced placement credit, independent study, part-time degree program, services for LD students, study abroad.

Computers: 49 computers/terminals are available on campus for general student use. Wireless service is available via entire campus.

STUDENT LIFE
Housing options: college housing not available.

Activities and organizations: student-run newspaper, Student Council, School Newspaper.

COSTS & FINANCIAL AID
Costs (2014–15) ***Tuition:*** $14,000 full-time, $460 per credit part-time. Full-time tuition and fees vary according to degree level. Part-time tuition and fees vary according to course load. ***Required fees:*** $360 full-time, $460 per credit part-time, $125 per semester part-time. ***Payment plan:*** installment.

Financial Aid Of all full-time matriculated undergraduates who enrolled in 1999, 102 applied for aid, 92 were judged to have need, 1 had their need fully met. ***Average percent of need met:*** 62. ***Average financial aid package:*** $6717. ***Average need-based loan:*** $3446. ***Average need-based gift aid:*** $3460. ***Average indebtedness upon graduation:*** $13,536.

APPLYING
Standardized Tests *Required:* SAT or ACT (for admission).

Required: high school transcript, minimum 2.0 GPA, 2 letters of recommendation, interview, Portfolio Interview. ***Recommended:*** essay or personal statement.

CONTACT
Mrs. Lynn Pascale, Admissions Secretary, Paier College of Art, Inc., 20 Gorham Avenue, Hamden, CT 06514 . *Phone:* 203-287-3031. *Fax:* 203-287-3021. *E-mail:* paier.admission@snet.net.

★ Post University
Waterbury, Connecticut
http://www.post.edu/

- **Independent** comprehensive, founded 1890
- **Suburban** 70-acre campus with easy access to Hartford
- **Coed** 731 undergraduate students, 97% full-time, 46% women, 54% men
- **Moderately difficult** entrance level, 54% of applicants were admitted

UNDERGRAD STUDENTS
708 full-time, 23 part-time. Students come from 25 states and territories; 17 other countries; 33% are from out of state; 23% Black or African American, non-Hispanic/Latino; 9% Hispanic/Latino; 2% Asian, non-Hispanic/Latino; 0.1% Native Hawaiian or other Pacific Islander, non-Hispanic/Latino; 0.7% American Indian or Alaska Native, non-Hispanic/Latino; 2% Two or more races, non-Hispanic/Latino; 18% Race/ethnicity unknown; 3% international; 8% transferred in; 52% live on campus.

Freshmen
Admission: 1,208 applied, 648 admitted, 185 enrolled. ***Average high school GPA:*** 2.63. ***Test scores:*** SAT critical reading scores over 500: 16%; SAT math scores over 500: 19%; SAT writing scores over 500: 19%; ACT scores over 18: 71%; SAT critical reading scores over 600: 2%; SAT math scores over 600: 2%; SAT writing scores over 600: 1%; ACT scores over 24: 41%; ACT scores over 30: 2%.

Retention: 57% of full-time freshmen returned.

FACULTY
Total: 133, 23% full-time, 38% with terminal degrees.

Student/faculty ratio: 9:1.

ACADEMICS
Calendar: semesters (modular courses offered in the evening). *Degrees:* certificates, associate, bachelor's, and master's.

Special study options: accelerated degree program, advanced placement credit, cooperative education, distance learning, double majors, English as a second language, freshman honors college, honors programs, independent study, internships, off-campus study, part-time degree program, services for LD students, summer session for credit.

Computers: 150 computers/terminals and 150 ports are available on campus for general student use. Students can access the following: campus intranet, computer help desk, free student e-mail accounts, online (class) grades, online (class) registration, online (class) schedules, software applications. Campuswide network is available. 100% of college-owned or -operated housing units are wired for high-speed Internet access. Wireless service is available via entire campus.

STUDENT LIFE
Housing options: coed. Campus housing is university owned. Freshman campus housing is guaranteed.

Activities and organizations: drama/theater group, choral group, Equine Club, Newman Club, GSA, Accounting Club, Choir.

Athletics Member NCAA. All Division II. ***Intercollegiate sports:*** baseball M(s), basketball M(s)/W(s), cross-country running M(s)/W(s), equestrian sports M(c)/W(c), football M(c), golf M(s)/W(s), lacrosse M(s)/W(s), soccer M(s)/W(s), softball W(s), tennis M(s)/W(s), track and field M(s)/W(s), volleyball W(s). ***Intramural sports:*** basketball M/W, bowling W.

Campus security: 24-hour emergency response devices and patrols, late-night transport/escort service, controlled dormitory access, Annual and Semi-annual Emergency Preparedness Training for students and staff.

Student services: health clinic, personal/psychological counseling.

COSTS & FINANCIAL AID
Costs (2014–15) ***Comprehensive fee:*** $37,850 includes full-time tuition ($26,250), mandatory fees ($1100), and room and board ($10,500). Part-time tuition: $875 per credit. Part-time tuition and fees vary according to class time. ***Room and board:*** Room and board charges vary according to housing facility. ***Payment plans:*** tuition prepayment, installment. ***Waivers:*** senior citizens and employees or children of employees.

Financial Aid Of all full-time matriculated undergraduates who enrolled in 2013, 647 applied for aid, 613 were judged to have need, 82 had their need fully met. In 2013, 19 non-need-based awards were made. ***Average percent of need met:*** 59. ***Average financial aid package:*** $19,779. ***Average need-based loan:*** $4443. ***Average need-based gift aid:*** $15,419. ***Average non-need-based aid:*** $8425. ***Average indebtedness upon graduation:*** $15,995.

APPLYING
Standardized Tests *Required:* SAT or ACT (for admission).

Options: electronic application, deferred entrance.

Application fee: $40.

Required: high school transcript, minimum 2.0 GPA, 1 letter of recommendation. ***Recommended:*** essay or personal statement, interview.

Application deadlines: rolling (freshmen), rolling (out-of-state freshmen), rolling (transfers).

Notification: continuous (freshmen), continuous (out-of-state freshmen), continuous (transfers).

CONTACT
Kathryn Reilly, Director of Admissions, Main Campus, Post University, PO Box 2540, Waterbury, CT 06723. *Phone:* 203-596-4630. *Toll-free phone:* 800-345-2562. *Fax:* 203-756-5810. *E-mail:* admiss@post.edu.

★ Quinnipiac University
Hamden, Connecticut
http://www.quinnipiac.edu/

- **Independent** comprehensive, founded 1929
- **Suburban** 600-acre campus with easy access to New Haven, Hartford
- **Endowment** $348.9 million
- **Coed** 6,553 undergraduate students, 97% full-time, 60% women, 40% men
- **Moderately difficult** entrance level, 66% of applicants were admitted

UNDERGRAD STUDENTS
6,335 full-time, 218 part-time. Students come from 30 states and territories; 30 other countries; 74% are from out of state; 5% Black or African American, non-Hispanic/Latino; 9% Hispanic/Latino; 3% Asian, non-Hispanic/Latino; 0.1% Native Hawaiian or other Pacific Islander, non-Hispanic/Latino; 0.2% American Indian or Alaska Native, non-Hispanic/Latino; 2% Two or more races, non-Hispanic/Latino; 3% Race/ethnicity unknown; 2% international; 3% transferred in; 78% live on campus.

Freshmen
Admission: 23,240 applied, 15,318 admitted, 1,656 enrolled. ***Average high school GPA:*** 3.4. ***Test scores:*** SAT critical reading scores over 500: 73%; SAT math scores over 500: 80%; ACT scores over 18: 99%; SAT critical reading scores over 600: 21%; SAT math scores over 600: 31%; ACT scores over 24: 65%; SAT critical reading scores over 700: 1%; SAT math scores over 700: 2%; ACT scores over 30: 7%.

Retention: 87% of full-time freshmen returned.

FACULTY
Total: 921, 43% full-time, 55% with terminal degrees.

Student/faculty ratio: 11:1.

ACADEMICS
Calendar: semesters. *Degrees:* bachelor's, master's, doctoral, post-master's, and postbachelor's certificates.

Special study options: accelerated degree program, advanced placement credit, distance learning, double majors, honors programs, independent study, internships, part-time degree program, services for LD students, study abroad, summer session for credit. ***ROTC:*** Army (c), Air Force (c).

Computers: 600 computers/terminals and 2,500 ports are available on campus for general student use. Students can access the following: campus intranet, computer help desk, free student e-mail accounts, online (class) grades, online (class) registration, online (class) schedules, e-commerce 'Q' card for local merchants, food service, dorm card access. Campuswide network is available. 100% of college-owned or -operated housing units are wired for high-speed Internet access. Wireless service is available via entire campus.

STUDENT LIFE
Housing options: coed. Campus housing is university owned. Freshman campus housing is guaranteed.

Activities and organizations: drama/theater group, student-run newspaper, radio and television station, choral group, student government,

Social Programming Board, Drama Club, Chronicle (student newspaper), dance company, national fraternities, national sororities.

Athletics Member NCAA. All Division I. ***Intercollegiate sports:*** baseball M(s), basketball M(s)/W(s), cross-country running M(s)/W(s), field hockey W(s), golf W(s), gymnastics W(s), ice hockey M(s)/W(s), lacrosse M(s)/W(s), rugby W(s), soccer M(s)/W(s), softball W(s), tennis M(s)/W(s), track and field W(s), volleyball W(s). ***Intramural sports:*** baseball M, basketball M/W, bowling M/W, field hockey W, soccer M/W, softball W, tennis M/W, volleyball M/W.

Campus security: 24-hour emergency response devices and patrols, late-night transport/escort service, controlled dormitory access, text message emergency notification system.

Student services: health clinic, personal/psychological counseling.

COSTS & FINANCIAL AID

Costs (2015–16) ***Comprehensive fee:*** $57,090 includes full-time tuition ($42,270) and room and board ($14,820). Part-time tuition: $965 per credit. Part-time tuition and fees vary according to class time and course load. ***Required fees:*** $38 per credit part-time. ***Room and board:*** Room and board charges vary according to housing facility. ***Payment plan:*** installment. ***Waivers:*** employees or children of employees.

Financial Aid Of all full-time matriculated undergraduates who enrolled in 2014, 4,595 applied for aid, 3,912 were judged to have need, 541 had their need fully met. 1,713 Federal Work-Study jobs (averaging $2047). In 2014, 1342 non-need-based awards were made. ***Average percent of need met:*** 65. ***Average financial aid package:*** $25,571. ***Average need-based loan:*** $4667. ***Average need-based gift aid:*** $19,741. ***Average non-need-based aid:*** $14,155. ***Average indebtedness upon graduation:*** $45,711.

APPLYING

Standardized Tests *Required:* SAT or ACT (for admission).

Options: electronic application, early decision, deferred entrance.

Application fee: $65.

Required: essay or personal statement, high school transcript, 1 letter of recommendation. ***Required for some:*** minimum 3.0 GPA. ***Recommended:*** minimum 3.0 GPA, interview.

Application deadlines: 2/1 (freshmen), 2/1 (out-of-state freshmen), 4/1 (transfers).

Early decision deadline: 11/1.

Notification: continuous (freshmen), continuous (out-of-state freshmen), continuous (transfers).

CONTACT

Ms. Joan Isaac-Mohr, Vice President for Admissions and Financial Aid, Quinnipiac University, 275 Mount Carmel Avenue, Hamden, CT 06518. *Phone:* 203-582-8600. *Toll-free phone:* 800-462-1944. *Fax:* 203-582-8906. *E-mail:* admissions@quinnipiac.edu.

See below for display ad and page 1572 for the College Close-Up.

Sacred Heart University

Fairfield, Connecticut

http://www.sacredheart.edu/

- **Independent Roman Catholic** comprehensive, founded 1963
- **Suburban** 100-acre campus with easy access to New York City
- **Endowment** $137.3 million
- **Coed** 4,997 undergraduate students, 85% full-time, 64% women, 36% men
- **Moderately difficult** entrance level, 57% of applicants were admitted

UNDERGRAD STUDENTS

4,232 full-time, 765 part-time. Students come from 43 states and territories; 18 other countries; 60% are from out of state; 4% Black or African American, non-Hispanic/Latino; 7% Hispanic/Latino; 2% Asian, non-Hispanic/Latino; 0.1% Native Hawaiian or other Pacific Islander, non-Hispanic/Latino; 0.2% American Indian or Alaska Native, non-Hispanic/Latino; 1% Two or more races, non-Hispanic/Latino; 16% Race/ethnicity unknown; 1% international; 2% transferred in; 53% live on campus.

Freshmen

Admission: 9,114 applied, 5,209 admitted, 1,385 enrolled. ***Average high school GPA:*** 3.3. ***Test scores:*** SAT critical reading scores over 500: 78%; SAT math scores over 500: 88%; ACT scores over 18: 190%; SAT critical

reading scores over 600: 13%; SAT math scores over 600: 22%; ACT scores over 24: 111%; SAT critical reading scores over 700: 1%; SAT math scores over 700: 1%; ACT scores over 30: 7%.

Retention: 82% of full-time freshmen returned.

FACULTY
Total: 733, 36% full-time, 44% with terminal degrees.

Student/faculty ratio: 15:1.

ACADEMICS
Calendar: semesters. *Degrees:* bachelor's, master's, doctoral, post-master's, and postbachelor's certificates (also offers part-time program with significant enrollment not reflected in profile).

Special study options: academic remediation for entering students, accelerated degree program, adult/continuing education programs, advanced placement credit, cooperative education, distance learning, double majors, English as a second language, honors programs, independent study, internships, off-campus study, part-time degree program, services for LD students, student-designed majors, study abroad, summer session for credit. ***ROTC:*** Army (c).

Unusual degree programs: 3-2 occupational therapy.

Computers: Students can access the following: campus intranet, computer help desk, free student e-mail accounts, online (class) grades, online (class) registration, online (class) schedules. Campuswide network is available. 100% of college-owned or -operated housing units are wired for high-speed Internet access. Wireless service is available via entire campus.

STUDENT LIFE
Housing options: on-campus residence required through sophomore year; coed, special housing for students with disabilities. Campus housing is university owned and leased by the school. Freshman campus housing is guaranteed.

Activities and organizations: drama/theater group, student-run newspaper, radio and television station, choral group, marching band, Student Nurses Association, Concert Choir, S.E.T., Pre-PT Club, SHU Dance Ensemble, national fraternities, national sororities.

Athletics Member NCAA. All Division I except football (Division I-AA). ***Intercollegiate sports:*** baseball M(s), basketball M(s)/W(s), bowling W(s), cheerleading W(c), crew W, cross-country running M(s)/W(s), equestrian sports W, fencing M/W, field hockey W(s), golf M(s)/W(s), ice hockey M(s)/W, lacrosse M(s)/W(s), soccer M(s)/W(s), softball W(s), swimming and diving W(s), tennis M(s)/W(s), track and field M(s)/W(s), volleyball M/W(s), wrestling M(s). ***Intramural sports:*** baseball M(c), basketball M(c)/W(c), bowling M(c), cross-country running M(c)/W(c), field hockey W(c), golf M(c)/W(c), gymnastics W(c), ice hockey M(c), lacrosse M(c)/W(c), rugby M(c)/W(c), sailing M(c)/W(c), soccer M(c)/W(c), softball W, tennis M(c)/W(c), ultimate Frisbee M(c)/W(c), volleyball M(c)/W(c), weight lifting W(c).

Campus security: 24-hour emergency response devices and patrols, late-night transport/escort service, controlled dormitory access, Campus Emergency Plan, Personal Safety Escort Program, Security Alarm Systems, Crime Prevention Announcements, Security Surveys.

Student services: health clinic, personal/psychological counseling.

COSTS & FINANCIAL AID
Costs (2014–15) ***Comprehensive fee:*** $49,264 includes full-time tuition ($35,500), mandatory fees ($250), and room and board ($13,514). Full-time tuition and fees vary according to location and program. Part-time tuition: $545 per credit hour. Part-time tuition and fees vary according to course load, location, and program. ***Required fees:*** $115 per term part-time. ***College room only:*** $9474. Room and board charges vary according to board plan and housing facility. ***Payment plan:*** installment. ***Waivers:*** employees or children of employees.

Financial Aid Of all full-time matriculated undergraduates who enrolled in 2013, 3,596 applied for aid, 2,579 were judged to have need, 374 had their need fully met. 933 Federal Work-Study jobs (averaging $732). 562 state and other part-time jobs (averaging $597). In 2013, 754 non-need-based awards were made. ***Average percent of need met:*** 57. ***Average financial aid package:*** $19,052. ***Average need-based loan:*** $5003. ***Average need-based gift aid:*** $15,037. ***Average non-need-based aid:*** $8572. ***Average indebtedness upon graduation:*** $45,746.

APPLYING
Standardized Tests *Recommended:* Test-Optional Admissions Policy, SAT/ACT scores will be considered if submitted.

Options: electronic application, early admission, early decision.

Application fee: $50.

Required: high school transcript, 1 letter of recommendation. ***Required for some:*** interview, interview for Early Decision candidates. ***Recommended:*** essay or personal statement, interview.

Early decision deadline: 12/1.

Notification: continuous (freshmen), continuous (transfers), 12/15 (early decision).

CONTACT
Mr. Kenneth Higgins, Director of Undergraduate Admissions, Sacred Heart University, 5151 Park Avenue, Fairfield, CT 06825-1000. *Phone:* 203-610-9388. *Fax:* 203-365-7607. *E-mail:* higginsk2288@sacredheart.edu.

★ Southern Connecticut State University

New Haven, Connecticut

http://www.southernct.edu/

- **State-supported** comprehensive, founded 1893, part of Connecticut State Colleges & Universities (ConnSCU)
- **Suburban** 168-acre campus with easy access to New York City
- **Endowment** $14.7 million
- **Coed** 8,133 undergraduate students, 84% full-time, 60% women, 40% men
- **Moderately difficult** entrance level, 72% of applicants were admitted

UNDERGRAD STUDENTS
6,802 full-time, 1,331 part-time. Students come from 32 states and territories; 14 other countries; 4% are from out of state; 16% Black or African American, non-Hispanic/Latino; 12% Hispanic/Latino; 3% Asian, non-Hispanic/Latino; 0.2% American Indian or Alaska Native, non-Hispanic/Latino; 2% Two or more races, non-Hispanic/Latino; 9% Race/ethnicity unknown; 0.4% international; 9% transferred in; 31% live on campus.

Freshmen
Admission: 4,568 applied, 3,268 admitted, 1,286 enrolled. ***Average high school GPA:*** 2.9. ***Test scores:*** SAT critical reading scores over 500: 36%; SAT math scores over 500: 33%; SAT writing scores over 500: 39%; ACT scores over 18: 72%; SAT critical reading scores over 600: 7%; SAT math scores over 600: 4%; SAT writing scores over 600: 7%; ACT scores over 24: 16%; ACT scores over 30: 1%.

Retention: 75% of full-time freshmen returned.

FACULTY
Total: 1,005, 44% full-time, 46% with terminal degrees.

Student/faculty ratio: 14:1.

ACADEMICS
Calendar: semesters. *Degrees:* bachelor's, master's, doctoral, post-master's, and postbachelor's certificates.

Special study options: academic remediation for entering students, accelerated degree program, advanced placement credit, cooperative education, distance learning, double majors, freshman honors college, honors programs, independent study, internships, off-campus study, part-time degree program, services for LD students, student-designed majors, study abroad, summer session for credit. ***ROTC:*** Army (c), Air Force (c).

Computers: 800 computers/terminals are available on campus for general student use. Students can access the following: computer help desk, free student e-mail accounts, online (class) grades, online (class) registration, online (class) schedules. Campuswide network is available. 100% of college-owned or -operated housing units are wired for high-speed Internet access. Wireless service is available via entire campus.

STUDENT LIFE
Housing options: coed, special housing for students with disabilities. Campus housing is university owned. Freshman campus housing is guaranteed.

Activities and organizations: drama/theater group, student-run newspaper, radio and television station, choral group, marching band, Student Government Association, Psychology Club, Habitat for Humanity, Crescent Players, Black Student Union, national fraternities, national sororities.

Athletics Member NCAA. All Division II. ***Intercollegiate sports:*** baseball M(s), basketball M(s)/W(s), cheerleading M(c)/W(c), cross-country running M(s)/W(s), field hockey W(s), football M(s), gymnastics W(s), lacrosse W(s), rugby M(c)/W(c), soccer M(s)/W(s), softball W(s), swimming and diving M(s)/W(s), track and field M(s)/W(s), ultimate Frisbee M(c)/W(c), volleyball W(s). ***Intramural sports:*** badminton M/W, basketball M/W, football M/W, ice hockey M(c)/W(c), soccer M/W, softball M/W, tennis M/W, volleyball M/W.

Campus security: 24-hour emergency response devices and patrols, late-night transport/escort service, controlled dormitory access.

Student services: health clinic, personal/psychological counseling, women's center.

COSTS & FINANCIAL AID

Costs (2014–15) ***Tuition:*** state resident $4600 full-time, $457 per credit hour part-time; nonresident $14,886 full-time, $471 per credit hour part-time. Full-time tuition and fees vary according to course load and reciprocity agreements. Part-time tuition and fees vary according to course load. ***Required fees:*** $4557 full-time, $55 per term part-time. ***Room and board:*** $11,289; room only: $6216. Room and board charges vary according to board plan and housing facility. ***Payment plans:*** installment, deferred payment. ***Waivers:*** senior citizens and employees or children of employees.

Financial Aid Of all full-time matriculated undergraduates who enrolled in 2014, 5,465 applied for aid, 4,609 were judged to have need, 737 had their need fully met. 128 Federal Work-Study jobs (averaging $3420). In 2014, 251 non-need-based awards were made. ***Average percent of need met:*** 69. ***Average financial aid package:*** $13,602. ***Average need-based loan:*** $4829. ***Average need-based gift aid:*** $6592. ***Average non-need-based aid:*** $5796. ***Average indebtedness upon graduation:*** $23,781. ***Financial aid deadline:*** 3/9.

APPLYING

Standardized Tests *Required:* SAT or ACT (for admission).

Options: electronic application, deferred entrance.

Application fee: $50.

Required: essay or personal statement, high school transcript.

Application deadlines: rolling (freshmen), 8/1 (transfers).

Notification: continuous (freshmen), continuous (transfers).

CONTACT

Mrs. Alexis S. Haakonsen, Associate Director of Admissions, Southern Connecticut State University, Admissions House, 131 Farnham Avenue, New Haven, CT 06515-1202. *Phone:* 203-392-5652. *Fax:* 203-392-5727. *E-mail:* haakonsena1@southernct.edu.

★ Trinity College

Hartford, Connecticut

http://www.trincoll.edu/

- **Independent** comprehensive, founded 1823
- **Urban** 100-acre campus
- **Endowment** $542.8 million
- **Coed** 2,255 undergraduate students, 95% full-time, 47% women, 53% men
- **Most difficult** entrance level, 33% of applicants were admitted

UNDERGRAD STUDENTS

2,146 full-time, 109 part-time. Students come from 44 states and territories; 62 other countries; 84% are from out of state; 6% Black or African American, non-Hispanic/Latino; 7% Hispanic/Latino; 4% Asian, non-Hispanic/Latino; 0.1% American Indian or Alaska Native, non-Hispanic/Latino; 3% Two or more races, non-Hispanic/Latino; 5% Race/ethnicity unknown; 10% international; 1% transferred in; 90% live on campus.

Freshmen

Admission: 7,507 applied, 2,480 admitted, 611 enrolled. ***Test scores:*** SAT critical reading scores over 500: 97%; SAT math scores over 500: 98%; SAT writing scores over 500: 96%; ACT scores over 18: 100%; SAT

critical reading scores over 600: 59%; SAT math scores over 600: 70%; SAT writing scores over 600: 68%; ACT scores over 24: 96%; SAT critical reading scores over 700: 13%; SAT math scores over 700: 20%; SAT writing scores over 700: 18%; ACT scores over 30: 37%.

Retention: 89% of full-time freshmen returned.

FACULTY

Total: 295, 65% full-time, 82% with terminal degrees.

Student/faculty ratio: 10:1.

ACADEMICS

Calendar: semesters. *Degrees:* bachelor's and master's.

Special study options: accelerated degree program, adult/continuing education programs, advanced placement credit, double majors, honors programs, independent study, internships, off-campus study, part-time degree program, student-designed majors, study abroad, summer session for credit. ***ROTC:*** Army (c).

Unusual degree programs: 3-2 engineering with Rensselaer Polytechnic Institute.

Computers: 249 computers/terminals and 3,000 ports are available on campus for general student use. Students can access the following: campus intranet, computer help desk, free student e-mail accounts, online (class) grades, online (class) registration, online (class) schedules, Web pages. Campuswide network is available. 100% of college-owned or -operated housing units are wired for high-speed Internet access. Wireless service is available via classrooms, computer centers, computer labs, learning centers, libraries, student centers.

STUDENT LIFE

Housing options: on-campus residence required for freshman year; coed, special housing for students with disabilities. Campus housing is university owned. Freshman campus housing is guaranteed.

Activities and organizations: drama/theater group, student-run newspaper, radio station, choral group, Friends Active in Community Engagement and Service (FACES), The Mill, Student Government Association, Relay for Life, Multi-Cultural Affairs Council, national fraternities, national sororities.

Athletics Member NCAA. All Division III. ***Intercollegiate sports:*** baseball M, basketball M/W, crew M/W, cross-country running M/W, equestrian sports M(c)/W(c), fencing M(c)/W(c), football M, golf M, ice hockey M/W, lacrosse M/W, rugby M(c)/W(c), sailing M(c)/W(c), skiing (downhill) M(c)/W(c), soccer M/W, softball W, squash M/W, swimming and diving M/W, tennis M/W, track and field M/W, ultimate Frisbee M(c)/W(c), volleyball W, water polo M(c)/W(c), wrestling M. ***Intramural sports:*** badminton M/W, basketball M/W, soccer M/W, softball M/W, squash M/W, tennis M/W.

Campus security: 24-hour emergency response devices and patrols, late-night transport/escort service, controlled dormitory access.

Student services: health clinic, personal/psychological counseling, women's center.

COSTS & FINANCIAL AID

Costs (2015–16) ***One-time required fee:*** $25. ***Comprehensive fee:*** $63,920 includes full-time tuition ($48,446), mandatory fees ($2330), and room and board ($13,144). Full-time tuition and fees vary according to course load and program. Part-time tuition and fees vary according to course load and program. ***College room only:*** $8550. Room and board charges vary according to board plan. ***Payment plan:*** installment. ***Waivers:*** adult students and employees or children of employees.

Financial Aid Of all full-time matriculated undergraduates who enrolled in 2014, 989 applied for aid, 913 were judged to have need, 913 had their need fully met. 791 Federal Work-Study jobs (averaging $1797). In 2014, 82 non-need-based awards were made. ***Average percent of need met:*** 100. ***Average financial aid package:*** $44,424. ***Average need-based loan:*** $4583. ***Average need-based gift aid:*** $41,684. ***Average non-need-based aid:*** $24,836. ***Average indebtedness upon graduation:*** $28,237. ***Financial aid deadline:*** 3/1.

APPLYING

Standardized Tests *Required for some:* SAT or ACT (for admission), SAT Subject Tests (for admission).

Options: electronic application, early admission, early decision, deferred entrance.

Application fee: $60.

Required: essay or personal statement, high school transcript, 3 letters of recommendation. ***Recommended:*** interview.

Application deadlines: 1/1 (freshmen), 4/1 (transfers).

Early decision deadline: 11/15 (for plan 1), 1/1 (for plan 2).

Notification: 4/1 (freshmen), 6/10 (transfers), 12/15 (early decision plan 1), 2/15 (early decision plan 2).

CONTACT

Trinity College, 300 Summit Street, Hartford, CT 06106-3100. *Phone:* 860-297-2180.

See previous page for display ad and page 1650 for the College Close-Up.

★ United States Coast Guard Academy

New London, Connecticut

http://www.uscga.edu/

- **Federally supported** 4-year, founded 1876
- **Suburban** 103-acre campus with easy access to Providence, Hartford
- **Endowment** $1.3 million
- **Coed** 902 undergraduate students, 100% full-time, 34% women, 66% men
- **Very difficult** entrance level, 16% of applicants were admitted

UNDERGRAD STUDENTS

902 full-time. Students come from 52 states and territories; 13 other countries; 94% are from out of state; 2% Black or African American, non-Hispanic/Latino; 13% Hispanic/Latino; 5% Asian, non-Hispanic/Latino; 0.7% Native Hawaiian or other Pacific Islander, non-Hispanic/Latino; 0.7% American Indian or Alaska Native, non-Hispanic/Latino; 7% Two or more races, non-Hispanic/Latino; 2% Race/ethnicity unknown; 3% international; 100% live on campus.

Freshmen

Admission: 1,992 applied, 328 admitted, 217 enrolled. ***Average high school GPA:*** 3.92. ***Test scores:*** SAT critical reading scores over 500: 96%; SAT math scores over 500: 100%; SAT writing scores over 500: 94%; ACT scores over 18: 100%; SAT critical reading scores over 600: 66%; SAT math scores over 600: 90%; SAT writing scores over 600: 58%; ACT scores over 24: 91%; SAT critical reading scores over 700: 15%; SAT math scores over 700: 25%; SAT writing scores over 700: 12%; ACT scores over 30: 29%.

Retention: 94% of full-time freshmen returned.

FACULTY

Total: 140, 90% full-time, 53% with terminal degrees.

Student/faculty ratio: 7:1.

ACADEMICS

Calendar: semesters. *Degree:* bachelor's.

Special study options: academic remediation for entering students, advanced placement credit, double majors, honors programs, independent study, internships, off-campus study, summer session for credit.

Computers: 280 computers/terminals are available on campus for general student use. Students can access the following: campus intranet, computer help desk, free student e-mail accounts, online (class) grades, online (class) schedules. Campuswide network is available. 100% of college-owned or -operated housing units are wired for high-speed Internet access. Wireless service is available via classrooms, dorm rooms, libraries, student centers.

STUDENT LIFE

Housing options: on-campus residence required through senior year; coed. Campus housing is university owned. Freshman campus housing is guaranteed.

Activities and organizations: drama/theater group, choral group, marching band, Club Sports, Musical activities, Multicultural Club, Officers Christian Fellowship, International Dance Club.

Athletics Member NCAA. All Division III. ***Intercollegiate sports:*** baseball M, basketball M/W, cheerleading W(c), crew M/W, cross-country running M/W, football M, ice hockey M(c)/W(c), lacrosse M(c)/W(c), riflery M/W, rugby M(c)/W(c), sailing M/W, soccer M/W, softball W, swimming and diving M/W, tennis M, track and field M/W, volleyball W, water polo M(c)/W(c), wrestling M. ***Intramural sports:*** basketball M/W, bowling M/W, equestrian sports M(c)/W(c), fencing M(c)/W(c), football M, golf M/W, racquetball M/W, sailing M/W, skiing (downhill) M/W, soccer M/W, softball M/W, table tennis M/W, track and field M/W, ultimate Frisbee M/W, volleyball M/W, water polo M/W, weight lifting M/W, wrestling M.

Campus security: 24-hour patrols, late-night transport/escort service, controlled dormitory access, Cadets staff a 24 hour Watch Office.

Student services: health clinic, personal/psychological counseling, legal services.

COSTS

Costs (2014–15) ***Comprehensive fee:*** Tuition, room and board, and medical and dental care are provided by the US government. Each cadet receives a salary from which to pay for uniforms, supplies, and personal expenses.

APPLYING

Standardized Tests *Required:* SAT or ACT (for admission).

Options: electronic application, early action, deferred entrance.

Required: essay or personal statement, high school transcript, 3 letters of recommendation, Medical examination, Physical Fitness examination. ***Recommended:*** interview.

Application deadlines: 2/1 (freshmen), 2/1 (out-of-state freshmen), 2/1 (transfers), 11/15 (early action).

Notification: continuous until 4/15 (freshmen), continuous until 4/15 (out-of-state freshmen), continuous until 4/15 (transfers), 2/1 (early action).

CONTACT

Mr. Daniel V. Pinch, Associate Director of Admissions for Outreach, United States Coast Guard Academy, 31 Mohegan Avenue, New London, CT 06320-4195. *Phone:* 860-444-8503. *Toll-free phone:* 800-883-8724. *Fax:* 860-701-6700. *E-mail:* daniel.v.pinch@uscga.edu.

University of Bridgeport

Bridgeport, Connecticut

http://www.bridgeport.edu/

- **Independent** comprehensive, founded 1927
- **Urban** 86-acre campus with easy access to New York City
- **Endowment** $30.7 million
- **Coed** 3,021 undergraduate students, 75% full-time, 65% women, 35% men
- **Moderately difficult** entrance level, 61% of applicants were admitted

UNDERGRAD STUDENTS

2,254 full-time, 767 part-time. Students come from 38 states and territories; 50 other countries; 36% are from out of state; 38% Black or African American, non-Hispanic/Latino; 17% Hispanic/Latino; 3% Asian, non-Hispanic/Latino; 0.3% Native Hawaiian or other Pacific Islander, non-Hispanic/Latino; 0.8% American Indian or Alaska Native, non-Hispanic/Latino; 2% Two or more races, non-Hispanic/Latino; 15% international; 8% transferred in; 42% live on campus.

Freshmen

Admission: 5,990 applied, 3,637 admitted, 537 enrolled. ***Average high school GPA:*** 2.91. ***Test scores:*** SAT critical reading scores over 500: 25%; SAT math scores over 500: 25%; SAT writing scores over 500: 25%; ACT scores over 18: 58%; SAT critical reading scores over 600: 4%; SAT math scores over 600: 4%; SAT writing scores over 600: 4%; ACT scores over 24: 16%; SAT critical reading scores over 700: 1%; SAT math scores over 700: 1%; SAT writing scores over 700: 1%.

Retention: 67% of full-time freshmen returned.

FACULTY

Total: 462, 27% full-time.

Student/faculty ratio: 17:1.

ACADEMICS

Calendar: semesters. *Degrees:* certificates, associate, bachelor's, master's, doctoral, post-master's, and postbachelor's certificates.

Special study options: academic remediation for entering students, accelerated degree program, adult/continuing education programs, advanced placement credit, cooperative education, distance learning, double majors, English as a second language, honors programs, independent study, internships, off-campus study, part-time degree program, services for LD students, student-designed majors, study abroad, summer session for credit.

Computers: 300 computers/terminals and 300 ports are available on campus for general student use. Students can access the following: computer help desk, free student e-mail accounts, online (class) grades, online (class) registration, online (class) schedules. Campuswide network is available. 100% of college-owned or -operated housing units are wired for high-speed Internet access. Wireless service is available via classrooms, computer centers, computer labs, dorm rooms, learning centers, libraries, student centers.

STUDENT LIFE

Housing options: on-campus residence required through sophomore year; coed. Campus housing is university owned. Freshman campus housing is guaranteed.

Activities and organizations: student-run newspaper, choral group, Student Congress, International Relations Club, Black Students Alliance, Latin America Club, Martial Arts Club, national fraternities, national sororities.

Athletics Member NCAA. All Division II. ***Intercollegiate sports:*** baseball M(s), basketball M(s)/W(s), cross-country running M(s)/W(s), gymnastics W(s), lacrosse W(s), soccer M(s)/W(s), softball W(s), swimming and diving M(s)/W(s), volleyball W(s). ***Intramural sports:*** basketball M/W, football M/W, golf M/W, racquetball M/W, soccer M/W, softball M/W, tennis M/W.

Campus security: 24-hour emergency response devices and patrols, student patrols, late-night transport/escort service, controlled dormitory access.

Student services: health clinic, personal/psychological counseling.

COSTS & FINANCIAL AID

Costs (2014–15) ***Comprehensive fee:*** $42,630 includes full-time tuition ($27,900), mandatory fees ($2020), and room and board ($12,710). Full-time tuition and fees vary according to course load and program. Part-time tuition: $930 per credit hour. Part-time tuition and fees vary according to course load and program. ***Required fees:*** $200 per term part-time. ***Room and board:*** Room and board charges vary according to board plan and housing facility. ***Payment plans:*** installment, deferred payment. ***Waivers:*** senior citizens and employees or children of employees.

Financial Aid Of all full-time matriculated undergraduates who enrolled in 2013, 1,709 applied for aid, 1,648 were judged to have need, 61 had their need fully met. 339 Federal Work-Study jobs (averaging $1100). In 2013, 265 non-need-based awards were made. ***Average percent of need met:*** 59. ***Average financial aid package:*** $24,745. ***Average need-based loan:*** $7167. ***Average need-based gift aid:*** $7750. ***Average non-need-based aid:*** $8815. ***Average indebtedness upon graduation:*** $22,900.

APPLYING

Standardized Tests *Required:* SAT or ACT (for admission).

Options: electronic application, early admission, deferred entrance.

Application fee: $25.

Required: essay or personal statement, high school transcript, minimum 2.0 GPA. ***Required for some:*** 2 letters of recommendation, interview, portfolio, audition. ***Recommended:*** 1 letter of recommendation, interview.

Application deadlines: rolling (freshmen), rolling (out-of-state freshmen), rolling (transfers).

Notification: continuous (freshmen), continuous (out-of-state freshmen), continuous (transfers).

CONTACT

Ms. Jessica N Crowley Goddu, Director of Undergraduate Admissions, University of Bridgeport, 126 Park Avenue, Bridgeport, CT 06604. *Phone:* 203-576-4812. *Toll-free phone:* 800-EXCEL-UB. *Fax:* 203-576-4941. *E-mail:* admit@bridgeport.edu.

University of Connecticut
Storrs, Connecticut
http://www.uconn.edu/

- **State-supported** university, founded 1881
- **Rural** 4093-acre campus
- **Endowment** $359.5 million
- **Coed**
- **Moderately difficult** entrance level

FACULTY
Student/faculty ratio: 16:1.

ACADEMICS
Calendar: semesters. *Degrees:* associate, bachelor's, master's, doctoral, post-master's, and postbachelor's certificates.

STUDENT LIFE
Housing options: coed, men-only, women-only, special housing for students with disabilities. Campus housing is university owned and is provided by a third party. Freshman campus housing is guaranteed.

Activities and organizations: drama/theater group, student-run newspaper, radio and television station, choral group, marching band, national fraternities, national sororities.

Athletics Member NCAA. All Division I except football (Division I-A).

Campus security: 24-hour emergency response devices, late-night transport/escort service.

Student services: health clinic, personal/psychological counseling, women's center.

COSTS & FINANCIAL AID
Costs (2014–15) ***Tuition:*** state resident $9858 full-time, $411 per credit part-time; nonresident $30,038 full-time, $1252 per credit part-time. Part-time tuition and fees vary according to course load. ***Required fees:*** $2842 full-time. ***Room and board:*** $12,074; room only: $6466. Room and board charges vary according to board plan and housing facility. ***Payment plans:*** installment, deferred payment.

Financial Aid Of all full-time matriculated undergraduates who enrolled in 2013, 12,646 applied for aid, 9,845 were judged to have need, 1,380 had their need fully met. 888 Federal Work-Study jobs (averaging $2092). 4,005 state and other part-time jobs (averaging $1841). In 2013, 1732 non-need-based awards were made. ***Average percent of need met:*** 62. ***Average financial aid package:*** $12,917. ***Average need-based loan:*** $4451. ***Average need-based gift aid:*** $8318. ***Average non-need-based aid:*** $6747. ***Average indebtedness upon graduation:*** $24,600.

APPLYING
Standardized Tests *Required:* SAT or ACT (for admission).

Options: electronic application, deferred entrance.

Application fee: $70.

Required: essay or personal statement, high school transcript. ***Recommended:*** 1 letter of recommendation.

CONTACT
Nathan Fuerst, Director of Undergraduate Admissions, University of Connecticut, 2131 Hillside Road, U-88, Storrs, CT 06269. *Phone:* 860-486-3137. *Fax:* 860-486-1476. *E-mail:* beahusky@uconn.edu.

★ University of Hartford
West Hartford, Connecticut
http://www.hartford.edu/

- **Independent** comprehensive, founded 1877
- **Suburban** 320-acre campus with easy access to Hartford
- **Endowment** $146.1 million
- **Coed** 5,180 undergraduate students, 86% full-time, 50% women, 50% men
- **Moderately difficult** entrance level, 72% of applicants were admitted

UNDERGRAD STUDENTS
4,446 full-time, 734 part-time. Students come from 50 states and territories; 42 other countries; 49% are from out of state; 15% Black or African American, non-Hispanic/Latino; 10% Hispanic/Latino; 3% Asian, non-Hispanic/Latino; 0.1% Native Hawaiian or other Pacific Islander, non-Hispanic/Latino; 0.3% American Indian or Alaska Native, non-Hispanic/Latino; 3% Two or more races, non-Hispanic/Latino; 8% Race/ethnicity unknown; 6% international; 4% transferred in; 61% live on campus.

Freshmen
Admission: 14,444 applied, 10,419 admitted, 1,217 enrolled. ***Test scores:*** SAT critical reading scores over 500: 61%; SAT math scores over 500: 63%; ACT scores over 18: 96%; SAT critical reading scores over 600: 16%; SAT math scores over 600: 19%; ACT scores over 24: 37%; SAT critical reading scores over 700: 2%; SAT math scores over 700: 3%; ACT scores over 30: 7%.

Retention: 76% of full-time freshmen returned.

FACULTY
Total: 788, 44% full-time.

Student/faculty ratio: 10:1.

ACADEMICS
Calendar: semesters. *Degrees:* certificates, diplomas, associate, bachelor's, master's, doctoral, post-master's, and postbachelor's certificates.

Special study options: academic remediation for entering students, adult/continuing education programs, advanced placement credit, cooperative education, distance learning, double majors, English as a second language, honors programs, independent study, internships, off-campus study, part-time degree program, services for LD students, student-designed majors, study abroad, summer session for credit. ***ROTC:*** Army (c), Air Force (c).

Computers: 400 computers/terminals are available on campus for general student use. Students can access the following: campus intranet, computer help desk, free student e-mail accounts, online (class) grades, online (class) registration, online (class) schedules, student Web pages. Campuswide network is available. 100% of college-owned or -operated housing units are wired for high-speed Internet access. Wireless service is available via entire campus.

STUDENT LIFE
Housing options: coed, women-only, special housing for students with disabilities. Campus housing is university owned and leased by the school. Freshman campus housing is guaranteed.

Activities and organizations: drama/theater group, student-run newspaper, radio and television station, choral group, Program Council, Brothers and Sisters United, Hillel, Student Government Association, Residence Hall Association, national fraternities, national sororities.

Athletics Member NCAA. All Division I. ***Intercollegiate sports:*** badminton M(c)/W(c), baseball M(s), basketball M(s)/W(s), cross-country running M(s)/W(s), golf M(s)/W(s), lacrosse M(s), racquetball M(c)/W(c), rugby M(c)/W(c), soccer M(s)/W(s), softball W(s), squash M(c)/W(c), tennis M(s)/W(s), track and field M/W, volleyball M(c)/W(s). ***Intramural sports:*** badminton M/W, basketball M/W, football M/W, racquetball M/W, soccer M/W, softball M/W, squash M/W, swimming and diving M/W, tennis M/W, ultimate Frisbee M/W, volleyball M/W, water polo M/W.

Campus security: 24-hour emergency response devices and patrols, late-night transport/escort service, controlled dormitory access, bicycle patrols.

Student services: health clinic, personal/psychological counseling, women's center, legal services.

COSTS & FINANCIAL AID
Costs (2015–16) ***Comprehensive fee:*** $48,098 includes full-time tuition ($33,740), mandatory fees ($2720), and room and board ($11,638). Full-time tuition and fees vary according to program. Part-time tuition: $500 per credit. Part-time tuition and fees vary according to course load and program. ***College room only:*** $7548. Room and board charges vary according to board plan and housing facility. ***Payment plans:*** tuition prepayment, installment. ***Waivers:*** senior citizens and employees or children of employees.

Financial Aid Of all full-time matriculated undergraduates who enrolled in 2014, 3,612 applied for aid, 3,355 were judged to have need, 391 had their need fully met. 611 Federal Work-Study jobs (averaging $1121). In 2014, 738 non-need-based awards were made. ***Average percent of need met:*** 65. ***Average financial aid package:*** $23,883. ***Average need-based loan:*** $4641. ***Average need-based gift aid:*** $18,654. ***Average non-need-based aid:*** $11,707.

APPLYING
Standardized Tests *Required:* SAT or ACT (for admission).

Options: electronic application, early admission, early action, deferred entrance.

Application fee: $40.

Required: high school transcript. ***Recommended:*** essay or personal statement, 2 letters of recommendation, interview.

Application deadlines: rolling (freshmen), rolling (transfers).

Notification: continuous (freshmen), continuous (transfers).

CONTACT
Mr. Richard Zeiser, Dean of Admissions, University of Hartford, 200 Bloomfield Avenue, West Hartford, CT 06117. *Phone:* 860-768-4296. *Toll-free phone:* 800-947-4303. *Fax:* 860-768-4961. *E-mail:* admissions@hartford.edu.

See previous page for display ad and page 1670 for the College Close-Up.

★ University of New Haven
West Haven, Connecticut
http://www.newhaven.edu/

- **Independent** comprehensive, founded 1920
- **Suburban** 82-acre campus with easy access to New Haven
- **Coed** 5,048 undergraduate students, 93% full-time, 50% women, 50% men
- **Moderately difficult** entrance level, 81% of applicants were admitted

UNDERGRAD STUDENTS
4,674 full-time, 374 part-time. Students come from 41 states and territories; 30 other countries; 58% are from out of state; 9% Black or African American, non-Hispanic/Latino; 10% Hispanic/Latino; 3% Asian, non-Hispanic/Latino; 0.2% Native Hawaiian or other Pacific Islander, non-Hispanic/Latino; 0.3% American Indian or Alaska Native, non-Hispanic/Latino; 2% Two or more races, non-Hispanic/Latino; 9% Race/ethnicity unknown; 8% international; 5% transferred in; 54% live on campus.

Freshmen
Admission: 9,006 applied, 7,282 admitted, 1,221 enrolled. ***Average high school GPA:*** 3.4. ***Test scores:*** SAT critical reading scores over 500: 64%; SAT math scores over 500: 67%; SAT writing scores over 500: 61%; ACT scores over 18: 94%; SAT critical reading scores over 600: 16%; SAT math scores over 600: 22%; SAT writing scores over 600: 16%; ACT scores over 24: 44%; SAT critical reading scores over 700: 1%; SAT math scores over 700: 3%; SAT writing scores over 700: 1%; ACT scores over 30: 8%.

Retention: 80% of full-time freshmen returned.

FACULTY
Total: 642, 41% full-time, 59% with terminal degrees.

Student/faculty ratio: 15:1.

ACADEMICS
Calendar: 4-1-4. *Degrees:* certificates, associate, bachelor's, master's, doctoral, post-master's, and postbachelor's certificates.

Special study options: academic remediation for entering students, accelerated degree program, adult/continuing education programs, advanced placement credit, cooperative education, distance learning, double majors, English as a second language, honors programs, independent study, internships, off-campus study, part-time degree program, services for LD students, study abroad, summer session for credit. ***ROTC:*** Army (b), Air Force (c).

Computers: 300 computers/terminals and 250 ports are available on campus for general student use. Students can access the following: campus intranet, computer help desk, free student e-mail accounts, online (class) grades, online (class) registration, online (class) schedules, computer repair services. Campuswide network is available. 100% of college-owned or -operated housing units are wired for high-speed Internet access. Wireless service is available via entire campus.

STUDENT LIFE
Housing options: coed, special housing for students with disabilities. Campus housing is university owned and leased by the school. Freshman applicants given priority for college housing.

Activities and organizations: student-run newspaper, radio and television station, marching band, Student government, Criminal Justice

Club, Music Entertainment and Industry Association, Black Student Union, Fire Science Club, national fraternities, national sororities.

Athletics Member NCAA. All Division II. ***Intercollegiate sports:*** baseball M(s), basketball M(s)/W(s), cross-country running M(s)/W(s), field hockey W(c), football M(s), ice hockey M(c), lacrosse M(c)/W(s), rugby M(c), soccer M(s)/W(s), softball W(s), tennis W(s), track and field M(s)/W(s), ultimate Frisbee M(c)/W(c), volleyball M(c)/W(s), wrestling M(c). ***Intramural sports:*** basketball M/W, cheerleading M/W, racquetball M/W, soccer M/W, softball M/W, tennis M/W, volleyball M/W.

Campus security: 24-hour emergency response devices and patrols, student patrols, late-night transport/escort service, controlled dormitory access, escort service, vehicle, bicycle and foot patrols, crime prevention programs.

Student services: health clinic, personal/psychological counseling.

COSTS & FINANCIAL AID

Costs (2014–15) ***Comprehensive fee:*** $49,040 includes full-time tuition ($33,330), mandatory fees ($1300), and room and board ($14,410). Full-time tuition and fees vary according to course load and program. Part-time tuition: $1110 per credit. Part-time tuition and fees vary according to class time, course load, and program. ***College room only:*** $9160. Room and board charges vary according to board plan and housing facility. ***Payment plan:*** installment. ***Waivers:*** senior citizens and employees or children of employees.

Financial Aid Of all full-time matriculated undergraduates who enrolled in 2014, 3,740 applied for aid, 3,433 were judged to have need, 550 had their need fully met. In 2014, 594 non-need-based awards were made. ***Average percent of need met:*** 61. ***Average financial aid package:*** $21,989. ***Average need-based loan:*** $4371. ***Average need-based gift aid:*** $18,345. ***Average non-need-based aid:*** $13,014. ***Average indebtedness upon graduation:*** $43,472.

APPLYING

Standardized Tests *Required:* SAT or ACT (for admission).

Options: electronic application, early decision, early action.

Application fee: $50.

Required: essay or personal statement, high school transcript, 1 letter of recommendation. ***Recommended:*** interview.

Application deadlines: rolling (freshmen), rolling (out-of-state freshmen), rolling (transfers), 12/15 (early action).

Early decision deadline: 12/1.

Notification: continuous (freshmen), continuous (out-of-state freshmen), continuous (transfers), 12/15 (early decision), 1/15 (early action).

CONTACT

Mr. Kevin J. Phillips, Associate Vice President for Enrollment Management, University of New Haven, Bayer Hall, 300 Boston Post Road, West Haven, CT 06516. *Phone:* 203-932-7318. *Toll-free phone:* 800-342-5864. *Fax:* 203-931-6093. *E-mail:* admissions@newhaven.edu.

See below for display ad and page 1690 for the College Close-Up.

University of Saint Joseph

West Hartford, Connecticut

http://www.usj.edu/

- **Independent Roman Catholic** comprehensive, founded 1932
- **Suburban** 90-acre campus with easy access to Hartford
- **Endowment** $25.6 million
- **Coed, primarily women** 987 undergraduate students, 77% full-time, 98% women, 2% men
- **Moderately difficult** entrance level, 80% of applicants were admitted

UNDERGRAD STUDENTS

761 full-time, 226 part-time. 5% are from out of state; 15% Black or African American, non-Hispanic/Latino; 15% Hispanic/Latino; 2% Asian, non-Hispanic/Latino; 0.2% Native Hawaiian or other Pacific Islander, non-Hispanic/Latino; 0.2% American Indian or Alaska Native, non-Hispanic/Latino; 1% Two or more races, non-Hispanic/Latino; 15% Race/ethnicity unknown; 0.2% international; 6% transferred in; 32% live on campus.

Freshmen

Admission: 724 applied, 579 admitted, 150 enrolled. ***Average high school GPA:*** 3.21. ***Test scores:*** SAT critical reading scores over 500: 42%; SAT math scores over 500: 39%; ACT scores over 18: 87%; SAT critical

reading scores over 600: 9%; SAT math scores over 600: 6%; ACT scores over 24: 22%.

Retention: 79% of full-time freshmen returned.

FACULTY

Total: 279, 44% full-time, 44% with terminal degrees.

Student/faculty ratio: 11:1.

ACADEMICS

Calendar: semesters. *Degrees:* certificates, bachelor's, master's, doctoral, post-master's, and postbachelor's certificates.

Special study options: accelerated degree program, adult/continuing education programs, advanced placement credit, distance learning, double majors, honors programs, independent study, internships, off-campus study, part-time degree program, services for LD students, student-designed majors, study abroad, summer session for credit.

Computers: 72 computers/terminals are available on campus for general student use. Students can access the following: campus intranet, computer help desk, free student e-mail accounts, online (class) grades, online (class) registration, online (class) schedules. Campuswide network is available. 100% of college-owned or -operated housing units are wired for high-speed Internet access. Wireless service is available via computer centers, computer labs, dorm rooms, libraries, student centers.

STUDENT LIFE

Housing options: women-only, special housing for students with disabilities. Campus housing is university owned.

Activities and organizations: drama/theater group, choral group.

Athletics Member NCAA. All Division III. ***Intercollegiate sports:*** basketball W, cross-country running W, lacrosse W, soccer W, softball W, swimming and diving W, tennis W, volleyball W.

Campus security: 24-hour emergency response devices and patrols, late-night transport/escort service, controlled dormitory access.

Student services: health clinic, personal/psychological counseling.

COSTS & FINANCIAL AID

Costs (2015–16) ***Comprehensive fee:*** $50,990 includes full-time tuition ($34,530), mandatory fees ($1610), and room and board ($14,850). Full-time tuition and fees vary according to course load, degree level, location, program, and student level. Part-time tuition: $751 per credit hour. Part-time tuition and fees vary according to course load, degree level, location, program, and student level. ***Required fees:*** $55 per credit hour part-time. ***College room only:*** $6850. Room and board charges vary according to board plan and housing facility. ***Payment plan:*** installment. ***Waivers:*** employees or children of employees.

Financial Aid Of all full-time matriculated undergraduates who enrolled in 2014, 720 applied for aid, 684 were judged to have need, 82 had their need fully met. 50 state and other part-time jobs (averaging $1806). In 2014, 61 non-need-based awards were made. ***Average percent of need met:*** 68. ***Average financial aid package:*** $24,930. ***Average need-based loan:*** $5878. ***Average need-based gift aid:*** $20,175. ***Average non-need-based aid:*** $12,380. ***Average indebtedness upon graduation:*** $37,557.

APPLYING

Standardized Tests *Required:* SAT or ACT (for admission). *Recommended:* SAT (for admission).

Options: electronic application, deferred entrance.

Application fee: $50.

Required: high school transcript. ***Recommended:*** essay or personal statement, interview.

Application deadlines: rolling (freshmen), rolling (out-of-state freshmen), rolling (transfers).

Notification: continuous (freshmen), continuous (out-of-state freshmen), continuous (transfers).

CONTACT

Office of Admissions, University of Saint Joseph, 1678 Asylum Avenue, West Hartford, CT 06117. *Phone:* 860-231-5216. *Toll-free phone:* 866-442-8752. *Fax:* 860-231-5744. *E-mail:* admissions@usj.edu.

Wesleyan University

Middletown, Connecticut

http://www.wesleyan.edu/

- **Independent** university, founded 1831
- **Suburban** 316-acre campus with easy access to Hartford, CT and New Haven, CT
- **Endowment** $793.3 million
- **Coed** 2,928 undergraduate students, 100% full-time, 52% women, 48% men
- **Most difficult** entrance level, 24% of applicants were admitted

UNDERGRAD STUDENTS

2,914 full-time, 14 part-time. Students come from 47 states and territories; 48 other countries; 92% are from out of state; 7% Black or African American, non-Hispanic/Latino; 10% Hispanic/Latino; 9% Asian, non-Hispanic/Latino; 0.1% Native Hawaiian or other Pacific Islander, non-Hispanic/Latino; 0.1% American Indian or Alaska Native, non-Hispanic/Latino; 6% Two or more races, non-Hispanic/Latino; 7% Race/ethnicity unknown; 9% international; 2% transferred in; 99% live on campus.

Freshmen

Admission: 9,390 applied, 2,245 admitted, 750 enrolled. ***Test scores:*** SAT critical reading scores over 500: 100%; SAT math scores over 500: 99%; SAT writing scores over 500: 100%; ACT scores over 18: 100%; SAT critical reading scores over 600: 88%; SAT math scores over 600: 91%; SAT writing scores over 600: 91%; ACT scores over 24: 99%; SAT critical reading scores over 700: 51%; SAT math scores over 700: 52%; SAT writing scores over 700: 59%; ACT scores over 30: 74%.

Retention: 96% of full-time freshmen returned.

FACULTY

Total: 396, 89% full-time, 91% with terminal degrees.

Student/faculty ratio: 8:1.

ACADEMICS

Calendar: semesters. *Degrees:* bachelor's, master's, doctoral, and post-master's certificates.

Special study options: accelerated degree program, adult/continuing education programs, advanced placement credit, double majors, honors programs, independent study, internships, off-campus study, services for LD students, student-designed majors, study abroad, summer session for credit. ***ROTC:*** Air Force (c).

Unusual degree programs: 3-2 engineering with Columbia University, California Institute of Technology, Dartmouth College.

Computers: 1,600 computers/terminals and 6,000 ports are available on campus for general student use. Students can access the following: campus intranet, computer help desk, free student e-mail accounts, online (class) grades, online (class) registration, online (class) schedules, Electronic Portfolio, Online Course Drop/Add, Blackboard Course Management System, Lynda.com. Campuswide network is available. 100% of college-owned or -operated housing units are wired for high-speed Internet access. Wireless service is available via entire campus.

STUDENT LIFE

Housing options: on-campus residence required through senior year; coed, men-only, women-only, cooperative, special housing for students with disabilities. Campus housing is university owned. Freshman campus housing is guaranteed.

Activities and organizations: drama/theater group, student-run newspaper, radio station, choral group, Environmental Organizers Network, WesDems, Ajuacampos (Latino affinity group), Ujima, Terpsichore, national fraternities, national sororities.

Athletics Member NCAA. All Division III. ***Intercollegiate sports:*** baseball M, basketball M/W, crew M/W, cross-country running M/W, equestrian sports M(c)/W(c), field hockey W, football M, golf M, ice hockey M/W, lacrosse M/W, rugby M(c)/W(c), sailing M(c)/W(c), skiing (cross-country) M(c)/W(c), skiing (downhill) M(c)/W(c), soccer M/W, softball W, squash M/W, swimming and diving M/W, tennis M/W, track and field M/W, volleyball M(c)/W, water polo M(c), wrestling M. ***Intramural sports:*** basketball M/W, ice hockey M/W, soccer M/W, softball M/W, squash M/W, ultimate Frisbee M/W, water polo M/W.

Campus security: 24-hour emergency response devices and patrols, student patrols, late-night transport/escort service, controlled dormitory access.

Student services: health clinic, personal/psychological counseling.

COSTS & FINANCIAL AID

Costs (2015–16) ***Comprehensive fee:*** $62,478 includes full-time tuition ($48,704), mandatory fees ($270), and room and board ($13,504). ***Room and board:*** Room and board charges vary according to board plan, housing facility, and student level. ***Payment plan:*** installment.

Financial Aid Of all full-time matriculated undergraduates who enrolled in 2013, 1,464 applied for aid, 1,361 were judged to have need, 1,361 had their need fully met. 1,200 Federal Work-Study jobs (averaging $2500). 1,200 state and other part-time jobs (averaging $2500). In 2013, 21 non-need-based awards were made. ***Average percent of need met:*** 100. ***Average financial aid package:*** $43,670. ***Average need-based loan:*** $4584. ***Average need-based gift aid:*** $39,476. ***Average non-need-based aid:*** $47,003. ***Average indebtedness upon graduation:*** $21,635. ***Financial aid deadline:*** 2/15.

APPLYING

Standardized Tests *Required for some:* SAT and SAT Subject Tests or ACT (for admission).

Options: electronic application, early admission, early decision, deferred entrance.

Application fee: $55.

Required: essay or personal statement, high school transcript, 2 letters of recommendation. ***Required for some:*** interview. ***Recommended:*** interview.

Application deadlines: 1/1 (freshmen), 3/15 (transfers).

Early decision deadline: 11/15 (for plan 1), 1/1 (for plan 2).

Notification: 4/1 (freshmen), 5/15 (transfers), 12/15 (early decision plan 1), 2/15 (early decision plan 2).

CONTACT

Ms. Nancy Hargrave Meislahn, Dean of Admission and Financial Aid, Wesleyan University, Stewart M. Reid House, 70 Wyllys Avenue, Middletown, CT 06459-0265. *Phone:* 860-685-3000. *Fax:* 860-685-3001. *E-mail:* admissions@wesleyan.edu.

★ Western Connecticut State University

Danbury, Connecticut

http://www.wcsu.edu/

- **State-supported** comprehensive, founded 1903, part of Connecticut State Colleges & Universities (ConnSCU)
- **Urban** 340-acre campus with easy access to New York City
- **Endowment** $10.5 million
- **Coed**
- **Moderately difficult** entrance level

FACULTY

Student/faculty ratio: 15:1.

ACADEMICS

Calendar: semesters. *Degrees:* associate, bachelor's, master's, doctoral, and post-master's certificates.

STUDENT LIFE

Housing options: coed, women-only. Campus housing is university owned. Freshman campus housing is guaranteed.

Activities and organizations: drama/theater group, student-run newspaper, radio station, choral group, National Society of Collegiate Scholars, Criminology Club, Jazz Club, American Marketing Club, Meteorology, national fraternities, national sororities.

Athletics Member NCAA. All Division III.

Campus security: 24-hour emergency response devices and patrols, student patrols, late-night transport/escort service, controlled dormitory access.

Student services: health clinic, personal/psychological counseling.

COSTS & FINANCIAL AID

Costs (2014–15) ***Tuition:*** state resident $4600 full-time, $192 per credit part-time; nonresident $14,886 full-time, $196 per credit part-time. Full-time tuition and fees vary according to course load, program, and reciprocity agreements. ***Required fees:*** $4477 full-time, $226 per credit part-time. ***Room and board:*** $11,311; room only: $6637. Room and board charges vary according to board plan and housing facility.

Financial Aid ***Financial aid deadline:*** 3/15.

APPLYING

Standardized Tests *Required:* SAT or ACT (for admission).

Options: electronic application, early admission, deferred entrance.

Application fee: $50.

Required: high school transcript, 2 letters of recommendation. ***Required for some:*** essay or personal statement, interview.

CONTACT

Office of University Admissions, Western Connecticut State University, 181 White Street, Danbury, CT 06810. *Phone:* 203-837-9000. *Toll-free phone:* 877-837-WCSU. *Fax:* 203-837-8338. *E-mail:* admissions@wcsu.edu.

See previous page for display ad and page 1730 for the College Close-Up.

Yale University

New Haven, Connecticut

http://www.yale.edu/

- **Independent** university, founded 1701
- **Urban** 342-acre campus with easy access to New York City
- **Endowment** $23.9 billion
- **Coed** 5,477 undergraduate students, 100% full-time, 49% women, 51% men
- **Most difficult** entrance level, 6% of applicants were admitted

UNDERGRAD STUDENTS

5,470 full-time, 7 part-time. Students come from 50 states and territories; 84 other countries; 94% are from out of state; 7% Black or African American, non-Hispanic/Latino; 11% Hispanic/Latino; 17% Asian, non-Hispanic/Latino; 0.6% American Indian or Alaska Native, non-Hispanic/Latino; 6% Two or more races, non-Hispanic/Latino; 2% Race/ethnicity unknown; 10% international; 0.5% transferred in; 87% live on campus.

Freshmen

Admission: 30,932 applied, 1,950 admitted, 1,360 enrolled. ***Test scores:*** SAT critical reading scores over 500: 100%; SAT math scores over 500: 100%; SAT writing scores over 500: 99%; SAT critical reading scores over 600: 98%; SAT math scores over 600: 99%; SAT writing scores over 600: 98%; SAT critical reading scores over 700: 79%; SAT math scores over 700: 79%; SAT writing scores over 700: 81%.

Retention: 98% of full-time freshmen returned.

FACULTY

Total: 1,687, 71% full-time, 89% with terminal degrees.

Student/faculty ratio: 6:1.

ACADEMICS

Calendar: semesters. *Degrees:* bachelor's, master's, doctoral, and post-master's certificates.

Special study options: advanced placement credit, double majors, independent study, part-time degree program, services for LD students, student-designed majors, study abroad, summer session for credit. ***ROTC:*** Army (c), Navy (b), Air Force (b).

Computers: 450 computers/terminals are available on campus for general student use. Students can access the following: campus intranet, computer help desk, free student e-mail accounts, online (class) grades, online (class) registration, online (class) schedules. Campuswide network is available. 100% of college-owned or -operated housing units are wired for high-speed Internet access. Wireless service is available via classrooms, computer centers, computer labs, dorm rooms, learning centers, libraries, student centers.

STUDENT LIFE

Housing options: on-campus residence required through sophomore year; coed, special housing for students with disabilities. Campus housing is university owned. Freshman campus housing is guaranteed.

Activities and organizations: drama/theater group, student-run newspaper, radio station, choral group, marching band, national fraternities, national sororities.

Athletics Member NCAA. All Division I except football (Division I-AA). ***Intercollegiate sports:*** archery M(c)/W(c), badminton M(c)/W(c), baseball M, basketball M/W, cheerleading M(c)/W, crew M/W, cross-country running M/W, equestrian sports M(c)/W(c), fencing M/W, field hockey W, golf M/W, gymnastics W, ice hockey M/W, lacrosse M/W, riflery M(c)/W(c), rock climbing M(c)/W(c), rugby M(c)/W(c), sailing M/W, skiing (cross-country) M(c)/W(c), skiing (downhill) M(c)/W(c), soccer M/W, softball W, squash M/W, swimming and diving M/W, table tennis M(c)/W(c), tennis M/W, track and field M/W, ultimate Frisbee M(c)/W(c), volleyball M(c)/W, water polo M(c)/W(c), wrestling M(c)/W(c). ***Intramural sports:*** badminton M(c)/W(c), baseball M, basketball M/W, bowling M/W, crew M/W, cross-country running M/W, field hockey W, football M/W, golf M/W, ice hockey M/W, racquetball M/W, soccer M/W, softball M/W, squash M/W, swimming and diving M/W, table tennis M/W, tennis M/W, ultimate Frisbee M/W, volleyball M/W, water polo M/W.

Campus security: 24-hour emergency response devices and patrols, late-night transport/escort service, controlled dormitory access.

Student services: health clinic, personal/psychological counseling, women's center.

COSTS & FINANCIAL AID

Costs (2015–16) ***Comprehensive fee:*** $62,200 includes full-time tuition ($47,600) and room and board ($14,600). ***College room only:*** $8200. Room and board charges vary according to board plan. ***Payment plan:*** installment. ***Waivers:*** employees or children of employees.

Financial Aid Of all full-time matriculated undergraduates who enrolled in 2013, 2,946 applied for aid, 2,825 were judged to have need, 2,825 had their need fully met. 681 Federal Work-Study jobs (averaging $2456). 1,483 state and other part-time jobs (averaging $2744). ***Average percent of need met:*** 100. ***Average financial aid package:*** $46,844. ***Average need-based loan:*** $3163. ***Average need-based gift aid:*** $44,268. ***Average indebtedness upon graduation:*** $13,009. ***Financial aid deadline:*** 3/1.

APPLYING

Standardized Tests *Required:* SAT and SAT Subject Tests or ACT (for admission).

Options: electronic application, early admission, early action, deferred entrance.

Application fee: $80.

Required: essay or personal statement, high school transcript, 3 letters of recommendation. ***Recommended:*** interview.

Application deadlines: 1/1 (freshmen), 3/1 (transfers), 11/1 (early action).

Notification: 4/1 (freshmen), 5/15 (transfers), 12/15 (early action).

CONTACT

Admissions Director, Yale University, PO Box 208234, New Haven, CT 06520. *Phone:* 203-432-9300. *E-mail:* student.questions@yale.edu.

DELAWARE

Delaware State University

Dover, Delaware

http://www.desu.edu/

- **State-supported** university, founded 1891, part of Delaware Higher Education Commission
- **Small-town** 400-acre campus
- **Coed** 4,012 undergraduate students, 87% full-time, 63% women, 37% men
- **Moderately difficult** entrance level, 44% of applicants were admitted

UNDERGRAD STUDENTS
3,479 full-time, 533 part-time. 44% are from out of state; 75% Black or African American, non-Hispanic/Latino; 6% Hispanic/Latino; 0.8% Asian, non-Hispanic/Latino; 0.1% Native Hawaiian or other Pacific Islander, non-Hispanic/Latino; 0.3% American Indian or Alaska Native, non-Hispanic/Latino; 4% Two or more races, non-Hispanic/Latino; 0.8% Race/ethnicity unknown; 2% international; 5% transferred in; 55% live on campus.

Freshmen
Admission: 7,191 applied, 3,145 admitted, 894 enrolled.
Retention: 69% of full-time freshmen returned.

ACADEMICS
Calendar: semesters. *Degrees:* bachelor's, master's, and doctoral.

Special study options: academic remediation for entering students, accelerated degree program, adult/continuing education programs, advanced placement credit, cooperative education, distance learning, double majors, English as a second language, honors programs, internships, off-campus study, part-time degree program, services for LD students, study abroad, summer session for credit. ***ROTC:*** Army (b), Air Force (c).

Computers: Students can access the following: campus intranet, computer help desk, free student e-mail accounts, online (class) grades, online (class) registration, online (class) schedules. Campuswide network is available. Wireless service is available via classrooms, computer centers, computer labs, learning centers, libraries, student centers.

STUDENT LIFE
Housing options: coed, men-only, women-only, special housing for students with disabilities. Campus housing is university owned. Freshman applicants given priority for college housing.

Activities and organizations: drama/theater group, student-run newspaper, radio and television station, choral group, marching band, SGA, NPHC, Women's Senate, RHA, Men's Council, national fraternities, national sororities.

Athletics Member NCAA. All Division I except football (Division I-AA). ***Intercollegiate sports:*** baseball M(s), basketball M(s)/W(s), bowling W(s), cheerleading M(s)/W(s), cross-country running M(s)/W(s), equestrian sports W(s), soccer W(s), softball W(s), tennis W(s), track and field M(s)/W(s), volleyball W(s). ***Intramural sports:*** basketball M/W, football M(c)/W(c), soccer M/W, softball M/W, swimming and diving M/W, table tennis M/W, tennis M/W, track and field M/W, volleyball W.

Campus security: 24-hour emergency response devices and patrols, student patrols, late-night transport/escort service, controlled dormitory access.

Student services: health clinic, personal/psychological counseling, women's center.

COSTS & FINANCIAL AID
Costs (2014–15) ***Tuition:*** state resident $7336 full-time, $272 per credit hour part-time; nonresident $15,692 full-time, $620 per credit hour part-time. Full-time tuition and fees vary according to course load. Part-time tuition and fees vary according to course load. ***Required fees:*** $300 per term part-time. ***Room and board:*** $10,708; room only: $6976. Room and board charges vary according to board plan and housing facility. ***Payment plan:*** deferred payment. ***Waivers:*** senior citizens and employees or children of employees.

Financial Aid Of all full-time matriculated undergraduates who enrolled in 2013, 3,277 applied for aid, 2,951 were judged to have need, 2,374 had their need fully met. In 2013, 41 non-need-based awards were made. ***Average percent of need met:*** 71. ***Average financial aid package:*** $11,479. ***Average need-based loan:*** $5423. ***Average need-based gift aid:*** $5011. ***Average non-need-based aid:*** $15,445. ***Average indebtedness upon graduation:*** $38,702.

APPLYING
Standardized Tests *Required:* SAT or ACT (for admission).

Options: electronic application, early admission, early action.

Application fee: $35.

Required: high school transcript, minimum 2.0 GPA.

CONTACT
Mrs. Erin Hill, Executive Director for Admissions, Delaware State University, 1200 North DuPont Highway, Dover, DE 19901-2277. *Phone:* 302-857-6351. *Toll-free phone:* 800-845-2544. *Fax:* 302-857-6352. *E-mail:* ehill@desu.edu.

University of Delaware
Newark, Delaware
http://www.udel.edu/

- **State-related** university, founded 1743
- **Small-town** 1000-acre campus with easy access to Philadelphia, Baltimore
- **Coed** 18,141 undergraduate students, 92% full-time, 58% women, 42% men
- **Moderately difficult** entrance level, 67% of applicants were admitted

UNDERGRAD STUDENTS
16,703 full-time, 1,438 part-time. 61% are from out of state; 5% Black or African American, non-Hispanic/Latino; 7% Hispanic/Latino; 4% Asian, non-Hispanic/Latino; 0.1% Native Hawaiian or other Pacific Islander, non-Hispanic/Latino; 0.1% American Indian or Alaska Native, non-Hispanic/Latino; 3% Two or more races, non-Hispanic/Latino; 0.9% Race/ethnicity unknown; 4% international; 2% transferred in; 45% live on campus.

Freshmen
Admission: 24,442 applied, 16,331 admitted, 4,179 enrolled. ***Average high school GPA:*** 3.65. ***Test scores:*** SAT critical reading scores over 500: 92%; SAT math scores over 500: 94%; SAT writing scores over 500: 91%; ACT scores over 18: 99%; SAT critical reading scores over 600: 49%; SAT math scores over 600: 58%; SAT writing scores over 600: 49%; ACT scores over 24: 83%; SAT critical reading scores over 700: 11%; SAT math scores over 700: 13%; SAT writing scores over 700: 8%; ACT scores over 30: 21%.
Retention: 92% of full-time freshmen returned.

FACULTY
Total: 1,654, 71% full-time, 75% with terminal degrees.
Student/faculty ratio: 15:1.

ACADEMICS
Calendar: 4-1-4. *Degrees:* associate, bachelor's, master's, and doctoral.

Special study options: academic remediation for entering students, accelerated degree program, adult/continuing education programs, advanced placement credit, distance learning, double majors, English as a second language, honors programs, independent study, internships, off-campus study, part-time degree program, services for LD students, student-designed majors, study abroad, summer session for credit. ***ROTC:*** Army (b), Air Force (b).

Computers: Students can access the following: campus intranet, computer help desk, free student e-mail accounts, online (class) grades, online (class) registration, online (class) schedules, personal Web page, Google apps. Campuswide network is available. 100% of college-owned or -operated housing units are wired for high-speed Internet access. Wireless service is available via entire campus.

STUDENT LIFE
Housing options: on-campus residence required for freshman year; coed, women-only, special housing for students with disabilities. Campus housing is university owned. Freshman campus housing is guaranteed.

Activities and organizations: drama/theater group, student-run newspaper, radio station, choral group, marching band, national fraternities, national sororities.

Athletics Member NCAA. All Division I except football (Division I-AA). ***Intercollegiate sports:*** baseball M(s), basketball M(s)/W(s), bowling M(c)/W(c), cheerleading M(s)/W(s), crew M(c)/W(s), cross-country running M(c)/W(s), equestrian sports M(c)/W(c), field hockey W(s), golf M(s)/W(s), ice hockey M(c)/W(c), lacrosse M(s)/W(s), rugby M(c)/W(c), sailing M(c)/W(c), soccer M(s)/W(s), softball W(s), swimming and diving M/W(s), tennis M(s)/W(s), track and field M(c)/W(s), volleyball W(s), wrestling M(c). ***Intramural sports:*** badminton M/W, basketball M/W, field hockey W(c), football M/W, golf M/W, lacrosse M(c)/W(c), racquetball M/W, rock climbing M(c)/W(c), soccer M(c)/W(c), softball M/W, squash M/W, swimming and diving M/W, table tennis M/W, tennis M/W, track and field M/W, ultimate Frisbee M/W, volleyball M(c)/W(c), water polo M/W.

Campus security: 24-hour emergency response devices and patrols, student patrols, late-night transport/escort service, controlled dormitory access.

Student services: health clinic, personal/psychological counseling, women's center.

COSTS & FINANCIAL AID

Costs (2014–15) ***Tuition:*** state resident $10,900 full-time, $454 per credit hour part-time; nonresident $29,250 full-time, $1219 per credit hour part-time. ***Required fees:*** $1442 full-time. ***Room and board:*** $11,558; room only: $7014. Room and board charges vary according to board plan, housing facility, and student level. ***Payment plan:*** installment. ***Waivers:*** senior citizens and employees or children of employees.

Financial Aid Of all full-time matriculated undergraduates who enrolled in 2013, 11,697 applied for aid, 8,191 were judged to have need, 3,595 had their need fully met. In 2013, 3228 non-need-based awards were made. ***Average percent of need met:*** 74. ***Average financial aid package:*** $15,357. ***Average need-based loan:*** $7991. ***Average need-based gift aid:*** $8522. ***Average non-need-based aid:*** $6762. ***Average indebtedness upon graduation:*** $32,571. ***Financial aid deadline:*** 3/15.

APPLYING

Standardized Tests *Required:* SAT or ACT (for admission). *Required for some:* SAT Subject Tests (for admission). *Recommended:* SAT Subject Tests (for admission).

Options: electronic application, early admission, deferred entrance.

Application fee: $75.

Required: essay or personal statement, high school transcript, 1 letter of recommendation.

CONTACT

Dr. Jose Aviles, Director of Admissions, University of Delaware, 122 University Visitors Center, Newark, DE 19716. *Phone:* 302-831-8123. *Fax:* 302-831-6905. *E-mail:* admissions@udel.edu.

Wesley College

Dover, Delaware

http://www.wesley.edu/

- **Independent United Methodist** comprehensive, founded 1873
- **Small-town** 40-acre campus
- **Coed**
- **Moderately difficult** entrance level

ACADEMICS

Calendar: semesters. *Degrees:* certificates, associate, bachelor's, master's, post-master's, and postbachelor's certificates.

STUDENT LIFE

Housing options: on-campus residence required for freshman year; coed, men-only, women-only. Campus housing is university owned. Freshman campus housing is guaranteed.

Activities and organizations: drama/theater group, student-run newspaper, choral group, Student Activity Board, Student Government Association, National Coeducation Community Service Organization, national fraternities, national sororities.

Athletics Member NCAA. All Division III.

Campus security: 24-hour patrols, controlled dormitory access.

Student services: health clinic, personal/psychological counseling.

COSTS & FINANCIAL AID

Costs (2014–15) ***Comprehensive fee:*** $34,770 includes full-time tuition ($23,150), mandatory fees ($950), and room and board ($10,670). Full-time tuition and fees vary according to class time. ***College room only:*** $5550. Room and board charges vary according to board plan and housing facility.

Financial Aid Of all full-time matriculated undergraduates who enrolled in 2011, 1,265 applied for aid, 1,265 were judged to have need, 2 had their need fully met. ***Average percent of need met:*** 39. ***Average financial aid package:*** $13,896. ***Average need-based loan:*** $1858. ***Average need-based gift aid:*** $13,896.

APPLYING

Standardized Tests *Required:* SAT (for admission). *Required for some:* special test for nursing.

Options: electronic application.

Application fee: $25.

Required: essay or personal statement, high school transcript, minimum 2.2 GPA, 1 letter of recommendation. ***Recommended:*** interview.

CONTACT

Mr. Christopher Jester, Assistant Director of Undergraduate Admissions, Wesley College, 120 North State Street, Dover, DE 19901-3875. *Phone:* 302-736-2468. *Toll-free phone:* 800-937-5398. *E-mail:* christopher.jester@wesley.edu.

Wilmington University

New Castle, Delaware

http://www.wilmu.edu/

- **Independent** university, founded 1967
- **Suburban** 17-acre campus with easy access to Philadelphia
- **Endowment** $28.9 million
- **Coed** 9,326 undergraduate students, 43% full-time, 65% women, 35% men
- **Noncompetitive** entrance level, 99% of applicants were admitted

UNDERGRAD STUDENTS

4,037 full-time, 5,289 part-time. Students come from 38 states and territories; 25 other countries; 31% are from out of state; 25% Black or African American, non-Hispanic/Latino; 3% Hispanic/Latino; 2% Asian, non-Hispanic/Latino; 0.3% Native Hawaiian or other Pacific Islander, non-Hispanic/Latino; 1% American Indian or Alaska Native, non-Hispanic/Latino; 0.4% Two or more races, non-Hispanic/Latino; 15% Race/ethnicity unknown; 2% international; 15% transferred in.

Freshmen

Admission: 1,271 applied, 1,257 admitted, 740 enrolled.

Retention: 64% of full-time freshmen returned.

FACULTY

Total: 1,636, 6% full-time, 23% with terminal degrees.

Student/faculty ratio: 17:1.

ACADEMICS

Calendar: semesters. *Degrees:* certificates, associate, bachelor's, master's, doctoral, post-master's, and postbachelor's certificates.

Special study options: academic remediation for entering students, accelerated degree program, adult/continuing education programs, cooperative education, distance learning, double majors, English as a second language, external degree program, independent study, internships, part-time degree program, study abroad, summer session for credit. ***ROTC:*** Army (c), Air Force (c).

Computers: 600 computers/terminals are available on campus for general student use. Students can access the following: free student e-mail accounts, online (class) grades, online (class) registration, online (class) schedules. Campuswide network is available. Wireless service is available via entire campus.

STUDENT LIFE

Housing options: college housing not available.

Activities and organizations: Student Government Association, Green Team, Photography Club, WU Student United Way, Wildcat Cheerleaders.

Athletics Member NCAA. All Division II. ***Intercollegiate sports:*** baseball M(s), basketball M(s)/W(s), cross-country running M(s)/W(s), softball W(s), volleyball W(s).

Campus security: 24-hour emergency response devices and patrols, late-night transport/escort service.

COSTS & FINANCIAL AID

Costs (2014–15) ***Tuition:*** $8112 full-time, $338 per credit part-time. Full-time tuition and fees vary according to location. Part-time tuition and fees vary according to location. ***Required fees:*** $50 full-time, $25 per term part-time. ***Payment plan:*** installment. ***Waivers:*** employees or children of employees.

Financial Aid Of all full-time matriculated undergraduates who enrolled in 2004, 1,217 applied for aid, 900 were judged to have need. 25 Federal Work-Study jobs (averaging $2000). In 2004, 74 non-need-based awards were made. ***Average percent of need met:*** 48. ***Average financial aid***

package: $5770. ***Average need-based loan:*** $3889. ***Average need-based gift aid:*** $2464. ***Average non-need-based aid:*** $1100. ***Average indebtedness upon graduation:*** $17,486.

APPLYING
Options: early admission, deferred entrance.
Application fee: $25.
Required: high school transcript. ***Recommended:*** interview.
Application deadlines: rolling (freshmen), rolling (transfers).
Notification: continuous (freshmen), continuous (transfers).

CONTACT
Ms. Laura Morris, Director of Admissions, Wilmington University, 320 North DuPont Highway, New Castle, DE 19720-6491. *Phone:* 302-295-1179. *Toll-free phone:* 877-967-5464. *E-mail:* undergradadmissions@wilmu.edu.

DISTRICT OF COLUMBIA

American University
Washington, District of Columbia
http://www.american.edu/

- **Independent Methodist** university, founded 1893
- **Suburban** 84-acre campus with easy access to Washington, DC
- **Endowment** $546.0 million
- **Coed** 7,706 undergraduate students, 96% full-time, 62% women, 38% men
- **Very difficult** entrance level, 46% of applicants were admitted

UNDERGRAD STUDENTS
7,386 full-time, 320 part-time. Students come from 55 states and territories; 122 other countries; 81% are from out of state; 6% Black or African American, non-Hispanic/Latino; 11% Hispanic/Latino; 7% Asian, non-Hispanic/Latino; 0.1% Native Hawaiian or other Pacific Islander, non-Hispanic/Latino; 0.2% American Indian or Alaska Native, non-Hispanic/Latino; 5% Two or more races, non-Hispanic/Latino; 6% Race/ethnicity unknown; 7% international; 4% transferred in.

Freshmen
Admission: 15,119 applied, 6,931 admitted, 1,787 enrolled. ***Average high school GPA:*** 3.71. ***Test scores:*** SAT critical reading scores over 500: 97%; SAT math scores over 500: 95%; SAT writing scores over 500: 95%; ACT scores over 18: 100%; SAT critical reading scores over 600: 71%; SAT math scores over 600: 58%; SAT writing scores over 600: 66%; ACT scores over 24: 90%; SAT critical reading scores over 700: 20%; SAT math scores over 700: 12%; SAT writing scores over 700: 16%; ACT scores over 30: 34%.
Retention: 89% of full-time freshmen returned.

FACULTY
Total: 1,386, 56% full-time.
Student/faculty ratio: 12:1.

ACADEMICS
Calendar: semesters. *Degrees:* certificates, associate, bachelor's, master's, doctoral, and postbachelor's certificates.
Special study options: accelerated degree program, advanced placement credit, cooperative education, distance learning, double majors, English as a second language, honors programs, independent study, internships, off-campus study, part-time degree program, services for LD students, student-designed majors, study abroad, summer session for credit. ***ROTC:*** Army (c), Air Force (c).
Unusual degree programs: 3-2 engineering with University of Maryland College Park.
Computers: 700 computers/terminals and 7,000 ports are available on campus for general student use. Students can access the following: campus intranet, computer help desk, free student e-mail accounts, online (class) grades, online (class) registration, online (class) schedules, online e-support through Blackboard platform. Campuswide network is available. 100% of college-owned or -operated housing units are wired for high-speed Internet access. Wireless service is available via entire campus.

STUDENT LIFE
Housing options: coed, special housing for students with disabilities. Campus housing is university owned and leased by the school. Freshman campus housing is guaranteed.
Activities and organizations: drama/theater group, student-run newspaper, radio and television station, choral group, Kennedy Political Union, Habitat for Humanity, Student government, Amnesty International, Multiple Ethnic and religious organizations, national fraternities, national sororities.
Athletics Member NCAA. All Division I. ***Intercollegiate sports:*** basketball M(s)/W(s), cross-country running M(s)/W(s), field hockey W(s), lacrosse W(s), soccer M(s)/W(s), swimming and diving M/W, track and field M(s)/W(s), volleyball W(s), wrestling M(s). ***Intramural sports:*** baseball M(c)/W(c), basketball M/W, crew M(c)/W(c), equestrian sports M(c)/W(c), field hockey M(c)/W(c), football M/W, golf M(c)/W(c), gymnastics M(c)/W(c), ice hockey M(c)/W(c), lacrosse M(c)/W(c), rugby M(c)/W(c), sailing M(c)/W(c), soccer M/W, table tennis M/W, tennis M/W, track and field M/W, ultimate Frisbee M(c)/W(c), volleyball M/W, water polo M/W, weight lifting M.
Campus security: 24-hour emergency response devices and patrols, late-night transport/escort service, controlled dormitory access, e-mail and text emergency notification system.
Student services: health clinic, personal/psychological counseling, women's center.

COSTS & FINANCIAL AID
Costs (2015–16) ***Comprehensive fee:*** $56,910 includes full-time tuition ($42,556) and room and board ($14,354). Full-time tuition and fees vary according to course load and location. Part-time tuition: $1417 per credit hour. Part-time tuition and fees vary according to course load and location. ***College room only:*** $9704. Room and board charges vary according to board plan, housing facility, and location. ***Payment plans:*** tuition prepayment, installment. ***Waivers:*** employees or children of employees.
Financial Aid Of all full-time matriculated undergraduates who enrolled in 2013, 4,459 applied for aid, 3,773 were judged to have need, 412 had their need fully met. In 2013, 837 non-need-based awards were made. ***Average percent of need met:*** 71. ***Average financial aid package:*** $29,054. ***Average need-based loan:*** $4380. ***Average need-based gift aid:*** $22,757. ***Average non-need-based aid:*** $13,989. ***Financial aid deadline:*** 2/15.

APPLYING
Standardized Tests *Required:* SAT or ACT (for admission).
Options: electronic application, early decision, deferred entrance.
Application fee: $70.
Required: essay or personal statement, high school transcript. ***Recommended:*** 2 letters of recommendation.
Application deadlines: 1/15 (freshmen), 7/1 (transfers).
Early decision deadline: 11/15 (for plan 1), 1/15 (for plan 2).
Notification: 4/1 (freshmen), continuous (transfers), 12/31 (early decision plan 1), 2/15 (early decision plan 2).

CONTACT
Mr. Greg Grauman, Assistant Vice Provost, Undergraduate Admissions, American University, 4400 Massachusetts Avenue, NW, Washington, DC 20016-8001. *Phone:* 202-885-6063. *E-mail:* admissions@american.edu.

★ The Catholic University of America
Washington, District of Columbia
http://www.cua.edu/

- **Independent** university, founded 1887, affiliated with Roman Catholic Church
- **Urban** 176-acre campus
- **Coed** 3,572 undergraduate students, 94% full-time, 53% women, 47% men
- **Moderately difficult** entrance level, 74% of applicants were admitted

UNDERGRAD STUDENTS
3,355 full-time, 217 part-time. Students come from 50 states and territories; 34 other countries; 96% are from out of state; 6% Black or African American, non-Hispanic/Latino; 12% Hispanic/Latino; 3% Asian, non-Hispanic/Latino; 0.1% Native Hawaiian or other Pacific Islander, non-Hispanic/Latino; 0.2% American Indian or Alaska Native, non-Hispanic/Latino; 4% Two or more races, non-Hispanic/Latino; 7% Race/ethnicity unknown; 5% international; 2% transferred in; 58% live on campus.

Freshmen
Admission: 6,363 applied, 4,703 admitted, 832 enrolled. ***Average high school GPA:*** 3.37. ***Test scores:*** SAT critical reading scores over 500: 81%; SAT math scores over 500: 80%; ACT scores over 18: 97%; SAT critical reading scores over 600: 33%; SAT math scores over 600: 33%; ACT scores over 24: 65%; SAT critical reading scores over 700: 5%; SAT math scores over 700: 4%; ACT scores over 30: 16%.

Retention: 82% of full-time freshmen returned.

FACULTY
Total: 808, 50% full-time, 48% with terminal degrees.

Student/faculty ratio: 7:1.

ACADEMICS
Calendar: semesters. *Degrees:* certificates, bachelor's, master's, doctoral, post-master's, and postbachelor's certificates.

Special study options: accelerated degree program, adult/continuing education programs, advanced placement credit, cooperative education, distance learning, double majors, English as a second language, honors programs, independent study, internships, off-campus study, part-time degree program, services for LD students, study abroad, summer session for credit. ***ROTC:*** Army (b), Navy (c), Air Force (c).

Unusual degree programs: 3-2 engineering; nursing; architecture, accounting, education, psychology.

Computers: 325 computers/terminals and 50 ports are available on campus for general student use. Students can access the following: campus intranet, computer help desk, free student e-mail accounts, online (class) grades, online (class) registration, online (class) schedules, Internet2, video streaming, online voting, pedagogical software. Campuswide network is available. 100% of college-owned or -operated housing units are wired for high-speed Internet access. Wireless service is available via classrooms, computer centers, computer labs, dorm rooms, libraries, student centers.

STUDENT LIFE
Housing options: on-campus residence required through sophomore year; coed, men-only, women-only. Campus housing is university owned. Freshman campus housing is guaranteed.

Activities and organizations: drama/theater group, student-run newspaper, radio station, choral group, Student Nursing Association, College Republicans, CU Film Society, Alpha Phi Omega, Program Board, national fraternities, national sororities.

Athletics Member NCAA. All Division III. ***Intercollegiate sports:*** baseball M, basketball M/W, cross-country running M/W, field hockey W, football M, lacrosse M/W, soccer M/W, softball W, swimming and diving M/W, tennis M/W, track and field M/W, volleyball W. ***Intramural sports:*** basketball M/W, cheerleading M(c)/W(c), crew M(c)/W(c), fencing M(c)/W(c), football M/W, ice hockey M(c), lacrosse M(c), rugby M(c)/W(c), sailing M(c)/W(c), soccer M/W, softball M/W, tennis M/W, ultimate Frisbee M(c)/W(c), volleyball M/W.

Campus security: 24-hour emergency response devices and patrols, late-night transport/escort service, controlled dormitory access, controlled access of academic buildings.

Student services: health clinic, personal/psychological counseling, legal services.

COSTS & FINANCIAL AID
Costs (2014–15) ***One-time required fee:*** $425. ***Comprehensive fee:*** $54,244 includes full-time tuition ($39,200), mandatory fees ($526), and room and board ($14,518). Full-time tuition and fees vary according to program. Part-time tuition: $1550 per credit hour. Part-time tuition and fees vary according to course load and program. ***Required fees:*** $303 per year part-time. ***Room and board:*** Room and board charges vary according to board plan and housing facility. ***Payment plan:*** installment. ***Waivers:*** children of alumni and employees or children of employees.

Financial Aid Of all full-time matriculated undergraduates who enrolled in 2014, 2,300 applied for aid, 1,961 were judged to have need, 842 had their need fully met. 318 Federal Work-Study jobs (averaging $1932). In 2014, 1024 non-need-based awards were made. ***Average percent of need met:*** 79. ***Average financial aid package:*** $25,560. ***Average need-based loan:*** $4937. ***Average need-based gift aid:*** $21,601. ***Average non-need-based aid:*** $15,620. ***Financial aid deadline:*** 4/10.

APPLYING
Standardized Tests *Required:* SAT or ACT (for admission). *Recommended:* SAT Subject Tests (for admission).

Options: electronic application, early action, deferred entrance.

Application fee: $55.

Required: essay or personal statement, high school transcript, 1 letter of recommendation. ***Required for some:*** interview. ***Recommended:*** minimum 3.0 GPA.

Application deadlines: 2/15 (freshmen), 7/15 (transfers), 11/15 (early action).

Notification: 3/15 (freshmen), 12/15 (early action).

CONTACT
TBD, Dean, University Admissions, The Catholic University of America, 102 McMahon Hall, 620 Michigan Avenue, NE, Washington, DC 20064. *Phone:* 202-319-5305. *Toll-free phone:* 800-673-2772. *Fax:* 202-319-6533. *E-mail:* cua-admissions@cua.edu.

Gallaudet University

Washington, District of Columbia

http://www.gallaudet.edu/

- **Independent** university, founded 1864
- **Urban** 99-acre campus
- **Coed** 1,031 undergraduate students, 92% full-time, 55% women, 45% men
- **Moderately difficult** entrance level, 65% of applicants were admitted

UNDERGRAD STUDENTS
951 full-time, 80 part-time. Students come from 50 states and territories; 22 other countries; 97% are from out of state; 12% Black or African American, non-Hispanic/Latino; 14% Hispanic/Latino; 4% Asian, non-Hispanic/Latino; 0.3% Native Hawaiian or other Pacific Islander, non-Hispanic/Latino; 0.3% American Indian or Alaska Native, non-Hispanic/Latino; 3% Two or more races, non-Hispanic/Latino; 0.7% Race/ethnicity unknown; 9% international; 10% transferred in; 72% live on campus.

Freshmen
Admission: 496 applied, 324 admitted, 182 enrolled. ***Average high school GPA:*** 3.19. ***Test scores:*** SAT critical reading scores over 500: 17%; SAT math scores over 500: 17%; ACT scores over 18: 40%; SAT critical reading scores over 600: 4%; SAT math scores over 600: 4%; ACT scores over 24: 8%; SAT critical reading scores over 700: 4%; SAT math scores over 700: 4%; ACT scores over 30: 2%.

Retention: 67% of full-time freshmen returned.

FACULTY
Total: 308, 59% full-time, 57% with terminal degrees.

Student/faculty ratio: 6:1.

ACADEMICS
Calendar: semesters. *Degrees:* bachelor's, master's, doctoral, post-master's, and postbachelor's certificates (Undergraduate programs are open primarily to the students with hearing-impairments).

Special study options: academic remediation for entering students, adult/continuing education programs, advanced placement credit, distance learning, double majors, English as a second language, honors programs, independent study, internships, off-campus study, part-time degree program, services for LD students, student-designed majors, study abroad, summer session for credit.

Computers: 400 computers/terminals are available on campus for general student use. Students can access the following: campus intranet, computer help desk, free student e-mail accounts, online (class) grades, online (class) registration, online (class) schedules. Campuswide network is available. 100% of college-owned or -operated housing units are wired for

high-speed Internet access. Wireless service is available via entire campus.

STUDENT LIFE

Housing options: coed, special housing for students with disabilities. Campus housing is university owned.

Activities and organizations: drama/theater group, student-run newspaper, television station, Student Body Government, The Buff and Blue, Rainbow Society, Green Grow, national fraternities, national sororities.

Athletics Member NCAA. All Division III. ***Intercollegiate sports:*** baseball M, basketball M/W, cheerleading M(c)/W(c), cross-country running M/W, football M, soccer M/W, softball W, swimming and diving M/W, track and field M/W, volleyball W. ***Intramural sports:*** basketball M/W, football M/W, soccer M/W, table tennis M/W, ultimate Frisbee M/W, volleyball M/W.

Campus security: 24-hour emergency response devices and patrols, late-night transport/escort service, controlled dormitory access.

Student services: health clinic, personal/psychological counseling.

COSTS & FINANCIAL AID

Costs (2015–16) ***Comprehensive fee:*** $28,234 includes full-time tuition ($15,078), mandatory fees ($526), and room and board ($12,630). Full-time tuition and fees vary according to course load. Part-time tuition: $628 per credit. Part-time tuition and fees vary according to course load. ***College room only:*** $7080. Room and board charges vary according to board plan. ***Payment plans:*** installment, deferred payment. ***Waivers:*** employees or children of employees.

Financial Aid Of all full-time matriculated undergraduates who enrolled in 2013, 918 applied for aid, 860 were judged to have need, 92 had their need fully met. 32 Federal Work-Study jobs (averaging $1622). In 2013, 17 non-need-based awards were made. ***Average percent of need met:*** 71. ***Average financial aid package:*** $18,975. ***Average need-based loan:*** $3792. ***Average need-based gift aid:*** $14,274. ***Average non-need-based aid:*** $7148. ***Average indebtedness upon graduation:*** $15,972.

APPLYING

Standardized Tests *Required:* SAT or ACT (for admission). *Recommended:* ACT (for admission).

Options: electronic application, deferred entrance.

Application fee: $50.

Required: essay or personal statement, high school transcript, 2 letters of recommendation, audiogram. ***Required for some:*** interview.

Notification: continuous (freshmen), continuous (transfers).

CONTACT

Gallaudet University, 800 Florida Avenue, NE, Washington, DC 20002-3625. *Phone:* 202-651-5750. *Toll-free phone:* 800-995-0550.

Georgetown University

Washington, District of Columbia

http://www.georgetown.edu/

- **Independent Roman Catholic (Jesuit)** university, founded 1789
- **Urban** 104-acre campus with easy access to Washington, DC
- **Coed** 7,595 undergraduate students, 95% full-time, 55% women, 45% men
- **Most difficult** entrance level, 17% of applicants were admitted

UNDERGRAD STUDENTS

7,226 full-time, 369 part-time. Students come from 52 states and territories; 109 other countries; 97% are from out of state; 6% Black or African American, non-Hispanic/Latino; 7% Hispanic/Latino; 9% Asian, non-Hispanic/Latino; 0.1% American Indian or Alaska Native, non-Hispanic/Latino; 4% Two or more races, non-Hispanic/Latino; 3% Race/ethnicity unknown; 14% international; 2% transferred in; 63% live on campus.

Freshmen

Admission: 19,505 applied, 3,384 admitted, 1,578 enrolled. ***Test scores:*** SAT critical reading scores over 500: 99%; SAT math scores over 500: 100%; ACT scores over 18: 100%; SAT critical reading scores over 600: 91%; SAT math scores over 600: 94%; ACT scores over 24: 98%; SAT critical reading scores over 700: 59%; SAT math scores over 700: 56%; ACT scores over 30: 76%.

Retention: 96% of full-time freshmen returned.

FACULTY

Total: 1,975, 51% full-time, 61% with terminal degrees.

Student/faculty ratio: 11:1.

ACADEMICS

Calendar: semesters. *Degrees:* certificates, bachelor's, master's, doctoral, post-master's, and postbachelor's certificates.

Special study options: academic remediation for entering students, adult/continuing education programs, advanced placement credit, distance learning, double majors, English as a second language, honors programs, independent study, internships, off-campus study, part-time degree program, services for LD students, student-designed majors, study abroad, summer session for credit. ***ROTC:*** Army (b), Navy (c), Air Force (c).

Unusual degree programs: 3-2 Foreign service.

Computers: 500 computers/terminals and 1,000 ports are available on campus for general student use. Students can access the following: computer help desk, free student e-mail accounts, online (class) grades, online (class) registration, online (class) schedules, online grade reports. Campuswide network is available. 100% of college-owned or -operated housing units are wired for high-speed Internet access. Wireless service is available via classrooms, computer centers, computer labs, dorm rooms, learning centers, libraries, student centers.

STUDENT LIFE

Housing options: on-campus residence required through sophomore year; coed, special housing for students with disabilities. Campus housing is university owned. Freshman campus housing is guaranteed.

Activities and organizations: drama/theater group, student-run newspaper, radio and television station, choral group, Georgetown University Student Association (Student Government), International Relations Club, College Democrats, Georgetown University Grilling Society, Black Student Alliance.

Athletics Member NCAA. All Division I except football (Division I-AA). ***Intercollegiate sports:*** baseball M(s), basketball M(s)/W(s), crew M(s)/W(s), cross-country running M(s)/W(s), field hockey W(s), golf M(s)/W(s), ice hockey M(c), lacrosse M(s)/W(s), rugby M(c)/W(c), sailing M/W, soccer M(s)/W(s), softball W(s), swimming and diving M/W(s), tennis M/W(s), track and field M(s)/W(s), ultimate Frisbee M(c)/W(c), volleyball M(c)/W(s), water polo M(c). ***Intramural sports:*** basketball M/W, cross-country running M/W, football M/W, golf M/W, racquetball M/W, soccer M/W, softball M/W, squash M/W, table tennis M/W, tennis M/W, track and field M/W, ultimate Frisbee M, volleyball M/W.

Campus security: 24-hour emergency response devices and patrols, late-night transport/escort service, controlled dormitory access, student guards at residence halls and academic facilities.

Student services: health clinic, personal/psychological counseling, women's center.

COSTS & FINANCIAL AID

Costs (2014–15) ***Comprehensive fee:*** $60,768 includes full-time tuition ($46,200), mandatory fees ($544), and room and board ($14,024). Full-time tuition and fees vary according to course load and program. Part-time tuition: $1925 per credit hour. Part-time tuition and fees vary according to course load and program. ***College room only:*** $9548. Room and board charges vary according to board plan and housing facility. ***Payment plan:*** installment.

Financial Aid Of all full-time matriculated undergraduates who enrolled in 2014, 4,017 applied for aid, 2,757 were judged to have need, 2,757 had their need fully met. 2,614 Federal Work-Study jobs (averaging $2933). ***Average percent of need met:*** 100. ***Average financial aid package:*** $39,693. ***Average need-based loan:*** $4318. ***Average need-based gift aid:*** $36,878. ***Average indebtedness upon graduation:*** $22,464. ***Financial aid deadline:*** 2/1.

APPLYING

Standardized Tests *Required:* SAT or ACT (for admission). *Recommended:* SAT Subject Tests (for admission).

Options: electronic application, early action, deferred entrance.

Application fee: $75.

Required: essay or personal statement, high school transcript, 2 letters of recommendation, interview.

Application deadlines: 1/10 (freshmen), 3/1 (transfers), 11/1 (early action).

Notification: 4/1 (freshmen), 6/1 (transfers), 12/15 (early action).

CONTACT
Dean Charles A. Deacon, Dean of Undergraduate Admissions, Georgetown University, 37th and O Street, NW, Washington, DC 20057. *Phone:* 202-687-3600. *Fax:* 202-687-5084.

The George Washington University

Washington, District of Columbia

http://www.gwu.edu/

- **Independent** university, founded 1821
- **Urban** 36-acre campus
- **Coed** 10,740 undergraduate students, 92% full-time, 56% women, 44% men
- **Very difficult** entrance level, 44% of applicants were admitted

UNDERGRAD STUDENTS
9,830 full-time, 910 part-time. Students come from 54 states and territories; 87 other countries; 98% are from out of state; 6% Black or African American, non-Hispanic/Latino; 8% Hispanic/Latino; 10% Asian, non-Hispanic/Latino; 0.1% Native Hawaiian or other Pacific Islander, non-Hispanic/Latino; 0.2% American Indian or Alaska Native, non-Hispanic/Latino; 3% Two or more races, non-Hispanic/Latino; 5% Race/ethnicity unknown; 10% international; 5% transferred in; 63% live on campus.

Freshmen
Admission: 19,069 applied, 8,351 admitted, 2,416 enrolled. ***Test scores:*** SAT critical reading scores over 500: 97%; SAT math scores over 500: 97%; SAT writing scores over 500: 98%; ACT scores over 18: 100%; SAT critical reading scores over 600: 74%; SAT math scores over 600: 79%; SAT writing scores over 600: 80%; ACT scores over 24: 98%; SAT critical reading scores over 700: 21%; SAT math scores over 700: 27%; SAT writing scores over 700: 25%; ACT scores over 30: 46%.

Retention: 93% of full-time freshmen returned.

ACADEMICS
Calendar: semesters. *Degrees:* certificates, associate, bachelor's, master's, doctoral, post-master's, and postbachelor's certificates.

Special study options: accelerated degree program, adult/continuing education programs, advanced placement credit, cooperative education, distance learning, double majors, honors programs, independent study, internships, off-campus study, part-time degree program, services for LD students, student-designed majors, study abroad, summer session for credit. ***ROTC:*** Army (c), Navy (b), Air Force (c).

Unusual degree programs: 3-2 business administration; engineering; chemical toxicology, art therapy, economics, engineering economics, operations research.

Computers: Campuswide network is available.

STUDENT LIFE
Housing options: on-campus residence required through sophomore year; coed. Campus housing is university owned. Freshman campus housing is guaranteed.

Activities and organizations: drama/theater group, student-run newspaper, radio and television station, choral group, marching band, Program Board, Student Association, Residence Hall Association, College Democrats, College Republicans, national fraternities, national sororities.

Athletics Member NCAA. All Division I. ***Intercollegiate sports:*** baseball M(s), basketball M(s)/W(s), crew M(s)/W(s), cross-country running M(s)/W(s), golf M(s), gymnastics W(s), soccer M(s)/W(s), swimming and diving M(s)/W(s), tennis M(s)/W(s), volleyball W(s), water polo M(s). ***Intramural sports:*** badminton M(c)/W(c), basketball M/W, bowling M(c)/W(c), equestrian sports M(c)/W(c), fencing M(c)/W(c), football M/W, lacrosse M(c), racquetball M/W, rugby M(c), sailing M(c)/W(c), soccer M/W, softball M/W, squash M(c)/W, swimming and diving M/W, tennis M/W, volleyball M(c)/W, water polo M/W.

Campus security: 24-hour emergency response devices and patrols, late-night transport/escort service, controlled dormitory access.

Student services: health clinic, personal/psychological counseling, legal services.

COSTS & FINANCIAL AID
Costs (2015–16) ***Comprehensive fee:*** $62,485 includes full-time tuition ($50,367), mandatory fees ($68), and room and board ($12,050). Full-time tuition and fees vary according to student level. Part-time tuition: $1430 per credit hour. Part-time tuition and fees vary according to course load. No tuition increase for student's term of enrollment. ***Required fees:*** $2 per credit hour part-time. ***Room and board:*** Room and board charges vary according to housing facility. ***Payment plan:*** installment. ***Waivers:*** employees or children of employees.

Financial Aid Of all full-time matriculated undergraduates who enrolled in 2013, 5,371 applied for aid, 4,525 were judged to have need, 2,461 had their need fully met. In 2013, 1943 non-need-based awards were made. ***Average percent of need met:*** 89. ***Average financial aid package:*** $42,335. ***Average need-based loan:*** $5758. ***Average need-based gift aid:*** $29,879. ***Average non-need-based aid:*** $18,780. ***Average indebtedness upon graduation:*** $31,337. ***Financial aid deadline:*** 2/1.

APPLYING
Standardized Tests *Required:* SAT or ACT (for admission).

Options: electronic application, early admission, early decision, deferred entrance.

Application fee: $75.

Required: essay or personal statement, high school transcript, 2 letters of recommendation. ***Recommended:*** interview.

Application deadlines: 1/10 (freshmen), rolling (transfers).

Early decision deadline: 11/10 (for plan 1), 1/10 (for plan 2).

Notification: 4/1 (freshmen), continuous (transfers), 12/15 (early decision plan 1), 2/1 (early decision plan 2).

CONTACT
The George Washington University, 2121 I Street, NW, Washington, DC 20052. *Phone:* 202-994-6040.

See page 1456 for the College Close-Up.

Howard University

Washington, District of Columbia

http://www.howard.edu/

- **Independent** university, founded 1867
- **Urban** 256-acre campus with easy access to Baltimore Metropolitan Area
- **Endowment** $586.1 million
- **Coed** 7,013 undergraduate students, 93% full-time, 67% women, 33% men
- **Moderately difficult** entrance level, 48% of applicants were admitted

UNDERGRAD STUDENTS
6,513 full-time, 500 part-time. Students come from 48 states and territories; 41 other countries; 95% are from out of state; 91% Black or African American, non-Hispanic/Latino; 0.4% Hispanic/Latino; 2% Asian, non-Hispanic/Latino; 0.2% Native Hawaiian or other Pacific Islander, non-Hispanic/Latino; 1% American Indian or Alaska Native, non-Hispanic/Latino; 4% international; 5% transferred in; 56% live on campus.

Freshmen
Admission: 13,760 applied, 6,661 admitted, 1,479 enrolled. ***Average high school GPA:*** 3.34. ***Test scores:*** SAT critical reading scores over 500: 78%; SAT math scores over 500: 75%; SAT writing scores over 500: 74%; ACT scores over 18: 97%; SAT critical reading scores over 600: 32%; SAT math scores over 600: 31%; SAT writing scores over 600: 29%; ACT scores over 24: 54%; SAT critical reading scores over 700: 4%; SAT math scores over 700: 6%; SAT writing scores over 700: 4%; ACT scores over 30: 7%.

Retention: 85% of full-time freshmen returned.

FACULTY
Total: 1,520, 76% full-time, 76% with terminal degrees.

Student/faculty ratio: 8:1.

ACADEMICS

Calendar: semesters. *Degrees:* certificates, bachelor's, master's, doctoral, and post-master's certificates.

Special study options: academic remediation for entering students, accelerated degree program, advanced placement credit, cooperative education, distance learning, double majors, honors programs, independent study, internships, off-campus study, part-time degree program, services for LD students, study abroad, summer session for credit. ***ROTC:*** Army (b), Air Force (b).

Computers: 6,343 computers/terminals are available on campus for general student use. Students can access the following: campus intranet, computer help desk, free student e-mail accounts, online (class) grades, online (class) registration, online (class) schedules, student residential network. Campuswide network is available. 100% of college-owned or -operated housing units are wired for high-speed Internet access. Wireless service is available via entire campus.

STUDENT LIFE

Housing options: on-campus residence required through sophomore year; coed, men-only, women-only, special housing for students with disabilities. Campus housing is university owned. Freshman applicants given priority for college housing.

Activities and organizations: drama/theater group, student-run newspaper, radio and television station, choral group, marching band, Howard University Student Association, Undergraduate Student Assembly, Campus Pals, International Student Organization, Entrepreneurial Society, Howard University, national fraternities, national sororities.

Athletics Member NCAA. All Division I except football (Division I-AA). ***Intercollegiate sports:*** basketball M(s)/W(s), bowling W(s), cross-country running M(s)/W(s), lacrosse W(s), soccer M(s)/W(s), softball W, swimming and diving M(s)/W(s), tennis M(s)/W(s), track and field M(s)/W(s), volleyball W(s). ***Intramural sports:*** basketball M/W, football M, soccer M/W, softball W, swimming and diving M/W, tennis M/W, track and field M/W, volleyball M/W.

Campus security: 24-hour emergency response devices and patrols, student patrols, late-night transport/escort service, controlled dormitory access, security lighting.

Student services: health clinic, personal/psychological counseling.

COSTS & FINANCIAL AID

Costs (2015–16) ***Comprehensive fee:*** $37,616 includes full-time tuition ($22,737), mandatory fees ($1233), and room and board ($13,646). Full-time tuition and fees vary according to course load. Part-time tuition: $980 per credit hour. Part-time tuition and fees vary according to course load. ***Required fees:*** $1233 per term part-time. ***College room only:*** $9506. Room and board charges vary according to board plan and housing facility. ***Payment plan:*** installment. ***Waivers:*** employees or children of employees.

Financial Aid Of all full-time matriculated undergraduates who enrolled in 2012, 5,626 applied for aid, 5,085 were judged to have need, 580 had their need fully met. 241 Federal Work-Study jobs (averaging $3739). 224 state and other part-time jobs (averaging $3796). In 2012, 366 non-need-based awards were made. ***Average percent of need met:*** 75. ***Average financial aid package:*** $15,268. ***Average need-based loan:*** $4285. ***Average need-based gift aid:*** $6478. ***Average non-need-based aid:*** $22,012. ***Average indebtedness upon graduation:*** $10,455. ***Financial aid deadline:*** 8/15.

APPLYING

Standardized Tests *Required:* SAT or ACT (for admission).

Options: electronic application, early admission, early action, deferred entrance.

Application fee: $45.

Required: essay or personal statement, high school transcript. ***Required for some:*** 2 letters of recommendation.

Application deadlines: 2/15 (freshmen), 4/1 (transfers), 11/1 (early action).

Notification: continuous until 4/1 (freshmen), continuous (transfers), 12/20 (early action).

CONTACT

Tammy McCants, Associate Director of Admissions, Howard University, 2400 Sixth Street N.W., Suite 111, Washington, DC 20059. *Phone:* 202-806-2763. *Toll-free phone:* 800-822-6363. *Fax:* 202-806-4465. *E-mail:* admission@howard.edu.

University of the District of Columbia

Washington, District of Columbia

http://www.udc.edu/

- **District-supported** comprehensive, founded 1976
- **Urban** 28-acre campus
- **Endowment** $41.5 million
- **Coed** 4,491 undergraduate students, 42% full-time, 63% women, 37% men
- **Minimally difficult** entrance level

UNDERGRAD STUDENTS

1,902 full-time, 2,589 part-time. 62% Black or African American, non-Hispanic/Latino; 9% Hispanic/Latino; 3% Asian, non-Hispanic/Latino; 0.1% Native Hawaiian or other Pacific Islander, non-Hispanic/Latino; 0.2% American Indian or Alaska Native, non-Hispanic/Latino; 2% Two or more races, non-Hispanic/Latino; 17% Race/ethnicity unknown; 3% international.

Freshmen

Admission: 521 enrolled.

Retention: 52% of full-time freshmen returned.

FACULTY

Total: 576, 45% full-time.

Student/faculty ratio: 11:1.

ACADEMICS

Calendar: semesters. *Degrees:* associate, bachelor's, master's, and doctoral.

Special study options: academic remediation for entering students, accelerated degree program, adult/continuing education programs, cooperative education, English as a second language, external degree program, honors programs, internships, off-campus study, part-time degree program, services for LD students, summer session for credit. ***ROTC:*** Army (c), Air Force (c).

Computers: 1,586 computers/terminals are available on campus for general student use. Students can access the following: campus intranet, computer help desk, free student e-mail accounts, online (class) grades, online (class) registration, online (class) schedules. Campuswide network is available. Wireless service is available via classrooms, computer labs, learning centers, libraries.

STUDENT LIFE

Housing options: Campus housing is leased by the school.

Activities and organizations: drama/theater group, student-run newspaper, choral group, marching band, Caribbean Student Association, Theater Arts Ensemble, National Association for the Advancement of Colored People, national fraternities, national sororities.

Athletics Member NCAA. All Division II. ***Intercollegiate sports:*** basketball M(s)/W(s), cross-country running W(s), lacrosse M(s)/W(s), soccer M(s), tennis M(s)/W(s), track and field W(s).

Campus security: 24-hour emergency response devices and patrols.

Student services: health clinic, personal/psychological counseling.

COSTS & FINANCIAL AID

Costs (2014–15) ***Tuition:*** district resident $4518 full-time, $188 per credit hour part-time; nonresident $10,354 full-time, $431 per credit hour part-time. Full-time tuition and fees vary according to course load and location. Part-time tuition and fees vary according to course load. ***Required fees:*** $610 full-time, $30 per credit hour part-time. ***Room and board:*** $10,300; room only: $8400. ***Payment plans:*** installment, deferred payment. ***Waivers:*** senior citizens and employees or children of employees.

Financial Aid Of all full-time matriculated undergraduates who enrolled in 2014, 1,503 applied for aid, 1,398 were judged to have need, 269 had their need fully met. 45 Federal Work-Study jobs (averaging $2500). 53 state and other part-time jobs (averaging $3000). In 2014, 9 non-need-based awards were made. ***Average percent of need met:*** 58. ***Average financial aid package:*** $8200. ***Average need-based loan:*** $4200. ***Average need-based gift aid:*** $5500. ***Average non-need-based aid:*** $3200.

APPLYING
Standardized Tests *Required for some:* SAT (for admission).
Options: electronic application, deferred entrance.
Application fee: $35.
Required: high school transcript. ***Required for some:*** GED.
Application deadlines: 8/1 (freshmen), 8/1 (transfers).
Notification: continuous until 8/15 (freshmen), continuous until 8/15 (transfers).

CONTACT
Ms. Nicole L Daniels, Director of Undergraduate Recruitment and Admissions, University of the District of Columbia, 4200 Connecticut Ave. NW, Washington, DC 20008. *Phone:* 202-274-6430. *Fax:* 202-274-5553. *E-mail:* nicole.daniels@udc.edu.

University of the Potomac

Washington, District of Columbia

http://www.potomac.edu/

- **Proprietary** comprehensive, founded 1991
- **Urban** campus with easy access to Washington, DC
- **Coed**
- **Noncompetitive** entrance level

FACULTY
Student/faculty ratio: 10:1.

ACADEMICS
Calendar: 6-week modules. *Degrees:* associate, bachelor's, and master's.

STUDENT LIFE
Housing options: college housing not available.
Campus security: late-night transport/escort service.

COSTS
Costs (2014–15) ***Tuition:*** $12,984 full-time, $541 per credit part-time. No tuition increase for student's term of enrollment. ***Required fees:*** $541 full-time, $541 per credit part-time, $450 per term part-time.

APPLYING
Options: electronic application.
Required: interview.

CONTACT
Niambi Green, Director of Admissions, University of the Potomac, 1401 H Street N.W. Suite 100, Washington, DC 20005. *Phone:* 202-734-4357. *Toll-free phone:* 888-686-0876. *E-mail:* admissions@potomac.edu.

FLORIDA

Adventist University of Health Sciences

Orlando, Florida

http://www.adu.edu/

- **Independent** comprehensive, founded 1913
- **Urban** 9-acre campus with easy access to Orlando
- **Endowment** $6.9 million
- **Coed** 1,950 undergraduate students, 35% full-time, 80% women, 20% men
- **Minimally difficult** entrance level, 100% of applicants were admitted

UNDERGRAD STUDENTS
674 full-time, 1,276 part-time. Students come from 46 states and territories; 4 other countries; 30% are from out of state; 14% Black or African American, non-Hispanic/Latino; 22% Hispanic/Latino; 6% Asian, non-Hispanic/Latino; 0.7% Native Hawaiian or other Pacific Islander, non-Hispanic/Latino; 0.3% American Indian or Alaska Native, non-Hispanic/Latino; 2% Two or more races, non-Hispanic/Latino; 9% Race/ethnicity unknown; 0.4% international; 16% transferred in.

Freshmen
Admission: 118 applied, 118 admitted, 88 enrolled. ***Test scores:*** ACT scores over 18: 82%; ACT scores over 24: 14%; ACT scores over 30: 1%.
Retention: 70% of full-time freshmen returned.

FACULTY
Total: 246, 33% full-time, 25% with terminal degrees.
Student/faculty ratio: 9:1.

ACADEMICS
Calendar: semesters. *Degrees:* associate, bachelor's, master's, and doctoral.
Special study options: academic remediation for entering students, cooperative education, distance learning, double majors, independent study, part-time degree program, services for LD students, summer session for credit.
Computers: 43 computers/terminals are available on campus for general student use. Students can access the following: campus intranet, computer help desk, free student e-mail accounts, online (class) grades, online (class) registration, online (class) schedules, online registration. Campuswide network is available. Wireless service is available via entire campus.

STUDENT LIFE
Housing options: coed. Campus housing is leased by the school.
Activities and organizations: drama/theater group, Student Nursing Association, Student Occupational Therapy Association, Pre Physician Assistant, Pre Medical School, Campus Ministries.
Campus security: 24-hour emergency response devices and patrols, late-night transport/escort service, controlled dormitory access.
Student services: personal/psychological counseling.

COSTS & FINANCIAL AID
Costs (2015–16) ***Tuition:*** $12,450 full-time, $415 per credit hour part-time. Full-time tuition and fees vary according to course load, degree level, and program. Part-time tuition and fees vary according to course load, degree level, and program. ***Required fees:*** $580 full-time, $290 per term part-time. ***Room only:*** $4000. ***Payment plans:*** installment, deferred payment. ***Waivers:*** employees or children of employees.
Financial Aid ***Financial aid deadline:*** 7/22.

APPLYING
Standardized Tests *Required:* SAT or ACT (for admission).
Options: electronic application, early admission, early decision.
Application fee: $20.
Required: minimum 2.5 GPA. ***Required for some:*** essay or personal statement, high school transcript, 3 letters of recommendation, interview.
Application deadlines: 7/1 (freshmen), 7/1 (out-of-state freshmen), 7/1 (transfers).
Early decision deadline: 2/1.
Notification: continuous until 8/15 (freshmen), continuous until 8/15 (out-of-state freshmen), continuous until 8/15 (transfers), 3/1 (early decision).

CONTACT
Adventist University of Health Sciences, 671 Winyah Drive, Orlando, FL 32803. *Phone:* 407-303-7742. *Toll-free phone:* 800-500-7747.

Argosy University, Sarasota

Sarasota, Florida

http://www.argosy.edu/locations/sarasota/

- **Proprietary** university, founded 1974, part of Education Management Corporation
- **Coed**

ACADEMICS
Calendar: semesters. *Degrees:* certificates, associate, bachelor's, master's, and doctoral.

CONTACT
Argosy University, Sarasota, 5250 17th Street, Sarasota, FL 34235. *Phone:* 941-379-0404. *Toll-free phone:* 800-331-5995.

Argosy University, Tampa

Tampa, Florida

http://www.argosy.edu/locations/tampa/

- **Proprietary** university, part of Education Management Corporation
- **Urban** campus
- **Coed**

ACADEMICS
Calendar: semesters. *Degrees:* certificates, associate, bachelor's, master's, and doctoral.

CONTACT
Argosy University, Tampa, 1403 North Howard Avenue, Tampa, FL 33607. *Phone:* 813-393-5290. *Toll-free phone:* 800-850-6488.

The Art Institute of Fort Lauderdale

Fort Lauderdale, Florida

http://www.artinstitutes.edu/fortlauderdale/

- **Proprietary** 4-year, founded 1968, part of Education Management Corporation
- **Urban** campus
- **Coed**

ACADEMICS
Calendar: quarters. *Degrees:* diplomas, associate, and bachelor's.

CONTACT
The Art Institute of Fort Lauderdale, 1799 Southeast 17th Street, Fort Lauderdale, FL 33316. *Phone:* 954-463-3000. *Toll-free phone:* 800-275-7603.

The Art Institute of Jacksonville, a branch of Miami International University of Art & Design

Jacksonville, Florida

http://www.artinstitutes.edu/jacksonville/

- **Proprietary** 4-year, founded 2006, part of Education Management Corporation
- **Suburban** campus
- **Coed**

ACADEMICS
Degrees: diplomas, associate, and bachelor's.

CONTACT
The Art Institute of Jacksonville, a branch of Miami International University of Art & Design, 8775 Baypine Road, Jacksonville, FL 32256. *Phone:* 904-486-3000. *Toll-free phone:* 800-924-1589.

The Art Institute of Tampa, a branch of Miami International University of Art & Design

Tampa, Florida

http://www.artinstitutes.edu/tampa/

- **Proprietary** 4-year, part of Education Management Corporation
- **Suburban** campus
- **Coed**

ACADEMICS
Calendar: quarters. *Degrees:* diplomas, associate, and bachelor's.

CONTACT
The Art Institute of Tampa, a branch of Miami International University of Art & Design, Parkside at Tampa Bay Park, 4401 North Himes Avenue, Suite 150, Tampa, FL 33614. *Phone:* 813-873-2112. *Toll-free phone:* 866-703-3277.

★ Ave Maria University

Ave Maria, Florida

http://www.avemaria.edu/

- **Independent Roman Catholic** comprehensive, founded 2002
- **Small-town** 790-acre campus
- **Endowment** $2.5 million
- **Coed** 1,028 undergraduate students, 98% full-time, 48% women, 52% men
- **Moderately difficult** entrance level, 56% of applicants were admitted

UNDERGRAD STUDENTS
1,012 full-time, 16 part-time. Students come from 48 states and territories; 15 other countries; 55% are from out of state; 5% Black or African American, non-Hispanic/Latino; 17% Hispanic/Latino; 3% Asian, non-Hispanic/Latino; 0.5% American Indian or Alaska Native, non-Hispanic/Latino; 5% Race/ethnicity unknown; 2% international; 7% transferred in; 90% live on campus.

Freshmen
Admission: 1,464 applied, 819 admitted, 304 enrolled. ***Average high school GPA:*** 3.6. ***Test scores:*** SAT critical reading scores over 500: 97%; SAT math scores over 500: 86%; SAT writing scores over 500: 98%; ACT scores over 18: 98%; SAT critical reading scores over 600: 73%; SAT math scores over 600: 51%; SAT writing scores over 600: 73%; ACT scores over 24: 54%; SAT critical reading scores over 700: 30%; SAT math scores over 700: 18%; SAT writing scores over 700: 28%; ACT scores over 30: 27%.

Retention: 74% of full-time freshmen returned.

FACULTY
Total: 84, 73% full-time, 75% with terminal degrees.
Student/faculty ratio: 15:1.

ACADEMICS
Calendar: semesters. *Degrees:* bachelor's, master's, and doctoral.
Special study options: accelerated degree program, double majors, honors programs, independent study, internships, services for LD students, study abroad, summer session for credit.
Unusual degree programs: 3-2 theology.
Computers: Students can access the following: campus intranet, computer help desk, free student e-mail accounts, online (class) grades, online (class) registration, online (class) schedules. Campuswide network is available. 100% of college-owned or -operated housing units are wired for high-speed Internet access. Wireless service is available via classrooms, computer labs, dorm rooms, libraries, student centers.

STUDENT LIFE
Housing options: on-campus residence required through senior year; men-only, women-only. Campus housing is university owned. Freshman campus housing is guaranteed.
Activities and organizations: drama/theater group, student-run newspaper, choral group, Students for Life, Drama Club, Student Government Association, Intercollegiate Studies Institute, Faith in Action Ministry.
Athletics Member NAIA. ***Intercollegiate sports:*** baseball M, basketball M/W, cheerleading W, cross-country running M/W, football M, golf M/W, lacrosse W, soccer M/W, softball W, tennis M/W, volleyball W. ***Intramural sports:*** basketball M(c)/W(c), football M(c), rugby M(c), soccer M(c)/W(c), ultimate Frisbee M(c)/W(c), volleyball M(c)/W(c).
Campus security: 24-hour patrols, controlled dormitory access, County Sheriff workstation on campus with deputy patrols.
Student services: health clinic, personal/psychological counseling.

COSTS & FINANCIAL AID
Costs (2014–15) ***Comprehensive fee:*** $28,616 includes full-time tuition ($17,712), mandatory fees ($767), and room and board ($10,137). ***Payment plan:*** installment. ***Waivers:*** employees or children of employees.
Financial Aid Of all full-time matriculated undergraduates who enrolled in 2014, 798 applied for aid, 678 were judged to have need, 154 had their need fully met. 97 Federal Work-Study jobs (averaging $1466). 1 state and other part-time job (averaging $1500). In 2014, 286 non-need-based awards were made. ***Average percent of need met:*** 72. ***Average financial***

aid package: $15,647. ***Average need-based loan:*** $3851. ***Average need-based gift aid:*** $12,226. ***Average non-need-based aid:*** $7477.

APPLYING
Standardized Tests *Required:* SAT or ACT (for admission).

Options: electronic application, deferred entrance.

Required: high school transcript, minimum 2.8 GPA, activities list. ***Required for some:*** essay or personal statement, 2 letters of recommendation, interview.

Application deadlines: rolling (freshmen), 12/1 (transfers).

Notification: continuous (freshmen), continuous (transfers).

CONTACT
Ave Maria University, 5050 Ave Maria Boulevard, Ave Maria, FL 34142. *Phone:* 239-280-2487. *Toll-free phone:* 877-283-8648. *Fax:* 239-280-2559.

The Baptist College of Florida

Graceville, Florida

http://www.baptistcollege.edu/

- **Independent Southern Baptist** comprehensive, founded 1943
- **Small-town** 250-acre campus
- **Endowment** $6.5 million
- **Coed** 462 undergraduate students, 76% full-time, 38% women, 62% men
- **Noncompetitive** entrance level, 56% of applicants were admitted

UNDERGRAD STUDENTS
350 full-time, 112 part-time. Students come from 15 states and territories; 26% are from out of state; 7% Black or African American, non-Hispanic/Latino; 4% Hispanic/Latino; 0.2% Asian, non-Hispanic/Latino; 0.2% Native Hawaiian or other Pacific Islander, non-Hispanic/Latino; 0.9% American Indian or Alaska Native, non-Hispanic/Latino; 3% Two or more races, non-Hispanic/Latino; 5% Race/ethnicity unknown; 13% transferred in; 39% live on campus.

Freshmen
Admission: 144 applied, 80 admitted, 35 enrolled.

Retention: 67% of full-time freshmen returned.

FACULTY
Total: 74, 35% full-time, 46% with terminal degrees.

Student/faculty ratio: 10:1.

ACADEMICS
Calendar: semesters. *Degrees:* certificates, associate, bachelor's, and master's.

Special study options: academic remediation for entering students, advanced placement credit, distance learning, double majors, independent study, internships, part-time degree program, services for LD students, summer session for credit.

Computers: 25 computers/terminals are available on campus for general student use. Students can access the following: free student e-mail accounts, online (class) grades, online (class) registration. Campuswide network is available. Wireless service is available via entire campus.

STUDENT LIFE
Housing options: on-campus residence required through sophomore year; men-only, women-only, special housing for students with disabilities. Campus housing is university owned. Freshman campus housing is guaranteed.

Activities and organizations: drama/theater group, choral group, Baptist Collegiate Ministry, College Choir, AACC.

Athletics ***Intramural sports:*** basketball M/W, fencing M/W, football M/W, soccer M/W, softball M/W, ultimate Frisbee M/W, volleyball M/W.

Campus security: student patrols, patrols by police officers 11 pm to 7 am.

Student services: personal/psychological counseling.

COSTS & FINANCIAL AID
Costs (2014–15) ***Comprehensive fee:*** $13,838 includes full-time tuition ($9300), mandatory fees ($400), and room and board ($4138). Full-time tuition and fees vary according to location and program. Part-time tuition: $310 per credit hour. Part-time tuition and fees vary according to location and program. ***Room and board:*** Room and board charges vary according to board plan and housing facility. ***Waivers:*** employees or children of employees.

Financial Aid Of all full-time matriculated undergraduates who enrolled in 2014, 399 applied for aid, 341 were judged to have need, 19 had their need fully met. 23 Federal Work-Study jobs (averaging $2268). In 2014, 28 non-need-based awards were made. ***Average percent of need met:*** 42. ***Average financial aid package:*** $8628. ***Average need-based loan:*** $3810. ***Average need-based gift aid:*** $6071. ***Average non-need-based aid:*** $1399. ***Average indebtedness upon graduation:*** $17,258. ***Financial aid deadline:*** 4/15.

APPLYING
Standardized Tests *Required:* SAT or ACT (for admission).

Options: electronic application, deferred entrance.

Application fee: $25.

Required: essay or personal statement, high school transcript, 2 letters of recommendation, Christian/Church Member for 1 year minimum. ***Recommended:*** interview.

Application deadlines: 8/11 (freshmen), 8/11 (transfers).

Notification: continuous (freshmen), continuous (transfers).

CONTACT
The Baptist College of Florida, 5400 College Drive, Graceville, FL 32440-1898. *Phone:* 850-263-3261 Ext. 460. *Toll-free phone:* 800-328-2660 Ext. 460.

Barry University

Miami Shores, Florida

http://www.barry.edu/

- **Independent Roman Catholic** university, founded 1940
- **Suburban** 122-acre campus with easy access to Miami
- **Coed** 3,996 undergraduate students, 84% full-time, 61% women, 39% men
- **Moderately difficult** entrance level, 47% of applicants were admitted

UNDERGRAD STUDENTS
3,365 full-time, 631 part-time. 31% Black or African American, non-Hispanic/Latino; 28% Hispanic/Latino; 2% Asian, non-Hispanic/Latino; 0.2% Native Hawaiian or other Pacific Islander, non-Hispanic/Latino; 0.4% American Indian or Alaska Native, non-Hispanic/Latino; 2% Two or more races, non-Hispanic/Latino; 9% Race/ethnicity unknown; 8% international.

Freshmen
Admission: 7,511 applied, 3,497 admitted, 460 enrolled. ***Test scores:*** SAT critical reading scores over 500: 37%; SAT math scores over 500: 34%; SAT writing scores over 500: 21%; ACT scores over 18: 75%; SAT critical reading scores over 600: 4%; SAT math scores over 600: 6%; ACT scores over 24: 10%; ACT scores over 30: 1%.

ACADEMICS
Calendar: semesters. *Degrees:* certificates, bachelor's, master's, doctoral, post-master's, and postbachelor's certificates.

Special study options: academic remediation for entering students, accelerated degree program, adult/continuing education programs, advanced placement credit, distance learning, double majors, English as a second language, honors programs, independent study, internships, off-campus study, part-time degree program, services for LD students, study abroad, summer session for credit. ***ROTC:*** Army (c), Air Force (c).

Unusual degree programs: 3-2 engineering with University of Miami.

Computers: 368 computers/terminals are available on campus for general student use. Students can access the following: campus intranet, computer help desk, free student e-mail accounts, online (class) grades, online (class) registration, online (class) schedules, Blackboard. Campuswide network is available. Wireless service is available via computer centers, computer labs, learning centers, student centers.

STUDENT LIFE
Housing options: on-campus residence required for freshman year; coed, men-only, women-only, special housing for students with disabilities. Campus housing is university owned.

Activities and organizations: drama/theater group, student-run newspaper, radio and television station, choral group, Student

Government Association, Campus Activities Board, SCUBA Society, Caribbean Students Association, Jamaican Association, national fraternities, national sororities.

Athletics Member NCAA. All Division II. ***Intercollegiate sports:*** baseball M(s), basketball M(s)/W(s), crew W(s), golf M(s)/W(s), soccer M(s)/W(s), softball W(s), tennis M(s)/W(s), volleyball W(s). ***Intramural sports:*** basketball M/W, football M/W, golf M/W, soccer M/W, softball M/W, volleyball M/W.

Campus security: 24-hour emergency response devices and patrols, late-night transport/escort service.

Student services: health clinic, personal/psychological counseling.

COSTS & FINANCIAL AID

Costs (2015–16) ***Comprehensive fee:*** $38,560 includes full-time tuition ($28,160) and room and board ($10,400). Part-time tuition: $845 per credit. Part-time tuition and fees vary according to course load. ***Room and board:*** Room and board charges vary according to board plan.

Financial Aid Of all full-time matriculated undergraduates who enrolled in 2014, 2,782 applied for aid, 2,704 were judged to have need, 104 had their need fully met. In 2014, 272 non-need-based awards were made. ***Average percent of need met:*** 49. ***Average financial aid package:*** $20,058. ***Average need-based loan:*** $4671. ***Average need-based gift aid:*** $7690. ***Average non-need-based aid:*** $8662. ***Average indebtedness upon graduation:*** $38,342.

APPLYING

Standardized Tests *Required:* SAT or ACT (for admission).

Options: electronic application, early admission, deferred entrance.

Application fee: $30.

Required: high school transcript, minimum 2.0 GPA. ***Required for some:*** essay or personal statement. ***Recommended:*** interview.

Application deadlines: rolling (freshmen), rolling (transfers).

Notification: continuous (freshmen), continuous (transfers).

CONTACT

Barry University, 11300 Northeast Second Avenue, Miami Shores, FL 33161-6695. *Phone:* 305-899-3051. *Toll-free phone:* 800-695-2279.

See below for display ad and page 1358 for the College Close-Up.

Beacon College

Leesburg, Florida

http://www.beaconcollege.edu/

- **Independent** 4-year, founded 1989
- **Small-town** 5-acre campus with easy access to Orlando
- **Endowment** $56,217
- **Coed** 223 undergraduate students, 99% full-time, 35% women, 65% men
- **Moderately difficult** entrance level, 59% of applicants were admitted

UNDERGRAD STUDENTS

221 full-time, 2 part-time. Students come from 31 states and territories; 5 other countries; 70% are from out of state; 15% Black or African American, non-Hispanic/Latino; 3% Hispanic/Latino; 2% Asian, non-Hispanic/Latino; 0.4% Native Hawaiian or other Pacific Islander, non-Hispanic/Latino; 1% American Indian or Alaska Native, non-Hispanic/Latino; 5% Two or more races, non-Hispanic/Latino; 2% international; 15% transferred in; 83% live on campus.

Freshmen

Admission: 161 applied, 95 admitted, 52 enrolled. ***Average high school GPA:*** 3.

Retention: 82% of full-time freshmen returned.

FACULTY

Total: 26, 73% full-time, 62% with terminal degrees.

Student/faculty ratio: 11:1.

ACADEMICS

Calendar: semesters. *Degrees:* associate and bachelor's.

Special study options: academic remediation for entering students, adult/continuing education programs, advanced placement credit, cooperative education, double majors, honors programs, independent study, internships, services for LD students, summer session for credit.

Computers: 113 computers/terminals and 432 ports are available on campus for general student use. Students can access the following: campus intranet, computer help desk, free student e-mail accounts, online (class) grades, online (class) schedules. Campuswide network is available. 100% of college-owned or -operated housing units are wired for high-speed Internet access. Wireless service is available via entire campus.

STUDENT LIFE

Housing options: coed, special housing for students with disabilities. Campus housing is university owned and leased by the school. Freshman campus housing is guaranteed.

Activities and organizations: drama/theater group, Gamma Beta Phi, Performance Clube, Comic Book Convention Club, PRIDE Alliance, Car Club, national fraternities, national sororities.

Athletics ***Intramural sports:*** basketball M/W, football M/W.

Campus security: 24-hour emergency response devices and patrols, student patrols, late-night transport/escort service.

Student services: health clinic, personal/psychological counseling.

COSTS & FINANCIAL AID

Costs (2015–16) ***One-time required fee:*** $300. ***Comprehensive fee:*** $44,929 includes full-time tuition ($33,480), mandatory fees ($1200), and room and board ($10,249). Part-time tuition: $940 per credit. Part-time tuition and fees vary according to course load. ***Required fees:*** $600 per term part-time. ***College room only:*** $6514. Room and board charges vary according to housing facility. ***Payment plan:*** installment. ***Waivers:*** employees or children of employees.

Financial Aid Of all full-time matriculated undergraduates who enrolled in 2014, 131 applied for aid, 57 were judged to have need. 10 Federal Work-Study jobs (averaging $15,144). 2 state and other part-time jobs (averaging $2687). In 2014, 17 non-need-based awards were made. ***Average percent of need met:*** 80. ***Average financial aid package:*** $3000. ***Average need-based loan:*** $5500. ***Average need-based gift aid:*** $1500. ***Average non-need-based aid:*** $6000. ***Average indebtedness upon graduation:*** $27,000.

APPLYING

Standardized Tests *Recommended:* SAT or ACT (for admission).

Options: electronic application, early admission, deferred entrance.

Application fee: $50.

Required: high school transcript, 3 letters of recommendation, Psycho-educational Evaluation showing diagnosed Learning Disability or ADHD. ***Recommended:*** minimum 2.0 GPA, interview.

Application deadlines: rolling (freshmen), rolling (transfers).

Notification: 8/1 (freshmen), 8/1 (transfers).

CONTACT

Ms. Dale Herold, Dean of Admissions and Enrollment Management, Beacon College, 105 East Main Street, Leesburg, FL 34748. *Phone:* 352-638-9778. *Fax:* 352-787-0796. *E-mail:* dherold@beaconcollege.edu.

Bethune-Cookman University

Daytona Beach, Florida

http://www.cookman.edu/

- **Independent Methodist** comprehensive, founded 1904
- **Urban** 60-acre campus with easy access to Orlando
- **Endowment** $53.6 million
- **Coed** 3,900 undergraduate students, 95% full-time, 59% women, 41% men
- **Minimally difficult** entrance level, 64% of applicants were admitted

UNDERGRAD STUDENTS

3,696 full-time, 204 part-time. Students come from 45 states and territories; 32 other countries; 28% are from out of state; 89% Black or African American, non-Hispanic/Latino; 3% Hispanic/Latino; 0.2% Asian, non-Hispanic/Latino; 0.2% Native Hawaiian or other Pacific Islander, non-Hispanic/Latino; 0.1% American Indian or Alaska Native, non-Hispanic/Latino; 2% Two or more races, non-Hispanic/Latino; 2% Race/ethnicity unknown; 2% international; 5% transferred in; 51% live on campus.

Freshmen

Admission: 7,936 applied, 5,056 admitted, 965 enrolled. ***Average high school GPA:*** 2.94.

Retention: 66% of full-time freshmen returned.

FACULTY

Total: 278, 71% full-time, 35% with terminal degrees.

Student/faculty ratio: 17:1.

ACADEMICS

Calendar: semesters. *Degrees:* bachelor's and master's.

Special study options: academic remediation for entering students, accelerated degree program, adult/continuing education programs, advanced placement credit, cooperative education, distance learning, double majors, honors programs, independent study, internships, part-time degree program, study abroad, summer session for credit. ***ROTC:*** Army (c), Air Force (c).

Unusual degree programs: 3-2 engineering with Tuskegee University, University of Florida, Florida Atlantic University, Florida Agricultural and Mechanical University, University of Central Florida.

Computers: 611 computers/terminals and 1,471 ports are available on campus for general student use. Students can access the following: campus intranet, computer help desk, free student e-mail accounts, online (class) grades, online (class) registration, online (class) schedules. Campuswide network is available. 100% of college-owned or -operated housing units are wired for high-speed Internet access. Wireless service is available via entire campus.

STUDENT LIFE

Housing options: on-campus residence required for freshman year; coed, men-only, women-only. Campus housing is university owned. Freshman campus housing is guaranteed.

Activities and organizations: drama/theater group, student-run newspaper, radio station, choral group, marching band, Concert Chorale, marching band, Inspirational Gospel Choir, Student Government Association, national fraternities, national sororities.

Athletics Member NCAA. All Division I except football (Division I-AA). ***Intercollegiate sports:*** baseball M(s), basketball M(s)/W(s), bowling W(s), cheerleading W, cross-country running M(s)/W(s), golf M(s)/W(s), softball W(s), tennis M(s)/W(s), track and field M(s)/W(s), volleyball W(s). ***Intramural sports:*** basketball M/W, bowling M/W, football M, racquetball W, soccer M/W, table tennis W.

Campus security: 24-hour emergency response devices and patrols, student patrols, late-night transport/escort service.

Student services: health clinic, personal/psychological counseling.

COSTS & FINANCIAL AID

Costs (2014–15) ***Comprehensive fee:*** $22,958 includes full-time tuition ($13,440), mandatory fees ($970), and room and board ($8548). Full-time tuition and fees vary according to course load and degree level. Part-time tuition: $50 per credit hour. Part-time tuition and fees vary according to course load and degree level. ***College room only:*** $6710. Room and board charges vary according to housing facility. ***Payment plan:*** installment. ***Waivers:*** employees or children of employees.

Financial Aid Of all full-time matriculated undergraduates who enrolled in 2014, 3,243 applied for aid, 3,140 were judged to have need, 143 had their need fully met. 200 Federal Work-Study jobs (averaging $2500). 100 state and other part-time jobs (averaging $2000). In 2014, 44 non-need-based awards were made. ***Average percent of need met:*** 50. ***Average financial aid package:*** $13,672. ***Average need-based loan:*** $4072. ***Average need-based gift aid:*** $10,070. ***Average non-need-based aid:*** $8387. ***Average indebtedness upon graduation:*** $23,525.

APPLYING

Standardized Tests *Required:* SAT or ACT (for admission).

Options: electronic application, early admission, deferred entrance.

Application fee: $25.

Required: high school transcript, minimum 2.3 GPA, 1 letter of recommendation, medical history. ***Required for some:*** interview. ***Recommended:*** essay or personal statement.

Application deadlines: 6/30 (freshmen), 6/30 (transfers).

Notification: continuous (freshmen), continuous (transfers).

CONTACT
Bethune-Cookman University, FL. *Phone:* 386-481-2607. *Toll-free phone:* 800-448-0228.

Broward College
Fort Lauderdale, Florida
http://www.broward.edu/

- **State-supported** primarily 2-year, founded 1960, part of Florida College System
- **Urban** campus with easy access to Miami
- **Coed**
- **Noncompetitive** entrance level

FACULTY
Student/faculty ratio: 30:1.

ACADEMICS
Calendar: trimesters. *Degrees:* certificates, diplomas, associate, and bachelor's.

STUDENT LIFE
Housing options: college housing not available.
Activities and organizations: drama/theater group, student-run newspaper, choral group.
Athletics Member NJCAA.
Campus security: 24-hour emergency response devices and patrols, late-night transport/escort service.
Student services: personal/psychological counseling, women's center.

FINANCIAL AID
Financial Aid ***Financial aid deadline:*** 7/1.

APPLYING
Options: electronic application, early admission, deferred entrance.
Application fee: $35.
Required for some: high school transcript.

CONTACT
Mr. Willie J. Alexander, Associate Vice President for Student Affairs/College Registrar, Broward College, 225 East Las Olas Boulevard, Fort Lauderdale, FL 33301. *Phone:* 954-201-7471. *Fax:* 954-201-7466. *E-mail:* walexand@broward.edu.

Brown Mackie College–Miami
Miramar, Florida
http://www.brownmackie.edu/miami/

- **Proprietary** primarily 2-year, part of Education Management Corporation
- **Coed**

ACADEMICS
Degrees: diplomas, associate, and bachelor's.

CONTACT
Brown Mackie College–Miami, 3700 Lakeside Drive, Miramar, FL 33027. *Phone:* 305-341-6600. *Toll-free phone:* 866-505-0335.

Carlos Albizu University, Miami Campus
Miami, Florida
http://www.albizu.edu/

- **Independent** comprehensive, founded 1980, part of Carlos Albizu University
- **Urban** 18-acre campus
- **Coed** 305 undergraduate students, 56% full-time, 72% women, 28% men
- **Moderately difficult** entrance level, 35% of applicants were admitted

UNDERGRAD STUDENTS
171 full-time, 134 part-time. 2% Black or African American, non-Hispanic/Latino; 81% Hispanic/Latino; 0.3% American Indian or Alaska Native, non-Hispanic/Latino; 3% Race/ethnicity unknown; 11% international; 17% transferred in.

Freshmen
Admission: 68 applied, 24 admitted, 12 enrolled. ***Average high school GPA:*** 2.7.
Retention: 50% of full-time freshmen returned.

FACULTY
Total: 55, 11% full-time, 33% with terminal degrees.
Student/faculty ratio: 10:1.

ACADEMICS
Calendar: trimesters. *Degrees:* certificates, diplomas, bachelor's, master's, and doctoral.
Special study options: academic remediation for entering students, accelerated degree program, adult/continuing education programs, advanced placement credit, cooperative education, distance learning, double majors, English as a second language, independent study, internships, part-time degree program, services for LD students, summer session for credit.
Computers: 268 computers/terminals are available on campus for general student use. Students can access the following: campus intranet, computer help desk, free student e-mail accounts, online (class) grades, online (class) registration, online (class) schedules, Campus Portal; Virtual Library; 24/7 Support; Cloud Computing; Learning Center. Campuswide network is available. Wireless service is available via entire campus.

STUDENT LIFE
Housing options: college housing not available.
Activities and organizations: student-run newspaper, Student Council, Psi Chi, Kappa Delta Pi, Nu Sigma Si, Future Educators of America.
Campus security: 24-hour emergency response devices and patrols, late-night transport/escort service.

COSTS & FINANCIAL AID
Costs (2014–15) ***Tuition:*** $11,628 full-time, $323 per credit part-time. Full-time tuition and fees vary according to course load, degree level, and program. Part-time tuition and fees vary according to course load, degree level, and program. ***Required fees:*** $756 full-time, $252 per term part-time. ***Payment plan:*** installment. ***Waivers:*** employees or children of employees.
Financial Aid Of all full-time matriculated undergraduates who enrolled in 2014, 170 applied for aid, 147 were judged to have need. ***Average percent of need met:*** 50. ***Average financial aid package:*** $7428. ***Average need-based loan:*** $4826. ***Average need-based gift aid:*** $4850. ***Average indebtedness upon graduation:*** $16,500.

APPLYING
Options: electronic application.
Application fee: $25.
Required: high school transcript, minimum 2.0 GPA, 2 letters of recommendation, interview. ***Recommended:*** interview.
Application deadlines: rolling (freshmen), rolling (transfers).
Notification: continuous (freshmen).

CONTACT
Ms. Dayanes Rodriguez, Admissions Officer, Carlos Albizu University, Miami Campus, 2173 NW 99 Avenue, Miami, FL 33172. *Phone:* 305-593-1223 Ext. 3218. *Toll-free phone:* 888-GO-TO-CAU (in-state); 800-GO-TO-CAU (out-of-state). *Fax:* 305-593-1854. *E-mail:* drodriguez@albizu.edu.

Chamberlain College of Nursing
Jacksonville, Florida
http://www.chamberlain.edu/

- **Proprietary** 4-year
- **Coed**

FACULTY
Student/faculty ratio: 9:1.

ACADEMICS
Calendar: semesters. *Degree:* bachelor's.

COSTS
Costs (2014–15) ***Tuition:*** $17,160 full-time, $665 per credit hour part-time. Full-time tuition and fees vary according to course load. Part-time

tuition and fees vary according to course load. ***Required fees:*** $600 full-time.

APPLYING

Standardized Tests *Required:* SAT or ACT (for admission).

CONTACT

Admissions, Chamberlain College of Nursing, 5200 Belfort Road, Jacksonville, FL 32256-6040. *Phone:* 904-251-8100. *Toll-free phone:* 888-556-8CCN.

Chamberlain College of Nursing

Miramar, Florida

http://www.chamberlain.edu/

- **Proprietary** 4-year
- **Coed**
- **Moderately difficult** entrance level

FACULTY

Student/faculty ratio: 9:1.

ACADEMICS

Degree: bachelor's.

STUDENT LIFE

Housing options: college housing not available.

COSTS

Costs (2014–15) ***Tuition:*** $17,160 full-time, $665 per credit hour part-time. Full-time tuition and fees vary according to course load. Part-time tuition and fees vary according to course load. ***Required fees:*** $600 full-time.

APPLYING

Standardized Tests *Required:* SAT or ACT (for admission).

Application fee: $95.

CONTACT

Director of Recruitment, Chamberlain College of Nursing, 2300 SW 145th Avenue, Miramar, FL 33027. *Phone:* 954-885-3510.

Chipola College

Marianna, Florida

http://www.chipola.edu/

- **State-supported** primarily 2-year, founded 1947
- **Rural** 105-acre campus
- **Coed** 2,090 undergraduate students, 42% full-time, 63% women, 37% men
- **Noncompetitive** entrance level, 85% of applicants were admitted

UNDERGRAD STUDENTS

881 full-time, 1,209 part-time. Students come from 7 states and territories; 6 other countries; 8% are from out of state; 15% Black or African American, non-Hispanic/Latino; 4% Hispanic/Latino; 0.6% Asian, non-Hispanic/Latino; 0.1% Native Hawaiian or other Pacific Islander, non-Hispanic/Latino; 0.7% American Indian or Alaska Native, non-Hispanic/Latino; 3% Two or more races, non-Hispanic/Latino; 7% transferred in.

Freshmen

Admission: 684 applied, 578 admitted, 188 enrolled. ***Average high school GPA:*** 2.5. ***Test scores:*** SAT critical reading scores over 500: 16%; SAT math scores over 500: 36%; ACT scores over 18: 81%; SAT critical reading scores over 600: 4%; SAT math scores over 600: 12%; ACT scores over 24: 25%; ACT scores over 30: 3%.

FACULTY

Total: 127, 31% full-time, 13% with terminal degrees.

Student/faculty ratio: 24:1.

ACADEMICS

Calendar: semesters. *Degrees:* certificates, associate, and bachelor's.

Special study options: academic remediation for entering students, adult/continuing education programs, advanced placement credit, distance learning, honors programs, independent study, part-time degree program, services for LD students, summer session for credit.

Computers: 80 computers/terminals are available on campus for general student use. Campuswide network is available.

STUDENT LIFE

Housing options: college housing not available.

Activities and organizations: drama/theater group, student-run newspaper, choral group, Drama/Theater Group.

Athletics Member NJCAA. ***Intercollegiate sports:*** baseball M(s), basketball M(s)/W(s), softball W(s).

Campus security: night security personnel.

COSTS

Costs (2014–15) ***Tuition:*** state resident $3060 full-time, $102 per semester hour part-time; nonresident $8891 full-time, $296 per semester hour part-time. Full-time tuition and fees vary according to degree level. Part-time tuition and fees vary according to degree level. ***Required fees:*** $40 full-time.

APPLYING

Options: early admission.

Required: high school transcript.

Application deadlines: rolling (freshmen), rolling (transfers).

Notification: continuous (freshmen), continuous (transfers).

CONTACT

Mrs. Kathy L. Rehberg, Registrar, Chipola College, 3094 Indian Circle, Marianna, FL 32446-3065. *Phone:* 850-718-2233. *Fax:* 850-718-2287. *E-mail:* rehbergk@chipola.edu.

Clearwater Christian College

Clearwater, Florida

http://www.clearwater.edu/

- **Independent nondenominational** comprehensive, founded 1966
- **Suburban** 138-acre campus with easy access to Tampa-St. Petersburg
- **Endowment** $1.1 million
- **Coed** 412 undergraduate students, 96% full-time, 48% women, 52% men
- **Minimally difficult** entrance level, 76% of applicants were admitted

UNDERGRAD STUDENTS

395 full-time, 17 part-time. Students come from 42 states and territories; 3 other countries; 42% are from out of state; 7% Black or African American, non-Hispanic/Latino; 12% Hispanic/Latino; 2% Asian, non-Hispanic/Latino; 0.2% Native Hawaiian or other Pacific Islander, non-Hispanic/Latino; 3% Two or more races, non-Hispanic/Latino; 1% international; 11% transferred in; 69% live on campus.

Freshmen

Admission: 98 applied, 74 admitted, 73 enrolled. ***Average high school GPA:*** 3.24. ***Test scores:*** SAT critical reading scores over 500: 55%; SAT math scores over 500: 45%; ACT scores over 18: 81%; SAT critical reading scores over 600: 7%; SAT math scores over 600: 10%; ACT scores over 24: 23%; SAT critical reading scores over 700: 2%; ACT scores over 30: 2%.

Retention: 60% of full-time freshmen returned.

FACULTY

Total: 56, 39% full-time, 55% with terminal degrees.

Student/faculty ratio: 12:1.

ACADEMICS

Calendar: semesters. *Degrees:* associate, bachelor's, and master's.

Special study options: academic remediation for entering students, advanced placement credit, distance learning, double majors, independent study, internships, off-campus study, part-time degree program, services for LD students, student-designed majors, study abroad, summer session for credit. ***ROTC:*** Army (c), Navy (c), Air Force (c).

Computers: 45 computers/terminals are available on campus for general student use. Students can access the following: campus intranet, computer help desk, free student e-mail accounts, online (class) grades, online (class) registration, online (class) schedules. Campuswide network is available. 100% of college-owned or -operated housing units are wired for high-speed Internet access. Wireless service is available via entire campus.

STUDENT LIFE
Housing options: on-campus residence required through senior year; men-only, women-only. Campus housing is university owned. Freshman campus housing is guaranteed.

Activities and organizations: drama/theater group, choral group, National Association of Music Education, Alpha Chi, Flag Football club, Praise and Worship, Social groups (Greeks) activities on campus.

Athletics Member NCCAA. ***Intercollegiate sports:*** baseball M, basketball M/W, soccer M/W, volleyball W. ***Intramural sports:*** basketball M/W, soccer M/W, softball M/W, ultimate Frisbee M/W, volleyball M/W.

Campus security: 24-hour emergency response devices and patrols.

Student services: personal/psychological counseling.

COSTS & FINANCIAL AID
Costs (2015–16) ***One-time required fee:*** $350. ***Comprehensive fee:*** $26,545 includes full-time tuition ($18,050), mandatory fees ($115), and room and board ($8380). Part-time tuition: $680 per semester hour. No tuition increase for student's term of enrollment. ***College room only:*** $5100. Room and board charges vary according to board plan. ***Payment plan:*** installment. ***Waivers:*** employees or children of employees.

Financial Aid Of all full-time matriculated undergraduates who enrolled in 2014, 361 applied for aid, 327 were judged to have need, 33 had their need fully met. In 2014, 64 non-need-based awards were made. ***Average percent of need met:*** 54. ***Average financial aid package:*** $14,300. ***Average need-based loan:*** $4647. ***Average need-based gift aid:*** $11,619. ***Average non-need-based aid:*** $4318. ***Average indebtedness upon graduation:*** $23,213.

APPLYING
Standardized Tests *Required:* SAT or ACT (for admission).

Options: electronic application, early admission, deferred entrance.

Application fee: $35.

Required: essay or personal statement, high school transcript, minimum 2.0 GPA, 2 letters of recommendation, Christian testimony. ***Recommended:*** interview.

Application deadlines: rolling (freshmen), rolling (transfers).

Notification: continuous (freshmen), continuous (transfers).

CONTACT
Miss Colleen Gumbert, Admissions Administrative Assistant, Clearwater Christian College, 3400 Gulf-to-Bay Boulevard, Clearwater, FL 33759-4595. *Phone:* 727-726-1153 Ext. 228. *Toll-free phone:* 800-348-4463. *Fax:* 813-726-8597. *E-mail:* admissions@clearwater.edu.

College of Central Florida

Ocala, Florida

http://www.cf.edu/

- **State and locally supported** primarily 2-year, founded 1957, part of Florida Community College System
- **Small-town** 139-acre campus
- **Endowment** $64.5 million
- **Coed** 8,210 undergraduate students, 37% full-time, 63% women, 37% men
- **Noncompetitive** entrance level, 62% of applicants were admitted

UNDERGRAD STUDENTS
3,066 full-time, 5,144 part-time. Students come from 61 other countries; 1% are from out of state; 14% Black or African American, non-Hispanic/Latino; 14% Hispanic/Latino; 2% Asian, non-Hispanic/Latino; 0.3% Native Hawaiian or other Pacific Islander, non-Hispanic/Latino; 0.4% American Indian or Alaska Native, non-Hispanic/Latino; 8% Race/ethnicity unknown; 1% international; 1% transferred in.

Freshmen
Admission: 3,452 applied, 2,132 admitted, 1,597 enrolled.

FACULTY
Total: 393, 34% full-time, 12% with terminal degrees.

Student/faculty ratio: 21:1.

ACADEMICS
Calendar: semesters. *Degrees:* certificates, diplomas, associate, and bachelor's.

Special study options: academic remediation for entering students, adult/continuing education programs, advanced placement credit, cooperative education, distance learning, English as a second language, freshman honors college, honors programs, independent study, internships, part-time degree program, services for LD students, summer session for credit.

Computers: 2,500 computers/terminals are available on campus for general student use. Students can access the following: campus intranet, computer help desk, online (class) grades, online (class) registration, online (class) schedules. Campuswide network is available. Wireless service is available via classrooms, computer centers, computer labs, learning centers, libraries, student centers.

STUDENT LIFE
Housing options: college housing not available.

Activities and organizations: drama/theater group, student-run newspaper, choral group, Inspirational Choir, Model United nations, Performing Arts, Phi Theta Kappa (PTK), Student Nurses Association.

Athletics Member NJCAA. ***Intercollegiate sports:*** baseball M(s), basketball M(s)/W(s), softball W(s), volleyball W(s). ***Intramural sports:*** bowling M/W.

Campus security: 24-hour emergency response devices and patrols, student patrols, late-night transport/escort service.

Student services: personal/psychological counseling.

COSTS & FINANCIAL AID
Costs (2014–15) ***Tuition:*** state resident $2388 full-time, $80 per credit part-time; nonresident $9552 full-time, $318 per credit part-time. Full-time tuition and fees vary according to course level, degree level, program, and student level. Part-time tuition and fees vary according to course level, degree level, program, and student level. ***Required fees:*** $825 full-time, $28 per credit hour part-time. ***Payment plan:*** deferred payment. ***Waivers:*** employees or children of employees.

Financial Aid Of all full-time matriculated undergraduates who enrolled in 2013, 85 Federal Work-Study jobs (averaging $1505).

APPLYING
Standardized Tests *Recommended:* SAT (for admission), ACT (for admission), SAT or ACT (for admission), SAT and SAT Subject Tests or ACT (for admission), SAT Subject Tests (for admission).

Options: electronic application, early admission.

Application fee: $30.

Required: high school transcript.

Application deadlines: rolling (freshmen), rolling (transfers).

Notification: continuous (freshmen), continuous (transfers).

CONTACT
Ms. Devona Sewell, Registrar, Admission and Records, College of Central Florida, 3001 SW College Road, Ocala, FL 34474. *Phone:* 352-237-2111 Ext. 1398. *Fax:* 352-873-5882. *E-mail:* sewelld@cf.edu.

Daytona State College

Daytona Beach, Florida

http://www.daytonastate.edu/

- **State-supported** primarily 2-year, founded 1958, part of Florida Community College System
- **Suburban** 100-acre campus with easy access to Orlando
- **Endowment** $6.3 million
- **Coed** 14,951 undergraduate students, 37% full-time, 60% women, 40% men
- **Noncompetitive** entrance level

UNDERGRAD STUDENTS
5,583 full-time, 9,368 part-time. Students come from 130 other countries; 4% are from out of state; 13% Black or African American, non-Hispanic/Latino; 13% Hispanic/Latino; 2% Asian, non-Hispanic/Latino; 0.2% Native Hawaiian or other Pacific Islander, non-Hispanic/Latino; 0.5% American Indian or Alaska Native, non-Hispanic/Latino; 2% Two or more races, non-Hispanic/Latino; 1% Race/ethnicity unknown; 0.4% international; 5% transferred in.

Freshmen
Admission: 1,805 admitted, 1,572 enrolled. ***Test scores:*** SAT critical reading scores over 500: 40%; SAT math scores over 500: 32%; SAT writing scores over 500: 25%; ACT scores over 18: 66%; SAT critical reading scores over 600: 8%; SAT math scores over 600: 7%; SAT writing scores over 600: 4%; ACT scores over 24: 14%; SAT critical reading scores over 700: 1%; SAT math scores over 700: 1%; ACT scores over 30: 1%.

FACULTY
Total: 879, 35% full-time, 17% with terminal degrees.

Student/faculty ratio: 21:1.

ACADEMICS
Calendar: semesters. *Degrees:* certificates, diplomas, associate, bachelor's, and postbachelor's certificates.

Special study options: academic remediation for entering students, adult/continuing education programs, advanced placement credit, cooperative education, distance learning, double majors, English as a second language, external degree program, freshman honors college, honors programs, independent study, internships, off-campus study, part-time degree program, services for LD students, study abroad, summer session for credit. ***ROTC:*** Army (c), Air Force (c).

Computers: 3,208 computers/terminals are available on campus for general student use. Students can access the following: campus intranet, computer help desk, free student e-mail accounts, online (class) grades, online (class) registration, online (class) schedules. Campuswide network is available. Wireless service is available via entire campus.

STUDENT LIFE
Housing options: college housing not available.

Activities and organizations: drama/theater group, student-run newspaper, choral group, Rotaract, Student Government Association, Student Occupational Therapy Club, Massage Therapy Club, Student Paralegal Club, national fraternities, national sororities.

Athletics Member NJCAA. ***Intercollegiate sports:*** baseball M(s), basketball M(s)/W(s), golf W(s), softball W(s), volleyball W(s). ***Intramural sports:*** basketball M/W, football M/W, soccer M/W, table tennis M/W, tennis M/W.

Campus security: 24-hour emergency response devices and patrols, late-night transport/escort service.

Student services: personal/psychological counseling, women's center.

COSTS & FINANCIAL AID
Costs (2014–15) ***Tuition:*** state resident $1940 full-time, $81 per credit hour part-time; nonresident $7621 full-time, $318 per credit hour part-time. Full-time tuition and fees vary according to course load and degree level. Part-time tuition and fees vary according to course load and degree level. ***Required fees:*** $740 full-time, $24 per credit hour part-time. ***Payment plan:*** installment.

Financial Aid Of all full-time matriculated undergraduates who enrolled in 2013, 4,148 applied for aid, 3,780 were judged to have need, 1,991 had their need fully met. 193 Federal Work-Study jobs (averaging $1299). In 2013, 334 non-need-based awards were made. ***Average need-based loan:*** $1839. ***Average need-based gift aid:*** $1479. ***Average non-need-based aid:*** $798.

APPLYING
Options: electronic application, early admission, deferred entrance.

Required: high school transcript.

Application deadlines: rolling (freshmen), rolling (transfers).

Notification: continuous (freshmen), continuous (transfers).

CONTACT
Dr. Karen Sanders, Director of Admissions and Recruitment, Daytona State College, 1200 International Speedway Boulevard, Daytona Beach, FL 32114. *Phone:* 386-506-3050. *E-mail:* SanderK@daytonastate.edu.

DeVry University
Jacksonville, Florida
http://www.devry.edu/

- **Proprietary** comprehensive
- **Coed**

ACADEMICS
Degrees: associate, bachelor's, and master's.

COSTS
Costs (2014–15) ***Tuition:*** $17,052 full-time, $609 per credit hour part-time. ***Required fees:*** $80 full-time.

CONTACT
Admissions Office, DeVry University, 5200 Belfort Road, Suite 175, Jacksonville, FL 32256-6040. *Phone:* 904-367-4942.

DeVry University
Miramar, Florida
http://www.devry.edu/

- **Proprietary** comprehensive, founded 2002, part of DeVry University
- **Coed** 503 undergraduate students, 41% full-time, 41% women, 59% men
- **Minimally difficult** entrance level

UNDERGRAD STUDENTS
206 full-time, 297 part-time. 9% are from out of state; 27% Black or African American, non-Hispanic/Latino; 47% Hispanic/Latino; 0.6% Asian, non-Hispanic/Latino; 5% Race/ethnicity unknown; 5% international; 29% transferred in.

Freshmen
Admission: 20 enrolled.

FACULTY
Total: 76, 17% full-time.

Student/faculty ratio: 11:1.

ACADEMICS
Calendar: semesters. *Degrees:* associate, bachelor's, master's, and postbachelor's certificates.

Special study options: part-time degree program.

STUDENT LIFE
Housing options: college housing not available.

COSTS & FINANCIAL AID
Costs (2014–15) ***Tuition:*** $17,052 full-time, $609 per credit hour part-time. ***Required fees:*** $80 full-time.

Financial Aid Of all full-time matriculated undergraduates who enrolled in 2007, 204 applied for aid, 197 were judged to have need, 2 had their need fully met. In 2007, 35 non-need-based awards were made. ***Average percent of need met:*** 38. ***Average financial aid package:*** $12,172. ***Average need-based loan:*** $7414. ***Average need-based gift aid:*** $7044. ***Average non-need-based aid:*** $12,256. ***Average indebtedness upon graduation:*** $51,131.

APPLYING
Application fee: $40.

Required: high school transcript, interview.

CONTACT
DeVry University, 2300 Southwest 145th Avenue, Miramar, FL 33027-4150. *Phone:* 954-499-9775. *Toll-free phone:* 866-338-7941.

DeVry University
Orlando, Florida
http://www.devry.edu/

- **Proprietary** comprehensive, founded 2000, part of DeVry University
- **Urban** campus
- **Coed** 914 undergraduate students, 45% full-time, 42% women, 58% men
- **Minimally difficult** entrance level

UNDERGRAD STUDENTS
411 full-time, 503 part-time. 7% are from out of state; 23% Black or African American, non-Hispanic/Latino; 23% Hispanic/Latino; 2% Asian, non-Hispanic/Latino; 0.2% Native Hawaiian or other Pacific Islander, non-Hispanic/Latino; 0.2% American Indian or Alaska Native, non-Hispanic/Latino; 0.8% Two or more races, non-Hispanic/Latino; 8% Race/ethnicity unknown; 2% international; 36% transferred in.

Freshmen
Admission: 57 enrolled.

FACULTY
Total: 48, 35% full-time.

Student/faculty ratio: 26:1.

ACADEMICS
Calendar: semesters. *Degrees:* associate, bachelor's, master's, and postbachelor's certificates.

Special study options: adult/continuing education programs, part-time degree program.

Computers: Students can access the following: online (class) registration.

STUDENT LIFE
Housing options: college housing not available.

COSTS & FINANCIAL AID
Costs (2014–15) ***Tuition:*** $17,052 full-time, $609 per credit hour part-time. ***Required fees:*** $80 full-time.

Financial Aid Of all full-time matriculated undergraduates who enrolled in 2007, 314 applied for aid, 294 were judged to have need, 2 had their need fully met. In 2007, 35 non-need-based awards were made. ***Average percent of need met:*** 33. ***Average financial aid package:*** $10,774. ***Average need-based loan:*** $7062. ***Average need-based gift aid:*** $5608. ***Average non-need-based aid:*** $18,240. ***Average indebtedness upon graduation:*** $23,511.

APPLYING
Application fee: $40.

Required: high school transcript, interview.

CONTACT
DeVry University, 4000 Millenia Boulevard, Orlando, FL 32839. *Phone:* 407-345-2800. *Toll-free phone:* 866-338-7941.

DeVry University
Tampa, Florida
http://www.devry.edu/

- **Proprietary** comprehensive
- **Coed**

ACADEMICS
Calendar: semesters. *Degrees:* associate, bachelor's, and master's.

COSTS
Costs (2014–15) ***Tuition:*** $17,052 full-time, $609 per credit hour part-time. ***Required fees:*** $80 full-time.

CONTACT
Admissions Office, DeVry University, 5540 W. Executive Drive, Suite 100, Tampa, FL 33609. *Phone:* 813-288-8994. *Toll-free phone:* 866-338-7941.

Eastern Florida State College
Cocoa, Florida
http://www.easternflorida.edu/

- **State-supported** primarily 2-year, founded 1960, part of Florida Community College System
- **Suburban** 100-acre campus with easy access to Orlando
- **Coed**
- **Noncompetitive** entrance level

FACULTY
Student/faculty ratio: 23:1.

ACADEMICS
Calendar: semesters. *Degrees:* certificates, associate, and bachelor's.

STUDENT LIFE
Housing options: college housing not available.

Activities and organizations: drama/theater group, student-run newspaper, television station, choral group, Phi Theta Kappa, The Green Team, African-American Student Union, Student Government Association, Cosmetology in Action.

Athletics Member NJCAA.

Campus security: 24-hour emergency response devices and patrols.

Student services: women's center.

COSTS & FINANCIAL AID
Costs (2014–15) ***Tuition:*** state resident $2496 full-time, $104 per credit part-time; nonresident $9738 full-time, $406 per credit part-time. Full-time tuition and fees vary according to degree level and program. Part-time tuition and fees vary according to degree level and program. ***Required fees:*** $20 full-time, $10 per term part-time.

Financial Aid Of all full-time matriculated undergraduates who enrolled in 2013, 200 Federal Work-Study jobs (averaging $2244). 200 state and other part-time jobs (averaging $2000).

APPLYING
Options: electronic application, early admission.

Application fee: $30.

Required: high school transcript.

CONTACT
Ms. Stephanie Burnette, Registrar, Eastern Florida State College, 1519 Clearlake Road, Cocoa, FL 32922-6597. *Phone:* 321-433-7271. *Fax:* 321-433-7172. *E-mail:* cocoaadmissions@brevardcc.edu.

Eckerd College
St. Petersburg, Florida
http://www.eckerd.edu/

- **Independent Presbyterian** 4-year, founded 1958
- **Suburban** 188-acre campus with easy access to Tampa
- **Coed** 1,802 undergraduate students, 98% full-time, 61% women, 39% men
- **Moderately difficult** entrance level, 76% of applicants were admitted

UNDERGRAD STUDENTS
1,768 full-time, 34 part-time. Students come from 48 states and territories; 40 other countries; 83% are from out of state; 2% Black or African American, non-Hispanic/Latino; 8% Hispanic/Latino; 2% Asian, non-Hispanic/Latino; 0.2% Native Hawaiian or other Pacific Islander, non-Hispanic/Latino; 0.3% American Indian or Alaska Native, non-Hispanic/Latino; 3% Two or more races, non-Hispanic/Latino; 0.8% Race/ethnicity unknown; 4% international; 2% transferred in; 86% live on campus.

Freshmen
Admission: 3,963 applied, 3,028 admitted, 512 enrolled. ***Average high school GPA:*** 3.39. ***Test scores:*** SAT critical reading scores over 500: 81%; SAT math scores over 500: 77%; ACT scores over 18: 100%; SAT critical reading scores over 600: 38%; SAT math scores over 600: 33%; ACT scores over 24: 69%; SAT critical reading scores over 700: 6%; SAT math scores over 700: 2%; ACT scores over 30: 18%.

Retention: 81% of full-time freshmen returned.

FACULTY
Total: 171, 67% full-time, 79% with terminal degrees.

Student/faculty ratio: 12:1.

ACADEMICS
Calendar: 4-1-4. *Degree:* bachelor's.

Special study options: accelerated degree program, adult/continuing education programs, advanced placement credit, double majors, external degree program, honors programs, independent study, internships, off-campus study, part-time degree program, services for LD students, student-designed majors, study abroad, summer session for credit. ***ROTC:*** Army (c), Air Force (c).

Unusual degree programs: 3-2 engineering with Columbia University.

Computers: 300 computers/terminals and 2,000 ports are available on campus for general student use. Students can access the following: campus intranet, computer help desk, free student e-mail accounts, online (class) grades, online (class) registration, online (class) schedules, free computer repair shop. Campuswide network is available. 100% of college-owned or -operated housing units are wired for high-speed Internet access. Wireless service is available via entire campus.

STUDENT LIFE
Housing options: on-campus residence required for freshman year; coed, women-only. Campus housing is university owned. Freshman campus housing is guaranteed.

Activities and organizations: drama/theater group, student-run newspaper, radio and television station, choral group, Earth Society, Water Search and Rescue Team, The Current (student newspaper), College Choir, Organization of Students.

Athletics Member NCAA. All Division II. ***Intercollegiate sports:*** baseball M(s), basketball M(s)/W(s), golf M(s)/W(s), sailing M/W, soccer M(s)/W(s), softball W(s), tennis M(s)/W(s), volleyball W(s). ***Intramural sports:*** baseball M, basketball M/W, bowling M/W, cheerleading M(c)/W(c), equestrian sports M(c)/W(c), field hockey M(c)/W(c), football M(c)/W(c), golf M(c)/W(c), lacrosse M(c)/W(c), rugby M(c)/W(c), sailing M/W, soccer M(c)/W(c), softball M/W, swimming and diving M(c)/W(c), table tennis M/W, tennis M(c)/W(c), ultimate Frisbee M(c)/W(c), volleyball M/W.

Campus security: 24-hour emergency response devices and patrols, student patrols, late-night transport/escort service, controlled dormitory access.

Student services: health clinic, personal/psychological counseling, women's center.

COSTS & FINANCIAL AID

Costs (2014–15) ***Comprehensive fee:*** $49,218 includes full-time tuition ($38,342), mandatory fees ($326), and room and board ($10,550). Part-time tuition: $4514 per course. ***College room only:*** $5310. Room and board charges vary according to board plan and housing facility. ***Payment plan:*** installment. ***Waivers:*** employees or children of employees.

Financial Aid Of all full-time matriculated undergraduates who enrolled in 2014, 1,234 applied for aid, 1,062 were judged to have need, 228 had their need fully met. In 2014, 631 non-need-based awards were made. ***Average percent of need met:*** 87. ***Average financial aid package:*** $31,297. ***Average need-based loan:*** $3836. ***Average need-based gift aid:*** $21,747. ***Average non-need-based aid:*** $14,326. ***Average indebtedness upon graduation:*** $33,697.

APPLYING

Standardized Tests *Required:* SAT or ACT (for admission). *Recommended:* SAT Subject Tests (for admission).

Options: electronic application, early action, deferred entrance.

Application fee: $40.

Required: essay or personal statement, high school transcript. ***Recommended:*** interview.

Application deadlines: rolling (freshmen), rolling (transfers), 11/15 (early action).

Notification: continuous (freshmen), continuous (transfers), 12/15 (early action).

CONTACT

Ms. Lucille Lopez, Eckerd College, 4200 54th Avenue South, St. Petersburg, FL 33711. *Phone:* 727-864-8331. *Toll-free phone:* 800-456-9009. *Fax:* 727-866-2304. *E-mail:* admissions@eckerd.edu.

★ Embry-Riddle Aeronautical University–Daytona

Daytona Beach, Florida

http://www.embryriddle.edu/

- **Independent** university, founded 1926
- **Suburban** 185-acre campus with easy access to Orlando
- **Coed** 4,967 undergraduate students, 94% full-time, 19% women, 81% men
- **Moderately difficult** entrance level, 73% of applicants were admitted

UNDERGRAD STUDENTS

4,647 full-time, 320 part-time. Students come from 51 states and territories; 97 other countries; 64% are from out of state; 6% Black or African American, non-Hispanic/Latino; 6% Hispanic/Latino; 4% Asian, non-Hispanic/Latino; 0.2% Native Hawaiian or other Pacific Islander, non-Hispanic/Latino; 0.4% American Indian or Alaska Native, non-Hispanic/Latino; 6% Two or more races, non-Hispanic/Latino; 9% Race/ethnicity unknown; 15% international; 5% transferred in; 41% live on campus.

Freshmen
Admission: 4,087 applied, 2,986 admitted, 1,217 enrolled. ***Average high school GPA:*** 3.61. ***Test scores:*** SAT critical reading scores over 500: 70%; SAT math scores over 500: 79%; SAT writing scores over 500: 64%; ACT scores over 18: 95%; SAT critical reading scores over 600: 27%; SAT math scores over 600: 43%; SAT writing scores over 600: 21%; ACT scores over 24: 63%; SAT critical reading scores over 700: 5%; SAT math scores over 700: 9%; SAT writing scores over 700: 2%; ACT scores over 30: 18%.

Retention: 79% of full-time freshmen returned.

ACADEMICS
Calendar: semesters. *Degrees:* associate, bachelor's, master's, and doctoral.

Special study options: academic remediation for entering students, accelerated degree program, advanced placement credit, cooperative education, distance learning, double majors, English as a second language, honors programs, internships, services for LD students, study abroad, summer session for credit. ***ROTC:*** Army (b), Navy (b), Air Force (b).

Computers: 1,049 computers/terminals are available on campus for general student use. Students can access the following: campus intranet, computer help desk, free student e-mail accounts, online (class) grades, online (class) registration, online (class) schedules. Campuswide network is available. 100% of college-owned or -operated housing units are wired for high-speed Internet access. Wireless service is available via entire campus.

STUDENT LIFE
Housing options: on-campus residence required for freshman year; coed. Campus housing is university owned. Freshman campus housing is guaranteed.

Activities and organizations: drama/theater group, student-run newspaper, radio station, choral group, Eagle Wing, Future Professional Pilots Association, African Student Association, Caribbean Student Association, Sigma Gamma Tau, national fraternities, national sororities.

Athletics Member NAIA. ***Intercollegiate sports:*** baseball M(s), basketball M(s), cheerleading M/W, cross-country running M(s)/W(s), golf M(s)/W(s), soccer M(s)/W(s), softball W(s), tennis M(s)/W(s), track and field M(s)/W(s), volleyball W(s). ***Intramural sports:*** basketball M/W, bowling M/W, crew M(c)/W(c), football M/W, golf M/W, ice hockey M(c), lacrosse M(c), racquetball M/W, rugby M(c), soccer M/W, softball M/W, swimming and diving M(c)/W(c), table tennis M/W, tennis M/W, ultimate Frisbee M(c)/W(c), volleyball M/W.

Campus security: 24-hour emergency response devices and patrols, student patrols, late-night transport/escort service, controlled dormitory access.

Student services: health clinic, personal/psychological counseling, women's center.

COSTS & FINANCIAL AID
Costs (2015–16) ***Comprehensive fee:*** $43,600 includes full-time tuition ($31,944), mandatory fees ($1274), and room and board ($10,382). Part-time tuition: $1331 per credit hour. ***College room only:*** $6160. Room and board charges vary according to board plan, housing facility, and location. ***Payment plan:*** installment. ***Waivers:*** employees or children of employees.

Financial Aid Of all full-time matriculated undergraduates who enrolled in 2014, 3,866 applied for aid, 3,154 were judged to have need. 163 Federal Work-Study jobs (averaging $1756). 1,658 state and other part-time jobs (averaging $3304). ***Average financial aid package:*** $15,986. ***Average need-based loan:*** $4849. ***Average need-based gift aid:*** $13,233.

APPLYING
Standardized Tests *Recommended:* SAT or ACT (for admission).

Options: electronic application, deferred entrance.

Application fee: $50.

Required: high school transcript, minimum 2.0 GPA, 2 letters of recommendation. ***Required for some:*** medical examination for flight students. ***Recommended:*** essay or personal statement, minimum 3.0 GPA, 3 letters of recommendation, interview.

Application deadlines: rolling (freshmen), rolling (out-of-state freshmen), 6/1 (transfers).

Notification: continuous (freshmen), continuous (out-of-state freshmen), continuous (transfers).

CONTACT
Embry-Riddle Aeronautical University–Daytona, 600 South Clyde Morris Boulevard, Daytona Beach, FL 32114-3900. *Phone:* 386-226-6100. *Toll-free phone:* 800-862-2416. *Fax:* 386-226-7070. *E-mail:* dbadmit@erau.edu.

See previous page for display ad and page 1432 for the College Close-Up.

Embry-Riddle Aeronautical University–Worldwide

Daytona Beach, Florida

http://www.embryriddle.edu/

- **Independent** comprehensive, founded 1970
- **Coed** 10,561 undergraduate students, 28% full-time, 12% women, 88% men
- **Minimally difficult** entrance level, 69% of applicants were admitted

UNDERGRAD STUDENTS
2,959 full-time, 7,602 part-time. 8% Black or African American, non-Hispanic/Latino; 6% Hispanic/Latino; 2% Asian, non-Hispanic/Latino; 0.7% Native Hawaiian or other Pacific Islander, non-Hispanic/Latino; 0.6% American Indian or Alaska Native, non-Hispanic/Latino; 5% Two or more races, non-Hispanic/Latino; 20% Race/ethnicity unknown; 4% international.

Freshmen
Admission: 938 applied, 645 admitted.

ACADEMICS
Calendar: 5 9-week terms. *Degrees:* certificates, associate, bachelor's, master's, and doctoral (programs offered at 100 military bases worldwide).

Special study options: accelerated degree program, advanced placement credit, cooperative education, distance learning, double majors, external degree program, independent study, off-campus study, part-time degree program, services for LD students, summer session for credit.

Computers: Students can access the following: free student e-mail accounts, online (class) grades, online (class) registration, online (class) schedules.

COSTS & FINANCIAL AID
Costs (2014–15) ***Comprehensive fee:*** $13,284 includes full-time tuition ($8040) and room and board ($5244). Part-time tuition: $335 per credit hour. ***College room only:*** $3400. ***Waivers:*** employees or children of employees.

Financial Aid Of all full-time matriculated undergraduates who enrolled in 2013, 1,089 applied for aid, 819 were judged to have need. ***Average financial aid package:*** $6384. ***Average need-based loan:*** $4649. ***Average need-based gift aid:*** $4396.

APPLYING
Standardized Tests *Required for some:* SAT or ACT (for admission).

Options: electronic application, deferred entrance.

Application fee: $50.

Required for some: essay or personal statement, high school transcript, minimum 2.0 GPA, 2 letters of recommendation.

Application deadlines: rolling (freshmen), rolling (transfers).

Notification: continuous (freshmen), continuous (transfers).

CONTACT
Embry-Riddle Aeronautical University–Worldwide, 600 South Clyde Morris Boulevard, Daytona Beach, FL 32114-3900. *Phone:* 800-522-6787. *Toll-free phone:* 800-522-6787. *Fax:* 386-226-6984. *E-mail:* worldwide@erau.edu.

Everglades University

Sarasota, Florida

http://www.evergladesuniversity.edu/

- **Independent** comprehensive, founded 2003
- **Urban** campus with easy access to Miami
- **Coed** 1,313 undergraduate students, 100% full-time, 53% women, 47% men
- **Minimally difficult** entrance level, 86% of applicants were admitted

UNDERGRAD STUDENTS

1,313 full-time. Students come from 20 states and territories; 3 other countries; 53% are from out of state; 17% Black or African American, non-Hispanic/Latino; 15% Hispanic/Latino; 2% Asian, non-Hispanic/Latino; 0.3% Native Hawaiian or other Pacific Islander, non-Hispanic/Latino; 0.7% American Indian or Alaska Native, non-Hispanic/Latino; 5% Two or more races, non-Hispanic/Latino; 1% Race/ethnicity unknown; 0.1% international.

Freshmen

Admission: 177 applied, 152 admitted, 53 enrolled.

Retention: 75% of full-time freshmen returned.

FACULTY

Total: 229, 40% full-time.

Student/faculty ratio: 7:1.

ACADEMICS

Calendar: continuous. *Degrees:* bachelor's and master's.

Special study options: academic remediation for entering students, advanced placement credit, cooperative education, distance learning, off-campus study, services for LD students, summer session for credit.

Computers: 55 computers/terminals are available on campus for general student use. Students can access the following: campus intranet, computer help desk, free student e-mail accounts, online (class) grades, online (class) schedules. Campuswide network is available. Wireless service is available via classrooms, computer centers, computer labs, libraries, student centers.

STUDENT LIFE

Housing options: college housing not available.

Campus security: 24-hour patrols.

Student services: personal/psychological counseling.

COSTS & FINANCIAL AID

Costs (2015–16) ***One-time required fee:*** $195. ***Tuition:*** $14,400 full-time. ***Required fees:*** $1600 full-time. ***Payment plan:*** installment.

Financial Aid Of all full-time matriculated undergraduates who enrolled in 2014, 190 applied for aid, 179 were judged to have need, 45 had their need fully met. In 2014, 1 non-need-based awards were made. ***Average percent of need met:*** 59. ***Average financial aid package:*** $8455. ***Average need-based loan:*** $4782. ***Average need-based gift aid:*** $5230. ***Average non-need-based aid:*** $60. ***Average indebtedness upon graduation:*** $52,777.

APPLYING

Options: electronic application.

Application fee: $50.

Required: high school transcript.

CONTACT

Everglades University, 6001 Lake Osprey Drive #110, Sarasota, FL 34240. *Phone:* 561-912-1211 Ext. 135. *Toll-free phone:* 866-907-2262.

Flagler College

St. Augustine, Florida

http://www.flagler.edu/

- **Independent** 4-year, founded 1968
- **Small-town** 47-acre campus with easy access to Jacksonville
- **Endowment** $63.2 million
- **Coed** 2,774 undergraduate students, 97% full-time, 60% women, 40% men
- **Moderately difficult** entrance level, 48% of applicants were admitted

UNDERGRAD STUDENTS

2,682 full-time, 92 part-time. Students come from 44 states and territories; 43 other countries; 39% are from out of state; 3% Black or African American, non-Hispanic/Latino; 10% Hispanic/Latino; 1% Asian, non-Hispanic/Latino; 0.3% American Indian or Alaska Native, non-Hispanic/Latino; 3% Two or more races, non-Hispanic/Latino; 5% Race/ethnicity unknown; 4% international; 6% transferred in; 37% live on campus.

Freshmen

Admission: 6,585 applied, 3,153 admitted, 673 enrolled. ***Average high school GPA:*** 3.39. ***Test scores:*** SAT critical reading scores over 500: 70%; SAT math scores over 500: 62%; SAT writing scores over 500: 58%; ACT scores over 18: 98%; SAT critical reading scores over 600: 18%; SAT math scores over 600: 12%; SAT writing scores over 600: 15%; ACT scores over 24: 42%; SAT critical reading scores over 700: 2%; SAT math scores over 700: 1%; SAT writing scores over 700: 1%; ACT scores over 30: 1%.

Retention: 69% of full-time freshmen returned.

FACULTY

Total: 228, 48% full-time, 46% with terminal degrees.

Student/faculty ratio: 19:1.

ACADEMICS

Calendar: semesters. *Degree:* bachelor's.

Special study options: academic remediation for entering students, advanced placement credit, cooperative education, double majors, independent study, internships, services for LD students, study abroad, summer session for credit.

Computers: 363 computers/terminals are available on campus for general student use. Students can access the following: campus intranet, computer help desk, free student e-mail accounts, online (class) grades, online (class) registration, online (class) schedules. Campuswide network is available. 100% of college-owned or -operated housing units are wired for high-speed Internet access. Wireless service is available via entire campus.

STUDENT LIFE

Housing options: on-campus residence required for freshman year; men-only, women-only. Campus housing is university owned. Freshman campus housing is guaranteed.

Activities and organizations: drama/theater group, student-run newspaper, radio station, choral group, Student Government Association, Inter-Varsity, CRU, Adventure Club, Phi Alpha Omega (women's service club).

Athletics Member NCAA. All Division II. ***Intercollegiate sports:*** baseball M(s), basketball M(s)/W(s), cheerleading M/W, cross-country running M(s)/W(s), golf M(s)/W(s), soccer M(s)/W(s), softball W(s), tennis M(s)/W(s), volleyball W(s). ***Intramural sports:*** basketball M/W, bowling M, cheerleading W, football M/W, lacrosse M(c)/W(c), soccer M/W, table tennis M/W, tennis M/W, volleyball M/W.

Campus security: 24-hour emergency response devices and patrols, late-night transport/escort service, controlled dormitory access, Transport/escort service is provided from 6:00 pm until 6:00 am daily.

Student services: health clinic, personal/psychological counseling.

COSTS & FINANCIAL AID

Costs (2015–16) ***Comprehensive fee:*** $26,250 includes full-time tuition ($16,800), mandatory fees ($100), and room and board ($9350). Full-time tuition and fees vary according to location. Part-time tuition: $560 per credit hour. Part-time tuition and fees vary according to location. ***College room only:*** $4450. Room and board charges vary according to board plan and housing facility. ***Payment plan:*** installment. ***Waivers:*** employees or children of employees.

Financial Aid Of all full-time matriculated undergraduates who enrolled in 2013, 2,344 applied for aid, 1,760 were judged to have need, 257 had their need fully met. 265 Federal Work-Study jobs (averaging $1106). 77 state and other part-time jobs (averaging $1074). In 2013, 904 non-need-based awards were made. ***Average percent of need met:*** 78. ***Average financial aid package:*** $11,619. ***Average need-based loan:*** $4073. ***Average need-based gift aid:*** $8082. ***Average non-need-based aid:*** $1402. ***Average indebtedness upon graduation:*** $27,408.

APPLYING
Standardized Tests *Required:* SAT or ACT (for admission).

Options: electronic application, early admission, early decision.

Application fee: $50.

Required: essay or personal statement, high school transcript, 1 letter of recommendation. ***Required for some:*** interview. ***Recommended:*** minimum 2.5 GPA.

Application deadlines: 3/1 (freshmen), 3/1 (transfers).

Early decision deadline: 11/1.

Notification: 3/31 (freshmen), 3/31 (transfers), 12/15 (early decision).

CONTACT
Ms. Rachel Branch, Director of Admissions, Flagler College, 74 King Street, St. Augustine, FL 32085. *Phone:* 904-819-6294. *Toll-free phone:* 800-304-4208. *Fax:* 904-819-6466. *E-mail:* RBranch@flagler.edu.

★ Florida Agricultural and Mechanical University
Tallahassee, Florida
http://www.famu.edu/

- **State-supported** university, founded 1887, part of State University System of Florida
- **Urban** 419-acre campus with easy access to Jacksonville
- **Endowment** $127.2 million
- **Coed** 8,495 undergraduate students, 85% full-time, 62% women, 38% men
- **Moderately difficult** entrance level, 49% of applicants were admitted

UNDERGRAD STUDENTS
7,230 full-time, 1,265 part-time. Students come from 43 states and territories; 57 other countries; 12% are from out of state; 90% Black or African American, non-Hispanic/Latino; 2% Hispanic/Latino; 0.9% Asian, non-Hispanic/Latino; 0.2% American Indian or Alaska Native, non-Hispanic/Latino; 0.2% Two or more races, non-Hispanic/Latino; 1% international; 5% transferred in; 28% live on campus.

Freshmen
Admission: 5,017 applied, 2,456 admitted, 1,400 enrolled. ***Average high school GPA:*** 3.29. ***Test scores:*** SAT critical reading scores over 500: 37%; SAT math scores over 500: 31%; SAT writing scores over 500: 28%; ACT scores over 18: 79%; SAT critical reading scores over 600: 8%; SAT math scores over 600: 9%; SAT writing scores over 600: 7%; ACT scores over 24: 16%; SAT critical reading scores over 700: 1%; ACT scores over 30: 1%.

Retention: 81% of full-time freshmen returned.

FACULTY
Total: 791, 69% full-time, 53% with terminal degrees.

Student/faculty ratio: 16:1.

ACADEMICS
Calendar: semesters. *Degrees:* associate, bachelor's, master's, doctoral, and post-master's certificates.

Special study options: academic remediation for entering students, accelerated degree program, adult/continuing education programs, advanced placement credit, cooperative education, distance learning, double majors, honors programs, independent study, internships, off-campus study, part-time degree program, services for LD students, study abroad, summer session for credit. ***ROTC:*** Army (b), Navy (b), Air Force (c).

Unusual degree programs: 3-2 business administration; occupational therapy, architecture.

Computers: 4,000 computers/terminals and 8,000 ports are available on campus for general student use. Students can access the following: campus intranet, computer help desk, free student e-mail accounts, online (class) grades, online (class) registration, online (class) schedules. Campuswide network is available. 100% of college-owned or -operated housing units are wired for high-speed Internet access. Wireless service is available via classrooms, computer centers, computer labs, dorm rooms, learning centers, libraries, student centers.

STUDENT LIFE
Housing options: on-campus residence required for freshman year; coed, men-only, women-only, special housing for students with disabilities. Campus housing is university owned. Freshman applicants given priority for college housing.

Activities and organizations: drama/theater group, student-run newspaper, radio and television station, choral group, marching band, National Council of Negro Women, FAMU Chapter, American Society of Mechanical Engineers, Psi Chi International Honor Society, Caribbean Student Association, Academy of Student Pharmacists/Student National Pharmaceutical Association, national fraternities, national sororities.

Athletics Member NCAA. All Division I except football (Division I-AA). ***Intercollegiate sports:*** baseball M(s), basketball M(s)/W(s), bowling W(s), cheerleading M/W, cross-country running M(s)/W(s), golf M(s)/W(s), softball W(s), swimming and diving M(s)/W(s), tennis M(s)/W(s), track and field M(s)/W(s), volleyball W(s). ***Intramural sports:*** badminton M/W, basketball M/W, bowling M/W, cheerleading W, football M, golf M/W, gymnastics M/W, racquetball M/W, skiing (downhill) M/W, soccer M/W, softball M/W, swimming and diving M/W, table tennis M/W, tennis M/W, track and field M/W, ultimate Frisbee M/W, volleyball M/W, weight lifting M/W, wrestling M/W.

Campus security: 24-hour emergency response devices and patrols, late-night transport/escort service, controlled dormitory access.

Student services: health clinic, personal/psychological counseling.

COSTS & FINANCIAL AID
Costs (2014–15) ***One-time required fee:*** $35. ***Tuition:*** state resident $5644 full-time, $188 per credit part-time; nonresident $17,586 full-time, $586 per credit part-time. ***Required fees:*** $140 full-time. ***Room and board:*** $9576; room only: $5558. Room and board charges vary according to board plan and housing facility. ***Payment plan:*** tuition prepayment. ***Waivers:*** senior citizens and employees or children of employees.

Financial Aid Of all full-time matriculated undergraduates who enrolled in 2013, 8,732 applied for aid, 7,735 were judged to have need, 1,033 had their need fully met. 263 Federal Work-Study jobs (averaging $1951). In 2013, 48 non-need-based awards were made. ***Average percent of need met:*** 70. ***Average financial aid package:*** $13,039. ***Average need-based loan:*** $4043. ***Average need-based gift aid:*** $6063. ***Average non-need-based aid:*** $4590. ***Average indebtedness upon graduation:*** $31,251.

APPLYING
Standardized Tests *Required:* SAT or ACT (for admission).

Options: electronic application, early admission.

Application fee: $30.

Required: essay or personal statement, high school transcript, minimum 2.5 GPA, 3 letters of recommendation. ***Required for some:*** interview, audition for music major applicants. ***Recommended:*** minimum 3.0 GPA.

Application deadlines: 5/15 (freshmen), 5/15 (out-of-state freshmen), 5/15 (transfers).

Notification: continuous (freshmen), continuous (out-of-state freshmen), continuous (transfers).

CONTACT
Ms. Barbara R. Cox, Director, Admissions, Florida Agricultural and Mechanical University, Office of Admissions, Florida A & M University, Tallahassee, FL 32307. *Phone:* 850-599-3796. *Toll-free phone:* 866-642-1198. *Fax:* 850-599-3069. *E-mail:* ugrdadmissions@famu.edu.

★ Florida Atlantic University
Boca Raton, Florida
http://www.fau.edu/

- **State-supported** university, founded 1961, part of State University System of Florida
- **Suburban** 850-acre campus with easy access to Miami, Fort Lauderdale, West Palm Beach
- **Endowment** $208.5 million
- **Coed** 25,209 undergraduate students, 62% full-time, 56% women, 44% men
- **Moderately difficult** entrance level, 66% of applicants were admitted

UNDERGRAD STUDENTS
15,524 full-time, 9,685 part-time. Students come from 45 states and territories; 120 other countries; 4% are from out of state; 19% Black or

African American, non-Hispanic/Latino; 25% Hispanic/Latino; 4% Asian, non-Hispanic/Latino; 0.1% Native Hawaiian or other Pacific Islander, non-Hispanic/Latino; 0.2% American Indian or Alaska Native, non-Hispanic/Latino; 3% Two or more races, non-Hispanic/Latino; 1% Race/ethnicity unknown; 2% international; 10% transferred in; 6% live on campus.

Freshmen

Admission: 14,944 applied, 9,867 admitted, 3,072 enrolled. ***Average high school GPA:*** 378. ***Test scores:*** SAT critical reading scores over 500: 67%; SAT math scores over 500: 65%; SAT writing scores over 500: 62%; ACT scores over 18: 99%; SAT critical reading scores over 600: 17%; SAT math scores over 600: 17%; SAT writing scores over 600: 12%; ACT scores over 24: 37%; SAT critical reading scores over 700: 2%; SAT math scores over 700: 2%; SAT writing scores over 700: 2%; ACT scores over 30: 4%.

Retention: 74% of full-time freshmen returned.

FACULTY

Total: 1,248, 61% full-time, 69% with terminal degrees.

Student/faculty ratio: 24:1.

ACADEMICS

Calendar: semesters. *Degrees:* certificates, associate, bachelor's, master's, doctoral, and post-master's certificates.

Special study options: accelerated degree program, adult/continuing education programs, advanced placement credit, cooperative education, distance learning, double majors, English as a second language, freshman honors college, honors programs, independent study, internships, off-campus study, part-time degree program, services for LD students, study abroad, summer session for credit. ***ROTC:*** Army (b), Air Force (c).

Unusual degree programs: business administration; engineering; nursing; Architecture, Mathematics.

Computers: 1,350 computers/terminals are available on campus for general student use. Students can access the following: campus intranet, computer help desk, free student e-mail accounts, online (class) grades, online (class) registration, online (class) schedules. Campuswide network is available. 100% of college-owned or -operated housing units are wired for high-speed Internet access. Wireless service is available via entire campus.

STUDENT LIFE

Housing options: on-campus residence required for freshman year; coed, women-only. Campus housing is university owned. Freshman campus housing is guaranteed.

Activities and organizations: drama/theater group, student-run newspaper, radio and television station, choral group, marching band, American Society of Civil Engineers, Dive Club, Pre-Law Society, Submarine Club, American Criminal Justice Society, national fraternities, national sororities.

Athletics Member NCAA. All Division I. ***Intercollegiate sports:*** baseball M(s), basketball M(s)/W(s), cheerleading M/W, cross-country running M/W, football M(s), golf M(s)/W(s), soccer M/W, softball W(s), swimming and diving M/W, tennis M/W, track and field W, volleyball W(s). ***Intramural sports:*** baseball M/W, bowling M/W, football M, ice hockey M(c)/W(c), lacrosse M(c), rock climbing M(c)/W(c), rugby M(c)/W(c), sailing M(c)/W(c), soccer M/W, softball W, table tennis M/W, ultimate Frisbee M/W, volleyball M/W, weight lifting M(c), wrestling M(c).

Campus security: 24-hour emergency response devices and patrols, student patrols, late-night transport/escort service, controlled dormitory access.

Student services: health clinic, personal/psychological counseling, women's center.

COSTS & FINANCIAL AID

Costs (2014–15) ***Tuition:*** state resident $6039 full-time, $105 per credit hour part-time; nonresident $21,595 full-time, $599 per credit hour part-time. Full-time tuition and fees vary according to course load. Part-time tuition and fees vary according to course load. ***Room and board:*** $11,924. Room and board charges vary according to board plan and housing facility. ***Payment plans:*** tuition prepayment, installment, deferred payment. ***Waivers:*** senior citizens and employees or children of employees.

Financial Aid Of all full-time matriculated undergraduates who enrolled in 2012, 12,645 applied for aid, 10,224 were judged to have need, 961 had

their need fully met. 160 Federal Work-Study jobs (averaging $3799). 3 state and other part-time jobs (averaging $2345). In 2012, 266 non-need-based awards were made. ***Average percent of need met:*** 61. ***Average financial aid package:*** $10,405. ***Average need-based loan:*** $6568. ***Average need-based gift aid:*** $5949. ***Average non-need-based aid:*** $2678. ***Average indebtedness upon graduation:*** $19,898. ***Financial aid deadline:*** 6/30.

APPLYING
Standardized Tests *Required:* SAT or ACT (for admission).

Options: electronic application, early admission, deferred entrance.

Application fee: $30.

Required: high school transcript.

Application deadlines: 5/1 (freshmen), 5/1 (out-of-state freshmen), 5/1 (transfers).

Notification: continuous (freshmen), continuous (out-of-state freshmen), continuous (transfers).

CONTACT
Ms. Mary Edmunds, Associate Director, Florida Atlantic University, 777 Glades Road, PO Box 3091, Boca Raton, FL 33431-0991. *Phone:* 561-297-3040. *Fax:* 561-297-2758. *E-mail:* Recruitment@fau.edu.

See previous page for display ad and page 1446 for the College Close-Up.

Florida College

Temple Terrace, Florida

http://www.floridacollege.edu/

- **Independent** 4-year, founded 1944
- **Small-town** 95-acre campus with easy access to Tampa
- **Endowment** $11.9 million
- **Coed** 555 undergraduate students, 96% full-time, 50% women, 50% men
- **Moderately difficult** entrance level, 72% of applicants were admitted

UNDERGRAD STUDENTS
533 full-time, 22 part-time. Students come from 34 states and territories; 5 other countries; 68% are from out of state; 5% Black or African American, non-Hispanic/Latino; 4% Hispanic/Latino; 0.7% Asian, non-Hispanic/Latino; 0.5% Native Hawaiian or other Pacific Islander, non-Hispanic/Latino; 1% American Indian or Alaska Native, non-Hispanic/Latino; 5% Two or more races, non-Hispanic/Latino; 0.2% Race/ethnicity unknown; 2% international; 5% transferred in; 81% live on campus.

Freshmen
Admission: 335 applied, 241 admitted, 199 enrolled. ***Test scores:*** SAT critical reading scores over 500: 75%; SAT math scores over 500: 64%; SAT writing scores over 500: 52%; ACT scores over 18: 127%; SAT critical reading scores over 600: 27%; SAT math scores over 600: 30%; SAT writing scores over 600: 16%; ACT scores over 24: 64%; SAT critical reading scores over 700: 9%; SAT math scores over 700: 3%; SAT writing scores over 700: 3%; ACT scores over 30: 10%.

FACULTY
Total: 55, 67% full-time, 33% with terminal degrees.

Student/faculty ratio: 13:1.

ACADEMICS
Calendar: semesters. *Degrees:* associate and bachelor's.

Special study options: academic remediation for entering students, advanced placement credit, independent study, summer session for credit. ***ROTC:*** Army (c), Air Force (c).

Computers: 36 computers/terminals are available on campus for general student use. Students can access the following: campus intranet, computer help desk, free student e-mail accounts, online (class) grades, online (class) schedules. Campuswide network is available. 100% of college-owned or -operated housing units are wired for high-speed Internet access. Wireless service is available via classrooms, computer centers, computer labs, dorm rooms, libraries, student centers.

STUDENT LIFE
Housing options: on-campus residence required through sophomore year; men-only, women-only. Campus housing is university owned. Freshman campus housing is guaranteed.

Activities and organizations: drama/theater group, choral group, Co-ed Societies, Circle K, NAFME, SBGA, Footlighters.

Athletics Member USCAA. ***Intercollegiate sports:*** basketball M(s)/W, cheerleading W, cross-country running M/W, soccer M(s)/W(s), volleyball W(s). ***Intramural sports:*** basketball M/W, football M/W, soccer M/W, softball M/W, ultimate Frisbee M/W, volleyball M/W.

Campus security: controlled dormitory access, evening patrols by trained security personnel.

Student services: health clinic, personal/psychological counseling.

COSTS & FINANCIAL AID
Costs (2014–15) ***Comprehensive fee:*** $23,290 includes full-time tuition ($14,490), mandatory fees ($840), and room and board ($7960). Part-time tuition: $572 per credit. Part-time tuition and fees vary according to course load. ***College room only:*** $4000. Room and board charges vary according to board plan and housing facility. ***Payment plan:*** installment. ***Waivers:*** employees or children of employees.

Financial Aid Of all full-time matriculated undergraduates who enrolled in 2012, 449 applied for aid, 382 were judged to have need, 38 had their need fully met. 34 Federal Work-Study jobs (averaging $685). In 2012, 97 non-need-based awards were made. ***Average percent of need met:*** 54. ***Average financial aid package:*** $11,823. ***Average need-based loan:*** $3142. ***Average need-based gift aid:*** $4349. ***Average non-need-based aid:*** $3154.

APPLYING
Standardized Tests *Required:* SAT or ACT (for admission).

Options: electronic application.

Application fee: $35.

Required: high school transcript, minimum 2.0 GPA, 2 letters of recommendation. ***Required for some:*** essay for international students.

Application deadlines: 8/1 (freshmen), 8/1 (transfers).

Notification: continuous (freshmen), continuous (transfers).

CONTACT
Mrs. Colleen Engel, Assistant Director of Admissions, Florida College, 119 North Glen Arven Avenue, Temple Terrace, FL 33617. *Phone:* 813-988-5131 Ext. 152. *Fax:* 813-899-6772. *E-mail:* admissions@floridacollege.edu.

Florida Gateway College

Lake City, Florida

http://www.fgc.edu/

- **State-supported** primarily 2-year, founded 1962, part of Florida Community College System
- **Small-town** 132-acre campus with easy access to Jacksonville
- **Coed**
- **Noncompetitive** entrance level

FACULTY
Student/faculty ratio: 16:1.

ACADEMICS
Calendar: semesters. *Degrees:* certificates, diplomas, associate, and bachelor's.

STUDENT LIFE
Housing options: college housing not available.

Activities and organizations: drama/theater group, choral group, Anime Club, Art Club, FGC Board Game Club, Gay Straight Alliance, Rotaract.

Campus security: 24-hour emergency response devices and patrols.

Student services: personal/psychological counseling.

COSTS
Costs (2014–15) ***Tuition:*** state resident $2368 full-time, $103 per credit hour part-time; nonresident $11,747 full-time, $392 per credit hour part-time. Full-time tuition and fees vary according to course level, course load, degree level, program, reciprocity agreements, and student level. Part-time tuition and fees vary according to course level, course load, degree level, program, reciprocity agreements, and student level. ***Required fees:*** $731 full-time. ***Payment plans:*** installment, deferred payment.

APPLYING
Required for some: high school transcript.

CONTACT
Admissions, Florida Gateway College, 149 SE College Place, Lake City, FL 32025-8703. *Phone:* 386-755-4236. *E-mail:* admissions@fgc.edu.

Florida Gulf Coast University

Fort Myers, Florida

http://www.fgcu.edu/

- **State-supported** comprehensive, founded 1991, part of State University System of Florida
- **Suburban** 760-acre campus
- **Endowment** $75.7 million
- **Coed** 13,300 undergraduate students, 79% full-time, 56% women, 44% men
- **Moderately difficult** entrance level, 59% of applicants were admitted

UNDERGRAD STUDENTS
10,564 full-time, 2,736 part-time. Students come from 44 states and territories; 81 other countries; 10% are from out of state; 8% Black or African American, non-Hispanic/Latino; 19% Hispanic/Latino; 2% Asian, non-Hispanic/Latino; 0.1% Native Hawaiian or other Pacific Islander, non-Hispanic/Latino; 0.2% American Indian or Alaska Native, non-Hispanic/Latino; 3% Two or more races, non-Hispanic/Latino; 1% Race/ethnicity unknown; 2% international; 7% transferred in; 36% live on campus.

Freshmen
Admission: 13,773 applied, 8,110 admitted, 2,782 enrolled. ***Average high school GPA:*** 3.57. ***Test scores:*** SAT critical reading scores over 500: 69%; SAT math scores over 500: 65%; SAT writing scores over 500: 59%; ACT scores over 18: 98%; SAT critical reading scores over 600: 14%; SAT math scores over 600: 14%; SAT writing scores over 600: 9%; ACT scores over 24: 37%; SAT critical reading scores over 700: 1%; SAT math scores over 700: 1%; ACT scores over 30: 3%.
Retention: 76% of full-time freshmen returned.

FACULTY
Total: 709, 63% full-time, 46% with terminal degrees.
Student/faculty ratio: 23:1.

ACADEMICS
Calendar: semesters. *Degrees:* certificates, associate, bachelor's, master's, doctoral, and post-master's certificates.
Special study options: academic remediation for entering students, accelerated degree program, advanced placement credit, cooperative education, distance learning, double majors, honors programs, independent study, internships, off-campus study, part-time degree program, services for LD students, study abroad, summer session for credit.
Computers: 942 computers/terminals are available on campus for general student use. Students can access the following: computer help desk, free student e-mail accounts, online (class) registration, online (class) schedules, online admissions and advising. Campuswide network is available. 100% of college-owned or -operated housing units are wired for high-speed Internet access. Wireless service is available via entire campus.

STUDENT LIFE
Housing options: coed. Campus housing is university owned.
Activities and organizations: drama/theater group, student-run newspaper, student government, Ignite (Religious Organization), International Club, Martial Arts Club, Physical Therapy Association, national fraternities, national sororities.
Athletics Member NCAA. All Division I. ***Intercollegiate sports:*** baseball M(s), basketball M(s)/W(s), cheerleading W, cross-country running M(s)/W(s), golf M(s)/W(s), soccer M(s)/W(s), softball W(s), swimming and diving W(s), tennis M(s)/W(s), volleyball W(s). ***Intramural sports:*** basketball M/W, cross-country running M(c)/W(c), fencing M(c)/W(c), football M/W, ice hockey M(c), lacrosse M(c)/W(c), sailing M(c)/W(c), skiing (downhill) M(c)/W(c), soccer M/W, softball M/W, swimming and diving M(c)/W(c), table tennis M/W, tennis M(c)/W(c), ultimate Frisbee M/W, volleyball M/W, water polo M/W, weight lifting M(c)/W(c), wrestling M(c)/W(c).
Campus security: 24-hour emergency response devices and patrols, late-night transport/escort service.
Student services: health clinic, personal/psychological counseling.

COSTS & FINANCIAL AID
Costs (2014–15) ***Tuition:*** state resident $4191 full-time; nonresident $22,381 full-time. Full-time tuition and fees vary according to course load. Part-time tuition and fees vary according to course load. ***Required fees:*** $1927 full-time. ***Room and board:*** $8359; room only: $4820. Room and board charges vary according to board plan and housing facility.
Financial Aid Of all full-time matriculated undergraduates who enrolled in 2013, 8,044 applied for aid, 5,505 were judged to have need, 350 had their need fully met. In 2013, 332 non-need-based awards were made. ***Average percent of need met:*** 59. ***Average financial aid package:*** $9386. ***Average need-based loan:*** $6982. ***Average need-based gift aid:*** $5250. ***Average non-need-based aid:*** $3562. ***Average indebtedness upon graduation:*** $22,718. ***Financial aid deadline:*** 6/30.

APPLYING
Standardized Tests *Required:* SAT or ACT (for admission).
Options: electronic application, deferred entrance.
Application fee: $30.
Required: high school transcript, minimum 2.0 GPA.
Application deadlines: 5/1 (freshmen), 7/1 (transfers).
Notification: continuous (freshmen), continuous (transfers).

CONTACT
Florida Gulf Coast University, 10501 FGCU Boulevard South, Fort Myers, FL 33965-6565. *Phone:* 239-590-7878. *Toll-free phone:* 888-889-1095.

★ Florida Institute of Technology

Melbourne, Florida

http://www.fit.edu/

- **Independent** university, founded 1958
- **Small-town** 130-acre campus with easy access to Orlando
- **Endowment** $61.1 million
- **Coed** 3,656 undergraduate students, 92% full-time, 28% women, 72% men
- **Moderately difficult** entrance level, 62% of applicants were admitted

UNDERGRAD STUDENTS
3,372 full-time, 284 part-time. Students come from 50 states and territories; 110 other countries; 45% are from out of state; 6% Black or African American, non-Hispanic/Latino; 7% Hispanic/Latino; 3% Asian, non-Hispanic/Latino; 0.4% Native Hawaiian or other Pacific Islander, non-Hispanic/Latino; 0.4% American Indian or Alaska Native, non-Hispanic/Latino; 2% Two or more races, non-Hispanic/Latino; 9% Race/ethnicity unknown; 33% international; 5% transferred in; 55% live on campus.

Freshmen
Admission: 8,573 applied, 5,278 admitted, 791 enrolled. ***Average high school GPA:*** 3.62. ***Test scores:*** SAT critical reading scores over 500: 81%; SAT math scores over 500: 86%; ACT scores over 18: 100%; SAT critical reading scores over 600: 32%; SAT math scores over 600: 51%; ACT scores over 24: 72%; SAT critical reading scores over 700: 5%; SAT math scores over 700: 11%; ACT scores over 30: 25%.
Retention: 76% of full-time freshmen returned.

FACULTY
Total: 517, 56% full-time, 72% with terminal degrees.
Student/faculty ratio: 9:1.

ACADEMICS
Calendar: semesters. *Degrees:* bachelor's, master's, doctoral, and post-master's certificates.
Special study options: academic remediation for entering students, accelerated degree program, adult/continuing education programs, advanced placement credit, cooperative education, distance learning, double majors, English as a second language, independent study, internships, part-time degree program, services for LD students, student-

designed majors, study abroad, summer session for credit. ***ROTC:*** Army (b).

Computers: 440 computers/terminals and 75 ports are available on campus for general student use. Students can access the following: campus intranet, computer help desk, free student e-mail accounts, online (class) grades, online (class) registration, online (class) schedules. Campuswide network is available. 100% of college-owned or -operated housing units are wired for high-speed Internet access. Wireless service is available via classrooms, computer centers, computer labs, dorm rooms, learning centers, libraries, student centers.

STUDENT LIFE

Housing options: on-campus residence required through sophomore year; coed. Campus housing is university owned. Freshman campus housing is guaranteed.

Activities and organizations: drama/theater group, student-run newspaper, radio and television station, choral group, Florida Institute of Technology Society for Science Fiction and Fantasy (FITSSFF), International Student Services Organization (ISSO), Student Government Association (SGA), ISA-Sanskriti, Campus Activities Board, national fraternities, national sororities.

Athletics Member NCAA. All Division II. ***Intercollegiate sports:*** baseball M(s), basketball M(s)/W(s), crew M(s)/W(s), cross-country running M(s)/W(s), football M(s), golf M(s)/W(s), lacrosse M(s)/W(s), soccer M(s)/W(s), softball W(s), swimming and diving M(s)/W(s), tennis M(s)/W(s), track and field M(s)/W(s), volleyball W(s), water polo M(c)/W(c). ***Intramural sports:*** badminton M/W, baseball M(c)/W(c), basketball M/W, bowling M/W, football M/W, ice hockey M(c)/W(c), racquetball M/W, rugby M/W, sailing M/W, soccer M/W, softball W, tennis M/W, ultimate Frisbee M/W, volleyball M/W.

Campus security: 24-hour emergency response devices and patrols, late-night transport/escort service, controlled dormitory access.

Student services: health clinic, personal/psychological counseling, women's center.

COSTS & FINANCIAL AID

Costs (2014–15) ***Comprehensive fee:*** $50,816 includes full-time tuition ($37,240), mandatory fees ($750), and room and board ($12,826). Full-time tuition and fees vary according to course load and program. Part-time tuition: $1075 per credit hour. ***College room only:*** $7510. Room and board charges vary according to board plan and housing facility. ***Payment plan:*** installment. ***Waivers:*** senior citizens and employees or children of employees.

Financial Aid Of all full-time matriculated undergraduates who enrolled in 2014, 1,852 applied for aid, 1,674 were judged to have need, 555 had their need fully met. 711 Federal Work-Study jobs (averaging $1975). 10 state and other part-time jobs (averaging $3092). In 2014, 907 non-need-based awards were made. ***Average percent of need met:*** 82. ***Average financial aid package:*** $34,092. ***Average need-based loan:*** $5235. ***Average need-based gift aid:*** $23,464. ***Average non-need-based aid:*** $14,171. ***Average indebtedness upon graduation:*** $40,383.

APPLYING

Standardized Tests *Required:* SAT or ACT (for admission).

Options: electronic application, deferred entrance.

Required: essay or personal statement, high school transcript, minimum 2.6 GPA, 1 letter of recommendation, SAT or ACT. ***Recommended:*** minimum 3.3 GPA, interview.

Application deadlines: rolling (freshmen), rolling (transfers).

Notification: continuous (freshmen), continuous (transfers).

CONTACT

Michael J. Perry, Director of Undergraduate Admission, Florida Institute of Technology, 150 West University Boulevard, Melbourne, FL 32901-6975. *Phone:* 321-674-8030. *Toll-free phone:* 800-888-4348. *Fax:* 321-723-9468. *E-mail:* admission@fit.edu.

Florida International University

Miami, Florida

http://www.fiu.edu/

- **State-supported** university, founded 1965, part of State University System of Florida
- **Urban** 582-acre campus with easy access to Miami
- **Endowment** $176.5 million
- **Coed** 40,974 undergraduate students, 63% full-time, 56% women, 44% men
- **Moderately difficult** entrance level, 48% of applicants were admitted

UNDERGRAD STUDENTS

25,645 full-time, 15,329 part-time. Students come from 49 states and territories; 144 other countries; 3% are from out of state; 12% Black or African American, non-Hispanic/Latino; 67% Hispanic/Latino; 3% Asian, non-Hispanic/Latino; 0.1% Native Hawaiian or other Pacific Islander, non-Hispanic/Latino; 0.1% American Indian or Alaska Native, non-Hispanic/Latino; 2% Two or more races, non-Hispanic/Latino; 1% Race/ethnicity unknown; 5% international; 12% transferred in; 8% live on campus.

Freshmen

Admission: 17,617 applied, 8,380 admitted, 4,144 enrolled. ***Average high school GPA:*** 3.91. ***Test scores:*** SAT critical reading scores over 500: 88%; SAT math scores over 500: 85%; SAT writing scores over 500: 84%; ACT scores over 18: 100%; SAT critical reading scores over 600: 28%; SAT math scores over 600: 27%; SAT writing scores over 600: 24%; ACT scores over 24: 62%; SAT critical reading scores over 700: 3%; SAT math scores over 700: 3%; SAT writing scores over 700: 2%; ACT scores over 30: 9%.

Retention: 84% of full-time freshmen returned.

FACULTY

Total: 2,255, 54% full-time, 68% with terminal degrees.

Student/faculty ratio: 26:1.

ACADEMICS

Calendar: semesters. *Degrees:* bachelor's, master's, doctoral, and postbachelor's certificates.

Special study options: accelerated degree program, adult/continuing education programs, advanced placement credit, cooperative education, distance learning, double majors, freshman honors college, honors programs, independent study, internships, off-campus study, part-time degree program, services for LD students, study abroad, summer session for credit. ***ROTC:*** Army (b), Air Force (b).

Computers: Students can access the following: computer help desk, free student e-mail accounts, online (class) grades, online (class) registration, online (class) schedules, online financial and cashier's information; class schedule, financial, campus maps information available on cell phones. Campuswide network is available. 100% of college-owned or -operated housing units are wired for high-speed Internet access. Wireless service is available via entire campus.

STUDENT LIFE

Housing options: coed. Campus housing is university owned.

Activities and organizations: drama/theater group, student-run newspaper, radio station, choral group, marching band, Students for Community Service, Black Student Leadership Council, Hospitality Management Student Club, Hispanic Students Association, Haitian Students Organization, national fraternities, national sororities.

Athletics Member NCAA. All Division I. ***Intercollegiate sports:*** baseball M(s), basketball M(s)/W(s), cross-country running M(s)/W(s), football M(s), golf W(s), soccer M(s)/W(s), softball W(s), swimming and diving W(s), tennis W(s), track and field M(s)/W(s), volleyball W(s). ***Intramural sports:*** badminton M(c)/W(c), baseball M(c), basketball M/W, crew M(c)/W(c), cross-country running M(c)/W(c), equestrian sports M(c)/W(c), football M/W, golf W, lacrosse M(c)/W(c), racquetball M/W, rugby M(c)/W(c), sailing M/W, soccer M/W, softball M/W, swimming and diving M(c)/W(c), table tennis M/W, tennis M(c)/W(c), ultimate Frisbee M/W, volleyball M/W, weight lifting M/W, wrestling M(c)/W(c).

Campus security: 24-hour emergency response devices and patrols, late-night transport/escort service, controlled dormitory access.

Student services: health clinic, personal/psychological counseling, women's center.

COSTS & FINANCIAL AID
Costs (2014–15) ***Tuition:*** state resident $6108 full-time, $204 per credit hour part-time; nonresident $18,507 full-time, $617 per credit hour part-time. ***Required fees:*** $389 full-time. ***Room and board:*** $10,702. Room and board charges vary according to board plan and housing facility. ***Payment plan:*** installment. ***Waivers:*** employees or children of employees.

Financial Aid Of all full-time matriculated undergraduates who enrolled in 2012, 18,131 applied for aid, 17,925 were judged to have need, 1,865 had their need fully met. 384 Federal Work-Study jobs (averaging $3905). 22 state and other part-time jobs (averaging $4362). In 2012, 1815 non-need-based awards were made. ***Average percent of need met:*** 17. ***Average financial aid package:*** $8086. ***Average need-based loan:*** $9345. ***Average need-based gift aid:*** $5813. ***Average non-need-based aid:*** $650. ***Average indebtedness upon graduation:*** $17,893. ***Financial aid deadline:*** 5/15.

APPLYING
Standardized Tests *Required:* SAT or ACT (for admission), TOEFL is required of all applicants whose native language is not English (for admission).

Options: electronic application.

Application fee: $30.

Required: high school transcript. ***Required for some:*** Some programs require portfolio or audition.

Application deadlines: 11/1 (freshmen), rolling (out-of-state freshmen), rolling (transfers).

Notification: continuous (freshmen), continuous (out-of-state freshmen), continuous (transfers).

CONTACT
Ms. Luisa Havens, Director of Admissions, Florida International University, 11200 SW Eighth Street, PC 140, Miami, FL 33199. *Phone:* 305-348-2363. *Fax:* 305-348-3648. *E-mail:* admiss@fiu.edu.

Florida National University
Hialeah, Florida
http://www.fnu.edu/

- **Proprietary** comprehensive, founded 1982
- **Urban** 4-acre campus with easy access to Miami
- **Coed** 2,376 undergraduate students, 84% full-time, 73% women, 27% men
- **Moderately difficult** entrance level, 96% of applicants were admitted

UNDERGRAD STUDENTS
2,006 full-time, 370 part-time. Students come from 18 states and territories; 21 other countries; 1% are from out of state; 2% Black or African American, non-Hispanic/Latino; 89% Hispanic/Latino; 0.2% Asian, non-Hispanic/Latino; 0.2% American Indian or Alaska Native, non-Hispanic/Latino; 0.3% Two or more races, non-Hispanic/Latino; 6% international; 0.8% transferred in.

Freshmen
Admission: 992 applied, 952 admitted, 472 enrolled.
Retention: 70% of full-time freshmen returned.

FACULTY
Total: 139, 63% full-time, 14% with terminal degrees.

Student/faculty ratio: 20:1.

ACADEMICS
Calendar: semesters. *Degrees:* certificates, diplomas, associate, bachelor's, and master's.

Special study options: academic remediation for entering students, accelerated degree program, adult/continuing education programs, advanced placement credit, cooperative education, distance learning, English as a second language, independent study, internships, part-time degree program, services for LD students, summer session for credit.

Computers: 287 computers/terminals are available on campus for general student use. Students can access the following: computer help desk, online (class) grades, online (class) registration, online (class) schedules. Campuswide network is available. Wireless service is available via entire campus.

STUDENT LIFE
Housing options: college housing not available.

Activities and organizations: student-run newspaper, Student Government Association, Bible Club, Salsa Club, W.I.C.S (Women Community Service), Criminal Justice Society, national fraternities.

Athletics Member USCAA. ***Intercollegiate sports:*** basketball M(s).

Campus security: 24-hour emergency response devices.

COSTS & FINANCIAL AID
Costs (2015–16) ***Tuition:*** $525 per credit part-time. No tuition increase for student's term of enrollment. ***Payment plans:*** tuition prepayment, installment. ***Waivers:*** employees or children of employees.

Financial Aid Of all full-time matriculated undergraduates who enrolled in 2013, 1,885 applied for aid, 1,866 were judged to have need. 14 Federal Work-Study jobs (averaging $8320). ***Average need-based gift aid:*** $5069. ***Average indebtedness upon graduation:*** $10,000.

APPLYING
Standardized Tests *Required:* SAT or ACT (for admission).

Options: electronic application, deferred entrance.

Required: high school transcript, interview.

Application deadlines: rolling (freshmen), rolling (transfers).

Notification: continuous (freshmen), continuous (transfers).

CONTACT
Mrs. Virginia Rabelo, Admissions Supervisor, Florida National University, 4425 W. Jose Regueiro (20th) Avenue, Hialeah, FL 33012. *Phone:* 305-821-3333 Ext. 1016. *Fax:* 305-362-0595. *E-mail:* vrabelo@fnu.edu.

★ Florida Southern College
Lakeland, Florida
http://www.flsouthern.edu/

- **Independent** comprehensive, founded 1885, affiliated with United Methodist Church
- **Suburban** 113-acre campus with easy access to Tampa, Orlando
- **Endowment** $82.4 million
- **Coed** 2,172 undergraduate students, 97% full-time, 61% women, 39% men
- **Moderately difficult** entrance level, 45% of applicants were admitted

UNDERGRAD STUDENTS
2,115 full-time, 57 part-time. Students come from 47 states and territories; 38 other countries; 36% are from out of state; 6% Black or African American, non-Hispanic/Latino; 10% Hispanic/Latino; 1% Asian, non-Hispanic/Latino; 0.1% Native Hawaiian or other Pacific Islander, non-Hispanic/Latino; 0.6% American Indian or Alaska Native, non-Hispanic/Latino; 4% Two or more races, non-Hispanic/Latino; 0.4% Race/ethnicity unknown; 5% international; 5% transferred in; 80% live on campus.

Freshmen
Admission: 5,590 applied, 2,505 admitted, 581 enrolled. ***Average high school GPA:*** 3.69. ***Test scores:*** SAT critical reading scores over 500: 86%; SAT math scores over 500: 86%; SAT writing scores over 500: 76%; ACT scores over 18: 100%; SAT critical reading scores over 600: 35%; SAT math scores over 600: 28%; SAT writing scores over 600: 21%; ACT scores over 24: 71%; SAT critical reading scores over 700: 7%; SAT math scores over 700: 3%; SAT writing scores over 700: 3%; ACT scores over 30: 6%.
Retention: 81% of full-time freshmen returned.

FACULTY
Total: 239, 54% full-time, 54% with terminal degrees.

Student/faculty ratio: 13:1.

ACADEMICS
Calendar: semesters. *Degrees:* bachelor's, master's, and doctoral.

Special study options: accelerated degree program, adult/continuing education programs, advanced placement credit, distance learning, double majors, external degree program, honors programs, independent study, internships, off-campus study, part-time degree program, student-designed

A ★ indicates that the school has detailed information with a Premium Profile on Petersons.com.

majors, study abroad, summer session for credit. ***ROTC:*** Army (b), Air Force (c).

Unusual degree programs: 3-2 business administration with BA/MBA in Business Administration; engineering with Washington University in St. Louis; Environmental Science, Duke University; BS in Accounting and Master of Accountancy, Florida Southern College; Pre-Med Honors Program/MD, USF College of Medicine; Lake Erie College of Osteopathic Medicine, 3/4 Pharmacy, 3+4/4+4 DO, 4+4 Dental.

Computers: 435 computers/terminals and 50 ports are available on campus for general student use. Students can access the following: campus intranet, computer help desk, free student e-mail accounts, online (class) grades, online (class) registration, online (class) schedules, campus portal. Campuswide network is available. 100% of college-owned or -operated housing units are wired for high-speed Internet access. Wireless service is available via entire campus.

STUDENT LIFE

Housing options: on-campus residence required through senior year; coed, men-only, women-only, special housing for students with disabilities. Campus housing is university owned. Freshman campus housing is guaranteed.

Activities and organizations: drama/theater group, student-run newspaper, television station, choral group, Student Government Association, Toastmasters, Association of Campus Entertainment, Beyond (Campus Ministry), Fellowship of Christian Athletes, national fraternities, national sororities.

Athletics Member NCAA. All Division II. ***Intercollegiate sports:*** baseball M(s), basketball M(s)/W(s), cheerleading W(c), cross-country running M(s)/W(s), golf M(s)/W(s), lacrosse M(s)/W(s), soccer M(s)/W(s), softball W(s), swimming and diving M(s)/W(s), tennis M(s)/W(s), track and field M(s)/W(s), volleyball W(s). ***Intramural sports:*** basketball M/W, bowling M/W, field hockey M/W, football M/W, soccer M/W, softball M/W, swimming and diving M/W, tennis M/W, ultimate Frisbee M/W, volleyball M/W, water polo M/W.

Campus security: 24-hour emergency response devices and patrols, student patrols, late-night transport/escort service, controlled dormitory access.

Student services: health clinic, personal/psychological counseling.

COSTS & FINANCIAL AID

Costs (2014–15) ***Comprehensive fee:*** $39,990 includes full-time tuition ($29,340), mandatory fees ($650), and room and board ($10,000). Part-time tuition: $840 per credit hour. Part-time tuition and fees vary according to class time and course load. ***College room only:*** $5740. Room and board charges vary according to board plan and housing facility. ***Payment plan:*** installment. ***Waivers:*** children of alumni and employees or children of employees.

Financial Aid Of all full-time matriculated undergraduates who enrolled in 2013, 1,838 applied for aid, 1,543 were judged to have need, 396 had their need fully met. 150 Federal Work-Study jobs (averaging $1757). 287 state and other part-time jobs (averaging $1746). In 2013, 540 non-need-based awards were made. ***Average percent of need met:*** 73. ***Average financial aid package:*** $23,599. ***Average need-based loan:*** $6174. ***Average need-based gift aid:*** $17,154. ***Average non-need-based aid:*** $14,522. ***Average indebtedness upon graduation:*** $33,191. ***Financial aid deadline:*** 7/1.

APPLYING

Standardized Tests *Required:* SAT or ACT (for admission).

Options: electronic application, early admission, early decision, deferred entrance.

Application fee: $30.

Required: high school transcript, minimum 2.0 GPA, 1 letter of recommendation. ***Recommended:*** essay or personal statement, interview.

Application deadlines: 3/1 (freshmen), rolling (transfers).

Early decision deadline: 12/1.

Notification: continuous (freshmen), continuous (transfers), 12/15 (early decision).

CONTACT

Florida Southern College, 111 Lake Hollingsworth Drive, Lakeland, FL 33801-5698. *Phone:* 863-680-4131. *Toll-free phone:* 800-274-4131.

See this page for display ad and page 1448 for the College Close-Up.

Florida SouthWestern State College

Fort Myers, Florida

http://www.fsw.edu/

- **State and locally supported** primarily 2-year, founded 1962, part of Florida College System
- **Urban** 413-acre campus
- **Endowment** $46.1 million
- **Coed** 15,705 undergraduate students, 34% full-time, 61% women, 39% men
- **Noncompetitive** entrance level, 80% of applicants were admitted

UNDERGRAD STUDENTS

5,387 full-time, 10,318 part-time. Students come from 39 states and territories; 95 other countries; 2% are from out of state; 11% Black or African American, non-Hispanic/Latino; 26% Hispanic/Latino; 2% Asian, non-Hispanic/Latino; 0.2% Native Hawaiian or other Pacific Islander, non-Hispanic/Latino; 0.3% American Indian or Alaska Native, non-Hispanic/Latino; 2% Two or more races, non-Hispanic/Latino; 5% Race/ethnicity unknown; 2% international; 3% transferred in; 3% live on campus.

Freshmen

Admission: 4,972 applied, 3,994 admitted, 2,993 enrolled. ***Average high school GPA:*** 2.93. ***Test scores:*** SAT critical reading scores over 500: 33%; SAT math scores over 500: 25%; SAT critical reading scores over 600: 5%; SAT math scores over 600: 5%.

Retention: 61% of full-time freshmen returned.

FACULTY

Total: 646, 27% full-time, 36% with terminal degrees.

Student/faculty ratio: 27:1.

ACADEMICS

Calendar: semesters. *Degrees:* certificates, associate, and bachelor's.

Special study options: academic remediation for entering students, accelerated degree program, advanced placement credit, cooperative education, distance learning, double majors, English as a second language, honors programs, independent study, internships, off-campus study, part-time degree program, services for LD students, study abroad, summer session for credit.

Computers: 2,700 computers/terminals are available on campus for general student use. Students can access the following: computer help desk, free student e-mail accounts, online (class) grades, online (class) registration, online (class) schedules. Campuswide network is available. 100% of college-owned or -operated housing units are wired for high-speed Internet access. Wireless service is available via entire campus.

STUDENT LIFE

Housing options: Campus housing is university owned.

Activities and organizations: drama/theater group, choral group.

Athletics Member NJCAA. ***Intramural sports:*** basketball M/W, soccer M/W, volleyball M/W.

Campus security: 24-hour emergency response devices and patrols, controlled dormitory access.

COSTS

Costs (2014–15) ***Tuition:*** state resident $2436 full-time, $81 per credit hour part-time; nonresident $9750 full-time, $325 per credit hour part-time. Full-time tuition and fees vary according to degree level. Part-time tuition and fees vary according to degree level. ***Required fees:*** $904 full-time, $30 per credit hour part-time. ***Room and board:*** $8860; room only: $6000. ***Payment plan:*** installment. ***Waivers:*** employees or children of employees.

APPLYING

Options: electronic application, early admission, deferred entrance.

Application fee: $30.

Required: high school transcript.

Application deadlines: 8/14 (freshmen), 8/14 (transfers).

Notification: continuous (freshmen), continuous (transfers).

CONTACT

Mr. Mark Bukowski, Director of Admissions, Florida SouthWestern State College, 8099 College Parkway, Fort Myers, FL 33919. *Phone:* 239-489-9362 Ext. 1362. *E-mail:* Lauren.Willison@edison.edu.

Florida State College at Jacksonville

Jacksonville, Florida

http://www.fscj.edu/

- **State-supported** primarily 2-year, founded 1963, part of Florida College System
- **Urban** 844-acre campus
- **Endowment** $44.6 million
- **Coed** 25,514 undergraduate students, 31% full-time, 60% women, 40% men
- **Noncompetitive** entrance level

UNDERGRAD STUDENTS

7,819 full-time, 17,695 part-time. 25% Black or African American, non-Hispanic/Latino; 7% Hispanic/Latino; 4% Asian, non-Hispanic/Latino; 0.5% Native Hawaiian or other Pacific Islander, non-Hispanic/Latino; 0.3% American Indian or Alaska Native, non-Hispanic/Latino; 2% Two or more races, non-Hispanic/Latino; 12% Race/ethnicity unknown; 0.8% international; 6% transferred in.

Freshmen

Admission: 3,195 enrolled.

FACULTY

Total: 1,180, 34% full-time, 29% with terminal degrees.

Student/faculty ratio: 21:1.

ACADEMICS

Calendar: semesters. *Degrees:* certificates, diplomas, associate, and bachelor's.

Special study options: academic remediation for entering students, accelerated degree program, adult/continuing education programs, advanced placement credit, cooperative education, distance learning, double majors, English as a second language, honors programs, independent study, internships, off-campus study, part-time degree program, services for LD students, study abroad, summer session for credit. ***ROTC:*** Navy (c).

Computers: 4,800 computers/terminals are available on campus for general student use. Students can access the following: campus intranet, computer help desk, free student e-mail accounts, online (class) grades, online (class) registration, online (class) schedules, 1 TB Online file storage, free MS office online. Campuswide network is available. Wireless service is available via entire campus.

STUDENT LIFE

Activities and organizations: drama/theater group, student-run newspaper, radio and television station, choral group, Phi Theta Kappa, Forensic Team, Brain Bowl Team, International Student Association, DramaWorks.

Athletics Member NJCAA. ***Intercollegiate sports:*** baseball M(s), basketball M(s)/W(s), softball W(s), tennis W(s), volleyball W(s). ***Intramural sports:*** badminton M/W, basketball M/W, bowling M/W, football M/W, golf M/W, soccer M/W, softball M/W, table tennis M/W, tennis M/W, volleyball M/W.

Campus security: 24-hour emergency response devices and patrols, late-night transport/escort service.

Student services: personal/psychological counseling, women's center.

COSTS

Costs (2014–15) ***Tuition:*** state resident $2470 full-time, $103 per credit hour part-time; nonresident $9583 full-time, $399 per credit hour part-time. Full-time tuition and fees vary according to degree level and program. Part-time tuition and fees vary according to degree level and program. ***Required fees:*** $320 full-time. ***Payment plan:*** installment. ***Waivers:*** employees or children of employees.

APPLYING

Options: electronic application, early admission, deferred entrance.

Application fee: $25.

Required for some: high school transcript.

Application deadlines: rolling (freshmen), rolling (out-of-state freshmen), rolling (transfers).

CONTACT
Dr. Peter Biegel, Registrar, Florida State College at Jacksonville, 501 West State Street, Jacksonville, FL 32202. *Phone:* 904-632-5112. *Toll-free phone:* 888-873-1145. *E-mail:* pbiegel@fscj.edu.

Florida State University

Tallahassee, Florida

http://www.fsu.edu/

- **State-supported** university, founded 1851, part of State University System of Florida
- **Suburban** 451-acre campus
- **Endowment** $624.6 million
- **Coed** 32,948 undergraduate students, 89% full-time, 55% women, 45% men
- **Very difficult** entrance level, 55% of applicants were admitted

UNDERGRAD STUDENTS
29,211 full-time, 3,737 part-time. Students come from 52 states and territories; 109 other countries; 10% are from out of state; 8% Black or African American, non-Hispanic/Latino; 18% Hispanic/Latino; 2% Asian, non-Hispanic/Latino; 0.2% Native Hawaiian or other Pacific Islander, non-Hispanic/Latino; 0.3% American Indian or Alaska Native, non-Hispanic/Latino; 3% Two or more races, non-Hispanic/Latino; 1% Race/ethnicity unknown; 2% international; 6% transferred in; 20% live on campus.

Freshmen
Admission: 30,266 applied, 16,763 admitted, 5,994 enrolled. ***Average high school GPA:*** 3.92. ***Test scores:*** SAT critical reading scores over 500: 98%; SAT math scores over 500: 97%; SAT writing scores over 500: 98%; ACT scores over 18: 100%; SAT critical reading scores over 600: 56%; SAT math scores over 600: 56%; SAT writing scores over 600: 53%; ACT scores over 24: 95%; SAT critical reading scores over 700: 8%; SAT math scores over 700: 8%; SAT writing scores over 700: 7%; ACT scores over 30: 21%.

Retention: 92% of full-time freshmen returned.

FACULTY
Total: 1,670, 76% full-time, 92% with terminal degrees.

Student/faculty ratio: 26:1.

ACADEMICS
Calendar: semesters. *Degrees:* certificates, associate, bachelor's, master's, doctoral, post-master's, and postbachelor's certificates.

Special study options: accelerated degree program, advanced placement credit, cooperative education, distance learning, double majors, English as a second language, honors programs, independent study, internships, off-campus study, part-time degree program, services for LD students, study abroad, summer session for credit. ***ROTC:*** Army (b), Navy (c), Air Force (b).

Computers: 3,821 computers/terminals are available on campus for general student use. Students can access the following: computer help desk, free student e-mail accounts, online (class) grades, online (class) registration, online (class) schedules, course home pages, course search, online fee payment. Campuswide network is available. 100% of college-owned or -operated housing units are wired for high-speed Internet access. Wireless service is available via entire campus.

STUDENT LIFE
Housing options: coed, women-only, cooperative, special housing for students with disabilities. Campus housing is university owned. Freshman applicants given priority for college housing.

Activities and organizations: drama/theater group, student-run newspaper, radio and television station, choral group, marching band, student government, honors program, Golden Key Honor Society, Marching Chiefs, intramural sports, national fraternities, national sororities.

Athletics Member NCAA. All Division I except football (Division I-A). ***Intercollegiate sports:*** baseball M(s), basketball M(s)/W(s), bowling M(c)/W(c), cheerleading M/W, cross-country running M(s)/W(s), golf M(s)/W(s), rugby M(c)/W(c), soccer M(c)/W(s), softball W(s), swimming and diving M(s)/W(s), table tennis M(c)/W(c), tennis M(s)/W(s), track and field M(s)/W(s), volleyball M(c)/W(s), wrestling M(c)/W(c). ***Intramural sports:*** badminton M(c)/W(c), baseball M(c), basketball M/W, bowling M/W, crew M(c)/W(c), equestrian sports M(c)/W(c), fencing M(c)/W(c), field hockey W(c), football M/W, golf M/W, gymnastics W(c), ice hockey M(c)/W(c), lacrosse M(c)/W(c), racquetball M/W, sailing M(c)/W(c), soccer M/W, softball M/W, squash M(c)/W(c), swimming and diving M/W, table tennis M/W, tennis M/W, track and field M/W, ultimate Frisbee M(c)/W(c), volleyball M/W, water polo M(c)/W(c), weight lifting M/W, wrestling M/W.

Campus security: 24-hour emergency response devices and patrols, late-night transport/escort service, controlled dormitory access.

Student services: health clinic, personal/psychological counseling, women's center, legal services.

COSTS & FINANCIAL AID
Costs (2014–15) ***Tuition:*** state resident $4640 full-time, $105 per credit hour part-time; nonresident $19,806 full-time, $611 per credit hour part-time. Full-time tuition and fees vary according to course load, degree level, and location. Part-time tuition and fees vary according to course load, degree level, and location. ***Required fees:*** $1867 full-time, $110 per credit hour part-time, $20 per term part-time. ***Room and board:*** $10,208; room only: $6160. Room and board charges vary according to board plan and housing facility. ***Payment plans:*** tuition prepayment, installment. ***Waivers:*** senior citizens and employees or children of employees.

Financial Aid Of all full-time matriculated undergraduates who enrolled in 2013, 24,098 applied for aid, 15,993 were judged to have need, 2,109 had their need fully met. 582 Federal Work-Study jobs (averaging $2400). 31 state and other part-time jobs (averaging $2400). In 2013, 1282 non-need-based awards were made. ***Average percent of need met:*** 49. ***Average financial aid package:*** $9033. ***Average need-based loan:*** $3585. ***Average need-based gift aid:*** $3946. ***Average non-need-based aid:*** $2595. ***Average indebtedness upon graduation:*** $23,782.

APPLYING
Standardized Tests *Required:* SAT or ACT (for admission).

Options: electronic application, early admission.

Application fee: $30.

Required: high school transcript. ***Recommended:*** essay or personal statement.

Application deadlines: 1/14 (freshmen), 1/14 (out-of-state freshmen), 7/1 (transfers).

Notification: 3/18 (freshmen), 3/18 (out-of-state freshmen), continuous (transfers).

CONTACT
Florida State University, Tallahassee, FL 32306. *Phone:* 850-644-6200.

Hobe Sound Bible College

Hobe Sound, Florida

http://www.hsbc.edu/

- **Independent nondenominational** 4-year, founded 1960
- **Small-town** 84-acre campus
- **Endowment** $2.1 million
- **Coed** 251 undergraduate students, 50% full-time, 46% women, 54% men
- **Noncompetitive** entrance level

UNDERGRAD STUDENTS
125 full-time, 126 part-time. Students come from 28 states and territories; 3 other countries; 63% are from out of state; 10% Black or African American, non-Hispanic/Latino; 3% Hispanic/Latino; 15% Race/ethnicity unknown; 2% international; 4% transferred in.

Freshmen
Admission: 51 enrolled.

Retention: 58% of full-time freshmen returned.

FACULTY
Total: 22, 36% full-time, 27% with terminal degrees.

Student/faculty ratio: 19:1.

ACADEMICS
Calendar: semesters. *Degrees:* certificates, associate, and bachelor's.

Special study options: academic remediation for entering students, advanced placement credit, distance learning, double majors, English as a second language, external degree program, independent study, internships, summer session for credit.

STUDENT LIFE
Housing options: on-campus residence required through senior year; men-only, women-only.

Activities and organizations: choral group.

Campus security: student patrols, late-night transport/escort service, controlled dormitory access.

COSTS & FINANCIAL AID
Costs (2014–15) ***Comprehensive fee:*** $11,520 includes full-time tuition ($5200), mandatory fees ($720), and room and board ($5600). Part-time tuition: $250 per credit hour. Part-time tuition and fees vary according to course load. ***Required fees:*** $720 per year part-time. ***College room only:*** $1070. ***Payment plans:*** installment, deferred payment. ***Waivers:*** employees or children of employees.

Financial Aid ***Average financial aid package:*** $3550. ***Average indebtedness upon graduation:*** $7000.

APPLYING
Standardized Tests *Required:* SAT or ACT (for admission).

Options: early admission.

Application fee: $25.

Required: essay or personal statement, high school transcript, 3 letters of recommendation, photograph, medical report.

Application deadlines: rolling (freshmen), rolling (transfers).

Notification: continuous until 8/30 (freshmen), continuous until 8/30 (transfers).

CONTACT
Mrs. Pamela S. Davis, Director of Admissions, Hobe Sound Bible College, PO Box 1065, Hobe Sound, FL 33475-1065. *Phone:* 772-545-1400. *E-mail:* pamdavis@hsbc.edu.

Hodges University

Naples, Florida

http://www.hodges.edu/

- **Independent** comprehensive, founded 1990
- **Suburban** 31-acre campus with easy access to Miami
- **Endowment** $2.8 million
- **Coed** 1,678 undergraduate students, 68% full-time, 63% women, 37% men
- **Minimally difficult** entrance level

UNDERGRAD STUDENTS
1,137 full-time, 541 part-time. Students come from 36 states and territories; 4% are from out of state; 13% Black or African American, non-Hispanic/Latino; 35% Hispanic/Latino; 2% Asian, non-Hispanic/Latino; 0.2% Native Hawaiian or other Pacific Islander, non-Hispanic/Latino; 0.6% American Indian or Alaska Native, non-Hispanic/Latino; 1% Two or more races, non-Hispanic/Latino; 2% Race/ethnicity unknown; 17% transferred in.

Freshmen
Admission: 134 enrolled.

FACULTY
Total: 127, 52% full-time, 40% with terminal degrees.

Student/faculty ratio: 15:1.

ACADEMICS
Calendar: trimesters. *Degrees:* certificates, associate, bachelor's, and master's.

Special study options: academic remediation for entering students, accelerated degree program, adult/continuing education programs, advanced placement credit, cooperative education, distance learning, double majors, English as a second language, external degree program, independent study, internships, part-time degree program, services for LD students, summer session for credit.

Computers: 1,500 computers/terminals are available on campus for general student use. Students can access the following: campus intranet, computer help desk, free student e-mail accounts, online (class) grades, online (class) registration, online (class) schedules, Our campus intranet takes the form of a student portal that is accessible via the internet. The portal provides single sign on access to all of the above as well as our Learning Management System, online storage, library resources, and a student calendar. Campuswide network is available. Wireless service is available via entire campus.

STUDENT LIFE
Housing options: college housing not available.

Activities and organizations: Ambassadors, Paralegal Club, Institute of Managerial Accountants, Sports club, Entrepreneurial Club.

Campus security: late-night transport/escort service, building security.

Student services: personal/psychological counseling.

COSTS & FINANCIAL AID
Costs (2014–15) ***Tuition:*** $12,720 full-time, $530 per credit hour part-time. ***Required fees:*** $500 full-time. ***Payment plan:*** installment. ***Waivers:*** employees or children of employees.

Financial Aid Of all full-time matriculated undergraduates who enrolled in 2014, 1,104 applied for aid, 1,082 were judged to have need, 194 had their need fully met. 45 Federal Work-Study jobs (averaging $3733). In 2014, 29 non-need-based awards were made. ***Average percent of need met:*** 80. ***Average financial aid package:*** $10,050. ***Average need-based loan:*** $2975. ***Average need-based gift aid:*** $2900. ***Average non-need-based aid:*** $300. ***Average indebtedness upon graduation:*** $17,775.

APPLYING
Standardized Tests *Required for some:* CPAt.

Options: electronic application, deferred entrance.

Application fee: $20.

Required: essay or personal statement, high school transcript, interview. ***Required for some:*** 2 letters of recommendation.

Application deadlines: rolling (freshmen), rolling (transfers).

Notification: continuous (freshmen), continuous (transfers).

CONTACT
Hodges University, 2655 Northbrooke Drive, Naples, FL 34119. *Phone:* 239-513-1122 Ext. 6104. *Toll-free phone:* 800-466-8017.

Indian River State College

Fort Pierce, Florida

http://www.irsc.edu/

- **State-supported** 4-year, founded 1960, part of Florida Community College System
- **Small-town** 713-acre campus
- **Coed** 17,665 undergraduate students, 34% full-time, 60% women, 40% men
- **Noncompetitive** entrance level, 100% of applicants were admitted

UNDERGRAD STUDENTS
5,950 full-time, 11,715 part-time. Students come from 19 states and territories; 110 other countries; 10% are from out of state; 18% Black or African American, non-Hispanic/Latino; 18% Hispanic/Latino; 2% Asian, non-Hispanic/Latino; 0.2% Native Hawaiian or other Pacific Islander, non-Hispanic/Latino; 0.3% American Indian or Alaska Native, non-Hispanic/Latino; 2% Two or more races, non-Hispanic/Latino; 3% Race/ethnicity unknown; 1% international; 14% transferred in.

Freshmen
Admission: 1,877 applied, 1,877 admitted, 1,877 enrolled.

FACULTY
Total: 859, 28% full-time, 23% with terminal degrees.

Student/faculty ratio: 22:1.

ACADEMICS
Calendar: semesters. *Degrees:* certificates, diplomas, associate, and bachelor's.

Special study options: academic remediation for entering students, adult/continuing education programs, advanced placement credit, distance learning, English as a second language, independent study, part-time degree program, services for LD students, summer session for credit.

Computers: 3,400 computers/terminals are available on campus for general student use. Students can access the following: computer help desk, free student e-mail accounts, online (class) grades, online (class) registration, online (class) schedules. Campuswide network is available. Wireless service is available via classrooms, computer centers, computer labs, learning centers, libraries, student centers.

STUDENT LIFE
Activities and organizations: drama/theater group, choral group.
Athletics Member NJCAA. ***Intercollegiate sports:*** baseball M(s), basketball M(s)/W(s), softball W(s), swimming and diving M(s)/W(s), volleyball W(s). ***Intramural sports:*** basketball M/W, racquetball M/W, soccer M, volleyball M/W.
Campus security: 24-hour emergency response devices and patrols.
Student services: health clinic, personal/psychological counseling, women's center.

COSTS
Costs (2015–16) ***Tuition:*** state resident $2492 full-time, $104 per credit hour part-time; nonresident $9372 full-time, $390 per credit hour part-time. Full-time tuition and fees vary according to course load and degree level. Part-time tuition and fees vary according to course load and degree level. ***Room and board:*** $5700; room only: $3150. ***Payment plans:*** installment, deferred payment.

APPLYING
Options: early admission, deferred entrance.
Required: high school transcript.
Application deadlines: rolling (freshmen), rolling (transfers).
Notification: continuous (freshmen), continuous (transfers).

CONTACT
Mr. Eileen Storck, Dean of Educational Services, Indian River State College, 3209 Virginia Avenue, Fort Pierce, FL 34981-5596. *Phone:* 772-462-7361. *Toll-free phone:* 866-792-4772. *E-mail:* estrock@irsc.edu.

ITT Technical Institute
Fort Lauderdale, Florida
http://www.itt-tech.edu/

- **Proprietary** primarily 2-year, founded 1991, part of ITT Educational Services, Inc.
- **Suburban** campus
- **Coed**
- **Minimally difficult** entrance level

ACADEMICS
Calendar: quarters. *Degrees:* associate and bachelor's.

STUDENT LIFE
Housing options: college housing not available.

CONTACT
Director of Recruitment, ITT Technical Institute, 3401 South University Drive, Fort Lauderdale, FL 33328-2021. *Phone:* 954-476-9300. *Toll-free phone:* 800-488-7797.

ITT Technical Institute
Fort Myers, Florida
http://www.itt-tech.edu/

- **Proprietary** primarily 2-year
- **Coed**
- **Minimally difficult** entrance level

ACADEMICS
Degrees: associate and bachelor's.

CONTACT
Director of Recruitment, ITT Technical Institute, 13500 Powers Court, Suite 100, Fort Myers, FL 33912. *Phone:* 239-603-8700. *Toll-free phone:* 877-485-5313.

ITT Technical Institute
Hialeah, Florida
http://www.itt-tech.edu/

- **Proprietary** primarily 2-year, founded 1996, part of ITT Educational Services, Inc.
- **Coed**
- **Minimally difficult** entrance level

ACADEMICS
Calendar: quarters. *Degrees:* associate and bachelor's.

STUDENT LIFE
Housing options: college housing not available.

CONTACT
Director of Recruitment, ITT Technical Institute, 5901 NW 183rd Street, Suite 100, Hialeah, FL 33015. *Phone:* 305-477-3080.

ITT Technical Institute
Jacksonville, Florida
http://www.itt-tech.edu/

- **Proprietary** primarily 2-year, founded 1991, part of ITT Educational Services, Inc.
- **Urban** campus
- **Coed**
- **Minimally difficult** entrance level

ACADEMICS
Calendar: quarters. *Degrees:* associate and bachelor's.

STUDENT LIFE
Housing options: college housing not available.

FINANCIAL AID
Financial Aid Of all full-time matriculated undergraduates who enrolled in 2013, 5 Federal Work-Study jobs.

CONTACT
Director of Recruitment, ITT Technical Institute, 7011 A.C. Skinner Parkway, Suite 140, Jacksonville, FL 32256. *Phone:* 904-573-9100. *Toll-free phone:* 800-318-1264.

ITT Technical Institute
Lake Mary, Florida
http://www.itt-tech.edu/

- **Proprietary** primarily 2-year, founded 1989, part of ITT Educational Services, Inc.
- **Suburban** campus
- **Coed**
- **Minimally difficult** entrance level

ACADEMICS
Calendar: quarters. *Degrees:* associate and bachelor's.

CONTACT
Director of Recruitment, ITT Technical Institute, 1400 South International Parkway, Lake Mary, FL 32746. *Phone:* 407-936-0600. *Toll-free phone:* 866-489-8441.

ITT Technical Institute
Orlando, Florida
http://www.itt-tech.edu/

- **Proprietary** primarily 2-year, part of ITT Educational Services, Inc.
- **Coed**

ACADEMICS
Calendar: quarters. *Degrees:* associate and bachelor's.

CONTACT
Director of Recruitment, ITT Technical Institute, 8301 Southpark Circle, Suite 100, Orlando, FL 32819. *Phone:* 407-371-6000. *Toll-free phone:* 877-201-4367.

ITT Technical Institute
St. Petersburg, Florida
http://www.itt-tech.edu/

- **Proprietary** primarily 2-year, part of ITT Educational Services, Inc.
- **Coed**
- **Minimally difficult** entrance level

ACADEMICS
Degrees: associate and bachelor's.

STUDENT LIFE
Housing options: college housing not available.

CONTACT
Director of Recruitment, ITT Technical Institute, 877 Executive Center Drive W., Suite 100, St. Petersburg, FL 33702. *Phone:* 727-209-4700. *Toll-free phone:* 866-488-5084.

ITT Technical Institute
Tallahassee, Florida
http://www.itt-tech.edu/

- **Proprietary** primarily 2-year
- **Coed**
- **Minimally difficult** entrance level

ACADEMICS
Degrees: associate and bachelor's.

CONTACT
Director of Recruitment, ITT Technical Institute, 2639 North Monroe Street, Building A, Suite 100, Tallahassee, FL 32303. *Phone:* 850-422-6300. *Toll-free phone:* 877-230-3559.

ITT Technical Institute
Tampa, Florida
http://www.itt-tech.edu/

- **Proprietary** primarily 2-year, founded 1981, part of ITT Educational Services, Inc.
- **Suburban** campus
- **Coed**
- **Minimally difficult** entrance level

ACADEMICS
Calendar: quarters. *Degrees:* associate and bachelor's.

STUDENT LIFE
Housing options: college housing not available.

CONTACT
Director of Recruitment, ITT Technical Institute, 4809 Memorial Highway, Tampa, FL 33634-7151. *Phone:* 813-885-2244. *Toll-free phone:* 800-825-2831.

ITT Technical Institute
West Palm Beach, Florida
http://www.itt-tech.edu/

- **Proprietary** 4-year
- **Coed**
- **Minimally difficult** entrance level

ACADEMICS
Degrees: associate and bachelor's.

CONTACT
Director of Recruitment, ITT Technical Institute, 1756 N. Congress Avenue, West Palm Beach, FL 33409. *Phone:* 561-233-4900. *Toll-free phone:* 877-236-8164.

Jacksonville University
Jacksonville, Florida
http://www.ju.edu/

- **Independent** comprehensive, founded 1934
- **Suburban** 198-acre campus with easy access to Jacksonville and Saint Augustine
- **Endowment** $35.4 million
- **Coed** 3,223 undergraduate students, 65% full-time, 64% women, 36% men
- **Moderately difficult** entrance level, 56% of applicants were admitted

UNDERGRAD STUDENTS
2,111 full-time, 1,112 part-time. Students come from 51 states and territories; 39 other countries; 37% are from out of state; 16% Black or African American, non-Hispanic/Latino; 7% Hispanic/Latino; 3% Asian, non-Hispanic/Latino; 0.3% Native Hawaiian or other Pacific Islander, non-Hispanic/Latino; 1% American Indian or Alaska Native, non-Hispanic/Latino; 18% Race/ethnicity unknown; 3% international; 11% transferred in; 28% live on campus.

Freshmen
Admission: 2,939 applied, 1,648 admitted, 394 enrolled. ***Average high school GPA:*** 3.39. ***Test scores:*** SAT critical reading scores over 500: 55%; SAT math scores over 500: 58%; ACT scores over 18: 87%; SAT critical reading scores over 600: 13%; SAT math scores over 600: 16%; ACT scores over 24: 38%; SAT critical reading scores over 700: 1%; SAT math scores over 700: 2%; ACT scores over 30: 4%.

Retention: 73% of full-time freshmen returned.

FACULTY
Total: 335, 60% full-time, 56% with terminal degrees.

Student/faculty ratio: 11:1.

ACADEMICS
Calendar: semesters. *Degrees:* bachelor's, master's, doctoral, and post-master's certificates.

Special study options: academic remediation for entering students, accelerated degree program, adult/continuing education programs, advanced placement credit, cooperative education, distance learning, double majors, English as a second language, honors programs, independent study, internships, off-campus study, part-time degree program, services for LD students, student-designed majors, study abroad, summer session for credit. ***ROTC:*** Army (b), Navy (b).

Unusual degree programs: 3-2 engineering; nursing; Pre-law: Florida Coastal School of Law.

Computers: 400 computers/terminals and 1,205 ports are available on campus for general student use. Students can access the following: campus intranet, computer help desk, free student e-mail accounts, online (class) grades, online (class) registration, online (class) schedules, Blackboard and Web Advisor. Campuswide network is available. 100% of college-owned or -operated housing units are wired for high-speed Internet access. Wireless service is available via entire campus.

STUDENT LIFE
Housing options: on-campus residence required through sophomore year; coed, men-only, women-only, special housing for students with disabilities. Campus housing is university owned. Freshman campus housing is guaranteed.

Activities and organizations: drama/theater group, student-run newspaper, radio and television station, choral group, marching band, Honors Student Association- Academic, International Student Association- Multicultural, JU Student Alliance - Special Interest, Student Veterans of America - Special Interest, The National Society of Leadership and Success - Honorary, national fraternities, national sororities.

Athletics Member NCAA. All Division I except football (Division I-AA). ***Intercollegiate sports:*** baseball M(s), basketball M(s)/W(s), crew M(s)/W(s), cross-country running M/W(s), golf M(s)/W(s), lacrosse M(s)/W(s), soccer M(s)/W(s), softball W(s), track and field W(s), volleyball W(s). ***Intramural sports:*** basketball M/W, cheerleading M(c)/W(c), football M/W, riflery M(c)/W(c), sailing M(c)/W(c), soccer M/W, softball M/W, ultimate Frisbee M/W, volleyball M/W.

Campus security: 24-hour emergency response devices and patrols, student patrols, late-night transport/escort service, controlled dormitory

access, code lock doors in residence halls, trained security patrols during evening hours.

Student services: health clinic, personal/psychological counseling.

COSTS & FINANCIAL AID

Costs (2014–15) ***Comprehensive fee:*** $42,190 includes full-time tuition ($31,370) and room and board ($10,820). Full-time tuition and fees vary according to course load, degree level, and program. Part-time tuition: $1042 per credit hour. Part-time tuition and fees vary according to course load, degree level, and program. ***Required fees:*** $523 per credit hour part-time. ***College room only:*** $6480. Room and board charges vary according to board plan and housing facility. ***Payment plan:*** deferred payment. ***Waivers:*** employees or children of employees.

Financial Aid Of all full-time matriculated undergraduates who enrolled in 2014, 2,058 applied for aid, 1,497 were judged to have need, 533 had their need fully met. 119 Federal Work-Study jobs (averaging $484). 155 state and other part-time jobs (averaging $645). In 2014, 441 non-need-based awards were made. ***Average percent of need met:*** 73. ***Average financial aid package:*** $23,040. ***Average need-based loan:*** $3545. ***Average need-based gift aid:*** $16,847. ***Average non-need-based aid:*** $10,435.

APPLYING

Standardized Tests *Recommended:* SAT or ACT (for admission).

Options: electronic application, early admission, deferred entrance.

Application fee: $30.

Required: high school transcript, minimum 2.0 GPA. ***Required for some:*** essay or personal statement. ***Recommended:*** interview.

Application deadlines: rolling (freshmen), rolling (transfers).

Notification: continuous (freshmen).

CONTACT

Mrs. Marisol Preston, Chief Admissions Officer, Jacksonville University, 2800 University Boulevard North, Office of Admissions, Jacksonville, FL 32211. *Phone:* 904-256-7663. *Toll-free phone:* 800-225-2027. *Fax:* 904-256-7012. *E-mail:* admissions@ju.edu.

Johnson & Wales University

North Miami, Florida

http://www.jwu.edu/northmiami/

- **Independent** 4-year, founded 1992
- **Suburban** 8-acre campus with easy access to Miami
- **Coed** 1,904 undergraduate students, 97% full-time, 63% women, 37% men
- **Moderately difficult** entrance level, 70% of applicants were admitted

UNDERGRAD STUDENTS

1,855 full-time, 49 part-time. 50% are from out of state; 30% Black or African American, non-Hispanic/Latino; 23% Hispanic/Latino; 0.7% Asian, non-Hispanic/Latino; 0.2% Native Hawaiian or other Pacific Islander, non-Hispanic/Latino; 0.1% American Indian or Alaska Native, non-Hispanic/Latino; 6% Two or more races, non-Hispanic/Latino; 7% Race/ethnicity unknown; 12% international; 7% transferred in; 54% live on campus.

Freshmen

Admission: 4,739 applied, 3,319 admitted, 498 enrolled.

FACULTY

Total: 109, 52% full-time.

Student/faculty ratio: 25:1.

ACADEMICS

Calendar: quarters. *Degrees:* associate and bachelor's.

Special study options: academic remediation for entering students, accelerated degree program, advanced placement credit, cooperative education, English as a second language, honors programs, independent study, internships, part-time degree program, services for LD students, study abroad, summer session for credit.

Computers: Campuswide network is available.

STUDENT LIFE

Housing options: on-campus residence required for freshman year; coed. Campus housing is university owned and leased by the school. Freshman campus housing is guaranteed.

Activities and organizations: national fraternities, national sororities.

Athletics Member NAIA. ***Intramural sports:*** basketball M/W, football M, golf M/W, soccer M/W, softball M/W, table tennis M/W, tennis M/W, volleyball M/W.

Campus security: 24-hour emergency response devices and patrols, video camera surveillance throughout campus.

Student services: personal/psychological counseling.

COSTS & FINANCIAL AID

Costs (2015–16) ***Tuition:*** $29,226 full-time, $196 per credit hour part-time. ***Required fees:*** $350 full-time.

Financial Aid Of all full-time matriculated undergraduates who enrolled in 2010, 1,776 applied for aid, 1,635 were judged to have need, 172 had their need fully met. In 2010, 247 non-need-based awards were made. ***Average percent of need met:*** 68. ***Average financial aid package:*** $18,719. ***Average need-based loan:*** $5150. ***Average need-based gift aid:*** $8710. ***Average non-need-based aid:*** $5454.

APPLYING

Standardized Tests *Required for some:* SAT or ACT (for admission).

Options: early admission, deferred entrance.

Required: high school transcript. ***Required for some:*** essay or personal statement, interview. ***Recommended:*** minimum 2.0 GPA.

Application deadlines: rolling (freshmen), rolling (transfers).

Notification: continuous (freshmen), continuous (transfers).

CONTACT

Jeff Greenip, Director of Admissions, Johnson & Wales University, 1701 Northeast 127th Street, North Miami, FL 33181. *Phone:* 305-892-7600. *Toll-free phone:* 866-598-3567. *Fax:* 305-892-7020. *E-mail:* mia@admissions.jwu.edu.

Jones College

Jacksonville, Florida

http://www.jones.edu/

- **Independent** 4-year, founded 1918
- **Urban** 3-acre campus
- **Coed**
- **Noncompetitive** entrance level

FACULTY

Student/faculty ratio: 6:1.

ACADEMICS

Calendar: trimesters. *Degrees:* associate and bachelor's.

STUDENT LIFE

Housing options: college housing not available.

Campus security: late-night transport/escort service, emergency notification system through email/texting/phones.

COSTS

Costs (2014–15) ***Tuition:*** $7320 full-time, $305 per credit part-time. ***Required fees:*** $90 full-time, $45 per term part-time.

APPLYING

Standardized Tests *Required for some:* CPAt/ACCUPLACER.

Options: electronic application.

Required: interview. ***Required for some:*** high school transcript.

CONTACT

Jones College, 5353 Arlington Expressway, Jacksonville, FL 32211-5588. *Phone:* 904-743-1122. *Toll-free phone:* 800-631-4056.

Keiser University

Fort Lauderdale, Florida

http://www.keiseruniversity.edu/

- **Independent** university, founded 1977, part of The main campus of Keiser University is located in Fort Lauderdale and branch campuses are located throughout the State of Florida and internationally
- **Urban** campus
- **Coed** 16,039 undergraduate students, 75% full-time, 68% women, 32% men

UNDERGRAD STUDENTS
12,007 full-time, 4,032 part-time. Students come from 53 states and territories; 11% are from out of state; 20% Black or African American, non-Hispanic/Latino; 31% Hispanic/Latino; 2% Asian, non-Hispanic/Latino; 0.3% American Indian or Alaska Native, non-Hispanic/Latino; 4% Two or more races, non-Hispanic/Latino; 3% Race/ethnicity unknown; 0.3% international.

Freshmen
Admission: 2,289 enrolled.
Retention: 74% of full-time freshmen returned.

FACULTY
Total: 1,597, 61% full-time.
Student/faculty ratio: 12:1.

ACADEMICS
Calendar: 3 semesters per year. *Degrees:* associate, bachelor's, master's, doctoral, and post-master's certificates (profile includes data from campuses located in Daytona Beach, Fort Lauderdale, Fort Myers, Jacksonville, Lakeland, Melbourne, Miami, Orlando, Pembroke Pines, Port St. Lucie, Sarasota, Tallahassee, Tampa, and West Palm Beach; not all programs offered at all locations, but many classes offered 100% online).
Special study options: advanced placement credit, distance learning, English as a second language, internships, part-time degree program, summer session for credit.
Computers: Students can access the following: free student e-mail accounts. Campuswide network is available.

STUDENT LIFE
Housing options: college housing not available.
Activities and organizations: Student Government Association, Phi Theta Kappa, Sigma Beta Delta International Honor Society, Alpha Phi Sigma National Honor Society, Student Nurses Association.
Campus security: AlertNow Rapid Communications Service, Campus Response Teams.

COSTS
Costs (2014–15) ***Tuition:*** $16,056 full-time, $669 per credit hour part-time. Full-time tuition and fees vary according to course load and program. Part-time tuition and fees vary according to course load and program. ***Required fees:*** $1540 full-time.

APPLYING
Standardized Tests *Required:* SAT or ACT or Wonderlic Test (for admission).
Options: electronic application.
Application fee: $50.
Required: Proof of high school graduation, or GED completion, or graduation from a foreign institution comparable to a US secondary school, or an earned degree from an accredited institution.
Application deadlines: rolling (freshmen), rolling (out-of-state freshmen), rolling (transfers).
Notification: continuous (freshmen), continuous (out-of-state freshmen), continuous (transfers).

CONTACT
Keiser University, 1500 NW 49th Street, Fort Lauderdale, FL 33309.
Phone: 954-275-1569. *Toll-free phone:* 888-534-7379.

Lynn University

Boca Raton, Florida

http://www.lynn.edu/

- **Independent** comprehensive, founded 1962
- **Suburban** 123-acre campus with easy access to Fort Lauderdale
- **Endowment** $24.4 million
- **Coed** 1,976 undergraduate students, 92% full-time, 47% women, 53% men
- **Moderately difficult** entrance level, 75% of applicants were admitted

UNDERGRAD STUDENTS
1,815 full-time, 161 part-time. Students come from 45 states and territories; 89 other countries; 61% are from out of state; 9% Black or African American, non-Hispanic/Latino; 13% Hispanic/Latino; 1% Asian, non-Hispanic/Latino; 0.2% Native Hawaiian or other Pacific Islander, non-Hispanic/Latino; 0.6% American Indian or Alaska Native, non-Hispanic/Latino; 0.8% Two or more races, non-Hispanic/Latino; 10% Race/ethnicity unknown; 23% international; 8% transferred in; 51% live on campus.

Freshmen
Admission: 3,557 applied, 2,663 admitted, 540 enrolled. ***Average high school GPA:*** 2.92. ***Test scores:*** SAT critical reading scores over 500: 42%; SAT math scores over 500: 45%; SAT writing scores over 500: 38%; ACT scores over 18: 88%; SAT critical reading scores over 600: 7%; SAT math scores over 600: 10%; SAT writing scores over 600: 10%; ACT scores over 24: 21%; SAT critical reading scores over 700: 1%; SAT math scores over 700: 1%; SAT writing scores over 700: 2%; ACT scores over 30: 1%.
Retention: 69% of full-time freshmen returned.

FACULTY
Total: 199, 51% full-time, 49% with terminal degrees.
Student/faculty ratio: 18:1.

ACADEMICS
Calendar: semesters 3 summer sessions, 6 8-week evening terms for undergraduate and graduate. *Degrees:* bachelor's, master's, doctoral, post-master's, and postbachelor's certificates.
Special study options: academic remediation for entering students, accelerated degree program, advanced placement credit, cooperative education, distance learning, double majors, independent study, internships, part-time degree program, services for LD students, study abroad, summer session for credit. ***ROTC:*** Air Force (c).
Computers: 200 computers/terminals are available on campus for general student use. Students can access the following: campus intranet, computer help desk, free student e-mail accounts, online (class) grades, online (class) schedules, online registration with advisor approval for juniors, seniors and MBA students. Campuswide network is available. 100% of college-owned or -operated housing units are wired for high-speed Internet access. Wireless service is available via entire campus.

STUDENT LIFE
Housing options: on-campus residence required through sophomore year; coed, special housing for students with disabilities. Campus housing is university owned. Freshman campus housing is guaranteed.
Activities and organizations: drama/theater group, student-run newspaper, radio and television station, Knights of the Round Table, intramural groups, student newspaper, Student Activities Board, Greek Life, national fraternities, national sororities.
Athletics Member NCAA. All Division II. ***Intercollegiate sports:*** baseball M(s), basketball M(s)/W(s), cross-country running W(s), golf M(s)/W(s), lacrosse M(s), soccer M(s)/W(s), softball W(s), swimming and diving W(s), tennis M(s)/W(s), volleyball W(s). ***Intramural sports:*** basketball M/W, cheerleading W(c), football M/W, golf M/W, soccer M/W, tennis M/W, ultimate Frisbee M/W, volleyball M(c).
Campus security: 24-hour emergency response devices and patrols, late-night transport/escort service, video monitor at residence entrances.
Student services: health clinic, personal/psychological counseling, women's center.

COSTS & FINANCIAL AID
Costs (2015–16) ***Comprehensive fee:*** $46,500 includes full-time tuition ($33,450), mandatory fees ($1750), and room and board ($11,300). Full-

time tuition and fees vary according to program. Part-time tuition: $970 per credit. Part-time tuition and fees vary according to course load and program. ***Room and board:*** Room and board charges vary according to board plan and housing facility. ***Payment plans:*** installment, deferred payment. ***Waivers:*** employees or children of employees.

Financial Aid Of all full-time matriculated undergraduates who enrolled in 2013, 1,235 applied for aid, 708 were judged to have need, 698 had their need fully met. 93 Federal Work-Study jobs (averaging $1965). 32 state and other part-time jobs (averaging $7642). In 2013, 313 non-need-based awards were made. ***Average percent of need met:*** 56. ***Average financial aid package:*** $20,042. ***Average need-based loan:*** $4705. ***Average need-based gift aid:*** $9808. ***Average non-need-based aid:*** $11,888. ***Average indebtedness upon graduation:*** $31,634.

APPLYING

Standardized Tests *Required:* SAT or ACT (for admission).

Options: electronic application, early admission, deferred entrance.

Application fee: $45.

Required: essay or personal statement, high school transcript. ***Required for some:*** Audition required for Conservatory of Music applicants. ***Recommended:*** interview.

Application deadlines: 3/1 (freshmen), rolling (transfers), 11/15 (early action).

Notification: continuous until 1/15 (freshmen), continuous (transfers), 12/15 (early action).

CONTACT

Stefano Papaleo, Director of Undergraduate Admission, Lynn University, Admission, 3601 North Military Trail, Boca Raton, FL 33431. *Phone:* 561-237-7831. *Toll-free phone:* 800-888-5966. *Fax:* 561-237-7100. *E-mail:* spapaleo@lynn.edu.

★ Miami Dade College

Miami, Florida

http://www.mdc.edu/

- **State and locally supported** primarily 2-year, founded 1960, part of Florida College System
- **Urban** campus
- **Endowment** $163.0 million
- **Coed** 66,046 undergraduate students, 40% full-time, 58% women, 42% men
- **Noncompetitive** entrance level, 100% of applicants were admitted

UNDERGRAD STUDENTS

26,157 full-time, 39,889 part-time. Students come from 43 states and territories; 180 other countries; 0.4% are from out of state; 16% Black or African American, non-Hispanic/Latino; 68% Hispanic/Latino; 1% Asian, non-Hispanic/Latino; 0.1% Native Hawaiian or other Pacific Islander, non-Hispanic/Latino; 0.1% American Indian or Alaska Native, non-Hispanic/Latino; 0.3% Two or more races, non-Hispanic/Latino; 3% Race/ethnicity unknown; 5% international; 2% transferred in.

Freshmen

Admission: 22,978 applied, 22,978 admitted, 12,860 enrolled.

FACULTY

Total: 2,566, 29% full-time, 22% with terminal degrees.

Student/faculty ratio: 29:1.

ACADEMICS

Calendar: 16-16-6-6. *Degrees:* certificates, associate, bachelor's, and postbachelor's certificates.

Special study options: academic remediation for entering students, accelerated degree program, adult/continuing education programs, advanced placement credit, cooperative education, distance learning, English as a second language, freshman honors college, honors programs, independent study, internships, off-campus study, part-time degree program, services for LD students, study abroad, summer session for credit. ***ROTC:*** Army (b), Air Force (b).

Computers: 9,655 computers/terminals and 1,500 ports are available on campus for general student use. Students can access the following: campus intranet, computer help desk, free student e-mail accounts, online (class) grades, online (class) registration, online (class) schedules, admissions; student feedback of faculty; financial aid; IRS Form 1098. Campuswide network is available. Wireless service is available via classrooms, computer centers, computer labs, learning centers, libraries, student centers.

STUDENT LIFE

Housing options: college housing not available.

Activities and organizations: drama/theater group, student-run newspaper, radio and television station, choral group, Student Government Association, Phi Theta Kappa, Phi Beta Lambda (Business), Future Educators of America Professional, Kappa Delta Pi Honor Society (Education), national fraternities.

Athletics Member NCAA, NJCAA. All NCAA Division I. ***Intercollegiate sports:*** baseball M(s), basketball M(s)/W(s), softball W(s), volleyball W(s).

Campus security: 24-hour emergency response devices and patrols, late-night transport/escort service, Emergency Mass Notification System (EMNS), campus sirens and public address systems, In Case of Crisis smart phone application.

Student services: health clinic, personal/psychological counseling.

COSTS & FINANCIAL AID

Costs (2015–16) ***One-time required fee:*** $30. ***Tuition:*** state resident $1987 full-time, $83 per credit hour part-time; nonresident $7947 full-time, $331 per credit hour part-time. Full-time tuition and fees vary according to course load, degree level, and program. Part-time tuition and fees vary according to course load, degree level, and program. ***Required fees:*** $803 full-time, $33 per credit hour part-time. ***Waivers:*** employees or children of employees.

Financial Aid Of all full-time matriculated undergraduates who enrolled in 2013, 800 Federal Work-Study jobs (averaging $5000). 125 state and other part-time jobs (averaging $5000).

APPLYING

Options: electronic application, early admission.

Application fee: $30.

Required: high school transcript. ***Required for some:*** Some programs such as Honors College and Medical programs have additional admissions requirements.

Application deadlines: rolling (freshmen), rolling (out-of-state freshmen), rolling (transfers).

Notification: continuous (freshmen), continuous (out-of-state freshmen), continuous (transfers).

CONTACT

Ms. Ferne Creary, Interim College Registrar, Miami Dade College, 11011 SW 104th Street, Miami, FL 33176. *Phone:* 305-237-2206. *Fax:* 305-237-2532. *E-mail:* fcreary@mdc.edu.

Miami International University of Art & Design

Miami, Florida

http://www.artinstitutes.edu/miami/

- **Proprietary** comprehensive, founded 1965, part of Education Management Corporation
- **Urban** campus
- **Coed**

ACADEMICS

Calendar: quarters. *Degrees:* diplomas, associate, bachelor's, and master's.

CONTACT

Miami International University of Art & Design, 1501 Biscayne Boulevard, Suite 100, Miami, FL 33132-1418. *Phone:* 305-428-5700. *Toll-free phone:* 800-225-9023.

New College of Florida

Sarasota, Florida

http://www.ncf.edu/

- **State-supported** comprehensive, founded 1960, part of State University System of Florida
- **Suburban** 119-acre campus with easy access to Tampa-St. Petersburg
- **Endowment** $36.4 million
- **Coed** 834 undergraduate students, 100% full-time, 59% women, 41% men
- **Very difficult** entrance level, 60% of applicants were admitted

UNDERGRAD STUDENTS
834 full-time. Students come from 38 states and territories; 10 other countries; 19% are from out of state; 3% Black or African American, non-Hispanic/Latino; 15% Hispanic/Latino; 2% Asian, non-Hispanic/Latino; 0.1% American Indian or Alaska Native, non-Hispanic/Latino; 5% Two or more races, non-Hispanic/Latino; 3% Race/ethnicity unknown; 2% international; 5% transferred in; 77% live on campus.

Freshmen
Admission: 1,570 applied, 940 admitted, 236 enrolled. ***Average high school GPA:*** 4. ***Test scores:*** SAT critical reading scores over 500: 100%; SAT math scores over 500: 98%; SAT writing scores over 500: 97%; ACT scores over 18: 100%; SAT critical reading scores over 600: 84%; SAT math scores over 600: 63%; SAT writing scores over 600: 69%; ACT scores over 24: 93%; SAT critical reading scores over 700: 30%; SAT math scores over 700: 14%; SAT writing scores over 700: 19%; ACT scores over 30: 32%.

Retention: 80% of full-time freshmen returned.

FACULTY
Total: 106, 69% full-time, 92% with terminal degrees.

Student/faculty ratio: 10:1.

ACADEMICS
Calendar: 4-1-4. *Degrees:* bachelor's and master's.

Special study options: cooperative education, double majors, honors programs, independent study, internships, off-campus study, services for LD students, student-designed majors, study abroad, summer session for credit.

Computers: 123 computers/terminals and 1,000 ports are available on campus for general student use. Students can access the following: campus intranet, computer help desk, free student e-mail accounts, online (class) grades, online (class) registration, online (class) schedules. Campuswide network is available. 100% of college-owned or -operated housing units are wired for high-speed Internet access. Wireless service is available via classrooms, dorm rooms, learning centers, libraries, student centers.

STUDENT LIFE
Housing options: on-campus residence required through senior year; coed, special housing for students with disabilities. Campus housing is university owned. Freshman campus housing is guaranteed.

Activities and organizations: drama/theater group, student-run newspaper, radio station, choral group, PRIDE, Interfaith groups, New College Student Alliance, Feminist Majority Leadership Alliance, Sailing Club.

Athletics ***Intercollegiate sports:*** sailing M/W. ***Intramural sports:*** basketball M/W, fencing M/W, golf M/W, racquetball M/W, sailing M(c)/W(c), soccer M(c)/W(c), softball M(c)/W(c), swimming and diving M(c)/W(c), table tennis M(c)/W(c), tennis M(c)/W(c), ultimate Frisbee M(c)/W(c), weight lifting M/W, wrestling M/W.

Campus security: 24-hour emergency response devices and patrols, student patrols, late-night transport/escort service, controlled dormitory access, campus police are state certified police officers and available 24/7.

Student services: health clinic, personal/psychological counseling, women's center.

COSTS & FINANCIAL AID
Costs (2015–16) ***Tuition:*** state resident $7040 full-time; nonresident $30,069 full-time. Full-time tuition and fees vary according to course load. ***Room and board:*** $9009; room only: $6348. Room and board charges vary according to board plan and housing facility. ***Payment plan:*** installment.

Financial Aid Of all full-time matriculated undergraduates who enrolled in 2014, 710 applied for aid, 464 were judged to have need, 154 had their

need fully met. 28 Federal Work-Study jobs (averaging $2010). In 2014, 298 non-need-based awards were made. ***Average percent of need met:*** 83. ***Average financial aid package:*** $12,940. ***Average need-based loan:*** $3083. ***Average need-based gift aid:*** $8481. ***Average non-need-based aid:*** $2293. ***Average indebtedness upon graduation:*** $17,553.

APPLYING

Standardized Tests *Required:* SAT or ACT (for admission).

Options: electronic application, early admission, deferred entrance.

Application fee: $30.

Required: essay or personal statement, high school transcript, 1 letter of recommendation. ***Recommended:*** minimum 3.0 GPA.

Application deadlines: 4/15 (freshmen), 4/15 (out-of-state freshmen), 4/15 (transfers).

Notification: 4/25 (freshmen), 4/25 (out-of-state freshmen), 4/25 (transfers).

CONTACT

Office of Admissions, New College of Florida, 5800 Bay Shore Road, Sarasota, FL 34243-2109. *Phone:* 941-487-5000. *Fax:* 941-487-5010. *E-mail:* admissions@ncf.edu.

See previous page for display ad and page 1544 for the College Close-Up.

Northwest Florida State College

Niceville, Florida

http://www.nwfsc.edu/

- **State and locally supported** primarily 2-year, founded 1963, part of Florida College System
- **Small-town** 264-acre campus
- **Endowment** $28.6 million
- **Coed**
- **Noncompetitive** entrance level

FACULTY

Student/faculty ratio: 26:1.

ACADEMICS

Calendar: semesters plus summer sessions. *Degrees:* certificates, associate, and bachelor's.

STUDENT LIFE

Housing options: college housing not available.

Activities and organizations: drama/theater group, choral group, Student Nurses Association, Ambassadors, Pre-Professional Educators Association, Campus Christian Fellowship, Film Club.

Athletics Member NJCAA.

Campus security: 24-hour patrols.

Student services: women's center.

COSTS

Costs (2014–15) ***Tuition:*** state resident $2313 full-time, $77 per credit part-time; nonresident $9252 full-time, $308 per credit part-time. Full-time tuition and fees vary according to course level, degree level, program, and reciprocity agreements. Part-time tuition and fees vary according to course level, degree level, program, and reciprocity agreements. ***Required fees:*** $811 full-time, $27 per credit part-time. ***Payment plans:*** tuition prepayment, deferred payment.

APPLYING

Standardized Tests *Required for some:* ACT, SAT I, ACT ASSET, MAPS, or PERT are used for placement not admission.

Options: electronic application.

Required: high school transcript.

CONTACT

Ms. Karen Cooper, Director of Admissions, Northwest Florida State College, 100 College Boulevard, Niceville, FL 32578. *Phone:* 850-729-4901. *Fax:* 850-729-5206. *E-mail:* cooperk@nwfsc.edu.

Nova Southeastern University

Fort Lauderdale, Florida

http://www.nova.edu/

- **Independent** university, founded 1964
- **Suburban** 300-acre campus
- **Coed** 4,699 undergraduate students, 67% full-time, 70% women, 30% men
- **Moderately difficult** entrance level, 49% of applicants were admitted

UNDERGRAD STUDENTS

3,162 full-time, 1,537 part-time. Students come from 48 states and territories; 74 other countries; 16% are from out of state; 18% Black or African American, non-Hispanic/Latino; 33% Hispanic/Latino; 8% Asian, non-Hispanic/Latino; 0.3% American Indian or Alaska Native, non-Hispanic/Latino; 2% Two or more races, non-Hispanic/Latino; 3% Race/ethnicity unknown; 5% international; 16% transferred in; 20% live on campus.

Freshmen

Admission: 4,364 applied, 2,130 admitted, 602 enrolled. ***Average high school GPA:*** 3.91. ***Test scores:*** SAT critical reading scores over 500: 81%; SAT math scores over 500: 78%; ACT scores over 18: 99%; SAT critical reading scores over 600: 33%; SAT math scores over 600: 40%; ACT scores over 24: 65%; SAT critical reading scores over 700: 3%; SAT math scores over 700: 7%; ACT scores over 30: 16%.

Retention: 74% of full-time freshmen returned.

FACULTY

Total: 1,725, 47% full-time, 75% with terminal degrees.

Student/faculty ratio: 16:1.

ACADEMICS

Calendar: trimesters. *Degrees:* certificates, associate, bachelor's, master's, doctoral, post-master's, and postbachelor's certificates.

Special study options: academic remediation for entering students, adult/continuing education programs, advanced placement credit, distance learning, double majors, honors programs, independent study, internships, off-campus study, part-time degree program, services for LD students, study abroad, summer session for credit.

Unusual degree programs: 3-2 business administration with Business Administration; Human Resource Management; International Business Administration; Leadership; Public Administration; Computer Science; Criminal Justice; Education.

Computers: 3,000 computers/terminals and 6,000 ports are available on campus for general student use. Students can access the following: campus intranet, computer help desk, free student e-mail accounts, online (class) grades, online (class) registration, online (class) schedules. Campuswide network is available. 100% of college-owned or -operated housing units are wired for high-speed Internet access. Wireless service is available via entire campus.

STUDENT LIFE

Housing options: on-campus residence required through sophomore year; coed, special housing for students with disabilities. Campus housing is university owned. Freshman campus housing is guaranteed.

Activities and organizations: drama/theater group, student-run newspaper, radio and television station, choral group, Kappa Delta Pi, Pre-Med, Sea Board, Delta Epsilon Iota, Commuter Student Organization, national fraternities, national sororities.

Athletics Member NCAA. All Division II. ***Intercollegiate sports:*** baseball M(s), basketball M(s)/W(s), cheerleading W, crew W(s), cross-country running M(s)/W(s), golf M(s)/W(s), soccer M(s)/W(s), softball W(s), swimming and diving M(s)/W(s), tennis W(s), track and field M(s)/W(s), volleyball W(s). ***Intramural sports:*** badminton M/W, basketball M/W, soccer M/W, softball W, volleyball M/W.

Campus security: 24-hour emergency response devices and patrols, late-night transport/escort service, controlled dormitory access, shuttle bus service.

Student services: health clinic, personal/psychological counseling.

COSTS & FINANCIAL AID

Costs (2014–15) ***Comprehensive fee:*** $37,280 includes full-time tuition ($25,950), mandatory fees ($750), and room and board ($10,580). Full-time tuition and fees vary according to class time and program. Part-time tuition: $865 per credit hour. Part-time tuition and fees vary according to class time, course load, and program. ***College room only:*** $7980. Room and board charges vary according to board plan and housing facility. ***Payment plans:*** installment, deferred payment. ***Waivers:*** employees or children of employees.

Financial Aid Of all full-time matriculated undergraduates who enrolled in 2014, 2,729 applied for aid, 2,395 were judged to have need, 254 had their need fully met. 966 Federal Work-Study jobs (averaging $4914). 380 state and other part-time jobs (averaging $1298). In 2014, 507 non-need-based awards were made. ***Average percent of need met:*** 65. ***Average financial aid package:*** $25,774. ***Average need-based loan:*** $4232. ***Average need-based gift aid:*** $13,847. ***Average non-need-based aid:*** $9515. ***Average indebtedness upon graduation:*** $31,022.

APPLYING

Standardized Tests *Required:* SAT or ACT (for admission).

Options: electronic application, deferred entrance.

Application fee: $50.

Recommended: high school transcript, minimum 3.0 GPA.

Application deadlines: rolling (freshmen), rolling (out-of-state freshmen), rolling (transfers).

Notification: continuous (freshmen), continuous (out-of-state freshmen), continuous (transfers).

CONTACT

Ms. Mensima Biney, Director of Undergraduate Admissions, Nova Southeastern University, Enrollment Processing Services, 3301 College Avenue, Ft. Lauderdale, FL 33329-9905. *Phone:* 954-262-8000. *Toll-free phone:* 800-541-NOVA. *Fax:* 954-262-3811. *E-mail:* nsuinfo@nova.edu.

Palm Beach Atlantic University

West Palm Beach, Florida

http://www.pba.edu/

- **Independent nondenominational** comprehensive, founded 1968
- **Urban** 100-acre campus with easy access to Miami-Dade County
- **Endowment** $80.1 million
- **Coed** 3,021 undergraduate students, 80% full-time, 65% women, 35% men
- **Moderately difficult** entrance level, 95% of applicants were admitted

UNDERGRAD STUDENTS

2,424 full-time, 597 part-time. Students come from 44 states and territories; 43 other countries; 36% are from out of state; 12% Black or African American, non-Hispanic/Latino; 16% Hispanic/Latino; 2% Asian, non-Hispanic/Latino; 0.3% Native Hawaiian or other Pacific Islander, non-Hispanic/Latino; 0.4% American Indian or Alaska Native, non-Hispanic/Latino; 3% Two or more races, non-Hispanic/Latino; 2% Race/ethnicity unknown; 3% international; 11% transferred in; 46% live on campus.

Freshmen

Admission: 1,564 applied, 1,490 admitted, 524 enrolled. ***Average high school GPA:*** 3.59. ***Test scores:*** SAT critical reading scores over 500: 58%; SAT math scores over 500: 57%; SAT writing scores over 500: 52%; ACT scores over 18: 93%; SAT critical reading scores over 600: 24%; SAT math scores over 600: 17%; SAT writing scores over 600: 16%; ACT scores over 24: 48%; SAT critical reading scores over 700: 3%; SAT math scores over 700: 1%; SAT writing scores over 700: 2%; ACT scores over 30: 10%.

Retention: 74% of full-time freshmen returned.

FACULTY

Total: 359, 45% full-time, 62% with terminal degrees.

Student/faculty ratio: 13:1.

ACADEMICS

Calendar: semesters. *Degrees:* associate, bachelor's, master's, and doctoral.

Special study options: academic remediation for entering students, accelerated degree program, adult/continuing education programs, advanced placement credit, distance learning, double majors, honors programs, independent study, internships, off-campus study, part-time degree program, services for LD students, student-designed majors, study abroad, summer session for credit. ***ROTC:*** Army (c).

Unusual degree programs: 3-2 M Div.

Computers: 340 computers/terminals are available on campus for general student use. Students can access the following: campus intranet, computer help desk, free student e-mail accounts, online (class) grades, online (class) registration, online (class) schedules. Campuswide network is available. 100% of college-owned or -operated housing units are wired for high-speed Internet access. Wireless service is available via entire campus.

STUDENT LIFE

Housing options: on-campus residence required through sophomore year; coed, men-only, women-only. Campus housing is university owned and leased by the school. Freshman campus housing is guaranteed.

Activities and organizations: drama/theater group, student-run newspaper, radio and television station, choral group, Impact Leadership Team, Nursing Student Association, Nurses Christian Fellowship, Student Government, Sigma Alpha Omega, national sororities.

Athletics Member NCAA, NCCAA. All NCAA Division II. ***Intercollegiate sports:*** baseball M(s), basketball M(s)/W(s), cheerleading M(c)/W(c), cross-country running W(s), golf M/W, lacrosse M(c)/W(c), soccer M(s)/W(s), softball W(s), tennis M(s)/W(s), volleyball W(s). ***Intramural sports:*** badminton M/W, basketball M/W, bowling M/W, racquetball M/W, soccer M/W, softball M/W, table tennis M/W, ultimate Frisbee M/W, volleyball M/W.

Campus security: 24-hour emergency response devices and patrols, late-night transport/escort service, controlled dormitory access, Security Escort Services; Lighted pathways/sidewalks; Self-defense education; Closed-circuit television system.

Student services: health clinic, personal/psychological counseling.

COSTS & FINANCIAL AID

Costs (2014–15) ***One-time required fee:*** $50. ***Comprehensive fee:*** $34,874 includes full-time tuition ($25,974), mandatory fees ($300), and room and board ($8600). Full-time tuition and fees vary according to course load, location, and program. Part-time tuition: $625 per credit hour. Part-time tuition and fees vary according to course load, location, and program. These charges are for the traditional day undergraduate program offered on the main campus in West Palm Beach, FL. Online and non-traditional evening undergraduate programs have other, per-credit-hour charges. ***Required fees:*** $99 per term part-time. ***College room only:*** $4430. Room and board charges vary according to board plan and housing facility. ***Payment plan:*** installment. ***Waivers:*** employees or children of employees.

Financial Aid Of all full-time matriculated undergraduates who enrolled in 2014, 2,112 applied for aid, 1,810 were judged to have need, 303 had their need fully met. 186 Federal Work-Study jobs (averaging $2955). 17 state and other part-time jobs (averaging $1441). In 2014, 585 non-need-based awards were made. ***Average percent of need met:*** 61. ***Average financial aid package:*** $17,688. ***Average need-based loan:*** $3910. ***Average need-based gift aid:*** $14,721. ***Average non-need-based aid:*** $9594. ***Average indebtedness upon graduation:*** $27,374. ***Financial aid deadline:*** 8/1.

APPLYING

Standardized Tests *Required:* SAT or ACT (for admission).

Options: electronic application, early admission, early action, deferred entrance.

Application fee: $50.

Required: essay or personal statement, high school transcript. ***Required for some:*** interview.

Application deadlines: rolling (freshmen), rolling (out-of-state freshmen), rolling (transfers), 3/31 (early action).

Notification: continuous (freshmen), continuous (out-of-state freshmen), continuous (transfers), 4/15 (early action).

CONTACT

Mr. James Zugelder, Director of Admissions, Palm Beach Atlantic University, 901 South Flagler Drive, PO Box 24708, West Palm Beach, FL 33416-4708. *Phone:* 561-803-2101. *Toll-free phone:* 888-GO-TO-PBA. *E-mail:* jamie_zugelder@pba.edu.

Palm Beach State College

Lake Worth, Florida

http://www.palmbeachstate.edu/

- **State-supported** 4-year, founded 1933, part of Florida College System
- **Urban** 150-acre campus with easy access to West Palm Beach
- **Endowment** $31.0 million
- **Coed** 29,174 undergraduate students, 32% full-time, 57% women, 43% men
- **Noncompetitive** entrance level, 100% of applicants were admitted

UNDERGRAD STUDENTS

9,410 full-time, 19,764 part-time. Students come from 49 states and territories; 146 other countries; 5% are from out of state; 23% Black or African American, non-Hispanic/Latino; 26% Hispanic/Latino; 3% Asian, non-Hispanic/Latino; 0.2% Native Hawaiian or other Pacific Islander, non-Hispanic/Latino; 0.1% American Indian or Alaska Native, non-Hispanic/Latino; 2% Two or more races, non-Hispanic/Latino; 5% Race/ethnicity unknown; 2% international; 4% transferred in.

Freshmen

Admission: 4,248 applied, 4,248 admitted, 4,248 enrolled.

FACULTY

Total: 1,185, 24% full-time.

Student/faculty ratio: 49:1.

ACADEMICS

Calendar: semesters. *Degrees:* certificates, diplomas, associate, and bachelor's.

Special study options: academic remediation for entering students, adult/continuing education programs, advanced placement credit, cooperative education, distance learning, double majors, English as a second language, freshman honors college, honors programs, independent study, internships, off-campus study, part-time degree program, services for LD students, student-designed majors, study abroad, summer session for credit.

Computers: 2,300 computers/terminals are available on campus for general student use. Students can access the following: computer help desk, free student e-mail accounts, online (class) registration. Campuswide network is available. Wireless service is available via entire campus.

STUDENT LIFE

Housing options: college housing not available.

Activities and organizations: drama/theater group, student-run newspaper, choral group, student government, Phi Theta Kappa, Students for International Understanding, Black Student Union, Drama Club, national fraternities.

Athletics Member NJCAA. ***Intercollegiate sports:*** baseball M(s), basketball M(s)/W(s), softball W(s), volleyball W(s).

Campus security: 24-hour emergency response devices and patrols.

Student services: health clinic, women's center.

COSTS

Costs (2014–15) ***Tuition:*** state resident $2358 full-time, $98 per credit part-time; nonresident $8592 full-time, $358 per credit part-time. ***Required fees:*** $20 full-time, $10 per year part-time, $10 per year part-time.

APPLYING

Standardized Tests *Recommended:* SAT and SAT Subject Tests or ACT (for admission).

Options: electronic application, early admission, deferred entrance.

Application fee: $30.

Required: high school transcript.

Application deadlines: 8/20 (freshmen), 8/20 (transfers).

Notification: continuous until 8/20 (freshmen), continuous until 8/20 (transfers).

CONTACT

Ms. Anne Guiler, Coordinator of Distance Learning, Palm Beach State College, Lake Worth, FL 33461. *Phone:* 561-868-3032. *Fax:* 561-868-3584. *E-mail:* enrollmt@palmbeachstate.edu.

Pensacola State College

Pensacola, Florida

http://www.pensacolastate.edu/

- **State-supported** primarily 2-year, founded 1948, part of Florida College System
- **Urban** 130-acre campus
- **Coed** 10,317 undergraduate students, 38% full-time, 60% women, 40% men
- **Noncompetitive** entrance level

UNDERGRAD STUDENTS

3,888 full-time, 6,429 part-time. Students come from 16 states and territories; 1% are from out of state; 15% Black or African American, non-Hispanic/Latino; 6% Hispanic/Latino; 3% Asian, non-Hispanic/Latino; 0.4% Native Hawaiian or other Pacific Islander, non-Hispanic/Latino; 0.8% American Indian or Alaska Native, non-Hispanic/Latino; 6% Two or more races, non-Hispanic/Latino; 1% Race/ethnicity unknown; 0.3% international; 2% transferred in.

Freshmen

Admission: 1,554 enrolled.

FACULTY

Total: 599, 30% full-time, 6% with terminal degrees.

Student/faculty ratio: 23:1.

ACADEMICS

Calendar: semesters. *Degrees:* certificates, diplomas, associate, and bachelor's.

Special study options: academic remediation for entering students, adult/continuing education programs, advanced placement credit, cooperative education, distance learning, double majors, English as a second language, external degree program, honors programs, independent study, part-time degree program, services for LD students, summer session for credit. ***ROTC:*** Army (b).

Computers: 1,700 computers/terminals are available on campus for general student use. Students can access the following: campus intranet, computer help desk, free student e-mail accounts, online (class) grades, online (class) registration, online (class) schedules. Campuswide network is available. Wireless service is available via entire campus.

STUDENT LIFE

Housing options: college housing not available.

Activities and organizations: drama/theater group, student-run newspaper, choral group.

Athletics Member NJCAA. ***Intercollegiate sports:*** baseball M(s), basketball M(s)/W(s), softball W(s), volleyball W. ***Intramural sports:*** archery M/W, badminton M/W, basketball M/W, bowling M/W, cross-country running M/W, gymnastics M/W, racquetball M/W, sailing M/W, swimming and diving M/W, tennis M/W, track and field M/W, volleyball M/W, weight lifting M/W, wrestling M.

Campus security: 24-hour emergency response devices and patrols, late-night transport/escort service.

Student services: health clinic, personal/psychological counseling.

COSTS & FINANCIAL AID

Costs (2014–15) ***One-time required fee:*** $30. ***Tuition:*** state resident $2510 full-time, $105 per credit hour part-time; nonresident $10,075 full-time, $420 per credit hour part-time. Full-time tuition and fees vary according to degree level. Part-time tuition and fees vary according to degree level. ***Payment plan:*** deferred payment. ***Waivers:*** senior citizens and employees or children of employees.

Financial Aid Of all full-time matriculated undergraduates who enrolled in 2013, 120 Federal Work-Study jobs (averaging $3000).

APPLYING

Options: electronic application, early admission.

Application fee: $30.

Required: high school transcript.

Application deadlines: 8/30 (freshmen), 8/30 (transfers).

Notification: continuous until 8/30 (freshmen), continuous until 8/30 (transfers).

CONTACT
Susan Desbrow, Registrar, Pensacola State College, 1000 College Blvd, Pensacola, FL 32504. *Phone:* 850-484-1605. *Fax:* 850-484-1020. *E-mail:* kdutremble@pensacolastate.edu.

Polk State College

Winter Haven, Florida

http://www.polk.edu/

- **State-supported** 4-year, founded 1964, part of Florida College System
- **Suburban** 98-acre campus with easy access to Orlando, Tampa
- **Endowment** $11.1 million
- **Coed** 11,887 undergraduate students, 29% full-time, 64% women, 36% men
- **Noncompetitive** entrance level

UNDERGRAD STUDENTS
3,486 full-time, 8,401 part-time. Students come from 7 states and territories; 9 other countries; 5% are from out of state; 17% Black or African American, non-Hispanic/Latino; 19% Hispanic/Latino; 3% Asian, non-Hispanic/Latino; 0.1% Native Hawaiian or other Pacific Islander, non-Hispanic/Latino; 0.2% American Indian or Alaska Native, non-Hispanic/Latino; 2% Two or more races, non-Hispanic/Latino; 4% Race/ethnicity unknown; 0.8% international; 7% transferred in.

Freshmen
Admission: 1,100 enrolled. *Test scores:* SAT critical reading scores over 500: 55%; SAT math scores over 500: 40%; SAT writing scores over 500: 58%; ACT scores over 18: 88%; SAT critical reading scores over 600: 20%; SAT math scores over 600: 3%; SAT writing scores over 600: 26%; ACT scores over 24: 7%; ACT scores over 30: 2%.

FACULTY
Total: 388, 39% full-time, 22% with terminal degrees.
Student/faculty ratio: 26:1.

ACADEMICS
Calendar: semesters 16-16-6-6. *Degrees:* certificates, diplomas, associate, and bachelor's.
Special study options: academic remediation for entering students, accelerated degree program, adult/continuing education programs, advanced placement credit, cooperative education, distance learning, double majors, English as a second language, honors programs, independent study, internships, off-campus study, part-time degree program, services for LD students, study abroad, summer session for credit. *ROTC:* Army (c).
Computers: 250 computers/terminals are available on campus for general student use. Students can access the following: computer help desk, free student e-mail accounts, online (class) grades, online (class) registration, online (class) schedules. Campuswide network is available. Wireless service is available via entire campus.

STUDENT LIFE
Housing options: college housing not available.
Activities and organizations: drama/theater group, choral group, Florida Student Nursing Association, SLAM (Student's Living a Message), Eagleteers, Student Government Association, SALO (Student Activities and Leadership Office).
Athletics Member NJCAA. *Intercollegiate sports:* baseball M(s), basketball M(s), cheerleading W, soccer W(s), softball W(s), volleyball W(s). *Intramural sports:* basketball M/W, bowling M/W, football M/W, volleyball M/W.
Campus security: 24-hour emergency response devices and patrols.
Student services: personal/psychological counseling.

COSTS
Costs (2014–15) *Tuition:* state resident $3367 full-time, $112 per credit hour part-time; nonresident $12,272 full-time, $409 per credit hour part-time. Full-time tuition and fees vary according to course level and degree level. Part-time tuition and fees vary according to course level and degree level. *Waivers:* employees or children of employees.

APPLYING
Options: electronic application, early admission, deferred entrance.
Required: high school transcript.
Application deadlines: rolling (freshmen), rolling (transfers).
Notification: continuous (freshmen), continuous (transfers).

CONTACT
Polk State College, 999 Avenue H, NE, Winter Haven, FL 33881-4299. *Phone:* 863-297-1021.

Rasmussen College Fort Myers

Fort Myers, Florida

http://www.rasmussen.edu/

- **Proprietary** 4-year, part of Rasmussen College System
- **Suburban** campus
- **Coed** 718 undergraduate students, 62% full-time, 69% women, 31% men
- **Minimally difficult** entrance level

UNDERGRAD STUDENTS
446 full-time, 272 part-time.

Freshmen
Admission: 64 enrolled.

FACULTY
Total: 34, 32% full-time.
Student/faculty ratio: 22:1.

ACADEMICS
Degrees: certificates, diplomas, associate, and bachelor's.
Special study options: academic remediation for entering students, accelerated degree program, adult/continuing education programs, distance learning, double majors, internships, part-time degree program, summer session for credit.
Computers: 129 computers/terminals are available on campus for general student use. Students can access the following: computer help desk, free student e-mail accounts, online (class) grades, online (class) schedules. Campuswide network is available. Wireless service is available via entire campus.

STUDENT LIFE
Housing options: college housing not available.

COSTS
Costs (2014–15) *Tuition:* $10,764 full-time, $310 per credit hour part-time. Full-time tuition and fees vary according to course level, course load, degree level, location, and program. Part-time tuition and fees vary according to course level, course load, degree level, location, and program. No tuition increase for student's term of enrollment. *Required fees:* $1350 full-time. *Payment plans:* installment, deferred payment. *Waivers:* employees or children of employees.

APPLYING
Standardized Tests *Required:* Internal Exam (for admission).
Options: electronic application, early admission, deferred entrance.
Required: high school transcript, minimum 2.0 GPA. *Required for some:* interview.
Application deadlines: rolling (freshmen), rolling (transfers).

CONTACT
Susan Hammerstrom, Director of Admissions, Rasmussen College Fort Myers, 9160 Forum Corporate Parkway, Suite 100, Fort Myers, FL 33905. *Phone:* 239-477-2100. *Toll-free phone:* 888-549-6755. *E-mail:* susan.hammerstrom@rasmussen.edu.

Rasmussen College Land O' Lakes

Land O' Lakes, Florida

http://www.rasmussen.edu/

- **Proprietary** 4-year, part of Rasmussen College System
- **Suburban** campus
- **Coed** 238 undergraduate students, 56% full-time, 73% women, 27% men
- **Minimally difficult** entrance level

UNDERGRAD STUDENTS
134 full-time, 104 part-time.

Freshmen
Admission: 36 enrolled.

FACULTY
Total: 13, 31% full-time.
Student/faculty ratio: 22:1.

ACADEMICS
Degrees: certificates, diplomas, associate, and bachelor's.
Special study options: academic remediation for entering students, accelerated degree program, adult/continuing education programs, distance learning, double majors, internships, part-time degree program, summer session for credit.
Computers: 61 computers/terminals are available on campus for general student use. Students can access the following: computer help desk, free student e-mail accounts, online (class) grades, online (class) schedules. Campuswide network is available. Wireless service is available via entire campus.

STUDENT LIFE
Housing options: college housing not available.

COSTS
Costs (2014–15) ***Tuition:*** $10,764 full-time, $310 per credit hour part-time. Full-time tuition and fees vary according to course level, course load, degree level, location, and program. Part-time tuition and fees vary according to course level, course load, degree level, location, and program. No tuition increase for student's term of enrollment. ***Required fees:*** $1350 full-time. ***Payment plans:*** installment, deferred payment. ***Waivers:*** employees or children of employees.

APPLYING
Standardized Tests *Required:* Internal Exam (for admission).
Options: electronic application, early admission, deferred entrance.
Required: high school transcript, minimum 2.0 GPA. ***Required for some:*** interview.
Application deadlines: rolling (freshmen), rolling (transfers).

CONTACT
Susan Hammerstrom, Director of Admissions, Rasmussen College Land O' Lakes, 18600 Fernview Street, Land O' Lakes, FL 34638. *Phone:* 813-435-3601. *Toll-free phone:* 888-549-6755. *E-mail:* susan.hammerstrom@rasmussen.edu.

Rasmussen College New Port Richey

New Port Richey, Florida

http://www.rasmussen.edu/

- **Proprietary** 4-year, part of Rasmussen College System
- **Suburban** campus
- **Coed** 815 undergraduate students, 56% full-time, 69% women, 31% men
- **Minimally difficult** entrance level

UNDERGRAD STUDENTS
453 full-time, 362 part-time.

Freshmen
Admission: 39 enrolled.

FACULTY
Total: 31, 58% full-time.
Student/faculty ratio: 22:1.

ACADEMICS
Degrees: certificates, diplomas, associate, and bachelor's.
Special study options: academic remediation for entering students, accelerated degree program, adult/continuing education programs, distance learning, double majors, internships, part-time degree program, summer session for credit.
Computers: 118 computers/terminals are available on campus for general student use. Students can access the following: computer help desk, free student e-mail accounts, online (class) grades, online (class) schedules. Campuswide network is available. Wireless service is available via entire campus.

STUDENT LIFE
Housing options: college housing not available.

COSTS & FINANCIAL AID
Costs (2014–15) ***Tuition:*** $10,764 full-time, $310 per credit hour part-time. Full-time tuition and fees vary according to course level, course load, degree level, location, and program. Part-time tuition and fees vary according to course level, course load, degree level, location, and program. No tuition increase for student's term of enrollment. ***Required fees:*** $1350 full-time. ***Payment plans:*** installment, deferred payment. ***Waivers:*** employees or children of employees.
Financial Aid Of all full-time matriculated undergraduates who enrolled in 2013, 6 Federal Work-Study jobs.

APPLYING
Standardized Tests *Required:* Internal Exam (for admission).
Options: electronic application, early admission, deferred entrance.
Required: high school transcript, minimum 2.0 GPA. ***Required for some:*** interview.
Application deadlines: rolling (freshmen), rolling (transfers).

CONTACT
Susan Hammerstrom, Director of Admissions, Rasmussen College New Port Richey, 8661 Citizens Drive, New Port Richey, FL 34654. *Phone:* 727-942-0069. *Toll-free phone:* 888-549-6755. *E-mail:* susan.hammerstrom@rasmussen.edu.

Rasmussen College Ocala

Ocala, Florida

http://www.rasmussen.edu/

- **Proprietary** 4-year, founded 1984, part of Rasmussen College System
- **Suburban** campus with easy access to Orlando
- **Coed** 1,194 undergraduate students, 62% full-time, 75% women, 25% men
- **Minimally difficult** entrance level

UNDERGRAD STUDENTS
745 full-time, 449 part-time.

Freshmen
Admission: 74 enrolled.

FACULTY
Total: 36, 25% full-time.
Student/faculty ratio: 22:1.

ACADEMICS
Calendar: quarters. *Degrees:* certificates, diplomas, associate, and bachelor's.
Special study options: academic remediation for entering students, accelerated degree program, adult/continuing education programs, distance learning, double majors, internships, part-time degree program, summer session for credit.
Computers: 124 computers/terminals are available on campus for general student use. Students can access the following: computer help desk, free student e-mail accounts, online (class) grades, online (class) schedules. Campuswide network is available. Wireless service is available via entire campus.

STUDENT LIFE
Housing options: college housing not available.

COSTS
Costs (2014–15) ***Tuition:*** $10,764 full-time, $310 per credit hour part-time. Full-time tuition and fees vary according to course level, course load, degree level, location, and program. Part-time tuition and fees vary according to course level, course load, degree level, location, and program. No tuition increase for student's term of enrollment. ***Required fees:*** $1350 full-time. ***Payment plans:*** installment, deferred payment. ***Waivers:*** employees or children of employees.

APPLYING
Standardized Tests *Required:* Internal Exam (for admission).
Options: electronic application, early admission, deferred entrance.
Required: high school transcript, minimum 2.0 GPA. ***Required for some:*** interview.
Application deadlines: rolling (freshmen), rolling (transfers).

CONTACT
Susan Hammerstrom, Director of Admissions, Rasmussen College Ocala, 4755 SW 46th Court, Ocala, FL 34471. *Phone:* 352-629-1941. *Toll-free phone:* 888-549-6755. *E-mail:* susan.hammerstrom@rasmussen.edu.

Rasmussen College Ocala School of Nursing

Ocala, Florida

http://www.rasmussen.edu/

- **Proprietary** 4-year, part of Rasmussen College System
- **Suburban** campus
- **Coed** 324 undergraduate students, 66% full-time, 88% women, 12% men
- **Minimally difficult** entrance level

UNDERGRAD STUDENTS
215 full-time, 109 part-time.

Freshmen
Admission: 2 enrolled.

FACULTY
Total: 24, 63% full-time.

Student/faculty ratio: 22:1.

ACADEMICS
Degrees: associate and bachelor's.

Special study options: academic remediation for entering students, accelerated degree program, adult/continuing education programs, distance learning, double majors, internships, part-time degree program, summer session for credit.

Computers: Students can access the following: computer help desk, free student e-mail accounts, online (class) grades, online (class) schedules. Campuswide network is available. Wireless service is available via entire campus.

STUDENT LIFE
Housing options: college housing not available.

COSTS
Costs (2014–15) ***Tuition:*** $14,220 full-time, $395 per credit hour part-time. Full-time tuition and fees vary according to course level, course load, degree level, location, and program. Part-time tuition and fees vary according to course level, course load, degree level, location, and program. No tuition increase for student's term of enrollment. ***Required fees:*** $1350 full-time. ***Payment plans:*** installment, deferred payment. ***Waivers:*** employees or children of employees.

APPLYING
Standardized Tests *Required:* Internal Exam (for admission).

Options: electronic application, early admission, deferred entrance.

Required: high school transcript, minimum 2.0 GPA. ***Required for some:*** interview.

Application deadlines: rolling (freshmen), rolling (transfers).

CONTACT
Susan Hammerstrom, Director of Admissions, Rasmussen College Ocala School of Nursing, 2100 SW 22nd Place, Ocala, FL 34471. *Phone:* 352-291-8560. *Toll-free phone:* 888-549-6755. *E-mail:* susan.hammerstrom@rasmussen.edu.

Rasmussen College Tampa/Brandon

Tampa, Florida

http://www.rasmussen.edu/

- **Proprietary** 4-year, part of Rasmussen College System
- **Suburban** campus
- **Coed** 444 undergraduate students, 66% full-time, 76% women, 24% men
- **Minimally difficult** entrance level

UNDERGRAD STUDENTS
291 full-time, 153 part-time.

Freshmen
Admission: 34 enrolled.

FACULTY
Total: 25, 44% full-time.

Student/faculty ratio: 22:1.

ACADEMICS
Degrees: certificates, diplomas, associate, and bachelor's.

Special study options: academic remediation for entering students, accelerated degree program, adult/continuing education programs, distance learning, double majors, internships, part-time degree program, summer session for credit.

Computers: 47 computers/terminals are available on campus for general student use. Students can access the following: computer help desk, free student e-mail accounts, online (class) grades, online (class) schedules. Campuswide network is available. Wireless service is available via entire campus.

STUDENT LIFE
Housing options: college housing not available.

COSTS
Costs (2014–15) ***Tuition:*** $10,764 full-time, $310 per credit hour part-time. Full-time tuition and fees vary according to course level, course load, degree level, location, and program. Part-time tuition and fees vary according to course level, course load, degree level, location, and program. No tuition increase for student's term of enrollment. ***Required fees:*** $1350 full-time. ***Payment plans:*** installment, deferred payment. ***Waivers:*** employees or children of employees.

APPLYING
Standardized Tests *Required:* Internal Exam (for admission).

Options: electronic application, early admission, deferred entrance.

Required: high school transcript, minimum 2.0 GPA. ***Required for some:*** interview.

Application deadlines: rolling (freshmen), rolling (transfers).

CONTACT
Susan Hammerstrom, Director of Admissions, Rasmussen College Tampa/Brandon, 4042 Park Oaks Boulevard, Tampa, FL 33610. *Phone:* 813-246-7600. *Toll-free phone:* 888-549-6755. *E-mail:* susan.hammerstrom@rasmussen.edu.

Ringling College of Art and Design

Sarasota, Florida

http://www.ringling.edu/

- **Independent** 4-year, founded 1931
- **Small-town** 49-acre campus with easy access to Tampa-St. Petersburg
- **Endowment** $43.1 million
- **Coed** 1,219 undergraduate students, 96% full-time, 60% women, 40% men
- **Moderately difficult** entrance level, 70% of applicants were admitted

UNDERGRAD STUDENTS
1,170 full-time, 49 part-time. Students come from 47 states and territories; 60 other countries; 57% are from out of state; 3% Black or African American, non-Hispanic/Latino; 15% Hispanic/Latino; 8% Asian, non-Hispanic/Latino; 0.3% Native Hawaiian or other Pacific Islander, non-Hispanic/Latino; 0.9% American Indian or Alaska Native, non-Hispanic/Latino; 2% Two or more races, non-Hispanic/Latino; 1% Race/ethnicity unknown; 16% international; 5% transferred in; 65% live on campus.

Freshmen
Admission: 1,409 applied, 980 admitted, 270 enrolled. ***Average high school GPA:*** 3.2.

Retention: 83% of full-time freshmen returned.

FACULTY
Total: 148, 62% full-time, 53% with terminal degrees.

Student/faculty ratio: 11:1.

ACADEMICS
Calendar: semesters. *Degree:* bachelor's.

Special study options: academic remediation for entering students, advanced placement credit, independent study, internships, off-campus study, part-time degree program, services for LD students, study abroad.

Computers: 879 computers/terminals are available on campus for general student use. Students can access the following: campus intranet, computer help desk, free student e-mail accounts, online (class) grades, online (class) registration, online (class) schedules, central file storage, high performance computing labs. Campuswide network is available. 100% of college-owned or -operated housing units are wired for high-speed Internet access. Wireless service is available via entire campus.

STUDENT LIFE
Housing options: coed, men-only, women-only. Campus housing is university owned. Freshman applicants given priority for college housing.

Activities and organizations: drama/theater group, student-run television station, Student Government Association, Digital Painting Sketch Club, Resident Student Association, MOSAIC, Quidditch Team.

Athletics ***Intramural sports:*** basketball M(c)/W(c), football M(c)/W(c), soccer M(c)/W(c), table tennis M(c)/W(c), ultimate Frisbee M(c)/W(c), volleyball M(c)/W(c), weight lifting M(c)/W(c).

Campus security: 24-hour emergency response devices and patrols, late-night transport/escort service, controlled dormitory access, lighted campus.

Student services: health clinic, personal/psychological counseling, legal services.

COSTS & FINANCIAL AID
Costs (2014–15) ***Comprehensive fee:*** $53,620 includes full-time tuition ($36,880), mandatory fees ($3160), and room and board ($13,580). Full-time tuition and fees vary according to course load, program, and student level. Part-time tuition: $1720 per credit hour. Part-time tuition and fees vary according to course load, program, and student level. ***College room only:*** $7220. Room and board charges vary according to board plan and housing facility. ***Payment plan:*** installment. ***Waivers:*** employees or children of employees.

Financial Aid Of all full-time matriculated undergraduates who enrolled in 2014, 790 applied for aid, 713 were judged to have need, 38 had their need fully met. In 2014, 162 non-need-based awards were made. ***Average percent of need met:*** 43. ***Average financial aid package:*** $20,276. ***Average need-based loan:*** $7648. ***Average need-based gift aid:*** $13,591. ***Average non-need-based aid:*** $15,603. ***Average indebtedness upon graduation:*** $43,685.

APPLYING
Options: electronic application, deferred entrance.

Application fee: $70.

Required: essay or personal statement, high school transcript, minimum 2.0 GPA, 2 letters of recommendation, portfolio, resume. ***Recommended:*** interview.

Application deadlines: rolling (freshmen), rolling (transfers).

Notification: continuous (freshmen), continuous (transfers).

CONTACT
Ringling College of Art and Design, . *Phone:* 941-359-7523. *Toll-free phone:* 800-255-7695. *Fax:* -. *E-mail:* admissions@ringling.edu.

Rollins College
Winter Park, Florida
http://www.rollins.edu/

- **Independent** comprehensive, founded 1885
- **Suburban** 80-acre campus with easy access to Orlando
- **Endowment** $374.7 million
- **Coed** 1,932 undergraduate students, 100% full-time, 59% women, 41% men
- **Moderately difficult** entrance level, 57% of applicants were admitted

UNDERGRAD STUDENTS
1,932 full-time. Students come from 44 states and territories; 52 other countries; 47% are from out of state; 3% Black or African American, non-Hispanic/Latino; 13% Hispanic/Latino; 3% Asian, non-Hispanic/Latino; 0.1% Native Hawaiian or other Pacific Islander, non-Hispanic/Latino; 0.2% American Indian or Alaska Native, non-Hispanic/Latino; 3% Two or more races, non-Hispanic/Latino; 3% Race/ethnicity unknown; 8% international; 4% transferred in; 60% live on campus.

Freshmen
Admission: 4,858 applied, 2,783 admitted, 540 enrolled. ***Average high school GPA:*** 3.33. ***Test scores:*** SAT critical reading scores over 500: 94%; SAT math scores over 500: 97%; SAT writing scores over 500: 90%; ACT scores over 18: 100%; SAT critical reading scores over 600: 48%; SAT math scores over 600: 50%; SAT writing scores over 600: 46%; ACT scores over 24: 88%; SAT critical reading scores over 700: 8%; SAT math scores over 700: 7%; SAT writing scores over 700: 8%; ACT scores over 30: 18%.

Retention: 83% of full-time freshmen returned.

FACULTY
Total: 219, 100% full-time, 89% with terminal degrees.

Student/faculty ratio: 10:1.

ACADEMICS
Calendar: semesters. *Degrees:* bachelor's, master's, and doctoral.

Special study options: academic remediation for entering students, accelerated degree program, adult/continuing education programs, advanced placement credit, double majors, honors programs, independent study, internships, off-campus study, part-time degree program, services for LD students, student-designed majors, study abroad, summer session for credit.

Unusual degree programs: 3-2 business administration with Crummer Graduate School of Business, Rollins College; engineering with Columbia University, Washington University in St. Louis, or Auburn University; forestry with Duke University School of the Environment; Environmental Management with Duke University School of the Environment.

Computers: 307 computers/terminals and 8,000 ports are available on campus for general student use. Students can access the following: campus intranet, computer help desk, free student e-mail accounts, online (class) grades, online (class) registration, online (class) schedules. Campuswide network is available. 100% of college-owned or -operated housing units are wired for high-speed Internet access. Wireless service is available via entire campus.

STUDENT LIFE
Housing options: on-campus residence required through sophomore year; coed, men-only, women-only, special housing for students with disabilities. Campus housing is university owned. Freshman campus housing is guaranteed.

Activities and organizations: drama/theater group, student-run newspaper, radio and television station, choral group, Interfraternity Council, Panhellenic Association, Student Government Association, Rollins Entertainment Programs, National Society of Collegiate Scholars, national fraternities, national sororities.

Athletics Member NCAA. All Division II. ***Intercollegiate sports:*** baseball M(s), basketball M(s)/W(s), crew M/W, cross-country running M/W, golf M(s)/W(s), lacrosse M/W, sailing M/W, skiing (downhill) M/W, soccer M(s)/W(s), softball W(s), swimming and diving M/W, tennis M(s)/W(s), volleyball W(s). ***Intramural sports:*** baseball M, basketball M/W, bowling M/W, equestrian sports W(c), ice hockey M(c), rock climbing M/W, soccer M/W, softball M/W, table tennis M/W, tennis M/W, ultimate Frisbee M/W, volleyball M/W.

Campus security: 24-hour emergency response devices and patrols, late-night transport/escort service, controlled dormitory access.

Student services: health clinic, personal/psychological counseling, women's center.

COSTS & FINANCIAL AID
Costs (2014–15) ***Comprehensive fee:*** $56,550 includes full-time tuition ($43,080) and room and board ($13,470). ***College room only:*** $7920. Room and board charges vary according to housing facility. ***Payment plan:*** installment. ***Waivers:*** employees or children of employees.

Financial Aid Of all full-time matriculated undergraduates who enrolled in 2014, 1,135 applied for aid, 976 were judged to have need, 255 had their need fully met. 240 Federal Work-Study jobs (averaging $1705). 2 state and other part-time jobs (averaging $2762). In 2014, 531 non-need-based awards were made. ***Average percent of need met:*** 78. ***Average financial aid package:*** $31,352. ***Average need-based loan:*** $4721. ***Average need-based gift aid:*** $26,635. ***Average non-need-based aid:*** $19,134. ***Average indebtedness upon graduation:*** $26,689.

APPLYING
Standardized Tests *Required for some:* SAT or ACT (for admission), Selection of Test Score Waived Option (TSWO) or official SAT/ACT scores (TSWO is not appropriate for applicants seeking academic merit scholarship, Honors Program, or 3/2 Accelerated Management Program consideration).

Options: electronic application, early admission, early decision, deferred entrance.

Application fee: $40.

Required: essay or personal statement, high school transcript, 1 letter of recommendation. ***Recommended:*** minimum 2.0 GPA, interview.

Application deadlines: 2/15 (freshmen), 4/15 (transfers).

Early decision deadline: 11/15 (for plan 1), 1/15 (for plan 2).

Notification: 4/1 (freshmen), continuous (transfers), 12/15 (early decision plan 1), 2/1 (early decision plan 2).

CONTACT
Ms. Holly Pohlig, Director of Admission, Rollins College, 1000 Holt Avenue, Campus Box 2720, Winter Park, FL 32789. *Phone:* 407-646-2161. *Fax:* 407-646-1502. *E-mail:* admission@rollins.edu.

★ Saint Leo University
Saint Leo, Florida
http://www.saintleo.edu/

- **Independent Roman Catholic** comprehensive, founded 1889
- **Rural** 297-acre campus with easy access to Tampa, Orlando
- **Endowment** $53.1 million
- **Coed** 2,290 undergraduate students, 96% full-time, 52% women, 48% men
- **Moderately difficult** entrance level, 72% of applicants were admitted

UNDERGRAD STUDENTS
2,193 full-time, 97 part-time. Students come from 45 states and territories; 61 other countries; 28% are from out of state; 13% Black or African American, non-Hispanic/Latino; 17% Hispanic/Latino; 1% Asian, non-Hispanic/Latino; 0.3% American Indian or Alaska Native, non-Hispanic/Latino; 2% Two or more races, non-Hispanic/Latino; 7% Race/ethnicity unknown; 13% international; 7% transferred in; 63% live on campus.

Freshmen
Admission: 3,490 applied, 2,511 admitted, 617 enrolled. ***Average high school GPA:*** 3.4. ***Test scores:*** SAT critical reading scores over 500: 52%; SAT math scores over 500: 51%; SAT writing scores over 500: 37%; ACT scores over 18: 97%; SAT critical reading scores over 600: 9%; SAT math scores over 600: 13%; SAT writing scores over 600: 5%; ACT scores over 24: 36%; SAT critical reading scores over 700: 1%; SAT math scores over 700: 1%; SAT writing scores over 700: 1%; ACT scores over 30: 2%.

Retention: 68% of full-time freshmen returned.

FACULTY
Total: 203, 60% full-time, 61% with terminal degrees.

Student/faculty ratio: 15:1.

ACADEMICS
Calendar: semesters. *Degrees:* associate, bachelor's, master's, doctoral, and postbachelor's certificates.

Special study options: academic remediation for entering students, accelerated degree program, adult/continuing education programs, advanced placement credit, distance learning, double majors, English as a second language, honors programs, independent study, internships, part-time degree program, services for LD students, study abroad, summer session for credit. ***ROTC:*** Army (b).

Computers: 150 computers/terminals are available on campus for general student use. Students can access the following: campus intranet, computer help desk, free student e-mail accounts, online (class) grades, online (class) registration, online (class) schedules, campus residents are issued a laptop for their personal use. Campuswide network is available. 100% of college-owned or -operated housing units are wired for high-speed Internet access. Wireless service is available via classrooms, computer centers, computer labs, dorm rooms, learning centers, libraries, student centers.

STUDENT LIFE
Housing options: on-campus residence required through junior year; coed, men-only, women-only, special housing for students with

disabilities. Campus housing is university owned. Freshman applicants given priority for college housing.

Activities and organizations: drama/theater group, student-run newspaper, choral group, Caribbean Student Association, Alphi Omega, Intercultural Student Association, Opus Fides, Pacioli Accounting Club, national fraternities, national sororities.

Athletics Member NCAA. All Division II. ***Intercollegiate sports:*** baseball M(s), basketball M(s)/W(s), cross-country running M(s)/W(s), golf M(s)/W(s), lacrosse M(s)/W(s), soccer M(s)/W(s), softball W(s), swimming and diving M(s)/W(s), tennis M(s)/W(s), track and field M(s)/W(s), volleyball W(s). ***Intramural sports:*** basketball M/W, field hockey M/W, football M/W, soccer M/W, tennis M/W, ultimate Frisbee M/W, water polo M/W.

Campus security: 24-hour emergency response devices and patrols, late-night transport/escort service, controlled dormitory access, surveillance cameras in parking lots.

Student services: health clinic, personal/psychological counseling.

COSTS & FINANCIAL AID

Costs (2015–16) ***Comprehensive fee:*** $30,390 includes full-time tuition ($20,150), mandatory fees ($370), and room and board ($9870). ***College room only:*** $5250. Room and board charges vary according to board plan and housing facility. ***Payment plans:*** installment, deferred payment. ***Waivers:*** employees or children of employees.

Financial Aid Of all full-time matriculated undergraduates who enrolled in 2014, 1,783 applied for aid, 1,555 were judged to have need, 262 had their need fully met. 419 Federal Work-Study jobs (averaging $3417). 4 state and other part-time jobs (averaging $3500). In 2014, 146 non-need-based awards were made. ***Average percent of need met:*** 69. ***Average financial aid package:*** $19,034. ***Average need-based loan:*** $3941. ***Average need-based gift aid:*** $14,433. ***Average non-need-based aid:*** $5911. ***Average indebtedness upon graduation:*** $27,436.

APPLYING

Standardized Tests *Recommended:* SAT or ACT (for admission).

Options: electronic application, early admission, deferred entrance.

Application fee: $40.

Required: high school transcript, 1 letter of recommendation. ***Recommended:*** interview.

Application deadlines: rolling (freshmen), rolling (transfers).

Notification: continuous (freshmen), continuous (transfers).

CONTACT

Mr. Peter Littlefield, Director of Undergraduate Admissions, Saint Leo University, MC 2008, PO Box 6665, Saint Leo, FL 33574-6665. *Phone:* 352-588-8283. *Toll-free phone:* 800-334-5532. *Fax:* 352-588-8257. *E-mail:* admissions@saintleo.edu.

See previous page for display ad and page 1602 for the College Close-Up.

St. Thomas University

Miami Gardens, Florida

http://www.stu.edu/

- **Independent Roman Catholic** comprehensive, founded 1961
- **Suburban** 140-acre campus
- **Coed** 936 undergraduate students, 94% full-time, 51% women, 49% men
- **Minimally difficult** entrance level, 85% of applicants were admitted

UNDERGRAD STUDENTS

883 full-time, 53 part-time. 22% Black or African American, non-Hispanic/Latino; 46% Hispanic/Latino; 0.4% Asian, non-Hispanic/Latino; 0.1% Native Hawaiian or other Pacific Islander, non-Hispanic/Latino; 0.1% American Indian or Alaska Native, non-Hispanic/Latino; 1% Two or more races, non-Hispanic/Latino; 4% Race/ethnicity unknown; 18% international; 14% transferred in; 27% live on campus.

Freshmen

Admission: 874 applied, 742 admitted, 163 enrolled. ***Average high school GPA:*** 3.1. ***Test scores:*** SAT critical reading scores over 500: 29%; SAT math scores over 500: 36%; SAT writing scores over 500: 23%; ACT scores over 18: 68%; SAT critical reading scores over 600: 6%; SAT math scores over 600: 9%; SAT writing scores over 600: 2%; ACT scores over 24: 15%.

Retention: 72% of full-time freshmen returned.

FACULTY

Total: 230, 45% full-time, 67% with terminal degrees.

Student/faculty ratio: 12:1.

ACADEMICS

Calendar: semesters. *Degrees:* certificates, bachelor's, master's, doctoral, post-master's, and postbachelor's certificates.

Special study options: academic remediation for entering students, adult/continuing education programs, advanced placement credit, distance learning, double majors, freshman honors college, honors programs, independent study, internships, part-time degree program, services for LD students, summer session for credit.

Computers: Students can access the following: campus intranet, free student e-mail accounts, online (class) grades, online (class) registration, online (class) schedules. Campuswide network is available. Wireless service is available via entire campus.

STUDENT LIFE

Housing options: men-only, women-only. Campus housing is university owned.

Activities and organizations: student-run television station, choral group, Psychology Club, National Society of Leadership and Success (NSLS), Criminal Justice, Kreyol Nation, Gay Strait Alliance (GSA).

Athletics Member NAIA. ***Intercollegiate sports:*** baseball M(s), cross-country running M(s)/W(s), golf M(s)/W(s), soccer M(s)/W(s), softball W(s), tennis M(s)/W(s), volleyball W(s). ***Intramural sports:*** baseball M, basketball M/W, cross-country running M/W, football M, golf M, soccer M/W, softball M/W, table tennis M/W, tennis M/W, volleyball M/W, water polo M/W, weight lifting M/W.

Campus security: 24-hour emergency response devices and patrols, late-night transport/escort service, controlled dormitory access.

Student services: health clinic, personal/psychological counseling.

COSTS & FINANCIAL AID

Costs (2014–15) ***Comprehensive fee:*** $32,300 includes full-time tuition ($27,150) and room and board ($5150). Full-time tuition and fees vary according to course load and program. Part-time tuition: $543 per credit hour. Part-time tuition and fees vary according to course load and program. ***College room only:*** $4120. Room and board charges vary according to board plan and housing facility. ***Payment plan:*** installment. ***Waivers:*** employees or children of employees.

Financial Aid Of all full-time matriculated undergraduates who enrolled in 2014, 712 applied for aid, 618 were judged to have need, 132 had their need fully met. In 2014, 176 non-need-based awards were made. ***Average need-based loan:*** $4416. ***Average need-based gift aid:*** $3482. ***Average non-need-based aid:*** $8000.

APPLYING

Standardized Tests *Required:* SAT or ACT (for admission).

Options: electronic application, deferred entrance.

Application fee: $40.

Required: high school transcript, minimum 2.0 GPA. ***Recommended:*** essay or personal statement, 1 letter of recommendation, interview.

CONTACT

Mr. Andre Lightbourne, Director of Admissions, St. Thomas University, 16401 Northwest 37th Avenue, Miami Gardens, FL 33054-6459. *Phone:* 305-628-6712. *Toll-free phone:* 800-367-9010. *Fax:* 305-628-6591. *E-mail:* signup@stu.edu.

Santa Fe College

Gainesville, Florida

http://www.sfcollege.edu/

- **State and locally supported** 4-year, founded 1966, part of Florida College System
- **Suburban** 187-acre campus with easy access to Jacksonville
- **Coed** 15,745 undergraduate students, 43% full-time, 55% women, 45% men
- **Noncompetitive** entrance level

UNDERGRAD STUDENTS

6,777 full-time, 8,968 part-time. Students come from 28 states and territories; 61 other countries; 2% are from out of state; 16% Black or

African American, non-Hispanic/Latino; 12% Hispanic/Latino; 2% Asian, non-Hispanic/Latino; 0.4% Native Hawaiian or other Pacific Islander, non-Hispanic/Latino; 0.5% American Indian or Alaska Native, non-Hispanic/Latino; 2% Two or more races, non-Hispanic/Latino; 8% Race/ethnicity unknown; 1% international; 11% transferred in.

Freshmen
Admission: 3,076 enrolled.

FACULTY
Total: 829, 30% full-time, 19% with terminal degrees.

Student/faculty ratio: 25:1.

ACADEMICS
Calendar: semesters. *Degrees:* certificates, associate, and bachelor's (offers bachelor's degrees in conjunction with Saint Leo College).

Special study options: academic remediation for entering students, adult/continuing education programs, advanced placement credit, cooperative education, distance learning, English as a second language, honors programs, independent study, internships, part-time degree program, services for LD students, study abroad, summer session for credit. ***ROTC:*** Army (c), Air Force (c).

Computers: Students can access the following: computer help desk, free student e-mail accounts, online (class) grades, online (class) registration, online (class) schedules, apply for financial aid and view the status of awards, pay tuition, view and print unofficial transcripts, apply for graduation, view degree audits to check progress toward completion of their degree requirements. Campuswide network is available. Wireless service is available via entire campus.

STUDENT LIFE
Housing options: college housing not available.

Activities and organizations: drama/theater group, student-run newspaper, choral group.

Athletics Member NJCAA. ***Intercollegiate sports:*** baseball M(s), basketball M(s)/W(s), softball W(s), volleyball W. ***Intramural sports:*** badminton M(c)/W(c), basketball M/W, bowling M(c)/W(c), cheerleading M(c)/W(c), fencing M(c)/W(c), football M, racquetball M/W, soccer M/W, softball W, tennis M/W, track and field M(c)/W(c), ultimate Frisbee M/W, volleyball M/W, weight lifting M/W.

Campus security: 24-hour emergency response devices and patrols.

Student services: health clinic, personal/psychological counseling, women's center, legal services.

FINANCIAL AID
Financial Aid Of all full-time matriculated undergraduates who enrolled in 2013, 190 Federal Work-Study jobs.

APPLYING
Options: electronic application, early admission.

Required: high school transcript. ***Required for some:*** essay or personal statement, high school transcript, interview.

Application deadlines: rolling (freshmen), rolling (transfers).

Notification: continuous (freshmen), continuous (transfers).

CONTACT
Santa Fe College, 3000 Northwest 83rd Street, Gainesville, FL 32606.
Phone: 352-395-4177.

Schiller International University
Largo, Florida
http://www.schiller.edu/

- **Independent** comprehensive, founded 1991, part of Schiller International University
- **Suburban** 4-acre campus with easy access to Tampa
- **Coed**
- **Minimally difficult** entrance level

FACULTY
Student/faculty ratio: 16:1.

ACADEMICS
Calendar: semesters. *Degrees:* diplomas, associate, bachelor's, and master's.

STUDENT LIFE
Housing options: coed. Campus housing is provided by a third party. Freshman applicants given priority for college housing.

Activities and organizations: student government, Model United Nations.

Campus security: night patrols.

Student services: personal/psychological counseling.

APPLYING
Options: electronic application, deferred entrance.

Application fee: $20.

Required: essay or personal statement, high school transcript.
Recommended: minimum 2.0 GPA, interview.

CONTACT
Admissions Officer, Schiller International University, Largo, FL 33770.
Toll-free phone: 800-261-9571 (in-state); 800-261-9751 (out-of-state).
Fax: 727-738-6376. *E-mail:* admissions@schiller.edu.

Seminole State College of Florida
Sanford, Florida
http://www.seminolestate.edu/

- **State and locally supported** primarily 2-year, founded 1966
- **Small-town** 200-acre campus with easy access to Orlando
- **Endowment** $14.6 million
- **Coed** 18,422 undergraduate students, 34% full-time, 56% women, 44% men
- **Noncompetitive** entrance level, 100% of applicants were admitted

UNDERGRAD STUDENTS
6,345 full-time, 12,077 part-time. Students come from 24 states and territories; 75 other countries; 0.2% are from out of state; 17% Black or African American, non-Hispanic/Latino; 23% Hispanic/Latino; 3% Asian, non-Hispanic/Latino; 0.3% Native Hawaiian or other Pacific Islander, non-Hispanic/Latino; 0.2% American Indian or Alaska Native, non-Hispanic/Latino; 3% Two or more races, non-Hispanic/Latino; 1% Race/ethnicity unknown; 2% international; 6% transferred in.

Freshmen
Admission: 2,689 applied, 2,689 admitted, 2,689 enrolled.

FACULTY
Total: 780, 30% full-time, 21% with terminal degrees.

Student/faculty ratio: 25:1.

ACADEMICS
Calendar: semesters. *Degrees:* certificates, diplomas, associate, bachelor's, and postbachelor's certificates.

Special study options: academic remediation for entering students, accelerated degree program, adult/continuing education programs, advanced placement credit, cooperative education, distance learning, double majors, English as a second language, external degree program, honors programs, independent study, internships, part-time degree program, services for LD students, study abroad, summer session for credit. ***ROTC:*** Army (b).

Computers: 250 computers/terminals are available on campus for general student use. Students can access the following: campus intranet, computer help desk, free student e-mail accounts, online (class) grades, online (class) registration, online (class) schedules, online syllabi. Campuswide network is available. Wireless service is available via entire campus.

STUDENT LIFE
Housing options: college housing not available.

Activities and organizations: drama/theater group, student-run newspaper, choral group, Phi Beta Lambda, Phi Theta Kappa, Student Government Association, Sigma Phi Gamma, Hispanic Student Association.

Athletics Member NJCAA. ***Intercollegiate sports:*** baseball M(s), golf W(s), softball W(s).

Campus security: 24-hour emergency response devices and patrols, late-night transport/escort service.

Student services: personal/psychological counseling.

COSTS
Costs (2014–15) ***Tuition:*** state resident $3131 full-time, $104 per credit hour part-time; nonresident $11,456 full-time, $382 per credit hour part-time. Full-time tuition and fees vary according to course level, course load, degree level, and program. Part-time tuition and fees vary according to course level, course load, degree level, and program. ***Payment plan:*** deferred payment. ***Waivers:*** senior citizens and employees or children of employees.

APPLYING
Standardized Tests *Recommended:* SAT (for admission), ACT (for admission), SAT or ACT (for admission), SAT and SAT Subject Tests or ACT (for admission), SAT Subject Tests (for admission), CPT, PERT.

Options: electronic application, early admission, deferred entrance.

Required: high school transcript, minimum 2.0 GPA.

Application deadlines: rolling (freshmen), rolling (transfers).

Notification: continuous (freshmen), continuous (transfers).

CONTACT
Ms. Pamela Mennechey, Associate Vice President - Student Recruitment and Enrollment, Seminole State College of Florida, Sanford, FL 32773-6199. *Phone:* 407-708-2050. *Fax:* 407-708-2395. *E-mail:* admissions@scc-fl.edu.

Southeastern University
Lakeland, Florida
http://www.seu.edu/

- **Independent** comprehensive, founded 1935, affiliated with Assemblies of God
- **Suburban** 87-acre campus with easy access to Tampa, Orlando
- **Endowment** $8.3 million
- **Coed** 3,436 undergraduate students, 79% full-time, 55% women, 45% men
- **Minimally difficult** entrance level, 44% of applicants were admitted

UNDERGRAD STUDENTS
2,715 full-time, 721 part-time. Students come from 48 states and territories; 47 other countries; 32% are from out of state; 14% Black or African American, non-Hispanic/Latino; 16% Hispanic/Latino; 1% Asian, non-Hispanic/Latino; 0.4% Native Hawaiian or other Pacific Islander, non-Hispanic/Latino; 0.4% American Indian or Alaska Native, non-Hispanic/Latino; 0.5% Two or more races, non-Hispanic/Latino; 8% Race/ethnicity unknown; 1% international; 9% transferred in; 52% live on campus.

Freshmen
Admission: 3,402 applied, 1,495 admitted, 905 enrolled. ***Test scores:*** SAT critical reading scores over 500: 49%; SAT math scores over 500: 35%; SAT writing scores over 500: 43%; ACT scores over 18: 75%; SAT critical reading scores over 600: 12%; SAT math scores over 600: 9%; SAT writing scores over 600: 11%; ACT scores over 24: 24%; SAT critical reading scores over 700: 1%; SAT math scores over 700: 1%; SAT writing scores over 700: 1%; ACT scores over 30: 2%.

Retention: 66% of full-time freshmen returned.

FACULTY
Total: 276, 43% full-time.

Student/faculty ratio: 18:1.

ACADEMICS
Calendar: semesters. *Degrees:* associate, bachelor's, master's, and doctoral.

Special study options: academic remediation for entering students, adult/continuing education programs, advanced placement credit, cooperative education, distance learning, double majors, honors programs, independent study, internships, off-campus study, part-time degree program, services for LD students, study abroad, summer session for credit. ***ROTC:*** Army (c).

Computers: 119 computers/terminals are available on campus for general student use. Students can access the following: campus intranet, computer help desk, free student e-mail accounts, online (class) grades, online (class) registration, online (class) schedules, network programs. Campuswide network is available. 100% of college-owned or -operated housing units are wired for high-speed Internet access. Wireless service is available via entire campus.

STUDENT LIFE
Housing options: on-campus residence required through junior year; men-only, women-only. Campus housing is university owned. Freshman campus housing is guaranteed.

Activities and organizations: drama/theater group, student-run newspaper, radio and television station, choral group.

Athletics Member NAIA, NCCAA. ***Intercollegiate sports:*** baseball M(s), basketball M(s)/W(s), cheerleading M/W, cross-country running M(s)/W(s), football M(s), golf M(s)/W(s), soccer M(s)/W(s), softball W(s), tennis M(s)/W(s), volleyball W(s), wrestling M(s). ***Intramural sports:*** basketball M/W, football M/W, soccer M/W, softball M/W, volleyball M/W.

Campus security: 24-hour emergency response devices and patrols, late-night transport/escort service.

Student services: health clinic, personal/psychological counseling.

COSTS & FINANCIAL AID
Costs (2014–15) ***Comprehensive fee:*** $31,499 includes full-time tuition ($21,202), mandatory fees ($1000), and room and board ($9297). Full-time tuition and fees vary according to class time, degree level, and reciprocity agreements. Part-time tuition: $883 per credit hour. Part-time tuition and fees vary according to class time, course load, degree level, and reciprocity agreements. ***Required fees:*** $200 per term part-time. ***Room and board:*** Room and board charges vary according to board plan and housing facility. ***Payment plan:*** installment. ***Waivers:*** employees or children of employees.

Financial Aid Of all full-time matriculated undergraduates who enrolled in 2011, 2,057 applied for aid, 1,814 were judged to have need, 172 had their need fully met. In 2011, 245 non-need-based awards were made. ***Average percent of need met:*** 2. ***Average financial aid package:*** $11,535. ***Average need-based loan:*** $3861. ***Average need-based gift aid:*** $8187. ***Average non-need-based aid:*** $3846. ***Average indebtedness upon graduation:*** $24,398.

APPLYING
Standardized Tests *Required:* SAT or ACT (for admission).

Options: electronic application, early admission, deferred entrance.

Application fee: $40.

Required: essay or personal statement, high school transcript, 2 letters of recommendation. ***Required for some:*** interview.

Application deadlines: 5/1 (freshmen), 7/1 (transfers).

Notification: 6/1 (freshmen), continuous (transfers).

CONTACT
Southeastern University, 1000 Longfellow Boulevard, Lakeland, FL 33801-6099. *Phone:* 800-500-8760. *Toll-free phone:* 800-500-8760.

South Florida State College
Avon Park, Florida
http://www.southflorida.edu/

- **State-supported** primarily 2-year, founded 1965, part of Florida State College System
- **Rural** 228-acre campus with easy access to Tampa-St. Petersburg, Orlando
- **Endowment** $5.0 million
- **Coed** 2,699 undergraduate students, 36% full-time, 62% women, 38% men
- **Noncompetitive** entrance level, 100% of applicants were admitted

UNDERGRAD STUDENTS
970 full-time, 1,729 part-time. 3% are from out of state; 10% Black or African American, non-Hispanic/Latino; 29% Hispanic/Latino; 2% Asian, non-Hispanic/Latino; 0.4% Native Hawaiian or other Pacific Islander, non-Hispanic/Latino; 0.1% American Indian or Alaska Native, non-Hispanic/Latino; 1% Two or more races, non-Hispanic/Latino; 2% Race/ethnicity unknown; 1% international; 0.9% transferred in.

Freshmen
Admission: 736 applied, 736 admitted, 568 enrolled. ***Average high school GPA:*** 3.03.

FACULTY
Total: 145, 45% full-time, 18% with terminal degrees.
Student/faculty ratio: 16:1.

ACADEMICS
Calendar: semesters. *Degrees:* certificates, diplomas, associate, and bachelor's.

Special study options: academic remediation for entering students, adult/continuing education programs, advanced placement credit, cooperative education, distance learning, English as a second language, internships, part-time degree program, services for LD students, summer session for credit.

Computers: 81 computers/terminals are available on campus for general student use. Students can access the following: campus intranet, computer help desk, free student e-mail accounts, online (class) grades, online (class) registration, online (class) schedules. Campuswide network is available. Wireless service is available via classrooms, computer centers, computer labs, learning centers, libraries, student centers.

STUDENT LIFE
Housing options: Campus housing is provided by a third party.

Activities and organizations: drama/theater group, student-run newspaper, choral group, Phi Theta Kappa, Phi Beta Lambda, Performing Arts Club, Anime & Gaming Club, Basketball Club.

Athletics Member NJCAA. ***Intercollegiate sports:*** baseball M(s), cheerleading M/W, softball W(s), volleyball W(s). ***Intramural sports:*** basketball M(c)/W(c), soccer M(c)/W(c).

Campus security: 24-hour emergency response devices and patrols, late-night transport/escort service.

Student services: personal/psychological counseling.

COSTS
Costs (2014–15) ***One-time required fee:*** $15. ***Tuition:*** state resident $2505 full-time, $105 per credit hour part-time; nonresident $9463 full-time, $394 per credit hour part-time. Full-time tuition and fees vary according to degree level. Part-time tuition and fees vary according to degree level. ***Room and board:*** $5821; room only: $1500. ***Payment plan:*** installment. ***Waivers:*** employees or children of employees.

APPLYING
Options: electronic application, early admission, deferred entrance.

Application fee: $15.

Required: high school transcript.

Notification: continuous (freshmen).

CONTACT
Ms. Lynn Hintz, Admissions Director, South Florida State College, 600 West College Drive, Avon Park, FL 33825. *Phone:* 863-453-6661.

South University
Royal Palm Beach, Florida
http://www.southuniversity.edu/west-palm-beach/

- **Proprietary** comprehensive, founded 1899, part of Education Management Corporation
- **Coed**

ACADEMICS
Calendar: quarters. *Degrees:* associate, bachelor's, and master's.

CONTACT
South University, University Centre, 9801 Belvedere Road, Royal Palm Beach, FL 33411. *Phone:* 561-273-6500. *Toll-free phone:* 866-629-2902.

South University
Tampa, Florida
http://www.southuniversity.edu/tampa/

- **Proprietary** comprehensive, part of Education Management Corporation
- **Coed**

ACADEMICS
Degrees: associate, bachelor's, master's, doctoral, and post-master's certificates.

CONTACT
South University, 4401 North Himes Avenue, Suite 175, Tampa, FL 33614. *Phone:* 813-393-3800. *Toll-free phone:* 800-846-1472.

State College of Florida Manatee-Sarasota
Bradenton, Florida
http://www.scf.edu/

- **State-supported** 4-year, founded 1957, part of Florida Community College System
- **Suburban** 100-acre campus with easy access to Tampa-St. Petersburg
- **Coed** 10,314 undergraduate students, 40% full-time, 62% women, 38% men
- **Noncompetitive** entrance level, 100% of applicants were admitted

UNDERGRAD STUDENTS
4,173 full-time, 6,141 part-time. Students come from 23 states and territories; 35 other countries; 3% are from out of state; 9% Black or African American, non-Hispanic/Latino; 14% Hispanic/Latino; 2% Asian, non-Hispanic/Latino; 0.1% Native Hawaiian or other Pacific Islander, non-Hispanic/Latino; 0.3% American Indian or Alaska Native, non-Hispanic/Latino; 2% Two or more races, non-Hispanic/Latino; 5% Race/ethnicity unknown; 1% international; 7% transferred in.

Freshmen
Admission: 2,912 applied, 2,912 admitted, 1,689 enrolled. ***Test scores:*** SAT critical reading scores over 500: 33%; SAT math scores over 500: 29%; SAT writing scores over 500: 34%; ACT scores over 18: 57%; SAT math scores over 600: 4%; SAT writing scores over 600: 4%; ACT scores over 24: 16%; ACT scores over 30: 3%.

FACULTY
Total: 442, 34% full-time.

ACADEMICS
Calendar: semesters. *Degrees:* certificates, associate, and bachelor's.

Special study options: academic remediation for entering students, advanced placement credit, cooperative education, distance learning, double majors, English as a second language, honors programs, independent study, part-time degree program, services for LD students, summer session for credit.

Computers: 1,000 computers/terminals are available on campus for general student use. Students can access the following: campus intranet, computer help desk, free student e-mail accounts, online (class) registration, online (class) schedules. Campuswide network is available. Wireless service is available via entire campus.

STUDENT LIFE
Housing options: college housing not available.

Activities and organizations: drama/theater group, student-run newspaper, choral group, Student Government Association, Phi Theta Kappa, American Chemical Society Student Affiliate, Campus Ministry, Medical Community Club.

Athletics Member NJCAA. ***Intercollegiate sports:*** baseball M(s), basketball M(s), softball W(s), volleyball W(s). ***Intramural sports:*** basketball M/W, softball M/W, volleyball M/W, weight lifting M/W.

Campus security: 24-hour emergency response devices and patrols, late-night transport/escort service.

COSTS & FINANCIAL AID
Costs (2015–16) ***One-time required fee:*** $40. ***Tuition:*** state resident $3074 full-time, $102 per credit part-time; nonresident $11,596 full-time, $387 per credit part-time. Full-time tuition and fees vary according to degree level. Part-time tuition and fees vary according to degree level. ***Payment plan:*** deferred payment. ***Waivers:*** employees or children of employees.

Financial Aid Of all full-time matriculated undergraduates who enrolled in 2013, 82 Federal Work-Study jobs (averaging $2800). ***Financial aid deadline:*** 8/15.

APPLYING
Options: electronic application, early admission.

Required: high school transcript.

Application deadlines: 8/20 (freshmen), 8/20 (transfers).

Notification: continuous (freshmen), continuous (transfers).

CONTACT

Ms. MariLynn Lewy, AVP, Student Services, State College of Florida Manatee-Sarasota, Bradenton, FL 34206. *Phone:* 941-752-5384. *Fax:* 941-727-6380. *E-mail:* lewym@scf.edu.

Stetson University

DeLand, Florida

http://www.stetson.edu/

- **Independent** comprehensive, founded 1883
- **Small-town** 155-acre campus with easy access to Orlando
- **Endowment** $207.8 million
- **Coed** 2,841 undergraduate students, 99% full-time, 58% women, 42% men
- **Moderately difficult** entrance level, 61% of applicants were admitted

UNDERGRAD STUDENTS

2,804 full-time, 37 part-time. Students come from 41 states and territories; 51 other countries; 28% are from out of state; 8% Black or African American, non-Hispanic/Latino; 14% Hispanic/Latino; 2% Asian, non-Hispanic/Latino; 0.5% American Indian or Alaska Native, non-Hispanic/Latino; 3% Two or more races, non-Hispanic/Latino; 2% Race/ethnicity unknown; 6% international; 4% transferred in; 64% live on campus.

Freshmen

Admission: 10,986 applied, 6,728 admitted, 773 enrolled. ***Average high school GPA:*** 3.79. ***Test scores:*** SAT critical reading scores over 500: 90%; SAT math scores over 500: 88%; SAT writing scores over 500: 83%; ACT scores over 18: 100%; SAT critical reading scores over 600: 48%; SAT math scores over 600: 42%; SAT writing scores over 600: 37%; ACT scores over 24: 77%; SAT critical reading scores over 700: 11%; SAT math scores over 700: 6%; SAT writing scores over 700: 7%; ACT scores over 30: 15%.

Retention: 79% of full-time freshmen returned.

FACULTY

Total: 424, 62% full-time, 83% with terminal degrees.

Student/faculty ratio: 12:1.

ACADEMICS

Calendar: semesters. *Degrees:* bachelor's, master's, doctoral, and post-master's certificates.

Special study options: accelerated degree program, advanced placement credit, distance learning, double majors, honors programs, independent study, internships, off-campus study, part-time degree program, services for LD students, student-designed majors, study abroad, summer session for credit. ***ROTC:*** Army (c).

Unusual degree programs: 3-2 engineering; forestry with Duke University; Master of Environmental Management with Duke University, Master of Public Administration with American University (guaranteed admission for Stetson graduates who meet specific criteria).

Computers: 500 computers/terminals are available on campus for general student use. Students can access the following: campus intranet, computer help desk, free student e-mail accounts, online (class) grades, online (class) registration, online (class) schedules. Campuswide network is available. 100% of college-owned or -operated housing units are wired for high-speed Internet access. Wireless service is available via entire campus.

STUDENT LIFE

Housing options: on-campus residence required through junior year; coed, men-only, women-only. Campus housing is university owned and leased by the school. Freshman campus housing is guaranteed.

Activities and organizations: drama/theater group, student-run newspaper, radio station, choral group, Caribbean Student Association, Fellowship of Christian Athletes, Kaleidoscope (promotes inclusivity), Enactus (social action), Model United Nations, national fraternities, national sororities.

Athletics Member NCAA. All Division I. ***Intercollegiate sports:*** baseball M(s), basketball M(s)/W(s), crew M/W(s), cross-country running M(s)/W(s), football M, golf M(s)/W(s), lacrosse W(s), soccer M(s)/W(s), softball W(s), tennis M(s)/W(s), volleyball W(s). ***Intramural sports:*** baseball M(c), basketball M(c)/W, crew M(c)/W(c), equestrian sports M(c)/W(c), lacrosse M(c)/W(c), riflery M(c)/W(c), soccer M(c)/W(c), softball M/W(c), tennis M(c)/W(c), ultimate Frisbee M(c)/W(c), volleyball M/W(c), water polo M(c)/W(c).

Campus security: 24-hour emergency response devices and patrols, late-night transport/escort service, controlled dormitory access.

Student services: health clinic, personal/psychological counseling.

COSTS & FINANCIAL AID

Costs (2015–16) ***Tuition:*** $41,240 full-time, $4274 per course part-time. Part-time tuition and fees vary according to course load. ***Required fees:*** $350 full-time. ***Room only:*** $6874. Room and board charges vary according to board plan and housing facility. ***Payment plan:*** installment. ***Waivers:*** employees or children of employees.

Financial Aid Of all full-time matriculated undergraduates who enrolled in 2014, 2,326 applied for aid, 2,053 were judged to have need, 416 had their need fully met. 904 Federal Work-Study jobs (averaging $2444). 277 state and other part-time jobs (averaging $2465). In 2014, 592 non-need-based awards were made. ***Average percent of need met:*** 76. ***Average financial aid package:*** $33,033. ***Average need-based loan:*** $5082. ***Average need-based gift aid:*** $26,057. ***Average non-need-based aid:*** $19,811. ***Average indebtedness upon graduation:*** $32,302.

APPLYING

Standardized Tests *Required for some:* SAT or ACT (for admission).

Options: electronic application, deferred entrance.

Application fee: $50.

Required: essay or personal statement, high school transcript, 1 letter of recommendation. ***Recommended:*** interview.

Application deadlines: rolling (freshmen), rolling (out-of-state freshmen), rolling (transfers).

Notification: continuous (freshmen), continuous (out-of-state freshmen), continuous (transfers).

CONTACT

Robert Andrews, Director of Admissions, Stetson University, 421 N Woodland Blvd, Unit 8378, DeLand, FL 32723. *Phone:* 386-822-7100. *Toll-free phone:* 800-688-0101. *Fax:* 386-822-7112. *E-mail:* admissions@stetson.edu.

Trinity College of Florida

Trinity, Florida

http://www.trinitycollege.edu/

- **Independent nondenominational** 4-year, founded 1932
- **Small-town** 40-acre campus with easy access to Tampa
- **Coed** 229 undergraduate students, 83% full-time, 43% women, 57% men
- **Minimally difficult** entrance level, 74% of applicants were admitted

UNDERGRAD STUDENTS

191 full-time, 38 part-time. Students come from 10 states and territories; 4 other countries; 8% are from out of state; 21% Black or African American, non-Hispanic/Latino; 14% Hispanic/Latino; 1% Asian, non-Hispanic/Latino; 2% Two or more races, non-Hispanic/Latino; 7% Race/ethnicity unknown; 2% international; 19% transferred in; 48% live on campus.

Freshmen

Admission: 61 applied, 45 admitted, 31 enrolled. ***Average high school GPA:*** 2.94. ***Test scores:*** SAT critical reading scores over 500: 13%; SAT math scores over 500: 19%; SAT writing scores over 500: 19%; ACT scores over 18: 55%; SAT critical reading scores over 600: 13%; SAT math scores over 600: 6%; SAT writing scores over 600: 6%; ACT scores over 24: 10%.

Retention: 45% of full-time freshmen returned.

FACULTY

Total: 37, 19% full-time, 46% with terminal degrees.

Student/faculty ratio: 8:1.

ACADEMICS

Calendar: semesters. *Degrees:* certificates, associate, and bachelor's.

Special study options: academic remediation for entering students, accelerated degree program, adult/continuing education programs,

advanced placement credit, cooperative education, distance learning, double majors, honors programs, independent study, internships, off-campus study, part-time degree program, services for LD students, summer session for credit.

Computers: 17 computers/terminals and 144 ports are available on campus for general student use. Students can access the following: campus intranet, computer help desk, free student e-mail accounts, online (class) grades, online (class) registration, online (class) schedules. Campuswide network is available. 100% of college-owned or -operated housing units are wired for high-speed Internet access. Wireless service is available via entire campus.

STUDENT LIFE

Housing options: on-campus residence required through senior year; men-only, women-only, special housing for students with disabilities. Campus housing is university owned and leased by the school. Freshman campus housing is guaranteed.

Activities and organizations: choral group, SGA, GCMF, Prayer Group, Trinity Against Trafficking, Film Crew.

Athletics Member NCCAA. except basketball (Division II), volleyball (Division II)***Intercollegiate sports:*** basketball M, volleyball W. ***Intramural sports:*** soccer M.

Campus security: student patrols.

Student services: personal/psychological counseling.

COSTS & FINANCIAL AID

Costs (2014–15) ***Comprehensive fee:*** $22,100 includes full-time tuition ($14,850), mandatory fees ($800), and room and board ($6450). Full-time tuition and fees vary according to program. Part-time tuition: $495 per credit hour. Part-time tuition and fees vary according to program. ***Required fees:*** $400 per term part-time. ***Payment plan:*** installment. ***Waivers:*** senior citizens and employees or children of employees.

Financial Aid Of all full-time matriculated undergraduates who enrolled in 2014, 175 applied for aid, 170 were judged to have need, 21 had their need fully met. 16 Federal Work-Study jobs (averaging $3055). 1 state and other part-time job (averaging $1903). In 2014, 14 non-need-based awards were made. ***Average percent of need met:*** 59. ***Average financial aid package:*** $14,321. ***Average need-based loan:*** $8915. ***Average need-based gift aid:*** $6747. ***Average non-need-based aid:*** $1596. ***Average indebtedness upon graduation:*** $28,201.

APPLYING

Standardized Tests *Required:* SAT or ACT (for admission).

Options: electronic application, deferred entrance.

Application fee: $35.

Required: essay or personal statement, high school transcript, 2 letters of recommendation. ***Required for some:*** interview. ***Recommended:*** minimum 2.0 GPA.

Application deadlines: 7/31 (freshmen), 7/31 (out-of-state freshmen), 7/31 (transfers).

Notification: continuous (freshmen), continuous (out-of-state freshmen), continuous (transfers).

CONTACT

Mr. Timothy Bettelli, Director of Admissions/Marketing Coordinator, Trinity College of Florida, 2430 Welbilt Boulevard, Trinity, FL 34655. *Phone:* 727-376-6911 Ext. 309. *Toll-free phone:* 800-388-0869. *Fax:* 727-569-1410. *E-mail:* timothy.bettelli@trinitycollege.edu.

University of Central Florida

Orlando, Florida

http://www.ucf.edu/

- **State-supported** university, founded 1963, part of State University System of Florida
- **Suburban** 1415-acre campus with easy access to Orlando
- **Endowment** $152.7 million
- **Coed** 52,532 undergraduate students, 69% full-time, 55% women, 45% men
- **Moderately difficult** entrance level, 50% of applicants were admitted

UNDERGRAD STUDENTS

36,428 full-time, 16,104 part-time. Students come from 50 states and territories; 140 other countries; 5% are from out of state; 11% Black or

African American, non-Hispanic/Latino; 23% Hispanic/Latino; 6% Asian, non-Hispanic/Latino; 0.2% Native Hawaiian or other Pacific Islander, non-Hispanic/Latino; 0.2% American Indian or Alaska Native, non-Hispanic/Latino; 3% Two or more races, non-Hispanic/Latino; 0.7% Race/ethnicity unknown; 1% international; 12% transferred in; 18% live on campus.

Freshmen
Admission: 33,226 applied, 16,483 admitted, 6,467 enrolled. ***Average high school GPA:*** 3.86. ***Test scores:*** SAT critical reading scores over 500: 92%; SAT math scores over 500: 94%; SAT writing scores over 500: 84%; ACT scores over 18: 100%; SAT critical reading scores over 600: 47%; SAT math scores over 600: 50%; SAT writing scores over 600: 32%; ACT scores over 24: 79%; SAT critical reading scores over 700: 7%; SAT math scores over 700: 7%; SAT writing scores over 700: 4%; ACT scores over 30: 14%.

Retention: 88% of full-time freshmen returned.

FACULTY
Total: 1,823, 73% full-time, 67% with terminal degrees.

Student/faculty ratio: 31:1.

ACADEMICS
Calendar: semesters. *Degrees:* certificates, associate, bachelor's, master's, doctoral, and postbachelor's certificates.

Special study options: accelerated degree program, adult/continuing education programs, advanced placement credit, cooperative education, distance learning, double majors, English as a second language, freshman honors college, honors programs, independent study, internships, off-campus study, part-time degree program, services for LD students, study abroad, summer session for credit. ***ROTC:*** Army (b), Air Force (b).

Unusual degree programs: 3-2 business administration; engineering; nursing; history; communicative sciences and disorders; computer science; law.

Computers: 4,260 computers/terminals and 450 ports are available on campus for general student use. Students can access the following: campus intranet, computer help desk, free student e-mail accounts, online (class) grades, online (class) registration, online (class) schedules. Campuswide network is available. 100% of college-owned or -operated housing units are wired for high-speed Internet access. Wireless service is available via entire campus.

STUDENT LIFE
Housing options: coed, men-only, women-only, special housing for students with disabilities. Campus housing is university owned and is provided by a third party. Freshman applicants given priority for college housing.

Activities and organizations: drama/theater group, student-run newspaper, radio and television station, choral group, marching band, Volunteer UCF, RWC Intramural Sports, Fraternity & Sorority Life, Multicultural Student Center and Organizations, Knight-thon Dance Marathon, national fraternities, national sororities.

Athletics Member NCAA. All Division I except football (Division I-A). ***Intercollegiate sports:*** baseball M(s), basketball M(s)/W(s), crew W(s), cross-country running W(s), golf M(s)/W(s), soccer M(s)/W(s), softball W(s), tennis M(s)/W(s), track and field W(s), volleyball W(s). ***Intramural sports:*** badminton M/W, baseball M, basketball M/W, bowling M/W, crew M(c), equestrian sports M(c)/W(c), fencing M(c), golf M, ice hockey M(c), lacrosse M(c)/W(c), racquetball M/W, rock climbing M(c)/W(c), rugby M(c)/W(c), soccer M/W, softball W(c), swimming and diving M(c)/W(c), table tennis M(c)/W(c), tennis M/W, ultimate Frisbee M(c)/W(c), volleyball M/W, water polo M(c)/W(c), wrestling M(c)/W(c).

Campus security: 24-hour emergency response devices and patrols, late-night transport/escort service, controlled dormitory access.

Student services: health clinic, personal/psychological counseling, women's center, legal services.

COSTS & FINANCIAL AID
Costs (2014–15) ***Tuition:*** state resident $6368 full-time, $212 per credit hour part-time; nonresident $22,467 full-time, $749 per credit hour part-time. Full-time tuition and fees vary according to course load. Part-time tuition and fees vary according to course load. ***Room and board:*** $9300; room only: $5400. Room and board charges vary according to board plan and housing facility. ***Payment plans:*** tuition prepayment, deferred payment. ***Waivers:*** senior citizens and employees or children of employees.

Financial Aid Of all full-time matriculated undergraduates who enrolled in 2013, 31,410 applied for aid, 23,714 were judged to have need, 1,650 had their need fully met. 563 Federal Work-Study jobs (averaging $3445). In 2013, 1544 non-need-based awards were made. ***Average percent of need met:*** 57. ***Average financial aid package:*** $8295. ***Average need-based loan:*** $4584. ***Average need-based gift aid:*** $4953. ***Average non-need-based aid:*** $3459. ***Average indebtedness upon graduation:*** $23,378. ***Financial aid deadline:*** 6/30.

APPLYING
Standardized Tests *Required:* SAT or ACT (for admission).

Options: electronic application, early admission.

Application fee: $30.

Required: high school transcript, minimum 2.0 GPA. ***Recommended:*** essay or personal statement.

Application deadlines: 5/1 (freshmen), 7/1 (transfers).

Notification: continuous (freshmen), continuous (transfers).

CONTACT
Dr. Gordon Chavis Jr., Associate Vice President, Undergraduate Admissions, Student Financial Assistance and Outreach Programs, University of Central Florida, PO Box 160111, Orlando, FL 32816-0111. *Phone:* 407-823-3000. *Fax:* 407-823-5625. *E-mail:* admission@ucf.edu.

See previous page for display ad and page 1658 for the College Close-Up.

University of Florida
Gainesville, Florida
http://www.ufl.edu/

- **State-supported** university, founded 1853, part of Board of Trustees
- **Suburban** 2000-acre campus with easy access to Jacksonville
- **Endowment** $1.5 billion
- **Coed** 33,720 undergraduate students, 90% full-time, 55% women, 45% men
- **Very difficult** entrance level, 47% of applicants were admitted

UNDERGRAD STUDENTS
30,248 full-time, 3,472 part-time. Students come from 51 states and territories; 130 other countries; 6% are from out of state; 7% Black or African American, non-Hispanic/Latino; 20% Hispanic/Latino; 8% Asian, non-Hispanic/Latino; 0.6% Native Hawaiian or other Pacific Islander, non-Hispanic/Latino; 0.3% American Indian or Alaska Native, non-Hispanic/Latino; 3% Two or more races, non-Hispanic/Latino; 3% Race/ethnicity unknown; 1% international; 6% transferred in; 23% live on campus.

Freshmen
Admission: 27,852 applied, 13,111 admitted, 6,524 enrolled. ***Test scores:*** SAT critical reading scores over 500: 96%; SAT math scores over 500: 97%; SAT writing scores over 500: 95%; ACT scores over 18: 98%; SAT critical reading scores over 600: 68%; SAT math scores over 600: 74%; SAT writing scores over 600: 67%; ACT scores over 24: 90%; SAT critical reading scores over 700: 16%; SAT math scores over 700: 22%; SAT writing scores over 700: 17%; ACT scores over 30: 38%.

ACADEMICS
Calendar: semesters. *Degrees:* certificates, bachelor's, master's, doctoral, post-master's, and postbachelor's certificates.

Special study options: accelerated degree program, adult/continuing education programs, advanced placement credit, cooperative education, distance learning, double majors, English as a second language, external degree program, honors programs, independent study, internships, off-campus study, part-time degree program, services for LD students, student-designed majors, study abroad, summer session for credit. ***ROTC:*** Army (b), Navy (b), Air Force (b).

Unusual degree programs: 3-2 business administration; engineering.

Computers: 2,071 computers/terminals and 741 ports are available on campus for general student use. Students can access the following: campus intranet, computer help desk, free student e-mail accounts, online (class) grades, online (class) registration, online (class) schedules, course management system. Campuswide network is available. 100% of college-owned or -operated housing units are wired for high-speed Internet access.

Wireless service is available via classrooms, computer centers, computer labs, dorm rooms, learning centers, libraries, student centers.

STUDENT LIFE

Housing options: coed, special housing for students with disabilities. Campus housing is university owned. Freshman applicants given priority for college housing.

Activities and organizations: drama/theater group, student-run newspaper, radio and television station, choral group, marching band, VISA - Volunteers for International Student Affairs, Fellowship of Christian Athletes, Black Student Union, Hispanic Student Association, Asian American Student Union, national fraternities, national sororities.

Athletics Member NCAA. All Division I. ***Intercollegiate sports:*** baseball M(s), basketball M(s)/W(s), bowling M(c)/W(c), cheerleading M(s)/W(s), cross-country running M(s)/W(s), football M(s), golf M(s)/W(s), gymnastics W(s), lacrosse W(s), racquetball M(c)/W(c), soccer M/W(s), softball W(s), swimming and diving M(s)/W(s), table tennis M(c)/W(c), tennis M(s)/W(s), track and field M(s)/W(s), ultimate Frisbee M(c)/W(c), volleyball M/W(s). ***Intramural sports:*** archery M(c)/W(c), badminton M(c)/W(c), baseball M(c), basketball M/W, bowling M/W, cheerleading W(c), crew M(c)/W(c), cross-country running M(c)/W(c), equestrian sports M(c)/W(c), fencing M(c)/W(c), football M/W, golf M/W, gymnastics W(c), ice hockey M(c), lacrosse M(c)/W(c), racquetball M/W, rock climbing M(c)/W(c), rugby M(c)/W(c), sailing M(c)/W(c), soccer M/W, softball M/W, swimming and diving M/W, table tennis M/W, tennis M/W, track and field M/W, ultimate Frisbee M/W, volleyball M/W, water polo M(c)/W(c), wrestling M(c)/W(c).

Campus security: 24-hour emergency response devices and patrols, student patrols, late-night transport/escort service, controlled dormitory access, crime and rape prevention programs.

Student services: health clinic, personal/psychological counseling, legal services.

COSTS & FINANCIAL AID

Costs (2014–15) ***Tuition:*** state resident $4477 full-time, $149 per credit hour part-time; nonresident $25,694 full-time, $856 per credit hour part-time. Full-time tuition and fees vary according to course level, location, and program. Part-time tuition and fees vary according to course level, location, and program. ***Room and board:*** $9630; room only: $5340. Room and board charges vary according to board plan and housing facility. ***Payment plan:*** deferred payment. ***Waivers:*** senior citizens and employees or children of employees.

Financial Aid Of all full-time matriculated undergraduates who enrolled in 2013, 27,502 applied for aid, 18,604 were judged to have need, 3,699 had their need fully met. 659 Federal Work-Study jobs (averaging $2277). 4,308 state and other part-time jobs (averaging $2043). In 2013, 1657 non-need-based awards were made. ***Average percent of need met:*** 96. ***Average financial aid package:*** $11,597. ***Average need-based loan:*** $4592. ***Average need-based gift aid:*** $6778. ***Average non-need-based aid:*** $2437. ***Average indebtedness upon graduation:*** $20,642.

APPLYING

Standardized Tests *Required:* SAT or ACT (for admission). *Required for some:* SAT Subject Tests (for admission).

Options: electronic application, early admission.

Application fee: $30.

Required: essay or personal statement, Self-reported academic record required for current high school students while applying; those already graduated send their final high school transcript. All admitted students will be asked to send their final high school transcript after graduation.

Application deadlines: 11/1 (freshmen), rolling (transfers).

Notification: 2/13 (freshmen), continuous (transfers).

CONTACT

Office of Admissions, University of Florida, PO Box 114000, Gainesville, FL 32611-4000. *Phone:* 352-392-1365.

University of Miami

Coral Gables, Florida

http://www.miami.edu/

- **Independent** university, founded 1925
- **Suburban** 239-acre campus with easy access to Miami
- **Endowment** $865.4 million
- **Coed** 11,273 undergraduate students, 94% full-time, 51% women, 49% men
- **Very difficult** entrance level, 38% of applicants were admitted

UNDERGRAD STUDENTS

10,619 full-time, 654 part-time. Students come from 54 states and territories; 106 other countries; 55% are from out of state; 7% Black or African American, non-Hispanic/Latino; 21% Hispanic/Latino; 6% Asian, non-Hispanic/Latino; 0.1% Native Hawaiian or other Pacific Islander, non-Hispanic/Latino; 0.1% American Indian or Alaska Native, non-Hispanic/Latino; 3% Two or more races, non-Hispanic/Latino; 5% Race/ethnicity unknown; 14% international; 5% transferred in; 37% live on campus.

Freshmen

Admission: 31,607 applied, 12,064 admitted, 2,076 enrolled. ***Average high school GPA:*** 4.3. ***Test scores:*** SAT critical reading scores over 500: 96%; SAT math scores over 500: 98%; SAT writing scores over 500: 96%; ACT scores over 18: 100%; SAT critical reading scores over 600: 76%; SAT math scores over 600: 84%; SAT writing scores over 600: 73%; ACT scores over 24: 95%; SAT critical reading scores over 700: 23%; SAT math scores over 700: 39%; SAT writing scores over 700: 25%; ACT scores over 30: 61%.

Retention: 93% of full-time freshmen returned.

FACULTY

Total: 1,542, 70% full-time, 81% with terminal degrees.

Student/faculty ratio: 12:1.

ACADEMICS

Calendar: semesters. *Degrees:* certificates, bachelor's, master's, doctoral, post-master's, and postbachelor's certificates.

Special study options: academic remediation for entering students, accelerated degree program, advanced placement credit, cooperative education, distance learning, double majors, English as a second language, honors programs, independent study, internships, off-campus study, part-time degree program, services for LD students, student-designed majors, study abroad, summer session for credit. ***ROTC:*** Army (b), Air Force (b).

Computers: 400 computers/terminals and 600 ports are available on campus for general student use. Students can access the following: campus intranet, computer help desk, free student e-mail accounts, online (class) grades, online (class) registration, online (class) schedules, online bill payment, online housing registration. Campuswide network is available. 100% of college-owned or -operated housing units are wired for high-speed Internet access. Wireless service is available via entire campus.

STUDENT LIFE

Housing options: on-campus residence required for freshman year; coed, special housing for students with disabilities. Campus housing is university owned. Freshman campus housing is guaranteed.

Activities and organizations: drama/theater group, student-run newspaper, radio and television station, choral group, marching band, Association of Greek Letter Organizations, Federation of Cuban Students, Association of Commuter Students, United Black Students, Chinese Students and Scholars Association, national fraternities, national sororities.

Athletics Member NCAA. All Division I except football (Division I-A). ***Intercollegiate sports:*** baseball M(s), basketball M(s)/W(s), cheerleading M/W, crew W(s), cross-country running M(s)/W(s), golf W(s), soccer W(s), swimming and diving M(s)/W(s), tennis M(s)/W(s), track and field M(s)/W(s), volleyball W(s). ***Intramural sports:*** badminton M(c)/W(c), baseball M(c), basketball M/W, cross-country running M(c)/W(c), equestrian sports M(c)/W(c), fencing M(c)/W(c), field hockey W(c), football M/W, golf M(c)/W(c), ice hockey M(c), lacrosse M(c)/W(c), racquetball M(c)/W(c), rock climbing M(c)/W(c), rugby M(c)/W(c), sailing M(c)/W(c), soccer M(c)/W(c), softball M/W, squash M(c)/W(c), swimming and diving M(c)/W(c), table tennis M(c)/W(c), tennis

M(c)/W(c), ultimate Frisbee M(c)/W(c), volleyball M(c)/W(c), water polo M(c)/W(c), weight lifting M/W, wrestling M(c)/W(c).

Campus security: 24-hour emergency response devices and patrols, student patrols, late-night transport/escort service, controlled dormitory access, programs, seminars, activities, classes and publications are available to students, faculty, staff, parents and friends.

Student services: health clinic, personal/psychological counseling, women's center.

COSTS & FINANCIAL AID

Costs (2014–15) ***Comprehensive fee:*** $57,034 includes full-time tuition ($43,040), mandatory fees ($1310), and room and board ($12,684). Full-time tuition and fees vary according to course load. Part-time tuition: $1790 per credit hour. Part-time tuition and fees vary according to course load and program. ***College room only:*** $7336. Room and board charges vary according to board plan and housing facility. ***Payment plan:*** installment. ***Waivers:*** employees or children of employees.

Financial Aid Of all full-time matriculated undergraduates who enrolled in 2014, 5,629 applied for aid, 4,540 were judged to have need, 1,345 had their need fully met. 2,010 Federal Work-Study jobs (averaging $3000). 1,700 state and other part-time jobs (averaging $3000). In 2014, 2397 non-need-based awards were made. ***Average percent of need met:*** 75. ***Average financial aid package:*** $33,539. ***Average need-based loan:*** $5770. ***Average need-based gift aid:*** $25,950. ***Average non-need-based aid:*** $18,846. ***Average indebtedness upon graduation:*** $26,793.

APPLYING

Standardized Tests *Required:* SAT or ACT (for admission). *Required for some:* SAT and SAT Subject Tests or ACT (for admission).

Options: electronic application, early admission, early decision, early action, deferred entrance.

Application fee: $70.

Required: essay or personal statement, 1 letter of recommendation, College transcript(s) and statement of good standing from prior institution(s). Standardized test scores are required of some. ***Required for some:*** high school transcript, interview.

Application deadlines: 1/1 (freshmen), 3/1 (transfers), 11/1 (early action).

Early decision deadline: 11/1.

Notification: 4/15 (freshmen), 3/1 (transfers), 12/20 (early decision), 2/1 (early action).

CONTACT

Ms. Deanna Lynn Voss, Executive Director of Undergraduate Admission, University of Miami, PO Box 248025, Coral Gables, FL 33124. *Phone:* 305-284-4323. *Fax:* 305-284-6605. *E-mail:* admission@miami.edu.

University of North Florida

Jacksonville, Florida

http://www.unf.edu/

- **State-supported** comprehensive, founded 1965, part of State University System of Florida
- **Urban** 1300-acre campus
- **Endowment** $94.9 million
- **Coed** 14,121 undergraduate students, 70% full-time, 55% women, 45% men
- **Moderately difficult** entrance level, 61% of applicants were admitted

UNDERGRAD STUDENTS

9,901 full-time, 4,220 part-time. Students come from 48 states and territories; 59 other countries; 3% are from out of state; 10% Black or African American, non-Hispanic/Latino; 10% Hispanic/Latino; 4% Asian, non-Hispanic/Latino; 0.1% Native Hawaiian or other Pacific Islander, non-Hispanic/Latino; 0.1% American Indian or Alaska Native, non-Hispanic/Latino; 5% Two or more races, non-Hispanic/Latino; 0.3% Race/ethnicity unknown; 1% international; 11% transferred in; 23% live on campus.

Freshmen

Admission: 11,154 applied, 6,756 admitted, 1,859 enrolled. ***Average high school GPA:*** 3.72. ***Test scores:*** SAT critical reading scores over 500: 92%; SAT math scores over 500: 90%; SAT writing scores over 500: 79%; ACT scores over 18: 99%; SAT critical reading scores over 600: 40%; SAT math scores over 600: 34%; SAT writing scores over 600: 26%; ACT scores over 24: 51%; SAT critical reading scores over 700: 6%; SAT math scores over 700: 4%; SAT writing scores over 700: 2%; ACT scores over 30: 6%.

Retention: 83% of full-time freshmen returned.

FACULTY

Total: 873, 60% full-time, 61% with terminal degrees.

Student/faculty ratio: 20:1.

ACADEMICS

Calendar: semesters. *Degrees:* associate, bachelor's, master's, doctoral, post-master's, and postbachelor's certificates (doctoral degree in education only).

Special study options: accelerated degree program, adult/continuing education programs, advanced placement credit, cooperative education, distance learning, double majors, English as a second language, honors programs, independent study, internships, off-campus study, part-time degree program, services for LD students, study abroad, summer session for credit. ***ROTC:*** Army (b), Navy (c).

Unusual degree programs: 3-2 Accelerated BS/MS Computer Science Program. The School of Computing offers an accelerated program which allows students to obtain both Bachelor's and Master's Degrees in Computer Science in as little as 5 years. You must apply to the School for acceptance into this accelerated program.

Computers: 700 computers/terminals are available on campus for general student use. Students can access the following: campus intranet, computer help desk, free student e-mail accounts, online (class) grades, online (class) registration, online (class) schedules, reduced prices for students on certain business and design software. Campuswide network is available. 100% of college-owned or -operated housing units are wired for high-speed Internet access. Wireless service is available via entire campus.

STUDENT LIFE

Housing options: on-campus residence required for freshman year; coed, special housing for students with disabilities. Campus housing is university owned. Freshman campus housing is guaranteed.

Activities and organizations: drama/theater group, student-run newspaper, radio and television station, choral group, Student Government Association, African American Student Association, International Student Association, Filipino Student Association, National Education Association, national fraternities, national sororities.

Athletics Member NCAA. All Division I. ***Intercollegiate sports:*** baseball M(s), basketball M(s)/W(s), cross-country running M(s)/W(s), golf M(s)/W, soccer M(s)/W(s), softball W(s), swimming and diving W(s), tennis M(s)/W(s), track and field M(s)/W(s), volleyball W(s). ***Intramural sports:*** badminton M/W, basketball M/W, bowling M/W, fencing M(c)/W(c), football M/W, golf M/W, lacrosse M(c)/W(c), racquetball M(c)/W(c), rugby M(c), sailing M(c)/W(c), soccer M/W, swimming and diving M/W, table tennis M/W, track and field M/W, ultimate Frisbee M(c)/W(c), volleyball M(c)/W(c).

Campus security: 24-hour emergency response devices and patrols, late-night transport/escort service, controlled dormitory access, electronic parking lot security.

Student services: health clinic, personal/psychological counseling, women's center.

COSTS & FINANCIAL AID

Costs (2014–15) ***Tuition:*** state resident $4281 full-time, $143 per credit hour part-time; nonresident $17,999 full-time, $600 per credit hour part-time. Full-time tuition and fees vary according to course load. Part-time tuition and fees vary according to course load. ***Required fees:*** $2104 full-time, $70 per credit hour part-time. ***Room and board:*** $9204. Room and board charges vary according to board plan and housing facility. ***Payment plan:*** installment. ***Waivers:*** senior citizens and employees or children of employees.

Financial Aid Of all full-time matriculated undergraduates who enrolled in 2014, 7,324 applied for aid, 5,662 were judged to have need, 507 had their need fully met. 184 Federal Work-Study jobs (averaging $2921). In 2014, 1398 non-need-based awards were made. ***Average percent of need met:*** 91. ***Average financial aid package:*** $8668. ***Average need-based loan:*** $4762. ***Average need-based gift aid:*** $6060. ***Average non-need-based aid:*** $2970. ***Average indebtedness upon graduation:*** $19,253.

APPLYING

Standardized Tests *Required:* SAT or ACT (for admission).

Options: electronic application, deferred entrance.

Application fee: $30.

Required: high school transcript, minimum 2.5 GPA, Meet minimum test score requirements (460 SAT Critical Reading, 460 SAT Math, 440 SAT Writing; or 19 ACT Reading, 19 ACT Math, 18 ACT English/Writing). Note: Meeting minimum requirements does not guarantee admission. ***Required for some:*** essay or personal statement. ***Recommended:*** minimum 3.0 GPA.

Application deadlines: rolling (freshmen), 8/8 (transfers).

Notification: continuous (freshmen), continuous (transfers).

CONTACT

Mr. John Yancey, Director of Admissions, University of North Florida, 1 UNF Drive, Jacksonville, FL 32224. *Phone:* 904-620-2624. *Fax:* 904-620-2014. *E-mail:* admissions@unf.edu.

University of South Florida

Tampa, Florida

http://www.usf.edu/

- **State-supported** university, founded 1956, part of State University System of Florida
- **Urban** 1562-acre campus
- **Endowment** $417.3 million
- **Coed** 31,067 undergraduate students, 77% full-time, 55% women, 45% men
- **Moderately difficult** entrance level, 47% of applicants were admitted

UNDERGRAD STUDENTS

23,783 full-time, 7,284 part-time. Students come from 51 states and territories; 140 other countries; 6% are from out of state; 11% Black or African American, non-Hispanic/Latino; 20% Hispanic/Latino; 6% Asian, non-Hispanic/Latino; 0.3% Native Hawaiian or other Pacific Islander, non-Hispanic/Latino; 0.2% American Indian or Alaska Native, non-Hispanic/Latino; 4% Two or more races, non-Hispanic/Latino; 1% Race/ethnicity unknown; 5% international; 11% transferred in; 18% live on campus.

Freshmen

Admission: 27,987 applied, 13,285 admitted, 4,116 enrolled. ***Average high school GPA:*** 3.9. ***Test scores:*** SAT critical reading scores over 500: 90%; SAT math scores over 500: 93%; SAT writing scores over 500: 82%; ACT scores over 18: 100%; SAT critical reading scores over 600: 37%; SAT math scores over 600: 44%; SAT writing scores over 600: 27%; ACT scores over 24: 80%; SAT critical reading scores over 700: 5%; SAT math scores over 700: 6%; SAT writing scores over 700: 3%; ACT scores over 30: 14%.

Retention: 88% of full-time freshmen returned.

FACULTY

Total: 1,698, 73% full-time, 74% with terminal degrees.

Student/faculty ratio: 24:1.

ACADEMICS

Calendar: semesters. *Degrees:* associate, bachelor's, master's, and doctoral.

Special study options: academic remediation for entering students, accelerated degree program, adult/continuing education programs, advanced placement credit, cooperative education, distance learning, double majors, freshman honors college, honors programs, internships, off-campus study, part-time degree program, services for LD students, student-designed majors, study abroad, summer session for credit. ***ROTC:*** Army (b), Navy (b), Air Force (b).

Computers: 825 computers/terminals and 2,000 ports are available on campus for general student use. Students can access the following: campus intranet, computer help desk, free student e-mail accounts, online (class) grades, online (class) registration, online (class) schedules. Campuswide network is available. 100% of college-owned or -operated housing units are wired for high-speed Internet access. Wireless service is available via entire campus.

STUDENT LIFE

Housing options: on-campus residence required for freshman year; coed, men-only, women-only, cooperative, special housing for students with disabilities. Campus housing is university owned. Freshman campus housing is guaranteed.

Activities and organizations: drama/theater group, student-run newspaper, radio and television station, choral group, marching band, student government, Campus Activities Board, USF Ambassadors, Student Admissions Representatives, national fraternities, national sororities.

Athletics Member NCAA. All Division I except football (Division I-A). ***Intercollegiate sports:*** badminton M(c)/W(c), baseball M(s), basketball M(s)/W(s), bowling M(s)(c)/W(s)(c), crew M(c)/W(c), cross-country running M(s)/W(s), fencing M(c)/W(c), golf M(s)/W(s), gymnastics W(c), ice hockey M(c)/W(c), lacrosse M(c)/W(c), rugby M(c)/W(c), soccer M(s)/W(s), softball W(s), tennis M(s)/W(s), track and field M(s)/W(s), ultimate Frisbee M(c)/W(c), volleyball M(c)/W(s). ***Intramural sports:*** badminton M/W, basketball M/W, bowling M/W, cross-country running M/W, football M, golf M/W, racquetball M/W, soccer M/W, swimming and diving M/W, tennis M/W, track and field M/W, volleyball M/W.

Campus security: 24-hour emergency response devices and patrols, student patrols, late-night transport/escort service, controlled dormitory access, residence hall lobby personnel 8 pm to 6 am.

Student services: health clinic, personal/psychological counseling, women's center, legal services.

COSTS & FINANCIAL AID

Costs (2014–15) ***Tuition:*** state resident $4559 full-time, $211 per credit hour part-time; nonresident $15,474 full-time, $575 per credit hour part-time. Full-time tuition and fees vary according to course level, course load, and location. Part-time tuition and fees vary according to course level, course load, and location. ***Required fees:*** $1851 full-time, $37 per credit hour part-time. ***Room and board:*** $9400; room only: $5750. Room and board charges vary according to board plan, housing facility, and location. ***Payment plan:*** installment. ***Waivers:*** senior citizens.

Financial Aid Of all full-time matriculated undergraduates who enrolled in 2013, 23,523 applied for aid, 19,404 were judged to have need, 726 had their need fully met. 704 Federal Work-Study jobs (averaging $3180). 311 state and other part-time jobs (averaging $1772). In 2013, 1728 non-need-based awards were made. ***Average percent of need met:*** 50. ***Average financial aid package:*** $9309. ***Average need-based loan:*** $6987. ***Average need-based gift aid:*** $6757. ***Average non-need-based aid:*** $2576. ***Average indebtedness upon graduation:*** $22,611.

APPLYING

Standardized Tests *Required:* SAT or ACT (for admission).

Options: electronic application, early admission.

Application fee: $30.

Required: minimum 2.0 GPA. ***Required for some:*** high school transcript, 1 letter of recommendation.

Application deadlines: 3/1 (freshmen), 3/5 (transfers).

Notification: continuous (freshmen), continuous (transfers).

CONTACT

Ms. Amanda Dale, Associate Director of Recruitment, University of South Florida, Office of Undergraduate Admissions, 4202 East Fowler Avenue, Tampa, FL 33620-9951. *Phone:* 813-974-3350. *Fax:* 813-974-9689. *E-mail:* admissions@usf.edu.

University of South Florida, St. Petersburg

St. Petersburg, Florida

http://www.stpt.usf.edu/

- **State-supported** comprehensive, founded 1965, part of University of South Florida System
- **Urban** 50-acre campus with easy access to Tampa
- **Endowment** $16.1 million
- **Coed** 3,994 undergraduate students, 64% full-time, 60% women, 40% men

UNDERGRAD STUDENTS
2,542 full-time, 1,452 part-time. Students come from 32 states and territories; 10 other countries; 2% are from out of state; 7% Black or African American, non-Hispanic/Latino; 15% Hispanic/Latino; 4% Asian, non-Hispanic/Latino; 0.4% Native Hawaiian or other Pacific Islander, non-Hispanic/Latino; 0.3% American Indian or Alaska Native, non-Hispanic/Latino; 3% Two or more races, non-Hispanic/Latino; 1% Race/ethnicity unknown; 0.4% international; 13% transferred in; 15% live on campus.

Freshmen
Admission: 272 enrolled. ***Average high school GPA:*** 3.85. ***Test scores:*** SAT critical reading scores over 500: 89%; SAT math scores over 500: 87%; ACT scores over 18: 100%; SAT critical reading scores over 600: 35%; SAT math scores over 600: 26%; ACT scores over 24: 68%; SAT critical reading scores over 700: 4%; SAT math scores over 700: 2%; ACT scores over 30: 10%.

Retention: 65% of full-time freshmen returned.

FACULTY
Total: 263, 48% full-time, 76% with terminal degrees.

Student/faculty ratio: 17:1.

ACADEMICS
Calendar: semesters. *Degrees:* bachelor's and master's.

Special study options: distance learning, double majors, freshman honors college, honors programs, independent study, internships, services for LD students, study abroad, summer session for credit. ***ROTC:*** Army (b).

Computers: 125 computers/terminals and 350 ports are available on campus for general student use. Students can access the following: computer help desk, free student e-mail accounts, online (class) grades, online (class) registration, online (class) schedules. Campuswide network is available. 100% of college-owned or -operated housing units are wired for high-speed Internet access. Wireless service is available via entire campus.

STUDENT LIFE
Housing options: on-campus residence required for freshman year; coed. Campus housing is university owned and is provided by a third party. Freshman applicants given priority for college housing.

Activities and organizations: drama/theater group, student-run newspaper.

Athletics ***Intercollegiate sports:*** baseball M(c), sailing W(c). ***Intramural sports:*** basketball M/W, football M/W, sailing M/W, soccer M/W, volleyball M/W.

Campus security: 24-hour emergency response devices and patrols, late-night transport/escort service, controlled dormitory access.

Student services: health clinic, personal/psychological counseling.

COSTS
Costs (2014–15) ***Tuition:*** state resident $4206 full-time, $194 per credit hour part-time; nonresident $14,601 full-time, $557 per credit hour part-time. Out-of-state tuition and fee waivers for honorably discharged veterans of the United States Armed Forces, United States Reserve Forces, or the National Guard who physically reside within the state of Florida. ***Required fees:*** $1615 full-time. ***Room and board:*** $9400. Room and board charges vary according to board plan and housing facility. ***Payment plan:*** installment. ***Waivers:*** employees or children of employees.

APPLYING
Standardized Tests *Required:* SAT or ACT (for admission).

Required: high school transcript, minimum 2.5 GPA.

CONTACT
Ms. Holly Kickliter, Director, Enrollment Services, University of South Florida, St. Petersburg, 140 Seventh Avenue South, St. Petersburg, FL 33701. *Phone:* 727-873-4142. *Fax:* 727-873-4525. *E-mail:* admissions@usfsp.edu.

University of South Florida Sarasota-Manatee

Sarasota, Florida

http://www.usfsm.edu/

- **State-supported** comprehensive, founded 1956, part of University of South Florida System
- **Urban** 31-acre campus with easy access to Tampa
- **Endowment** $9.6 million
- **Coed** 1,770 undergraduate students, 50% full-time, 59% women, 41% men

UNDERGRAD STUDENTS
887 full-time, 883 part-time. Students come from 14 states and territories; 3 other countries; 2% are from out of state; 7% Black or African American, non-Hispanic/Latino; 14% Hispanic/Latino; 2% Asian, non-Hispanic/Latino; 0.1% Native Hawaiian or other Pacific Islander, non-Hispanic/Latino; 0.4% American Indian or Alaska Native, non-Hispanic/Latino; 2% Two or more races, non-Hispanic/Latino; 2% Race/ethnicity unknown; 0.5% international; 22% transferred in.

Freshmen
Admission: 91 enrolled. ***Average high school GPA:*** 3.7. ***Test scores:*** SAT critical reading scores over 500: 76%; SAT math scores over 500: 78%; SAT writing scores over 500: 70%; ACT scores over 18: 99%; SAT critical reading scores over 600: 29%; SAT math scores over 600: 19%; SAT writing scores over 600: 14%; ACT scores over 24: 51%; SAT critical reading scores over 700: 3%; SAT math scores over 700: 1%; ACT scores over 30: 3%.

Retention: 72% of full-time freshmen returned.

FACULTY
Total: 135, 56% full-time, 63% with terminal degrees.

Student/faculty ratio: 13:1.

ACADEMICS
Calendar: semesters. *Degrees:* certificates, associate, bachelor's, master's, and post-master's certificates.

Special study options: advanced placement credit, distance learning, double majors, honors programs, independent study, internships, part-time degree program, services for LD students, study abroad, summer session for credit. ***ROTC:*** Army (c), Navy (c), Air Force (c).

Computers: 41 computers/terminals and 57 ports are available on campus for general student use. Students can access the following: campus intranet, computer help desk, free student e-mail accounts, online (class) grades, online (class) registration, online (class) schedules. Campuswide network is available. Wireless service is available via entire campus.

STUDENT LIFE
Housing options: college housing not available.

Activities and organizations: Accounting Society, Campus Activities Board, Psychology Club, Educator's Alliance, Adventure Club.

Campus security: 24-hour emergency response devices and patrols, late-night transport/escort service.

Student services: health clinic, personal/psychological counseling.

COSTS
Costs (2014–15) ***Tuition:*** state resident $4206 full-time, $186 per credit hour part-time; nonresident $15,120 full-time, $550 per credit hour part-time. Full-time tuition and fees vary according to course load and program. Part-time tuition and fees vary according to course load and program. ***Required fees:*** $1381 full-time, $5 per term part-time. ***Waivers:*** employees or children of employees.

APPLYING
Standardized Tests *Required:* SAT or ACT (for admission). *Required for some:* SAT Subject Tests (for admission). *Recommended:* SAT Subject Tests (for admission).

Required: high school transcript, minimum 3.3 GPA. ***Required for some:*** minimum 3.3 GPA, interview. ***Recommended:*** essay or personal statement, minimum 3.3 GPA, 2 letters of recommendation.

CONTACT
Mr. Andy Telatovich, Director, Admissions, University of South Florida Sarasota-Manatee, 8350 N. Tamiami Trail, C107, Sarasota, FL 34232.

Phone: 941-359-4330. *Fax:* 941-359-4236. *E-mail:* atelatovich@sar.usf.edu.

The University of Tampa

Tampa, Florida

http://www.ut.edu/

- **Independent** comprehensive, founded 1931
- **Urban** 100-acre campus with easy access to Tampa-St. Petersburg, Clearwater
- **Coed** 8,045 undergraduate students, 96% full-time, 63% women, 37% men
- **Moderately difficult** entrance level, 52% of applicants were admitted

UNDERGRAD STUDENTS

7,752 full-time, 293 part-time. Students come from 50 states and territories; 137 other countries; 67% are from out of state; 5% Black or African American, non-Hispanic/Latino; 12% Hispanic/Latino; 1% Asian, non-Hispanic/Latino; 0.1% Native Hawaiian or other Pacific Islander, non-Hispanic/Latino; 0.2% American Indian or Alaska Native, non-Hispanic/Latino; 3% Two or more races, non-Hispanic/Latino; 8% Race/ethnicity unknown; 10% international; 6% transferred in; 61% live on campus.

Freshmen

Admission: 17,208 applied, 8,927 admitted, 1,753 enrolled. ***Average high school GPA:*** 3.3. ***Test scores:*** SAT critical reading scores over 500: 71%; SAT math scores over 500: 78%; SAT writing scores over 500: 69%; ACT scores over 18: 99%; SAT critical reading scores over 600: 19%; SAT math scores over 600: 20%; SAT writing scores over 600: 16%; ACT scores over 24: 56%; SAT critical reading scores over 700: 1%; SAT math scores over 700: 1%; SAT writing scores over 700: 1%; ACT scores over 30: 6%.

Retention: 72% of full-time freshmen returned.

FACULTY

Total: 675, 42% full-time, 56% with terminal degrees.

Student/faculty ratio: 17:1.

ACADEMICS

Calendar: semesters. *Degrees:* certificates, associate, bachelor's, master's, and post-master's certificates.

Special study options: academic remediation for entering students, adult/continuing education programs, advanced placement credit, cooperative education, double majors, English as a second language, honors programs, independent study, internships, part-time degree program, services for LD students, study abroad, summer session for credit. ***ROTC:*** Army (b), Navy (c), Air Force (c).

Unusual degree programs: 3-2 chemistry/MBA joint program.

Computers: 800 computers/terminals and 8,000 ports are available on campus for general student use. Students can access the following: campus intranet, computer help desk, free student e-mail accounts, online (class) grades, online (class) registration, online (class) schedules. Campuswide network is available. 100% of college-owned or -operated housing units are wired for high-speed Internet access. Wireless service is available via entire campus.

STUDENT LIFE

Housing options: coed, special housing for students with disabilities. Campus housing is university owned.

Activities and organizations: drama/theater group, student-run newspaper, radio and television station, choral group, Greek Life, student government, PEACE (volunteer organization), Student Productions, Minaret, national fraternities, national sororities.

Athletics Member NCAA. All Division II. ***Intercollegiate sports:*** baseball M(s), basketball M(s)/W(s), crew W(s), cross-country running M(s)/W(s), golf M(s)/W(s), lacrosse M(s), soccer M(s)/W(s), softball W(s), swimming and diving M(s)/W(s), tennis W(s), volleyball W(s). ***Intramural sports:*** basketball M/W, cheerleading W(c), crew M(c), field hockey W, football M/W, golf M/W, soccer M/W, softball M/W, swimming and diving M/W, table tennis W, tennis M/W, track and field M/W, ultimate Frisbee M/W, volleyball M/W.

Campus security: 24-hour emergency response devices and patrols, student patrols, late-night transport/escort service, controlled dormitory access.

Student services: health clinic, personal/psychological counseling, women's center.

COSTS & FINANCIAL AID

Costs (2014–15) ***One-time required fee:*** $85. ***Comprehensive fee:*** $35,954 includes full-time tuition ($24,528), mandatory fees ($1802), and room and board ($9624). Full-time tuition and fees vary according to class time, course load, and program. Part-time tuition: $522 per credit hour. Part-time tuition and fees vary according to class time, course load, and program. ***Required fees:*** $40 per term part-time. ***College room only:*** $5100. Room and board charges vary according to board plan and housing facility. ***Payment plan:*** installment. ***Waivers:*** employees or children of employees.

Financial Aid Of all full-time matriculated undergraduates who enrolled in 2014, 4,769 applied for aid, 3,922 were judged to have need, 364 had their need fully met. 301 Federal Work-Study jobs (averaging $2000). 4 state and other part-time jobs (averaging $2000). In 2014, 1810 non-need-based awards were made. ***Average percent of need met:*** 64. ***Average financial aid package:*** $16,667. ***Average need-based loan:*** $4368. ***Average need-based gift aid:*** $13,058. ***Average non-need-based aid:*** $7249. ***Average indebtedness upon graduation:*** $33,673.

APPLYING

Standardized Tests *Required:* SAT or ACT (for admission).

Options: electronic application, early admission, early action, deferred entrance.

Application fee: $40.

Required: essay or personal statement, high school transcript, minimum 2.0 GPA. ***Required for some:*** 1 letter of recommendation. ***Recommended:*** interview.

Application deadlines: rolling (freshmen), rolling (out-of-state freshmen), rolling (transfers), 5/1 (early action).

Notification: continuous (freshmen), continuous (out-of-state freshmen), continuous (transfers), 12/15 (early action).

CONTACT

Mr. Dennis Nostrand, Vice President for Enrollment, The University of Tampa, 401 West Kennedy Boulevard, Tampa, FL 33606-1480. *Phone:* 813-257-1808. *Toll-free phone:* 888-646-2738 (in-state); 888-MINARET (out-of-state). *Fax:* 813-258-7398. *E-mail:* admissions@ut.edu.

University of West Florida

Pensacola, Florida

http://www.uwf.edu/

- **State-supported** comprehensive, founded 1963, part of State University System of Florida
- **Suburban** 1600-acre campus
- **Endowment** $64.3 million
- **Coed** 10,072 undergraduate students, 73% full-time, 57% women, 43% men
- **Moderately difficult** entrance level, 42% of applicants were admitted

UNDERGRAD STUDENTS

7,394 full-time, 2,678 part-time. Students come from 50 states and territories; 80 other countries; 8% are from out of state; 12% Black or African American, non-Hispanic/Latino; 9% Hispanic/Latino; 3% Asian, non-Hispanic/Latino; 0.4% Native Hawaiian or other Pacific Islander, non-Hispanic/Latino; 0.6% American Indian or Alaska Native, non-Hispanic/Latino; 5% Two or more races, non-Hispanic/Latino; 2% Race/ethnicity unknown; 2% international; 11% transferred in; 18% live on campus.

Freshmen

Admission: 10,138 applied, 4,229 admitted, 1,237 enrolled. ***Average high school GPA:*** 3.51. ***Test scores:*** SAT critical reading scores over 500: 38%; SAT math scores over 500: 46%; SAT writing scores over 500: 52%; ACT scores over 18: 97%; SAT critical reading scores over 600: 2%; SAT math scores over 600: 2%; SAT writing scores over 600: 5%; ACT scores over 24: 47%; ACT scores over 30: 5%.

Retention: 74% of full-time freshmen returned.

FACULTY
Total: 598, 53% full-time.
Student/faculty ratio: 23:1.

ACADEMICS
Calendar: semesters. *Degrees:* associate, bachelor's, master's, doctoral, and post-master's certificates.

Special study options: advanced placement credit, cooperative education, distance learning, English as a second language, honors programs, independent study, internships, off-campus study, part-time degree program, services for LD students, study abroad, summer session for credit. ***ROTC:*** Army (b), Air Force (b).

Unusual degree programs: 3-2 business administration.

Computers: 1,246 computers/terminals and 50 ports are available on campus for general student use. Students can access the following: campus intranet, computer help desk, free student e-mail accounts, online (class) grades, online (class) registration, online (class) schedules. Campuswide network is available. 100% of college-owned or -operated housing units are wired for high-speed Internet access. Wireless service is available via entire campus.

STUDENT LIFE
Housing options: coed. Campus housing is university owned.

Activities and organizations: drama/theater group, student-run newspaper, choral group, Florida Engineering Society, Gay-Straight Alliance, Alpha Chi Omega, Baptist Collegiate Ministries, Kappa Delta, national fraternities, national sororities.

Athletics Member NCAA. All Division II. ***Intercollegiate sports:*** baseball M(s), basketball M(s)/W(s), cross-country running M(s)/W(s), golf M(s)/W(s), soccer M(s)/W(s), softball W(s), swimming and diving W(s), tennis M(s)/W(s), volleyball W(s). ***Intramural sports:*** basketball M/W, bowling M/W, cheerleading W, fencing M/W, football M/W, sailing M/W, soccer M/W, softball W, swimming and diving M/W, tennis M/W, volleyball M/W.

Campus security: 24-hour emergency response devices and patrols, student patrols, late-night transport/escort service, controlled dormitory access.

Student services: health clinic, personal/psychological counseling.

COSTS & FINANCIAL AID
Costs (2014–15) ***Tuition:*** state resident $6359 full-time, $212 per semester hour part-time; nonresident $19,241 full-time, $642 per semester hour part-time. Full-time tuition and fees vary according to location and reciprocity agreements. Part-time tuition and fees vary according to location and reciprocity agreements. ***Required fees:*** $2041 full-time. ***Room and board:*** $9912. Room and board charges vary according to board plan, housing facility, and student level. ***Payment plans:*** tuition prepayment, deferred payment. ***Waivers:*** senior citizens and employees or children of employees.

Financial Aid Of all full-time matriculated undergraduates who enrolled in 2013, 6,202 applied for aid, 4,964 were judged to have need, 686 had their need fully met. 369 Federal Work-Study jobs (averaging $1943). In 2013, 417 non-need-based awards were made. ***Average percent of need met:*** 60. ***Average financial aid package:*** $8868. ***Average need-based loan:*** $4203. ***Average need-based gift aid:*** $5563. ***Average non-need-based aid:*** $2891.

APPLYING
Standardized Tests *Required:* SAT or ACT (for admission), SAT and SAT Subject Tests or ACT (for admission).

Options: electronic application, early admission, deferred entrance.

Application fee: $30.

Required: high school transcript, minimum 2.5 GPA.

Application deadlines: 6/1 (freshmen), 6/1 (transfers).

Notification: continuous (freshmen), continuous (transfers).

CONTACT
Katie Condon, Director of Admissions, University of West Florida, Admissions, 11000 University Parkway, Pensacola, FL 32514. *Phone:* 850-474-2230. *Toll-free phone:* 800-263-1074. *Fax:* 850-474-3460. *E-mail:* admissions@uwf.edu.

Valencia College
Orlando, Florida
http://valenciacollege.edu/

- **State-supported** 4-year, founded 1967, part of Florida College System
- **Urban** 629-acre campus with easy access to Orlando
- **Endowment** $55.6 million
- **Coed** 42,915 undergraduate students, 40% full-time, 57% women, 43% men
- 90% of applicants were admitted

UNDERGRAD STUDENTS
16,998 full-time, 25,917 part-time. Students come from 59 other countries; 3% are from out of state; 17% Black or African American, non-Hispanic/Latino; 31% Hispanic/Latino; 4% Asian, non-Hispanic/Latino; 0.3% Native Hawaiian or other Pacific Islander, non-Hispanic/Latino; 0.3% American Indian or Alaska Native, non-Hispanic/Latino; 2% Two or more races, non-Hispanic/Latino; 9% Race/ethnicity unknown; 1% international; 9% transferred in.

Freshmen
Admission: 11,235 applied, 10,111 admitted, 8,055 enrolled.
Retention: 65% of full-time freshmen returned.

FACULTY
Total: 1,602, 25% full-time, 6% with terminal degrees.
Student/faculty ratio: 16:1.

ACADEMICS
Calendar: semesters. *Degrees:* certificates, diplomas, associate, and bachelor's.

Special study options: academic remediation for entering students, accelerated degree program, adult/continuing education programs, advanced placement credit, cooperative education, distance learning, double majors, English as a second language, external degree program, freshman honors college, honors programs, independent study, internships, part-time degree program, services for LD students, study abroad, summer session for credit. ***ROTC:*** Army (c), Navy (c).

Computers: Students can access the following: campus intranet, computer help desk, free student e-mail accounts, online (class) grades, online (class) registration, online (class) schedules, Emergency Alert System. Campuswide network is available. Wireless service is available via entire campus.

STUDENT LIFE
Housing options: college housing not available.

Activities and organizations: drama/theater group, student-run newspaper, choral group.

Athletics ***Intramural sports:*** baseball M/W, basketball M/W, racquetball M/W, rock climbing M/W, soccer M/W, softball M/W, tennis M/W, volleyball M/W, weight lifting M/W.

Campus security: 24-hour emergency response devices and patrols, student patrols, late-night transport/escort service.

Student services: personal/psychological counseling, legal services.

COSTS & FINANCIAL AID
Costs (2014–15) ***Tuition:*** state resident $2473 full-time, $103 per credit hour part-time; nonresident $9383 full-time, $391 per credit hour part-time. Full-time tuition and fees vary according to degree level. Part-time tuition and fees vary according to degree level. ***Payment plans:*** tuition prepayment, installment. ***Waivers:*** senior citizens and employees or children of employees.

Financial Aid Of all full-time matriculated undergraduates who enrolled in 2010, 21,366 applied for aid, 17,532 were judged to have need, 485 had their need fully met. 242 Federal Work-Study jobs (averaging $2608). 27 state and other part-time jobs (averaging $2738). In 2010, 93 non-need-based awards were made. ***Average percent of need met:*** 46. ***Average financial aid package:*** $7383. ***Average need-based loan:*** $3242. ***Average need-based gift aid:*** $3430. ***Average non-need-based aid:*** $642.

APPLYING
Options: electronic application, early admission, deferred entrance.

Application fee: $35.

Required: $35 Application fee for lower level (1000 and 2000 level courses) students and $50 application fee for Bachelor level students. ***Required for some:*** high school transcript.

Application deadlines: 8/12 (freshmen), 8/12 (out-of-state freshmen), 8/12 (transfers).

CONTACT

Dr. Renee Simpson, Assistant Vice President of Admissions and Records, Valencia College, Orlando, FL 32802-3028. *Phone:* 407-582-1511. *Fax:* 407-582-1866. *E-mail:* rsimpson@valenciacollege.edu.

★ Webber International University

Babson Park, Florida

http://www.webber.edu/

- **Independent** comprehensive, founded 1927
- **Small-town** 110-acre campus with easy access to Orlando
- **Coed** 681 undergraduate students, 95% full-time, 32% women, 68% men
- **Moderately difficult** entrance level, 51% of applicants were admitted

UNDERGRAD STUDENTS

647 full-time, 34 part-time. 13% are from out of state; 22% Black or African American, non-Hispanic/Latino; 11% Hispanic/Latino; 1% Asian, non-Hispanic/Latino; 0.3% American Indian or Alaska Native, non-Hispanic/Latino; 2% Two or more races, non-Hispanic/Latino; 0.6% Race/ethnicity unknown; 24% international; 16% transferred in; 52% live on campus.

Freshmen

Admission: 710 applied, 359 admitted, 178 enrolled. ***Average high school GPA:*** 3.14. ***Test scores:*** SAT critical reading scores over 500: 31%; ACT scores over 18: 77%; SAT critical reading scores over 600: 4%; ACT scores over 24: 10%.

FACULTY

Total: 44, 48% full-time, 50% with terminal degrees.

Student/faculty ratio: 23:1.

ACADEMICS

Calendar: semesters. *Degrees:* associate, bachelor's, and master's.

Special study options: academic remediation for entering students, accelerated degree program, adult/continuing education programs, advanced placement credit, cooperative education, distance learning, double majors, English as a second language, internships, part-time degree program, services for LD students, study abroad, summer session for credit.

Computers: Students can access the following: campus intranet, free student e-mail accounts, online (class) grades, online (class) schedules. Campuswide network is available. 100% of college-owned or -operated housing units are wired for high-speed Internet access. Wireless service is available via computer labs, libraries, student centers.

STUDENT LIFE

Housing options: on-campus residence required for freshman year; men-only, women-only. Campus housing is university owned and leased by the school. Freshman campus housing is guaranteed.

Activities and organizations: student-run newspaper, marching band, Student Leadership Association, Phi Beta Lambda, Society of International Students, Fellowship of Christian Athletes, Marketing Club.

Athletics Member NAIA. ***Intercollegiate sports:*** baseball M(s), basketball M(s)/W(s), bowling M(s)/W(s), cheerleading M(s)/W(s), cross-country running M(s)/W(s), football M(s), golf M(s)/W(s), soccer M(s)/W(s), softball W(s), tennis M(s)/W(s), track and field M(s)/W(s), volleyball W(s). ***Intramural sports:*** basketball M/W, football M/W, soccer M/W, softball W, table tennis M/W, tennis M/W, volleyball M(c)/W(c).

Campus security: 24-hour emergency response devices and patrols, late-night transport/escort service, controlled dormitory access.

Student services: health clinic, personal/psychological counseling.

COSTS & FINANCIAL AID

Costs (2014–15) ***Comprehensive fee:*** $32,278 includes full-time tuition ($21,686), mandatory fees ($2130), and room and board ($8462). Full-time tuition and fees vary according to class time and course load. Part-time tuition: $316 per credit hour. Part-time tuition and fees vary according to course load. ***College room only:*** $5432. Room and board charges vary according to board plan, gender, and housing facility.

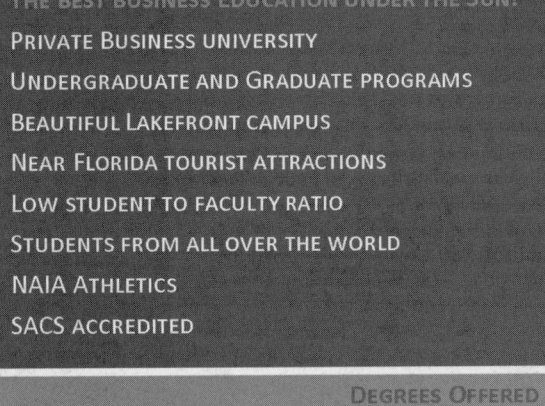

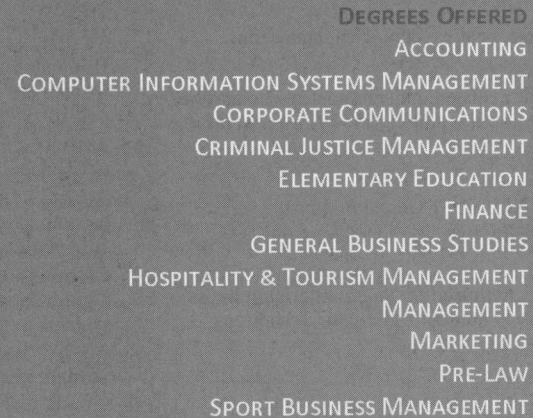

Payment plan: installment. ***Waivers:*** children of alumni, adult students, senior citizens, and employees or children of employees.

Financial Aid Of all full-time matriculated undergraduates who enrolled in 2014, 502 applied for aid, 462 were judged to have need, 36 had their need fully met. 35 Federal Work-Study jobs (averaging $1066). 38 state and other part-time jobs (averaging $952). In 2014, 187 non-need-based awards were made. ***Average percent of need met:*** 62. ***Average financial aid package:*** $19,410. ***Average need-based loan:*** $4132. ***Average need-based gift aid:*** $16,117. ***Average non-need-based aid:*** $10,302. ***Average indebtedness upon graduation:*** $24,578. ***Financial aid deadline:*** 8/1.

APPLYING

Standardized Tests *Required:* SAT or ACT (for admission).

Options: electronic application, early action.

Application fee: $35.

Required: high school transcript, minimum 2.0 GPA. ***Required for some:*** interview. ***Recommended:*** essay or personal statement.

CONTACT

Office of Admissions, Webber International University, P. O. Box 96, Babson Park, FL 33827. *Phone:* 863-638-2910. *Toll-free phone:* 800-741-1844. *Fax:* 863-638-1591. *E-mail:* admissions@webber.edu.

See previous page for display ad and page 1720 for the College Close-Up.

GEORGIA

Abraham Baldwin Agricultural College

Tifton, Georgia

http://www.abac.edu/

- **State-supported** 4-year, founded 1933, part of University System of Georgia
- **Small-town** 421-acre campus
- **Coed**
- **Minimally difficult** entrance level

FACULTY

Student/faculty ratio: 24:1.

ACADEMICS

Calendar: semesters. *Degrees:* certificates, associate, and bachelor's.

STUDENT LIFE

Housing options: on-campus residence required for freshman year; coed, special housing for students with disabilities. Campus housing is university owned. Freshman applicants given priority for college housing.

Activities and organizations: drama/theater group, student-run newspaper, radio station, choral group, Campus Activities Board, Baptist Collegiate Ministry, Forestry/Wildlife Club, Agriculture Engineering Technology, Residence Hall Association, national fraternities, national sororities.

Athletics Member NJCAA.

Campus security: 24-hour emergency response devices and patrols, controlled dormitory access.

Student services: health clinic, personal/psychological counseling.

FINANCIAL AID

Financial Aid Of all full-time matriculated undergraduates who enrolled in 2013, 133 Federal Work-Study jobs (averaging $1539). ***Financial aid deadline:*** 7/1.

APPLYING

Standardized Tests *Required:* SAT or ACT (for admission).

Options: electronic application, early admission, deferred entrance.

Application fee: $20.

Required: high school transcript. ***Required for some:*** minimum high school GPA of 2.0 for College Prep Diploma and 2.2 for Tech Prep Diploma.

CONTACT

Mrs. Donna Webb, Director of Enrollment Services, Abraham Baldwin Agricultural College, Box 4, 2802 Moore Highway, Tifton, GA 31793-2601. *Phone:* 229-391-5004. *Toll-free phone:* 800-733-3653. *Fax:* 229-391-5002. *E-mail:* dwebb@abac.edu.

Agnes Scott College

Decatur, Georgia

http://www.agnesscott.edu/

- **Independent** 4-year, founded 1889, affiliated with Presbyterian Church (U.S.A.)
- **Urban** 100-acre campus with easy access to Atlanta
- **Endowment** $272.3 million
- **Women only** 873 undergraduate students, 97% full-time
- **Moderately difficult** entrance level, 68% of applicants were admitted

UNDERGRAD STUDENTS

847 full-time, 26 part-time. Students come from 36 states and territories; 33 other countries; 42% are from out of state; 33% Black or African American, non-Hispanic/Latino; 9% Hispanic/Latino; 5% Asian, non-Hispanic/Latino; 0.2% Native Hawaiian or other Pacific Islander, non-Hispanic/Latino; 0.1% American Indian or Alaska Native, non-Hispanic/Latino; 6% Two or more races, non-Hispanic/Latino; 3% Race/ethnicity unknown; 12% international; 1% transferred in; 84% live on campus.

Freshmen

Admission: 1,394 applied, 944 admitted, 225 enrolled. ***Average high school GPA:*** 3.66. ***Test scores:*** SAT critical reading scores over 500: 92%; SAT math scores over 500: 89%; SAT writing scores over 500: 91%; ACT scores over 18: 100%; SAT critical reading scores over 600: 48%; SAT math scores over 600: 28%; SAT writing scores over 600: 46%; ACT scores over 24: 69%; SAT critical reading scores over 700: 13%; SAT math scores over 700: 3%; SAT writing scores over 700: 10%; ACT scores over 30: 16%.

Retention: 82% of full-time freshmen returned.

FACULTY

Total: 111, 66% full-time, 86% with terminal degrees.

Student/faculty ratio: 10:1.

ACADEMICS

Calendar: semesters. *Degree:* bachelor's.

Special study options: accelerated degree program, adult/continuing education programs, advanced placement credit, double majors, independent study, internships, off-campus study, part-time degree program, services for LD students, student-designed majors, study abroad, summer session for credit. ***ROTC:*** Army (c), Air Force (c).

Unusual degree programs: 3-2 engineering with Georgia Institute of Technology; nursing with Emory University; computer science with Emory University.

Computers: Students can access the following: campus intranet, computer help desk, free student e-mail accounts, online (class) grades, online (class) registration, online (class) schedules. Campuswide network is available. 100% of college-owned or -operated housing units are wired for high-speed Internet access. Wireless service is available via entire campus.

STUDENT LIFE

Housing options: on-campus residence required through senior year; women-only. Campus housing is university owned. Freshman campus housing is guaranteed.

Activities and organizations: drama/theater group, student-run newspaper, television station, choral group, marching band.

Athletics Member NCAA. All Division III. ***Intercollegiate sports:*** basketball W, cross-country running W, soccer W, softball W, tennis W, volleyball W. ***Intramural sports:*** swimming and diving W(c), tennis W.

Campus security: 24-hour emergency response devices and patrols, late-night transport/escort service, controlled dormitory access, security systems in apartments, public safety facility, surveillance equipment, key required for residence hall entry.

Student services: health clinic, personal/psychological counseling.

COSTS & FINANCIAL AID
Costs (2015–16) ***Comprehensive fee:*** $48,386 includes full-time tuition ($36,996), mandatory fees ($240), and room and board ($11,150). Part-time tuition and fees vary according to course load. ***Room and board:*** Room and board charges vary according to board plan and housing facility. ***Payment plan:*** installment. ***Waivers:*** employees or children of employees.

Financial Aid Of all full-time matriculated undergraduates who enrolled in 2013, 716 applied for aid, 656 were judged to have need, 153 had their need fully met. 290 Federal Work-Study jobs (averaging $2300). 30 state and other part-time jobs (averaging $2300). In 2013, 194 non-need-based awards were made. ***Average percent of need met:*** 87. ***Average financial aid package:*** $32,875. ***Average need-based loan:*** $4471. ***Average need-based gift aid:*** $26,590. ***Average non-need-based aid:*** $19,796. ***Average indebtedness upon graduation:*** $30,139. ***Financial aid deadline:*** 5/1.

APPLYING
Standardized Tests *Required for some:* SAT or ACT (for admission), SAT and SAT Subject Tests or ACT (for admission).

Options: electronic application, early admission, early decision, early action, deferred entrance.

Required: essay or personal statement, high school transcript. ***Recommended:*** interview.

Application deadlines: 3/15 (freshmen), 3/15 (transfers), 11/15 (early action).

Early decision deadline: 11/1.

Notification: continuous (transfers), 12/1 (early decision), 12/15 (early action).

CONTACT
Agnes Scott College, 141 East College Avenue, Decatur, GA 30030-3797. *Phone:* 404-471-6285. *Toll-free phone:* 800-868-8602.

Albany State University

Albany, Georgia

http://www.asurams.edu/

- **State-supported** comprehensive, founded 1903, part of University System of Georgia
- **Urban** 232-acre campus
- **Endowment** $1.8 million
- **Coed** 3,316 undergraduate students, 84% full-time, 67% women, 33% men
- **Minimally difficult** entrance level, 47% of applicants were admitted

UNDERGRAD STUDENTS
2,780 full-time, 536 part-time. 2% are from out of state; 89% Black or African American, non-Hispanic/Latino; 1% Hispanic/Latino; 0.1% Asian, non-Hispanic/Latino; 0.2% American Indian or Alaska Native, non-Hispanic/Latino; 1% Two or more races, non-Hispanic/Latino; 2% Race/ethnicity unknown; 0.4% international.

Freshmen
Admission: 2,381 applied, 1,126 admitted, 426 enrolled. ***Average high school GPA:*** 2.92. ***Test scores:*** SAT critical reading scores over 500: 16%; SAT math scores over 500: 13%; ACT scores over 18: 55%; SAT critical reading scores over 600: 1%; SAT math scores over 600: 1%; ACT scores over 24: 2%.

Retention: 69% of full-time freshmen returned.

FACULTY
Total: 220, 89% full-time.

Student/faculty ratio: 16:1.

ACADEMICS
Calendar: semesters. *Degrees:* bachelor's, master's, and post-master's certificates.

Special study options: academic remediation for entering students, adult/continuing education programs, advanced placement credit, cooperative education, distance learning, double majors, honors programs, independent study, internships, off-campus study, part-time degree program, services for LD students, study abroad, summer session for credit. ***ROTC:*** Army (b).

Unusual degree programs: 3-2 engineering with Georgia Institute of Technology.

Computers: Students can access the following: campus intranet, computer help desk, free student e-mail accounts, online (class) grades, online (class) registration, online (class) schedules, academic advising tools, online payment, and campus one stop portal. Campuswide network is available. 100% of college-owned or -operated housing units are wired for high-speed Internet access. Wireless service is available via entire campus.

STUDENT LIFE
Housing options: on-campus residence required for freshman year; coed, men-only, women-only. Campus housing is university owned. Freshman applicants given priority for college housing.

Activities and organizations: drama/theater group, student-run newspaper, radio and television station, choral group, marching band, ASU Anointed Gospel Choir, ASU Pan-Hellenic Council (Greeks), Peer Educators, SIFE (Students In Free Enterprise), Student Government Association, national fraternities, national sororities.

Athletics Member NCAA. All Division II. ***Intercollegiate sports:*** baseball M(s), basketball M(s)/W(s), cheerleading M/W, cross-country running M(s)/W(s), football M(s), softball W(s), tennis W(s), track and field M(s)/W(s), volleyball W(s). ***Intramural sports:*** basketball M/W, football M.

Campus security: 24-hour emergency response devices and patrols, late-night transport/escort service, controlled dormitory access, Connect Ed.-Emergency E-mail, Emergency sirens, Active Shooter Team, Certified Police Officers.

Student services: health clinic, personal/psychological counseling.

COSTS & FINANCIAL AID
Costs (2014–15) ***Tuition:*** state resident $3792 full-time, $158 per credit hour part-time; nonresident $13,797 full-time, $575 per credit hour part-time. Full-time tuition and fees vary according to course load and degree level. Part-time tuition and fees vary according to course load and degree level. ***Required fees:*** $1400 full-time. ***Room and board:*** $7522; room only: $4674. Room and board charges vary according to board plan and housing facility. ***Payment plan:*** installment. ***Waivers:*** senior citizens and employees or children of employees.

Financial Aid Of all full-time matriculated undergraduates who enrolled in 2011, 3,608 applied for aid, 3,462 were judged to have need, 63 had their need fully met. In 2011, 2 non-need-based awards were made. ***Average percent of need met:*** 67. ***Average financial aid package:*** $4910. ***Average need-based loan:*** $2336. ***Average need-based gift aid:*** $2532. ***Average non-need-based aid:*** $2750. ***Average indebtedness upon graduation:*** $32,034. ***Financial aid deadline:*** 6/1.

APPLYING
Standardized Tests *Required:* SAT or ACT (for admission).

Options: electronic application, early admission, deferred entrance.

Application fee: $25.

Required: high school transcript, minimum 2.2 GPA. ***Required for some:*** COMPASS Test.

Application deadlines: 6/1 (freshmen), 6/1 (out-of-state freshmen), 6/1 (transfers).

Notification: continuous (freshmen), continuous (out-of-state freshmen), continuous (transfers).

CONTACT
Interim Director, Enrollment Services, Albany State University, 504 College Drive, Albany, GA 31705-2717. *Phone:* 229-430-4646. *Toll-free phone:* 866-579-3498. *Fax:* 229-430-4105. *E-mail:* enrollmentservices@asurams.edu.

Argosy University, Atlanta

Atlanta, Georgia

http://www.argosy.edu/locations/atlanta/

- **Proprietary** university, founded 1990, part of Education Management Corporation
- **Suburban** campus
- **Coed**

ACADEMICS
Calendar: semesters. *Degrees:* certificates, associate, bachelor's, master's, and doctoral.

CONTACT
Argosy University, Atlanta, 980 Hammond Drive, Suite 100, Atlanta, GA 30328. *Phone:* 770-671-1200. *Toll-free phone:* 888-671-4777.

Armstrong State University

Savannah, Georgia

http://www.armstrong.edu/

- **State-supported** comprehensive, founded 1935, part of University System of Georgia
- **Suburban** 267-acre campus
- **Endowment** $9.8 million
- **Coed** 6,346 undergraduate students, 74% full-time, 67% women, 33% men

UNDERGRAD STUDENTS
4,702 full-time, 1,644 part-time. Students come from 44 states and territories; 70 other countries; 6% are from out of state; 25% Black or African American, non-Hispanic/Latino; 7% Hispanic/Latino; 3% Asian, non-Hispanic/Latino; 0.2% Native Hawaiian or other Pacific Islander, non-Hispanic/Latino; 0.2% American Indian or Alaska Native, non-Hispanic/Latino; 4% Two or more races, non-Hispanic/Latino; 0.3% Race/ethnicity unknown; 2% international; 10% transferred in; 19% live on campus.

Freshmen
Admission: 812 enrolled. ***Average high school GPA:*** 3.25. ***Test scores:*** SAT critical reading scores over 500: 57%; SAT math scores over 500: 44%; SAT writing scores over 500: 42%; ACT scores over 18: 91%; SAT critical reading scores over 600: 14%; SAT math scores over 600: 9%; SAT writing scores over 600: 7%; ACT scores over 24: 24%; SAT critical reading scores over 700: 1%; SAT math scores over 700: 1%; SAT writing scores over 700: 1%; ACT scores over 30: 2%.

Retention: 70% of full-time freshmen returned.

FACULTY
Total: 421, 62% full-time.
Student/faculty ratio: 18:1.

ACADEMICS
Calendar: semesters. *Degrees:* certificates, associate, bachelor's, master's, doctoral, post-master's, and postbachelor's certificates.

Special study options: academic remediation for entering students, adult/continuing education programs, advanced placement credit, cooperative education, distance learning, double majors, honors programs, independent study, internships, off-campus study, part-time degree program, services for LD students, study abroad, summer session for credit. ***ROTC:*** Army (b), Navy (c).

Computers: 300 computers/terminals are available on campus for general student use. Students can access the following: campus intranet, computer help desk, free student e-mail accounts, online (class) grades, online (class) registration, online (class) schedules. Campuswide network is available. 100% of college-owned or -operated housing units are wired for high-speed Internet access. Wireless service is available via entire campus.

STUDENT LIFE
Housing options: on-campus residence required for freshman year; coed. Campus housing is leased by the school and is provided by a third party. Freshman applicants given priority for college housing.

Activities and organizations: drama/theater group, student-run newspaper, choral group, Hispanic Outreach and Leadership at Armstrong (HOLA), Student Government Association, Campus Union Board, Gay Straight Alliance, Collegiate 100, national fraternities, national sororities.

Athletics Member NCAA. All Division II. ***Intercollegiate sports:*** baseball M(s), basketball M(s)/W(s), cheerleading M(c)/W(c), cross-country running M(s), golf M(s)/W(s), soccer W(s), softball W(s), tennis M(s)/W(s), volleyball W(s). ***Intramural sports:*** baseball M(c), basketball M(c)/W(c), bowling M/W, cross-country running M(c)/W(c), lacrosse M(c), rugby M(c), sailing M(c)/W(c), soccer M(c)/W, softball M/W, table tennis M/W, tennis M(c)/W(c), track and field M/W, ultimate Frisbee M(c), volleyball M/W, water polo M/W, wrestling M(c).

Campus security: 24-hour emergency response devices and patrols, student patrols, late-night transport/escort service, controlled dormitory access, Personal safety app. We operate the largest digital forensics lab in GA so police from around the state are on our campus daily.

Student services: health clinic, personal/psychological counseling.

COSTS & FINANCIAL AID
Costs (2014–15) ***Tuition:*** state resident $4740 full-time, $158 per credit hour part-time; nonresident $17,246 full-time, $575 per credit hour part-time. Full-time tuition and fees vary according to course load, location, and program. Part-time tuition and fees vary according to course load, location, and program. ***Required fees:*** $1474 full-time, $612 per term part-time. ***Room and board:*** $10,266; room only: $6288. Room and board charges vary according to board plan and housing facility. ***Waivers:*** senior citizens and employees or children of employees.

Financial Aid Of all full-time matriculated undergraduates who enrolled in 2014, 3,069 applied for aid, 1,503 were judged to have need. 63 Federal Work-Study jobs (averaging $2000). In 2014, 108 non-need-based awards were made. ***Average percent of need met:*** 86. ***Average financial aid package:*** $8499. ***Average need-based loan:*** $4750. ***Average need-based gift aid:*** $1500. ***Average non-need-based aid:*** $1500. ***Average indebtedness upon graduation:*** $6602.

APPLYING
Standardized Tests *Required:* SAT or ACT (for admission). *Required for some:* SAT Subject Tests (for admission).

Required: high school transcript, minimum 2.5 GPA, ACT/SAT score.

CONTACT
Armstrong State University, 11935 Abercorn Street, Savannah, GA 31419-1997. *Phone:* 912-344-2514. *Toll-free phone:* 800-633-2349.

The Art Institute of Atlanta

Atlanta, Georgia

http://www.artinstitutes.edu/atlanta/

- **Proprietary** 4-year, founded 1949, part of Education Management Corporation
- **Suburban** 7-acre campus
- **Coed**

ACADEMICS
Calendar: quarters. *Degrees:* diplomas, associate, and bachelor's.

CONTACT
The Art Institute of Atlanta, 6600 Peachtree Dunwoody Road, NE, 100 Embassy Row, Atlanta, GA 30328. *Phone:* 770-394-8300. *Toll-free phone:* 800-275-4242.

The Art Institute of Atlanta–Decatur, a branch of The Art Institute of Atlanta

Decatur, Georgia

http://www.artinstitutes.edu/decatur/

- **Proprietary** 4-year, founded 2007, part of Education Management Corporation
- **Coed**

ACADEMICS
Calendar: quarters. *Degrees:* diplomas, associate, and bachelor's.

CONTACT
The Art Institute of Atlanta–Decatur, a branch of The Art Institute of Atlanta, One West Court Square, Suite 110, Decatur, GA 30030. *Phone:* 404-942-1800. *Toll-free phone:* 866-856-6203.

Berry College
Mount Berry, Georgia
http://www.berry.edu/

- **Independent interdenominational** comprehensive, founded 1902
- **Suburban** 27,000-acre campus with easy access to Atlanta
- **Endowment** $925.7 million
- **Coed** 2,085 undergraduate students, 99% full-time, 61% women, 39% men
- **Moderately difficult** entrance level, 61% of applicants were admitted

UNDERGRAD STUDENTS
2,060 full-time, 25 part-time. Students come from 35 states and territories; 13 other countries; 29% are from out of state; 4% Black or African American, non-Hispanic/Latino; 6% Hispanic/Latino; 1% Asian, non-Hispanic/Latino; 0.1% Native Hawaiian or other Pacific Islander, non-Hispanic/Latino; 0.1% American Indian or Alaska Native, non-Hispanic/Latino; 3% Two or more races, non-Hispanic/Latino; 1% Race/ethnicity unknown; 0.7% international; 2% transferred in; 87% live on campus.

Freshmen
Admission: 3,801 applied, 2,312 admitted, 568 enrolled. ***Average high school GPA:*** 3.73. ***Test scores:*** SAT critical reading scores over 500: 90%; SAT math scores over 500: 90%; SAT writing scores over 500: 84%; ACT scores over 18: 99%; SAT critical reading scores over 600: 39%; SAT math scores over 600: 41%; SAT writing scores over 600: 34%; ACT scores over 24: 75%; SAT critical reading scores over 700: 6%; SAT math scores over 700: 7%; SAT writing scores over 700: 7%; ACT scores over 30: 15%.
Retention: 79% of full-time freshmen returned.

FACULTY
Total: 225, 73% full-time, 76% with terminal degrees.
Student/faculty ratio: 12:1.

ACADEMICS
Calendar: semesters. *Degrees:* bachelor's and master's.
Special study options: adult/continuing education programs, advanced placement credit, double majors, honors programs, independent study, internships, part-time degree program, services for LD students, student-designed majors, study abroad, summer session for credit.
Unusual degree programs: 3-2 engineering with Georgia Institute of Technology; nursing with Emory University.
Computers: 200 computers/terminals and 80 ports are available on campus for general student use. Students can access the following: campus intranet, computer help desk, free student e-mail accounts, online (class) grades, online (class) registration, online (class) schedules. Campuswide network is available. 100% of college-owned or -operated housing units are wired for high-speed Internet access. Wireless service is available via classrooms, computer centers, computer labs, dorm rooms, learning centers, libraries, student centers.

STUDENT LIFE
Housing options: on-campus residence required through senior year; coed, men-only, women-only. Campus housing is university owned. Freshman campus housing is guaranteed.
Activities and organizations: drama/theater group, student-run newspaper, choral group, Student Government Association, Campus Outreach, Block-n-Bridle, Allied Health, Athletes Bettering the Community.
Athletics Member NCAA. All Division III. ***Intercollegiate sports:*** baseball M, basketball M/W, cross-country running M/W, equestrian sports W, football M, golf M/W, lacrosse M/W, soccer M/W, softball W, swimming and diving M/W, tennis M/W, track and field M/W, volleyball W. ***Intramural sports:*** basketball M/W, bowling M/W, cheerleading M(c)/W(c), crew M(c)/W(c), cross-country running M/W, football M/W, golf M/W, racquetball M/W, rock climbing M/W, soccer M/W, softball M/W, swimming and diving M/W, tennis M/W, ultimate Frisbee M/W, volleyball M/W, water polo M/W.
Campus security: 24-hour emergency response devices and patrols, controlled dormitory access, lighted pathways, gated campus, mobile police patrols, identification of valuables, limited access to campus, on campus police officers.
Student services: health clinic, personal/psychological counseling.

COSTS & FINANCIAL AID
Costs (2014–15) ***Comprehensive fee:*** $41,190 includes full-time tuition ($30,330), mandatory fees ($200), and room and board ($10,660). Part-time tuition: $1011 per credit hour. ***College room only:*** $6020. Room and board charges vary according to board plan and housing facility. ***Payment plan:*** installment. ***Waivers:*** senior citizens and employees or children of employees.
Financial Aid Of all full-time matriculated undergraduates who enrolled in 2014, 1,802 applied for aid, 1,490 were judged to have need, 432 had their need fully met. 398 Federal Work-Study jobs (averaging $2101). 144 state and other part-time jobs (averaging $4390). In 2014, 557 non-need-based awards were made. ***Average percent of need met:*** 82. ***Average financial aid package:*** $25,079. ***Average need-based loan:*** $5083. ***Average need-based gift aid:*** $20,510. ***Average non-need-based aid:*** $11,976. ***Average indebtedness upon graduation:*** $23,997.

APPLYING
Standardized Tests *Required:* SAT or ACT (for admission).
Options: electronic application.
Required: essay or personal statement, high school transcript, 1 letter of recommendation. ***Required for some:*** 2 letters of recommendation, Home-school applicants must meet or exceed academic profile of previous freshmen class. ***Recommended:*** interview.
Application deadlines: 7/24 (freshmen), 7/24 (transfers).
Notification: continuous (freshmen), continuous (transfers).

CONTACT
Mr. Timothy Tarpley, Director of Operations, Enrollment Management, Berry College, PO Box 490159, 2277 Martha Berry Highway, NW, Mount Berry, GA 30149-0159. *Phone:* 706-236-2215. *Toll-free phone:* 800-237-7942. *E-mail:* admissions@berry.edu.

Beulah Heights University
Atlanta, Georgia
http://www.beulah.org/

- **Independent Pentecostal** comprehensive, founded 1918
- **Urban** 10-acre campus with easy access to Atlanta
- **Coed** 454 undergraduate students, 37% full-time, 56% women, 44% men
- **Noncompetitive** entrance level

UNDERGRAD STUDENTS
170 full-time, 284 part-time. Students come from 22 states and territories; 12 other countries; 30% are from out of state; 73% Black or African American, non-Hispanic/Latino; 2% Hispanic/Latino; 10% Asian, non-Hispanic/Latino; 8% Race/ethnicity unknown; 0.8% international; 11% transferred in; 10% live on campus.

Freshmen
Admission: 52 enrolled. ***Average high school GPA:*** 3.
Retention: 57% of full-time freshmen returned.

FACULTY
Total: 82, 21% full-time, 56% with terminal degrees.
Student/faculty ratio: 8:1.

ACADEMICS
Calendar: semesters. *Degrees:* associate, bachelor's, master's, and doctoral.
Special study options: academic remediation for entering students, accelerated degree program, adult/continuing education programs, advanced placement credit, cooperative education, distance learning, double majors, independent study, internships, off-campus study, part-time degree program, services for LD students, summer session for credit.
Unusual degree programs: Bachelor of Arts in religious studies, BA in leadership studies, Master of Divinity, MA in leadership and MA in religious studies can be complete at the Griffin campus extension.
Computers: 28 computers/terminals are available on campus for general student use. Students can access the following: campus intranet, computer help desk, free student e-mail accounts, online (class) registration, online (class) schedules. Campuswide network is available. 100% of college-owned or -operated housing units are wired for high-speed Internet access. Wireless service is available via entire campus.

STUDENT LIFE
Housing options: men-only, women-only. Campus housing is university owned.
Activities and organizations: student-run newspaper, choral group, Chapel Choir, student government, Club Give.
Campus security: 24-hour emergency response devices and patrols.
Student services: personal/psychological counseling.

COSTS & FINANCIAL AID
Costs (2015–16) ***Tuition:*** $7272 full-time, $303 per credit hour part-time. Full-time tuition and fees vary according to course load. ***Required fees:*** $300 full-time, $100 per year part-time. ***Room only:*** $2500. Room and board charges vary according to housing facility. ***Payment plans:*** installment, deferred payment. ***Waivers:*** employees or children of employees.
Financial Aid Of all full-time matriculated undergraduates who enrolled in 2009, 113 applied for aid, 113 were judged to have need. 13 Federal Work-Study jobs (averaging $4335). ***Average percent of need met:*** 75. ***Average financial aid package:*** $5619. ***Average need-based loan:*** $2250. ***Average need-based gift aid:*** $3500. ***Average indebtedness upon graduation:*** $40,000.

APPLYING
Standardized Tests *Required:* TOEFL required for international students (for admission). *Recommended:* SAT or ACT (for admission).
Options: electronic application, early admission.
Application fee: $30.
Required: essay or personal statement, high school transcript, minimum 2.0 GPA, 2 letters of recommendation, Statement of Faith. ***Recommended:*** interview.
Application deadlines: rolling (freshmen), rolling (transfers).
Notification: continuous (freshmen), continuous (transfers).

CONTACT
Arthur Breland, Admissions Coordinator, Beulah Heights University, 892 Berne Street, SE, Atlanta, GA 30316. *Phone:* 404-627-2681 Ext. 158. *Toll-free phone:* 888-777-BHBC. *E-mail:* arthur.breland@beulah.edu.

Brenau University
Gainesville, Georgia
http://www.brenau.edu/

- **Independent** comprehensive, founded 1878
- **Small-town** 57-acre campus with easy access to Atlanta
- **Women only** 1,596 undergraduate students, 63% full-time
- **Moderately difficult** entrance level, 76% of applicants were admitted

UNDERGRAD STUDENTS
1,000 full-time, 596 part-time. Students come from 20 states and territories; 18 other countries; 5% are from out of state; 32% Black or African American, non-Hispanic/Latino; 8% Hispanic/Latino; 2% Asian, non-Hispanic/Latino; 0.2% Native Hawaiian or other Pacific Islander, non-Hispanic/Latino; 3% Two or more races, non-Hispanic/Latino; 3% Race/ethnicity unknown; 3% international; 20% transferred in.

Freshmen
Admission: 2,563 applied, 1,943 admitted, 231 enrolled. ***Test scores:*** SAT writing scores over 700: 1%.
Retention: 66% of full-time freshmen returned.

FACULTY
Total: 326, 34% full-time, 54% with terminal degrees.
Student/faculty ratio: 11:1.

ACADEMICS
Calendar: semesters. *Degrees:* associate, bachelor's, and master's (also offers coed evening and weekend programs with significant enrollment not reflected in profile).
Special study options: academic remediation for entering students, advanced placement credit, distance learning, double majors, English as a second language, honors programs, independent study, internships, part-time degree program, services for LD students, student-designed majors, study abroad, summer session for credit.
Computers: Students can access the following: campus intranet, computer help desk, free student e-mail accounts, online (class) grades, online (class) registration, online (class) schedules. Campuswide network is available. 100% of college-owned or -operated housing units are wired for high-speed Internet access. Wireless service is available via classrooms, computer centers, computer labs, dorm rooms, learning centers, libraries, student centers.

STUDENT LIFE
Housing options: on-campus residence required through junior year; women-only, special housing for students with disabilities. Campus housing is university owned. Freshman campus housing is guaranteed.
Activities and organizations: drama/theater group, student-run newspaper, radio station, choral group, Sigma Alpha Pi Leadership Society, Student Government Association/Student Activities Board, Circle K, Silhouettes, International Club, national sororities.
Athletics Member NAIA. ***Intercollegiate sports:*** basketball W(s), cheerleading W(c), crew W(c), cross-country running W(s), soccer W(s), softball W(s), swimming and diving W(s), tennis W(s), volleyball W(s).
Campus security: 24-hour emergency response devices and patrols, late-night transport/escort service.
Student services: health clinic, personal/psychological counseling.

COSTS & FINANCIAL AID
Costs (2015–16) ***Comprehensive fee:*** $37,476 includes full-time tuition ($25,478) and room and board ($11,998). Full-time tuition and fees vary according to course load, location, and program. Part-time tuition: $849 per credit. Part-time tuition and fees vary according to course load, location, and program. ***Payment plan:*** installment. ***Waivers:*** employees or children of employees.
Financial Aid Of all full-time matriculated undergraduates who enrolled in 2013, 961 applied for aid, 903 were judged to have need, 10 had their need fully met. 120 Federal Work-Study jobs (averaging $2002). In 2013, 88 non-need-based awards were made. ***Average percent of need met:*** 60. ***Average financial aid package:*** $16,844. ***Average need-based loan:*** $4932. ***Average need-based gift aid:*** $15,073. ***Average non-need-based aid:*** $12,001. ***Average indebtedness upon graduation:*** $31,672.

APPLYING
Standardized Tests *Required:* SAT or ACT (for admission).
Options: electronic application, deferred entrance.
Application fee: $35.
Required: high school transcript. ***Required for some:*** interview.
Application deadlines: rolling (freshmen), rolling (out-of-state freshmen), rolling (transfers).
Notification: continuous (freshmen), continuous (out-of-state freshmen), continuous (transfers).

CONTACT
Mr. Ray Tatum, Senior Vice President, Enrollment Management and Student Services, Brenau University, Admissions, 500 Washington Street, SE, Gainesville, GA 30501. *Phone:* 770-538-4704. *Toll-free phone:* 800-252-5119. *Fax:* 770-538-4701. *E-mail:* admissions@brenau.edu.

Chamberlain College of Nursing
Atlanta, Georgia
http://www.chamberlain.edu/

- **Proprietary** 4-year
- **Coed**

FACULTY
Student/faculty ratio: 11:1.

ACADEMICS
Degree: bachelor's.

APPLYING
Standardized Tests *Required:* SAT or ACT (for admission).
Application fee: $95.

CONTACT
Chamberlain College of Nursing, 5775 Peachtree-Dunwoody Road, NE, Suite A100, Atlanta, GA 30342.

Clark Atlanta University

Atlanta, Georgia

http://www.cau.edu/

- **Independent United Methodist** university, founded 1865
- **Urban** 126-acre campus
- **Endowment** $66.7 million
- **Coed** 2,567 undergraduate students, 95% full-time, 75% women, 25% men
- **Moderately difficult** entrance level, 85% of applicants were admitted

UNDERGRAD STUDENTS

2,441 full-time, 126 part-time. Students come from 43 states and territories; 9 other countries; 63% are from out of state; 87% Black or African American, non-Hispanic/Latino; 0.4% Hispanic/Latino; 0.2% Asian, non-Hispanic/Latino; 0.4% American Indian or Alaska Native, non-Hispanic/Latino; 11% Race/ethnicity unknown; 1% international; 4% transferred in; 61% live on campus.

Freshmen

Admission: 5,140 applied, 4,352 admitted, 717 enrolled. ***Average high school GPA:*** 3. ***Test scores:*** SAT critical reading scores over 500: 14%; SAT math scores over 500: 14%; SAT critical reading scores over 600: 1%; SAT math scores over 600: 2%.

Retention: 60% of full-time freshmen returned.

FACULTY

Total: 281, 60% full-time, 64% with terminal degrees.

Student/faculty ratio: 17:1.

ACADEMICS

Calendar: semesters. *Degrees:* bachelor's, master's, doctoral, post-master's, and postbachelor's certificates.

Special study options: academic remediation for entering students, accelerated degree program, adult/continuing education programs, advanced placement credit, cooperative education, double majors, honors programs, independent study, internships, off-campus study, part-time degree program, services for LD students, study abroad, summer session for credit. ***ROTC:*** Army (c), Navy (c).

Unusual degree programs: 3-2 engineering with Georgia Institute of Technology, Boston University, North Carolina Agricultural and Technical State University.

Computers: 741 computers/terminals and 2,000 ports are available on campus for general student use. Students can access the following: computer help desk, free student e-mail accounts, online (class) grades, online (class) registration, online (class) schedules. Campuswide network is available. 100% of college-owned or -operated housing units are wired for high-speed Internet access. Wireless service is available via entire campus.

STUDENT LIFE

Housing options: on-campus residence required through sophomore year; coed, men-only, women-only. Campus housing is university owned and is provided by a third party. Freshman applicants given priority for college housing.

Activities and organizations: drama/theater group, student-run newspaper, radio and television station, choral group, marching band, Spirit Boosters, Pre-Alumni Council, Campus Activities Board, Orientation Guides, National Association for the Advancement of Colored People, national fraternities, national sororities.

Athletics Member NCAA. All Division II. ***Intercollegiate sports:*** baseball M(s), basketball M(s)/W(s), cross-country running M(s)/W(s), football M(s), softball W(s), tennis W(s), track and field M(s)/W(s), volleyball W(s). ***Intramural sports:*** basketball M/W, football M, softball W, tennis W, track and field M/W, volleyball M/W.

Campus security: 24-hour emergency response devices and patrols, late-night transport/escort service, controlled dormitory access.

Student services: health clinic, personal/psychological counseling.

COSTS & FINANCIAL AID

Costs (2014–15) ***Comprehensive fee:*** $31,596 includes full-time tuition ($19,682), mandatory fees ($1652), and room and board ($10,262). Part-time tuition: $820 per credit hour. ***Required fees:*** $753 per term part-time. ***Room and board:*** Room and board charges vary according to board plan and housing facility. ***Payment plan:*** installment. ***Waivers:*** employees or children of employees.

Financial Aid Of all full-time matriculated undergraduates who enrolled in 2005, 3,883 applied for aid, 3,712 were judged to have need, 1,567 had their need fully met. 229 Federal Work-Study jobs (averaging $1335). ***Average percent of need met:*** 8. ***Average financial aid package:*** $10,935. ***Average need-based loan:*** $4526. ***Average need-based gift aid:*** $3818. ***Average indebtedness upon graduation:*** $17,751.

APPLYING

Standardized Tests *Required:* SAT or ACT (for admission).

Options: electronic application, early admission, deferred entrance.

Application fee: $35.

Required: essay or personal statement, high school transcript, minimum 2.5 GPA, 2 letters of recommendation. ***Required for some:*** interview.

Application deadlines: 6/1 (freshmen), 6/1 (out-of-state freshmen), 6/1 (transfers).

Notification: continuous (freshmen), continuous (out-of-state freshmen), continuous (transfers).

CONTACT

Mr. lorri Rice, Interim Director, Office of Admissions, Clark Atlanta University, 223 James P. Brawley Drive, SW, Atlanta, GA 30314. *Phone:* 404-880-8043. *Toll-free phone:* 800-688-3228. *Fax:* 404-880-6174. *E-mail:* cauadmissions@cau.edu.

Clayton State University

Morrow, Georgia

http://www.clayton.edu/

- **State-supported** comprehensive, founded 1969, part of University System of Georgia
- **Suburban** 163-acre campus with easy access to Atlanta
- **Endowment** $2.1 million
- **Coed** 6,632 undergraduate students, 56% full-time, 69% women, 31% men
- **Minimally difficult** entrance level, 41% of applicants were admitted

UNDERGRAD STUDENTS

3,711 full-time, 2,921 part-time. Students come from 34 states and territories; 118 other countries; 3% are from out of state; 62% Black or African American, non-Hispanic/Latino; 2% Hispanic/Latino; 5% Asian, non-Hispanic/Latino; 0.2% American Indian or Alaska Native, non-Hispanic/Latino; 3% Two or more races, non-Hispanic/Latino; 4% Race/ethnicity unknown; 1% international; 11% transferred in; 14% live on campus.

Freshmen

Admission: 2,321 applied, 943 admitted, 532 enrolled. ***Average high school GPA:*** 3. ***Test scores:*** SAT critical reading scores over 500: 29%; SAT math scores over 500: 27%; SAT writing scores over 500: 20%; ACT scores over 18: 86%; SAT critical reading scores over 600: 5%; SAT math scores over 600: 4%; SAT writing scores over 600: 3%; ACT scores over 24: 11%; SAT critical reading scores over 700: 1%.

Retention: 67% of full-time freshmen returned.

FACULTY

Total: 369, 66% full-time, 67% with terminal degrees.

Student/faculty ratio: 17:1.

ACADEMICS

Calendar: semesters. *Degrees:* certificates, associate, bachelor's, and master's.

Special study options: academic remediation for entering students, adult/continuing education programs, advanced placement credit, cooperative education, distance learning, double majors, English as a second language, freshman honors college, honors programs, independent study, internships, off-campus study, part-time degree program, services for LD students, student-designed majors, study abroad, summer session for credit. ***ROTC:*** Army (b), Navy (c), Air Force (c).

Computers: 3,500 computers/terminals are available on campus for general student use. Students can access the following: computer help desk, free student e-mail accounts, online (class) grades, online (class) registration, online (class) schedules. Campuswide network is available.

100% of college-owned or -operated housing units are wired for high-speed Internet access. Wireless service is available via entire campus.

STUDENT LIFE
Housing options: on-campus residence required for freshman year; coed. Campus housing is university owned. Freshman applicants given priority for college housing.

Activities and organizations: drama/theater group, student-run newspaper, radio station, choral group, Accounting Club, International Awareness Club, Black Cultural Awareness Association, Student Government Association, music club, national fraternities, national sororities.

Athletics Member NCAA. All Division II. ***Intercollegiate sports:*** basketball M(s)/W(s), cheerleading W(s)(c), cross-country running M(s)/W(s), golf M(s), soccer M(s)/W(s), tennis W(s), track and field M(s)/W(s). ***Intramural sports:*** bowling M/W, softball M/W, table tennis M/W, volleyball M/W.

Campus security: 24-hour emergency response devices and patrols, late-night transport/escort service, controlled dormitory access, lighted pathways.

Student services: health clinic, personal/psychological counseling.

COSTS & FINANCIAL AID
Costs (2015–16) ***Tuition:*** state resident $4740 full-time; nonresident $17,246 full-time. Full-time tuition and fees vary according to course load. Part-time tuition and fees vary according to course load. ***Required fees:*** $1454 full-time. ***Room and board:*** $9240. Room and board charges vary according to board plan and housing facility. ***Waivers:*** senior citizens and employees or children of employees.

Financial Aid Of all full-time matriculated undergraduates who enrolled in 2014, 3,344 applied for aid, 3,151 were judged to have need, 101 had their need fully met. 62 Federal Work-Study jobs (averaging $4733). In 2014, 29 non-need-based awards were made. ***Average percent of need met:*** 46. ***Average financial aid package:*** $9007. ***Average need-based loan:*** $4179. ***Average need-based gift aid:*** $5947. ***Average non-need-based aid:*** $2321. ***Average indebtedness upon graduation:*** $30,423.

APPLYING
Standardized Tests *Required:* SAT or ACT (for admission).

Options: electronic application, early admission, deferred entrance.

Application fee: $40.

Required: high school transcript, proof of immunization.

Notification: continuous (freshmen), continuous (transfers).

CONTACT
Ms. Theadora Riley, Admissions, Clayton State University, 2000 Clayton State Boulevard, Morrow, GA 30260-0285. *Phone:* 678-466-4115. *Fax:* 678-466-4149. *E-mail:* csc-info@clayton.edu.

College of Coastal Georgia
Brunswick, Georgia
http://www.ccga.edu/

- **State-supported** 4-year, founded 1961, part of University System of Georgia
- **Small-town** 193-acre campus with easy access to Jacksonville
- **Endowment** $7.8 million
- **Coed** 3,008 undergraduate students, 62% full-time, 66% women, 34% men
- **Minimally difficult** entrance level, 92% of applicants were admitted

UNDERGRAD STUDENTS
1,858 full-time, 1,150 part-time. Students come from 42 states and territories; 33 other countries; 8% are from out of state; 17% Black or African American, non-Hispanic/Latino; 5% Hispanic/Latino; 2% Asian, non-Hispanic/Latino; 0.1% Native Hawaiian or other Pacific Islander, non-Hispanic/Latino; 0.4% American Indian or Alaska Native, non-Hispanic/Latino; 4% Two or more races, non-Hispanic/Latino; 4% Race/ethnicity unknown; 1% international; 6% transferred in; 15% live on campus.

Freshmen
Admission: 1,072 applied, 990 admitted, 638 enrolled. ***Average high school GPA:*** 3.04. ***Test scores:*** SAT critical reading scores over 500: 31%; SAT math scores over 500: 30%; ACT scores over 18: 79%; SAT critical reading scores over 600: 5%; SAT math scores over 600: 4%; ACT scores over 24: 12%.

Retention: 62% of full-time freshmen returned.

FACULTY
Total: 195, 45% full-time, 44% with terminal degrees.

Student/faculty ratio: 18:1.

ACADEMICS
Calendar: semesters. *Degrees:* associate and bachelor's.

Special study options: academic remediation for entering students, advanced placement credit, distance learning, double majors, honors programs, internships, part-time degree program, services for LD students, study abroad, summer session for credit.

Computers: 395 computers/terminals and 300 ports are available on campus for general student use. Students can access the following: computer help desk, free student e-mail accounts, online (class) grades, online (class) registration, online (class) schedules. Campuswide network is available. 100% of college-owned or -operated housing units are wired for high-speed Internet access. Wireless service is available via entire campus.

STUDENT LIFE
Housing options: on-campus residence required for freshman year; coed. Campus housing is university owned. Freshman campus housing is guaranteed.

Activities and organizations: student-run newspaper, International Association, Coastal Georgia Association of Nursing Students, Urban Gaming Club, Association of Coastal Educators, CCGA Biology Club.

Athletics Member NAIA. ***Intercollegiate sports:*** basketball M(s)/W(s), golf M(s)/W(s), softball W(s), tennis M(s)/W(s), volleyball W(s). ***Intramural sports:*** baseball M(c), basketball M/W, bowling M, cheerleading W(c), football M/W, golf M/W, lacrosse W(c), sailing M(c)/W(c), soccer M/W, softball M/W, ultimate Frisbee M/W.

Campus security: 24-hour emergency response devices and patrols, late-night transport/escort service, controlled dormitory access.

Student services: health clinic, personal/psychological counseling.

COSTS & FINANCIAL AID
Costs (2014–15) ***Tuition:*** state resident $2990 full-time, $100 per credit hour part-time; nonresident $11,046 full-time, $368 per credit hour part-time. Full-time tuition and fees vary according to course load and location. Part-time tuition and fees vary according to course load and location. ***Required fees:*** $1370 full-time, $685 per term part-time. ***Room and board:*** $8404; room only: $5104. Room and board charges vary according to board plan, housing facility, and location. ***Waivers:*** senior citizens and employees or children of employees.

Financial Aid Of all full-time matriculated undergraduates who enrolled in 2013, 80 Federal Work-Study jobs (averaging $1500).

APPLYING
Standardized Tests *Required:* SAT or ACT (for admission).

Options: electronic application, early admission, deferred entrance.

Application fee: $25.

Required: high school transcript, minimum 2.0 GPA, Immunization records, proof of residency and SAT or ACT scores(for applicants graduating from high school within the last five years).

Application deadlines: 7/15 (freshmen), 7/15 (transfers).

Notification: continuous (freshmen), continuous (transfers).

CONTACT
Mr. Clayton Daniels, Assistant Vice President for Enrollment Management, College of Coastal Georgia, One College Drive, Brunswick, GA 31520. *Phone:* 912-279-5730. *Toll-free phone:* 800-675-7235. *Fax:* 912-262-3072. *E-mail:* admiss@ccga.edu.

Columbus State University

Columbus, Georgia

http://www.columbusstate.edu/

- **State-supported** comprehensive, founded 1958, part of University System of Georgia
- **Suburban** 132-acre campus with easy access to Atlanta
- **Coed** 7,021 undergraduate students, 71% full-time, 60% women, 40% men
- **Minimally difficult** entrance level, 56% of applicants were admitted

UNDERGRAD STUDENTS

4,979 full-time, 2,042 part-time. Students come from 46 states and territories; 40 other countries; 15% are from out of state; 36% Black or African American, non-Hispanic/Latino; 5% Hispanic/Latino; 2% Asian, non-Hispanic/Latino; 0.3% Native Hawaiian or other Pacific Islander, non-Hispanic/Latino; 0.5% American Indian or Alaska Native, non-Hispanic/Latino; 3% Two or more races, non-Hispanic/Latino; 1% international; 9% transferred in; 19% live on campus.

Freshmen

Admission: 3,172 applied, 1,775 admitted, 1,044 enrolled. ***Average high school GPA:*** 3.15. ***Test scores:*** SAT critical reading scores over 500: 47%; SAT math scores over 500: 43%; SAT writing scores over 500: 39%; ACT scores over 18: 80%; SAT critical reading scores over 600: 13%; SAT math scores over 600: 12%; SAT writing scores over 600: 8%; ACT scores over 24: 15%; SAT critical reading scores over 700: 2%; SAT math scores over 700: 2%; SAT writing scores over 700: 1%; ACT scores over 30: 1%.

Retention: 67% of full-time freshmen returned.

FACULTY

Total: 500, 57% full-time, 55% with terminal degrees.

Student/faculty ratio: 17:1.

ACADEMICS

Calendar: semesters. *Degrees:* certificates, associate, bachelor's, master's, doctoral, post-master's, and postbachelor's certificates.

Special study options: academic remediation for entering students, adult/continuing education programs, advanced placement credit, cooperative education, distance learning, double majors, English as a second language, freshman honors college, honors programs, independent study, internships, off-campus study, part-time degree program, services for LD students, study abroad, summer session for credit. ***ROTC:*** Army (b).

Unusual degree programs: 3-2 engineering with Georgia Institute of Technology.

Computers: Students can access the following: campus intranet, computer help desk, free student e-mail accounts, online (class) grades, online (class) registration, online (class) schedules. Campuswide network is available. 100% of college-owned or -operated housing units are wired for high-speed Internet access. Wireless service is available via entire campus.

STUDENT LIFE

Housing options: on-campus residence required for freshman year; coed, men-only, women-only, special housing for students with disabilities. Campus housing is university owned. Freshman applicants given priority for college housing.

Activities and organizations: drama/theater group, student-run newspaper, choral group, Student Government Association, Student Activities Council, Campus Ministry Association, African Students Association, SABER Student Newspaper, national fraternities, national sororities.

Athletics Member NCAA. All Division II except men's and women's riflery (Division I). ***Intercollegiate sports:*** baseball M(s), basketball M(s)/W(s), cheerleading M(s)/W(s), cross-country running M(s)/W(s), golf M(s)/W(s), riflery M(s)/W(s), soccer W(s), softball W(s), tennis M(s)/W(s), volleyball W(s). ***Intramural sports:*** badminton M/W, basketball M/W, bowling M/W, cross-country running M/W, football M, golf M/W, racquetball M/W, skiing (downhill) M/W, soccer M/W, softball M/W, table tennis M/W, tennis M/W, track and field M/W, volleyball M/W.

Campus security: 24-hour emergency response devices and patrols, late-night transport/escort service, controlled dormitory access.

Student services: health clinic, personal/psychological counseling.

COSTS & FINANCIAL AID

Costs (2014–15) ***Tuition:*** state resident $5098 full-time, $109 per credit hour part-time; nonresident $17,994 full-time, $601 per credit hour part-time. Full-time tuition and fees vary according to course load, degree level, and program. Part-time tuition and fees vary according to course load, degree level, and program. ***Required fees:*** $1800 full-time, $768 per term part-time. ***Room and board:*** $8880; room only: $4080. Room and board charges vary according to board plan and housing facility.

Financial Aid Of all full-time matriculated undergraduates who enrolled in 2014, 4,175 applied for aid, 3,549 were judged to have need, 482 had their need fully met. In 2014, 235 non-need-based awards were made. ***Average percent of need met:*** 68. ***Average financial aid package:*** $9057. ***Average need-based loan:*** $4249. ***Average need-based gift aid:*** $4833. ***Average non-need-based aid:*** $1874. ***Average indebtedness upon graduation:*** $30,142.

APPLYING

Standardized Tests *Required:* SAT or ACT (for admission).

Options: electronic application, early admission, deferred entrance.

Application fee: $40.

Required: high school transcript, minimum 2.4 GPA, proof of immunization.

Application deadlines: 6/30 (freshmen), 6/30 (transfers).

Notification: continuous (freshmen), continuous (transfers).

CONTACT

Columbus State University, 4225 University Avenue, Columbus, GA 31907-5645. *Phone:* 706-507-8806. *Toll-free phone:* 866-264-2035.

Covenant College

Lookout Mountain, Georgia

http://www.covenant.edu/

- **Independent** comprehensive, founded 1955, affiliated with Presbyterian Church in America
- **Suburban** 350-acre campus
- **Coed** 1,105 undergraduate students, 95% full-time, 58% women, 42% men
- **Moderately difficult** entrance level, 97% of applicants were admitted

UNDERGRAD STUDENTS

1,049 full-time, 56 part-time. 78% are from out of state; 3% Black or African American, non-Hispanic/Latino; 3% Hispanic/Latino; 2% Asian, non-Hispanic/Latino; 0.2% Native Hawaiian or other Pacific Islander, non-Hispanic/Latino; 0.4% American Indian or Alaska Native, non-Hispanic/Latino; 2% Two or more races, non-Hispanic/Latino; 2% international; 4% transferred in; 85% live on campus.

Freshmen

Admission: 655 applied, 633 admitted, 265 enrolled. ***Average high school GPA:*** 3.6. ***Test scores:*** SAT critical reading scores over 500: 90%; SAT math scores over 500: 83%; SAT writing scores over 500: 81%; ACT scores over 18: 100%; SAT critical reading scores over 600: 52%; SAT math scores over 600: 38%; SAT writing scores over 600: 46%; ACT scores over 24: 75%; SAT critical reading scores over 700: 17%; SAT math scores over 700: 6%; SAT writing scores over 700: 9%; ACT scores over 30: 20%.

Retention: 85% of full-time freshmen returned.

FACULTY

Total: 95, 69% full-time, 71% with terminal degrees.

Student/faculty ratio: 14:1.

ACADEMICS

Calendar: semesters. *Degrees:* bachelor's and master's (master's degree in education only).

Special study options: academic remediation for entering students, adult/continuing education programs, advanced placement credit, double majors, independent study, internships, off-campus study, part-time degree program, services for LD students, student-designed majors, study abroad, summer session for credit. ***ROTC:*** Army (c).

Computers: Students can access the following: computer help desk, free student e-mail accounts, online (class) registration, online student information system. Campuswide network is available. 100% of college-owned or -operated housing units are wired for high-speed Internet access. Wireless service is available via classrooms, computer labs, dorm rooms, libraries.

STUDENT LIFE
Housing options: on-campus residence required through junior year; coed. Campus housing is university owned. Freshman campus housing is guaranteed.

Activities and organizations: drama/theater group, student-run newspaper, radio station, choral group.

Athletics Member NCAA, NAIA, NCCAA. All NCAA Division III. ***Intercollegiate sports:*** baseball M, basketball M/W, cross-country running M/W, golf M/W, soccer M/W, softball W, tennis M/W, volleyball W. ***Intramural sports:*** badminton M/W, basketball M/W, football M, soccer M/W, volleyball M/W.

Campus security: controlled dormitory access, night security guards.

Student services: health clinic, personal/psychological counseling, women's center.

COSTS & FINANCIAL AID
Costs (2014–15) ***Comprehensive fee:*** $38,990 includes full-time tuition ($29,300), mandatory fees ($860), and room and board ($8830). Full-time tuition and fees vary according to course load. Part-time tuition: $1245 per credit hour. Part-time tuition and fees vary according to course load. ***Room and board:*** Room and board charges vary according to board plan and housing facility. ***Payment plan:*** installment. ***Waivers:*** senior citizens and employees or children of employees.

Financial Aid Of all full-time matriculated undergraduates who enrolled in 2012, 708 applied for aid, 608 were judged to have need, 202 had their need fully met. In 2012, 292 non-need-based awards were made. ***Average percent of need met:*** 83. ***Average financial aid package:*** $23,826. ***Average need-based loan:*** $6448. ***Average need-based gift aid:*** $17,264. ***Average non-need-based aid:*** $10,837. ***Average indebtedness upon graduation:*** $22,790.

APPLYING
Standardized Tests *Required:* SAT or ACT (for admission).

Options: electronic application, early admission, deferred entrance.

Application fee: $35.

Required: essay or personal statement, high school transcript, minimum 2.5 GPA, 2 letters of recommendation, interview.

CONTACT
Mr. Philip Howlett, Assistant Director of Admissions, Covenant College, 14049 Scenic Highway, Lookout Mountain, GA 30750. *Phone:* 706-419-1145. *Toll-free phone:* 888-451-2683. *Fax:* 706-820-0893. *E-mail:* admissions@covenant.edu.

Darton State College

Albany, Georgia

http://www.darton.edu/

- **State-supported** primarily 2-year, founded 1965, part of University System of Georgia
- **Urban** 185-acre campus
- **Endowment** $1.9 million
- **Coed** 5,620 undergraduate students, 46% full-time, 71% women, 29% men
- **Minimally difficult** entrance level, 48% of applicants were admitted

UNDERGRAD STUDENTS
2,577 full-time, 3,043 part-time. Students come from 29 states and territories; 6 other countries; 3% are from out of state; 45% Black or African American, non-Hispanic/Latino; 3% Hispanic/Latino; 1% Asian, non-Hispanic/Latino; 0.1% Native Hawaiian or other Pacific Islander, non-Hispanic/Latino; 0.3% American Indian or Alaska Native, non-Hispanic/Latino; 0.8% Two or more races, non-Hispanic/Latino; 0.5% Race/ethnicity unknown; 0.1% international; 12% transferred in.

Freshmen
Admission: 1,825 applied, 878 admitted, 886 enrolled. ***Average high school GPA:*** 2.08. ***Test scores:*** SAT critical reading scores over 500: 29%; SAT math scores over 500: 23%; SAT writing scores over 500: 18%; ACT scores over 18: 41%; SAT critical reading scores over 600: 5%; SAT math scores over 600: 3%; SAT writing scores over 600: 3%; ACT scores over 24: 9%; SAT critical reading scores over 700: 1%.

Retention: 40% of full-time freshmen returned.

FACULTY
Total: 265, 50% full-time.

Student/faculty ratio: 25:1.

ACADEMICS
Calendar: semesters. *Degrees:* certificates, associate, bachelor's, and postbachelor's certificates.

Special study options: academic remediation for entering students, accelerated degree program, adult/continuing education programs, advanced placement credit, cooperative education, distance learning, double majors, English as a second language, honors programs, independent study, off-campus study, part-time degree program, services for LD students, summer session for credit. ***ROTC:*** Army (c).

Computers: 653 computers/terminals and 4 ports are available on campus for general student use. Students can access the following: campus intranet, computer help desk, free student e-mail accounts, online (class) grades, online (class) registration, online (class) schedules. Campuswide network is available. 100% of college-owned or -operated housing units are wired for high-speed Internet access. Wireless service is available via entire campus.

STUDENT LIFE
Housing options: coed. Campus housing is provided by a third party.

Activities and organizations: drama/theater group, choral group, Cultural Exchange Club, Democratic, Independent, & Republican Team (D.I.R.T.), Human Services Club, Outdoor Adventure Club (OAC), Music Club.

Athletics Member NJCAA. ***Intercollegiate sports:*** baseball M(s), basketball W(s), cross-country running M(s)/W(s), golf M(s), soccer M(s)/W(s), softball W(s), swimming and diving M(s)/W(s), wrestling M. ***Intramural sports:*** badminton M/W, basketball M/W, bowling M/W, football M, racquetball M/W, table tennis M, volleyball M/W.

Campus security: 24-hour emergency response devices and patrols, student patrols, late-night transport/escort service, controlled dormitory access.

Student services: health clinic, personal/psychological counseling.

COSTS
Costs (2014–15) ***Tuition:*** state resident $2660 full-time, $89 per credit hour part-time; nonresident $9822 full-time, $335 per credit hour part-time. ***Required fees:*** $992 full-time, $587 per term part-time. ***Room and board:*** $9340. Room and board charges vary according to board plan and housing facility. ***Waivers:*** senior citizens and employees or children of employees.

APPLYING
Standardized Tests *Required:* non-traditional students must take the ACT Compass test (for admission). *Required for some:* SAT or ACT (for admission), SAT Subject Tests (for admission). *Recommended:* SAT or ACT (for admission), SAT Subject Tests (for admission).

Options: electronic application, deferred entrance.

Application fee: $20.

Required: minimum 2.0 GPA, proof of immunization. ***Required for some:*** high school transcript.

Application deadlines: 8/1 (freshmen), 8/1 (transfers).

Notification: continuous until 8/8 (freshmen), continuous until 8/8 (transfers).

CONTACT
Darton State College, 2400 Gillionville Road, Albany, GA 31707-3098. *Phone:* 229-430-6740. *Toll-free phone:* 866-775-1214.

DeVry University

Alpharetta, Georgia

http://www.devry.edu/

- **Proprietary** comprehensive, founded 1997, part of DeVry University
- **Suburban** campus with easy access to Atlanta
- **Coed**

ACADEMICS
Calendar: semesters. *Degrees:* associate, bachelor's, and master's.

COSTS & FINANCIAL AID
Costs (2014–15) ***Tuition:*** $17,052 full-time, $609 per credit hour part-time. ***Required fees:*** $80 full-time.

Financial Aid Of all full-time matriculated undergraduates who enrolled in 2007, 171 applied for aid, 159 were judged to have need, 11 had their need fully met. In 2007, 17 non-need-based awards were made. ***Average percent of need met:*** 45. ***Average financial aid package:*** $13,554. ***Average need-based loan:*** $8238. ***Average need-based gift aid:*** $5898. ***Average non-need-based aid:*** $13,569. ***Average indebtedness upon graduation:*** $32,836.

CONTACT
Admissions Office, DeVry University, 2555 Northwinds Parkway, Alpharetta, GA 30009. *Phone:* 770-619-3600. *Toll-free phone:* 866-338-7941.

DeVry University

Decatur, Georgia

http://www.devry.edu/

- **Proprietary** comprehensive, founded 1969, part of DeVry University
- **Suburban** campus
- **Coed** 1,684 undergraduate students, 36% full-time, 59% women, 41% men
- **Minimally difficult** entrance level

UNDERGRAD STUDENTS
598 full-time, 1,086 part-time. 4% are from out of state; 54% Black or African American, non-Hispanic/Latino; 5% Hispanic/Latino; 1% Asian, non-Hispanic/Latino; 0.1% Native Hawaiian or other Pacific Islander, non-Hispanic/Latino; 0.2% American Indian or Alaska Native, non-Hispanic/Latino; 1% Two or more races, non-Hispanic/Latino; 15% Race/ethnicity unknown; 0.9% international; 29% transferred in.

Freshmen
Admission: 81 enrolled.

FACULTY
Total: 148, 19% full-time.
Student/faculty ratio: 16:1.

ACADEMICS
Calendar: semesters. *Degrees:* associate, bachelor's, master's, and postbachelor's certificates.

Special study options: adult/continuing education programs, part-time degree program.

STUDENT LIFE
Housing options: college housing not available.

Athletics ***Intramural sports:*** basketball M/W, football M/W, softball M/W, volleyball M/W.

COSTS
Costs (2014–15) ***Tuition:*** $17,052 full-time, $609 per credit hour part-time. ***Required fees:*** $80 full-time.

APPLYING
Application fee: $40.
Required: high school transcript, interview.

CONTACT
DeVry University, 1 West Court Square, Suite 100, Decatur, GA 30030-2556. *Phone:* 404-270-2700. *Toll-free phone:* 866-338-7941.

DeVry University

Duluth, Georgia

http://www.devry.edu/

- **Proprietary** comprehensive
- **Coed**

ACADEMICS
Calendar: semesters. *Degrees:* associate, bachelor's, and master's.

COSTS
Costs (2014–15) ***Tuition:*** $17,052 full-time, $609 per credit hour part-time. ***Required fees:*** $80 full-time.

CONTACT
Admissions Office, DeVry University, 3505 Koger Boulevard, Suite 170, Duluth, GA 30096-7671. *Phone:* 770-381-4400. *Toll-free phone:* 866-338-7941.

Emmanuel College

Franklin Springs, Georgia

http://www.ec.edu/

- **Independent** 4-year, founded 1919, affiliated with Pentecostal Holiness Church
- **Rural** 90-acre campus with easy access to Atlanta, GA
- **Endowment** $3.9 million
- **Coed** 816 undergraduate students, 89% full-time, 50% women, 50% men
- **Moderately difficult** entrance level, 49% of applicants were admitted

UNDERGRAD STUDENTS
723 full-time, 93 part-time. Students come from 18 states and territories; 14 other countries; 25% are from out of state; 16% Black or African American, non-Hispanic/Latino; 4% Hispanic/Latino; 1% Asian, non-Hispanic/Latino; 0.2% Native Hawaiian or other Pacific Islander, non-Hispanic/Latino; 0.9% Two or more races, non-Hispanic/Latino; 4% international; 9% transferred in; 60% live on campus.

Freshmen
Admission: 1,480 applied, 727 admitted, 193 enrolled. ***Average high school GPA:*** 3.32.

Retention: 62% of full-time freshmen returned.

FACULTY
Total: 89, 54% full-time, 34% with terminal degrees.
Student/faculty ratio: 12:1.

ACADEMICS
Calendar: semesters. *Degrees:* associate and bachelor's.

Special study options: academic remediation for entering students, accelerated degree program, advanced placement credit, distance learning, honors programs, independent study, internships, part-time degree program, services for LD students, study abroad, summer session for credit.

Unusual degree programs: 3-2 Psychology: Richmont University, Atlanta, Georgia.

Computers: 80 computers/terminals are available on campus for general student use. Students can access the following: campus intranet, computer help desk, free student e-mail accounts, online (class) grades, online (class) registration, online (class) schedules. Campuswide network is available. 100% of college-owned or -operated housing units are wired for high-speed Internet access. Wireless service is available via entire campus.

STUDENT LIFE
Housing options: on-campus residence required through sophomore year; men-only, women-only. Campus housing is university owned. Freshman campus housing is guaranteed.

Activities and organizations: drama/theater group, choral group, Students in Free Enterprise (SIFE), Fellowship of Christian Athletes, SOS, BSU, International Students Club.

Athletics Member NCAA, NCCAA. All NCAA Division II. ***Intercollegiate sports:*** archery M(s)/W(s), baseball M(s), basketball M(s)/W(s), bowling M(s)/W(s), cheerleading M(s)/W(s), cross-country running M(s)/W(s), golf M(s)/W(s), lacrosse M(s)/W(s), riflery M(s)/W(s), soccer M(s)/W(s), softball W(s), swimming and diving M(s)/W(s), tennis M(s)/W(s), track and field M(s)/W(s), volleyball M(s)/W(s), wrestling M(s)/W(s). ***Intramural sports:*** basketball M/W, football M/W, golf M/W, soccer M/W, tennis M/W, track and field M/W, volleyball M/W, weight lifting M/W.

Campus security: 24-hour patrols.

Student services: personal/psychological counseling.

COSTS & FINANCIAL AID

Costs (2014–15) ***Comprehensive fee:*** $25,370 includes full-time tuition ($18,000), mandatory fees ($170), and room and board ($7200). Part-time tuition: $750 per credit hour. ***Room and board:*** Room and board charges vary according to housing facility. ***Payment plan:*** installment. ***Waivers:*** senior citizens and employees or children of employees.

Financial Aid Of all full-time matriculated undergraduates who enrolled in 2014, 605 applied for aid, 544 were judged to have need, 100 had their need fully met. 120 Federal Work-Study jobs (averaging $883). 132 state and other part-time jobs (averaging $939). In 2014, 119 non-need-based awards were made. ***Average percent of need met:*** 68. ***Average financial aid package:*** $15,519. ***Average need-based loan:*** $3762. ***Average need-based gift aid:*** $11,770. ***Average non-need-based aid:*** $4930. ***Average indebtedness upon graduation:*** $29,202. ***Financial aid deadline:*** 6/15.

APPLYING

Standardized Tests *Required:* SAT or ACT (for admission).

Options: electronic application, early admission, deferred entrance.

Application fee: $25.

Required: essay or personal statement, high school transcript. ***Required for some:*** interview.

Application deadlines: 8/1 (freshmen), 8/1 (transfers).

Notification: continuous until 8/1 (freshmen), continuous until 8/1 (transfers).

CONTACT

Mrs. Kay Clifton, Director of Admissions, Emmanuel College, PO Box 129, 181 Spring Street, Franklin Springs, GA 30639-0129. *Phone:* 706-245-7226 Ext. 2814. *Toll-free phone:* 800-860-8800. *E-mail:* admissions@ec.edu.

Emory University

Atlanta, Georgia

http://www.emory.edu/

- **Independent Methodist** university, founded 1836
- **Suburban** 634-acre campus with easy access to Atlanta
- **Endowment** $5.8 billion
- **Coed**
- **Most difficult** entrance level

FACULTY

Student/faculty ratio: 8:1.

ACADEMICS

Calendar: semesters. *Degrees:* associate, bachelor's, master's, doctoral, post-master's, and postbachelor's certificates (enrollment figures include Emory University, Oxford College; application data for main campus only).

STUDENT LIFE

Housing options: on-campus residence required through sophomore year; coed. Campus housing is university owned. Freshman campus housing is guaranteed.

Activities and organizations: drama/theater group, student-run newspaper, radio and television station, choral group, Volunteer Emory, music/theater, student government, Outdoor Emory, Hillel, national fraternities, national sororities.

Athletics Member NCAA. All Division III.

Campus security: 24-hour emergency response devices and patrols, student patrols, late-night transport/escort service, controlled dormitory access.

Student services: health clinic, personal/psychological counseling, women's center, legal services.

COSTS & FINANCIAL AID

Costs (2014–15) ***Comprehensive fee:*** $57,768 includes full-time tuition ($44,400), mandatory fees ($608), and room and board ($12,760). Full-time tuition and fees vary according to degree level and location. Part-time tuition: $1850 per credit hour. ***College room only:*** $7560. Room and board charges vary according to board plan, housing facility, location, and student level.

Financial Aid Of all full-time matriculated undergraduates who enrolled in 2014, 2,813 applied for aid, 2,491 were judged to have need, 2,329 had their need fully met. In 2014, 260 non-need-based awards were made. ***Average percent of need met:*** 97. ***Average financial aid package:*** $40,309. ***Average need-based loan:*** $4620. ***Average need-based gift aid:*** $37,657. ***Average non-need-based aid:*** $22,538. ***Average indebtedness upon graduation:*** $24,741. ***Financial aid deadline:*** 3/1.

APPLYING

Standardized Tests *Required:* SAT or ACT (for admission). *Recommended:* SAT Subject Tests (for admission).

Options: electronic application, early admission, early decision, deferred entrance.

Application fee: $75.

Required: essay or personal statement, high school transcript, 2 letters of recommendation.

CONTACT

Dr. John Latting PhD, Dean of Admission, Emory University, 1390 Oxford Road NE, 3rd Floor, Atlanta, GA 30322-1100. *Phone:* 404-727-6036. *Toll-free phone:* 800-727-6036. *Fax:* 404-727-4303. *E-mail:* admiss@emory.edu.

Fort Valley State University

Fort Valley, Georgia

http://www.fvsu.edu/

- **State-supported** comprehensive, founded 1895, part of University System of Georgia
- **Small-town** 1365-acre campus
- **Coed**
- **Moderately difficult** entrance level

FACULTY

Student/faculty ratio: 19:1.

ACADEMICS

Calendar: semesters. *Degrees:* bachelor's and master's.

STUDENT LIFE

Housing options: men-only, women-only. Campus housing is university owned and leased by the school.

Activities and organizations: drama/theater group, student-run newspaper, radio and television station, choral group, marching band, Drama Group, Christian Student Organization, Habitat for Humanity, Debate Club, national fraternities, national sororities.

Athletics Member NCAA. All Division II.

Campus security: 24-hour emergency response devices and patrols, student patrols, late-night transport/escort service.

Student services: health clinic, personal/psychological counseling.

COSTS & FINANCIAL AID

Costs (2014–15) ***Tuition:*** state resident $4740 full-time, $158 per credit hour part-time; nonresident $17,246 full-time, $575 per credit hour part-time. Full-time tuition and fees vary according to course load, degree level, and student level. Part-time tuition and fees vary according to course load, degree level, and student level. ***Required fees:*** $1708 full-time. ***Room and board:*** $7920. Room and board charges vary according to board plan, housing facility, and student level.

Financial Aid Of all full-time matriculated undergraduates who enrolled in 2013, 2,570 applied for aid, 2,382 were judged to have need, 2,328 had their need fully met. 264 Federal Work-Study jobs (averaging $1500). In 2013, 2186 non-need-based awards were made. ***Average percent of need met:*** 48. ***Average financial aid package:*** $14,962. ***Average need-based loan:*** $2086. ***Average need-based gift aid:*** $7601. ***Average non-need-based aid:*** $2955. ***Average indebtedness upon graduation:*** $9301.

APPLYING

Standardized Tests *Required:* SAT or ACT (for admission).

Options: electronic application, early admission, deferred entrance.

Application fee: $20.

Required: high school transcript.

CONTACT

Mr. Donald Moore, Director of Admissions and Recruitment, Fort Valley State University, 1005 State University Drive, Fort Valley, GA 31030.

Phone: 478-825-6307. *Toll-free phone:* 877-462-3878. *Fax:* 478-825-6169. *E-mail:* admissap@fvsu.edu.

Georgia College & State University

Milledgeville, Georgia

http://www.gcsu.edu/

- **State-supported** comprehensive, founded 1889, part of University System of Georgia
- **Small-town** 602-acre campus
- **Endowment** $33.2 million
- **Coed** 5,927 undergraduate students, 93% full-time, 61% women, 39% men
- **Moderately difficult** entrance level, 76% of applicants were admitted

UNDERGRAD STUDENTS

5,521 full-time, 406 part-time. Students come from 21 states and territories; 26 other countries; 1% are from out of state; 5% Black or African American, non-Hispanic/Latino; 5% Hispanic/Latino; 1% Asian, non-Hispanic/Latino; 0.1% Native Hawaiian or other Pacific Islander, non-Hispanic/Latino; 0.2% American Indian or Alaska Native, non-Hispanic/Latino; 2% Two or more races, non-Hispanic/Latino; 0.3% Race/ethnicity unknown; 1% international; 5% transferred in; 38% live on campus.

Freshmen

Admission: 3,978 applied, 3,033 admitted, 1,465 enrolled. ***Average high school GPA:*** 3.45. ***Test scores:*** SAT critical reading scores over 500: 89%; SAT math scores over 500: 87%; SAT writing scores over 500: 81%; ACT scores over 18: 99%; SAT critical reading scores over 600: 36%; SAT math scores over 600: 32%; SAT writing scores over 600: 27%; ACT scores over 24: 63%; SAT critical reading scores over 700: 3%; SAT math scores over 700: 2%; SAT writing scores over 700: 1%; ACT scores over 30: 4%.

Retention: 86% of full-time freshmen returned.

FACULTY

Total: 411, 79% full-time, 62% with terminal degrees.

Student/faculty ratio: 17:1.

ACADEMICS

Calendar: semesters. *Degrees:* bachelor's, master's, doctoral, and post-master's certificates.

Special study options: accelerated degree program, advanced placement credit, distance learning, double majors, English as a second language, external degree program, freshman honors college, honors programs, independent study, internships, part-time degree program, services for LD students, student-designed majors, study abroad, summer session for credit. ***ROTC:*** Army (c).

Unusual degree programs: 3-2 engineering with Georgia Institute of Technology.

Computers: 900 computers/terminals and 6,295 ports are available on campus for general student use. Students can access the following: campus intranet, computer help desk, free student e-mail accounts, online (class) grades, online (class) registration, online (class) schedules. Campuswide network is available. 100% of college-owned or -operated housing units are wired for high-speed Internet access. Wireless service is available via entire campus.

STUDENT LIFE

Housing options: on-campus residence required for freshman year; coed, special housing for students with disabilities. Campus housing is university owned and leased by the school. Freshman applicants given priority for college housing.

Activities and organizations: drama/theater group, student-run newspaper, radio station, choral group, National Society of Collegiate Scholars, International Club, Campus Activities Board, Wesley Foundation of Campus Ministries, Gamma Sigma Sigma, national fraternities, national sororities.

Athletics Member NCAA. All Division II. ***Intercollegiate sports:*** baseball M(s), basketball M(s)/W(s), cheerleading M/W, cross-country running M(s)/W(s), golf M(s), soccer W(s), softball W(s), tennis M(s)/W(s), volleyball W(s). ***Intramural sports:*** basketball M/W, equestrian sports M(c)/W(c), golf M(c), lacrosse M(c)/W(c), rugby M(c), soccer M(c)/W(c), softball W(c), swimming and diving M(c)/W(c), table tennis M(c)/W(c), tennis M(c)/W(c), ultimate Frisbee M/W(c), volleyball M/W(c).

Campus security: 24-hour emergency response devices and patrols, student patrols, late-night transport/escort service, controlled dormitory access.

Student services: health clinic, personal/psychological counseling, women's center.

COSTS & FINANCIAL AID

Costs (2014–15) ***Tuition:*** state resident $6970 full-time; nonresident $25,318 full-time. Full-time tuition and fees vary according to course load, location, and program. Part-time tuition and fees vary according to course load, location, and program. ***Required fees:*** $1990 full-time. ***Room and board:*** $9940; room only: $5860. Room and board charges vary according to board plan and housing facility. ***Payment plan:*** installment. ***Waivers:*** senior citizens and employees or children of employees.

Financial Aid Of all full-time matriculated undergraduates who enrolled in 2013, 4,258 applied for aid, 2,949 were judged to have need. In 2013, 116 non-need-based awards were made. ***Average percent of need met:*** 30. ***Average financial aid package:*** $9534. ***Average need-based loan:*** $4248. ***Average need-based gift aid:*** $4346. ***Average non-need-based aid:*** $1613. ***Average indebtedness upon graduation:*** $21,919.

APPLYING

Standardized Tests *Required:* SAT or ACT (for admission). *Required for some:* SAT Subject Tests (for admission).

Options: electronic application, early admission, early action, deferred entrance.

Application fee: $40.

Required: essay or personal statement, proof of immunization. ***Required for some:*** high school transcript.

Application deadlines: 4/1 (freshmen), 4/1 (out-of-state freshmen), 7/1 (transfers), 11/1 (early action).

Notification: continuous (freshmen), continuous (out-of-state freshmen), continuous (transfers), 12/15 (early action).

CONTACT

Mr. Ramon Blakley, Director of Admissions, Georgia College & State University, CPO Box 023, Milledgeville, GA 31061. *Phone:* 478-445-1283. *Toll-free phone:* 800-342-0471. *Fax:* 478-445-3653. *E-mail:* admissions@gcsu.edu.

Georgia Gwinnett College

Lawrenceville, Georgia

http://www.ggc.edu/

- **State-supported** 4-year, part of University System of Georgia
- **Suburban** 260-acre campus with easy access to Atlanta
- **Coed** 10,828 undergraduate students, 70% full-time, 55% women, 45% men
- **Noncompetitive** entrance level, 91% of applicants were admitted

UNDERGRAD STUDENTS

7,527 full-time, 3,301 part-time. Students come from 32 states and territories; 104 other countries; 1% are from out of state; 31% Black or African American, non-Hispanic/Latino; 15% Hispanic/Latino; 9% Asian, non-Hispanic/Latino; 0.1% Native Hawaiian or other Pacific Islander, non-Hispanic/Latino; 0.1% American Indian or Alaska Native, non-Hispanic/Latino; 4% Two or more races, non-Hispanic/Latino; 1% Race/ethnicity unknown; 2% international; 7% transferred in; 7% live on campus.

Freshmen

Admission: 3,817 applied, 3,472 admitted, 2,445 enrolled. ***Test scores:*** SAT critical reading scores over 500: 36%; SAT math scores over 500: 33%; SAT writing scores over 500: 26%; ACT scores over 18: 61%; SAT critical reading scores over 600: 7%; SAT math scores over 600: 7%; SAT writing scores over 600: 4%; ACT scores over 24: 11%.

Retention: 68% of full-time freshmen returned.

FACULTY

Total: 602, 65% full-time, 66% with terminal degrees.

Student/faculty ratio: 19:1.

ACADEMICS
Degrees: associate and bachelor's.

Special study options: academic remediation for entering students, advanced placement credit, double majors, English as a second language, honors programs, internships, part-time degree program, services for LD students, study abroad, summer session for credit. ***ROTC:*** Army (b).

Computers: 243 computers/terminals are available on campus for general student use. Students can access the following: campus intranet, computer help desk, free student e-mail accounts, online (class) grades, online (class) registration, online (class) schedules. Campuswide network is available. 100% of college-owned or -operated housing units are wired for high-speed Internet access. Wireless service is available via entire campus.

STUDENT LIFE
Housing options: coed. Campus housing is university owned. Freshman campus housing is guaranteed.

Athletics Member NAIA. ***Intercollegiate sports:*** baseball M, soccer M/W, softball W, tennis M/W.

Campus security: 24-hour emergency response devices and patrols, student patrols, controlled dormitory access.

Student services: health clinic, personal/psychological counseling.

COSTS
Costs (2014–15) ***Tuition:*** state resident $3458 full-time, $118 per credit hour part-time; nonresident $13,244 full-time, $441 per credit hour part-time. Full-time tuition and fees vary according to reciprocity agreements. Part-time tuition and fees vary according to reciprocity agreements. ***Required fees:*** $1804 full-time, $642 per term part-time. ***Room and board:*** $11,494; room only: $8230. Room and board charges vary according to board plan. ***Payment plans:*** installment, deferred payment. ***Waivers:*** senior citizens.

APPLYING
Standardized Tests *Recommended:* SAT or ACT (for admission).

Options: electronic application, deferred entrance.

Application fee: $20.

Required: high school transcript, minimum 2.0 GPA.

Application deadlines: 6/1 (freshmen), 6/1 (out-of-state freshmen), rolling (transfers).

CONTACT
Admissions Office, Georgia Gwinnett College, 1000 University Center Lane, Lawrenceville, GA 30043. *Phone:* 678-407-5313. *Toll-free phone:* 877-704-4422. *E-mail:* ggcadmissions@ggc.edu.

Georgia Highlands College
Rome, Georgia
http://www.highlands.edu/

- **State-supported** primarily 2-year, founded 1970, part of University System of Georgia
- **Suburban** 226-acre campus with easy access to Atlanta
- **Endowment** $33,299
- **Coed**
- **Noncompetitive** entrance level

FACULTY
Student/faculty ratio: 22:1.

ACADEMICS
Calendar: semesters. *Degrees:* associate and bachelor's.

STUDENT LIFE
Housing options: college housing not available.

Activities and organizations: drama/theater group, student-run newspaper, Highlands Association of Nursing Students, Green Highlands, Black Awareness Society, Political Science Association, Phi Theta Kappa.

Athletics Member NJCAA.

Campus security: 24-hour emergency response devices and patrols, emergency phone/email alert system.

Student services: personal/psychological counseling.

COSTS & FINANCIAL AID
Costs (2014–15) ***Tuition:*** state resident $2660 full-time, $89 per hour part-time; nonresident $10,068 full-time, $336 per hour part-time. Full-time tuition and fees vary according to course load. Part-time tuition and fees vary according to course load. ***Required fees:*** $934 full-time, $467 per term part-time.

Financial Aid Of all full-time matriculated undergraduates who enrolled in 2013, 50 Federal Work-Study jobs (averaging $3500).

APPLYING
Standardized Tests *Required:* ACT Compass (for admission).

Options: electronic application, deferred entrance.

Application fee: $20.

Required: high school transcript, minimum 2.0 GPA. ***Required for some:*** Additional requirements for Nursing.

CONTACT
Sandra Davis, Director of Admissions, Georgia Highlands College, 3175 Cedartown Highway, Rome, GA 30161. *Phone:* 706-295-6339. *Toll-free phone:* 800-332-2406. *Fax:* 706-295-6341. *E-mail:* sdavis@highlands.edu.

Georgia Institute of Technology
Atlanta, Georgia
http://www.gatech.edu/

- **State-supported** university, founded 1885, part of University System of Georgia
- **Urban** 400-acre campus
- **Endowment** $1.9 billion
- **Coed** 14,682 undergraduate students, 90% full-time, 34% women, 66% men
- **Most difficult** entrance level, 33% of applicants were admitted

UNDERGRAD STUDENTS
13,253 full-time, 1,429 part-time. Students come from 53 states and territories; 95 other countries; 31% are from out of state; 6% Black or African American, non-Hispanic/Latino; 6% Hispanic/Latino; 19% Asian, non-Hispanic/Latino; 0.1% Native Hawaiian or other Pacific Islander, non-Hispanic/Latino; 0.1% American Indian or Alaska Native, non-Hispanic/Latino; 4% Two or more races, non-Hispanic/Latino; 1% Race/ethnicity unknown; 11% international; 3% transferred in; 54% live on campus.

Freshmen
Admission: 25,884 applied, 8,641 admitted, 2,809 enrolled. ***Average high school GPA:*** 3.95. ***Test scores:*** SAT critical reading scores over 500: 99%; SAT math scores over 500: 99%; SAT writing scores over 500: 99%; ACT scores over 18: 100%; SAT critical reading scores over 600: 90%; SAT math scores over 600: 96%; SAT writing scores over 600: 90%; ACT scores over 24: 99%; SAT critical reading scores over 700: 37%; SAT math scores over 700: 67%; SAT writing scores over 700: 42%; ACT scores over 30: 76%.

Retention: 96% of full-time freshmen returned.

FACULTY
Total: 1,153, 91% full-time, 84% with terminal degrees.
Student/faculty ratio: 19:1.

ACADEMICS
Calendar: semesters. *Degrees:* bachelor's, master's, and doctoral.

Special study options: academic remediation for entering students, accelerated degree program, advanced placement credit, cooperative education, distance learning, English as a second language, honors programs, independent study, internships, off-campus study, part-time degree program, services for LD students, student-designed majors, study abroad, summer session for credit. ***ROTC:*** Army (b), Navy (b), Air Force (b).

Unusual degree programs: 3-2 engineering with Many of the schools in the University System of Georgia, Morehouse College, Spelman College, Clark Atlanta University, and other liberal arts colleges, historically black colleges, and women's colleges in the Southeast.

Computers: 1,000 computers/terminals and 16,776 ports are available on campus for general student use. Students can access the following: campus intranet, computer help desk, free student e-mail accounts, online (class) grades, online (class) registration, online (class) schedules. Campuswide network is available. 100% of college-owned or -operated housing units are wired for high-speed Internet access. Wireless service is available via entire campus.

STUDENT LIFE

Housing options: coed, men-only, women-only, special housing for students with disabilities. Campus housing is university owned. Freshman campus housing is guaranteed.

Activities and organizations: drama/theater group, student-run newspaper, radio and television station, choral group, marching band, national fraternities, national sororities.

Athletics Member NCAA. All Division I except football (Division I-A). ***Intercollegiate sports:*** baseball M(s), basketball M(s)/W(s), cross-country running M(s)/W(s), golf M(s), softball W(s), swimming and diving M(s)/W(s), tennis M(s)/W(s), track and field M(s)/W(s), volleyball W(s). ***Intramural sports:*** archery M(c)/W(c), badminton M(c)/W(c), baseball M(c)/W(c), basketball M/W, cheerleading M(c)/W(c), crew M(c)/W(c), equestrian sports M(c)/W(c), fencing M(c)/W(c), field hockey M(c)/W(c), football M/W, golf M(c)/W(c), gymnastics M(c)/W(c), ice hockey M(c), lacrosse M(c)/W(c), racquetball M/W, rugby M(c)/W(c), sailing M(c)/W(c), soccer M/W, softball M/W, swimming and diving M(c)/W(c), table tennis M(c)/W(c), tennis M(c)/W(c), ultimate Frisbee M/W, volleyball M/W, water polo M(c)/W(c), weight lifting M(c), wrestling M(c).

Campus security: 24-hour emergency response devices and patrols, late-night transport/escort service, controlled dormitory access, self defense education, lighted pathways and walks, video cameras, email and phone alerts of emergency situations.

Student services: health clinic, personal/psychological counseling, women's center, legal services.

COSTS & FINANCIAL AID

Costs (2014–15) ***Tuition:*** state resident $9002 full-time, $2675 per term part-time; nonresident $28,306 full-time, $8399 per term part-time. Part-time tuition and fees vary according to course load. ***Required fees:*** $2392 full-time, $1196 per term part-time, $1196 per term part-time. ***Room and board:*** $12,840; room only: $8488. Room and board charges vary according to board plan and housing facility. ***Payment plan:*** deferred payment. ***Waivers:*** senior citizens and employees or children of employees.

Financial Aid Of all full-time matriculated undergraduates who enrolled in 2013, 9,371 applied for aid, 6,003 were judged to have need, 1,410 had their need fully met. 386 Federal Work-Study jobs (averaging $2191). In 2013, 936 non-need-based awards were made. ***Average percent of need met:*** 50. ***Average financial aid package:*** $11,566. ***Average need-based loan:*** $6446. ***Average need-based gift aid:*** $9522. ***Average non-need-based aid:*** $4367. ***Average indebtedness upon graduation:*** $24,891. ***Financial aid deadline:*** 2/15.

APPLYING

Standardized Tests *Required:* SAT or ACT (for admission).

Options: electronic application, early admission, early action, deferred entrance.

Application fee: $75.

Required: essay or personal statement, high school transcript.

Application deadlines: 1/10 (freshmen), 3/1 (transfers), 10/15 (early action).

Notification: 3/14 (freshmen), 6/15 (transfers), 1/10 (early action).

CONTACT

Mr. Rick A. Clark Jr., Director of Undergraduate Admissions, Georgia Institute of Technology, Office of Undergraduate Admission, Atlanta, GA 30332-0320. *Phone:* 404-894-4154. *Fax:* 404-894-9511. *E-mail:* admission@gatech.edu.

Georgia Regents University

Augusta, Georgia

http://www.gru.edu/

- **State-supported** comprehensive, founded 1828, part of University System of Georgia
- **Urban** 670-acre campus
- **Endowment** $9.4 million
- **Coed** 5,224 undergraduate students, 78% full-time, 64% women, 36% men

UNDERGRAD STUDENTS

4,077 full-time, 1,147 part-time. 25% Black or African American, non-Hispanic/Latino; 5% Hispanic/Latino; 0.8% Asian, non-Hispanic/Latino; 0.5% Native Hawaiian or other Pacific Islander, non-Hispanic/Latino; 0.4% American Indian or Alaska Native, non-Hispanic/Latino; 4% Two or more races, non-Hispanic/Latino; 6% Race/ethnicity unknown; 1% international.

Freshmen

Admission: 745 enrolled.

Retention: 70% of full-time freshmen returned.

FACULTY

Total: 1,483, 65% full-time, 97% with terminal degrees.

ACADEMICS

Calendar: semesters. *Degrees:* associate, bachelor's, master's, doctoral, post-master's, and postbachelor's certificates.

Special study options: academic remediation for entering students, adult/continuing education programs, advanced placement credit, cooperative education, distance learning, double majors, honors programs, independent study, internships, off-campus study, services for LD students, study abroad, summer session for credit. ***ROTC:*** Army (b).

Computers: Students can access the following: campus intranet, computer help desk, free student e-mail accounts, online (class) grades, online (class) registration, online (class) schedules. Campuswide network is available. 100% of college-owned or -operated housing units are wired for high-speed Internet access. Wireless service is available via classrooms, computer centers, computer labs, dorm rooms, learning centers, libraries, student centers.

STUDENT LIFE

Housing options: coed. Campus housing is university owned.

Activities and organizations: drama/theater group, student-run newspaper, choral group, national fraternities, national sororities.

Athletics Member NCAA. All Division II except men's and women's golf (Division I). ***Intercollegiate sports:*** baseball M(s), basketball M(s)/W(s), cross-country running M(s)/W(s), golf M(s)/W(s), softball W(s), tennis M(s)/W(s), track and field M/W. ***Intramural sports:*** badminton M/W, basketball M/W, football M/W, racquetball M/W, soccer M/W, softball M/W, table tennis M/W, volleyball M/W.

Campus security: 24-hour emergency response devices and patrols, late-night transport/escort service.

Student services: health clinic, personal/psychological counseling.

FINANCIAL AID

Financial Aid Of all full-time matriculated undergraduates who enrolled in 2013, 3,290 applied for aid, 2,724 were judged to have need, 121 had their need fully met. 73 Federal Work-Study jobs (averaging $4005). In 2013, 38 non-need-based awards were made. ***Average financial aid package:*** $2186. ***Average need-based loan:*** $1960. ***Average need-based gift aid:*** $2262. ***Average non-need-based aid:*** $1533. ***Average indebtedness upon graduation:*** $4839.

APPLYING

Options: electronic application.

Application fee: $50.

CONTACT

Georgia Regents University, 1120 15th Street, Augusta, GA 30912. *Phone:* 706-737-1632. *Toll-free phone:* 800-519-3388.

Georgia Southern University

Statesboro, Georgia

http://www.georgiasouthern.edu/

- **State-supported** university, founded 1906, part of University System of Georgia
- **Small-town** 900-acre campus
- **Endowment** $46.2 million
- **Coed** 18,004 undergraduate students, 88% full-time, 50% women, 50% men
- **Moderately difficult** entrance level, 63% of applicants were admitted

UNDERGRAD STUDENTS

15,844 full-time, 2,160 part-time. Students come from 48 states and territories; 65 other countries; 3% are from out of state; 26% Black or African American, non-Hispanic/Latino; 5% Hispanic/Latino; 1% Asian, non-Hispanic/Latino; 0.1% Native Hawaiian or other Pacific Islander, non-Hispanic/Latino; 0.5% American Indian or Alaska Native, non-Hispanic/Latino; 2% Two or more races, non-Hispanic/Latino; 1% Race/ethnicity unknown; 1% international; 6% transferred in; 28% live on campus.

Freshmen

Admission: 9,679 applied, 6,107 admitted, 3,498 enrolled. ***Average high school GPA:*** 3.27. ***Test scores:*** SAT critical reading scores over 500: 87%; SAT math scores over 500: 87%; SAT writing scores over 500: 67%; ACT scores over 18: 100%; SAT critical reading scores over 600: 24%; SAT math scores over 600: 23%; SAT writing scores over 600: 15%; ACT scores over 24: 41%; SAT critical reading scores over 700: 2%; SAT math scores over 700: 2%; SAT writing scores over 700: 1%; ACT scores over 30: 4%.

Retention: 81% of full-time freshmen returned.

FACULTY

Total: 889, 89% full-time, 78% with terminal degrees.

Student/faculty ratio: 21:1.

ACADEMICS

Calendar: semesters. *Degrees:* bachelor's, master's, doctoral, post-master's, and postbachelor's certificates.

Special study options: academic remediation for entering students, accelerated degree program, adult/continuing education programs, advanced placement credit, cooperative education, distance learning, double majors, English as a second language, honors programs, independent study, internships, off-campus study, part-time degree program, services for LD students, student-designed majors, study abroad, summer session for credit. ***ROTC:*** Army (b).

Unusual degree programs: 3-2 engineering with Georgia Institute of Technology; nursing.

Computers: 3,320 computers/terminals and 5,200 ports are available on campus for general student use. Students can access the following: campus intranet, computer help desk, free student e-mail accounts, online (class) grades, online (class) registration, online (class) schedules, online degree audit, online career services, and online healthcare. Campuswide network is available. 100% of college-owned or -operated housing units are wired for high-speed Internet access. Wireless service is available via entire campus.

STUDENT LIFE

Housing options: on-campus residence required for freshman year; coed, special housing for students with disabilities. Campus housing is university owned. Freshman applicants given priority for college housing.

Activities and organizations: drama/theater group, student-run newspaper, radio station, choral group, marching band, Residence Hall Association, Campus Religious Ministries, Student Government Association, Club Sports and Recreation, Greek Life, national fraternities, national sororities.

Athletics Member NCAA. All Division I. ***Intercollegiate sports:*** baseball M(s), basketball M(s)/W(s), cheerleading M/W, cross-country running W(s), football M(s), golf M(s), riflery M/W(s), soccer M(s)/W(s), softball W(s), swimming and diving W(s), tennis M(s)/W(s), track and field W(s), volleyball W(s). ***Intramural sports:*** archery M/W, baseball M, basketball M/W, bowling M/W, equestrian sports M/W, fencing M/W, football M/W, golf M/W, lacrosse M/W, riflery M/W, soccer M/W, softball M/W, swimming and diving M/W, table tennis M/W, tennis M/W, ultimate Frisbee M/W, volleyball M/W, weight lifting M/W.

Campus security: 24-hour emergency response devices and patrols, student patrols, late-night transport/escort service, controlled dormitory access, bike police and environmental safety services.

Student services: health clinic, personal/psychological counseling, women's center, legal services.

COSTS & FINANCIAL AID

Costs (2014–15) ***Tuition:*** state resident $5098 full-time, $170 per credit hour part-time; nonresident $17,994 full-time, $600 per credit hour part-time. Full-time tuition and fees vary according to course load, degree level, location, and program. Part-time tuition and fees vary according to course load, degree level, location, and program. ***Required fees:*** $2092 full-time, $1046 per term part-time. ***Room and board:*** $9752; room only: $6052. Room and board charges vary according to board plan and housing facility. ***Payment plan:*** installment. ***Waivers:*** senior citizens and employees or children of employees.

Financial Aid Of all full-time matriculated undergraduates who enrolled in 2013, 14,243 applied for aid, 10,959 were judged to have need, 904 had their need fully met. 261 Federal Work-Study jobs (averaging $1768). In 2013, 207 non-need-based awards were made. ***Average percent of need met:*** 49. ***Average financial aid package:*** $9309. ***Average need-based loan:*** $4765. ***Average need-based gift aid:*** $6347. ***Average non-need-based aid:*** $1775. ***Average indebtedness upon graduation:*** $24,201.

APPLYING

Standardized Tests *Required:* SAT or ACT (for admission).

Options: electronic application, early admission, deferred entrance.

Application fee: $30.

Required: minimum 2.0 GPA, proof of immunization prior to enrollment. ***Required for some:*** high school transcript.

Application deadlines: 5/1 (freshmen), 5/1 (out-of-state freshmen), 8/1 (transfers).

Notification: continuous (freshmen), continuous (out-of-state freshmen), continuous (transfers).

CONTACT

Miss Amy Smith, Director, Georgia Southern University, PO Box 8024, Statesboro, GA 30460. *Phone:* 912-478-5391. *Fax:* 912-478-7240. *E-mail:* admissions@georgiasouthern.edu.

★ Georgia Southwestern State University

Americus, Georgia

http://www.gsw.edu/

- **State-supported** comprehensive, founded 1906, part of University System of Georgia
- **Small-town** 400-acre campus
- **Endowment** $29.6 million
- **Coed** 2,527 undergraduate students, 69% full-time, 63% women, 37% men
- **Moderately difficult** entrance level, 70% of applicants were admitted

UNDERGRAD STUDENTS

1,752 full-time, 775 part-time. Students come from 24 states and territories; 34 other countries; 3% are from out of state; 28% Black or African American, non-Hispanic/Latino; 4% Hispanic/Latino; 1% Asian, non-Hispanic/Latino; 0.2% Native Hawaiian or other Pacific Islander, non-Hispanic/Latino; 0.1% American Indian or Alaska Native, non-Hispanic/Latino; 2% Two or more races, non-Hispanic/Latino; 0.4% Race/ethnicity unknown; 2% international; 13% transferred in; 31% live on campus.

Freshmen

Admission: 1,179 applied, 821 admitted, 392 enrolled. ***Average high school GPA:*** 3.24. ***Test scores:*** SAT critical reading scores over 500: 44%; SAT math scores over 500: 42%; SAT writing scores over 500: 34%; ACT scores over 18: 85%; SAT critical reading scores over 600: 10%; SAT math scores over 600: 6%; SAT writing scores over 600: 5%; ACT scores over 24: 18%; SAT critical reading scores over 700: 1%; ACT scores over 30: 1%.

Retention: 70% of full-time freshmen returned.

FACULTY

Total: 154, 71% full-time, 60% with terminal degrees.

Student/faculty ratio: 17:1.

ACADEMICS

Calendar: semesters. *Degrees:* bachelor's, master's, post-master's, and postbachelor's certificates.

Special study options: academic remediation for entering students, accelerated degree program, advanced placement credit, distance learning, double majors, English as a second language, honors programs, internships, off-campus study, part-time degree program, services for LD students, study abroad, summer session for credit.

Unusual degree programs: 3-2 engineering with Georgia Institute of Technology.

Computers: 260 computers/terminals are available on campus for general student use. Students can access the following: free student e-mail accounts, online (class) grades, online (class) registration, online (class) schedules. Campuswide network is available. 100% of college-owned or -operated housing units are wired for high-speed Internet access. Wireless service is available via dorm rooms, libraries.

STUDENT LIFE

Housing options: on-campus residence required through sophomore year; coed. Campus housing is university owned. Freshman campus housing is guaranteed.

Activities and organizations: drama/theater group, student-run newspaper, choral group, National sororities and fraternities, Orientation Team, Students in Free Enterprise, GSW Association of Nursing Students, Student African American Brotherhood, national fraternities, national sororities.

Athletics Member NCAA. All Division II. ***Intercollegiate sports:*** baseball M(s), basketball M(s)/W(s), cross-country running W(s), golf M(s), soccer M(s)/W(s), softball W(s), tennis M(s)/W(s). ***Intramural sports:*** badminton M/W, basketball M/W, racquetball M/W, softball M/W, table tennis M/W, ultimate Frisbee M/W, volleyball M/W, weight lifting M/W.

Campus security: 24-hour emergency response devices and patrols, late-night transport/escort service, controlled dormitory access.

Student services: health clinic, personal/psychological counseling.

COSTS & FINANCIAL AID

Costs (2014–15) ***Tuition:*** state resident $4740 full-time, $158 per credit hour part-time; nonresident $17,246 full-time, $575 per credit hour part-time. Full-time tuition and fees vary according to course load and location. Part-time tuition and fees vary according to course load and location. ***Required fees:*** $1330 full-time, $665 per term part-time. ***Room and board:*** $8350; room only: $4830. Room and board charges vary according to board plan and housing facility.

Financial Aid Of all full-time matriculated undergraduates who enrolled in 2014, 1,551 applied for aid, 1,320 were judged to have need, 130 had their need fully met. 52 Federal Work-Study jobs (averaging $2054). In 2014, 106 non-need-based awards were made. ***Average percent of need met:*** 58. ***Average financial aid package:*** $9373. ***Average need-based loan:*** $4205. ***Average need-based gift aid:*** $4751. ***Average non-need-based aid:*** $1444. ***Average indebtedness upon graduation:*** $23,450. ***Financial aid deadline:*** 6/15.

APPLYING

Standardized Tests *Required:* SAT or ACT (for admission).

Options: electronic application, early admission, deferred entrance.

Application fee: $25.

Required: high school transcript, minimum 2.0 GPA, SAT or ACT scores. ***Recommended:*** interview.

Application deadlines: 7/21 (freshmen), 7/21 (transfers).

Early decision deadline: 12/15.

Notification: continuous (freshmen), continuous (transfers), 1/15 (early decision).

CONTACT

Mr. David Jenkins, Assistant Director of Admissions, Georgia Southwestern State University, Americus, GA 31709. *Phone:* 229-928-1273. *Toll-free phone:* 800-338-0082. *Fax:* 229-931-2983. *E-mail:* admissions@gsw.edu.

Georgia State University

Atlanta, Georgia

http://www.gsu.edu/

- **State-supported** university, founded 1913, part of University System of Georgia
- **Urban** 72-acre campus with easy access to Atlanta
- **Endowment** $133.3 million
- **Coed** 25,315 undergraduate students, 75% full-time, 59% women, 41% men
- **Moderately difficult** entrance level, 57% of applicants were admitted

UNDERGRAD STUDENTS

18,976 full-time, 6,339 part-time. Students come from 53 states and territories; 136 other countries; 4% are from out of state; 41% Black or African American, non-Hispanic/Latino; 9% Hispanic/Latino; 12% Asian, non-Hispanic/Latino; 0.1% Native Hawaiian or other Pacific Islander, non-Hispanic/Latino; 0.2% American Indian or Alaska Native, non-Hispanic/Latino; 5% Two or more races, non-Hispanic/Latino; 3% Race/ethnicity unknown; 2% international; 11% transferred in; 17% live on campus.

Freshmen

Admission: 12,518 applied, 7,144 admitted, 3,696 enrolled. ***Average high school GPA:*** 3.34. ***Test scores:*** SAT critical reading scores over 500: 65%; SAT math scores over 500: 64%; ACT scores over 18: 95%; SAT critical reading scores over 600: 19%; SAT math scores over 600: 21%; ACT scores over 24: 34%; SAT critical reading scores over 700: 2%; SAT math scores over 700: 3%; ACT scores over 30: 3%.

Retention: 82% of full-time freshmen returned.

FACULTY

Total: 1,711, 70% full-time, 80% with terminal degrees.

Student/faculty ratio: 21:1.

ACADEMICS

Calendar: semesters. *Degrees:* certificates, bachelor's, master's, doctoral, post-master's, and postbachelor's certificates.

Special study options: advanced placement credit, cooperative education, distance learning, double majors, English as a second language, honors programs, independent study, internships, part-time degree program, services for LD students, study abroad, summer session for credit. ***ROTC:*** Army (b), Navy (c), Air Force (c).

Computers: 982 computers/terminals and 14,295 ports are available on campus for general student use. Students can access the following: computer help desk, free student e-mail accounts, online (class) grades, online (class) registration, online (class) schedules. Campuswide network is available. 100% of college-owned or -operated housing units are wired for high-speed Internet access. Wireless service is available via entire campus.

STUDENT LIFE

Housing options: coed, special housing for students with disabilities. Campus housing is university owned and leased by the school. Freshman applicants given priority for college housing.

Activities and organizations: drama/theater group, student-run newspaper, radio and television station, choral group, marching band, Spotlight Programs Board, Fraternities/Sororities, Service Organizations, Academic Organizations, Sports Clubs, national fraternities, national sororities.

Athletics Member NCAA. All Division I. ***Intercollegiate sports:*** baseball M(s), basketball M(s)/W(s), cheerleading M/W, crew M(c)/W(c), cross-country running M(s)/W, equestrian sports M(c)/W(c), football M(s), golf M(s)/W(s), ice hockey M(c), lacrosse M(c), rugby M(c), soccer M(s)/W(s), softball W(s), squash M(c)/W(c), swimming and diving M(c)/W(c), table tennis M(c)/W(c), tennis M(s)/W(s), track and field W(s), ultimate Frisbee M(c)/W(c), volleyball W(s). ***Intramural sports:*** badminton M/W, basketball M/W, bowling M/W, crew M(c)/W(c), equestrian sports M(c)/W(c), football M/W, golf M/W, racquetball M/W, rock climbing M(c)/W(c), soccer M/W, table tennis M/W, ultimate Frisbee M/W, volleyball M/W, wrestling M(c)/W(c).

Campus security: 24-hour emergency response devices and patrols, late-night transport/escort service, controlled dormitory access, Emergency Notification System.

Student services: health clinic, personal/psychological counseling.

COSTS & FINANCIAL AID
Costs (2014–15) ***Tuition:*** state resident $8112 full-time, $270 per credit hour part-time; nonresident $26,322 full-time, $867 per credit hour part-time. Part-time tuition and fees vary according to course load. ***Required fees:*** $2128 full-time, $1064 per term part-time. ***Room and board:*** $13,342; room only: $9616. Room and board charges vary according to housing facility. ***Waivers:*** senior citizens and employees or children of employees.

Financial Aid Of all full-time matriculated undergraduates who enrolled in 2013, 16,435 applied for aid, 14,430 were judged to have need, 966 had their need fully met. ***Average percent of need met:*** 58. ***Average financial aid package:*** $10,659. ***Average need-based gift aid:*** $4855. ***Average indebtedness upon graduation:*** $27,295. ***Financial aid deadline:*** 4/1.

APPLYING
Standardized Tests *Required:* SAT or ACT (for admission).

Options: electronic application, early admission, early action, deferred entrance.

Application fee: $60.

Required: essay or personal statement, high school transcript, minimum 2.8 GPA, 1 letter of recommendation, College preparatory curriculum as specified by the University System of Georgia Board of Regents. Combined SAT of 830. Freshman Index of 2500 or higher.

Application deadlines: 3/1 (freshmen), 8/1 (transfers), 11/15 (early action).

Notification: 5/1 (freshmen), continuous (transfers), 1/30 (early action).

CONTACT
Scott Burke, Director of Admissions, Georgia State University, PO Box 4009, Atlanta, GA 30302-4009. *Phone:* 404-413-2500. *Fax:* 404-413-2002. *E-mail:* onestopshop@gsu.edu.

Gordon State College

Barnesville, Georgia

http://www.gordonstate.edu/

- **State-supported** primarily 2-year, founded 1852, part of University System of Georgia
- **Small-town** 125-acre campus with easy access to Atlanta
- **Endowment** $7.8 million
- **Coed**
- **Minimally difficult** entrance level

FACULTY
Student/faculty ratio: 23:1.

ACADEMICS
Calendar: semesters. *Degrees:* certificates, associate, and bachelor's.

STUDENT LIFE
Housing options: on-campus residence required for freshman year; coed. Campus housing is university owned. Freshman applicants given priority for college housing.

Activities and organizations: drama/theater group, student-run newspaper, choral group, Campus Activity Board, Student Government Association, Earth wind fire (Science Club), Student African American Brotherhood (SAAB), Swazi Step Team.

Athletics Member NJCAA.

Campus security: 24-hour emergency response devices and patrols, student patrols, late-night transport/escort service, controlled dormitory access, RA's and RDs (housing) and Parking Patrol (Public Safety).

Student services: health clinic, personal/psychological counseling.

COSTS & FINANCIAL AID
Costs (2014–15) ***Tuition:*** state resident $3073 full-time; nonresident $9207 full-time. ***Required fees:*** $1074 full-time. ***Room and board:*** $9772; room only: $4410.

Financial Aid Of all full-time matriculated undergraduates who enrolled in 2013, 75 Federal Work-Study jobs (averaging $1850).

APPLYING
Standardized Tests *Required for some:* SAT and SAT Subject Tests or ACT (for admission).

Options: electronic application, early admission, deferred entrance.

Application fee: $30.

Required: high school transcript.

CONTACT
Gordon State College, 419 College Drive, Barnesville, GA 30204-1762. *Phone:* 678-359-5021. *Toll-free phone:* 800-282-6504.

ITT Technical Institute

Atlanta, Georgia

http://www.itt-tech.edu/

- **Proprietary** primarily 2-year, part of ITT Educational Services, Inc.
- **Coed**
- **Minimally difficult** entrance level

ACADEMICS
Degrees: associate and bachelor's.

STUDENT LIFE
Housing options: college housing not available.

CONTACT
Director of Recruitment, ITT Technical Institute, 485 Oak Place, Suite 800, Atlanta, GA 30349. *Phone:* 404-765-4600. *Toll-free phone:* 877-488-6102 (in-state); 877-788-6102 (out-of-state).

ITT Technical Institute

Douglasville, Georgia

http://www.itt-tech.edu/

- **Proprietary** 4-year
- **Coed**

CONTACT
Director of Recruiting, ITT Technical Institute, 5905 Stewart Parkway, Douglasville, GA 30135. *Phone:* 678-715-2100. *Toll-free phone:* 877-215-1173.

ITT Technical Institute

Duluth, Georgia

http://www.itt-tech.edu/

- **Proprietary** primarily 2-year, founded 2003, part of ITT Educational Services, Inc.
- **Coed**
- **Minimally difficult** entrance level

ACADEMICS
Calendar: quarters. *Degrees:* associate and bachelor's.

STUDENT LIFE
Housing options: college housing not available.

CONTACT
Director of Recruitment, ITT Technical Institute, 10700 Abbotts Bridge Road, Duluth, GA 30097. *Phone:* 678-957-8510. *Toll-free phone:* 866-489-8818.

ITT Technical Institute

Kennesaw, Georgia

http://www.itt-tech.edu/

- **Proprietary** primarily 2-year, founded 2004, part of ITT Educational Services, Inc.
- **Coed**
- **Minimally difficult** entrance level

ACADEMICS
Calendar: quarters. *Degrees:* associate and bachelor's.

CONTACT
Director of Recruitment, ITT Technical Institute, 2065 ITT Tech Way NW, Kennesaw, GA 30144. *Phone:* 770-426-2300. *Toll-free phone:* 877-231-6415 (in-state); 800-231-6415 (out-of-state).

Kennesaw State University

Kennesaw, Georgia

http://www.kennesaw.edu/

- **State-supported** comprehensive, founded 1963, part of University System of Georgia
- **Suburban** 384-acre campus with easy access to Atlanta
- **Endowment** $26.0 million
- **Coed** 23,592 undergraduate students, 75% full-time, 57% women, 43% men
- **Moderately difficult** entrance level, 54% of applicants were admitted

UNDERGRAD STUDENTS

17,732 full-time, 5,860 part-time. 6% are from out of state; 19% Black or African American, non-Hispanic/Latino; 7% Hispanic/Latino; 3% Asian, non-Hispanic/Latino; 0.2% Native Hawaiian or other Pacific Islander, non-Hispanic/Latino; 0.2% American Indian or Alaska Native, non-Hispanic/Latino; 4% Two or more races, non-Hispanic/Latino; 3% Race/ethnicity unknown; 2% international; 9% transferred in; 16% live on campus.

Freshmen

Admission: 11,309 applied, 6,073 admitted, 3,674 enrolled. ***Average high school GPA:*** 3.23. ***Test scores:*** SAT critical reading scores over 500: 81%; SAT math scores over 500: 74%; SAT writing scores over 500: 57%; ACT scores over 18: 98%; SAT critical reading scores over 600: 21%; SAT math scores over 600: 19%; SAT writing scores over 600: 12%; ACT scores over 24: 34%; SAT critical reading scores over 700: 2%; SAT math scores over 700: 1%; SAT writing scores over 700: 1%; ACT scores over 30: 2%.

Retention: 79% of full-time freshmen returned.

FACULTY

Total: 1,438, 53% full-time, 56% with terminal degrees.

Student/faculty ratio: 21:1.

ACADEMICS

Calendar: semesters. *Degrees:* certificates, bachelor's, master's, doctoral, post-master's, and postbachelor's certificates.

Special study options: adult/continuing education programs, advanced placement credit, cooperative education, distance learning, double majors, English as a second language, honors programs, internships, off-campus study, part-time degree program, services for LD students, study abroad, summer session for credit. ***ROTC:*** Army (c), Air Force (c).

Computers: 2,625 computers/terminals and 12,000 ports are available on campus for general student use. Students can access the following: campus intranet, computer help desk, free student e-mail accounts, online (class) grades, online (class) registration, online (class) schedules. Campuswide network is available. 100% of college-owned or -operated housing units are wired for high-speed Internet access. Wireless service is available via classrooms, computer centers, computer labs, dorm rooms, learning centers, libraries, student centers.

STUDENT LIFE

Housing options: coed. Campus housing is provided by a third party. Freshman applicants given priority for college housing.

Activities and organizations: drama/theater group, student-run newspaper, radio station, choral group, Global Society, Student Government Association, Kennesaw Activities Board, African-American Student Alliance, International Student Association, national fraternities, national sororities.

Athletics Member NCAA. All Division I except football (Division I-AA). ***Intercollegiate sports:*** baseball M(s), basketball M(s)/W(s), cross-country running M(s)/W(s), golf M(s)/W(s), lacrosse W(s), soccer W(s), softball W(s), tennis M(s)/W(s), track and field M(s)/W(s), volleyball W(s). ***Intramural sports:*** archery M(c)/W(c), badminton M(c)/W(c), baseball M(c)/W(c), basketball M/W, bowling M/W, cheerleading W(c), cross-country running M(c)/W(c), equestrian sports M(c)/W(c), fencing M(c)/W(c), football M, golf M/W, gymnastics M(c)/W(c), ice hockey M(c), lacrosse M(c)/W(c), rugby M(c)/W(c), soccer M/W, softball M/W, swimming and diving M(c)/W(c), tennis M/W, ultimate Frisbee M/W, volleyball M/W, weight lifting M(c)/W(c), wrestling M(c).

Campus security: 24-hour emergency response devices and patrols, student patrols, late-night transport/escort service, controlled dormitory access, Campus Advisory Webpage, Early Notification System that will send rapid email, text, and phone messages to all staff and students.

Student services: health clinic, personal/psychological counseling.

COSTS & FINANCIAL AID

Costs (2014–15) ***Tuition:*** state resident $5098 full-time, $170 per credit hour part-time; nonresident $17,994 full-time, $600 per credit hour part-time. Part-time tuition and fees vary according to course load. ***Required fees:*** $1834 full-time, $917 per term part-time. ***Room and board:*** $7914. Room and board charges vary according to board plan, housing facility, and student level. ***Payment plan:*** deferred payment. ***Waivers:*** senior citizens and employees or children of employees.

Financial Aid Of all full-time matriculated undergraduates who enrolled in 2014, 14,813 applied for aid, 12,119 were judged to have need, 2,042 had their need fully met. 162 Federal Work-Study jobs (averaging $2817). In 2014, 77 non-need-based awards were made. ***Average percent of need met:*** 67. ***Average financial aid package:*** $4322. ***Average need-based loan:*** $1789. ***Average need-based gift aid:*** $3407. ***Average non-need-based aid:*** $1218. ***Average indebtedness upon graduation:*** $24,740.

APPLYING

Standardized Tests *Required:* SAT or ACT (for admission). *Required for some:* SAT Subject Tests (for admission).

Options: electronic application, early admission, deferred entrance.

Application fee: $40.

Required: high school transcript, minimum 2.5 GPA, proof of immunization.

Application deadlines: 5/8 (freshmen), 6/19 (transfers).

Notification: continuous (freshmen), continuous (transfers).

CONTACT

Admissions Office, Kennesaw State University, 3391 Town Point Drive, Suite 1000, Mail Drop #9111, Kennesaw, GA 30144. *Phone:* 770-423-6300. *Fax:* 470-578-9169. *E-mail:* ksuadmit@kennesaw.edu.

LaGrange College

LaGrange, Georgia

http://www.lagrange.edu/

- **Independent United Methodist** comprehensive, founded 1831
- **Small-town** 120-acre campus with easy access to Atlanta
- **Endowment** $56.2 million
- **Coed** 880 undergraduate students, 91% full-time, 53% women, 47% men
- **Moderately difficult** entrance level, 55% of applicants were admitted

UNDERGRAD STUDENTS

804 full-time, 76 part-time. Students come from 18 states and territories; 4 other countries; 16% are from out of state; 23% Black or African American, non-Hispanic/Latino; 2% Hispanic/Latino; 0.9% Asian, non-Hispanic/Latino; 0.8% American Indian or Alaska Native, non-Hispanic/Latino; 4% Two or more races, non-Hispanic/Latino; 0.3% Race/ethnicity unknown; 0.6% international; 10% transferred in; 60% live on campus.

Freshmen

Admission: 1,343 applied, 742 admitted, 238 enrolled. ***Average high school GPA:*** 3.5. ***Test scores:*** SAT critical reading scores over 500: 63%; SAT math scores over 500: 58%; SAT writing scores over 500: 49%; ACT scores over 18: 97%; SAT critical reading scores over 600: 12%; SAT math scores over 600: 15%; SAT writing scores over 600: 11%; ACT scores over 24: 28%; SAT critical reading scores over 700: 1%; SAT math scores over 700: 1%; SAT writing scores over 700: 1%; ACT scores over 30: 3%.

Retention: 61% of full-time freshmen returned.

FACULTY

Total: 113, 64% full-time, 60% with terminal degrees.

Student/faculty ratio: 10:1.

ACADEMICS

Calendar: 4-1-4. *Degrees:* certificates, bachelor's, and master's.

Special study options: accelerated degree program, adult/continuing education programs, advanced placement credit, distance learning, double majors, independent study, internships, part-time degree program, services for LD students, student-designed majors, study abroad, summer session for credit.

Unusual degree programs: 3-2 engineering with Georgia Institute of Technology, Auburn University.

Computers: 116 computers/terminals and 960 ports are available on campus for general student use. Students can access the following: campus intranet, free student e-mail accounts, online (class) grades, online (class) registration, online (class) schedules. Campuswide network is available. 100% of college-owned or -operated housing units are wired for high-speed Internet access. Wireless service is available via entire campus.

STUDENT LIFE

Housing options: on-campus residence required through senior year; coed, men-only, women-only, special housing for students with disabilities. Campus housing is university owned. Freshman campus housing is guaranteed.

Activities and organizations: drama/theater group, student-run newspaper, choral group, Student Government Association, Greek Life, Baptist Collegiate Ministries, Wesley Fellowship, Fellowship of Christian Athletes, national fraternities, national sororities.

Athletics Member NCAA. All Division III. ***Intercollegiate sports:*** baseball M, basketball M/W, cheerleading W, cross-country running M/W, football M, golf M, lacrosse W, soccer M/W, softball W, swimming and diving M/W, tennis M/W, volleyball W. ***Intramural sports:*** basketball M/W, softball M/W, table tennis M/W, water polo M/W.

Campus security: 24-hour patrols, controlled dormitory access, A mass notification system, called e2Campus, allows the college to automatically send emergency messages to students and employees.

Student services: health clinic, personal/psychological counseling.

COSTS

Costs (2014–15) ***One-time required fee:*** $150. ***Comprehensive fee:*** $37,670 includes full-time tuition ($26,290), mandatory fees ($330), and room and board ($11,050). Full-time tuition and fees vary according to class time, course load, and program. Part-time tuition: $1080 per semester hour. Part-time tuition and fees vary according to class time, course load, and program. ***College room only:*** $6310. Room and board charges vary according to board plan and housing facility. ***Payment plan:*** installment. ***Waivers:*** senior citizens and employees or children of employees.

APPLYING

Standardized Tests *Required:* SAT or ACT (for admission). *Required for some:* SAT (for admission), ACT (for admission).

Options: electronic application, deferred entrance.

Required: essay or personal statement, high school transcript, SAT or ACT. ***Required for some:*** minimum 2.5 GPA, 3 letters of recommendation, interview.

Application deadlines: rolling (freshmen), rolling (transfers).

Notification: continuous (freshmen), continuous (transfers).

CONTACT

Mr. David McGreal, Director of Admission, LaGrange College, 601 Broad Street, LaGrange, GA 30240-2999. *Phone:* 706-880-8069. *Toll-free phone:* 800-593-2885. *Fax:* 706-880-8010. *E-mail:* dmcgreal@lagrange.edu.

Life University

Marietta, Georgia

http://www.life.edu/

- **Independent** comprehensive, founded 1974
- **Suburban** 96-acre campus
- **Coed** 774 undergraduate students, 69% full-time, 50% women, 50% men
- **Minimally difficult** entrance level, 57% of applicants were admitted

UNDERGRAD STUDENTS

534 full-time, 240 part-time. Students come from 44 states and territories; 14 other countries; 59% are from out of state; 22% Black or African American, non-Hispanic/Latino; 8% Hispanic/Latino; 2% Asian, non-Hispanic/Latino; 0.9% American Indian or Alaska Native, non-Hispanic/Latino; 33% Race/ethnicity unknown; 3% international; 13% transferred in; 17% live on campus.

Freshmen

Admission: 331 applied, 189 admitted, 98 enrolled. ***Average high school GPA:*** 2.81.

Retention: 64% of full-time freshmen returned.

FACULTY

Total: 199, 69% full-time, 79% with terminal degrees.

Student/faculty ratio: 16:1.

ACADEMICS

Calendar: quarters. *Degrees:* certificates, associate, bachelor's, master's, and doctoral.

Special study options: academic remediation for entering students, accelerated degree program, advanced placement credit, cooperative education, distance learning, double majors, English as a second language, independent study, internships, off-campus study, part-time degree program, services for LD students, student-designed majors, study abroad, summer session for credit.

Computers: Students can access the following: campus intranet, computer help desk, free student e-mail accounts, online (class) grades, online (class) registration. Campuswide network is available. 100% of college-owned or -operated housing units are wired for high-speed Internet access. Wireless service is available via classrooms, computer centers, computer labs, learning centers, libraries.

STUDENT LIFE

Housing options: coed. Campus housing is university owned.

Activities and organizations: student-run newspaper, Student Ambassadors, Jewish Life, Student Nutrition and Dietetics Association, Gay Straight Alliance, Hispanic Club.

Athletics Member NAIA. ***Intercollegiate sports:*** cross-country running W(s), ice hockey M, rugby M(s)/W(s), swimming and diving W(s), track and field W, wrestling M(s)/W(s). ***Intramural sports:*** basketball M/W, cross-country running M/W, football M, rugby M/W, soccer M, softball M/W, table tennis M, tennis M/W, volleyball M/W, weight lifting M/W.

Campus security: 24-hour emergency response devices and patrols, controlled dormitory access.

Student services: health clinic, personal/psychological counseling.

COSTS & FINANCIAL AID

Costs (2014–15) ***Comprehensive fee:*** $23,070 includes full-time tuition ($9540), mandatory fees ($1050), and room and board ($12,480). Full-time tuition and fees vary according to course load, degree level, and student level. Part-time tuition: $210 per credit hour. Part-time tuition and fees vary according to degree level and student level. ***Required fees:*** $350 per term part-time. ***Payment plan:*** installment. ***Waivers:*** employees or children of employees.

Financial Aid Of all full-time matriculated undergraduates who enrolled in 2013, 468 applied for aid, 441 were judged to have need. 111 Federal Work-Study jobs (averaging $2000). ***Average percent of need met:*** 32. ***Average financial aid package:*** $10,600. ***Average need-based loan:*** $4900. ***Average need-based gift aid:*** $5300. ***Average indebtedness upon graduation:*** $30,000.

APPLYING

Standardized Tests *Recommended:* SAT or ACT (for admission).

Options: electronic application.

Application fee: $50.

Required: high school transcript, minimum 2.0 GPA.

Notification: continuous (freshmen), continuous (transfers).

CONTACT

Miss Stephanie Buchanan, Office of New Student Development, Life University, 1269 Barclay Circle, Marietta, GA 30060. *Phone:* 800-543-3202. *Toll-free phone:* 800-543-3202. *Fax:* 770-426-2895. *E-mail:* admissions@life.edu.

Mercer University

Macon, Georgia

http://www.mercer.edu/

- **Independent Baptist** university, founded 1833
- **Suburban** 150-acre campus with easy access to Atlanta
- **Endowment** $256.9 million
- **Coed** 2,747 undergraduate students, 97% full-time, 49% women, 51% men
- **Moderately difficult** entrance level, 67% of applicants were admitted

UNDERGRAD STUDENTS
2,677 full-time, 70 part-time. Students come from 40 states and territories; 38 other countries; 19% are from out of state; 19% Black or African American, non-Hispanic/Latino; 5% Hispanic/Latino; 7% Asian, non-Hispanic/Latino; 0.2% Native Hawaiian or other Pacific Islander, non-Hispanic/Latino; 0.5% American Indian or Alaska Native, non-Hispanic/Latino; 3% Two or more races, non-Hispanic/Latino; 3% Race/ethnicity unknown; 4% international; 3% transferred in; 74% live on campus.

Freshmen
Admission: 4,375 applied, 2,919 admitted, 807 enrolled. ***Average high school GPA:*** 3.75. ***Test scores:*** SAT critical reading scores over 500: 93%; SAT math scores over 500: 96%; SAT writing scores over 500: 84%; ACT scores over 18: 100%; SAT critical reading scores over 600: 44%; SAT math scores over 600: 50%; SAT writing scores over 600: 33%; ACT scores over 24: 84%; SAT critical reading scores over 700: 10%; SAT math scores over 700: 7%; SAT writing scores over 700: 5%; ACT scores over 30: 24%.

Retention: 80% of full-time freshmen returned.

FACULTY
Total: 720, 56% full-time, 75% with terminal degrees.

Student/faculty ratio: 13:1.

ACADEMICS
Calendar: semesters. *Degrees:* bachelor's, master's, doctoral, and post-master's certificates.

Special study options: accelerated degree program, adult/continuing education programs, advanced placement credit, cooperative education, distance learning, double majors, English as a second language, honors programs, independent study, internships, off-campus study, part-time degree program, services for LD students, student-designed majors, study abroad, summer session for credit. ***ROTC:*** Army (b).

Unusual degree programs: pharmacy, physical therapy, physicians assistant.

Computers: Students can access the following: campus intranet, computer help desk, free student e-mail accounts, online (class) grades, online (class) registration, online (class) schedules. Campuswide network is available. 100% of college-owned or -operated housing units are wired for high-speed Internet access. Wireless service is available via entire campus.

STUDENT LIFE
Housing options: on-campus residence required through sophomore year; coed, men-only, women-only, special housing for students with disabilities. Campus housing is university owned and is provided by a third party. Freshman campus housing is guaranteed.

Activities and organizations: drama/theater group, student-run newspaper, radio and television station, choral group, marching band, national fraternities, national sororities.

Athletics Member NCAA. All Division I. ***Intercollegiate sports:*** baseball M(s), basketball M(s)/W(s), cross-country running M(s)/W(s), football M, golf M(s)/W(s), lacrosse M(s)/W(s), soccer M(s)/W(s), softball W(s), tennis M(s)/W(s), track and field W, volleyball W(s). ***Intramural sports:*** basketball M/W, cheerleading M/W, equestrian sports W(c), golf M/W, lacrosse M(c)/W(c), soccer M/W, softball M/W, swimming and diving M(c)/W(c), table tennis M(c)/W(c), tennis M/W, volleyball M/W, wrestling M(c).

Campus security: 24-hour emergency response devices and patrols, student patrols, late-night transport/escort service, controlled dormitory access, patrols by police officers.

Student services: health clinic, personal/psychological counseling.

COSTS & FINANCIAL AID
Costs (2014–15) ***Comprehensive fee:*** $44,458 includes full-time tuition ($33,480), mandatory fees ($300), and room and board ($10,678). Full-time tuition and fees vary according to location. Part-time tuition: $1116 per credit hour. Part-time tuition and fees vary according to course load and location. ***Required fees:*** $10 per credit hour part-time. ***College room only:*** $4880. Room and board charges vary according to board plan, housing facility, location, and student level. ***Payment plan:*** installment. ***Waivers:*** employees or children of employees.

Financial Aid Of all full-time matriculated undergraduates who enrolled in 2014, 2,604 applied for aid, 1,920 were judged to have need, 667 had their need fully met. In 2014, 613 non-need-based awards were made. ***Average percent of need met:*** 82. ***Average financial aid package:*** $32,468. ***Average need-based loan:*** $9226. ***Average need-based gift aid:*** $24,043. ***Average non-need-based aid:*** $19,145. ***Average indebtedness upon graduation:*** $30,018.

APPLYING
Standardized Tests *Required:* SAT or ACT (for admission).

Options: electronic application, early admission, early action, deferred entrance.

Application fee: $50.

Required: essay or personal statement, high school transcript, minimum 3.0 GPA. ***Required for some:*** 2 letters of recommendation, interview. ***Recommended:*** interview, counselor's evaluation.

Application deadlines: 7/1 (freshmen), rolling (transfers), 11/1 (early action).

Notification: continuous (freshmen), continuous (transfers), 11/15 (early action).

CONTACT
Ms. Alejandra Sosa, Director of Freshman Admissions, Mercer University, 1400 Coleman Avenue, Macon, GA 31207-0003. *Phone:* 478-301-5125. *Toll-free phone:* 800-MERCER-U. *E-mail:* sosa_ac@mercer.edu.

Morehouse College

Atlanta, Georgia

http://www.morehouse.edu/

- **Independent** 4-year, founded 1867
- **Urban** 61-acre campus
- **Endowment** $125.8 million
- **Men only**
- **Moderately difficult** entrance level

FACULTY
Student/faculty ratio: 12:1.

ACADEMICS
Calendar: semesters. *Degree:* bachelor's.

STUDENT LIFE
Housing options: on-campus residence required for freshman year; men-only. Campus housing is university owned. Freshman campus housing is guaranteed.

Activities and organizations: drama/theater group, student-run newspaper, choral group, marching band, Morehouse College Glee Club, Morehouse Business Association, NAACP, Morehouse Public Health Association, Pre-Law Society, national fraternities.

Athletics Member NCAA. All Division II.

Campus security: 24-hour emergency response devices and patrols, late-night transport/escort service, controlled dormitory access.

Student services: health clinic, personal/psychological counseling.

COSTS & FINANCIAL AID
Costs (2014–15) ***Comprehensive fee:*** $39,049 includes full-time tuition ($23,966), mandatory fees ($2373), and room and board ($12,710). Full-time tuition and fees vary according to course load and student level. Part-time tuition: $988 per hour. Part-time tuition and fees vary according to course load. ***College room only:*** $7510. Room and board charges vary according to board plan.

Financial Aid Of all full-time matriculated undergraduates who enrolled in 2012, 2,221 applied for aid, 2,221 were judged to have need, 466 had their need fully met. 201 Federal Work-Study jobs (averaging $1189). 60 state and other part-time jobs (averaging $1572). ***Average percent of need met:*** 61. ***Average financial aid package:*** $21,418. ***Average need-based loan:*** $5410. ***Average need-based gift aid:*** $18,253. ***Average indebtedness upon graduation:*** $37,559. ***Financial aid deadline:*** 4/1.

APPLYING

Standardized Tests *Required:* SAT or ACT (for admission).

Options: electronic application, early admission, early decision, early action, deferred entrance.

Application fee: $50.

Required: essay or personal statement, high school transcript. ***Recommended:*** minimum 3.0 GPA, interview.

CONTACT

Morehouse College, 830 Westview Drive, SW, Atlanta, GA 30314. *Phone:* 404-215-6272. *Toll-free phone:* 800-851-1254.

Oglethorpe University

Atlanta, Georgia

http://www.oglethorpe.edu/

- **Independent** 4-year, founded 1835
- **Suburban** 102-acre campus with easy access to Atlanta
- **Endowment** $19.7 million
- **Coed** 1,095 undergraduate students, 95% full-time, 58% women, 42% men
- **Very difficult** entrance level, 78% of applicants were admitted

UNDERGRAD STUDENTS

1,035 full-time, 60 part-time. Students come from 33 states and territories; 15 other countries; 26% are from out of state; 18% Black or African American, non-Hispanic/Latino; 10% Hispanic/Latino; 4% Asian, non-Hispanic/Latino; 0.3% American Indian or Alaska Native, non-Hispanic/Latino; 3% Two or more races, non-Hispanic/Latino; 25% Race/ethnicity unknown; 6% international; 8% transferred in; 65% live on campus.

Freshmen

Admission: 2,770 applied, 2,167 admitted, 277 enrolled. ***Average high school GPA:*** 3.51. ***Test scores:*** SAT critical reading scores over 500: 92%; SAT math scores over 500: 80%; SAT writing scores over 500: 76%; ACT scores over 18: 100%; SAT critical reading scores over 600: 40%; SAT math scores over 600: 28%; SAT writing scores over 600: 27%; ACT scores over 24: 58%; SAT critical reading scores over 700: 6%; SAT math scores over 700: 4%; SAT writing scores over 700: 3%; ACT scores over 30: 10%.

Retention: 71% of full-time freshmen returned.

FACULTY

Total: 96, 58% full-time, 74% with terminal degrees.

Student/faculty ratio: 15:1.

ACADEMICS

Calendar: semesters. *Degree:* bachelor's.

Special study options: accelerated degree program, adult/continuing education programs, advanced placement credit, cooperative education, double majors, honors programs, independent study, internships, off-campus study, part-time degree program, services for LD students, student-designed majors, study abroad, summer session for credit. ***ROTC:*** Air Force (c).

Unusual degree programs: 3-2 engineering with Auburn University, Georgia Institute of Technology, University of Florida, University of Southern California.

Computers: 575 ports are available on campus for general student use. Students can access the following: campus intranet, computer help desk, free student e-mail accounts, online (class) grades, online (class) registration, online (class) schedules. Campuswide network is available. 100% of college-owned or -operated housing units are wired for high-speed Internet access. Wireless service is available via classrooms, computer centers, computer labs, learning centers, libraries, student centers.

STUDENT LIFE

Housing options: on-campus residence required through sophomore year; coed. Campus housing is university owned. Freshman campus housing is guaranteed.

Activities and organizations: drama/theater group, student-run newspaper, choral group, national fraternities, national sororities.

Athletics Member NCAA. All Division III. ***Intercollegiate sports:*** baseball M, basketball M/W, cross-country running M/W, golf M/W, lacrosse M/W, soccer M/W, tennis M/W, track and field M/W, volleyball W. ***Intramural sports:*** badminton M/W, basketball M/W, football M/W, softball M/W, table tennis M/W, ultimate Frisbee M/W, volleyball M/W.

Campus security: 24-hour emergency response devices and patrols, late-night transport/escort service, controlled dormitory access.

Student services: health clinic, personal/psychological counseling.

COSTS & FINANCIAL AID

Costs (2014–15) ***Comprehensive fee:*** $44,200 includes full-time tuition ($32,200), mandatory fees ($300), and room and board ($11,700). Full-time tuition and fees vary according to degree level. Part-time tuition: $1350 per credit hour. Part-time tuition and fees vary according to class time, course load, and degree level. ***Room and board:*** Room and board charges vary according to housing facility and location. ***Payment plans:*** tuition prepayment, installment. ***Waivers:*** employees or children of employees.

Financial Aid Of all full-time matriculated undergraduates who enrolled in 2013, 746 applied for aid, 678 were judged to have need, 94 had their need fully met. In 2013, 242 non-need-based awards were made. ***Average percent of need met:*** 72. ***Average financial aid package:*** $25,722. ***Average need-based loan:*** $3266. ***Average need-based gift aid:*** $22,239. ***Average non-need-based aid:*** $14,279. ***Average indebtedness upon graduation:*** $23,777.

APPLYING

Standardized Tests *Required:* SAT or ACT (for admission).

Options: electronic application, early admission, early action, deferred entrance.

Application fee: $50.

Required: essay or personal statement, high school transcript, 1 letter of recommendation. ***Required for some:*** interview. ***Recommended:*** minimum 2.5 GPA, interview.

Application deadlines: rolling (freshmen), rolling (transfers), 12/5 (early action).

Notification: continuous (freshmen), continuous (transfers), 12/20 (early action).

CONTACT

Ms. Lucy Leusch, Vice President for Enrollment and Financial Aid, Oglethorpe University, 4484 Peachtree Road, NE, Atlanta, GA 30319. *Phone:* 404-364-8307. *Toll-free phone:* 800-428-4484. *Fax:* 404-364-8491. *E-mail:* admission@oglethorpe.edu.

Paine College

Augusta, Georgia

http://www.paine.edu/

- **Independent Methodist** 4-year, founded 1882
- **Urban** 65-acre campus with easy access to Columbia, SC
- **Endowment** $8.4 million
- **Coed**
- **Minimally difficult** entrance level

FACULTY

Student/faculty ratio: 14:1.

ACADEMICS

Calendar: semesters. *Degree:* bachelor's.

STUDENT LIFE

Housing options: men-only, women-only. Campus housing is university owned. Freshman applicants given priority for college housing.

Activities and organizations: drama/theater group, student-run newspaper, choral group, Wesley Fellowship, Alpha Kappa Mu National Honor Society, International Student Association, National Association for the Advancement of Colored People, Creme de la Creme Models, national fraternities, national sororities.

Athletics Member NCAA. All Division II.

Campus security: 24-hour emergency response devices and patrols, late-night transport/escort service.

Student services: health clinic, personal/psychological counseling.

COSTS & FINANCIAL AID

Costs (2014–15) ***One-time required fee:*** $23. ***Comprehensive fee:*** $19,826 includes full-time tuition ($11,880), mandatory fees ($1452), and room and board ($6494). Full-time tuition and fees vary according to class time, course load, and location. Part-time tuition: $495 per semester hour. Part-time tuition and fees vary according to class time, course load, and location. ***Room and board:*** Room and board charges vary according to housing facility. ***Payment plans:*** installment, deferred payment.

Financial Aid ***Average indebtedness upon graduation:*** $2304.

APPLYING

Standardized Tests *Required:* SAT or ACT (for admission).

Options: electronic application, early admission, deferred entrance.

Application fee: $35.

Required: essay or personal statement, high school transcript, minimum 2.0 GPA, 3 letters of recommendation. ***Required for some:*** score of 500 on each Georgia high school exit exam.

CONTACT

Mr. Reginald Beaty, Dean of Students, Paine College, 1235 15th Street, Augusta, GA 30901-3182. *Phone:* 706-821-8320. *Toll-free phone:* 800-476-7703. *Fax:* 706-821-8691. *E-mail:* rbeaty@paine.edu.

Piedmont College

Demorest, Georgia

http://www.piedmont.edu/

- **Independent** comprehensive, founded 1897, affiliated with United Church of Christ
- **Rural** 186-acre campus with easy access to Atlanta
- **Endowment** $54.5 million
- **Coed** 1,286 undergraduate students, 88% full-time, 66% women, 34% men
- **Moderately difficult** entrance level, 58% of applicants were admitted

UNDERGRAD STUDENTS

1,137 full-time, 149 part-time. Students come from 19 states and territories; 8 other countries; 7% are from out of state; 9% Black or African American, non-Hispanic/Latino; 4% Hispanic/Latino; 1% Asian, non-Hispanic/Latino; 0.1% Native Hawaiian or other Pacific Islander, non-Hispanic/Latino; 0.6% American Indian or Alaska Native, non-Hispanic/Latino; 2% Two or more races, non-Hispanic/Latino; 9% Race/ethnicity unknown; 0.2% international; 9% transferred in; 45% live on campus.

Freshmen

Admission: 994 applied, 572 admitted, 271 enrolled. ***Average high school GPA:*** 3.4. ***Test scores:*** SAT critical reading scores over 500: 42%; SAT math scores over 500: 36%; ACT scores over 18: 84%; SAT critical reading scores over 600: 6%; SAT math scores over 600: 9%; ACT scores over 24: 23%; SAT math scores over 700: 1%; ACT scores over 30: 2%.

Retention: 73% of full-time freshmen returned.

FACULTY

Total: 251, 47% full-time, 69% with terminal degrees.

Student/faculty ratio: 14:1.

ACADEMICS

Calendar: semesters. *Degrees:* bachelor's, master's, doctoral, and post-master's certificates.

Special study options: accelerated degree program, adult/continuing education programs, advanced placement credit, cooperative education, distance learning, double majors, honors programs, independent study, internships, off-campus study, part-time degree program, services for LD students, student-designed majors, study abroad, summer session for credit.

Unusual degree programs: 3-2 engineering with Georgia Institute of Technology; Engineering Physics (Primarily for Mechanical Engineering).

Computers: 150 computers/terminals are available on campus for general student use. Students can access the following: campus intranet, computer help desk, free student e-mail accounts, online (class) grades, online (class) registration, online (class) schedules. Campuswide network is available. Wireless service is available via classrooms, computer centers, computer labs, dorm rooms, learning centers, libraries, student centers.

STUDENT LIFE

Housing options: on-campus residence required through sophomore year; coed, men-only, women-only, special housing for students with disabilities. Campus housing is university owned. Freshman campus housing is guaranteed.

Activities and organizations: drama/theater group, student-run newspaper, radio and television station, choral group, Campus Activity Board, Residence Hall Council, Outdoor Club, Team Piedmont, Student Leadership Council.

Athletics Member NCAA. All Division III. ***Intercollegiate sports:*** baseball M, basketball M/W, cross-country running M/W, golf M/W, lacrosse M/W, soccer M/W, softball W, tennis M/W, track and field M/W, volleyball W. ***Intramural sports:*** cheerleading W.

Campus security: 24-hour emergency response devices and patrols, late-night transport/escort service.

Student services: personal/psychological counseling.

COSTS & FINANCIAL AID

Costs (2014–15) ***Comprehensive fee:*** $30,136 includes full-time tuition ($21,350) and room and board ($8786). Full-time tuition and fees vary according to course load, degree level, location, and program. Part-time tuition: $890 per credit. Part-time tuition and fees vary according to course load, degree level, location, and program. ***College room only:*** $4886. Room and board charges vary according to board plan. ***Payment plan:*** installment. ***Waivers:*** employees or children of employees.

Financial Aid Of all full-time matriculated undergraduates who enrolled in 2014, 1,102 applied for aid, 909 were judged to have need, 143 had their need fully met. 82 Federal Work-Study jobs (averaging $2606). 343 state and other part-time jobs (averaging $3132). In 2014, 200 non-need-based awards were made. ***Average percent of need met:*** 70. ***Average financial aid package:*** $18,169. ***Average need-based loan:*** $4196. ***Average need-based gift aid:*** $14,047. ***Average non-need-based aid:*** $11,292. ***Average indebtedness upon graduation:*** $23,481.

APPLYING

Standardized Tests *Required:* SAT or ACT (for admission).

Options: electronic application, early admission, deferred entrance.

Required: high school transcript, minimum 2.8 GPA. ***Required for some:*** interview. ***Recommended:*** essay or personal statement.

Application deadlines: 7/1 (freshmen), 7/1 (transfers).

CONTACT

Ms. Brenda Boonstra, Director of Undergraduate Admissions, Piedmont College, PO Box 10, 165 Central Avenue, Demorest, GA 30535. *Phone:* 706-776-0103 Ext. 1188. *Toll-free phone:* 800-277-7020. *Fax:* 706-776-6635. *E-mail:* bboonstra@piedmont.edu.

Point University

West Point, Georgia

http://point.edu/

- **Independent Christian** 4-year, founded 1937
- **Small-town** campus with easy access to Atlanta, GA and Montgomery, AL
- **Coed** 1,522 undergraduate students, 77% full-time, 56% women, 44% men
- **Moderately difficult** entrance level, 52% of applicants were admitted

UNDERGRAD STUDENTS

1,173 full-time, 349 part-time. Students come from 8 other countries; 24% are from out of state; 38% Black or African American, non-Hispanic/Latino; 3% Hispanic/Latino; 0.6% Asian, non-Hispanic/Latino; 0.1% Native Hawaiian or other Pacific Islander, non-Hispanic/Latino; 0.2% American Indian or Alaska Native, non-Hispanic/Latino; 5% Two or more races, non-Hispanic/Latino; 10% Race/ethnicity unknown; 0.7% international; 11% transferred in; 72% live on campus.

Freshmen

Admission: 954 applied, 495 admitted, 281 enrolled. ***Average high school GPA:*** 3.35. ***Test scores:*** SAT critical reading scores over 500: 31%; SAT math scores over 500: 33%; ACT scores over 18: 73%; SAT critical reading scores over 600: 3%; SAT math scores over 600: 3%; ACT scores over 24: 14%; ACT scores over 30: 2%.

Retention: 52% of full-time freshmen returned.

FACULTY

Total: 120, 28% full-time, 30% with terminal degrees.

Student/faculty ratio: 20:1.

ACADEMICS

Calendar: semesters. *Degrees:* certificates, associate, and bachelor's.

Special study options: accelerated degree program, adult/continuing education programs, advanced placement credit, distance learning, double majors, independent study, part-time degree program, services for LD students, summer session for credit.

Computers: 115 computers/terminals and 50 ports are available on campus for general student use. Students can access the following: campus intranet, computer help desk, free student e-mail accounts, online (class) grades, online (class) registration, online (class) schedules, free access to Wi-Fi campus wide. Campuswide network is available. 100% of college-owned or -operated housing units are wired for high-speed Internet access. Wireless service is available via entire campus.

STUDENT LIFE

Housing options: on-campus residence required through sophomore year; men-only, women-only. Campus housing is leased by the school. Freshman applicants given priority for college housing.

Activities and organizations: choral group, marching band, Student Government Association, Global Mission Conference, Campus Life Ministers, Campus Activities Board, Sunday Night Live.

Athletics Member NAIA, NCCAA. ***Intercollegiate sports:*** baseball M(s), basketball M(s)/W(s), cheerleading W(s), cross-country running M(s)/W(s), football M(s), golf M(s)/W(s), lacrosse M(s)/W(s), soccer M(s)/W(s), softball W(s), swimming and diving M(s)/W(s), tennis M(s)/W(s), volleyball W(s). ***Intramural sports:*** basketball M/W, football M/W, softball M/W, table tennis M/W, ultimate Frisbee M/W, volleyball M/W, weight lifting M/W.

Campus security: 24-hour patrols.

Student services: personal/psychological counseling.

COSTS

Costs (2014–15) ***Comprehensive fee:*** $24,000 includes full-time tuition ($16,700), mandatory fees ($950), and room and board ($6350). Full-time tuition and fees vary according to course load. Part-time tuition and fees vary according to course load. ***College room only:*** $3750. ***Payment plan:*** installment. ***Waivers:*** employees or children of employees.

APPLYING

Standardized Tests *Required:* SAT or ACT (for admission).

Options: electronic application, deferred entrance.

Application fee: $25.

Required: minimum 2.0 GPA, 1 letter of recommendation, SAT or ACT for some, COMPASS for some, college transcript if applicable. ***Required for some:*** essay or personal statement, high school transcript, interview. ***Recommended:*** high school transcript.

Application deadlines: 8/1 (freshmen), 8/1 (out-of-state freshmen), 8/1 (transfers).

Notification: continuous (freshmen), continuous (out-of-state freshmen), continuous (transfers).

CONTACT

Mr. Rusty Hassell, Director of Admission, Point University, 507 West 10th Street, West Point, GA 31833. *Phone:* 706-385-1503. *Toll-free phone:* 855-37-POINT. *Fax:* 706-645-9473. *E-mail:* admissions@point.edu.

Reinhardt University

Waleska, Georgia

http://www.reinhardt.edu/

- **Independent** comprehensive, founded 1883, affiliated with United Methodist Church
- **Rural** 600-acre campus with easy access to Atlanta
- **Coed** 1,334 undergraduate students, 92% full-time, 48% women, 52% men
- **Moderately difficult** entrance level, 90% of applicants were admitted

UNDERGRAD STUDENTS

1,231 full-time, 103 part-time. 5% are from out of state; 6% Black or African American, non-Hispanic/Latino; 18% Hispanic/Latino; 0.6% Asian, non-Hispanic/Latino; 0.4% American Indian or Alaska Native, non-Hispanic/Latino; 6% Race/ethnicity unknown; 0.2% international; 11% transferred in; 43% live on campus.

Freshmen

Admission: 1,172 applied, 1,055 admitted, 310 enrolled. ***Average high school GPA:*** 3.11. ***Test scores:*** SAT critical reading scores over 500: 48%; SAT math scores over 500: 47%; ACT scores over 18: 88%; SAT critical reading scores over 600: 13%; SAT math scores over 600: 10%; ACT scores over 24: 16%; SAT critical reading scores over 700: 1%; SAT math scores over 700: 1%; ACT scores over 30: 2%.

Retention: 63% of full-time freshmen returned.

FACULTY

Total: 172, 40% full-time, 33% with terminal degrees.

Student/faculty ratio: 12:1.

ACADEMICS

Calendar: semesters. *Degrees:* associate, bachelor's, and master's.

Special study options: academic remediation for entering students, adult/continuing education programs, advanced placement credit, cooperative education, distance learning, double majors, freshman honors college, honors programs, independent study, internships, off-campus study, part-time degree program, services for LD students, student-designed majors, study abroad, summer session for credit.

Computers: Students can access the following: campus intranet, computer help desk, free student e-mail accounts, online (class) grades, online (class) registration, online (class) schedules. Campuswide network is available. 100% of college-owned or -operated housing units are wired for high-speed Internet access. Wireless service is available via classrooms, computer centers, computer labs, dorm rooms, learning centers, libraries, student centers.

STUDENT LIFE

Housing options: on-campus residence required for freshman year; coed, men-only, women-only, special housing for students with disabilities. Campus housing is university owned. Freshman campus housing is guaranteed.

Activities and organizations: drama/theater group, student-run newspaper, television station, choral group, Real Deal, International and Historical Film Society, Student Government Association, SOAR (Student Orientation Leaders), Communication Club.

Athletics Member NAIA. ***Intercollegiate sports:*** baseball M(s), basketball M(s)/W(s), cross-country running M(s)/W(s), football M(s), golf M(s), lacrosse M(s)/W(s), soccer M(s)/W(s), softball W(s), tennis M(s)/W(s), volleyball W(s). ***Intramural sports:*** basketball M/W, cheerleading M/W, football M/W, soccer M/W, softball M/W, volleyball M/W.

Campus security: 24-hour emergency response devices and patrols, late-night transport/escort service, controlled dormitory access.

Student services: health clinic, personal/psychological counseling.

COSTS & FINANCIAL AID

Costs (2015–16) ***Comprehensive fee:*** $27,834 includes full-time tuition ($19,946), mandatory fees ($320), and room and board ($7568). Part-time tuition: $665 per credit hour.

Financial Aid Of all full-time matriculated undergraduates who enrolled in 2009, 1,601 applied for aid, 1,382 were judged to have need, 56 had their need fully met. In 2009, 235 non-need-based awards were made. ***Average percent of need met:*** 27. ***Average financial aid package:*** $9523. ***Average need-based loan:*** $3631. ***Average need-based gift aid:*** $7417.

Average non-need-based aid: $4221. *Average indebtedness upon graduation:* $21,096.

APPLYING

Standardized Tests *Required:* SAT or ACT (for admission).

Options: electronic application, early admission, deferred entrance.

Required: high school transcript, minimum 2.0 GPA.

CONTACT

Ms. Julie Fleming, Director of Admissions, Reinhardt University, 7300 Reinhardt College Circle, Waleska, GA 30183-0128. *Phone:* 770-720-5526. *Fax:* 770-720-5602. *E-mail:* admissions@mail.reinhardt.edu.

Savannah College of Art and Design

Savannah, Georgia

http://www.scad.edu/

- **Independent** comprehensive, founded 1978
- **Urban** campus
- **Coed** 9,695 undergraduate students, 83% full-time, 65% women, 35% men
- **Moderately difficult** entrance level, 66% of applicants were admitted

UNDERGRAD STUDENTS

8,043 full-time, 1,652 part-time. Students come from 54 states and territories; 93 other countries; 78% are from out of state; 11% Black or African American, non-Hispanic/Latino; 8% Hispanic/Latino; 8% Asian, non-Hispanic/Latino; 0.3% Native Hawaiian or other Pacific Islander, non-Hispanic/Latino; 0.5% American Indian or Alaska Native, non-Hispanic/Latino; 0.2% Two or more races, non-Hispanic/Latino; 5% Race/ethnicity unknown; 14% international; 6% transferred in; 41% live on campus.

Freshmen

Admission: 9,656 applied, 6,344 admitted, 1,925 enrolled. *Average high school GPA:* 3.44. *Test scores:* SAT critical reading scores over 500: 71%; SAT math scores over 500: 61%; SAT writing scores over 500: 61%; ACT scores over 18: 93%; SAT critical reading scores over 600: 28%; SAT math scores over 600: 20%; SAT writing scores over 600: 21%; ACT scores over 24: 50%; SAT critical reading scores over 700: 5%; SAT math scores over 700: 2%; SAT writing scores over 700: 3%; ACT scores over 30: 7%.

Retention: 82% of full-time freshmen returned.

FACULTY

Total: 655, 78% full-time, 78% with terminal degrees.

Student/faculty ratio: 19:1.

ACADEMICS

Calendar: quarters. *Degrees:* certificates, bachelor's, master's, and postbachelor's certificates.

Special study options: advanced placement credit, distance learning, double majors, English as a second language, independent study, internships, off-campus study, part-time degree program, services for LD students, study abroad, summer session for credit.

Computers: 3,464 computers/terminals are available on campus for general student use. Students can access the following: campus intranet, computer help desk, free student e-mail accounts, online (class) grades, online (class) registration, online (class) schedules. Campuswide network is available. 100% of college-owned or -operated housing units are wired for high-speed Internet access. Wireless service is available via entire campus.

STUDENT LIFE

Housing options: coed, women-only, special housing for students with disabilities. Campus housing is university owned and leased by the school. Freshman applicants given priority for college housing.

Activities and organizations: drama/theater group, student-run newspaper, radio station, choral group, Queers and Allies, HvZ (Humans vs. Zombies), Colleges Against Cancer, IDSA/ASID, MOME Love.

Athletics Member NAIA. *Intercollegiate sports:* cross-country running M(s)/W(s), equestrian sports M(s)/W(s), golf M(s)/W(s), lacrosse M(s)/W(s), soccer M(s)/W(s), swimming and diving M(s)/W(s), tennis M(s)/W(s), track and field M(s)/W(s). *Intramural sports:* badminton M/W, basketball M/W, football M/W, soccer M/W, tennis M/W, ultimate Frisbee M/W, volleyball M/W.

Campus security: 24-hour emergency response devices and patrols, student patrols, late-night transport/escort service, controlled dormitory access, video camera surveillance.

Student services: health clinic, personal/psychological counseling.

COSTS & FINANCIAL AID

Costs (2014–15) *Comprehensive fee:* $48,005 includes full-time tuition ($33,795), mandatory fees ($500), and room and board ($13,710). Full-time tuition and fees vary according to course load and degree level. Part-time tuition: $751 per quarter hour. Part-time tuition and fees vary according to course load and degree level. *College room only:* $8715. Room and board charges vary according to board plan, housing facility, and location. *Payment plan:* installment. *Waivers:* employees or children of employees.

Financial Aid Of all full-time matriculated undergraduates who enrolled in 2014, 4,837 applied for aid, 4,225 were judged to have need, 342 had their need fully met. In 2014, 2982 non-need-based awards were made. *Average percent of need met:* 18. *Average financial aid package:* $27,795. *Average need-based loan:* $4097. *Average need-based gift aid:* $6013. *Average non-need-based aid:* $9891. *Average indebtedness upon graduation:* $36,088.

APPLYING

Standardized Tests *Required:* SAT or ACT (for admission).

Options: electronic application, early admission, deferred entrance.

Application fee: $40.

Required for some: essay or personal statement, high school transcript, College transcripts required for transfer students; Portfolio/audition recommended for all performing arts, riding, writing, or visual arts applicants. *Recommended:* essay or personal statement, minimum 3.0 GPA, 3 letters of recommendation, interview.

Application deadlines: rolling (freshmen), rolling (transfers).

Notification: continuous (freshmen), continuous (transfers).

CONTACT

Ms. Jenny Jaquillard, Executive Director of Admissions, Recruitment and Events, Savannah College of Art and Design, 342 Bull Street, PO Box 3146, Savannah, GA 31402-3146. *Phone:* 912-525-5100. *Toll-free phone:* 800-869-7223. *Fax:* 912-525-5983. *E-mail:* admission@scad.edu.

Savannah State University

Savannah, Georgia

http://www.savannahstate.edu/

- **State-supported** comprehensive, founded 1890, part of University System of Georgia
- **Suburban** 173-acre campus
- **Endowment** $3.9 million
- **Coed** 4,769 undergraduate students, 88% full-time, 56% women, 44% men
- **Minimally difficult** entrance level, 34% of applicants were admitted

UNDERGRAD STUDENTS

4,196 full-time, 573 part-time. Students come from 37 states and territories; 43 other countries; 7% are from out of state; 88% Black or African American, non-Hispanic/Latino; 3% Hispanic/Latino; 0.1% Asian, non-Hispanic/Latino; 0.1% Native Hawaiian or other Pacific Islander, non-Hispanic/Latino; 0.3% American Indian or Alaska Native, non-Hispanic/Latino; 3% Two or more races, non-Hispanic/Latino; 0.7% Race/ethnicity unknown; 0.8% international; 3% transferred in.

Freshmen

Admission: 7,916 applied, 2,706 admitted, 1,204 enrolled. *Average high school GPA:* 2.77. *Test scores:* SAT critical reading scores over 500: 13%; SAT math scores over 500: 11%; ACT scores over 18: 42%; SAT critical reading scores over 600: 2%; SAT math scores over 600: 1%; ACT scores over 24: 2%.

Retention: 67% of full-time freshmen returned.

FACULTY

Total: 252, 83% full-time.

Student/faculty ratio: 21:1.

ACADEMICS
Calendar: semesters. *Degrees:* certificates, associate, bachelor's, master's, and postbachelor's certificates.

Special study options: academic remediation for entering students, accelerated degree program, adult/continuing education programs, advanced placement credit, cooperative education, distance learning, double majors, English as a second language, honors programs, independent study, internships, off-campus study, part-time degree program, services for LD students, study abroad, summer session for credit. ***ROTC:*** Army (b), Navy (b).

Unusual degree programs: 3-2 engineering with Georgia Institute of Technology.

Computers: 200 computers/terminals are available on campus for general student use. Students can access the following: campus intranet, computer help desk, free student e-mail accounts, online (class) grades, online (class) registration, online (class) schedules, Office 2013 (free download for students), virtual computer lab, loaner laptops during semester. Campuswide network is available. 100% of college-owned or -operated housing units are wired for high-speed Internet access. Wireless service is available via entire campus.

STUDENT LIFE
Housing options: coed, men-only, women-only. Campus housing is university owned.

Activities and organizations: drama/theater group, student-run newspaper, radio and television station, choral group, marching band, Marching band, Gospel Choir, Concert Choir, Student Orientation Leaders, Tiger Ambassadors, national fraternities, national sororities.

Athletics Member NCAA. All Division I. ***Intercollegiate sports:*** baseball M(s), basketball M(s)/W(s), cheerleading M(s)/W(s), cross-country running M(s)/W(s), football M(s), golf M(s)/W(s), softball W(s), tennis W(s), track and field M(s)/W(s), volleyball W(s). ***Intramural sports:*** basketball M/W, football M/W, softball M/W, swimming and diving M/W, table tennis M/W, tennis M/W, volleyball M/W, weight lifting M/W.

Campus security: 24-hour emergency response devices and patrols, late-night transport/escort service, controlled dormitory access.

Student services: health clinic, personal/psychological counseling, women's center.

COSTS
Costs (2015–16) ***One-time required fee:*** $125. ***Tuition:*** state resident $4740 full-time, $158 per credit hour part-time; nonresident $17,246 full-time, $548 per credit hour part-time. Full-time tuition and fees vary according to course load and program. Part-time tuition and fees vary according to course load and program. ***Required fees:*** $1758 full-time, $879 per term part-time. ***Room and board:*** $7330; room only: $3386. Room and board charges vary according to board plan and housing facility. ***Payment plan:*** installment. ***Waivers:*** senior citizens and employees or children of employees.

APPLYING
Standardized Tests *Required:* SAT or ACT (for admission). *Required for some:* SAT Subject Tests (for admission). *Recommended:* SAT (for admission).

Options: electronic application, early admission, deferred entrance.

Required: high school transcript, minimum 2.3 GPA. ***Required for some:*** essay or personal statement, interview.

Application deadlines: 7/15 (freshmen), 7/15 (transfers).

Notification: continuous (freshmen), continuous (transfers).

CONTACT
Mr. Descatur Potier, Assistant Vice President of Academic Affairs for Enrollment Services/Director of Admission, Savannah State University, PO Box 20209, 3219 College St., Savannah, GA 31404. *Phone:* 912-358-4014. *Toll-free phone:* 800-788-0478. *Fax:* 912-650-8009. *E-mail:* potierd@savannahstate.edu.

South Georgia State College
Douglas, Georgia
http://www.sgc.edu/

- **State-supported** primarily 2-year, founded 1906, part of University System of Georgia
- **Small-town** 340-acre campus
- **Endowment** $286,240
- **Coed**
- **Minimally difficult** entrance level

FACULTY
Student/faculty ratio: 27:1.

ACADEMICS
Calendar: semesters. *Degrees:* associate and bachelor's.

STUDENT LIFE
Housing options: on-campus residence required for freshman year; men-only, women-only. Campus housing is university owned. Freshman applicants given priority for college housing.

Activities and organizations: drama/theater group, student-run newspaper, choral group, Intramural Sports, Cultural Exchange Club, Georgia Association of Nursing Students, Student Government Association, Phi Theta Kappa Honors Society.

Athletics Member NJCAA.

Campus security: 24-hour emergency response devices and patrols, controlled dormitory access.

Student services: personal/psychological counseling.

APPLYING
Options: electronic application, early admission, deferred entrance.

Application fee: $20.

Required: high school transcript.

CONTACT
South Georgia State College, 100 West College Park Drive, Douglas, GA 31533-5098. *Phone:* 912-260-4409. *Toll-free phone:* 800-342-6364.

South University
Savannah, Georgia
http://www.southuniversity.edu/savannah/

- **Proprietary** comprehensive, founded 1899, part of Education Management Corporation
- **Coed**

ACADEMICS
Calendar: quarters. *Degrees:* associate, bachelor's, master's, doctoral, and post-master's certificates.

CONTACT
South University, 709 Mall Boulevard, Savannah, GA 31406. *Phone:* 912-201-8000. *Toll-free phone:* 866-629-2901.

Spelman College
Atlanta, Georgia
http://www.spelman.edu/

- **Independent** 4-year, founded 1881
- **Urban** 39-acre campus with easy access to Atlanta
- **Endowment** $327.2 million
- **Women only** 2,135 undergraduate students, 97% full-time
- **Very difficult** entrance level, 54% of applicants were admitted

UNDERGRAD STUDENTS
2,072 full-time, 63 part-time. Students come from 43 states and territories; 13 other countries; 73% are from out of state; 87% Black or African American, non-Hispanic/Latino; 0.3% Hispanic/Latino; 0.1% Asian, non-Hispanic/Latino; 0.1% American Indian or Alaska Native, non-Hispanic/Latino; 3% Two or more races, non-Hispanic/Latino; 8% Race/ethnicity unknown; 1% international; 1% transferred in; 71% live on campus.

Freshmen

Admission: 4,324 applied, 2,335 admitted, 552 enrolled. ***Average high school GPA:*** 3.55. ***Test scores:*** SAT critical reading scores over 500: 61%; SAT math scores over 500: 50%; ACT scores over 18: 91%; SAT critical reading scores over 600: 16%; SAT math scores over 600: 9%; ACT scores over 24: 32%; SAT critical reading scores over 700: 2%; SAT math scores over 700: 1%; ACT scores over 30: 1%.

Retention: 89% of full-time freshmen returned.

FACULTY

Total: 244, 74% full-time, 76% with terminal degrees.

Student/faculty ratio: 10:1.

ACADEMICS

Calendar: semesters. *Degree:* bachelor's.

Special study options: adult/continuing education programs, advanced placement credit, double majors, honors programs, independent study, internships, off-campus study, part-time degree program, services for LD students, student-designed majors, study abroad. ***ROTC:*** Army (c), Navy (c), Air Force (c).

Unusual degree programs: 3-2 engineering with North Carolina Agricultural and Technical State University, Rensselaer Polytechnic Institute, Georgia Institute of Technology, Boston University, The University of Alabama in Huntsville, Auburn University.

Computers: 240 computers/terminals and 1,500 ports are available on campus for general student use. Students can access the following: computer help desk, free student e-mail accounts, online (class) grades, online (class) registration, online (class) schedules. Campuswide network is available. 100% of college-owned or -operated housing units are wired for high-speed Internet access. Wireless service is available via entire campus.

STUDENT LIFE

Housing options: on-campus residence required through sophomore year; women-only. Campus housing is university owned and leased by the school. Freshman applicants given priority for college housing.

Activities and organizations: drama/theater group, student-run newspaper, choral group, marching band.

Campus security: 24-hour emergency response devices and patrols, late-night transport/escort service, controlled dormitory access, lighted pathways/sidewalks.

Student services: health clinic, personal/psychological counseling, women's center.

COSTS & FINANCIAL AID

Costs (2015–16) ***Comprehensive fee:*** $37,441 includes full-time tuition ($22,055), mandatory fees ($3441), and room and board ($11,945). Full-time tuition and fees vary according to course load. Part-time tuition and fees vary according to course load. ***Room and board:*** Room and board charges vary according to board plan and housing facility. ***Payment plans:*** installment, deferred payment. ***Waivers:*** employees or children of employees.

Financial Aid Of all full-time matriculated undergraduates who enrolled in 2013, 1,878 applied for aid, 1,725 were judged to have need, 250 had their need fully met. 181 Federal Work-Study jobs (averaging $1280). ***Average percent of need met:*** 44. ***Average financial aid package:*** $18,184. ***Average need-based loan:*** $7666. ***Average need-based gift aid:*** $13,427. ***Average indebtedness upon graduation:*** $35,516.

APPLYING

Standardized Tests *Required:* SAT or ACT (for admission).

Options: electronic application, early admission, early decision, early action, deferred entrance.

Application fee: $35.

Required: essay or personal statement, high school transcript, minimum 2.0 GPA, 2 letters of recommendation, SAT or ACT scores. ***Required for some:*** interview.

Application deadlines: 2/1 (freshmen), 4/1 (transfers), 11/15 (early action).

Early decision deadline: 11/1.

Notification: 4/1 (freshmen), 5/1 (transfers), 12/15 (early decision), 12/31 (early action).

CONTACT

Ms. Ingrid Hayes, Vice President for Enrollment Management, Spelman College, 350 Spelman Lane, SW, Atlanta, GA 30314-4399. *Phone:* 800-982-2411. *Toll-free phone:* 800-982-2411. *Fax:* 404-270-5201. *E-mail:* admiss@spelman.edu.

Toccoa Falls College

Toccoa Falls, Georgia

http://www.tfc.edu/

- **Independent interdenominational** 4-year, founded 1907
- **Small-town** 1100-acre campus with easy access to Atlanta, GA metro area
- **Endowment** $2.5 million
- **Coed** 920 undergraduate students, 85% full-time, 53% women, 47% men
- **Moderately difficult** entrance level, 37% of applicants were admitted

UNDERGRAD STUDENTS

779 full-time, 141 part-time. Students come from 35 states and territories; 10 other countries; 41% are from out of state; 7% Black or African American, non-Hispanic/Latino; 4% Hispanic/Latino; 8% Asian, non-Hispanic/Latino; 0.1% Native Hawaiian or other Pacific Islander, non-Hispanic/Latino; 0.1% American Indian or Alaska Native, non-Hispanic/Latino; 1% Two or more races, non-Hispanic/Latino; 4% Race/ethnicity unknown; 2% international; 8% transferred in; 68% live on campus.

Freshmen

Admission: 583 applied, 216 admitted, 164 enrolled. ***Average high school GPA:*** 3.37. ***Test scores:*** SAT critical reading scores over 500: 51%; SAT math scores over 500: 41%; ACT scores over 18: 79%; SAT critical reading scores over 600: 17%; SAT math scores over 600: 12%; ACT scores over 24: 26%; SAT critical reading scores over 700: 3%; SAT math scores over 700: 1%; ACT scores over 30: 4%.

Retention: 71% of full-time freshmen returned.

FACULTY

Total: 86, 48% full-time, 43% with terminal degrees.

Student/faculty ratio: 15:1.

ACADEMICS

Calendar: 4-1-4. *Degrees:* certificates, associate, and bachelor's.

Special study options: accelerated degree program, advanced placement credit, distance learning, double majors, independent study, internships, part-time degree program, services for LD students, study abroad, summer session for credit.

Computers: 40 computers/terminals and 25 ports are available on campus for general student use. Students can access the following: campus intranet, computer help desk, free student e-mail accounts, online (class) grades, online (class) registration, online (class) schedules. Campuswide network is available. 90% of college-owned or -operated housing units are wired for high-speed Internet access. Wireless service is available via entire campus.

STUDENT LIFE

Housing options: on-campus residence required through junior year; men-only, women-only. Campus housing is university owned. Freshman campus housing is guaranteed.

Activities and organizations: drama/theater group, student-run newspaper, radio station, choral group, Outdoor Club, Hmong Student Fellowship, Theatrical Society, Student Missions Fellowship, Fellowship of Christian Athletes.

Athletics Member NCCAA. ***Intercollegiate sports:*** baseball M, basketball M/W, cross-country running M/W, soccer M/W, volleyball W. ***Intramural sports:*** basketball M/W, football M/W, soccer M/W, softball M/W.

Campus security: student patrols.

Student services: health clinic, personal/psychological counseling.

COSTS & FINANCIAL AID

Costs (2015–16) ***Comprehensive fee:*** $27,920 includes full-time tuition ($20,110), mandatory fees ($550), and room and board ($7260). Full-time tuition and fees vary according to location. Part-time tuition: $840 per credit hour. Part-time tuition and fees vary according to location. ***Required fees:*** $550 per year part-time. ***Room and board:*** Room and board charges vary according to board plan. ***Payment plan:*** installment. ***Waivers:*** employees or children of employees.

Financial Aid Of all full-time matriculated undergraduates who enrolled in 2005, 765 applied for aid, 675 were judged to have need, 83 had their need fully met. 369 Federal Work-Study jobs (averaging $1336). 154 state and other part-time jobs (averaging $1351). In 2005, 173 non-need-based awards were made. ***Average percent of need met:*** 60. ***Average financial aid package:*** $9653. ***Average need-based loan:*** $3110. ***Average need-based gift aid:*** $6486. ***Average non-need-based aid:*** $7595. ***Average indebtedness upon graduation:*** $17,273.

APPLYING

Standardized Tests *Required:* SAT or ACT (for admission).

Options: electronic application, early admission, deferred entrance.

Application fee: $25.

Required: essay or personal statement, high school transcript, minimum 2.0 GPA, 1 letter of recommendation. ***Required for some:*** interview.

Application deadlines: rolling (freshmen), rolling (transfers).

Notification: continuous (freshmen), continuous (transfers).

CONTACT

Mrs. Kelsey Council, Toccoa Falls College, 107 Kincaid Dr., MSC 899, Toccoa Falls, GA 30598. *Phone:* 706-886-6831 Ext. 5382. *Toll-free phone:* 888-785-5624. *Fax:* 706-282-6012. *E-mail:* kcouncil@tfc.edu@tfc.edu.

Truett-McConnell College

Cleveland, Georgia

http://www.truett.edu/

- **Independent Baptist** comprehensive, founded 1946
- **Rural** 310-acre campus with easy access to Atlanta
- **Coed** 1,663 undergraduate students, 45% full-time, 53% women, 47% men
- **Minimally difficult** entrance level, 96% of applicants were admitted

UNDERGRAD STUDENTS

752 full-time, 911 part-time. Students come from 14 states and territories; 4 other countries; 9% are from out of state; 7% Black or African American, non-Hispanic/Latino; 5% Hispanic/Latino; 0.1% Asian, non-Hispanic/Latino; 3% Race/ethnicity unknown; 1% international; 3% transferred in; 30% live on campus.

Freshmen

Admission: 490 applied, 472 admitted, 209 enrolled. ***Average high school GPA:*** 3.39. ***Test scores:*** SAT critical reading scores over 500: 46%; SAT math scores over 500: 40%; SAT writing scores over 500: 41%; ACT scores over 18: 77%; SAT critical reading scores over 600: 11%; SAT math scores over 600: 8%; SAT writing scores over 600: 10%; ACT scores over 24: 24%; SAT math scores over 700: 1%.

Retention: 67% of full-time freshmen returned.

FACULTY

Total: 128.

Student/faculty ratio: 13:1.

ACADEMICS

Calendar: semesters. *Degrees:* bachelor's and master's.

Special study options: academic remediation for entering students, accelerated degree program, advanced placement credit, distance learning, double majors, services for LD students, summer session for credit.

Computers: 40 computers/terminals are available on campus for general student use. Students can access the following: computer help desk, free student e-mail accounts, online (class) grades, online (class) registration, online (class) schedules. Campuswide network is available. 100% of college-owned or -operated housing units are wired for high-speed Internet access. Wireless service is available via classrooms, computer labs, dorm rooms, libraries, student centers.

STUDENT LIFE

Housing options: on-campus residence required through senior year; men-only, women-only. Campus housing is university owned.

Activities and organizations: choral group.

Athletics Member NAIA. ***Intercollegiate sports:*** baseball M(s), basketball M(s)/W(s), cross-country running M(s)/W(s), golf M(s)/W(s), lacrosse W(s), soccer M(s)/W(s), softball W(s), volleyball W(s), wrestling M(s). ***Intramural sports:*** football M/W.

Campus security: 24-hour weekday patrols, 10-hour weekend patrols by trained security personnel.

COSTS & FINANCIAL AID

Costs (2014–15) ***Comprehensive fee:*** $24,420 includes full-time tuition ($16,650), mandatory fees ($650), and room and board ($7120). Full-time tuition and fees vary according to course load and location. Part-time tuition: $555 per credit hour. Part-time tuition and fees vary according to course load and location. ***Room and board:*** Room and board charges vary according to housing facility. ***Payment plan:*** installment. ***Waivers:*** employees or children of employees.

Financial Aid Of all full-time matriculated undergraduates who enrolled in 2014, 642 applied for aid, 587 were judged to have need, 65 had their need fully met. 32 Federal Work-Study jobs (averaging $1059). In 2014, 89 non-need-based awards were made. ***Average percent of need met:*** 65. ***Average financial aid package:*** $14,314. ***Average need-based loan:*** $4236. ***Average need-based gift aid:*** $11,309. ***Average non-need-based aid:*** $6015. ***Average indebtedness upon graduation:*** $13,508.

APPLYING

Standardized Tests *Required:* SAT or ACT (for admission).

Options: electronic application, early admission, deferred entrance.

Application fee: $25.

Required: essay or personal statement, high school transcript, minimum 2.0 GPA. ***Required for some:*** 1 letter of recommendation, interview.

Application deadlines: 8/1 (freshmen), 8/1 (out-of-state freshmen), 8/1 (transfers).

Notification: continuous (freshmen), continuous (out-of-state freshmen), continuous (transfers).

CONTACT

Truett-McConnell College, 100 Alumni Drive, Cleveland, GA 30528. *Phone:* 706-865-2134 Ext. 210. *Toll-free phone:* 800-226-8621.

University of Georgia

Athens, Georgia

http://www.uga.edu/

- **State-supported** comprehensive, founded 1785, part of University System of Georgia
- **Suburban** 759-acre campus with easy access to Atlanta
- **Endowment** $939.0 million
- **Coed** 26,882 undergraduate students, 94% full-time, 57% women, 43% men
- **Moderately difficult** entrance level, 56% of applicants were admitted

UNDERGRAD STUDENTS

25,371 full-time, 1,511 part-time. Students come from 54 states and territories; 122 other countries; 9% are from out of state; 7% Black or African American, non-Hispanic/Latino; 5% Hispanic/Latino; 9% Asian, non-Hispanic/Latino; 0.1% Native Hawaiian or other Pacific Islander, non-Hispanic/Latino; 0.1% American Indian or Alaska Native, non-Hispanic/Latino; 3% Two or more races, non-Hispanic/Latino; 1% Race/ethnicity unknown; 2% international; 4% transferred in; 28% live on campus.

Freshmen

Admission: 20,877 applied, 11,644 admitted, 5,348 enrolled. ***Average high school GPA:*** 3.9. ***Test scores:*** SAT critical reading scores over 500: 96%; SAT math scores over 500: 96%; SAT writing scores over 500: 96%; ACT scores over 18: 100%; SAT critical reading scores over 600: 62%; SAT math scores over 600: 66%; SAT writing scores over 600: 63%; ACT scores over 24: 91%; SAT critical reading scores over 700: 12%; SAT math scores over 700: 16%; SAT writing scores over 700: 14%; ACT scores over 30: 34%.

Retention: 94% of full-time freshmen returned.

FACULTY

Total: 1,774.

Student/faculty ratio: 17:1.

ACADEMICS

Calendar: semesters. *Degrees:* certificates, bachelor's, master's, doctoral, post-master's, and postbachelor's certificates.

Special study options: academic remediation for entering students, accelerated degree program, adult/continuing education programs, advanced placement credit, cooperative education, distance learning, double majors, honors programs, independent study, internships, off-campus study, part-time degree program, services for LD students, student-designed majors, study abroad, summer session for credit. ***ROTC:*** Army (b), Air Force (b).

Computers: 3,046 computers/terminals are available on campus for general student use. Students can access the following: campus intranet, computer help desk, free student e-mail accounts, online (class) grades, online (class) registration, online (class) schedules. Campuswide network is available. 100% of college-owned or -operated housing units are wired for high-speed Internet access. Wireless service is available via classrooms, computer centers, computer labs, dorm rooms, learning centers, libraries, student centers.

STUDENT LIFE

Housing options: on-campus residence required for freshman year; coed, women-only, special housing for students with disabilities. Campus housing is university owned. Freshman campus housing is guaranteed.

Activities and organizations: drama/theater group, student-run newspaper, radio and television station, choral group, marching band, Intramural Sports, Recreational sports program, Communiversity, University Union, Red Coat Band, national fraternities, national sororities.

Athletics Member NCAA. All Division I except football (Division I-A). ***Intercollegiate sports:*** badminton M(c)/W(c), baseball M(s), basketball M(s)/W(s), cheerleading M(c)/W(c), crew M(c)/W(c), cross-country running M(s)/W(s), equestrian sports W(s), fencing M(c)/W(c), golf M(s)/W(s), gymnastics W(s), ice hockey M(c), lacrosse M(c)/W(c), racquetball M(c)/W(c), rugby M(c)/W(c), sailing M(c)/W(c), soccer W(s), softball W(s), swimming and diving M(s)/W(s), tennis M(s)/W(s), track and field M(s)/W(s), ultimate Frisbee M(c)/W(c), volleyball W(s), water polo M(c)/W(c), wrestling M(c). ***Intramural sports:*** badminton M/W, basketball M/W, football M/W, golf M/W, racquetball M/W, soccer M/W, softball M/W, tennis M/W, ultimate Frisbee M/W, volleyball M/W.

Campus security: 24-hour emergency response devices and patrols, late-night transport/escort service, controlled dormitory access.

Student services: health clinic, personal/psychological counseling, women's center, legal services.

COSTS & FINANCIAL AID

Costs (2014–15) ***Tuition:*** state resident $8590 full-time; nonresident $26,800 full-time. Full-time tuition and fees vary according to course load, location, and program. Part-time tuition and fees vary according to course load, location, and program. ***Required fees:*** $2246 full-time. ***Room and board:*** $9246; room only: $5290. Room and board charges vary according to board plan and housing facility. ***Waivers:*** senior citizens.

Financial Aid Of all full-time matriculated undergraduates who enrolled in 2014, 18,161 applied for aid, 11,074 were judged to have need, 2,649 had their need fully met. 378 Federal Work-Study jobs (averaging $2640). In 2014, 1601 non-need-based awards were made. ***Average percent of need met:*** 75. ***Average financial aid package:*** $11,395. ***Average need-based loan:*** $4154. ***Average need-based gift aid:*** $8623. ***Average non-need-based aid:*** $2141. ***Average indebtedness upon graduation:*** $21,638.

APPLYING

Standardized Tests *Required:* SAT or ACT (for admission).

Options: electronic application, early admission, early action, deferred entrance.

Application fee: $60.

Required: high school transcript, counselor evaluation. ***Recommended:*** essay or personal statement, minimum 2.0 GPA.

Application deadlines: 1/15 (freshmen), 4/1 (transfers), 10/15 (early action).

Notification: 4/1 (freshmen), continuous (transfers), 12/1 (early action).

CONTACT

Mr. Charles Carabello, Associate Director for Enrollment Management, University of Georgia, Terrell Hall, Athens, GA 30602. *Phone:* 706-542-8776. *Fax:* 706-542-1466. *E-mail:* admproc@uga.edu.

University of North Georgia

Dahlonega, Georgia

http://www.ung.edu/

- **State-supported** comprehensive, founded 1873, part of University System of Georgia
- **Small-town** campus with easy access to Atlanta
- **Coed** 15,507 undergraduate students, 69% full-time, 55% women, 45% men
- **Moderately difficult** entrance level, 65% of applicants were admitted

UNDERGRAD STUDENTS

10,745 full-time, 4,762 part-time. 3% are from out of state; 4% Black or African American, non-Hispanic/Latino; 9% Hispanic/Latino; 3% Asian, non-Hispanic/Latino; 0.1% Native Hawaiian or other Pacific Islander, non-Hispanic/Latino; 0.2% American Indian or Alaska Native, non-Hispanic/Latino; 3% Two or more races, non-Hispanic/Latino; 1% Race/ethnicity unknown; 1% international; 4% transferred in; 14% live on campus.

Freshmen

Admission: 4,904 applied, 3,180 admitted, 3,261 enrolled. ***Average high school GPA:*** 3.25. ***Test scores:*** SAT critical reading scores over 500: 82%; SAT math scores over 500: 75%; ACT scores over 18: 100%; SAT critical reading scores over 600: 26%; SAT math scores over 600: 25%; ACT scores over 24: 56%; SAT critical reading scores over 700: 1%; SAT math scores over 700: 2%; ACT scores over 30: 6%.

Retention: 83% of full-time freshmen returned.

FACULTY

Total: 779, 65% full-time, 63% with terminal degrees.

Student/faculty ratio: 21:1.

ACADEMICS

Calendar: semesters. *Degrees:* certificates, associate, bachelor's, master's, doctoral, and post-master's certificates.

Special study options: academic remediation for entering students, accelerated degree program, advanced placement credit, cooperative education, distance learning, double majors, English as a second language, external degree program, freshman honors college, honors programs, independent study, internships, part-time degree program, services for LD students, study abroad, summer session for credit. ***ROTC:*** Army (b).

Unusual degree programs: 3-2 engineering with Georgia Institute of Technology, Clemson University; industrial management, computer science with Georgia Institute of Technology.

Computers: 2,400 computers/terminals are available on campus for general student use. Students can access the following: computer help desk, free student e-mail accounts, online (class) grades, online (class) registration, online (class) schedules. Campuswide network is available. 100% of college-owned or -operated housing units are wired for high-speed Internet access. Wireless service is available via classrooms, computer centers, computer labs, dorm rooms, learning centers, libraries.

STUDENT LIFE

Housing options: on-campus residence required through sophomore year; coed, men-only, women-only. Campus housing is university owned. Freshman campus housing is guaranteed.

Activities and organizations: drama/theater group, student-run newspaper, radio station, choral group, marching band, Student Government Association, Commuter Council, Graduate Student Senate, Student Activities Board, Greek organizations, national fraternities, national sororities.

Athletics Member NCAA. All Division II. ***Intercollegiate sports:*** baseball M(s), basketball M(s)/W(s), cheerleading M/W, cross-country running M(c)/W(s), equestrian sports W(c), golf M(s)/W(s), lacrosse M(c)/W(c), riflery M(s)/W(s), soccer M(s)/W(s), softball W(s), tennis M(s)/W(s), wrestling M(c). ***Intramural sports:*** basketball M/W, football M/W, golf M(c)/W(c), rugby M/W, soccer M/W, softball M/W, table tennis M/W, ultimate Frisbee M/W, volleyball M/W, water polo M/W.

Campus security: 24-hour emergency response devices and patrols, late-night transport/escort service, controlled dormitory access.

Student services: health clinic, personal/psychological counseling.

COSTS & FINANCIAL AID
Costs (2015–16) ***Tuition:*** state resident $5098 full-time, $194 per credit hour part-time; nonresident $17,994 full-time, $600 per credit hour part-time. Full-time tuition and fees vary according to course load, degree level, and location. Part-time tuition and fees vary according to course load, degree level, and location. ***Required fees:*** $1718 full-time. ***Room and board:*** $9162; room only: $5090. Room and board charges vary according to board plan and housing facility. ***Waivers:*** senior citizens and employees or children of employees.

Financial Aid Of all full-time matriculated undergraduates who enrolled in 2013, 7,877 applied for aid, 5,691 were judged to have need, 2,001 had their need fully met. In 2013, 224 non-need-based awards were made. ***Average percent of need met:*** 69. ***Average financial aid package:*** $12,752. ***Average need-based loan:*** $5155. ***Average need-based gift aid:*** $5055. ***Average non-need-based aid:*** $1100. ***Average indebtedness upon graduation:*** $12,072.

APPLYING
Standardized Tests *Required:* SAT or ACT (for admission). *Required for some:* SAT and SAT Subject Tests or ACT (for admission).

Options: electronic application, early admission.

Application fee: $30.

Required: high school transcript, minimum 2.0 GPA, proof of immunization.

Application deadlines: 7/1 (freshmen), rolling (transfers).

Notification: continuous (freshmen), continuous (transfers).

CONTACT
Keith Antonia, Director of Admissions, University of North Georgia, Admissions Center, Dahlonega, GA 30533. *Phone:* 706-864-1800. *Toll-free phone:* 800-498-9581. *Fax:* 706-864-1478. *E-mail:* bacheloradmissions@ung.edu.

★ University of West Georgia
Carrollton, Georgia
http://www.westga.edu/

- **State-supported** comprehensive, founded 1933, part of University System of Georgia
- **Rural** 645-acre campus with easy access to Atlanta
- **Endowment** $25.9 million
- **Coed** 10,249 undergraduate students, 83% full-time, 63% women, 37% men
- **Minimally difficult** entrance level, 49% of applicants were admitted

UNDERGRAD STUDENTS
8,531 full-time, 1,718 part-time. Students come from 38 states and territories; 57 other countries; 3% are from out of state; 36% Black or African American, non-Hispanic/Latino; 4% Hispanic/Latino; 1% Asian, non-Hispanic/Latino; 0.1% Native Hawaiian or other Pacific Islander, non-Hispanic/Latino; 0.1% American Indian or Alaska Native, non-Hispanic/Latino; 4% Two or more races, non-Hispanic/Latino; 3% Race/ethnicity unknown; 1% international; 7% transferred in; 29% live on campus.

Freshmen
Admission: 7,868 applied, 3,825 admitted, 2,231 enrolled. ***Average high school GPA:*** 3.13. ***Test scores:*** SAT math scores over 500: 31%; SAT writing scores over 500: 29%; ACT scores over 18: 85%; SAT math scores over 600: 5%; SAT writing scores over 600: 4%; ACT scores over 24: 13%; SAT math scores over 700: 1%; SAT writing scores over 700: 1%; ACT scores over 30: 1%.

Retention: 74% of full-time freshmen returned.

FACULTY
Total: 635, 65% full-time, 64% with terminal degrees.

Student/faculty ratio: 21:1.

ACADEMICS
Calendar: semesters. *Degrees:* bachelor's, master's, doctoral, post-master's, and postbachelor's certificates.

Special study options: accelerated degree program, adult/continuing education programs, advanced placement credit, cooperative education, distance learning, double majors, external degree program, freshman honors college, honors programs, independent study, internships, off-campus study, part-time degree program, services for LD students, study abroad, summer session for credit. ***ROTC:*** Air Force (c).

Unusual degree programs: 3-2 engineering with Georgia Institute of Technology, Auburn University, Mercer University, University of Georgia.

Computers: 1,200 computers/terminals are available on campus for general student use. Students can access the following: campus intranet, computer help desk, free student e-mail accounts, online (class) grades, online (class) registration, online (class) schedules. Campuswide network is available. 100% of college-owned or -operated housing units are wired for high-speed Internet access. Wireless service is available via entire campus.

STUDENT LIFE
Housing options: on-campus residence required for freshman year; coed, special housing for students with disabilities. Campus housing is university owned and leased by the school. Freshman campus housing is guaranteed.

Activities and organizations: drama/theater group, student-run newspaper, radio and television station, choral group, marching band, Black Student Alliance, Student Activities Council, Baptist Collegiate Ministries, Campus Outreach, United Voices Gospel Choir, national fraternities, national sororities.

Athletics Member NCAA. All Division II. ***Intercollegiate sports:*** baseball M(s), basketball M(s)/W(s), cheerleading W(s), cross-country running M(s)/W(s), football M(s), golf M(s)/W(s), soccer W(s), softball W(s), tennis W(s), track and field W(s), volleyball W(s). ***Intramural sports:*** basketball M/W, football M/W, soccer M/W, softball M/W, volleyball M/W.

Campus security: 24-hour emergency response devices and patrols, student patrols, late-night transport/escort service, controlled dormitory access.

Student services: health clinic, personal/psychological counseling.

COSTS & FINANCIAL AID
Costs (2014–15) ***Tuition:*** state resident $5098 full-time, $170 per semester hour part-time; nonresident $17,994 full-time, $600 per semester hour part-time. Full-time tuition and fees vary according to course load and location. Part-time tuition and fees vary according to course load and location. ***Required fees:*** $1858 full-time, $83 per semester hour part-time, $512 per term part-time. ***Room and board:*** $8532; room only: $4700. Room and board charges vary according to board plan and housing facility. ***Waivers:*** senior citizens and employees or children of employees.

Financial Aid Of all full-time matriculated undergraduates who enrolled in 2014, 7,618 applied for aid, 6,474 were judged to have need, 2,937 had their need fully met. In 2014, 258 non-need-based awards were made. ***Average percent of need met:*** 45. ***Average financial aid package:*** $8242. ***Average need-based loan:*** $3933. ***Average need-based gift aid:*** $4875. ***Average non-need-based aid:*** $2200. ***Average indebtedness upon graduation:*** $27,494.

APPLYING
Standardized Tests *Required:* SAT or ACT (for admission).

Options: electronic application, early admission, deferred entrance.

Application fee: $40.

Required: high school transcript, minimum 2.4 GPA, proof of immunization.

Application deadlines: 6/1 (freshmen), 6/1 (out-of-state freshmen), 6/1 (transfers).

Notification: continuous (freshmen), continuous (out-of-state freshmen), continuous (transfers).

CONTACT
Ms. Ketty Ballard, Associate Director (Recruiting), University of West Georgia, 1601 Maple Street, Carrollton, GA 30118. *Phone:* 678-839-5600. *Fax:* 678-839-4747. *E-mail:* admiss@westga.edu.

Valdosta State University

Valdosta, Georgia

http://www.valdosta.edu/

- **State-supported** university, founded 1906, part of University System of Georgia
- **Small-town** 180-acre campus
- **Endowment** $35.5 million
- **Coed** 9,328 undergraduate students, 84% full-time, 59% women, 41% men
- **Moderately difficult** entrance level, 54% of applicants were admitted

UNDERGRAD STUDENTS

7,815 full-time, 1,513 part-time. Students come from 46 states and territories; 61 other countries; 5% are from out of state; 36% Black or African American, non-Hispanic/Latino; 5% Hispanic/Latino; 1% Asian, non-Hispanic/Latino; 0.1% Native Hawaiian or other Pacific Islander, non-Hispanic/Latino; 0.2% American Indian or Alaska Native, non-Hispanic/Latino; 3% Two or more races, non-Hispanic/Latino; 1% Race/ethnicity unknown; 2% international; 6% transferred in; 27% live on campus.

Freshmen

Admission: 5,427 applied, 2,938 admitted, 1,555 enrolled. ***Average high school GPA:*** 3.17. ***Test scores:*** SAT critical reading scores over 500: 48%; SAT math scores over 500: 39%; SAT writing scores over 500: 36%; ACT scores over 18: 99%; SAT critical reading scores over 600: 9%; SAT math scores over 600: 7%; SAT writing scores over 600: 6%; ACT scores over 24: 17%; SAT critical reading scores over 700: 1%; ACT scores over 30: 1%.

Retention: 71% of full-time freshmen returned.

FACULTY

Total: 616, 79% full-time, 66% with terminal degrees.

Student/faculty ratio: 19:1.

ACADEMICS

Calendar: semesters. *Degrees:* certificates, associate, bachelor's, master's, doctoral, post-master's, and postbachelor's certificates.

Special study options: accelerated degree program, adult/continuing education programs, advanced placement credit, cooperative education, distance learning, double majors, English as a second language, external degree program, honors programs, independent study, internships, off-campus study, part-time degree program, services for LD students, study abroad, summer session for credit. ***ROTC:*** Air Force (b).

Unusual degree programs: 3-2 engineering with Georgia Institute of Technology.

Computers: 1,225 computers/terminals are available on campus for general student use. Students can access the following: campus intranet, computer help desk, free student e-mail accounts, online (class) grades, online (class) registration, online (class) schedules. Campuswide network is available. 100% of college-owned or -operated housing units are wired for high-speed Internet access. Wireless service is available via entire campus.

STUDENT LIFE

Housing options: on-campus residence required for freshman year; coed, special housing for students with disabilities. Campus housing is university owned. Freshman applicants given priority for college housing.

Activities and organizations: drama/theater group, student-run newspaper, radio and television station, choral group, marching band, Interfraternity Council, College Panhellenic Council, Black Student League, Enactus, Alpha Lambda Delta Freshmen Honor Society, national fraternities, national sororities.

Athletics Member NCAA. All Division II. ***Intercollegiate sports:*** baseball M(s), basketball M(s)/W(s), cheerleading M/W, cross-country running M(s)/W(s), football M(s), golf M(s), soccer W(s), softball W(s), tennis M(s)/W(s), volleyball W(s). ***Intramural sports:*** basketball M/W, bowling M/W, golf M/W, lacrosse M(c)/W(c), racquetball M/W, rugby M(c), soccer M(c)/W(c), softball M/W, swimming and diving M(c)/W(c), table tennis M(c)/W(c), tennis M/W, ultimate Frisbee M(c)/W(c), volleyball M/W.

Campus security: 24-hour emergency response devices and patrols, late-night transport/escort service, controlled dormitory access, bicycle patrols, security cameras.

Student services: health clinic, personal/psychological counseling.

COSTS & FINANCIAL AID

Costs (2014–15) ***Tuition:*** state resident $4078 full-time, $170 per credit hour part-time; nonresident $14,395 full-time, $600 per credit hour part-time. Full-time tuition and fees vary according to course load, location, program, and reciprocity agreements. Part-time tuition and fees vary according to course load, location, program, and reciprocity agreements. ***Required fees:*** $2064 full-time, $1032 per term part-time. ***Room and board:*** $7864; room only: $4072. Room and board charges vary according to board plan and housing facility. ***Payment plan:*** installment. ***Waivers:*** employees or children of employees.

Financial Aid Of all full-time matriculated undergraduates who enrolled in 2013, 7,895 applied for aid, 6,884 were judged to have need, 1,720 had their need fully met. 165 Federal Work-Study jobs (averaging $3105). In 2013, 90 non-need-based awards were made. ***Average percent of need met:*** 81. ***Average financial aid package:*** $13,861. ***Average need-based loan:*** $4365. ***Average need-based gift aid:*** $6068. ***Average non-need-based aid:*** $1955. ***Average indebtedness upon graduation:*** $25,108.

APPLYING

Standardized Tests *Required:* SAT or ACT (for admission).

Options: electronic application, deferred entrance.

Application fee: $40.

Required: high school transcript.

Application deadlines: 6/15 (freshmen), 6/15 (out-of-state freshmen), 6/15 (transfers).

Notification: continuous until 8/1 (freshmen), continuous until 8/1 (out-of-state freshmen), continuous until 8/1 (transfers).

CONTACT

Mr. Ryan M. Hogan, Associate Director of Admissions, Valdosta State University, Office of Admissions, 1500 North Patterson Street, Valdosta, GA 31698. *Phone:* 229-333-5791. *Toll-free phone:* 800-618-1878. *Fax:* 229-333-5482. *E-mail:* admissions@valdosta.edu.

Wesleyan College

Macon, Georgia

http://www.wesleyancollege.edu/

- **Independent United Methodist** comprehensive, founded 1836
- **Suburban** 200-acre campus with easy access to Atlanta
- **Endowment** $63.3 million
- **Undergraduate: women only; graduate: coed** 665 undergraduate students, 74% full-time, 100% women
- **Moderately difficult** entrance level, 45% of applicants were admitted

UNDERGRAD STUDENTS

489 full-time, 176 part-time. Students come from 15 states and territories; 25 other countries; 8% are from out of state; 28% Black or African American, non-Hispanic/Latino; 4% Hispanic/Latino; 2% Asian, non-Hispanic/Latino; 0.4% Native Hawaiian or other Pacific Islander, non-Hispanic/Latino; 2% Two or more races, non-Hispanic/Latino; 2% Race/ethnicity unknown; 20% international; 5% transferred in; 82% live on campus.

Freshmen

Admission: 829 applied, 369 admitted, 106 enrolled. ***Test scores:*** SAT critical reading scores over 500: 55%; SAT math scores over 500: 46%; SAT writing scores over 500: 35%; ACT scores over 18: 81%; SAT critical reading scores over 600: 17%; SAT math scores over 600: 13%; SAT writing scores over 600: 9%; ACT scores over 24: 23%; SAT math scores over 700: 5%; SAT writing scores over 700: 1%.

Retention: 67% of full-time freshmen returned.

FACULTY

Total: 52, 98% full-time, 90% with terminal degrees.

Student/faculty ratio: 13:1.

ACADEMICS

Calendar: semesters. *Degrees:* bachelor's and master's.

Special study options: adult/continuing education programs, advanced placement credit, cooperative education, double majors, honors programs, independent study, internships, part-time degree program, services for LD students, student-designed majors, study abroad, summer session for credit. ***ROTC:*** Army (c).

Unusual degree programs: 3-2 engineering with Georgia Tech, Auburn University and Mercer University.

Computers: 63 computers/terminals are available on campus for general student use. Students can access the following: campus intranet, computer help desk, free student e-mail accounts, online (class) grades, online (class) registration, online (class) schedules, online payment. Campuswide network is available. 100% of college-owned or -operated housing units are wired for high-speed Internet access. Wireless service is available via classrooms, computer centers, computer labs, learning centers, libraries, student centers.

STUDENT LIFE

Housing options: on-campus residence required for freshman year; women-only, special housing for students with disabilities. Campus housing is university owned. Freshman campus housing is guaranteed.

Activities and organizations: drama/theater group, student-run newspaper, choral group, Student Recreation Council, Campus Activities Board, Student Government Association, Council on Religious Concerns, Christian Fellowship.

Athletics Member NCAA. All Division III. ***Intercollegiate sports:*** basketball W, cross-country running W, equestrian sports W, soccer W, softball W, tennis W, volleyball W. ***Intramural sports:*** basketball W, cross-country running W, equestrian sports W, soccer W, softball W, tennis W, volleyball W.

Campus security: 24-hour emergency response devices and patrols, late-night transport/escort service.

Student services: health clinic, women's center.

COSTS & FINANCIAL AID

Costs (2014–15) ***One-time required fee:*** $250. ***Comprehensive fee:*** $28,700 includes full-time tuition ($19,750), mandatory fees ($150), and room and board ($8800). Full-time tuition and fees vary according to degree level, program, and reciprocity agreements. Part-time tuition: $470 per credit hour. Part-time tuition and fees vary according to class time, degree level, program, and reciprocity agreements. ***Required fees:*** $5 per credit hour part-time. ***Room and board:*** Room and board charges vary according to board plan and housing facility. ***Payment plans:*** installment, deferred payment. ***Waivers:*** senior citizens and employees or children of employees.

Financial Aid Of all full-time matriculated undergraduates who enrolled in 2013, 277 applied for aid, 259 were judged to have need, 29 had their need fully met. 25 Federal Work-Study jobs (averaging $1472). 172 state and other part-time jobs (averaging $1433). In 2013, 132 non-need-based awards were made. ***Average percent of need met:*** 71. ***Average financial aid package:*** $19,067. ***Average need-based loan:*** $4771. ***Average need-based gift aid:*** $14,845. ***Average non-need-based aid:*** $11,617. ***Average indebtedness upon graduation:*** $32,755. ***Financial aid deadline:*** 6/15.

APPLYING

Standardized Tests *Required:* SAT or ACT (for admission).

Options: electronic application, early admission, early decision, early action, deferred entrance.

Application fee: $30.

Required: high school transcript, minimum 2.0 GPA, 1 letter of recommendation. ***Required for some:*** interview. ***Recommended:*** essay or personal statement, 2 letters of recommendation.

Application deadlines: 2/15 (freshmen), rolling (transfers), 1/15 (early action).

Early decision deadline: 11/15.

Notification: continuous (freshmen), continuous (transfers), 12/15 (early decision).

CONTACT

Mr. Stephen Farr, Vice President for Enrollment Services, Wesleyan College, 4760 Forsyth Road, Macon, GA 31210-4462. *Phone:* 478-757-3700. *Toll-free phone:* 800-447-6610. *Fax:* 478-757-4030. *E-mail:* admissions@wesleyancollege.edu.

HAWAII

Argosy University, Hawai`i

Honolulu, Hawaii

http://www.argosy.edu/locations/hawaii/

- **Proprietary** university, founded 1994, part of Education Management Corporation
- **Coed**

ACADEMICS

Calendar: semesters. *Degrees:* associate, bachelor's, master's, and doctoral.

CONTACT

Argosy University, Hawai`i, 1001 Bishop Street, Suite 400, Honolulu, HI 96813. *Phone:* 808-536-5555. *Toll-free phone:* 888-323-2777.

Chaminade University of Honolulu

Honolulu, Hawaii

http://www.chaminade.edu/

- **Independent Roman Catholic** comprehensive, founded 1955
- **Urban** 62-acre campus with easy access to Honolulu
- **Endowment** $11.3 million
- **Coed** 1,306 undergraduate students, 97% full-time, 68% women, 32% men
- **Moderately difficult** entrance level, 85% of applicants were admitted

UNDERGRAD STUDENTS

1,270 full-time, 36 part-time. Students come from 35 states and territories; 23 other countries; 32% are from out of state; 3% Black or African American, non-Hispanic/Latino; 5% Hispanic/Latino; 37% Asian, non-Hispanic/Latino; 18% Native Hawaiian or other Pacific Islander, non-Hispanic/Latino; 0.5% American Indian or Alaska Native, non-Hispanic/Latino; 17% Two or more races, non-Hispanic/Latino; 3% Race/ethnicity unknown; 2% international; 10% transferred in; 27% live on campus.

Freshmen

Admission: 918 applied, 784 admitted, 239 enrolled. ***Average high school GPA:*** 3.38. ***Test scores:*** SAT critical reading scores over 500: 35%; SAT math scores over 500: 37%; ACT scores over 18: 94%; SAT critical reading scores over 600: 4%; SAT math scores over 600: 6%; ACT scores over 24: 12%.

Retention: 78% of full-time freshmen returned.

FACULTY

Total: 148, 59% full-time.

Student/faculty ratio: 12:1.

ACADEMICS

Calendar: semesters. *Degrees:* associate, bachelor's, master's, and postbachelor's certificates.

Special study options: academic remediation for entering students, accelerated degree program, adult/continuing education programs, advanced placement credit, distance learning, double majors, independent study, internships, off-campus study, part-time degree program, study abroad, summer session for credit. ***ROTC:*** Army (c), Air Force (c).

Computers: 200 computers/terminals are available on campus for general student use. Students can access the following: computer help desk, free student e-mail accounts, online (class) grades, online (class) registration, online (class) schedules. Campuswide network is available. 100% of college-owned or -operated housing units are wired for high-speed Internet access. Wireless service is available via entire campus.

STUDENT LIFE

Housing options: coed, women-only, special housing for students with disabilities. Campus housing is university owned and leased by the school.

Activities and organizations: drama/theater group, student-run newspaper, radio station, choral group, Lumana O Samoa (Samoan Club), Kaimi Lalakea (Hawaiian Club), Rotaract, Residence Hall Association, Chaminade Student Government Association.

Athletics Member NCAA. All Division II. ***Intercollegiate sports:*** basketball M(s)/W(s), cross-country running M(s)/W(s), golf M(s), soccer M(s)/W(s), softball W(s), tennis W(s), volleyball W(s). ***Intramural sports:*** basketball M/W.

Campus security: 24-hour emergency response devices and patrols, late-night transport/escort service, controlled dormitory access.

Student services: personal/psychological counseling.

COSTS & FINANCIAL AID

Costs (2014–15) ***Comprehensive fee:*** $32,580 includes full-time tuition ($20,810), mandatory fees ($130), and room and board ($11,640). Full-time tuition and fees vary according to course load and program. Part-time tuition: $694 per credit. Part-time tuition and fees vary according to course load and program. ***Room and board:*** Room and board charges vary according to board plan and housing facility. ***Payment plan:*** installment.

Financial Aid Of all full-time matriculated undergraduates who enrolled in 2013, 971 applied for aid, 879 were judged to have need, 143 had their need fully met. 813 Federal Work-Study jobs (averaging $2615). In 2013, 227 non-need-based awards were made. ***Average percent of need met:*** 71. ***Average financial aid package:*** $18,271. ***Average need-based loan:*** $4217. ***Average need-based gift aid:*** $4802. ***Average non-need-based aid:*** $6631. ***Average indebtedness upon graduation:*** $26,323.

APPLYING

Standardized Tests *Required:* SAT or ACT (for admission), TOEFL for international students (for admission).

Options: electronic application, deferred entrance.

Application fee: $50.

Required: essay or personal statement, high school transcript, minimum 2.5 GPA. ***Required for some:*** minimum 2.8 GPA, 2 letters of recommendation, interview. ***Recommended:*** minimum 3.0 GPA.

Application deadlines: rolling (freshmen), rolling (transfers).

Notification: continuous (freshmen), continuous (transfers).

CONTACT

Office of Admissions, Chaminade University of Honolulu, 3140 Waialae Avenue, Honolulu, HI 96816-1578. *Phone:* 808-739-8340. *Toll-free phone:* 800-735-3733. *Fax:* 808-739-4647. *E-mail:* admissions@chaminade.edu.

Hawai`i Pacific University

Honolulu, Hawaii

http://www.hpu.edu/

- **Independent** comprehensive, founded 1965
- **Urban** 140-acre campus
- **Endowment** $63.8 million
- **Coed** 4,835 undergraduate students, 65% full-time, 57% women, 43% men
- **Moderately difficult** entrance level, 63% of applicants were admitted

UNDERGRAD STUDENTS

3,145 full-time, 1,690 part-time. Students come from 56 states and territories; 66 other countries; 36% are from out of state; 6% Black or African American, non-Hispanic/Latino; 14% Hispanic/Latino; 17% Asian, non-Hispanic/Latino; 2% Native Hawaiian or other Pacific Islander, non-Hispanic/Latino; 0.5% American Indian or Alaska Native, non-Hispanic/Latino; 18% Two or more races, non-Hispanic/Latino; 3% Race/ethnicity unknown; 11% international; 11% transferred in.

Freshmen

Admission: 4,477 applied, 2,811 admitted, 590 enrolled. ***Average high school GPA:*** 3.4. ***Test scores:*** SAT critical reading scores over 500: 54%; SAT math scores over 500: 56%; SAT writing scores over 500: 47%; ACT scores over 18: 89%; SAT critical reading scores over 600: 16%; SAT math scores over 600: 17%; SAT writing scores over 600: 12%; ACT scores over 24: 41%; SAT critical reading scores over 700: 2%; SAT math scores over 700: 1%; SAT writing scores over 700: 1%; ACT scores over 30: 7%.

Retention: 70% of full-time freshmen returned.

FACULTY

Total: 515, 41% full-time, 42% with terminal degrees.

Student/faculty ratio: 12:1.

ACADEMICS

Calendar: semesters. *Degrees:* certificates, associate, bachelor's, master's, post-master's, and postbachelor's certificates.

Special study options: academic remediation for entering students, accelerated degree program, adult/continuing education programs, advanced placement credit, cooperative education, distance learning, double majors, English as a second language, freshman honors college, honors programs, independent study, internships, off-campus study, part-time degree program, services for LD students, student-designed majors, study abroad, summer session for credit. ***ROTC:*** Army (c), Air Force (c).

Unusual degree programs: 3-2 engineering with Washington University in St. Louis, University of Southern California.

Computers: 200 computers/terminals are available on campus for general student use. Students can access the following: campus intranet, computer help desk, free student e-mail accounts, online (class) grades, online (class) registration, online (class) schedules. Campuswide network is available. Wireless service is available via entire campus.

STUDENT LIFE

Housing options: coed. Campus housing is university owned and is provided by a third party. Freshman applicants given priority for college housing.

Activities and organizations: drama/theater group, student-run newspaper, choral group, Student Government Association, Circle K International, Campus Activities Board, Student Nurses Association, Christian Student Organization.

Athletics Member NCAA. All Division II. ***Intercollegiate sports:*** baseball M(s), basketball M(s)/W(s), cheerleading M(s)/W(s), cross-country running M(s)/W(s), golf M(s), soccer M(s)/W(s), softball W(s), tennis M(s)/W(s), volleyball W(s). ***Intramural sports:*** basketball M/W, football M/W, soccer M/W, softball M/W, table tennis M/W, tennis M/W, ultimate Frisbee M/W, volleyball M/W.

Campus security: 24-hour emergency response devices and patrols, late-night transport/escort service, controlled dormitory access, Emergency telephone: Informacast. Emergency Notification: Rave Alert. Detex Patrol system and Emergency Exit Alarms in residence hall.

Student services: personal/psychological counseling.

COSTS & FINANCIAL AID

Costs (2015–16) ***Comprehensive fee:*** $35,970 includes full-time tuition ($22,160), mandatory fees ($200), and room and board ($13,610). Full-time tuition and fees vary according to course level, course load, degree level, location, program, and student level. Part-time tuition: $740 per credit. Part-time tuition and fees vary according to course level, course load, degree level, location, program, and student level. ***Required fees:*** $25 per term part-time. ***Room and board:*** Room and board charges vary according to housing facility. ***Payment plan:*** installment. ***Waivers:*** employees or children of employees.

Financial Aid Of all full-time matriculated undergraduates who enrolled in 2013, 2,262 applied for aid, 1,452 were judged to have need, 225 had their need fully met. 242 Federal Work-Study jobs (averaging $3000). In 2013, 109 non-need-based awards were made. ***Average percent of need met:*** 70. ***Average financial aid package:*** $20,234. ***Average need-based loan:*** $6080. ***Average need-based gift aid:*** $1766. ***Average non-need-based aid:*** $889.

APPLYING

Standardized Tests *Required:* SAT or ACT (for admission). *Required for some:* TOEFL/IELTS.

Options: electronic application, deferred entrance.

Application fee: $50.

Required: high school transcript, minimum 2.5 GPA. ***Required for some:*** interview. ***Recommended:*** essay or personal statement, 2 letters of recommendation.

Application deadlines: rolling (freshmen), rolling (out-of-state freshmen), rolling (transfers).

Notification: continuous (transfers).

CONTACT

Marissa Bratton, Director of Admissions, Hawai`i Pacific University, 1164 Bishop Street, Suite 1100, Honolulu, HI 96813-2785. *Phone:* 808-544-0249. *Toll-free phone:* 866-225-5478. *Fax:* 808-543-8065. *E-mail:* mbratton@hpu.edu.

University of Hawaii at Hilo
Hilo, Hawaii
http://hilo.hawaii.edu/

- **State-supported** comprehensive, founded 1970, part of University of Hawaii System
- **Small-town** 115-acre campus
- **Coed** 3,362 undergraduate students, 81% full-time, 60% women, 40% men
- **Moderately difficult** entrance level, 71% of applicants were admitted

UNDERGRAD STUDENTS
2,726 full-time, 636 part-time. 28% are from out of state; 1% Black or African American, non-Hispanic/Latino; 13% Hispanic/Latino; 17% Asian, non-Hispanic/Latino; 11% Native Hawaiian or other Pacific Islander, non-Hispanic/Latino; 0.6% American Indian or Alaska Native, non-Hispanic/Latino; 30% Two or more races, non-Hispanic/Latino; 0.3% Race/ethnicity unknown; 5% international; 18% transferred in.

Freshmen
Admission: 1,679 applied, 1,195 admitted, 432 enrolled. ***Average high school GPA:*** 3.36. ***Test scores:*** SAT critical reading scores over 500: 36%; SAT math scores over 500: 43%; SAT writing scores over 500: 28%; ACT scores over 18: 59%; SAT critical reading scores over 600: 8%; SAT math scores over 600: 7%; SAT writing scores over 600: 5%; ACT scores over 24: 16%; SAT critical reading scores over 700: 1%; ACT scores over 30: 3%.
Retention: 66% of full-time freshmen returned.

FACULTY
Total: 338, 71% full-time, 58% with terminal degrees.
Student/faculty ratio: 13:1.

ACADEMICS
Calendar: semesters. *Degrees:* certificates, bachelor's, master's, doctoral, and postbachelor's certificates.
Special study options: advanced placement credit, distance learning, double majors, English as a second language, honors programs, independent study, internships, off-campus study, part-time degree program, services for LD students, student-designed majors, study abroad, summer session for credit. ***ROTC:*** Army (b).
Computers: Students can access the following: free student e-mail accounts, online (class) grades, online (class) registration, online (class) schedules. Campuswide network is available. Wireless service is available via entire campus.

STUDENT LIFE
Housing options: coed, special housing for students with disabilities. Campus housing is university owned.
Activities and organizations: drama/theater group, student-run newspaper, radio station, choral group, International Student Association, Hawaiian Leadership and Development, Delta Sigma Pi Business Fraternity, University Canoe Club, Samoan Club, national fraternities, national sororities.
Athletics Member NCAA. All Division II except baseball (Division I), soccer (Division I). ***Intercollegiate sports:*** baseball M(s), basketball M(s)/W(s), cross-country running M(s)/W(s), golf M(s)/W(s), soccer M(s)/W(s), softball W(s), tennis M(s)/W(s), volleyball W(s). ***Intramural sports:*** basketball M/W, football M/W, rugby M/W, sailing M/W, soccer M/W, volleyball M/W.
Campus security: 24-hour emergency response devices and patrols, controlled dormitory access.
Student services: health clinic, personal/psychological counseling, women's center.

COSTS & FINANCIAL AID
Costs (2015–16) ***Tuition:*** state resident $7128 full-time, $297 per credit hour part-time; nonresident $19,368 full-time, $807 per credit hour part-time. Full-time tuition and fees vary according to program and reciprocity agreements. Part-time tuition and fees vary according to course load and program. ***Required fees:*** $420 full-time. ***Room and board:*** $9970. Room and board charges vary according to board plan, housing facility, and location.
Financial Aid Of all full-time matriculated undergraduates who enrolled in 2013, 1,785 applied for aid, 1,780 were judged to have need, 512 had their need fully met. In 2013, 29 non-need-based awards were made. ***Average percent of need met:*** 77. ***Average financial aid package:*** $12,761. ***Average need-based loan:*** $4450. ***Average need-based gift aid:*** $3649. ***Average non-need-based aid:*** $1949. ***Average indebtedness upon graduation:*** $23,515.

APPLYING
Standardized Tests *Required:* SAT or ACT (for admission).
Options: electronic application, deferred entrance.
Application fee: $50.
Required: high school transcript. ***Recommended:*** minimum 3.0 GPA.
Application deadlines: 7/1 (freshmen), 7/1 (transfers).
Notification: 7/31 (freshmen), 7/31 (transfers).

CONTACT
University of Hawaii at Hilo, Admissions, 200 W. Kawili St., Hilo, HI 96720. *Phone:* 808-932-7446. *Toll-free phone:* 800-897-4456. *Fax:* 808-932-7459. *E-mail:* uhhadm@hawaii.edu.

★ University of Hawaii at Manoa
Honolulu, Hawaii
http://manoa.hawaii.edu/

- **State-supported** university, founded 1907, part of University of Hawaii System
- **Urban** 320,300-acre campus with easy access to Honolulu
- **Coed** 14,126 undergraduate students, 83% full-time, 55% women, 45% men
- **Moderately difficult** entrance level, 78% of applicants were admitted

UNDERGRAD STUDENTS
11,741 full-time, 2,385 part-time. Students come from 51 states and territories; 45 other countries; 25% are from out of state; 2% Black or African American, non-Hispanic/Latino; 2% Hispanic/Latino; 41% Asian, non-Hispanic/Latino; 18% Native Hawaiian or other Pacific Islander, non-Hispanic/Latino; 0.3% American Indian or Alaska Native, non-Hispanic/Latino; 15% Two or more races, non-Hispanic/Latino; 0.2% Race/ethnicity unknown; 3% international; 12% transferred in; 25% live on campus.

Freshmen
Admission: 7,604 applied, 5,920 admitted, 1,841 enrolled. ***Average high school GPA:*** 3.5. ***Test scores:*** SAT critical reading scores over 500: 67%; SAT math scores over 500: 78%; SAT writing scores over 500: 62%; ACT scores over 18: 97%; SAT critical reading scores over 600: 18%; SAT math scores over 600: 31%; SAT writing scores over 600: 16%; ACT scores over 24: 44%; SAT critical reading scores over 700: 2%; SAT math scores over 700: 5%; SAT writing scores over 700: 2%; ACT scores over 30: 6%.
Retention: 79% of full-time freshmen returned.

FACULTY
Total: 1,512, 82% full-time, 89% with terminal degrees.
Student/faculty ratio: 13:1.

ACADEMICS
Calendar: semesters. *Degrees:* bachelor's, master's, doctoral, and postbachelor's certificates.
Special study options: accelerated degree program, advanced placement credit, cooperative education, distance learning, double majors, English as a second language, honors programs, independent study, internships, off-campus study, part-time degree program, services for LD students, student-designed majors, study abroad, summer session for credit. ***ROTC:*** Army (b), Air Force (b).
Computers: Students can access the following: campus intranet, computer help desk, free student e-mail accounts, online (class) grades, online (class) registration, online (class) schedules. Campuswide network is available. 100% of college-owned or -operated housing units are wired for high-speed Internet access. Wireless service is available via entire campus.

STUDENT LIFE
Housing options: coed, special housing for students with disabilities. Campus housing is university owned. Freshman applicants given priority for college housing.

Activities and organizations: drama/theater group, student-run newspaper, radio station, choral group, marching band, Biology Club, Pre-Medical Association, International Student Association, Katipunan, Timpuyog, national fraternities, national sororities.

Athletics Member NCAA. All Division I except football (Division I-A). ***Intercollegiate sports:*** archery M, baseball M(s), basketball M(s)/W(s), cheerleading M/W, cross-country running W, golf M(s)/W(s), sailing M/W, soccer W(s), softball W(s), swimming and diving M(s)/W(s), tennis M(s)/W(s), track and field W(s), volleyball M(s)/W(s), water polo W(s). ***Intramural sports:*** badminton M/W, basketball M/W, crew M/W, cross-country running M/W, golf M/W, rugby M, sailing M/W, soccer M, softball M, swimming and diving M/W, table tennis M/W, tennis M/W, track and field M/W, ultimate Frisbee M/W, volleyball M/W, weight lifting M/W, wrestling M/W.

Campus security: 24-hour emergency response devices and patrols, student patrols, late-night transport/escort service, controlled dormitory access.

Student services: health clinic, personal/psychological counseling, women's center.

COSTS & FINANCIAL AID

Costs (2015–16) ***Tuition:*** state resident $10,584 full-time, $410 per credit hour part-time; nonresident $30,696 full-time, $1193 per credit hour part-time. Full-time tuition and fees vary according to class time, course level, course load, degree level, program, reciprocity agreements, and student level. Part-time tuition and fees vary according to class time, course level, course load, degree level, program, reciprocity agreements, and student level. ***Room and board:*** Room and board charges vary according to board plan and housing facility. ***Payment plan:*** installment. ***Waivers:*** minority students, adult students, senior citizens, and employees or children of employees.

Financial Aid Of all full-time matriculated undergraduates who enrolled in 2014, 9,514 applied for aid, 6,819 were judged to have need, 1,983 had their need fully met. 479 Federal Work-Study jobs (averaging $2739). In 2014, 2303 non-need-based awards were made. ***Average percent of need met:*** 71. ***Average financial aid package:*** $13,718. ***Average need-based loan:*** $4829. ***Average need-based gift aid:*** $8846. ***Average non-need-based aid:*** $10,405. ***Average indebtedness upon graduation:*** $24,277.

APPLYING

Standardized Tests *Required:* SAT or ACT (for admission). *Recommended:* SAT (for admission), ACT (for admission).

Options: electronic application.

Application fee: $70.

Required: minimum 2.8 GPA. ***Required for some:*** high school transcript.

Application deadlines: 3/1 (freshmen), 3/1 (transfers).

Notification: continuous (freshmen), continuous (transfers).

CONTACT

Ms. Lisa Buto, Student Services Specialist, University of Hawaii at Manoa, 2600 Campus Road, Room 001, Honolulu, HI 96822. *Phone:* 808-956-8975. *Toll-free phone:* 800-823-9771. *Fax:* 808-956-4148. *E-mail:* uhmanoa.admissions@hawaii.edu.

University of Hawaii Maui College

Kahului, Hawaii

http://maui.hawaii.edu/

- **State-supported** primarily 2-year, founded 1967, part of University of Hawaii System
- **Rural** 77-acre campus
- **Coed**
- **Noncompetitive** entrance level

ACADEMICS

Calendar: semesters. *Degrees:* certificates, associate, and bachelor's.

STUDENT LIFE

Housing options: coed.

Activities and organizations: student-run newspaper.

Campus security: 24-hour emergency response devices and patrols.

Student services: health clinic, personal/psychological counseling.

COSTS & FINANCIAL AID

Costs (2014–15) ***Tuition:*** state resident $2736 full-time, $114 per credit part-time; nonresident $7584 full-time, $316 per credit part-time. Full-time tuition and fees vary according to course level, course load, and location. Part-time tuition and fees vary according to course level, course load, and location. ***Required fees:*** $126 full-time. ***Room and board:*** $14,766.

Financial Aid Of all full-time matriculated undergraduates who enrolled in 2013, 40 Federal Work-Study jobs (averaging $4000).

APPLYING

Options: electronic application, early admission.

Application fee: $25.

Required for some: high school transcript.

CONTACT

Mr. Stephen Kameda, Director of Admissions and Records, University of Hawaii Maui College, 310 Kaahumanu Avenue, Kahului, HI 96732. *Phone:* 808-984-3267. *Toll-free phone:* 800-479-6692. *Fax:* 808-984-3872. *E-mail:* skameda@hawaii.edu.

University of Hawaii–West Oahu

Kapolei, Hawaii

http://www.uhwo.hawaii.edu/

- **State-supported** 4-year, founded 1976, part of University of Hawaii System
- **Small-town** campus with easy access to Honolulu
- **Coed** 2,661 undergraduate students, 45% full-time, 66% women, 34% men
- **Moderately difficult** entrance level, 70% of applicants were admitted

UNDERGRAD STUDENTS

1,209 full-time, 1,452 part-time. 3% are from out of state; 2% Black or African American, non-Hispanic/Latino; 1% Hispanic/Latino; 39% Asian, non-Hispanic/Latino; 29% Native Hawaiian or other Pacific Islander, non-Hispanic/Latino; 0.3% American Indian or Alaska Native, non-Hispanic/Latino; 15% Two or more races, non-Hispanic/Latino; 0.9% Race/ethnicity unknown; 0.5% international; 22% transferred in.

Freshmen

Admission: 948 applied, 667 admitted, 266 enrolled. ***Average high school GPA:*** 3.18. ***Test scores:*** SAT critical reading scores over 500: 20%; SAT math scores over 500: 24%; SAT writing scores over 500: 14%; ACT scores over 18: 54%; SAT critical reading scores over 600: 3%; SAT math scores over 600: 2%; SAT writing scores over 600: 2%; ACT scores over 24: 9%; ACT scores over 30: 1%.

Retention: 61% of full-time freshmen returned.

FACULTY

Total: 71, 89% full-time, 83% with terminal degrees.

Student/faculty ratio: 26:1.

ACADEMICS

Calendar: semesters. *Degree:* certificates and bachelor's.

Special study options: part-time degree program. ***ROTC:*** Army (c), Air Force (c).

Computers: Students can access the following: computer help desk, free student e-mail accounts, online (class) grades, online (class) registration, online (class) schedules. Campuswide network is available. Wireless service is available via classrooms.

STUDENT LIFE

Housing options: college housing not available.

Campus security: 24-hour emergency response devices and patrols, late-night transport/escort service.

Student services: personal/psychological counseling.

COSTS & FINANCIAL AID

Costs (2015–16) ***Tuition:*** state resident $7128 full-time, $297 per credit part-time; nonresident $19,368 full-time, $807 per credit part-time. ***Required fees:*** $252 full-time, $252 per term part-time. ***Payment plan:*** installment. ***Waivers:*** employees or children of employees.

Financial Aid Of all full-time matriculated undergraduates who enrolled in 2012, 240 applied for aid, 240 were judged to have need. In 2012, 6 non-need-based awards were made. ***Average percent of need met:*** 50. ***Average financial aid package:*** $8380. ***Average need-based loan:*** $4346. ***Average need-based gift aid:*** $5326. ***Average non-need-based aid:*** $917.

APPLYING
Standardized Tests *Required for some:* SAT (for admission), ACT (for admission), SAT or ACT (for admission).

Options: deferred entrance.

Application fee: $50.

Required: minimum 2.7 GPA. ***Required for some:*** high school transcript, 2 letters of recommendation, college transcripts.

Application deadlines: 8/1 (freshmen), 8/1 (transfers).

Notification: continuous until 12/15 (freshmen), continuous until 12/1 (transfers).

CONTACT
Craig Morimoto, University of Hawaii–West Oahu, HI. *Phone:* 808-689-2916. *Toll-free phone:* 866-299-8656. *E-mail:* uhwoadm@hawaii.edu.

IDAHO

Boise State University

Boise, Idaho

http://www.boisestate.edu/

- **State-supported** university, founded 1932, part of Idaho System of Higher Education
- **Urban** 216-acre campus
- **Coed**
- **Moderately difficult** entrance level

FACULTY
Student/faculty ratio: 20:1.

ACADEMICS
Calendar: semesters. *Degrees:* associate, bachelor's, master's, doctoral, and postbachelor's certificates.

STUDENT LIFE
Housing options: coed, men-only, women-only. Campus housing is university owned. Freshman applicants given priority for college housing.

Activities and organizations: drama/theater group, student-run newspaper, radio station, choral group, marching band, Latter-Day Saints Student Association, Residence Hall Association, Organization of Student Social Workers, Marching Band Association, Teacher Education Association, national fraternities, national sororities.

Athletics Member NCAA. All Division I except football (Division I-A).

Campus security: 24-hour emergency response devices and patrols, late-night transport/escort service.

Student services: health clinic, personal/psychological counseling, women's center, legal services.

COSTS & FINANCIAL AID
Costs (2014–15) ***One-time required fee:*** $175. ***Tuition:*** state resident $4621 full-time, $169 per credit hour part-time; nonresident $17,473 full-time, $369 per credit hour part-time. Full-time tuition and fees vary according to course load and reciprocity agreements. Part-time tuition and fees vary according to course load. ***Required fees:*** $2020 full-time, $95 per credit hour part-time. ***Room and board:*** $6829; room only: $3609. Room and board charges vary according to board plan and housing facility.

Financial Aid Of all full-time matriculated undergraduates who enrolled in 2013, 8,120 applied for aid, 7,360 were judged to have need, 2,839 had their need fully met. 213 Federal Work-Study jobs (averaging $3655). 214 state and other part-time jobs (averaging $3666). In 2013, 1102 non-need-based awards were made. ***Average percent of need met:*** 20. ***Average financial aid package:*** $10,072. ***Average need-based loan:*** $7175. ***Average need-based gift aid:*** $4965. ***Average non-need-based aid:*** $1201. ***Average indebtedness upon graduation:*** $27,948. ***Financial aid deadline:*** 6/30.

APPLYING
Standardized Tests *Required:* SAT or ACT (for admission).

Options: electronic application.

Application fee: $60.

Required for some: high school transcript.

CONTACT
Ms. Niki Callison, Associate Director/Admissions, Boise State University, 1910 University Drive, Boise, ID 83725. *Phone:* 208-426-2715. *Toll-free phone:* 800-824-7017. *E-mail:* bsuinfo@boisestate.edu.

Broadview University–Boise

Meridian, Idaho

http://www.broadviewuniversity.edu/

- **Proprietary** 4-year, part of Globe Education Network (GEN) which is composed of Globe University, Minnesota School of Business, Broadview University, The Institute of Production and Recording and Minnesota School of Cosmetology
- **Small-town** 4-acre campus
- **Coed**

ACADEMICS
Degrees: certificates, diplomas, associate, and bachelor's.

STUDENT LIFE
Campus security: 24-hour emergency response devices, late-night transport/escort service.

APPLYING
Standardized Tests *Required:* ACCUPLACER is required of most applicants unless documentation of a minimum ACT composite score of 21 or documentation of a minimum composite score of 1485 on the SAT is presented (for admission).

Options: electronic application.

Application fee: $50.

Required: interview. ***Required for some:*** Certification of high school graduation or GED.

CONTACT
Broadview University–Boise, 2750 East Gala Court, Meridian, ID 83642. *Toll-free phone:* 877-572-5757.

Brown Mackie College–Boise

Boise, Idaho

http://www.brownmackie.edu/boise/

- **Proprietary** primarily 2-year, part of Education Management Corporation
- **Coed**

ACADEMICS
Degrees: diplomas, associate, and bachelor's.

CONTACT
Brown Mackie College–Boise, 9050 West Overland Road, Suite 100, Boise, ID 83709. *Phone:* 208-321-8800.

The College of Idaho

Caldwell, Idaho

http://www.collegeofidaho.edu/

- **Independent** comprehensive, founded 1891
- **Suburban** 50-acre campus
- **Endowment** $91.7 million
- **Coed** 1,120 undergraduate students, 97% full-time, 52% women, 48% men
- **Moderately difficult** entrance level, 93% of applicants were admitted

UNDERGRAD STUDENTS
1,085 full-time, 35 part-time. Students come from 29 states and territories; 53 other countries; 17% are from out of state; 2% Black or African American, non-Hispanic/Latino; 15% Hispanic/Latino; 3% Asian, non-Hispanic/Latino; 0.4% Native Hawaiian or other Pacific Islander, non-Hispanic/Latino; 0.5% American Indian or Alaska Native, non-Hispanic/Latino; 2% Two or more races, non-Hispanic/Latino; 5% Race/ethnicity unknown; 7% international; 6% transferred in; 62% live on campus.

Freshmen
Admission: 944 applied, 877 admitted, 336 enrolled. ***Average high school GPA:*** 3.51. ***Test scores:*** SAT critical reading scores over 500: 52%; SAT math scores over 500: 54%; SAT writing scores over 500: 50%; ACT scores over 18: 92%; SAT critical reading scores over 600: 21%; SAT math scores over 600: 19%; SAT writing scores over 600: 14%; ACT scores over 24: 46%; SAT critical reading scores over 700: 3%; SAT math scores over 700: 1%; SAT writing scores over 700: 3%; ACT scores over 30: 8%.
Retention: 86% of full-time freshmen returned.

FACULTY
Total: 131, 66% full-time, 62% with terminal degrees.
Student/faculty ratio: 11:1.

ACADEMICS
Calendar: 12-6-12 week calendar. *Degrees:* bachelor's and master's.
Special study options: advanced placement credit, cooperative education, double majors, English as a second language, honors programs, independent study, internships, off-campus study, part-time degree program, services for LD students, study abroad. ***ROTC:*** Army (c).
Unusual degree programs: 3-2 nursing with Idaho State University; law, speech language pathology, pharmacy, medical laboratory science.
Computers: 475 computers/terminals are available on campus for general student use. Students can access the following: campus intranet, computer help desk, free student e-mail accounts, online (class) grades, online (class) registration, online (class) schedules, online course syllabi, course assignments, course discussion, College of Idaho catalog. Campuswide network is available. 100% of college-owned or -operated housing units are wired for high-speed Internet access. Wireless service is available via entire campus.

STUDENT LIFE
Housing options: on-campus residence required through junior year; coed, special housing for students with disabilities. Campus housing is university owned. Freshman campus housing is guaranteed.
Activities and organizations: drama/theater group, student-run newspaper, choral group, ISO- International Student Organization, ALAS- Association of Latino American Students, Potter's Clay, GSCA- Gay-Straight Campus Alliance, AFRO- Africans Friends Relatives and Others, national fraternities, national sororities.
Athletics Member NAIA. ***Intercollegiate sports:*** baseball M(s), basketball M(s)/W(s), cross-country running M(s)/W(s), golf M(s)/W(s), skiing (downhill) M(s)/W(s), soccer M(s)/W(s), softball W(s), swimming and diving M(s)/W(s), tennis W(s), track and field M(s)/W(s), volleyball W(s). ***Intramural sports:*** badminton M/W, basketball M/W, football M/W, soccer M/W, softball M/W, ultimate Frisbee M/W, volleyball M/W.
Campus security: 24-hour emergency response devices and patrols, student patrols, late-night transport/escort service, controlled dormitory access.
Student services: health clinic, personal/psychological counseling, women's center.

COSTS & FINANCIAL AID
Costs (2015–16) ***Comprehensive fee:*** $35,155 includes full-time tuition ($25,410), mandatory fees ($755), and room and board ($8990). Part-time tuition: $1009 per credit.
Financial Aid Of all full-time matriculated undergraduates who enrolled in 2014, 884 applied for aid, 783 were judged to have need, 133 had their need fully met. 215 Federal Work-Study jobs (averaging $1000). 57 state and other part-time jobs (averaging $1000). In 2014, 311 non-need-based awards were made. ***Average percent of need met:*** 93. ***Average financial aid package:*** $25,976. ***Average need-based loan:*** $4763. ***Average need-based gift aid:*** $7833. ***Average non-need-based aid:*** $14,708. ***Average indebtedness upon graduation:*** $29,998.

APPLYING
Standardized Tests *Required:* SAT or ACT (for admission).
Options: electronic application, early admission, early action, deferred entrance.
Required: essay or personal statement, high school transcript, 1 letter of recommendation. ***Recommended:*** interview, class rank, extracurricular resume.
Application deadlines: 8/1 (freshmen), 8/1 (transfers), 11/15 (early action).
Notification: continuous (freshmen), continuous (transfers), 11/15 (early action).

CONTACT
Lorna Hunter, Vice President of Enrollment Management, The College of Idaho, 2112 Cleveland Boulevard, Caldwell, ID 83605-4432. *Phone:* 208-459-5319. *Toll-free phone:* 800-244-3246. *Fax:* 208-459-. *E-mail:* admission@collegeofidaho.edu.

ITT Technical Institute
Boise, Idaho
http://www.itt-tech.edu/

- **Proprietary** primarily 2-year, founded 1906, part of ITT Educational Services, Inc.
- **Urban** campus
- **Coed**
- **Minimally difficult** entrance level

ACADEMICS
Calendar: quarters. *Degrees:* associate and bachelor's.

STUDENT LIFE
Housing options: college housing not available.

FINANCIAL AID
Financial Aid Of all full-time matriculated undergraduates who enrolled in 2013, 9 Federal Work-Study jobs (averaging $5500).

CONTACT
Director of Recruitment, ITT Technical Institute, 12302 West Explorer Drive, Boise, ID 83713. *Phone:* 208-322-8844. *Toll-free phone:* 800-666-4888.

Lewis-Clark State College
Lewiston, Idaho
http://www.lcsc.edu/

- **State-supported** 4-year, founded 1893
- **Small-town** 44-acre campus
- **Coed**
- **Minimally difficult** entrance level

ACADEMICS
Calendar: semesters. *Degrees:* certificates, associate, and bachelor's.

STUDENT LIFE
Housing options: coed. Campus housing is university owned, leased by the school and is provided by a third party.
Athletics Member NAIA.
Campus security: 24-hour emergency response devices and patrols, student patrols, late-night transport/escort service.

COSTS & FINANCIAL AID
Costs (2014–15) ***Tuition:*** state resident $5900 full-time, $302 per credit hour part-time; nonresident $16,418 full-time, $302 per credit hour part-time. Full-time tuition and fees vary according to course load and reciprocity agreements. ***Room and board:*** $6194; room only: $3200. Room and board charges vary according to board plan and housing facility.
Financial Aid Of all full-time matriculated undergraduates who enrolled in 2013, 2,070 applied for aid, 1,277 were judged to have need, 244 had their need fully met. 80 Federal Work-Study jobs (averaging $1305). 79 state and other part-time jobs (averaging $1290). In 2013, 189 non-need-based awards were made. ***Average percent of need met:*** 72. ***Average financial aid package:*** $8602. ***Average need-based loan:*** $3938. ***Average need-based gift aid:*** $5713. ***Average non-need-based aid:*** $2921. ***Average indebtedness upon graduation:*** $18,065.

APPLYING
Standardized Tests *Required for some:* SAT or ACT (for admission).
Options: electronic application, deferred entrance.
Required: high school transcript, minimum 2.0 GPA. ***Required for some:*** interview.

CONTACT
Soo Lee Bruce-Smith, Coordinator of New Student Recruitment, Lewis-Clark State College, 500 Eighth Avenue, Lewiston, ID 83501-2698. *Phone:* 208-792-2210. *Toll-free phone:* 800-933-5272. *Fax:* 208-792-2876. *E-mail:* admissions@lcsc.edu.

New Saint Andrews College

Moscow, Idaho

http://www.nsa.edu/

- **Independent Christian** comprehensive, founded 1993
- **Small-town** campus
- **Coed** 140 undergraduate students, 91% full-time, 58% women, 42% men
- **Moderately difficult** entrance level, 72% of applicants were admitted

UNDERGRAD STUDENTS
128 full-time, 12 part-time. Students come from 28 states and territories; 5 other countries; 93% are from out of state; 4% Hispanic/Latino; 2% Asian, non-Hispanic/Latino; 0.8% American Indian or Alaska Native, non-Hispanic/Latino; 0.8% Two or more races, non-Hispanic/Latino; 8% Race/ethnicity unknown; 7% international.

Freshmen
Admission: 88 applied, 63 admitted, 31 enrolled. ***Test scores:*** SAT critical reading scores over 500: 92%; SAT math scores over 500: 71%; SAT writing scores over 500: 82%; ACT scores over 18: 99%; SAT critical reading scores over 600: 69%; SAT math scores over 600: 37%; SAT writing scores over 600: 48%; ACT scores over 24: 81%; SAT critical reading scores over 700: 31%; SAT math scores over 700: 3%; SAT writing scores over 700: 10%; ACT scores over 30: 36%.
Retention: 76% of full-time freshmen returned.

FACULTY
Total: 18, 33% full-time, 50% with terminal degrees.
Student/faculty ratio: 12:1.

ACADEMICS
Calendar: 4 8-week terms. *Degrees:* associate, bachelor's, master's, and postbachelor's certificates.
Special study options: advanced placement credit, independent study, part-time degree program, summer session for credit.
Computers: 4 computers/terminals are available on campus for general student use. Students can access the following: campus intranet, free student e-mail accounts, online (class) grades, online (class) registration, online (class) schedules. Campuswide network is available. Wireless service is available via entire campus.

STUDENT LIFE
Housing options: college housing not available.
Activities and organizations: drama/theater group, choral group, Students for the Relief of the Oppressed, Nursing Home Visits and Elderly Assistance (snow and leaf removal, firewood distribution), Blood Drives, Fall Carnival, St. Andrews Day Food Bank Drive.
Athletics ***Intramural sports:*** rugby M(c), soccer M(c), volleyball W(c).
Campus security: 24-hour emergency response devices.
Student services: personal/psychological counseling.

COSTS
Costs (2015–16) ***Tuition:*** $11,800 full-time, $950 per course part-time. Full-time tuition and fees vary according to program. Part-time tuition and fees vary according to program. No tuition increase for student's term of enrollment. ***Payment plan:*** installment. ***Waivers:*** employees or children of employees.

APPLYING
Standardized Tests *Required:* SAT or ACT (for admission).
Options: electronic application, deferred entrance.
Application fee: $40.
Required: essay or personal statement, high school transcript, 2 letters of recommendation. ***Required for some:*** interview.
Application deadlines: 2/15 (freshmen), 2/15 (transfers).
Notification: 3/15 (freshmen), 3/15 (transfers).

CONTACT
Mr. John Sawyer, Director of Student Recruitment, New Saint Andrews College, PO Box 9025, Moscow, ID 83843. *Phone:* 208-882-1566 Ext. 100. *Fax:* 208-882-4293. *E-mail:* info@nsa.edu.

Northwest Nazarene University

Nampa, Idaho

http://www.nnu.edu/

- **Independent** comprehensive, founded 1913, affiliated with Church of the Nazarene
- **Small-town** 85-acre campus with easy access to Boise
- **Coed** 1,524 undergraduate students, 77% full-time, 57% women, 43% men
- **Moderately difficult** entrance level, 65% of applicants were admitted

UNDERGRAD STUDENTS
1,167 full-time, 357 part-time. 42% are from out of state; 1% Black or African American, non-Hispanic/Latino; 9% Hispanic/Latino; 1% Asian, non-Hispanic/Latino; 0.3% Native Hawaiian or other Pacific Islander, non-Hispanic/Latino; 0.7% American Indian or Alaska Native, non-Hispanic/Latino; 2% Two or more races, non-Hispanic/Latino; 7% Race/ethnicity unknown; 3% international; 5% transferred in; 71% live on campus.

Freshmen
Admission: 1,603 applied, 1,043 admitted, 276 enrolled. ***Average high school GPA:*** 3.51. ***Test scores:*** SAT critical reading scores over 500: 61%; SAT math scores over 500: 56%; SAT writing scores over 500: 51%; ACT scores over 18: 93%; SAT critical reading scores over 600: 24%; SAT math scores over 600: 21%; SAT writing scores over 600: 18%; ACT scores over 24: 40%; SAT critical reading scores over 700: 5%; SAT math scores over 700: 4%; SAT writing scores over 700: 4%; ACT scores over 30: 12%.
Retention: 75% of full-time freshmen returned.

FACULTY
Total: 106, 99% full-time, 70% with terminal degrees.
Student/faculty ratio: 17:1.

ACADEMICS
Calendar: semesters. *Degrees:* bachelor's, master's, doctoral, and post-master's certificates.
Special study options: academic remediation for entering students, accelerated degree program, adult/continuing education programs, advanced placement credit, cooperative education, distance learning, double majors, English as a second language, freshman honors college, honors programs, independent study, internships, off-campus study, part-time degree program, services for LD students, student-designed majors, study abroad, summer session for credit. ***ROTC:*** Army (b).
Computers: Students can access the following: campus intranet, computer help desk, free student e-mail accounts, online (class) grades, online (class) registration, online (class) schedules. Campuswide network is available. 99% of college-owned or -operated housing units are wired for high-speed Internet access. Wireless service is available via entire campus.

STUDENT LIFE
Housing options: on-campus residence required through sophomore year; men-only, women-only, special housing for students with disabilities. Campus housing is university owned. Freshman campus housing is guaranteed.
Activities and organizations: drama/theater group, student-run newspaper, choral group, Students in Free Enterprise (SIFE), Student Government Association, Fellowship of Christian Athletes, The Crusader newspaper, The Oasis yearbook.
Athletics Member NCAA. All Division II. ***Intercollegiate sports:*** baseball M(s), basketball M(s)/W(s), cheerleading W(c), cross-country running M(s)/W(s), golf M(s)/W(s), soccer M/W(s), softball W(s), track and field M(s)/W(s), volleyball W(s). ***Intramural sports:*** basketball M/W, cross-country running M/W, football M/W, lacrosse W, softball M/W, table tennis M/W, tennis M/W, ultimate Frisbee M/W, volleyball M/W.
Campus security: 24-hour emergency response devices and patrols, student patrols, late-night transport/escort service, controlled dormitory access, residence hall check-in system, on-campus police hub.

Student services: health clinic, personal/psychological counseling.

COSTS & FINANCIAL AID
Costs (2015–16) ***Comprehensive fee:*** $34,550 includes full-time tuition ($27,750), mandatory fees ($200), and room and board ($6600). Full-time tuition and fees vary according to course load, degree level, program, and reciprocity agreements. ***Room and board:*** Room and board charges vary according to board plan. ***Payment plans:*** tuition prepayment, installment. ***Waivers:*** employees or children of employees.

Financial Aid Of all full-time matriculated undergraduates who enrolled in 2014, 1,060 applied for aid, 970 were judged to have need, 166 had their need fully met. 161 Federal Work-Study jobs (averaging $987). 507 state and other part-time jobs (averaging $1401). In 2014, 180 non-need-based awards were made. ***Average percent of need met:*** 70. ***Average financial aid package:*** $19,993. ***Average need-based loan:*** $4813. ***Average need-based gift aid:*** $6512. ***Average non-need-based aid:*** $9729. ***Average indebtedness upon graduation:*** $27,657.

APPLYING
Standardized Tests *Required:* SAT or ACT (for admission).

Options: electronic application, early action, deferred entrance.

Application fee: $25.

Required: essay or personal statement, high school transcript, minimum 2.5 GPA, 2 letters of recommendation. ***Required for some:*** interview.

Application deadlines: 8/15 (freshmen), 8/15 (transfers), 12/15 (early action).

Notification: continuous (freshmen), continuous (transfers), 1/15 (early action).

CONTACT
Northwest Nazarene University, 623 S. University Blvd., Nampa, ID 83686-5897. *Phone:* 208-467-8950. *Toll-free phone:* 877-668-4968.

University of Idaho

Moscow, Idaho

http://www.uidaho.edu/

- **State-supported** university, founded 1889
- **Small-town** 1354-acre campus
- **Endowment** $239.6 million
- **Coed** 9,388 undergraduate students, 83% full-time, 48% women, 52% men
- **Moderately difficult** entrance level, 67% of applicants were admitted

UNDERGRAD STUDENTS
7,824 full-time, 1,564 part-time. Students come from 50 states and territories; 45 other countries; 23% are from out of state; 1% Black or African American, non-Hispanic/Latino; 9% Hispanic/Latino; 1% Asian, non-Hispanic/Latino; 0.2% Native Hawaiian or other Pacific Islander, non-Hispanic/Latino; 0.7% American Indian or Alaska Native, non-Hispanic/Latino; 3% Two or more races, non-Hispanic/Latino; 3% Race/ethnicity unknown; 5% international; 6% transferred in; 23% live on campus.

Freshmen
Admission: 8,515 applied, 5,746 admitted, 1,590 enrolled. ***Average high school GPA:*** 3.41. ***Test scores:*** SAT critical reading scores over 500: 59%; SAT math scores over 500: 62%; SAT writing scores over 500: 53%; ACT scores over 18: 91%; SAT critical reading scores over 600: 22%; SAT math scores over 600: 24%; SAT writing scores over 600: 17%; ACT scores over 24: 50%; SAT critical reading scores over 700: 5%; SAT math scores over 700: 6%; SAT writing scores over 700: 3%; ACT scores over 30: 10%.

Retention: 77% of full-time freshmen returned.

FACULTY
Total: 696, 80% full-time, 66% with terminal degrees.

Student/faculty ratio: 17:1.

ACADEMICS
Calendar: semesters. *Degrees:* certificates, bachelor's, master's, doctoral, post-master's, and postbachelor's certificates.

Special study options: academic remediation for entering students, accelerated degree program, adult/continuing education programs, advanced placement credit, cooperative education, distance learning, double majors, English as a second language, honors programs, independent study, internships, off-campus study, part-time degree program, services for LD students, study abroad, summer session for credit. ***ROTC:*** Army (b), Navy (b), Air Force (c).

Computers: 510 computers/terminals are available on campus for general student use. Students can access the following: campus intranet, computer help desk, free student e-mail accounts, online (class) grades, online (class) registration, online (class) schedules. Campuswide network is available. 100% of college-owned or -operated housing units are wired for high-speed Internet access. Wireless service is available via entire campus.

STUDENT LIFE
Housing options: on-campus residence required for freshman year; coed, men-only, women-only, cooperative, special housing for students with disabilities. Campus housing is university owned. Freshman campus housing is guaranteed.

Activities and organizations: drama/theater group, student-run newspaper, radio and television station, choral group, marching band, Pre-Med club, Vandal Volunteers Club, Associate Students University of Idaho, Photography Club, UI Polo Club, National Society of Collegiate Scholars, Gender Sexuality Alliance, national fraternities, national sororities.

Athletics Member NCAA. All Division I except football (Division I-A). ***Intercollegiate sports:*** basketball M(s)/W(s), cross-country running M(s)/W(s), golf M(s)/W(s), soccer W(s), swimming and diving W(s), tennis M(s)/W(s), track and field M(s)/W(s), volleyball W(s). ***Intramural sports:*** badminton M/W, basketball M/W, bowling M/W, equestrian sports M(c)/W(c), football M, golf M/W, ice hockey M(c)/W(c), lacrosse M(c)/W(c), racquetball M/W, rock climbing M(c)/W(c), rugby M(c)/W(c), skiing (cross-country) M/W, skiing (downhill) M(c)/W(c), soccer M/W, softball M/W, swimming and diving M/W, table tennis M/W, tennis M/W, track and field M/W, ultimate Frisbee M/W, volleyball M/W, water polo M(c)/W(c), weight lifting M/W, wrestling M.

Campus security: 24-hour emergency response devices and patrols, late-night transport/escort service, controlled dormitory access, contracted services with the city of Moscow police department.

Student services: health clinic, personal/psychological counseling, women's center.

COSTS & FINANCIAL AID
Costs (2014–15) ***Tuition:*** state resident $4784 full-time, $281 per credit hour part-time; nonresident $18,314 full-time, $958 per credit hour part-time. Full-time tuition and fees vary according to degree level and program. Part-time tuition and fees vary according to degree level and program. ***Required fees:*** $2000 full-time, $59 per credit hour part-time. ***Room and board:*** $8022. Room and board charges vary according to board plan and housing facility. ***Payment plans:*** installment, deferred payment. ***Waivers:*** senior citizens and employees or children of employees.

Financial Aid Of all full-time matriculated undergraduates who enrolled in 2013, 6,809 applied for aid, 5,651 were judged to have need, 1,645 had their need fully met. 374 Federal Work-Study jobs (averaging $1783). 185 state and other part-time jobs (averaging $1889). In 2013, 1526 non-need-based awards were made. ***Average percent of need met:*** 75. ***Average financial aid package:*** $13,279. ***Average need-based loan:*** $6931. ***Average need-based gift aid:*** $4753. ***Average non-need-based aid:*** $3910. ***Average indebtedness upon graduation:*** $25,753.

APPLYING
Standardized Tests *Required:* SAT or ACT (for admission).

Options: electronic application, deferred entrance.

Application fee: $60.

Required: high school transcript, minimum 2.2 GPA. ***Required for some:*** essay or personal statement.

Application deadlines: 8/1 (freshmen), rolling (transfers).

Notification: continuous (freshmen), continuous (transfers).

CONTACT
Ms. Melissa Goodwin, Associate Director, Admissions, University of Idaho, 875 Perimeter Drive MS 4264, Moscow, ID 83844-4264. *Phone:* 208-885-6326. *Toll-free phone:* 888-884-3246. *Fax:* 208-885-9119. *E-mail:* admissions@uidaho.edu.

ILLINOIS

American Academy of Art

Chicago, Illinois

http://www.aaart.edu/

- **Proprietary** 4-year, founded 1923
- **Urban** campus with easy access to Chicago
- **Coed** 432 undergraduate students
- **Moderately difficult** entrance level

UNDERGRAD STUDENTS
20% are from out of state.

FACULTY
Student/faculty ratio: 15:1.

ACADEMICS
Calendar: trimesters. *Degree:* bachelor's.

Special study options: academic remediation for entering students, accelerated degree program, adult/continuing education programs, independent study, internships, part-time degree program, study abroad, summer session for credit.

STUDENT LIFE
Housing options: college housing not availableCampus housing is provided by a third party.

Campus security: 24-hour emergency response devices.

COSTS & FINANCIAL AID
Costs (2014–15) ***Tuition:*** $14,900 full-time, $7450 per term part-time. Full-time tuition and fees vary according to course load. Part-time tuition and fees vary according to course load. ***Required fees:*** $500 full-time. ***Payment plan:*** installment. ***Waivers:*** employees or children of employees.

Financial Aid ***Average percent of need met:*** 70.

APPLYING
Options: electronic application.

Application fee: $25.

Required: high school transcript, interview.

Application deadlines: rolling (freshmen), rolling (transfers).

CONTACT
Mr. Stuart Rosenbloom, Director of Admissions, American Academy of Art, 332 South Michigan Avenue, Suite 300, Chicago, IL 60604-4302. *Phone:* 312-461-0600 Ext. 159. *Toll-free phone:* 888-461-0600. *E-mail:* srosenbloom@aaart.edu.

Argosy University, Chicago

Chicago, Illinois

http://www.argosy.edu/chicago-illinois/default.aspx

- **Proprietary** university, founded 1976
- **Urban** campus
- **Coed**

ACADEMICS
Calendar: semesters. *Degrees:* certificates, bachelor's, master's, and doctoral.

CONTACT
Argosy University, Chicago, 225 North Michigan Avenue, Suite 1300, Chicago, IL 60601. *Phone:* 312-777-7600. *Toll-free phone:* 800-626-4123.

Argosy University, Schaumburg

Schaumburg, Illinois

http://www.argosy.edu/locations/chicago-schaumburg/

- **Proprietary** university, founded 1979
- **Coed**

ACADEMICS
Calendar: semesters. *Degrees:* bachelor's, master's, doctoral, and post-master's certificates.

CONTACT
Argosy University, Schaumburg, 999 North Plaza Drive, Suite 111, Schaumburg, IL 60173-5403. *Phone:* 847-969-4900. *Toll-free phone:* 866-290-2777.

Augustana College

Rock Island, Illinois

http://www.augustana.edu/

- **Independent** 4-year, founded 1860, affiliated with Evangelical Lutheran Church in America
- **Suburban** 115-acre campus
- **Endowment** $142.0 million
- **Coed** 2,500 undergraduate students, 99% full-time, 58% women, 42% men
- **Moderately difficult** entrance level, 54% of applicants were admitted

UNDERGRAD STUDENTS
2,475 full-time, 25 part-time. Students come from 34 states and territories; 28 other countries; 16% are from out of state; 4% Black or African American, non-Hispanic/Latino; 10% Hispanic/Latino; 2% Asian, non-Hispanic/Latino; 0.1% Native Hawaiian or other Pacific Islander, non-Hispanic/Latino; 0.2% American Indian or Alaska Native, non-Hispanic/Latino; 4% Two or more races, non-Hispanic/Latino; 2% Race/ethnicity unknown; 2% international; 2% transferred in; 70% live on campus.

Freshmen
Admission: 6,053 applied, 3,245 admitted, 726 enrolled. ***Average high school GPA:*** 3.29. ***Test scores:*** SAT critical reading scores over 500: 85%; SAT math scores over 500: 93%; SAT writing scores over 500: 70%; ACT scores over 18: 99%; SAT critical reading scores over 600: 23%; SAT math scores over 600: 60%; SAT writing scores over 600: 30%; ACT scores over 24: 73%; SAT critical reading scores over 700: 3%; SAT math scores over 700: 18%; SAT writing scores over 700: 3%; ACT scores over 30: 17%.

Retention: 83% of full-time freshmen returned.

FACULTY
Total: 267, 73% full-time, 75% with terminal degrees.

Student/faculty ratio: 11:1.

ACADEMICS
Calendar: quarters. *Degree:* bachelor's.

Special study options: advanced placement credit, double majors, English as a second language, honors programs, independent study, internships, off-campus study, part-time degree program, services for LD students, student-designed majors, study abroad, summer session for credit.

Unusual degree programs: 3-2 engineering with formal agreements with Washington University in St. Louis, Northern Illinois University; 3-2 approval may be given for any ABET accredited institution; forestry with Duke University; occupational therapy with Washington University in St. Louis, landscape architecture with University of Illinois, environmental studies with Duke University.

Computers: 600 computers/terminals and 1,800 ports are available on campus for general student use. Students can access the following: campus intranet, computer help desk, free student e-mail accounts, online (class) grades, online (class) registration, online (class) schedules. Campuswide network is available. 100% of college-owned or -operated housing units are wired for high-speed Internet access. Wireless service is available via classrooms, computer centers, computer labs, dorm rooms, libraries, student centers.

STUDENT LIFE
Housing options: on-campus residence required through junior year; coed. Campus housing is university owned. Freshman campus housing is guaranteed.

Activities and organizations: drama/theater group, student-run newspaper, radio station, choral group, College Union Board of Managers, Student Government Association, student newspaper, student radio station, service organizations (APO, Dance Marathon committee).

Athletics Member NCAA. All Division III. ***Intercollegiate sports:*** baseball M, basketball M/W, cheerleading M(c)/W(c), crew M(c)/W(c), cross-country running M/W, equestrian sports M(c)/W(c), fencing

M(c)/W(c), football M, golf M/W, ice hockey M(c), lacrosse M/W, soccer M/W, softball W, swimming and diving M/W, tennis M/W, track and field M/W, ultimate Frisbee M(c)/W(c), volleyball M(c)/W, water polo M(c)/W(c), wrestling M. ***Intramural sports:*** badminton M/W, basketball M/W, bowling M/W, cross-country running M/W, football M/W, golf M/W, racquetball M/W, rugby M, skiing (cross-country) M/W, skiing (downhill) M/W, soccer M/W, softball M/W, swimming and diving M/W, table tennis M/W, tennis M/W, track and field M/W, ultimate Frisbee M/W, volleyball M/W, wrestling M.

Campus security: 24-hour emergency response devices and patrols, late-night transport/escort service, controlled dormitory access.

Student services: personal/psychological counseling.

COSTS & FINANCIAL AID

Costs (2015–16) ***Comprehensive fee:*** $48,212 includes full-time tuition ($38,466) and room and board ($9746). Part-time tuition: $1650 per credit. Part-time tuition and fees vary according to course load. ***Room and board:*** Room and board charges vary according to board plan and housing facility. ***Payment plans:*** tuition prepayment, installment. ***Waivers:*** employees or children of employees.

Financial Aid Of all full-time matriculated undergraduates who enrolled in 2013, 2,283 applied for aid, 1,937 were judged to have need, 358 had their need fully met. 1,344 Federal Work-Study jobs (averaging $2331). In 2013, 535 non-need-based awards were made. ***Average percent of need met:*** 84. ***Average financial aid package:*** $25,989. ***Average need-based loan:*** $4649. ***Average need-based gift aid:*** $20,527. ***Average non-need-based aid:*** $16,568. ***Average indebtedness upon graduation:*** $31,612.

APPLYING

Standardized Tests *Recommended:* SAT or ACT (for admission).

Options: electronic application, deferred entrance.

Required: high school transcript. ***Required for some:*** essay or personal statement, interview. ***Recommended:*** essay or personal statement, 1 letter of recommendation, interview.

Application deadlines: rolling (freshmen), rolling (out-of-state freshmen), rolling (transfers).

Notification: continuous (freshmen), continuous (out-of-state freshmen), continuous (transfers).

CONTACT

W. Kent Barnds, Vice President of Enrollment Management, Augustana College, 639 38th St, Rock Island, IL 61201. *Phone:* 309-794-7662. *Toll-free phone:* 800-798-8100. *Fax:* 309-794-8797. *E-mail:* admissions@augustana.edu.

Aurora University

Aurora, Illinois

http://www.aurora.edu/

- **Independent** comprehensive, founded 1893
- **Suburban** 32-acre campus with easy access to Chicago
- **Endowment** $38.5 million
- **Coed**
- **Moderately difficult** entrance level

FACULTY

Student/faculty ratio: 17:1.

ACADEMICS

Calendar: semesters. *Degrees:* bachelor's, master's, doctoral, post-master's, and postbachelor's certificates.

STUDENT LIFE

Housing options: coed. Campus housing is university owned. Freshman applicants given priority for college housing.

Activities and organizations: drama/theater group, student-run newspaper, radio station, choral group, Aurora University Student Association, Latin American Student Organization, Student Nursing Association, Social Work Association, Future Educators Association, national fraternities, national sororities.

Athletics Member NCAA. All Division III.

Campus security: 24-hour emergency response devices and patrols, late-night transport/escort service, controlled dormitory access.

Student services: health clinic, personal/psychological counseling.

COSTS & FINANCIAL AID

Costs (2014–15) ***Comprehensive fee:*** $30,882 includes full-time tuition ($21,120), mandatory fees ($220), and room and board ($9542). Full-time tuition and fees vary according to location. Part-time tuition: $610 per semester hour. Part-time tuition and fees vary according to course load, location, and program. ***Room and board:*** Room and board charges vary according to board plan, housing facility, and location. ***Payment plans:*** installment, deferred payment.

Financial Aid Of all full-time matriculated undergraduates who enrolled in 2013, 2,554 applied for aid, 2,311 were judged to have need, 599 had their need fully met. 1,456 Federal Work-Study jobs (averaging $1609). 32 state and other part-time jobs (averaging $7648). In 2013, 478 non-need-based awards were made. ***Average percent of need met:*** 85. ***Average financial aid package:*** $18,159. ***Average need-based loan:*** $4429. ***Average need-based gift aid:*** $6912. ***Average non-need-based aid:*** $8400. ***Average indebtedness upon graduation:*** $27,672.

APPLYING

Standardized Tests *Required:* SAT or ACT (for admission).

Options: electronic application, deferred entrance.

Application fee: $25.

Required: high school transcript, minimum 2.0 GPA. ***Required for some:*** 2 letters of recommendation, interview. ***Recommended:*** essay or personal statement, interview.

CONTACT

Mr. James Lancaster, Director, Freshman Admission, Aurora University, 347 South Gladstone Avenue, Aurora, IL 60506-4892. *Phone:* 630-844-5533. *Toll-free phone:* 800-742-5281. *Fax:* 630-844-5535. *E-mail:* admission@aurora.edu.

Benedictine University

Lisle, Illinois

http://www.ben.edu/

- **Independent Roman Catholic** comprehensive, founded 1887
- **Suburban** 108-acre campus with easy access to Chicago
- **Coed** 3,818 undergraduate students, 80% full-time, 58% women, 42% men
- **Moderately difficult** entrance level, 77% of applicants were admitted

UNDERGRAD STUDENTS

3,071 full-time, 747 part-time. 10% are from out of state; 9% Black or African American, non-Hispanic/Latino; 11% Hispanic/Latino; 15% Asian, non-Hispanic/Latino; 0.2% Native Hawaiian or other Pacific Islander, non-Hispanic/Latino; 0.2% American Indian or Alaska Native, non-Hispanic/Latino; 17% Race/ethnicity unknown; 1% international; 10% transferred in; 18% live on campus.

Freshmen

Admission: 2,558 applied, 1,974 admitted, 672 enrolled. ***Average high school GPA:*** 3.27. ***Test scores:*** ACT scores over 18: 89%; ACT scores over 24: 37%; ACT scores over 30: 5%.

Retention: 73% of full-time freshmen returned.

FACULTY

Total: 719, 23% full-time, 34% with terminal degrees.

Student/faculty ratio: 13:1.

ACADEMICS

Calendar: semesters. *Degrees:* certificates, associate, bachelor's, master's, doctoral, and postbachelor's certificates.

Special study options: academic remediation for entering students, accelerated degree program, adult/continuing education programs, advanced placement credit, distance learning, double majors, English as a second language, honors programs, independent study, internships, off-campus study, part-time degree program, services for LD students, study abroad, summer session for credit. ***ROTC:*** Army (c).

Unusual degree programs: 3-2 engineering with University of Illinois at Urbana–Champaign, Illinois Institute of Technology, Purdue University; nursing with Rush University-Clinical Life Science, Respiratory Care and Perfusion Technology.

Computers: Students can access the following: computer help desk, free student e-mail accounts, online (class) grades, online (class) registration, online (class) schedules. Campuswide network is available. 100% of college-owned or -operated housing units are wired for high-speed Internet access. Wireless service is available via computer centers, dorm rooms, libraries, student centers.

STUDENT LIFE

Housing options: coed, men-only, women-only. Campus housing is university owned and is provided by a third party. Freshman campus housing is guaranteed.

Activities and organizations: student-run newspaper, television station, choral group, Student Senate, MSA-Muslim Student Association, AMSA-American Medical Student Association, The Candor-Student Newspaper, Programming Board.

Athletics Member NCAA. All Division III. ***Intercollegiate sports:*** baseball M, basketball M/W, cross-country running M/W, football M, golf M/W, lacrosse M/W, soccer M/W, softball W, tennis W, track and field M/W, volleyball W. ***Intramural sports:*** basketball M/W, bowling M/W, cheerleading W(c), football M/W, lacrosse M(c), softball M/W, table tennis M/W, volleyball M/W.

Campus security: 24-hour emergency response devices and patrols, late-night transport/escort service, controlled dormitory access.

Student services: health clinic, personal/psychological counseling.

COSTS & FINANCIAL AID

Costs (2014–15) ***Comprehensive fee:*** $36,766 includes full-time tuition ($27,140), mandatory fees ($1100), and room and board ($8526). Full-time tuition and fees vary according to course load, degree level, and location. Part-time tuition: $905 per hour. Part-time tuition and fees vary according to course load, degree level, and location. ***Required fees:*** $55 per credit hour part-time. ***College room only:*** $5846. Room and board charges vary according to board plan, housing facility, and location. ***Waivers:*** employees or children of employees.

Financial Aid Of all full-time matriculated undergraduates who enrolled in 2013, 2,022 applied for aid, 1,884 were judged to have need. 166 Federal Work-Study jobs (averaging $1806). In 2013, 276 non-need-based awards were made. ***Average financial aid package:*** $18,064. ***Average need-based loan:*** $4132. ***Average need-based gift aid:*** $7781. ***Average non-need-based aid:*** $11,026. ***Average indebtedness upon graduation:*** $23,260.

APPLYING

Standardized Tests *Required:* SAT or ACT (for admission).

Options: electronic application, deferred entrance.

Application fee: $40.

Required: essay or personal statement, high school transcript. ***Required for some:*** interview. ***Recommended:*** rank in upper 50% of high school class.

CONTACT

Ms. Kari Gibbons, Dean of Enrollment, Benedictine University, 5700 College Road, Lisle, IL 60532-0900. *Phone:* 630-829-6300. *Toll-free phone:* 888-829-6363. *Fax:* 630-829-6301. *E-mail:* admissions@ben.edu.

Benedictine University at Springfield

Springfield, Illinois

http://www1.ben.edu/springfield/

- **Independent** comprehensive, founded 1929, affiliated with Roman Catholic Church
- **Small-town** 8-acre campus
- **Coed**

FACULTY

Student/faculty ratio: 7:1.

ACADEMICS

Calendar: semesters. *Degrees:* diplomas, bachelor's, master's, and doctoral (The college partners with Benedictine University, offering baccalaureate and master degree programs at Springfield College's campus).

STUDENT LIFE

Housing options: coed. Campus housing is university owned.

Activities and organizations: student-run newspaper, choral group, Literary Magazine, Choral Groups, Student Government, International Student Organization, Campus Ministries.

Athletics Member NAIA.

Campus security: 24-hour emergency response devices, late-night transport/escort service.

Student services: personal/psychological counseling.

COSTS & FINANCIAL AID

Costs (2014–15) ***Comprehensive fee:*** $24,100 includes full-time tuition ($16,500), mandatory fees ($100), and room and board ($7500). Full-time tuition and fees vary according to program. Part-time tuition: $690 per credit hour. Part-time tuition and fees vary according to course load and program. No tuition increase for student's term of enrollment. ***Required fees:*** $50 per term part-time. ***Room and board:*** Room and board charges vary according to housing facility. ***Payment plans:*** installment, deferred payment.

Financial Aid Of all full-time matriculated undergraduates who enrolled in 2013, 30 Federal Work-Study jobs (averaging $1700).

APPLYING

Standardized Tests *Required:* SAT and SAT Subject Tests or ACT (for admission).

Required: high school transcript. ***Required for some:*** interview. ***Recommended:*** minimum 2.0 GPA.

CONTACT

Michelle Meyer, Associate Director of Admissions, Benedictine University at Springfield, 1500 North Fifth Street, Springfield, IL 62702. *Phone:* 217-525-1420 Ext. 3321. *Toll-free phone:* 800-635-7289. *Fax:* 217-528-9871. *E-mail:* mmeyer@ben.edu.

Blackburn College

Carlinville, Illinois

http://www.blackburn.edu/

- **Independent Presbyterian** 4-year, founded 1837
- **Small-town** 80-acre campus with easy access to St. Louis
- **Endowment** $13.9 million
- **Coed** 585 undergraduate students, 95% full-time, 55% women, 45% men
- **Moderately difficult** entrance level, 65% of applicants were admitted

UNDERGRAD STUDENTS

554 full-time, 31 part-time. Students come from 19 states and territories; 4 other countries; 10% are from out of state; 11% Black or African American, non-Hispanic/Latino; 2% Hispanic/Latino; 1% Asian, non-Hispanic/Latino; 0.5% American Indian or Alaska Native, non-Hispanic/Latino; 2% Two or more races, non-Hispanic/Latino; 1% Race/ethnicity unknown; 9% transferred in; 68% live on campus.

Freshmen

Admission: 788 applied, 513 admitted, 171 enrolled. ***Average high school GPA:*** 3.26. ***Test scores:*** ACT scores over 18: 75%; ACT scores over 24: 27%; ACT scores over 30: 3%.

Retention: 62% of full-time freshmen returned.

FACULTY

Total: 73, 51% full-time, 49% with terminal degrees.

Student/faculty ratio: 12:1.

ACADEMICS

Calendar: semesters. *Degree:* bachelor's.

Special study options: advanced placement credit, cooperative education, double majors, honors programs, independent study, internships, off-campus study, services for LD students, student-designed majors, study abroad, summer session for credit.

Unusual degree programs: 3-2 engineering with Washington University in St. Louis or University of Missouri, Kansas City; nursing with St. John's in Springfield, IL.

Computers: 202 computers/terminals are available on campus for general student use. Students can access the following: computer help desk, free student e-mail accounts, online (class) grades, online (class) registration, online (class) schedules. Campuswide network is available. 100% of college-owned or -operated housing units are wired for high-speed Internet access. Wireless service is available via libraries, student centers.

STUDENT LIFE

Housing options: on-campus residence required through junior year; coed, men-only, women-only. Campus housing is university owned. Freshman campus housing is guaranteed.

Activities and organizations: drama/theater group, student-run newspaper, radio station, choral group, Habitat for Humanity, Pre-Health Professions, Running Club, Trading Card Games, Spectrum.

Athletics Member NCAA. All Division III. ***Intercollegiate sports:*** baseball M, basketball M/W, cross-country running M/W, golf M, soccer M/W, softball W, tennis W, volleyball W. ***Intramural sports:*** badminton M/W, basketball M/W, football M/W, golf M/W, racquetball M/W, soccer M/W, softball M/W, table tennis M/W, tennis M/W, ultimate Frisbee M/W, volleyball M/W.

Campus security: student patrols, late-night transport/escort service.

Student services: personal/psychological counseling.

COSTS & FINANCIAL AID

Costs (2015–16) ***Comprehensive fee:*** $27,398 includes full-time tuition ($19,954), mandatory fees ($410), and room and board ($7034). Full-time tuition and fees vary according to student level. Part-time tuition: $665 per quarter hour. Part-time tuition and fees vary according to student level. ***College room only:*** $4064. Room and board charges vary according to board plan and housing facility. ***Payment plan:*** installment. ***Waivers:*** employees or children of employees.

Financial Aid Of all full-time matriculated undergraduates who enrolled in 2009, 581 applied for aid, 502 were judged to have need, 194 had their need fully met. 388 Federal Work-Study jobs (averaging $2653). 113 state and other part-time jobs (averaging $2337). In 2009, 62 non-need-based awards were made. ***Average percent of need met:*** 80. ***Average financial aid package:*** $13,873. ***Average need-based loan:*** $4107. ***Average need-based gift aid:*** $11,209. ***Average non-need-based aid:*** $5163. ***Average indebtedness upon graduation:*** $20,077.

APPLYING

Standardized Tests *Required:* SAT or ACT (for admission).

Options: electronic application, deferred entrance.

Application fee: $20.

Required: high school transcript, minimum 2.0 GPA. ***Required for some:*** essay or personal statement, 3 letters of recommendation, interview. ***Recommended:*** minimum 2.5 GPA.

Application deadlines: rolling (freshmen), rolling (out-of-state freshmen), rolling (transfers).

Notification: continuous (freshmen), continuous (out-of-state freshmen), continuous (transfers).

CONTACT

Mrs. Alisha Kapp, Director of Admission, Blackburn College, 700 College Avenue, Carlinville, IL 62626. *Phone:* 217-854-5110. *Toll-free phone:* 800-233-3550. *E-mail:* alisha.kapp@blackburn.edu.

Blessing-Rieman College of Nursing

Quincy, Illinois

http://www.brcn.edu/

- **Independent** comprehensive, founded 1985
- **Small-town** 1-acre campus
- **Endowment** $7.7 million
- **Coed, primarily women** 234 undergraduate students, 82% full-time, 84% women, 16% men
- **Moderately difficult** entrance level, 66% of applicants were admitted

UNDERGRAD STUDENTS

193 full-time, 41 part-time. Students come from 10 states and territories; 30% are from out of state; 3% Black or African American, non-Hispanic/Latino; 0.9% Hispanic/Latino; 2% Asian, non-Hispanic/Latino; 1% American Indian or Alaska Native, non-Hispanic/Latino; 12% transferred in; 82% live on campus.

Freshmen

Admission: 546 applied, 362 admitted. ***Average high school GPA:*** 3.29. ***Test scores:*** ACT scores over 18: 100%; ACT scores over 24: 49%.

FACULTY

Total: 18, 100% full-time, 28% with terminal degrees.

Student/faculty ratio: 12:1.

ACADEMICS

Calendar: semesters. *Degrees:* bachelor's and master's.

Special study options: academic remediation for entering students, adult/continuing education programs, advanced placement credit, distance learning, double majors, honors programs, internships, part-time degree program, summer session for credit.

Computers: 28 computers/terminals are available on campus for general student use. Students can access the following: campus intranet, computer help desk, free student e-mail accounts. Campuswide network is available. 100% of college-owned or -operated housing units are wired for high-speed Internet access.

STUDENT LIFE

Housing options: on-campus residence required through sophomore year; coed. Campus housing is university owned. Freshman campus housing is guaranteed.

Activities and organizations: drama/theater group, student-run newspaper, radio station, choral group, Student Nurses Organization, national fraternities, national sororities.

Athletics ***Intercollegiate sports:*** baseball M(s)/W(s), basketball M(s)/W(s), football M(s), soccer M(s)/W(s), volleyball M(s)/W(s). ***Intramural sports:*** baseball M/W, basketball M/W, football M, soccer M/W, volleyball M/W.

Campus security: 24-hour patrols, late-night transport/escort service, controlled dormitory access.

Student services: health clinic, personal/psychological counseling.

COSTS & FINANCIAL AID

Costs (2015–16) ***Tuition:*** $21,810 full-time, $727 per credit hour part-time. Full-time tuition and fees vary according to course load, degree level, and student level. Part-time tuition and fees vary according to course load, degree level, and student level. ***Room only:*** Room and board charges vary according to student level. ***Payment plan:*** installment.

Financial Aid Of all full-time matriculated undergraduates who enrolled in 2014, 177 applied for aid, 177 were judged to have need, 177 had their need fully met. ***Average percent of need met:*** 100. ***Average financial aid package:*** $12,429. ***Average need-based gift aid:*** $4294. ***Average indebtedness upon graduation:*** $8475.

APPLYING

Standardized Tests *Required:* SAT or ACT (for admission).

Options: electronic application, deferred entrance.

Required: high school transcript, minimum 3.0 GPA. ***Recommended:*** essay or personal statement, interview.

Application deadlines: rolling (freshmen), rolling (transfers).

CONTACT

Ms. Heather Mutter, Admissions Counselor, Blessing-Rieman College of Nursing, Broadway at 11th Street, POB 7005, Quincy, IL 62305-7005. *Phone:* 217-228-5520 Ext. 6979. *Toll-free phone:* 800-877-9140 Ext. 6964. *Fax:* 217-223-4661. *E-mail:* admissions@brcn.edu.

★ Bradley University

Peoria, Illinois

http://www.bradley.edu/

- **Independent** comprehensive, founded 1897
- **Suburban** 85-acre campus
- **Endowment** $293.7 million
- **Coed** 4,589 undergraduate students, 95% full-time, 51% women, 49% men
- **Moderately difficult** entrance level, 61% of applicants were admitted

UNDERGRAD STUDENTS

4,373 full-time, 216 part-time. Students come from 44 states and territories; 31 other countries; 17% are from out of state; 5% Black or African American, non-Hispanic/Latino; 6% Hispanic/Latino; 3% Asian, non-Hispanic/Latino; 0.1% Native Hawaiian or other Pacific Islander, non-Hispanic/Latino; 0.2% American Indian or Alaska Native, non-Hispanic/Latino; 1% Two or more races, non-Hispanic/Latino; 13%

Race/ethnicity unknown; 1% international; 5% transferred in; 68% live on campus.

Freshmen

Admission: 9,575 applied, 5,793 admitted, 948 enrolled. ***Average high school GPA:*** 3.6. ***Test scores:*** SAT critical reading scores over 500: 71%; SAT math scores over 500: 83%; SAT writing scores over 500: 65%; ACT scores over 18: 100%; SAT critical reading scores over 600: 37%; SAT math scores over 600: 45%; SAT writing scores over 600: 26%; ACT scores over 24: 70%; SAT critical reading scores over 700: 7%; SAT math scores over 700: 13%; SAT writing scores over 700: 5%; ACT scores over 30: 13%.

Retention: 88% of full-time freshmen returned.

FACULTY

Total: 583, 60% full-time, 60% with terminal degrees.

Student/faculty ratio: 12:1.

ACADEMICS

Calendar: semesters. *Degrees:* certificates, bachelor's, master's, and doctoral.

Special study options: advanced placement credit, cooperative education, distance learning, double majors, honors programs, independent study, internships, off-campus study, part-time degree program, services for LD students, student-designed majors, study abroad, summer session for credit. ***ROTC:*** Army (b).

Computers: 2,500 computers/terminals are available on campus for general student use. Students can access the following: computer help desk, free student e-mail accounts, online (class) grades, online (class) registration, online (class) schedules. Campuswide network is available. 100% of college-owned or -operated housing units are wired for high-speed Internet access. Wireless service is available via entire campus.

STUDENT LIFE

Housing options: on-campus residence required through sophomore year; coed. Campus housing is university owned, leased by the school and is provided by a third party. Freshman campus housing is guaranteed.

Activities and organizations: drama/theater group, student-run newspaper, radio station, choral group, Fraternity/Sorority Life, Service on Saturday, Activities Council of Bradley University, Up 'Til Dawn, CRU (Campus Christian group), national fraternities, national sororities.

Athletics Member NCAA. All Division I. ***Intercollegiate sports:*** baseball M(s), basketball M(s)/W, cheerleading M/W, cross-country running M(s)/W(s), golf M(s)/W(s), soccer M(s), softball W(s), tennis W(s), track and field M(s)/W(s), volleyball W(s). ***Intramural sports:*** badminton M/W, baseball M, basketball M/W, bowling M/W, fencing M/W, football M, ice hockey M(c), racquetball M/W, rock climbing M/W, soccer M(c)/W(c), softball M/W, table tennis M/W, tennis M/W, ultimate Frisbee M/W, volleyball M(c).

Campus security: 24-hour emergency response devices and patrols, late-night transport/escort service, controlled dormitory access, emergency text messaging, mass notification/emergency communication system in 20 academic buildings.

Student services: health clinic, personal/psychological counseling.

COSTS & FINANCIAL AID

Costs (2014–15) ***One-time required fee:*** $200. ***Comprehensive fee:*** $40,264 includes full-time tuition ($30,500), mandatory fees ($344), and room and board ($9420). Full-time tuition and fees vary according to course load and program. Part-time tuition: $940 per credit hour. Part-time tuition and fees vary according to course load and program. ***Required fees:*** $810 per credit hour part-time. ***College room only:*** $5460. Room and board charges vary according to board plan. ***Payment plans:*** installment, deferred payment. ***Waivers:*** senior citizens and employees or children of employees.

Financial Aid Of all full-time matriculated undergraduates who enrolled in 2014, 4,087 applied for aid, 3,480 were judged to have need, 499 had their need fully met. 280 Federal Work-Study jobs (averaging $2000). In 2014, 805 non-need-based awards were made. ***Average percent of need met:*** 67. ***Average financial aid package:*** $20,117. ***Average need-based loan:*** $6379. ***Average need-based gift aid:*** $15,016. ***Average non-need-based aid:*** $10,012. ***Average indebtedness upon graduation:*** $27,277.

APPLYING

Standardized Tests *Required:* SAT or ACT (for admission).

Options: electronic application, early admission, deferred entrance.

Application fee: $35.

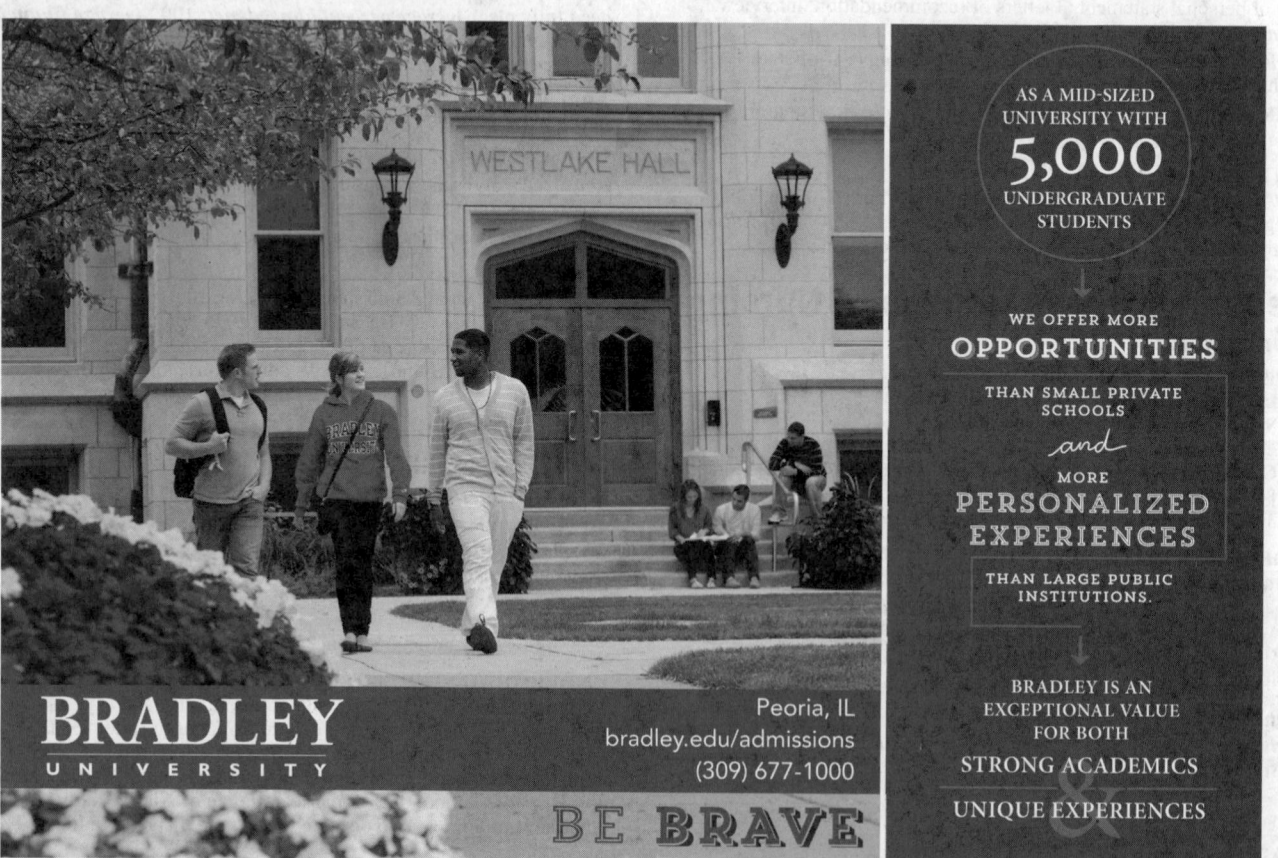

Required: essay or personal statement, high school transcript. ***Recommended:*** 1 letter of recommendation, interview.

Application deadlines: rolling (freshmen), rolling (out-of-state freshmen), rolling (transfers).

CONTACT

Dr. Justin Ball, Director of Admissions, Bradley University, 1501 West Bradley Avenue, Peoria, IL 61625-0002. *Phone:* 309-677-1000. *Toll-free phone:* 800-447-6460. *Fax:* 309-677-2797. *E-mail:* admissions@bradley.edu.

See previous page for display ad and page 1372 for the College Close-Up.

Chamberlain College of Nursing

Addison, Illinois

http://www.chamberlain.edu/

- **Proprietary** 4-year
- **Coed**

FACULTY

Student/faculty ratio: 28:1.

ACADEMICS

Calendar: semesters. *Degree:* bachelor's.

COSTS

Costs (2014–15) ***Tuition:*** $17,160 full-time, $665 per credit hour part-time. Full-time tuition and fees vary according to course load. Part-time tuition and fees vary according to course load. ***Required fees:*** $600 full-time.

APPLYING

Standardized Tests *Required:* SAT or ACT (for admission).

CONTACT

Admissions, Chamberlain College of Nursing, 1221 N. Swift Road, Addison, IL 60101-6106. *Phone:* 630-953-3680. *Toll-free phone:* 888-556-8CCN.

Chamberlain College of Nursing

Chicago, Illinois

http://www.chamberlain.edu/

- **Proprietary** 4-year
- **Coed**

FACULTY

Student/faculty ratio: 13:1.

ACADEMICS

Calendar: semesters. *Degree:* bachelor's.

COSTS

Costs (2014–15) ***Tuition:*** $17,160 full-time, $665 per credit hour part-time. Full-time tuition and fees vary according to course load. Part-time tuition and fees vary according to course load. ***Required fees:*** $600 full-time.

APPLYING

Standardized Tests *Required:* SAT or ACT (for admission).

CONTACT

Admissions, Chamberlain College of Nursing, 3300 N. Campbell Avenue, Chicago, IL 60618. *Phone:* 773-961-3000. *Toll-free phone:* 888-556-8CCN.

Chicago State University

Chicago, Illinois

http://www.csu.edu/

- **State-supported** comprehensive, founded 1867
- **Urban** 161-acre campus
- **Coed** 3,912 undergraduate students, 64% full-time, 71% women, 29% men
- **Minimally difficult** entrance level, 30% of applicants were admitted

UNDERGRAD STUDENTS

2,498 full-time, 1,414 part-time. Students come from 25 states and territories; 23 other countries; 3% are from out of state; 74% Black or African American, non-Hispanic/Latino; 7% Hispanic/Latino; 0.6% Asian, non-Hispanic/Latino; 12% Race/ethnicity unknown; 4% international; 13% transferred in.

Freshmen

Admission: 5,517 applied, 1,653 admitted, 260 enrolled. ***Average high school GPA:*** 3.03. ***Test scores:*** ACT scores over 18: 66%; ACT scores over 24: 8%.

Retention: 53% of full-time freshmen returned.

FACULTY

Total: 366, 73% full-time, 30% with terminal degrees.

Student/faculty ratio: 13:1.

ACADEMICS

Calendar: semesters. *Degrees:* bachelor's, master's, doctoral, and postbachelor's certificates.

Special study options: academic remediation for entering students, accelerated degree program, adult/continuing education programs, advanced placement credit, cooperative education, distance learning, double majors, external degree program, freshman honors college, honors programs, independent study, internships, off-campus study, part-time degree program, services for LD students, student-designed majors, study abroad, summer session for credit. ***ROTC:*** Army (b), Navy (c), Air Force (c).

Computers: 75 computers/terminals and 250 ports are available on campus for general student use. Students can access the following: free student e-mail accounts, online (class) grades, online (class) registration, online (class) schedules. Campuswide network is available. 100% of college-owned or -operated housing units are wired for high-speed Internet access. Wireless service is available via libraries.

STUDENT LIFE

Housing options: coed. Campus housing is university owned.

Activities and organizations: drama/theater group, student-run newspaper, radio station, choral group, national fraternities, national sororities.

Athletics Member NCAA. All Division I. ***Intercollegiate sports:*** baseball M(s), basketball M(s)/W(s), cross-country running M(s)/W(s), golf M(s)/W(s), tennis M(s)/W(s), track and field M(s)/W(s), volleyball W(s).

Campus security: 24-hour emergency response devices and patrols, student patrols, late-night transport/escort service, controlled dormitory access.

Student services: health clinic, personal/psychological counseling, women's center.

COSTS & FINANCIAL AID

Costs (2015–16) ***Tuition:*** state resident $7056 full-time, $294 per credit hour part-time; nonresident $14,016 full-time, $584 per credit hour part-time. Full-time tuition and fees vary according to course load, degree level, location, program, reciprocity agreements, and student level. Part-time tuition and fees vary according to course load, degree level, location, program, reciprocity agreements, and student level. No tuition increase for student's term of enrollment. ***Required fees:*** $2790 full-time, $460 per term part-time. ***Room and board:*** $8724. Room and board charges vary according to housing facility. ***Payment plans:*** tuition prepayment, installment. ***Waivers:*** employees or children of employees.

Financial Aid Of all full-time matriculated undergraduates who enrolled in 2013, 2,703 applied for aid, 2,701 were judged to have need. In 2013, 22 non-need-based awards were made. ***Average percent of need met:*** 40. ***Average financial aid package:*** $11,606. ***Average need-based loan:*** $4343. ***Average need-based gift aid:*** $7724. ***Average non-need-based aid:*** $5931. ***Average indebtedness upon graduation:*** $29,731. ***Financial aid deadline:*** 6/30.

APPLYING

Standardized Tests *Required:* SAT or ACT (for admission).

Options: electronic application.

Application fee: $25.

Required: high school transcript, minimum 2.5 GPA. ***Required for some:*** essay or personal statement, interview.

Notification: continuous (freshmen), continuous (transfers).

CONTACT

Mr. John Martinez, Associate Director of Admissions, Chicago State University, 95th Street at King Drive, ADM 200, Chicago, IL 60628. *Phone:* 773-995-3578. *Fax:* 773-995-3820. *E-mail:* jmarti21@csu.edu.

Christian Life College

Mount Prospect, Illinois

http://www.christianlifecollege.edu/

- **Independent Christian** 4-year, founded 1950
- **Suburban** 5-acre campus with easy access to Chicago
- **Coed** 40 undergraduate students, 83% full-time, 45% women, 55% men
- **Noncompetitive** entrance level

UNDERGRAD STUDENTS

33 full-time, 7 part-time. Students come from 5 states and territories; 3 other countries; 10% are from out of state; 10% Black or African American, non-Hispanic/Latino; 15% Hispanic/Latino; 13% Asian, non-Hispanic/Latino; 5% Two or more races, non-Hispanic/Latino; 30% international; 13% transferred in.

Freshmen

Admission: 6 enrolled. ***Average high school GPA:*** 3.61.

FACULTY

Total: 7, 14% full-time, 43% with terminal degrees.

Student/faculty ratio: 4:1.

ACADEMICS

Degrees: diplomas, associate, and bachelor's.

Special study options: academic remediation for entering students, adult/continuing education programs, cooperative education, external degree program, independent study, internships, off-campus study, part-time degree program.

Computers: 7 computers/terminals are available on campus for general student use. Students can access the following: free student e-mail accounts. 100% of college-owned or -operated housing units are wired for high-speed Internet access. Wireless service is available via entire campus.

STUDENT LIFE

Housing options: Campus housing is university owned. Freshman campus housing is guaranteed.

Campus security: controlled dormitory access.

COSTS & FINANCIAL AID

Costs (2014–15) ***Tuition:*** $10,400 full-time, $390 per credit hour part-time. Full-time tuition and fees vary according to class time, course load, and program. Part-time tuition and fees vary according to class time, course load, and program. ***Required fees:*** $600 full-time, $450 per year part-time. ***Room only:*** $3700. ***Payment plans:*** installment, deferred payment. ***Waivers:*** employees or children of employees.

Financial Aid Of all full-time matriculated undergraduates who enrolled in 2012, 23 applied for aid, 22 were judged to have need. 3 Federal Work-Study jobs (averaging $7603). ***Average percent of need met:*** 89. ***Average financial aid package:*** $8483. ***Average need-based loan:*** $3937. ***Average need-based gift aid:*** $5476.

APPLYING

Standardized Tests *Required:* SAT or ACT (for admission).

Options: early admission, deferred entrance.

Application fee: $40.

Required: high school transcript, minimum 2.0 GPA. ***Required for some:*** essay or personal statement, minimum 2.5 GPA, interview. ***Recommended:*** minimum 2.5 GPA.

Application deadlines: rolling (freshmen), rolling (out-of-state freshmen), rolling (transfers).

Notification: continuous (freshmen), continuous (out-of-state freshmen), continuous (transfers).

CONTACT

Christian Life College, 400 East Gregory Street, Mount Prospect, IL 60056. *Phone:* 847-259-1840 Ext. 100.

Columbia College Chicago

Chicago, Illinois

http://www.colum.edu/

- **Independent** comprehensive, founded 1890
- **Urban** campus with easy access to Chicago
- **Coed** 9,003 undergraduate students, 91% full-time, 56% women, 44% men
- **Moderately difficult** entrance level, 82% of applicants were admitted

UNDERGRAD STUDENTS

8,172 full-time, 831 part-time. 40% are from out of state; 16% Black or African American, non-Hispanic/Latino; 10% Hispanic/Latino; 3% Asian, non-Hispanic/Latino; 0.4% American Indian or Alaska Native, non-Hispanic/Latino; 5% Two or more races, non-Hispanic/Latino; 6% Race/ethnicity unknown; 3% international; 7% transferred in; 27% live on campus.

Freshmen

Admission: 8,953 applied, 7,370 admitted, 1,820 enrolled. ***Average high school GPA:*** 3.25. ***Test scores:*** SAT critical reading scores over 500: 71%; SAT math scores over 500: 54%; SAT writing scores over 500: 65%; ACT scores over 18: 89%; SAT critical reading scores over 600: 29%; SAT math scores over 600: 16%; SAT writing scores over 600: 23%; ACT scores over 24: 41%; SAT critical reading scores over 700: 5%; SAT math scores over 700: 1%; SAT writing scores over 700: 3%; ACT scores over 30: 7%.

Retention: 71% of full-time freshmen returned.

FACULTY

Total: 1,460, 26% full-time.

Student/faculty ratio: 11:1..

ACADEMICS

Calendar: semesters. *Degrees:* bachelor's and master's.

Special study options: academic remediation for entering students, adult/continuing education programs, advanced placement credit, cooperative education, distance learning, double majors, English as a second language, honors programs, independent study, internships, off-campus study, part-time degree program, services for LD students, student-designed majors, study abroad, summer session for credit.

Computers: Students can access the following: campus intranet, computer help desk, free student e-mail accounts, online (class) grades, online (class) registration, online (class) schedules. Campuswide network is available. 100% of college-owned or -operated housing units are wired for high-speed Internet access. Wireless service is available via entire campus.

STUDENT LIFE

Housing options: coed. Campus housing is university owned and leased by the school. Freshman applicants given priority for college housing.

Activities and organizations: drama/theater group, student-run newspaper, radio and television station, choral group, Columbia Urban Music Association, International Student Organization, Acianza Latina, Marketing Club.

Athletics ***Intercollegiate sports:*** baseball M(c), basketball M(c), lacrosse M(c). ***Intramural sports:*** cheerleading M/W, cross-country running M/W, fencing M/W, football M/W, rugby M/W, soccer M/W, softball W, swimming and diving M/W, tennis M/W, ultimate Frisbee M/W, volleyball M/W.

Campus security: 24-hour emergency response devices and patrols, late-night transport/escort service, controlled dormitory access, escort upon request.

Student services: health clinic, personal/psychological counseling.

COSTS & FINANCIAL AID

Costs (2014–15) ***Comprehensive fee:*** $36,079 includes full-time tuition ($22,884), mandatory fees ($745), and room and board ($12,450). Full-time tuition and fees vary according to course load. Part-time tuition: $790 per credit hour. Part-time tuition and fees vary according to course load.

Room and board: Room and board charges vary according to housing facility. ***Waivers:*** employees or children of employees.

Financial Aid Of all full-time matriculated undergraduates who enrolled in 2009, 7,243 applied for aid, 6,428 were judged to have need, 5,780 had their need fully met. ***Average percent of need met:*** 29. ***Average financial aid package:*** $8922. ***Average need-based loan:*** $4337. ***Average need-based gift aid:*** $2347.

APPLYING
Standardized Tests *Recommended:* SAT (for admission), ACT (for admission), SAT or ACT (for admission), SAT and SAT Subject Tests or ACT (for admission), SAT Subject Tests (for admission).

Options: electronic application, deferred entrance.

Application fee: $35.

Required: essay or personal statement, high school transcript, 1 letter of recommendation. ***Recommended:*** minimum 2.0 GPA, interview.

CONTACT
Mr. Murphy Monroe, Executive Director of Admissions, Columbia College Chicago, 600 South Michigan Avenue, Chicago, IL 60605-1996. *Phone:* 312-369-7133. *Fax:* 312-344-8024. *E-mail:* admissions@colum.edu.

Concordia University Chicago

River Forest, Illinois

http://www.cuchicago.edu/

- **Independent** comprehensive, founded 1864, affiliated with Lutheran Church–Missouri Synod, part of Concordia University System
- **Suburban** 40-acre campus with easy access to Chicago
- **Coed** 1,538 undergraduate students, 91% full-time, 61% women, 39% men
- **Moderately difficult** entrance level, 54% of applicants were admitted

UNDERGRAD STUDENTS
1,397 full-time, 141 part-time. 22% are from out of state; 13% Black or African American, non-Hispanic/Latino; 24% Hispanic/Latino; 2% Asian, non-Hispanic/Latino; 0.1% Native Hawaiian or other Pacific Islander, non-Hispanic/Latino; 0.1% American Indian or Alaska Native, non-Hispanic/Latino; 3% Two or more races, non-Hispanic/Latino; 1% Race/ethnicity unknown; 0.9% international; 6% transferred in; 36% live on campus.

Freshmen
Admission: 3,723 applied, 2,005 admitted, 300 enrolled. ***Average high school GPA:*** 3.01. ***Test scores:*** SAT critical reading scores over 500: 50%; SAT math scores over 500: 54%; ACT scores over 18: 93%; SAT critical reading scores over 600: 25%; SAT math scores over 600: 18%; ACT scores over 24: 33%; SAT critical reading scores over 700: 7%; SAT math scores over 700: 5%; ACT scores over 30: 5%.

FACULTY
Total: 426, 60% full-time, 38% with terminal degrees.

Student/faculty ratio: 17:1.

ACADEMICS
Calendar: semesters. *Degrees:* certificates, bachelor's, master's, doctoral, and post-master's certificates.

Special study options: adult/continuing education programs, part-time degree program.

Computers: Students can access the following: campus intranet, computer help desk, free student e-mail accounts, online (class) grades, online (class) registration, online (class) schedules. Campuswide network is available. Wireless service is available via libraries, student centers.

STUDENT LIFE
Housing options: coed. Campus housing is university owned.

Athletics Member NCAA. All Division III. ***Intercollegiate sports:*** baseball M, basketball M/W, cheerleading M/W, cross-country running M/W, football M, golf M, soccer M/W, softball W, tennis M/W, track and field M/W, volleyball W. ***Intramural sports:*** badminton M/W, basketball M/W, bowling M/W, football W, swimming and diving M/W, table tennis M/W, tennis M/W, volleyball M/W.

Campus security: 24-hour emergency response devices and patrols, student patrols, late-night transport/escort service, controlled dormitory access, emergency call boxes.

COSTS & FINANCIAL AID
Costs (2015–16) ***Comprehensive fee:*** $38,442 includes full-time tuition ($28,660), mandatory fees ($790), and room and board ($8992). Full-time tuition and fees vary according to course load, degree level, program, and reciprocity agreements. Part-time tuition: $895 per credit hour. Part-time tuition and fees vary according to course load, degree level, program, and reciprocity agreements. ***College room only:*** $4374. Room and board charges vary according to board plan and housing facility. ***Payment plan:*** installment. ***Waivers:*** children of alumni, senior citizens, and employees or children of employees.

Financial Aid Of all full-time matriculated undergraduates who enrolled in 2013, 1,402 applied for aid, 1,282 were judged to have need, 221 had their need fully met. In 2013, 157 non-need-based awards were made. ***Average percent of need met:*** 74. ***Average financial aid package:*** $19,289. ***Average need-based loan:*** $4222. ***Average need-based gift aid:*** $14,880. ***Average non-need-based aid:*** $11,656. ***Average indebtedness upon graduation:*** $32,408. ***Financial aid deadline:*** 6/1.

APPLYING
Standardized Tests *Required:* SAT or ACT (for admission).

Options: electronic application, deferred entrance.

Required: high school transcript, minimum 2.0 GPA, 1 letter of recommendation. ***Required for some:*** essay or personal statement, interview.

CONTACT
Ms. Gwen Kanelos, Director of Admission, Concordia University Chicago, 7400 Augusta Street, River Forest, IL 60305. *Phone:* 708-209-3101. *Toll-free phone:* 800-285-2668. *Fax:* 708-209-3473. *E-mail:* gwen.kanelos@cuchicago.edu.

DePaul University

Chicago, Illinois

http://www.depaul.edu/

- **Independent Roman Catholic** university, founded 1898
- **Urban** 38-acre campus with easy access to Chicago
- **Endowment** $447.2 million
- **Coed** 16,153 undergraduate students, 84% full-time, 53% women, 47% men
- **Moderately difficult** entrance level, 70% of applicants were admitted

UNDERGRAD STUDENTS
13,643 full-time, 2,510 part-time. Students come from 52 states and territories; 86 other countries; 21% are from out of state; 8% Black or African American, non-Hispanic/Latino; 17% Hispanic/Latino; 8% Asian, non-Hispanic/Latino; 0.2% Native Hawaiian or other Pacific Islander, non-Hispanic/Latino; 0.1% American Indian or Alaska Native, non-Hispanic/Latino; 4% Two or more races, non-Hispanic/Latino; 4% Race/ethnicity unknown; 3% international; 10% transferred in; 16% live on campus.

Freshmen
Admission: 19,533 applied, 13,649 admitted, 2,544 enrolled. ***Average high school GPA:*** 3.56. ***Test scores:*** SAT critical reading scores over 500: 84%; SAT math scores over 500: 83%; ACT scores over 18: 98%; SAT critical reading scores over 600: 43%; SAT math scores over 600: 40%; ACT scores over 24: 68%; SAT critical reading scores over 700: 8%; SAT math scores over 700: 7%; ACT scores over 30: 14%.

Retention: 87% of full-time freshmen returned.

FACULTY
Total: 1,872, 49% full-time, 44% with terminal degrees.

Student/faculty ratio: 17:1.

ACADEMICS
Calendar: quarters College of Law on semester system. *Degrees:* certificates, bachelor's, master's, doctoral, post-master's, and postbachelor's certificates.

Special study options: academic remediation for entering students, accelerated degree program, adult/continuing education programs, advanced placement credit, distance learning, double majors, English as a second language, freshman honors college, honors programs, independent study, internships, off-campus study, part-time degree program, services for LD students, study abroad, summer session for credit. ***ROTC:*** Army (b).

Unusual degree programs: 3-2 engineering with Illinois Institute of Technology; Accountancy, Animation, Anthropology, Biological Science, Chemistry, Communications & Media, Communications Studies, Computer Game Development, Computer Science, Digital Cinema, Economics, English, Environmental Science, Environmental Studies, Geography, Health Science, History, Journalism, Math.

Computers: Students can access the following: campus intranet, computer help desk, free student e-mail accounts, online (class) grades, online (class) registration, online (class) schedules, tuition payments, degree progress, financial aid, transcript requests, housing services, student employment information. Campuswide network is available. 100% of college-owned or -operated housing units are wired for high-speed Internet access. Wireless service is available via entire campus.

STUDENT LIFE

Housing options: coed, special housing for students with disabilities. Campus housing is university owned, leased by the school and is provided by a third party. Freshman applicants given priority for college housing.

Activities and organizations: drama/theater group, student-run newspaper, radio station, choral group, DePaul Activities Board (DAB), DePaul Community Service Association (DCSA), DePaul Fundamental Research in Academic Gaming, DePaul's Voices for the Animals, National Society of Collegiate Scholars (NSCS), national fraternities, national sororities.

Athletics Member NCAA. All Division I. ***Intercollegiate sports:*** basketball M(s)/W(s), cross-country running M(s)/W(s), golf M(s), soccer M(s)/W(s), softball W(s), tennis M(s)/W(s), track and field M(s)/W(s), volleyball W(s). ***Intramural sports:*** badminton M/W, baseball M(c), basketball M(c)/W(c), cross-country running M(c)/W(c), football M/W, golf M(c)/W(c), ice hockey M(c)/W(c), lacrosse M(c)/W(c), racquetball M/W, rock climbing M(c)/W(c), rugby M(c)/W(c), sailing M(c)/W(c), skiing (downhill) M(c)/W(c), soccer M(c)/W, softball M(c)/W(c), table tennis M(c)/W(c), tennis M/W(c), ultimate Frisbee M(c)/W(c), volleyball M(c)/W(c), water polo M(c)/W.

Campus security: 24-hour emergency response devices and patrols, late-night transport/escort service, controlled dormitory access, security lighting, prevention/awareness programs, on-campus police officers, video cameras, smoke detectors in residence halls.

Student services: health clinic, personal/psychological counseling, women's center, legal services.

COSTS & FINANCIAL AID

Costs (2014–15) ***Comprehensive fee:*** $47,623 includes full-time tuition ($34,390), mandatory fees ($681), and room and board ($12,552). Full-time tuition and fees vary according to course load and program. Part-time tuition: $570 per credit hour. Part-time tuition and fees vary according to course load and program. ***College room only:*** $9027. Room and board charges vary according to board plan, housing facility, and location. ***Payment plans:*** installment, deferred payment. ***Waivers:*** employees or children of employees.

Financial Aid Of all full-time matriculated undergraduates who enrolled in 2013, 10,613 applied for aid, 9,559 were judged to have need, 1,149 had their need fully met. 471 Federal Work-Study jobs (averaging $3132). 2,568 state and other part-time jobs (averaging $3101). In 2013, 1951 non-need-based awards were made. ***Average percent of need met:*** 61. ***Average financial aid package:*** $21,294. ***Average need-based loan:*** $4558. ***Average need-based gift aid:*** $12,719. ***Average non-need-based aid:*** $10,011. ***Average indebtedness upon graduation:*** $27,498.

APPLYING

Standardized Tests *Required for some:* SAT or ACT (for admission).

Options: electronic application, early action, deferred entrance.

Application fee: $25.

Required: essay or personal statement, high school transcript, minimum 2.0 GPA. ***Required for some:*** minimum 3.0 GPA, interview, Audition/Interviews for the School of Music and Theatre School applicants. ***Recommended:*** minimum 2.8 GPA.

Application deadlines: 2/1 (freshmen), rolling (transfers), 11/15 (early action).

Notification: 3/15 (freshmen), continuous (transfers), 1/15 (early action).

CONTACT

Carlene Klaas-Kennelly, Dean of Undergraduate Admission, DePaul University, 1 East Jackson Boulevard, Suite 9000, Chicago, IL 60604. *Phone:* 312-362-8300. *Toll-free phone:* 800-4DE-PAUL. *E-mail:* admission@depaul.edu.

DeVry University

Addison, Illinois

http://www.devry.edu/

- **Proprietary** 4-year, founded 1982, part of DeVry University
- **Suburban** campus with easy access to Chicago
- **Coed**

ACADEMICS

Calendar: semesters. *Degrees:* associate and bachelor's.

COSTS & FINANCIAL AID

Costs (2014–15) ***Tuition:*** $17,052 full-time, $609 per credit hour part-time. ***Required fees:*** $80 full-time.

Financial Aid Of all full-time matriculated undergraduates who enrolled in 2007, 481 applied for aid, 447 were judged to have need, 18 had their need fully met. In 2007, 57 non-need-based awards were made. ***Average percent of need met:*** 47. ***Average financial aid package:*** $13,134. ***Average need-based loan:*** $8478. ***Average need-based gift aid:*** $6727. ***Average non-need-based aid:*** $15,985. ***Average indebtedness upon graduation:*** $31,740.

CONTACT

Admissions Office, DeVry University, 1221 North Swift Road, Addison, IL 60101-6106. *Phone:* 630-953-1300. *Toll-free phone:* 866-338-7941.

DeVry University

Chicago, Illinois

http://www.devry.edu/

- **Proprietary** comprehensive, founded 1931, part of DeVry University
- **Urban** campus
- **Coed** 1,149 undergraduate students, 64% full-time, 40% women, 60% men
- **Minimally difficult** entrance level

UNDERGRAD STUDENTS

738 full-time, 411 part-time. 2% are from out of state; 27% Black or African American, non-Hispanic/Latino; 43% Hispanic/Latino; 8% Asian, non-Hispanic/Latino; 0.2% Native Hawaiian or other Pacific Islander, non-Hispanic/Latino; 0.4% American Indian or Alaska Native, non-Hispanic/Latino; 0.6% Two or more races, non-Hispanic/Latino; 1% Race/ethnicity unknown; 2% international; 20% transferred in.

Freshmen

Admission: 63 enrolled.

FACULTY

Total: 164, 17% full-time.

Student/faculty ratio: 13:1.

ACADEMICS

Calendar: semesters. *Degrees:* associate, bachelor's, master's, and postbachelor's certificates.

Special study options: adult/continuing education programs, part-time degree program.

STUDENT LIFE

Housing options: college housing not available.

COSTS & FINANCIAL AID

Costs (2014–15) ***Tuition:*** $17,052 full-time, $609 per credit hour part-time. ***Required fees:*** $80 full-time.

Financial Aid Of all full-time matriculated undergraduates who enrolled in 2007, 479 applied for aid, 467 were judged to have need, 5 had their need fully met. In 2007, 14 non-need-based awards were made. ***Average percent of need met:*** 48. ***Average financial aid package:*** $16,145.

Average need-based loan: $8033. ***Average need-based gift aid:*** $8371. ***Average non-need-based aid:*** $11,220. ***Average indebtedness upon graduation:*** $49,157.

APPLYING
Application fee: $40.
Required: high school transcript, interview.

CONTACT
DeVry University, 3300 North Campbell Avenue, Chicago, IL 60618-5994. *Phone:* 773-929-8500. *Toll-free phone:* 866-338-7941.

DeVry University
Downers Grove, Illinois
http://www.devry.edu/

- **Proprietary** comprehensive, founded 1973
- **Coed**

ACADEMICS
Calendar: semesters. *Degrees:* bachelor's and master's.

COSTS
Costs (2014–15) ***Tuition:*** $17,052 full-time, $609 per credit hour part-time. ***Required fees:*** $80 full-time.

CONTACT
Admissions Office, DeVry University, 3005 Highland Parkway, Suite 100, Downers Grove, IL 60515. *Phone:* 630-515-3000. *Toll-free phone:* 866-338-7941.

DeVry University
Elgin, Illinois
http://www.devry.edu/

- **Proprietary** comprehensive
- **Coed**

ACADEMICS
Calendar: semesters. *Degrees:* bachelor's and master's.

COSTS
Costs (2014–15) ***Tuition:*** $17,052 full-time, $609 per credit hour part-time. ***Required fees:*** $80 full-time.

CONTACT
Admissions Office, DeVry University, Randall Point, 2250 Point Boulevard, Suite 250, Elgin, IL 60123. *Phone:* 847-649-3980. *Toll-free phone:* 866-338-7941.

DeVry University
Gurnee, Illinois
http://www.devry.edu/

- **Proprietary** comprehensive
- **Coed**

ACADEMICS
Calendar: semesters. *Degrees:* associate, bachelor's, and master's.

COSTS
Costs (2014–15) ***Tuition:*** $17,052 full-time, $609 per credit hour part-time. ***Required fees:*** $80 full-time.

CONTACT
Admissions Office, DeVry University, 1075 Tri-State Parkway, Suite 800, Gurnee, IL 60031-9126. *Phone:* 847-855-2649. *Toll-free phone:* 866-338-7941.

DeVry University
Naperville, Illinois
http://www.devry.edu/

- **Proprietary** comprehensive
- **Coed**

ACADEMICS
Calendar: semesters. *Degrees:* bachelor's and master's.

COSTS
Costs (2014–15) ***Tuition:*** $17,052 full-time, $609 per credit hour part-time. ***Required fees:*** $80 full-time.

CONTACT
Admissions Office, DeVry University, 2056 Westings Avenue, Suite 40, Naperville, IL 60563-2361. *Phone:* 630-428-9086. *Toll-free phone:* 866-338-7941.

DeVry University
Tinley Park, Illinois
http://www.devry.edu/

- **Proprietary** comprehensive, founded 2000, part of DeVry University
- **Suburban** campus
- **Coed**

ACADEMICS
Calendar: semesters. *Degrees:* associate, bachelor's, and master's.

COSTS & FINANCIAL AID
Costs (2014–15) ***Tuition:*** $17,052 full-time, $609 per credit hour part-time. ***Required fees:*** $80 full-time.

Financial Aid Of all full-time matriculated undergraduates who enrolled in 2007, 379 applied for aid, 366 were judged to have need, 18 had their need fully met. In 2007, 24 non-need-based awards were made. ***Average percent of need met:*** 45. ***Average financial aid package:*** $12,346. ***Average need-based loan:*** $7379. ***Average need-based gift aid:*** $6916. ***Average non-need-based aid:*** $14,254. ***Average indebtedness upon graduation:*** $4375.

CONTACT
Admissions Office, DeVry University, 18624 West Creek Drive, Tinley Park, IL 60477 . *Phone:* 708-342-3300. *Toll-free phone:* 866-338-7941.

DeVry University Online
Addison, Illinois
http://www.devry.edu/

- **Proprietary** comprehensive, founded 2000
- **Coed** 15,795 undergraduate students, 29% full-time, 55% women, 45% men

UNDERGRAD STUDENTS
4,535 full-time, 11,260 part-time. 83% are from out of state; 17% Black or African American, non-Hispanic/Latino; 10% Hispanic/Latino; 2% Asian, non-Hispanic/Latino; 0.4% Native Hawaiian or other Pacific Islander, non-Hispanic/Latino; 0.6% American Indian or Alaska Native, non-Hispanic/Latino; 1% Two or more races, non-Hispanic/Latino; 18% Race/ethnicity unknown; 0.9% international; 38% transferred in.

Freshmen
Admission: 975 enrolled.

FACULTY
Total: 2,500, 4% full-time.
Student/faculty ratio: 11:1.

ACADEMICS
Calendar: semesters. *Degrees:* associate, bachelor's, master's, and postbachelor's certificates.

COSTS & FINANCIAL AID
Costs (2014–15) ***Tuition:*** $17,052 full-time, $609 per credit hour part-time. ***Required fees:*** $80 full-time.

Financial Aid Of all full-time matriculated undergraduates who enrolled in 2006, 810 applied for aid, 785 were judged to have need, 9 had their need fully met. In 2006, 146 non-need-based awards were made. ***Average percent of need met:*** 36. ***Average financial aid package:*** $10,560. ***Average need-based loan:*** $6201. ***Average need-based gift aid:*** $7114. ***Average non-need-based aid:*** $10,591. ***Average indebtedness upon graduation:*** $35,423.

APPLYING
Application fee: $40.
Required: high school transcript, interview.

Application deadlines: rolling (freshmen), rolling (transfers).
Notification: continuous (freshmen), continuous (transfers).

CONTACT
DeVry University Online, 1221 North Swift Road, Addison, IL 60101-6106. *Phone:* 877-496-9050. *Toll-free phone:* 866-338-7941.

Dominican University

River Forest, Illinois

http://www.dom.edu/

- **Independent Roman Catholic** comprehensive, founded 1901
- **Suburban** 30-acre campus with easy access to Chicago
- **Endowment** $23.3 million
- **Coed** 2,180 undergraduate students, 92% full-time, 66% women, 34% men
- **Moderately difficult** entrance level, 61% of applicants were admitted

UNDERGRAD STUDENTS
1,996 full-time, 184 part-time. Students come from 27 states and territories; 8 other countries; 7% are from out of state; 6% Black or African American, non-Hispanic/Latino; 44% Hispanic/Latino; 3% Asian, non-Hispanic/Latino; 0.2% Native Hawaiian or other Pacific Islander, non-Hispanic/Latino; 0.1% American Indian or Alaska Native, non-Hispanic/Latino; 1% Two or more races, non-Hispanic/Latino; 0.9% Race/ethnicity unknown; 3% international; 7% transferred in; 27% live on campus.

Freshmen
Admission: 3,692 applied, 2,240 admitted, 473 enrolled. ***Average high school GPA:*** 3.59. ***Test scores:*** SAT critical reading scores over 500: 28%; SAT math scores over 500: 46%; SAT writing scores over 500: 43%; ACT scores over 18: 96%; SAT critical reading scores over 600: 14%; SAT math scores over 600: 17%; SAT writing scores over 600: 29%; ACT scores over 24: 30%; SAT math scores over 700: 17%; ACT scores over 30: 1%.

Retention: 81% of full-time freshmen returned.

FACULTY
Total: 431, 37% full-time, 59% with terminal degrees.

Student/faculty ratio: 10:1.

ACADEMICS
Calendar: semesters. *Degrees:* certificates, bachelor's, master's, doctoral, post-master's, and postbachelor's certificates.

Special study options: accelerated degree program, adult/continuing education programs, advanced placement credit, distance learning, double majors, English as a second language, honors programs, independent study, internships, off-campus study, part-time degree program, services for LD students, student-designed majors, study abroad, summer session for credit.

Unusual degree programs: 3-2 business administration; engineering with Illinois Institute of Technology; nursing; social work; library science, pharmacy (Midwestern).

Computers: 550 computers/terminals are available on campus for general student use. Students can access the following: campus intranet, computer help desk, free student e-mail accounts, online (class) grades, online (class) registration, online (class) schedules. Campuswide network is available. 100% of college-owned or -operated housing units are wired for high-speed Internet access. Wireless service is available via entire campus.

STUDENT LIFE
Housing options: coed, special housing for students with disabilities. Campus housing is university owned and leased by the school. Freshman campus housing is guaranteed.

Activities and organizations: drama/theater group, student-run newspaper, choral group, Polish Club, Commuter Student Association, Nutrition Club, Organization of Latin American Students, Fashion Club.

Athletics Member NCAA. All Division III. ***Intercollegiate sports:*** baseball M, basketball M/W, cross-country running M/W, golf M, soccer M/W, softball W, tennis M/W, volleyball M/W. ***Intramural sports:*** basketball M/W, bowling M/W, football M/W, racquetball M/W, soccer M, ultimate Frisbee M/W, volleyball W.

Campus security: 24-hour emergency response devices and patrols, student patrols, late-night transport/escort service, controlled dormitory access, door alarms.

Student services: health clinic, personal/psychological counseling.

COSTS & FINANCIAL AID
Costs (2015–16) ***One-time required fee:*** $150. ***Comprehensive fee:*** $40,050 includes full-time tuition ($30,300), mandatory fees ($370), and room and board ($9380). Full-time tuition and fees vary according to course load, program, and reciprocity agreements. Part-time tuition: $1010 per credit hour. Part-time tuition and fees vary according to course load, program, and reciprocity agreements. ***Required fees:*** $90 per term part-time. ***Room and board:*** Room and board charges vary according to board plan and housing facility. ***Payment plan:*** deferred payment. ***Waivers:*** employees or children of employees.

Financial Aid Of all full-time matriculated undergraduates who enrolled in 2014, 1,552 applied for aid, 1,459 were judged to have need, 156 had their need fully met. In 2014, 124 non-need-based awards were made. ***Average percent of need met:*** 71. ***Average financial aid package:*** $22,638. ***Average need-based loan:*** $4276. ***Average need-based gift aid:*** $19,096. ***Average non-need-based aid:*** $7108. ***Average indebtedness upon graduation:*** $29,235.

APPLYING
Standardized Tests *Required:* SAT or ACT (for admission).

Options: electronic application, deferred entrance.

Application fee: $25.

Required: high school transcript. ***Required for some:*** interview. ***Recommended:*** essay or personal statement, minimum 2.8 GPA.

Application deadlines: rolling (freshmen), rolling (out-of-state freshmen), rolling (transfers).

Notification: continuous (freshmen), continuous (out-of-state freshmen), continuous (transfers).

CONTACT
Mr. Glenn Hamilton, Assistant Vice President, Enrollment Management, Dominican University, 7900 West Division Street, River Forest, IL 60305. *Phone:* 708-524-6800. *Toll-free phone:* 800-828-8475. *Fax:* 708-524-6864. *E-mail:* domadmis@dom.edu.

Eastern Illinois University

Charleston, Illinois

http://www.eiu.edu/

- **State-supported** comprehensive, founded 1895
- **Small-town** 320-acre campus
- **Endowment** $69.3 million
- **Coed** 7,640 undergraduate students, 87% full-time, 60% women, 40% men
- **Moderately difficult** entrance level, 50% of applicants were admitted

UNDERGRAD STUDENTS
6,676 full-time, 964 part-time. Students come from 37 states and territories; 31 other countries; 4% are from out of state; 19% Black or African American, non-Hispanic/Latino; 5% Hispanic/Latino; 0.8% Asian, non-Hispanic/Latino; 0.1% Native Hawaiian or other Pacific Islander, non-Hispanic/Latino; 0.2% American Indian or Alaska Native, non-Hispanic/Latino; 2% Two or more races, non-Hispanic/Latino; 2% Race/ethnicity unknown; 1% international; 12% transferred in; 38% live on campus.

Freshmen
Admission: 8,918 applied, 4,438 admitted, 1,126 enrolled. ***Average high school GPA:*** 3.05. ***Test scores:*** ACT scores over 18: 89%; ACT scores over 24: 28%; ACT scores over 30: 4%.

Retention: 76% of full-time freshmen returned.

FACULTY
Total: 665, 79% full-time, 60% with terminal degrees.

Student/faculty ratio: 14:1.

ACADEMICS
Calendar: semesters. *Degrees:* bachelor's, master's, post-master's, and postbachelor's certificates.

Special study options: academic remediation for entering students, accelerated degree program, adult/continuing education programs, advanced placement credit, distance learning, double majors, English as a second language, freshman honors college, honors programs, independent study, internships, off-campus study, part-time degree program, services for LD students, study abroad, summer session for credit. ***ROTC:*** Army (b).

Unusual degree programs: 3-2 engineering with University of Illinois at Urbana-Champaign and Southern Illinois University at Carbondale.

Computers: 664 computers/terminals and 10,000 ports are available on campus for general student use. Students can access the following: computer help desk, free student e-mail accounts, online (class) grades, online (class) registration, online (class) schedules. Campuswide network is available. 100% of college-owned or -operated housing units are wired for high-speed Internet access. Wireless service is available via classrooms, computer centers, computer labs, dorm rooms, learning centers, libraries, student centers.

STUDENT LIFE

Housing options: on-campus residence required for freshman year; coed, men-only, women-only, special housing for students with disabilities. Campus housing is university owned. Freshman campus housing is guaranteed.

Activities and organizations: drama/theater group, student-run newspaper, radio and television station, choral group, marching band, Greek Organizations, Black Student Union, Intramural Sports, University Board, Religious Student Organizations, national fraternities, national sororities.

Athletics Member NCAA. All Division I except football (Division I-AA). ***Intercollegiate sports:*** badminton M(c)/W(c), baseball M(s)/W(c), basketball M(s)/W(s), cross-country running M(s)/W(s), equestrian sports M(c)/W(c), golf M(s)/W(s), ice hockey M(c), lacrosse M(c)/W(c), racquetball M(c)/W(c), rugby M(c)/W(s), soccer M(s)/W(s), softball M(c)/W(s), swimming and diving M(s)/W(s), tennis M(s)/W(s), track and field M(s)/W(s), ultimate Frisbee M(c)/W(c), volleyball M(c)/W(s). ***Intramural sports:*** badminton M/W, basketball M/W, bowling M/W, racquetball M/W, soccer M/W, softball M/W, table tennis M/W, tennis M/W, volleyball M/W.

Campus security: 24-hour emergency response devices and patrols, student patrols, late-night transport/escort service, controlled dormitory access, AlertEIU and warning sirens; Self-defense education; Shuttle buses; Lighted pathways and sidewalks.

Student services: health clinic, personal/psychological counseling, women's center, legal services.

COSTS & FINANCIAL AID

Costs (2014–15) ***Tuition:*** state resident $8490 full-time, $283 per credit hour part-time; nonresident $25,470 full-time, $849 per credit hour part-time. Full-time tuition and fees vary according to course load and student level. Part-time tuition and fees vary according to course load and student level. No tuition increase for student's term of enrollment. ***Required fees:*** $2618 full-time, $96 per credit hour part-time. ***Room and board:*** $9358. Room and board charges vary according to board plan and housing facility. ***Payment plan:*** installment. ***Waivers:*** senior citizens and employees or children of employees.

Financial Aid Of all full-time matriculated undergraduates who enrolled in 2014, 6,483 applied for aid, 4,625 were judged to have need, 396 had their need fully met. 208 Federal Work-Study jobs (averaging $980). 2,342 state and other part-time jobs (averaging $1489). In 2014, 763 non-need-based awards were made. ***Average percent of need met:*** 64. ***Average financial aid package:*** $11,392. ***Average need-based loan:*** $4201. ***Average need-based gift aid:*** $3447. ***Average non-need-based aid:*** $3537. ***Average indebtedness upon graduation:*** $31,219.

APPLYING

Standardized Tests *Required:* SAT or ACT (for admission).

Options: electronic application, deferred entrance.

Application fee: $30.

Required: high school transcript, minimum 2.3 GPA, standardized test scores, audition for music program. ***Required for some:*** essay or personal statement, 2 letters of recommendation, standardized test scores, audition for music program.

Application deadlines: rolling (freshmen), rolling (out-of-state freshmen), rolling (transfers).

Notification: continuous (freshmen), continuous (out-of-state freshmen), continuous (transfers).

CONTACT

Denise Lee, Assistant Director of Admissions, Eastern Illinois University, 600 Lincoln Avenue, Charleston, IL 61920. *Phone:* 217-581-7975. *Toll-free phone:* 877-581-2348. *Fax:* 217-581-7060. *E-mail:* dalee@eiu.edu.

Ellis University

Oakbrook Terrace, Illinois

http://www.ellis.edu/

- **Proprietary** comprehensive
- **Coed** 15 undergraduate students, 60% full-time, 73% women, 27% men

UNDERGRAD STUDENTS

9 full-time, 6 part-time. Students come from 28 states and territories; 93% are from out of state; 14% Black or African American, non-Hispanic/Latino; 7% Hispanic/Latino; 11% Asian, non-Hispanic/Latino; 18% Race/ethnicity unknown.

FACULTY

Student/faculty ratio: 8:1.

ACADEMICS

Degrees: certificates, associate, bachelor's, and master's.

COSTS

Costs (2014–15) ***Tuition:*** $6000 full-time, $3000 per year part-time.

APPLYING

Application fee: $75.

CONTACT

Office of Admissions, Ellis University, 2 Mid America Plaza, Suite 824AB, Oakbrook Terrace, IL 60181. *Phone:* 312-669-5000. *Toll-free phone:* 877-355-4762. *E-mail:* admissions@ellis.edu.

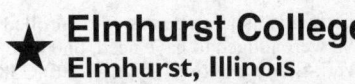

★ Elmhurst College

Elmhurst, Illinois

http://www.elmhurst.edu/

- **Independent** comprehensive, founded 1871, affiliated with United Church of Christ
- **Suburban** 38-acre campus with easy access to Chicago
- **Endowment** $97.0 million
- **Coed** 2,853 undergraduate students, 95% full-time, 60% women, 40% men
- **Moderately difficult** entrance level, 68% of applicants were admitted

UNDERGRAD STUDENTS

2,699 full-time, 154 part-time. Students come from 36 states and territories; 31 other countries; 10% are from out of state; 4% Black or African American, non-Hispanic/Latino; 16% Hispanic/Latino; 5% Asian, non-Hispanic/Latino; 0.1% Native Hawaiian or other Pacific Islander, non-Hispanic/Latino; 0.1% American Indian or Alaska Native, non-Hispanic/Latino; 3% Two or more races, non-Hispanic/Latino; 2% Race/ethnicity unknown; 0.1% international; 10% transferred in; 40% live on campus.

Freshmen

Admission: 3,193 applied, 2,162 admitted, 510 enrolled. ***Average high school GPA:*** 3.38.

Retention: 82% of full-time freshmen returned.

FACULTY

Total: 360, 44% full-time.

Student/faculty ratio: 12:1.

ACADEMICS

Calendar: 4-1-4. *Degrees:* bachelor's and master's.

Special study options: academic remediation for entering students, accelerated degree program, adult/continuing education programs, advanced placement credit, cooperative education, double majors, honors programs, independent study, internships, off-campus study, part-time degree program, services for LD students, study abroad, summer session for credit. ***ROTC:*** Army (c), Air Force (c).

Unusual degree programs: 3-2 engineering with University of Illinois at Urbana-Champaign, University of Southern California.

Computers: 800 computers/terminals are available on campus for general student use. Students can access the following: campus intranet, computer help desk, free student e-mail accounts, online (class) grades, online (class) registration, online (class) schedules. Campuswide network is available. 100% of college-owned or -operated housing units are wired for high-speed Internet access. Wireless service is available via classrooms, computer labs, dorm rooms, libraries, student centers.

STUDENT LIFE

Housing options: coed. Campus housing is university owned, leased by the school and is provided by a third party. Freshman applicants given priority for college housing.

Activities and organizations: drama/theater group, student-run newspaper, radio station, choral group, Programming Board and Student Government, theater and music groups, Black Student Union, residence life groups, Hablamos, national fraternities, national sororities.

Athletics Member NCAA. All Division III. ***Intercollegiate sports:*** baseball M, basketball M/W, bowling W, cross-country running M/W, football M, golf M/W, lacrosse M/W, soccer M/W, softball W, tennis M/W, track and field M/W, volleyball W, wrestling M. ***Intramural sports:*** basketball M/W, football M, golf M/W, racquetball M/W, soccer M/W, softball W, volleyball M/W.

Campus security: 24-hour emergency response devices and patrols, late-night transport/escort service, controlled dormitory access.

Student services: health clinic, personal/psychological counseling.

COSTS & FINANCIAL AID

Costs (2015–16) ***Comprehensive fee:*** $44,116 includes full-time tuition ($34,200), mandatory fees ($250), and room and board ($9666). Part-time tuition and fees vary according to course load. ***College room only:*** $5856. Room and board charges vary according to board plan and housing facility. ***Payment plan:*** installment. ***Waivers:*** senior citizens and employees or children of employees.

Financial Aid Of all full-time matriculated undergraduates who enrolled in 2014, 2,323 applied for aid, 1,890 were judged to have need, 660 had their need fully met. 372 Federal Work-Study jobs (averaging $1236). 238 state and other part-time jobs (averaging $1607). In 2014, 448 non-need-based awards were made. ***Average percent of need met:*** 76. ***Average financial aid package:*** $27,279. ***Average need-based loan:*** $4634. ***Average need-based gift aid:*** $22,002. ***Average non-need-based aid:*** $13,248. ***Average indebtedness upon graduation:*** $28,068.

APPLYING

Standardized Tests *Required:* SAT or ACT (for admission).

Options: electronic application, deferred entrance.

Required: high school transcript. ***Required for some:*** essay or personal statement, interview. ***Recommended:*** essay or personal statement, interview.

Application deadlines: rolling (freshmen), rolling (transfers).

Notification: continuous (freshmen), continuous (transfers).

CONTACT

Mrs. Stephanie Levenson, Executive Director of Admission, Elmhurst College, Elmhurst College, Admission Office, 190 South Prospect Avenue, Elmhurst, IL 60126-3296. *Phone:* 630-617-3400. *Toll-free phone:* 800-697-1871. *Fax:* 630-617-5501. *E-mail:* admit@elmhurst.edu.

Eureka College

Eureka, Illinois

http://www.eureka.edu/

- **Independent** 4-year, founded 1855, affiliated with Christian Church (Disciples of Christ)
- **Small-town** 64-acre campus
- **Endowment** $16.6 million
- **Coed** 664 undergraduate students, 96% full-time, 56% women, 44% men
- **Minimally difficult** entrance level, 65% of applicants were admitted

UNDERGRAD STUDENTS

639 full-time, 25 part-time. Students come from 9 states and territories; 1 other country; 7% are from out of state; 5% Black or African American, non-Hispanic/Latino; 2% Hispanic/Latino; 0.8% Asian, non-Hispanic/Latino; 0.5% Native Hawaiian or other Pacific Islander, non-Hispanic/Latino; 0.3% American Indian or Alaska Native, non-Hispanic/Latino; 3% Two or more races, non-Hispanic/Latino; 3% Race/ethnicity unknown; 0.8% international; 9% transferred in; 59% live on campus.

Freshmen

Admission: 1,164 applied, 759 admitted, 168 enrolled. ***Average high school GPA:*** 3.2. ***Test scores:*** SAT critical reading scores over 500: 100%; SAT math scores over 500: 75%; SAT writing scores over 500: 100%; ACT scores over 18: 89%; SAT critical reading scores over 600: 50%; SAT math scores over 600: 25%; SAT writing scores over 600: 50%; ACT scores over 24: 42%; ACT scores over 30: 7%.

Retention: 65% of full-time freshmen returned.

FACULTY

Total: 75, 53% full-time, 60% with terminal degrees.

Student/faculty ratio: 12:1.

ACADEMICS

Calendar: 4 8-week terms. *Degree:* bachelor's.

Special study options: adult/continuing education programs, advanced placement credit, cooperative education, double majors, honors programs, independent study, internships, student-designed majors, study abroad, summer session for credit.

Unusual degree programs: 3-2 Physical Science - University of Missouri-Kansas City (UM-KC), Psychology/Occupational Therapy - Washington University (St. Louis).

Computers: 80 computers/terminals are available on campus for general student use. Students can access the following: campus intranet, computer help desk, free student e-mail accounts, online (class) grades, online (class) registration, online (class) schedules, online bill payments, online 1098T access. Campuswide network is available. 100% of college-owned or -operated housing units are wired for high-speed Internet access. Wireless service is available via classrooms, computer centers, computer labs, dorm rooms, learning centers, libraries, student centers.

STUDENT LIFE

Housing options: on-campus residence required through senior year; coed, men-only, women-only. Campus housing is university owned. Freshman campus housing is guaranteed.

Activities and organizations: drama/theater group, student-run newspaper, choral group, national fraternities, national sororities.

Athletics Member NCAA. All Division III. ***Intercollegiate sports:*** baseball M, basketball M/W, football M, golf M, soccer M/W, softball W, swimming and diving M/W, tennis M/W, volleyball W.

Campus security: 24-hour emergency response devices, controlled dormitory access, late night patrols.

Student services: personal/psychological counseling.

COSTS & FINANCIAL AID

Costs (2015–16) ***Tuition:*** $550 per semester hour part-time. Full-time tuition and fees vary according to course load and program. Part-time tuition and fees vary according to course load and program. ***Room only:*** Room and board charges vary according to board plan and housing facility. ***Payment plan:*** installment. ***Waivers:*** senior citizens and employees or children of employees.

Financial Aid Of all full-time matriculated undergraduates who enrolled in 2014, 564 applied for aid, 504 were judged to have need, 95 had their need fully met. 103 Federal Work-Study jobs (averaging $823). 98 state and other part-time jobs (averaging $1066). In 2014, 132 non-need-based awards were made. ***Average percent of need met:*** 72. ***Average financial aid package:*** $15,558. ***Average need-based loan:*** $4396. ***Average need-based gift aid:*** $11,278. ***Average non-need-based aid:*** $6773. ***Average indebtedness upon graduation:*** $30,194.

APPLYING

Standardized Tests *Required:* SAT or ACT (for admission).

Options: electronic application.

Required: high school transcript, minimum 2.3 GPA, 1 letter of recommendation. ***Required for some:*** essay or personal statement. ***Recommended:*** essay or personal statement, interview.

Application deadlines: 8/1 (freshmen), 8/15 (transfers).

Notification: continuous (freshmen), continuous (transfers).

CONTACT

Mr. Kurt Krile, Dean of Admissions and Financial Aid, Eureka College, 300 East College Avenue, Eureka, IL 61530. *Phone:* 309-467-6350. *Toll-free phone:* 888-4-EUREKA. *Fax:* 309-467-6576. *E-mail:* admissions@eureka.edu.

Governors State University

University Park, Illinois

http://www.govst.edu/

- **State-supported** university, founded 1969
- **Suburban** 750-acre campus with easy access to Chicago
- **Endowment** $1.7 million
- **Coed** 3,585 undergraduate students, 48% full-time, 67% women, 33% men
- 94% of applicants were admitted

UNDERGRAD STUDENTS

1,713 full-time, 1,872 part-time. Students come from 14 states and territories; 15 other countries; 2% are from out of state; 37% Black or African American, non-Hispanic/Latino; 11% Hispanic/Latino; 2% Asian, non-Hispanic/Latino; 0.1% Native Hawaiian or other Pacific Islander, non-Hispanic/Latino; 0.3% American Indian or Alaska Native, non-Hispanic/Latino; 2% Two or more races, non-Hispanic/Latino; 9% Race/ethnicity unknown; 0.8% international; 27% transferred in; 5% live on campus.

Freshmen

Admission: 389 applied, 366 admitted, 160 enrolled. ***Average high school GPA:*** 2.97. ***Test scores:*** ACT scores over 18: 64%; ACT scores over 24: 8%.

FACULTY

Total: 443, 51% full-time, 40% with terminal degrees.

Student/faculty ratio: 10:1.

ACADEMICS

Calendar: trimesters. *Degrees:* certificates, bachelor's, master's, doctoral, post-master's, and postbachelor's certificates.

Special study options: adult/continuing education programs, advanced placement credit, distance learning, double majors, English as a second language, honors programs, independent study, internships, off-campus study, part-time degree program, services for LD students, student-designed majors, study abroad, summer session for credit.

Computers: 150 computers/terminals and 400 ports are available on campus for general student use. Students can access the following: campus intranet, computer help desk, free student e-mail accounts, online (class) grades, online (class) registration, online (class) schedules, student portal. Campuswide network is available. 100% of college-owned or -operated housing units are wired for high-speed Internet access. Wireless service is available via entire campus.

STUDENT LIFE

Housing options: coed. Campus housing is university owned.

Activities and organizations: drama/theater group, student-run newspaper, choral group, Physical Therapy Club, Social Work Club, Criminal Justice Club, International Club, Public Administration Club.

Athletics ***Intercollegiate sports:*** basketball M(s)/W(s), cross-country running M(s)/W(s), golf M(s)/W(s), volleyball W(s). ***Intramural sports:*** basketball M/W, bowling M/W, golf M/W, racquetball M/W, softball M/W, table tennis M/W, volleyball M/W.

Campus security: 24-hour emergency response devices and patrols, late-night transport/escort service, controlled dormitory access.

Student services: personal/psychological counseling.

COSTS

Costs (2014–15) ***Tuition:*** state resident $7650 full-time, $255 per credit hour part-time; nonresident $15,300 full-time, $510 per credit hour part-time. Full-time tuition and fees vary according to course load, degree level, reciprocity agreements, and student level. Part-time tuition and fees vary according to course load, degree level, reciprocity agreements, and student level. No tuition increase for student's term of enrollment. ***Required fees:*** $1736 full-time, $49 per credit hour part-time, $133 per term part-time. ***Room and board:*** $9000; room only: $5238. Room and board charges vary according to housing facility. ***Payment plans:*** installment, deferred payment. ***Waivers:*** senior citizens and employees or children of employees.

APPLYING

Standardized Tests *Required:* SAT and SAT Subject Tests or ACT (for admission).

Options: electronic application, early admission, early decision, early action, deferred entrance.

Application fee: $25.

Required: high school transcript, minimum 2.5 GPA. ***Recommended:*** essay or personal statement.

Early decision deadline: 11/15.

Notification: 1/31 (early decision).

CONTACT

Ms. Yakeea Daniels, Assistant Vice President for Enrollment Services and Admissions, Governors State University, One University Parkway, University Park, IL 60466. *Phone:* 708-534-4510. *Toll-free phone:* 800-478-8478. *Fax:* 708-235-7455. *E-mail:* ydaniels@govst.edu.

Greenville College

Greenville, Illinois

http://www.greenville.edu/

- **Independent Free Methodist** comprehensive, founded 1892
- **Small-town** 50-acre campus with easy access to St. Louis
- **Endowment** $16.9 million
- **Coed** 1,103 undergraduate students, 93% full-time, 48% women, 52% men
- **Moderately difficult** entrance level, 56% of applicants were admitted

UNDERGRAD STUDENTS

1,031 full-time, 72 part-time. Students come from 38 states and territories; 4 other countries; 33% are from out of state; 10% Black or African American, non-Hispanic/Latino; 5% Hispanic/Latino; 0.9% Asian, non-Hispanic/Latino; 0.1% Native Hawaiian or other Pacific Islander, non-Hispanic/Latino; 2% Two or more races, non-Hispanic/Latino; 5% Race/ethnicity unknown; 3% international; 6% transferred in; 73% live on campus.

Freshmen

Admission: 2,321 applied, 1,292 admitted, 269 enrolled. ***Average high school GPA:*** 3.38. ***Test scores:*** SAT critical reading scores over 500: 50%; SAT math scores over 500: 36%; SAT writing scores over 500: 34%; ACT scores over 18: 92%; SAT critical reading scores over 600: 12%; SAT math scores over 600: 7%; SAT writing scores over 600: 5%; ACT scores over 24: 42%; ACT scores over 30: 6%.

Retention: 70% of full-time freshmen returned.

FACULTY

Total: 182, 34% full-time, 37% with terminal degrees.

Student/faculty ratio: 14:1.

ACADEMICS

Calendar: 4-1-4. *Degrees:* bachelor's and master's.

Special study options: academic remediation for entering students, accelerated degree program, adult/continuing education programs, advanced placement credit, cooperative education, distance learning, double majors, external degree program, honors programs, independent study, internships, off-campus study, part-time degree program, student-designed majors, study abroad, summer session for credit.

Unusual degree programs: 3-2 engineering with University of Illinois at Urbana-Champaign; Washington University in St. Louis; nursing with St. John's College of Nursing; chiropractic at Logan College of Chiropractic.

Computers: 50 computers/terminals are available on campus for general student use. Students can access the following: campus intranet, computer help desk, free student e-mail accounts, online (class) grades, online (class) registration, online (class) schedules. Campuswide network is

available. 100% of college-owned or -operated housing units are wired for high-speed Internet access. Wireless service is available via entire campus.

STUDENT LIFE

Housing options: on-campus residence required through senior year; men-only, women-only. Campus housing is university owned. Freshman campus housing is guaranteed.

Activities and organizations: drama/theater group, student-run newspaper, radio station, choral group, marching band, Campus Activity Board, Panther Corps Marching Band, Greenville College Student Association, Circle K, Music and Entertainment Industry Student Association.

Athletics Member NCAA, NCCAA. All NCAA Division III. ***Intercollegiate sports:*** baseball M, basketball M/W, cross-country running M/W, football M, soccer M/W, softball W, tennis M/W, track and field M/W, volleyball W. ***Intramural sports:*** basketball M/W, cheerleading W, football M/W, softball M/W, ultimate Frisbee M/W, volleyball M/W.

Campus security: 24-hour emergency response devices and patrols, late-night transport/escort service, controlled dormitory access.

Student services: personal/psychological counseling.

COSTS & FINANCIAL AID

Costs (2015–16) ***Comprehensive fee:*** $33,376 includes full-time tuition ($24,864), mandatory fees ($224), and room and board ($8288). Full-time tuition and fees vary according to degree level. Part-time tuition: $526 per credit. Part-time tuition and fees vary according to course load and degree level. ***College room only:*** $4012. Room and board charges vary according to housing facility. ***Waivers:*** senior citizens and employees or children of employees.

Financial Aid Of all full-time matriculated undergraduates who enrolled in 2014, 847 applied for aid, 780 were judged to have need, 108 had their need fully met. In 2014, 122 non-need-based awards were made. ***Average percent of need met:*** 74. ***Average financial aid package:*** $19,031. ***Average need-based loan:*** $4353. ***Average need-based gift aid:*** $15,526. ***Average non-need-based aid:*** $9208. ***Average indebtedness upon graduation:*** $28,452.

APPLYING

Standardized Tests *Required:* SAT or ACT (for admission).

Options: electronic application, early admission, deferred entrance.

Application fee: $30.

Required: essay or personal statement, high school transcript, minimum 2.3 GPA, agreement to lifestyle statement. ***Required for some:*** interview.

Application deadlines: rolling (freshmen), rolling (transfers).

Notification: continuous (freshmen), continuous (transfers).

CONTACT

Mr. John R. Massena, Director of Undergraduate Admissions, Greenville College, 315 East College Avenue, Greenville, IL 62246. *Phone:* 618-664-7100. *Toll-free phone:* 800-345-4440. *Fax:* 618-664-9841. *E-mail:* admissions@greenville.edu.

Illinois College

Jacksonville, Illinois

http://www.ic.edu/

- **Independent interdenominational** comprehensive, founded 1829
- **Small-town** 62-acre campus with easy access to St. Louis
- **Coed** 957 undergraduate students, 99% full-time, 50% women, 50% men
- **Moderately difficult** entrance level, 54% of applicants were admitted

UNDERGRAD STUDENTS

952 full-time, 5 part-time. 14% are from out of state; 13% Black or African American, non-Hispanic/Latino; 9% Hispanic/Latino; 0.9% Asian, non-Hispanic/Latino; 0.2% Native Hawaiian or other Pacific Islander, non-Hispanic/Latino; 0.2% American Indian or Alaska Native, non-Hispanic/Latino; 3% Two or more races, non-Hispanic/Latino; 0.3% Race/ethnicity unknown; 3% international; 3% transferred in; 83% live on campus.

Freshmen

Admission: 2,749 applied, 1,488 admitted, 253 enrolled. ***Average high school GPA:*** 3.57. ***Test scores:*** SAT critical reading scores over 500: 38%; SAT math scores over 500: 48%; SAT writing scores over 500: 52%; ACT scores over 18: 86%; SAT critical reading scores over 600: 10%; SAT math scores over 600: 19%; SAT writing scores over 600: 10%; ACT scores over 24: 38%; ACT scores over 30: 5%.

Retention: 77% of full-time freshmen returned.

FACULTY

Total: 99, 82% full-time, 76% with terminal degrees.

Student/faculty ratio: 11:1.

ACADEMICS

Calendar: semesters. *Degrees:* bachelor's and master's.

Computers: Students can access the following: computer help desk, free student e-mail accounts, online (class) grades, online (class) registration, online (class) schedules. Campuswide network is available. Wireless service is available via entire campus.

STUDENT LIFE

Housing options: on-campus residence required through sophomore year; coed, men-only, women-only. Campus housing is university owned. Freshman campus housing is guaranteed.

Athletics Member NCAA. All Division III. ***Intercollegiate sports:*** baseball M, cheerleading W, cross-country running M/W, football M, golf M/W, soccer M/W, softball W, swimming and diving M/W, tennis M/W, track and field M/W, volleyball W. ***Intramural sports:*** badminton M/W, basketball M/W, fencing M/W, football M, racquetball M/W, softball M/W, swimming and diving M/W, volleyball M/W, water polo M/W, weight lifting M/W.

Campus security: 24-hour emergency response devices and patrols, late-night transport/escort service, controlled dormitory access.

COSTS & FINANCIAL AID

Costs (2014–15) ***Comprehensive fee:*** $38,400 includes full-time tuition ($28,660), mandatory fees ($550), and room and board ($9190). Part-time tuition: $890 per credit hour. ***Required fees:*** $138 per term part-time. ***College room only:*** $4890. Room and board charges vary according to board plan and housing facility. ***Payment plans:*** installment, deferred payment. ***Waivers:*** employees or children of employees.

Financial Aid Of all full-time matriculated undergraduates who enrolled in 2014, 853 applied for aid, 789 were judged to have need, 170 had their need fully met. 559 Federal Work-Study jobs (averaging $1960). In 2014, 148 non-need-based awards were made. ***Average percent of need met:*** 86. ***Average financial aid package:*** $26,431. ***Average need-based loan:*** $5192. ***Average need-based gift aid:*** $20,864. ***Average non-need-based aid:*** $15,492. ***Average indebtedness upon graduation:*** $22,958.

APPLYING

Options: electronic application, early admission, early action, deferred entrance.

Required: high school transcript, 1 letter of recommendation. ***Required for some:*** essay or personal statement. ***Recommended:*** essay or personal statement, minimum 2.5 GPA, interview.

CONTACT

Mr. Rick Bystry, Associate Director of Admission, Illinois College, 1101 West College, Jacksonville, IL 62650. *Phone:* 217-245-3030. *Toll-free phone:* 866-464-5265. *Fax:* 217-245-3034. *E-mail:* admissions@ic.edu.

The Illinois Institute of Art–Chicago

Chicago, Illinois

http://www.artinstitutes.edu/chicago/

- **Proprietary** 4-year, founded 1916, part of Education Management Corporation
- **Urban** campus
- **Coed**

ACADEMICS

Calendar: quarters. *Degrees:* diplomas, associate, and bachelor's.

CONTACT

The Illinois Institute of Art–Chicago, 350 North Orleans Street, Chicago, IL 60654. *Phone:* 312-280-3500. *Toll-free phone:* 800-351-3450.

The Illinois Institute of Art–Schaumburg

Schaumburg, Illinois

http://www.artinstitutes.edu/schaumburg/

- **Proprietary** 4-year, part of Education Management Corporation
- **Suburban** campus
- **Coed**

ACADEMICS

Calendar: quarters. *Degrees:* diplomas, associate, and bachelor's.

CONTACT

The Illinois Institute of Art–Schaumburg, 1000 North Plaza Drive, Suite 100, Schaumburg, IL 60173. *Phone:* 847-619-3450. *Toll-free phone:* 800-314-3450.

The Illinois Institute of Art–Tinley Park

Tinley Park, Illinois

http://www.artinstitutes.edu/tinleypark

- **Proprietary** 4-year, part of Education Management Corporation
- **Coed**

ACADEMICS

Degrees: diplomas, associate, and bachelor's.

CONTACT

The Illinois Institute of Art–Tinley Park, 18670 Graphic Drive, Tinley Park, IL 60477. *Phone:* 708-781-4200. *Toll-free phone:* 877-342-3298.

Illinois Institute of Technology

Chicago, Illinois

http://www.iit.edu/

- **Independent** university, founded 1890
- **Urban** 120-acre campus with easy access to Chicago
- **Endowment** $223.0 million
- **Coed** 3,099 undergraduate students, 94% full-time, 31% women, 69% men
- **Moderately difficult** entrance level, 51% of applicants were admitted

UNDERGRAD STUDENTS

2,922 full-time, 177 part-time. Students come from 46 states and territories; 73 other countries; 20% are from out of state; 6% Black or African American, non-Hispanic/Latino; 14% Hispanic/Latino; 11% Asian, non-Hispanic/Latino; 0.3% Native Hawaiian or other Pacific Islander, non-Hispanic/Latino; 0.3% American Indian or Alaska Native, non-Hispanic/Latino; 0.8% Two or more races, non-Hispanic/Latino; 4% Race/ethnicity unknown; 30% international; 7% transferred in.

Freshmen

Admission: 3,559 applied, 1,801 admitted, 440 enrolled. ***Average high school GPA:*** 3.62. ***Test scores:*** SAT critical reading scores over 500: 86%; SAT math scores over 500: 100%; SAT writing scores over 500: 57%; ACT scores over 18: 100%; SAT critical reading scores over 600: 42%; SAT math scores over 600: 92%; SAT writing scores over 600: 17%; ACT scores over 24: 90%; SAT critical reading scores over 700: 11%; SAT math scores over 700: 48%; SAT writing scores over 700: 7%; ACT scores over 30: 37%.

Retention: 91% of full-time freshmen returned.

FACULTY

Total: 824, 51% full-time.

Student/faculty ratio: 13:1.

ACADEMICS

Calendar: semesters. *Degrees:* bachelor's, master's, doctoral, post-master's, and postbachelor's certificates.

Special study options: advanced placement credit, cooperative education, distance learning, double majors, English as a second language, independent study, internships, off-campus study, part-time degree program, services for LD students, study abroad, summer session for credit. ***ROTC:*** Army (b), Navy (b), Air Force (b).

Unusual degree programs: 3-2 engineering; BS in Political Science/Master of Public Administration; BS in Psychology/MS in Personnel and Human Resources Development; BS in Psychology/MS in Rehabilitation Counseling Dual Degree Program.

Computers: 586 computers/terminals are available on campus for general student use. Students can access the following: campus intranet, computer help desk, free student e-mail accounts, online (class) grades, online (class) registration, online (class) schedules. Campuswide network is available. 100% of college-owned or -operated housing units are wired for high-speed Internet access. Wireless service is available via classrooms, computer centers, computer labs, dorm rooms, learning centers, libraries, student centers.

STUDENT LIFE

Housing options: on-campus residence required for freshman year; coed. Campus housing is university owned and is provided by a third party. Freshman applicants given priority for college housing.

Activities and organizations: drama/theater group, student-run newspaper, radio station, choral group, Union Board, International Students Association, Student Government Association, Greek Council, Commuter Student Associate, national fraternities, national sororities.

Athletics Member NCAA. All Division III. ***Intercollegiate sports:*** badminton M(c)/W(c), baseball M(s), basketball M/W, bowling M(c)/W(c), cross-country running M(s)/W(s), lacrosse M(c)/W, rugby M(c)/W(c), soccer M(s)/W(s), swimming and diving M(s)/W(s), track and field M/W, ultimate Frisbee M(c)/W(c), volleyball M(c)/W(s). ***Intramural sports:*** badminton M/W, basketball M/W, bowling M/W, field hockey M/W, football M/W, racquetball M/W, soccer M/W, softball M/W, squash M/W, table tennis M/W, tennis M(c)/W(c), track and field M(c)/W(c), ultimate Frisbee M/W, volleyball M/W.

Campus security: 24-hour emergency response devices and patrols, late-night transport/escort service, controlled dormitory access.

Student services: health clinic, personal/psychological counseling, women's center, legal services.

COSTS & FINANCIAL AID

Costs (2015–16) ***Tuition:*** $42,000 full-time, $1313 per credit hour part-time. Full-time tuition and fees vary according to student level. Part-time tuition and fees vary according to course load and student level. ***Room only:*** Room and board charges vary according to board plan and housing facility. ***Payment plan:*** installment. ***Waivers:*** employees or children of employees.

Financial Aid Of all full-time matriculated undergraduates who enrolled in 2013, 1,797 applied for aid, 1,714 were judged to have need, 250 had their need fully met. In 2013, 908 non-need-based awards were made. ***Average percent of need met:*** 78. ***Average financial aid package:*** $33,649. ***Average need-based loan:*** $4918. ***Average need-based gift aid:*** $28,262. ***Average non-need-based aid:*** $19,854. ***Average indebtedness upon graduation:*** $32,691.

APPLYING

Standardized Tests *Required:* SAT or ACT (for admission).

Options: electronic application, early admission, early action, deferred entrance.

Required: essay or personal statement, high school transcript, 1 letter of recommendation. ***Recommended:*** interview.

Application deadlines: 8/1 (freshmen), 6/1 (transfers), 12/1 (early action).

Notification: continuous (freshmen), continuous (transfers), 11/15 (early action).

CONTACT

Ms. Toni Riley, Director, Undergraduate Admissions Office, Illinois Institute of Technology, Office of Undergraduate Admission, Perlstein 101, 10 West 33rd Street, Chicago, IL 60616. *Phone:* 312-567-5239. *Toll-free phone:* 800-448-2329. *E-mail:* admission@iit.edu.

Illinois State University
Normal, Illinois
http://www.illinoisstate.edu/

- **State-supported** university, founded 1857
- **Urban** 490-acre campus
- **Endowment** $86.1 million
- **Coed** 18,155 undergraduate students, 94% full-time, 55% women, 45% men
- **Moderately difficult** entrance level, 74% of applicants were admitted

UNDERGRAD STUDENTS
17,040 full-time, 1,115 part-time. Students come from 44 states and territories; 38 other countries; 3% are from out of state; 7% Black or African American, non-Hispanic/Latino; 9% Hispanic/Latino; 2% Asian, non-Hispanic/Latino; 0.1% Native Hawaiian or other Pacific Islander, non-Hispanic/Latino; 0.1% American Indian or Alaska Native, non-Hispanic/Latino; 2% Two or more races, non-Hispanic/Latino; 0.4% Race/ethnicity unknown; 0.4% international; 10% transferred in; 34% live on campus.

Freshmen
Admission: 15,297 applied, 11,301 admitted, 3,589 enrolled. ***Average high school GPA:*** 3.39. ***Test scores:*** ACT scores over 18: 100%; ACT scores over 24: 50%; ACT scores over 30: 6%.

Retention: 81% of full-time freshmen returned.

FACULTY
Total: 1,247, 71% full-time, 65% with terminal degrees.

Student/faculty ratio: 17:1.

ACADEMICS
Calendar: semesters. *Degrees:* bachelor's, master's, doctoral, post-master's, and postbachelor's certificates.

Special study options: academic remediation for entering students, accelerated degree program, adult/continuing education programs, advanced placement credit, cooperative education, distance learning, double majors, English as a second language, honors programs, independent study, internships, off-campus study, part-time degree program, services for LD students, student-designed majors, study abroad, summer session for credit. ***ROTC:*** Army (b).

Unusual degree programs: 3-2 engineering with University of Illinois or Bradley University.

Computers: 2,445 computers/terminals and 2,445 ports are available on campus for general student use. Students can access the following: campus intranet, computer help desk, free student e-mail accounts, online (class) grades, online (class) registration, online (class) schedules. Campuswide network is available. 100% of college-owned or -operated housing units are wired for high-speed Internet access. Wireless service is available via entire campus.

STUDENT LIFE
Housing options: on-campus residence required through sophomore year; coed, special housing for students with disabilities. Campus housing is university owned. Freshman campus housing is guaranteed.

Activities and organizations: drama/theater group, student-run newspaper, radio and television station, choral group, marching band, national fraternities, national sororities.

Athletics Member NCAA. All Division I except football (Division I-AA). ***Intercollegiate sports:*** baseball M(s), basketball M(s)/W(s), cross-country running M(s)/W(s), golf M(s)/W(s), gymnastics W(s), soccer W(s), softball W(s), swimming and diving W(s), tennis M(s)/W(s), track and field M(s)/W(s), volleyball W(s). ***Intramural sports:*** badminton M(c)/W(c), baseball M(c), basketball M/W(c), bowling M(c)/W(c), cheerleading M(c)/W(c), cross-country running M(c)/W(c), equestrian sports W(c), fencing M(c)/W(c), golf M/W, ice hockey M(c), lacrosse M(c)/W(c), rugby M(c)/W(c), soccer M(c)/W(c), softball M/W(c), tennis M(c)/W(c), ultimate Frisbee M(c)/W(c), volleyball M(c)/W(c), water polo M(c)/W(c).

Campus security: 24-hour emergency response devices and patrols, late-night transport/escort service, controlled dormitory access.

Student services: health clinic, personal/psychological counseling, women's center, legal services.

COSTS & FINANCIAL AID
Costs (2014–15) ***Tuition:*** state resident $10,470 full-time, $349 per credit hour part-time; nonresident $18,060 full-time, $602 per credit hour part-time. Full-time tuition and fees vary according to course load and degree level. Part-time tuition and fees vary according to course load and degree level. No tuition increase for student's term of enrollment. ***Required fees:*** $2826 full-time, $79 per credit hour part-time. ***Room and board:*** $9816; room only: $5282. Room and board charges vary according to board plan, housing facility, and location. ***Payment plan:*** installment. ***Waivers:*** minority students, senior citizens, and employees or children of employees.

Financial Aid Of all full-time matriculated undergraduates who enrolled in 2014, 13,132 applied for aid, 11,013 were judged to have need, 3,119 had their need fully met. 307 Federal Work-Study jobs (averaging $2034). 51 state and other part-time jobs (averaging $2462). In 2014, 866 non-need-based awards were made. ***Average percent of need met:*** 72. ***Average financial aid package:*** $10,482. ***Average need-based loan:*** $4517. ***Average need-based gift aid:*** $9785. ***Average non-need-based aid:*** $2706. ***Average indebtedness upon graduation:*** $30,373.

APPLYING
Standardized Tests *Required:* SAT or ACT (for admission).

Options: electronic application, deferred entrance.

Application fee: $40.

Required: essay or personal statement. ***Recommended:*** high school transcript.

Application deadlines: 4/1 (freshmen), 4/1 (out-of-state freshmen), 5/1 (transfers).

Notification: continuous (freshmen), continuous (transfers).

CONTACT
Mr. Jeff Mavros, Director of Admissions, Illinois State University, Campus Box 2200, Normal, IL 61790-2200. *Phone:* 309-438-2181. *Toll-free phone:* 800-366-2478. *Fax:* 309-438-3932. *E-mail:* admissions@ilstu.edu.

Illinois Wesleyan University
Bloomington, Illinois
http://www.iwu.edu/

- **Independent** 4-year, founded 1850
- **Suburban** 79-acre campus
- **Coed** 1,893 undergraduate students, 100% full-time, 56% women, 44% men
- **Very difficult** entrance level, 58% of applicants were admitted

UNDERGRAD STUDENTS
1,885 full-time, 8 part-time. 11% are from out of state; 5% Black or African American, non-Hispanic/Latino; 7% Hispanic/Latino; 4% Asian, non-Hispanic/Latino; 0.1% Native Hawaiian or other Pacific Islander, non-Hispanic/Latino; 0.3% American Indian or Alaska Native, non-Hispanic/Latino; 2% Two or more races, non-Hispanic/Latino; 3% Race/ethnicity unknown; 8% international; 2% transferred in; 71% live on campus.

Freshmen
Admission: 3,556 applied, 2,076 admitted, 455 enrolled. ***Average high school GPA:*** 3.77. ***Test scores:*** SAT critical reading scores over 500: 74%; SAT math scores over 500: 100%; ACT scores over 18: 100%; SAT critical reading scores over 600: 30%; SAT math scores over 600: 83%; ACT scores over 24: 88%; SAT critical reading scores over 700: 5%; SAT math scores over 700: 58%; ACT scores over 30: 27%.

Retention: 92% of full-time freshmen returned.

FACULTY
Total: 214, 72% full-time, 77% with terminal degrees.

Student/faculty ratio: 11:1.

ACADEMICS
Calendar: 4-4-1. *Degree:* bachelor's.

ROTC: Army (c).

Unusual degree programs: 3-2 engineering with Case Western Reserve University, Northwestern University, Washington University in St. Louis,

Dartmouth College, University of Illinois; forestry with Duke University; occupational therapy.

Computers: Students can access the following: campus intranet, computer help desk, free student e-mail accounts, online (class) grades, online (class) registration, online (class) schedules. Campuswide network is available. Wireless service is available via entire campus.

STUDENT LIFE
Housing options: on-campus residence required through sophomore year; coed, special housing for students with disabilities. Campus housing is university owned. Freshman campus housing is guaranteed.

Athletics Member NCAA. All Division III. ***Intercollegiate sports:*** baseball M, basketball M/W, cheerleading M(c)/W(c), cross-country running M/W, football M, golf M/W, lacrosse M(c), soccer M/W, softball W, swimming and diving M/W, tennis M/W, track and field M/W, ultimate Frisbee M(c)/W(c), volleyball M(c)/W, water polo M(c). ***Intramural sports:*** badminton M/W, basketball M/W, football M/W, golf M/W, racquetball M/W, soccer M/W, softball M/W, tennis M/W, volleyball M/W.

Campus security: 24-hour emergency response devices and patrols, late-night transport/escort service, controlled dormitory access, emergency response team.

COSTS & FINANCIAL AID
Costs (2014–15) ***Comprehensive fee:*** $50,290 includes full-time tuition ($40,664), mandatory fees ($180), and room and board ($9446). Part-time tuition: $1271 per unit. ***Required fees:*** $4892 per unit part-time. ***College room only:*** $5926. Room and board charges vary according to housing facility. ***Payment plan:*** installment. ***Waivers:*** employees or children of employees.

Financial Aid Of all full-time matriculated undergraduates who enrolled in 2014, 1,457 applied for aid, 1,195 were judged to have need, 459 had their need fully met. In 2014, 633 non-need-based awards were made. ***Average percent of need met:*** 85. ***Average financial aid package:*** $29,999. ***Average need-based loan:*** $5594. ***Average need-based gift aid:*** $23,480. ***Average non-need-based aid:*** $15,760. ***Average indebtedness upon graduation:*** $32,101.

APPLYING
Standardized Tests *Required:* SAT or ACT (for admission).

Options: electronic application, early admission, early action, deferred entrance.

Required: essay or personal statement, high school transcript, minimum 2.0 GPA, 1 letter of recommendation. ***Recommended:*** minimum 3.0 GPA, 2 letters of recommendation, interview.

CONTACT
Mr. Tony Bankston, Dean of Admissions, Illinois Wesleyan University, PO Box 2900, Bloomington, IL 61702-2900. *Phone:* 309-556-3031. *Toll-free phone:* 800-332-2498. *Fax:* 309-556-3820. *E-mail:* iwuadmit@iwu.edu.

ITT Technical Institute
Arlington Heights, Illinois
http://www.itt-tech.edu/

- **Proprietary** primarily 2-year, founded 1986, part of ITT Educational Services, Inc.
- **Suburban** campus
- **Coed**
- **Minimally difficult** entrance level

ACADEMICS
Calendar: quarters. *Degrees:* associate and bachelor's.

STUDENT LIFE
Housing options: college housing not available.

CONTACT
Director of Recruitment, ITT Technical Institute, 3800 N. Wilke Road, Arlington Heights, IL 60004. *Phone:* 847-454-1800.

ITT Technical Institute
Oak Brook, Illinois
http://www.itt-tech.edu/

- **Proprietary** primarily 2-year, founded 1998, part of ITT Educational Services, Inc.
- **Coed**
- **Minimally difficult** entrance level

ACADEMICS
Calendar: quarters. *Degrees:* associate and bachelor's.

STUDENT LIFE
Housing options: college housing not available.

CONTACT
Director of Recruitment, ITT Technical Institute, 800 Jorie Boulevard, Suite 100, Oak Brook, IL 60523. *Phone:* 630-472-7000. *Toll-free phone:* 877-488-0001.

ITT Technical Institute
Orland Park, Illinois
http://www.itt-tech.edu/

- **Proprietary** primarily 2-year, founded 1993, part of ITT Educational Services, Inc.
- **Suburban** campus
- **Coed**
- **Minimally difficult** entrance level

ACADEMICS
Calendar: quarters. *Degrees:* associate and bachelor's.

STUDENT LIFE
Housing options: college housing not available.

FINANCIAL AID
Financial Aid Of all full-time matriculated undergraduates who enrolled in 2013, 6 Federal Work-Study jobs (averaging $4000).

CONTACT
Director of Recruitment, ITT Technical Institute, 11551 184th Place, Orland Park, IL 60467. *Phone:* 708-326-3200.

ITT Technical Institute
Springfield, Illinois
http://www.itt-tech.edu/

- **Proprietary** 4-year
- **Coed**
- **Minimally difficult** entrance level

ACADEMICS
Degrees: associate and bachelor's.

CONTACT
Director of Recruitment, ITT Technical Institute, 2501 Wabash Avenue, Springfield, IL 62704. *Phone:* 217-547-5700. *Toll-free phone:* 877-263-2374.

Judson University
Elgin, Illinois
http://www.judsonu.edu/

- **Independent Baptist** comprehensive, founded 1963
- **Suburban** 90-acre campus with easy access to Chicago
- **Endowment** $15.2 million
- **Coed** 1,154 undergraduate students, 68% full-time, 60% women, 40% men
- **Moderately difficult** entrance level, 73% of applicants were admitted

UNDERGRAD STUDENTS
781 full-time, 373 part-time. Students come from 34 states and territories; 20 other countries; 17% are from out of state; 8% Black or African American, non-Hispanic/Latino; 13% Hispanic/Latino; 2% Asian, non-Hispanic/Latino; 0.2% Native Hawaiian or other Pacific Islander, non-Hispanic/Latino; 0.2% American Indian or Alaska Native, non-Hispanic/Latino; 2% Two or more races, non-Hispanic/Latino; 11%

Race/ethnicity unknown; 3% international; 15% transferred in; 48% live on campus.

Freshmen

Admission: 703 applied, 514 admitted, 201 enrolled. ***Average high school GPA:*** 3.39. ***Test scores:*** SAT critical reading scores over 500: 74%; SAT math scores over 500: 77%; ACT scores over 18: 90%; SAT critical reading scores over 600: 37%; SAT math scores over 600: 30%; ACT scores over 24: 48%; SAT critical reading scores over 700: 7%; SAT math scores over 700: 17%; ACT scores over 30: 8%.

Retention: 69% of full-time freshmen returned.

FACULTY

Total: 159, 42% full-time.

Student/faculty ratio: 10:1.

ACADEMICS

Calendar: semesters. *Degrees:* certificates, diplomas, bachelor's, master's, doctoral, and postbachelor's certificates.

Special study options: academic remediation for entering students, accelerated degree program, adult/continuing education programs, advanced placement credit, distance learning, double majors, honors programs, independent study, internships, off-campus study, part-time degree program, services for LD students, student-designed majors, study abroad, summer session for credit. ***ROTC:*** Army (c).

Computers: 90 computers/terminals are available on campus for general student use. Students can access the following: campus intranet, computer help desk, free student e-mail accounts, online (class) grades, online (class) registration, online (class) schedules. Campuswide network is available. 100% of college-owned or -operated housing units are wired for high-speed Internet access. Wireless service is available via entire campus.

STUDENT LIFE

Housing options: on-campus residence required through senior year; coed, men-only, women-only, special housing for students with disabilities. Campus housing is university owned. Freshman campus housing is guaranteed.

Activities and organizations: drama/theater group, choral group, Judson Student Organization, University Ministries, Judson Choir, Fellowship of Christian Athletes, Judson Business Network.

Athletics Member NAIA, NCCAA. ***Intercollegiate sports:*** baseball M(s), basketball M(s)/W(s), cheerleading W(s), cross-country running M(s)/W(s), golf M(s)/W(s), lacrosse M(s), soccer M(s)/W(s), softball W(s), tennis M(s)/W(s), track and field M(s)/W(s), volleyball W(s). ***Intramural sports:*** basketball M/W, football M, racquetball M/W, soccer M/W, ultimate Frisbee M/W, volleyball M/W.

Campus security: 24-hour emergency response devices and patrols, controlled dormitory access.

Student services: health clinic, personal/psychological counseling.

COSTS & FINANCIAL AID

Costs (2015–16) ***Comprehensive fee:*** $37,520 includes full-time tuition ($27,290), mandatory fees ($780), and room and board ($9450). Full-time tuition and fees vary according to course load and program. Part-time tuition: $1115 per credit. Part-time tuition and fees vary according to course load and program. ***Room and board:*** Room and board charges vary according to board plan. ***Payment plan:*** deferred payment. ***Waivers:*** adult students, senior citizens, and employees or children of employees.

Financial Aid Of all full-time matriculated undergraduates who enrolled in 2013, 615 applied for aid, 615 were judged to have need, 88 had their need fully met. 100 Federal Work-Study jobs (averaging $1075). In 2013, 38 non-need-based awards were made. ***Average percent of need met:*** 55. ***Average financial aid package:*** $18,828. ***Average need-based loan:*** $4993. ***Average need-based gift aid:*** $8976. ***Average non-need-based aid:*** $8514. ***Average indebtedness upon graduation:*** $33,921. ***Financial aid deadline:*** 8/1.

APPLYING

Standardized Tests *Required:* SAT or ACT (for admission).

Options: electronic application.

Application fee: $50.

Required: high school transcript, minimum 2.5 GPA, Minimum 21 ACT; lifestyle statement; portfolios for some majors. ***Required for some:*** essay or personal statement, 1 letter of recommendation.

Application deadlines: rolling (freshmen), rolling (out-of-state freshmen), rolling (transfers).

Notification: continuous (freshmen), continuous (out-of-state freshmen), continuous (transfers).

CONTACT

Mrs. Nancy Binger, Executive Director of Enrollment Services, Judson University, 1151 North State Street, Elgin, IL 60123. *Phone:* 847-628-2512. *Toll-free phone:* 800-879-5376. *Fax:* 847-628-2526. *E-mail:* nbinger@judsonu.edu.

★ Kendall College

Chicago, Illinois

http://www.kendall.edu/

CONTACT

Mr. Thomas Marigliano, Director of Enrollment, Kendall College, 900 North Branch Street, Chicago, IL 60642. *Toll-free phone:* 888-90-KENDALL. *E-mail:* admissions@kendall.edu.

Knox College

Galesburg, Illinois

http://www.knox.edu/

- **Independent** 4-year, founded 1837
- **Small-town** 82-acre campus with easy access to Peoria; Quad Cities
- **Endowment** $124.4 million
- **Coed** 1,399 undergraduate students, 98% full-time, 58% women, 42% men
- **Very difficult** entrance level, 68% of applicants were admitted

UNDERGRAD STUDENTS

1,367 full-time, 32 part-time. Students come from 39 states and territories; 45 other countries; 43% are from out of state; 8% Black or African American, non-Hispanic/Latino; 13% Hispanic/Latino; 6% Asian, non-Hispanic/Latino; 0.2% American Indian or Alaska Native, non-Hispanic/Latino; 4% Two or more races, non-Hispanic/Latino; 4% Race/ethnicity unknown; 13% international; 3% transferred in; 80% live on campus.

Freshmen

Admission: 3,221 applied, 2,198 admitted, 362 enrolled. ***Test scores:*** SAT critical reading scores over 500: 95%; SAT math scores over 500: 96%; SAT writing scores over 500: 96%; ACT scores over 18: 100%; SAT critical reading scores over 600: 67%; SAT math scores over 600: 56%; SAT writing scores over 600: 69%; ACT scores over 24: 73%; SAT critical reading scores over 700: 23%; SAT math scores over 700: 17%; SAT writing scores over 700: 14%; ACT scores over 30: 26%.

Retention: 88% of full-time freshmen returned.

FACULTY

Total: 145, 80% full-time, 82% with terminal degrees.

Student/faculty ratio: 11:1.

ACADEMICS

Calendar: trimesters. *Degree:* bachelor's.

Special study options: advanced placement credit, double majors, English as a second language, honors programs, independent study, internships, off-campus study, part-time degree program, services for LD students, student-designed majors, study abroad.

Unusual degree programs: 3-2 engineering with University of Illinois at Urbana, Washington University, Columbia University, Rensselaer Polytechnic Institute (not Masters work - Bachelor of Engineering); forestry with Duke University; nursing with Rush University's College of Nursing.

Computers: 250 computers/terminals are available on campus for general student use. Students can access the following: campus intranet, computer help desk, free student e-mail accounts, online (class) grades, online (class) registration, online (class) schedules, Transcripts, EDR, Moodle. Campuswide network is available. 100% of college-owned or -operated

housing units are wired for high-speed Internet access. Wireless service is available via entire campus.

STUDENT LIFE
Housing options: on-campus residence required through sophomore year; coed, men-only, women-only, special housing for students with disabilities. Campus housing is university owned. Freshman campus housing is guaranteed.

Activities and organizations: drama/theater group, student-run newspaper, radio station, choral group, Student-Run Radio Station (WVKC), International Club, Student Newspaper (The Knox Student), Common Ground, Terpsichore (Dance Collective), national fraternities, national sororities.

Athletics Member NCAA. All Division III. ***Intercollegiate sports:*** baseball M, basketball M/W, cross-country running M/W, football M, golf M/W, soccer M/W, softball W, swimming and diving M/W, tennis M/W, track and field M/W, volleyball W, wrestling M. ***Intramural sports:*** basketball M/W, equestrian sports W(c), fencing M(c)/W(c), lacrosse M(c)/W(c), soccer M/W, ultimate Frisbee M(c)/W(c), volleyball M/W, water polo M(c)/W(c).

Campus security: 24-hour emergency response devices and patrols, late-night transport/escort service.

Student services: health clinic, personal/psychological counseling.

COSTS & FINANCIAL AID
Costs (2015–16) ***Comprehensive fee:*** $50,859 includes full-time tuition ($41,094), mandatory fees ($753), and room and board ($9012). Full-time tuition and fees vary according to course load. Part-time tuition: $4566 per credit. Part-time tuition and fees vary according to course load. ***College room only:*** $4512. Room and board charges vary according to housing facility. ***Payment plan:*** installment. ***Waivers:*** employees or children of employees.

Financial Aid Of all full-time matriculated undergraduates who enrolled in 2013, 1,176 applied for aid, 1,092 were judged to have need, 257 had their need fully met. In 2013, 256 non-need-based awards were made. ***Average percent of need met:*** 87. ***Average financial aid package:*** $32,942. ***Average need-based loan:*** $5168. ***Average need-based gift aid:*** $27,887. ***Average non-need-based aid:*** $15,785. ***Average indebtedness upon graduation:*** $29,085.

APPLYING
Standardized Tests *Required for some:* SAT or ACT (for admission). *Recommended:* SAT or ACT (for admission).

Options: electronic application, early admission, early action, deferred entrance.

Application fee: $40.

Required: essay or personal statement, high school transcript, 2 letters of recommendation, All students apply using the Common Application. First-year students must submit the Common Application, High School Transcript, School Report form, and Teacher Evaluation Form. Scholarships auditions or portfolios and ACT/SAT scores are optional for most students. ***Recommended:*** interview.

Application deadlines: 2/1 (freshmen), 4/1 (transfers), 12/1 (early action).

Notification: 3/31 (freshmen), 5/15 (transfers), 12/31 (early action).

CONTACT
Mr. Paul Steenis, Dean of Admission, Knox College, 2 East South Street, Campus Box148, Galesburg, IL 61401. *Phone:* 309-341-7100. *Toll-free phone:* 800-678-KNOX. *Fax:* 309-341-7070. *E-mail:* admission@knox.edu.

Lake Forest College

Lake Forest, Illinois

http://www.lakeforest.edu/

- **Independent** comprehensive, founded 1857
- **Suburban** 107-acre campus with easy access to Chicago
- **Endowment** $83.3 million
- **Coed** 1,607 undergraduate students, 99% full-time, 57% women, 43% men
- **Moderately difficult** entrance level, 55% of applicants were admitted

UNDERGRAD STUDENTS
1,589 full-time, 18 part-time. Students come from 45 states and territories; 73 other countries; 36% are from out of state; 7% Black or African American, non-Hispanic/Latino; 15% Hispanic/Latino; 5% Asian, non-Hispanic/Latino; 0.3% American Indian or Alaska Native, non-Hispanic/Latino; 4% Two or more races, non-Hispanic/Latino; 3% Race/ethnicity unknown; 9% international; 5% transferred in; 72% live on campus.

Freshmen
Admission: 3,451 applied, 1,905 admitted, 410 enrolled. ***Average high school GPA:*** 3.67.

Retention: 85% of full-time freshmen returned.

FACULTY
Total: 182, 55% full-time, 77% with terminal degrees.

Student/faculty ratio: 12:1.

ACADEMICS
Calendar: semesters. *Degrees:* bachelor's, master's, and postbachelor's certificates.

Special study options: accelerated degree program, advanced placement credit, double majors, honors programs, independent study, internships, off-campus study, part-time degree program, services for LD students, student-designed majors, study abroad, summer session for credit.

Unusual degree programs: 3-2 engineering with Washington University in St. Louis.

Computers: 175 computers/terminals are available on campus for general student use. Students can access the following: campus intranet, computer help desk, free student e-mail accounts, online (class) grades, online (class) registration, online (class) schedules, file storage. Campuswide network is available. 100% of college-owned or -operated housing units are wired for high-speed Internet access. Wireless service is available via entire campus.

STUDENT LIFE
Housing options: on-campus residence required through junior year; coed. Campus housing is university owned. Freshman applicants given priority for college housing.

Activities and organizations: drama/theater group, student-run newspaper, radio station, choral group, Student Government, Athletic Council, United Black Association, Alpha Phi, PRIDE, national fraternities, national sororities.

Athletics Member NCAA. All Division III. ***Intercollegiate sports:*** archery M(c)/W(c), baseball M(c), basketball M/W, cheerleading M(c)/W(c), cross-country running M/W, equestrian sports M/W, fencing M(c)/W(c), football M, golf M/W, ice hockey M/W, lacrosse M(c)/W(c), rugby M(c)/W(c), sailing M(c)/W(c), soccer M/W, softball W, swimming and diving M/W, tennis M/W, track and field M(c)/W(c), ultimate Frisbee M(c)/W(c), volleyball M(c)/W, water polo M(c)/W(c). ***Intramural sports:*** badminton M/W, basketball M/W, soccer M/W, table tennis M/W, volleyball M/W.

Campus security: 24-hour emergency response devices and patrols, student patrols, late-night transport/escort service, controlled dormitory access.

Student services: health clinic, personal/psychological counseling.

COSTS & FINANCIAL AID
Costs (2015–16) ***Comprehensive fee:*** $52,214 includes full-time tuition ($41,920), mandatory fees ($724), and room and board ($9570). Part-time tuition: $5240 per course. ***College room only:*** $4570. Room and board charges vary according to board plan and housing facility. ***Payment plan:*** installment. ***Waivers:*** employees or children of employees.

Financial Aid ***Financial aid deadline:*** 5/1.

APPLYING
Standardized Tests *Required for some:* SAT or ACT (for admission).

Options: electronic application, early decision, early action, deferred entrance.

Required: essay or personal statement, high school transcript, 2 letters of recommendation. ***Recommended:*** 2 letters of recommendation, interview.

Application deadlines: 2/15 (freshmen), rolling (transfers), 11/15 (early action).

Early decision deadline: 11/15 (for plan 1), 1/15 (for plan 2).

Notification: 3/20 (freshmen), continuous (transfers), 12/15 (early decision plan 1), 1/31 (early decision plan 2), 12/15 (early action).

CONTACT

Vice President for Admissions and Career Services, Lake Forest College, 555 North Sheridan Road, Lake Forest, IL 60045-2338. *Phone:* 847-735-5000. *Toll-free phone:* 800-828-4751. *Fax:* 847-735-6271. *E-mail:* admissions@lakeforest.edu.

Lakeview College of Nursing

Danville, Illinois

http://www.lakeviewcol.edu/

- **Independent** upper-level, founded 1987
- **Small-town** 1-acre campus
- **Endowment** $6.5 million
- **Coed, primarily women** 322 undergraduate students, 79% full-time, 85% women, 15% men
- **Moderately difficult** entrance level

UNDERGRAD STUDENTS

255 full-time, 67 part-time. 9% Black or African American, non-Hispanic/Latino; 2% Hispanic/Latino; 2% Asian, non-Hispanic/Latino; 0.9% Native Hawaiian or other Pacific Islander, non-Hispanic/Latino; 0.6% American Indian or Alaska Native, non-Hispanic/Latino; 1% Two or more races, non-Hispanic/Latino; 0.6% Race/ethnicity unknown.

FACULTY

Total: 35, 57% full-time, 3% with terminal degrees.

Student/faculty ratio: 10:1.

ACADEMICS

Calendar: semesters. *Degree:* bachelor's.

Special study options: academic remediation for entering students, off-campus study, part-time degree program, summer session for credit. ***ROTC:*** Army (c).

Computers: 61 computers/terminals are available on campus for general student use. Students can access the following: free student e-mail accounts, online (class) grades, online (class) schedules. Campuswide network is available. Wireless service is available via classrooms, computer centers, computer labs, libraries, student centers.

STUDENT LIFE

Housing options: college housing not available.

Campus security: 24-hour emergency response devices.

COSTS & FINANCIAL AID

Costs (2014–15) ***Tuition:*** $13,120 full-time, $410 per credit hour part-time. Full-time tuition and fees vary according to course load and location. Part-time tuition and fees vary according to course load and location. ***Required fees:*** $1920 full-time, $60 per credit hour part-time. ***Payment plan:*** installment. ***Waivers:*** employees or children of employees.

Financial Aid Of all full-time matriculated undergraduates who enrolled in 2014, 392 applied for aid, 360 were judged to have need, 307 had their need fully met. ***Average percent of need met:*** 82. ***Average financial aid package:*** $20,500. ***Average need-based loan:*** $5500. ***Average need-based gift aid:*** $2500. ***Average indebtedness upon graduation:*** $25,000.

APPLYING

Standardized Tests *Required:* HESI A2 pre-admission test (for admission).

Options: early admission, early decision, deferred entrance.

Application fee: $100.

CONTACT

Admissions Office, Lakeview College of Nursing, 903 North Logan Avenue, Danville, IL 61832. *Phone:* 217-709-0920. *Fax:* 217-709-0953. *E-mail:* admission@lakeviewcol.edu.

Lewis University

Romeoville, Illinois

http://www.lewisu.edu/

- **Independent** comprehensive, founded 1932, affiliated with Roman Catholic Church
- **Suburban** 410-acre campus with easy access to Chicago
- **Endowment** $52.6 million
- **Coed** 4,752 undergraduate students, 80% full-time, 56% women, 44% men
- **Moderately difficult** entrance level, 62% of applicants were admitted

UNDERGRAD STUDENTS

3,816 full-time, 936 part-time. Students come from 34 states and territories; 19 other countries; 6% are from out of state; 7% Black or African American, non-Hispanic/Latino; 18% Hispanic/Latino; 3% Asian, non-Hispanic/Latino; 0.2% Native Hawaiian or other Pacific Islander, non-Hispanic/Latino; 0.1% American Indian or Alaska Native, non-Hispanic/Latino; 3% Two or more races, non-Hispanic/Latino; 3% Race/ethnicity unknown; 0.8% international; 13% transferred in; 28% live on campus.

Freshmen

Admission: 5,786 applied, 3,582 admitted, 744 enrolled. ***Average high school GPA:*** 3.38. ***Test scores:*** SAT critical reading scores over 500: 78%; SAT math scores over 500: 72%; SAT writing scores over 500: 59%; ACT scores over 18: 96%; SAT critical reading scores over 600: 17%; SAT math scores over 600: 11%; ACT scores over 24: 43%; ACT scores over 30: 4%.

Retention: 83% of full-time freshmen returned.

FACULTY

Total: 694, 32% full-time, 37% with terminal degrees.

Student/faculty ratio: 13:1.

ACADEMICS

Calendar: semesters. *Degrees:* certificates, associate, bachelor's, master's, doctoral, post-master's, and postbachelor's certificates.

Special study options: academic remediation for entering students, accelerated degree program, adult/continuing education programs, advanced placement credit, distance learning, double majors, English as a second language, honors programs, independent study, internships, off-campus study, part-time degree program, services for LD students, student-designed majors, study abroad, summer session for credit. ***ROTC:*** Army (c), Air Force (c).

Computers: 600 computers/terminals are available on campus for general student use. Students can access the following: campus intranet, computer help desk, free student e-mail accounts, online (class) grades, online (class) registration, online (class) schedules, online help, online billing, online financial aid, online payments, online application for admission, online housing application, online application for graduation, Blackboard course management system. Campuswide network is available. 100% of college-owned or -operated housing units are wired for high-speed Internet access. Wireless service is available via entire campus.

STUDENT LIFE

Housing options: coed. Campus housing is university owned. Freshman campus housing is guaranteed.

Activities and organizations: drama/theater group, student-run newspaper, radio and television station, choral group, Student Governing Board, Student Nurses Association, Latin American Student Organization, Theta Kappa Pi Sorority, Delta Sigma Pi (business fraternity), national fraternities, national sororities.

Athletics Member NCAA. All Division II except volleyball (Division I). ***Intercollegiate sports:*** baseball M(s), basketball M(s)/W(s), cheerleading W(s)(c), cross-country running M(s)/W(s), golf M(s)/W(s), ice hockey M(c), lacrosse M(c)/W(c), rugby M(c), skiing (downhill) M(c)/W(c), soccer M(s)/W(s), softball W(s), swimming and diving M(s)/W(s), tennis M(s)/W(s), track and field M(s)/W(s), ultimate Frisbee M(c)/W(c), volleyball M(s)/W(s), water polo M(c)/W(c). ***Intramural sports:*** badminton M/W, baseball M(c), basketball M(c)/W, bowling M/W, football M/W, rugby W(c), soccer M/W(c), softball M/W, table tennis M/W, volleyball M(c)/W.

Campus security: 24-hour emergency response devices and patrols, student patrols, late-night transport/escort service, controlled dormitory access.

Student services: health clinic, personal/psychological counseling.

COSTS & FINANCIAL AID

Costs (2015–16) ***Comprehensive fee:*** $38,970 includes full-time tuition ($28,940), mandatory fees ($100), and room and board ($9930). Full-time tuition and fees vary according to course load, location, and program. Part-time tuition: $852 per credit. Part-time tuition and fees vary according to course load, location, and program. ***Required fees:*** $50 per term part-time. ***College room only:*** $6310. Room and board charges vary according to board plan and housing facility. ***Payment plan:*** installment. ***Waivers:*** children of alumni, adult students, and employees or children of employees.

Financial Aid Of all full-time matriculated undergraduates who enrolled in 2014, 3,273 applied for aid, 2,916 were judged to have need, 638 had their need fully met. 2,169 Federal Work-Study jobs (averaging $3283). 267 state and other part-time jobs (averaging $4247). In 2014, 661 non-need-based awards were made. ***Average percent of need met:*** 75. ***Average financial aid package:*** $20,334. ***Average need-based loan:*** $4421. ***Average need-based gift aid:*** $14,019. ***Average non-need-based aid:*** $9998. ***Average indebtedness upon graduation:*** $33,748. ***Financial aid deadline:*** 5/1.

APPLYING

Standardized Tests *Required:* SAT or ACT (for admission).

Options: electronic application, deferred entrance.

Application fee: $40.

Required: high school transcript, minimum 2.0 GPA. ***Required for some:*** interview.

Application deadlines: 8/1 (freshmen), 8/1 (out-of-state freshmen), rolling (transfers).

Notification: continuous (freshmen), continuous (out-of-state freshmen), continuous (transfers).

CONTACT

Mr. Ryan Cockerill, Director of Admission, Lewis University, Box 297, One University Parkway, Romeoville, IL 60446. *Phone:* 815-836-5237. *Toll-free phone:* 800-897-9000. *Fax:* 815-836-5002. *E-mail:* admissions@lewisu.edu.

Lincoln Christian University

Lincoln, Illinois

http://www.lincolnchristian.edu/

- **Independent** comprehensive, founded 1944, affiliated with Christian Churches and Churches of Christ
- **Small-town** 100-acre campus
- **Endowment** $4.4 million
- **Coed** 557 undergraduate students, 80% full-time, 53% women, 47% men
- **Moderately difficult** entrance level, 48% of applicants were admitted

UNDERGRAD STUDENTS

444 full-time, 113 part-time. Students come from 23 states and territories; 4 other countries; 29% are from out of state; 9% Black or African American, non-Hispanic/Latino; 4% Hispanic/Latino; 3% Asian, non-Hispanic/Latino; 0.2% Native Hawaiian or other Pacific Islander, non-Hispanic/Latino; 1% American Indian or Alaska Native, non-Hispanic/Latino; 2% Two or more races, non-Hispanic/Latino; 0.2% Race/ethnicity unknown; 5% transferred in; 51% live on campus.

Freshmen

Admission: 227 applied, 108 admitted, 64 enrolled. ***Average high school GPA:*** 3.17. ***Test scores:*** SAT critical reading scores over 500: 100%; SAT math scores over 500: 100%; SAT writing scores over 500: 83%; ACT scores over 18: 83%; SAT critical reading scores over 600: 100%; SAT math scores over 600: 100%; SAT writing scores over 600: 25%; ACT scores over 24: 25%; SAT writing scores over 700: 1%; ACT scores over 30: 1%.

Retention: 83% of full-time freshmen returned.

FACULTY

Total: 145, 35% full-time, 46% with terminal degrees.

Student/faculty ratio: 8:1.

ACADEMICS

Calendar: semesters. *Degrees:* certificates, associate, bachelor's, master's, and doctoral.

Special study options: academic remediation for entering students, adult/continuing education programs, advanced placement credit, distance learning, double majors, external degree program, honors programs, independent study, internships, off-campus study, part-time degree program, services for LD students, study abroad, summer session for credit.

Unusual degree programs: 3-2 teacher education.

Computers: 51 computers/terminals are available on campus for general student use. Students can access the following: campus intranet, computer help desk, free student e-mail accounts, online (class) grades, online (class) registration, online (class) schedules. Campuswide network is available. 100% of college-owned or -operated housing units are wired for high-speed Internet access. Wireless service is available via entire campus.

STUDENT LIFE

Housing options: on-campus residence required through senior year; men-only, women-only. Campus housing is university owned. Freshman campus housing is guaranteed.

Activities and organizations: drama/theater group, choral group, Chorale, Student Cabinet, American Association of Christian Counselors (AACC) - Student Chapter, Cheerleading.

Athletics Member NAIA, NCCAA. ***Intercollegiate sports:*** baseball M(s), basketball M(s)/W(s), soccer M(s)/W(s), volleyball W(s). ***Intramural sports:*** badminton M/W, basketball M/W, soccer M/W, ultimate Frisbee M/W, volleyball M/W.

Campus security: 24-hour emergency response devices, student patrols, controlled dormitory access.

Student services: personal/psychological counseling.

COSTS & FINANCIAL AID

Costs (2014–15) ***Comprehensive fee:*** $23,484 includes full-time tuition ($15,810), mandatory fees ($240), and room and board ($7434). Full-time tuition and fees vary according to location and program. Part-time tuition: $527 per credit hour. Part-time tuition and fees vary according to location and program. ***College room only:*** $5434. ***Payment plans:*** installment, deferred payment. ***Waivers:*** senior citizens and employees or children of employees.

Financial Aid Of all full-time matriculated undergraduates who enrolled in 2013, 598 applied for aid, 561 were judged to have need, 39 had their need fully met. 65 Federal Work-Study jobs (averaging $1590). 125 state and other part-time jobs (averaging $1572). In 2013, 60 non-need-based awards were made. ***Average percent of need met:*** 60. ***Average financial aid package:*** $10,673. ***Average need-based loan:*** $3887. ***Average need-based gift aid:*** $7085. ***Average non-need-based aid:*** $4461. ***Average indebtedness upon graduation:*** $25,578.

APPLYING

Standardized Tests *Required:* SAT or ACT (for admission).

Options: electronic application, deferred entrance.

Application fee: $25.

Required: essay or personal statement, high school transcript, 3 letters of recommendation. ***Required for some:*** interview.

Application deadlines: rolling (freshmen), rolling (out-of-state freshmen), rolling (transfers).

Notification: continuous (freshmen), continuous (out-of-state freshmen), continuous (transfers).

CONTACT

Mrs. Mary K. Davis, Admissions Office Manager, Lincoln Christian University, 100 Campus View Drive, Lincoln, IL 62656. *Phone:* 217-732-3168 Ext. 2251. *Toll-free phone:* 888-522-5228. *Fax:* 217-732-4199. *E-mail:* admissions@lincolnchristian.edu.

Loyola University Chicago

Chicago, Illinois

http://www.luc.edu/

- **Independent Roman Catholic (Jesuit)** university, founded 1870
- **Urban** 105-acre campus
- **Endowment** $538.5 million
- **Coed** 10,322 undergraduate students, 90% full-time, 64% women, 36% men
- **Moderately difficult** entrance level, 63% of applicants were admitted

UNDERGRAD STUDENTS
9,331 full-time, 991 part-time. Students come from 54 states and territories; 87 other countries; 35% are from out of state; 4% Black or African American, non-Hispanic/Latino; 13% Hispanic/Latino; 11% Asian, non-Hispanic/Latino; 0.2% Native Hawaiian or other Pacific Islander, non-Hispanic/Latino; 0.1% American Indian or Alaska Native, non-Hispanic/Latino; 6% Two or more races, non-Hispanic/Latino; 2% Race/ethnicity unknown; 4% international; 5% transferred in; 44% live on campus.

Freshmen
Admission: 20,414 applied, 12,931 admitted, 2,292 enrolled. ***Average high school GPA:*** 3.8. ***Test scores:*** SAT critical reading scores over 500: 86%; SAT math scores over 500: 88%; SAT writing scores over 500: 86%; ACT scores over 18: 100%; SAT critical reading scores over 600: 39%; SAT math scores over 600: 42%; SAT writing scores over 600: 39%; ACT scores over 24: 85%; SAT critical reading scores over 700: 5%; SAT math scores over 700: 7%; SAT writing scores over 700: 5%; ACT scores over 30: 21%.

Retention: 86% of full-time freshmen returned.

FACULTY
Total: 1,530, 49% full-time.

Student/faculty ratio: 14:1.

ACADEMICS
Calendar: semesters. *Degrees:* certificates, bachelor's, master's, doctoral, post-master's, and postbachelor's certificates (also offers adult part-time program with significant enrollment not reflected in profile).

Special study options: accelerated degree program, adult/continuing education programs, advanced placement credit, cooperative education, distance learning, double majors, English as a second language, freshman honors college, honors programs, independent study, internships, off-campus study, part-time degree program, services for LD students, study abroad, summer session for credit. ***ROTC:*** Army (b), Navy (c), Air Force (c).

Unusual degree programs: 3-2 business administration; engineering with BS Physics and Engineering, Columbia University in NYC; BS Physics and Engineering, Washington University, St. Louis; BS Physics and Engineering, Notre Dame University; social work; political science, sociology, psychology, computer science, biology, education, accounting, information technology, criminal justice, environmental studies, women's studies, applied human perception.

Computers: 1,300 computers/terminals are available on campus for general student use. Students can access the following: campus intranet, computer help desk, free student e-mail accounts, online (class) grades, online (class) registration, online (class) schedules. Campuswide network is available. 100% of college-owned or -operated housing units are wired for high-speed Internet access. Wireless service is available via entire campus.

STUDENT LIFE
Housing options: on-campus residence required through sophomore year; coed, special housing for students with disabilities. Campus housing is university owned. Freshman campus housing is guaranteed.

Activities and organizations: drama/theater group, student-run newspaper, radio station, Department of Programming, Panhellenic Sororities, American Medical Association, South Asian Student Alliance, Habitat for Humanity, national fraternities, national sororities.

Athletics Member NCAA. All Division I. ***Intercollegiate sports:*** basketball M(s)/W(s), cross-country running M(s)/W(s), golf M(s)/W(s), soccer M(s)/W(s), softball W(s), track and field M(s)/W(s), volleyball M(s)/W(s). ***Intramural sports:*** badminton M/W, baseball M(c), basketball M/W, cheerleading M(c)/W(c), cross-country running M(c)/W(c), fencing M(c)/W(c), field hockey W(c), football M(c)/W(c), ice hockey M(c)/W(c), lacrosse M(c)/W(c), racquetball M/W, rugby M(c)/W(c), soccer M(c)/W(c), softball W(c), swimming and diving M(c)/W(c), table tennis M/W, tennis M(c)/W(c), ultimate Frisbee M(c)/W(c), volleyball M(c)/W(c), water polo M(c)/W(c).

Campus security: 24-hour emergency response devices and patrols, late-night transport/escort service, controlled dormitory access, Loyola Alert (special service to provide personalized, time-sensitive alerts to students, faculty, staff and other personnel at Loyola).

Student services: health clinic, personal/psychological counseling, women's center.

COSTS & FINANCIAL AID
Costs (2015–16) ***Comprehensive fee:*** $52,489 includes full-time tuition ($37,883), mandatory fees ($1296), and room and board ($13,310). Full-time tuition and fees vary according to location, program, and student level. Part-time tuition: $722 per credit. Part-time tuition and fees vary according to course load. ***College room only:*** $8380. Room and board charges vary according to board plan, housing facility, and location. ***Payment plans:*** installment, deferred payment. ***Waivers:*** senior citizens and employees or children of employees.

Financial Aid Of all full-time matriculated undergraduates who enrolled in 2014, 7,284 applied for aid, 6,371 were judged to have need, 795 had their need fully met. 4,649 Federal Work-Study jobs (averaging $2196). In 2014, 2091 non-need-based awards were made. ***Average percent of need met:*** 78. ***Average financial aid package:*** $30,916. ***Average need-based loan:*** $4763. ***Average need-based gift aid:*** $18,875. ***Average non-need-based aid:*** $13,220. ***Average indebtedness upon graduation:*** $31,089.

APPLYING
Standardized Tests *Required:* SAT or ACT (for admission).

Options: electronic application.

Required: essay or personal statement, high school transcript, minimum 2.0 GPA. ***Recommended:*** interview.

Notification: continuous (freshmen), continuous (out-of-state freshmen), continuous (transfers).

CONTACT
Ms. Lori Greene, Director of Undergraduate Admissions, Loyola University Chicago, 1032 West Sheridan Road, Chicago, IL 60660. *Phone:* 773-508-3079. *Toll-free phone:* 800-262-2373. *E-mail:* admission@luc.edu.

McKendree University

Lebanon, Illinois

http://www.mckendree.edu/

- **Independent** comprehensive, founded 1828, affiliated with United Methodist Church
- **Suburban** 234-acre campus with easy access to St. Louis, MO; Belleville, IL
- **Endowment** $30.9 million
- **Coed** 2,521 undergraduate students, 77% full-time, 56% women, 44% men
- **Moderately difficult** entrance level, 61% of applicants were admitted

UNDERGRAD STUDENTS
1,950 full-time, 571 part-time. Students come from 29 states and territories; 25 other countries; 15% are from out of state; 14% Black or African American, non-Hispanic/Latino; 4% Hispanic/Latino; 1% Asian, non-Hispanic/Latino; 0.4% Native Hawaiian or other Pacific Islander, non-Hispanic/Latino; 1% American Indian or Alaska Native, non-Hispanic/Latino; 2% Two or more races, non-Hispanic/Latino; 6% Race/ethnicity unknown; 2% international; 6% transferred in; 73% live on campus.

Freshmen
Admission: 1,965 applied, 1,201 admitted, 421 enrolled. ***Average high school GPA:*** 3.4. ***Test scores:*** SAT critical reading scores over 500: 52%; SAT math scores over 500: 58%; SAT writing scores over 500: 49%; ACT scores over 18: 95%; SAT critical reading scores over 600: 12%; SAT math scores over 600: 12%; SAT writing scores over 600: 12%; ACT

scores over 24: 39%; SAT critical reading scores over 700: 6%; SAT math scores over 700: 3%; ACT scores over 30: 3%.

Retention: 76% of full-time freshmen returned.

FACULTY
Total: 271, 38% full-time, 54% with terminal degrees.

Student/faculty ratio: 13:1.

ACADEMICS
Calendar: semesters. *Degrees:* associate, bachelor's, master's, doctoral, and post-master's certificates.

Special study options: academic remediation for entering students, accelerated degree program, adult/continuing education programs, advanced placement credit, cooperative education, distance learning, double majors, honors programs, independent study, internships, off-campus study, part-time degree program, services for LD students, student-designed majors, study abroad, summer session for credit. ***ROTC:*** Army (c), Air Force (c).

Unusual degree programs: 3-2 engineering with Missouri University of Science and Technology or University of Illinois-Champaign; Occupational Therapy with Washington University in St. Louis.

Computers: 205 computers/terminals and 1,096 ports are available on campus for general student use. Students can access the following: campus intranet, computer help desk, free student e-mail accounts, online (class) grades, online (class) registration, online (class) schedules. Campuswide network is available. 100% of college-owned or -operated housing units are wired for high-speed Internet access. Wireless service is available via entire campus.

STUDENT LIFE
Housing options: on-campus residence required through junior year; coed, special housing for students with disabilities. Campus housing is university owned and leased by the school. Freshman campus housing is guaranteed.

Activities and organizations: drama/theater group, student-run newspaper, radio station, choral group, marching band, Center for Public Service, Wonders of Wellness, Campus Ministries, APO, Debate, national fraternities, national sororities.

Athletics Member NCAA. All Division II except volleyball (Division I). ***Intercollegiate sports:*** baseball M(s), basketball M(s)/W(s), bowling M(c)/W(s), cheerleading M(s)(c)/W(s)(c), cross-country running M(s)/W(s), fencing M/W, football M(s), golf M(s)/W(s), ice hockey M(c), lacrosse W(s), soccer M(s)/W(s), softball W(s), tennis M(s)/W(s), track and field M(s)/W(s), volleyball M(s)/W(s), wrestling M(s)/W(s). ***Intramural sports:*** basketball M/W, football M/W, softball M/W, table tennis M/W, ultimate Frisbee M/W, volleyball M/W.

Campus security: 24-hour emergency response devices and patrols, student patrols, late-night transport/escort service, controlled dormitory access.

Student services: health clinic, personal/psychological counseling.

COSTS & FINANCIAL AID
Costs (2015–16) ***Comprehensive fee:*** $36,950 includes full-time tuition ($26,930), mandatory fees ($1000), and room and board ($9020). Full-time tuition and fees vary according to course load, degree level, and location. Part-time tuition: $870 per credit hour. Part-time tuition and fees vary according to course load, degree level, and location. ***College room only:*** $4820. Room and board charges vary according to board plan and housing facility. ***Payment plans:*** installment, deferred payment. ***Waivers:*** children of alumni and employees or children of employees.

Financial Aid Of all full-time matriculated undergraduates who enrolled in 2014, 1,531 applied for aid, 1,411 were judged to have need, 280 had their need fully met. 893 Federal Work-Study jobs (averaging $1255). 65 state and other part-time jobs (averaging $1052). In 2014, 227 non-need-based awards were made. ***Average percent of need met:*** 75. ***Average financial aid package:*** $20,754. ***Average need-based loan:*** $4165. ***Average need-based gift aid:*** $17,344. ***Average non-need-based aid:*** $11,109. ***Average indebtedness upon graduation:*** $21,731.

APPLYING
Standardized Tests *Required:* SAT or ACT (for admission).

Options: electronic application, deferred entrance.

Required: essay or personal statement, high school transcript, minimum 2.5 GPA, 1 letter of recommendation, rank in upper 50% of high school class, ACT score of 20 or higher. ***Required for some:*** interview.

Application deadlines: rolling (freshmen), rolling (transfers).

Notification: continuous (freshmen), continuous (transfers).

CONTACT
Mrs. Josie Blasdel, Director of Undergraduate Admission, McKendree University, 701 College Road, Lebanon, IL 62254. *Phone:* 618-537-6836. *Toll-free phone:* 800-232-7228. *Fax:* 618-537-6496. *E-mail:* jlblasdel@mckendree.edu.

Millikin University
Decatur, Illinois
http://www.millikin.edu/

- **Independent** comprehensive, founded 1901, affiliated with Presbyterian Church (U.S.A.)
- **Suburban** 75-acre campus
- **Endowment** $124.9 million
- **Coed** 2,112 undergraduate students, 96% full-time, 59% women, 41% men
- **Moderately difficult** entrance level, 63% of applicants were admitted

UNDERGRAD STUDENTS
2,018 full-time, 94 part-time. Students come from 35 states and territories; 19 other countries; 13% are from out of state; 14% Black or African American, non-Hispanic/Latino; 6% Hispanic/Latino; 0.8% Asian, non-Hispanic/Latino; 0.2% American Indian or Alaska Native, non-Hispanic/Latino; 4% Two or more races, non-Hispanic/Latino; 0.4% Race/ethnicity unknown; 0.9% international; 5% transferred in; 67% live on campus.

Freshmen
Admission: 3,255 applied, 2,042 admitted, 477 enrolled. ***Average high school GPA:*** 3.3. ***Test scores:*** SAT critical reading scores over 500: 48%; SAT math scores over 500: 41%; SAT writing scores over 500: 47%; ACT scores over 18: 92%; SAT critical reading scores over 600: 19%; SAT math scores over 600: 29%; SAT writing scores over 600: 21%; ACT scores over 24: 40%; SAT critical reading scores over 700: 5%; SAT math scores over 700: 5%; SAT writing scores over 700: 3%; ACT scores over 30: 7%.

Retention: 82% of full-time freshmen returned.

FACULTY
Total: 279, 52% full-time, 50% with terminal degrees.

Student/faculty ratio: 11:1.

ACADEMICS
Calendar: semesters. *Degrees:* bachelor's, master's, and doctoral.

Special study options: accelerated degree program, adult/continuing education programs, advanced placement credit, double majors, English as a second language, honors programs, independent study, internships, off-campus study, part-time degree program, services for LD students, student-designed majors, study abroad, summer session for credit.

Unusual degree programs: 3-2 engineering with Washington University in St. Louis; occupational therapy with Washington University; pharmacy with Midwestern University.

Computers: 282 computers/terminals and 318 ports are available on campus for general student use. Students can access the following: computer help desk, free student e-mail accounts, online (class) grades, online (class) registration, online (class) schedules, online degree audit; online financials (view and pay bills; view financial aid). Campuswide network is available. 100% of college-owned or -operated housing units are wired for high-speed Internet access. Wireless service is available via classrooms, computer centers, computer labs, dorm rooms, learning centers, libraries, student centers.

STUDENT LIFE
Housing options: on-campus residence required through junior year; coed, women-only, special housing for students with disabilities. Campus housing is university owned, leased by the school and is provided by a third party. Freshman campus housing is guaranteed.

Activities and organizations: drama/theater group, student-run newspaper, radio station, choral group, University Center Board,

Multicultural Student Council, Student Housing Council, Panhellenic Council, Interfraternity Council, national fraternities, national sororities.

Athletics Member NCAA. All Division III. ***Intercollegiate sports:*** baseball M, basketball M/W, cheerleading M/W, cross-country running M/W, football M, golf M/W, soccer M/W, softball W, swimming and diving M/W, tennis W, track and field M/W, volleyball W, wrestling M. ***Intramural sports:*** basketball M/W, bowling M/W, football M, soccer M/W, softball M/W, volleyball M/W, wrestling M.

Campus security: 24-hour emergency response devices and patrols, late-night transport/escort service, controlled dormitory access, emergency notification program provides communication of a critical event to the campus community.

Student services: health clinic, personal/psychological counseling.

COSTS & FINANCIAL AID

Costs (2014–15) ***Comprehensive fee:*** $38,860 includes full-time tuition ($28,828), mandatory fees ($792), and room and board ($9240). Part-time tuition: $964 per credit hour. ***Required fees:*** $22 per credit hour part-time. ***College room only:*** $4820. Room and board charges vary according to board plan and housing facility. ***Payment plan:*** installment. ***Waivers:*** employees or children of employees.

Financial Aid Of all full-time matriculated undergraduates who enrolled in 2013, 1,898 applied for aid, 1,667 were judged to have need, 898 had their need fully met. 496 Federal Work-Study jobs (averaging $1027). 344 state and other part-time jobs (averaging $814). In 2013, 207 non-need-based awards were made. ***Average percent of need met:*** 92. ***Average financial aid package:*** $23,190. ***Average need-based loan:*** $4599. ***Average need-based gift aid:*** $9054. ***Average non-need-based aid:*** $13,037. ***Average indebtedness upon graduation:*** $31,989.

APPLYING

Standardized Tests *Required:* SAT or ACT (for admission).

Options: electronic application, deferred entrance.

Required: high school transcript, minimum 2.0 GPA, 2 letters of recommendation. ***Required for some:*** audition for music/theatre, art portfolio review. ***Recommended:*** interview.

Application deadlines: rolling (freshmen), rolling (out-of-state freshmen), rolling (transfers).

Notification: continuous (freshmen), continuous (out-of-state freshmen), continuous (transfers).

CONTACT

Mr. Lin Stoner, Director, Office of Admission, Millikin University, 1184 West Main Street, Decatur, IL 62522-2084. *Phone:* 217-424-6210. *Toll-free phone:* 800-373-7733. *Fax:* 217-425-4669. *E-mail:* admis@millikin.edu.

Monmouth College

Monmouth, Illinois

http://www.monmouthcollege.edu/

- **Independent** 4-year, founded 1853, affiliated with Presbyterian Church
- **Small-town** 112-acre campus
- **Endowment** $99.2 million
- **Coed** 1,300 undergraduate students, 98% full-time, 54% women, 46% men
- **Moderately difficult** entrance level, 69% of applicants were admitted

UNDERGRAD STUDENTS

1,278 full-time, 22 part-time. Students come from 29 states and territories; 23 other countries; 8% are from out of state; 11% Black or African American, non-Hispanic/Latino; 13% Hispanic/Latino; 1% Asian, non-Hispanic/Latino; 0.1% Native Hawaiian or other Pacific Islander, non-Hispanic/Latino; 0.6% American Indian or Alaska Native, non-Hispanic/Latino; 1% Two or more races, non-Hispanic/Latino; 5% Race/ethnicity unknown; 4% international; 3% transferred in; 92% live on campus.

Freshmen

Admission: 2,849 applied, 1,969 admitted, 394 enrolled. ***Average high school GPA:*** 3.2. ***Test scores:*** ACT scores over 18: 93%; ACT scores over 24: 35%; ACT scores over 30: 5%.

Retention: 78% of full-time freshmen returned.

FACULTY

Total: 133, 69% full-time, 74% with terminal degrees.

Student/faculty ratio: 12:1.

ACADEMICS

Calendar: semesters. *Degree:* bachelor's.

Special study options: academic remediation for entering students, advanced placement credit, double majors, English as a second language, honors programs, independent study, internships, off-campus study, part-time degree program, services for LD students, student-designed majors, study abroad. ***ROTC:*** Army (c).

Unusual degree programs: engineering with Case Western Reserve University; University of Southern California (joint five-year and six-year coordinated programs); Illinois Institute of Technology; nursing with Rush University College of Nursing; 3-2 Architecture program with Washington University - St. Louis; joint five-year and six-year occupational therapy and medical technology Masters programs with Rush University; atmospheric science with Creighton University.

Computers: 140 computers/terminals are available on campus for general student use. Students can access the following: campus intranet, computer help desk, free student e-mail accounts, online (class) grades, online (class) registration, online (class) schedules, 11 PC labs and 3 specialized Mac labs. Campuswide network is available. 100% of college-owned or -operated housing units are wired for high-speed Internet access. Wireless service is available via entire campus.

STUDENT LIFE

Housing options: on-campus residence required through senior year; coed, men-only, women-only, special housing for students with disabilities. Campus housing is university owned. Freshman campus housing is guaranteed.

Activities and organizations: drama/theater group, student-run newspaper, radio and television station, choral group, marching band, Fighting Scots Marching Band and Jazz Band, Associated Students of Monmouth College, Crimson Masque (theatre), Alternative Spring Break, Coalition for Ethnic Awareness, national fraternities, national sororities.

Athletics Member NCAA. All Division III. ***Intercollegiate sports:*** baseball M, basketball M/W, cross-country running M/W, football M, golf M/W, lacrosse M/W, soccer M/W, softball W, swimming and diving M/W, tennis M/W, track and field M/W, volleyball W, water polo M/W. ***Intramural sports:*** archery M/W, badminton M/W, baseball M, cheerleading W(c), soccer M/W, swimming and diving M/W, table tennis M/W, tennis M/W, ultimate Frisbee M/W, volleyball M/W, water polo M(c)/W(c), wrestling M.

Campus security: 24-hour emergency response devices, late-night transport/escort service, controlled dormitory access, night security.

Student services: personal/psychological counseling.

COSTS & FINANCIAL AID

Costs (2014–15) ***One-time required fee:*** $190. ***Comprehensive fee:*** $42,260 includes full-time tuition ($34,200) and room and board ($8060). Full-time tuition and fees vary according to course load. ***Room and board:*** Room and board charges vary according to board plan and housing facility. ***Payment plan:*** installment. ***Waivers:*** employees or children of employees.

Financial Aid Of all full-time matriculated undergraduates who enrolled in 2014, 1,175 applied for aid, 1,100 were judged to have need, 199 had their need fully met. In 2014, 75 non-need-based awards were made. ***Average percent of need met:*** 87. ***Average financial aid package:*** $30,380. ***Average need-based loan:*** $4553. ***Average need-based gift aid:*** $25,285. ***Average non-need-based aid:*** $15,703. ***Average indebtedness upon graduation:*** $31,154.

APPLYING

Standardized Tests *Required:* SAT or ACT (for admission).

Options: electronic application, deferred entrance.

Required: high school transcript. ***Required for some:*** interview. ***Recommended:*** essay or personal statement, minimum 2.7 GPA, interview.

Application deadlines: rolling (freshmen), rolling (transfers).

Notification: continuous (freshmen), continuous (transfers).

CONTACT
Mr. Michael Blaesing, Director of Admissions, Monmouth College, 700 East Broadway, Monmouth, IL 61462-1988. *Phone:* 309-457-2132. *Toll-free phone:* 800-747-2687. *Fax:* 309-457-2141. *E-mail:* admissions@monmouthcollege.edu.

North Central College

Naperville, Illinois

http://www.northcentralcollege.edu/

- **Independent United Methodist** comprehensive, founded 1861
- **Suburban** 65-acre campus with easy access to Chicago
- **Endowment** $109.5 million
- **Coed** 2,782 undergraduate students, 93% full-time, 55% women, 45% men
- **Moderately difficult** entrance level, 60% of applicants were admitted

UNDERGRAD STUDENTS
2,599 full-time, 183 part-time. Students come from 33 states and territories; 32 other countries; 7% are from out of state; 4% Black or African American, non-Hispanic/Latino; 9% Hispanic/Latino; 2% Asian, non-Hispanic/Latino; 0.1% Native Hawaiian or other Pacific Islander, non-Hispanic/Latino; 0.1% American Indian or Alaska Native, non-Hispanic/Latino; 3% Two or more races, non-Hispanic/Latino; 8% Race/ethnicity unknown; 2% international; 10% transferred in; 55% live on campus.

Freshmen
Admission: 5,807 applied, 3,475 admitted, 576 enrolled. ***Average high school GPA:*** 3.59. ***Test scores:*** ACT scores over 18: 100%; ACT scores over 24: 66%; ACT scores over 30: 10%.
Retention: 78% of full-time freshmen returned.

FACULTY
Total: 267, 52% full-time, 70% with terminal degrees.
Student/faculty ratio: 15:1.

ACADEMICS
Calendar: quarters. *Degrees:* bachelor's, master's, and postbachelor's certificates.
Special study options: academic remediation for entering students, accelerated degree program, advanced placement credit, double majors, English as a second language, honors programs, independent study, internships, off-campus study, part-time degree program, services for LD students, student-designed majors, study abroad, summer session for credit. ***ROTC:*** Army (c), Air Force (c).
Unusual degree programs: 3-2 engineering with Washington University in St. Louis; University of Illinois at Urbana-Champaign; Marquette University; University of Minnesota, Twin Cities Campus.
Computers: 325 computers/terminals are available on campus for general student use. Students can access the following: campus intranet, computer help desk, free student e-mail accounts, online (class) grades, online (class) registration, online (class) schedules, software packages. Campuswide network is available. 100% of college-owned or -operated housing units are wired for high-speed Internet access. Wireless service is available via classrooms, computer centers, computer labs, dorm rooms, learning centers, libraries, student centers.

STUDENT LIFE
Housing options: on-campus residence required through sophomore year; coed, men-only, women-only, special housing for students with disabilities. Campus housing is university owned. Freshman applicants given priority for college housing.
Activities and organizations: drama/theater group, student-run newspaper, radio station, choral group, College Union Activities Board, WONC (student radio station), Cardinals in Action (service group), ENACTUS (Students in Free Enterprise SIFE), Residence Hall Association.
Athletics Member NCAA. All Division III. ***Intercollegiate sports:*** baseball M, basketball M/W, cheerleading W, cross-country running M/W, football M, golf M/W, lacrosse W, soccer M/W, softball W, swimming and diving M/W, tennis M/W, track and field M/W, volleyball W, wrestling M. ***Intramural sports:*** badminton M/W, basketball M/W, football M/W, golf M/W, racquetball M/W, soccer M/W, softball M/W, ultimate Frisbee M/W, volleyball M/W.
Campus security: 24-hour emergency response devices and patrols, late-night transport/escort service, controlled dormitory access.
Student services: health clinic, personal/psychological counseling.

COSTS & FINANCIAL AID
Costs (2014–15) ***Comprehensive fee:*** $44,025 includes full-time tuition ($34,050), mandatory fees ($180), and room and board ($9795). Part-time tuition: $825 per credit hour. Part-time tuition and fees vary according to course load. ***Required fees:*** $20 per term part-time. ***College room only:*** $6795. Room and board charges vary according to housing facility. ***Payment plan:*** installment. ***Waivers:*** senior citizens and employees or children of employees.
Financial Aid Of all full-time matriculated undergraduates who enrolled in 2013, 2,191 applied for aid, 1,959 were judged to have need, 372 had their need fully met. 1,395 Federal Work-Study jobs (averaging $172). In 2013, 533 non-need-based awards were made. ***Average percent of need met:*** 73. ***Average financial aid package:*** $23,286. ***Average need-based loan:*** $4766. ***Average need-based gift aid:*** $18,092. ***Average non-need-based aid:*** $13,048. ***Average indebtedness upon graduation:*** $29,047.

APPLYING
Standardized Tests *Required:* SAT or ACT (for admission). *Recommended:* ACT (for admission).
Options: electronic application, deferred entrance.
Application fee: $25.
Required: high school transcript, minimum 2.5 GPA. ***Required for some:*** interview. ***Recommended:*** essay or personal statement, 1 letter of recommendation.
Application deadlines: rolling (freshmen), rolling (out-of-state freshmen), rolling (transfers).
Notification: continuous (freshmen), continuous (out-of-state freshmen), continuous (transfers).

CONTACT
Ms. Martha Stolze, Dean of Admission, North Central College, 30 North Brainard Street, PO Box 3063, Naperville, IL 60566-7063. *Phone:* 630-637-5800. *Toll-free phone:* 800-411-1861. *Fax:* 630-637-5819. *E-mail:* admissions@noctrl.edu.

Northeastern Illinois University

Chicago, Illinois

http://www.neiu.edu/

- **State-supported** comprehensive, founded 1961
- **Urban** 67-acre campus with easy access to Chicago
- **Coed** 8,943 undergraduate students, 57% full-time, 55% women, 45% men
- **Minimally difficult** entrance level, 60% of applicants were admitted

UNDERGRAD STUDENTS
5,065 full-time, 3,878 part-time. 1% are from out of state; 10% Black or African American, non-Hispanic/Latino; 35% Hispanic/Latino; 9% Asian, non-Hispanic/Latino; 0.3% Native Hawaiian or other Pacific Islander, non-Hispanic/Latino; 0.2% American Indian or Alaska Native, non-Hispanic/Latino; 2% Two or more races, non-Hispanic/Latino; 2% Race/ethnicity unknown; 4% international; 15% transferred in.

Freshmen
Admission: 5,291 applied, 3,181 admitted, 805 enrolled. ***Average high school GPA:*** 2.84. ***Test scores:*** ACT scores over 18: 60%; ACT scores over 24: 10%; ACT scores over 30: 1%.
Retention: 61% of full-time freshmen returned.

FACULTY
Total: 631, 63% full-time, 62% with terminal degrees.
Student/faculty ratio: 15:1.

ACADEMICS
Calendar: semesters. *Degrees:* bachelor's and master's.
Special study options: academic remediation for entering students, adult/continuing education programs, advanced placement credit, cooperative education, distance learning, double majors, English as a second language, external degree program, honors programs, independent study, internships, off-campus study, part-time degree program, services

for LD students, study abroad, summer session for credit. ***ROTC:*** Army (c), Air Force (c).

Computers: 560 computers/terminals are available on campus for general student use. Students can access the following: computer help desk, free student e-mail accounts, online (class) grades, online (class) registration, online (class) schedules, productivity software. Campuswide network is available. Wireless service is available via classrooms, computer centers, computer labs, learning centers, libraries, student centers.

STUDENT LIFE

Housing options: college housing not available.

Activities and organizations: drama/theater group, student-run newspaper, radio station, choral group, Student Government Association, United Greek Council, Anime Club, Honors Society, Latinas in Power, national fraternities, national sororities.

Athletics ***Intramural sports:*** badminton M(c)/W(c), baseball M(c), basketball M(c)/W(c), crew M(c)/W(c), cross-country running M(c)/W(c), football M(c)/W(c), ice hockey M(c)/W(c), racquetball M(c)/W(c), rock climbing M(c)/W(c), soccer M(c)/W(c), softball M(c)/W(c), table tennis M(c)/W(c), tennis M(c)/W(c), volleyball M(c)/W(c), weight lifting M(c)/W(c), wrestling M(c).

Campus security: 24-hour emergency response devices and patrols, late-night transport/escort service.

Student services: health clinic, personal/psychological counseling, women's center.

COSTS & FINANCIAL AID

Costs (2014–15) ***One-time required fee:*** $10. ***Tuition:*** state resident $7296 full-time, $304 per credit hour part-time; nonresident $14,592 full-time, $608 per credit hour part-time. Full-time tuition and fees vary according to course load and degree level. Part-time tuition and fees vary according to course load and degree level. No tuition increase for student's term of enrollment. ***Required fees:*** $1316 full-time, $55 per credit hour part-time, $3 per term part-time. ***Payment plan:*** deferred payment. ***Waivers:*** senior citizens and employees or children of employees.

Financial Aid Of all full-time matriculated undergraduates who enrolled in 2014, 3,825 applied for aid, 3,378 were judged to have need, 120 had their need fully met. In 2014, 79 non-need-based awards were made. ***Average percent of need met:*** 18. ***Average financial aid package:*** $8284. ***Average need-based loan:*** $4278. ***Average need-based gift aid:*** $6730. ***Average non-need-based aid:*** $1956. ***Average indebtedness upon graduation:*** $13,366.

APPLYING

Standardized Tests *Required:* SAT or ACT (for admission).

Options: electronic application, deferred entrance.

Application fee: $30.

Required: high school transcript.

Application deadlines: 7/1 (freshmen), 7/1 (transfers).

Notification: 9/1 (freshmen), continuous (transfers).

CONTACT

Ms. Zarrin Kerwell, Admissions Counselor, Northeastern Illinois University, 5500 North St. Louis Avenue, Chicago, IL 60625. *Phone:* 773-442-4026. *Fax:* 773-794-6243. *E-mail:* admrec@neiu.edu.

Northern Illinois University

De Kalb, Illinois

http://www.niu.edu/

- **State-supported** university, founded 1895
- **Small-town** 650-acre campus with easy access to Chicago
- **Endowment** $3.5 million
- **Coed** 15,435 undergraduate students, 87% full-time, 49% women, 51% men
- **Moderately difficult** entrance level, 51% of applicants were admitted

UNDERGRAD STUDENTS

13,489 full-time, 1,946 part-time. Students come from 36 states and territories; 45 other countries; 3% are from out of state; 16% Black or African American, non-Hispanic/Latino; 14% Hispanic/Latino; 5% Asian, non-Hispanic/Latino; 0.1% Native Hawaiian or other Pacific Islander, non-Hispanic/Latino; 0.1% American Indian or Alaska Native, non-Hispanic/Latino; 3% Two or more races, non-Hispanic/Latino; 1% Race/ethnicity unknown; 2% international; 12% transferred in; 28% live on campus.

Freshmen

Admission: 19,814 applied, 10,083 admitted, 2,542 enrolled. ***Average high school GPA:*** 3.15. ***Test scores:*** ACT scores over 18: 89%; ACT scores over 24: 34%; ACT scores over 30: 4%.

Retention: 71% of full-time freshmen returned.

FACULTY

Total: 1,099, 77% full-time, 74% with terminal degrees.

Student/faculty ratio: 15:1.

ACADEMICS

Calendar: semesters. *Degrees:* bachelor's, master's, and doctoral.

Special study options: accelerated degree program, adult/continuing education programs, advanced placement credit, cooperative education, double majors, honors programs, independent study, internships, off-campus study, part-time degree program, services for LD students, student-designed majors, study abroad, summer session for credit. ***ROTC:*** Army (b), Air Force (c).

Computers: 1,500 computers/terminals are available on campus for general student use. Students can access the following: computer help desk, free student e-mail accounts, online (class) grades, online (class) registration, online (class) schedules. Campuswide network is available. 90% of college-owned or -operated housing units are wired for high-speed Internet access. Wireless service is available via entire campus.

STUDENT LIFE

Housing options: on-campus residence required for freshman year; coed. Campus housing is university owned. Freshman applicants given priority for college housing.

Activities and organizations: drama/theater group, student-run newspaper, radio station, choral group, marching band, American Marketing Association, Delta Sigma Pi, Pi Sigma Epsilon, Black Choir, Student Volunteer Choir, national fraternities, national sororities.

Athletics Member NCAA. All Division I except football (Division I-A). ***Intercollegiate sports:*** baseball M(s), basketball M(s)/W(s), cross-country running W, golf M(s)/W(s), gymnastics W(s), soccer M(s)/W(s), softball W(s), swimming and diving M(s)/W(s), tennis M(s)/W(s), volleyball W(s), wrestling M(s). ***Intramural sports:*** archery M(c)/W(c), badminton M/W, basketball M/W, bowling M(c)/W(c), cross-country running W, football M/W, golf M/W, ice hockey M(c)/W(c), lacrosse M(c)/W(c), racquetball M/W, rugby M(c)/W(c), skiing (downhill) M(c)/W(c), soccer M/W, softball M/W, table tennis M/W, tennis M/W, track and field M(c)/W(c), volleyball M/W, water polo M(c)/W(c), weight lifting M(c)/W(c).

Campus security: 24-hour emergency response devices and patrols, student patrols, late-night transport/escort service, controlled dormitory access.

Student services: health clinic, personal/psychological counseling, women's center, legal services.

COSTS & FINANCIAL AID

Costs (2014–15) ***Tuition:*** state resident $9253 full-time; nonresident $18,506 full-time. ***Required fees:*** $2739 full-time. ***Room and board:*** $11,790. Room and board charges vary according to board plan and housing facility.

Financial Aid Of all full-time matriculated undergraduates who enrolled in 2013, 12,180 applied for aid, 10,754 were judged to have need, 572 had their need fully met. 7,082 Federal Work-Study jobs (averaging $2689). In 2013, 1041 non-need-based awards were made. ***Average percent of need met:*** 59. ***Average financial aid package:*** $12,284. ***Average need-based loan:*** $4418. ***Average need-based gift aid:*** $8067. ***Average non-need-based aid:*** $3867. ***Average indebtedness upon graduation:*** $33,234.

APPLYING

Standardized Tests *Required:* SAT or ACT (for admission).

Options: electronic application.

Application fee: $40.

Required: high school transcript, high school rank.

Application deadlines: 8/1 (freshmen), 8/1 (transfers).

Notification: continuous (freshmen), continuous (transfers).

CONTACT
Dr. Dani Rollins, Director of Admissions, Northern Illinois University, Student Affairs & Enrollment Management, DeKalb, IL 60115-2857. *Phone:* 815-753-0446. *Toll-free phone:* 800-892-3050. *E-mail:* admissions@niu.edu.

North Park University

Chicago, Illinois

http://www.northpark.edu/

- **Independent** comprehensive, founded 1891, affiliated with Evangelical Covenant Church
- **Urban** 30-acre campus
- **Coed**
- **Moderately difficult** entrance level

FACULTY
Student/faculty ratio: 13:1.

ACADEMICS
Calendar: semesters. *Degrees:* bachelor's, master's, doctoral, and post-master's certificates.

STUDENT LIFE
Housing options: on-campus residence required through junior year; men-only, women-only. Campus housing is university owned. Freshman campus housing is guaranteed.

Activities and organizations: drama/theater group, student-run newspaper, choral group.

Athletics Member NCAA. All Division III.

Campus security: 24-hour emergency response devices and patrols, late-night transport/escort service, controlled dormitory access.

Student services: health clinic, personal/psychological counseling.

COSTS & FINANCIAL AID
Costs (2014–15) ***Comprehensive fee:*** $32,820 includes full-time tuition ($24,540), mandatory fees ($60), and room and board ($8220). Part-time tuition: $735 per credit. ***College room only:*** $4400. Room and board charges vary according to board plan and housing facility.

Financial Aid Of all full-time matriculated undergraduates who enrolled in 2008, 158 Federal Work-Study jobs (averaging $1500).

APPLYING
Standardized Tests *Required:* SAT or ACT (for admission).

Options: electronic application, early admission.

Application fee: $40.

Required: essay or personal statement, high school transcript, minimum 2.8 GPA, 2 letters of recommendation. ***Required for some:*** interview. ***Recommended:*** minimum 3.0 GPA.

CONTACT
Office of Admissions, North Park University, 3225 West Foster Avenue, Chicago, IL 60625-4895. *Phone:* 773-244-5500. *Toll-free phone:* 800-888-NPC8. *Fax:* 773-583-0858. *E-mail:* afao@northpark.edu.

Northwestern University

Evanston, Illinois

http://www.northwestern.edu/

- **Independent** university, founded 1851
- **Suburban** 250-acre campus with easy access to Chicago
- **Coed** 9,177 undergraduate students, 92% full-time, 51% women, 49% men
- **Most difficult** entrance level, 13% of applicants were admitted

UNDERGRAD STUDENTS
8,419 full-time, 758 part-time. Students come from 76 other countries; 67% are from out of state; 6% Black or African American, non-Hispanic/Latino; 11% Hispanic/Latino; 17% Asian, non-Hispanic/Latino; 0.1% American Indian or Alaska Native, non-Hispanic/Latino; 5% Two or more races, non-Hispanic/Latino; 2% Race/ethnicity unknown; 7% international; 0.6% transferred in; 88% live on campus.

Freshmen
Admission: 33,673 applied, 4,415 admitted, 2,043 enrolled. ***Test scores:*** SAT critical reading scores over 500: 100%; SAT math scores over 500: 100%; ACT scores over 18: 100%; SAT critical reading scores over 600: 95%; SAT math scores over 600: 96%; ACT scores over 24: 99%; SAT critical reading scores over 700: 72%; SAT math scores over 700: 78%; ACT scores over 30: 85%.

Retention: 97% of full-time freshmen returned.

FACULTY
Total: 1,629, 87% full-time.

Student/faculty ratio: 7:1.

ACADEMICS
Calendar: semesters. *Degrees:* certificates, bachelor's, master's, doctoral, and post-master's certificates.

Special study options: accelerated degree program, adult/continuing education programs, advanced placement credit, cooperative education, double majors, honors programs, independent study, internships, part-time degree program, services for LD students, student-designed majors, study abroad, summer session for credit. ***ROTC:*** Army (c), Navy (b), Air Force (c).

Computers: Students can access the following: campus intranet, computer help desk, free student e-mail accounts, online (class) grades, online (class) registration, online (class) schedules. Campuswide network is available. 100% of college-owned or -operated housing units are wired for high-speed Internet access. Wireless service is available via entire campus.

STUDENT LIFE
Housing options: coed, men-only, women-only. Campus housing is university owned. Freshman campus housing is guaranteed.

Activities and organizations: drama/theater group, student-run newspaper, radio and television station, choral group, marching band, national fraternities, national sororities.

Athletics Member NCAA. All Division I.

Campus security: 24-hour emergency response devices and patrols, late-night transport/escort service, controlled dormitory access.

Student services: health clinic, personal/psychological counseling, women's center.

COSTS & FINANCIAL AID
Costs (2014–15) ***Comprehensive fee:*** $61,640 includes full-time tuition ($46,836), mandatory fees ($415), and room and board ($14,389). ***Room and board:*** Room and board charges vary according to board plan and housing facility. ***Payment plan:*** installment.

Financial Aid Of all full-time matriculated undergraduates who enrolled in 2013, 4,109 applied for aid, 3,720 were judged to have need, 3,720 had their need fully met. In 2013, 386 non-need-based awards were made. ***Average percent of need met:*** 100. ***Average financial aid package:*** $40,978. ***Average need-based loan:*** $4926. ***Average need-based gift aid:*** $37,674. ***Average non-need-based aid:*** $2480. ***Average indebtedness upon graduation:*** $19,864. ***Financial aid deadline:*** 3/5.

APPLYING
Standardized Tests *Required:* SAT or ACT (for admission). *Required for some:* SAT Subject Tests (for admission).

Options: electronic application, early admission, early decision, deferred entrance.

Application fee: $75.

Required: essay or personal statement, high school transcript, 1 letter of recommendation. ***Required for some:*** Audition for music program.

Application deadlines: 1/1 (freshmen), 3/15 (transfers).

Early decision deadline: 11/1.

Notification: 4/1 (freshmen), continuous (transfers), 12/15 (early decision).

CONTACT
Mr. Christopher Watson, Dean of Undergraduate Admission, Northwestern University, PO Box 3060, Evanston, IL 60208. *Phone:* 847-491-7271. *E-mail:* ug-admission@northwestern.edu.

★ Olivet Nazarene University

Bourbonnais, Illinois

http://www.olivet.edu/

- **Independent** comprehensive, founded 1907, affiliated with Church of the Nazarene
- **Small-town** 200-acre campus with easy access to Chicago
- **Endowment** $24.0 million
- **Coed** 3,521 undergraduate students, 88% full-time, 62% women, 38% men
- **Minimally difficult** entrance level, 74% of applicants were admitted

UNDERGRAD STUDENTS

3,082 full-time, 439 part-time. Students come from 45 states and territories; 14 other countries; 32% are from out of state; 7% Black or African American, non-Hispanic/Latino; 7% Hispanic/Latino; 2% Asian, non-Hispanic/Latino; 0.2% Native Hawaiian or other Pacific Islander, non-Hispanic/Latino; 0.1% American Indian or Alaska Native, non-Hispanic/Latino; 2% Two or more races, non-Hispanic/Latino; 0.9% international; 10% transferred in.

Freshmen

Admission: 4,783 applied, 3,563 admitted, 780 enrolled.

Retention: 77% of full-time freshmen returned.

FACULTY

Total: 463, 30% full-time.

Student/faculty ratio: 16:1.

ACADEMICS

Calendar: semesters. *Degrees:* associate, bachelor's, master's, and doctoral.

Special study options: academic remediation for entering students, adult/continuing education programs, advanced placement credit, cooperative education, distance learning, double majors, honors programs, independent study, internships, off-campus study, part-time degree program, services for LD students, study abroad, summer session for credit. ***ROTC:*** Army (b).

Computers: Students can access the following: campus intranet, computer help desk, free student e-mail accounts, online (class) grades, online (class) registration, online (class) schedules. Campuswide network is available. Wireless service is available via entire campus.

STUDENT LIFE

Housing options: on-campus residence required through senior year; men-only, women-only. Campus housing is university owned. Freshman campus housing is guaranteed.

Activities and organizations: drama/theater group, student-run newspaper, radio station, choral group, Fellowship of Christian Athletes, C.A.U.S.E. (College and University Serving and Enabling), Diakonia, Student Education Association, Women's Residence Association.

Athletics Member NAIA, NCCAA. ***Intercollegiate sports:*** baseball M(s), basketball M(s)/W(s), cheerleading M(s)/W(s), cross-country running M(s)/W(s), football M(s), golf M(s), soccer M(s)/W(s), softball W(s), tennis M(s)/W(s), track and field M(s)/W(s), volleyball W(s). ***Intramural sports:*** baseball M, basketball M/W, football M/W, golf M/W, racquetball M/W, soccer M/W, softball M/W, table tennis M/W, tennis M/W, track and field M/W, volleyball M/W.

Campus security: 24-hour patrols, late-night transport/escort service.

Student services: health clinic, personal/psychological counseling.

COSTS & FINANCIAL AID

Costs (2015–16) ***Comprehensive fee:*** $40,690 includes full-time tuition ($31,950), mandatory fees ($840), and room and board ($7900). Full-time tuition and fees vary according to course load. Part-time tuition: $1332 per semester hour. Part-time tuition and fees vary according to course load. ***Room and board:*** Room and board charges vary according to board plan. ***Payment plan:*** installment. ***Waivers:*** employees or children of employees.

Financial Aid Of all full-time matriculated undergraduates who enrolled in 2014, 2,698 applied for aid, 2,473 were judged to have need, 612 had their need fully met. 353 Federal Work-Study jobs (averaging $1380). 911 state and other part-time jobs (averaging $1302). In 2014, 524 non-need-based awards were made. ***Average percent of need met:*** 80. ***Average financial aid package:*** $24,719. ***Average need-based loan:*** $4522.

Average need-based gift aid: $19,925. ***Average non-need-based aid:*** $12,655. ***Average indebtedness upon graduation:*** $32,906.

APPLYING

Standardized Tests *Required:* ACT (for admission).

Options: electronic application, deferred entrance.

Application fee: $25.

Required: high school transcript, minimum 2.0 GPA, 2 letters of recommendation. ***Recommended:*** essay or personal statement, interview.

Application deadlines: rolling (freshmen), rolling (transfers).

Notification: continuous (freshmen), continuous (transfers).

CONTACT

Brian Robbins SAC, Associate Director of Admissions, Olivet Nazarene University, One University Avenue, Bourbonnais, IL 60914. *Phone:* 815-928-5572. *Toll-free phone:* 800-648-1463. *E-mail:* blrobbins@olivet.edu.

See previous page for display ad and page 1560 for the College Close-Up.

Principia College

Elsah, Illinois

http://www.principiacollege.edu/

- **Independent Christian Science** 4-year, founded 1910
- **Rural** 2600-acre campus with easy access to St. Louis
- **Endowment** $557.2 million
- **Coed** 495 undergraduate students, 99% full-time, 51% women, 49% men
- **Moderately difficult** entrance level, 79% of applicants were admitted

UNDERGRAD STUDENTS

488 full-time, 7 part-time. Students come from 36 states and territories; 32 other countries; 94% are from out of state; 1% Black or African American, non-Hispanic/Latino; 2% Hispanic/Latino; 0.8% Asian, non-Hispanic/Latino; 0.6% Native Hawaiian or other Pacific Islander, non-Hispanic/Latino; 0.4% American Indian or Alaska Native, non-Hispanic/Latino; 2% Two or more races, non-Hispanic/Latino; 4% Race/ethnicity unknown; 19% international; 3% transferred in; 100% live on campus.

Freshmen

Admission: 211 applied, 167 admitted, 117 enrolled. ***Average high school GPA:*** 3.4. ***Test scores:*** SAT critical reading scores over 500: 61%; SAT math scores over 500: 68%; SAT writing scores over 500: 50%; ACT scores over 18: 96%; SAT critical reading scores over 600: 34%; SAT math scores over 600: 28%; SAT writing scores over 600: 25%; ACT scores over 24: 59%; SAT critical reading scores over 700: 6%; SAT math scores over 700: 6%; SAT writing scores over 700: 4%; ACT scores over 30: 17%.

Retention: 89% of full-time freshmen returned.

FACULTY

Total: 76, 82% full-time, 55% with terminal degrees.

Student/faculty ratio: 7:1.

ACADEMICS

Calendar: quarters. *Degree:* bachelor's.

Special study options: advanced placement credit, double majors, honors programs, independent study, internships, off-campus study, part-time degree program, student-designed majors, study abroad, summer session for credit.

Unusual degree programs: 3-2 engineering with Washington University in St. Louis, Southern Illinois University at Edwardsville, University of Southern California.

Computers: 100 computers/terminals are available on campus for general student use. Students can access the following: campus intranet, computer help desk, free student e-mail accounts, online (class) grades, online (class) registration, online (class) schedules. Campuswide network is available. 100% of college-owned or -operated housing units are wired for high-speed Internet access. Wireless service is available via classrooms, computer centers, computer labs, dorm rooms, libraries, student centers.

STUDENT LIFE

Housing options: on-campus residence required through senior year; men-only, women-only. Campus housing is university owned. Freshman campus housing is guaranteed.

Activities and organizations: drama/theater group, student-run newspaper, radio and television station, choral group, Christian Science Organization, Community Service Team, International Students Association (Friendship Around the World), Rugby, student government.

Athletics Member NCAA. All Division III. ***Intercollegiate sports:*** baseball M, basketball M/W, cross-country running M/W, lacrosse W(c), rugby M(c), soccer M/W, softball W, swimming and diving M/W, tennis M/W, track and field M/W, volleyball W. ***Intramural sports:*** basketball M/W, soccer M/W, softball M/W.

Campus security: 24-hour emergency response devices and patrols, controlled dormitory access.

Student services: health clinic.

COSTS & FINANCIAL AID

Costs (2015–16) ***Comprehensive fee:*** $38,250 includes full-time tuition ($26,940), mandatory fees ($500), and room and board ($10,810). Full-time tuition and fees vary according to course load. Part-time tuition and fees vary according to course load. ***College room only:*** $5130. Room and board charges vary according to board plan. ***Payment plan:*** installment.

Financial Aid Of all full-time matriculated undergraduates who enrolled in 2014, 382 applied for aid, 349 were judged to have need, 180 had their need fully met. In 2014, 133 non-need-based awards were made. ***Average percent of need met:*** 91. ***Average financial aid package:*** $28,728. ***Average need-based loan:*** $5536. ***Average need-based gift aid:*** $24,591. ***Average non-need-based aid:*** $22,664. ***Average indebtedness upon graduation:*** $23,732.

APPLYING

Standardized Tests *Required:* SAT or ACT (for admission). *Recommended:* SAT Subject Tests (for admission).

Options: electronic application, deferred entrance.

Required: essay or personal statement, high school transcript, minimum 2.3 GPA, 3 letters of recommendation, Christian Science commitment. ***Required for some:*** interview. ***Recommended:*** interview.

Application deadlines: rolling (freshmen), rolling (transfers).

Notification: continuous (freshmen), continuous (transfers).

CONTACT

Mrs. Tami Gavaletz, Director of Admissions and Financial Aid, Principia College, 1 Maybeck Place, Elsah, IL 62028. *Phone:* 618-374-5187. *Toll-free phone:* 800-277-4648 Ext. 2804.

Quincy University

Quincy, Illinois

http://www.quincy.edu/

- **Independent Roman Catholic** comprehensive, founded 1860
- **Small-town** 70-acre campus
- **Endowment** $18.1 million
- **Coed** 1,097 undergraduate students, 93% full-time, 56% women, 44% men
- **Moderately difficult** entrance level, 89% of applicants were admitted

UNDERGRAD STUDENTS

1,019 full-time, 78 part-time. Students come from 24 states and territories; 5 other countries; 28% are from out of state; 10% Black or African American, non-Hispanic/Latino; 3% Hispanic/Latino; 2% Asian, non-Hispanic/Latino; 0.6% Native Hawaiian or other Pacific Islander, non-Hispanic/Latino; 0.6% American Indian or Alaska Native, non-Hispanic/Latino; 1% Two or more races, non-Hispanic/Latino; 10% Race/ethnicity unknown; 0.5% international; 8% transferred in; 57% live on campus.

Freshmen

Admission: 903 applied, 803 admitted, 214 enrolled. ***Average high school GPA:*** 3.41. ***Test scores:*** SAT critical reading scores over 500: 23%; SAT math scores over 500: 23%; ACT scores over 18: 89%; ACT scores over 24: 36%.

Retention: 76% of full-time freshmen returned.

FACULTY

Total: 124, 44% full-time, 48% with terminal degrees.

Student/faculty ratio: 13:1.

ACADEMICS
Calendar: semesters. *Degrees:* associate, bachelor's, and master's.
Special study options: academic remediation for entering students, accelerated degree program, adult/continuing education programs, advanced placement credit, distance learning, double majors, honors programs, independent study, internships, off-campus study, part-time degree program, student-designed majors, study abroad, summer session for credit.
Computers: 179 computers/terminals are available on campus for general student use. Students can access the following: campus intranet, computer help desk, free student e-mail accounts, online (class) grades, online (class) registration, online (class) schedules. Campuswide network is available. 100% of college-owned or -operated housing units are wired for high-speed Internet access. Wireless service is available via classrooms, computer centers, computer labs, dorm rooms, learning centers, libraries, student centers.

STUDENT LIFE
Housing options: on-campus residence required through junior year; coed, special housing for students with disabilities. Campus housing is university owned. Freshman campus housing is guaranteed.
Activities and organizations: drama/theater group, student-run newspaper, choral group, marching band, Student Senate, Kappa Kappa Psi, Student Programming Board, Minority Student Association, Students in Free Enterprise (SIFE), national fraternities, national sororities.
Athletics Member NCAA. All Division II except volleyball (Division I). ***Intercollegiate sports:*** baseball M(s), basketball M(s)/W(s), cheerleading M(c)/W(c), cross-country running M(s)/W(s), football M(s), golf M(s)/W(s), soccer M(s)/W(s), softball W(s), tennis M(s)/W(s), volleyball M(s)/W(s). ***Intramural sports:*** basketball M/W, bowling M/W, football M/W, racquetball M/W, soccer M/W, softball M/W, table tennis M/W, ultimate Frisbee M/W, volleyball M/W.
Campus security: 24-hour emergency response devices and patrols, student patrols, late-night transport/escort service, controlled dormitory access, self-defense education, shuttle buses, lighted pathways/sidewalks.
Student services: health clinic, personal/psychological counseling.

COSTS & FINANCIAL AID
Costs (2015–16) ***Comprehensive fee:*** $36,998 includes full-time tuition ($25,998), mandatory fees ($1000), and room and board ($10,000). Part-time tuition: $700 per semester hour. Part-time tuition and fees vary according to course load. ***Required fees:*** $30 per semester hour part-time. ***College room only:*** $5500. Room and board charges vary according to board plan, housing facility, and student level. ***Payment plan:*** installment. ***Waivers:*** senior citizens and employees or children of employees.
Financial Aid Of all full-time matriculated undergraduates who enrolled in 2014, 944 applied for aid, 880 were judged to have need, 754 had their need fully met. 279 Federal Work-Study jobs (averaging $2000). 153 state and other part-time jobs (averaging $1104). In 2014, 64 non-need-based awards were made. ***Average percent of need met:*** 79. ***Average financial aid package:*** $24,349. ***Average need-based loan:*** $4243. ***Average need-based gift aid:*** $18,114. ***Average non-need-based aid:*** $14,220. ***Average indebtedness upon graduation:*** $27,857.

APPLYING
Standardized Tests *Required:* SAT or ACT (for admission).
Options: electronic application, deferred entrance.
Application fee: $25.
Required: essay or personal statement, high school transcript, minimum 2.5 GPA. ***Required for some:*** 1 letter of recommendation, audition for music majors, portfolio recommended for art majors. ***Recommended:*** interview.
Application deadlines: rolling (freshmen), rolling (out-of-state freshmen), rolling (transfers).
Notification: continuous (freshmen), continuous (out-of-state freshmen), continuous (transfers).

CONTACT
Ms. Abby Wayman, Associate Director, Admissions, Quincy University, Admissions Office, 1800 College Avenue, Quincy, IL 62301-2699. *Phone:* 217-228-5432 Ext. 3414. *Toll-free phone:* 800-688-4295. *E-mail:* admissions@quincy.edu.

Rasmussen College Aurora

Aurora, Illinois

http://www.rasmussen.edu/

- **Proprietary** 4-year, part of Rasmussen College System
- **Suburban** campus
- **Coed** 326 undergraduate students, 57% full-time, 78% women, 22% men
- **Minimally difficult** entrance level

UNDERGRAD STUDENTS
185 full-time, 141 part-time.

Freshmen
Admission: 12 enrolled.

FACULTY
Total: 13, 23% full-time.
Student/faculty ratio: 22:1.

ACADEMICS
Degrees: certificates, diplomas, associate, and bachelor's.
Special study options: academic remediation for entering students, accelerated degree program, adult/continuing education programs, distance learning, double majors, internships, part-time degree program, summer session for credit.
Computers: 87 computers/terminals are available on campus for general student use. Students can access the following: computer help desk, free student e-mail accounts, online (class) grades, online (class) schedules. Campuswide network is available. Wireless service is available via entire campus.

STUDENT LIFE
Housing options: college housing not available.

COSTS
Costs (2014–15) ***Tuition:*** $10,764 full-time, $350 per credit hour part-time. Full-time tuition and fees vary according to course level, course load, degree level, location, and program. Part-time tuition and fees vary according to course level, course load, degree level, location, and program. No tuition increase for student's term of enrollment. ***Required fees:*** $1350 full-time. ***Payment plans:*** installment, deferred payment. ***Waivers:*** employees or children of employees.

APPLYING
Standardized Tests *Required:* Internal Exam (for admission).
Options: electronic application, early admission, deferred entrance.
Required: high school transcript, minimum 2.0 GPA. ***Required for some:*** interview.
Application deadlines: rolling (freshmen), rolling (transfers).

CONTACT
Susan Hammerstrom, Director of Admissions, Rasmussen College Aurora, 2363 Sequoia Drive, Aurora, IL 60506. *Phone:* 630-888-3500. *Toll-free phone:* 888-549-6755. *E-mail:* susan.hammerstrom@rasmussen.edu.

Rasmussen College Mokena/Tinley Park

Mokena, Illinois

http://www.rasmussen.edu/

- **Proprietary** 4-year, part of Rasmussen College System
- **Suburban** campus
- **Coed** 281 undergraduate students, 63% full-time, 86% women, 14% men
- **Minimally difficult** entrance level

UNDERGRAD STUDENTS
178 full-time, 103 part-time.

Freshmen
Admission: 8 enrolled.

FACULTY
Total: 12, 8% full-time.
Student/faculty ratio: 22:1.

ACADEMICS
Degrees: certificates, diplomas, associate, and bachelor's.
Special study options: academic remediation for entering students, accelerated degree program, adult/continuing education programs, distance learning, double majors, internships, part-time degree program, summer session for credit.
Computers: 73 computers/terminals are available on campus for general student use. Students can access the following: computer help desk, free student e-mail accounts, online (class) grades, online (class) schedules. Campuswide network is available. Wireless service is available via entire campus.

STUDENT LIFE
Housing options: college housing not available.

COSTS
Costs (2014–15) ***Tuition:*** $10,764 full-time, $310 per credit hour part-time. Full-time tuition and fees vary according to course level, course load, degree level, location, and program. Part-time tuition and fees vary according to course level, course load, degree level, location, and program. No tuition increase for student's term of enrollment. ***Required fees:*** $1350 full-time. ***Payment plans:*** installment, deferred payment. ***Waivers:*** employees or children of employees.

APPLYING
Standardized Tests *Required:* Internal Exam (for admission).
Options: electronic application, early admission, deferred entrance.
Required: high school transcript, minimum 2.0 GPA. ***Required for some:*** interview.
Application deadlines: rolling (freshmen), rolling (transfers).

CONTACT
Susan Hammerstrom, Director of Admissions, Rasmussen College Mokena/Tinley Park, 8650 West Spring Lake Road, Mokena, IL 60448. *Phone:* 815-534-3300. *Toll-free phone:* 888-549-6755.

Rasmussen College Rockford

Rockford, Illinois

http://www.rasmussen.edu/

- **Proprietary** 4-year, part of Rasmussen College System
- **Suburban** campus
- **Coed** 690 undergraduate students, 55% full-time, 79% women, 21% men
- **Minimally difficult** entrance level

UNDERGRAD STUDENTS
377 full-time, 313 part-time.

Freshmen
Admission: 41 enrolled.

FACULTY
Total: 27, 44% full-time.
Student/faculty ratio: 22:1.

ACADEMICS
Degrees: certificates, diplomas, associate, and bachelor's.
Special study options: academic remediation for entering students, accelerated degree program, adult/continuing education programs, distance learning, double majors, internships, part-time degree program, summer session for credit.
Computers: 103 computers/terminals are available on campus for general student use. Students can access the following: computer help desk, free student e-mail accounts, online (class) grades, online (class) schedules. Campuswide network is available. Wireless service is available via entire campus.

STUDENT LIFE
Housing options: college housing not available.

COSTS
Costs (2014–15) ***Tuition:*** $10,764 full-time, $310 per credit hour part-time. Full-time tuition and fees vary according to course level, course load, degree level, location, and program. Part-time tuition and fees vary according to course level, course load, degree level, location, and program. No tuition increase for student's term of enrollment. ***Required fees:*** $1350 full-time. ***Payment plans:*** installment, deferred payment. ***Waivers:*** employees or children of employees.

APPLYING
Standardized Tests *Required:* Internal Exam (for admission).
Options: electronic application, early admission, deferred entrance.
Required: high school transcript, minimum 2.0 GPA. ***Required for some:*** interview.
Application deadlines: rolling (freshmen), rolling (transfers).

CONTACT
Susan Hammerstrom, Director of Admissions, Rasmussen College Rockford, 6000 East State Street, Fourth Floor, Rockford, IL 61108-2513. *Phone:* 815-316-4800. *Toll-free phone:* 888-549-6755. *E-mail:* susan.hammerstrom@rasmussen.edu.

Rasmussen College Romeoville/Joliet

Romeoville, Illinois

http://www.rasmussen.edu/

- **Proprietary** 4-year, part of Rasmussen College System
- **Suburban** campus
- **Coed** 554 undergraduate students, 49% full-time, 80% women, 20% men
- **Minimally difficult** entrance level

UNDERGRAD STUDENTS
270 full-time, 284 part-time.

Freshmen
Admission: 24 enrolled.

FACULTY
Total: 31, 32% full-time.
Student/faculty ratio: 22:1.

ACADEMICS
Degrees: certificates, diplomas, associate, and bachelor's.
Special study options: academic remediation for entering students, accelerated degree program, adult/continuing education programs, distance learning, double majors, internships, part-time degree program, summer session for credit.
Computers: 87 computers/terminals are available on campus for general student use. Students can access the following: computer help desk, free student e-mail accounts, online (class) grades, online (class) schedules. Campuswide network is available. Wireless service is available via entire campus.

STUDENT LIFE
Housing options: college housing not available.

COSTS
Costs (2014–15) ***Tuition:*** $10,764 full-time, $310 per credit hour part-time. Full-time tuition and fees vary according to course level, course load, degree level, location, and program. Part-time tuition and fees vary according to course level, course load, degree level, location, and program. No tuition increase for student's term of enrollment. ***Required fees:*** $1350 full-time. ***Payment plans:*** installment, deferred payment. ***Waivers:*** employees or children of employees.

APPLYING
Standardized Tests *Required:* Internal Exam (for admission).
Options: electronic application, early admission, deferred entrance.
Required: high school transcript, minimum 2.0 GPA. ***Required for some:*** interview.
Application deadlines: rolling (freshmen), rolling (transfers).

CONTACT
Susan Hammerstrom, Director of Admissions, Rasmussen College Romeoville/Joliet, 1400 W. Normantown Road, Romeoville, IL 60446. *Phone:* 815-306-2600. *Toll-free phone:* 888-549-6755. *E-mail:* susan.hammerstrom@rasmussen.edu.

Resurrection University

Chicago, Illinois

http://www.resu.edu/

- **Independent** upper-level, founded 1982
- **Urban** 10-acre campus with easy access to Chicago
- **Endowment** $1.5 million
- **Coed**
- **Moderately difficult** entrance level

FACULTY
Student/faculty ratio: 10:1.

ACADEMICS
Calendar: semesters. *Degrees:* certificates, bachelor's, and master's.

STUDENT LIFE
Housing options: college housing not available.

Campus security: 24-hour emergency response devices and patrols, late-night transport/escort service.

Student services: personal/psychological counseling.

COSTS & FINANCIAL AID
Costs (2014–15) ***Tuition:*** $11,923 full-time, $808 per credit hour part-time. ***Required fees:*** $290 full-time, $140 per term part-time. ***Payment plans:*** installment, deferred payment.

Financial Aid Of all full-time matriculated undergraduates who enrolled in 2013, 257 applied for aid, 257 were judged to have need, 186 had their need fully met. 11 Federal Work-Study jobs (averaging $3000). In 2013, 8 non-need-based awards were made. ***Average percent of need met:*** 80. ***Average financial aid package:*** $15,809. ***Average need-based loan:*** $5500. ***Average need-based gift aid:*** $10,365. ***Average non-need-based aid:*** $11,000.

APPLYING
Options: electronic application, deferred entrance.

Application fee: $50.

CONTACT
Resurrection University, 1431 N. Claremont Avenue, Chicago, IL 60622.

Robert Morris University Illinois

Chicago, Illinois

http://www.robertmorris.edu/

- **Independent** comprehensive, founded 1913
- **Urban** campus with easy access to Chicago
- **Endowment** $42.5 million
- **Coed** 2,779 undergraduate students, 96% full-time, 50% women, 50% men
- **Minimally difficult** entrance level, 24% of applicants were admitted

UNDERGRAD STUDENTS
2,666 full-time, 113 part-time. Students come from 28 states and territories; 11 other countries; 8% are from out of state; 27% Black or African American, non-Hispanic/Latino; 29% Hispanic/Latino; 3% Asian, non-Hispanic/Latino; 0.1% Native Hawaiian or other Pacific Islander, non-Hispanic/Latino; 0.1% American Indian or Alaska Native, non-Hispanic/Latino; 2% Two or more races, non-Hispanic/Latino; 1% Race/ethnicity unknown; 1% international; 15% transferred in; 9% live on campus.

Freshmen
Admission: 3,412 applied, 830 admitted, 727 enrolled. ***Average high school GPA:*** 2.78. ***Test scores:*** ACT scores over 18: 57%; ACT scores over 24: 12%; ACT scores over 30: 1%.

Retention: 47% of full-time freshmen returned.

FACULTY
Total: 234, 38% full-time, 21% with terminal degrees.

Student/faculty ratio: 21:1.

ACADEMICS
Calendar: 5 10-week academic sessions per year. *Degrees:* associate, bachelor's, and master's.

Special study options: accelerated degree program, adult/continuing education programs, advanced placement credit, double majors, honors programs, internships, part-time degree program, services for LD students, study abroad, summer session for credit. ***ROTC:*** Army (c).

Computers: 1,220 computers/terminals are available on campus for general student use. Students can access the following: computer help desk, free student e-mail accounts, online (class) grades, online (class) registration, online (class) schedules, online credentials, online payments, online student accounts, online degree audit. Campuswide network is available. Wireless service is available via entire campus.

STUDENT LIFE
Housing options: coed. Campus housing is leased by the school.

Activities and organizations: drama/theater group, student-run newspaper, choral group, marching band, Eagle Newspaper, Warriors to Scholars, Culinary Society, UNA-USA, Student Council.

Athletics Member NAIA, USCAA. ***Intercollegiate sports:*** baseball M(s), basketball M(s)/W(s), bowling M(s)/W(s), cheerleading M(s)/W(s), cross-country running M(s)/W(s), field hockey W(s)(c), football M(s), golf M(s)/W(s), ice hockey M/W, lacrosse M(s)/W(s), soccer M(s)/W(s), softball W(s), tennis W(s), track and field M(s)/W(s), volleyball M(s)/W(s). ***Intramural sports:*** bowling M/W, cross-country running M/W, golf M/W, softball M/W, volleyball M/W.

Campus security: late-night transport/escort service, controlled dormitory access.

Student services: personal/psychological counseling.

COSTS & FINANCIAL AID
Costs (2015–16) ***Comprehensive fee:*** $37,800 includes full-time tuition ($25,200) and room and board ($12,600). Part-time tuition: $700 per credit hour. Part-time tuition and fees vary according to course load. ***Payment plan:*** installment. ***Waivers:*** employees or children of employees.

Financial Aid Of all full-time matriculated undergraduates who enrolled in 2014, 3,380 applied for aid, 3,244 were judged to have need, 118 had their need fully met. 164 Federal Work-Study jobs (averaging $1168). In 2014, 77 non-need-based awards were made. ***Average percent of need met:*** 49. ***Average financial aid package:*** $16,097. ***Average need-based loan:*** $4152. ***Average need-based gift aid:*** $12,298. ***Average non-need-based aid:*** $11,374. ***Average indebtedness upon graduation:*** $31,562.

APPLYING
Standardized Tests *Required for some:* SAT or ACT (for admission).

Options: electronic application, deferred entrance.

Application fee: $20.

Required: ACT scores (Nursing and Surgical Tech applicants). ***Required for some:*** high school transcript. ***Recommended:*** interview.

Application deadlines: rolling (freshmen), rolling (out-of-state freshmen), rolling (transfers).

Notification: continuous (freshmen), continuous (out-of-state freshmen), continuous (transfers).

CONTACT
Danielle Naffziger, Vice President of Marketing and Recruitment, Robert Morris University Illinois, 401 South State Street, Chicago, IL 60605. *Phone:* 312-935-4532. *Toll-free phone:* 800-762-5960. *Fax:* 312-935-4182. *E-mail:* dnaffziger@robertmorris.edu.

Rockford University

Rockford, Illinois

http://www.rockford.edu/

- **Independent** comprehensive, founded 1847
- **Suburban** 150-acre campus with easy access to Chicago
- **Coed** 1,032 undergraduate students, 87% full-time, 62% women, 38% men

UNDERGRAD STUDENTS
901 full-time, 131 part-time. Students come from 25 states and territories; 5 other countries; 13% are from out of state; 9% Black or African American, non-Hispanic/Latino; 5% Hispanic/Latino; 2% Asian, non-Hispanic/Latino; 9% Two or more races, non-Hispanic/Latino; 8% Race/ethnicity unknown; 1% international; 17% transferred in; 31% live on campus.

Freshmen
Admission: 147 enrolled. ***Average high school GPA:*** 3.25. ***Test scores:*** SAT critical reading scores over 500: 44%; SAT math scores over 500: 30%; SAT writing scores over 500: 29%; ACT scores over 18: 94%; SAT critical reading scores over 600: 15%; SAT math scores over 600: 15%; ACT scores over 24: 29%; SAT critical reading scores over 700: 15%; ACT scores over 30: 7%.

Retention: 64% of full-time freshmen returned.

FACULTY
Total: 166, 46% full-time, 43% with terminal degrees.

Student/faculty ratio: 10:1.

ACADEMICS
Calendar: semesters. *Degrees:* bachelor's, master's, and postbachelor's certificates.

Special study options: academic remediation for entering students, accelerated degree program, adult/continuing education programs, advanced placement credit, distance learning, double majors, English as a second language, honors programs, independent study, internships, off-campus study, part-time degree program, services for LD students, study abroad, summer session for credit.

Computers: 75 computers/terminals are available on campus for general student use. Students can access the following: campus intranet, computer help desk, free student e-mail accounts, online (class) grades, online (class) registration, online (class) schedules, online bill payment. Campuswide network is available. 100% of college-owned or -operated housing units are wired for high-speed Internet access. Wireless service is available via entire campus.

STUDENT LIFE
Housing options: coed, special housing for students with disabilities. Campus housing is university owned.

Activities and organizations: drama/theater group, student-run newspaper, radio station, choral group, Campus Activities Board, Multicultural Club, Muslim Student Association, Nursing Student Organization, Psychology Society.

Athletics Member NCAA. All Division III. ***Intercollegiate sports:*** baseball M, basketball M/W, cross-country running M/W, football M, golf M, soccer M/W, softball W, track and field M/W, volleyball W. ***Intramural sports:*** basketball M/W, football M/W, ultimate Frisbee M/W, volleyball M/W.

Campus security: 24-hour emergency response devices and patrols, student patrols, late-night transport/escort service, controlled dormitory access.

Student services: health clinic, personal/psychological counseling.

COSTS & FINANCIAL AID
Costs (2014–15) ***Comprehensive fee:*** $35,240 includes full-time tuition ($27,400), mandatory fees ($130), and room and board ($7710). Full-time tuition and fees vary according to course load. Part-time tuition: $735 per credit. Part-time tuition and fees vary according to course load. ***College room only:*** $4190. Room and board charges vary according to board plan and housing facility. ***Payment plan:*** installment. ***Waivers:*** employees or children of employees.

Financial Aid Of all full-time matriculated undergraduates who enrolled in 2013, 723 applied for aid, 696 were judged to have need, 80 had their need fully met. 120 Federal Work-Study jobs (averaging $734). 172 state and other part-time jobs (averaging $771). In 2013, 55 non-need-based awards were made. ***Average percent of need met:*** 66. ***Average financial aid package:*** $18,844. ***Average need-based loan:*** $5191. ***Average need-based gift aid:*** $13,997. ***Average non-need-based aid:*** $9444. ***Average indebtedness upon graduation:*** $39,619.

APPLYING
Standardized Tests *Required:* SAT or ACT (for admission).

Required: high school transcript, SAT/ACT score. ***Required for some:*** essay or personal statement, minimum 2.7 GPA, 2 letters of recommendation. ***Recommended:*** minimum 2.7 GPA.

CONTACT
Ms. Jennifer Nordstrom, Associate Vice President for Undergraduate Admission, Rockford University, 5050 East State Street, Rockford, IL 61108-2393. *Phone:* 815-226-4050. *Toll-free phone:* 800-892-2984. *Fax:* 815-226-2822. *E-mail:* admissions@rockford.edu.

Roosevelt University
Chicago, Illinois
http://www.roosevelt.edu/

- **Independent** comprehensive, founded 1945
- **Urban** campus with easy access to Chicago
- **Endowment** $89.8 million
- **Coed** 3,793 undergraduate students, 78% full-time, 63% women, 37% men
- **Moderately difficult** entrance level, 76% of applicants were admitted

UNDERGRAD STUDENTS
2,953 full-time, 840 part-time. Students come from 40 states and territories; 42 other countries; 8% are from out of state; 19% Black or African American, non-Hispanic/Latino; 22% Hispanic/Latino; 5% Asian, non-Hispanic/Latino; 0.2% Native Hawaiian or other Pacific Islander, non-Hispanic/Latino; 0.2% American Indian or Alaska Native, non-Hispanic/Latino; 3% Two or more races, non-Hispanic/Latino; 2% Race/ethnicity unknown; 3% international; 17% transferred in; 23% live on campus.

Freshmen
Admission: 5,409 applied, 4,122 admitted, 607 enrolled. ***Average high school GPA:*** 3.3. ***Test scores:*** SAT critical reading scores over 500: 67%; SAT math scores over 500: 60%; SAT writing scores over 500: 68%; ACT scores over 18: 98%; SAT critical reading scores over 600: 27%; SAT math scores over 600: 16%; SAT writing scores over 600: 28%; ACT scores over 24: 36%; SAT critical reading scores over 700: 7%; SAT math scores over 700: 3%; SAT writing scores over 700: 3%; ACT scores over 30: 5%.

Retention: 65% of full-time freshmen returned.

FACULTY
Total: 723, 34% full-time.

Student/faculty ratio: 11:1.

ACADEMICS
Calendar: semesters. *Degrees:* bachelor's, master's, doctoral, and postbachelor's certificates.

Special study options: academic remediation for entering students, accelerated degree program, adult/continuing education programs, advanced placement credit, distance learning, double majors, English as a second language, honors programs, independent study, internships, off-campus study, part-time degree program, services for LD students, student-designed majors, study abroad, summer session for credit.

Computers: 646 computers/terminals are available on campus for general student use. Students can access the following: campus intranet, computer help desk, free student e-mail accounts, online (class) grades, online (class) registration, online (class) schedules. Campuswide network is available. 100% of college-owned or -operated housing units are wired for high-speed Internet access. Wireless service is available via classrooms, computer centers, computer labs, dorm rooms, libraries, student centers.

STUDENT LIFE
Housing options: on-campus residence required through sophomore year; coed. Campus housing is university owned, leased by the school and is provided by a third party. Freshman campus housing is guaranteed.

Activities and organizations: student-run newspaper, radio station, International Student Union, RU Proud, Association of Latin Americans (ALAS), student government, Residence Hall Council, national fraternities, national sororities.

Athletics Member NAIA. ***Intercollegiate sports:*** baseball M, basketball M/W, cross-country running M/W, golf M, soccer M/W, softball W, tennis M/W, volleyball W.

Campus security: 24-hour emergency response devices and patrols, late-night transport/escort service, controlled dormitory access.

Student services: personal/psychological counseling.

COSTS & FINANCIAL AID
Costs (2014–15) ***Comprehensive fee:*** $39,832 includes full-time tuition ($27,300) and room and board ($12,532). Full-time tuition and fees vary according to program. Part-time tuition: $737 per credit. Part-time tuition and fees vary according to program.

Financial Aid Of all full-time matriculated undergraduates who enrolled in 2013, 2,660 applied for aid, 2,268 were judged to have need, 170 had their need fully met. In 2013, 500 non-need-based awards were made. ***Average percent of need met:*** 75. ***Average financial aid package:*** $22,090. ***Average need-based loan:*** $8900. ***Average need-based gift aid:*** $9000. ***Average non-need-based aid:*** $7000. ***Average indebtedness upon graduation:*** $16,887.

APPLYING

Standardized Tests *Required:* SAT or ACT (for admission).

Options: electronic application, deferred entrance.

Application fee: $25.

Required: high school transcript, minimum 2.5 GPA, audition for music and theater programs. ***Required for some:*** essay or personal statement, interview. ***Recommended:*** essay or personal statement.

Application deadlines: 8/15 (freshmen), rolling (transfers).

Notification: continuous (freshmen), continuous (transfers).

CONTACT

Director of Admission, Roosevelt University, IL. *Phone:* 312-341-2107. *Toll-free phone:* 877-APPLYRU. *Fax:* 312-341-3253. *E-mail:* admission@roosevelt.edu.

Saint Anthony College of Nursing

Rockford, Illinois

http://www.sacn.edu/

- **Independent Roman Catholic** upper-level, founded 1915
- **Suburban** 7-acre campus with easy access to Chicago
- **Endowment** $4.9 million
- **Coed, primarily women** 235 undergraduate students, 65% full-time, 88% women, 12% men
- **Moderately difficult** entrance level

UNDERGRAD STUDENTS

152 full-time, 83 part-time. Students come from 2 states and territories; 8% are from out of state; 6% Black or African American, non-Hispanic/Latino; 8% Hispanic/Latino; 5% Asian, non-Hispanic/Latino; 0.4% Native Hawaiian or other Pacific Islander, non-Hispanic/Latino; 1% Two or more races, non-Hispanic/Latino; 2% Race/ethnicity unknown; 23% transferred in.

FACULTY

Total: 43, 47% full-time, 23% with terminal degrees.

Student/faculty ratio: 7:1.

ACADEMICS

Calendar: semesters. *Degrees:* bachelor's, master's, doctoral, and post-master's certificates.

Special study options: advanced placement credit, independent study, internships, off-campus study, part-time degree program, services for LD students, summer session for credit.

Computers: 104 computers/terminals are available on campus for general student use. Students can access the following: computer help desk, free student e-mail accounts, online (class) grades, online (class) registration, online (class) schedules. Campuswide network is available. Wireless service is available via entire campus.

STUDENT LIFE

Housing options: college housing not available.

Activities and organizations: Student Organization.

Campus security: 24-hour emergency response devices and patrols, late-night transport/escort service.

Student services: health clinic, personal/psychological counseling, legal services.

COSTS & FINANCIAL AID

Costs (2014–15) ***Tuition:*** $22,144 full-time, $692 per credit hour part-time. Full-time tuition and fees vary according to course load and student level. Part-time tuition and fees vary according to course load and student level. ***Required fees:*** $746 full-time, $403 per year part-time. ***Payment plans:*** installment, deferred payment.

Financial Aid Of all full-time matriculated undergraduates who enrolled in 2013, 144 applied for aid, 138 were judged to have need, 3 had their need fully met. 42 state and other part-time jobs (averaging $4457). In 2013, 1 non-need-based awards were made. ***Average percent of need met:*** 36. ***Average financial aid package:*** $8775. ***Average need-based loan:*** $4457. ***Average need-based gift aid:*** $6475. ***Average non-need-based aid:*** $1000.

APPLYING

Application fee: $50.

Notification: 3/18 (transfers).

CONTACT

Ms. April Lipnitzky, Supervisor of Enrollment Management, Saint Anthony College of Nursing, 5658 East State Street, Rockford, IL 61108-2468. *Phone:* 815-227-2141. *Fax:* 815-227-2730. *E-mail:* admissions@sacn.edu.

Saint Francis Medical Center College of Nursing

Peoria, Illinois

http://www.sfmccon.edu/

- **Independent Roman Catholic** upper-level, founded 1986
- **Urban** campus
- **Coed, primarily women** 405 undergraduate students, 76% full-time, 90% women, 10% men
- 59% of applicants were admitted

UNDERGRAD STUDENTS

306 full-time, 99 part-time. Students come from 2 states and territories; 1 other country; 1% are from out of state; 2% Black or African American, non-Hispanic/Latino; 2% Hispanic/Latino; 5% Asian, non-Hispanic/Latino; 0.3% Native Hawaiian or other Pacific Islander, non-Hispanic/Latino; 0.3% Two or more races, non-Hispanic/Latino; 0.8% Race/ethnicity unknown; 0.3% international; 21% transferred in; 18% live on campus.

Freshmen

Admission: 239 applied, 142 admitted.

FACULTY

Total: 57, 63% full-time, 25% with terminal degrees.

Student/faculty ratio: 9:1.

ACADEMICS

Calendar: semesters. *Degrees:* bachelor's, master's, doctoral, and post-master's certificates.

Special study options: academic remediation for entering students, accelerated degree program, adult/continuing education programs, advanced placement credit, distance learning, independent study, part-time degree program, summer session for credit.

Computers: 62 computers/terminals and 53 ports are available on campus for general student use. Students can access the following: computer help desk, online (class) grades, online (class) registration, online (class) schedules. Campuswide network is available. 100% of college-owned or -operated housing units are wired for high-speed Internet access. Wireless service is available via entire campus.

STUDENT LIFE

Housing options: coed. Campus housing is university owned.

Activities and organizations: Student Senate, SNAI, Minority Student Association, Tau Omicron.

Campus security: 24-hour emergency response devices and patrols, controlled dormitory access.

Student services: health clinic, personal/psychological counseling.

COSTS & FINANCIAL AID

Costs (2015–16) ***Tuition:*** $18,016 full-time, $563 per hour part-time. Full-time tuition and fees vary according to course load, degree level, and student level. Part-time tuition and fees vary according to course load, degree level, and student level. ***Required fees:*** $865 full-time. ***Room only:*** $3400. ***Payment plan:*** installment. ***Waivers:*** employees or children of employees.

Financial Aid Of all full-time matriculated undergraduates who enrolled in 2014, 254 applied for aid, 201 were judged to have need, 14 had their need fully met. In 2014, 18 non-need-based awards were made. ***Average percent of need met:*** 41. ***Average financial aid package:*** $9346. ***Average need-based loan:*** $4924. ***Average need-based gift aid:*** $6526. ***Average non-need-based aid:*** $1547.

APPLYING
Options: deferred entrance.
Application fee: $50.
Notification: 10/15 (transfers).

CONTACT
Saint Francis Medical Center College of Nursing, 511 Northeast Greenleaf Street, Peoria, IL 61603-3783. *Phone:* 309-624-8980.

St. John's College

Springfield, Illinois

http://www.stjohnscollegespringfield.edu/

- **Independent Roman Catholic** upper-level, founded 1886
- **Urban** campus
- **Coed, primarily women**
- **Moderately difficult** entrance level

FACULTY
Student/faculty ratio: 6:1.

ACADEMICS
Calendar: semesters. *Degree:* bachelor's.

STUDENT LIFE
Housing options: college housing not available.
Campus security: 24-hour emergency response devices and patrols, late-night transport/escort service.

COSTS & FINANCIAL AID
Costs (2014–15) ***Tuition:*** $15,228 full-time, $710 per credit hour part-time. Full-time tuition and fees vary according to course load, program, and student level. Part-time tuition and fees vary according to course load, program, and student level. ***Required fees:*** $1802 full-time.
Financial Aid Of all full-time matriculated undergraduates who enrolled in 2009, 67 applied for aid, 55 were judged to have need, 43 had their need fully met. 5 Federal Work-Study jobs (averaging $1717). ***Average percent of need met:*** 78. ***Average financial aid package:*** $16,202. ***Average need-based loan:*** $4953. ***Average need-based gift aid:*** $6211.

APPLYING
Application fee: $60.
Required: TEAS V test.

CONTACT
St. John's College, 729 East Carpenter Street, Springfield, IL 62702. *Phone:* 217-525-5628.

School of the Art Institute of Chicago

Chicago, Illinois

http://www.saic.edu/

- **Independent** comprehensive, founded 1866
- **Urban** 1-acre campus with easy access to Chicago
- **Coed** 2,783 undergraduate students, 93% full-time, 72% women, 28% men
- **Very difficult** entrance level, 69% of applicants were admitted

UNDERGRAD STUDENTS
2,599 full-time, 184 part-time. Students come from 54 other countries; 3% Black or African American, non-Hispanic/Latino; 7% Hispanic/Latino; 13% Asian, non-Hispanic/Latino; 0.4% American Indian or Alaska Native, non-Hispanic/Latino; 2% Two or more races, non-Hispanic/Latino; 3% Race/ethnicity unknown; 31% international; 8% transferred in; 17% live on campus.

Freshmen
Admission: 3,737 applied, 2,584 admitted, 604 enrolled.
Retention: 82% of full-time freshmen returned.

FACULTY
Total: 853, 18% full-time, 74% with terminal degrees.
Student/faculty ratio: 9:1.

ACADEMICS
Calendar: semesters. *Degrees:* certificates, bachelor's, master's, and postbachelor's certificates.
Special study options: academic remediation for entering students, advanced placement credit, cooperative education, double majors, English as a second language, independent study, internships, off-campus study, part-time degree program, services for LD students, student-designed majors, study abroad, summer session for credit.
Computers: 300 computers/terminals and 945 ports are available on campus for general student use. Students can access the following: campus intranet, computer help desk, free student e-mail accounts, online (class) grades, online (class) registration, online (class) schedules. Campuswide network is available. 100% of college-owned or -operated housing units are wired for high-speed Internet access. Wireless service is available via entire campus.

STUDENT LIFE
Housing options: coed, special housing for students with disabilities. Campus housing is university owned.
Activities and organizations: drama/theater group, student-run newspaper, radio and television station, Student Association/Student Union Galleries, Korean Student Association, InterVarsity, Curatorial Community, Good 'Ol Futbol.
Campus security: 24-hour emergency response devices and patrols, late-night transport/escort service, controlled dormitory access.
Student services: health clinic, personal/psychological counseling.

COSTS & FINANCIAL AID
Costs (2014–15) ***One-time required fee:*** $150. ***Comprehensive fee:*** $54,730 includes full-time tuition ($41,430), mandatory fees ($800), and room and board ($12,500). Full-time tuition and fees vary according to course load, degree level, and program. Part-time tuition: $1381 per credit hour. Part-time tuition and fees vary according to course load, degree level, and program. ***Required fees:*** $265 per term part-time. ***College room only:*** $11,000. Room and board charges vary according to board plan. ***Payment plan:*** installment. ***Waivers:*** employees or children of employees.
Financial Aid Of all full-time matriculated undergraduates who enrolled in 2013, 1,367 applied for aid, 1,231 were judged to have need, 83 had their need fully met. In 2013, 1154 non-need-based awards were made. ***Average percent of need met:*** 74. ***Average financial aid package:*** $31,573. ***Average need-based loan:*** $5233. ***Average need-based gift aid:*** $16,633. ***Average non-need-based aid:*** $7766. ***Average indebtedness upon graduation:*** $42,097.

APPLYING
Standardized Tests *Required:* SAT or ACT (for admission).
Options: electronic application, early action, deferred entrance.
Application fee: $65.
Required: essay or personal statement, high school transcript. ***Recommended:*** interview.
Application deadlines: 6/1 (freshmen), 8/15 (transfers), 1/3 (early action).
Notification: continuous (freshmen), continuous (transfers), 2/15 (early action).

CONTACT
Ms. Asia Mitchell, Director, Undergraduate Admissions, School of the Art Institute of Chicago, 36 South Wabash, Chicago, IL 60603. *Phone:* 312-629-6100. *Toll-free phone:* 800-232-SAIC. *Fax:* 312-629-6101. *E-mail:* ugadmiss@saic.edu.

Shimer College

Chicago, Illinois

http://www.shimer.edu/

- **Independent** 4-year, founded 1853
- **Urban** 3-acre campus with easy access to Chicago, Milwaukee
- **Coed** 77 undergraduate students, 87% full-time, 47% women, 53% men
- **Moderately difficult** entrance level, 84% of applicants were admitted

UNDERGRAD STUDENTS
67 full-time, 10 part-time. 50% are from out of state; 9% Black or African American, non-Hispanic/Latino; 12% Hispanic/Latino; 7% Asian, non-Hispanic/Latino; 4% Race/ethnicity unknown; 9% transferred in; 10% live on campus.

Freshmen
Admission: 31 applied, 26 admitted, 11 enrolled. ***Average high school GPA:*** 2.99. ***Test scores:*** SAT critical reading scores over 500: 100%; SAT math scores over 500: 100%; SAT writing scores over 500: 100%; SAT critical reading scores over 600: 100%; SAT math scores over 600: 34%; SAT writing scores over 600: 67%; SAT critical reading scores over 700: 67%.

Retention: 63% of full-time freshmen returned.

FACULTY
Total: 12, 75% full-time, 92% with terminal degrees.

Student/faculty ratio: 7:1.

ACADEMICS
Calendar: semesters. *Degree:* bachelor's.

Special study options: adult/continuing education programs, cooperative education, double majors, independent study, internships, off-campus study, part-time degree program, student-designed majors, study abroad, summer session for credit.

Computers: Students can access the following: campus intranet, computer help desk, free student e-mail accounts, online (class) schedules. Campuswide network is available. 100% of college-owned or -operated housing units are wired for high-speed Internet access. Wireless service is available via entire campus.

STUDENT LIFE
Housing options: coed, special housing for students with disabilities. Campus housing is university owned and leased by the school. Freshman campus housing is guaranteed.

Activities and organizations: drama/theater group, student-run newspaper, radio station, choral group.

Athletics ***Intramural sports:*** baseball M, basketball M/W, cross-country running M/W, soccer M/W, softball W, track and field M/W, volleyball M/W.

Campus security: 24-hour emergency response devices, late-night transport/escort service.

Student services: personal/psychological counseling.

COSTS & FINANCIAL AID
Costs (2014–15) ***Comprehensive fee:*** $43,303 includes full-time tuition ($28,454), mandatory fees ($4045), and room and board ($10,804). Part-time tuition: $1035 per credit hour. ***Required fees:*** $1700 per year part-time. ***Room and board:*** Room and board charges vary according to board plan and housing facility. ***Payment plan:*** installment. ***Waivers:*** senior citizens and employees or children of employees.

Financial Aid Of all full-time matriculated undergraduates who enrolled in 2013, 67 applied for aid, 56 were judged to have need, 3 had their need fully met. In 2013, 12 non-need-based awards were made. ***Average percent of need met:*** 64. ***Average financial aid package:*** $22,684. ***Average need-based loan:*** $5428. ***Average need-based gift aid:*** $14,257. ***Average non-need-based aid:*** $8775. ***Average indebtedness upon graduation:*** $25,125.

APPLYING
Standardized Tests *Required for some:* SAT and SAT Subject Tests or ACT (for admission).

Options: electronic application.

Application fee: $25.

Required: essay or personal statement, high school transcript, 1 letter of recommendation, interview.

CONTACT
Ms. Amy Pritts, Director of Admission, Shimer College, 3424 South State Street, Chicago, IL 60616. *Phone:* 312-235-3504. *Toll-free phone:* 800-215-7173. *Fax:* 888-808-3133. *E-mail:* admission@shimer.edu.

★ Southern Illinois University Carbondale

Carbondale, Illinois

http://www.siuc.edu/

- **State-supported** university, founded 1869, part of Southern Illinois University
- **Rural** 1136-acre campus with easy access to St. Louis
- **Coed** 13,461 undergraduate students, 88% full-time, 46% women, 54% men
- **Moderately difficult** entrance level, 82% of applicants were admitted

UNDERGRAD STUDENTS
11,873 full-time, 1,588 part-time. Students come from 55 other countries; 15% are from out of state; 20% Black or African American, non-Hispanic/Latino; 8% Hispanic/Latino; 2% Asian, non-Hispanic/Latino; 0.1% Native Hawaiian or other Pacific Islander, non-Hispanic/Latino; 0.2% American Indian or Alaska Native, non-Hispanic/Latino; 3% Two or more races, non-Hispanic/Latino; 0.1% Race/ethnicity unknown; 3% international; 11% transferred in; 33% live on campus.

Freshmen
Admission: 10,877 applied, 8,883 admitted, 2,775 enrolled. ***Average high school GPA:*** 2.91. ***Test scores:*** SAT critical reading scores over 500: 68%; SAT math scores over 500: 71%; ACT scores over 18: 85%; SAT critical reading scores over 600: 38%; SAT math scores over 600: 38%; ACT scores over 24: 39%; SAT critical reading scores over 700: 8%; SAT math scores over 700: 10%; ACT scores over 30: 8%.

Retention: 68% of full-time freshmen returned.

FACULTY
Total: 928, 89% full-time, 78% with terminal degrees.

Student/faculty ratio: 15:1.

ACADEMICS
Calendar: semesters plus 8-week summer session. *Degrees:* certificates, associate, bachelor's, master's, doctoral, and postbachelor's certificates.

Special study options: academic remediation for entering students, accelerated degree program, adult/continuing education programs, advanced placement credit, cooperative education, distance learning, double majors, English as a second language, honors programs, independent study, internships, off-campus study, part-time degree program, services for LD students, student-designed majors, study abroad, summer session for credit. ***ROTC:*** Army (b), Air Force (b).

Computers: 1,856 computers/terminals are available on campus for general student use. Students can access the following: campus intranet, computer help desk, free student e-mail accounts, online (class) grades, online (class) registration, online (class) schedules. Campuswide network is available. 100% of college-owned or -operated housing units are wired for high-speed Internet access. Wireless service is available via classrooms, computer centers, computer labs, dorm rooms, learning centers, libraries, student centers.

STUDENT LIFE
Housing options: on-campus residence required for freshman year; coed, men-only, women-only, special housing for students with disabilities. Campus housing is university owned. Freshman campus housing is guaranteed.

Activities and organizations: drama/theater group, student-run newspaper, radio and television station, choral group, marching band, Inter-Greek Council, Black Affairs Council, Residence Hall Association, Collegiate FFA, Equestrian Club, national fraternities, national sororities.

Athletics Member NCAA. All Division I except football (Division I-AA). ***Intercollegiate sports:*** baseball M(s), basketball M(s)/W(s), cheerleading M/W, cross-country running M(s)/W(s), golf M(s)/W(s), softball W(s), swimming and diving M(s)/W(s), tennis M(s)/W(s), track and field M(s)/W(s), volleyball W(s). ***Intramural sports:*** archery M(c)/W(c), badminton M(c)/W(c), baseball M(c), basketball M/W, bowling M(c)/W(c), equestrian sports M(c)/W(c), fencing M(c)/W(c), football M, gymnastics M(c)/W(c), lacrosse M(c)/W(c), racquetball M/W, rock climbing M(c)/W(c), rugby M(c)/W(c), sailing M(c)/W(c), skiing (downhill) M(c)/W(c), soccer M(c)/W(c), softball M/W(c), swimming and diving M/W, table tennis M(c)/W(c), tennis M(c)/W(c), track and field M/W, ultimate Frisbee M(c)/W(c), volleyball M(c)/W(c), water polo M(c)/W(c), weight lifting M(c)/W(c), wrestling M(c)/W(c).

Campus security: 24-hour emergency response devices and patrols, student patrols, late-night transport/escort service, controlled dormitory access, well-lit pathways, night safety vans, student transit system.

Student services: health clinic, personal/psychological counseling, women's center, legal services.

COSTS & FINANCIAL AID

Costs (2014–15) ***Tuition:*** state resident $8415 full-time, $281 per credit hour part-time; nonresident $21,038 full-time, $701 per credit hour part-time. Full-time tuition and fees vary according to course load, program, reciprocity agreements, and student level. Part-time tuition and fees vary according to course load, program, reciprocity agreements, and student level. No tuition increase for student's term of enrollment. ***Required fees:*** $3833 full-time, $172 per credit hour part-time. ***Room and board:*** $9694. Room and board charges vary according to board plan and housing facility. ***Payment plan:*** installment. ***Waivers:*** children of alumni, senior citizens, and employees or children of employees.

Financial Aid Of all full-time matriculated undergraduates who enrolled in 2014, 9,681 applied for aid, 8,319 were judged to have need, 463 had their need fully met. 1,633 Federal Work-Study jobs (averaging $1165). In 2014, 509 non-need-based awards were made. ***Average percent of need met:*** 60. ***Average financial aid package:*** $14,366. ***Average need-based loan:*** $4368. ***Average need-based gift aid:*** $7931. ***Average non-need-based aid:*** $6057. ***Average indebtedness upon graduation:*** $30,138.

APPLYING

Standardized Tests *Required:* SAT or ACT (for admission).

Options: electronic application, deferred entrance.

Application fee: $40.

Required: high school transcript, SAT or ACT.

Application deadlines: rolling (freshmen), rolling (out-of-state freshmen), rolling (transfers).

Notification: continuous until 9/1 (freshmen), continuous until 9/1 (out-of-state freshmen), continuous (transfers).

CONTACT

Rachel Richey, Interim Director Undergraduate Admissions, Southern Illinois University Carbondale, Undergraduate Admissions, 1263 Lincoln Dr, Carbondale, IL 62901. *Phone:* 618-536-4405. *Fax:* 618-453-4609. *E-mail:* admissions@siu.edu.

See below for display ad and page 1624 for the College Close-Up.

Southern Illinois University Edwardsville

Edwardsville, Illinois

http://www.siue.edu/

- **State-supported** comprehensive, founded 1957, part of Southern Illinois University
- **Suburban** 2660-acre campus with easy access to St. Louis
- **Endowment** $20.9 million
- **Coed** 11,421 undergraduate students, 85% full-time, 53% women, 47% men
- **Moderately difficult** entrance level, 87% of applicants were admitted

UNDERGRAD STUDENTS

9,714 full-time, 1,707 part-time. Students come from 41 states and territories; 45 other countries; 8% are from out of state; 15% Black or African American, non-Hispanic/Latino; 4% Hispanic/Latino; 2% Asian, non-Hispanic/Latino; 0.1% Native Hawaiian or other Pacific Islander, non-Hispanic/Latino; 0.2% American Indian or Alaska Native, non-Hispanic/Latino; 3% Two or more races, non-Hispanic/Latino; 1% Race/ethnicity unknown; 1% international; 12% transferred in; 30% live on campus.

Freshmen

Admission: 7,594 applied, 6,604 admitted, 2,126 enrolled. ***Test scores:*** ACT scores over 18: 96%; ACT scores over 24: 49%; ACT scores over 30: 7%.

Retention: 73% of full-time freshmen returned.

FACULTY
Total: 907, 69% full-time, 68% with terminal degrees.

Student/faculty ratio: 19:1.

ACADEMICS
Calendar: semesters. *Degrees:* bachelor's, master's, doctoral, post-master's, and postbachelor's certificates.

Special study options: academic remediation for entering students, accelerated degree program, advanced placement credit, cooperative education, distance learning, double majors, English as a second language, honors programs, independent study, internships, off-campus study, part-time degree program, services for LD students, student-designed majors, study abroad, summer session for credit. ***ROTC:*** Army (b), Air Force (c).

Unusual degree programs: 3-2 engineering.

Computers: 767 computers/terminals are available on campus for general student use. Students can access the following: campus intranet, computer help desk, free student e-mail accounts, online (class) grades, online (class) registration, online (class) schedules, online job finder. Campuswide network is available. 100% of college-owned or -operated housing units are wired for high-speed Internet access. Wireless service is available via entire campus.

STUDENT LIFE
Housing options: coed, special housing for students with disabilities. Campus housing is university owned. Freshman applicants given priority for college housing.

Activities and organizations: drama/theater group, student-run newspaper, radio and television station, choral group, Fraternity & Sorority Life, Campus Activities Board, Sports Clubs/Intramurals, Dance Marathon, Student Government, national fraternities, national sororities.

Athletics Member NCAA. All Division I. ***Intercollegiate sports:*** baseball M(s), basketball M(s)/W(s), cross-country running M(s)/W(s), golf M(s)/W(s), soccer M(s)/W(s), softball W(s), tennis M(s)/W(s), track and field M(s)/W(s), volleyball W(s), wrestling M(s). ***Intramural sports:*** archery M/W, badminton M/W, basketball M/W, bowling M/W, cheerleading M/W, fencing M/W, football M, ice hockey M, racquetball M/W, rock climbing M/W, soccer M/W, softball M/W, swimming and diving M/W, table tennis M/W, tennis M/W, ultimate Frisbee M/W, volleyball M/W, water polo M/W, weight lifting M/W.

Campus security: 24-hour emergency response devices and patrols, student patrols, late-night transport/escort service, controlled dormitory access, 24-hour ID check at residence hall entrances, emergency call boxes located throughout campus.

Student services: health clinic, personal/psychological counseling, legal services.

COSTS & FINANCIAL AID
Costs (2014–15) ***Tuition:*** state resident $7296 full-time, $243 per credit hour part-time; nonresident $18,240 full-time, $608 per credit hour part-time. Full-time tuition and fees vary according to course load. Part-time tuition and fees vary according to course load. No tuition increase for student's term of enrollment. ***Required fees:*** $2442 full-time, $872 per term part-time. ***Room and board:*** $8781. Room and board charges vary according to board plan and housing facility. ***Payment plan:*** installment. ***Waivers:*** senior citizens and employees or children of employees.

Financial Aid Of all full-time matriculated undergraduates who enrolled in 2013, 7,968 applied for aid, 6,690 were judged to have need, 1,463 had their need fully met. In 2013, 119 non-need-based awards were made. ***Average percent of need met:*** 53. ***Average financial aid package:*** $11,179. ***Average need-based loan:*** $4346. ***Average need-based gift aid:*** $8502. ***Average non-need-based aid:*** $6712. ***Average indebtedness upon graduation:*** $27,681.

APPLYING
Standardized Tests *Required:* SAT or ACT (for admission).

Options: electronic application, deferred entrance.

Application fee: $30.

Required: high school transcript. ***Recommended:*** minimum 2.5 GPA.

Notification: continuous (freshmen), continuous (transfers).

CONTACT
Mr. Todd Burrell, Director of Admissions, Southern Illinois University Edwardsville, Campus Box 1600, Rendleman Hall, Edwardsville, IL 62026-1600. *Phone:* 618-650-3705. *Toll-free phone:* 800-447-SIUE. *Fax:* 618-650-5013. *E-mail:* admissions@siue.edu.

Trinity Christian College

Palos Heights, Illinois

http://www.trnty.edu/

- **Independent Christian Reformed** comprehensive, founded 1959
- **Suburban** 53-acre campus with easy access to Chicago
- **Endowment** $10.3 million
- **Coed** 1,337 undergraduate students, 83% full-time, 65% women, 35% men
- **Moderately difficult** entrance level, 78% of applicants were admitted

UNDERGRAD STUDENTS
1,114 full-time, 223 part-time. Students come from 25 states and territories; 8 other countries; 35% are from out of state; 10% Black or African American, non-Hispanic/Latino; 11% Hispanic/Latino; 2% Asian, non-Hispanic/Latino; 0.1% Native Hawaiian or other Pacific Islander, non-Hispanic/Latino; 0.4% American Indian or Alaska Native, non-Hispanic/Latino; 2% Two or more races, non-Hispanic/Latino; 2% Race/ethnicity unknown; 4% international; 8% transferred in; 49% live on campus.

Freshmen
Admission: 805 applied, 627 admitted, 190 enrolled. ***Average high school GPA:*** 3.5. ***Test scores:*** SAT critical reading scores over 500: 79%; SAT math scores over 500: 95%; ACT scores over 18: 96%; SAT critical reading scores over 600: 37%; SAT math scores over 600: 42%; ACT scores over 24: 43%; SAT critical reading scores over 700: 16%; SAT math scores over 700: 11%; ACT scores over 30: 12%.

Retention: 84% of full-time freshmen returned.

FACULTY
Total: 154, 55% full-time, 42% with terminal degrees.

Student/faculty ratio: 11:1.

ACADEMICS
Calendar: semesters plus 2 week interim term. *Degrees:* bachelor's and master's.

Special study options: academic remediation for entering students, accelerated degree program, adult/continuing education programs, advanced placement credit, cooperative education, distance learning, double majors, English as a second language, honors programs, independent study, internships, off-campus study, part-time degree program, services for LD students, study abroad, summer session for credit.

Computers: 170 computers/terminals are available on campus for general student use. Students can access the following: campus intranet, computer help desk, free student e-mail accounts, online (class) grades, online (class) registration, online (class) schedules. Campuswide network is available. 100% of college-owned or -operated housing units are wired for high-speed Internet access. Wireless service is available via entire campus.

STUDENT LIFE
Housing options: coed. Campus housing is university owned. Freshman campus housing is guaranteed.

Activities and organizations: drama/theater group, student-run newspaper, choral group, Student Association, Student ministries, Campus newspaper, Pro-Life Task Force, PACE (prison tutoring program).

Athletics Member NAIA, NCCAA. ***Intercollegiate sports:*** baseball M(s), basketball M(s)/W(s), cross-country running M(s)/W(s), golf M(s)/W, soccer M(s)/W(s), softball M/W(s), track and field M(s)/W(s), volleyball M/W(s). ***Intramural sports:*** badminton M/W, basketball M/W, football M/W, soccer M/W, volleyball M/W.

Campus security: 24-hour emergency response devices and patrols, student patrols, late-night transport/escort service, security cameras, Code Blue Emergency Phones.

Student services: health clinic, personal/psychological counseling.

COSTS & FINANCIAL AID
Costs (2014–15) ***One-time required fee:*** $225. ***Comprehensive fee:*** $34,680 includes full-time tuition ($25,060), mandatory fees ($230), and

room and board ($9390). Part-time tuition: $836 per credit hour. ***College room only:*** $4960. Room and board charges vary according to board plan. ***Payment plan:*** installment. ***Waivers:*** employees or children of employees.

Financial Aid Of all full-time matriculated undergraduates who enrolled in 2014, 840 applied for aid, 761 were judged to have need, 101 had their need fully met. 76 Federal Work-Study jobs (averaging $1426). 367 state and other part-time jobs (averaging $1190). In 2014, 110 non-need-based awards were made. ***Average percent of need met:*** 68. ***Average financial aid package:*** $17,489. ***Average need-based loan:*** $4679. ***Average need-based gift aid:*** $13,796. ***Average non-need-based aid:*** $8260. ***Average indebtedness upon graduation:*** $30,996.

APPLYING

Standardized Tests *Required:* SAT or ACT (for admission). *Required for some:* SAT (for admission), SAT and SAT Subject Tests or ACT (for admission), SAT Subject Tests (for admission). *Recommended:* ACT (for admission).

Options: electronic application, deferred entrance.

Application fee: $30.

Required: essay or personal statement, high school transcript, minimum 2.5 GPA, interview. ***Required for some:*** 1 letter of recommendation, Composite ACT 19 or Combined SAT 910.

Application deadlines: rolling (freshmen), rolling (transfers).

Notification: continuous (freshmen), continuous (transfers).

CONTACT

Jeremy Klyn, Director of Admissions, Trinity Christian College, 6601 West College Drive, Palos Heights, IL 60463. *Phone:* 708-239-4708. *Toll-free phone:* 866-TRIN-4-ME. *Fax:* 708-239-4826. *E-mail:* admissions@trnty.edu.

University of Chicago

Chicago, Illinois

http://www.uchicago.edu/

- **Independent** university, founded 1891
- **Urban** 217-acre campus
- **Endowment** $6.5 billion
- **Coed** 5,681 undergraduate students, 99% full-time, 47% women, 53% men
- **Most difficult** entrance level, 9% of applicants were admitted

UNDERGRAD STUDENTS

5,616 full-time, 65 part-time. 83% are from out of state; 5% Black or African American, non-Hispanic/Latino; 9% Hispanic/Latino; 17% Asian, non-Hispanic/Latino; 0.1% Native Hawaiian or other Pacific Islander, non-Hispanic/Latino; 0.2% American Indian or Alaska Native, non-Hispanic/Latino; 4% Two or more races, non-Hispanic/Latino; 11% Race/ethnicity unknown; 10% international; 0.4% transferred in; 54% live on campus.

Freshmen

Admission: 27,500 applied, 2,409 admitted, 1,445 enrolled. ***Average high school GPA:*** 4.16. ***Test scores:*** SAT critical reading scores over 500: 100%; SAT math scores over 500: 100%; SAT writing scores over 500: 100%; ACT scores over 18: 100%; SAT critical reading scores over 600: 99%; SAT math scores over 600: 99%; SAT writing scores over 600: 99%; ACT scores over 24: 100%; SAT critical reading scores over 700: 83%; SAT math scores over 700: 82%; SAT writing scores over 700: 80%; ACT scores over 30: 95%.

Retention: 99% of full-time freshmen returned.

FACULTY

Total: 1,748, 75% full-time, 90% with terminal degrees.

Student/faculty ratio: 6:1.

ACADEMICS

Calendar: quarters. *Degrees:* bachelor's, master's, and doctoral.

Special study options: accelerated degree program, advanced placement credit, double majors, independent study, internships, off-campus study, services for LD students, student-designed majors, study abroad, summer session for credit. ***ROTC:*** Army (c), Air Force (c).

Unusual degree programs: 3-2 social work; public policy, social sciences (MAPSS), international relations.

Computers: 300 computers/terminals are available on campus for general student use. Students can access the following: campus intranet, computer help desk, free student e-mail accounts, online (class) grades, online (class) registration, online (class) schedules. Campuswide network is available. 100% of college-owned or -operated housing units are wired for high-speed Internet access. Wireless service is available via entire campus.

STUDENT LIFE

Housing options: on-campus residence required for freshman year; coed, special housing for students with disabilities. Campus housing is university owned. Freshman campus housing is guaranteed.

Activities and organizations: drama/theater group, student-run newspaper, radio and television station, choral group, marching band, University Theatre, Model United Nations, Council on University Programming, South Asian Students Association, Splash, national fraternities, national sororities.

Athletics Member NCAA. All Division III. ***Intercollegiate sports:*** baseball M, basketball M/W, cross-country running M/W, football M, soccer M/W, softball W, swimming and diving M/W, tennis M/W, track and field M/W, volleyball W, wrestling M. ***Intramural sports:*** archery M/W, badminton M/W, basketball M/W, bowling M/W, cheerleading W, crew M/W, fencing M/W, field hockey M/W, football M/W, golf M/W, gymnastics M/W, ice hockey M/W, lacrosse M/W, racquetball M/W, rock climbing M/W, rugby M/W, sailing M/W, soccer M/W, softball M/W, squash M/W, swimming and diving M/W, table tennis M/W, tennis M/W, track and field M/W, ultimate Frisbee M/W, volleyball M/W, water polo M/W.

Campus security: 24-hour emergency response devices and patrols, student patrols, late-night transport/escort service, controlled dormitory access.

Student services: health clinic, personal/psychological counseling, women's center.

COSTS & FINANCIAL AID

Costs (2014–15) ***One-time required fee:*** $1128. ***Comprehensive fee:*** $62,458 includes full-time tuition ($47,139), mandatory fees ($1114), and room and board ($14,205). Full-time tuition and fees vary according to course load and program. Part-time tuition and fees vary according to course load and program. ***Room and board:*** Room and board charges vary according to board plan and housing facility. ***Payment plans:*** tuition prepayment, installment. ***Waivers:*** employees or children of employees.

Financial Aid Of all full-time matriculated undergraduates who enrolled in 2014, 3,032 applied for aid, 2,565 were judged to have need, 2,565 had their need fully met. ***Average percent of need met:*** 100. ***Average financial aid package:*** $43,220. ***Average need-based loan:*** $4196. ***Average need-based gift aid:*** $39,784. ***Average indebtedness upon graduation:*** $23,223.

APPLYING

Standardized Tests *Required:* SAT or ACT (for admission).

Options: electronic application, early admission, early action, deferred entrance.

Application fee: $75.

Required: essay or personal statement, high school transcript, 2 letters of recommendation, 2 teacher recommendations.

Application deadlines: 1/1 (freshmen), 3/1 (transfers), 11/15 (early action).

Notification: 4/1 (freshmen), 5/9 (transfers), 12/17 (early action).

CONTACT

Mr. James G. Nondorf, Vice President for Enrollment and Student Advancement and Dean of Admissions and Financial Aid, University of Chicago, Rosenwald Hall, 1101 East 58th Street, Suite 105, Chicago, IL 60637. *Phone:* 773-702-8650. *Fax:* 773-702-4199. *E-mail:* collegeadmissions@uchicago.edu.

University of Illinois at Chicago
Chicago, Illinois
http://www.uic.edu/

- **State-supported** university, founded 1946, part of University of Illinois System
- **Urban** 240-acre campus with easy access to Chicago
- **Endowment** $299.5 million
- **Coed** 16,707 undergraduate students, 93% full-time, 50% women, 50% men
- **Moderately difficult** entrance level, 73% of applicants were admitted

UNDERGRAD STUDENTS
15,459 full-time, 1,248 part-time. 2% are from out of state; 8% Black or African American, non-Hispanic/Latino; 26% Hispanic/Latino; 23% Asian, non-Hispanic/Latino; 0.3% Native Hawaiian or other Pacific Islander, non-Hispanic/Latino; 0.1% American Indian or Alaska Native, non-Hispanic/Latino; 2% Two or more races, non-Hispanic/Latino; 2% Race/ethnicity unknown; 2% international; 10% transferred in; 17% live on campus.

Freshmen
Admission: 15,949 applied, 11,598 admitted, 3,030 enrolled. ***Average high school GPA:*** 3.3. ***Test scores:*** SAT critical reading scores over 500: 64%; SAT math scores over 500: 84%; SAT writing scores over 500: 64%; ACT scores over 18: 99%; SAT critical reading scores over 600: 21%; SAT math scores over 600: 55%; SAT writing scores over 600: 19%; ACT scores over 24: 57%; SAT critical reading scores over 700: 9%; SAT math scores over 700: 18%; SAT writing scores over 700: 8%; ACT scores over 30: 10%.

Retention: 80% of full-time freshmen returned.

FACULTY
Total: 1,856, 73% full-time, 82% with terminal degrees.

Student/faculty ratio: 17:1.

ACADEMICS
Calendar: semesters. *Degrees:* bachelor's, master's, doctoral, post-master's, and postbachelor's certificates.

Special study options: academic remediation for entering students, accelerated degree program, advanced placement credit, cooperative education, distance learning, double majors, freshman honors college, honors programs, independent study, internships, off-campus study, part-time degree program, services for LD students, student-designed majors, study abroad, summer session for credit. ***ROTC:*** Army (b), Navy (c), Air Force (c).

Computers: 910 computers/terminals are available on campus for general student use. Students can access the following: campus intranet, computer help desk, free student e-mail accounts, online (class) grades, online (class) registration, online (class) schedules. Campuswide network is available. 100% of college-owned or -operated housing units are wired for high-speed Internet access. Wireless service is available via classrooms, computer centers, computer labs, dorm rooms, learning centers, libraries, student centers.

STUDENT LIFE
Housing options: coed. Campus housing is university owned.

Activities and organizations: drama/theater group, student-run newspaper, radio station, choral group, Alternative Spring Break, Muslim Student Association, Society of Future Physicians, Ski and Snowboard Club, Accounting Club, national fraternities, national sororities.

Athletics Member NCAA. All Division I. ***Intercollegiate sports:*** baseball M(s), basketball M(s)/W(s), cross-country running M(s)/W(s), gymnastics M(s)/W(s), soccer M(s), softball W(s), swimming and diving M(s)/W(s), tennis M(s)/W(s), track and field M(s)/W(s), volleyball W(s). ***Intramural sports:*** badminton M/W, basketball M/W, bowling M/W, fencing M(c)/W(c), field hockey W, football M/W, golf M/W, racquetball M/W, rugby M(c)/W(c), soccer M/W, softball M/W, squash M/W, table tennis M/W, tennis M/W, volleyball M(c)/W, water polo M(c)/W(c), wrestling M.

Campus security: 24-hour emergency response devices and patrols, student patrols, late-night transport/escort service, controlled dormitory access, housing ID stickers, guest escort policy, 24-hour closed circuit videos for exits and entrances, security screen for first floor.

Student services: health clinic, personal/psychological counseling, women's center, legal services.

COSTS & FINANCIAL AID
Costs (2015–16) ***Tuition:*** state resident $10,584 full-time; nonresident $22,974 full-time. Full-time tuition and fees vary according to degree level and program. Part-time tuition and fees vary according to course load, degree level, and program. No tuition increase for student's term of enrollment. ***Required fees:*** $3050 full-time. ***Room and board:*** $10,871; room only: $7808. Room and board charges vary according to board plan and housing facility. ***Payment plan:*** installment. ***Waivers:*** senior citizens and employees or children of employees.

Financial Aid Of all full-time matriculated undergraduates who enrolled in 2013, 12,920 applied for aid, 11,712 were judged to have need, 852 had their need fully met. 1,041 Federal Work-Study jobs (averaging $2000). 2,602 state and other part-time jobs (averaging $2500). In 2013, 474 non-need-based awards were made. ***Average percent of need met:*** 60. ***Average financial aid package:*** $14,024. ***Average need-based loan:*** $4592. ***Average need-based gift aid:*** $12,863. ***Average non-need-based aid:*** $5027. ***Average indebtedness upon graduation:*** $23,158.

APPLYING
Standardized Tests *Required:* SAT or ACT (for admission).

Options: electronic application, early decision.

Application fee: $50.

Required: essay or personal statement, high school transcript, auditions for music and theater majors; portfolios for art majors.

Application deadlines: 1/15 (freshmen), 3/31 (transfers).

Notification: continuous until 11/30 (freshmen), continuous (transfers).

CONTACT
Ms. Maureen Woods SAC, Associate Director, Admissions Undergraduate, University of Illinois at Chicago, 1100 SSB, m/c 018, Chicago, IL 60607-7128. *Phone:* 312-996-4111. *Fax:* 312-413-7628. *E-mail:* uic.admit@uic.edu.

University of Illinois at Springfield
Springfield, Illinois
http://www.uis.edu/

- **State-supported** comprehensive, founded 1969, part of University of Illinois System
- **Suburban** 746-acre campus
- **Endowment** $15.1 million
- **Coed** 3,038 undergraduate students, 64% full-time, 51% women, 49% men
- **Moderately difficult** entrance level, 62% of applicants were admitted

UNDERGRAD STUDENTS
1,935 full-time, 1,103 part-time. Students come from 47 states and territories; 17 other countries; 14% are from out of state; 15% Black or African American, non-Hispanic/Latino; 6% Hispanic/Latino; 4% Asian, non-Hispanic/Latino; 0.1% Native Hawaiian or other Pacific Islander, non-Hispanic/Latino; 0.1% American Indian or Alaska Native, non-Hispanic/Latino; 3% Two or more races, non-Hispanic/Latino; 3% Race/ethnicity unknown; 4% international; 20% transferred in; 30% live on campus.

Freshmen
Admission: 1,460 applied, 899 admitted, 305 enrolled. ***Average high school GPA:*** 3.42. ***Test scores:*** ACT scores over 18: 95%; ACT scores over 24: 46%; ACT scores over 30: 10%.

Retention: 79% of full-time freshmen returned.

FACULTY
Total: 379, 56% full-time.

Student/faculty ratio: 14:1.

ACADEMICS
Calendar: semesters. *Degrees:* bachelor's, master's, doctoral, post-master's, and postbachelor's certificates.

Special study options: academic remediation for entering students, advanced placement credit, cooperative education, distance learning, English as a second language, honors programs, independent study, internships, off-campus study, part-time degree program, services for LD students, study abroad, summer session for credit.

Computers: 550 computers/terminals and 39 ports are available on campus for general student use. Students can access the following: campus intranet, computer help desk, free student e-mail accounts, online (class) grades, online (class) registration, online (class) schedules. Campuswide network is available. 100% of college-owned or -operated housing units are wired for high-speed Internet access. Wireless service is available via entire campus.

STUDENT LIFE
Housing options: on-campus residence required for freshman year; coed, special housing for students with disabilities. Campus housing is university owned. Freshman campus housing is guaranteed.

Activities and organizations: drama/theater group, student-run newspaper, radio station, choral group, Student Activities Committee, Black Student Union, Christian Student Fellowship, Dance Marathon, Club Dodgeball, national sororities.

Athletics Member NCAA. All Division II. ***Intercollegiate sports:*** baseball M(s), basketball M(s)/W(s), golf M(s)/W(s), soccer M(s)/W(s), softball W(s), tennis M(s)/W(s), volleyball W(s). ***Intramural sports:*** badminton M(c)/W(c), basketball M/W, bowling M(c)/W(c), cheerleading M(c)/W(c), football M/W, racquetball M/W, sailing M(c)/W(c), soccer M/W, softball M/W, squash M(c)/W(c), table tennis M/W, track and field M/W, ultimate Frisbee M/W, volleyball M(c)/W(c).

Campus security: 24-hour emergency response devices and patrols, late-night transport/escort service, controlled dormitory access.

Student services: health clinic, personal/psychological counseling, women's center.

COSTS & FINANCIAL AID
Costs (2015–16) ***Tuition:*** state resident $9405 full-time, $314 per credit hour part-time; nonresident $18,930 full-time, $631 per credit hour part-time. Full-time tuition and fees vary according to course load. Part-time tuition and fees vary according to course load. No tuition increase for student's term of enrollment. ***Required fees:*** $2008 full-time, $18 per credit hour part-time, $1005 per term part-time. ***Room and board:*** $11,550; room only: $7350. Room and board charges vary according to board plan and housing facility. ***Payment plan:*** installment. ***Waivers:*** senior citizens and employees or children of employees.

Financial Aid Of all full-time matriculated undergraduates who enrolled in 2013, 1,656 applied for aid, 1,400 were judged to have need, 136 had their need fully met. In 2013, 259 non-need-based awards were made. ***Average percent of need met:*** 68. ***Average financial aid package:*** $12,320. ***Average need-based loan:*** $4250. ***Average need-based gift aid:*** $9451. ***Average non-need-based aid:*** $5932. ***Average indebtedness upon graduation:*** $23,507. ***Financial aid deadline:*** 11/15.

APPLYING
Standardized Tests *Required:* SAT or ACT (for admission).

Options: electronic application, deferred entrance.

Application fee: $50.

Required: high school transcript.

Application deadlines: rolling (freshmen), rolling (transfers).

Notification: continuous (transfers).

CONTACT
Fernando Planas, Director of Admissions, University of Illinois at Springfield, One University Plaza, MS UHB 1080, Springfield, IL 62703-5407. *Phone:* 217-206-4847. *Toll-free phone:* 888-977-4847. *E-mail:* admissions@uis.edu.

University of Illinois at Urbana–Champaign

Champaign, Illinois

http://www.illinois.edu/

- **State-supported** university, founded 1867, part of University of Illinois System
- **Urban** 1783-acre campus
- **Coed**
- **Very difficult** entrance level

FACULTY
Student/faculty ratio: 18:1.

ACADEMICS
Calendar: semesters. *Degrees:* certificates, bachelor's, master's, doctoral, post-master's, and postbachelor's certificates.

STUDENT LIFE
Housing options: on-campus residence required for freshman year; coed, men-only, women-only, cooperative, special housing for students with disabilities. Campus housing is university owned and is provided by a third party. Freshman campus housing is guaranteed.

Activities and organizations: drama/theater group, student-run newspaper, radio and television station, choral group, marching band, Volunteer Illini Project, October Lovers, Illini Pride Student Board, National Society of Collegiate Scholars, Phi Eta Sigma Freshman Honor Society, national fraternities, national sororities.

Athletics Member NCAA. All Division I except football (Division I-A).

Campus security: 24-hour emergency response devices and patrols, student patrols, late-night transport/escort service, controlled dormitory access, safety training classes, ID cards with safety numbers.

Student services: health clinic, personal/psychological counseling, women's center, legal services.

COSTS & FINANCIAL AID
Costs (2014–15) ***Tuition:*** state resident $12,036 full-time; nonresident $26,662 full-time. Full-time tuition and fees vary according to program and student level. No tuition increase for student's term of enrollment. ***Required fees:*** $3566 full-time. ***Room and board:*** $10,848. Room and board charges vary according to board plan, housing facility, and location.

Financial Aid Of all full-time matriculated undergraduates who enrolled in 2011, 18,852 applied for aid, 14,910 were judged to have need, 3,890 had their need fully met. In 2011, 3324 non-need-based awards were made. ***Average percent of need met:*** 63. ***Average financial aid package:*** $13,533. ***Average need-based loan:*** $4588. ***Average need-based gift aid:*** $11,557. ***Average non-need-based aid:*** $4073. ***Average indebtedness upon graduation:*** $24,657.

APPLYING
Standardized Tests *Required:* SAT or ACT (for admission).

Options: electronic application, early admission, deferred entrance.

Application fee: $50.

Required: essay or personal statement, high school transcript. ***Required for some:*** application essay is required for all potential students. Auditions or portfolios may be required of some applicants depending on their field of study.

CONTACT
Stacey Kostell, Director of Admissions, University of Illinois at Urbana–Champaign, 901 West Illinois, Urbana, IL 61801. *Phone:* 217-333-0302. *Fax:* 217-244-4614. *E-mail:* ugradadmissions@uiuc.edu.

University of St. Francis

Joliet, Illinois

http://www.stfrancis.edu/

- **Independent Roman Catholic** comprehensive, founded 1920
- **Suburban** 34-acre campus with easy access to Chicago
- **Endowment** $15.4 million
- **Coed** 1,381 undergraduate students, 95% full-time, 64% women, 36% men
- **Moderately difficult** entrance level, 51% of applicants were admitted

UNDERGRAD STUDENTS
1,316 full-time, 65 part-time. Students come from 15 states and territories; 16 other countries; 5% are from out of state; 8% Black or African American, non-Hispanic/Latino; 17% Hispanic/Latino; 2% Asian, non-Hispanic/Latino; 0.4% Native Hawaiian or other Pacific Islander, non-Hispanic/Latino; 0.4% American Indian or Alaska Native, non-Hispanic/Latino; 3% Two or more races, non-Hispanic/Latino; 0.3% Race/ethnicity unknown; 2% international; 14% transferred in; 26% live on campus.

Freshmen
Admission: 1,509 applied, 763 admitted, 216 enrolled. ***Average high school GPA:*** 3.43. ***Test scores:*** SAT critical reading scores over 500: 50%; SAT math scores over 500: 50%; SAT writing scores over 500: 29%; ACT scores over 18: 98%; SAT critical reading scores over 600: 14%; SAT math scores over 600: 7%; SAT writing scores over 600: 7%; ACT scores over 24: 43%; SAT writing scores over 700: 7%; ACT scores over 30: 4%.

Retention: 81% of full-time freshmen returned.

FACULTY
Total: 294, 35% full-time, 37% with terminal degrees.

Student/faculty ratio: 11:1.

ACADEMICS
Calendar: semesters. *Degrees:* certificates, bachelor's, master's, doctoral, post-master's, and postbachelor's certificates.

Special study options: academic remediation for entering students, accelerated degree program, adult/continuing education programs, advanced placement credit, distance learning, double majors, English as a second language, honors programs, independent study, internships, off-campus study, part-time degree program, services for LD students, student-designed majors, study abroad, summer session for credit. ***ROTC:*** Army (c).

Computers: 560 computers/terminals and 2,000 ports are available on campus for general student use. Students can access the following: campus intranet, computer help desk, free student e-mail accounts, online (class) grades, online (class) registration, online (class) schedules, billing/payment. Campuswide network is available. 100% of college-owned or -operated housing units are wired for high-speed Internet access. Wireless service is available via entire campus.

STUDENT LIFE
Housing options: coed. Campus housing is university owned. Freshman campus housing is guaranteed.

Activities and organizations: drama/theater group, student-run newspaper, radio and television station, choral group, Justice League, Unidos Vamos Alcanzar (UVA), International Club, Student Nurses Association, Student Activities Board, national sororities.

Athletics Member NAIA. ***Intercollegiate sports:*** baseball M(s), basketball M(s)/W(s), bowling M(s)/W(s), cheerleading M(s)/W(s), cross-country running M(s)/W(s), football M(s), golf M(s)/W(s), soccer M(s)/W(s), softball W(s), tennis M(s)/W(s), track and field M(s)/W(s), volleyball W(s). ***Intramural sports:*** badminton M/W, basketball M/W, bowling M/W, volleyball M/W.

Campus security: 24-hour emergency response devices and patrols, student patrols, late-night transport/escort service, controlled dormitory access, First Response trained security personnel.

Student services: health clinic, personal/psychological counseling.

COSTS & FINANCIAL AID
Costs (2015–16) ***Tuition:*** $29,630 full-time, $825 per credit hour part-time. Full-time tuition and fees vary according to degree level, location, and program. Part-time tuition and fees vary according to degree level and program. ***Required fees:*** $320 full-time, $75 per term part-time. ***Room only:*** Room and board charges vary according to housing facility. ***Payment plans:*** installment, deferred payment. ***Waivers:*** children of alumni and employees or children of employees.

Financial Aid Of all full-time matriculated undergraduates who enrolled in 2013, 1,268 applied for aid, 1,172 were judged to have need, 834 had their need fully met. 174 Federal Work-Study jobs (averaging $1421). 243 state and other part-time jobs (averaging $1473). In 2013, 171 non-need-based awards were made. ***Average percent of need met:*** 77. ***Average financial aid package:*** $22,137. ***Average need-based loan:*** $4589. ***Average need-based gift aid:*** $8213. ***Average non-need-based aid:*** $10,061. ***Average indebtedness upon graduation:*** $27,373.

APPLYING
Standardized Tests *Required:* SAT or ACT (for admission).

Options: electronic application, deferred entrance.

Required: high school transcript, minimum 2.5 GPA. ***Required for some:*** essay or personal statement, 2 letters of recommendation, interview.

Notification: continuous (freshmen), continuous (transfers).

CONTACT
Ms. Cynthia Lambert, Director of Undergraduate Admissions, University of St. Francis, 500 North Wilcox Street, Joliet, IL 60435-6188. *Phone:* 800-735-7500. *Toll-free phone:* 800-735-7500. *Fax:* 815-740-5032. *E-mail:* clambert@stfrancis.edu.

VanderCook College of Music

Chicago, Illinois

http://www.vandercook.edu/

- **Independent** comprehensive, founded 1909
- **Urban** 1-acre campus with easy access to Chicago
- **Endowment** $929,237
- **Coed** 148 undergraduate students, 71% full-time, 47% women, 53% men

UNDERGRAD STUDENTS
105 full-time, 43 part-time. Students come from 13 states and territories; 2 other countries; 24% are from out of state; 6% Black or African American, non-Hispanic/Latino; 21% Hispanic/Latino; 0.9% Asian, non-Hispanic/Latino; 4% Two or more races, non-Hispanic/Latino; 0.9% Race/ethnicity unknown; 2% international; 8% transferred in; 21% live on campus.

Freshmen
Admission: 25 enrolled. ***Average high school GPA:*** 3.68. ***Test scores:*** ACT scores over 18: 96%; ACT scores over 24: 53%; ACT scores over 30: 24%.

Retention: 87% of full-time freshmen returned.

FACULTY
Total: 35, 26% full-time, 29% with terminal degrees.

Student/faculty ratio: 8:1.

ACADEMICS
Calendar: semesters. *Degrees:* bachelor's and master's.

Special study options: advanced placement credit, distance learning, independent study, internships, part-time degree program.

Computers: 21 computers/terminals are available on campus for general student use. Students can access the following: campus intranet, free student e-mail accounts. Campuswide network is available. Wireless service is available via entire campus.

STUDENT LIFE
Housing options: coed, special housing for students with disabilities. Campus housing is provided by a third party.

Activities and organizations: choral group, NAfME (National Association for Music Education), ACDA (American Choral Directors Association), NBA (National Band Association), ASTA (American String Teachers Association), national fraternities, national sororities.

Campus security: 24-hour emergency response devices and patrols, late-night transport/escort service, controlled dormitory access.

COSTS & FINANCIAL AID
Costs (2014–15) ***Comprehensive fee:*** $36,870 includes full-time tuition ($24,150), mandatory fees ($1540), and room and board ($11,180). Full-time tuition and fees vary according to course level, course load, degree level, and program. Part-time tuition: $1000 per semester hour. Part-time tuition and fees vary according to course level, course load, degree level, and program. ***Required fees:*** $1190 per year part-time. ***College room only:*** $5712. Room and board charges vary according to board plan and housing facility. ***Payment plan:*** installment. ***Waivers:*** employees or children of employees.

Financial Aid Of all full-time matriculated undergraduates who enrolled in 2013, 97 applied for aid, 86 were judged to have need. 18 Federal Work-Study jobs (averaging $706). 15 state and other part-time jobs (averaging $1026). In 2013, 11 non-need-based awards were made. ***Average financial aid package:*** $16,671. ***Average need-based loan:*** $4699. ***Average need-based gift aid:*** $9722. ***Average non-need-based aid:*** $5550. ***Average indebtedness upon graduation:*** $38,861.

APPLYING
Standardized Tests *Required for some:* SAT or ACT (for admission).

Required: essay or personal statement, high school transcript, 3 letters of recommendation, interview, Audition on their primary instrument or voice. ***Required for some:*** minimum 3.0 GPA. ***Recommended:*** minimum 3.0 GPA.

CONTACT
Ms. Amy L. Lenting, Director of Admissions and Retention, VanderCook College of Music, 3140 South Federal Street, Chicago, IL 60616. *Phone:* 312-788-1120 Ext. 230. *Fax:* 312-225-5211. *E-mail:* alenting@vandercook.edu.

Western Illinois University

Macomb, Illinois

http://www.wiu.edu/

- **State-supported** comprehensive, founded 1899
- **Small-town** 1050-acre campus
- **Endowment** $43.2 million
- **Coed** 9,645 undergraduate students, 89% full-time, 49% women, 51% men
- **Moderately difficult** entrance level, 70% of applicants were admitted

UNDERGRAD STUDENTS
8,607 full-time, 1,038 part-time. Students come from 37 states and territories; 57 other countries; 12% are from out of state; 19% Black or African American, non-Hispanic/Latino; 9% Hispanic/Latino; 0.9% Asian, non-Hispanic/Latino; 0.1% Native Hawaiian or other Pacific Islander, non-Hispanic/Latino; 0.1% American Indian or Alaska Native, non-Hispanic/Latino; 2% Two or more races, non-Hispanic/Latino; 3% Race/ethnicity unknown; 2% international; 13% transferred in; 44% live on campus.

Freshmen
Admission: 10,671 applied, 7,431 admitted, 1,605 enrolled. ***Average high school GPA:*** 3.15. ***Test scores:*** ACT scores over 18: 79%; ACT scores over 24: 21%; ACT scores over 30: 4%.
Retention: 72% of full-time freshmen returned.

FACULTY
Total: 705, 90% full-time, 67% with terminal degrees.
Student/faculty ratio: 15:1.

ACADEMICS
Calendar: semesters. *Degrees:* bachelor's, master's, doctoral, and postbachelor's certificates.
Special study options: academic remediation for entering students, adult/continuing education programs, advanced placement credit, distance learning, double majors, English as a second language, external degree program, freshman honors college, honors programs, independent study, internships, off-campus study, part-time degree program, services for LD students, student-designed majors, study abroad, summer session for credit. ***ROTC:*** Army (b).
Computers: 1,100 computers/terminals are available on campus for general student use. Students can access the following: computer help desk, free student e-mail accounts, online (class) grades, online (class) registration, online (class) schedules. Campuswide network is available. 100% of college-owned or -operated housing units are wired for high-speed Internet access. Wireless service is available via entire campus.

STUDENT LIFE
Housing options: on-campus residence required through sophomore year; coed, men-only, women-only, special housing for students with disabilities. Campus housing is university owned. Freshman campus housing is guaranteed.
Activities and organizations: drama/theater group, student-run newspaper, radio and television station, choral group, marching band, Student Government Association, Black Student Association, University Union Board, International Friendship Club, Bureau of Cultural Affairs, national fraternities, national sororities.
Athletics Member NCAA. All Division I except football (Division I-AA). ***Intercollegiate sports:*** baseball M(s), basketball M(s)/W(s), cross-country running M(s)/W(s), golf M(s)/W, soccer M(s)/W(s), softball W(s), swimming and diving M(s)/W(s), tennis M(s)/W(s), track and field M(s)/W(s), volleyball W(s). ***Intramural sports:*** archery M/W, badminton M/W, basketball M/W, bowling M, cheerleading M/W, cross-country running M/W, equestrian sports M/W, fencing M/W, football M/W, golf M/W, lacrosse M, racquetball M/W, rugby M/W, soccer M/W, softball M/W, swimming and diving M/W, tennis M/W, ultimate Frisbee M/W, volleyball M/W, water polo M/W, wrestling M.
Campus security: 24-hour emergency response devices and patrols, student patrols, late-night transport/escort service, controlled dormitory access.
Student services: health clinic, personal/psychological counseling, women's center, legal services.

COSTS & FINANCIAL AID
Costs (2014–15) ***Tuition:*** state resident $8632 full-time, $288 per credit hour part-time; nonresident $12,948 full-time, $432 per credit hour part-time. Full-time tuition and fees vary according to course load and student level. Part-time tuition and fees vary according to course load and student level. No tuition increase for student's term of enrollment. ***Required fees:*** $2650 full-time, $88 per credit hour part-time. ***Room and board:*** $9450; room only: $5800. Room and board charges vary according to board plan, housing facility, and student level. ***Payment plan:*** installment. ***Waivers:*** senior citizens and employees or children of employees.
Financial Aid Of all full-time matriculated undergraduates who enrolled in 2014, 7,363 applied for aid, 6,444 were judged to have need, 1,813 had their need fully met. In 2014, 211 non-need-based awards were made. ***Average percent of need met:*** 59. ***Average financial aid package:*** $11,221. ***Average need-based loan:*** $4316. ***Average need-based gift aid:*** $8595. ***Average non-need-based aid:*** $2851. ***Average indebtedness upon graduation:*** $28,785.

APPLYING
Standardized Tests *Required:* SAT or ACT (for admission).
Options: electronic application, deferred entrance.
Application fee: $30.
Required: high school transcript, minimum 2.5 GPA.
Application deadlines: 5/15 (freshmen), rolling (transfers).
Notification: continuous (freshmen), continuous (transfers).

CONTACT
Western Illinois University, 1 University Circle, Macomb, IL 61455-1390. *Phone:* 309-298-3157. *Toll-free phone:* 877-742-5948.

Wheaton College

Wheaton, Illinois

http://www.wheaton.edu/

- **Independent nondenominational** comprehensive, founded 1860
- **Suburban** 80-acre campus with easy access to Chicago
- **Endowment** $405.0 million
- **Coed** 2,432 undergraduate students, 97% full-time, 52% women, 48% men
- **Very difficult** entrance level, 69% of applicants were admitted

UNDERGRAD STUDENTS
2,368 full-time, 64 part-time. Students come from 51 states and territories; 39 other countries; 74% are from out of state; 2% Black or African American, non-Hispanic/Latino; 5% Hispanic/Latino; 9% Asian, non-Hispanic/Latino; 0.1% American Indian or Alaska Native, non-Hispanic/Latino; 5% Two or more races, non-Hispanic/Latino; 3% international; 3% transferred in; 90% live on campus.

Freshmen
Admission: 2,010 applied, 1,390 admitted, 607 enrolled. ***Average high school GPA:*** 3.68. ***Test scores:*** SAT critical reading scores over 500: 98%; SAT math scores over 500: 96%; SAT writing scores over 500: 95%; ACT scores over 18: 100%; SAT critical reading scores over 600: 78%; SAT math scores over 600: 73%; SAT writing scores over 600: 78%; ACT scores over 24: 93%; SAT critical reading scores over 700: 34%; SAT math scores over 700: 27%; SAT writing scores over 700: 27%; ACT scores over 30: 53%.
Retention: 93% of full-time freshmen returned.

FACULTY
Total: 314, 65% full-time, 76% with terminal degrees.
Student/faculty ratio: 11:1.

ACADEMICS
Calendar: semesters. *Degrees:* bachelor's, master's, doctoral, and postbachelor's certificates.

Special study options: advanced placement credit, double majors, independent study, internships, off-campus study, services for LD students, student-designed majors, study abroad, summer session for credit. ***ROTC:*** Army (b), Air Force (c).

Unusual degree programs: 3-2 engineering with University of Illinois - Urbana Champaign, University of Minnesota, Washington University. A special arrangement is in place with the nearby Illinois Institute of Technology in Chicago which allows students to spend all 5 years living at Wheaton; nursing with Emory University, Vanderbilt University.

Computers: 125 computers/terminals and 3,500 ports are available on campus for general student use. Students can access the following: campus intranet, computer help desk, free student e-mail accounts, online (class) grades, online (class) registration, online (class) schedules, financial information, degree requirements evaluation. Campuswide network is available. 100% of college-owned or -operated housing units are wired for high-speed Internet access. Wireless service is available via entire campus.

STUDENT LIFE

Housing options: on-campus residence required through senior year; coed, men-only, women-only, cooperative, special housing for students with disabilities. Campus housing is university owned. Freshman campus housing is guaranteed.

Activities and organizations: drama/theater group, student-run newspaper, radio station, choral group, Discipleship small groups, intramurals, Club Sports, Christian Service Council, New Student Orientation.

Athletics Member NCAA. All Division III. ***Intercollegiate sports:*** baseball M, basketball M/W, cheerleading W(c), crew M(c)/W(c), cross-country running M/W, football M, golf M/W, ice hockey M(c), lacrosse M(c)/W(c), soccer M/W, softball W, swimming and diving M/W, tennis M/W, track and field M/W, volleyball M(c)/W, water polo W(c), wrestling M. ***Intramural sports:*** basketball M/W, golf M/W, soccer M/W, softball M, ultimate Frisbee M/W, volleyball M/W.

Campus security: 24-hour emergency response devices and patrols, student patrols, late-night transport/escort service, controlled dormitory access.

Student services: health clinic, personal/psychological counseling.

COSTS & FINANCIAL AID

Costs (2014–15) ***Comprehensive fee:*** $40,720 includes full-time tuition ($31,900) and room and board ($8820). Full-time tuition and fees vary according to program. Part-time tuition: $1329 per credit hour. Part-time tuition and fees vary according to course load and program. ***College room only:*** $5120. Room and board charges vary according to board plan and housing facility. ***Payment plans:*** installment, deferred payment.

Financial Aid Of all full-time matriculated undergraduates who enrolled in 2014, 1,607 applied for aid, 1,238 were judged to have need, 394 had their need fully met. 184 Federal Work-Study jobs (averaging $1227). In 2014, 449 non-need-based awards were made. ***Average percent of need met:*** 89. ***Average financial aid package:*** $24,003. ***Average need-based loan:*** $4858. ***Average need-based gift aid:*** $20,255. ***Average non-need-based aid:*** $6428. ***Average indebtedness upon graduation:*** $25,939.

APPLYING

Standardized Tests *Required:* SAT or ACT (for admission).

Options: electronic application, early action, deferred entrance.

Application fee: $50.

Required: essay or personal statement, high school transcript, 2 letters of recommendation. ***Recommended:*** interview.

Application deadlines: 1/10 (freshmen), 3/1 (transfers), 11/1 (early action).

Notification: 4/1 (freshmen), 4/1 (transfers), 12/31 (early action).

CONTACT

Ms. Shawn Leftwich, Director of Admissions, Wheaton College, 501 College Avenue, Wheaton, IL 60187-5593. *Phone:* 630-752-5011. *Toll-free phone:* 800-222-2419. *Fax:* 630-752-5285. *E-mail:* admissions@wheaton.edu.

See below for display ad and page 1736 for the College Close-Up.

INDIANA

Anderson University

Anderson, Indiana

http://www.anderson.edu/

- **Independent** comprehensive, founded 1917, affiliated with Church of God
- **Suburban** 163-acre campus with easy access to Indianapolis
- **Endowment** $30.3 million
- **Coed** 1,976 undergraduate students, 85% full-time, 60% women, 40% men
- **Moderately difficult** entrance level, 55% of applicants were admitted

UNDERGRAD STUDENTS
1,674 full-time, 302 part-time. Students come from 40 states and territories; 20 other countries; 26% are from out of state; 9% Black or African American, non-Hispanic/Latino; 2% Hispanic/Latino; 0.8% Asian, non-Hispanic/Latino; 0.3% Native Hawaiian or other Pacific Islander, non-Hispanic/Latino; 0.3% American Indian or Alaska Native, non-Hispanic/Latino; 1% Two or more races, non-Hispanic/Latino; 6% Race/ethnicity unknown; 3% international; 5% transferred in; 60% live on campus.

Freshmen
Admission: 2,659 applied, 1,460 admitted, 441 enrolled. ***Average high school GPA:*** 3.4. ***Test scores:*** SAT critical reading scores over 500: 57%; SAT math scores over 500: 59%; ACT scores over 18: 94%; SAT critical reading scores over 600: 18%; SAT math scores over 600: 18%; ACT scores over 24: 47%; SAT critical reading scores over 700: 3%; SAT math scores over 700: 2%; ACT scores over 30: 6%.
Retention: 75% of full-time freshmen returned.

FACULTY
Total: 264, 48% full-time, 33% with terminal degrees.
Student/faculty ratio: 11:1.

ACADEMICS
Calendar: semesters. *Degrees:* associate, bachelor's, master's, and doctoral.
Special study options: academic remediation for entering students, accelerated degree program, adult/continuing education programs, advanced placement credit, distance learning, double majors, honors programs, independent study, internships, off-campus study, part-time degree program, services for LD students, student-designed majors, study abroad, summer session for credit.
Unusual degree programs: 3-2 engineering with Purdue University.
Computers: 300 computers/terminals are available on campus for general student use. Students can access the following: campus intranet, computer help desk, free student e-mail accounts, online (class) grades, online (class) registration, online (class) schedules, microcomputer software. Campuswide network is available. 100% of college-owned or -operated housing units are wired for high-speed Internet access. Wireless service is available via entire campus.

STUDENT LIFE
Housing options: on-campus residence required through junior year; men-only, women-only. Campus housing is university owned. Freshman campus housing is guaranteed.
Activities and organizations: drama/theater group, student-run newspaper, radio station, choral group, Adult and Continuing Education Students Association, Multicultural Student Union, Campus Ministries.
Athletics Member NCAA. All Division III. ***Intercollegiate sports:*** baseball M, basketball M/W, cross-country running M/W, football M, golf M/W, soccer M/W, softball W, tennis M/W, track and field M/W, volleyball W. ***Intramural sports:*** badminton M/W, basketball M/W, bowling M/W, cheerleading M(c)/W(c), rugby M(c), soccer M/W, softball M/W, tennis M/W, volleyball M/W.
Campus security: 24-hour emergency response devices and patrols, student patrols, late-night transport/escort service, controlled dormitory access, 24-hour crime line.
Student services: health clinic, personal/psychological counseling.

COSTS & FINANCIAL AID
Costs (2014–15) ***Comprehensive fee:*** $36,100 includes full-time tuition ($26,770), mandatory fees ($80), and room and board ($9250). Part-time tuition: $1116 per semester hour. Part-time tuition and fees vary according to course load. ***College room only:*** $5920. Room and board charges vary according to board plan and housing facility. ***Payment plan:*** installment. ***Waivers:*** employees or children of employees.
Financial Aid Of all full-time matriculated undergraduates who enrolled in 2013, 1,594 applied for aid, 1,445 were judged to have need, 602 had their need fully met. 920 Federal Work-Study jobs (averaging $3094). In 2013, 340 non-need-based awards were made. ***Average percent of need met:*** 84. ***Average financial aid package:*** $21,552. ***Average need-based loan:*** $4886. ***Average need-based gift aid:*** $15,101. ***Average non-need-based aid:*** $13,948. ***Average indebtedness upon graduation:*** $30,404.

APPLYING
Standardized Tests *Required:* SAT or ACT (for admission).
Options: electronic application, deferred entrance.
Application fee: $25.
Required: high school transcript, minimum 2.0 GPA, 2 letters of recommendation, lifestyle statement. ***Required for some:*** interview. ***Recommended:*** essay or personal statement.
Application deadlines: 7/1 (freshmen), rolling (transfers).
Notification: 9/1 (freshmen), continuous until 9/1 (transfers).

CONTACT
Mr. Joe Davis, Director of Admissions, Anderson University, 1100 East 5th Street, Anderson, IN 46012-3495. *Phone:* 765-641-4076. *Toll-free phone:* 800-428-6414. *Fax:* 765-641-3851. *E-mail:* info@anderson.edu.

The Art Institute of Indianapolis

Indianapolis, Indiana

http://www.artinstitutes.edu/indianapolis/

- **Proprietary** 4-year, part of Education Management Corporation
- **Suburban** campus
- **Coed**

ACADEMICS
Degrees: certificates, associate, and bachelor's.

CONTACT
The Art Institute of Indianapolis, 3500 Depauw Boulevard, Suite 1010, Indianapolis, IN 46268. *Phone:* 317-613-4800. *Toll-free phone:* 866-441-9031.

Ball State University

Muncie, Indiana

http://www.bsu.edu/

- **State-supported** university, founded 1918
- **Suburban** 1140-acre campus with easy access to Indianapolis
- **Endowment** $192.2 million
- **Coed** 16,415 undergraduate students, 91% full-time, 58% women, 42% men
- **Moderately difficult** entrance level, 60% of applicants were admitted

UNDERGRAD STUDENTS
15,018 full-time, 1,397 part-time. 12% are from out of state; 7% Black or African American, non-Hispanic/Latino; 4% Hispanic/Latino; 1% Asian, non-Hispanic/Latino; 0.1% Native Hawaiian or other Pacific Islander, non-Hispanic/Latino; 0.1% American Indian or Alaska Native, non-Hispanic/Latino; 2% Two or more races, non-Hispanic/Latino; 2% Race/ethnicity unknown; 3% international; 4% transferred in; 41% live on campus.

Freshmen
Admission: 18,107 applied, 10,842 admitted, 3,597 enrolled. ***Average high school GPA:*** 3.45. ***Test scores:*** SAT critical reading scores over 500: 66%; SAT math scores over 500: 65%; SAT writing scores over 500: 56%; ACT scores over 18: 98%; SAT critical reading scores over 600: 18%; SAT math scores over 600: 16%; SAT writing scores over 600: 13%; ACT scores over 24: 37%; SAT critical reading scores over 700: 2%; SAT math

scores over 700: 1%; SAT writing scores over 700: 1%; ACT scores over 30: 5%.

Retention: 82% of full-time freshmen returned.

FACULTY
Total: 1,230, 80% full-time, 65% with terminal degrees.

Student/faculty ratio: 15:1.

ACADEMICS
Calendar: semesters. *Degrees:* certificates, associate, bachelor's, master's, doctoral, post-master's, and postbachelor's certificates.

Special study options: accelerated degree program, adult/continuing education programs, advanced placement credit, cooperative education, distance learning, double majors, English as a second language, external degree program, freshman honors college, honors programs, independent study, internships, part-time degree program, services for LD students, student-designed majors, study abroad, summer session for credit. ***ROTC:*** Army (b).

Unusual degree programs: 3-2 engineering with Purdue University, Tri-State University.

Computers: 635 computers/terminals and 21,135 ports are available on campus for general student use. Students can access the following: campus intranet, computer help desk, free student e-mail accounts, online (class) grades, online (class) registration, online (class) schedules, room reservations, testing and test results, manage and pay tuition, order/buy textbooks, request room repairs, order transcripts, manage meal plan, manage and prepay long distance service, undergraduate degree progress report. Campuswide network is available. 100% of college-owned or -operated housing units are wired for high-speed Internet access. Wireless service is available via entire campus.

STUDENT LIFE
Housing options: on-campus residence required for freshman year; coed, men-only, women-only, special housing for students with disabilities. Campus housing is university owned. Freshman campus housing is guaranteed.

Activities and organizations: drama/theater group, student-run newspaper, radio and television station, choral group, marching band, Epsilon Sigma Alpha International, WCRD- Student Radio Station, Golden Key Honor Society, Excellence in Leadership (EIL), Student Voluntary Services, national fraternities, national sororities.

Athletics Member NCAA. All Division I except football (Division I-A). ***Intercollegiate sports:*** baseball M(s)/W(c), basketball M(s)/W(s), bowling M(c)/W(c), cheerleading M/W, cross-country running W(s), equestrian sports M(c)/W(c), fencing M(c)/W(c), field hockey W(s), golf M(s)/W(s), gymnastics W(s), lacrosse M(c)/W(c), racquetball M(c)/W(c), rock climbing M(c)/W(c), rugby M(c)/W(c), soccer M(c)/W(s), softball W(s), swimming and diving M(s)/W(s), tennis M(s)/W(s), track and field W(s), ultimate Frisbee M(c)/W(c), volleyball M(s)/W(s), water polo M(c)/W(c), wrestling M(c). ***Intramural sports:*** badminton M/W, basketball M/W, bowling M/W, golf M/W, racquetball M/W, soccer M/W, softball M/W, swimming and diving M/W, table tennis M/W, tennis M/W, track and field M/W, ultimate Frisbee M/W, volleyball M/W.

Campus security: 24-hour emergency response devices and patrols, late-night transport/escort service, controlled dormitory access.

Student services: health clinic, personal/psychological counseling, women's center, legal services.

COSTS & FINANCIAL AID
Costs (2015–16) ***Tuition:*** state resident $8722 full-time, $327 per credit part-time; nonresident $23,948 full-time, $989 per credit part-time. Full-time tuition and fees vary according to course load, program, and reciprocity agreements. Part-time tuition and fees vary according to course load and reciprocity agreements. ***Required fees:*** $662 full-time. ***Room and board:*** $9537; room only: $4343. Room and board charges vary according to board plan and housing facility. ***Payment plan:*** installment. ***Waivers:*** senior citizens and employees or children of employees.

Financial Aid Of all full-time matriculated undergraduates who enrolled in 2013, 12,856 applied for aid, 10,203 were judged to have need, 2,825 had their need fully met. In 2013, 1553 non-need-based awards were made. ***Average percent of need met:*** 67. ***Average financial aid package:*** $11,337. ***Average need-based loan:*** $4377. ***Average need-based gift aid:*** $5843. ***Average non-need-based aid:*** $6979. ***Average indebtedness upon graduation:*** $25,918.

APPLYING
Standardized Tests *Required for some:* SAT or ACT (for admission).

Options: electronic application, deferred entrance.

Application fee: $55.

Required: high school transcript. ***Required for some:*** essay or personal statement.

Application deadlines: 8/10 (freshmen), rolling (transfers).

Notification: continuous (freshmen), continuous (transfers).

CONTACT
Ball State University, 2000 West University Avenue, Muncie, IN 47306-1099. *Phone:* 765-285-5608. *Toll-free phone:* 800-482-4BSU.

Bethel College
Mishawaka, Indiana
http://www.bethelcollege.edu/

- **Independent** comprehensive, founded 1947, affiliated with Missionary Church
- **Suburban** 80-acre campus
- **Endowment** $10.4 million
- **Coed** 1,600 undergraduate students, 77% full-time, 65% women, 35% men
- **Minimally difficult** entrance level, 70% of applicants were admitted

UNDERGRAD STUDENTS
1,227 full-time, 373 part-time. Students come from 31 states and territories; 11 other countries; 29% are from out of state; 10% Black or African American, non-Hispanic/Latino; 6% Hispanic/Latino; 0.8% Asian, non-Hispanic/Latino; 0.5% Native Hawaiian or other Pacific Islander, non-Hispanic/Latino; 0.3% American Indian or Alaska Native, non-Hispanic/Latino; 3% Two or more races, non-Hispanic/Latino; 0.4% Race/ethnicity unknown; 2% international; 12% transferred in; 48% live on campus.

Freshmen
Admission: 1,211 applied, 853 admitted, 224 enrolled. ***Average high school GPA:*** 3.46. ***Test scores:*** SAT critical reading scores over 500: 55%; SAT math scores over 500: 56%; SAT writing scores over 500: 48%; ACT scores over 18: 89%; SAT critical reading scores over 600: 18%; SAT math scores over 600: 25%; SAT writing scores over 600: 12%; ACT scores over 24: 43%; SAT critical reading scores over 700: 3%; SAT math scores over 700: 3%; SAT writing scores over 700: 3%; ACT scores over 30: 8%.

Retention: 80% of full-time freshmen returned.

FACULTY
Total: 197, 41% full-time, 35% with terminal degrees.

Student/faculty ratio: 12:1.

ACADEMICS
Calendar: semesters. *Degrees:* associate, bachelor's, and master's.

Special study options: academic remediation for entering students, accelerated degree program, adult/continuing education programs, advanced placement credit, distance learning, double majors, honors programs, independent study, internships, off-campus study, part-time degree program, services for LD students, student-designed majors, study abroad, summer session for credit. ***ROTC:*** Army (c), Air Force (c).

Unusual degree programs: 3-2 engineering with University of Notre Dame, Trine University.

Computers: 160 computers/terminals are available on campus for general student use. Students can access the following: computer help desk, free student e-mail accounts, online (class) grades, online (class) registration, online (class) schedules. Campuswide network is available. 100% of college-owned or -operated housing units are wired for high-speed Internet access. Wireless service is available via entire campus.

STUDENT LIFE
Housing options: on-campus residence required through sophomore year; men-only, women-only. Campus housing is university owned.

Activities and organizations: drama/theater group, student-run newspaper, radio station, choral group, International Student Fellowship, Students for Life, Student Council, Spiritual Life Team.

Athletics Member NAIA, NCCAA. ***Intercollegiate sports:*** baseball M(s), basketball M(s)/W(s), cheerleading M(s)/W(s), cross-country running M(s)/W(s), golf M(s)/W(s), lacrosse M(s), rugby M(s), soccer M(s)/W(s), softball W(s), tennis M(s)/W(s), track and field M(s)/W(s), volleyball W(s). ***Intramural sports:*** badminton M/W, basketball M/W, soccer M/W, softball M/W, table tennis M/W, tennis M/W, ultimate Frisbee M/W, volleyball M/W.

Campus security: 24-hour emergency response devices and patrols, late-night transport/escort service, controlled dormitory access.

Student services: health clinic, personal/psychological counseling.

COSTS & FINANCIAL AID

Costs (2015–16) ***Comprehensive fee:*** $34,930 includes full-time tuition ($26,240), mandatory fees ($350), and room and board ($8340). Full-time tuition and fees vary according to program. Part-time tuition: $834 per credit. Part-time tuition and fees vary according to course load and program. ***College room only:*** $4040. Room and board charges vary according to board plan and housing facility. ***Payment plan:*** installment. ***Waivers:*** employees or children of employees.

Financial Aid Of all full-time matriculated undergraduates who enrolled in 2013, 1,208 applied for aid, 1,113 were judged to have need, 122 had their need fully met. In 2013, 127 non-need-based awards were made. ***Average percent of need met:*** 64. ***Average financial aid package:*** $17,321. ***Average need-based loan:*** $4451. ***Average need-based gift aid:*** $8313. ***Average non-need-based aid:*** $7674. ***Average indebtedness upon graduation:*** $25,703. ***Financial aid deadline:*** 3/10.

APPLYING

Standardized Tests *Required:* SAT or ACT (for admission).

Options: electronic application, early admission, deferred entrance.

Required: high school transcript, minimum 2.0 GPA, 1 letter of recommendation. ***Recommended:*** essay or personal statement, minimum 2.5 GPA, interview.

Application deadlines: 8/15 (freshmen), 8/15 (transfers).

Notification: continuous (freshmen), continuous (transfers).

CONTACT

Ms. Stephanie Hochstetler, Associate Director of Admission, Bethel College, 1001 Bethel Circle, Mishawaka, IN 46545. *Phone:* 574-807-7600. *Toll-free phone:* 800-422-4101. *Fax:* 574-807-7650. *E-mail:* admissions@bethelcollege.edu.

Brown Mackie College–Fort Wayne

Fort Wayne, Indiana

http://www.brownmackie.edu/fortwayne/

- **Proprietary** primarily 2-year, part of Education Management Corporation
- **Coed**

ACADEMICS

Calendar: quarters. *Degrees:* certificates, associate, and bachelor's.

CONTACT

Brown Mackie College–Fort Wayne, 3000 East Coliseum Boulevard, Fort Wayne, IN 46805. *Phone:* 260-484-4400. *Toll-free phone:* 866-433-2289.

Brown Mackie College–Indianapolis

Indianapolis, Indiana

http://www.brownmackie.edu/indianapolis/

- **Proprietary** primarily 2-year, part of Education Management Corporation
- **Coed**

ACADEMICS

Degrees: certificates, diplomas, associate, and bachelor's.

CONTACT

Brown Mackie College–Indianapolis, 1200 North Meridian Street, Suite 100, Indianapolis, IN 46204. *Phone:* 317-554-8300. *Toll-free phone:* 866-255-0279.

Brown Mackie College–Merrillville

Merrillville, Indiana

http://www.brownmackie.edu/merrillville/

- **Proprietary** primarily 2-year, founded 1890, part of Education Management Corporation
- **Small-town** campus
- **Coed**

ACADEMICS

Calendar: quarters. *Degrees:* certificates, associate, and bachelor's.

CONTACT

Brown Mackie College–Merrillville, 1000 East 80th Place, Suite 205S, Merrillville, IN 46410. *Phone:* 219-769-3321. *Toll-free phone:* 800-258-3321.

Brown Mackie College–Michigan City

Michigan City, Indiana

http://www.brownmackie.edu/michigancity/

- **Proprietary** primarily 2-year, part of Education Management Corporation
- **Rural** campus
- **Coed**

ACADEMICS

Calendar: quarters. *Degrees:* certificates, associate, and bachelor's.

CONTACT

Brown Mackie College–Michigan City, 1001 East US Highway 20, Michigan City, IN 46360. *Phone:* 219-877-3100. *Toll-free phone:* 800-519-2416.

Brown Mackie College–South Bend

South Bend, Indiana

http://www.brownmackie.edu/southbend/

- **Proprietary** primarily 2-year, founded 1882, part of Education Management Corporation
- **Urban** campus
- **Coed, primarily women**

ACADEMICS

Calendar: quarters. *Degrees:* certificates, diplomas, associate, and bachelor's.

CONTACT

Brown Mackie College–South Bend, 3454 Douglas Road, South Bend, IN 46635. *Phone:* 574-237-0774. *Toll-free phone:* 800-743-2447.

Butler University

Indianapolis, Indiana

http://www.butler.edu/

- **Independent** comprehensive, founded 1855
- **Urban** 290-acre campus with easy access to Indianapolis
- **Endowment** $186.0 million
- **Coed** 4,062 undergraduate students, 98% full-time, 60% women, 40% men
- **Very difficult** entrance level, 68% of applicants were admitted

UNDERGRAD STUDENTS

3,980 full-time, 82 part-time. Students come from 46 states and territories; 56 other countries; 51% are from out of state; 4% Black or African American, non-Hispanic/Latino; 3% Hispanic/Latino; 3% Asian, non-Hispanic/Latino; 0.2% American Indian or Alaska Native, non-Hispanic/Latino; 2% Two or more races, non-Hispanic/Latino; 4% Race/ethnicity unknown; 3% international; 2% transferred in; 66% live on campus.

Freshmen

Admission: 10,103 applied, 6,917 admitted, 971 enrolled. ***Average high school GPA:*** 3.81. ***Test scores:*** SAT critical reading scores over 500: 90%; SAT math scores over 500: 90%; SAT writing scores over 500: 84%; ACT scores over 18: 99%; SAT critical reading scores over 600: 43%; SAT math scores over 600: 52%; SAT writing scores over 600: 38%; ACT

scores over 24: 87%; SAT critical reading scores over 700: 7%; SAT math scores over 700: 9%; SAT writing scores over 700: 4%; ACT scores over 30: 30%.

Retention: 91% of full-time freshmen returned.

FACULTY

Total: 557, 63% full-time.

Student/faculty ratio: 12:1.

ACADEMICS

Calendar: semesters. *Degrees:* associate, bachelor's, master's, and doctoral.

Special study options: adult/continuing education programs, advanced placement credit, cooperative education, double majors, honors programs, independent study, internships, off-campus study, part-time degree program, services for LD students, student-designed majors, study abroad, summer session for credit. ***ROTC:*** Army (b), Air Force (c).

Unusual degree programs: 3-2 engineering with Indiana University-Purdue University Indianapolis.

Computers: 450 computers/terminals are available on campus for general student use. Students can access the following: campus intranet, computer help desk, free student e-mail accounts, online (class) grades, online (class) registration, online (class) schedules. Campuswide network is available. 100% of college-owned or -operated housing units are wired for high-speed Internet access. Wireless service is available via entire campus.

STUDENT LIFE

Housing options: on-campus residence required through junior year; coed, women-only. Campus housing is university owned. Freshman campus housing is guaranteed.

Activities and organizations: drama/theater group, student-run newspaper, radio and television station, choral group, marching band, Delta Delta Delta, Alpha Kappa Psi (professional business fraternity), Engineering Dual Degree Club (EDDC), Kappa Delta Pi, Pre-Pharmacy Club, national fraternities, national sororities.

Athletics Member NCAA. All Division I except football (Division I-AA). ***Intercollegiate sports:*** baseball M(s), basketball M(s)/W(s), crew M(c)/W(c), cross-country running M(s)/W(s), equestrian sports W(c), golf M(s)/W(s), ice hockey M(c), lacrosse M(c)/W(c), rugby M(c), soccer M(s)/W(s), softball W(s), swimming and diving M(c)/W, tennis M(s)/W(s), track and field M(s)/W(s), ultimate Frisbee M(c)/W(c), volleyball M(c)/W(s). ***Intramural sports:*** badminton M/W, baseball M, basketball M/W, bowling M/W, football M, soccer M/W, softball M/W, swimming and diving M/W, table tennis M/W, tennis M/W, track and field M/W, volleyball M/W, weight lifting M/W.

Campus security: 24-hour emergency response devices and patrols, late-night transport/escort service, controlled dormitory access.

Student services: health clinic, personal/psychological counseling.

COSTS & FINANCIAL AID

Costs (2014–15) ***Comprehensive fee:*** $47,272 includes full-time tuition ($34,750), mandatory fees ($902), and room and board ($11,620). Full-time tuition and fees vary according to course load, degree level, and program. Part-time tuition: $1450 per credit hour. Part-time tuition and fees vary according to course load, degree level, and program. ***College room only:*** $5460. Room and board charges vary according to housing facility. ***Payment plan:*** installment. ***Waivers:*** employees or children of employees.

Financial Aid Of all full-time matriculated undergraduates who enrolled in 2014, 3,853 applied for aid, 2,670 were judged to have need, 338 had their need fully met. 193 Federal Work-Study jobs (averaging $962). In 2014, 1141 non-need-based awards were made. ***Average percent of need met:*** 68. ***Average financial aid package:*** $23,034. ***Average need-based loan:*** $5192. ***Average need-based gift aid:*** $18,704. ***Average non-need-based aid:*** $11,979. ***Average indebtedness upon graduation:*** $35,797.

APPLYING

Standardized Tests *Required:* SAT or ACT (for admission).

Options: electronic application, early action, deferred entrance.

Application fee: $35.

Required: essay or personal statement, high school transcript, 1 letter of recommendation. ***Required for some:*** Audition/interview/portfolio required for applicants to JCFA. Four years of math and science STRONGLY recommended for students interested in COPHS majors and natural sciences. ***Recommended:*** 1 letter of recommendation.

Application deadlines: rolling (freshmen), rolling (out-of-state freshmen), 8/15 (transfers), 11/1 (early action).

Notification: continuous (freshmen), continuous (out-of-state freshmen), continuous (transfers), 12/20 (early action).

CONTACT

Mrs. Aimee Scheuermann, Director of Admission, Butler University, 4600 Sunset Avenue, Indianapolis, IN 46208-3485. *Phone:* 317-940-8100. *Toll-free phone:* 888-940-8100. *Fax:* 317-940-8150. *E-mail:* admission@butler.edu.

Calumet College of Saint Joseph

Whiting, Indiana

http://www.ccsj.edu/

- **Independent Roman Catholic** comprehensive, founded 1951
- **Urban** 25-acre campus with easy access to Chicago
- **Endowment** $4.4 million
- **Coed** 907 undergraduate students, 59% full-time, 47% women, 53% men
- **Noncompetitive** entrance level, 34% of applicants were admitted

UNDERGRAD STUDENTS

532 full-time, 375 part-time. Students come from 19 states and territories; 11 other countries; 38% are from out of state; 27% Black or African American, non-Hispanic/Latino; 29% Hispanic/Latino; 0.9% Asian, non-Hispanic/Latino; 3% American Indian or Alaska Native, non-Hispanic/Latino; 0.9% Two or more races, non-Hispanic/Latino; 0.1% international; 14% transferred in.

Freshmen

Admission: 524 applied, 177 admitted, 126 enrolled. ***Average high school GPA:*** 2.57. ***Test scores:*** SAT critical reading scores over 500: 11%; SAT math scores over 500: 25%; SAT writing scores over 500: 10%; ACT scores over 18: 47%; SAT critical reading scores over 600: 2%; SAT math scores over 600: 2%; ACT scores over 24: 10%.

Retention: 56% of full-time freshmen returned.

FACULTY

Total: 125, 25% full-time, 37% with terminal degrees.

Student/faculty ratio: 12:1.

ACADEMICS

Calendar: semesters. *Degrees:* certificates, associate, bachelor's, and master's.

Special study options: academic remediation for entering students, accelerated degree program, adult/continuing education programs, advanced placement credit, cooperative education, distance learning, double majors, external degree program, honors programs, independent study, internships, part-time degree program, services for LD students, summer session for credit.

Computers: 173 computers/terminals are available on campus for general student use. Students can access the following: computer help desk, free student e-mail accounts, online (class) grades, online (class) registration, online (class) schedules. Campuswide network is available. Wireless service is available via classrooms, computer labs, learning centers, libraries, student centers.

STUDENT LIFE

Housing options: college housing not available.

Activities and organizations: drama/theater group, student-run newspaper, student government, Los Amigos Hispanic Club, Criminal Justice Club, Drama Club, GIVE.

Athletics Member NAIA. ***Intercollegiate sports:*** baseball M(s), basketball M(s)/W(s), bowling M(s)/W(s), cross-country running M(s)/W(s), golf M(s)/W(s), soccer M(s)/W(s), softball W(s), tennis M(s)/W(s), track and field M(s)/W(s), volleyball M(s)/W(s), wrestling M(s).

Campus security: day and night security, emergency alert system.

Student services: personal/psychological counseling.

COSTS & FINANCIAL AID

Costs (2014–15) ***Tuition:*** $16,170 full-time, $510 per credit hour part-time. Full-time tuition and fees vary according to course load and program. Part-time tuition and fees vary according to course load and program. No tuition increase for student's term of enrollment. ***Required fees:*** $270 full-time, $135 per term part-time. ***Payment plan:*** deferred payment. ***Waivers:*** children of alumni, senior citizens, and employees or children of employees.

Financial Aid Of all full-time matriculated undergraduates who enrolled in 2013, 557 applied for aid, 502 were judged to have need, 63 had their need fully met. 23 Federal Work-Study jobs (averaging $1816). 1 state and other part-time job (averaging $1284). In 2013, 19 non-need-based awards were made. ***Average percent of need met:*** 60. ***Average financial aid package:*** $12,417. ***Average need-based loan:*** $2984. ***Average need-based gift aid:*** $7738. ***Average non-need-based aid:*** $2959. ***Average indebtedness upon graduation:*** $30,847.

APPLYING

Standardized Tests *Required:* ACCUPLACER (for admission). *Recommended:* SAT or ACT (for admission).

Options: electronic application, deferred entrance.

Required: high school transcript. ***Required for some:*** essay or personal statement, 1 letter of recommendation. ***Recommended:*** minimum 2.0 GPA, interview.

Application deadlines: rolling (freshmen), rolling (out-of-state freshmen), rolling (transfers).

Notification: continuous (freshmen), continuous (out-of-state freshmen), continuous (transfers).

CONTACT

Mr. Carl Cuttone, Director of Recruitment and Enrollment, Calumet College of Saint Joseph, 2400 New York Avenue, Whiting, IN 46394. *Phone:* 219-473-4295. *Toll-free phone:* 877-700-9100. *Fax:* 219-473-4336. *E-mail:* admissions@ccsj.edu.

Chamberlain College of Nursing

Indianapolis, Indiana

http://www.chamberlain.edu/

- **Proprietary** 4-year
- **Coed**

FACULTY

Student/faculty ratio: 18:1.

ACADEMICS

Degree: bachelor's.

APPLYING

Standardized Tests *Required:* SAT or ACT (for admission).

Application fee: $95.

CONTACT

Chamberlain College of Nursing, 9100 Keystone Crossing, Suite 600, Indianapolis, IN 46240.

DePauw University

Greencastle, Indiana

http://www.depauw.edu/

- **Independent** 4-year, founded 1837, affiliated with United Methodist Church
- **Small-town** 655-acre campus with easy access to Indianapolis
- **Coed** 2,216 undergraduate students, 99% full-time, 54% women, 46% men
- **Moderately difficult** entrance level, 61% of applicants were admitted

UNDERGRAD STUDENTS

2,186 full-time, 30 part-time. 63% are from out of state; 6% Black or African American, non-Hispanic/Latino; 3% Hispanic/Latino; 3% Asian, non-Hispanic/Latino; 0.3% American Indian or Alaska Native, non-Hispanic/Latino; 7% Two or more races, non-Hispanic/Latino; 2% Race/ethnicity unknown; 9% international; 0.7% transferred in; 96% live on campus.

Freshmen

Admission: 5,086 applied, 3,113 admitted, 514 enrolled. ***Average high school GPA:*** 3.86. ***Test scores:*** SAT critical reading scores over 500: 87%; SAT math scores over 500: 96%; SAT writing scores over 500: 88%; ACT scores over 18: 100%; SAT critical reading scores over 600: 44%; SAT math scores over 600: 58%; SAT writing scores over 600: 42%; ACT scores over 24: 85%; SAT critical reading scores over 700: 10%; SAT math scores over 700: 11%; SAT writing scores over 700: 7%; ACT scores over 30: 21%.

Retention: 93% of full-time freshmen returned.

FACULTY

Total: 239, 87% full-time, 87% with terminal degrees.

Student/faculty ratio: 10:1.

ACADEMICS

Calendar: 4-1-4. *Degree:* bachelor's.

Special study options: part-time degree program. ***ROTC:*** Army (c), Air Force (c).

Unusual degree programs: 3-2 engineering with Columbia University, Washington University in St. Louis.

Computers: Students can access the following: online (class) registration. Campuswide network is available.

STUDENT LIFE

Housing options: on-campus residence required through senior year; coed, special housing for students with disabilities. Campus housing is university owned. Freshman campus housing is guaranteed.

Activities and organizations: drama/theater group, student-run newspaper, radio and television station, choral group, national fraternities, national sororities.

Athletics Member NCAA. All Division III. ***Intercollegiate sports:*** baseball M, basketball M/W, cheerleading M(c)/W(c), crew M(c)/W(c), cross-country running M/W, field hockey W, football M, golf M/W, rugby M(c), soccer M/W, softball W, swimming and diving M/W, tennis M/W, track and field M/W, volleyball W. ***Intramural sports:*** badminton M/W, basketball M/W, bowling M/W, football M/W, golf M, racquetball M/W, soccer M/W, softball M/W, table tennis M/W, tennis M/W, ultimate Frisbee M/W, volleyball M/W.

Campus security: 24-hour emergency response devices and patrols, student patrols, late-night transport/escort service, controlled dormitory access.

Student services: health clinic, personal/psychological counseling, women's center.

COSTS & FINANCIAL AID

Costs (2014–15) ***Comprehensive fee:*** $53,946 includes full-time tuition ($42,050), mandatory fees ($696), and room and board ($11,200). Part-time tuition: $1314 per credit hour. ***Room and board:*** Room and board charges vary according to board plan. ***Payment plan:*** installment. ***Waivers:*** employees or children of employees.

Financial Aid Of all full-time matriculated undergraduates who enrolled in 2013, 1,422 applied for aid, 1,213 were judged to have need, 322 had their need fully met. In 2013, 203 non-need-based awards were made. ***Average percent of need met:*** 89. ***Average financial aid package:*** $34,151. ***Average need-based loan:*** $4444. ***Average need-based gift aid:*** $29,557. ***Average non-need-based aid:*** $16,638. ***Average indebtedness upon graduation:*** $25,305. ***Financial aid deadline:*** 3/1.

APPLYING

Standardized Tests *Required:* SAT or ACT (for admission).

Options: electronic application, early admission, early decision, early action, deferred entrance.

Application fee: $40.

Required: essay or personal statement, high school transcript, 1 letter of recommendation. ***Recommended:*** interview.

CONTACT

Earl Macam, Director of Admission, DePauw University, 313 South Locust Street, Greencastle, IN 46135. *Phone:* 765-658-4006. *Toll-free phone:* 800-447-2495. *Fax:* 765-658-4007. *E-mail:* emacam@depauw.edu.

DeVry University

Indianapolis, Indiana

http://www.devry.edu/

- **Proprietary** comprehensive
- **Coed**

ACADEMICS

Calendar: semesters. *Degrees:* associate, bachelor's, and master's.

STUDENT LIFE

Housing options: college housing not available.

COSTS & FINANCIAL AID

Costs (2014–15) ***Tuition:*** $17,052 full-time, $609 per credit hour part-time. ***Required fees:*** $80 full-time.

Financial Aid Of all full-time matriculated undergraduates who enrolled in 2007, 19 applied for aid, 19 were judged to have need. In 2007, 1 non-need-based awards were made. ***Average percent of need met:*** 42. ***Average financial aid package:*** $14,132. ***Average need-based loan:*** $10,993. ***Average need-based gift aid:*** $6728. ***Average non-need-based aid:*** $20,854.

CONTACT

Admissions Office, DeVry University, 9100 Keystone Crossing, Suite 100, Indianapolis, IN 46240-2158. *Phone:* 317-581-8854. *Toll-free phone:* 866-338-7941.

DeVry University

Merrillville, Indiana

http://www.devry.edu/

- **Proprietary** comprehensive
- **Coed**

ACADEMICS

Calendar: semesters. *Degrees:* associate, bachelor's, and master's.

COSTS

Costs (2014–15) ***Tuition:*** $17,052 full-time, $609 per credit hour part-time. ***Required fees:*** $80 full-time.

CONTACT

Admissions Office, DeVry University, Twin Towers 1000 East 80th Place, Suite 222 Mall, Merrillville, IN 46410-5673. *Phone:* 219-736-7440. *Toll-free phone:* 866-338-7941.

Earlham College

Richmond, Indiana

http://www.earlham.edu/

- **Independent** comprehensive, founded 1847, affiliated with Society of Friends
- **Small-town** 800-acre campus with easy access to Cincinnati, Indianapolis, Dayton
- **Endowment** $405.0 million
- **Coed** 993 undergraduate students, 99% full-time, 55% women, 45% men
- **Very difficult** entrance level, 65% of applicants were admitted

UNDERGRAD STUDENTS

981 full-time, 12 part-time. Students come from 47 states and territories; 62 other countries; 80% are from out of state; 13% Black or African American, non-Hispanic/Latino; 6% Hispanic/Latino; 6% Asian, non-Hispanic/Latino; 1% American Indian or Alaska Native, non-Hispanic/Latino; 0.1% Two or more races, non-Hispanic/Latino; 2% Race/ethnicity unknown; 18% international; 2% transferred in; 96% live on campus.

Freshmen

Admission: 2,001 applied, 1,291 admitted, 270 enrolled. ***Average high school GPA:*** 3.5. ***Test scores:*** SAT critical reading scores over 500: 92%; SAT math scores over 500: 95%; SAT writing scores over 500: 96%; ACT scores over 18: 100%; SAT critical reading scores over 600: 67%; SAT math scores over 600: 68%; SAT writing scores over 600: 59%; ACT scores over 24: 91%; SAT critical reading scores over 700: 20%; SAT math scores over 700: 17%; SAT writing scores over 700: 13%; ACT scores over 30: 32%.

Retention: 84% of full-time freshmen returned.

FACULTY

Total: 120, 88% full-time, 92% with terminal degrees.
Student/faculty ratio: 9:1.

ACADEMICS

Calendar: semesters. *Degrees:* bachelor's and master's.

Special study options: accelerated degree program, advanced placement credit, double majors, English as a second language, independent study, internships, off-campus study, services for LD students, student-designed majors, study abroad.

Unusual degree programs: 3-2 engineering with Columbia University, University of Minnesota, Rensselaer Polytechnic Institute.

Computers: 180 computers/terminals are available on campus for general student use. Students can access the following: campus intranet, computer help desk, free student e-mail accounts, online (class) grades, online (class) registration, online (class) schedules. Campuswide network is available. 100% of college-owned or -operated housing units are wired for high-speed Internet access. Wireless service is available via entire campus.

STUDENT LIFE

Housing options: on-campus residence required through senior year; coed, men-only, women-only, special housing for students with disabilities. Campus housing is university owned. Freshman campus housing is guaranteed.

Activities and organizations: drama/theater group, student-run newspaper, radio station, choral group, Gospel Revelations Chorus, Dance Alloy, club sports, student government, Black Student Union.

Athletics Member NCAA. All Division III. ***Intercollegiate sports:*** baseball M, basketball M/W, cheerleading W(c), cross-country running M/W, equestrian sports W(c), field hockey W, football M, lacrosse M(c)/W(c), rugby M(c)/W(c), soccer M/W, tennis M/W, track and field M/W, ultimate Frisbee M(c)/W(c), volleyball M(c)/W. ***Intramural sports:*** basketball M/W, bowling M/W, football M, racquetball M/W, soccer M/W.

Campus security: 24-hour emergency response devices and patrols, student patrols, late-night transport/escort service, controlled dormitory access.

Student services: health clinic, personal/psychological counseling, women's center.

COSTS & FINANCIAL AID

Costs (2014–15) ***Comprehensive fee:*** $51,470 includes full-time tuition ($42,000), mandatory fees ($870), and room and board ($8600). Part-time tuition: $1400 per credit. ***College room only:*** $4400. Room and board charges vary according to board plan. ***Payment plans:*** tuition prepayment, installment, deferred payment. ***Waivers:*** employees or children of employees.

Financial Aid Of all full-time matriculated undergraduates who enrolled in 2013, 697 applied for aid, 669 were judged to have need, 155 had their need fully met. 676 Federal Work-Study jobs (averaging $2086). 37 state and other part-time jobs (averaging $600). In 2013, 105 non-need-based awards were made. ***Average percent of need met:*** 88. ***Average financial aid package:*** $38,857. ***Average need-based loan:*** $5147. ***Average need-based gift aid:*** $30,350. ***Average non-need-based aid:*** $12,143. ***Average indebtedness upon graduation:*** $27,421. ***Financial aid deadline:*** 3/1.

APPLYING

Standardized Tests *Recommended:* SAT or ACT (for admission).

Options: electronic application, early admission, early decision, early action, deferred entrance.

Required: essay or personal statement, high school transcript, minimum 3.0 GPA, 2 letters of recommendation. ***Recommended:*** interview.

Application deadlines: 2/15 (freshmen), 4/1 (transfers), 12/1 (early action).

Early decision deadline: 11/1.

Notification: 4/1 (freshmen), continuous until 4/15 (transfers), 12/1 (early decision), 2/1 (early action).

CONTACT
Ms. Shenita Piper, Director of Admissions, Earlham College, 801 National Road West, Richmond, IN 47374. *Phone:* 765-983-1600. *Toll-free phone:* 800-327-5426. *Fax:* 765-983-1560. *E-mail:* admission@earlham.edu.

Franklin College

Franklin, Indiana

http://www.franklincollege.edu/

- **Independent** comprehensive, founded 1834, affiliated with American Baptist Churches in the U.S.A.
- **Suburban** 207-acre campus with easy access to Indianapolis
- **Endowment** $80.1 million
- **Coed** 1,075 undergraduate students, 94% full-time, 54% women, 46% men
- **Moderately difficult** entrance level, 60% of applicants were admitted

UNDERGRAD STUDENTS
1,008 full-time, 67 part-time. Students come from 19 states and territories; 14 other countries; 11% are from out of state; 4% Black or African American, non-Hispanic/Latino; 2% Hispanic/Latino; 0.6% Asian, non-Hispanic/Latino; 0.2% American Indian or Alaska Native, non-Hispanic/Latino; 3% Two or more races, non-Hispanic/Latino; 4% Race/ethnicity unknown; 2% international; 2% transferred in; 76% live on campus.

Freshmen
Admission: 2,221 applied, 1,333 admitted, 328 enrolled. ***Average high school GPA:*** 3.4. ***Test scores:*** SAT critical reading scores over 500: 54%; SAT math scores over 500: 59%; SAT writing scores over 500: 46%; ACT scores over 18: 90%; SAT critical reading scores over 600: 11%; SAT math scores over 600: 15%; SAT writing scores over 600: 8%; ACT scores over 24: 28%; ACT scores over 30: 4%.

Retention: 79% of full-time freshmen returned.

FACULTY
Total: 109, 71% full-time, 59% with terminal degrees.

Student/faculty ratio: 12:1.

ACADEMICS
Calendar: 4-1-4. *Degrees:* bachelor's and master's.

Special study options: academic remediation for entering students, advanced placement credit, cooperative education, double majors, English as a second language, independent study, internships, off-campus study, part-time degree program, services for LD students, student-designed majors, study abroad, summer session for credit. ***ROTC:*** Army (c).

Unusual degree programs: 3-2 engineering with Indiana University - Purdue University Indianapolis.

Computers: 150 computers/terminals are available on campus for general student use. Students can access the following: campus intranet, computer help desk, free student e-mail accounts, online (class) grades, online (class) registration, online (class) schedules. Campuswide network is available. 100% of college-owned or -operated housing units are wired for high-speed Internet access. Wireless service is available via classrooms, computer centers, computer labs, dorm rooms, learning centers, libraries, student centers.

STUDENT LIFE
Housing options: on-campus residence required through junior year; coed. Campus housing is university owned. Freshman campus housing is guaranteed.

Activities and organizations: drama/theater group, student-run newspaper, radio and television station, choral group, FLOW, FC Volunteers, Student Entertainment Board, Student Congress, national fraternities, national sororities.

Athletics Member NCAA. All Division III. ***Intercollegiate sports:*** baseball M, basketball M/W, cheerleading W(c), cross-country running M/W, football M, golf M/W, lacrosse W, soccer M/W, softball W, swimming and diving M/W, tennis M/W, track and field M/W, volleyball W. ***Intramural sports:*** basketball M/W, softball W, volleyball W.

Campus security: 24-hour emergency response devices and patrols, late-night transport/escort service.

Student services: health clinic, personal/psychological counseling.

COSTS & FINANCIAL AID
Costs (2015–16) ***Comprehensive fee:*** $37,675 includes full-time tuition ($28,840), mandatory fees ($185), and room and board ($8650). ***College***

room only: $5150. Room and board charges vary according to board plan. ***Payment plan:*** installment. ***Waivers:*** senior citizens and employees or children of employees.

Financial Aid Of all full-time matriculated undergraduates who enrolled in 2013, 883 applied for aid, 794 were judged to have need, 74 had their need fully met. In 2013, 143 non-need-based awards were made. ***Average percent of need met:*** 71. ***Average financial aid package:*** $21,465. ***Average need-based loan:*** $4660. ***Average need-based gift aid:*** $17,058. ***Average non-need-based aid:*** $12,648. ***Average indebtedness upon graduation:*** $32,451.

APPLYING

Standardized Tests *Required:* SAT or ACT (for admission).

Options: electronic application, deferred entrance.

Required: high school transcript. ***Required for some:*** interview. ***Recommended:*** essay or personal statement.

Notification: continuous (freshmen), continuous (transfers).

CONTACT

Ms. Jennifer Bostrom, Director of Admissions, Franklin College, 101 Branigin Boulevard, Franklin, IN 46131-2623. *Phone:* 317-738-8075. *Toll-free phone:* 800-852-0232. *Fax:* 317-738-8075. *E-mail:* admissions@franklincollege.edu.

See previous page for display ad and page 1450 for the College Close-Up.

★ Goshen College

Goshen, Indiana

http://www.goshen.edu/

- **Independent Mennonite** comprehensive, founded 1894
- **Small-town** 135-acre campus
- **Endowment** $117.5 million
- **Coed** 774 undergraduate students, 91% full-time, 58% women, 42% men
- **Moderately difficult** entrance level, 54% of applicants were admitted

UNDERGRAD STUDENTS

702 full-time, 72 part-time. Students come from 32 states and territories; 24 other countries; 48% are from out of state; 4% Black or African American, non-Hispanic/Latino; 11% Hispanic/Latino; 1% Asian, non-Hispanic/Latino; 3% Two or more races, non-Hispanic/Latino; 0.9% Race/ethnicity unknown; 8% international; 3% transferred in; 66% live on campus.

Freshmen

Admission: 900 applied, 486 admitted, 159 enrolled. ***Average high school GPA:*** 3.5. ***Test scores:*** SAT critical reading scores over 500: 68%; SAT math scores over 500: 68%; SAT writing scores over 500: 54%; SAT critical reading scores over 600: 33%; SAT math scores over 600: 37%; SAT writing scores over 600: 31%; SAT critical reading scores over 700: 13%; SAT math scores over 700: 11%; SAT writing scores over 700: 8%. ***Retention:*** 77% of full-time freshmen returned.

FACULTY

Total: 92, 71% full-time, 55% with terminal degrees.

Student/faculty ratio: 10:1.

ACADEMICS

Calendar: semesters. *Degrees:* bachelor's and master's.

Special study options: academic remediation for entering students, accelerated degree program, adult/continuing education programs, advanced placement credit, distance learning, double majors, independent study, internships, off-campus study, part-time degree program, services for LD students, student-designed majors, study abroad, summer session for credit.

Unusual degree programs: 3-2 engineering with Case Western Reserve University, University of Illinois at Urbana-Champaign, University of Notre Dame, Washington University in St. Louis.

Computers: 160 computers/terminals and 2,000 ports are available on campus for general student use. Students can access the following: campus intranet, computer help desk, free student e-mail accounts, online (class) grades, online (class) registration, online (class) schedules. Campuswide network is available. 100% of college-owned or -operated housing units are wired for high-speed Internet access. Wireless service is available via entire campus.

STUDENT LIFE

Housing options: on-campus residence required through junior year; coed, men-only, women-only, special housing for students with disabilities. Campus housing is university owned. Freshman campus housing is guaranteed.

Activities and organizations: drama/theater group, student-run newspaper, radio and television station, choral group, International Student Club, Latino Student Union, PAX - Peace Club, Goshen Student Women's Organization, Business Club.

Athletics Member NAIA. ***Intercollegiate sports:*** baseball M(s), basketball M(s)/W(s), cross-country running M(s)/W(s), soccer M(s)/W(s), softball W(s), tennis M(s)/W(s), track and field M(s)/W(s), volleyball W(s). ***Intramural sports:*** badminton M/W, baseball M, basketball M/W, cross-country running M/W, racquetball M/W, soccer M/W, softball W, table tennis M/W, tennis M/W, ultimate Frisbee M/W, volleyball M/W.

Campus security: 24-hour emergency response devices and patrols, late-night transport/escort service, controlled dormitory access.

Student services: health clinic, personal/psychological counseling.

COSTS & FINANCIAL AID

Costs (2015–16) ***Comprehensive fee:*** $40,575 includes full-time tuition ($30,590) and room and board ($9985). Full-time tuition and fees vary according to degree level and program. Part-time tuition: $1250 per credit hour. Part-time tuition and fees vary according to course load, degree level, and program. ***College room only:*** $5350. Room and board charges vary according to board plan and housing facility. ***Payment plan:*** installment. ***Waivers:*** employees or children of employees.

Financial Aid Of all full-time matriculated undergraduates who enrolled in 2014, 541 applied for aid, 491 were judged to have need, 96 had their need fully met. 282 Federal Work-Study jobs (averaging $1090). 49 state and other part-time jobs (averaging $1678). In 2014, 176 non-need-based awards were made. ***Average percent of need met:*** 82. ***Average financial aid package:*** $24,844. ***Average need-based loan:*** $5498. ***Average need-based gift aid:*** $20,195. ***Average non-need-based aid:*** $13,569. ***Average indebtedness upon graduation:*** $26,586.

APPLYING

Standardized Tests *Required:* SAT or ACT (for admission).

Options: electronic application, deferred entrance.

Application fee: $25.

Required: minimum 2.0 GPA. ***Required for some:*** essay or personal statement, high school transcript. ***Recommended:*** minimum 2.8 GPA, 1 letter of recommendation, interview, rank in upper 50% of high school class.

Application deadlines: 8/15 (freshmen), 8/15 (transfers).

Notification: continuous (freshmen), continuous (transfers).

CONTACT

Adela Hufford, Director of Admission, Goshen College, 1700 South Main Street, Goshen, IN 46526-4794. *Phone:* 574-535-7535. *Toll-free phone:* 800-348-7422. *Fax:* 574-535-7609. *E-mail:* ahufford@goshen.edu.

Grace College

Winona Lake, Indiana

http://www.grace.edu/

- **Independent** comprehensive, founded 1948, affiliated with Fellowship of Grace Brethren Churches
- **Small-town** 160-acre campus
- **Endowment** $10.8 million
- **Coed** 1,857 undergraduate students, 73% full-time, 55% women, 45% men
- **Moderately difficult** entrance level, 80% of applicants were admitted

UNDERGRAD STUDENTS

1,347 full-time, 510 part-time. Students come from 35 states and territories; 5 other countries; 28% are from out of state; 5% Black or African American, non-Hispanic/Latino; 4% Hispanic/Latino; 0.9% Asian, non-Hispanic/Latino; 0.3% Native Hawaiian or other Pacific Islander, non-Hispanic/Latino; 0.3% American Indian or Alaska Native, non-Hispanic/Latino; 2% Two or more races, non-Hispanic/Latino; 15% Race/ethnicity unknown; 0.7% international; 4% transferred in; 61% live on campus.

Freshmen
Admission: 3,511 applied, 2,803 admitted, 356 enrolled. ***Average high school GPA:*** 3.52. ***Test scores:*** SAT critical reading scores over 500: 63%; SAT math scores over 500: 62%; ACT scores over 18: 96%; SAT critical reading scores over 600: 21%; SAT math scores over 600: 23%; ACT scores over 24: 50%; SAT critical reading scores over 700: 1%; SAT math scores over 700: 2%; ACT scores over 30: 11%.

Retention: 81% of full-time freshmen returned.

FACULTY
Total: 164, 29% full-time, 38% with terminal degrees.

Student/faculty ratio: 21:1.

ACADEMICS
Calendar: semesters. *Degrees:* certificates, diplomas, associate, bachelor's, master's, and doctoral.

Special study options: academic remediation for entering students, accelerated degree program, adult/continuing education programs, advanced placement credit, cooperative education, distance learning, double majors, honors programs, independent study, internships, off-campus study, part-time degree program, services for LD students, study abroad, summer session for credit.

Computers: 150 computers/terminals are available on campus for general student use. Students can access the following: campus intranet, computer help desk, free student e-mail accounts, online (class) grades, online (class) registration, online (class) schedules. Campuswide network is available. 100% of college-owned or -operated housing units are wired for high-speed Internet access. Wireless service is available via entire campus.

STUDENT LIFE
Housing options: on-campus residence required through senior year; men-only, women-only. Campus housing is university owned. Freshman campus housing is guaranteed.

Activities and organizations: drama/theater group, student-run newspaper, choral group, Grace Ministries in Action, Student Activities Board, Funfest, women's ministries, Breakout.

Athletics Member NAIA, NCCAA. ***Intercollegiate sports:*** baseball M(s), basketball M(s)/W(s), cheerleading M(s)/W(s), cross-country running M(s)/W(s), golf M(s), soccer M(s)/W(s), softball W(s), tennis M(s)/W(s), track and field M(s)/W(s), volleyball W(s). ***Intramural sports:*** basketball M/W, soccer M/W, volleyball M/W.

Campus security: student patrols, late-night transport/escort service, controlled dormitory access, evening patrols by trained security personnel.

Student services: health clinic, personal/psychological counseling.

COSTS & FINANCIAL AID
Costs (2014–15) ***Comprehensive fee:*** $32,600 includes full-time tuition ($24,670) and room and board ($7930). Full-time tuition and fees vary according to degree level and location. Part-time tuition: $820 per credit hour. Part-time tuition and fees vary according to degree level and location. ***College room only:*** $4130. Room and board charges vary according to board plan and housing facility. ***Payment plan:*** installment. ***Waivers:*** senior citizens and employees or children of employees.

Financial Aid Of all full-time matriculated undergraduates who enrolled in 2009, 1,276 applied for aid, 1,273 were judged to have need. ***Average financial aid package:*** $11,338.

APPLYING
Standardized Tests *Required:* SAT or ACT (for admission).

Options: electronic application, early admission, early action, deferred entrance.

Application fee: $30.

Required: essay or personal statement, high school transcript, minimum 2.3 GPA, 2 letters of recommendation, personal statement of faith. ***Required for some:*** interview.

Application deadlines: 8/1 (freshmen), 8/1 (transfers), 12/1 (early action).

Notification: 8/15 (freshmen), continuous until 8/15 (transfers).

CONTACT
Miss niki Barlow, Admissions Office, Grace College, 200 Seminary Drive, Winona Lake, IN 46590. *Phone:* 574-372-5100 Ext. 6008. *Toll-free phone:* 800-54-GRACE. *Fax:* 574-372-5120. *E-mail:* enroll@grace.edu.

Hanover College
Hanover, Indiana
http://www.hanover.edu/

- **Independent Presbyterian** 4-year, founded 1827
- **Rural** 630-acre campus with easy access to Louisville
- **Endowment** $151.1 million
- **Coed** 1,145 undergraduate students, 99% full-time, 58% women, 42% men
- **Moderately difficult** entrance level, 64% of applicants were admitted

UNDERGRAD STUDENTS
1,134 full-time, 11 part-time. Students come from 23 states and territories; 25 other countries; 29% are from out of state; 5% Black or African American, non-Hispanic/Latino; 2% Hispanic/Latino; 1% Asian, non-Hispanic/Latino; 0.6% American Indian or Alaska Native, non-Hispanic/Latino; 2% Two or more races, non-Hispanic/Latino; 2% Race/ethnicity unknown; 5% international; 1% transferred in; 95% live on campus.

Freshmen
Admission: 2,888 applied, 1,862 admitted, 293 enrolled. ***Average high school GPA:*** 3.62. ***Test scores:*** SAT critical reading scores over 500: 64%; SAT math scores over 500: 71%; SAT writing scores over 500: 55%; ACT scores over 18: 97%; SAT critical reading scores over 600: 20%; SAT math scores over 600: 22%; SAT writing scores over 600: 16%; ACT scores over 24: 62%; SAT critical reading scores over 700: 2%; SAT math scores over 700: 2%; SAT writing scores over 700: 1%; ACT scores over 30: 13%.

Retention: 82% of full-time freshmen returned.

FACULTY
Total: 104, 94% full-time, 97% with terminal degrees.

Student/faculty ratio: 12:1.

ACADEMICS
Calendar: 4-4-1. *Degree:* bachelor's.

Special study options: advanced placement credit, cooperative education, double majors, independent study, internships, off-campus study, services for LD students, student-designed majors, study abroad.

Computers: 120 computers/terminals and 1,550 ports are available on campus for general student use. Students can access the following: campus intranet, computer help desk, free student e-mail accounts, online (class) grades, online (class) registration, online (class) schedules. Campuswide network is available. 100% of college-owned or -operated housing units are wired for high-speed Internet access. Wireless service is available via entire campus.

STUDENT LIFE
Housing options: on-campus residence required through senior year; coed, men-only, women-only. Campus housing is university owned and leased by the school. Freshman campus housing is guaranteed.

Activities and organizations: drama/theater group, student-run newspaper, radio and television station, choral group, marching band, Student Senate, Campus Crusade for Christ, Campus Activities Board, People for Peace, Love Out Loud, national fraternities, national sororities.

Athletics Member NCAA. All Division III. ***Intercollegiate sports:*** baseball M, basketball M/W, cross-country running M/W, football M, golf M/W, lacrosse M/W, soccer M/W, softball W, tennis M/W, track and field M/W, volleyball W. ***Intramural sports:*** archery W(c), basketball M/W, football M/W, rugby M(c)/W(c), soccer M/W, softball M/W, ultimate Frisbee M(c), volleyball M/W.

Campus security: 24-hour emergency response devices and patrols, late-night transport/escort service, controlled dormitory access.

Student services: health clinic, personal/psychological counseling.

COSTS & FINANCIAL AID
Costs (2015–16) ***One-time required fee:*** $250. ***Comprehensive fee:*** $44,966 includes full-time tuition ($33,744), mandatory fees ($770), and room and board ($10,452). Full-time tuition and fees vary according to reciprocity agreements. Part-time tuition: $3750 per unit. Part-time tuition and fees vary according to course load and reciprocity agreements.

College room only: $5200. Room and board charges vary according to housing facility. ***Payment plan:*** installment. ***Waivers:*** senior citizens and employees or children of employees.

Financial Aid Of all full-time matriculated undergraduates who enrolled in 2013, 964 applied for aid, 865 were judged to have need, 216 had their need fully met. 528 Federal Work-Study jobs (averaging $1311). In 2013, 252 non-need-based awards were made. ***Average percent of need met:*** 82. ***Average financial aid package:*** $27,889. ***Average need-based loan:*** $4292. ***Average need-based gift aid:*** $23,577. ***Average non-need-based aid:*** $18,221. ***Average indebtedness upon graduation:*** $31,004.

APPLYING

Standardized Tests *Required:* SAT or ACT (for admission).

Options: electronic application, early admission, early action, deferred entrance.

Application fee: $40.

Required: essay or personal statement, high school transcript, 1 letter of recommendation. ***Recommended:*** interview.

Application deadlines: 3/1 (freshmen), rolling (transfers), 12/1 (early action).

Notification: continuous (freshmen), continuous (transfers), 12/20 (early action).

CONTACT

Mr. Christopher Gage, Dean of Admission, Hanover College, PO Box 108, Hanover, IN 47243-0108. *Phone:* 812-866-7021. *Toll-free phone:* 800-213-2178. *Fax:* 812-866-7098. *E-mail:* admission@hanover.edu.

Harrison College

Indianapolis, Indiana

http://www.harrison.edu/

- **Proprietary** 4-year, founded 1902, part of Additional Indiana locations in Anderson, Columbus, Indianapolis East Side, Evansville, Fort Wayne, Lafayette, Indianapolis Northwest side, Terre Haute, and a fully online campus
- **Urban** 1-acre campus with easy access to Indianapolis
- **Coed**
- **Moderately difficult** entrance level

FACULTY

Student/faculty ratio: 13:1.

ACADEMICS

Calendar: quarters. *Degrees:* certificates, diplomas, associate, and bachelor's.

STUDENT LIFE

Housing options: college housing not available.

Activities and organizations: Student Advisory Board, Student Ambassadors, Phi Beta Lambda.

Campus security: 24-hour patrols.

APPLYING

Standardized Tests *Required:* Wonderlic Scholastic Level Exam (SLE) (for admission).

Options: electronic application.

Required: high school transcript, interview.

CONTACT

Mr. Jason Howanec, Vice President of Enrollment, Harrison College, 500 N. Meridian St., Indianapolis, IN 46204. *Phone:* 888-544-4422. *Toll-free phone:* 888-544-4422. *E-mail:* Admissions@harrison.edu.

Holy Cross College

Notre Dame, Indiana

http://www.hcc-nd.edu/

- **Independent Roman Catholic** 4-year, founded 1966
- **Suburban** 150-acre campus with easy access to Chicago, Indianapolis
- **Coed** 553 undergraduate students, 91% full-time, 37% women, 63% men
- **Moderately difficult** entrance level, 93% of applicants were admitted

UNDERGRAD STUDENTS

502 full-time, 51 part-time. Students come from 32 states and territories; 12 other countries; 55% are from out of state; 9% Black or African American, non-Hispanic/Latino; 11% Hispanic/Latino; 2% Asian, non-Hispanic/Latino; 0.2% Native Hawaiian or other Pacific Islander, non-Hispanic/Latino; 0.4% American Indian or Alaska Native, non-Hispanic/Latino; 3% Two or more races, non-Hispanic/Latino; 0.6% Race/ethnicity unknown; 6% international; 7% transferred in.

Freshmen

Admission: 585 applied, 545 admitted, 156 enrolled. ***Average high school GPA:*** 3.2.

Retention: 70% of full-time freshmen returned.

ACADEMICS

Calendar: semesters. *Degrees:* associate and bachelor's.

Special study options: academic remediation for entering students, advanced placement credit, double majors, freshman honors college, honors programs, independent study, internships, off-campus study, student-designed majors, study abroad, summer session for credit. ***ROTC:*** Army (c), Air Force (c).

Computers: 91 computers/terminals are available on campus for general student use. Students can access the following: campus intranet, free student e-mail accounts, online (class) registration, online (class) schedules. Campuswide network is available. 100% of college-owned or -operated housing units are wired for high-speed Internet access. Wireless service is available via entire campus.

STUDENT LIFE

Housing options: on-campus residence required for freshman year; men-only, women-only, special housing for students with disabilities. Campus housing is university owned. Freshman applicants given priority for college housing.

Activities and organizations: drama/theater group, student-run newspaper, choral group, marching band, Student Government Association, Campus Ministry, Intramural athletics, Commuter Student Organization, SAGE.

Athletics Member NAIA. ***Intercollegiate sports:*** basketball M(s), crew M, golf M(s)/W(s), ice hockey M(c), lacrosse M(c), soccer M(s)/W(s), track and field M/W, water polo M/W. ***Intramural sports:*** basketball M/W, cheerleading M/W, football M/W, rugby M, skiing (downhill) M(c)/W(c), softball M/W, table tennis M/W, tennis W, ultimate Frisbee M/W, volleyball M/W, weight lifting M/W.

Campus security: 24-hour emergency response devices and patrols, late-night transport/escort service, controlled dormitory access.

Student services: personal/psychological counseling.

COSTS

Costs (2015–16) ***Comprehensive fee:*** $37,925 includes full-time tuition ($27,000), mandatory fees ($950), and room and board ($9975). Full-time tuition and fees vary according to course load. Part-time tuition: $900 per credit hour. Part-time tuition and fees vary according to course load. ***Payment plan:*** installment. ***Waivers:*** employees or children of employees.

APPLYING

Standardized Tests *Required:* SAT or ACT (for admission).

Options: electronic application, deferred entrance.

Required: high school transcript, Freshmen applicants and Transfer applicants with fewer than 24 transferable credits are required to submit ACT or SAT scores. ***Required for some:*** essay or personal statement. ***Recommended:*** 2 letters of recommendation, interview.

Application deadlines: rolling (freshmen), rolling (out-of-state freshmen), rolling (transfers).

Notification: continuous (freshmen), continuous (out-of-state freshmen), continuous (transfers).

CONTACT

Mr. Adam DeBeck, Associate Director of Admissions, Holy Cross College, 54515 SR 933 N, PO Box 308, Notre Dame, IN 46556. *Phone:* 574-239-8400. *E-mail:* admissions@hcc-nd.edu.

Huntington University

Huntington, Indiana

http://www.huntington.edu/

- **Independent** comprehensive, founded 1897, affiliated with Church of the United Brethren in Christ
- **Small-town** 170-acre campus with easy access to Fort Wayne
- **Endowment** $22.7 million
- **Coed**
- **Moderately difficult** entrance level

FACULTY

Student/faculty ratio: 13:1.

ACADEMICS

Calendar: 4-1-4. *Degrees:* associate, bachelor's, and master's.

STUDENT LIFE

Housing options: on-campus residence required through junior year; men-only, women-only, special housing for students with disabilities. Campus housing is university owned. Freshman campus housing is guaranteed.

Activities and organizations: drama/theater group, student-run newspaper, radio and television station, choral group, Film Club, Friesen Center for Volunteer Service, Mu Kappa, Social Work Student Council, Investment Club.

Athletics Member NAIA, NCCAA.

Campus security: 24-hour emergency response devices, late-night transport/escort service, campus police on duty from 6 pm to 6 am.

COSTS & FINANCIAL AID

Costs (2014–15) ***Comprehensive fee:*** $33,077 includes full-time tuition ($23,976), mandatory fees ($795), and room and board ($8306). Full-time tuition and fees vary according to course load, degree level, and program. Part-time tuition and fees vary according to course load, degree level, and program. ***Room and board:*** Room and board charges vary according to board plan.

Financial Aid Of all full-time matriculated undergraduates who enrolled in 2013, 832 applied for aid, 754 were judged to have need, 83 had their need fully met. 144 Federal Work-Study jobs (averaging $1926). In 2013, 139 non-need-based awards were made. ***Average percent of need met:*** 72. ***Average financial aid package:*** $18,334. ***Average need-based loan:*** $4820. ***Average need-based gift aid:*** $15,017. ***Average non-need-based aid:*** $11,515. ***Average indebtedness upon graduation:*** $34,662.

APPLYING

Standardized Tests *Required:* SAT or ACT (for admission).

Options: electronic application, deferred entrance.

Application fee: $20.

Required: essay or personal statement, high school transcript, minimum 2.3 GPA. ***Recommended:*** interview.

CONTACT

Huntington University, 2303 College Avenue, Huntington, IN 46750-1299. *Phone:* 260-356-6000. *Toll-free phone:* 800-642-6493.

Indiana State University

Terre Haute, Indiana

http://www.indstate.edu/

- **State-supported** university, founded 1865
- **Small-town** 91-acre campus with easy access to Indianapolis
- **Endowment** $40.3 million
- **Coed** 10,881 undergraduate students, 87% full-time, 54% women, 46% men
- **Moderately difficult** entrance level, 83% of applicants were admitted

UNDERGRAD STUDENTS

9,459 full-time, 1,422 part-time. Students come from 47 states and territories; 61 other countries; 15% are from out of state; 19% Black or African American, non-Hispanic/Latino; 3% Hispanic/Latino; 1% Asian, non-Hispanic/Latino; 0.1% Native Hawaiian or other Pacific Islander, non-Hispanic/Latino; 0.3% American Indian or Alaska Native, non-Hispanic/Latino; 3% Two or more races, non-Hispanic/Latino; 0.7% Race/ethnicity unknown; 6% international; 6% transferred in; 33% live on campus.

Freshmen

Admission: 11,258 applied, 9,292 admitted, 2,739 enrolled. ***Average high school GPA:*** 3.07. ***Test scores:*** SAT critical reading scores over 500: 32%; SAT math scores over 500: 32%; SAT writing scores over 500: 21%; ACT scores over 18: 61%; SAT critical reading scores over 600: 6%; SAT math scores over 600: 6%; SAT writing scores over 600: 3%; ACT scores over 24: 17%; ACT scores over 30: 2%.

Retention: 64% of full-time freshmen returned.

FACULTY

Total: 703, 67% full-time, 60% with terminal degrees.

Student/faculty ratio: 20:1.

ACADEMICS

Calendar: semesters. *Degrees:* certificates, associate, bachelor's, master's, doctoral, post-master's, and postbachelor's certificates.

Special study options: academic remediation for entering students, accelerated degree program, adult/continuing education programs, advanced placement credit, cooperative education, distance learning, double majors, English as a second language, freshman honors college, honors programs, independent study, internships, off-campus study, part-time degree program, services for LD students, study abroad, summer session for credit. ***ROTC:*** Army (b), Air Force (b).

Computers: 395 computers/terminals are available on campus for general student use. Students can access the following: campus intranet, computer help desk, free student e-mail accounts, online (class) grades, online (class) registration, online (class) schedules. Campuswide network is available. 100% of college-owned or -operated housing units are wired for high-speed Internet access. Wireless service is available via entire campus.

STUDENT LIFE

Housing options: on-campus residence required for freshman year; coed, men-only, women-only, special housing for students with disabilities. Campus housing is university owned. Freshman campus housing is guaranteed.

Activities and organizations: drama/theater group, student-run newspaper, radio station, choral group, marching band, Union Board, Student Government Association, Panhellenic Council (sororities), Interfraternity Council (fraternities), Residence Hall Association, national fraternities, national sororities.

Athletics Member NCAA. All Division I except football (Division I-AA). ***Intercollegiate sports:*** baseball M(s), basketball M(s)/W(s), cross-country running M(s)/W(s), golf W(s), soccer W(s), softball W(s), track and field M(s)/W(s), volleyball W(s). ***Intramural sports:*** badminton M/W, basketball M/W, racquetball M/W, soccer M/W, softball M/W, swimming and diving M/W, track and field M/W, ultimate Frisbee M/W, volleyball M/W.

Campus security: 24-hour emergency response devices and patrols, student patrols, late-night transport/escort service.

Student services: health clinic, personal/psychological counseling, women's center.

COSTS & FINANCIAL AID

Costs (2014–15) ***Tuition:*** state resident $8216 full-time, $298 per credit hour part-time; nonresident $18,146 full-time, $643 per credit hour part-time. Full-time tuition and fees vary according to reciprocity agreements. Part-time tuition and fees vary according to course load and reciprocity agreements. ***Required fees:*** $200 full-time, $100 per term part-time. ***Room and board:*** $9182. Room and board charges vary according to board plan and housing facility. ***Payment plans:*** installment, deferred payment. ***Waivers:*** senior citizens and employees or children of employees.

Financial Aid Of all full-time matriculated undergraduates who enrolled in 2013, 7,883 applied for aid, 6,742 were judged to have need, 691 had their need fully met. In 2013, 1003 non-need-based awards were made. ***Average percent of need met:*** 80. ***Average financial aid package:*** $9995. ***Average need-based loan:*** $3971. ***Average need-based gift aid:*** $5625. ***Average non-need-based aid:*** $3462. ***Average indebtedness upon graduation:*** $26,256. ***Financial aid deadline:*** 7/1.

APPLYING

Standardized Tests *Required:* SAT or ACT (for admission).

Options: electronic application, deferred entrance.

Application fee: $25.

Required: high school transcript. ***Required for some:*** interview. ***Recommended:*** minimum 2.5 GPA.

Notification: continuous (freshmen), continuous (transfers).

CONTACT

Mr. Richard Toomey, Assistant Vice President of Enrollment Management, Indiana State University, 218 North Sixth Street, Erickson Hall, Terre Haute, IN 47809-9989. *Phone:* 812-237-2121. *Toll-free phone:* 800-468-6478. *Fax:* 812-237-8023. *E-mail:* admissions@indstate.edu.

Indiana Tech

Fort Wayne, Indiana

http://www.indianatech.edu/

- **Independent** comprehensive, founded 1930
- **Urban** 42-acre campus
- **Coed**
- **Moderately difficult** entrance level

FACULTY

Student/faculty ratio: 19:1.

ACADEMICS

Calendar: semesters. *Degrees:* associate, bachelor's, master's, and doctoral.

STUDENT LIFE

Housing options: on-campus residence required through sophomore year; coed. Campus housing is university owned.

Activities and organizations: student-run newspaper, Multicultural Club, NSBE, Indiana Tech Gaming Society, Tech LOL, Cyber Defense Club of Indiana Tech, national fraternities.

Athletics Member NAIA.

Campus security: 24-hour emergency response devices and patrols, student patrols, late-night transport/escort service, controlled dormitory access.

Student services: personal/psychological counseling.

COSTS & FINANCIAL AID

Costs (2014–15) ***Comprehensive fee:*** $34,381 includes full-time tuition ($24,450), mandatory fees ($410), and room and board ($9521). Full-time tuition and fees vary according to class time, course load, and program. Part-time tuition: $480 per credit hour. Part-time tuition and fees vary according to class time, course load, and program. ***Room and board:*** Room and board charges vary according to board plan and housing facility. ***Payment plans:*** installment, deferred payment.

Financial Aid Of all full-time matriculated undergraduates who enrolled in 2014, 3,776 applied for aid, 3,634 were judged to have need. 124 Federal Work-Study jobs (averaging $188,419). In 2014, 48 non-need-based awards were made. ***Average percent of need met:*** 39. ***Average financial aid package:*** $18,712. ***Average need-based loan:*** $3813. ***Average need-based gift aid:*** $8419. ***Average non-need-based aid:*** $8490. ***Average indebtedness upon graduation:*** $41,844.

APPLYING

Standardized Tests *Required:* SAT or ACT (for admission).

Options: electronic application.

Application fee: $50.

Required: high school transcript, minimum 2.0 GPA. ***Required for some:*** essay or personal statement, high school transcript, minimum 3.0 GPA, 2 letters of recommendation, interview, Interview with the Director of Software Engineering and college-level math courses for the Software Engineering program, Interview with the Director for the Pre-Law program. ***Recommended:*** Interview with the Director of Software Engineering and college-level math courses for the Software Engineering program, Interview with the Director for the Pre-Law program.

CONTACT

Mrs. Monica L Chamberlain, Associate Vice President of Enrollment Management, Indiana Tech, 1600 East Washington Boulevard, Fort Wayne, IN 46803. *Phone:* 260-422-5561 Ext. 2348. *Toll-free phone:* 800-937-2448. *Fax:* 260-422-7696. *E-mail:* admissions@indianatech.edu.

Indiana University Bloomington

Bloomington, Indiana

http://www.iub.edu/

- **State-supported** university, founded 1820, part of Indiana University System
- **Small-town** 1929-acre campus with easy access to Indianapolis
- **Endowment** $1.1 billion
- **Coed** 36,419 undergraduate students, 86% full-time, 51% women, 49% men
- **Moderately difficult** entrance level, 76% of applicants were admitted

UNDERGRAD STUDENTS

31,370 full-time, 5,049 part-time. Students come from 51 states and territories; 148 other countries; 27% are from out of state; 4% Black or African American, non-Hispanic/Latino; 5% Hispanic/Latino; 4% Asian, non-Hispanic/Latino; 0.1% Native Hawaiian or other Pacific Islander, non-Hispanic/Latino; 0.1% American Indian or Alaska Native, non-Hispanic/Latino; 3% Two or more races, non-Hispanic/Latino; 0.6% Race/ethnicity unknown; 10% international; 3% transferred in; 37% live on campus.

Freshmen

Admission: 36,362 applied, 27,668 admitted, 6,985 enrolled. ***Average high school GPA:*** 3.63. ***Test scores:*** SAT critical reading scores over 500: 83%; SAT math scores over 500: 91%; SAT writing scores over 500: 82%; ACT scores over 18: 99%; SAT critical reading scores over 600: 38%; SAT math scores over 600: 52%; SAT writing scores over 600: 34%; ACT scores over 24: 82%; SAT critical reading scores over 700: 7%; SAT math scores over 700: 14%; SAT writing scores over 700: 6%; ACT scores over 30: 29%.

Retention: 89% of full-time freshmen returned.

FACULTY

Total: 2,404, 85% full-time, 71% with terminal degrees.

Student/faculty ratio: 17:1.

ACADEMICS

Calendar: semesters plus 2 summer sessions. *Degrees:* certificates, associate, bachelor's, master's, doctoral, and postbachelor's certificates.

Special study options: academic remediation for entering students, accelerated degree program, adult/continuing education programs, advanced placement credit, cooperative education, distance learning, double majors, English as a second language, external degree program, freshman honors college, honors programs, independent study, internships, off-campus study, part-time degree program, services for LD students, student-designed majors, study abroad, summer session for credit. ***ROTC:*** Army (b), Air Force (b).

Unusual degree programs: 3-2 business administration with accounting.

Computers: 2,016 computers/terminals are available on campus for general student use. Students can access the following: campus intranet, computer help desk, free student e-mail accounts, online (class) grades, online (class) registration, online (class) schedules. Campuswide network is available. 100% of college-owned or -operated housing units are wired for high-speed Internet access. Wireless service is available via entire campus.

STUDENT LIFE

Housing options: on-campus residence required for freshman year; coed, men-only, women-only, cooperative, special housing for students with disabilities. Campus housing is university owned. Freshman applicants given priority for college housing.

Activities and organizations: drama/theater group, student-run newspaper, radio and television station, choral group, marching band, Union Board, Student Association, Student Foundation, Habitat for Humanity, Student Athletic Board, national fraternities, national sororities.

Athletics Member NCAA. All Division I except football (Division I-A). ***Intercollegiate sports:*** baseball M(s), basketball M(s)/W(s), crew W(s), cross-country running M(s)/W(s), field hockey W, golf M(s)/W(s), soccer M(s)/W(s), softball W(s), swimming and diving M(s)/W(s), tennis M(s)/W(s), track and field M(s)/W(s), volleyball W(s), water polo W(s), wrestling M(s). ***Intramural sports:*** archery M/W, badminton M(c)/W(c), baseball M/W, basketball M/W, bowling M(c)/W(c), crew M(c)/W(c), cross-country running M/W, equestrian sports M(c)/W(c), fencing

M(c)/W(c), field hockey W(c), golf M/W, gymnastics M(c)/W(c), ice hockey M(c)/W(c), lacrosse M(c)/W, racquetball M(c)/W(c), riflery M(c)/W(c), rugby M(c)/W(c), sailing M(c)/W(c), skiing (downhill) M(c)/W(c), soccer M(c)/W(c), softball M/W, squash M/W, swimming and diving M/W, table tennis M/W, tennis M(c)/W(c), track and field M/W, ultimate Frisbee M(c)/W(c), volleyball M/W, water polo M(c)/W, weight lifting M(c)/W(c), wrestling M(c).

Campus security: 24-hour emergency response devices and patrols, late-night transport/escort service, safety seminars, lighted pathways, escort service, shuttle bus service, emergency telephones.

Student services: health clinic, personal/psychological counseling, women's center, legal services.

COSTS & FINANCIAL AID

Costs (2014–15) ***Tuition:*** state resident $9087 full-time, $284 per credit hour part-time; nonresident $31,940 full-time, $998 per credit hour part-time. Full-time tuition and fees vary according to location and program. Part-time tuition and fees vary according to course load, location, and program. ***Required fees:*** $1301 full-time. ***Room and board:*** $9493. Room and board charges vary according to board plan and housing facility. ***Payment plans:*** installment, deferred payment. ***Waivers:*** employees or children of employees.

Financial Aid Of all full-time matriculated undergraduates who enrolled in 2013, 18,540 applied for aid, 13,558 were judged to have need, 2,500 had their need fully met. In 2013, 8426 non-need-based awards were made. ***Average percent of need met:*** 64. ***Average financial aid package:*** $11,998. ***Average need-based loan:*** $4356. ***Average need-based gift aid:*** $10,137. ***Average non-need-based aid:*** $5446. ***Average indebtedness upon graduation:*** $27,300.

APPLYING

Standardized Tests *Required:* SAT or ACT (for admission). *Recommended:* SAT Subject Tests (for admission).

Options: electronic application, deferred entrance.

Application fee: $60.

Required: high school transcript. ***Recommended:*** interview.

Application deadlines: rolling (freshmen), rolling (transfers).

Notification: continuous (freshmen), continuous (transfers).

CONTACT

Ms. Sacha Thieme, Executive Director of Admissions, Indiana University Bloomington, 300 North Jordan Avenue, Bloomington, IN 47405-1106. *Phone:* 812-855-0661. *Fax:* 812-855-5102. *E-mail:* iuadmit@indiana.edu.

Indiana University East

Richmond, Indiana

http://www.iue.edu/

- **State-supported** comprehensive, founded 1971, part of Indiana University System
- **Small-town** 182-acre campus with easy access to Indianapolis
- **Endowment** $4.5 million
- **Coed** 4,430 undergraduate students, 45% full-time, 63% women, 37% men
- **Moderately difficult** entrance level, 64% of applicants were admitted

UNDERGRAD STUDENTS

2,015 full-time, 2,415 part-time. Students come from 42 states and territories; 37 other countries; 25% are from out of state; 3% Black or African American, non-Hispanic/Latino; 3% Hispanic/Latino; 1% Asian, non-Hispanic/Latino; 0.2% American Indian or Alaska Native, non-Hispanic/Latino; 2% Two or more races, non-Hispanic/Latino; 2% Race/ethnicity unknown; 0.7% international; 10% transferred in.

Freshmen

Admission: 1,388 applied, 885 admitted, 397 enrolled. ***Average high school GPA:*** 3.2. ***Test scores:*** SAT critical reading scores over 500: 34%; SAT math scores over 500: 36%; SAT writing scores over 500: 24%; ACT scores over 18: 76%; SAT critical reading scores over 600: 6%; SAT math scores over 600: 6%; SAT writing scores over 600: 3%; ACT scores over 24: 22%; SAT critical reading scores over 700: 1%; ACT scores over 30: 1%.

Retention: 63% of full-time freshmen returned.

FACULTY

Total: 299, 35% full-time, 33% with terminal degrees.

Student/faculty ratio: 15:1.

ACADEMICS

Calendar: semesters. *Degrees:* certificates, bachelor's, master's, and postbachelor's certificates.

Special study options: academic remediation for entering students, accelerated degree program, adult/continuing education programs, advanced placement credit, cooperative education, distance learning, double majors, external degree program, honors programs, independent study, internships, off-campus study, part-time degree program, services for LD students, study abroad, summer session for credit.

Computers: 187 computers/terminals are available on campus for general student use. Students can access the following: campus intranet, computer help desk, free student e-mail accounts, online (class) grades, online (class) registration, online (class) schedules. Campuswide network is available. Wireless service is available via entire campus.

STUDENT LIFE

Housing options: college housing not available.

Activities and organizations: drama/theater group, student-run newspaper, television station, choral group, Student Government Association, Psychology Club, Sociology Club, Humanities Club, Business Club.

Athletics Member NAIA. ***Intercollegiate sports:*** basketball M/W, cross-country running M/W, golf M/W, tennis M/W, track and field M/W, volleyball W. ***Intramural sports:*** basketball M(c)/W(c), cheerleading W(c), cross-country running M(c)/W(c), golf M(c)/W(c), tennis M(c)/W(c), track and field M(c)/W(c), volleyball M/W.

Campus security: 24-hour emergency response devices, late-night transport/escort service, safety awareness, lighted pathways, 14-hour foot and vehicle patrol.

Student services: personal/psychological counseling.

COSTS & FINANCIAL AID

Costs (2014–15) ***Tuition:*** state resident $6196 full-time, $207 per credit hour part-time; nonresident $17,490 full-time, $583 per credit hour part-time. Full-time tuition and fees vary according to course load, location, program, and reciprocity agreements. Part-time tuition and fees vary according to course load, location, program, and reciprocity agreements. ***Required fees:*** $591 full-time. ***Payment plans:*** installment, deferred payment. ***Waivers:*** employees or children of employees.

Financial Aid Of all full-time matriculated undergraduates who enrolled in 2013, 1,791 applied for aid, 1,604 were judged to have need, 85 had their need fully met. In 2013, 99 non-need-based awards were made. ***Average percent of need met:*** 63. ***Average financial aid package:*** $8834. ***Average need-based loan:*** $3776. ***Average need-based gift aid:*** $6834. ***Average non-need-based aid:*** $2148. ***Average indebtedness upon graduation:*** $29,952.

APPLYING

Standardized Tests *Required:* SAT or ACT (for admission).

Options: electronic application, early admission, deferred entrance.

Application fee: $35.

Required: high school transcript, Recent high school graduates from Indiana are expected to complete the Core 40 curriculum. Out-of-state students are expected to complete a minimum of 28 semester hours of college prep courses. ***Recommended:*** minimum 2.0 GPA.

Application deadlines: rolling (freshmen), rolling (transfers).

Notification: continuous (freshmen), continuous (transfers).

CONTACT

Ms. Molly Vanderpool, Director of Admissions, Indiana University East, 2325 Chester Boulevard, Whitewater Hall 151J, Richmond, IN 47374-1289. *Phone:* 765-973-8208. *Toll-free phone:* 800-959-EAST. *Fax:* 765-973-8209. *E-mail:* applynow@iue.edu.

Indiana University Kokomo

Kokomo, Indiana

http://www.iuk.edu/

- **State-supported** comprehensive, founded 1945, part of Indiana University System
- **Small-town** 51-acre campus with easy access to Indianapolis
- **Endowment** $4.6 million
- **Coed** 4,004 undergraduate students, 52% full-time, 66% women, 34% men
- **Minimally difficult** entrance level, 67% of applicants were admitted

UNDERGRAD STUDENTS

2,077 full-time, 1,927 part-time. Students come from 7 states and territories; 25 other countries; 0.2% are from out of state; 4% Black or African American, non-Hispanic/Latino; 5% Hispanic/Latino; 1% Asian, non-Hispanic/Latino; 0.2% Native Hawaiian or other Pacific Islander, non-Hispanic/Latino; 0.5% American Indian or Alaska Native, non-Hispanic/Latino; 2% Two or more races, non-Hispanic/Latino; 2% Race/ethnicity unknown; 0.3% international; 6% transferred in.

Freshmen

Admission: 1,408 applied, 947 admitted, 523 enrolled. ***Average high school GPA:*** 3.08. ***Test scores:*** SAT critical reading scores over 500: 32%; SAT math scores over 500: 36%; SAT writing scores over 500: 24%; ACT scores over 18: 75%; SAT critical reading scores over 600: 7%; SAT math scores over 600: 5%; SAT writing scores over 600: 4%; ACT scores over 24: 15%; ACT scores over 30: 1%.

Retention: 64% of full-time freshmen returned.

FACULTY

Total: 220, 52% full-time, 36% with terminal degrees.

Student/faculty ratio: 16:1.

ACADEMICS

Calendar: semesters. *Degrees:* certificates, associate, bachelor's, master's, and postbachelor's certificates.

Special study options: academic remediation for entering students, accelerated degree program, adult/continuing education programs, advanced placement credit, distance learning, double majors, English as a second language, external degree program, freshman honors college, honors programs, independent study, internships, part-time degree program, services for LD students, study abroad, summer session for credit. ***ROTC:*** Army (b).

Computers: Students can access the following: campus intranet, computer help desk, free student e-mail accounts, online (class) grades, online (class) registration, online (class) schedules. Campuswide network is available. Wireless service is available via entire campus.

STUDENT LIFE

Housing options: college housing not available.

Activities and organizations: drama/theater group, student-run newspaper, radio station, choral group, national sororities.

Athletics Member NAIA. ***Intercollegiate sports:*** basketball M/W, cross-country running M/W, golf M/W, volleyball W. ***Intramural sports:*** basketball M, soccer M/W, softball M/W, volleyball M/W.

Campus security: 24-hour patrols, late-night transport/escort service, campus police, lighted pathways.

Student services: personal/psychological counseling.

COSTS & FINANCIAL AID

Costs (2014–15) ***Tuition:*** state resident $6220 full-time, $207 per credit hour part-time; nonresident $17,490 full-time, $583 per credit hour part-time. Full-time tuition and fees vary according to course load, location, and program. Part-time tuition and fees vary according to course load, location, and program. ***Required fees:*** $591 full-time. ***Payment plans:*** installment, deferred payment. ***Waivers:*** employees or children of employees.

Financial Aid Of all full-time matriculated undergraduates who enrolled in 2013, 1,807 applied for aid, 1,495 were judged to have need, 45 had their need fully met. In 2013, 98 non-need-based awards were made. ***Average percent of need met:*** 62. ***Average financial aid package:*** $8311. ***Average need-based loan:*** $3689. ***Average need-based gift aid:*** $6627. ***Average non-need-based aid:*** $1194. ***Average indebtedness upon graduation:*** $26,651. ***Financial aid deadline:*** 6/30.

APPLYING

Standardized Tests *Required:* SAT or ACT (for admission).

Options: electronic application, deferred entrance.

Application fee: $35.

Required: high school transcript.

Notification: continuous (freshmen), continuous (transfers).

CONTACT

Ms. Angie Siders, Director of Admissions, Indiana University Kokomo, Kelley Student Center, Room 230, 2300 South Washington Street, Kokomo, IN 46904-9003. *Phone:* 765-455-9217. *Toll-free phone:* 888-875-4485. *Fax:* 765-455-9537. *E-mail:* iuadmis@iuk.edu.

Indiana University Northwest

Gary, Indiana

http://www.iun.edu/

- **State-supported** comprehensive, founded 1959, part of Indiana University System
- **Urban** 42-acre campus with easy access to Chicago
- **Endowment** $7.8 million
- **Coed** 5,661 undergraduate students, 55% full-time, 67% women, 33% men
- **Minimally difficult** entrance level, 77% of applicants were admitted

UNDERGRAD STUDENTS

3,114 full-time, 2,547 part-time. Students come from 12 states and territories; 34 other countries; 2% are from out of state; 16% Black or African American, non-Hispanic/Latino; 18% Hispanic/Latino; 2% Asian, non-Hispanic/Latino; 0.1% Native Hawaiian or other Pacific Islander, non-Hispanic/Latino; 0.2% American Indian or Alaska Native, non-Hispanic/Latino; 2% Two or more races, non-Hispanic/Latino; 9% Race/ethnicity unknown; 0.1% international; 5% transferred in.

Freshmen

Admission: 1,658 applied, 1,273 admitted, 711 enrolled. ***Average high school GPA:*** 2.88. ***Test scores:*** SAT critical reading scores over 500: 29%; SAT math scores over 500: 29%; SAT writing scores over 500: 22%; ACT scores over 18: 68%; SAT critical reading scores over 600: 5%; SAT math scores over 600: 4%; SAT writing scores over 600: 4%; ACT scores over 24: 18%; ACT scores over 30: 2%.

Retention: 67% of full-time freshmen returned.

FACULTY

Total: 386, 46% full-time, 41% with terminal degrees.

Student/faculty ratio: 15:1.

ACADEMICS

Calendar: semesters. *Degrees:* certificates, associate, bachelor's, master's, and postbachelor's certificates.

Special study options: academic remediation for entering students, accelerated degree program, adult/continuing education programs, advanced placement credit, cooperative education, distance learning, double majors, external degree program, honors programs, independent study, internships, off-campus study, part-time degree program, services for LD students, student-designed majors, study abroad, summer session for credit. ***ROTC:*** Army (b).

Computers: Students can access the following: campus intranet, computer help desk, free student e-mail accounts, online (class) grades, online (class) registration, online (class) schedules. Campuswide network is available. Wireless service is available via entire campus.

STUDENT LIFE

Housing options: college housing not available.

Activities and organizations: drama/theater group, student-run newspaper, radio station, choral group, Student Government Association, Student Ambassadors, Student Nurses Association, Art Club, Modern Languages Club, national fraternities, national sororities.

Athletics Member NAIA. ***Intercollegiate sports:*** basketball M(s)/W(s), cross-country running M/W, golf M/W, volleyball W. ***Intramural sports:*** baseball M(c), basketball M(c)/W(c), cheerleading W, football M(c)/W(c), golf M/W, ice hockey M(c)/W(c), softball M(c)/W(c), tennis M(c)/W(c), volleyball M/W.

Campus security: 24-hour emergency response devices and patrols, late-night transport/escort service, lighted pathways.

Student services: health clinic, personal/psychological counseling.

COSTS & FINANCIAL AID
Costs (2014–15) ***Tuition:*** state resident $6263 full-time, $209 per credit hour part-time; nonresident $17,490 full-time, $583 per credit hour part-time. Full-time tuition and fees vary according to course load, location, and program. Part-time tuition and fees vary according to course load, location, and program. ***Required fees:*** $591 full-time. ***Payment plans:*** installment, deferred payment. ***Waivers:*** employees or children of employees.

Financial Aid Of all full-time matriculated undergraduates who enrolled in 2013, 2,795 applied for aid, 2,314 were judged to have need, 74 had their need fully met. In 2013, 194 non-need-based awards were made. ***Average percent of need met:*** 62. ***Average financial aid package:*** $8186. ***Average need-based loan:*** $3618. ***Average need-based gift aid:*** $6589. ***Average non-need-based aid:*** $3485. ***Average indebtedness upon graduation:*** $33,790.

APPLYING
Standardized Tests *Required:* SAT or ACT (for admission).

Options: electronic application, deferred entrance.

Application fee: $35.

Required: high school transcript, minimum 2.0 GPA.

Application deadlines: rolling (freshmen), rolling (transfers).

Notification: continuous (freshmen), continuous (transfers).

CONTACT
., Indiana University Northwest, Hawthorn Hall 101, 3400 Broadway, Gary, IN 46408-1197. *Phone:* 219-980-6991. *Toll-free phone:* 800-968-7486. *Fax:* 219-981-4219. *E-mail:* admit@iun.edu.

Indiana University–Purdue University Fort Wayne

Fort Wayne, Indiana

http://www.ipfw.edu/

- **State-supported** comprehensive, founded 1917, part of Indiana University System and Purdue University System
- **Urban** 683-acre campus
- **Endowment** $57.1 million
- **Coed** 12,674 undergraduate students, 55% full-time, 55% women, 45% men
- **Minimally difficult** entrance level, 91% of applicants were admitted

UNDERGRAD STUDENTS
6,971 full-time, 5,703 part-time. Students come from 37 states and territories; 45 other countries; 5% are from out of state; 5% Black or African American, non-Hispanic/Latino; 5% Hispanic/Latino; 2% Asian, non-Hispanic/Latino; 0.3% American Indian or Alaska Native, non-Hispanic/Latino; 3% Two or more races, non-Hispanic/Latino; 0.6% Race/ethnicity unknown; 1% international; 5% transferred in; 8% live on campus.

Freshmen
Admission: 3,386 applied, 3,077 admitted, 1,559 enrolled. ***Average high school GPA:*** 3.2. ***Test scores:*** SAT critical reading scores over 500: 47%; SAT math scores over 500: 48%; SAT writing scores over 500: 36%; ACT scores over 18: 88%; SAT critical reading scores over 600: 12%; SAT math scores over 600: 13%; SAT writing scores over 600: 7%; ACT scores over 24: 35%; SAT critical reading scores over 700: 2%; SAT math scores over 700: 1%; SAT writing scores over 700: 1%; ACT scores over 30: 8%.

Retention: 68% of full-time freshmen returned.

FACULTY
Total: 801, 50% full-time, 47% with terminal degrees.

Student/faculty ratio: 17:1.

ACADEMICS
Calendar: semesters. *Degrees:* certificates, associate, bachelor's, master's, and postbachelor's certificates.

Special study options: academic remediation for entering students, accelerated degree program, adult/continuing education programs, advanced placement credit, cooperative education, distance learning, double majors, English as a second language, honors programs, independent study, internships, off-campus study, part-time degree program, services for LD students, student-designed majors, study abroad, summer session for credit. ***ROTC:*** Army (b).

Computers: 642 computers/terminals are available on campus for general student use. Students can access the following: computer help desk, free student e-mail accounts, online (class) grades, online (class) registration, online (class) schedules, student academic records. Campuswide network is available. 100% of college-owned or -operated housing units are wired for high-speed Internet access. Wireless service is available via entire campus.

STUDENT LIFE
Housing options: coed. Campus housing is provided by a third party.

Activities and organizations: drama/theater group, student-run newspaper, television station, choral group, Live Action Combat Club, Active Minds, InterVarsity Christian Fellowship, Student Athlete Leadership Team, League of Legends (LOL).

Athletics Member NCAA. All Division I. ***Intercollegiate sports:*** baseball M(s), basketball M(s)/W(s), cross-country running M(s)/W(s), golf M(s)/W(s), soccer M(s)/W(s), softball W(s), tennis M(s)/W(s), track and field W(s), volleyball M(s)/W(s). ***Intramural sports:*** basketball M/W, golf M/W, racquetball M/W, soccer M/W, softball W, tennis M/W, ultimate Frisbee M/W, volleyball M/W.

Campus security: 24-hour emergency response devices and patrols, late-night transport/escort service, controlled dormitory access.

Student services: health clinic, personal/psychological counseling, women's center.

COSTS & FINANCIAL AID
Costs (2014–15) ***Tuition:*** state resident $6938 full-time, $231 per credit hour part-time; nonresident $18,081 full-time, $603 per credit hour part-time. Full-time tuition and fees vary according to course load. Part-time tuition and fees vary according to course load. ***Required fees:*** $1011 full-time, $34 per credit hour part-time. ***Room only:*** $7632. Room and board charges vary according to housing facility. ***Payment plans:*** installment, deferred payment. ***Waivers:*** senior citizens and employees or children of employees.

Financial Aid Of all full-time matriculated undergraduates who enrolled in 2014, 6,395 applied for aid, 5,469 were judged to have need, 116 had their need fully met. 200 Federal Work-Study jobs (averaging $3000). In 2014, 84 non-need-based awards were made. ***Average percent of need met:*** 47. ***Average financial aid package:*** $9525. ***Average need-based loan:*** $3870. ***Average need-based gift aid:*** $5437. ***Average non-need-based aid:*** $3660. ***Average indebtedness upon graduation:*** $29,452.

APPLYING
Standardized Tests *Required:* SAT or ACT (for admission).

Options: electronic application, deferred entrance.

Application fee: $50.

Required: high school transcript, minimum 2.8 GPA. ***Recommended:*** rank in upper 50% of high school class.

Application deadlines: 8/1 (freshmen), 8/1 (out-of-state freshmen), 8/1 (transfers).

Notification: continuous (freshmen), continuous (out-of-state freshmen), continuous (transfers).

CONTACT
Angela Morren, Undergraduate Applications Coordinator, Indiana University–Purdue University Fort Wayne, 2101 East Coliseum Boulevard, Fort Wayne, IN 46805-1499. *Phone:* 260-481-6142. *Toll-free phone:* 800-324-4739. *Fax:* 260-481-6880. *E-mail:* morrena@ipfw.edu.

Indiana University–Purdue University Indianapolis

Indianapolis, Indiana

http://www.iupui.edu/

- **State-supported** university, founded 1969, part of Indiana University System
- **Urban** 534-acre campus
- **Endowment** $717.3 million
- **Coed** 22,525 undergraduate students, 77% full-time, 56% women, 44% men
- **Moderately difficult** entrance level, 70% of applicants were admitted

UNDERGRAD STUDENTS

17,262 full-time, 5,263 part-time. Students come from 49 states and territories; 149 other countries; 2% are from out of state; 10% Black or African American, non-Hispanic/Latino; 6% Hispanic/Latino; 4% Asian, non-Hispanic/Latino; 0.1% Native Hawaiian or other Pacific Islander, non-Hispanic/Latino; 0.1% American Indian or Alaska Native, non-Hispanic/Latino; 4% Two or more races, non-Hispanic/Latino; 1% Race/ethnicity unknown; 4% international; 8% transferred in; 9% live on campus.

Freshmen

Admission: 12,920 applied, 9,107 admitted, 3,779 enrolled. ***Average high school GPA:*** 3.34. ***Test scores:*** SAT critical reading scores over 500: 50%; SAT math scores over 500: 52%; SAT writing scores over 500: 41%; ACT scores over 18: 86%; SAT critical reading scores over 600: 13%; SAT math scores over 600: 17%; SAT writing scores over 600: 10%; ACT scores over 24: 36%; SAT critical reading scores over 700: 1%; SAT math scores over 700: 2%; SAT writing scores over 700: 1%; ACT scores over 30: 5%.

Retention: 71% of full-time freshmen returned.

FACULTY

Total: 3,302, 67% full-time, 65% with terminal degrees.

Student/faculty ratio: 19:1.

ACADEMICS

Calendar: semesters. *Degrees:* certificates, associate, bachelor's, master's, doctoral, post-master's, and postbachelor's certificates.

Special study options: academic remediation for entering students, accelerated degree program, adult/continuing education programs, advanced placement credit, cooperative education, distance learning, double majors, English as a second language, external degree program, freshman honors college, honors programs, independent study, internships, off-campus study, part-time degree program, services for LD students, student-designed majors, study abroad, summer session for credit. ***ROTC:*** Army (b), Air Force (c).

Computers: 1,158 computers/terminals are available on campus for general student use. Students can access the following: campus intranet, computer help desk, free student e-mail accounts, online (class) grades, online (class) registration, online (class) schedules. Campuswide network is available. 100% of college-owned or -operated housing units are wired for high-speed Internet access. Wireless service is available via entire campus.

STUDENT LIFE

Housing options: coed. Campus housing is university owned.

Activities and organizations: drama/theater group, student-run newspaper, national fraternities, national sororities.

Athletics Member NCAA. All Division I. ***Intercollegiate sports:*** basketball M(s)/W(s), cross-country running M(s)/W(s), golf M(s)/W(s), soccer M(s)/W(s), softball W(s), swimming and diving M(s)/W(s), tennis M(s)/W(s), track and field M/W, volleyball W(s). ***Intramural sports:*** baseball M, basketball M/W, cross-country running M/W, equestrian sports M(c)/W(c), football M/W, golf M/W, gymnastics M(c)/W(c), ice hockey M(c)/W(c), lacrosse M(c), racquetball M/W, soccer M/W, softball M/W, swimming and diving M(c)/W(c), table tennis M(c)/W(c), tennis M/W, track and field M/W, ultimate Frisbee M/W, volleyball M/W, water polo M/W.

Campus security: 24-hour emergency response devices and patrols, late-night transport/escort service, controlled dormitory access, lighted pathways, self-defense education.

Student services: health clinic, personal/psychological counseling, women's center.

COSTS & FINANCIAL AID

Costs (2014–15) ***Tuition:*** state resident $7878 full-time, $263 per credit hour part-time; nonresident $29,058 full-time, $969 per credit hour part-time. Full-time tuition and fees vary according to course load, location, and program. Part-time tuition and fees vary according to course load, location, and program. ***Required fees:*** $1031 full-time. ***Room and board:*** $7981. Room and board charges vary according to board plan and housing facility. ***Payment plan:*** deferred payment. ***Waivers:*** employees or children of employees.

Financial Aid Of all full-time matriculated undergraduates who enrolled in 2013, 13,984 applied for aid, 11,784 were judged to have need, 644 had their need fully met. In 2013, 1332 non-need-based awards were made. ***Average percent of need met:*** 61. ***Average financial aid package:*** $9862. ***Average need-based loan:*** $4196. ***Average need-based gift aid:*** $7816. ***Average non-need-based aid:*** $4658. ***Average indebtedness upon graduation:*** $31,010.

APPLYING

Standardized Tests *Required:* SAT or ACT (for admission).

Options: electronic application, deferred entrance.

Application fee: $55.

Required: high school transcript. ***Required for some:*** interview. ***Recommended:*** portfolio for art program.

Application deadlines: 5/1 (freshmen), rolling (transfers).

Notification: continuous (freshmen), continuous (transfers).

CONTACT

Mr. Chris J. Foley, Director of Admissions, Indiana University–Purdue University Indianapolis, 420 University Boulevard, Campus Center 255, Indianapolis, IN 46202-5143. *Phone:* 317-274-4591. *Fax:* 317-278-1862. *E-mail:* apply@iupui.edu.

Indiana University South Bend

South Bend, Indiana

http://www.iusb.edu/

- **State-supported** comprehensive, founded 1922, part of Indiana University System
- **Suburban** 104-acre campus with easy access to Chicago
- **Endowment** $11.4 million
- **Coed** 7,293 undergraduate students, 53% full-time, 61% women, 39% men
- **Moderately difficult** entrance level, 73% of applicants were admitted

UNDERGRAD STUDENTS

3,857 full-time, 3,436 part-time. Students come from 14 states and territories; 76 other countries; 3% are from out of state; 7% Black or African American, non-Hispanic/Latino; 8% Hispanic/Latino; 2% Asian, non-Hispanic/Latino; 0.2% American Indian or Alaska Native, non-Hispanic/Latino; 3% Two or more races, non-Hispanic/Latino; 2% Race/ethnicity unknown; 2% international; 6% transferred in; 9% live on campus.

Freshmen

Admission: 2,430 applied, 1,782 admitted, 938 enrolled. ***Average high school GPA:*** 3.07. ***Test scores:*** SAT critical reading scores over 500: 39%; SAT math scores over 500: 36%; SAT writing scores over 500: 27%; ACT scores over 18: 75%; SAT critical reading scores over 600: 7%; SAT math scores over 600: 7%; SAT writing scores over 600: 4%; ACT scores over 24: 23%; SAT critical reading scores over 700: 1%; SAT math scores over 700: 1%; ACT scores over 30: 4%.

Retention: 66% of full-time freshmen returned.

FACULTY

Total: 485, 58% full-time, 46% with terminal degrees.

Student/faculty ratio: 13:1.

ACADEMICS

Calendar: semesters. *Degrees:* certificates, diplomas, associate, bachelor's, master's, and postbachelor's certificates.

Special study options: accelerated degree program, adult/continuing education programs, advanced placement credit, distance learning, double

majors, English as a second language, external degree program, freshman honors college, honors programs, independent study, internships, off-campus study, part-time degree program, services for LD students, study abroad, summer session for credit. ***ROTC:*** Army (c), Navy (c), Air Force (c).

Computers: Students can access the following: campus intranet, computer help desk, free student e-mail accounts, online (class) grades, online (class) registration, online (class) schedules. Campuswide network is available. Wireless service is available via entire campus.

STUDENT LIFE

Housing options: coed. Campus housing is university owned.

Activities and organizations: drama/theater group, student-run newspaper, choral group, national fraternities, national sororities.

Athletics Member NAIA. ***Intercollegiate sports:*** baseball M, basketball M(s)/W(s), cross-country running M/W, golf M, volleyball W. ***Intramural sports:*** basketball M/W, bowling M(c)/W(c), cheerleading W(c), cross-country running M(c)/W(c), equestrian sports M(c)/W(c), football M/W, golf M(c)/W(c), soccer M(c)/W(c), softball W(c), tennis M/W, volleyball M(c)/W(c).

Campus security: 24-hour emergency response devices and patrols, late-night transport/escort service, safety seminars, lighted pathways.

Student services: health clinic, personal/psychological counseling, women's center.

COSTS & FINANCIAL AID

Costs (2014–15) ***Tuition:*** state resident $6314 full-time, $210 per credit hour part-time; nonresident $17,490 full-time, $583 per credit hour part-time. Full-time tuition and fees vary according to course load, location, and program. Part-time tuition and fees vary according to course load, location, and program. ***Required fees:*** $591 full-time. ***Room only:*** $7150. Room and board charges vary according to housing facility. ***Payment plans:*** installment, deferred payment. ***Waivers:*** employees or children of employees.

Financial Aid Of all full-time matriculated undergraduates who enrolled in 2013, 3,501 applied for aid, 3,090 were judged to have need, 114 had their need fully met. In 2013, 175 non-need-based awards were made. ***Average percent of need met:*** 61. ***Average financial aid package:*** $8661. ***Average need-based loan:*** $3833. ***Average need-based gift aid:*** $6688. ***Average non-need-based aid:*** $1709. ***Average indebtedness upon graduation:*** $29,919.

APPLYING

Standardized Tests *Required:* SAT or ACT (for admission).

Options: electronic application, deferred entrance.

Application fee: $35.

Required: high school transcript, minimum 2.0 GPA. ***Required for some:*** interview.

Application deadlines: rolling (freshmen), rolling (transfers).

Notification: continuous (freshmen), continuous (transfers).

CONTACT

Ms. Connie Peterson-Miller, Director of Admissions, Indiana University South Bend, 1700 Mishawaka Avenue, PO Box 7111, South Bend, IN 46634-7111. *Phone:* 574-520-4839. *Toll-free phone:* 877-GO-2-IUSB. *Fax:* 574-520-4834. *E-mail:* admissions@iusb.edu.

★ Indiana University Southeast

New Albany, Indiana

http://www.ius.edu/

- **State-supported** comprehensive, founded 1941, part of Indiana University System
- **Suburban** 179-acre campus with easy access to Louisville
- **Endowment** $11.8 million
- **Coed** 5,989 undergraduate students, 60% full-time, 59% women, 41% men
- **Minimally difficult** entrance level, 80% of applicants were admitted

UNDERGRAD STUDENTS

3,587 full-time, 2,402 part-time. Students come from 15 states and territories; 43 other countries; 28% are from out of state; 6% Black or African American, non-Hispanic/Latino; 3% Hispanic/Latino; 1% Asian, non-Hispanic/Latino; 0.2% Native Hawaiian or other Pacific Islander, non-Hispanic/Latino; 0.1% American Indian or Alaska Native, non-Hispanic/Latino; 2% Two or more races, non-Hispanic/Latino; 3% Race/ethnicity unknown; 0.4% international; 8% transferred in; 11% live on campus.

Freshmen

Admission: 2,038 applied, 1,637 admitted, 923 enrolled. ***Average high school GPA:*** 3.04. ***Test scores:*** SAT critical reading scores over 500: 42%; SAT math scores over 500: 38%; SAT writing scores over 500: 28%; ACT scores over 18: 80%; SAT critical reading scores over 600: 7%; SAT math scores over 600: 5%; SAT writing scores over 600: 5%; ACT scores over 24: 21%; ACT scores over 30: 1%.

Retention: 62% of full-time freshmen returned.

FACULTY

Total: 499, 43% full-time, 40% with terminal degrees.

Student/faculty ratio: 14:1.

ACADEMICS

Calendar: semesters. *Degrees:* certificates, associate, bachelor's, master's, and postbachelor's certificates.

Special study options: academic remediation for entering students, accelerated degree program, adult/continuing education programs, advanced placement credit, distance learning, double majors, English as a second language, external degree program, honors programs, independent study, internships, off-campus study, part-time degree program, services for LD students, student-designed majors, study abroad, summer session for credit. ***ROTC:*** Army (c), Air Force (c).

Computers: 885 computers/terminals are available on campus for general student use. Students can access the following: campus intranet, computer help desk, free student e-mail accounts, online (class) grades, online (class) registration, online (class) schedules. Campuswide network is available. Wireless service is available via entire campus.

STUDENT LIFE

Housing options: coed. Campus housing is university owned.

Activities and organizations: drama/theater group, student-run newspaper, choral group, national fraternities, national sororities.

Athletics Member NAIA. ***Intercollegiate sports:*** baseball M(s), basketball M(s)/W(s), softball W, tennis M/W, volleyball W(s). ***Intramural sports:*** basketball M/W, football M/W, golf M/W, soccer M/W, softball M/W, ultimate Frisbee M/W, volleyball M/W.

Campus security: 24-hour emergency response devices and patrols, self-defense education, lighted pathways, police department on campus.

Student services: personal/psychological counseling.

COSTS & FINANCIAL AID

Costs (2014–15) ***Tuition:*** state resident $6236 full-time, $208 per credit hour part-time; nonresident $17,490 full-time, $583 per credit hour part-time. Full-time tuition and fees vary according to course load, location, program, and reciprocity agreements. Part-time tuition and fees vary according to course load, location, program, and reciprocity agreements. ***Required fees:*** $591 full-time. ***Room only:*** $6280. Room and board charges vary according to board plan and housing facility. ***Payment plans:*** installment, deferred payment. ***Waivers:*** employees or children of employees.

Financial Aid Of all full-time matriculated undergraduates who enrolled in 2013, 3,081 applied for aid, 2,527 were judged to have need, 115 had their need fully met. In 2013, 336 non-need-based awards were made. ***Average percent of need met:*** 58. ***Average financial aid package:*** $7667. ***Average need-based loan:*** $3708. ***Average need-based gift aid:*** $5876. ***Average non-need-based aid:*** $1056. ***Average indebtedness upon graduation:*** $26,594.

APPLYING

Standardized Tests *Required:* SAT or ACT (for admission).

Options: electronic application, early admission, deferred entrance.

Application fee: $35.

Required: high school transcript. ***Required for some:*** interview.

Application deadlines: rolling (freshmen), rolling (transfers).

Notification: continuous (freshmen), continuous (transfers).

CONTACT
Ms. Chris Crews, Director of Recruitment and Admission, Indiana University Southeast, University Center South Room 102, 4201 Grant Line Road, New Albany, IN 47150. *Phone:* 812-941-2212. *Toll-free phone:* 800-852-8835. *Fax:* 812-941-2595. *E-mail:* admissions@ius.edu.

Indiana Wesleyan University

Marion, Indiana

http://www.indwes.edu/

- **Independent Wesleyan** comprehensive, founded 1920
- **Small-town** 300-acre campus with easy access to Indianapolis
- **Coed**
- **Moderately difficult** entrance level

FACULTY
Student/faculty ratio: 14:1.

ACADEMICS
Calendar: semesters. *Degrees:* associate, bachelor's, master's, doctoral, post-master's, and postbachelor's certificates (also offers adult program with significant enrollment not reflected in profile).

STUDENT LIFE
Housing options: on-campus residence required through junior year; men-only, women-only. Campus housing is university owned. Freshman campus housing is guaranteed.

Activities and organizations: drama/theater group, student-run newspaper, radio and television station, choral group, Student Government Organization, Student Activities Council, University Players, World Christian Fellowship, Sixth Man Club.

Athletics Member NAIA, NCCAA.

Campus security: 24-hour emergency response devices and patrols, late-night transport/escort service, controlled dormitory access.

Student services: health clinic, personal/psychological counseling.

COSTS & FINANCIAL AID
Costs (2014–15) ***Tuition:*** $24,102 full-time, $803 per credit hour part-time. Full-time tuition and fees vary according to course load and degree level. Part-time tuition and fees vary according to course load and degree level. ***Room only:*** $3797. Room and board charges vary according to board plan.

Financial Aid Of all full-time matriculated undergraduates who enrolled in 2012, 2,716 applied for aid, 2,247 were judged to have need, 860 had their need fully met. 1,522 Federal Work-Study jobs (averaging $515). In 2012, 428 non-need-based awards were made. ***Average percent of need met:*** 79. ***Average financial aid package:*** $21,370. ***Average need-based loan:*** $6888. ***Average need-based gift aid:*** $13,851. ***Average non-need-based aid:*** $5185.

APPLYING
Standardized Tests *Required:* SAT or ACT (for admission), TOEFL for non-English speaking, and some non-resident alien students (for admission).

Options: electronic application, deferred entrance.

Required: essay or personal statement, high school transcript, minimum 2.5 GPA, 2 letters of recommendation.

CONTACT
Mr. Daniel Solms, Director of Admissions, Indiana Wesleyan University, 4201 South Washington Street, Marion, IN 46953. *Phone:* 866-468-6498 Ext. 2138. *Toll-free phone:* 866-468-6498. *Fax:* 765-677-2333. *E-mail:* admissions@indwes.edu.

International Business College

Fort Wayne, Indiana

http://www.ibcfortwayne.edu/

- **Private** 4-year, founded 1889
- **Suburban** campus
- **Coed** 406 undergraduate students
- 77% of applicants were admitted

Freshmen
Admission: 752 applied, 577 admitted.

ACADEMICS
Calendar: semesters. *Degrees:* diplomas, associate, and bachelor's.

CONTACT
Admissions Office, International Business College, 5699 Coventry Lane, Fort Wayne, IN 46804. *Phone:* 260-459-4500. *Toll-free phone:* 800-589-6363.

ITT Technical Institute

Fort Wayne, Indiana

http://www.itt-tech.edu/

- **Proprietary** primarily 2-year, founded 1967, part of ITT Educational Services, Inc.
- **Coed**
- **Minimally difficult** entrance level

ACADEMICS
Calendar: quarters. *Degrees:* associate and bachelor's.

STUDENT LIFE
Housing options: college housing not available.

CONTACT
Director of Recruitment, ITT Technical Institute, 2810 Dupont Commerce Court, Fort Wayne, IN 46825. *Phone:* 260-497-6200. *Toll-free phone:* 800-866-4488.

ITT Technical Institute

Indianapolis, Indiana

http://www.itt-tech.edu/

- **Proprietary** 4-year
- **Coed**
- **Minimally difficult** entrance level

ACADEMICS
Degrees: associate and bachelor's.

CONTACT
Director of Recruitment, ITT Technical Institute, 2525 N. Shadeland Avenue, Suite 103, Indianapolis, IN 46219. *Phone:* 317-351-3800. *Toll-free phone:* 877-264-1057.

ITT Technical Institute

Indianapolis, Indiana

http://www.itt-tech.edu/

- **Proprietary** comprehensive, founded 1966, part of ITT Educational Services, Inc.
- **Suburban** campus
- **Coed**
- **Minimally difficult** entrance level

ACADEMICS
Calendar: quarters. *Degrees:* associate, bachelor's, and master's.

CONTACT
Director of Recruitment, ITT Technical Institute, 9511 Angola Court, Indianapolis, IN 46268-1119. *Phone:* 317-875-8640. *Toll-free phone:* 800-937-4488.

ITT Technical Institute

Merrillville, Indiana

http://www.itt-tech.edu/

- **Proprietary** primarily 2-year
- **Coed**
- **Minimally difficult** entrance level

ACADEMICS
Degrees: associate and bachelor's.

CONTACT
Director of Recruitment, ITT Technical Institute, 8488 Georgia Street, Merrillville, IN 46410. *Phone:* 219-738-6100. *Toll-free phone:* 877-418-8134.

ITT Technical Institute

Newburgh, Indiana

http://www.itt-tech.edu/

- **Proprietary** primarily 2-year, founded 1966, part of ITT Educational Services, Inc.
- **Coed**
- **Minimally difficult** entrance level

ACADEMICS
Calendar: quarters. *Degrees:* associate and bachelor's.

STUDENT LIFE
Housing options: college housing not available.

CONTACT
Director of Recruitment, ITT Technical Institute, 10999 Stahl Road, Newburgh, IN 47630-7430. *Phone:* 812-858-1600. *Toll-free phone:* 800-832-4488.

ITT Technical Institute

South Bend, Indiana

http://www.itt-tech.edu/

- **Proprietary** 4-year, part of ITT Educational Services, Inc.
- **Coed**
- **Minimally difficult** entrance level

ACADEMICS
Calendar: quarters. *Degrees:* associate and bachelor's.

STUDENT LIFE
Housing options: college housing not available.

CONTACT
Director of Recruitment, ITT Technical Institute, 17390 Dugdale Drive, Suite 100, South Bend, IN 46635. *Phone:* 574-247-8300. *Toll-free phone:* 877-474-1926.

Manchester University

North Manchester, Indiana

http://www.manchester.edu/

- **Independent** comprehensive, founded 1889, affiliated with Church of the Brethren
- **Small-town** 125-acre campus
- **Endowment** $54.4 million
- **Coed** 1,257 undergraduate students, 98% full-time, 52% women, 48% men
- **Moderately difficult** entrance level, 74% of applicants were admitted

UNDERGRAD STUDENTS
1,233 full-time, 24 part-time. Students come from 22 states and territories; 15 other countries; 12% are from out of state; 4% Black or African American, non-Hispanic/Latino; 5% Hispanic/Latino; 1% Asian, non-Hispanic/Latino; 0.1% American Indian or Alaska Native, non-Hispanic/Latino; 3% Two or more races, non-Hispanic/Latino; 1% Race/ethnicity unknown; 2% international; 2% transferred in; 75% live on campus.

Freshmen
Admission: 2,551 applied, 1,895 admitted, 441 enrolled. ***Average high school GPA:*** 3.36. ***Test scores:*** SAT critical reading scores over 500: 48%; SAT math scores over 500: 54%; SAT writing scores over 500: 37%; ACT scores over 18: 86%; SAT critical reading scores over 600: 8%; SAT math scores over 600: 13%; SAT writing scores over 600: 6%; ACT scores over 24: 33%; SAT critical reading scores over 700: 1%; SAT writing scores over 700: 1%; ACT scores over 30: 4%.
Retention: 69% of full-time freshmen returned.

FACULTY
Total: 97, 76% full-time, 70% with terminal degrees.
Student/faculty ratio: 17:1.

ACADEMICS
Calendar: 4-1-4. *Degrees:* associate, bachelor's, master's, and doctoral.
Special study options: accelerated degree program, advanced placement credit, distance learning, double majors, honors programs, independent study, internships, off-campus study, part-time degree program, services for LD students, student-designed majors, study abroad, summer session for credit.
Unusual degree programs: 3-2 engineering with institutions such as Washington University in St. Louis, Purdue University, Ohio State University, Columbia University.
Computers: 250 computers/terminals are available on campus for general student use. Students can access the following: campus intranet, computer help desk, free student e-mail accounts, online (class) grades, online (class) registration, online (class) schedules. Campuswide network is available. 100% of college-owned or -operated housing units are wired for high-speed Internet access. Wireless service is available via classrooms, computer centers, computer labs, dorm rooms, learning centers, libraries, student centers.

STUDENT LIFE
Housing options: on-campus residence required through junior year; coed, special housing for students with disabilities. Campus housing is university owned. Freshman campus housing is guaranteed.
Activities and organizations: drama/theater group, student-run newspaper, radio station, choral group, Accounting and Business Club, Athletic Training Club, Pre-Professionals of Science, Student Education Association, Swim Club.
Athletics Member NCAA. All Division III. ***Intercollegiate sports:*** baseball M, basketball M/W, cheerleading W, cross-country running M/W, football M, golf M/W, soccer M/W, softball W, swimming and diving M/W, tennis M/W, track and field M/W, volleyball W, wrestling M. ***Intramural sports:*** basketball M/W, football M/W, soccer M/W, softball M/W, volleyball M/W.
Campus security: 24-hour emergency response devices and patrols, student patrols, late-night transport/escort service, alarm system, locked residence hall entrances.
Student services: health clinic, personal/psychological counseling.

COSTS & FINANCIAL AID
Costs (2014–15) ***One-time required fee:*** $250. ***Tuition:*** $700 per credit hour part-time. Part-time tuition and fees vary according to course load. ***Required fees:*** $30 per credit hour part-time. ***Room only:*** Room and board charges vary according to board plan and housing facility. ***Payment plan:*** installment. ***Waivers:*** employees or children of employees.
Financial Aid Of all full-time matriculated undergraduates who enrolled in 2014, 1,160 applied for aid, 1,085 were judged to have need, 250 had their need fully met. In 2014, 101 non-need-based awards were made. ***Average percent of need met:*** 67. ***Average financial aid package:*** $25,265. ***Average need-based loan:*** $4315. ***Average need-based gift aid:*** $20,939. ***Average non-need-based aid:*** $16,865. ***Average indebtedness upon graduation:*** $30,141.

APPLYING
Standardized Tests *Required:* SAT or ACT (for admission).
Options: electronic application.
Application fee: $25.
Required: high school transcript, 1 letter of recommendation, rank in upper 50% of high school class. ***Required for some:*** essay or personal statement, minimum 3.0 GPA. ***Recommended:*** minimum 2.3 GPA.
Application deadlines: rolling (freshmen), rolling (out-of-state freshmen), rolling (transfers).
Notification: continuous (freshmen), continuous (out-of-state freshmen), continuous (transfers).

CONTACT
Mr. Adam Hohman, Associate Director of Admissions, Manchester University, 604 East College Avenue, North Manchester, IN 46962-1225. *Phone:* 260-982-5235. *Toll-free phone:* 800-852-3648. *Fax:* 260-982-5239. *E-mail:* arhohman@manchester.edu.

Marian University

Indianapolis, Indiana

http://www.marian.edu/

- **Independent Roman Catholic** comprehensive, founded 1851
- **Suburban** 114-acre campus with easy access to Indianapolis
- **Endowment** $31.8 million
- **Coed** 2,150 undergraduate students, 80% full-time, 64% women, 36% men
- **Moderately difficult** entrance level, 75% of applicants were admitted

UNDERGRAD STUDENTS

1,711 full-time, 439 part-time. Students come from 30 states and territories; 10 other countries; 14% are from out of state; 13% Black or African American, non-Hispanic/Latino; 5% Hispanic/Latino; 1% Asian, non-Hispanic/Latino; 0.2% Native Hawaiian or other Pacific Islander, non-Hispanic/Latino; 0.2% American Indian or Alaska Native, non-Hispanic/Latino; 3% Two or more races, non-Hispanic/Latino; 3% Race/ethnicity unknown; 1% international; 5% transferred in; 34% live on campus.

Freshmen

Admission: 1,825 applied, 1,377 admitted, 321 enrolled. ***Average high school GPA:*** 3.38. ***Test scores:*** SAT critical reading scores over 500: 56%; SAT math scores over 500: 64%; SAT writing scores over 500: 37%; ACT scores over 18: 96%; SAT critical reading scores over 600: 15%; SAT math scores over 600: 15%; SAT writing scores over 600: 8%; ACT scores over 24: 40%; SAT critical reading scores over 700: 1%; SAT math scores over 700: 1%; SAT writing scores over 700: 1%; ACT scores over 30: 6%.

Retention: 74% of full-time freshmen returned.

FACULTY

Total: 273, 50% full-time, 41% with terminal degrees.

Student/faculty ratio: 13:1.

ACADEMICS

Calendar: semesters. *Degrees:* associate, bachelor's, master's, and doctoral.

Special study options: academic remediation for entering students, accelerated degree program, adult/continuing education programs, advanced placement credit, cooperative education, distance learning, double majors, honors programs, independent study, internships, off-campus study, part-time degree program, services for LD students, study abroad, summer session for credit. ***ROTC:*** Army (c).

Computers: 118 computers/terminals are available on campus for general student use. Students can access the following: computer help desk, free student e-mail accounts, online (class) grades, online (class) registration, online (class) schedules. Campuswide network is available. 100% of college-owned or -operated housing units are wired for high-speed Internet access. Wireless service is available via entire campus.

STUDENT LIFE

Housing options: on-campus residence required through junior year; coed. Campus housing is university owned. Freshman campus housing is guaranteed.

Activities and organizations: drama/theater group, student-run newspaper, choral group, marching band, Student Government Association, College Mentors for Kids, Best Buddies, Knight Nation, Sophia Club.

Athletics Member NAIA. ***Intercollegiate sports:*** baseball M(s), basketball M(s)/W(s), bowling M(s)/W(s), cheerleading M(s)/W(s), cross-country running M(s)/W(s), football M(s), golf M(s)/W(s), soccer M(s)/W(s), softball W(s), tennis M(s)/W(s), track and field M(s)/W(s), volleyball W(s). ***Intramural sports:*** basketball M/W, cheerleading M/W, football M/W, racquetball M/W, softball W, table tennis M/W, tennis M/W, ultimate Frisbee M/W, volleyball M/W, weight lifting M/W.

Campus security: 24-hour emergency response devices and patrols, student patrols, late-night transport/escort service, controlled dormitory access.

Student services: health clinic, personal/psychological counseling.

COSTS & FINANCIAL AID

Costs (2014–15) ***Comprehensive fee:*** $38,540 includes full-time tuition ($29,400) and room and board ($9140). Part-time tuition: $1305 per credit. ***Room and board:*** Room and board charges vary according to board plan and housing facility. ***Payment plan:*** installment. ***Waivers:*** children of alumni and employees or children of employees.

Financial Aid Of all full-time matriculated undergraduates who enrolled in 2008, 1,192 applied for aid, 1,068 were judged to have need, 231 had their need fully met. 200 Federal Work-Study jobs (averaging $1500). In 2008, 185 non-need-based awards were made. ***Average percent of need met:*** 75. ***Average financial aid package:*** $19,509. ***Average need-based loan:*** $4478. ***Average need-based gift aid:*** $11,188. ***Average non-need-based aid:*** $12,191. ***Average indebtedness upon graduation:*** $23,467.

APPLYING

Standardized Tests *Required:* SAT or ACT (for admission).

Options: electronic application, deferred entrance.

Application fee: $35.

Required: high school transcript, minimum 2.3 GPA, college transcripts. ***Required for some:*** essay or personal statement, letters of recommendation, interview.

Application deadlines: 8/1 (freshmen), 8/1 (out-of-state freshmen), 8/1 (transfers).

Notification: continuous (freshmen), continuous (out-of-state freshmen), continuous (transfers).

CONTACT

Ms. Luann Brames, Director of Freshmen Admission, Marian University, 3200 Cold Spring Road, Indianapolis, IN 46222-1997. *Phone:* 317-955-6300. *Toll-free phone:* 800-772-7264. *Fax:* 317-955-6401. *E-mail:* admissions@marian.edu.

Oakland City University

Oakland City, Indiana

http://www.oak.edu/

- **Independent General Baptist** comprehensive, founded 1885
- **Rural** 20-acre campus
- **Endowment** $4.6 million
- **Coed** 2,011 undergraduate students, 29% full-time, 57% women, 43% men
- **Minimally difficult** entrance level, 55% of applicants were admitted

UNDERGRAD STUDENTS

576 full-time, 1,435 part-time. Students come from 20 states and territories; 9 other countries; 19% are from out of state; 7% Black or African American, non-Hispanic/Latino; 2% Hispanic/Latino; 0.2% Asian, non-Hispanic/Latino; 0.3% American Indian or Alaska Native, non-Hispanic/Latino; 1% Two or more races, non-Hispanic/Latino; 14% Race/ethnicity unknown; 3% international; 4% transferred in; 50% live on campus.

Freshmen

Admission: 675 applied, 371 admitted, 87 enrolled. ***Average high school GPA:*** 3.15. ***Test scores:*** SAT critical reading scores over 500: 32%; SAT math scores over 500: 38%; SAT writing scores over 500: 32%; ACT scores over 18: 69%; SAT critical reading scores over 600: 5%; SAT math scores over 600: 8%; SAT writing scores over 600: 4%; ACT scores over 24: 25%; SAT critical reading scores over 700: 2%; SAT math scores over 700: 1%; ACT scores over 30: 2%.

Retention: 70% of full-time freshmen returned.

FACULTY

Total: 97, 85% full-time, 73% with terminal degrees.

Student/faculty ratio: 12:1.

ACADEMICS

Calendar: semesters. *Degrees:* certificates, associate, bachelor's, master's, and doctoral.

Special study options: academic remediation for entering students, accelerated degree program, adult/continuing education programs, advanced placement credit, distance learning, external degree program, part-time degree program, services for LD students, summer session for credit.

Computers: Students can access the following: campus intranet, free student e-mail accounts, online (class) grades, online (class) schedules.

Campuswide network is available. Wireless service is available via entire campus.

STUDENT LIFE

Housing options: on-campus residence required for freshman year; men-only, women-only. Campus housing is university owned. Freshman campus housing is guaranteed.

Activities and organizations: drama/theater group, student-run newspaper, choral group, Student Government Association, Good News Players, Art Guild, FOCUS, intramural sports.

Athletics Member NCAA, NCCAA. All NCAA Division II. ***Intercollegiate sports:*** baseball M(s), basketball M(s)/W(s), cheerleading W(s), cross-country running M(s)/W(s), golf M(s)/W(s), soccer M(s)/W(s), softball W(s), tennis M(s)/W(s), volleyball W(s). ***Intramural sports:*** archery M/W, badminton M/W, basketball M/W, bowling M/W, football M, golf M/W, soccer M/W, softball M/W, table tennis M/W, tennis M/W, volleyball M/W.

Campus security: 24-hour patrols, student patrols.

Student services: personal/psychological counseling.

COSTS & FINANCIAL AID

Costs (2015–16) ***Comprehensive fee:*** $31,830 includes full-time tuition ($22,800) and room and board ($9030). Full-time tuition and fees vary according to degree level. Part-time tuition: $760 per credit hour. ***Room and board:*** Room and board charges vary according to board plan and housing facility. ***Payment plan:*** deferred payment.

Financial Aid Of all full-time matriculated undergraduates who enrolled in 2007, 150 Federal Work-Study jobs (averaging $1600). 4 state and other part-time jobs (averaging $1500). ***Average percent of need met:*** 90.

APPLYING

Standardized Tests *Required for some:* SAT or ACT (for admission).

Options: electronic application, early admission, deferred entrance.

Application fee: $35.

Required: high school transcript, minimum 2.0 GPA. ***Recommended:*** essay or personal statement, interview.

CONTACT

Mr. Caleb Fendrich, Director of Admissions, Oakland City University, 138 North Lucretia Street, Oakland City, IN 47660. *Phone:* 812-749-1216. *Toll-free phone:* 800-737-5125. *E-mail:* cfendrich@oak.edu.

Purdue University

West Lafayette, Indiana

http://www.purdue.edu/

- **State-supported** university, founded 1869, part of Purdue University System
- **Suburban** 2660-acre campus with easy access to Indianapolis
- **Endowment** $2.5 billion
- **Coed** 29,255 undergraduate students, 95% full-time, 43% women, 57% men
- **Moderately difficult** entrance level, 59% of applicants were admitted

UNDERGRAD STUDENTS

27,881 full-time, 1,374 part-time. Students come from 52 states and territories; 89 other countries; 33% are from out of state; 3% Black or African American, non-Hispanic/Latino; 4% Hispanic/Latino; 6% Asian, non-Hispanic/Latino; 0.1% Native Hawaiian or other Pacific Islander, non-Hispanic/Latino; 0.1% American Indian or Alaska Native, non-Hispanic/Latino; 2% Two or more races, non-Hispanic/Latino; 2% Race/ethnicity unknown; 18% international; 2% transferred in; 37% live on campus.

Freshmen

Admission: 39,706 applied, 23,506 admitted, 6,422 enrolled. ***Average high school GPA:*** 3.72. ***Test scores:*** SAT critical reading scores over 500: 85%; SAT math scores over 500: 93%; SAT writing scores over 500: 84%; ACT scores over 18: 100%; SAT critical reading scores over 600: 41%; SAT math scores over 600: 65%; SAT writing scores over 600: 41%; ACT scores over 24: 83%; SAT critical reading scores over 700: 9%; SAT math scores over 700: 28%; SAT writing scores over 700: 7%; ACT scores over 30: 32%.

Retention: 93% of full-time freshmen returned.

FACULTY

Total: 2,243, 87% full-time, 96% with terminal degrees.

Student/faculty ratio: 14:1.

ACADEMICS

Calendar: semesters. *Degrees:* certificates, associate, bachelor's, master's, doctoral, post-master's, and postbachelor's certificates.

Special study options: accelerated degree program, adult/continuing education programs, cooperative education, distance learning, double majors, English as a second language, honors programs, independent study, internships, part-time degree program, services for LD students, study abroad, summer session for credit. ***ROTC:*** Army (b), Navy (b), Air Force (b).

Unusual degree programs: 3-2 business administration; engineering; forestry; nursing; social work; pharmacy.

Computers: 5,178 computers/terminals are available on campus for general student use. Students can access the following: campus intranet, computer help desk, free student e-mail accounts, online (class) grades, online (class) registration, online (class) schedules. Campuswide network is available. 100% of college-owned or -operated housing units are wired for high-speed Internet access. Wireless service is available via classrooms, computer centers, computer labs, learning centers, libraries, student centers.

STUDENT LIFE

Housing options: coed, men-only, women-only, cooperative, special housing for students with disabilities. Campus housing is university owned. Freshman applicants given priority for college housing.

Activities and organizations: drama/theater group, student-run newspaper, radio and television station, choral group, marching band, student government, Golden Key National Honor Society, Society of Women Engineers, Purdue student union board, Krannert Graduate Student Association, national fraternities, national sororities.

Athletics Member NCAA. All Division I except football (Division I-A). ***Intercollegiate sports:*** baseball M(s), basketball M(s)/W(s), cross-country running M(s)/W(s), golf M(s)/W(s), soccer W(s), softball W(s), swimming and diving M(s)/W(s), tennis M(s)/W(s), track and field M(s)/W(s), volleyball W(s), wrestling M(s). ***Intramural sports:*** archery M(c)/W(c), badminton M(c)/W(c), baseball M(c), basketball M(c)/W(c), bowling M(c)/W(c), crew M(c)/W(c), cross-country running M(c)/W(c), equestrian sports M(c)/W(c), fencing M(c)/W(c), gymnastics M(c)/W(c), ice hockey M(c), lacrosse M(c)/W(c), racquetball M(c)/W(c), riflery M(c)/W(c), rock climbing M(c)/W(c), rugby M(c)/W(c), sailing M(c)/W(c), soccer M(c)/W(c), squash M(c)/W(c), swimming and diving M(c)/W(c), table tennis M(c)/W(c), tennis M(c)/W(c), track and field M(c)/W(c), ultimate Frisbee M(c)/W(c), volleyball M(c)/W(c), water polo M(c)/W(c).

Campus security: 24-hour emergency response devices and patrols, student patrols, late-night transport/escort service, controlled dormitory access.

Student services: health clinic, personal/psychological counseling, women's center, legal services.

COSTS & FINANCIAL AID

Costs (2014–15) ***Tuition:*** state resident $9208 full-time, $348 per credit hour part-time; nonresident $28,010 full-time, $948 per credit hour part-time. Full-time tuition and fees vary according to course load and program. Part-time tuition and fees vary according to course load. ***Required fees:*** $794 full-time. ***Room and board:*** $10,030; room only: $4860. Room and board charges vary according to board plan and housing facility. ***Payment plan:*** installment. ***Waivers:*** senior citizens and employees or children of employees.

Financial Aid Of all full-time matriculated undergraduates who enrolled in 2014, 16,551 applied for aid, 12,079 were judged to have need, 4,668 had their need fully met. 1,975 Federal Work-Study jobs (averaging $2321). In 2014, 2963 non-need-based awards were made. ***Average percent of need met:*** 85. ***Average financial aid package:*** $13,076. ***Average need-based loan:*** $4543. ***Average need-based gift aid:*** $11,744. ***Average non-need-based aid:*** $6697. ***Average indebtedness upon graduation:*** $28,343.

APPLYING

Standardized Tests *Required:* SAT or ACT (for admission).

Options: electronic application, early admission, early action, deferred entrance.

Application fee: $60.

Required: essay or personal statement, high school transcript.

Application deadlines: rolling (freshmen), rolling (transfers), 11/1 (early action).

Notification: 12/12 (freshmen), 12/12 (early action).

CONTACT

Ms. Pamela T. Horne, Assistant Vice President for Enrollment Management and Dean of Admissions, Purdue University, 475 Stadium Mall Drive, Schleman Hall, West Lafayette, IN 47907-2050. *Phone:* 765-494-1776. *Fax:* 765-494-0544. *E-mail:* admissions@purdue.edu.

Purdue University Calumet

Hammond, Indiana

http://www.purduecal.edu/

- **State-supported** comprehensive, founded 1951, part of Purdue University System
- **Urban** 185-acre campus with easy access to Chicago
- **Endowment** $15.6 million
- **Coed** 8,491 undergraduate students, 58% full-time, 56% women, 44% men
- **Moderately difficult** entrance level, 60% of applicants were admitted

UNDERGRAD STUDENTS

4,905 full-time, 3,586 part-time. Students come from 34 states and territories; 36 other countries; 22% are from out of state; 13% Black or African American, non-Hispanic/Latino; 18% Hispanic/Latino; 2% Asian, non-Hispanic/Latino; 0.2% Native Hawaiian or other Pacific Islander, non-Hispanic/Latino; 0.2% American Indian or Alaska Native, non-Hispanic/Latino; 2% Two or more races, non-Hispanic/Latino; 2% Race/ethnicity unknown; 7% international; 9% transferred in; 7% live on campus.

Freshmen

Admission: 2,351 applied, 1,403 admitted, 945 enrolled. ***Average high school GPA:*** 3.1. ***Test scores:*** SAT critical reading scores over 500: 39%; SAT math scores over 500: 44%; SAT writing scores over 500: 32%; SAT critical reading scores over 600: 9%; SAT math scores over 600: 10%; SAT writing scores over 600: 4%; SAT critical reading scores over 700: 1%; SAT math scores over 700: 1%.

Retention: 74% of full-time freshmen returned.

FACULTY

Total: 504, 55% full-time, 44% with terminal degrees.

Student/faculty ratio: 19:1.

ACADEMICS

Calendar: semesters. *Degrees:* certificates, associate, bachelor's, master's, post-master's, and postbachelor's certificates.

Special study options: academic remediation for entering students, accelerated degree program, adult/continuing education programs, advanced placement credit, cooperative education, distance learning, double majors, English as a second language, freshman honors college, honors programs, independent study, internships, part-time degree program, services for LD students, study abroad, summer session for credit. ***ROTC:*** Army (b).

Computers: 1,500 computers/terminals are available on campus for general student use. Students can access the following: campus intranet, computer help desk, free student e-mail accounts, online (class) grades, online (class) registration, online (class) schedules. Campuswide network is available. 100% of college-owned or -operated housing units are wired for high-speed Internet access. Wireless service is available via entire campus.

STUDENT LIFE

Housing options: coed. Campus housing is university owned.

Activities and organizations: drama/theater group, student-run newspaper, choral group, marching band, Purdue University Gamers Guild, Finance and Accounting Club, Environmental Club, Spanish Club, Society for Human Resources Management, national fraternities, national sororities.

Athletics Member NAIA. ***Intercollegiate sports:*** baseball M(s), basketball M(s)/W(s), cross-country running M(s)/W(s), golf M(s), soccer M(s)/W(s), softball W(s), tennis M(s)/W(s), volleyball W(s). ***Intramural sports:*** badminton M/W, basketball M/W, bowling M/W, football M/W, golf M/W, racquetball M/W, soccer M/W, softball M/W, table tennis M/W, ultimate Frisbee M/W, volleyball M/W, weight lifting M/W.

Campus security: 24-hour emergency response devices and patrols, student patrols, late-night transport/escort service.

Student services: health clinic, personal/psychological counseling.

COSTS & FINANCIAL AID

Costs (2014–15) ***Tuition:*** state resident $6758 full-time, $241 per credit hour part-time; nonresident $15,266 full-time, $545 per credit hour part-time. Full-time tuition and fees vary according to course load and program. Part-time tuition and fees vary according to course load and program. ***Room only:*** $5485. Room and board charges vary according to housing facility. ***Payment plan:*** installment. ***Waivers:*** employees or children of employees.

Financial Aid Of all full-time matriculated undergraduates who enrolled in 2013, 4,173 applied for aid, 3,657 were judged to have need, 56 had their need fully met. 111 Federal Work-Study jobs (averaging $1853). In 2013, 158 non-need-based awards were made. ***Average percent of need met:*** 10. ***Average financial aid package:*** $7282. ***Average need-based loan:*** $3507. ***Average need-based gift aid:*** $5378. ***Average non-need-based aid:*** $4570. ***Average indebtedness upon graduation:*** $28,600.

APPLYING

Standardized Tests *Required:* SAT or ACT (for admission).

Options: electronic application.

Application fee: $25.

Required: high school transcript, minimum 2.0 GPA.

Application deadlines: 8/1 (freshmen), 8/1 (out-of-state freshmen), 8/1 (transfers).

Notification: continuous (freshmen), continuous (out-of-state freshmen), continuous (transfers).

CONTACT

Purdue University Calumet, 2200 169th Street, Hammond, IN 46323-2094. *Phone:* 219-989-2768. *Toll-free phone:* 800-447-8738.

Purdue University North Central

Westville, Indiana

http://www.pnc.edu/

- **State-supported** comprehensive, founded 1967, part of Purdue University System
- **Rural** 305-acre campus with easy access to Chicago
- **Coed**
- **Minimally difficult** entrance level

FACULTY

Student/faculty ratio: 17:1.

ACADEMICS

Calendar: semesters. *Degrees:* certificates, associate, bachelor's, master's, and postbachelor's certificates.

STUDENT LIFE

Housing options: college housing not available.

Activities and organizations: drama/theater group, student-run newspaper, choral group, Dean's Leadership Group, Society of Human Resource Management, PLAYCE (Early Childhood Education), Astronomy Club, PNC Veteran's.

Athletics Member NAIA.

Campus security: 24-hour emergency response devices and patrols, late-night transport/escort service.

Student services: personal/psychological counseling.

FINANCIAL AID

Financial Aid Of all full-time matriculated undergraduates who enrolled in 2011, 2,552 applied for aid, 1,891 were judged to have need, 35 had their need fully met. In 2011, 17 non-need-based awards were made. ***Average percent of need met:*** 48. ***Average financial aid package:*** $7588. ***Average need-based loan:*** $3619. ***Average need-based gift aid:*** $6297.

Average non-need-based aid: $1728. *Average indebtedness upon graduation:* $22,952. *Financial aid deadline:* 6/30.

APPLYING
Standardized Tests *Recommended:* SAT or ACT (for admission).

Options: electronic application, deferred entrance.

Required: high school transcript. ***Required for some:*** minimum 2.0 GPA.

CONTACT
Ms. Janice Whisler, Director Enrollment/Outreach Recruitment, Purdue University North Central, 1401 South U.S. Highway 421, Westville, IN 46391. *Phone:* 219-785-5415. *Toll-free phone:* 800-872-1231. *Fax:* 219-785-5538. *E-mail:* jwhisler@pnc.edu.

Rose-Hulman Institute of Technology

Terre Haute, Indiana

http://www.rose-hulman.edu/

- **Independent** comprehensive, founded 1874
- **Suburban** 200-acre campus with easy access to Indianapolis
- **Endowment** $199.8 million
- **Coed, primarily men** 2,280 undergraduate students, 99% full-time, 22% women, 78% men
- **Very difficult** entrance level, 59% of applicants were admitted

UNDERGRAD STUDENTS
2,258 full-time, 22 part-time. Students come from 48 states and territories; 15 other countries; 64% are from out of state; 2% Black or African American, non-Hispanic/Latino; 3% Hispanic/Latino; 4% Asian, non-Hispanic/Latino; 0.1% Native Hawaiian or other Pacific Islander, non-Hispanic/Latino; 4% Two or more races, non-Hispanic/Latino; 0.2% Race/ethnicity unknown; 11% international; 0.4% transferred in; 59% live on campus.

Freshmen
Admission: 4,404 applied, 2,589 admitted, 582 enrolled. *Average high school GPA:* 3.96. *Test scores:* SAT critical reading scores over 500: 92%; SAT math scores over 500: 100%; SAT writing scores over 500: 89%; ACT scores over 18: 100%; SAT critical reading scores over 600: 50%; SAT math scores over 600: 89%; SAT writing scores over 600: 47%; ACT scores over 24: 96%; SAT critical reading scores over 700: 14%; SAT math scores over 700: 48%; SAT writing scores over 700: 9%; ACT scores over 30: 50%.

Retention: 94% of full-time freshmen returned.

FACULTY
Total: 197, 92% full-time, 99% with terminal degrees.

Student/faculty ratio: 13:1.

ACADEMICS
Calendar: quarters. *Degrees:* bachelor's and master's.

Special study options: accelerated degree program, adult/continuing education programs, advanced placement credit, cooperative education, distance learning, double majors, independent study, internships, off-campus study, services for LD students, study abroad, summer session for credit. ***ROTC:*** Army (b), Air Force (b).

Computers: 45 computers/terminals and 8,000 ports are available on campus for general student use. Students can access the following: campus intranet, computer help desk, free student e-mail accounts, online (class) grades, online (class) registration, online (class) schedules. Campuswide network is available. 100% of college-owned or -operated housing units are wired for high-speed Internet access. Wireless service is available via classrooms, computer centers, computer labs, learning centers, libraries, student centers.

STUDENT LIFE
Housing options: on-campus residence required for freshman year; coed, men-only. Campus housing is university owned. Freshman campus housing is guaranteed.

Activities and organizations: drama/theater group, student-run newspaper, radio station, choral group, Paintball Club, Rose Innovative Student Entrepreneurs (RISE), Bowling Club, Drama Club, International Students Association, national fraternities, national sororities.

Athletics Member NCAA. All Division III. ***Intercollegiate sports:*** baseball M, basketball M/W, cross-country running M/W, football M, golf M/W, riflery M/W, soccer M/W, softball W, swimming and diving M/W, tennis M/W, track and field M/W, volleyball W. ***Intramural sports:*** basketball M/W, bowling M/W, cross-country running M/W, fencing M(c)/W(c), football M/W, golf M/W, lacrosse M(c)/W(c), racquetball M/W, soccer M/W, softball M/W, swimming and diving M/W, table tennis M/W, tennis M/W, track and field M/W, ultimate Frisbee M/W, volleyball M/W.

Campus security: 24-hour emergency response devices and patrols, late-night transport/escort service, controlled dormitory access.

Student services: health clinic, personal/psychological counseling.

COSTS & FINANCIAL AID
Costs (2014–15) ***One-time required fee:*** $2400. ***Comprehensive fee:*** $53,340 includes full-time tuition ($40,449), mandatory fees ($834), and room and board ($12,057). Full-time tuition and fees vary according to course load. Part-time tuition: $1181 per credit hour. Part-time tuition and fees vary according to course load. ***College room only:*** $7392. Room and board charges vary according to board plan. ***Payment plans:*** tuition prepayment, installment. ***Waivers:*** employees or children of employees.

Financial Aid Of all full-time matriculated undergraduates who enrolled in 2014, 1,587 applied for aid, 1,387 were judged to have need, 247 had their need fully met. 417 Federal Work-Study jobs (averaging $1257). 487 state and other part-time jobs (averaging $1266). In 2014, 781 non-need-based awards were made. ***Average percent of need met:*** 74. ***Average financial aid package:*** $28,720. ***Average need-based loan:*** $5288. ***Average need-based gift aid:*** $23,950. ***Average non-need-based aid:*** $11,295. ***Average indebtedness upon graduation:*** $35,420.

APPLYING
Standardized Tests *Required:* SAT or ACT (for admission).

Options: electronic application, early action, deferred entrance.

Application fee: $40.

Required: high school transcript, 1 letter of recommendation, curricular; minimum math and verbal standardized test scores. ***Recommended:*** essay or personal statement.

Notification: continuous (freshmen), continuous (transfers).

CONTACT
Mrs. Lisa Norton, Director of Admissions, Rose-Hulman Institute of Technology, 5500 Wabash Avenue, CM 1, Terre Haute, IN 47803-3920. *Phone:* 812-877-8213. *Toll-free phone:* 800-248-7448. *Fax:* 812-877-8941. *E-mail:* admissions@rose-hulman.edu.

Saint Joseph's College

Rensselaer, Indiana

http://www.saintjoe.edu/

- **Independent Roman Catholic** comprehensive, founded 1889
- **Small-town** 180-acre campus
- **Endowment** $24.2 million
- **Coed** 1,142 undergraduate students, 89% full-time, 60% women, 40% men
- **Moderately difficult** entrance level, 66% of applicants were admitted

UNDERGRAD STUDENTS
1,012 full-time, 130 part-time. Students come from 19 states and territories; 8 other countries; 23% are from out of state; 9% Black or African American, non-Hispanic/Latino; 4% Hispanic/Latino; 0.5% Asian, non-Hispanic/Latino; 0.6% American Indian or Alaska Native, non-Hispanic/Latino; 3% Two or more races, non-Hispanic/Latino; 2% Race/ethnicity unknown; 0.9% international; 3% transferred in; 68% live on campus.

Freshmen
Admission: 1,572 applied, 1,044 admitted, 216 enrolled. *Average high school GPA:* 3.19. *Test scores:* SAT critical reading scores over 500: 53%; SAT math scores over 500: 53%; ACT scores over 18: 89%; SAT critical reading scores over 600: 10%; SAT math scores over 600: 17%; ACT scores over 24: 26%; SAT math scores over 700: 1%; ACT scores over 30: 5%.

Retention: 74% of full-time freshmen returned.

FACULTY
Total: 125, 63% full-time, 55% with terminal degrees.

Student/faculty ratio: 11:1.

ACADEMICS

Calendar: semesters. *Degrees:* diplomas, associate, bachelor's, and master's.

Special study options: academic remediation for entering students, accelerated degree program, advanced placement credit, double majors, honors programs, independent study, internships, part-time degree program, services for LD students, student-designed majors, study abroad, summer session for credit.

Computers: 66 computers/terminals and 156 ports are available on campus for general student use. Students can access the following: campus intranet, computer help desk, free student e-mail accounts, online (class) grades, online (class) registration, online (class) schedules. Campuswide network is available. 100% of college-owned or -operated housing units are wired for high-speed Internet access. Wireless service is available via entire campus.

STUDENT LIFE

Housing options: on-campus residence required through senior year; coed, men-only, women-only, special housing for students with disabilities. Campus housing is university owned. Freshman campus housing is guaranteed.

Activities and organizations: drama/theater group, student-run newspaper, radio and television station, choral group, marching band, Gallagher Charitable Society, Cup O' Joe, Habitat for Humanity, Science Club, Alpha Lambda Delta.

Athletics Member NCAA. All Division II. ***Intercollegiate sports:*** baseball M(s), basketball M(s)/W(s), cheerleading M(s)(c)/W(s)(c), cross-country running M(s)/W(s), football M(s), golf M(s)/W(s), soccer M(s)/W(s), softball W(s), tennis M(s)/W(s), track and field M(s)/W(s), volleyball W(s). ***Intramural sports:*** basketball M/W, rugby M(c)/W(c), soccer M/W, softball M/W, ultimate Frisbee M/W, volleyball M/W.

Campus security: 24-hour emergency response devices and patrols, student patrols, late-night transport/escort service.

Student services: health clinic, personal/psychological counseling.

COSTS & FINANCIAL AID

Costs (2014–15) ***Comprehensive fee:*** $36,095 includes full-time tuition ($27,295), mandatory fees ($190), and room and board ($8610). Full-time tuition and fees vary according to reciprocity agreements and student level. Part-time tuition: $925 per credit. Part-time tuition and fees vary according to course load and reciprocity agreements. No tuition increase for student's term of enrollment. ***College room only:*** $4180. Room and board charges vary according to board plan and housing facility. ***Payment plan:*** installment. ***Waivers:*** minority students, children of alumni, and employees or children of employees.

Financial Aid Of all full-time matriculated undergraduates who enrolled in 2013, 825 applied for aid, 721 were judged to have need, 240 had their need fully met. 229 Federal Work-Study jobs (averaging $1441). In 2013, 97 non-need-based awards were made. ***Average percent of need met:*** 85. ***Average financial aid package:*** $27,622. ***Average need-based loan:*** $4607. ***Average need-based gift aid:*** $19,209. ***Average non-need-based aid:*** $16,896. ***Average indebtedness upon graduation:*** $30,899.

APPLYING

Standardized Tests *Required:* SAT or ACT (for admission).

Options: electronic application, deferred entrance.

Application fee: $25.

Required: high school transcript, minimum 2.0 GPA. ***Required for some:*** essay or personal statement. ***Recommended:*** interview.

Application deadlines: rolling (freshmen), rolling (transfers).

Notification: continuous (freshmen), continuous (transfers).

CONTACT

Michael Ramian, Director of Admissions, Saint Joseph's College, PO Box 815, Rensselaer, IN 47978-0850. *Phone:* 219-866-6170. *Toll-free phone:* 800-447-8781. *Fax:* 219-866-6122. *E-mail:* admissions@saintjoe.edu.

Saint Mary-of-the-Woods College

Saint Mary of the Woods, Indiana

http://www.smwc.edu/

- **Independent Roman Catholic** comprehensive, founded 1840
- **Rural** 67-acre campus with easy access to Indianapolis
- **Coed, primarily women** 746 undergraduate students, 55% full-time, 93% women, 7% men
- **Minimally difficult** entrance level, 100% of applicants were admitted

UNDERGRAD STUDENTS

407 full-time, 339 part-time. 80% are from out of state; 4% Black or African American, non-Hispanic/Latino; 1% Hispanic/Latino; 0.4% Asian, non-Hispanic/Latino; 0.1% Native Hawaiian or other Pacific Islander, non-Hispanic/Latino; 1% American Indian or Alaska Native, non-Hispanic/Latino; 20% Race/ethnicity unknown; 0.6% international.

Freshmen

Admission: 284 applied, 284 admitted, 94 enrolled.

Retention: 82% of full-time freshmen returned.

FACULTY

Total: 167, 28% full-time.

Student/faculty ratio: 8:1.

ACADEMICS

Calendar: semesters. *Degrees:* certificates, associate, bachelor's, and master's (also offers external degree program with significant enrollment not reflected in profile).

Special study options: academic remediation for entering students, accelerated degree program, adult/continuing education programs, advanced placement credit, distance learning, double majors, external degree program, honors programs, independent study, internships, off-campus study, part-time degree program, services for LD students, student-designed majors, study abroad, summer session for credit.

Unusual degree programs: 3-2 business administration.

Computers: Students can access the following: campus intranet, computer help desk, free student e-mail accounts, online (class) grades, online (class) schedules. Campuswide network is available. 100% of college-owned or -operated housing units are wired for high-speed Internet access. Wireless service is available via entire campus.

STUDENT LIFE

Housing options: on-campus residence required through senior year; women-only, special housing for students with disabilities. Campus housing is university owned. Freshman campus housing is guaranteed.

Activities and organizations: drama/theater group, student-run newspaper, choral group, Student Activities Committee, Chorale, Student Senate, Woods Newspaper.

Athletics Member USCAA. ***Intercollegiate sports:*** basketball W(s), cross-country running W(s), equestrian sports W(s), golf W(s), soccer W(s), softball W(s).

Campus security: 24-hour emergency response devices and patrols, late-night transport/escort service, Resident Assistants (RAs) patrol the residence hall 3-4 times per night.

Student services: health clinic, personal/psychological counseling.

COSTS & FINANCIAL AID

Costs (2015–16) ***Comprehensive fee:*** $37,922 includes full-time tuition ($27,672) and room and board ($10,250). Part-time tuition and fees vary according to course load. No tuition increase for student's term of enrollment. ***College room only:*** $6375. Room and board charges vary according to housing facility. ***Payment plan:*** installment. ***Waivers:*** employees or children of employees.

Financial Aid Of all full-time matriculated undergraduates who enrolled in 2012, 429 applied for aid, 384 were judged to have need, 168 had their need fully met. 65 Federal Work-Study jobs (averaging $887). In 2012, 13 non-need-based awards were made. ***Average percent of need met:*** 41. ***Average financial aid package:*** $17,771. ***Average need-based loan:*** $3804. ***Average need-based gift aid:*** $7551. ***Average non-need-based aid:*** $7356. ***Average indebtedness upon graduation:*** $20,354.

APPLYING

Standardized Tests *Required:* SAT or ACT (for admission).

Options: electronic application, early admission, deferred entrance.

Required: high school transcript, minimum 2.0 GPA. ***Required for some:*** essay or personal statement, minimum 1.0 GPA, Transfer students must provide official transcripts from all previous institutions; students in RN-to-BSN program must provide proof of RN license, valid driver's license, and background check; Teacher Licensure students must have background check and Praxis II scores. ***Recommended:*** essay or personal statement.

CONTACT

Ryan McDonald, Director of Campus Admissions, Saint Mary-of-the-Woods College, Rooney Library, 1 St Mary of the Woods Coll, St Mary of the Woods, IN 47876. *Phone:* 812-535-5106. *Toll-free phone:* 800-926-SMWC. *Fax:* 812-535-5010. *E-mail:* rmcdonald@smwc.edu.

Saint Mary's College

Notre Dame, Indiana

http://www.saintmarys.edu/

- **Independent Roman Catholic** 4-year, founded 1844
- **Suburban** 100-acre campus
- **Endowment** $148.1 million
- **Women only** 1,519 undergraduate students, 99% full-time
- **Moderately difficult** entrance level, 83% of applicants were admitted

UNDERGRAD STUDENTS

1,501 full-time, 18 part-time. Students come from 40 states and territories; 16 other countries; 74% are from out of state; 1% Black or African American, non-Hispanic/Latino; 11% Hispanic/Latino; 2% Asian, non-Hispanic/Latino; 0.1% American Indian or Alaska Native, non-Hispanic/Latino; 3% Two or more races, non-Hispanic/Latino; 3% Race/ethnicity unknown; 2% international; 1% transferred in; 87% live on campus.

Freshmen

Admission: 1,687 applied, 1,406 admitted, 378 enrolled. ***Average high school GPA:*** 3.75. ***Test scores:*** SAT critical reading scores over 500: 80%; SAT math scores over 500: 76%; SAT writing scores over 500: 77%; ACT scores over 18: 100%; SAT critical reading scores over 600: 32%; SAT math scores over 600: 28%; SAT writing scores over 600: 32%; ACT scores over 24: 68%; SAT critical reading scores over 700: 2%; SAT math scores over 700: 2%; SAT writing scores over 700: 3%; ACT scores over 30: 15%.

Retention: 89% of full-time freshmen returned.

FACULTY

Total: 195, 66% full-time, 65% with terminal degrees.

Student/faculty ratio: 10:1.

ACADEMICS

Calendar: semesters. *Degree:* bachelor's.

Special study options: academic remediation for entering students, advanced placement credit, distance learning, double majors, English as a second language, independent study, internships, off-campus study, part-time degree program, services for LD students, student-designed majors, study abroad, summer session for credit. ***ROTC:*** Army (c), Navy (c), Air Force (c).

Computers: 285 computers/terminals are available on campus for general student use. Students can access the following: campus intranet, computer help desk, free student e-mail accounts, online (class) grades, online (class) registration, online (class) schedules. Campuswide network is available. 100% of college-owned or -operated housing units are wired for high-speed Internet access. Wireless service is available via classrooms, computer centers, computer labs, dorm rooms, learning centers, libraries, student centers.

STUDENT LIFE

Housing options: on-campus residence required through junior year; women-only, special housing for students with disabilities. Campus housing is university owned. Freshman campus housing is guaranteed.

Activities and organizations: drama/theater group, student-run newspaper, radio and television station, choral group, marching band, Student Government Association, Dance Marathon, Class Boards, Residence Hall Association, Student Diversity Board.

Athletics Member NCAA. All Division III. ***Intercollegiate sports:*** basketball W, cross-country running W, golf W, lacrosse W, soccer W, softball W, tennis W, volleyball W. ***Intramural sports:*** cheerleading W(c), field hockey W(c), volleyball W(c).

Campus security: 24-hour emergency response devices and patrols, late-night transport/escort service, controlled dormitory access.

Student services: health clinic, personal/psychological counseling, women's center.

COSTS & FINANCIAL AID

Costs (2014–15) ***Comprehensive fee:*** $46,900 includes full-time tuition ($35,210), mandatory fees ($760), and room and board ($10,930). Part-time tuition: $1390 per credit hour. ***Required fees:*** $380 per term part-time. ***College room only:*** $6760. Room and board charges vary according to board plan and housing facility. ***Payment plan:*** installment. ***Waivers:*** employees or children of employees.

Financial Aid Of all full-time matriculated undergraduates who enrolled in 2014, 1,138 applied for aid, 865 were judged to have need, 166 had their need fully met. In 2014, 567 non-need-based awards were made. ***Average percent of need met:*** 84. ***Average financial aid package:*** $29,773. ***Average need-based loan:*** $4937. ***Average need-based gift aid:*** $25,675. ***Average non-need-based aid:*** $13,874. ***Average indebtedness upon graduation:*** $30,910. ***Financial aid deadline:*** 3/1.

APPLYING

Standardized Tests *Required:* SAT or ACT (for admission).

Options: electronic application, early admission, early decision, deferred entrance.

Required: essay or personal statement, high school transcript, 1 letter of recommendation, 16 high school academic units; at least two years of study of the same foreign language. ***Recommended:*** interview.

Application deadlines: 2/15 (freshmen), 4/15 (transfers).

Early decision deadline: 11/15.

Notification: continuous (freshmen), continuous (transfers), 12/15 (early decision).

CONTACT

Sarah Dvorak, Director of Admission, Saint Mary's College, Notre Dame, IN 46556. *Phone:* 574-284-4587. *Toll-free phone:* 800-551-7621. *Fax:* 574-284-4841. *E-mail:* admission@saintmarys.edu.

See previous page for display ad and page 1606 for the College Close-Up.

Taylor University

Upland, Indiana

http://www.taylor.edu/

- **Independent interdenominational** comprehensive, founded 1846
- **Rural** 950-acre campus with easy access to Indianapolis
- **Endowment** $74.6 million
- **Coed** 2,103 undergraduate students, 87% full-time, 56% women, 44% men
- **Moderately difficult** entrance level, 88% of applicants were admitted

UNDERGRAD STUDENTS

1,825 full-time, 278 part-time. Students come from 42 states and territories; 30 other countries; 63% are from out of state; 3% Black or African American, non-Hispanic/Latino; 3% Hispanic/Latino; 2% Asian, non-Hispanic/Latino; 0.3% Native Hawaiian or other Pacific Islander, non-Hispanic/Latino; 0.3% American Indian or Alaska Native, non-Hispanic/Latino; 0.6% Two or more races, non-Hispanic/Latino; 5% international; 1% transferred in; 85% live on campus.

Freshmen

Admission: 1,496 applied, 1,317 admitted, 438 enrolled. ***Average high school GPA:*** 3.65. ***Test scores:*** SAT critical reading scores over 500: 74%; SAT math scores over 500: 76%; SAT writing scores over 500: 70%; ACT scores over 18: 96%; SAT critical reading scores over 600: 41%; SAT math scores over 600: 43%; SAT writing scores over 600: 29%; ACT scores over 24: 76%; SAT critical reading scores over 700: 12%; SAT math scores over 700: 6%; SAT writing scores over 700: 4%; ACT scores over 30: 26%.

Retention: 88% of full-time freshmen returned.

FACULTY

Total: 210, 60% full-time, 70% with terminal degrees.

Student/faculty ratio: 13:1.

ACADEMICS

Calendar: 4-1-4. *Degrees:* certificates, diplomas, associate, bachelor's, and master's.

Special study options: academic remediation for entering students, advanced placement credit, cooperative education, distance learning, double majors, English as a second language, honors programs, independent study, internships, off-campus study, part-time degree program, services for LD students, student-designed majors, study abroad, summer session for credit.

Computers: 370 computers/terminals are available on campus for general student use. Students can access the following: campus intranet, computer help desk, free student e-mail accounts, online (class) grades, online (class) registration, online (class) schedules. Campuswide network is available. 100% of college-owned or -operated housing units are wired for high-speed Internet access. Wireless service is available via entire campus.

STUDENT LIFE

Housing options: on-campus residence required through junior year; men-only, women-only. Campus housing is university owned and is provided by a third party. Freshman campus housing is guaranteed.

Activities and organizations: drama/theater group, student-run newspaper, radio and television station, choral group, Spring Break Missions, Lighthouse, Alpha Pi Lota, Encounter, Kappa Delta Pi.

Athletics Member NAIA. ***Intercollegiate sports:*** baseball M(s), basketball M(s)/W(s), cross-country running M(s)/W(s), football M(s), golf M(s)/W(s), soccer M(s)/W(s), softball W(s), tennis M(s)/W(s), track and field M(s)/W(s), volleyball W(s). ***Intramural sports:*** badminton M/W, basketball M/W, equestrian sports W(c), lacrosse M(c)/W(c), racquetball M/W, soccer M/W, softball M/W, tennis M/W, ultimate Frisbee M/W, volleyball M/W.

Campus security: 24-hour patrols, student patrols, late-night transport/escort service.

Student services: health clinic, personal/psychological counseling.

COSTS & FINANCIAL AID

Costs (2014–15) ***Comprehensive fee:*** $37,821 includes full-time tuition ($29,298), mandatory fees ($240), and room and board ($8283). Full-time tuition and fees vary according to course load. Part-time tuition: $1032 per credit hour. Part-time tuition and fees vary according to course load. ***Required fees:*** $38 per term part-time. ***College room only:*** $4346. Room and board charges vary according to board plan and housing facility. ***Payment plan:*** installment. ***Waivers:*** senior citizens and employees or children of employees.

Financial Aid Of all full-time matriculated undergraduates who enrolled in 2014, 1,310 applied for aid, 1,085 were judged to have need, 252 had their need fully met. 819 Federal Work-Study jobs (averaging $541). In 2014, 517 non-need-based awards were made. ***Average percent of need met:*** 72. ***Average financial aid package:*** $19,626. ***Average need-based loan:*** $4681. ***Average need-based gift aid:*** $15,416. ***Average non-need-based aid:*** $9342. ***Average indebtedness upon graduation:*** $25,125. ***Financial aid deadline:*** 3/10.

APPLYING

Standardized Tests *Required:* SAT or ACT (for admission).

Options: electronic application, deferred entrance.

Application fee: $25.

Required: essay or personal statement, high school transcript, 2 letters of recommendation, interview. ***Recommended:*** minimum 2.8 GPA.

Application deadlines: rolling (freshmen), rolling (transfers), 12/1 (early action).

Notification: continuous (freshmen), continuous (transfers), 12/20 (early action).

CONTACT

Mr. Jonny Rupp, Visit Coordinator, Taylor University, 236 West Reade Avenue, Upland, IN 46989-1001. *Phone:* 765-998-5134. *Toll-free phone:* 800-882-3456. *Fax:* 765-998-4925. *E-mail:* admissions@taylor.edu.

★ Trine University
Angola, Indiana
http://www.trine.edu/

- **Independent** comprehensive, founded 1884
- **Small-town** 400-acre campus
- **Endowment** $26.8 million
- **Coed** 2,791 undergraduate students, 58% full-time, 42% women, 58% men
- **Moderately difficult** entrance level, 76% of applicants were admitted

UNDERGRAD STUDENTS
1,622 full-time, 1,169 part-time. Students come from 30 states and territories; 16 other countries; 39% are from out of state; 2% Black or African American, non-Hispanic/Latino; 4% Hispanic/Latino; 0.4% Asian, non-Hispanic/Latino; 0.1% Native Hawaiian or other Pacific Islander, non-Hispanic/Latino; 0.4% American Indian or Alaska Native, non-Hispanic/Latino; 3% Two or more races, non-Hispanic/Latino; 4% Race/ethnicity unknown; 8% international; 2% transferred in; 56% live on campus.

Freshmen
Admission: 2,890 applied, 2,196 admitted, 523 enrolled. ***Average high school GPA:*** 3.47. ***Test scores:*** SAT critical reading scores over 500: 54%; SAT math scores over 500: 72%; ACT scores over 18: 95%; SAT critical reading scores over 600: 13%; SAT math scores over 600: 28%; ACT scores over 24: 52%; SAT critical reading scores over 700: 1%; SAT math scores over 700: 4%; ACT scores over 30: 7%.

Retention: 72% of full-time freshmen returned.

FACULTY
Total: 358, 30% full-time, 15% with terminal degrees.

Student/faculty ratio: 11:1.

ACADEMICS
Calendar: semesters. *Degrees:* associate, bachelor's, and master's.

Special study options: academic remediation for entering students, adult/continuing education programs, advanced placement credit, cooperative education, distance learning, double majors, English as a second language, honors programs, internships, part-time degree program, services for LD students, student-designed majors, study abroad, summer session for credit. ***ROTC:*** Air Force (c).

Unusual degree programs: 3-2 engineering.

Computers: 400 computers/terminals and 1,100 ports are available on campus for general student use. Students can access the following: computer help desk, free student e-mail accounts, online (class) grades, online (class) registration, online (class) schedules, online campus billing accounts; online course management system. Campuswide network is available. 100% of college-owned or -operated housing units are wired for high-speed Internet access. Wireless service is available via entire campus.

STUDENT LIFE
Housing options: on-campus residence required through senior year; coed, men-only, women-only. Campus housing is university owned and is provided by a third party. Freshman campus housing is guaranteed.

Activities and organizations: drama/theater group, student-run newspaper, radio station, choral group, marching band, Campus Christian House, Fellowship of Christian Athletes, Multicultural Student Organization, Math Club, Trine Disc Golf Collective, national fraternities, national sororities.

Athletics Member NCAA. All Division III. ***Intercollegiate sports:*** baseball M, basketball M/W, cross-country running M/W, field hockey W, football M, golf M/W, lacrosse M/W, soccer M/W, softball W, tennis M/W, track and field M/W, volleyball W, wrestling M. ***Intramural sports:*** badminton M/W, basketball M/W, football M, golf M/W, racquetball M/W, softball M/W, table tennis M/W, volleyball M/W.

Campus security: 24-hour emergency response devices and patrols, late-night transport/escort service, controlled dormitory access.

Student services: health clinic, personal/psychological counseling.

COSTS & FINANCIAL AID
Costs (2015–16) ***Comprehensive fee:*** $40,550 includes full-time tuition ($29,900), mandatory fees ($450), and room and board ($10,200). Full-

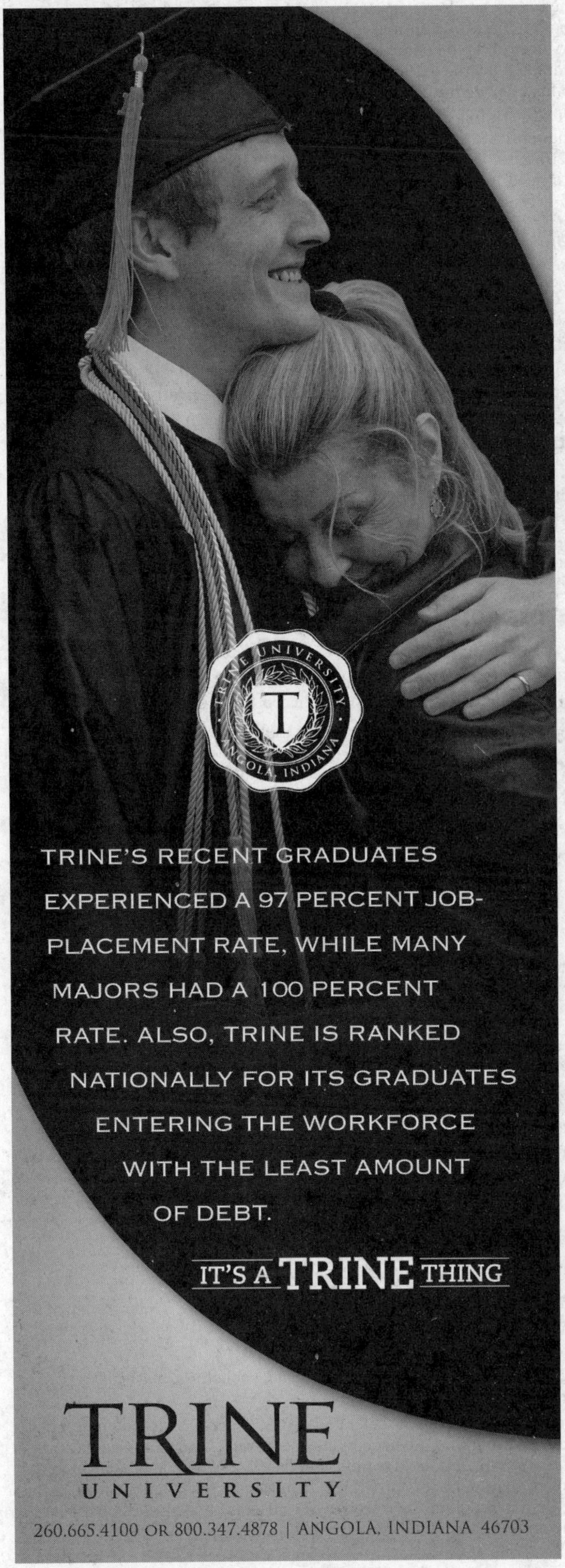

time tuition and fees vary according to degree level, location, and program. Part-time tuition: $935 per credit hour. Part-time tuition and fees vary according to degree level, location, and program. ***Room and board:*** Room and board charges vary according to board plan and housing facility. ***Payment plan:*** installment. ***Waivers:*** senior citizens and employees or children of employees.

Financial Aid Of all full-time matriculated undergraduates who enrolled in 2014, 1,442 applied for aid, 1,304 were judged to have need, 207 had their need fully met. 990 Federal Work-Study jobs (averaging $1861). In 2014, 183 non-need-based awards were made. ***Average percent of need met:*** 78. ***Average financial aid package:*** $25,519. ***Average need-based loan:*** $5572. ***Average need-based gift aid:*** $4596. ***Average non-need-based aid:*** $12,318. ***Average indebtedness upon graduation:*** $32,641.

APPLYING

Standardized Tests *Required:* SAT or ACT (for admission).

Options: electronic application, deferred entrance.

Required: high school transcript, minimum 2.5 GPA. ***Recommended:*** essay or personal statement, 2 letters of recommendation, interview.

Application deadlines: 8/1 (freshmen), 8/1 (transfers).

Notification: 8/15 (freshmen), continuous until 8/15 (transfers).

CONTACT

Dr. Stuart Jones, Dean of Admission, Trine University, 1 University Avenue, Angola, IN 46703. *Phone:* 260-665-4365. *Toll-free phone:* 800-347-4878. *Fax:* 260-665-4578. *E-mail:* admit@trine.edu.

See previous page for display ad and page 1648 for the College Close-Up.

University of Evansville

Evansville, Indiana

http://www.evansville.edu/

- **Independent** comprehensive, founded 1854, affiliated with United Methodist Church
- **Urban** 75-acre campus
- **Endowment** $130.9 million
- **Coed** 2,420 undergraduate students, 94% full-time, 55% women, 45% men
- **Moderately difficult** entrance level, 83% of applicants were admitted

UNDERGRAD STUDENTS

2,265 full-time, 155 part-time. Students come from 41 states and territories; 52 other countries; 41% are from out of state; 3% Black or African American, non-Hispanic/Latino; 3% Hispanic/Latino; 1% Asian, non-Hispanic/Latino; 0.2% American Indian or Alaska Native, non-Hispanic/Latino; 2% Two or more races, non-Hispanic/Latino; 3% Race/ethnicity unknown; 14% international; 4% transferred in; 64% live on campus.

Freshmen

Admission: 2,762 applied, 2,291 admitted, 532 enrolled. ***Average high school GPA:*** 3.62. ***Test scores:*** SAT critical reading scores over 500: 79%; SAT math scores over 500: 82%; SAT writing scores over 500: 66%; ACT scores over 18: 98%; SAT critical reading scores over 600: 30%; SAT math scores over 600: 38%; SAT writing scores over 600: 24%; ACT scores over 24: 69%; SAT critical reading scores over 700: 7%; SAT math scores over 700: 6%; SAT writing scores over 700: 2%; ACT scores over 30: 16%.

Retention: 85% of full-time freshmen returned.

FACULTY

Total: 233, 76% full-time.

Student/faculty ratio: 14:1.

ACADEMICS

Calendar: semesters. *Degrees:* associate, bachelor's, master's, and doctoral.

Special study options: accelerated degree program, adult/continuing education programs, advanced placement credit, cooperative education, distance learning, double majors, English as a second language, external degree program, honors programs, independent study, internships, part-time degree program, services for LD students, student-designed majors, study abroad, summer session for credit. ***ROTC:*** Army (c).

Computers: 385 computers/terminals and 3,000 ports are available on campus for general student use. Students can access the following: campus intranet, computer help desk, free student e-mail accounts, online (class) grades, online (class) registration, online (class) schedules. Campuswide network is available. 100% of college-owned or -operated housing units are wired for high-speed Internet access. Wireless service is available via entire campus.

STUDENT LIFE

Housing options: on-campus residence required through sophomore year; coed, men-only, women-only. Campus housing is university owned. Freshman campus housing is guaranteed.

Activities and organizations: drama/theater group, student-run newspaper, radio station, choral group, Phi Eta Sigma, International Club, PT Club, Student Christian Fellowship, Alpha Omicron Pi, national fraternities, national sororities.

Athletics Member NCAA. All Division I. ***Intercollegiate sports:*** baseball M(s), basketball M(s)/W(s), cross-country running M(s)/W(s), golf M(s)/W(s), soccer M(s)/W(s), softball W(s), swimming and diving M(s)/W(s), tennis W(s), volleyball W(s). ***Intramural sports:*** badminton M/W, basketball M/W, cross-country running M/W, racquetball M/W, soccer M/W, tennis M/W, ultimate Frisbee M/W, volleyball M/W.

Campus security: 24-hour emergency response devices and patrols, student patrols, late-night transport/escort service, controlled dormitory access.

Student services: health clinic, personal/psychological counseling.

COSTS & FINANCIAL AID

Costs (2014–15) ***Comprehensive fee:*** $42,656 includes full-time tuition ($30,900), mandatory fees ($876), and room and board ($10,880). Part-time tuition: $860 per credit hour. Part-time tuition and fees vary according to course load. ***Required fees:*** $130 per term part-time. ***College room only:*** $5690. Room and board charges vary according to board plan and housing facility. ***Payment plan:*** installment. ***Waivers:*** minority students, children of alumni, adult students, senior citizens, and employees or children of employees.

Financial Aid Of all full-time matriculated undergraduates who enrolled in 2014, 1,632 applied for aid, 1,449 were judged to have need, 387 had their need fully met. 310 Federal Work-Study jobs (averaging $1514). 15 state and other part-time jobs (averaging $1525). In 2014, 579 non-need-based awards were made. ***Average percent of need met:*** 83. ***Average financial aid package:*** $26,090. ***Average need-based loan:*** $4962. ***Average need-based gift aid:*** $22,778. ***Average non-need-based aid:*** $17,045. ***Average indebtedness upon graduation:*** $29,441.

APPLYING

Standardized Tests *Required:* SAT or ACT (for admission).

Options: electronic application, early action, deferred entrance.

Required: essay or personal statement, high school transcript. ***Required for some:*** interview. ***Recommended:*** minimum 3.0 GPA, 1 letter of recommendation, interview.

Application deadlines: 2/1 (freshmen), rolling (transfers), 12/1 (early action).

Notification: 2/15 (freshmen), continuous (transfers), 12/15 (early action).

CONTACT

Scott Henne, Dean of Admission, University of Evansville, 1800 Lincoln Avenue, Evansville, IN 47722. *Phone:* 812-488-2468. *Toll-free phone:* 800-423-8633 Ext. 2468. *Fax:* 812-488-4076. *E-mail:* admission@evansville.edu.

★ University of Indianapolis

Indianapolis, Indiana

http://www.uindy.edu/

- **Independent** comprehensive, founded 1902, affiliated with United Methodist Church
- **Urban** 65-acre campus with easy access to Indianapolis
- **Endowment** $93.1 million
- **Coed** 4,169 undergraduate students, 81% full-time, 65% women, 35% men
- **Moderately difficult** entrance level, 66% of applicants were admitted

UNDERGRAD STUDENTS
3,364 full-time, 805 part-time. Students come from 39 states and territories; 52 other countries; 7% are from out of state; 9% Black or African American, non-Hispanic/Latino; 4% Hispanic/Latino; 1% Asian, non-Hispanic/Latino; 0.1% Native Hawaiian or other Pacific Islander, non-Hispanic/Latino; 0.1% American Indian or Alaska Native, non-Hispanic/Latino; 2% Two or more races, non-Hispanic/Latino; 8% Race/ethnicity unknown; 8% international; 6% transferred in; 36% live on campus.

Freshmen
Admission: 6,796 applied, 4,518 admitted, 992 enrolled. ***Average high school GPA:*** 3.5. ***Test scores:*** SAT critical reading scores over 500: 44%; SAT math scores over 500: 50%; SAT writing scores over 500: 40%; ACT scores over 18: 88%; SAT critical reading scores over 600: 11%; SAT math scores over 600: 13%; SAT writing scores over 600: 9%; ACT scores over 24: 37%; SAT critical reading scores over 700: 1%; SAT math scores over 700: 1%; SAT writing scores over 700: 1%; ACT scores over 30: 5%.
Retention: 74% of full-time freshmen returned.

FACULTY
Total: 542, 45% full-time, 46% with terminal degrees.
Student/faculty ratio: 11:1.

ACADEMICS
Calendar: semesters. *Degrees:* associate, bachelor's, master's, and doctoral.
Special study options: academic remediation for entering students, accelerated degree program, adult/continuing education programs, advanced placement credit, cooperative education, distance learning, double majors, English as a second language, freshman honors college, honors programs, independent study, internships, off-campus study, part-time degree program, services for LD students, student-designed majors, study abroad, summer session for credit. ***ROTC:*** Army (c).
Unusual degree programs: 3-2 business administration with BS/MBA (Accounting); engineering with Indiana University - Purdue University Indianapolis; physical therapy, occupational therapy.

Computers: 255 computers/terminals are available on campus for general student use. Students can access the following: campus intranet, computer help desk, free student e-mail accounts, online (class) grades, online (class) schedules. Campuswide network is available. 100% of college-owned or -operated housing units are wired for high-speed Internet access. Wireless service is available via entire campus.

STUDENT LIFE
Housing options: coed, women-only. Campus housing is university owned.
Activities and organizations: drama/theater group, student-run newspaper, radio and television station, choral group, Fellowship of Christian Athletes, Intercultural Association, Circle K, Indianapolis Student Government, Residence Hall Association.
Athletics Member NCAA. All Division II. ***Intercollegiate sports:*** baseball M(s), basketball M(s)/W(s), cross-country running M(s)/W(s), football M(s), golf M(s)/W(s), lacrosse M/W, soccer M(s)/W(s), softball W(s), swimming and diving M(s)/W(s), tennis M(s)/W(s), track and field M(s)/W(s), volleyball W(s), wrestling M(s). ***Intramural sports:*** badminton M/W, basketball M/W, cheerleading M/W, football M/W, racquetball M/W, softball M/W, table tennis M/W, tennis M/W, volleyball M/W.
Campus security: 24-hour emergency response devices and patrols, student patrols, late-night transport/escort service, controlled dormitory access, emergency call boxes.
Student services: health clinic, personal/psychological counseling.

COSTS & FINANCIAL AID
Costs (2015–16) ***Comprehensive fee:*** $35,494 includes full-time tuition ($25,910), mandatory fees ($260), and room and board ($9324). Full-time tuition and fees vary according to class time. Part-time tuition: $1080 per credit hour. Part-time tuition and fees vary according to class time and course load. ***College room only:*** $5340. Room and board charges vary according to board plan and housing facility. ***Payment plan:*** installment. ***Waivers:*** employees or children of employees.
Financial Aid Of all full-time matriculated undergraduates who enrolled in 2014, 3,261 applied for aid, 2,876 were judged to have need, 389 had their need fully met. 379 Federal Work-Study jobs (averaging $739). 147

state and other part-time jobs (averaging $7344). In 2014, 552 non-need-based awards were made. ***Average percent of need met:*** 66. ***Average financial aid package:*** $17,983. ***Average need-based loan:*** $4249. ***Average need-based gift aid:*** $7968. ***Average non-need-based aid:*** $9629. ***Average indebtedness upon graduation:*** $35,689.

APPLYING

Standardized Tests *Required:* SAT or ACT (for admission).

Options: electronic application, deferred entrance.

Application fee: $25.

Required: high school transcript, minimum 2.0 GPA. ***Required for some:*** interview.

Application deadlines: rolling (freshmen), rolling (out-of-state freshmen), rolling (transfers).

Notification: continuous (freshmen), continuous (out-of-state freshmen), continuous (transfers).

CONTACT

Mr. Ronald Wilks, Associate Vice President of Admissions, University of Indianapolis, 1400 East Hanna Avenue, Indianapolis, IN 46227-3697. *Phone:* 317-788-3216. *Toll-free phone:* 800-232-8634 Ext. 3216. *Fax:* 317-788-3300. *E-mail:* admissions@uindy.edu.

See previous page for display ad and page 1672 for the College Close-Up.

University of Notre Dame

Notre Dame, Indiana

http://www.nd.edu/

- **Independent Roman Catholic** university, founded 1842
- **Suburban** 1250-acre campus
- **Endowment** $10.0 billion
- **Coed** 8,448 undergraduate students, 100% full-time, 48% women, 52% men
- **Most difficult** entrance level, 21% of applicants were admitted

UNDERGRAD STUDENTS

8,430 full-time, 18 part-time. Students come from 54 states and territories; 49 other countries; 92% are from out of state; 4% Black or African American, non-Hispanic/Latino; 10% Hispanic/Latino; 6% Asian, non-Hispanic/Latino; 0.2% American Indian or Alaska Native, non-Hispanic/Latino; 4% Two or more races, non-Hispanic/Latino; 0.6% Race/ethnicity unknown; 5% international; 1% transferred in; 80% live on campus.

Freshmen

Admission: 17,901 applied, 3,785 admitted, 2,011 enrolled. ***Test scores:*** SAT critical reading scores over 500: 99%; SAT math scores over 500: 100%; SAT writing scores over 500: 99%; ACT scores over 18: 100%; SAT critical reading scores over 600: 92%; SAT math scores over 600: 95%; SAT writing scores over 600: 91%; ACT scores over 24: 99%; SAT critical reading scores over 700: 58%; SAT math scores over 700: 66%; SAT writing scores over 700: 55%; ACT scores over 30: 91%.

Retention: 98% of full-time freshmen returned.

FACULTY

Total: 1,309, 85% full-time, 86% with terminal degrees.

Student/faculty ratio: 10:1.

ACADEMICS

Calendar: semesters. *Degrees:* bachelor's, master's, and doctoral.

Special study options: advanced placement credit, distance learning, double majors, honors programs, independent study, internships, off-campus study, services for LD students, student-designed majors, study abroad, summer session for credit. ***ROTC:*** Army (b), Navy (b), Air Force (b).

Computers: 236 computers/terminals are available on campus for general student use. Students can access the following: computer help desk, free student e-mail accounts, online (class) grades, online (class) registration, online (class) schedules. Campuswide network is available. Wireless service is available via entire campus.

STUDENT LIFE

Housing options: on-campus residence required for freshman year; men-only, women-only. Campus housing is university owned. Freshman campus housing is guaranteed.

Activities and organizations: drama/theater group, student-run newspaper, radio station, choral group, marching band, marching band, Circle K, Finance Club, Notre Dame/St. Mary's Right to Life.

Athletics Member NCAA. All Division I except football (Division I-A). ***Intercollegiate sports:*** baseball M(s), basketball M(s)/W(s), crew W(s), cross-country running M(s)/W(s), fencing M(s)/W(s), golf M(s)/W(s), ice hockey M(s), lacrosse M(s)/W(s), soccer M(s)/W(s), softball W(s), swimming and diving M(s)/W(s), tennis M(s)/W(s), track and field M(s)/W(s), volleyball W(s). ***Intramural sports:*** badminton M/W, baseball M, basketball M/W, bowling M(c)/W(c), crew M(c), cross-country running M/W, equestrian sports M(c)/W(c), field hockey M(c)/W(c), football M/W, golf M/W, gymnastics M(c)/W(c), ice hockey M/W(c), lacrosse M/W, racquetball M/W, rock climbing M(c)/W(c), rugby M(c)/W(c), sailing M(c)/W(c), skiing (cross-country) M(c)/W(c), skiing (downhill) M(c)/W(c), soccer M/W, softball M/W, squash M(c)/W(c), tennis M/W, ultimate Frisbee M/W, volleyball M(c)/W(c), water polo M(c)/W(c), wrestling M(c).

Campus security: 24-hour emergency response devices and patrols, student patrols, late-night transport/escort service, controlled dormitory access, crime prevention and personal safety workshops, full-time trained police investigators, fire sprinklers in all residence halls.

Student services: health clinic, personal/psychological counseling, women's center.

COSTS & FINANCIAL AID

Costs (2014–15) ***Comprehensive fee:*** $59,461 includes full-time tuition ($45,730), mandatory fees ($507), and room and board ($13,224). Part-time tuition: $1905 per credit hour. ***Payment plan:*** installment. ***Waivers:*** employees or children of employees.

Financial Aid Of all full-time matriculated undergraduates who enrolled in 2014, 4,945 applied for aid, 3,804 were judged to have need, 3,768 had their need fully met. 1,681 Federal Work-Study jobs (averaging $2526). 3,073 state and other part-time jobs (averaging $3237). In 2014, 575 non-need-based awards were made. ***Average percent of need met:*** 100. ***Average financial aid package:*** $41,932. ***Average need-based loan:*** $5496. ***Average need-based gift aid:*** $33,025. ***Average non-need-based aid:*** $15,804. ***Average indebtedness upon graduation:*** $26,674.

APPLYING

Standardized Tests *Required:* SAT or ACT (for admission). *Required for some:* SAT Subject Tests (for admission).

Options: electronic application, early action, deferred entrance.

Application fee: $75.

Required: essay or personal statement, high school transcript, 1 letter of recommendation.

Application deadlines: 1/1 (freshmen), 3/15 (transfers), 11/1 (early action).

Notification: 4/10 (freshmen), 12/21 (early action).

CONTACT

Office of Undergraduate Admissions, University of Notre Dame, 220 Main Building, Notre Dame, IN 46556-5612. *Phone:* 574-631-7505. *Fax:* 574-631-8865. *E-mail:* admissions@nd.edu.

University of Saint Francis

Fort Wayne, Indiana

http://www.sf.edu/

- **Independent Roman Catholic** comprehensive, founded 1890
- **Suburban** 110-acre campus
- **Endowment** $20.1 million
- **Coed** 1,861 undergraduate students, 84% full-time, 70% women, 30% men
- **Minimally difficult** entrance level, 97% of applicants were admitted

UNDERGRAD STUDENTS

1,558 full-time, 303 part-time. Students come from 20 states and territories; 15 other countries; 10% are from out of state; 6% Black or African American, non-Hispanic/Latino; 6% Hispanic/Latino; 0.9% Asian, non-Hispanic/Latino; 0.3% Native Hawaiian or other Pacific Islander, non-Hispanic/Latino; 0.5% American Indian or Alaska Native, non-Hispanic/Latino; 2% Two or more races, non-Hispanic/Latino; 4% Race/ethnicity unknown; 0.6% international; 12% transferred in; 20% live on campus.

Freshmen
Admission: 954 applied, 924 admitted, 345 enrolled. ***Average high school GPA:*** 3.23. ***Test scores:*** SAT critical reading scores over 500: 44%; SAT math scores over 500: 44%; SAT writing scores over 500: 34%; ACT scores over 18: 86%; SAT critical reading scores over 600: 10%; SAT math scores over 600: 9%; SAT writing scores over 600: 6%; ACT scores over 24: 31%; SAT critical reading scores over 700: 1%; ACT scores over 30: 3%.

Retention: 72% of full-time freshmen returned.

FACULTY
Total: 274, 46% full-time, 27% with terminal degrees.

Student/faculty ratio: 12:1.

ACADEMICS
Calendar: semesters. *Degrees:* certificates, associate, bachelor's, master's, post-master's, and postbachelor's certificates.

Special study options: academic remediation for entering students, advanced placement credit, cooperative education, distance learning, double majors, honors programs, independent study, internships, off-campus study, part-time degree program, services for LD students, student-designed majors, summer session for credit.

Computers: 498 computers/terminals are available on campus for general student use. Students can access the following: campus intranet, computer help desk, free student e-mail accounts, online (class) grades, online (class) registration, online (class) schedules. Campuswide network is available. 100% of college-owned or -operated housing units are wired for high-speed Internet access. Wireless service is available via entire campus.

STUDENT LIFE
Housing options: on-campus residence required through sophomore year; coed. Campus housing is university owned. Freshman applicants given priority for college housing.

Activities and organizations: drama/theater group, student-run newspaper, choral group, Student Activities Council, Art Club, Student Government Organization, Student Nursing Association, Residence Hall Council.

Athletics Member NAIA. ***Intercollegiate sports:*** baseball M(s), basketball M(s)/W(s), cheerleading M(s)/W(s), cross-country running M(s)/W(s), football M(s), golf M(s)/W(s), soccer M(s)/W(s), softball W(s), tennis M(s)/W(s), track and field M(s)/W(s), volleyball W(s). ***Intramural sports:*** basketball M/W, bowling M/W, soccer M/W, ultimate Frisbee M/W, volleyball W.

Campus security: 24-hour emergency response devices and patrols, late-night transport/escort service, controlled dormitory access.

Student services: personal/psychological counseling.

COSTS & FINANCIAL AID
Costs (2015–16) ***One-time required fee:*** $100. ***Comprehensive fee:*** $36,496 includes full-time tuition ($26,250), mandatory fees ($970), and room and board ($9276). Full-time tuition and fees vary according to course load. Part-time tuition: $830 per credit hour. Part-time tuition and fees vary according to course load. ***Required fees:*** $47 per credit hour part-time. ***Room and board:*** Room and board charges vary according to board plan and housing facility. ***Payment plan:*** installment. ***Waivers:*** employees or children of employees.

Financial Aid Of all full-time matriculated undergraduates who enrolled in 2009, 1,477 applied for aid, 1,316 were judged to have need, 258 had their need fully met. 629 Federal Work-Study jobs (averaging $1411). In 2009, 146 non-need-based awards were made. ***Average percent of need met:*** 72. ***Average financial aid package:*** $16,158. ***Average need-based loan:*** $4028. ***Average need-based gift aid:*** $12,247. ***Average non-need-based aid:*** $5446. ***Average indebtedness upon graduation:*** $28,428. ***Financial aid deadline:*** 6/30.

APPLYING
Standardized Tests *Required:* SAT or ACT (for admission).

Options: electronic application, deferred entrance.

Required: high school transcript, minimum 2.3 GPA. ***Required for some:*** interview. ***Recommended:*** essay or personal statement.

Application deadlines: rolling (freshmen), rolling (transfers).

Notification: 8/15 (freshmen), continuous until 8/15 (transfers).

CONTACT
Mrs. Maria Gerber, Director of Admissions, University of Saint Francis, 2701 Spring Street, Fort Wayne, IN 46808. *Phone:* 260-399-7700 Ext. 6308. *Toll-free phone:* 800-729-4732. *E-mail:* admis@sf.edu.

★ University of Southern Indiana
Evansville, Indiana
http://www.usi.edu/

- **State-supported** comprehensive, founded 1965, part of Indiana Commission for Higher Education
- **Suburban** 1400-acre campus
- **Coed** 8,414 undergraduate students, 83% full-time, 60% women, 40% men
- **Moderately difficult** entrance level, 61% of applicants were admitted

UNDERGRAD STUDENTS
6,980 full-time, 1,434 part-time. Students come from 33 states and territories; 31 other countries; 11% are from out of state; 4% Black or African American, non-Hispanic/Latino; 2% Hispanic/Latino; 1% Asian, non-Hispanic/Latino; 0.1% Native Hawaiian or other Pacific Islander, non-Hispanic/Latino; 0.2% American Indian or Alaska Native, non-Hispanic/Latino; 2% Two or more races, non-Hispanic/Latino; 2% Race/ethnicity unknown; 2% international; 7% transferred in; 30% live on campus.

Freshmen
Admission: 5,831 applied, 3,576 admitted, 1,613 enrolled. ***Average high school GPA:*** 3.27. ***Test scores:*** SAT critical reading scores over 500: 61%; SAT math scores over 500: 56%; SAT writing scores over 500: 37%; ACT scores over 18: 87%; SAT critical reading scores over 600: 22%; SAT math scores over 600: 19%; SAT writing scores over 600: 7%; ACT scores over 24: 30%; SAT critical reading scores over 700: 12%; SAT math scores over 700: 6%; ACT scores over 30: 3%.

Retention: 72% of full-time freshmen returned.

FACULTY
Total: 664, 53% full-time, 46% with terminal degrees.

Student/faculty ratio: 17:1.

ACADEMICS
Calendar: semesters. *Degrees:* certificates, associate, bachelor's, master's, doctoral, and postbachelor's certificates.

Special study options: academic remediation for entering students, adult/continuing education programs, advanced placement credit, cooperative education, distance learning, double majors, English as a second language, honors programs, independent study, internships, part-time degree program, services for LD students, study abroad, summer session for credit. ***ROTC:*** Army (b).

Computers: 306 computers/terminals are available on campus for general student use. Students can access the following: computer help desk, free student e-mail accounts, online (class) grades, online (class) registration, online (class) schedules. Campuswide network is available. 100% of college-owned or -operated housing units are wired for high-speed Internet access. Wireless service is available via entire campus.

STUDENT LIFE
Housing options: coed, special housing for students with disabilities. Campus housing is university owned.

Activities and organizations: drama/theater group, student-run newspaper, radio and television station, choral group, Humans vs. Zombies, Honors Student Assembly, Colleges Against Cancer, Student Alumni Association, Habitat for Humanity, national fraternities, national sororities.

Athletics Member NCAA. All Division II. ***Intercollegiate sports:*** baseball M(s), basketball M(s)/W(s), cheerleading M/W, cross-country running M(s)/W(s), golf M(s)/W(s), rugby M(c)/W(c), soccer M(s)/W(s), softball W(s), tennis M(s)/W(s), track and field M/W, ultimate Frisbee M(c)/W(c), volleyball W(s). ***Intramural sports:*** badminton M/W, basketball M/W, bowling M/W, football M/W, golf M/W, soccer M/W, softball W, table tennis M/W, tennis M/W, volleyball M/W.

Campus security: 24-hour emergency response devices and patrols, student patrols, late-night transport/escort service, controlled dormitory access.

A ★ indicates that the school has detailed information with a Premium Profile on Petersons.com.

Student services: health clinic, personal/psychological counseling.

COSTS & FINANCIAL AID

Costs (2014–15) ***One-time required fee:*** $100. ***Tuition:*** state resident $6637 full-time, $221 per credit hour part-time; nonresident $15,977 full-time, $533 per credit hour part-time. Full-time tuition and fees vary according to course load, program, and reciprocity agreements. Part-time tuition and fees vary according to course load, program, and reciprocity agreements. ***Required fees:*** $320 full-time, $23 per term part-time. ***Room and board:*** $7928; room only: $4140. Room and board charges vary according to board plan and housing facility. ***Payment plan:*** installment. ***Waivers:*** employees or children of employees.

Financial Aid Of all full-time matriculated undergraduates who enrolled in 2014, 6,347 applied for aid, 4,433 were judged to have need, 262 had their need fully met. 119 Federal Work-Study jobs (averaging $1210). In 2014, 818 non-need-based awards were made. ***Average percent of need met:*** 76. ***Average financial aid package:*** $9015. ***Average need-based loan:*** $4019. ***Average need-based gift aid:*** $7062. ***Average non-need-based aid:*** $1970. ***Average indebtedness upon graduation:*** $25,732.

APPLYING

Standardized Tests *Required:* SAT or ACT (for admission).

Options: electronic application.

Application fee: $40.

Required: high school transcript. ***Required for some:*** interview. ***Recommended:*** essay or personal statement, minimum 2.0 GPA.

Notification: continuous (freshmen), continuous (transfers).

CONTACT

Mr. Mark Rusk, Interim Director of Admission, University of Southern Indiana, 8600 University Boulevard, Evansville, IN 47712-3590. *Phone:* 812-464-1765. *Toll-free phone:* 800-467-1965. *Fax:* 812-465-7154. *E-mail:* enroll@usi.edu.

See below for display ad and page 1702 for the College Close-Up.

Valparaiso University

Valparaiso, Indiana

http://www.valpo.edu/

- **Independent** university, founded 1859, affiliated with Lutheran Church
- **Small-town** 320-acre campus with easy access to Chicago
- **Endowment** $202.7 million
- **Coed** 3,260 undergraduate students, 97% full-time, 52% women, 48% men
- **Moderately difficult** entrance level, 82% of applicants were admitted

UNDERGRAD STUDENTS

3,159 full-time, 101 part-time. Students come from 40 states and territories; 33 other countries; 59% are from out of state; 5% Black or African American, non-Hispanic/Latino; 8% Hispanic/Latino; 2% Asian, non-Hispanic/Latino; 0.3% American Indian or Alaska Native, non-Hispanic/Latino; 2% Two or more races, non-Hispanic/Latino; 1% Race/ethnicity unknown; 8% international; 6% transferred in; 65% live on campus.

Freshmen

Admission: 6,491 applied, 5,346 admitted, 714 enrolled. ***Average high school GPA:*** 3.67. ***Test scores:*** SAT critical reading scores over 500: 76%; SAT math scores over 500: 78%; SAT writing scores over 500: 66%; ACT scores over 18: 99%; SAT critical reading scores over 600: 26%; SAT math scores over 600: 33%; SAT writing scores over 600: 22%; ACT scores over 24: 73%; SAT critical reading scores over 700: 4%; SAT math scores over 700: 4%; SAT writing scores over 700: 2%; ACT scores over 30: 23%.

Retention: 84% of full-time freshmen returned.

FACULTY

Total: 391, 71% full-time, 70% with terminal degrees.

Student/faculty ratio: 13:1.

ACADEMICS

Calendar: semesters. *Degrees:* certificates, associate, bachelor's, master's, doctoral, post-master's, and postbachelor's certificates.

Special study options: accelerated degree program, adult/continuing education programs, advanced placement credit, cooperative education, distance learning, double majors, English as a second language, freshman honors college, honors programs, independent study, internships, off-campus study, part-time degree program, services for LD students, student-designed majors, study abroad, summer session for credit. ***ROTC:*** Army (c), Air Force (c).

Unusual degree programs: 3-2 Physician Assistant.

Computers: 500 computers/terminals are available on campus for general student use. Students can access the following: campus intranet, computer help desk, free student e-mail accounts, online (class) grades, online (class) registration, online (class) schedules, Web academic information, degree audit. Campuswide network is available. 100% of college-owned or -operated housing units are wired for high-speed Internet access. Wireless service is available via classrooms, computer centers, computer labs, dorm rooms, learning centers, libraries, student centers.

STUDENT LIFE

Housing options: on-campus residence required through junior year; coed, women-only. Campus housing is university owned and leased by the school. Freshman campus housing is guaranteed.

Activities and organizations: drama/theater group, student-run newspaper, radio station, choral group, student government, student volunteer organization, chapel programs, Union Board, national fraternities, national sororities.

Athletics Member NCAA. All Division I except football (Division I-AA). ***Intercollegiate sports:*** baseball M(s), basketball M(s)/W(s), bowling W(s), cross-country running M(s)/W(s), golf M(s)/W(s), soccer M(s)/W(s), softball W(s), swimming and diving M(s)/W(s), tennis M(s)/W(s), track and field M(s)/W(s), volleyball W(s). ***Intramural sports:*** badminton M/W, basketball M/W, bowling M/W, cheerleading M/W, football M/W, golf M/W, racquetball M/W, soccer M(c)/W(c), softball M/W, table tennis M/W, tennis M(c)/W(c), ultimate Frisbee M(c)/W(c), volleyball M/W.

Campus security: 24-hour emergency response devices and patrols, late-night transport/escort service, controlled dormitory access.

Student services: health clinic, personal/psychological counseling, legal services.

COSTS & FINANCIAL AID

Costs (2014–15) ***Comprehensive fee:*** $44,940 includes full-time tuition ($33,680), mandatory fees ($1080), and room and board ($10,180). Full-time tuition and fees vary according to course load and program. Part-time tuition: $1505 per credit hour. Part-time tuition and fees vary according to course load and program. ***Required fees:*** $96 per term part-time. ***College room only:*** $6200. Room and board charges vary according to housing facility and student level. ***Payment plans:*** tuition prepayment, installment. ***Waivers:*** employees or children of employees.

Financial Aid Of all full-time matriculated undergraduates who enrolled in 2013, 2,552 applied for aid, 2,286 were judged to have need, 844 had their need fully met. 546 Federal Work-Study jobs (averaging $1245). 779 state and other part-time jobs (averaging $1698). In 2013, 601 non-need-based awards were made. ***Average percent of need met:*** 84. ***Average financial aid package:*** $29,768. ***Average need-based loan:*** $5330. ***Average need-based gift aid:*** $22,433. ***Average non-need-based aid:*** $13,003. ***Average indebtedness upon graduation:*** $35,449.

APPLYING

Standardized Tests *Required:* SAT or ACT (for admission).

Options: electronic application, deferred entrance.

Required: essay or personal statement, high school transcript. ***Required for some:*** interview. ***Recommended:*** 2 letters of recommendation, interview.

Application deadlines: rolling (freshmen), rolling (out-of-state freshmen), rolling (transfers).

Notification: continuous (freshmen), continuous (out-of-state freshmen), continuous (transfers).

CONTACT

Mr. Bart Harvey, Director of Freshman Admission and Operations, Valparaiso University, Kretzmann Hall, 1700 Chapel Drive, Valparaiso, IN 46383-6493. *Phone:* 219-464-5011. *Toll-free phone:* 888-GO-VALPO. *Fax:* 219-464-6898. *E-mail:* undergrad.admission@valpo.edu.

Vincennes University

Vincennes, Indiana

http://www.vinu.edu/

- **State-supported** primarily 2-year, founded 1801
- **Small-town** 160-acre campus
- **Coed** 19,205 undergraduate students, 32% full-time, 45% women, 55% men
- **Noncompetitive** entrance level, 81% of applicants were admitted

UNDERGRAD STUDENTS

6,175 full-time, 13,030 part-time. 13% Black or African American, non-Hispanic/Latino; 3% Hispanic/Latino; 0.6% Asian, non-Hispanic/Latino; 0.2% Native Hawaiian or other Pacific Islander, non-Hispanic/Latino; 0.3% American Indian or Alaska Native, non-Hispanic/Latino; 2% Two or more races, non-Hispanic/Latino; 9% Race/ethnicity unknown; 0.4% international.

Freshmen

Admission: 5,965 applied, 4,860 admitted, 3,089 enrolled.

ACADEMICS

Calendar: semesters. *Degrees:* certificates, associate, and bachelor's.

Special study options: academic remediation for entering students, accelerated degree program, adult/continuing education programs, advanced placement credit, distance learning, double majors, English as a second language, external degree program, freshman honors college, honors programs, independent study, internships, off-campus study, part-time degree program, services for LD students, student-designed majors, summer session for credit. ***ROTC:*** Army (b), Air Force (c).

Computers: 1,500 computers/terminals are available on campus for general student use. Campuswide network is available.

STUDENT LIFE

Housing options: on-campus residence required for freshman year; coed, men-only, women-only, special housing for students with disabilities. Campus housing is university owned. Freshman campus housing is guaranteed.

Activities and organizations: drama/theater group, student-run newspaper, radio and television station, choral group, national fraternities, national sororities.

Athletics Member NJCAA. ***Intercollegiate sports:*** baseball M, basketball M/W, bowling M, cross-country running M/W, golf M, tennis M, track and field M/W, volleyball W.

Campus security: 24-hour emergency response devices and patrols, student patrols, late-night transport/escort service, controlled dormitory access, surveillance cameras.

Student services: health clinic, personal/psychological counseling.

COSTS

Costs (2014–15) ***Tuition:*** state resident $5174 full-time, $2209 per year part-time; nonresident $12,234 full-time, $5033 per year part-time. Full-time tuition and fees vary according to course level, course load, location, program, reciprocity agreements, and student level. Part-time tuition and fees vary according to course level, course load, location, program, reciprocity agreements, and student level. ***Room and board:*** $8732. Room and board charges vary according to board plan, gender, and housing facility. ***Payment plan:*** installment. ***Waivers:*** senior citizens and employees or children of employees.

APPLYING

Options: electronic application, early admission, deferred entrance.

Application fee: $20.

Required: high school transcript. ***Required for some:*** interview.

Application deadlines: rolling (freshmen), rolling (transfers).

Notification: continuous until 8/1 (freshmen), continuous (transfers).

CONTACT

Vincennes University, 1002 North First Street, Vincennes, IN 47591-5202. *Phone:* 812-888-4313. *Toll-free phone:* 800-742-9198.

Wabash College
Crawfordsville, Indiana
http://www.wabash.edu/

- **Independent** 4-year, founded 1832
- **Small-town** 60-acre campus with easy access to Indianapolis
- **Endowment** $371.2 million
- **Men only** 926 undergraduate students, 100% full-time
- **Moderately difficult** entrance level, 70% of applicants were admitted

UNDERGRAD STUDENTS
924 full-time, 2 part-time. Students come from 36 states and territories; 12 other countries; 25% are from out of state; 6% Black or African American, non-Hispanic/Latino; 6% Hispanic/Latino; 1% Asian, non-Hispanic/Latino; 0.1% Native Hawaiian or other Pacific Islander, non-Hispanic/Latino; 0.5% American Indian or Alaska Native, non-Hispanic/Latino; 3% Two or more races, non-Hispanic/Latino; 1% Race/ethnicity unknown; 7% international; 0.4% transferred in; 86% live on campus.

Freshmen
Admission: 1,259 applied, 881 admitted, 256 enrolled. ***Average high school GPA:*** 3.6. ***Test scores:*** SAT critical reading scores over 500: 76%; SAT math scores over 500: 83%; SAT writing scores over 500: 63%; ACT scores over 18: 97%; SAT critical reading scores over 600: 29%; SAT math scores over 600: 44%; SAT writing scores over 600: 24%; ACT scores over 24: 63%; SAT critical reading scores over 700: 4%; SAT math scores over 700: 11%; SAT writing scores over 700: 3%; ACT scores over 30: 13%.

Retention: 89% of full-time freshmen returned.

FACULTY
Total: 103, 83% full-time, 94% with terminal degrees.

Student/faculty ratio: 10:1.

ACADEMICS
Calendar: semesters. *Degree:* bachelor's.

Special study options: advanced placement credit, double majors, independent study, internships, off-campus study, services for LD students, student-designed majors, study abroad.

Unusual degree programs: 3-2 business administration with accounting with Indiana University; engineering with Purdue University, Columbia University, Washington University in St. Louis.

Computers: 335 computers/terminals are available on campus for general student use. Students can access the following: campus intranet, computer help desk, free student e-mail accounts, online (class) grades, online (class) schedules, online course management, degree audit, expenses. Campuswide network is available. 100% of college-owned or -operated housing units are wired for high-speed Internet access. Wireless service is available via entire campus.

STUDENT LIFE
Housing options: on-campus residence required through sophomore year; men-only. Campus housing is university owned. Freshman campus housing is guaranteed.

Activities and organizations: drama/theater group, student-run newspaper, radio station, choral group, College Mentors for Kids, Alpha Phi Omega, Malcolm X Institute for Black Studies, Inter-Fraternity Council, Independent Men's Association, national fraternities.

Athletics Member NCAA. All Division III. ***Intercollegiate sports:*** baseball M, basketball M, cross-country running M, football M, golf M, lacrosse M, rugby M(c), soccer M, swimming and diving M, tennis M, track and field M, ultimate Frisbee M(c), volleyball M(c), wrestling M. ***Intramural sports:*** badminton M, basketball M, bowling M, cross-country running M, football M, golf M, racquetball M, soccer M, softball M, swimming and diving M, table tennis M, tennis M, track and field M, volleyball M, weight lifting M, wrestling M.

Campus security: 24-hour patrols, late-night transport/escort service.

Student services: health clinic, personal/psychological counseling.

COSTS & FINANCIAL AID
Costs (2014–15) ***Comprehensive fee:*** $46,880 includes full-time tuition ($37,100), mandatory fees ($650), and room and board ($9130). Part-time tuition: $6183 per course. Part-time tuition and fees vary according to course load. ***College room only:*** $4530. Room and board charges vary according to board plan and housing facility. ***Payment plans:*** tuition prepayment, installment. ***Waivers:*** employees or children of employees.

Financial Aid Of all full-time matriculated undergraduates who enrolled in 2014, 882 applied for aid, 736 were judged to have need, 467 had their need fully met. 75 Federal Work-Study jobs (averaging $2943). 550 state and other part-time jobs (averaging $2672). In 2014, 163 non-need-based awards were made. ***Average percent of need met:*** 88. ***Average financial aid package:*** $31,886. ***Average need-based loan:*** $5919. ***Average need-based gift aid:*** $23,621. ***Average non-need-based aid:*** $19,235. ***Average indebtedness upon graduation:*** $30,734. ***Financial aid deadline:*** 3/1.

APPLYING
Standardized Tests *Required:* SAT or ACT (for admission).

Options: electronic application, early admission, early decision, early action, deferred entrance.

Application fee: $40.

Required: essay or personal statement, high school transcript, High School Report. ***Required for some:*** interview. ***Recommended:*** 1 letter of recommendation, interview.

Application deadlines: rolling (freshmen), rolling (out-of-state freshmen), rolling (transfers), 12/1 (early action).

Early decision deadline: 11/15.

Notification: continuous (freshmen), continuous (out-of-state freshmen), continuous (transfers), 12/1 (early decision), 12/19 (early action).

CONTACT
Mr. Charles Timmons, Associate Director of Admissions, Wabash College, PO Box 362, Crawfordsville, IN 47933-0352. *Phone:* 765-361-6225. *Toll-free phone:* 800-345-5385. *Fax:* 765-361-6437. *E-mail:* admissions@wabash.edu.

IOWA

Allen College
Waterloo, Iowa
http://www.allencollege.edu/

- **Independent** comprehensive, founded 1989
- **Suburban** 20-acre campus
- **Endowment** $5.7 million
- **Coed, primarily women** 397 undergraduate students, 65% full-time, 93% women, 7% men
- **Moderately difficult** entrance level, 50% of applicants were admitted

UNDERGRAD STUDENTS
257 full-time, 140 part-time. Students come from 8 states and territories; 2 other countries; 5% are from out of state; 2% Black or African American, non-Hispanic/Latino; 0.5% Hispanic/Latino; 1% Asian, non-Hispanic/Latino; 1% Two or more races, non-Hispanic/Latino; 0.5% international; 33% transferred in; 4% live on campus.

Freshmen
Admission: 4 applied, 2 admitted, 1 enrolled.

FACULTY
Total: 53, 62% full-time, 36% with terminal degrees.

Student/faculty ratio: 12:1.

ACADEMICS
Calendar: semesters. *Degrees:* certificates, associate, bachelor's, master's, doctoral, and post-master's certificates (liberal arts and general education courses offered at either University of North Iowa or Wartburg College).

Special study options: accelerated degree program, advanced placement credit, cooperative education, distance learning, honors programs, independent study, internships, off-campus study, part-time degree program. ***ROTC:*** Army (c).

Unusual degree programs: 3-2 nursing with Wartburg College, Loras College, Central College, Simpson College.

Computers: 32 computers/terminals are available on campus for general student use. Students can access the following: campus intranet, computer help desk, free student e-mail accounts, online (class) grades, online (class) schedules. Campuswide network is available. 100% of college-owned or -operated housing units are wired for high-speed Internet access. Wireless service is available via entire campus.

STUDENT LIFE

Housing options: coed. Campus housing is university owned.

Activities and organizations: choral group, Allen Student Nurses' Association, Nurses' Christian Fellowship.

Campus security: 24-hour patrols, controlled dormitory access.

Student services: health clinic, personal/psychological counseling.

COSTS & FINANCIAL AID

Costs (2014–15) ***Comprehensive fee:*** $26,576 includes full-time tuition ($17,262), mandatory fees ($2033), and room and board ($7281). Full-time tuition and fees vary according to course load and program. Part-time tuition: $557 per credit hour. Part-time tuition and fees vary according to course load and program. ***Required fees:*** $75 per credit part-time. ***College room only:*** $3641. ***Payment plan:*** deferred payment. ***Waivers:*** employees or children of employees.

Financial Aid Of all full-time matriculated undergraduates who enrolled in 2013, 294 applied for aid, 265 were judged to have need, 18 had their need fully met. 9 Federal Work-Study jobs (averaging $2177). In 2013, 16 non-need-based awards were made. ***Average percent of need met:*** 51. ***Average financial aid package:*** $12,215. ***Average need-based loan:*** $5119. ***Average need-based gift aid:*** $6977. ***Average non-need-based aid:*** $2071.

APPLYING

Standardized Tests *Required for some:* SAT or ACT (for admission).

Options: electronic application.

Application fee: $50.

Required: minimum 3.0 GPA. ***Required for some:*** essay or personal statement, high school transcript, 1 letter of recommendation, interview. ***Recommended:*** GPA requirements are based on grades in specific general education courses, not on a cumulative GPA.

Application deadlines: 2/1 (freshmen), 2/1 (transfers).

Notification: continuous until 3/1 (freshmen), continuous until 3/1 (transfers).

CONTACT

Ashlee Gilstrap, Education Secretary, Student Services, Allen College, Barrett Forum, 1825 Logan Avenue, Waterloo, IA 50703. *Phone:* 319-226-2014. *Fax:* 319-226-2010. *E-mail:* Admissions@AllenCollege.edu.

Briar Cliff University

Sioux City, Iowa

http://www.briarcliff.edu/

- **Independent Roman Catholic** comprehensive, founded 1930
- **Suburban** 75-acre campus
- **Coed**
- **Moderately difficult** entrance level

FACULTY

Student/faculty ratio: 12:1.

ACADEMICS

Calendar: (3 10-week terms plus 2 5-week summer sessions). *Degrees:* associate, bachelor's, master's, post-master's, and postbachelor's certificates.

STUDENT LIFE

Housing options: on-campus residence required through junior year; coed. Campus housing is university owned. Freshman campus housing is guaranteed.

Activities and organizations: drama/theater group, student-run newspaper, radio station, choral group, Residence Hall Association, Briar Cliff Student Government, Choices, Blue Crew, Catholic Daughters of America.

Athletics Member NAIA.

Campus security: 24-hour emergency response devices and patrols, student patrols, late-night transport/escort service, controlled dormitory access.

Student services: health clinic, personal/psychological counseling.

COSTS & FINANCIAL AID

Costs (2014–15) ***Comprehensive fee:*** $35,100 includes full-time tuition ($26,228), mandatory fees ($984), and room and board ($7888). Part-time

tuition: $865 per credit hour. ***College room only:*** $3840. Room and board charges vary according to board plan and housing facility. ***Payment plans:*** installment, deferred payment.

Financial Aid Of all full-time matriculated undergraduates who enrolled in 2012, 819 applied for aid, 819 were judged to have need, 655 had their need fully met. 313 Federal Work-Study jobs (averaging $1339). 255 state and other part-time jobs (averaging $1333). In 2012, 60 non-need-based awards were made. ***Average percent of need met:*** 80. ***Average financial aid package:*** $20,651. ***Average need-based loan:*** $3230. ***Average need-based gift aid:*** $10,878. ***Average non-need-based aid:*** $4318. ***Average indebtedness upon graduation:*** $34,312. ***Financial aid deadline:*** 3/15.

APPLYING

Standardized Tests *Required:* SAT or ACT (for admission).

Options: electronic application, early admission, deferred entrance.

Application fee: $20.

Required: high school transcript, minimum 2.0 GPA. ***Required for some:*** essay or personal statement, 3 letters of recommendation, interview.

CONTACT

Mr. Brian Eben, Assistant Vice President for Enrollment Management, Briar Cliff University, 3303 Rebecca Street, Sioux City, IA 51104. *Phone:* 712-279-5200. *Toll-free phone:* 800-662-3303. *Fax:* 712-279-1632. *E-mail:* admissions@briarcliff.edu.

See below for display ad and page 1374 for the College Close-Up.

Buena Vista University

Storm Lake, Iowa

http://www.bvu.edu/

- **Independent** comprehensive, founded 1891, affiliated with Presbyterian Church (U.S.A.)
- **Small-town** 60-acre campus
- **Endowment** $135.6 million
- **Coed** 861 undergraduate students, 98% full-time, 51% women, 49% men
- **Moderately difficult** entrance level, 68% of applicants were admitted

UNDERGRAD STUDENTS

844 full-time, 17 part-time. Students come from 25 states and territories; 11 other countries; 23% are from out of state; 2% Black or African American, non-Hispanic/Latino; 8% Hispanic/Latino; 3% Asian, non-Hispanic/Latino; 0.1% Native Hawaiian or other Pacific Islander, non-Hispanic/Latino; 0.4% American Indian or Alaska Native, non-Hispanic/Latino; 2% Two or more races, non-Hispanic/Latino; 4% Race/ethnicity unknown; 6% international; 5% transferred in; 88% live on campus.

Freshmen

Admission: 1,227 applied, 833 admitted, 201 enrolled. ***Average high school GPA:*** 3.5. ***Test scores:*** ACT scores over 18: 95%; ACT scores over 24: 39%; ACT scores over 30: 4%.

Retention: 73% of full-time freshmen returned.

FACULTY

Total: 114, 74% full-time, 54% with terminal degrees.

Student/faculty ratio: 9:1.

ACADEMICS

Calendar: 4-1-4. *Degrees:* bachelor's and master's.

Special study options: academic remediation for entering students, adult/continuing education programs, advanced placement credit, distance learning, double majors, English as a second language, external degree program, honors programs, independent study, internships, off-campus study, part-time degree program, services for LD students, student-designed majors, study abroad, summer session for credit. ***ROTC:*** Army (b).

Unusual degree programs: 3-2 engineering with Washington University in St. Louis.

Computers: 400 computers/terminals are available on campus for general student use. Students can access the following: computer help desk, free student e-mail accounts, online (class) grades, online (class) registration, online (class) schedules. Campuswide network is available. 100% of college-owned or -operated housing units are wired for high-speed Internet access. Wireless service is available via entire campus.

STUDENT LIFE

Housing options: on-campus residence required through senior year; coed, men-only, women-only. Campus housing is university owned. Freshman campus housing is guaranteed.

Activities and organizations: drama/theater group, student-run newspaper, radio and television station, choral group, Student Activities Board, student orientation staff, Esprit De Corps, Student Senate, Marketing Association.

Athletics Member NCAA. All Division III. ***Intercollegiate sports:*** baseball M, basketball M/W, cross-country running M/W, football M, golf M/W, soccer M/W, softball W, tennis M/W, track and field M/W, volleyball W, wrestling M. ***Intramural sports:*** basketball M/W, football M, racquetball M/W, softball M/W, volleyball M/W.

Campus security: 24-hour emergency response devices, late-night transport/escort service, controlled dormitory access, night security patrols.

Student services: health clinic, personal/psychological counseling.

COSTS & FINANCIAL AID

Costs (2015–16) ***Comprehensive fee:*** $40,364 includes full-time tuition ($31,318) and room and board ($9046). Full-time tuition and fees vary according to location. Part-time tuition and fees vary according to location. ***Room and board:*** Room and board charges vary according to board plan. ***Payment plan:*** installment. ***Waivers:*** employees or children of employees.

Financial Aid Of all full-time matriculated undergraduates who enrolled in 2014, 750 applied for aid, 691 were judged to have need, 52 had their need fully met. In 2014, 127 non-need-based awards were made. ***Average percent of need met:*** 100. ***Average financial aid package:*** $28,602. ***Average need-based loan:*** $5165. ***Average need-based gift aid:*** $8375. ***Average non-need-based aid:*** $18,061. ***Average indebtedness upon graduation:*** $34,173.

APPLYING

Standardized Tests *Required:* SAT or ACT (for admission). *Recommended:* ACT (for admission).

Options: electronic application, deferred entrance.

Required: high school transcript. ***Required for some:*** essay or personal statement, interview. ***Recommended:*** minimum 3.0 GPA.

Notification: continuous (freshmen), continuous (transfers).

CONTACT

Michael Fox, Director of Admissions, Buena Vista University, 610 West Fourth Street, Storm Lake, IA 50588. *Phone:* 712-749-2078. *Toll-free phone:* 800-383-9600. *E-mail:* admissions@bvu.edu.

Central College

Pella, Iowa

http://www.central.edu/

- **Independent** 4-year, founded 1853, affiliated with Reformed Church in America
- **Small-town** 169-acre campus with easy access to Des Moines
- **Endowment** $71.1 million
- **Coed** 1,411 undergraduate students, 97% full-time, 52% women, 48% men
- **Moderately difficult** entrance level, 66% of applicants were admitted

UNDERGRAD STUDENTS

1,365 full-time, 46 part-time. Students come from 28 states and territories; 2 other countries; 20% are from out of state; 2% Black or African American, non-Hispanic/Latino; 3% Hispanic/Latino; 1% Asian, non-Hispanic/Latino; 0.1% Native Hawaiian or other Pacific Islander, non-Hispanic/Latino; 0.4% American Indian or Alaska Native, non-Hispanic/Latino; 1% Two or more races, non-Hispanic/Latino; 3% Race/ethnicity unknown; 1% international; 2% transferred in; 94% live on campus.

Freshmen

Admission: 3,068 applied, 2,024 admitted, 429 enrolled. ***Average high school GPA:*** 3.56. ***Test scores:*** SAT critical reading scores over 500: 70%; SAT math scores over 500: 53%; ACT scores over 18: 96%; SAT

critical reading scores over 600: 6%; SAT math scores over 600: 12%; ACT scores over 24: 52%; ACT scores over 30: 11%.

Retention: 78% of full-time freshmen returned.

FACULTY

Total: 101, 95% full-time, 82% with terminal degrees.

Student/faculty ratio: 13:1.

ACADEMICS

Calendar: semesters. *Degree:* bachelor's.

Special study options: cooperative education, double majors, honors programs, independent study, internships, off-campus study, part-time degree program, services for LD students, student-designed majors, study abroad, summer session for credit.

Unusual degree programs: 3-2 engineering with Washington University in St. Louis, University of Iowa, and Iowa State University; nursing with Allen College; Palmer College of Chiropractic.

Computers: 288 computers/terminals and 1,600 ports are available on campus for general student use. Students can access the following: campus intranet, computer help desk, free student e-mail accounts, online (class) grades, online (class) registration, online (class) schedules. Campuswide network is available. 100% of college-owned or -operated housing units are wired for high-speed Internet access. Wireless service is available via entire campus.

STUDENT LIFE

Housing options: on-campus residence required through senior year; coed, men-only, women-only, special housing for students with disabilities. Campus housing is university owned. Freshman campus housing is guaranteed.

Activities and organizations: drama/theater group, student-run newspaper, choral group, Campus Activities Board, Fellowship of Christian Athletes, Central Volunteer Center, Health Professions, Economics, Accounting, Management (EAM) Club.

Athletics Member NCAA. All Division III. ***Intercollegiate sports:*** baseball M, basketball M/W, cross-country running M/W, football M, golf M/W, soccer M/W, softball W, tennis M/W, track and field M/W, volleyball W, wrestling M. ***Intramural sports:*** basketball M/W, football M, racquetball M/W, rugby M, soccer M/W, softball M/W, volleyball M/W.

Campus security: 24-hour emergency response devices and patrols, late-night transport/escort service, controlled dormitory access.

Student services: health clinic, personal/psychological counseling.

COSTS & FINANCIAL AID

Costs (2015–16) ***Comprehensive fee:*** $43,325 includes full-time tuition ($33,345) and room and board ($9980). Part-time tuition: $1389 per credit hour. Part-time tuition and fees vary according to course load. ***College room only:*** $4892. Room and board charges vary according to board plan. ***Payment plan:*** installment. ***Waivers:*** employees or children of employees.

Financial Aid Of all full-time matriculated undergraduates who enrolled in 2014, 1,164 applied for aid, 1,056 were judged to have need, 196 had their need fully met. In 2014, 251 non-need-based awards were made. ***Average percent of need met:*** 80. ***Average financial aid package:*** $24,872. ***Average need-based loan:*** $3045. ***Average need-based gift aid:*** $22,088. ***Average non-need-based aid:*** $16,292. ***Average indebtedness upon graduation:*** $29,440.

APPLYING

Standardized Tests *Required:* SAT or ACT (for admission).

Options: electronic application, deferred entrance.

Application fee: $25.

Required: high school transcript. ***Required for some:*** essay or personal statement, 3 letters of recommendation, interview. ***Recommended:*** minimum 2.7 GPA.

Application deadlines: 8/15 (freshmen), rolling (transfers).

Notification: continuous (freshmen), continuous (transfers).

CONTACT

Chevy Freiburger, Director of Admissions, Central College, 812 University, Pella, IA 50112. *Phone:* 641-628-7637. *Toll-free phone:* 877-462-3687. *Fax:* 641-628-5983. *E-mail:* freiburgerc@central.edu.

Clarke University

Dubuque, Iowa

http://www.clarke.edu/

- **Independent Roman Catholic** comprehensive, founded 1843
- **Urban** 55-acre campus
- **Endowment** $33.4 million
- **Coed** 949 undergraduate students, 88% full-time, 68% women, 32% men
- **Moderately difficult** entrance level, 70% of applicants were admitted

UNDERGRAD STUDENTS

835 full-time, 114 part-time. Students come from 28 states and territories; 7 other countries; 38% are from out of state; 4% Black or African American, non-Hispanic/Latino; 5% Hispanic/Latino; 0.9% Asian, non-Hispanic/Latino; 0.1% American Indian or Alaska Native, non-Hispanic/Latino; 0.2% Two or more races, non-Hispanic/Latino; 1% international; 6% transferred in; 56% live on campus.

Freshmen

Admission: 1,359 applied, 958 admitted, 183 enrolled. ***Average high school GPA:*** 3.51. ***Test scores:*** SAT critical reading scores over 500: 55%; SAT math scores over 500: 55%; ACT scores over 18: 91%; SAT critical reading scores over 600: 10%; SAT math scores over 600: 10%; ACT scores over 24: 31%; ACT scores over 30: 5%.

Retention: 73% of full-time freshmen returned.

FACULTY

Total: 156, 57% full-time, 41% with terminal degrees.

Student/faculty ratio: 10:1.

ACADEMICS

Calendar: semesters. *Degrees:* associate, bachelor's, master's, and doctoral.

Special study options: accelerated degree program, adult/continuing education programs, advanced placement credit, cooperative education, distance learning, double majors, English as a second language, honors programs, independent study, internships, off-campus study, part-time degree program, student-designed majors, study abroad, summer session for credit. ***ROTC:*** Army (c).

Unusual degree programs: 3-2 business administration.

Computers: 237 computers/terminals are available on campus for general student use. Students can access the following: campus intranet, computer help desk, free student e-mail accounts, online (class) grades, online (class) registration, online (class) schedules. Campuswide network is available. 100% of college-owned or -operated housing units are wired for high-speed Internet access. Wireless service is available via entire campus.

STUDENT LIFE

Housing options: on-campus residence required through sophomore year; coed, men-only, women-only. Campus housing is university owned. Freshman campus housing is guaranteed.

Activities and organizations: drama/theater group, student-run newspaper, radio station, choral group, Admissions Student Team, Student Multicultural Organization, concert choir, campus ministry, student government.

Athletics Member NAIA. ***Intercollegiate sports:*** baseball M(s), basketball M(s)/W(s), bowling M(s)/W(s), cheerleading W, cross-country running M(s)/W(s), golf M(s)/W(s), lacrosse M(s)/W(s), soccer M(s)/W(s), softball W(s), track and field M(s)/W(s), volleyball M(s)/W(s). ***Intramural sports:*** badminton M/W, basketball M/W, bowling M/W, football M/W, golf M/W, skiing (cross-country) M/W, skiing (downhill) M/W, softball M/W, table tennis M/W, tennis M/W, track and field M/W, volleyball M/W, weight lifting M/W.

Campus security: 24-hour emergency response devices and patrols, late-night transport/escort service, controlled dormitory access.

Student services: health clinic, personal/psychological counseling.

COSTS & FINANCIAL AID

Costs (2015–16) ***Comprehensive fee:*** $38,940 includes full-time tuition ($29,000), mandatory fees ($940), and room and board ($9000). Part-time tuition: $690 per credit. ***College room only:*** $4300. Room and board charges vary according to housing facility. ***Payment plans:*** installment, deferred payment. ***Waivers:*** children of alumni, adult students, senior citizens, and employees or children of employees.

Financial Aid Of all full-time matriculated undergraduates who enrolled in 2014, 752 applied for aid, 696 were judged to have need, 144 had their need fully met. 343 Federal Work-Study jobs (averaging $1840). In 2014, 99 non-need-based awards were made. ***Average percent of need met:*** 71. ***Average financial aid package:*** $23,657. ***Average need-based loan:*** $4582. ***Average need-based gift aid:*** $18,750. ***Average non-need-based aid:*** $18,107. ***Average indebtedness upon graduation:*** $37,200.

APPLYING
Standardized Tests *Required:* SAT or ACT (for admission).

Options: electronic application, deferred entrance.

Application fee: $25.

Required: high school transcript, minimum 2.0 GPA.

Application deadlines: rolling (freshmen), rolling (transfers).

Notification: 7/15 (freshmen), continuous until 8/15 (transfers).

CONTACT
Ms. Emily Kruse, Assistant Director of Admissions, Clarke University, 1550 Clarke Drive, Dubuque, IA 52001-3198. *Phone:* 563-588-6436. *Toll-free phone:* 800-383-2345. *E-mail:* admissions@clarke.edu.

Coe College

Cedar Rapids, Iowa

http://www.coe.edu/

- **Independent** 4-year, founded 1851, affiliated with Presbyterian Church
- **Urban** 53-acre campus
- **Endowment** $97.1 million
- **Coed** 1,435 undergraduate students, 95% full-time, 56% women, 44% men
- **Moderately difficult** entrance level, 55% of applicants were admitted

UNDERGRAD STUDENTS
1,360 full-time, 75 part-time. Students come from 38 states and territories; 24 other countries; 51% are from out of state; 5% Black or African American, non-Hispanic/Latino; 8% Hispanic/Latino; 2% Asian, non-Hispanic/Latino; 0.1% Native Hawaiian or other Pacific Islander, non-Hispanic/Latino; 0.2% American Indian or Alaska Native, non-Hispanic/Latino; 3% Two or more races, non-Hispanic/Latino; 4% Race/ethnicity unknown; 5% international; 3% transferred in; 89% live on campus.

Freshmen
Admission: 3,403 applied, 1,882 admitted, 376 enrolled. ***Average high school GPA:*** 3.65. ***Test scores:*** SAT critical reading scores over 500: 80%; SAT math scores over 500: 88%; SAT writing scores over 500: 68%; ACT scores over 18: 100%; SAT critical reading scores over 600: 39%; SAT math scores over 600: 42%; SAT writing scores over 600: 30%; ACT scores over 24: 65%; SAT critical reading scores over 700: 5%; SAT math scores over 700: 10%; SAT writing scores over 700: 3%; ACT scores over 30: 17%.

Retention: 78% of full-time freshmen returned.

FACULTY
Total: 171, 56% full-time, 68% with terminal degrees.

Student/faculty ratio: 12:1.

ACADEMICS
Calendar: 4-4-1. *Degree:* bachelor's.

Special study options: advanced placement credit, double majors, English as a second language, honors programs, independent study, internships, off-campus study, part-time degree program, services for LD students, student-designed majors, study abroad, summer session for credit. ***ROTC:*** Army (b), Air Force (c).

Computers: 450 computers/terminals and 1,850 ports are available on campus for general student use. Students can access the following: campus intranet, computer help desk, free student e-mail accounts, online (class) grades, online (class) registration, online (class) schedules. Campuswide network is available. 100% of college-owned or -operated housing units are wired for high-speed Internet access. Wireless service is available via entire campus.

STUDENT LIFE
Housing options: on-campus residence required through senior year; coed, men-only, women-only, special housing for students with disabilities. Campus housing is university owned. Freshman campus housing is guaranteed.

Activities and organizations: drama/theater group, student-run newspaper, radio station, choral group, Student Activities Committee, Psychology Club, International Club, Coe Alliance, Student Athlete Advisory Committee, national fraternities, national sororities.

Athletics Member NCAA. All Division III. ***Intercollegiate sports:*** baseball M, basketball M/W, cheerleading W, cross-country running M/W, football M, golf M/W, soccer M/W, softball W, swimming and diving M/W, tennis M/W, track and field M/W, volleyball W, wrestling M. ***Intramural sports:*** badminton M/W, basketball M/W, cross-country running M(c)/W(c), football M/W, racquetball M/W, rock climbing M/W, rugby M(c)/W(c), soccer M/W, softball M/W, squash M/W, swimming and diving M(c)/W(c), table tennis M/W, tennis M/W, ultimate Frisbee M(c)/W(c), volleyball M/W.

Campus security: 24-hour emergency response devices and patrols, late-night transport/escort service, controlled dormitory access.

Student services: health clinic, personal/psychological counseling.

COSTS & FINANCIAL AID
Costs (2014–15) ***Comprehensive fee:*** $45,550 includes full-time tuition ($36,990), mandatory fees ($330), and room and board ($8230). Part-time tuition: $4155 per course. Part-time tuition and fees vary according to course load. ***College room only:*** $3730. Room and board charges vary according to board plan and housing facility. ***Payment plan:*** installment. ***Waivers:*** adult students, senior citizens, and employees or children of employees.

Financial Aid Of all full-time matriculated undergraduates who enrolled in 2014, 1,210 applied for aid, 1,124 were judged to have need, 224 had their need fully met. 651 Federal Work-Study jobs (averaging $1668). 224 state and other part-time jobs (averaging $1449). In 2014, 200 non-need-based awards were made. ***Average percent of need met:*** 83. ***Average financial aid package:*** $30,351. ***Average need-based loan:*** $5491. ***Average need-based gift aid:*** $25,079. ***Average non-need-based aid:*** $20,313. ***Average indebtedness upon graduation:*** $31,992.

APPLYING
Standardized Tests *Required:* SAT or ACT (for admission).

Options: electronic application, early admission, early action, deferred entrance.

Application fee: $30.

Required: essay or personal statement, high school transcript, 1 letter of recommendation. ***Recommended:*** minimum 3.0 GPA, interview.

Application deadlines: 3/1 (freshmen), rolling (transfers), 12/10 (early action).

Notification: 3/15 (freshmen), continuous (transfers).

CONTACT
Ms. Julie Staker, Dean of Admission, Coe College, 1220 1st Avenue NE, Cedar Rapids, IA 52402-5070. *Phone:* 319-399-8500. *Toll-free phone:* 877-225-5263. *Fax:* 319-399-8816. *E-mail:* admission@coe.edu.

Cornell College

Mount Vernon, Iowa

http://www.cornellcollege.edu/

- **Independent Methodist** 4-year, founded 1853
- **Small-town** 129-acre campus
- **Endowment** $67.0 million
- **Coed** 1,077 undergraduate students, 100% full-time, 53% women, 47% men
- **Moderately difficult** entrance level, 74% of applicants were admitted

UNDERGRAD STUDENTS
1,072 full-time, 5 part-time. Students come from 47 states and territories; 15 other countries; 82% are from out of state; 5% Black or African American, non-Hispanic/Latino; 13% Hispanic/Latino; 2% Asian, non-Hispanic/Latino; 0.3% Native Hawaiian or other Pacific Islander, non-Hispanic/Latino; 0.4% American Indian or Alaska Native, non-Hispanic/Latino; 4% Two or more races, non-Hispanic/Latino; 4% Race/ethnicity unknown; 4% international; 3% transferred in; 92% live on campus.

Freshmen
Admission: 1,915 applied, 1,410 admitted, 262 enrolled. ***Average high school GPA:*** 3.54. ***Test scores:*** SAT critical reading scores over 500: 84%; SAT math scores over 500: 80%; SAT writing scores over 500: 75%; ACT scores over 18: 99%; SAT critical reading scores over 600: 51%; SAT math scores over 600: 48%; SAT writing scores over 600: 36%; ACT scores over 24: 72%; SAT critical reading scores over 700: 20%; SAT math scores over 700: 10%; SAT writing scores over 700: 8%; ACT scores over 30: 25%.
Retention: 83% of full-time freshmen returned.

FACULTY
Total: 118, 73% full-time, 70% with terminal degrees.

Student/faculty ratio: 11:1.

ACADEMICS
Calendar: 8 3.5 week terms. *Degree:* bachelor's.

Special study options: advanced placement credit, double majors, English as a second language, independent study, internships, off-campus study, services for LD students, student-designed majors, study abroad.

Unusual degree programs: 3-2 engineering with University of Minnesota; forestry with Duke University (Forestry or Environmental Management); Architecture with Washington University–St. Louis; Cooperative Program in Medical Technology with St. Luke's Hospital in Cedar Rapids, Iowa; Deferred Admit Program in Dentistry with the University of Iowa.

Computers: 259 computers/terminals and 1,200 ports are available on campus for general student use. Students can access the following: campus intranet, computer help desk, free student e-mail accounts, online (class) grades, online (class) registration, online (class) schedules. Campuswide network is available. 100% of college-owned or -operated housing units are wired for high-speed Internet access. Wireless service is available via entire campus.

STUDENT LIFE
Housing options: on-campus residence required through senior year; coed, women-only. Campus housing is university owned and leased by the school. Freshman campus housing is guaranteed.

Activities and organizations: drama/theater group, student-run newspaper, radio station, choral group, Student-initiated Living-Learning Community, Chess and Games, Environmental Club, Performing Arts and Activities Council, Alliance.

Athletics Member NCAA. All Division III. ***Intercollegiate sports:*** baseball M, basketball M/W, cheerleading M/W, cross-country running M/W, football M, lacrosse M/W, soccer M/W, softball W, tennis M/W, track and field M/W, ultimate Frisbee M(c)/W(c), volleyball M(c)/W, wrestling M. ***Intramural sports:*** badminton M/W, basketball M/W, bowling M/W, fencing M(c)/W(c), football M/W, golf M/W, ice hockey M/W, lacrosse M(c)/W(c), racquetball M/W, soccer M/W, softball M/W, table tennis M/W, tennis M/W, track and field M/W, ultimate Frisbee M/W, volleyball M/W, weight lifting M/W, wrestling M/W.

Campus security: 24-hour emergency response devices and patrols, late-night transport/escort service, controlled dormitory access.

Student services: health clinic, personal/psychological counseling.

COSTS & FINANCIAL AID
Costs (2015–16) ***Comprehensive fee:*** $46,225 includes full-time tuition ($37,500), mandatory fees ($225), and room and board ($8500). Part-time tuition: $1520 per credit. Part-time tuition and fees vary according to course load. ***College room only:*** $3800. Room and board charges vary according to board plan and housing facility. ***Payment plan:*** installment. ***Waivers:*** employees or children of employees.

Financial Aid Of all full-time matriculated undergraduates who enrolled in 2014, 895 applied for aid, 813 were judged to have need, 116 had their need fully met. 493 Federal Work-Study jobs (averaging $1521). 87 state and other part-time jobs (averaging $1141). In 2014, 234 non-need-based awards were made. ***Average percent of need met:*** 80. ***Average financial aid package:*** $32,245. ***Average need-based loan:*** $4805. ***Average need-based gift aid:*** $23,447. ***Average non-need-based aid:*** $18,292. ***Average indebtedness upon graduation:*** $25,004. ***Financial aid deadline:*** 3/1.

APPLYING
Standardized Tests *Required:* SAT or ACT (for admission).

Options: electronic application, early admission, early decision, early action, deferred entrance.

Application fee: $30.

Required: essay or personal statement, high school transcript, 1 letter of recommendation. ***Recommended:*** interview.

Application deadlines: 2/1 (freshmen), 3/1 (transfers), 12/1 (early action).

Early decision deadline: 11/1 (for plan 1), 2/1 (for plan 2).

Notification: 3/20 (freshmen), continuous (transfers), 12/15 (early decision plan 1), 3/15 (early decision plan 2), 2/1 (early action).

CONTACT
Ms. Marie Schofer, Director of Admissions, Cornell College, 600 First Street SW, Mount Vernon, IA 52314-1098. *Phone:* 319-895-4159. *Toll-free phone:* 800-747-1112. *Fax:* 319-895-4451. *E-mail:* admission@cornellcollege.edu.

Divine Word College

Epworth, Iowa

http://www.dwci.edu/

- **Independent Roman Catholic** 4-year, founded 1912
- **Rural** 35-acre campus
- **Coed**

ACADEMICS
Calendar: semesters. *Degrees:* associate and bachelor's.

STUDENT LIFE
Housing options: on-campus residence required through senior year; men-only, women-only.

Activities and organizations: choral group.

Campus security: controlled dormitory access.

Student services: personal/psychological counseling.

COSTS
Costs (2014–15) ***Comprehensive fee:*** $15,750 includes full-time tuition ($12,250), mandatory fees ($100), and room and board ($3400). Part-time tuition: $410 per credit.

APPLYING
Standardized Tests *Recommended:* SAT or ACT (for admission).

Options: early admission.

Application fee: $25.

Required: essay or personal statement, high school transcript, 3 letters of recommendation, interview.

CONTACT
Divine Word College, 102 Jacoby Drive SW, Epworth, IA 52045-0380. *Phone:* 563-876-3353. *Toll-free phone:* 800-553-3321.

Dordt College

Sioux Center, Iowa

http://www.dordt.edu/

- **Independent Christian Reformed** comprehensive, founded 1955
- **Small-town** 110-acre campus
- **Endowment** $26.0 million
- **Coed**
- **Moderately difficult** entrance level

FACULTY
Student/faculty ratio: 15:1.

ACADEMICS
Calendar: semesters. *Degrees:* associate, bachelor's, and master's.

STUDENT LIFE
Housing options: on-campus residence required through senior year; men-only, women-only, special housing for students with disabilities. Campus housing is university owned. Freshman campus housing is guaranteed.

Activities and organizations: drama/theater group, student-run newspaper, radio station, choral group, PLIA, Future Teachers, Ag Club, Lacrosse Club, Defenders of Life.

Athletics Member NAIA.

Campus security: 24-hour emergency response devices, student patrols, late-night transport/escort service, controlled dormitory access.

Student services: health clinic, personal/psychological counseling.

FINANCIAL AID

Financial Aid Of all full-time matriculated undergraduates who enrolled in 2014, 1,079 applied for aid, 928 were judged to have need, 293 had their need fully met. 400 Federal Work-Study jobs (averaging $1600). 500 state and other part-time jobs (averaging $1600). In 2014, 297 non-need-based awards were made. ***Average percent of need met:*** 76. ***Average financial aid package:*** $21,965. ***Average need-based loan:*** $5367. ***Average need-based gift aid:*** $14,967. ***Average non-need-based aid:*** $18,363. ***Average indebtedness upon graduation:*** $27,867.

APPLYING

Standardized Tests *Required:* SAT or ACT (for admission).

Options: electronic application, deferred entrance.

Required: high school transcript, minimum 2.3 GPA. ***Required for some:*** essay or personal statement, interview.

CONTACT

Mr. Howard Wislon, Vice President for Enrollment, Dordt College, 498 4th Avenue, NE, Sioux Center, IA 51250-1697. *Phone:* 712-722-6080. *Toll-free phone:* 800-343-6738. *Fax:* 712-722-6035. *E-mail:* admissions@dordt.edu.

★ Drake University

Des Moines, Iowa

http://www.drake.edu/

- **Independent** university, founded 1881
- **Urban** 120-acre campus
- **Endowment** $186.3 million
- **Coed** 3,364 undergraduate students, 94% full-time, 56% women, 44% men
- **Moderately difficult** entrance level, 69% of applicants were admitted

UNDERGRAD STUDENTS

3,177 full-time, 187 part-time. Students come from 40 states and territories; 34 other countries; 68% are from out of state; 4% Black or African American, non-Hispanic/Latino; 3% Hispanic/Latino; 4% Asian, non-Hispanic/Latino; 0.1% Native Hawaiian or other Pacific Islander, non-Hispanic/Latino; 0.2% American Indian or Alaska Native, non-Hispanic/Latino; 2% Two or more races, non-Hispanic/Latino; 1% Race/ethnicity unknown; 7% international; 5% transferred in; 72% live on campus.

Freshmen

Admission: 6,476 applied, 4,485 admitted, 870 enrolled. ***Average high school GPA:*** 3.7. ***Test scores:*** SAT critical reading scores over 500: 59%; SAT math scores over 500: 86%; ACT scores over 18: 100%; SAT critical reading scores over 600: 55%; SAT math scores over 600: 50%; ACT scores over 24: 82%; SAT critical reading scores over 700: 10%; SAT math scores over 700: 15%; ACT scores over 30: 28%.

Retention: 89% of full-time freshmen returned.

FACULTY

Total: 430, 65% full-time, 64% with terminal degrees.

Student/faculty ratio: 12:1.

ACADEMICS

Calendar: semesters. *Degrees:* bachelor's, master's, doctoral, post-master's, and postbachelor's certificates.

Special study options: accelerated degree program, advanced placement credit, cooperative education, distance learning, double majors, English as a second language, honors programs, independent study, internships, off-campus study, part-time degree program, services for LD students, student-designed majors, study abroad, summer session for credit. ***ROTC:*** Army (c), Air Force (c).

Unusual degree programs: 3-2 journalism and law, arts and sciences and law, accounting.

Computers: 1,000 computers/terminals are available on campus for general student use. Students can access the following: campus intranet, computer help desk, free student e-mail accounts, online (class) grades, online (class) registration, online (class) schedules. Campuswide network is available. 100% of college-owned or -operated housing units are wired for high-speed Internet access. Wireless service is available via classrooms, computer centers, computer labs, dorm rooms, libraries, student centers.

STUDENT LIFE

Housing options: on-campus residence required through sophomore year; coed, special housing for students with disabilities. Campus housing is university owned and is provided by a third party. Freshman campus housing is guaranteed.

Activities and organizations: drama/theater group, student-run newspaper, radio and television station, choral group, marching band, Student Activities Board, Drake Magazine, Dog Pound Pep Squad, Alpha Phi Omega, Residence Hall Association, national fraternities, national sororities.

Athletics Member NCAA. All Division I except football (Division I-AA). ***Intercollegiate sports:*** basketball M(s)/W(s), cheerleading M(s)/W(s), crew W, cross-country running M(s)/W(s), golf M(s)/W, soccer M(s)/W(s), softball W(s), tennis M(s)/W(s), track and field M(s)/W(s), volleyball W(s). ***Intramural sports:*** badminton M/W, basketball M/W, football M/W, golf M/W, racquetball M/W, soccer M(c)/W, softball M/W, swimming and diving M/W, tennis M/W, volleyball M/W(c).

Campus security: 24-hour emergency response devices and patrols, late-night transport/escort service, controlled dormitory access, 24-hour desk attendants in residence halls.

Student services: health clinic, personal/psychological counseling, legal services.

COSTS & FINANCIAL AID

Costs (2014–15) ***Comprehensive fee:*** $41,516 includes full-time tuition ($32,100), mandatory fees ($146), and room and board ($9270). Full-time tuition and fees vary according to course load, degree level, program, and student level. Part-time tuition: $635 per credit hour. Part-time tuition and fees vary according to class time, degree level, and program. ***College room only:*** $4950. Room and board charges vary according to board plan. ***Payment plan:*** installment. ***Waivers:*** children of alumni, senior citizens, and employees or children of employees.

Financial Aid Of all full-time matriculated undergraduates who enrolled in 2014, 2,301 applied for aid, 1,880 were judged to have need, 465 had their need fully met. 1,529 Federal Work-Study jobs (averaging $1915). In 2014, 1068 non-need-based awards were made. ***Average percent of need met:*** 79. ***Average financial aid package:*** $25,015. ***Average need-based loan:*** $6152. ***Average need-based gift aid:*** $16,669. ***Average non-need-based aid:*** $12,889. ***Average indebtedness upon graduation:*** $31,546.

APPLYING

Standardized Tests *Required:* SAT or ACT (for admission).

Options: electronic application, early admission, deferred entrance.

Application fee: $25.

Required: essay or personal statement, high school transcript. ***Recommended:*** interview.

Application deadlines: 3/1 (freshmen), rolling (transfers).

Notification: continuous (freshmen), continuous (transfers).

CONTACT

Ms. Laura Linn, Director of Admission, Drake University, 2507 University Avenue, Des Moines, IA 50311. *Phone:* 515-271-3181 Ext. 3182. *Toll-free phone:* 800-44-DRAKE Ext. 3181. *Fax:* 515-271-2831. *E-mail:* admission@drake.edu.

Emmaus Bible College

Dubuque, Iowa

http://www.emmaus.edu/

- **Independent nondenominational** 4-year, founded 1941
- **Small-town** 22-acre campus
- **Coed**
- **Noncompetitive** entrance level

FACULTY

Student/faculty ratio: 9:1.

ACADEMICS
Calendar: semesters. *Degrees:* certificates, associate, and bachelor's.

STUDENT LIFE
Housing options: on-campus residence required through senior year; men-only, women-only. Campus housing is university owned. Freshman campus housing is guaranteed.

Activities and organizations: choral group.

Athletics Member NCCAA.

Campus security: 24-hour emergency response devices, student patrols, controlled dormitory access.

Student services: personal/psychological counseling.

COSTS
Costs (2014–15) ***Comprehensive fee:*** $21,950 includes full-time tuition ($14,600), mandatory fees ($790), and room and board ($6560). Part-time tuition: $642 per credit.

APPLYING
Standardized Tests *Required:* SAT or ACT (for admission).

Options: electronic application, deferred entrance.

Application fee: $25.

Required: essay or personal statement, high school transcript, 2 letters of recommendation.

CONTACT
Emmaus Bible College, 2570 Asbury Road, Dubuque, IA 52001-3097. *Phone:* 563-588-8000 Ext. 1310. *Toll-free phone:* 800-397-2425.

Faith Baptist Bible College and Theological Seminary

Ankeny, Iowa

http://www.faith.edu/

- **Independent** comprehensive, founded 1921, affiliated with General Association of Regular Baptist Churches
- **Suburban** 52-acre campus
- **Endowment** $4.0 million
- **Coed** 229 undergraduate students, 90% full-time, 54% women, 46% men
- **Minimally difficult** entrance level, 67% of applicants were admitted

UNDERGRAD STUDENTS
206 full-time, 23 part-time. Students come from 29 states and territories; 7 other countries; 52% are from out of state; 2% Black or African American, non-Hispanic/Latino; 1% Hispanic/Latino; 0.9% Asian, non-Hispanic/Latino; 0.4% Native Hawaiian or other Pacific Islander, non-Hispanic/Latino; 2% American Indian or Alaska Native, non-Hispanic/Latino; 0.4% Two or more races, non-Hispanic/Latino; 6% transferred in; 75% live on campus.

Freshmen
Admission: 127 applied, 85 admitted, 60 enrolled. ***Average high school GPA:*** 3.39. ***Test scores:*** SAT critical reading scores over 500: 72%; SAT math scores over 500: 43%; SAT writing scores over 500: 57%; ACT scores over 18: 82%; SAT critical reading scores over 600: 29%; SAT writing scores over 600: 14%; ACT scores over 24: 33%; ACT scores over 30: 2%.

Retention: 70% of full-time freshmen returned.

FACULTY
Total: 28, 64% full-time, 50% with terminal degrees.

Student/faculty ratio: 10:1.

ACADEMICS
Calendar: semesters. *Degrees:* associate, bachelor's, and master's.

Special study options: academic remediation for entering students, adult/continuing education programs, advanced placement credit, double majors, independent study, internships, part-time degree program, summer session for credit.

Computers: 45 computers/terminals and 250 ports are available on campus for general student use. Students can access the following: free student e-mail accounts. Campuswide network is available. 100% of college-owned or -operated housing units are wired for high-speed Internet access. Wireless service is available via entire campus.

STUDENT LIFE
Housing options: on-campus residence required through senior year; men-only, women-only, special housing for students with disabilities. Campus housing is university owned. Freshman campus housing is guaranteed.

Activities and organizations: drama/theater group, choral group, Student Association, Student Missionary Fellowship, Intramural Sports, Photo Club, Chapel Orchestra.

Athletics Member NCCAA. ***Intercollegiate sports:*** basketball M/W, cross-country running M/W, soccer M/W, track and field M/W, volleyball W. ***Intramural sports:*** basketball M/W, football M, ultimate Frisbee M/W, volleyball M/W.

Campus security: 24-hour emergency response devices and patrols, late-night transport/escort service.

Student services: personal/psychological counseling.

FINANCIAL AID
Financial Aid Of all full-time matriculated undergraduates who enrolled in 2004, 311 applied for aid, 290 were judged to have need, 5 had their need fully met. In 2004, 21 non-need-based awards were made. ***Average percent of need met:*** 48. ***Average financial aid package:*** $7124. ***Average need-based loan:*** $3142. ***Average need-based gift aid:*** $6299. ***Average non-need-based aid:*** $2465. ***Average indebtedness upon graduation:*** $15,006.

APPLYING
Standardized Tests *Required:* SAT or ACT (for admission).

Options: electronic application, deferred entrance.

Required: essay or personal statement, high school transcript, 2 letters of recommendation. ***Required for some:*** interview. ***Recommended:*** minimum 2.0 GPA.

Application deadlines: 8/1 (freshmen), 8/1 (transfers).

Notification: 9/1 (freshmen), continuous until 9/1 (transfers).

CONTACT
Mrs. Krisanna Sternquist, Admissions Secretary, Faith Baptist Bible College and Theological Seminary, 1900 NW 4th Street, Ankeny, IA 50023. *Phone:* 515-964-0601. *Toll-free phone:* 888-FAITH 4U. *Fax:* 515-964-1638. *E-mail:* admissions@faith.edu.

★ Graceland University

Lamoni, Iowa

http://www.graceland.edu/

- **Independent Community of Christ** comprehensive, founded 1895
- **Rural** 170-acre campus with easy access to Des Moines
- **Endowment** $43.8 million
- **Coed** 1,594 undergraduate students, 79% full-time, 56% women, 44% men
- **Moderately difficult** entrance level, 50% of applicants were admitted

UNDERGRAD STUDENTS
1,255 full-time, 339 part-time. Students come from 46 states and territories; 26 other countries; 75% are from out of state; 9% Black or African American, non-Hispanic/Latino; 8% Hispanic/Latino; 0.7% Asian, non-Hispanic/Latino; 1% Native Hawaiian or other Pacific Islander, non-Hispanic/Latino; 0.3% American Indian or Alaska Native, non-Hispanic/Latino; 3% Two or more races, non-Hispanic/Latino; 6% Race/ethnicity unknown; 5% international; 13% transferred in; 71% live on campus.

Freshmen
Admission: 2,169 applied, 1,081 admitted, 282 enrolled. ***Average high school GPA:*** 3.08. ***Test scores:*** SAT critical reading scores over 500: 18%; SAT math scores over 500: 25%; ACT scores over 18: 77%; SAT critical reading scores over 600: 5%; SAT math scores over 600: 5%; ACT scores over 24: 22%; ACT scores over 30: 2%.

Retention: 60% of full-time freshmen returned.

FACULTY
Total: 192, 47% full-time, 51% with terminal degrees.

Student/faculty ratio: 13:1.

ACADEMICS
Calendar: 4-1-4. *Degrees:* bachelor's, master's, doctoral, and post-master's certificates.

Special study options: academic remediation for entering students, accelerated degree program, adult/continuing education programs, advanced placement credit, cooperative education, distance learning, double majors, English as a second language, freshman honors college, honors programs, independent study, internships, off-campus study, part-time degree program, services for LD students, student-designed majors, study abroad, summer session for credit.

Computers: 240 computers/terminals and 1,068 ports are available on campus for general student use. Students can access the following: campus intranet, computer help desk, free student e-mail accounts, online (class) grades, online (class) registration, online (class) schedules. Campuswide network is available. 100% of college-owned or -operated housing units are wired for high-speed Internet access. Wireless service is available via classrooms, computer centers, computer labs, dorm rooms, learning centers, libraries, student centers.

STUDENT LIFE
Housing options: on-campus residence required through sophomore year; men-only, women-only. Campus housing is university owned. Freshman campus housing is guaranteed.

Activities and organizations: drama/theater group, student-run newspaper, radio station, choral group, International Club, Student Athletic Trainers, Outreach International, Art Student Society, Students in Free Enterprise (ENACTUS).

Athletics Member NAIA. ***Intercollegiate sports:*** baseball M(s), basketball M(s)/W(s), bowling M(s)/W(s), cheerleading M(s)/W(s), cross-country running M(s)/W(s), football M(s), golf M(s)/W(s), soccer M(s)/W(s), softball W(s), tennis M(s)/W(s), track and field M(s)/W(s), volleyball M(s)/W(s), wrestling M(s). ***Intramural sports:*** basketball M/W, football M/W, golf M/W, racquetball M/W, soccer M/W, softball M/W, swimming and diving M/W, table tennis M/W, ultimate Frisbee M/W, volleyball M/W.

Campus security: 24-hour emergency response devices and patrols, late-night transport/escort service, controlled dormitory access.

Student services: health clinic, personal/psychological counseling.

COSTS & FINANCIAL AID
Costs (2015–16) ***Comprehensive fee:*** $33,990 includes full-time tuition ($25,420), mandatory fees ($470), and room and board ($8100). Full-time tuition and fees vary according to course load. Part-time tuition: $775 per credit. Part-time tuition and fees vary according to course load. ***Room and board:*** Room and board charges vary according to board plan, housing facility, and location. ***Payment plan:*** installment. ***Waivers:*** senior citizens and employees or children of employees.

Financial Aid Of all full-time matriculated undergraduates who enrolled in 2014, 1,150 applied for aid, 1,073 were judged to have need, 176 had their need fully met. 163 Federal Work-Study jobs (averaging $1522). 652 state and other part-time jobs (averaging $1558). In 2014, 169 non-need-based awards were made. ***Average percent of need met:*** 75. ***Average financial aid package:*** $22,106. ***Average need-based loan:*** $5108. ***Average need-based gift aid:*** $17,148. ***Average non-need-based aid:*** $12,039. ***Average indebtedness upon graduation:*** $35,077.

APPLYING
Standardized Tests *Required:* SAT or ACT (for admission), TOEFL for all students whose first language is not English (for admission).

Options: electronic application.

Required: high school transcript, minimum 2.5 GPA, Students who do not meet 2 out of the following 3 requirements to be considered for admission: rank in top half of class; score a minimum of 21 on ACT or 960 on the SAT; have a 2.5 high school GPA (on a 4.0 scale) will be considered for admission on an individual basis. ***Required for some:*** essay or personal statement, 2 letters of recommendation, interview.

Application deadlines: rolling (freshmen), rolling (out-of-state freshmen), rolling (transfers).

Notification: continuous (freshmen), continuous (out-of-state freshmen), continuous (transfers).

CONTACT
Mr. Kevin Brown, Director of Admissions, Graceland University, 1 University Place, Lamoni, IA 50140. *Phone:* 641-784-5149. *Toll-free phone:* 866-GRACELAND. *Fax:* 641-784-5480. *E-mail:* admissions@graceland.edu.

See below for display ad and page 1460 for the College Close-Up.

★ Grand View University

Des Moines, Iowa

http://www.grandview.edu/

- **Independent** comprehensive, founded 1896, affiliated with Evangelical Lutheran Church in America
- **Urban** 25-acre campus
- **Endowment** $20.3 million
- **Coed** 2,005 undergraduate students, 84% full-time, 56% women, 44% men
- **Minimally difficult** entrance level, 99% of applicants were admitted

UNDERGRAD STUDENTS

1,679 full-time, 326 part-time. Students come from 39 states and territories; 19 other countries; 15% are from out of state; 8% Black or African American, non-Hispanic/Latino; 4% Hispanic/Latino; 3% Asian, non-Hispanic/Latino; 0.0% Native Hawaiian or other Pacific Islander, non-Hispanic/Latino; 0.3% American Indian or Alaska Native, non-Hispanic/Latino; 3% Two or more races, non-Hispanic/Latino; 8% Race/ethnicity unknown; 2% international; 39% live on campus.

Freshmen

Admission: 772 applied, 762 admitted, 279 enrolled. ***Average high school GPA:*** 3.2. ***Test scores:*** SAT critical reading scores over 500: 19%; SAT math scores over 500: 43%; SAT writing scores over 500: 16%; ACT scores over 18: 85%; SAT critical reading scores over 600: 4%; SAT math scores over 600: 8%; SAT writing scores over 600: 4%; ACT scores over 24: 21%; SAT math scores over 700: 4%; ACT scores over 30: 2%.

Retention: 71% of full-time freshmen returned.

FACULTY

Total: 216, 45% full-time, 48% with terminal degrees.

Student/faculty ratio: 13:1.

ACADEMICS

Calendar: semesters. *Degrees:* bachelor's, master's, and postbachelor's certificates.

Special study options: academic remediation for entering students, accelerated degree program, adult/continuing education programs, advanced placement credit, cooperative education, distance learning, double majors, English as a second language, freshman honors college, honors programs, independent study, internships, off-campus study, part-time degree program, services for LD students, student-designed majors, study abroad, summer session for credit. ***ROTC:*** Army (c), Air Force (c).

Unusual degree programs: 3-2 engineering with Iowa State University.

Computers: 331 computers/terminals are available on campus for general student use. Students can access the following: campus intranet, computer help desk, free student e-mail accounts, online (class) grades, online (class) registration, online (class) schedules. Campuswide network is available. 100% of college-owned or -operated housing units are wired for high-speed Internet access. Wireless service is available via classrooms, computer labs, libraries, student centers.

STUDENT LIFE

Housing options: on-campus residence required through junior year; coed. Campus housing is university owned. Freshman applicants given priority for college housing.

Activities and organizations: drama/theater group, student-run newspaper, radio and television station, choral group, Nursing Student Association, Art Club, Science Club, Education Club, Business Club.

Athletics Member NAIA. ***Intercollegiate sports:*** baseball M(s), basketball M(s)/W(s), bowling M(s)/W(s), cheerleading W(s), cross-country running M(s)/W(s), football M(s), golf M(s)/W(s), soccer M(s)/W(s), softball W(s), tennis M(s)/W(s), track and field M(s)/W(s), volleyball M(s)/W(s), wrestling M(s). ***Intramural sports:*** basketball M/W, football M/W, soccer M/W, table tennis M/W, ultimate Frisbee M/W, volleyball M/W.

Campus security: 24-hour emergency response devices and patrols, late-night transport/escort service, controlled dormitory access, night security patrols.

Student services: health clinic, personal/psychological counseling.

COSTS & FINANCIAL AID

Costs (2015–16) ***Comprehensive fee:*** $32,320 includes full-time tuition ($23,864), mandatory fees ($590), and room and board ($7866). Full-time tuition and fees vary according to class time and course load. Part-time tuition: $593 per credit hour. Part-time tuition and fees vary according to

class time and course load. ***Room and board:*** Room and board charges vary according to board plan and housing facility. ***Payment plan:*** installment. ***Waivers:*** children of alumni, senior citizens, and employees or children of employees.

Financial Aid Of all full-time matriculated undergraduates who enrolled in 2014, 1,522 applied for aid, 1,361 were judged to have need, 284 had their need fully met. 330 Federal Work-Study jobs (averaging $1386). In 2014, 268 non-need-based awards were made. ***Average percent of need met:*** 74. ***Average financial aid package:*** $17,223. ***Average need-based loan:*** $4470. ***Average need-based gift aid:*** $15,092. ***Average non-need-based aid:*** $8180. ***Average indebtedness upon graduation:*** $38,160.

APPLYING

Standardized Tests *Required:* SAT or ACT (for admission).

Options: electronic application.

Required: high school transcript. ***Recommended:*** minimum 2.0 GPA.

Application deadlines: 8/15 (freshmen), 8/15 (transfers).

Notification: 9/15 (freshmen), continuous until 9/15 (transfers).

CONTACT

Mr. Ryan Thompson, Director of Admissions, Grand View University, 1200 Grandview Avenue, Des Moines, IA 50316-1599. *Phone:* 515-263-2810. *Toll-free phone:* 800-444-6083. *Fax:* 515-263-2974. *E-mail:* admissions@grandview.edu.

See previous page for display ad and page 1462 for the College Close-Up.

Grinnell College

Grinnell, Iowa

http://www.grinnell.edu/

- **Independent** 4-year, founded 1846
- **Small-town** 120-acre campus
- **Endowment** $1.8 billion
- **Coed** 1,734 undergraduate students, 96% full-time, 55% women, 45% men
- **Very difficult** entrance level, 28% of applicants were admitted

UNDERGRAD STUDENTS

1,672 full-time, 62 part-time. Students come from 47 states and territories; 46 other countries; 92% are from out of state; 6% Black or African American, non-Hispanic/Latino; 8% Hispanic/Latino; 7% Asian, non-Hispanic/Latino; 0.2% American Indian or Alaska Native, non-Hispanic/Latino; 4% Two or more races, non-Hispanic/Latino; 4% Race/ethnicity unknown; 13% international; 0.3% transferred in; 82% live on campus.

Freshmen

Admission: 6,058 applied, 1,697 admitted, 435 enrolled. ***Test scores:*** SAT critical reading scores over 500: 98%; SAT math scores over 500: 99%; ACT scores over 18: 100%; SAT critical reading scores over 600: 87%; SAT math scores over 600: 90%; ACT scores over 24: 100%; SAT critical reading scores over 700: 43%; SAT math scores over 700: 53%; ACT scores over 30: 75%.

Retention: 94% of full-time freshmen returned.

FACULTY

Total: 199, 84% full-time, 90% with terminal degrees.

Student/faculty ratio: 9:1.

ACADEMICS

Calendar: semesters. *Degree:* bachelor's.

Special study options: accelerated degree program, advanced placement credit, double majors, independent study, internships, off-campus study, services for LD students, student-designed majors, study abroad.

Unusual degree programs: 3-2 engineering with Columbia University, California Institute of Technology, Rensselaer Polytechnic Institute, Washington University in St. Louis; Architecture with Washington University in St. Louis, Law at Columbia University.

Computers: 200 computers/terminals are available on campus for general student use. Students can access the following: campus intranet, computer help desk, free student e-mail accounts, online (class) grades, online (class) registration, online (class) schedules. Campuswide network is available. 100% of college-owned or -operated housing units are wired for high-speed Internet access. Wireless service is available via entire campus.

STUDENT LIFE

Housing options: on-campus residence required through sophomore year; coed, cooperative, special housing for students with disabilities. Campus housing is university owned. Freshman campus housing is guaranteed.

Activities and organizations: drama/theater group, student-run newspaper, radio station, choral group, Concerned Black Students, International Student Organization, Student Organization of Latinas/Latinos, Campus Democrats, Ultimate Frisbee.

Athletics Member NCAA. All Division III. ***Intercollegiate sports:*** baseball M, basketball M/W, cross-country running M/W, football M, golf M/W, soccer M/W, softball W, swimming and diving M/W, tennis M/W, track and field M/W, volleyball W. ***Intramural sports:*** archery M(c)/W(c), badminton M/W, baseball M(c)/W(c), basketball M/W, equestrian sports M(c)/W(c), fencing M(c)/W(c), rugby M(c)/W(c), sailing M(c)/W(c), soccer M/W, softball M/W, tennis M/W, ultimate Frisbee M(c)/W, volleyball M/W, water polo M/W.

Campus security: 24-hour emergency response devices and patrols, student patrols, late-night transport/escort service, controlled dormitory access.

Student services: health clinic, personal/psychological counseling.

COSTS & FINANCIAL AID

Costs (2014–15) ***Comprehensive fee:*** $57,020 includes full-time tuition ($45,620), mandatory fees ($403), and room and board ($10,997). Part-time tuition: $1413 per credit hour. ***College room only:*** $5152. Room and board charges vary according to board plan and housing facility. ***Payment plan:*** installment. ***Waivers:*** employees or children of employees.

Financial Aid Of all full-time matriculated undergraduates who enrolled in 2014, 1,263 applied for aid, 1,172 were judged to have need, 1,172 had their need fully met. 711 Federal Work-Study jobs (averaging $1863). 390 state and other part-time jobs (averaging $2141). In 2014, 255 non-need-based awards were made. ***Average percent of need met:*** 100. ***Average financial aid package:*** $43,287. ***Average need-based loan:*** $3894. ***Average need-based gift aid:*** $37,153. ***Average non-need-based aid:*** $16,968. ***Average indebtedness upon graduation:*** $16,315. ***Financial aid deadline:*** 2/1.

APPLYING

Standardized Tests *Required:* SAT or ACT (for admission).

Options: electronic application, early admission, early decision, deferred entrance.

Required: essay or personal statement, high school transcript, 3 letters of recommendation. ***Recommended:*** interview.

Application deadlines: 1/15 (freshmen), 4/1 (transfers).

Early decision deadline: 11/15 (for plan 1), 1/1 (for plan 2).

Notification: 4/1 (freshmen), 5/20 (transfers), 12/15 (early decision plan 1), 2/1 (early decision plan 2).

CONTACT

Mr. Gregory Sneed, Director of Admission, Grinnell College, 1103 Park Street, Grinnell, IA 50112. *Phone:* 641-269-3600. *Toll-free phone:* 800-247-0113. *Fax:* 641-269-4800. *E-mail:* askgrin@grinnell.edu.

Iowa State University of Science and Technology

Ames, Iowa

http://www.iastate.edu/

- **State-supported** university, founded 1858
- **Suburban** 1795-acre campus with easy access to Des Moines
- **Endowment** $777.0 million
- **Coed** 28,893 undergraduate students, 95% full-time, 43% women, 57% men
- **Moderately difficult** entrance level, 87% of applicants were admitted

UNDERGRAD STUDENTS

27,436 full-time, 1,457 part-time. Students come from 53 states and territories; 110 other countries; 28% are from out of state; 3% Black or African American, non-Hispanic/Latino; 4% Hispanic/Latino; 3% Asian, non-Hispanic/Latino; 0.1% Native Hawaiian or other Pacific Islander, non-Hispanic/Latino; 0.2% American Indian or Alaska Native, non-

Hispanic/Latino; 2% Two or more races, non-Hispanic/Latino; 4% Race/ethnicity unknown; 8% international; 7% transferred in; 33% live on campus.

Freshmen

Admission: 18,399 applied, 15,990 admitted, 6,041 enrolled. ***Average high school GPA:*** 3.57. ***Test scores:*** SAT critical reading scores over 500: 65%; SAT math scores over 500: 85%; ACT scores over 18: 97%; SAT critical reading scores over 600: 32%; SAT math scores over 600: 60%; ACT scores over 24: 62%; SAT critical reading scores over 700: 9%; SAT math scores over 700: 18%; ACT scores over 30: 15%.

Retention: 86% of full-time freshmen returned.

FACULTY

Total: 1,802, 84% full-time, 87% with terminal degrees.

Student/faculty ratio: 19:1.

ACADEMICS

Calendar: semesters. *Degrees:* bachelor's, master's, doctoral, post-master's, and postbachelor's certificates.

Special study options: academic remediation for entering students, accelerated degree program, adult/continuing education programs, advanced placement credit, cooperative education, distance learning, double majors, English as a second language, external degree program, freshman honors college, honors programs, independent study, internships, off-campus study, part-time degree program, services for LD students, student-designed majors, study abroad, summer session for credit. ***ROTC:*** Army (b), Navy (b), Air Force (b).

Unusual degree programs: 3-2 engineering with William Penn College.

Computers: 2,400 computers/terminals are available on campus for general student use. Students can access the following: campus intranet, computer help desk, free student e-mail accounts, online (class) grades, online (class) registration, online (class) schedules, network services. Campuswide network is available. 100% of college-owned or -operated housing units are wired for high-speed Internet access. Wireless service is available via entire campus.

STUDENT LIFE

Housing options: coed, men-only, women-only, special housing for students with disabilities. Campus housing is university owned. Freshman applicants given priority for college housing.

Activities and organizations: drama/theater group, student-run newspaper, radio and television station, choral group, marching band, Student Government, Student Alumni Association, Residence Hall Associations, national fraternities, national sororities.

Athletics Member NCAA. All Division I except football (Division I-A). ***Intercollegiate sports:*** basketball M(s)/W(s), cross-country running M(s)/W(s), golf M(s)/W(s), gymnastics W(s), soccer W(s), softball W(s), swimming and diving M(s)/W(s), tennis W(s), track and field M(s)/W(s), volleyball W(s), wrestling M(s). ***Intramural sports:*** archery M(c)/W(c), badminton M(c)/W(c), basketball M/W, bowling M(c)/W(c), cross-country running M/W, equestrian sports M(c)/W(c), fencing M(c)/W(c), football M/W, golf M/W, ice hockey M(c)/W(c), lacrosse M(c)/W(c), racquetball M(c)/W(c), riflery M(c)/W(c), rugby M(c)/W(c), sailing M(c)/W(c), skiing (cross-country) M(c)/W(c), skiing (downhill) M(c)/W(c), soccer M(c)/W(c), softball M/W, squash M/W, swimming and diving M/W, table tennis M(c)/W(c), tennis M/W, volleyball M(c)/W(c), water polo M(c)/W(c), weight lifting M(c)/W(c), wrestling M/W.

Campus security: 24-hour emergency response devices and patrols, student patrols, late-night transport/escort service, controlled dormitory access, crime prevention programs, threat assessment team, motor vehicle help van.

Student services: health clinic, personal/psychological counseling, women's center, legal services.

COSTS & FINANCIAL AID

Costs (2015–16) ***Tuition:*** state resident $6648 full-time, $277 per semester hour part-time; nonresident $19,768 full-time, $824 per semester hour part-time. Full-time tuition and fees vary according to class time, degree level, and program. Part-time tuition and fees vary according to class time, course load, degree level, and program. ***Required fees:*** $1088 full-time. ***Room and board:*** $8070; room only: $4279. Room and board charges vary according to board plan and housing facility. ***Payment plans:*** installment, deferred payment.

Financial Aid Of all full-time matriculated undergraduates who enrolled in 2013, 19,967 applied for aid, 13,671 were judged to have need, 4,596 had their need fully met. In 2013, 8071 non-need-based awards were made. ***Average percent of need met:*** 80. ***Average financial aid package:*** $11,793. ***Average need-based loan:*** $4420. ***Average need-based gift aid:*** $6814. ***Average non-need-based aid:*** $2916. ***Average indebtedness upon graduation:*** $28,880.

APPLYING

Standardized Tests *Required:* SAT or ACT (for admission).

Options: electronic application, early admission, deferred entrance.

Application fee: $40.

Required: high school transcript, Regent Admission Index (RAI) of at least 245 and meet minimum HS course requirements.

Application deadlines: rolling (freshmen), rolling (transfers).

Notification: continuous (freshmen), continuous (transfers).

CONTACT

Mr. Phillip B Caffrey, Associate Director for Freshman Admissions, Iowa State University of Science and Technology, 100 Enrollment Services Center, Ames, IA 50011-2010. *Phone:* 515-294-5836. *Toll-free phone:* 800-262-3810. *Fax:* 515-294-2592. *E-mail:* admissions@iastate.edu.

Iowa Wesleyan College

Mount Pleasant, Iowa

http://www.iwc.edu/

- **Independent United Methodist** 4-year, founded 1842
- **Small-town** 60-acre campus
- **Endowment** $12.7 million
- **Coed** 473 undergraduate students, 82% full-time, 60% women, 40% men
- **Moderately difficult** entrance level, 41% of applicants were admitted

UNDERGRAD STUDENTS

386 full-time, 87 part-time. Students come from 26 states and territories; 2 other countries; 36% are from out of state; 6% Black or African American, non-Hispanic/Latino; 4% Hispanic/Latino; 1% Asian, non-Hispanic/Latino; 0.2% Native Hawaiian or other Pacific Islander, non-Hispanic/Latino; 0.8% American Indian or Alaska Native, non-Hispanic/Latino; 2% Two or more races, non-Hispanic/Latino; 21% Race/ethnicity unknown; 5% international; 11% transferred in; 68% live on campus.

Freshmen

Admission: 1,696 applied, 700 admitted, 75 enrolled. ***Average high school GPA:*** 3.02. ***Test scores:*** SAT critical reading scores over 500: 40%; SAT math scores over 500: 80%; SAT writing scores over 500: 80%; ACT scores over 18: 87%; SAT critical reading scores over 600: 20%; SAT math scores over 600: 20%; ACT scores over 24: 27%.

Retention: 58% of full-time freshmen returned.

FACULTY

Total: 84, 43% full-time, 25% with terminal degrees.

Student/faculty ratio: 10:1.

ACADEMICS

Calendar: semesters. *Degree:* bachelor's.

Special study options: academic remediation for entering students, adult/continuing education programs, advanced placement credit, cooperative education, distance learning, double majors, honors programs, independent study, internships, off-campus study, part-time degree program, services for LD students, student-designed majors, study abroad, summer session for credit.

Unusual degree programs: 3-2 Medical technology program with St. Luke's Hospital in Cedar Rapids, IA.

Computers: 97 computers/terminals are available on campus for general student use. Students can access the following: campus intranet, computer help desk, free student e-mail accounts, online (class) grades, online (class) schedules. Campuswide network is available. 100% of college-owned or -operated housing units are wired for high-speed Internet access. Wireless service is available via entire campus.

STUDENT LIFE

Housing options: on-campus residence required through senior year; coed, men-only, women-only. Campus housing is university owned. Freshman campus housing is guaranteed.

Activities and organizations: choral group, Student Union Board, Student Government Association, Behavioral Science Club, Student Nurses Association, Homecoming Committee.

Athletics Member NCAA. All Division III. ***Intercollegiate sports:*** baseball M, basketball M/W, football M, golf M/W, soccer M/W, softball W, volleyball W. ***Intramural sports:*** badminton M/W, basketball M/W, cheerleading M/W, football M/W, soccer M/W, softball M/W, table tennis M/W, tennis M/W, volleyball M/W, weight lifting M/W.

Campus security: late-night transport/escort service, controlled dormitory access, evening patrols by trained security personnel.

Student services: personal/psychological counseling.

COSTS & FINANCIAL AID

Costs (2015–16) ***Comprehensive fee:*** $36,862 includes full-time tuition ($26,806), mandatory fees ($480), and room and board ($9576). Part-time tuition: $675 per credit hour. Part-time tuition and fees vary according to class time, course load, and location. ***Required fees:*** $20 per credit hour part-time. ***College room only:*** $3644. Room and board charges vary according to housing facility. ***Payment plans:*** installment, deferred payment. ***Waivers:*** employees or children of employees.

Financial Aid Of all full-time matriculated undergraduates who enrolled in 2013, 423 applied for aid, 399 were judged to have need, 58 had their need fully met. 115 Federal Work-Study jobs (averaging $2000). In 2013, 59 non-need-based awards were made. ***Average percent of need met:*** 68. ***Average financial aid package:*** $19,292. ***Average need-based loan:*** $4016. ***Average need-based gift aid:*** $15,275. ***Average non-need-based aid:*** $11,362. ***Average indebtedness upon graduation:*** $36,797.

APPLYING

Standardized Tests *Required:* SAT or ACT (for admission).

Options: electronic application, early admission, deferred entrance.

Application fee: $20.

Required: high school transcript, minimum 2.5 GPA, minimum ACT score of 19 or SAT of 890. ***Required for some:*** essay or personal statement, 1 letter of recommendation, interview.

Application deadlines: 8/15 (freshmen), 8/15 (transfers).

CONTACT

Scott A. Briell, Senior Vice President for Enrollment and Communications, Iowa Wesleyan College, 601 N Main Street, Mount Pleasant, IA 52641. *Phone:* 319-385-6231. *Toll-free phone:* 800-582-2383. *Fax:* 319-385-6240. *E-mail:* scott.briell@iwc.edu.

ITT Technical Institute

Clive, Iowa

http://www.itt-tech.edu/

- **Proprietary** primarily 2-year, part of ITT Educational Services, Inc.
- **Coed**
- **Minimally difficult** entrance level

ACADEMICS

Degrees: associate and bachelor's.

STUDENT LIFE

Housing options: college housing not available.

CONTACT

Director of Recruitment, ITT Technical Institute, 1860 Northwest 118th Street, Suite 110, Clive, IA 50325. *Phone:* 515-327-5500. *Toll-free phone:* 877-526-7312.

Loras College

Dubuque, Iowa

http://www.loras.edu/

- **Independent Roman Catholic** comprehensive, founded 1839
- **Suburban** 64-acre campus
- **Endowment** $29.2 million
- **Coed** 1,490 undergraduate students, 97% full-time, 48% women, 52% men
- **Moderately difficult** entrance level, 95% of applicants were admitted

UNDERGRAD STUDENTS

1,446 full-time, 44 part-time. Students come from 24 states and territories; 10 other countries; 63% are from out of state; 3% Black or African American, non-Hispanic/Latino; 6% Hispanic/Latino; 0.8% Asian, non-Hispanic/Latino; 0.1% Native Hawaiian or other Pacific Islander, non-Hispanic/Latino; 0.1% American Indian or Alaska Native, non-Hispanic/Latino; 1% Two or more races, non-Hispanic/Latino; 3% Race/ethnicity unknown; 2% international; 4% transferred in; 68% live on campus.

Freshmen

Admission: 1,293 applied, 1,230 admitted, 374 enrolled. ***Average high school GPA:*** 3.37. ***Test scores:*** SAT critical reading scores over 500: 45%; SAT math scores over 500: 56%; ACT scores over 18: 98%; SAT math scores over 600: 22%; ACT scores over 24: 47%; ACT scores over 30: 4%.

Retention: 81% of full-time freshmen returned.

FACULTY

Total: 153, 72% full-time, 74% with terminal degrees.

Student/faculty ratio: 12:1.

ACADEMICS

Calendar: semesters. *Degrees:* associate, bachelor's, and master's.

Special study options: academic remediation for entering students, advanced placement credit, cooperative education, distance learning, double majors, honors programs, independent study, internships, off-campus study, part-time degree program, services for LD students, student-designed majors, study abroad, summer session for credit. ***ROTC:*** Army (c).

Unusual degree programs: 3-2 nursing with Allen College of Nursing; PharmD with Creighton College (3+4 plan).

Computers: 20 computers/terminals and 991 ports are available on campus for general student use. Students can access the following: campus intranet, computer help desk, free student e-mail accounts, online (class) grades, online (class) registration, online (class) schedules. Campuswide network is available. 100% of college-owned or -operated housing units are wired for high-speed Internet access. Wireless service is available via entire campus.

STUDENT LIFE

Housing options: on-campus residence required through junior year; coed, men-only, women-only. Campus housing is university owned. Freshman campus housing is guaranteed.

Activities and organizations: drama/theater group, student-run newspaper, radio and television station, choral group, Dance Marathon, College Activities Board, Student Union, Social Work Club, Alpha Sigma Alpha, national fraternities, national sororities.

Athletics Member NCAA. All Division III. ***Intercollegiate sports:*** baseball M, basketball M/W, cheerleading M(c)/W(c), cross-country running M/W, football M, golf M/W, ice hockey M(c)/W(c), lacrosse W, rugby M(c)/W(c), soccer M/W, softball W, swimming and diving M/W, tennis M/W, track and field M/W, ultimate Frisbee M(c)/W(c), volleyball M/W, wrestling M. ***Intramural sports:*** badminton M/W, basketball M/W, cheerleading M/W, football M/W, golf M/W, lacrosse M/W, racquetball M/W, soccer M/W, softball M/W, table tennis M/W, tennis M/W, track and field M/W, volleyball M/W.

Campus security: 24-hour emergency response devices and patrols, student patrols, late-night transport/escort service, controlled dormitory access, online anonymous reporting system.

Student services: health clinic, personal/psychological counseling.

COSTS & FINANCIAL AID

Costs (2014–15) ***Comprehensive fee:*** $38,082 includes full-time tuition ($28,340), mandatory fees ($1389), and room and board ($8353). Full-time tuition and fees vary according to course load and degree level. Part-time tuition: $590 per credit. ***Required fees:*** $25 per credit part-time. ***College room only:*** $3953. Room and board charges vary according to board plan and housing facility. ***Payment plan:*** installment. ***Waivers:*** employees or children of employees.

Financial Aid Of all full-time matriculated undergraduates who enrolled in 2014, 1,251 applied for aid, 1,094 were judged to have need, 856 had their need fully met. 600 Federal Work-Study jobs (averaging $1932). 177 state and other part-time jobs (averaging $1951). In 2014, 389 non-need-based awards were made. ***Average percent of need met:*** 84. ***Average financial aid package:*** $20,971. ***Average need-based loan:*** $4580. ***Average need-based gift aid:*** $17,647. ***Average non-need-based aid:*** $15,082. ***Average indebtedness upon graduation:*** $34,514.

APPLYING

Standardized Tests *Required:* SAT or ACT (for admission). *Recommended:* ACT (for admission).

Options: electronic application, deferred entrance.

Application fee: $25.

Required: high school transcript, minimum 2.5 GPA. ***Recommended:*** essay or personal statement, 1 letter of recommendation.

Application deadlines: rolling (freshmen), rolling (out-of-state freshmen), rolling (transfers).

Notification: continuous (freshmen), continuous (out-of-state freshmen), continuous (transfers).

CONTACT

Dr. Jason L. Woods, Dean of Admissions, Loras College, 1450 Alta Vista, Dubuque, IA 52004-0178. *Phone:* 800-245-6727. *Toll-free phone:* 800-245-6727. *Fax:* 563-588-7119. *E-mail:* admissions@loras.edu.

★ Luther College

Decorah, Iowa

http://www.luther.edu/

- **Independent** 4-year, founded 1861, affiliated with Evangelical Lutheran Church in America
- **Small-town** 200-acre campus
- **Endowment** $147.1 million
- **Coed** 2,385 undergraduate students, 98% full-time, 56% women, 44% men
- **Moderately difficult** entrance level, 71% of applicants were admitted

UNDERGRAD STUDENTS

2,339 full-time, 46 part-time. Students come from 40 states and territories; 61 other countries; 67% are from out of state; 1% Black or African American, non-Hispanic/Latino; 3% Hispanic/Latino; 2% Asian, non-Hispanic/Latino; 0.3% American Indian or Alaska Native, non-Hispanic/Latino; 2% Two or more races, non-Hispanic/Latino; 0.6% Race/ethnicity unknown; 6% international; 2% transferred in; 85% live on campus.

Freshmen

Admission: 3,440 applied, 2,448 admitted, 559 enrolled. ***Average high school GPA:*** 3.71. ***Test scores:*** SAT critical reading scores over 500: 62%; SAT math scores over 500: 80%; SAT writing scores over 500: 58%; ACT scores over 18: 100%; SAT critical reading scores over 600: 31%; SAT math scores over 600: 43%; SAT writing scores over 600: 26%; ACT scores over 24: 73%; SAT critical reading scores over 700: 9%; SAT math scores over 700: 11%; SAT writing scores over 700: 9%; ACT scores over 30: 15%.

Retention: 85% of full-time freshmen returned.

FACULTY

Total: 246, 73% full-time, 77% with terminal degrees.

Student/faculty ratio: 12:1.

ACADEMICS

Calendar: 4-1-4. *Degree:* bachelor's.

Special study options: academic remediation for entering students, advanced placement credit, double majors, honors programs, independent study, internships, off-campus study, part-time degree program, services for LD students, student-designed majors, study abroad, summer session for credit.

Unusual degree programs: 3-2 engineering with Washington University in St. Louis; University of Minnesota, Twin Cities Campus.

Computers: 592 computers/terminals are available on campus for general student use. Students can access the following: campus intranet, computer help desk, free student e-mail accounts, online (class) grades, online (class) registration, online (class) schedules. Campuswide network is available. 100% of college-owned or -operated housing units are wired for high-speed Internet access. Wireless service is available via entire campus.

STUDENT LIFE

Housing options: on-campus residence required through senior year; coed, special housing for students with disabilities. Campus housing is university owned. Freshman campus housing is guaranteed.

Activities and organizations: drama/theater group, student-run newspaper, radio station, choral group, Alpha Phi Omega, college ministries, recreational sports, Student Activities Council, Diversity groups.

Athletics Member NCAA. All Division III. ***Intercollegiate sports:*** baseball M, basketball M/W, cross-country running M/W, football M, golf M/W, soccer M/W, softball W, swimming and diving M/W, tennis M/W, track and field M/W, ultimate Frisbee M(c)/W(c), volleyball W, wrestling M. ***Intramural sports:*** archery M/W, badminton M/W, basketball M/W, bowling M/W, football M/W, golf M/W, lacrosse W(c), racquetball M/W, rugby M(c)/W(c), soccer M/W, softball M/W, table tennis M/W, tennis M/W, track and field M/W, ultimate Frisbee M(c)/W(c), volleyball M/W.

Campus security: 24-hour emergency response devices and patrols, late-night transport/escort service, controlled dormitory access.

Student services: health clinic, personal/psychological counseling, women's center.

COSTS & FINANCIAL AID

Costs (2015–16) ***Comprehensive fee:*** $47,110 includes full-time tuition ($38,940), mandatory fees ($250), and room and board ($7920). Full-time tuition and fees vary according to course load. Part-time tuition: $1392 per credit hour. Part-time tuition and fees vary according to course load. ***College room only:*** $3570. Room and board charges vary according to board plan and housing facility. ***Payment plan:*** installment. ***Waivers:*** employees or children of employees.

Financial Aid Of all full-time matriculated undergraduates who enrolled in 2014, 1,882 applied for aid, 1,604 were judged to have need, 428 had their need fully met. 1,014 Federal Work-Study jobs (averaging $2046). 1,071 state and other part-time jobs (averaging $1960). In 2014, 259 non-need-based awards were made. ***Average percent of need met:*** 86. ***Average financial aid package:*** $30,365. ***Average need-based loan:*** $5017. ***Average need-based gift aid:*** $22,197. ***Average non-need-based aid:*** $16,062. ***Average indebtedness upon graduation:*** $36,918.

APPLYING

Standardized Tests *Required:* SAT or ACT (for admission).

Options: electronic application, deferred entrance.

Required: essay or personal statement, high school transcript, 1 letter of recommendation. ***Recommended:*** interview.

Notification: continuous (freshmen), continuous (transfers).

CONTACT

Mr. Kirk Neubauer, Director of Recruiting Services, Luther College, 700 College Drive, Decorah, IA 52101. *Phone:* 563-387-1287. *Toll-free phone:* 800-458-8437. *Fax:* 563-387-2159. *E-mail:* neubauki@luther.edu.

See previous page for display ad and page 1508 for the College Close-Up.

Maharishi University of Management

Fairfield, Iowa

http://www.mum.edu/

- **Independent** university, founded 1971
- **Small-town** campus
- **Coed** 287 undergraduate students, 97% full-time, 46% women, 54% men
- **Moderately difficult** entrance level, 38% of applicants were admitted

UNDERGRAD STUDENTS

278 full-time, 9 part-time. 82% are from out of state; 13% Black or African American, non-Hispanic/Latino; 12% Hispanic/Latino; 5% Asian, non-Hispanic/Latino; 0.7% American Indian or Alaska Native, non-Hispanic/Latino; 5% Two or more races, non-Hispanic/Latino; 0.7% Race/ethnicity unknown; 13% international; 18% transferred in; 49% live on campus.

Freshmen

Admission: 63 applied, 24 admitted, 21 enrolled. ***Average high school GPA:*** 3.19.

Retention: 72% of full-time freshmen returned.

FACULTY

Total: 139, 54% full-time, 61% with terminal degrees.

Student/faculty ratio: 11:1.

ACADEMICS

Calendar: semesters. *Degrees:* bachelor's, master's, doctoral, post-master's, and postbachelor's certificates.

Special study options: adult/continuing education programs.

Computers: Students can access the following: campus intranet, computer help desk, free student e-mail accounts, online (class) grades, online (class) schedules. Campuswide network is available. 100% of college-owned or -operated housing units are wired for high-speed Internet access.

STUDENT LIFE

Housing options: on-campus residence required through senior year; men-only, women-only. Campus housing is university owned. Freshman campus housing is guaranteed.

Athletics ***Intercollegiate sports:*** soccer M(c)/W(c), ultimate Frisbee M(c)/W(c), volleyball M(c)/W(c). ***Intramural sports:*** archery M/W, badminton M/W, basketball M/W, football M/W, gymnastics M/W, rock climbing M/W, sailing M/W, soccer M/W, table tennis M/W, tennis M/W, ultimate Frisbee M/W, volleyball M/W.

Campus security: 24-hour emergency response devices and patrols, late-night transport/escort service, controlled dormitory access.

COSTS & FINANCIAL AID

Costs (2015–16) ***Comprehensive fee:*** $33,930 includes full-time tuition ($26,000), mandatory fees ($530), and room and board ($7400).

Financial Aid Of all full-time matriculated undergraduates who enrolled in 2006, 150 applied for aid, 148 were judged to have need, 32 had their need fully met. 120 Federal Work-Study jobs (averaging $1422). 7 state and other part-time jobs (averaging $2729). In 2006, 5 non-need-based awards were made. ***Average percent of need met:*** 89. ***Average financial aid package:*** $23,963. ***Average need-based loan:*** $8281. ***Average need-based gift aid:*** $14,082. ***Average non-need-based aid:*** $9300. ***Average indebtedness upon graduation:*** $22,691.

APPLYING

Options: electronic application, early admission, deferred entrance.

Application fee: $25.

Required: essay or personal statement, high school transcript, minimum 2.5 GPA, 2 letters of recommendation. ***Recommended:*** interview.

CONTACT

Maharishi University of Management, Office of Admissions, Fairfield, IA 52557. *Phone:* 641-472-1110. *Toll-free phone:* 800-369-6480. *Fax:* 641-472-1179. *E-mail:* admissions@mum.edu.

Mercy College of Health Sciences

Des Moines, Iowa

http://www.mchs.edu/

- **Independent** 4-year, founded 1995, affiliated with Roman Catholic Church
- **Urban** 5-acre campus
- **Endowment** $3.4 million
- **Coed** 774 undergraduate students, 48% full-time, 88% women, 12% men

UNDERGRAD STUDENTS
373 full-time, 401 part-time. Students come from 14 states and territories; 4% are from out of state; 5% Black or African American, non-Hispanic/Latino; 2% Hispanic/Latino; 3% Asian, non-Hispanic/Latino; 0.3% American Indian or Alaska Native, non-Hispanic/Latino; 0.4% Two or more races, non-Hispanic/Latino; 1% Race/ethnicity unknown; 86% transferred in.

Freshmen
Admission: 46 enrolled. ***Test scores:*** ACT scores over 18: 85%; ACT scores over 24: 24%.

FACULTY
Total: 111, 40% full-time, 14% with terminal degrees.

Student/faculty ratio: 8:1.

ACADEMICS
Calendar: semesters. *Degrees:* certificates, associate, and bachelor's.

Special study options: academic remediation for entering students, accelerated degree program, adult/continuing education programs, advanced placement credit, distance learning, English as a second language, independent study, off-campus study, part-time degree program, services for LD students, study abroad, summer session for credit.

Computers: 46 computers/terminals are available on campus for general student use. Students can access the following: campus intranet, computer help desk, free student e-mail accounts, online (class) grades, online (class) registration, online (class) schedules. Campuswide network is available. Wireless service is available via classrooms, computer centers, computer labs, libraries.

STUDENT LIFE
Housing options: college housing not available.

Activities and organizations: student senate, Campus Ministry, Science Club, Mercy College Association of Nursing Students, Zeta Chi—At Large Chapter.

Campus security: 24-hour emergency response devices and patrols, late-night transport/escort service.

Student services: personal/psychological counseling.

COSTS
Costs (2014–15) ***Tuition:*** $15,642 full-time, $541 per credit hour part-time. Full-time tuition and fees vary according to program. Part-time tuition and fees vary according to course load. ***Payment plan:*** installment.

APPLYING
Standardized Tests *Required for some:* ACT (for admission).

Required: high school transcript, minimum 2.3 GPA. ***Required for some:*** interview.

CONTACT
Melinda Tingle-Williams, Director of Admissions, Mercy College of Health Sciences, 921 Sixth Avenue, Des Moines, IA 50309-1200. *Phone:* 515-643-6604. *Toll-free phone:* 800-637-2994. *Fax:* 515-643-6698. *E-mail:* mtingle-williams@mercydesmoines.org.

Morningside College

Sioux City, Iowa

http://www.morningside.edu/

- **Independent** comprehensive, founded 1894, affiliated with United Methodist Church
- **Suburban** 69-acre campus
- **Endowment** $46.6 million
- **Coed** 1,321 undergraduate students, 97% full-time, 52% women, 48% men
- **Moderately difficult** entrance level, 57% of applicants were admitted

UNDERGRAD STUDENTS
1,279 full-time, 42 part-time. Students come from 27 states and territories; 8 other countries; 35% are from out of state; 2% Black or African American, non-Hispanic/Latino; 6% Hispanic/Latino; 0.7% Asian, non-Hispanic/Latino; 0.2% Native Hawaiian or other Pacific Islander, non-Hispanic/Latino; 0.6% American Indian or Alaska Native, non-Hispanic/Latino; 2% Two or more races, non-Hispanic/Latino; 3% Race/ethnicity unknown; 2% international; 6% transferred in; 62% live on campus.

Freshmen
Admission: 4,150 applied, 2,358 admitted, 353 enrolled. ***Average high school GPA:*** 3.45. ***Test scores:*** ACT scores over 18: 95%; ACT scores over 24: 44%; ACT scores over 30: 7%.

Retention: 75% of full-time freshmen returned.

FACULTY
Total: 237, 35% full-time, 40% with terminal degrees.

Student/faculty ratio: 13:1.

ACADEMICS
Calendar: semesters. *Degrees:* bachelor's and master's.

Special study options: academic remediation for entering students, adult/continuing education programs, advanced placement credit, distance learning, double majors, English as a second language, honors programs, independent study, internships, off-campus study, part-time degree program, services for LD students, student-designed majors, study abroad, summer session for credit. ***ROTC:*** Army (c).

Computers: 150 computers/terminals are available on campus for general student use. Students can access the following: campus intranet, computer help desk, free student e-mail accounts, online (class) grades, online (class) registration, online (class) schedules, academic and financial records. Campuswide network is available. 100% of college-owned or -operated housing units are wired for high-speed Internet access. Wireless service is available via entire campus.

STUDENT LIFE
Housing options: on-campus residence required through junior year; coed. Campus housing is university owned. Freshman campus housing is guaranteed.

Activities and organizations: drama/theater group, student-run newspaper, radio and television station, choral group, Student Government/Activities Council, Student Ambassadors, Homecoming Committee, national fraternities, national sororities.

Athletics Member NCAA, NAIA. All NCAA Division II. ***Intercollegiate sports:*** baseball M(s), basketball M(s)/W(s), bowling M/W, cross-country running M(s)/W(s), football M(s), golf M(s)/W(s), soccer M(s)/W(s), softball W(s), swimming and diving M(s)/W(s), tennis M(s)/W(s), track and field M(s)/W(s), volleyball W(s), wrestling M(s). ***Intramural sports:*** basketball M/W, bowling M/W, ultimate Frisbee M/W, volleyball M/W.

Campus security: 24-hour emergency response devices and patrols, student patrols, late-night transport/escort service, controlled dormitory access.

Student services: health clinic, personal/psychological counseling, women's center.

COSTS & FINANCIAL AID
Costs (2014–15) ***Comprehensive fee:*** $35,430 includes full-time tuition ($25,710), mandatory fees ($1470), and room and board ($8250). Full-time tuition and fees vary according to program. Part-time tuition: $820 per credit hour. Part-time tuition and fees vary according to course load and program. ***College room only:*** $4220. Room and board charges vary according to housing facility. ***Payment plan:*** installment. ***Waivers:*** children of alumni, senior citizens, and employees or children of employees.

Financial Aid Of all full-time matriculated undergraduates who enrolled in 2014, 1,190 applied for aid, 1,076 were judged to have need, 366 had their need fully met. 560 Federal Work-Study jobs (averaging $1112). 310 state and other part-time jobs (averaging $1862). In 2014, 249 non-need-based awards were made. ***Average percent of need met:*** 80. ***Average financial aid package:*** $21,392. ***Average need-based loan:*** $4609. ***Average need-based gift aid:*** $6562. ***Average non-need-based aid:*** $8821. ***Average indebtedness upon graduation:*** $34,667.

APPLYING
Standardized Tests *Required:* SAT or ACT (for admission).

Options: electronic application, deferred entrance.

Required: high school transcript, 20 ACT/1410 SAT and either rank in top half of class or 2.5 GPA. ***Recommended:*** minimum 2.5 GPA, interview.

Application deadlines: rolling (freshmen), rolling (out-of-state freshmen), rolling (transfers).

Notification: continuous (freshmen), continuous (out-of-state freshmen), continuous (transfers).

CONTACT
Mrs. Stephanie Peters, Director of Admissions, Morningside College, 1501 Morningside Avenue, Sioux City, IA 51106. *Phone:* 712-274-5111. *Toll-free phone:* 800-831-0806 Ext. 5111. *Fax:* 712-274-5101. *E-mail:* mscadm@morningside.edu.

See previous page for display ad and page 1534 for the College Close-Up.

Mount Mercy University
Cedar Rapids, Iowa
http://www.mtmercy.edu/

- **Independent Roman Catholic** comprehensive, founded 1928
- **Suburban** 40-acre campus with easy access to Iowa City
- **Endowment** $26.4 million
- **Coed** 1,444 undergraduate students, 59% full-time, 70% women, 30% men
- **Moderately difficult** entrance level, 57% of applicants were admitted

UNDERGRAD STUDENTS
858 full-time, 586 part-time. Students come from 19 states and territories; 27 other countries; 4% are from out of state; 4% Black or African American, non-Hispanic/Latino; 1% Hispanic/Latino; 1% Asian, non-Hispanic/Latino; 0.1% Native Hawaiian or other Pacific Islander, non-Hispanic/Latino; 0.3% American Indian or Alaska Native, non-Hispanic/Latino; 2% Two or more races, non-Hispanic/Latino; 4% Race/ethnicity unknown; 3% international; 45% live on campus.

Freshmen
Admission: 695 applied, 395 admitted, 134 enrolled. ***Average high school GPA:*** 3.4. ***Test scores:*** ACT scores over 18: 89%; ACT scores over 24: 33%; ACT scores over 30: 4%.

Retention: 81% of full-time freshmen returned.

FACULTY
Total: 152, 55% full-time, 39% with terminal degrees.

Student/faculty ratio: 14:1.

ACADEMICS
Calendar: 4-1-4. *Degrees:* bachelor's and master's.

Special study options: academic remediation for entering students, accelerated degree program, adult/continuing education programs, advanced placement credit, double majors, honors programs, independent study, internships, off-campus study, part-time degree program, services for LD students, study abroad, summer session for credit.

Computers: 120 computers/terminals and 200 ports are available on campus for general student use. Students can access the following: campus intranet, computer help desk, free student e-mail accounts, online (class) grades, online (class) registration, online (class) schedules. Campuswide network is available. 100% of college-owned or -operated housing units are wired for high-speed Internet access. Wireless service is available via entire campus.

STUDENT LIFE
Housing options: on-campus residence required through sophomore year; coed, men-only, women-only. Campus housing is university owned. Freshman campus housing is guaranteed.

Activities and organizations: drama/theater group, student-run newspaper, choral group, Student Ambassadors, Mount Mercy University Association of Nursing Students, Cheerleaders, Best Buddies, Student Government Association.

Athletics Member NAIA. ***Intercollegiate sports:*** baseball M(s), basketball M(s)/W(s), bowling M/W, cross-country running M(s)/W(s), golf M(s)/W(s), soccer M(s)/W(s), softball W(s), track and field

M(s)/W(s), volleyball W(s). ***Intramural sports:*** baseball M, basketball M/W, bowling M/W, cheerleading W, football M/W, racquetball M/W, tennis M/W, volleyball M/W, weight lifting M/W.

Campus security: 24-hour emergency response devices and patrols, student patrols, late-night transport/escort service, controlled dormitory access, Mount Mercy University Department of Public Safety is operational 24 hours a day, seven days a week.

Student services: health clinic, personal/psychological counseling.

COSTS & FINANCIAL AID
Costs (2015–16) ***Comprehensive fee:*** $36,826 includes full-time tuition ($28,226) and room and board ($8600). Full-time tuition and fees vary according to course load. Part-time tuition: $768 per credit. Part-time tuition and fees vary according to course load. ***Room and board:*** Room and board charges vary according to board plan and housing facility. ***Payment plan:*** installment. ***Waivers:*** employees or children of employees.

Financial Aid Of all full-time matriculated undergraduates who enrolled in 2013, 666 applied for aid, 612 were judged to have need, 96 had their need fully met. 246 Federal Work-Study jobs (averaging $1453). 225 state and other part-time jobs (averaging $998). In 2013, 127 non-need-based awards were made. ***Average percent of need met:*** 71. ***Average financial aid package:*** $19,750. ***Average need-based loan:*** $4127. ***Average need-based gift aid:*** $15,859. ***Average non-need-based aid:*** $11,238. ***Average indebtedness upon graduation:*** $27,442.

APPLYING
Standardized Tests *Required:* SAT or ACT (for admission).

Options: electronic application, deferred entrance.

Required: high school transcript, minimum 2.5 GPA. ***Required for some:*** 1 letter of recommendation.

Application deadlines: 8/15 (freshmen), 8/15 (transfers).

Notification: continuous (freshmen), continuous (transfers).

CONTACT
Ms. Lauren Garcia, Associate Director of Admissions, Mount Mercy University, 1330 Elmhurst Drive, NE, Cedar Rapids, IA 52402. *Phone:* 319-368-6460. *Toll-free phone:* 800-248-4504. *Fax:* 319-363-5270. *E-mail:* lgarcia@mtmercy.edu.

Northwestern College
Orange City, Iowa
http://www.nwciowa.edu/

- **Independent** comprehensive, founded 1882, affiliated with Reformed Church in America
- **Small-town** 100-acre campus
- **Endowment** $46.7 million
- **Coed** 1,205 undergraduate students, 91% full-time, 59% women, 41% men
- **Moderately difficult** entrance level, 78% of applicants were admitted

UNDERGRAD STUDENTS
1,100 full-time, 105 part-time. Students come from 34 states and territories; 23 other countries; 47% are from out of state; 1% Black or African American, non-Hispanic/Latino; 5% Hispanic/Latino; 1% Asian, non-Hispanic/Latino; 0.2% American Indian or Alaska Native, non-Hispanic/Latino; 2% Two or more races, non-Hispanic/Latino; 4% Race/ethnicity unknown; 3% international; 3% transferred in; 89% live on campus.

Freshmen
Admission: 1,254 applied, 976 admitted, 315 enrolled. ***Average high school GPA:*** 3.6. ***Test scores:*** SAT critical reading scores over 500: 67%; SAT math scores over 500: 74%; SAT writing scores over 500: 55%; ACT scores over 18: 98%; SAT critical reading scores over 600: 27%; SAT math scores over 600: 41%; SAT writing scores over 600: 24%; ACT scores over 24: 55%; SAT critical reading scores over 700: 11%; SAT math scores over 700: 5%; SAT writing scores over 700: 3%; ACT scores over 30: 11%.

Retention: 77% of full-time freshmen returned.

FACULTY
Total: 138, 60% full-time, 50% with terminal degrees.

Student/faculty ratio: 11:1.

ACADEMICS
Calendar: semesters. *Degrees:* certificates, bachelor's, master's, and postbachelor's certificates.

Special study options: academic remediation for entering students, advanced placement credit, cooperative education, distance learning, double majors, English as a second language, honors programs, independent study, internships, off-campus study, services for LD students, student-designed majors, study abroad, summer session for credit.

Unusual degree programs: 3-2 engineering with University of Minnesota.

Computers: 250 computers/terminals are available on campus for general student use. Students can access the following: campus intranet, computer help desk, free student e-mail accounts, online (class) grades, online (class) registration, online (class) schedules, online degree audits. Campuswide network is available. 100% of college-owned or -operated housing units are wired for high-speed Internet access. Wireless service is available via entire campus.

STUDENT LIFE
Housing options: on-campus residence required through senior year; men-only, women-only, special housing for students with disabilities. Campus housing is university owned. Freshman campus housing is guaranteed.

Activities and organizations: drama/theater group, student-run newspaper, television station, choral group, Drama Ministries Ensemble, Acappella Choir, Discipleship Groups, Fellowship of Christian Athletes, International Club.

Athletics Member NAIA. ***Intercollegiate sports:*** baseball M(s), basketball M(s)/W(s), cheerleading M(s)/W(s), cross-country running M(s)/W(s), football M(s), golf M(s)/W(s), soccer M(s)/W(s), softball W(s), tennis W(s), track and field M(s)/W(s), volleyball W(s), wrestling M(s). ***Intramural sports:*** badminton M/W, basketball M/W, bowling M/W, football M/W, golf M/W, racquetball M/W, soccer M/W, softball M/W, table tennis M/W, tennis M/W, ultimate Frisbee M/W, volleyball M/W.

Campus security: 24-hour emergency response devices, controlled dormitory access.

Student services: health clinic, personal/psychological counseling.

COSTS & FINANCIAL AID
Costs (2015–16) ***Comprehensive fee:*** $37,800 includes full-time tuition ($28,750), mandatory fees ($300), and room and board ($8750). Part-time tuition: $620 per credit hour. Part-time tuition and fees vary according to course load. ***Required fees:*** $75 per term part-time. ***Room and board:*** Room and board charges vary according to board plan and housing facility. ***Payment plans:*** tuition prepayment, installment. ***Waivers:*** employees or children of employees.

Financial Aid Of all full-time matriculated undergraduates who enrolled in 2007, 997 applied for aid, 997 were judged to have need, 418 had their need fully met. 354 Federal Work-Study jobs (averaging $1120). 412 state and other part-time jobs (averaging $1120). In 2007, 229 non-need-based awards were made. ***Average percent of need met:*** 87. ***Average financial aid package:*** $16,330. ***Average need-based loan:*** $4453. ***Average need-based gift aid:*** $6289. ***Average non-need-based aid:*** $5562. ***Average indebtedness upon graduation:*** $23,817.

APPLYING
Standardized Tests *Required:* SAT or ACT (for admission).

Options: electronic application, early admission, deferred entrance.

Application fee: $25.

Required: essay or personal statement, high school transcript, minimum 2.0 GPA, 1 letter of recommendation. ***Recommended:*** minimum 2.5 GPA, interview.

Application deadlines: rolling (freshmen), rolling (transfers).

Notification: continuous (freshmen), continuous (transfers).

CONTACT
Mr. Kenton Pauls, Dean of Enrollment Management, Northwestern College, 101 7th Street SW, Orange City, IA 51041-1996. *Phone:* 712-737-7130. *Toll-free phone:* 800-747-4757. *Fax:* 712-707-7164. *E-mail:* admissions@nwciowa.edu.

St. Luke's College

Sioux City, Iowa

http://stlukescollege.edu/

- **Independent** primarily 2-year, founded 1967, part of UnityPoint Health - St. Luke's (formerly St. Luke's Regional Medical Center and Iowa Health System)
- **Rural** 3-acre campus with easy access to Omaha
- **Endowment** $1.1 million
- **Coed** 251 undergraduate students, 62% full-time, 88% women, 12% men
- **Minimally difficult** entrance level, 25% of applicants were admitted

UNDERGRAD STUDENTS
156 full-time, 95 part-time. Students come from 19 states and territories; 3 other countries; 41% are from out of state; 4% Black or African American, non-Hispanic/Latino; 6% Hispanic/Latino; 4% Asian, non-Hispanic/Latino; 0.4% Native Hawaiian or other Pacific Islander, non-Hispanic/Latino; 0.4% American Indian or Alaska Native, non-Hispanic/Latino; 2% Two or more races, non-Hispanic/Latino.

Freshmen
Admission: 24 applied, 6 admitted, 5 enrolled. ***Average high school GPA:*** 3.51.

FACULTY
Total: 40, 63% full-time, 10% with terminal degrees.

Student/faculty ratio: 8:1.

ACADEMICS
Calendar: semesters. *Degrees:* certificates, associate, and bachelor's.

Special study options: advanced placement credit, cooperative education, distance learning, summer session for credit.

Computers: 9 computers/terminals are available on campus for general student use. Students can access the following: campus intranet, computer help desk, free student e-mail accounts, online (class) grades, online (class) registration, online (class) schedules. Campuswide network is available. Wireless service is available via entire campus.

STUDENT LIFE
Housing options: college housing not available.

Campus security: 24-hour emergency response devices and patrols, late-night transport/escort service.

Student services: health clinic, personal/psychological counseling.

COSTS & FINANCIAL AID
Costs (2015–16) ***Tuition:*** $18,000 full-time, $500 per credit hour part-time. Full-time tuition and fees vary according to course load, degree level, and program. Part-time tuition and fees vary according to course load, degree level, and program. ***Required fees:*** $1440 full-time. ***Payment plans:*** installment, deferred payment.

Financial Aid Of all full-time matriculated undergraduates who enrolled in 2013, 108 applied for aid, 108 were judged to have need, 5 had their need fully met. 9 Federal Work-Study jobs (averaging $837). 4 state and other part-time jobs (averaging $522). In 2013, 3 non-need-based awards were made. ***Average percent of need met:*** 60. ***Average financial aid package:*** $14,950. ***Average need-based loan:*** $5100. ***Average need-based gift aid:*** $5227. ***Average non-need-based aid:*** $1800. ***Average indebtedness upon graduation:*** $52,799.

APPLYING
Standardized Tests *Required:* SAT or ACT (for admission).

Options: electronic application.

Application fee: $50.

Required: essay or personal statement, high school transcript, minimum 2.5 GPA, interview.

Notification: continuous (transfers).

CONTACT
Ms. Sherry McCarthy, Admissions Coordinator, St. Luke's College, 2800 Pierce St, Sioux City, IA 51104. *Phone:* 712-279-3149. *Toll-free phone:* 800-352-4660 Ext. 3149. *Fax:* 712-233-8017. *E-mail:* sherry.mccarthy@stlukescollege.edu.

Shiloh University

Kalona, Iowa

http://www.shilohuniversity.edu/

- **Independent** comprehensive, founded 2007
- **Small-town** 200-acre campus
- **Coed** 13 undergraduate students, 8% full-time, 54% women, 46% men
- **Noncompetitive** entrance level

UNDERGRAD STUDENTS
1 full-time, 12 part-time. Students come from 5 states and territories; 1 other country; 76% are from out of state; 18% Native Hawaiian or other Pacific Islander, non-Hispanic/Latino; 9% international; 385% transferred in.

Freshmen
Admission: 1 enrolled.

Retention: 100% of full-time freshmen returned.

FACULTY
Total: 23, 9% full-time.

Student/faculty ratio: 1:1.

ACADEMICS
Degrees: certificates, associate, bachelor's, master's, and post-master's certificates.

Special study options: distance learning, off-campus study, part-time degree program, summer session for credit.

COSTS
Costs (2015–16) ***Tuition:*** $4500 full-time, $150 per credit part-time. ***Required fees:*** $10 full-time, $10 per year part-time. ***Payment plan:*** installment.

APPLYING
Standardized Tests *Recommended:* SAT and SAT Subject Tests or ACT (for admission).

Options: electronic application, early admission, deferred entrance.

Required: essay or personal statement, high school transcript, minimum 2.0 GPA.

Application deadlines: 7/6 (freshmen), 6/30 (out-of-state freshmen), 7/6 (transfers).

Notification: 7/20 (freshmen), 7/20 (out-of-state freshmen), 7/20 (transfers).

CONTACT
Andrew R Thompson, Admissions Coordinator, Shiloh University, 100 Shiloh Drive, Kalona, IA 52247. *Phone:* 319-656-2447. *Fax:* 319-656-2448. *E-mail:* admissions@shilohuniversity.edu.

★ Simpson College

Indianola, Iowa

http://www.simpson.edu/

- **Independent United Methodist** comprehensive, founded 1860
- **Suburban** 80-acre campus with easy access to Des Moines
- **Endowment** $85.4 million
- **Coed** 1,660 undergraduate students, 88% full-time, 56% women, 44% men
- **Moderately difficult** entrance level, 85% of applicants were admitted

UNDERGRAD STUDENTS
1,466 full-time, 194 part-time. Students come from 27 states and territories; 8 other countries; 14% are from out of state; 2% Black or African American, non-Hispanic/Latino; 2% Hispanic/Latino; 1% Asian, non-Hispanic/Latino; 0.7% American Indian or Alaska Native, non-Hispanic/Latino; 2% Two or more races, non-Hispanic/Latino; 14% Race/ethnicity unknown; 0.9% international; 4% transferred in; 85% live on campus.

Freshmen
Admission: 1,313 applied, 1,122 admitted, 345 enrolled. ***Test scores:*** ACT scores over 18: 99%; ACT scores over 24: 58%; ACT scores over 30: 12%.

Retention: 82% of full-time freshmen returned.

FACULTY

Total: 188, 51% full-time, 55% with terminal degrees.

Student/faculty ratio: 12:1.

ACADEMICS

Calendar: 4-4-1. *Degrees:* bachelor's, master's, and postbachelor's certificates.

Special study options: accelerated degree program, adult/continuing education programs, advanced placement credit, cooperative education, double majors, independent study, internships, off-campus study, part-time degree program, services for LD students, student-designed majors, study abroad, summer session for credit.

Unusual degree programs: 3-2 engineering with Washington University in St. Louis, MO; Iowa State University in Ames, IA; Institute of Technology (University of Minnesota) in Minneapolis, MN; nursing with Allen College (Waterloo, IA).

Computers: 377 computers/terminals are available on campus for general student use. Students can access the following: campus intranet, computer help desk, free student e-mail accounts, online (class) grades, online (class) registration, online (class) schedules, wireless campus. Campuswide network is available. 100% of college-owned or -operated housing units are wired for high-speed Internet access. Wireless service is available via entire campus.

STUDENT LIFE

Housing options: on-campus residence required through junior year; coed, men-only, women-only. Campus housing is university owned. Freshman campus housing is guaranteed.

Activities and organizations: drama/theater group, student-run newspaper, radio station, choral group, Religious Life Community, Campus Activities Board, Student Government Association, Residence Hall Association, intramurals, national fraternities, national sororities.

Athletics Member NCAA. All Division III. ***Intercollegiate sports:*** baseball M, basketball M/W, cheerleading M/W, cross-country running M/W, football M, golf M/W, soccer M/W, softball W, swimming and diving M/W, tennis M/W, track and field M/W, volleyball W, wrestling M. ***Intramural sports:*** badminton M/W, basketball M/W, bowling M/W, football M/W, golf M/W, racquetball M/W, rugby M, soccer M/W, softball M/W, swimming and diving M/W, table tennis M/W, tennis M/W, ultimate Frisbee M/W, volleyball M/W.

Campus security: 24-hour emergency response devices and patrols, student patrols, late-night transport/escort service, controlled dormitory access, Safe (Simpson Alert for Emergencies) Students and staff/faculty will receive phone calls in case of campus emergency, including weather.

Student services: health clinic, personal/psychological counseling, women's center.

COSTS & FINANCIAL AID

Costs (2014–15) ***One-time required fee:*** $200. ***Comprehensive fee:*** $40,513 includes full-time tuition ($31,935), mandatory fees ($615), and room and board ($7963). Full-time tuition and fees vary according to class time, course load, degree level, and program. Part-time tuition: $365 per credit hour. Part-time tuition and fees vary according to class time, course load, degree level, and program. ***College room only:*** $3860. Room and board charges vary according to board plan and housing facility. ***Payment plan:*** installment. ***Waivers:*** children of alumni, senior citizens, and employees or children of employees.

Financial Aid Of all full-time matriculated undergraduates who enrolled in 2014, 1,459 applied for aid, 1,205 were judged to have need, 281 had their need fully met. 408 Federal Work-Study jobs (averaging $1047). 409 state and other part-time jobs (averaging $1369). In 2014, 240 non-need-based awards were made. ***Average percent of need met:*** 86. ***Average financial aid package:*** $29,037. ***Average need-based loan:*** $3845. ***Average need-based gift aid:*** $19,883. ***Average non-need-based aid:*** $18,070. ***Average indebtedness upon graduation:*** $35,205.

APPLYING

Standardized Tests *Required:* SAT or ACT (for admission).

Options: electronic application, deferred entrance.

Required: high school transcript, online or paper application, guidance counselor recommendation form. ***Recommended:*** minimum 3.0 GPA, interview.

Application deadlines: 8/15 (freshmen), 8/15 (transfers).
Notification: continuous (freshmen), continuous (transfers).

CONTACT
Deborah Tierney, Vice President for Enrollment, Simpson College, 701 North C Street, Indianola, IA 50125. *Phone:* 515-961-1624. *Toll-free phone:* 800-362-2454. *Fax:* 515-961-1870. *E-mail:* admiss@simpson.edu.

See previous page for display ad and page 1620 for the College Close-Up.

★ University of Dubuque

Dubuque, Iowa
http://www.dbq.edu/

- **Independent Presbyterian** comprehensive, founded 1852
- **Suburban** 77-acre campus
- **Endowment** $87.1 million
- **Coed** 1,764 undergraduate students, 90% full-time, 42% women, 58% men
- **Minimally difficult** entrance level, 78% of applicants were admitted

UNDERGRAD STUDENTS
1,590 full-time, 174 part-time. Students come from 43 states and territories; 22 other countries; 55% are from out of state; 12% Black or African American, non-Hispanic/Latino; 8% Hispanic/Latino; 2% Asian, non-Hispanic/Latino; 0.1% Native Hawaiian or other Pacific Islander, non-Hispanic/Latino; 0.5% American Indian or Alaska Native, non-Hispanic/Latino; 2% Two or more races, non-Hispanic/Latino; 6% Race/ethnicity unknown; 1% international; 9% transferred in; 42% live on campus.

Freshmen
Admission: 1,451 applied, 1,130 admitted, 447 enrolled. ***Average high school GPA:*** 2.95. ***Test scores:*** SAT critical reading scores over 500: 24%; SAT math scores over 500: 38%; ACT scores over 18: 71%; SAT critical reading scores over 600: 3%; SAT math scores over 600: 3%; ACT scores over 24: 20%; ACT scores over 30: 1%.
Retention: 65% of full-time freshmen returned.

FACULTY
Total: 216, 40% full-time, 23% with terminal degrees.
Student/faculty ratio: 13:1.

ACADEMICS
Calendar: semesters. *Degrees:* associate, bachelor's, and master's.
Special study options: academic remediation for entering students, accelerated degree program, adult/continuing education programs, advanced placement credit, distance learning, double majors, English as a second language, honors programs, independent study, internships, off-campus study, part-time degree program, services for LD students, student-designed majors, study abroad, summer session for credit. ***ROTC:*** Army (b).
Unusual degree programs: 3-2 business administration; communications, theology.
Computers: 220 computers/terminals are available on campus for general student use. Students can access the following: campus intranet, computer help desk, free student e-mail accounts, online (class) grades, online (class) registration, online (class) schedules. Campuswide network is available. 100% of college-owned or -operated housing units are wired for high-speed Internet access. Wireless service is available via libraries, student centers.

STUDENT LIFE
Housing options: on-campus residence required through junior year; coed, special housing for students with disabilities. Campus housing is university owned. Freshman campus housing is guaranteed.
Activities and organizations: drama/theater group, student-run newspaper, choral group, Black Student Union, Flight Team, Fellowship of Christian Athletes, Teacher Education Student Organization, Students in Free Enterprise (SIFE).
Athletics Member NCAA. All Division III. ***Intercollegiate sports:*** baseball M, basketball M/W, cross-country running M/W, football M, golf M/W, soccer M/W, softball W, tennis M/W, track and field M/W, volleyball W, wrestling M. ***Intramural sports:*** archery M/W, badminton M/W, baseball M, basketball M/W, bowling M/W, cheerleading M/W, football M, golf M/W, racquetball M/W, soccer M/W, softball M/W, table

tennis M/W, tennis M/W, track and field M/W, ultimate Frisbee M/W, volleyball M/W, wrestling M.

Campus security: 24-hour patrols, late-night transport/escort service, controlled dormitory access.

Student services: health clinic, personal/psychological counseling.

COSTS & FINANCIAL AID

Costs (2014–15) ***Comprehensive fee:*** $35,440 includes full-time tuition ($25,730), mandatory fees ($1220), and room and board ($8490). ***Required fees:*** $570 per credit hour part-time. ***College room only:*** $4230. Room and board charges vary according to board plan, housing facility, and location. ***Payment plan:*** installment. ***Waivers:*** employees or children of employees.

Financial Aid Of all full-time matriculated undergraduates who enrolled in 2014, 1,401 applied for aid, 1,301 were judged to have need, 222 had their need fully met. 185 Federal Work-Study jobs (averaging $2000). 150 state and other part-time jobs (averaging $2000). In 2014, 160 non-need-based awards were made. ***Average percent of need met:*** 71. ***Average financial aid package:*** $22,959. ***Average need-based loan:*** $6843. ***Average need-based gift aid:*** $16,807. ***Average non-need-based aid:*** $9822. ***Average indebtedness upon graduation:*** $22,894.

APPLYING

Standardized Tests *Required:* SAT or ACT (for admission).

Options: electronic application.

Application fee: $25.

Required: essay or personal statement, high school transcript, 2 letters of recommendation. ***Recommended:*** interview.

Application deadlines: rolling (freshmen), rolling (transfers).

Notification: continuous (freshmen), continuous (transfers).

CONTACT

Mr. Bob Broshous, Director of Admissions, University of Dubuque, 2000 University Avenue, Dubuque, IA 52001-5099. *Phone:* 563-589-3199. *Toll-free phone:* 800-722-5583. *Fax:* 563-589-3690. *E-mail:* admissns@dbq.edu.

See previous page for display ad and page 1664 for the College Close-Up.

The University of Iowa

Iowa City, Iowa

http://www.uiowa.edu/

- **State-supported** university, founded 1847
- **Small-town** 1700-acre campus
- **Endowment** $1.3 billion
- **Coed** 22,354 undergraduate students, 87% full-time, 52% women, 48% men
- **Moderately difficult** entrance level, 81% of applicants were admitted

UNDERGRAD STUDENTS

19,546 full-time, 2,808 part-time. Students come from 53 states and territories; 61 other countries; 34% are from out of state; 3% Black or African American, non-Hispanic/Latino; 6% Hispanic/Latino; 3% Asian, non-Hispanic/Latino; 0.1% Native Hawaiian or other Pacific Islander, non-Hispanic/Latino; 0.1% American Indian or Alaska Native, non-Hispanic/Latino; 2% Two or more races, non-Hispanic/Latino; 6% Race/ethnicity unknown; 11% international; 5% transferred in; 26% live on campus.

Freshmen

Admission: 24,097 applied, 19,506 admitted, 4,666 enrolled. ***Average high school GPA:*** 3.63. ***Test scores:*** SAT critical reading scores over 500: 65%; SAT math scores over 500: 86%; ACT scores over 18: 99%; SAT critical reading scores over 600: 34%; SAT math scores over 600: 60%; ACT scores over 24: 67%; SAT critical reading scores over 700: 9%; SAT math scores over 700: 26%; ACT scores over 30: 16%.

Retention: 89% of full-time freshmen returned.

FACULTY

Total: 1,616, 92% full-time, 97% with terminal degrees.

Student/faculty ratio: 16:1.

ACADEMICS

Calendar: semesters. *Degrees:* bachelor's, master's, doctoral, post-master's, and postbachelor's certificates.

Special study options: accelerated degree program, adult/continuing education programs, advanced placement credit, cooperative education, distance learning, double majors, English as a second language, external degree program, honors programs, independent study, internships, off-campus study, part-time degree program, services for LD students, student-designed majors, study abroad, summer session for credit. ***ROTC:*** Army (b), Air Force (b).

Unusual degree programs: engineering; Urban & Regional Planning, Education, Computer Science, Public Health, Law, Biochemistry, Epidemiology, Occupational & Environmental Health, Linguistics, Microbiology.

Computers: 1,468 computers/terminals are available on campus for general student use. Students can access the following: computer help desk, free student e-mail accounts, online (class) grades, online (class) registration, online (class) schedules, online degree process, financial aid summary, university bill. Campuswide network is available. 100% of college-owned or -operated housing units are wired for high-speed Internet access. Wireless service is available via classrooms, computer centers, computer labs, dorm rooms, learning centers, libraries, student centers.

STUDENT LIFE

Housing options: coed, special housing for students with disabilities. Campus housing is university owned and leased by the school.

Activities and organizations: drama/theater group, student-run newspaper, radio and television station, choral group, marching band, Association of Residence Halls, Graduate Student Senate, National Society of Collegiate Scholars, Organization for the Active Support of International Students (OASIS), Dance Marathon, national fraternities, national sororities.

Athletics Member NCAA. All Division I except football (Division I-A). ***Intercollegiate sports:*** baseball M(s), basketball M(s)/W(s), cheerleading M/W, crew M(c)/W(s), cross-country running M(s)/W(s), field hockey W(s), golf M(s)/W(s), gymnastics M(s)/W(s), ice hockey M(c)/W(c), lacrosse M(c)/W(c), rugby M(c)/W(c), sailing M(c)/W(c), soccer M(c)/W(s), softball W(s), swimming and diving M(s)/W(s), table tennis M(c)/W(c), tennis M(s)/W(s), track and field M(s)/W(s), ultimate Frisbee M(c)/W(c), volleyball M(c)/W(s), wrestling M(s). ***Intramural sports:*** archery M(c)/W(c), badminton M/W, basketball M/W, bowling M/W, fencing M(c)/W(c), field hockey W(c), football M/W, golf M/W, racquetball M/W, rugby M(c)/W(c), sailing M(c)/W(c), skiing (cross-country) M(c)/W(c), skiing (downhill) M(c)/W(c), soccer M/W, softball M/W, swimming and diving M/W, table tennis M/W, tennis M/W, track and field M/W, ultimate Frisbee M/W, volleyball M/W, water polo M(c)/W(c), weight lifting M(c)/W(c), wrestling M/W.

Campus security: 24-hour emergency response devices and patrols, late-night transport/escort service, controlled dormitory access.

Student services: health clinic, personal/psychological counseling, women's center, legal services.

COSTS & FINANCIAL AID

Costs (2015–16) ***Tuition:*** state resident $6678 full-time, $279 per semester hour part-time; nonresident $26,464 full-time, $1101 per semester hour part-time. Full-time tuition and fees vary according to program and student level. Part-time tuition and fees vary according to course load, program, and student level. ***Required fees:*** $1426 full-time, $73 per semester hour part-time. ***Room and board:*** $9728. Room and board charges vary according to board plan and housing facility. ***Payment plan:*** installment.

Financial Aid Of all full-time matriculated undergraduates who enrolled in 2013, 12,619 applied for aid, 8,930 were judged to have need, 2,099 had their need fully met. In 2013, 3051 non-need-based awards were made. ***Average percent of need met:*** 60. ***Average financial aid package:*** $13,515. ***Average need-based loan:*** $5147. ***Average need-based gift aid:*** $7623. ***Average non-need-based aid:*** $4739. ***Average indebtedness upon graduation:*** $28,716.

APPLYING

Standardized Tests *Required:* SAT or ACT (for admission).

Options: electronic application, early admission, deferred entrance.

Application fee: $40.

Required: high school transcript, Must submit ACT or SAT score; must meet Regent Admission Index (RAI) requirement: residents 245 or above; nonresidents 255 or above.

Application deadlines: 4/1 (freshmen), 4/1 (transfers).

Notification: continuous (freshmen), continuous (transfers).

CONTACT

Debra Miller, Sr. Associate Director, Undergraduate Evaluation, The University of Iowa, 108 Calvin Hall, Iowa City, IA 52242. *Phone:* 319-335-3847. *Toll-free phone:* 800-553-4692. *Fax:* 319-335-1535. *E-mail:* admissions@uiowa.edu.

University of Northern Iowa

Cedar Falls, Iowa

http://www.uni.edu/

- **State-supported** comprehensive, founded 1876, part of Board of Regents, State of Iowa
- **Small-town** 916-acre campus
- **Endowment** $109.9 million
- **Coed** 10,142 undergraduate students, 90% full-time, 56% women, 44% men
- **Moderately difficult** entrance level, 54% of applicants were admitted

UNDERGRAD STUDENTS

9,122 full-time, 1,020 part-time. 6% are from out of state; 3% Black or African American, non-Hispanic/Latino; 3% Hispanic/Latino; 0.9% Asian, non-Hispanic/Latino; 0.1% Native Hawaiian or other Pacific Islander, non-Hispanic/Latino; 0.2% American Indian or Alaska Native, non-Hispanic/Latino; 2% Two or more races, non-Hispanic/Latino; 2% Race/ethnicity unknown; 5% international; 9% transferred in; 40% live on campus.

Freshmen

Admission: 5,509 applied, 2,960 admitted, 1,797 enrolled. ***Average high school GPA:*** 3.48. ***Test scores:*** ACT scores over 18: 94%; ACT scores over 24: 39%; ACT scores over 30: 5%.

Retention: 85% of full-time freshmen returned.

FACULTY

Total: 790, 72% full-time, 61% with terminal degrees.

Student/faculty ratio: 16:1.

ACADEMICS

Calendar: semesters. *Degrees:* bachelor's, master's, and doctoral.

Special study options: academic remediation for entering students, accelerated degree program, adult/continuing education programs, advanced placement credit, cooperative education, distance learning, double majors, English as a second language, external degree program, honors programs, independent study, internships, off-campus study, part-time degree program, services for LD students, student-designed majors, study abroad, summer session for credit. ***ROTC:*** Army (b).

Unusual degree programs: 3-2 nursing with Allen College; University of Iowa; medical technology with St. Luke's Hospital/University of Iowa Medical School, cytotechnology with Mayo School of Health-Related Sciences, Wisconsin State Laboratory of Hygiene and Mercy School of Cytotechnology, chiropractic with Logan College of Chiropractic.

Computers: 1,900 computers/terminals are available on campus for general student use. Students can access the following: campus intranet, computer help desk, free student e-mail accounts, online (class) grades, online (class) registration, online (class) schedules, course registration, student account, degree audit, program of study. Campuswide network is available. 100% of college-owned or -operated housing units are wired for high-speed Internet access. Wireless service is available via entire campus.

STUDENT LIFE

Housing options: coed, women-only, special housing for students with disabilities. Campus housing is university owned. Freshman campus housing is guaranteed.

Activities and organizations: drama/theater group, student-run newspaper, radio station, choral group, marching band, Dance Marathon, Colleges Against Cancer/Relay for Life, Accounting Club, Phi Eta Sigma, Students Today Alumni Tomorrow, national fraternities, national sororities.

Athletics Member NCAA. All Division I except football (Division I-AA). ***Intercollegiate sports:*** basketball M(s)/W(s), cross-country running M(s)/W(s), golf M(s)/W(s), soccer W(s), softball W(s), swimming and diving W(s), tennis W(s), track and field M(s)/W(s), volleyball W(s), wrestling M(s). ***Intramural sports:*** badminton M/W, baseball M(c), basketball M/W, bowling M(c)/W(c), cheerleading M/W, crew M(c)/W(c), cross-country running M(c)/W(c), football M(c), golf M(c)/W(c), ice hockey M(c), racquetball M(c)/W(c), rugby M(c)/W(c), skiing (cross-country) M(c)/W(c), skiing (downhill) M(c)/W(c), soccer M(c)/W(c), softball M(c)/W(c), swimming and diving M(c)/W(c), table tennis M/W, tennis M(c)/W(c), track and field M(c)/W(c), ultimate Frisbee M(c)/W(c), volleyball M/W(c), weight lifting M/W, wrestling M.

Campus security: 24-hour emergency response devices and patrols, student patrols, late-night transport/escort service, controlled dormitory access, automatic external defibrillators, silent witness online, vehicle help, and loan engravers.

Student services: health clinic, personal/psychological counseling.

COSTS & FINANCIAL AID

Costs (2014–15) ***Tuition:*** state resident $6648 full-time, $277 per credit hour part-time; nonresident $16,546 full-time, $689 per credit hour part-time. Full-time tuition and fees vary according to course load and program. Part-time tuition and fees vary according to course load and program. ***Required fees:*** $1101 full-time. ***Room and board:*** $8046; room only: $3962. Room and board charges vary according to board plan and housing facility. ***Payment plan:*** installment.

Financial Aid Of all full-time matriculated undergraduates who enrolled in 2012, 7,639 applied for aid, 6,172 were judged to have need, 1,036 had their need fully met. 465 Federal Work-Study jobs (averaging $1462). In 2012, 806 non-need-based awards were made. ***Average percent of need met:*** 70. ***Average financial aid package:*** $7642. ***Average need-based loan:*** $4210. ***Average need-based gift aid:*** $4559. ***Average non-need-based aid:*** $3589. ***Average indebtedness upon graduation:*** $23,151.

APPLYING

Standardized Tests *Required:* SAT or ACT (for admission). *Recommended:* SAT (for admission), ACT (for admission).

Options: electronic application, deferred entrance.

Application fee: $40.

Required: high school transcript, Regent Admission Index (RAI) score of 245 guarantees admission. High school requirements include 4 years of English; 3 years each of math, science and social studies, and 2 or more years of electives, which may include foreign language and fine arts. ***Required for some:*** interview.

Application deadlines: 8/15 (freshmen), 8/15 (transfers).

Notification: 9/1 (freshmen), 9/1 (transfers).

CONTACT

Amy Schipper, Associate Director, University of Northern Iowa, 002 Gilchrist, Cedar Falls, IA 50614. *Phone:* 319-273-2281. *Toll-free phone:* 800-772-2037. *Fax:* 319-273-2885. *E-mail:* admissions@uni.edu.

Upper Iowa University

Fayette, Iowa

http://www.uiu.edu/

- **Independent** comprehensive, founded 1857
- **Rural** 80-acre campus with easy access to Minneapolis-St. Paul, Chicago
- **Endowment** $11.5 million
- **Coed** 4,439 undergraduate students, 60% full-time, 60% women, 40% men
- **Moderately difficult** entrance level, 70% of applicants were admitted

UNDERGRAD STUDENTS

2,684 full-time, 1,755 part-time. Students come from 49 states and territories; 35 other countries; 60% are from out of state; 18% Black or African American, non-Hispanic/Latino; 5% Hispanic/Latino; 1% Asian, non-Hispanic/Latino; 0.2% Native Hawaiian or other Pacific Islander, non-Hispanic/Latino; 0.4% American Indian or Alaska Native, non-Hispanic/Latino; 2% Two or more races, non-Hispanic/Latino; 3% Race/ethnicity unknown; 5% international; 76% transferred in; 96% live on campus.

Freshmen
Admission: 1,397 applied, 977 admitted, 355 enrolled. ***Average high school GPA:*** 3.19. ***Test scores:*** ACT scores over 18: 90%; ACT scores over 24: 42%; ACT scores over 30: 1%.
Retention: 60% of full-time freshmen returned.

FACULTY
Total: 659, 11% full-time, 35% with terminal degrees.
Student/faculty ratio: 18:1.

ACADEMICS
Calendar: 6 8-week terms. *Degrees:* certificates, associate, bachelor's, and master's (enrollment figures include extended learning centers and online and distance education programs).
Special study options: academic remediation for entering students, accelerated degree program, adult/continuing education programs, advanced placement credit, cooperative education, distance learning, double majors, English as a second language, external degree program, freshman honors college, honors programs, independent study, internships, off-campus study, part-time degree program, services for LD students, student-designed majors, study abroad, summer session for credit.
Computers: 630 computers/terminals and 630 ports are available on campus for general student use. Students can access the following: campus intranet, computer help desk, free student e-mail accounts, online (class) grades, online (class) registration, online (class) schedules. Campuswide network is available. 100% of college-owned or -operated housing units are wired for high-speed Internet access. Wireless service is available via classrooms, computer centers, computer labs, dorm rooms, learning centers, libraries, student centers.

STUDENT LIFE
Housing options: on-campus residence required through junior year; coed, men-only, women-only. Campus housing is university owned. Freshman campus housing is guaranteed.
Activities and organizations: drama/theater group, student-run newspaper, choral group, Student Athlete Advisory Committee, Peacock Alumni for Student Traditions, UIU Science and Environment Club, Student Government Association, Peacocks for Progress.
Athletics Member NCAA. All Division II. ***Intercollegiate sports:*** baseball M(s), basketball M(s)/W(s), cross-country running W(s), football M(s), golf M(s)/W(s), soccer M(s)/W(s), softball W(s), tennis W(s), track and field W(s), volleyball W(s), wrestling M(s). ***Intramural sports:*** badminton M/W, basketball M/W, bowling M/W, cheerleading M(c)/W(c), football M, golf M/W, soccer M/W, softball M/W, table tennis M/W, ultimate Frisbee M/W, volleyball M/W.
Campus security: late-night transport/escort service, controlled dormitory access.
Student services: health clinic, personal/psychological counseling.

COSTS & FINANCIAL AID
Costs (2015–16) ***Comprehensive fee:*** $35,983 includes full-time tuition ($27,323), mandatory fees ($750), and room and board ($7910). Full-time tuition and fees vary according to degree level, location, and program. ***College room only:*** $3213. Room and board charges vary according to board plan, housing facility, and location. ***Payment plan:*** installment. ***Waivers:*** employees or children of employees.
Financial Aid Of all full-time matriculated undergraduates who enrolled in 2014, 2,459 applied for aid, 2,459 were judged to have need, 3 had their need fully met. 213 Federal Work-Study jobs (averaging $1930). In 2014, 3 non-need-based awards were made. ***Average percent of need met:*** 54. ***Average financial aid package:*** $12,097. ***Average need-based loan:*** $2764. ***Average need-based gift aid:*** $10,426. ***Average non-need-based aid:*** $1000. ***Average indebtedness upon graduation:*** $30,401.

APPLYING
Standardized Tests *Required:* SAT or ACT (for admission).
Options: electronic application.
Required: high school transcript, minimum 2.0 GPA. ***Required for some:*** essay or personal statement, interview.
Application deadlines: rolling (freshmen), rolling (out-of-state freshmen), rolling (transfers).

CONTACT
Mr. Storm M Schmitt, Dean of Enrollment Management, Upper Iowa University, 605 Washington Street, Parker Fox Hall, Fayette, IA 52142. *Phone:* 563-425-5857. *Toll-free phone:* 800-553-4150. *Fax:* 563-4255323. *E-mail:* schmitts@uiu.edu.

Waldorf College
Forest City, Iowa
http://www.waldorf.edu/

- **Independent Lutheran** 4-year, founded 1903, part of Columbia Southern Education Group
- **Rural** 51-acre campus
- **Coed** 1,425 undergraduate students, 79% full-time, 37% women, 63% men
- **Moderately difficult** entrance level, 69% of applicants were admitted

UNDERGRAD STUDENTS
1,119 full-time, 306 part-time. Students come from 50 states and territories; 24 other countries; 83% are from out of state; 18% Black or African American, non-Hispanic/Latino; 8% Hispanic/Latino; 1% Asian, non-Hispanic/Latino; 0.8% Native Hawaiian or other Pacific Islander, non-Hispanic/Latino; 0.5% American Indian or Alaska Native, non-Hispanic/Latino; 1% Two or more races, non-Hispanic/Latino; 1% Race/ethnicity unknown; 0.1% international; 19% transferred in; 70% live on campus.

Freshmen
Admission: 748 applied, 515 admitted, 146 enrolled. ***Average high school GPA:*** 3. ***Test scores:*** ACT scores over 18: 70%; ACT scores over 24: 15%.
Retention: 44% of full-time freshmen returned.

FACULTY
Total: 46, 91% full-time, 59% with terminal degrees.
Student/faculty ratio: 12:1.

ACADEMICS
Calendar: semesters. *Degrees:* associate and bachelor's.
Special study options: academic remediation for entering students, adult/continuing education programs, advanced placement credit, cooperative education, distance learning, double majors, freshman honors college, honors programs, independent study, internships, part-time degree program, services for LD students, summer session for credit.
Computers: 621 computers/terminals are available on campus for general student use. Students can access the following: campus intranet, computer help desk, free student e-mail accounts, online (class) grades, online (class) schedules, all full-time students receive laptops. Campuswide network is available. 100% of college-owned or -operated housing units are wired for high-speed Internet access. Wireless service is available via entire campus.

STUDENT LIFE
Housing options: on-campus residence required through junior year; coed, men-only, women-only, cooperative, special housing for students with disabilities. Campus housing is university owned and leased by the school. Freshman campus housing is guaranteed.
Activities and organizations: drama/theater group, student-run newspaper, radio and television station, choral group, Student Activities Team, Education Club, Campus Ministry groups, intramurals, Radio/TV/Newspaper.
Athletics Member NAIA. ***Intercollegiate sports:*** baseball M(s), basketball M(s)/W(s), bowling M(s)/W(s), cheerleading W(s), cross-country running M(s)/W(s), football M(s), golf M(s)/W(s), ice hockey M(c), soccer M(s)/W(s), softball W(s), volleyball W(s), wrestling M(s)/W(s). ***Intramural sports:*** basketball M/W, bowling M/W, football M, racquetball M/W, soccer M/W, softball M/W, table tennis M/W, tennis M/W, ultimate Frisbee M/W, volleyball M/W.
Campus security: 24-hour emergency response devices, student patrols, late-night transport/escort service, controlled dormitory access, evening and night patrols by trained security personnel, camera surveillance system.
Student services: health clinic, personal/psychological counseling.

COSTS & FINANCIAL AID
Costs (2015–16) ***Comprehensive fee:*** $27,878 includes full-time tuition ($19,804), mandatory fees ($1080), and room and board ($6994). Full-time tuition and fees vary according to class time, course load, and program. ***Room and board:*** Room and board charges vary according to board plan and housing facility. ***Payment plans:*** installment, deferred payment. ***Waivers:*** employees or children of employees.

Financial Aid Of all full-time matriculated undergraduates who enrolled in 2014, 947 applied for aid, 781 were judged to have need, 85 had their need fully met. In 2014, 115 non-need-based awards were made. ***Average percent of need met:*** 60. ***Average financial aid package:*** $13,082. ***Average need-based loan:*** $4488. ***Average need-based gift aid:*** $9802. ***Average non-need-based aid:*** $6833. ***Average indebtedness upon graduation:*** $33,494.

APPLYING
Standardized Tests *Required:* SAT or ACT (for admission).

Options: electronic application.

Required: high school transcript, ACT or SAT scores. ***Required for some:*** 1 letter of recommendation, interview. ***Recommended:*** minimum 2.0 GPA.

Application deadlines: rolling (freshmen), rolling (out-of-state freshmen), rolling (transfers).

Notification: continuous (freshmen), continuous (out-of-state freshmen), continuous (transfers).

CONTACT
Scott Pitcher, Director for Admissions, Waldorf College, 106 South 6th Street, Forest City, IA 50436. *Phone:* 641-585-8112. *Toll-free phone:* 800-292-1903. *Fax:* 641-585-8125. *E-mail:* admissions@waldorf.edu.

Wartburg College

Waverly, Iowa

http://www.wartburg.edu/

- **Independent Lutheran** 4-year, founded 1852
- **Small-town** 118-acre campus
- **Endowment** $59.1 million
- **Coed** 1,661 undergraduate students, 96% full-time, 52% women, 48% men
- **Moderately difficult** entrance level, 79% of applicants were admitted

UNDERGRAD STUDENTS
1,596 full-time, 65 part-time. Students come from 27 states and territories; 68 other countries; 27% are from out of state; 5% Black or African American, non-Hispanic/Latino; 3% Hispanic/Latino; 1% Asian, non-Hispanic/Latino; 0.1% Native Hawaiian or other Pacific Islander, non-Hispanic/Latino; 0.1% American Indian or Alaska Native, non-Hispanic/Latino; 2% Two or more races, non-Hispanic/Latino; 2% Race/ethnicity unknown; 10% international; 2% transferred in; 78% live on campus.

Freshmen
Admission: 2,310 applied, 1,821 admitted, 464 enrolled. ***Average high school GPA:*** 3.5. ***Test scores:*** SAT critical reading scores over 500: 57%; SAT math scores over 500: 80%; SAT writing scores over 500: 57%; ACT scores over 18: 92%; SAT critical reading scores over 600: 20%; SAT math scores over 600: 29%; SAT writing scores over 600: 23%; ACT scores over 24: 53%; SAT critical reading scores over 700: 3%; SAT math scores over 700: 6%; SAT writing scores over 700: 3%; ACT scores over 30: 9%.

Retention: 74% of full-time freshmen returned.

FACULTY
Total: 166, 66% full-time, 63% with terminal degrees.

Student/faculty ratio: 11:1.

ACADEMICS
Calendar: 4-4-1. *Degree:* bachelor's.

Special study options: academic remediation for entering students, accelerated degree program, advanced placement credit, double majors, honors programs, independent study, internships, off-campus study, part-time degree program, services for LD students, student-designed majors, study abroad, summer session for credit.

Unusual degree programs: 3-2 nursing with Allen College.

Computers: 250 computers/terminals are available on campus for general student use. Students can access the following: campus intranet, computer help desk, free student e-mail accounts, online (class) grades, online (class) registration, online (class) schedules. Campuswide network is available. 100% of college-owned or -operated housing units are wired for high-speed Internet access. Wireless service is available via entire campus.

STUDENT LIFE
Housing options: on-campus residence required through senior year; coed, men-only, women-only, special housing for students with disabilities. Campus housing is university owned. Freshman campus housing is guaranteed.

Activities and organizations: drama/theater group, student-run newspaper, radio and television station, choral group, Entertainment To Knight, Student Senate, Campus Ministry, Symphonic Band, Wartburg Choir.

Athletics Member NCAA. All Division III. ***Intercollegiate sports:*** baseball M, basketball M/W, cheerleading W, cross-country running M/W, football M, golf M/W, lacrosse W, soccer M/W, softball W, tennis M/W, track and field M/W, volleyball W, wrestling M. ***Intramural sports:*** badminton M/W, basketball M/W, bowling M/W, golf M/W, racquetball M/W, rugby W(c), softball M/W, tennis M/W, ultimate Frisbee M/W, volleyball M/W.

Campus security: 24-hour emergency response devices and patrols, late-night transport/escort service, controlled dormitory access.

Student services: health clinic, personal/psychological counseling.

COSTS & FINANCIAL AID
Costs (2015–16) ***Comprehensive fee:*** $46,200 includes full-time tuition ($36,210), mandatory fees ($980), and room and board ($9010). Part-time tuition and fees vary according to course load. ***College room only:*** $4325. Room and board charges vary according to board plan and housing facility. ***Payment plan:*** installment. ***Waivers:*** employees or children of employees.

Financial Aid Of all full-time matriculated undergraduates who enrolled in 2013, 1,392 applied for aid, 1,235 were judged to have need, 230 had their need fully met. 423 Federal Work-Study jobs (averaging $1230). 900 state and other part-time jobs (averaging $1668). In 2013, 400 non-need-based awards were made. ***Average percent of need met:*** 81. ***Average financial aid package:*** $25,732. ***Average need-based loan:*** $5055. ***Average need-based gift aid:*** $20,830. ***Average non-need-based aid:*** $18,077. ***Average indebtedness upon graduation:*** $39,414.

APPLYING
Standardized Tests *Required:* SAT or ACT (for admission).

Options: electronic application, early action, deferred entrance.

Required: high school transcript, minimum 2.0 GPA. ***Required for some:*** interview. ***Recommended:*** secondary school report.

Application deadlines: rolling (freshmen), rolling (transfers), 12/1 (early action).

Notification: continuous (freshmen), continuous (transfers).

CONTACT
Mr. Todd Coleman, Assistant Vice President for Admissions, Wartburg College, 100 Wartburg Boulevard, PO Box 1003, Waverly, IA 50677-0903. *Phone:* 319-352-8264. *Toll-free phone:* 800-772-2085. *Fax:* 319-352-8579. *E-mail:* admissions@wartburg.edu.

William Penn University

Oskaloosa, Iowa

http://www.wmpenn.edu/

- **Independent** comprehensive, founded 1873, affiliated with Society of Friends
- **Rural** 60-acre campus with easy access to Des Moines
- **Endowment** $6.6 million
- **Coed** 1,698 undergraduate students, 88% full-time, 50% women, 50% men
- **Moderately difficult** entrance level, 54% of applicants were admitted

UNDERGRAD STUDENTS
1,493 full-time, 205 part-time. Students come from 48 states and territories; 19 other countries; 36% are from out of state; 16% Black or

African American, non-Hispanic/Latino; 8% Hispanic/Latino; 1% Asian, non-Hispanic/Latino; 0.3% Native Hawaiian or other Pacific Islander, non-Hispanic/Latino; 0.6% American Indian or Alaska Native, non-Hispanic/Latino; 2% Two or more races, non-Hispanic/Latino; 3% Race/ethnicity unknown; 3% international; 11% transferred in; 40% live on campus.

Freshmen
Admission: 841 applied, 450 admitted, 337 enrolled. ***Average high school GPA:*** 2.88. ***Test scores:*** ACT scores over 18: 69%; ACT scores over 24: 11%; ACT scores over 30: 1%.

Retention: 63% of full-time freshmen returned.

FACULTY
Total: 215, 19% full-time, 17% with terminal degrees.

Student/faculty ratio: 15:1.

ACADEMICS
Calendar: semesters. *Degrees:* associate, bachelor's, and master's.

Special study options: academic remediation for entering students, adult/continuing education programs, advanced placement credit, cooperative education, distance learning, double majors, honors programs, independent study, internships, part-time degree program, services for LD students, study abroad, summer session for credit.

Unusual degree programs: 3-2 engineering with Iowa State University College of Engineering.

Computers: 85 computers/terminals are available on campus for general student use. Students can access the following: computer help desk, free student e-mail accounts, online (class) grades, online (class) schedules. Campuswide network is available. 100% of college-owned or -operated housing units are wired for high-speed Internet access. Wireless service is available via classrooms, computer labs, libraries.

STUDENT LIFE
Housing options: on-campus residence required through sophomore year; coed, men-only, women-only. Campus housing is university owned. Freshman campus housing is guaranteed.

Activities and organizations: drama/theater group, student-run newspaper, radio and television station, choral group, marching band, Student Government Association, Computer Club, InterVarsity/Campus Ministries, College Republicans, Education Club.

Athletics Member NAIA. ***Intercollegiate sports:*** baseball M(s), basketball M(s)/W(s), bowling M(s)/W(s), cheerleading M(s)/W(s), cross-country running M(s)/W(s), football M(s), golf M(s)/W(s), soccer M(s)/W(s), softball W(s), track and field M(s)/W(s), volleyball W(s), wrestling M(s). ***Intramural sports:*** basketball M/W, football M, table tennis M/W, volleyball M/W, weight lifting M/W.

Campus security: 24-hour emergency response devices and patrols, late-night transport/escort service, controlled dormitory access.

Student services: health clinic, personal/psychological counseling.

COSTS & FINANCIAL AID
Costs (2014–15) ***Comprehensive fee:*** $29,432 includes full-time tuition ($22,750), mandatory fees ($460), and room and board ($6222). ***College room only:*** $2752. Room and board charges vary according to board plan and housing facility. ***Payment plan:*** installment. ***Waivers:*** senior citizens and employees or children of employees.

Financial Aid Of all full-time matriculated undergraduates who enrolled in 2005, 808 applied for aid, 768 were judged to have need, 238 had their need fully met. 511 Federal Work-Study jobs (averaging $1287). 1 state and other part-time job (averaging $1103). In 2005, 2 non-need-based awards were made. ***Average percent of need met:*** 82. ***Average financial aid package:*** $17,782. ***Average need-based loan:*** $4600. ***Average need-based gift aid:*** $11,300. ***Average non-need-based aid:*** $4500. ***Average indebtedness upon graduation:*** $22,169.

APPLYING
Standardized Tests *Required:* SAT or ACT (for admission).

Options: electronic application, deferred entrance.

Application fee: $20.

Required: high school transcript, minimum 2.0 GPA. ***Required for some:*** essay or personal statement, interview.

Notification: continuous (freshmen), continuous (out-of-state freshmen), continuous (transfers).

CONTACT
Kerra Strong, Director of Admissions, William Penn University, 201 Trueblood Avenue, Oskaloosa, IA 52577-1799. *Phone:* 641-673-1012. *Fax:* 641-673-2113. *E-mail:* admissions@wmpenn.edu.

KANSAS

The Art Institutes International–Kansas City

Lenexa, Kansas

http://www.artinstitutes.edu/kansascity/

- **Proprietary** 4-year, founded 2008, part of Education Management Corporation
- **Coed**

ACADEMICS
Degrees: diplomas, associate, and bachelor's.

CONTACT
The Art Institutes International–Kansas City, 8208 Melrose Drive, Lenexa, KS 66214. *Phone:* 913-217-4600. *Toll-free phone:* 866-530-8508.

Baker University

Baldwin City, Kansas

http://www.bakeru.edu/

- **Independent United Methodist** comprehensive, founded 1858
- **Small-town** 26-acre campus with easy access to Kansas City
- **Endowment** $39.0 million
- **Coed** 1,010 undergraduate students, 81% full-time, 50% women, 50% men
- **Moderately difficult** entrance level, 76% of applicants were admitted

UNDERGRAD STUDENTS
818 full-time, 192 part-time. Students come from 26 states and territories; 13 other countries; 32% are from out of state; 8% Black or African American, non-Hispanic/Latino; 5% Hispanic/Latino; 1% Asian, non-Hispanic/Latino; 0.4% Native Hawaiian or other Pacific Islander, non-Hispanic/Latino; 3% American Indian or Alaska Native, non-Hispanic/Latino; 1% Two or more races, non-Hispanic/Latino; 3% Race/ethnicity unknown; 2% international; 3% transferred in; 80% live on campus.

Freshmen
Admission: 971 applied, 737 admitted, 224 enrolled. ***Average high school GPA:*** 3.4. ***Test scores:*** ACT scores over 18: 95%; ACT scores over 24: 43%; ACT scores over 30: 4%.

Retention: 80% of full-time freshmen returned.

FACULTY
Total: 106, 60% full-time, 62% with terminal degrees.

Student/faculty ratio: 11:1.

ACADEMICS
Calendar: 4-1-4, semesters for nursing program. *Degrees:* bachelor's, master's, and doctoral (profile includes information primarily for undergraduate residential campus in Baldwin City, KS).

Special study options: advanced placement credit, double majors, honors programs, independent study, internships, services for LD students, student-designed majors, study abroad, summer session for credit. ***ROTC:*** Army (c), Air Force (c).

Unusual degree programs: 3-2 engineering with Washington University in St. Louis, University of Kansas, University of Missouri Kansas City.

Computers: 140 computers/terminals are available on campus for general student use. Students can access the following: computer help desk, free student e-mail accounts, online (class) grades, online (class) registration, online (class) schedules. Campuswide network is available. 100% of college-owned or -operated housing units are wired for high-speed Internet access. Wireless service is available via classrooms, computer labs, libraries, student centers.

STUDENT LIFE

Housing options: on-campus residence required through senior year; coed, men-only, women-only, special housing for students with disabilities. Campus housing is university owned. Freshman campus housing is guaranteed.

Activities and organizations: drama/theater group, student-run newspaper, radio and television station, choral group, Cardinal Key, Baker University Speech Choir, Mungano, Fellowship of Christian Athletes, Student Activities Council, national fraternities, national sororities.

Athletics Member NAIA. ***Intercollegiate sports:*** baseball M(s), basketball M(s)/W(s), bowling W(s), cheerleading M(s)/W(s), cross-country running M(s)/W(s), football M(s), golf M(s)/W(s), soccer M(s)/W(s), softball W(s), tennis M(s)/W(s), track and field M(s)/W(s), volleyball W(s), wrestling M(s). ***Intramural sports:*** basketball M/W, football M/W, softball M/W, table tennis M/W, volleyball M/W.

Campus security: 24-hour emergency response devices and patrols, controlled dormitory access.

Student services: health clinic, personal/psychological counseling.

COSTS & FINANCIAL AID

Costs (2014–15) ***One-time required fee:*** $80. ***Comprehensive fee:*** $34,330 includes full-time tuition ($25,950), mandatory fees ($340), and room and board ($8040). Full-time tuition and fees vary according to course load, degree level, location, and program. Part-time tuition: $790 per credit hour. Part-time tuition and fees vary according to course load, degree level, location, and program. ***College room only:*** $3740. Room and board charges vary according to board plan and housing facility. ***Payment plan:*** installment. ***Waivers:*** senior citizens and employees or children of employees.

Financial Aid Of all full-time matriculated undergraduates who enrolled in 2008, 839 applied for aid, 713 were judged to have need, 268 had their need fully met. In 2008, 180 non-need-based awards were made. ***Average percent of need met:*** 84. ***Average financial aid package:*** $13,600. ***Average need-based loan:*** $5622. ***Average need-based gift aid:*** $6787. ***Average non-need-based aid:*** $9006. ***Average indebtedness upon graduation:*** $26,869.

APPLYING

Standardized Tests *Required:* SAT or ACT (for admission).

Options: electronic application, deferred entrance.

Required: high school transcript, 1 letter of recommendation. ***Required for some:*** essay or personal statement, interview.

Application deadlines: rolling (freshmen), rolling (transfers).

CONTACT

Mr. Kevin Kropf, Director of Enrollment Management, Baker University, PO Box 65, Baldwin City, KS 66006-0065. *Phone:* 785-594-8327. *Toll-free phone:* 800-873-4282. *Fax:* 785-594-8353. *E-mail:* admissions@bakeru.edu.

Barclay College

Haviland, Kansas

http://www.barclaycollege.edu/

- **Independent** comprehensive, founded 1917, affiliated with Society of Friends
- **Rural** 17-acre campus
- **Endowment** $1.4 million
- **Coed** 229 undergraduate students, 83% full-time, 48% women, 52% men
- **Minimally difficult** entrance level, 54% of applicants were admitted

UNDERGRAD STUDENTS

189 full-time, 40 part-time. Students come from 32 states and territories; 2 other countries; 66% are from out of state; 11% Black or African American, non-Hispanic/Latino; 6% Hispanic/Latino; 0.4% Asian, non-Hispanic/Latino; 2% American Indian or Alaska Native, non-Hispanic/Latino; 1% Two or more races, non-Hispanic/Latino; 4% Race/ethnicity unknown; 0.9% international; 10% transferred in; 78% live on campus.

Freshmen

Admission: 140 applied, 75 admitted, 52 enrolled. ***Test scores:*** SAT critical reading scores over 500: 20%; SAT math scores over 500: 40%; SAT writing scores over 500: 20%; ACT scores over 18: 68%; SAT critical reading scores over 600: 20%; ACT scores over 24: 9%.

Retention: 62% of full-time freshmen returned.

FACULTY

Total: 33, 42% full-time, 27% with terminal degrees.

Student/faculty ratio: 11:1.

ACADEMICS

Calendar: semesters. *Degrees:* certificates, associate, bachelor's, and master's.

Special study options: academic remediation for entering students, adult/continuing education programs, advanced placement credit, distance learning, double majors, external degree program, independent study, internships, off-campus study, part-time degree program.

Unusual degree programs: 3-2 nursing with Pratt Community College.

Computers: 28 computers/terminals are available on campus for general student use. Students can access the following: campus intranet, computer help desk, free student e-mail accounts, online (class) grades, online (class) registration, online (class) schedules. Campuswide network is available. 100% of college-owned or -operated housing units are wired for high-speed Internet access. Wireless service is available via entire campus.

STUDENT LIFE

Housing options: on-campus residence required through senior year; men-only, women-only. Campus housing is university owned. Freshman campus housing is guaranteed.

Activities and organizations: drama/theater group, choral group, Pep Club, Drama Club, Missions Club.

Athletics ***Intercollegiate sports:*** basketball M/W, cheerleading M/W, soccer M, tennis M/W, volleyball W. ***Intramural sports:*** basketball M/W, volleyball M/W.

Campus security: student patrols.

Student services: personal/psychological counseling.

COSTS & FINANCIAL AID

Costs (2015–16) ***Comprehensive fee:*** $22,990 includes full-time tuition ($11,000), mandatory fees ($3990), and room and board ($8000). Part-time tuition: $295 per credit hour. Part-time tuition and fees vary according to course load. ***Required fees:*** $295 per credit hour part-time. ***Room and board:*** Room and board charges vary according to board plan and housing facility. ***Payment plan:*** installment. ***Waivers:*** employees or children of employees.

Financial Aid Of all full-time matriculated undergraduates who enrolled in 2013, 232 applied for aid, 232 were judged to have need, 17 had their need fully met. In 2013, 18 non-need-based awards were made. ***Average percent of need met:*** 92. ***Average financial aid package:*** $6288. ***Average need-based loan:*** $3016. ***Average need-based gift aid:*** $2965. ***Average non-need-based aid:*** $1166. ***Average indebtedness upon graduation:*** $9287.

APPLYING

Standardized Tests *Required:* SAT or ACT (for admission).

Options: electronic application, early admission, deferred entrance.

Application fee: $15.

Required: essay or personal statement, high school transcript, minimum 2.3 GPA, 2 letters of recommendation, interview.

Application deadlines: 9/1 (freshmen), 9/1 (transfers).

Notification: continuous (freshmen), continuous (transfers).

CONTACT

Mr. Justin Kendall, Admissions Recruiter, Barclay College, 607 North Kingman, Haviland, KS 67059. *Phone:* 620-862-5252 Ext. 21. *Toll-free phone:* 800-862-0226. *Fax:* 620-862-5242. *E-mail:* jkendall@barclaycollege.edu.

Benedictine College
Atchison, Kansas
http://www.benedictine.edu/

- **Independent Roman Catholic** comprehensive, founded 1859
- **Small-town** 225-acre campus with easy access to Kansas City
- **Endowment** $18.2 million
- **Coed** 2,100 undergraduate students, 88% full-time, 52% women, 48% men
- **Minimally difficult** entrance level, 98% of applicants were admitted

UNDERGRAD STUDENTS
1,838 full-time, 262 part-time. Students come from 47 states and territories; 13 other countries; 76% are from out of state; 4% Black or African American, non-Hispanic/Latino; 6% Hispanic/Latino; 1% Asian, non-Hispanic/Latino; 0.4% Native Hawaiian or other Pacific Islander, non-Hispanic/Latino; 0.4% American Indian or Alaska Native, non-Hispanic/Latino; 4% Two or more races, non-Hispanic/Latino; 3% Race/ethnicity unknown; 3% international; 4% transferred in; 85% live on campus.

Freshmen
Admission: 2,249 applied, 2,199 admitted, 488 enrolled. ***Average high school GPA:*** 3.5. ***Test scores:*** SAT critical reading scores over 500: 73%; SAT math scores over 500: 62%; ACT scores over 18: 97%; SAT critical reading scores over 600: 48%; SAT math scores over 600: 28%; ACT scores over 24: 60%; SAT critical reading scores over 700: 17%; SAT math scores over 700: 8%; ACT scores over 30: 14%.

Retention: 77% of full-time freshmen returned.

FACULTY
Total: 181, 58% full-time, 44% with terminal degrees.

Student/faculty ratio: 14:1.

ACADEMICS
Calendar: semesters. *Degrees:* bachelor's and master's.

Special study options: academic remediation for entering students, advanced placement credit, cooperative education, distance learning, double majors, English as a second language, honors programs, independent study, internships, off-campus study, part-time degree program, services for LD students, student-designed majors, study abroad, summer session for credit. ***ROTC:*** Army (c).

Computers: 100 computers/terminals and 1,800 ports are available on campus for general student use. Students can access the following: computer help desk, free student e-mail accounts, online (class) grades, online (class) registration, online (class) schedules. Campuswide network is available. 100% of college-owned or -operated housing units are wired for high-speed Internet access. Wireless service is available via entire campus.

STUDENT LIFE
Housing options: on-campus residence required through senior year; men-only, women-only. Campus housing is university owned. Freshman campus housing is guaranteed.

Activities and organizations: drama/theater group, student-run newspaper, choral group, marching band, student government, ENACTUS, Knights of Columbus, Concert Chorale/Chamber Singers, Ravens Respect Life.

Athletics Member NAIA. ***Intercollegiate sports:*** baseball M(s), basketball M(s)/W(s), cheerleading W(s), cross-country running M(s)/W(s), football M(s), lacrosse M/W, soccer M(s)/W(s), softball W(s), track and field M(s)/W(s), volleyball W(s), wrestling M(s). ***Intramural sports:*** basketball M/W, football M/W, golf M/W, lacrosse M/W, racquetball M/W, rugby M/W, soccer M/W, softball M/W, table tennis M/W, ultimate Frisbee M/W, volleyball M/W.

Campus security: 24-hour emergency response devices and patrols, late-night transport/escort service, controlled dormitory access.

Student services: health clinic, personal/psychological counseling.

COSTS & FINANCIAL AID
Costs (2014–15) ***Comprehensive fee:*** $34,640 includes full-time tuition ($24,850), mandatory fees ($740), and room and board ($9050). Full-time tuition and fees vary according to course load and degree level. Part-time tuition: $665 per credit hour. Part-time tuition and fees vary according to course load and degree level. ***College room only:*** $4985. Room and board charges vary according to board plan and housing facility. ***Payment plan:*** installment. ***Waivers:*** senior citizens and employees or children of employees.

Financial Aid Of all full-time matriculated undergraduates who enrolled in 2013, 1,408 applied for aid, 1,214 were judged to have need, 256 had their need fully met. 335 Federal Work-Study jobs (averaging $606). In 2013, 368 non-need-based awards were made. ***Average percent of need met:*** 76. ***Average financial aid package:*** $19,766. ***Average need-based loan:*** $4877. ***Average need-based gift aid:*** $15,377. ***Average non-need-based aid:*** $10,769. ***Average indebtedness upon graduation:*** $24,667.

APPLYING
Standardized Tests *Required:* SAT or ACT (for admission).

Options: electronic application, deferred entrance.

Application fee: $50.

Required: high school transcript, minimum 2.0 GPA, 1 letter of recommendation. ***Required for some:*** interview.

Application deadlines: rolling (freshmen), rolling (out-of-state freshmen), rolling (transfers).

Notification: continuous (freshmen), continuous (transfers).

CONTACT
Mr. Pete Helgesen, Dean of Enrollment Management, Benedictine College, 1020 North 2nd Street, Atchison, KS 66002-1499. *Phone:* 913-367-5340 Ext. 2476. *Toll-free phone:* 800-467-5340. *E-mail:* phelgesen@benedictine.edu.

Bethany College
Lindsborg, Kansas
http://www.bethanylb.edu/

- **Independent Lutheran** 4-year, founded 1881
- **Small-town** 80-acre campus
- **Endowment** $24.1 million
- **Coed**
- **Moderately difficult** entrance level

FACULTY
Student/faculty ratio: 12:1.

ACADEMICS
Calendar: 4-1-4. *Degree:* bachelor's.

STUDENT LIFE
Housing options: on-campus residence required through junior year; coed, women-only. Campus housing is university owned. Freshman campus housing is guaranteed.

Activities and organizations: drama/theater group, student-run newspaper, choral group, Student Activities Board (SAB), Alpha Theta Chi, Alpha Sigma Nu, Fellowship of Christian Athletes (FCA), Bethany Youth Ministries Team.

Athletics Member NAIA.

Campus security: 24-hour emergency response devices, controlled dormitory access, night patrols by security personnel.

Student services: health clinic, personal/psychological counseling.

FINANCIAL AID
Financial Aid Of all full-time matriculated undergraduates who enrolled in 2011, 541 applied for aid, 466 were judged to have need, 188 had their need fully met. 381 Federal Work-Study jobs (averaging $1342). In 2011, 1 non-need-based awards were made. ***Average percent of need met:*** 91. ***Average financial aid package:*** $22,887. ***Average need-based loan:*** $7529. ***Average need-based gift aid:*** $6935. ***Average non-need-based aid:*** $4800. ***Average indebtedness upon graduation:*** $22,015.

APPLYING
Standardized Tests *Required:* SAT or ACT (for admission).

Options: electronic application, deferred entrance.

Required: high school transcript, minimum 2.0 GPA. ***Required for some:*** essay or personal statement, .

CONTACT
Katie Laier, Dean of Admissions and Financial Aid, Bethany College, 335 East Swensson Avenue, Lindsborg, KS 67456-1895. *Phone:* 785-227-

3311 Ext. 8344. *Toll-free phone:* 800-826-2281. *Fax:* 785-227-8993. *E-mail:* admissions@bethanylb.edu.

Bethel College
North Newton, Kansas
http://www.bethelks.edu/

- **Independent** 4-year, founded 1887, affiliated with Mennonite Church USA
- **Small-town** 60-acre campus with easy access to Wichita
- **Coed** 483 undergraduate students, 97% full-time, 51% women, 49% men
- **Moderately difficult** entrance level, 49% of applicants were admitted

UNDERGRAD STUDENTS
468 full-time, 15 part-time. 38% are from out of state; 15% Black or African American, non-Hispanic/Latino; 10% Hispanic/Latino; 0.4% Asian, non-Hispanic/Latino; 0.4% American Indian or Alaska Native, non-Hispanic/Latino; 2% Two or more races, non-Hispanic/Latino; 2% international; 13% transferred in; 71% live on campus.

Freshmen
Admission: 833 applied, 409 admitted, 110 enrolled. ***Average high school GPA:*** 3.38. ***Test scores:*** SAT critical reading scores over 500: 5%; SAT math scores over 500: 10%; ACT scores over 18: 86%; ACT scores over 24: 37%; ACT scores over 30: 8%.

Retention: 63% of full-time freshmen returned.

FACULTY
Total: 62, 61% full-time, 48% with terminal degrees.

Student/faculty ratio: 10:1.

ACADEMICS
Calendar: 4-1-4. *Degree:* certificates and bachelor's.

Special study options: part-time degree program.

Unusual degree programs: 3-2 engineering with Kansas State University, University of Kansas, Wichita State University.

Computers: Students can access the following: campus intranet, computer help desk, free student e-mail accounts, online (class) grades, online (class) registration, online (class) schedules. Campuswide network is available. Wireless service is available via entire campus.

STUDENT LIFE
Housing options: on-campus residence required through senior year; coed. Campus housing is university owned. Freshman campus housing is guaranteed.

Activities and organizations: drama/theater group, student-run newspaper, radio and television station, choral group.

Athletics Member NAIA. ***Intercollegiate sports:*** basketball M(s)/W(s), cross-country running M(s)/W(s), football M(s), golf M(s)/W(s), soccer M(s)/W(s), tennis M(s)/W(s), track and field M(s)/W(s), volleyball W(s). ***Intramural sports:*** badminton M/W, baseball M, basketball M/W, bowling M/W, cross-country running M/W, golf M/W, soccer M/W, softball M/W, table tennis M/W, tennis M/W, ultimate Frisbee M/W, volleyball M/W.

Student services: health clinic, personal/psychological counseling.

COSTS & FINANCIAL AID
Costs (2014–15) ***One-time required fee:*** $200. ***Comprehensive fee:*** $32,440 includes full-time tuition ($24,200) and room and board ($8240). Part-time tuition: $865 per credit hour. Part-time tuition and fees vary according to course load. ***College room only:*** $4420. Room and board charges vary according to board plan, housing facility, and student level. ***Payment plans:*** installment, deferred payment. ***Waivers:*** senior citizens and employees or children of employees.

Financial Aid Of all full-time matriculated undergraduates who enrolled in 2013, 443 applied for aid, 414 were judged to have need, 131 had their need fully met. 154 Federal Work-Study jobs (averaging $1239). 195 state and other part-time jobs (averaging $1331). In 2013, 66 non-need-based awards were made. ***Average percent of need met:*** 89. ***Average financial aid package:*** $23,801. ***Average need-based loan:*** $7969. ***Average need-based gift aid:*** $4859. ***Average non-need-based aid:*** $9154. ***Average indebtedness upon graduation:*** $24,132.

APPLYING
Standardized Tests *Required:* SAT or ACT (for admission).

Options: deferred entrance.

Application fee: $20.

Required: high school transcript, minimum 2.5 GPA. ***Required for some:*** essay or personal statement, 2 letters of recommendation. ***Recommended:*** interview.

CONTACT
Mr. Todd H. Moore, Vice President for Admissions, Bethel College, 300 East 27th Street, North Newton, KS 67117-0531. *Phone:* 316-284-5230. *Toll-free phone:* 800-522-1887 Ext. 230. *Fax:* 316-284-5870. *E-mail:* admissions@bethelks.edu.

Brown Mackie College–Kansas City
Lenexa, Kansas
http://www.brownmackie.edu/kansascity/

- **Proprietary** primarily 2-year, founded 1892, part of Education Management Corporation
- **Suburban** campus
- **Coed**

ACADEMICS
Calendar: quarters. *Degrees:* certificates, diplomas, associate, and bachelor's.

CONTACT
Brown Mackie College–Kansas City, 9705 Lenexa Drive, Lenexa, KS 66215. *Phone:* 913-768-1900. *Toll-free phone:* 800-635-9101.

Brown Mackie College–Salina
Salina, Kansas
http://www.brownmackie.edu/salina/

- **Proprietary** primarily 2-year, founded 1892, part of Education Management Corporation
- **Small-town** campus
- **Coed**

ACADEMICS
Calendar: modular. *Degrees:* certificates, diplomas, associate, and bachelor's.

CONTACT
Brown Mackie College–Salina, 2106 South 9th Street, Salina, KS 67401-2810. *Phone:* 785-825-5422. *Toll-free phone:* 800-365-0433.

Cleveland University–Kansas City
Overland Park, Kansas
http://www.cleveland.edu/

- **Independent** comprehensive, founded 1922
- **Suburban** 34-acre campus with easy access to Kansas City
- **Coed**
- **Noncompetitive** entrance level

FACULTY
Student/faculty ratio: 11:1.

ACADEMICS
Calendar: trimesters. *Degrees:* associate, bachelor's, master's, and doctoral.

STUDENT LIFE
Housing options: college housing not available.

Campus security: 24-hour patrols.

Student services: health clinic, personal/psychological counseling.

COSTS
Costs (2014–15) ***Tuition:*** $7050 full-time, $235 per credit hour part-time. Full-time tuition and fees vary according to course load and program. Part-time tuition and fees vary according to course load and program. ***Required fees:*** $440 full-time, $220 per term part-time.

APPLYING
Standardized Tests *Required for some:* SAT or ACT (for admission).

Options: electronic application, deferred entrance.

Application fee: $50.

Required: high school transcript, minimum 2.5 GPA. ***Required for some:*** interview.

CONTACT

Ms. Melissa Denton, Director of Admissions, Cleveland University–Kansas City, 10850 Lowell Avenue, Overland Park, KS 66210. *Phone:* 913-234-0750. *Toll-free phone:* 800-467-2252. *Fax:* 913-234-0906. *E-mail:* kc.admissions@cleveland.edu.

Donnelly College

Kansas City, Kansas

http://www.donnelly.edu/

- **Independent Roman Catholic** primarily 2-year, founded 1949
- **Urban** 4-acre campus
- **Endowment** $4.9 million
- **Coed** 463 undergraduate students, 67% full-time, 71% women, 29% men
- **Noncompetitive** entrance level

UNDERGRAD STUDENTS

310 full-time, 153 part-time. Students come from 2 states and territories; 35 other countries; 25% are from out of state; 29% Black or African American, non-Hispanic/Latino; 40% Hispanic/Latino; 10% Asian, non-Hispanic/Latino; 0.4% American Indian or Alaska Native, non-Hispanic/Latino; 5% Two or more races, non-Hispanic/Latino; 6% international; 6% transferred in; 9% live on campus.

Freshmen

Admission: 185 enrolled.

Retention: 45% of full-time freshmen returned.

FACULTY

Total: 56, 36% full-time.

Student/faculty ratio: 11:1.

ACADEMICS

Calendar: semesters. *Degrees:* certificates, associate, and bachelor's.

Special study options: academic remediation for entering students, advanced placement credit, distance learning, English as a second language, external degree program, honors programs, independent study, part-time degree program, services for LD students, summer session for credit.

Computers: 75 computers/terminals and 75 ports are available on campus for general student use. Students can access the following: campus intranet, computer help desk, free student e-mail accounts, online (class) grades, online (class) schedules. Campuswide network is available. Wireless service is available via entire campus.

STUDENT LIFE

Housing options: men-only, women-only. Campus housing is university owned and is provided by a third party.

Activities and organizations: Organization of Student Leadership, Student Ambassadors, Healthy Student Task Force, Men's Soccer Club, Women's Soccer Club.

Campus security: 24-hour emergency response devices.

Student services: personal/psychological counseling.

COSTS

Costs (2015–16) ***Comprehensive fee:*** $12,244 includes full-time tuition ($5920), mandatory fees ($100), and room and board ($6224). Full-time tuition and fees vary according to course level, course load, degree level, and program. Part-time tuition and fees vary according to course level. ***Room and board:*** Room and board charges vary according to housing facility. ***Payment plan:*** installment. ***Waivers:*** employees or children of employees.

APPLYING

Standardized Tests *Recommended:* ACT (for admission).

Options: electronic application, early admission, deferred entrance.

Recommended: high school transcript.

Application deadlines: rolling (freshmen), rolling (transfers).

CONTACT

Ms. Sydney Beeler, Vice President of Enrollment and Student Affairs, Donnelly College, 608 North 18th Street, Kansas City, KS 66102. *Phone:* 913-621-8713. *Fax:* 913-621-8719. *E-mail:* admissions@donnelly.edu.

Emporia State University

Emporia, Kansas

http://www.emporia.edu/

- **State-supported** comprehensive, founded 1863, part of Kansas State Board of Regents
- **Small-town** 207-acre campus with easy access to Wichita
- **Endowment** $68.5 million
- **Coed** 3,924 undergraduate students, 90% full-time, 60% women, 40% men
- **Noncompetitive** entrance level, 77% of applicants were admitted

UNDERGRAD STUDENTS

3,527 full-time, 397 part-time. Students come from 20 states and territories; 41 other countries; 11% are from out of state; 6% Black or African American, non-Hispanic/Latino; 6% Hispanic/Latino; 0.7% Asian, non-Hispanic/Latino; 0.1% Native Hawaiian or other Pacific Islander, non-Hispanic/Latino; 0.5% American Indian or Alaska Native, non-Hispanic/Latino; 6% Two or more races, non-Hispanic/Latino; 1% Race/ethnicity unknown; 8% international; 10% transferred in; 28% live on campus.

Freshmen

Admission: 1,979 applied, 1,515 admitted, 755 enrolled. ***Average high school GPA:*** 3.33. ***Test scores:*** SAT critical reading scores over 500: 27%; ACT scores over 18: 87%; SAT critical reading scores over 600: 18%; ACT scores over 24: 32%; SAT critical reading scores over 700: 9%; ACT scores over 30: 3%.

Retention: 73% of full-time freshmen returned.

FACULTY

Total: 276, 90% full-time, 75% with terminal degrees.

Student/faculty ratio: 17:1.

ACADEMICS

Calendar: semesters. *Degrees:* bachelor's, master's, doctoral, post-master's, and postbachelor's certificates.

Special study options: academic remediation for entering students, accelerated degree program, adult/continuing education programs, advanced placement credit, cooperative education, distance learning, double majors, English as a second language, freshman honors college, honors programs, independent study, internships, off-campus study, part-time degree program, services for LD students, study abroad, summer session for credit.

Unusual degree programs: 3-2 engineering with Kansas State University, University of Kansas, Wichita State University.

Computers: 410 computers/terminals are available on campus for general student use. Students can access the following: campus intranet, computer help desk, free student e-mail accounts, online (class) grades, online (class) registration, online (class) schedules. Campuswide network is available. 100% of college-owned or -operated housing units are wired for high-speed Internet access. Wireless service is available via entire campus.

STUDENT LIFE

Housing options: on-campus residence required for freshman year; coed, men-only, women-only, special housing for students with disabilities. Campus housing is university owned. Freshman campus housing is guaranteed.

Activities and organizations: drama/theater group, student-run newspaper, radio station, choral group, marching band, Phi Eta Sigma, Student Chapter of the American Library Association of ESU, TradPlus Student Organization, Arabic Culture Student Organization, Emporia Kansas Association of Nursing Students, national fraternities, national sororities.

Athletics Member NCAA. All Division II. ***Intercollegiate sports:*** baseball M(s), basketball M(s)/W(s), cheerleading M(s)/W(s), cross-country running M(s)/W(s), football M(s), soccer W(s), softball W(s), tennis M(s)/W(s), track and field M(s)/W(s), volleyball W(s). ***Intramural sports:*** badminton M/W, basketball M/W, fencing M(c)/W(c), football M/W, rugby M(c), soccer M(c)/W(c), softball M/W, table tennis M/W, tennis M/W, volleyball M/W.

Campus security: 24-hour emergency response devices and patrols, student patrols, late-night transport/escort service, controlled dormitory

access, 24-hour residence hall monitoring, safety and self-awareness programs.

Student services: health clinic, personal/psychological counseling, women's center, legal services.

COSTS & FINANCIAL AID

Costs (2014–15) ***Tuition:*** state resident $4500 full-time, $150 per credit hour part-time; nonresident $16,650 full-time, $555 per credit hour part-time. Full-time tuition and fees vary according to course load, degree level, and location. Part-time tuition and fees vary according to course load, degree level, and location. ***Required fees:*** $1246 full-time, $75 per credit hour part-time. ***Room and board:*** $7582; room only: $4182. Room and board charges vary according to board plan, housing facility, and location. ***Payment plans:*** installment, deferred payment. ***Waivers:*** senior citizens and employees or children of employees.

Financial Aid Of all full-time matriculated undergraduates who enrolled in 2014, 2,740 applied for aid, 2,284 were judged to have need, 308 had their need fully met. 224 Federal Work-Study jobs (averaging $1904). 13 state and other part-time jobs (averaging $2241). In 2014, 530 non-need-based awards were made. ***Average percent of need met:*** 62. ***Average financial aid package:*** $8805. ***Average need-based loan:*** $6240. ***Average need-based gift aid:*** $5833. ***Average non-need-based aid:*** $2315. ***Average indebtedness upon graduation:*** $30,488.

APPLYING

Standardized Tests *Required:* SAT or ACT (for admission).

Options: electronic application, early admission, deferred entrance.

Application fee: $30.

Required: high school transcript, 21 ACT, or Rank in the Top 1/3 of your class, AND completed QA core classes with cum 2.0 GPA, 22 Math subscore, OR completed 4th year of math. ***Recommended:*** minimum 2.0 GPA.

Application deadlines: rolling (freshmen), rolling (out-of-state freshmen), rolling (transfers).

Notification: continuous (freshmen), continuous (out-of-state freshmen), continuous (transfers).

CONTACT

Ms. Laura Eddy, Director of Admissions, Emporia State University, 1 Kellogg Circle, Campus Box 4034, Emporia, KS 66801-5087. *Phone:* 620-341-5465. *Toll-free phone:* 877-GOTOESU (in-state); 877-468-6378 (out-of-state). *Fax:* 620-341-5599. *E-mail:* go2esu@emporia.edu.

Fort Hays State University

Hays, Kansas

http://www.fhsu.edu/

- **State-supported** comprehensive, founded 1902
- **Small-town** 200-acre campus
- **Coed** 11,643 undergraduate students, 48% full-time, 60% women, 40% men

UNDERGRAD STUDENTS

5,644 full-time, 5,999 part-time. 29% are from out of state; 4% Black or African American, non-Hispanic/Latino; 7% Hispanic/Latino; 0.9% Asian, non-Hispanic/Latino; 0.1% Native Hawaiian or other Pacific Islander, non-Hispanic/Latino; 0.4% American Indian or Alaska Native, non-Hispanic/Latino; 2% Two or more races, non-Hispanic/Latino; 1% Race/ethnicity unknown; 29% international; 19% transferred in; 12% live on campus.

Freshmen

Admission: 1,025 enrolled. ***Average high school GPA:*** 3.3. ***Test scores:*** ACT scores over 18: 84%; ACT scores over 24: 29%; ACT scores over 30: 3%.

Retention: 65% of full-time freshmen returned.

FACULTY

Total: 522, 58% full-time, 50% with terminal degrees.

Student/faculty ratio: 17:1.

ACADEMICS

Calendar: semesters. *Degrees:* certificates, associate, bachelor's, master's, and post-master's certificates.

Special study options: academic remediation for entering students, distance learning, double majors, English as a second language, honors programs, independent study, internships, part-time degree program, student-designed majors, study abroad.

Computers: Students can access the following: campus intranet, computer help desk, free student e-mail accounts, online (class) grades, online (class) registration, online (class) schedules. Campuswide network is available. Wireless service is available via entire campus.

STUDENT LIFE

Housing options: on-campus residence required for freshman year; coed, men-only, women-only. Campus housing is university owned and leased by the school.

Activities and organizations: marching band, Students for Life, Honors Society, Panhellenic Council, Residents Hall Association, Catholic Disciples.

Athletics ***Intercollegiate sports:*** soccer M(s)/W(s). ***Intramural sports:*** badminton M/W, basketball M/W, fencing M/W, softball M/W, swimming and diving M/W, volleyball M/W.

Campus security: 24-hour emergency response devices and patrols.

Student services: health clinic.

FINANCIAL AID

Financial Aid Of all full-time matriculated undergraduates who enrolled in 2012, 4,926 applied for aid, 4,204 were judged to have need, 371 had their need fully met. In 2012, 459 non-need-based awards were made. ***Average percent of need met:*** 54. ***Average financial aid package:*** $6966. ***Average need-based loan:*** $3720. ***Average need-based gift aid:*** $4528. ***Average non-need-based aid:*** $1535. ***Average indebtedness upon graduation:*** $25,945.

APPLYING

Standardized Tests *Required for some:* SAT or ACT (for admission).

Required: high school transcript.

CONTACT

Tricia Cline, Director, Admissions, Fort Hays State University, 600 Park Street, Hays, KS 67601-4099. *Phone:* 785-628-4091. *Toll-free phone:* 800-628-FHSU. *E-mail:* tcline@fhsu.edu.

Friends University

Wichita, Kansas

http://www.friends.edu/

- **Independent** comprehensive, founded 1898, affiliated with Christian non-denominational
- **Urban** 55-acre campus
- **Endowment** $44.7 million
- **Coed** 1,344 undergraduate students, 76% full-time, 53% women, 47% men
- **Moderately difficult** entrance level, 84% of applicants were admitted

UNDERGRAD STUDENTS

1,024 full-time, 320 part-time. Students come from 40 states and territories; 18 other countries; 17% are from out of state; 10% Black or African American, non-Hispanic/Latino; 4% Hispanic/Latino; 2% Asian, non-Hispanic/Latino; 0.5% Native Hawaiian or other Pacific Islander, non-Hispanic/Latino; 1% American Indian or Alaska Native, non-Hispanic/Latino; 7% Two or more races, non-Hispanic/Latino; 5% Race/ethnicity unknown; 13% transferred in; 46% live on campus.

Freshmen

Admission: 487 applied, 410 admitted, 182 enrolled. ***Average high school GPA:*** 3.29. ***Test scores:*** SAT critical reading scores over 500: 23%; SAT math scores over 500: 50%; ACT scores over 18: 82%; SAT critical reading scores over 600: 4%; SAT math scores over 600: 12%; ACT scores over 24: 29%; ACT scores over 30: 3%.

Retention: 68% of full-time freshmen returned.

FACULTY

Total: 231, 32% full-time.

Student/faculty ratio: 19:1.

ACADEMICS

Calendar: semesters. *Degrees:* associate, bachelor's, and master's.

Special study options: academic remediation for entering students, accelerated degree program, adult/continuing education programs, advanced placement credit, cooperative education, distance learning, double majors, honors programs, independent study, internships, off-campus study, part-time degree program, services for LD students, student-designed majors, study abroad, summer session for credit.

Computers: 360 computers/terminals are available on campus for general student use. Students can access the following: campus intranet, computer help desk, free student e-mail accounts, online (class) grades, online (class) registration, online (class) schedules. Campuswide network is available. 90% of college-owned or -operated housing units are wired for high-speed Internet access. Wireless service is available via entire campus.

STUDENT LIFE

Housing options: coed. Campus housing is university owned.

Activities and organizations: drama/theater group, choral group, Concert Choir, Singing Quakers, Zoo Science Club, Psychology Club, Spanish Club.

Athletics Member NAIA. ***Intercollegiate sports:*** baseball M(s), basketball M(s)/W(s), cheerleading M(s)/W(s), cross-country running M(s)/W(s), football M(s), golf M(s), soccer M(s)/W(s), softball W(s), tennis M(s)/W(s), track and field M(s)/W(s), volleyball W(s). ***Intramural sports:*** basketball M/W, football M/W, racquetball M/W, soccer M/W, table tennis M/W, tennis M/W, ultimate Frisbee M/W, volleyball M/W.

Campus security: 24-hour patrols, late-night transport/escort service, controlled dormitory access.

Student services: health clinic, personal/psychological counseling.

COSTS & FINANCIAL AID

Costs (2015–16) ***Comprehensive fee:*** $31,950 includes full-time tuition ($24,450), mandatory fees ($180), and room and board ($7320). Full-time tuition and fees vary according to class time, course load, degree level, and location. Part-time tuition: $855 per credit hour. Part-time tuition and fees vary according to class time, course load, degree level, and location. ***College room only:*** $3550. Room and board charges vary according to board plan and housing facility. ***Payment plan:*** installment. ***Waivers:*** senior citizens and employees or children of employees.

Financial Aid Of all full-time matriculated undergraduates who enrolled in 2013, 919 applied for aid, 869 were judged to have need, 208 had their need fully met. 174 Federal Work-Study jobs (averaging $1720). 223 state and other part-time jobs (averaging $1427). In 2013, 147 non-need-based awards were made. ***Average percent of need met:*** 69. ***Average financial aid package:*** $16,311. ***Average need-based loan:*** $4334. ***Average need-based gift aid:*** $12,584. ***Average non-need-based aid:*** $12,508. ***Average indebtedness upon graduation:*** $22,305.

APPLYING

Standardized Tests *Required for some:* SAT or ACT (for admission). *Recommended:* ACT (for admission), SAT and SAT Subject Tests or ACT (for admission).

Options: electronic application.

Application fee: $35.

Required: High school transcripts are not required for adult students enrolling in degree completion programs. Auditions are required for music, dance and theater programs. Portfolios are required for art program. Admission for traditional undergraduate students is based on student's HS GPA x ACT score. ***Required for some:*** high school transcript, interview.

Application deadlines: rolling (freshmen), rolling (out-of-state freshmen), rolling (transfers).

Notification: continuous (freshmen), continuous (out-of-state freshmen), continuous (transfers).

CONTACT

Mr. Brandon Pierce, Director of Traditional Undergraduate Admissions, Friends University, 2100 West University Avenue, Wichita, KS 67213. *Phone:* 316-295-5100. *Toll-free phone:* 800-794-6945. *Fax:* 316-295-5101. *E-mail:* learn@friends.edu.

ITT Technical Institute

Overland Park, Kansas

http://www.itt-tech.edu/

- **Proprietary** 4-year
- **Coed**
- **Minimally difficult** entrance level

ACADEMICS

Degrees: associate and bachelor's.

CONTACT

Director of Recruitment, ITT Technical Institute, 7600 West 119th Street, Suite 100, Overland Park, KS 66213. *Phone:* 913-253-1300. *Toll-free phone:* 877-327-9026.

ITT Technical Institute

Wichita, Kansas

http://www.itt-tech.edu/

- **Proprietary** 4-year, part of ITT Educational Services, Inc.
- **Coed**
- **Minimally difficult** entrance level

ACADEMICS

Calendar: quarters. *Degrees:* associate and bachelor's.

STUDENT LIFE

Housing options: college housing not available.

CONTACT

Director of Recruitment, ITT Technical Institute, 8111 E. 32nd Street North, Suite 103, Wichita, KS 67226. *Phone:* 316-609-4100. *Toll-free phone:* 877-207-1047.

Kansas State University

Manhattan, Kansas

http://www.k-state.edu/

- **State-supported** university, founded 1863, part of Kansas Board of Regents
- **Suburban** 668-acre campus
- **Endowment** $474.0 million
- **Coed** 20,327 undergraduate students, 90% full-time, 48% women, 52% men
- **Noncompetitive** entrance level, 95% of applicants were admitted

UNDERGRAD STUDENTS

18,258 full-time, 2,069 part-time. Students come from 52 states and territories; 76 other countries; 17% are from out of state; 4% Black or African American, non-Hispanic/Latino; 6% Hispanic/Latino; 1% Asian, non-Hispanic/Latino; 0.1% Native Hawaiian or other Pacific Islander, non-Hispanic/Latino; 0.4% American Indian or Alaska Native, non-Hispanic/Latino; 3% Two or more races, non-Hispanic/Latino; 1% Race/ethnicity unknown; 7% international; 7% transferred in.

Freshmen

Admission: 9,614 applied, 9,127 admitted, 3,757 enrolled. ***Average high school GPA:*** 3.49. ***Test scores:*** ACT scores over 18: 96%; ACT scores over 24: 56%; ACT scores over 30: 13%.

Retention: 83% of full-time freshmen returned.

FACULTY

Total: 1,291, 84% full-time, 78% with terminal degrees.

Student/faculty ratio: 19:1.

ACADEMICS

Calendar: semesters. *Degrees:* certificates, associate, bachelor's, master's, doctoral, and postbachelor's certificates.

Special study options: academic remediation for entering students, accelerated degree program, adult/continuing education programs, advanced placement credit, cooperative education, distance learning, double majors, English as a second language, freshman honors college, honors programs, independent study, internships, off-campus study, part-time degree program, services for LD students, study abroad, summer session for credit. ***ROTC:*** Army (b), Air Force (b).

Unusual degree programs: 3-2 engineering; biology, kinesiology, horticulture, master of public health, biochemistry.

Computers: Students can access the following: computer help desk, free student e-mail accounts, online (class) grades, online (class) registration, online (class) schedules. Campuswide network is available. Wireless service is available via entire campus.

STUDENT LIFE
Housing options: coed, men-only, women-only, cooperative. Campus housing is university owned.

Activities and organizations: drama/theater group, student-run newspaper, radio and television station, choral group, marching band, athletic department groups, marching band, Union Governing Board, theater productions, debate team, national fraternities, national sororities.

Athletics Member NCAA. All Division I except football (Division I-A). ***Intercollegiate sports:*** baseball M(s), basketball M(s)/W(s), crew W(s), cross-country running M(s)/W(s), golf M(s)/W(s), soccer W, tennis W(s), track and field M(s)/W(s), volleyball W(s). ***Intramural sports:*** badminton M/W, basketball M/W, bowling M/W, crew M/W, cross-country running M/W, football M/W, golf M/W, ice hockey M, lacrosse M, racquetball M/W, soccer M/W, softball M/W, table tennis M/W, tennis M/W, track and field M/W, volleyball M/W, water polo M/W, weight lifting M/W, wrestling M.

Campus security: 24-hour emergency response devices and patrols, late-night transport/escort service, controlled dormitory access.

Student services: health clinic, personal/psychological counseling, women's center, legal services.

COSTS & FINANCIAL AID
Costs (2014–15) ***Tuition:*** state resident $8223 full-time; nonresident $21,813 full-time. Full-time tuition and fees vary according to course load, degree level, location, program, and reciprocity agreements. Part-time tuition and fees vary according to course load, degree level, location, program, and reciprocity agreements. ***Required fees:*** $811 full-time. ***Room and board:*** $8060. Room and board charges vary according to board plan, housing facility, and location. ***Payment plans:*** installment, deferred payment. ***Waivers:*** employees or children of employees.

Financial Aid Of all full-time matriculated undergraduates who enrolled in 2013, 12,227 applied for aid, 9,454 were judged to have need, 1,542 had their need fully met. In 2013, 1299 non-need-based awards were made. ***Average percent of need met:*** 77. ***Average financial aid package:*** $11,773. ***Average need-based loan:*** $4247. ***Average need-based gift aid:*** $4298. ***Average non-need-based aid:*** $3736. ***Average indebtedness upon graduation:*** $26,779.

APPLYING
Standardized Tests *Required for some:* SAT or ACT (for admission). *Recommended:* SAT or ACT (for admission).

Options: electronic application, early admission.

Application fee: $30.

Required: high school transcript, minimum 2.0 GPA.

Application deadlines: rolling (freshmen), rolling (out-of-state freshmen), rolling (transfers).

Notification: continuous (freshmen), continuous (out-of-state freshmen), continuous (transfers).

CONTACT
Ms. Molly McGaughey, Associate Director of Admissions, Kansas State University, 119 Anderson Hall, Manhattan, KS 66506. *Phone:* 785-532-6250. *Toll-free phone:* 800-432-8270. *Fax:* 785-532-6393. *E-mail:* k-state@k-state.edu.

Kansas Wesleyan University

Salina, Kansas

http://www.kwu.edu/

- **Independent United Methodist** comprehensive, founded 1886
- **Urban** 28-acre campus
- **Endowment** $29.0 million
- **Coed** 667 undergraduate students, 89% full-time, 55% women, 45% men
- **Moderately difficult** entrance level, 62% of applicants were admitted

UNDERGRAD STUDENTS
593 full-time, 74 part-time. Students come from 23 states and territories; 11 other countries; 41% are from out of state; 6% Black or African American, non-Hispanic/Latino; 13% Hispanic/Latino; 0.8% Asian, non-Hispanic/Latino; 0.7% American Indian or Alaska Native, non-Hispanic/Latino; 2% Two or more races, non-Hispanic/Latino; 0.2% Race/ethnicity unknown; 3% international; 15% transferred in; 63% live on campus.

Freshmen
Admission: 605 applied, 373 admitted, 144 enrolled. ***Average high school GPA:*** 3.41. ***Test scores:*** ACT scores over 18: 94%; ACT scores over 24: 40%; ACT scores over 30: 3%.

Retention: 63% of full-time freshmen returned.

FACULTY
Total: 90, 47% full-time, 33% with terminal degrees.
Student/faculty ratio: 11:1.

ACADEMICS
Calendar: 2 semesters with a summer term. *Degrees:* associate, bachelor's, and master's.

Special study options: academic remediation for entering students, adult/continuing education programs, advanced placement credit, cooperative education, distance learning, double majors, honors programs, independent study, internships, off-campus study, part-time degree program, student-designed majors, study abroad, summer session for credit.

Unusual degree programs: 3-2 engineering with Washington University in St. Louis.

Computers: 130 computers/terminals are available on campus for general student use. Students can access the following: campus intranet, free student e-mail accounts, online (class) grades, online (class) registration, online (class) schedules. Campuswide network is available. 100% of college-owned or -operated housing units are wired for high-speed Internet access. Wireless service is available via classrooms, dorm rooms, learning centers, libraries, student centers.

STUDENT LIFE
Housing options: on-campus residence required through sophomore year; coed, men-only, women-only. Campus housing is university owned. Freshman campus housing is guaranteed.

Activities and organizations: drama/theater group, student-run newspaper, radio and television station, choral group, marching band, Fellowship of Christian Athletes, Student Government, Wesleyan Chorale, Student Nurses Organization, Coyote Activities Board.

Athletics Member NAIA. ***Intercollegiate sports:*** baseball M(s), basketball M(s)/W(s), bowling M(s)/W(s), cheerleading M(s)/W(s), cross-country running M(s)/W(s), football M(s), golf M(s)/W(s), soccer M(s)/W(s), softball W(s), tennis M(s)/W(s), track and field M(s)/W(s), volleyball W(s), wrestling M(s). ***Intramural sports:*** basketball M/W, bowling M/W, fencing M/W, football W, golf M/W, racquetball M/W, softball M/W, table tennis M/W, volleyball M/W, weight lifting M/W.

Campus security: 24-hour emergency response devices, student patrols, late-night transport/escort service, controlled dormitory access, evening patrols by security.

Student services: personal/psychological counseling.

COSTS & FINANCIAL AID
Costs (2015–16) ***One-time required fee:*** $200. ***Comprehensive fee:*** $34,800 includes full-time tuition ($26,600) and room and board ($8200). Part-time tuition: $2400 per term. Part-time tuition and fees vary according to course load. ***College room only:*** $2800. Room and board charges vary according to housing facility. ***Payment plan:*** installment. ***Waivers:*** children of alumni, senior citizens, and employees or children of employees.

Financial Aid Of all full-time matriculated undergraduates who enrolled in 2013, 634 applied for aid, 530 were judged to have need, 91 had their need fully met. 98 Federal Work-Study jobs (averaging $1336). 75 state and other part-time jobs (averaging $1336). In 2013, 70 non-need-based awards were made. ***Average percent of need met:*** 70. ***Average financial aid package:*** $18,644. ***Average need-based loan:*** $4582. ***Average need-based gift aid:*** $7608. ***Average non-need-based aid:*** $7874. ***Average indebtedness upon graduation:*** $33,809.

APPLYING
Standardized Tests *Required:* SAT or ACT (for admission).

Options: electronic application, deferred entrance.

Application fee: $20.

Required: high school transcript, minimum 2.5 GPA. ***Required for some:*** essay or personal statement, interview.

Application deadlines: rolling (freshmen), rolling (out-of-state freshmen), rolling (transfers).

Notification: continuous (freshmen), continuous (out-of-state freshmen), continuous (transfers).

CONTACT
Kansas Wesleyan University, 100 East Claflin Avenue, Salina, KS 67401-6196. *Phone:* 785-827-5541 Ext. 1289. *Toll-free phone:* 800-874-1154 Ext. 1285.

Manhattan Christian College

Manhattan, Kansas

http://www.mccks.edu/

- **Independent** 4-year, founded 1927, affiliated with Christian Churches and Churches of Christ
- **Small-town** 10-acre campus
- **Coed** 327 undergraduate students, 68% full-time, 45% women, 55% men
- **Minimally difficult** entrance level, 60% of applicants were admitted

UNDERGRAD STUDENTS
222 full-time, 105 part-time. 1% are from out of state; 2% Black or African American, non-Hispanic/Latino; 4% Hispanic/Latino; 0.9% American Indian or Alaska Native, non-Hispanic/Latino; 2% Two or more races, non-Hispanic/Latino; 13% Race/ethnicity unknown; 5% international.

Freshmen
Admission: 162 applied, 97 admitted.

Retention: 75% of full-time freshmen returned.

FACULTY
Total: 34, 71% full-time.

Student/faculty ratio: 12:1.

ACADEMICS
Calendar: semesters. *Degrees:* certificates, diplomas, associate, and bachelor's.

Special study options: academic remediation for entering students, adult/continuing education programs, advanced placement credit, cooperative education, distance learning, double majors, independent study, internships, part-time degree program, summer session for credit. ***ROTC:*** Army (c), Air Force (c).

Unusual degree programs: 3-2 business administration with Kansas State University; engineering with Kansas State University; forestry with Kansas State University; nursing with Manhattan Area Technical College; social work with Kansas State University; Education with Kansas State University.

Computers: Students can access the following: campus intranet, computer help desk, free student e-mail accounts, online (class) grades, online (class) registration, online (class) schedules. Campuswide network is available. 100% of college-owned or -operated housing units are wired for high-speed Internet access. Wireless service is available via entire campus.

STUDENT LIFE
Housing options: on-campus residence required through sophomore year; men-only, women-only. Campus housing is university owned. Freshman campus housing is guaranteed.

Activities and organizations: drama/theater group, student-run newspaper, choral group, Campus Planning Committee, Drama Club, Nursing Home Ministry.

Athletics Member NCCAA. ***Intercollegiate sports:*** baseball M, basketball M/W, cross-country running M/W, soccer M/W, volleyball W. ***Intramural sports:*** basketball M/W, volleyball M/W.

Student services: personal/psychological counseling.

COSTS & FINANCIAL AID
Costs (2014–15) ***One-time required fee:*** $25. ***Comprehensive fee:*** $20,792 includes full-time tuition ($13,152), mandatory fees ($560), and room and board ($7080). Part-time tuition: $548 per credit hour. Part-time tuition and fees vary according to course load. ***Room and board:*** Room and board charges vary according to board plan. ***Payment plan:*** deferred payment. ***Waivers:*** employees or children of employees.

Financial Aid Of all full-time matriculated undergraduates who enrolled in 2009, 299 applied for aid, 270 were judged to have need, 184 had their need fully met. 56 Federal Work-Study jobs (averaging $1293). In 2009, 48 non-need-based awards were made. ***Average percent of need met:*** 70. ***Average financial aid package:*** $12,278. ***Average need-based loan:*** $3731. ***Average need-based gift aid:*** $4459. ***Average non-need-based aid:*** $3201. ***Average indebtedness upon graduation:*** $16,572.

APPLYING
Standardized Tests *Required:* SAT or ACT (for admission).

Options: electronic application.

Application fee: $25.

Required: essay or personal statement, high school transcript, minimum 2.0 GPA, 2 letters of recommendation, ACT of 18, SAT of 1290.

Application deadlines: 8/11 (freshmen), 8/11 (out-of-state freshmen), 8/11 (transfers).

Notification: continuous (freshmen), continuous (out-of-state freshmen), continuous (transfers).

CONTACT
Teka Wilson, Admissions Office Manager, Manhattan Christian College, 1415 Anderson Avenue, Manhattan, KS 66502. *Phone:* 877-246-4622 Ext. 212. *Toll-free phone:* 877-246-4622. *E-mail:* teka.wilson@mccks.edu.

McPherson College

McPherson, Kansas

http://www.mcpherson.edu/

- **Independent** comprehensive, founded 1887, affiliated with Church of the Brethren
- **Small-town** 26-acre campus
- **Coed**
- **Moderately difficult** entrance level

FACULTY
Student/faculty ratio: 14:1.

ACADEMICS
Calendar: 4-1-4. *Degrees:* bachelor's and master's.

STUDENT LIFE
Housing options: on-campus residence required through senior year; coed, men-only, women-only, special housing for students with disabilities. Campus housing is university owned. Freshman campus housing is guaranteed.

Activities and organizations: drama/theater group, student-run newspaper.

Athletics Member NAIA.

Campus security: student patrols, controlled dormitory access.

Student services: personal/psychological counseling.

COSTS & FINANCIAL AID
Costs (2014–15) ***Comprehensive fee:*** $32,446 includes full-time tuition ($23,390), mandatory fees ($645), and room and board ($8411). Full-time tuition and fees vary according to course load. Part-time tuition: $250 per hour. Part-time tuition and fees vary according to course load. ***Required fees:*** $30 per term part-time. ***Room and board:*** Room and board charges vary according to board plan, housing facility, and location.

Financial Aid Of all full-time matriculated undergraduates who enrolled in 2012, 524 applied for aid, 472 were judged to have need, 128 had their need fully met. 335 Federal Work-Study jobs (averaging $960). In 2012, 89 non-need-based awards were made. ***Average percent of need met:*** 85. ***Average financial aid package:*** $22,852. ***Average need-based loan:*** $8843. ***Average need-based gift aid:*** $6194. ***Average non-need-based aid:*** $9145. ***Average indebtedness upon graduation:*** $28,615.

APPLYING
Standardized Tests *Required:* SAT or ACT (for admission).
Options: electronic application, deferred entrance.
Application fee: $25.
Required: high school transcript, minimum 2.0 GPA.

CONTACT
Mr. Matt Pfannenstiel, Director of Admissions, McPherson College, 1600 East Euclid, McPherson, KS 67460. *Phone:* 800-365-7402. *Toll-free phone:* 800-365-7402. *E-mail:* admiss@mcpherson.edu.

★ MidAmerica Nazarene University
Olathe, Kansas
http://www.mnu.edu/

- **Independent** comprehensive, founded 1966, affiliated with Church of the Nazarene
- **Suburban** 105-acre campus with easy access to Kansas City
- **Endowment** $7.9 million
- **Coed** 1,393 undergraduate students, 81% full-time, 61% women, 39% men
- **Minimally difficult** entrance level, 72% of applicants were admitted

UNDERGRAD STUDENTS
1,132 full-time, 261 part-time. Students come from 35 states and territories; 4 other countries; 40% are from out of state; 10% Black or African American, non-Hispanic/Latino; 5% Hispanic/Latino; 2% Asian, non-Hispanic/Latino; 0.2% Native Hawaiian or other Pacific Islander, non-Hispanic/Latino; 1% American Indian or Alaska Native, non-Hispanic/Latino; 0.9% Two or more races, non-Hispanic/Latino; 14% Race/ethnicity unknown; 0.1% international; 24% transferred in; 63% live on campus.

Freshmen
Admission: 1,012 applied, 731 admitted, 202 enrolled. ***Average high school GPA:*** 3.3. ***Test scores:*** ACT scores over 18: 88%; ACT scores over 24: 37%; ACT scores over 30: 4%.
Retention: 62% of full-time freshmen returned.

FACULTY
Total: 82, 94% full-time.
Student/faculty ratio: 23:1.

ACADEMICS
Calendar: semesters. *Degrees:* associate, bachelor's, master's, post-master's, and postbachelor's certificates.
Special study options: academic remediation for entering students, accelerated degree program, adult/continuing education programs, advanced placement credit, distance learning, double majors, honors programs, independent study, internships, off-campus study, part-time degree program, services for LD students, study abroad, summer session for credit. ***ROTC:*** Army (c), Air Force (c).
Computers: Students can access the following: campus intranet, computer help desk, free student e-mail accounts, online (class) grades, online (class) registration, online (class) schedules. Campuswide network is available. 100% of college-owned or -operated housing units are wired for high-speed Internet access. Wireless service is available via entire campus.

STUDENT LIFE
Housing options: men-only, women-only, special housing for students with disabilities. Campus housing is university owned. Freshman campus housing is guaranteed.
Activities and organizations: drama/theater group, student-run newspaper, radio and television station, choral group.
Athletics Member NAIA. ***Intercollegiate sports:*** baseball M(s), basketball M(s)/W(s), cheerleading M(s)/W(s), football M(s), soccer M(s)/W(s), softball W(s), track and field M(s)/W(s), volleyball W(s). ***Intramural sports:*** basketball M/W, soccer M/W, softball M/W, tennis M/W, volleyball M/W.
Campus security: 24-hour emergency response devices and patrols, student patrols, late-night transport/escort service, controlled dormitory access.
Student services: personal/psychological counseling.

COSTS & FINANCIAL AID

Costs (2014–15) ***Comprehensive fee:*** $31,800 includes full-time tuition ($24,250) and room and board ($7550). Full-time tuition and fees vary according to course load and degree level. Part-time tuition: $800 per credit hour. Part-time tuition and fees vary according to course load, degree level, and program. ***Room and board:*** Room and board charges vary according to board plan. ***Payment plan:*** installment. ***Waivers:*** senior citizens and employees or children of employees.

Financial Aid Of all full-time matriculated undergraduates who enrolled in 2008, 796 applied for aid, 692 were judged to have need, 97 had their need fully met. In 2008, 187 non-need-based awards were made. ***Average percent of need met:*** 65. ***Average financial aid package:*** $13,686. ***Average need-based loan:*** $5638. ***Average need-based gift aid:*** $8989. ***Average non-need-based aid:*** $4891. ***Average indebtedness upon graduation:*** $28,859.

APPLYING

Standardized Tests *Required:* SAT or ACT (for admission).

Options: electronic application, deferred entrance.

Required: high school transcript, minimum 2.0 GPA. ***Recommended:*** TOEFL for international applicants.

Application deadlines: 8/1 (freshmen), 8/1 (transfers).

Notification: continuous (freshmen), continuous (transfers).

CONTACT

MidAmerica Nazarene University, 2030 East College Way, Olathe, KS 66062-1899. *Phone:* 913-971-3380. *Toll-free phone:* 800-800-8887.

See previous page for display ad and page 1520 for the College Close-Up.

Newman University

Wichita, Kansas

http://www.newmanu.edu/

- **Independent Roman Catholic** comprehensive, founded 1933
- **Urban** 61-acre campus
- **Endowment** $21.3 million
- **Coed** 2,732 undergraduate students, 38% full-time, 62% women, 38% men
- **Minimally difficult** entrance level, 53% of applicants were admitted

UNDERGRAD STUDENTS

1,045 full-time, 1,687 part-time. Students come from 21 states and territories; 26 other countries; 8% are from out of state; 3% Black or African American, non-Hispanic/Latino; 11% Hispanic/Latino; 6% Asian, non-Hispanic/Latino; 0.1% Native Hawaiian or other Pacific Islander, non-Hispanic/Latino; 1% American Indian or Alaska Native, non-Hispanic/Latino; 3% Two or more races, non-Hispanic/Latino; 0.9% Race/ethnicity unknown; 3% international; 6% transferred in; 11% live on campus.

Freshmen

Admission: 2,494 applied, 1,316 admitted, 174 enrolled. ***Average high school GPA:*** 3.62. ***Test scores:*** SAT critical reading scores over 500: 54%; SAT math scores over 500: 69%; SAT writing scores over 500: 54%; ACT scores over 18: 99%; SAT critical reading scores over 600: 8%; SAT math scores over 600: 31%; SAT writing scores over 600: 8%; ACT scores over 24: 46%; SAT critical reading scores over 700: 8%; SAT writing scores over 700: 8%; ACT scores over 30: 13%.

Retention: 71% of full-time freshmen returned.

FACULTY

Total: 267, 31% full-time, 25% with terminal degrees.

Student/faculty ratio: 15:1.

ACADEMICS

Calendar: semesters. *Degrees:* associate, bachelor's, and master's.

Special study options: academic remediation for entering students, accelerated degree program, adult/continuing education programs, advanced placement credit, cooperative education, distance learning, double majors, honors programs, independent study, internships, off-campus study, part-time degree program, services for LD students, student-designed majors, study abroad, summer session for credit.

Unusual degree programs: 3-2 occupational therapy with Washington University in St. Louis.

Computers: 90 computers/terminals and 300 ports are available on campus for general student use. Students can access the following: computer help desk, free student e-mail accounts, online (class) grades, online (class) registration, online (class) schedules. Campuswide network is available. 100% of college-owned or -operated housing units are wired for high-speed Internet access. Wireless service is available via entire campus.

STUDENT LIFE

Housing options: on-campus residence required through sophomore year; coed, men-only, women-only, special housing for students with disabilities. Campus housing is university owned. Freshman campus housing is guaranteed.

Activities and organizations: drama/theater group, student-run newspaper, choral group, Newman University Medical Professionals Club (NUMPC), Jets for Life, Ambassadors for Christ, Nursing Club, Hispanic American Leadership Organization (HALO).

Athletics Member NCAA. All Division II. ***Intercollegiate sports:*** baseball M(s)/W, basketball M(s)/W(s), bowling M(s)(c)/W(s)(c), cross-country running M(s)/W(s), golf M(s)/W(s), soccer M(s)/W(s), softball W(s), tennis M(s)/W(s), volleyball W(s), wrestling M(s). ***Intramural sports:*** baseball M, basketball M/W, bowling M/W, football M/W, golf M/W, soccer M/W, softball M/W, table tennis M/W, volleyball M/W, weight lifting M/W.

Campus security: 24-hour emergency response devices and patrols, student patrols, late-night transport/escort service, controlled dormitory access.

Student services: personal/psychological counseling.

COSTS & FINANCIAL AID

Costs (2014–15) ***Comprehensive fee:*** $31,790 includes full-time tuition ($23,790), mandatory fees ($940), and room and board ($7060). Part-time tuition: $793 per credit hour. Part-time tuition and fees vary according to course load. ***Required fees:*** $17 per credit hour part-time, $35 per term part-time. ***Room and board:*** Room and board charges vary according to board plan and housing facility. ***Payment plan:*** installment. ***Waivers:*** employees or children of employees.

Financial Aid Of all full-time matriculated undergraduates who enrolled in 2013, 1,027 applied for aid, 877 were judged to have need, 225 had their need fully met. 59 Federal Work-Study jobs (averaging $2000). 89 state and other part-time jobs (averaging $2000). In 2013, 55 non-need-based awards were made. ***Average percent of need met:*** 67. ***Average financial aid package:*** $19,844. ***Average need-based loan:*** $4051. ***Average need-based gift aid:*** $4844. ***Average non-need-based aid:*** $8927. ***Average indebtedness upon graduation:*** $23,843.

APPLYING

Standardized Tests *Required for some:* SAT or ACT (for admission).

Options: electronic application, early admission, deferred entrance.

Required: high school transcript, minimum 2.0 GPA. ***Recommended:*** interview.

Application deadlines: rolling (freshmen), rolling (out-of-state freshmen), rolling (transfers).

Notification: continuous (freshmen), continuous (out-of-state freshmen), continuous (transfers).

CONTACT

Quinn Bowman, Associate Director of admissions, Newman University, 3100 McCormick Avenue, Wichita, KS 67213. *Phone:* 316-942-4291 Ext. 2125. *Toll-free phone:* 877-NEWMANU. *Fax:* 316-942-4483. *E-mail:* reusserj@newmanu.edu.

Pittsburg State University

Pittsburg, Kansas

http://www.pittstate.edu/

- **State-supported** comprehensive, founded 1903, part of Kansas State Board of Regents
- **Small-town** 630-acre campus
- **Coed** 6,270 undergraduate students, 89% full-time, 48% women, 52% men
- **Minimally difficult** entrance level, 79% of applicants were admitted

UNDERGRAD STUDENTS
5,586 full-time, 684 part-time. Students come from 31 states and territories; 46 other countries; 34% are from out of state; 4% Black or African American, non-Hispanic/Latino; 5% Hispanic/Latino; 0.8% Asian, non-Hispanic/Latino; 0.2% Native Hawaiian or other Pacific Islander, non-Hispanic/Latino; 1% American Indian or Alaska Native, non-Hispanic/Latino; 5% Two or more races, non-Hispanic/Latino; 0.4% Race/ethnicity unknown; 6% international; 9% transferred in; 19% live on campus.

Freshmen
Admission: 2,758 applied, 2,184 admitted, 1,027 enrolled. ***Average high school GPA:*** 3.3. ***Test scores:*** ACT scores over 18: 86%; ACT scores over 24: 30%; ACT scores over 30: 3%.

Retention: 74% of full-time freshmen returned.

FACULTY
Total: 412, 77% full-time, 60% with terminal degrees.

Student/faculty ratio: 19:1.

ACADEMICS
Calendar: semesters. *Degrees:* certificates, associate, bachelor's, master's, and post-master's certificates.

Special study options: accelerated degree program, adult/continuing education programs, distance learning, double majors, freshman honors college, honors programs, independent study, internships, off-campus study, part-time degree program, services for LD students, student-designed majors, study abroad, summer session for credit. ***ROTC:*** Army (b).

Computers: 425 computers/terminals are available on campus for general student use. Students can access the following: campus intranet, computer help desk, free student e-mail accounts, online (class) grades, online (class) registration, online (class) schedules. Campuswide network is available. 100% of college-owned or -operated housing units are wired for high-speed Internet access. Wireless service is available via entire campus.

STUDENT LIFE
Housing options: on-campus residence required for freshman year; coed, special housing for students with disabilities. Campus housing is university owned. Freshman applicants given priority for college housing.

Activities and organizations: drama/theater group, student-run newspaper, radio and television station, choral group, marching band, Student Government Association, student yearbook, student newspaper, Student Activities Council, Students in Free Enterprise (SIFE), national fraternities, national sororities.

Athletics Member NCAA. All Division II. ***Intercollegiate sports:*** baseball M(s), basketball M(s)/W(s), cheerleading M(s)/W(s), cross-country running M(s)/W(s), football M(s), golf M(s), softball W(s), track and field M(s)/W(s), volleyball W(s). ***Intramural sports:*** badminton M/W, basketball M/W, football M/W, lacrosse M(c), racquetball M/W, rugby M(c), soccer M(c)/W(c), softball M/W, table tennis M/W, tennis M/W, ultimate Frisbee M/W, volleyball M/W.

Campus security: 24-hour emergency response devices and patrols, late-night transport/escort service, controlled dormitory access.

Student services: health clinic, personal/psychological counseling, legal services.

COSTS & FINANCIAL AID
Costs (2014–15) ***Tuition:*** state resident $4936 full-time, $165 per credit hour part-time; nonresident $15,042 full-time, $502 per credit hour part-time. Part-time tuition and fees vary according to course load. ***Required fees:*** $1294 full-time, $56 per credit hour part-time. ***Room and board:*** $6936. Room and board charges vary according to board plan and housing facility. ***Payment plan:*** installment. ***Waivers:*** employees or children of employees.

Financial Aid Of all full-time matriculated undergraduates who enrolled in 2014, 4,411 applied for aid, 3,551 were judged to have need, 440 had their need fully met. 270 Federal Work-Study jobs (averaging $1680). 8 state and other part-time jobs (averaging $1423). In 2014, 381 non-need-based awards were made. ***Average percent of need met:*** 6. ***Average financial aid package:*** $6505. ***Average need-based loan:*** $3973. ***Average need-based gift aid:*** $4422. ***Average non-need-based aid:*** $2094. ***Average indebtedness upon graduation:*** $23,307.

APPLYING
Standardized Tests *Required:* SAT or ACT (for admission).

Options: electronic application, deferred entrance.

Application fee: $30.

Required: high school transcript. ***Required for some:*** minimum 2.0 GPA.

Application deadlines: rolling (freshmen), rolling (transfers).

CONTACT
Director of Admission, Pittsburg State University, 1701 South Broadway, Pittsburg, KS 66762. *Phone:* 620-235-4251. *Toll-free phone:* 800-854-7488. *Fax:* 620-235-6003. *E-mail:* psuadmit@pittstate.edu.

Rasmussen College Kansas City/Overland Park

Overland Park, Kansas

http://www.rasmussen.edu/

- **Proprietary** 4-year, founded 2013, part of Rasmussen College System
- **Suburban** campus
- **Coed** 36 undergraduate students, 83% full-time, 75% women, 25% men
- **Minimally difficult** entrance level

UNDERGRAD STUDENTS
30 full-time, 6 part-time.

Freshmen
Admission: 7 enrolled.

FACULTY
Total: 3, 67% full-time.

Student/faculty ratio: 22:1.

ACADEMICS
Degrees: certificates, diplomas, associate, bachelor's, and postbachelor's certificates.

Special study options: academic remediation for entering students, accelerated degree program, adult/continuing education programs, distance learning, double majors, internships, part-time degree program, summer session for credit.

Computers: Students can access the following: computer help desk, free student e-mail accounts, online (class) grades, online (class) schedules. Campuswide network is available. Wireless service is available via entire campus.

STUDENT LIFE
Housing options: college housing not available.

COSTS
Costs (2014–15) ***Tuition:*** $10,764 full-time, $310 per credit part-time. Full-time tuition and fees vary according to course level, course load, degree level, location, and program. Part-time tuition and fees vary according to course level, course load, degree level, location, and program. No tuition increase for student's term of enrollment. ***Required fees:*** $1350 full-time. ***Payment plans:*** installment, deferred payment. ***Waivers:*** employees or children of employees.

APPLYING
Standardized Tests *Required:* Internal Exam (for admission).

Options: electronic application, early admission, deferred entrance.

Required: high school transcript, minimum 2.0 GPA. ***Required for some:*** interview.

Application deadlines: rolling (freshmen), rolling (transfers).

CONTACT
Susan Hammerstrom, Director of Admissions, Rasmussen College Kansas City/Overland Park, 11600 College Boulevard, Overland Park, KS 66210. *Phone:* 913-491-7870. *Toll-free phone:* 888-549-6755. *E-mail:* susan.hammerstrom@rasmussen.edu.

Rasmussen College Topeka

Topeka, Kansas

http://www.rasmussen.edu/

- **Proprietary** 4-year, founded 2013, part of Rasmussen College System
- **Suburban** campus
- **Coed** 99 undergraduate students, 74% full-time, 78% women, 22% men
- **Minimally difficult** entrance level

UNDERGRAD STUDENTS
73 full-time, 26 part-time.

Freshmen
Admission: 25 enrolled.

FACULTY
Total: 7, 14% full-time.

Student/faculty ratio: 22:1.

ACADEMICS
Degrees: certificates, diplomas, associate, bachelor's, and postbachelor's certificates.

Special study options: academic remediation for entering students, accelerated degree program, adult/continuing education programs, distance learning, double majors, internships, part-time degree program, summer session for credit.

Computers: Students can access the following: computer help desk, free student e-mail accounts, online (class) grades, online (class) schedules. Campuswide network is available. Wireless service is available via entire campus.

STUDENT LIFE
Housing options: college housing not available.

COSTS
Costs (2014–15) ***Tuition:*** $10,764 full-time, $310 per credit hour part-time. Full-time tuition and fees vary according to course level, course load, degree level, location, and program. Part-time tuition and fees vary according to course level, course load, degree level, location, and program. No tuition increase for student's term of enrollment. ***Required fees:*** $1350 full-time. ***Payment plans:*** installment, deferred payment. ***Waivers:*** employees or children of employees.

APPLYING
Standardized Tests *Required:* Internal Exam (for admission).

Options: electronic application, early admission, deferred entrance.

Required: high school transcript, minimum 2.0 GPA. ***Required for some:*** interview.

Application deadlines: rolling (freshmen), rolling (transfers).

CONTACT
Susan Hammerstrom, Director of Admissions, Rasmussen College Topeka, 620 SW Governor View, Topeka, KS 66606. *Phone:* 785-228-7320. *Toll-free phone:* 888-549-6755. *E-mail:* susan.hammerstrom@rasmussen.edu.

Southwestern College

Winfield, Kansas

http://www.sckans.edu/

- **Independent United Methodist** comprehensive, founded 1885
- **Small-town** 70-acre campus with easy access to Wichita
- **Endowment** $30.8 million
- **Coed** 1,323 undergraduate students, 42% full-time, 42% women, 58% men
- **Minimally difficult** entrance level, 88% of applicants were admitted

UNDERGRAD STUDENTS
557 full-time, 766 part-time. Students come from 46 states and territories; 10 other countries; 45% are from out of state; 10% Black or African American, non-Hispanic/Latino; 7% Hispanic/Latino; 1% Asian, non-Hispanic/Latino; 0.2% Native Hawaiian or other Pacific Islander, non-Hispanic/Latino; 2% American Indian or Alaska Native, non-Hispanic/Latino; 4% Two or more races, non-Hispanic/Latino; 9% Race/ethnicity unknown; 5% international; 5% transferred in; 69% live on campus.

Freshmen
Admission: 439 applied, 386 admitted, 123 enrolled. ***Average high school GPA:*** 3.39. ***Test scores:*** SAT critical reading scores over 500: 18%; SAT math scores over 500: 36%; SAT writing scores over 500: 10%; ACT scores over 18: 90%; SAT critical reading scores over 600: 5%; SAT math scores over 600: 9%; ACT scores over 24: 30%; ACT scores over 30: 2%. ***Retention:*** 66% of full-time freshmen returned.

FACULTY
Total: 167, 28% full-time, 34% with terminal degrees.

Student/faculty ratio: 10:1.

ACADEMICS
Calendar: semesters. *Degrees:* certificates, bachelor's, master's, doctoral, and postbachelor's certificates.

Special study options: accelerated degree program, adult/continuing education programs, advanced placement credit, distance learning, double majors, honors programs, independent study, internships, off-campus study, part-time degree program, student-designed majors, study abroad, summer session for credit.

Computers: 50 computers/terminals are available on campus for general student use. Students can access the following: campus intranet, computer help desk, free student e-mail accounts, online (class) grades, online (class) registration, online (class) schedules. Campuswide network is available. 100% of college-owned or -operated housing units are wired for high-speed Internet access. Wireless service is available via classrooms, computer centers, computer labs, dorm rooms, learning centers, libraries, student centers.

STUDENT LIFE
Housing options: on-campus residence required through sophomore year; coed, men-only, women-only. Campus housing is university owned. Freshman campus housing is guaranteed.

Activities and organizations: drama/theater group, student-run newspaper, radio and television station, choral group, Discipleship SC, Leadership SC, Acappella Choir, Concert Band, Southwestern Singers, national fraternities, national sororities.

Athletics Member NAIA. ***Intercollegiate sports:*** basketball M(s)/W(s), cross-country running M(s)/W(s), football M(s), golf M(s)/W(s), soccer M(s)/W(s), softball W(s), tennis M(s)/W(s), track and field M(s)/W(s), volleyball W(s). ***Intramural sports:*** basketball M/W, softball M/W, swimming and diving M(c)/W(c), tennis M/W, ultimate Frisbee M(c)/W(c), volleyball M/W.

Campus security: 24-hour emergency response devices and patrols, late-night transport/escort service, controlled dormitory access.

Student services: health clinic, personal/psychological counseling.

COSTS & FINANCIAL AID
Costs (2015–16) ***Comprehensive fee:*** $33,026 includes full-time tuition ($25,796), mandatory fees ($150), and room and board ($7080). Full-time tuition and fees vary according to class time, course load, degree level, location, and program. Part-time tuition: $1075 per credit hour. Part-time tuition and fees vary according to class time, course load, degree level, location, and program. ***College room only:*** $3200. Room and board charges vary according to board plan and housing facility. ***Payment plan:*** installment. ***Waivers:*** senior citizens and employees or children of employees.

Financial Aid Of all full-time matriculated undergraduates who enrolled in 2013, 479 applied for aid, 442 were judged to have need, 64 had their need fully met. 140 Federal Work-Study jobs (averaging $1640). 91 state and other part-time jobs (averaging $1322). In 2013, 93 non-need-based awards were made. ***Average percent of need met:*** 71. ***Average financial aid package:*** $20,531. ***Average need-based loan:*** $6337. ***Average need-based gift aid:*** $14,101. ***Average non-need-based aid:*** $7729. ***Average indebtedness upon graduation:*** $33,478. ***Financial aid deadline:*** 8/15.

APPLYING
Standardized Tests *Required:* SAT or ACT (for admission).

Options: electronic application.

Application fee: $25.

Required: high school transcript, minimum 2.5 GPA. ***Required for some:*** 2 letters of recommendation, interview. ***Recommended:*** essay or personal statement.

Application deadlines: 8/1 (freshmen), 8/1 (out-of-state freshmen), 8/1 (transfers).

Notification: continuous (freshmen), continuous (out-of-state freshmen), continuous (transfers).

CONTACT

Southwestern College, 100 College Street, Winfield, KS 67156-2499. *Phone:* 620-229-6364. *Toll-free phone:* 800-846-1543.

Sterling College

Sterling, Kansas

http://www.sterling.edu/

- **Independent Presbyterian** 4-year, founded 1887
- **Rural** 46-acre campus
- **Endowment** $12.6 million
- **Coed** 718 undergraduate students, 86% full-time, 46% women, 54% men
- **Minimally difficult** entrance level, 44% of applicants were admitted

UNDERGRAD STUDENTS

620 full-time, 98 part-time. Students come from 30 states and territories; 4 other countries; 50% are from out of state; 11% Black or African American, non-Hispanic/Latino; 11% Hispanic/Latino; 2% Native Hawaiian or other Pacific Islander, non-Hispanic/Latino; 3% American Indian or Alaska Native, non-Hispanic/Latino; 6% Race/ethnicity unknown; 1% international; 8% transferred in; 80% live on campus.

Freshmen

Admission: 883 applied, 389 admitted, 188 enrolled. *Average high school GPA:* 3.2. *Test scores:* SAT critical reading scores over 500: 41%; SAT math scores over 500: 39%; SAT writing scores over 500: 35%; ACT scores over 18: 86%; SAT critical reading scores over 600: 5%; SAT math scores over 600: 7%; SAT writing scores over 600: 5%; ACT scores over 24: 33%; ACT scores over 30: 7%.

Retention: 65% of full-time freshmen returned.

FACULTY

Total: 63, 62% full-time, 30% with terminal degrees.

Student/faculty ratio: 14:1.

ACADEMICS

Calendar: 4-1-4. *Degree:* bachelor's.

Special study options: advanced placement credit, distance learning, double majors, honors programs, independent study, internships, off-campus study, services for LD students, student-designed majors, study abroad, summer session for credit.

Unusual degree programs: 3-2 biology/medical technology with Wichita State University.

Computers: 50 computers/terminals are available on campus for general student use. Students can access the following: campus intranet, computer help desk, free student e-mail accounts, online (class) grades, online (class) registration, online (class) schedules. Campuswide network is available. 100% of college-owned or -operated housing units are wired for high-speed Internet access. Wireless service is available via entire campus.

STUDENT LIFE

Housing options: on-campus residence required through senior year; men-only, women-only. Campus housing is university owned. Freshman campus housing is guaranteed.

Activities and organizations: drama/theater group, student-run newspaper, radio and television station, choral group, Fellowship of Christian Athletes, Student Activities Council, Bible study groups, theatre, Mission teams.

Athletics Member NAIA. *Intercollegiate sports:* baseball M(s), basketball M(s)/W(s), cross-country running M(s)/W(s), football M(s), golf M(s)/W(s), soccer M(s)/W(s), softball W(s), track and field M(s)/W(s), volleyball W(s). *Intramural sports:* basketball M/W, softball M/W, ultimate Frisbee M/W, volleyball M/W.

Campus security: controlled dormitory access, late night security patrol.

Student services: health clinic, personal/psychological counseling.

COSTS & FINANCIAL AID

Costs (2014–15) *Comprehensive fee:* $29,921 includes full-time tuition ($21,700), mandatory fees ($290), and room and board ($7931). Part-time tuition: $406 per credit. *Room and board:* Room and board charges vary according to board plan and housing facility. *Payment plan:* installment. *Waivers:* senior citizens and employees or children of employees.

Financial Aid Of all full-time matriculated undergraduates who enrolled in 2013, 588 applied for aid, 511 were judged to have need, 162 had their need fully met. 206 Federal Work-Study jobs (averaging $712). In 2013, 75 non-need-based awards were made. *Average percent of need met:* 89. *Average financial aid package:* $21,107. *Average need-based loan:* $5297. *Average need-based gift aid:* $11,050. *Average non-need-based aid:* $9778. *Average indebtedness upon graduation:* $28,221.

APPLYING

Standardized Tests *Required:* SAT or ACT (for admission).

Options: electronic application, deferred entrance.

Application fee: $25.

Required: high school transcript, minimum 2.2 GPA. *Required for some:* 2 letters of recommendation. *Recommended:* essay or personal statement, interview.

Application deadlines: rolling (freshmen), rolling (transfers).

Notification: continuous (freshmen), continuous (transfers).

CONTACT

Marge Jones, Admissions Office Manager, Sterling College, 125 West Cooper, Sterling, KS 67579. *Phone:* 620-278-4275. *Toll-free phone:* 800-346-1017. *Fax:* 620-278-4416. *E-mail:* admissions@sterling.edu.

Tabor College

Hillsboro, Kansas

http://www.tabor.edu/

- **Independent Mennonite Brethren** comprehensive, founded 1908
- **Small-town** 87-acre campus with easy access to Wichita
- **Endowment** $8.5 million
- **Coed** 735 undergraduate students, 77% full-time, 50% women, 50% men
- **Moderately difficult** entrance level, 86% of applicants were admitted

UNDERGRAD STUDENTS

569 full-time, 166 part-time. Students come from 33 states and territories; 8 other countries; 49% are from out of state; 8% Black or African American, non-Hispanic/Latino; 11% Hispanic/Latino; 0.7% Asian, non-Hispanic/Latino; 0.3% Native Hawaiian or other Pacific Islander, non-Hispanic/Latino; 0.4% American Indian or Alaska Native, non-Hispanic/Latino; 3% Two or more races, non-Hispanic/Latino; 6% Race/ethnicity unknown; 2% international; 16% transferred in; 86% live on campus.

Freshmen

Admission: 482 applied, 413 admitted, 159 enrolled. *Average high school GPA:* 3.38. *Test scores:* SAT critical reading scores over 500: 42%; SAT math scores over 500: 39%; ACT scores over 18: 96%; SAT critical reading scores over 600: 12%; SAT math scores over 600: 12%; ACT scores over 24: 37%; SAT critical reading scores over 700: 6%; SAT math scores over 700: 6%; ACT scores over 30: 7%.

Retention: 61% of full-time freshmen returned.

FACULTY

Total: 102, 32% full-time, 34% with terminal degrees.

Student/faculty ratio: 12:1.

ACADEMICS

Calendar: 4-1-4. *Degrees:* associate, bachelor's, and master's.

Special study options: academic remediation for entering students, accelerated degree program, adult/continuing education programs, advanced placement credit, cooperative education, distance learning, double majors, honors programs, independent study, internships, off-campus study, part-time degree program, services for LD students, student-designed majors, study abroad.

Computers: 39 computers/terminals are available on campus for general student use. Students can access the following: computer help desk, free student e-mail accounts, online (class) grades, online (class) schedules. Campuswide network is available. 100% of college-owned or -operated housing units are wired for high-speed Internet access. Wireless service is available via entire campus.

STUDENT LIFE
Housing options: on-campus residence required through senior year; men-only, women-only, special housing for students with disabilities. Campus housing is university owned. Freshman campus housing is guaranteed.

Activities and organizations: drama/theater group, student-run newspaper, choral group, Student Activities Board, CHUMS (Challenging, Helping and Understanding through Mentorship), Intramurals, WUMP (Wichita Urban Ministries Plunge), Multi-Cultural Student Union.

Athletics Member NAIA. ***Intercollegiate sports:*** baseball M(s), basketball M(s)/W(s), bowling M(s)/W(s), cheerleading M(s)/W(s), cross-country running M(s)/W(s), football M(s), soccer M(s)/W(s), softball W(s), swimming and diving M(s)/W(s), tennis M(s)/W(s), track and field M(s)/W(s), volleyball W(s). ***Intramural sports:*** basketball M/W, racquetball M/W, soccer M/W, volleyball M/W.

Campus security: Emergency Alert System (voluntary individual sign-up).

Student services: personal/psychological counseling.

COSTS & FINANCIAL AID
Costs (2014–15) ***Comprehensive fee:*** $32,520 includes full-time tuition ($23,100), mandatory fees ($800), and room and board ($8620). Full-time tuition and fees vary according to course load and program. Part-time tuition: $482 per hour. Part-time tuition and fees vary according to course load and program. ***Required fees:*** $480 per term part-time. ***Room and board:*** Room and board charges vary according to housing facility and location. ***Payment plan:*** installment. ***Waivers:*** employees or children of employees.

Financial Aid Of all full-time matriculated undergraduates who enrolled in 2013, 581 applied for aid, 499 were judged to have need, 62 had their need fully met. 235 Federal Work-Study jobs (averaging $914). In 2013, 81 non-need-based awards were made. ***Average percent of need met:*** 72. ***Average financial aid package:*** $19,268. ***Average need-based loan:*** $4656. ***Average need-based gift aid:*** $4696. ***Average non-need-based aid:*** $9458. ***Average indebtedness upon graduation:*** $26,588. ***Financial aid deadline:*** 8/15.

APPLYING
Standardized Tests *Required:* SAT or ACT (for admission).

Options: electronic application, early admission, deferred entrance.

Application fee: $30.

Required: essay or personal statement, high school transcript, minimum 2.0 GPA, ACT or SAT required; transfers must validate high school graduation date. ***Recommended:*** interview.

Application deadlines: rolling (freshmen), rolling (out-of-state freshmen), rolling (transfers).

Notification: continuous (freshmen), continuous (out-of-state freshmen), continuous (transfers).

CONTACT
Mr. Lee Waldron, Director of Admissions, Tabor College, 400 South Jefferson, Hillsboro, KS 67063. *Phone:* 620-947-3121 Ext. 1727. *Toll-free phone:* 800-822-6799. *Fax:* 620-947-3789. *E-mail:* leew@tabor.edu.

The University of Kansas
Lawrence, Kansas
http://www.ku.edu/

- **State-supported** university, founded 1866, part of Kansas Board of Regents System
- **Suburban** 1000-acre campus with easy access to Kansas City
- **Endowment** $2.0 billion
- **Coed** 19,343 undergraduate students, 90% full-time, 50% women, 50% men
- **Moderately difficult** entrance level, 91% of applicants were admitted

UNDERGRAD STUDENTS
17,335 full-time, 2,008 part-time. Students come from 53 states and territories; 73 other countries; 24% are from out of state; 5% Black or African American, non-Hispanic/Latino; 7% Hispanic/Latino; 4% Asian, non-Hispanic/Latino; 0.1% Native Hawaiian or other Pacific Islander, non-Hispanic/Latino; 0.4% American Indian or Alaska Native, non-Hispanic/Latino; 5% Two or more races, non-Hispanic/Latino; 0.9% Race/ethnicity unknown; 6% international; 6% transferred in; 25% live on campus.

Freshmen
Admission: 15,767 applied, 14,414 admitted, 4,084 enrolled. ***Average high school GPA:*** 3.5. ***Test scores:*** ACT scores over 18: 96%; ACT scores over 24: 64%; ACT scores over 30: 16%.

Retention: 80% of full-time freshmen returned.

FACULTY
Total: 1,773, 78% full-time, 80% with terminal degrees.

Student/faculty ratio: 17:1.

ACADEMICS
Calendar: semesters. *Degrees:* certificates, bachelor's, master's, doctoral, and postbachelor's certificates (University of Kansas is a single institution with academic programs and facilities at two primary locations: Lawrence and Kansas City).

Special study options: academic remediation for entering students, accelerated degree program, advanced placement credit, cooperative education, distance learning, double majors, English as a second language, honors programs, independent study, internships, part-time degree program, services for LD students, study abroad, summer session for credit. ***ROTC:*** Army (b), Navy (b), Air Force (b).

Computers: 1,500 computers/terminals are available on campus for general student use. Students can access the following: campus intranet, computer help desk, free student e-mail accounts, online (class) grades, online (class) registration, online (class) schedules, online payments, wireless network. Campuswide network is available. 100% of college-owned or -operated housing units are wired for high-speed Internet access. Wireless service is available via entire campus.

STUDENT LIFE
Housing options: coed, women-only, cooperative. Campus housing is university owned.

Activities and organizations: drama/theater group, student-run newspaper, radio and television station, choral group, marching band, Adventure Club, Entrepreneurship Club, Panhellenic Association, Center for Community Outreach, KU Running Club, national fraternities, national sororities.

Athletics Member NCAA. All Division I except football (Division I-A). ***Intercollegiate sports:*** baseball M(s), basketball M(s)/W(s), crew W(s), cross-country running M(s)/W(s), golf M(s)/W(s), rugby M(c), soccer W(s), softball W(s), swimming and diving W(s), tennis W(s), track and field M(s)/W(s), volleyball W(s). ***Intramural sports:*** badminton M(c)/W(c), baseball M(c), basketball M/W, bowling M(c)/W(c), crew M(c)/W(c), football M/W, golf M/W, lacrosse M(c)/W(c), racquetball M(c)/W(c), rock climbing M(c)/W(c), rugby W(c), sailing M(c)/W(c), soccer M(c)/W(c), softball W(c), swimming and diving M(c)/W(c), table tennis M(c)/W(c), tennis M(c)/W(c), ultimate Frisbee M(c)/W(c), volleyball W(c).

Campus security: 24-hour emergency response devices and patrols, late-night transport/escort service, controlled dormitory access, University police department.

Student services: health clinic, personal/psychological counseling, women's center, legal services.

COSTS & FINANCIAL AID
Costs (2014–15) ***Tuition:*** state resident $8807 full-time, $294 per credit hour part-time; nonresident $22,947 full-time, $765 per credit hour part-time. Full-time tuition and fees vary according to program, reciprocity agreements, and student level. Part-time tuition and fees vary according to program, reciprocity agreements, and student level. No tuition increase for student's term of enrollment. ***Required fees:*** $900 full-time, $75 per credit hour part-time. ***Room and board:*** $7896; room only: $4262. Room and board charges vary according to board plan and housing facility. ***Payment plan:*** installment. ***Waivers:*** employees or children of employees.

Financial Aid Of all full-time matriculated undergraduates who enrolled in 2013, 11,117 applied for aid, 8,258 were judged to have need, 835 had their need fully met. 440 Federal Work-Study jobs (averaging $2136). 63 state and other part-time jobs (averaging $4121). In 2013, 2041 non-need-based awards were made. ***Average percent of need met:*** 50. ***Average financial aid package:*** $8965. ***Average need-based loan:*** $4253. ***Average need-based gift aid:*** $5096. ***Average non-need-based aid:*** $3744. ***Average indebtedness upon graduation:*** $25,268.

APPLYING
Standardized Tests *Required:* SAT or ACT (for admission).
Options: electronic application.
Application fee: $30.
Required: high school transcript, minimum 2.0 GPA, Kansas Qualified Admissions college-prep curriculum; ACT or SAT scores (in-state ACT 21/SAT 980; out-of-state ACT 24/SAT 1090); class rank. ***Required for some:*** minimum 2.5 GPA.
Notification: continuous (freshmen), continuous (out-of-state freshmen), continuous (transfers).

CONTACT
Ms. Lisa Pinamonti Kress, Director of Admissions, The University of Kansas, KU Visitor Center, 1502 Iowa Street, Lawrence, KS 66045-7576. *Phone:* 785-864-3911. *Toll-free phone:* 888-686-7323. *Fax:* 785-864-5006. *E-mail:* adm@ku.edu.

University of Saint Mary

Leavenworth, Kansas

http://www.stmary.edu/

- **Independent Roman Catholic** comprehensive, founded 1923
- **Small-town** 240-acre campus with easy access to Kansas City
- **Endowment** $18.5 million
- **Coed** 917 undergraduate students, 65% full-time, 64% women, 36% men
- **Moderately difficult** entrance level, 47% of applicants were admitted

UNDERGRAD STUDENTS
593 full-time, 324 part-time. Students come from 26 states and territories; 4 other countries; 42% are from out of state; 10% Black or African American, non-Hispanic/Latino; 11% Hispanic/Latino; 0.7% Asian, non-Hispanic/Latino; 1% Native Hawaiian or other Pacific Islander, non-Hispanic/Latino; 0.6% American Indian or Alaska Native, non-Hispanic/Latino; 3% Two or more races, non-Hispanic/Latino; 12% Race/ethnicity unknown; 0.9% international; 11% transferred in; 43% live on campus.

Freshmen
Admission: 737 applied, 350 admitted, 107 enrolled. ***Average high school GPA:*** 3.32. ***Test scores:*** SAT critical reading scores over 500: 35%; SAT math scores over 500: 31%; ACT scores over 18: 95%; SAT critical reading scores over 600: 4%; ACT scores over 24: 26%; ACT scores over 30: 1%.
Retention: 72% of full-time freshmen returned.

FACULTY
Total: 245, 25% full-time, 26% with terminal degrees.
Student/faculty ratio: 9:1.

ACADEMICS
Calendar: semesters. *Degrees:* associate, bachelor's, master's, and doctoral.
Special study options: academic remediation for entering students, adult/continuing education programs, advanced placement credit, cooperative education, distance learning, double majors, honors programs, independent study, internships, off-campus study, part-time degree program, services for LD students, student-designed majors, study abroad, summer session for credit. ***ROTC:*** Army (c), Air Force (c).
Computers: 45 computers/terminals are available on campus for general student use. Students can access the following: campus intranet, computer help desk, free student e-mail accounts, online (class) grades, online (class) registration, online (class) schedules. Campuswide network is available. 100% of college-owned or -operated housing units are wired for high-speed Internet access. Wireless service is available via entire campus.

STUDENT LIFE
Housing options: on-campus residence required through sophomore year; coed. Campus housing is university owned. Freshman campus housing is guaranteed.
Activities and organizations: drama/theater group, choral group, Student Government Association, BACCHUS, Theatrical Union, campus ministry, Amnesty International.
Athletics Member NAIA. ***Intercollegiate sports:*** baseball M(s), basketball M(s)/W(s), cheerleading M(s)/W(s), cross-country running M(s)/W(s), football M(s), soccer M(s)/W(s), softball W(s), track and field M(s)/W(s), volleyball W(s). ***Intramural sports:*** badminton M/W, basketball M/W, bowling M/W, football M, lacrosse M/W, racquetball M/W, soccer M/W, softball W, table tennis M/W, ultimate Frisbee M/W, volleyball M/W, weight lifting M/W.
Campus security: 24-hour patrols, late-night transport/escort service, controlled dormitory access.
Student services: personal/psychological counseling.

COSTS & FINANCIAL AID
Costs (2014–15) ***Comprehensive fee:*** $32,898 includes full-time tuition ($23,750), mandatory fees ($700), and room and board ($8448). Full-time tuition and fees vary according to class time, course load, degree level, location, program, and reciprocity agreements. Part-time tuition: $460 per credit. Part-time tuition and fees vary according to class time, course load, degree level, location, program, and reciprocity agreements. ***Required fees:*** $155 per term part-time. ***Room and board:*** Room and board charges vary according to board plan and housing facility. ***Payment plan:*** installment. ***Waivers:*** senior citizens and employees or children of employees.
Financial Aid ***Average percent of need met:*** 82.

APPLYING
Standardized Tests *Required:* SAT or ACT (for admission).
Options: electronic application.
Application fee: $25.
Required: high school transcript, minimum 2.5 GPA. ***Recommended:*** 1 letter of recommendation, interview.
Application deadlines: rolling (freshmen), rolling (transfers).
Notification: continuous (freshmen), continuous (transfers).

CONTACT
Ms. Kitti O'Donnell, Director of Operations, University of Saint Mary, 4100 South Fourth Street, Leavenworth, KS 66048. *Phone:* 913-758-6415. *Toll-free phone:* 800-752-7043. *Fax:* 913-758-6140. *E-mail:* admiss@stmary.edu.

Washburn University

Topeka, Kansas

http://www.washburn.edu/

- **City-supported** comprehensive, founded 1865
- **Urban** 160-acre campus with easy access to Kansas City
- **Endowment** $143.7 million
- **Coed** 5,901 undergraduate students, 66% full-time, 59% women, 41% men
- **Noncompetitive** entrance level, 98% of applicants were admitted

UNDERGRAD STUDENTS
3,903 full-time, 1,998 part-time. Students come from 37 states and territories; 38 other countries; 9% are from out of state; 9% transferred in; 16% live on campus.

Freshmen
Admission: 1,416 applied, 1,390 admitted, 801 enrolled. ***Average high school GPA:*** 3.4. ***Test scores:*** ACT scores over 18: 90%; ACT scores over 24: 36%; ACT scores over 30: 4%.
Retention: 66% of full-time freshmen returned.

FACULTY
Total: 537, 52% full-time, 62% with terminal degrees.
Student/faculty ratio: 14:1.

ACADEMICS
Calendar: semesters. *Degrees:* certificates, associate, bachelor's, master's, doctoral, post-master's, and postbachelor's certificates.
Special study options: academic remediation for entering students, adult/continuing education programs, advanced placement credit, cooperative education, distance learning, double majors, English as a second language, honors programs, independent study, internships, off-campus study, part-time degree program, services for LD students, student-designed majors, study abroad, summer session for credit. ***ROTC:*** Army (b), Navy (c), Air Force (c).

Unusual degree programs: 3-2 engineering with University of Kansas, Kansas State University.

Computers: 560 computers/terminals are available on campus for general student use. Students can access the following: campus intranet, computer help desk, free student e-mail accounts, online (class) grades, online (class) registration, online (class) schedules. Campuswide network is available. 100% of college-owned or -operated housing units are wired for high-speed Internet access. Wireless service is available via entire campus.

STUDENT LIFE
Housing options: coed. Campus housing is university owned.

Activities and organizations: drama/theater group, student-run newspaper, television station, choral group, marching band, national fraternities, national sororities.

Athletics Member NCAA. All Division II. ***Intercollegiate sports:*** baseball M(s), basketball M(s)/W(s), cheerleading M(s)/W(s), football M(s), golf M(s), soccer W(s), softball W(s), tennis M(s)/W(s), volleyball W(s). ***Intramural sports:*** badminton M/W, basketball M/W, crew M(c)/W(c), football M/W, rugby M(c), soccer M/W, softball M/W, table tennis M/W, tennis M/W, volleyball M/W.

Campus security: 24-hour emergency response devices and patrols, student patrols, late-night transport/escort service.

Student services: health clinic, personal/psychological counseling, legal services.

COSTS & FINANCIAL AID
Costs (2014–15) ***Tuition:*** state resident $5952 full-time, $248 per credit hour part-time; nonresident $13,440 full-time, $560 per credit hour part-time. Full-time tuition and fees vary according to program. Part-time tuition and fees vary according to program. ***Required fees:*** $86 full-time, $21 per term part-time. ***Room and board:*** $6541; room only: $3701. Room and board charges vary according to board plan and housing facility. ***Payment plan:*** installment. ***Waivers:*** senior citizens and employees or children of employees.

Financial Aid Of all full-time matriculated undergraduates who enrolled in 2014, 3,462 applied for aid, 2,425 were judged to have need, 337 had their need fully met. 707 Federal Work-Study jobs (averaging $2601). 16 state and other part-time jobs (averaging $1753). In 2014, 556 non-need-based awards were made. ***Average percent of need met:*** 43. ***Average financial aid package:*** $9613. ***Average need-based loan:*** $4216. ***Average need-based gift aid:*** $5090. ***Average non-need-based aid:*** $3111. ***Average indebtedness upon graduation:*** $27,383.

APPLYING
Standardized Tests *Required:* ACT (for admission).

Options: electronic application.

Application fee: $20.

Required: high school transcript.

Application deadlines: 8/1 (freshmen), 8/1 (transfers).

Notification: continuous (freshmen), continuous (transfers).

CONTACT
Ms. Kris Klima, Director of Admissions, Washburn University, 1700 SW College, MO 114, Topeka, KS 66621. *Phone:* 785-670-1030. *Toll-free phone:* 800-332-0291. *Fax:* 785-670-1113. *E-mail:* admissions@washburn.edu.

Wichita State University

Wichita, Kansas

http://www.wichita.edu/

- **State-supported** university, founded 1895, part of Kansas Board of Regents
- **Urban** 335-acre campus
- **Coed** 11,979 undergraduate students, 74% full-time, 52% women, 48% men
- **Noncompetitive** entrance level, 96% of applicants were admitted

UNDERGRAD STUDENTS
8,909 full-time, 3,070 part-time. Students come from 45 states and territories; 96 other countries; 6% are from out of state; 6% Black or African American, non-Hispanic/Latino; 10% Hispanic/Latino; 7% Asian, non-Hispanic/Latino; 0.1% Native Hawaiian or other Pacific Islander, non-Hispanic/Latino; 0.9% American Indian or Alaska Native, non-Hispanic/Latino; 3% Two or more races, non-Hispanic/Latino; 4% Race/ethnicity unknown; 8% international; 12% transferred in; 9% live on campus.

Freshmen
Admission: 4,517 applied, 4,315 admitted, 1,481 enrolled. ***Average high school GPA:*** 3.45. ***Test scores:*** SAT critical reading scores over 500: 67%; SAT math scores over 500: 81%; ACT scores over 18: 92%; SAT critical reading scores over 600: 35%; SAT math scores over 600: 32%; ACT scores over 24: 44%; SAT critical reading scores over 700: 6%; SAT math scores over 700: 4%; ACT scores over 30: 7%.

Retention: 70% of full-time freshmen returned.

FACULTY
Total: 857, 61% full-time, 53% with terminal degrees.

Student/faculty ratio: 18:1.

ACADEMICS
Calendar: semesters. *Degrees:* certificates, associate, bachelor's, master's, doctoral, post-master's, and postbachelor's certificates.

Special study options: academic remediation for entering students, accelerated degree program, adult/continuing education programs, advanced placement credit, cooperative education, distance learning, double majors, English as a second language, freshman honors college, honors programs, independent study, internships, off-campus study, part-time degree program, services for LD students, study abroad, summer session for credit.

Computers: 1,500 computers/terminals are available on campus for general student use. Students can access the following: computer help desk, free student e-mail accounts, online (class) grades, online (class) registration, online (class) schedules, online Blackboard. Campuswide network is available. 100% of college-owned or -operated housing units are wired for high-speed Internet access. Wireless service is available via entire campus.

STUDENT LIFE
Housing options: on-campus residence required for freshman year; coed, special housing for students with disabilities. Campus housing is university owned. Freshman applicants given priority for college housing.

Activities and organizations: drama/theater group, student-run newspaper, radio and television station, choral group, Golden Key Honor Society, WSU Green Group, Criminal Justice Society, Future Health Care Professionals, Students in Free Enterprise (SIFE), national fraternities, national sororities.

Athletics Member NCAA. All Division I. ***Intercollegiate sports:*** baseball M(s), basketball M(s)/W(s), bowling M(s)/W(s), cheerleading M/W, cross-country running M(s)/W(s), golf M(s)/W(s), ice hockey M(c), softball W(s), tennis M(s)/W(s), track and field M(s)/W(s), volleyball M(c)/W(s), wrestling M(c)/W(c). ***Intramural sports:*** badminton M/W, basketball M/W, bowling M/W, crew M/W, football M, golf M/W, racquetball M/W, soccer M/W, softball M/W, swimming and diving M/W, table tennis M/W, tennis M/W, track and field M/W, volleyball M/W.

Campus security: 24-hour emergency response devices and patrols, student patrols, late-night transport/escort service, controlled dormitory access, bicycle patrols by campus security.

Student services: health clinic, personal/psychological counseling, women's center, legal services.

COSTS & FINANCIAL AID
Costs (2014–15) ***Tuition:*** state resident $5869 full-time, $196 per credit hour part-time; nonresident $13,903 full-time, $463 per credit hour part-time. Full-time tuition and fees vary according to course level, course load, degree level, program, and student level. Part-time tuition and fees vary according to course level, course load, degree level, program, and student level. ***Required fees:*** $1396 full-time, $47 per credit hour part-time. ***Room and board:*** $8373. Room and board charges vary according to board plan and housing facility. ***Payment plan:*** installment. ***Waivers:*** senior citizens and employees or children of employees.

Financial Aid Of all full-time matriculated undergraduates who enrolled in 2013, 7,560 applied for aid, 4,474 were judged to have need, 2,859 had their need fully met. In 2013, 1260 non-need-based awards were made. ***Average percent of need met:*** 63. ***Average financial aid package:*** $7684. ***Average need-based loan:*** $4292. ***Average need-based gift aid:*** $4314.

Average non-need-based aid: $1911. ***Average indebtedness upon graduation:*** $23,534.

APPLYING

Standardized Tests *Required for some:* SAT or ACT (for admission). *Recommended:* SAT or ACT (for admission).

Options: electronic application, deferred entrance.

Application fee: $30.

Required for some: minimum 2.5 GPA, rank in upper one-third of high school class or complete the pre-college curriculum with a minimum 2.0 GPA (2.5 GPA for nonresidents). ***Recommended:*** high school transcript.

Application deadlines: rolling (freshmen), rolling (out-of-state freshmen), rolling (transfers).

Notification: continuous (freshmen), continuous (out-of-state freshmen), continuous (transfers).

CONTACT

Wichita State University, 1845 North Fairmount, Wichita, KS 67260. *Phone:* 316-978-3085. *Toll-free phone:* 800-362-2594.

Wright Career College

Overland Park, Kansas

http://www.wrightcc.edu/

- **Proprietary** primarily 2-year
- **Suburban** 5-acre campus with easy access to Kansas City
- **Coed**
- **Noncompetitive** entrance level

ACADEMICS

Degrees: associate and bachelor's.

STUDENT LIFE

Housing options: college housing not available.

CONTACT

Wright Career College, 10700 Metcalf Avenue, Overland Park, KS 66210. *Phone:* 913-385-7700. *E-mail:* info@wrightcc.edu.

Wright Career College

Wichita, Kansas

http://www.wrightcc.edu/

- **Proprietary** primarily 2-year, founded 2011
- **Suburban** campus with easy access to Wichita
- **Coed**
- **Noncompetitive** entrance level

ACADEMICS

Degrees: diplomas, associate, and bachelor's.

STUDENT LIFE

Housing options: college housing not available.

CONTACT

Wright Career College, 7700 East Kellogg, Wichita, KS 67207. *Phone:* 316-927-7700. *Toll-free phone:* 800-555-4003. *E-mail:* info@wrightcc.edu.

KENTUCKY

Alice Lloyd College

Pippa Passes, Kentucky

http://www.alc.edu/

- **Independent** 4-year, founded 1923
- **Rural** 175-acre campus
- **Endowment** $35.8 million
- **Coed** 619 undergraduate students, 95% full-time, 54% women, 46% men

UNDERGRAD STUDENTS

589 full-time, 30 part-time. Students come from 9 states and territories; 1 other country; 19% are from out of state; 0.6% Black or African American, non-Hispanic/Latino; 0.3% Hispanic/Latino; 0.3% Native Hawaiian or other Pacific Islander, non-Hispanic/Latino; 0.3% American Indian or Alaska Native, non-Hispanic/Latino; 0.2% Two or more races, non-Hispanic/Latino; 1% Race/ethnicity unknown; 0.2% international; 9% transferred in; 80% live on campus.

Freshmen

Admission: 184 enrolled. ***Average high school GPA:*** 3.52. ***Test scores:*** SAT critical reading scores over 500: 17%; SAT math scores over 500: 33%; ACT scores over 18: 85%; SAT critical reading scores over 600: 17%; SAT math scores over 600: 33%; ACT scores over 24: 28%; ACT scores over 30: 5%.

Retention: 66% of full-time freshmen returned.

FACULTY

Total: 49, 59% full-time, 45% with terminal degrees.

Student/faculty ratio: 17:1.

ACADEMICS

Calendar: semesters. *Degree:* bachelor's.

Special study options: academic remediation for entering students, advanced placement credit, double majors, independent study, internships, part-time degree program, study abroad.

Unusual degree programs: 3-2 nursing with University of Kentucky, Eastern Kentucky University.

Computers: 124 computers/terminals and 550 ports are available on campus for general student use. Students can access the following: campus intranet, computer help desk, free student e-mail accounts. Campuswide network is available. 100% of college-owned or -operated housing units are wired for high-speed Internet access. Wireless service is available via classrooms, computer centers, computer labs, dorm rooms, learning centers, libraries, student centers.

STUDENT LIFE

Housing options: on-campus residence required through senior year; men-only, women-only. Campus housing is university owned.

Activities and organizations: drama/theater group, student-run newspaper, radio and television station, choral group, Voices of Appalachia, Intramurals, Baptist Collegiate Ministries, Allied Health Sciences Club, Alpha Chi National Honor Society.

Athletics Member NAIA. ***Intercollegiate sports:*** baseball M(s), basketball M(s)/W(s), cheerleading W, cross-country running M/W, golf M/W, softball W, tennis M/W, track and field M/W, volleyball W. ***Intramural sports:*** basketball M/W, volleyball M/W.

Campus security: 24-hour patrols, late-night transport/escort service.

Student services: health clinic, personal/psychological counseling.

COSTS & FINANCIAL AID

Costs (2015–16) ***Comprehensive fee:*** $17,400 includes full-time tuition ($9600), mandatory fees ($1860), and room and board ($5940). Part-time tuition: $212 per credit hour. Part-time tuition and fees vary according to course load. ***College room only:*** $2850. ***Payment plan:*** installment. ***Waivers:*** employees or children of employees.

Financial Aid Of all full-time matriculated undergraduates who enrolled in 2013, 613 applied for aid, 563 were judged to have need, 57 had their need fully met. 463 Federal Work-Study jobs (averaging $2320). 152 state and other part-time jobs (averaging $2320). In 2013, 79 non-need-based awards were made. ***Average percent of need met:*** 71. ***Average financial aid package:*** $12,574. ***Average need-based loan:*** $2291. ***Average need-based gift aid:*** $8780. ***Average non-need-based aid:*** $6392. ***Average indebtedness upon graduation:*** $8314.

APPLYING

Standardized Tests *Required:* SAT or ACT (for admission).

Required: high school transcript, minimum 2.3 GPA, interview. ***Required for some:*** essay or personal statement, 2 letters of recommendation.

CONTACT

Ms. Angie Phipps, Director of Admissions, Alice Lloyd College, 100 Purpose Road, Pippa Passes, KY 41844. *Phone:* 606-368-6134. *Toll-free phone:* 888-280-4252. *Fax:* 606-368-6038. *E-mail:* angiephipps@alc.edu.

Asbury University

Wilmore, Kentucky

http://www.asbury.edu/

- **Independent nondenominational** comprehensive, founded 1890
- **Small-town** 400-acre campus with easy access to Lexington
- **Endowment** $47.6 million
- **Coed** 1,622 undergraduate students, 82% full-time, 59% women, 41% men
- **Moderately difficult** entrance level, 69% of applicants were admitted

UNDERGRAD STUDENTS
1,326 full-time, 296 part-time. Students come from 44 states and territories; 25 other countries; 48% are from out of state; 3% Black or African American, non-Hispanic/Latino; 2% Hispanic/Latino; 0.8% Asian, non-Hispanic/Latino; 0.3% Native Hawaiian or other Pacific Islander, non-Hispanic/Latino; 0.2% American Indian or Alaska Native, non-Hispanic/Latino; 6% Two or more races, non-Hispanic/Latino; 4% Race/ethnicity unknown; 2% international; 3% transferred in; 86% live on campus.

Freshmen
Admission: 1,328 applied, 913 admitted, 303 enrolled. ***Average high school GPA:*** 3.66. ***Test scores:*** SAT critical reading scores over 500: 70%; SAT math scores over 500: 75%; ACT scores over 18: 96%; SAT critical reading scores over 600: 35%; SAT math scores over 600: 31%; ACT scores over 24: 59%; SAT critical reading scores over 700: 5%; SAT math scores over 700: 2%; ACT scores over 30: 17%.

Retention: 81% of full-time freshmen returned.

FACULTY
Total: 183, 51% full-time.

Student/faculty ratio: 13:1.

ACADEMICS
Calendar: semesters. *Degrees:* associate, bachelor's, and master's.

Special study options: adult/continuing education programs, advanced placement credit, distance learning, double majors, off-campus study, study abroad, summer session for credit. ***ROTC:*** Army (c), Air Force (c).

Unusual degree programs: 3-2 engineering with University of Kentucky.

Computers: 250 computers/terminals and 950 ports are available on campus for general student use. Students can access the following: campus intranet, computer help desk, free student e-mail accounts, online (class) grades, online (class) registration, online (class) schedules. Campuswide network is available. 100% of college-owned or -operated housing units are wired for high-speed Internet access. Wireless service is available via classrooms, computer centers, computer labs, dorm rooms, learning centers, libraries, student centers.

STUDENT LIFE
Housing options: on-campus residence required through senior year; men-only, women-only. Campus housing is university owned. Freshman campus housing is guaranteed.

Activities and organizations: drama/theater group, student-run newspaper, radio and television station, choral group, Fellowship of Christian Athletes, Impact (community service), Christian Service Association, ministry teams, Student-Faculty Council.

Athletics Member NAIA, NCCAA. ***Intercollegiate sports:*** baseball M(s), basketball M(s)/W(s), cross-country running M(s)/W(s), golf M(s)/W(s), lacrosse M(s)/W(s), soccer M(s)/W(s), softball W(s), swimming and diving M(s)/W(s), tennis M(s)/W(s), volleyball W(s). ***Intramural sports:*** basketball M/W, football M/W, golf M/W, racquetball M/W, soccer M/W, softball M/W, ultimate Frisbee M/W, volleyball M/W.

Campus security: 24-hour emergency response devices, late-night transport/escort service, controlled dormitory access, late night security personnel.

Student services: health clinic, personal/psychological counseling.

COSTS & FINANCIAL AID
Costs (2015–16) ***Comprehensive fee:*** $34,072 includes full-time tuition ($27,538), mandatory fees ($198), and room and board ($6336). Full-time tuition and fees vary according to course load, location, and program. Part-time tuition: $1059 per credit hour. Part-time tuition and fees vary according to course load, location, and program. ***Room and board:*** Room and board charges vary according to board plan, housing facility, and location. ***Payment plan:*** installment. ***Waivers:*** senior citizens and employees or children of employees.

Financial Aid Of all full-time matriculated undergraduates who enrolled in 2013, 1,167 applied for aid, 1,057 were judged to have need, 199 had their need fully met. 593 Federal Work-Study jobs (averaging $1622). In 2013, 106 non-need-based awards were made. ***Average percent of need met:*** 75. ***Average financial aid package:*** $19,467. ***Average need-based loan:*** $3958. ***Average need-based gift aid:*** $12,989. ***Average non-need-based aid:*** $13,758. ***Average indebtedness upon graduation:*** $30,123.

APPLYING
Standardized Tests *Required:* SAT or ACT (for admission).

Options: electronic application, early admission, deferred entrance.

Required: essay or personal statement, high school transcript, minimum 2.5 GPA, 1 letter of recommendation. ***Required for some:*** interview.

Application deadlines: rolling (freshmen), rolling (out-of-state freshmen), rolling (transfers).

Notification: continuous (freshmen), continuous (out-of-state freshmen), continuous (transfers).

CONTACT
Mr. Brandon Combs, Director of Undergraduate Admissions, Asbury University, One Macklem Drive, Wilmore, KY 40390. *Phone:* 800-888-1818. *Toll-free phone:* 800-888-1818. *Fax:* -. *E-mail:* admissions@asbury.edu.

Bellarmine University

Louisville, Kentucky

http://www.bellarmine.edu/

- **Independent Roman Catholic** comprehensive, founded 1950
- **Suburban** 175-acre campus with easy access to Louisville
- **Endowment** $45.7 million
- **Coed**
- **Moderately difficult** entrance level

FACULTY
Student/faculty ratio: 12:1.

ACADEMICS
Calendar: semesters. *Degrees:* bachelor's, master's, doctoral, and postbachelor's certificates.

STUDENT LIFE
Housing options: on-campus residence required through junior year; coed, men-only, women-only, special housing for students with disabilities. Campus housing is university owned. Freshman campus housing is guaranteed.

Activities and organizations: drama/theater group, student-run newspaper, radio station, choral group, student government, Bellarmine Activities Council, Knights Nation, Fellowship of Christian Athletes, Delta Sigma Pi, national fraternities, national sororities.

Athletics Member NCAA. All Division II except lacrosse (Division I).

Campus security: 24-hour emergency response devices and patrols, student patrols, late-night transport/escort service, controlled dormitory access, 24-hour locked residence hall entrances, security cameras.

Student services: health clinic, personal/psychological counseling.

COSTS & FINANCIAL AID
Costs (2014–15) ***One-time required fee:*** $400. ***Comprehensive fee:*** $47,366 includes full-time tuition ($34,900), mandatory fees ($1390), and room and board ($11,076). Part-time tuition: $820 per credit hour. ***College room only:*** $6956. Room and board charges vary according to board plan and housing facility.

Financial Aid Of all full-time matriculated undergraduates who enrolled in 2014, 2,053 applied for aid, 1,827 were judged to have need, 372 had their need fully met. 259 Federal Work-Study jobs (averaging $1844). In 2014, 501 non-need-based awards were made. ***Average percent of need met:*** 75. ***Average financial aid package:*** $28,838. ***Average need-based loan:*** $4237. ***Average need-based gift aid:*** $21,414. ***Average non-need-based aid:*** $19,958. ***Average indebtedness upon graduation:*** $31,381.

APPLYING
Standardized Tests *Required:* SAT or ACT (for admission).

Options: electronic application, early admission, early action, deferred entrance.

Application fee: $25.

Required: high school transcript, minimum 2.5 GPA, 1 letter of recommendation. ***Required for some:*** essay or personal statement. ***Recommended:*** interview.

CONTACT

Mr. Timothy A. Sturgeon, Dean of Admission, Bellarmine University, 2001 Newburg Road, Louisville, KY 40205-0671. *Phone:* 502-272-8131. *Toll-free phone:* 800-274-4723 Ext. 8131. *E-mail:* admissions@bellarmine.edu.

Berea College

Berea, Kentucky

http://www.berea.edu/

- **Independent** 4-year, founded 1855
- **Small-town** 140-acre campus
- **Endowment** $1.2 billion
- **Coed** 1,621 undergraduate students, 97% full-time, 56% women, 44% men
- **Moderately difficult** entrance level, 34% of applicants were admitted

UNDERGRAD STUDENTS

1,578 full-time, 43 part-time. Students come from 45 states and territories; 62 other countries; 53% are from out of state; 15% Black or African American, non-Hispanic/Latino; 6% Hispanic/Latino; 2% Asian, non-Hispanic/Latino; 0.2% Native Hawaiian or other Pacific Islander, non-Hispanic/Latino; 0.1% American Indian or Alaska Native, non-Hispanic/Latino; 6% Two or more races, non-Hispanic/Latino; 1% Race/ethnicity unknown; 8% international; 3% transferred in; 82% live on campus.

Freshmen

Admission: 1,648 applied, 555 admitted, 416 enrolled. ***Average high school GPA:*** 3.45. ***Test scores:*** SAT critical reading scores over 500: 80%; SAT math scores over 500: 80%; SAT writing scores over 500: 79%; ACT scores over 18: 99%; SAT critical reading scores over 600: 29%; SAT math scores over 600: 43%; SAT writing scores over 600: 25%; ACT scores over 24: 56%; SAT critical reading scores over 700: 5%; SAT math scores over 700: 7%; SAT writing scores over 700: 5%; ACT scores over 30: 8%.

Retention: 84% of full-time freshmen returned.

FACULTY

Total: 185, 71% full-time, 79% with terminal degrees.

Student/faculty ratio: 10:1.

ACADEMICS

Calendar: 4-1-4. *Degree:* bachelor's.

Special study options: academic remediation for entering students, advanced placement credit, double majors, English as a second language, honors programs, independent study, internships, off-campus study, services for LD students, student-designed majors, study abroad, summer session for credit.

Unusual degree programs: 3-2 engineering with University of Kentucky.

Computers: 60 computers/terminals and 7,000 ports are available on campus for general student use. Students can access the following: campus intranet, computer help desk, free student e-mail accounts, online (class) grades, online (class) registration, online (class) schedules. Campuswide network is available. 100% of college-owned or -operated housing units are wired for high-speed Internet access. Wireless service is available via entire campus.

STUDENT LIFE

Housing options: on-campus residence required through senior year; men-only, women-only. Campus housing is university owned. Freshman campus housing is guaranteed.

Activities and organizations: drama/theater group, student-run newspaper, choral group, Campus Activities Board, Cosmopolitan Club, CELTS (Center for Excellence in Learning through Service), Black Cultural Center, African Student Association.

Athletics Member NCAA. All Division III. ***Intercollegiate sports:*** baseball M, basketball M/W, cross-country running M/W, golf M, soccer M/W, softball W, tennis M/W, track and field M/W, volleyball W. ***Intramural sports:*** basketball M/W, football M/W, racquetball M/W, soccer M/W, softball M/W, ultimate Frisbee M/W, volleyball M/W.

Campus security: 24-hour emergency response devices and patrols, late-night transport/escort service, controlled dormitory access, crime prevention programs.

Student services: health clinic, personal/psychological counseling, women's center.

COSTS & FINANCIAL AID

Costs (2014–15) ***Comprehensive fee:*** includes mandatory fees ($870) and room and board ($6322). Financial aid is provided to all students for tuition costs. ***Room and board:*** Room and board charges vary according to board plan.

Financial Aid Of all full-time matriculated undergraduates who enrolled in 2014, 1,577 applied for aid, 1,577 were judged to have need. ***Average percent of need met:*** 91. ***Average financial aid package:*** $30,448. ***Average need-based loan:*** $181. ***Average need-based gift aid:*** $28,182. ***Average indebtedness upon graduation:*** $6186. ***Financial aid deadline:*** 3/1.

APPLYING

Standardized Tests *Required:* SAT or ACT (for admission).

Options: electronic application.

Required: essay or personal statement, high school transcript, interview, financial aid application. ***Recommended:*** 2 letters of recommendation.

Application deadlines: 4/30 (freshmen), 3/31 (transfers).

Notification: continuous (freshmen), continuous until 4/15 (transfers).

CONTACT

Mr. Luke Hodson, Director of Admissions, Berea College, CPO 2220, Berea, KY 40404. *Phone:* 859-985-3500. *Toll-free phone:* 800-326-5948. *Fax:* 859-985-3512. *E-mail:* admissions@berea.edu.

Brown Mackie College–Louisville

Louisville, Kentucky

http://www.brownmackie.edu/louisville/

- **Proprietary** primarily 2-year, founded 1972, part of Education Management Corporation
- **Suburban** campus
- **Coed**

ACADEMICS

Calendar: quarters. *Degrees:* certificates, diplomas, associate, and bachelor's.

CONTACT

Brown Mackie College–Louisville, 3605 Fern Valley Road, Louisville, KY 40219. *Phone:* 502-968-7191. *Toll-free phone:* 800-999-7387.

Brown Mackie College–Northern Kentucky

Fort Mitchell, Kentucky

http://www.brownmackie.edu/northernkentucky/

- **Proprietary** primarily 2-year, founded 1927, part of Education Management Corporation
- **Suburban** campus
- **Coed**

ACADEMICS

Calendar: quarters. *Degrees:* diplomas, associate, and bachelor's.

CONTACT

Brown Mackie College–Northern Kentucky, 309 Buttermilk Pike, Fort Mitchell, KY 41017-2191. *Phone:* 859-341-5627. *Toll-free phone:* 800-888-1445.

Campbellsville University

Campbellsville, Kentucky

http://www.campbellsville.edu/

- **Independent** comprehensive, founded 1906, affiliated with Kentucky Baptist Convention
- **Small-town** 90-acre campus
- **Endowment** $13.8 million
- **Coed** 3,062 undergraduate students, 63% full-time, 58% women, 42% men
- **Moderately difficult** entrance level, 73% of applicants were admitted

UNDERGRAD STUDENTS

1,920 full-time, 1,142 part-time. Students come from 42 states and territories; 47 other countries; 16% are from out of state; 14% Black or African American, non-Hispanic/Latino; 2% Hispanic/Latino; 0.2% Asian, non-Hispanic/Latino; 0.1% Native Hawaiian or other Pacific Islander, non-Hispanic/Latino; 0.2% American Indian or Alaska Native, non-Hispanic/Latino; 2% Two or more races, non-Hispanic/Latino; 0.6% Race/ethnicity unknown; 8% international; 7% transferred in; 47% live on campus.

Freshmen

Admission: 2,672 applied, 1,943 admitted, 523 enrolled. ***Average high school GPA:*** 3.19. ***Test scores:*** ACT scores over 18: 77%; ACT scores over 24: 21%; ACT scores over 30: 2%.

Retention: 57% of full-time freshmen returned.

FACULTY

Total: 310, 49% full-time, 31% with terminal degrees.

Student/faculty ratio: 13:1.

ACADEMICS

Calendar: semesters. *Degrees:* certificates, associate, bachelor's, master's, post-master's, and postbachelor's certificates.

Special study options: academic remediation for entering students, accelerated degree program, adult/continuing education programs, advanced placement credit, distance learning, double majors, English as a second language, honors programs, independent study, internships, off-campus study, part-time degree program, study abroad, summer session for credit. ***ROTC:*** Army (c).

Unusual degree programs: 3-2 engineering with University of Kentucky.

Computers: 220 computers/terminals are available on campus for general student use. Students can access the following: campus intranet, computer help desk, free student e-mail accounts, online (class) grades, online (class) registration, online (class) schedules. Campuswide network is available. Wireless service is available via classrooms, computer centers, computer labs, dorm rooms, learning centers, libraries, student centers.

STUDENT LIFE

Housing options: on-campus residence required through sophomore year; men-only, women-only. Campus housing is university owned. Freshman campus housing is guaranteed.

Activities and organizations: drama/theater group, student-run newspaper, radio and television station, choral group, marching band, Student Government Association, Baptist Student Union, Phi Beta Lambda, African-American Leadership League, Fellowship of Christian Athletes.

Athletics Member NAIA, NCCAA. ***Intercollegiate sports:*** baseball M(s), basketball M(s)/W(s), bowling M(s)/W(s), cheerleading M(s)/W(s), cross-country running M(s)/W(s), football M(s), golf M(s)/W(s), soccer M(s)/W(s), softball W(s), swimming and diving M(s)/W(s), tennis M(s)/W(s), track and field M(s)/W(s), volleyball W(s), wrestling M(s)/W(s). ***Intramural sports:*** basketball M/W, bowling M/W, football M/W, racquetball M/W, soccer M/W, softball M/W, swimming and diving M/W, table tennis M/W, tennis M/W, volleyball M/W, weight lifting M/W.

Campus security: 24-hour emergency response devices and patrols, student patrols, late-night transport/escort service, controlled dormitory access.

Student services: health clinic, personal/psychological counseling.

COSTS & FINANCIAL AID

Costs (2015–16) ***Comprehensive fee:*** $31,598 includes full-time tuition ($23,328), mandatory fees ($500), and room and board ($7770). Full-time tuition and fees vary according to location. Part-time tuition: $972 per credit hour. Part-time tuition and fees vary according to location. ***Room and board:*** Room and board charges vary according to housing facility. ***Payment plan:*** installment. ***Waivers:*** adult students, senior citizens, and employees or children of employees.

Financial Aid Of all full-time matriculated undergraduates who enrolled in 2013, 1,597 applied for aid, 1,515 were judged to have need, 263 had their need fully met. 275 Federal Work-Study jobs (averaging $1400). 30 state and other part-time jobs (averaging $1200). In 2013, 111 non-need-based awards were made. ***Average percent of need met:*** 79. ***Average financial aid package:*** $18,861. ***Average need-based loan:*** $3580. ***Average need-based gift aid:*** $16,117. ***Average non-need-based aid:*** $10,046. ***Average indebtedness upon graduation:*** $22,261.

APPLYING

Standardized Tests *Required:* SAT or ACT (for admission).

Options: electronic application, deferred entrance.

Application fee: $20.

Required: high school transcript, minimum 2.0 GPA. ***Recommended:*** essay or personal statement, minimum 3.0 GPA, interview.

Application deadlines: rolling (freshmen), rolling (transfers).

Notification: continuous (freshmen), continuous (transfers).

CONTACT

Mr. David Walters, Vice President for Admissions and Student Services, Campbellsville University, 1 University Drive, Campbellsville, KY 42718-2799. *Phone:* 270-789-5220 Ext. 5007. *Toll-free phone:* 800-264-6014. *Fax:* 270-789-5071. *E-mail:* admissions@campbellsville.edu.

Centre College

Danville, Kentucky

http://www.centre.edu/

- **Independent** 4-year, founded 1819, affiliated with Presbyterian Church (U.S.A.)
- **Small-town** 152-acre campus
- **Endowment** $263.8 million
- **Coed** 1,387 undergraduate students, 100% full-time, 52% women, 48% men
- **Very difficult** entrance level, 72% of applicants were admitted

UNDERGRAD STUDENTS

1,386 full-time, 1 part-time. Students come from 44 states and territories; 8 other countries; 44% are from out of state; 5% Black or African American, non-Hispanic/Latino; 2% Hispanic/Latino; 3% Asian, non-Hispanic/Latino; 0.1% Native Hawaiian or other Pacific Islander, non-Hispanic/Latino; 3% Two or more races, non-Hispanic/Latino; 0.4% Race/ethnicity unknown; 6% international; 0.7% transferred in; 98% live on campus.

Freshmen

Admission: 2,494 applied, 1,785 admitted, 386 enrolled. ***Average high school GPA:*** 3.71. ***Test scores:*** SAT critical reading scores over 500: 92%; SAT math scores over 500: 95%; SAT writing scores over 500: 92%; ACT scores over 18: 100%; SAT critical reading scores over 600: 57%; SAT math scores over 600: 58%; SAT writing scores over 600: 55%; ACT scores over 24: 95%; SAT critical reading scores over 700: 16%; SAT math scores over 700: 23%; SAT writing scores over 700: 9%; ACT scores over 30: 39%.

Retention: 90% of full-time freshmen returned.

FACULTY

Total: 146, 84% full-time, 89% with terminal degrees.

Student/faculty ratio: 10:1.

ACADEMICS

Calendar: 4-1-4. *Degree:* bachelor's.

Special study options: advanced placement credit, cooperative education, double majors, honors programs, independent study, internships, off-campus study, services for LD students, student-designed majors, study abroad. ***ROTC:*** Army (c), Air Force (c).

Unusual degree programs: 3-2 engineering with Washington University in St. Louis, Columbia University, Vanderbilt University, University of Kentucky.

Computers: 425 computers/terminals and 1,500 ports are available on campus for general student use. Students can access the following: campus intranet, computer help desk, free student e-mail accounts, online (class) grades, online (class) registration, online (class) schedules. Campuswide network is available. 100% of college-owned or -operated housing units are wired for high-speed Internet access. Wireless service is available via entire campus.

STUDENT LIFE

Housing options: on-campus residence required through senior year; coed, men-only, women-only, special housing for students with disabilities. Campus housing is university owned. Freshman campus housing is guaranteed.

Activities and organizations: drama/theater group, student-run newspaper, radio station, choral group, Student Government Association, Centre Action Reaches Everyone, Student Activities Council, Christian fellowship group, Diversity Student Union, national fraternities, national sororities.

Athletics Member NCAA. All Division III. ***Intercollegiate sports:*** baseball M, basketball M/W, cheerleading W, cross-country running M/W, field hockey W, football M, golf M/W, lacrosse M/W, soccer M/W, softball W, swimming and diving M/W, tennis M/W, track and field M/W, volleyball W. ***Intramural sports:*** badminton M/W, basketball M/W, bowling M/W, equestrian sports M/W, football M/W, golf M/W, racquetball M/W, soccer M/W, softball M/W, swimming and diving M/W, table tennis M/W, tennis M/W, track and field M/W, ultimate Frisbee M/W, volleyball M/W, weight lifting M/W.

Campus security: 24-hour emergency response devices and patrols, late-night transport/escort service, controlled dormitory access.

Student services: health clinic, personal/psychological counseling.

COSTS & FINANCIAL AID

Costs (2015–16) ***Comprehensive fee:*** $47,820 includes full-time tuition ($38,200) and room and board ($9620). Part-time tuition: $1375 per credit hour. ***College room only:*** $4810. ***Payment plan:*** installment. ***Waivers:*** employees or children of employees.

Financial Aid Of all full-time matriculated undergraduates who enrolled in 2013, 1,007 applied for aid, 816 were judged to have need, 216 had their need fully met. 385 Federal Work-Study jobs (averaging $1510). 2 state and other part-time jobs (averaging $2790). In 2013, 503 non-need-based awards were made. ***Average percent of need met:*** 83. ***Average financial aid package:*** $27,581. ***Average need-based loan:*** $4551. ***Average need-based gift aid:*** $24,278. ***Average non-need-based aid:*** $17,742. ***Average indebtedness upon graduation:*** $25,269. ***Financial aid deadline:*** 1/31.

APPLYING

Standardized Tests *Required:* SAT or ACT (for admission).

Options: electronic application, early admission, early decision, early action, deferred entrance.

Required: essay or personal statement, high school transcript, 1 letter of recommendation. ***Recommended:*** interview.

Application deadlines: 1/15 (freshmen), 1/15 (out-of-state freshmen), rolling (transfers), 12/1 (early action).

Early decision deadline: 12/1 (for plan 1), 1/15 (for plan 2).

Notification: 3/15 (freshmen), 3/15 (out-of-state freshmen), 12/31 (early decision plan 1), 2/15 (early decision plan 2), 1/15 (early action).

CONTACT

Mr. Bob Nesmith, Dean of Admission and Student Financial Planning, Centre College, 600 West Walnut Street, Danville, KY 40422-1394. *Phone:* 859-238-5350. *Toll-free phone:* 800-423-6236. *Fax:* 859-238-5373. *E-mail:* admission@centre.edu.

DeVry University

Louisville, Kentucky

http://www.devry.edu/

- **Proprietary** comprehensive
- **Coed**

ACADEMICS

Degrees: associate, bachelor's, and master's.

CONTACT

Admissions Office, DeVry University, 10172 Linn Station Road, Suite 300, Louisville, KY 40223. *Phone:* 502-326-2860. *Toll-free phone:* 866-338-7941.

Eastern Kentucky University

Richmond, Kentucky

http://www.eku.edu/

- **State-supported** comprehensive, founded 1906
- **Small-town** 500-acre campus with easy access to Lexington
- **Endowment** $61.4 million
- **Coed** 13,949 undergraduate students, 80% full-time, 56% women, 44% men
- **Minimally difficult** entrance level, 74% of applicants were admitted

UNDERGRAD STUDENTS

11,167 full-time, 2,782 part-time. Students come from 50 states and territories; 35 other countries; 13% are from out of state; 6% Black or African American, non-Hispanic/Latino; 2% Hispanic/Latino; 0.9% Asian, non-Hispanic/Latino; 0.1% Native Hawaiian or other Pacific Islander, non-Hispanic/Latino; 0.3% American Indian or Alaska Native, non-Hispanic/Latino; 2% Two or more races, non-Hispanic/Latino; 3% Race/ethnicity unknown; 2% international; 8% transferred in; 32% live on campus.

Freshmen

Admission: 9,776 applied, 7,222 admitted, 2,608 enrolled. ***Average high school GPA:*** 3.22. ***Test scores:*** SAT critical reading scores over 500: 47%; SAT math scores over 500: 44%; SAT writing scores over 500: 34%; ACT scores over 18: 83%; SAT critical reading scores over 600: 10%; SAT math scores over 600: 12%; SAT writing scores over 600: 7%; ACT scores over 24: 32%; SAT math scores over 700: 1%; SAT writing scores over 700: 1%; ACT scores over 30: 3%.

Retention: 68% of full-time freshmen returned.

FACULTY

Total: 1,178, 59% full-time, 46% with terminal degrees.

Student/faculty ratio: 14:1.

ACADEMICS

Calendar: semesters. *Degrees:* certificates, associate, bachelor's, master's, doctoral, post-master's, and postbachelor's certificates.

Special study options: academic remediation for entering students, accelerated degree program, adult/continuing education programs, advanced placement credit, cooperative education, distance learning, double majors, English as a second language, external degree program, honors programs, independent study, internships, part-time degree program, services for LD students, student-designed majors, study abroad, summer session for credit. ***ROTC:*** Army (b), Air Force (c).

Unusual degree programs: 3-2 engineering with University of Kentucky, Auburn University.

Computers: 1,800 computers/terminals and 2,000 ports are available on campus for general student use. Students can access the following: campus intranet, computer help desk, free student e-mail accounts, online (class) grades, online (class) registration, online (class) schedules. Campuswide network is available. 90% of college-owned or -operated housing units are wired for high-speed Internet access. Wireless service is available via entire campus.

STUDENT LIFE

Housing options: on-campus residence required through sophomore year; coed, men-only, women-only. Campus housing is university owned and leased by the school. Freshman campus housing is guaranteed.

Activities and organizations: drama/theater group, student-run newspaper, radio station, choral group, marching band, Honor Society, Regular Society, national fraternities, national sororities.

Athletics Member NCAA. All Division I. ***Intercollegiate sports:*** baseball M(s), basketball M(s)/W(s), cheerleading M/W, cross-country running M(s)/W(s), football M(s), golf M(s)/W(s), softball W(s), tennis M(s)/W(s), track and field M(s)/W(s), volleyball W(s). ***Intramural sports:*** archery M(c)/W(c), baseball M(c), basketball M/W, bowling M/W, equestrian sports W(c), fencing M(c)/W(c), football M/W, golf M/W, ice hockey M(c), lacrosse M(c), racquetball M/W, riflery M(c)/W(c), rock climbing M(c)/W(c), rugby M(c)/W(c), soccer M(c)/W(c), softball M/W, table tennis M/W, tennis M/W, track and field M/W, ultimate Frisbee M/W, volleyball M/W, water polo M/W, weight lifting M/W.

Campus security: 24-hour emergency response devices and patrols, student patrols, late-night transport/escort service, controlled dormitory access.

Student services: health clinic, personal/psychological counseling.

COSTS & FINANCIAL AID

Costs (2015–16) ***Tuition:*** state resident $8150 full-time, $340 per credit hour part-time; nonresident $17,640 full-time, $735 per credit hour part-time. Full-time tuition and fees vary according to degree level and location. Part-time tuition and fees vary according to course load. ***Room only:*** $4562. Room and board charges vary according to board plan and housing facility. ***Payment plan:*** installment. ***Waivers:*** senior citizens and employees or children of employees.

Financial Aid Of all full-time matriculated undergraduates who enrolled in 2014, 9,375 applied for aid, 8,121 were judged to have need, 3,186 had their need fully met. 1,200 Federal Work-Study jobs (averaging $2400). 1,200 state and other part-time jobs (averaging $2400). In 2014, 1187 non-need-based awards were made. ***Average percent of need met:*** 84. ***Average financial aid package:*** $10,970. ***Average need-based loan:*** $3876. ***Average need-based gift aid:*** $5765. ***Average non-need-based aid:*** $5455. ***Average indebtedness upon graduation:*** $27,438.

APPLYING

Standardized Tests *Required:* SAT or ACT (for admission). *Required for some:* SAT and SAT Subject Tests or ACT (for admission).

Options: electronic application, deferred entrance.

Application fee: $35.

Required: high school transcript, minimum 2.0 GPA, All new freshman must take a standardize test (ACT/SAT). Only adults over the age of 21 may use Placement Exam for admission. ***Recommended:*** minimum 2.5 GPA.

Application deadlines: 8/1 (freshmen), 8/1 (out-of-state freshmen), 8/1 (transfers).

Notification: continuous (freshmen), continuous (out-of-state freshmen), continuous (transfers).

CONTACT

Ms. Kimberly Merritt, Director of Admissions, Eastern Kentucky University, SSB CPO 54, 521 Lancaster Avenue, Richmond, KY 40475-3102. *Phone:* 859-622-2106. *Toll-free phone:* 800-465-9191. *Fax:* 859-622-8024. *E-mail:* admissions@eku.edu.

Georgetown College

Georgetown, Kentucky

http://www.georgetowncollege.edu/

- **Independent** comprehensive, founded 1829, affiliated with Baptist Church
- **Suburban** 104-acre campus with easy access to Cincinnati, OH; Louisville, KY
- **Endowment** $33.7 million
- **Coed** 979 undergraduate students, 97% full-time, 54% women, 46% men
- **Moderately difficult** entrance level, 89% of applicants were admitted

UNDERGRAD STUDENTS

952 full-time, 27 part-time. Students come from 30 states and territories; 12 other countries; 26% are from out of state; 9% Black or African American, non-Hispanic/Latino; 3% Hispanic/Latino; 0.8% Asian, non-Hispanic/Latino; 0.2% American Indian or Alaska Native, non-Hispanic/Latino; 3% Two or more races, non-Hispanic/Latino; 3% Race/ethnicity unknown; 2% international; 4% transferred in; 91% live on campus.

Freshmen

Admission: 2,089 applied, 1,854 admitted, 273 enrolled. ***Average high school GPA:*** 3.37. ***Test scores:*** SAT critical reading scores over 500: 63%; SAT math scores over 500: 77%; ACT scores over 18: 98%; SAT critical reading scores over 600: 23%; SAT math scores over 600: 8%; ACT scores over 24: 51%; ACT scores over 30: 9%.

Retention: 67% of full-time freshmen returned.

FACULTY

Total: 155, 63% full-time, 76% with terminal degrees.

Student/faculty ratio: 9:1.

ACADEMICS

Calendar: semesters. *Degrees:* bachelor's, master's, and post-master's certificates.

Special study options: advanced placement credit, cooperative education, distance learning, double majors, English as a second language, honors programs, independent study, internships, off-campus study, part-time degree program, services for LD students, student-designed majors, study abroad, summer session for credit. ***ROTC:*** Army (c), Air Force (c).

Unusual degree programs: 3-2 engineering with University of Kentucky; nursing with University of Kentucky; University of Kentucky, Patterson School of Diplomacy.

Computers: 175 computers/terminals are available on campus for general student use. Students can access the following: campus intranet, computer help desk, free student e-mail accounts, online (class) grades, online (class) registration, online (class) schedules, Library apps for iPhone and Android available from the LRC Homepage. Campuswide network is available. 100% of college-owned or -operated housing units are wired for high-speed Internet access. Wireless service is available via entire campus.

STUDENT LIFE

Housing options: on-campus residence required through senior year; men-only, women-only. Campus housing is university owned and leased by the school. Freshman campus housing is guaranteed.

Activities and organizations: drama/theater group, student-run newspaper, radio station, choral group, Campus Ministries, Association of Georgetown Students, Harper-Gatton Leadership Center, Phi Beta Lambda, Outdoor High Adventure Club, national fraternities, national sororities.

Athletics Member NAIA. ***Intercollegiate sports:*** baseball M(s), basketball M(s)/W(s), cheerleading W(s), cross-country running M(s)/W(s), football M(s), golf M(s)/W(s), lacrosse W(s), soccer M(s)/W(s), softball W(s), tennis M(s)/W(s), track and field M(s)/W(s), volleyball W(s). ***Intramural sports:*** basketball M/W, football M/W, golf M/W, racquetball M/W, soccer M/W, softball M/W, table tennis M/W, tennis M/W, ultimate Frisbee M/W, volleyball M/W.

Campus security: 24-hour patrols, late-night transport/escort service, controlled dormitory access.

Student services: health clinic, personal/psychological counseling.

COSTS & FINANCIAL AID

Costs (2014–15) ***Comprehensive fee:*** $41,440 includes full-time tuition ($32,960) and room and board ($8480). Full-time tuition and fees vary according to course load and degree level. Part-time tuition: $1020 per credit hour. Part-time tuition and fees vary according to degree level. ***College room only:*** $4090. Room and board charges vary according to board plan and housing facility. ***Payment plan:*** installment. ***Waivers:*** employees or children of employees.

Financial Aid Of all full-time matriculated undergraduates who enrolled in 2013, 936 applied for aid, 833 were judged to have need, 457 had their need fully met. 575 Federal Work-Study jobs (averaging $555,227). In 2013, 194 non-need-based awards were made. ***Average percent of need met:*** 76. ***Average financial aid package:*** $32,160. ***Average need-based loan:*** $4775. ***Average need-based gift aid:*** $17,764. ***Average non-need-based aid:*** $15,594. ***Average indebtedness upon graduation:*** $19,076.

APPLYING

Standardized Tests *Required:* SAT or ACT (for admission). *Recommended:* ACT (for admission).

Options: electronic application, deferred entrance.

Required: high school transcript, minimum 2.0 GPA, ACT or SAT scores. ***Required for some:*** essay or personal statement, interview.

Application deadlines: 8/15 (freshmen), rolling (transfers).

Notification: continuous (freshmen), continuous (transfers).

CONTACT

Mr. Jeremiah Tudor, Senior Associate Director of Admissions, Georgetown College, 400 East College Street, Georgetown, KY 40324. *Phone:* 502-863-8727. *Toll-free phone:* 800-788-9985. *Fax:* 502-868-7733. *E-mail:* admissions@georgetowncollege.edu.

ITT Technical Institute
Lexington, Kentucky
http://www.itt-tech.edu/

- **Proprietary** 4-year, founded 2006, part of ITT Educational Services, Inc.
- **Coed**
- **Minimally difficult** entrance level

ACADEMICS
Degrees: associate and bachelor's.

STUDENT LIFE
Housing options: college housing not available.

CONTACT
Director of Recruitment, ITT Technical Institute, 2473 Fortune Drive, Suite 180, Lexington, KY 40509. *Phone:* 859-246-3300. *Toll-free phone:* 800-519-8151.

ITT Technical Institute
Louisville, Kentucky
http://www.itt-tech.edu/

- **Proprietary** primarily 2-year, founded 1993, part of ITT Educational Services, Inc.
- **Suburban** campus
- **Coed**
- **Minimally difficult** entrance level

ACADEMICS
Calendar: quarters. *Degrees:* associate and bachelor's.

STUDENT LIFE
Housing options: college housing not available.

CONTACT
Director of Recruitment, ITT Technical Institute, 9500 Ormsby Station Road, Suite 100, Louisville, KY 40223. *Phone:* 502-327-7424. *Toll-free phone:* 888-790-7427.

Kentucky Christian University
Grayson, Kentucky
http://www.kcu.edu/

- **Independent** comprehensive, founded 1919, affiliated with Christian Churches and Churches of Christ
- **Small-town** 121-acre campus
- **Endowment** $6.2 million
- **Coed** 602 undergraduate students, 83% full-time, 49% women, 51% men
- **Moderately difficult** entrance level, 48% of applicants were admitted

UNDERGRAD STUDENTS
497 full-time, 105 part-time. Students come from 29 states and territories; 3 other countries; 51% are from out of state; 10% Black or African American, non-Hispanic/Latino; 1% Hispanic/Latino; 0.7% Asian, non-Hispanic/Latino; 0.2% American Indian or Alaska Native, non-Hispanic/Latino; 0.7% Two or more races, non-Hispanic/Latino; 18% Race/ethnicity unknown; 2% international; 5% transferred in; 68% live on campus.

Freshmen
Admission: 886 applied, 423 admitted, 171 enrolled. ***Average high school GPA:*** 3.16. ***Test scores:*** SAT critical reading scores over 500: 50%; SAT math scores over 500: 30%; SAT writing scores over 500: 34%; ACT scores over 18: 93%; SAT critical reading scores over 600: 10%; SAT math scores over 600: 7%; SAT writing scores over 600: 10%; ACT scores over 24: 22%; SAT critical reading scores over 700: 3%; SAT writing scores over 700: 3%; ACT scores over 30: 2%.
Retention: 73% of full-time freshmen returned.

FACULTY
Total: 64, 53% full-time, 39% with terminal degrees.
Student/faculty ratio: 12:1.

ACADEMICS
Calendar: semesters. *Degrees:* bachelor's and master's.
Special study options: academic remediation for entering students, accelerated degree program, adult/continuing education programs, advanced placement credit, cooperative education, distance learning, double majors, external degree program, independent study, internships, off-campus study, part-time degree program, services for LD students, study abroad, summer session for credit.
Computers: 72 computers/terminals and 48 ports are available on campus for general student use. Students can access the following: computer help desk, free student e-mail accounts, online (class) grades, online (class) registration, online (class) schedules. Campuswide network is available. 100% of college-owned or -operated housing units are wired for high-speed Internet access. Wireless service is available via entire campus.

STUDENT LIFE
Housing options: on-campus residence required through sophomore year; men-only, women-only, special housing for students with disabilities. Campus housing is university owned. Freshman campus housing is guaranteed.
Activities and organizations: drama/theater group, choral group, marching band, Congressional Award Society, Laos Protos (Social Work), Herodotus Society (History), Elevate (Musical Touring Group), Student Council.
Athletics Member NCAA, NAIA, NCCAA. All NCAA Division II. ***Intercollegiate sports:*** archery M/W, basketball M/W, cheerleading M(c)/W(c), football M, soccer M/W, softball W, volleyball W. ***Intramural sports:*** skiing (downhill) M(c)/W(c).
Campus security: 24-hour emergency response devices, late-night transport/escort service, controlled dormitory access.
Student services: health clinic, personal/psychological counseling.

COSTS & FINANCIAL AID
Costs (2015–16) ***Comprehensive fee:*** $25,610 includes full-time tuition ($17,400), mandatory fees ($410), and room and board ($7800). Full-time tuition and fees vary according to course load. Part-time tuition: $580 per credit. Part-time tuition and fees vary according to class time, course load, and program. ***Room and board:*** Room and board charges vary according to housing facility. ***Payment plan:*** installment. ***Waivers:*** employees or children of employees.
Financial Aid Of all full-time matriculated undergraduates who enrolled in 2013, 485 applied for aid, 453 were judged to have need, 41 had their need fully met. 234 Federal Work-Study jobs (averaging $1261). 44 state and other part-time jobs (averaging $1495). In 2013, 52 non-need-based awards were made. ***Average percent of need met:*** 62. ***Average financial aid package:*** $14,428. ***Average need-based loan:*** $3986. ***Average need-based gift aid:*** $5354. ***Average non-need-based aid:*** $7313. ***Average indebtedness upon graduation:*** $30,578.

APPLYING
Standardized Tests *Required:* SAT or ACT (for admission).
Options: electronic application.
Application fee: $30.
Required: essay or personal statement, high school transcript, minimum 2.0 GPA, 2 letters of recommendation. ***Required for some:*** 3 letters of recommendation, interview.
Application deadlines: rolling (freshmen), rolling (transfers).
Notification: continuous (freshmen), continuous (transfers).

CONTACT
Ms. Heather Stacy, Director of Admissions, Kentucky Christian University, 100 Academic Parkway, Grayson, KY 41143. *Phone:* 606-474-3284. *Toll-free phone:* 800-522-3181. *Fax:* 606-474-3155. *E-mail:* sgreer@kcu.edu.

Kentucky Mountain Bible College
Vancleve, Kentucky
http://www.kmbc.edu/

- **Independent interdenominational** 4-year, founded 1931
- **Rural** 500-acre campus with easy access to Lexington
- **Coed** 84 undergraduate students, 69% full-time, 48% women, 42% men
- **Minimally difficult** entrance level, 44% of applicants were admitted

UNDERGRAD STUDENTS
58 full-time, 17 part-time. Students come from 17 states and territories; 3 other countries; 56% are from out of state; 1% Hispanic/Latino; 7% international; 3% transferred in; 92% live on campus.

Freshmen
Admission: 50 applied, 22 admitted, 14 enrolled. ***Average high school GPA:*** 3.23.

Retention: 61% of full-time freshmen returned.

FACULTY
Total: 17, 6% with terminal degrees.

Student/faculty ratio: 11:1.

ACADEMICS
Calendar: semesters. *Degrees:* associate and bachelor's.

Special study options: academic remediation for entering students, cooperative education, distance learning, independent study, internships, part-time degree program.

Computers: 4 computers/terminals are available on campus for general student use. Students can access the following: campus intranet, free student e-mail accounts, online (class) grades, online (class) schedules, Wi-Fi. Campuswide network is available. 100% of college-owned or -operated housing units are wired for high-speed Internet access. Wireless service is available via entire campus.

STUDENT LIFE
Housing options: on-campus residence required through senior year; men-only, women-only. Campus housing is university owned. Freshman campus housing is guaranteed.

Activities and organizations: drama/theater group, student-run newspaper, choral group, Missionary Involvement, Class Organizations.

Athletics *Intramural sports:* basketball M, volleyball W.

Campus security: student patrols.

Student services: personal/psychological counseling.

COSTS
Costs (2014–15) *One-time required fee:* $640. ***Comprehensive fee:*** $12,330 includes full-time tuition ($7040), mandatory fees ($690), and room and board ($4600). Full-time tuition and fees vary according to program. Part-time tuition: $220 per credit hour. Part-time tuition and fees vary according to program. ***Required fees:*** $175 per year part-time. ***College room only:*** $1650. Room and board charges vary according to board plan and housing facility. ***Payment plan:*** installment. ***Waivers:*** employees or children of employees.

APPLYING
Standardized Tests *Required:* ACT (for admission).

Application fee: $25.

Required: essay or personal statement, high school transcript, minimum 2.0 GPA, testimony of Christian belief and practice. ***Recommended:*** minimum 2.0 GPA, interview.

Application deadlines: rolling (freshmen), rolling (transfers).

Notification: continuous (freshmen), continuous (transfers).

CONTACT
Mr. David Lorimer, Director of Recruiting, Kentucky Mountain Bible College, PO Box 10, Vancleve, KY 41385. *Phone:* 606-693-5000 Ext. 138. *Toll-free phone:* 800-879-KMBC. *Fax:* 606-693-4884. *E-mail:* dlorimer@kmbc.edu.

Kentucky State University

Frankfort, Kentucky

http://www.kysu.edu/

- **State-related** comprehensive, founded 1886
- **Small-town** 916-acre campus with easy access to Louisville
- **Endowment** $15.1 million
- **Coed** 1,754 undergraduate students, 80% full-time, 61% women, 39% men

UNDERGRAD STUDENTS
1,397 full-time, 357 part-time. Students come from 36 states and territories; 4 other countries; 42% are from out of state; 58% Black or African American, non-Hispanic/Latino; 2% Hispanic/Latino; 0.5% Asian, non-Hispanic/Latino; 0.2% Native Hawaiian or other Pacific Islander, non-Hispanic/Latino; 0.2% American Indian or Alaska Native, non-Hispanic/Latino; 2% Two or more races, non-Hispanic/Latino; 12% Race/ethnicity unknown; 0.3% international; 10% transferred in; 34% live on campus.

Freshmen
Admission: 289 enrolled. ***Average high school GPA:*** 2.78. ***Test scores:*** SAT critical reading scores over 500: 18%; SAT math scores over 500: 9%; SAT writing scores over 500: 10%; ACT scores over 18: 52%; SAT math scores over 600: 3%; ACT scores over 24: 11%; ACT scores over 30: 1%.

Retention: 44% of full-time freshmen returned.

FACULTY
Total: 150, 83% full-time, 58% with terminal degrees.

Student/faculty ratio: 12:1.

ACADEMICS
Calendar: semesters. *Degrees:* associate, bachelor's, master's, and doctoral.

Special study options: academic remediation for entering students, adult/continuing education programs, advanced placement credit, cooperative education, distance learning, double majors, external degree program, freshman honors college, honors programs, independent study, internships, services for LD students, student-designed majors, study abroad, summer session for credit. ***ROTC:*** Army (c), Air Force (c).

Unusual degree programs: 3-2 engineering with University of Kentucky, University of Maryland at College Park, Vanderbilt University, Florida A&M University.

Computers: 94 computers/terminals and 24 ports are available on campus for general student use. Students can access the following: campus intranet, computer help desk, free student e-mail accounts, online (class) grades, online (class) registration, online (class) schedules, review grades, pay student bill, verify address, and accept financial aid awards. Campuswide network is available. 100% of college-owned or -operated housing units are wired for high-speed Internet access. Wireless service is available via entire campus.

STUDENT LIFE
Housing options: on-campus residence required through sophomore year; coed, men-only, women-only. Campus housing is university owned. Freshman applicants given priority for college housing.

Activities and organizations: student-run newspaper, marching band, Collegiate100, Alpha Phi Omega, Drive Our Peer's Education DOPE, Student Ambassador's, Alpha Phi Alpha, national fraternities, national sororities.

Athletics Member NCAA. All Division II. ***Intercollegiate sports:*** baseball M(s), basketball M(s)/W(s), cross-country running M(s)/W(s), football M(s), golf M(s), softball W(s), track and field M(s)/W(s), volleyball W(s). ***Intramural sports:*** cheerleading W(c).

Campus security: 24-hour emergency response devices and patrols, controlled dormitory access.

Student services: health clinic, personal/psychological counseling.

COSTS & FINANCIAL AID
Costs (2014–15) *Tuition:* state resident $7014 full-time, $292 per credit hour part-time; nonresident $16,824 full-time, $701 per credit hour part-time. Full-time tuition and fees vary according to course load and degree level. Part-time tuition and fees vary according to course load and degree level. ***Required fees:*** $390 full-time, $13 per credit hour part-time. ***Room and board:*** $6690; room only: $3340. Room and board charges vary according to board plan and housing facility. ***Payment plan:*** installment. ***Waivers:*** senior citizens and employees or children of employees.

Financial Aid Of all full-time matriculated undergraduates who enrolled in 2014, 1,300 applied for aid, 1,238 were judged to have need, 151 had their need fully met. 115 Federal Work-Study jobs (averaging $4584). 96 state and other part-time jobs (averaging $1594). In 2014, 46 non-need-based awards were made. ***Average percent of need met:*** 59. ***Average financial aid package:*** $12,182. ***Average need-based loan:*** $4132. ***Average need-based gift aid:*** $8090. ***Average non-need-based aid:*** $9663. ***Average indebtedness upon graduation:*** $34,110.

APPLYING
Standardized Tests *Required:* SAT or ACT (for admission).

Required: minimum 2.5 GPA, ACT greater than or equal to 18. ***Required for some:*** high school transcript.

CONTACT

Ms. Jameelah Means, Director of Admission, Kentucky State University, 400 East Main Street, Academic Suite Building 312, Frankfort, KY 40601. *Phone:* 502- 597-6813. *Toll-free phone:* 877-367-5978. *Fax:* 502-597-5814. *E-mail:* jameelah.means@kysu.edu.

Kentucky Wesleyan College

Owensboro, Kentucky

http://www.kwc.edu/

- **Independent Methodist** 4-year, founded 1858
- **Suburban** 52-acre campus
- **Endowment** $32.6 million
- **Coed** 709 undergraduate students, 93% full-time, 46% women, 54% men
- **Moderately difficult** entrance level, 61% of applicants were admitted

UNDERGRAD STUDENTS

662 full-time, 47 part-time. Students come from 28 states and territories; 12 other countries; 29% are from out of state; 14% Black or African American, non-Hispanic/Latino; 2% Hispanic/Latino; 0.4% Asian, non-Hispanic/Latino; 0.1% American Indian or Alaska Native, non-Hispanic/Latino; 15% Race/ethnicity unknown; 0.7% international; 7% transferred in; 46% live on campus.

Freshmen

Admission: 1,087 applied, 660 admitted, 239 enrolled. ***Average high school GPA:*** 3.3. ***Test scores:*** SAT critical reading scores over 500: 8%; SAT math scores over 500: 13%; ACT scores over 18: 163%; SAT critical reading scores over 600: 2%; SAT math scores over 600: 4%; ACT scores over 24: 69%; ACT scores over 30: 8%.

Retention: 66% of full-time freshmen returned.

FACULTY

Total: 92, 51% full-time.

Student/faculty ratio: 11:1.

ACADEMICS

Calendar: semesters. *Degree:* bachelor's.

Special study options: academic remediation for entering students, accelerated degree program, adult/continuing education programs, advanced placement credit, cooperative education, distance learning, double majors, independent study, internships, off-campus study, part-time degree program, services for LD students, study abroad, summer session for credit. ***ROTC:*** Army (c).

Unusual degree programs: 3-2 engineering with Auburn University, University of Kentucky; nursing with University of Louisville.

Computers: 125 computers/terminals are available on campus for general student use. Students can access the following: campus intranet, computer help desk, free student e-mail accounts, online (class) grades, online (class) registration, online (class) schedules. Campuswide network is available. 100% of college-owned or -operated housing units are wired for high-speed Internet access. Wireless service is available via entire campus.

STUDENT LIFE

Housing options: on-campus residence required through senior year; coed, men-only, women-only, special housing for students with disabilities. Campus housing is university owned. Freshman campus housing is guaranteed.

Activities and organizations: drama/theater group, student-run newspaper, radio station, choral group, Student Government Association, Student Activities Programming Board, Campus Ministries, Pre Professional, St Jude Up 'Til Dawn Executive Board, national fraternities, national sororities.

Athletics Member NCAA. All Division II. ***Intercollegiate sports:*** baseball M(s), basketball M(s)/W(s), bowling W(s), cheerleading M/W, cross-country running M(s)/W(s), football M(s), golf M(s)/W(s), soccer M(s)/W(s), softball W(s), tennis W(s), track and field M(s)/W(s), volleyball W(s). ***Intramural sports:*** basketball M/W, soccer M/W, volleyball M/W.

Campus security: 24-hour emergency response devices, late-night transport/escort service, 12-hour patrols by trained security personnel.

Student services: health clinic, personal/psychological counseling, women's center.

COSTS & FINANCIAL AID

Costs (2014–15) ***Comprehensive fee:*** $29,830 includes full-time tuition ($21,400), mandatory fees ($630), and room and board ($7800). Full-time tuition and fees vary according to course load. Part-time tuition: $610 per credit. Part-time tuition and fees vary according to course load. ***Room and board:*** Room and board charges vary according to board plan and housing facility. ***Payment plans:*** installment, deferred payment. ***Waivers:*** children of alumni, senior citizens, and employees or children of employees.

Financial Aid Of all full-time matriculated undergraduates who enrolled in 2012, 657 applied for aid, 605 were judged to have need, 121 had their need fully met. In 2012, 85 non-need-based awards were made. ***Average percent of need met:*** 72. ***Average financial aid package:*** $16,223. ***Average need-based loan:*** $3914. ***Average need-based gift aid:*** $13,036. ***Average non-need-based aid:*** $9746. ***Financial aid deadline:*** 3/15.

APPLYING

Standardized Tests *Required:* SAT or ACT (for admission).

Options: electronic application, early admission, deferred entrance.

Required: high school transcript.

Notification: continuous (freshmen), continuous (transfers).

CONTACT

Kentucky Wesleyan College, 3000 Frederica Street, Owensboro, KY 42301. *Phone:* 270-852-3120. *Toll-free phone:* 800-999-0592 (in-state); 800-990-0592 (out-of-state).

Lindsey Wilson College

Columbia, Kentucky

http://www.lindsey.edu/

- **Independent United Methodist** comprehensive, founded 1903
- **Rural** 225-acre campus
- **Endowment** $19.4 million
- **Coed** 2,205 undergraduate students, 94% full-time, 58% women, 42% men
- **Minimally difficult** entrance level, 71% of applicants were admitted

UNDERGRAD STUDENTS

2,079 full-time, 126 part-time. Students come from 33 states and territories; 37 other countries; 22% are from out of state; 10% Black or African American, non-Hispanic/Latino; 1% Hispanic/Latino; 0.5% Asian, non-Hispanic/Latino; 0.4% American Indian or Alaska Native, non-Hispanic/Latino; 1% Two or more races, non-Hispanic/Latino; 19% Race/ethnicity unknown; 14% transferred in; 53% live on campus.

Freshmen

Admission: 3,103 applied, 2,213 admitted, 526 enrolled. ***Average high school GPA:*** 3.21. ***Test scores:*** ACT scores over 18: 87%; ACT scores over 24: 27%; ACT scores over 30: 1%.

Retention: 62% of full-time freshmen returned.

FACULTY

Total: 245, 44% full-time, 44% with terminal degrees.

Student/faculty ratio: 14:1.

ACADEMICS

Calendar: semesters. *Degrees:* associate, bachelor's, master's, and doctoral.

Special study options: academic remediation for entering students, accelerated degree program, adult/continuing education programs, advanced placement credit, cooperative education, double majors, English as a second language, independent study, internships, off-campus study, part-time degree program, services for LD students, student-designed majors, study abroad, summer session for credit.

Computers: 120 computers/terminals are available on campus for general student use. Students can access the following: campus intranet, computer help desk, free student e-mail accounts, online (class) grades, online (class) registration, online (class) schedules. Campuswide network is available. 100% of college-owned or -operated housing units are wired for high-speed Internet access. Wireless service is available via entire campus.

STUDENT LIFE
Housing options: on-campus residence required through senior year; men-only, women-only. Campus housing is university owned. Freshman campus housing is guaranteed.

Activities and organizations: drama/theater group, student-run newspaper, choral group, marching band.

Athletics Member NAIA. ***Intercollegiate sports:*** baseball M(s), basketball M(s)/W(s), bowling M(s)/W(s), cheerleading M(s)/W(s), cross-country running M(s)/W(s), football M(s)/W(s), golf M(s)/W(s), soccer M(s)/W(s), softball W(s), swimming and diving M(s)/W(s), tennis M(s)/W(s), track and field M(s)/W(s), volleyball W(s), wrestling M(s). ***Intramural sports:*** basketball M/W, football M/W, softball M/W, table tennis M/W, tennis M/W, volleyball M/W, weight lifting M/W.

Campus security: 24-hour emergency response devices and patrols.

Student services: health clinic, personal/psychological counseling, women's center.

COSTS & FINANCIAL AID
Costs (2015–16) ***Comprehensive fee:*** $32,062 includes full-time tuition ($22,920), mandatory fees ($242), and room and board ($8900). Full-time tuition and fees vary according to class time, degree level, and location. Part-time tuition: $955 per credit hour. Part-time tuition and fees vary according to class time, degree level, and location. ***Required fees:*** $48 per term part-time. ***College room only:*** $3225. ***Payment plan:*** installment. ***Waivers:*** senior citizens and employees or children of employees.

Financial Aid Of all full-time matriculated undergraduates who enrolled in 2014, 2,121 applied for aid, 2,005 were judged to have need, 460 had their need fully met. 282 Federal Work-Study jobs (averaging $2145). 23 state and other part-time jobs (averaging $2375). ***Average need-based loan:*** $4522. ***Average need-based gift aid:*** $17,472. ***Average indebtedness upon graduation:*** $26,249.

APPLYING
Standardized Tests *Required for some:* SAT or ACT (for admission).

Options: electronic application.

Required: high school transcript. ***Recommended:*** interview.

Application deadlines: rolling (freshmen), rolling (transfers).

Notification: continuous (freshmen), continuous (transfers).

CONTACT
Mrs. Charity Ferguson, Assistant Director of Admissions, Lindsey Wilson College, 210 Lindsey Wilson Street, Columbia, KY 42728-1298. *Phone:* 270-384-8100. *Toll-free phone:* 800-264-0138. *Fax:* 270-384-8591.

Morehead State University

Morehead, Kentucky

http://www.moreheadstate.edu/

- **State-supported** comprehensive, founded 1922
- **Small-town** 1187-acre campus
- **Endowment** $43.0 million
- **Coed** 9,952 undergraduate students, 63% full-time, 60% women, 40% men
- **Minimally difficult** entrance level, 84% of applicants were admitted

UNDERGRAD STUDENTS
6,258 full-time, 3,694 part-time. Students come from 37 states and territories; 24 other countries; 14% are from out of state; 4% Black or African American, non-Hispanic/Latino; 1% Hispanic/Latino; 0.3% Asian, non-Hispanic/Latino; 0.1% Native Hawaiian or other Pacific Islander, non-Hispanic/Latino; 0.2% American Indian or Alaska Native, non-Hispanic/Latino; 1% Two or more races, non-Hispanic/Latino; 1% Race/ethnicity unknown; 1% international; 5% transferred in; 40% live on campus.

Freshmen
Admission: 5,236 applied, 4,421 admitted, 1,513 enrolled. ***Average high school GPA:*** 3.32. ***Test scores:*** SAT critical reading scores over 500: 51%; SAT math scores over 500: 47%; SAT writing scores over 500: 35%; ACT scores over 18: 91%; SAT critical reading scores over 600: 12%; SAT math scores over 600: 15%; SAT writing scores over 600: 10%; ACT scores over 24: 33%; SAT critical reading scores over 700: 2%; SAT math scores over 700: 3%; ACT scores over 30: 4%.

Retention: 69% of full-time freshmen returned.

FACULTY
Total: 492, 73% full-time.

Student/faculty ratio: 18:1.

ACADEMICS
Calendar: semesters. *Degrees:* certificates, associate, bachelor's, master's, doctoral, post-master's, and postbachelor's certificates.

Special study options: academic remediation for entering students, accelerated degree program, adult/continuing education programs, advanced placement credit, cooperative education, distance learning, double majors, English as a second language, honors programs, independent study, internships, off-campus study, part-time degree program, services for LD students, student-designed majors, study abroad, summer session for credit. ***ROTC:*** Army (b).

Unusual degree programs: 3-2 engineering with Chemical Engineering: 3 years (96 hours) at Morehead State University, transfer to University of Kentucky to an approved engineering program.

Computers: 1,000 computers/terminals and 1,820 ports are available on campus for general student use. Students can access the following: campus intranet, computer help desk, free student e-mail accounts, online (class) grades, online (class) registration, online (class) schedules. Campuswide network is available. 100% of college-owned or -operated housing units are wired for high-speed Internet access. Wireless service is available via entire campus.

STUDENT LIFE
Housing options: on-campus residence required through sophomore year; coed, special housing for students with disabilities. Campus housing is university owned. Freshman applicants given priority for college housing.

Activities and organizations: drama/theater group, student-run newspaper, radio and television station, choral group, marching band, Delta Tau Delta Fraternity, Delta Gamma, Phi Sigma Pi (Honors), Baptist Campus Ministries (BCM), Collegiate Future Farmers of America (FFA), national fraternities, national sororities.

Athletics Member NCAA. All Division I except football (Division I-AA). ***Intercollegiate sports:*** baseball M(s), basketball M(s)/W(s), bowling M(c)/W(c), cheerleading M(s)/W(s), cross-country running M(s)/W(s), equestrian sports M(c)/W(c), golf M(s)/W(s), riflery M(s)/W(s), soccer W(s), softball W(s), tennis M(s)/W(s), track and field M(s)/W(s), volleyball W(s). ***Intramural sports:*** badminton M/W, basketball M/W, bowling M/W, football M/W, golf M/W, racquetball M/W, soccer M(c), softball M/W, table tennis M/W, tennis M/W, ultimate Frisbee M/W, volleyball M/W.

Campus security: 24-hour emergency response devices and patrols, student patrols, late-night transport/escort service, controlled dormitory access.

Student services: health clinic, personal/psychological counseling.

COSTS & FINANCIAL AID
Costs (2014–15) ***Tuition:*** state resident $7866 full-time, $328 per credit hour part-time; nonresident $19,666 full-time, $820 per credit hour part-time. Full-time tuition and fees vary according to course load, degree level, location, reciprocity agreements, and student level. Part-time tuition and fees vary according to course load, degree level, location, reciprocity agreements, and student level. ***Room and board:*** $7888; room only: $4328. Room and board charges vary according to board plan and housing facility. ***Payment plans:*** installment, deferred payment. ***Waivers:*** minority students, children of alumni, senior citizens, and employees or children of employees.

Financial Aid Of all full-time matriculated undergraduates who enrolled in 2014, 5,481 applied for aid, 4,803 were judged to have need, 1,063 had their need fully met. 526 Federal Work-Study jobs (averaging $1927). 768 state and other part-time jobs (averaging $2484). In 2014, 885 non-need-based awards were made. ***Average percent of need met:*** 64. ***Average financial aid package:*** $10,961. ***Average need-based loan:*** $3644. ***Average need-based gift aid:*** $5421. ***Average non-need-based aid:*** $6347. ***Average indebtedness upon graduation:*** $28,147.

APPLYING
Standardized Tests *Required:* SAT or ACT (for admission).

Options: electronic application, early admission, deferred entrance.

Application fee: $30.

Required: high school transcript. ***Required for some:*** essay or personal statement, 1 letter of recommendation, interview.

Application deadlines: rolling (freshmen), rolling (out-of-state freshmen), rolling (transfers).

Notification: continuous (freshmen), continuous (out-of-state freshmen), continuous (transfers).

CONTACT
Mr. Jeffrey R Liles, Assistant Vice President for Enrollment Services, Morehead State University, 100 Admissions Center, Morehead, KY 40351. *Phone:* 606-783-2000. *Toll-free phone:* 800-585-6781. *Fax:* 606-783-5038. *E-mail:* admissions@moreheadstate.edu.

Murray State University

Murray, Kentucky

http://www.murraystate.edu/

- **State-supported** comprehensive, founded 1922
- **Small-town** 261-acre campus
- **Endowment** $21.5 million
- **Coed** 9,444 undergraduate students, 78% full-time, 56% women, 44% men
- **Moderately difficult** entrance level, 80% of applicants were admitted

UNDERGRAD STUDENTS
7,370 full-time, 2,074 part-time. Students come from 44 states and territories; 43 other countries; 31% are from out of state; 8% Black or African American, non-Hispanic/Latino; 2% Hispanic/Latino; 0.7% Asian, non-Hispanic/Latino; 0.1% Native Hawaiian or other Pacific Islander, non-Hispanic/Latino; 0.2% American Indian or Alaska Native, non-Hispanic/Latino; 2% Two or more races, non-Hispanic/Latino; 2% Race/ethnicity unknown; 4% international; 8% transferred in.

Freshmen
Admission: 4,760 applied, 3,806 admitted, 1,508 enrolled. ***Average high school GPA:*** 3.4. ***Test scores:*** SAT critical reading scores over 500: 47%; SAT math scores over 500: 54%; ACT scores over 18: 91%; SAT critical reading scores over 600: 12%; SAT math scores over 600: 15%; ACT scores over 24: 39%; SAT critical reading scores over 700: 2%; SAT math scores over 700: 2%; ACT scores over 30: 7%.

Retention: 72% of full-time freshmen returned.

FACULTY
Total: 681, 65% full-time, 58% with terminal degrees.

Student/faculty ratio: 16:1.

ACADEMICS
Calendar: semesters. *Degrees:* certificates, associate, bachelor's, master's, doctoral, and postbachelor's certificates.

Special study options: academic remediation for entering students, adult/continuing education programs, advanced placement credit, cooperative education, distance learning, double majors, English as a second language, external degree program, honors programs, independent study, internships, off-campus study, part-time degree program, services for LD students, student-designed majors, study abroad, summer session for credit. ***ROTC:*** Army (b).

Computers: 230 computers/terminals are available on campus for general student use. Students can access the following: campus intranet, computer help desk, free student e-mail accounts, online (class) grades, online (class) registration, online (class) schedules, billing accounts, course evaluation forms, reserve library material, receive instant campus alerts, secure on-campus housing, and pre-order food or take-out. Campuswide network is available. 100% of college-owned or -operated housing units are wired for high-speed Internet access. Wireless service is available via entire campus.

STUDENT LIFE
Housing options: on-campus residence required through sophomore year; coed, women-only, special housing for students with disabilities. Campus housing is university owned.

Activities and organizations: drama/theater group, student-run newspaper, television station, choral group, marching band, Student Government Association, Black Student Council, Agriculture Leadership Council, Future Business Leaders of America, American Society of Safety Engineers, national fraternities, national sororities.

Athletics Member NCAA. All Division I except football (Division I-AA). ***Intercollegiate sports:*** baseball M(s), basketball M(s)/W(s), cheerleading W(c), crew M(c)/W(c), cross-country running M/W(s), equestrian sports M(c)/W(c), golf M(s)/W(s), riflery M(s)/W(s), soccer W(s), softball W(s), tennis M(s)/W(s), track and field W(s), volleyball W(s). ***Intramural sports:*** basketball M/W, fencing M(c)/W(c), football M/W, golf M/W, racquetball M(c)/W(c), rugby M(c), soccer M/W, softball M/W, tennis M/W, ultimate Frisbee M/W, volleyball M/W, water polo M/W.

Campus security: 24-hour emergency response devices and patrols, student patrols, late-night transport/escort service, controlled dormitory access.

Student services: health clinic, personal/psychological counseling, women's center.

COSTS & FINANCIAL AID
Costs (2014–15) ***Tuition:*** state resident $6360 full-time, $265 per hour part-time; nonresident $19,080 full-time, $795 per hour part-time. Full-time tuition and fees vary according to reciprocity agreements. Part-time tuition and fees vary according to reciprocity agreements. ***Required fees:*** $1032 full-time, $43 per hour part-time. ***Room and board:*** $7912; room only: $4576. Room and board charges vary according to board plan and housing facility. ***Payment plan:*** installment. ***Waivers:*** children of alumni, senior citizens, and employees or children of employees.

Financial Aid Of all full-time matriculated undergraduates who enrolled in 2013, 5,412 applied for aid, 4,660 were judged to have need, 1,202 had their need fully met. 339 Federal Work-Study jobs (averaging $1625). 2,121 state and other part-time jobs (averaging $2138). In 2013, 414 non-need-based awards were made. ***Average percent of need met:*** 29. ***Average financial aid package:*** $11,339. ***Average need-based loan:*** $6367. ***Average need-based gift aid:*** $5850. ***Average non-need-based aid:*** $4381. ***Average indebtedness upon graduation:*** $24,554.

APPLYING
Standardized Tests *Required:* SAT or ACT (for admission). *Recommended:* ACT (for admission).

Options: electronic application, early admission.

Application fee: $40.

Required: high school transcript, minimum 3.0 GPA, For unconditional admission, applicants must have a minimum composite score of 18 on the ACT and rank in the top half of their class or have at least a 3.0 GPA on a 4.0 scale. They must complete 22 academic high school course units.

Application deadlines: rolling (freshmen), rolling (out-of-state freshmen), rolling (transfers).

Notification: continuous (freshmen), continuous (out-of-state freshmen), continuous (transfers).

CONTACT
Ms. Stacy Bell, Assistant Director of Undergraduate Admissions, Murray State University, 102 Curris Center, Murray, KY 42701-0009. *Phone:* 270-809-3741. *Toll-free phone:* 800-272-4678. *Fax:* 270-809-3780. *E-mail:* msu.admissions@murraystate.edu.

Northern Kentucky University

Highland Heights, Kentucky

http://www.nku.edu/

- **State-supported** comprehensive, founded 1968
- **Suburban** 430-acre campus with easy access to Cincinnati
- **Endowment** $94.9 million
- **Coed** 12,809 undergraduate students, 74% full-time, 55% women, 45% men
- **Moderately difficult** entrance level, 93% of applicants were admitted

UNDERGRAD STUDENTS
9,433 full-time, 3,376 part-time. Students come from 37 states and territories; 45 other countries; 31% are from out of state; 7% Black or African American, non-Hispanic/Latino; 3% Hispanic/Latino; 1% Asian, non-Hispanic/Latino; 0.1% Native Hawaiian or other Pacific Islander, non-Hispanic/Latino; 0.4% American Indian or Alaska Native, non-Hispanic/Latino; 2% Two or more races, non-Hispanic/Latino; 1% Race/ethnicity unknown; 3% international; 5% transferred in; 16% live on campus.

Freshmen
Admission: 6,957 applied, 6,489 admitted, 2,193 enrolled. ***Average high school GPA:*** 3.23. ***Test scores:*** SAT critical reading scores over 500:

52%; SAT math scores over 500: 52%; SAT writing scores over 500: 44%; ACT scores over 18: 96%; SAT critical reading scores over 600: 15%; SAT math scores over 600: 17%; SAT writing scores over 600: 11%; ACT scores over 24: 41%; SAT critical reading scores over 700: 3%; SAT math scores over 700: 3%; SAT writing scores over 700: 4%; ACT scores over 30: 7%.

Retention: 69% of full-time freshmen returned.

FACULTY

Total: 978, 57% full-time, 57% with terminal degrees.

Student/faculty ratio: 17:1.

ACADEMICS

Calendar: semesters. *Degrees:* certificates, associate, bachelor's, master's, doctoral, post-master's, and postbachelor's certificates.

Special study options: academic remediation for entering students, accelerated degree program, adult/continuing education programs, advanced placement credit, cooperative education, distance learning, double majors, English as a second language, honors programs, independent study, internships, off-campus study, part-time degree program, services for LD students, student-designed majors, study abroad, summer session for credit. ***ROTC:*** Army (c), Air Force (c).

Computers: 235 computers/terminals are available on campus for general student use. Students can access the following: campus intranet, computer help desk, free student e-mail accounts, online (class) grades, online (class) registration, online (class) schedules. Campuswide network is available. 100% of college-owned or -operated housing units are wired for high-speed Internet access. Wireless service is available via entire campus.

STUDENT LIFE

Housing options: coed, special housing for students with disabilities. Campus housing is university owned. Freshman applicants given priority for college housing.

Activities and organizations: drama/theater group, student-run newspaper, radio and television station, choral group, Sororities, Fraternities, Freshmen Service Leadership Committee, Student Alumni Association, Activities Programming Board, national sororities.

Athletics Member NCAA. All Division I except volleyball (Division II). ***Intercollegiate sports:*** baseball M(s), basketball M(s)/W(s), cheerleading M/W, cross-country running M(s)/W(s), golf M(s)/W(s), soccer M(s)/W(s), softball W(s), tennis M(s)/W(s), track and field M/W, volleyball W(s). ***Intramural sports:*** badminton M(c)/W(c), basketball M/W(c), bowling M/W, equestrian sports M(c)/W(c), football M/W, gymnastics W(c), ice hockey M(c), lacrosse M(c), racquetball M/W, soccer M(c)/W(c), softball M(c)/W(c), tennis M/W, ultimate Frisbee M(c)/W(c), volleyball M(c)/W(c), water polo M/W, weight lifting M/W.

Campus security: 24-hour emergency response devices and patrols, late-night transport/escort service, controlled dormitory access.

Student services: health clinic, personal/psychological counseling.

COSTS & FINANCIAL AID

Costs (2014–15) ***Tuition:*** state resident $8472 full-time, $353 per credit hour part-time; nonresident $16,944 full-time, $706 per credit hour part-time. Full-time tuition and fees vary according to course load and reciprocity agreements. Part-time tuition and fees vary according to course load and reciprocity agreements. ***Required fees:*** $384 full-time, $353 per credit hour part-time. ***Room and board:*** $8964. Room and board charges vary according to board plan and housing facility. ***Payment plan:*** installment. ***Waivers:*** senior citizens and employees or children of employees.

Financial Aid Of all full-time matriculated undergraduates who enrolled in 2013, 7,820 applied for aid, 6,408 were judged to have need, 1,336 had their need fully met. In 2013, 870 non-need-based awards were made. ***Average percent of need met:*** 59. ***Average financial aid package:*** $10,447. ***Average need-based loan:*** $4400. ***Average need-based gift aid:*** $5325. ***Average non-need-based aid:*** $5039. ***Average indebtedness upon graduation:*** $27,594.

APPLYING

Standardized Tests *Required:* SAT or ACT (for admission).

Options: electronic application, deferred entrance.

Application fee: $40.

Required: high school transcript. ***Required for some:*** some programs require separate applications.

Application deadlines: 8/19 (freshmen), 8/19 (out-of-state freshmen), 8/1 (transfers).

Notification: continuous (freshmen), continuous (out-of-state freshmen), continuous (transfers).

CONTACT

Ms. Melissa Gorbandt, Office of Admissions, Northern Kentucky University, Lucas Administrative Center, 400 Nunn Drive, Highland Heights, KY 41099. *Phone:* 859-572-5744. *Toll-free phone:* 800-637-9948. *Fax:* 859-572-6665. *E-mail:* admitnku@nku.edu.

See previous page for display ad and page 1552 for the College Close-Up.

St. Catharine College

St. Catharine, Kentucky

http://www.sccky.edu/

- **Independent Roman Catholic** comprehensive, founded 1931
- **Rural** 643-acre campus with easy access to Louisville
- **Endowment** $300,000
- **Coed** 939 undergraduate students, 61% full-time, 60% women, 40% men
- **Minimally difficult** entrance level, 45% of applicants were admitted

UNDERGRAD STUDENTS

571 full-time, 368 part-time. Students come from 23 states and territories; 11 other countries; 14% are from out of state; 11% Black or African American, non-Hispanic/Latino; 6% Hispanic/Latino; 0.3% Asian, non-Hispanic/Latino; 0.3% American Indian or Alaska Native, non-Hispanic/Latino; 3% Two or more races, non-Hispanic/Latino; 0.3% Race/ethnicity unknown; 2% international; 1% transferred in.

Freshmen

Admission: 700 applied, 317 admitted, 146 enrolled.

Retention: 86% of full-time freshmen returned.

FACULTY

Total: 63.

Student/faculty ratio: 8:1.

ACADEMICS

Calendar: semesters. *Degrees:* certificates, associate, bachelor's, and master's.

Special study options: academic remediation for entering students, advanced placement credit, cooperative education, distance learning, double majors, honors programs, independent study, internships, part-time degree program, services for LD students, study abroad, summer session for credit.

Computers: 60 computers/terminals are available on campus for general student use. Students can access the following: free student e-mail accounts, online (class) grades, online (class) registration.

STUDENT LIFE

Housing options: coed. Campus housing is university owned and is provided by a third party.

Activities and organizations: drama/theater group, student-run newspaper, choral group, Phi Theta Kappa National Honor Society, Alpha Chi Omega National Honor Society, Student Government Association, STARS, Drama Club.

Athletics Member NAIA. ***Intercollegiate sports:*** baseball M(s), basketball M(s)/W(s), bowling M/W, cheerleading W(s), golf M(s)/W(s), soccer M(s)/W(s), softball W(s), swimming and diving M/W, tennis M(s), track and field M(s)/W(s), volleyball W(s), wrestling M(s). ***Intramural sports:*** volleyball M/W.

Campus security: 24-hour emergency response devices, night security guard.

Student services: personal/psychological counseling.

COSTS & FINANCIAL AID

Costs (2015–16) ***Comprehensive fee:*** $29,194 includes full-time tuition ($19,732), mandatory fees ($50), and room and board ($9412). Full-time tuition and fees vary according to course level, course load, and program. Part-time tuition: $660 per credit hour. Part-time tuition and fees vary according to course level, course load, and program. ***College room only:*** $4912. Room and board charges vary according to housing facility.

Payment plan: installment. ***Waivers:*** senior citizens and employees or children of employees.

Financial Aid Of all full-time matriculated undergraduates who enrolled in 2013, 45 Federal Work-Study jobs (averaging $1000).

APPLYING

Standardized Tests *Recommended:* SAT or ACT (for admission).

Options: electronic application, early admission.

Application fee: $15.

Required for some: high school transcript.

Application deadlines: rolling (freshmen), rolling (transfers).

CONTACT

Ms. Stacey Garrett, Assistant Director of Admissions, St. Catharine College, 2735 Bardstown Rd, St. Catharine, KY 40061. *Phone:* 859-336-8082 Ext. 1259. *Fax:* 859-336-9381. *E-mail:* staceygarrett@sccky.edu.

Spalding University

Louisville, Kentucky

http://www.spalding.edu/

- **Independent** comprehensive, founded 1814, affiliated with Roman Catholic Church
- **Urban** 16-acre campus with easy access to Louisville
- **Endowment** $15.3 million
- **Coed** 1,312 undergraduate students, 70% full-time, 69% women, 31% men
- **Moderately difficult** entrance level, 46% of applicants were admitted

UNDERGRAD STUDENTS

921 full-time, 391 part-time. Students come from 15 states and territories; 4 other countries; 10% are from out of state; 20% Black or African American, non-Hispanic/Latino; 4% Hispanic/Latino; 1% Asian, non-Hispanic/Latino; 0.2% Native Hawaiian or other Pacific Islander, non-Hispanic/Latino; 0.2% American Indian or Alaska Native, non-Hispanic/Latino; 3% Two or more races, non-Hispanic/Latino; 3% Race/ethnicity unknown; 0.2% international; 8% transferred in; 8% live on campus.

Freshmen

Admission: 1,061 applied, 485 admitted, 205 enrolled. ***Average high school GPA:*** 3.28. ***Test scores:*** SAT critical reading scores over 500: 38%; SAT math scores over 500: 20%; ACT scores over 18: 87%; SAT critical reading scores over 600: 5%; SAT math scores over 600: 10%; ACT scores over 24: 18%; ACT scores over 30: 2%.

Retention: 74% of full-time freshmen returned.

ACADEMICS

Calendar: other. *Degrees:* associate, bachelor's, master's, doctoral, post-master's, and postbachelor's certificates.

Special study options: academic remediation for entering students, accelerated degree program, adult/continuing education programs, advanced placement credit, cooperative education, distance learning, double majors, independent study, internships, off-campus study, part-time degree program, services for LD students, study abroad, summer session for credit. ***ROTC:*** Army (c), Air Force (c).

Computers: 203 computers/terminals are available on campus for general student use. Students can access the following: computer help desk, free student e-mail accounts, online (class) grades, online (class) registration, online (class) schedules. Campuswide network is available. 100% of college-owned or -operated housing units are wired for high-speed Internet access. Wireless service is available via entire campus.

STUDENT LIFE

Housing options: coed, special housing for students with disabilities. Campus housing is university owned.

Activities and organizations: student-run radio station, choral group, Egan Service Learning Program, Student Occupational Therapy Association, Spalding University Nursing Students, Campus Activities Board, Best Buddies, national sororities.

Athletics Member NCAA, USCAA. All Division III. ***Intercollegiate sports:*** baseball M, basketball M/W, bowling W, cross-country running M/W, golf M/W, soccer M/W, softball W, track and field M/W, volleyball W.

Campus security: 24-hour emergency response devices and patrols, late-night transport/escort service, controlled dormitory access, outdoor emergency call stations located in various locations around campus.

Student services: personal/psychological counseling.

COSTS & FINANCIAL AID

Costs (2015–16) ***Comprehensive fee:*** $32,287 includes full-time tuition ($23,887) and room and board ($8400). Full-time tuition and fees vary according to class time, course load, and program. Part-time tuition and fees vary according to class time, course load, and program. ***College room only:*** $5600. Room and board charges vary according to board plan. ***Payment plans:*** installment, deferred payment. ***Waivers:*** senior citizens and employees or children of employees.

Financial Aid ***Average percent of need met:*** 75. ***Average financial aid package:*** $11,500.

APPLYING

Standardized Tests *Required:* SAT or ACT (for admission).

Options: electronic application, early admission, deferred entrance.

Application fee: $20.

Required: high school transcript, minimum 2.5 GPA. ***Required for some:*** essay or personal statement. ***Recommended:*** interview.

Application deadlines: rolling (freshmen), rolling (out-of-state freshmen), rolling (transfers).

Notification: continuous (freshmen), continuous (out-of-state freshmen), continuous (transfers).

CONTACT

Mr. Matt Elder, Associate Director of Admissions, Spalding University, 845 South Third Street, Louisville, KY 40203. *Phone:* 502-873-4177. *Toll-free phone:* 800-896-8941. *Fax:* 502-992-2418. *E-mail:* admissions@spalding.edu.

Spencerian College

Louisville, Kentucky

http://www.spencerian.edu/

- **Proprietary** primarily 2-year, founded 1892
- **Urban** 10-acre campus
- **Coed** 500 undergraduate students, 61% full-time, 87% women, 13% men
- **Moderately difficult** entrance level

UNDERGRAD STUDENTS

303 full-time, 197 part-time. Students come from 3 states and territories; 19% Black or African American, non-Hispanic/Latino; 3% Hispanic/Latino; 0.8% Asian, non-Hispanic/Latino; 0.4% Native Hawaiian or other Pacific Islander, non-Hispanic/Latino; 11% Two or more races, non-Hispanic/Latino; 6% Race/ethnicity unknown; 1% live on campus.

Freshmen

Admission: 81 enrolled.

ACADEMICS

Calendar: quarters. *Degrees:* certificates, diplomas, associate, and bachelor's.

Special study options: distance learning, summer session for credit.

Computers: 142 computers/terminals are available on campus for general student use. Students can access the following: free student e-mail accounts, online (class) grades, online (class) schedules. Campuswide network is available.

STUDENT LIFE

Housing options: coed. Campus housing is university owned.

COSTS

Costs (2014–15) ***Comprehensive fee:*** $28,545 includes full-time tuition ($17,940), mandatory fees ($1680), and room and board ($8925). Full-time tuition and fees vary according to class time and program. Part-time tuition: $299 per credit hour. Part-time tuition and fees vary according to class time and program. ***Required fees:*** $60 per course part-time. ***College room only:*** $5940. Room and board charges vary according to housing facility. ***Waivers:*** employees or children of employees.

APPLYING

Application fee: $50.

Required: high school transcript. ***Required for some:*** essay or personal statement, interview, Some medical programs have specific selective admission criteria.

Notification: continuous (freshmen), continuous (out-of-state freshmen), continuous (transfers).

CONTACT

Spencerian College, 4627 Dixie Highway, Louisville, KY 40216. *Phone:* 502-447-1000 Ext. 7808. *Toll-free phone:* 800-264-1799.

Sullivan College of Technology and Design

Louisville, Kentucky

http://www.sctd.edu/

- **Proprietary** primarily 2-year, founded 1961, part of The Sullivan University System, Inc.
- **Suburban** 10-acre campus with easy access to Louisville
- **Coed** 365 undergraduate students, 62% full-time, 30% women, 70% men
- **Moderately difficult** entrance level

UNDERGRAD STUDENTS

228 full-time, 137 part-time. Students come from 3 states and territories; 13% are from out of state; 12% Black or African American, non-Hispanic/Latino; 0.3% Hispanic/Latino; 2% Asian, non-Hispanic/Latino; 0.5% Native Hawaiian or other Pacific Islander, non-Hispanic/Latino; 0.3% American Indian or Alaska Native, non-Hispanic/Latino; 13% Two or more races, non-Hispanic/Latino; 4% Race/ethnicity unknown; 5% transferred in.

Freshmen

Admission: 52 enrolled.

FACULTY

Total: 75, 33% full-time.

Student/faculty ratio: 9:1.

ACADEMICS

Calendar: quarters. *Degrees:* associate and bachelor's.

Special study options: academic remediation for entering students, accelerated degree program, adult/continuing education programs, advanced placement credit, double majors, independent study, internships, part-time degree program, services for LD students, summer session for credit.

Computers: 268 computers/terminals are available on campus for general student use. Students can access the following: campus intranet, computer help desk, free student e-mail accounts, online (class) grades, online (class) schedules, wireless Internet. Campuswide network is available. 50% of college-owned or -operated housing units are wired for high-speed Internet access. Wireless service is available via classrooms, computer centers, computer labs, dorm rooms, learning centers, libraries, student centers.

STUDENT LIFE

Housing options: coed. Campus housing is university owned. Freshman campus housing is guaranteed.

Activities and organizations: ASID, IIDA, ADDA, MAKE Club, Skills USA.

Campus security: late-night transport/escort service, controlled dormitory access, patrols by trained security personnel while classes are in session.

COSTS

Costs (2015–16) ***Comprehensive fee:*** $32,005 includes full-time tuition ($20,460), mandatory fees ($1735), and room and board ($9810). Full-time tuition and fees vary according to course load, degree level, and program. Part-time tuition and fees vary according to course load, degree level, and program. No tuition increase for student's term of enrollment. ***Room and board:*** Room and board charges vary according to board plan. ***Payment plan:*** installment. ***Waivers:*** employees or children of employees.

APPLYING

Standardized Tests *Required:* ACT Compass or ACT or SAT Language and Math scores in place of Compass results (for admission). *Recommended:* SAT or ACT (for admission).

Options: electronic application, deferred entrance.

Application fee: $50.

Required: high school transcript, interview, Compass Exam or ACT/SAT Scores.

Application deadlines: rolling (freshmen), rolling (out-of-state freshmen), rolling (transfers).

Notification: continuous (freshmen), continuous (out-of-state freshmen), continuous (transfers).

CONTACT

Ms. Heather Wilson, Director of Admissions, Sullivan College of Technology and Design, 3901 Atkinson Square Drive, Louisville, KY 40218. *Phone:* 502-456-6509 Ext. 8220. *Toll-free phone:* 800-884-6528. *Fax:* 502-456-2341. *E-mail:* hwilson@sctd.edu.

Sullivan University

Louisville, Kentucky

http://www.sullivan.edu/

- **Proprietary** comprehensive, founded 1864
- **Urban** 15-acre campus
- **Coed** 3,027 undergraduate students, 58% full-time, 61% women, 39% men
- **Minimally difficult** entrance level, 80% of applicants were admitted

UNDERGRAD STUDENTS

1,759 full-time, 1,268 part-time. Students come from 41 states and territories; 40 other countries; 22% are from out of state; 19% Black or African American, non-Hispanic/Latino; 0.1% Hispanic/Latino; 1% Asian, non-Hispanic/Latino; 0.2% Native Hawaiian or other Pacific Islander, non-Hispanic/Latino; 0.6% American Indian or Alaska Native, non-Hispanic/Latino; 9% Two or more races, non-Hispanic/Latino; 19% Race/ethnicity unknown; 0.2% international; 9% live on campus.

Freshmen

Admission: 1,042 applied, 834 admitted, 289 enrolled.

FACULTY

Total: 319, 44% full-time, 41% with terminal degrees.

Student/faculty ratio: 19:1.

ACADEMICS

Calendar: quarters. *Degrees:* certificates, diplomas, associate, bachelor's, master's, doctoral, post-master's, and postbachelor's certificates.

Special study options: academic remediation for entering students, accelerated degree program, adult/continuing education programs, cooperative education, distance learning, double majors, independent study, internships, part-time degree program, services for LD students, student-designed majors, summer session for credit.

Computers: 93 computers/terminals are available on campus for general student use. Students can access the following: campus intranet, computer help desk, free student e-mail accounts, online (class) grades, online (class) schedules. Campuswide network is available. Wireless service is available via entire campus.

STUDENT LIFE

Housing options: coed, men-only, women-only, special housing for students with disabilities. Campus housing is university owned. Freshman campus housing is guaranteed.

Activities and organizations: drama/theater group, choral group, Student Activities Committee, Student Veterans Association, Sullivan Christian Fellowship, Sullivan Film Society, Phi Beta Lambda.

Athletics ***Intramural sports:*** basketball M/W, bowling M/W, soccer M/W, softball M/W, volleyball M/W.

Campus security: 24-hour patrols, late-night transport/escort service, controlled dormitory access.

Student services: personal/psychological counseling.

FINANCIAL AID

Financial Aid Of all full-time matriculated undergraduates who enrolled in 2002, 6,028 applied for aid, 5,247 were judged to have need. 31 Federal Work-Study jobs (averaging $2065). In 2002, 374 non-need-based awards were made. ***Average non-need-based aid:*** $2000. ***Average indebtedness upon graduation:*** $15,000.

APPLYING

Standardized Tests *Required:* Acceptable SAT, ACT, Sullivan Admissions Placement Assessment Scores Required (for admission).

Options: electronic application, deferred entrance.

Application fee: $50.

Required: high school transcript, interview. ***Required for some:*** essay or personal statement, Certain programs require criminal background checks and no felony convictions. Some drug and abuse related misdemeanors will exclude applicants from being accepted into several programs.

Application deadlines: rolling (freshmen), rolling (transfers).

Notification: continuous (freshmen), continuous (transfers).

CONTACT

Ms. Nina Martinez, Vice President of Admissions, Sullivan University, 3101 Bardstown Road, Louisville, KY 40205. *Phone:* 502-456-6505. *Toll-free phone:* 800-844-1354. *Fax:* 502-456-0040. *E-mail:* admissions@sullivan.edu.

★ Thomas More College

Crestview Hills, Kentucky

http://www.thomasmore.edu/

- **Independent Roman Catholic** comprehensive, founded 1921
- **Suburban** 100-acre campus with easy access to Cincinnati
- **Endowment** $17.4 million
- **Coed** 1,497 undergraduate students, 81% full-time, 51% women, 49% men
- **Moderately difficult** entrance level, 93% of applicants were admitted

UNDERGRAD STUDENTS

1,214 full-time, 283 part-time. Students come from 19 states and territories; 6 other countries; 52% are from out of state; 8% Black or African American, non-Hispanic/Latino; 2% Hispanic/Latino; 0.6% Asian, non-Hispanic/Latino; 0.2% American Indian or Alaska Native, non-Hispanic/Latino; 2% Two or more races, non-Hispanic/Latino; 14% Race/ethnicity unknown; 0.6% international; 5% transferred in; 31% live on campus.

Freshmen

Admission: 1,190 applied, 1,109 admitted, 276 enrolled. ***Average high school GPA:*** 3.2. ***Test scores:*** SAT critical reading scores over 500: 17%; SAT math scores over 500: 20%; ACT scores over 18: 90%; SAT critical reading scores over 600: 3%; SAT math scores over 600: 3%; ACT scores over 24: 25%; SAT math scores over 700: 1%; ACT scores over 30: 3%.

Retention: 71% of full-time freshmen returned.

FACULTY

Total: 128, 59% full-time, 52% with terminal degrees.

Student/faculty ratio: 15:1.

ACADEMICS

Calendar: semesters. *Degrees:* certificates, associate, bachelor's, and master's.

Special study options: academic remediation for entering students, accelerated degree program, adult/continuing education programs, advanced placement credit, cooperative education, distance learning, double majors, honors programs, independent study, internships, off-campus study, part-time degree program, services for LD students, student-designed majors, study abroad, summer session for credit. ***ROTC:*** Army (c), Air Force (c).

Unusual degree programs: 3-2 engineering.

Computers: 100 computers/terminals are available on campus for general student use. Students can access the following: campus intranet, computer help desk, free student e-mail accounts, online (class) grades, online (class) registration, online (class) schedules. Campuswide network is available. 100% of college-owned or -operated housing units are wired for high-speed Internet access. Wireless service is available via entire campus.

STUDENT LIFE

Housing options: coed, men-only, women-only, special housing for students with disabilities. Campus housing is university owned.

Activities and organizations: drama/theater group, choral group, marching band, Student Government Association, Student Activities

Board, More Ministry, Outdoors Adventure Club, Education Club, national fraternities, national sororities.

Athletics Member NCAA. All Division III. ***Intercollegiate sports:*** baseball M, basketball M/W, bowling M/W, cross-country running M/W, football M, golf M/W, lacrosse W, soccer M/W, softball W, tennis M/W, track and field M/W, volleyball W. ***Intramural sports:*** basketball M/W, football M/W, volleyball M/W.

Campus security: 24-hour emergency response devices and patrols, late-night transport/escort service, controlled dormitory access.

Student services: health clinic, personal/psychological counseling.

COSTS & FINANCIAL AID

Costs (2015–16) ***Comprehensive fee:*** $36,923 includes full-time tuition ($27,628), mandatory fees ($1525), and room and board ($7770). Part-time tuition: $605 per semester hour. ***Required fees:*** $70 per semester hour part-time. ***College room only:*** $3570. Room and board charges vary according to board plan and housing facility. ***Payment plans:*** installment, deferred payment. ***Waivers:*** senior citizens and employees or children of employees.

Financial Aid Of all full-time matriculated undergraduates who enrolled in 2013, 973 applied for aid, 665 were judged to have need, 164 had their need fully met. 139 Federal Work-Study jobs (averaging $916). 205 state and other part-time jobs (averaging $858). In 2013, 150 non-need-based awards were made. ***Average percent of need met:*** 74. ***Average financial aid package:*** $20,151. ***Average need-based loan:*** $4544. ***Average need-based gift aid:*** $15,681. ***Average non-need-based aid:*** $14,474. ***Average indebtedness upon graduation:*** $31,014.

APPLYING

Standardized Tests *Required:* SAT or ACT (for admission).

Options: electronic application, deferred entrance.

Application fee: $25.

Required: high school transcript, minimum 2.5 GPA.

Application deadlines: 8/1 (freshmen), 8/1 (transfers).

Notification: continuous (freshmen), continuous (transfers).

CONTACT

Ms. Kristin Lehmer, Executive Director of Enrollment Management, Thomas More College, 333 Thomas More Parkway, Crestview Hills, KY 41017-3495. *Phone:* 859-344-3332. *Toll-free phone:* 800-825-4557. *Fax:* 859-344-3444. *E-mail:* admissions@thomasmore.edu.

Transylvania University

Lexington, Kentucky

http://www.transy.edu/

- **Independent** 4-year, founded 1780, affiliated with Christian Church (Disciples of Christ)
- **Urban** 40-acre campus with easy access to Cincinnati, Louisville
- **Endowment** $169.0 million
- **Coed** 1,014 undergraduate students, 100% full-time, 58% women, 42% men
- **Very difficult** entrance level, 83% of applicants were admitted

UNDERGRAD STUDENTS

1,010 full-time, 4 part-time. Students come from 25 states and territories; 7 other countries; 23% are from out of state; 3% Black or African American, non-Hispanic/Latino; 5% Hispanic/Latino; 2% Asian, non-Hispanic/Latino; 0.1% Native Hawaiian or other Pacific Islander, non-Hispanic/Latino; 0.1% American Indian or Alaska Native, non-Hispanic/Latino; 3% Two or more races, non-Hispanic/Latino; 3% Race/ethnicity unknown; 4% international; 1% transferred in; 76% live on campus.

Freshmen

Admission: 1,444 applied, 1,193 admitted, 261 enrolled. ***Average high school GPA:*** 3.74. ***Test scores:*** SAT critical reading scores over 500: 77%; SAT math scores over 500: 87%; ACT scores over 18: 100%; SAT critical reading scores over 600: 44%; SAT math scores over 600: 47%; ACT scores over 24: 86%; SAT critical reading scores over 700: 10%; SAT math scores over 700: 19%; ACT scores over 30: 34%.

Retention: 83% of full-time freshmen returned.

FACULTY

Total: 110, 79% full-time, 85% with terminal degrees.

Student/faculty ratio: 11:1.

ACADEMICS

Calendar: 4-4-1. *Degree:* bachelor's.

Special study options: advanced placement credit, double majors, independent study, internships, off-campus study, part-time degree program, services for LD students, student-designed majors, study abroad, summer session for credit. ***ROTC:*** Army (c), Air Force (c).

Unusual degree programs: 3-2 engineering with University of Kentucky, Vanderbilt University.

Computers: 200 computers/terminals and 200 ports are available on campus for general student use. Students can access the following: campus intranet, computer help desk, free student e-mail accounts, online (class) grades, online (class) registration, online (class) schedules. Campuswide network is available. 100% of college-owned or -operated housing units are wired for high-speed Internet access. Wireless service is available via classrooms, computer centers, computer labs, dorm rooms, learning centers, libraries, student centers.

STUDENT LIFE

Housing options: on-campus residence required through junior year; coed, men-only, women-only, special housing for students with disabilities. Campus housing is university owned. Freshman campus housing is guaranteed.

Activities and organizations: drama/theater group, student-run newspaper, radio station, choral group, Student Government Association, Delta Sigma Phi, Phi Mu, Delta Delta Delta, Chi Omega, national fraternities, national sororities.

Athletics Member NCAA. All Division III. ***Intercollegiate sports:*** baseball M, basketball M/W, cheerleading M/W, cross-country running M/W, equestrian sports M/W, field hockey W, golf M/W, lacrosse M/W, soccer M/W, softball W, swimming and diving M/W, tennis M/W, track and field M/W, volleyball W. ***Intramural sports:*** badminton M/W, basketball M/W, bowling M/W, golf M/W, racquetball M/W, soccer M/W, swimming and diving M/W, tennis M/W, ultimate Frisbee M/W, volleyball M/W.

Campus security: 24-hour emergency response devices and patrols, late-night transport/escort service, controlled dormitory access.

Student services: health clinic, personal/psychological counseling.

COSTS & FINANCIAL AID

Costs (2014–15) ***Comprehensive fee:*** $42,660 includes full-time tuition ($32,010), mandatory fees ($1350), and room and board ($9300). Part-time tuition: $3560 per course. Part-time tuition and fees vary according to course load. ***Room and board:*** Room and board charges vary according to board plan and housing facility. ***Payment plan:*** installment. ***Waivers:*** employees or children of employees.

Financial Aid Of all full-time matriculated undergraduates who enrolled in 2014, 785 applied for aid, 678 were judged to have need, 166 had their need fully met. 377 Federal Work-Study jobs (averaging $1719). 44 state and other part-time jobs (averaging $5453). In 2014, 314 non-need-based awards were made. ***Average percent of need met:*** 82. ***Average financial aid package:*** $27,365. ***Average need-based loan:*** $4921. ***Average need-based gift aid:*** $22,883. ***Average non-need-based aid:*** $15,372. ***Average indebtedness upon graduation:*** $28,079.

APPLYING

Standardized Tests *Required for some:* SAT or ACT (for admission).

Options: electronic application, early admission, early action, deferred entrance.

Required: essay or personal statement, high school transcript, minimum 2.8 GPA, 2 letters of recommendation. ***Required for some:*** interview. ***Recommended:*** interview.

Application deadlines: 2/1 (freshmen), rolling (transfers), 12/1 (early action).

Notification: 3/1 (freshmen), 1/15 (early action).

CONTACT

Mr. Bradley Goan, Vice President for Enrollment and Dean of Admissions, Transylvania University, 300 North Broadway, Lexington, KY 40508-1797. *Phone:* 859-233-4242. *Toll-free phone:* 800-872-6798. *Fax:* 859-281-3649. *E-mail:* admissions@transy.edu.

Union College

Barbourville, Kentucky

http://www.unionky.edu/

- **Independent United Methodist** comprehensive, founded 1879
- **Small-town** 100-acre campus
- **Coed** 870 undergraduate students, 90% full-time, 48% women, 52% men
- **Moderately difficult** entrance level, 75% of applicants were admitted

UNDERGRAD STUDENTS

782 full-time, 88 part-time. Students come from 28 states and territories; 14 other countries; 27% are from out of state; 10% Black or African American, non-Hispanic/Latino; 2% Hispanic/Latino; 0.7% Asian, non-Hispanic/Latino; 0.2% Native Hawaiian or other Pacific Islander, non-Hispanic/Latino; 0.5% American Indian or Alaska Native, non-Hispanic/Latino; 3% Two or more races, non-Hispanic/Latino; 1% Race/ethnicity unknown; 6% international; 8% transferred in; 48% live on campus.

Freshmen

Admission: 1,385 applied, 1,042 admitted, 240 enrolled. ***Average high school GPA:*** 3.26. ***Test scores:*** ACT scores over 18: 87%; ACT scores over 24: 21%.

Retention: 62% of full-time freshmen returned.

FACULTY

Total: 107, 50% full-time, 49% with terminal degrees.

Student/faculty ratio: 13:1.

ACADEMICS

Calendar: semesters. *Degrees:* bachelor's, master's, post-master's, and postbachelor's certificates.

Special study options: academic remediation for entering students, accelerated degree program, advanced placement credit, double majors, English as a second language, honors programs, independent study, off-campus study, part-time degree program, services for LD students, student-designed majors, study abroad, summer session for credit.

Computers: 290 computers/terminals and 550 ports are available on campus for general student use. Students can access the following: campus intranet, computer help desk, free student e-mail accounts, online (class) grades, online (class) registration, online (class) schedules. Campuswide network is available. 100% of college-owned or -operated housing units are wired for high-speed Internet access. Wireless service is available via classrooms, computer centers, computer labs, dorm rooms, learning centers, libraries, student centers.

STUDENT LIFE

Housing options: on-campus residence required through sophomore year; men-only, women-only. Campus housing is university owned. Freshman campus housing is guaranteed.

Activities and organizations: drama/theater group, choral group.

Athletics Member NAIA. ***Intercollegiate sports:*** baseball M(s), basketball M(s)/W(s), bowling M(s)/W(s), cheerleading M(s)/W(s), cross-country running M(s)/W(s), football M(s), golf M(s)/W(s), soccer M(s)/W(s), softball W(s), swimming and diving M(s)/W(s), tennis M(s)/W(s), track and field M(s)/W(s), volleyball W(s). ***Intramural sports:*** basketball M/W, football M, soccer M/W, softball M/W, table tennis M/W, ultimate Frisbee M/W, volleyball M/W, water polo W.

Campus security: 24-hour emergency response devices and patrols, late-night transport/escort service, controlled dormitory access.

Student services: health clinic, personal/psychological counseling.

COSTS & FINANCIAL AID

Costs (2015–16) ***Comprehensive fee:*** $31,075 includes full-time tuition ($22,720), mandatory fees ($1355), and room and board ($7000). Part-time tuition: $340 per credit. ***Required fees:*** $25 per credit hour part-time. ***College room only:*** $3100. Room and board charges vary according to housing facility. ***Payment plan:*** installment. ***Waivers:*** employees or children of employees.

Financial Aid Of all full-time matriculated undergraduates who enrolled in 2014, 767 applied for aid, 731 were judged to have need, 105 had their need fully met. 111 Federal Work-Study jobs (averaging $1500). 33 state and other part-time jobs (averaging $1500). In 2014, 82 non-need-based awards were made. ***Average percent of need met:*** 68. ***Average financial aid package:*** $21,434. ***Average need-based loan:*** $4316. ***Average need-based gift aid:*** $17,682. ***Average non-need-based aid:*** $15,252. ***Average indebtedness upon graduation:*** $32,691.

APPLYING

Standardized Tests *Required:* SAT or ACT (for admission).

Options: electronic application, deferred entrance.

Application fee: $10.

Required: high school transcript, minimum 2.0 GPA. ***Required for some:*** interview.

Application deadlines: rolling (freshmen), rolling (out-of-state freshmen), rolling (transfers).

Notification: continuous (freshmen), continuous (out-of-state freshmen), continuous (transfers).

CONTACT

Mr. Craig Grooms, Director: Undergraduate Enrollment, Union College, 310 College Street, Barbourville, KY 40906. *Phone:* 606-546-4151 Ext. 1709. *Toll-free phone:* 800-489-8646. *Fax:* 606-546-1667. *E-mail:* cgrooms@unionky.edu.

University of Kentucky

Lexington, Kentucky

http://www.uky.edu/

- **State-supported** university, founded 1865
- **Urban** 685-acre campus with easy access to Cincinnati, Louisville
- **Endowment** $1.1 billion
- **Coed** 22,223 undergraduate students, 93% full-time, 52% women, 48% men
- **Moderately difficult** entrance level, 92% of applicants were admitted

UNDERGRAD STUDENTS

20,690 full-time, 1,533 part-time. Students come from 52 states and territories; 80 other countries; 27% are from out of state; 8% Black or African American, non-Hispanic/Latino; 4% Hispanic/Latino; 3% Asian, non-Hispanic/Latino; 0.1% Native Hawaiian or other Pacific Islander, non-Hispanic/Latino; 0.2% American Indian or Alaska Native, non-Hispanic/Latino; 3% Two or more races, non-Hispanic/Latino; 3% Race/ethnicity unknown; 3% international; 5% transferred in.

Freshmen

Admission: 16,299 applied, 14,930 admitted, 5,185 enrolled. ***Average high school GPA:*** 3.63. ***Test scores:*** SAT critical reading scores over 500: 75%; SAT math scores over 500: 81%; SAT writing scores over 500: 70%; ACT scores over 18: 99%; SAT critical reading scores over 600: 32%; SAT math scores over 600: 39%; SAT writing scores over 600: 29%; ACT scores over 24: 66%; SAT critical reading scores over 700: 10%; SAT math scores over 700: 11%; SAT writing scores over 700: 7%; ACT scores over 30: 18%.

Retention: 82% of full-time freshmen returned.

ACADEMICS

Calendar: semesters. *Degrees:* certificates, bachelor's, master's, doctoral, post-master's, and postbachelor's certificates.

Special study options: academic remediation for entering students, accelerated degree program, adult/continuing education programs, advanced placement credit, cooperative education, distance learning, double majors, English as a second language, honors programs, independent study, internships, off-campus study, part-time degree program, services for LD students, study abroad, summer session for credit. ***ROTC:*** Army (b), Air Force (b).

Unusual degree programs: 3-2 business administration.

Computers: 1,000 computers/terminals are available on campus for general student use. Students can access the following: campus intranet, computer help desk, free student e-mail accounts, online (class) grades, online (class) registration, online (class) schedules. Campuswide network is available. 100% of college-owned or -operated housing units are wired for high-speed Internet access. Wireless service is available via entire campus.

STUDENT LIFE

Housing options: coed, men-only, women-only, special housing for students with disabilities. Campus housing is university owned, leased by the school and is provided by a third party. Freshman applicants given priority for college housing.

Activities and organizations: drama/theater group, student-run newspaper, radio station, choral group, marching band, Student Activities Board, Student Government Association, Campus Progressive Coalition, Ski and Snowboard Club, Society of Women Engineers, national fraternities, national sororities.

Athletics Member NCAA. All Division I except football (Division I-A). ***Intercollegiate sports:*** baseball M(s), basketball M(s)/W(s), cross-country running M(s)/W(s), golf M(s)/W(s), gymnastics W(s), riflery M(s)/W(s), soccer M(s)/W(s), softball W(s), swimming and diving M(s)/W(s), tennis M(s)/W(s), track and field M(s)/W(s), volleyball W(s). ***Intramural sports:*** archery M/W, badminton M/W, basketball M/W, fencing M/W, football M/W, golf M/W, ice hockey M, lacrosse M, rugby M, soccer M/W, softball M/W, swimming and diving M/W, table tennis M/W, tennis M/W, track and field M/W, volleyball M/W.

Campus security: 24-hour emergency response devices and patrols, late-night transport/escort service, controlled dormitory access.

Student services: health clinic, personal/psychological counseling, women's center, legal services.

COSTS & FINANCIAL AID

Costs (2014–15) ***Tuition:*** state resident $10,616 full-time, $421 per credit hour part-time; nonresident $22,888 full-time, $931 per credit hour part-time. Full-time tuition and fees vary according to location, program, reciprocity agreements, and student level. Part-time tuition and fees vary according to course load, location, program, reciprocity agreements, and student level. ***Room and board:*** $10,506. Room and board charges vary according to board plan and housing facility.

Financial Aid Of all full-time matriculated undergraduates who enrolled in 2013, 13,018 applied for aid, 10,344 were judged to have need, 1,737 had their need fully met. In 2013, 3892 non-need-based awards were made. ***Average percent of need met:*** 60. ***Average financial aid package:*** $10,872. ***Average need-based loan:*** $4403. ***Average need-based gift aid:*** $5457. ***Average non-need-based aid:*** $7487. ***Average indebtedness upon graduation:*** $25,102.

APPLYING

Standardized Tests *Required:* SAT or ACT (for admission).

Options: electronic application, deferred entrance.

Application fee: $50.

Required: high school transcript, minimum 2.0 GPA.

CONTACT

Ms. Michelle R. Nordin, Associate Director of Admissions, University of Kentucky, 100 W.D. Funkhouser Building, Lexington, KY 40506-0054. *Phone:* 859-257-2000. *Toll-free phone:* 866-900-GO-UK. *E-mail:* admissio@uky.edu.

University of Louisville

Louisville, Kentucky

http://www.louisville.edu/

- **State-supported** university, founded 1798
- **Urban** 345-acre campus with easy access to Louisville
- **Coed** 15,959 undergraduate students, 78% full-time, 51% women, 49% men
- **Moderately difficult** entrance level, 72% of applicants were admitted

UNDERGRAD STUDENTS

12,491 full-time, 3,468 part-time. Students come from 53 states and territories; 53 other countries; 15% are from out of state; 11% Black or African American, non-Hispanic/Latino; 4% Hispanic/Latino; 3% Asian, non-Hispanic/Latino; 0.1% Native Hawaiian or other Pacific Islander, non-Hispanic/Latino; 0.1% American Indian or Alaska Native, non-Hispanic/Latino; 4% Two or more races, non-Hispanic/Latino; 0.2% Race/ethnicity unknown; 1% international; 6% transferred in; 17% live on campus.

Freshmen

Admission: 9,711 applied, 6,979 admitted, 2,887 enrolled. ***Average high school GPA:*** 3.55. ***Test scores:*** SAT critical reading scores over 500: 77%; SAT math scores over 500: 78%; ACT scores over 18: 99%; SAT critical reading scores over 600: 34%; SAT math scores over 600: 39%; ACT scores over 24: 63%; SAT critical reading scores over 700: 6%; SAT math scores over 700: 8%; ACT scores over 30: 17%.

Retention: 81% of full-time freshmen returned.

FACULTY

Total: 1,288, 63% full-time, 68% with terminal degrees.

Student/faculty ratio: 17:1.

ACADEMICS

Calendar: semesters. *Degrees:* certificates, associate, bachelor's, master's, doctoral, post-master's, and postbachelor's certificates.

Special study options: academic remediation for entering students, accelerated degree program, adult/continuing education programs, advanced placement credit, cooperative education, distance learning, double majors, English as a second language, honors programs, independent study, internships, off-campus study, part-time degree program, services for LD students, student-designed majors, study abroad, summer session for credit. ***ROTC:*** Army (b), Air Force (b).

Unusual degree programs: 3-2 engineering; Bachelor of Arts/Science and Master of Public Health.

Computers: 400 computers/terminals and 400 ports are available on campus for general student use. Students can access the following: campus intranet, computer help desk, free student e-mail accounts, online (class) grades, online (class) registration, online (class) schedules. Campuswide network is available. 100% of college-owned or -operated housing units are wired for high-speed Internet access. Wireless service is available via entire campus.

STUDENT LIFE

Housing options: on-campus residence required for freshman year; coed, cooperative, special housing for students with disabilities. Campus housing is university owned and is provided by a third party. Freshman applicants given priority for college housing.

Activities and organizations: drama/theater group, student-run newspaper, radio station, choral group, marching band, Baptist Campus Ministry, Society of Porter Scholars, Association of Black Students, Common Ground, Raise Red Dance Marathon, national fraternities, national sororities.

Athletics Member NCAA. All Division I except football (Division I-A). ***Intercollegiate sports:*** baseball M(s), basketball M(s)/W(s), cheerleading M/W, crew W(s), cross-country running M(s)/W(s), field hockey W(s), golf M(s)/W(s), lacrosse W(s), soccer M(s)/W(s), softball W(s), swimming and diving M(s)/W(s), tennis M(s)/W(s), track and field M(s)/W(s), volleyball W(s). ***Intramural sports:*** badminton M/W, basketball M/W, bowling M/W, cross-country running M/W, equestrian sports W(c), fencing M/W, football M/W, golf M/W, gymnastics W(c), ice hockey M, lacrosse M(c)/W(c), racquetball M/W, rugby M(c), soccer M/W, softball W, swimming and diving M/W, table tennis M/W, tennis M/W, track and field M/W, ultimate Frisbee M/W, volleyball M/W.

Campus security: 24-hour emergency response devices and patrols, late-night transport/escort service, controlled dormitory access, The University of Louisville Alert notification system.

Student services: health clinic, personal/psychological counseling, women's center.

COSTS & FINANCIAL AID

Costs (2014–15) ***Tuition:*** state resident $10,236 full-time, $427 per credit hour part-time; nonresident $24,124 full-time, $1006 per credit hour part-time. Full-time tuition and fees vary according to reciprocity agreements. Part-time tuition and fees vary according to reciprocity agreements. ***Room and board:*** $7710; room only: $4790. Room and board charges vary according to board plan and housing facility. ***Payment plan:*** installment. ***Waivers:*** senior citizens and employees or children of employees.

Financial Aid Of all full-time matriculated undergraduates who enrolled in 2014, 9,455 applied for aid, 7,703 were judged to have need, 1,640 had their need fully met. 375 Federal Work-Study jobs (averaging $3196). In 2014, 1719 non-need-based awards were made. ***Average percent of need met:*** 61. ***Average financial aid package:*** $11,342. ***Average need-based loan:*** $4074. ***Average need-based gift aid:*** $8705. ***Average non-need-based aid:*** $7908. ***Average indebtedness upon graduation:*** $23,375.

APPLYING

Standardized Tests *Required:* SAT or ACT (for admission). *Required for some:* TOEFL for students whose primary language is not English.

Options: electronic application, deferred entrance.

Application fee: $50.

Required: high school transcript, minimum 2.5 GPA.

Application deadlines: 2/15 (freshmen), 7/1 (transfers).

Notification: continuous (freshmen), continuous (transfers).

CONTACT

Ms. Jenny L. Sawyer, Executive Director of Admissions, University of Louisville, 2301 South Third Street, Houchens Room 150, Louisville, KY 40292-0001. *Phone:* 502-852-6531. *Toll-free phone:* 800-334-8635. *Fax:* 502-852-4776. *E-mail:* admitme@louisville.edu.

University of Pikeville

Pikeville, Kentucky

http://www.upike.edu/

- **Independent** comprehensive, founded 1889, affiliated with Presbyterian Church (U.S.A.)
- **Small-town** 25-acre campus
- **Endowment** $12.0 million
- **Coed** 1,929 undergraduate students, 67% full-time, 54% women, 46% men
- **Noncompetitive** entrance level, 100% of applicants were admitted

UNDERGRAD STUDENTS

1,295 full-time, 634 part-time. Students come from 36 states and territories; 22 other countries; 20% are from out of state; 12% Black or African American, non-Hispanic/Latino; 2% Hispanic/Latino; 0.5% Asian, non-Hispanic/Latino; 0.4% American Indian or Alaska Native, non-Hispanic/Latino; 3% international; 5% transferred in; 60% live on campus.

Freshmen

Admission: 2,278 applied, 2,278 admitted, 352 enrolled. ***Average high school GPA:*** 3.13. ***Test scores:*** SAT math scores over 500: 29%; SAT writing scores over 500: 24%; ACT scores over 18: 78%; SAT math scores over 600: 6%; ACT scores over 24: 22%; ACT scores over 30: 3%. ***Retention:*** 55% of full-time freshmen returned.

FACULTY

Total: 150, 45% full-time, 31% with terminal degrees.

Student/faculty ratio: 16:1.

ACADEMICS

Calendar: semesters. *Degrees:* associate, bachelor's, master's, and doctoral.

Special study options: academic remediation for entering students, advanced placement credit, double majors, English as a second language, internships, part-time degree program, services for LD students, student-designed majors, study abroad, summer session for credit. ***ROTC:*** Army (b).

Computers: 149 computers/terminals are available on campus for general student use. Students can access the following: computer help desk, free student e-mail accounts, online (class) grades, online (class) schedules. Campuswide network is available. 100% of college-owned or -operated housing units are wired for high-speed Internet access. Wireless service is available via entire campus.

STUDENT LIFE

Housing options: coed, men-only, women-only. Campus housing is university owned.

Activities and organizations: drama/theater group, student-run newspaper, choral group, student government, Phi Beta Lambda, Lambda Sigma, Concert Choir, Student Nurses at PC.

Athletics Member NAIA. ***Intercollegiate sports:*** baseball M(s), basketball M(s)/W(s), bowling M(s)/W(s), cheerleading M(s)/W(s), cross-country running M(s)/W(s), football M(s), golf M(s)/W(s), lacrosse W(s), soccer M(s)/W(s), softball W(s), tennis M(s)/W(s), track and field M(s)/W(s), volleyball W(s).

Campus security: 24-hour emergency response devices and patrols, controlled dormitory access.

Student services: personal/psychological counseling.

COSTS & FINANCIAL AID

Costs (2015–16) ***Comprehensive fee:*** $26,050 includes full-time tuition ($18,840) and room and board ($7210). Full-time tuition and fees vary according to course load. Part-time tuition: $785 per semester hour. Part-time tuition and fees vary according to course load. ***Room and board:*** Room and board charges vary according to housing facility. ***Payment plan:*** installment. ***Waivers:*** senior citizens and employees or children of employees.

Financial Aid Of all full-time matriculated undergraduates who enrolled in 2014, 1,283 applied for aid, 1,283 were judged to have need, 541 had their need fully met. 176 Federal Work-Study jobs (averaging $1943). ***Average percent of need met:*** 84. ***Average financial aid package:*** $20,661. ***Average need-based loan:*** $4104. ***Average need-based gift aid:*** $17,286. ***Average indebtedness upon graduation:*** $20,087.

APPLYING

Standardized Tests *Required:* SAT or ACT (for admission).

Options: electronic application, deferred entrance.

Required: high school transcript.

Application deadlines: 8/15 (freshmen), 8/15 (out-of-state freshmen), 8/15 (transfers).

Notification: continuous (freshmen), continuous (out-of-state freshmen), continuous (transfers).

CONTACT

Ms. Amber Collins, Director of Admissions, University of Pikeville, 147 Sycamore Street, Pikeville, KY 41501. *Phone:* 606-218-5251. *Toll-free phone:* 866-232-7700. *Fax:* 606-218-5255. *E-mail:* wewantyou@pc.edu.

University of the Cumberlands

Williamsburg, Kentucky

http://www.ucumberlands.edu/

- **Independent Kentucky Baptist** university, founded 1889
- **Rural** 150-acre campus with easy access to Knoxville
- **Endowment** $76.5 million
- **Coed** 2,655 undergraduate students, 64% full-time, 55% women, 45% men
- **Moderately difficult** entrance level, 66% of applicants were admitted

UNDERGRAD STUDENTS

1,697 full-time, 958 part-time. Students come from 38 states and territories; 26 other countries; 32% are from out of state; 7% Black or African American, non-Hispanic/Latino; 2% Hispanic/Latino; 0.2% Asian, non-Hispanic/Latino; 0.1% Native Hawaiian or other Pacific Islander, non-Hispanic/Latino; 0.4% American Indian or Alaska Native, non-Hispanic/Latino; 1% Two or more races, non-Hispanic/Latino; 6% Race/ethnicity unknown; 6% international; 4% transferred in; 70% live on campus.

Freshmen

Admission: 2,322 applied, 1,539 admitted, 405 enrolled. ***Average high school GPA:*** 3.4. ***Test scores:*** SAT critical reading scores over 500: 41%; SAT math scores over 500: 52%; ACT scores over 18: 93%; SAT critical reading scores over 600: 12%; SAT math scores over 600: 13%; ACT scores over 24: 35%; SAT critical reading scores over 700: 2%; ACT scores over 30: 8%.

Retention: 63% of full-time freshmen returned.

FACULTY

Total: 324, 43% full-time, 63% with terminal degrees.

Student/faculty ratio: 14:1.

ACADEMICS

Calendar: semesters. *Degrees:* associate, bachelor's, master's, doctoral, post-master's, and postbachelor's certificates.

Special study options: academic remediation for entering students, accelerated degree program, adult/continuing education programs, advanced placement credit, cooperative education, distance learning, double majors, honors programs, independent study, internships, part-time degree program, student-designed majors, study abroad, summer session for credit.

Unusual degree programs: 3-2 engineering with University of Kentucky; physician assistant.

Computers: 176 computers/terminals are available on campus for general student use. Students can access the following: campus intranet, computer help desk, free student e-mail accounts, online (class) grades, online (class) registration, online (class) schedules. Campuswide network is available. 100% of college-owned or -operated housing units are wired for high-speed Internet access. Wireless service is available via entire campus.

STUDENT LIFE

Housing options: on-campus residence required through senior year; men-only, women-only. Campus housing is university owned. Freshman campus housing is guaranteed.

Activities and organizations: drama/theater group, student-run newspaper, radio and television station, choral group, marching band, Baptist Campus Ministries, Student Government Association, Campus Activity Board, Mountain Outreach, Fellowship of Christian Athletes.

Athletics Member NAIA. ***Intercollegiate sports:*** archery M(s)/W(s), baseball M(s), basketball M(s)/W(s), bowling M(s)/W(s), cheerleading M(s)/W(s), cross-country running M(s)/W(s), football M(s), golf M(s)/W(s), lacrosse M(s)/W(s), soccer M(s)/W(s), softball W(s), swimming and diving M(s)/W(s), tennis M(s)/W(s), track and field M(s)/W(s), volleyball W(s), wrestling M(s)/W(s). ***Intramural sports:*** badminton M/W, basketball M/W, football M/W, golf M/W, softball M/W, table tennis M/W, ultimate Frisbee M/W, volleyball M/W.

Campus security: 24-hour emergency response devices and patrols, student patrols, late-night transport/escort service.

Student services: health clinic.

COSTS & FINANCIAL AID

Costs (2015–16) ***Comprehensive fee:*** $30,500 includes full-time tuition ($21,640), mandatory fees ($360), and room and board ($8500). Part-time tuition: $690 per credit. Part-time tuition and fees vary according to course load. No tuition increase for student's term of enrollment. ***Payment plan:*** installment. ***Waivers:*** senior citizens and employees or children of employees.

Financial Aid Of all full-time matriculated undergraduates who enrolled in 2014, 1,441 applied for aid, 1,339 were judged to have need, 230 had their need fully met. 830 Federal Work-Study jobs (averaging $1954). 11 state and other part-time jobs (averaging $2095). In 2014, 184 non-need-based awards were made. ***Average percent of need met:*** 77. ***Average financial aid package:*** $19,233. ***Average need-based loan:*** $3622. ***Average need-based gift aid:*** $15,543. ***Average non-need-based aid:*** $9564. ***Average indebtedness upon graduation:*** $18,777.

APPLYING

Standardized Tests *Required:* SAT or ACT (for admission).

Options: electronic application, deferred entrance.

Application fee: $30.

Required: high school transcript, minimum 2.0 GPA.

Application deadlines: 8/15 (freshmen), 8/15 (transfers).

Notification: 8/15 (freshmen), 8/15 (transfers).

CONTACT

Mrs. Erica Harris, Director of Admissions, University of the Cumberlands, 6178 College Station Drive, Williamsburg, KY 40769. *Phone:* 606-539-4241. *Toll-free phone:* 800-343-1609. *Fax:* 606-539-4303. *E-mail:* admiss@ucumberlands.edu.

See below for display ad and page 1704 for the College Close-Up.

Western Kentucky University
Bowling Green, Kentucky
http://www.wku.edu/

- **State-supported** comprehensive, founded 1906
- **Suburban** 235-acre campus with easy access to Nashville
- **Endowment** $135.1 million
- **Coed** 17,452 undergraduate students, 76% full-time, 57% women, 43% men
- **Minimally difficult** entrance level, 93% of applicants were admitted

UNDERGRAD STUDENTS

13,297 full-time, 4,155 part-time. Students come from 45 states and territories; 72 other countries; 18% are from out of state; 10% Black or African American, non-Hispanic/Latino; 3% Hispanic/Latino; 1% Asian, non-Hispanic/Latino; 0.1% Native Hawaiian or other Pacific Islander, non-Hispanic/Latino; 0.2% American Indian or Alaska Native, non-

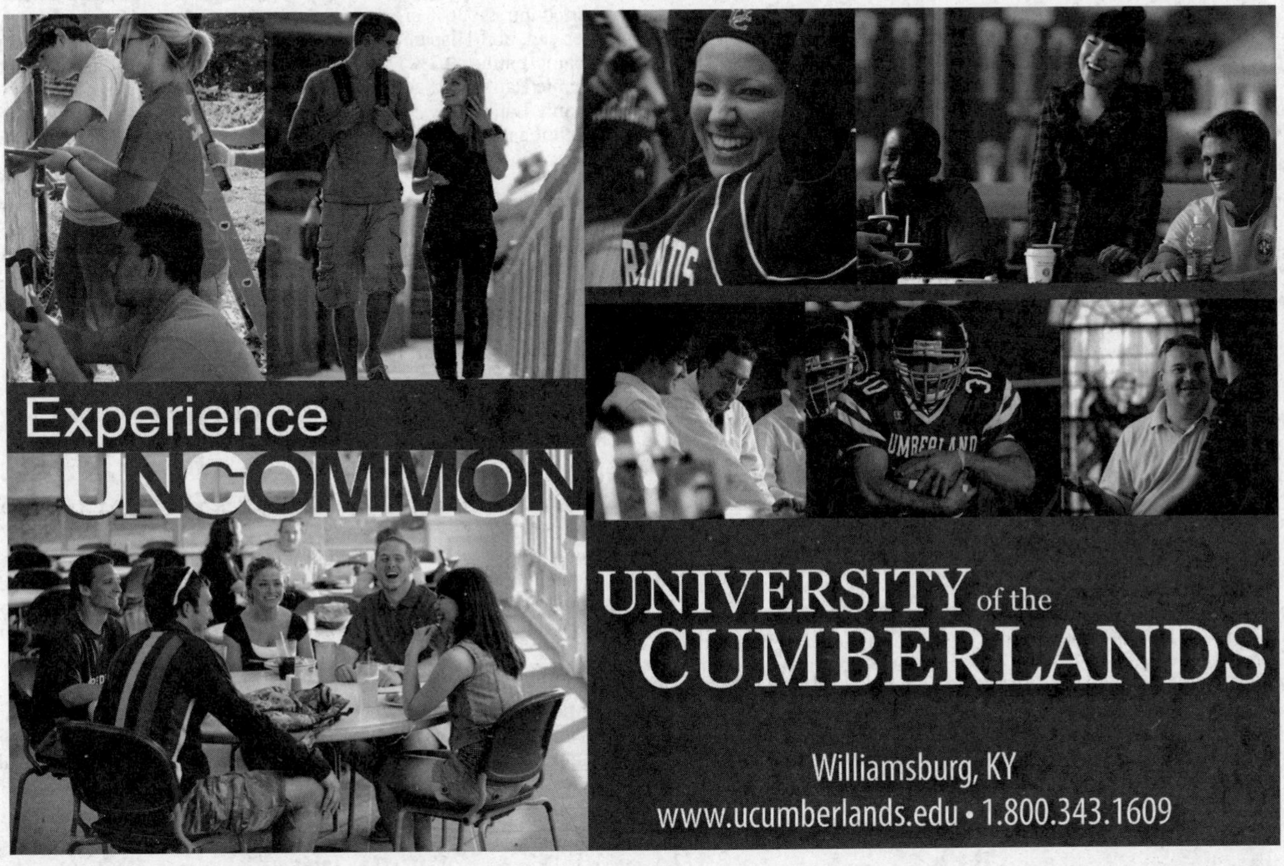

Hispanic/Latino; 2% Two or more races, non-Hispanic/Latino; 1% Race/ethnicity unknown; 7% international; 6% transferred in; 32% live on campus.

Freshmen

Admission: 8,462 applied, 7,897 admitted, 3,136 enrolled. ***Average high school GPA:*** 3.26. ***Test scores:*** SAT critical reading scores over 500: 50%; SAT math scores over 500: 54%; ACT scores over 18: 86%; SAT critical reading scores over 600: 15%; SAT math scores over 600: 21%; ACT scores over 24: 42%; SAT critical reading scores over 700: 3%; SAT math scores over 700: 4%; ACT scores over 30: 9%.

Retention: 73% of full-time freshmen returned.

FACULTY

Total: 1,195, 65% full-time, 57% with terminal degrees.

Student/faculty ratio: 18:1.

ACADEMICS

Calendar: semesters. *Degrees:* certificates, associate, bachelor's, master's, doctoral, post-master's, and postbachelor's certificates.

Special study options: academic remediation for entering students, accelerated degree program, adult/continuing education programs, advanced placement credit, cooperative education, distance learning, double majors, English as a second language, freshman honors college, honors programs, independent study, internships, off-campus study, part-time degree program, services for LD students, student-designed majors, study abroad, summer session for credit. ***ROTC:*** Army (b), Air Force (c).

Unusual degree programs: 3-2 engineering with Western Kentucky University has cooperative agreements with a number of engineering schools; 3-2 Dual-Degree (Physics / Applied Sciences / Engineering) option requires three years of study at WKU and two years at a science / engineering school, leading to two degrees, one in physics and astronomy at WKU and one in engineering or applied science.

Computers: 3,400 computers/terminals are available on campus for general student use. Students can access the following: campus intranet, computer help desk, free student e-mail accounts, online (class) grades, online (class) registration, online (class) schedules. Campuswide network is available. 100% of college-owned or -operated housing units are wired for high-speed Internet access. Wireless service is available via entire campus.

STUDENT LIFE

Housing options: on-campus residence required through sophomore year; coed, men-only, women-only. Campus housing is university owned. Freshman applicants given priority for college housing.

Activities and organizations: drama/theater group, student-run newspaper, radio and television station, choral group, marching band, Student Government Association, Campus Activities Board, Campus Crusade for Christ, Campus Ministries, Residence Hall Association, national fraternities, national sororities.

Athletics Member NCAA. All Division I except football (Division I-A). ***Intercollegiate sports:*** baseball M(s), basketball M(s)/W(s), cross-country running M(s)/W(s), golf M(s)/W(s), soccer W, softball W(s), swimming and diving M(s)/W(s), tennis M(s)/W(s), track and field M(s)/W(s), volleyball W(s). ***Intramural sports:*** badminton M/W, basketball M/W, bowling M(c)/W(c), fencing M(c)/W(c), field hockey M(c)/W(c), football M/W, golf M/W, lacrosse M(c)/W(c), racquetball M/W, rugby M(c)/W(c), soccer M/W, softball M/W, swimming and diving M(c)/W(c), tennis M(c)/W(c), ultimate Frisbee M/W, volleyball M/W.

Campus security: 24-hour emergency response devices and patrols, student patrols, late-night transport/escort service, controlled dormitory access.

Student services: health clinic, personal/psychological counseling, women's center.

COSTS & FINANCIAL AID

Costs (2014–15) ***Tuition:*** state resident $9140 full-time, $381 per credit hour part-time; nonresident $23,352 full-time, $973 per credit hour part-time. Full-time tuition and fees vary according to course load, location, program, and reciprocity agreements. Part-time tuition and fees vary according to course load, location, program, and reciprocity agreements. ***Room and board:*** $7171; room only: $4180. Room and board charges vary according to board plan and housing facility. ***Payment plan:*** installment. ***Waivers:*** children of alumni, senior citizens, and employees or children of employees.

Financial Aid Of all full-time matriculated undergraduates who enrolled in 2013, 10,622 applied for aid, 8,662 were judged to have need, 2,427 had their need fully met. 751 Federal Work-Study jobs (averaging $2648). 1,787 state and other part-time jobs (averaging $2563). In 2013, 1360 non-need-based awards were made. ***Average percent of need met:*** 28. ***Average financial aid package:*** $13,904. ***Average need-based loan:*** $3937. ***Average need-based gift aid:*** $4941. ***Average non-need-based aid:*** $5812. ***Average indebtedness upon graduation:*** $26,768.

APPLYING

Standardized Tests *Required:* SAT or ACT (for admission).

Options: electronic application.

Application fee: $40.

Required: high school transcript, minimum 2.5 GPA. ***Required for some:*** minimum 2.0 GPA. ***Recommended:*** minimum 2.5 GPA.

Application deadlines: 8/1 (freshmen), 8/1 (transfers).

Notification: continuous (freshmen), continuous (transfers).

CONTACT

Western Kentucky University, 1906 College Heights Boulevard, Bowling Green, KY 42101. *Phone:* 270-7452551. *Toll-free phone:* 800-495-8463.

LOUISIANA

Centenary College of Louisiana

Shreveport, Louisiana

http://www.centenary.edu/

- **Independent United Methodist** comprehensive, founded 1825
- **Suburban** 65-acre campus with easy access to Shreveport
- **Coed** 553 undergraduate students, 98% full-time, 57% women, 43% men
- **Moderately difficult** entrance level, 66% of applicants were admitted

UNDERGRAD STUDENTS

544 full-time, 9 part-time. Students come from 28 states and territories; 7 other countries; 36% are from out of state; 15% Black or African American, non-Hispanic/Latino; 6% Hispanic/Latino; 4% Asian, non-Hispanic/Latino; 0.2% Native Hawaiian or other Pacific Islander, non-Hispanic/Latino; 1% American Indian or Alaska Native, non-Hispanic/Latino; 4% Two or more races, non-Hispanic/Latino; 2% international; 3% transferred in; 60% live on campus.

Freshmen

Admission: 769 applied, 505 admitted, 141 enrolled. ***Average high school GPA:*** 3.52. ***Test scores:*** SAT critical reading scores over 500: 59%; SAT math scores over 500: 68%; ACT scores over 18: 98%; SAT critical reading scores over 600: 21%; SAT math scores over 600: 12%; ACT scores over 24: 57%; SAT math scores over 700: 3%; ACT scores over 30: 17%.

Retention: 80% of full-time freshmen returned.

FACULTY

Total: 88, 67% full-time, 76% with terminal degrees.

Student/faculty ratio: 8:1.

ACADEMICS

Calendar: Hybrid Semester/Immersion Calendar. *Degrees:* bachelor's and master's.

Special study options: adult/continuing education programs, advanced placement credit, double majors, honors programs, independent study, internships, off-campus study, part-time degree program, services for LD students, student-designed majors, study abroad, summer session for credit.

Unusual degree programs: 3-2 engineering; Psychology.

Computers: Students can access the following: free student e-mail accounts, online (class) grades, online (class) registration, online (class) schedules. Campuswide network is available. Wireless service is available via classrooms, dorm rooms, libraries, student centers.

STUDENT LIFE

Housing options: on-campus residence required through senior year; coed. Campus housing is university owned. Freshman campus housing is guaranteed.

Activities and organizations: drama/theater group, student-run newspaper, radio station, choral group, Intramural sports, Residence Life, FCA, Church Career/Campus Ministries, student media, national fraternities, national sororities.

Athletics Member NCAA. All Division III. ***Intercollegiate sports:*** baseball M, basketball M/W, cross-country running M/W, golf M/W, gymnastics W, lacrosse M(c), soccer M/W, softball W, swimming and diving M/W, tennis M/W, volleyball W. ***Intramural sports:*** basketball M/W, football M/W, soccer M/W, softball M/W, volleyball M/W.

Campus security: 24-hour emergency response devices and patrols, late-night transport/escort service, controlled dormitory access.

Student services: health clinic, personal/psychological counseling.

COSTS & FINANCIAL AID

Costs (2015–16) ***One-time required fee:*** $250. ***Comprehensive fee:*** $46,250 includes full-time tuition ($33,900) and room and board ($12,350). Full-time tuition and fees vary according to course load, degree level, and student level. Part-time tuition and fees vary according to course load, degree level, and student level. ***Room and board:*** Room and board charges vary according to board plan, housing facility, and student level. ***Payment plan:*** installment. ***Waivers:*** employees or children of employees.

Financial Aid Of all full-time matriculated undergraduates who enrolled in 2014, 479 applied for aid, 424 were judged to have need, 80 had their need fully met. 184 Federal Work-Study jobs (averaging $2184). 42 state and other part-time jobs (averaging $1396). In 2014, 126 non-need-based awards were made. ***Average percent of need met:*** 75. ***Average financial aid package:*** $25,657. ***Average need-based loan:*** $4398. ***Average need-based gift aid:*** $21,909. ***Average non-need-based aid:*** $15,863. ***Average indebtedness upon graduation:*** $27,692.

APPLYING

Standardized Tests *Required:* SAT or ACT (for admission).

Options: electronic application, early admission, early action, deferred entrance.

Required: essay or personal statement, high school transcript, minimum 2.0 GPA, 1 letter of recommendation. ***Required for some:*** interview. ***Recommended:*** class rank.

Application deadlines: 8/1 (freshmen), 8/1 (out-of-state freshmen), 8/15 (transfers), 12/15 (early action).

Notification: continuous (freshmen), continuous (out-of-state freshmen), continuous (transfers).

CONTACT

Mr. Thomas Newton, Director of Admission, Centenary College of Louisiana, Office of Admission, 2911 Centenary Boulevard, Shreveport, LA 71104. *Phone:* 318-869-5701. *Toll-free phone:* 800-234-4448. *Fax:* 318-869-5005.

Dillard University

New Orleans, Louisiana

http://www.dillard.edu/

- **Independent interdenominational** 4-year, founded 1869
- **Urban** 55-acre campus
- **Endowment** $54.8 million
- **Coed**
- **Moderately difficult** entrance level

FACULTY

Student/faculty ratio: 13:1.

ACADEMICS

Calendar: semesters. *Degree:* bachelor's.

STUDENT LIFE

Housing options: on-campus residence required for freshman year; coed, men-only, women-only, special housing for students with disabilities. Campus housing is university owned and leased by the school. Freshman campus housing is guaranteed.

Activities and organizations: drama/theater group, student-run newspaper, radio and television station, choral group, Student Government Association, Student Activities Board, National Pan-Hellenic Council, Collegiate 100, Class Councils, national fraternities, national sororities.

Athletics Member NAIA.

Campus security: 24-hour emergency response devices and patrols, late-night transport/escort service, controlled dormitory access.

Student services: health clinic, personal/psychological counseling, legal services.

COSTS & FINANCIAL AID

Costs (2014–15) ***Comprehensive fee:*** $25,408 includes full-time tuition ($14,600), mandatory fees ($1494), and room and board ($9314). Part-time tuition: $609 per unit. Part-time tuition and fees vary according to course load. ***College room only:*** $5976. Room and board charges vary according to housing facility and student level.

Financial Aid Of all full-time matriculated undergraduates who enrolled in 2013, 1,129 applied for aid, 1,096 were judged to have need, 55 had their need fully met. 204 Federal Work-Study jobs (averaging $1632). In 2013, 43 non-need-based awards were made. ***Average percent of need met:*** 59. ***Average financial aid package:*** $14,972. ***Average need-based loan:*** $5244. ***Average need-based gift aid:*** $9946. ***Average non-need-based aid:*** $8078. ***Average indebtedness upon graduation:*** $30,095.

APPLYING

Standardized Tests *Required:* SAT or ACT (for admission), minimum SAT score of 870 (math and verbal) or minimum ACT composite score of 18 (for admission).

Options: electronic application, early admission.

Application fee: $35.

Required: high school transcript, minimum 2.5 GPA. ***Required for some:*** essay or personal statement, 2 letters of recommendation.

CONTACT

Mr. Thomas W. Steffen, Assistant Vice President of Enrollment Management, Dillard University, 2601 Gentilly Boulevard, New Orleans, LA 70122-3097. *Phone:* 504-816-4951. *Toll-free phone:* 800-216-8094. *Fax:* 504-816-4895. *E-mail:* acyprian@dillard.edu.

Grambling State University

Grambling, Louisiana

http://www.gram.edu/

- **State-supported** university, founded 1901, part of University of Louisiana System
- **Small-town** 590-acre campus with easy access to Shreveport
- **Endowment** $7.2 million
- **Coed** 3,524 undergraduate students, 93% full-time, 60% women, 40% men
- **Noncompetitive** entrance level, 44% of applicants were admitted

UNDERGRAD STUDENTS

3,264 full-time, 260 part-time. 27% are from out of state; 91% Black or African American, non-Hispanic/Latino; 0.9% Hispanic/Latino; 0.2% Asian, non-Hispanic/Latino; 0.1% Native Hawaiian or other Pacific Islander, non-Hispanic/Latino; 0.4% American Indian or Alaska Native, non-Hispanic/Latino; 2% Two or more races, non-Hispanic/Latino; 0.8% Race/ethnicity unknown; 4% international; 7% transferred in; 75% live on campus.

Freshmen

Admission: 2,894 applied, 1,272 admitted, 406 enrolled. ***Average high school GPA:*** 2.86. ***Test scores:*** SAT math scores over 500: 17%; SAT writing scores over 500: 19%; ACT scores over 18: 61%; ACT scores over 24: 5%.

Retention: 68% of full-time freshmen returned.

FACULTY

Total: 225, 94% full-time.

Student/faculty ratio: 20:1.

ACADEMICS

Calendar: semesters. *Degrees:* bachelor's, master's, doctoral, and post-master's certificates.

Special study options: academic remediation for entering students, adult/continuing education programs, advanced placement credit, cooperative education, distance learning, double majors, honors programs, internships, off-campus study, part-time degree program, services for LD students, summer session for credit. ***ROTC:*** Army (b), Air Force (c).

Computers: Students can access the following: campus intranet, computer help desk, free student e-mail accounts, online (class) grades, online (class) registration, online (class) schedules. Campuswide network is available. Wireless service is available via classrooms, computer centers, computer labs, dorm rooms, learning centers, libraries, student centers.

STUDENT LIFE
Housing options: on-campus residence required for freshman year; coed, men-only, women-only, special housing for students with disabilities. Campus housing is provided by a third party. Freshman applicants given priority for college housing.

Activities and organizations: drama/theater group, student-run newspaper, radio and television station, choral group, marching band, Tiger Marching Band, Black Dynasty Modeling Troupe, Academic and Professional Clubs, sororities, fraternities, national fraternities, national sororities.

Athletics Member NCAA. All Division I except football (Division I-AA). ***Intercollegiate sports:*** baseball M(s), basketball M(s)/W(s), bowling W(s), cross-country running M/W, soccer W, softball W(s), tennis W(s), track and field M(s)/W(s), volleyball W(s). ***Intramural sports:*** badminton M/W, basketball M/W, bowling M(c)/W(c), racquetball M(c)/W(c), soccer M(c)/W(c), softball W, table tennis M/W, tennis M(c)/W(c), volleyball M(c)/W(c), weight lifting M/W.

Campus security: 24-hour patrols, student patrols, controlled dormitory access.

Student services: health clinic, personal/psychological counseling.

COSTS & FINANCIAL AID
Costs (2014–15) ***Tuition:*** state resident $4895 full-time, $204 per credit hour part-time; nonresident $14,114 full-time, $204 per credit hour part-time. Full-time tuition and fees vary according to course load, degree level, and student level. Part-time tuition and fees vary according to course load, degree level, and student level. ***Required fees:*** $1749 full-time, $204 per credit hour part-time. ***Room and board:*** $9372; room only: $5948. Room and board charges vary according to housing facility. ***Payment plans:*** installment, deferred payment. ***Waivers:*** children of alumni, senior citizens, and employees or children of employees.

Financial Aid Of all full-time matriculated undergraduates who enrolled in 2014, 3,076 applied for aid, 3,076 were judged to have need. In 2014, 447 non-need-based awards were made. ***Average financial aid package:*** $3935. ***Average need-based loan:*** $4064. ***Average need-based gift aid:*** $3852. ***Average non-need-based aid:*** $3386. ***Financial aid deadline:*** 6/1.

APPLYING
Standardized Tests *Required:* SAT or ACT (for admission).

Options: electronic application, early admission.

Application fee: $20.

Required: high school transcript, minimum 2.0 GPA, 19 Units from Required Core 4 Curriculum; no more than one developmental course allowed; minimum test score of ACT English-18 and ACT Math-19 or SAT Critical Reading-450 and SAT Math-460 or COMPASS Writing-68 and COMPASS Algebra-40.

Application deadlines: 8/15 (freshmen), 7/15 (transfers).

Notification: 4/1 (freshmen), continuous until 6/15 (transfers).

CONTACT
Director of Admissions and Recruitment, Grambling State University, GSU Box 4200, Grambling, LA 71245. *Phone:* 318-274-6423. *Toll-free phone:* 800-569-4714. *Fax:* 318-274-3292. *E-mail:* mossa@gram.edu.

ITT Technical Institute

Baton Rouge, Louisiana

http://www.itt-tech.edu/

- **Proprietary** primarily 2-year
- **Coed**

ACADEMICS
Degrees: associate and bachelor's.

STUDENT LIFE
Housing options: college housing not available.

CONTACT
Director of Recruitment, ITT Technical Institute, 14111 Airline Highway, Suite 101, Baton Rouge, LA 70817. *Phone:* 225-754-5800. *Toll-free phone:* 800-295-8485.

ITT Technical Institute

St. Rose, Louisiana

http://www.itt-tech.edu/

- **Proprietary** primarily 2-year, founded 1998, part of ITT Educational Services, Inc.
- **Coed**
- **Minimally difficult** entrance level

ACADEMICS
Calendar: quarters. *Degrees:* associate and bachelor's.

STUDENT LIFE
Housing options: college housing not available.

CONTACT
Director of Recruitment, ITT Technical Institute, 140 James Drive East, St. Rose, LA 70087. *Phone:* 504-463-0338. *Toll-free phone:* 866-463-0338.

Louisiana College

Pineville, Louisiana

http://www.lacollege.edu/

- **Independent Southern Baptist** comprehensive, founded 1906
- **Small-town** 81-acre campus
- **Endowment** $35.8 million
- **Coed** 985 undergraduate students, 95% full-time, 48% women, 52% men
- **Moderately difficult** entrance level, 61% of applicants were admitted

UNDERGRAD STUDENTS
931 full-time, 54 part-time. Students come from 29 states and territories; 13 other countries; 10% are from out of state; 21% Black or African American, non-Hispanic/Latino; 3% Hispanic/Latino; 0.7% Asian, non-Hispanic/Latino; 0.1% Native Hawaiian or other Pacific Islander, non-Hispanic/Latino; 0.6% American Indian or Alaska Native, non-Hispanic/Latino; 1% Two or more races, non-Hispanic/Latino; 1% Race/ethnicity unknown; 7% international; 5% transferred in; 55% live on campus.

Freshmen
Admission: 809 applied, 494 admitted, 236 enrolled. ***Average high school GPA:*** 3.17. ***Test scores:*** ACT scores over 18: 87%; ACT scores over 24: 23%; ACT scores over 30: 1%.

Retention: 54% of full-time freshmen returned.

FACULTY
Total: 108, 69% full-time, 49% with terminal degrees.

Student/faculty ratio: 11:1.

ACADEMICS
Calendar: semesters. *Degrees:* associate, bachelor's, and master's.

Special study options: academic remediation for entering students, accelerated degree program, adult/continuing education programs, advanced placement credit, cooperative education, distance learning, double majors, English as a second language, honors programs, independent study, internships, part-time degree program, services for LD students, student-designed majors, summer session for credit. ***ROTC:*** Army (b).

Computers: 269 computers/terminals are available on campus for general student use. Students can access the following: campus intranet, computer help desk, free student e-mail accounts, online (class) grades, online (class) registration, online (class) schedules. Campuswide network is available. 100% of college-owned or -operated housing units are wired for high-speed Internet access. Wireless service is available via entire campus.

STUDENT LIFE
Housing options: on-campus residence required through junior year; men-only, women-only. Campus housing is university owned. Freshman campus housing is guaranteed.

Activities and organizations: drama/theater group, student-run newspaper, radio station, choral group, marching band, Baptist Student Union, Delta Xi Omega, Student Government Association, Union Board, Lambda Chi Beta.

Athletics Member NCAA. All Division III. ***Intercollegiate sports:*** baseball M, basketball M/W, cheerleading M/W, cross-country running M/W, football M, golf M/W, soccer M/W, softball W, tennis M/W. ***Intramural sports:*** badminton M/W, basketball M/W, football M/W, racquetball M/W, soccer M/W, softball M/W, table tennis M/W, tennis M/W, ultimate Frisbee M/W, volleyball M/W, water polo M/W.

Campus security: 24-hour emergency response devices and patrols, student patrols, late-night transport/escort service, controlled dormitory access.

Student services: health clinic, personal/psychological counseling.

COSTS & FINANCIAL AID
Costs (2014–15) ***Comprehensive fee:*** $19,644 includes full-time tuition ($12,750), mandatory fees ($1820), and room and board ($5074). Full-time tuition and fees vary according to course load. Part-time tuition: $425 per credit hour. Part-time tuition and fees vary according to course load. ***Required fees:*** $364 per term part-time. ***Room and board:*** Room and board charges vary according to board plan and housing facility. ***Payment plan:*** installment. ***Waivers:*** employees or children of employees.

Financial Aid Of all full-time matriculated undergraduates who enrolled in 2012, 1,033 applied for aid, 844 were judged to have need, 170 had their need fully met. 114 Federal Work-Study jobs (averaging $1800). In 2012, 239 non-need-based awards were made. ***Average percent of need met:*** 64. ***Average financial aid package:*** $11,275. ***Average need-based loan:*** $3180. ***Average need-based gift aid:*** $9022. ***Average non-need-based aid:*** $5214. ***Average indebtedness upon graduation:*** $22,969.

APPLYING
Standardized Tests *Required:* SAT or ACT (for admission).

Options: electronic application, early admission.

Application fee: $25.

Required: high school transcript, minimum 2.0 GPA, class rank. ***Required for some:*** 3 letters of recommendation. ***Recommended:*** interview.

Notification: continuous (freshmen), continuous (transfers).

CONTACT
Mr. Byron McGee, Interim Vice President of Enrollment Management, Louisiana College, LC Box 566, Pineville, LA 71359. *Phone:* 318-487-7439. *Toll-free phone:* 800-487-1906. *Fax:* 318-487-7550. *E-mail:* admissions@lacollege.edu.

Louisiana State University and Agricultural & Mechanical College

Baton Rouge, Louisiana

http://www.lsu.edu/

- **State-supported** university, founded 1860, part of Louisiana State University System
- **Urban** 2000-acre campus with easy access to New Orleans
- **Endowment** $414.1 million
- **Coed** 25,572 undergraduate students, 91% full-time, 51% women, 49% men
- **Moderately difficult** entrance level, 77% of applicants were admitted

UNDERGRAD STUDENTS
23,195 full-time, 2,377 part-time. Students come from 51 states and territories; 76 other countries; 18% are from out of state; 11% Black or African American, non-Hispanic/Latino; 6% Hispanic/Latino; 4% Asian, non-Hispanic/Latino; 0.1% Native Hawaiian or other Pacific Islander, non-Hispanic/Latino; 0.3% American Indian or Alaska Native, non-Hispanic/Latino; 2% Two or more races, non-Hispanic/Latino; 0.2% Race/ethnicity unknown; 2% international; 4% transferred in; 25% live on campus.

Freshmen
Admission: 16,580 applied, 12,706 admitted, 5,655 enrolled. ***Average high school GPA:*** 3.46. ***Test scores:*** SAT critical reading scores over 500: 80%; SAT math scores over 500: 81%; ACT scores over 18: 100%; SAT critical reading scores over 600: 29%; SAT math scores over 600: 40%; ACT scores over 24: 70%; SAT critical reading scores over 700: 5%; SAT math scores over 700: 8%; ACT scores over 30: 16%.
Retention: 85% of full-time freshmen returned.

FACULTY
Total: 1,467, 87% full-time, 85% with terminal degrees.

Student/faculty ratio: 22:1.

ACADEMICS
Calendar: semesters. *Degrees:* bachelor's, master's, doctoral, post-master's, and postbachelor's certificates.

Special study options: accelerated degree program, adult/continuing education programs, advanced placement credit, cooperative education, distance learning, double majors, English as a second language, freshman honors college, honors programs, independent study, internships, off-campus study, part-time degree program, services for LD students, student-designed majors, study abroad, summer session for credit. ***ROTC:*** Army (b), Navy (c), Air Force (b).

Computers: 1,189 computers/terminals and 8,300 ports are available on campus for general student use. Students can access the following: computer help desk, free student e-mail accounts, online (class) grades, online (class) registration, online (class) schedules, free software for download, personal Web sites, storage, discounts on hardware, virtual computer lab. Campuswide network is available. 100% of college-owned or -operated housing units are wired for high-speed Internet access. Wireless service is available via entire campus.

STUDENT LIFE
Housing options: coed, men-only, women-only, special housing for students with disabilities. Campus housing is university owned.

Activities and organizations: drama/theater group, student-run newspaper, radio and television station, choral group, marching band, intramural athletics, student political organizations, student professional organizations, religious organizations, cultural organizations, national fraternities, national sororities.

Athletics Member NCAA. All Division I except football (Division I-A). ***Intercollegiate sports:*** baseball M(s), basketball M(s)/W(s), cheerleading M/W, cross-country running M(s)/W(s), golf M(s)/W(s), gymnastics W(s), soccer W(s), softball W(s), swimming and diving M(s)/W(s), tennis M(s)/W(s), track and field M(s)/W(s), volleyball W(s). ***Intramural sports:*** badminton M/W, basketball M/W, bowling M(c)/W(c), crew M(c)/W(c), equestrian sports W(c), football M/W, golf M/W, ice hockey M(c)/W(c), lacrosse M(c)/W(c), racquetball M/W, rugby M(c)/W(c), soccer M(c)/W(c), softball M/W, table tennis M/W, tennis M(c)/W(c), ultimate Frisbee M(c)/W(c), volleyball M(c)/W(c), water polo M(c)/W(c), weight lifting M(c)/W(c).

Campus security: 24-hour emergency response devices and patrols, late-night transport/escort service, controlled dormitory access, self-defense education, crime prevention programs.

Student services: health clinic, personal/psychological counseling, women's center, legal services.

COSTS & FINANCIAL AID
Costs (2014–15) ***Tuition:*** state resident $6678 full-time; nonresident $24,395 full-time. Part-time tuition and fees vary according to course load. ***Required fees:*** $2072 full-time. ***Room and board:*** $10,804; room only: $6900. Room and board charges vary according to board plan and housing facility. ***Payment plan:*** deferred payment. ***Waivers:*** employees or children of employees.

Financial Aid Of all full-time matriculated undergraduates who enrolled in 2013, 12,945 applied for aid, 9,842 were judged to have need, 2,201 had their need fully met. 770 Federal Work-Study jobs (averaging $2200). 4,700 state and other part-time jobs (averaging $2400). In 2013, 3100 non-need-based awards were made. ***Average percent of need met:*** 68. ***Average financial aid package:*** $14,798. ***Average need-based loan:*** $6354. ***Average need-based gift aid:*** $10,097. ***Average non-need-based aid:*** $5098. ***Average indebtedness upon graduation:*** $22,294.

APPLYING
Standardized Tests *Required:* SAT or ACT (for admission).

Options: electronic application, early admission, deferred entrance.

Application fee: $40.

Required: high school transcript, minimum 3.0 GPA, 22 ACT (1030 SAT) with a minimum critical reading score of 18 ACT (450 SAT), and a math score of 19 ACT (460 SAT). ***Required for some:*** essay or personal statement.

Application deadlines: 4/15 (freshmen), 4/15 (transfers).

Notification: continuous (freshmen), continuous (transfers).

CONTACT

Ms. Guadalupe Lamadrid, Associate Director, Undergraduate Admissions, Louisiana State University and Agricultural & Mechanical College, 1146 Pleasant Hall, Baton Rouge, LA 70803. *Phone:* 225-578-1175. *Fax:* 225-578-4433. *E-mail:* glamadrid@lsu.edu.

Louisiana State University Health Sciences Center

New Orleans, Louisiana

http://www.lsuhsc.edu/

- **State-supported** university, founded 1931, part of Louisiana State University System
- **Urban** 80-acre campus
- **Endowment** $68.5 million
- **Coed** 911 undergraduate students, 69% full-time, 85% women, 15% men

UNDERGRAD STUDENTS

633 full-time, 278 part-time. Students come from 10 states and territories; 4 other countries; 1% are from out of state; 10% live on campus.

FACULTY

Total: 893, 81% full-time, 100% with terminal degrees.

ACADEMICS

Calendar: varies by academic program. *Degrees:* associate, bachelor's, master's, doctoral, and post-master's certificates.

Special study options: accelerated degree program, advanced placement credit, cooperative education, distance learning, double majors, independent study, internships, services for LD students, summer session for credit. ***ROTC:*** Army (c), Navy (c), Air Force (c).

Computers: 120 computers/terminals and 1,800 ports are available on campus for general student use. Students can access the following: campus intranet, computer help desk, free student e-mail accounts. Campuswide network is available. 100% of college-owned or -operated housing units are wired for high-speed Internet access. Wireless service is available via classrooms, learning centers, libraries, student centers.

STUDENT LIFE

Housing options: coed. Campus housing is university owned.

Campus security: 24-hour emergency response devices and patrols, late-night transport/escort service, controlled dormitory access.

Student services: health clinic, personal/psychological counseling.

COSTS

Costs (2015–16) ***Tuition:*** state resident $4638 full-time, $296 per semester hour part-time; nonresident $9287 full-time, $587 per semester hour part-time. Full-time tuition and fees vary according to degree level, program, and reciprocity agreements. Part-time tuition and fees vary according to course load, degree level, program, and reciprocity agreements. ***Required fees:*** $902 full-time, $50 part-time. ***Room only:*** $3708. Room and board charges vary according to housing facility. ***Waivers:*** employees or children of employees.

APPLYING

Application fee: $50.

Notification: 8/1 (transfers).

CONTACT

Louisiana State University Health Sciences Center, 433 Bolivar Street, New Orleans, LA 70112-2223. *Phone:* 504-568-4829.

Louisiana State University in Shreveport

Shreveport, Louisiana

http://www.lsus.edu/

- **State-supported** comprehensive, founded 1965, part of Louisiana State University System
- **Urban** 250-acre campus
- **Endowment** $16.5 million
- **Coed** 3,220 undergraduate students, 61% full-time, 60% women, 40% men
- **Moderately difficult** entrance level, 77% of applicants were admitted

UNDERGRAD STUDENTS

1,967 full-time, 1,253 part-time. Students come from 43 states and territories; 12 other countries; 9% are from out of state; 23% Black or African American, non-Hispanic/Latino; 4% Hispanic/Latino; 2% Asian, non-Hispanic/Latino; 0.1% Native Hawaiian or other Pacific Islander, non-Hispanic/Latino; 0.7% American Indian or Alaska Native, non-Hispanic/Latino; 4% Two or more races, non-Hispanic/Latino; 6% Race/ethnicity unknown; 2% international; 11% transferred in.

Freshmen

Admission: 690 applied, 529 admitted, 348 enrolled. ***Average high school GPA:*** 3.29. ***Test scores:*** ACT scores over 18: 99%; ACT scores over 24: 43%; ACT scores over 30: 4%.

Retention: 66% of full-time freshmen returned.

FACULTY

Total: 178, 67% full-time, 61% with terminal degrees.

Student/faculty ratio: 19:1.

ACADEMICS

Calendar: semesters plus 8-week and two 4-week summer terms. *Degrees:* certificates, bachelor's, master's, doctoral, and post-master's certificates.

Special study options: academic remediation for entering students, accelerated degree program, adult/continuing education programs, advanced placement credit, cooperative education, distance learning, double majors, English as a second language, honors programs, independent study, internships, off-campus study, part-time degree program, services for LD students, student-designed majors, summer session for credit. ***ROTC:*** Army (b).

Computers: Students can access the following: computer help desk, free student e-mail accounts, online (class) grades, online (class) registration, online (class) schedules. Campuswide network is available. Wireless service is available via entire campus.

STUDENT LIFE

Housing options: college housing not availableCampus housing is provided by a third party.

Activities and organizations: drama/theater group, student-run newspaper, national fraternities, national sororities.

Athletics Member NAIA. ***Intercollegiate sports:*** baseball M(s), basketball M(s)/W(s), cross-country running M/W, soccer W(s), tennis W(s). ***Intramural sports:*** basketball M/W, soccer M/W, softball M/W, volleyball M/W.

Campus security: 24-hour emergency response devices and patrols, student patrols, controlled dormitory access.

Student services: personal/psychological counseling.

COSTS

Costs (2014–15) ***Tuition:*** state resident $4964 full-time, $201 per credit hour part-time; nonresident $17,466 full-time, $720 per credit hour part-time. Full-time tuition and fees vary according to course load. Part-time tuition and fees vary according to course load. ***Required fees:*** $1273 full-time, $51 per credit hour part-time. ***Payment plan:*** installment. ***Waivers:*** employees or children of employees.

APPLYING

Standardized Tests *Required:* SAT or ACT (for admission).

Options: electronic application.

Application fee: $20.

Required: high school transcript, minimum 2.0 GPA.

CONTACT
Louisiana State University in Shreveport, 1 University Place, Shreveport, LA 71115-2399. *Phone:* 318-797-5063. *Toll-free phone:* 800-229-5957.

Louisiana Tech University

Ruston, Louisiana

http://www.latech.edu/

- **State-supported** university, founded 1894, part of University of Louisiana System
- **Small-town** 247-acre campus
- **Coed**
- **Moderately difficult** entrance level

FACULTY
Student/faculty ratio: 23:1.

ACADEMICS
Calendar: quarters. *Degrees:* associate, bachelor's, master's, doctoral, post-master's, and postbachelor's certificates.

STUDENT LIFE
Housing options: on-campus residence required through sophomore year; men-only, women-only, special housing for students with disabilities. Campus housing is university owned and is provided by a third party.

Activities and organizations: drama/theater group, student-run newspaper, radio and television station, choral group, marching band, Student Government Association, Association of Women's Studies, Union Board, national fraternities, national sororities.

Athletics Member NCAA. All Division I except football (Division I-A).

Campus security: 24-hour emergency response devices and patrols, student patrols, late-night transport/escort service, controlled dormitory access.

Student services: health clinic, personal/psychological counseling, legal services.

COSTS & FINANCIAL AID
Costs (2014–15) ***Tuition:*** state resident $6233 full-time, $336 per credit hour part-time; nonresident $20,816 full-time, $943 per credit hour part-time. Full-time tuition and fees vary according to course load, location, and program. Part-time tuition and fees vary according to course load, location, and program. ***Required fees:*** $1819 full-time. ***Room and board:*** $5520. Room and board charges vary according to board plan and housing facility. ***Payment plans:*** installment, deferred payment.

Financial Aid Of all full-time matriculated undergraduates who enrolled in 2013, 3,715 applied for aid, 2,581 were judged to have need, 541 had their need fully met. 280 Federal Work-Study jobs (averaging $2067). 1,008 state and other part-time jobs (averaging $2356). In 2013, 1159 non-need-based awards were made. ***Average percent of need met:*** 62. ***Average financial aid package:*** $9757. ***Average need-based loan:*** $3348. ***Average need-based gift aid:*** $8375. ***Average non-need-based aid:*** $3011. ***Average indebtedness upon graduation:*** $16,855.

APPLYING
Standardized Tests *Required:* SAT or ACT (for admission). *Recommended:* ACT (for admission).

Options: early admission.

Application fee: $20.

Required: high school transcript, minimum 2.2 GPA.

CONTACT
Mrs. Jan B. Albritton, Director of Admissions, Louisiana Tech University, PO Box 3168, Ruston, LA 71272. *Phone:* 318-257-3036. *Toll-free phone:* 800-528-3241. *Fax:* 318-257-2499. *E-mail:* bulldog@latech.edu.

★ Loyola University New Orleans

New Orleans, Louisiana

http://www.loyno.edu/

- **Independent Roman Catholic (Jesuit)** comprehensive, founded 1912
- **Suburban** 26-acre campus with easy access to New Orleans
- **Endowment** $249.0 million
- **Coed** 2,946 undergraduate students, 93% full-time, 59% women, 41% men
- **Moderately difficult** entrance level, 87% of applicants were admitted

UNDERGRAD STUDENTS
2,741 full-time, 205 part-time. Students come from 53 states and territories; 44 other countries; 54% are from out of state; 16% Black or African American, non-Hispanic/Latino; 16% Hispanic/Latino; 4% Asian, non-Hispanic/Latino; 0.6% American Indian or Alaska Native, non-Hispanic/Latino; 4% Two or more races, non-Hispanic/Latino; 6% Race/ethnicity unknown; 4% international; 5% transferred in; 43% live on campus.

Freshmen
Admission: 4,827 applied, 4,203 admitted, 624 enrolled. ***Average high school GPA:*** 3.54. ***Test scores:*** SAT critical reading scores over 500: 85%; SAT math scores over 500: 79%; ACT scores over 18: 100%; SAT critical reading scores over 600: 41%; SAT math scores over 600: 31%; ACT scores over 24: 65%; SAT critical reading scores over 700: 8%; SAT math scores over 700: 4%; ACT scores over 30: 15%.
Retention: 80% of full-time freshmen returned.

FACULTY
Total: 441, 68% full-time, 76% with terminal degrees.

Student/faculty ratio: 11:1.

ACADEMICS
Calendar: semesters. *Degrees:* bachelor's, master's, doctoral, post-master's, and postbachelor's certificates.

Special study options: accelerated degree program, adult/continuing education programs, advanced placement credit, cooperative education, distance learning, double majors, English as a second language, external degree program, honors programs, independent study, internships, off-campus study, part-time degree program, services for LD students, student-designed majors, study abroad, summer session for credit. ***ROTC:*** Army (c), Navy (c), Air Force (c).

Unusual degree programs: 3-2 engineering with The Pre-Engineering Physics track is a 3-2 dual degree program with students completing their engineering degrees at another institution while earning a Physics degree from Loyola.

Computers: 626 computers/terminals and 2,500 ports are available on campus for general student use. Students can access the following: campus intranet, computer help desk, free student e-mail accounts, online (class) grades, online (class) registration, online (class) schedules. Campuswide network is available. 100% of college-owned or -operated housing units are wired for high-speed Internet access. Wireless service is available via entire campus.

STUDENT LIFE
Housing options: on-campus residence required through sophomore year; coed, special housing for students with disabilities. Campus housing is university owned. Freshman campus housing is guaranteed.

Activities and organizations: drama/theater group, student-run newspaper, radio station, choral group, University Programming Board, Student Government Association, Black Student Union, Loyola University Community Action Program (LUCAP), Panhellenic Council, national fraternities, national sororities.

Athletics Member NAIA. ***Intercollegiate sports:*** baseball M, basketball M(s)/W(s), cross-country running M/W, golf M(c)/W(c), rugby M(c), sailing M(c)/W(c), swimming and diving M/W, table tennis M/W, tennis M/W, track and field M/W, volleyball W. ***Intramural sports:*** basketball M/W, racquetball M/W, soccer M/W, softball M/W, swimming and diving M/W, volleyball M/W, weight lifting M/W.

Campus security: 24-hour emergency response devices and patrols, student patrols, late-night transport/escort service, controlled dormitory access, self-defense education, bicycle patrols, closed circuit TV monitors, door alarms, crime prevention programs, card access control.

Student services: health clinic, personal/psychological counseling, women's center.

COSTS & FINANCIAL AID
Costs (2014–15) ***Comprehensive fee:*** $49,270 includes full-time tuition ($35,504), mandatory fees ($1106), and room and board ($12,660). Part-time tuition: $1012 per credit. ***Required fees:*** $294 per term part-time. ***College room only:*** $7430. Room and board charges vary according to board plan and housing facility. ***Payment plan:*** installment. ***Waivers:*** senior citizens and employees or children of employees.

A ★ indicates that the school has detailed information with a Premium Profile on Petersons.com.

Financial Aid Of all full-time matriculated undergraduates who enrolled in 2014, 1,940 applied for aid, 1,707 were judged to have need, 193 had their need fully met. In 2014, 660 non-need-based awards were made. ***Average percent of need met:*** 72. ***Average financial aid package:*** $29,614. ***Average need-based loan:*** $4879. ***Average need-based gift aid:*** $25,182. ***Average non-need-based aid:*** $14,876. ***Average indebtedness upon graduation:*** $25,133.

APPLYING

Standardized Tests *Required:* SAT or ACT (for admission).

Options: electronic application, early admission.

Application fee: $20.

Required: essay or personal statement, high school transcript, 1 letter of recommendation. ***Required for some:*** interview. ***Recommended:*** interview.

Application deadlines: rolling (freshmen), rolling (out-of-state freshmen), rolling (transfers).

Notification: continuous (freshmen), continuous (out-of-state freshmen).

CONTACT

Ms. Roberta E. Kaskel, Interim Vice President for Enrollment Management, Loyola University New Orleans, 6363 St. Charles Avenue, Campus Box 18, New Orleans, LA 70118. *Phone:* 504-865-3240. *Toll-free phone:* 800-4-LOYOLA. *Fax:* 504-865-3383. *E-mail:* rekaskel@loyno.edu.

McNeese State University

Lake Charles, Louisiana

http://www.mcneese.edu/

- **State-supported** comprehensive, founded 1939, part of University of Louisiana System
- **Suburban** 766-acre campus
- **Coed** 7,431 undergraduate students, 78% full-time, 61% women, 39% men
- **Moderately difficult** entrance level, 75% of applicants were admitted

UNDERGRAD STUDENTS

5,831 full-time, 1,600 part-time. Students come from 35 states and territories; 53 other countries; 8% are from out of state; 19% Black or African American, non-Hispanic/Latino; 3% Hispanic/Latino; 2% Asian, non-Hispanic/Latino; 0.1% Native Hawaiian or other Pacific Islander, non-Hispanic/Latino; 0.6% American Indian or Alaska Native, non-Hispanic/Latino; 2% Two or more races, non-Hispanic/Latino; 0.1% Race/ethnicity unknown; 4% international; 4% transferred in.

Freshmen

Admission: 2,734 applied, 2,058 admitted, 1,260 enrolled. ***Average high school GPA:*** 3.38.

Retention: 70% of full-time freshmen returned.

FACULTY

Total: 435, 61% full-time, 48% with terminal degrees.

Student/faculty ratio: 21:1.

ACADEMICS

Calendar: semesters. *Degrees:* associate, bachelor's, master's, post-master's, and postbachelor's certificates.

Special study options: academic remediation for entering students, accelerated degree program, advanced placement credit, cooperative education, distance learning, double majors, English as a second language, freshman honors college, honors programs, independent study, internships, off-campus study, part-time degree program, services for LD students, study abroad, summer session for credit.

Computers: Students can access the following: computer help desk, free student e-mail accounts, online (class) grades, online (class) registration, online (class) schedules. Campuswide network is available. Wireless service is available via entire campus.

STUDENT LIFE

Housing options: coed. Campus housing is provided by a third party.

Activities and organizations: drama/theater group, student-run newspaper, choral group, marching band, Student Government Association, International Students Association, Resident Student Association, national fraternities, national sororities.

Athletics Member NCAA. All Division I except football (Division I-AA). ***Intercollegiate sports:*** baseball M(s), basketball M(s)/W(s), cross-country running M(s)/W(s), golf M(s)/W(s), soccer W(s), softball W(s), tennis W(s), track and field M(s)/W(s), volleyball W(s). ***Intramural sports:*** badminton M/W, baseball M, basketball M/W, football M/W, golf M/W, racquetball M/W, soccer M/W, softball W, swimming and diving M/W, table tennis M/W, tennis M/W, ultimate Frisbee M/W, volleyball M/W, water polo M/W, weight lifting M/W.

Campus security: 24-hour emergency response devices and patrols, late-night transport/escort service, controlled dormitory access.

Student services: health clinic, personal/psychological counseling, women's center.

COSTS

Costs (2014–15) ***Tuition:*** $529 per credit hour part-time; state resident $4679 full-time; nonresident $15,749 full-time. Full-time tuition and fees vary according to course load. Part-time tuition and fees vary according to course load. ***Required fees:*** $1655 full-time. ***Room and board:*** $6536; room only: $3760. Room and board charges vary according to board plan and housing facility. ***Waivers:*** senior citizens and employees or children of employees.

APPLYING

Standardized Tests *Required:* SAT or ACT (for admission).

Options: electronic application, early admission, deferred entrance.

Application fee: $20.

Required: high school transcript, minimum 2.0 GPA, Complete Louisiana Board of Regents high school core 4 curriculum, need no more than one developmental course, and minimum high school GPA of 2.35 and meet one of the following: minimum high school core GPA of 2.0 or minimum ACT composite 20 (SAT critical reading/math combined scores 940).

Application deadlines: rolling (freshmen), rolling (transfers).

Notification: continuous (freshmen), continuous (transfers).

CONTACT

Ms. Kara Smith, Director of Admissions and Recruiting, McNeese State University, Box 91740, Lake Charles, LA 70609. *Phone:* 337-475-5504. *Toll-free phone:* 800-622-3352. *Fax:* 337-475-5978. *E-mail:* ksmith2@mcneese.edu.

Nicholls State University

Thibodaux, Louisiana

http://www.nicholls.edu/

- **State-supported** comprehensive, founded 1948, part of University of Louisiana System
- **Small-town** 210-acre campus with easy access to New Orleans
- **Coed** 5,695 undergraduate students, 84% full-time, 62% women, 38% men
- **Noncompetitive** entrance level, 88% of applicants were admitted

UNDERGRAD STUDENTS

4,769 full-time, 926 part-time. Students come from 36 states and territories; 38 other countries; 5% are from out of state; 20% Black or African American, non-Hispanic/Latino; 3% Hispanic/Latino; 1% Asian, non-Hispanic/Latino; 0.1% Native Hawaiian or other Pacific Islander, non-Hispanic/Latino; 2% American Indian or Alaska Native, non-Hispanic/Latino; 3% Two or more races, non-Hispanic/Latino; 2% Race/ethnicity unknown; 2% international; 5% transferred in; 18% live on campus.

Freshmen

Admission: 2,424 applied, 2,142 admitted, 1,210 enrolled. ***Average high school GPA:*** 3.22. ***Test scores:*** SAT critical reading scores over 500: 50%; SAT math scores over 500: 64%; SAT writing scores over 500: 36%; ACT scores over 18: 94%; SAT critical reading scores over 600: 11%; SAT math scores over 600: 32%; SAT writing scores over 600: 7%; ACT scores over 24: 28%; SAT math scores over 700: 7%; ACT scores over 30: 1%.

Retention: 67% of full-time freshmen returned.

FACULTY

Total: 311, 83% full-time, 54% with terminal degrees.

Student/faculty ratio: 20:1.

ACADEMICS
Calendar: semesters. *Degrees:* certificates, associate, bachelor's, master's, post-master's, and postbachelor's certificates.

Special study options: academic remediation for entering students, accelerated degree program, adult/continuing education programs, advanced placement credit, cooperative education, distance learning, double majors, English as a second language, honors programs, independent study, internships, off-campus study, part-time degree program, services for LD students, study abroad, summer session for credit.

Computers: 285 computers/terminals are available on campus for general student use. Students can access the following: campus intranet, free student e-mail accounts, online (class) grades, online (class) registration, online (class) schedules, course management system—Moodle. Campuswide network is available. 100% of college-owned or -operated housing units are wired for high-speed Internet access. Wireless service is available via entire campus.

STUDENT LIFE
Housing options: on-campus residence required for freshman year; coed. Campus housing is university owned. Freshman campus housing is guaranteed.

Activities and organizations: drama/theater group, student-run newspaper, radio and television station, choral group, marching band, Student Government Association, Student Programming Association, Residence Hall Association, Food Advisory Association, national fraternities, national sororities.

Athletics Member NCAA. All Division I except football (Division I-AA). ***Intercollegiate sports:*** baseball M(s), basketball M(s)/W(s), cross-country running M(s)/W(s), golf M(s), soccer W(s), softball W(s), tennis M/W(s), track and field W(s), volleyball W(s). ***Intramural sports:*** basketball M/W, football M/W, softball M/W, volleyball M/W.

Campus security: 24-hour emergency response devices and patrols, student patrols, late-night transport/escort service.

Student services: health clinic, personal/psychological counseling, women's center, legal services.

COSTS & FINANCIAL AID
Costs (2014–15) ***Tuition:*** state resident $4992 full-time; nonresident $15,169 full-time. Full-time tuition and fees vary according to program. Part-time tuition and fees vary according to course load and program. ***Required fees:*** $2312 full-time. ***Room and board:*** $8580; room only: $5400. Room and board charges vary according to board plan, housing facility, and location. ***Payment plans:*** installment, deferred payment. ***Waivers:*** employees or children of employees.

Financial Aid Of all full-time matriculated undergraduates who enrolled in 2012, 4,146 applied for aid, 3,070 were judged to have need, 476 had their need fully met. In 2012, 371 non-need-based awards were made. ***Average percent of need met:*** 59. ***Average financial aid package:*** $9075. ***Average need-based loan:*** $2733. ***Average need-based gift aid:*** $6218. ***Average non-need-based aid:*** $4004. ***Average indebtedness upon graduation:*** $30,069. ***Financial aid deadline:*** 6/30.

APPLYING
Standardized Tests *Required:* SAT or ACT (for admission).

Options: electronic application, early admission, deferred entrance.

Application fee: $20.

Required: high school transcript, minimum 2.0 GPA, Minimum State Core Curriculum (19 units) and 2.0 Minimum Overall GPA and no more than 1 developmental need and (Core curriculum GPA 2.0 or higher or ACT Composite 20).

Application deadlines: rolling (freshmen), rolling (transfers).

Notification: 9/1 (freshmen), continuous until 8/28 (transfers).

CONTACT
Mrs. Becky L. Durocher, Director of Admissions, Nicholls State University, PO Box 2004-NSU, Thibodaux, LA 70310. *Phone:* 985-448-4507. *Toll-free phone:* 877-NICHOLLS. *Fax:* 985-448-4929. *E-mail:* nicholls@nicholls.edu.

Northwestern State University of Louisiana

Natchitoches, Louisiana

http://www.nsula.edu/

- **State-supported** comprehensive, founded 1884, part of University of Louisiana System
- **Small-town** 916-acre campus
- **Endowment** $12.4 million
- **Coed**
- **Moderately difficult** entrance level

FACULTY
Student/faculty ratio: 19:1.

ACADEMICS
Calendar: semesters. *Degrees:* associate, bachelor's, master's, doctoral, post-master's, and postbachelor's certificates.

STUDENT LIFE
Housing options: on-campus residence required through junior year; coed, special housing for students with disabilities. Campus housing is university owned and is provided by a third party. Freshman applicants given priority for college housing.

Activities and organizations: drama/theater group, student-run newspaper, radio and television station, choral group, marching band, Student Activities Board, Student Government Associate, College Panhellenic Council, national fraternities, national sororities.

Athletics Member NCAA. All Division I except football (Division I-AA).

Campus security: 24-hour emergency response devices and patrols, student patrols, late-night transport/escort service, controlled dormitory access.

Student services: health clinic, personal/psychological counseling.

COSTS & FINANCIAL AID
Costs (2014–15) ***Tuition:*** state resident $4934 full-time; nonresident $15,722 full-time. Full-time tuition and fees vary according to course load and location. Part-time tuition and fees vary according to course load and location. ***Required fees:*** $1873 full-time. ***Room and board:*** $8397; room only: $5223. Room and board charges vary according to board plan, housing facility, and location.

Financial Aid Of all full-time matriculated undergraduates who enrolled in 2012, 4,793 applied for aid, 4,045 were judged to have need, 125 had their need fully met. 167 Federal Work-Study jobs (averaging $2359). 204 state and other part-time jobs (averaging $1961). In 2012, 423 non-need-based awards were made. ***Average percent of need met:*** 64. ***Average financial aid package:*** $10,000. ***Average need-based loan:*** $3943. ***Average need-based gift aid:*** $6483. ***Average non-need-based aid:*** $3170. ***Average indebtedness upon graduation:*** $22,953.

APPLYING
Standardized Tests *Required:* SAT or ACT (for admission).

Options: electronic application, deferred entrance.

Application fee: $20.

Required: high school transcript, minimum 2.0 GPA, college preparatory curriculum.

CONTACT
Ms. Jana Lucky, Director of University Recruiting, Northwestern State University of Louisiana, 175 Sam Sibley Drive, Recruiting Office, Student Services Center, 1st Floor, Natchitoches, LA 71497. *Phone:* 318-357-4503. *Toll-free phone:* 800-327-1903. *Fax:* 318-357-5567. *E-mail:* recruiting@nsula.edu.

Our Lady of the Lake College

Baton Rouge, Louisiana

http://www.ololcollege.edu/

- **Independent Roman Catholic** comprehensive, founded 1990
- **Suburban** 5-acre campus with easy access to New Orleans
- **Endowment** $7.5 million
- **Coed**
- **Minimally difficult** entrance level

ACADEMICS
Calendar: semesters. *Degrees:* certificates, diplomas, associate, bachelor's, master's, and postbachelor's certificates.

STUDENT LIFE
Housing options: college housing not available.

Activities and organizations: Student Government Association, Cultural Arts Association, Christian Fellowship Association, Mathematics/Science Association.

Campus security: 24-hour patrols.

Student services: health clinic, personal/psychological counseling.

COSTS & FINANCIAL AID
Costs (2014–15) ***Tuition:*** $10,134 full-time, $422 per credit hour part-time. Full-time tuition and fees vary according to course load and program. Part-time tuition and fees vary according to course load and program. ***Required fees:*** $1016 full-time, $23 per credit hour part-time, $135 per term part-time.

Financial Aid Of all full-time matriculated undergraduates who enrolled in 2008, 684 applied for aid, 546 were judged to have need, 10 had their need fully met. ***Average financial aid package:*** $5175. ***Average need-based loan:*** $3664. ***Average need-based gift aid:*** $2486. ***Average indebtedness upon graduation:*** $12,019.

APPLYING
Standardized Tests *Required:* SAT or ACT (for admission), ACT ASSET (for admission).

Options: electronic application, early admission, deferred entrance.

Application fee: $35.

Required: high school transcript, minimum 2.5 GPA.

CONTACT
Mrs. Rebecca Cannon, Director of Enrollment Management, Our Lady of the Lake College, 7434 Perkins Road, Baton Rouge, LA 70808. *Phone:* 225-768-1718. *E-mail:* admissions@ololcollege.edu.

Saint Joseph Seminary College

Saint Benedict, Louisiana

http://www.sjasc.edu/

- **Independent Roman Catholic** 4-year, founded 1891
- **Rural** 1800-acre campus with easy access to New Orleans
- **Endowment** $1.1 million
- **Men only**
- **Minimally difficult** entrance level

FACULTY
Student/faculty ratio: 3:1.

ACADEMICS
Calendar: semesters. *Degrees:* bachelor's (Religious Studies Institute is coed).

STUDENT LIFE
Housing options: on-campus residence required through senior year; men-only. Campus housing is university owned. Freshman campus housing is guaranteed.

Activities and organizations: drama/theater group, student-run newspaper, choral group, student government, yearbook.

Campus security: 24-hour emergency response devices, controlled dormitory access, entrance gate.

Student services: health clinic, personal/psychological counseling.

COSTS
Costs (2014–15) ***One-time required fee:*** $350. ***Comprehensive fee:*** $30,070 includes full-time tuition ($14,320), mandatory fees ($1920), and room and board ($13,830). Full-time tuition and fees vary according to student level. Part-time tuition: $260 per semester hour. Part-time tuition and fees vary according to course load. ***Required fees:*** $600 per year part-time. ***College room only:*** $7266.

APPLYING
Standardized Tests *Required:* ACT (for admission).

Options: early admission, deferred entrance.

Required: high school transcript, minimum 2.0 GPA.

CONTACT
Saint Joseph Seminary College, 75376 River Road, St. Benedict, LA 70457. *Phone:* 985-867-2273. *Fax:* 985-327-1085. *E-mail:* registrar@sjasc.edu.

Southeastern Louisiana University

Hammond, Louisiana

http://www.selu.edu/

- **State-supported** comprehensive, founded 1925, part of University of Louisiana System
- **Small-town** 375-acre campus with easy access to New Orleans
- **Coed** 13,376 undergraduate students, 73% full-time, 61% women, 39% men
- **Moderately difficult** entrance level, 87% of applicants were admitted

UNDERGRAD STUDENTS
9,732 full-time, 3,644 part-time. 2% are from out of state; 15% Black or African American, non-Hispanic/Latino; 6% Hispanic/Latino; 0.9% Asian, non-Hispanic/Latino; 0.1% Native Hawaiian or other Pacific Islander, non-Hispanic/Latino; 0.3% American Indian or Alaska Native, non-Hispanic/Latino; 6% Two or more races, non-Hispanic/Latino; 6% Race/ethnicity unknown; 2% international; 4% transferred in; 21% live on campus.

Freshmen
Admission: 3,725 applied, 3,229 admitted, 2,428 enrolled. ***Average high school GPA:*** 3.17. ***Test scores:*** ACT scores over 18: 94%; ACT scores over 24: 29%; ACT scores over 30: 2%.

Retention: 62% of full-time freshmen returned.

FACULTY
Total: 610, 81% full-time, 64% with terminal degrees.

Student/faculty ratio: 20:1.

ACADEMICS
Calendar: semesters. *Degrees:* associate, bachelor's, master's, doctoral, post-master's, and postbachelor's certificates.

Special study options: adult/continuing education programs, advanced placement credit, distance learning, double majors, English as a second language, honors programs, independent study, internships, off-campus study, part-time degree program, services for LD students, study abroad, summer session for credit. ***ROTC:*** Army (c).

Computers: 1,031 computers/terminals and 600 ports are available on campus for general student use. Students can access the following: campus intranet, computer help desk, free student e-mail accounts, online (class) grades, online (class) registration, online (class) schedules, campus Webmail, student newspaper, transcripts, bookstore. Campuswide network is available. 100% of college-owned or -operated housing units are wired for high-speed Internet access. Wireless service is available via classrooms, computer centers, computer labs, dorm rooms, learning centers, libraries, student centers.

STUDENT LIFE
Housing options: on-campus residence required through sophomore year; coed, women-only, special housing for students with disabilities. Campus housing is university owned.

Activities and organizations: drama/theater group, student-run newspaper, radio and television station, choral group, marching band, Catholic Student Association, National Society of Collegiate Scholars, Sigma Alpha Lambda, Student Nurses' Association, national fraternities, national sororities.

Athletics Member NCAA. All Division I except football (Division I-AA). ***Intercollegiate sports:*** baseball M(s), basketball M(s)/W(s), cross-country running M(s)/W(s), golf M(s), soccer W(s), softball W(s), tennis W(s), track and field M(s)/W(s), volleyball W(s). ***Intramural sports:*** baseball M/W, basketball M/W, football M/W, racquetball M/W, rugby M(c), soccer M/W, softball M/W, tennis M/W, volleyball M/W, weight lifting M/W.

Campus security: 24-hour emergency response devices and patrols, student patrols, late-night transport/escort service, controlled dormitory access, video cameras, motorist assistance.

Student services: health clinic, personal/psychological counseling.

COSTS & FINANCIAL AID
Costs (2014–15) ***Tuition:*** state resident $4798 full-time, $273 per credit hour part-time; nonresident $17,362 full-time, $796 per credit hour part-time. Full-time tuition and fees vary according to course load. Part-time tuition and fees vary according to course load. ***Required fees:*** $1749 full-time, $273 per credit hour part-time. ***Room and board:*** $7100; room only: $4520. Room and board charges vary according to board plan and housing facility. ***Payment plan:*** installment. ***Waivers:*** employees or children of employees.

Financial Aid Of all full-time matriculated undergraduates who enrolled in 2013, 7,976 applied for aid, 6,054 were judged to have need, 960 had their need fully met. 165 Federal Work-Study jobs (averaging $2045). 1,074 state and other part-time jobs (averaging $2163). In 2013, 911 non-need-based awards were made. ***Average financial aid package:*** $9093. ***Average need-based loan:*** $3778. ***Average need-based gift aid:*** $4916. ***Average non-need-based aid:*** $3210. ***Average indebtedness upon graduation:*** $18,433.

APPLYING
Standardized Tests *Required:* SAT or ACT (for admission).

Options: electronic application, early admission, deferred entrance.

Application fee: $20.

Required: proof of immunization required for all, college transcripts and statement of good standing required for some. ***Required for some:*** high school transcript.

Application deadlines: 8/1 (freshmen), 8/1 (out-of-state freshmen), 8/1 (transfers).

Notification: continuous (freshmen), continuous (out-of-state freshmen), continuous (transfers).

CONTACT
Southeastern Louisiana University, LA. *Phone:* 985-549-5629. *Toll-free phone:* 800-222-7358.

Tulane University

New Orleans, Louisiana

http://www.tulane.edu/

- **Independent** university, founded 1834
- **Urban** 110-acre campus
- **Endowment** $1.4 billion
- **Coed** 8,353 undergraduate students, 79% full-time, 58% women, 42% men
- **Very difficult** entrance level, 28% of applicants were admitted

UNDERGRAD STUDENTS
6,606 full-time, 1,747 part-time. Students come from 53 states and territories; 79 other countries; 87% are from out of state; 9% Black or African American, non-Hispanic/Latino; 6% Hispanic/Latino; 3% Asian, non-Hispanic/Latino; 0.1% Native Hawaiian or other Pacific Islander, non-Hispanic/Latino; 0.3% American Indian or Alaska Native, non-Hispanic/Latino; 3% Two or more races, non-Hispanic/Latino; 4% Race/ethnicity unknown; 3% international; 1% transferred in; 44% live on campus.

Freshmen
Admission: 28,901 applied, 8,078 admitted, 1,647 enrolled. ***Average high school GPA:*** 3.49. ***Test scores:*** SAT critical reading scores over 500: 98%; SAT math scores over 500: 99%; SAT writing scores over 500: 98%; ACT scores over 18: 99%; SAT critical reading scores over 600: 83%; SAT math scores over 600: 88%; SAT writing scores over 600: 90%; ACT scores over 24: 97%; SAT critical reading scores over 700: 30%; SAT math scores over 700: 30%; SAT writing scores over 700: 38%; ACT scores over 30: 65%.

Retention: 92% of full-time freshmen returned.

FACULTY
Total: 1,211, 57% full-time, 75% with terminal degrees.

Student/faculty ratio: 9:1.

ACADEMICS
Calendar: semesters plus 3 summer sessions. *Degrees:* certificates, associate, bachelor's, master's, doctoral, and postbachelor's certificates.

Special study options: accelerated degree program, adult/continuing education programs, advanced placement credit, cooperative education, distance learning, double majors, English as a second language, freshman honors college, honors programs, independent study, internships, off-campus study, part-time degree program, services for LD students, student-designed majors, study abroad, summer session for credit. ***ROTC:*** Army (b), Navy (b), Air Force (b).

Unusual degree programs: 3-2 business administration; public health tropical medicine, science and engineering.

Computers: 556 computers/terminals are available on campus for general student use. Students can access the following: campus intranet, computer help desk, free student e-mail accounts, online (class) grades, online (class) registration, online (class) schedules. Campuswide network is available. 100% of college-owned or -operated housing units are wired for high-speed Internet access. Wireless service is available via entire campus.

STUDENT LIFE
Housing options: on-campus residence required through sophomore year; coed, women-only, special housing for students with disabilities. Campus housing is university owned. Freshman campus housing is guaranteed.

Activities and organizations: drama/theater group, student-run newspaper, radio and television station, choral group, marching band, Community Action Council of Tulane Students (CACTUS), Associated Student Body, Tulane University Campus Programming (TUCP), Association of Club Sports (ACS), National Pan-Hellenic Council, national fraternities, national sororities.

Athletics Member NCAA. All Division I except football (Division I-A). ***Intercollegiate sports:*** baseball M(s), basketball M(s)/W(s), crew M(c)/W(c), cross-country running M(s)/W(s), golf W(s), gymnastics M(c)/W(c), ice hockey M(c)/W(c), lacrosse M(c)/W(c), rugby M(c), sailing M(c)/W(c), soccer M(c)/W(s), swimming and diving M(c)/W(s), tennis M(s)/W(s), track and field M(c)/W(s), volleyball M(c)/W(s), water polo M(c)/W(c). ***Intramural sports:*** baseball M(c), cheerleading M(c)/W(c), crew M(c)/W(c), cross-country running M(c), fencing M(c)/W(c), field hockey M(c)/W(c), gymnastics M(c)/W(c), ice hockey M(c), lacrosse M(c)/W(c), racquetball M(c)/W(c), rock climbing M(c)/W(c), rugby M(c), sailing M(c)/W(c), soccer M(c)/W(c), swimming and diving M(c)/W(c), tennis M(c)/W(c), track and field M(c)/W, ultimate Frisbee M(c)/W(c), volleyball M(c)/W(c), water polo M(c)/W(c).

Campus security: 24-hour emergency response devices and patrols, student patrols, late-night transport/escort service, controlled dormitory access, on and off-campus shuttle service, crime prevention programs, lighted pathways.

Student services: health clinic, personal/psychological counseling, women's center, legal services.

COSTS & FINANCIAL AID
Costs (2014–15) ***Comprehensive fee:*** $60,862 includes full-time tuition ($44,426), mandatory fees ($3880), and room and board ($12,556). ***College room only:*** $7206. Room and board charges vary according to board plan and housing facility. ***Payment plans:*** tuition prepayment, installment. ***Waivers:*** employees or children of employees.

Financial Aid Of all full-time matriculated undergraduates who enrolled in 2013, 3,278 applied for aid, 2,461 were judged to have need, 1,679 had their need fully met. 1,083 Federal Work-Study jobs (averaging $2440). In 2013, 2168 non-need-based awards were made. ***Average percent of need met:*** 93. ***Average financial aid package:*** $34,605. ***Average need-based loan:*** $8600. ***Average need-based gift aid:*** $28,233. ***Average non-need-based aid:*** $21,325. ***Average indebtedness upon graduation:*** $31,653.

APPLYING
Standardized Tests *Required:* SAT or ACT (for admission).

Options: electronic application, early action, deferred entrance.

Required: essay or personal statement, high school transcript, 1 letter of recommendation.

Application deadlines: 1/15 (freshmen), 6/1 (transfers), 11/15 (early action).

Notification: 4/1 (freshmen), 12/15 (early action).

CONTACT
Earl Retif, Vice President for Enrollment Management, Tulane University, Office of Admissions, 210 Gibson Hall, New Orleans, LA 70118. *Phone:* 504-865-5731. *Toll-free phone:* 800-873-9283. *Fax:* 504-862-8715. *E-mail:* undergrad.admission@tulane.edu.

University of Louisiana at Lafayette

Lafayette, Louisiana

http://www.louisiana.edu/

- **State-supported** university, founded 1898, part of University of Louisiana System
- **Urban** 1375-acre campus
- **Endowment** $138.9 million
- **Coed** 15,574 undergraduate students, 80% full-time, 56% women, 44% men
- **Moderately difficult** entrance level, 56% of applicants were admitted

UNDERGRAD STUDENTS

12,498 full-time, 3,076 part-time. Students come from 49 states and territories; 66 other countries; 8% are from out of state; 21% Black or African American, non-Hispanic/Latino; 3% Hispanic/Latino; 2% Asian, non-Hispanic/Latino; 0.1% Native Hawaiian or other Pacific Islander, non-Hispanic/Latino; 0.5% American Indian or Alaska Native, non-Hispanic/Latino; 2% Two or more races, non-Hispanic/Latino; 1% Race/ethnicity unknown; 2% international; 5% transferred in; 18% live on campus.

Freshmen

Admission: 9,386 applied, 5,297 admitted, 2,922 enrolled. ***Average high school GPA:*** 3.3. ***Test scores:*** SAT critical reading scores over 500: 60%; SAT math scores over 500: 71%; ACT scores over 18: 97%; SAT critical reading scores over 600: 20%; SAT math scores over 600: 24%; ACT scores over 24: 38%; SAT critical reading scores over 700: 6%; SAT math scores over 700: 7%; ACT scores over 30: 4%.

Retention: 76% of full-time freshmen returned.

FACULTY

Total: 748, 80% full-time, 53% with terminal degrees.

Student/faculty ratio: 23:1.

ACADEMICS

Calendar: semesters. *Degrees:* bachelor's, master's, doctoral, post-master's, and postbachelor's certificates.

Special study options: academic remediation for entering students, accelerated degree program, adult/continuing education programs, advanced placement credit, cooperative education, distance learning, double majors, honors programs, independent study, internships, part-time degree program, services for LD students, student-designed majors, study abroad, summer session for credit. ***ROTC:*** Army (b).

Computers: 413 computers/terminals and 800 ports are available on campus for general student use. Students can access the following: campus intranet, computer help desk, free student e-mail accounts, online (class) grades, online (class) registration, online (class) schedules. Campuswide network is available. 98% of college-owned or -operated housing units are wired for high-speed Internet access. Wireless service is available via libraries.

STUDENT LIFE

Housing options: on-campus residence required for freshman year; coed, men-only, women-only. Campus housing is university owned. Freshman campus housing is guaranteed.

Activities and organizations: drama/theater group, student-run newspaper, radio station, choral group, marching band, Union Program Council, Chi Alpha, Student Government Association, Greek Council, Newman Club, national fraternities, national sororities.

Athletics Member NCAA. All Division I except football (Division I-A). ***Intercollegiate sports:*** baseball M(s), basketball M(s)/W(s), cross-country running M(s)/W(s), golf M(s), soccer W, softball W(s), tennis M(s)/W(s), track and field M(s)/W(s), volleyball W(s). ***Intramural sports:*** badminton M/W, baseball M, basketball M/W, bowling M/W, football M/W, ice hockey M, lacrosse M, racquetball M/W, rugby M, soccer M, softball M/W, tennis M/W, ultimate Frisbee M/W, volleyball M/W, weight lifting M/W.

Campus security: 24-hour emergency response devices and patrols, late-night transport/escort service, controlled dormitory access.

Student services: health clinic, personal/psychological counseling, women's center, legal services.

COSTS & FINANCIAL AID

Costs (2014–15) ***Tuition:*** state resident $4915 full-time, $290 per credit hour part-time; nonresident $17,315 full-time, $764 per credit hour part-time. Full-time tuition and fees vary according to course load. Part-time tuition and fees vary according to course load. ***Required fees:*** $2033 full-time. ***Room and board:*** $8566. Room and board charges vary according to board plan and housing facility. ***Waivers:*** children of alumni and employees or children of employees.

Financial Aid Of all full-time matriculated undergraduates who enrolled in 2013, 9,951 applied for aid, 6,997 were judged to have need, 652 had their need fully met. 510 Federal Work-Study jobs (averaging $1574). 303 state and other part-time jobs (averaging $1419). In 2013, 1082 non-need-based awards were made. ***Average percent of need met:*** 52. ***Average financial aid package:*** $8507. ***Average need-based loan:*** $3697. ***Average need-based gift aid:*** $6609. ***Average non-need-based aid:*** $3050.

APPLYING

Standardized Tests *Required:* SAT or ACT (for admission).

Options: electronic application, early admission, deferred entrance.

Application fee: $25.

Required: high school transcript, minimum 2.0 GPA, core requirements, no remedial courses.

Application deadlines: rolling (freshmen), rolling (transfers).

CONTACT

Mr. Andy Benoit Jr., Assistant Vice President for Enrollment Management and Director of Enrollment Services and Recruitment, University of Louisiana at Lafayette, PO Drawer 41210, Lafayette, LA 70504. *Phone:* 337-482-6473. *Toll-free phone:* 800-752-6553. *Fax:* 337-482-1317. *E-mail:* admissions@louisiana.edu.

University of Louisiana at Monroe

Monroe, Louisiana

http://www.ulm.edu/

- **State-supported** university, founded 1931, part of University of Louisiana System
- **Urban** 238-acre campus
- **Coed**
- **Moderately difficult** entrance level

FACULTY

Student/faculty ratio: 23:1.

ACADEMICS

Calendar: semesters. *Degrees:* associate, bachelor's, master's, doctoral, post-master's, and postbachelor's certificates.

STUDENT LIFE

Housing options: on-campus residence required through sophomore year; coed, men-only, women-only. Campus housing is university owned and leased by the school. Freshman applicants given priority for college housing.

Activities and organizations: drama/theater group, student-run newspaper, radio station, marching band, Maroon Platoon, Alpha Lambda Delta, Louisiana Pharmacist Alliance, Association for Students in Kinesiology, Pre-Pharmacy Organization/Sound of Today, national fraternities, national sororities.

Athletics Member NCAA. All Division I except football (Division I-A).

Campus security: 24-hour emergency response devices and patrols, student patrols, late-night transport/escort service.

Student services: health clinic, personal/psychological counseling.

COSTS

Costs (2014–15) ***Tuition:*** state resident $4986 full-time, $314 per credit hour part-time; nonresident $17,144 full-time, $314 per credit hour part-time. Full-time tuition and fees vary according to course load, degree level, and program. Part-time tuition and fees vary according to course load, degree level, and program. ***Required fees:*** $1977 full-time, $244 per credit hour part-time. ***Room and board:*** $6830; room only: $4030. Room and board charges vary according to board plan and housing facility.

APPLYING

Standardized Tests *Required:* SAT or ACT (for admission).

Options: electronic application, early admission.

Application fee: $20.

Required: high school transcript.

CONTACT

Ms. Diana Gooden, Coordinator of Enrollment Services, University of Louisiana at Monroe, Office of Recruitment and Admissions, University Library, 202, Monroe, LA 71209. *Phone:* 318-342-3095. *Toll-free phone:* 800-372-5127. *Fax:* 318-342-1915. *E-mail:* gooden@ulm.edu.

University of New Orleans

New Orleans, Louisiana

http://www.uno.edu/

- **State-supported** university, founded 1958, part of University of Louisiana System
- **Urban** 345-acre campus
- **Endowment** $23.3 million
- **Coed** 7,152 undergraduate students, 74% full-time, 51% women, 49% men
- **Moderately difficult** entrance level, 44% of applicants were admitted

UNDERGRAD STUDENTS

5,280 full-time, 1,872 part-time. Students come from 42 states and territories; 60 other countries; 5% are from out of state; 16% Black or African American, non-Hispanic/Latino; 10% Hispanic/Latino; 8% Asian, non-Hispanic/Latino; 0.4% American Indian or Alaska Native, non-Hispanic/Latino; 4% Two or more races, non-Hispanic/Latino; 3% Race/ethnicity unknown; 5% international; 12% transferred in; 10% live on campus.

Freshmen

Admission: 3,828 applied, 1,674 admitted, 865 enrolled. ***Average high school GPA:*** 3.25. ***Test scores:*** SAT critical reading scores over 500: 77%; SAT math scores over 500: 78%; ACT scores over 18: 96%; SAT critical reading scores over 600: 39%; SAT math scores over 600: 45%; ACT scores over 24: 39%; SAT critical reading scores over 700: 7%; SAT math scores over 700: 19%; ACT scores over 30: 5%.

Retention: 69% of full-time freshmen returned.

FACULTY

Total: 397, 71% full-time, 68% with terminal degrees.

Student/faculty ratio: 21:1.

ACADEMICS

Calendar: semesters. *Degrees:* bachelor's, master's, doctoral, post-master's, and postbachelor's certificates.

Special study options: advanced placement credit, cooperative education, distance learning, double majors, English as a second language, honors programs, independent study, internships, off-campus study, part-time degree program, services for LD students, study abroad, summer session for credit. ***ROTC:*** Army (c), Navy (c), Air Force (c).

Unusual degree programs: 3-2 engineering with Xavier University of Louisiana; Southern University at New Orleans; Loyola University, New Orleans; Dillard University.

Computers: 1,208 computers/terminals and 1,191 ports are available on campus for general student use. Students can access the following: campus intranet, computer help desk, free student e-mail accounts, online (class) grades, online (class) registration, online (class) schedules, classes in Moodle. Campuswide network is available. 100% of college-owned or -operated housing units are wired for high-speed Internet access. Wireless service is available via entire campus.

STUDENT LIFE

Housing options: coed, special housing for students with disabilities. Campus housing is university owned and is provided by a third party.

Activities and organizations: drama/theater group, student-run newspaper, choral group, Student Activities Council, Student Government, International Student Organization, Vietnamese American Student Association, Greek Life, national fraternities, national sororities.

Athletics Member NCAA. All Division I. ***Intercollegiate sports:*** baseball M(s), basketball M(s)/W(s), cross-country running M(s)/W(s), golf M(s), tennis M(s)/W(s), track and field M(s)/W(s), volleyball W(s). ***Intramural sports:*** basketball M/W, football M/W, racquetball M/W, rugby M(c), sailing M(c)/W(c), soccer M/W, swimming and diving M(c)/W(c), table tennis M(c)/W(c), weight lifting M(c)/W(c), wrestling M(c).

Campus security: 24-hour emergency response devices and patrols, late-night transport/escort service, controlled dormitory access.

Student services: health clinic, personal/psychological counseling, women's center, legal services.

COSTS & FINANCIAL AID

Costs (2014–15) ***Tuition:*** state resident $5537 full-time; nonresident $19,147 full-time. Full-time tuition and fees vary according to course load. Part-time tuition and fees vary according to course load. ***Required fees:*** $1945 full-time. ***Room and board:*** $9274. Room and board charges vary according to board plan and housing facility. ***Waivers:*** senior citizens and employees or children of employees.

Financial Aid Of all full-time matriculated undergraduates who enrolled in 2014, 4,410 applied for aid, 3,808 were judged to have need, 226 had their need fully met. 202 Federal Work-Study jobs (averaging $2001). 317 state and other part-time jobs (averaging $1666). In 2014, 8 non-need-based awards were made. ***Average percent of need met:*** 57. ***Average financial aid package:*** $9359. ***Average need-based loan:*** $4079. ***Average need-based gift aid:*** $5575. ***Average non-need-based aid:*** $1450. ***Average indebtedness upon graduation:*** $18,850.

APPLYING

Standardized Tests *Required:* SAT or ACT (for admission).

Options: electronic application, early admission, deferred entrance.

Application fee: $20.

Required: high school transcript, Core Requirements (19 units); ACT Composite Score of 23 or greater (SAT 1060) or High School Core GPA of 2.5 or greater.

Application deadlines: 7/25 (freshmen), 7/25 (out-of-state freshmen), 7/25 (transfers).

CONTACT

Mr. Carlos Gooden, Assistant Director for Recruitment, University of New Orleans, Privateer Enrollment Center, University of New Orleans, 105 Earl K. Long Library, New Orleans, LA 70148. *Phone:* 504-280-6598. *Toll-free phone:* 800-256-5866. *Fax:* 504-280-5522. *E-mail:* cagooden@uno.edu.

Xavier University of Louisiana

New Orleans, Louisiana

http://www.xula.edu/

- **Independent Roman Catholic** comprehensive, founded 1925
- **Urban** 23-acre campus
- **Coed** 2,359 undergraduate students, 95% full-time, 73% women, 27% men
- **Moderately difficult** entrance level, 66% of applicants were admitted

UNDERGRAD STUDENTS

2,238 full-time, 121 part-time. 49% are from out of state; 77% Black or African American, non-Hispanic/Latino; 3% Hispanic/Latino; 10% Asian, non-Hispanic/Latino; 0.1% American Indian or Alaska Native, non-Hispanic/Latino; 3% Two or more races, non-Hispanic/Latino; 0.9% Race/ethnicity unknown; 2% international; 5% transferred in; 47% live on campus.

Freshmen

Admission: 3,963 applied, 2,615 admitted, 579 enrolled. ***Average high school GPA:*** 3.41. ***Test scores:*** SAT critical reading scores over 500: 48%; SAT math scores over 500: 50%; SAT writing scores over 500: 41%; ACT scores over 18: 95%; SAT critical reading scores over 600: 12%; SAT math scores over 600: 13%; SAT writing scores over 600: 7%; ACT scores over 24: 39%; SAT math scores over 700: 1%; SAT writing scores over 700: 1%; ACT scores over 30: 2%.

Retention: 71% of full-time freshmen returned.

FACULTY

Total: 245, 89% full-time, 90% with terminal degrees.

Student/faculty ratio: 14:1.

ACADEMICS

Calendar: semesters. *Degrees:* bachelor's, master's, and doctoral.

Special study options: academic remediation for entering students, accelerated degree program, adult/continuing education programs, advanced placement credit, cooperative education, double majors, freshman honors college, honors programs, independent study, internships, off-campus study, part-time degree program, services for LD students, study abroad, summer session for credit. ***ROTC:*** Army (c), Navy (c), Air Force (c).

Unusual degree programs: 3-2 business administration with Tulane University; engineering with Tulane University, University of Maryland, University of New Orleans, Georgia Institute of Technology, University of Wisconsin-Madison, Morgan State University, Southern University and Agricultural and Mechanical College; biostatistics with Louisiana State University Medical Center.

Computers: Students can access the following: computer help desk, free student e-mail accounts, online (class) grades, online (class) registration, online (class) schedules. Campuswide network is available. 100% of college-owned or -operated housing units are wired for high-speed Internet access. Wireless service is available via entire campus.

STUDENT LIFE

Housing options: coed, men-only, women-only, special housing for students with disabilities. Campus housing is university owned. Freshman applicants given priority for college housing.

Activities and organizations: drama/theater group, student-run newspaper, television station, choral group, Mobilization at Xavier, AWARE, NAACP, California Club, Beta Beta Beta (Biology Club), national fraternities, national sororities.

Athletics Member NAIA. ***Intercollegiate sports:*** basketball M(s)/W(s), cross-country running M/W, tennis M(s)/W(s). ***Intramural sports:*** badminton M/W, basketball M/W, football M/W, golf M/W, softball M/W, swimming and diving M/W, table tennis M/W, tennis M/W, track and field M/W, volleyball M/W.

Campus security: 24-hour emergency response devices and patrols, student patrols, bicycle patrols.

Student services: health clinic, personal/psychological counseling.

COSTS & FINANCIAL AID

Costs (2014–15) ***One-time required fee:*** $150. ***Comprehensive fee:*** $30,052 includes full-time tuition ($19,100), mandatory fees ($2452), and room and board ($8500). Part-time tuition: $800 per credit hour. Part-time tuition and fees vary according to course load. ***Required fees:*** $150 per term part-time. ***Room and board:*** Room and board charges vary according to housing facility. ***Payment plan:*** installment. ***Waivers:*** employees or children of employees.

Financial Aid Of all full-time matriculated undergraduates who enrolled in 2012, 2,265 applied for aid, 1,985 were judged to have need, 11 had their need fully met. In 2012, 81 non-need-based awards were made. ***Average percent of need met:*** 14. ***Average financial aid package:*** $17,678. ***Average need-based loan:*** $4715. ***Average need-based gift aid:*** $5783. ***Average non-need-based aid:*** $11,446. ***Average indebtedness upon graduation:*** $27,338.

APPLYING

Standardized Tests *Required:* SAT or ACT (for admission).

Options: electronic application.

Application fee: $25.

Required: high school transcript, minimum 2.0 GPA, 1 letter of recommendation. ***Required for some:*** interview.

CONTACT

Mr. Winston Brown, Dean of Admissions, Xavier University of Louisiana, 7325 Palmetto Street, New Orleans, LA 70125. *Phone:* 504-520-7388. *Toll-free phone:* 877-XAVIERU. *Fax:* 504-520-7941. *E-mail:* apply@xula.edu.

MAINE

Bates College
Lewiston, Maine
http://www.bates.edu/

- **Independent** 4-year, founded 1855
- **Small-town** 133-acre campus
- **Endowment** $263.9 million
- **Coed** 1,773 undergraduate students, 100% full-time, 50% women, 50% men
- **Very difficult** entrance level, 25% of applicants were admitted

UNDERGRAD STUDENTS

1,773 full-time. Students come from 46 states and territories; 56 other countries; 89% are from out of state; 5% Black or African American, non-Hispanic/Latino; 7% Hispanic/Latino; 5% Asian, non-Hispanic/Latino; 0.2% American Indian or Alaska Native, non-Hispanic/Latino; 4% Two or more races, non-Hispanic/Latino; 0.8% Race/ethnicity unknown; 7% international; 0.3% transferred in; 91% live on campus.

Freshmen

Admission: 5,044 applied, 1,282 admitted, 491 enrolled. ***Test scores:*** SAT critical reading scores over 500: 100%; SAT math scores over 500: 100%; SAT writing scores over 500: 99%; ACT scores over 18: 100%; SAT critical reading scores over 600: 92%; SAT math scores over 600: 91%; SAT writing scores over 600: 89%; ACT scores over 24: 99%; SAT critical reading scores over 700: 32%; SAT math scores over 700: 34%; SAT writing scores over 700: 40%; ACT scores over 30: 75%.

Retention: 95% of full-time freshmen returned.

FACULTY

Total: 187, 87% full-time, 89% with terminal degrees.

Student/faculty ratio: 10:1.

ACADEMICS

Calendar: 4-4-1. *Degree:* bachelor's.

Special study options: accelerated degree program, advanced placement credit, cooperative education, double majors, honors programs, independent study, internships, off-campus study, services for LD students, student-designed majors, study abroad.

Unusual degree programs: 3-2 engineering with Columbia University, Rensselaer Polytechnic Institute, Case Western Reserve University, Washington University in St. Louis, Dartmouth College.

Computers: 400 computers/terminals and 2,075 ports are available on campus for general student use. Students can access the following: computer help desk, free student e-mail accounts, online (class) grades, online (class) registration, online (class) schedules, course web pages; Google apps for education; Moodle and other web-based services; 200+ software applications for learning, teaching and research; available online: course evaluation, transcripts, major declaration, degree audit, financial records. Campuswide network is available. 100% of college-owned or -operated housing units are wired for high-speed Internet access. Wireless service is available via classrooms, computer labs, dorm rooms, learning centers, libraries, student centers.

STUDENT LIFE

Housing options: on-campus residence required through senior year; coed, men-only, women-only. Campus housing is university owned. Freshman campus housing is guaranteed.

Activities and organizations: drama/theater group, student-run newspaper, radio station, choral group, Outing Club (outdoor recreation), International Club, Chase Hall Committee (student activities planning), Representative Assembly, WRBC (student radio station).

Athletics Member NCAA. All Division III. ***Intercollegiate sports:*** baseball M, basketball M/W, crew M/W, cross-country running M/W, equestrian sports M(c)/W(c), fencing M(c)/W(c), field hockey W, football M, golf M/W, ice hockey M(c)/W(c), lacrosse M/W, rugby M(c)/W(c), sailing M(c)/W(c), skiing (cross-country) M/W, skiing (downhill) M/W, soccer M/W, softball W, squash M/W, swimming and diving M/W, tennis M/W, track and field M/W, ultimate Frisbee M(c)/W(c), volleyball M(c)/W, water polo M(c)/W(c). ***Intramural sports:*** basketball M/W, bowling M/W, ice hockey M/W, racquetball M/W, soccer M/W, softball M/W, squash M/W, tennis M/W, volleyball M/W.

Campus security: 24-hour emergency response devices and patrols, student patrols, late-night transport/escort service, controlled dormitory access, emergency contact/notification system.

Student services: health clinic, personal/psychological counseling, women's center.

COSTS & FINANCIAL AID

Costs (2014–15) ***Comprehensive fee:*** $60,720. ***Payment plans:*** tuition prepayment, installment. ***Waivers:*** employees or children of employees.

Financial Aid Of all full-time matriculated undergraduates who enrolled in 2014, 876 applied for aid, 781 were judged to have need, 781 had their need fully met. 465 Federal Work-Study jobs (averaging $1774). 289 state and other part-time jobs (averaging $1749). ***Average percent of need met:*** 100. ***Average financial aid package:*** $42,718. ***Average need-based loan:*** $3169. ***Average need-based gift aid:*** $38,921. ***Average indebtedness upon graduation:*** $18,929. ***Financial aid deadline:*** 2/15.

APPLYING

Options: electronic application, early admission, early decision, deferred entrance.

Application fee: $60.

Required: essay or personal statement, high school transcript, 3 letters of recommendation. ***Recommended:*** interview.

Application deadlines: 1/1 (freshmen), 3/1 (transfers).

Early decision deadline: 11/15 (for plan 1), 1/1 (for plan 2).

Notification: 4/1 (freshmen), 6/1 (transfers), 12/20 (early decision plan 1), 2/15 (early decision plan 2).

CONTACT

Leigh Weisenburger, Dean of Admission and Financial Aid, Bates College, 23 Campus Ave, Lindholm House, Bates College, Lewiston, ME 04240-6028. *Phone:* 855-228-3755. *Toll-free phone:* 855-228-3755. *Fax:* 207-786-6025. *E-mail:* admission@bates.edu.

Bowdoin College

Brunswick, Maine

http://www.bowdoin.edu/

- **Independent** 4-year, founded 1794
- **Small-town** 207-acre campus with easy access to Portland
- **Endowment** $1.2 billion
- **Coed** 1,805 undergraduate students, 100% full-time, 50% women, 50% men
- **Most difficult** entrance level, 15% of applicants were admitted

UNDERGRAD STUDENTS

1,802 full-time, 3 part-time. Students come from 50 states and territories; 28 other countries; 89% are from out of state; 5% Black or African American, non-Hispanic/Latino; 13% Hispanic/Latino; 6% Asian, non-Hispanic/Latino; 0.1% American Indian or Alaska Native, non-Hispanic/Latino; 7% Two or more races, non-Hispanic/Latino; 0.6% Race/ethnicity unknown; 5% international; 0.1% transferred in; 92% live on campus.

Freshmen

Admission: 6,935 applied, 1,034 admitted, 501 enrolled. ***Average high school GPA:*** 3.8. ***Test scores:*** SAT critical reading scores over 500: 100%; SAT math scores over 500: 100%; SAT writing scores over 500: 100%; ACT scores over 18: 100%; SAT critical reading scores over 600: 97%; SAT math scores over 600: 99%; SAT writing scores over 600: 97%; ACT scores over 24: 100%; SAT critical reading scores over 700: 70%; SAT math scores over 700: 67%; SAT writing scores over 700: 68%; ACT scores over 30: 90%.

Retention: 98% of full-time freshmen returned.

FACULTY

Total: 235, 80% full-time, 97% with terminal degrees.

Student/faculty ratio: 9:1.

ACADEMICS

Calendar: semesters. *Degree:* bachelor's.

Special study options: accelerated degree program, advanced placement credit, double majors, independent study, off-campus study, services for LD students, student-designed majors, study abroad.

Unusual degree programs: 3-2 engineering with California Institute of Technology, Columbia University, Dartmouth College, University of Maine Orono; Law with Columbia University.

Computers: 500 computers/terminals and 650 ports are available on campus for general student use. Students can access the following: campus intranet, computer help desk, free student e-mail accounts, online (class) grades, online (class) registration, online (class) schedules, Training classes on a variety of desktop and academic software, 24/7 software support, free equipment loaner pool: laptops, video and digital cameras, sound and lighting systems, iPads, iPods. Campuswide network is available. 100% of college-owned or -operated housing units are wired for high-speed Internet access. Wireless service is available via entire campus.

STUDENT LIFE

Housing options: on-campus residence required through sophomore year; coed, special housing for students with disabilities. Campus housing is university owned. Freshman campus housing is guaranteed.

Activities and organizations: drama/theater group, student-run newspaper, radio and television station, choral group, Outing Club, Intramural sports, Community Service Volunteer Programs, WBOR 91.1 FM, Bowdoin Orient.

Athletics Member NCAA. All Division III except men's and women's sailing (Division I), men's and women's skiing (cross-country) (Division I), men's and women's squash (Division I). ***Intercollegiate sports:*** baseball M, basketball M/W, crew M(c)/W(c), cross-country running M/W, equestrian sports W(c), fencing M(c)/W(c), field hockey W, football M, golf M/W, ice hockey M/W, lacrosse M/W, rugby M(c)/W, sailing M/W, skiing (cross-country) M/W, soccer M/W, softball W, squash M/W, swimming and diving M/W, tennis M/W, track and field M/W, ultimate Frisbee M(c)/W(c), volleyball M(c)/W, water polo M(c)/W(c). ***Intramural sports:*** badminton M/W, basketball M/W, cheerleading M(c)/W(c), ice hockey M/W, lacrosse M(c)/W(c), rock climbing M(c)/W(c), skiing (cross-country) M(c)/W(c), skiing (downhill) M(c)/W(c), soccer M/W, softball M/W, table tennis M(c)/W(c), tennis M(c)/W(c), volleyball W(c).

Campus security: 24-hour emergency response devices and patrols, late-night transport/escort service, controlled dormitory access, self-defense education, safe ride service, emergency notification system.

Student services: health clinic, personal/psychological counseling, women's center.

COSTS & FINANCIAL AID

Costs (2014–15) ***Comprehensive fee:*** $59,568 includes full-time tuition ($46,354), mandatory fees ($454), and room and board ($12,760). ***College room only:*** $5964. Room and board charges vary according to board plan. ***Payment plans:*** installment, deferred payment. ***Waivers:*** employees or children of employees.

Financial Aid Of all full-time matriculated undergraduates who enrolled in 2013, 911 applied for aid, 803 were judged to have need, 803 had their need fully met. 341 Federal Work-Study jobs (averaging $1839). 391 state and other part-time jobs (averaging $1860). In 2013, 70 non-need-based awards were made. ***Average percent of need met:*** 100. ***Average financial aid package:*** $41,712. ***Average need-based gift aid:*** $40,025. ***Average non-need-based aid:*** $1000. ***Average indebtedness upon graduation:*** $21,292. ***Financial aid deadline:*** 2/15.

APPLYING

Options: electronic application, early admission, early decision, deferred entrance.

Application fee: $60.

Required: essay or personal statement, high school transcript, 3 letters of recommendation. ***Recommended:*** interview.

Application deadlines: 1/1 (freshmen), 1/1 (out-of-state freshmen), 3/1 (transfers).

Early decision deadline: 11/15 (for plan 1), 1/1 (for plan 2).

Notification: 4/5 (freshmen), 4/5 (out-of-state freshmen), 5/1 (transfers), 12/15 (early decision plan 1), 2/15 (early decision plan 2).

CONTACT

Jacob Daly, Assistant Dean of Admissions, Bowdoin College, 5000 College Station, Brunswick, ME 04011-8411. *Phone:* 207-725-3730. *Fax:* 207-725-3101. *E-mail:* admissions@bowdoin.edu.

Colby College

Waterville, Maine

http://www.colby.edu/

- **Independent** 4-year, founded 1813
- **Small-town** 714-acre campus with easy access to Portland
- **Endowment** $740.6 million
- **Coed** 1,847 undergraduate students, 100% full-time, 53% women, 47% men
- **Most difficult** entrance level, 28% of applicants were admitted

UNDERGRAD STUDENTS

1,847 full-time. Students come from 45 states and territories; 74 other countries; 86% are from out of state; 3% Black or African American, non-Hispanic/Latino; 6% Hispanic/Latino; 6% Asian, non-Hispanic/Latino; 0.2% American Indian or Alaska Native, non-Hispanic/Latino; 5% Two or more races, non-Hispanic/Latino; 9% Race/ethnicity unknown; 11% international; 0.8% transferred in; 95% live on campus.

Freshmen

Admission: 5,148 applied, 1,444 admitted, 480 enrolled. ***Test scores:*** SAT critical reading scores over 500: 98%; SAT math scores over 500: 99%; SAT writing scores over 500: 99%; ACT scores over 18: 100%; SAT critical reading scores over 600: 82%; SAT math scores over 600: 85%; SAT writing scores over 600: 85%; ACT scores over 24: 98%; SAT critical reading scores over 700: 31%; SAT math scores over 700: 36%; SAT writing scores over 700: 34%; ACT scores over 30: 62%.

Retention: 92% of full-time freshmen returned.

FACULTY

Total: 205, 83% full-time, 95% with terminal degrees.

Student/faculty ratio: 10:1.

ACADEMICS

Calendar: 4-1-4. *Degree:* bachelor's.

Special study options: advanced placement credit, double majors, honors programs, independent study, internships, off-campus study, services for LD students, student-designed majors, study abroad. ***ROTC:*** Army (c).

Unusual degree programs: 3-2 engineering with Dartmouth College and Columbia University.

Computers: 380 computers/terminals and 7,000 ports are available on campus for general student use. Students can access the following: campus intranet, computer help desk, free student e-mail accounts, online (class) grades, online (class) registration, online (class) schedules, Microsoft Office license for every student computer, Google Apps for Education suite of services, unlimited technology training from Lynda.com, video editing lab, high performance natural science research computing, GIS lab. Campuswide network is available. 100% of college-owned or -operated housing units are wired for high-speed Internet access. Wireless service is available via entire campus.

STUDENT LIFE

Housing options: on-campus residence required through senior year; coed. Campus housing is university owned. Freshman campus housing is guaranteed.

Activities and organizations: drama/theater group, student-run newspaper, radio station, choral group, Outing Club, volunteer center, WMHB-FM (College Radio Station), student government, Powder and Wig (theater).

Athletics Member NCAA. All Division III except men's and women's skiing (cross-country) (Division I), men's and women's skiing (downhill) (Division I). ***Intercollegiate sports:*** archery M(c)/W(c), badminton M(c)/W(c), baseball M, basketball M/W, crew M/W, cross-country running M/W, equestrian sports M(c)/W(c), fencing M(c)/W(c), field hockey W, football M, golf M/W, ice hockey M/W, lacrosse M/W, rugby M(c)/W(c), skiing (cross-country) M/W, skiing (downhill) M/W, soccer M/W, softball W, squash M/W, swimming and diving M/W, tennis M/W, track and field M/W, ultimate Frisbee M(c)/W(c), volleyball M(c)/W, water polo M(c)/W(c). ***Intramural sports:*** basketball M/W, field hockey M/W, football M/W, soccer M/W, softball M/W, tennis M/W.

Campus security: 24-hour emergency response devices and patrols, student patrols, late-night transport/escort service, controlled dormitory access, campus lighting, student emergency response team, self-defense class, property id program, party monitors.

Student services: health clinic, personal/psychological counseling, women's center.

COSTS & FINANCIAL AID

Costs (2014–15) ***Comprehensive fee:*** $59,500 includes full-time tuition ($45,360), mandatory fees ($1990), and room and board ($12,150). Part-time tuition and fees vary according to course load. ***Required fees:*** $1740 per credit hour part-time. ***Room and board:*** Room and board charges vary according to housing facility. ***Payment plan:*** installment. ***Waivers:*** employees or children of employees.

Financial Aid Of all full-time matriculated undergraduates who enrolled in 2014, 915 applied for aid, 712 were judged to have need, 712 had their need fully met. 370 Federal Work-Study jobs (averaging $1706). 146 state and other part-time jobs (averaging $1733). In 2014, 4 non-need-based awards were made. ***Average percent of need met:*** 100. ***Average financial aid package:*** $42,858. ***Average need-based loan:*** $3942. ***Average need-based gift aid:*** $41,033. ***Average non-need-based aid:*** $500. ***Average indebtedness upon graduation:*** $21,958. ***Financial aid deadline:*** 2/1.

APPLYING

Standardized Tests *Required:* Students must submit either (a) SAT, (b) ACT, or (c) three SAT Subject Tests of their choice (for admission). *Required for some:* SAT (for admission), ACT (for admission), SAT or ACT (for admission), SAT and SAT Subject Tests or ACT (for admission), SAT Subject Tests (for admission).

Options: electronic application, early admission, early decision, deferred entrance.

Required: essay or personal statement, high school transcript, 2 letters of recommendation, Must submit SAT, ACT, and/or three Subject Tests. *Recommended:* interview.

Application deadlines: 1/1 (freshmen), 1/1 (out-of-state freshmen), 3/1 (transfers).

Early decision deadline: 11/15 (for plan 1), 1/1 (for plan 2).

Notification: 4/1 (freshmen), 4/1 (out-of-state freshmen), 5/15 (transfers), 12/15 (early decision plan 1), 2/15 (early decision plan 2).

CONTACT

Ms. K.C. Ford, Associate Director of Admissions and Financial Aid, Colby College, 4000 Mayflower Hill, Waterville, ME 04901-8840. *Phone:* 207-859-4800. *Toll-free phone:* 800-723-3032. *Fax:* 207-859-4828. *E-mail:* admissions@colby.edu.

College of the Atlantic

Bar Harbor, Maine

http://www.coa.edu/

- **Independent** comprehensive, founded 1969
- **Small-town** 35-acre campus
- **Endowment** $46.2 million
- **Coed** 378 undergraduate students, 96% full-time, 70% women, 30% men
- **Very difficult** entrance level, 71% of applicants were admitted

UNDERGRAD STUDENTS

364 full-time, 14 part-time. Students come from 40 states and territories; 37 other countries; 80% are from out of state; 0.8% Black or African American, non-Hispanic/Latino; 6% Hispanic/Latino; 2% Asian, non-Hispanic/Latino; 0.5% American Indian or Alaska Native, non-Hispanic/Latino; 1% Two or more races, non-Hispanic/Latino; 5% Race/ethnicity unknown; 16% international; 6% transferred in; 42% live on campus.

Freshmen

Admission: 429 applied, 305 admitted, 79 enrolled. ***Average high school GPA:*** 3.68. ***Test scores:*** SAT critical reading scores over 500: 98%; SAT math scores over 500: 90%; SAT writing scores over 500: 90%; ACT scores over 18: 100%; SAT critical reading scores over 600: 65%; SAT math scores over 600: 39%; SAT writing scores over 600: 54%; ACT scores over 24: 81%; SAT critical reading scores over 700: 21%; SAT math scores over 700: 11%; SAT writing scores over 700: 10%; ACT scores over 30: 24%.

Retention: 81% of full-time freshmen returned.

FACULTY

Total: 50, 58% full-time, 76% with terminal degrees.

Student/faculty ratio: 10:1.

ACADEMICS
Calendar: trimesters. *Degrees:* bachelor's and master's.

Special study options: academic remediation for entering students, accelerated degree program, advanced placement credit, cooperative education, independent study, internships, off-campus study, part-time degree program, services for LD students, student-designed majors, study abroad, summer session for credit.

Computers: 45 computers/terminals and 85 ports are available on campus for general student use. Students can access the following: computer help desk, free student e-mail accounts, online (class) grades, online (class) registration, online (class) schedules, online billing, grades, transcript, financial aid and course management system. Campuswide network is available. 100% of college-owned or -operated housing units are wired for high-speed Internet access. Wireless service is available via entire campus.

STUDENT LIFE
Housing options: on-campus residence required for freshman year; coed. Campus housing is university owned. Freshman campus housing is guaranteed.

Activities and organizations: drama/theater group, student-run newspaper, choral group, All College Meeting, Open Mic, Outdoor Program, Campus Committee on Sustainability, Theater Club.

Athletics ***Intramural sports:*** badminton M/W, basketball M/W, bowling M/W, fencing M/W(c), ice hockey M/W, rock climbing M/W, sailing M/W, skiing (cross-country) M/W, soccer M/W, softball M/W, table tennis M/W, ultimate Frisbee M/W, volleyball M/W, water polo M/W.

Campus security: 24-hour emergency response devices and patrols, late-night transport/escort service.

Student services: health clinic, personal/psychological counseling.

COSTS & FINANCIAL AID
Costs (2015–16) ***Comprehensive fee:*** $51,516 includes full-time tuition ($41,535), mandatory fees ($549), and room and board ($9432). Full-time tuition and fees vary according to course load and degree level. Part-time tuition: $4615 per credit. Part-time tuition and fees vary according to course load and degree level. ***Required fees:*** $183 per term part-time. ***College room only:*** $6000. Room and board charges vary according to board plan. ***Payment plan:*** installment. ***Waivers:*** employees or children of employees.

Financial Aid Of all full-time matriculated undergraduates who enrolled in 2014, 322 applied for aid, 305 were judged to have need, 274 had their need fully met. 245 Federal Work-Study jobs (averaging $2795). 80 state and other part-time jobs (averaging $2884). In 2014, 32 non-need-based awards were made. ***Average percent of need met:*** 92. ***Average financial aid package:*** $37,812. ***Average need-based loan:*** $4722. ***Average need-based gift aid:*** $31,578. ***Average non-need-based aid:*** $9693. ***Average indebtedness upon graduation:*** $23,926.

APPLYING
Standardized Tests *Recommended:* SAT or ACT (for admission).

Options: electronic application, early admission, early decision, deferred entrance.

Application fee: $50.

Required: essay or personal statement, high school transcript, 3 letters of recommendation. ***Required for some:*** interview. ***Recommended:*** minimum 3.0 GPA, interview.

Application deadlines: 2/15 (freshmen), 4/1 (transfers).

Early decision deadline: 12/1 (for plan 1), 1/15 (for plan 2).

Notification: 4/1 (freshmen), 4/25 (transfers), 12/15 (early decision plan 1), 1/30 (early decision plan 2).

CONTACT
Ms. Heather Albert-Knopp, Dean of Admission, College of the Atlantic, 105 Eden Street, Bar Harbor, ME 04609-1198. *Phone:* 207-288-5015. *Toll-free phone:* 800-528-0025. *Fax:* 207-288-4126. *E-mail:* inquiry@coa.edu.

Husson University

Bangor, Maine

http://www.husson.edu/

- **Independent** comprehensive, founded 1898
- **Suburban** 208-acre campus
- **Endowment** $13.4 million
- **Coed** 2,704 undergraduate students, 82% full-time, 54% women, 46% men
- **Moderately difficult** entrance level, 72% of applicants were admitted

UNDERGRAD STUDENTS
2,230 full-time, 474 part-time. Students come from 39 states and territories; 37 other countries; 20% are from out of state; 3% Black or African American, non-Hispanic/Latino; 1% Hispanic/Latino; 0.5% Asian, non-Hispanic/Latino; 0.2% Native Hawaiian or other Pacific Islander, non-Hispanic/Latino; 0.5% American Indian or Alaska Native, non-Hispanic/Latino; 1% Two or more races, non-Hispanic/Latino; 1% Race/ethnicity unknown; 2% international; 7% transferred in; 39% live on campus.

Freshmen
Admission: 2,150 applied, 1,547 admitted, 517 enrolled. ***Average high school GPA:*** 3.22. ***Test scores:*** SAT critical reading scores over 500: 42%; SAT math scores over 500: 41%; SAT writing scores over 500: 37%; ACT scores over 18: 74%; SAT critical reading scores over 600: 4%; SAT math scores over 600: 7%; SAT writing scores over 600: 4%; ACT scores over 24: 11%; SAT math scores over 700: 1%.

Retention: 76% of full-time freshmen returned.

FACULTY
Total: 355, 43% full-time, 41% with terminal degrees.

Student/faculty ratio: 16:1.

ACADEMICS
Calendar: semesters. *Degrees:* certificates, associate, bachelor's, master's, doctoral, post-master's, and postbachelor's certificates.

Special study options: academic remediation for entering students, adult/continuing education programs, advanced placement credit, cooperative education, distance learning, double majors, English as a second language, independent study, internships, off-campus study, part-time degree program, services for LD students, student-designed majors, study abroad, summer session for credit. ***ROTC:*** Army (b), Navy (c).

Unusual degree programs: 3-2 business administration; occupational therapy.

Computers: 116 computers/terminals and 116 ports are available on campus for general student use. Students can access the following: campus intranet, computer help desk, free student e-mail accounts, online (class) grades, online (class) registration, online (class) schedules. Campuswide network is available. 100% of college-owned or -operated housing units are wired for high-speed Internet access. Wireless service is available via entire campus.

STUDENT LIFE
Housing options: on-campus residence required through sophomore year; coed. Campus housing is university owned and leased by the school. Freshman campus housing is guaranteed.

Activities and organizations: drama/theater group, student-run radio station, choral group, Student Government, Organization of Student Nurses, Organization of Physical Therapy Students, Accounting Society, Criminal Justice Club, national sororities.

Athletics Member NCAA. All Division III. ***Intercollegiate sports:*** baseball M, basketball M/W, cross-country running M/W, field hockey W, football M, golf M, lacrosse M/W, soccer M/W, softball W, swimming and diving M/W, track and field W, volleyball W. ***Intramural sports:*** basketball M/W, cheerleading M(c)/W(c), football M/W, ice hockey M(c), lacrosse M/W, soccer M/W, softball M/W, swimming and diving M/W, tennis M/W, ultimate Frisbee M/W, volleyball M/W.

Campus security: 24-hour emergency response devices and patrols, late-night transport/escort service, controlled dormitory access.

Student services: health clinic, personal/psychological counseling.

COSTS & FINANCIAL AID
Costs (2015–16) ***One-time required fee:*** $100. ***Comprehensive fee:*** $24,982 includes full-time tuition ($15,660), mandatory fees ($400), and

room and board ($8922). Full-time tuition and fees vary according to class time and location. Part-time tuition: $522 per credit. Part-time tuition and fees vary according to class time, course load, and location. ***Room and board:*** Room and board charges vary according to board plan and housing facility. ***Payment plans:*** tuition prepayment, installment. ***Waivers:*** senior citizens and employees or children of employees.

Financial Aid Of all full-time matriculated undergraduates who enrolled in 2013, 1,537 applied for aid, 1,376 were judged to have need, 87 had their need fully met. In 2013, 159 non-need-based awards were made. ***Average percent of need met:*** 66. ***Average financial aid package:*** $13,469. ***Average need-based loan:*** $4069. ***Average need-based gift aid:*** $9215. ***Average non-need-based aid:*** $2749. ***Average indebtedness upon graduation:*** $32,343. ***Financial aid deadline:*** 4/15.

APPLYING

Standardized Tests *Required:* SAT or ACT (for admission).

Options: electronic application, deferred entrance.

Application fee: $40.

Required: essay or personal statement, high school transcript, 2 letters of recommendation. ***Required for some:*** GED required for financial aid to be awarded. ***Recommended:*** minimum 3.0 GPA, interview.

Application deadlines: 8/15 (freshmen), 8/15 (transfers).

Notification: continuous (freshmen), continuous (transfers).

CONTACT

Ms. Carlena Bean, Director of Admissions, Husson University, 1 College Circle, Bangor, ME 04401-2999. *Phone:* 207-941-7067. *Toll-free phone:* 800-4-HUSSON. *Fax:* 207-941-7935. *E-mail:* beanc@husson.edu.

Maine Maritime Academy

Castine, Maine

http://www.mainemaritime.edu/

- **State-supported** comprehensive, founded 1941
- **Small-town** 35-acre campus
- **Endowment** $17.7 million
- **Coed, primarily men** 1,037 undergraduate students, 99% full-time, 13% women, 87% men
- **Moderately difficult** entrance level, 79% of applicants were admitted

UNDERGRAD STUDENTS

1,024 full-time, 13 part-time. Students come from 32 states and territories; 3 other countries; 27% are from out of state; 0.5% Black or African American, non-Hispanic/Latino; 0.8% Hispanic/Latino; 0.8% Asian, non-Hispanic/Latino; 0.2% Native Hawaiian or other Pacific Islander, non-Hispanic/Latino; 0.3% American Indian or Alaska Native, non-Hispanic/Latino; 3% Race/ethnicity unknown; 6% transferred in; 78% live on campus.

Freshmen

Admission: 805 applied, 633 admitted, 234 enrolled. ***Test scores:*** SAT critical reading scores over 500: 52%; SAT math scores over 500: 66%; SAT writing scores over 500: 41%; ACT scores over 18: 96%; SAT critical reading scores over 600: 11%; SAT math scores over 600: 19%; SAT writing scores over 600: 7%; ACT scores over 24: 36%; SAT critical reading scores over 700: 1%; SAT math scores over 700: 2%; ACT scores over 30: 4%.

Retention: 79% of full-time freshmen returned.

FACULTY

Total: 93, 70% full-time, 25% with terminal degrees.

Student/faculty ratio: 13:1.

ACADEMICS

Calendar: semesters. *Degrees:* associate, bachelor's, and master's.

Special study options: academic remediation for entering students, adult/continuing education programs, advanced placement credit, cooperative education, double majors, honors programs, independent study, internships, off-campus study, student-designed majors, study abroad. ***ROTC:*** Army (c), Navy (b).

Computers: Students can access the following: computer help desk, free student e-mail accounts, online (class) grades, online (class) registration, online (class) schedules. Campuswide network is available. 100% of college-owned or -operated housing units are wired for high-speed Internet access. Wireless service is available via entire campus.

STUDENT LIFE

Housing options: on-campus residence required through junior year; coed. Campus housing is university owned. Freshman campus housing is guaranteed.

Activities and organizations: drama/theater group, choral group, marching band, Rugby Club, yacht club, Alpha Phi Omega (community service), Chess Club, Drill Team.

Athletics Member NCAA. All Division III. ***Intercollegiate sports:*** basketball M/W, cross-country running M/W, football M, lacrosse M, sailing M/W, soccer M/W, softball W, volleyball W. ***Intramural sports:*** basketball M/W, golf M/W, ice hockey M, racquetball M/W, riflery M/W, rock climbing M, rugby M/W, sailing M/W, skiing (downhill) M/W, softball M/W, squash M/W, swimming and diving M/W, tennis M/W, volleyball M, weight lifting M/W.

Campus security: 24-hour emergency response devices and patrols, late-night transport/escort service, controlled dormitory access.

Student services: health clinic, personal/psychological counseling, women's center.

COSTS & FINANCIAL AID

Costs (2014–15) ***Tuition:*** area resident $14,160 full-time; state resident $9440 full-time; nonresident $21,080 full-time. ***Required fees:*** $2960 full-time. ***Room and board:*** $9830; room only: $3880. ***Payment plan:*** installment. ***Waivers:*** employees or children of employees.

Financial Aid Of all full-time matriculated undergraduates who enrolled in 2013, 866 applied for aid, 751 were judged to have need, 70 had their need fully met. 153 Federal Work-Study jobs (averaging $619). In 2013, 41 non-need-based awards were made. ***Average percent of need met:*** 43. ***Average financial aid package:*** $9245. ***Average need-based loan:*** $4924. ***Average need-based gift aid:*** $6318. ***Average non-need-based aid:*** $4369. ***Average indebtedness upon graduation:*** $40,909.

APPLYING

Standardized Tests *Required:* SAT or ACT (for admission).

Options: electronic application, early admission, early action, deferred entrance.

Required: high school transcript, 1 letter of recommendation. ***Recommended:*** interview.

Application deadlines: rolling (freshmen), 7/1 (transfers), 10/30 (early action).

Notification: 2/1 (early action).

CONTACT

Maine Maritime Academy, Castine, ME 04420. *Phone:* 207-326-2215. *Toll-free phone:* 800-464-6565 (in-state); 800-227-8465 (out-of-state).

Unity College

Unity, Maine

http://www.unity.edu/

- **Independent** 4-year, founded 1965
- **Rural** 265-acre campus
- **Endowment** $14.2 million
- **Coed** 577 undergraduate students, 99% full-time, 51% women, 49% men
- **Moderately difficult** entrance level, 93% of applicants were admitted

UNDERGRAD STUDENTS

574 full-time, 3 part-time. Students come from 33 states and territories; 73% are from out of state; 0.9% Black or African American, non-Hispanic/Latino; 3% Hispanic/Latino; 1% Asian, non-Hispanic/Latino; 0.2% Native Hawaiian or other Pacific Islander, non-Hispanic/Latino; 0.7% American Indian or Alaska Native, non-Hispanic/Latino; 3% Two or more races, non-Hispanic/Latino; 0.2% Race/ethnicity unknown; 7% transferred in; 70% live on campus.

Freshmen

Admission: 638 applied, 594 admitted, 183 enrolled. ***Average high school GPA:*** 3.25. ***Test scores:*** SAT critical reading scores over 500: 65%; SAT math scores over 500: 60%; SAT writing scores over 500: 50%; ACT scores over 18: 23%; SAT critical reading scores over 600: 16%; SAT math scores over 600: 11%; SAT writing scores over 600: 9%; ACT scores over 24: 6%; SAT critical reading scores over 700: 2%.

Retention: 74% of full-time freshmen returned.

FACULTY

Total: 70, 61% full-time, 76% with terminal degrees.

Student/faculty ratio: 11:1.

ACADEMICS

Calendar: semesters. *Degrees:* associate and bachelor's.

Special study options: academic remediation for entering students, accelerated degree program, advanced placement credit, cooperative education, double majors, honors programs, independent study, internships, off-campus study, part-time degree program, services for LD students, study abroad. ***ROTC:*** Army (c).

Unusual degree programs: 3-2 business administration with Husson University in Bangor (ME); MS in criminal justice with Husson University Bangor Maine.

Computers: 100 computers/terminals and 150 ports are available on campus for general student use. Students can access the following: campus intranet, computer help desk, free student e-mail accounts, online (class) grades, online (class) registration, online (class) schedules. Campuswide network is available. 100% of college-owned or -operated housing units are wired for high-speed Internet access. Wireless service is available via entire campus.

STUDENT LIFE

Housing options: on-campus residence required through sophomore year; coed, men-only, women-only, cooperative. Campus housing is university owned. Freshman campus housing is guaranteed.

Activities and organizations: drama/theater group, Woodsmen Team, Ultimate Frisbee, Outing Club.

Athletics *Intercollegiate sports:* basketball M/W, cross-country running M/W, soccer M/W, volleyball W. ***Intramural sports:*** baseball M, basketball M/W, cross-country running M/W, golf M/W, ice hockey M/W, soccer W, softball M/W, table tennis M/W, tennis M/W, ultimate Frisbee M/W, volleyball M/W, weight lifting M/W.

Campus security: 24-hour emergency response devices and patrols.

Student services: health clinic, personal/psychological counseling.

COSTS & FINANCIAL AID

Costs (2014–15) *Comprehensive fee:* $35,150 includes full-time tuition ($24,620), mandatory fees ($1200), and room and board ($9330). Part-time tuition: $890 per credit hour. Part-time tuition and fees vary according to course load. ***Room and board:*** Room and board charges vary according to board plan and housing facility. ***Payment plan:*** installment. ***Waivers:*** employees or children of employees.

Financial Aid Of all full-time matriculated undergraduates who enrolled in 2013, 515 applied for aid, 480 were judged to have need, 30 had their need fully met. 398 Federal Work-Study jobs (averaging $1244). 9 state and other part-time jobs (averaging $1056). In 2013, 53 non-need-based awards were made. ***Average percent of need met:*** 72. ***Average financial aid package:*** $18,932. ***Average need-based loan:*** $5797. ***Average need-based gift aid:*** $12,796. ***Average non-need-based aid:*** $4906.

APPLYING

Standardized Tests *Recommended:* SAT or ACT (for admission).

Options: electronic application, early admission, early action, deferred entrance.

Required: essay or personal statement, high school transcript, 2 letters of recommendation. ***Required for some:*** interview. ***Recommended:*** minimum 2.4 GPA, interview.

Application deadlines: 6/15 (freshmen), 6/15 (out-of-state freshmen), 6/15 (transfers), 12/15 (early action).

CONTACT

Mr. Joe Saltalamachia, Director of Admissions, Unity College, 90 Quaker Hill Road, Unity, ME 04988. *Phone:* 207-509-7205. *E-mail:* jsalty@unity.edu.

University of Maine

Orono, Maine

http://www.umaine.edu/

- **State-supported** university, founded 1865, part of University of Maine System
- **Small-town** 3300-acre campus
- **Coed** 9,339 undergraduate students, 87% full-time, 48% women, 52% men
- **Moderately difficult** entrance level, 83% of applicants were admitted

UNDERGRAD STUDENTS

8,129 full-time, 1,210 part-time. Students come from 46 states and territories; 41 other countries; 24% are from out of state; 2% Black or African American, non-Hispanic/Latino; 2% Hispanic/Latino; 1% Asian, non-Hispanic/Latino; 1% American Indian or Alaska Native, non-Hispanic/Latino; 3% Two or more races, non-Hispanic/Latino; 6% Race/ethnicity unknown; 2% international; 5% transferred in; 38% live on campus.

Freshmen

Admission: 11,552 applied, 9,539 admitted, 2,068 enrolled. ***Average high school GPA:*** 3.27. ***Test scores:*** SAT critical reading scores over 500: 68%; SAT math scores over 500: 72%; SAT writing scores over 500: 60%; ACT scores over 18: 97%; SAT critical reading scores over 600: 24%; SAT math scores over 600: 28%; SAT writing scores over 600: 18%; ACT scores over 24: 54%; SAT critical reading scores over 700: 3%; SAT math scores over 700: 4%; SAT writing scores over 700: 2%; ACT scores over 30: 9%.

Retention: 77% of full-time freshmen returned.

FACULTY

Total: 845, 58% full-time, 59% with terminal degrees.

Student/faculty ratio: 16:1.

ACADEMICS

Calendar: semesters. *Degrees:* bachelor's, master's, doctoral, post-master's, and postbachelor's certificates.

Special study options: accelerated degree program, advanced placement credit, cooperative education, distance learning, double majors, English as a second language, freshman honors college, honors programs, independent study, internships, off-campus study, part-time degree program, services for LD students, student-designed majors, study abroad, summer session for credit. ***ROTC:*** Army (b), Navy (c).

Computers: 600 computers/terminals are available on campus for general student use. Students can access the following: campus intranet, computer help desk, free student e-mail accounts, online (class) grades, online (class) registration, online (class) schedules, online housing and financial aid information. Campuswide network is available. 100% of college-owned or -operated housing units are wired for high-speed Internet access. Wireless service is available via classrooms, computer centers, computer labs, learning centers, libraries, student centers.

STUDENT LIFE

Housing options: on-campus residence required for freshman year; coed, special housing for students with disabilities. Campus housing is university owned. Freshman campus housing is guaranteed.

Activities and organizations: drama/theater group, student-run newspaper, radio and television station, choral group, marching band, Fraternity and Sorority Life, Alternative Breaks, UMaine Student Government, Campus Activities Board, Wilde Stein, national fraternities, national sororities.

Athletics Member NCAA. All Division I except football (Division I-AA). ***Intercollegiate sports:*** baseball M(s), basketball M(s)/W(s), cheerleading M(c)/W(c), cross-country running M(s)/W(s), field hockey W(s), ice hockey M(s)/W(s), soccer W(s), softball W(s), swimming and diving M/W(s), track and field M(s)/W(s). ***Intramural sports:*** badminton M/W, basketball M/W, crew M(c)/W(c), equestrian sports M(c)/W(c), fencing M(c)/W(c), field hockey M(c)/W(c), football M(c), golf M(c)/W(c), ice hockey M(c)/W(c), lacrosse M(c)/W(c), racquetball M/W, rock climbing M(c)/W(c), rugby M(c)/W(c), skiing (cross-country) M/W, skiing (downhill) M(c)/W(c), soccer M/W, softball M/W, swimming and diving M/W, table tennis M/W, tennis M/W, track and field M/W, ultimate Frisbee M(c)/W(c), volleyball M(c)/W(c), water polo M/W, wrestling M(c).

Campus security: 24-hour emergency response devices and patrols, late-night transport/escort service, controlled dormitory access, area emergency text and email message system.

Student services: health clinic, personal/psychological counseling, women's center, legal services.

COSTS & FINANCIAL AID
Costs (2014–15) ***Tuition:*** state resident $8370 full-time, $279 per credit hour part-time; nonresident $26,250 full-time, $875 per credit hour part-time. Full-time tuition and fees vary according to course load. Part-time tuition and fees vary according to course load. ***Required fees:*** $2236 full-time. ***Room and board:*** $9296; room only: $4858. Room and board charges vary according to board plan and housing facility. ***Payment plan:*** installment. ***Waivers:*** senior citizens and employees or children of employees.

Financial Aid Of all full-time matriculated undergraduates who enrolled in 2014, 6,887 applied for aid, 5,728 were judged to have need, 870 had their need fully met. 1,330 Federal Work-Study jobs (averaging $2343). In 2014, 577 non-need-based awards were made. ***Average percent of need met:*** 80. ***Average financial aid package:*** $16,083. ***Average need-based loan:*** $4569. ***Average need-based gift aid:*** $8332. ***Average non-need-based aid:*** $4679. ***Average indebtedness upon graduation:*** $33,875. ***Financial aid deadline:*** 5/15.

APPLYING
Standardized Tests *Required:* SAT or ACT (for admission).

Options: electronic application, early admission, early action, deferred entrance.

Application fee: $40.

Required: essay or personal statement, high school transcript, 1 letter of recommendation. ***Required for some:*** audition for music majors.

Application deadlines: rolling (freshmen), rolling (out-of-state freshmen), rolling (transfers), 12/15 (early action).

Notification: continuous (freshmen), continuous (out-of-state freshmen), continuous (transfers), 1/31 (early action).

CONTACT
Ms. Sharon Oliver, Director of Admissions, University of Maine, 5713 Chadbourne Hall, Orono, ME 04469-5713. *Phone:* 207-581-1561. *Toll-free phone:* 877-486-2364. *Fax:* 207-581-1213. *E-mail:* um-admit@maine.edu.

See below for display ad and page 1674 for the College Close-Up.

University of Maine at Augusta
Augusta, Maine
http://www.uma.maine.edu/

- **State-supported** 4-year, founded 1965, part of University of Maine System
- **Small-town** 159-acre campus
- **Coed** 4,664 undergraduate students, 35% full-time, 72% women, 28% men
- **Noncompetitive** entrance level, 97% of applicants were admitted

UNDERGRAD STUDENTS
1,641 full-time, 3,023 part-time. 3% are from out of state; 1% Black or African American, non-Hispanic/Latino; 2% Hispanic/Latino; 0.5% Asian, non-Hispanic/Latino; 0.1% Native Hawaiian or other Pacific Islander, non-Hispanic/Latino; 2% American Indian or Alaska Native, non-Hispanic/Latino; 2% Two or more races, non-Hispanic/Latino; 6% Race/ethnicity unknown; 0.5% international; 13% transferred in.

Freshmen
Admission: 856 applied, 830 admitted, 405 enrolled.
Retention: 49% of full-time freshmen returned.

FACULTY
Total: 282, 32% full-time, 34% with terminal degrees.
Student/faculty ratio: 17:1.

ACADEMICS
Calendar: semesters. *Degrees:* certificates, associate, and bachelor's (also offers some graduate courses and continuing education programs with significant enrollment not reflected in profile).

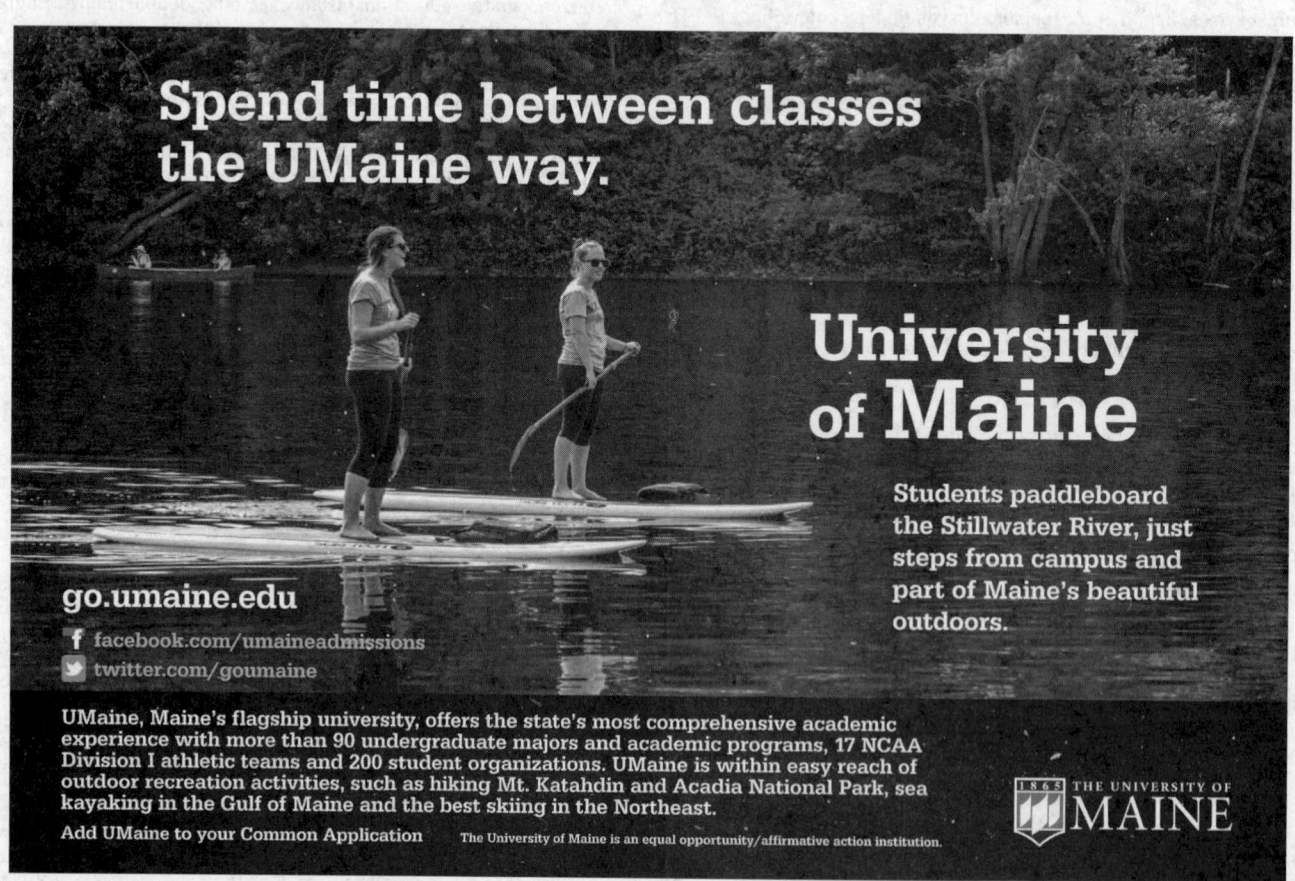

Special study options: academic remediation for entering students, adult/continuing education programs, advanced placement credit, distance learning, double majors, honors programs, independent study, internships, off-campus study, part-time degree program, services for LD students, student-designed majors, study abroad, summer session for credit. ***ROTC:*** Army (c).

Computers: Students can access the following: computer help desk, free student e-mail accounts, online (class) grades, online (class) registration, online (class) schedules, wireless internet available everywhere on campus. Campuswide network is available. Wireless service is available via entire campus.

STUDENT LIFE
Housing options: college housing not available.

Activities and organizations: drama/theater group, student-run newspaper, Honors Program Student Association, Arts and Architecture Students of UMA, Student Nurse Association, Student American Dental Hygiene Association, International Student Club.

Athletics Member USCAA. ***Intercollegiate sports:*** basketball M(s)/W(s), golf M/W, soccer M/W(s). ***Intramural sports:*** racquetball M/W, soccer M, softball M/W, tennis M/W, volleyball M/W.

Campus security: 24-hour emergency response devices, late-night transport/escort service.

Student services: personal/psychological counseling.

COSTS & FINANCIAL AID
Costs (2014–15) ***Tuition:*** state resident $6510 full-time, $217 per credit hour part-time; nonresident $15,750 full-time, $525 per credit hour part-time. Full-time tuition and fees vary according to course load, location, program, and reciprocity agreements. Part-time tuition and fees vary according to course load, location, program, and reciprocity agreements. ***Required fees:*** $938 full-time, $31 per credit hour part-time. ***Payment plan:*** installment. ***Waivers:*** minority students, senior citizens, and employees or children of employees.

Financial Aid Of all full-time matriculated undergraduates who enrolled in 2014, 1,609 applied for aid, 1,526 were judged to have need, 48 had their need fully met. In 2014, 1 non-need-based awards were made. ***Average percent of need met:*** 52. ***Average financial aid package:*** $9172. ***Average need-based loan:*** $7755. ***Average need-based gift aid:*** $5749. ***Average non-need-based aid:*** $1000. ***Average indebtedness upon graduation:*** $30,827.

APPLYING
Options: electronic application, early admission, deferred entrance.

Application fee: $40.

Required: high school transcript. ***Required for some:*** interview, music audition. ***Recommended:*** essay or personal statement.

CONTACT
Jonathan H. Henry, Vice President of Enrollment Management and Director of Admissions, University of Maine at Augusta, 46 University Drive, Robinson Hall, Augusta, ME 04330. *Phone:* 207-621-3136. *Toll-free phone:* 877-862-1234 Ext. 3185 (in-state); 877-862-1234 (out-of-state). *Fax:* 207-621-3333. *E-mail:* umaadm@maine.edu.

University of Maine at Fort Kent

Fort Kent, Maine

http://www.umfk.maine.edu/

- **State-supported** 4-year, founded 1878, part of University of Maine System
- **Rural** 52-acre campus
- **Endowment** $3.1 million
- **Coed** 1,327 undergraduate students, 44% full-time, 68% women, 32% men
- **Minimally difficult** entrance level, 90% of applicants were admitted

UNDERGRAD STUDENTS
578 full-time, 749 part-time. Students come from 21 states and territories; 12 other countries; 10% are from out of state; 3% Black or African American, non-Hispanic/Latino; 2% Hispanic/Latino; 0.5% Asian, non-Hispanic/Latino; 0.2% Native Hawaiian or other Pacific Islander, non-Hispanic/Latino; 0.8% American Indian or Alaska Native, non-Hispanic/Latino; 2% Two or more races, non-Hispanic/Latino; 21% Race/ethnicity unknown; 8% international; 16% transferred in; 23% live on campus.

Freshmen
Admission: 231 applied, 207 admitted, 138 enrolled. ***Average high school GPA:*** 3. ***Test scores:*** SAT critical reading scores over 500: 24%; SAT math scores over 500: 29%; SAT writing scores over 500: 15%; SAT critical reading scores over 600: 2%; SAT math scores over 600: 2%; SAT writing scores over 600: 1%.

Retention: 64% of full-time freshmen returned.

FACULTY
Total: 93, 33% full-time, 20% with terminal degrees.

Student/faculty ratio: 16:1.

ACADEMICS
Calendar: semesters. *Degrees:* certificates, associate, and bachelor's.

Special study options: academic remediation for entering students, accelerated degree program, advanced placement credit, cooperative education, distance learning, double majors, English as a second language, external degree program, honors programs, independent study, internships, part-time degree program, services for LD students, student-designed majors, summer session for credit.

Computers: 100 computers/terminals are available on campus for general student use. Students can access the following: campus intranet, computer help desk, free student e-mail accounts, online (class) grades, online (class) registration, online (class) schedules. Campuswide network is available. Wireless service is available via entire campus.

STUDENT LIFE
Housing options: on-campus residence required for freshman yearCampus housing is university owned. Freshman applicants given priority for college housing.

Activities and organizations: drama/theater group, choral group, Student Nurses Organization, Student Teachers Educational Professional Society, Student Senate, Student Activities Board, Dorm Council, national fraternities, national sororities.

Athletics Member USCAA. ***Intercollegiate sports:*** basketball M/W, soccer M/W, volleyball W. ***Intramural sports:*** basketball M/W, racquetball M/W, soccer M/W, softball M/W, volleyball M/W.

Campus security: controlled dormitory access, 8-hour night patrols by security personnel 11pm-7am.

Student services: health clinic, personal/psychological counseling.

COSTS & FINANCIAL AID
Costs (2014–15) ***Tuition:*** state resident $6600 full-time, $220 per credit part-time; nonresident $9900 full-time, $330 per credit part-time. Full-time tuition and fees vary according to program. Part-time tuition and fees vary according to program. ***Required fees:*** $975 full-time, $33 per credit part-time. ***Room and board:*** $7720; room only: $4150. Room and board charges vary according to board plan and housing facility. ***Payment plan:*** installment. ***Waivers:*** senior citizens and employees or children of employees.

Financial Aid Of all full-time matriculated undergraduates who enrolled in 2013, 524 applied for aid, 457 were judged to have need, 260 had their need fully met. 80 Federal Work-Study jobs (averaging $680). In 2013, 20 non-need-based awards were made. ***Average percent of need met:*** 80. ***Average financial aid package:*** $11,455. ***Average need-based loan:*** $6278. ***Average need-based gift aid:*** $5670. ***Average non-need-based aid:*** $2675. ***Average indebtedness upon graduation:*** $24,028.

APPLYING
Standardized Tests *Required for some:* SAT (for admission), SAT and SAT Subject Tests or ACT (for admission). *Recommended:* SAT and SAT Subject Tests or ACT (for admission).

Options: electronic application, deferred entrance.

Application fee: $40.

Required: essay or personal statement, high school transcript. ***Required for some:*** interview.

Application deadlines: rolling (freshmen), rolling (out-of-state freshmen), rolling (transfers).

Notification: continuous (freshmen), continuous (out-of-state freshmen), continuous (transfers).

CONTACT
University of Maine at Fort Kent, 23 University Drive, Fort Kent, ME 04743-1292. *Phone:* 207-834-7600. *Toll-free phone:* 888-TRY-UMFK.

★ University of Maine at Machias

Machias, Maine

http://umm.maine.edu/

- **State-supported** 4-year, founded 1909, part of University of Maine System
- **Rural** 42-acre campus
- **Coed** 810 undergraduate students, 54% full-time, 68% women, 32% men
- **Moderately difficult** entrance level, 87% of applicants were admitted

UNDERGRAD STUDENTS
434 full-time, 376 part-time. 19% are from out of state; 4% Black or African American, non-Hispanic/Latino; 4% Hispanic/Latino; 0.9% Asian, non-Hispanic/Latino; 3% American Indian or Alaska Native, non-Hispanic/Latino; 2% Two or more races, non-Hispanic/Latino; 6% Race/ethnicity unknown; 2% international; 6% transferred in; 37% live on campus.

Freshmen
Admission: 363 applied, 317 admitted, 118 enrolled. ***Test scores:*** SAT critical reading scores over 500: 34%; SAT math scores over 500: 32%; SAT writing scores over 500: 27%; ACT scores over 18: 70%; SAT critical reading scores over 600: 6%; SAT math scores over 600: 4%; SAT writing scores over 600: 3%; ACT scores over 24: 20%; SAT critical reading scores over 700: 2%; ACT scores over 30: 10%.

Retention: 76% of full-time freshmen returned.

ACADEMICS
Calendar: semesters. *Degrees:* certificates, associate, bachelor's, and postbachelor's certificates.

Special study options: academic remediation for entering students, advanced placement credit, cooperative education, distance learning, double majors, independent study, internships, off-campus study, part-time degree program, services for LD students, student-designed majors, study abroad, summer session for credit.

STUDENT LIFE
Housing options: on-campus residence required through sophomore year; coed, special housing for students with disabilities. Campus housing is university owned.

Athletics Member NAIA. ***Intercollegiate sports:*** basketball M/W, cross-country running M/W, lacrosse M(c)/W(c), soccer M/W, volleyball W. ***Intramural sports:*** basketball M/W, cheerleading W, fencing M/W, football M/W, soccer M/W, softball W, water polo M/W.

COSTS & FINANCIAL AID
Costs (2014–15) ***Tuition:*** state resident $6660 full-time, $222 per credit part-time; nonresident $18,480 full-time, $616 per credit part-time. ***Required fees:*** $820 full-time. ***Room and board:*** $8178.

Financial Aid Of all full-time matriculated undergraduates who enrolled in 2002, 512 applied for aid, 419 were judged to have need, 108 had their need fully met. 140 Federal Work-Study jobs (averaging $1621). 83 state and other part-time jobs (averaging $1660). In 2002, 44 non-need-based awards were made. ***Average percent of need met:*** 83. ***Average financial aid package:*** $8182. ***Average need-based loan:*** $3356. ***Average need-based gift aid:*** $4847. ***Average non-need-based aid:*** $5051. ***Average indebtedness upon graduation:*** $14,873.

APPLYING
Standardized Tests *Required:* SAT or ACT (for admission).

Options: electronic application, early admission, early action, deferred entrance.

Application fee: $40.

Required: essay or personal statement, high school transcript, 1 letter of recommendation. ***Required for some:*** minimum 2.0 GPA, interview. ***Recommended:*** minimum 2.5 GPA, 2 letters of recommendation, interview.

CONTACT
Director of Admissions, University of Maine at Machias, 9 O'Brien Avenue, Machias, ME 04654. *Phone:* 207-255-1318. *Toll-free phone:* 888-GOTOUMM (in-state); 888-468-6866 (out-of-state). *Fax:* 207-255-1363. *E-mail:* ummadmissions@maine.edu.

See below for display ad and page 1676 for the College Close-Up.

University of Maine at Presque Isle

Presque Isle, Maine

http://www.umpi.edu/

- **State-supported** 4-year, founded 1903, part of University of Maine System
- **Small-town** 150-acre campus
- **Coed** 1,138 undergraduate students, 58% full-time, 64% women, 36% men
- **Minimally difficult** entrance level, 83% of applicants were admitted

UNDERGRAD STUDENTS

659 full-time, 479 part-time. 4% are from out of state; 1% Black or African American, non-Hispanic/Latino; 1% Hispanic/Latino; 0.2% Asian, non-Hispanic/Latino; 3% American Indian or Alaska Native, non-Hispanic/Latino; 3% Two or more races, non-Hispanic/Latino; 4% Race/ethnicity unknown; 8% international; 7% transferred in; 22% live on campus.

Freshmen

Admission: 580 applied, 480 admitted, 197 enrolled. ***Average high school GPA:*** 2.91. ***Test scores:*** SAT critical reading scores over 500: 33%; SAT math scores over 500: 40%; SAT writing scores over 500: 19%; ACT scores over 18: 67%; SAT critical reading scores over 600: 5%; SAT math scores over 600: 5%; SAT writing scores over 600: 3%; ACT scores over 24: 33%; SAT math scores over 700: 1%; ACT scores over 30: 33%.

Retention: 61% of full-time freshmen returned.

FACULTY

Total: 98, 45% full-time, 47% with terminal degrees.

Student/faculty ratio: 13:1.

ACADEMICS

Calendar: semesters. *Degrees:* certificates, associate, and bachelor's.

Special study options: academic remediation for entering students, accelerated degree program, adult/continuing education programs, advanced placement credit, cooperative education, distance learning, double majors, honors programs, independent study, internships, off-campus study, part-time degree program, services for LD students, student-designed majors, study abroad, summer session for credit.

Computers: Students can access the following: campus intranet, computer help desk, free student e-mail accounts, online (class) grades, online (class) registration, online (class) schedules. Campuswide network is available. Wireless service is available via entire campus.

STUDENT LIFE

Housing options: coed, special housing for students with disabilities. Campus housing is university owned and leased by the school. Freshman campus housing is guaranteed.

Activities and organizations: student-run newspaper, radio station, PE Majors Club, Student Senate, Athletic Training Student Club, Student Organization of Social Workers, Criminal Justice Club, national fraternities, national sororities.

Athletics Member NCAA, USCAA. All Division III except men's and women's skiing (cross-country) (Division I). ***Intercollegiate sports:*** baseball M, basketball M/W, cross-country running M/W, golf M, skiing (cross-country) M/W, soccer M/W, softball W, volleyball W. ***Intramural sports:*** archery M/W, badminton M/W, basketball M/W, bowling M/W, cross-country running M/W, football M/W, ice hockey M(c)/W(c), skiing (cross-country) M/W, skiing (downhill) M/W, soccer M/W, softball M/W, table tennis M/W, tennis M/W, track and field M/W, volleyball M/W, weight lifting M/W.

Campus security: student patrols, controlled dormitory access, crime prevention programs, lighted pathways, security cameras.

Student services: health clinic, personal/psychological counseling.

COSTS & FINANCIAL AID

Costs (2014–15) ***Tuition:*** state resident $6600 full-time, $220 per credit hour part-time; nonresident $9900 full-time, $330 per credit hour part-time. Full-time tuition and fees vary according to course load, location, and reciprocity agreements. Part-time tuition and fees vary according to course load, location, and reciprocity agreements. ***Required fees:*** $835 full-time. ***Room and board:*** $7656. Room and board charges vary according to board plan and housing facility. ***Payment plans:*** installment, deferred payment. ***Waivers:*** minority students, senior citizens, and employees or children of employees.

Financial Aid Of all full-time matriculated undergraduates who enrolled in 2014, 575 applied for aid, 519 were judged to have need, 325 had their need fully met. 232 Federal Work-Study jobs (averaging $2573). In 2014, 31 non-need-based awards were made. ***Average percent of need met:*** 88. ***Average financial aid package:*** $11,575. ***Average need-based loan:*** $5019. ***Average need-based gift aid:*** $6568. ***Average non-need-based aid:*** $2344. ***Average indebtedness upon graduation:*** $23,777.

APPLYING

Options: electronic application, early admission, deferred entrance.

Required: essay or personal statement, high school transcript, minimum 2.0 GPA. ***Required for some:*** 1 letter of recommendation, interview.

CONTACT

University of Maine at Presque Isle, 181 Main Street, Presque Isle, ME 04769-2888. *Phone:* 207-768-9453.

★ University of New England

Biddeford, Maine

http://www.une.edu/

- **Independent** comprehensive, founded 1831
- **Small-town** 540-acre campus
- **Endowment** $32.6 million
- **Coed** 2,749 undergraduate students, 80% full-time, 71% women, 29% men
- **Moderately difficult** entrance level, 86% of applicants were admitted

UNDERGRAD STUDENTS

2,202 full-time, 547 part-time. Students come from 37 states and territories; 10 other countries; 67% are from out of state; 1% Black or African American, non-Hispanic/Latino; 0.1% Hispanic/Latino; 3% Asian, non-Hispanic/Latino; 0.2% Native Hawaiian or other Pacific Islander, non-Hispanic/Latino; 0.4% American Indian or Alaska Native, non-Hispanic/Latino; 0.8% Two or more races, non-Hispanic/Latino; 19% Race/ethnicity unknown; 0.6% international; 3% transferred in; 63% live on campus.

Freshmen

Admission: 4,317 applied, 3,699 admitted, 576 enrolled. ***Average high school GPA:*** 3.26. ***Test scores:*** SAT critical reading scores over 500: 68%; SAT math scores over 500: 74%; ACT scores over 18: 96%; SAT critical reading scores over 600: 19%; SAT math scores over 600: 21%; ACT scores over 24: 40%; SAT critical reading scores over 700: 2%; SAT math scores over 700: 2%; ACT scores over 30: 6%.

Retention: 80% of full-time freshmen returned.

FACULTY

Total: 499, 53% full-time, 56% with terminal degrees.

Student/faculty ratio: 13:1.

ACADEMICS

Calendar: semesters. *Degrees:* bachelor's, master's, doctoral, post-master's, and postbachelor's certificates.

Special study options: academic remediation for entering students, accelerated degree program, adult/continuing education programs, advanced placement credit, cooperative education, distance learning, double majors, honors programs, independent study, internships, off-campus study, part-time degree program, services for LD students, study abroad, summer session for credit. ***ROTC:*** Army (c).

Unusual degree programs: 3-2 physician assistant.

Computers: 91 computers/terminals are available on campus for general student use. Students can access the following: campus intranet, computer help desk, free student e-mail accounts, online (class) grades, online (class) registration, online (class) schedules. Campuswide network is available. 100% of college-owned or -operated housing units are wired for high-speed Internet access. Wireless service is available via classrooms, computer centers, computer labs, dorm rooms, learning centers, libraries, student centers.

STUDENT LIFE

Housing options: on-campus residence required through junior year; coed, women-only, special housing for students with disabilities. Campus housing is university owned.

Activities and organizations: drama/theater group, student-run newspaper, choral group, student government, Outing Club, Campus Programming Board, Earth's Eco, Dance Team.

Athletics Member NCAA. All Division III. ***Intercollegiate sports:*** basketball M/W, cross-country running M/W, field hockey W, golf M, ice hockey M/W, lacrosse M/W, soccer M/W, softball W, swimming and diving W, volleyball W. ***Intramural sports:*** baseball M(c), basketball M/W, cheerleading M(c)/W(c), equestrian sports M(c)/W(c), gymnastics M(c)/W(c), ice hockey M/W, racquetball M/W, rugby M(c)/W(c), soccer M/W, softball M/W, swimming and diving M(c), table tennis M/W, tennis M/W, ultimate Frisbee M/W, volleyball M(c)/W, water polo M/W.

Campus security: 24-hour emergency response devices and patrols, late-night transport/escort service, controlled dormitory access.

Student services: health clinic, personal/psychological counseling.

COSTS

Costs (2014–15) ***Comprehensive fee:*** $46,750 includes full-time tuition ($32,880), mandatory fees ($1200), and room and board ($12,670). Full-time tuition and fees vary according to course load and program. Part-time tuition: $1160 per credit hour. Part-time tuition and fees vary according to course load and program. ***Room and board:*** Room and board charges vary according to board plan and housing facility. ***Payment plan:*** installment. ***Waivers:*** children of alumni and employees or children of employees.

APPLYING

Standardized Tests *Required:* SAT or ACT (for admission).

Options: electronic application, early admission, early action, deferred entrance.

Application fee: $40.

Required: essay or personal statement, high school transcript. ***Recommended:*** 1 letter of recommendation.

Application deadlines: 2/15 (freshmen), rolling (transfers).

Notification: continuous (freshmen), continuous (transfers).

CONTACT

Peter Heeley, Senior Associate Director of Undergraduate Admission, University of New England, 11 Hills Beach Road, Biddeford, ME 04005-9526. *Phone:* 800-477-4863. *Toll-free phone:* 800-477-4UNE. *Fax:* 207-602-5900. *E-mail:* admissions@une.edu.

See below for display ad and page 1686 for the College Close-Up.

★ University of Southern Maine

Portland, Maine

http://www.usm.maine.edu/

- **State-supported** comprehensive, founded 1878, part of University of Maine System
- **Urban** 144-acre campus
- **Endowment** $40.0 million
- **Coed** 6,628 undergraduate students, 60% full-time, 57% women, 43% men
- **Moderately difficult** entrance level, 84% of applicants were admitted

UNDERGRAD STUDENTS

3,985 full-time, 2,643 part-time. Students come from 32 states and territories; 9 other countries; 8% are from out of state; 3% Black or African American, non-Hispanic/Latino; 2% Hispanic/Latino; 2% Asian, non-Hispanic/Latino; 0.1% Native Hawaiian or other Pacific Islander, non-Hispanic/Latino; 0.9% American Indian or Alaska Native, non-Hispanic/Latino; 3% Two or more races, non-Hispanic/Latino; 6% Race/ethnicity unknown; 1% international; 11% transferred in; 18% live on campus.

Freshmen

Admission: 3,781 applied, 3,174 admitted, 737 enrolled. ***Average high school GPA:*** 3.04. ***Test scores:*** SAT critical reading scores over 500: 49%; SAT math scores over 500: 48%; SAT writing scores over 500: 44%; ACT scores over 18: 86%; SAT critical reading scores over 600: 14%; SAT math scores over 600: 10%; SAT writing scores over 600: 11%; ACT scores over 24: 35%; SAT critical reading scores over 700: 1%; SAT math scores over 700: 1%; SAT writing scores over 700: 1%; ACT scores over 30: 5%.

Retention: 65% of full-time freshmen returned.

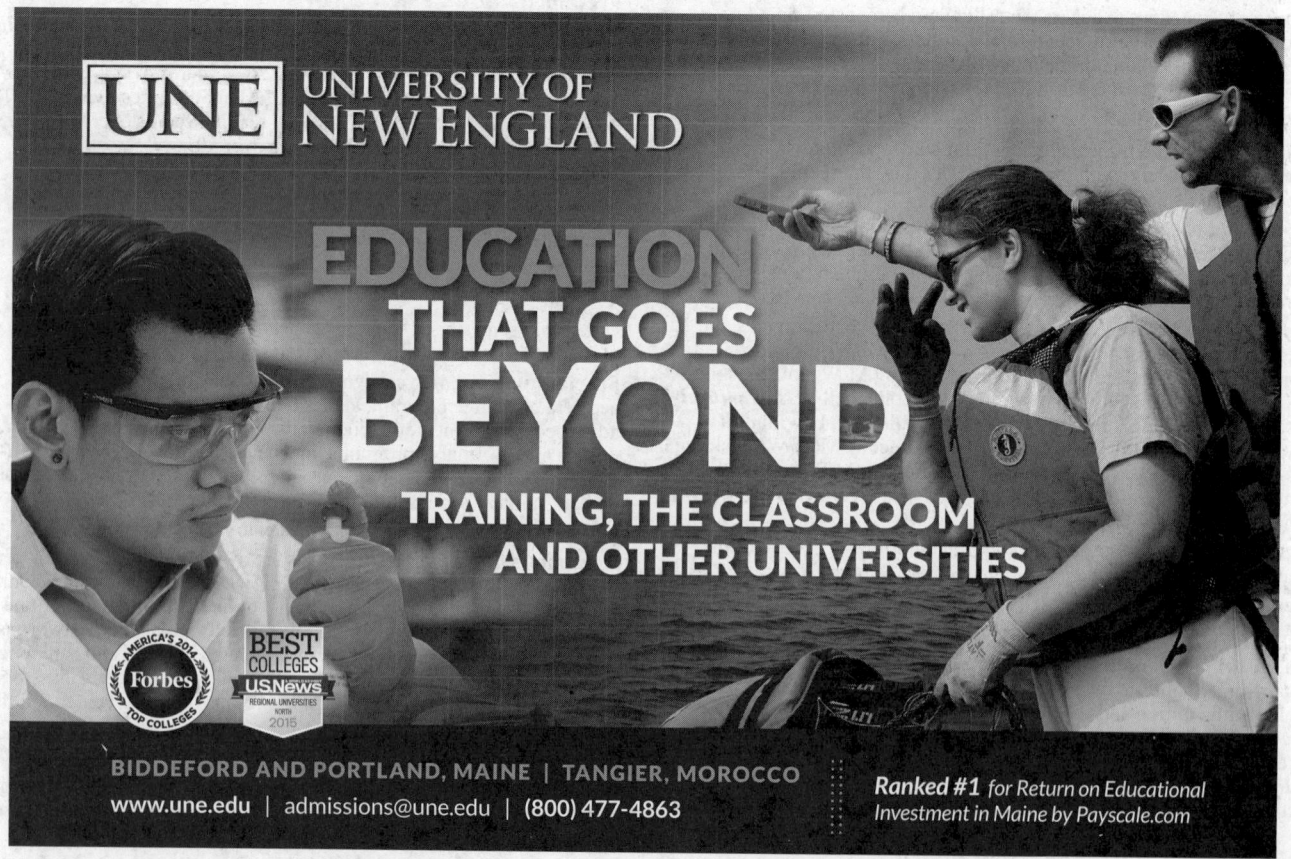

FACULTY
Total: 622, 50% full-time, 54% with terminal degrees.

Student/faculty ratio: 15:1.

ACADEMICS
Calendar: semesters. *Degrees:* certificates, bachelor's, master's, doctoral, post-master's, and postbachelor's certificates.

Special study options: academic remediation for entering students, accelerated degree program, adult/continuing education programs, advanced placement credit, cooperative education, distance learning, double majors, English as a second language, honors programs, independent study, internships, off-campus study, part-time degree program, services for LD students, student-designed majors, study abroad, summer session for credit. ***ROTC:*** Army (c), Air Force (c).

Unusual degree programs: 3-2 business administration.

Computers: 219 computers/terminals are available on campus for general student use. Students can access the following: campus intranet, computer help desk, free student e-mail accounts, online (class) grades, online (class) registration, online (class) schedules. Campuswide network is available. 100% of college-owned or -operated housing units are wired for high-speed Internet access. Wireless service is available via entire campus.

STUDENT LIFE
Housing options: coed, special housing for students with disabilities. Campus housing is university owned. Freshman applicants given priority for college housing.

Activities and organizations: drama/theater group, student-run newspaper, radio station, choral group, Outing and Ski Clubs, Gorham Events Board, Commuter Student Group, Circle K, national fraternities, national sororities.

Athletics Member NCAA. All Division III. ***Intercollegiate sports:*** baseball M, basketball M/W, cross-country running M/W, fencing M/W(c), field hockey W, golf M/W, ice hockey M/W, lacrosse M/W, sailing M/W, soccer M/W, softball W, tennis M/W, track and field M/W, volleyball W, wrestling M. ***Intramural sports:*** baseball M, basketball M/W, cheerleading M(c)/W(c), football M/W, ice hockey M/W, lacrosse M(c)/W(c), racquetball M/W, rugby M(c)/W(c), skiing (downhill) M(c)/W(c), soccer M/W, softball M/W, squash M/W, table tennis M/W, tennis M/W, ultimate Frisbee M/W, volleyball M/W, weight lifting M/W.

Campus security: 24-hour emergency response devices and patrols, late-night transport/escort service, controlled dormitory access, security lighting, preventive programs within residence halls.

Student services: health clinic, personal/psychological counseling, women's center, legal services.

COSTS & FINANCIAL AID
Costs (2015–16) ***Tuition:*** state resident $7590 full-time, $253 per credit hour part-time; nonresident $19,950 full-time, $665 per credit hour part-time. Full-time tuition and fees vary according to course load, degree level, and reciprocity agreements. Part-time tuition and fees vary according to course load, degree level, and reciprocity agreements. ***Required fees:*** $1330 full-time. ***Room and board:*** $9150; room only: $4700. Room and board charges vary according to board plan, housing facility, and location. ***Payment plan:*** installment.

Financial Aid Of all full-time matriculated undergraduates who enrolled in 2013, 3,751 applied for aid, 3,248 were judged to have need, 1,569 had their need fully met. In 2013, 118 non-need-based awards were made. ***Average percent of need met:*** 75. ***Average financial aid package:*** $13,146. ***Average need-based loan:*** $7479. ***Average need-based gift aid:*** $6385. ***Average non-need-based aid:*** $3934.

APPLYING
Standardized Tests *Required:* SAT or ACT (for admission).

Options: electronic application, early admission, deferred entrance.

Application fee: $40.

Required: essay or personal statement, high school transcript. ***Required for some:*** interview, auditions for music majors. ***Recommended:*** 1 letter of recommendation, interview.

Notification: continuous (freshmen), continuous (out-of-state freshmen), continuous (transfers).

CONTACT
Rachel Morales, Interim Director of Undergraduate Admission, University of Southern Maine, Portland, ME 04104-9300. *Phone:* 207-780-5770. *Toll-free phone:* 800-800-4USM Ext. 5670. *E-mail:* usmadm@usm.maine.edu.

MARYLAND

Bowie State University

Bowie, Maryland

http://www.bowiestate.edu/

- **State-supported** comprehensive, founded 1865, part of University System of Maryland
- **Small-town** 295-acre campus with easy access to Baltimore and Washington, DC
- **Endowment** $5.7 million
- **Coed** 4,358 undergraduate students, 81% full-time, 62% women, 38% men
- **Minimally difficult** entrance level, 52% of applicants were admitted

UNDERGRAD STUDENTS
3,521 full-time, 837 part-time. Students come from 31 states and territories; 9% are from out of state; 89% Black or African American, non-Hispanic/Latino; 3% Hispanic/Latino; 1% Asian, non-Hispanic/Latino; 0.1% Native Hawaiian or other Pacific Islander, non-Hispanic/Latino; 0.1% American Indian or Alaska Native, non-Hispanic/Latino; 3% Two or more races, non-Hispanic/Latino; 0.9% Race/ethnicity unknown; 0.8% international; 11% transferred in; 34% live on campus.

Freshmen
Admission: 3,986 applied, 2,063 admitted, 629 enrolled. ***Average high school GPA:*** 2.53. ***Test scores:*** SAT critical reading scores over 500: 23%; SAT math scores over 500: 18%; SAT critical reading scores over 600: 2%; SAT math scores over 600: 2%.

Retention: 67% of full-time freshmen returned.

FACULTY
Total: 408, 53% full-time, 88% with terminal degrees.

Student/faculty ratio: 16:1.

ACADEMICS
Calendar: semesters. *Degrees:* certificates, bachelor's, master's, doctoral, and postbachelor's certificates.

Special study options: academic remediation for entering students, adult/continuing education programs, advanced placement credit, cooperative education, distance learning, double majors, external degree program, honors programs, independent study, internships, off-campus study, part-time degree program, services for LD students, study abroad, summer session for credit. ***ROTC:*** Army (b).

Unusual degree programs: 3-2 engineering with George Washington University, University of Maryland College Park, Howard University.

Computers: 3,500 computers/terminals are available on campus for general student use. Students can access the following: computer help desk, free student e-mail accounts, online (class) grades, online (class) registration. Campuswide network is available. Wireless service is available via entire campus.

STUDENT LIFE
Housing options: coed, men-only, women-only. Campus housing is university owned and is provided by a third party. Freshman applicants given priority for college housing.

Activities and organizations: drama/theater group, student-run newspaper, radio and television station, choral group, marching band, Honda Campus All-Star Challenge, national fraternities, national sororities.

Athletics Member NCAA. All Division II. ***Intercollegiate sports:*** basketball M(s)/W(s), bowling W, cross-country running M(s)/W(s), football M(s), softball W(s), tennis W(s), track and field M(s)/W(s), volleyball W(s).

Campus security: 24-hour emergency response devices and patrols, student patrols, late-night transport/escort service, controlled dormitory access.

Student services: health clinic, personal/psychological counseling.

COSTS & FINANCIAL AID

Costs (2014–15) ***Tuition:*** state resident $4969 full-time, $219 per credit hour part-time; nonresident $15,545 full-time, $653 per credit hour part-time. Part-time tuition and fees vary according to course load. ***Required fees:*** $2330 full-time, $91 per credit hour part-time. ***Room and board:*** $10,432; room only: $6702. Room and board charges vary according to board plan and housing facility. ***Payment plans:*** installment, deferred payment. ***Waivers:*** senior citizens and employees or children of employees.

Financial Aid Of all full-time matriculated undergraduates who enrolled in 2013, 2,580 applied for aid, 2,577 were judged to have need, 1,020 had their need fully met. 76 Federal Work-Study jobs (averaging $2567). In 2013, 76 non-need-based awards were made. ***Average percent of need met:*** 45. ***Average financial aid package:*** $8993. ***Average need-based loan:*** $4098. ***Average need-based gift aid:*** $6825. ***Average non-need-based aid:*** $92. ***Average indebtedness upon graduation:*** $29,737.

APPLYING

Standardized Tests *Required:* SAT or ACT (for admission).

Options: electronic application.

Application fee: $40.

Required: high school transcript, minimum 2.5 GPA.

Application deadlines: 4/1 (freshmen), 4/1 (transfers).

Notification: continuous (freshmen), continuous (transfers).

CONTACT

Mrs. Shirley Holt, Assistant Director of Admissions, Bowie State University, Administration Building, 1st Floor. *Phone:* 301-860-3415. *Toll-free phone:* 877-772-6943. *Fax:* 301-860-3438. *E-mail:* sholt@bowiestate.edu.

Capitol Technology University

Laurel, Maryland

http://www.captechu.edu/

- **Independent** comprehensive, founded 1964
- **Suburban** 52-acre campus with easy access to Baltimore and Washington, DC
- **Coed** 309 undergraduate students
- **Minimally difficult** entrance level

UNDERGRAD STUDENTS

Students come from 11 states and territories.

Freshmen

Admission: 384 applied.

FACULTY

Student/faculty ratio: 12:1.

ACADEMICS

Calendar: semesters. *Degrees:* certificates, associate, bachelor's, master's, doctoral, and postbachelor's certificates.

Special study options: academic remediation for entering students, accelerated degree program, adult/continuing education programs, advanced placement credit, cooperative education, English as a second language, part-time degree program, summer session for credit. ***ROTC:*** Army (c).

Computers: Students can access the following: campus intranet, computer help desk, free student e-mail accounts, online (class) grades, online (class) registration, online (class) schedules. Campuswide network is available.

STUDENT LIFE

Housing options: coed. Campus housing is university owned. Freshman campus housing is guaranteed.

Activities and organizations: student-run newspaper.

Athletics ***Intramural sports:*** basketball M, bowling M/W, football M, soccer M, table tennis M/W, volleyball M/W.

Campus security: night security patrols.

Student services: personal/psychological counseling.

FINANCIAL AID

Financial Aid Of all full-time matriculated undergraduates who enrolled in 2011, 317 applied for aid, 231 were judged to have need, 21 had their need fully met. 39 Federal Work-Study jobs (averaging $1647). 67 state and other part-time jobs (averaging $1124). In 2011, 11 non-need-based awards were made. ***Average percent of need met:*** 47. ***Average financial aid package:*** $13,929. ***Average need-based loan:*** $3597. ***Average need-based gift aid:*** $4153. ***Average non-need-based aid:*** $5864. ***Average indebtedness upon graduation:*** $34,609.

APPLYING

Standardized Tests *Required:* SAT or ACT (for admission).

Options: electronic application, deferred entrance.

Application fee: $25.

Required: high school transcript. ***Required for some:*** essay or personal statement, 2 letters of recommendation, interview. ***Recommended:*** minimum 2.2 GPA, interview.

Application deadlines: rolling (freshmen), rolling (transfers).

CONTACT

Capitol Technology University, 11301 Springfield Road, Laurel, MD 20708-9759. *Phone:* 301-953-3200 Ext. 3033. *Toll-free phone:* 800-950-1992.

DeVry University

Bethesda, Maryland

http://www.devry.edu/

- **Proprietary** comprehensive, part of DeVry University
- **Coed**

ACADEMICS

Calendar: semesters. *Degrees:* bachelor's and master's.

COSTS & FINANCIAL AID

Costs (2014–15) ***Tuition:*** $17,052 full-time, $609 per credit hour part-time. ***Required fees:*** $80 full-time.

Financial Aid Of all full-time matriculated undergraduates who enrolled in 2007, 5 applied for aid, 4 were judged to have need. In 2007, 2 non-need-based awards were made. ***Average percent of need met:*** 24. ***Average financial aid package:*** $11,820. ***Average need-based loan:*** $9900. ***Average need-based gift aid:*** $5760. ***Average non-need-based aid:*** $22,795.

CONTACT

Admissions Office, DeVry University, 4550 Montgomery Avenue, Suite 100 North, Bethesda, MD 20814-3304. *Phone:* 301-652-8477. *Toll-free phone:* 866-338-7941.

Frostburg State University

Frostburg, Maryland

http://www.frostburg.edu/

- **State-supported** comprehensive, founded 1898, part of University System of Maryland
- **Small-town** 260-acre campus with easy access to Baltimore and Washington, DC
- **Endowment** $17.4 million
- **Coed** 4,915 undergraduate students, 86% full-time, 51% women, 49% men
- **Moderately difficult** entrance level, 59% of applicants were admitted

UNDERGRAD STUDENTS

4,228 full-time, 687 part-time. Students come from 31 states and territories; 41 other countries; 8% are from out of state; 29% Black or African American, non-Hispanic/Latino; 5% Hispanic/Latino; 2% Asian, non-Hispanic/Latino; 0.1% Native Hawaiian or other Pacific Islander, non-Hispanic/Latino; 0.1% American Indian or Alaska Native, non-Hispanic/Latino; 4% Two or more races, non-Hispanic/Latino; 1% Race/ethnicity unknown; 2% international; 12% transferred in; 32% live on campus.

Freshmen
Admission: 4,252 applied, 2,488 admitted, 958 enrolled. ***Average high school GPA:*** 3.18. ***Test scores:*** SAT critical reading scores over 500: 45%; SAT math scores over 500: 44%; SAT writing scores over 500: 37%; ACT scores over 18: 76%; SAT critical reading scores over 600: 11%; SAT math scores over 600: 11%; SAT writing scores over 600: 6%; ACT scores over 24: 15%; SAT critical reading scores over 700: 1%; SAT math scores over 700: 1%; SAT writing scores over 700: 1%; ACT scores over 30: 3%.

Retention: 76% of full-time freshmen returned.

FACULTY
Total: 386, 66% full-time, 60% with terminal degrees.

Student/faculty ratio: 16:1.

ACADEMICS
Calendar: semesters. *Degrees:* certificates, bachelor's, master's, doctoral, and postbachelor's certificates.

Special study options: adult/continuing education programs, advanced placement credit, cooperative education, distance learning, double majors, freshman honors college, honors programs, independent study, internships, off-campus study, part-time degree program, services for LD students, study abroad, summer session for credit.

Unusual degree programs: business administration with Management/Accounting; engineering with University of Maryland.

Computers: 577 computers/terminals are available on campus for general student use. Students can access the following: campus intranet, computer help desk, free student e-mail accounts, online (class) grades, online (class) registration, online (class) schedules. Campuswide network is available. 100% of college-owned or -operated housing units are wired for high-speed Internet access. Wireless service is available via entire campus.

STUDENT LIFE
Housing options: coed, men-only, women-only. Campus housing is university owned and is provided by a third party.

Activities and organizations: drama/theater group, student-run newspaper, radio and television station, choral group, marching band, Student Government Association, Black Student Association, Campus Activities Board, Residence Hall Association, University Programming Council, national fraternities, national sororities.

Athletics Member NCAA. All Division III. ***Intercollegiate sports:*** baseball M, basketball M/W, cross-country running M/W, field hockey W, football M, lacrosse M/W, soccer M/W, softball W, swimming and diving M/W, tennis M/W, track and field M/W, volleyball W. ***Intramural sports:*** basketball M/W, football M/W, lacrosse M(c), racquetball M/W, rugby M(c), soccer M/W, softball M/W, tennis M/W, volleyball M(c)/W, wrestling M.

Campus security: 24-hour emergency response devices and patrols, student patrols, late-night transport/escort service, controlled dormitory access, bicycle patrols.

Student services: health clinic, personal/psychological counseling, women's center.

COSTS & FINANCIAL AID
Costs (2015–16) ***Tuition:*** state resident $6214 full-time, $257 per credit part-time; nonresident $18,314 full-time, $514 per credit part-time. Full-time tuition and fees vary according to location. Part-time tuition and fees vary according to course load and location. ***Required fees:*** $2274 full-time, $106 per credit part-time, $25 per term part-time. ***Room and board:*** $8574; room only: $4110. Room and board charges vary according to board plan and housing facility. ***Payment plans:*** installment, deferred payment. ***Waivers:*** senior citizens and employees or children of employees.

Financial Aid Of all full-time matriculated undergraduates who enrolled in 2014, 3,698 applied for aid, 3,077 were judged to have need, 418 had their need fully met. 156 Federal Work-Study jobs (averaging $664). In 2014, 803 non-need-based awards were made. ***Average percent of need met:*** 61. ***Average financial aid package:*** $9335. ***Average need-based loan:*** $3865. ***Average need-based gift aid:*** $6870. ***Average non-need-based aid:*** $3108. ***Average indebtedness upon graduation:*** $24,916.

APPLYING
Standardized Tests *Required:* SAT or ACT (for admission).

Options: electronic application, early admission.

Application fee: $30.

Required: high school transcript, minimum 2.0 GPA. ***Required for some:*** essay or personal statement. ***Recommended:*** interview.

Application deadlines: 2/15 (freshmen), 2/30 (out-of-state freshmen), 6/1 (transfers).

CONTACT
Frostburg State University, 101 Braddock Road, Frostburg, MD 21532-1099. *Phone:* 301-687-4201.

★ Goucher College
Baltimore, Maryland
http://www.goucher.edu/

- **Independent** comprehensive, founded 1885
- **Suburban** 287-acre campus with easy access to Baltimore and Washington, DC
- **Endowment** $227.6 million
- **Coed** 1,471 undergraduate students, 98% full-time, 67% women, 33% men
- **Moderately difficult** entrance level, 76% of applicants were admitted

UNDERGRAD STUDENTS
1,447 full-time, 24 part-time. Students come from 49 states and territories; 16 other countries; 73% are from out of state; 10% Black or African American, non-Hispanic/Latino; 8% Hispanic/Latino; 3% Asian, non-Hispanic/Latino; 0.1% Native Hawaiian or other Pacific Islander, non-Hispanic/Latino; 0.2% American Indian or Alaska Native, non-Hispanic/Latino; 4% Two or more races, non-Hispanic/Latino; 4% Race/ethnicity unknown; 3% international; 3% transferred in; 81% live on campus.

Freshmen
Admission: 3,340 applied, 2,528 admitted, 403 enrolled. ***Average high school GPA:*** 3.17. ***Test scores:*** SAT critical reading scores over 500: 83%; SAT math scores over 500: 77%; SAT writing scores over 500: 79%; ACT scores over 18: 97%; SAT critical reading scores over 600: 48%; SAT math scores over 600: 37%; SAT writing scores over 600: 38%; ACT scores over 24: 76%; SAT critical reading scores over 700: 14%; SAT math scores over 700: 6%; SAT writing scores over 700: 9%; ACT scores over 30: 18%.

Retention: 77% of full-time freshmen returned.

FACULTY
Total: 179, 76% full-time, 83% with terminal degrees.

Student/faculty ratio: 10:1.

ACADEMICS
Calendar: semesters. *Degrees:* bachelor's, master's, and postbachelor's certificates.

Special study options: accelerated degree program, adult/continuing education programs, advanced placement credit, distance learning, double majors, independent study, internships, off-campus study, part-time degree program, services for LD students, student-designed majors, study abroad, summer session for credit. ***ROTC:*** Army (c), Air Force (c).

Unusual degree programs: 3-2 engineering with Johns Hopkins University, Columbia University FU Foundation School of Engineering and Applied Science.

Computers: 246 computers/terminals are available on campus for general student use. Students can access the following: campus intranet, computer help desk, free student e-mail accounts, online (class) grades, online (class) registration, online (class) schedules, transcripts, financial aid information, billing, ePortfolios, academic progress reports, study abroad plan. Campuswide network is available. 100% of college-owned or -operated housing units are wired for high-speed Internet access. Wireless service is available via entire campus.

STUDENT LIFE
Housing options: on-campus residence required through sophomore year; coed, men-only, women-only, special housing for students with disabilities. Campus housing is university owned. Freshman campus housing is guaranteed.

Activities and organizations: drama/theater group, student-run newspaper, radio station, choral group, Goucher Student Government,

The Quindecim, Food Recovery Network/ Ag Co-op / Gear (Environmental action clubs), Hillel, Umoja: The Black Student Union.

Athletics Member NCAA. All Division III. ***Intercollegiate sports:*** basketball M/W, cross-country running M/W, equestrian sports M/W, field hockey W, lacrosse M/W, soccer M/W, swimming and diving M/W, tennis M/W, track and field M/W, volleyball W. ***Intramural sports:*** basketball M/W, fencing M(c)/W(c), soccer M/W, ultimate Frisbee M/W.

Campus security: 24-hour emergency response devices and patrols, late-night transport/escort service, controlled dormitory access, e2 campus alerts.

Student services: health clinic, personal/psychological counseling.

COSTS & FINANCIAL AID

Costs (2014–15) ***Comprehensive fee:*** $52,040 includes full-time tuition ($39,808), mandatory fees ($750), and room and board ($11,482). Part-time tuition: $1327 per credit hour. ***College room only:*** $6798. Room and board charges vary according to board plan and housing facility. ***Payment plans:*** tuition prepayment, installment. ***Waivers:*** employees or children of employees.

Financial Aid Of all full-time matriculated undergraduates who enrolled in 2014, 1,040 applied for aid, 929 were judged to have need, 189 had their need fully met. 418 Federal Work-Study jobs (averaging $1095). In 2014, 333 non-need-based awards were made. ***Average percent of need met:*** 61. ***Average financial aid package:*** $31,019. ***Average need-based loan:*** $4609. ***Average need-based gift aid:*** $26,977. ***Average non-need-based aid:*** $15,740. ***Average indebtedness upon graduation:*** $25,580.

APPLYING

Options: electronic application, early admission, early decision, early action, deferred entrance.

Application fee: $55.

Required: essay or personal statement, high school transcript except for those applying via the Goucher Video Application which requires a short video, digital application, signed statement of academic integrity, two works from your high school years (one of which must be a graded writing assignment). ***Required for some:*** high school transcript. ***Recommended:*** 3 letters of recommendation, interview.

Application deadlines: 2/1 (freshmen), 4/1 (transfers), 12/1 (early action).

Early decision deadline: 11/15.

Notification: 4/1 (freshmen), 5/1 (transfers), 12/15 (early decision), 2/1 (early action).

CONTACT

Mr. Carlton E. Surbeck, Director of Admissions, Goucher College, 1021 Dulaney Valley Road, Baltimore, MD 21204. *Phone:* 410-337-6100. *Toll-free phone:* 800-468-2437. *Fax:* 410-337-6354. *E-mail:* admissions@goucher.edu.

Hood College

Frederick, Maryland

http://www.hood.edu/

- **Independent** comprehensive, founded 1893
- **Suburban** 50-acre campus with easy access to Baltimore and Washington, DC
- **Endowment** $69.4 million
- **Coed**
- **Moderately difficult** entrance level

FACULTY

Student/faculty ratio: 12:1.

ACADEMICS

Calendar: semesters. *Degrees:* certificates, bachelor's, master's, and postbachelor's certificates (also offers adult program with significant enrollment not reflected in profile).

STUDENT LIFE

Housing options: on-campus residence required through sophomore year; coed, women-only. Campus housing is university owned and leased by the school. Freshman campus housing is guaranteed.

Activities and organizations: drama/theater group, student-run newspaper, radio station, choral group, Education Club, Black Student Union, Campus Activities Board, International Club, Hood Today (newspaper).

Athletics Member NCAA. All Division III.

Campus security: 24-hour emergency response devices and patrols, late-night transport/escort service, controlled dormitory access.

Student services: health clinic, personal/psychological counseling.

COSTS & FINANCIAL AID

Costs (2014–15) ***Comprehensive fee:*** $45,730 includes full-time tuition ($33,620), mandatory fees ($500), and room and board ($11,610). Part-time tuition: $975 per credit. ***Required fees:*** $160 per term part-time. ***College room only:*** $6080. Room and board charges vary according to board plan and housing facility.

Financial Aid Of all full-time matriculated undergraduates who enrolled in 2013, 1,143 applied for aid, 1,068 were judged to have need, 159 had their need fully met. 307 Federal Work-Study jobs (averaging $1475). 40 state and other part-time jobs (averaging $1455). In 2013, 166 non-need-based awards were made. ***Average percent of need met:*** 74. ***Average financial aid package:*** $26,534. ***Average need-based loan:*** $5531. ***Average need-based gift aid:*** $21,564. ***Average non-need-based aid:*** $15,665. ***Average indebtedness upon graduation:*** $29,760.

APPLYING

Standardized Tests *Required:* SAT or ACT (for admission).

Options: electronic application, early decision, early action, deferred entrance.

Application fee: $35.

Required: essay or personal statement, high school transcript, minimum 2.0 GPA. ***Required for some:*** test scores (ACT/SAT) unless applying SAT Optional with a minimum high school GPA of 3.26 on a 4.0 scale. ***Recommended:*** 1 letter of recommendation, interview.

CONTACT

Ms. Jennifer Decker, Freshman Counselor, Hood College, 401 Rosemont Avenue, Frederick, MD 21701. *Phone:* 301-696-3400. *Toll-free phone:* 800-922-1599. *Fax:* 301-696-3819. *E-mail:* admission@hood.edu.

ITT Technical Institute

Hanover, Maryland

http://www.itt-tech.edu/

- **Proprietary** 4-year
- **Coed**
- **Minimally difficult** entrance level

ACADEMICS

Degrees: associate and bachelor's.

CONTACT

Director of Recruitment, ITT Technical Institute, 7030 Dorsey Road, Suite 100, Hanover, MD 21076. *Phone:* 410-694-4700. *Toll-free phone:* 877-243-6993.

ITT Technical Institute

Owings Mills, Maryland

http://www.itt-tech.edu/

- **Proprietary** primarily 2-year, founded 2005
- **Coed**
- **Minimally difficult** entrance level

ACADEMICS

Calendar: quarters. *Degrees:* associate and bachelor's.

STUDENT LIFE

Housing options: college housing not available.

CONTACT

Director of Recruitment, ITT Technical Institute, 11301 Red Run Boulevard, Owings Mills, MD 21117. *Phone:* 443-394-7115. *Toll-free phone:* 877-411-6782.

★ Johns Hopkins University

Baltimore, Maryland

http://www.jhu.edu/

- **Independent** university, founded 1876
- **Urban** 140-acre campus with easy access to Baltimore and Washington, DC
- **Endowment** $3.5 billion
- **Coed** 5,365 undergraduate students, 99% full-time, 49% women, 51% men
- **Most difficult** entrance level, 15% of applicants were admitted

UNDERGRAD STUDENTS
5,335 full-time, 30 part-time. Students come from 54 states and territories; 62 other countries; 88% are from out of state; 5% Black or African American, non-Hispanic/Latino; 13% Hispanic/Latino; 21% Asian, non-Hispanic/Latino; 0.1% Native Hawaiian or other Pacific Islander, non-Hispanic/Latino; 0.1% American Indian or Alaska Native, non-Hispanic/Latino; 5% Two or more races, non-Hispanic/Latino; 2% Race/ethnicity unknown; 9% international; 0.7% transferred in; 52% live on campus.

Freshmen
Admission: 23,877 applied, 3,587 admitted, 1,414 enrolled. ***Average high school GPA:*** 3.88. ***Test scores:*** SAT critical reading scores over 500: 100%; SAT math scores over 500: 100%; SAT writing scores over 500: 99%; ACT scores over 18: 100%; SAT critical reading scores over 600: 97%; SAT math scores over 600: 98%; SAT writing scores over 600: 96%; ACT scores over 24: 100%; SAT critical reading scores over 700: 62%; SAT math scores over 700: 75%; SAT writing scores over 700: 67%; ACT scores over 30: 95%.

Retention: 97% of full-time freshmen returned.

FACULTY
Total: 640, 90% full-time, 92% with terminal degrees.

Student/faculty ratio: 12:1.

ACADEMICS
Calendar: 4-1-4. *Degrees:* certificates, diplomas, bachelor's, master's, doctoral, post-master's, and postbachelor's certificates.

Special study options: advanced placement credit, double majors, independent study, internships, off-campus study, services for LD students, student-designed majors, study abroad, summer session for credit. ***ROTC:*** Army (b), Air Force (c).

Unusual degree programs: 3-2 engineering; International Studies with Johns Hopkins University, School of Advanced International Studies (Washington, DC); Biology; Classics; German; History; Neuroscience; Public Policy; Mathematics; Education.

Computers: 200 computers/terminals and 4,000 ports are available on campus for general student use. Students can access the following: campus intranet, computer help desk, free student e-mail accounts, online (class) grades, online (class) registration, online (class) schedules. Campuswide network is available. 100% of college-owned or -operated housing units are wired for high-speed Internet access. Wireless service is available via classrooms, computer centers, computer labs, dorm rooms, libraries.

STUDENT LIFE
Housing options: on-campus residence required through sophomore year; coed, special housing for students with disabilities. Campus housing is university owned. Freshman campus housing is guaranteed.

Activities and organizations: drama/theater group, student-run newspaper, radio station, choral group, Hopkins Organization for Programming (The Hop), Johns Hopkins Model United Nations Conference (JHUMUNC), The Outdoors Club, JHU Tutorial Project, JHU Student Government Association (SGA), national fraternities, national sororities.

Athletics Member NCAA. All Division III except men's and women's lacrosse (Division I). ***Intercollegiate sports:*** baseball M, basketball M/W, cross-country running M/W, fencing M/W, field hockey W, football M, lacrosse M(s)/W(s), soccer M/W, swimming and diving M/W, tennis M/W, track and field M/W, volleyball W, water polo M, wrestling M. ***Intramural sports:*** badminton M(c)/W(c), baseball M(c), basketball M/W, cheerleading W(c), equestrian sports M(c)/W(c), field hockey W(c), football M/W, golf M(c)/W(c), gymnastics M(c)/W(c), ice hockey M(c)/W(c), lacrosse M(c)/W(c), rock climbing M/W, rugby M(c)/W(c), soccer M/W, softball W(c), squash M(c)/W(c), table tennis M(c)/W(c), tennis M(c)/W(c), ultimate Frisbee M(c)/W(c), volleyball M(c)/W(c), water polo M(c)/W(c), wrestling M(c).

Campus security: 24-hour emergency response devices and patrols, student patrols, late-night transport/escort service, controlled dormitory access, CCTV monitoring of public areas.

Student services: health clinic, personal/psychological counseling.

COSTS & FINANCIAL AID

Costs (2014–15) ***One-time required fee:*** $500. ***Comprehensive fee:*** $61,306 includes full-time tuition ($47,060) and room and board ($14,246). Part-time tuition: $1570 per credit hour. ***College room only:*** $8168. Room and board charges vary according to board plan and housing facility. ***Payment plan:*** installment. ***Waivers:*** employees or children of employees.

Financial Aid Of all full-time matriculated undergraduates who enrolled in 2013, 1,878 Federal Work-Study jobs (averaging $2280). ***Financial aid deadline:*** 3/1.

APPLYING

Standardized Tests *Required:* SAT or ACT (for admission). *Recommended:* SAT and SAT Subject Tests or ACT (for admission), SAT Subject Tests (for admission), Strongly recommend 2 SAT Subject Tests. SAT Math Level 2 and at least one SAT science subject test strongly recommended for students applying to the school of engineering.

Options: electronic application, early admission, early decision, deferred entrance.

Application fee: $70.

Required: essay or personal statement, high school transcript, 2 letters of recommendation. ***Recommended:*** interview.

Application deadlines: 1/1 (freshmen), 3/15 (transfers).

Early decision deadline: 11/1.

Notification: 4/1 (freshmen), 5/31 (transfers), 12/15 (early decision).

CONTACT

Ms. Susan Muller, Application Coordinator, Johns Hopkins University, Mason Hall, 3400 North Charles Street, Baltimore, MD 21218-2699. *Phone:* 410-516-8171. *Fax:* 410-516-6025. *E-mail:* gotojhu@jhu.edu.

See previous page for display ad and page 1482 for the College Close-Up.

★ Loyola University Maryland
Baltimore, Maryland
http://www.loyola.edu/

- **Independent Roman Catholic (Jesuit)** university, founded 1852
- **Urban** 89-acre campus with easy access to Washington, DC
- **Endowment** $159.3 million
- **Coed**
- **Moderately difficult** entrance level

FACULTY

Student/faculty ratio: 12:1.

ACADEMICS

Calendar: semesters. *Degrees:* bachelor's, master's, doctoral, post-master's, and postbachelor's certificates.

STUDENT LIFE

Housing options: coed, cooperative. Freshman campus housing is guaranteed.

Activities and organizations: drama/theater group, student-run newspaper, radio and television station, choral group, Student Government Association, Resident Affairs Council (RAC), Relay for Life, Resident Assistants (RA), The Evergreens.

Athletics Member NCAA. All Division I.

Campus security: 24-hour emergency response devices and patrols, late-night transport/escort service, controlled dormitory access.

Student services: health clinic, personal/psychological counseling, women's center.

COSTS & FINANCIAL AID

Costs (2014–15) ***Comprehensive fee:*** $57,045 includes full-time tuition ($42,690), mandatory fees ($1565), and room and board ($12,790). Full-

time tuition and fees vary according to course load. Part-time tuition: $692 per credit. Part-time tuition and fees vary according to course load. ***Room and board:*** Room and board charges vary according to housing facility.

Financial Aid Of all full-time matriculated undergraduates who enrolled in 2012, 2,557 applied for aid, 2,219 were judged to have need, 1,997 had their need fully met. In 2012, 325 non-need-based awards were made. ***Average percent of need met:*** 94. ***Average financial aid package:*** $27,655. ***Average need-based loan:*** $4645. ***Average need-based gift aid:*** $21,620. ***Average non-need-based aid:*** $15,875. ***Average indebtedness upon graduation:*** $34,012. ***Financial aid deadline:*** 2/15.

APPLYING
Options: electronic application, early admission, early action, deferred entrance.

Application fee: $50.

Required: essay or personal statement, high school transcript.

CONTACT
Loyola University Maryland, 4501 North Charles Street, Baltimore, MD 21210-2699. *Phone:* 410-617-2000. *Toll-free phone:* 800-221-9107.

See previous page for display ad and page 1506 for the College Close-Up.

Maryland Institute College of Art

Baltimore, Maryland

http://www.mica.edu/

- **Independent** comprehensive, founded 1826
- **Urban** 16-acre campus with easy access to Washington, DC
- **Endowment** $72.9 million
- **Coed**
- **Very difficult** entrance level

FACULTY
Student/faculty ratio: 10:1.

ACADEMICS
Calendar: semesters. *Degrees:* bachelor's, master's, and postbachelor's certificates.

STUDENT LIFE
Housing options: coed, special housing for students with disabilities. Campus housing is university owned. Freshman campus housing is guaranteed.

Activities and organizations: drama/theater group, student-run radio station, choral group, Soccer Club, Urban Gaming Club, Black Student Union, Students of Sustainability, National Art Educators Association.

Campus security: 24-hour emergency response devices and patrols, student patrols, late-night transport/escort service, controlled dormitory access, self-defense education, 24-hour building security, safety awareness programs, campus patrols by city police.

Student services: health clinic, personal/psychological counseling.

FINANCIAL AID
Financial Aid ***Average indebtedness upon graduation:*** $17,472.

APPLYING
Standardized Tests *Required:* SAT or ACT (for admission).

Options: electronic application, early admission, early decision, deferred entrance.

Application fee: $60.

Required: essay or personal statement, high school transcript, 3 letters of recommendation, art portfolio. ***Recommended:*** interview.

CONTACT
Ms. Christine Seese, Director of Undergraduate Admission, Maryland Institute College of Art, 1300 Mount Royal Avenue, Baltimore, MD 21217. *Phone:* 410-225-2222. *Fax:* 410-225-2337. *E-mail:* cgyland@mica.edu.

★ McDaniel College

Westminster, Maryland

http://www.mcdaniel.edu/

- **Independent** comprehensive, founded 1867
- **Suburban** 160-acre campus with easy access to Baltimore and Washington, DC
- **Endowment** $113.5 million
- **Coed** 1,706 undergraduate students, 98% full-time, 53% women, 47% men
- **Moderately difficult** entrance level, 76% of applicants were admitted

UNDERGRAD STUDENTS
1,665 full-time, 41 part-time. Students come from 35 states and territories; 15 other countries; 64% are from out of state; 11% Black or African American, non-Hispanic/Latino; 6% Hispanic/Latino; 3% Asian, non-Hispanic/Latino; 0.1% Native Hawaiian or other Pacific Islander, non-Hispanic/Latino; 0.4% American Indian or Alaska Native, non-Hispanic/Latino; 3% Two or more races, non-Hispanic/Latino; 2% Race/ethnicity unknown; 1% international; 4% transferred in; 78% live on campus.

Freshmen
Admission: 2,966 applied, 2,258 admitted, 412 enrolled. ***Average high school GPA:*** 3.46. ***Test scores:*** SAT critical reading scores over 500: 75%; SAT math scores over 500: 75%; ACT scores over 18: 99%; SAT critical reading scores over 600: 28%; SAT math scores over 600: 30%; ACT scores over 24: 51%; SAT critical reading scores over 700: 6%; SAT math scores over 700: 4%; ACT scores over 30: 14%.

Retention: 83% of full-time freshmen returned.

FACULTY
Total: 378, 29% full-time, 50% with terminal degrees.

Student/faculty ratio: 11:1.

ACADEMICS
Calendar: 4-1-4. *Degrees:* bachelor's, master's, and postbachelor's certificates.

Special study options: academic remediation for entering students, adult/continuing education programs, advanced placement credit, distance learning, double majors, honors programs, independent study, internships, off-campus study, part-time degree program, services for LD students, student-designed majors, study abroad, summer session for credit. ***ROTC:*** Army (b).

Computers: 138 computers/terminals and 1,500 ports are available on campus for general student use. Students can access the following: campus intranet, computer help desk, free student e-mail accounts, online (class) grades, online (class) registration, online (class) schedules, online billing summaries, financial aid letter, tax information. Campuswide network is available. 100% of college-owned or -operated housing units are wired for high-speed Internet access. Wireless service is available via entire campus.

STUDENT LIFE
Housing options: on-campus residence required through junior year; coed, special housing for students with disabilities. Campus housing is university owned. Freshman campus housing is guaranteed.

Activities and organizations: drama/theater group, student-run newspaper, radio and television station, choral group, Student Government Association, Black Student Union, International Club, Maryland State Legislature, Up 'til Dawn, national fraternities, national sororities.

Athletics Member NCAA. All Division III. ***Intercollegiate sports:*** baseball M, basketball M/W, cross-country running M/W, field hockey W, football M, golf M/W, lacrosse M/W, soccer M/W, softball W, swimming and diving M/W, tennis M/W, track and field M/W, volleyball W, wrestling M. ***Intramural sports:*** badminton M/W, basketball M/W, cheerleading M(c)/W(c), equestrian sports W(c), football M, golf M/W, skiing (downhill) M(c)/W(c), soccer M/W, softball M/W, ultimate Frisbee M(c)/W(c), volleyball M/W.

Campus security: 24-hour emergency response devices and patrols, late-night transport/escort service, About half patrol force sworn as campus police. All are certified to US DOT First Responder standards.

Student services: health clinic, personal/psychological counseling.

COSTS & FINANCIAL AID

Costs (2014–15) ***Comprehensive fee:*** $47,450 includes full-time tuition ($38,350) and room and board ($9100). Full-time tuition and fees vary according to course load. Part-time tuition: $1198 per credit hour. Part-time tuition and fees vary according to course load and reciprocity agreements. ***College room only:*** $4550. Room and board charges vary according to board plan and housing facility. ***Payment plans:*** tuition prepayment, installment. ***Waivers:*** employees or children of employees.

Financial Aid Of all full-time matriculated undergraduates who enrolled in 2013, 1,339 applied for aid, 1,217 were judged to have need, 390 had their need fully met. 350 Federal Work-Study jobs (averaging $1500). In 2013, 361 non-need-based awards were made. ***Average percent of need met:*** 86. ***Average financial aid package:*** $31,352. ***Average need-based loan:*** $4732. ***Average need-based gift aid:*** $25,562. ***Average non-need-based aid:*** $17,787. ***Average indebtedness upon graduation:*** $29,554.

APPLYING

Standardized Tests *Required for some:* SAT or ACT (for admission).

Options: electronic application, early admission, early action, deferred entrance.

Application fee: $50.

Required: essay or personal statement, high school transcript, minimum 2.5 GPA, 2 letters of recommendation. ***Required for some:*** interview. ***Recommended:*** interview.

Application deadlines: 2/15 (freshmen), 2/15 (out-of-state freshmen), 6/1 (transfers), 12/1 (early action).

Notification: 3/7 (freshmen), 3/7 (out-of-state freshmen), 6/15 (transfers), 12/22 (early action).

CONTACT

Ms. Florence Hines, Vice President for Enrollment Management and Dean of Admissions, McDaniel College, 2 College Hill, Westminster, MD 21157-4390. *Phone:* 410-857-2230. *Toll-free phone:* 800-638-5005. *Fax:* 410-857-2757. *E-mail:* admissions@mcdaniel.edu.

Mount St. Mary's University

Emmitsburg, Maryland

http://www.msmary.edu/

- **Independent Roman Catholic** comprehensive, founded 1808
- **Rural** 1400-acre campus with easy access to Baltimore and Washington, DC
- **Endowment** $52.3 million
- **Coed** 1,810 undergraduate students, 95% full-time, 56% women, 44% men
- **Moderately difficult** entrance level, 67% of applicants were admitted

UNDERGRAD STUDENTS

1,723 full-time, 87 part-time. Students come from 36 states and territories; 13 other countries; 49% are from out of state; 11% Black or African American, non-Hispanic/Latino; 9% Hispanic/Latino; 2% Asian, non-Hispanic/Latino; 0.1% Native Hawaiian or other Pacific Islander, non-Hispanic/Latino; 0.3% American Indian or Alaska Native, non-Hispanic/Latino; 4% Two or more races, non-Hispanic/Latino; 2% Race/ethnicity unknown; 0.9% international; 2% transferred in; 83% live on campus.

Freshmen

Admission: 6,142 applied, 4,107 admitted, 510 enrolled. ***Average high school GPA:*** 3.39. ***Test scores:*** SAT critical reading scores over 500: 66%; SAT math scores over 500: 66%; SAT writing scores over 500: 58%; ACT scores over 18: 88%; SAT critical reading scores over 600: 21%; SAT math scores over 600: 16%; SAT writing scores over 600: 15%; ACT scores over 24: 27%; SAT critical reading scores over 700: 3%; SAT math scores over 700: 2%; SAT writing scores over 700: 2%.

Retention: 79% of full-time freshmen returned.

FACULTY

Total: 203, 58% full-time, 63% with terminal degrees.

Student/faculty ratio: 13:1.

ACADEMICS

Calendar: semesters. *Degrees:* bachelor's, master's, post-master's, and postbachelor's certificates.

Special study options: academic remediation for entering students, accelerated degree program, adult/continuing education programs, advanced placement credit, double majors, honors programs, independent study, internships, off-campus study, part-time degree program, services for LD students, student-designed majors, study abroad, summer session for credit. ***ROTC:*** Army (c).

Unusual degree programs: 3-2 nursing with University of MD, Shenandoah University.

Computers: 80 computers/terminals are available on campus for general student use. Students can access the following: campus intranet, computer help desk, free student e-mail accounts, online (class) grades, online (class) registration, online (class) schedules, tuition payment, course management system. Campuswide network is available. 100% of college-owned or -operated housing units are wired for high-speed Internet access. Wireless service is available via entire campus.

STUDENT LIFE

Housing options: on-campus residence required for freshman year; coed, special housing for students with disabilities. Campus housing is university owned. Freshman campus housing is guaranteed.

Activities and organizations: drama/theater group, student-run newspaper, radio and television station, choral group, Mount Students for Life, CRUX - Outdoor Adventures, Campus Ministry Student Organization, Circle K, Mount Chorale.

Athletics Member NCAA. All Division I. ***Intercollegiate sports:*** baseball M(s), basketball M(s)/W(s), cheerleading W(c), cross-country running M(s)/W(s), equestrian sports M(c)/W(c), ice hockey M(c)/W(c), lacrosse M(s)/W(s), rugby M(c)/W(c), soccer W(s), softball W(s), swimming and diving W(s), tennis M(s)/W(s), track and field M(s)/W(s). ***Intramural sports:*** basketball M, field hockey M/W, skiing (downhill) M/W, soccer M/W, softball M/W, tennis M/W, ultimate Frisbee M/W, volleyball W.

Campus security: 24-hour emergency response devices and patrols, late-night transport/escort service, controlled dormitory access.

Student services: health clinic, personal/psychological counseling.

COSTS & FINANCIAL AID

Costs (2015–16) ***Comprehensive fee:*** $49,900 includes full-time tuition ($36,250), mandatory fees ($1250), and room and board ($12,400). Full-time tuition and fees vary according to location and program. Part-time tuition: $1210 per credit. Part-time tuition and fees vary according to location and program. ***College room only:*** $6070. Room and board charges vary according to housing facility. ***Payment plan:*** installment. ***Waivers:*** employees or children of employees.

Financial Aid Of all full-time matriculated undergraduates who enrolled in 2014, 1,351 applied for aid, 1,187 were judged to have need, 280 had their need fully met. 130 Federal Work-Study jobs (averaging $1800). 680 state and other part-time jobs (averaging $1200). In 2014, 471 non-need-based awards were made. ***Average percent of need met:*** 73. ***Average financial aid package:*** $24,665. ***Average need-based loan:*** $4615. ***Average need-based gift aid:*** $20,282. ***Average non-need-based aid:*** $15,923. ***Average indebtedness upon graduation:*** $36,130. ***Financial aid deadline:*** 3/1.

APPLYING

Standardized Tests *Required:* SAT or ACT (for admission).

Options: electronic application, early action, deferred entrance.

Application fee: $45.

Required: high school transcript, minimum 2.0 GPA, 1 letter of recommendation. ***Recommended:*** essay or personal statement, minimum 3.0 GPA, interview.

Application deadlines: 3/1 (freshmen), 6/1 (transfers), 12/1 (early action).

Notification: continuous (freshmen), continuous (transfers), 12/25 (early action).

CONTACT

Mr. Michael Post, Dean of Admissions and Enrollment Management, Mount St. Mary's University, 16300 Old Emmitsburg Road, Emmitsburg, MD 21727. *Phone:* 301-447-5214. *Toll-free phone:* 800-448-4347. *Fax:* 301-447-5860. *E-mail:* admissions@msmary.edu.

Notre Dame of Maryland University

Baltimore, Maryland

http://www.ndm.edu/

- **Independent Roman Catholic** comprehensive, founded 1873
- **Urban** 58-acre campus with easy access to Baltimore and Washington, DC
- **Coed, primarily women** 1,169 undergraduate students, 46% full-time, 95% women, 5% men
- **Moderately difficult** entrance level, 49% of applicants were admitted

UNDERGRAD STUDENTS
538 full-time, 631 part-time. Students come from 18 states and territories; 12 other countries; 7% are from out of state; 27% Black or African American, non-Hispanic/Latino; 6% Hispanic/Latino; 5% Asian, non-Hispanic/Latino; 0.3% Native Hawaiian or other Pacific Islander, non-Hispanic/Latino; 3% American Indian or Alaska Native, non-Hispanic/Latino; 1% Race/ethnicity unknown; 1% international; 5% transferred in.

Freshmen
Admission: 827 applied, 409 admitted, 107 enrolled. ***Average high school GPA:*** 3.66. ***Test scores:*** SAT critical reading scores over 500: 67%; SAT math scores over 500: 58%; ACT scores over 18: 100%; SAT critical reading scores over 600: 17%; SAT math scores over 600: 18%; ACT scores over 24: 53%; SAT critical reading scores over 700: 3%; SAT math scores over 700: 7%; ACT scores over 30: 6%.

Retention: 85% of full-time freshmen returned.

FACULTY
Total: 136, 93% full-time.

Student/faculty ratio: 11:1.

ACADEMICS
Calendar: 4-1-4. *Degrees:* certificates, bachelor's, master's, doctoral, post-master's, and postbachelor's certificates (offers coed undergraduate program for adult students).

Special study options: accelerated degree program, adult/continuing education programs, advanced placement credit, distance learning, double majors, English as a second language, honors programs, independent study, internships, off-campus study, part-time degree program, services for LD students, student-designed majors, study abroad, summer session for credit. ***ROTC:*** Army (c).

Unusual degree programs: 3-2 engineering with University of Maryland, College Park; Johns Hopkins University; radiological science with Johns Hopkins University.

Computers: 100 computers/terminals are available on campus for general student use. Students can access the following: campus intranet, computer help desk, free student e-mail accounts, online (class) grades, online (class) registration, online (class) schedules, online classroom assignments and information. Campuswide network is available. 100% of college-owned or -operated housing units are wired for high-speed Internet access. Wireless service is available via entire campus.

STUDENT LIFE
Housing options: on-campus residence required through sophomore year; women-only, special housing for students with disabilities. Campus housing is university owned. Freshman campus housing is guaranteed.

Activities and organizations: drama/theater group, student-run newspaper, radio and television station, choral group, Omega Phi Alpha Service Sorority, Maryland Student Legislature, Business and Economics Society, Sigma Tau Delta Honor Society, Residence Hall Council.

Athletics Member NCAA. All Division III. ***Intercollegiate sports:*** basketball W, field hockey W, lacrosse W, soccer W, softball W, swimming and diving W, tennis W, volleyball W.

Campus security: 24-hour emergency response devices and patrols, late-night transport/escort service, controlled dormitory access, emergency call boxes.

Student services: health clinic, personal/psychological counseling, women's center.

COSTS & FINANCIAL AID
Costs (2015–16) ***Comprehensive fee:*** $44,600 includes full-time tuition ($32,548), mandatory fees ($1122), and room and board ($10,930). Part-time tuition: $485 per credit. Part-time tuition and fees vary according to course load and reciprocity agreements. ***Required fees:*** $130 per term part-time. ***Payment plans:*** installment, deferred payment. ***Waivers:*** employees or children of employees.

Financial Aid Of all full-time matriculated undergraduates who enrolled in 2013, 469 applied for aid, 440 were judged to have need, 67 had their need fully met. 90 Federal Work-Study jobs (averaging $1091). In 2013, 68 non-need-based awards were made. ***Average percent of need met:*** 67. ***Average financial aid package:*** $23,572. ***Average need-based loan:*** $4401. ***Average need-based gift aid:*** $19,711. ***Average non-need-based aid:*** $16,044. ***Average indebtedness upon graduation:*** $32,346.

APPLYING
Standardized Tests *Required:* SAT or ACT (for admission).

Options: electronic application, early admission, early action, deferred entrance.

Application fee: $45.

Required: essay or personal statement, high school transcript, minimum 2.5 GPA, 2 letters of recommendation. ***Recommended:*** minimum 3.0 GPA, interview, resume.

Application deadlines: rolling (freshmen), rolling (out-of-state freshmen), rolling (transfers).

Notification: continuous (freshmen), continuous (out-of-state freshmen), continuous (transfers).

CONTACT
Angela Baumler, Director of Admissions (Women's College), Notre Dame of Maryland University, 4701 N Charles Street, Baltimore, MD 21210. *Phone:* -410-532-5330. *Toll-free phone:* 800-435-0200. *E-mail:* abaumler@ndm.edu.

Peabody Conservatory of The Johns Hopkins University

Baltimore, Maryland

http://www.peabody.jhu.edu/

- **Independent** comprehensive, founded 1857
- **Urban** 1-acre campus with easy access to Washington, DC
- **Endowment** $106.2 million
- **Coed** 269 undergraduate students, 97% full-time, 49% women, 51% men
- **Very difficult** entrance level, 52% of applicants were admitted

UNDERGRAD STUDENTS
262 full-time, 7 part-time. Students come from 33 states and territories; 16 other countries; 72% are from out of state; 5% Black or African American, non-Hispanic/Latino; 4% Hispanic/Latino; 27% Asian, non-Hispanic/Latino; 1% American Indian or Alaska Native, non-Hispanic/Latino; 18% international; 5% transferred in; 40% live on campus.

Freshmen
Admission: 711 applied, 367 admitted, 54 enrolled.

Retention: 87% of full-time freshmen returned.

FACULTY
Total: 178, 46% full-time, 21% with terminal degrees.

Student/faculty ratio: 6:1.

ACADEMICS
Calendar: semesters. *Degrees:* certificates, diplomas, bachelor's, master's, doctoral, post-master's, and postbachelor's certificates.

Special study options: academic remediation for entering students, accelerated degree program, advanced placement credit, double majors, English as a second language, honors programs, independent study, internships, off-campus study, services for LD students.

Computers: 40 computers/terminals are available on campus for general student use. Students can access the following: campus intranet, computer help desk, free student e-mail accounts, online (class) grades, online (class) registration, online (class) schedules, word processing, music processing. Campuswide network is available. 100% of college-owned or -operated housing units are wired for high-speed Internet access. Wireless service is available via entire campus.

STUDENT LIFE
Housing options: on-campus residence required through sophomore year; coed. Campus housing is university owned. Freshman campus housing is guaranteed.

Activities and organizations: choral group.

Campus security: 24-hour emergency response devices and patrols, late-night transport/escort service, controlled dormitory access.

Student services: health clinic, personal/psychological counseling.

COSTS & FINANCIAL AID
Costs (2014–15) ***One-time required fee:*** $700. ***Comprehensive fee:*** $55,390 includes full-time tuition ($41,190), mandatory fees ($680), and room and board ($13,520). Full-time tuition and fees vary according to program. Part-time tuition: $1175 per semester hour. Part-time tuition and fees vary according to course load. ***Room and board:*** Room and board charges vary according to board plan. ***Payment plan:*** installment.

Financial Aid Of all full-time matriculated undergraduates who enrolled in 2013, 207 applied for aid, 169 were judged to have need, 36 had their need fully met. In 2013, 81 non-need-based awards were made. ***Average percent of need met:*** 72. ***Average financial aid package:*** $16,268. ***Average need-based loan:*** $5679. ***Average need-based gift aid:*** $12,396. ***Average non-need-based aid:*** $18,543. ***Average indebtedness upon graduation:*** $30,960.

APPLYING
Standardized Tests *Required for some:* SAT or ACT (for admission).

Application fee: $100.

Required: essay or personal statement, high school transcript, 3 letters of recommendation, interview, audition. ***Recommended:*** minimum 3.0 GPA.

Application deadlines: 12/1 (freshmen), 12/1 (transfers).

Notification: 4/1 (freshmen), 4/1 (transfers).

CONTACT
Mr. David Lane, Director of Admissions, Peabody Conservatory of The Johns Hopkins University, Peabody Conservatory Admissions Office, One East Mount Vernon Place, Baltimore, MD 21202-2397. *Phone:* 410-234-4848. *Toll-free phone:* 800-368-2521.

★ St. John's College

Annapolis, Maryland

http://www.stjohnscollege.edu/

- **Independent** comprehensive, founded 1784
- **Urban** 36-acre campus with easy access to Baltimore and Washington, DC
- **Endowment** $89.3 million
- **Coed** 426 undergraduate students, 100% full-time, 45% women, 55% men
- **Moderately difficult** entrance level, 87% of applicants were admitted

UNDERGRAD STUDENTS
426 full-time. Students come from 39 states and territories; 18 other countries; 81% are from out of state; 1% Black or African American, non-Hispanic/Latino; 5% Hispanic/Latino; 3% Asian, non-Hispanic/Latino; 0.2% American Indian or Alaska Native, non-Hispanic/Latino; 3% Two or more races, non-Hispanic/Latino; 1% Race/ethnicity unknown; 10% international; 5% transferred in; 80% live on campus.

Freshmen
Admission: 345 applied, 299 admitted, 133 enrolled. ***Test scores:*** SAT critical reading scores over 500: 99%; SAT math scores over 500: 98%; SAT writing scores over 500: 99%; ACT scores over 18: 100%; SAT critical reading scores over 600: 86%; SAT math scores over 600: 61%; SAT writing scores over 600: 81%; ACT scores over 24: 97%; SAT critical reading scores over 700: 51%; SAT math scores over 700: 25%; SAT writing scores over 700: 27%; ACT scores over 30: 53%.
Retention: 83% of full-time freshmen returned.

FACULTY
Total: 78, 90% full-time, 74% with terminal degrees.

Student/faculty ratio: 7:1.

ACADEMICS
Calendar: semesters. *Degrees:* bachelor's and master's.

Special study options: internships, off-campus study.

Computers: 22 computers/terminals are available on campus for general student use. Students can access the following: computer help desk, free student e-mail accounts. Campuswide network is available. 100% of college-owned or -operated housing units are wired for high-speed Internet access. Wireless service is available via entire campus.

STUDENT LIFE
Housing options: on-campus residence required through senior year; coed. Campus housing is university owned. Freshman campus housing is guaranteed.

Activities and organizations: drama/theater group, student-run newspaper, choral group, King William's Players (drama), Reality (social), Delegate Council (student government), Waltz (social), Student Committee on Instruction (advisory).

Athletics Member USCAA. ***Intercollegiate sports:*** crew M(c)/W(c), fencing M(c)/W(c), sailing M(c)/W(c). ***Intramural sports:*** badminton M(c)/W(c), basketball M/W, fencing M(c)/W(c), football M/W, sailing M(c)/W(c), soccer M(c)/W(c), swimming and diving M(c)/W(c), tennis M(c)/W(c), track and field M(c)/W(c), volleyball M/W, weight lifting M(c)/W(c).

Campus security: 24-hour emergency response devices and patrols, late-night transport/escort service, controlled dormitory access, Personal Whistle Safety Program; Operation ID (Identification of Valuables).

Student services: health clinic, personal/psychological counseling.

COSTS & FINANCIAL AID
Costs (2015–16) ***Comprehensive fee:*** includes mandatory fees ($450) and room and board ($11,270). ***Room and board:*** Room and board charges vary according to board plan and housing facility. ***Payment plans:*** tuition prepayment, installment. ***Waivers:*** employees or children of employees.

Financial Aid Of all full-time matriculated undergraduates who enrolled in 2014, 348 applied for aid, 313 were judged to have need, 65 had their need fully met. 101 Federal Work-Study jobs (averaging $2712). 95 state and other part-time jobs (averaging $2668). In 2014, 80 non-need-based awards were made. ***Average percent of need met:*** 81. ***Average financial aid package:*** $35,892. ***Average need-based loan:*** $4855. ***Average need-based gift aid:*** $30,564. ***Average non-need-based aid:*** $19,258. ***Average indebtedness upon graduation:*** $28,730.

APPLYING
Standardized Tests *Required for some:* SAT or ACT (for admission), International applicants must submit the results of the SAT or ACT, unless they currently participate in an IB program. We also require the TOEFL if the applicant's first language is not English.

Options: electronic application, early admission, early action, deferred entrance.

Required: essay or personal statement, high school transcript, 2 letters of recommendation. ***Required for some:*** Home-schooled applicants must submit a GED or its equivalent, or the results of the SAT or ACT. They should also submit an outline of the curriculum they have followed, with brief descriptions of the course content and texts used. ***Recommended:*** interview.

Application deadlines: rolling (freshmen), 11/15 (early action).

Notification: continuous (freshmen), 12/15 (early action).

CONTACT
Mr. Thomas Weede, Director of Admissions, St. John's College, 60 College Avenue, Annapolis, MD 21401. *Phone:* 410-626-2522. *Toll-free phone:* 800-727-9238. *Fax:* 410-269-7916. *E-mail:* annapolis.admissions@sjc.edu.

St. Mary's College of Maryland

St. Mary's City, Maryland

http://www.smcm.edu/

- **State-supported** comprehensive, founded 1840
- **Rural** 361-acre campus
- **Endowment** $33.0 million
- **Coed** 1,771 undergraduate students, 96% full-time, 57% women, 43% men
- **Moderately difficult** entrance level, 79% of applicants were admitted

UNDERGRAD STUDENTS
1,709 full-time, 62 part-time. Students come from 30 states and territories; 22 other countries; 9% are from out of state; 8% Black or African American, non-Hispanic/Latino; 7% Hispanic/Latino; 3% Asian, non-Hispanic/Latino; 0.3% American Indian or Alaska Native, non-Hispanic/Latino; 5% Two or more races, non-Hispanic/Latino; 3% Race/ethnicity unknown; 2% international; 5% transferred in; 82% live on campus.

Freshmen
Admission: 1,874 applied, 1,478 admitted, 379 enrolled. ***Average high school GPA:*** 3.39. ***Test scores:*** SAT critical reading scores over 500: 88%; SAT math scores over 500: 86%; SAT writing scores over 500: 83%; ACT scores over 18: 95%; SAT critical reading scores over 600: 47%; SAT math scores over 600: 43%; SAT writing scores over 600: 41%; ACT scores over 24: 70%; SAT critical reading scores over 700: 10%; SAT math scores over 700: 5%; SAT writing scores over 700: 6%; ACT scores over 30: 22%.

Retention: 86% of full-time freshmen returned.

FACULTY
Total: 214, 66% full-time, 81% with terminal degrees.

Student/faculty ratio: 11:1.

ACADEMICS
Calendar: semesters. *Degrees:* bachelor's and master's.

Special study options: advanced placement credit, cooperative education, double majors, freshman honors college, honors programs, independent study, internships, off-campus study, part-time degree program, services for LD students, student-designed majors, study abroad, summer session for credit.

Computers: 390 computers/terminals and 500 ports are available on campus for general student use. Students can access the following: campus intranet, computer help desk, free student e-mail accounts, online (class) grades, online (class) registration, online (class) schedules, Blackboard. Campuswide network is available. 100% of college-owned or -operated housing units are wired for high-speed Internet access. Wireless service is available via entire campus.

STUDENT LIFE
Housing options: coed, men-only, women-only, cooperative, special housing for students with disabilities. Campus housing is university owned. Freshman campus housing is guaranteed.

Activities and organizations: drama/theater group, student-run newspaper, radio station, choral group, Crew, Acappella groups, SEAC (Student Environmental Action Coalition), Dance Club, Outdoors Club.

Athletics Member NCAA. All Division III. ***Intercollegiate sports:*** badminton M/W, baseball M, basketball M/W, cheerleading M/W, crew M(c)/W(c), cross-country running M/W, equestrian sports M(c)/W(c), fencing M(c)/W(c), field hockey W, lacrosse M/W, rock climbing M(c)/W(c), rugby M(c)/W(c), sailing M/W, soccer M/W, swimming and diving M/W, tennis M/W, ultimate Frisbee M(c)/W(c), volleyball W. ***Intramural sports:*** badminton M/W, basketball M/W, football M/W, lacrosse M/W, soccer M/W, softball M/W, volleyball M/W.

Campus security: 24-hour emergency response devices and patrols, late-night transport/escort service, controlled dormitory access.

Student services: health clinic, personal/psychological counseling.

COSTS & FINANCIAL AID
Costs (2014–15) ***Tuition:*** state resident $11,195 full-time, $195 per credit hour part-time; nonresident $26,045 full-time, $195 per credit hour part-time. Full-time tuition and fees vary according to course load. Part-time tuition and fees vary according to course load. ***Required fees:*** $2629 full-time. ***Room and board:*** $11,930; room only: $6770. Room and board charges vary according to board plan and housing facility. ***Payment plan:*** installment. ***Waivers:*** senior citizens and employees or children of employees.

Financial Aid Of all full-time matriculated undergraduates who enrolled in 2013, 1,226 applied for aid, 824 were judged to have need, 62 had their need fully met. 117 Federal Work-Study jobs (averaging $861). In 2013, 288 non-need-based awards were made. ***Average percent of need met:*** 70. ***Average financial aid package:*** $14,332. ***Average need-based loan:*** $4198. ***Average need-based gift aid:*** $10,944. ***Average non-need-based aid:*** $4021. ***Average indebtedness upon graduation:*** $24,621.

APPLYING
Standardized Tests *Required:* SAT or ACT (for admission).

Options: electronic application, early admission, early decision, deferred entrance.

Application fee: $50.

Required: essay or personal statement, high school transcript, 2 letters of recommendation, Prospective students should apply online through the Common Application. ***Recommended:*** interview.

Application deadlines: 2/15 (freshmen), 4/1 (transfers).

Early decision deadline: 11/1 (for plan 1), 12/1 (for plan 2).

Notification: 3/1 (freshmen), 5/1 (transfers), 11/25 (early decision plan 1), 12/25 (early decision plan 2).

CONTACT
Mr. Gary Sherman, Vice President of Enrollment Management and Dean of Admissions, St. Mary's College of Maryland, 18952 East Fisher Road, St. Mary's City, MD 20686-3001. *Phone:* 240-895-5000. *Toll-free phone:* 800-492-7181. *Fax:* 240-895-5001. *E-mail:* admissions@smcm.edu.

Salisbury University
Salisbury, Maryland
http://www.salisbury.edu/

- **State-supported** comprehensive, founded 1925, part of University System of Maryland
- **Small-town** 183-acre campus
- **Endowment** $62.3 million
- **Coed** 7,997 undergraduate students, 92% full-time, 57% women, 43% men
- **Moderately difficult** entrance level, 55% of applicants were admitted

UNDERGRAD STUDENTS
7,350 full-time, 647 part-time. Students come from 35 states and territories; 68 other countries; 14% are from out of state; 12% Black or African American, non-Hispanic/Latino; 4% Hispanic/Latino; 3% Asian, non-Hispanic/Latino; 0.1% Native Hawaiian or other Pacific Islander, non-Hispanic/Latino; 0.4% American Indian or Alaska Native, non-Hispanic/Latino; 4% Two or more races, non-Hispanic/Latino; 3% Race/ethnicity unknown; 2% international; 12% transferred in; 28% live on campus.

Freshmen
Admission: 8,730 applied, 4,778 admitted, 1,157 enrolled. ***Average high school GPA:*** 3.75. ***Test scores:*** SAT critical reading scores over 500: 95%; SAT math scores over 500: 93%; SAT writing scores over 500: 93%; ACT scores over 18: 100%; SAT critical reading scores over 600: 36%; SAT math scores over 600: 37%; SAT writing scores over 600: 31%; ACT scores over 24: 52%; SAT critical reading scores over 700: 3%; SAT math scores over 700: 2%; SAT writing scores over 700: 2%; ACT scores over 30: 4%.

Retention: 82% of full-time freshmen returned.

FACULTY
Total: 660, 63% full-time, 57% with terminal degrees.

Student/faculty ratio: 16:1.

ACADEMICS
Calendar: 4-1-4. *Degrees:* bachelor's, master's, doctoral, and postbachelor's certificates.

Special study options: accelerated degree program, advanced placement credit, cooperative education, distance learning, double majors, English as a second language, freshman honors college, honors programs, independent study, internships, off-campus study, part-time degree program, services for LD students, student-designed majors, study abroad, summer session for credit. ***ROTC:*** Army (b), Air Force (c).

Unusual degree programs: 3-2 engineering with Pre-Engineering Program with University of Maryland College Park, Old Dominion University, and Widener University; social work with Social Work and Sociology Dual Degree Program with University of Maryland Eastern Shore; Biology and Environmental Marine Science with University of Maryland Eastern Shore.

Computers: 500 computers/terminals and 3,552 ports are available on campus for general student use. Students can access the following: campus intranet, computer help desk, free student e-mail accounts, online (class) grades, online (class) registration, online (class) schedules, University accounts. Campuswide network is available. 100% of college-owned or -operated housing units are wired for high-speed Internet access. Wireless service is available via entire campus.

STUDENT LIFE

Housing options: on-campus residence required through sophomore year; coed, special housing for students with disabilities. Campus housing is university owned. Freshman applicants given priority for college housing.

Activities and organizations: drama/theater group, student-run newspaper, radio and television station, choral group, Student Government Association, Radio (WXSU) / SU TV / The Flyer Newspaper, Student Organization for Activity Planning (SOAP), Campus Crusade for Christ, Union of African American Students, national fraternities, national sororities.

Athletics Member NCAA. All Division III. ***Intercollegiate sports:*** baseball M, basketball M/W, cross-country running M/W, field hockey W, football M, lacrosse M/W, soccer M/W, softball M/W, swimming and diving M/W, tennis M/W, track and field M/W, volleyball W. ***Intramural sports:*** archery M(c)/W(c), basketball M/W, cheerleading M(c)/W(c), equestrian sports W(c), fencing M(c)/W(c), field hockey W(c), gymnastics W(c), ice hockey M(c), lacrosse M(c)/W(c), racquetball M/W, rock climbing M(c)/W(c), rugby M(c)/W(c), sailing M(c)/W(c), soccer M/W, softball W, table tennis M(c)/W(c), ultimate Frisbee M(c)/W(c), volleyball M/W.

Campus security: 24-hour emergency response devices and patrols, student patrols, late-night transport/escort service, controlled dormitory access, lighted pathways, sidewalks, 24-hour university police protection, shuttle buses, emergency notification system, self-defense education.

Student services: health clinic, personal/psychological counseling.

COSTS & FINANCIAL AID

Costs (2014–15) ***Tuition:*** state resident $6268 full-time, $258 per credit hour part-time; nonresident $14,614 full-time, $605 per credit hour part-time. Full-time tuition and fees vary according to course load and degree level. Part-time tuition and fees vary according to course load and degree level. ***Required fees:*** $2292 full-time, $76 per credit hour part-time. ***Room and board:*** $10,620; room only: $6150. Room and board charges vary according to board plan and housing facility. ***Payment plan:*** installment. ***Waivers:*** senior citizens and employees or children of employees.

Financial Aid Of all full-time matriculated undergraduates who enrolled in 2013, 5,417 applied for aid, 3,926 were judged to have need, 451 had their need fully met. 73 Federal Work-Study jobs (averaging $1779). In 2013, 871 non-need-based awards were made. ***Average percent of need met:*** 53. ***Average financial aid package:*** $8174. ***Average need-based loan:*** $4297. ***Average need-based gift aid:*** $5881. ***Average non-need-based aid:*** $2322. ***Average indebtedness upon graduation:*** $24,567. ***Financial aid deadline:*** 12/31.

APPLYING

Standardized Tests *Required for some:* SAT or ACT (for admission), SAT/ACT not required for students who have been out of high school for more than 3 years or for whom TOEFL is required. Students earning a weighted grade point average of 3.5 or higher on a 4.0 scale may decide if they wish to submit standardized test scores.

Options: electronic application, early admission, early decision, early action, deferred entrance.

Application fee: $50.

Required: essay or personal statement, minimum 2.0 GPA. ***Required for some:*** high school transcript.

Application deadlines: 1/15 (freshmen), rolling (transfers), 12/1 (early action).

Early decision deadline: 11/15.

Notification: 3/15 (freshmen), continuous (transfers), 12/15 (early decision), 1/15 (early action).

CONTACT

Elizabeth Skoglund, Director of Admissions, Salisbury University, Admissions House, 1101 Camden Avenue, Salisbury, MD 21801. *Phone:* 410-543-6161. *Toll-free phone:* 888-543-0148. *Fax:* 410-546-6016. *E-mail:* admissions@salisbury.edu.

★ Stevenson University

Stevenson, Maryland

http://www.stevenson.edu/

- **Independent** comprehensive, founded 1952
- **Suburban** 168-acre campus with easy access to Baltimore
- **Endowment** $77.4 million
- **Coed** 3,808 undergraduate students, 84% full-time, 65% women, 35% men
- **Moderately difficult** entrance level, 62% of applicants were admitted

UNDERGRAD STUDENTS

3,203 full-time, 605 part-time. Students come from 36 states and territories; 14 other countries; 26% are from out of state; 29% Black or African American, non-Hispanic/Latino; 5% Hispanic/Latino; 3% Asian, non-Hispanic/Latino; 0.2% Native Hawaiian or other Pacific Islander, non-Hispanic/Latino; 0.1% American Indian or Alaska Native, non-Hispanic/Latino; 3% Two or more races, non-Hispanic/Latino; 4% Race/ethnicity unknown; 0.4% international; 18% transferred in; 48% live on campus.

Freshmen

Admission: 5,086 applied, 3,169 admitted, 690 enrolled. ***Average high school GPA:*** 3.45. ***Test scores:*** SAT critical reading scores over 500: 51%; SAT math scores over 500: 53%; SAT writing scores over 500: 49%; ACT scores over 18: 79%; SAT critical reading scores over 600: 9%; SAT math scores over 600: 13%; SAT writing scores over 600: 9%; ACT scores over 24: 23%; SAT writing scores over 700: 1%; ACT scores over 30: 1%.

Retention: 79% of full-time freshmen returned.

FACULTY

Total: 461, 29% full-time, 49% with terminal degrees.

Student/faculty ratio: 15:1.

ACADEMICS

Calendar: semesters. *Degrees:* bachelor's and master's.

Special study options: academic remediation for entering students, accelerated degree program, adult/continuing education programs, advanced placement credit, cooperative education, distance learning, independent study, internships, off-campus study, part-time degree program, services for LD students, student-designed majors, study abroad, summer session for credit. ***ROTC:*** Army (c), Air Force (c).

Computers: 300 computers/terminals and 1,000 ports are available on campus for general student use. Students can access the following: campus intranet, computer help desk, free student e-mail accounts, online (class) grades, online (class) registration, online (class) schedules. Campuswide network is available. 100% of college-owned or -operated housing units are wired for high-speed Internet access. Wireless service is available via entire campus.

STUDENT LIFE

Housing options: coed. Campus housing is university owned. Freshman applicants given priority for college housing.

Activities and organizations: drama/theater group, student-run newspaper, radio station, choral group, marching band, Student Government Association, Mustang Activities Programming, Black Student Union, CRU, Phi Sigma Sigma.

Athletics Member NCAA. All Division III. ***Intercollegiate sports:*** baseball M, basketball M/W, cheerleading M/W, cross-country running M/W, field hockey W, football M, golf M/W, ice hockey W, lacrosse M/W, soccer M/W, softball W, tennis M/W, track and field M/W, volleyball M/W. ***Intramural sports:*** badminton M/W, baseball M, basketball M/W, fencing M(c)/W(c), field hockey W, football M/W, skiing (downhill) M/W, softball W, table tennis M/W, tennis M/W, volleyball M.

Campus security: 24-hour emergency response devices and patrols, late-night transport/escort service, controlled dormitory access, patrols by trained security personnel during campus hours.

Student services: health clinic, personal/psychological counseling.

COSTS & FINANCIAL AID

Costs (2014–15) ***Comprehensive fee:*** $41,470 includes full-time tuition ($26,976), mandatory fees ($2004), and room and board ($12,490). Full-time tuition and fees vary according to degree level. Part-time tuition:

$682 per credit hour. Part-time tuition and fees vary according to course load and degree level. ***Required fees:*** $75 per credit part-time. ***College room only:*** $8718. Room and board charges vary according to board plan and housing facility. ***Payment plans:*** installment, deferred payment. ***Waivers:*** employees or children of employees.

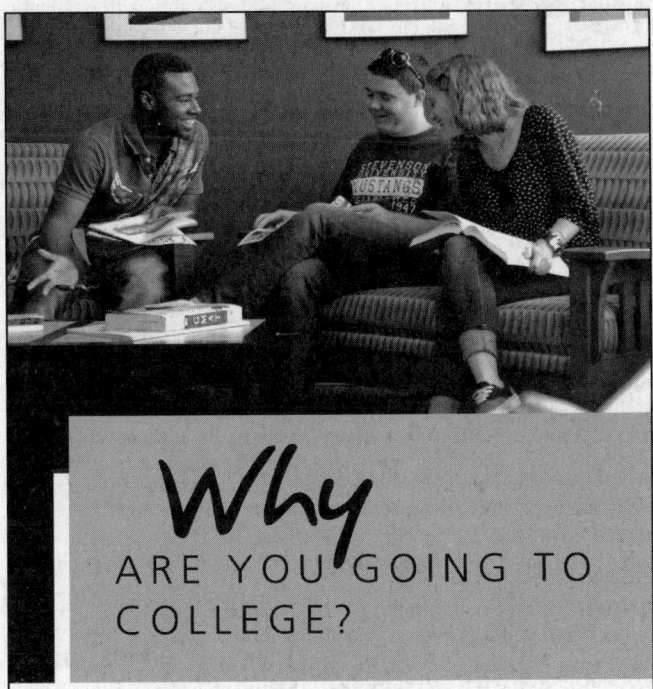

Financial Aid Of all full-time matriculated undergraduates who enrolled in 2013, 2,826 applied for aid, 2,509 were judged to have need, 226 had their need fully met. 124 Federal Work-Study jobs (averaging $2348). In 2013, 651 non-need-based awards were made. ***Average percent of need met:*** 59. ***Average financial aid package:*** $18,305. ***Average need-based loan:*** $4235. ***Average need-based gift aid:*** $14,720. ***Average non-need-based aid:*** $9013. ***Average indebtedness upon graduation:*** $31,736.

APPLYING

Standardized Tests *Required:* SAT or ACT (for admission).

Options: electronic application, deferred entrance.

Application fee: $40.

Required: essay or personal statement, high school transcript, 2 letters of recommendation. ***Recommended:*** interview.

Application deadlines: rolling (freshmen), rolling (transfers).

Notification: continuous (freshmen), continuous (transfers).

CONTACT

Mr. Mark Hergan, Vice President, Enrollment Management, Stevenson University, 1525 Greenspring Valley Road, Stevenson, MD 21153. *Phone:* 410-486-7001. *Toll-free phone:* 877-468-6852 (in-state); 877-468-3852 (out-of-state). *Fax:* 410-352-4440. *E-mail:* admissions@stevenson.edu.

See this page for display ad and page 1636 for the College Close-Up.

Stratford University

Baltimore, Maryland

http://www.stratford.edu/

- **Proprietary** comprehensive, founded 1972
- **Urban** 6-acre campus with easy access to Baltimore and Washington, DC
- **Coed** 347 undergraduate students, 21% full-time, 54% women, 46% men
- **Minimally difficult** entrance level, 71% of applicants were admitted

UNDERGRAD STUDENTS

72 full-time, 275 part-time. 12% are from out of state; 70% Black or African American, non-Hispanic/Latino; 2% Hispanic/Latino; 1% Asian, non-Hispanic/Latino; 0.9% Two or more races, non-Hispanic/Latino; 2% Race/ethnicity unknown; 14% transferred in.

Freshmen

Admission: 162 applied, 115 admitted. ***Average high school GPA:*** 2.

Retention: 87% of full-time freshmen returned.

FACULTY

Total: 31, 42% full-time, 23% with terminal degrees.

Student/faculty ratio: 20:1.

ACADEMICS

Calendar: semesters. *Degrees:* certificates, associate, bachelor's, and master's.

Special study options: academic remediation for entering students, accelerated degree program, adult/continuing education programs, advanced placement credit, cooperative education, internships, off-campus study, part-time degree program, services for LD students, summer session for credit.

Computers: 40 computers/terminals are available on campus for general student use. Students can access the following: campus intranet, computer help desk, free student e-mail accounts, online (class) grades, online (class) schedules. Campuswide network is available. Wireless service is available via entire campus.

STUDENT LIFE

Housing options: on-campus residence required for freshman yearCampus housing is provided by a third party.

Activities and organizations: student-run newspaper, Chai Eta Psi / Eta Psi Xi, Gardening Club, Epicurean Club, Enactus, Event Planning Club.

Campus security: late-night transport/escort service, controlled dormitory access.

Student services: personal/psychological counseling.

COSTS
Costs (2015–16) ***Tuition:*** $370 per quarter hour part-time. Full-time tuition and fees vary according to course level, degree level, and program. Part-time tuition and fees vary according to course level, degree level, and program. ***Required fees:*** $100 per degree program part-time. ***Payment plan:*** installment. ***Waivers:*** employees or children of employees.

APPLYING
Options: electronic application, early action, deferred entrance.

Application fee: $50.

Required: essay or personal statement, high school transcript, minimum 2.0 GPA, interview. ***Required for some:*** 1 letter of recommendation.

Application deadlines: rolling (freshmen), rolling (out-of-state freshmen), rolling (transfers).

Notification: continuous (freshmen), continuous (out-of-state freshmen), continuous (transfers).

CONTACT
Stratford University, Baltimore, MD. *Phone:* 410-752-4710 Ext. 5390. *Toll-free phone:* 800-624-9926 (in-state); 800-624-9926 Ext. 120 (out-of-state).

Towson University

Towson, Maryland

http://www.towson.edu/

- **State-supported** university, founded 1866, part of University System of Maryland
- **Suburban** 329-acre campus with easy access to Baltimore and Washington, DC
- **Endowment** $71.0 million
- **Coed** 18,807 undergraduate students, 88% full-time, 60% women, 40% men
- **Moderately difficult** entrance level, 59% of applicants were admitted

UNDERGRAD STUDENTS
16,575 full-time, 2,232 part-time. Students come from 46 states and territories; 64 other countries; 15% are from out of state; 16% Black or African American, non-Hispanic/Latino; 6% Hispanic/Latino; 5% Asian, non-Hispanic/Latino; 0.1% Native Hawaiian or other Pacific Islander, non-Hispanic/Latino; 0.2% American Indian or Alaska Native, non-Hispanic/Latino; 4% Two or more races, non-Hispanic/Latino; 4% Race/ethnicity unknown; 2% international; 11% transferred in; 26% live on campus.

Freshmen
Admission: 18,134 applied, 10,738 admitted, 2,712 enrolled. ***Average high school GPA:*** 3.61. ***Test scores:*** SAT critical reading scores over 500: 75%; SAT math scores over 500: 78%; SAT writing scores over 500: 75%; ACT scores over 18: 97%; SAT critical reading scores over 600: 17%; SAT math scores over 600: 22%; SAT writing scores over 600: 19%; ACT scores over 24: 44%; SAT critical reading scores over 700: 1%; SAT math scores over 700: 2%; SAT writing scores over 700: 2%; ACT scores over 30: 2%.

Retention: 85% of full-time freshmen returned.

FACULTY
Total: 1,671, 52% full-time, 54% with terminal degrees.

Student/faculty ratio: 17:1.

ACADEMICS
Calendar: semesters. *Degrees:* bachelor's, master's, doctoral, post-master's, and postbachelor's certificates.

Special study options: academic remediation for entering students, accelerated degree program, adult/continuing education programs, advanced placement credit, cooperative education, distance learning, double majors, English as a second language, freshman honors college, honors programs, independent study, internships, off-campus study, part-time degree program, services for LD students, student-designed majors, study abroad, summer session for credit. ***ROTC:*** Army (c), Air Force (c).

Unusual degree programs: 3-2 business administration with Accounting BA/MS; engineering with University of Maryland College Park; Occupational Therapy BS-MS Towson University; Geography and Environmental Planning BA/BS - MS Towson University; JD Law with University of Baltimore; MS Aquaculture with University of Tasmania; MS Antarctic and Southern Studies with University of Tasmania.

Computers: 3,047 computers/terminals and 8,445 ports are available on campus for general student use. Students can access the following: computer help desk, free student e-mail accounts, online (class) grades, online (class) registration, online (class) schedules. Campuswide network is available. 100% of college-owned or -operated housing units are wired for high-speed Internet access. Wireless service is available via entire campus.

STUDENT LIFE
Housing options: coed, special housing for students with disabilities. Campus housing is university owned and is provided by a third party. Freshman campus housing is guaranteed.

Activities and organizations: drama/theater group, student-run newspaper, radio and television station, choral group, marching band, University Residence Government, Latin American Student Organization, Black Student Union, Hillel, African Diaspora Club, national fraternities, national sororities.

Athletics Member NCAA. All Division I except football (Division I-A). ***Intercollegiate sports:*** badminton M(c)/W(c), baseball M(s), basketball M(s)/W(s), cross-country running W(s), equestrian sports W(c), field hockey W(s), golf M(s)/W(s), gymnastics W(s), ice hockey M(c)/W(c), lacrosse M(s)/W(s), rock climbing M(c)/W(c), rugby M(c)/W(c), skiing (downhill) M(c)/W(c), soccer M(c)/W(s), softball W(s), swimming and diving M(s)/W(s), tennis W(s), track and field M(c)/W(s), ultimate Frisbee M(c)/W(c), volleyball W(s), water polo M(c)/W(c), wrestling M(c). ***Intramural sports:*** basketball M(c)/W(c), cheerleading W(c), field hockey W(c), golf M(c), lacrosse M(c)/W(c), soccer M(c)/W(c), softball M/W(c), swimming and diving M(c)/W(c), tennis M(c)/W(c), track and field W(c), ultimate Frisbee M/W, volleyball M(c)/W(c).

Campus security: 24-hour emergency response devices and patrols, late-night transport/escort service, controlled dormitory access.

Student services: health clinic, personal/psychological counseling, women's center.

COSTS & FINANCIAL AID
Costs (2014–15) ***Tuition:*** state resident $6064 full-time, $260 per credit hour part-time; nonresident $17,742 full-time, $740 per credit hour part-time. Full-time tuition and fees vary according to course load. Part-time tuition and fees vary according to course load. ***Required fees:*** $2586 full-time, $111 per credit hour part-time. ***Room and board:*** $11,260; room only: $6238. Room and board charges vary according to board plan and housing facility. ***Payment plan:*** installment. ***Waivers:*** senior citizens and employees or children of employees.

Financial Aid Of all full-time matriculated undergraduates who enrolled in 2014, 11,899 applied for aid, 8,934 were judged to have need, 1,006 had their need fully met. 544 Federal Work-Study jobs (averaging $1704). In 2014, 1025 non-need-based awards were made. ***Average percent of need met:*** 60. ***Average financial aid package:*** $9675. ***Average need-based loan:*** $4010. ***Average need-based gift aid:*** $8316. ***Average non-need-based aid:*** $4867. ***Average indebtedness upon graduation:*** $25,926.

APPLYING
Standardized Tests *Required:* SAT or ACT (for admission).

Options: electronic application, early admission, deferred entrance.

Application fee: $45.

Required: essay or personal statement, high school transcript. ***Required for some:*** interview. ***Recommended:*** minimum 3.0 GPA, 2 letters of recommendation.

Application deadlines: 1/15 (freshmen), 1/15 (transfers).

Notification: continuous (freshmen), continuous (transfers).

CONTACT
Dr. David Fedorchak, Director of University Admissions, Towson University, 8000 York Road, Towson, MD 21252. *Phone:* 410-704-2113. *Fax:* 410-704-3030. *E-mail:* admissions@towson.edu.

United States Naval Academy

Annapolis, Maryland

http://www.usna.edu/

- **Federally supported** 4-year, founded 1845
- **Small-town** 338-acre campus with easy access to Baltimore and Washington, DC
- **Endowment** $223.0 million
- **Coed** 4,511 undergraduate students, 100% full-time, 23% women, 77% men
- **Very difficult** entrance level, 8% of applicants were admitted

UNDERGRAD STUDENTS

4,511 full-time. Students come from 54 states and territories; 30 other countries; 94% are from out of state; 7% Black or African American, non-Hispanic/Latino; 11% Hispanic/Latino; 7% Asian, non-Hispanic/Latino; 0.5% Native Hawaiian or other Pacific Islander, non-Hispanic/Latino; 0.4% American Indian or Alaska Native, non-Hispanic/Latino; 8% Two or more races, non-Hispanic/Latino; 1% Race/ethnicity unknown; 1% international; 100% live on campus.

Freshmen

Admission: 17,618 applied, 1,398 admitted, 1,175 enrolled. ***Test scores:*** SAT critical reading scores over 500: 95%; SAT math scores over 500: 99%; SAT critical reading scores over 600: 63%; SAT math scores over 600: 80%; SAT critical reading scores over 700: 19%; SAT math scores over 700: 29%.

Retention: 97% of full-time freshmen returned.

FACULTY

Total: 582, 94% full-time, 61% with terminal degrees.

Student/faculty ratio: 8:1.

ACADEMICS

Calendar: semesters. *Degree:* bachelor's.

Special study options: academic remediation for entering students, advanced placement credit, double majors, honors programs, independent study, off-campus study, study abroad, summer session for credit.

Computers: 1,000 computers/terminals and 1,000 ports are available on campus for general student use. Students can access the following: campus intranet, computer help desk, free student e-mail accounts, online (class) grades, online (class) registration, online (class) schedules. Campuswide network is available. Wireless service is available via classrooms, computer labs, libraries.

STUDENT LIFE

Housing options: on-campus residence required through senior year; coed. Campus housing is university owned. Freshman campus housing is guaranteed.

Activities and organizations: drama/theater group, student-run radio station, choral group, marching band, Mountaineering Club, Semper Fi, Black Studies Club, Midshipmen Action Club, Martial Arts Club.

Athletics Member NCAA. All Division I except football (Division I-A). ***Intercollegiate sports:*** baseball M, basketball M/W, cheerleading M(c)/W(c), crew M/W, cross-country running M/W, fencing M(c)/W(c), field hockey W(c), golf M/W, gymnastics M/W(c), ice hockey M(c)/W(c), lacrosse M/W, riflery M/W, rugby M(c)/W(c), sailing M/W, skiing (downhill) M(c)/W(c), soccer M/W, softball W(c), squash M, swimming and diving M/W, tennis M/W, track and field M/W, volleyball M(c)/W, water polo M, weight lifting M(c)/W(c), wrestling M. ***Intramural sports:*** basketball M/W, cross-country running M/W, football M/W, lacrosse M(c)/W(c), racquetball M/W, sailing M/W, soccer M/W, softball M/W, ultimate Frisbee M(c)/W(c), volleyball M/W, weight lifting M/W.

Campus security: 24-hour emergency response devices and patrols, campus gate security.

Student services: health clinic, personal/psychological counseling, women's center, legal services.

COSTS

Costs (2015–16) ***Tuition:*** area resident $0 full-time. No tuition increase for student's term of enrollment.

APPLYING

Standardized Tests *Required:* SAT or ACT (for admission).

Options: electronic application, early action.

Required: essay or personal statement, high school transcript, 2 letters of recommendation, interview, age 17-22, medical exam, authorized nomination, candidate fitness test.

Notification: continuous until 4/15 (freshmen).

CONTACT

Capt. Ann Kubera, Director of Admissions, United States Naval Academy, 52 King George Street, United States Naval Academy, Annapolis, MD 21402. *Phone:* 410-293-4361. *Toll-free phone:* 888-249-7707. *Fax:* 410-293-4348. *E-mail:* webmail@usna.edu.

University of Maryland, Baltimore County

Baltimore, Maryland

http://www.umbc.edu/

- **State-supported** university, founded 1963, part of University System of Maryland
- **Suburban** 530-acre campus with easy access to Washington, DC
- **Endowment** $72.8 million
- **Coed** 11,379 undergraduate students, 85% full-time, 45% women, 55% men
- **Moderately difficult** entrance level, 60% of applicants were admitted

UNDERGRAD STUDENTS

9,653 full-time, 1,726 part-time. Students come from 40 states and territories; 90 other countries; 6% are from out of state; 16% Black or African American, non-Hispanic/Latino; 6% Hispanic/Latino; 20% Asian, non-Hispanic/Latino; 0.2% Native Hawaiian or other Pacific Islander, non-Hispanic/Latino; 0.2% American Indian or Alaska Native, non-Hispanic/Latino; 4% Two or more races, non-Hispanic/Latino; 5% Race/ethnicity unknown; 5% international; 11% transferred in; 34% live on campus.

Freshmen

Admission: 10,217 applied, 6,090 admitted, 1,629 enrolled. ***Average high school GPA:*** 3.78. ***Test scores:*** SAT critical reading scores over 500: 92%; SAT math scores over 500: 97%; SAT writing scores over 500: 54%; ACT scores over 18: 98%; SAT critical reading scores over 600: 46%; SAT math scores over 600: 62%; SAT writing scores over 600: 10%; ACT scores over 24: 79%; SAT critical reading scores over 700: 10%; SAT math scores over 700: 16%; ACT scores over 30: 26%.

Retention: 89% of full-time freshmen returned.

FACULTY

Total: 785, 66% full-time, 69% with terminal degrees.

Student/faculty ratio: 20:1.

ACADEMICS

Calendar: 4-1-4. *Degrees:* bachelor's, master's, doctoral, and postbachelor's certificates.

Special study options: academic remediation for entering students, adult/continuing education programs, advanced placement credit, cooperative education, distance learning, double majors, English as a second language, external degree program, freshman honors college, honors programs, independent study, internships, off-campus study, part-time degree program, services for LD students, student-designed majors, study abroad, summer session for credit. ***ROTC:*** Army (c), Air Force (c).

Computers: 1,065 computers/terminals and 4,000 ports are available on campus for general student use. Students can access the following: campus intranet, computer help desk, free student e-mail accounts, online (class) grades, online (class) registration, online (class) schedules, Billing, Housing, Parking, Degree Audit and Advising, Career Placement and Community Service Learning. Campuswide network is available. 100% of college-owned or -operated housing units are wired for high-speed Internet access. Wireless service is available via entire campus.

STUDENT LIFE

Housing options: coed, special housing for students with disabilities. Campus housing is university owned and is provided by a third party. Freshman campus housing is guaranteed.

Activities and organizations: drama/theater group, student-run newspaper, radio station, choral group, Student Government Association, Student Events Board, Retriever Weekly, Resident Student Association, Freedom Alliance, national fraternities, national sororities.

Athletics Member NCAA. All Division I. ***Intercollegiate sports:*** badminton M(c)/W(c), baseball M(s), basketball M(s)/W(s), bowling M(c)/W(c), crew M(c)/W(c), cross-country running M(s)/W(s), fencing M(c)/W(c), field hockey W(c), ice hockey M(c), lacrosse M(s)/W(s), rugby M(c)/W(c), sailing M(c)/W(c), skiing (downhill) M(c)/W(c), soccer M(s)/W(s), softball W(s), swimming and diving M(s)/W(s), tennis M(s)/W(s), track and field M(s)/W(s), ultimate Frisbee M(c)/W(c), volleyball M(c)/W(s), wrestling M(c). ***Intramural sports:*** basketball M/W, football M/W, lacrosse M(c)/W(c), soccer M(c)/W(c), softball M/W, tennis M(c)/W(c), volleyball M/W(c).

Campus security: 24-hour emergency response devices and patrols, late-night transport/escort service.

Student services: health clinic, personal/psychological counseling, women's center, legal services.

COSTS & FINANCIAL AID

Costs (2014–15) ***One-time required fee:*** $125. ***Tuition:*** state resident $7518 full-time, $313 per credit hour part-time; nonresident $19,816 full-time, $823 per credit hour part-time. Full-time tuition and fees vary according to location and program. Part-time tuition and fees vary according to location and program. ***Required fees:*** $2866 full-time, $122 per credit hour part-time. ***Room and board:*** $10,562; room only: $6376. Room and board charges vary according to board plan and housing facility. ***Payment plan:*** installment. ***Waivers:*** senior citizens and employees or children of employees.

Financial Aid Of all full-time matriculated undergraduates who enrolled in 2014, 6,363 applied for aid, 5,071 were judged to have need, 609 had their need fully met. 89 Federal Work-Study jobs (averaging $2017). 94 state and other part-time jobs (averaging $9647). In 2014, 1288 non-need-based awards were made. ***Average percent of need met:*** 58. ***Average financial aid package:*** $10,641. ***Average need-based loan:*** $4377. ***Average need-based gift aid:*** $8292. ***Average non-need-based aid:*** $8555. ***Average indebtedness upon graduation:*** $25,925.

APPLYING

Standardized Tests *Required:* SAT or ACT (for admission).

Options: electronic application, early admission, early action, deferred entrance.

Application fee: $50.

Required: essay or personal statement, high school transcript. ***Recommended:*** minimum 3.0 GPA, 2 letters of recommendation.

Application deadlines: 2/1 (freshmen), 5/31 (transfers), 11/1 (early action).

Notification: continuous (freshmen), continuous (transfers), 12/15 (early action).

CONTACT

Mr. Dale Bittinger, Director of Admissions, University of Maryland, Baltimore County, 1000 Hilltop Circle, Baltimore, MD 21250. *Phone:* 410-455-2291. *Toll-free phone:* 800-UMBC-4U2 (in-state); 800-862-2402 (out-of-state). *Fax:* 410-455-1094. *E-mail:* admissions@umbc.edu.

University of Maryland, College Park

College Park, Maryland

http://www.maryland.edu/

- **State-supported** university, founded 1856, part of University System of Maryland
- **Suburban** 1500-acre campus with easy access to Baltimore and Washington, DC
- **Endowment** $437.6 million
- **Coed** 27,056 undergraduate students, 93% full-time, 46% women, 54% men
- **Moderately difficult** entrance level, 48% of applicants were admitted

UNDERGRAD STUDENTS

25,027 full-time, 2,029 part-time. Students come from 46 states and territories; 79 other countries; 20% are from out of state; 13% Black or African American, non-Hispanic/Latino; 9% Hispanic/Latino; 16% Asian, non-Hispanic/Latino; 0.1% Native Hawaiian or other Pacific Islander, non-Hispanic/Latino; 0.1% American Indian or Alaska Native, non-Hispanic/Latino; 4% Two or more races, non-Hispanic/Latino; 2% Race/ethnicity unknown; 3% international; 7% transferred in; 44% live on campus.

Freshmen

Admission: 26,268 applied, 12,556 admitted, 4,129 enrolled. ***Average high school GPA:*** 4.15. ***Test scores:*** SAT critical reading scores over 500: 95%; SAT math scores over 500: 97%; SAT critical reading scores over 600: 72%; SAT math scores over 600: 82%; SAT critical reading scores over 700: 22%; SAT math scores over 700: 40%.

Retention: 95% of full-time freshmen returned.

FACULTY

Total: 2,442, 72% full-time, 81% with terminal degrees.

Student/faculty ratio: 17:1.

ACADEMICS

Calendar: semesters. *Degrees:* certificates, bachelor's, master's, doctoral, post-master's, and postbachelor's certificates.

Special study options: academic remediation for entering students, accelerated degree program, adult/continuing education programs, advanced placement credit, cooperative education, distance learning, double majors, English as a second language, external degree program, honors programs, independent study, internships, off-campus study, part-time degree program, services for LD students, student-designed majors, study abroad, summer session for credit. ***ROTC:*** Army (b), Navy (c), Air Force (b).

Computers: 3,890 computers/terminals are available on campus for general student use. Students can access the following: campus intranet, computer help desk, free student e-mail accounts, online (class) grades, online (class) registration, online (class) schedules, student account information, financial aid summary. Campuswide network is available. 100% of college-owned or -operated housing units are wired for high-speed Internet access. Wireless service is available via entire campus.

STUDENT LIFE

Housing options: coed, women-only, cooperative, special housing for students with disabilities. Campus housing is university owned and is provided by a third party. Freshman campus housing is guaranteed.

Activities and organizations: drama/theater group, student-run newspaper, radio and television station, choral group, marching band, Student Government Association, Residence Hall Association, Black Student Union, Asian-American Student Union/Jewish Student Union, Commuter Students Association, national fraternities, national sororities.

Athletics Member NCAA. All Division I except football (Division I-A). ***Intercollegiate sports:*** baseball M(s), basketball M(s)/W(s), cross-country running W(s), field hockey W(s), golf M(s)/W(s), gymnastics W, lacrosse M(s)/W(s), soccer M(s)/W(s), softball W(s), swimming and diving M/W, tennis M/W, track and field M/W(s), volleyball W(s), water polo W(s), wrestling M(s). ***Intramural sports:*** badminton M(c)/W(c), baseball M(c), basketball M(c)/W(c), crew M(c)/W(c), cross-country running M(c)/W(c), equestrian sports M(c)/W(c), fencing M(c)/W(c), field hockey W(c), football M/W, golf M(c)/W(c), ice hockey M(c)/W(c), lacrosse M(c)/W(c), racquetball M(c)/W(c), rock climbing M(c)/W(c), rugby M(c)/W(c), sailing M(c)/W(c), soccer M(c)/W(c), softball W(c), swimming and diving M(c)/W(c), table tennis M(c)/W(c), tennis M(c)/W(c), ultimate Frisbee M/W, volleyball M(c)/W(c), water polo M(c)/W(c), wrestling M(c).

Campus security: 24-hour emergency response devices and patrols, student patrols, late-night transport/escort service, controlled dormitory access, campus police, video camera surveillance.

Student services: health clinic, personal/psychological counseling, women's center, legal services.

COSTS & FINANCIAL AID

Costs (2014–15) ***Tuition:*** state resident $7612 full-time, $317 per credit hour part-time; nonresident $27,905 full-time, $1163 per credit hour part-time. Part-time tuition and fees vary according to course load. ***Required fees:*** $1815 full-time, $420 per term part-time. ***Room and board:*** $10,633; room only: $6424. Room and board charges vary according to board plan and housing facility. ***Payment plans:*** installment, deferred payment. ***Waivers:*** employees or children of employees.

Financial Aid Of all full-time matriculated undergraduates who enrolled in 2012, 14,574 applied for aid, 10,742 were judged to have need, 2,262 had their need fully met. 2,528 Federal Work-Study jobs (averaging $2107). In 2012, 3032 non-need-based awards were made. ***Average percent of need met:*** 69. ***Average financial aid package:*** $12,889. ***Average need-based loan:*** $6233. ***Average need-based gift aid:*** $8295.

Average non-need-based aid: $6589. *Average indebtedness upon graduation:* $25,254.

APPLYING

Standardized Tests *Required:* SAT or ACT (for admission).

Options: electronic application, early admission, early action, deferred entrance.

Application fee: $65.

Required: essay or personal statement, high school transcript. *Required for some:* Resume of activities; audition for music applicants; drawing requirement for architecture applicants. *Recommended:* 2 letters of recommendation.

Application deadlines: 1/20 (freshmen), 6/1 (transfers), 11/1 (early action).

Notification: 4/1 (freshmen), continuous (transfers), 1/31 (early action).

CONTACT

Ms. Barbara Gill, Director of Undergraduate Admissions, University of Maryland, College Park, College Park, MD 20742. *Phone:* 301-314-8385. *Toll-free phone:* 800-422-5867. *Fax:* 301-314-9693.

University of Maryland University College

Adelphi, Maryland

http://www.umuc.edu/

- **State-supported** comprehensive, founded 1947, part of University System of Maryland
- **Suburban** campus with easy access to Washington, DC
- **Coed** 35,154 undergraduate students, 23% full-time, 47% women, 53% men
- **Noncompetitive** entrance level, 100% of applicants were admitted

UNDERGRAD STUDENTS

8,261 full-time, 26,893 part-time. Students come from 54 states and territories; 61 other countries; 54% are from out of state; 27% Black or African American, non-Hispanic/Latino; 11% Hispanic/Latino; 4% Asian, non-Hispanic/Latino; 0.7% Native Hawaiian or other Pacific Islander, non-Hispanic/Latino; 0.5% American Indian or Alaska Native, non-Hispanic/Latino; 4% Two or more races, non-Hispanic/Latino; 9% Race/ethnicity unknown; 1% international; 12% transferred in.

Freshmen

Admission: 1,789 applied, 1,789 admitted, 1,143 enrolled.

FACULTY

Total: 2,599, 7% full-time, 63% with terminal degrees.

Student/faculty ratio: 22:1.

ACADEMICS

Calendar: semesters. *Degrees:* certificates, associate, bachelor's, master's, doctoral, post-master's, and postbachelor's certificates (offers primarily part-time evening and weekend degree programs at more than 30 off-campus locations in Maryland and the Washington, DC area, and more than 180 military communities in Europe and Asia with military enrollment not reflected in this profile; associate of arts program available to military students only).

Special study options: academic remediation for entering students, accelerated degree program, advanced placement credit, cooperative education, distance learning, double majors, external degree program, independent study, internships, off-campus study, part-time degree program, services for LD students, summer session for credit.

Computers: 356 computers/terminals are available on campus for general student use. Students can access the following: campus intranet, computer help desk, free student e-mail accounts, online (class) grades, online (class) registration, online (class) schedules. Campuswide network is available. Wireless service is available via entire campus.

STUDENT LIFE

Housing options: college housing not available.

Campus security: 24-hour emergency response devices and patrols, late-night transport/escort service.

COSTS & FINANCIAL AID

Costs (2015–16) *Tuition:* state resident $6384 full-time, $266 per credit hour part-time; nonresident $11,976 full-time, $499 per credit hour part-time. *Required fees:* $360 full-time. *Payment plan:* installment. *Waivers:* senior citizens and employees or children of employees.

Financial Aid Of all full-time matriculated undergraduates who enrolled in 2013, 3,742 applied for aid, 3,599 were judged to have need, 16 had their need fully met. *Average percent of need met:* 28. *Average financial aid package:* $7752. *Average need-based loan:* $4451. *Average need-based gift aid:* $4741.

APPLYING

Options: electronic application, deferred entrance.

Application fee: $50.

Required: high school transcript.

Application deadlines: rolling (freshmen), rolling (transfers).

Notification: continuous (freshmen), continuous (transfers).

CONTACT

University of Maryland University College, 3501 University Boulevard East, Adelphi, MD 20783. *Phone:* 800-888-UMUC (8682). *Toll-free phone:* 800-888-8682. *E-mail:* enroll@umuc.edu.

Washington College

Chestertown, Maryland

http://www.washcoll.edu/

- **Independent** comprehensive, founded 1782
- **Small-town** 140-acre campus with easy access to Baltimore and Washington, DC
- **Endowment** $205.0 million
- **Coed** 1,463 undergraduate students, 97% full-time, 57% women, 43% men
- **Moderately difficult** entrance level, 56% of applicants were admitted

UNDERGRAD STUDENTS

1,417 full-time, 46 part-time. Students come from 30 states and territories; 32 other countries; 54% are from out of state; 4% Black or African American, non-Hispanic/Latino; 4% Hispanic/Latino; 2% Asian, non-Hispanic/Latino; 0.5% American Indian or Alaska Native, non-Hispanic/Latino; 2% Two or more races, non-Hispanic/Latino; 5% Race/ethnicity unknown; 8% international; 2% transferred in; 85% live on campus.

Freshmen

Admission: 5,318 applied, 2,960 admitted, 388 enrolled. *Average high school GPA:* 3.56. *Test scores:* SAT critical reading scores over 500: 92%; SAT math scores over 500: 87%; ACT scores over 18: 100%; SAT critical reading scores over 600: 46%; SAT math scores over 600: 45%; ACT scores over 24: 84%; SAT critical reading scores over 700: 6%; SAT math scores over 700: 4%; ACT scores over 30: 19%.

Retention: 85% of full-time freshmen returned.

FACULTY

Total: 184, 55% full-time, 73% with terminal degrees.

Student/faculty ratio: 11:1.

ACADEMICS

Calendar: semesters. *Degrees:* bachelor's and master's.

Special study options: accelerated degree program, advanced placement credit, double majors, English as a second language, honors programs, independent study, internships, off-campus study, part-time degree program, services for LD students, student-designed majors, study abroad, summer session for credit.

Unusual degree programs: 3-2 engineering with Columbia University (NY); nursing with Johns Hopkins University; Pharmacy.

Computers: 100 computers/terminals and 225 ports are available on campus for general student use. Students can access the following: campus intranet, computer help desk, free student e-mail accounts, online (class) grades, online (class) registration, online (class) schedules, thousands of wireless addresses available for students. Campuswide network is available. 100% of college-owned or -operated housing units are wired for high-speed Internet access. Wireless service is available via entire campus.

STUDENT LIFE

Housing options: on-campus residence required through sophomore year; coed, men-only, women-only, special housing for students with disabilities. Campus housing is university owned. Freshman campus housing is guaranteed.

Activities and organizations: drama/theater group, student-run newspaper, radio station, choral group, Writers Union, Student Government Association, Hands Out, Omicron Delta Kappa, Dale Adams Society, national fraternities, national sororities.

Athletics Member NCAA. All Division III. ***Intercollegiate sports:*** baseball M, basketball M/W, cheerleading W(c), crew M/W, equestrian sports M(c)/W(c), field hockey W, ice hockey M(c), lacrosse M/W, rugby M(c)/W(c), sailing M/W, soccer M/W, softball W, swimming and diving M/W, tennis M/W, volleyball W, water polo M(c)/W(c). ***Intramural sports:*** basketball M/W, football M/W, lacrosse M(c), racquetball M/W, rugby M/W, sailing M/W, soccer M/W, squash M/W, table tennis M/W, tennis M/W, ultimate Frisbee M/W.

Campus security: 24-hour emergency response devices and patrols, student patrols, late-night transport/escort service, controlled dormitory access, LiveSafe mobile app.

Student services: health clinic, personal/psychological counseling.

COSTS & FINANCIAL AID

Costs (2015–16) ***Comprehensive fee:*** $54,452 includes full-time tuition ($42,844), mandatory fees ($996), and room and board ($10,612). Part-time tuition and fees vary according to course load. ***College room only:*** $5390. Room and board charges vary according to board plan, housing facility, and location. ***Payment plans:*** tuition prepayment, installment. ***Waivers:*** employees or children of employees.

Financial Aid Of all full-time matriculated undergraduates who enrolled in 2014, 921 applied for aid, 819 were judged to have need, 167 had their need fully met. 138 Federal Work-Study jobs (averaging $1200). In 2014, 456 non-need-based awards were made. ***Average percent of need met:*** 79. ***Average financial aid package:*** $29,263. ***Average need-based loan:*** $4481. ***Average need-based gift aid:*** $23,935. ***Average non-need-based aid:*** $16,794. ***Average indebtedness upon graduation:*** $35,833.

APPLYING

Standardized Tests *Recommended:* SAT or ACT (for admission).

Options: electronic application, early admission, early decision, early action, deferred entrance.

Application fee: $50.

Required: essay or personal statement, high school transcript, 1 letter of recommendation. ***Required for some:*** interview. ***Recommended:*** interview.

Application deadlines: 2/15 (freshmen), rolling (transfers), 12/1 (early action).

Early decision deadline: 11/15 (for plan 1), 12/15 (for plan 2).

Notification: continuous (freshmen), continuous (transfers), 12/15 (early decision plan 1), 1/15 (early decision plan 2), 1/15 (early action).

CONTACT

Mr. Bradly Booke, Director of Admissions, Washington College, 300 Washington Avenue, Chestertown, MD 21620. *Phone:* 410-778-7700. *Toll-free phone:* 800-422-1782. *Fax:* 410-778-7287. *E-mail:* wc_admissions@washcoll.edu.

Yeshiva College of the Nation's Capital

Silver Spring, Maryland

http://www.yeshiva.edu/

- **Independent Jewish** 4-year, founded 1963, part of Yeshiva of Greater Washington
- **Suburban** campus
- **Men only**

ACADEMICS

Degree: bachelor's.

APPLYING

Application fee: $50.

CONTACT

Yeshiva College of the Nation's Capital, 1216 Arcola Avenue, Silver Spring, MD 20902.

MASSACHUSETTS

American International College

Springfield, Massachusetts

http://www.aic.edu/

- **Independent** comprehensive, founded 1885
- **Urban** 58-acre campus
- **Endowment** $12.1 million
- **Coed** 1,473 undergraduate students, 93% full-time, 59% women, 41% men
- **Moderately difficult** entrance level, 68% of applicants were admitted

UNDERGRAD STUDENTS

1,376 full-time, 97 part-time. Students come from 36 states and territories; 27 other countries; 35% are from out of state; 25% Black or African American, non-Hispanic/Latino; 10% Hispanic/Latino; 2% Asian, non-Hispanic/Latino; 0.5% Native Hawaiian or other Pacific Islander, non-Hispanic/Latino; 0.3% American Indian or Alaska Native, non-Hispanic/Latino; 4% Two or more races, non-Hispanic/Latino; 15% Race/ethnicity unknown; 0.3% international; 10% transferred in; 47% live on campus.

Freshmen

Admission: 2,026 applied, 1,369 admitted, 309 enrolled. ***Test scores:*** SAT critical reading scores over 500: 22%; SAT math scores over 500: 26%; SAT writing scores over 500: 16%; ACT scores over 18: 63%; SAT critical reading scores over 600: 2%; SAT math scores over 600: 5%; SAT writing scores over 600: 4%; ACT scores over 24: 23%; SAT math scores over 700: 1%; ACT scores over 30: 3%.

Retention: 68% of full-time freshmen returned.

FACULTY

Total: 404, 19% full-time.

Student/faculty ratio: 13:1.

ACADEMICS

Calendar: semesters. *Degrees:* associate, bachelor's, master's, doctoral, and post-master's certificates.

Special study options: academic remediation for entering students, accelerated degree program, adult/continuing education programs, advanced placement credit, double majors, honors programs, independent study, internships, off-campus study, part-time degree program, services for LD students, study abroad, summer session for credit. ***ROTC:*** Army (c), Air Force (c).

Computers: 244 computers/terminals and 75 ports are available on campus for general student use. Students can access the following: campus intranet, computer help desk, free student e-mail accounts, online (class) grades, online (class) registration, online (class) schedules. Campuswide network is available. 100% of college-owned or -operated housing units are wired for high-speed Internet access. Wireless service is available via entire campus.

STUDENT LIFE

Housing options: on-campus residence required for freshman year; coed, women-only. Campus housing is university owned. Freshman campus housing is guaranteed.

Activities and organizations: drama/theater group, student-run newspaper, choral group, Student Activities Committee, Best Buddies Program, PRIDE (Persons Ready in Defense of Ebony), student government, School newspaper.

Athletics Member NCAA. All Division II except ice hockey (Division I). ***Intercollegiate sports:*** baseball M(s), basketball M(s)/W(s), cross-country running M(s)/W(s), field hockey W(s), football M(s), golf M, ice hockey M(s), lacrosse M(s)/W(s), rugby M(s)(c)/W(s)(c), soccer M(s)/W(s), softball W(s), tennis M/W, track and field M(s)/W(s), volleyball W(s), wrestling M(s). ***Intramural sports:*** basketball M/W, cheerleading M/W, golf M, soccer M/W, softball M/W, volleyball M/W, wrestling W(c).

Campus security: 24-hour emergency response devices and patrols, late-night transport/escort service, controlled dormitory access.

Student services: health clinic, personal/psychological counseling.

COSTS & FINANCIAL AID

Costs (2015–16) ***Comprehensive fee:*** $44,770 includes full-time tuition ($31,870) and room and board ($12,900). Full-time tuition and fees vary according to course load and program. Part-time tuition: $660 per credit hour. Part-time tuition and fees vary according to course load. ***Required fees:*** $30 per term part-time. ***Room and board:*** Room and board charges vary according to board plan and housing facility. ***Payment plan:*** installment. ***Waivers:*** employees or children of employees.

Financial Aid Of all full-time matriculated undergraduates who enrolled in 2013, 1,394 applied for aid, 1,333 were judged to have need, 159 had their need fully met. 466 Federal Work-Study jobs (averaging $640). 161 state and other part-time jobs (averaging $1190). ***Average percent of need met:*** 70. ***Average financial aid package:*** $23,969. ***Average need-based loan:*** $4133. ***Average need-based gift aid:*** $19,916. ***Average indebtedness upon graduation:*** $35,587.

APPLYING

Standardized Tests *Required:* SAT or ACT (for admission).

Options: electronic application, deferred entrance.

Application fee: $25.

Required: high school transcript. ***Required for some:*** interview. ***Recommended:*** essay or personal statement, 1 letter of recommendation.

Application deadlines: rolling (freshmen), rolling (out-of-state freshmen), rolling (transfers).

Notification: continuous (freshmen), continuous (transfers).

CONTACT

Mr. Jonathan Scully, Director of Undergraduate Admissions, American International College, 1000 State Street, Springfield, MA 01109-3189. *Phone:* 413-205-3270. *Toll-free phone:* 800-242-3142. *Fax:* 413-205-3051. *E-mail:* jonathan.scully@aic.edu.

Amherst College

Amherst, Massachusetts

http://www.amherst.edu/

- **Independent** 4-year, founded 1821
- **Small-town** 1020-acre campus
- **Endowment** $2.2 billion
- **Coed** 1,792 undergraduate students, 100% full-time, 48% women, 52% men
- **Most difficult** entrance level, 14% of applicants were admitted

UNDERGRAD STUDENTS

1,792 full-time. Students come from 50 states and territories; 55 other countries; 88% are from out of state; 12% Black or African American, non-Hispanic/Latino; 13% Hispanic/Latino; 13% Asian, non-Hispanic/Latino; 0.1% Native Hawaiian or other Pacific Islander, non-Hispanic/Latino; 0.3% American Indian or Alaska Native, non-Hispanic/Latino; 5% Two or more races, non-Hispanic/Latino; 5% Race/ethnicity unknown; 10% international; 0.8% transferred in; 99% live on campus.

Freshmen

Admission: 8,478 applied, 1,173 admitted, 469 enrolled. ***Test scores:*** SAT critical reading scores over 500: 100%; SAT math scores over 500: 100%; SAT writing scores over 500: 100%; ACT scores over 18: 100%; SAT critical reading scores over 600: 97%; SAT math scores over 600: 95%; SAT writing scores over 600: 94%; ACT scores over 24: 99%; SAT critical reading scores over 700: 67%; SAT math scores over 700: 69%; SAT writing scores over 700: 64%; ACT scores over 30: 82%.

Retention: 98% of full-time freshmen returned.

FACULTY

Total: 271, 81% full-time, 94% with terminal degrees.

Student/faculty ratio: 8:1.

ACADEMICS

Calendar: semesters. *Degree:* bachelor's.

Special study options: double majors, honors programs, independent study, off-campus study, student-designed majors, study abroad. ***ROTC:*** Army (c), Air Force (c).

Computers: 450 computers/terminals are available on campus for general student use. Students can access the following: campus intranet, computer help desk, free student e-mail accounts, online (class) grades, online (class) registration, online (class) schedules. Campuswide network is available. 100% of college-owned or -operated housing units are wired for high-speed Internet access. Wireless service is available via entire campus.

STUDENT LIFE

Housing options: on-campus residence required through senior year; coed, cooperative, special housing for students with disabilities. Campus housing is university owned. Freshman campus housing is guaranteed.

Activities and organizations: drama/theater group, student-run newspaper, radio station, choral group, choral groups, WAMH (campus radio station), OUTREACH (community service), literary magazines, The Amherst Student (school newspaper).

Athletics Member NCAA. All Division III. ***Intercollegiate sports:*** baseball M, basketball M/W, cheerleading W(c), crew M(c)/W(c), cross-country running M/W, equestrian sports M(c)/W(c), fencing M(c)/W(c), field hockey W, football M, golf M/W, ice hockey M/W, lacrosse M/W, rugby M(c)/W(c), sailing M(c)/W(c), skiing (downhill) M(c)/W(c), soccer M/W, softball W, squash M/W, swimming and diving M/W, tennis M/W, track and field M/W, ultimate Frisbee M(c)/W(c), volleyball M(c)/W, water polo M(c)/W(c), wrestling M(c)/W(c). ***Intramural sports:*** badminton M/W, basketball M/W, golf M/W, ice hockey M/W, soccer M/W, softball M/W, squash M/W, table tennis M/W, tennis M/W, track and field M/W, volleyball M/W.

Campus security: 24-hour emergency response devices and patrols, student patrols, late-night transport/escort service, controlled dormitory access.

Student services: health clinic, personal/psychological counseling, women's center.

COSTS & FINANCIAL AID

Costs (2014–15) ***Comprehensive fee:*** $61,206 includes full-time tuition ($47,720), mandatory fees ($806), and room and board ($12,680). ***College room only:*** $6870. ***Payment plans:*** installment, deferred payment.

Financial Aid Of all full-time matriculated undergraduates who enrolled in 2014, 1,245 applied for aid, 1,103 were judged to have need, 1,103 had their need fully met. 694 Federal Work-Study jobs (averaging $1602). 227 state and other part-time jobs (averaging $1658). ***Average percent of need met:*** 100. ***Average financial aid package:*** $48,535. ***Average need-based loan:*** $330. ***Average need-based gift aid:*** $47,243. ***Average indebtedness upon graduation:*** $14,490.

APPLYING

Standardized Tests *Required:* SAT and SAT Subject Tests or ACT (for admission).

Options: electronic application, early admission, early decision, deferred entrance.

Application fee: $60.

Required: essay or personal statement, high school transcript, 3 letters of recommendation, Amherst College Supplement.

Application deadlines: 1/1 (freshmen), 3/1 (transfers).

Early decision deadline: 11/15.

Notification: 4/1 (freshmen), 6/1 (transfers), 12/15 (early decision).

CONTACT

Ms. Katie L. Fretwell, Dean of Admission and Financial Aid, Amherst College, PO Box 5000, Amherst, MA 01002-5000. *Phone:* 413-542-2328. *Fax:* 413-542-2040. *E-mail:* admission@amherst.edu.

★ Anna Maria College

Paxton, Massachusetts

http://www.annamaria.edu/

- **Independent Roman Catholic** comprehensive, founded 1946
- **Rural** 192-acre campus with easy access to Boston
- **Endowment** $3.5 million
- **Coed** 1,116 undergraduate students, 69% full-time, 60% women, 40% men
- **Minimally difficult** entrance level, 78% of applicants were admitted

UNDERGRAD STUDENTS
769 full-time, 347 part-time. Students come from 36 states and territories; 2 other countries; 37% are from out of state; 8% Black or African American, non-Hispanic/Latino; 6% Hispanic/Latino; 2% Asian, non-Hispanic/Latino; 0.3% Native Hawaiian or other Pacific Islander, non-Hispanic/Latino; 0.3% American Indian or Alaska Native, non-Hispanic/Latino; 2% Two or more races, non-Hispanic/Latino; 10% Race/ethnicity unknown; 0.5% international; 3% transferred in; 60% live on campus.

Freshmen
Admission: 1,944 applied, 1,508 admitted, 169 enrolled. ***Average high school GPA:*** 3.
Retention: 66% of full-time freshmen returned.

FACULTY
Total: 42.
Student/faculty ratio: 10:1.

ACADEMICS
Calendar: semesters. *Degrees:* certificates, bachelor's, master's, doctoral, post-master's, and postbachelor's certificates.
Special study options: academic remediation for entering students, accelerated degree program, adult/continuing education programs, advanced placement credit, cooperative education, distance learning, double majors, honors programs, independent study, internships, off-campus study, part-time degree program, services for LD students, student-designed majors, study abroad, summer session for credit. ***ROTC:*** Air Force (c).
Computers: 86 computers/terminals are available on campus for general student use. Students can access the following: campus intranet, computer help desk, free student e-mail accounts, online (class) grades, online (class) registration, online (class) schedules, student account information. Campuswide network is available. 100% of college-owned or -operated housing units are wired for high-speed Internet access. Wireless service is available via entire campus.

STUDENT LIFE
Housing options: coed, special housing for students with disabilities. Campus housing is university owned. Freshman campus housing is guaranteed.
Activities and organizations: drama/theater group, choral group, marching band, Habitat for Humanity, Social Action Group, Chorus Club, Alana, Programming Board - AMCAB.
Athletics Member NCAA. All Division III. ***Intercollegiate sports:*** baseball M, basketball M/W, cross-country running M/W, field hockey W, football M, golf M, lacrosse M/W, soccer M/W, softball W, tennis M/W, volleyball W. ***Intramural sports:*** basketball M/W, football M, soccer M/W, softball M/W, volleyball M/W.
Campus security: 24-hour emergency response devices and patrols, late-night transport/escort service, controlled dormitory access.
Student services: health clinic, personal/psychological counseling.

COSTS & FINANCIAL AID
Costs (2014–15) ***Comprehensive fee:*** $46,790 includes full-time tuition ($31,920), mandatory fees ($2140), and room and board ($12,730). Part-time tuition: $1185 per course.
Financial Aid Of all full-time matriculated undergraduates who enrolled in 2014, 721 applied for aid, 674 were judged to have need, 18 had their need fully met. In 2014, 37 non-need-based awards were made. ***Average percent of need met:*** 23. ***Average financial aid package:*** $14,551. ***Average need-based loan:*** $4381. ***Average need-based gift aid:*** $8998. ***Average non-need-based aid:*** $9947. ***Average indebtedness upon graduation:*** $51,934.

APPLYING
Standardized Tests *Recommended:* SAT or ACT (for admission).
Options: electronic application, deferred entrance.
Application fee: $40.
Required: high school transcript, minimum 2.0 GPA. ***Required for some:*** essay or personal statement, audition for music programs, portfolio for art programs. ***Recommended:*** 1 letter of recommendation, interview.
Application deadlines: rolling (freshmen), rolling (transfers).
Notification: continuous (freshmen), continuous (transfers).

CONTACT
Mr. Peter Miller, Dean of Admissions and Financial Aid, Anna Maria College, 50 Sunset Lane, Paxton, MA 01612. *Phone:* 508-849-3586. *Fax:* 508-849-3362. *E-mail:* admissions@annamaria.edu.

See previous page for display ad and page 1342 for the College Close-Up.

★ Assumption College
Worcester, Massachusetts
http://www.assumption.edu/

- **Independent Roman Catholic** comprehensive, founded 1904
- **Suburban** 180-acre campus with easy access to Boston
- **Endowment** $100.8 million
- **Coed** 2,008 undergraduate students, 99% full-time, 58% women, 42% men
- **Moderately difficult** entrance level, 81% of applicants were admitted

UNDERGRAD STUDENTS
1,997 full-time, 11 part-time. Students come from 27 states and territories; 23 other countries; 34% are from out of state; 5% Black or African American, non-Hispanic/Latino; 7% Hispanic/Latino; 2% Asian, non-Hispanic/Latino; 0.1% Native Hawaiian or other Pacific Islander, non-Hispanic/Latino; 0.2% American Indian or Alaska Native, non-Hispanic/Latino; 2% Two or more races, non-Hispanic/Latino; 7% Race/ethnicity unknown; 2% international; 2% transferred in; 89% live on campus.

Freshmen
Admission: 4,402 applied, 3,579 admitted, 571 enrolled. ***Average high school GPA:*** 3.43. ***Test scores:*** SAT critical reading scores over 500: 81%; SAT math scores over 500: 82%; ACT scores over 18: 97%; SAT critical reading scores over 600: 27%; SAT math scores over 600: 28%; ACT scores over 24: 68%; SAT critical reading scores over 700: 4%; SAT math scores over 700: 3%; ACT scores over 30: 11%.
Retention: 83% of full-time freshmen returned.

FACULTY
Total: 226, 63% full-time, 80% with terminal degrees.
Student/faculty ratio: 12:1.

ACADEMICS
Calendar: semesters. *Degrees:* bachelor's, master's, post-master's, and postbachelor's certificates.
Special study options: advanced placement credit, double majors, honors programs, independent study, internships, off-campus study, part-time degree program, services for LD students, student-designed majors, study abroad, summer session for credit. ***ROTC:*** Army (c), Air Force (c).
Unusual degree programs: 3-2 business administration; engineering with University of Notre Dame; forestry with Duke University; nursing with Massachusetts College of Pharmacy and Health Sciences; special education, rehabilitation counseling, school counseling; law (JD) with Duquesne U School of Law, Western NE College School of Law, Vermont Law School; optometry with New England College of Optometry; osteopathic medicine with Des Moines U; environmental science management with Duke U.
Computers: 360 computers/terminals and 1,900 ports are available on campus for general student use. Students can access the following: campus intranet, computer help desk, free student e-mail accounts, online (class) grades, online (class) registration, online (class) schedules. Campuswide network is available. 100% of college-owned or -operated housing units are wired for high-speed Internet access. Wireless service is available via entire campus.

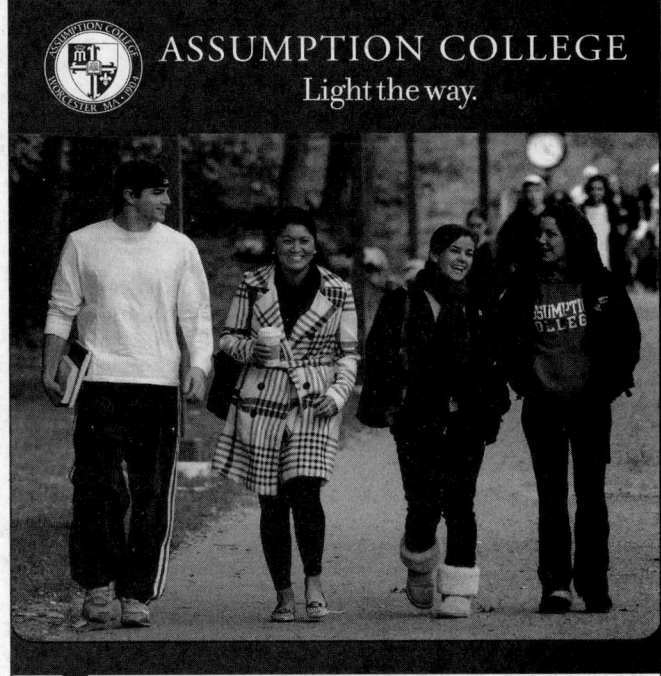

STUDENT LIFE
Housing options: coed, women-only, special housing for students with disabilities. Campus housing is university owned. Freshman campus housing is guaranteed.

Activities and organizations: drama/theater group, student-run newspaper, television station, choral group, Volunteer center, Campus Activities Board, student government, Campus Ministry, intramural sports.

Athletics Member NCAA. All Division II. ***Intercollegiate sports:*** baseball M, basketball M(s)/W(s), crew W, cross-country running M/W, field hockey W, football M, golf M, ice hockey M, lacrosse M/W, soccer M/W, softball W, swimming and diving W, tennis M/W, track and field M/W, volleyball W. ***Intramural sports:*** badminton M/W, basketball M(c)/W(c), cheerleading M(c)/W(c), equestrian sports M(c)/W(c), football M, golf M/W, ice hockey M/W, racquetball M/W, soccer M/W, softball M/W, swimming and diving M/W, table tennis M/W, tennis M/W, ultimate Frisbee M/W, volleyball M(c)/W(c).

Campus security: 24-hour emergency response devices and patrols, student patrols, late-night transport/escort service, controlled dormitory access, front gate security, well-lit pathways.

Student services: health clinic, personal/psychological counseling.

COSTS & FINANCIAL AID
Costs (2014–15) ***Comprehensive fee:*** $47,122 includes full-time tuition ($35,510), mandatory fees ($650), and room and board ($10,962). Full-time tuition and fees vary according to course load and reciprocity agreements. Part-time tuition: $1184 per credit hour. Part-time tuition and fees vary according to course load. No tuition increase for student's term of enrollment. ***College room only:*** $6914. Room and board charges vary according to housing facility. ***Waivers:*** employees or children of employees.

Financial Aid Of all full-time matriculated undergraduates who enrolled in 2014, 1,718 applied for aid, 1,546 were judged to have need, 293 had their need fully met. 393 Federal Work-Study jobs (averaging $1398). In 2014, 354 non-need-based awards were made. ***Average percent of need met:*** 74. ***Average financial aid package:*** $26,459. ***Average need-based loan:*** $4937. ***Average need-based gift aid:*** $21,039. ***Average non-need-based aid:*** $13,158. ***Average indebtedness upon graduation:*** $34,417. ***Financial aid deadline:*** 2/15.

APPLYING
Options: electronic application, early action, deferred entrance.

Application fee: $50.

Required: essay or personal statement, high school transcript, 1 letter of recommendation. ***Recommended:*** interview.

Application deadlines: 2/15 (freshmen), 7/1 (transfers), 11/1 (early action).

Notification: continuous (freshmen), continuous (transfers), 12/15 (early action).

CONTACT
Ms. Kathleen Murphy, Dean of Enrollment, Assumption College, 500 Salisbury Street, Worcester, MA 01609-1296. *Phone:* 508-767-7110. *Toll-free phone:* 866-477-7776. *Fax:* 508-799-4412. *E-mail:* admiss@assumption.edu.

See previous page for display ad and page 1348 for the College Close-Up.

★ Babson College
Wellesley, Massachusetts
http://www.babson.edu/

- **Independent** comprehensive, founded 1919
- **Suburban** 370-acre campus with easy access to Boston
- **Endowment** $332.0 million
- **Coed** 2,107 undergraduate students, 100% full-time, 47% women, 53% men
- **Very difficult** entrance level, 26% of applicants were admitted

UNDERGRAD STUDENTS
2,107 full-time. Students come from 45 states and territories; 71 other countries; 72% are from out of state; 5% Black or African American, non-Hispanic/Latino; 10% Hispanic/Latino; 11% Asian, non-Hispanic/Latino; 0.2% American Indian or Alaska Native, non-Hispanic/Latino; 2% Two or more races, non-Hispanic/Latino; 6% Race/ethnicity unknown; 27% international; 2% transferred in.

Freshmen

Admission: 6,199 applied, 1,631 admitted, 506 enrolled. ***Test scores:*** SAT critical reading scores over 500: 99%; SAT math scores over 500: 100%; SAT writing scores over 500: 98%; ACT scores over 18: 99%; SAT critical reading scores over 600: 54%; SAT math scores over 600: 80%; SAT writing scores over 600: 66%; ACT scores over 24: 93%; SAT critical reading scores over 700: 10%; SAT math scores over 700: 33%; SAT writing scores over 700: 14%; ACT scores over 30: 35%.

Retention: 94% of full-time freshmen returned.

FACULTY

Total: 254, 67% full-time, 74% with terminal degrees.

Student/faculty ratio: 14:1.

ACADEMICS

Calendar: semesters. *Degrees:* bachelor's, master's, and post-master's certificates.

Special study options: advanced placement credit, freshman honors college, honors programs, independent study, internships, off-campus study, services for LD students, student-designed majors, study abroad, summer session for credit. ***ROTC:*** Army (c), Navy (c), Air Force (c).

Computers: Students can access the following: campus intranet, computer help desk, free student e-mail accounts, online (class) grades, online (class) registration, online (class) schedules, network drives and folders; students are also issued an IBM Thinkpad. Campuswide network is available. Wireless service is available via entire campus.

STUDENT LIFE

Housing options: on-campus residence required for freshman year; coed, men-only, special housing for students with disabilities. Campus housing is university owned. Freshman campus housing is guaranteed.

Activities and organizations: drama/theater group, student-run newspaper, radio station, choral group, Student Government Association, Free Press, Dance Ensemble, Asian Pacific Student Association, College Radio, national fraternities, national sororities.

Athletics Member NCAA. All Division III. ***Intercollegiate sports:*** baseball M, basketball M/W, cheerleading W(c), cross-country running M/W, field hockey W, golf M, ice hockey M/W(c), lacrosse M/W, rugby M(c)/W(c), skiing (downhill) M/W, soccer M/W, softball W, swimming and diving M/W, tennis M/W, track and field M/W, volleyball W. ***Intramural sports:*** basketball M/W, football M, ice hockey M/W, racquetball M/W, soccer M/W, softball M/W, squash M/W, tennis M/W, ultimate Frisbee M/W, volleyball M/W, wrestling M(c).

Campus security: 24-hour emergency response devices and patrols, late-night transport/escort service, controlled dormitory access.

Student services: health clinic, personal/psychological counseling, women's center.

COSTS & FINANCIAL AID

Costs (2015–16) ***Comprehensive fee:*** $61,712 includes full-time tuition ($46,784) and room and board ($14,928). ***College room only:*** $9634. Room and board charges vary according to board plan and housing facility. ***Payment plan:*** installment. ***Waivers:*** employees or children of employees.

Financial Aid Of all full-time matriculated undergraduates who enrolled in 2014, 1,013 applied for aid, 903 were judged to have need, 449 had their need fully met. In 2014, 156 non-need-based awards were made. ***Average percent of need met:*** 96. ***Average financial aid package:*** $38,749. ***Average need-based loan:*** $4532. ***Average need-based gift aid:*** $35,332. ***Average non-need-based aid:*** $19,462. ***Average indebtedness upon graduation:*** $35,290. ***Financial aid deadline:*** 2/15.

APPLYING

Standardized Tests *Required:* SAT or ACT (for admission). *Recommended:* TOEFL or IELTS for non-native English speakers.

Options: electronic application, early decision, early action, deferred entrance.

Application fee: $75.

Required: essay or personal statement, high school transcript, 2 letters of recommendation. ***Recommended:*** interview.

Application deadlines: 1/4 (freshmen), 3/15 (transfers), 11/1 (early action).

Early decision deadline: 11/1.

Notification: 4/1 (freshmen), 5/15 (transfers), 12/15 (early decision), 1/1 (early action).

CONTACT

Mrs. Adrienne Ramsey, Associate Director of Undergraduate Admission, Babson College, Lunder Undergraduate Admission Center, Babson Park, MA 02457-0310. *Phone:* 781-239-5522. *Toll-free phone:* 800-488-3696. *Fax:* 781-239-4135. *E-mail:* ugradadmission@babson.edu.

See previous page for display ad and page 1350 for the College Close-Up.

Bard College at Simon's Rock

Great Barrington, Massachusetts

http://www.simons-rock.edu/

- **Independent** 4-year, founded 1964
- **Small-town** 210-acre campus with easy access to Boston, New York City
- **Coed** 329 undergraduate students, 98% full-time, 59% women, 41% men
- **Moderately difficult** entrance level, 89% of applicants were admitted

UNDERGRAD STUDENTS

322 full-time, 7 part-time. Students come from 35 states and territories; 14 other countries; 88% are from out of state; 6% Black or African American, non-Hispanic/Latino; 2% Hispanic/Latino; 2% Asian, non-Hispanic/Latino; 5% Native Hawaiian or other Pacific Islander, non-Hispanic/Latino; 4% American Indian or Alaska Native, non-Hispanic/Latino; 10% Two or more races, non-Hispanic/Latino; 4% Race/ethnicity unknown; 15% international; 88% live on campus.

Freshmen

Admission: 198 applied, 177 admitted, 116 enrolled. ***Average high school GPA:*** 3.51. ***Test scores:*** SAT critical reading scores over 500: 99%; SAT math scores over 500: 100%; SAT writing scores over 500: 88%; ACT scores over 18: 99%; SAT critical reading scores over 600: 87%; SAT math scores over 600: 88%; SAT writing scores over 600: 88%; ACT scores over 24: 99%; SAT critical reading scores over 700: 25%; SAT math scores over 700: 50%; SAT writing scores over 700: 25%; ACT scores over 30: 66%.

Retention: 80% of full-time freshmen returned.

FACULTY

Total: 68, 65% full-time, 68% with terminal degrees.

Student/faculty ratio: 6:1.

ACADEMICS

Calendar: semesters. *Degrees:* associate and bachelor's.

Special study options: cooperative education, double majors, English as a second language, independent study, internships, off-campus study, services for LD students, student-designed majors, study abroad.

Unusual degree programs: 3-2 engineering with Columbia University, Dartmouth College; Bard College's Center for Environmental Policy.

Computers: 50 computers/terminals and 250 ports are available on campus for general student use. Students can access the following: campus intranet, computer help desk, free student e-mail accounts, online (class) grades, online (class) schedules. Campuswide network is available. 100% of college-owned or -operated housing units are wired for high-speed Internet access. Wireless service is available via entire campus.

STUDENT LIFE

Housing options: on-campus residence required through senior year; coed, men-only, women-only. Campus housing is university owned. Freshman campus housing is guaranteed.

Activities and organizations: drama/theater group, student-run newspaper, choral group, Black Student Union, QueerSA, Student Action Service Learning, U.S.O. (Untitled Student Organization), Boffing.

Athletics ***Intercollegiate sports:*** basketball M/W, racquetball M/W, soccer M/W, swimming and diving M/W. ***Intramural sports:*** cross-country running M/W, soccer M/W, squash M/W, swimming and diving M/W, tennis M/W, weight lifting M/W.

Campus security: 24-hour emergency response devices and patrols, controlled dormitory access, Security Department is available for escorts or late night transport whenever needed.

Student services: health clinic, personal/psychological counseling, women's center.

COSTS & FINANCIAL AID

Costs (2014–15) ***Comprehensive fee:*** $61,749 includes full-time tuition ($47,442), mandatory fees ($1109), and room and board ($13,198). Full-time tuition and fees vary according to course load. Part-time tuition: $2025 per credit hour. Part-time tuition and fees vary according to course load. ***Payment plan:*** installment. ***Waivers:*** employees or children of employees.

Financial Aid Of all full-time matriculated undergraduates who enrolled in 2011, 271 applied for aid, 245 were judged to have need, 38 had their need fully met. 156 Federal Work-Study jobs (averaging $1000). In 2011, 73 non-need-based awards were made. ***Average percent of need met:*** 77. ***Average financial aid package:*** $34,687. ***Average need-based loan:*** $4721. ***Average need-based gift aid:*** $17,845. ***Average non-need-based aid:*** $16,504. ***Average indebtedness upon graduation:*** $30,000.

APPLYING

Options: electronic application.

Application fee: $50.

Required: essay or personal statement, high school transcript, 3 letters of recommendation, interview, school report, parent supplement.

Application deadlines: 5/1 (freshmen), 5/1 (out-of-state freshmen), 5/1 (transfers).

Notification: continuous (freshmen), continuous (out-of-state freshmen), continuous (transfers).

CONTACT

Director of Admissions, Bard College at Simon's Rock, 84 Alford Road, Great Barrington, MA 01230-9702. *Phone:* 800-235-7186. *Toll-free phone:* 800-235-7186. *Fax:* 413-541-0081. *E-mail:* admit@simons-rock.edu.

See this page for display ad and page 1354 for the College Close-Up.

Bay Path University

Longmeadow, Massachusetts

http://www.baypath.edu/

- **Independent** comprehensive, founded 1897
- **Suburban** 48-acre campus with easy access to Hartford, CT and Boston, MA
- **Endowment** $40.9 million
- **Undergraduate: women only; graduate: coed** 1,590 undergraduate students, 81% full-time, 100% women
- **Moderately difficult** entrance level, 63% of applicants were admitted

UNDERGRAD STUDENTS

1,293 full-time, 297 part-time. Students come from 24 states and territories; 5 other countries; 43% are from out of state; 14% Black or African American, non-Hispanic/Latino; 16% Hispanic/Latino; 2% Asian, non-Hispanic/Latino; 0.1% Native Hawaiian or other Pacific Islander, non-Hispanic/Latino; 0.3% American Indian or Alaska Native, non-Hispanic/Latino; 2% Two or more races, non-Hispanic/Latino; 8% Race/ethnicity unknown; 0.5% international; 5% transferred in; 50% live on campus.

Freshmen

Admission: 893 applied, 563 admitted, 129 enrolled. ***Average high school GPA:*** 3.28. ***Test scores:*** SAT critical reading scores over 500: 43%; SAT math scores over 500: 40%; SAT writing scores over 500: 40%; ACT scores over 18: 70%; SAT critical reading scores over 600: 9%; SAT math scores over 600: 4%; SAT writing scores over 600: 8%; ACT scores over 24: 20%.

Retention: 77% of full-time freshmen returned.

FACULTY

Total: 335, 16% full-time, 37% with terminal degrees.

Student/faculty ratio: 12:1.

ACADEMICS

Calendar: semesters. *Degrees:* certificates, associate, bachelor's, master's, post-master's, and postbachelor's certificates.

Special study options: academic remediation for entering students, accelerated degree program, adult/continuing education programs, advanced placement credit, cooperative education, distance learning, double majors, English as a second language, external degree program, honors programs, independent study, internships, off-campus study, part-time degree program, services for LD students, student-designed majors, study abroad, summer session for credit. ***ROTC:*** Army (c), Air Force (c).

Unusual degree programs: 3-2 Occupational Therapy.

Computers: 286 computers/terminals are available on campus for general student use. Students can access the following: campus intranet, computer help desk, free student e-mail accounts, online (class) grades, online (class) registration, online (class) schedules, Learning commons for iPad initiative. Campuswide network is available. 100% of college-owned or -operated housing units are wired for high-speed Internet access. Wireless service is available via entire campus.

STUDENT LIFE

Housing options: women-only. Campus housing is university owned. Freshman campus housing is guaranteed.

Activities and organizations: drama/theater group, choral group, Psychology Club, Body Positive Club, CEO Club, Alliance Club, Dance Company.

Athletics Member NCAA. All Division III. ***Intercollegiate sports:*** basketball W, cross-country running W, field hockey W, lacrosse W, soccer W, softball W, tennis W, volleyball W. ***Intramural sports:*** ice hockey W(c), swimming and diving W(c), track and field W(c).

Campus security: 24-hour emergency response devices and patrols, late-night transport/escort service, controlled dormitory access.

Student services: health clinic, personal/psychological counseling.

COSTS & FINANCIAL AID

Costs (2014–15) ***Comprehensive fee:*** $43,099 includes full-time tuition ($30,859) and room and board ($12,240). Part-time tuition: $490 per credit hour. Part-time tuition and fees vary according to course load. ***Room and board:*** Room and board charges vary according to board plan. ***Payment plan:*** installment. ***Waivers:*** children of alumni and employees or children of employees.

Financial Aid Of all full-time matriculated undergraduates who enrolled in 2014, 585 applied for aid, 559 were judged to have need, 44 had their need fully met. In 2014, 55 non-need-based awards were made. ***Average percent of need met:*** 73. ***Average financial aid package:*** $24,708. ***Average need-based loan:*** $5193. ***Average need-based gift aid:*** $19,475. ***Average non-need-based aid:*** $14,177.

APPLYING

Standardized Tests *Required:* SAT or ACT (for admission).

Options: electronic application, early action, deferred entrance.

Application fee: $25.

Required: high school transcript. ***Required for some:*** interview. ***Recommended:*** essay or personal statement, minimum 2.0 GPA, interview.

Application deadlines: rolling (freshmen), rolling (transfers), 12/15 (early action).

Notification: continuous (freshmen), continuous (transfers), 1/2 (early action).

CONTACT

Dawn Bryden, Associate Dean of Admissions, Bay Path University, 588 Longmeadow Street, Longmeadow, MA 01106-2292. *Phone:* 413-565-1000. *Toll-free phone:* 800-782-7284 Ext. 1331. *E-mail:* dbryden@baypath.edu.

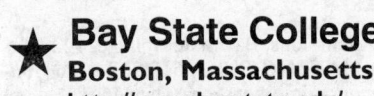

★ Bay State College

Boston, Massachusetts

http://www.baystate.edu/

- **Independent** primarily 2-year, founded 1946
- **Urban** campus
- **Coed**
- **Minimally difficult** entrance level

FACULTY

Student/faculty ratio: 20:1.

ACADEMICS

Calendar: semesters. *Degrees:* certificates, diplomas, associate, and bachelor's.

STUDENT LIFE

Housing options: coed, women-only. Campus housing is provided by a third party.

Activities and organizations: student-run radio station.

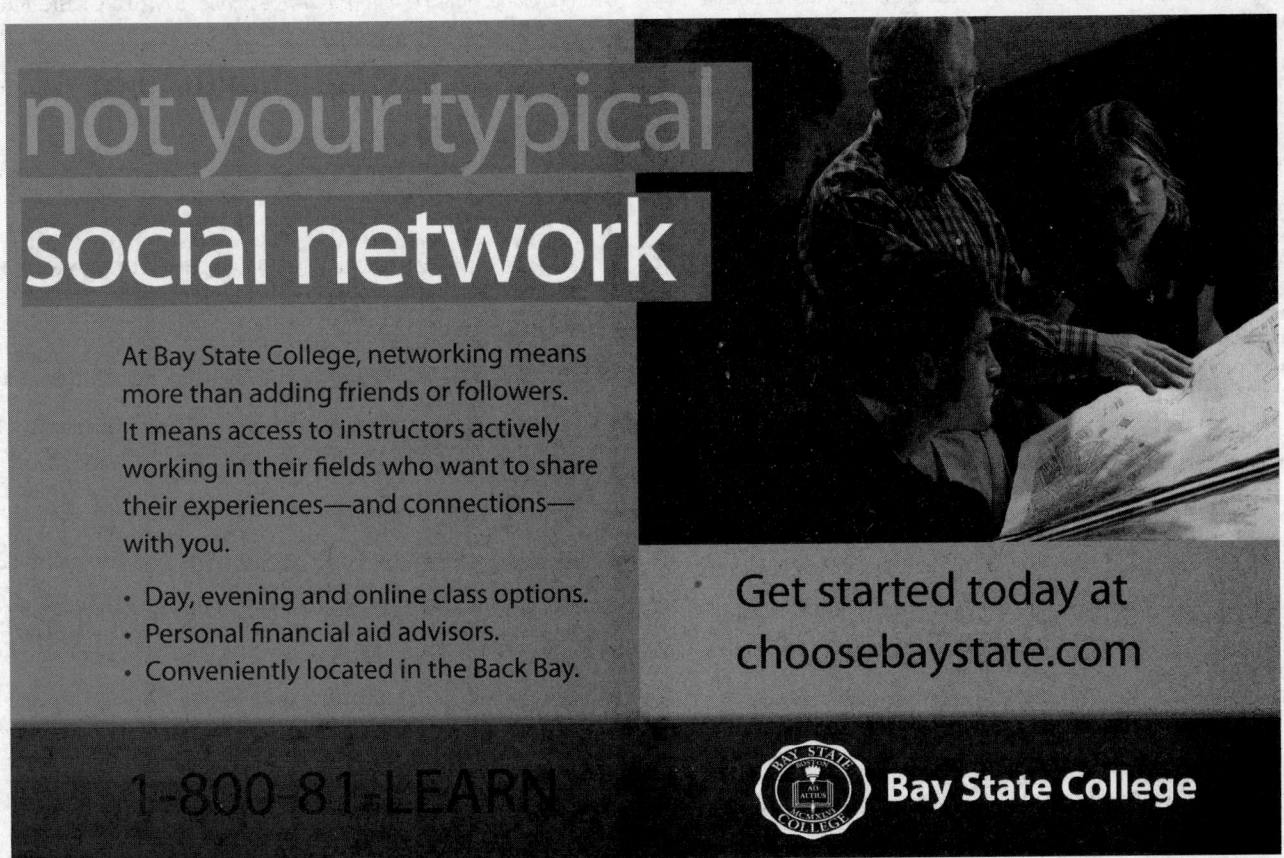

Campus security: late-night transport/escort service, controlled dormitory access, 14-hour patrols by trained security personnel.

Student services: personal/psychological counseling.

COSTS & FINANCIAL AID

Costs (2014–15) ***Comprehensive fee:*** $36,580 includes full-time tuition ($24,780) and room and board ($11,800). Full-time tuition and fees vary according to class time, location, and program. Part-time tuition: $826 per credit. Part-time tuition and fees vary according to class time, location, and program.

Financial Aid Of all full-time matriculated undergraduates who enrolled in 2013, 20 Federal Work-Study jobs (averaging $2600).

APPLYING

Standardized Tests *Recommended:* SAT or ACT (for admission).

Options: electronic application, early admission.

Required: high school transcript, minimum 2.3 GPA. ***Recommended:*** interview.

CONTACT

Kimberly Odusami, Director of Admissions, Bay State College, 122 Commonwealth Avenue, Boston, MA 02116. *Phone:* 617-217-9186. *Toll-free phone:* 800-81-LEARN. *E-mail:* admissions@baystate.edu.

See previous page for display ad and page 1360 for the College Close-Up.

Becker College

Worcester, Massachusetts

http://www.becker.edu/

- **Independent** 4-year, founded 1784
- **Urban** 100-acre campus with easy access to Boston
- **Coed** 2,021 undergraduate students, 78% full-time, 59% women, 41% men
- **Moderately difficult** entrance level, 65% of applicants were admitted

UNDERGRAD STUDENTS

1,567 full-time, 454 part-time. 34% are from out of state; 8% Black or African American, non-Hispanic/Latino; 7% Hispanic/Latino; 2% Asian, non-Hispanic/Latino; 0.1% Native Hawaiian or other Pacific Islander, non-Hispanic/Latino; 0.1% American Indian or Alaska Native, non-Hispanic/Latino; 2% Two or more races, non-Hispanic/Latino; 8% Race/ethnicity unknown; 0.9% international; 8% transferred in; 51% live on campus.

Freshmen

Admission: 3,040 applied, 1,985 admitted, 407 enrolled.

Retention: 67% of full-time freshmen returned.

FACULTY

Total: 177, 25% full-time, 29% with terminal degrees.

Student/faculty ratio: 16:1.

ACADEMICS

Calendar: semesters. *Degrees:* certificates, associate, and bachelor's (also includes Leicester, MA small town campus).

Special study options: academic remediation for entering students, accelerated degree program, adult/continuing education programs, advanced placement credit, cooperative education, distance learning, honors programs, independent study, internships, off-campus study, part-time degree program, services for LD students, study abroad. ***ROTC:*** Army (c), Air Force (c).

Computers: Students can access the following: campus intranet, computer help desk, free student e-mail accounts, online (class) grades, online (class) registration, online (class) schedules. Campuswide network is available. 100% of college-owned or -operated housing units are wired for high-speed Internet access. Wireless service is available via entire campus.

STUDENT LIFE

Housing options: coed, men-only, women-only. Campus housing is university owned and leased by the school. Freshman applicants given priority for college housing.

Activities and organizations: drama/theater group, student-run newspaper, television station, choral group, student government, Student Activities Committee, Black Student Union, Animal Health Club, Drama Club.

Athletics Member NCAA. ***Intercollegiate sports:*** baseball M, basketball M/W, cheerleading M/W, equestrian sports M/W, field hockey W, football M, golf M, ice hockey M, lacrosse M/W, soccer M/W, softball W, tennis M/W, volleyball W. ***Intramural sports:*** basketball M/W, bowling M/W, skiing (downhill) M(c)/W(c), soccer M/W, table tennis M/W, volleyball M/W.

Campus security: 24-hour emergency response devices and patrols, late-night transport/escort service, controlled dormitory access.

Student services: health clinic, personal/psychological counseling.

COSTS & FINANCIAL AID

Costs (2014–15) ***Comprehensive fee:*** $44,870 includes full-time tuition ($31,320), mandatory fees ($1550), and room and board ($12,000). Full-time tuition and fees vary according to class time, course load, program, and student level. Part-time tuition: $1305 per credit. Part-time tuition and fees vary according to class time, course load, program, and student level. No tuition increase for student's term of enrollment. ***College room only:*** $5850. Room and board charges vary according to board plan and housing facility. ***Payment plan:*** installment. ***Waivers:*** senior citizens and employees or children of employees.

Financial Aid Of all full-time matriculated undergraduates who enrolled in 2014, 1,330 applied for aid, 1,238 were judged to have need, 124 had their need fully met. 255 Federal Work-Study jobs (averaging $1227). In 2014, 210 non-need-based awards were made. ***Average percent of need met:*** 64. ***Average financial aid package:*** $21,776. ***Average need-based loan:*** $4292. ***Average need-based gift aid:*** $8675. ***Average non-need-based aid:*** $17,224.

APPLYING

Options: electronic application, early admission, early action, deferred entrance.

Required: high school transcript, minimum 2.0 GPA, 1 letter of recommendation. ***Required for some:*** interview. ***Recommended:*** essay or personal statement.

CONTACT

Office of Admissions, Becker College, 61 Sever Street, Worcester, MA 01609. *Phone:* 508-373-9400. *Toll-free phone:* 877-5BECKER. *Fax:* 508-890-1500. *E-mail:* admissions@becker.edu.

Benjamin Franklin Institute of Technology

Boston, Massachusetts

http://www.bfit.edu/

- **Independent** primarily 2-year, founded 1908
- **Urban** 3-acre campus
- **Coed** 493 undergraduate students, 87% full-time, 10% women, 90% men
- **Minimally difficult** entrance level, 64% of applicants were admitted

UNDERGRAD STUDENTS

428 full-time, 65 part-time. 29% Black or African American, non-Hispanic/Latino; 21% Hispanic/Latino; 9% Asian, non-Hispanic/Latino; 0.2% Native Hawaiian or other Pacific Islander, non-Hispanic/Latino; 0.4% American Indian or Alaska Native, non-Hispanic/Latino; 3% Two or more races, non-Hispanic/Latino; 6% Race/ethnicity unknown; 0.8% international.

Freshmen

Admission: 635 applied, 407 admitted, 210 enrolled. ***Test scores:*** SAT critical reading scores over 500: 13%; SAT math scores over 500: 24%; SAT writing scores over 500: 11%; SAT critical reading scores over 600: 5%; SAT math scores over 600: 5%; SAT writing scores over 600: 5%; SAT critical reading scores over 700: 3%; SAT writing scores over 700: 2%.

ACADEMICS

Calendar: semesters. *Degrees:* certificates, associate, and bachelor's.

Special study options: academic remediation for entering students, adult/continuing education programs, advanced placement credit, cooperative education, English as a second language, internships, off-campus study, part-time degree program, services for LD students, summer session for credit.

Computers: Students can access the following: free student e-mail accounts, online (class) grades, online (class) schedules, online payments. Campuswide network is available. 100% of college-owned or -operated housing units are wired for high-speed Internet access. Wireless service is available via classrooms, computer labs, dorm rooms, learning centers, libraries, student centers.

STUDENT LIFE

Housing options: coed. Campus housing is provided by a third party. Freshman campus housing is guaranteed.

Activities and organizations: Phi Theta Kappa, Student Government and Leadership, yearbook and video club, Green Technology Club, Women's Forum.

Athletics Member NJCAA. ***Intercollegiate sports:*** soccer M. ***Intramural sports:*** basketball M/W, table tennis M/W.

Campus security: 24-hour emergency response devices.

Student services: personal/psychological counseling.

COSTS & FINANCIAL AID

Costs (2014–15) ***Comprehensive fee:*** $32,050 includes full-time tuition ($16,950), mandatory fees ($1200), and room and board ($13,900). Full-time tuition and fees vary according to course load, degree level, and program. Part-time tuition: $707 per credit hour. Part-time tuition and fees vary according to course load, degree level, and program. ***Room and board:*** Room and board charges vary according to housing facility. ***Payment plan:*** installment. ***Waivers:*** employees or children of employees.

Financial Aid Of all full-time matriculated undergraduates who enrolled in 2009, 470 applied for aid, 430 were judged to have need, 12 had their need fully met. 22 Federal Work-Study jobs (averaging $1635). In 2009, 3 non-need-based awards were made. ***Average percent of need met:*** 41. ***Average financial aid package:*** $5094. ***Average need-based loan:*** $1979. ***Average need-based gift aid:*** $3239. ***Average non-need-based aid:*** $917.

APPLYING

Standardized Tests *Recommended:* SAT or ACT (for admission).

Options: electronic application, deferred entrance.

Application fee: $25.

Required: high school transcript. ***Recommended:*** essay or personal statement, minimum 2.0 GPA, interview.

CONTACT

Ms. Brittainy Johnson, Associate Director of Admissions, Benjamin Franklin Institute of Technology, Boston, MA 02116. *Phone:* 617-423-4630 Ext. 122. *Toll-free phone:* 877-400-BFIT. *Fax:* 617-482-3706. *E-mail:* bjohnson@bfit.edu.

★ Bentley University

Waltham, Massachusetts

http://www.bentley.edu/

- **Independent** comprehensive, founded 1917
- **Suburban** 163-acre campus with easy access to Boston
- **Endowment** $268.0 million
- **Coed** 4,264 undergraduate students, 98% full-time, 40% women, 60% men
- **Very difficult** entrance level, 46% of applicants were admitted

UNDERGRAD STUDENTS

4,170 full-time, 94 part-time. Students come from 45 states and territories; 78 other countries; 54% are from out of state; 3% Black or African American, non-Hispanic/Latino; 7% Hispanic/Latino; 8% Asian, non-Hispanic/Latino; 0.1% American Indian or Alaska Native, non-Hispanic/Latino; 2% Two or more races, non-Hispanic/Latino; 4% Race/ethnicity unknown; 15% international; 3% transferred in; 78% live on campus.

Freshmen

Admission: 7,477 applied, 3,448 admitted, 978 enrolled. ***Test scores:*** SAT critical reading scores over 500: 91%; SAT math scores over 500: 98%; SAT writing scores over 500: 93%; ACT scores over 18: 100%; SAT critical reading scores over 600: 48%; SAT math scores over 600: 80%; SAT writing scores over 600: 54%; ACT scores over 24: 92%; SAT

critical reading scores over 700: 5%; SAT math scores over 700: 24%; SAT writing scores over 700: 9%; ACT scores over 30: 30%.
Retention: 94% of full-time freshmen returned.

FACULTY
Total: 465, 61% full-time, 62% with terminal degrees.
Student/faculty ratio: 12:1.

ACADEMICS
Calendar: semesters. *Degrees:* bachelor's, master's, doctoral, post-master's, and postbachelor's certificates.
Special study options: accelerated degree program, adult/continuing education programs, advanced placement credit, distance learning, double majors, English as a second language, honors programs, independent study, internships, off-campus study, part-time degree program, services for LD students, study abroad, summer session for credit. ***ROTC:*** Army (c), Air Force (c).
Computers: 4,522 computers/terminals and 10,754 ports are available on campus for general student use. Students can access the following: campus intranet, computer help desk, free student e-mail accounts, online (class) grades, online (class) registration, online (class) schedules, grade checking, online admission, Blackboard, resume review, student employment, interlibrary loan, free software. Campuswide network is available. 100% of college-owned or -operated housing units are wired for high-speed Internet access. Wireless service is available via entire campus.

STUDENT LIFE
Housing options: coed, special housing for students with disabilities. Campus housing is university owned. Freshman campus housing is guaranteed.
Activities and organizations: drama/theater group, student-run newspaper, radio and television station, choral group, Bentley Entrepreneurship Society, Campus Activities Board, Delta Sigma Pi, Bentley Investment Group, National Association of Black Accountants, national fraternities, national sororities.
Athletics Member NCAA. All Division II except ice hockey (Division I). ***Intercollegiate sports:*** baseball M, basketball M(s)/W(s), cross-country running M/W, field hockey W, football M, golf M, ice hockey M(s), lacrosse M/W, soccer M/W, softball W, swimming and diving M/W, tennis M/W, track and field M/W, volleyball W. ***Intramural sports:*** basketball M/W, cheerleading W(c), football M, golf M(c)/W(c), racquetball M(c)/W(c), rugby M(c)/W(c), sailing M(c)/W(c), skiing (downhill) M(c)/W(c), soccer M/W, softball M/W, ultimate Frisbee M/W, volleyball M/W, water polo M(c), wrestling M(c).
Campus security: 24-hour emergency response devices and patrols, late-night transport/escort service, controlled dormitory access, security cameras, Community Policing Team, self-defense classes, CPR and first-aid training, anonymous crime reporting, fire drills.
Student services: health clinic, personal/psychological counseling, women's center.

COSTS & FINANCIAL AID
Costs (2014–15) ***Comprehensive fee:*** $56,460 includes full-time tuition ($40,990), mandatory fees ($1521), and room and board ($13,949). Part-time tuition: $2080 per course. Part-time tuition and fees vary according to class time and course load. ***Required fees:*** $26 per year part-time. ***College room only:*** $8449. Room and board charges vary according to board plan and housing facility. ***Payment plan:*** installment. ***Waivers:*** employees or children of employees.
Financial Aid Of all full-time matriculated undergraduates who enrolled in 2013, 2,486 applied for aid, 1,842 were judged to have need, 722 had their need fully met. 839 Federal Work-Study jobs (averaging $1637). 733 state and other part-time jobs (averaging $956). In 2013, 799 non-need-based awards were made. ***Average percent of need met:*** 94. ***Average financial aid package:*** $33,956. ***Average need-based loan:*** $5370. ***Average need-based gift aid:*** $29,025. ***Average non-need-based aid:*** $16,761. ***Average indebtedness upon graduation:*** $30,602. ***Financial aid deadline:*** 2/1.

APPLYING
Standardized Tests *Required:* SAT or ACT (for admission). *Required for some:* TOEFL (or IELTS) is required form non-native English speakers unless the student receives at least 577 (paper-based) or 90 (Internet-based) on the writing section of the SAT.
Options: electronic application, early admission, early decision, early action, deferred entrance.
Application fee: $50.
Required: essay or personal statement, high school transcript, 2 letters of recommendation. ***Required for some:*** TOEFL or IELTS required of non-native English speakers. ***Recommended:*** interview.
Application deadlines: 1/7 (freshmen), 1/7 (out-of-state freshmen), 4/15 (transfers), 11/1 (early action).
Early decision deadline: 11/1.
Notification: 3/31 (freshmen), 3/31 (out-of-state freshmen), continuous (transfers), 12/22 (early decision), 1/31 (early action).

CONTACT
Office of Undergraduate Admissions, Bentley University, 175 Forest Street, Waltham, MA 02452. *Phone:* 781-891-2244. *Toll-free phone:* 800-523-2354. *Fax:* 781-891-3414. *E-mail:* ugadmission@bentley.edu.

See previous page for display ad and page 1364 for the College Close-Up.

★ Berklee College of Music
Boston, Massachusetts
http://www.berklee.edu/

CONTACT
Mr. Damien Bracken, Director of Admissions, Berklee College of Music, 1140 Boylston Street, Boston, MA 02215-3693. *Phone:* 617-747-2222. *Toll-free phone:* 800-BERKLEE. *Fax:* 617-747-2047. *E-mail:* admissions@berklee.edu.

See next page for display ad and page 1366 for the College Close-Up.

Boston Architectural College
Boston, Massachusetts
http://www.the-bac.edu/

- **Independent** comprehensive, founded 1889
- **Urban** 1-acre campus with easy access to Boston
- **Endowment** $10.7 million
- **Coed** 472 undergraduate students, 75% full-time, 42% women, 58% men
- **Noncompetitive** entrance level, 16% of applicants were admitted

UNDERGRAD STUDENTS
354 full-time, 118 part-time. 6% Black or African American, non-Hispanic/Latino; 17% Hispanic/Latino; 9% Asian, non-Hispanic/Latino; 0.3% Native Hawaiian or other Pacific Islander, non-Hispanic/Latino; 0.3% American Indian or Alaska Native, non-Hispanic/Latino; 4% Two or more races, non-Hispanic/Latino; 8% Race/ethnicity unknown; 5% international.

Freshmen
Admission: 152 applied, 24 admitted, 24 enrolled.
Retention: 67% of full-time freshmen returned.

FACULTY
Total: 371, 6% full-time, 39% with terminal degrees.
Student/faculty ratio: 2:1.

ACADEMICS
Calendar: semesters. *Degrees:* certificates, bachelor's, and master's.
Special study options: adult/continuing education programs, advanced placement credit, distance learning, independent study, internships, off-campus study, summer session for credit.
Computers: 84 computers/terminals are available on campus for general student use. Students can access the following: campus intranet, computer help desk, free student e-mail accounts, online (class) grades, online (class) registration, online (class) schedules. Campuswide network is available. Wireless service is available via entire campus.

STUDENT LIFE
Activities and organizations: Atelier, Student Government, American Institute of Architectural Students, BAC Interior Design Society (IIDA and ASID), National Organization of Minority Architecture Students (NOMAS), Student American Society of Landscape Architects.

Campus security: 24-hour emergency response devices and patrols, late-night transport/escort service, electronically operated building access and CCTV systems.

Student services: personal/psychological counseling, legal services.

COSTS & FINANCIAL AID

Costs (2014–15) ***Tuition:*** $19,056 full-time, $1588 per credit hour part-time. Full-time tuition and fees vary according to course load, degree level, and program. Part-time tuition and fees vary according to course load, degree level, and program. ***Required fees:*** $650 full-time, $175 part-time. ***Payment plan:*** deferred payment. ***Waivers:*** employees or children of employees.

Financial Aid Of all full-time matriculated undergraduates who enrolled in 2013, 139 applied for aid, 136 were judged to have need. 24 Federal Work-Study jobs (averaging $78,623). In 2013, 3 non-need-based awards were made. ***Average percent of need met:*** 31. ***Average financial aid package:*** $10,194. ***Average need-based loan:*** $5362. ***Average need-based gift aid:*** $6255. ***Average non-need-based aid:*** $2622. ***Average indebtedness upon graduation:*** $50,520.

APPLYING

Options: electronic application.

Required: essay or personal statement, high school transcript, resumes, creative exercise. ***Recommended:*** interview.

CONTACT

Admission Office, Boston Architectural College, 320 Newbury Street, Boston, MA 02115-2795. *Phone:* 617-585-0123. *Fax:* 617-585-0121. *E-mail:* admissions@the-bac.edu.

Boston Baptist College

Boston, Massachusetts

http://www.boston.edu/

- **Independent Baptist** 4-year, founded 1976
- **Suburban** 8-acre campus with easy access to Boston, Providence
- **Coed**
- **Moderately difficult** entrance level

ACADEMICS

Calendar: semesters. *Degrees:* certificates, diplomas, associate, and bachelor's.

STUDENT LIFE

Housing options: on-campus residence required through senior year; men-only, women-only, special housing for students with disabilities. Campus housing is university owned. Freshman campus housing is guaranteed.

Activities and organizations: choral group, Community Service Organization, Recruitment, Campus Life.

Campus security: 24-hour emergency response devices, student patrols, late-night transport/escort service, controlled dormitory access.

Student services: personal/psychological counseling.

APPLYING

Standardized Tests *Required for some:* SAT or ACT (for admission), Students who have been out of high school more than 3 years are no longer required to submit standardized test scores.

Options: deferred entrance.

Application fee: $50.

Required: essay or personal statement, high school transcript, 1 letter of recommendation. ***Recommended:*** 1 letter of recommendation.

CONTACT

Mrs. Kim Melton, Director of Admissions, Boston Baptist College, 950 Metropolitan Avenue, Boston, MA 02136. *Phone:* 617-364-3510 Ext. 233. *Toll-free phone:* 888-235-2014. *Fax:* 617-399-8220. *E-mail:* kmelton@boston.edu.

Boston College

Chestnut Hill, Massachusetts

http://www.bc.edu/

- **Independent Roman Catholic (Jesuit)** university, founded 1863
- **Suburban** 338-acre campus with easy access to Boston
- **Endowment** $2.2 billion
- **Coed** 9,154 undergraduate students, 100% full-time, 54% women, 46% men
- **Very difficult** entrance level, 34% of applicants were admitted

UNDERGRAD STUDENTS

9,154 full-time. Students come from 53 states and territories; 61 other countries; 74% are from out of state; 4% Black or African American, non-Hispanic/Latino; 10% Hispanic/Latino; 10% Asian, non-Hispanic/Latino; 0.1% American Indian or Alaska Native, non-Hispanic/Latino; 3% Two or more races, non-Hispanic/Latino; 5% Race/ethnicity unknown; 6% international; 2% transferred in; 85% live on campus.

Freshmen

Admission: 23,223 applied, 7,875 admitted, 2,344 enrolled. ***Test scores:*** SAT critical reading scores over 500: 98%; SAT math scores over 500: 99%; SAT writing scores over 500: 98%; ACT scores over 18: 100%; SAT critical reading scores over 600: 88%; SAT math scores over 600: 91%; SAT writing scores over 600: 90%; ACT scores over 24: 98%; SAT critical reading scores over 700: 34%; SAT math scores over 700: 46%; SAT writing scores over 700: 47%; ACT scores over 30: 78%.
Retention: 96% of full-time freshmen returned.

FACULTY

Total: 1,477, 51% full-time, 95% with terminal degrees.
Student/faculty ratio: 13:1.

ACADEMICS

Calendar: semesters. *Degrees:* bachelor's, master's, doctoral, and post-master's certificates (also offers continuing education program with significant enrollment not reflected in profile).

Special study options: accelerated degree program, advanced placement credit, double majors, honors programs, independent study, internships, off-campus study, part-time degree program, services for LD students, student-designed majors, study abroad, summer session for credit. ***ROTC:*** Army (c), Navy (c), Air Force (c).

Computers: 1,000 computers/terminals are available on campus for general student use. Students can access the following: campus intranet, computer help desk, free student e-mail accounts, online (class) grades, online (class) registration, online (class) schedules. Campuswide network is available. 100% of college-owned or -operated housing units are wired for high-speed Internet access. Wireless service is available via entire campus.

STUDENT LIFE

Housing options: coed, women-only. Campus housing is university owned. Freshman campus housing is guaranteed.

Activities and organizations: drama/theater group, student-run newspaper, radio and television station, choral group, marching band, UGBC and individual School Senates, Asian Caucus, Appalachia Volunteers, Dance Marathon, 4Boston.

Athletics Member NCAA. All Division I except football (Division I-A). ***Intercollegiate sports:*** baseball M(s), basketball M(s)/W(s), cheerleading M(c)/W(c), crew W(s), cross-country running M(s)/W(s), fencing M/W, field hockey W(s), golf M(s)/W(s), ice hockey M(s)/W(s), lacrosse W(s), sailing M/W, skiing (downhill) M/W, soccer M(s)/W(s), softball W(s), swimming and diving M(s)/W(s), tennis M(s)/W(s), track and field M(s)/W(s), volleyball W(s). ***Intramural sports:*** badminton M/W, basketball M(c)/W(c), crew M(c), cross-country running M(c)/W(c), equestrian sports M(c)/W(c), field hockey W(c), golf M(c)/W(c), ice hockey M/W, lacrosse M(c)/W(c), racquetball M/W, rugby M(c)/W(c), soccer M(c)/W(c), softball M/W, squash M/W, tennis M/W, track and field M(c)/W(c), ultimate Frisbee M(c)/W(c), volleyball M(c)/W, water polo M(c)/W(c).

Campus security: 24-hour emergency response devices and patrols, late-night transport/escort service, controlled dormitory access, Students, Faculty/Staff can sign up to receive text Alerts of Emergencies on their phone.

Student services: health clinic, personal/psychological counseling, women's center.

COSTS & FINANCIAL AID

Costs (2014–15) ***One-time required fee:*** $474. ***Comprehensive fee:*** $60,622 includes full-time tuition ($46,670), mandatory fees ($766), and room and board ($13,186). ***College room only:*** $8180. Room and board charges vary according to housing facility. ***Payment plan:*** installment. ***Waivers:*** employees or children of employees.

Financial Aid Of all full-time matriculated undergraduates who enrolled in 2013, 4,346 applied for aid, 3,887 were judged to have need, 3,887 had their need fully met. In 2013, 167 non-need-based awards were made. ***Average percent of need met:*** 100. ***Average financial aid package:*** $36,793. ***Average need-based loan:*** $5182. ***Average need-based gift aid:*** $32,330. ***Average non-need-based aid:*** $18,337. ***Average indebtedness upon graduation:*** $21,139.

APPLYING

Standardized Tests *Required:* SAT or ACT (for admission).

Options: electronic application, early admission, early action, deferred entrance.

Application fee: $70.

Required: essay or personal statement, high school transcript, 2 letters of recommendation.

Application deadlines: 1/1 (freshmen), 3/15 (transfers), 11/1 (early action).

Notification: 4/15 (freshmen), 6/1 (transfers), 12/25 (early action).

CONTACT

Office of Undergraduate Admissions, Boston College, 140 Commonwealth Avenue, Devlin 208, Chestnut Hill, MA 02467-3809. *Phone:* 617-552-3100. *Toll-free phone:* 800-360-2522. *Fax:* 617-552-0798.

See page 1368 for the College Close-Up.

The Boston Conservatory

Boston, Massachusetts

http://www.bostonconservatory.edu/

- **Independent** comprehensive, founded 1867
- **Urban** campus with easy access to Boston
- **Coed**
- **Moderately difficult** entrance level

FACULTY

Student/faculty ratio: 6:1.

ACADEMICS

Calendar: semesters. *Degrees:* certificates, diplomas, bachelor's, master's, post-master's, and postbachelor's certificates.

STUDENT LIFE

Housing options: on-campus residence required for freshman year; coed. Campus housing is university owned. Freshman campus housing is guaranteed.

Activities and organizations: drama/theater group, student-run radio station, choral group, Student Government Association, BoCo Cares, The Tent, Sigma Alpha Iota, Phi Mu Alpha, national fraternities, national sororities.

Campus security: 24-hour emergency response devices and patrols, late-night transport/escort service, controlled dormitory access.

Student services: health clinic, personal/psychological counseling.

COSTS & FINANCIAL AID

Costs (2014–15) ***Comprehensive fee:*** $59,506 includes full-time tuition ($40,150), mandatory fees ($2176), and room and board ($17,180). Full-time tuition and fees vary according to course load, degree level, and program. Part-time tuition: $1615 per credit hour. Part-time tuition and fees vary according to course load, degree level, and program. ***College room only:*** $11,100. Room and board charges vary according to board plan and housing facility.

Financial Aid Of all full-time matriculated undergraduates who enrolled in 2008, 335 applied for aid, 293 were judged to have need, 23 had their need fully met. In 2008, 20 non-need-based awards were made. ***Average percent of need met:*** 0. ***Average financial aid package:*** $13,967. ***Average***

need-based loan: $4257. ***Average need-based gift aid:*** $12,772. ***Average non-need-based aid:*** $9235. ***Average indebtedness upon graduation:*** $34,931.

APPLYING

Standardized Tests *Required:* SAT or ACT (for admission).

Options: electronic application.

Application fee: $110.

Required: essay or personal statement, high school transcript, minimum 2.7 GPA, 2 letters of recommendation, audition. ***Required for some:*** interview.

CONTACT

Ms. Meghan Cadwallader, The Boston Conservatory, 8 The Fenway, Boston, MA 02215. *Phone:* 617-912-9153.

Boston University

Boston, Massachusetts

http://www.bu.edu/

- **Independent** university, founded 1839
- **Urban** 135-acre campus
- **Endowment** $1.4 billion
- **Coed** 18,017 undergraduate students, 92% full-time, 60% women, 40% men
- **Very difficult** entrance level, 35% of applicants were admitted

UNDERGRAD STUDENTS

16,619 full-time, 1,398 part-time. Students come from 52 states and territories; 103 other countries; 74% are from out of state; 3% Black or African American, non-Hispanic/Latino; 10% Hispanic/Latino; 13% Asian, non-Hispanic/Latino; 0.1% Native Hawaiian or other Pacific Islander, non-Hispanic/Latino; 0.1% American Indian or Alaska Native, non-Hispanic/Latino; 4% Two or more races, non-Hispanic/Latino; 5% Race/ethnicity unknown; 19% international; 3% transferred in; 75% live on campus.

Freshmen

Admission: 54,190 applied, 18,701 admitted, 3,915 enrolled. ***Average high school GPA:*** 3.6. ***Test scores:*** SAT critical reading scores over 500: 101%; SAT math scores over 500: 100%; SAT writing scores over 500: 99%; ACT scores over 18: 100%; SAT critical reading scores over 600: 72%; SAT math scores over 600: 86%; SAT writing scores over 600: 79%; ACT scores over 24: 98%; SAT critical reading scores over 700: 17%; SAT math scores over 700: 39%; SAT writing scores over 700: 24%; ACT scores over 30: 48%.

Retention: 93% of full-time freshmen returned.

FACULTY

Total: 2,650, 63% full-time.

Student/faculty ratio: 13:1.

ACADEMICS

Calendar: semesters. *Degrees:* certificates, bachelor's, master's, doctoral, post-master's, and postbachelor's certificates.

Special study options: accelerated degree program, adult/continuing education programs, advanced placement credit, cooperative education, distance learning, double majors, English as a second language, honors programs, independent study, internships, off-campus study, part-time degree program, services for LD students, student-designed majors, study abroad, summer session for credit. ***ROTC:*** Army (b), Navy (b), Air Force (b).

Computers: 250 computers/terminals and 1,650 ports are available on campus for general student use. Students can access the following: campus intranet, computer help desk, free student e-mail accounts, online (class) grades, online (class) registration, online (class) schedules, research and educational networks. Campuswide network is available. 100% of college-owned or -operated housing units are wired for high-speed Internet access. Wireless service is available via classrooms, computer labs, dorm rooms, libraries, student centers.

STUDENT LIFE

Housing options: on-campus residence required for freshman year; coed, women-only, cooperative, special housing for students with disabilities.

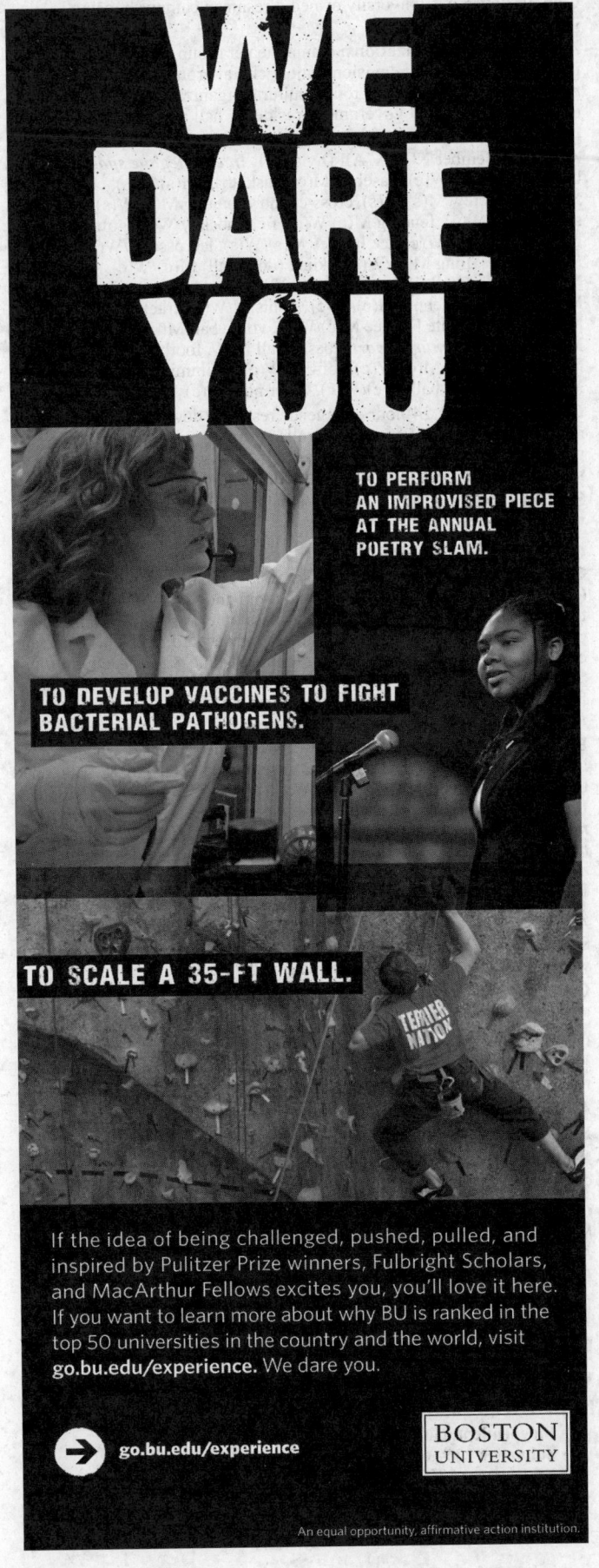

Campus housing is university owned. Freshman campus housing is guaranteed.

Activities and organizations: drama/theater group, student-run newspaper, radio and television station, choral group, marching band, performing and Acappella groups, cultural organizations, service organizations, student government, residence hall associations, national fraternities, national sororities.

Athletics Member NCAA. All Division I. ***Intercollegiate sports:*** badminton M(c)/W(c), baseball M(c), basketball M(s)/W(s), cheerleading M(c)/W(c), crew M(s)/W(s), cross-country running M(s)/W(s), equestrian sports M(c)/W(c), fencing M(c)/W(c), field hockey W(s), golf M(c)/W, gymnastics M(c)/W(c), ice hockey M(s)/W(s), lacrosse M/W(s), rugby M(c)/W(c), sailing M(c)/W(c), skiing (downhill) M(c)/W(c), soccer M(s)/W(s), softball W(s), squash M(c)/W(c), swimming and diving M(s)/W(s), table tennis M(c)/W(c), tennis M/W(s), track and field M(s)/W(s), ultimate Frisbee M(c)/W(c), volleyball M(c)/W(c), water polo M(c)/W(c). ***Intramural sports:*** basketball M/W, football M(c)/W(c), ice hockey W, soccer M(c)/W(c), softball W(c), swimming and diving M(c)/W(c), volleyball M(c)/W(c), water polo M(c)/W(c).

Campus security: 24-hour emergency response devices and patrols, late-night transport/escort service, controlled dormitory access, security personnel at residence hall entrances, self-defense education, well-lit sidewalks, Emergency Alert System, Blue Light System.

Student services: health clinic, personal/psychological counseling, women's center.

COSTS & FINANCIAL AID

Costs (2014–15) ***Comprehensive fee:*** $60,694 includes full-time tuition ($45,686), mandatory fees ($978), and room and board ($14,030). Full-time tuition and fees vary according to class time. Part-time tuition: $1428 per credit hour. Part-time tuition and fees vary according to class time and course load. ***Required fees:*** $60 per term part-time. ***College room only:*** $9200. Room and board charges vary according to board plan, housing facility, and location. ***Payment plans:*** tuition prepayment, installment. ***Waivers:*** employees or children of employees.

Financial Aid Of all full-time matriculated undergraduates who enrolled in 2014, 7,037 applied for aid, 6,262 were judged to have need, 1,803 had their need fully met. 3,129 Federal Work-Study jobs (averaging $1934). In 2014, 1338 non-need-based awards were made. ***Average percent of need met:*** 86. ***Average financial aid package:*** $35,766. ***Average need-based loan:*** $5526. ***Average need-based gift aid:*** $29,854. ***Average non-need-based aid:*** $17,594. ***Average indebtedness upon graduation:*** $39,166. ***Financial aid deadline:*** 2/15.

APPLYING

Standardized Tests *Required:* SAT or ACT (for admission). *Required for some:* SAT Subject Tests (for admission).

Options: electronic application, early admission, early decision, deferred entrance.

Application fee: $80.

Required: essay or personal statement, high school transcript, 2 letters of recommendation. ***Required for some:*** interview, audition, portfolio.

Application deadlines: 1/1 (freshmen), 3/1 (transfers).

Early decision deadline: 11/1.

Notification: 4/1 (freshmen), continuous until 6/1 (transfers), 12/15 (early decision).

CONTACT

Ms. Kelly A. Walter, Associate Vice-President and Executive Director of Admissions, Boston University, 233 Bay State Road, Boston, MA 02215. *Phone:* 617-353-2300. *Fax:* 617-353-9695. *E-mail:* admissions@bu.edu.

See previous page for display ad and page 1370 for the College Close-Up.

Brandeis University

Waltham, Massachusetts

http://www.brandeis.edu/

- **Independent** university, founded 1948
- **Suburban** 235-acre campus with easy access to Boston
- **Endowment** $861.2 million
- **Coed** 3,729 undergraduate students, 100% full-time, 57% women, 43% men
- **Most difficult** entrance level, 35% of applicants were admitted

UNDERGRAD STUDENTS

3,711 full-time, 18 part-time. Students come from 47 states and territories; 90 other countries; 72% are from out of state; 5% Black or African American, non-Hispanic/Latino; 7% Hispanic/Latino; 13% Asian, non-Hispanic/Latino; 0.1% American Indian or Alaska Native, non-Hispanic/Latino; 3% Two or more races, non-Hispanic/Latino; 6% Race/ethnicity unknown; 18% international; 2% transferred in; 77% live on campus.

Freshmen

Admission: 10,004 applied, 3,523 admitted, 859 enrolled. ***Average high school GPA:*** 3.84. ***Test scores:*** SAT critical reading scores over 500: 98%; SAT math scores over 500: 98%; SAT writing scores over 500: 98%; ACT scores over 18: 88%; SAT critical reading scores over 600: 74%; SAT math scores over 600: 92%; SAT writing scores over 600: 90%; ACT scores over 24: 85%; SAT critical reading scores over 700: 30%; SAT math scores over 700: 60%; SAT writing scores over 700: 35%; ACT scores over 30: 56%.

Retention: 93% of full-time freshmen returned.

FACULTY

Total: 535, 68% full-time, 87% with terminal degrees.

Student/faculty ratio: 10:1.

ACADEMICS

Calendar: semesters. *Degrees:* bachelor's, master's, and doctoral.

Special study options: adult/continuing education programs, advanced placement credit, double majors, English as a second language, honors programs, independent study, internships, off-campus study, services for LD students, student-designed majors, study abroad, summer session for credit. ***ROTC:*** Army (c), Air Force (c).

Unusual degree programs: 3-2 engineering with Columbia University.

Computers: 130 computers/terminals are available on campus for general student use. Students can access the following: computer help desk, free student e-mail accounts, online (class) grades, online (class) registration, online (class) schedules, educational software. Campuswide network is available. 100% of college-owned or -operated housing units are wired for high-speed Internet access. Wireless service is available via entire campus.

STUDENT LIFE

Housing options: on-campus residence required for freshman year; coed, men-only, women-only, special housing for students with disabilities. Campus housing is university owned. Freshman campus housing is guaranteed.

Activities and organizations: drama/theater group, student-run newspaper, radio and television station, choral group, Waltham Group, Undergraduate Theater Collective, Student Union, Student Events (Programming Board), BEMCo - student EMTs.

Athletics Member NCAA. All Division III. ***Intercollegiate sports:*** baseball M, basketball M/W, cross-country running M/W, fencing M/W, soccer M/W, softball W, swimming and diving M(c)/W(c), tennis M/W, track and field M/W, volleyball W. ***Intramural sports:*** archery M(c)/W(c), cheerleading M(c)/W(c), crew M(c)/W(c), equestrian sports M(c)/W(c), field hockey M(c)/W(c), gymnastics M(c)/W(c), lacrosse W(c), rugby M(c)/W(c), sailing M(c)/W(c), skiing (downhill) M(c)/W(c), squash M/W, table tennis M/W, ultimate Frisbee M(c)/W(c), volleyball M.

Campus security: 24-hour emergency response devices and patrols, late-night transport/escort service, controlled dormitory access.

Student services: health clinic, personal/psychological counseling.

COSTS & FINANCIAL AID

Costs (2014–15) ***One-time required fee:*** $275. ***Comprehensive fee:*** $60,750 includes full-time tuition ($46,022), mandatory fees ($1536), and room and board ($13,192). Full-time tuition and fees vary according to student level. Part-time tuition: $5753 per course. Part-time tuition and fees vary according to course load. ***Required fees:*** $768 per term part-time. ***College room only:*** $7492. Room and board charges vary according to board plan and housing facility. ***Payment plans:*** tuition prepayment, installment. ***Waivers:*** employees or children of employees.

Financial Aid Of all full-time matriculated undergraduates who enrolled in 2013, 2,174 applied for aid, 1,909 were judged to have need, 435 had their need fully met. In 2013, 175 non-need-based awards were made. ***Average percent of need met:*** 91. ***Average financial aid package:***

$37,276. ***Average need-based loan:*** $5007. ***Average need-based gift aid:*** $32,276. ***Average non-need-based aid:*** $17,895. ***Average indebtedness upon graduation:*** $30,848.

APPLYING

Standardized Tests *Required:* SAT or ACT (for admission).

Options: electronic application, early admission, early decision, deferred entrance.

Application fee: $75.

Required: essay or personal statement, high school transcript, 1 letter of recommendation. ***Recommended:*** interview.

Application deadlines: 1/1 (freshmen), 4/1 (transfers).

Early decision deadline: 11/1 (for plan 1), 1/1 (for plan 2).

Notification: 4/1 (freshmen), 5/25 (transfers), 12/15 (early decision plan 1), 2/1 (early decision plan 2).

CONTACT

Jennifer Walker, Dean of Admissions, Brandeis University, 415 South Street, PO Box 549110, Waltham, MA 02454-9110. *Phone:* 781-736-3500. *Toll-free phone:* 800-622-0622. *Fax:* 781-736-3536. *E-mail:* admissions@brandeis.edu.

Bridgewater State University

Bridgewater, Massachusetts

http://www.bridgew.edu/

- **State-supported** comprehensive, founded 1840, part of Massachusetts Department of Higher Education
- **Suburban** 278-acre campus with easy access to Boston
- **Endowment** $34.2 million
- **Coed** 9,628 undergraduate students, 83% full-time, 59% women, 41% men
- **Moderately difficult** entrance level, 79% of applicants were admitted

UNDERGRAD STUDENTS

8,019 full-time, 1,609 part-time. Students come from 27 states and territories; 22 other countries; 4% are from out of state; 9% Black or African American, non-Hispanic/Latino; 6% Hispanic/Latino; 2% Asian, non-Hispanic/Latino; 0.1% Native Hawaiian or other Pacific Islander, non-Hispanic/Latino; 0.3% American Indian or Alaska Native, non-Hispanic/Latino; 3% Two or more races, non-Hispanic/Latino; 2% Race/ethnicity unknown; 0.4% international; 10% transferred in; 41% live on campus.

Freshmen

Admission: 5,799 applied, 4,599 admitted, 1,540 enrolled. ***Average high school GPA:*** 3.1. ***Test scores:*** SAT critical reading scores over 500: 47%; SAT math scores over 500: 55%; ACT scores over 18: 93%; SAT critical reading scores over 600: 10%; SAT math scores over 600: 10%; ACT scores over 24: 27%; SAT critical reading scores over 700: 1%; SAT math scores over 700: 1%; ACT scores over 30: 2%.

Retention: 81% of full-time freshmen returned.

FACULTY

Total: 810, 41% full-time, 61% with terminal degrees.

Student/faculty ratio: 19:1.

ACADEMICS

Calendar: semesters. *Degrees:* bachelor's, master's, post-master's, and postbachelor's certificates.

Special study options: academic remediation for entering students, accelerated degree program, adult/continuing education programs, advanced placement credit, distance learning, double majors, English as a second language, honors programs, independent study, internships, off-campus study, part-time degree program, services for LD students, study abroad, summer session for credit. ***ROTC:*** Army (c), Air Force (c).

Computers: 780 computers/terminals and 14 ports are available on campus for general student use. Students can access the following: campus intranet, computer help desk, free student e-mail accounts, online (class) grades, online (class) registration, online (class) schedules, student account information, application software. Campuswide network is available. 100% of college-owned or -operated housing units are wired for high-speed Internet access. Wireless service is available via entire campus.

STUDENT LIFE

Housing options: coed, special housing for students with disabilities. Campus housing is university owned. Freshman applicants given priority for college housing.

Activities and organizations: drama/theater group, student-run newspaper, radio station, choral group, Dance Company, African American Society (Afro-Am), Program Committee, Panhellenic Association, Inter-Fraternity Council, national fraternities, national sororities.

Athletics Member NCAA. All Division III. ***Intercollegiate sports:*** baseball M, basketball M/W, cross-country running M/W, field hockey W, football M, lacrosse W, soccer M/W, softball W, swimming and diving M/W, tennis M/W, track and field M/W, volleyball W, wrestling M. ***Intramural sports:*** badminton M/W, basketball M/W, cheerleading W(c), equestrian sports M(c)/W(c), field hockey W, football M/W, ice hockey M(c), lacrosse M(c), rugby W(c), soccer M/W, softball M/W, tennis M/W, ultimate Frisbee M(c)/W(c), volleyball M/W.

Campus security: 24-hour emergency response devices and patrols, late-night transport/escort service, controlled dormitory access, 24-hour patrols by Bridgewater State University Police.

Student services: health clinic, personal/psychological counseling.

COSTS & FINANCIAL AID

Costs (2014–15) ***Tuition:*** state resident $910 full-time, $38 per credit hour part-time; nonresident $7050 full-time, $294 per credit hour part-time. Full-time tuition and fees vary according to course load. ***Required fees:*** $7443 full-time, $305 per credit hour part-time. ***Room and board:*** $11,400; room only: $7500. Room and board charges vary according to board plan and housing facility. ***Payment plan:*** installment. ***Waivers:*** senior citizens and employees or children of employees.

Financial Aid Of all full-time matriculated undergraduates who enrolled in 2011, 7,601 applied for aid, 5,041 were judged to have need, 351 had their need fully met. 526 Federal Work-Study jobs (averaging $1710). In 2011, 31 non-need-based awards were made. ***Average financial aid package:*** $10,368. ***Average need-based loan:*** $3997. ***Average need-based gift aid:*** $4146. ***Average non-need-based aid:*** $5278. ***Average indebtedness upon graduation:*** $30,189.

APPLYING

Standardized Tests *Required:* SAT or ACT (for admission).

Options: electronic application, early action, deferred entrance.

Application fee: $40.

Required: high school transcript, minimum 2.0 GPA, SAT or ACT scores. ***Recommended:*** essay or personal statement, .

Application deadlines: 2/15 (freshmen), 2/15 (out-of-state freshmen), 2/15 (transfers), 11/15 (early action).

Notification: continuous until 4/15 (freshmen), continuous until 4/15 (out-of-state freshmen), continuous until 4/15 (transfers), 12/15 (early action).

CONTACT

Mr. Gregg Meyer, Dean of University Admissions, Bridgewater State University, Gates House, 40 Cedar Street, Bridgewater, MA 02325. *Phone:* 508-531-1237. *Fax:* 508-531-1746. *E-mail:* admission@bridgew.edu.

Clark University

Worcester, Massachusetts

http://www.clarku.edu/

- **Independent** university, founded 1887
- **Urban** 50-acre campus with easy access to Boston
- **Endowment** $406.4 million
- **Coed** 2,301 undergraduate students, 96% full-time, 58% women, 42% men
- **Moderately difficult** entrance level, 54% of applicants were admitted

UNDERGRAD STUDENTS

2,213 full-time, 88 part-time. Students come from 39 states and territories; 63 other countries; 62% are from out of state; 4% Black or African American, non-Hispanic/Latino; 6% Hispanic/Latino; 7% Asian, non-Hispanic/Latino; 0.1% Native Hawaiian or other Pacific Islander, non-Hispanic/Latino; 2% Two or more races, non-Hispanic/Latino; 7%

Race/ethnicity unknown; 14% international; 2% transferred in; 70% live on campus.

Freshmen

Admission: 7,304 applied, 3,946 admitted, 548 enrolled. ***Average high school GPA:*** 3.6. ***Test scores:*** SAT critical reading scores over 500: 91%; SAT math scores over 500: 93%; SAT writing scores over 500: 91%; ACT scores over 18: 100%; SAT critical reading scores over 600: 59%; SAT math scores over 600: 60%; SAT writing scores over 600: 59%; ACT scores over 24: 87%; SAT critical reading scores over 700: 16%; SAT math scores over 700: 14%; SAT writing scores over 700: 13%; ACT scores over 30: 36%.

Retention: 88% of full-time freshmen returned.

FACULTY

Total: 300, 66% full-time.

Student/faculty ratio: 10:1.

ACADEMICS

Calendar: semesters. *Degrees:* bachelor's, master's, doctoral, and post-master's certificates.

Special study options: academic remediation for entering students, accelerated degree program, adult/continuing education programs, advanced placement credit, double majors, English as a second language, honors programs, independent study, internships, off-campus study, part-time degree program, services for LD students, student-designed majors, study abroad, summer session for credit. ***ROTC:*** Army (c), Navy (c), Air Force (c).

Unusual degree programs: 3-2 business administration; engineering with Columbia University, Washington University in St. Louis, Worcester Polytechnic Institute; environmental studies, international development, community planning, biology, biochemistry, chemistry, physics, economics, history, communications, public administration, geographic information systems.

Computers: 319 computers/terminals and 4,000 ports are available on campus for general student use. Students can access the following: campus intranet, computer help desk, free student e-mail accounts, online (class) grades, online (class) registration, online (class) schedules, online course support. Campuswide network is available. 100% of college-owned or -operated housing units are wired for high-speed Internet access. Wireless service is available via entire campus.

STUDENT LIFE

Housing options: on-campus residence required through sophomore year; coed, women-only, special housing for students with disabilities. Campus housing is university owned. Freshman campus housing is guaranteed.

Activities and organizations: drama/theater group, student-run newspaper, radio and television station, choral group, marching band, International Students Association, Science Fiction People of Clark, Outing Club, Hillel, Clark Musical Theater.

Athletics Member NCAA, NAIA. All NCAA Division III. ***Intercollegiate sports:*** baseball M, basketball M/W, crew M/W, cross-country running M/W, field hockey W, lacrosse M, soccer M/W, softball W, swimming and diving M/W, tennis M/W, volleyball W. ***Intramural sports:*** basketball M/W, equestrian sports M(c)/W(c), football M/W, ice hockey M(c), lacrosse W(c), racquetball M/W, soccer M(c)/W, softball M/W, track and field M(c)/W(c), ultimate Frisbee M(c)/W(c), volleyball M(c)/W(c), water polo M/W.

Campus security: 24-hour emergency response devices and patrols, student patrols, late-night transport/escort service, controlled dormitory access.

Student services: health clinic, personal/psychological counseling, women's center.

COSTS & FINANCIAL AID

Costs (2015–16) ***Comprehensive fee:*** $50,140 includes full-time tuition ($41,590), mandatory fees ($350), and room and board ($8200). Part-time tuition: $1300 per credit. ***College room only:*** $4700. Room and board charges vary according to board plan and housing facility. ***Payment plans:*** tuition prepayment, installment. ***Waivers:*** employees or children of employees.

Financial Aid Of all full-time matriculated undergraduates who enrolled in 2014, 1,647 applied for aid, 1,310 were judged to have need, 896 had their need fully met. 1,000 Federal Work-Study jobs (averaging $2000). In 2014, 680 non-need-based awards were made. ***Average percent of need met:*** 95. ***Average financial aid package:*** $33,231. ***Average need-based loan:*** $4089. ***Average need-based gift aid:*** $25,826. ***Average non-need-based aid:*** $16,362. ***Average indebtedness upon graduation:*** $24,990. ***Financial aid deadline:*** 2/1.

APPLYING

Options: electronic application, early admission, early decision, early action, deferred entrance.

Application fee: $55.

Required: essay or personal statement, high school transcript, 2 letters of recommendation. ***Recommended:*** interview.

Application deadlines: 1/15 (freshmen), 4/15 (transfers), 11/1 (early action).

Notification: 4/1 (freshmen), 6/1 (transfers), 12/15 (early action).

CONTACT

Mr. Donald Honeman, Dean of Admissions, Clark University, Admissions House, 950 Main Street, Worcester, MA 01610. *Phone:* 508-793-7431. *Toll-free phone:* 800-GO-CLARK. *Fax:* 508-793-8821. *E-mail:* admissions@clarku.edu.

College of the Holy Cross

Worcester, Massachusetts

http://www.holycross.edu/

- **Independent Roman Catholic (Jesuit)** 4-year, founded 1843
- **Suburban** 174-acre campus with easy access to Boston
- **Endowment** $726.1 million
- **Coed** 2,937 undergraduate students, 99% full-time, 50% women, 50% men
- **Very difficult** entrance level, 43% of applicants were admitted

UNDERGRAD STUDENTS

2,904 full-time, 33 part-time. Students come from 49 states and territories; 16 other countries; 63% are from out of state; 4% Black or African American, non-Hispanic/Latino; 11% Hispanic/Latino; 5% Asian, non-Hispanic/Latino; 0.2% American Indian or Alaska Native, non-Hispanic/Latino; 3% Two or more races, non-Hispanic/Latino; 7% Race/ethnicity unknown; 1% international; 0.3% transferred in; 91% live on campus.

Freshmen

Admission: 5,302 applied, 2,298 admitted, 773 enrolled. ***Test scores:*** SAT critical reading scores over 500: 99%; SAT math scores over 500: 99%; SAT writing scores over 500: 98%; ACT scores over 18: 100%; SAT critical reading scores over 600: 80%; SAT math scores over 600: 86%; SAT writing scores over 600: 84%; ACT scores over 24: 96%; SAT critical reading scores over 700: 22%; SAT math scores over 700: 24%; SAT writing scores over 700: 30%; ACT scores over 30: 47%.

Retention: 94% of full-time freshmen returned.

FACULTY

Total: 332, 86% full-time, 93% with terminal degrees.

Student/faculty ratio: 10:1.

ACADEMICS

Calendar: semesters. *Degree:* bachelor's.

Special study options: accelerated degree program, advanced placement credit, double majors, honors programs, independent study, internships, off-campus study, services for LD students, student-designed majors, study abroad. ***ROTC:*** Army (c), Navy (b), Air Force (c).

Unusual degree programs: 3-2 engineering with Columbia University.

Computers: 485 computers/terminals are available on campus for general student use. Students can access the following: computer help desk, free student e-mail accounts, online (class) registration. Campuswide network is available. 100% of college-owned or -operated housing units are wired for high-speed Internet access. Wireless service is available via classrooms, computer centers, computer labs, dorm rooms, learning centers, libraries, student centers.

STUDENT LIFE

Housing options: on-campus residence required through sophomore year; coed, special housing for students with disabilities. Campus housing is university owned. Freshman campus housing is guaranteed.

Activities and organizations: drama/theater group, student-run newspaper, radio station, choral group, marching band, SPUD (community service organization), choral and music groups, Campus Activities Board, Student Government Association, Purple Key Society.

Athletics Member NCAA. All Division I except football (Division I-AA). ***Intercollegiate sports:*** baseball M, basketball M(s)/W(s), crew M/W(s), cross-country running M/W(s), field hockey W(s), golf M/W, ice hockey M(s)/W, lacrosse M(s)/W(s), soccer M(s)/W(s), softball W(s), swimming and diving M/W(s), tennis M/W, track and field M/W(s), volleyball W(s). ***Intramural sports:*** baseball M(c), basketball M(c)/W(c), equestrian sports M(c)/W(c), field hockey W(c), football M/W, golf M(c)/W(c), ice hockey M(c), lacrosse M(c)/W(c), rugby M(c)/W(c), sailing M(c)/W(c), skiing (downhill) M(c)/W(c), soccer M(c)/W(c), softball M/W, swimming and diving M(c)/W(c), tennis M(c)/W(c), ultimate Frisbee M(c)/W(c), volleyball M(c)/W(c), water polo M/W.

Campus security: 24-hour emergency response devices and patrols, late-night transport/escort service, controlled dormitory access.

Student services: health clinic, personal/psychological counseling.

COSTS & FINANCIAL AID

Costs (2015–16) ***Comprehensive fee:*** $59,924 includes full-time tuition ($46,550), mandatory fees ($626), and room and board ($12,748). ***College room only:*** $6878. Room and board charges vary according to housing facility. ***Payment plan:*** installment. ***Waivers:*** employees or children of employees.

Financial Aid Of all full-time matriculated undergraduates who enrolled in 2014, 1,909 applied for aid, 1,603 were judged to have need, 1,603 had their need fully met. 1,106 Federal Work-Study jobs (averaging $1620). In 2014, 55 non-need-based awards were made. ***Average percent of need met:*** 100. ***Average financial aid package:*** $35,279. ***Average need-based loan:*** $5441. ***Average need-based gift aid:*** $32,207. ***Average non-need-based aid:*** $33,308. ***Average indebtedness upon graduation:*** $28,354. ***Financial aid deadline:*** 2/1.

APPLYING

Options: electronic application, early admission, early decision, deferred entrance.

Application fee: $60.

Required: essay or personal statement, high school transcript, 2 letters of recommendation. ***Recommended:*** interview.

Application deadlines: 1/15 (freshmen), 3/1 (transfers).

Early decision deadline: 12/15.

Notification: 4/1 (freshmen), continuous (transfers), 1/15 (early decision).

CONTACT

College of the Holy Cross, 1 College Street, Worcester, MA 01610-2395. *Phone:* 508-793-2443. *Toll-free phone:* 800-442-2421.

★ Curry College

Milton, Massachusetts

http://www.curry.edu/

- **Independent** comprehensive, founded 1879
- **Suburban** 131-acre campus with easy access to Boston
- **Endowment** $92.4 million
- **Coed** 2,900 undergraduate students, 73% full-time, 63% women, 37% men
- **Moderately difficult** entrance level, 87% of applicants were admitted

UNDERGRAD STUDENTS

2,103 full-time, 797 part-time. Students come from 30 states and territories; 12 other countries; 22% are from out of state; 9% Black or African American, non-Hispanic/Latino; 5% Hispanic/Latino; 2% Asian, non-Hispanic/Latino; 0.4% American Indian or Alaska Native, non-Hispanic/Latino; 2% Two or more races, non-Hispanic/Latino; 12% Race/ethnicity unknown; 1% international; 2% transferred in; 75% live on campus.

Freshmen

Admission: 5,448 applied, 4,733 admitted, 649 enrolled. ***Average high school GPA:*** 2.8. ***Test scores:*** SAT critical reading scores over 500: 35%; SAT math scores over 500: 42%; SAT writing scores over 500: 35%; ACT scores over 18: 77%; SAT critical reading scores over 600: 3%; SAT math scores over 600: 5%; SAT writing scores over 600: 3%; ACT scores over 24: 12%.

Retention: 71% of full-time freshmen returned.

FACULTY
Total: 484, 25% full-time, 40% with terminal degrees.

Student/faculty ratio: 11:1.

ACADEMICS
Calendar: semesters. *Degrees:* bachelor's and master's.

Special study options: academic remediation for entering students, accelerated degree program, adult/continuing education programs, advanced placement credit, double majors, English as a second language, honors programs, independent study, internships, off-campus study, part-time degree program, services for LD students, student-designed majors, study abroad, summer session for credit. ***ROTC:*** Army (c), Air Force (c).

Computers: 245 computers/terminals and 2,500 ports are available on campus for general student use. Students can access the following: campus intranet, computer help desk, free student e-mail accounts, online (class) grades, online (class) registration, online (class) schedules, library online catalog and research databases. Campuswide network is available. 100% of college-owned or -operated housing units are wired for high-speed Internet access. Wireless service is available via entire campus.

STUDENT LIFE
Housing options: coed, men-only, women-only. Campus housing is university owned.

Activities and organizations: drama/theater group, student-run newspaper, radio and television station, choral group, Student radio station, Student government, Student Program Board, Curry Cares: Community Service, Theatre.

Athletics Member NCAA. All Division III. ***Intercollegiate sports:*** baseball M, basketball M/W, cross-country running W, equestrian sports M(c)/W(c), football M, ice hockey M/W(c), lacrosse M/W, rugby M(c), soccer M/W, softball W, tennis M/W, volleyball W. ***Intramural sports:*** badminton M/W, basketball M/W, cheerleading M/W, equestrian sports M/W, field hockey W, ice hockey W, skiing (downhill) M/W, soccer M/W, softball M/W, tennis M/W, ultimate Frisbee M/W, volleyball M/W.

Campus security: 24-hour emergency response devices and patrols, late-night transport/escort service, controlled dormitory access, A campus safety office offers security services.

Student services: health clinic, personal/psychological counseling.

COSTS & FINANCIAL AID
Costs (2015–16) ***One-time required fee:*** $320. ***Comprehensive fee:*** $50,345 includes full-time tuition ($34,730), mandatory fees ($1715), and room and board ($13,900). Full-time tuition and fees vary according to class time, course load, location, and program. Part-time tuition: $1158 per credit. Part-time tuition and fees vary according to class time, course load, location, and program. ***College room only:*** $7800. Room and board charges vary according to board plan and housing facility. ***Payment plan:*** installment. ***Waivers:*** children of alumni and employees or children of employees.

Financial Aid Of all full-time matriculated undergraduates who enrolled in 2014, 1,591 applied for aid, 1,590 were judged to have need, 134 had their need fully met. 910 Federal Work-Study jobs (averaging $1971). In 2014, 365 non-need-based awards were made. ***Average percent of need met:*** 69. ***Average financial aid package:*** $24,327. ***Average need-based loan:*** $4474. ***Average need-based gift aid:*** $12,318. ***Average non-need-based aid:*** $9572. ***Average indebtedness upon graduation:*** $43,388.

APPLYING
Standardized Tests *Required for some:* SAT or ACT (for admission), TOEFL for international applicants whose native language is not English. The College's Program for the Advancement of Learning does not require nor does it consider SAT or ACT scores during the admissions process.

Options: electronic application, early admission, early action, deferred entrance.

Application fee: $50.

Required: essay or personal statement, high school transcript, minimum 2.0 GPA, 1 letter of recommendation, There is a supplemental form for Common Application subscribers and Program for Advancement of Learning (PAL). Students applying to the PAL Program must submit Cognitive and Achievement Testing. ***Required for some:*** interview.

Application deadlines: 4/1 (freshmen), 7/1 (transfers), 12/1 (early action).

Notification: continuous (freshmen), continuous (transfers), 12/15 (early action).

CONTACT
Ms. Jane P. Fidler, Dean of Admission, Curry College, 1071 Blue Hill Avenue, Milton, MA 02186. *Phone:* 617-333-2210. *Toll-free phone:* 800-669-0686. *Fax:* 617-333-2114. *E-mail:* curryadm@curry.edu.

See previous page for display ad and page 1414 for the College Close-Up.

★ Dean College
Franklin, Massachusetts
http://www.dean.edu/

- **Independent** primarily 2-year, founded 1865
- **Small-town** 100-acre campus with easy access to Boston, Providence
- **Coed**
- **Minimally difficult** entrance level

FACULTY
Student/faculty ratio: 16:1.

ACADEMICS
Calendar: semesters. *Degrees:* certificates, diplomas, associate, and bachelor's.

STUDENT LIFE
Housing options: on-campus residence required through sophomore year; coed, men-only, women-only, special housing for students with disabilities. Campus housing is university owned. Freshman campus housing is guaranteed.

Activities and organizations: drama/theater group, student-run radio station, choral group, Emerging Leaders, College Success Staff, Student Ambassadors, student government, Phi Theta Kappa.

Athletics Member NJCAA.

Campus security: 24-hour emergency response devices and patrols, late-night transport/escort service, controlled dormitory access.

Student services: health clinic, personal/psychological counseling.

COSTS & FINANCIAL AID
Costs (2014–15) ***Comprehensive fee:*** $47,790 includes full-time tuition ($33,230), mandatory fees ($300), and room and board ($14,260). ***College room only:*** $9010.

Financial Aid Of all full-time matriculated undergraduates who enrolled in 2014, 821 applied for aid, 751 were judged to have need. 211 Federal Work-Study jobs (averaging $1440). In 2014, 185 non-need-based awards were made. ***Average financial aid package:*** $27,361. ***Average need-based loan:*** $16,651. ***Average need-based gift aid:*** $14,615. ***Average non-need-based aid:*** $15,012. ***Average indebtedness upon graduation:*** $34,243.

APPLYING
Standardized Tests *Required:* SAT or ACT (for admission).

Options: electronic application, early action, deferred entrance.

Application fee: $35.

Required: essay or personal statement, high school transcript. ***Recommended:*** minimum 2.0 GPA, interview.

CONTACT
Iris Godes, Assistant Vice President for Enrollment/Dean of Admissions, Dean College, 99 Main Street, Franklin, MA 02038. *Phone:* 508-541-1547. *Toll-free phone:* 877-TRY-DEAN. *Fax:* 508-541-8726. *E-mail:* igodes@dean.edu.

See page 1418 for the College Close-Up.

Elms College
Chicopee, Massachusetts
http://www.elms.edu/

- **Independent Roman Catholic** comprehensive, founded 1928
- **Suburban** 32-acre campus
- **Coed** 1,396 undergraduate students, 73% full-time, 76% women, 24% men
- **Moderately difficult** entrance level, 79% of applicants were admitted

UNDERGRAD STUDENTS
1,023 full-time, 373 part-time. Students come from 24 states and territories; 5 other countries; 20% are from out of state; 8% Black or African American, non-Hispanic/Latino; 9% Hispanic/Latino; 3% Asian, non-Hispanic/Latino; 0.7% American Indian or Alaska Native, non-Hispanic/Latino; 29% Race/ethnicity unknown; 1% international; 20% transferred in.

Freshmen
Admission: 851 applied, 672 admitted, 187 enrolled.
Retention: 85% of full-time freshmen returned.

FACULTY
Total: 181, 32% full-time.
Student/faculty ratio: 13:1.

ACADEMICS
Calendar: semesters. *Degrees:* associate, bachelor's, master's, doctoral, post-master's, and postbachelor's certificates.
Special study options: academic remediation for entering students, accelerated degree program, adult/continuing education programs, advanced placement credit, double majors, English as a second language, honors programs, internships, off-campus study, part-time degree program, student-designed majors, study abroad, summer session for credit. ***ROTC:*** Army (c), Air Force (c).
Computers: Campuswide network is available.

STUDENT LIFE
Housing options: coed, women-only. Campus housing is university owned. Freshman campus housing is guaranteed.
Activities and organizations: drama/theater group, student-run newspaper, radio station, choral group.
Athletics Member NCAA. All Division III. ***Intercollegiate sports:*** baseball M, basketball M/W, cross-country running M/W, field hockey W, golf M, lacrosse W, soccer M/W, softball W, swimming and diving M/W, volleyball M/W. ***Intramural sports:*** basketball M/W, bowling M/W, cross-country running M/W, field hockey W, golf W, lacrosse M/W, racquetball M/W, skiing (cross-country) M/W, soccer M/W, softball M/W, swimming and diving M/W, volleyball M/W, water polo M/W, weight lifting M/W.
Campus security: 24-hour emergency response devices and patrols, late-night transport/escort service, controlled dormitory access.
Student services: health clinic, personal/psychological counseling.

COSTS & FINANCIAL AID
Costs (2015–16) ***Comprehensive fee:*** $44,043 includes full-time tuition ($30,768), mandatory fees ($1567), and room and board ($11,708). Part-time tuition and fees vary according to location and program. ***Room and board:*** Room and board charges vary according to board plan. ***Payment plan:*** installment. ***Waivers:*** senior citizens and employees or children of employees.
Financial Aid Of all full-time matriculated undergraduates who enrolled in 2014, 953 applied for aid, 910 were judged to have need, 70 had their need fully met. 114 Federal Work-Study jobs (averaging $1164). In 2014, 89 non-need-based awards were made. ***Average percent of need met:*** 63. ***Average financial aid package:*** $22,246. ***Average need-based loan:*** $4714. ***Average need-based gift aid:*** $18,179. ***Average non-need-based aid:*** $14,164. ***Average indebtedness upon graduation:*** $35,089.

APPLYING
Standardized Tests *Required:* SAT or ACT (for admission).
Options: early admission, deferred entrance.
Application fee: $30.
Required: essay or personal statement, high school transcript, 2 letters of recommendation. ***Recommended:*** interview.
Application deadlines: rolling (freshmen), rolling (transfers).
Notification: continuous (freshmen), continuous (transfers).

CONTACT
Mr. Joseph Wagner, Director of Admissions, Elms College, Chicopee, MA 01013-2839. *Phone:* 413-592-3189 Ext. 350. *Toll-free phone:* 800-255-ELMS. *Fax:* 413-594-2781. *E-mail:* admissions@elms.edu.

★ Emerson College
Boston, Massachusetts
http://www.emerson.edu/

- **Independent** comprehensive, founded 1880
- **Urban** campus
- **Endowment** $146.2 million
- **Coed** 3,765 undergraduate students, 98% full-time, 61% women, 39% men
- **Very difficult** entrance level, 49% of applicants were admitted

UNDERGRAD STUDENTS
3,707 full-time, 58 part-time. Students come from 51 states and territories; 48 other countries; 76% are from out of state; 3% Black or African American, non-Hispanic/Latino; 10% Hispanic/Latino; 4% Asian, non-Hispanic/Latino; 0.1% Native Hawaiian or other Pacific Islander, non-Hispanic/Latino; 0.1% American Indian or Alaska Native, non-Hispanic/Latino; 5% Two or more races, non-Hispanic/Latino; 6% Race/ethnicity unknown; 5% international; 6% transferred in; 58% live on campus.

Freshmen
Admission: 8,709 applied, 4,283 admitted, 857 enrolled. ***Average high school GPA:*** 3.66. ***Test scores:*** SAT critical reading scores over 500: 98%; SAT math scores over 500: 95%; SAT writing scores over 500: 97%; ACT scores over 18: 100%; SAT critical reading scores over 600: 71%; SAT math scores over 600: 58%; SAT writing scores over 600: 69%; ACT scores over 24: 91%; SAT critical reading scores over 700: 18%; SAT math scores over 700: 9%; SAT writing scores over 700: 15%; ACT scores over 30: 26%.
Retention: 89% of full-time freshmen returned.

FACULTY
Total: 456, 43% full-time, 55% with terminal degrees.
Student/faculty ratio: 13:1.

ACADEMICS
Calendar: semesters. *Degrees:* certificates, bachelor's, master's, and doctoral.
Special study options: adult/continuing education programs, advanced placement credit, double majors, honors programs, independent study, internships, off-campus study, part-time degree program, services for LD students, student-designed majors, study abroad, summer session for credit.
Computers: 480 computers/terminals and 1,900 ports are available on campus for general student use. Students can access the following: computer help desk, free student e-mail accounts, online (class) grades, online (class) registration, online (class) schedules. Campuswide network is available. 100% of college-owned or -operated housing units are wired for high-speed Internet access. Wireless service is available via entire campus.

STUDENT LIFE
Housing options: on-campus residence required through sophomore year; coed. Campus housing is university owned. Freshman campus housing is guaranteed.
Activities and organizations: drama/theater group, student-run newspaper, radio and television station, choral group, EIV (Emerson Independent Video), National Broadcasting Society (student chapter), SPEC (Screenwriting), Emertainment Monthly (entertainment news), Emerson International (international student group), national fraternities, national sororities.
Athletics Member NCAA. All Division III. ***Intercollegiate sports:*** baseball M, basketball M/W, cross-country running M/W, golf M(c)/W(c), ice hockey M(c), lacrosse M/W, soccer M/W, softball W, tennis M/W, track and field W, volleyball M/W. ***Intramural sports:*** basketball M/W, soccer M/W, volleyball M/W.
Campus security: 24-hour emergency response devices and patrols, late-night transport/escort service, controlled dormitory access.
Student services: health clinic, personal/psychological counseling.

COSTS & FINANCIAL AID
Costs (2015–16) ***Comprehensive fee:*** $54,736 includes full-time tuition ($38,304), mandatory fees ($732), and room and board ($15,700). Full-time tuition and fees vary according to student level. Part-time tuition:

$1197 per credit. Part-time tuition and fees vary according to student level. ***Room and board:*** Room and board charges vary according to board plan. ***Payment plan:*** installment. ***Waivers:*** employees or children of employees.

Financial Aid Of all full-time matriculated undergraduates who enrolled in 2014, 2,552 applied for aid, 1,994 were judged to have need, 279 had their need fully met. 402 Federal Work-Study jobs (averaging $1409). 75 state and other part-time jobs (averaging $13,065). In 2014, 321 non-need-based awards were made. ***Average percent of need met:*** 59. ***Average financial aid package:*** $20,840. ***Average need-based loan:*** $4857. ***Average need-based gift aid:*** $17,140. ***Average non-need-based aid:*** $14,675. ***Average indebtedness upon graduation:*** $23,606.

APPLYING

Standardized Tests *Required:* SAT or ACT (for admission).

Options: electronic application, early admission, early action, deferred entrance.

Application fee: $65.

Required: essay or personal statement, high school transcript, 1 letter of recommendation. ***Required for some:*** interview.

Application deadlines: 1/15 (freshmen), 3/1 (transfers), 11/1 (early action).

Notification: 4/1 (freshmen), 5/1 (transfers), 12/15 (early action).

CONTACT

Emerson College, 120 Boylston Street, Boston, MA 02116-4624. *Phone:* 617-824-8600.

★ Emmanuel College

Boston, Massachusetts

http://www.emmanuel.edu/

- **Independent Roman Catholic** comprehensive, founded 1919
- **Urban** 17-acre campus
- **Endowment** $96.5 million
- **Coed** 2,082 undergraduate students, 87% full-time, 74% women, 26% men
- **Moderately difficult** entrance level, 69% of applicants were admitted

UNDERGRAD STUDENTS

1,817 full-time, 265 part-time. Students come from 33 states and territories; 48 other countries; 44% are from out of state; 5% Black or African American, non-Hispanic/Latino; 7% Hispanic/Latino; 3% Asian, non-Hispanic/Latino; 0.1% Native Hawaiian or other Pacific Islander, non-Hispanic/Latino; 0.2% American Indian or Alaska Native, non-Hispanic/Latino; 3% Two or more races, non-Hispanic/Latino; 12% Race/ethnicity unknown; 1% international; 2% transferred in; 72% live on campus.

Freshmen

Admission: 5,899 applied, 4,088 admitted, 524 enrolled. ***Average high school GPA:*** 3.62. ***Test scores:*** SAT critical reading scores over 500: 73%; SAT math scores over 500: 80%; SAT writing scores over 500: 77%; ACT scores over 18: 95%; SAT critical reading scores over 600: 24%; SAT math scores over 600: 28%; SAT writing scores over 600: 26%; ACT scores over 24: 55%; SAT critical reading scores over 700: 3%; SAT math scores over 700: 2%; SAT writing scores over 700: 2%; ACT scores over 30: 4%.

Retention: 79% of full-time freshmen returned.

FACULTY

Total: 231, 40% full-time, 56% with terminal degrees.

Student/faculty ratio: 14:1.

ACADEMICS

Calendar: semesters. *Degrees:* bachelor's, master's, and postbachelor's certificates.

Special study options: academic remediation for entering students, accelerated degree program, adult/continuing education programs, advanced placement credit, distance learning, double majors, honors programs, independent study, internships, off-campus study, part-time degree program, services for LD students, student-designed majors, study abroad, summer session for credit. ***ROTC:*** Army (c), Air Force (c).

Computers: 284 computers/terminals are available on campus for general student use. Students can access the following: campus intranet, computer help desk, free student e-mail accounts, online (class) grades, online (class) registration, online (class) schedules, software/applications. Campuswide network is available. 100% of college-owned or -operated housing units are wired for high-speed Internet access. Wireless service is available via entire campus.

STUDENT LIFE

Housing options: coed, special housing for students with disabilities. Campus housing is university owned and leased by the school. Freshman campus housing is guaranteed.

Activities and organizations: drama/theater group, student-run newspaper, radio station, choral group, Student Government Association, Black Student Union, OUTSpoken (LGBTQ Club), Model UN, EC Programming Board.

Athletics Member NCAA. All Division III. ***Intercollegiate sports:*** basketball M/W, cross-country running M/W, golf M, lacrosse M/W, soccer M/W, softball W, track and field M/W, volleyball M/W. ***Intramural sports:*** baseball M(c), basketball M/W, field hockey W(c), racquetball M/W, sailing M(c)/W(c), soccer M/W, softball M/W, swimming and diving M(c)/W(c), tennis M/W, ultimate Frisbee M/W, volleyball M/W.

Campus security: 24-hour emergency response devices and patrols, student patrols, late-night transport/escort service, controlled dormitory access, 24-hour staffed residence hall desks and security office, closed-circuit surveillance in public areas, off-campus escorts, bike patrol.

Student services: health clinic, personal/psychological counseling.

COSTS & FINANCIAL AID

Costs (2014–15) ***One-time required fee:*** $280. ***Comprehensive fee:*** $49,112 includes full-time tuition ($35,312), mandatory fees ($220), and room and board ($13,580). Part-time tuition: $1104 per credit hour. ***Room and board:*** Room and board charges vary according to housing facility. ***Payment plan:*** installment. ***Waivers:*** children of alumni and employees or children of employees.

Financial Aid Of all full-time matriculated undergraduates who enrolled in 2014, 1,604 applied for aid, 1,478 were judged to have need, 812 had their need fully met. 453 Federal Work-Study jobs (averaging $1993). In 2014, 305 non-need-based awards were made. ***Average percent of need met:*** 75. ***Average financial aid package:*** $27,346. ***Average need-based loan:*** $4869. ***Average need-based gift aid:*** $19,872. ***Average non-need-based aid:*** $12,505. ***Average indebtedness upon graduation:*** $35,679.

APPLYING

Options: electronic application, early admission, early action, deferred entrance.

Application fee: $60.

Required: essay or personal statement, high school transcript, 2 letters of recommendation. ***Recommended:*** interview.

Application deadlines: 2/15 (freshmen), 4/1 (transfers), 11/1 (early action).

Notification: continuous until 12/15 (freshmen), continuous until 12/15 (transfers), 12/15 (early action).

CONTACT

Ms. Sandra Robbins, Dean for Enrollment, Emmanuel College, Admission Office, 400 The Fenway, Boston, MA 02115. *Phone:* 617-735-9715. *Fax:* 617-735-9801. *E-mail:* enroll@emmanuel.edu.

Endicott College

Beverly, Massachusetts

http://www.endicott.edu/

- **Independent** comprehensive, founded 1939
- **Suburban** 235-acre campus with easy access to Boston
- **Endowment** $62.2 million
- **Coed** 2,963 undergraduate students, 88% full-time, 62% women, 38% men
- **Moderately difficult** entrance level, 73% of applicants were admitted

UNDERGRAD STUDENTS

2,618 full-time, 345 part-time. Students come from 30 states and territories; 31 other countries; 52% are from out of state; 3% Black or African American, non-Hispanic/Latino; 4% Hispanic/Latino; 1% Asian,

non-Hispanic/Latino; 0.1% Native Hawaiian or other Pacific Islander, non-Hispanic/Latino; 0.1% American Indian or Alaska Native, non-Hispanic/Latino; 1% Two or more races, non-Hispanic/Latino; 9% Race/ethnicity unknown; 1% international; 2% transferred in; 86% live on campus.

Freshmen

Admission: 3,848 applied, 2,815 admitted, 763 enrolled. ***Average high school GPA:*** 3.22. ***Test scores:*** SAT critical reading scores over 500: 71%; SAT math scores over 500: 77%; SAT writing scores over 500: 69%; ACT scores over 18: 96%; SAT critical reading scores over 600: 18%; SAT math scores over 600: 24%; SAT writing scores over 600: 18%; ACT scores over 24: 47%; SAT critical reading scores over 700: 1%; SAT math scores over 700: 2%; SAT writing scores over 700: 1%; ACT scores over 30: 3%.

Retention: 83% of full-time freshmen returned.

FACULTY

Total: 429, 22% full-time, 44% with terminal degrees.

Student/faculty ratio: 14:1.

ACADEMICS

Calendar: semesters. *Degrees:* certificates, associate, bachelor's, master's, doctoral, and postbachelor's certificates.

Special study options: accelerated degree program, adult/continuing education programs, advanced placement credit, cooperative education, distance learning, double majors, honors programs, independent study, internships, off-campus study, part-time degree program, services for LD students, student-designed majors, study abroad, summer session for credit. ***ROTC:*** Army (c).

Computers: 276 computers/terminals are available on campus for general student use. Students can access the following: campus intranet, computer help desk, free student e-mail accounts, online (class) grades, online (class) registration, online (class) schedules. Campuswide network is available. 100% of college-owned or -operated housing units are wired for high-speed Internet access. Wireless service is available via entire campus.

STUDENT LIFE

Housing options: coed, women-only, special housing for students with disabilities. Campus housing is university owned. Freshman campus housing is guaranteed.

Activities and organizations: drama/theater group, student-run newspaper, radio and television station, choral group, Campus Activities Board, Student Senate, Intramurals, Sailing Club, Shipmates.

Athletics Member NCAA. All Division III. ***Intercollegiate sports:*** baseball M, basketball M/W, cheerleading W(c), crew M(c)/W(c), cross-country running M/W, equestrian sports M/W, field hockey W, football M, golf M/W(c), ice hockey M(c)/W(c), lacrosse M/W, rugby M(c)/W(c), sailing M(c)/W(c), soccer M/W, softball W, tennis M/W, volleyball M/W. ***Intramural sports:*** basketball M/W, football M/W, racquetball M/W, soccer M/W, softball M/W, tennis M/W, volleyball M/W.

Campus security: 24-hour emergency response devices and patrols, student patrols, late-night transport/escort service, controlled dormitory access, license plate recognition, crime prevention programs, rape awareness defense, property identification, security cameras, front gate.

Student services: health clinic, personal/psychological counseling.

COSTS & FINANCIAL AID

Costs (2014–15) ***Comprehensive fee:*** $43,228 includes full-time tuition ($28,994), mandatory fees ($500), and room and board ($13,734). Full-time tuition and fees vary according to location. Part-time tuition: $890 per credit hour. Part-time tuition and fees vary according to location. ***College room only:*** $9468. Room and board charges vary according to board plan and housing facility. ***Payment plans:*** tuition prepayment, installment. ***Waivers:*** employees or children of employees.

Financial Aid Of all full-time matriculated undergraduates who enrolled in 2014, 2,302 applied for aid, 1,707 were judged to have need, 175 had their need fully met. 625 Federal Work-Study jobs (averaging $2000). In 2014, 459 non-need-based awards were made. ***Average percent of need met:*** 65. ***Average financial aid package:*** $20,277. ***Average need-based loan:*** $4573. ***Average need-based gift aid:*** $10,925. ***Average non-need-based aid:*** $8248. ***Average indebtedness upon graduation:*** $39,187.

APPLYING

Standardized Tests *Required for some:* SAT or ACT (for admission).

Options: electronic application.

Application fee: $50.

Required: essay or personal statement, high school transcript, minimum 2.5 GPA, 1 letter of recommendation. ***Required for some:*** interview. ***Recommended:*** interview.

Application deadlines: 2/15 (freshmen), 3/15 (transfers).

Notification: continuous (freshmen), continuous (transfers).

CONTACT

Mr. Thomas J. Redman, Vice President of Admission and Financial Aid, Endicott College, 376 Hale Street, Beverly, MA 01915. *Phone:* 978-921-1000. *Toll-free phone:* 800-325-1114. *Fax:* 978-232-2520. *E-mail:* admissio@endicott.edu.

Fisher College

Boston, Massachusetts

http://www.fisher.edu/

- **Independent** comprehensive, founded 1903
- **Urban** 1-acre campus with easy access to Boston
- **Endowment** $30.0 million
- **Coed** 1,875 undergraduate students, 62% full-time, 73% women, 27% men

UNDERGRAD STUDENTS

1,161 full-time, 714 part-time. 18% are from out of state; 9% Black or African American, non-Hispanic/Latino; 8% Hispanic/Latino; 1% Asian, non-Hispanic/Latino; 0.2% Native Hawaiian or other Pacific Islander, non-Hispanic/Latino; 0.3% American Indian or Alaska Native, non-Hispanic/Latino; 1% Two or more races, non-Hispanic/Latino; 40% Race/ethnicity unknown; 7% international; 3% transferred in; 16% live on campus.

Freshmen

Admission: 429 enrolled. ***Average high school GPA:*** 2.33. ***Test scores:*** SAT critical reading scores over 500: 13%; SAT math scores over 500: 15%; ACT scores over 18: 44%; SAT critical reading scores over 600: 2%; SAT math scores over 600: 3%; ACT scores over 24: 1%.

Retention: 60% of full-time freshmen returned.

FACULTY

Total: 183, 23% full-time, 22% with terminal degrees.

Student/faculty ratio: 16:1.

ACADEMICS

Calendar: semesters. *Degrees:* certificates, associate, bachelor's, and master's.

Special study options: academic remediation for entering students, adult/continuing education programs, advanced placement credit, distance learning, English as a second language, honors programs, independent study, internships, off-campus study, part-time degree program, services for LD students, study abroad, summer session for credit. ***ROTC:*** Army (c).

Computers: 137 computers/terminals are available on campus for general student use. Students can access the following: campus intranet, computer help desk, free student e-mail accounts, online (class) grades, online (class) registration, online (class) schedules. Campuswide network is available. 100% of college-owned or -operated housing units are wired for high-speed Internet access. Wireless service is available via entire campus.

STUDENT LIFE

Housing options: coed, women-only. Campus housing is university owned and leased by the school.

Activities and organizations: drama/theater group, choral group, National Society of Leadership and Success (NSLS), Psychology Club, Criminal Justice Club, Fashion Club, Multi-Cultural Club.

Athletics Member NAIA. ***Intercollegiate sports:*** baseball M, basketball M/W, soccer M/W, softball W.

Campus security: 24-hour emergency response devices and patrols, controlled dormitory access.

Student services: health clinic, personal/psychological counseling, women's center.

COSTS & FINANCIAL AID

Costs (2015–16) ***Comprehensive fee:*** $45,019 includes full-time tuition ($28,942), mandatory fees ($995), and room and board ($15,082). Part-time tuition and fees vary according to course load. ***Room and board:*** Room and board charges vary according to housing facility. ***Payment plan:*** installment.

Financial Aid Of all full-time matriculated undergraduates who enrolled in 2013, 980 applied for aid, 810 were judged to have need.

APPLYING

Standardized Tests *Required for some:* SAT or ACT (for admission).

Required: high school transcript. ***Required for some:*** essay or personal statement, interview. ***Recommended:*** minimum 2.0 GPA.

CONTACT

Mr. Robert Melaragni, Vice President of Enrollment Management, Fisher College, Boston, MA 02116. *Phone:* 617-236-8818. *Fax:* 617-236-5473. *E-mail:* admissions@fisher.edu.

★ Fitchburg State University

Fitchburg, Massachusetts

http://www.fitchburgstate.edu/

- **State-supported** comprehensive, founded 1894, part of Massachusetts Public Higher Education System
- **Suburban** 78-acre campus with easy access to Boston
- **Endowment** $11.9 million
- **Coed** 4,212 undergraduate students, 81% full-time, 56% women, 44% men
- **Moderately difficult** entrance level, 72% of applicants were admitted

UNDERGRAD STUDENTS

3,419 full-time, 793 part-time. Students come from 26 states and territories; 4 other countries; 8% are from out of state; 7% Black or African American, non-Hispanic/Latino; 10% Hispanic/Latino; 2% Asian, non-Hispanic/Latino; 0.1% American Indian or Alaska Native, non-Hispanic/Latino; 3% Two or more races, non-Hispanic/Latino; 3% Race/ethnicity unknown; 0.5% international; 9% transferred in; 41% live on campus.

Freshmen

Admission: 3,814 applied, 2,758 admitted, 727 enrolled. ***Average high school GPA:*** 3.1. ***Test scores:*** SAT critical reading scores over 500: 47%; SAT math scores over 500: 51%; SAT writing scores over 500: 41%; ACT scores over 18: 84%; SAT critical reading scores over 600: 10%; SAT math scores over 600: 9%; SAT writing scores over 600: 7%; ACT scores over 24: 23%; SAT critical reading scores over 700: 1%; SAT math scores over 700: 1%; ACT scores over 30: 3%.

Retention: 77% of full-time freshmen returned.

FACULTY

Total: 304, 63% full-time, 67% with terminal degrees.

Student/faculty ratio: 16:1.

ACADEMICS

Calendar: semesters. *Degrees:* certificates, bachelor's, master's, post-master's, and postbachelor's certificates.

Special study options: academic remediation for entering students, accelerated degree program, adult/continuing education programs, advanced placement credit, distance learning, double majors, honors programs, independent study, internships, off-campus study, part-time degree program, services for LD students, student-designed majors, study abroad, summer session for credit. ***ROTC:*** Army (b).

Computers: 500 computers/terminals are available on campus for general student use. Students can access the following: computer help desk, free student e-mail accounts, online (class) grades, online (class) registration, online (class) schedules. Campuswide network is available. 100% of college-owned or -operated housing units are wired for high-speed Internet access. Wireless service is available via entire campus.

STUDENT LIFE

Housing options: coed, special housing for students with disabilities. Campus housing is university owned. Freshman applicants given priority for college housing.

Activities and organizations: drama/theater group, student-run newspaper, radio station, choral group, Student Government Association, Dance Club, Activities Board, Greek Council, MASSPIRG, national fraternities, national sororities.

Athletics Member NCAA. All Division III. ***Intercollegiate sports:*** baseball M, basketball M/W, cross-country running M/W, field hockey W, football M, ice hockey M, lacrosse W, soccer M/W, softball W, track and field M/W. ***Intramural sports:*** basketball M/W, football M/W, racquetball M/W, soccer M/W, softball M/W, swimming and diving M/W, table tennis M/W, ultimate Frisbee M/W, volleyball M/W, water polo M/W.

Campus security: 24-hour emergency response devices and patrols, student patrols, late-night transport/escort service, controlled dormitory access.

Student services: health clinic, personal/psychological counseling.

COSTS & FINANCIAL AID
Costs (2014–15) ***Tuition:*** state resident $970 full-time, $40 per credit part-time; nonresident $7050 full-time, $294 per credit part-time. Full-time tuition and fees vary according to class time and reciprocity agreements. Part-time tuition and fees vary according to class time and reciprocity agreements. ***Required fees:*** $8290 full-time. ***Room and board:*** $8840; room only: $5890. Room and board charges vary according to board plan and housing facility. ***Payment plan:*** installment. ***Waivers:*** senior citizens and employees or children of employees.

Financial Aid Of all full-time matriculated undergraduates who enrolled in 2013, 3,077 applied for aid, 2,181 were judged to have need, 2,126 had their need fully met. 192 Federal Work-Study jobs (averaging $1760). In 2013, 54 non-need-based awards were made. ***Average percent of need met:*** 90. ***Average financial aid package:*** $9970. ***Average need-based loan:*** $3965. ***Average need-based gift aid:*** $5007. ***Average non-need-based aid:*** $1458. ***Average indebtedness upon graduation:*** $25,524.

APPLYING
Standardized Tests *Required:* SAT or ACT (for admission).

Options: electronic application, deferred entrance.

Application fee: $25.

Required: essay or personal statement, high school transcript, minimum 2.0 GPA, 16 core courses.

Application deadlines: rolling (freshmen), rolling (out-of-state freshmen), rolling (transfers).

Notification: continuous (freshmen), continuous (out-of-state freshmen), continuous (transfers).

CONTACT
Sean Ganas SAC, Director of Admissions, Fitchburg State University, 160 Pearl Street, Fitchburg, MA 01420-2697. *Phone:* 978-665-3140. *Toll-free phone:* 800-705-9692. *Fax:* 978-665-4540. *E-mail:* admissions@fitchburgstate.edu.

See previous page for display ad and page 1444 for the College Close-Up.

★ Framingham State University

Framingham, Massachusetts

http://www.framingham.edu/

- **State-supported** comprehensive, founded 1839, part of Massachusetts Public Higher Education System
- **Suburban** 52-acre campus with easy access to Boston
- **Endowment** $23.6 million
- **Coed** 4,609 undergraduate students, 85% full-time, 63% women, 37% men
- **Moderately difficult** entrance level, 62% of applicants were admitted

UNDERGRAD STUDENTS
3,925 full-time, 684 part-time. Students come from 22 states and territories; 4% are from out of state; 8% Black or African American, non-Hispanic/Latino; 9% Hispanic/Latino; 3% Asian, non-Hispanic/Latino; 0.1% Native Hawaiian or other Pacific Islander, non-Hispanic/Latino; 0.2% American Indian or Alaska Native, non-Hispanic/Latino; 3% Two or more races, non-Hispanic/Latino; 3% Race/ethnicity unknown; 0.3% international; 9% transferred in; 50% live on campus.

Freshmen
Admission: 5,207 applied, 3,241 admitted, 808 enrolled. ***Average high school GPA:*** 3.23. ***Test scores:*** SAT critical reading scores over 500: 55%; SAT math scores over 500: 59%; SAT writing scores over 500: 50%; ACT scores over 18: 96%; SAT critical reading scores over 600: 12%; SAT math scores over 600: 11%; SAT writing scores over 600: 8%; ACT scores over 24: 28%; SAT critical reading scores over 700: 1%; SAT math scores over 700: 1%.

Retention: 75% of full-time freshmen returned.

FACULTY
Total: 359, 52% full-time, 42% with terminal degrees.

Student/faculty ratio: 16:1.

ACADEMICS
Calendar: semesters. *Degrees:* bachelor's, master's, and postbachelor's certificates.

Special study options: advanced placement credit, cooperative education, distance learning, double majors, English as a second language, honors programs, independent study, internships, off-campus study, part-time degree program, services for LD students, student-designed majors, study abroad, summer session for credit.

Computers: 216 computers/terminals and 3,500 ports are available on campus for general student use. Students can access the following: computer help desk, free student e-mail accounts, online (class) grades, online (class) registration, online (class) schedules. Campuswide network is available. 100% of college-owned or -operated housing units are wired for high-speed Internet access. Wireless service is available via entire campus.

STUDENT LIFE
Housing options: coed, women-only, special housing for students with disabilities. Campus housing is university owned. Freshman applicants given priority for college housing.

Activities and organizations: drama/theater group, student-run newspaper, radio station, choral group, Dance Club, Student Union Activities Board, Gatepost (student newspaper), Student Government Association, Hilltop Players (theater group).

Athletics Member NCAA. All Division III. ***Intercollegiate sports:*** baseball M, basketball M/W, cross-country running M/W, field hockey W, football M, ice hockey M, lacrosse W, soccer M/W, softball W, volleyball W. ***Intramural sports:*** basketball M/W, cheerleading W(c), football M/W, golf M/W, lacrosse M(c), rugby M(c)/W(c), soccer M/W, volleyball M/W, weight lifting M/W.

Campus security: 24-hour emergency response devices and patrols, student patrols, late-night transport/escort service, controlled dormitory access.

Student services: health clinic, personal/psychological counseling.

COSTS & FINANCIAL AID
Costs (2014–15) ***Tuition:*** state resident $970 full-time, $162 per course part-time; nonresident $7050 full-time, $1175 per course part-time. Full-time tuition and fees vary according to class time and degree level. Part-time tuition and fees vary according to class time, course load, and degree level. ***Required fees:*** $7350 full-time, $1290 per course part-time. ***Room and board:*** $10,543; room only: $7114. Room and board charges vary according to board plan and housing facility. ***Payment plans:*** tuition prepayment, installment. ***Waivers:*** senior citizens and employees or children of employees.

Financial Aid Of all full-time matriculated undergraduates who enrolled in 2012, 3,310 applied for aid, 2,506 were judged to have need, 63 had their need fully met. In 2012, 186 non-need-based awards were made. ***Average percent of need met:*** 59. ***Average financial aid package:*** $8272. ***Average need-based loan:*** $4178. ***Average need-based gift aid:*** $4945. ***Average non-need-based aid:*** $1110. ***Average indebtedness upon graduation:*** $18,027.

APPLYING
Standardized Tests *Required:* SAT or ACT (for admission).

Options: electronic application, early action, deferred entrance.

Application fee: $45.

Required: high school transcript, minimum 2.0 GPA, Minimum of 16 college preparatory courses in specified areas. ***Recommended:*** minimum 3.0 GPA.

Application deadlines: 2/15 (freshmen), 11/15 (early action).

Notification: continuous (freshmen), continuous (transfers), 12/15 (early action).

CONTACT
Ms. Shayna Eddy, Associate Dean of Admissions, Framingham State University, 100 State Street, PO Box 9101, Framingham, MA 01701-9101. *Phone:* 508-626-4500. *Fax:* 508-626-4017. *E-mail:* admissions@framingham.edu.

Franklin W. Olin College of Engineering

Needham, Massachusetts

http://www.olin.edu/

- **Independent** 4-year, founded 2002
- **Suburban** 75-acre campus with easy access to Boston
- **Endowment** $379.9 million
- **Coed** 370 undergraduate students, 94% full-time, 49% women, 51% men
- **Most difficult** entrance level, 12% of applicants were admitted

UNDERGRAD STUDENTS
348 full-time, 22 part-time. Students come from 38 states and territories; 13 other countries; 85% are from out of state; 0.8% Black or African American, non-Hispanic/Latino; 3% Hispanic/Latino; 14% Asian, non-Hispanic/Latino; 0.3% American Indian or Alaska Native, non-Hispanic/Latino; 6% Two or more races, non-Hispanic/Latino; 15% Race/ethnicity unknown; 11% international; 2% transferred in; 100% live on campus.

Freshmen
Admission: 983 applied, 118 admitted, 79 enrolled. ***Average high school GPA:*** 4. ***Test scores:*** SAT critical reading scores over 500: 100%; SAT math scores over 500: 100%; SAT writing scores over 500: 100%; ACT scores over 18: 100%; SAT critical reading scores over 600: 99%; SAT math scores over 600: 100%; SAT writing scores over 600: 98%; ACT scores over 24: 100%; SAT critical reading scores over 700: 74%; SAT math scores over 700: 85%; SAT writing scores over 700: 63%; ACT scores over 30: 97%.

Retention: 96% of full-time freshmen returned.

FACULTY
Total: 55, 64% full-time, 82% with terminal degrees.
Student/faculty ratio: 8:1.

ACADEMICS
Degree: bachelor's.
Special study options: independent study, internships, off-campus study, services for LD students, student-designed majors, study abroad.
Computers: 410 computers/terminals and 2,364 ports are available on campus for general student use. Students can access the following: campus intranet, computer help desk, free student e-mail accounts, online (class) grades, online (class) registration, online (class) schedules. Campuswide network is available. 100% of college-owned or -operated housing units are wired for high-speed Internet access. Wireless service is available via entire campus.

STUDENT LIFE
Housing options: on-campus residence required through senior year; coed, special housing for students with disabilities. Campus housing is university owned. Freshman campus housing is guaranteed.
Activities and organizations: drama/theater group, student-run newspaper, choral group, Greening Olin, Olin Fire Arts Club, Support, Encourage and Recognize Volunteerism (SERV), Olin Entrepreneurial Group, Open.
Athletics ***Intercollegiate sports:*** soccer M(c)/W(c), ultimate Frisbee M(c)/W(c). ***Intramural sports:*** basketball M/W, softball M/W, volleyball M/W.
Campus security: 24-hour emergency response devices and patrols, controlled dormitory access.
Student services: health clinic, personal/psychological counseling.

COSTS & FINANCIAL AID
Costs (2015–16) ***One-time required fee:*** $2656. ***Comprehensive fee:*** $61,125 includes full-time tuition ($45,000), mandatory fees ($525), and room and board ($15,600). ***College room only:*** $9300. ***Payment plan:*** installment.
Financial Aid Of all full-time matriculated undergraduates who enrolled in 2014, 192 applied for aid, 167 were judged to have need, 156 had their need fully met. In 2014, 177 non-need-based awards were made. ***Average percent of need met:*** 99. ***Average financial aid package:*** $41,000. ***Average need-based loan:*** $3417. ***Average need-based gift aid:*** $36,611. ***Average non-need-based aid:*** $21,749. ***Average indebtedness upon graduation:*** $19,992. ***Financial aid deadline:*** 2/15.

APPLYING
Standardized Tests *Required:* SAT or ACT (for admission). *Recommended:* SAT Subject Tests (for admission).
Options: electronic application, deferred entrance.
Application fee: $80.
Required: essay or personal statement, high school transcript, 3 letters of recommendation, interview.
Notification: 3/21 (freshmen).

CONTACT
Franklin W. Olin College of Engineering, 1000 Olin Way, Needham, MA 02492-1200. *Phone:* 781-292-2250. *Fax:* 781-292-2310. *E-mail:* info@olin.edu.

Gordon College

Wenham, Massachusetts

http://www.gordon.edu/

- **Independent nondenominational** comprehensive, founded 1889
- **Suburban** 480-acre campus with easy access to Boston
- **Endowment** $44.0 million
- **Coed** 1,736 undergraduate students, 98% full-time, 62% women, 38% men
- **Moderately difficult** entrance level, 88% of applicants were admitted

UNDERGRAD STUDENTS
1,697 full-time, 39 part-time. Students come from 41 states and territories; 39 other countries; 66% are from out of state; 4% Black or African American, non-Hispanic/Latino; 7% Hispanic/Latino; 4% Asian, non-Hispanic/Latino; 0.5% Native Hawaiian or other Pacific Islander, non-Hispanic/Latino; 0.2% American Indian or Alaska Native, non-Hispanic/Latino; 3% Two or more races, non-Hispanic/Latino; 7% international; 3% transferred in; 86% live on campus.

Freshmen
Admission: 1,892 applied, 1,672 admitted, 402 enrolled. ***Average high school GPA:*** 3.6. ***Test scores:*** SAT critical reading scores over 500: 83%; SAT math scores over 500: 81%; SAT writing scores over 500: 83%; ACT scores over 18: 97%; SAT critical reading scores over 600: 45%; SAT math scores over 600: 41%; SAT writing scores over 600: 41%; ACT scores over 24: 68%; SAT critical reading scores over 700: 9%; SAT math scores over 700: 9%; SAT writing scores over 700: 8%; ACT scores over 30: 19%.

Retention: 81% of full-time freshmen returned.

FACULTY
Total: 196, 49% full-time, 43% with terminal degrees.
Student/faculty ratio: 13:1.

ACADEMICS
Calendar: semesters. *Degrees:* bachelor's and master's.
Special study options: advanced placement credit, cooperative education, double majors, honors programs, independent study, internships, off-campus study, part-time degree program, services for LD students, student-designed majors, study abroad, summer session for credit. ***ROTC:*** Army (c).
Unusual degree programs: 3-2 engineering with University of Southern California.
Computers: 100 computers/terminals are available on campus for general student use. Students can access the following: campus intranet, computer help desk, free student e-mail accounts, online (class) grades, online (class) registration, online (class) schedules. Campuswide network is available. 100% of college-owned or -operated housing units are wired for high-speed Internet access. Wireless service is available via entire campus.

STUDENT LIFE

Housing options: coed, men-only, women-only, special housing for students with disabilities. Campus housing is university owned. Freshman campus housing is guaranteed.

Activities and organizations: drama/theater group, student-run newspaper, radio station, choral group, Student Government Association, Student ministries and volunteer programs, Diverse music ensembles, Intramural sports, Short-term missions.

Athletics Member NCAA. All Division III. ***Intercollegiate sports:*** baseball M, basketball M/W, cross-country running M/W, field hockey W, lacrosse M/W, soccer M/W, softball W, swimming and diving M/W, tennis M/W, track and field M/W, volleyball W. ***Intramural sports:*** badminton M/W, basketball M/W, football M/W, ice hockey M(c)/W(c), soccer M/W, table tennis M/W, ultimate Frisbee M/W, volleyball M/W, water polo M/W.

Campus security: 24-hour emergency response devices and patrols, late-night transport/escort service, controlled dormitory access, gated entrance.

Student services: health clinic, personal/psychological counseling.

COSTS & FINANCIAL AID

Costs (2014–15) ***Comprehensive fee:*** $44,320 includes full-time tuition ($32,930), mandatory fees ($1460), and room and board ($9930). Full-time tuition and fees vary according to course load and program. Part-time tuition: $1165 per credit. Part-time tuition and fees vary according to course load and program. ***College room only:*** $6560. Room and board charges vary according to board plan and housing facility. ***Payment plan:*** installment. ***Waivers:*** employees or children of employees.

Financial Aid Of all full-time matriculated undergraduates who enrolled in 2014, 1,305 applied for aid, 1,134 were judged to have need, 186 had their need fully met. 488 Federal Work-Study jobs (averaging $504). In 2014, 447 non-need-based awards were made. ***Average percent of need met:*** 68. ***Average financial aid package:*** $22,562. ***Average need-based loan:*** $4826. ***Average need-based gift aid:*** $17,663. ***Average non-need-based aid:*** $13,460. ***Average indebtedness upon graduation:*** $38,456.

APPLYING

Standardized Tests *Required:* SAT or ACT (for admission).

Options: electronic application, early admission, early decision, early action, deferred entrance.

Application fee: $50.

Required: essay or personal statement, high school transcript, 2 letters of recommendation, interview, Pastoral recommendation and statement of Christian faith. ***Recommended:*** minimum 3.0 GPA.

Application deadlines: rolling (freshmen), rolling (transfers), 11/15 (early action).

Early decision deadline: 11/1.

Notification: continuous until 9/15 (freshmen), continuous until 9/15 (out-of-state freshmen), continuous (transfers), 12/1 (early decision), 12/1 (early action).

CONTACT

Miss June Bodoni, Associate Vice President for Enrollment, Gordon College, 255 Grapevine Road, Wenham, MA 01984. *Phone:* 978-867-4218. *Toll-free phone:* 866-464-6736. *Fax:* 978-867-4682. *E-mail:* admissions@gordon.edu.

Hampshire College

Amherst, Massachusetts

http://www.hampshire.edu/

- **Independent** 4-year, founded 1965
- **Small-town** 800-acre campus
- **Endowment** $28.9 million
- **Coed** 1,376 undergraduate students, 100% full-time, 59% women, 41% men
- **Moderately difficult** entrance level, 67% of applicants were admitted

UNDERGRAD STUDENTS

1,376 full-time. 4% Black or African American, non-Hispanic/Latino; 10% Hispanic/Latino; 2% Asian, non-Hispanic/Latino; 0.1% Native Hawaiian or other Pacific Islander, non-Hispanic/Latino; 0.1% American Indian or Alaska Native, non-Hispanic/Latino; 6% Two or more races, non-Hispanic/Latino; 5% Race/ethnicity unknown; 5% international; 83% live on campus.

Freshmen

Admission: 2,671 applied, 1,780 admitted, 324 enrolled. ***Test scores:*** SAT critical reading scores over 500: 95%; SAT math scores over 500: 87%; SAT writing scores over 500: 93%; ACT scores over 18: 100%; SAT critical reading scores over 600: 71%; SAT math scores over 600: 49%; SAT writing scores over 600: 61%; ACT scores over 24: 87%; SAT critical reading scores over 700: 25%; SAT math scores over 700: 9%; SAT writing scores over 700: 14%; ACT scores over 30: 30%.

Retention: 78% of full-time freshmen returned.

FACULTY

Total: 158, 71% full-time.

Student/faculty ratio: 11:1.

ACADEMICS

Calendar: 4-1-4. *Degree:* bachelor's.

Special study options: advanced placement credit, independent study, internships, off-campus study, services for LD students, student-designed majors, study abroad. ***ROTC:*** Army (c).

Computers: 205 computers/terminals are available on campus for general student use. Students can access the following: campus intranet, computer help desk, free student e-mail accounts, online (class) grades, online (class) registration, online (class) schedules. Campuswide network is available. 100% of college-owned or -operated housing units are wired for high-speed Internet access. Wireless service is available via entire campus.

STUDENT LIFE

Housing options: on-campus residence required through senior year; coed, men-only, women-only, special housing for students with disabilities. Campus housing is university owned. Freshman campus housing is guaranteed.

Activities and organizations: drama/theater group, student-run newspaper, radio station, choral group, Red Scare Frisbee, Queer Community Alliance, Excalibur (fantasy/role playing), Sports Coop, Circus Folks Unite.

Athletics Member USCAA. ***Intercollegiate sports:*** basketball M(c)/W(c), cross-country running M/W, equestrian sports M(c)/W(c), fencing M/W, soccer M/W, ultimate Frisbee M/W. ***Intramural sports:*** basketball M/W, equestrian sports M(c)/W(c), rock climbing M(c)/W(c), soccer M/W, table tennis M(c)/W(c), ultimate Frisbee M/W.

Campus security: 24-hour emergency response devices and patrols.

Student services: health clinic, personal/psychological counseling, women's center.

COSTS & FINANCIAL AID

Costs (2014–15) ***Comprehensive fee:*** $62,310 includes full-time tuition ($47,620), mandatory fees ($1740), and room and board ($12,950). ***College room only:*** $8110. Room and board charges vary according to board plan. ***Payment plan:*** installment. ***Waivers:*** employees or children of employees.

Financial Aid Of all full-time matriculated undergraduates who enrolled in 2014, 941 applied for aid, 805 were judged to have need, 125 had their need fully met. 763 Federal Work-Study jobs (averaging $2600). In 2014, 370 non-need-based awards were made. ***Average percent of need met:*** 86. ***Average financial aid package:*** $35,078. ***Average need-based loan:*** $4246. ***Average need-based gift aid:*** $30,256. ***Average non-need-based aid:*** $13,583. ***Average indebtedness upon graduation:*** $20,432.

APPLYING

Options: electronic application, early admission, early decision, early action, deferred entrance.

Application fee: $60.

Required: essay or personal statement, high school transcript, 1 letter of recommendation. ***Recommended:*** interview.

Application deadlines: 1/15 (freshmen), 3/15 (transfers), 12/1 (early action).

Early decision deadline: 11/15 (for plan 1), 1/1 (for plan 2).

Notification: 4/1 (freshmen), 4/15 (transfers), 12/15 (early decision plan 1), 2/1 (early decision plan 2), 2/1 (early action).

CONTACT
Hampshire College, 893 West Street, Amherst, MA 01002. *Phone:* 413-559-5471. *Toll-free phone:* 877-937-4267. *E-mail:* admissions@hampshire.edu.

Harvard University

Cambridge, Massachusetts

http://www.harvard.edu/

- **Independent** university, founded 1636
- **Urban** 380-acre campus with easy access to Boston
- **Endowment** $36.4 billion
- **Coed** 6,694 undergraduate students, 100% full-time, 47% women, 53% men
- **Most difficult** entrance level, 6% of applicants were admitted

UNDERGRAD STUDENTS
6,688 full-time, 6 part-time. Students come from 54 states and territories; 110 other countries; 84% are from out of state; 7% Black or African American, non-Hispanic/Latino; 10% Hispanic/Latino; 19% Asian, non-Hispanic/Latino; 0.2% American Indian or Alaska Native, non-Hispanic/Latino; 7% Two or more races, non-Hispanic/Latino; 3% Race/ethnicity unknown; 11% international; 0.2% transferred in; 98% live on campus.

Freshmen
Admission: 34,919 applied, 1,944 admitted, 1,650 enrolled. ***Average high school GPA:*** 4.03. ***Test scores:*** SAT critical reading scores over 500: 100%; SAT math scores over 500: 100%; SAT writing scores over 500: 100%; SAT critical reading scores over 600: 96%; SAT math scores over 600: 99%; SAT writing scores over 600: 97%; ACT scores over 24: 100%; SAT critical reading scores over 700: 79%; SAT math scores over 700: 81%; SAT writing scores over 700: 80%; ACT scores over 30: 90%. ***Retention:*** 97% of full-time freshmen returned.

FACULTY
Total: 1,164, 83% full-time, 82% with terminal degrees.
Student/faculty ratio: 7:1.

ACADEMICS
Calendar: semesters. *Degrees:* bachelor's, master's, and doctoral.
Special study options: accelerated degree program, advanced placement credit, double majors, honors programs, independent study, internships, off-campus study, services for LD students, student-designed majors, study abroad, summer session for credit. ***ROTC:*** Army (c), Navy (b), Air Force (c).
Computers: 605 computers/terminals are available on campus for general student use. Students can access the following: computer help desk, free student e-mail accounts, online (class) grades, online (class) registration, online (class) schedules. Campuswide network is available. 100% of college-owned or -operated housing units are wired for high-speed Internet access. Wireless service is available via entire campus.

STUDENT LIFE
Housing options: on-campus residence required for freshman year; coed, cooperative, special housing for students with disabilities. Campus housing is university owned. Freshman campus housing is guaranteed.
Activities and organizations: drama/theater group, student-run newspaper, radio and television station, choral group, marching band, Phillips Brooks House Association, Asian-American Association, International Relations Council, Harvard Crimson (newspaper), Harvard/Radcliffe Chorus.
Athletics Member NCAA. All Division I except football (Division I-AA). ***Intercollegiate sports:*** baseball M, basketball M/W, crew M/W, cross-country running M/W, fencing M/W, field hockey W, golf M/W, ice hockey M/W, lacrosse M/W, rugby W, sailing M/W, skiing (cross-country) M/W, skiing (downhill) M/W, soccer M/W, softball W, squash M/W, swimming and diving M/W, tennis M/W, track and field M/W, volleyball M/W, water polo M/W, wrestling M. ***Intramural sports:*** archery M(c)/W(c), badminton M(c)/W(c), baseball M(c), basketball M/W, cheerleading M(c)/W(c), cross-country running M/W, fencing M/W, field hockey W(c), golf M(c)/W(c), ice hockey M/W, lacrosse M(c)/W(c), riflery M(c)/W(c), rugby M(c), skiing (cross-country) M(c)/W(c), skiing (downhill) M(c)/W(c), soccer M/W, squash M/W, swimming and diving M/W, table tennis M/W, tennis M/W, ultimate Frisbee M/W, volleyball M/W, water polo M(c)/W(c), weight lifting M(c)/W(c), wrestling M(c)/W(c).
Campus security: 24-hour emergency response devices and patrols, late-night transport/escort service, controlled dormitory access, required and optional safety courses.
Student services: health clinic, personal/psychological counseling, women's center.

COSTS & FINANCIAL AID
Costs (2014–15) ***Comprehensive fee:*** $58,607 includes full-time tuition ($40,418), mandatory fees ($3520), and room and board ($14,669). ***College room only:*** $9009. ***Payment plans:*** tuition prepayment, installment.
Financial Aid Of all full-time matriculated undergraduates who enrolled in 2013, 4,291 applied for aid, 3,986 were judged to have need, 3,960 had their need fully met. 1,024 Federal Work-Study jobs (averaging $2781). 2,128 state and other part-time jobs (averaging $2855). In 2013, 9 non-need-based awards were made. ***Average percent of need met:*** 100. ***Average financial aid package:*** $47,475. ***Average need-based loan:*** $4462. ***Average need-based gift aid:*** $44,430. ***Average non-need-based aid:*** $20,827. ***Average indebtedness upon graduation:*** $15,117.

APPLYING
Standardized Tests *Required:* SAT or ACT (for admission), SAT Subject Tests (for admission).
Options: electronic application, early action, deferred entrance.
Application fee: $75.
Required: essay or personal statement, high school transcript. ***Recommended:*** 2 letters of recommendation, interview.
Application deadlines: 1/1 (freshmen), 3/1 (transfers).
Notification: 4/1 (freshmen), 6/15 (transfers).

CONTACT
Harvard University, Cambridge, MA 02138. *Phone:* 617-495-1551.

ITT Technical Institute

Norwood, Massachusetts

http://www.itt-tech.edu/

- **Proprietary** primarily 2-year, founded 1990, part of ITT Educational Services, Inc.
- **Suburban** campus
- **Coed**
- **Minimally difficult** entrance level

ACADEMICS
Calendar: quarters. *Degrees:* associate and bachelor's.

STUDENT LIFE
Housing options: college housing not available.

CONTACT
Director of Recruitment, ITT Technical Institute, 333 Providence Highway, Norwood, MA 02062. *Phone:* 781-278-7200. *Toll-free phone:* 800-879-8324.

ITT Technical Institute

Wilmington, Massachusetts

http://www.itt-tech.edu/

- **Proprietary** primarily 2-year, founded 2000, part of ITT Educational Services, Inc.
- **Coed**
- **Minimally difficult** entrance level

ACADEMICS
Calendar: quarters. *Degrees:* associate and bachelor's.

STUDENT LIFE
Housing options: college housing not available.

CONTACT
Director of Recruitment, ITT Technical Institute, 200 Ballardvale Street, Suite 200, Wilmington, MA 01887. *Phone:* 978-658-2636. *Toll-free phone:* 800-430-5097.

Lasell College

Newton, Massachusetts

http://www.lasell.edu/

- **Independent** comprehensive, founded 1851
- **Suburban** 53-acre campus with easy access to Boston
- **Endowment** $40.1 million
- **Coed** 1,737 undergraduate students, 98% full-time, 65% women, 35% men
- **Moderately difficult** entrance level, 76% of applicants were admitted

UNDERGRAD STUDENTS

1,706 full-time, 31 part-time. Students come from 30 states and territories; 17 other countries; 47% are from out of state; 6% Black or African American, non-Hispanic/Latino; 9% Hispanic/Latino; 2% Asian, non-Hispanic/Latino; 0.1% Native Hawaiian or other Pacific Islander, non-Hispanic/Latino; 0.3% American Indian or Alaska Native, non-Hispanic/Latino; 3% Two or more races, non-Hispanic/Latino; 1% Race/ethnicity unknown; 4% international; 4% transferred in; 79% live on campus.

Freshmen

Admission: 3,121 applied, 2,382 admitted, 501 enrolled. ***Average high school GPA:*** 2.87. ***Test scores:*** SAT critical reading scores over 500: 43%; SAT math scores over 500: 44%; SAT writing scores over 500: 39%; ACT scores over 18: 78%; SAT critical reading scores over 600: 7%; SAT math scores over 600: 9%; SAT writing scores over 600: 6%; ACT scores over 24: 22%; SAT critical reading scores over 700: 1%; ACT scores over 30: 3%.

Retention: 75% of full-time freshmen returned.

FACULTY

Total: 237, 37% full-time, 74% with terminal degrees.

Student/faculty ratio: 13:1.

ACADEMICS

Calendar: semesters. *Degrees:* bachelor's and master's.

Special study options: accelerated degree program, advanced placement credit, cooperative education, distance learning, double majors, English as a second language, honors programs, independent study, internships, part-time degree program, services for LD students, student-designed majors, study abroad, summer session for credit.

Unusual degree programs: business administration with Lasell College.

Computers: 225 computers/terminals are available on campus for general student use. Students can access the following: campus intranet, computer help desk, free student e-mail accounts, online (class) grades, online (class) registration, online (class) schedules, online tutoring in various subjects. Campuswide network is available. 100% of college-owned or -operated housing units are wired for high-speed Internet access. Wireless service is available via entire campus.

STUDENT LIFE

Housing options: coed, women-only, cooperative. Campus housing is university owned. Freshman campus housing is guaranteed.

Activities and organizations: drama/theater group, student-run newspaper, radio station, choral group, Campus Activities Board, Fashion Connection, Lasell College Radio Station, Students Advocating for Equality, Rugby Club.

Athletics Member NCAA. All Division III. ***Intercollegiate sports:*** baseball M, basketball M/W, cross-country running M/W, field hockey W, lacrosse M/W, soccer M/W, softball W, track and field M/W, volleyball M/W. ***Intramural sports:*** basketball M/W, cheerleading M(c)/W(c), crew M(c)/W(c), golf M(c)/W(c), rugby M(c)/W(c), skiing (downhill) M(c)/W(c), tennis M(c)/W(c), ultimate Frisbee M(c).

Campus security: 24-hour emergency response devices and patrols, late-night transport/escort service, controlled dormitory access, 24/7 Academy trained police officers who are trained first responders and have the power of arrest.

Student services: health clinic, personal/psychological counseling.

COSTS & FINANCIAL AID

Costs (2014–15) ***Comprehensive fee:*** $43,750 includes full-time tuition ($29,800), mandatory fees ($1200), and room and board ($12,750). Part-time tuition: $980 per credit hour. Part-time tuition and fees vary according to course load. ***Required fees:*** $310 per term part-time. ***Room and board:*** Room and board charges vary according to board plan and housing facility. ***Payment plan:*** installment. ***Waivers:*** children of alumni and employees or children of employees.

Financial Aid Of all full-time matriculated undergraduates who enrolled in 2014, 1,510 applied for aid, 1,401 were judged to have need, 230 had their need fully met. 901 Federal Work-Study jobs (averaging $1800). In 2014, 234 non-need-based awards were made. ***Average percent of need met:*** 72. ***Average financial aid package:*** $24,392. ***Average need-based loan:*** $4281. ***Average need-based gift aid:*** $19,754. ***Average non-need-based aid:*** $12,241. ***Average indebtedness upon graduation:*** $37,302.

APPLYING

Standardized Tests *Required:* SAT or ACT (for admission).

Options: electronic application, early action, deferred entrance.

Application fee: $40.

Required: essay or personal statement, high school transcript, 2 letters of recommendation, college preparatory program. ***Recommended:*** interview.

Application deadlines: 9/1 (freshmen), rolling (transfers), 11/15 (early action).

Notification: continuous until 12/15 (freshmen), continuous (transfers), 12/1 (early action).

CONTACT

Dean James Tweed, Dean of Undergraduate Admission, Lasell College, 1844 Commonwealth Avenue, Newton, MA 02466. *Phone:* 617-243-2225. *Toll-free phone:* 888-LASELL-4. *Fax:* 617-243-2380. *E-mail:* info@lasell.edu.

Lesley University

Cambridge, Massachusetts

http://www.lesley.edu/

- **Independent** comprehensive, founded 1909
- **Urban** campus with easy access to Boston
- **Coed, primarily women** 1,492 undergraduate students, 88% full-time, 78% women, 22% men
- 71% of applicants were admitted

UNDERGRAD STUDENTS

1,307 full-time, 185 part-time. 42% are from out of state; 3% Black or African American, non-Hispanic/Latino; 10% Hispanic/Latino; 4% Asian, non-Hispanic/Latino; 0.1% Native Hawaiian or other Pacific Islander, non-Hispanic/Latino; 0.2% American Indian or Alaska Native, non-Hispanic/Latino; 4% Two or more races, non-Hispanic/Latino; 7% Race/ethnicity unknown; 2% international; 6% transferred in; 65% live on campus.

Freshmen

Admission: 2,827 applied, 2,021 admitted, 306 enrolled. ***Average high school GPA:*** 3.02. ***Test scores:*** SAT critical reading scores over 500: 79%; SAT writing scores over 500: 72%; ACT scores over 18: 98%; SAT critical reading scores over 600: 29%; SAT writing scores over 600: 28%; ACT scores over 24: 50%; SAT critical reading scores over 700: 3%; SAT writing scores over 700: 4%; ACT scores over 30: 2%.

Retention: 76% of full-time freshmen returned.

FACULTY

Total: 249, 34% full-time, 49% with terminal degrees.

Student/faculty ratio: 10:1.

ACADEMICS

Calendar: semesters. *Degrees:* associate, bachelor's, master's, doctoral, post-master's, and postbachelor's certificates.

Special study options: academic remediation for entering students, accelerated degree program, adult/continuing education programs, advanced placement credit, distance learning, double majors, external degree program, freshman honors college, honors programs, independent study, internships, off-campus study, part-time degree program, services for LD students, student-designed majors, study abroad, summer session for credit.

Computers: Students can access the following: free student e-mail accounts, online (class) registration. Campuswide network is available. Wireless service is available via classrooms, student centers.

STUDENT LIFE
Housing options: coed, women-only. Campus housing is university owned and leased by the school. Freshman applicants given priority for college housing.

Activities and organizations: drama/theater group, choral group.

Athletics Member NCAA. All Division III except baseball (Division II). ***Intercollegiate sports:*** baseball M, basketball M/W, cross-country running M/W, soccer M/W, softball W, volleyball M/W. ***Intramural sports:*** swimming and diving M/W, tennis M.

Campus security: 24-hour emergency response devices and patrols, late-night transport/escort service, controlled dormitory access.

Student services: health clinic, personal/psychological counseling.

COSTS & FINANCIAL AID
Costs (2015–16) ***Comprehensive fee:*** $40,380 includes full-time tuition ($24,720), mandatory fees ($830), and room and board ($14,830). Full-time tuition and fees vary according to class time, course level, course load, degree level, location, program, reciprocity agreements, and student level. Part-time tuition: $1030 per credit hour. ***College room only:*** $9060. Room and board charges vary according to housing facility. ***Payment plan:*** installment. ***Waivers:*** employees or children of employees.

Financial Aid Of all full-time matriculated undergraduates who enrolled in 2014, 1,036 applied for aid, 888 were judged to have need, 151 had their need fully met. In 2014, 373 non-need-based awards were made. ***Average percent of need met:*** 70. ***Average financial aid package:*** $14,007. ***Average need-based loan:*** $4679. ***Average need-based gift aid:*** $9020. ***Average non-need-based aid:*** $5775. ***Average indebtedness upon graduation:*** $23,000.

APPLYING
Standardized Tests *Required:* SAT or ACT (for admission).

Options: electronic application, early action, deferred entrance.

Required: essay or personal statement, high school transcript. ***Recommended:*** interview.

Application deadlines: rolling (freshmen), rolling (transfers).

Notification: continuous (freshmen), continuous (transfers).

CONTACT
Lesley University, 29 Everett Street, Cambridge, MA 02138-2790. *Phone:* 617-349-8800. *Toll-free phone:* 800-999-1959 Ext. 8800.

Massachusetts College of Art and Design

Boston, Massachusetts

http://www.massart.edu/

- **State-supported** comprehensive, founded 1873, part of Massachusetts Public Higher Education System
- **Urban** 5-acre campus
- **Coed** 1,965 undergraduate students, 83% full-time, 70% women, 30% men
- **Very difficult** entrance level, 73% of applicants were admitted

UNDERGRAD STUDENTS
1,628 full-time, 337 part-time. Students come from 26 states and territories; 49 other countries; 34% are from out of state; 3% Black or African American, non-Hispanic/Latino; 8% Hispanic/Latino; 7% Asian, non-Hispanic/Latino; 0.2% Native Hawaiian or other Pacific Islander, non-Hispanic/Latino; 0.4% American Indian or Alaska Native, non-Hispanic/Latino; 1% Two or more races, non-Hispanic/Latino; 15% Race/ethnicity unknown; 3% international; 6% transferred in; 38% live on campus.

Freshmen
Admission: 1,345 applied, 981 admitted, 328 enrolled. ***Average high school GPA:*** 3.42. ***Test scores:*** SAT critical reading scores over 500: 73%; SAT math scores over 500: 64%; SAT writing scores over 500: 65%; SAT critical reading scores over 600: 30%; SAT math scores over 600: 23%; SAT writing scores over 600: 25%; SAT critical reading scores over 700: 8%; SAT math scores over 700: 1%; SAT writing scores over 700: 4%.

Retention: 89% of full-time freshmen returned.

FACULTY
Total: 269, 38% full-time.

Student/faculty ratio: 10:1.

ACADEMICS
Calendar: semesters. *Degrees:* certificates, bachelor's, master's, and postbachelor's certificates.

Special study options: double majors, independent study, internships, off-campus study, part-time degree program, student-designed majors, study abroad, summer session for credit.

Computers: 370 computers/terminals are available on campus for general student use. Students can access the following: campus intranet, computer help desk, free student e-mail accounts, online (class) grades, online (class) registration, online (class) schedules. Campuswide network is available. 100% of college-owned or -operated housing units are wired for high-speed Internet access. Wireless service is available via entire campus.

STUDENT LIFE
Housing options: coed. Campus housing is university owned. Freshman campus housing is guaranteed.

Activities and organizations: drama/theater group, student-run newspaper, radio station, International Students' Club, Design Research Unit, Spectrum, film society, Event Works.

Athletics ***Intramural sports:*** basketball M/W, ice hockey M, sailing M/W, softball M/W, table tennis M/W, volleyball M/W.

Campus security: 24-hour emergency response devices and patrols, late-night transport/escort service, security lighting, self-defense workshops.

Student services: health clinic, personal/psychological counseling, women's center.

COSTS & FINANCIAL AID
Costs (2014–15) ***Tuition:*** state resident $11,225 full-time; nonresident $29,925 full-time. Part-time tuition and fees vary according to course load. ***Room and board:*** $13,000. Room and board charges vary according to board plan and housing facility. ***Payment plan:*** installment. ***Waivers:*** senior citizens and employees or children of employees.

Financial Aid Of all full-time matriculated undergraduates who enrolled in 2014, 1,345 applied for aid, 992 were judged to have need. 201 Federal Work-Study jobs (averaging $1304). In 2014, 214 non-need-based awards were made. ***Average financial aid package:*** $10,544. ***Average need-based loan:*** $4389. ***Average need-based gift aid:*** $7198. ***Average non-need-based aid:*** $5737. ***Average indebtedness upon graduation:*** $26,792.

APPLYING
Standardized Tests *Required:* SAT or ACT (for admission).

Options: electronic application, early action, deferred entrance.

Application fee: $50.

Required: essay or personal statement, high school transcript, 2 letters of recommendation, portfolio required; for GPA between 2.0 and 2.9, SAT/ACT scores considered with GPA on sliding scale. ***Recommended:*** minimum 3.0 GPA.

Application deadlines: 2/1 (freshmen), 2/1 (transfers), 12/1 (early action).

Notification: 1/5 (early action).

CONTACT
Massachusetts College of Art and Design, 621 Huntington Avenue, Boston, MA 02115. *Phone:* 617-879-7230. *Fax:* 617-879-7250. *E-mail:* admissions@massart.edu.

Massachusetts College of Liberal Arts

North Adams, Massachusetts

http://www.mcla.edu/

- **State-supported** comprehensive, founded 1894, part of Massachusetts State University System
- **Small-town** 105-acre campus with easy access to Albany-Schenectady-Troy New York Metro Area
- **Coed** 1,562 undergraduate students, 88% full-time, 63% women, 37% men
- **Moderately difficult** entrance level, 72% of applicants were admitted

UNDERGRAD STUDENTS
1,378 full-time, 184 part-time. Students come from 21 states and territories; 1 other country; 25% are from out of state; 9% Black or African American, non-Hispanic/Latino; 7% Hispanic/Latino; 2% Asian, non-Hispanic/Latino; 0.4% American Indian or Alaska Native, non-Hispanic/Latino; 3% Two or more races, non-Hispanic/Latino; 4% Race/ethnicity unknown; 10% transferred in; 61% live on campus.

Freshmen
Admission: 2,066 applied, 1,493 admitted, 352 enrolled. ***Average high school GPA:*** 3.03. ***Test scores:*** SAT critical reading scores over 500: 48%; SAT math scores over 500: 44%; ACT scores over 18: 78%; SAT critical reading scores over 600: 15%; SAT math scores over 600: 9%; ACT scores over 24: 25%; SAT critical reading scores over 700: 2%; SAT math scores over 700: 1%; ACT scores over 30: 5%.

Retention: 78% of full-time freshmen returned.

FACULTY
Total: 172, 51% full-time, 56% with terminal degrees.

Student/faculty ratio: 13:1.

ACADEMICS
Calendar: semesters. *Degrees:* certificates, bachelor's, master's, post-master's, and postbachelor's certificates.

Special study options: academic remediation for entering students, accelerated degree program, adult/continuing education programs, advanced placement credit, cooperative education, distance learning, double majors, honors programs, independent study, internships, off-campus study, part-time degree program, services for LD students, student-designed majors, study abroad, summer session for credit.

Unusual degree programs: 3-2 engineering with University of Massachusetts at Amherst; podiatric medicine with the New York School of Podiatric Medicine.

Computers: 140 computers/terminals are available on campus for general student use. Students can access the following: campus intranet, computer help desk, free student e-mail accounts, online (class) grades, online (class) registration, online (class) schedules. Campuswide network is available. 100% of college-owned or -operated housing units are wired for high-speed Internet access. Wireless service is available via entire campus.

STUDENT LIFE
Housing options: on-campus residence required through junior year; coed, special housing for students with disabilities. Campus housing is university owned. Freshman campus housing is guaranteed.

Activities and organizations: drama/theater group, student-run newspaper, radio and television station, choral group, Student Activities Council, Student Government Association, The Beacon (Student Newspaper), Harlequin-Musical Theatre Company, Dance Company, national fraternities, national sororities.

Athletics Member NCAA. All Division III. ***Intercollegiate sports:*** baseball M, basketball M/W, cross-country running M/W, golf M, lacrosse W, soccer M/W, softball W, tennis M/W, volleyball W. ***Intramural sports:*** basketball M/W, cheerleading W(c), equestrian sports M(c)/W(c), football M/W, golf M/W, lacrosse M(c), racquetball M/W, rugby M(c)/W(c), skiing (cross-country) M/W, skiing (downhill) M(c)/W(c), soccer M/W, softball M/W, squash M/W, swimming and diving M/W, tennis M/W, ultimate Frisbee M/W, volleyball M/W.

Campus security: 24-hour emergency response devices and patrols, late-night transport/escort service, controlled dormitory access.

Student services: health clinic, personal/psychological counseling, women's center.

COSTS & FINANCIAL AID
Costs (2014–15) ***Tuition:*** state resident $1030 full-time, $43 per credit part-time; nonresident $9975 full-time, $416 per credit part-time. Part-time tuition and fees vary according to course load. ***Required fees:*** $7945 full-time, $268 per credit part-time. ***Room and board:*** $9638. Room and board charges vary according to board plan and housing facility. ***Payment plan:*** installment. ***Waivers:*** senior citizens and employees or children of employees.

Financial Aid Of all full-time matriculated undergraduates who enrolled in 2014, 1,252 applied for aid, 1,030 were judged to have need, 795 had their need fully met. In 2014, 58 non-need-based awards were made. ***Average percent of need met:*** 79. ***Average financial aid package:*** $14,445. ***Average need-based loan:*** $3978. ***Average need-based gift aid:*** $6370. ***Average non-need-based aid:*** $2715. ***Average indebtedness upon graduation:*** $28,817.

APPLYING
Standardized Tests *Required:* SAT or ACT (for admission).

Options: electronic application, early admission, early action, deferred entrance.

Application fee: $40.

Required: essay or personal statement, high school transcript, minimum 3.0 GPA, 1 letter of recommendation. ***Required for some:*** interview, sliding scale applies (GPA and SAT) if below 3.0.

Application deadlines: rolling (freshmen), rolling (transfers), 12/1 (early action).

Notification: continuous (freshmen), continuous (transfers), 12/15 (early action).

CONTACT
Massachusetts College of Liberal Arts, 375 Church Street, North Adams, MA 01247-4100. *Phone:* 413-662-5410. *Toll-free phone:* 800-989-MCLA.

Massachusetts Institute of Technology

Cambridge, Massachusetts

http://web.mit.edu/

- **Independent** university, founded 1861
- **Urban** 168-acre campus with easy access to Boston
- **Endowment** $12.4 billion
- **Coed** 4,512 undergraduate students, 99% full-time, 46% women, 54% men
- **Most difficult** entrance level, 8% of applicants were admitted

UNDERGRAD STUDENTS
4,476 full-time, 36 part-time. Students come from 54 states and territories; 98 other countries; 91% are from out of state; 6% Black or African American, non-Hispanic/Latino; 16% Hispanic/Latino; 25% Asian, non-Hispanic/Latino; 0.2% American Indian or Alaska Native, non-Hispanic/Latino; 5% Two or more races, non-Hispanic/Latino; 2% Race/ethnicity unknown; 10% international; 0.4% transferred in; 88% live on campus.

Freshmen
Admission: 18,356 applied, 1,447 admitted, 1,043 enrolled. ***Test scores:*** SAT critical reading scores over 500: 100%; SAT math scores over 500: 100%; SAT writing scores over 500: 100%; ACT scores over 18: 100%; SAT critical reading scores over 600: 96%; SAT math scores over 600: 100%; SAT writing scores over 600: 97%; ACT scores over 24: 100%; SAT critical reading scores over 700: 67%; SAT math scores over 700: 96%; SAT writing scores over 700: 71%; ACT scores over 30: 95%.

Retention: 99% of full-time freshmen returned.

FACULTY
Total: 1,504, 82% full-time, 88% with terminal degrees.

Student/faculty ratio: 8:1.

ACADEMICS
Calendar: 4-1-4. *Degrees:* bachelor's, master's, and doctoral.

Special study options: advanced placement credit, cooperative education, double majors, English as a second language, independent study, internships, off-campus study, services for LD students, study abroad. ***ROTC:*** Army (b), Navy (b), Air Force (b).

Computers: 1,100 computers/terminals and 50,000 ports are available on campus for general student use. Students can access the following: campus intranet, computer help desk, free student e-mail accounts, online (class) grades, online (class) registration, online (class) schedules. Campuswide network is available. 100% of college-owned or -operated housing units are wired for high-speed Internet access. Wireless service is available via entire campus.

STUDENT LIFE
Housing options: on-campus residence required for freshman year; coed, women-only, cooperative, special housing for students with disabilities. Campus housing is university owned. Freshman campus housing is guaranteed.

Activities and organizations: drama/theater group, student-run newspaper, radio and television station, choral group, marching band, Educational Studies Program, Dance Troupe, Science Fiction Society, The Tech (student newspaper), Anime Club, national fraternities, national sororities.

Athletics Member NCAA. All Division III except men's and women's crew (Division I). ***Intercollegiate sports:*** baseball M, basketball M/W, crew M/W, cross-country running M/W, fencing M/W, field hockey W, football M, lacrosse M/W, riflery M/W, sailing M/W, soccer M/W, softball W, squash M, swimming and diving M/W, tennis M/W, track and field M/W, volleyball M/W, water polo M. ***Intramural sports:*** archery M(c)/W(c), badminton M/W, basketball M/W, cheerleading M(c)/W(c), crew M(c)/W(c), golf M(c)/W(c), gymnastics M(c)/W(c), ice hockey M/W, rugby M(c)/W(c), soccer M/W, softball M/W, table tennis M/W, tennis M/W, ultimate Frisbee M/W, volleyball M/W, water polo M/W, wrestling M(c).

Campus security: 24-hour emergency response devices and patrols, late-night transport/escort service, controlled dormitory access.

Student services: health clinic, personal/psychological counseling.

COSTS & FINANCIAL AID
Costs (2014–15) ***Comprehensive fee:*** $58,240 includes full-time tuition ($44,720), mandatory fees ($296), and room and board ($13,224). Part-time tuition: $699 per unit. Part-time tuition and fees vary according to course load. ***College room only:*** $8330. Room and board charges vary according to board plan and housing facility. ***Payment plan:*** installment. ***Waivers:*** employees or children of employees.

Financial Aid Of all full-time matriculated undergraduates who enrolled in 2013, 2,965 applied for aid, 2,643 were judged to have need, 2,643 had their need fully met. 1,096 Federal Work-Study jobs (averaging $2169). 963 state and other part-time jobs (averaging $2697). ***Average percent of need met:*** 100. ***Average financial aid package:*** $40,118. ***Average need-based loan:*** $3005. ***Average need-based gift aid:*** $37,090. ***Average indebtedness upon graduation:*** $19,064. ***Financial aid deadline:*** 2/15.

APPLYING
Standardized Tests *Required:* SAT or ACT (for admission), SAT Subject Tests (for admission).

Options: electronic application, early action, deferred entrance.

Application fee: $75.

Required: essay or personal statement, high school transcript, 2 letters of recommendation, SAT, ACT or TOEFL. Two SAT II Subject tests: one in math and one in science. ***Recommended:*** interview.

Application deadlines: 1/1 (freshmen), 2/15 (transfers), 11/1 (early action).

Notification: 3/20 (freshmen), 5/1 (transfers), 12/20 (early action).

CONTACT
Admissions Counselors, Massachusetts Institute of Technology, 77 Massachusetts Avenue, Building 3-108, Cambridge, MA 02139-4307. *Phone:* 617-253-3400. *Fax:* 617-258-8304. *E-mail:* admissions@mit.edu.

Massachusetts Maritime Academy

Buzzards Bay, Massachusetts

http://www.maritime.edu/

- **State-supported** comprehensive, founded 1891, part of Massachusetts State University System
- **Small-town** 55-acre campus with easy access to Boston, Providence
- **Endowment** $10.4 million
- **Coed, primarily men** 1,401 undergraduate students, 98% full-time, 12% women, 88% men
- **Moderately difficult** entrance level, 62% of applicants were admitted

UNDERGRAD STUDENTS
1,373 full-time, 28 part-time. Students come from 30 states and territories; 8 other countries; 21% are from out of state; 2% Black or African American, non-Hispanic/Latino; 3% Hispanic/Latino; 3% Asian, non-Hispanic/Latino; 0.1% Native Hawaiian or other Pacific Islander, non-Hispanic/Latino; 1% American Indian or Alaska Native, non-Hispanic/Latino; 0.1% Two or more races, non-Hispanic/Latino; 2% Race/ethnicity unknown; 0.5% international; 3% transferred in; 95% live on campus.

Freshmen
Admission: 810 applied, 499 admitted, 321 enrolled. ***Average high school GPA:*** 3.18. ***Test scores:*** SAT critical reading scores over 500: 58%; SAT math scores over 500: 83%; SAT writing scores over 500: 53%; ACT scores over 18: 43%; SAT critical reading scores over 600: 15%; SAT math scores over 600: 26%; SAT writing scores over 600: 12%; ACT scores over 24: 24%; SAT critical reading scores over 700: 2%; SAT math scores over 700: 2%; SAT writing scores over 700: 2%; ACT scores over 30: 3%.

Retention: 89% of full-time freshmen returned.

FACULTY
Total: 114, 69% full-time, 46% with terminal degrees.

Student/faculty ratio: 15:1.

ACADEMICS
Calendar: semesters plus sea term. *Degrees:* bachelor's and master's.

Special study options: academic remediation for entering students, advanced placement credit, cooperative education, distance learning, double majors, internships, off-campus study, part-time degree program, services for LD students, study abroad, summer session for credit. ***ROTC:*** Army (c), Navy (b).

Computers: 150 computers/terminals and 1,000 ports are available on campus for general student use. Students can access the following: campus intranet, computer help desk, free student e-mail accounts, online (class) grades, online (class) registration, online (class) schedules, course-supported e-learning, wireless available campus wide. Campuswide network is available. 100% of college-owned or -operated housing units are wired for high-speed Internet access. Wireless service is available via entire campus.

STUDENT LIFE
Housing options: on-campus residence required for freshman year; coed, special housing for students with disabilities. Campus housing is university owned. Freshman campus housing is guaranteed.

Activities and organizations: drama/theater group, student-run newspaper, choral group, marching band, club hockey, water sports, sailing/crew, rugby club, scuba club.

Athletics Member NCAA. All Division III. ***Intercollegiate sports:*** baseball M, crew M/W, cross-country running M/W, football M, lacrosse M/W, riflery M/W, sailing M/W, soccer M/W, softball W, track and field M/W, volleyball W. ***Intramural sports:*** basketball M/W, golf M(c)/W(c), ice hockey M(c), racquetball M/W, rugby M(c), skiing (cross-country) M(c)/W(c), skiing (downhill) M(c)/W(c), soccer M, softball M/W, squash M/W, swimming and diving M/W, table tennis M/W, tennis M/W, ultimate Frisbee M/W, volleyball M/W, water polo M/W, weight lifting M(c)/W(c).

Campus security: 24-hour emergency response devices and patrols, student patrols, late-night transport/escort service, controlled dormitory access.

Student services: health clinic, personal/psychological counseling, women's center.

COSTS & FINANCIAL AID
Costs (2014–15) ***Tuition:*** state resident $1480 full-time, $297 per credit part-time; nonresident $16,534 full-time, $924 per credit part-time. ***Required fees:*** $5800 full-time. ***Room and board:*** $11,120; room only: $6440.

Financial Aid Of all full-time matriculated undergraduates who enrolled in 2014, 1,057 applied for aid, 752 were judged to have need, 286 had their need fully met. 450 Federal Work-Study jobs (averaging $1500). In 2014, 125 non-need-based awards were made. ***Average percent of need met:*** 78. ***Average financial aid package:*** $12,158. ***Average need-based loan:*** $4180. ***Average need-based gift aid:*** $8844. ***Average non-need-based aid:*** $4008. ***Average indebtedness upon graduation:*** $37,582.

APPLYING
Standardized Tests *Required:* SAT and SAT Subject Tests or ACT (for admission).

Options: electronic application, early action, deferred entrance.

Application fee: $50.

Required: essay or personal statement, high school transcript, minimum 2.0 GPA, 2 letters of recommendation, for students transferring between 12 and 23 credits minimum college GPA 2.5; for less than 23 transferable credits minimum college GPA 2.0 and meet admission standards for freshman applicants; for more than 24 transferable credits minimum college GPA 2.0. ***Recommended:*** interview.

Application deadlines: rolling (freshmen), rolling (out-of-state freshmen), rolling (transfers), 11/1 (early action).

Notification: continuous (freshmen), continuous (out-of-state freshmen), continuous (transfers).

CONTACT

Capt. Elizabeth Daly AIA, Director of Admissions, Massachusetts Maritime Academy, 101 Academy Drive, Blinn Hall, Buzzards Bay, MA 02532. *Phone:* 508-830-5031. *Toll-free phone:* 800-544-3411. *Fax:* 508-830-5077. *E-mail:* edaly@maritime.edu.

MCPHS University

Boston, Massachusetts

http://www.mcphs.edu/

- **Independent** university, founded 1823
- **Urban** 3-acre campus
- **Endowment** $514.0 million
- **Coed** 4,338 undergraduate students, 95% full-time, 68% women, 32% men
- 84% of applicants were admitted

UNDERGRAD STUDENTS

4,135 full-time, 203 part-time. Students come from 48 states and territories; 42 other countries; 44% are from out of state; 5% Black or African American, non-Hispanic/Latino; 3% Hispanic/Latino; 22% Asian, non-Hispanic/Latino; 0.1% American Indian or Alaska Native, non-Hispanic/Latino; 0.3% Two or more races, non-Hispanic/Latino; 24% Race/ethnicity unknown; 12% international; 9% transferred in; 20% live on campus.

Freshmen

Admission: 4,885 applied, 4,104 admitted, 875 enrolled.

Retention: 87% of full-time freshmen returned.

ACADEMICS

Calendar: semesters. *Degrees:* certificates, bachelor's, master's, doctoral, post-master's, and postbachelor's certificates.

Special study options: accelerated degree program, adult/continuing education programs, advanced placement credit, distance learning, double majors, independent study, internships, off-campus study, part-time degree program, services for LD students, study abroad, summer session for credit.

Computers: 507 computers/terminals are available on campus for general student use. Students can access the following: computer help desk, free student e-mail accounts, online (class) grades, online (class) registration, online (class) schedules. Campuswide network is available. 100% of college-owned or -operated housing units are wired for high-speed Internet access. Wireless service is available via entire campus.

STUDENT LIFE

Housing options: coed. Campus housing is university owned, leased by the school and is provided by a third party. Freshman campus housing is guaranteed.

Activities and organizations: drama/theater group, student-run newspaper, choral group, Residence Hall Council, Vietnamese Student Association, Student Government Association, Campus Activities Board, Student Indian Organization, national fraternities.

Athletics ***Intramural sports:*** basketball M/W, bowling M/W, cross-country running M/W, field hockey M/W, football M/W, racquetball M/W, soccer M/W, softball M/W, tennis M/W, ultimate Frisbee M/W, volleyball M/W.

Campus security: 24-hour emergency response devices and patrols, late-night transport/escort service, controlled dormitory access, electronically operated academic area entrances, security guards at entrance.

Student services: health clinic, personal/psychological counseling.

COSTS & FINANCIAL AID

Costs (2015–16) ***Comprehensive fee:*** $45,770 includes full-time tuition ($29,600), mandatory fees ($930), and room and board ($15,240). Full-time tuition and fees vary according to course load, degree level, location, program, and student level. Part-time tuition: $1090 per credit. ***Required fees:*** $245 per term part-time. ***College room only:*** $12,100. Room and board charges vary according to board plan, housing facility, and location. ***Payment plan:*** installment. ***Waivers:*** employees or children of employees.

Financial Aid Of all full-time matriculated undergraduates who enrolled in 2013, 3,046 applied for aid, 2,864 were judged to have need, 102 had their need fully met. In 2013, 142 non-need-based awards were made. ***Average percent of need met:*** 33. ***Average financial aid package:*** $14,078. ***Average need-based loan:*** $5751. ***Average need-based gift aid:*** $7540. ***Average non-need-based aid:*** $8508. ***Average indebtedness upon graduation:*** $14,618.

APPLYING

Standardized Tests *Required:* SAT or ACT (for admission).

Options: electronic application, early action, deferred entrance.

Required: essay or personal statement, 2 letters of recommendation. ***Required for some:*** high school transcript, interview.

Application deadlines: rolling (freshmen), 2/1 (transfers), 11/15 (early action).

Notification: continuous until 2/15 (freshmen), continuous (transfers), 12/19 (early action).

CONTACT

Sandra Hernandez, Visit Concierge, MCPHS University, 179 Longwood Avenue, Boston, MA 02115. *Phone:* 617-732-2850. *Fax:* 617-732-2118. *E-mail:* admissions@mcphs.edu.

Merrimack College

North Andover, Massachusetts

http://www.merrimack.edu/

- **Independent Roman Catholic** comprehensive, founded 1947
- **Suburban** 220-acre campus with easy access to Boston
- **Endowment** $46.6 million
- **Coed** 3,051 undergraduate students, 94% full-time, 51% women, 49% men
- **Moderately difficult** entrance level, 78% of applicants were admitted

UNDERGRAD STUDENTS

2,877 full-time, 174 part-time. Students come from 30 states and territories; 23 other countries; 28% are from out of state; 3% Black or African American, non-Hispanic/Latino; 6% Hispanic/Latino; 1% Asian, non-Hispanic/Latino; 0.1% American Indian or Alaska Native, non-Hispanic/Latino; 1% Two or more races, non-Hispanic/Latino; 14% Race/ethnicity unknown; 6% international; 2% transferred in; 75% live on campus.

Freshmen

Admission: 7,044 applied, 5,478 admitted, 858 enrolled. ***Average high school GPA:*** 3.09.

Retention: 83% of full-time freshmen returned.

FACULTY

Total: 357, 46% full-time.

Student/faculty ratio: 13:1.

ACADEMICS

Calendar: semesters. *Degrees:* bachelor's, master's, and post-master's certificates.

Special study options: academic remediation for entering students, adult/continuing education programs, advanced placement credit, cooperative education, double majors, English as a second language, honors programs, independent study, internships, off-campus study, part-time degree program, services for LD students, student-designed majors, study abroad, summer session for credit. ***ROTC:*** Air Force (c).

Computers: Students can access the following: campus intranet, computer help desk, free student e-mail accounts, online (class) grades, online (class) registration, online (class) schedules. Campuswide network is available. 100% of college-owned or -operated housing units are wired

for high-speed Internet access. Wireless service is available via entire campus.

STUDENT LIFE

Housing options: coed, special housing for students with disabilities. Campus housing is university owned. Freshman applicants given priority for college housing.

Activities and organizations: drama/theater group, student-run newspaper, television station, choral group, Merrimack Programming Board, Best Buddies, Greek Life, ALANA, Live 2 Give, national fraternities, national sororities.

Athletics Member NCAA. All Division II except men's and women's ice hockey (Division I). ***Intercollegiate sports:*** baseball M(s), basketball M(s)/W(s), crew W(s), cross-country running M(s)/W(s), field hockey W(s), football M(s), golf W(s), ice hockey M(s)/W(s), lacrosse M(s)/W(s), soccer M(s)/W(s), softball W(s), swimming and diving W(s), tennis M(s)/W(s), track and field M(s)/W(s), volleyball W(s). ***Intramural sports:*** badminton M/W, baseball M(c), basketball M/W, cheerleading W(c), golf M(c), ice hockey M/W, lacrosse M(c), rugby M(c)/W(c), soccer M/W, softball M/W, ultimate Frisbee M(c)/W(c), volleyball M/W.

Campus security: 24-hour emergency response devices and patrols, student patrols, late-night transport/escort service, controlled dormitory access, staffed dorm entrances.

Student services: health clinic, personal/psychological counseling.

COSTS & FINANCIAL AID

Costs (2014–15) ***Comprehensive fee:*** $49,470 includes full-time tuition ($34,615), mandatory fees ($1600), and room and board ($13,255). Full-time tuition and fees vary according to degree level. Part-time tuition: $1240 per credit. Part-time tuition and fees vary according to class time, course load, and degree level. ***Room and board:*** Room and board charges vary according to board plan and housing facility. ***Payment plan:*** installment. ***Waivers:*** senior citizens and employees or children of employees.

Financial Aid Of all full-time matriculated undergraduates who enrolled in 2014, 2,298 applied for aid, 2,064 were judged to have need, 239 had their need fully met. In 2014, 549 non-need-based awards were made. ***Average percent of need met:*** 64. ***Average financial aid package:*** $22,246. ***Average need-based loan:*** $4635. ***Average need-based gift aid:*** $18,377. ***Average non-need-based aid:*** $9798. ***Financial aid deadline:*** 2/15.

APPLYING

Options: electronic application, early admission, early decision, early action, deferred entrance.

Required: essay or personal statement, high school transcript, 1 letter of recommendation, first quarter senior grades. ***Required for some:*** interview. ***Recommended:*** interview.

Application deadlines: 2/15 (freshmen), 8/15 (transfers), 11/15 (early action).

Early decision deadline: 11/15.

Notification: continuous until 3/15 (freshmen), continuous (transfers), 12/15 (early decision), 12/15 (early action).

CONTACT

Admissions Office, Merrimack College, 510 Turnpike St, North Andover, MA 01845. *Phone:* 978-837-5100. *Fax:* 978-837-5133. *E-mail:* admission@merrimack.edu.

Mount Holyoke College

South Hadley, Massachusetts

http://www.mtholyoke.edu/

- **Independent** comprehensive, founded 1837
- **Small-town** 800-acre campus with easy access to Springfield
- **Endowment** $713.5 million
- **Women only** 2,189 undergraduate students, 99% full-time
- **Very difficult** entrance level, 55% of applicants were admitted

UNDERGRAD STUDENTS

2,161 full-time, 28 part-time. Students come from 45 states and territories; 74 other countries; 77% are from out of state; 6% Black or African American, non-Hispanic/Latino; 8% Hispanic/Latino; 10% Asian, non-Hispanic/Latino; 3% Two or more races, non-Hispanic/Latino; 1% Race/ethnicity unknown; 25% international; 4% transferred in; 95% live on campus.

Freshmen

Admission: 3,201 applied, 1,751 admitted, 531 enrolled. ***Average high school GPA:*** 3.75. ***Test scores:*** SAT critical reading scores over 500: 99%; SAT math scores over 500: 99%; SAT writing scores over 500: 99%; ACT scores over 18: 100%; SAT critical reading scores over 600: 81%; SAT math scores over 600: 83%; SAT writing scores over 600: 83%; ACT scores over 24: 97%; SAT critical reading scores over 700: 36%; SAT math scores over 700: 39%; SAT writing scores over 700: 36%; ACT scores over 30: 52%.

Retention: 91% of full-time freshmen returned.

FACULTY

Total: 240, 87% full-time, 96% with terminal degrees.

Student/faculty ratio: 10:1.

ACADEMICS

Calendar: semesters. *Degrees:* bachelor's, master's, and postbachelor's certificates.

Special study options: adult/continuing education programs, advanced placement credit, cooperative education, distance learning, double majors, independent study, internships, off-campus study, part-time degree program, services for LD students, student-designed majors, study abroad, summer session for credit. ***ROTC:*** Army (c), Air Force (c).

Unusual degree programs: 3-2 engineering with Dartmouth College, University of Massachusetts, California Institute of Technology.

Computers: 552 computers/terminals and 3,000 ports are available on campus for general student use. Students can access the following: campus intranet, computer help desk, free student e-mail accounts, online (class) grades, online (class) registration, online (class) schedules, personal Web pages. Campuswide network is available. 100% of college-owned or -operated housing units are wired for high-speed Internet access. Wireless service is available via classrooms, computer centers, computer labs, dorm rooms, learning centers, libraries, student centers.

STUDENT LIFE

Housing options: on-campus residence required through senior year; women-only, special housing for students with disabilities. Campus housing is university owned. Freshman campus housing is guaranteed.

Activities and organizations: drama/theater group, student-run newspaper, radio station, choral group, Student Government Association, C.A.U.S.E. (Creating Awareness and Unity for Social Equality), WMHC Radio 91.5 FM, Model UN, MHC Outing Club.

Athletics Member NCAA. All Division III. ***Intercollegiate sports:*** basketball W, crew W, cross-country running W, equestrian sports W, field hockey W, golf W, lacrosse W, soccer W, squash W, swimming and diving W, tennis W, track and field W, volleyball W. ***Intramural sports:*** equestrian sports W(c), fencing W(c), ice hockey W(c), rugby W(c), ultimate Frisbee W(c).

Campus security: 24-hour emergency response devices and patrols, student patrols, late-night transport/escort service, controlled dormitory access, police officers on-campus.

Student services: health clinic, personal/psychological counseling.

COSTS & FINANCIAL AID

Costs (2015–16) ***Comprehensive fee:*** $56,746 includes full-time tuition ($43,700), mandatory fees ($186), and room and board ($12,860). Part-time tuition: $1370 per credit hour. ***College room only:*** $6280. ***Payment plan:*** installment. ***Waivers:*** employees or children of employees.

Financial Aid Of all full-time matriculated undergraduates who enrolled in 2014, 1,729 applied for aid, 1,482 were judged to have need, 1,482 had their need fully met. 764 Federal Work-Study jobs (averaging $1883). 368 state and other part-time jobs (averaging $1959). In 2014, 292 non-need-based awards were made. ***Average percent of need met:*** 100. ***Average financial aid package:*** $36,761. ***Average need-based loan:*** $5375. ***Average need-based gift aid:*** $30,707. ***Average non-need-based aid:*** $16,888. ***Average indebtedness upon graduation:*** $23,914. ***Financial aid deadline:*** 3/1.

APPLYING

Standardized Tests *Required for some:* SAT Subject Tests (for admission).

Options: electronic application, early admission, early decision, deferred entrance.

Application fee: $60.

Required: essay or personal statement, high school transcript, 2 letters of recommendation. ***Recommended:*** interview.

Application deadlines: 1/15 (freshmen), 5/15 (transfers).

Early decision deadline: 11/15 (for plan 1), 1/1 (for plan 2).

Notification: 4/1 (freshmen), continuous (transfers), 1/1 (early decision plan 1), 2/1 (early decision plan 2).

CONTACT

Ms. Diane Anci, Vice President of Enrollment and Dean of Admission, Mount Holyoke College, Office of Admission, Mount Holyoke College, South Hadley, MA 01075. *Phone:* 413-538-2023. *Fax:* 413-538-2409. *E-mail:* admission@mtholyoke.edu.

Newbury College

Brookline, Massachusetts

http://www.newbury.edu/

- **Independent** 4-year, founded 1962
- **Suburban** 10-acre campus with easy access to Boston
- **Endowment** $2.1 million
- **Coed** 873 undergraduate students, 92% full-time, 57% women, 43% men
- **Minimally difficult** entrance level, 70% of applicants were admitted

UNDERGRAD STUDENTS

800 full-time, 73 part-time. Students come from 27 states and territories; 17 other countries; 21% are from out of state; 38% Black or African American, non-Hispanic/Latino; 15% Hispanic/Latino; 6% Asian, non-Hispanic/Latino; 0.2% American Indian or Alaska Native, non-Hispanic/Latino; 3% international; 3% transferred in; 40% live on campus.

Freshmen

Admission: 3,162 applied, 2,216 admitted, 266 enrolled. ***Average high school GPA:*** 2.45. ***Test scores:*** SAT critical reading scores over 500: 19%; SAT math scores over 500: 21%; SAT writing scores over 500: 17%; SAT critical reading scores over 600: 3%; SAT math scores over 600: 3%; SAT writing scores over 600: 3%; SAT critical reading scores over 700: 1%.

Retention: 59% of full-time freshmen returned.

FACULTY

Total: 106, 32% full-time, 30% with terminal degrees.

Student/faculty ratio: 14:1.

ACADEMICS

Calendar: semesters. *Degrees:* certificates, associate, and bachelor's.

Special study options: academic remediation for entering students, accelerated degree program, adult/continuing education programs, advanced placement credit, cooperative education, distance learning, double majors, honors programs, independent study, internships, off-campus study, part-time degree program, services for LD students, student-designed majors, study abroad, summer session for credit.

Computers: Students can access the following: campus intranet, computer help desk, free student e-mail accounts, online (class) grades, online (class) registration, online (class) schedules. Campuswide network is available. 100% of college-owned or -operated housing units are wired for high-speed Internet access. Wireless service is available via entire campus.

STUDENT LIFE

Housing options: coed. Campus housing is university owned and leased by the school. Freshman applicants given priority for college housing.

Activities and organizations: drama/theater group, student-run radio and television station, choral group, Campus Activities Board, Innkeeper's Club, Games Club, Commuter Council, Quidditch Club.

Athletics Member NCAA. All Division III. ***Intercollegiate sports:*** baseball M, basketball M/W, cross-country running M/W, golf M, soccer M/W, softball W, tennis M/W, volleyball M/W.

Campus security: 24-hour emergency response devices and patrols, late-night transport/escort service.

Student services: personal/psychological counseling.

COSTS & FINANCIAL AID

Costs (2014–15) ***Comprehensive fee:*** $43,270 includes full-time tuition ($28,830), mandatory fees ($1100), and room and board ($13,340). Full-time tuition and fees vary according to program and reciprocity agreements. Part-time tuition: $960 per credit hour. Part-time tuition and fees vary according to class time, course load, program, and reciprocity agreements. ***Room and board:*** Room and board charges vary according to housing facility. ***Payment plan:*** installment. ***Waivers:*** employees or children of employees.

Financial Aid Of all full-time matriculated undergraduates who enrolled in 2012, 837 applied for aid, 792 were judged to have need, 3 had their need fully met. 208 Federal Work-Study jobs (averaging $1582). In 2012, 27 non-need-based awards were made. ***Average percent of need met:*** 47. ***Average financial aid package:*** $13,034. ***Average need-based loan:*** $4180. ***Average need-based gift aid:*** $11,702. ***Average non-need-based aid:*** $9778. ***Average indebtedness upon graduation:*** $30,802.

APPLYING

Options: electronic application.

Required: essay or personal statement, high school transcript, 2 letters of recommendation.

Application deadlines: 9/1 (freshmen), 9/1 (transfers).

Notification: continuous (freshmen), continuous (transfers).

CONTACT

Mrs. Jill Hall, Director of Admissions, Newbury College, 129 Fisher Avenue, Brookline, MA 02445-5796. *Phone:* 617-730-7105. *Toll-free phone:* 800-NEWBURY. *Fax:* 617-731-9618. *E-mail:* jill.hall@newbury.edu.

New England Conservatory of Music

Boston, Massachusetts

http://necmusic.edu/

- **Independent** comprehensive, founded 1867
- **Urban** 2-acre campus
- **Endowment** $120.3 million
- **Coed** 413 undergraduate students, 91% full-time, 43% women, 57% men
- **Very difficult** entrance level, 29% of applicants were admitted

UNDERGRAD STUDENTS

376 full-time, 37 part-time. Students come from 34 states and territories; 19 other countries; 87% are from out of state; 1% Black or African American, non-Hispanic/Latino; 5% Hispanic/Latino; 11% Asian, non-Hispanic/Latino; 5% Two or more races, non-Hispanic/Latino; 7% Race/ethnicity unknown; 32% international; 4% transferred in; 30% live on campus.

Freshmen

Admission: 1,249 applied, 364 admitted, 75 enrolled.

Retention: 92% of full-time freshmen returned.

FACULTY

Total: 243, 46% full-time, 21% with terminal degrees.

Student/faculty ratio: 5:1.

ACADEMICS

Calendar: semesters. *Degrees:* certificates, diplomas, bachelor's, master's, doctoral, post-master's, and postbachelor's certificates.

Special study options: advanced placement credit, double majors, English as a second language, independent study, internships, off-campus study, services for LD students, study abroad, summer session for credit.

Computers: 70 computers/terminals and 200 ports are available on campus for general student use. Students can access the following: campus intranet, computer help desk, free student e-mail accounts, online (class) grades, online (class) registration, online (class) schedules. Campuswide network is available. 100% of college-owned or -operated housing units are wired for high-speed Internet access. Wireless service is available via classrooms, computer labs, dorm rooms, libraries.

STUDENT LIFE

Housing options: on-campus residence required for freshman year; coed. Campus housing is university owned. Freshman campus housing is guaranteed.

Activities and organizations: drama/theater group, student-run newspaper, choral group, The Penguin (newspaper).

Campus security: 24-hour patrols, late-night transport/escort service.

Student services: health clinic, personal/psychological counseling.

COSTS & FINANCIAL AID

Costs (2014–15) ***Comprehensive fee:*** $54,255 includes full-time tuition ($40,950), mandatory fees ($455), and room and board ($12,850). Part-time tuition: $1310 per credit. ***Room and board:*** Room and board charges vary according to board plan. ***Waivers:*** employees or children of employees.

Financial Aid Of all full-time matriculated undergraduates who enrolled in 2014, 244 applied for aid, 192 were judged to have need, 27 had their need fully met. 168 Federal Work-Study jobs (averaging $1561). In 2014, 189 non-need-based awards were made. ***Average percent of need met:*** 59. ***Average financial aid package:*** $25,463. ***Average need-based loan:*** $5112. ***Average need-based gift aid:*** $19,776. ***Average non-need-based aid:*** $14,234. ***Average indebtedness upon graduation:*** $25,288.

APPLYING

Options: electronic application, deferred entrance.

Application fee: $115.

Required: essay or personal statement, high school transcript, minimum 2.8 GPA, 2 letters of recommendation, audition recording, repertoire list.

Application deadlines: 12/1 (freshmen), 12/1 (transfers).

Notification: 4/1 (freshmen), 4/1 (transfers).

CONTACT

New England Conservatory of Music, 290 Huntington Avenue, Boston, MA 02115-5000. *Phone:* 617-585-1103.

The New England Institute of Art

Brookline, Massachusetts

http://www.artinstitutes.edu/boston/

- **Proprietary** 4-year, part of Education Management Corporation
- **Urban** campus
- **Coed**

ACADEMICS

Calendar: semesters. *Degrees:* certificates, associate, and bachelor's.

CONTACT

The New England Institute of Art, 10 Brookline Place West, Brookline, MA 02445. *Phone:* 617-739-1700. *Toll-free phone:* 800-903-4425.

Nichols College

Dudley, Massachusetts

http://www.nichols.edu/

- **Independent** comprehensive, founded 1815
- **Suburban** 250-acre campus with easy access to Boston
- **Endowment** $11.9 million
- **Coed** 1,330 undergraduate students, 89% full-time, 39% women, 61% men

UNDERGRAD STUDENTS

1,180 full-time, 150 part-time. Students come from 31 states and territories; 11 other countries; 38% are from out of state; 6% Black or African American, non-Hispanic/Latino; 7% Hispanic/Latino; 1% Asian, non-Hispanic/Latino; 0.2% Native Hawaiian or other Pacific Islander, non-Hispanic/Latino; 0.2% American Indian or Alaska Native, non-Hispanic/Latino; 3% Two or more races, non-Hispanic/Latino; 0.8% international; 2% transferred in; 80% live on campus.

Freshmen

Admission: 400 enrolled. ***Average high school GPA:*** 2.7. ***Test scores:*** SAT critical reading scores over 500: 29%; SAT math scores over 500: 40%; SAT writing scores over 500: 27%; ACT scores over 18: 75%; SAT critical reading scores over 600: 2%; SAT math scores over 600: 5%; SAT writing scores over 600: 3%; ACT scores over 24: 16%.

FACULTY

Total: 81, 54% full-time, 31% with terminal degrees.

Student/faculty ratio: 18:1.

ACADEMICS

Calendar: semesters. *Degrees:* certificates, associate, bachelor's, master's, and postbachelor's certificates.

Special study options: academic remediation for entering students, accelerated degree program, adult/continuing education programs, advanced placement credit, cooperative education, distance learning, double majors, honors programs, independent study, internships, off-campus study, part-time degree program, services for LD students, study abroad, summer session for credit. ***ROTC:*** Army (c), Air Force (c).

Unusual degree programs: 3-2 business administration.

Computers: 43 computers/terminals are available on campus for general student use. Students can access the following: computer help desk, free student e-mail accounts, online (class) grades, online (class) registration, online (class) schedules. Campuswide network is available. 100% of college-owned or -operated housing units are wired for high-speed Internet access. Wireless service is available via entire campus.

STUDENT LIFE

Housing options: coed, men-only, women-only, special housing for students with disabilities. Campus housing is university owned.

Activities and organizations: drama/theater group, student-run radio station, Campus Activities Board, Club Hockey, Sport Management, Student Athletic Advisory Council, History.

Athletics Member NCAA. All Division III. ***Intercollegiate sports:*** baseball M, basketball M/W, field hockey W, football M, golf M, ice hockey M/W, lacrosse M/W, soccer M/W, softball W, tennis M/W, track and field M(c)/W(c), volleyball W(c). ***Intramural sports:*** basketball M/W, cheerleading M/W, ice hockey M(c)/W(c), racquetball M(c)/W(c), rugby M, soccer M/W, volleyball M(c)/W(c).

Campus security: 24-hour emergency response devices and patrols, student patrols, late-night transport/escort service, controlled dormitory access.

Student services: health clinic, personal/psychological counseling, women's center.

COSTS & FINANCIAL AID

Costs (2015–16) ***Comprehensive fee:*** $45,900 includes full-time tuition ($33,000), mandatory fees ($300), and room and board ($12,600). Part-time tuition: $1100 per credit. ***Required fees:*** $150 per term part-time. ***College room only:*** $7000. Room and board charges vary according to board plan, housing facility, and student level. ***Payment plan:*** installment. ***Waivers:*** employees or children of employees.

Financial Aid Of all full-time matriculated undergraduates who enrolled in 2013, 970 applied for aid, 898 were judged to have need, 156 had their need fully met. 449 Federal Work-Study jobs (averaging $1640). In 2013, 71 non-need-based awards were made. ***Average percent of need met:*** 75. ***Average financial aid package:*** $25,024. ***Average need-based loan:*** $4088. ***Average need-based gift aid:*** $17,573. ***Average non-need-based aid:*** $14,120. ***Average indebtedness upon graduation:*** $32,747.

APPLYING

Standardized Tests *Required for some:* SAT or ACT (for admission).

Required: essay or personal statement, high school transcript, 1 letter of recommendation. ***Required for some:*** interview. ***Recommended:*** 2 letters of recommendation.

CONTACT

Ms. Emily Reardon, Associate Director of Admissions, Nichols College, 129 Center Road, Dudley, MA 01571. *Phone:* 508-213-2275. *Toll-free phone:* 800-470-3379. *E-mail:* emily.reardon@nichols.edu.

Northeastern University

Boston, Massachusetts

http://www.northeastern.edu/

- **Independent** university, founded 1898
- **Urban** 73-acre campus
- **Coed** 17,445 undergraduate students, 100% full-time, 50% women, 50% men
- **Very difficult** entrance level, 32% of applicants were admitted

UNDERGRAD STUDENTS

17,427 full-time, 18 part-time. 68% are from out of state; 3% Black or African American, non-Hispanic/Latino; 7% Hispanic/Latino; 11% Asian, non-Hispanic/Latino; 4% Two or more races, non-Hispanic/Latino; 7% Race/ethnicity unknown; 18% international; 3% transferred in.

Freshmen
Admission: 49,822 applied, 16,052 admitted, 2,944 enrolled. ***Test scores:*** SAT critical reading scores over 500: 98%; SAT math scores over 500: 99%; SAT writing scores over 500: 98%; ACT scores over 18: 100%; SAT critical reading scores over 600: 93%; SAT math scores over 600: 95%; SAT writing scores over 600: 89%; ACT scores over 24: 99%; SAT critical reading scores over 700: 51%; SAT math scores over 700: 66%; SAT writing scores over 700: 43%; ACT scores over 30: 91%.

Retention: 96% of full-time freshmen returned.

ACADEMICS
Calendar: semesters. *Degrees:* bachelor's, master's, doctoral, and post-master's certificates.

Special study options: accelerated degree program, cooperative education, double majors, honors programs, independent study, internships, services for LD students, student-designed majors, study abroad, summer session for credit. ***ROTC:*** Army (b), Navy (c), Air Force (c).

Computers: Students can access the following: campus intranet, computer help desk, free student e-mail accounts, online (class) grades, online (class) registration, online (class) schedules. Campuswide network is available. 100% of college-owned or -operated housing units are wired for high-speed Internet access. Wireless service is available via entire campus.

STUDENT LIFE
Housing options: on-campus residence required through sophomore year; coed, special housing for students with disabilities. Campus housing is university owned and leased by the school. Freshman campus housing is guaranteed.

Activities and organizations: drama/theater group, student-run newspaper, radio and television station, choral group, Student Government Association, Council for University Programs, Resident Student Association, Downhillers Ski and Snowboard Club, Northeastern University Huskiers & Outing Club, national fraternities, national sororities.

Athletics Member NCAA. All Division I. ***Intercollegiate sports:*** baseball M(s), basketball M(s)/W(s), cheerleading M(c)/W(c), crew M(s)/W(s), cross-country running M(s)/W(s), field hockey W(s), golf M(c)/W(c), ice hockey M(s)/W(s), lacrosse M(c)/W(c), riflery M(c)/W(c), rugby M(c)/W(c), sailing M(c)/W(c), soccer M(s)/W(s), softball M(c)/W(c), squash M(c)/W(c), swimming and diving W(s), table tennis M(c)/W(c), tennis M(c)/W(c), track and field M(s)/W(s), ultimate Frisbee M(c)/W(c), volleyball W(s), water polo M(c)/W(c), weight lifting M(c)/W(c), wrestling M(c). ***Intramural sports:*** basketball M/W, field hockey W(c), ice hockey M/W, lacrosse M/W, racquetball M/W, skiing (cross-country) M(c)/W(c), skiing (downhill) M(c)/W(c), soccer M/W, softball M/W, swimming and diving M(c)/W(c), tennis M/W, track and field M(c)/W(c), volleyball M(c)/W(c), water polo M/W.

Campus security: 24-hour emergency response devices and patrols, student patrols, late-night transport/escort service, controlled dormitory access, public safety website.

Student services: health clinic, personal/psychological counseling.

COSTS & FINANCIAL AID
Costs (2014–15) ***Comprehensive fee:*** $58,010 includes full-time tuition ($42,534), mandatory fees ($906), and room and board ($14,570). ***College room only:*** $7780. Room and board charges vary according to board plan and housing facility. ***Payment plan:*** installment. ***Waivers:*** employees or children of employees.

Financial Aid Of all full-time matriculated undergraduates who enrolled in 2014, 8,877 applied for aid, 6,601 were judged to have need, 2,285 had their need fully met. In 2014, 4329 non-need-based awards were made. ***Average percent of need met:*** 81. ***Average financial aid package:*** $26,669. ***Average need-based loan:*** $4880. ***Average need-based gift aid:*** $22,445. ***Average non-need-based aid:*** $14,130.

APPLYING
Standardized Tests *Required:* SAT or ACT (for admission).

Options: electronic application, early admission, early decision, early action, deferred entrance.

Application fee: $75.

Application deadlines: 1/1 (freshmen), 4/1 (transfers), 11/1 (early action).

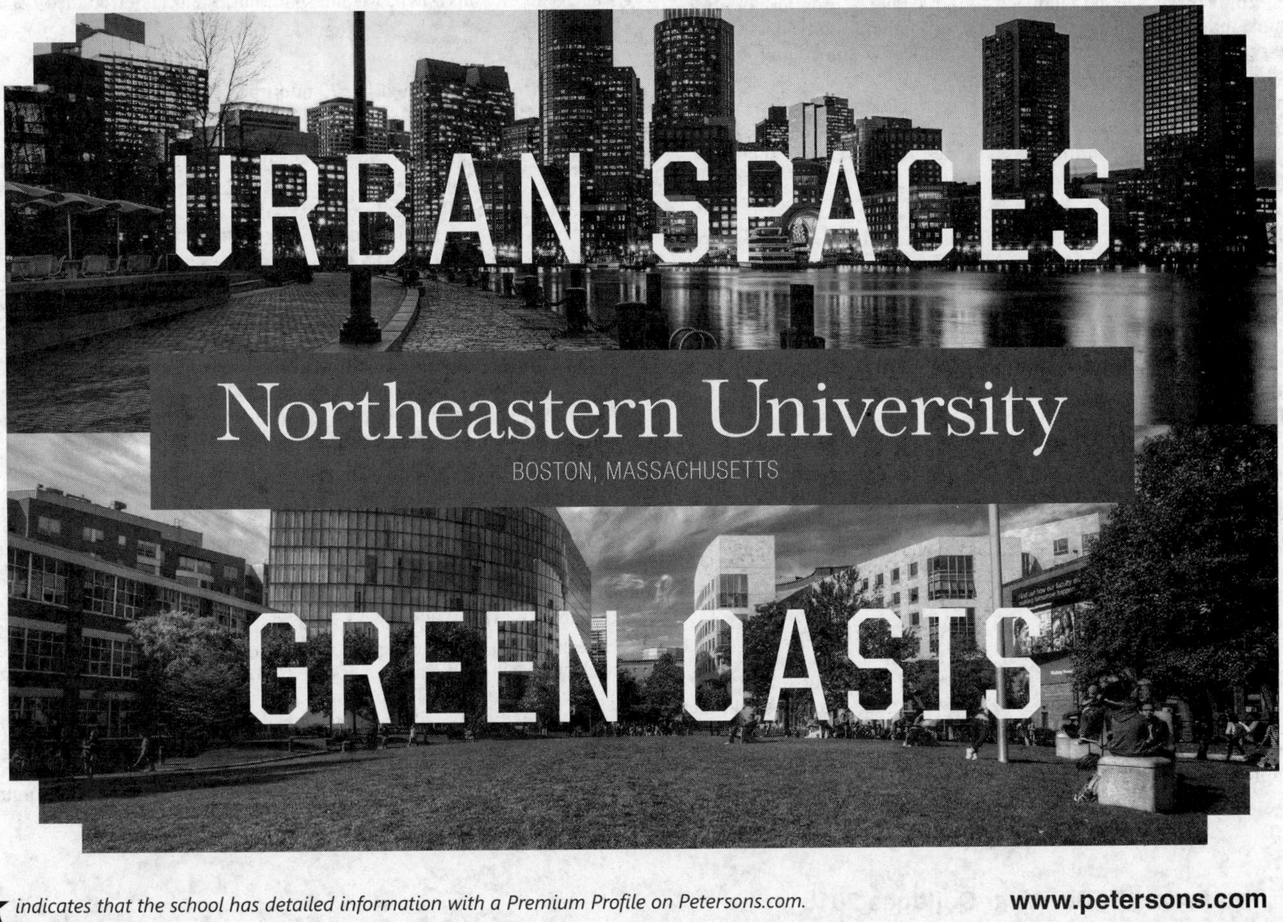

Early decision deadline: 11/1.

Notification: continuous until 4/1 (freshmen), continuous (transfers), 12/15 (early decision), 12/31 (early action).

CONTACT

Ronne Patrick Turner, Associate Vice President for Enrollment and Dean of Admissions, Northeastern University, 360 Huntington Avenue, Boston, MA 02115. *Phone:* 617-373-2200. *E-mail:* admissions@neu.edu.

See previous page for display ad and page 1550 for the College Close-Up.

Pine Manor College

Chestnut Hill, Massachusetts

http://www.pmc.edu/

- **Independent** comprehensive, founded 1911
- **Suburban** 50-acre campus
- **Endowment** $8.5 million
- **Coed** 403 undergraduate students, 99% full-time, 64% women, 36% men
- **Moderately difficult** entrance level, 68% of applicants were admitted

UNDERGRAD STUDENTS

399 full-time, 4 part-time. Students come from 20 states and territories; 14 other countries; 44% are from out of state; 28% Black or African American, non-Hispanic/Latino; 16% Hispanic/Latino; 2% Asian, non-Hispanic/Latino; 0.7% American Indian or Alaska Native, non-Hispanic/Latino; 9% Two or more races, non-Hispanic/Latino; 10% Race/ethnicity unknown; 28% international; 2% transferred in.

Freshmen

Admission: 908 applied, 616 admitted, 122 enrolled.

Retention: 70% of full-time freshmen returned.

FACULTY

Total: 72, 32% full-time, 57% with terminal degrees.

Student/faculty ratio: 10:1.

ACADEMICS

Calendar: semesters. *Degrees:* associate, bachelor's, and master's.

Special study options: academic remediation for entering students, adult/continuing education programs, advanced placement credit, double majors, English as a second language, external degree program, honors programs, independent study, internships, off-campus study, part-time degree program, services for LD students, student-designed majors, study abroad, summer session for credit.

Computers: 85 computers/terminals are available on campus for general student use. Students can access the following: computer help desk, free student e-mail accounts, online (class) grades, online (class) schedules. Campuswide network is available.

STUDENT LIFE

Housing options: coed. Campus housing is university owned.

Activities and organizations: drama/theater group, student-run newspaper, radio station, choral group, African American, Latina, Asian, Native American and All (ALANA), Community Service Committee, International Student Club, The Model UN, Student Government Association (SGA).

Athletics Member NCAA. All Division III. ***Intercollegiate sports:*** basketball M/W, cross-country running W, soccer M/W, softball W, volleyball W.

Campus security: 24-hour emergency response devices and patrols, student patrols, late-night transport/escort service, controlled dormitory access.

Student services: health clinic, personal/psychological counseling, women's center.

COSTS & FINANCIAL AID

Costs (2014–15) ***One-time required fee:*** $664. ***Comprehensive fee:*** $38,336 includes full-time tuition ($25,516) and room and board ($12,820). Full-time tuition and fees vary according to course load. Part-time tuition: $760 per credit. Part-time tuition and fees vary according to course load. ***Room and board:*** Room and board charges vary according to housing facility. ***Payment plan:*** installment. ***Waivers:*** children of alumni and employees or children of employees.

Financial Aid Of all full-time matriculated undergraduates who enrolled in 2013, 198 applied for aid, 194 were judged to have need, 8 had their need fully met. 170 Federal Work-Study jobs (averaging $880). In 2013, 32 non-need-based awards were made. ***Average percent of need met:*** 72. ***Average financial aid package:*** $24,014. ***Average need-based loan:*** $4086. ***Average need-based gift aid:*** $18,525. ***Average non-need-based aid:*** $13,400. ***Average indebtedness upon graduation:*** $31,016.

APPLYING

Standardized Tests *Required:* SAT or ACT (for admission).

Options: electronic application, deferred entrance.

Application fee: $25.

Required: essay or personal statement, high school transcript, SAT or ACT scores. ***Recommended:*** minimum 2.0 GPA, interview.

Application deadlines: rolling (freshmen), rolling (transfers).

Notification: continuous (freshmen), continuous (transfers).

CONTACT

Pine Manor College, 400 Heath Street, Chestnut Hill, MA 02467. *Phone:* 617-731-7107. *Toll-free phone:* 800-762-1357.

★ Regis College

Weston, Massachusetts

http://www.regiscollege.edu/

- **Independent Roman Catholic** comprehensive, founded 1927
- **Small-town** 131-acre campus with easy access to Boston
- **Endowment** $32.1 million
- **Coed** 1,166 undergraduate students, 78% full-time, 77% women, 23% men
- **Moderately difficult** entrance level, 76% of applicants were admitted

UNDERGRAD STUDENTS

911 full-time, 255 part-time. Students come from 22 states and territories; 9 other countries; 16% are from out of state; 20% Black or African American, non-Hispanic/Latino; 10% Hispanic/Latino; 6% Asian, non-Hispanic/Latino; 0.2% Native Hawaiian or other Pacific Islander, non-Hispanic/Latino; 0.3% American Indian or Alaska Native, non-Hispanic/Latino; 2% Two or more races, non-Hispanic/Latino; 12% Race/ethnicity unknown; 1% international; 3% transferred in; 59% live on campus.

Freshmen

Admission: 2,204 applied, 1,673 admitted, 249 enrolled. ***Average high school GPA:*** 3.01. ***Test scores:*** SAT critical reading scores over 500: 40%; SAT math scores over 500: 44%; SAT writing scores over 500: 40%; ACT scores over 18: 85%; SAT critical reading scores over 600: 5%; SAT math scores over 600: 6%; SAT writing scores over 600: 7%; ACT scores over 24: 15%; SAT critical reading scores over 700: 1%; SAT math scores over 700: 1%; SAT writing scores over 700: 1%; ACT scores over 30: 4%.

Retention: 84% of full-time freshmen returned.

FACULTY

Total: 211, 43% full-time, 51% with terminal degrees.

Student/faculty ratio: 12:1.

ACADEMICS

Calendar: semesters. *Degrees:* associate, bachelor's, master's, doctoral, and post-master's certificates.

Special study options: academic remediation for entering students, accelerated degree program, adult/continuing education programs, advanced placement credit, double majors, English as a second language, honors programs, independent study, internships, off-campus study, part-time degree program, services for LD students, student-designed majors, study abroad, summer session for credit. ***ROTC:*** Army (c).

Unusual degree programs: 3-2 business administration; communication.

Computers: 196 computers/terminals are available on campus for general student use. Students can access the following: campus intranet, computer help desk, free student e-mail accounts, online (class) grades, online (class) registration, online (class) schedules, online bills, financial aid award letters and check-in requirements. Campuswide network is available. 100% of college-owned or -operated housing units are wired for high-speed Internet access. Wireless service is available via computer labs, dorm rooms, learning centers, libraries, student centers.

STUDENT LIFE
Housing options: coed, women-only. Campus housing is university owned. Freshman campus housing is guaranteed.

Activities and organizations: drama/theater group, student-run newspaper, radio station, choral group, Campus Ministry, SGA-Student Government Association, Asian American Student Organization, Dynasty Step Squad, Black Student Organization.

Athletics Member NCAA. All Division III. ***Intercollegiate sports:*** basketball M/W, field hockey W, lacrosse M/W, soccer M/W, softball W, swimming and diving M/W, tennis M/W, track and field M/W, volleyball M/W.

Campus security: 24-hour emergency response devices and patrols, late-night transport/escort service, controlled dormitory access.

Student services: health clinic, personal/psychological counseling.

COSTS & FINANCIAL AID
Costs (2014–15) ***One-time required fee:*** $200. ***Comprehensive fee:*** $49,450 includes full-time tuition ($35,750) and room and board ($13,700). Full-time tuition and fees vary according to course load. Part-time tuition: $1191 per credit hour. Part-time tuition and fees vary according to class time. ***Payment plan:*** installment. ***Waivers:*** employees or children of employees.

Financial Aid Of all full-time matriculated undergraduates who enrolled in 2008, 695 applied for aid, 644 were judged to have need, 93 had their need fully met. 436 Federal Work-Study jobs (averaging $2000). 40 state and other part-time jobs (averaging $1500). In 2008, 66 non-need-based awards were made. ***Average percent of need met:*** 59. ***Average financial aid package:*** $22,111. ***Average need-based loan:*** $4849. ***Average need-based gift aid:*** $12,529. ***Average non-need-based aid:*** $8231. ***Average indebtedness upon graduation:*** $24,178.

APPLYING
Standardized Tests *Required for some:* SAT or ACT (for admission).

Options: electronic application, early admission, early action, deferred entrance.

Application fee: $50.

Required: essay or personal statement, high school transcript, minimum 2.0 GPA, 2 letters of recommendation. ***Required for some:*** interview. ***Recommended:*** minimum 3.0 GPA, interview, rank in upper 50% of high school class.

Application deadlines: rolling (freshmen), rolling (transfers), 12/1 (early action).

Notification: 12/23 (early action).

CONTACT
Mr. Paul Vaccaro, Vice President Enrollment and Marketing, Regis College, 235 Wellesley Street, Weston, MA 02493. *Phone:* 781-768-7100. *Toll-free phone:* 866-438-7344. *Fax:* 781-768-7071. *E-mail:* admission@regiscollege.edu.

Salem State University

Salem, Massachusetts

http://www.salemstate.edu/

- **State-supported** comprehensive, founded 1854, part of Massachusetts Public Higher Education System
- **Urban** 62-acre campus with easy access to Boston
- **Coed**
- **Minimally difficult** entrance level

FACULTY
Student/faculty ratio: 15:1.

ACADEMICS
Calendar: semesters. *Degrees:* certificates, bachelor's, master's, and post-master's certificates.

STUDENT LIFE
Housing options: coed. Campus housing is university owned. Freshman applicants given priority for college housing.

Activities and organizations: drama/theater group, student-run newspaper, radio station, choral group, Student Government Association, Program Council, Residence Hall Association, Multicultural Student Association, International Student Association, national fraternities, national sororities.

Athletics Member NCAA. All Division III.

Campus security: 24-hour emergency response devices and patrols, late-night transport/escort service, controlled dormitory access.

Student services: health clinic, personal/psychological counseling, women's center, legal services.

COSTS & FINANCIAL AID
Costs (2014–15) ***Tuition:*** state resident $910 full-time, $38 per credit part-time; nonresident $7050 full-time, $294 per credit part-time. Full-time tuition and fees vary according to class time and course load. Part-time tuition and fees vary according to class time and course load. ***Required fees:*** $7736 full-time. ***Room and board:*** $11,956; room only: $8660. Room and board charges vary according to board plan and housing facility.

Financial Aid Of all full-time matriculated undergraduates who enrolled in 2009, 286 Federal Work-Study jobs (averaging $3000).

APPLYING
Standardized Tests *Required:* SAT or ACT (for admission).

Options: electronic application, early action.

Application fee: $40.

Required: high school transcript. ***Required for some:*** interview.

CONTACT
Dr. Mary Dunn, Assistant Dean for Undergraduate Admissions, Salem State University, 352 Lafayette Street, Salem, MA 01970. *Phone:* 978-542-6202. *Fax:* 978-542-6893. *E-mail:* admissions@salemstate.edu.

School of the Museum of Fine Arts, Boston

Boston, Massachusetts

http://www.smfa.edu/

- **Independent** comprehensive, founded 1876
- **Urban** 14-acre campus with easy access to Boston
- **Endowment** $27.1 million
- **Coed** 397 undergraduate students, 86% full-time, 73% women, 27% men
- **Moderately difficult** entrance level, 84% of applicants were admitted

UNDERGRAD STUDENTS
342 full-time, 55 part-time. Students come from 33 states and territories; 31 other countries; 62% are from out of state; 3% Black or African American, non-Hispanic/Latino; 11% Hispanic/Latino; 4% Asian, non-Hispanic/Latino; 0.5% American Indian or Alaska Native, non-Hispanic/Latino; 4% Two or more races, non-Hispanic/Latino; 18% Race/ethnicity unknown; 11% international; 15% transferred in; 13% live on campus.

Freshmen
Admission: 487 applied, 411 admitted, 70 enrolled. ***Average high school GPA:*** 3.16.
Retention: 77% of full-time freshmen returned.

FACULTY
Total: 107, 44% full-time, 76% with terminal degrees.

Student/faculty ratio: 8:1.

ACADEMICS
Calendar: semesters. *Degrees:* certificates, diplomas, bachelor's, master's, and postbachelor's certificates.

Special study options: adult/continuing education programs, double majors, independent study, internships, off-campus study, part-time degree program, services for LD students, student-designed majors, study abroad, summer session for credit.

Unusual degree programs: 3-2 Visual/Fine Art and Liberal Arts.

Computers: 100 computers/terminals are available on campus for general student use. Students can access the following: campus intranet, computer help desk, free student e-mail accounts, online (class) grades, online (class) registration, online (class) schedules. Campuswide network is available. 100% of college-owned or -operated housing units are wired for high-speed Internet access. Wireless service is available via entire campus.

STUDENT LIFE

Housing options: on-campus residence required for freshman year; coed. Campus housing is leased by the school. Freshman campus housing is guaranteed.

Activities and organizations: GLBT Group, Student Body, Inc and Student Voice, Bikes Are Really Fun, Film Screenings/Movie nights, CRU @ SMFA.

Campus security: 24-hour emergency response devices and patrols, late night taxis service between buildings.

Student services: health clinic, personal/psychological counseling.

COSTS & FINANCIAL AID

Costs (2014–15) ***Tuition:*** $39,068 full-time, $1452 per credit hour part-time. Full-time tuition and fees vary according to course load, degree level, program, and student level. Part-time tuition and fees vary according to class time, course load, program, and student level. ***Required fees:*** $1280 full-time. ***Room only:*** $10,950. Room and board charges vary according to board plan and housing facility. ***Payment plan:*** installment. ***Waivers:*** employees or children of employees.

Financial Aid Of all full-time matriculated undergraduates who enrolled in 2014, 267 applied for aid, 252 were judged to have need, 19 had their need fully met. In 2014, 14 non-need-based awards were made. ***Average percent of need met:*** 57. ***Average financial aid package:*** $23,317. ***Average need-based loan:*** $4966. ***Average need-based gift aid:*** $7351. ***Average non-need-based aid:*** $7786. ***Average indebtedness upon graduation:*** $34,081.

APPLYING

Standardized Tests *Recommended:* Test scores are considered if submitted.

Options: electronic application, early admission, deferred entrance.

Application fee: $65.

Required: essay or personal statement, high school transcript, 2 letters of recommendation, portfolio. ***Recommended:*** interview.

Application deadlines: rolling (freshmen), rolling (out-of-state freshmen), rolling (transfers).

Notification: continuous (freshmen), continuous (out-of-state freshmen), continuous (transfers).

CONTACT

Ms. Angela Jones, Director of Admissions, School of the Museum of Fine Arts, Boston, 230 The Fenway, Boston, MA 02115. *Phone:* 617-369-3626. *Toll-free phone:* 800-643-6078. *Fax:* 617-369-4264. *E-mail:* admissions@smfa.edu.

★ Simmons College

Boston, Massachusetts

http://www.simmons.edu/

- **Independent** university, founded 1899
- **Urban** 12-acre campus with easy access to Boston
- **Endowment** $180.0 million
- **Undergraduate: women only; graduate: coed** 1,622 undergraduate students, 91% full-time, 100% women, 0% men
- **Moderately difficult** entrance level, 52% of applicants were admitted

UNDERGRAD STUDENTS

1,484 full-time, 138 part-time. Students come from 37 states and territories; 48 other countries; 39% are from out of state; 6% Black or African American, non-Hispanic/Latino; 6% Hispanic/Latino; 10% Asian, non-Hispanic/Latino; 0.2% American Indian or Alaska Native, non-Hispanic/Latino; 3% Two or more races, non-Hispanic/Latino; 4% Race/ethnicity unknown; 3% international; 2% transferred in; 60% live on campus.

Freshmen

Admission: 3,999 applied, 2,086 admitted, 303 enrolled. ***Average high school GPA:*** 3.3. ***Test scores:*** SAT critical reading scores over 500: 93%; SAT math scores over 500: 94%; SAT writing scores over 500: 91%; ACT scores over 18: 99%; SAT critical reading scores over 600: 45%; SAT math scores over 600: 40%; SAT writing scores over 600: 50%; ACT scores over 24: 81%; SAT critical reading scores over 700: 10%; SAT math scores over 700: 4%; SAT writing scores over 700: 8%; ACT scores over 30: 13%.

Retention: 86% of full-time freshmen returned.

FACULTY

Total: 710, 29% full-time.

Student/faculty ratio: 11:1.

ACADEMICS

Calendar: semesters. *Degrees:* certificates, bachelor's, master's, doctoral, post-master's, and postbachelor's certificates.

Special study options: accelerated degree program, adult/continuing education programs, advanced placement credit, distance learning, double majors, honors programs, independent study, internships, off-campus study, part-time degree program, services for LD students, student-designed majors, study abroad, summer session for credit. ***ROTC:*** Army (c).

Unusual degree programs: 3-2 business administration; nursing; social work; Nutrition, Teaching, Physical Therapy, Pharmacy with Massachusetts College of Pharmacy and Health Sciences.

Computers: 350 computers/terminals are available on campus for general student use. Students can access the following: campus intranet, computer help desk, free student e-mail accounts, online (class) grades, online (class) registration, online (class) schedules. Campuswide network is available. 100% of college-owned or -operated housing units are wired for high-speed Internet access. Wireless service is available via entire campus.

STUDENT LIFE

Housing options: on-campus residence required for freshman year; coed, women-only. Campus housing is university owned. Freshman applicants given priority for college housing.

Activities and organizations: drama/theater group, student-run newspaper, radio station, choral group, Simmons College Dance Company, Student Government Association, Campus Activities Board, Simmons Nursing Student Association, Black Student Organization.

Athletics Member NCAA. All Division III. ***Intercollegiate sports:*** basketball W, crew W, cross-country running W, field hockey W, lacrosse W, soccer W, softball W, swimming and diving W, tennis W, volleyball W. ***Intramural sports:*** basketball M/W, rugby W(c), soccer M/W, softball M/W, tennis M/W, volleyball M/W.

Campus security: 24-hour emergency response devices and patrols, late-night transport/escort service, controlled dormitory access.

Student services: health clinic, personal/psychological counseling, women's center.

COSTS & FINANCIAL AID

Costs (2014–15) ***Comprehensive fee:*** $49,966 includes full-time tuition ($35,200), mandatory fees ($1030), and room and board ($13,736). Full-time tuition and fees vary according to course load and program. Part-time tuition: $1100 per credit hour. Part-time tuition and fees vary according to course load and program. ***Required fees:*** $260 per term part-time. ***Room and board:*** Room and board charges vary according to location. ***Payment plan:*** installment. ***Waivers:*** employees or children of employees.

Financial Aid Of all full-time matriculated undergraduates who enrolled in 2014, 1,220 applied for aid, 1,148 were judged to have need, 110 had their need fully met. 860 Federal Work-Study jobs (averaging $2365). In 2014, 231 non-need-based awards were made. ***Average percent of need met:*** 72. ***Average financial aid package:*** $27,978. ***Average need-based loan:*** $4602. ***Average need-based gift aid:*** $23,636. ***Average non-need-based aid:*** $14,030.

APPLYING

Standardized Tests *Required:* SAT or ACT (for admission).

Options: electronic application, early action, deferred entrance.

Application fee: $55.

Required: essay or personal statement, high school transcript, 2 letters of recommendation, test scores. ***Recommended:*** minimum 3.0 GPA, interview.

Application deadlines: 2/1 (freshmen), 2/1 (out-of-state freshmen), 4/1 (transfers), 11/1 (early action).

Notification: 3/15 (freshmen), 3/15 (out-of-state freshmen), 12/15 (early action).

CONTACT
Ellen Johnson, Director of Undergraduate Admission, Simmons College, 300 The Fenway, Boston, MA 02115. *Phone:* 617-521-2515. *Toll-free phone:* 800-345-8468. *Fax:* 617-521-3190. *E-mail:* ellen.johnson3@simmons.edu.

★ Smith College
Northampton, Massachusetts
http://www.smith.edu/

- **Independent** comprehensive, founded 1871
- **Small-town** 147-acre campus with easy access to Hartford
- **Undergraduate: women only; graduate: coed** 2,563 undergraduate students, 99% full-time, 100% women
- **Very difficult** entrance level, 42% of applicants were admitted

UNDERGRAD STUDENTS
2,544 full-time, 19 part-time. 78% are from out of state; 5% Black or African American, non-Hispanic/Latino; 9% Hispanic/Latino; 13% Asian, non-Hispanic/Latino; 0.1% Native Hawaiian or other Pacific Islander, non-Hispanic/Latino; 0.2% American Indian or Alaska Native, non-Hispanic/Latino; 4% Two or more races, non-Hispanic/Latino; 8% Race/ethnicity unknown; 14% international; 2% transferred in; 95% live on campus.

Freshmen
Admission: 4,466 applied, 1,885 admitted, 616 enrolled. ***Average high school GPA:*** 3.9. ***Test scores:*** SAT critical reading scores over 500: 99%; SAT math scores over 500: 99%; SAT writing scores over 500: 100%; ACT scores over 18: 100%; SAT critical reading scores over 600: 84%; SAT math scores over 600: 85%; SAT writing scores over 600: 88%; ACT scores over 24: 96%; SAT critical reading scores over 700: 34%; SAT math scores over 700: 37%; SAT writing scores over 700: 41%; ACT scores over 30: 60%.

Retention: 94% of full-time freshmen returned.

FACULTY
Total: 298, 92% full-time, 98% with terminal degrees.

Student/faculty ratio: 9:1.

ACADEMICS
Calendar: semesters. *Degrees:* bachelor's, master's, doctoral, post-master's, and postbachelor's certificates.

Special study options: adult/continuing education programs, part-time degree program. ***ROTC:*** Army (c), Air Force (c).

Computers: Students can access the following: campus intranet, computer help desk, free student e-mail accounts, online (class) grades, online (class) registration, online (class) schedules. Campuswide network is available. 100% of college-owned or -operated housing units are wired for high-speed Internet access. Wireless service is available via classrooms, computer centers, computer labs, dorm rooms, learning centers, libraries, student centers.

STUDENT LIFE
Housing options: on-campus residence required through senior year; women-only, cooperative. Campus housing is university owned. Freshman campus housing is guaranteed.

Athletics Member NCAA. All Division III. ***Intercollegiate sports:*** basketball W, crew W, cross-country running W, equestrian sports W, field hockey W, lacrosse W, soccer W, softball W, squash W, swimming and diving W, tennis W, track and field W, volleyball W. ***Intramural sports:*** badminton W(c), cheerleading W(c), crew W, equestrian sports W(c), fencing W(c), golf W(c), ice hockey W(c), rock climbing W, rugby W(c), soccer W, squash W, ultimate Frisbee W(c).

Campus security: 24-hour emergency response devices and patrols, late-night transport/escort service, self-defense workshops, emergency telephones, programs in crime and sexual assault prevention.

COSTS & FINANCIAL AID
Costs (2014–15) ***Comprehensive fee:*** $59,674 includes full-time tuition ($44,450), mandatory fees ($274), and room and board ($14,950). Part-time tuition: $1390 per credit hour. ***College room only:*** $7480. ***Payment plans:*** tuition prepayment, installment. ***Waivers:*** employees or children of employees.

Financial Aid Of all full-time matriculated undergraduates who enrolled in 2014, 1,772 applied for aid, 1,588 were judged to have need, 1,588 had their need fully met. In 2014, 117 non-need-based awards were made. ***Average percent of need met:*** 100. ***Average financial aid package:*** $43,182. ***Average need-based loan:*** $4960. ***Average need-based gift aid:*** $38,417. ***Average non-need-based aid:*** $15,982. ***Average indebtedness upon graduation:*** $24,758. ***Financial aid deadline:*** 2/15.

APPLYING
Standardized Tests *Required for some:* SAT or ACT (for admission).

Options: electronic application, early admission, early decision, deferred entrance.

Application fee: $60.

Required: essay or personal statement, high school transcript, 3 letters of recommendation. ***Recommended:*** interview.

CONTACT
Ms. Debra Shaver, Dean of Admissions, Smith College, 7 College Lane, Northampton, MA 01063. *Phone:* 413-585-2500. *Toll-free phone:* 800-383-3232. *Fax:* 413-585-2527. *E-mail:* admission@smith.edu.

★ Springfield College
Springfield, Massachusetts
http://www.springfieldcollege.edu/

- **Independent** comprehensive, founded 1885
- **Suburban** 150-acre campus
- **Coed**
- **Moderately difficult** entrance level

FACULTY
Student/faculty ratio: 13:1.

ACADEMICS
Calendar: semesters. *Degrees:* bachelor's, master's, doctoral, and postbachelor's certificates.

STUDENT LIFE
Housing options: on-campus residence required through junior year; coed, men-only, women-only. Campus housing is university owned. Freshman campus housing is guaranteed.

Activities and organizations: drama/theater group, student-run newspaper, radio station, choral group.

Athletics Member NCAA. All Division III.

Student services: health clinic, personal/psychological counseling.

COSTS
Costs (2014–15) ***Comprehensive fee:*** $44,665 includes full-time tuition ($32,980), mandatory fees ($475), and room and board ($11,210). Part-time tuition: $992 per credit hour. ***College room only:*** $6100. Room and board charges vary according to board plan and housing facility.

APPLYING
Standardized Tests *Required:* SAT or ACT (for admission).

Options: electronic application, early admission, early decision, deferred entrance.

Application fee: $50.

Required: high school transcript, 1 letter of recommendation. ***Required for some:*** portfolio. ***Recommended:*** interview.

CONTACT
Richard K. Veres, Director of Undergraduate Admissions, Springfield College, 263 Alden Street, Springfield, MA 01109. *Phone:* 413-748-3136. *Toll-free phone:* 800-343-1257. *Fax:* 413-748-3694. *E-mail:* admissions@spfldcol.edu.

See next page for display ad and page 1628 for the College Close-Up.

Stonehill College
Easton, Massachusetts
http://www.stonehill.edu/

- **Independent Roman Catholic** 4-year, founded 1948
- **Suburban** 384-acre campus with easy access to Boston
- **Endowment** $191.0 million
- **Coed** 2,401 undergraduate students, 99% full-time, 60% women, 40% men
- **Very difficult** entrance level, 77% of applicants were admitted

UNDERGRAD STUDENTS
2,373 full-time, 28 part-time. Students come from 32 states and territories; 9 other countries; 44% are from out of state; 4% Black or African American, non-Hispanic/Latino; 5% Hispanic/Latino; 2% Asian, non-Hispanic/Latino; 2% Two or more races, non-Hispanic/Latino; 2% Race/ethnicity unknown; 0.8% international; 1% transferred in; 91% live on campus.

Freshmen
Admission: 6,006 applied, 4,622 admitted, 610 enrolled. ***Average high school GPA:*** 3.3. ***Test scores:*** SAT critical reading scores over 500: 77%; SAT math scores over 500: 79%; SAT writing scores over 500: 79%; ACT scores over 18: 98%; SAT critical reading scores over 600: 29%; SAT math scores over 600: 39%; SAT writing scores over 600: 31%; ACT scores over 24: 67%; SAT critical reading scores over 700: 3%; SAT math scores over 700: 5%; SAT writing scores over 700: 4%; ACT scores over 30: 9%.
Retention: 90% of full-time freshmen returned.

FACULTY
Total: 274, 58% full-time, 68% with terminal degrees.
Student/faculty ratio: 12:1.

ACADEMICS
Calendar: semesters. *Degree:* bachelor's.
Special study options: advanced placement credit, double majors, honors programs, independent study, internships, off-campus study, part-time degree program, services for LD students, student-designed majors, study abroad, summer session for credit. ***ROTC:*** Army (b).
Unusual degree programs: 3-2 engineering with University of Notre Dame.
Computers: 403 computers/terminals and 300 ports are available on campus for general student use. Students can access the following: campus intranet, computer help desk, free student e-mail accounts, online (class) grades, online (class) registration, online (class) schedules, Learning Management System; online degree evaluation/planning; add funds to ID online and use at off campus locations; online housing contracts and room lottery; online financial aid awards; online time sheets and payments for campus jobs; ebill. Campuswide network is available. 100% of college-owned or -operated housing units are wired for high-speed Internet access. Wireless service is available via entire campus.

STUDENT LIFE
Housing options: coed, women-only, special housing for students with disabilities. Campus housing is university owned.
Activities and organizations: drama/theater group, student-run newspaper, radio station, choral group, Into the Streets, Recreation/Intramural Sports Teams, Dance Club, Student Government Association, Education Society.
Athletics Member NCAA. All Division II. ***Intercollegiate sports:*** baseball M(s), basketball M(s)/W(s), bowling M(c)/W(c), cheerleading M(c)/W(c), cross-country running M(s)/W(s), equestrian sports W, field hockey W(s), football M(s), golf M(c)/W(c), ice hockey M, lacrosse M(c)/W(s), rugby M(c)/W(c), soccer M(s)/W(s), softball W(s), tennis M(s)/W(s), track and field M(s)/W(s), ultimate Frisbee M(c)/W(c), volleyball M(c)/W(s), wrestling M(c). ***Intramural sports:*** basketball M/W, field hockey M/W, soccer M/W, softball M/W, tennis M/W, volleyball M/W.
Campus security: 24-hour emergency response devices and patrols, late-night transport/escort service, controlled dormitory access, Vehicles entering campus check point (Fri./Sat. 6pm-2am) are stopped, IDs checked, only community members and guests allowed on campus.
Student services: health clinic, personal/psychological counseling, women's center.

COSTS & FINANCIAL AID

Costs (2014–15) ***Comprehensive fee:*** $51,716 includes full-time tuition ($37,426) and room and board ($14,290). Part-time tuition: $1247 per credit. Part-time tuition and fees vary according to course load. ***Room and board:*** Room and board charges vary according to board plan. ***Payment plans:*** tuition prepayment, installment. ***Waivers:*** employees or children of employees.

Financial Aid Of all full-time matriculated undergraduates who enrolled in 2014, 1,969 applied for aid, 1,694 were judged to have need, 813 had their need fully met. In 2014, 453 non-need-based awards were made. ***Average percent of need met:*** 91. ***Average financial aid package:*** $28,514. ***Average need-based loan:*** $4732. ***Average need-based gift aid:*** $23,001. ***Average non-need-based aid:*** $13,797. ***Average indebtedness upon graduation:*** $31,622.

APPLYING

Options: electronic application, early decision, early action, deferred entrance.

Application fee: $60.

Required: essay or personal statement, high school transcript, 2 letters of recommendation. ***Recommended:*** interview.

Application deadlines: 1/15 (freshmen), 4/1 (transfers), 11/1 (early action).

Early decision deadline: 12/1.

Notification: 3/15 (freshmen), continuous until 5/31 (transfers), 12/31 (early decision), 12/31 (early action).

CONTACT

Stonehill College, 320 Washington Street, Easton, MA 02357-5610. *Phone:* 508-565-1373. *Fax:* 508-565-1545. *E-mail:* admission@stonehill.edu.

See below for display ad and page 1640 for the College Close-Up.

Suffolk University

Boston, Massachusetts

http://www.suffolk.edu/

- **Independent** comprehensive, founded 1906
- **Urban** 2-acre campus
- **Endowment** $194.5 million
- **Coed** 5,496 undergraduate students; 93% full-time, 55% women, 45% men
- **Moderately difficult** entrance level, 84% of applicants were admitted

UNDERGRAD STUDENTS

5,130 full-time, 366 part-time. Students come from 45 states and territories; 108 other countries; 29% are from out of state; 6% Black or African American, non-Hispanic/Latino; 5% Hispanic/Latino; 8% Asian, non-Hispanic/Latino; 0.1% American Indian or Alaska Native, non-Hispanic/Latino; 2% Two or more races, non-Hispanic/Latino; 12% Race/ethnicity unknown; 22% international; 8% transferred in; 23% live on campus.

Freshmen

Admission: 8,921 applied, 7,486 admitted, 1,113 enrolled. ***Average high school GPA:*** 3.12. ***Test scores:*** SAT critical reading scores over 500: 53%; SAT math scores over 500: 56%; SAT writing scores over 500: 59%; ACT scores over 18: 90%; SAT critical reading scores over 600: 15%; SAT math scores over 600: 15%; SAT writing scores over 600: 17%; ACT scores over 24: 38%; SAT critical reading scores over 700: 1%; SAT math scores over 700: 1%; SAT writing scores over 700: 2%; ACT scores over 30: 5%.

Retention: 76% of full-time freshmen returned.

FACULTY

Total: 765, 44% full-time, 62% with terminal degrees.

Student/faculty ratio: 11:1.

ACADEMICS

Calendar: semesters. *Degrees:* certificates, diplomas, associate, bachelor's, master's, doctoral, post-master's, and postbachelor's certificates (doctoral degree in law).

Special study options: academic remediation for entering students, accelerated degree program, adult/continuing education programs, advanced placement credit, cooperative education, distance learning, double majors, English as a second language, honors programs, independent study, internships, off-campus study, part-time degree program, services for LD students, study abroad, summer session for credit. ***ROTC:*** Army (c).

Computers: 384 computers/terminals are available on campus for general student use. Students can access the following: campus intranet, computer help desk, free student e-mail accounts, online (class) grades, online (class) registration, online (class) schedules. Campuswide network is available. 100% of college-owned or -operated housing units are wired for high-speed Internet access. Wireless service is available via entire campus.

STUDENT LIFE

Housing options: coed. Campus housing is university owned. Freshman applicants given priority for college housing.

Activities and organizations: drama/theater group, student-run newspaper, radio and television station, choral group, Student Government Association, Program Committee, Suffolk Free Radio, Black Student Union, Journey Leadership Program, national fraternities, national sororities.

Athletics Member NCAA. All Division III. ***Intercollegiate sports:*** baseball M, basketball M/W, cross-country running M/W, golf M, ice hockey M, soccer M, softball W, tennis M/W, volleyball W. ***Intramural sports:*** basketball M/W, soccer M/W, softball M/W, volleyball M/W.

Campus security: 24-hour emergency response devices, late-night transport/escort service, controlled dormitory access.

Student services: health clinic, personal/psychological counseling, women's center.

COSTS & FINANCIAL AID

Costs (2014–15) ***One-time required fee:*** $200. ***Comprehensive fee:*** $47,298 includes full-time tuition ($32,530), mandatory fees ($130), and room and board ($14,638). Full-time tuition and fees vary according to reciprocity agreements. Part-time tuition: $798 per credit hour. Part-time tuition and fees vary according to course load and reciprocity agreements. ***Room and board:*** Room and board charges vary according to board plan and housing facility. ***Payment plans:*** installment, deferred payment. ***Waivers:*** children of alumni, senior citizens, and employees or children of employees.

Financial Aid Of all full-time matriculated undergraduates who enrolled in 2014, 3,299 applied for aid, 3,057 were judged to have need, 484 had their need fully met. 855 Federal Work-Study jobs (averaging $2275). 579 state and other part-time jobs (averaging $3049). In 2014, 830 non-need-based awards were made. ***Average percent of need met:*** 72. ***Average financial aid package:*** $26,333. ***Average need-based loan:*** $3954. ***Average need-based gift aid:*** $13,106. ***Average non-need-based aid:*** $10,647. ***Average indebtedness upon graduation:*** $29,535. ***Financial aid deadline:*** 3/1.

APPLYING

Standardized Tests *Required:* SAT or ACT (for admission).

Options: electronic application, early action, deferred entrance.

Application fee: $50.

Required: essay or personal statement, high school transcript, 2 letters of recommendation. ***Required for some:*** interview.

Application deadlines: 2/15 (freshmen), 6/30 (transfers), 11/15 (early action).

Notification: continuous until 3/20 (freshmen), continuous (transfers), 12/15 (early action).

CONTACT

Mr. John Hamel, Associate Vice President/Director Undergraduate Admissions, Suffolk University, 8 Ashburton Place, Boston, MA 02108. *Phone:* 617-573-8460. *Toll-free phone:* 800-6-SUFFOLK. *Fax:* 617-742-4291. *E-mail:* admission@suffolk.edu.

Tufts University

Medford, Massachusetts

http://www.tufts.edu/

- **Independent** university, founded 1852
- **Suburban** 150-acre campus with easy access to Boston
- **Endowment** $1.5 billion
- **Coed** 5,177 undergraduate students, 99% full-time, 51% women, 49% men
- **Most difficult** entrance level, 17% of applicants were admitted

UNDERGRAD STUDENTS

5,127 full-time, 50 part-time. Students come from 52 states and territories; 72 other countries; 77% are from out of state; 4% Black or African American, non-Hispanic/Latino; 7% Hispanic/Latino; 11% Asian, non-Hispanic/Latino; 4% Two or more races, non-Hispanic/Latino; 9% Race/ethnicity unknown; 8% international; 0.4% transferred in; 63% live on campus.

Freshmen

Admission: 19,059 applied, 3,287 admitted, 1,347 enrolled. ***Test scores:*** SAT critical reading scores over 500: 100%; SAT math scores over 500: 100%; SAT writing scores over 500: 100%; ACT scores over 18: 100%; SAT critical reading scores over 600: 95%; SAT math scores over 600: 97%; SAT writing scores over 600: 97%; ACT scores over 24: 100%; SAT critical reading scores over 700: 64%; SAT math scores over 700: 70%; SAT writing scores over 700: 70%; ACT scores over 30: 83%.

Retention: 96% of full-time freshmen returned.

FACULTY

Total: 1,061, 68% full-time, 83% with terminal degrees.

Student/faculty ratio: 9:1.

ACADEMICS

Calendar: semesters. *Degrees:* bachelor's, master's, doctoral, post-master's, and postbachelor's certificates.

Special study options: adult/continuing education programs, advanced placement credit, double majors, independent study, internships, off-campus study, services for LD students, student-designed majors, study abroad, summer session for credit. ***ROTC:*** Army (c), Navy (c), Air Force (c).

Unusual degree programs: 3-2 New England Conservatory of Music (BA or BS and BM), School of the Museum of Fine Arts (BA or BS and BFA).

Computers: 110 computers/terminals are available on campus for general student use. Students can access the following: campus intranet, computer help desk, free student e-mail accounts, online (class) grades, online (class) registration, online (class) schedules, Cloud storage for all students, staff, and faculty. Campuswide network is available. 100% of college-owned or -operated housing units are wired for high-speed Internet access. Wireless service is available via entire campus.

STUDENT LIFE

Housing options: on-campus residence required through sophomore year; coed, men-only, women-only, cooperative, special housing for students with disabilities. Campus housing is university owned. Freshman campus housing is guaranteed.

Activities and organizations: drama/theater group, student-run newspaper, radio and television station, choral group, Leonard Carmichael Society (community service), Pen, Paint, and Pretzels (student directed theater umbrella organization), intramural sports, Tufts Daily (newspaper), Tufts Mountain Club, national fraternities, national sororities.

Athletics Member NCAA. All Division III. ***Intercollegiate sports:*** baseball M, basketball M/W, crew M/W, cross-country running M/W, equestrian sports M(c)/W(c), fencing W, field hockey W, football M, golf M, ice hockey M, lacrosse M/W, rugby M(c)/W(c), sailing M/W, soccer M/W, softball W, squash M/W, swimming and diving M/W, tennis M/W, track and field M/W, ultimate Frisbee M(c)/W(c), volleyball M(c)/W, water polo M(c)/W(c). ***Intramural sports:*** badminton M/W, baseball M(c), basketball M/W, cheerleading W, fencing M(c), field hockey W(c), football M(c)/W(c), ice hockey M(c), lacrosse M(c)/W(c), racquetball M/W, rock climbing M(c)/W(c), skiing (downhill) M/W, soccer M/W, softball M/W(c), table tennis M(c)/W(c), tennis M/W, volleyball M/W.

Campus security: 24-hour emergency response devices and patrols, late-night transport/escort service, controlled dormitory access, security lighting, call boxes to campus police.

Student services: health clinic, personal/psychological counseling, women's center, legal services.

COSTS & FINANCIAL AID

Costs (2014–15) ***Comprehensive fee:*** $61,277 includes full-time tuition ($47,596), mandatory fees ($1047), and room and board ($12,634). ***College room only:*** $6876. Room and board charges vary according to board plan. ***Payment plans:*** tuition prepayment, installment. ***Waivers:*** employees or children of employees.

Financial Aid Of all full-time matriculated undergraduates who enrolled in 2014, 2,337 applied for aid, 2,026 were judged to have need, 1,995 had their need fully met. 1,537 Federal Work-Study jobs (averaging $1866). 125 state and other part-time jobs (averaging $1782). In 2014, 100 non-need-based awards were made. ***Average percent of need met:*** 100. ***Average financial aid package:*** $40,168. ***Average need-based loan:*** $3869. ***Average need-based gift aid:*** $37,147. ***Average non-need-based aid:*** $500. ***Average indebtedness upon graduation:*** $26,616. ***Financial aid deadline:*** 2/15.

APPLYING

Standardized Tests *Required:* SAT and SAT Subject Tests or ACT (for admission).

Options: electronic application, early decision, deferred entrance.

Application fee: $70.

Required: essay or personal statement, high school transcript, 2 letters of recommendation, Common Application, the Tufts Supplement, and standardized testing. ***Recommended:*** interview.

Application deadlines: 1/1 (freshmen), 3/15 (transfers).

Early decision deadline: 11/1 (for plan 1), 1/1 (for plan 2).

Notification: 4/1 (freshmen), 5/15 (transfers), 12/15 (early decision plan 1), 2/15 (early decision plan 2).

CONTACT

Mr. Lee Coffin, Office of Undergraduate Admissions, Tufts University, Bendetson Hall, Medford, MA 02155. *Phone:* 617-627-3170. *Fax:* 617-627-3860. *E-mail:* admissions.inquiry@ase.tufts.edu.

University of Massachusetts Amherst

Amherst, Massachusetts

http://www.umass.edu/

- **State-supported** university, founded 1863, part of University of Massachusetts
- **Small-town** 1463-acre campus with easy access to Hartford
- **Endowment** $307.1 million
- **Coed** 22,252 undergraduate students, 93% full-time, 49% women, 51% men
- **Moderately difficult** entrance level, 61% of applicants were admitted

UNDERGRAD STUDENTS

20,684 full-time, 1,568 part-time. Students come from 51 states and territories; 71 other countries; 21% are from out of state; 4% Black or African American, non-Hispanic/Latino; 5% Hispanic/Latino; 8% Asian, non-Hispanic/Latino; 0.1% American Indian or Alaska Native, non-Hispanic/Latino; 2% Two or more races, non-Hispanic/Latino; 10% Race/ethnicity unknown; 3% international; 5% transferred in; 65% live on campus.

Freshmen

Admission: 37,183 applied, 22,804 admitted, 4,694 enrolled. ***Average high school GPA:*** 3.78. ***Test scores:*** SAT critical reading scores over 500: 92%; SAT math scores over 500: 97%; ACT scores over 18: 99%; SAT critical reading scores over 600: 48%; SAT math scores over 600: 65%; ACT scores over 24: 87%; SAT critical reading scores over 700: 9%; SAT math scores over 700: 16%; ACT scores over 30: 27%.

Retention: 90% of full-time freshmen returned.

FACULTY

Total: 1,470, 87% full-time, 92% with terminal degrees.

Student/faculty ratio: 17:1.

ACADEMICS

Calendar: semesters. *Degrees:* certificates, associate, bachelor's, master's, doctoral, post-master's, and postbachelor's certificates.

Special study options: academic remediation for entering students, accelerated degree program, adult/continuing education programs, advanced placement credit, cooperative education, distance learning, double majors, English as a second language, freshman honors college, honors programs, independent study, internships, off-campus study, part-time degree program, services for LD students, student-designed majors, study abroad, summer session for credit. ***ROTC:*** Army (b), Air Force (b).

Computers: 616 computers/terminals and 296 ports are available on campus for general student use. Students can access the following: computer help desk, free student e-mail accounts, online (class) grades, online (class) registration, online (class) schedules, online housing assignments, bill payment, Learning Management System, file storage, web hosting, blogs. Campuswide network is available. 100% of college-owned or -operated housing units are wired for high-speed Internet access. Wireless service is available via entire campus.

STUDENT LIFE

Housing options: on-campus residence required for freshman year; coed, men-only, women-only, special housing for students with disabilities. Campus housing is university owned. Freshman campus housing is guaranteed.

Activities and organizations: drama/theater group, student-run newspaper, radio and television station, choral group, marching band, Minutemen Marching Band, Ski Club, Outing Club, University Programming Council, Student Government Association, national fraternities, national sororities.

Athletics Member NCAA. All Division I except football (Division I-A). ***Intercollegiate sports:*** baseball M(s), basketball M(s)/W(s), crew W(s), cross-country running M(s)/W(s), field hockey W(s), ice hockey M(s), lacrosse M(s)/W(s), soccer M(s)/W(s), softball W(s), swimming and diving M(s)/W(s), tennis W(s), track and field M(s)/W(s). ***Intramural sports:*** archery M(c)/W(c), badminton M/W, baseball M(c), basketball M/W, cheerleading M/W, equestrian sports M(c)/W(c), fencing M(c)/W(c), field hockey W, football M/W, golf M(c), gymnastics W(c), ice hockey M/W(c), lacrosse M(c)/W(c), racquetball M/W, rugby M(c)/W(c), sailing M(c)/W(c), skiing (downhill) M(c)/W(c), soccer M/W, softball M/W, swimming and diving M(c)/W(c), table tennis M/W, tennis M/W, ultimate Frisbee M(c)/W(c), volleyball M/W, water polo M(c)/W(c), wrestling M(c)/W(c).

Campus security: 24-hour emergency response devices and patrols, student patrols, late-night transport/escort service, controlled dormitory access.

Student services: health clinic, personal/psychological counseling, women's center, legal services.

COSTS & FINANCIAL AID

Costs (2014–15) ***One-time required fee:*** $185. ***Tuition:*** state resident $1714 full-time, $72 per credit hour part-time; nonresident $9937 full-time, $414 per credit hour part-time. Full-time tuition and fees vary according to class time, course load, location, program, reciprocity agreements, and student level. Part-time tuition and fees vary according to class time, course load, location, program, reciprocity agreements, and student level. Mandatory fees: $11,729 for first-year state residents; $19,061 for first year out-of-state students. ***Room and board:*** $6137; room only: $5320. Room and board charges vary according to board plan and housing facility. ***Payment plan:*** installment. ***Waivers:*** senior citizens and employees or children of employees.

Financial Aid Of all full-time matriculated undergraduates who enrolled in 2013, 16,961 applied for aid, 12,273 were judged to have need, 1,475 had their need fully met. 2,254 Federal Work-Study jobs (averaging $1244). In 2013, 2079 non-need-based awards were made. ***Average percent of need met:*** 81. ***Average financial aid package:*** $15,526. ***Average need-based loan:*** $4642. ***Average need-based gift aid:*** $9653. ***Average non-need-based aid:*** $4310. ***Average indebtedness upon graduation:*** $30,453.

APPLYING

Standardized Tests *Required:* SAT or ACT (for admission).

Options: electronic application, early action, deferred entrance.

Application fee: $75.

Required: essay or personal statement, high school transcript, 1 letter of recommendation, SAT or ACT. ***Recommended:*** minimum 3.0 GPA.

Application deadlines: 1/15 (freshmen), 1/15 (out-of-state freshmen), 4/15 (transfers), 11/1 (early action).

Notification: continuous (freshmen), continuous (out-of-state freshmen), continuous (transfers), 12/15 (early action).

CONTACT

Mr. Kevin Kelly, Director, Undergraduate Admissions, University of Massachusetts Amherst, 37 Mather Drive, Amherst, MA 01003. *Phone:* 413-545-0222. *Fax:* 413-545-4312. *E-mail:* mail@admissions.umass.edu.

★ University of Massachusetts Boston

Boston, Massachusetts

http://www.umb.edu/

- **State-supported** university, founded 1964, part of University of Massachusetts
- **Urban** 187-acre campus
- **Endowment** $78.9 million
- **Coed** 12,700 undergraduate students, 72% full-time, 55% women, 45% men
- **Moderately difficult** entrance level, 71% of applicants were admitted

UNDERGRAD STUDENTS

9,178 full-time, 3,522 part-time. Students come from 39 states and territories; 156 other countries; 5% are from out of state; 15% Black or African American, non-Hispanic/Latino; 12% Hispanic/Latino; 12% Asian, non-Hispanic/Latino; 0.1% American Indian or Alaska Native, non-Hispanic/Latino; 2% Two or more races, non-Hispanic/Latino; 9% Race/ethnicity unknown; 11% international; 13% transferred in.

Freshmen

Admission: 8,453 applied, 5,981 admitted, 1,542 enrolled. ***Average high school GPA:*** 3.19. ***Test scores:*** SAT critical reading scores over 500: 57%; SAT math scores over 500: 71%; SAT critical reading scores over 600: 18%; SAT math scores over 600: 22%; SAT critical reading scores over 700: 3%; SAT math scores over 700: 3%.

Retention: 80% of full-time freshmen returned.

FACULTY

Total: 1,219, 53% full-time, 67% with terminal degrees.

Student/faculty ratio: 16:1.

ACADEMICS

Calendar: semesters. *Degrees:* certificates, bachelor's, master's, doctoral, post-master's, and postbachelor's certificates.

Special study options: academic remediation for entering students, accelerated degree program, adult/continuing education programs, advanced placement credit, cooperative education, distance learning, double majors, English as a second language, freshman honors college, honors programs, independent study, internships, off-campus study, part-time degree program, services for LD students, student-designed majors, study abroad, summer session for credit. ***ROTC:*** Army (c), Navy (c), Air Force (c).

Computers: 350 computers/terminals are available on campus for general student use. Students can access the following: computer help desk, free student e-mail accounts, online (class) grades, online (class) registration, online (class) schedules. Campuswide network is available. Wireless service is available via entire campus.

STUDENT LIFE

Housing options: college housing not available.

Activities and organizations: drama/theater group, student-run newspaper, radio station, choral group, Student Arts & Events Council, Haitian Student Association, Golden Key Honor Society, Campus Kitchens, Mass Media.

Athletics Member NCAA. All Division III. ***Intercollegiate sports:*** baseball M, basketball M/W, cross-country running M/W, ice hockey M/W, lacrosse M, soccer M/W, softball W, tennis M/W, track and field M/W, volleyball W. ***Intramural sports:*** basketball M/W, bowling M/W, football M/W, golf M/W, racquetball M/W, soccer M/W, softball M/W, volleyball M/W.

Campus security: 24-hour emergency response devices and patrols, late-night transport/escort service, crime prevention program, bicycle patrols.

Student services: health clinic, personal/psychological counseling, women's center.

COSTS & FINANCIAL AID

Costs (2014–15) ***Tuition:*** state resident $11,966 full-time; nonresident $28,390 full-time. Full-time tuition and fees vary according to program. Part-time tuition and fees vary according to program.

Financial Aid Of all full-time matriculated undergraduates who enrolled in 2012, 6,357 applied for aid, 5,628 were judged to have need, 2,793 had their need fully met. 561 Federal Work-Study jobs (averaging $3801). In 2012, 234 non-need-based awards were made. ***Average percent of need met:*** 90. ***Average financial aid package:*** $15,265. ***Average need-based loan:*** $7082. ***Average need-based gift aid:*** $8894. ***Average non-need-based aid:*** $4141. ***Average indebtedness upon graduation:*** $26,078.

APPLYING

Standardized Tests *Required:* SAT (for admission), ACT (for admission), SAT or ACT (for admission). *Recommended:* SAT and SAT Subject Tests or ACT (for admission), SAT Subject Tests (for admission).

Options: electronic application, early action, deferred entrance.

Application fee: $60.

Required: high school transcript, minimum 2.5 GPA. ***Required for some:*** essay or personal statement, minimum 2.8 GPA, interview. ***Recommended:*** essay or personal statement.

Application deadlines: 4/1 (freshmen), 6/15 (transfers).

Notification: continuous (freshmen), continuous (transfers).

CONTACT

Mr. John Drew, Director of Undergraduate Admissions, University of Massachusetts Boston, 100 Morrissey Boulevard, Boston, MA 02125-3393. *Phone:* 617-287-6000. *Fax:* 617-287-5999. *E-mail:* enrollment.info@umb.edu.

See previous page for display ad and page 1678 for the College Close-Up.

University of Massachusetts Dartmouth

North Dartmouth, Massachusetts

http://www.umassd.edu/

- **State-supported** university, founded 1895, part of University of Massachusetts
- **Suburban** 710-acre campus with easy access to Boston, Providence
- **Endowment** $49.0 million
- **Coed** 7,454 undergraduate students, 85% full-time, 48% women, 52% men
- **Moderately difficult** entrance level, 77% of applicants were admitted

UNDERGRAD STUDENTS

6,361 full-time, 1,093 part-time. Students come from 31 states and territories; 44 other countries; 5% are from out of state; 12% Black or African American, non-Hispanic/Latino; 8% Hispanic/Latino; 3% Asian, non-Hispanic/Latino; 0.2% American Indian or Alaska Native, non-Hispanic/Latino; 3% Two or more races, non-Hispanic/Latino; 7% Race/ethnicity unknown; 2% international; 7% transferred in; 55% live on campus.

Freshmen

Admission: 7,472 applied, 5,740 admitted, 1,509 enrolled. ***Average high school GPA:*** 3.15. ***Test scores:*** SAT critical reading scores over 500: 53%; SAT math scores over 500: 65%; SAT writing scores over 500: 47%; ACT scores over 18: 83%; SAT critical reading scores over 600: 14%; SAT math scores over 600: 19%; SAT writing scores over 600: 10%; ACT scores over 24: 31%; SAT critical reading scores over 700: 1%; SAT math scores over 700: 1%; SAT writing scores over 700: 1%; ACT scores over 30: 1%.

Retention: 79% of full-time freshmen returned.

FACULTY

Total: 594, 64% full-time, 66% with terminal degrees.

Student/faculty ratio: 19:1.

ACADEMICS
Calendar: semesters. *Degrees:* certificates, bachelor's, master's, doctoral, post-master's, and postbachelor's certificates.

Special study options: academic remediation for entering students, advanced placement credit, cooperative education, distance learning, double majors, honors programs, independent study, internships, off-campus study, part-time degree program, services for LD students, study abroad, summer session for credit. ***ROTC:*** Army (c).

Unusual degree programs: 3-2 Liberal Arts BA/MAT.

Computers: 368 computers/terminals and 5,000 ports are available on campus for general student use. Students can access the following: campus intranet, computer help desk, free student e-mail accounts, online (class) grades, online (class) registration, online (class) schedules. Campuswide network is available. 100% of college-owned or -operated housing units are wired for high-speed Internet access. Wireless service is available via classrooms, computer centers, computer labs, learning centers, libraries, student centers.

STUDENT LIFE
Housing options: coed, special housing for students with disabilities. Campus housing is university owned.

Activities and organizations: drama/theater group, student-run newspaper, radio station, choral group, Outdoor Club, Ski & Snowboard Club, DECA, Relay for Life, Model UN, national fraternities, national sororities.

Athletics Member NCAA. All Division III. ***Intercollegiate sports:*** baseball M, basketball M/W, cross-country running M/W, equestrian sports W(c), field hockey W, football M, golf M, ice hockey M, lacrosse M/W, sailing W, soccer M/W, softball W, swimming and diving M/W, tennis M/W, track and field M/W, volleyball W. ***Intramural sports:*** badminton M/W, basketball M/W, rugby M/W, skiing (downhill) M(c)/W(c), soccer M/W, table tennis M/W, tennis M/W, ultimate Frisbee M/W, volleyball M/W, water polo M.

Campus security: 24-hour emergency response devices and patrols, student patrols, late-night transport/escort service, controlled dormitory access.

Student services: health clinic, personal/psychological counseling, women's center, legal services.

COSTS & FINANCIAL AID
Costs (2014–15) ***One-time required fee:*** $100. ***Tuition:*** state resident $1417 full-time, $59 per credit part-time; nonresident $8099 full-time, $337 per credit part-time. Full-time tuition and fees vary according to class time and reciprocity agreements. Part-time tuition and fees vary according to class time, course load, and reciprocity agreements. Out-of-state mandatory fees $16,520. ***Required fees:*** $10,264 full-time, $428 per credit part-time. ***Room and board:*** $11,435; room only: $7247. Room and board charges vary according to board plan and housing facility. ***Payment plan:*** installment. ***Waivers:*** senior citizens and employees or children of employees.

Financial Aid Of all full-time matriculated undergraduates who enrolled in 2014, 5,451 applied for aid, 4,607 were judged to have need, 2,337 had their need fully met. 1,150 Federal Work-Study jobs (averaging $1304). In 2014, 391 non-need-based awards were made. ***Average percent of need met:*** 90. ***Average financial aid package:*** $16,379. ***Average need-based loan:*** $4157. ***Average need-based gift aid:*** $9550. ***Average non-need-based aid:*** $4542. ***Average indebtedness upon graduation:*** $31,070.

APPLYING
Standardized Tests *Required:* SAT or ACT (for admission).

Options: electronic application, early admission, early action, deferred entrance.

Application fee: $60.

Required: high school transcript, minimum 3.0 GPA. ***Recommended:*** essay or personal statement, 1 letter of recommendation.

Application deadlines: rolling (freshmen), rolling (transfers), 11/15 (early action).

Notification: continuous (freshmen), continuous (transfers), 12/15 (early action).

CONTACT
University of Massachusetts Dartmouth, 285 Old Westport Road, North Dartmouth, MA 02747-2300. *Phone:* 508-999-8605. *Fax:* 508-999-8755. *E-mail:* admissions@umassd.edu.

See previous page for display ad and page 1680 for the College Close-Up.

★ University of Massachusetts Lowell
Lowell, Massachusetts
http://www.uml.edu/

- **State-supported** university, founded 1894, part of University of Massachusetts
- **Urban** 100-acre campus with easy access to Boston
- **Endowment** $78.4 million
- **Coed** 12,986 undergraduate students, 73% full-time, 38% women, 62% men
- **Moderately difficult** entrance level, 62% of applicants were admitted

UNDERGRAD STUDENTS
9,443 full-time, 3,543 part-time. Students come from 37 states and territories; 64 other countries; 10% are from out of state; 6% Black or African American, non-Hispanic/Latino; 9% Hispanic/Latino; 8% Asian, non-Hispanic/Latino; 0.2% American Indian or Alaska Native, non-Hispanic/Latino; 3% Two or more races, non-Hispanic/Latino; 5% Race/ethnicity unknown; 2% international; 9% transferred in; 38% live on campus.

Freshmen
Admission: 9,394 applied, 5,825 admitted, 1,642 enrolled. ***Average high school GPA:*** 3.43. ***Test scores:*** SAT critical reading scores over 500: 84%; SAT math scores over 500: 91%; SAT writing scores over 500: 72%; ACT scores over 18: 98%; SAT critical reading scores over 600: 29%; SAT math scores over 600: 46%; SAT writing scores over 600: 24%; ACT scores over 24: 66%; SAT critical reading scores over 700: 4%; SAT math scores over 700: 7%; SAT writing scores over 700: 3%; ACT scores over 30: 13%.

Retention: 84% of full-time freshmen returned.

FACULTY
Total: 1,043, 53% full-time, 65% with terminal degrees.

Student/faculty ratio: 18:1.

ACADEMICS
Calendar: semesters. *Degrees:* certificates, associate, bachelor's, master's, doctoral, post-master's, and postbachelor's certificates.

Special study options: accelerated degree program, adult/continuing education programs, advanced placement credit, cooperative education, distance learning, double majors, honors programs, independent study, internships, off-campus study, part-time degree program, services for LD students, study abroad, summer session for credit. ***ROTC:*** Army (b), Air Force (b).

Computers: 450 computers/terminals and 4,100 ports are available on campus for general student use. Students can access the following: campus intranet, computer help desk, free student e-mail accounts, online (class) grades, online (class) registration, online (class) schedules. Campuswide network is available. 100% of college-owned or -operated housing units are wired for high-speed Internet access. Wireless service is available via entire campus.

STUDENT LIFE
Housing options: coed. Campus housing is university owned and leased by the school.

Activities and organizations: drama/theater group, student-run newspaper, radio station, choral group, marching band, Student Government Association, Recreational Sports Club, Association of Students of African Origin, WUML (radio station), Campus Activities Programming Association, national fraternities, national sororities.

Athletics Member NCAA. All Division I. ***Intercollegiate sports:*** baseball M(s), basketball M(s)/W(s), cross-country running M(s)/W(s), field hockey W(s), golf M(s), ice hockey M(s), lacrosse M(s)/W(s), soccer M(s)/W(s), softball W(s), track and field M(s)/W(s), volleyball W(s). ***Intramural sports:*** badminton M/W, basketball M/W, cheerleading M(c)/W(c), crew M(c)/W(c), cross-country running M(c)/W(c), field hockey W(c), football M/W, golf M(c)/W(c), ice hockey M(c)/W(c), lacrosse M(c)/W(c), racquetball M/W, rock climbing M/W, rugby M(c)/W(c), skiing (cross-country) M/W, skiing (downhill) M/W, soccer M/W, softball M/W, squash M/W, swimming and diving M(c)/W(c), table tennis M/W, tennis M(c)/W(c), track and field M(c)/W(c), ultimate Frisbee M(c)/W(c), volleyball M(c)/W(c), weight lifting M/W.

Campus security: 24-hour emergency response devices and patrols, student patrols, late-night transport/escort service, controlled dormitory access.

Student services: health clinic, personal/psychological counseling.

COSTS & FINANCIAL AID

Costs (2014–15) ***One-time required fee:*** $200. ***Tuition:*** state resident $1454 full-time, $61 per credit hour part-time; nonresident $8567 full-time, $357 per credit hour part-time. Part-time tuition and fees vary according to course load. ***Required fees:*** $10,993 full-time, $458 per credit hour part-time. ***Room and board:*** $11,278; room only: $7450. Room and board charges vary according to board plan and housing facility. ***Payment plan:*** installment. ***Waivers:*** senior citizens and employees or children of employees.

Financial Aid Of all full-time matriculated undergraduates who enrolled in 2012, 6,878 applied for aid, 5,522 were judged to have need, 2,935 had their need fully met. 176 Federal Work-Study jobs (averaging $2024). 621 state and other part-time jobs (averaging $3218). In 2012, 599 non-need-based awards were made. ***Average percent of need met:*** 91. ***Average financial aid package:*** $13,921. ***Average need-based loan:*** $7215. ***Average need-based gift aid:*** $7604. ***Average non-need-based aid:*** $4097. ***Average indebtedness upon graduation:*** $28,482.

APPLYING

Standardized Tests *Required:* SAT or ACT (for admission).

Options: electronic application, early action, deferred entrance.

Application fee: $60.

Required: essay or personal statement, high school transcript, minimum 3.0 GPA, 1 letter of recommendation. ***Required for some:*** audition for music students, art portfolio for art majors.

Application deadlines: 2/15 (freshmen), 2/15 (out-of-state freshmen), 8/15 (transfers), 11/15 (early action).

Notification: continuous (freshmen), continuous (out-of-state freshmen), continuous (transfers), rolling (early action).

CONTACT

Admissions Office, University of Massachusetts Lowell, University Crossing, Suite 420, 220 Pawtucket Street, Lowell, MA 01854-2874. *Phone:* 978-934-3931. *Fax:* 978-934-3086. *E-mail:* admissions@uml.edu.

See below for display ad and page 1682 for the College Close-Up.

Wellesley College

Wellesley, Massachusetts

http://www.wellesley.edu/

- **Independent** 4-year, founded 1870
- **Suburban** 500-acre campus with easy access to Boston
- **Endowment** $1.6 billion
- **Women only**
- **Most difficult** entrance level

FACULTY

Student/faculty ratio: 7:1.

ACADEMICS

Calendar: semesters. *Degrees:* bachelor's (double bachelor's degree with Massachusetts Institute of Technology).

STUDENT LIFE

Housing options: women-only, cooperative. Campus housing is university owned. Freshman campus housing is guaranteed.

Activities and organizations: drama/theater group, student-run newspaper, radio and television station, choral group, student government, community service organizations, cultural clubs, societies, theater groups.

Athletics Member NCAA. All Division III.

Campus security: 24-hour emergency response devices and patrols, late-night transport/escort service, controlled dormitory access.

Student services: health clinic, personal/psychological counseling, women's center.

COSTS & FINANCIAL AID

Costs (2014–15) ***Comprehensive fee:*** $59,038 includes full-time tuition ($44,802), mandatory fees ($276), and room and board ($13,960). Part-time tuition: $5411 per course. Part-time tuition and fees vary according to course load. ***College room only:*** $7086. ***Payment plans:*** tuition prepayment, installment.

Financial Aid Of all full-time matriculated undergraduates who enrolled in 2014, 1,532 applied for aid, 1,392 were judged to have need, 1,392 had their need fully met. 856 Federal Work-Study jobs (averaging $2022). 311 state and other part-time jobs (averaging $2070). ***Average percent of need met:*** 100. ***Average financial aid package:*** $42,400. ***Average need-based loan:*** $3352. ***Average need-based gift aid:*** $39,988. ***Average indebtedness upon graduation:*** $12,956.

APPLYING

Standardized Tests *Required:* SAT and SAT Subject Tests or ACT (for admission).

Options: electronic application, early admission, early decision, deferred entrance.

Required: essay or personal statement, high school transcript, 3 letters of recommendation, first senior marking period grades and mid-year report. ***Required for some:*** interview. ***Recommended:*** interview.

CONTACT

Director of Admission, Wellesley College, 106 Central Street, Wellesley, MA 02481. *Phone:* 781-283-2270. *Fax:* 781-283-3678. *E-mail:* admission@wellesley.edu.

★ Wentworth Institute of Technology

Boston, Massachusetts

http://www.wit.edu/

- **Independent** comprehensive, founded 1904
- **Urban** 31-acre campus
- **Endowment** $81.9 million
- **Coed** 4,329 undergraduate students, 89% full-time, 19% women, 81% men
- **Moderately difficult** entrance level, 83% of applicants were admitted

UNDERGRAD STUDENTS

3,871 full-time, 458 part-time. Students come from 30 states and territories; 53 other countries; 37% are from out of state; 5% Black or African American, non-Hispanic/Latino; 3% Hispanic/Latino; 7% Asian, non-Hispanic/Latino; 0.2% American Indian or Alaska Native, non-Hispanic/Latino; 6% Two or more races, non-Hispanic/Latino; 13% Race/ethnicity unknown; 6% international; 4% transferred in; 51% live on campus.

Freshmen

Admission: 5,316 applied, 4,393 admitted, 1,085 enrolled. ***Average high school GPA:*** 3.05. ***Test scores:*** SAT critical reading scores over 500: 69%; SAT math scores over 500: 87%; SAT writing scores over 500: 62%; ACT scores over 18: 98%; SAT critical reading scores over 600: 20%; SAT math scores over 600: 41%; SAT writing scores over 600: 17%; ACT scores over 24: 62%; SAT critical reading scores over 700: 3%; SAT math scores over 700: 6%; SAT writing scores over 700: 1%; ACT scores over 30: 10%.

Retention: 85% of full-time freshmen returned.

FACULTY

Total: 355, 43% full-time, 24% with terminal degrees.

Student/faculty ratio: 16:1.

ACADEMICS

Calendar: semesters for freshmen and sophomores, trimesters for juniors and seniors. *Degrees:* certificates, associate, bachelor's, and master's.

Special study options: academic remediation for entering students, advanced placement credit, cooperative education, internships, off-campus study, part-time degree program, services for LD students, study abroad, summer session for credit. ***ROTC:*** Army (c), Air Force (c).

Computers: 320 computers/terminals and 200 ports are available on campus for general student use. Students can access the following: campus intranet, computer help desk, free student e-mail accounts, online (class) grades, online (class) registration, online (class) schedules. Campuswide network is available. 100% of college-owned or -operated housing units are wired for high-speed Internet access. Wireless service is available via entire campus.

STUDENT LIFE

Housing options: on-campus residence required through sophomore year; coed. Campus housing is university owned. Freshman campus housing is guaranteed.

Activities and organizations: student-run radio station, Intramural Sports, Wentworth Events Board, Multicultural Student Association, Phi Sigma Pi, Major Particular Professional Student Associations.

Athletics Member NCAA. All Division III. ***Intercollegiate sports:*** baseball M, basketball M/W, crew M, cross-country running M, golf M, ice hockey M, lacrosse M/W, rugby M(c)/W(c), soccer M/W, softball W, tennis M/W, ultimate Frisbee M(c)/W(c), volleyball M/W.

Campus security: 24-hour emergency response devices and patrols, student patrols, late-night transport/escort service, controlled dormitory access.

Student services: health clinic, personal/psychological counseling, women's center.

COSTS

Costs (2014–15) ***Comprehensive fee:*** $43,605 includes full-time tuition ($29,320), mandatory fees ($1445), and room and board ($12,840). Part-time tuition: $915 per credit hour. Part-time tuition and fees vary according to course load and degree level. ***Required fees:*** $465 per credit hour part-time. ***Room and board:*** Room and board charges vary according to board plan and housing facility. ***Payment plan:*** installment. ***Waivers:*** employees or children of employees.

APPLYING

Standardized Tests *Required:* SAT or ACT (for admission).

Options: electronic application, deferred entrance.

Application fee: $50.

Required: essay or personal statement, high school transcript, 1 letter of recommendation. ***Recommended:*** minimum 2.0 GPA, interview.

Application deadlines: 2/15 (freshmen), 2/15 (out-of-state freshmen), 5/1 (transfers).

Notification: continuous (freshmen), continuous (transfers).

CONTACT

Ms. Amy Dufour, Senior Associate Director of Admissions, Wentworth Institute of Technology, 550 Huntington Avenue, Boston, MA 02115. *Phone:* 617-989-4116. *Toll-free phone:* 800-556-0610. *Fax:* 617-989-4010. *E-mail:* dufoura@wit.edu.

See previous page for display ad and page 1726 for the College Close-Up.

Western New England University

Springfield, Massachusetts

http://www.wne.edu/

- **Independent** comprehensive, founded 1919
- **Suburban** 215-acre campus
- **Endowment** $64.8 million
- **Coed** 2,732 undergraduate students, 94% full-time, 40% women, 60% men
- **Moderately difficult** entrance level, 80% of applicants were admitted

UNDERGRAD STUDENTS

2,576 full-time, 156 part-time. Students come from 33 states and territories; 17 other countries; 52% are from out of state; 6% Black or African American, non-Hispanic/Latino; 8% Hispanic/Latino; 3% Asian, non-Hispanic/Latino; 0.1% Native Hawaiian or other Pacific Islander, non-Hispanic/Latino; 0.2% American Indian or Alaska Native, non-Hispanic/Latino; 1% Two or more races, non-Hispanic/Latino; 5% Race/ethnicity unknown; 3% international; 5% transferred in; 66% live on campus.

Freshmen

Admission: 6,216 applied, 4,982 admitted, 757 enrolled. ***Average high school GPA:*** 3.3. ***Test scores:*** SAT critical reading scores over 500: 62%; SAT math scores over 500: 75%; ACT scores over 18: 99%; SAT critical reading scores over 600: 16%; SAT math scores over 600: 26%; ACT scores over 24: 58%; SAT critical reading scores over 700: 1%; SAT math scores over 700: 3%; ACT scores over 30: 1%.

Retention: 75% of full-time freshmen returned.

FACULTY

Total: 352, 65% full-time.

Student/faculty ratio: 12:1.

ACADEMICS

Calendar: semesters. *Degrees:* certificates, associate, bachelor's, master's, doctoral, and postbachelor's certificates.

Special study options: accelerated degree program, adult/continuing education programs, advanced placement credit, distance learning, double majors, English as a second language, honors programs, independent study, internships, off-campus study, part-time degree program, services for LD students, student-designed majors, study abroad, summer session for credit. ***ROTC:*** Army (b), Air Force (c).

Unusual degree programs: 3-2 business administration; engineering.

Computers: 530 computers/terminals are available on campus for general student use. Students can access the following: computer help desk, free student e-mail accounts, online (class) grades, online (class) registration, online (class) schedules. Campuswide network is available. 100% of college-owned or -operated housing units are wired for high-speed Internet access. Wireless service is available via entire campus.

STUDENT LIFE

Housing options: coed, special housing for students with disabilities. Campus housing is university owned. Freshman campus housing is guaranteed.

Activities and organizations: drama/theater group, student-run newspaper, radio and television station, choral group, Student Senate, Residence Hall Association, Campus Activities Board, student radio station, The Westerner (student newspaper).

Athletics Member NCAA. All Division III. ***Intercollegiate sports:*** baseball M, basketball M/W, cross-country running M/W, field hockey W, football M, golf M, ice hockey M, lacrosse M/W, soccer M/W, softball W, swimming and diving W, tennis M/W, volleyball W, wrestling M. ***Intramural sports:*** badminton M/W, basketball M/W, bowling M(c)/W(c), football M/W, rock climbing M/W, rugby M(c), soccer M/W, softball M/W, table tennis M/W, ultimate Frisbee M/W, volleyball M/W, water polo M/W.

Campus security: 24-hour emergency response devices and patrols, student patrols, late-night transport/escort service, controlled dormitory access, security cameras.

Student services: health clinic, personal/psychological counseling.

COSTS & FINANCIAL AID

Costs (2014–15) ***Comprehensive fee:*** $46,154 includes full-time tuition ($31,200), mandatory fees ($2266), and room and board ($12,688). Full-time tuition and fees vary according to course load and program. Part-time tuition: $588 per credit hour. Part-time tuition and fees vary according to course load and program. ***Room and board:*** Room and board charges vary according to board plan and housing facility. ***Payment plans:*** tuition prepayment, installment. ***Waivers:*** senior citizens and employees or children of employees.

Financial Aid Of all full-time matriculated undergraduates who enrolled in 2014, 2,474 applied for aid, 2,053 were judged to have need, 224 had their need fully met. 894 Federal Work-Study jobs (averaging $1548). 590 state and other part-time jobs (averaging $1068). In 2014, 376 non-need-based awards were made. ***Average percent of need met:*** 70. ***Average financial aid package:*** $23,667. ***Average need-based loan:*** $4184. ***Average need-based gift aid:*** $18,377. ***Average non-need-based aid:*** $11,817.

APPLYING

Standardized Tests *Required:* SAT or ACT (for admission).

Options: electronic application, early admission, deferred entrance.

Application fee: $40.

Required: high school transcript, 1 letter of recommendation. ***Recommended:*** essay or personal statement, interview.

Application deadlines: rolling (freshmen), rolling (transfers).

Notification: continuous (freshmen), continuous (transfers).

CONTACT

Mr. Bryan Gross, Vice President for Enrollment Management, Western New England University, 1215 Wilbraham Road, Springfield, MA 01119. *Phone:* 413-782-1321. *Toll-free phone:* 800-325-1122 Ext. 1321. *Fax:* 413-782-1777. *E-mail:* learn@wne.edu.

Westfield State University

Westfield, Massachusetts

http://www.wsc.ma.edu/

- **State-supported** comprehensive, founded 1838, part of Massachusetts Public Higher Education System
- **Suburban** 256-acre campus
- **Coed** 5,590 undergraduate students, 87% full-time, 53% women, 47% men
- **Moderately difficult** entrance level, 75% of applicants were admitted

UNDERGRAD STUDENTS

4,890 full-time, 700 part-time. Students come from 26 states and territories; 7 other countries; 8% are from out of state; 4% Black or African American, non-Hispanic/Latino; 8% Hispanic/Latino; 1% Asian, non-Hispanic/Latino; 0.1% Native Hawaiian or other Pacific Islander, non-Hispanic/Latino; 0.2% American Indian or Alaska Native, non-Hispanic/Latino; 4% Two or more races, non-Hispanic/Latino; 3% Race/ethnicity unknown; 0.3% international; 8% transferred in; 54% live on campus.

Freshmen

Admission: 5,163 applied, 3,848 admitted, 1,224 enrolled. ***Average high school GPA:*** 3.1. ***Test scores:*** SAT critical reading scores over 500: 48%; SAT math scores over 500: 57%; SAT writing scores over 500: 45%; ACT scores over 18: 76%; SAT critical reading scores over 600: 9%; SAT math scores over 600: 11%; SAT writing scores over 600: 8%; ACT scores over 24: 24%; SAT critical reading scores over 700: 1%; SAT math scores over 700: 1%; SAT writing scores over 700: 1%; ACT scores over 30: 3%.

Retention: 77% of full-time freshmen returned.

FACULTY

Total: 482, 48% full-time, 51% with terminal degrees.

Student/faculty ratio: 16:1.

ACADEMICS

Calendar: semesters. *Degrees:* bachelor's, master's, post-master's, and postbachelor's certificates.

Special study options: adult/continuing education programs, advanced placement credit, distance learning, double majors, honors programs, independent study, internships, off-campus study, part-time degree program, services for LD students, student-designed majors, study abroad, summer session for credit. ***ROTC:*** Army (c), Air Force (c).

Computers: 642 computers/terminals are available on campus for general student use. Students can access the following: computer help desk, free student e-mail accounts, online (class) grades, online (class) registration, online (class) schedules, online transcripts and billing information, web portal. Campuswide network is available. 100% of college-owned or -operated housing units are wired for high-speed Internet access. Wireless service is available via entire campus.

STUDENT LIFE

Housing options: coed, special housing for students with disabilities. Campus housing is university owned. Freshman applicants given priority for college housing.

Activities and organizations: drama/theater group, student-run newspaper, radio and television station, choral group, Student National Education Association, Student Government Association, Campus Activities Board, The Dance Company, Multicultural Student Association.

Athletics Member NCAA. All Division III. ***Intercollegiate sports:*** baseball M, basketball M/W, cheerleading W, cross-country running M/W, field hockey W, football M, golf M/W, ice hockey M, lacrosse W, soccer M/W, softball W, swimming and diving W, track and field M/W, volleyball W. ***Intramural sports:*** basketball M, equestrian sports M(c)/W(c), football M/W, ice hockey M(c)/W(c), lacrosse M(c), rugby M(c)/W(c), soccer M/W, softball M, table tennis M/W, ultimate Frisbee M(c)/W(c), volleyball M/W.

Campus security: 24-hour emergency response devices and patrols, student patrols, late-night transport/escort service, controlled dormitory access.

Student services: health clinic, personal/psychological counseling, legal services.

COSTS & FINANCIAL AID

Costs (2014–15) ***Tuition:*** state resident $970 full-time, $260 per credit hour part-time; nonresident $7050 full-time, $260 per credit hour part-time. Full-time tuition and fees vary according to program and reciprocity agreements. Part-time tuition and fees vary according to course load. ***Required fees:*** $7712 full-time, $75 per term part-time. ***Room and board:*** $10,236. Room and board charges vary according to board plan and housing facility. ***Payment plan:*** installment. ***Waivers:*** senior citizens and employees or children of employees.

Financial Aid Of all full-time matriculated undergraduates who enrolled in 2013, 4,549 applied for aid, 3,083 were judged to have need, 185 had their need fully met. 332 Federal Work-Study jobs (averaging $1304). In 2013, 85 non-need-based awards were made. ***Average percent of need met:*** 66. ***Average financial aid package:*** $6893. ***Average need-based loan:*** $4047. ***Average need-based gift aid:*** $4621. ***Average non-need-based aid:*** $3277. ***Average indebtedness upon graduation:*** $26,326.

APPLYING

Standardized Tests *Required:* SAT or ACT (for admission).

Options: electronic application, deferred entrance.

Application fee: $50.

Required: high school transcript, minimum 3.0 GPA. ***Required for some:*** interview, audition for music major, portfolio for art major, essay and interview may be required of nursing majors, also sliding scale minimum high school GPA using SAT/ACT scores for GPAs between 2.0 and 3.0.

Application deadlines: 3/1 (freshmen), 3/1 (out-of-state freshmen), 3/1 (transfers).

Notification: continuous until 3/15 (freshmen), continuous until 3/15 (out-of-state freshmen), continuous until 3/15 (transfers).

CONTACT

Dr. Kelly Hart, Director of Admissions, Westfield State University, 333 Western Avenue, Westfield, MA 01002. *Phone:* 413-572-5218. *Fax:* 413-572-0520. *E-mail:* admission@westfield.ma.edu.

Wheaton College

Norton, Massachusetts

http://www.wheatoncollege.edu/

- **Independent** 4-year, founded 1834
- **Suburban** 400-acre campus with easy access to Boston
- **Endowment** $193.5 million
- **Coed** 1,587 undergraduate students, 99% full-time, 64% women, 36% men
- **Very difficult** entrance level, 70% of applicants were admitted

UNDERGRAD STUDENTS

1,577 full-time, 10 part-time. Students come from 41 states and territories; 42 other countries; 66% are from out of state; 6% Black or African American, non-Hispanic/Latino; 7% Hispanic/Latino; 4% Asian, non-Hispanic/Latino; 0.1% Native Hawaiian or other Pacific Islander, non-Hispanic/Latino; 0.1% American Indian or Alaska Native, non-Hispanic/Latino; 3% Two or more races, non-Hispanic/Latino; 2% Race/ethnicity unknown; 10% international; 0.4% transferred in; 96% live on campus.

Freshmen

Admission: 4,047 applied, 2,818 admitted, 423 enrolled. ***Average high school GPA:*** 3.33. ***Test scores:*** SAT critical reading scores over 500: 94%; SAT math scores over 500: 91%; SAT writing scores over 500: 92%; ACT scores over 18: 98%; SAT critical reading scores over 600: 57%; SAT math scores over 600: 55%; SAT writing scores over 600: 58%; ACT scores over 24: 85%; SAT critical reading scores over 700: 15%; SAT math scores over 700: 12%; SAT writing scores over 700: 15%; ACT scores over 30: 15%.

Retention: 83% of full-time freshmen returned.

FACULTY
Total: 188, 70% full-time, 78% with terminal degrees.

Student/faculty ratio: 10:1.

ACADEMICS
Calendar: semesters. *Degree:* bachelor's.

Special study options: advanced placement credit, cooperative education, double majors, English as a second language, external degree program, honors programs, independent study, internships, off-campus study, services for LD students, student-designed majors, study abroad, summer session for credit. ***ROTC:*** Army (c).

Unusual degree programs: 3-2 engineering with Thayer School of Engineering, Dartmouth College; Theology with Andover Newton Theological School, Optometry with New England School of Optometry, Integrated Marketing Communication Studies with Emerson College, Clark University Graduate School of Management.

Computers: 253 computers/terminals are available on campus for general student use. Students can access the following: campus intranet, computer help desk, free student e-mail accounts, online (class) grades, online (class) registration, online (class) schedules, assistive technology; online software training; media equipment loan program. Campuswide network is available. 100% of college-owned or -operated housing units are wired for high-speed Internet access. Wireless service is available via entire campus.

STUDENT LIFE
Housing options: on-campus residence required through senior year; coed, men-only, women-only, special housing for students with disabilities. Campus housing is university owned. Freshman campus housing is guaranteed.

Activities and organizations: drama/theater group, student-run newspaper, radio station, choral group, Student Government Association, Community Service Council, Amnesty International, Acappella singing groups, Programming Council.

Athletics Member NCAA. All Division III. ***Intercollegiate sports:*** baseball M, basketball M/W, cross-country running M/W, field hockey W, lacrosse M/W, soccer M/W, softball W, swimming and diving M/W, tennis M/W, track and field M/W, volleyball W. ***Intramural sports:*** archery M(c)/W, badminton M/W, basketball M/W, equestrian sports M(c)/W(c), fencing M/W, field hockey W(c), golf M(c)/W(c), ice hockey M(c)/W(c), rugby M(c)/W(c), sailing M(c)/W(c), soccer M/W, softball M/W, tennis M/W, ultimate Frisbee M(c)/W(c), volleyball M/W, wrestling M(c)/W(c).

Campus security: 24-hour emergency response devices and patrols, student patrols, late-night transport/escort service, controlled dormitory access.

Student services: health clinic, personal/psychological counseling, women's center.

COSTS & FINANCIAL AID
Costs (2014–15) ***Comprehensive fee:*** $58,263 includes full-time tuition ($46,120), mandatory fees ($303), and room and board ($11,840). Part-time tuition: $1441 per credit hour. ***College room only:*** $6320. ***Payment plans:*** tuition prepayment, installment. ***Waivers:*** employees or children of employees.

Financial Aid Of all full-time matriculated undergraduates who enrolled in 2014, 1,171 applied for aid, 1,022 were judged to have need, 466 had their need fully met. 771 Federal Work-Study jobs (averaging $1670). 321 state and other part-time jobs (averaging $1650). In 2014, 403 non-need-based awards were made. ***Average percent of need met:*** 92. ***Average financial aid package:*** $36,699. ***Average need-based loan:*** $4969. ***Average need-based gift aid:*** $31,090. ***Average non-need-based aid:*** $12,486. ***Average indebtedness upon graduation:*** $29,651. ***Financial aid deadline:*** 2/1.

APPLYING
Standardized Tests *Recommended:* SAT or ACT (for admission).

Options: electronic application, early admission, early decision, early action, deferred entrance.

Application fee: $50.

Required: essay or personal statement, high school transcript, 2 letters of recommendation. ***Recommended:*** interview.

Application deadlines: 1/15 (freshmen), 1/15 (out-of-state freshmen), 4/1 (transfers), 11/15 (early action).

Early decision deadline: 11/15.

Notification: 4/1 (freshmen), 4/1 (out-of-state freshmen), 5/1 (transfers), 12/15 (early decision), 1/1 (early action).

CONTACT
Grant M. Gosselin, Vice President for Enrollment and Dean of Admission and Student Aid, Wheaton College, 26 East Main Street, Norton, MA 02766. *Phone:* 508-286-8251. *Toll-free phone:* 800-394-6003. *Fax:* 508-286-8271. *E-mail:* admission@wheatoncollege.edu.

Wheelock College

Boston, Massachusetts

http://www.wheelock.edu/

- **Independent** comprehensive, founded 1888
- **Urban** 6-acre campus with easy access to Boston
- **Endowment** $43.7 million
- **Coed, primarily women** 869 undergraduate students, 96% full-time, 88% women, 12% men
- **Minimally difficult** entrance level, 88% of applicants were admitted

UNDERGRAD STUDENTS
836 full-time, 33 part-time. Students come from 27 states and territories; 15 other countries; 39% are from out of state; 11% Black or African American, non-Hispanic/Latino; 12% Hispanic/Latino; 3% Asian, non-Hispanic/Latino; 0.1% American Indian or Alaska Native, non-Hispanic/Latino; 3% Two or more races, non-Hispanic/Latino; 9% Race/ethnicity unknown; 2% international; 5% transferred in; 65% live on campus.

Freshmen
Admission: 1,458 applied, 1,276 admitted, 266 enrolled. ***Average high school GPA:*** 3.11. ***Test scores:*** SAT critical reading scores over 500: 50%; SAT math scores over 500: 43%; SAT writing scores over 500: 49%; SAT critical reading scores over 600: 14%; SAT math scores over 600: 6%; SAT writing scores over 600: 13%; SAT critical reading scores over 700: 1%; SAT writing scores over 700: 1%.

Retention: 76% of full-time freshmen returned.

FACULTY
Total: 180, 38% full-time, 47% with terminal degrees.

Student/faculty ratio: 11:1.

ACADEMICS
Calendar: semesters. *Degrees:* bachelor's, master's, and postbachelor's certificates.

Special study options: advanced placement credit, distance learning, double majors, honors programs, independent study, internships, off-campus study, part-time degree program, services for LD students, study abroad, summer session for credit.

Computers: 100 computers/terminals and 1,100 ports are available on campus for general student use. Students can access the following: campus intranet, computer help desk, free student e-mail accounts, online (class) grades, online (class) registration, online (class) schedules. Campuswide network is available. Wireless service is available via classrooms, computer labs, dorm rooms, learning centers, libraries, student centers.

STUDENT LIFE
Housing options: coed, women-only, special housing for students with disabilities. Campus housing is university owned. Freshman campus housing is guaranteed.

Activities and organizations: drama/theater group, choral group.

Athletics Member NCAA. All Division III. ***Intercollegiate sports:*** basketball M/W, cross-country running M/W, field hockey W, lacrosse M/W, soccer M/W, softball W, tennis M. ***Intramural sports:*** basketball M/W, racquetball M/W, soccer M, softball M/W, squash M/W, table tennis M/W, ultimate Frisbee M/W, volleyball M/W, water polo M/W.

Campus security: 24-hour patrols, late-night transport/escort service, controlled dormitory access.

Student services: personal/psychological counseling, women's center.

COSTS & FINANCIAL AID

Costs (2014–15) ***Comprehensive fee:*** $46,430 includes full-time tuition ($31,675), mandatory fees ($1155), and room and board ($13,600). Part-time tuition: $990 per credit hour. ***Payment plan:*** installment. ***Waivers:*** employees or children of employees.

Financial Aid Of all full-time matriculated undergraduates who enrolled in 2014, 747 applied for aid, 692 were judged to have need, 97 had their need fully met. 198 Federal Work-Study jobs (averaging $1800). In 2014, 133 non-need-based awards were made. ***Average percent of need met:*** 64. ***Average financial aid package:*** $22,967. ***Average need-based loan:*** $4010. ***Average need-based gift aid:*** $19,060. ***Average non-need-based aid:*** $13,232. ***Average indebtedness upon graduation:*** $46,690.

APPLYING

Standardized Tests *Required:* SAT or ACT (for admission).

Options: electronic application, early admission, early action, deferred entrance.

Required: essay or personal statement, high school transcript, minimum 2.0 GPA, 1 letter of recommendation. ***Recommended:*** interview.

Application deadlines: 5/1 (freshmen), 6/1 (transfers), 12/1 (early action).

Notification: continuous (freshmen), continuous (transfers), 12/20 (early action).

CONTACT

Ms. Lisa Slavin, Director of Undergraduate Admissions, Wheelock College, 200 The Riverway, Boston, MA 02215. *Phone:* 617-879-2209. *Toll-free phone:* 800-734-5212. *Fax:* 617-879-2449. *E-mail:* lslavin@wheelock.edu.

Williams College

Williamstown, Massachusetts

http://www.williams.edu/

- **Independent** comprehensive, founded 1793
- **Small-town** 450-acre campus with easy access to Albany, NY
- **Endowment** $2.1 billion
- **Coed** 2,045 undergraduate students, 99% full-time, 51% women, 49% men
- **Most difficult** entrance level, 19% of applicants were admitted

UNDERGRAD STUDENTS

2,015 full-time, 30 part-time. Students come from 49 states and territories; 54 other countries; 88% are from out of state; 7% Black or African American, non-Hispanic/Latino; 12% Hispanic/Latino; 11% Asian, non-Hispanic/Latino; 0.1% American Indian or Alaska Native, non-Hispanic/Latino; 7% Two or more races, non-Hispanic/Latino; 7% international; 0.3% transferred in; 94% live on campus.

Freshmen

Admission: 6,316 applied, 1,220 admitted, 546 enrolled. ***Test scores:*** SAT critical reading scores over 500: 100%; SAT math scores over 500: 100%; SAT writing scores over 500: 100%; ACT scores over 18: 100%; SAT critical reading scores over 600: 95%; SAT math scores over 600: 95%; SAT writing scores over 600: 97%; ACT scores over 24: 100%; SAT critical reading scores over 700: 69%; SAT math scores over 700: 65%; SAT writing scores over 700: 73%; ACT scores over 30: 82%.

Retention: 98% of full-time freshmen returned.

FACULTY

Total: 346, 80% full-time, 90% with terminal degrees.

Student/faculty ratio: 7:1.

ACADEMICS

Calendar: 4-1-4. *Degrees:* bachelor's and master's.

Special study options: double majors, independent study, internships, off-campus study, student-designed majors, study abroad. ***ROTC:*** Air Force (c).

Unusual degree programs: 3-2 engineering with Columbia University.

Computers: 252 computers/terminals are available on campus for general student use. Students can access the following: computer help desk, free student e-mail accounts, online (class) grades, online (class) registration. Campuswide network is available. 100% of college-owned or -operated housing units are wired for high-speed Internet access. Wireless service is available via entire campus.

STUDENT LIFE

Housing options: on-campus residence required for freshman year; coed, cooperative. Campus housing is university owned.

Activities and organizations: drama/theater group, student-run newspaper, radio station, choral group, marching band.

Athletics Member NCAA. All Division III except men's and women's skiing (cross-country) (Division I), men's and women's skiing (downhill) (Division I). ***Intercollegiate sports:*** baseball M, basketball M/W, crew M/W, cross-country running M/W, equestrian sports M(c)/W(c), field hockey W, football M, golf M/W(c), ice hockey M/W, lacrosse M/W, rugby M(c)/W(c), sailing M(c)/W(c), skiing (cross-country) M/W, skiing (downhill) M/W, soccer M/W, softball W, squash M/W, swimming and diving M/W, tennis M/W, track and field M/W, ultimate Frisbee M(c)/W(c), volleyball M(c)/W, water polo M(c)/W(c), wrestling M. ***Intramural sports:*** badminton M/W, baseball M(c), basketball M/W, fencing M(c)/W(c), gymnastics M(c)/W(c), ice hockey M/W, skiing (cross-country) M/W, skiing (downhill) M/W, soccer M/W, softball M/W, ultimate Frisbee M(c)/W(c), volleyball M/W, water polo M/W.

Campus security: 24-hour emergency response devices and patrols, student patrols, late-night transport/escort service, controlled dormitory access.

Student services: health clinic, personal/psychological counseling.

COSTS & FINANCIAL AID

Costs (2014–15) ***Comprehensive fee:*** $61,070 includes full-time tuition ($48,030), mandatory fees ($280), and room and board ($12,760). ***College room only:*** $6460. Room and board charges vary according to board plan. ***Payment plan:*** installment.

Financial Aid Of all full-time matriculated undergraduates who enrolled in 2014, 1,136 applied for aid, 1,001 were judged to have need, 1,001 had their need fully met. 439 Federal Work-Study jobs (averaging $1900). 467 state and other part-time jobs (averaging $1876). ***Average percent of need met:*** 100. ***Average financial aid package:*** $47,404. ***Average need-based loan:*** $2965. ***Average need-based gift aid:*** $43,689. ***Average indebtedness upon graduation:*** $12,627. ***Financial aid deadline:*** 2/1.

APPLYING

Standardized Tests *Required:* SAT and SAT Subject Tests or ACT (for admission).

Options: electronic application, early admission, early decision, deferred entrance.

Application fee: $65.

Required: essay or personal statement, high school transcript, 2 letters of recommendation.

Application deadlines: 1/1 (freshmen), 1/1 (out-of-state freshmen), 4/1 (transfers).

Early decision deadline: 11/15.

Notification: 4/7 (freshmen), 4/7 (out-of-state freshmen), 5/15 (transfers), 12/15 (early decision).

CONTACT

Mr. Richard L. Nesbitt, Director of Admission, Williams College, 33 Stetson Court, Williamstown, MA 01267. *Phone:* 413-597-2211. *Fax:* 413-597-4052. *E-mail:* admission@williams.edu.

★ Worcester Polytechnic Institute

Worcester, Massachusetts

http://www.wpi.edu/

- **Independent** university, founded 1865
- **Suburban** 80-acre campus with easy access to Boston
- **Endowment** $389.3 million
- **Coed** 4,235 undergraduate students, 97% full-time, 32% women, 68% men
- **Very difficult** entrance level, 44% of applicants were admitted

UNDERGRAD STUDENTS

4,096 full-time, 139 part-time. Students come from 52 states and territories; 68 other countries; 55% are from out of state; 2% Black or

African American, non-Hispanic/Latino; 8% Hispanic/Latino; 5% Asian, non-Hispanic/Latino; 0.1% American Indian or Alaska Native, non-Hispanic/Latino; 3% Two or more races, non-Hispanic/Latino; 7% Race/ethnicity unknown; 13% international; 1% transferred in; 49% live on campus.

Freshmen

Admission: 10,233 applied, 4,480 admitted, 1,056 enrolled. ***Average high school GPA:*** 3.8. ***Test scores:*** SAT critical reading scores over 500: 94%; SAT math scores over 500: 100%; SAT writing scores over 500: 95%; ACT scores over 18: 100%; SAT critical reading scores over 600: 63%; SAT math scores over 600: 93%; SAT writing scores over 600: 64%; ACT scores over 24: 97%; SAT critical reading scores over 700: 16%; SAT math scores over 700: 48%; SAT writing scores over 700: 15%; ACT scores over 30: 56%.

Retention: 97% of full-time freshmen returned.

FACULTY

Total: 485, 69% full-time, 78% with terminal degrees.

Student/faculty ratio: 14:1.

ACADEMICS

Calendar: 4 7-week terms. *Degrees:* bachelor's, master's, and doctoral.

Special study options: accelerated degree program, advanced placement credit, cooperative education, distance learning, double majors, English as a second language, independent study, internships, off-campus study, part-time degree program, services for LD students, student-designed majors, study abroad, summer session for credit. ***ROTC:*** Army (b), Navy (c), Air Force (b).

Computers: 500 computers/terminals and 775 ports are available on campus for general student use. Students can access the following: campus intranet, computer help desk, free student e-mail accounts, online (class) grades, online (class) registration, online (class) schedules, online course content. Campuswide network is available. 100% of college-owned or -operated housing units are wired for high-speed Internet access. Wireless service is available via entire campus.

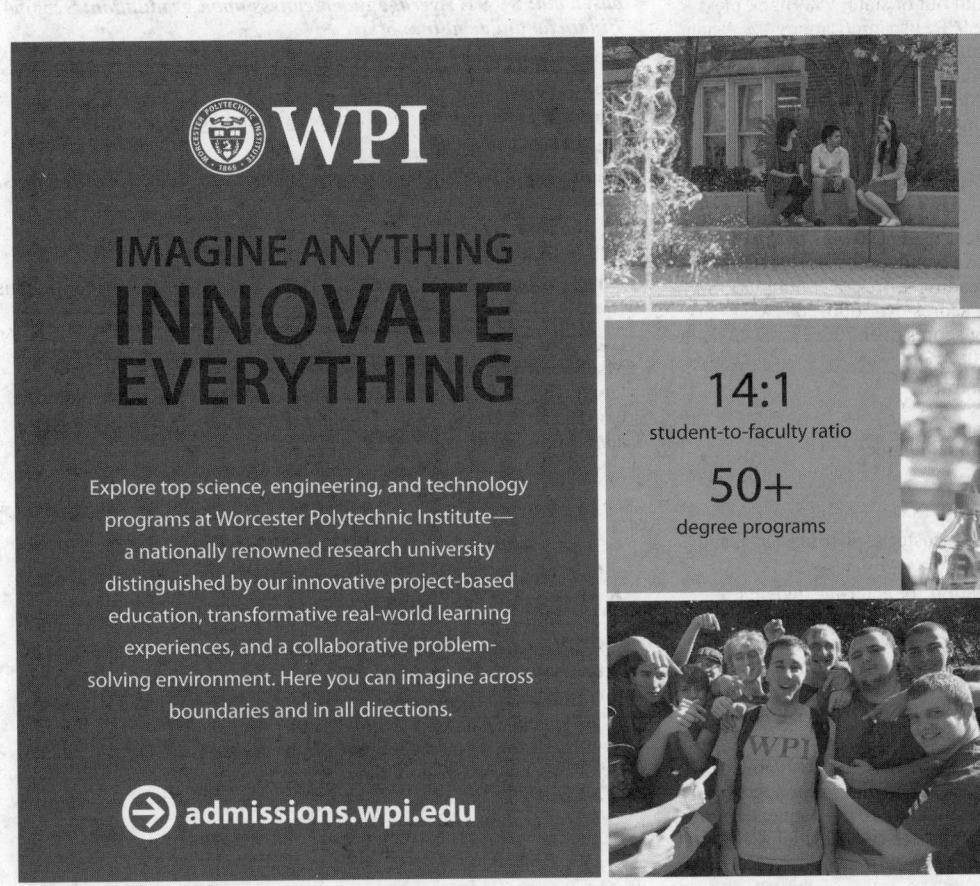

STUDENT LIFE

Housing options: coed, men-only, women-only, special housing for students with disabilities. Campus housing is university owned. Freshman campus housing is guaranteed.

Activities and organizations: drama/theater group, student-run newspaper, radio station, choral group, marching band, Student Government Association, Social Committee (Student Events Programming Board), Music Association (all music-performing groups), intramural and club sports, International Student Council, national fraternities, national sororities.

Athletics Member NCAA. All Division III. ***Intercollegiate sports:*** baseball M, basketball M/W, crew M/W, cross-country running M/W, field hockey W, football M, soccer M/W, softball W, swimming and diving M/W, track and field M/W, volleyball W, water polo M(c)/W(c), wrestling M. ***Intramural sports:*** baseball M/W, basketball M/W, cheerleading M(c)/W(c), cross-country running M(c)/W(c), fencing M(c)/W(c), golf M(c)/W(c), ice hockey M(c)/W(c), lacrosse M(c)/W(c), racquetball M/W, rugby M(c)/W(c), sailing M(c)/W(c), skiing (cross-country) M(c)/W(c), skiing (downhill) M(c)/W(c), soccer M/W, softball M/W, squash M/W, swimming and diving M/W, table tennis M/W, tennis M(c)/W(c), track and field M/W, ultimate Frisbee M(c)/W(c), volleyball M(c)/W, water polo M(c)/W(c), wrestling M(c).

Campus security: 24-hour emergency response devices and patrols, student patrols, late-night transport/escort service, controlled dormitory access.

Student services: health clinic, personal/psychological counseling.

COSTS & FINANCIAL AID

Costs (2014–15) ***One-time required fee:*** $200. ***Comprehensive fee:*** $57,304 includes full-time tuition ($43,612), mandatory fees ($610), and room and board ($13,082). Part-time tuition: $1211 per credit hour. Part-time tuition and fees vary according to course load. ***College room only:*** $7466. Room and board charges vary according to board plan and housing facility. ***Payment plans:*** tuition prepayment, installment, deferred payment. ***Waivers:*** employees or children of employees.

Financial Aid Of all full-time matriculated undergraduates who enrolled in 2013, 3,015 applied for aid, 2,676 were judged to have need, 1,204 had their need fully met. 700 Federal Work-Study jobs (averaging $951). In

2013, 1208 non-need-based awards were made. ***Average percent of need met:*** 77. ***Average financial aid package:*** $33,762. ***Average need-based loan:*** $2617. ***Average need-based gift aid:*** $21,119. ***Average non-need-based aid:*** $15,783.

APPLYING

Standardized Tests *Required for some:* SAT or ACT (for admission), IELTS or TOEFL.

Options: electronic application, early admission, early action, deferred entrance.

Application fee: $65.

Required: essay or personal statement, high school transcript, 2 letters of recommendation. ***Required for some:*** interview.

Application deadlines: 2/1 (freshmen), 4/15 (transfers), 11/1 (early action).

Notification: 4/1 (freshmen), continuous (transfers), 12/20 (early action).

CONTACT

Mrs. Jennifer A. Cluett, Interim Dean of Admissions, Worcester Polytechnic Institute, 100 Institute Road, Worcester, MA 01609-2280. *Phone:* 508-831-5286. *Fax:* 508-831-5875. *E-mail:* admissions@wpi.edu.

See previous page for display ad and page 1744 for the College Close-Up.

Worcester State University

Worcester, Massachusetts

http://www.worcester.edu/

- **State-supported** comprehensive, founded 1874, part of Massachusetts Public Higher Education System
- **Urban** 58-acre campus with easy access to Boston
- **Endowment** $23.0 million
- **Coed** 5,563 undergraduate students, 75% full-time, 60% women, 40% men
- **Moderately difficult** entrance level, 61% of applicants were admitted

UNDERGRAD STUDENTS

4,157 full-time, 1,406 part-time. Students come from 24 states and territories; 25 other countries; 3% are from out of state; 7% Black or African American, non-Hispanic/Latino; 9% Hispanic/Latino; 4% Asian, non-Hispanic/Latino; 0.1% Native Hawaiian or other Pacific Islander, non-Hispanic/Latino; 0.6% American Indian or Alaska Native, non-Hispanic/Latino; 2% Two or more races, non-Hispanic/Latino; 7% Race/ethnicity unknown; 0.8% international; 10% transferred in; 25% live on campus.

Freshmen

Admission: 4,158 applied, 2,549 admitted, 794 enrolled. ***Average high school GPA:*** 3.19. ***Test scores:*** SAT critical reading scores over 500: 48%; SAT math scores over 500: 56%; SAT writing scores over 500: 43%; ACT scores over 18: 91%; SAT critical reading scores over 600: 9%; SAT math scores over 600: 11%; SAT writing scores over 600: 7%; ACT scores over 24: 40%; SAT critical reading scores over 700: 1%; SAT math scores over 700: 1%; ACT scores over 30: 2%.

Retention: 82% of full-time freshmen returned.

FACULTY

Total: 512, 40% full-time, 45% with terminal degrees.

Student/faculty ratio: 16:1.

ACADEMICS

Calendar: semesters. *Degrees:* bachelor's, master's, post-master's, and postbachelor's certificates.

Special study options: academic remediation for entering students, accelerated degree program, adult/continuing education programs, advanced placement credit, distance learning, double majors, English as a second language, honors programs, independent study, internships, off-campus study, part-time degree program, services for LD students, study abroad, summer session for credit. ***ROTC:*** Army (c), Navy (c), Air Force (c).

Computers: 500 computers/terminals and 1,700 ports are available on campus for general student use. Students can access the following: campus intranet, computer help desk, free student e-mail accounts, online (class) grades, online (class) registration, online (class) schedules. Campuswide network is available. 100% of college-owned or -operated housing units are wired for high-speed Internet access. Wireless service is available via entire campus.

STUDENT LIFE

Housing options: coed, men-only, women-only, special housing for students with disabilities. Campus housing is university owned.

Activities and organizations: drama/theater group, student-run newspaper, radio and television station, choral group, Senate, SEC (Student Events Committee), TWA (Third World Alliance), WSCW (radio station), Dance Company/Club.

Athletics Member NCAA. All Division III. ***Intercollegiate sports:*** baseball M, basketball M/W, cheerleading W, cross-country running M/W, field hockey W, football M, golf M, ice hockey M, lacrosse W, soccer M/W, softball W, tennis W, track and field M/W, volleyball W. ***Intramural sports:*** basketball M/W, football M, lacrosse W, soccer M/W, softball W, ultimate Frisbee M/W.

Campus security: 24-hour emergency response devices and patrols, late-night transport/escort service, controlled dormitory access, well-lit campus and limited access to campus at night.

Student services: health clinic, personal/psychological counseling.

COSTS & FINANCIAL AID

Costs (2014–15) ***Tuition:*** state resident $970 full-time, $40 per credit hour part-time; nonresident $7050 full-time, $294 per credit hour part-time. Full-time tuition and fees vary according to class time, course load, degree level, and reciprocity agreements. Part-time tuition and fees vary according to class time, course load, degree level, and reciprocity agreements. ***Required fees:*** $7587 full-time. ***Room and board:*** $11,255; room only: $7735. Room and board charges vary according to board plan and housing facility. ***Payment plan:*** installment. ***Waivers:*** senior citizens and employees or children of employees.

Financial Aid Of all full-time matriculated undergraduates who enrolled in 2013, 3,479 applied for aid, 2,529 were judged to have need, 960 had their need fully met. 200 Federal Work-Study jobs (averaging $1500). In 2013, 72 non-need-based awards were made. ***Average percent of need met:*** 80. ***Average financial aid package:*** $11,055. ***Average need-based loan:*** $3151. ***Average need-based gift aid:*** $4696. ***Average non-need-based aid:*** $2691. ***Average indebtedness upon graduation:*** $25,654. ***Financial aid deadline:*** 5/1.

APPLYING

Standardized Tests *Required:* SAT or ACT (for admission).

Options: electronic application, early action, deferred entrance.

Application fee: $50.

Required: high school transcript, minimum 2.0 GPA. ***Required for some:*** essay or personal statement.

Application deadlines: 5/1 (freshmen), 5/1 (out-of-state freshmen), rolling (transfers), 11/15 (early action).

Notification: 1/2 (freshmen), 1/2 (out-of-state freshmen), continuous (transfers), 12/15 (early action).

CONTACT

Ms. Sabine Dupoux, Admissions Receptionist, Worcester State University, 486 Chandler Street, Administration Building, Worcester, MA 01602-2597. *Phone:* 508-929-8040. *Fax:* 508-929-8183. *E-mail:* admissions@worcester.edu.

MICHIGAN

Adrian College

Adrian, Michigan

http://www.adrian.edu/

- **Independent** comprehensive, founded 1859, affiliated with United Methodist Church
- **Small-town** 100-acre campus with easy access to Detroit, Toledo
- **Endowment** $27.4 million
- **Coed**
- **Moderately difficult** entrance level

FACULTY
Student/faculty ratio: 10:1.

ACADEMICS
Calendar: semesters. *Degrees:* associate, bachelor's, and master's.

STUDENT LIFE
Housing options: on-campus residence required through senior year; coed, men-only, women-only, special housing for students with disabilities. Campus housing is university owned. Freshman campus housing is guaranteed.

Activities and organizations: drama/theater group, student-run newspaper, radio station, choral group, marching band, Student Government Association, Adrian College Business Club, Circle K, Campus Activities Network, Adrian College Mortar Board, national fraternities, national sororities.

Athletics Member NCAA. All Division III.

Campus security: 24-hour patrols, student patrols, late-night transport/escort service, controlled dormitory access.

Student services: health clinic, personal/psychological counseling.

COSTS & FINANCIAL AID
Costs (2014–15) ***Comprehensive fee:*** $42,400 includes full-time tuition ($31,870), mandatory fees ($790), and room and board ($9740). Part-time tuition: $890 per credit. ***College room only:*** $4680. Room and board charges vary according to board plan and housing facility.

Financial Aid Of all full-time matriculated undergraduates who enrolled in 2013, 1,408 applied for aid, 1,332 were judged to have need, 141 had their need fully met. 1,275 Federal Work-Study jobs (averaging $1500). 75 state and other part-time jobs (averaging $1500). In 2013, 196 non-need-based awards were made. ***Average percent of need met:*** 76. ***Average financial aid package:*** $26,336. ***Average need-based loan:*** $4368. ***Average need-based gift aid:*** $21,336. ***Average non-need-based aid:*** $14,942. ***Average indebtedness upon graduation:*** $27,741.

APPLYING
Standardized Tests *Required:* SAT or ACT (for admission). *Recommended:* ACT (for admission).

Options: electronic application, deferred entrance.

Required: high school transcript, ACT or SAT. ***Required for some:*** essay or personal statement, interview.

CONTACT
Mr. Frank Hribar, Vice President for Enrollment, Adrian College, 110 S. Madison St., Adrian, MI 49221. *Phone:* 800-877-2246. *Toll-free phone:* 800-877-2246. *Fax:* 517-264-3331. *E-mail:* admissions@adrian.edu.

Albion College
Albion, Michigan
http://www.albion.edu/

- **Independent Methodist** 4-year, founded 1835
- **Small-town** 565-acre campus with easy access to Detroit
- **Endowment** $187.7 million
- **Coed** 1,268 undergraduate students, 98% full-time, 50% women, 50% men
- **Moderately difficult** entrance level, 61% of applicants were admitted

UNDERGRAD STUDENTS
1,242 full-time, 26 part-time. Students come from 19 states and territories; 18 other countries; 8% are from out of state; 4% Black or African American, non-Hispanic/Latino; 4% Hispanic/Latino; 2% Asian, non-Hispanic/Latino; 0.1% Native Hawaiian or other Pacific Islander, non-Hispanic/Latino; 0.2% American Indian or Alaska Native, non-Hispanic/Latino; 3% Two or more races, non-Hispanic/Latino; 5% Race/ethnicity unknown; 2% international; 2% transferred in; 89% live on campus.

Freshmen
Admission: 4,886 applied, 2,970 admitted, 357 enrolled. ***Average high school GPA:*** 3.49. ***Test scores:*** ACT scores over 18: 99%; ACT scores over 24: 58%; ACT scores over 30: 12%.

Retention: 84% of full-time freshmen returned.

FACULTY
Total: 144, 68% full-time, 79% with terminal degrees.

Student/faculty ratio: 11:1.

ACADEMICS
Calendar: semesters. *Degree:* bachelor's.

Special study options: advanced placement credit, double majors, honors programs, independent study, internships, off-campus study, part-time degree program, services for LD students, student-designed majors, study abroad, summer session for credit.

Unusual degree programs: 3-2 engineering with Columbia University, University of Michigan, Michigan Technological University; forestry with Duke University; nursing with Oakland University.

Computers: 185 computers/terminals and 2,000 ports are available on campus for general student use. Students can access the following: computer help desk, free student e-mail accounts, online (class) grades, online (class) registration, online (class) schedules, online student account and financial aid. Campuswide network is available. 100% of college-owned or -operated housing units are wired for high-speed Internet access. Wireless service is available via classrooms, computer centers, computer labs, dorm rooms, learning centers, libraries, student centers.

STUDENT LIFE
Housing options: on-campus residence required through senior year; coed, men-only, women-only, cooperative, special housing for students with disabilities. Campus housing is university owned. Freshman campus housing is guaranteed.

Activities and organizations: drama/theater group, student-run newspaper, radio station, choral group, marching band, Greek Life (Fraternities and Sororities), Student Senate (Student Government), Umbrella (Diversity Groups), Union Board (Programming Board), Spiritual Life (Religious Centered groups), national fraternities, national sororities.

Athletics Member NCAA. All Division III. ***Intercollegiate sports:*** baseball M, basketball M/W, cross-country running M/W, equestrian sports M/W, football M, golf M/W, lacrosse M/W, soccer M/W, softball W, swimming and diving M/W, tennis M/W, track and field M/W, volleyball W. ***Intramural sports:*** basketball M/W, cheerleading M(c)/W(c), equestrian sports M(c)/W(c), ice hockey M(c)/W(c), sailing M(c)/W(c), ultimate Frisbee M(c)/W(c), volleyball M, water polo M(c)/W(c).

Campus security: 24-hour emergency response devices and patrols, late-night transport/escort service, controlled dormitory access.

Student services: health clinic, personal/psychological counseling, women's center.

COSTS & FINANCIAL AID
Costs (2014–15) ***One-time required fee:*** $185. ***Comprehensive fee:*** $47,850 includes full-time tuition ($36,872), mandatory fees ($428), and room and board ($10,550). Full-time tuition and fees vary according to course load. Part-time tuition: $1560 per semester hour. Part-time tuition and fees vary according to course load. ***College room only:*** $5160. Room and board charges vary according to board plan and housing facility. ***Payment plans:*** installment, deferred payment. ***Waivers:*** employees or children of employees.

Financial Aid Of all full-time matriculated undergraduates who enrolled in 2014, 1,016 applied for aid, 907 were judged to have need, 191 had their need fully met. 312 Federal Work-Study jobs (averaging $1317). 68 state and other part-time jobs (averaging $955). In 2014, 331 non-need-based awards were made. ***Average percent of need met:*** 82. ***Average financial aid package:*** $29,076. ***Average need-based loan:*** $5301. ***Average need-based gift aid:*** $24,065. ***Average non-need-based aid:*** $17,458. ***Average indebtedness upon graduation:*** $37,151.

APPLYING
Standardized Tests *Required:* SAT or ACT (for admission).

Options: electronic application, early action, deferred entrance.

Required: essay or personal statement, high school transcript, minimum 2.7 GPA, 1 letter of recommendation. ***Recommended:*** interview.

Application deadlines: rolling (freshmen), rolling (out-of-state freshmen), rolling (transfers), 12/1 (early action).

Notification: continuous (freshmen), continuous (out-of-state freshmen), continuous (transfers), 1/15 (early action).

CONTACT
Shar Sanders, Admissions Assistant, Albion College, 611 East Porter Street, Albion, MI 49224-1831. *Phone:* 517-629-0466. *Toll-free phone:* 800-858-6770. *Fax:* 517-629-0569. *E-mail:* ssanders@albion.edu.

Alma College

Alma, Michigan

http://www.alma.edu/

- **Independent Presbyterian** 4-year, founded 1886
- **Small-town** 128-acre campus with easy access to Lansing
- **Endowment** $116.5 million
- **Coed** 1,396 undergraduate students, 97% full-time, 55% women, 45% men
- **Moderately difficult** entrance level, 72% of applicants were admitted

UNDERGRAD STUDENTS
1,353 full-time, 43 part-time. Students come from 30 states and territories; 9 other countries; 9% are from out of state; 3% Black or African American, non-Hispanic/Latino; 4% Hispanic/Latino; 2% Asian, non-Hispanic/Latino; 0.1% Native Hawaiian or other Pacific Islander, non-Hispanic/Latino; 0.6% American Indian or Alaska Native, non-Hispanic/Latino; 3% Two or more races, non-Hispanic/Latino; 4% Race/ethnicity unknown; 1% international; 3% transferred in; 93% live on campus.

Freshmen
Admission: 2,338 applied, 1,683 admitted, 356 enrolled. ***Average high school GPA:*** 3.5. ***Test scores:*** SAT critical reading scores over 500: 60%; SAT math scores over 500: 44%; SAT writing scores over 500: 44%; ACT scores over 18: 99%; SAT critical reading scores over 600: 20%; SAT math scores over 600: 11%; SAT writing scores over 600: 11%; ACT scores over 24: 52%; ACT scores over 30: 5%.

Retention: 78% of full-time freshmen returned.

FACULTY
Total: 154, 60% full-time, 61% with terminal degrees.

Student/faculty ratio: 12:1.

ACADEMICS
Calendar: 4-4-1. *Degree:* bachelor's.

Special study options: cooperative education, double majors, honors programs, independent study, internships, off-campus study, services for LD students, student-designed majors, study abroad. ***ROTC:*** Army (c).

Unusual degree programs: 3-2 engineering with University of Michigan, Kettering University.

Computers: 340 computers/terminals are available on campus for general student use. Students can access the following: campus intranet, computer help desk, free student e-mail accounts, online (class) grades, online (class) registration, online (class) schedules. Campuswide network is available. Wireless service is available via entire campus.

STUDENT LIFE
Housing options: on-campus residence required through senior year; coed, special housing for students with disabilities. Campus housing is university owned. Freshman campus housing is guaranteed.

Activities and organizations: drama/theater group, student-run newspaper, radio station, choral group, marching band, Alma Ambassadors, Alma College Union Board, New Life Campus Ministries, Student Congress, Alpha Phi Omega, national fraternities, national sororities.

Athletics Member NCAA. All Division III. ***Intercollegiate sports:*** baseball M, basketball M/W, bowling W, cheerleading M/W, equestrian sports W(c), football M, golf M/W, lacrosse M/W, soccer M/W, softball W, swimming and diving M/W, tennis M/W, track and field M/W, volleyball W, wrestling M. ***Intramural sports:*** basketball M/W, equestrian sports W(c), soccer M/W, softball M/W, volleyball M/W.

Campus security: 24-hour emergency response devices, late-night transport/escort service, controlled dormitory access.

Student services: health clinic, personal/psychological counseling.

COSTS & FINANCIAL AID
Costs (2014–15) ***Comprehensive fee:*** $44,075 includes full-time tuition ($34,190), mandatory fees ($395), and room and board ($9490). Full-time tuition and fees vary according to student level. Part-time tuition: $1100 per credit hour. Part-time tuition and fees vary according to course load and student level. ***College room only:*** $4745. Room and board charges vary according to board plan. ***Payment plans:*** installment, deferred payment. ***Waivers:*** employees or children of employees.

Financial Aid Of all full-time matriculated undergraduates who enrolled in 2014, 1,248 applied for aid, 1,118 were judged to have need, 195 had their need fully met. 372 Federal Work-Study jobs (averaging $1086). In 2014, 230 non-need-based awards were made. ***Average percent of need met:*** 68. ***Average financial aid package:*** $23,452. ***Average need-based loan:*** $4959. ***Average need-based gift aid:*** $22,473. ***Average non-need-based aid:*** $17,604. ***Average indebtedness upon graduation:*** $32,389.

APPLYING
Standardized Tests *Required:* SAT or ACT (for admission).

Options: electronic application.

Application fee: $25.

Required: essay or personal statement, high school transcript. ***Required for some:*** interview.

Application deadlines: rolling (freshmen), rolling (out-of-state freshmen), rolling (transfers).

Notification: continuous (freshmen), continuous (out-of-state freshmen), continuous (transfers).

CONTACT
Amanda Slenski, Director of Admissions, Alma College, 614 W. Superior St., Alma, MI 48801-1599. *Phone:* 800-321-2562. *Toll-free phone:* 800-321-ALMA. *E-mail:* admissions@alma.edu.

Andrews University

Berrien Springs, Michigan

http://www.andrews.edu/

- **Independent Seventh-day Adventist** university, founded 1874
- **Small-town** 1650-acre campus
- **Endowment** $43.1 million
- **Coed** 1,805 undergraduate students, 84% full-time, 56% women, 44% men
- **Moderately difficult** entrance level, 37% of applicants were admitted

UNDERGRAD STUDENTS
1,517 full-time, 288 part-time. Students come from 50 states and territories; 61 other countries; 67% are from out of state; 20% Black or African American, non-Hispanic/Latino; 13% Hispanic/Latino; 14% Asian, non-Hispanic/Latino; 0.4% Native Hawaiian or other Pacific Islander, non-Hispanic/Latino; 0.2% American Indian or Alaska Native, non-Hispanic/Latino; 3% Two or more races, non-Hispanic/Latino; 2% Race/ethnicity unknown; 20% international; 9% transferred in; 62% live on campus.

Freshmen
Admission: 2,311 applied, 863 admitted, 273 enrolled. ***Average high school GPA:*** 3.51. ***Test scores:*** SAT critical reading scores over 500: 66%; SAT math scores over 500: 75%; SAT writing scores over 500: 61%; ACT scores over 18: 91%; SAT critical reading scores over 600: 33%; SAT math scores over 600: 37%; SAT writing scores over 600: 21%; ACT scores over 24: 55%; SAT critical reading scores over 700: 7%; SAT math scores over 700: 7%; SAT writing scores over 700: 3%; ACT scores over 30: 16%.

Retention: 78% of full-time freshmen returned.

FACULTY
Total: 346, 68% full-time, 58% with terminal degrees.

Student/faculty ratio: 9:1.

ACADEMICS
Calendar: semesters. *Degrees:* associate, bachelor's, master's, doctoral, post-master's, and postbachelor's certificates.

Special study options: academic remediation for entering students, accelerated degree program, adult/continuing education programs, advanced placement credit, cooperative education, distance learning, double majors, English as a second language, freshman honors college, honors programs, internships, off-campus study, part-time degree program, student-designed majors, study abroad, summer session for credit.

Unusual degree programs: 3-2 physical therapy and architecture.

Computers: 151 computers/terminals are available on campus for general student use. Students can access the following: campus intranet, computer help desk, free student e-mail accounts, online (class) grades, online (class) registration, online (class) schedules, degree audit. Campuswide network is available. 99% of college-owned or -operated housing units are wired for high-speed Internet access. Wireless service is available via entire campus.

STUDENT LIFE

Housing options: on-campus residence required through senior year; men-only, women-only. Campus housing is university owned. Freshman campus housing is guaranteed.

Activities and organizations: drama/theater group, student-run newspaper, radio station, choral group.

Athletics ***Intramural sports:*** basketball M/W, football M/W, golf M/W, gymnastics M/W, racquetball M/W, soccer M/W, softball M/W, volleyball M/W, water polo M/W.

Campus security: 24-hour emergency response devices and patrols, controlled dormitory access.

Student services: health clinic, personal/psychological counseling.

COSTS & FINANCIAL AID

Costs (2014–15) ***Comprehensive fee:*** $34,564 includes full-time tuition ($25,416), mandatory fees ($846), and room and board ($8302). Full-time tuition and fees vary according to course load. Part-time tuition: $1059 per semester hour. Part-time tuition and fees vary according to course load. ***College room only:*** $4302. Room and board charges vary according to board plan. ***Payment plan:*** installment. ***Waivers:*** senior citizens and employees or children of employees.

Financial Aid Of all full-time matriculated undergraduates who enrolled in 2014, 1,007 applied for aid, 938 were judged to have need, 132 had their need fully met. 695 Federal Work-Study jobs (averaging $938). In 2014, 579 non-need-based awards were made. ***Average percent of need met:*** 83. ***Average financial aid package:*** $27,265. ***Average need-based loan:*** $4807. ***Average need-based gift aid:*** $7285. ***Average non-need-based aid:*** $9580. ***Average indebtedness upon graduation:*** $36,536.

APPLYING

Standardized Tests *Required:* SAT or ACT (for admission).

Options: electronic application, deferred entrance.

Application fee: $30.

Required: high school transcript, minimum 2.3 GPA, 2 letters of recommendation.

Application deadlines: rolling (freshmen), rolling (transfers).

Notification: continuous (freshmen), continuous (transfers).

CONTACT

Shanna Leak, Undergraduate Admissions Coordinator, Andrews University, Berrien Springs, MI 49104. *Phone:* 800-253-2874. *Toll-free phone:* 800-253-2874. *Fax:* 269-471-3228. *E-mail:* enroll@andrews.edu.

Aquinas College

Grand Rapids, Michigan

http://www.aquinas.edu/

- **Independent Roman Catholic** comprehensive, founded 1886
- **Suburban** 107-acre campus with easy access to Grand Rapids
- **Coed** 1,789 undergraduate students, 88% full-time, 61% women, 39% men
- **Moderately difficult** entrance level, 65% of applicants were admitted

UNDERGRAD STUDENTS

1,570 full-time, 219 part-time. Students come from 28 states and territories; 8 other countries; 6% are from out of state; 3% Black or African American, non-Hispanic/Latino; 6% Hispanic/Latino; 1% Asian, non-Hispanic/Latino; 0.5% American Indian or Alaska Native, non-Hispanic/Latino; 2% Two or more races, non-Hispanic/Latino; 3% Race/ethnicity unknown; 0.9% international; 4% transferred in; 46% live on campus.

Freshmen

Admission: 2,572 applied, 1,674 admitted, 354 enrolled. ***Average high school GPA:*** 3.44. ***Test scores:*** ACT scores over 18: 98%; ACT scores over 24: 49%; ACT scores over 30: 5%.

Retention: 79% of full-time freshmen returned.

FACULTY
Total: 232, 38% full-time, 42% with terminal degrees.

Student/faculty ratio: 12:1.

ACADEMICS
Calendar: semesters. *Degrees:* associate, bachelor's, and master's.

Special study options: academic remediation for entering students, accelerated degree program, adult/continuing education programs, advanced placement credit, cooperative education, distance learning, double majors, external degree program, honors programs, independent study, internships, off-campus study, part-time degree program, services for LD students, student-designed majors, study abroad, summer session for credit. ***ROTC:*** Army (c).

Computers: 210 computers/terminals are available on campus for general student use. Students can access the following: campus intranet, computer help desk, free student e-mail accounts, online (class) grades, online (class) registration, online (class) schedules. Campuswide network is available. 100% of college-owned or -operated housing units are wired for high-speed Internet access. Wireless service is available via entire campus.

STUDENT LIFE
Housing options: on-campus residence required through junior year; coed, women-only. Campus housing is university owned. Freshman campus housing is guaranteed.

Activities and organizations: drama/theater group, student-run newspaper, radio station, choral group, Community Senate Programming Board, The Saint (newspaper), Insignis Honors Group, Community Action Volunteers of Aquinas (CAVA), RHC.

Athletics Member NAIA. ***Intercollegiate sports:*** baseball M, basketball M/W, bowling M/W, cheerleading W, cross-country running M/W, golf M/W, ice hockey M/W, lacrosse M/W, soccer M/W, softball W, tennis M/W, track and field M/W, volleyball W. ***Intramural sports:*** basketball M/W, football M/W, golf M, skiing (cross-country) M/W, skiing (downhill) M/W, soccer M/W, softball M/W, tennis M/W, volleyball M/W.

Campus security: 24-hour emergency response devices and patrols, student patrols, late-night transport/escort service, controlled dormitory access.

Student services: health clinic, personal/psychological counseling, women's center.

COSTS & FINANCIAL AID
Costs (2015–16) ***Comprehensive fee:*** $37,378 includes full-time tuition ($28,426), mandatory fees ($394), and room and board ($8558). Full-time tuition and fees vary according to course load. Part-time tuition: $498 per credit hour. Part-time tuition and fees vary according to course load. ***College room only:*** $4014. Room and board charges vary according to board plan and housing facility. ***Payment plans:*** installment, deferred payment. ***Waivers:*** children of alumni and employees or children of employees.

Financial Aid Of all full-time matriculated undergraduates who enrolled in 2013, 1,400 applied for aid, 1,296 were judged to have need, 530 had their need fully met. In 2013, 311 non-need-based awards were made. ***Average percent of need met:*** 78. ***Average financial aid package:*** $20,130. ***Average need-based loan:*** $2707. ***Average need-based gift aid:*** $17,422. ***Average non-need-based aid:*** $12,422. ***Average indebtedness upon graduation:*** $23,469. ***Financial aid deadline:*** 8/15.

APPLYING
Standardized Tests *Required:* SAT or ACT (for admission).

Options: electronic application, early admission, deferred entrance.

Required: high school transcript, minimum 2.0 GPA. ***Required for some:*** essay or personal statement, interview.

Application deadlines: rolling (freshmen), rolling (transfers).

CONTACT
Ms. Rebecca Roberts, Admissions Office Applications Specialist, Aquinas College, 1607 Robinson Road, SE, Grand Rapids, MI 49506-1799. *Phone:* 616-632-2900. *Toll-free phone:* 800-678-9593. *Fax:* 616-732-4469. *E-mail:* admissions@aquinas.edu.

See previous page for display ad and page 1344 for the College Close-Up.

The Art Institute of Michigan
Novi, Michigan
http://www.artinstitutes.edu/detroit/

- **Proprietary** 4-year, part of Education Management Corporation
- **Coed**

ACADEMICS
Degrees: diplomas, associate, and bachelor's.

CONTACT
The Art Institute of Michigan, 28125 Cabot Drive, Suite 120, Novi, MI 48377. *Phone:* 248-675-3800. *Toll-free phone:* 800-479-0087.

The Art Institute of Michigan–Troy
Troy, Michigan
http://www.artinstitutes.edu/troy

- **Proprietary** 4-year
- **Coed**

ACADEMICS
Degrees: diplomas, associate, and bachelor's.

CONTACT
The Art Institute of Michigan–Troy, 1414 East Maple Avenue, Suite 150, Troy, MI 48083. *Phone:* 248-837-3200. *Toll-free phone:* 877-320-3275.

Baker College
Flint, Michigan
http://www.baker.edu/

- **Independent** comprehensive, founded 1911, part of The Baker College System is made up of 9 main campuses, Flint, Muskegon, Owosso, Clinton Township, Allen Park, Auburn Hills, Jackson, Cadillac, and Port Huron; The Center for Graduate Studies, Baker College Online, and three satellite locations, Fremont, Cass City and Coldwater
- **Suburban** with easy access to Detroit
- **Coed** 27,737 undergraduate students, 54% full-time, 68% women, 32% men
- **Minimally difficult** entrance level, 100% of applicants were admitted

UNDERGRAD STUDENTS
14,913 full-time, 12,824 part-time. Students come from 40 states and territories; 6 other countries; 1% are from out of state; 17% Black or African American, non-Hispanic/Latino; 4% Hispanic/Latino; 0.4% Asian, non-Hispanic/Latino; 0.5% American Indian or Alaska Native, non-Hispanic/Latino; 1% Race/ethnicity unknown; 8% live on campus.

Freshmen
Admission: 14,369 applied, 14,369 admitted.

FACULTY
Total: 2,170.

Student/faculty ratio: 13:1.

ACADEMICS
Calendar: quarters. *Degrees:* certificates, diplomas, associate, bachelor's, master's, doctoral, and postbachelor's certificates.

Special study options: academic remediation for entering students, accelerated degree program, advanced placement credit, cooperative education, distance learning, double majors, external degree program, independent study, internships, part-time degree program, services for LD students, summer session for credit.

Computers: 412 computers/terminals are available on campus for general student use. Students can access the following: online (class) registration. Campuswide network is available. 90% of college-owned or -operated housing units are wired for high-speed Internet access. Wireless service is available via entire campus.

STUDENT LIFE
Housing options: on-campus residence required for freshman year; coed. Campus housing is university owned.

Activities and organizations: Occupational Therapy Club, Interior Design Society, Medical Assistants Student Organization, Physical Therapist Assistant Club, Cyber Defense Team.

Campus security: 24-hour emergency response devices, late-night transport/escort service, video monitoring of high traffic areas.

Student services: personal/psychological counseling.

COSTS

Costs (2015–16) ***Tuition:*** $8460 full-time, $4230 per year part-time. Full-time tuition and fees vary according to program. Part-time tuition and fees vary according to program. ***Room only:*** $3000. ***Waivers:*** employees or children of employees.

APPLYING

Standardized Tests *Recommended:* SAT or ACT (for admission).

Options: electronic application, early admission, deferred entrance.

Application fee: $20.

Required: high school transcript.

Application deadlines: 9/19 (freshmen), 9/19 (out-of-state freshmen), 9/19 (transfers).

CONTACT

Mr. Mark Heaton, System Marketing/Admission, Baker College, 1050 West Bristol Road, Flint, MI 48507-5508. *Phone:* 810-766-4280. *Toll-free phone:* 800-964-4299. *Fax:* 810-766-4279. *E-mail:* mark.heaton@baker.edu.

Calvin College

Grand Rapids, Michigan

http://www.calvin.edu/

- **Independent Christian Reformed** comprehensive, founded 1876
- **Suburban** 400-acre campus with easy access to Grand Rapids
- **Endowment** $126.3 million
- **Coed** 3,894 undergraduate students, 97% full-time, 55% women, 45% men
- **Moderately difficult** entrance level, 73% of applicants were admitted

UNDERGRAD STUDENTS

3,760 full-time, 134 part-time. Students come from 47 states and territories; 56 other countries; 44% are from out of state; 2% Black or African American, non-Hispanic/Latino; 3% Hispanic/Latino; 4% Asian, non-Hispanic/Latino; 0.4% American Indian or Alaska Native, non-Hispanic/Latino; 3% Two or more races, non-Hispanic/Latino; 2% Race/ethnicity unknown; 10% international; 2% transferred in; 60% live on campus.

Freshmen

Admission: 3,677 applied, 2,691 admitted, 951 enrolled. ***Average high school GPA:*** 3.69. ***Test scores:*** SAT critical reading scores over 500: 81%; SAT math scores over 500: 87%; ACT scores over 18: 98%; SAT critical reading scores over 600: 45%; SAT math scores over 600: 53%; ACT scores over 24: 73%; SAT critical reading scores over 700: 10%; SAT math scores over 700: 13%; ACT scores over 30: 22%.

Retention: 87% of full-time freshmen returned.

FACULTY

Total: 345, 80% full-time, 71% with terminal degrees.

Student/faculty ratio: 13:1.

ACADEMICS

Calendar: 4-1-4. *Degrees:* bachelor's and master's.

Special study options: academic remediation for entering students, accelerated degree program, advanced placement credit, distance learning, double majors, honors programs, independent study, internships, off-campus study, part-time degree program, services for LD students, student-designed majors, study abroad, summer session for credit. ***ROTC:*** Army (c).

Unusual degree programs: 3-2 occupational therapy with Washington University in St. Louis.

Computers: 1,025 computers/terminals and 2,656 ports are available on campus for general student use. Students can access the following: campus intranet, computer help desk, free student e-mail accounts, online (class) grades, online (class) registration, online (class) schedules. Campuswide network is available. 100% of college-owned or -operated housing units are wired for high-speed Internet access. Wireless service is available via classrooms, computer centers, computer labs, dorm rooms, learning centers, libraries, student centers.

STUDENT LIFE

Housing options: on-campus residence required through sophomore year; men-only, women-only. Campus housing is university owned. Freshman campus housing is guaranteed.

Activities and organizations: drama/theater group, student-run newspaper, choral group, Dance Guild, Airband (Lip-syncing contest), Chimes (Student Newspaper), International Reconciliation Organization, Knight Investment Management Organization.

Athletics Member NCAA. All Division III. ***Intercollegiate sports:*** baseball M, basketball M/W, cross-country running M/W, equestrian sports M(c)/W(c), golf M/W, ice hockey M(c), lacrosse M/W, rugby M(c)/W(c), soccer M/W, softball W, swimming and diving M/W, tennis M/W, track and field M/W, ultimate Frisbee M(c)/W(c), volleyball M(c)/W. ***Intramural sports:*** badminton M/W, basketball M/W, cross-country running M/W, football M/W, golf M/W, racquetball M/W, rock climbing M/W, soccer M/W, softball M/W, swimming and diving M/W, tennis M/W, track and field M/W, volleyball M/W, water polo M/W.

Campus security: 24-hour emergency response devices and patrols, student patrols, late-night transport/escort service, controlled dormitory access, crime prevention programs, crime alert bulletins.

Student services: health clinic, personal/psychological counseling.

COSTS & FINANCIAL AID

Costs (2014–15) ***Comprehensive fee:*** $39,120 includes full-time tuition ($29,400), mandatory fees ($235), and room and board ($9485). Full-time tuition and fees vary according to degree level and program. Part-time tuition: $700 per credit hour. Part-time tuition and fees vary according to course load and degree level. ***Room and board:*** Room and board charges vary according to board plan and housing facility. ***Payment plans:*** tuition prepayment, installment. ***Waivers:*** employees or children of employees.

Financial Aid Of all full-time matriculated undergraduates who enrolled in 2014, 3,063 applied for aid, 2,327 were judged to have need, 337 had their need fully met. 1,306 Federal Work-Study jobs (averaging $1344). 1,073 state and other part-time jobs (averaging $1220). In 2014, 1226 non-need-based awards were made. ***Average percent of need met:*** 72. ***Average financial aid package:*** $21,920. ***Average need-based loan:*** $6919. ***Average need-based gift aid:*** $15,097. ***Average non-need-based aid:*** $7640. ***Average indebtedness upon graduation:*** $29,403.

APPLYING

Standardized Tests *Required:* SAT or ACT (for admission).

Options: electronic application, deferred entrance.

Application fee: $35.

Required: essay or personal statement, high school transcript, minimum 2.5 GPA, 1 letter of recommendation. ***Recommended:*** interview.

Application deadlines: 8/15 (freshmen), rolling (transfers).

Notification: continuous (freshmen).

CONTACT

Dr. Ben Arendt, Director of Admissions, Calvin College, 3201 Burton Street, SE, Grand Rapids, MI 49546. *Phone:* 616-526-6106. *Toll-free phone:* 800-688-0122. *Fax:* 616-526-6777. *E-mail:* admissions@calvin.edu.

Central Michigan University

Mount Pleasant, Michigan

http://www.cmich.edu/

- **State-supported** university, founded 1892
- **Small-town** 854-acre campus
- **Endowment** $108.0 million
- **Coed** 20,794 undergraduate students, 87% full-time, 56% women, 44% men
- **Moderately difficult** entrance level, 70% of applicants were admitted

UNDERGRAD STUDENTS

18,059 full-time, 2,735 part-time. Students come from 50 states and territories; 48 other countries; 4% are from out of state; 8% Black or African American, non-Hispanic/Latino; 3% Hispanic/Latino; 1% Asian, non-Hispanic/Latino; 0.1% Native Hawaiian or other Pacific Islander, non-Hispanic/Latino; 0.7% American Indian or Alaska Native, non-Hispanic/Latino; 2% Two or more races, non-Hispanic/Latino; 4% Race/ethnicity unknown; 3% international; 5% transferred in; 34% live on campus.

Freshmen
Admission: 17,999 applied, 12,565 admitted, 3,811 enrolled. ***Average high school GPA:*** 3.34. ***Test scores:*** SAT critical reading scores over 500: 54%; SAT math scores over 500: 65%; ACT scores over 18: 95%; SAT critical reading scores over 600: 18%; SAT math scores over 600: 25%; ACT scores over 24: 37%; SAT critical reading scores over 700: 4%; SAT math scores over 700: 7%; ACT scores over 30: 4%.

Retention: 76% of full-time freshmen returned.

FACULTY
Total: 1,136, 70% full-time, 67% with terminal degrees.

Student/faculty ratio: 20:1.

ACADEMICS
Calendar: semesters. *Degrees:* bachelor's, master's, doctoral, post-master's, and postbachelor's certificates.

Special study options: academic remediation for entering students, accelerated degree program, adult/continuing education programs, advanced placement credit, distance learning, double majors, English as a second language, freshman honors college, honors programs, independent study, internships, off-campus study, part-time degree program, services for LD students, student-designed majors, study abroad, summer session for credit. ***ROTC:*** Army (b), Air Force (c).

Unusual degree programs: 3-2 apparel product development and merchandising technology; computer science; economics; experimental psychology; geographic information science; accounting (MBA); master of science in administration; Spanish; mathematics; political science; human development and family studies.

Computers: 490 computers/terminals and 26,902 ports are available on campus for general student use. Students can access the following: campus intranet, computer help desk, free student e-mail accounts, online (class) grades, online (class) registration, online (class) schedules, Blackboard. Campuswide network is available. 100% of college-owned or -operated housing units are wired for high-speed Internet access. Wireless service is available via entire campus.

STUDENT LIFE
Housing options: on-campus residence required through sophomore year; coed, special housing for students with disabilities. Campus housing is university owned. Freshman campus housing is guaranteed.

Activities and organizations: drama/theater group, student-run newspaper, radio and television station, choral group, marching band, national fraternities, national sororities.

Athletics Member NCAA. All Division I except football (Division I-A). ***Intercollegiate sports:*** baseball M(s), basketball M(s)/W(s), cross-country running M(s)/W(s), field hockey W(s), golf W(s), gymnastics W(s), lacrosse W(s), soccer W(s), softball W(s), track and field M(s)/W(s), volleyball W(s), wrestling M(s). ***Intramural sports:*** basketball M/W, bowling M/W, cross-country running M/W, equestrian sports M(c)/W(c), football M/W, golf M(c)/W(c), ice hockey M(c)/W(c), lacrosse M(c)/W(c), racquetball M/W, rugby M(c)/W(c), skiing (downhill) M(c)/W(c), soccer M(c)/W(c), softball M/W, swimming and diving M(c)/W(c), tennis M(c)/W(c), ultimate Frisbee M(c)/W(c), volleyball M(c)/W(c), water polo M(c)/W(c), wrestling M.

Campus security: 24-hour emergency response devices and patrols, student patrols, late-night transport/escort service, controlled dormitory access.

Student services: health clinic, personal/psychological counseling, women's center.

COSTS & FINANCIAL AID
Costs (2014–15) ***Tuition:*** state resident $11,550 full-time, $385 per credit hour part-time; nonresident $23,670 full-time, $789 per credit hour part-time. Full-time tuition and fees vary according to location. Part-time tuition and fees vary according to location. ***Room and board:*** $8780; room only: $4390. Room and board charges vary according to board plan and housing facility. ***Payment plan:*** installment. ***Waivers:*** children of alumni, senior citizens, and employees or children of employees.

Financial Aid Of all full-time matriculated undergraduates who enrolled in 2013, 14,115 applied for aid, 11,295 were judged to have need, 5,444 had their need fully met. 861 Federal Work-Study jobs (averaging $1471). 4,468 state and other part-time jobs (averaging $2334). In 2013, 1589 non-need-based awards were made. ***Average percent of need met:*** 79. ***Average financial aid package:*** $12,940. ***Average need-based loan:*** $7296. ***Average need-based gift aid:*** $5961. ***Average non-need-based aid:*** $3838. ***Average indebtedness upon graduation:*** $33,545.

APPLYING
Standardized Tests *Required:* SAT or ACT (for admission). *Recommended:* ACT (for admission).

Options: electronic application, early admission, early action, deferred entrance.

Application fee: $35.

Required: high school transcript. ***Required for some:*** essay or personal statement, interview.

Application deadlines: 7/1 (freshmen), rolling (transfers).

Notification: continuous (freshmen), continuous (transfers).

CONTACT
Central Michigan University, Warriner Hall 102, Mt Pleasant, MI 48859. *Phone:* 989-774-3076. *Toll-free phone:* 888-292-5366. *Fax:* 989-774-7267. *E-mail:* cmuadmit@cmich.edu.

★ College for Creative Studies
Detroit, Michigan
http://www.collegeforcreativestudies.edu/

- **Independent** comprehensive, founded 1926
- **Urban** campus
- **Coed** 1,401 undergraduate students, 80% full-time, 50% women, 50% men
- **Moderately difficult** entrance level, 46% of applicants were admitted

UNDERGRAD STUDENTS
1,120 full-time, 281 part-time. 8% are from out of state; 9% Black or African American, non-Hispanic/Latino; 4% Hispanic/Latino; 4% Asian, non-Hispanic/Latino; 0.3% Native Hawaiian or other Pacific Islander, non-Hispanic/Latino; 0.2% American Indian or Alaska Native, non-Hispanic/Latino; 4% Two or more races, non-Hispanic/Latino; 14% Race/ethnicity unknown; 7% international; 9% transferred in; 38% live on campus.

Freshmen
Admission: 1,388 applied, 633 admitted, 251 enrolled. ***Average high school GPA:*** 3.19.

Retention: 82% of full-time freshmen returned.

FACULTY
Total: 289, 17% full-time.

Student/faculty ratio: 9:1.

ACADEMICS
Calendar: semesters. *Degrees:* bachelor's, master's, and postbachelor's certificates.

Special study options: part-time degree program.

Computers: Campuswide network is available.

STUDENT LIFE
Housing options: coed. Campus housing is university owned.

Campus security: 24-hour patrols, late-night transport/escort service, controlled dormitory access.

COSTS
Costs (2015–16) ***Comprehensive fee:*** $47,400 includes full-time tuition ($37,560), mandatory fees ($1390), and room and board ($8450). Part-time tuition: $1252 per credit hour. ***College room only:*** $5550. Room and board charges vary according to board plan and housing facility. ***Payment plan:*** installment. ***Waivers:*** employees or children of employees.

APPLYING
Standardized Tests *Required:* SAT or ACT (for admission).

Options: electronic application, early action, deferred entrance.

Application fee: $35.

Required: essay or personal statement, high school transcript, portfolio. ***Required for some:*** interview. ***Recommended:*** minimum 2.5 GPA.

CONTACT
Office of Admissions, College for Creative Studies, 201 East Kirby, Detroit, MI 48202-4034. *Phone:* 800-952-2787. *Toll-free phone:* 800-

952-ARTS. *Fax:* 313-872-2739. *E-mail:* admissions@collegeforcreativestudies.edu.

Cornerstone University

Grand Rapids, Michigan

http://www.cornerstone.edu/

- **Independent nondenominational** comprehensive, founded 1941
- **Suburban** 132-acre campus
- **Endowment** $6.6 million
- **Coed** 2,153 undergraduate students, 69% full-time, 60% women, 40% men
- **Minimally difficult** entrance level, 69% of applicants were admitted

UNDERGRAD STUDENTS

1,481 full-time, 672 part-time. Students come from 35 states and territories; 17 other countries; 25% are from out of state; 12% Black or African American, non-Hispanic/Latino; 4% Hispanic/Latino; 1% Asian, non-Hispanic/Latino; 0.1% Native Hawaiian or other Pacific Islander, non-Hispanic/Latino; 0.7% American Indian or Alaska Native, non-Hispanic/Latino; 0.4% Two or more races, non-Hispanic/Latino; 2% international; 3% transferred in; 55% live on campus.

Freshmen

Admission: 2,394 applied, 1,648 admitted, 323 enrolled. ***Average high school GPA:*** 3.5. ***Test scores:*** SAT critical reading scores over 500: 64%; SAT math scores over 500: 64%; ACT scores over 18: 92%; SAT critical reading scores over 600: 31%; SAT math scores over 600: 16%; ACT scores over 24: 42%; SAT critical reading scores over 700: 2%; SAT math scores over 700: 2%; ACT scores over 30: 5%.

Retention: 76% of full-time freshmen returned.

FACULTY

Total: 121, 49% full-time, 29% with terminal degrees.

Student/faculty ratio: 18:1.

ACADEMICS

Calendar: semesters. *Degrees:* diplomas, associate, bachelor's, and master's.

Special study options: academic remediation for entering students, accelerated degree program, adult/continuing education programs, advanced placement credit, distance learning, double majors, English as a second language, honors programs, independent study, internships, off-campus study, part-time degree program, services for LD students, study abroad, summer session for credit. ***ROTC:*** Army (c).

Computers: 93 computers/terminals are available on campus for general student use. Students can access the following: campus intranet, computer help desk, free student e-mail accounts, online (class) grades, online (class) registration, online (class) schedules. Campuswide network is available. 100% of college-owned or -operated housing units are wired for high-speed Internet access. Wireless service is available via entire campus.

STUDENT LIFE

Housing options: on-campus residence required through sophomore year; men-only, women-only, special housing for students with disabilities. Campus housing is university owned. Freshman campus housing is guaranteed.

Activities and organizations: drama/theater group, student-run newspaper, choral group, student government, Student Education Association, Breakpoint, Student Activities Council, International Justice Mission.

Athletics Member NAIA. ***Intercollegiate sports:*** baseball M(s), basketball M(s)/W(s), cheerleading W(s), cross-country running M(s)/W(s), golf M(s)/W(s), soccer M(s)/W(s), softball W(s), track and field M(s)/W(s), volleyball W(s). ***Intramural sports:*** basketball M/W, football M, soccer M/W, softball M/W, volleyball M/W.

Campus security: 24-hour emergency response devices and patrols, student patrols, late-night transport/escort service, controlled dormitory access.

Student services: health clinic, personal/psychological counseling.

COSTS & FINANCIAL AID

Costs (2014–15) ***Comprehensive fee:*** $33,338 includes full-time tuition ($24,542), mandatory fees ($570), and room and board ($8226). Full-time tuition and fees vary according to course load and reciprocity agreements. Part-time tuition: $941 per credit hour. Part-time tuition and fees vary according to course load. ***Required fees:*** $185 per term part-time. ***Room and board:*** Room and board charges vary according to board plan and housing facility. ***Payment plan:*** installment. ***Waivers:*** employees or children of employees.

Financial Aid Of all full-time matriculated undergraduates who enrolled in 2014, 1,056 applied for aid, 956 were judged to have need, 132 had their need fully met. 241 Federal Work-Study jobs (averaging $1426). In 2014, 197 non-need-based awards were made. ***Average percent of need met:*** 68. ***Average financial aid package:*** $19,871. ***Average need-based loan:*** $4232. ***Average need-based gift aid:*** $15,814. ***Average non-need-based aid:*** $9356. ***Average indebtedness upon graduation:*** $27,919.

APPLYING

Standardized Tests *Required:* SAT or ACT (for admission).

Options: electronic application.

Application fee: $25.

Required: essay or personal statement, high school transcript, minimum 2.5 GPA, 1 letter of recommendation, pastoral letter.

Application deadlines: rolling (freshmen), rolling (transfers).

Notification: continuous (freshmen), continuous (transfers).

CONTACT

Mrs. Lisa Link, Office of Admissions, Cornerstone University, 1001 East Beltline Avenue, NE, Grand Rapids, MI 49525. *Phone:* 616-222-1426. *Toll-free phone:* 800-787-9778. *Fax:* 616-222-1418. *E-mail:* admissions@cornerstone.edu.

Davenport University

Grand Rapids, Michigan

http://www.davenport.edu/

- **Independent** comprehensive, founded 1866
- **Suburban** campus
- **Endowment** $16.1 million
- **Coed** 7,876 undergraduate students, 29% full-time, 62% women, 38% men
- **Minimally difficult** entrance level, 93% of applicants were admitted

UNDERGRAD STUDENTS

2,316 full-time, 5,560 part-time. Students come from 52 states and territories; 25 other countries; 4% are from out of state; 15% Black or African American, non-Hispanic/Latino; 1% Hispanic/Latino; 2% Asian, non-Hispanic/Latino; 0.1% Native Hawaiian or other Pacific Islander, non-Hispanic/Latino; 0.5% American Indian or Alaska Native, non-Hispanic/Latino; 2% Two or more races, non-Hispanic/Latino; 16% Race/ethnicity unknown; 2% international; 12% transferred in; 6% live on campus.

Freshmen

Admission: 1,537 applied, 1,435 admitted, 653 enrolled.

Retention: 73% of full-time freshmen returned.

FACULTY

Total: 874, 20% full-time, 26% with terminal degrees.

Student/faculty ratio: 12:1.

ACADEMICS

Calendar: semesters. *Degrees:* certificates, diplomas, associate, bachelor's, master's, post-master's, and postbachelor's certificates.

Special study options: academic remediation for entering students, accelerated degree program, adult/continuing education programs, advanced placement credit, cooperative education, distance learning, English as a second language, independent study, internships, part-time degree program, services for LD students, study abroad, summer session for credit. ***ROTC:*** Army (c).

Computers: 3,098 computers/terminals and 315 ports are available on campus for general student use. Students can access the following: campus intranet, computer help desk, free student e-mail accounts, online (class) grades, online (class) registration, online (class) schedules. Campuswide network is available. 100% of college-owned or -operated housing units are wired for high-speed Internet access. Wireless service is available via entire campus.

STUDENT LIFE
Housing options: coed. Campus housing is university owned. Freshman applicants given priority for college housing.

Activities and organizations: student-run newspaper, marching band, Business Professionals of America, Delta Epsilon Chi, Student Government, Health Occupations Students of America, Connect.

Athletics Member NAIA. ***Intercollegiate sports:*** baseball M(s), basketball M(s)/W(s), bowling M(s)/W(s), cheerleading W(s), cross-country running M(s)/W(s), football M(s), golf M(s)/W(s), ice hockey M(s)/W(s), lacrosse M(s)/W(s), rugby M(s)/W(s), soccer M(s)/W(s), softball M(s)/W(s), tennis M(s)/W(s), track and field M(s)/W(s), volleyball W(s).

Campus security: 24-hour emergency response devices and patrols, late-night transport/escort service, controlled dormitory access.

Student services: personal/psychological counseling.

COSTS
Costs (2014–15) ***Comprehensive fee:*** $24,912 includes full-time tuition ($14,472), mandatory fees ($600), and room and board ($9840). Full-time tuition and fees vary according to location and program. Part-time tuition: $603 per credit. Part-time tuition and fees vary according to location and program. ***College room only:*** $5700. Room and board charges vary according to board plan and housing facility. ***Payment plan:*** installment. ***Waivers:*** employees or children of employees.

APPLYING
Standardized Tests *Required for some:* SAT or ACT (for admission).

Options: electronic application, deferred entrance.

Application fee: $25.

Required: high school transcript. ***Recommended:*** interview.

Application deadlines: rolling (freshmen), rolling (out-of-state freshmen), rolling (transfers).

Notification: continuous (freshmen), continuous (out-of-state freshmen), continuous (transfers).

CONTACT
Ms. Amy Lucas, Interim Executive Director of Admissions, Davenport University, 6191 Kraft Avenue SE, Grand Rapids, MI 49512. *Phone:* 616-451-3511. *Toll-free phone:* 800-925-3884 (in-state); 866-925-3884 (out-of-state). *Fax:* 616-732-1145. *E-mail:* amy.lucas@davenport.edu.

DeVry University

Southfield, Michigan

http://www.devry.edu/

- **Proprietary** 4-year, founded 2008
- **Coed**

ACADEMICS
Calendar: semesters. *Degrees:* associate and bachelor's.

COSTS & FINANCIAL AID
Costs (2014–15) ***Tuition:*** $17,052 full-time, $609 per credit hour part-time. ***Required fees:*** $80 full-time.

Financial Aid Of all full-time matriculated undergraduates who enrolled in 2007, 2 applied for aid, 2 were judged to have need. ***Average percent of need met:*** 38. ***Average financial aid package:*** $8705. ***Average need-based loan:*** $5750. ***Average need-based gift aid:*** $5910.

CONTACT
Admissions Office, DeVry University, 26999 Central Park Boulevard, Suite 125, Southfield, MI 48076. *Phone:* 248-213-1610. *Toll-free phone:* 866-338-7941.

Eastern Michigan University

Ypsilanti, Michigan

http://www.emich.edu/

- **State-supported** comprehensive, founded 1849
- **Suburban** 460-acre campus with easy access to Detroit
- **Endowment** $67.2 million
- **Coed** 18,208 undergraduate students, 72% full-time, 59% women, 41% men
- **Moderately difficult** entrance level, 69% of applicants were admitted

UNDERGRAD STUDENTS
13,051 full-time, 5,157 part-time. Students come from 55 states and territories; 52 other countries; 9% are from out of state; 20% Black or African American, non-Hispanic/Latino; 4% Hispanic/Latino; 2% Asian, non-Hispanic/Latino; 0.1% Native Hawaiian or other Pacific Islander, non-Hispanic/Latino; 0.2% American Indian or Alaska Native, non-Hispanic/Latino; 3% Two or more races, non-Hispanic/Latino; 2% Race/ethnicity unknown; 2% international; 10% transferred in; 29% live on campus.

Freshmen
Admission: 12,353 applied, 8,500 admitted, 2,630 enrolled. ***Average high school GPA:*** 3.27. ***Test scores:*** SAT critical reading scores over 500: 43%; SAT math scores over 500: 59%; SAT writing scores over 500: 43%; ACT scores over 18: 89%; SAT critical reading scores over 600: 17%; SAT math scores over 600: 19%; SAT writing scores over 600: 9%; ACT scores over 24: 35%; SAT critical reading scores over 700: 3%; SAT math scores over 700: 2%; SAT writing scores over 700: 1%; ACT scores over 30: 3%.

Retention: 72% of full-time freshmen returned.

FACULTY
Total: 1,342, 56% full-time, 49% with terminal degrees.

Student/faculty ratio: 18:1.

ACADEMICS
Calendar: semesters. *Degrees:* bachelor's, master's, doctoral, post-master's, and postbachelor's certificates.

Special study options: academic remediation for entering students, accelerated degree program, advanced placement credit, cooperative education, distance learning, double majors, English as a second language, external degree program, honors programs, independent study, internships, part-time degree program, services for LD students, student-designed majors, study abroad, summer session for credit. ***ROTC:*** Army (b), Navy (c), Air Force (c).

Unusual degree programs: accounting, occupational therapy.

Computers: 1,600 computers/terminals and 200 ports are available on campus for general student use. Students can access the following: campus intranet, computer help desk, free student e-mail accounts, online (class) grades, online (class) registration, online (class) schedules, Wireless internet connections are available for all students. Campuswide network is available. 100% of college-owned or -operated housing units are wired for high-speed Internet access. Wireless service is available via entire campus.

STUDENT LIFE
Housing options: on-campus residence required through sophomore year; coed, special housing for students with disabilities. Campus housing is university owned.

Activities and organizations: drama/theater group, student-run newspaper, radio and television station, choral group, marching band, International Student Association, Golden Key International Honor Society, Psychology Club, Indian Student Association, GREEN (Gathering Resources to Educate about our Environment and Nature), national fraternities, national sororities.

Athletics Member NCAA. All Division I except football (Division I-A). ***Intercollegiate sports:*** baseball M(s), basketball M(s)/W(s), crew W(s), cross-country running M(s)/W(s), golf M(s)/W(s), gymnastics W(s), soccer W(s), softball W(s), swimming and diving M(s)/W(s), tennis W(s), track and field M(s)/W(s), volleyball W(s), wrestling M(s). ***Intramural sports:*** badminton M/W, basketball M/W, bowling M/W, cross-country running M/W, golf M/W, racquetball M/W, rock climbing M/W, soccer M/W, softball M/W, swimming and diving M/W, table tennis M/W, track and field M/W, ultimate Frisbee M/W, volleyball M/W, weight lifting M/W.

Campus security: 24-hour emergency response devices and patrols, student patrols, late-night transport/escort service, controlled dormitory access, bicycle patrols, local police in dormitories, self-defense education, lighted pathways, bike lock lease program.

Student services: health clinic, personal/psychological counseling, women's center, legal services.

COSTS & FINANCIAL AID
Costs (2014–15) ***One-time required fee:*** $310. ***Tuition:*** state resident $8244 full-time, $275 per credit hour part-time; nonresident $24,287 full-

time, $810 per credit hour part-time. Full-time tuition and fees vary according to course level and reciprocity agreements. Part-time tuition and fees vary according to course level and reciprocity agreements. ***Required fees:*** $1419 full-time, $44 per credit hour part-time, $52 per term part-time. ***Room and board:*** $8940; room only: $4676. Room and board charges vary according to board plan, housing facility, and location. ***Payment plan:*** installment. ***Waivers:*** employees or children of employees.

Financial Aid Of all full-time matriculated undergraduates who enrolled in 2013, 11,263 applied for aid, 9,545 were judged to have need, 257 had their need fully met. 675 Federal Work-Study jobs (averaging $1612). In 2013, 1848 non-need-based awards were made. ***Average percent of need met:*** 48. ***Average financial aid package:*** $9291. ***Average need-based loan:*** $4112. ***Average need-based gift aid:*** $4845. ***Average non-need-based aid:*** $4785. ***Average indebtedness upon graduation:*** $25,781.

APPLYING

Standardized Tests *Required:* SAT or ACT (for admission).

Options: electronic application, deferred entrance.

Application fee: $35.

Required: high school transcript, minimum 2.0 GPA. ***Required for some:*** 1 letter of recommendation, interview.

Application deadlines: rolling (freshmen), rolling (out-of-state freshmen), rolling (transfers).

Notification: continuous (freshmen), continuous (out-of-state freshmen), continuous (transfers).

CONTACT

Eastern Michigan University, Ypsilanti, MI 48197. *Phone:* 734-487-3060. *Toll-free phone:* 800-GO TO EMU.

Ferris State University

Big Rapids, Michigan

http://www.ferris.edu/

- **State-supported** comprehensive, founded 1884
- **Small-town** 941-acre campus with easy access to Grand Rapids
- **Endowment** $46.3 million
- **Coed** 13,357 undergraduate students, 68% full-time, 53% women, 47% men
- **Minimally difficult** entrance level, 78% of applicants were admitted

UNDERGRAD STUDENTS

9,105 full-time, 4,252 part-time. Students come from 47 states and territories; 42 other countries; 6% are from out of state; 7% Black or African American, non-Hispanic/Latino; 4% Hispanic/Latino; 2% Asian, non-Hispanic/Latino; 0.6% American Indian or Alaska Native, non-Hispanic/Latino; 3% Two or more races, non-Hispanic/Latino; 2% Race/ethnicity unknown; 2% international; 10% transferred in; 26% live on campus.

Freshmen

Admission: 10,426 applied, 8,176 admitted, 1,926 enrolled. ***Average high school GPA:*** 3.23. ***Test scores:*** ACT scores over 18: 85%; ACT scores over 24: 32%; ACT scores over 30: 4%.

Retention: 72% of full-time freshmen returned.

FACULTY

Total: 798, 63% full-time, 35% with terminal degrees.

Student/faculty ratio: 16:1.

ACADEMICS

Calendar: semesters. *Degrees:* certificates, associate, bachelor's, master's, doctoral, and postbachelor's certificates.

Special study options: academic remediation for entering students, accelerated degree program, adult/continuing education programs, advanced placement credit, cooperative education, distance learning, double majors, English as a second language, external degree program, freshman honors college, honors programs, independent study, internships, off-campus study, part-time degree program, services for LD students, student-designed majors, study abroad, summer session for credit. ***ROTC:*** Army (c).

Computers: 1,889 computers/terminals are available on campus for general student use. Students can access the following: campus intranet, computer help desk, free student e-mail accounts, online (class) grades, online (class) registration, online (class) schedules. Campuswide network is available. 100% of college-owned or -operated housing units are wired for high-speed Internet access. Wireless service is available via entire campus.

STUDENT LIFE

Housing options: on-campus residence required for freshman year; coed, women-only, special housing for students with disabilities. Campus housing is university owned. Freshman campus housing is guaranteed.

Activities and organizations: drama/theater group, student-run newspaper, radio and television station, choral group, Music Industry Management, Crafter's Anonymous, Pre-Pharmacy D Club, American Marketing Association, Social Work Association, national fraternities, national sororities.

Athletics Member NCAA. All Division II. ***Intercollegiate sports:*** basketball M(s)/W(s), cross-country running M(s)/W(s), football M(s), golf M(s)/W(s), ice hockey M(s), soccer W(s), softball W(s), tennis M(s)/W(s), track and field M(s)/W(s), volleyball W(s). ***Intramural sports:*** badminton M/W, baseball M(c), basketball M(c)/W, bowling M/W, cheerleading M(c)/W(c), cross-country running M(c)/W(c), equestrian sports M(c)/W(c), golf M/W, ice hockey M/W, lacrosse M(c)/W(c), rugby M(c)/W(c), soccer M/W, softball M/W, table tennis M/W, tennis M(c)/W(c), ultimate Frisbee M/W, volleyball M/W, weight lifting M/W.

Campus security: 24-hour emergency response devices, student patrols, late-night transport/escort service, controlled dormitory access.

Student services: health clinic, personal/psychological counseling.

COSTS & FINANCIAL AID

Costs (2014–15) ***One-time required fee:*** $162. ***Tuition:*** state resident $11,190 full-time, $373 per credit hour part-time; nonresident $16,800 full-time, $560 per credit hour part-time. Full-time tuition and fees vary according to location, program, and student level. Part-time tuition and fees vary according to location and student level. ***Room and board:*** $9208. Room and board charges vary according to board plan and housing facility. ***Payment plan:*** installment. ***Waivers:*** employees or children of employees.

Financial Aid Of all full-time matriculated undergraduates who enrolled in 2014, 8,749 applied for aid, 7,087 were judged to have need, 1,005 had their need fully met. 448 Federal Work-Study jobs (averaging $2250). 245 state and other part-time jobs (averaging $1780). In 2014, 1140 non-need-based awards were made. ***Average percent of need met:*** 64. ***Average financial aid package:*** $10,950. ***Average need-based loan:*** $4450. ***Average need-based gift aid:*** $5030. ***Average non-need-based aid:*** $4270. ***Average indebtedness upon graduation:*** $35,720.

APPLYING

Standardized Tests *Required:* SAT or ACT (for admission).

Options: electronic application.

Application fee: $30.

Required: high school transcript, minimum 2.5 GPA, SAT or ACT.

Application deadlines: 8/1 (freshmen), 7/1 (transfers).

Notification: continuous (freshmen), continuous (transfers).

CONTACT

Mr. Jason Daday, Associate Director of Admissions, Ferris State University, 1201 South State Street, CSS201, Big Rapids, MI 49307-2742. *Phone:* 231-591-3106. *Toll-free phone:* 800-433-7747. *Fax:* 231-591-2242. *E-mail:* dadayja@ferris.edu.

Grand Valley State University

Allendale, Michigan

http://www.gvsu.edu/

- **State-supported** comprehensive, founded 1960
- **Small-town** 1337-acre campus with easy access to Grand Rapids
- **Endowment** $100.1 million
- **Coed** 21,636 undergraduate students, 88% full-time, 58% women, 42% men
- **Moderately difficult** entrance level, 80% of applicants were admitted

UNDERGRAD STUDENTS

19,084 full-time, 2,552 part-time. Students come from 41 states and territories; 66 other countries; 6% are from out of state; 5% Black or

African American, non-Hispanic/Latino; 5% Hispanic/Latino; 2% Asian, non-Hispanic/Latino; 0.4% American Indian or Alaska Native, non-Hispanic/Latino; 3% Two or more races, non-Hispanic/Latino; 0.4% Race/ethnicity unknown; 1% international; 8% transferred in; 31% live on campus.

Freshmen
Admission: 16,884 applied, 13,580 admitted, 4,199 enrolled. ***Average high school GPA:*** 3.3. ***Test scores:*** ACT scores over 18: 98%; ACT scores over 24: 50%; ACT scores over 30: 7%.

Retention: 83% of full-time freshmen returned.

FACULTY
Total: 1,726, 64% full-time, 53% with terminal degrees.

Student/faculty ratio: 17:1.

ACADEMICS
Calendar: semesters. *Degrees:* certificates, bachelor's, master's, doctoral, post-master's, and postbachelor's certificates.

Special study options: academic remediation for entering students, accelerated degree program, adult/continuing education programs, advanced placement credit, cooperative education, distance learning, double majors, English as a second language, freshman honors college, honors programs, independent study, internships, part-time degree program, services for LD students, study abroad, summer session for credit.

Computers: 2,600 computers/terminals are available on campus for general student use. Students can access the following: campus intranet, computer help desk, free student e-mail accounts, online (class) grades, online (class) registration, online (class) schedules, transcript, degree audit, credit card payments. Campuswide network is available. 100% of college-owned or -operated housing units are wired for high-speed Internet access. Wireless service is available via entire campus.

STUDENT LIFE
Housing options: coed. Campus housing is university owned. Freshman campus housing is guaranteed.

Activities and organizations: drama/theater group, student-run newspaper, radio and television station, choral group, marching band, Habitat for Humanity, Alternative Breaks, Hospitality and tourism Management Club, Dance Troupe, Colleges Against Cancer, national fraternities, national sororities.

Athletics Member NCAA. All Division II. ***Intercollegiate sports:*** baseball M(s), basketball M(s)/W(s), cheerleading M(c)/W(c), crew M(c)/W(c), cross-country running M(s)/W(s), football M(s), golf M(s)/W(s), ice hockey M(c), lacrosse M(c)/W, rugby M(c)/W(c), sailing M(c)/W(c), skiing (downhill) M(c)/W(c), soccer M(c)/W(s), softball W(s), swimming and diving M(s)/W(s), tennis M(s)/W(s), track and field M(s)/W(s), volleyball M(c)/W(s), water polo M(c)/W(c), wrestling M(c). ***Intramural sports:*** archery M/W, badminton M/W, basketball M/W, bowling M/W, cheerleading M/W, crew M/W, cross-country running M/W, fencing M/W, field hockey M/W, football M/W, golf M/W, gymnastics M/W, lacrosse M/W, racquetball M/W, skiing (cross-country) M/W, skiing (downhill) M/W, soccer M/W, softball M/W, squash M/W, swimming and diving M/W, tennis M/W, volleyball M/W, water polo M/W, weight lifting M/W, wrestling M.

Campus security: 24-hour emergency response devices and patrols, student patrols, late-night transport/escort service, controlled dormitory access.

Student services: health clinic, personal/psychological counseling, women's center.

COSTS & FINANCIAL AID
Costs (2014–15) ***Tuition:*** state resident $10,752 full-time, $448 per credit hour part-time; nonresident $15,408 full-time, $642 per credit hour part-time. Full-time tuition and fees vary according to course load, program, and student level. Part-time tuition and fees vary according to course load, program, and student level. ***Room and board:*** $8200. Room and board charges vary according to board plan and housing facility. ***Payment plans:*** installment, deferred payment. ***Waivers:*** employees or children of employees.

Financial Aid Of all full-time matriculated undergraduates who enrolled in 2014, 15,525 applied for aid, 11,590 were judged to have need, 1,783 had their need fully met. 1,487 Federal Work-Study jobs (averaging $2452). In 2014, 2802 non-need-based awards were made. ***Average percent of need met:*** 66. ***Average financial aid package:*** $9357. ***Average need-based loan:*** $4340. ***Average need-based gift aid:*** $6277. ***Average non-need-based aid:*** $2676. ***Average indebtedness upon graduation:*** $30,222.

APPLYING
Standardized Tests *Required:* SAT or ACT (for admission).

Options: electronic application.

Application fee: $30.

Required: high school transcript. ***Required for some:*** essay or personal statement, interview.

Application deadlines: 5/1 (freshmen), 7/24 (transfers).

Notification: 5/1 (freshmen), continuous (transfers).

CONTACT
Ms. Jodi Chycinski, Director of Admissions, Grand Valley State University, 1 Campus Drive, Allendale, MI 49401. *Phone:* 616-331-2025. *Toll-free phone:* 800-748-0246. *Fax:* 616-331-2000. *E-mail:* go2gvsu@gvsu.edu.

Great Lakes Christian College
Lansing, Michigan
http://www.glcc.edu/

- **Independent** 4-year, founded 1949, affiliated with Christian Churches and Churches of Christ
- **Suburban** 47-acre campus
- **Endowment** $514,831
- **Coed** 225 undergraduate students, 74% full-time, 41% women, 59% men
- **Minimally difficult** entrance level

UNDERGRAD STUDENTS
166 full-time, 59 part-time. Students come from 4 states and territories; 3 other countries; 2% are from out of state; 23% Black or African American, non-Hispanic/Latino; 2% Hispanic/Latino; 0.5% Asian, non-Hispanic/Latino; 0.5% American Indian or Alaska Native, non-Hispanic/Latino; 3% Two or more races, non-Hispanic/Latino; 4% Race/ethnicity unknown; 3% international.

Freshmen
Test scores: ACT scores over 18: 79%; ACT scores over 24: 19%; ACT scores over 30: 2%.

Retention: 53% of full-time freshmen returned.

FACULTY
Total: 23, 43% full-time, 35% with terminal degrees.

Student/faculty ratio: 10:1.

ACADEMICS
Calendar: semesters. *Degrees:* associate and bachelor's.

Special study options: academic remediation for entering students, advanced placement credit, double majors, independent study, internships, off-campus study, part-time degree program, services for LD students.

Computers: 24 computers/terminals and 190 ports are available on campus for general student use. Students can access the following: campus intranet, computer help desk, free student e-mail accounts, online (class) grades, online (class) schedules. Campuswide network is available. 100% of college-owned or -operated housing units are wired for high-speed Internet access. Wireless service is available via entire campus.

STUDENT LIFE
Housing options: on-campus residence required through senior year; men-only, women-only. Campus housing is university owned.

Activities and organizations: drama/theater group, student-run newspaper, choral group.

Athletics Member NCCAA. ***Intercollegiate sports:*** basketball M/W, soccer M, volleyball W.

Campus security: controlled dormitory access, evening security patrols.

Student services: personal/psychological counseling.

COSTS
Costs (2014–15) ***Comprehensive fee:*** $22,990 includes full-time tuition ($13,110), mandatory fees ($1780), and room and board ($8100). Part-time tuition: $437 per credit hour. ***Payment plan:*** installment.

APPLYING

Standardized Tests *Required:* SAT or ACT (for admission).

Options: electronic application.

Application fee: $30.

Required: essay or personal statement, high school transcript, minimum 2.3 GPA, 3 letters of recommendation.

Application deadlines: 8/1 (freshmen), 8/1 (transfers).

Notification: 8/15 (freshmen), continuous until 8/15 (transfers).

CONTACT

Mrs. Judy Carter, Admissions Office Manager, Great Lakes Christian College, 6211 West Willow Highway, Lansing, MI 48917-1299. *Phone:* 517-321-0242 Ext. 221. *Toll-free phone:* 800-YES-GLCC. *Fax:* 517-321-5902. *E-mail:* jcarter@glcc.edu.

Griggs University

Berrien Springs, Michigan

http://www.andrews.edu/distance/

- **Independent Seventh-day Adventist** 4-year, founded 1990
- **Suburban** campus with easy access to Chicago
- **Coed**
- **Minimally difficult** entrance level

ACADEMICS

Calendar: continuous. *Degrees:* associate and bachelor's (offers only external degree programs).

STUDENT LIFE

Housing options: college housing not available.

APPLYING

Options: early admission, deferred entrance.

Application fee: $80.

Required: essay or personal statement, high school transcript, minimum 2.0 GPA.

CONTACT

Ms. Linda Lundberg, Enrollment Officer, Griggs University, PO Box 4437, Silver Spring, MD 20914-4437. *Phone:* 301-680-6590. *Toll-free phone:* 800-782-4769. *Fax:* 301-680-6577. *E-mail:* LLundberg@griggs.edu.

Hillsdale College

Hillsdale, Michigan

http://www.hillsdale.edu/

- **Independent** comprehensive, founded 1844
- **Small-town** 400-acre campus
- **Endowment** $456.0 million
- **Coed** 1,472 undergraduate students, 98% full-time, 52% women, 48% men
- **Very difficult** entrance level, 53% of applicants were admitted

UNDERGRAD STUDENTS

1,437 full-time, 35 part-time. Students come from 50 states and territories; 9 other countries; 66% are from out of state; 2% transferred in; 74% live on campus.

Freshmen

Admission: 1,833 applied, 972 admitted, 360 enrolled. ***Average high school GPA:*** 3.81. ***Test scores:*** SAT critical reading scores over 500: 98%; SAT math scores over 500: 97%; SAT writing scores over 500: 98%; ACT scores over 18: 100%; SAT critical reading scores over 600: 81%; SAT math scores over 600: 70%; SAT writing scores over 600: 78%; ACT scores over 24: 96%; SAT critical reading scores over 700: 44%; SAT math scores over 700: 23%; SAT writing scores over 700: 27%; ACT scores over 30: 50%.

Retention: 94% of full-time freshmen returned.

FACULTY

Total: 173, 77% full-time, 74% with terminal degrees.

Student/faculty ratio: 10:1.

ACADEMICS

Calendar: semesters. *Degrees:* bachelor's, master's, and doctoral.

Special study options: advanced placement credit, double majors, honors programs, independent study, internships, off-campus study, part-time degree program, student-designed majors, study abroad, summer session for credit.

Unusual degree programs: 3-2 engineering.

Computers: 368 computers/terminals and 1,058 ports are available on campus for general student use. Students can access the following: campus intranet, computer help desk, free student e-mail accounts, online (class) grades, online (class) registration, online (class) schedules. Campuswide network is available. 90% of college-owned or -operated housing units are wired for high-speed Internet access. Wireless service is available via entire campus.

STUDENT LIFE

Housing options: on-campus residence required through sophomore year; men-only, women-only, cooperative. Campus housing is university owned. Freshman campus housing is guaranteed.

Activities and organizations: drama/theater group, student-run newspaper, choral group, Students for Life, Praxis, InterVarsity, American Chemical Society, College Republicans and YAF, national fraternities, national sororities.

Athletics Member NCAA. All Division II. ***Intercollegiate sports:*** baseball M(s), basketball M(s)/W(s), cheerleading M/W, cross-country running M(s)/W(s), equestrian sports W, football M(s), riflery M(s)/W(s), rugby M(c), soccer M/W, softball W(s), swimming and diving W(s), tennis W(s), track and field M(s)/W(s), volleyball W(s). ***Intramural sports:*** basketball M/W, cheerleading W(c), crew M(c)/W(c), equestrian sports M(c)/W(c), football M/W, golf M, racquetball M/W, rugby M(c), soccer M(c)/W(c), swimming and diving M(c), table tennis M/W, tennis M(c)/W(c), volleyball M(c)/W(c).

Campus security: 24-hour emergency response devices and patrols, student patrols, late-night transport/escort service, controlled dormitory access.

Student services: health clinic, personal/psychological counseling.

COSTS & FINANCIAL AID

Costs (2015–16) ***One-time required fee:*** $300. ***Comprehensive fee:*** $34,351 includes full-time tuition ($23,840), mandatory fees ($751), and room and board ($9760). Full-time tuition and fees vary according to degree level. Part-time tuition: $950 per credit. Part-time tuition and fees vary according to degree level. ***Required fees:*** $85 per credit part-time, $751 per year part-time. ***College room only:*** $4800. Room and board charges vary according to board plan. ***Payment plans:*** tuition prepayment, installment. ***Waivers:*** children of alumni and employees or children of employees.

Financial Aid Of all full-time matriculated undergraduates who enrolled in 2014, 811 applied for aid, 781 were judged to have need, 311 had their need fully met. In 2014, 722 non-need-based awards were made. ***Average percent of need met:*** 65. ***Average financial aid package:*** $16,245. ***Average need-based loan:*** $6189. ***Average need-based gift aid:*** $7905. ***Average non-need-based aid:*** $5531. ***Average indebtedness upon graduation:*** $25,502.

APPLYING

Standardized Tests *Required:* SAT or ACT (for admission). *Recommended:* SAT Subject Tests (for admission).

Options: electronic application, early admission, early decision, early action.

Application fee: $35.

Required: essay or personal statement, high school transcript, 2 letters of recommendation. ***Recommended:*** minimum 3.5 GPA, interview.

Application deadlines: 2/15 (freshmen), 2/15 (out-of-state freshmen), 2/15 (transfers), 12/15 (early action).

Early decision deadline: 11/15.

Notification: 4/1 (freshmen), 4/1 (out-of-state freshmen), 4/1 (transfers), 12/1 (early decision), 2/15 (early action).

CONTACT

Mr. Douglas Banbury, Associate Vice President Admissions, Hillsdale College, 33 East College Street, Hillsdale, MI 49242-1298. *Phone:* 517-607-2327. *Fax:* 517-607-2223. *E-mail:* admissions@hillsdale.edu.

See previous page for display ad and page 1472 for the College Close-Up.

Hope College

Holland, Michigan

http://www.hope.edu/

- **Independent** 4-year, founded 1866, affiliated with Reformed Church in America
- **Suburban** 91-acre campus with easy access to Grand Rapids
- **Endowment** $196.0 million
- **Coed** 3,455 undergraduate students, 94% full-time, 60% women, 40% men
- **Moderately difficult** entrance level, 82% of applicants were admitted

UNDERGRAD STUDENTS

3,259 full-time, 196 part-time. Students come from 40 states and territories; 24 other countries; 32% are from out of state; 2% Black or African American, non-Hispanic/Latino; 8% Hispanic/Latino; 2% Asian, non-Hispanic/Latino; 0.1% American Indian or Alaska Native, non-Hispanic/Latino; 2% Two or more races, non-Hispanic/Latino; 0.1% Race/ethnicity unknown; 2% international; 1% transferred in; 81% live on campus.

Freshmen

Admission: 4,167 applied, 3,402 admitted, 830 enrolled. ***Average high school GPA:*** 3.71. ***Test scores:*** SAT critical reading scores over 500: 85%; SAT math scores over 500: 86%; ACT scores over 18: 99%; SAT critical reading scores over 600: 48%; SAT math scores over 600: 49%; ACT scores over 24: 73%; SAT critical reading scores over 700: 11%; SAT math scores over 700: 9%; ACT scores over 30: 21%.

Retention: 91% of full-time freshmen returned.

FACULTY

Total: 382, 62% full-time.

Student/faculty ratio: 12:1.

ACADEMICS

Calendar: semesters. *Degree:* bachelor's.

Special study options: advanced placement credit, double majors, English as a second language, independent study, internships, off-campus study, part-time degree program, services for LD students, student-designed majors, study abroad, summer session for credit. ***ROTC:*** Army (c).

Computers: 300 computers/terminals and 5,000 ports are available on campus for general student use. Students can access the following: campus intranet, computer help desk, free student e-mail accounts, online (class) grades, online (class) registration, online (class) schedules. Campuswide network is available. 100% of college-owned or -operated housing units are wired for high-speed Internet access. Wireless service is available via entire campus.

STUDENT LIFE

Housing options: on-campus residence required through junior year; coed, men-only, women-only, special housing for students with disabilities. Campus housing is university owned and leased by the school. Freshman campus housing is guaranteed.

Activities and organizations: drama/theater group, student-run newspaper, radio station, choral group, Social Activities Committee, Greek Life, Dance Marathon, Hockey Club, Relay for Life, national fraternities, national sororities.

Athletics Member NCAA. All Division III. ***Intercollegiate sports:*** baseball M, basketball M/W, cheerleading M/W, cross-country running M/W, football M, golf M/W, ice hockey M(c), lacrosse M/W, sailing M(c)/W(c), soccer M/W, softball W, swimming and diving M/W, tennis M/W, track and field M/W, volleyball W. ***Intramural sports:*** badminton M/W, basketball M/W, football M/W, ice hockey M(c), rugby M(c), sailing M(c)/W(c), soccer M/W, softball M/W, tennis M/W, ultimate Frisbee M/W, volleyball M/W, water polo M/W.

Campus security: 24-hour emergency response devices and patrols, late-night transport/escort service, controlled dormitory access.

Student services: health clinic, personal/psychological counseling.

COSTS & FINANCIAL AID

Costs (2015–16) ***Comprehensive fee:*** $39,940 includes full-time tuition ($30,370), mandatory fees ($180), and room and board ($9390). Part-time tuition and fees vary according to course load and program. ***College room only:*** $4310. Room and board charges vary according to board plan.

Payment plan: installment. ***Waivers:*** employees or children of employees.

Financial Aid Of all full-time matriculated undergraduates who enrolled in 2014, 2,353 applied for aid, 1,924 were judged to have need, 429 had their need fully met. 179 Federal Work-Study jobs (averaging $1534). 577 state and other part-time jobs (averaging $909). In 2014, 855 non-need-based awards were made. ***Average percent of need met:*** 79. ***Average financial aid package:*** $23,850. ***Average need-based loan:*** $5114. ***Average need-based gift aid:*** $18,044. ***Average non-need-based aid:*** $8286. ***Average indebtedness upon graduation:*** $31,717.

APPLYING

Standardized Tests *Required:* SAT or ACT (for admission).

Options: electronic application, early admission, deferred entrance.

Application fee: $35.

Required: essay or personal statement, high school transcript. ***Required for some:*** 1 letter of recommendation. ***Recommended:*** interview.

Application deadlines: rolling (freshmen), rolling (transfers).

Notification: continuous (freshmen), continuous (transfers).

CONTACT

Admissions Office, Hope College, 69 East 10th Street, PO Box 9000, Holland, MI 49422-9000. *Phone:* 616-395-7850. *Toll-free phone:* 800-968-7850. *E-mail:* admissions@hope.edu.

ITT Technical Institute

Canton, Michigan

http://www.itt-tech.edu/

- **Proprietary** primarily 2-year, founded 2002, part of ITT Educational Services, Inc.
- **Coed**
- **Minimally difficult** entrance level

ACADEMICS

Calendar: quarters. *Degrees:* associate and bachelor's.

STUDENT LIFE

Housing options: college housing not available.

CONTACT

Director of Recruitment, ITT Technical Institute, 1905 South Haggerty Road, Canton, MI 48188-2025. *Phone:* 784-397-7800. *Toll-free phone:* 800-247-4477.

ITT Technical Institute

Dearborn, Michigan

http://www.itt-tech.edu/

- **Proprietary** primarily 2-year, part of ITT Educational Services, Inc.
- **Coed**

ACADEMICS

Calendar: quarters. *Degrees:* associate and bachelor's.

CONTACT

Director of Recruitment, ITT Technical Institute, 19855 W. Outer Drive, Suite L10W, Dearborn, MI 48124. *Phone:* 313-278-5208. *Toll-free phone:* 800-605-0801.

ITT Technical Institute

Swartz Creek, Michigan

http://www.itt-tech.edu/

- **Proprietary** primarily 2-year, founded 2005, part of ITT Educational Services, Inc.
- **Coed**
- **Minimally difficult** entrance level

ACADEMICS

Calendar: quarters. *Degrees:* associate and bachelor's.

CONTACT

Director of Recruitment, ITT Technical Institute, 6359 Miller Road, Swartz Creek, MI 48473. *Phone:* 810-628-2500. *Toll-free phone:* 800-514-6564.

ITT Technical Institute

Troy, Michigan

http://www.itt-tech.edu/

- **Proprietary** primarily 2-year, founded 1987, part of ITT Educational Services, Inc.
- **Coed**
- **Minimally difficult** entrance level

ACADEMICS

Calendar: quarters. *Degrees:* associate and bachelor's.

STUDENT LIFE

Housing options: college housing not available.

CONTACT

Director of Recruitment, ITT Technical Institute, 1522 East Big Beaver Road, Troy, MI 48083-1905. *Phone:* 248-524-1800. *Toll-free phone:* 800-832-6817.

ITT Technical Institute

Wyoming, Michigan

http://www.itt-tech.edu/

- **Proprietary** primarily 2-year, part of ITT Educational Services, Inc.
- **Coed**
- **Minimally difficult** entrance level

ACADEMICS

Calendar: quarters. *Degrees:* associate and bachelor's.

STUDENT LIFE

Housing options: college housing not available.

CONTACT

Director of Recruitment, ITT Technical Institute, 1980 Metro Court SW, Wyoming, MI 49519. *Phone:* 616-406-1200. *Toll-free phone:* 800-632-4676.

Kalamazoo College

Kalamazoo, Michigan

http://www.kzoo.edu/

- **Independent** 4-year, founded 1833, affiliated with American Baptist Churches in the U.S.A.
- **Suburban** 60-acre campus with easy access to Grand Rapids
- **Endowment** $222.0 million
- **Coed** 1,461 undergraduate students, 99% full-time, 57% women, 43% men
- **Very difficult** entrance level, 70% of applicants were admitted

UNDERGRAD STUDENTS

1,448 full-time, 13 part-time. Students come from 42 states and territories; 28 other countries; 31% are from out of state; 5% Black or African American, non-Hispanic/Latino; 9% Hispanic/Latino; 6% Asian, non-Hispanic/Latino; 0.2% Native Hawaiian or other Pacific Islander, non-Hispanic/Latino; 0.1% American Indian or Alaska Native, non-Hispanic/Latino; 5% Two or more races, non-Hispanic/Latino; 6% Race/ethnicity unknown; 6% international; 1% transferred in; 65% live on campus.

Freshmen

Admission: 2,366 applied, 1,648 admitted, 357 enrolled. ***Average high school GPA:*** 3.78. ***Test scores:*** SAT critical reading scores over 500: 87%; SAT math scores over 500: 94%; SAT writing scores over 500: 89%; ACT scores over 18: 100%; SAT critical reading scores over 600: 52%; SAT math scores over 600: 60%; SAT writing scores over 600: 56%; ACT scores over 24: 87%; SAT critical reading scores over 700: 15%; SAT math scores over 700: 27%; SAT writing scores over 700: 17%; ACT scores over 30: 30%.

Retention: 92% of full-time freshmen returned.

FACULTY

Total: 124, 82% full-time, 84% with terminal degrees.

Student/faculty ratio: 12:1.

ACADEMICS
Calendar: quarters. *Degree:* bachelor's.

Special study options: advanced placement credit, double majors, independent study, internships, off-campus study, services for LD students, student-designed majors, study abroad. ***ROTC:*** Army (c).

Unusual degree programs: 3-2 engineering with The University of Michigan and Washington University in St. Louis, Missouri, but any ABET accredited program is acceptable for the 3/2 engineering program.

Computers: 250 computers/terminals are available on campus for general student use. Students can access the following: campus intranet, computer help desk, free student e-mail accounts, online (class) grades, online (class) registration, online (class) schedules, Residential computer consultant. Campuswide network is available. 100% of college-owned or -operated housing units are wired for high-speed Internet access. Wireless service is available via entire campus.

STUDENT LIFE
Housing options: on-campus residence required through sophomore year; coed, special housing for students with disabilities. Campus housing is university owned. Freshman campus housing is guaranteed.

Activities and organizations: drama/theater group, student-run newspaper, radio station, choral group, Frelon Dance Company, Acappella groups, Environmental Student Organization, Kaleidoscope - LGBT, Student Commission - Student Government.

Athletics Member NCAA. All Division III. ***Intercollegiate sports:*** baseball M, basketball M/W, cross-country running M/W, football M, golf M/W, lacrosse M/W, soccer M/W, softball W, swimming and diving M/W, tennis M/W, volleyball W. ***Intramural sports:*** badminton M/W, basketball M/W, cheerleading M(c)/W(c), lacrosse M(c)/W(c), racquetball M/W, soccer M/W, softball M/W, table tennis M/W, tennis M/W, ultimate Frisbee M(c)/W(c), volleyball M/W.

Campus security: 24-hour emergency response devices and patrols, late-night transport/escort service, controlled dormitory access.

Student services: health clinic, personal/psychological counseling.

COSTS & FINANCIAL AID
Costs (2014–15) ***Comprehensive fee:*** $49,740 includes full-time tuition ($40,728), mandatory fees ($333), and room and board ($8679). ***College room only:*** $4233. Room and board charges vary according to board plan and housing facility. ***Payment plan:*** installment. ***Waivers:*** employees or children of employees.

Financial Aid Of all full-time matriculated undergraduates who enrolled in 2014, 1,074 applied for aid, 957 were judged to have need, 444 had their need fully met. 491 Federal Work-Study jobs (averaging $2440). In 2014, 429 non-need-based awards were made. ***Average percent of need met:*** 91. ***Average financial aid package:*** $34,463. ***Average need-based loan:*** $5747. ***Average need-based gift aid:*** $26,990. ***Average non-need-based aid:*** $16,358. ***Average indebtedness upon graduation:*** $28,405.

APPLYING
Standardized Tests *Required:* SAT or ACT (for admission).

Options: electronic application, early decision, early action, deferred entrance.

Required: essay or personal statement, high school transcript, 2 letters of recommendation. ***Recommended:*** minimum 3.0 GPA, interview.

Application deadlines: 1/15 (freshmen), 5/1 (transfers), 11/15 (early action).

Early decision deadline: 11/15 (for plan 1), 2/15 (for plan 2).

Notification: 4/1 (freshmen), 5/15 (transfers), 12/1 (early decision plan 1), 3/1 (early decision plan 2), 12/20 (early action).

CONTACT
Records Processing Team, Kalamazoo College, Mandelle Hall, 1200 Academy Street, Kalamazoo, MI 49006-3295. *Phone:* 269-337-5759. *Toll-free phone:* 800-253-3602. *Fax:* 269-337-7390. *E-mail:* admission.records@kzoo.edu.

★ Kettering University
Flint, Michigan
http://www.kettering.edu/

- **Independent** comprehensive, founded 1919
- **Urban** 85-acre campus with easy access to Detroit
- **Endowment** $81.3 million
- **Coed** 1,741 undergraduate students, 92% full-time, 18% women, 82% men
- **Very difficult** entrance level, 72% of applicants were admitted

UNDERGRAD STUDENTS
1,608 full-time, 133 part-time. Students come from 39 states and territories; 18 other countries; 18% are from out of state; 4% Black or African American, non-Hispanic/Latino; 3% Hispanic/Latino; 3% Asian, non-Hispanic/Latino; 0.1% Native Hawaiian or other Pacific Islander, non-Hispanic/Latino; 0.2% American Indian or Alaska Native, non-Hispanic/Latino; 3% Two or more races, non-Hispanic/Latino; 6% Race/ethnicity unknown; 7% international; 2% transferred in; 34% live on campus.

Freshmen
Admission: 1,587 applied, 1,137 admitted, 364 enrolled. ***Average high school GPA:*** 3.65. ***Test scores:*** SAT critical reading scores over 500: 85%; SAT math scores over 500: 100%; ACT scores over 18: 100%; SAT critical reading scores over 600: 42%; SAT math scores over 600: 73%; ACT scores over 24: 87%; SAT critical reading scores over 700: 4%; SAT math scores over 700: 11%; ACT scores over 30: 23%.

Retention: 92% of full-time freshmen returned.

FACULTY
Total: 134, 89% full-time, 75% with terminal degrees.

Student/faculty ratio: 13:1.

ACADEMICS
Calendar: semesters (11 weeks of full-time study plus 12 weeks of paid co-op experience per semester). *Degrees:* bachelor's and master's.

Special study options: advanced placement credit, cooperative education, distance learning, double majors, external degree program, independent study, internships, services for LD students, study abroad, summer session for credit.

Computers: 450 computers/terminals and 800 ports are available on campus for general student use. Students can access the following: campus intranet, computer help desk, free student e-mail accounts, online (class) grades, online (class) registration, online (class) schedules. Campuswide network is available. 100% of college-owned or -operated housing units are wired for high-speed Internet access. Wireless service is available via entire campus.

STUDENT LIFE
Housing options: on-campus residence required for freshman year; coed. Campus housing is university owned and is provided by a third party. Freshman campus housing is guaranteed.

Activities and organizations: student-run newspaper, radio station, choral group, student government, Dance Club, Firebirds, Outdoors Club, International Club, national fraternities, national sororities.

Athletics ***Intramural sports:*** baseball M(c)/W(c), basketball M/W, bowling M/W, football M/W, golf M(c)/W(c), ice hockey M(c)/W(c), lacrosse M(c)/W(c), racquetball M/W, riflery M(c)/W(c), soccer M/W, softball M/W, squash M/W, table tennis M(c)/W(c), tennis M/W, ultimate Frisbee M(c)/W(c), volleyball M/W, water polo M/W.

Campus security: 24-hour emergency response devices and patrols, late-night transport/escort service, controlled dormitory access, security card access to all campus buildings 24/7 except the campus center main entrance which is secure 11pm-7am.

Student services: health clinic, personal/psychological counseling, women's center.

COSTS & FINANCIAL AID
Costs (2014–15) ***One-time required fee:*** $300. ***Comprehensive fee:*** $44,220 includes full-time tuition ($36,980) and room and board ($7240). Part-time tuition: $1233 per credit hour. No tuition increase for student's term of enrollment. ***College room only:*** $4420. ***Payment plan:*** installment. ***Waivers:*** employees or children of employees.

Financial Aid Of all full-time matriculated undergraduates who enrolled in 2013, 1,274 applied for aid, 1,190 were judged to have need, 145 had their need fully met. In 2013, 362 non-need-based awards were made. ***Average percent of need met:*** 64. ***Average financial aid package:*** $19,146. ***Average need-based loan:*** $4333. ***Average need-based gift aid:*** $11,658. ***Average non-need-based aid:*** $12,757.

APPLYING

Standardized Tests *Required:* SAT or ACT (for admission).

Options: electronic application, deferred entrance.

Required: high school transcript. ***Required for some:*** essay or personal statement. ***Recommended:*** minimum 3.0 GPA, interview.

Application deadlines: rolling (freshmen), rolling (out-of-state freshmen), rolling (transfers).

Notification: continuous (freshmen), continuous (out-of-state freshmen), continuous (transfers).

CONTACT

Mr. Kip Darcy, Vice President of Marketing, Communications and Enrollment, Kettering University, 1700 University Avenue, Flint, MI 48504-6214. *Phone:* 810-762-9511. *Toll-free phone:* 800-955-4464 Ext. 7865 (in-state); 800-955-4464 (out-of-state). *Fax:* 810-762-9837. *E-mail:* kdarcy@kettering.edu.

See below for display ad and page 1484 for the College Close-Up.

Kuyper College

Grand Rapids, Michigan

http://www.kuyper.edu/

- **Independent Christian** 4-year, founded 1939
- **Suburban** 34-acre campus with easy access to Grand Rapids
- **Endowment** $7.4 million
- **Coed** 272 undergraduate students, 86% full-time, 51% women, 49% men
- **Moderately difficult** entrance level, 71% of applicants were admitted

UNDERGRAD STUDENTS

235 full-time, 37 part-time. Students come from 16 states and territories; 10 other countries; 10% are from out of state; 7% Black or African American, non-Hispanic/Latino; 1% Hispanic/Latino; 3% Asian, non-Hispanic/Latino; 0.7% American Indian or Alaska Native, non-Hispanic/Latino; 4% Two or more races, non-Hispanic/Latino; 7% Race/ethnicity unknown; 5% international; 42% live on campus.

Freshmen

Admission: 201 applied, 142 admitted, 54 enrolled. ***Average high school GPA:*** 3.26.

Retention: 59% of full-time freshmen returned.

FACULTY

Total: 39, 33% full-time, 31% with terminal degrees.

Student/faculty ratio: 12:1.

ACADEMICS

Calendar: semesters. *Degrees:* certificates, associate, bachelor's, and postbachelor's certificates.

Special study options: academic remediation for entering students, advanced placement credit, cooperative education, distance learning, double majors, independent study, internships, off-campus study, part-time degree program, services for LD students, study abroad, summer session for credit. ***ROTC:*** Army (c).

Computers: 70 computers/terminals and 70 ports are available on campus for general student use. Students can access the following: campus intranet, computer help desk, free student e-mail accounts, online (class) grades, online (class) registration, online (class) schedules. Campuswide network is available. 100% of college-owned or -operated housing units are wired for high-speed Internet access. Wireless service is available via entire campus.

STUDENT LIFE

Housing options: on-campus residence required through sophomore year; coed. Campus housing is university owned. Freshman campus housing is guaranteed.

Activities and organizations: drama/theater group, choral group, intramurals, Student Activities Club, Helping and Nurturing During Service, yearbook, Roots.

Athletics Member NCCAA. ***Intercollegiate sports:*** basketball M/W, cross-country running M/W, soccer M, volleyball W. ***Intramural sports:***

basketball M/W, football M/W, soccer M/W, softball M/W, table tennis M/W, ultimate Frisbee M/W, volleyball M/W.

Campus security: 24-hour emergency response devices, student patrols, late-night transport/escort service, controlled dormitory access.

Student services: health clinic, personal/psychological counseling.

COSTS & FINANCIAL AID

Costs (2014–15) ***One-time required fee:*** $544. ***Comprehensive fee:*** $25,584 includes full-time tuition ($18,400), mandatory fees ($584), and room and board ($6600). Full-time tuition and fees vary according to course load and reciprocity agreements. Part-time tuition: $880 per credit hour. Part-time tuition and fees vary according to course load and reciprocity agreements. ***Required fees:*** $295 per year part-time. ***Room and board:*** Room and board charges vary according to board plan, housing facility, and student level. ***Payment plans:*** installment, deferred payment. ***Waivers:*** employees or children of employees.

Financial Aid Of all full-time matriculated undergraduates who enrolled in 2013, 239 applied for aid, 228 were judged to have need, 14 had their need fully met. 12 Federal Work-Study jobs (averaging $2487). 110 state and other part-time jobs (averaging $2636). In 2013, 3 non-need-based awards were made. ***Average percent of need met:*** 71. ***Average financial aid package:*** $14,146. ***Average need-based loan:*** $5313. ***Average need-based gift aid:*** $8763. ***Average non-need-based aid:*** $7000. ***Average indebtedness upon graduation:*** $35,753.

APPLYING

Options: electronic application, deferred entrance.

Required: essay or personal statement, high school transcript, minimum 2.5 GPA. ***Recommended:*** interview.

Application deadlines: rolling (freshmen), rolling (transfers).

Notification: continuous (freshmen), continuous (transfers).

CONTACT

Admissions Office, Kuyper College, 3333 East Beltline Avenue, NE, Grand Rapids, MI 49525. *Phone:* 616-222-3000 Ext. 632. *Fax:* 616-222-3045. *E-mail:* admissions@kuyper.edu.

Lake Superior State University

Sault Sainte Marie, Michigan

http://www.lssu.edu/

- **State-supported** comprehensive, founded 1946
- **Small-town** 115-acre campus
- **Endowment** $9.0 million
- **Coed**
- **Moderately difficult** entrance level

FACULTY

Student/faculty ratio: 15:1.

ACADEMICS

Calendar: semesters. *Degrees:* certificates, associate, bachelor's, master's, and postbachelor's certificates.

STUDENT LIFE

Housing options: on-campus residence required through sophomore year; coed, men-only, women-only. Campus housing is university owned. Freshman campus housing is guaranteed.

Activities and organizations: drama/theater group, student-run newspaper, radio station, choral group, Activities Board, SAILS - Student Alumni Involved in Lake State, Fisheries and Wildlife, Enactus (Formally known as SIFE), Chemistry and Environmental Science Club, national fraternities, national sororities.

Athletics Member NCAA. All Division II except ice hockey (Division I).

Campus security: 24-hour emergency response devices and patrols, student patrols, late-night transport/escort service.

Student services: health clinic, personal/psychological counseling.

COSTS & FINANCIAL AID

Costs (2014–15) ***One-time required fee:*** $125. ***Tuition:*** state resident $10,128 full-time, $422 per credit hour part-time; nonresident $15,192 full-time, $633 per credit hour part-time. Full-time tuition and fees vary according to program and reciprocity agreements. Part-time tuition and fees vary according to course load, location, program, and reciprocity agreements. ***Required fees:*** $120 full-time, $60 per term part-time. ***Room and board:*** $8987. Room and board charges vary according to board plan and housing facility. ***Payment plans:*** installment, deferred payment.

Financial Aid Of all full-time matriculated undergraduates who enrolled in 2012, 1,728 applied for aid, 1,443 were judged to have need, 224 had their need fully met. In 2012, 233 non-need-based awards were made. ***Average percent of need met:*** 60. ***Average financial aid package:*** $9515. ***Average need-based loan:*** $4103. ***Average need-based gift aid:*** $5732. ***Average non-need-based aid:*** $3635. ***Average indebtedness upon graduation:*** $28,479.

APPLYING

Standardized Tests *Required:* SAT or ACT (for admission).

Options: electronic application, deferred entrance.

Application fee: $25.

Required: high school transcript. ***Required for some:*** SAT or ACT for students out of high school for less than 26 months or have less than 19 transferable credits.

CONTACT

Lake Superior State University, 650 West Easterday Avenue, Sault Sainte Marie, MI 49783. *Phone:* 906-635-2231. *Toll-free phone:* 888-800-LSSU Ext. 2231.

★ Lawrence Technological University

Southfield, Michigan

http://www.ltu.edu/

- **Independent** university, founded 1932
- **Suburban** 102-acre campus with easy access to Detroit
- **Endowment** $57.9 million
- **Coed** 2,798 undergraduate students, 57% full-time, 24% women, 76% men
- **Moderately difficult** entrance level, 57% of applicants were admitted

UNDERGRAD STUDENTS

1,596 full-time, 1,202 part-time. Students come from 21 states and territories; 43 other countries; 4% are from out of state; 6% Black or African American, non-Hispanic/Latino; 3% Hispanic/Latino; 17% Asian, non-Hispanic/Latino; 0.3% American Indian or Alaska Native, non-Hispanic/Latino; 20% Race/ethnicity unknown; 6% international; 6% transferred in; 24% live on campus.

Freshmen

Admission: 2,285 applied, 1,312 admitted, 337 enrolled. ***Average high school GPA:*** 3.43. ***Test scores:*** SAT critical reading scores over 500: 75%; SAT math scores over 500: 83%; SAT writing scores over 500: 62%; ACT scores over 18: 91%; SAT critical reading scores over 600: 18%; SAT math scores over 600: 56%; SAT writing scores over 600: 16%; ACT scores over 24: 66%; SAT critical reading scores over 700: 8%; SAT math scores over 700: 6%; ACT scores over 30: 14%.

Retention: 82% of full-time freshmen returned.

FACULTY

Total: 413, 30% full-time, 36% with terminal degrees.

Student/faculty ratio: 11:1.

ACADEMICS

Calendar: semesters. *Degrees:* certificates, associate, bachelor's, master's, doctoral, and postbachelor's certificates.

Special study options: academic remediation for entering students, accelerated degree program, adult/continuing education programs, advanced placement credit, cooperative education, distance learning, double majors, English as a second language, honors programs, independent study, internships, off-campus study, part-time degree program, services for LD students, study abroad, summer session for credit. ***ROTC:*** Air Force (c).

Computers: 126 computers/terminals and 3,170 ports are available on campus for general student use. Students can access the following: campus intranet, computer help desk, free student e-mail accounts, online (class) grades, online (class) registration, online (class) schedules, degree audit, Blackboard, SCT Banner (student information), Personal websites, Document collection. Campuswide network is available. 50% of college-owned or -operated housing units are wired for high-speed Internet access. Wireless service is available via entire campus.

STUDENT LIFE
Housing options: coed, special housing for students with disabilities. Campus housing is university owned. Freshman applicants given priority for college housing.

Activities and organizations: drama/theater group, student-run newspaper, American Institute of Architecture Students, American Society of Mechanical Engineers, Institute of Electric and Electronic Engineers, American Society of Civil Engineers, student government, national fraternities, national sororities.

Athletics Member NAIA. ***Intercollegiate sports:*** basketball M(s)/W(s), bowling M(s)/W(s), cross-country running M(s)/W(s), ice hockey M, lacrosse M(s)/W(s), soccer M(s)/W(s), volleyball W(s). ***Intramural sports:*** badminton M/W, basketball M/W, bowling M/W, cross-country running M/W, football M/W, golf M/W, ice hockey M(c), racquetball M/W, skiing (downhill) M/W, soccer M/W, softball M/W, table tennis M/W, tennis M/W, ultimate Frisbee M(c), volleyball M/W.

Campus security: 24-hour emergency response devices and patrols, late-night transport/escort service, controlled dormitory access.

Student services: personal/psychological counseling.

COSTS & FINANCIAL AID
Costs (2014–15) ***Comprehensive fee:*** $39,186 includes full-time tuition ($29,580), mandatory fees ($620), and room and board ($8986). Full-time tuition and fees vary according to course level, degree level, location, program, and student level. Part-time tuition: $986 per credit hour. Part-time tuition and fees vary according to course level, degree level, location, program, and student level. ***Required fees:*** $310 per term part-time. ***College room only:*** $5095. Room and board charges vary according to board plan and housing facility. ***Payment plan:*** installment. ***Waivers:*** employees or children of employees.

Financial Aid Of all full-time matriculated undergraduates who enrolled in 2013, 1,230 applied for aid, 915 were judged to have need, 130 had their need fully met. 80 Federal Work-Study jobs (averaging $2259). In 2013, 266 non-need-based awards were made. ***Average percent of need met:*** 68. ***Average financial aid package:*** $23,443. ***Average need-based loan:*** $7382. ***Average need-based gift aid:*** $14,033. ***Average non-need-based aid:*** $12,603. ***Average indebtedness upon graduation:*** $38,966.

APPLYING
Standardized Tests *Required:* SAT or ACT (for admission).

Options: electronic application, deferred entrance.

Application fee: $30.

Required: high school transcript, minimum 2.5 GPA. ***Required for some:*** essay or personal statement, minimum 2.8 GPA, 1 letter of recommendation, interview.

Application deadlines: 8/15 (freshmen), 8/15 (transfers).

Notification: continuous until 8/26 (freshmen), continuous until 8/26 (transfers).

CONTACT
Jane Rohrback, Director of Admissions, Lawrence Technological University, 21000 West Ten Mile Road, Southfield, MI 48075. *Phone:* 248-204-3160. *Toll-free phone:* 800-225-5588. *Fax:* 248-204-2228. *E-mail:* admissions@ltu.edu.

Madonna University

Livonia, Michigan

http://www.madonna.edu/

- **Independent Roman Catholic** comprehensive, founded 1947
- **Suburban** 97-acre campus with easy access to Detroit
- **Endowment** $38.6 million
- **Coed** 3,008 undergraduate students, 52% full-time, 67% women, 33% men
- **Moderately difficult** entrance level, 59% of applicants were admitted

UNDERGRAD STUDENTS
1,550 full-time, 1,458 part-time. Students come from 10 states and territories; 47 other countries; 1% are from out of state; 13% Black or African American, non-Hispanic/Latino; 4% Hispanic/Latino; 0.7% Asian, non-Hispanic/Latino; 0.1% Native Hawaiian or other Pacific Islander, non-Hispanic/Latino; 0.2% American Indian or Alaska Native, non-Hispanic/Latino; 2% Two or more races, non-Hispanic/Latino; 0.6% Race/ethnicity unknown; 16% international; 15% transferred in; 8% live on campus.

Freshmen
Admission: 838 applied, 491 admitted, 174 enrolled. ***Average high school GPA:*** 3.1. ***Test scores:*** SAT critical reading scores over 500: 50%; SAT math scores over 500: 50%; SAT writing scores over 500: 50%; ACT scores over 18: 86%; SAT critical reading scores over 600: 25%; SAT math scores over 600: 50%; ACT scores over 24: 40%; SAT critical reading scores over 700: 25%; ACT scores over 30: 7%.

Retention: 80% of full-time freshmen returned.

FACULTY
Total: 327, 34% full-time, 32% with terminal degrees.

Student/faculty ratio: 11:1.

ACADEMICS
Calendar: semesters. *Degrees:* certificates, diplomas, associate, bachelor's, master's, doctoral, post-master's, and postbachelor's certificates.

Special study options: academic remediation for entering students, accelerated degree program, adult/continuing education programs, advanced placement credit, cooperative education, distance learning, double majors, English as a second language, independent study, internships, off-campus study, part-time degree program, services for LD students, student-designed majors, study abroad, summer session for credit. ***ROTC:*** Army (c).

Computers: 262 computers/terminals and 262 ports are available on campus for general student use. Students can access the following: campus intranet, computer help desk, free student e-mail accounts, online (class) grades, online (class) registration, online (class) schedules, online payments, online statements, online Unofficial Transcripts. Campuswide network is available. 100% of college-owned or -operated housing units are wired for high-speed Internet access. Wireless service is available via classrooms, computer labs, dorm rooms, learning centers, libraries, student centers.

STUDENT LIFE
Housing options: men-only, women-only. Campus housing is university owned. Freshman campus housing is guaranteed.

Activities and organizations: drama/theater group, student-run newspaper, radio station, choral group, Campus Ministry, Red Cross Club, Madonna University Nursing Student Association, Broadcast & Film Club, Society of Future Teachers.

Athletics Member NAIA. ***Intercollegiate sports:*** baseball M(s), basketball M(s)/W(s), cross-country running M(s)/W(s), golf M(s)/W(s), soccer M(s)/W(s), softball W(s), volleyball W(s). ***Intramural sports:*** basketball M/W, volleyball M/W.

Campus security: 24-hour emergency response devices and patrols, late-night transport/escort service, controlled dormitory access.

Student services: personal/psychological counseling.

COSTS & FINANCIAL AID
Costs (2014–15) ***Comprehensive fee:*** $26,000 includes full-time tuition ($17,250), mandatory fees ($140), and room and board ($8610). Full-time tuition and fees vary according to course load. Part-time tuition: $575 per credit hour. Part-time tuition and fees vary according to course load. ***Required fees:*** $70 per term part-time. ***College room only:*** $4140. Room and board charges vary according to board plan. ***Payment plan:*** deferred payment. ***Waivers:*** senior citizens and employees or children of employees.

Financial Aid Of all full-time matriculated undergraduates who enrolled in 2007, 862 applied for aid, 698 were judged to have need, 122 had their need fully met. In 2007, 172 non-need-based awards were made. ***Average percent of need met:*** 56. ***Average financial aid package:*** $7396. ***Average need-based loan:*** $3862. ***Average need-based gift aid:*** $4508. ***Average non-need-based aid:*** $2427.

APPLYING
Standardized Tests *Required:* SAT or ACT (for admission).

Options: electronic application, deferred entrance.

Application fee: $25.

Required: essay or personal statement, high school transcript, minimum 2.8 GPA. ***Required for some:*** 2 letters of recommendation, Pre-Nursing requires 3.0 GPA. ***Recommended:*** interview.

Application deadlines: rolling (freshmen), rolling (transfers).

Notification: continuous (freshmen), continuous (transfers).

CONTACT

Mr. Mike Quattro, Director of Enrollment Management, Madonna University, 36600 Schoolcraft Road, Livonia, MI 48150-1173. *Phone:* 734-432-5341. *Toll-free phone:* 800-852-4951. *Fax:* 734-432-5424. *E-mail:* admissions@madonna.edu.

Michigan State University

East Lansing, Michigan

http://www.msu.edu/

- **State-supported** university, founded 1855
- **Suburban** 5192-acre campus with easy access to Detroit
- **Endowment** $2.1 billion
- **Coed** 38,786 undergraduate students, 91% full-time, 50% women, 50% men
- **Moderately difficult** entrance level, 66% of applicants were admitted

UNDERGRAD STUDENTS

35,341 full-time, 3,445 part-time. Students come from 55 states and territories; 99 other countries; 11% are from out of state; 7% Black or African American, non-Hispanic/Latino; 4% Hispanic/Latino; 4% Asian, non-Hispanic/Latino; 0.1% Native Hawaiian or other Pacific Islander, non-Hispanic/Latino; 0.2% American Indian or Alaska Native, non-Hispanic/Latino; 3% Two or more races, non-Hispanic/Latino; 1% Race/ethnicity unknown; 13% international; 4% transferred in; 39% live on campus.

Freshmen

Admission: 33,211 applied, 21,950 admitted, 8,055 enrolled. ***Average high school GPA:*** 3.66. ***Test scores:*** SAT critical reading scores over 500: 52%; SAT math scores over 500: 88%; SAT writing scores over 500: 61%; ACT scores over 18: 98%; SAT critical reading scores over 600: 22%; SAT math scores over 600: 58%; SAT writing scores over 600: 19%; ACT scores over 24: 74%; SAT critical reading scores over 700: 6%; SAT math scores over 700: 21%; SAT writing scores over 700: 4%; ACT scores over 30: 16%.

Retention: 92% of full-time freshmen returned.

FACULTY

Total: 2,793, 86% full-time, 84% with terminal degrees.

Student/faculty ratio: 17:1.

ACADEMICS

Calendar: semesters. *Degrees:* certificates, bachelor's, master's, doctoral, and post-master's certificates.

Special study options: academic remediation for entering students, accelerated degree program, adult/continuing education programs, advanced placement credit, cooperative education, distance learning, double majors, English as a second language, freshman honors college, honors programs, independent study, internships, off-campus study, part-time degree program, services for LD students, student-designed majors, study abroad, summer session for credit. ***ROTC:*** Army (b), Air Force (b).

Unusual degree programs: 3-2 engineering.

Computers: Students can access the following: campus intranet, computer help desk, free student e-mail accounts, online (class) grades, online (class) registration, online (class) schedules. Campuswide network is available. 100% of college-owned or -operated housing units are wired for high-speed Internet access. Wireless service is available via classrooms, computer centers, computer labs, dorm rooms, learning centers, libraries, student centers.

STUDENT LIFE

Housing options: on-campus residence required for freshman year; coed, women-only, cooperative, special housing for students with disabilities. Campus housing is university owned. Freshman campus housing is guaranteed.

Activities and organizations: drama/theater group, student-run newspaper, radio and television station, choral group, marching band, national fraternities, national sororities.

Athletics Member NCAA. All Division I except football (Division I-A). ***Intercollegiate sports:*** baseball M(s), basketball M(s)/W(s), cheerleading M/W, crew M(c)/W(s), cross-country running M(s)/W(s), equestrian sports M(c)/W(c), fencing M(c)/W(c), field hockey W(s), golf M(s)/W(s), gymnastics W(s), ice hockey M(s)/W(c), lacrosse M(c)/W(c), rugby M(c)/W(c), sailing M(c)/W(c), skiing (downhill) M(c)/W(c), soccer M(s)/W(s), softball W(s), swimming and diving M(s)/W(s), table tennis M(c)/W(c), tennis M(s)/W(s), track and field M(s)/W(s), volleyball M(c)/W(s), water polo M(c)/W(c), wrestling M(s). ***Intramural sports:*** archery M/W, badminton M/W, baseball M(c), basketball M/W, bowling M/W, cheerleading W(c), crew M(c)/W(c), cross-country running M/W, fencing M/W, football M/W, golf M/W, ice hockey M/W, lacrosse M/W, racquetball M/W, riflery M/W, rugby M/W, soccer M/W, softball M/W, squash M/W, table tennis M/W, tennis M/W, ultimate Frisbee M(c)/W(c), volleyball M/W.

Campus security: 24-hour emergency response devices and patrols, late-night transport/escort service, controlled dormitory access, self-defense workshops.

Student services: health clinic, personal/psychological counseling, women's center, legal services.

COSTS & FINANCIAL AID

Costs (2014–15) ***Tuition:*** state resident $13,200 full-time, $440 per credit hour part-time; nonresident $34,965 full-time, $1166 per credit hour part-time. Full-time tuition and fees vary according to course load, program, and student level. Part-time tuition and fees vary according to course load, program, and student level. ***Room and board:*** $9154; room only: $3780. Room and board charges vary according to board plan and housing facility. ***Payment plan:*** deferred payment. ***Waivers:*** employees or children of employees.

Financial Aid Of all full-time matriculated undergraduates who enrolled in 2014, 21,555 applied for aid, 16,673 were judged to have need, 2,254 had their need fully met. In 2014, 2534 non-need-based awards were made. ***Average percent of need met:*** 62. ***Average financial aid package:*** $12,712. ***Average need-based loan:*** $4166. ***Average need-based gift aid:*** $9587. ***Average non-need-based aid:*** $8241. ***Average indebtedness upon graduation:*** $26,122.

APPLYING

Standardized Tests *Required:* SAT or ACT (for admission).

Options: electronic application, early action.

Application fee: $50.

Required: essay or personal statement, high school transcript.

Application deadlines: rolling (freshmen), rolling (out-of-state freshmen), rolling (transfers).

Notification: continuous (freshmen), continuous (out-of-state freshmen), continuous (transfers).

CONTACT

James Cotter, Director of Admissions, Michigan State University, 250 Administration Building, East Lansing, MI 48824. *Phone:* 517-355-8332. *Fax:* 517-353-1647. *E-mail:* admis@msu.edu.

Michigan Technological University

Houghton, Michigan

http://www.mtu.edu/

- **State-supported** university, founded 1885
- **Small-town** 925-acre campus
- **Endowment** $93.0 million
- **Coed** 5,662 undergraduate students, 93% full-time, 26% women, 74% men
- **Moderately difficult** entrance level, 76% of applicants were admitted

UNDERGRAD STUDENTS

5,242 full-time, 420 part-time. Students come from 43 states and territories; 33 other countries; 23% are from out of state; 1% Black or African American, non-Hispanic/Latino; 2% Hispanic/Latino; 1% Asian, non-Hispanic/Latino; 0.1% Native Hawaiian or other Pacific Islander, non-Hispanic/Latino; 0.6% American Indian or Alaska Native, non-Hispanic/Latino; 2% Two or more races, non-Hispanic/Latino; 3% Race/ethnicity unknown; 5% international; 4% transferred in; 48% live on campus.

Freshmen

Admission: 5,111 applied, 3,859 admitted, 1,199 enrolled. ***Average high school GPA:*** 3.69. ***Test scores:*** SAT critical reading scores over 500: 85%; SAT math scores over 500: 99%; SAT writing scores over 500: 75%; ACT scores over 18: 100%; SAT critical reading scores over 600: 51%; SAT math scores over 600: 69%; SAT writing scores over 600: 46%; ACT scores over 24: 84%; SAT critical reading scores over 700: 17%; SAT math scores over 700: 21%; SAT writing scores over 700: 6%; ACT scores over 30: 26%.

Retention: 85% of full-time freshmen returned.

FACULTY

Total: 453, 91% full-time, 84% with terminal degrees.

Student/faculty ratio: 13:1.

ACADEMICS

Calendar: semesters. *Degrees:* certificates, associate, bachelor's, master's, doctoral, and postbachelor's certificates.

Special study options: advanced placement credit, cooperative education, distance learning, double majors, English as a second language, honors programs, independent study, internships, off-campus study, part-time degree program, services for LD students, study abroad, summer session for credit. ***ROTC:*** Army (b), Air Force (b).

Unusual degree programs: 3-2 engineering with Adrian College, MI; Albion College, MI; Augsburg College, MN; Northland College, WI; Olivet College, MI; and University of Wisconsin-Superior; forestry with Northland College, WI and University of Wisconsin-Superior.

Computers: 880 computers/terminals and 10 ports are available on campus for general student use. Students can access the following: campus intranet, computer help desk, free student e-mail accounts, online (class) grades, online (class) registration, online (class) schedules. Campuswide network is available. 100% of college-owned or -operated housing units are wired for high-speed Internet access. Wireless service is available via entire campus.

STUDENT LIFE

Housing options: on-campus residence required for freshman year; coed, cooperative, special housing for students with disabilities. Campus housing is university owned. Freshman campus housing is guaranteed.

Activities and organizations: drama/theater group, student-run newspaper, radio station, choral group, Huskies Pep Band, American Society of Mechanical Engineers, WMTU Radio Station, Indian Students Association, Society for Women Engineers, national fraternities, national sororities.

Athletics Member NCAA. All Division II except ice hockey (Division I). ***Intercollegiate sports:*** archery M(c)/W(c), badminton M(c)/W(c), baseball M(c), basketball M(s)/W(s), cheerleading M(c)/W(c), crew M(c)/W(c), cross-country running M(s)/W(s), fencing M(c)/W(c), football M(s), golf M(c)/W(c), gymnastics M(c)/W(c), ice hockey M(s)/W(c), lacrosse M(c)/W(c), racquetball M(c)/W(c), riflery M(c)/W(c), rugby M(c)/W(c), sailing M(c)/W(c), skiing (cross-country) M(s)/W(s), skiing (downhill) M(c)/W(c), soccer M(c)/W(s), softball W(c), swimming and diving M(c)/W(c), tennis M(s)/W(s), track and field M(s)/W(s), ultimate Frisbee M(c)/W(c), volleyball M(c)/W(s), water polo M(c)/W(c), wrestling M(c)/W(c). ***Intramural sports:*** badminton M/W, basketball M/W, bowling M/W, cross-country running M/W, golf M/W, ice hockey M/W, racquetball M/W, riflery M/W, soccer M/W, softball M/W, swimming and diving M/W, table tennis M/W, tennis M/W, ultimate Frisbee M/W, volleyball M/W, water polo M/W.

Campus security: 24-hour emergency response devices and patrols, late-night transport/escort service, controlled dormitory access.

Student services: health clinic, personal/psychological counseling, women's center.

COSTS & FINANCIAL AID

Costs (2014–15) ***Tuition:*** state resident $13,740 full-time, $520 per credit hour part-time; nonresident $29,220 full-time, $1082 per credit hour part-time. Full-time tuition and fees vary according to program and student level. Part-time tuition and fees vary according to course load, program, and student level. ***Required fees:*** $300 full-time, $150 per term part-time. ***Room and board:*** $9516; room only: $5145. Room and board charges vary according to board plan and housing facility. ***Payment plans:*** installment, deferred payment. ***Waivers:*** children of alumni, senior citizens, and employees or children of employees.

Financial Aid Of all full-time matriculated undergraduates who enrolled in 2014, 4,157 applied for aid, 3,401 were judged to have need, 592 had their need fully met. 153 Federal Work-Study jobs (averaging $866). In 2014, 1280 non-need-based awards were made. ***Average percent of need met:*** 72. ***Average financial aid package:*** $13,900. ***Average need-based loan:*** $4800. ***Average need-based gift aid:*** $7198. ***Average non-need-based aid:*** $5301. ***Average indebtedness upon graduation:*** $36,041.

APPLYING

Standardized Tests *Required:* SAT or ACT (for admission).

Options: electronic application, deferred entrance.

Required: high school transcript. ***Required for some:*** essay or personal statement. ***Recommended:*** minimum 2.8 GPA.

Application deadlines: rolling (freshmen), rolling (transfers).

Notification: continuous (freshmen), continuous (transfers).

CONTACT

Ms. Allison Carter, Director of Admissions, Michigan Technological University, 1400 Townsend Drive, Houghton, MI 49931-1295. *Phone:* 906-487-2335. *Toll-free phone:* 888-MTU-1885. *Fax:* 906-487-2125. *E-mail:* mtu4u@mtu.edu.

Northern Michigan University

Marquette, Michigan

http://www.nmu.edu/

- **State-supported** comprehensive, founded 1899
- **Small-town** 360-acre campus
- **Coed** 8,001 undergraduate students, 88% full-time, 54% women, 46% men
- **Minimally difficult** entrance level, 72% of applicants were admitted

UNDERGRAD STUDENTS

7,002 full-time, 999 part-time. Students come from 54 states and territories; 39 other countries; 19% are from out of state; 2% Black or African American, non-Hispanic/Latino; 3% Hispanic/Latino; 0.5% Asian, non-Hispanic/Latino; 0.1% Native Hawaiian or other Pacific Islander, non-Hispanic/Latino; 2% American Indian or Alaska Native, non-Hispanic/Latino; 2% Two or more races, non-Hispanic/Latino; 3% Race/ethnicity unknown; 1% international; 5% transferred in; 38% live on campus.

Freshmen

Admission: 6,848 applied, 4,937 admitted, 1,595 enrolled. ***Average high school GPA:*** 3.16. ***Test scores:*** ACT scores over 18: 86%; ACT scores over 24: 32%; ACT scores over 30: 4%.

Retention: 73% of full-time freshmen returned.

FACULTY

Total: 456, 67% full-time, 52% with terminal degrees.

Student/faculty ratio: 21:1.

ACADEMICS

Calendar: semesters. *Degrees:* certificates, diplomas, associate, bachelor's, master's, doctoral, post-master's, and postbachelor's certificates.

Special study options: accelerated degree program, adult/continuing education programs, advanced placement credit, cooperative education, distance learning, double majors, English as a second language, honors programs, internships, off-campus study, part-time degree program, services for LD students, study abroad, summer session for credit. ***ROTC:*** Army (b).

Computers: Students can access the following: campus intranet, computer help desk, free student e-mail accounts, online (class) grades, online (class) registration, online (class) schedules. Campuswide network is available. 100% of college-owned or -operated housing units are wired for high-speed Internet access. Wireless service is available via entire campus.

STUDENT LIFE

Housing options: on-campus residence required through sophomore year; coed, men-only, women-only, special housing for students with disabilities. Campus housing is university owned. Freshman campus housing is guaranteed.

Activities and organizations: drama/theater group, student-run newspaper, radio and television station, choral group, marching band, national sororities.

Athletics Member NCAA. All Division II except ice hockey (Division I). ***Intercollegiate sports:*** baseball M(c), basketball M(s)/W(s), crew M(c)/W(c), cross-country running W(s), football M(s), golf M(s)/W(s), ice hockey M(s)/W(c), lacrosse M(c)/W(s), rugby M(c)/W(c), sailing M(c)/W(c), skiing (cross-country) M(s)/W(s), skiing (downhill) M(c)/W(c), soccer M(s)/W(s), swimming and diving M(s)/W(s), track and field M(c)/W(s), ultimate Frisbee M(c)/W(c), volleyball W(s). ***Intramural sports:*** badminton M/W, basketball M/W, football M/W, ice hockey M/W, soccer M/W, ultimate Frisbee M/W, volleyball M/W, water polo M/W.

Campus security: 24-hour emergency response devices and patrols, student patrols, late-night transport/escort service.

Student services: health clinic.

COSTS & FINANCIAL AID

Costs (2014–15) ***One-time required fee:*** $235. ***Tuition:*** state resident $9324 full-time, $361 per credit hour part-time; nonresident $14,556 full-time, $579 per credit hour part-time. Full-time tuition and fees vary according to course level and program. Part-time tuition and fees vary according to course level, course load, and program. ***Required fees:*** $64 full-time. ***Room and board:*** $8954; room only: $4566. Room and board charges vary according to board plan and housing facility. ***Payment plans:*** installment, deferred payment. ***Waivers:*** senior citizens and employees or children of employees.

Financial Aid Of all full-time matriculated undergraduates who enrolled in 2013, 6,864 applied for aid, 5,080 were judged to have need, 501 had their need fully met. 570 Federal Work-Study jobs (averaging $1.0 million). In 2013, 489 non-need-based awards were made. ***Average percent of need met:*** 58. ***Average financial aid package:*** $9303. ***Average need-based loan:*** $4084. ***Average need-based gift aid:*** $5202. ***Average non-need-based aid:*** $2970. ***Average indebtedness upon graduation:*** $29,618.

APPLYING

Standardized Tests *Required:* SAT or ACT (for admission).

Options: electronic application, deferred entrance.

Application fee: $35.

Required: high school transcript. ***Required for some:*** minimum 2.3 GPA.

Application deadlines: rolling (freshmen), rolling (out-of-state freshmen), rolling (transfers).

Notification: continuous (freshmen), continuous (out-of-state freshmen), continuous (transfers).

CONTACT

Ms. Gerri Daniels, Director of Admissions, Northern Michigan University, 1401 Presque Isle Avenue, Marquette, MI 49855. *Phone:* 906-227-2650. *Toll-free phone:* 800-682-9797. *Fax:* 906-227-1747. *E-mail:* admiss@nmu.edu.

Northwestern Michigan College

Traverse City, Michigan

http://www.nmc.edu/

- **State and locally supported** primarily 2-year, founded 1951
- **Small-town** 180-acre campus
- **Coed** 4,609 undergraduate students, 44% full-time, 59% women, 41% men
- **Noncompetitive** entrance level, 55% of applicants were admitted

UNDERGRAD STUDENTS

2,011 full-time, 2,598 part-time. Students come from 19 states and territories; 21 other countries; 2% are from out of state; 11% transferred in.

Freshmen

Admission: 1,909 applied, 1,054 admitted, 1,036 enrolled.

Retention: 61% of full-time freshmen returned.

FACULTY

Total: 280, 33% full-time.

Student/faculty ratio: 18:1.

ACADEMICS

Calendar: semesters. *Degrees:* certificates, associate, and bachelor's.

Special study options: academic remediation for entering students, adult/continuing education programs, advanced placement credit, cooperative education, distance learning, honors programs, independent study, internships, part-time degree program, services for LD students, summer session for credit.

Computers: 553 computers/terminals are available on campus for general student use. Students can access the following: campus intranet, computer help desk, free student e-mail accounts, online (class) grades, online (class) registration, online (class) schedules. Campuswide network is available. 100% of college-owned or -operated housing units are wired for high-speed Internet access. Wireless service is available via entire campus.

STUDENT LIFE

Housing options: coed. Campus housing is university owned and leased by the school.

Activities and organizations: drama/theater group, student-run newspaper, radio station, choral group, Residence Hall Council, Honors fraternity, student newspaper, student magazine, NMC I-dance.

Athletics ***Intramural sports:*** basketball M/W, football M/W, golf M/W, sailing M(c)/W(c), skiing (downhill) M(c)/W(c), softball M/W, volleyball M/W.

Campus security: 24-hour emergency response devices and patrols, student patrols, late-night transport/escort service, controlled dormitory access, well-lit campus.

Student services: health clinic, personal/psychological counseling.

COSTS & FINANCIAL AID

Costs (2014–15) ***Tuition:*** area resident $2727 full-time, $91 per contact hour part-time; state resident $5400 full-time, $180 per contact hour part-time; nonresident $7040 full-time, $235 per contact hour part-time. Full-time tuition and fees vary according to course load and program. Part-time tuition and fees vary according to course load, program, and reciprocity agreements. ***Required fees:*** $859 full-time, $26 per contact hour part-time, $26 per term part-time. ***Room and board:*** $8725; room only: $5325. Room and board charges vary according to board plan, housing facility, and student level. ***Payment plan:*** installment. ***Waivers:*** employees or children of employees.

Financial Aid Of all full-time matriculated undergraduates who enrolled in 2013, 58 Federal Work-Study jobs (averaging $2068). 39 state and other part-time jobs (averaging $1718).

APPLYING

Options: electronic application, early admission, deferred entrance.

Application fee: $20.

Required for some: high school transcript. ***Recommended:*** minimum 2.0 GPA.

Application deadlines: rolling (freshmen), rolling (transfers).

Notification: continuous until 8/22 (freshmen), continuous until 8/22 (transfers).

CONTACT

Catheryn Claerhout, Director of Admissions, Northwestern Michigan College, 1701 E. Front St., Traverse City, MI 49686. *Phone:* 231-995-1034. *Toll-free phone:* 800-748-0566. *E-mail:* c.claerhout@nmc.edu.

Northwood University, Michigan Campus

Midland, Michigan

http://www.northwood.edu/

- **Independent** comprehensive, founded 1959
- **Small-town** 434-acre campus
- **Endowment** $31.1 million
- **Coed** 1,416 undergraduate students, 96% full-time, 37% women, 63% men
- **Moderately difficult** entrance level, 70% of applicants were admitted

UNDERGRAD STUDENTS

1,363 full-time, 53 part-time. Students come from 24 other countries; 13% are from out of state; 6% Black or African American, non-

Hispanic/Latino; 3% Hispanic/Latino; 0.5% Asian, non-Hispanic/Latino; 0.5% Native Hawaiian or other Pacific Islander, non-Hispanic/Latino; 0.3% American Indian or Alaska Native, non-Hispanic/Latino; 2% Two or more races, non-Hispanic/Latino; 9% Race/ethnicity unknown; 7% international; 9% transferred in; 49% live on campus.

Freshmen
Admission: 1,417 applied, 990 admitted, 331 enrolled. ***Average high school GPA:*** 3.16. ***Test scores:*** ACT scores over 18: 90%; ACT scores over 24: 33%; ACT scores over 30: 1%.

Retention: 79% of full-time freshmen returned.

FACULTY
Total: 143, 34% full-time, 25% with terminal degrees.

Student/faculty ratio: 19:1.

ACADEMICS
Calendar: quarters. *Degrees:* associate, bachelor's, and master's.

Special study options: academic remediation for entering students, accelerated degree program, adult/continuing education programs, advanced placement credit, cooperative education, distance learning, double majors, external degree program, honors programs, internships, off-campus study, part-time degree program, services for LD students, study abroad, summer session for credit.

Computers: 215 computers/terminals are available on campus for general student use. Students can access the following: campus intranet, computer help desk, free student e-mail accounts, online (class) grades, online (class) registration, online (class) schedules. Campuswide network is available. 100% of college-owned or -operated housing units are wired for high-speed Internet access. Wireless service is available via entire campus.

STUDENT LIFE
Housing options: on-campus residence required for freshman year; coed, men-only, women-only, special housing for students with disabilities. Campus housing is university owned. Freshman campus housing is guaranteed.

Activities and organizations: drama/theater group, student-run newspaper, Student Senate, intramural sports/club sports, campus art, Northwood University International Auto Show (NUTAS), national fraternities, national sororities.

Athletics Member NCAA. All Division II. ***Intercollegiate sports:*** baseball M(s), basketball M(s)/W(s), cheerleading M(s)/W(s), cross-country running M(s)/W(s), football M(s), golf M(s)/W(s), soccer M(s)/W(s), softball W(s), tennis M(s)/W(s), track and field M(s)/W(s), volleyball W(s). ***Intramural sports:*** badminton M/W, baseball M(c), basketball M/W, football M, ice hockey M(c), lacrosse M(c), soccer M(c)/W, softball M/W, table tennis M/W, tennis M/W, ultimate Frisbee M/W, volleyball M/W.

Campus security: 24-hour emergency response devices and patrols, late-night transport/escort service, controlled dormitory access.

Student services: health clinic, personal/psychological counseling.

COSTS & FINANCIAL AID
Costs (2014–15) ***Comprehensive fee:*** $32,442 includes full-time tuition ($21,950), mandatory fees ($1182), and room and board ($9310). Full-time tuition and fees vary according to course load. Part-time tuition: $845 per credit hour. Part-time tuition and fees vary according to course load. ***Room and board:*** Room and board charges vary according to board plan. ***Payment plan:*** installment. ***Waivers:*** employees or children of employees.

Financial Aid Of all full-time matriculated undergraduates who enrolled in 2013, 1,115 applied for aid, 996 were judged to have need, 219 had their need fully met. 99 Federal Work-Study jobs (averaging $1577). In 2013, 247 non-need-based awards were made. ***Average percent of need met:*** 62. ***Average financial aid package:*** $18,737. ***Average need-based loan:*** $4323. ***Average need-based gift aid:*** $5159. ***Average non-need-based aid:*** $8057. ***Average indebtedness upon graduation:*** $30,857.

APPLYING
Standardized Tests *Required:* SAT or ACT (for admission).

Options: electronic application, early admission, deferred entrance.

Application fee: $30.

Required: essay or personal statement, high school transcript, minimum 2.0 GPA. ***Recommended:*** 1 letter of recommendation, interview.

Application deadlines: 8/1 (freshmen), 8/1 (out-of-state freshmen), rolling (transfers).

Notification: continuous (freshmen), continuous (out-of-state freshmen), continuous (transfers).

CONTACT
Miss Keri Nieto, Director of Admission, Northwood University, Michigan Campus, 4000 Whiting Drive, Midland, MI 48640. *Phone:* 989-837-4342. *Toll-free phone:* 800-457-7878. *Fax:* 989-837-4490. *E-mail:* miadmit@northwood.edu.

Oakland University
Rochester, Michigan
http://www.oakland.edu/

- **State-supported** university, founded 1957
- **Suburban** 1444-acre campus with easy access to Detroit
- **Endowment** $75.3 million
- **Coed** 16,935 undergraduate students, 74% full-time, 58% women, 42% men
- **Moderately difficult** entrance level, 67% of applicants were admitted

UNDERGRAD STUDENTS
12,454 full-time, 4,481 part-time. Students come from 39 states and territories; 46 other countries; 1% are from out of state; 8% Black or African American, non-Hispanic/Latino; 3% Hispanic/Latino; 4% Asian, non-Hispanic/Latino; 0.1% Native Hawaiian or other Pacific Islander, non-Hispanic/Latino; 0.4% American Indian or Alaska Native, non-Hispanic/Latino; 3% Two or more races, non-Hispanic/Latino; 5% Race/ethnicity unknown; 2% international; 11% transferred in; 16% live on campus.

Freshmen
Admission: 12,403 applied, 8,354 admitted, 2,559 enrolled. ***Average high school GPA:*** 3.4. ***Test scores:*** ACT scores over 18: 94%; ACT scores over 24: 43%; ACT scores over 30: 7%.

Retention: 78% of full-time freshmen returned.

FACULTY
Total: 1,129, 50% full-time, 59% with terminal degrees.

Student/faculty ratio: 22:1.

ACADEMICS
Calendar: semesters. *Degrees:* bachelor's, master's, doctoral, post-master's, and postbachelor's certificates.

Special study options: academic remediation for entering students, accelerated degree program, advanced placement credit, cooperative education, distance learning, double majors, English as a second language, honors programs, independent study, internships, off-campus study, part-time degree program, services for LD students, student-designed majors, study abroad, summer session for credit. ***ROTC:*** Air Force (c).

Computers: Students can access the following: computer help desk, free student e-mail accounts, online (class) grades, online (class) registration, online (class) schedules. Campuswide network is available. 100% of college-owned or -operated housing units are wired for high-speed Internet access. Wireless service is available via entire campus.

STUDENT LIFE
Housing options: coed, cooperative, special housing for students with disabilities. Campus housing is university owned. Freshman applicants given priority for college housing.

Activities and organizations: drama/theater group, student-run newspaper, radio and television station, choral group, Beta Alpha Psi, OASIS, AMA, InterVarsity Christian Fellowship, Alternative Spring Break & Global Brigades, Greek Life (Sororities and Fraternities), Grizz Gang, Club Sports (Recreational), national fraternities, national sororities.

Athletics Member NCAA. All Division I. ***Intercollegiate sports:*** baseball M(s), basketball M(s)/W(s), cross-country running M(s)/W(s), golf M(s)/W(s), soccer M(s)/W(s), softball W(s), swimming and diving M(s)/W(s), tennis W(s), track and field M(s)/W(s), volleyball W(s). ***Intramural sports:*** badminton M/W, basketball M/W, bowling M/W, cross-country running M(c)/W(c), equestrian sports M(c)/W(c), fencing M(c)/W(c), football M(c), ice hockey M(c), lacrosse M(c)/W(c), racquetball M/W, rugby M(c)/W(c), soccer M/W, softball M/W, table tennis M/W, tennis M(c)/W(c), volleyball M/W, water polo M(c)/W(c), wrestling M(c).

Campus security: 24-hour emergency response devices and patrols, student patrols, late-night transport/escort service, controlled dormitory access, state certified police officers, security lighting, extensive camera system, self-defense/alcohol abuse classes.

Student services: health clinic, personal/psychological counseling.

COSTS & FINANCIAL AID

Costs (2014–15) ***Tuition:*** state resident $10,613 full-time, $354 per credit hour part-time; nonresident $23,873 full-time, $795 per credit hour part-time. Full-time tuition and fees vary according to student level. Part-time tuition and fees vary according to student level. ***Room and board:*** $8895. Room and board charges vary according to housing facility. ***Payment plans:*** installment, deferred payment. ***Waivers:*** senior citizens and employees or children of employees.

Financial Aid Of all full-time matriculated undergraduates who enrolled in 2012, 9,139 applied for aid, 7,728 were judged to have need, 676 had their need fully met. In 2012, 1433 non-need-based awards were made. ***Average percent of need met:*** 71. ***Average financial aid package:*** $12,636. ***Average need-based loan:*** $4094. ***Average need-based gift aid:*** $4825. ***Average non-need-based aid:*** $3615. ***Average indebtedness upon graduation:*** $27,840.

APPLYING

Standardized Tests *Required:* SAT or ACT (for admission).

Options: electronic application, deferred entrance.

Required: high school transcript, minimum 2.5 GPA. ***Required for some:*** interview, Students interested in Music, Theatre, or Dance must audition for admission to the major.

Application deadlines: rolling (freshmen), rolling (out-of-state freshmen), rolling (transfers).

Notification: continuous until 9/1 (freshmen), continuous until 9/1 (out-of-state freshmen), continuous (transfers).

CONTACT

Ms. Dawn M Aubry, Interim Assistant Vice President Student Affairs, Admissions, Oakland University, Rochester, MI 48309-4401. *Phone:* 248-370-3228. *Toll-free phone:* 800-OAK-UNIV. *Fax:* 248-370-4462. *E-mail:* ouinfo@oakland.edu.

Olivet College

Olivet, Michigan

http://www.olivetcollege.edu/

- **Independent** comprehensive, founded 1844, affiliated with Congregational Christian Church
- **Small-town** 92-acre campus with easy access to Lansing, Battle Creek
- **Coed** 1,456 undergraduate students, 92% full-time, 57% women, 43% men
- **Minimally difficult** entrance level, 61% of applicants were admitted

UNDERGRAD STUDENTS

1,338 full-time, 118 part-time. Students come from 8 states and territories; 6 other countries; 5% are from out of state; 10% Black or African American, non-Hispanic/Latino; 6% Hispanic/Latino; 0.7% Asian, non-Hispanic/Latino; 0.4% American Indian or Alaska Native, non-Hispanic/Latino; 3% Two or more races, non-Hispanic/Latino; 0.4% Race/ethnicity unknown; 1% international; 49% live on campus.

Freshmen

Admission: 3,017 applied, 1,853 admitted, 228 enrolled.

Retention: 59% of full-time freshmen returned.

FACULTY

Total: 90, 49% full-time.

Student/faculty ratio: 17:1.

ACADEMICS

Calendar: 4-4-1. *Degrees:* bachelor's and master's.

Special study options: advanced placement credit, cooperative education, double majors, honors programs, independent study, internships, part-time degree program, student-designed majors, summer session for credit. ***ROTC:*** Air Force (c).

Computers: 118 computers/terminals are available on campus for general student use. Students can access the following: campus intranet, computer help desk, free student e-mail accounts, online (class) grades, online (class) registration, online (class) schedules. Campuswide network is available. Wireless service is available via entire campus.

STUDENT LIFE

Housing options: on-campus residence required through junior year; coed, men-only, women-only. Campus housing is university owned. Freshman campus housing is guaranteed.

Activities and organizations: drama/theater group, student-run newspaper, radio station, choral group, marching band, Black Student Union, Olivet College Veterans Advocates, Mathletes, Earthbound, Alpha Omega.

Athletics Member NCAA. All Division III. ***Intercollegiate sports:*** baseball M, basketball M/W, cross-country running M/W, football M, golf M/W, lacrosse M/W, soccer M/W, softball W, swimming and diving M/W, tennis W, track and field M/W, volleyball W, wrestling M. ***Intramural sports:*** basketball M/W, bowling M/W, cheerleading M/W, football M/W, softball M/W, volleyball M/W.

Campus security: 24-hour emergency response devices and patrols, student patrols, late-night transport/escort service, security cameras in all dorms and campus surveillance.

Student services: health clinic, personal/psychological counseling, women's center.

COSTS & FINANCIAL AID

Costs (2015–16) ***Tuition:*** $22,950 full-time, $750 per semester hour part-time. ***Required fees:*** $851 full-time. ***Room only:*** $3950. Room and board charges vary according to board plan and housing facility.

Financial Aid Of all full-time matriculated undergraduates who enrolled in 2013, 1,075 applied for aid, 1,006 were judged to have need, 201 had their need fully met. 206 Federal Work-Study jobs (averaging $864). In 2013, 120 non-need-based awards were made. ***Average percent of need met:*** 80. ***Average financial aid package:*** $17,650. ***Average need-based loan:*** $4612. ***Average need-based gift aid:*** $11,725. ***Average non-need-based aid:*** $10,675. ***Average indebtedness upon graduation:*** $26,222.

APPLYING

Standardized Tests *Required:* SAT or ACT (for admission).

Options: electronic application, deferred entrance.

Application fee: $25.

Required: high school transcript. ***Required for some:*** essay or personal statement, interview. ***Recommended:*** minimum 2.6 GPA.

Application deadlines: rolling (freshmen), rolling (transfers).

Notification: continuous (freshmen), continuous (transfers).

CONTACT

Olivet College, 320 South Main Street, Olivet, MI 49076-9701. *Phone:* 800-456-7189. *Toll-free phone:* 800-456-7189.

Saginaw Valley State University

University Center, Michigan

http://www.svsu.edu/

- **State-supported** comprehensive, founded 1963
- **Small-town** 782-acre campus
- **Endowment** $62.2 million
- **Coed** 8,797 undergraduate students, 84% full-time, 58% women, 42% men
- **Moderately difficult** entrance level, 79% of applicants were admitted

UNDERGRAD STUDENTS

7,411 full-time, 1,386 part-time. Students come from 22 states and territories; 25 other countries; 1% are from out of state; 11% Black or African American, non-Hispanic/Latino; 4% Hispanic/Latino; 0.7% Asian, non-Hispanic/Latino; 0.4% American Indian or Alaska Native, non-Hispanic/Latino; 2% Two or more races, non-Hispanic/Latino; 6% Race/ethnicity unknown; 5% international; 7% transferred in; 31% live on campus.

Freshmen
Admission: 6,266 applied, 4,960 admitted, 1,507 enrolled. ***Average high school GPA:*** 3.2. ***Test scores:*** ACT scores over 18: 90%; ACT scores over 24: 38%; ACT scores over 30: 5%.

Retention: 71% of full-time freshmen returned.

FACULTY
Total: 756, 41% full-time.

Student/faculty ratio: 18:1.

ACADEMICS
Calendar: semesters plus summer session. *Degrees:* bachelor's, master's, doctoral, and post-master's certificates.

Special study options: academic remediation for entering students, accelerated degree program, adult/continuing education programs, advanced placement credit, cooperative education, distance learning, double majors, English as a second language, honors programs, independent study, internships, part-time degree program, services for LD students, student-designed majors, study abroad, summer session for credit.

Computers: Students can access the following: computer help desk, free student e-mail accounts, online (class) grades, online (class) registration, online (class) schedules. Campuswide network is available. 100% of college-owned or -operated housing units are wired for high-speed Internet access. Wireless service is available via classrooms, dorm rooms, libraries, student centers.

STUDENT LIFE
Housing options: coed, special housing for students with disabilities. Campus housing is university owned.

Activities and organizations: drama/theater group, student-run newspaper, radio station, choral group, marching band, His House Christian Fellowship, Criminal Justice Society, Delta Sigma Pi, Alpha Phi Omega, International Students Club, national fraternities, national sororities.

Athletics Member NCAA. All Division II. ***Intercollegiate sports:*** baseball M(s), basketball M(s)/W(s), bowling M(c)/W(c), cheerleading M(c)/W(c), cross-country running M(s)/W(s), equestrian sports M(c)/W(c), football M(s), golf M(s), gymnastics M(c)/W(c), ice hockey M(c)/W(c), lacrosse M(c)/W(c), rugby M(c)/W(c), soccer M(s)/W(s), softball W(s), swimming and diving M(s)/W(s), tennis M(c)/W(s), track and field M(s)/W(s), volleyball W(s), wrestling M(c). ***Intramural sports:*** badminton M/W, basketball M/W, football M/W, golf M/W, ice hockey M/W, racquetball M/W, soccer M/W, softball M/W, table tennis M/W, tennis M/W, volleyball M/W, water polo M/W.

Campus security: 24-hour emergency response devices and patrols, student patrols, late-night transport/escort service, controlled dormitory access, rape prevention program.

Student services: health clinic, personal/psychological counseling.

COSTS & FINANCIAL AID
Costs (2014–15) ***Tuition:*** state resident $8253 full-time, $275 per credit hour part-time; nonresident $19,971 full-time, $666 per credit hour part-time. Full-time tuition and fees vary according to course level, degree level, location, and program. Part-time tuition and fees vary according to course level, degree level, location, and program. ***Required fees:*** $438 full-time, $15 per credit hour part-time. ***Room and board:*** $8400; room only: $4750. Room and board charges vary according to board plan and housing facility. ***Payment plan:*** installment. ***Waivers:*** employees or children of employees.

Financial Aid Of all full-time matriculated undergraduates who enrolled in 2014, 4,908 applied for aid, 4,848 were judged to have need.

APPLYING
Standardized Tests *Required:* SAT or ACT (for admission).

Options: electronic application, deferred entrance.

Application fee: $30.

Required: high school transcript, minimum 2.5 GPA. ***Recommended:*** high school transcript, minimum 2.5 GPA.

Application deadlines: rolling (freshmen), rolling (transfers).

Notification: continuous (freshmen), continuous (transfers).

CONTACT
Jennifer Pahl, Director of Admissions, Saginaw Valley State University, 7400 Bay Road, University Center, MI 48710-0001. *Phone:* 989-964-4200. *Toll-free phone:* 800-968-9500. *Fax:* 989-790-0180. *E-mail:* admissions@svsu.edu.

Siena Heights University
Adrian, Michigan
http://www.sienaheights.edu/

- **Independent Roman Catholic** comprehensive, founded 1919
- **Small-town** 140-acre campus with easy access to Detroit, Toledo
- **Coed** 2,402 undergraduate students, 52% full-time, 56% women, 44% men
- **Moderately difficult** entrance level, 74% of applicants were admitted

UNDERGRAD STUDENTS
1,245 full-time, 1,157 part-time. Students come from 39 states and territories; 30 other countries; 16% are from out of state; 12% Black or African American, non-Hispanic/Latino; 4% Hispanic/Latino; 1% Asian, non-Hispanic/Latino; 0.2% Native Hawaiian or other Pacific Islander, non-Hispanic/Latino; 0.5% American Indian or Alaska Native, non-Hispanic/Latino; 2% Two or more races, non-Hispanic/Latino; 12% Race/ethnicity unknown; 3% international; 5% transferred in; 25% live on campus.

Freshmen
Admission: 1,545 applied, 1,147 admitted, 273 enrolled. ***Average high school GPA:*** 3.2.

Retention: 63% of full-time freshmen returned.

FACULTY
Total: 268, 32% full-time.

Student/faculty ratio: 12:1.

ACADEMICS
Calendar: semesters. *Degrees:* associate, bachelor's, and master's.

Special study options: academic remediation for entering students, accelerated degree program, adult/continuing education programs, advanced placement credit, cooperative education, distance learning, double majors, English as a second language, independent study, internships, off-campus study, part-time degree program, services for LD students, student-designed majors, study abroad, summer session for credit.

Computers: 180 computers/terminals are available on campus for general student use. Students can access the following: campus intranet, computer help desk, free student e-mail accounts, online (class) grades, online (class) registration, online (class) schedules. Campuswide network is available. 100% of college-owned or -operated housing units are wired for high-speed Internet access. Wireless service is available via entire campus.

STUDENT LIFE
Housing options: on-campus residence required through junior year; coed, special housing for students with disabilities. Campus housing is university owned. Freshman campus housing is guaranteed.

Activities and organizations: drama/theater group, student-run newspaper, choral group, marching band, national fraternities, national sororities.

Athletics Member NAIA. ***Intercollegiate sports:*** baseball M(s), basketball M(s)/W(s), bowling M(s)/W(s), cheerleading M/W, cross-country running M(s)/W(s), football M(s), golf M(s)/W(s), lacrosse M(s)/W(s), soccer M(s)/W(s), softball W(s), track and field M(s)/W(s), volleyball M(s)/W(s). ***Intramural sports:*** basketball M/W, softball M/W, volleyball M/W.

Campus security: 24-hour emergency response devices and patrols, student patrols, late-night transport/escort service.

Student services: health clinic, personal/psychological counseling.

COSTS & FINANCIAL AID
Costs (2014–15) ***Comprehensive fee:*** $32,040 includes full-time tuition ($22,100), mandatory fees ($640), and room and board ($9300). Full-time tuition and fees vary according to course load, location, and program. Part-time tuition: $460 per semester hour. Part-time tuition and fees vary according to course load, location, and program. ***Required fees:*** $130 per

year part-time. ***Room and board:*** Room and board charges vary according to board plan, housing facility, and location. ***Payment plans:*** installment, deferred payment. ***Waivers:*** senior citizens and employees or children of employees.

Financial Aid In 2002, 166 non-need-based awards were made. ***Average percent of need met:*** 66. ***Average financial aid package:*** $12,200. ***Average indebtedness upon graduation:*** $13,500.

APPLYING

Standardized Tests *Required:* SAT or ACT (for admission).

Options: electronic application, deferred entrance.

Required: high school transcript.

Application deadlines: rolling (freshmen), rolling (out-of-state freshmen), rolling (transfers).

CONTACT

Ms. Trudy Mohre, Director of Admissions, Siena Heights University, 1247 East Siena Heights Drive, Adrian, MI 49221. *Phone:* 517-264-7185. *Toll-free phone:* 800-521-0009. *E-mail:* tmohre@sienaheights.edu.

South University

Novi, Michigan

http://www.southuniversity.edu/novi.aspx

- **Proprietary** comprehensive, part of Education Management Corporation
- **Coed**

ACADEMICS

Degrees: associate, bachelor's, and master's.

CONTACT

South University, 41555 Twelve Mile Road, Novi, MI 48377. *Phone:* 248-675-0200. *Toll-free phone:* 877-693-2085.

Spring Arbor University

Spring Arbor, Michigan

http://www.arbor.edu/

- **Independent Free Methodist** comprehensive, founded 1873
- **Rural** 100-acre campus
- **Endowment** $10.8 million
- **Coed**
- **Moderately difficult** entrance level

FACULTY

Student/faculty ratio: 15:1.

ACADEMICS

Calendar: 4-1-4. *Degrees:* associate, bachelor's, master's, and postbachelor's certificates.

STUDENT LIFE

Housing options: on-campus residence required through senior year; men-only, women-only, special housing for students with disabilities. Campus housing is university owned. Freshman campus housing is guaranteed.

Activities and organizations: drama/theater group, student-run newspaper, radio and television station, choral group, Inter-faith Shelter Ministries, Band of Brothers, Action Jackson, Circle of Sisters, Heartside Homeless.

Athletics Member NAIA, NCCAA.

Campus security: 24-hour emergency response devices and patrols, student patrols, late-night transport/escort service, controlled dormitory access.

Student services: health clinic, personal/psychological counseling.

COSTS & FINANCIAL AID

Costs (2014–15) ***Comprehensive fee:*** $32,810 includes full-time tuition ($23,750), mandatory fees ($600), and room and board ($8460). Full-time tuition and fees vary according to course load, degree level, and program. Part-time tuition: $575 per credit hour. Part-time tuition and fees vary according to course load, degree level, program, and reciprocity agreements. ***Required fees:*** $280 per term part-time. ***College room only:*** $3940. Room and board charges vary according to board plan and housing facility.

Financial Aid Of all full-time matriculated undergraduates who enrolled in 2013, 1,299 applied for aid, 1,215 were judged to have need, 239 had their need fully met. In 2013, 2 non-need-based awards were made. ***Average percent of need met:*** 81. ***Average financial aid package:*** $21,465. ***Average need-based loan:*** $4716. ***Average need-based gift aid:*** $13,630. ***Average non-need-based aid:*** $1702. ***Average indebtedness upon graduation:*** $32,577.

APPLYING

Standardized Tests *Required:* SAT or ACT (for admission). *Recommended:* ACT (for admission).

Options: electronic application, early admission, deferred entrance.

Application fee: $30.

Required: high school transcript. ***Required for some:*** essay or personal statement, interview. ***Recommended:*** minimum 2.6 GPA, Guidance counselor's form and ACT score of 20 or SAT score of 930 recommended.

CONTACT

Office of Admissions, Spring Arbor University, 106 East Main Street, Spring Arbor, MI 49283-9799. *Phone:* 517-750-1200 Ext. 1468. *Toll-free phone:* 800-968-0011. *Fax:* 517-750-6620. *E-mail:* admissions@arbor.edu.

University of Michigan

Ann Arbor, Michigan

http://www.umich.edu/

- **State-supported** university, founded 1817
- **Urban** 3211-acre campus with easy access to Detroit
- **Endowment** $9.6 billion
- **Coed** 28,413 undergraduate students, 96% full-time, 49% women, 51% men
- **Very difficult** entrance level, 32% of applicants were admitted

UNDERGRAD STUDENTS

27,413 full-time, 1,000 part-time. Students come from 56 states and territories; 91 other countries; 37% are from out of state; 4% Black or African American, non-Hispanic/Latino; 4% Hispanic/Latino; 13% Asian, non-Hispanic/Latino; 0.2% American Indian or Alaska Native, non-Hispanic/Latino; 3% Two or more races, non-Hispanic/Latino; 7% Race/ethnicity unknown; 7% international; 4% transferred in; 34% live on campus.

Freshmen

Admission: 49,776 applied, 16,047 admitted, 6,523 enrolled. ***Average high school GPA:*** 3.81. ***Test scores:*** SAT critical reading scores over 500: 99%; SAT math scores over 500: 99%; SAT writing scores over 500: 98%; ACT scores over 18: 100%; SAT critical reading scores over 600: 85%; SAT math scores over 600: 92%; SAT writing scores over 600: 88%; ACT scores over 24: 97%; SAT critical reading scores over 700: 33%; SAT math scores over 700: 60%; SAT writing scores over 700: 46%; ACT scores over 30: 67%.

Retention: 97% of full-time freshmen returned.

FACULTY

Total: 3,259, 82% full-time, 88% with terminal degrees.

Student/faculty ratio: 15:1.

ACADEMICS

Calendar: trimesters. *Degrees:* bachelor's, master's, doctoral, post-master's, and postbachelor's certificates.

Special study options: accelerated degree program, adult/continuing education programs, advanced placement credit, cooperative education, distance learning, double majors, English as a second language, external degree program, honors programs, independent study, internships, off-campus study, part-time degree program, services for LD students, student-designed majors, study abroad, summer session for credit. ***ROTC:*** Army (b), Navy (b), Air Force (b).

Unusual degree programs: 3-2 business administration; engineering; architecture.

Computers: 2,674 computers/terminals are available on campus for general student use. Students can access the following: campus intranet, computer help desk, free student e-mail accounts, online (class) grades, online (class) registration, online (class) schedules, file storage, personal web pages, printing. Campuswide network is available. 100% of college-owned or -operated housing units are wired for high-speed Internet access. Wireless service is available via entire campus.

STUDENT LIFE

Housing options: coed, women-only, cooperative. Campus housing is university owned and leased by the school. Freshman campus housing is guaranteed.

Activities and organizations: drama/theater group, student-run newspaper, radio and television station, choral group, marching band, Hillel Society, K-Grams (Kids' Program), M-Powered Entrepreneurial Club, Dance Marathon, Alternative Spring Break, national fraternities, national sororities.

Athletics Member NCAA. All Division I except football (Division I-AA). ***Intercollegiate sports:*** baseball M(s), basketball M(s)/W(s), cheerleading M(s)(c)/W(s)(c), crew M(c)/W(s), cross-country running M(s)/W(s), fencing M(c)/W(c), field hockey W(s), golf M(s)/W(s), gymnastics M(s)/W(s), ice hockey M(s), lacrosse M(s)/W(s), riflery M(c)/W(c), rugby M(c)/W(c), sailing M(c)/W(c), soccer M(s)/W(s), softball W(s), swimming and diving M(s)/W(s), table tennis M(c)/W(c), tennis M(s)/W(s), track and field M(s)/W(s), ultimate Frisbee M(c)/W(c), volleyball M(c)/W(s), water polo M(c)/W(s), wrestling M(s). ***Intramural sports:*** badminton M/W, baseball M, basketball M/W, cross-country running M(c)/W(c), field hockey M/W, gymnastics W(c), ice hockey M(c)/W(c), lacrosse W(c), racquetball M/W, soccer M(c)/W(c), softball W(c), squash M/W, swimming and diving M/W(c), table tennis M/W, tennis M(c)/W(c), track and field M/W, ultimate Frisbee M/W, volleyball M/W(c), water polo W(c), wrestling M(c).

Campus security: 24-hour emergency response devices and patrols, student patrols, late-night transport/escort service, controlled dormitory access, Safewalk (no-cost night-time escorts), SafeRide (no-cost night-time ride service), Violence Prevention in College (for-credit course).

Student services: health clinic, personal/psychological counseling, women's center, legal services.

COSTS & FINANCIAL AID

Costs (2014–15) ***Tuition:*** state resident $13,158 full-time, $519 per credit hour part-time; nonresident $41,578 full-time, $1703 per credit hour part-time. Full-time tuition and fees vary according to course load, program, and student level. Part-time tuition and fees vary according to course load, program, and student level. ***Required fees:*** $328 full-time, $164 per term part-time. ***Room and board:*** $10,246. Room and board charges vary according to board plan and housing facility. ***Payment plan:*** installment.

Financial Aid Of all full-time matriculated undergraduates who enrolled in 2013, 13,311 applied for aid, 10,417 were judged to have need, 8,191 had their need fully met. 2,864 Federal Work-Study jobs (averaging $1602). In 2013, 4476 non-need-based awards were made. ***Average percent of need met:*** 82. ***Average financial aid package:*** $21,422. ***Average need-based loan:*** $5205. ***Average need-based gift aid:*** $15,050. ***Average non-need-based aid:*** $7536. ***Average indebtedness upon graduation:*** $26,510. ***Financial aid deadline:*** 4/30.

APPLYING

Standardized Tests *Required:* SAT or ACT (for admission). *Required for some:* SAT Subject Tests (for admission).

Options: electronic application, early action, deferred entrance.

Application fee: $75.

Required: essay or personal statement, high school transcript, 1 letter of recommendation. ***Required for some:*** interview, audition for School of Music, Theatre and Dance; portfolio for School of Art and Design.

Application deadlines: 2/1 (freshmen), 2/1 (out-of-state freshmen), 2/1 (transfers), 11/1 (early action).

Notification: continuous (freshmen), continuous (out-of-state freshmen), continuous (transfers), 12/24 (early action).

CONTACT

University of Michigan, Ann Arbor, MI 48109. *Phone:* 734-764-7433.

University of Michigan–Dearborn

Dearborn, Michigan

http://www.umd.umich.edu/

- **State-supported** comprehensive, founded 1959, part of University of Michigan System
- **Suburban** 210-acre campus with easy access to Detroit
- **Endowment** $32.6 million
- **Coed** 7,171 undergraduate students, 68% full-time, 49% women, 51% men
- **Moderately difficult** entrance level, 64% of applicants were admitted

UNDERGRAD STUDENTS

4,843 full-time, 2,328 part-time. Students come from 27 other countries; 10% Black or African American, non-Hispanic/Latino; 6% Hispanic/Latino; 6% Asian, non-Hispanic/Latino; 0.1% Native Hawaiian or other Pacific Islander, non-Hispanic/Latino; 0.4% American Indian or Alaska Native, non-Hispanic/Latino; 3% Two or more races, non-Hispanic/Latino; 3% Race/ethnicity unknown; 1% international; 10% transferred in.

Freshmen

Admission: 5,174 applied, 3,292 admitted, 951 enrolled. ***Test scores:*** ACT scores over 18: 55%; ACT scores over 24: 11%; ACT scores over 30: 11%.

FACULTY

Total: 563, 59% full-time, 66% with terminal degrees.

Student/faculty ratio: 15:1.

ACADEMICS

Calendar: semesters. *Degrees:* bachelor's, master's, and doctoral.

Special study options: academic remediation for entering students, accelerated degree program, adult/continuing education programs, advanced placement credit, cooperative education, distance learning, double majors, English as a second language, honors programs, independent study, internships, off-campus study, part-time degree program, services for LD students, study abroad, summer session for credit. ***ROTC:*** Army (b), Navy (b), Air Force (b).

Computers: 975 computers/terminals are available on campus for general student use. Students can access the following: campus intranet, computer help desk, free student e-mail accounts, online (class) grades, online (class) registration, online (class) schedules, tuition and application payments accepted online. Campuswide network is available. Wireless service is available via entire campus.

STUDENT LIFE

Housing options: college housing not available.

Activities and organizations: student-run newspaper, radio station, choral group, Greek Life, Student Government, Pre-Professional Health Society, Intervarsity Christian Fellowship, Student Activities Board, national sororities.

Athletics Member NAIA. ***Intercollegiate sports:*** basketball M(s)/W(s), bowling M(c)/W(c), cheerleading M(c)/W(c), cross-country running M(s)/W(s), ice hockey M(c), lacrosse M(s), rugby M(c), soccer M/W(c), softball W(s), tennis M(c)/W(c), ultimate Frisbee M(c), volleyball W(s), wrestling M(c). ***Intramural sports:*** basketball M/W, cross-country running M(c)/W(c), fencing M(c)/W(c), volleyball W.

Campus security: 24-hour emergency response devices and patrols, late-night transport/escort service.

Student services: personal/psychological counseling, women's center.

COSTS & FINANCIAL AID

Costs (2014–15) ***One-time required fee:*** $75. ***Tuition:*** state resident $10,542 full-time, $417 per credit hour part-time; nonresident $22,740 full-time, $905 per credit hour part-time. Full-time tuition and fees vary according to course level, course load, degree level, program, and student level. Part-time tuition and fees vary according to course level, course load, degree level, program, and student level. ***Required fees:*** $680 full-time, $323 per term part-time. ***Payment plan:*** installment. ***Waivers:*** senior citizens and employees or children of employees.

Financial Aid Of all full-time matriculated undergraduates who enrolled in 2013, 3,762 applied for aid, 3,193 were judged to have need, 178 had their need fully met. 152 Federal Work-Study jobs (averaging $1309). 703 state and other part-time jobs (averaging $1.1 million). In 2013, 531 non-need-based awards were made. ***Average percent of need met:*** 55. ***Average financial aid package:*** $9427. ***Average need-based loan:*** $4571. ***Average need-based gift aid:*** $5344. ***Average non-need-based aid:*** $5038. ***Average indebtedness upon graduation:*** $22,168.

APPLYING

Standardized Tests *Required:* SAT or ACT (for admission).

Options: electronic application, deferred entrance.

Application fee: $30.

Required: high school transcript. ***Required for some:*** interview. ***Recommended:*** minimum 2.5 GPA.

Application deadlines: rolling (freshmen), rolling (transfers).

Notification: continuous (freshmen), continuous (transfers).

CONTACT

Ms. Deb Peffer, Director of Admissions and Orientation, University of Michigan–Dearborn, 4901 Evergreen Road, Room 1145 UC, Dearborn, MI 48128-1491. *Phone:* 313-593-5100. *Fax:* 313-436-9167. *E-mail:* admissions@umd.umich.edu.

University of Michigan–Flint

Flint, Michigan

http://www.umflint.edu/

- **State-supported** comprehensive, founded 1956, part of University of Michigan System
- **Urban** 72-acre campus with easy access to Detroit, Lansing
- **Endowment** $95.0 million
- **Coed** 7,078 undergraduate students, 60% full-time, 60% women, 40% men
- **Moderately difficult** entrance level, 79% of applicants were admitted

UNDERGRAD STUDENTS

4,240 full-time, 2,838 part-time. Students come from 42 states and territories; 50 other countries; 2% are from out of state; 13% Black or African American, non-Hispanic/Latino; 4% Hispanic/Latino; 2% Asian, non-Hispanic/Latino; 0.1% Native Hawaiian or other Pacific Islander, non-Hispanic/Latino; 0.7% American Indian or Alaska Native, non-Hispanic/Latino; 3% Two or more races, non-Hispanic/Latino; 4% Race/ethnicity unknown; 6% international; 11% transferred in; 4% live on campus.

Freshmen

Admission: 3,160 applied, 2,485 admitted, 662 enrolled. ***Average high school GPA:*** 3.22. ***Test scores:*** SAT critical reading scores over 500: 67%; SAT math scores over 500: 75%; SAT writing scores over 500: 83%; ACT scores over 18: 79%; SAT critical reading scores over 600: 17%; SAT math scores over 600: 50%; SAT writing scores over 600: 17%; ACT scores over 24: 30%; SAT critical reading scores over 700: 17%; SAT math scores over 700: 17%; SAT writing scores over 700: 17%; ACT scores over 30: 5%.

Retention: 72% of full-time freshmen returned.

FACULTY

Total: 576, 55% full-time, 48% with terminal degrees.

Student/faculty ratio: 15:1.

ACADEMICS

Calendar: semesters. *Degrees:* bachelor's, master's, doctoral, post-master's, and postbachelor's certificates.

Special study options: academic remediation for entering students, accelerated degree program, adult/continuing education programs, advanced placement credit, cooperative education, distance learning, double majors, English as a second language, honors programs, independent study, internships, off-campus study, part-time degree program, services for LD students, student-designed majors, study abroad, summer session for credit. ***ROTC:*** Army (c).

Unusual degree programs: 3-2 engineering with 3 year University of Michigan Flint (Science/Math Bachelors); 2 year University of Michigan Ann Arbor (Engineering Bachelors).

Computers: 532 computers/terminals are available on campus for general student use. Students can access the following: campus intranet, computer help desk, free student e-mail accounts, online (class) grades, online (class) registration, online (class) schedules. Campuswide network is available. 100% of college-owned or -operated housing units are wired for high-speed Internet access. Wireless service is available via entire campus.

STUDENT LIFE

Housing options: coed. Campus housing is university owned.

Activities and organizations: drama/theater group, student-run newspaper, choral group, International Student Organization, Kappa Sigma Fraternity, Student Government, Campus Activities Board, Video Gamers Club, national fraternities, national sororities.

Athletics ***Intramural sports:*** badminton M(c)/W(c), basketball M(c)/W(c), cheerleading W(c), football M(c), golf M(c)/W(c), ice hockey M(c)/W(c), lacrosse M(c), soccer M(c)/W(c), table tennis M(c)/W(c), ultimate Frisbee M(c)/W(c), volleyball M(c)/W(c).

Campus security: 24-hour emergency response devices and patrols, student patrols, late-night transport/escort service, controlled dormitory access.

Student services: health clinic, personal/psychological counseling, women's center.

COSTS & FINANCIAL AID

Costs (2014–15) ***Tuition:*** state resident $9720 full-time, $384 per credit hour part-time; nonresident $18,942 full-time, $766 per credit hour part-time. Full-time tuition and fees vary according to course level, course load, degree level, program, and student level. Part-time tuition and fees vary according to course level, course load, degree level, program, and student level. ***Required fees:*** $418 full-time, $160 per term part-time. ***Room and board:*** $7911; room only: $4978. Room and board charges vary according to housing facility. ***Payment plan:*** installment. ***Waivers:*** senior citizens.

Financial Aid Of all full-time matriculated undergraduates who enrolled in 2013, 3,673 applied for aid, 3,279 were judged to have need, 119 had their need fully met. 231 Federal Work-Study jobs (averaging $2355). In 2013, 76 non-need-based awards were made. ***Average percent of need met:*** 72. ***Average financial aid package:*** $12,405. ***Average need-based loan:*** $4193. ***Average need-based gift aid:*** $5780. ***Average non-need-based aid:*** $3755. ***Average indebtedness upon graduation:*** $32,107.

APPLYING

Standardized Tests *Required:* SAT or ACT (for admission).

Options: electronic application, deferred entrance.

Application fee: $30.

Required: high school transcript.

Application deadlines: 8/18 (freshmen), rolling (out-of-state freshmen), 8/18 (transfers).

Notification: continuous (freshmen), continuous (out-of-state freshmen), continuous (transfers).

CONTACT

University of Michigan–Flint, 303 East Kearsley Street, Flint, MI 48502-1950. *Phone:* 810-762-3300. *Toll-free phone:* 800-942-5636.

Walsh College of Accountancy and Business Administration

Troy, Michigan

http://www.walshcollege.edu/

- **Independent** upper-level, founded 1922
- **Suburban** 29-acre campus with easy access to Detroit
- **Endowment** $5.1 million
- **Coed** 950 undergraduate students, 9% full-time, 47% women, 53% men
- **Noncompetitive** entrance level

UNDERGRAD STUDENTS

88 full-time, 862 part-time. Students come from 3 states and territories; 28 other countries; 0.3% are from out of state; 6% Black or African American, non-Hispanic/Latino; 2% Hispanic/Latino; 4% Asian, non-Hispanic/Latino; 0.1% Native Hawaiian or other Pacific Islander, non-Hispanic/Latino; 0.1% American Indian or Alaska Native, non-Hispanic/Latino; 1% Two or more races, non-Hispanic/Latino; 1% Race/ethnicity unknown; 2% international; 98% transferred in.

FACULTY
Total: 185, 12% full-time.
Student/faculty ratio: 15:1.

ACADEMICS
Calendar: 4-11week terms. *Degrees:* bachelor's and master's.
Special study options: adult/continuing education programs, advanced placement credit, distance learning, double majors, independent study, internships, off-campus study, part-time degree program, services for LD students, summer session for credit.
Computers: 300 computers/terminals are available on campus for general student use. Students can access the following: campus intranet, computer help desk, free student e-mail accounts, online (class) grades, online (class) registration, online (class) schedules. Campuswide network is available. Wireless service is available via entire campus.

STUDENT LIFE
Housing options: college housing not available.
Activities and organizations: student government, American Marketing Association, Economics/Finance Club, Accounting Club, National Association of Black Accountants.
Campus security: 24-hour emergency response devices.

COSTS & FINANCIAL AID
Costs (2014–15) ***Tuition:*** $14,400 full-time, $7200 per year part-time. Full-time tuition and fees vary according to course level and degree level. Part-time tuition and fees vary according to course level and degree level. ***Required fees:*** $375 full-time, $375 per year part-time. ***Payment plan:*** deferred payment. ***Waivers:*** employees or children of employees.
Financial Aid Of all full-time matriculated undergraduates who enrolled in 2009, 199 applied for aid, 177 were judged to have need. In 2009, 14 non-need-based awards were made. ***Average percent of need met:*** 36. ***Average financial aid package:*** $8986. ***Average need-based loan:*** $5034. ***Average need-based gift aid:*** $5700. ***Average non-need-based aid:*** $1689. ***Average indebtedness upon graduation:*** $13,100.

APPLYING
Options: electronic application, deferred entrance.
Application fee: $35.
Notification: continuous (transfers).

CONTACT
Walsh College of Accountancy and Business Administration, 3838 Livernois Road, PO Box 7006, Troy, MI 48007-7006. *Phone:* 248-823-1610. *Toll-free phone:* 800-925-7401.

Wayne State University

Detroit, Michigan

http://www.wayne.edu/

- **State-supported** university, founded 1868
- **Urban** 169-acre campus with easy access to Detroit
- **Endowment** $306.2 million
- **Coed** 18,347 undergraduate students, 66% full-time, 55% women, 45% men
- **Moderately difficult** entrance level, 77% of applicants were admitted

UNDERGRAD STUDENTS
12,030 full-time, 6,317 part-time. Students come from 48 states and territories; 62 other countries; 1% are from out of state; 21% Black or African American, non-Hispanic/Latino; 4% Hispanic/Latino; 8% Asian, non-Hispanic/Latino; 0.1% Native Hawaiian or other Pacific Islander, non-Hispanic/Latino; 0.3% American Indian or Alaska Native, non-Hispanic/Latino; 3% Two or more races, non-Hispanic/Latino; 6% Race/ethnicity unknown; 2% international; 11% transferred in; 12% live on campus.

Freshmen
Admission: 12,199 applied, 9,433 admitted, 2,195 enrolled. ***Average high school GPA:*** 3.3. ***Test scores:*** ACT scores over 18: 91%; ACT scores over 24: 45%; ACT scores over 30: 9%.
Retention: 76% of full-time freshmen returned.

FACULTY
Total: 1,804, 58% full-time.
Student/faculty ratio: 15:1.

ACADEMICS
Calendar: semesters. *Degrees:* certificates, bachelor's, master's, doctoral, post-master's, and postbachelor's certificates.
Special study options: academic remediation for entering students, accelerated degree program, adult/continuing education programs, advanced placement credit, cooperative education, distance learning, double majors, English as a second language, freshman honors college, honors programs, independent study, internships, off-campus study, part-time degree program, services for LD students, study abroad, summer session for credit. ***ROTC:*** Army (b), Air Force (c).
Unusual degree programs: 3-2 engineering with Students must complete three years of study in Engineering or Computer Science disciplines at their home institution. Study fourth and fifth years as MS students at Wayne State University to earn a BS and MS in five years.
Computers: Students can access the following: computer help desk, free student e-mail accounts, online (class) grades, online (class) registration, online (class) schedules. Campuswide network is available. 100% of college-owned or -operated housing units are wired for high-speed Internet access. Wireless service is available via entire campus.

STUDENT LIFE
Housing options: coed, special housing for students with disabilities. Campus housing is university owned. Freshman applicants given priority for college housing.
Activities and organizations: drama/theater group, student-run newspaper, radio station, choral group, marching band, Muslim Students Association, Honors Students Association, Indian Students Association, American Medical Students Association-Pre-Med Chapter, national fraternities, national sororities.
Athletics Member NCAA. All Division II. ***Intercollegiate sports:*** baseball M(s), basketball M(s)/W(s), cheerleading M(s)/W(s), cross-country running M(s)/W(s), fencing M(s)/W(s), football M(s), golf M(s)/W(s), lacrosse M(c)/W(c), soccer M(c)/W(c), softball W(s), swimming and diving M(s)/W(s), tennis M(s)/W(s), track and field W(s), volleyball W(s). ***Intramural sports:*** badminton M/W, basketball M(c)/W(c), football M/W, rock climbing M/W, soccer M/W, softball M/W, table tennis M/W, tennis M/W, ultimate Frisbee M/W, volleyball M(c)/W(c).
Campus security: 24-hour emergency response devices and patrols, late-night transport/escort service, controlled dormitory access, VIN etching, bike patrol, safety and defense classes, K-9 unit, victim assistance, confidential tip line.
Student services: health clinic, personal/psychological counseling, legal services.

COSTS & FINANCIAL AID
Costs (2014–15) ***One-time required fee:*** $250. ***Tuition:*** state resident $10,995 full-time, $336 per credit hour part-time; nonresident $25,237 full-time, $841 per credit hour part-time. Full-time tuition and fees vary according to course load, program, reciprocity agreements, and student level. Part-time tuition and fees vary according to course load, program, reciprocity agreements, and student level. ***Required fees:*** $1355 full-time, $30 per credit hour part-time, $224 per term part-time. ***Room and board:*** $9713; room only: $5723. Room and board charges vary according to board plan and housing facility. ***Payment plan:*** installment. ***Waivers:*** senior citizens and employees or children of employees.
Financial Aid Of all full-time matriculated undergraduates who enrolled in 2013, 10,093 applied for aid, 9,243 were judged to have need, 401 had their need fully met. 361 Federal Work-Study jobs (averaging $2577). In 2013, 1058 non-need-based awards were made. ***Average percent of need met:*** 50. ***Average financial aid package:*** $10,291. ***Average need-based loan:*** $4348. ***Average need-based gift aid:*** $6496. ***Average non-need-based aid:*** $6556. ***Average indebtedness upon graduation:*** $23,785.

APPLYING
Standardized Tests *Required:* SAT or ACT (for admission).
Options: electronic application, deferred entrance.
Application fee: $25.
Required: high school transcript. ***Required for some:*** ACT or SAT and high school transcript or GED required.

Application deadlines: 8/1 (freshmen), 8/1 (out-of-state freshmen), 8/1 (transfers).

Notification: continuous (freshmen), continuous (out-of-state freshmen), continuous (transfers).

CONTACT

Ms. La Joyce Brown, Interim Senior Director of Undergraduate Admissions and Orientation, Wayne State University, 42 West Warren, Undergraduate Admissions, Student Development and Campus Life, Detroit 48202. *Phone:* 313-577-2100. *Toll-free phone:* 877-WSU-INFO. *E-mail:* admissions@wayne.edu.

Western Michigan University

Kalamazoo, Michigan

http://www.wmich.edu/

- **State-supported** university, founded 1903
- **Urban** 1200-acre campus
- **Endowment** $320.0 million
- **Coed** 18,889 undergraduate students, 83% full-time, 50% women, 50% men
- **Moderately difficult** entrance level, 84% of applicants were admitted

UNDERGRAD STUDENTS

15,713 full-time, 3,176 part-time. Students come from 42 states and territories; 64 other countries; 7% are from out of state; 12% Black or African American, non-Hispanic/Latino; 5% Hispanic/Latino; 2% Asian, non-Hispanic/Latino; 0.1% Native Hawaiian or other Pacific Islander, non-Hispanic/Latino; 0.4% American Indian or Alaska Native, non-Hispanic/Latino; 3% Two or more races, non-Hispanic/Latino; 1% Race/ethnicity unknown; 3% international; 9% transferred in; 28% live on campus.

Freshmen

Admission: 14,008 applied, 11,775 admitted, 3,012 enrolled. ***Average high school GPA:*** 3.35. ***Test scores:*** ACT scores over 18: 88%; ACT scores over 24: 36%; ACT scores over 30: 4%.

Retention: 78% of full-time freshmen returned.

FACULTY

Total: 1,466, 64% full-time, 50% with terminal degrees.

Student/faculty ratio: 17:1.

ACADEMICS

Calendar: semesters. *Degrees:* bachelor's, master's, doctoral, post-master's, and postbachelor's certificates.

Special study options: academic remediation for entering students, accelerated degree program, adult/continuing education programs, advanced placement credit, cooperative education, distance learning, double majors, English as a second language, freshman honors college, honors programs, independent study, internships, off-campus study, part-time degree program, services for LD students, student-designed majors, study abroad, summer session for credit. ***ROTC:*** Army (b).

Computers: 2,387 computers/terminals are available on campus for general student use. Students can access the following: computer help desk, free student e-mail accounts, online (class) grades, online (class) registration, online (class) schedules. Campuswide network is available. 100% of college-owned or -operated housing units are wired for high-speed Internet access. Wireless service is available via entire campus.

STUDENT LIFE

Housing options: coed, men-only, women-only, special housing for students with disabilities. Campus housing is university owned. Freshman campus housing is guaranteed.

Activities and organizations: drama/theater group, student-run newspaper, radio station, choral group, marching band, Campus Activities Board, Western Student Association, Young Black Male Support Network, Drive Safe Kalamazoo, Alternative Spring Break, national fraternities, national sororities.

Athletics Member NCAA. All Division I except football (Division I-A). ***Intercollegiate sports:*** baseball M(s), basketball M(s)/W(s), cross-country running W(s), golf W(s), gymnastics W(s), ice hockey M(s), soccer M(s)/W(s), softball W(s), tennis M(s)/W(s), track and field W(s), volleyball W(s). ***Intramural sports:*** baseball M(c)/W(c), basketball M(c)/W(c), equestrian sports M/W, golf M(c)/W(c), ice hockey M, lacrosse M(c)/W(c), racquetball M/W, rugby M(c)/W(c), sailing M(c)/W(c), skiing (downhill) M(c)/W(c), soccer M/W, softball M/W, swimming and diving M(c)/W(c), tennis M/W, ultimate Frisbee M/W, volleyball M/W.

Campus security: 24-hour emergency response devices and patrols, student patrols, late-night transport/escort service, controlled dormitory access.

Student services: health clinic, personal/psychological counseling, women's center.

COSTS & FINANCIAL AID

Costs (2014–15) ***One-time required fee:*** $300. ***Tuition:*** state resident $9794 full-time, $339 per credit hour part-time; nonresident $24,026 full-time, $831 per credit hour part-time. Full-time tuition and fees vary according to course load, location, program, and student level. Part-time tuition and fees vary according to course load, location, program, and student level. ***Required fees:*** $891 full-time, $243 per term part-time. ***Room and board:*** $8943; room only: $4613. Room and board charges vary according to board plan. ***Payment plan:*** installment. ***Waivers:*** senior citizens and employees or children of employees.

Financial Aid Of all full-time matriculated undergraduates who enrolled in 2013, 14,150 applied for aid, 11,750 were judged to have need, 2,400 had their need fully met. In 2013, 625 non-need-based awards were made. ***Average percent of need met:*** 75. ***Average financial aid package:*** $14,400. ***Average need-based loan:*** $3700. ***Average need-based gift aid:*** $5300. ***Average non-need-based aid:*** $3300. ***Average indebtedness upon graduation:*** $32,720.

APPLYING

Standardized Tests *Required:* SAT or ACT (for admission).

Options: electronic application.

Application fee: $40.

Required: high school transcript. ***Required for some:*** interview.

Application deadlines: rolling (freshmen), 9/1 (transfers).

Notification: continuous (freshmen), continuous (transfers).

CONTACT

Western Michigan University, 1903 West Michigan Avenue, Kalamazoo, MI 49008. *Phone:* 269-387-2000. *E-mail:* ask-wmu@wmich.edu.

MINNESOTA

Argosy University, Twin Cities

Eagan, Minnesota

http://www.argosy.edu/locations/twin-cities/

- **Proprietary** university, founded 1961, part of Education Management Corporation
- **Suburban** campus
- **Coed**

ACADEMICS

Calendar: semesters. *Degrees:* associate, bachelor's, master's, doctoral, and post-master's certificates.

CONTACT

Argosy University, Twin Cities, 1515 Central Parkway, Eagan, MN 55121. *Phone:* 651-846-2882. *Toll-free phone:* 888-844-2004.

The Art Institutes International Minnesota

Minneapolis, Minnesota

http://www.artinstitutes.edu/minneapolis/

- **Proprietary** 4-year, founded 1964, part of Education Management Corporation
- **Urban** campus
- **Coed**

ACADEMICS

Calendar: quarters. *Degrees:* diplomas, associate, and bachelor's.

CONTACT
The Art Institutes International Minnesota, 15 South 9th Street, Minneapolis, MN 55402. *Phone:* 612-332-3361. *Toll-free phone:* 800-777-3643.

Augsburg College

Minneapolis, Minnesota

http://www.augsburg.edu/

- **Independent Lutheran** comprehensive, founded 1869
- **Urban** 23-acre campus with easy access to Minneapolis-St. Paul
- **Endowment** $37.8 million
- **Coed** 2,620 undergraduate students, 76% full-time, 54% women, 46% men
- **Moderately difficult** entrance level, 68% of applicants were admitted

UNDERGRAD STUDENTS
2,002 full-time, 618 part-time. Students come from 37 states and territories; 47 other countries; 20% are from out of state; 11% Black or African American, non-Hispanic/Latino; 5% Hispanic/Latino; 8% Asian, non-Hispanic/Latino; 1% American Indian or Alaska Native, non-Hispanic/Latino; 4% Two or more races, non-Hispanic/Latino; 11% Race/ethnicity unknown; 2% international; 8% transferred in; 37% live on campus.

Freshmen
Admission: 2,824 applied, 1,921 admitted, 393 enrolled. ***Average high school GPA:*** 3.25. ***Test scores:*** ACT scores over 18: 90%; ACT scores over 24: 40%; ACT scores over 30: 6%.

Retention: 75% of full-time freshmen returned.

FACULTY
Total: 371, 45% full-time, 65% with terminal degrees.

Student/faculty ratio: 12:1.

ACADEMICS
Calendar: semesters for undergraduate programs; trimesters for graduate programs and weekend college. *Degrees:* certificates, bachelor's, master's, doctoral, post-master's, and postbachelor's certificates.

Special study options: academic remediation for entering students, adult/continuing education programs, advanced placement credit, cooperative education, double majors, English as a second language, freshman honors college, honors programs, independent study, internships, off-campus study, part-time degree program, services for LD students, student-designed majors, study abroad, summer session for credit. ***ROTC:*** Army (c), Navy (c), Air Force (c).

Unusual degree programs: 3-2 engineering with Michigan Technological University, University of Minnesota, Twin Cities Campus.

Computers: 252 computers/terminals are available on campus for general student use. Students can access the following: campus intranet, computer help desk, free student e-mail accounts, online (class) grades, online (class) registration, online (class) schedules. Campuswide network is available. 100% of college-owned or -operated housing units are wired for high-speed Internet access. Wireless service is available via entire campus.

STUDENT LIFE
Housing options: coed, men-only, women-only, special housing for students with disabilities. Campus housing is university owned. Freshman applicants given priority for college housing.

Activities and organizations: drama/theater group, student-run newspaper, radio station, choral group, Student Activities Council, student government, newspaper/yearbook, campus ministry, intramurals.

Athletics Member NCAA. All Division III. ***Intercollegiate sports:*** baseball M, basketball M/W, cross-country running M/W, football M, golf M/W, ice hockey M/W, lacrosse W, soccer M/W, softball W, swimming and diving W, track and field M/W, volleyball W, wrestling M. ***Intramural sports:*** basketball M/W, football M, skiing (cross-country) M(c)/W(c), skiing (downhill) M(c)/W(c), softball M/W, volleyball M/W, wrestling M.

Campus security: 24-hour emergency response devices and patrols, student patrols, late-night transport/escort service, controlled dormitory access.

Student services: health clinic, personal/psychological counseling, women's center.

COSTS & FINANCIAL AID
Costs (2015–16) ***Comprehensive fee:*** $44,845 includes full-time tuition ($34,800), mandatory fees ($665), and room and board ($9380). Part-time tuition: $1088 per credit. ***Required fees:*** $182 per term part-time. ***College room only:*** $4850. Room and board charges vary according to board plan and housing facility. ***Payment plan:*** installment. ***Waivers:*** employees or children of employees.

Financial Aid Of all full-time matriculated undergraduates who enrolled in 2012, 2,326 applied for aid, 2,141 were judged to have need, 309 had their need fully met. 174 Federal Work-Study jobs (averaging $1938). 825 state and other part-time jobs (averaging $2892). In 2012, 351 non-need-based awards were made. ***Average percent of need met:*** 65. ***Average financial aid package:*** $21,349. ***Average need-based loan:*** $5706. ***Average need-based gift aid:*** $16,603. ***Average non-need-based aid:*** $10,489. ***Average indebtedness upon graduation:*** $27,081. ***Financial aid deadline:*** 8/15.

APPLYING
Standardized Tests *Required:* SAT or ACT (for admission).

Options: electronic application, deferred entrance.

Required: essay or personal statement, high school transcript, minimum 2.5 GPA, 1 letter of recommendation.

Application deadlines: 8/15 (freshmen), 8/15 (transfers).

Notification: continuous (freshmen), continuous (transfers).

CONTACT
Ms. Marissa Machado, Senior Associate Director of Admissions, Augsburg College, 2211 Riverside Avenue, Minneapolis, MN 55454-1351. *Phone:* 612-330-1586. *Toll-free phone:* 800-788-5678. *Fax:* 612-330-1590. *E-mail:* admissions@augsburg.edu.

Bemidji State University

Bemidji, Minnesota

http://www.bemidjistate.edu/

- **State-supported** comprehensive, founded 1919, part of Minnesota State Colleges and Universities System
- **Small-town** 89-acre campus
- **Coed** 4,697 undergraduate students, 75% full-time, 56% women, 44% men
- **Moderately difficult** entrance level, 94% of applicants were admitted

UNDERGRAD STUDENTS
3,504 full-time, 1,193 part-time. 10% are from out of state; 2% Black or African American, non-Hispanic/Latino; 2% Hispanic/Latino; 0.9% Asian, non-Hispanic/Latino; 3% American Indian or Alaska Native, non-Hispanic/Latino; 3% Two or more races, non-Hispanic/Latino; 2% Race/ethnicity unknown; 2% international; 6% transferred in; 30% live on campus.

Freshmen
Admission: 2,132 applied, 1,994 admitted, 802 enrolled. ***Average high school GPA:*** 3.1. ***Test scores:*** ACT scores over 18: 90%; ACT scores over 24: 26%; ACT scores over 30: 2%.

Retention: 68% of full-time freshmen returned.

FACULTY
Total: 253, 62% full-time, 47% with terminal degrees.

Student/faculty ratio: 21:1.

ACADEMICS
Calendar: semesters. *Degrees:* certificates, associate, bachelor's, master's, and postbachelor's certificates.

Special study options: adult/continuing education programs, part-time degree program.

Computers: Students can access the following: computer help desk, free student e-mail accounts, online (class) grades, online (class) registration, online (class) schedules. Wireless service is available via entire campus.

STUDENT LIFE
Housing options: coed, special housing for students with disabilities. Campus housing is university owned. Freshman applicants given priority for college housing.

Athletics Member NCAA. All Division II except men's and women's ice hockey (Division I). ***Intercollegiate sports:*** baseball M(s), basketball M(s)/W(s), cross-country running W(s), football M(s), golf M(s)/W(s), ice hockey M(s)/W(s), soccer W(s), softball W(s), tennis W(s), track and field W(s), volleyball W(s). ***Intramural sports:*** basketball M/W, football M, ice hockey M/W, soccer M/W, softball M/W, volleyball M/W.

Campus security: 24-hour emergency response devices and patrols, late-night transport/escort service, controlled dormitory access.

COSTS & FINANCIAL AID

Costs (2014–15) ***Tuition:*** state resident $7146 full-time, $250 per credit part-time; nonresident $7146 full-time, $250 per credit part-time. Full-time tuition and fees vary according to course load, location, program, and reciprocity agreements. Part-time tuition and fees vary according to course load, location, program, and reciprocity agreements. ***Required fees:*** $988 full-time, $22 per credit part-time. ***Room and board:*** $7470. Room and board charges vary according to board plan and housing facility. ***Payment plan:*** installment. ***Waivers:*** senior citizens and employees or children of employees.

Financial Aid Of all full-time matriculated undergraduates who enrolled in 2013, 2,890 applied for aid, 2,284 were judged to have need, 311 had their need fully met. 285 Federal Work-Study jobs (averaging $1693). 176 state and other part-time jobs (averaging $1863). In 2013, 564 non-need-based awards were made. ***Average percent of need met:*** 61. ***Average financial aid package:*** $8764. ***Average need-based loan:*** $4104. ***Average need-based gift aid:*** $5339. ***Average non-need-based aid:*** $10,309.

APPLYING

Standardized Tests *Required:* SAT or ACT (for admission).

Options: electronic application, early action, deferred entrance.

Application fee: $20.

Required: high school transcript. ***Required for some:*** essay or personal statement, interview.

CONTACT

Bemidji State University, 1500 Birchmont Drive, NE, Bemidji, MN 56601-2699. *Phone:* 218-755-2602. *Toll-free phone:* 800-475-2001.

Bethany Lutheran College

Mankato, Minnesota

http://www.blc.edu/

- **Independent Lutheran** 4-year, founded 1927
- **Small-town** 50-acre campus with easy access to Minneapolis-St. Paul
- **Endowment** $43.2 million
- **Coed** 533 undergraduate students, 94% full-time, 53% women, 47% men
- **Moderately difficult** entrance level, 78% of applicants were admitted

UNDERGRAD STUDENTS

503 full-time, 30 part-time. Students come from 30 states and territories; 6 other countries; 26% are from out of state; 3% Black or African American, non-Hispanic/Latino; 3% Hispanic/Latino; 0.9% Asian, non-Hispanic/Latino; 0.2% Native Hawaiian or other Pacific Islander, non-Hispanic/Latino; 0.6% American Indian or Alaska Native, non-Hispanic/Latino; 2% Two or more races, non-Hispanic/Latino; 3% Race/ethnicity unknown; 0.8% international; 3% transferred in; 66% live on campus.

Freshmen

Admission: 457 applied, 355 admitted, 142 enrolled. ***Average high school GPA:*** 3.39. ***Test scores:*** ACT scores over 18: 91%; ACT scores over 24: 43%; ACT scores over 30: 9%.

Retention: 71% of full-time freshmen returned.

FACULTY

Total: 73, 56% full-time, 32% with terminal degrees.

Student/faculty ratio: 10:1.

ACADEMICS

Calendar: semesters. *Degree:* bachelor's.

Special study options: academic remediation for entering students, advanced placement credit, cooperative education, double majors, independent study, internships, services for LD students, student-designed majors, study abroad, summer session for credit. ***ROTC:*** Army (c).

Unusual degree programs: 3-2 engineering with University of Minnesota-Twin Cities.

Computers: 100 computers/terminals are available on campus for general student use. Students can access the following: computer help desk, free student e-mail accounts, online (class) grades, online (class) registration, online (class) schedules. Campuswide network is available. 100% of college-owned or -operated housing units are wired for high-speed Internet access. Wireless service is available via entire campus.

STUDENT LIFE

Housing options: on-campus residence required through sophomore year; men-only, women-only. Campus housing is university owned. Freshman campus housing is guaranteed.

Activities and organizations: drama/theater group, student-run newspaper, choral group, Bethany Activities Committee, Student Senate, Scholastic Leadership Society, PAMA (Promoting Awareness, spurring Motivation, and encouraging Action), Bethany Society of Royal Scientists.

Athletics Member NCAA. All Division III. ***Intercollegiate sports:*** baseball M, basketball M/W, cross-country running M/W, equestrian sports M(c)/W(c), golf M/W, soccer M/W, softball W, tennis M/W, track and field M/W, volleyball W. ***Intramural sports:*** basketball M/W, football M/W, racquetball M/W, table tennis M/W, tennis M/W, ultimate Frisbee M/W, volleyball M/W.

Campus security: 24-hour emergency response devices and patrols, late-night transport/escort service, controlled dormitory access.

Student services: personal/psychological counseling.

COSTS & FINANCIAL AID

Costs (2015–16) ***One-time required fee:*** $130. ***Comprehensive fee:*** $32,880 includes full-time tuition ($24,720), mandatory fees ($450), and room and board ($7710). Part-time tuition: $1050 per credit hour. Part-time tuition and fees vary according to course load. ***Required fees:*** $225 part-time. ***Room and board:*** Room and board charges vary according to board plan, housing facility, and student level. ***Payment plan:*** installment. ***Waivers:*** senior citizens and employees or children of employees.

Financial Aid Of all full-time matriculated undergraduates who enrolled in 2013, 518 applied for aid, 489 were judged to have need, 95 had their need fully met. 27 Federal Work-Study jobs (averaging $1620). 273 state and other part-time jobs (averaging $787). In 2013, 47 non-need-based awards were made. ***Average percent of need met:*** 81. ***Average financial aid package:*** $19,087. ***Average need-based loan:*** $5039. ***Average need-based gift aid:*** $14,155. ***Average non-need-based aid:*** $5862. ***Average indebtedness upon graduation:*** $33,384.

APPLYING

Standardized Tests *Required:* SAT or ACT (for admission).

Options: electronic application.

Required: essay or personal statement, high school transcript, minimum 2.4 GPA. ***Required for some:*** interview. ***Recommended:*** minimum 3.2 GPA, interview.

Notification: continuous (transfers).

CONTACT

Mr. Daniel Tomhave, Director of Admissions, Bethany Lutheran College, 700 Luther Drive, Mankato, MN 56001. *Phone:* 507-344-7000 Ext. 451. *Toll-free phone:* 800-944-3066. *Fax:* 507-344-7376. *E-mail:* dtomhave@blc.edu.

★ Bethel University

St. Paul, Minnesota

http://www.bethel.edu/

- **Independent** comprehensive, founded 1871, affiliated with Baptist General Conference
- **Suburban** 289-acre campus with easy access to Minneapolis-St. Paul
- **Endowment** $28.4 million
- **Coed** 3,051 undergraduate students, 85% full-time, 62% women, 38% men
- **Moderately difficult** entrance level, 95% of applicants were admitted

UNDERGRAD STUDENTS

2,579 full-time, 472 part-time. Students come from 38 states and territories; 6 other countries; 22% are from out of state; 5% Black or

African American, non-Hispanic/Latino; 3% Hispanic/Latino; 3% Asian, non-Hispanic/Latino; 0.1% American Indian or Alaska Native, non-Hispanic/Latino; 2% Two or more races, non-Hispanic/Latino; 2% Race/ethnicity unknown; 0.4% international; 4% transferred in; 71% live on campus.

Freshmen
Admission: 2,059 applied, 1,965 admitted, 604 enrolled. ***Average high school GPA:*** 3.5. ***Test scores:*** ACT scores over 18: 97%; ACT scores over 24: 60%; ACT scores over 30: 15%.

Retention: 83% of full-time freshmen returned.

FACULTY
Total: 285, 62% full-time, 59% with terminal degrees.

Student/faculty ratio: 12:1.

ACADEMICS
Calendar: 4-1-4. *Degrees:* associate, bachelor's, master's, doctoral, post-master's, and postbachelor's certificates.

Special study options: academic remediation for entering students, accelerated degree program, adult/continuing education programs, advanced placement credit, double majors, honors programs, independent study, internships, off-campus study, part-time degree program, services for LD students, student-designed majors, study abroad, summer session for credit. ***ROTC:*** Army (c), Air Force (c).

Unusual degree programs: 3-2 engineering with University of Minnesota; other institutions by arrangement.

Computers: 420 computers/terminals are available on campus for general student use. Students can access the following: campus intranet, computer help desk, free student e-mail accounts, online (class) grades, online (class) registration, online (class) schedules. Campuswide network is available. 100% of college-owned or -operated housing units are wired for high-speed Internet access. Wireless service is available via classrooms, computer centers, computer labs, dorm rooms, learning centers, libraries, student centers.

STUDENT LIFE
Housing options: on-campus residence required through sophomore year; special housing for students with disabilities. Campus housing is university owned. Freshman campus housing is guaranteed.

Activities and organizations: drama/theater group, student-run newspaper, radio station, choral group.

Athletics Member NCAA. All Division III. ***Intercollegiate sports:*** baseball M, basketball M/W, cross-country running M/W, football M, golf M/W, ice hockey M/W, soccer M/W, softball W, tennis M/W, track and field M/W, volleyball M(c)/W. ***Intramural sports:*** badminton M/W, basketball M/W, football M, ice hockey M(c), lacrosse M(c)/W(c), rugby M(c), softball M/W, volleyball W.

Campus security: 24-hour emergency response devices and patrols, student patrols, late-night transport/escort service, controlled dormitory access, video surveillance for residence halls, academic buildings, and parking lots.

Student services: health clinic, personal/psychological counseling.

COSTS & FINANCIAL AID
Costs (2014–15) ***Comprehensive fee:*** $42,430 includes full-time tuition ($32,840), mandatory fees ($150), and room and board ($9440). Part-time tuition: $1370 per credit. Part-time tuition and fees vary according to course load. ***College room only:*** $5400. Room and board charges vary according to board plan. ***Payment plans:*** tuition prepayment, installment. ***Waivers:*** employees or children of employees.

Financial Aid Of all full-time matriculated undergraduates who enrolled in 2014, 2,150 applied for aid, 1,798 were judged to have need, 311 had their need fully met. 350 Federal Work-Study jobs (averaging $2500). 1,500 state and other part-time jobs (averaging $2500). In 2014, 616 non-need-based awards were made. ***Average percent of need met:*** 78. ***Average financial aid package:*** $24,292. ***Average need-based loan:*** $4368. ***Average need-based gift aid:*** $18,217. ***Average non-need-based aid:*** $10,497. ***Average indebtedness upon graduation:*** $33,685.

APPLYING
Standardized Tests *Required:* SAT or ACT (for admission).

Options: electronic application, early admission.

Required: essay or personal statement, high school transcript, rank in upper 50% of high school class. ***Required for some:*** 2 letters of recommendation. ***Recommended:*** minimum 2.5 GPA, interview.

Application deadlines: rolling (freshmen), rolling (out-of-state freshmen), rolling (transfers).

Notification: continuous (freshmen), continuous (out-of-state freshmen), continuous (transfers).

CONTACT
Office of Admissions, Bethel University, 3900 Bethel Drive, St. Paul, MN 55112. *Phone:* 651-638-6242. *Toll-free phone:* 800-255-8706 Ext. 6242. *Fax:* 651-635-1490. *E-mail:* buadmissions-cas@bethel.edu.

Carleton College
Northfield, Minnesota
http://www.carleton.edu/

- **Independent** 4-year, founded 1866
- **Small-town** 955-acre campus with easy access to Minneapolis-St. Paul
- **Endowment** $792.7 million
- **Coed** 2,057 undergraduate students, 99% full-time, 53% women, 47% men
- **Very difficult** entrance level, 23% of applicants were admitted

UNDERGRAD STUDENTS
2,044 full-time, 13 part-time. Students come from 50 states and territories; 38 other countries; 81% are from out of state; 4% Black or African American, non-Hispanic/Latino; 6% Hispanic/Latino; 9% Asian, non-Hispanic/Latino; 0.1% Native Hawaiian or other Pacific Islander, non-Hispanic/Latino; 0.1% American Indian or Alaska Native, non-Hispanic/Latino; 5% Two or more races, non-Hispanic/Latino; 2% Race/ethnicity unknown; 9% international; 96% live on campus.

Freshmen
Admission: 6,297 applied, 1,434 admitted, 521 enrolled. ***Test scores:*** SAT critical reading scores over 500: 100%; SAT math scores over 500: 99%; SAT writing scores over 500: 99%; ACT scores over 18: 100%; SAT critical reading scores over 600: 94%; SAT math scores over 600: 93%; SAT writing scores over 600: 92%; ACT scores over 24: 98%; SAT critical reading scores over 700: 58%; SAT math scores over 700: 58%; SAT writing scores over 700: 60%; ACT scores over 30: 77%.

Retention: 97% of full-time freshmen returned.

FACULTY
Total: 242, 87% full-time, 94% with terminal degrees.

Student/faculty ratio: 9:1.

ACADEMICS
Calendar: three courses for each of three terms. *Degree:* bachelor's.

Special study options: accelerated degree program, advanced placement credit, double majors, independent study, internships, off-campus study, services for LD students, student-designed majors, study abroad.

Unusual degree programs: 3-2 engineering with Columbia University (3-2 Program)and Washington University in St. Louis (4-2 Program).

Computers: 250 computers/terminals and 220 ports are available on campus for general student use. Students can access the following: campus intranet, computer help desk, free student e-mail accounts, online (class) grades, online (class) registration, online (class) schedules. Campuswide network is available. 100% of college-owned or -operated housing units are wired for high-speed Internet access. Wireless service is available via classrooms, computer centers, computer labs, dorm rooms, learning centers, libraries, student centers.

STUDENT LIFE
Housing options: on-campus residence required through senior year; coed, special housing for students with disabilities. Campus housing is university owned. Freshman campus housing is guaranteed.

Activities and organizations: drama/theater group, student-run newspaper, radio station, choral group, CANOE (Carleton Association of Nature and Outdoor Enthusiasts), Farm Club, Ebony II, WHIMS (Women in Math and Science), Amnesty International.

Athletics Member NCAA. All Division III. ***Intercollegiate sports:*** badminton M(c)/W(c), baseball M, basketball M/W, crew M(c)/W(c), cross-country running M/W, equestrian sports M(c)/W(c), fencing M(c)/W(c), field hockey W(c), football M, golf M/W, gymnastics W(c), ice hockey M(c)/W(c), lacrosse M(c)/W(c), rugby M(c)/W(c), sailing M(c)/W(c), skiing (cross-country) M(c)/W(c), skiing (downhill) M(c)/W(c), soccer M/W, softball W, swimming and diving M/W, tennis M/W, track and field M/W, ultimate Frisbee M(c)/W(c), volleyball M(c)/W, water polo M(c)/W(c). ***Intramural sports:*** badminton M/W, basketball M/W, soccer M/W, softball M/W, table tennis M/W, tennis M/W, ultimate Frisbee M/W, volleyball M/W.

Campus security: 24-hour emergency response devices and patrols, student patrols, late-night transport/escort service, controlled dormitory access, Emergency Notification Service (cell phone text and email alerts).

Student services: health clinic, personal/psychological counseling, women's center.

COSTS & FINANCIAL AID

Costs (2014–15) ***Comprehensive fee:*** $60,102 includes full-time tuition ($47,460), mandatory fees ($276), and room and board ($12,366). ***College room only:*** $6468. Room and board charges vary according to board plan. ***Payment plan:*** installment. ***Waivers:*** employees or children of employees.

Financial Aid Of all full-time matriculated undergraduates who enrolled in 2013, 1,763 applied for aid, 1,129 were judged to have need, 1,129 had their need fully met. 350 Federal Work-Study jobs (averaging $25,310). 1,342 state and other part-time jobs (averaging $2539). In 2013, 135 non-need-based awards were made. ***Average percent of need met:*** 100. ***Average financial aid package:*** $38,623. ***Average need-based loan:*** $5281. ***Average need-based gift aid:*** $34,050. ***Average non-need-based aid:*** $3095. ***Average indebtedness upon graduation:*** $18,302. ***Financial aid deadline:*** 2/15.

APPLYING

Standardized Tests *Required:* SAT or ACT (for admission). *Recommended:* SAT Subject Tests (for admission).

Options: electronic application, early admission, early decision, deferred entrance.

Application fee: $30.

Required: essay or personal statement, high school transcript, 2 letters of recommendation, common application supplement. ***Recommended:*** interview.

Application deadlines: 1/15 (freshmen), 3/31 (transfers).

Early decision deadline: 11/15 (for plan 1), 1/15 (for plan 2).

Notification: 4/15 (freshmen), 5/15 (transfers), 12/15 (early decision plan 1), 2/15 (early decision plan 2).

CONTACT

Carleton College, One North College Street, Northfield, MN 55057-4001. *Phone:* 507-222-4190. *Toll-free phone:* 800-995-2275.

★ College of Saint Benedict

Saint Joseph, Minnesota

http://www.csbsju.edu/

- **Independent Roman Catholic** 4-year, founded 1887
- **Small-town** 600-acre campus with easy access to Minneapolis-St. Paul
- **Endowment** $57.3 million
- **Women only** 2,020 undergraduate students, 99% full-time
- **Moderately difficult** entrance level, 82% of applicants were admitted

UNDERGRAD STUDENTS

1,992 full-time, 28 part-time. Students come from 32 states and territories; 16 other countries; 16% are from out of state; 2% Black or African American, non-Hispanic/Latino; 5% Hispanic/Latino; 6% Asian, non-Hispanic/Latino; 0.1% Native Hawaiian or other Pacific Islander, non-Hispanic/Latino; 0.7% American Indian or Alaska Native, non-Hispanic/Latino; 0.6% Two or more races, non-Hispanic/Latino; 5% international; 1% transferred in; 89% live on campus.

Freshmen

Admission: 1,768 applied, 1,453 admitted, 542 enrolled. ***Average high school GPA:*** 3.68. ***Test scores:*** SAT critical reading scores over 500: 80%; SAT math scores over 500: 72%; SAT writing scores over 500: 70%; ACT scores over 18: 98%; SAT critical reading scores over 600: 27%; SAT math scores over 600: 31%; SAT writing scores over 600: 30%; ACT scores over 24: 71%; SAT critical reading scores over 700: 6%; SAT math scores over 700: 8%; SAT writing scores over 700: 4%; ACT scores over 30: 20%.

Retention: 88% of full-time freshmen returned.

FACULTY
Total: 168, 86% full-time, 84% with terminal degrees.

Student/faculty ratio: 12:1.

ACADEMICS
Calendar: semesters. *Degrees:* bachelor's (coordinate with Saint John's University for men).

Special study options: advanced placement credit, double majors, English as a second language, honors programs, independent study, internships, off-campus study, services for LD students, student-designed majors, study abroad. ***ROTC:*** Army (c).

Unusual degree programs: 3-2 engineering with University of Minnesota.

Computers: 1,024 computers/terminals and 3,000 ports are available on campus for general student use. Students can access the following: campus intranet, computer help desk, free student e-mail accounts, online (class) grades, online (class) registration, online (class) schedules, online student accounts. Campuswide network is available. 100% of college-owned or -operated housing units are wired for high-speed Internet access. Wireless service is available via entire campus.

STUDENT LIFE
Housing options: on-campus residence required through senior year; women-only, special housing for students with disabilities. Campus housing is university owned. Freshman campus housing is guaranteed.

Activities and organizations: drama/theater group, student-run newspaper, radio and television station, choral group, Alpha Kappa Sigma Service Sorority (AKS), Allied Health Club, College Republicans, Fides et Ratio, Spanish Club.

Athletics Member NCAA. All Division III. ***Intercollegiate sports:*** basketball W, crew W(c), cross-country running W, golf W, ice hockey W, lacrosse W(c), riflery W(c), rugby W(c), skiing (cross-country) W(c), soccer W, softball W, swimming and diving W, tennis W, track and field W, ultimate Frisbee W(c), volleyball W, water polo W(c). ***Intramural sports:*** badminton W, basketball W, football W, golf W(c), racquetball W, rock climbing W(c), skiing (downhill) W(c), soccer W, softball W, table tennis W, tennis W, volleyball W.

Campus security: 24-hour emergency response devices and patrols, student patrols, late-night transport/escort service, controlled dormitory access, well-lit pathways.

Student services: health clinic, personal/psychological counseling, women's center.

COSTS & FINANCIAL AID
Costs (2014–15) ***Comprehensive fee:*** $49,358 includes full-time tuition ($38,428), mandatory fees ($974), and room and board ($9956). Part-time tuition: $1601 per credit hour. Part-time tuition and fees vary according to course load. ***College room only:*** $4782. Room and board charges vary according to board plan and housing facility. ***Payment plan:*** installment. ***Waivers:*** employees or children of employees.

Financial Aid Of all full-time matriculated undergraduates who enrolled in 2014, 1,608 applied for aid, 1,406 were judged to have need, 595 had their need fully met. 423 Federal Work-Study jobs (averaging $2691). 1,102 state and other part-time jobs (averaging $2689). In 2014, 481 non-need-based awards were made. ***Average percent of need met:*** 89. ***Average financial aid package:*** $31,995. ***Average need-based loan:*** $4287. ***Average need-based gift aid:*** $25,770. ***Average non-need-based aid:*** $15,708. ***Average indebtedness upon graduation:*** $39,437.

APPLYING
Standardized Tests *Required:* SAT or ACT (for admission).

Options: electronic application, early action, deferred entrance.

Required: essay or personal statement, high school transcript, 1 letter of recommendation. ***Recommended:*** minimum 3.0 GPA, interview.

Application deadlines: rolling (freshmen), rolling (transfers), 11/15 (early action).

Notification: continuous (freshmen), continuous (transfers), 12/15 (early action).

CONTACT
Ms. Karen Backes, Dean of Admissions, College of Saint Benedict, 37 South College Avenue, St. Joseph, MN 56374. *Phone:* 320-363-5055. *Toll-free phone:* 800-544-1489. *Fax:* 320-363-5650. *E-mail:* admissions@csbsju.edu.

See previous page for display ad and page 1404 for the College Close-Up.

The College of St. Scholastica
Duluth, Minnesota
http://www.css.edu/

- **Independent** comprehensive, founded 1912, affiliated with Roman Catholic Church
- **Suburban** 186-acre campus
- **Endowment** $54.5 million
- **Coed** 2,859 undergraduate students, 81% full-time, 70% women, 30% men
- **Moderately difficult** entrance level, 66% of applicants were admitted

UNDERGRAD STUDENTS
2,317 full-time, 542 part-time. Students come from 49 states and territories; 37 other countries; 16% are from out of state; 3% Black or African American, non-Hispanic/Latino; 2% Hispanic/Latino; 2% Asian, non-Hispanic/Latino; 2% American Indian or Alaska Native, non-Hispanic/Latino; 2% Two or more races, non-Hispanic/Latino; 2% Race/ethnicity unknown; 4% international; 14% transferred in; 53% live on campus.

Freshmen
Admission: 3,368 applied, 2,229 admitted, 461 enrolled. ***Average high school GPA:*** 3.51. ***Test scores:*** SAT critical reading scores over 500: 65%; SAT math scores over 500: 74%; SAT writing scores over 500: 70%; ACT scores over 18: 97%; SAT critical reading scores over 600: 17%; SAT math scores over 600: 39%; SAT writing scores over 600: 17%; ACT scores over 24: 53%; SAT math scores over 700: 4%; SAT writing scores over 700: 4%; ACT scores over 30: 6%.

Retention: 85% of full-time freshmen returned.

FACULTY
Total: 389, 47% full-time, 43% with terminal degrees.

Student/faculty ratio: 14:1.

ACADEMICS
Calendar: semesters. *Degrees:* certificates, bachelor's, master's, doctoral, post-master's, and postbachelor's certificates.

Special study options: accelerated degree program, adult/continuing education programs, advanced placement credit, distance learning, double majors, honors programs, independent study, internships, off-campus study, part-time degree program, services for LD students, student-designed majors, study abroad, summer session for credit. ***ROTC:*** Air Force (c).

Unusual degree programs: 3-2 occupational therapy.

Computers: 517 computers/terminals are available on campus for general student use. Students can access the following: campus intranet, computer help desk, free student e-mail accounts, online (class) grades, online (class) registration, online (class) schedules, student account information and transcripts online. Campuswide network is available. 100% of college-owned or -operated housing units are wired for high-speed Internet access. Wireless service is available via classrooms, computer centers, computer labs, dorm rooms, learning centers, libraries, student centers.

STUDENT LIFE
Housing options: on-campus residence required through sophomore year; coed, special housing for students with disabilities. Campus housing is university owned. Freshman campus housing is guaranteed.

Activities and organizations: drama/theater group, student-run newspaper, television station, choral group, Campus Activity Board, Inter-Varsity, Habitat for Humanity, SHIMA, Volunteers Involved Through Action.

Athletics Member NCAA. All Division III. ***Intercollegiate sports:*** baseball M, basketball M/W, cross-country running M/W, football M, ice hockey M/W, skiing (cross-country) M/W, soccer M/W, softball W, tennis M/W, track and field M/W, volleyball W. ***Intramural sports:*** basketball M/W, football M/W, soccer M/W, tennis M/W, volleyball M/W.

Campus security: 24-hour emergency response devices and patrols, late-night transport/escort service, controlled dormitory access, student door monitor at night.

Student services: health clinic, personal/psychological counseling.

COSTS & FINANCIAL AID

Costs (2015–16) ***Comprehensive fee:*** $42,926 includes full-time tuition ($33,784), mandatory fees ($210), and room and board ($8932). Full-time tuition and fees vary according to class time and program. Part-time tuition: $1056 per credit. Part-time tuition and fees vary according to class time, course load, and program. ***College room only:*** $4928. Room and board charges vary according to board plan and housing facility. ***Payment plan:*** installment. ***Waivers:*** senior citizens and employees or children of employees.

Financial Aid Of all full-time matriculated undergraduates who enrolled in 2014, 1,993 applied for aid, 1,812 were judged to have need, 365 had their need fully met. In 2014, 149 non-need-based awards were made. ***Average percent of need met:*** 70. ***Average financial aid package:*** $21,774. ***Average need-based loan:*** $4693. ***Average need-based gift aid:*** $7093. ***Average non-need-based aid:*** $14,630. ***Average indebtedness upon graduation:*** $42,792.

APPLYING

Standardized Tests *Required:* SAT or ACT (for admission).

Options: electronic application, deferred entrance.

Required: high school transcript. ***Required for some:*** minimum 2.0 GPA, interview. ***Recommended:*** interview.

Application deadlines: rolling (freshmen), rolling (transfers).

Notification: continuous (freshmen), continuous (transfers).

CONTACT

Mr. Eric Berg, Vice President for Enrollment Management, The College of St. Scholastica, 1200 Kenwood Avenue, Duluth, MN 55811-4199. *Phone:* 218-723-6053. *Toll-free phone:* 800-249-6412. *E-mail:* admissions@css.edu.

Concordia College

Moorhead, Minnesota

http://www.concordiacollege.edu/

- **Independent** comprehensive, founded 1891, affiliated with Evangelical Lutheran Church in America
- **Suburban** 113-acre campus
- **Coed** 2,381 undergraduate students, 98% full-time, 60% women, 40% men
- **Moderately difficult** entrance level, 64% of applicants were admitted

UNDERGRAD STUDENTS

2,332 full-time, 49 part-time. Students come from 36 states and territories; 29 other countries; 28% are from out of state; 2% Black or African American, non-Hispanic/Latino; 2% Hispanic/Latino; 2% Asian, non-Hispanic/Latino; 0.5% American Indian or Alaska Native, non-Hispanic/Latino; 1% Two or more races, non-Hispanic/Latino; 6% Race/ethnicity unknown; 4% international; 2% transferred in; 62% live on campus.

Freshmen

Admission: 2,948 applied, 1,895 admitted, 540 enrolled. ***Average high school GPA:*** 3.59. ***Test scores:*** SAT critical reading scores over 500: 100%; SAT math scores over 500: 100%; SAT writing scores over 500: 83%; ACT scores over 18: 99%; SAT critical reading scores over 600: 83%; SAT math scores over 600: 100%; SAT writing scores over 600: 50%; ACT scores over 24: 67%; SAT math scores over 700: 17%; SAT writing scores over 700: 17%; ACT scores over 30: 17%.

Retention: 83% of full-time freshmen returned.

FACULTY

Total: 257, 68% full-time, 68% with terminal degrees.

Student/faculty ratio: 12:1.

ACADEMICS

Calendar: semesters. *Degrees:* bachelor's and master's.

Special study options: advanced placement credit, cooperative education, double majors, honors programs, independent study, internships, off-campus study, part-time degree program, services for LD students, student-designed majors, study abroad, summer session for credit. ***ROTC:*** Army (c), Air Force (c).

Unusual degree programs: 3-2 engineering with Institute of Technology (IT) at the University of Minnesota.

Computers: 570 computers/terminals and 87 ports are available on campus for general student use. Students can access the following: campus intranet, computer help desk, free student e-mail accounts, online (class) grades, online (class) registration, online (class) schedules, online degree audit. Campuswide network is available. 100% of college-owned or -operated housing units are wired for high-speed Internet access. Wireless service is available via entire campus.

STUDENT LIFE

Housing options: on-campus residence required through sophomore year; coed, women-only. Campus housing is university owned. Freshman applicants given priority for college housing.

Activities and organizations: drama/theater group, student-run newspaper, radio and television station, choral group, Campus Entertainment Commission, Habitat for Humanity, Dance Marathon, Colleges Against Cancer (Relay for Life), Campus Ministry Commission.

Athletics Member NCAA. All Division III. ***Intercollegiate sports:*** baseball M, basketball M/W, cheerleading M(c)/W(c), cross-country running M/W, football M, golf M/W, ice hockey M/W, soccer M/W, softball W, swimming and diving W, tennis M/W, track and field M/W, volleyball M(c)/W, wrestling M. ***Intramural sports:*** basketball M/W, bowling M/W, football M, ice hockey M(c)/W(c), lacrosse M(c)/W(c), rugby W(c), skiing (cross-country) M(c)/W(c), skiing (downhill) M(c)/W(c), swimming and diving M(c)/W(c), tennis M(c)/W(c), ultimate Frisbee M(c)/W(c), volleyball M/W.

Campus security: 24-hour emergency response devices and patrols, late-night transport/escort service, controlled dormitory access, well-lighted campus.

Student services: health clinic, personal/psychological counseling, women's center.

COSTS & FINANCIAL AID

Costs (2015–16) ***Comprehensive fee:*** $43,064 includes full-time tuition ($35,250), mandatory fees ($214), and room and board ($7600). Full-time tuition and fees vary according to course load and degree level. Part-time tuition: $1380 per credit hour. Part-time tuition and fees vary according to course load and degree level. ***College room only:*** $3260. Room and board charges vary according to board plan and housing facility. ***Payment plan:*** installment. ***Waivers:*** employees or children of employees.

Financial Aid Of all full-time matriculated undergraduates who enrolled in 2013, 2,069 applied for aid, 1,815 were judged to have need, 293 had their need fully met. In 2013, 609 non-need-based awards were made. ***Average percent of need met:*** 90. ***Average financial aid package:*** $27,360. ***Average need-based loan:*** $8730. ***Average need-based gift aid:*** $18,955. ***Average non-need-based aid:*** $12,974.

APPLYING

Standardized Tests *Required:* SAT or ACT (for admission).

Options: electronic application, early admission, deferred entrance.

Application fee: $20.

Required: high school transcript, 2 letters of recommendation.

Application deadlines: rolling (freshmen), rolling (transfers).

Notification: continuous (freshmen), continuous (transfers).

CONTACT

Mr. Scott D. Ellingson, Dean of Admissions, Concordia College, 901 8th Street South, Moorhead, MN 56562. *Phone:* 218-299-3004. *Toll-free phone:* 800-699-9897. *Fax:* 218-299-4720. *E-mail:* sellings@cord.edu.

Concordia University, St. Paul

St. Paul, Minnesota

http://www.csp.edu/

- **Independent** comprehensive, founded 1893, affiliated with Lutheran Church–Missouri Synod
- **Urban** 37-acre campus with easy access to Minneapolis/St. Paul
- **Endowment** $39.6 million
- **Coed** 2,420 undergraduate students, 57% full-time, 59% women, 41% men
- **Minimally difficult** entrance level, 43% of applicants were admitted

UNDERGRAD STUDENTS
1,374 full-time, 1,046 part-time. Students come from 45 states and territories; 9 other countries; 17% are from out of state; 12% Black or African American, non-Hispanic/Latino; 4% Hispanic/Latino; 7% Asian, non-Hispanic/Latino; 0.6% American Indian or Alaska Native, non-Hispanic/Latino; 4% Two or more races, non-Hispanic/Latino; 6% Race/ethnicity unknown; 4% international; 22% transferred in; 23% live on campus.

Freshmen
Admission: 1,443 applied, 617 admitted, 242 enrolled. ***Average high school GPA:*** 3.12. ***Test scores:*** ACT scores over 18: 85%; ACT scores over 24: 29%; ACT scores over 30: 2%.
Retention: 71% of full-time freshmen returned.

FACULTY
Total: 419, 21% full-time, 36% with terminal degrees.
Student/faculty ratio: 19:1.

ACADEMICS
Calendar: semesters. *Degrees:* certificates, associate, bachelor's, master's, doctoral, post-master's, and postbachelor's certificates.
Special study options: academic remediation for entering students, accelerated degree program, adult/continuing education programs, advanced placement credit, distance learning, double majors, honors programs, independent study, internships, off-campus study, part-time degree program, services for LD students, student-designed majors, study abroad, summer session for credit. ***ROTC:*** Army (c), Air Force (c).
Unusual degree programs: 3-2 engineering with University of Minnesota.
Computers: 10 computers/terminals are available on campus for general student use. Students can access the following: campus intranet, computer help desk, free student e-mail accounts, online (class) grades, online (class) registration, online (class) schedules. Campuswide network is available. 100% of college-owned or -operated housing units are wired for high-speed Internet access. Wireless service is available via entire campus.

STUDENT LIFE
Housing options: on-campus residence required for freshman year; coed, men-only, women-only, special housing for students with disabilities. Campus housing is university owned. Freshman campus housing is guaranteed.
Activities and organizations: drama/theater group, student-run newspaper, choral group.
Athletics Member NCAA. All Division II. ***Intercollegiate sports:*** baseball M(s), basketball M(s)/W(s), cross-country running M(s)/W(s), football M(s), golf M(s)/W(s), soccer W(s), softball W(s), track and field M(s)/W(s), volleyball W(s). ***Intramural sports:*** basketball M/W, football M/W, soccer M/W, volleyball M/W.
Campus security: 24-hour emergency response devices and patrols, student patrols, late-night transport/escort service, controlled dormitory access.

COSTS & FINANCIAL AID
Costs (2015–16) ***Comprehensive fee:*** $29,050 includes full-time tuition ($20,750) and room and board ($8300). Full-time tuition and fees vary according to degree level and program. Part-time tuition: $650 per credit. Part-time tuition and fees vary according to course load, degree level, and program. ***Room and board:*** Room and board charges vary according to board plan and housing facility. ***Payment plan:*** installment. ***Waivers:*** employees or children of employees.
Financial Aid Of all full-time matriculated undergraduates who enrolled in 2014, 1,123 applied for aid, 997 were judged to have need, 94 had their need fully met. 99 Federal Work-Study jobs (averaging $2351). 219 state and other part-time jobs (averaging $2377). In 2014, 112 non-need-based awards were made. ***Average percent of need met:*** 58. ***Average financial aid package:*** $13,706. ***Average need-based loan:*** $4447. ***Average need-based gift aid:*** $9632. ***Average non-need-based aid:*** $4316. ***Average indebtedness upon graduation:*** $30,747.

APPLYING
Standardized Tests *Required:* SAT or ACT (for admission).
Options: electronic application, early admission, deferred entrance.
Application fee: $30.
Required: high school transcript, 2 letters of recommendation. ***Required for some:*** essay or personal statement. ***Recommended:*** minimum 2.0 GPA.
Application deadlines: 8/1 (freshmen), 8/1 (transfers).
Notification: continuous (freshmen), continuous (transfers).

CONTACT
Ms. Briana Eicheldinger, Director of Traditional Admission, Concordia University, St. Paul, 1282 Concordia Ave, St. Paul, MN 55104-5494. *Phone:* 651-641-8230. *Toll-free phone:* 800-333-4705. *Fax:* 651-603-6320. *E-mail:* admission@csp.edu.

Crossroads College

Rochester, Minnesota

http://www.crossroadscollege.edu/

- **Independent** 4-year, founded 1913, affiliated with Christian Churches and Churches of Christ
- **Suburban** 40-acre campus with easy access to Minneapolis-St. Paul
- **Coed** 109 undergraduate students, 89% full-time, 50% women, 50% men
- **Noncompetitive** entrance level, 90% of applicants were admitted

UNDERGRAD STUDENTS
97 full-time, 12 part-time. Students come from 20 states and territories; 2 other countries; 36% are from out of state; 17% Black or African American, non-Hispanic/Latino; 6% Hispanic/Latino; 0.9% Asian, non-Hispanic/Latino; 0.9% American Indian or Alaska Native, non-Hispanic/Latino; 0.9% Two or more races, non-Hispanic/Latino; 10% Race/ethnicity unknown; 3% international; 17% transferred in.

Freshmen
Admission: 31 applied, 28 admitted, 22 enrolled.
Retention: 55% of full-time freshmen returned.

FACULTY
Student/faculty ratio: 7:1.

ACADEMICS
Calendar: semesters. *Degrees:* associate and bachelor's.
Special study options: academic remediation for entering students, accelerated degree program, adult/continuing education programs, advanced placement credit, cooperative education, distance learning, double majors, external degree program, independent study, internships, student-designed majors, summer session for credit.
Computers: 15 computers/terminals are available on campus for general student use. Students can access the following: campus intranet, free student e-mail accounts, online (class) grades, online (class) registration, online (class) schedules. Campuswide network is available. 80% of college-owned or -operated housing units are wired for high-speed Internet access. Wireless service is available via entire campus.

STUDENT LIFE
Housing options: on-campus residence required through senior year; men-only, women-only, special housing for students with disabilities. Campus housing is university owned. Freshman campus housing is guaranteed.
Activities and organizations: drama/theater group, choral group, Musical Outreach Concert Choir, Adoration, Ambassadors Mission Group, Staged Reactions (drama group).
Athletics Member NCCAA. ***Intercollegiate sports:*** basketball M/W, golf M/W, racquetball M/W, soccer M/W, tennis M/W, volleyball W, weight lifting M/W.

Campus security: student patrols, late-night transport/escort service.

Student services: personal/psychological counseling.

COSTS

Costs (2014–15) ***Tuition:*** $15,100 full-time. Full-time tuition and fees vary according to class time and course load. Part-time tuition and fees vary according to class time and course load. ***Required fees:*** $435 per semester hour part-time. ***Room only:*** Room and board charges vary according to housing facility. ***Payment plan:*** installment. ***Waivers:*** employees or children of employees.

APPLYING

Standardized Tests *Required:* SAT or ACT (for admission).

Options: electronic application, deferred entrance.

Required: essay or personal statement, high school transcript, minimum 2.0 GPA, 3 letters of recommendation. ***Recommended:*** interview.

Application deadlines: 8/15 (freshmen), 8/15 (transfers).

Notification: continuous until 9/1 (freshmen), continuous until 9/1 (transfers).

CONTACT

Mr. Todd Looney, Director of Admissions, Crossroads College, 920 Mayowood Road, SW, Rochester, MN 55902-2382. *Phone:* 507-288-4563. *Toll-free phone:* 800-456-7651. *Fax:* 507-288-9046. *E-mail:* admissions@crossroadscollege.edu.

Crown College

St. Bonifacius, Minnesota

http://www.crown.edu/

- **Independent** comprehensive, founded 1916, affiliated with The Christian and Missionary Alliance
- **Small-town** 215-acre campus with easy access to Minneapolis-St. Paul
- **Endowment** $6.5 million
- **Coed**
- **Minimally difficult** entrance level

FACULTY

Student/faculty ratio: 15:1.

ACADEMICS

Calendar: semesters. *Degrees:* certificates, associate, bachelor's, master's, and postbachelor's certificates.

STUDENT LIFE

Housing options: on-campus residence required through senior year; men-only, women-only. Campus housing is university owned. Freshman campus housing is guaranteed.

Activities and organizations: drama/theater group, student-run newspaper, radio station, choral group, Hmong Student Fellowship, Global Impact Team, Student Activities Board, Student Senate, Storm Chaser Newspaper.

Athletics Member NCAA. All Division III.

Campus security: 24-hour emergency response devices, student patrols, late-night transport/escort service, controlled dormitory access.

Student services: health clinic, personal/psychological counseling.

FINANCIAL AID

Financial Aid ***Average indebtedness upon graduation:*** $33,239. ***Financial aid deadline:*** 8/1.

APPLYING

Standardized Tests *Required:* SAT or ACT (for admission).

Options: electronic application, early admission, deferred entrance.

Application fee: $20.

Required: essay or personal statement, high school transcript, minimum 2.0 GPA. ***Required for some:*** interview.

CONTACT

Mr. Bret Hyder, Assistant Director of Admissions, Crown College, 8700 College View Drive, St. Bonifacius, MN 55375-9001. *Phone:* 952-446-4142. *Toll-free phone:* 800-68-CROWN. *Fax:* 952-446-4149. *E-mail:* admissions@crown.edu.

DeVry University

Edina, Minnesota

http://www.devry.edu/

- **Proprietary** comprehensive
- **Coed**

ACADEMICS

Degrees: associate, bachelor's, and master's.

COSTS & FINANCIAL AID

Costs (2014–15) ***Tuition:*** $17,052 full-time, $609 per credit hour part-time. ***Required fees:*** $80 full-time.

Financial Aid Of all full-time matriculated undergraduates who enrolled in 2007, 31 applied for aid, 29 were judged to have need. In 2007, 2 non-need-based awards were made. ***Average percent of need met:*** 38. ***Average financial aid package:*** $10,797. ***Average need-based loan:*** $8696. ***Average need-based gift aid:*** $5538. ***Average non-need-based aid:*** $10,606.

CONTACT

Admissions Office, DeVry University, 7700 France Avenue South, Suite 575, Edina, MN 55435. *Phone:* 952-838-1860. *Toll-free phone:* 866-338-7941.

Dunwoody College of Technology

Minneapolis, Minnesota

http://www.dunwoody.edu/

- **Independent** primarily 2-year, founded 1914
- **Urban** 12-acre campus with easy access to Minneapolis-St. Paul
- **Endowment** $21.6 million
- **Coed, primarily men** 1,070 undergraduate students, 82% full-time, 14% women, 86% men
- **Minimally difficult** entrance level, 68% of applicants were admitted

UNDERGRAD STUDENTS

873 full-time, 197 part-time. 1% are from out of state; 7% Black or African American, non-Hispanic/Latino; 2% Hispanic/Latino; 4% Asian, non-Hispanic/Latino; 0.2% Native Hawaiian or other Pacific Islander, non-Hispanic/Latino; 0.6% American Indian or Alaska Native, non-Hispanic/Latino; 5% Two or more races, non-Hispanic/Latino; 3% Race/ethnicity unknown.

Freshmen

Admission: 741 applied, 501 admitted, 180 enrolled. ***Average high school GPA:*** 2.48.

Retention: 100% of full-time freshmen returned.

FACULTY

Total: 145, 54% full-time, 9% with terminal degrees.

Student/faculty ratio: 9:1.

ACADEMICS

Calendar: semesters. *Degrees:* certificates, associate, and bachelor's.

Special study options: academic remediation for entering students, cooperative education, distance learning, independent study, internships, study abroad, summer session for credit.

Computers: 300 computers/terminals and 1,000 ports are available on campus for general student use. Students can access the following: campus intranet, computer help desk, free student e-mail accounts, online (class) grades, online (class) registration, online (class) schedules. Campuswide network is available. Wireless service is available via entire campus.

STUDENT LIFE

Housing options: college housing not available.

Activities and organizations: Phi Theta Kappa, Historic Green.

Campus security: 24-hour emergency response devices, late-night transport/escort service.

Student services: personal/psychological counseling, women's center.

COSTS & FINANCIAL AID

Costs (2014–15) ***Tuition:*** $17,645 full-time. Full-time tuition and fees vary according to course level, course load, and program. Part-time tuition and fees vary according to course level, course load, and program.

Required fees: $1446 full-time. ***Payment plans:*** installment, deferred payment.

Financial Aid Of all full-time matriculated undergraduates who enrolled in 2013, 635 applied for aid, 584 were judged to have need, 14 had their need fully met. 22 Federal Work-Study jobs (averaging $3410). 44 state and other part-time jobs (averaging $2369). In 2013, 7 non-need-based awards were made. ***Average percent of need met:*** 32. ***Average financial aid package:*** $8339. ***Average need-based loan:*** $3770. ***Average need-based gift aid:*** $5698. ***Average non-need-based aid:*** $1333. ***Average indebtedness upon graduation:*** $9798.

APPLYING

Standardized Tests *Recommended:* SAT or ACT (for admission).

Options: electronic application.

Application fee: $50.

Required: essay or personal statement, high school transcript, minimum 2.5 GPA. ***Required for some:*** minimum 3.0 GPA, . ***Recommended:*** interview.

Application deadlines: rolling (freshmen), rolling (out-of-state freshmen), rolling (transfers).

Notification: continuous (freshmen), continuous (out-of-state freshmen), continuous (transfers).

CONTACT

Cynthia Olson, Director of Admissions and Student Services, Dunwoody College of Technology, 818 Dunwoody Boulevard, Minneapolis, MN 55403. *Phone:* 612-374-5800. *Toll-free phone:* 800-292-4625.

Globe University–Minneapolis

Minneapolis, Minnesota

http://www.globeuniversity.edu/

- **Proprietary** comprehensive, part of Globe Education Network (GEN) which is composed of Globe University, Minnesota School of Business, Broadview University, The Institute of Production and Recording and Minnesota School of Cosmetology
- **Urban** campus
- **Coed**

ACADEMICS

Degrees: certificates, diplomas, associate, bachelor's, master's, and doctoral.

STUDENT LIFE

Housing options: college housing not available.

Campus security: 24-hour emergency response devices.

APPLYING

Standardized Tests *Required:* ACCUPLACER is required of most applicants unless documentation of a minimum ACT composite score of 21 or documentation of a minimum composite score of 1485 on the SAT is presented (for admission).

Options: electronic application.

Application fee: $50.

Required: interview. ***Required for some:*** essay or personal statement, Certification of high school graduation or GED.

CONTACT

Globe University–Minneapolis, 80 South 8th Street, Suite 51, Minneapolis, MN 55402.

Globe University–Moorhead

Moorhead, Minnesota

http://www.globeuniversity.edu/

- **Proprietary** 4-year, part of Globe Education Network (GEN) which is composed of Globe University, Minnesota School of Business, Broadview University, The Institute of Production and Recording and Minnesota School of Cosmetology
- **Small-town** 5-acre campus
- **Coed**

ACADEMICS

Degrees: certificates, diplomas, associate, and bachelor's.

STUDENT LIFE

Housing options: college housing not available.

Campus security: 24-hour emergency response devices.

APPLYING

Standardized Tests *Required:* ACCUPLACER is required of most applicants unless documentation of a minimum ACT composite score of 21 or documentation of a minimum composite score of 1485 on the SAT is presented (for admission).

Options: electronic application.

Application fee: $50.

Required: interview, Certification of high school graduation or GED.

CONTACT

Globe University–Moorhead, 2777 34th Street South, Moorhead, MN 56560.

Globe University–Woodbury

Woodbury, Minnesota

http://www.globeuniversity.edu/

- **Proprietary** comprehensive, founded 1885, part of Globe Education Network (GEN) which is composed of Globe University, Minnesota School of Business, Broadview University, The Institute of Production and Recording and Minnesota School of Cosmetology
- **Suburban** 5-acre campus with easy access to Minneapolis-St. Paul
- **Coed**

ACADEMICS

Calendar: quarters. *Degrees:* certificates, diplomas, associate, bachelor's, and master's.

STUDENT LIFE

Campus security: 24-hour emergency response devices.

APPLYING

Standardized Tests *Required:* ACCUPLACER is required of most applicants unless documentation of a minimum ACT composite score of 21 or documentation of a minimum composite score of 1485 on the SAT is presented (for admission).

Options: electronic application.

Application fee: $50.

Required: interview. ***Required for some:*** essay or personal statement, Certification of high school graduation or GED.

CONTACT

Globe University–Woodbury, 8089 Globe Drive, Woodbury, MN 55125. *Toll-free phone:* 800-231-0660.

Gustavus Adolphus College

St. Peter, Minnesota

http://www.gustavus.edu/

- **Independent** 4-year, founded 1862, affiliated with Evangelical Lutheran Church in America
- **Small-town** 340-acre campus with easy access to Minneapolis-St. Paul
- **Coed** 2,456 undergraduate students, 99% full-time, 54% women, 46% men
- **Very difficult** entrance level, 61% of applicants were admitted

UNDERGRAD STUDENTS

2,425 full-time, 31 part-time. 19% are from out of state; 2% Black or African American, non-Hispanic/Latino; 3% Hispanic/Latino; 4% Asian, non-Hispanic/Latino; 0.1% American Indian or Alaska Native, non-Hispanic/Latino; 4% Two or more races, non-Hispanic/Latino; 2% Race/ethnicity unknown; 3% international; 1% transferred in; 85% live on campus.

Freshmen

Admission: 5,199 applied, 3,175 admitted, 599 enrolled. ***Average high school GPA:*** 3.63. ***Test scores:*** SAT critical reading scores over 500: 88%; SAT math scores over 500: 93%; ACT scores over 18: 99%; SAT critical reading scores over 600: 62%; SAT math scores over 600: 57%;

ACT scores over 24: 83%; SAT critical reading scores over 700: 13%; SAT math scores over 700: 18%; ACT scores over 30: 28%.
Retention: 90% of full-time freshmen returned.

FACULTY
Total: 255, 76% full-time, 85% with terminal degrees.
Student/faculty ratio: 11:1.

ACADEMICS
Calendar: 4-1-4. *Degree:* bachelor's.
Special study options: accelerated degree program, advanced placement credit, cooperative education, double majors, honors programs, independent study, internships, off-campus study, services for LD students, student-designed majors, study abroad, summer session for credit. ***ROTC:*** Army (c).
Unusual degree programs: 3-2 engineering with Minnesota State University, Mankato; University of Minnesota; social work; occupational therapy with Washington University in St. Louis.
Computers: Students can access the following: computer help desk, free student e-mail accounts, online (class) grades, online (class) registration, online (class) schedules. Campuswide network is available. 100% of college-owned or -operated housing units are wired for high-speed Internet access. Wireless service is available via entire campus.

STUDENT LIFE
Housing options: on-campus residence required through senior year; coed, special housing for students with disabilities. Campus housing is university owned. Freshman campus housing is guaranteed.
Activities and organizations: drama/theater group, student-run newspaper, radio and television station, choral group, Proclaim, Big Partner/Little Partner, Study Buddies, I am...We are, Pound Pals, national fraternities, national sororities.
Athletics Member NCAA. All Division III. ***Intercollegiate sports:*** baseball M, basketball M/W, cross-country running M/W, football M, golf M/W, gymnastics W, ice hockey M/W, lacrosse M(c), rugby M(c)/W(c), skiing (cross-country) M/W, soccer M/W, softball W, swimming and diving M/W, tennis M/W, track and field M/W, ultimate Frisbee M(c)/W(c), volleyball M(c)/W. ***Intramural sports:*** badminton M/W, basketball M/W, football M, golf M/W, ice hockey M/W, racquetball M/W, rugby M/W, skiing (cross-country) M/W, skiing (downhill) M/W, soccer M/W, softball M/W, swimming and diving M/W, tennis M/W, track and field M/W, ultimate Frisbee M/W, volleyball M/W, water polo M/W, weight lifting M/W.
Campus security: 24-hour emergency response devices and patrols, late-night transport/escort service, controlled dormitory access.
Student services: health clinic, personal/psychological counseling, women's center.

COSTS & FINANCIAL AID
Costs (2014–15) ***One-time required fee:*** $460. ***Comprehensive fee:*** $49,330 includes full-time tuition ($39,550), mandatory fees ($530), and room and board ($9250). Part-time tuition: $5400 per course. ***College room only:*** $5950. Room and board charges vary according to board plan and housing facility. ***Payment plans:*** tuition prepayment, installment. ***Waivers:*** employees or children of employees.
Financial Aid Of all full-time matriculated undergraduates who enrolled in 2013, 1,971 applied for aid, 1,774 were judged to have need, 420 had their need fully met. In 2013, 694 non-need-based awards were made. ***Average percent of need met:*** 89. ***Average financial aid package:*** $33,495. ***Average need-based loan:*** $4060. ***Average need-based gift aid:*** $26,393. ***Average non-need-based aid:*** $16,668. ***Average indebtedness upon graduation:*** $36,636. ***Financial aid deadline:*** 4/15.

APPLYING
Options: electronic application, early admission, early action, deferred entrance.
Required: essay or personal statement, high school transcript, 1 letter of recommendation. ***Recommended:*** interview.

CONTACT
Dr. Tom M. Crady, Vice President for Enrollment Management, Gustavus Adolphus College, 800 West College Avenue, St. Peter, MN 56082-1498. *Phone:* 507-933-7676. *Toll-free phone:* 800-GUSTAVU(S). *Fax:* 507-933-7474. *E-mail:* admission@gac.edu.

Hamline University
St. Paul, Minnesota
http://www.hamline.edu/

- **Independent** comprehensive, founded 1854, affiliated with United Methodist Church
- **Urban** 60-acre campus with easy access to Minneapolis-St. Paul
- **Coed** 2,242 undergraduate students, 96% full-time, 58% women, 42% men
- **Moderately difficult** entrance level, 70% of applicants were admitted

UNDERGRAD STUDENTS
2,162 full-time, 80 part-time. Students come from 44 states and territories; 34 other countries; 21% are from out of state; 6% Black or African American, non-Hispanic/Latino; 6% Hispanic/Latino; 6% Asian, non-Hispanic/Latino; 0.2% Native Hawaiian or other Pacific Islander, non-Hispanic/Latino; 0.4% American Indian or Alaska Native, non-Hispanic/Latino; 5% Two or more races, non-Hispanic/Latino; 3% Race/ethnicity unknown; 2% international; 6% transferred in; 42% live on campus.

Freshmen
Admission: 3,417 applied, 2,378 admitted, 521 enrolled. ***Average high school GPA:*** 3.37. ***Test scores:*** SAT critical reading scores over 500: 64%; SAT math scores over 500: 73%; SAT writing scores over 500: 70%; ACT scores over 18: 97%; SAT critical reading scores over 600: 32%; SAT math scores over 600: 22%; SAT writing scores over 600: 34%; ACT scores over 24: 56%; SAT critical reading scores over 700: 10%; SAT math scores over 700: 3%; SAT writing scores over 700: 3%; ACT scores over 30: 11%.
Retention: 83% of full-time freshmen returned.

FACULTY
Total: 426, 40% full-time, 61% with terminal degrees.
Student/faculty ratio: 13:1.

ACADEMICS
Calendar: 4-1-4. *Degrees:* certificates, bachelor's, master's, doctoral, post-master's, and postbachelor's certificates.
Special study options: academic remediation for entering students, advanced placement credit, distance learning, double majors, English as a second language, honors programs, independent study, internships, off-campus study, part-time degree program, services for LD students, student-designed majors, study abroad, summer session for credit. ***ROTC:*** Army (c), Air Force (c).
Unusual degree programs: 3-2 engineering with University of Minnesota, Washington University in St. Louis.
Computers: 300 computers/terminals are available on campus for general student use. Students can access the following: campus intranet, computer help desk, free student e-mail accounts, online (class) grades, online (class) registration, online (class) schedules. Campuswide network is available. 99% of college-owned or -operated housing units are wired for high-speed Internet access. Wireless service is available via entire campus.

STUDENT LIFE
Housing options: coed. Campus housing is university owned. Freshman campus housing is guaranteed.
Activities and organizations: drama/theater group, student-run newspaper, radio and television station, choral group, Theta Chi, Habitat for Humanity, Omicron Delta Kappa Leadership Honor Society, Mock Trial, Intervarsity Christian Fellowship, national fraternities, national sororities.
Athletics Member NCAA. All Division III. ***Intercollegiate sports:*** baseball M, basketball M/W, cheerleading W(c), cross-country running M/W, football M, golf M(c)/W(c), gymnastics W, ice hockey M/W, lacrosse M(c)/W, soccer M/W, softball W, swimming and diving M/W, tennis M/W, track and field M/W, ultimate Frisbee M(c)/W(c), volleyball W. ***Intramural sports:*** basketball M/W, racquetball M(c)/W(c), rock climbing M(c)/W(c), volleyball M/W.
Campus security: 24-hour emergency response devices and patrols, student patrols, late-night transport/escort service, controlled dormitory access, security cameras on campus and in residence halls. Security officers are trained as first responders.

Student services: health clinic, personal/psychological counseling, women's center.

COSTS & FINANCIAL AID

Costs (2014–15) ***Comprehensive fee:*** $45,662 includes full-time tuition ($35,710), mandatory fees ($560), and room and board ($9392). Part-time tuition: $1116 per credit. Part-time tuition and fees vary according to course load. ***Required fees:*** $486 per year part-time. ***College room only:*** $4794. Room and board charges vary according to board plan and housing facility. ***Payment plan:*** installment. ***Waivers:*** employees or children of employees.

Financial Aid Of all full-time matriculated undergraduates who enrolled in 2014, 1,909 applied for aid, 1,761 were judged to have need, 303 had their need fully met. 489 Federal Work-Study jobs (averaging $2398). 884 state and other part-time jobs (averaging $2731). In 2014, 308 non-need-based awards were made. ***Average percent of need met:*** 79. ***Average financial aid package:*** $28,520. ***Average need-based loan:*** $4955. ***Average need-based gift aid:*** $21,916. ***Average non-need-based aid:*** $15,238. ***Average indebtedness upon graduation:*** $36,006.

APPLYING

Standardized Tests *Required:* SAT or ACT (for admission).

Options: electronic application, early admission, early decision, early action, deferred entrance.

Required: essay or personal statement, high school transcript, 1 letter of recommendation, ACT or SAT. ***Recommended:*** interview.

Application deadlines: rolling (freshmen), rolling (out-of-state freshmen), rolling (transfers), 12/1 (early action).

Early decision deadline: 11/1.

Notification: continuous (freshmen), continuous (out-of-state freshmen), continuous (transfers), 11/15 (early decision), 12/20 (early action).

CONTACT

Admissions Office, Hamline University, 1536 Hewitt Avenue, St. Paul, MN 55104-1284. *Phone:* 651-523-2207. *Toll-free phone:* 800-753-9753. *E-mail:* admission@hamline.edu.

ITT Technical Institute

Brooklyn Center, Minnesota

http://www.itt-tech.edu/

- **Proprietary** primarily 2-year, part of ITT Educational Services, Inc.
- **Coed**

ACADEMICS

Calendar: quarters. *Degrees:* associate and bachelor's.

CONTACT

Director of Recruitment, ITT Technical Institute, 6120 Earle Brown Drive, Suite 100, Brooklyn Center, MN 55430. *Phone:* 763-549-5900. *Toll-free phone:* 800-216-8883.

ITT Technical Institute

Eden Prairie, Minnesota

http://www.itt-tech.edu/

- **Proprietary** primarily 2-year, founded 2003, part of ITT Educational Services, Inc.
- **Coed**
- **Minimally difficult** entrance level

ACADEMICS

Calendar: quarters. *Degrees:* associate and bachelor's.

CONTACT

Director of Recruitment, ITT Technical Institute, 7905 Golden Triangle Drive, Eden Prairie, MN 55344. *Phone:* 952-914-5300. *Toll-free phone:* 888-488-9646.

Macalester College

St. Paul, Minnesota

http://www.macalester.edu/

- **Independent Presbyterian** 4-year, founded 1874
- **Urban** 53-acre campus
- **Endowment** $689,096
- **Coed** 2,039 undergraduate students, 99% full-time, 61% women, 39% men
- **Very difficult** entrance level, 34% of applicants were admitted

UNDERGRAD STUDENTS

2,011 full-time, 28 part-time. Students come from 90 other countries; 82% are from out of state; 3% Black or African American, non-Hispanic/Latino; 6% Hispanic/Latino; 7% Asian, non-Hispanic/Latino; 0.1% American Indian or Alaska Native, non-Hispanic/Latino; 5% Two or more races, non-Hispanic/Latino; 12% international; 0.6% transferred in; 72% live on campus.

Freshmen

Admission: 6,683 applied, 2,283 admitted, 555 enrolled. ***Test scores:*** SAT critical reading scores over 500: 98%; SAT math scores over 500: 99%; SAT writing scores over 500: 98%; ACT scores over 18: 100%; SAT critical reading scores over 600: 82%; SAT math scores over 600: 80%; SAT writing scores over 600: 87%; ACT scores over 24: 99%; SAT critical reading scores over 700: 43%; SAT math scores over 700: 34%; SAT writing scores over 700: 41%; ACT scores over 30: 69%.

Retention: 95% of full-time freshmen returned.

FACULTY

Total: 238, 75% full-time, 85% with terminal degrees.

Student/faculty ratio: 10:1.

ACADEMICS

Calendar: semesters. *Degree:* bachelor's.

Special study options: advanced placement credit, double majors, honors programs, independent study, internships, off-campus study, part-time degree program, services for LD students, student-designed majors, study abroad, summer session for credit. ***ROTC:*** Army (c), Navy (c), Air Force (c).

Unusual degree programs: 3-2 engineering with Washington University in St. Louis, University of Minnesota; Architecture with Washington University in St. Louis.

Computers: 510 computers/terminals and 1,000 ports are available on campus for general student use. Students can access the following: campus intranet, computer help desk, free student e-mail accounts, online (class) grades, online (class) registration, online (class) schedules, online applications, public printing, specialized software, 24 hour/7 day lab. Campuswide network is available. 100% of college-owned or -operated housing units are wired for high-speed Internet access. Wireless service is available via entire campus.

STUDENT LIFE

Housing options: on-campus residence required through sophomore year; coed, men-only, women-only, cooperative. Campus housing is university owned. Freshman campus housing is guaranteed.

Activities and organizations: drama/theater group, student-run newspaper, radio station, choral group, Multicultural Organization, Outdoor Recreation Club, Macalester International Organization (M10), campus publications, Leaders in Service.

Athletics Member NCAA. All Division III. ***Intercollegiate sports:*** baseball M, basketball M/W, crew M(c)/W(c), cross-country running M/W, football M, golf M/W, ice hockey M(c)/W(c), lacrosse W(c), rugby M(c)/W(c), skiing (cross-country) M(c)/W(c), soccer M/W, softball W, swimming and diving M/W, tennis M/W, track and field M/W, ultimate Frisbee M(c)/W(c), volleyball M(c)/W, water polo M(c)/W. ***Intramural sports:*** basketball M/W, racquetball M/W, soccer M/W, softball M/W, table tennis M/W, ultimate Frisbee M/W.

Campus security: 24-hour emergency response devices and patrols, late-night transport/escort service, controlled dormitory access.

Student services: health clinic, personal/psychological counseling.

COSTS & FINANCIAL AID

Costs (2015–16) ***Tuition:*** $1521 per credit hour part-time. Full-time tuition and fees vary according to course load. Part-time tuition and fees vary according to course load. ***Room only:*** Room and board charges vary according to board plan and housing facility. ***Payment plan:*** installment. ***Waivers:*** employees or children of employees.

Financial Aid Of all full-time matriculated undergraduates who enrolled in 2014, 1,548 applied for aid, 1,413 were judged to have need, 1,413 had their need fully met. In 2014, 174 non-need-based awards were made. ***Average percent of need met:*** 100. ***Average financial aid package:*** $40,694. ***Average need-based loan:*** $4662. ***Average need-based gift aid:*** $34,527. ***Average non-need-based aid:*** $11,856. ***Average indebtedness upon graduation:*** $24,156. ***Financial aid deadline:*** 3/1.

APPLYING

Standardized Tests *Required:* SAT or ACT (for admission).

Options: electronic application, early admission, early decision, deferred entrance.

Application fee: $40.

Required: essay or personal statement, high school transcript, 2 letters of recommendation. ***Recommended:*** interview.

Application deadlines: 1/15 (freshmen), 1/15 (out-of-state freshmen), 4/15 (transfers).

Early decision deadline: 11/15 (for plan 1), 1/1 (for plan 2).

Notification: 3/30 (freshmen), 3/30 (out-of-state freshmen), 5/15 (transfers), 12/15 (early decision plan 1), 2/7 (early decision plan 2).

CONTACT

Mr. Lorne T. Robinson, Dean of Admissions and Financial Aid, Macalester College, 1600 Grand Avenue, St. Paul, MN 55105-1899. *Phone:* 651-696-6357. *Toll-free phone:* 800-231-7974. *Fax:* 651-696-6724. *E-mail:* admissions@macalester.edu.

Martin Luther College

New Ulm, Minnesota

http://www.mlc-wels.edu/

- **Independent** comprehensive, founded 1995, affiliated with Wisconsin Evangelical Lutheran Synod
- **Small-town** 50-acre campus
- **Coed** 783 undergraduate students, 90% full-time, 52% women, 48% men
- **Moderately difficult** entrance level, 97% of applicants were admitted

UNDERGRAD STUDENTS

708 full-time, 75 part-time. 80% are from out of state; 0.8% Black or African American, non-Hispanic/Latino; 0.9% Hispanic/Latino; 0.5% Asian, non-Hispanic/Latino; 0.1% American Indian or Alaska Native, non-Hispanic/Latino; 1% Two or more races, non-Hispanic/Latino; 2% international; 2% transferred in; 92% live on campus.

Freshmen

Admission: 224 applied, 218 admitted, 189 enrolled. ***Average high school GPA:*** 3.51. ***Test scores:*** ACT scores over 18: 99%; ACT scores over 24: 61%; ACT scores over 30: 13%.

Retention: 80% of full-time freshmen returned.

FACULTY

Total: 72, 67% full-time, 42% with terminal degrees.

Student/faculty ratio: 14:1.

ACADEMICS

Calendar: semesters. *Degrees:* certificates, diplomas, bachelor's, and master's.

Special study options: advanced placement credit, distance learning, double majors, summer session for credit.

Computers: Campuswide network is available.

STUDENT LIFE

Housing options: on-campus residence required through junior year; men-only, women-only. Campus housing is university owned.

Activities and organizations: drama/theater group, choral group.

Athletics Member NCAA, NAIA. All NCAA Division III. ***Intercollegiate sports:*** baseball M, basketball M/W, cross-country running M/W, football M, golf M, soccer M/W, softball W, tennis M/W, track and field M/W, volleyball W. ***Intramural sports:*** badminton M/W, basketball M/W, bowling M/W, football M, soccer M/W, softball M/W, tennis M/W, volleyball M/W.

Student services: health clinic, personal/psychological counseling.

COSTS & FINANCIAL AID

Costs (2015–16) ***Comprehensive fee:*** $18,920 includes full-time tuition ($13,565) and room and board ($5355). ***Payment plan:*** installment.

Financial Aid Of all full-time matriculated undergraduates who enrolled in 2012, 613 applied for aid, 529 were judged to have need, 80 had their need fully met. In 2012, 113 non-need-based awards were made. ***Average percent of need met:*** 73. ***Average financial aid package:*** $10,322. ***Average need-based loan:*** $4323. ***Average need-based gift aid:*** $6445. ***Average non-need-based aid:*** $2670. ***Average indebtedness upon graduation:*** $15,895. ***Financial aid deadline:*** 4/15.

APPLYING

Standardized Tests *Required:* ACT (for admission).

Options: deferred entrance.

Required: high school transcript, minimum 2.0 GPA.

CONTACT

Prof. Mark A Stein, Director of Admissions, Martin Luther College, 1995 Luther Court, New Ulm, MN 56073. *Phone:* 507-354-8221 Ext. 280. *Toll-free phone:* 877-MLC-1995. *E-mail:* brutlaro@mlc-wels.edu.

★ McNally Smith College of Music

Saint Paul, Minnesota

http://www.mcnallysmith.edu/

- **Proprietary** comprehensive, founded 1985
- **Urban** 1-acre campus with easy access to Minneapolis-St. Paul
- **Coed**
- **Moderately difficult** entrance level

FACULTY

Student/faculty ratio: 9:1.

ACADEMICS

Calendar: semesters. *Degrees:* diplomas, associate, bachelor's, and master's.

STUDENT LIFE

Housing options: coed. Campus housing is leased by the school. Freshman applicants given priority for college housing.

Activities and organizations: student-run newspaper, choral group, Student Advisory Board, Audio Engineering Society, Minnesota Songwriters Association, Jazz Club, Intramural sports.

Campus security: 24-hour emergency response devices and patrols.

Student services: personal/psychological counseling.

COSTS & FINANCIAL AID

Costs (2014–15) ***Comprehensive fee:*** $30,310 includes full-time tuition ($24,310), mandatory fees ($900), and room and board ($5100). Full-time tuition and fees vary according to course load and program. Part-time tuition: $935 per credit. Part-time tuition and fees vary according to course load and program. ***Required fees:*** $450 per term part-time. ***College room only:*** $3900. Room and board charges vary according to board plan. ***Payment plans:*** tuition prepayment, installment, deferred payment.

Financial Aid Of all full-time matriculated undergraduates who enrolled in 2013, 331 applied for aid, 318 were judged to have need. 31 Federal Work-Study jobs (averaging $1954). 21 state and other part-time jobs (averaging $1521). In 2013, 8 non-need-based awards were made. ***Average percent of need met:*** 33. ***Average financial aid package:*** $10,708. ***Average need-based loan:*** $4527. ***Average need-based gift aid:*** $6703. ***Average non-need-based aid:*** $8927. ***Average indebtedness upon graduation:*** $46,230. ***Financial aid deadline:*** 8/1.

APPLYING

Standardized Tests *Recommended:* ACT (for admission), SAT or ACT (for admission).

Options: electronic application.

Application fee: $75.

Required: essay or personal statement, high school transcript, minimum 2.0 GPA. ***Required for some:*** audition or demo recording. ***Recommended:*** minimum 2.5 GPA, interview.

CONTACT
Mrs. Katie Marshall, Admissions Representative, McNally Smith College of Music, 19 Exchange Street East, St. Paul, MN 55101. *Phone:* 651-361-3451. *Toll-free phone:* 800-594-9500. *Fax:* 651-291-0366. *E-mail:* katie.marshall@mcnallysmith.edu.

Metropolitan State University

St. Paul, Minnesota

http://www.metrostate.edu/

- **State-supported** comprehensive, founded 1971, part of Minnesota State Colleges and Universities System
- **Urban** campus with easy access to Minneapolis-St. Paul
- **Coed** 7,593 undergraduate students, 36% full-time, 56% women, 44% men
- **Minimally difficult** entrance level, 100% of applicants were admitted

UNDERGRAD STUDENTS
2,714 full-time, 4,879 part-time. 19% Black or African American, non-Hispanic/Latino; 5% Hispanic/Latino; 12% Asian, non-Hispanic/Latino; 0.1% Native Hawaiian or other Pacific Islander, non-Hispanic/Latino; 0.7% American Indian or Alaska Native, non-Hispanic/Latino; 4% Two or more races, non-Hispanic/Latino; 1% Race/ethnicity unknown; 2% international; 91% transferred in.

Freshmen
Admission: 376 applied, 376 admitted, 95 enrolled.
Retention: 60% of full-time freshmen returned.

ACADEMICS
Calendar: semesters. *Degrees:* certificates, bachelor's, master's, doctoral, and postbachelor's certificates (offers primarily part-time evening degree programs).

Special study options: adult/continuing education programs, advanced placement credit, distance learning, double majors, English as a second language, external degree program, independent study, internships, off-campus study, part-time degree program, student-designed majors, study abroad, summer session for credit.

Computers: Students can access the following: computer help desk, free student e-mail accounts, online (class) grades, online (class) registration, online (class) schedules. Campuswide network is available. Wireless service is available via entire campus.

STUDENT LIFE
Housing options: college housing not available.
Activities and organizations: drama/theater group, student-run newspaper.
Campus security: 24-hour emergency response devices, late-night transport/escort service.
Student services: personal/psychological counseling.

COSTS
Costs (2014–15) ***Tuition:*** state resident $6329 full-time, $211 per credit hour part-time; nonresident $12,914 full-time, $430 per credit hour part-time. Full-time tuition and fees vary according to degree level, program, and reciprocity agreements. Part-time tuition and fees vary according to degree level, program, and reciprocity agreements. ***Required fees:*** $313 full-time, $10 per credit hour part-time. ***Waivers:*** senior citizens and employees or children of employees.

APPLYING
Standardized Tests *Recommended:* SAT or ACT (for admission).
Options: electronic application, deferred entrance.
Application fee: $20.
Required: high school transcript, minimum 2.0 GPA.
Application deadlines: 6/15 (freshmen), 6/15 (transfers).

CONTACT
Mr. Daryl Johnson, Director, Metropolitan State University, 700 East 7th Street, St. Paul, MN 55106. *Phone:* 651-793-1227. *Fax:* 651-793-1546. *E-mail:* daryl.johnson@metrostate.edu.

Minneapolis College of Art and Design

Minneapolis, Minnesota

http://www.mcad.edu/

- **Independent** comprehensive, founded 1886
- **Urban** 7-acre campus
- **Coed**
- **Moderately difficult** entrance level

FACULTY
Student/faculty ratio: 10:1.

ACADEMICS
Calendar: semesters. *Degrees:* bachelor's, master's, and postbachelor's certificates.

STUDENT LIFE
Housing options: coed. Campus housing is university owned, leased by the school and is provided by a third party. Freshman applicants given priority for college housing.
Activities and organizations: student-run radio station.
Campus security: 24-hour emergency response devices and patrols, late-night transport/escort service, controlled dormitory access.
Student services: personal/psychological counseling.

COSTS & FINANCIAL AID
Costs (2014–15) ***Comprehensive fee:*** $41,176 includes full-time tuition ($33,696), mandatory fees ($450), and room and board ($7030). Part-time tuition: $1404 per credit hour. Part-time tuition and fees vary according to course load. ***Required fees:*** $225 per hour part-time. ***College room only:*** $4960. Room and board charges vary according to housing facility.

Financial Aid Of all full-time matriculated undergraduates who enrolled in 2012, 565 applied for aid, 523 were judged to have need, 52 had their need fully met. In 2012, 73 non-need-based awards were made. ***Average percent of need met:*** 65. ***Average financial aid package:*** $19,544. ***Average need-based loan:*** $4533. ***Average need-based gift aid:*** $14,824. ***Average non-need-based aid:*** $9162. ***Average indebtedness upon graduation:*** $43,650. ***Financial aid deadline:*** 4/1.

APPLYING
Standardized Tests *Required for some:* SAT or ACT (for admission).
Options: electronic application, early action.
Application fee: $50.
Required: essay or personal statement, high school transcript, 1 letter of recommendation. ***Required for some:*** portfolio of visual artwork. ***Recommended:*** minimum 2.8 GPA, interview.

CONTACT
Minneapolis College of Art and Design, 2501 Stevens Avenue, Minneapolis, MN 55404-4347. *Phone:* 612-874-3764. *Toll-free phone:* 800-874-6223.

Minnesota School of Business–Blaine

Blaine, Minnesota

http://www.msbcollege.edu/

- **Proprietary** 4-year, part of Globe Education Network (GEN) which is composed of Globe University, Minnesota School of Business, Broadview University, The Institute of Production and Recording and Minnesota School of Cosmetology
- **Suburban** 7-acre campus with easy access to Minneapolis-St. Paul
- **Coed**

ACADEMICS
Degrees: certificates, diplomas, associate, and bachelor's.

STUDENT LIFE
Housing options: college housing not available.
Campus security: 24-hour emergency response devices.

APPLYING
Options: electronic application.
Application fee: $50.

Required: interview. ***Required for some:*** Certification of high school graduation or GED.

CONTACT
Minnesota School of Business–Blaine, 3680 Pheasant Ridge Drive NE, Blaine, MN 55449.

Minnesota School of Business–Brooklyn Center

Brooklyn Center, Minnesota

http://www.msbcollege.edu/

- **Proprietary** primarily 2-year, founded 1989, part of Globe Education Network (GEN) which is composed of Globe University, Minnesota School of Business, Broadview University, The Institute of Production and Recording and Minnesota School of Cosmetology
- **Suburban** 4-acre campus with easy access to Minneapolis-St. Paul
- **Coed**

ACADEMICS
Calendar: quarters. *Degrees:* certificates, diplomas, associate, and bachelor's.

STUDENT LIFE
Housing options: college housing not available.

Campus security: 24-hour emergency response devices.

APPLYING
Standardized Tests *Required:* ACCUPLACER is required of most applicants unless documentation of a minimum ACT composite score of 21 or documentation of a minimum composite score of 1485 on the SAT is presented (for admission).

Options: electronic application.

Application fee: $50.

Required: interview, Certification of high school graduation or GED.

CONTACT
Minnesota School of Business–Brooklyn Center, 5910 Shingle Creek Parkway, Brooklyn Center, MN 55430.

Minnesota School of Business–Elk River

Elk River, Minnesota

http://www.msbcollege.edu/

- **Proprietary** 4-year, part of Globe Education Network (GEN) which is composed of Globe University, Minnesota School of Business, Broadview University, The Institute of Production and Recording and Minnesota School of Cosmetology
- **Suburban** 4-acre campus with easy access to Minneapolis-St. Paul
- **Coed**

ACADEMICS
Degrees: certificates, diplomas, associate, and bachelor's.

STUDENT LIFE
Housing options: college housing not available.

Campus security: 24-hour emergency response devices.

APPLYING
Standardized Tests *Required:* ACCUPLACER is required of most applicants unless documentation of a minimum ACT composite score of 21 or documentation of a minimum composite score of 1485 on the SAT is presented (for admission).

Options: electronic application.

Application fee: $50.

Required: interview, Certification of high school graduation or GED.

CONTACT
Minnesota School of Business–Elk River, 11500 193rd Avenue NW, Elk River, MN 55330.

Minnesota School of Business–Lakeville

Lakeville, Minnesota

http://www.msbcollege.edu/

- **Proprietary** 4-year, part of Globe Education Network (GEN) which is composed of Globe University, Minnesota School of Business, Broadview University, The Institute of Production and Recording and Minnesota School of Cosmetology
- **Small-town** 3-acre campus with easy access to Minneapolis-St. Paul
- **Coed**

ACADEMICS
Degrees: certificates, diplomas, associate, and bachelor's.

STUDENT LIFE
Housing options: college housing not available.

Campus security: 24-hour emergency response devices.

APPLYING
Standardized Tests *Required:* ACCUPLACER is required of most applicants unless documentation of a minimum ACT composite score of 21 or documentation of a minimum composite score of 1485 on the SAT is presented (for admission).

Options: electronic application.

Application fee: $50.

Required: high school transcript. ***Required for some:*** Certification of high school graduation or GED.

CONTACT
Minnesota School of Business–Lakeville, 17685 Juniper Path, Lakeville, MN 55044.

Minnesota School of Business–Plymouth

Plymouth, Minnesota

http://www.msbcollege.edu/

- **Proprietary** primarily 2-year, founded 2002, part of Globe Education Network (GEN) which is composed of Globe University, Minnesota School of Business, Broadview University, The Institute of Production and Recording and Minnesota School of Cosmetology
- **Suburban** 7-acre campus with easy access to Minneapolis-St. Paul
- **Coed**

ACADEMICS
Calendar: quarters. *Degrees:* certificates, diplomas, associate, and bachelor's.

STUDENT LIFE
Housing options: college housing not available.

Campus security: 24-hour emergency response devices.

APPLYING
Standardized Tests *Required:* ACCUPLACER is required of most applicants unless documentation of a minimum ACT composite score of 21 or documentation of a minimum composite score of 1485 on the SAT is presented (for admission).

Options: electronic application.

Application fee: $50.

Required: interview, Certification of high school graduation or GED.

CONTACT
Minnesota School of Business–Plymouth, 1455 Country Road 101 North, Plymouth, MN 55447.

Minnesota School of Business–Richfield

Richfield, Minnesota

http://www.msbcollege.edu/

- **Proprietary** 4-year, founded 1877, part of Globe Education Network (GEN) which is composed of Globe University, Minnesota School of

Business, Broadview University, The Institute of Production and Recording and Minnesota School of Cosmetology
- **Urban** 3-acre campus with easy access to Minneapolis-St. Paul
- **Coed**

ACADEMICS
Calendar: quarters. *Degrees:* certificates, diplomas, associate, and bachelor's.

STUDENT LIFE
Housing options: college housing not available.

Campus security: 24-hour emergency response devices.

APPLYING
Standardized Tests *Required:* ACCUPLACER is required of most applicants unless documentation of a minimum ACT composite score of 21 or documentation of a minimum composite score of 1485 on the SAT is presented (for admission).

Options: electronic application.

Application fee: $50.

Required: interview, Certification of high school graduation or GED. ***Required for some:*** essay or personal statement, 2 letters of recommendation.

CONTACT
Minnesota School of Business–Richfield, 1401 West 76th Street, Suite 500, Richfield, MN 55423. *Toll-free phone:* 800-752-4223.

Minnesota School of Business–Rochester

Rochester, Minnesota

http://www.msbcollege.edu/

- **Proprietary** 4-year, part of Globe Education Network (GEN) which is composed of Globe University, Minnesota School of Business, Broadview University, The Institute of Production and Recording and Minnesota School of Cosmetology
- **Small-town** 5-acre campus
- **Coed**

ACADEMICS
Calendar: quarters. *Degrees:* certificates, diplomas, associate, and bachelor's.

STUDENT LIFE
Housing options: college housing not available.

Campus security: 24-hour emergency response devices.

APPLYING
Standardized Tests *Required:* ACCUPLACER is required of most applicants unless documentation of a minimum ACT composite score of 21 or documentation of a minimum composite score of 1485 on the SAT is presented (for admission).

Options: electronic application.

Application fee: $50.

Required: interview, Certification of high school graduation or GED.

CONTACT
Minnesota School of Business–Rochester, 2521 Pennington Drive, NW, Rochester, MN 55901. *Toll-free phone:* 888-662-8772.

Minnesota School of Business–St. Cloud

Waite Park, Minnesota

http://www.msbcollege.edu/

- **Proprietary** 4-year, founded 2004, part of Globe Education Network (GEN) which is composed of Globe University, Minnesota School of Business, Broadview University, The Institute of Production and Recording and Minnesota School of Cosmetology
- **Small-town** 2-acre campus
- **Coed**

ACADEMICS
Calendar: quarters. *Degrees:* certificates, diplomas, associate, and bachelor's.

STUDENT LIFE
Housing options: college housing not available.

Campus security: 24-hour emergency response devices.

APPLYING
Standardized Tests *Required:* ACCUPLACER is required of most applicants unless documentation of a minimum ACT composite score of 21 or documentation of a minimum composite score of 1485 on the SAT is presented (for admission).

Options: electronic application.

Application fee: $50.

Required: interview, Certification of high school graduation or GED.

CONTACT
Minnesota School of Business–St. Cloud, 1201 2nd Street South, Waite Park, MN 56387. *Toll-free phone:* 866-403-3333.

Minnesota State University Mankato

Mankato, Minnesota

http://www.mnsu.edu/

- **State-supported** university, founded 1868, part of Minnesota State Colleges and Universities System
- **Small-town** 303-acre campus with easy access to Minneapolis-St. Paul
- **Coed** 13,459 undergraduate students, 85% full-time, 52% women, 48% men
- **Moderately difficult** entrance level, 66% of applicants were admitted

UNDERGRAD STUDENTS
11,412 full-time, 2,047 part-time. Students come from 90 other countries; 12% are from out of state; 5% Black or African American, non-Hispanic/Latino; 3% Hispanic/Latino; 3% Asian, non-Hispanic/Latino; 0.2% American Indian or Alaska Native, non-Hispanic/Latino; 2% Two or more races, non-Hispanic/Latino; 3% Race/ethnicity unknown; 5% international; 8% transferred in; 25% live on campus.

Freshmen
Admission: 9,938 applied, 6,514 admitted, 2,456 enrolled. ***Average high school GPA:*** 3.17. ***Test scores:*** ACT scores over 18: 91%; ACT scores over 24: 30%; ACT scores over 30: 2%.

Retention: 74% of full-time freshmen returned.

FACULTY
Total: 754, 58% full-time.

Student/faculty ratio: 20:1.

ACADEMICS
Calendar: semesters. *Degrees:* certificates, associate, bachelor's, master's, doctoral, and post-master's certificates.

Special study options: academic remediation for entering students, accelerated degree program, adult/continuing education programs, advanced placement credit, cooperative education, distance learning, double majors, English as a second language, external degree program, honors programs, independent study, internships, off-campus study, part-time degree program, services for LD students, student-designed majors, study abroad, summer session for credit. ***ROTC:*** Army (b).

Computers: 900 computers/terminals are available on campus for general student use. Students can access the following: campus intranet, computer help desk, free student e-mail accounts, online (class) grades, online (class) registration, online (class) schedules. Campuswide network is available. Wireless service is available via entire campus.

STUDENT LIFE
Housing options: coed. Campus housing is university owned and leased by the school. Freshman applicants given priority for college housing.

Activities and organizations: drama/theater group, student-run newspaper, radio station, choral group, marching band, national fraternities, national sororities.

Athletics Member NCAA. All Division II except men's and women's ice hockey (Division I). ***Intercollegiate sports:*** baseball M(s), basketball M(s)/W(s), bowling W, cheerleading M/W, cross-country running

M(s)/W(s), football M(s), golf M(s)/W(s), ice hockey M(s)/W(s), soccer W(s), softball W(s), swimming and diving W(s), tennis M(s)/W(s), track and field M(s)/W(s), volleyball W(s), wrestling M(s). ***Intramural sports:*** archery M/W, basketball M/W, bowling M/W, fencing M/W, football M/W, golf M/W, ice hockey M/W, lacrosse M/W, racquetball M/W, rock climbing M/W, rugby M(c)/W(c), sailing M/W, skiing (downhill) M/W, soccer M/W, softball M/W, swimming and diving W, table tennis M/W, tennis M/W, track and field M/W, volleyball M/W, wrestling M.

Campus security: 24-hour emergency response devices and patrols, student patrols, late-night transport/escort service, controlled dormitory access, Night Owl security program in residence halls, closed circuit cameras in parking lots.

Student services: health clinic, personal/psychological counseling, women's center, legal services.

COSTS & FINANCIAL AID

Costs (2014–15) ***Tuition:*** state resident $7574 full-time, $262 per credit hour part-time; nonresident $15,052 full-time, $564 per credit hour part-time. Full-time tuition and fees vary according to course load, location, program, and reciprocity agreements. Part-time tuition and fees vary according to course load, location, program, and reciprocity agreements. ***Required fees:*** $907 full-time, $38 per credit hour part-time. ***Room and board:*** $8042. Room and board charges vary according to board plan and housing facility. ***Payment plan:*** installment. ***Waivers:*** senior citizens and employees or children of employees.

Financial Aid Of all full-time matriculated undergraduates who enrolled in 2013, 9,027 applied for aid, 6,670 were judged to have need, 1,396 had their need fully met. 294 Federal Work-Study jobs (averaging $3840). 494 state and other part-time jobs (averaging $3840). In 2013, 383 non-need-based awards were made. ***Average percent of need met:*** 72. ***Average financial aid package:*** $9117. ***Average need-based loan:*** $4381. ***Average need-based gift aid:*** $5265. ***Average non-need-based aid:*** $3262. ***Average indebtedness upon graduation:*** $29,245.

APPLYING

Standardized Tests *Required:* SAT or ACT (for admission). *Required for some:* SAT or ACT (for admission).

Options: electronic application, early admission, deferred entrance.

Application fee: $20.

Required: high school transcript. ***Required for some:*** essay or personal statement, 1 letter of recommendation.

Application deadlines: rolling (freshmen), rolling (transfers).

Notification: continuous (freshmen), continuous (transfers).

CONTACT

Office of Admissions, Minnesota State University Mankato, 122 Taylor Center, Mankato, MN 56001. *Phone:* 507-389-1822. *Toll-free phone:* 800-722-0544. *Fax:* 507-389-1511. *E-mail:* admissions@mnsu.edu.

Minnesota State University Moorhead

Moorhead, Minnesota

http://www.mnstate.edu/

- **State-supported** comprehensive, founded 1885, part of Minnesota State Colleges and Universities System
- **Urban** 119-acre campus
- **Coed** 5,738 undergraduate students, 82% full-time, 61% women, 39% men
- **Moderately difficult** entrance level, 84% of applicants were admitted

UNDERGRAD STUDENTS

4,731 full-time, 1,007 part-time. 34% are from out of state; 3% Black or African American, non-Hispanic/Latino; 3% Hispanic/Latino; 1% Asian, non-Hispanic/Latino; 0.8% American Indian or Alaska Native, non-Hispanic/Latino; 2% Two or more races, non-Hispanic/Latino; 5% Race/ethnicity unknown; 7% international; 9% transferred in; 25% live on campus.

Freshmen

Admission: 2,992 applied, 2,519 admitted, 894 enrolled.

Retention: 71% of full-time freshmen returned.

ACADEMICS

Calendar: semesters. *Degrees:* certificates, associate, bachelor's, master's, post-master's, and postbachelor's certificates.

Special study options: academic remediation for entering students, adult/continuing education programs, advanced placement credit, distance learning, double majors, English as a second language, honors programs, independent study, internships, off-campus study, part-time degree program, services for LD students, student-designed majors, study abroad, summer session for credit. ***ROTC:*** Army (c), Air Force (c).

Computers: 2,200 computers/terminals are available on campus for general student use. Students can access the following: computer help desk, free student e-mail accounts, online (class) grades, online (class) registration, online (class) schedules. Campuswide network is available. 100% of college-owned or -operated housing units are wired for high-speed Internet access. Wireless service is available via entire campus.

STUDENT LIFE

Housing options: coed, men-only, women-only, special housing for students with disabilities. Campus housing is university owned.

Activities and organizations: drama/theater group, student-run newspaper, radio and television station, choral group, Chi Alpha, International Students Organization, Student Orientation Counselor & Friends, Education Minnesota Student Program, Student Senate, national fraternities, national sororities.

Athletics Member NCAA. All Division II. ***Intercollegiate sports:*** basketball M(s)/W(s), cheerleading M/W, cross-country running M(s)/W(s), football M(s), golf W(s), soccer W(s), softball W(s), swimming and diving W(s), tennis W(s), track and field M(s)/W(s), volleyball W(s), wrestling M(s). ***Intramural sports:*** badminton M/W, basketball M/W, football M/W, golf W, ice hockey M/W, soccer M(c)/W(c), softball M/W, tennis M/W, ultimate Frisbee M/W, volleyball M/W.

Campus security: 24-hour emergency response devices and patrols, student patrols, late-night transport/escort service, controlled dormitory access.

Student services: health clinic, personal/psychological counseling, women's center.

COSTS & FINANCIAL AID

Costs (2014–15) ***Tuition:*** state resident $6898 full-time, $222 per credit hour part-time; nonresident $13,796 full-time, $445 per credit hour part-time. Full-time tuition and fees vary according to course load, program, and reciprocity agreements. Part-time tuition and fees vary according to course load, program, and reciprocity agreements. ***Required fees:*** $931 full-time, $465 per term part-time. ***Room and board:*** $7398. Room and board charges vary according to board plan and housing facility. ***Payment plan:*** installment. ***Waivers:*** senior citizens and employees or children of employees.

Financial Aid Of all full-time matriculated undergraduates who enrolled in 2013, 4,443 applied for aid, 3,147 were judged to have need. 258 Federal Work-Study jobs (averaging $2447). 254 state and other part-time jobs (averaging $2348). ***Average need-based loan:*** $4206. ***Average need-based gift aid:*** $4416. ***Average indebtedness upon graduation:*** $29,786.

APPLYING

Standardized Tests *Required:* SAT or ACT (for admission).

Options: electronic application, early admission, deferred entrance.

Application fee: $20.

Required: high school transcript.

Application deadlines: 8/1 (freshmen), 8/1 (out-of-state freshmen), 8/1 (transfers).

CONTACT

Admissions Office, Minnesota State University Moorhead, Owens Hall, Moorhead, MN 56563-0002. *Phone:* 218-477-2161. *Toll-free phone:* 800-593-7246. *Fax:* 218-477-4374. *E-mail:* admissionsoffice@mnstate.edu.

★ North Central University

Minneapolis, Minnesota

http://www.northcentral.edu/

CONTACT

Ms. Sigi Shawa, Assistant Director, North Central University, 910 Elliot Avenue, Minneapolis, MN 55404-1322. *Phone:* 612-343-4460. *Toll-free phone:* 800-289-6222. *Fax:* 612-343-4146. *E-mail:* admissions@northcentral.edu.

Rasmussen College Blaine

Blaine, Minnesota

http://www.rasmussen.edu/

- **Proprietary** 4-year, part of Rasmussen College System
- **Suburban** campus with easy access to Minneapolis-St. Paul
- **Coed** 492 undergraduate students, 59% full-time, 68% women, 32% men
- **Minimally difficult** entrance level

UNDERGRAD STUDENTS
289 full-time, 203 part-time.

Freshmen
Admission: 26 enrolled.

FACULTY
Total: 21, 29% full-time.

Student/faculty ratio: 22:1.

ACADEMICS
Degrees: certificates, diplomas, associate, and bachelor's.

Special study options: academic remediation for entering students, accelerated degree program, adult/continuing education programs, distance learning, double majors, internships, part-time degree program, summer session for credit.

Computers: 81 computers/terminals are available on campus for general student use. Students can access the following: computer help desk, free student e-mail accounts, online (class) grades, online (class) schedules. Campuswide network is available. Wireless service is available via entire campus.

STUDENT LIFE
Housing options: college housing not available.

COSTS
Costs (2014–15) ***Tuition:*** $10,764 full-time, $350 per credit hour part-time. Full-time tuition and fees vary according to course level, course load, degree level, location, and program. Part-time tuition and fees vary according to course level, course load, degree level, location, and program. No tuition increase for student's term of enrollment. ***Required fees:*** $1350 full-time. ***Payment plans:*** installment, deferred payment. ***Waivers:*** employees or children of employees.

APPLYING
Standardized Tests *Required:* Internal Exam (for admission).

Options: electronic application, early admission, deferred entrance.

Required: high school transcript, minimum 2.0 GPA. ***Required for some:*** interview.

Application deadlines: rolling (freshmen), rolling (transfers).

CONTACT
Susan Hammerstrom, Director of Admissions, Rasmussen College Blaine, 3629 95th Avenue NE, Blaine, MN 55014. *Phone:* 763-795-4720. *Toll-free phone:* 888-549-6755. *E-mail:* susan.hammerstrom@rasmussen.edu.

Rasmussen College Bloomington

Bloomington, Minnesota

http://www.rasmussen.edu/

- **Proprietary** 4-year, founded 1904, part of Rasmussen College System
- **Suburban** campus with easy access to Minneapolis-St. Paul
- **Coed** 612 undergraduate students, 56% full-time, 73% women, 27% men
- **Minimally difficult** entrance level

UNDERGRAD STUDENTS
345 full-time, 267 part-time.

Freshmen
Admission: 31 enrolled.

FACULTY
Total: 26, 50% full-time.

Student/faculty ratio: 22:1.

ACADEMICS
Calendar: quarters. *Degrees:* certificates, diplomas, associate, bachelor's, and postbachelor's certificates.

Special study options: academic remediation for entering students, accelerated degree program, adult/continuing education programs, distance learning, double majors, internships, part-time degree program, summer session for credit.

Computers: 68 computers/terminals are available on campus for general student use. Students can access the following: computer help desk, free student e-mail accounts, online (class) grades, online (class) schedules. Campuswide network is available. Wireless service is available via entire campus.

STUDENT LIFE
Housing options: college housing not available.

COSTS & FINANCIAL AID
Costs (2014–15) ***Tuition:*** $10,764 full-time, $350 per credit hour part-time. Full-time tuition and fees vary according to course level, course load, degree level, location, and program. Part-time tuition and fees vary according to course level, course load, degree level, location, and program. No tuition increase for student's term of enrollment. ***Required fees:*** $1350 full-time. ***Payment plans:*** installment, deferred payment. ***Waivers:*** employees or children of employees.

Financial Aid Of all full-time matriculated undergraduates who enrolled in 2013, 3 state and other part-time jobs (averaging $4338).

APPLYING
Standardized Tests *Required:* Internal Exam (for admission).

Options: electronic application, early admission, deferred entrance.

Required: high school transcript, minimum 2.0 GPA. ***Required for some:*** interview.

Application deadlines: rolling (freshmen), rolling (transfers).

CONTACT
Susan Hammerstrom, Director of Admissions, Rasmussen College Bloomington, 4400 West 78th Street, Bloomington, MN 55435. *Phone:* 952-545-2000. *Toll-free phone:* 888-549-6755.

Rasmussen College Brooklyn Park

Brooklyn Park, Minnesota

http://www.rasmussen.edu/

- **Proprietary** 4-year, part of Rasmussen College System
- **Suburban** campus with easy access to Minneapolis-St. Paul
- **Coed** 824 undergraduate students, 58% full-time, 71% women, 29% men
- **Minimally difficult** entrance level

UNDERGRAD STUDENTS
477 full-time, 347 part-time.

Freshmen
Admission: 32 enrolled.

FACULTY
Total: 28, 46% full-time.

Student/faculty ratio: 22:1.

ACADEMICS
Degrees: certificates, diplomas, associate, and bachelor's.

Special study options: academic remediation for entering students, accelerated degree program, adult/continuing education programs, distance learning, double majors, internships, part-time degree program, summer session for credit.

Computers: 80 computers/terminals are available on campus for general student use. Students can access the following: computer help desk, free student e-mail accounts, online (class) grades, online (class) schedules. Campuswide network is available. Wireless service is available via entire campus.

STUDENT LIFE
Housing options: college housing not available.

COSTS
Costs (2014–15) ***Tuition:*** $10,764 full-time, $310 per credit hour part-time. Full-time tuition and fees vary according to course level, course load, degree level, location, and program. Part-time tuition and fees vary according to course level, course load, degree level, location, and program. No tuition increase for student's term of enrollment. ***Required***

fees: $1350 full-time. ***Payment plans:*** installment, deferred payment. ***Waivers:*** employees or children of employees.

APPLYING
Standardized Tests *Required:* Internal Exam (for admission).

Options: electronic application, early admission, deferred entrance.

Required: high school transcript, minimum 2.0 GPA. ***Required for some:*** interview.

Application deadlines: rolling (freshmen), rolling (transfers).

CONTACT
Susan Hammerstrom, Director of Admissions, Rasmussen College Brooklyn Park, 8301 93rd Avenue North, Brooklyn Park, MN 55445-1512. *Phone:* 763-493-4500. *Toll-free phone:* 888-549-6755. *E-mail:* susan.hammerstrom@rasmussen.edu.

Rasmussen College Eagan

Eagan, Minnesota

http://www.rasmussen.edu/

- **Proprietary** 4-year, founded 1904, part of Rasmussen College System
- **Suburban** campus with easy access to Minneapolis-St. Paul
- **Coed** 704 undergraduate students, 54% full-time, 69% women, 31% men
- **Minimally difficult** entrance level

UNDERGRAD STUDENTS
378 full-time, 326 part-time.

Freshmen
Admission: 24 enrolled.

FACULTY
Total: 26, 42% full-time.
Student/faculty ratio: 22:1.

ACADEMICS
Calendar: quarters. *Degrees:* certificates, diplomas, associate, bachelor's, and postbachelor's certificates.

Special study options: academic remediation for entering students, accelerated degree program, adult/continuing education programs, distance learning, double majors, internships, part-time degree program, summer session for credit.

Computers: 93 computers/terminals are available on campus for general student use. Students can access the following: computer help desk, free student e-mail accounts, online (class) grades, online (class) schedules. Campuswide network is available. Wireless service is available via entire campus.

STUDENT LIFE
Housing options: college housing not available.

COSTS
Costs (2014–15) ***Tuition:*** $10,764 full-time, $310 per credit hour part-time. Full-time tuition and fees vary according to course level, course load, degree level, location, and program. Part-time tuition and fees vary according to course level, course load, degree level, location, and program. No tuition increase for student's term of enrollment. ***Required fees:*** $1350 full-time. ***Payment plans:*** installment, deferred payment. ***Waivers:*** employees or children of employees.

APPLYING
Standardized Tests *Required:* Internal Exam (for admission).

Options: electronic application, early admission, deferred entrance.

Required: high school transcript, minimum 2.0 GPA. ***Required for some:*** interview.

Application deadlines: rolling (freshmen), rolling (transfers).

CONTACT
Susan Hammerstrom, Director of Admissions, Rasmussen College Eagan, 3500 Federal Drive, Eagan, MN 55122-1346. *Phone:* 651-687-9000. *Toll-free phone:* 888-549-6755. *E-mail:* susan.hammerstrom@rasmussen.edu.

Rasmussen College Lake Elmo/Woodbury

Lake Elmo, Minnesota

http://www.rasmussen.edu/

- **Proprietary** 4-year, part of Rasmussen College System
- **Suburban** campus with easy access to Minneapolis-St. Paul
- **Coed** 1,360 undergraduate students, 29% full-time, 87% women, 13% men
- **Minimally difficult** entrance level

UNDERGRAD STUDENTS
401 full-time, 959 part-time.

Freshmen
Admission: 33 enrolled.

FACULTY
Total: 23, 22% full-time.
Student/faculty ratio: 22:1.

ACADEMICS
Degrees: certificates, diplomas, associate, and bachelor's.

Special study options: academic remediation for entering students, accelerated degree program, adult/continuing education programs, distance learning, double majors, internships, part-time degree program, summer session for credit.

Computers: 85 computers/terminals are available on campus for general student use. Students can access the following: computer help desk, free student e-mail accounts, online (class) grades, online (class) schedules. Campuswide network is available. Wireless service is available via entire campus.

STUDENT LIFE
Housing options: college housing not available.

COSTS
Costs (2014–15) ***Tuition:*** $10,764 full-time, $310 per credit hour part-time. Full-time tuition and fees vary according to course level, course load, degree level, location, and program. Part-time tuition and fees vary according to course level, course load, degree level, location, and program. No tuition increase for student's term of enrollment. ***Required fees:*** $1350 full-time. ***Payment plans:*** installment, deferred payment. ***Waivers:*** employees or children of employees.

APPLYING
Standardized Tests *Required:* Internal Exam (for admission).

Options: electronic application, early admission, deferred entrance.

Required: high school transcript, minimum 2.0 GPA. ***Required for some:*** interview.

Application deadlines: rolling (freshmen), rolling (transfers).

CONTACT
Susan Hammerstrom, Director of Admissions, Rasmussen College Lake Elmo/Woodbury, 8565 Eagle Point Circle, Lake Elmo, MN 55042. *Phone:* 651-259-6600. *Toll-free phone:* 888-549-6755. *E-mail:* susan.hammerstrom@rasmussen.edu.

Rasmussen College Mankato

Mankato, Minnesota

http://www.rasmussen.edu/

- **Proprietary** 4-year, founded 1904, part of Rasmussen College System
- **Suburban** campus with easy access to Minneapolis-St. Paul
- **Coed** 667 undergraduate students, 57% full-time, 78% women, 22% men
- **Minimally difficult** entrance level

UNDERGRAD STUDENTS
378 full-time, 289 part-time.

Freshmen
Admission: 21 enrolled.

FACULTY
Total: 34, 50% full-time.
Student/faculty ratio: 22:1.

ACADEMICS
Calendar: quarters. *Degrees:* certificates, diplomas, associate, bachelor's, and postbachelor's certificates.

Special study options: academic remediation for entering students, accelerated degree program, adult/continuing education programs, distance learning, double majors, internships, part-time degree program, summer session for credit.

Computers: 116 computers/terminals are available on campus for general student use. Students can access the following: computer help desk, free student e-mail accounts, online (class) grades, online (class) schedules. Campuswide network is available. Wireless service is available via entire campus.

STUDENT LIFE
Housing options: college housing not available.

COSTS & FINANCIAL AID
Costs (2014–15) ***Tuition:*** $10,764 full-time, $310 per credit hour part-time. Full-time tuition and fees vary according to course level, course load, degree level, location, and program. Part-time tuition and fees vary according to course level, course load, degree level, location, and program. No tuition increase for student's term of enrollment. ***Required fees:*** $1350 full-time. ***Payment plans:*** installment, deferred payment. ***Waivers:*** employees or children of employees.

Financial Aid Of all full-time matriculated undergraduates who enrolled in 2013, 15 Federal Work-Study jobs (averaging $4000). 13 state and other part-time jobs (averaging $4000).

APPLYING
Standardized Tests *Required:* Internal Exam (for admission).

Options: electronic application, early admission, deferred entrance.

Required: high school transcript, minimum 2.0 GPA. ***Required for some:*** interview.

Application deadlines: rolling (freshmen), rolling (transfers).

CONTACT
Susan Hammerstrom, Director of Admissions, Rasmussen College Mankato, 130 Saint Andrews Drive, Mankato, MN 56001. *Phone:* 507-625-6556. *Toll-free phone:* 888-549-6755. *E-mail:* susan.hammerstrom@rasmussen.edu.

Rasmussen College Moorhead

Moorhead, Minnesota

http://www.rasmussen.edu/

- **Proprietary** 4-year, part of Rasmussen College System
- **Suburban** campus
- **Coed** 754 undergraduate students, 57% full-time, 73% women, 27% men
- **Minimally difficult** entrance level

UNDERGRAD STUDENTS
428 full-time, 326 part-time.

Freshmen
Admission: 40 enrolled.

FACULTY
Total: 33, 21% full-time.

Student/faculty ratio: 22:1.

ACADEMICS
Degrees: certificates, diplomas, associate, and bachelor's.

Special study options: academic remediation for entering students, accelerated degree program, adult/continuing education programs, distance learning, double majors, internships, part-time degree program, summer session for credit.

Computers: 31 computers/terminals are available on campus for general student use. Students can access the following: computer help desk, free student e-mail accounts, online (class) grades, online (class) schedules. Campuswide network is available. Wireless service is available via entire campus.

STUDENT LIFE
Housing options: college housing not available.

COSTS
Costs (2014–15) ***Tuition:*** $10,764 full-time, $310 per credit hour part-time. Full-time tuition and fees vary according to course level, course load, degree level, location, and program. Part-time tuition and fees vary according to course level, course load, degree level, location, and program. No tuition increase for student's term of enrollment. ***Required fees:*** $1350 full-time. ***Payment plans:*** installment, deferred payment. ***Waivers:*** employees or children of employees.

APPLYING
Standardized Tests *Required:* Internal Exam (for admission).

Options: electronic application, early admission, deferred entrance.

Required: high school transcript, minimum 2.0 GPA. ***Required for some:*** interview.

Application deadlines: rolling (freshmen), rolling (transfers).

CONTACT
Susan Hammerstrom, Director of Admissions, Rasmussen College Moorhead, 1250 29th Avenue South, Moorhead, MN 56560. *Phone:* 218-304-6200. *Toll-free phone:* 888-549-6755. *E-mail:* susan.hammerstrom@rasmussen.edu.

Rasmussen College St. Cloud

St. Cloud, Minnesota

http://www.rasmussen.edu/

- **Proprietary** 4-year, founded 1904, part of Rasmussen College System
- **Suburban** campus
- **Coed** 826 undergraduate students, 63% full-time, 78% women, 22% men
- **Minimally difficult** entrance level

UNDERGRAD STUDENTS
519 full-time, 307 part-time.

Freshmen
Admission: 40 enrolled.

FACULTY
Total: 40, 38% full-time.

Student/faculty ratio: 22:1.

ACADEMICS
Calendar: quarters. *Degrees:* certificates, diplomas, associate, bachelor's, and postbachelor's certificates.

Special study options: academic remediation for entering students, accelerated degree program, adult/continuing education programs, distance learning, double majors, internships, part-time degree program, summer session for credit.

Computers: 91 computers/terminals are available on campus for general student use. Students can access the following: computer help desk, free student e-mail accounts, online (class) grades, online (class) schedules. Campuswide network is available. Wireless service is available via entire campus.

STUDENT LIFE
Housing options: college housing not available.

COSTS & FINANCIAL AID
Costs (2014–15) ***Tuition:*** $10,764 full-time, $310 per credit hour part-time. Full-time tuition and fees vary according to course level, course load, degree level, location, and program. Part-time tuition and fees vary according to course level, course load, degree level, location, and program. No tuition increase for student's term of enrollment. ***Required fees:*** $1350 full-time. ***Payment plans:*** installment, deferred payment. ***Waivers:*** employees or children of employees.

Financial Aid Of all full-time matriculated undergraduates who enrolled in 2013, 34 Federal Work-Study jobs (averaging $866). 51 state and other part-time jobs (averaging $700).

APPLYING
Standardized Tests *Required:* Internal Exam (for admission).

Options: electronic application, early admission, deferred entrance.

Required: high school transcript, minimum 2.0 GPA. ***Required for some:*** interview.

Application deadlines: rolling (freshmen), rolling (transfers).

CONTACT
Susan Hammerstrom, Director of Admissions, Rasmussen College St. Cloud, 226 Park Avenue South, St. Cloud, MN 56301-3713. *Phone:* 320-251-5600. *Toll-free phone:* 888-549-6755. *E-mail:* susan.hammerstrom@rasmussen.edu.

St. Catherine University

St. Paul, Minnesota

http://www.stkate.edu/

- **Independent Roman Catholic** comprehensive, founded 1905
- **Urban** 110-acre campus with easy access to Minneapolis-St. Paul
- **Undergraduate: women only; graduate: coed** 3,491 undergraduate students, 60% full-time, 96% women, 4% men
- **Moderately difficult** entrance level, 67% of applicants were admitted

UNDERGRAD STUDENTS
2,093 full-time, 1,398 part-time. 12% are from out of state; 10% Black or African American, non-Hispanic/Latino; 6% Hispanic/Latino; 11% Asian, non-Hispanic/Latino; 0.2% Native Hawaiian or other Pacific Islander, non-Hispanic/Latino; 0.5% American Indian or Alaska Native, non-Hispanic/Latino; 2% Two or more races, non-Hispanic/Latino; 4% Race/ethnicity unknown; 0.9% international; 17% transferred in; 43% live on campus.

Freshmen
Admission: 2,961 applied, 1,990 admitted, 478 enrolled. ***Average high school GPA:*** 3.6. ***Test scores:*** SAT critical reading scores over 500: 73%; SAT math scores over 500: 64%; SAT writing scores over 500: 73%; ACT scores over 18: 93%; SAT critical reading scores over 600: 36%; SAT math scores over 600: 36%; SAT writing scores over 600: 18%; ACT scores over 24: 41%; ACT scores over 30: 5%.
Retention: 78% of full-time freshmen returned.

FACULTY
Total: 525, 56% full-time, 66% with terminal degrees.
Student/faculty ratio: 10:1.

ACADEMICS
Calendar: 4-1-4. *Degrees:* certificates, associate, bachelor's, master's, doctoral, and postbachelor's certificates.
Special study options: adult/continuing education programs, part-time degree program. ***ROTC:*** Army (c), Air Force (c).
Computers: Students can access the following: campus intranet, computer help desk, free student e-mail accounts, online (class) grades, online (class) registration, online (class) schedules, transcript. Campuswide network is available. Wireless service is available via entire campus.

STUDENT LIFE
Housing options: women-only. Campus housing is university owned. Freshman campus housing is guaranteed.
Athletics Member NCAA. All Division III. ***Intercollegiate sports:*** basketball W, cross-country running W, ice hockey W, soccer W, softball W, swimming and diving W, tennis W, track and field W, volleyball W. ***Intramural sports:*** basketball W, cheerleading W, cross-country running W, football W, golf W, lacrosse W, racquetball W, soccer W, softball W, swimming and diving W, tennis W, track and field W, volleyball W.
Campus security: 24-hour emergency response devices and patrols, student patrols, late-night transport/escort service, controlled dormitory access.

COSTS & FINANCIAL AID
Costs (2014–15) ***One-time required fee:*** $100. ***Comprehensive fee:*** $45,314 includes full-time tuition ($35,840), mandatory fees ($580), and room and board ($8894). Full-time tuition and fees vary according to class time and degree level. Part-time tuition: $1120 per credit hour. Part-time tuition and fees vary according to class time and degree level. ***Required fees:*** $290 per term part-time. ***College room only:*** $5000. Room and board charges vary according to board plan and housing facility. ***Payment plan:*** installment. ***Waivers:*** senior citizens and employees or children of employees.
Financial Aid Of all full-time matriculated undergraduates who enrolled in 2012, 1,752 applied for aid, 1,655 were judged to have need, 179 had their need fully met. In 2012, 87 non-need-based awards were made. ***Average percent of need met:*** 80. ***Average financial aid package:*** $30,592. ***Average need-based loan:*** $5215. ***Average need-based gift aid:*** $10,581. ***Average non-need-based aid:*** $11,278. ***Average indebtedness upon graduation:*** $39,607.

APPLYING
Standardized Tests *Required:* SAT or ACT (for admission).
Options: deferred entrance.
Required: high school transcript, 1 letter of recommendation. ***Required for some:*** essay or personal statement, interview. ***Recommended:*** interview.

CONTACT
Ms. Cory Piper-Hauswirth, Associate Director of Admission and Financial Aid, St. Catherine University, 2004 Randolph Avenue, St. Paul, MN 55105. *Phone:* 651-690-6047. *Toll-free phone:* 800-945-4599. *E-mail:* stkate@stkate.edu.

St. Cloud State University

St. Cloud, Minnesota

http://www.stcloudstate.edu/

- **State-supported** comprehensive, founded 1869, part of Minnesota State Colleges and Universities System
- **Suburban** 100-acre campus with easy access to Minneapolis-St. Paul
- **Endowment** $23.1 million
- **Coed**
- **Moderately difficult** entrance level

FACULTY
Student/faculty ratio: 19:1.

ACADEMICS
Calendar: semesters. *Degrees:* certificates, diplomas, associate, bachelor's, master's, doctoral, post-master's, and postbachelor's certificates.

STUDENT LIFE
Housing options: coed, men-only, women-only, special housing for students with disabilities. Campus housing is university owned. Freshman applicants given priority for college housing.
Activities and organizations: drama/theater group, student-run newspaper, radio and television station, choral group, Nepalese Student Association, Residence Hall Association, International Student Association, American Marketing Association, KVSC - Campus Radio Station, national fraternities, national sororities.
Athletics Member NCAA. All Division II except men's and women's ice hockey (Division I).
Campus security: 24-hour emergency response devices and patrols, student patrols, late-night transport/escort service.
Student services: health clinic, personal/psychological counseling, women's center, legal services.

COSTS & FINANCIAL AID
Costs (2014–15) ***Tuition:*** state resident $6584 full-time, $219 per credit hour part-time; nonresident $14,226 full-time, $474 per credit hour part-time. Full-time tuition and fees vary according to course load, location, and reciprocity agreements. Part-time tuition and fees vary according to course load, location, and reciprocity agreements. ***Required fees:*** $970 full-time, $39 per credit hour part-time. ***Room and board:*** $7560; room only: $4700. Room and board charges vary according to board plan and housing facility.
Financial Aid Of all full-time matriculated undergraduates who enrolled in 2013, 7,523 applied for aid, 6,025 were judged to have need, 734 had their need fully met. 439 Federal Work-Study jobs (averaging $2990). 462 state and other part-time jobs (averaging $3017). In 2013, 1491 non-need-based awards were made. ***Average percent of need met:*** 61. ***Average financial aid package:*** $9220. ***Average need-based loan:*** $4108. ***Average need-based gift aid:*** $5322. ***Average non-need-based aid:*** $9027. ***Average indebtedness upon graduation:*** $31,219.

APPLYING
Standardized Tests *Required:* SAT or ACT (for admission).
Options: electronic application, deferred entrance.
Application fee: $20.

Required: high school transcript. ***Required for some:*** ACT/SAT score.

CONTACT
Mr. Richard Shearer, Director of Admissions, St. Cloud State University, 720 4th Avenue South, AS 115, St. Cloud, MN 56301-4498. *Phone:* 320-308-4046. *Toll-free phone:* 877-654-7278. *Fax:* 320-308-2243. *E-mail:* scsu4u@stcloudstate.edu.

Saint John's University

Collegeville, Minnesota

http://www.csbsju.edu/

- **Independent Roman Catholic** comprehensive, founded 1857
- **Rural** 2500-acre campus with easy access to Minneapolis-St. Paul
- **Endowment** $168.9 million
- **Undergraduate: men only; graduate: coed** 1,789 undergraduate students, 98% full-time, 100% men
- **Moderately difficult** entrance level, 79% of applicants were admitted

UNDERGRAD STUDENTS
1,758 full-time, 31 part-time. Students come from 40 states and territories; 22 other countries; 20% are from out of state; 3% Black or African American, non-Hispanic/Latino; 5% Hispanic/Latino; 3% Asian, non-Hispanic/Latino; 0.2% Native Hawaiian or other Pacific Islander, non-Hispanic/Latino; 0.8% American Indian or Alaska Native, non-Hispanic/Latino; 0.6% Two or more races, non-Hispanic/Latino; 6% international; 1% transferred in; 87% live on campus.

Freshmen
Admission: 1,469 applied, 1,157 admitted, 450 enrolled. ***Average high school GPA:*** 3.43. ***Test scores:*** SAT critical reading scores over 500: 67%; SAT math scores over 500: 74%; SAT writing scores over 500: 66%; ACT scores over 18: 99%; SAT critical reading scores over 600: 27%; SAT math scores over 600: 25%; SAT writing scores over 600: 20%; ACT scores over 24: 67%; SAT critical reading scores over 700: 6%; SAT math scores over 700: 11%; SAT writing scores over 700: 5%; ACT scores over 30: 15%.
Retention: 88% of full-time freshmen returned.

FACULTY
Total: 168, 83% full-time, 81% with terminal degrees.
Student/faculty ratio: 12:1.

ACADEMICS
Calendar: semesters. *Degrees:* bachelor's and master's (coordinate with College of Saint Benedict for women).
Special study options: advanced placement credit, double majors, English as a second language, honors programs, independent study, internships, off-campus study, services for LD students, student-designed majors, study abroad. ***ROTC:*** Army (b).
Unusual degree programs: 3-2 engineering with University of Minnesota.
Computers: 1,024 computers/terminals and 3,000 ports are available on campus for general student use. Students can access the following: campus intranet, computer help desk, free student e-mail accounts, online (class) grades, online (class) registration, online (class) schedules, online student accounts. Campuswide network is available. 100% of college-owned or -operated housing units are wired for high-speed Internet access. Wireless service is available via entire campus.

STUDENT LIFE
Housing options: on-campus residence required through senior year; men-only, special housing for students with disabilities. Campus housing is university owned. Freshman campus housing is guaranteed.
Activities and organizations: drama/theater group, student-run newspaper, radio and television station, choral group, Alpha Kappa Sigma Service Sorority (AKS), Allied Health Club, College Republicans, Fides et Ratio, Spanish Club.
Athletics Member NCAA. All Division III. ***Intercollegiate sports:*** baseball M, basketball M, crew M(c), cross-country running M, football M, golf M, ice hockey M, lacrosse M(c), riflery M(c), rugby M(c), skiing (cross-country) M(c), soccer M, swimming and diving M, tennis M, track and field M, ultimate Frisbee M(c), volleyball M(c), water polo M(c), wrestling M. ***Intramural sports:*** basketball M, football M, racquetball M, rock climbing M(c), skiing (downhill) M(c), soccer M, softball M, table tennis M, ultimate Frisbee M, volleyball M.
Campus security: 24-hour emergency response devices and patrols, student patrols, late-night transport/escort service, controlled dormitory access, well-lit pathways, 911 center on campus.
Student services: health clinic, personal/psychological counseling.

COSTS & FINANCIAL AID
Costs (2014–15) ***Comprehensive fee:*** $47,984 includes full-time tuition ($38,024), mandatory fees ($680), and room and board ($9280). Part-time tuition: $1584 per credit hour. Part-time tuition and fees vary according to course load. ***College room only:*** $4640. Room and board charges vary according to board plan and housing facility. ***Payment plan:*** installment. ***Waivers:*** employees or children of employees.
Financial Aid Of all full-time matriculated undergraduates who enrolled in 2014, 1,354 applied for aid, 1,169 were judged to have need, 448 had their need fully met. In 2014, 459 non-need-based awards were made. ***Average percent of need met:*** 89. ***Average financial aid package:*** $30,327. ***Average need-based loan:*** $3935. ***Average need-based gift aid:*** $25,274. ***Average non-need-based aid:*** $15,184. ***Average indebtedness upon graduation:*** $38,089.

APPLYING
Standardized Tests *Required:* SAT or ACT (for admission).
Options: electronic application, early action, deferred entrance.
Required: essay or personal statement, high school transcript, 1 letter of recommendation. ***Recommended:*** minimum 3.0 GPA, interview.
Application deadlines: rolling (freshmen), rolling (transfers), 11/15 (early action).
Notification: continuous (freshmen), continuous (transfers), 12/15 (early action).

CONTACT
Mr. Matt Beirne, Director of Admission, Saint John's University, 2850 Abbey Plaza, Collegeville, MN 56321-7155. *Phone:* 320-363-5055. *Toll-free phone:* 800-544-1489. *Fax:* 320-363-5650. *E-mail:* admissions@csbsju.edu.

See page 564 for display ad and page 1404 for the College Close-Up.

Saint Mary's University of Minnesota

Winona, Minnesota

http://www.smumn.edu/

- **Independent Roman Catholic** comprehensive, founded 1912
- **Small-town** 350-acre campus
- **Endowment** $53.2 million
- **Coed** 1,904 undergraduate students, 68% full-time, 53% women, 47% men
- **Moderately difficult** entrance level, 74% of applicants were admitted

UNDERGRAD STUDENTS
1,298 full-time, 606 part-time. Students come from 32 states and territories; 15 other countries; 46% are from out of state; 4% Black or African American, non-Hispanic/Latino; 6% Hispanic/Latino; 2% Asian, non-Hispanic/Latino; 0.4% American Indian or Alaska Native, non-Hispanic/Latino; 0.7% Two or more races, non-Hispanic/Latino; 29% Race/ethnicity unknown; 2% international; 10% transferred in; 93% live on campus.

Freshmen
Admission: 1,743 applied, 1,294 admitted, 334 enrolled. ***Average high school GPA:*** 3.34. ***Test scores:*** SAT critical reading scores over 500: 56%; SAT math scores over 500: 63%; SAT writing scores over 500: 53%; ACT scores over 18: 90%; SAT critical reading scores over 600: 25%; SAT math scores over 600: 13%; SAT writing scores over 600: 13%; ACT scores over 24: 47%; SAT critical reading scores over 700: 3%; SAT math scores over 700: 3%; SAT writing scores over 700: 3%; ACT scores over 30: 7%.
Retention: 79% of full-time freshmen returned.

FACULTY
Total: 631, 16% full-time, 45% with terminal degrees.
Student/faculty ratio: 16:1.

ACADEMICS
Calendar: semesters. *Degrees:* certificates, diplomas, bachelor's, master's, doctoral, post-master's, and postbachelor's certificates.

Special study options: academic remediation for entering students, accelerated degree program, adult/continuing education programs, advanced placement credit, cooperative education, distance learning, double majors, English as a second language, honors programs, independent study, internships, off-campus study, part-time degree program, services for LD students, student-designed majors, study abroad, summer session for credit. ***ROTC:*** Army (c).

Computers: 200 computers/terminals and 50 ports are available on campus for general student use. Students can access the following: campus intranet, computer help desk, free student e-mail accounts, online (class) grades, online (class) registration, online (class) schedules. Campuswide network is available. 100% of college-owned or -operated housing units are wired for high-speed Internet access. Wireless service is available via computer centers, computer labs, dorm rooms, libraries, student centers.

STUDENT LIFE
Housing options: on-campus residence required through sophomore year; coed, men-only, women-only, special housing for students with disabilities. Campus housing is university owned. Freshman campus housing is guaranteed.

Activities and organizations: drama/theater group, student-run newspaper, radio station, choral group, Student Activity Committee, PR Business Club, Serving Others United in Love (Soul) - Mission Trips, Colleges Against Cancer, Club Hockey, national fraternities, national sororities.

Athletics Member NCAA. All Division III. ***Intercollegiate sports:*** baseball M, basketball M/W, cross-country running M/W, golf M/W, ice hockey M/W, soccer M/W, softball W, swimming and diving M/W, tennis M/W, track and field M/W, volleyball W. ***Intramural sports:*** basketball M/W, cheerleading W(c), fencing M(c)/W(c), field hockey M/W, football M/W, ice hockey M, lacrosse M(c)/W(c), rugby M(c), skiing (downhill) M(c)/W(c), soccer M/W, softball M/W, tennis M/W, ultimate Frisbee M/W, volleyball M/W, water polo M(c)/W(c).

Campus security: 24-hour emergency response devices and patrols, late-night transport/escort service, controlled dormitory access.

Student services: health clinic, personal/psychological counseling.

COSTS & FINANCIAL AID
Costs (2014–15) ***Comprehensive fee:*** $39,575 includes full-time tuition ($30,830), mandatory fees ($505), and room and board ($8240). Full-time tuition and fees vary according to course load. Part-time tuition: $1026 per credit. Part-time tuition and fees vary according to course load. ***Required fees:*** $505 per year part-time. ***College room only:*** $4610. Room and board charges vary according to board plan and housing facility. ***Payment plan:*** installment. ***Waivers:*** employees or children of employees.

Financial Aid Of all full-time matriculated undergraduates who enrolled in 2014, 1,072 applied for aid, 961 were judged to have need, 182 had their need fully met. 175 Federal Work-Study jobs (averaging $1716). 256 state and other part-time jobs (averaging $1813). In 2014, 269 non-need-based awards were made. ***Average percent of need met:*** 73. ***Average financial aid package:*** $23,158. ***Average need-based loan:*** $4822. ***Average need-based gift aid:*** $18,700. ***Average non-need-based aid:*** $13,667. ***Average indebtedness upon graduation:*** $33,216.

APPLYING
Standardized Tests *Required:* SAT or ACT (for admission).

Options: electronic application, early admission, deferred entrance.

Application fee: $25.

Required: essay or personal statement, high school transcript, minimum 2.5 GPA. ***Required for some:*** interview. ***Recommended:*** 2 letters of recommendation.

Application deadlines: 5/1 (freshmen), rolling (transfers).

Notification: continuous (freshmen), continuous (transfers).

CONTACT
Mr. John Pyle, Vice President for Enrollment, Marketing, and Strategic Initiatives, Saint Mary's University of Minnesota, 700 Terrace Heights, Winona, MN 55987. *Phone:* 507-457-1743. *Toll-free phone:* 800-635-5987. *Fax:* 507-457-1722. *E-mail:* jpyle@smumn.edu.

St. Olaf College

Northfield, Minnesota

http://www.stolaf.edu/

- **Independent Lutheran** 4-year, founded 1874
- **Small-town** 300-acre campus with easy access to Minneapolis-St. Paul
- **Endowment** $446.8 million
- **Coed** 3,034 undergraduate students, 99% full-time, 58% women, 42% men
- **Very difficult** entrance level, 51% of applicants were admitted

UNDERGRAD STUDENTS
2,989 full-time, 45 part-time. Students come from 50 states and territories; 73 other countries; 52% are from out of state; 2% Black or African American, non-Hispanic/Latino; 5% Hispanic/Latino; 6% Asian, non-Hispanic/Latino; 0.1% American Indian or Alaska Native, non-Hispanic/Latino; 4% Two or more races, non-Hispanic/Latino; 0.8% Race/ethnicity unknown; 7% international; 0.9% transferred in; 93% live on campus.

Freshmen
Admission: 4,875 applied, 2,500 admitted, 765 enrolled. ***Average high school GPA:*** 3.62. ***Test scores:*** SAT critical reading scores over 500: 90%; SAT math scores over 500: 93%; ACT scores over 18: 101%; SAT critical reading scores over 600: 66%; SAT math scores over 600: 68%; ACT scores over 24: 93%; SAT critical reading scores over 700: 27%; SAT math scores over 700: 25%; ACT scores over 30: 50%.

Retention: 93% of full-time freshmen returned.

FACULTY
Total: 334, 64% full-time, 78% with terminal degrees.

Student/faculty ratio: 12:1.

ACADEMICS
Calendar: 4-1-4. *Degree:* bachelor's.

Special study options: advanced placement credit, double majors, English as a second language, independent study, internships, off-campus study, part-time degree program, services for LD students, student-designed majors, study abroad, summer session for credit.

Unusual degree programs: 3-2 engineering with Washington University in St. Louis and University of Minnesota in Minneapolis.

Computers: 1,022 computers/terminals and 3,300 ports are available on campus for general student use. Students can access the following: campus intranet, computer help desk, free student e-mail accounts, online (class) grades, online (class) registration, online (class) schedules. Campuswide network is available. 100% of college-owned or -operated housing units are wired for high-speed Internet access. Wireless service is available via entire campus.

STUDENT LIFE
Housing options: on-campus residence required through senior year; coed, special housing for students with disabilities. Campus housing is university owned. Freshman campus housing is guaranteed.

Activities and organizations: drama/theater group, student-run newspaper, radio station, choral group, Student Government Association, Ultimate Frisbee Teams, Ole Spring Relief, Taiko Drumming, Fellowship of Christian Oles.

Athletics Member NCAA. All Division III. ***Intercollegiate sports:*** baseball M, basketball M/W, cross-country running M/W, football M, golf M/W, ice hockey M/W, skiing (cross-country) M/W, skiing (downhill) M/W, soccer M/W, softball W, swimming and diving M/W, tennis M/W, track and field M/W, volleyball W, wrestling M. ***Intramural sports:*** badminton M(c)/W(c), basketball M/W, bowling M/W, crew M(c)/W(c), equestrian sports M(c)/W(c), fencing M(c)/W(c), football M/W, golf M/W, ice hockey M(c), lacrosse M(c)/W(c), rugby M(c)/W(c), soccer M/W, softball M/W, swimming and diving M/W, table tennis M/W, tennis M/W, ultimate Frisbee M/W, volleyball M(c)/W.

Campus security: 24-hour emergency response devices and patrols, late-night transport/escort service, controlled dormitory access, lighted pathways and sidewalks, first-year only dorms, quiet halls.

Student services: health clinic, personal/psychological counseling.

COSTS & FINANCIAL AID
Costs (2015–16) ***Comprehensive fee:*** $52,730 includes full-time tuition ($42,940) and room and board ($9790). Full-time tuition and fees vary

according to course load. Part-time tuition and fees vary according to course load. ***College room only:*** $4720. Room and board charges vary according to board plan. ***Payment plan:*** installment. ***Waivers:*** senior citizens and employees or children of employees.

Financial Aid Of all full-time matriculated undergraduates who enrolled in 2014, 2,165 applied for aid, 1,973 were judged to have need, 1,667 had their need fully met. 294 Federal Work-Study jobs (averaging $2120). 1,600 state and other part-time jobs (averaging $2100). In 2014, 667 non-need-based awards were made. ***Average percent of need met:*** 97. ***Average financial aid package:*** $33,883. ***Average need-based loan:*** $4149. ***Average need-based gift aid:*** $28,644. ***Average non-need-based aid:*** $13,290. ***Average indebtedness upon graduation:*** $28,396. ***Financial aid deadline:*** 3/1.

APPLYING

Standardized Tests *Required:* SAT or ACT (for admission).

Options: electronic application, early decision, deferred entrance.

Required: essay or personal statement, high school transcript, 1 letter of recommendation. ***Recommended:*** 2 letters of recommendation, interview.

Application deadlines: 1/15 (freshmen), 4/1 (transfers).

Early decision deadline: 11/15 (for plan 1), 1/1 (for plan 2).

Notification: 3/20 (freshmen), 5/1 (transfers), 12/15 (early decision plan 1), 2/1 (early decision plan 2).

CONTACT

Dave Wagner, Director of Admissions, St. Olaf College, 1520 St. Olaf Avenue, Northfield, MN 55057. *Phone:* 507-786-3025. *Toll-free phone:* 800-800-3025. *Fax:* 507-786-3832. *E-mail:* admissions@stolaf.edu.

Southwest Minnesota State University

Marshall, Minnesota

http://www.smsu.edu/

- **State-supported** comprehensive, founded 1963, part of Minnesota State Colleges and Universities System
- **Small-town** 216-acre campus
- **Coed** 6,451 undergraduate students, 32% full-time, 58% women, 42% men
- **Minimally difficult** entrance level, 64% of applicants were admitted

UNDERGRAD STUDENTS

2,080 full-time, 4,371 part-time. Students come from 26 states and territories; 25 other countries; 21% are from out of state; 4% Black or African American, non-Hispanic/Latino; 2% Hispanic/Latino; 2% Asian, non-Hispanic/Latino; 0.9% American Indian or Alaska Native, non-Hispanic/Latino; 0.2% Race/ethnicity unknown; 4% international; 4% transferred in; 40% live on campus.

Freshmen

Admission: 1,839 applied, 1,174 admitted, 467 enrolled. ***Test scores:*** ACT scores over 18: 89%; ACT scores over 24: 25%; ACT scores over 30: 1%.

Retention: 69% of full-time freshmen returned.

FACULTY

Total: 194, 56% full-time, 62% with terminal degrees.

Student/faculty ratio: 16:1.

ACADEMICS

Calendar: semesters. *Degrees:* associate, bachelor's, master's, and postbachelor's certificates.

Special study options: academic remediation for entering students, accelerated degree program, adult/continuing education programs, advanced placement credit, distance learning, double majors, English as a second language, external degree program, freshman honors college, honors programs, independent study, internships, off-campus study, part-time degree program, services for LD students, student-designed majors, study abroad, summer session for credit.

Computers: 420 computers/terminals and 500 ports are available on campus for general student use. Students can access the following: campus intranet, computer help desk, free student e-mail accounts, online (class) grades, online (class) registration, online (class) schedules. Campuswide network is available. 100% of college-owned or -operated housing units are wired for high-speed Internet access. Wireless service is available via classrooms, computer centers, computer labs, dorm rooms, learning centers, libraries, student centers.

STUDENT LIFE

Housing options: on-campus residence required for freshman year; coed, men-only, women-only, special housing for students with disabilities. Campus housing is university owned.

Activities and organizations: drama/theater group, student-run newspaper, radio and television station, choral group, marching band, Students in Free Enterprise (SIFE), Society of Leadership & Success, Family and Child Educators (FACE), Habitat for Humanity, Education Minnesota Student Program.

Athletics Member NCAA. All Division II. ***Intercollegiate sports:*** baseball M(s), basketball M(s)/W(s), football M(s), golf W(s), soccer W(s), softball W(s), tennis W(s), volleyball W(s), wrestling M(s). ***Intramural sports:*** badminton M/W, basketball M/W, football M, ice hockey M, racquetball M/W, softball M/W, tennis M/W, volleyball M/W.

Campus security: 24-hour emergency response devices and patrols, student patrols, late-night transport/escort service, controlled dormitory access.

Student services: health clinic, personal/psychological counseling, women's center.

COSTS & FINANCIAL AID

Costs (2014–15) ***Tuition:*** state resident $6974 full-time, $226 per credit part-time; nonresident $6974 full-time, $226 per credit part-time. Full-time tuition and fees vary according to course load, location, program, and reciprocity agreements. Part-time tuition and fees vary according to location, program, and reciprocity agreements. ***Required fees:*** $1088 full-time. ***Room and board:*** $7352. Room and board charges vary according to board plan and housing facility. ***Payment plan:*** installment. ***Waivers:*** senior citizens and employees or children of employees.

Financial Aid Of all full-time matriculated undergraduates who enrolled in 2013, 1,782 applied for aid, 1,441 were judged to have need, 181 had their need fully met. 93 Federal Work-Study jobs (averaging $2203). 154 state and other part-time jobs (averaging $2325). In 2013, 315 non-need-based awards were made. ***Average percent of need met:*** 52. ***Average financial aid package:*** $8146. ***Average need-based loan:*** $3940. ***Average need-based gift aid:*** $4866. ***Average non-need-based aid:*** $2442. ***Average indebtedness upon graduation:*** $25,493.

APPLYING

Standardized Tests *Required:* SAT or ACT (for admission). *Recommended:* ACT (for admission).

Options: electronic application, early admission, deferred entrance.

Application fee: $20.

Required: high school transcript, minimum 3.0 GPA, top half of graduating class or 21 ACT. ***Required for some:*** interview.

Application deadlines: 9/1 (freshmen), 9/1 (out-of-state freshmen), 9/1 (transfers).

CONTACT

Mr. Andrew Hlubeck, Director of Admissions, Southwest Minnesota State University, 1501 State Street, Marshall, MN 56258. *Phone:* 507-537-6286. *Toll-free phone:* 800-642-0684. *Fax:* 507-537-7145. *E-mail:* andrew.hlubek@smsu.edu.

University of Minnesota, Crookston

Crookston, Minnesota

http://www.umcrookston.edu/

- **State-supported** 4-year, founded 1966, part of University of Minnesota System
- **Rural** 237-acre campus
- **Endowment** $14.0 million
- **Coed** 2,850 undergraduate students, 47% full-time, 53% women, 47% men
- **Minimally difficult** entrance level, 71% of applicants were admitted

UNDERGRAD STUDENTS

1,349 full-time, 1,501 part-time. Students come from 43 states and territories; 12 other countries; 28% are from out of state; 7% Black or African American, non-Hispanic/Latino; 3% Hispanic/Latino; 2% Asian, non-Hispanic/Latino; 0.2% Native Hawaiian or other Pacific Islander, non-Hispanic/Latino; 0.4% American Indian or Alaska Native, non-Hispanic/Latino; 1% Two or more races, non-Hispanic/Latino; 2% Race/ethnicity unknown; 4% international; 8% transferred in; 39% live on campus.

Freshmen
Admission: 927 applied, 662 admitted, 274 enrolled. ***Average high school GPA:*** 3.15. ***Test scores:*** SAT critical reading scores over 500: 17%; SAT math scores over 500: 44%; SAT writing scores over 500: 11%; ACT scores over 18: 92%; ACT scores over 24: 29%; ACT scores over 30: 5%.
Retention: 66% of full-time freshmen returned.

FACULTY
Total: 87, 76% full-time, 43% with terminal degrees.
Student/faculty ratio: 20:1.

ACADEMICS
Calendar: semesters. *Degree:* bachelor's.
Special study options: academic remediation for entering students, advanced placement credit, cooperative education, distance learning, double majors, English as a second language, external degree program, honors programs, independent study, internships, off-campus study, part-time degree program, services for LD students, student-designed majors, study abroad, summer session for credit. ***ROTC:*** Air Force (c).
Computers: 25 computers/terminals are available on campus for general student use. Students can access the following: campus intranet, computer help desk, free student e-mail accounts, online (class) grades, online (class) registration, online (class) schedules, personal Web pages. Campuswide network is available. 100% of college-owned or -operated housing units are wired for high-speed Internet access. Wireless service is available via entire campus.

STUDENT LIFE
Housing options: coed, special housing for students with disabilities. Campus housing is university owned. Freshman applicants given priority for college housing.
Activities and organizations: drama/theater group, choral group, National Society for Leadership & Success, Archery Club, Crookston Futbol Club, Choir, Student Athletic Advisory Council, national fraternities.
Athletics Member NCAA. All Division II. ***Intercollegiate sports:*** baseball M(s), basketball M(s)/W(s), equestrian sports W(s), football M(s), golf M(s)/W(s), soccer W(s), softball W(s), tennis W(s), volleyball W(s). ***Intramural sports:*** basketball M/W, football M/W, golf M/W, ice hockey M(c), racquetball M/W, soccer M(c)/W, softball M/W, table tennis M/W, tennis M/W, volleyball M/W.
Campus security: 24-hour emergency response devices, student patrols, controlled dormitory access.
Student services: health clinic, personal/psychological counseling, women's center.

COSTS & FINANCIAL AID
Costs (2014–15) ***Tuition:*** state resident $10,030 full-time, $386 per credit part-time; nonresident $10,030 full-time, $386 per credit part-time. Full-time tuition and fees vary according to course load and location. Part-time tuition and fees vary according to course load and location. ***Required fees:*** $1438 full-time, $719 per term part-time. ***Room and board:*** $7350; room only: $3480. Room and board charges vary according to board plan and housing facility. ***Payment plan:*** installment. ***Waivers:*** senior citizens.
Financial Aid Of all full-time matriculated undergraduates who enrolled in 2013, 1,021 applied for aid, 869 were judged to have need, 151 had their need fully met. In 2013, 76 non-need-based awards were made. ***Average percent of need met:*** 73. ***Average financial aid package:*** $11,205. ***Average need-based loan:*** $4177. ***Average need-based gift aid:*** $8130. ***Average non-need-based aid:*** $2369. ***Average indebtedness upon graduation:*** $23,621.

APPLYING
Standardized Tests *Required:* SAT or ACT (for admission). *Recommended:* ACT (for admission).
Options: electronic application, deferred entrance.
Application fee: $30.
Required: high school transcript, minimum 2.0 GPA, ACT composite 21 or SAT 980.
Application deadlines: rolling (freshmen), rolling (out-of-state freshmen), rolling (transfers).
Notification: continuous (freshmen), continuous (out-of-state freshmen), continuous (transfers).

CONTACT
Carola Thorson, Director of Admissions, University of Minnesota, Crookston, 2900 University Avenue, Crookston, MN 56716-5001. *Phone:* 218-281-8568. *Toll-free phone:* 800-862-6466. *E-mail:* cthorson@umn.edu.

University of Minnesota, Duluth
Duluth, Minnesota
http://www.d.umn.edu/

- **State-supported** comprehensive, founded 1947, part of University of Minnesota System
- **Suburban** 250-acre campus
- **Endowment** $130.3 million
- **Coed** 9,987 undergraduate students, 89% full-time, 46% women, 54% men
- **Moderately difficult** entrance level, 77% of applicants were admitted

UNDERGRAD STUDENTS
8,869 full-time, 1,118 part-time. Students come from 34 states and territories; 35 other countries; 10% are from out of state; 2% Black or African American, non-Hispanic/Latino; 2% Hispanic/Latino; 3% Asian, non-Hispanic/Latino; 0.1% Native Hawaiian or other Pacific Islander, non-Hispanic/Latino; 0.6% American Indian or Alaska Native, non-Hispanic/Latino; 3% Two or more races, non-Hispanic/Latino; 1% Race/ethnicity unknown; 2% international; 5% transferred in; 33% live on campus.

Freshmen
Admission: 7,738 applied, 5,942 admitted, 2,196 enrolled. ***Average high school GPA:*** 3.44. ***Test scores:*** SAT critical reading scores over 500: 68%; SAT math scores over 500: 82%; SAT writing scores over 500: 64%; ACT scores over 18: 98%; SAT critical reading scores over 600: 38%; SAT math scores over 600: 38%; SAT writing scores over 600: 16%; ACT scores over 24: 52%; SAT critical reading scores over 700: 4%; SAT math scores over 700: 7%; SAT writing scores over 700: 2%; ACT scores over 30: 6%.
Retention: 77% of full-time freshmen returned.

FACULTY
Total: 615, 80% full-time, 64% with terminal degrees.
Student/faculty ratio: 19:1.

ACADEMICS
Calendar: semesters. *Degrees:* certificates, bachelor's, master's, doctoral, and postbachelor's certificates.
Special study options: academic remediation for entering students, accelerated degree program, adult/continuing education programs, advanced placement credit, cooperative education, distance learning, double majors, English as a second language, honors programs, independent study, internships, off-campus study, part-time degree program, services for LD students, student-designed majors, study abroad, summer session for credit. ***ROTC:*** Air Force (b).
Computers: 465 computers/terminals are available on campus for general student use. Students can access the following: campus intranet, computer help desk, free student e-mail accounts, online (class) grades, online (class) registration, online (class) schedules. Campuswide network is available. 100% of college-owned or -operated housing units are wired for high-speed Internet access. Wireless service is available via entire campus.

STUDENT LIFE
Housing options: coed, men-only, women-only, special housing for students with disabilities. Campus housing is university owned. Freshman applicants given priority for college housing.
Activities and organizations: drama/theater group, student-run newspaper, radio station, choral group, marching band, national fraternities, national sororities.

Athletics Member NCAA. All Division II except men's and women's ice hockey (Division I). ***Intercollegiate sports:*** badminton M(c)/W(c), baseball M(s), basketball M(s)/W(s), cheerleading W(c), crew M(c)/W(c), cross-country running M(s)/W(s), football M(s), ice hockey M(s)/W(s), lacrosse M(s)(c)/W(s)(c), rugby M(c)/W(c), skiing (downhill) M(c)/W(c), soccer M(c)/W(s), softball W(s), swimming and diving M(c)/W(c), table tennis M(c)/W(c), tennis W(s), track and field M(s)/W(s), ultimate Frisbee M(c)/W(c), volleyball M(c)/W(s), water polo M(c)/W(c), wrestling M(c). ***Intramural sports:*** badminton M/W, basketball M/W, bowling M/W, football M/W, golf M/W, ice hockey M/W, rock climbing M(c)/W(c), soccer M/W, softball M/W, table tennis M(c)/W(c), tennis M/W, volleyball M/W, water polo M/W.

Campus security: 24-hour emergency response devices and patrols, late-night transport/escort service, Campus housing assigns keys specific to residence area, doors are locked late hours of the night and opened in the early morning.

Student services: health clinic, personal/psychological counseling, women's center.

COSTS & FINANCIAL AID

Costs (2014–15) ***Tuition:*** state resident $11,720 full-time, $451 per credit part-time; nonresident $15,385 full-time, $592 per credit part-time. Full-time tuition and fees vary according to course load, program, and reciprocity agreements. Part-time tuition and fees vary according to course load, program, and reciprocity agreements. ***Required fees:*** $1082 full-time. ***Room and board:*** $7004. Room and board charges vary according to board plan and housing facility. ***Payment plan:*** installment. ***Waivers:*** children of alumni.

Financial Aid Of all full-time matriculated undergraduates who enrolled in 2013, 7,242 applied for aid, 5,381 were judged to have need, 1,088 had their need fully met. 348 Federal Work-Study jobs (averaging $1819). 734 state and other part-time jobs (averaging $1301). In 2013, 879 non-need-based awards were made. ***Average percent of need met:*** 68. ***Average financial aid package:*** $11,043. ***Average need-based loan:*** $4772. ***Average need-based gift aid:*** $7686. ***Average non-need-based aid:*** $2655. ***Average indebtedness upon graduation:*** $31,244.

APPLYING

Standardized Tests *Required:* SAT or ACT (for admission).

Options: electronic application.

Application fee: $35.

Required: high school transcript. ***Required for some:*** interview. ***Recommended:*** essay or personal statement.

Application deadlines: 12/15 (freshmen), 6/15 (transfers).

Notification: continuous (freshmen), continuous (transfers).

CONTACT

Office of Admissions, University of Minnesota, Duluth, 25 Solon Campus Center, 1117 University Drive, Duluth, MN 55812-3000. *Phone:* 218-726-7171. *Toll-free phone:* 800-232-1339. *Fax:* 218-726-6394. *E-mail:* umdadmis@d.umn.edu.

University of Minnesota, Morris

Morris, Minnesota

http://www.morris.umn.edu/

- **State-supported** 4-year, founded 1959, part of University of Minnesota System
- **Small-town** 130-acre campus
- **Endowment** $11.2 million
- **Coed** 1,899 undergraduate students, 93% full-time, 54% women, 46% men
- **Moderately difficult** entrance level, 64% of applicants were admitted

UNDERGRAD STUDENTS

1,761 full-time, 138 part-time. Students come from 34 states and territories; 17 other countries; 14% are from out of state; 1% Black or African American, non-Hispanic/Latino; 4% Hispanic/Latino; 3% Asian, non-Hispanic/Latino; 7% American Indian or Alaska Native, non-Hispanic/Latino; 11% Two or more races, non-Hispanic/Latino; 0.6% Race/ethnicity unknown; 9% international; 6% transferred in; 51% live on campus.

Freshmen

Admission: 2,867 applied, 1,823 admitted, 413 enrolled. ***Average high school GPA:*** 3.59. ***Test scores:*** SAT critical reading scores over 500: 85%; SAT math scores over 500: 81%; SAT writing scores over 500: 67%; ACT scores over 18: 99%; SAT critical reading scores over 600: 48%; SAT math scores over 600: 44%; SAT writing scores over 600: 22%; ACT scores over 24: 63%; SAT critical reading scores over 700: 7%; SAT math scores over 700: 4%; SAT writing scores over 700: 4%; ACT scores over 30: 14%.

Retention: 79% of full-time freshmen returned.

FACULTY

Total: 154, 77% full-time, 72% with terminal degrees.

Student/faculty ratio: 13:1.

ACADEMICS

Calendar: semesters. *Degree:* bachelor's.

Special study options: advanced placement credit, distance learning, double majors, English as a second language, freshman honors college, honors programs, independent study, internships, off-campus study, part-time degree program, services for LD students, student-designed majors, study abroad, summer session for credit.

Unusual degree programs: 3-2 engineering with University of Minnesota, Twin Cities.

Computers: 124 computers/terminals are available on campus for general student use. Students can access the following: campus intranet, computer help desk, free student e-mail accounts, online (class) grades, online (class) registration, online (class) schedules. Campuswide network is available. 100% of college-owned or -operated housing units are wired for high-speed Internet access. Wireless service is available via classrooms, computer labs, dorm rooms, learning centers, libraries, student centers.

STUDENT LIFE

Housing options: coed, special housing for students with disabilities. Campus housing is university owned. Freshman campus housing is guaranteed.

Activities and organizations: drama/theater group, student-run newspaper, radio station, choral group, student radio station, Inter-Varsity Christian Fellowship, jazz ensemble/concert choir, Big Friend, Little Friend, student newspaper.

Athletics Member NCAA. All Division III. ***Intercollegiate sports:*** baseball M, basketball M/W, cross-country running M/W, football M, golf M/W, soccer M/W, softball W, swimming and diving W, tennis M/W, track and field M/W, volleyball W. ***Intramural sports:*** baseball M, basketball M/W, cheerleading M(c)/W(c), equestrian sports M(c)/W(c), fencing M(c)/W(c), football M/W, racquetball M/W, rugby M(c)/W(c), skiing (cross-country) M/W, soccer M(c)/W(c), softball M/W, swimming and diving M/W, table tennis M/W, ultimate Frisbee M(c)/W(c), volleyball M(c)/W(c).

Campus security: 24-hour emergency response devices and patrols, late-night transport/escort service, controlled dormitory access.

Student services: health clinic, personal/psychological counseling, women's center, legal services.

COSTS & FINANCIAL AID

Costs (2014–15) ***Tuition:*** state resident $11,720 full-time, $451 per credit hour part-time; nonresident $11,720 full-time, $451 per credit hour part-time. Full-time tuition and fees vary according to reciprocity agreements. Part-time tuition and fees vary according to course load and reciprocity agreements. ***Required fees:*** $863 full-time. ***Room and board:*** $7626; room only: $3576. Room and board charges vary according to board plan and housing facility. ***Payment plan:*** installment. ***Waivers:*** senior citizens.

Financial Aid Of all full-time matriculated undergraduates who enrolled in 2013, 1,441 applied for aid, 1,140 were judged to have need, 527 had their need fully met. In 2013, 328 non-need-based awards were made. ***Average percent of need met:*** 81. ***Average financial aid package:*** $16,276. ***Average need-based loan:*** $8682. ***Average need-based gift aid:*** $9767. ***Average non-need-based aid:*** $3756. ***Average indebtedness upon graduation:*** $24,313.

APPLYING

Standardized Tests *Required:* SAT or ACT (for admission).

Options: electronic application, deferred entrance.

Application fee: $35.

Required: high school transcript. ***Required for some:*** essay or personal statement, 1 letter of recommendation, interview.

Application deadlines: 3/15 (freshmen), 5/1 (transfers).

Notification: continuous (freshmen), continuous (transfers).

CONTACT

University of Minnesota, Morris, 600 East 4th Street, Morris, MN 56267-2134. *Phone:* 320-539-6035. *Toll-free phone:* 800-992-8863. *Fax:* 320-589-6051. *E-mail:* admissions@morris.umn.edu.

University of Minnesota, Twin Cities Campus

Minneapolis, Minnesota

http://www.umn.edu/tc/

- **State-supported** comprehensive, founded 1851, part of University of Minnesota System
- **Urban** 2000-acre campus
- **Coed** 34,351 undergraduate students, 84% full-time, 51% women, 49% men
- **Moderately difficult** entrance level, 45% of applicants were admitted

UNDERGRAD STUDENTS

28,904 full-time, 5,447 part-time. Students come from 51 states and territories; 88 other countries; 27% are from out of state; 4% Black or African American, non-Hispanic/Latino; 3% Hispanic/Latino; 9% Asian, non-Hispanic/Latino; 0.1% Native Hawaiian or other Pacific Islander, non-Hispanic/Latino; 0.3% American Indian or Alaska Native, non-Hispanic/Latino; 3% Two or more races, non-Hispanic/Latino; 0.6% Race/ethnicity unknown; 9% international; 6% transferred in; 23% live on campus.

Freshmen

Admission: 44,761 applied, 20,300 admitted, 5,530 enrolled. ***Test scores:*** SAT critical reading scores over 500: 91%; SAT math scores over 500: 97%; SAT writing scores over 500: 93%; ACT scores over 18: 100%; SAT critical reading scores over 600: 62%; SAT math scores over 600: 82%; SAT writing scores over 600: 67%; ACT scores over 24: 90%; SAT critical reading scores over 700: 24%; SAT math scores over 700: 46%; SAT writing scores over 700: 19%; ACT scores over 30: 34%.

Retention: 92% of full-time freshmen returned.

FACULTY

Total: 2,913, 67% full-time, 68% with terminal degrees.

Student/faculty ratio: 21:1.

ACADEMICS

Calendar: semesters. *Degrees:* certificates, diplomas, bachelor's, master's, doctoral, post-master's, and postbachelor's certificates.

Special study options: academic remediation for entering students, accelerated degree program, adult/continuing education programs, advanced placement credit, cooperative education, distance learning, double majors, English as a second language, external degree program, freshman honors college, honors programs, independent study, internships, off-campus study, part-time degree program, services for LD students, student-designed majors, study abroad, summer session for credit. ***ROTC:*** Army (b), Navy (b), Air Force (b).

Computers: Students can access the following: computer help desk, free student e-mail accounts, online (class) grades, online (class) registration, online (class) schedules. Campuswide network is available.

STUDENT LIFE

Housing options: coed, cooperative, special housing for students with disabilities. Campus housing is university owned. Freshman campus housing is guaranteed.

Activities and organizations: drama/theater group, student-run newspaper, radio and television station, choral group, marching band, student government, national fraternities, national sororities.

Athletics Member NCAA. All Division I except football (Division I-A). ***Intercollegiate sports:*** baseball M(s), basketball M(s)/W(s), cross-country running M(s)/W(s), golf M(s)/W(s), gymnastics M(s)/W(s), ice hockey M(s)/W(s), soccer W(s), softball W(s), swimming and diving M(s)/W(s), tennis M(s)/W(s), track and field M(s)/W(s), volleyball W(s), wrestling M(s). ***Intramural sports:*** baseball M/W, basketball M/W, bowling M/W, crew M/W, football M/W, golf M/W, ice hockey M/W, rugby M/W, skiing (cross-country) M/W, skiing (downhill) M/W, soccer M/W, softball M/W, tennis M/W, volleyball M/W, water polo M/W, wrestling M/W.

Campus security: 24-hour emergency response devices and patrols, student patrols, late-night transport/escort service, controlled dormitory access, safety/security orientation, security lighting.

Student services: health clinic, personal/psychological counseling, women's center, legal services.

COSTS & FINANCIAL AID

Costs (2014–15) ***Tuition:*** state resident $12,060 full-time, $464 per credit part-time; nonresident $19,310 full-time, $743 per credit part-time. Full-time tuition and fees vary according to program and reciprocity agreements. Part-time tuition and fees vary according to course load, program, and reciprocity agreements. ***Required fees:*** $1566 full-time. ***Room and board:*** $8920; room only: $4920. Room and board charges vary according to board plan, housing facility, and location. ***Payment plan:*** installment. ***Waivers:*** senior citizens.

Financial Aid Of all full-time matriculated undergraduates who enrolled in 2014, 19,106 applied for aid, 13,915 were judged to have need, 3,088 had their need fully met. In 2014, 1995 non-need-based awards were made. ***Average percent of need met:*** 72. ***Average financial aid package:*** $12,397. ***Average need-based loan:*** $4624. ***Average need-based gift aid:*** $9388. ***Average non-need-based aid:*** $4992. ***Average indebtedness upon graduation:*** $26,796.

APPLYING

Standardized Tests *Required:* SAT or ACT (for admission).

Options: electronic application, early admission, deferred entrance.

Application fee: $55.

Required: high school transcript. ***Recommended:*** minimum 2.0 GPA.

Application deadlines: rolling (freshmen), rolling (transfers).

Notification: continuous (freshmen), continuous (transfers).

CONTACT

Rachelle Hernandez, Director of Admissions, University of Minnesota, Twin Cities Campus, 240 Williamson, Minneapolis, MN 55455-0213. *Phone:* 612-625-2008. *Toll-free phone:* 800-752-1000. *Fax:* 612-626-1693. *E-mail:* admissions@tc.umn.edu.

University of Northwestern–St. Paul

St. Paul, Minnesota

http://www.unwsp.edu/

- **Independent nondenominational** comprehensive, founded 1902
- **Suburban** 107-acre campus with easy access to Minneapolis-St. Paul
- **Endowment** $16.1 million
- **Coed** 3,222 undergraduate students, 60% full-time, 60% women, 40% men
- **Moderately difficult** entrance level, 70% of applicants were admitted

UNDERGRAD STUDENTS

1,931 full-time, 1,291 part-time. Students come from 30 states and territories; 6 other countries; 23% are from out of state; 3% Black or African American, non-Hispanic/Latino; 3% Hispanic/Latino; 4% Asian, non-Hispanic/Latino; 0.1% American Indian or Alaska Native, non-Hispanic/Latino; 2% Two or more races, non-Hispanic/Latino; 2% Race/ethnicity unknown; 0.5% international; 3% transferred in; 65% live on campus.

Freshmen

Admission: 1,356 applied, 943 admitted, 331 enrolled. ***Average high school GPA:*** 3.5. ***Test scores:*** SAT critical reading scores over 500: 90%; SAT math scores over 500: 79%; ACT scores over 18: 97%; SAT critical reading scores over 600: 55%; SAT math scores over 600: 38%; ACT scores over 24: 55%; SAT critical reading scores over 700: 7%; SAT math scores over 700: 3%; ACT scores over 30: 15%.

Retention: 80% of full-time freshmen returned.

FACULTY

Total: 208, 45% full-time, 79% with terminal degrees.

Student/faculty ratio: 18:1.

ACADEMICS
Calendar: semesters. *Degrees:* certificates, associate, bachelor's, master's, and postbachelor's certificates.

Special study options: academic remediation for entering students, adult/continuing education programs, advanced placement credit, distance learning, double majors, honors programs, independent study, internships, off-campus study, part-time degree program, services for LD students, student-designed majors, study abroad, summer session for credit. ***ROTC:*** Army (c), Air Force (c).

Unusual degree programs: 3-2 engineering with University of Minnesota-Twin Cities; BA/MDiv in pastoral studies.

Computers: 200 computers/terminals and 1,350 ports are available on campus for general student use. Students can access the following: campus intranet, computer help desk, free student e-mail accounts, online (class) grades, online (class) registration, online (class) schedules, network file space, personal web site, integrated student portal, b/w and color printing, virtual labs. Campuswide network is available. 100% of college-owned or -operated housing units are wired for high-speed Internet access. Wireless service is available via classrooms, computer centers, computer labs, dorm rooms, learning centers, libraries, student centers.

STUDENT LIFE
Housing options: on-campus residence required through junior year; men-only, women-only, special housing for students with disabilities. Campus housing is university owned. Freshman campus housing is guaranteed.

Activities and organizations: drama/theater group, student-run newspaper, radio and television station, choral group, Northwestern Student Association (student government), The Gathering (religious group), Student Missions Fellowship, Guardian Angels, Outreach Ministries.

Athletics Member NCAA, NCCAA. All NCAA Division III. ***Intercollegiate sports:*** baseball M, basketball M/W, cross-country running M/W, football M, golf M/W, ice hockey M(c), lacrosse W, soccer M/W, softball W, tennis M/W, track and field M/W, volleyball M(c)/W. ***Intramural sports:*** basketball M/W, football M/W, softball M/W, table tennis M/W, tennis M/W, volleyball M/W.

Campus security: 24-hour emergency response devices and patrols, late-night transport/escort service, controlled dormitory access, gated access to main campus, emergency notification system.

Student services: health clinic, personal/psychological counseling.

COSTS & FINANCIAL AID
Costs (2015–16) ***Comprehensive fee:*** $37,824 includes full-time tuition ($28,390), mandatory fees ($480), and room and board ($8954). Full-time tuition and fees vary according to course load. Part-time tuition: $1210 per credit. Part-time tuition and fees vary according to course load. ***College room only:*** $5350. Room and board charges vary according to board plan and student level. ***Payment plan:*** installment. ***Waivers:*** children of alumni and employees or children of employees.

Financial Aid Of all full-time matriculated undergraduates who enrolled in 2012, 1,661 applied for aid, 1,529 were judged to have need, 166 had their need fully met. 187 Federal Work-Study jobs (averaging $4151). 281 state and other part-time jobs (averaging $4267). In 2012, 272 non-need-based awards were made. ***Average percent of need met:*** 67. ***Average financial aid package:*** $18,390. ***Average need-based loan:*** $4468. ***Average need-based gift aid:*** $13,504. ***Average non-need-based aid:*** $8213. ***Average indebtedness upon graduation:*** $24,299.

APPLYING
Standardized Tests *Required:* SAT or ACT (for admission).

Options: electronic application, early admission, deferred entrance.

Required: essay or personal statement, high school transcript, minimum 2.0 GPA, 2 letters of recommendation, lifestyle agreement, statement of Christian faith. ***Required for some:*** interview. ***Recommended:*** minimum 3.0 GPA.

Application deadlines: 8/1 (freshmen), 8/1 (out-of-state freshmen), 8/1 (transfers).

Notification: continuous (freshmen), continuous (out-of-state freshmen), continuous (transfers).

CONTACT
Admissions, Admissions, University of Northwestern–St. Paul, Officer of Admissions, 3003 Snelling Avenue North, 212 Nazareth Hall, St. Paul, MN 55113-1598. *Phone:* 651-631-5111. *Toll-free phone:* 800-827-6827. *Fax:* 651-631-5680. *E-mail:* admissions@unwsp.edu.

University of St. Thomas
St. Paul, Minnesota
http://www.stthomas.edu/

- **Independent Roman Catholic** university, founded 1885
- **Urban** 78-acre campus with easy access to Minneapolis-St. Paul
- **Coed** 6,234 undergraduate students, 96% full-time, 46% women, 54% men
- **Moderately difficult** entrance level, 87% of applicants were admitted

UNDERGRAD STUDENTS
5,969 full-time, 265 part-time. 20% are from out of state; 2% Black or African American, non-Hispanic/Latino; 5% Hispanic/Latino; 3% Asian, non-Hispanic/Latino; 0.1% American Indian or Alaska Native, non-Hispanic/Latino; 3% Two or more races, non-Hispanic/Latino; 1% Race/ethnicity unknown; 3% international; 4% transferred in; 41% live on campus.

Freshmen
Admission: 5,343 applied, 4,628 admitted, 1,409 enrolled. ***Average high school GPA:*** 3.6. ***Test scores:*** SAT critical reading scores over 500: 95%; SAT math scores over 500: 82%; ACT scores over 18: 100%; SAT critical reading scores over 600: 51%; SAT math scores over 600: 54%; ACT scores over 24: 78%; SAT critical reading scores over 700: 19%; SAT math scores over 700: 14%; ACT scores over 30: 19%.

Retention: 85% of full-time freshmen returned.

FACULTY
Student/faculty ratio: 15:1.

ACADEMICS
Calendar: 4-1-4. *Degrees:* certificates, bachelor's, master's, doctoral, post-master's, and postbachelor's certificates.

Special study options: advanced placement credit, double majors, English as a second language, honors programs, independent study, internships, off-campus study, part-time degree program, services for LD students, student-designed majors, study abroad, summer session for credit. ***ROTC:*** Army (c), Navy (c), Air Force (b).

Unusual degree programs: 3-2 engineering with University of Notre Dame, Washington University in St. Louis, University of Minnesota-Twin Cities, Kettering University.

Computers: Students can access the following: online (class) registration. Campuswide network is available. Wireless service is available via entire campus.

STUDENT LIFE
Housing options: men-only, women-only. Campus housing is university owned. Freshman applicants given priority for college housing.

Activities and organizations: drama/theater group, student-run newspaper, radio and television station, choral group.

Athletics Member NCAA. All Division III. ***Intercollegiate sports:*** baseball M, basketball M/W, cross-country running M/W, football M, golf M/W, ice hockey M/W, lacrosse M(c)/W(c), soccer M/W, softball W, swimming and diving M/W, tennis M/W, volleyball W. ***Intramural sports:*** badminton M/W, basketball M/W, crew M(c)/W(c), golf M/W, racquetball M/W, sailing M(c)/W, skiing (downhill) M(c)/W(c), soccer M/W, table tennis M/W, tennis M/W, track and field M(c)/W(c), volleyball M/W.

Campus security: 24-hour emergency response devices and patrols, late-night transport/escort service, controlled dormitory access.

Student services: health clinic, personal/psychological counseling, women's center, legal services.

COSTS & FINANCIAL AID
Costs (2014–15) ***Tuition:*** $35,872 full-time, $1121 per credit hour part-time. ***Required fees:*** $810 full-time. ***Room only:*** $5770. Room and board charges vary according to board plan and housing facility. ***Payment plan:*** installment. ***Waivers:*** senior citizens and employees or children of employees.

Financial Aid Of all full-time matriculated undergraduates who enrolled in 2014, 4,178 applied for aid, 3,411 were judged to have need, 505 had their need fully met. 1,348 Federal Work-Study jobs (averaging $2904). 810 state and other part-time jobs (averaging $2671). In 2014, 678 non-need-based awards were made. ***Average percent of need met:*** 82. ***Average financial aid package:*** $24,513. ***Average need-based loan:*** $8135. ***Average need-based gift aid:*** $18,352. ***Average non-need-based aid:*** $15,098. ***Average indebtedness upon graduation:*** $37,131.

APPLYING

Standardized Tests *Required:* SAT or ACT (for admission).

Options: electronic application, deferred entrance.

Required: essay or personal statement, high school transcript. *Recommended:* interview.

Application deadlines: rolling (freshmen), rolling (transfers).

Notification: continuous (freshmen), continuous (transfers).

CONTACT

University of St. Thomas, 2115 Summit Avenue, St. Paul, MN 55105-1096. *Phone:* 651-962-6150. *Toll-free phone:* 800-328-6819.

Walden University

Minneapolis, Minnesota

http://www.waldenu.edu/

- **Proprietary** university, founded 1970, part of Laureate
- **Coed** 8,960 undergraduate students, 9% full-time, 76% women, 24% men
- 98% of applicants were admitted

UNDERGRAD STUDENTS

817 full-time, 8,143 part-time. Students come from 57 states and territories; 80 other countries; 97% are from out of state; 33% Black or African American, non-Hispanic/Latino; 7% Hispanic/Latino; 2% Asian, non-Hispanic/Latino; 0.2% Native Hawaiian or other Pacific Islander, non-Hispanic/Latino; 0.4% American Indian or Alaska Native, non-Hispanic/Latino; 2% Two or more races, non-Hispanic/Latino; 15% Race/ethnicity unknown; 1% international; 20% transferred in.

Freshmen

Admission: 696 applied, 682 admitted, 359 enrolled.

FACULTY

Total: 3,222, 10% full-time, 90% with terminal degrees.

ACADEMICS

Calendar: quarter/semester depending on program. *Degrees:* certificates, bachelor's, master's, doctoral, post-master's, and postbachelor's certificates.

Special study options: academic remediation for entering students, accelerated degree program, distance learning, honors programs, internships, off-campus study, part-time degree program, services for LD students, student-designed majors, study abroad, summer session for credit.

Computers: Students can access the following: free student e-mail accounts, online (class) grades, online (class) registration, online (class) schedules.

STUDENT LIFE

Student services: personal/psychological counseling, legal services.

COSTS & FINANCIAL AID

Costs (2014–15) ***Tuition:*** $13,950 full-time, $310 per credit hour part-time. Full-time tuition and fees vary according to course level, course load, degree level, and program. Part-time tuition and fees vary according to course level, course load, degree level, and program. ***Required fees:*** $360 full-time, $120 per term part-time. ***Payment plan:*** installment. ***Waivers:*** employees or children of employees.

Financial Aid Of all full-time matriculated undergraduates who enrolled in 2009, 908 applied for aid, 878 were judged to have need, 7 had their need fully met. In 2009, 17 non-need-based awards were made. ***Average percent of need met:*** 26. ***Average financial aid package:*** $6301. ***Average need-based loan:*** $3755. ***Average need-based gift aid:*** $3222. ***Average non-need-based aid:*** $1225.

APPLYING

Options: electronic application, deferred entrance.

Required: high school transcript.

Application deadlines: rolling (freshmen), rolling (out-of-state freshmen), rolling (transfers).

Notification: continuous (freshmen), continuous (out-of-state freshmen), continuous (transfers).

CONTACT

Walden University, 100 Washington South, Suite 900, Minneapolis, MN 55401. *Phone:* 480-289-2149. *Toll-free phone:* 866-492-5336.

Winona State University

Winona, Minnesota

http://www.winona.edu/

- **State-supported** comprehensive, founded 1858, part of Minnesota State Colleges and Universities System
- **Small-town** 125-acre campus
- **Coed** 8,109 undergraduate students, 89% full-time, 62% women, 38% men
- **Moderately difficult** entrance level, 63% of applicants were admitted

UNDERGRAD STUDENTS

7,202 full-time, 907 part-time. Students come from 46 other countries; 31% are from out of state; 2% Black or African American, non-Hispanic/Latino; 2% Hispanic/Latino; 2% Asian, non-Hispanic/Latino; 0.1% Native Hawaiian or other Pacific Islander, non-Hispanic/Latino; 0.1% American Indian or Alaska Native, non-Hispanic/Latino; 2% Two or more races, non-Hispanic/Latino; 1% Race/ethnicity unknown; 3% international; 8% transferred in; 28% live on campus.

Freshmen

Admission: 7,099 applied, 4,475 admitted, 1,648 enrolled. ***Average high school GPA:*** 3.28. ***Test scores:*** ACT scores over 18: 97%; ACT scores over 24: 37%; ACT scores over 30: 2%.

Retention: 76% of full-time freshmen returned.

FACULTY

Total: 620, 48% full-time, 39% with terminal degrees.

Student/faculty ratio: 20:1.

ACADEMICS

Calendar: semesters. *Degrees:* associate, bachelor's, master's, doctoral, post-master's, and postbachelor's certificates.

Special study options: academic remediation for entering students, accelerated degree program, adult/continuing education programs, advanced placement credit, distance learning, double majors, English as a second language, independent study, internships, off-campus study, part-time degree program, services for LD students, student-designed majors, study abroad, summer session for credit. ***ROTC:*** Army (c).

Computers: 50 computers/terminals and 19,500 ports are available on campus for general student use. Students can access the following: campus intranet, computer help desk, free student e-mail accounts, online (class) grades, online (class) registration, online (class) schedules. Campuswide network is available. 100% of college-owned or -operated housing units are wired for high-speed Internet access. Wireless service is available via entire campus.

STUDENT LIFE

Housing options: coed, men-only, women-only, special housing for students with disabilities. Campus housing is university owned and leased by the school. Freshman campus housing is guaranteed.

Activities and organizations: drama/theater group, student-run newspaper, radio station, choral group, University Program Activities Committee, Student Senate, Residence Hall Association, Inter Varsity, national fraternities, national sororities.

Athletics Member NCAA. All Division II. ***Intercollegiate sports:*** baseball M(s), basketball M(s)/W(s), cross-country running M(s)/W(s), football M(s), golf M(s)/W(s), gymnastics W, soccer W(s), softball W(s), tennis W(s), track and field W(s), volleyball W(s). ***Intramural sports:*** badminton M/W, baseball W(c), basketball M/W, bowling M(c)/W(c), cheerleading M(c)/W(c), fencing M(c)/W(c), ice hockey M(c)/W(c), racquetball M(c)/W(c), rugby M/W, skiing (cross-country) M/W, skiing (downhill) M/W, soccer M/W, softball M/W, swimming and diving M/W, tennis M(c)/W(c), ultimate Frisbee M(c)/W(c), volleyball M/W, wrestling M(c)/W(c).

Campus security: 24-hour emergency response devices and patrols, student patrols, late-night transport/escort service, controlled dormitory access, security cameras.

Student services: health clinic, personal/psychological counseling.

COSTS & FINANCIAL AID

Costs (2014–15) ***Tuition:*** state resident $6860 full-time, $227 per credit part-time; nonresident $12,360 full-time, $412 per credit part-time. Full-time tuition and fees vary according to location, program, and reciprocity agreements. Part-time tuition and fees vary according to course load, location, program, and reciprocity agreements. ***Required fees:*** $1890 full-time. ***Room and board:*** $7890. Room and board charges vary according to board plan, housing facility, and location. ***Payment plan:*** installment. ***Waivers:*** employees or children of employees.

Financial Aid Of all full-time matriculated undergraduates who enrolled in 2013, 5,913 applied for aid, 4,456 were judged to have need, 500 had their need fully met. 184 Federal Work-Study jobs (averaging $2138). 321 state and other part-time jobs (averaging $2330). In 2013, 802 non-need-based awards were made. ***Average percent of need met:*** 50. ***Average financial aid package:*** $7426. ***Average need-based loan:*** $3968. ***Average need-based gift aid:*** $4979. ***Average non-need-based aid:*** $3145. ***Average indebtedness upon graduation:*** $35,131.

APPLYING

Standardized Tests *Required:* SAT or ACT (for admission).

Options: electronic application, deferred entrance.

Application fee: $20.

Required: high school transcript, class rank. ***Required for some:*** minimum 3.0 GPA.

Application deadlines: 7/1 (freshmen), 7/1 (out-of-state freshmen), 7/1 (transfers).

Notification: continuous (freshmen), continuous (out-of-state freshmen), continuous (transfers).

CONTACT

Carl Stange, Director of Admissions, Winona State University, 170 West Sanborn, Winona, MN 55987. *Phone:* 507-457-5100. *Toll-free phone:* 800-DIAL WSU. *Fax:* 507-457-5620. *E-mail:* admissions@winona.edu.

MISSISSIPPI

Alcorn State University

Lorman, Mississippi

http://www.alcorn.edu/

- **State-supported** comprehensive, founded 1871, part of Mississippi Institutions of Higher Learning
- **Rural** 1756-acre campus
- **Endowment** $13.1 million
- **Coed** 3,006 undergraduate students, 85% full-time, 64% women, 36% men
- **Moderately difficult** entrance level, 78% of applicants were admitted

UNDERGRAD STUDENTS

2,570 full-time, 436 part-time. Students come from 33 states and territories; 15 other countries; 13% are from out of state; 94% Black or African American, non-Hispanic/Latino; 0.4% Hispanic/Latino; 0.2% Asian, non-Hispanic/Latino; 0.3% Native Hawaiian or other Pacific Islander, non-Hispanic/Latino; 0.1% American Indian or Alaska Native, non-Hispanic/Latino; 2% Two or more races, non-Hispanic/Latino; 1% international; 4% transferred in; 53% live on campus.

Freshmen

Admission: 2,078 applied, 1,630 admitted, 517 enrolled. ***Average high school GPA:*** 2.99. ***Test scores:*** SAT critical reading scores over 500: 19%; SAT math scores over 500: 27%; ACT scores over 18: 52%; SAT critical reading scores over 600: 3%; SAT math scores over 600: 5%; ACT scores over 24: 8%.

Retention: 76% of full-time freshmen returned.

FACULTY

Total: 218, 75% full-time, 64% with terminal degrees.

Student/faculty ratio: 17:1.

ACADEMICS

Calendar: semesters. *Degrees:* associate, bachelor's, master's, and post-master's certificates.

Special study options: academic remediation for entering students, accelerated degree program, adult/continuing education programs, advanced placement credit, cooperative education, distance learning, double majors, honors programs, independent study, internships, off-campus study, part-time degree program, study abroad, summer session for credit. ***ROTC:*** Army (b).

Computers: 500 computers/terminals and 2,500 ports are available on campus for general student use. Students can access the following: campus intranet, computer help desk, free student e-mail accounts, online (class) grades, online (class) registration, online (class) schedules, online payment; online transcript request. Campuswide network is available. 100% of college-owned or -operated housing units are wired for high-speed Internet access. Wireless service is available via classrooms, computer centers, computer labs, dorm rooms, learning centers, libraries, student centers.

STUDENT LIFE

Housing options: men-only, women-only. Campus housing is university owned. Freshman campus housing is guaranteed.

Activities and organizations: drama/theater group, student-run newspaper, radio and television station, choral group, marching band, marching band, Gospel Choir, inter-faith choir, national fraternities, national sororities.

Athletics Member NCAA. All Division I. ***Intercollegiate sports:*** baseball M(s), basketball M(s)/W(s), cross-country running M(s)/W(s), football M(s), golf M(s)/W(s), soccer W(s), softball W(s), tennis M(s)/W(s), track and field M(s)/W(s), volleyball W(s). ***Intramural sports:*** basketball M/W, football M.

Campus security: 24-hour emergency response devices and patrols, late-night transport/escort service.

Student services: health clinic, personal/psychological counseling.

COSTS & FINANCIAL AID

Costs (2014–15) ***Tuition:*** state resident $6192 full-time; nonresident $15,426 full-time. ***Room and board:*** $8650; room only: $5902. ***Payment plan:*** installment. ***Waivers:*** employees or children of employees.

Financial Aid Of all full-time matriculated undergraduates who enrolled in 2014, 1,650 applied for aid, 1,591 were judged to have need, 138 had their need fully met. 276 Federal Work-Study jobs (averaging $1172). In 2014, 491 non-need-based awards were made. ***Average percent of need met:*** 48. ***Average financial aid package:*** $15,322. ***Average need-based loan:*** $4168. ***Average need-based gift aid:*** $5388. ***Average non-need-based aid:*** $7556. ***Average indebtedness upon graduation:*** $34,725.

APPLYING

Standardized Tests *Required:* SAT or ACT (for admission).

Options: electronic application, deferred entrance.

Required: high school transcript, minimum 2.0 GPA.

Application deadlines: rolling (freshmen), rolling (transfers).

Notification: continuous (freshmen), continuous (transfers).

CONTACT

Mrs. Kantangelia Tenner, Director of Admissions, Alcorn State University, 1000 ASU Drive, #300, Alcorn State, MS 39096-7500. *Phone:* 601-877-6147. *Toll-free phone:* 800-222-6790. *Fax:* 601-877-6347. *E-mail:* ksampson@alcorn.edu.

Belhaven University

Jackson, Mississippi

http://www.belhaven.edu/

- **Independent Presbyterian** comprehensive, founded 1883
- **Urban** 42-acre campus
- **Endowment** $5.0 million
- **Coed** 2,567 undergraduate students, 50% full-time, 64% women, 36% men
- **Moderately difficult** entrance level, 72% of applicants were admitted

UNDERGRAD STUDENTS
1,289 full-time, 1,278 part-time. Students come from 49 states and territories; 38% are from out of state; 48% Black or African American, non-Hispanic/Latino; 5% Hispanic/Latino; 2% Asian, non-Hispanic/Latino; 0.2% Native Hawaiian or other Pacific Islander, non-Hispanic/Latino; 0.6% American Indian or Alaska Native, non-Hispanic/Latino; 2% Two or more races, non-Hispanic/Latino; 7% Race/ethnicity unknown; 18% transferred in; 22% live on campus.

Freshmen
Admission: 2,264 applied, 1,623 admitted, 343 enrolled. ***Average high school GPA:*** 3.1. ***Test scores:*** SAT critical reading scores over 500: 81%; SAT math scores over 500: 65%; ACT scores over 18: 84%; SAT critical reading scores over 600: 20%; SAT math scores over 600: 8%; ACT scores over 24: 24%; SAT critical reading scores over 700: 9%; ACT scores over 30: 2%.

Retention: 66% of full-time freshmen returned.

FACULTY
Total: 356, 29% full-time, 19% with terminal degrees.

Student/faculty ratio: 10:1.

ACADEMICS
Calendar: semesters. *Degrees:* certificates, associate, bachelor's, and master's.

Special study options: academic remediation for entering students, accelerated degree program, adult/continuing education programs, advanced placement credit, distance learning, double majors, English as a second language, honors programs, independent study, internships, off-campus study, part-time degree program, student-designed majors, study abroad, summer session for credit. ***ROTC:*** Army (c), Air Force (c).

Unusual degree programs: 3-2 engineering with Mississippi State University.

Computers: 36 computers/terminals are available on campus for general student use. Students can access the following: campus intranet, computer help desk, free student e-mail accounts, online (class) grades, online (class) registration, online (class) schedules. Campuswide network is available. 100% of college-owned or -operated housing units are wired for high-speed Internet access. Wireless service is available via classrooms, computer labs, dorm rooms, libraries, student centers.

STUDENT LIFE
Housing options: on-campus residence required through sophomore year; men-only, women-only. Campus housing is university owned. Freshman campus housing is guaranteed.

Activities and organizations: drama/theater group, student-run newspaper, choral group, marching band, Belhaven Activities Team, intramurals, Reformed University Fellowship, Quartertone, Sports Medicine: Exercise Science Club.

Athletics Member NAIA. ***Intercollegiate sports:*** baseball M(s), basketball M(s)/W(s), cross-country running M(s)/W(s), football M(s), golf M(s)/W(s), soccer M(s)/W(s), softball W(s), tennis M(s)/W(s), volleyball W(s). ***Intramural sports:*** basketball M/W, football M/W, soccer M/W, softball M/W, volleyball M/W.

Campus security: 24-hour emergency response devices and patrols, late-night transport/escort service, controlled dormitory access.

Student services: health clinic, personal/psychological counseling.

COSTS & FINANCIAL AID
Costs (2015–16) ***Comprehensive fee:*** $29,626 includes full-time tuition ($21,626) and room and board ($8000). Part-time tuition: $425 per hour. Part-time tuition and fees vary according to course load. ***Room and board:*** Room and board charges vary according to housing facility. ***Payment plan:*** installment. ***Waivers:*** employees or children of employees.

Financial Aid Of all full-time matriculated undergraduates who enrolled in 2014, 1,051 applied for aid, 986 were judged to have need, 67 had their need fully met. In 2014, 257 non-need-based awards were made. ***Average percent of need met:*** 57. ***Average financial aid package:*** $17,067. ***Average need-based loan:*** $4203. ***Average need-based gift aid:*** $12,178. ***Average non-need-based aid:*** $13,190. ***Average indebtedness upon graduation:*** $26,800.

APPLYING
Standardized Tests *Required:* SAT or ACT (for admission).

Options: electronic application, early admission, deferred entrance.

Application fee: $25.

Required: high school transcript, minimum 2.0 GPA, 1 letter of recommendation. ***Required for some:*** essay or personal statement, interview.

Application deadlines: rolling (freshmen), rolling (out-of-state freshmen), rolling (transfers).

Notification: continuous (freshmen), continuous (out-of-state freshmen), continuous (transfers).

CONTACT
Ms. Suzanne T. Sullivan, Assistant Vice President for Traditional and Online Admissions, Belhaven University, 1500 Peachtree Street, Jackson, MS 39202. *Phone:* 601-968-5940. *Toll-free phone:* 800-960-5940. *Fax:* 601-968-8946. *E-mail:* admission@belhaven.edu.

Blue Mountain College
Blue Mountain, Mississippi
http://www.bmc.edu/

- **Independent Southern Baptist** comprehensive, founded 1873
- **Rural** 44-acre campus with easy access to Memphis
- **Endowment** $13.3 million
- **Coed** 520 undergraduate students, 89% full-time, 59% women, 41% men
- **Moderately difficult** entrance level, 55% of applicants were admitted

UNDERGRAD STUDENTS
463 full-time, 57 part-time. Students come from 13 states and territories; 4 other countries; 21% are from out of state; 10% Black or African American, non-Hispanic/Latino; 2% Hispanic/Latino; 0.8% Asian, non-Hispanic/Latino; 0.2% American Indian or Alaska Native, non-Hispanic/Latino; 0.4% Two or more races, non-Hispanic/Latino; 0.2% Race/ethnicity unknown; 2% international; 18% transferred in; 56% live on campus.

Freshmen
Admission: 298 applied, 164 admitted, 76 enrolled. ***Average high school GPA:*** 3.51. ***Test scores:*** ACT scores over 18: 76%; ACT scores over 24: 33%; ACT scores over 30: 7%.

Retention: 63% of full-time freshmen returned.

FACULTY
Total: 49, 69% full-time, 69% with terminal degrees.

Student/faculty ratio: 14:1.

ACADEMICS
Calendar: semesters. *Degrees:* bachelor's and master's.

Special study options: academic remediation for entering students, accelerated degree program, advanced placement credit, distance learning, double majors, honors programs, internships, part-time degree program, summer session for credit.

Unusual degree programs: 3-2 nursing with Baptist College of Health Sciences, Union University; Baptist College of Health Sciences (Other Medical Related Fields).

Computers: 52 computers/terminals are available on campus for general student use. Students can access the following: computer help desk, free student e-mail accounts, online (class) grades, online (class) registration, online (class) schedules. Campuswide network is available. 100% of college-owned or -operated housing units are wired for high-speed Internet access. Wireless service is available via classrooms, computer centers, computer labs, dorm rooms, learning centers, libraries, student centers.

STUDENT LIFE
Housing options: on-campus residence required through senior year; men-only, women-only. Campus housing is university owned.

Activities and organizations: drama/theater group, choral group, Baptist Student Union, Student Body Association, Intramural Association, Ministerial Association, Mississippi Association of Educators/Student Program.

Athletics Member NAIA. ***Intercollegiate sports:*** baseball M(s), basketball M(s)/W(s), cross-country running M(s)/W(s), golf M(s)/W(s), softball W(s). ***Intramural sports:*** basketball M/W, football M, soccer M, softball M/W, swimming and diving W, table tennis W, tennis W, track and field M/W, ultimate Frisbee M, volleyball M/W.

Campus security: 24-hour emergency response devices and patrols, controlled dormitory access.

COSTS & FINANCIAL AID

Costs (2014–15) ***Comprehensive fee:*** $15,334 includes full-time tuition ($9240), mandatory fees ($1294), and room and board ($4800). Full-time tuition and fees vary according to course load, degree level, and program. Part-time tuition: $308 per hour. Part-time tuition and fees vary according to course load, degree level, and program. ***Required fees:*** $509 per term part-time. ***Room and board:*** Room and board charges vary according to gender, housing facility, and location. ***Payment plans:*** installment, deferred payment. ***Waivers:*** employees or children of employees.

Financial Aid Of all full-time matriculated undergraduates who enrolled in 2014, 451 applied for aid, 374 were judged to have need, 324 had their need fully met. 49 Federal Work-Study jobs (averaging $812). 52 state and other part-time jobs (averaging $834). In 2014, 385 non-need-based awards were made. ***Average percent of need met:*** 59. ***Average financial aid package:*** $10,156. ***Average need-based loan:*** $5005. ***Average need-based gift aid:*** $3700. ***Average non-need-based aid:*** $2616. ***Average indebtedness upon graduation:*** $24,571.

APPLYING

Standardized Tests *Required:* SAT or ACT (for admission).

Options: electronic application, deferred entrance.

Application fee: $10.

Required for some: high school transcript. ***Recommended:*** minimum 2.0 GPA.

Application deadlines: rolling (freshmen), rolling (out-of-state freshmen), rolling (transfers).

Notification: continuous (freshmen), continuous (out-of-state freshmen), continuous (transfers).

CONTACT

Mr. Lynn Gibson, Vice President for Enrollment Services, Blue Mountain College, PO Box 160, Blue Mountain, MS 38610-0160. *Phone:* 662-685-4771 Ext. 176. *Toll-free phone:* 800-235-0136. *Fax:* 662-685-4776. *E-mail:* lgibson@bmc.edu.

Delta State University

Cleveland, Mississippi

http://www.deltastate.edu/

- **State-supported** comprehensive, founded 1924, part of Mississippi Institutions of Higher Learning
- **Small-town** 274-acre campus
- **Coed** 2,778 undergraduate students, 83% full-time, 61% women, 39% men
- **Noncompetitive** entrance level, 92% of applicants were admitted

UNDERGRAD STUDENTS

2,308 full-time, 470 part-time. Students come from 31 states and territories; 31 other countries; 10% are from out of state; 35% Black or African American, non-Hispanic/Latino; 1% Hispanic/Latino; 0.7% Asian, non-Hispanic/Latino; 0.1% Native Hawaiian or other Pacific Islander, non-Hispanic/Latino; 0.1% American Indian or Alaska Native, non-Hispanic/Latino; 0.7% Two or more races, non-Hispanic/Latino; 0.4% Race/ethnicity unknown; 3% international; 17% transferred in; 25% live on campus.

Freshmen

Admission: 496 applied, 458 admitted, 419 enrolled.

Retention: 67% of full-time freshmen returned.

FACULTY

Total: 256, 71% full-time, 58% with terminal degrees.

Student/faculty ratio: 14:1.

ACADEMICS

Calendar: semesters. *Degrees:* bachelor's, master's, doctoral, and post-master's certificates.

Special study options: academic remediation for entering students, adult/continuing education programs, advanced placement credit, cooperative education, distance learning, double majors, freshman honors college, honors programs, independent study, internships, part-time degree program, services for LD students, summer session for credit.

ROTC: Army (b).

Computers: 533 computers/terminals are available on campus for general student use. Students can access the following: campus intranet, computer help desk, free student e-mail accounts, online (class) grades, online (class) registration, online (class) schedules. Campuswide network is available. 100% of college-owned or -operated housing units are wired for high-speed Internet access. Wireless service is available via classrooms, computer centers, dorm rooms, libraries, student centers.

STUDENT LIFE

Housing options: on-campus residence required for freshman year; men-only, women-only, special housing for students with disabilities. Campus housing is university owned. Freshman campus housing is guaranteed.

Activities and organizations: drama/theater group, student-run newspaper, choral group, marching band, Student Government Association, Student Alumni Association, Baptist Student Union, Union Program Council, Delta Volunteers, national fraternities, national sororities.

Athletics Member NCAA. All Division II. ***Intercollegiate sports:*** baseball M(s), basketball M(s)/W(s), cheerleading M(s)/W(s), cross-country running W(s), football M(s), golf M(s), soccer M(s)/W(s), softball W(s), swimming and diving M(s)/W(s), tennis M(s)/W(s). ***Intramural sports:*** archery M/W, badminton M/W, basketball M/W, bowling M/W, cross-country running M/W, football M/W, golf M/W, racquetball M/W, soccer M/W, softball M/W, swimming and diving M/W, table tennis M/W, tennis M/W, ultimate Frisbee M/W, volleyball M/W.

Campus security: 24-hour emergency response devices and patrols, late-night transport/escort service, controlled dormitory access.

Student services: health clinic, personal/psychological counseling.

COSTS & FINANCIAL AID

Costs (2014–15) ***Tuition:*** state resident $6012 full-time, $251 per hour part-time; nonresident $6012 full-time, $251 per hour part-time. Part-time tuition and fees vary according to course load. ***Required fees:*** $550 full-time, $376 per year part-time. ***Room and board:*** $7200; room only: $7200. Room and board charges vary according to housing facility. ***Payment plan:*** installment. ***Waivers:*** children of alumni, senior citizens, and employees or children of employees.

Financial Aid Of all full-time matriculated undergraduates who enrolled in 2014, 219 Federal Work-Study jobs (averaging $635). 126 state and other part-time jobs (averaging $4348). ***Average financial aid package:*** $4288. ***Average need-based gift aid:*** $2552.

APPLYING

Standardized Tests *Required:* ACT (for admission). *Recommended:* SAT or ACT (for admission).

Options: electronic application, deferred entrance.

Application fee: $25.

Required: high school transcript, minimum 2.0 GPA. ***Required for some:*** interview for art, music majors.

Application deadlines: rolling (freshmen), rolling (out-of-state freshmen), rolling (transfers).

Notification: continuous (freshmen), continuous (out-of-state freshmen), continuous (transfers).

CONTACT

Mr. Chris Gaines, Director of Recruiting, Delta State University, 1003 West Sunflower Road, Kent Wyatt Hall Office of Admissions, Cleveland, MS 38733. *Phone:* 662-8464020. *Toll-free phone:* 800-468-6378. *E-mail:* admissions@deltastate.edu.

ITT Technical Institute

Madison, Mississippi

http://www.itt-tech.edu/

- **Proprietary** 4-year, part of ITT Educational Services, Inc.
- **Coed**
- **Minimally difficult** entrance level

ACADEMICS

Calendar: quarters. *Degrees:* associate and bachelor's.

STUDENT LIFE
Housing options: college housing not available.

CONTACT
Director of Recruitment, ITT Technical Institute, 382 Galleria Parkway, Suite 100, Madison, MS 39110. *Phone:* 601-607-4500. *Toll-free phone:* 800-209-2521.

Jackson State University

Jackson, Mississippi

http://www.jsums.edu/

- **State-supported** university, founded 1877, part of Mississippi Institutions of Higher Learning
- **Urban** 250-acre campus
- **Endowment** $16.6 million
- **Coed** 7,199 undergraduate students, 83% full-time, 63% women, 37% men
- **Minimally difficult** entrance level, 26% of applicants were admitted

UNDERGRAD STUDENTS
5,959 full-time, 1,240 part-time. Students come from 41 states and territories; 60 other countries; 16% are from out of state; 91% Black or African American, non-Hispanic/Latino; 0.4% Hispanic/Latino; 0.3% Asian, non-Hispanic/Latino; 0.5% American Indian or Alaska Native, non-Hispanic/Latino; 1% Two or more races, non-Hispanic/Latino; 2% international; 11% transferred in; 32% live on campus.

Freshmen
Admission: 9,543 applied, 2,486 admitted, 1,196 enrolled. ***Average high school GPA:*** 2.85. ***Test scores:*** ACT scores over 18: 51%; ACT scores over 24: 14%; ACT scores over 30: 1%.

Retention: 78% of full-time freshmen returned.

FACULTY
Total: 535, 72% full-time, 69% with terminal degrees.

Student/faculty ratio: 17:1.

ACADEMICS
Calendar: semesters. *Degrees:* bachelor's, master's, doctoral, and post-master's certificates.

Special study options: academic remediation for entering students, adult/continuing education programs, advanced placement credit, cooperative education, distance learning, double majors, English as a second language, external degree program, honors programs, independent study, internships, off-campus study, part-time degree program, services for LD students, study abroad, summer session for credit. ***ROTC:*** Army (b), Air Force (b).

Computers: 1,119 computers/terminals are available on campus for general student use. Students can access the following: free student e-mail accounts, online (class) grades, online (class) registration, online (class) schedules. Campuswide network is available. 100% of college-owned or -operated housing units are wired for high-speed Internet access. Wireless service is available via classrooms, computer centers, computer labs, dorm rooms, learning centers, libraries, student centers.

STUDENT LIFE
Housing options: men-only, women-only, special housing for students with disabilities. Campus housing is university owned and leased by the school. Freshman applicants given priority for college housing.

Activities and organizations: drama/theater group, student-run newspaper, choral group, marching band, Student Government Association, Sonic Boom of the South, MADDRAMA, Interfaith, NAACP, national fraternities, national sororities.

Athletics Member NCAA. All Division I except football (Division I-AA). ***Intercollegiate sports:*** baseball M(s), basketball M(s)/W(s), bowling W(s), cross-country running M(s)/W(s), golf M(s)/W(s), soccer W(s), softball W(s), tennis M(s)/W(s), track and field M(s)/W(s), volleyball W(s). ***Intramural sports:*** basketball M/W, swimming and diving M/W, tennis M/W, volleyball W.

Campus security: 24-hour emergency response devices and patrols, late-night transport/escort service, controlled dormitory access.

Student services: health clinic, personal/psychological counseling.

COSTS & FINANCIAL AID
Costs (2014–15) ***Tuition:*** state resident $6602 full-time; nonresident $16,174 full-time. ***Room and board:*** Room and board charges vary according to housing facility. ***Payment plans:*** installment, deferred payment. ***Waivers:*** children of alumni and employees or children of employees.

Financial Aid Of all full-time matriculated undergraduates who enrolled in 2013, 5,606 applied for aid, 5,186 were judged to have need, 42 had their need fully met. 1,080 Federal Work-Study jobs (averaging $2368). In 2013, 195 non-need-based awards were made. ***Average percent of need met:*** 37. ***Average financial aid package:*** $10,504. ***Average need-based loan:*** $4032. ***Average need-based gift aid:*** $4724. ***Average non-need-based aid:*** $7004. ***Average indebtedness upon graduation:*** $31,576.

APPLYING
Standardized Tests *Required:* SAT or ACT (for admission).

Options: electronic application.

Required: high school transcript, minimum 2.0 GPA.

Application deadlines: 8/1 (freshmen), rolling (transfers).

Notification: continuous (freshmen), continuous (transfers).

CONTACT
Dr. Juanita M Morris, Director of Undergraduate Recruitment, Jackson State University, PO Box 18389, 1400 John R. Lynch Street, Jackson, MS 39217. *Phone:* 601-979-5845. *Toll-free phone:* 800-848-6817. *Fax:* 601-979-0360. *E-mail:* juanita.m.morris@jsums.edu.

Millsaps College

Jackson, Mississippi

http://www.millsaps.edu/

- **Independent United Methodist** comprehensive, founded 1890
- **Urban** 100-acre campus
- **Endowment** $123.3 million
- **Coed** 771 undergraduate students, 98% full-time, 49% women, 51% men
- **Moderately difficult** entrance level, 57% of applicants were admitted

UNDERGRAD STUDENTS
757 full-time, 14 part-time. Students come from 26 states and territories; 16 other countries; 55% are from out of state; 11% Black or African American, non-Hispanic/Latino; 2% Hispanic/Latino; 4% Asian, non-Hispanic/Latino; 0.8% American Indian or Alaska Native, non-Hispanic/Latino; 0.8% Two or more races, non-Hispanic/Latino; 3% Race/ethnicity unknown; 4% international; 4% transferred in; 88% live on campus.

Freshmen
Admission: 2,861 applied, 1,636 admitted, 236 enrolled. ***Average high school GPA:*** 3.68. ***Test scores:*** SAT critical reading scores over 500: 85%; SAT math scores over 500: 91%; ACT scores over 18: 100%; SAT critical reading scores over 600: 42%; SAT math scores over 600: 45%; ACT scores over 24: 71%; SAT critical reading scores over 700: 4%; SAT math scores over 700: 9%; ACT scores over 30: 19%.

Retention: 80% of full-time freshmen returned.

FACULTY
Total: 109, 79% full-time, 85% with terminal degrees.

Student/faculty ratio: 8:1.

ACADEMICS
Calendar: semesters. *Degrees:* bachelor's and master's.

Special study options: accelerated degree program, advanced placement credit, double majors, honors programs, independent study, internships, off-campus study, part-time degree program, services for LD students, student-designed majors, study abroad, summer session for credit. ***ROTC:*** Army (c), Air Force (c).

Unusual degree programs: 3-2 engineering with Auburn University, Columbia University, Vanderbilt University; nursing with University of Mississippi Medical Center School of Nursing, Vanderbilt University.

Computers: 150 computers/terminals are available on campus for general student use. Students can access the following: campus intranet, computer help desk, free student e-mail accounts, online (class) grades, online (class) registration, online (class) schedules, online transcripts. Campuswide network is available. 100% of college-owned or -operated

housing units are wired for high-speed Internet access. Wireless service is available via entire campus.

STUDENT LIFE

Housing options: on-campus residence required through sophomore year; coed, men-only, women-only, special housing for students with disabilities. Campus housing is university owned. Freshman campus housing is guaranteed.

Activities and organizations: drama/theater group, student-run newspaper, choral group, Campus Ministry Team, Student Body Association, SAPS (Campus Programming Board), Inter-fraternity/Panhellenic Councils, intramural sports, national fraternities, national sororities.

Athletics Member NCAA. All Division III. ***Intercollegiate sports:*** baseball M, basketball M/W, cross-country running M/W, football M, golf M/W, lacrosse M/W, soccer M/W, softball W, tennis M/W, track and field M/W, volleyball W. ***Intramural sports:*** basketball M/W, cheerleading W(c), fencing M(c)/W(c), football M/W, lacrosse W(c), soccer M/W, softball M/W, swimming and diving M(c)/W(c), ultimate Frisbee M(c)/W(c), volleyball M/W.

Campus security: 24-hour emergency response devices and patrols, student patrols, late-night transport/escort service, controlled dormitory access, self-defense education, lighted pathways.

Student services: health clinic, personal/psychological counseling.

COSTS & FINANCIAL AID

Costs (2014–15) ***Comprehensive fee:*** $45,860 includes full-time tuition ($31,872), mandatory fees ($2110), and room and board ($11,878). Part-time tuition: $982 per semester hour. Part-time tuition and fees vary according to course load. ***Required fees:*** $32 per semester hour part-time. ***College room only:*** $6704. Room and board charges vary according to housing facility. ***Payment plan:*** installment. ***Waivers:*** employees or children of employees.

Financial Aid Of all full-time matriculated undergraduates who enrolled in 2013, 508 applied for aid, 421 were judged to have need, 125 had their need fully met. In 2013, 293 non-need-based awards were made. ***Average percent of need met:*** 78. ***Average financial aid package:*** $27,915. ***Average need-based loan:*** $4965. ***Average need-based gift aid:*** $21,828. ***Average non-need-based aid:*** $19,564. ***Average indebtedness upon graduation:*** $27,926.

APPLYING

Standardized Tests *Required:* SAT or ACT (for admission).

Options: electronic application, early admission, early action, deferred entrance.

Required: essay or personal statement, high school transcript, minimum 2.5 GPA, 1 letter of recommendation, secondary school report. ***Required for some:*** interview.

Application deadlines: 2/1 (freshmen), 2/1 (out-of-state freshmen), 7/1 (transfers), 11/15 (early action).

Notification: continuous until 3/15 (freshmen), continuous until 3/15 (out-of-state freshmen), continuous until 3/15 (transfers), 1/15 (early action).

CONTACT

Dr. Robert Alexander, Millsaps College, 1701 North State Street, Jackson, MS 39210-0001. *Phone:* 601-974-1050. *Toll-free phone:* 800-352-1050. *Fax:* 601-974-1059. *E-mail:* admissions@millsaps.edu.

Mississippi State University

Mississippi State, Mississippi

http://www.msstate.edu/

- **State-supported** university, founded 1878, part of Mississippi Institutions of Higher Learning
- **Small-town** 4200-acre campus
- **Endowment** $433.7 million
- **Coed** 16,536 undergraduate students, 92% full-time, 48% women, 52% men
- **Moderately difficult** entrance level, 71% of applicants were admitted

UNDERGRAD STUDENTS

15,146 full-time, 1,390 part-time. Students come from 51 states and territories; 60 other countries; 26% are from out of state; 21% Black or African American, non-Hispanic/Latino; 2% Hispanic/Latino; 1% Asian, non-Hispanic/Latino; 0.1% Native Hawaiian or other Pacific Islander, non-Hispanic/Latino; 0.5% American Indian or Alaska Native, non-Hispanic/Latino; 1% Two or more races, non-Hispanic/Latino; 0.7% Race/ethnicity unknown; 2% international; 10% transferred in; 27% live on campus.

Freshmen

Admission: 10,766 applied, 7,646 admitted, 2,974 enrolled. ***Average high school GPA:*** 3.35. ***Test scores:*** SAT critical reading scores over 500: 72%; SAT math scores over 500: 76%; ACT scores over 18: 93%; SAT critical reading scores over 600: 36%; SAT math scores over 600: 42%; ACT scores over 24: 54%; SAT critical reading scores over 700: 10%; SAT math scores over 700: 10%; ACT scores over 30: 13%.

Retention: 80% of full-time freshmen returned.

FACULTY

Total: 1,005, 86% full-time, 76% with terminal degrees.

Student/faculty ratio: 19:1.

ACADEMICS

Calendar: semesters. *Degrees:* associate, bachelor's, master's, doctoral, and post-master's certificates.

Special study options: academic remediation for entering students, accelerated degree program, adult/continuing education programs, advanced placement credit, cooperative education, distance learning, double majors, English as a second language, freshman honors college, honors programs, independent study, internships, off-campus study, part-time degree program, services for LD students, student-designed majors, study abroad, summer session for credit. ***ROTC:*** Army (b), Air Force (b).

Computers: 1,000 computers/terminals and 1,000 ports are available on campus for general student use. Students can access the following: campus intranet, computer help desk, free student e-mail accounts, online (class) grades, online (class) registration, online (class) schedules, campus-wide wireless Internet access. Campuswide network is available. 100% of college-owned or -operated housing units are wired for high-speed Internet access. Wireless service is available via entire campus.

STUDENT LIFE

Housing options: on-campus residence required for freshman year; coed, men-only, women-only, special housing for students with disabilities. Campus housing is university owned. Freshman applicants given priority for college housing.

Activities and organizations: drama/theater group, student-run newspaper, radio and television station, choral group, marching band, Student Association, Black Student Alliance, Residence Hall Association, Fashion Board, Campus Activities Board, national fraternities, national sororities.

Athletics Member NCAA. All Division I except football (Division I-A). ***Intercollegiate sports:*** baseball M(s), basketball M(s)/W(s), cheerleading M(s)/W(s), cross-country running M(s)/W(s), golf M(s)/W(s), soccer W(s), softball W(s), tennis M(s)/W(s), track and field M(s)/W(s), volleyball W(s). ***Intramural sports:*** badminton M(c)/W(c), basketball M/W, bowling M/W, cross-country running M(c)/W(c), fencing M(c)/W(c), football M/W, golf M/W, ice hockey M(c), lacrosse M(c), racquetball M/W, riflery M/W, rugby M(c)/W(c), soccer M(c)/W(c), softball M(c)/W(c), swimming and diving M(c)/W(c), table tennis M(c)/W(c), tennis M(c)/W(c), ultimate Frisbee M/W, volleyball M(c)/W(c), water polo M/W.

Campus security: 24-hour emergency response devices and patrols, late-night transport/escort service, controlled dormitory access, bicycle patrols, crime prevention program, RAD program, general law enforcement services.

Student services: health clinic, personal/psychological counseling.

COSTS & FINANCIAL AID

Costs (2014–15) ***Tuition:*** state resident $7140 full-time, $294 per credit hour part-time; nonresident $18,478 full-time, $766 per credit hour part-time. Full-time tuition and fees vary according to degree level and location. Part-time tuition and fees vary according to course load, degree level, and location. ***Room and board:*** $8954; room only: $5404. Room and board charges vary according to board plan, housing facility, and student level. ***Payment plans:*** tuition prepayment, installment. ***Waivers:*** children of alumni, senior citizens, and employees or children of employees.

Financial Aid Of all full-time matriculated undergraduates who enrolled in 2013, 10,902 applied for aid, 9,383 were judged to have need, 2,117 had their need fully met. 713 Federal Work-Study jobs (averaging $3741). In 2013, 2782 non-need-based awards were made. ***Average percent of need met:*** 60. ***Average financial aid package:*** $13,208. ***Average need-based loan:*** $3999. ***Average need-based gift aid:*** $5435. ***Average non-need-based aid:*** $3930. ***Average indebtedness upon graduation:*** $29,365.

APPLYING

Standardized Tests *Required:* SAT or ACT (for admission).

Options: electronic application.

Application fee: $40.

Required: high school transcript, minimum 2.0 GPA.

Application deadlines: 8/1 (freshmen), 8/1 (transfers).

Notification: continuous (freshmen), continuous (transfers).

CONTACT

Ms. Lori Ball, Director of Undergraduate Admissions, Mississippi State University, PO Box 6334, Mississippi State, MS 39762. *Phone:* 662-325-2224. *Fax:* 662-325-1MSU. *E-mail:* admit@msstate.edu.

Mississippi University for Women

Columbus, Mississippi

http://www.muw.edu/

- **State-supported** comprehensive, founded 1884, part of Mississippi Institutions of Higher Learning
- **Small-town** 110-acre campus
- **Endowment** $49.0 million
- **Coed** 2,527 undergraduate students, 82% full-time, 81% women, 19% men
- **Moderately difficult** entrance level, 94% of applicants were admitted

UNDERGRAD STUDENTS

2,065 full-time, 462 part-time. Students come from 25 states and territories; 10 other countries; 10% are from out of state; 37% Black or African American, non-Hispanic/Latino; 0.7% Hispanic/Latino; 2% Asian, non-Hispanic/Latino; 0.1% Native Hawaiian or other Pacific Islander, non-Hispanic/Latino; 0.2% American Indian or Alaska Native, non-Hispanic/Latino; 0.4% Two or more races, non-Hispanic/Latino; 2% international; 26% transferred in; 27% live on campus.

Freshmen

Admission: 720 applied, 674 admitted, 243 enrolled. ***Average high school GPA:*** 3.43. ***Test scores:*** SAT critical reading scores over 500: 35%; SAT math scores over 500: 90%; ACT scores over 18: 78%; SAT critical reading scores over 600: 9%; SAT math scores over 600: 64%; ACT scores over 24: 21%; SAT critical reading scores over 700: 3%; SAT math scores over 700: 10%; ACT scores over 30: 2%.

Retention: 69% of full-time freshmen returned.

FACULTY

Total: 216, 64% full-time, 53% with terminal degrees.

Student/faculty ratio: 14:1.

ACADEMICS

Calendar: semesters. *Degrees:* associate, bachelor's, master's, doctoral, and post-master's certificates.

Special study options: academic remediation for entering students, adult/continuing education programs, advanced placement credit, distance learning, double majors, freshman honors college, honors programs, independent study, internships, off-campus study, part-time degree program, services for LD students, study abroad, summer session for credit. ***ROTC:*** Army (c), Air Force (c).

Computers: 393 computers/terminals and 1,220 ports are available on campus for general student use. Students can access the following: campus intranet, computer help desk, free student e-mail accounts, online (class) grades, online (class) registration, online (class) schedules. Campuswide network is available. 100% of college-owned or -operated housing units are wired for high-speed Internet access. Wireless service is available via entire campus.

STUDENT LIFE

Housing options: men-only, women-only, special housing for students with disabilities. Campus housing is university owned. Freshman campus housing is guaranteed.

Activities and organizations: drama/theater group, student-run newspaper, radio station, choral group, Student Government Association, Wesley Foundation, Modeling Squad, Baptist Student Union, International Justice Mission, national fraternities, national sororities.

Athletics ***Intramural sports:*** badminton M/W, basketball M/W, football M/W, racquetball M/W, soccer M/W, softball M/W, table tennis M/W, tennis M/W, ultimate Frisbee M/W, volleyball M/W.

Campus security: 24-hour emergency response devices and patrols, controlled dormitory access, Tornado and Voice-over Sirens, Voice Mail and Text Messaging Emergency Notification System.

Student services: health clinic, personal/psychological counseling, women's center.

COSTS & FINANCIAL AID

Costs (2015–16) ***Tuition:*** state resident $5640 full-time, $235 per credit hour part-time; nonresident $15,360 full-time, $640 per credit hour part-time. Part-time tuition and fees vary according to course load. ***Room and board:*** $6381. Room and board charges vary according to housing facility. ***Payment plan:*** installment. ***Waivers:*** employees or children of employees.

Financial Aid Of all full-time matriculated undergraduates who enrolled in 2013, 1,651 applied for aid, 1,468 were judged to have need, 574 had their need fully met. 88 Federal Work-Study jobs (averaging $1690). 243 state and other part-time jobs (averaging $1812). In 2013, 280 non-need-based awards were made. ***Average percent of need met:*** 74. ***Average financial aid package:*** $8948. ***Average need-based loan:*** $5194. ***Average need-based gift aid:*** $5527. ***Average non-need-based aid:*** $5458. ***Average indebtedness upon graduation:*** $21,095.

APPLYING

Standardized Tests *Required for some:* SAT or ACT (for admission). *Recommended:* SAT or ACT (for admission).

Options: electronic application, early admission.

Required: high school transcript. ***Required for some:*** minimum 2.0 GPA, rank in upper 50% of high school class.

Application deadlines: rolling (freshmen), rolling (out-of-state freshmen), rolling (transfers).

Notification: continuous (freshmen), continuous (out-of-state freshmen), continuous (transfers).

CONTACT

Mississippi University for Women, 1100 College Street, MUW-1600, Columbus, MS 39701-9998. *Phone:* 662-329-7106. *Toll-free phone:* 877-GO 2 THE W.

Mississippi Valley State University

Itta Bena, Mississippi

http://www.mvsu.edu/

- **State-supported** comprehensive, founded 1946, part of Mississippi Institutions of Higher Learning
- **Small-town** 450-acre campus
- **Endowment** $1.4 million
- **Coed** 1,889 undergraduate students, 87% full-time, 57% women, 43% men
- **Minimally difficult** entrance level, 16% of applicants were admitted

UNDERGRAD STUDENTS

1,652 full-time, 237 part-time. Students come from 34 states and territories; 10 other countries; 22% are from out of state; 91% Black or African American, non-Hispanic/Latino; 1% Hispanic/Latino; 0.6% Asian, non-Hispanic/Latino; 0.1% American Indian or Alaska Native, non-Hispanic/Latino; 4% Race/ethnicity unknown; 11% transferred in; 51% live on campus.

Freshmen

Admission: 7,216 applied, 1,143 admitted, 400 enrolled. ***Average high school GPA:*** 2.81. ***Test scores:*** ACT scores over 18: 42%; ACT scores over 24: 6%.

Retention: 65% of full-time freshmen returned.

FACULTY
Total: 146, 79% full-time, 60% with terminal degrees.

Student/faculty ratio: 16:1.

ACADEMICS
Calendar: semesters. *Degrees:* bachelor's and master's.

Special study options: academic remediation for entering students, cooperative education, distance learning, double majors, freshman honors college, honors programs, internships, part-time degree program, summer session for credit. ***ROTC:*** Army (b).

Computers: 285 computers/terminals are available on campus for general student use. Students can access the following: computer help desk, free student e-mail accounts, online (class) registration. Campuswide network is available.

STUDENT LIFE
Housing options: men-only, women-only. Campus housing is university owned.

Activities and organizations: drama/theater group, student-run newspaper, radio and television station, choral group, marching band, Student Government Association, Baptist Student Union, Black Student Fellowship, National Education Association, national fraternities, national sororities.

Athletics Member NCAA. All Division I except football (Division I-AA). ***Intercollegiate sports:*** baseball M(s), basketball M(s)/W(s), bowling W, cross-country running M(s)/W(s), golf M(s)/W(s), softball W(s), tennis M(s)/W(s), track and field M(s)/W(s). ***Intramural sports:*** baseball M, basketball M/W, cross-country running M/W, football M, golf M/W, softball M/W, tennis M/W, track and field M/W.

Campus security: 24-hour emergency response devices and patrols, controlled dormitory access.

Student services: health clinic, personal/psychological counseling.

COSTS
Costs (2014–15) ***Tuition:*** state resident $5916 full-time, $246 per hour part-time; nonresident $5916 full-time, $246 per hour part-time. Full-time tuition and fees vary according to course load. Part-time tuition and fees vary according to course load. ***Required fees:*** $150 full-time. ***Room and board:*** $7177; room only: $3936. ***Payment plan:*** installment. ***Waivers:*** employees or children of employees.

APPLYING
Standardized Tests *Required:* SAT or ACT (for admission).

Options: deferred entrance.

Required: high school transcript. ***Required for some:*** 2.5 letters of recommendation. ***Recommended:*** interview.

Application deadlines: rolling (freshmen), rolling (transfers).

Notification: continuous (freshmen), continuous (transfers).

CONTACT
Mississippi Valley State University, 14000 Highway 82 West, Itta Bena, MS 38941-1400. *Phone:* 662-254-3345. *Toll-free phone:* 800-844-6885.

Rust College
Holly Springs, Mississippi
http://www.rustcollege.edu/

- **Independent United Methodist** 4-year, founded 1866
- **Rural** 126-acre campus with easy access to Memphis
- **Coed** 1,031 undergraduate students, 93% full-time, 58% women, 42% men
- **Minimally difficult** entrance level, 6% of applicants were admitted

UNDERGRAD STUDENTS
963 full-time, 68 part-time. 96% Black or African American, non-Hispanic/Latino; 0.2% Asian, non-Hispanic/Latino; 1% Race/ethnicity unknown; 3% international; 93% live on campus.

Freshmen
Admission: 5,186 applied, 286 admitted, 286 enrolled. ***Average high school GPA:*** 2.7. ***Test scores:*** ACT scores over 18: 10%.

Retention: 73% of full-time freshmen returned.

FACULTY
Total: 50, 96% full-time, 54% with terminal degrees.

Student/faculty ratio: 17:1.

ACADEMICS
Calendar: semesters. *Degrees:* associate and bachelor's.

Special study options: academic remediation for entering students, accelerated degree program, adult/continuing education programs, advanced placement credit, double majors, honors programs, independent study, internships, part-time degree program, study abroad, summer session for credit.

Computers: 339 computers/terminals are available on campus for general student use. Students can access the following: campus intranet, computer help desk, free student e-mail accounts, online (class) grades. Campuswide network is available. 100% of college-owned or -operated housing units are wired for high-speed Internet access. Wireless service is available via computer centers, computer labs, dorm rooms, libraries.

STUDENT LIFE
Housing options: on-campus residence required for freshman year; men-only, women-only. Campus housing is university owned. Freshman campus housing is guaranteed.

Activities and organizations: drama/theater group, student-run newspaper, radio and television station, choral group, marching band, Acappella Choir, Pre-Med Club, DOBSAC (Division of Business Students' Advisory Council), MAE (Mississippi Association for Educators), Pre-Alumni Council, national fraternities, national sororities.

Athletics Member NCAA. All Division III. ***Intercollegiate sports:*** baseball M, basketball M/W, cheerleading M/W, cross-country running M/W, softball W, tennis M/W, track and field M/W, volleyball M/W. ***Intramural sports:*** badminton M/W, basketball M/W, swimming and diving M/W, volleyball M/W.

Campus security: 24-hour emergency response devices and patrols, late-night transport/escort service, controlled dormitory access.

Student services: health clinic, personal/psychological counseling.

COSTS & FINANCIAL AID
Costs (2014–15) ***Comprehensive fee:*** $13,286 includes full-time tuition ($9286) and room and board ($4000). Full-time tuition and fees vary according to course load. Part-time tuition: $396 per credit hour. Part-time tuition and fees vary according to course load. ***College room only:*** $1820. ***Payment plan:*** installment. ***Waivers:*** senior citizens and employees or children of employees.

Financial Aid Of all full-time matriculated undergraduates who enrolled in 2004, 806 applied for aid, 806 were judged to have need, 481 had their need fully met. 492 Federal Work-Study jobs (averaging $714). 189 state and other part-time jobs (averaging $546). In 2004, 112 non-need-based awards were made. ***Average percent of need met:*** 60. ***Average financial aid package:*** $5067. ***Average need-based loan:*** $2158. ***Average need-based gift aid:*** $4281. ***Average non-need-based aid:*** $2795. ***Average indebtedness upon graduation:*** $9314.

APPLYING
Standardized Tests *Required:* ACT (for admission).

Application fee: $10.

Required: high school transcript, minimum 2.3 GPA, 2 letters of recommendation.

Application deadlines: rolling (freshmen), rolling (out-of-state freshmen), rolling (transfers).

Notification: continuous (freshmen), continuous (out-of-state freshmen), continuous (transfers).

CONTACT
Mr. Braque Talley, Director of Enrollment Services, Rust College, 150 Rust Avenue, Holly Springs, MS 38635-2328. *Phone:* 601-252-8000 Ext. 4059. *Toll-free phone:* 888-886-8492 Ext. 4065. *Fax:* 662-252-8895. *E-mail:* admissions@rustcollege.edu.

Tougaloo College

Tougaloo, Mississippi

http://www.tougaloo.edu/

- **Independent** 4-year, founded 1869, affiliated with United Church of Christ
- **Suburban** 500-acre campus
- **Endowment** $4.7 million
- **Coed** 900 undergraduate students, 97% full-time, 65% women, 35% men
- **Minimally difficult** entrance level, 40% of applicants were admitted

UNDERGRAD STUDENTS

872 full-time, 28 part-time. Students come from 17 states and territories; 4 other countries; 19% are from out of state; 99% Black or African American, non-Hispanic/Latino; 0.3% Hispanic/Latino; 0.1% American Indian or Alaska Native, non-Hispanic/Latino; 0.4% international; 9% transferred in; 66% live on campus.

Freshmen

Admission: 2,551 applied, 1,028 admitted, 170 enrolled. ***Average high school GPA:*** 2.8. ***Test scores:*** ACT scores over 18: 58%; ACT scores over 24: 8%.

Retention: 82% of full-time freshmen returned.

FACULTY

Total: 103, 68% full-time.

Student/faculty ratio: 13:1.

ACADEMICS

Calendar: semesters. *Degrees:* associate and bachelor's.

Special study options: academic remediation for entering students, accelerated degree program, adult/continuing education programs, advanced placement credit, cooperative education, double majors, honors programs, independent study, internships, off-campus study, part-time degree program, student-designed majors, study abroad, summer session for credit. ***ROTC:*** Army (b).

Unusual degree programs: 3-2 engineering with Brown University, Georgia Institute of Technology.

Computers: 100 computers/terminals are available on campus for general student use. Students can access the following: campus intranet, computer help desk, free student e-mail accounts, online (class) grades, online (class) registration, online (class) schedules. Campuswide network is available. Wireless service is available via entire campus.

STUDENT LIFE

Housing options: men-only, women-only. Campus housing is university owned.

Activities and organizations: drama/theater group, student-run newspaper, choral group, concert choir, Student Government Association, gospel choir, NAACP, Pre-Alumni Club, national fraternities, national sororities.

Athletics Member NAIA. ***Intercollegiate sports:*** baseball M(s), basketball M(s)/W(s), cross-country running M(s)/W(s), golf M, tennis M(s)/W(s), volleyball W. ***Intramural sports:*** basketball M/W, cheerleading W, cross-country running M/W, golf M/W, softball M/W, tennis M/W, volleyball M/W.

Campus security: 24-hour emergency response devices and patrols.

Student services: health clinic, personal/psychological counseling.

COSTS & FINANCIAL AID

Costs (2015–16) ***One-time required fee:*** $95. ***Comprehensive fee:*** $17,000 includes full-time tuition ($10,130), mandatory fees ($470), and room and board ($6400). Full-time tuition and fees vary according to course load. Part-time tuition: $423 per credit hour. Part-time tuition and fees vary according to course load. ***Required fees:*** $423 per credit hour part-time. ***College room only:*** $2000. Room and board charges vary according to housing facility. ***Payment plans:*** installment, deferred payment. ***Waivers:*** senior citizens and employees or children of employees.

Financial Aid In 2002, 110 non-need-based awards were made. ***Average percent of need met:*** 80. ***Average financial aid package:*** $10,500. ***Average indebtedness upon graduation:*** $25,000.

APPLYING

Standardized Tests *Required:* SAT or ACT (for admission).

Options: early admission.

Application fee: $25.

Required: high school transcript, minimum 2.0 GPA.

Application deadlines: rolling (freshmen), rolling (transfers).

Notification: continuous (freshmen), continuous (transfers).

CONTACT

Dr. Juno Jacobs, Director of Admissions, Tougaloo College, 500 West County Line Road, Tougaloo, MS 39174. *Phone:* 601-977-7765. *Toll-free phone:* 888-42GALOO. *Fax:* 601-977-4501. *E-mail:* jjacobs@tougaloo.edu.

University of Mississippi

Oxford, Mississippi

http://www.olemiss.edu/

- **State-supported** university, founded 1844, part of Mississippi Institutions of Higher Learning
- **Small-town** 3902-acre campus with easy access to Memphis
- **Endowment** $666.7 million
- **Coed** 18,101 undergraduate students, 92% full-time, 56% women, 44% men
- **Moderately difficult** entrance level, 81% of applicants were admitted

UNDERGRAD STUDENTS

16,665 full-time, 1,436 part-time. Students come from 50 states and territories; 92 other countries; 43% are from out of state; 14% Black or African American, non-Hispanic/Latino; 3% Hispanic/Latino; 2% Asian, non-Hispanic/Latino; 0.1% Native Hawaiian or other Pacific Islander, non-Hispanic/Latino; 0.3% American Indian or Alaska Native, non-Hispanic/Latino; 2% Two or more races, non-Hispanic/Latino; 0.2% Race/ethnicity unknown; 3% international; 10% transferred in.

Freshmen

Admission: 16,101 applied, 13,077 admitted, 3,809 enrolled. ***Average high school GPA:*** 3.49. ***Test scores:*** SAT critical reading scores over 500: 68%; SAT math scores over 500: 70%; ACT scores over 18: 96%; SAT critical reading scores over 600: 23%; SAT math scores over 600: 24%; ACT scores over 24: 56%; SAT critical reading scores over 700: 4%; SAT math scores over 700: 4%; ACT scores over 30: 14%.

Retention: 85% of full-time freshmen returned.

FACULTY

Total: 2,063, 82% full-time.

Student/faculty ratio: 18:1.

ACADEMICS

Calendar: semesters. *Degrees:* bachelor's, master's, doctoral, post-master's, and postbachelor's certificates.

Special study options: academic remediation for entering students, accelerated degree program, adult/continuing education programs, advanced placement credit, cooperative education, distance learning, double majors, English as a second language, freshman honors college, honors programs, independent study, internships, part-time degree program, services for LD students, student-designed majors, study abroad, summer session for credit. ***ROTC:*** Army (b), Navy (b), Air Force (b).

Computers: Students can access the following: campus intranet, computer help desk, free student e-mail accounts, online (class) grades, online (class) registration, online (class) schedules, application for admission, registration for orientation. Campuswide network is available. 100% of college-owned or -operated housing units are wired for high-speed Internet access. Wireless service is available via classrooms, computer centers, computer labs, learning centers, libraries, student centers.

STUDENT LIFE

Housing options: on-campus residence required for freshman year; men-only, women-only. Campus housing is university owned, leased by the school and is provided by a third party. Freshman campus housing is guaranteed.

Activities and organizations: drama/theater group, student-run newspaper, radio and television station, choral group, marching band, Associated Student Body, Gospel Choir, sport clubs, Black Student Union, Student Programming Board, national fraternities, national sororities.

Athletics Member NCAA. All Division I except football (Division I-A). ***Intercollegiate sports:*** baseball M(s), basketball M(s)/W(s), cheerleading M(s)/W(s), cross-country running M(s)/W(s), fencing M(c)/W(c), golf M(s)/W(s), ice hockey M, lacrosse M/W, riflery W(s), soccer M(c)/W(s), softball W(s), tennis M(s)/W(s), track and field M(s)/W(s), volleyball M(c)/W(s).

Campus security: 24-hour emergency response devices and patrols, late-night transport/escort service, controlled dormitory access, crime prevention programs.

Student services: health clinic, personal/psychological counseling, women's center.

COSTS & FINANCIAL AID

Costs (2014–15) ***Tuition:*** state resident $6996 full-time, $292 per credit hour part-time; nonresident $19,044 full-time, $794 per credit hour part-time. Full-time tuition and fees vary according to course load and program. Part-time tuition and fees vary according to course load and program. ***Required fees:*** $100 full-time, $4 per credit hour part-time. ***Room and board:*** $9908. Room and board charges vary according to board plan and housing facility. ***Waivers:*** children of alumni, senior citizens, and employees or children of employees.

Financial Aid Of all full-time matriculated undergraduates who enrolled in 2013, 10,475 applied for aid, 8,227 were judged to have need, 880 had their need fully met. 388 Federal Work-Study jobs (averaging $1389). In 2013, 3322 non-need-based awards were made. ***Average percent of need met:*** 72. ***Average financial aid package:*** $8728. ***Average need-based loan:*** $4604. ***Average need-based gift aid:*** $7563. ***Average non-need-based aid:*** $7363. ***Average indebtedness upon graduation:*** $26,443.

APPLYING

Standardized Tests *Required:* SAT or ACT (for admission).

Options: electronic application, deferred entrance.

Application fee: $40.

Required: high school transcript, minimum 2.0 GPA.

Application deadlines: rolling (freshmen), rolling (out-of-state freshmen), rolling (transfers).

Notification: continuous (freshmen), continuous (out-of-state freshmen), continuous (transfers).

CONTACT

Mr. Whitman Smith, Director of Enrollment Services, University of Mississippi, 145 Martindale Student Services Center, University, MS 38677. *Phone:* 662-915-7226. *Toll-free phone:* 800-653-6477. *Fax:* 662-915-5869. *E-mail:* admissions@olemiss.edu.

University of Southern Mississippi

Hattiesburg, Mississippi

http://www.usm.edu/

- **State-supported** university, founded 1910, part of Mississippi Institutions of Higher Learning
- **Suburban** 1090-acre campus
- **Endowment** $64.7 million
- **Coed** 12,005 undergraduate students, 88% full-time, 64% women, 36% men
- **Moderately difficult** entrance level, 67% of applicants were admitted

UNDERGRAD STUDENTS

10,577 full-time, 1,428 part-time. Students come from 49 states and territories; 35 other countries; 16% are from out of state; 30% Black or African American, non-Hispanic/Latino; 3% Hispanic/Latino; 1% Asian, non-Hispanic/Latino; 0.1% Native Hawaiian or other Pacific Islander, non-Hispanic/Latino; 0.3% American Indian or Alaska Native, non-Hispanic/Latino; 2% Two or more races, non-Hispanic/Latino; 0.5% Race/ethnicity unknown; 0.7% international; 13% transferred in; 26% live on campus.

Freshmen

Admission: 5,850 applied, 3,904 admitted, 1,607 enrolled. ***Average high school GPA:*** 3.26. ***Test scores:*** SAT critical reading scores over 500: 56%; SAT math scores over 500: 49%; ACT scores over 18: 90%; SAT critical reading scores over 600: 13%; SAT math scores over 600: 14%; ACT scores over 24: 38%; SAT math scores over 700: 3%; ACT scores over 30: 8%.

Retention: 74% of full-time freshmen returned.

FACULTY

Total: 942, 76% full-time, 70% with terminal degrees.

Student/faculty ratio: 17:1.

ACADEMICS

Calendar: semesters. *Degrees:* certificates, bachelor's, master's, doctoral, post-master's, and postbachelor's certificates.

Special study options: academic remediation for entering students, accelerated degree program, adult/continuing education programs, advanced placement credit, cooperative education, distance learning, double majors, English as a second language, honors programs, independent study, internships, off-campus study, part-time degree program, services for LD students, study abroad, summer session for credit. ***ROTC:*** Army (c), Air Force (b).

Computers: 500 computers/terminals and 1,470 ports are available on campus for general student use. Students can access the following: campus intranet, computer help desk, free student e-mail accounts, online (class) grades, online (class) registration, online (class) schedules. Campuswide network is available. 100% of college-owned or -operated housing units are wired for high-speed Internet access. Wireless service is available via entire campus.

STUDENT LIFE

Housing options: men-only, women-only, special housing for students with disabilities. Campus housing is university owned. Freshman applicants given priority for college housing.

Activities and organizations: drama/theater group, student-run newspaper, radio station, choral group, marching band, national fraternities, national sororities.

Athletics Member NCAA. All Division I. ***Intercollegiate sports:*** baseball M(s), basketball M(s)/W(s), cheerleading M/W, cross-country running W(s), football M(s), golf M(s)/W(s), soccer W(s), softball W(s), tennis M(s)/W(s), track and field M(s)/W(s), volleyball W(s). ***Intramural sports:*** badminton M/W, basketball M/W, bowling M/W, racquetball M/W, rugby M, soccer M/W, softball W, tennis M/W, track and field M/W, ultimate Frisbee M/W, volleyball M/W.

Campus security: 24-hour emergency response devices and patrols, late-night transport/escort service, controlled dormitory access.

Student services: health clinic, personal/psychological counseling, women's center, legal services.

COSTS & FINANCIAL AID

Costs (2015–16) ***Tuition:*** state resident $7224 full-time, $291 per credit hour part-time; nonresident $16,094 full-time, $358 per credit hour part-time. Part-time tuition and fees vary according to course load and degree level. ***Room and board:*** $7640; room only: $4646. Room and board charges vary according to board plan and housing facility. ***Payment plan:*** installment. ***Waivers:*** children of alumni, senior citizens, and employees or children of employees.

Financial Aid Of all full-time matriculated undergraduates who enrolled in 2013, 9,243 applied for aid, 8,221 were judged to have need, 1,538 had their need fully met. In 2013, 5995 non-need-based awards were made. ***Average percent of need met:*** 68. ***Average financial aid package:*** $10,338. ***Average need-based loan:*** $4542. ***Average need-based gift aid:*** $4500. ***Average non-need-based aid:*** $4702. ***Average indebtedness upon graduation:*** $17,806.

APPLYING

Standardized Tests *Required:* SAT or ACT (for admission).

Options: electronic application, early admission.

Application fee: $35.

Required: minimum 2.0 GPA. ***Required for some:*** high school transcript.

Application deadlines: 6/30 (freshmen), 8/14 (transfers).

CONTACT

Dr. Allison Bruton, Director of Recruitment, University of Southern Mississippi, 118 College Drive, #5166, Hattiesburg, MS 39406-1000. *Phone:* 601-266-5000. *Fax:* 601-266-5148. *E-mail:* admissions@usm.edu.

MISSOURI

The Art Institute of St. Louis

St. Charles, Missouri

http://www.artinstitutes.edu/st-louis/

- **Proprietary** 4-year
- **Coed**

ACADEMICS

Degrees: associate and bachelor's.

CONTACT

The Art Institute of St. Louis, 1520 South Fifth Street, St. Charles, MO 63303. *Phone:* 636-688-3012.

Avila University

Kansas City, Missouri

http://www.avila.edu/

- **Independent Roman Catholic** comprehensive, founded 1916
- **Suburban** 50-acre campus
- **Coed** 1,407 undergraduate students, 82% full-time, 63% women, 37% men
- **Minimally difficult** entrance level, 53% of applicants were admitted

UNDERGRAD STUDENTS

1,151 full-time, 256 part-time. Students come from 25 states and territories; 20 other countries; 31% are from out of state; 19% Black or African American, non-Hispanic/Latino; 8% Hispanic/Latino; 2% Asian, non-Hispanic/Latino; 0.4% Native Hawaiian or other Pacific Islander, non-Hispanic/Latino; 0.8% American Indian or Alaska Native, non-Hispanic/Latino; 3% Two or more races, non-Hispanic/Latino; 7% international; 11% transferred in; 28% live on campus.

Freshmen

Admission: 1,946 applied, 1,029 admitted, 204 enrolled. ***Average high school GPA:*** 3.34. ***Test scores:*** SAT critical reading scores over 500: 50%; SAT math scores over 500: 11%; ACT scores over 18: 98%; SAT critical reading scores over 600: 17%; ACT scores over 24: 33%; ACT scores over 30: 3%.

Retention: 71% of full-time freshmen returned.

FACULTY

Total: 246, 28% full-time, 45% with terminal degrees.

Student/faculty ratio: 13:1.

ACADEMICS

Calendar: semesters. *Degrees:* bachelor's, master's, and postbachelor's certificates.

Special study options: academic remediation for entering students, accelerated degree program, adult/continuing education programs, advanced placement credit, cooperative education, distance learning, double majors, English as a second language, independent study, internships, off-campus study, part-time degree program, services for LD students, study abroad, summer session for credit. ***ROTC:*** Army (c).

Unusual degree programs: 3-2 occupational therapy, physical therapy, law with Rockhurst University, University of Missouri-Kansas City.

Computers: 118 computers/terminals and 225 ports are available on campus for general student use. Students can access the following: campus intranet, computer help desk, free student e-mail accounts, online (class) grades, online (class) registration, online (class) schedules, 60 laptops available for library checkout. Campuswide network is available. 100% of college-owned or -operated housing units are wired for high-speed Internet access. Wireless service is available via entire campus.

STUDENT LIFE

Housing options: on-campus residence required through sophomore year; coed, men-only, women-only. Campus housing is university owned. Freshman campus housing is guaranteed.

Activities and organizations: drama/theater group, student-run newspaper, choral group, Avila Ambassadors, Avila Student Nurses Association, Campus Ministries, Saudi Arabian Student Association, Avila University Theatre Company.

Athletics Member NAIA. ***Intercollegiate sports:*** baseball M(s), basketball M(s)/W(s), cheerleading W(s), cross-country running M(s)/W(s), football M(s), golf M(s)/W(s), soccer M(s)/W(s), softball W(s), track and field M(s)/W(s), volleyball W(s). ***Intramural sports:*** bowling M/W, table tennis M/W.

Campus security: 24-hour emergency response devices and patrols, student patrols, late-night transport/escort service, controlled dormitory access.

Student services: health clinic, personal/psychological counseling.

COSTS & FINANCIAL AID

Costs (2015–16) ***Tuition:*** $650 per credit hour part-time. Full-time tuition and fees vary according to course load and program. Part-time tuition and fees vary according to course load and program. No tuition increase for student's term of enrollment. ***Required fees:*** $38 per credit hour part-time. ***Room only:*** Room and board charges vary according to board plan and housing facility. ***Payment plans:*** installment, deferred payment. ***Waivers:*** children of alumni, senior citizens, and employees or children of employees.

Financial Aid Of all full-time matriculated undergraduates who enrolled in 2008, 1,927 applied for aid, 1,852 were judged to have need, 1,846 had their need fully met. 161 Federal Work-Study jobs (averaging $903). 55 state and other part-time jobs (averaging $885). In 2008, 60 non-need-based awards were made. ***Average percent of need met:*** 35. ***Average financial aid package:*** $12,976. ***Average need-based loan:*** $5465. ***Average need-based gift aid:*** $7854. ***Average non-need-based aid:*** $9152. ***Average indebtedness upon graduation:*** $16,508.

APPLYING

Standardized Tests *Required:* SAT or ACT (for admission).

Options: electronic application, early admission.

Required: high school transcript, minimum 2.5 GPA, secondary school report. ***Required for some:*** essay or personal statement. ***Recommended:*** interview.

Application deadlines: 8/15 (freshmen), 8/15 (transfers).

Notification: 8/15 (freshmen), 8/15 (transfers).

CONTACT

Ms. Bethany Bauer, Associate Director of Admissions, Avila University, 11901 Wornall Road, Kansas City, MO 64145. *Phone:* 816-501-2400. *Toll-free phone:* 800-GO-AVILA. *Fax:* 816-501-2453. *E-mail:* bethany.bauer@avila.edu.

Brown Mackie College–St. Louis

Fenton, Missouri

http://www.brownmackie.edu/st-louis/

- **Proprietary** primarily 2-year, part of Education Management Corporation
- **Coed**

ACADEMICS

Degrees: diplomas, associate, and bachelor's.

CONTACT

Brown Mackie College–St. Louis, #2 Soccer Park Road, Fenton, MO 63026. *Phone:* 636-651-3290.

Calvary Bible College and Theological Seminary

Kansas City, Missouri

http://www.calvary.edu/

- **Independent nondenominational** comprehensive, founded 1932
- **Suburban** 55-acre campus with easy access to Kansas City
- **Endowment** $1.2 million
- **Coed** 250 undergraduate students, 65% full-time, 50% women, 50% men
- **Minimally difficult** entrance level, 100% of applicants were admitted

UNDERGRAD STUDENTS

163 full-time, 87 part-time. Students come from 22 states and territories; 4 other countries; 46% are from out of state; 10% Black or African American, non-Hispanic/Latino; 3% Hispanic/Latino; 1% Asian, non-Hispanic/Latino; 1% American Indian or Alaska Native, non-

Hispanic/Latino; 2% Two or more races, non-Hispanic/Latino; 0.4% international; 11% transferred in; 52% live on campus.

Freshmen
Admission: 48 applied, 48 admitted, 38 enrolled. ***Average high school GPA:*** 3.4. ***Test scores:*** SAT critical reading scores over 500: 75%; SAT math scores over 500: 75%; SAT writing scores over 500: 75%; ACT scores over 18: 83%; SAT critical reading scores over 600: 25%; SAT writing scores over 600: 50%; ACT scores over 24: 28%; SAT writing scores over 700: 25%; ACT scores over 30: 3%.

Retention: 54% of full-time freshmen returned.

FACULTY
Total: 48, 33% full-time, 21% with terminal degrees.

Student/faculty ratio: 7:1.

ACADEMICS
Calendar: semesters. *Degrees:* certificates, associate, bachelor's, and master's.

Special study options: accelerated degree program, adult/continuing education programs, advanced placement credit, distance learning, double majors, external degree program, independent study, internships, part-time degree program, services for LD students, student-designed majors, summer session for credit. ***ROTC:*** Army (c).

Computers: 32 computers/terminals are available on campus for general student use. Students can access the following: campus intranet, computer help desk, free student e-mail accounts, online (class) grades, online (class) registration, online (class) schedules. Campuswide network is available. Wireless service is available via entire campus.

STUDENT LIFE
Housing options: on-campus residence required through senior year; men-only, women-only. Campus housing is university owned and leased by the school. Freshman campus housing is guaranteed.

Activities and organizations: drama/theater group, student-run radio station, choral group, Missions Encounter, Masterworks (Fine Arts).

Athletics Member NCCAA. ***Intercollegiate sports:*** basketball M/W, soccer M, volleyball W.

Campus security: 24-hour emergency response devices and patrols, late-night transport/escort service, controlled dormitory access, night patrols by trained security personnel, monitored closed circuit cameras.

Student services: personal/psychological counseling.

COSTS & FINANCIAL AID
Costs (2014–15) ***One-time required fee:*** $100. ***Comprehensive fee:*** $15,800 includes full-time tuition ($9520), mandatory fees ($840), and room and board ($5440). Full-time tuition and fees vary according to course load. Part-time tuition: $340 per credit hour. Part-time tuition and fees vary according to course load. ***Required fees:*** $30 per credit hour part-time, $60 per term part-time. ***Room and board:*** Room and board charges vary according to housing facility. ***Payment plan:*** installment. ***Waivers:*** employees or children of employees.

Financial Aid ***Financial aid deadline:*** 4/1.

APPLYING
Standardized Tests *Required:* SAT (for admission), ACT (for admission), SAT or ACT (for admission).

Options: electronic application.

Required: essay or personal statement, high school transcript, 2 letters of recommendation, statement of faith.

Application deadlines: 7/15 (freshmen), 7/15 (transfers).

CONTACT
Admissions Secretary, Admissions Office Assistant, Calvary Bible College and Theological Seminary, 15800 Calvary Road, Kansas City, MO 64147-1341. *Phone:* 816-322-3960. *Toll-free phone:* 800-326-3960. *Fax:* 816-331-4474. *E-mail:* admissions@calvary.edu.

Central Methodist University

Fayette, Missouri

http://www.centralmethodist.edu/

- **Independent Methodist** comprehensive, founded 1854
- **Small-town** 80-acre campus
- **Endowment** $37.0 million
- **Coed** 1,185 undergraduate students, 92% full-time, 52% women, 48% men
- **Moderately difficult** entrance level, 61% of applicants were admitted

UNDERGRAD STUDENTS
1,087 full-time, 98 part-time. Students come from 27 states and territories; 17 other countries; 7% are from out of state; 8% Black or African American, non-Hispanic/Latino; 3% Hispanic/Latino; 0.1% Asian, non-Hispanic/Latino; 0.1% Native Hawaiian or other Pacific Islander, non-Hispanic/Latino; 0.6% American Indian or Alaska Native, non-Hispanic/Latino; 3% Two or more races, non-Hispanic/Latino; 3% Race/ethnicity unknown; 3% international; 10% transferred in; 61% live on campus.

Freshmen
Admission: 1,533 applied, 928 admitted, 331 enrolled. ***Average high school GPA:*** 3.45. ***Test scores:*** ACT scores over 18: 95%; ACT scores over 24: 34%; ACT scores over 30: 3%.

Retention: 64% of full-time freshmen returned.

FACULTY
Total: 98, 65% full-time, 45% with terminal degrees.

Student/faculty ratio: 15:1.

ACADEMICS
Calendar: semesters. *Degrees:* associate, bachelor's, and master's.

Special study options: academic remediation for entering students, advanced placement credit, cooperative education, double majors, honors programs, independent study, internships, part-time degree program, services for LD students, student-designed majors, study abroad, summer session for credit. ***ROTC:*** Army (c), Air Force (c).

Unusual degree programs: 3-2 engineering with University of Missouri-Rolla.

Computers: 100 computers/terminals and 816 ports are available on campus for general student use. Students can access the following: computer help desk, free student e-mail accounts, online (class) grades, online (class) registration, online (class) schedules, over 175 wireless access points on campus. Campuswide network is available. 100% of college-owned or -operated housing units are wired for high-speed Internet access. Wireless service is available via entire campus.

STUDENT LIFE
Housing options: on-campus residence required through senior year; coed, men-only, women-only. Campus housing is university owned. Freshman applicants given priority for college housing.

Activities and organizations: drama/theater group, student-run newspaper, radio and television station, choral group, marching band, Student Government Association, Enactus, Alpha Phi Omega, Beta Beta Beta, Campus Ministries, national fraternities, national sororities.

Athletics Member NAIA. ***Intercollegiate sports:*** baseball M(s), basketball M(s)/W(s), cross-country running M(s)/W(s), football M(s), soccer M(s)/W(s), softball W(s), track and field M(s)/W(s), volleyball W(s). ***Intramural sports:*** basketball M/W, football M/W, racquetball M/W, soccer M/W, softball M/W, tennis M/W, track and field M/W, volleyball M/W, water polo M/W.

Campus security: 24-hour emergency response devices, late-night transport/escort service, controlled dormitory access.

Student services: health clinic, personal/psychological counseling.

COSTS
Costs (2015–16) ***One-time required fee:*** $100. ***Comprehensive fee:*** $29,700 includes full-time tuition ($21,630), mandatory fees ($730), and room and board ($7340). Full-time tuition and fees vary according to program and reciprocity agreements. Part-time tuition: $210 per credit hour. Part-time tuition and fees vary according to course load and program. ***Required fees:*** $30 part-time. ***Room and board:*** Room and board charges vary according to board plan and housing facility. ***Payment***

plan: installment. ***Waivers:*** children of alumni and employees or children of employees.

APPLYING
Standardized Tests *Required:* SAT or ACT (for admission).

Options: electronic application, deferred entrance.

Required: high school transcript, minimum 2.5 GPA. ***Required for some:*** 2 letters of recommendation.

Application deadlines: rolling (freshmen), rolling (out-of-state freshmen), rolling (transfers).

Notification: continuous (freshmen), continuous (out-of-state freshmen), continuous (transfers).

CONTACT
Mr. Adam Jenkins, Director of Admissions, Central Methodist University, 411 Central Methodist Square, Fayette, MO 65248. *Phone:* 660-248-6247. *Toll-free phone:* 888-CMU-1854 (in-state); 877-CMU-1854 (out-of-state). *Fax:* 660-248-1872. *E-mail:* admissions@centralmethodist.edu.

Chamberlain College of Nursing

St. Louis, Missouri

http://www.chamberlain.edu/

- **Proprietary** 4-year, founded 1889, part of DeVry University
- **Urban** campus
- **Coed**
- **Moderately difficult** entrance level

FACULTY
Student/faculty ratio: 9:1.

ACADEMICS
Calendar: semesters. *Degree:* bachelor's.

STUDENT LIFE
Campus security: 24-hour patrols, late-night transport/escort service, controlled dormitory access.

COSTS
Costs (2014–15) ***Tuition:*** $17,160 full-time, $665 per credit hour part-time. ***Required fees:*** $600 full-time.

APPLYING
Standardized Tests *Required:* SAT or ACT (for admission).

Application fee: $95.

Required: essay or personal statement, high school transcript. ***Required for some:*** interview.

CONTACT
Admissions, Chamberlain College of Nursing, 11830 Westline Industrial Drive, Suite 106, St. Louis, MO 63146. *Phone:* 314-991-6200. *Toll-free phone:* 888-556-8CCN.

City Vision College

Kansas City, Missouri

http://www.cityvision.edu/

- **Independent Christian** upper-level
- **Coed** 72 undergraduate students, 33% full-time, 61% women, 39% men
- **Noncompetitive** entrance level

UNDERGRAD STUDENTS
24 full-time, 48 part-time. Students come from 24 states and territories; 1 other country; 93% are from out of state; 29% Black or African American, non-Hispanic/Latino; 6% Hispanic/Latino; 1% Asian, non-Hispanic/Latino; 1% American Indian or Alaska Native, non-Hispanic/Latino; 4% Two or more races, non-Hispanic/Latino; 4% Race/ethnicity unknown; 6% transferred in.

FACULTY
Total: 19, 32% with terminal degrees.

Student/faculty ratio: 6:1.

ACADEMICS
Degrees: certificates, bachelor's, and master's.

Special study options: adult/continuing education programs, distance learning, double majors, internships, part-time degree program, services for LD students, summer session for credit.

Computers: Students can access the following: computer help desk, free student e-mail accounts, online (class) grades, online (class) registration, online (class) schedules.

COSTS & FINANCIAL AID
Costs (2015–16) ***One-time required fee:*** $25. ***Tuition:*** $6000 full-time, $3000 per year part-time. Full-time tuition and fees vary according to course load and degree level. Part-time tuition and fees vary according to course load and degree level. ***Payment plan:*** installment. ***Waivers:*** employees or children of employees.

Financial Aid Of all full-time matriculated undergraduates who enrolled in 2013, 67 applied for aid, 67 were judged to have need, 51 had their need fully met. In 2013, 26 non-need-based awards were made. ***Average percent of need met:*** 100. ***Average financial aid package:*** $3653. ***Average need-based loan:*** $4814. ***Average need-based gift aid:*** $1468. ***Average non-need-based aid:*** $1041.

APPLYING
Options: electronic application.

Application fee: $25.

Notification: continuous (transfers).

CONTACT
Mrs. Nancy Young, Student Admissions Representative, City Vision College, 3101 Troost Ave. Suite 200, Kansas City, MO 64109-1845. *Phone:* 816-960-2008 Ext. 3. *Fax:* 816-256-8471. *E-mail:* newstudents@cityvision.edu.

College of the Ozarks

Point Lookout, Missouri

http://www.cofo.edu/

- **Independent Presbyterian** 4-year, founded 1906
- **Small-town** 1000-acre campus
- **Endowment** $427.5 million
- **Coed** 1,433 undergraduate students, 99% full-time, 51% women, 49% men
- **Moderately difficult** entrance level, 8% of applicants were admitted

UNDERGRAD STUDENTS
1,422 full-time, 11 part-time. Students come from 29 states and territories; 16 other countries; 22% are from out of state; 1% Black or African American, non-Hispanic/Latino; 2% Hispanic/Latino; 0.5% Asian, non-Hispanic/Latino; 0.5% American Indian or Alaska Native, non-Hispanic/Latino; 2% Two or more races, non-Hispanic/Latino; 0.1% Race/ethnicity unknown; 2% international; 2% transferred in; 85% live on campus.

Freshmen
Admission: 3,407 applied, 283 admitted, 255 enrolled. ***Average high school GPA:*** 3.59. ***Test scores:*** SAT critical reading scores over 500: 100%; SAT math scores over 500: 78%; SAT writing scores over 500: 100%; ACT scores over 18: 96%; SAT critical reading scores over 600: 67%; SAT math scores over 600: 34%; SAT writing scores over 600: 56%; ACT scores over 24: 39%; SAT math scores over 700: 12%; SAT writing scores over 700: 12%; ACT scores over 30: 3%.

Retention: 87% of full-time freshmen returned.

FACULTY
Total: 136, 61% full-time, 38% with terminal degrees.

Student/faculty ratio: 15:1.

ACADEMICS
Calendar: semesters. *Degree:* bachelor's.

Special study options: academic remediation for entering students, advanced placement credit, double majors, independent study, internships, off-campus study, services for LD students, student-designed majors. ***ROTC:*** Army (b).

Unusual degree programs: 3-2 engineering with Missouri University Science and Technology; JD with University of Missouri; Medical Technology with Cox Medical Center Springfield Missouri.

Computers: 166 computers/terminals and 1,326 ports are available on campus for general student use. Students can access the following: campus intranet, computer help desk, free student e-mail accounts, online (class) grades, online (class) registration, online (class) schedules. Campuswide network is available. 100% of college-owned or -operated housing units are wired for high-speed Internet access. Wireless service is available via classrooms, dorm rooms, libraries, student centers.

STUDENT LIFE
Housing options: on-campus residence required through senior year; men-only, women-only. Campus housing is university owned.

Activities and organizations: drama/theater group, student-run newspaper, radio station, choral group, Young Americans for Freedom, Student Senate, Baptist Student Union, ROTC, Business Undergraduate Society.

Athletics Member NAIA. ***Intercollegiate sports:*** baseball M(s), basketball M(s)/W(s), cheerleading M/W, cross-country running M/W, volleyball W(s). ***Intramural sports:*** basketball M/W, football M/W, racquetball M/W, soccer M/W, softball M/W, table tennis M/W, tennis M/W, ultimate Frisbee M/W, volleyball M/W.

Campus security: 24-hour emergency response devices and patrols, controlled dormitory access, front gate closed 6 p.m. to 5 a.m., Security checks cars for proper credentials for entry.

Student services: health clinic, personal/psychological counseling.

COSTS & FINANCIAL AID
Costs (2015–16) ***Tuition:*** $310 per credit hour part-time. Part-time tuition and fees vary according to course load. ***Payment plan:*** installment.

Financial Aid Of all full-time matriculated undergraduates who enrolled in 2012, 1,471 applied for aid, 1,428 were judged to have need, 403 had their need fully met. In 2012, 95 non-need-based awards were made. ***Average percent of need met:*** 84. ***Average financial aid package:*** $17,434. ***Average need-based loan:*** $19. ***Average need-based gift aid:*** $14,414. ***Average non-need-based aid:*** $13,103. ***Average indebtedness upon graduation:*** $6424.

APPLYING
Standardized Tests *Required:* SAT or ACT (for admission).

Options: electronic application.

Required: high school transcript, 2 letters of recommendation, interview, medical history, financial statement. ***Recommended:*** minimum 3.0 GPA.

Application deadlines: 2/15 (freshmen), 2/15 (transfers).

Notification: continuous (freshmen), continuous (transfers).

CONTACT
Mrs. Gayle Groves, Admissions Secretary, College of the Ozarks, PO Box 17, Point Lookout, MO 65726. *Phone:* 417-690-2636. *Toll-free phone:* 800-222-0525. *Fax:* 417-335-2618. *E-mail:* admiss4@cofo.edu.

Columbia College
Columbia, Missouri
http://www.ccis.edu/

- **Independent** comprehensive, founded 1851, affiliated with Christian Church (Disciples of Christ)
- **Urban** 33-acre campus
- **Endowment** $108.4 million
- **Coed** 966 undergraduate students, 84% full-time, 58% women, 42% men
- **Moderately difficult** entrance level, 71% of applicants were admitted

UNDERGRAD STUDENTS
808 full-time, 158 part-time. Students come from 57 states and territories; 35 other countries; 13% are from out of state; 5% Black or African American, non-Hispanic/Latino; 3% Hispanic/Latino; 1% Asian, non-Hispanic/Latino; 0.8% American Indian or Alaska Native, non-Hispanic/Latino; 2% Two or more races, non-Hispanic/Latino; 5% Race/ethnicity unknown; 11% international; 18% transferred in; 34% live on campus.

Freshmen
Admission: 616 applied, 439 admitted, 133 enrolled. ***Average high school GPA:*** 3.59. ***Test scores:*** SAT critical reading scores over 500: 40%; SAT math scores over 500: 67%; ACT scores over 18: 93%; SAT critical reading scores over 600: 20%; SAT math scores over 600: 50%; ACT scores over 24: 54%; SAT critical reading scores over 700: 20%; SAT math scores over 700: 17%; ACT scores over 30: 2%.

Retention: 75% of full-time freshmen returned.

FACULTY
Total: 121, 58% full-time, 60% with terminal degrees.

Student/faculty ratio: 11:1.

ACADEMICS
Calendar: semesters. *Degrees:* associate, bachelor's, and master's (offers continuing education program with significant enrollment not reflected in profile).

Special study options: adult/continuing education programs, advanced placement credit, cooperative education, distance learning, double majors, English as a second language, honors programs, independent study, internships, off-campus study, part-time degree program, services for LD students, student-designed majors, study abroad, summer session for credit. ***ROTC:*** Army (c), Navy (c), Air Force (c).

Unusual degree programs: 3-2 Education.

Computers: 128 computers/terminals and 728 ports are available on campus for general student use. Students can access the following: campus intranet, computer help desk, free student e-mail accounts, online (class) grades, online (class) registration, online (class) schedules. Campuswide network is available. 100% of college-owned or -operated housing units are wired for high-speed Internet access. Wireless service is available via entire campus.

STUDENT LIFE
Housing options: on-campus residence required through sophomore year; coed, women-only, special housing for students with disabilities. Campus housing is university owned. Freshman campus housing is guaranteed.

Activities and organizations: drama/theater group, choral group, Elysium Players, Student Government Association, International Club, Chi Alpha Christian Fellowship, The Pride.

Athletics Member NAIA. ***Intercollegiate sports:*** basketball M(s)/W(s), cross-country running M(s)/W(s), golf M(s)/W(s), soccer M(s)/W(s), softball W(s), volleyball W(s). ***Intramural sports:*** basketball M/W, football M/W, soccer M/W, softball M/W, volleyball M/W.

Campus security: 24-hour emergency response devices and patrols, late-night transport/escort service, controlled dormitory access.

Student services: health clinic, personal/psychological counseling.

COSTS & FINANCIAL AID
Costs (2014–15) ***Comprehensive fee:*** $29,176 includes full-time tuition ($20,936) and room and board ($8240). Full-time tuition and fees vary according to class time, course load, degree level, program, and reciprocity agreements. Part-time tuition: $450 per credit hour. Part-time tuition and fees vary according to class time, course load, degree level, location, and reciprocity agreements. No tuition increase for student's term of enrollment. ***College room only:*** $5462. Room and board charges vary according to board plan and housing facility. ***Payment plans:*** installment, deferred payment. ***Waivers:*** children of alumni, senior citizens, and employees or children of employees.

Financial Aid Of all full-time matriculated undergraduates who enrolled in 2013, 574 applied for aid, 528 were judged to have need, 63 had their need fully met. 200 Federal Work-Study jobs (averaging $2528). 224 state and other part-time jobs (averaging $1666). In 2013, 79 non-need-based awards were made. ***Average percent of need met:*** 56. ***Average financial aid package:*** $14,981. ***Average need-based loan:*** $3691. ***Average need-based gift aid:*** $5063. ***Average non-need-based aid:*** $9926. ***Average indebtedness upon graduation:*** $14,591.

APPLYING
Standardized Tests *Required:* SAT or ACT (for admission).

Options: electronic application, deferred entrance.

Application fee: $35.

Required: high school transcript, minimum 2.5 GPA. ***Required for some:*** essay or personal statement, interview.

Application deadlines: 8/13 (freshmen), 8/13 (transfers).

Notification: continuous (freshmen), continuous (transfers).

CONTACT
Admissions Office, Columbia College, 1001 Rogers Street, Columbia, MO 65216. *Phone:* 573-875-7352. *Toll-free phone:* 800-231-2391. *Fax:* 573-875-7506. *E-mail:* admissions@ccis.edu.

Conception Seminary College

Conception, Missouri

http://www.conception.edu/

- **Independent Roman Catholic** 4-year, founded 1886
- **Rural** 30-acre campus
- **Men only** 86 undergraduate students, 100% full-time
- **Noncompetitive** entrance level, 100% of applicants were admitted

UNDERGRAD STUDENTS
86 full-time. Students come from 7 states and territories; 5 other countries; 83% are from out of state; 1% Black or African American, non-Hispanic/Latino; 16% Hispanic/Latino; 7% Asian, non-Hispanic/Latino; 1% American Indian or Alaska Native, non-Hispanic/Latino; 15% Race/ethnicity unknown; 17% transferred in.

Freshmen
Admission: 16 applied, 16 admitted, 16 enrolled.
Retention: 85% of full-time freshmen returned.

FACULTY
Student/faculty ratio: 4:1.

ACADEMICS
Calendar: semesters. *Degrees:* bachelor's and postbachelor's certificates.

Special study options: academic remediation for entering students, advanced placement credit, English as a second language, independent study, off-campus study.

Computers: 20 computers/terminals and 20 ports are available on campus for general student use. Students can access the following: free student e-mail accounts. Campuswide network is available.

STUDENT LIFE
Housing options: on-campus residence required through senior year; men-only. Campus housing is university owned.

Activities and organizations: drama/theater group, student-run newspaper, choral group.

Campus security: 24-hour emergency response devices.

Student services: health clinic, personal/psychological counseling.

COSTS & FINANCIAL AID
Costs (2015–16) ***Comprehensive fee:*** $32,378 includes full-time tuition ($20,104), mandatory fees ($200), and room and board ($12,074). Part-time tuition: $200 per credit hour. ***College room only:*** $5050. ***Payment plan:*** installment. ***Waivers:*** employees or children of employees.

Financial Aid Of all full-time matriculated undergraduates who enrolled in 2005, 34 applied for aid, 30 were judged to have need, 16 had their need fully met. 13 Federal Work-Study jobs (averaging $729). 35 state and other part-time jobs (averaging $691). In 2005, 11 non-need-based awards were made. ***Average percent of need met:*** 78. ***Average financial aid package:*** $16,500. ***Average need-based loan:*** $2254. ***Average need-based gift aid:*** $5825. ***Average non-need-based aid:*** $1708. ***Average indebtedness upon graduation:*** $16,375.

APPLYING
Standardized Tests *Required:* SAT or ACT (for admission).

Options: electronic application, early admission, deferred entrance.

Required: essay or personal statement, high school transcript, minimum 2.0 GPA, 2 letters of recommendation, church certificate, medical history.

Application deadlines: 7/31 (freshmen), 7/31 (transfers).

Notification: continuous until 8/15 (freshmen), continuous until 8/15 (transfers).

CONTACT
Br. Macario Martinez OSB, Director of Recruitment and Admissions, Conception Seminary College, PO Box 502, Conception, MO 64433-0502. *Phone:* 660-944-2886. *Fax:* 660-944-2829. *E-mail:* vocations@conception.edu.

Cottey College

Nevada, Missouri

http://www.cottey.edu/

- **Independent** primarily 2-year, founded 1884
- **Small-town** 51-acre campus
- **Endowment** $95,497
- **Women only**

FACULTY
Student/faculty ratio: 8:1.

ACADEMICS
Calendar: semesters. *Degrees:* associate and bachelor's.

STUDENT LIFE
Housing options: women-only. Campus housing is university owned.

Activities and organizations: drama/theater group, student-run newspaper, choral group, International Friendship Circle, Cottey Intramural Association, Ozarks Explorers Club, Inter-Varsity Club, Golden Keys.

Athletics Member NJCAA.

Campus security: 24-hour emergency response devices and patrols, late-night transport/escort service, controlled dormitory access.

Student services: health clinic, personal/psychological counseling.

COSTS & FINANCIAL AID
Costs (2014–15) ***Comprehensive fee:*** $26,950 includes full-time tuition ($18,400), mandatory fees ($900), and room and board ($7650). Part-time tuition: $125 per hour. Part-time tuition and fees vary according to course load. ***Required fees:*** $76 per credit hour part-time. ***College room only:*** $4000. Room and board charges vary according to housing facility.

Financial Aid Of all full-time matriculated undergraduates who enrolled in 2013, 236 applied for aid, 211 were judged to have need, 53 had their need fully met. In 2013, 59 non-need-based awards were made. ***Average percent of need met:*** 83. ***Average financial aid package:*** $19,014. ***Average need-based loan:*** $3376. ***Average need-based gift aid:*** $15,208. ***Average non-need-based aid:*** $10,607. ***Average indebtedness upon graduation:*** $13,066.

APPLYING
Standardized Tests *Required:* SAT or ACT (for admission).

Required: essay or personal statement, high school transcript, 1 letter of recommendation. ***Recommended:*** minimum 2.6 GPA, interview.

CONTACT
Ms. Judi Steege, Director of Admission, Cottey College, 1000 West Austin Boulevard, Nevada, MO 64772. *Phone:* 417-667-8181. *Toll-free phone:* 888-526-8839. *Fax:* 417-667-8103. *E-mail:* enrollmgt@cottey.edu.

Culver-Stockton College

Canton, Missouri

http://www.culver.edu/

- **Independent** comprehensive, founded 1853, affiliated with Christian Church (Disciples of Christ)
- **Rural** 143-acre campus
- **Endowment** $23.1 million
- **Coed** 957 undergraduate students, 93% full-time, 48% women, 52% men
- **Moderately difficult** entrance level, 58% of applicants were admitted

UNDERGRAD STUDENTS
892 full-time, 65 part-time. Students come from 33 states and territories; 11 other countries; 45% are from out of state; 13% Black or African American, non-Hispanic/Latino; 5% Hispanic/Latino; 0.4% Asian, non-Hispanic/Latino; 0.8% Native Hawaiian or other Pacific Islander, non-Hispanic/Latino; 0.3% American Indian or Alaska Native, non-Hispanic/Latino; 2% Two or more races, non-Hispanic/Latino; 5% international; 8% transferred in; 79% live on campus.

Freshmen
Admission: 2,372 applied, 1,369 admitted, 290 enrolled. ***Average high school GPA:*** 3.18. ***Test scores:*** SAT critical reading scores over 500: 31%; SAT math scores over 500: 49%; ACT scores over 18: 92%; SAT

critical reading scores over 600: 2%; SAT math scores over 600: 7%; ACT scores over 24: 23%; ACT scores over 30: 2%.

Retention: 76% of full-time freshmen returned.

FACULTY

Total: 92, 53% full-time, 39% with terminal degrees.

Student/faculty ratio: 15:1.

ACADEMICS

Calendar: semesters. *Degrees:* bachelor's and master's.

Special study options: academic remediation for entering students, accelerated degree program, adult/continuing education programs, advanced placement credit, distance learning, double majors, honors programs, independent study, internships, off-campus study, part-time degree program, services for LD students, student-designed majors, study abroad, summer session for credit.

Unusual degree programs: 3-2 occupational therapy with Washington University in St. Louis.

Computers: 100 computers/terminals and 50 ports are available on campus for general student use. Students can access the following: campus intranet, computer help desk, free student e-mail accounts, online (class) grades, online (class) registration, online (class) schedules. Campuswide network is available. 100% of college-owned or -operated housing units are wired for high-speed Internet access. Wireless service is available via entire campus.

STUDENT LIFE

Housing options: on-campus residence required through senior year; coed. Campus housing is university owned. Freshman campus housing is guaranteed.

Activities and organizations: drama/theater group, student-run newspaper, radio and television station, choral group, Up 'til Dawn (benefiting St. Jude's Hospital), Interfraternity Council/Panhellenic Council, Student Government Association, ENACTUS, Campus Programming Council, national fraternities, national sororities.

Athletics Member NAIA. ***Intercollegiate sports:*** baseball M(s), basketball M(s)/W(s), bowling M(s)/W(s), cheerleading M(s)/W(s), cross-country running M(s)/W(s), football M(s), golf M(s)/W(s), soccer M(s)/W(s), softball W(s), track and field M(s)/W(s), volleyball M(s)/W(s). ***Intramural sports:*** baseball M/W, basketball M/W, football M/W, soccer M/W, softball M/W, volleyball M/W.

Campus security: 24-hour emergency response devices and patrols, late-night transport/escort service, controlled dormitory access, lighted pathways/sidewalks; self defense education is currently offered on campus.

Student services: personal/psychological counseling.

COSTS & FINANCIAL AID

Costs (2015–16) ***One-time required fee:*** $200. ***Comprehensive fee:*** $32,850 includes full-time tuition ($24,500), mandatory fees ($400), and room and board ($7950). Part-time tuition: $570 per credit hour. ***Required fees:*** $17 per credit hour part-time. ***College room only:*** $3560. Room and board charges vary according to board plan and housing facility. ***Payment plan:*** installment. ***Waivers:*** senior citizens and employees or children of employees.

Financial Aid Of all full-time matriculated undergraduates who enrolled in 2014, 769 applied for aid, 722 were judged to have need, 121 had their need fully met. 115 Federal Work-Study jobs (averaging $655). 341 state and other part-time jobs (averaging $1047). In 2014, 109 non-need-based awards were made. ***Average percent of need met:*** 74. ***Average financial aid package:*** $20,407. ***Average need-based loan:*** $4173. ***Average need-based gift aid:*** $16,673. ***Average non-need-based aid:*** $8765. ***Average indebtedness upon graduation:*** $24,487. ***Financial aid deadline:*** 6/1.

APPLYING

Standardized Tests *Required:* SAT or ACT (for admission).

Options: electronic application, deferred entrance.

Required: high school transcript, minimum 2.0 GPA, ACT or SAT scores. ***Recommended:*** essay or personal statement, 1 letter of recommendation, interview.

Application deadlines: rolling (freshmen), rolling (transfers).

Notification: continuous (freshmen), continuous (transfers).

CONTACT

Misty McBee, Director of Admission, Culver-Stockton College, One College Hill, Canton, MO 63435-1299. *Phone:* 573-288-6507. *Toll-free phone:* 800-537-1883. *Fax:* 573-288-6618. *E-mail:* admissions@culver.edu.

DeVry University

Kansas City, Missouri

http://www.devry.edu/

- **Proprietary** comprehensive, founded 1931, part of DeVry University
- **Urban** campus
- **Coed** 423 undergraduate students, 41% full-time, 30% women, 70% men
- **Minimally difficult** entrance level

UNDERGRAD STUDENTS

173 full-time, 250 part-time. 32% are from out of state; 23% Black or African American, non-Hispanic/Latino; 4% Hispanic/Latino; 4% Asian, non-Hispanic/Latino; 0.5% Native Hawaiian or other Pacific Islander, non-Hispanic/Latino; 1% American Indian or Alaska Native, non-Hispanic/Latino; 1% Two or more races, non-Hispanic/Latino; 31% transferred in.

Freshmen

Admission: 28 enrolled.

FACULTY

Total: 75, 12% full-time.

Student/faculty ratio: 10:1.

ACADEMICS

Calendar: semesters. *Degrees:* associate, bachelor's, master's, and postbachelor's certificates.

COSTS & FINANCIAL AID

Costs (2014–15) ***Tuition:*** $17,052 full-time, $609 per credit hour part-time. ***Required fees:*** $80 full-time.

Financial Aid Of all full-time matriculated undergraduates who enrolled in 2007, 294 applied for aid, 281 were judged to have need, 12 had their need fully met. In 2007, 30 non-need-based awards were made. ***Average percent of need met:*** 40. ***Average financial aid package:*** $11,948. ***Average need-based loan:*** $8396. ***Average need-based gift aid:*** $5419. ***Average non-need-based aid:*** $13,609. ***Average indebtedness upon graduation:*** $8969.

APPLYING

Application fee: $40.

CONTACT

Admissions Office, DeVry University, 11224 Holmes Rd., Kansas City, MO 64131. *Phone:* 816-943-7300. *Toll-free phone:* 866-338-7941.

DeVry University

Kansas City, Missouri

http://www.devry.edu/

- **Proprietary** comprehensive
- **Coed**

ACADEMICS

Calendar: semesters. *Degrees:* associate, bachelor's, and master's.

COSTS

Costs (2014–15) ***Tuition:*** $17,052 full-time, $609 per credit hour part-time. ***Required fees:*** $80 full-time.

CONTACT

Admissions Office, DeVry University, City Center Square, 1100 Main Street, Suite 118, Kansas City, MO 64105-2112. *Phone:* 816-943-7300. *Toll-free phone:* 866-338-7941.

DeVry University

St. Louis, Missouri

http://www.devry.edu/

- **Proprietary** comprehensive
- **Coed**

ACADEMICS
Calendar: semesters. *Degrees:* associate, bachelor's, and master's.

COSTS
Costs (2014–15) ***Tuition:*** $17,052 full-time, $609 per credit hour part-time. ***Required fees:*** $80 full-time.

CONTACT
Admissions Office, DeVry University, 11830 Westline Industrial Drive, Suite 100, St. Louis, MO 63146. *Phone:* 314-991-6400. *Toll-free phone:* 866-338-7941.

Drury University
Springfield, Missouri
http://www.drury.edu/

- **Independent** comprehensive, founded 1873
- **Urban** 80-acre campus
- **Endowment** $86.6 million
- **Coed** 1,454 undergraduate students, 98% full-time, 52% women, 48% men
- **Moderately difficult** entrance level, 81% of applicants were admitted

UNDERGRAD STUDENTS
1,425 full-time, 29 part-time. Students come from 28 states and territories; 51 other countries; 15% are from out of state; 3% Black or African American, non-Hispanic/Latino; 4% Hispanic/Latino; 2% Asian, non-Hispanic/Latino; 0.1% Native Hawaiian or other Pacific Islander, non-Hispanic/Latino; 0.4% American Indian or Alaska Native, non-Hispanic/Latino; 2% Two or more races, non-Hispanic/Latino; 12% international; 5% transferred in; 59% live on campus.

Freshmen
Admission: 1,016 applied, 823 admitted, 310 enrolled. ***Average high school GPA:*** 3.8. ***Test scores:*** ACT scores over 18: 99%; ACT scores over 24: 70%; ACT scores over 30: 20%.

Retention: 82% of full-time freshmen returned.

FACULTY
Total: 174, 80% full-time, 73% with terminal degrees.

Student/faculty ratio: 10:1.

ACADEMICS
Calendar: semesters. *Degrees:* bachelor's and master's (also offers evening program with significant enrollment not reflected in profile).

Special study options: academic remediation for entering students, accelerated degree program, adult/continuing education programs, advanced placement credit, cooperative education, distance learning, double majors, English as a second language, honors programs, independent study, internships, off-campus study, part-time degree program, services for LD students, student-designed majors, study abroad, summer session for credit. ***ROTC:*** Army (c).

Unusual degree programs: 3-2 engineering with Washington University in St. Louis; international management with American Graduate School of International Management, occupational therapy with Washington University in St. Louis.

Computers: 389 computers/terminals are available on campus for general student use. Students can access the following: campus intranet, computer help desk, free student e-mail accounts, online (class) grades, online (class) registration, online (class) schedules, digital imaging lab, online bill payment/student information. Campuswide network is available. 100% of college-owned or -operated housing units are wired for high-speed Internet access. Wireless service is available via entire campus.

STUDENT LIFE
Housing options: on-campus residence required through junior year; coed, men-only, women-only. Campus housing is university owned and leased by the school. Freshman campus housing is guaranteed.

Activities and organizations: drama/theater group, student-run newspaper, radio and television station, choral group, Drury Volunteer Corps (DVC), International Student Association, Lambda Chi Alpha, Zeta Tau Alpha, Kappa Delta, national fraternities, national sororities.

Athletics Member NCAA. All Division II. ***Intercollegiate sports:*** baseball M(s), basketball M(s)/W(s), cheerleading M(s)/W(s), cross-country running M(s)/W(s), golf M(s)/W(s), soccer M(s)/W(s), softball W(s), swimming and diving M(s)/W(s), tennis M(s)/W(s), track and field M(s)/W(s), volleyball W(s). ***Intramural sports:*** basketball M/W, cross-country running M(c)/W(c), football M/W, ice hockey M(c), soccer M/W, softball M/W, tennis M/W, ultimate Frisbee M/W, volleyball M/W.

Campus security: 24-hour emergency response devices and patrols, student patrols, late-night transport/escort service, controlled dormitory access, security cameras in parking areas, police substation on campus, well-lit campus.

Student services: health clinic, personal/psychological counseling.

COSTS & FINANCIAL AID
Costs (2014–15) ***One-time required fee:*** $150. ***Comprehensive fee:*** $31,279 includes full-time tuition ($22,750), mandatory fees ($1135), and room and board ($7394). Full-time tuition and fees vary according to class time. Part-time tuition and fees vary according to class time. ***Room and board:*** Room and board charges vary according to board plan and housing facility. ***Payment plans:*** tuition prepayment, installment, deferred payment. ***Waivers:*** minority students, children of alumni, and employees or children of employees.

Financial Aid Of all full-time matriculated undergraduates who enrolled in 2014, 1,007 applied for aid, 876 were judged to have need, 173 had their need fully met. 177 Federal Work-Study jobs (averaging $2338). In 2014, 445 non-need-based awards were made. ***Average percent of need met:*** 73. ***Average financial aid package:*** $19,321. ***Average need-based loan:*** $5073. ***Average need-based gift aid:*** $14,987. ***Average non-need-based aid:*** $8263. ***Average indebtedness upon graduation:*** $25,336.

APPLYING
Standardized Tests *Required:* SAT or ACT (for admission).

Options: electronic application, deferred entrance.

Application fee: $50.

Required: essay or personal statement, high school transcript, minimum 2.7 GPA, 1 letter of recommendation. ***Recommended:*** interview.

Application deadlines: 5/1 (freshmen), rolling (transfers).

Notification: continuous (freshmen), continuous (transfers).

CONTACT
Mr. Jay Fedje, Dean of Enrollment, Drury University, 900 North Benton Ave., Springfield, MO 65802. *Phone:* 417-873-7205. *Toll-free phone:* 800-922-2274. *Fax:* 417-866-3873. *E-mail:* druryad@drury.edu.

Evangel University
Springfield, Missouri
http://www.evangel.edu/

- **Independent** comprehensive, founded 1955, affiliated with Assemblies of God
- **Urban** 80-acre campus
- **Coed** 1,788 undergraduate students, 90% full-time, 54% women, 46% men
- **Moderately difficult** entrance level, 65% of applicants were admitted

UNDERGRAD STUDENTS
1,603 full-time, 185 part-time. 43% are from out of state; 39% Black or African American, non-Hispanic/Latino; 48% Hispanic/Latino; 16% Asian, non-Hispanic/Latino; 9% American Indian or Alaska Native, non-Hispanic/Latino; 35% Two or more races, non-Hispanic/Latino; 85% Race/ethnicity unknown; 5% international; 6% transferred in; 68% live on campus.

Freshmen
Admission: 1,249 applied, 806 admitted, 329 enrolled.

ACADEMICS
Calendar: semesters. *Degrees:* associate, bachelor's, master's, and doctoral.

ROTC: Army (c).

Computers: Students can access the following: computer help desk, free student e-mail accounts, online (class) grades, online (class) registration, online (class) schedules, online payment. Campuswide network is available. Wireless service is available via classrooms, computer labs, learning centers, libraries, student centers.

STUDENT LIFE
Housing options: on-campus residence required through senior year; coed, men-only, women-only. Campus housing is university owned.

Activities and organizations: drama/theater group, student-run newspaper, radio and television station, choral group, marching band, Activities Board, student government, CrossWalk Student Ministries, Honor Societies, Music Ensembles.

Athletics Member NAIA. ***Intercollegiate sports:*** baseball M(s), basketball M(s)/W(s), cross-country running M(s)/W(s), football M(s), golf M(s)/W(s), softball W(s), tennis M(s)/W(s), track and field M(s)/W(s), volleyball W(s). ***Intramural sports:*** baseball M, basketball M/W, football M, golf M/W, soccer M/W, softball W, tennis M/W, volleyball W.

Campus security: 24-hour emergency response devices and patrols, student patrols, late-night transport/escort service, controlled dormitory access.

Student services: health clinic, personal/psychological counseling.

COSTS & FINANCIAL AID

Costs (2014–15) ***Comprehensive fee:*** $27,996 includes full-time tuition ($19,676), mandatory fees ($1120), and room and board ($7200). Full-time tuition and fees vary according to course load. Part-time tuition: $820 per credit hour. Part-time tuition and fees vary according to course load. ***College room only:*** $3720. Room and board charges vary according to board plan. ***Payment plan:*** installment. ***Waivers:*** employees or children of employees.

Financial Aid Of all full-time matriculated undergraduates who enrolled in 2013, 1,804 applied for aid, 1,588 were judged to have need, 143 had their need fully met. 1,273 Federal Work-Study jobs (averaging $1652). In 2013, 151 non-need-based awards were made. ***Average percent of need met:*** 64. ***Average financial aid package:*** $16,429. ***Average need-based loan:*** $4781. ***Average need-based gift aid:*** $11,073. ***Average non-need-based aid:*** $4879. ***Average indebtedness upon graduation:*** $30,179. ***Financial aid deadline:*** 7/1.

APPLYING

Standardized Tests *Required:* SAT or ACT (for admission).

Options: electronic application, deferred entrance.

Application fee: $25.

Required: essay or personal statement, high school transcript, interview. ***Recommended:*** minimum 2.0 GPA.

CONTACT

Evangel University, 1111 North Glenstone, Springfield, MO 65802. *Phone:* 417-865-2811 Ext. 7205. *Toll-free phone:* 800-382-6435. *Fax:* 417-865-9599. *E-mail:* admissions@evangel.edu.

See below for display ad and page 1436 for the College Close-Up.

Fontbonne University

St. Louis, Missouri

http://www.fontbonne.edu/

- **Independent Roman Catholic** comprehensive, founded 1917
- **Suburban** 13-acre campus with easy access to St. Louis
- **Endowment** $22.7 million
- **Coed** 1,213 undergraduate students, 74% full-time, 66% women, 34% men
- **Moderately difficult** entrance level, 65% of applicants were admitted

UNDERGRAD STUDENTS

899 full-time, 314 part-time. Students come from 25 states and territories; 19 other countries; 16% are from out of state; 16% Black or African American, non-Hispanic/Latino; 3% Hispanic/Latino; 1% Asian, non-Hispanic/Latino; 0.1% Native Hawaiian or other Pacific Islander, non-Hispanic/Latino; 0.3% American Indian or Alaska Native, non-Hispanic/Latino; 2% Two or more races, non-Hispanic/Latino; 1% Race/ethnicity unknown; 7% international; 13% transferred in.

Freshmen

Admission: 676 applied, 441 admitted, 113 enrolled. ***Average high school GPA:*** 3.41. ***Test scores:*** ACT scores over 18: 98%; ACT scores over 24: 41%; ACT scores over 30: 4%.

Retention: 68% of full-time freshmen returned.

FACULTY

Total: 250, 31% full-time, 44% with terminal degrees.

Student/faculty ratio: 10:1.

ACADEMICS

Calendar: semesters. *Degrees:* certificates, bachelor's, master's, post-master's, and postbachelor's certificates.

Special study options: academic remediation for entering students, accelerated degree program, adult/continuing education programs, advanced placement credit, cooperative education, distance learning, double majors, English as a second language, honors programs, independent study, internships, off-campus study, part-time degree program, services for LD students, student-designed majors, study abroad, summer session for credit. ***ROTC:*** Army (c), Air Force (c).

Unusual degree programs: 3-2 engineering with Washington University in St. Louis; social work with Washington University in St. Louis; Saint Louis University; occupational therapy with Washington University in St. Louis.

Computers: 215 computers/terminals are available on campus for general student use. Students can access the following: campus intranet, computer help desk, free student e-mail accounts, online (class) grades, online (class) registration, online (class) schedules. Campuswide network is available. Wireless service is available via entire campus.

STUDENT LIFE

Housing options: coed, men-only, women-only, special housing for students with disabilities. Campus housing is university owned. Freshman campus housing is guaranteed.

Activities and organizations: drama/theater group, student-run newspaper, choral group, Future Teachers Association, Students for the Enhancement of Black Awareness, Fontbonne Athletic Association, Fontbonne in Service and Humility, Student Government Association.

Athletics Member NCAA, NAIA. All NCAA Division III. ***Intercollegiate sports:*** baseball M, basketball M/W, bowling W, cheerleading W, cross-country running M/W, field hockey W, golf M/W, lacrosse M/W, soccer M/W, softball W, tennis M/W, track and field M/W, volleyball M/W. ***Intramural sports:*** basketball M/W, bowling M, soccer M, volleyball M/W.

Campus security: 24-hour patrols, late-night transport/escort service, controlled dormitory access.

Student services: health clinic, personal/psychological counseling.

COSTS & FINANCIAL AID

Costs (2015–16) ***Comprehensive fee:*** $32,601 includes full-time tuition ($23,430), mandatory fees ($360), and room and board ($8811). Full-time tuition and fees vary according to course load and program. Part-time tuition: $626 per credit. Part-time tuition and fees vary according to course load and program. ***Required fees:*** $18 per credit part-time. ***Room and board:*** Room and board charges vary according to board plan and housing facility. ***Payment plan:*** installment. ***Waivers:*** employees or children of employees.

Financial Aid In 2003, 502 non-need-based awards were made. ***Average percent of need met:*** 86. ***Average financial aid package:*** $15,600.

APPLYING

Standardized Tests *Required:* SAT or ACT (for admission).

Options: electronic application, deferred entrance.

Application fee: $25.

Required: high school transcript, minimum 2.5 GPA. ***Required for some:*** essay or personal statement. ***Recommended:*** 2 letters of recommendation, interview.

Application deadlines: rolling (freshmen), rolling (transfers).

Notification: continuous (freshmen), continuous (transfers).

CONTACT

Mr. Joseph Havis, Vice President of Enrollment Management, Fontbonne University, 6800 Wydown Boulevard, St. Louis, MO 63105. *Phone:* 314-889-1400. *Toll-free phone:* 800-205-5862. *Fax:* 314-889-1451. *E-mail:* FBU-Admissions@fontbonne.edu.

Goldfarb School of Nursing at Barnes-Jewish College

St. Louis, Missouri

http://www.barnesjewishcollege.edu/

- **Independent** comprehensive, founded 1902
- **Urban** campus
- **Endowment** $25.2 million
- **Coed, primarily women** 630 undergraduate students, 93% full-time, 88% women, 12% men
- **Moderately difficult** entrance level

UNDERGRAD STUDENTS

584 full-time, 46 part-time. Students come from 16 states and territories; 10 other countries; 27% are from out of state; 6% Black or African American, non-Hispanic/Latino; 2% Hispanic/Latino; 3% Asian, non-Hispanic/Latino; 2% Two or more races, non-Hispanic/Latino; 4% Race/ethnicity unknown; 100% transferred in.

FACULTY

Total: 48, 88% full-time, 35% with terminal degrees.

Student/faculty ratio: 16:1.

ACADEMICS

Calendar: trimesters. *Degrees:* bachelor's, master's, doctoral, and post-master's certificates.

Special study options: accelerated degree program, advanced placement credit, independent study, off-campus study, services for LD students, summer session for credit.

Computers: 160 computers/terminals are available on campus for general student use. Students can access the following: campus intranet, computer help desk, free student e-mail accounts, software, research databases. Campuswide network is available. Wireless service is available via entire campus.

STUDENT LIFE

Housing options: college housing not available.

Activities and organizations: student-run newspaper, Student Nurses Association.

Campus security: 24-hour patrols, late-night transport/escort service.

Student services: health clinic, personal/psychological counseling.

COSTS & FINANCIAL AID

Costs (2015–16) ***Tuition:*** $698 per credit hour part-time. Full-time tuition and fees vary according to course load and degree level. Part-time tuition and fees vary according to course load and degree level. ***Payment plan:*** installment.

Financial Aid Of all full-time matriculated undergraduates who enrolled in 2013, 19 Federal Work-Study jobs (averaging $24,500).

APPLYING

Options: deferred entrance.

Application fee: $50.

Notification: continuous (transfers).

CONTACT

Goldfarb School of Nursing at Barnes-Jewish College, 4483 Duncan Avenue, St. Louis, MO 63110. *Phone:* 314-362-9155. *Toll-free phone:* 800-832-9009.

Hannibal-LaGrange University

Hannibal, Missouri

http://www.hlg.edu/

- **Independent Southern Baptist** comprehensive, founded 1858
- **Small-town** 110-acre campus
- **Endowment** $8.4 million
- **Coed** 1,195 undergraduate students
- **Minimally difficult** entrance level

UNDERGRAD STUDENTS

Students come from 27 states and territories; 25 other countries; 26% are from out of state; 1% Black or African American, non-Hispanic/Latino; 1% Hispanic/Latino; 0.2% Asian, non-Hispanic/Latino; 0.6% Native Hawaiian or other Pacific Islander, non-Hispanic/Latino; 0.4% American

Indian or Alaska Native, non-Hispanic/Latino; 1% Two or more races, non-Hispanic/Latino; 0.7% Race/ethnicity unknown; 8% international; 47% live on campus.

FACULTY
Total: 138, 45% full-time.

ACADEMICS
Calendar: semesters. *Degrees:* certificates, associate, bachelor's, and master's.

Special study options: academic remediation for entering students, accelerated degree program, adult/continuing education programs, advanced placement credit, distance learning, double majors, English as a second language, honors programs, independent study, internships, off-campus study, part-time degree program, services for LD students, student-designed majors, study abroad, summer session for credit.

Computers: 170 computers/terminals are available on campus for general student use. Students can access the following: free student e-mail accounts, online (class) grades, online (class) registration, online (class) schedules. Campuswide network is available. 100% of college-owned or -operated housing units are wired for high-speed Internet access. Wireless service is available via classrooms, computer centers, computer labs, dorm rooms, learning centers, libraries, student centers.

STUDENT LIFE
Housing options: on-campus residence required through junior year; men-only, women-only. Campus housing is university owned. Freshman applicants given priority for college housing.

Activities and organizations: drama/theater group, student-run newspaper, choral group, Phi Beta Lambda, Student Nursing Association, Student Teachers Organization, Phi Beta Delta, Alpha Tau Beta.

Athletics Member NAIA. ***Intercollegiate sports:*** baseball M(s), basketball M(s)/W(s), cheerleading M(s)/W(s), cross-country running M(s)/W(s), golf M(s)/W(s), soccer M(s)/W(s), softball W(s), track and field M(s)/W(s), volleyball M(s)/W(s), wrestling M(s). ***Intramural sports:*** basketball M/W, bowling M/W, racquetball M/W, table tennis M/W, ultimate Frisbee M/W, volleyball M/W.

Campus security: 24-hour emergency response devices and patrols, student patrols, late-night transport/escort service, controlled dormitory access, Camera Surveillance, Alert System.

COSTS & FINANCIAL AID
Costs (2014–15) ***One-time required fee:*** $150. ***Comprehensive fee:*** $28,318 includes full-time tuition ($20,010), mandatory fees ($700), and room and board ($7608). Full-time tuition and fees vary according to course load, degree level, program, and student level. Part-time tuition: $622 per credit. Part-time tuition and fees vary according to course load, degree level, program, and student level. Online, Concurrent, Master, and Innovative Program tuition and/or fees are different from traditional undergraduate programs. ***Required fees:*** $350 per year part-time. ***Room and board:*** Room and board charges vary according to housing facility. ***Payment plan:*** installment. ***Waivers:*** employees or children of employees.

Financial Aid Of all full-time matriculated undergraduates who enrolled in 2013, 80 Federal Work-Study jobs (averaging $750).

APPLYING
Standardized Tests *Required:* SAT or ACT (for admission).

Options: electronic application, early admission, deferred entrance.

Application fee: $25.

Required: high school transcript, minimum 2.0 GPA. ***Required for some:*** GED.

Application deadlines: 9/10 (freshmen), 8/10 (out-of-state freshmen), rolling (transfers).

Notification: continuous until 9/10 (freshmen), 9/10 (out-of-state freshmen), continuous (transfers).

CONTACT
Dr. Ray Summerlin, Vice President for Enrollment Management, Hannibal-LaGrange University, 2800 Palmyra Road, Hannibal, MO 63401-1999. *Phone:* 573-6293089. *Toll-free phone:* 800-HLG-1119. *E-mail:* admissions@hlg.edu.

Harris-Stowe State University

St. Louis, Missouri

http://www.hssu.edu/

- **State-supported** 4-year, founded 1857, part of Missouri Coordinating Board for Higher Education
- **Urban** 22-acre campus
- **Endowment** $1.2 million
- **Coed** 1,280 undergraduate students, 76% full-time, 68% women, 32% men
- **Noncompetitive** entrance level, 94% of applicants were admitted

UNDERGRAD STUDENTS
969 full-time, 311 part-time. Students come from 14 states and territories; 10 other countries; 11% are from out of state; 83% Black or African American, non-Hispanic/Latino; 2% Hispanic/Latino; 0.2% Asian, non-Hispanic/Latino; 0.1% American Indian or Alaska Native, non-Hispanic/Latino; 2% Two or more races, non-Hispanic/Latino; 5% Race/ethnicity unknown; 0.6% international; 12% transferred in; 21% live on campus.

Freshmen
Admission: 590 applied, 553 admitted, 243 enrolled. ***Average high school GPA:*** 2.47. ***Test scores:*** ACT scores over 18: 30%; ACT scores over 24: 1%.

Retention: 51% of full-time freshmen returned.

FACULTY
Total: 166, 26% full-time.

Student/faculty ratio: 13:1.

ACADEMICS
Calendar: semesters. *Degree:* bachelor's.

Special study options: academic remediation for entering students, advanced placement credit, cooperative education, internships, off-campus study, part-time degree program, services for LD students, student-designed majors, summer session for credit. ***ROTC:*** Army (c), Air Force (c).

Unusual degree programs: 3-2 engineering with Saint Louis University.

Computers: 333 computers/terminals are available on campus for general student use. Students can access the following: computer help desk, free student e-mail accounts, online (class) grades, online (class) registration, online (class) schedules. Campuswide network is available. 100% of college-owned or -operated housing units are wired for high-speed Internet access. Wireless service is available via entire campus.

STUDENT LIFE
Housing options: coed. Campus housing is university owned. Freshman applicants given priority for college housing.

Activities and organizations: drama/theater group, choral group, Drama Club, Concert chorale, Student Government Association, Multicultural Council, Student Ambassadors, national fraternities, national sororities.

Athletics Member NAIA. ***Intercollegiate sports:*** baseball M(s), basketball M(s)/W(s), cheerleading M(s)/W(s), soccer M(s)/W(s), softball W(s), volleyball W(s).

Campus security: 24-hour emergency response devices and patrols, late-night transport/escort service, controlled dormitory access.

Student services: health clinic, personal/psychological counseling.

COSTS & FINANCIAL AID
Costs (2014–15) ***Tuition:*** state resident $4776 full-time, $199 per credit hour part-time; nonresident $9409 full-time, $392 per credit hour part-time. Full-time tuition and fees vary according to course load. ***Required fees:*** $444 full-time, $222 per term part-time. ***Room and board:*** $9250; room only: $6500. Room and board charges vary according to housing facility. ***Payment plan:*** installment. ***Waivers:*** employees or children of employees.

Financial Aid Of all full-time matriculated undergraduates who enrolled in 2008, 990 applied for aid, 890 were judged to have need, 200 had their need fully met. 86 Federal Work-Study jobs (averaging $2000). 80 state and other part-time jobs (averaging $2000). ***Average percent of need met:*** 90. ***Average financial aid package:*** $9500. ***Average need-based loan:*** $5000. ***Average need-based gift aid:*** $4500. ***Average non-need-based aid:*** $3000. ***Average indebtedness upon graduation:*** $16,000.

APPLYING

Standardized Tests *Required for some:* institutional placement test. *Recommended:* SAT or ACT (for admission).

Options: electronic application, early admission, deferred entrance.

Application fee: $20.

Required: high school transcript.

Application deadlines: 7/31 (freshmen), rolling (transfers).

Notification: continuous (freshmen), continuous (transfers).

CONTACT

Reynolda Brown, Director of Admissions and Retention, Harris-Stowe State University, 3026 Laclede Avenue, St. Louis, MO 63103. *Phone:* 314-340-3300. *Fax:* 314-340-3555. *E-mail:* admissions@hssu.edu.

Hickey College

St. Louis, Missouri

http://www.hickeycollege.edu/

- **Private** 4-year, founded 1933
- **Suburban** campus with easy access to St. Louis
- **Coed** 372 undergraduate students
- 72% of applicants were admitted

Freshmen

Admission: 822 applied, 590 admitted.

ACADEMICS

Calendar: semesters. *Degrees:* diplomas, associate, and bachelor's.

CONTACT

Admissions Office, Hickey College, 940 West Port Plaza, Suite 101, St. Louis, MO 63146. *Phone:* 314-434-2212. *Toll-free phone:* 800-777-1544.

ITT Technical Institute

Arnold, Missouri

http://www.itt-tech.edu/

- **Proprietary** primarily 2-year, founded 1997, part of ITT Educational Services, Inc.
- **Coed**
- **Minimally difficult** entrance level

ACADEMICS

Calendar: quarters. *Degrees:* associate and bachelor's.

STUDENT LIFE

Housing options: college housing not available.

CONTACT

Director of Recruitment, ITT Technical Institute, 1930 Meyer Drury Drive, Arnold, MO 63010. *Phone:* 636-464-6600. *Toll-free phone:* 888-488-1082.

ITT Technical Institute

Earth City, Missouri

http://www.itt-tech.edu/

- **Proprietary** primarily 2-year, founded 1936, part of ITT Educational Services, Inc.
- **Suburban** campus
- **Coed**
- **Minimally difficult** entrance level

ACADEMICS

Calendar: quarters. *Degrees:* associate and bachelor's.

STUDENT LIFE

Housing options: college housing not available.

CONTACT

Director of Recruitment, ITT Technical Institute, 3640 Corporate Trail Drive, Earth City, MO 63045. *Phone:* 314-298-7800. *Toll-free phone:* 800-235-5488.

ITT Technical Institute

Kansas City, Missouri

http://www.itt-tech.edu/

- **Proprietary** primarily 2-year, founded 2004, part of ITT Educational Services, Inc.
- **Coed**
- **Minimally difficult** entrance level

ACADEMICS

Calendar: quarters. *Degrees:* associate and bachelor's.

CONTACT

Director of Recruitment, ITT Technical Institute, 9150 East 41st Terrace, Kansas City, MO 64133. *Phone:* 816-276-1400. *Toll-free phone:* 877-488-1442.

ITT Technical Institute

Springfield, Missouri

http://www.itt-tech.edu/

- **Proprietary** 4-year, part of ITT Educational Services, Inc.
- **Coed**
- **Minimally difficult** entrance level

ACADEMICS

Calendar: quarters. *Degrees:* associate and bachelor's.

CONTACT

Director of Recruitment, ITT Technical Institute, 3216 South National Avenue, Springfield, MO 65807. *Phone:* 417-877-4800. *Toll-free phone:* 877-219-4387.

Kansas City Art Institute

Kansas City, Missouri

http://www.kcai.edu/

- **Independent** 4-year, founded 1885
- **Urban** 18-acre campus
- **Endowment** $55.0 million
- **Coed** 655 undergraduate students, 98% full-time, 65% women, 35% men
- **Moderately difficult** entrance level, 60% of applicants were admitted

UNDERGRAD STUDENTS

644 full-time, 11 part-time. Students come from 35 states and territories; 9 other countries; 62% are from out of state; 6% Black or African American, non-Hispanic/Latino; 8% Hispanic/Latino; 2% Asian, non-Hispanic/Latino; 0.2% American Indian or Alaska Native, non-Hispanic/Latino; 10% Two or more races, non-Hispanic/Latino; 12% Race/ethnicity unknown; 3% transferred in; 31% live on campus.

Freshmen

Admission: 612 applied, 367 admitted, 134 enrolled. ***Average high school GPA:*** 3.2. ***Test scores:*** SAT critical reading scores over 500: 87%; SAT math scores over 500: 65%; SAT writing scores over 500: 62%; ACT scores over 18: 97%; SAT critical reading scores over 600: 35%; SAT math scores over 600: 16%; SAT writing scores over 600: 10%; ACT scores over 24: 52%; ACT scores over 30: 10%.

Retention: 77% of full-time freshmen returned.

FACULTY

Total: 116, 45% full-time, 5% with terminal degrees.

ACADEMICS

Calendar: semesters. *Degrees:* bachelor's and postbachelor's certificates.

Special study options: academic remediation for entering students, advanced placement credit, cooperative education, double majors, English as a second language, independent study, internships, off-campus study, services for LD students, study abroad, summer session for credit.

Computers: 120 computers/terminals and 1,000 ports are available on campus for general student use. Students can access the following: campus intranet, computer help desk, free student e-mail accounts, online (class) grades, online (class) registration, online (class) schedules. Campuswide network is available. 100% of college-owned or -operated housing units are wired for high-speed Internet access. Wireless service is available via entire campus.

STUDENT LIFE
Housing options: on-campus residence required for freshman year; coed. Campus housing is university owned. Freshman applicants given priority for college housing.

Activities and organizations: ArtPlay, Black Artist Culture and Community, Quiltbag app (LGBTQIA), Illustration Student Committee, KCAIR.

Campus security: 24-hour emergency response devices and patrols, late-night transport/escort service, controlled dormitory access.

Student services: personal/psychological counseling.

COSTS & FINANCIAL AID
Costs (2015–16) ***Comprehensive fee:*** $45,510 includes full-time tuition ($35,120), mandatory fees ($150), and room and board ($10,240). Full-time tuition and fees vary according to program. Part-time tuition: $1465 per credit hour. Part-time tuition and fees vary according to program. ***Room and board:*** Room and board charges vary according to board plan. ***Payment plan:*** installment. ***Waivers:*** employees or children of employees.

Financial Aid Of all full-time matriculated undergraduates who enrolled in 2014, 637 applied for aid, 584 were judged to have need, 77 had their need fully met. 119 Federal Work-Study jobs (averaging $1026). 219 state and other part-time jobs (averaging $1200). In 2014, 109 non-need-based awards were made. ***Average percent of need met:*** 59. ***Average financial aid package:*** $23,526. ***Average need-based loan:*** $4740. ***Average need-based gift aid:*** $19,266. ***Average non-need-based aid:*** $15,298. ***Average indebtedness upon graduation:*** $25,000.

APPLYING
Standardized Tests *Required:* SAT or ACT (for admission).

Options: electronic application, early admission, deferred entrance.

Application fee: $45.

Required: essay or personal statement, high school transcript, minimum 2.5 GPA, 1 letter of recommendation, portfolio. ***Required for some:*** essay or personal statement. ***Recommended:*** interview.

Application deadlines: 8/1 (freshmen), 8/1 (out-of-state freshmen), 8/1 (transfers).

Notification: 8/15 (freshmen), 8/15 (out-of-state freshmen), 8/15 (transfers).

CONTACT
Mr. Gerald Valet, Director of Admission Technology, Kansas City Art Institute, 4415 Warwick Boulevard, Kansas City, MO 64111-1874. *Phone:* 816-474-5224. *Toll-free phone:* 800-522-5224. *Fax:* 816-802-3309. *E-mail:* admiss@kcai.edu.

Lincoln University
Jefferson City, Missouri
http://www.lincolnu.edu/

- **State-supported** comprehensive, founded 1866, part of Missouri Coordinating Board for Higher Education
- **Small-town** 170-acre campus
- **Endowment** $1.5 million
- **Coed** 2,977 undergraduate students, 68% full-time, 56% women, 44% men
- **Noncompetitive** entrance level, 54% of applicants were admitted

UNDERGRAD STUDENTS
2,032 full-time, 945 part-time. Students come from 35 states and territories; 18 other countries; 15% are from out of state; 40% Black or African American, non-Hispanic/Latino; 2% Hispanic/Latino; 0.6% Asian, non-Hispanic/Latino; 0.3% American Indian or Alaska Native, non-Hispanic/Latino; 2% Two or more races, non-Hispanic/Latino; 5% Race/ethnicity unknown; 2% international; 6% transferred in; 27% live on campus.

Freshmen
Admission: 3,940 applied, 2,139 admitted, 534 enrolled. ***Average high school GPA:*** 2.65. ***Test scores:*** SAT critical reading scores over 500: 7%; SAT math scores over 500: 13%; ACT scores over 18: 37%; ACT scores over 24: 7%; ACT scores over 30: 1%.

Retention: 64% of full-time freshmen returned.

FACULTY
Total: 194, 59% full-time.

Student/faculty ratio: 17:1.

ACADEMICS
Calendar: semesters. *Degrees:* associate, bachelor's, master's, and post-master's certificates.

Special study options: academic remediation for entering students, accelerated degree program, adult/continuing education programs, advanced placement credit, cooperative education, distance learning, double majors, honors programs, independent study, internships, off-campus study, part-time degree program, services for LD students, study abroad, summer session for credit. ***ROTC:*** Army (b), Navy (c), Air Force (c).

Computers: 315 computers/terminals and 1,100 ports are available on campus for general student use. Students can access the following: campus intranet, computer help desk, free student e-mail accounts, online (class) grades, online (class) registration, online (class) schedules. Campuswide network is available. 100% of college-owned or -operated housing units are wired for high-speed Internet access. Wireless service is available via entire campus.

STUDENT LIFE
Housing options: on-campus residence required through sophomore year; coed, men-only, women-only. Campus housing is university owned.

Activities and organizations: drama/theater group, student-run newspaper, radio and television station, choral group, marching band, Student Government Association (SGA), Lincoln University Band, Alpha Kappa Mu, Army ROTC, International Students Association, national fraternities, national sororities.

Athletics Member NCAA. All Division II. ***Intercollegiate sports:*** baseball M(s), basketball M(s)/W(s), bowling W(s), cheerleading W(s), cross-country running W(s), football M(s), golf M(s)/W(s), softball W(s), tennis W(s), track and field M(s)/W(s). ***Intramural sports:*** basketball M/W, bowling M/W, volleyball M/W, weight lifting M/W.

Campus security: 24-hour emergency response devices and patrols, student patrols, late-night transport/escort service, controlled dormitory access, security-related training upon request, Operation ID-ent, Timely Warnings, text message safety alerts, webpage with helpful tips.

Student services: health clinic, personal/psychological counseling.

COSTS & FINANCIAL AID
Costs (2014–15) ***Tuition:*** state resident $6150 full-time, $205 per credit hour part-time; nonresident $12,540 full-time, $418 per credit hour part-time. Full-time tuition and fees vary according to location and reciprocity agreements. Part-time tuition and fees vary according to location and reciprocity agreements. ***Required fees:*** $688 full-time, $17 per credit hour part-time, $93 per term part-time. ***Room and board:*** $5531; room only: $2786. Room and board charges vary according to board plan and housing facility. ***Payment plans:*** installment, deferred payment. ***Waivers:*** senior citizens and employees or children of employees.

Financial Aid Of all full-time matriculated undergraduates who enrolled in 2014, 1,837 applied for aid, 1,654 were judged to have need, 60 had their need fully met. 169 Federal Work-Study jobs (averaging $1214). 156 state and other part-time jobs (averaging $3956). In 2014, 3 non-need-based awards were made. ***Average percent of need met:*** 62. ***Average financial aid package:*** $10,788. ***Average need-based loan:*** $4058. ***Average need-based gift aid:*** $5762. ***Average non-need-based aid:*** $4333. ***Average indebtedness upon graduation:*** $30,225.

APPLYING
Standardized Tests *Required:* SAT or ACT (for admission).

Options: electronic application, deferred entrance.

Required: high school transcript. ***Required for some:*** minimum 2.0 GPA, audition for sacred music and music education.

Notification: continuous (freshmen), continuous (out-of-state freshmen), continuous (transfers).

CONTACT
Annette Crowder, Director of Admissions, Lincoln University, Office of Admissions, 820 Chestnut Street, B-7 Young Hall, Jefferson City, MO 65101. *Phone:* 573-681-5599. *Fax:* 573-681-5889. *E-mail:* enroll@lincolnu.edu.

★ Lindenwood University

St. Charles, Missouri

http://www.lindenwood.edu/

- **Independent Presbyterian** comprehensive, founded 1827
- **Suburban** 550-acre campus with easy access to St. Louis
- **Endowment** $122.2 million
- **Coed** 8,541 undergraduate students, 87% full-time, 54% women, 46% men
- **Moderately difficult** entrance level, 53% of applicants were admitted

UNDERGRAD STUDENTS

7,443 full-time, 1,098 part-time. Students come from 48 states and territories; 90 other countries; 33% are from out of state; 14% Black or African American, non-Hispanic/Latino; 4% Hispanic/Latino; 0.5% Asian, non-Hispanic/Latino; 0.3% Native Hawaiian or other Pacific Islander, non-Hispanic/Latino; 0.3% American Indian or Alaska Native, non-Hispanic/Latino; 3% Two or more races, non-Hispanic/Latino; 6% Race/ethnicity unknown; 12% international; 10% transferred in; 53% live on campus.

Freshmen

Admission: 4,595 applied, 2,430 admitted, 1,201 enrolled. ***Average high school GPA:*** 3.16. ***Test scores:*** SAT critical reading scores over 500: 42%; SAT math scores over 500: 56%; SAT writing scores over 500: 33%; ACT scores over 18: 97%; SAT critical reading scores over 600: 9%; SAT math scores over 600: 14%; SAT writing scores over 600: 11%; ACT scores over 24: 33%; SAT critical reading scores over 700: 2%; SAT math scores over 700: 2%; SAT writing scores over 700: 1%; ACT scores over 30: 5%.

Retention: 70% of full-time freshmen returned.

FACULTY

Total: 1,064, 28% full-time, 38% with terminal degrees.

Student/faculty ratio: 14:1.

ACADEMICS

Calendar: 4-1-4 for daytime programs; quarters for evening programs, and 5 term MBA programs. *Degrees:* bachelor's, master's, doctoral, post-master's, and postbachelor's certificates.

Special study options: academic remediation for entering students, accelerated degree program, adult/continuing education programs, advanced placement credit, distance learning, double majors, English as a second language, external degree program, freshman honors college, honors programs, independent study, internships, off-campus study, part-time degree program, services for LD students, student-designed majors, study abroad, summer session for credit. ***ROTC:*** Army (b), Air Force (c).

Unusual degree programs: 3-2 engineering with University of Missouri-Columbia.

Computers: 286 computers/terminals are available on campus for general student use. Students can access the following: campus intranet, computer help desk, free student e-mail accounts, online (class) grades, online (class) registration, online (class) schedules, Blackboard. Campuswide network is available. 100% of college-owned or -operated housing units are wired for high-speed Internet access. Wireless service is available via classrooms, computer centers, computer labs, dorm rooms, learning centers, libraries, student centers.

STUDENT LIFE

Housing options: on-campus residence required for freshman year; men-only, women-only. Campus housing is university owned and leased by the school. Freshman applicants given priority for college housing.

Activities and organizations: drama/theater group, student-run newspaper, radio and television station, choral group, marching band, Advertisers Desiring Success, Psychology Interest Club, Honors Society, Black Student Union, Accounting and Finance Club, national fraternities, national sororities.

Athletics Member NCAA, NAIA, USCAA. All NCAA Division II. ***Intercollegiate sports:*** baseball M(s), basketball M(s)/W(s), bowling M(s)/W(s), cheerleading M(s)/W(s), cross-country running M(s)/W(s), field hockey W(s), football M(s), golf M(s)/W(s), gymnastics W(s), ice hockey M(s)/W(s), lacrosse M(s)/W(s), riflery M(s)/W(s), rugby M(s)/W(s), soccer M(s)/W(s), softball W(s), swimming and diving M(s)/W(s), table tennis M(s)/W(s), tennis M(s)/W(s), track and field

M(s)/W(s), volleyball M(s)/W(s), water polo M(s)/W(s), weight lifting M(s)/W(s), wrestling M(s)/W(s). ***Intramural sports:*** baseball M/W, soccer M/W, softball W, volleyball M/W.

Campus security: 24-hour emergency response devices and patrols, late-night transport/escort service, controlled dormitory access, surveillance cameras throughout the campus and facilities.

Student services: health clinic, personal/psychological counseling.

COSTS & FINANCIAL AID

Costs (2014–15) ***Comprehensive fee:*** $23,460 includes full-time tuition ($15,230), mandatory fees ($350), and room and board ($7880). Part-time tuition: $440 per credit hour. Part-time tuition and fees vary according to course load. ***College room only:*** $4290. ***Payment plans:*** installment, deferred payment. ***Waivers:*** senior citizens and employees or children of employees.

Financial Aid Of all full-time matriculated undergraduates who enrolled in 2014, 5,089 applied for aid, 4,326 were judged to have need, 3,058 had their need fully met. 237 Federal Work-Study jobs (averaging $2209). 733 state and other part-time jobs (averaging $2222). In 2014, 3660 non-need-based awards were made. ***Average percent of need met:*** 90. ***Average financial aid package:*** $10,874. ***Average need-based loan:*** $4382. ***Average need-based gift aid:*** $6427. ***Average non-need-based aid:*** $4785.

APPLYING

Standardized Tests *Required:* SAT or ACT (for admission).

Options: electronic application.

Application fee: $30.

Required: high school transcript, minimum 2.5 GPA, Personal resume indicating community service, youth leadership, clubs, organizations, and non-academic experience. ***Recommended:*** essay or personal statement, 3 letters of recommendation, interview.

Application deadlines: rolling (freshmen), rolling (out-of-state freshmen), rolling (transfers).

Notification: continuous (freshmen), continuous (out-of-state freshmen), continuous (transfers).

CONTACT

Mrs. Rachel South, Director of Day Admissions, Lindenwood University, 209 S Kingshighway, St. Charles, MO 63301. *Phone:* 636-949-4946. *Fax:* 636-949-4989. *E-mail:* RSouth@lindenwood.edu.

See previous page for display ad and page 1502 for the College Close-Up.

Logan University

Chesterfield, Missouri

http://www.logan.edu/

- **Independent** upper-level, founded 1935
- **Suburban** 111-acre campus with easy access to St. Louis
- **Coed** 48 undergraduate students, 69% full-time, 52% women, 48% men
- **Moderately difficult** entrance level

UNDERGRAD STUDENTS

33 full-time, 15 part-time. Students come from 14 states and territories; 49% are from out of state; 2% Black or African American, non-Hispanic/Latino; 2% Hispanic/Latino; 4% Asian, non-Hispanic/Latino; 2% Two or more races, non-Hispanic/Latino; 27% Race/ethnicity unknown; 98% transferred in.

FACULTY

Total: 100, 52% full-time.

Student/faculty ratio: 12:1.

ACADEMICS

Calendar: trimesters. *Degrees:* bachelor's, master's, and doctoral.

Special study options: accelerated degree program, adult/continuing education programs, advanced placement credit, distance learning, independent study, internships, part-time degree program, services for LD students.

Computers: 100 computers/terminals and 1,000 ports are available on campus for general student use. Students can access the following: computer help desk, free student e-mail accounts, online (class) grades, online (class) registration, online (class) schedules, Student portal, LMS, online storage, Wi-Fi, specialty health care software, high-speed printing. Campuswide network is available. Wireless service is available via entire campus.

STUDENT LIFE

Housing options: college housing not available.

Activities and organizations: Pi Kappa Chi, Lambda Kappa Chi, Chiro Rho Sigma, Student American Chiropractic Association, Omega Sigma Pi, national fraternities, national sororities.

Athletics ***Intercollegiate sports:*** basketball M(c)/W(c), golf M(c), soccer M(c), tennis M(c). ***Intramural sports:*** basketball M/W, football M, ice hockey M, softball M/W, volleyball M/W.

Campus security: 24-hour patrols, late-night transport/escort service.

Student services: health clinic, personal/psychological counseling.

COSTS & FINANCIAL AID

Costs (2015–16) ***Tuition:*** $6600 full-time, $275 per credit hour part-time. Full-time tuition and fees vary according to course load and degree level. Part-time tuition and fees vary according to course load and degree level. ***Required fees:*** $280 full-time, $140 per term part-time. ***Waivers:*** employees or children of employees.

Financial Aid Of all full-time matriculated undergraduates who enrolled in 1999, 160 applied for aid, 160 were judged to have need, 130 had their need fully met. 130 Federal Work-Study jobs (averaging $2693). ***Average percent of need met:*** 100. ***Average need-based loan:*** $3500. ***Average need-based gift aid:*** $3000.

APPLYING

Options: electronic application, deferred entrance.

Application fee: $50.

Required: specific preparatory undergraduate coursework.

Notification: continuous (transfers).

CONTACT

Logan University, 1851 Schoettler Road, Chesterfield, MO 63017. *Phone:* 636-227-2100. *Toll-free phone:* 800-533-9210.

Maryville University of Saint Louis

St. Louis, Missouri

http://www.maryville.edu/

- **Independent** comprehensive, founded 1872
- **Suburban** 130-acre campus with easy access to St. Louis
- **Endowment** $42.5 million
- **Coed** 2,818 undergraduate students, 66% full-time, 71% women, 29% men
- **Moderately difficult** entrance level, 72% of applicants were admitted

UNDERGRAD STUDENTS

1,852 full-time, 966 part-time. Students come from 33 states and territories; 23 other countries; 21% are from out of state; 8% Black or African American, non-Hispanic/Latino; 3% Hispanic/Latino; 2% Asian, non-Hispanic/Latino; 0.2% Native Hawaiian or other Pacific Islander, non-Hispanic/Latino; 0.3% American Indian or Alaska Native, non-Hispanic/Latino; 3% Two or more races, non-Hispanic/Latino; 6% Race/ethnicity unknown; 3% international; 12% transferred in; 24% live on campus.

Freshmen

Admission: 1,576 applied, 1,134 admitted, 412 enrolled. ***Average high school GPA:*** 3.7. ***Test scores:*** SAT critical reading scores over 500: 45%; SAT math scores over 500: 76%; ACT scores over 18: 100%; SAT critical reading scores over 600: 12%; SAT math scores over 600: 21%; ACT scores over 24: 71%; SAT critical reading scores over 700: 6%; SAT math scores over 700: 6%; ACT scores over 30: 9%.

Retention: 87% of full-time freshmen returned.

FACULTY

Total: 559, 22% full-time, 51% with terminal degrees.

Student/faculty ratio: 13:1.

ACADEMICS

Calendar: semesters. *Degrees:* bachelor's, master's, doctoral, and postbachelor's certificates.

Special study options: accelerated degree program, adult/continuing education programs, advanced placement credit, cooperative education, distance learning, double majors, English as a second language, honors programs, independent study, internships, off-campus study, part-time degree program, services for LD students, study abroad, summer session for credit. ***ROTC:*** Army (c).

Unusual degree programs: 3-2 business administration; engineering with Washington University in St. Louis; social work with Saint Louis University; education.

Computers: 565 computers/terminals are available on campus for general student use. Students can access the following: campus intranet, computer help desk, free student e-mail accounts, online (class) grades, online (class) registration, online (class) schedules, specialized software, university catalog. Campuswide network is available. 100% of college-owned or -operated housing units are wired for high-speed Internet access. Wireless service is available via entire campus.

STUDENT LIFE

Housing options: coed. Campus housing is university owned.

Activities and organizations: drama/theater group, student-run newspaper, choral group, Campus Activities Board, Physical Therapy Club, Student Nurses Association, Community Service Club, Pediatric Enthusiasts Delivering Smiles.

Athletics Member NCAA. All Division II. ***Intercollegiate sports:*** baseball M(s), basketball M(s)/W(s), cross-country running M(s)/W(s), golf M(s)/W(s), soccer M(s)/W(s), softball W(s), swimming and diving W(s), tennis M/W(s), track and field M(s)/W(s), volleyball W(s), wrestling M(s). ***Intramural sports:*** basketball M/W, cheerleading M/W, football M/W, soccer M/W, softball W, volleyball M/W.

Campus security: 24-hour emergency response devices and patrols, late-night transport/escort service, controlled dormitory access, video security system in residence halls, self-defense and education programs.

Student services: health clinic, personal/psychological counseling.

COSTS & FINANCIAL AID

Costs (2014–15) ***Comprehensive fee:*** $35,856 includes full-time tuition ($24,694), mandatory fees ($1190), and room and board ($9972). Full-time tuition and fees vary according to course load. Part-time tuition: $740 per credit hour. Part-time tuition and fees vary according to class time. ***Required fees:*** $297 per term part-time. ***College room only:*** $7684. Room and board charges vary according to board plan and housing facility. ***Payment plans:*** installment, deferred payment. ***Waivers:*** senior citizens and employees or children of employees.

Financial Aid Of all full-time matriculated undergraduates who enrolled in 2014, 1,428 applied for aid, 1,291 were judged to have need, 173 had their need fully met. 340 Federal Work-Study jobs (averaging $618). 339 state and other part-time jobs (averaging $992). In 2014, 487 non-need-based awards were made. ***Average percent of need met:*** 70. ***Average financial aid package:*** $22,812. ***Average need-based loan:*** $3958. ***Average need-based gift aid:*** $14,323. ***Average non-need-based aid:*** $9559. ***Average indebtedness upon graduation:*** $31,696.

APPLYING

Standardized Tests *Required:* SAT or ACT (for admission).

Options: electronic application, deferred entrance.

Application fee: $30.

Required: high school transcript, minimum 2.5 GPA. ***Required for some:*** essay or personal statement, interview, audition, portfolio.

Application deadlines: 8/15 (freshmen), rolling (transfers).

Notification: continuous (freshmen), continuous (transfers).

CONTACT

Ms. Shani Lenore-Jenkins, Associate Vice President of Enrollment, Maryville University of Saint Louis, 650 Maryville University Drive, St. Louis, MO 63141-7299. *Phone:* 314-529-9350. *Toll-free phone:* 800-627-9855. *Fax:* 314-529-9927. *E-mail:* admissions@maryville.edu.

Missouri Baptist University

St. Louis, Missouri

http://www.mobap.edu/

- **Independent Southern Baptist** comprehensive, founded 1964
- **Suburban** 65-acre campus with easy access to St. Louis
- **Endowment** $4.7 million
- **Coed** 4,091 undergraduate students, 34% full-time, 60% women, 40% men
- **Moderately difficult** entrance level, 60% of applicants were admitted

UNDERGRAD STUDENTS

1,389 full-time, 2,702 part-time. Students come from 37 states and territories; 20 other countries; 25% are from out of state; 12% Black or African American, non-Hispanic/Latino; 3% Hispanic/Latino; 1% Asian, non-Hispanic/Latino; 0.4% American Indian or Alaska Native, non-Hispanic/Latino; 3% Two or more races, non-Hispanic/Latino; 5% Race/ethnicity unknown; 2% international; 9% transferred in; 25% live on campus.

Freshmen

Admission: 865 applied, 521 admitted, 224 enrolled. ***Average high school GPA:*** 3.09.

Retention: 57% of full-time freshmen returned.

FACULTY

Total: 286, 25% full-time, 28% with terminal degrees.

Student/faculty ratio: 20:1.

ACADEMICS

Calendar: semesters. *Degrees:* certificates, associate, bachelor's, master's, doctoral, post-master's, and postbachelor's certificates.

Special study options: academic remediation for entering students, accelerated degree program, adult/continuing education programs, advanced placement credit, distance learning, double majors, honors programs, independent study, internships, off-campus study, part-time degree program, services for LD students, student-designed majors, study abroad, summer session for credit. ***ROTC:*** Army (c).

Computers: 100 computers/terminals are available on campus for general student use. Students can access the following: campus intranet, computer help desk, free student e-mail accounts, online (class) grades, online (class) registration, online (class) schedules. Campuswide network is available. 100% of college-owned or -operated housing units are wired for high-speed Internet access. Wireless service is available via entire campus.

STUDENT LIFE

Housing options: men-only, women-only. Campus housing is university owned. Freshman applicants given priority for college housing.

Activities and organizations: drama/theater group, student-run radio station, choral group, Enactus: Students in Free Enterprise, Amp Ministries, Student Missouri State Teacher's Association, Gamma Delta Sigma, Ministerial Alliance.

Athletics Member NAIA. ***Intercollegiate sports:*** baseball M(s), basketball M(s)/W(s), bowling M(s)(c)/W(s)(c), cheerleading M(s)/W(s), cross-country running M(s)/W(s), football M(s), golf M(s)/W(s), lacrosse M(s)(c)/W(s)(c), soccer M(s)/W(s), softball W(s), tennis M(s)/W(s), track and field M(s)/W(s), volleyball M(s)/W(s), wrestling M(s)/W(s). ***Intramural sports:*** basketball M/W, bowling M/W, football M/W, soccer M/W, softball M/W, volleyball M/W.

Campus security: 24-hour emergency response devices and patrols, late-night transport/escort service, controlled dormitory access, self-defense classes.

Student services: health clinic, personal/psychological counseling.

COSTS & FINANCIAL AID

Costs (2014–15) ***Comprehensive fee:*** $31,830 includes full-time tuition ($21,620), mandatory fees ($1140), and room and board ($9070). Full-time tuition and fees vary according to course load and location. Part-time tuition: $745 per credit hour. Part-time tuition and fees vary according to course load and location. ***Required fees:*** $24 per credit hour part-time, $65 per term part-time. ***Room and board:*** Room and board charges vary according to board plan and housing facility. ***Payment plan:*** installment. ***Waivers:*** children of alumni, senior citizens, and employees or children of employees.

Financial Aid Of all full-time matriculated undergraduates who enrolled in 2014, 1,224 applied for aid, 1,116 were judged to have need, 193 had their need fully met. 555 Federal Work-Study jobs (averaging $1805). In 2014, 24 non-need-based awards were made. ***Average financial aid package:*** $16,719. ***Average need-based loan:*** $4168. ***Average need-based gift aid:*** $4988. ***Average non-need-based aid:*** $14,720. ***Average indebtedness upon graduation:*** $25,337.

APPLYING
Standardized Tests *Required:* SAT or ACT (for admission).

Options: electronic application.

Application fee: $35.

Required: high school transcript, minimum 2.0 GPA, 1 letter of recommendation.

Application deadlines: rolling (freshmen), rolling (out-of-state freshmen), rolling (transfers).

Notification: continuous (freshmen), continuous (out-of-state freshmen), continuous (transfers).

CONTACT
Ms. Beth Kinsey, Missouri Baptist University, One College Park Drive, St. Louis, MO 63141-8660. *Phone:* 877-434-1115. *Toll-free phone:* 877-434-1115 Ext. 2290. *Fax:* 314-434-7596. *E-mail:* admissions@mobap.edu.

Missouri Southern State University

Joplin, Missouri

http://www.mssu.edu/

- **State-supported** comprehensive, founded 1937
- **Small-town** 365-acre campus
- **Coed** 5,561 undergraduate students, 74% full-time, 57% women, 43% men
- **Moderately difficult** entrance level, 96% of applicants were admitted

UNDERGRAD STUDENTS
4,140 full-time, 1,421 part-time. Students come from 46 states and territories; 30 other countries; 17% are from out of state; 6% Black or African American, non-Hispanic/Latino; 4% Hispanic/Latino; 2% Asian, non-Hispanic/Latino; 0.1% Native Hawaiian or other Pacific Islander, non-Hispanic/Latino; 3% American Indian or Alaska Native, non-Hispanic/Latino; 0.7% Two or more races, non-Hispanic/Latino; 4% Race/ethnicity unknown; 3% international; 10% transferred in; 13% live on campus.

Freshmen
Admission: 2,002 applied, 1,922 admitted, 856 enrolled. ***Average high school GPA:*** 3.26. ***Test scores:*** ACT scores over 18: 64%; ACT scores over 24: 26%; ACT scores over 30: 1%.

Retention: 65% of full-time freshmen returned.

FACULTY
Total: 354, 56% full-time, 43% with terminal degrees.

Student/faculty ratio: 18:1.

ACADEMICS
Calendar: semesters. *Degrees:* certificates, associate, bachelor's, and master's.

Special study options: academic remediation for entering students, accelerated degree program, adult/continuing education programs, advanced placement credit, cooperative education, distance learning, double majors, English as a second language, honors programs, independent study, internships, off-campus study, part-time degree program, services for LD students, study abroad, summer session for credit.

Computers: 550 computers/terminals are available on campus for general student use. Students can access the following: campus intranet, computer help desk, free student e-mail accounts, online (class) grades, online (class) registration, online (class) schedules. Campuswide network is available. 100% of college-owned or -operated housing units are wired for high-speed Internet access. Wireless service is available via entire campus.

STUDENT LIFE
Housing options: on-campus residence required for freshman year; coed, men-only, women-only. Campus housing is university owned. Freshman campus housing is guaranteed.

Activities and organizations: drama/theater group, student-run newspaper, radio and television station, choral group, marching band, national fraternities, national sororities.

Athletics Member NCAA. All Division II. ***Intercollegiate sports:*** baseball M(s), basketball M(s)/W(s), cross-country running M(s)/W(s), football M(s), golf M(s), soccer M(s)/W(s), softball W(s), tennis W(s), track and field M(s)/W(s), volleyball W(s). ***Intramural sports:*** basketball M/W, football M/W, golf M/W, soccer M/W, softball M/W, tennis M/W, volleyball M/W.

Campus security: 24-hour emergency response devices and patrols, late-night transport/escort service, controlled dormitory access, security at campus events, emergency vehicle assistance, safety awareness information to students.

Student services: health clinic, personal/psychological counseling.

COSTS & FINANCIAL AID
Costs (2014–15) ***Tuition:*** state resident $5196 full-time, $173 per term part-time; nonresident $10,590 full-time, $353 per term part-time. Full-time tuition and fees vary according to course load. ***Required fees:*** $566 full-time. ***Room and board:*** $6299. Room and board charges vary according to board plan and housing facility. ***Payment plan:*** installment. ***Waivers:*** senior citizens and employees or children of employees.

Financial Aid Of all full-time matriculated undergraduates who enrolled in 2013, 2,836 applied for aid, 2,331 were judged to have need, 160 had their need fully met. 81 Federal Work-Study jobs (averaging $2020). 263 state and other part-time jobs (averaging $4116). In 2013, 252 non-need-based awards were made. ***Average percent of need met:*** 65. ***Average financial aid package:*** $7413. ***Average need-based loan:*** $2163. ***Average need-based gift aid:*** $4121. ***Average non-need-based aid:*** $2105. ***Average indebtedness upon graduation:*** $29,405.

APPLYING
Standardized Tests *Required:* SAT or ACT (for admission), SAT and SAT Subject Tests or ACT (for admission). *Recommended:* ACT (for admission).

Options: electronic application, deferred entrance.

Application fee: $25.

Required: high school transcript, minimum 2.3 GPA, class rank of at least 50% and a recommended ACT score of at least 21. ***Required for some:*** 2 letters of recommendation.

Application deadlines: 8/1 (freshmen), 8/1 (transfers).

Notification: continuous (freshmen), continuous (transfers).

CONTACT
Mr. Derek Skaggs, Director of Enrollment Services, Missouri Southern State University, 3950 East Newman Road, Hearnes 106B, Joplin, MO 64801-1595. *Phone:* 417-625-9537. *Toll-free phone:* 866-818-MSSU. *Fax:* 417-659-4429. *E-mail:* admissions@mssu.edu.

Missouri State University

Springfield, Missouri

http://www.missouristate.edu/

- **State-supported** comprehensive, founded 1905
- **Suburban** 225-acre campus
- **Coed** 18,517 undergraduate students, 76% full-time, 57% women, 43% men
- **Moderately difficult** entrance level, 85% of applicants were admitted

UNDERGRAD STUDENTS
14,097 full-time, 4,420 part-time. 11% are from out of state; 4% Black or African American, non-Hispanic/Latino; 3% Hispanic/Latino; 1% Asian, non-Hispanic/Latino; 0.2% Native Hawaiian or other Pacific Islander, non-Hispanic/Latino; 0.6% American Indian or Alaska Native, non-Hispanic/Latino; 3% Two or more races, non-Hispanic/Latino; 1% Race/ethnicity unknown; 5% international; 9% transferred in; 27% live on campus.

Freshmen

Admission: 8,044 applied, 6,840 admitted, 2,870 enrolled. ***Average high school GPA:*** 3.61. ***Test scores:*** SAT critical reading scores over 500: 68%; SAT math scores over 500: 68%; ACT scores over 18: 98%; SAT critical reading scores over 600: 30%; SAT math scores over 600: 28%; ACT scores over 24: 53%; SAT critical reading scores over 700: 5%; SAT math scores over 700: 1%; ACT scores over 30: 9%.

Retention: 77% of full-time freshmen returned.

FACULTY

Total: 1,128, 65% full-time, 59% with terminal degrees.

Student/faculty ratio: 20:1.

ACADEMICS

Calendar: semesters. *Degrees:* certificates, bachelor's, master's, doctoral, post-master's, and postbachelor's certificates.

Special study options: accelerated degree program, advanced placement credit, cooperative education, distance learning, double majors, English as a second language, freshman honors college, honors programs, independent study, internships, off-campus study, part-time degree program, services for LD students, student-designed majors, study abroad, summer session for credit. ***ROTC:*** Army (b).

Computers: Students can access the following: campus intranet, computer help desk, free student e-mail accounts, online (class) grades, online (class) registration, online (class) schedules. Campuswide network is available. 100% of college-owned or -operated housing units are wired for high-speed Internet access. Wireless service is available via classrooms, computer centers, computer labs, learning centers, libraries, student centers.

STUDENT LIFE

Housing options: on-campus residence required for freshman year; coed, special housing for students with disabilities. Campus housing is university owned. Freshman campus housing is guaranteed.

Activities and organizations: drama/theater group, student-run newspaper, radio and television station, choral group, marching band, Residence Hall Association, Campus Ministries, Fraternity and Sorority Life, Student Government Association, Student Activities Council, national fraternities, national sororities.

Athletics Member NCAA. All Division I except football (Division I-AA). ***Intercollegiate sports:*** baseball M(s), basketball M(s)/W(s), bowling M(c)/W(c), cross-country running W(s), equestrian sports M(c)/W(c), field hockey W(s), golf M(s)/W(s), ice hockey M(c), lacrosse M(c), racquetball M(c)/W(c), soccer M(s)/W(s), softball W(s), swimming and diving M(s)/W(s), track and field W(s), ultimate Frisbee M(c)/W(c), volleyball M(c)/W(s), wrestling M(c). ***Intramural sports:*** basketball M/W, bowling M/W, football M/W, golf M/W, racquetball M/W, soccer M/W, softball M/W, table tennis M/W, tennis M/W, track and field W, ultimate Frisbee M/W, volleyball M/W, weight lifting M/W.

Campus security: 24-hour emergency response devices and patrols, late-night transport/escort service, controlled dormitory access, on-campus police substation.

Student services: health clinic, personal/psychological counseling, legal services.

COSTS & FINANCIAL AID

Costs (2014–15) ***Tuition:*** state resident $6908 full-time, $204 per credit hour part-time; nonresident $13,668 full-time, $426 per credit hour part-time. Full-time tuition and fees vary according to course level, course load, and program. Part-time tuition and fees vary according to course level, course load, and program. ***Required fees:*** $888 full-time. ***Room and board:*** $7678. Room and board charges vary according to board plan, housing facility, and location. ***Payment plan:*** deferred payment. ***Waivers:*** children of alumni, senior citizens, and employees or children of employees.

Financial Aid Of all full-time matriculated undergraduates who enrolled in 2014, 11,079 applied for aid, 8,792 were judged to have need, 1,308 had their need fully met. In 2014, 1407 non-need-based awards were made. ***Average percent of need met:*** 59. ***Average financial aid package:*** $8892. ***Average need-based loan:*** $4173. ***Average need-based gift aid:*** $5632. ***Average non-need-based aid:*** $3427. ***Average indebtedness upon graduation:*** $24,655.

APPLYING

Standardized Tests *Required:* SAT or ACT (for admission).

Options: electronic application.

Application fee: $35.

Required: high school transcript. ***Required for some:*** essay or personal statement, interview.

CONTACT

Mr. Andrew Wright, Director of Admissions, Missouri State University, 901 South National Avenue, Springfield, MO 65897. *Phone:* 417-836-5517. *Toll-free phone:* 800-492-7900. *Fax:* 417-836-5137. *E-mail:* info@missouristate.edu.

Missouri University of Science and Technology

Rolla, Missouri

http://www.mst.edu/

- **State-supported** university, founded 1870, part of University of Missouri System
- **Small-town** 284-acre campus
- **Coed** 6,522 undergraduate students, 89% full-time, 23% women, 77% men
- **Very difficult** entrance level, 86% of applicants were admitted

UNDERGRAD STUDENTS

5,825 full-time, 697 part-time. 19% are from out of state; 4% Black or African American, non-Hispanic/Latino; 2% Hispanic/Latino; 3% Asian, non-Hispanic/Latino; 0.4% Native Hawaiian or other Pacific Islander, non-Hispanic/Latino; 0.4% American Indian or Alaska Native, non-Hispanic/Latino; 3% Race/ethnicity unknown; 7% international; 7% transferred in; 40% live on campus.

Freshmen

Admission: 3,577 applied, 3,071 admitted, 1,288 enrolled. ***Average high school GPA:*** 3.85. ***Test scores:*** SAT critical reading scores over 500: 86%; SAT math scores over 500: 96%; ACT scores over 18: 100%; SAT critical reading scores over 600: 56%; SAT math scores over 600: 75%; ACT scores over 24: 93%; SAT critical reading scores over 700: 14%; SAT math scores over 700: 30%; ACT scores over 30: 40%.

FACULTY

Total: 491, 77% full-time, 79% with terminal degrees.

Student/faculty ratio: 18:1.

ACADEMICS

Calendar: semesters. *Degrees:* certificates, bachelor's, master's, doctoral, and postbachelor's certificates.

Special study options: adult/continuing education programs, advanced placement credit, cooperative education, distance learning, double majors, English as a second language, freshman honors college, honors programs, independent study, internships, off-campus study, part-time degree program, services for LD students, study abroad, summer session for credit. ***ROTC:*** Army (b), Air Force (b).

Computers: Students can access the following: campus intranet, computer help desk, free student e-mail accounts, online (class) grades, online (class) registration, online (class) schedules. Campuswide network is available. 100% of college-owned or -operated housing units are wired for high-speed Internet access. Wireless service is available via entire campus.

STUDENT LIFE

Housing options: on-campus residence required through sophomore year; coed, cooperative, special housing for students with disabilities. Campus housing is university owned and leased by the school. Freshman campus housing is guaranteed.

Activities and organizations: drama/theater group, student-run newspaper, radio station, choral group, marching band, academic organizations, Honor Society, Special Interest Group, Greek Organizations, Recreational and Sports Club, national fraternities, national sororities.

Athletics Member NCAA. All Division II. ***Intercollegiate sports:*** baseball M(s), basketball M(s)/W(s), cross-country running M(s)/W(s), football M(s), soccer M(s)/W(s), softball W(s), swimming and diving M(s), track and field M(s)/W(s), volleyball W(s). ***Intramural sports:*** badminton M/W, basketball M/W, bowling M/W, football M/W, golf

M/W, racquetball M/W, soccer M/W, softball M/W, swimming and diving M/W, table tennis M/W, tennis M/W, track and field M/W, ultimate Frisbee M/W, volleyball M/W, water polo M/W, weight lifting M.

Campus security: 24-hour emergency response devices and patrols, student patrols, late-night transport/escort service, controlled dormitory access, crime prevention programs.

Student services: health clinic, personal/psychological counseling.

COSTS & FINANCIAL AID

Costs (2014–15) ***Tuition:*** state resident $8220 full-time, $274 per credit hour part-time; nonresident $24,087 full-time, $803 per credit hour part-time. Full-time tuition and fees vary according to course load, degree level, and program. Part-time tuition and fees vary according to course load, degree level, and program. ***Required fees:*** $1317 full-time, $146 per credit hour part-time. ***Room and board:*** $9540; room only: $6090. Room and board charges vary according to board plan, housing facility, and location. ***Payment plan:*** installment. ***Waivers:*** employees or children of employees.

Financial Aid Of all full-time matriculated undergraduates who enrolled in 2013, 3,286 applied for aid, 3,171 were judged to have need, 2,988 had their need fully met. 226 Federal Work-Study jobs (averaging $1176). In 2013, 579 non-need-based awards were made. ***Average percent of need met:*** 36. ***Average financial aid package:*** $15,253. ***Average need-based loan:*** $7776. ***Average need-based gift aid:*** $7460. ***Average non-need-based aid:*** $5080. ***Average indebtedness upon graduation:*** $27,591.

APPLYING

Standardized Tests *Required:* SAT or ACT (for admission). *Recommended:* ACT (for admission).

Options: electronic application, deferred entrance.

Application fee: $50.

Required: high school transcript. ***Recommended:*** essay or personal statement.

CONTACT

Ms. Lynn Stichnote, Admissions Office, Missouri University of Science and Technology, 300 West 13th Street, 106 Parker Hall, Rolla, MO 65409. *Phone:* 573-341-4075. *Toll-free phone:* 800-522-0938. *Fax:* 573-341-4082. *E-mail:* admissions@mst.edu.

Missouri Valley College

Marshall, Missouri

http://www.moval.edu/

- **Independent** comprehensive, founded 1889, affiliated with Presbyterian Church
- **Small-town** 140-acre campus with easy access to Kansas City
- **Endowment** $3.4 million
- **Coed** 1,653 undergraduate students, 85% full-time, 43% women, 57% men
- **Minimally difficult** entrance level, 44% of applicants were admitted

UNDERGRAD STUDENTS

1,409 full-time, 244 part-time. Students come from 42 states and territories; 29 other countries; 28% are from out of state; 15% Black or African American, non-Hispanic/Latino; 5% Hispanic/Latino; 0.7% Asian, non-Hispanic/Latino; 1% Native Hawaiian or other Pacific Islander, non-Hispanic/Latino; 0.5% American Indian or Alaska Native, non-Hispanic/Latino; 0.8% Two or more races, non-Hispanic/Latino; 2% Race/ethnicity unknown; 13% international; 7% transferred in; 73% live on campus.

Freshmen

Admission: 2,049 applied, 897 admitted, 403 enrolled. ***Average high school GPA:*** 2.9. ***Test scores:*** SAT critical reading scores over 500: 29%; ACT scores over 18: 68%; SAT critical reading scores over 600: 3%; ACT scores over 24: 9%; ACT scores over 30: 1%.

Retention: 56% of full-time freshmen returned.

FACULTY

Total: 90, 66% full-time, 44% with terminal degrees.

Student/faculty ratio: 18:1.

ACADEMICS

Calendar: semesters plus 2 summer sessions. *Degrees:* associate, bachelor's, and master's.

Special study options: academic remediation for entering students, adult/continuing education programs, advanced placement credit, cooperative education, distance learning, double majors, English as a second language, honors programs, independent study, internships, part-time degree program, services for LD students, student-designed majors, study abroad, summer session for credit. ***ROTC:*** Army (b).

Computers: 250 computers/terminals are available on campus for general student use. Students can access the following: campus intranet, computer help desk, free student e-mail accounts, online (class) grades, online (class) registration, online (class) schedules. Campuswide network is available. Wireless service is available via entire campus.

STUDENT LIFE

Housing options: coed, men-only, women-only. Campus housing is university owned. Freshman campus housing is guaranteed.

Activities and organizations: drama/theater group, student-run newspaper, radio and television station, choral group, student government, Valley players, American Humanics, national fraternities, national sororities.

Athletics Member NAIA. ***Intercollegiate sports:*** baseball M(s), basketball M(s)/W(s), cheerleading M(s)/W(s), cross-country running M(s)/W(s), football M(s), golf M(s)/W(s), soccer M(s)/W(s), softball W(s), tennis M(s)/W(s), track and field M(s)/W(s), volleyball M(s)/W(s), wrestling M(s)/W(s). ***Intramural sports:*** badminton M/W, baseball M, basketball M/W, bowling M/W, football M/W, soccer M/W, softball M/W, table tennis M/W, tennis M/W, volleyball M/W.

Campus security: 24-hour emergency response devices, student patrols, late-night transport/escort service, controlled dormitory access, evening patrol by trained security personnel.

Student services: health clinic, personal/psychological counseling.

COSTS & FINANCIAL AID

Costs (2014–15) ***Comprehensive fee:*** $27,450 includes full-time tuition ($18,200), mandatory fees ($1150), and room and board ($8100). Part-time tuition: $350 per credit hour. ***College room only:*** $4300.

Financial Aid Of all full-time matriculated undergraduates who enrolled in 2013, 1,290 applied for aid, 1,275 were judged to have need, 512 had their need fully met. 161 Federal Work-Study jobs (averaging $1860). 626 state and other part-time jobs (averaging $1860). In 2013, 430 non-need-based awards were made. ***Average percent of need met:*** 85. ***Average financial aid package:*** $11,900. ***Average need-based loan:*** $3750. ***Average need-based gift aid:*** $11,900. ***Average non-need-based aid:*** $11,900. ***Average indebtedness upon graduation:*** $24,000.

APPLYING

Standardized Tests *Required:* SAT or ACT (for admission).

Options: electronic application, early admission, deferred entrance.

Application fee: $15.

Required: high school transcript. ***Required for some:*** essay or personal statement, 3 letters of recommendation, interview. ***Recommended:*** minimum 2.0 GPA, interview.

Application deadlines: rolling (freshmen), rolling (transfers).

Notification: continuous (freshmen), continuous (transfers).

CONTACT

Ms. Debi Bultmann, Admissions Office Manager, Missouri Valley College, 500 East College, Marshall, MO 65340-3197. *Phone:* 660-831-4125. *Fax:* 660-831-4233. *E-mail:* admissions@moval.edu.

Missouri Western State University

St. Joseph, Missouri

http://www.missouriwestern.edu/

- **State-supported** comprehensive, founded 1915
- **Suburban** 744-acre campus with easy access to Kansas City
- **Coed** 5,650 undergraduate students, 69% full-time, 58% women, 42% men
- **Noncompetitive** entrance level, 74% of applicants were admitted

UNDERGRAD STUDENTS
3,875 full-time, 1,775 part-time. Students come from 36 states and territories; 31 other countries; 10% are from out of state; 12% Black or African American, non-Hispanic/Latino; 1% Hispanic/Latino; 1% Asian, non-Hispanic/Latino; 0.2% Native Hawaiian or other Pacific Islander, non-Hispanic/Latino; 0.6% American Indian or Alaska Native, non-Hispanic/Latino; 3% Two or more races, non-Hispanic/Latino; 3% Race/ethnicity unknown; 1% international; 7% transferred in; 23% live on campus.

Freshmen
Admission: 3,508 applied, 2,609 admitted, 1,042 enrolled. ***Average high school GPA:*** 3.1. ***Test scores:*** ACT scores over 18: 73%; ACT scores over 24: 22%; ACT scores over 30: 2%.
Retention: 64% of full-time freshmen returned.

FACULTY
Total: 407, 49% full-time, 47% with terminal degrees.
Student/faculty ratio: 17:1.

ACADEMICS
Calendar: semesters. *Degrees:* certificates, associate, bachelor's, master's, and postbachelor's certificates.
Special study options: academic remediation for entering students, accelerated degree program, adult/continuing education programs, advanced placement credit, distance learning, double majors, English as a second language, freshman honors college, honors programs, independent study, internships, off-campus study, part-time degree program, services for LD students, student-designed majors, study abroad, summer session for credit. ***ROTC:*** Army (b).
Computers: 648 computers/terminals are available on campus for general student use. Students can access the following: campus intranet, computer help desk, free student e-mail accounts, online (class) grades, online (class) registration, online (class) schedules, personal online storage. Campuswide network is available. 100% of college-owned or -operated housing units are wired for high-speed Internet access. Wireless service is available via entire campus.

STUDENT LIFE
Housing options: on-campus residence required for freshman year; coed, special housing for students with disabilities. Campus housing is university owned.
Activities and organizations: drama/theater group, student-run newspaper, television station, choral group, marching band, national fraternities, national sororities.
Athletics Member NCAA. All Division II. ***Intercollegiate sports:*** baseball M(s), basketball M(s)/W(s), football M(s), golf M(s)/W(s), soccer W(s), softball W(s), tennis W(s), volleyball W(s). ***Intramural sports:*** badminton M/W, basketball M/W, football M/W, racquetball M/W, soccer M/W, tennis M/W, volleyball M/W.
Campus security: 24-hour emergency response devices and patrols, student patrols, late-night transport/escort service, controlled dormitory access.
Student services: health clinic, personal/psychological counseling, women's center.

COSTS & FINANCIAL AID
Costs (2014–15) ***Tuition:*** state resident $5780 full-time, $193 per credit hour part-time; nonresident $11,771 full-time, $392 per credit hour part-time. Full-time tuition and fees vary according to course load, location, and program. Part-time tuition and fees vary according to course load, location, and program. ***Required fees:*** $718 full-time. ***Room and board:*** $7346; room only: $4248. Room and board charges vary according to board plan and housing facility. ***Payment plan:*** installment. ***Waivers:*** senior citizens and employees or children of employees.
Financial Aid Of all full-time matriculated undergraduates who enrolled in 2014, 3,534 applied for aid, 2,807 were judged to have need, 266 had their need fully met. 354 Federal Work-Study jobs (averaging $1328). 740 state and other part-time jobs (averaging $1502). In 2014, 405 non-need-based awards were made. ***Average percent of need met:*** 62. ***Average financial aid package:*** $8428. ***Average need-based loan:*** $3636. ***Average need-based gift aid:*** $5596. ***Average non-need-based aid:*** $3189. ***Average indebtedness upon graduation:*** $26,015.

APPLYING
Standardized Tests *Required:* SAT or ACT (for admission).
Options: electronic application, early admission.
Required: high school transcript.
Application deadlines: 5/1 (freshmen), 6/1 (transfers).
Notification: continuous (freshmen), continuous (transfers).

CONTACT
Mr. Howard McCauley, Dean of Enrollment Management, Missouri Western State University, 4525 Downs Drive, St. Joseph, MO 64507-2294. *Phone:* 816-271-4266. *Toll-free phone:* 800-662-7041. *Fax:* 816-271-5833. *E-mail:* admission@missouriwestern.edu.

Northwest Missouri State University

Maryville, Missouri

http://www.nwmissouri.edu/

- **State-supported** comprehensive, founded 1905, part of Missouri Coordinating Board for Higher Education
- **Small-town** 370-acre campus with easy access to Kansas City
- **Endowment** $18.9 million
- **Coed** 5,491 undergraduate students, 91% full-time, 55% women, 45% men
- **Moderately difficult** entrance level, 74% of applicants were admitted

UNDERGRAD STUDENTS
4,980 full-time, 511 part-time. Students come from 44 states and territories; 24 other countries; 32% are from out of state; 6% Black or African American, non-Hispanic/Latino; 3% Hispanic/Latino; 0.6% Asian, non-Hispanic/Latino; 0.1% Native Hawaiian or other Pacific Islander, non-Hispanic/Latino; 0.3% American Indian or Alaska Native, non-Hispanic/Latino; 3% Two or more races, non-Hispanic/Latino; 2% Race/ethnicity unknown; 4% international; 4% transferred in; 39% live on campus.

Freshmen
Admission: 4,516 applied, 3,334 admitted, 1,379 enrolled. ***Average high school GPA:*** 3.35. ***Test scores:*** ACT scores over 18: 93%; ACT scores over 24: 36%; ACT scores over 30: 4%.
Retention: 71% of full-time freshmen returned.

FACULTY
Total: 308, 81% full-time, 62% with terminal degrees.
Student/faculty ratio: 22:1.

ACADEMICS
Calendar: trimesters. *Degrees:* certificates, bachelor's, master's, post-master's, and postbachelor's certificates.
Special study options: academic remediation for entering students, advanced placement credit, distance learning, double majors, English as a second language, honors programs, independent study, internships, off-campus study, part-time degree program, services for LD students, study abroad, summer session for credit. ***ROTC:*** Army (b).
Computers: 6,465 computers/terminals and 6,000 ports are available on campus for general student use. Students can access the following: campus intranet, computer help desk, free student e-mail accounts, online (class) grades, online (class) registration, online (class) schedules, online courses with library and databases. Campuswide network is available. 100% of college-owned or -operated housing units are wired for high-speed Internet access. Wireless service is available via classrooms, computer centers, computer labs, dorm rooms, learning centers, libraries, student centers.

STUDENT LIFE
Housing options: on-campus residence required for freshman year; coed, special housing for students with disabilities. Campus housing is university owned. Freshman campus housing is guaranteed.
Activities and organizations: drama/theater group, student-run newspaper, radio and television station, choral group, marching band, student government, Residence Hall Association, Greek Life, national fraternities, national sororities.
Athletics Member NCAA. All Division II. ***Intercollegiate sports:*** baseball M(s), basketball M(s)/W(s), cheerleading M(s)/W(s), cross-country running M(s)/W(s), football M(s), golf W(s), soccer W(s), softball

W(s), tennis M(s)/W(s), track and field M(s)/W(s), volleyball W(s). ***Intramural sports:*** badminton M/W, basketball M/W, cross-country running M/W, football M/W, golf M/W, racquetball M/W, skiing (cross-country) M/W, soccer M(c)/W(c), softball W, swimming and diving M/W, table tennis M/W, tennis M/W, track and field M/W, volleyball M/W, wrestling M(c).

Campus security: 24-hour emergency response devices and patrols, student patrols, late-night transport/escort service, controlled dormitory access, security personnel are all police officers.

Student services: health clinic, personal/psychological counseling, women's center.

COSTS & FINANCIAL AID

Costs (2014–15) ***Tuition:*** state resident $5360 full-time, $179 per credit hour part-time; nonresident $11,611 full-time, $387 per credit hour part-time. Full-time tuition and fees vary according to course load, location, and reciprocity agreements. Part-time tuition and fees vary according to course load and location. ***Required fees:*** $2916 full-time, $97 per credit hour part-time. ***Room and board:*** $9192; room only: $5902. Room and board charges vary according to board plan and housing facility. ***Payment plans:*** installment, deferred payment. ***Waivers:*** senior citizens and employees or children of employees.

Financial Aid Of all full-time matriculated undergraduates who enrolled in 2013, 4,268 applied for aid, 3,436 were judged to have need, 1,840 had their need fully met. 409 Federal Work-Study jobs (averaging $1195). 1,153 state and other part-time jobs (averaging $1605). In 2013, 377 non-need-based awards were made. ***Average percent of need met:*** 68. ***Average financial aid package:*** $9380. ***Average need-based loan:*** $4021. ***Average need-based gift aid:*** $5602. ***Average non-need-based aid:*** $2759. ***Average indebtedness upon graduation:*** $24,710.

APPLYING

Standardized Tests *Required:* SAT or ACT (for admission).

Options: electronic application, deferred entrance.

Application fee: $25.

Required: high school transcript, minimum 2.0 GPA. ***Required for some:*** interview.

Application deadlines: rolling (freshmen), rolling (out-of-state freshmen), rolling (transfers).

Notification: continuous (freshmen), continuous (out-of-state freshmen), continuous (transfers).

CONTACT

Mrs. Tammi Grow, Associate Director of Admissions, Northwest Missouri State University, 800 University Drive, Maryville, MO 64468-6001. *Phone:* 660-562-1146. *Toll-free phone:* 800-633-1175. *Fax:* 660-562-1146. *E-mail:* admissions@nwmissouri.edu.

★ Park University

Parkville, Missouri

http://www.park.edu/

- **Independent** comprehensive, founded 1875
- **Suburban** 800-acre campus with easy access to Kansas City
- **Endowment** $52.3 million
- **Coed** 8,946 undergraduate students, 12% full-time, 47% women, 53% men
- **Minimally difficult** entrance level, 25% of applicants were admitted

UNDERGRAD STUDENTS

1,089 full-time, 7,857 part-time. Students come from 50 states and territories; 101 other countries; 20% are from out of state; 18% Black or African American, non-Hispanic/Latino; 3% Hispanic/Latino; 4% Asian, non-Hispanic/Latino; 0.1% Native Hawaiian or other Pacific Islander, non-Hispanic/Latino; 1% American Indian or Alaska Native, non-Hispanic/Latino; 2% Two or more races, non-Hispanic/Latino; 5% international; 3% transferred in; 20% live on campus.

Freshmen

Admission: 576 applied, 143 admitted, 165 enrolled. ***Average high school GPA:*** 3.2.

Retention: 58% of full-time freshmen returned.

FACULTY

Total: 174, 79% full-time.

Student/faculty ratio: 12:1.

ACADEMICS

Calendar: semesters. *Degrees:* associate, bachelor's, master's, and postbachelor's certificates.

Special study options: academic remediation for entering students, adult/continuing education programs, advanced placement credit, distance learning, double majors, English as a second language, external degree program, honors programs, independent study, internships, off-campus study, part-time degree program, services for LD students, student-designed majors, summer session for credit. ***ROTC:*** Army (b).

Computers: 1,240 computers/terminals are available on campus for general student use. Students can access the following: campus intranet, computer help desk, free student e-mail accounts, online (class) grades, online (class) registration, online (class) schedules, virtual applications; electronic portfolios, virtual helpdesk. Campuswide network is available. 100% of college-owned or -operated housing units are wired for high-speed Internet access. Wireless service is available via classrooms, computer centers, computer labs, dorm rooms, learning centers, libraries, student centers.

STUDENT LIFE

Housing options: on-campus residence required through junior year; coed. Campus housing is university owned. Freshman campus housing is guaranteed.

Activities and organizations: drama/theater group, student-run newspaper, radio and television station, World Student Union, Park Student Government Association, National Society of Leadership and Success, Student Nurses Association, Students in Interior Design.

Athletics Member NAIA. ***Intercollegiate sports:*** baseball M(s), basketball M(s)/W(s), cross-country running M(s)/W(s), golf W(s), soccer M(s)/W(s), softball W(s), track and field M(s)/W(s), volleyball M(s)/W(s). ***Intramural sports:*** basketball M/W, softball M/W, volleyball M/W.

Campus security: 24-hour patrols, student patrols, late-night transport/escort service.

Student services: health clinic, personal/psychological counseling.

COSTS & FINANCIAL AID

Costs (2014–15) ***Comprehensive fee:*** $18,580 includes full-time tuition ($10,500), mandatory fees ($100), and room and board ($7980). Full-time tuition and fees vary according to course load. Part-time tuition: $369 per credit. Part-time tuition and fees vary according to course load. ***College room only:*** $3713. Room and board charges vary according to housing facility. ***Waivers:*** senior citizens and employees or children of employees.

Financial Aid Of all full-time matriculated undergraduates who enrolled in 2013, 698 applied for aid, 559 were judged to have need, 83 had their need fully met. 110 Federal Work-Study jobs (averaging $2875). 91 state and other part-time jobs (averaging $3107). In 2013, 94 non-need-based awards were made. ***Average percent of need met:*** 63. ***Average financial aid package:*** $10,619. ***Average need-based loan:*** $4562. ***Average need-based gift aid:*** $4823. ***Average non-need-based aid:*** $8041. ***Average indebtedness upon graduation:*** $24,768.

APPLYING

Standardized Tests *Required:* SAT or ACT (for admission). ***Required for some:*** SAT or ACT (for admission).

Options: electronic application, early admission, deferred entrance.

Application fee: $25.

Required: high school transcript, minimum 2.0 GPA. ***Required for some:*** 2 letters of recommendation.

Application deadlines: 8/1 (freshmen), 8/1 (transfers).

Notification: continuous (freshmen), continuous (transfers).

CONTACT

Eric Blair, Director of Undergraduate Admissions, Park University, 8700 NW River Park Drive, Campus Box 1, Parkville, MO 64152. *Phone:* 816-584-6858. *Toll-free phone:* 800-745-7275. *Fax:* 816-741-4462. *E-mail:* admissions@mail.park.edu.

A ★ indicates that the school has detailed information with a Premium Profile on Petersons.com.

Research College of Nursing

Kansas City, Missouri

http://www.researchcollege.edu/

- **Independent** comprehensive, founded 1980, part of Rockhurst University
- **Urban** 66-acre campus with easy access to Kansas City
- **Coed, primarily women** 340 undergraduate students, 100% full-time, 90% women, 10% men
- **Moderately difficult** entrance level, 73% of applicants were admitted

UNDERGRAD STUDENTS

339 full-time, 1 part-time. Students come from 7 states and territories; 5% Black or African American, non-Hispanic/Latino; 3% Hispanic/Latino; 3% Asian, non-Hispanic/Latino; 0.3% Native Hawaiian or other Pacific Islander, non-Hispanic/Latino; 0.3% American Indian or Alaska Native, non-Hispanic/Latino; 0.6% Two or more races, non-Hispanic/Latino; 15% Race/ethnicity unknown; 2% transferred in.

Freshmen

Admission: 339 applied, 249 admitted, 78 enrolled. ***Average high school GPA:*** 3.53. ***Test scores:*** ACT scores over 18: 100%; ACT scores over 24: 56%; ACT scores over 30: 4%.

FACULTY

Total: 29, 90% full-time, 14% with terminal degrees.

Student/faculty ratio: 7:1.

ACADEMICS

Calendar: semesters. *Degrees:* bachelor's, master's, and post-master's certificates (bachelor's degree offered jointly with Rockhurst College).

Special study options: accelerated degree program, advanced placement credit, double majors, honors programs, independent study, services for LD students, study abroad, summer session for credit. ***ROTC:*** Army (c).

Computers: 125 computers/terminals are available on campus for general student use. Students can access the following: online (class) registration. Campuswide network is available.

STUDENT LIFE

Housing options: coed, men-only, women-only. Campus housing is university owned. Freshman campus housing is guaranteed.

Activities and organizations: drama/theater group, student-run newspaper, radio station, choral group, national fraternities, national sororities.

Athletics Member NCAA. All Division II. ***Intercollegiate sports:*** baseball M(s), basketball M(s)/W(s), golf M(s)/W(s), soccer M(s)/W(s), softball W(s), tennis M(s)/W(s), volleyball W(s). ***Intramural sports:*** badminton M/W, basketball M/W, cross-country running M/W, field hockey M/W, golf M/W, lacrosse M/W, racquetball M/W, rugby M/W, soccer M/W, softball M/W, table tennis M/W, tennis M/W, volleyball M/W, weight lifting M.

Campus security: 24-hour emergency response devices and patrols, late-night transport/escort service, controlled dormitory access.

Student services: health clinic, personal/psychological counseling.

COSTS

Costs (2014–15) ***Comprehensive fee:*** $41,695 includes full-time tuition ($32,075), mandatory fees ($820), and room and board ($8800). Part-time tuition: $1070 per credit hour. Part-time tuition and fees vary according to class time. ***College room only:*** $5800. Room and board charges vary according to board plan, housing facility, and location. ***Payment plans:*** installment, deferred payment. ***Waivers:*** senior citizens and employees or children of employees.

APPLYING

Standardized Tests *Required:* SAT or ACT (for admission).

Options: electronic application, deferred entrance.

Required: high school transcript, 1 letter of recommendation, ACT or SAT. ***Recommended:*** minimum 2.8 GPA, interview.

Application deadlines: 6/30 (freshmen), 2/15 (transfers).

Notification: 8/15 (freshmen), 6/20 (out-of-state freshmen), 3/15 (transfers).

CONTACT

Mr. Lane Ramey, Vice President for Enrollment Services, Research College of Nursing, 1100 Rockhurst Road, Kansas City, MO 64110. *Phone:* 816-501-2012. *E-mail:* lane.ramey@rockhurst.edu.

Rockhurst University

Kansas City, Missouri

http://www.rockhurst.edu/

- **Independent Roman Catholic (Jesuit)** comprehensive, founded 1910
- **Urban** 35-acre campus
- **Endowment** $37.2 million
- **Coed** 2,276 undergraduate students, 67% full-time, 59% women, 41% men
- **Moderately difficult** entrance level, 77% of applicants were admitted

UNDERGRAD STUDENTS

1,536 full-time, 740 part-time. Students come from 29 states and territories; 17 other countries; 32% are from out of state; 4% Black or African American, non-Hispanic/Latino; 6% Hispanic/Latino; 3% Asian, non-Hispanic/Latino; 0.2% Native Hawaiian or other Pacific Islander, non-Hispanic/Latino; 0.2% American Indian or Alaska Native, non-Hispanic/Latino; 2% Two or more races, non-Hispanic/Latino; 8% Race/ethnicity unknown; 1% international; 3% transferred in; 56% live on campus.

Freshmen

Admission: 2,494 applied, 1,919 admitted, 399 enrolled. ***Average high school GPA:*** 3.6. ***Test scores:*** SAT critical reading scores over 500: 78%; SAT math scores over 500: 71%; ACT scores over 18: 99%; SAT critical reading scores over 600: 48%; SAT math scores over 600: 49%; ACT scores over 24: 67%; SAT math scores over 700: 19%; ACT scores over 30: 16%.

Retention: 89% of full-time freshmen returned.

FACULTY

Total: 244, 52% full-time, 50% with terminal degrees.

Student/faculty ratio: 12:1.

ACADEMICS

Calendar: semesters. *Degrees:* certificates, bachelor's, master's, doctoral, and postbachelor's certificates.

Special study options: academic remediation for entering students, accelerated degree program, advanced placement credit, cooperative education, distance learning, double majors, freshman honors college, honors programs, independent study, internships, off-campus study, part-time degree program, services for LD students, study abroad, summer session for credit. ***ROTC:*** Army (c).

Computers: 250 computers/terminals are available on campus for general student use. Students can access the following: campus intranet, computer help desk, free student e-mail accounts, online (class) grades, online (class) registration, online (class) schedules, Campus Portal and Mobile Application. Campuswide network is available. 100% of college-owned or -operated housing units are wired for high-speed Internet access. Wireless service is available via entire campus.

STUDENT LIFE

Housing options: on-campus residence required through sophomore year; coed, men-only, women-only, special housing for students with disabilities. Campus housing is university owned. Freshman campus housing is guaranteed.

Activities and organizations: drama/theater group, student-run newspaper, choral group, Social Activities Board, Student Senate, Colleges Against Cancer, Panhellenic Sororities, IFC Fraternities, national fraternities, national sororities.

Athletics Member NCAA. All Division II except cross-country running (Division I). ***Intercollegiate sports:*** baseball M(s), basketball M(s)/W(s), cross-country running W(s), golf M(s)/W(s), lacrosse M(s)/W(s), soccer M(s)/W(s), softball W(s), tennis M(s)/W(s), volleyball W(s). ***Intramural sports:*** basketball M/W, bowling M/W, soccer M/W, softball M/W, ultimate Frisbee M/W, volleyball M/W.

Campus security: 24-hour emergency response devices and patrols, late-night transport/escort service, controlled dormitory access, closed-circuit TV monitors.

Student services: health clinic, personal/psychological counseling.

COSTS & FINANCIAL AID

Costs (2014–15) ***Comprehensive fee:*** $41,945 includes full-time tuition ($32,075), mandatory fees ($790), and room and board ($9080). Full-time tuition and fees vary according to class time and course load. Part-time tuition: $535 per credit hour. Part-time tuition and fees vary according to class time and course load. ***Required fees:*** $25 per credit hour part-time. ***College room only:*** $5480. Room and board charges vary according to board plan and housing facility. ***Payment plans:*** installment, deferred payment. ***Waivers:*** senior citizens and employees or children of employees.

Financial Aid Of all full-time matriculated undergraduates who enrolled in 2013, 1,287 applied for aid, 978 were judged to have need, 176 had their need fully met. In 2013, 266 non-need-based awards were made. ***Average percent of need met:*** 77. ***Average financial aid package:*** $24,834. ***Average need-based loan:*** $5561. ***Average need-based gift aid:*** $3209. ***Average non-need-based aid:*** $20,636. ***Average indebtedness upon graduation:*** $24,852.

APPLYING

Standardized Tests *Required:* SAT or ACT (for admission).

Options: electronic application, deferred entrance.

Application fee: $25.

Required: high school transcript, minimum 2.0 GPA, 1 letter of recommendation. ***Required for some:*** essay or personal statement, interview.

Application deadlines: 6/30 (freshmen), rolling (transfers).

Notification: continuous (freshmen), continuous (transfers).

CONTACT

Kyle Johnson, Director of Freshman Admissions, Rockhurst University, 1100 Rockhurst Road, Kansas City, MO 64110-2561. *Phone:* 816-501-4100. *Toll-free phone:* 800-842-6776. *Fax:* 816-501-4142. *E-mail:* admission@rockhurst.edu.

Saint Louis Christian College

Florissant, Missouri

http://www.slcconline.edu/

- **Independent Christian** 4-year, founded 1956
- **Suburban** 30-acre campus with easy access to St. Louis
- **Endowment** $1.1 million
- **Coed** 179 undergraduate students, 70% full-time, 45% women, 55% men
- **Minimally difficult** entrance level, 41% of applicants were admitted

UNDERGRAD STUDENTS

126 full-time, 53 part-time. Students come from 13 states and territories; 23% are from out of state; 33% Black or African American, non-Hispanic/Latino; 4% Hispanic/Latino; 0.6% American Indian or Alaska Native, non-Hispanic/Latino; 3% Two or more races, non-Hispanic/Latino; 48% live on campus.

Freshmen

Admission: 69 applied, 28 admitted, 14 enrolled. ***Average high school GPA:*** 3.3.

Retention: 53% of full-time freshmen returned.

FACULTY

Total: 34, 35% full-time, 18% with terminal degrees.

Student/faculty ratio: 9:1.

ACADEMICS

Calendar: semesters. *Degrees:* associate and bachelor's.

Special study options: academic remediation for entering students, accelerated degree program, adult/continuing education programs, advanced placement credit, double majors, independent study, internships, part-time degree program, services for LD students, study abroad, summer session for credit.

Computers: 10 computers/terminals are available on campus for general student use. Students can access the following: computer help desk, free student e-mail accounts, online (class) grades, online (class) registration, online (class) schedules. Campuswide network is available. 100% of college-owned or -operated housing units are wired for high-speed Internet access. Wireless service is available via entire campus.

STUDENT LIFE

Housing options: on-campus residence required through senior year; men-only, women-only. Campus housing is university owned.

Activities and organizations: drama/theater group, choral group, World Christians Unlimited, Drama Club, pep band.

Athletics Member NCCAA. ***Intercollegiate sports:*** baseball M, basketball M/W, cross-country running W, volleyball W. ***Intramural sports:*** basketball M/W, ultimate Frisbee M/W, volleyball M/W.

Campus security: 24-hour emergency response devices and patrols, controlled dormitory access, night security.

Student services: personal/psychological counseling.

COSTS & FINANCIAL AID

Costs (2015–16) ***Comprehensive fee:*** $14,675 includes full-time tuition ($10,075) and room and board ($4600). ***Room and board:*** Room and board charges vary according to housing facility. ***Waivers:*** employees or children of employees.

Financial Aid Of all full-time matriculated undergraduates who enrolled in 2014, 122 applied for aid, 113 were judged to have need, 4 had their need fully met. In 2014, 4 non-need-based awards were made. ***Average percent of need met:*** 59. ***Average financial aid package:*** $7966. ***Average need-based loan:*** $3797. ***Average need-based gift aid:*** $4828. ***Average non-need-based aid:*** $3257. ***Average indebtedness upon graduation:*** $32,975.

APPLYING

Standardized Tests *Required:* SAT or ACT (for admission).

Options: electronic application.

Required: essay or personal statement, high school transcript, 2 letters of recommendation, 18+ on ACT, 1270+ on SAT. ***Required for some:*** interview. ***Recommended:*** minimum 2.0 GPA.

Application deadlines: 8/7 (freshmen), 8/7 (out-of-state freshmen), 8/7 (transfers).

Notification: continuous (freshmen), continuous (transfers).

CONTACT

Hayley Womble, Admissions Director, Saint Louis Christian College, 1360 Grandview Drive, Florissant, MO 63033. *Phone:* 314-837-6777 Ext. 1305. *Toll-free phone:* 800-887-SLCC. *E-mail:* hwomble@stlchristian.edu.

★ St. Louis College of Pharmacy

St. Louis, Missouri

http://www.stlcop.edu/

- **Independent** comprehensive, founded 1864
- **Urban** 8-acre campus with easy access to St. Louis
- **Endowment** $147.1 million
- **Coed** 698 undergraduate students, 99% full-time, 60% women, 40% men
- **Moderately difficult** entrance level, 69% of applicants were admitted

UNDERGRAD STUDENTS

693 full-time, 5 part-time. Students come from 30 states and territories; 5 other countries; 52% are from out of state; 5% Black or African American, non-Hispanic/Latino; 0.3% Hispanic/Latino; 20% Asian, non-Hispanic/Latino; 0.3% Native Hawaiian or other Pacific Islander, non-Hispanic/Latino; 0.1% American Indian or Alaska Native, non-Hispanic/Latino; 2% Two or more races, non-Hispanic/Latino; 11% Race/ethnicity unknown; 2% international; 9% transferred in; 32% live on campus.

Freshmen

Admission: 445 applied, 309 admitted, 193 enrolled. ***Average high school GPA:*** 3.6. ***Test scores:*** SAT critical reading scores over 500: 79%; SAT math scores over 500: 95%; ACT scores over 18: 100%; SAT critical reading scores over 600: 31%; SAT math scores over 600: 74%; ACT scores over 24: 78%; SAT critical reading scores over 700: 5%; SAT math scores over 700: 26%; ACT scores over 30: 17%.

Retention: 89% of full-time freshmen returned.

FACULTY

Total: 151, 67% full-time, 82% with terminal degrees.

Student/faculty ratio: 9:1.

ACADEMICS

Calendar: semesters. *Degree:* doctoral.

Special study options: academic remediation for entering students, advanced placement credit, independent study, internships, study abroad, summer session for credit. ***ROTC:*** Army (c), Navy (c), Air Force (c).

Computers: 1,367 computers/terminals and 2,200 ports are available on campus for general student use. Students can access the following: campus intranet, computer help desk, free student e-mail accounts, online (class) grades, online (class) registration, online (class) schedules. Campuswide network is available. 100% of college-owned or -operated housing units are wired for high-speed Internet access. Wireless service is available via entire campus.

STUDENT LIFE

Housing options: on-campus residence required through sophomore year; coed. Campus housing is university owned. Freshman applicants given priority for college housing.

Activities and organizations: drama/theater group, student-run newspaper, choral group, Outdoor Club, Student Body Union, International Student Organization, Student Pharmacists Association, Student Organization for Drug and Alcohol Awareness, national fraternities, national sororities.

Athletics Member NAIA. ***Intercollegiate sports:*** basketball M(s)/W(s), cross-country running M(s)/W(s), soccer M(s)/W(s), softball W(s), tennis M(s)/W(s), track and field M(s)/W(s), volleyball W(s). ***Intramural sports:*** basketball M/W, football M/W, golf M(c)/W(c), soccer M/W, softball M(c)/W(c), table tennis M/W, tennis M(c)/W, volleyball M(c)/W.

Campus security: 24-hour emergency response devices and patrols, late-night transport/escort service, controlled dormitory access.

Student services: personal/psychological counseling.

COSTS & FINANCIAL AID

Costs (2015–16) ***Comprehensive fee:*** $38,047 includes full-time tuition ($27,502), mandatory fees ($762), and room and board ($9783). Full-time tuition and fees vary according to student level. Part-time tuition: $908 per credit. ***Room and board:*** Room and board charges vary according to board plan and housing facility. ***Payment plan:*** deferred payment. ***Waivers:*** employees or children of employees.

Financial Aid Of all full-time matriculated undergraduates who enrolled in 2013, 499 applied for aid, 441 were judged to have need, 29 had their need fully met. 285 Federal Work-Study jobs (averaging $431). In 2013, 115 non-need-based awards were made. ***Average percent of need met:*** 45. ***Average financial aid package:*** $13,868. ***Average need-based loan:*** $5669. ***Average need-based gift aid:*** $9351. ***Average non-need-based aid:*** $6712. ***Average indebtedness upon graduation:*** $104,713.

APPLYING

Standardized Tests *Required:* SAT or ACT (for admission).

Options: electronic application, early decision.

Application fee: $55.

Required: essay or personal statement, high school transcript, minimum 3.0 GPA, 2 letters of recommendation, letter of reference from science teacher. ***Required for some:*** interview.

Application deadlines: 2/1 (freshmen), 2/1 (transfers).

Early decision deadline: 12/15.

Notification: 3/1 (freshmen), 5/1 (transfers), 1/15 (early decision).

CONTACT

Connie Horrall, Administrative Assistant, St. Louis College of Pharmacy, 4588 Parkview Place, St. Louis, MO 63110-1088. *Phone:* 314-446-8328. *Toll-free phone:* 800-278-5267. *Fax:* 314-446-8310. *E-mail:* chorrall@stlcop.edu.

See this page for display ad and page 1604 for the College Close-Up.

Saint Louis University
St. Louis, Missouri
http://www.slu.edu/

- **Independent Roman Catholic (Jesuit)** university, founded 1818
- **Urban** 271-acre campus
- **Endowment** $1.1 billion
- **Coed** 8,564 undergraduate students, 90% full-time, 58% women, 42% men
- **Moderately difficult** entrance level, 60% of applicants were admitted

UNDERGRAD STUDENTS
7,703 full-time, 861 part-time. Students come from 50 states and territories; 53 other countries; 63% are from out of state; 6% Black or African American, non-Hispanic/Latino; 5% Hispanic/Latino; 8% Asian, non-Hispanic/Latino; 0.1% American Indian or Alaska Native, non-Hispanic/Latino; 5% Two or more races, non-Hispanic/Latino; 3% Race/ethnicity unknown; 8% international; 3% transferred in; 52% live on campus.

Freshmen
Admission: 13,911 applied, 8,383 admitted, 1,691 enrolled. ***Average high school GPA:*** 3.83. ***Test scores:*** SAT critical reading scores over 500: 87%; SAT math scores over 500: 91%; ACT scores over 18: 100%; SAT critical reading scores over 600: 52%; SAT math scores over 600: 58%; ACT scores over 24: 89%; SAT critical reading scores over 700: 11%; SAT math scores over 700: 18%; ACT scores over 30: 35%.

Retention: 88% of full-time freshmen returned.

FACULTY
Total: 1,301, 57% full-time, 60% with terminal degrees.

Student/faculty ratio: 12:1.

ACADEMICS
Calendar: semesters. *Degrees:* certificates, bachelor's, master's, doctoral, post-master's, and postbachelor's certificates.

Special study options: academic remediation for entering students, accelerated degree program, adult/continuing education programs, advanced placement credit, cooperative education, distance learning, double majors, English as a second language, honors programs, independent study, internships, off-campus study, part-time degree program, services for LD students, student-designed majors, study abroad, summer session for credit. ***ROTC:*** Army (c), Air Force (b).

Unusual degree programs: 3-2 engineering with Washington University in St. Louis.

Computers: 1,264 computers/terminals and 5,510 ports are available on campus for general student use. Students can access the following: campus intranet, computer help desk, free student e-mail accounts, online (class) grades, online (class) registration, online (class) schedules. Campuswide network is available. 100% of college-owned or -operated housing units are wired for high-speed Internet access. Wireless service is available via entire campus.

STUDENT LIFE
Housing options: on-campus residence required through sophomore year; coed, men-only, women-only, special housing for students with disabilities. Campus housing is university owned and leased by the school. Freshman campus housing is guaranteed.

Activities and organizations: drama/theater group, student-run newspaper, radio and television station, choral group, Alpha Phi Omega, Oriflamme, Student Activities Board, Interfraternity Council, Panhellenic Council, national fraternities, national sororities.

Athletics Member NCAA. All Division I. ***Intercollegiate sports:*** badminton M(c)/W(c), baseball M(s), basketball M(s)/W(s), bowling M(c)/W(c), crew M(c)/W(c), cross-country running M(s)/W(s), equestrian sports M(c)/W(c), fencing M(c)/W(c), field hockey W(s), golf M(c)/W(c), ice hockey M(c), lacrosse M(c)/W(c), racquetball M(c)/W(c), rugby M(c), soccer M(s)/W(s), softball W(s), squash M(c)/W(c), swimming and diving M(s)/W(s), table tennis M(c)/W(c), tennis M(s)/W(s), track and field M(s)/W(s), ultimate Frisbee M(c)/W(c), volleyball M(c)/W(s), water polo M(c)/W(c). ***Intramural sports:*** badminton M/W, basketball M/W, bowling M/W, football M/W, golf M/W, racquetball M/W, soccer M/W, softball M/W, squash M/W, table tennis M/W, tennis M/W, ultimate Frisbee M/W, volleyball M/W.

Campus security: 24-hour emergency response devices and patrols, late-night transport/escort service, controlled dormitory access, prevention awareness program, bike patrol, self-defense classes, shuttles, video cameras, notice of emergency.

Student services: health clinic, personal/psychological counseling, women's center.

COSTS & FINANCIAL AID
Costs (2014–15) ***Comprehensive fee:*** $48,346 includes full-time tuition ($37,350), mandatory fees ($616), and room and board ($10,380). Full-time tuition and fees vary according to course level, course load, degree level, location, program, and reciprocity agreements. Part-time tuition: $1305 per credit hour. Part-time tuition and fees vary according to course level, course load, degree level, location, program, and reciprocity agreements. ***Required fees:*** $153 per term part-time. ***College room only:*** $5676. Room and board charges vary according to board plan, housing facility, and location. ***Payment plan:*** installment. ***Waivers:*** children of alumni and employees or children of employees.

Financial Aid Of all full-time matriculated undergraduates who enrolled in 2013, 5,183 applied for aid, 4,523 were judged to have need, 831 had their need fully met. In 2013, 2084 non-need-based awards were made. ***Average percent of need met:*** 69. ***Average financial aid package:*** $25,135. ***Average need-based loan:*** $5010. ***Average need-based gift aid:*** $20,291. ***Average non-need-based aid:*** $13,880. ***Average indebtedness upon graduation:*** $35,615.

APPLYING
Standardized Tests *Required:* SAT or ACT (for admission).

Options: electronic application, deferred entrance.

Required: essay or personal statement, high school transcript, minimum 2.5 GPA. ***Recommended:*** 2 letters of recommendation, interview, secondary school report form and health examination.

Application deadlines: 8/20 (freshmen), 8/20 (out-of-state freshmen), 8/20 (transfers).

Notification: continuous until 10/15 (freshmen), continuous until 10/15 (out-of-state freshmen), continuous until 2/1 (transfers).

CONTACT
Jean M. Gilman, Assistant Vice President of Enrollment and Dean of Admission, Saint Louis University, One North Grand Boulevard, DuBourg Hall, Room 119, St. Louis, MO 63103-2097. *Phone:* 314-977-2500. *Toll-free phone:* 800-758-3678. *Fax:* 314-977-7136. *E-mail:* admission@slu.edu.

Southeast Missouri State University
Cape Girardeau, Missouri
http://www.semo.edu/

- **State-supported** comprehensive, founded 1873, part of Missouri Coordinating Board for Higher Education
- **Small-town** 400-acre campus
- **Endowment** $76.8 million
- **Coed** 10,848 undergraduate students, 75% full-time, 57% women, 43% men
- **Moderately difficult** entrance level, 85% of applicants were admitted

UNDERGRAD STUDENTS
8,168 full-time, 2,680 part-time. Students come from 37 states and territories; 46 other countries; 15% are from out of state; 9% Black or African American, non-Hispanic/Latino; 2% Hispanic/Latino; 1% Asian, non-Hispanic/Latino; 0.5% American Indian or Alaska Native, non-Hispanic/Latino; 0.1% Two or more races, non-Hispanic/Latino; 6% Race/ethnicity unknown; 7% international; 6% transferred in; 31% live on campus.

Freshmen
Admission: 4,750 applied, 4,027 admitted, 1,849 enrolled. ***Average high school GPA:*** 3.36. ***Test scores:*** SAT critical reading scores over 500: 56%; SAT math scores over 500: 50%; ACT scores over 18: 96%; SAT critical reading scores over 600: 25%; SAT math scores over 600: 33%; ACT scores over 24: 38%; SAT critical reading scores over 700: 8%; SAT math scores over 700: 14%; ACT scores over 30: 6%.

Retention: 73% of full-time freshmen returned.

FACULTY
Total: 560, 71% full-time, 61% with terminal degrees.
Student/faculty ratio: 21:1.

ACADEMICS
Calendar: semesters. *Degrees:* certificates, associate, bachelor's, master's, post-master's, and postbachelor's certificates.

Special study options: academic remediation for entering students, accelerated degree program, adult/continuing education programs, advanced placement credit, distance learning, double majors, English as a second language, honors programs, independent study, internships, off-campus study, part-time degree program, services for LD students, student-designed majors, study abroad, summer session for credit. ***ROTC:*** Air Force (b).

Computers: 1,241 computers/terminals and 2,000 ports are available on campus for general student use. Students can access the following: campus intranet, computer help desk, free student e-mail accounts, online (class) grades, online (class) registration, online (class) schedules. Campuswide network is available. 100% of college-owned or -operated housing units are wired for high-speed Internet access. Wireless service is available via classrooms, computer centers, computer labs, dorm rooms, learning centers, libraries, student centers.

STUDENT LIFE
Housing options: on-campus residence required through sophomore year; coed, special housing for students with disabilities. Campus housing is university owned. Freshman campus housing is guaranteed.

Activities and organizations: drama/theater group, student-run newspaper, radio and television station, choral group, marching band, Student Government, Student Activities Council, Greek Life, Residence Hall Association, International Students Association, national fraternities, national sororities.

Athletics Member NCAA. All Division I. ***Intercollegiate sports:*** baseball M(s), basketball M(s)/W(s), cheerleading M(s)/W(s), cross-country running M(s)/W(s), football M(s), gymnastics W(s), soccer W(s), softball W(s), tennis W(s), track and field M(s)/W(s), volleyball W(s). ***Intramural sports:*** basketball M/W, bowling M/W, equestrian sports M/W, fencing M/W, football M/W, golf M/W, racquetball M/W, riflery M/W, rock climbing M/W, rugby M/W, soccer M/W, softball M/W, swimming and diving M/W, table tennis M/W, tennis M/W, ultimate Frisbee M/W, volleyball M/W, weight lifting M/W.

Campus security: 24-hour emergency response devices and patrols, late-night transport/escort service, controlled dormitory access.

Student services: health clinic, personal/psychological counseling.

COSTS & FINANCIAL AID
Costs (2014–15) ***Tuition:*** state resident $5927 full-time, $198 per credit hour part-time; nonresident $11,259 full-time, $375 per credit hour part-time. Full-time tuition and fees vary according to course load and location. Part-time tuition and fees vary according to course load and location. ***Required fees:*** $1011 full-time, $34 per credit hour part-time. ***Room and board:*** $8432. Room and board charges vary according to board plan and housing facility. ***Payment plans:*** installment, deferred payment. ***Waivers:*** senior citizens and employees or children of employees.

Financial Aid Of all full-time matriculated undergraduates who enrolled in 2013, 6,146 applied for aid, 4,924 were judged to have need, 568 had their need fully met. 219 Federal Work-Study jobs (averaging $1556). 1,642 state and other part-time jobs (averaging $1935). In 2013, 1307 non-need-based awards were made. ***Average percent of need met:*** 56. ***Average financial aid package:*** $8388. ***Average need-based loan:*** $4066. ***Average need-based gift aid:*** $5365. ***Average non-need-based aid:*** $3944. ***Average indebtedness upon graduation:*** $26,508.

APPLYING
Standardized Tests *Required:* SAT or ACT (for admission).

Options: electronic application, deferred entrance.

Application fee: $30.

Required: high school transcript, minimum 2.0 GPA.

Application deadlines: 7/1 (freshmen), 7/1 (out-of-state freshmen), 7/1 (transfers).

Notification: 9/1 (freshmen), 9/1 (out-of-state freshmen), continuous until 9/1 (transfers).

CONTACT
Southeast Missouri State University, One University Plaza, Cape Girardeau, MO 63701-4799. *Phone:* 573-651-2590.

Southwest Baptist University

Bolivar, Missouri

http://www.sbuniv.edu/

- **Independent Southern Baptist** comprehensive, founded 1878
- **Small-town** 152-acre campus
- **Endowment** $23.5 million
- **Coed** 2,952 undergraduate students, 68% full-time, 64% women, 36% men
- **Moderately difficult** entrance level, 62% of applicants were admitted

UNDERGRAD STUDENTS
2,011 full-time, 941 part-time. Students come from 37 states and territories; 18 other countries; 28% are from out of state; 4% Black or African American, non-Hispanic/Latino; 2% Hispanic/Latino; 0.8% Asian, non-Hispanic/Latino; 1% American Indian or Alaska Native, non-Hispanic/Latino; 26% Race/ethnicity unknown; 0.9% international; 2% transferred in; 63% live on campus.

Freshmen
Admission: 1,604 applied, 992 admitted, 439 enrolled. ***Average high school GPA:*** 3.51. ***Test scores:*** ACT scores over 18: 87%; ACT scores over 24: 39%; ACT scores over 30: 5%.

Retention: 68% of full-time freshmen returned.

FACULTY
Total: 287, 47% full-time.
Student/faculty ratio: 16:1.

ACADEMICS
Calendar: 4-1-4. *Degrees:* associate, bachelor's, master's, doctoral, and post-master's certificates.

Special study options: academic remediation for entering students, advanced placement credit, cooperative education, distance learning, double majors, honors programs, independent study, internships, off-campus study, part-time degree program, services for LD students, student-designed majors, study abroad, summer session for credit. ***ROTC:*** Army (c).

Computers: 345 computers/terminals are available on campus for general student use. Students can access the following: campus intranet, computer help desk, free student e-mail accounts, online (class) grades, online (class) registration, online (class) schedules. Campuswide network is available. 100% of college-owned or -operated housing units are wired for high-speed Internet access. Wireless service is available via entire campus.

STUDENT LIFE
Housing options: on-campus residence required through junior year; men-only, women-only, special housing for students with disabilities. Campus housing is university owned. Freshman campus housing is guaranteed.

Activities and organizations: drama/theater group, student-run newspaper, choral group, Enactus, Student Government Association, Fellowship of Christian Athletes, Student Missouri State Teachers Association, PSY CHI.

Athletics Member NCAA. All Division II. ***Intercollegiate sports:*** baseball M(s), basketball M(s)/W(s), cheerleading M/W, cross-country running M(s)/W(s), football M(s), golf M(s), soccer M/W(s), softball W(s), tennis M(s)/W(s), track and field M(s)/W(s), volleyball W(s). ***Intramural sports:*** basketball M/W, football M/W, soccer M/W, softball M/W, table tennis M/W, volleyball M/W.

Campus security: 24-hour emergency response devices and patrols, controlled dormitory access.

Student services: health clinic, personal/psychological counseling.

COSTS & FINANCIAL AID
Costs (2014–15) ***Comprehensive fee:*** $27,640 includes full-time tuition ($20,000), mandatory fees ($840), and room and board ($6800). Full-time tuition and fees vary according to course load and location. Part-time tuition: $775 per credit hour. Part-time tuition and fees vary according to course load and location. ***Required fees:*** $145 per term part-time. ***College***

room only: $3300. Room and board charges vary according to board plan and housing facility. ***Payment plan:*** installment. ***Waivers:*** employees or children of employees.

Financial Aid Of all full-time matriculated undergraduates who enrolled in 2014, 1,748 applied for aid, 1,595 were judged to have need, 267 had their need fully met. 382 Federal Work-Study jobs (averaging $1878). In 2014, 292 non-need-based awards were made. ***Average percent of need met:*** 68. ***Average financial aid package:*** $16,305. ***Average need-based loan:*** $4367. ***Average need-based gift aid:*** $4885. ***Average non-need-based aid:*** $9934. ***Average indebtedness upon graduation:*** $26,615.

APPLYING

Standardized Tests *Required:* SAT or ACT (for admission).

Options: electronic application.

Application fee: $30.

Required: high school transcript, minimum 2.5 GPA. ***Required for some:*** 3 letters of recommendation. ***Recommended:*** essay or personal statement, interview.

Application deadlines: rolling (freshmen), rolling (transfers).

Notification: continuous (freshmen), continuous (transfers).

CONTACT

Mr. Darren Crowder, Director of Admissions, Southwest Baptist University, 1600 University Avenue, Bolivar, MO 65613-2597. *Phone:* 417-328-1817. *Toll-free phone:* 800-526-5859. *Fax:* 417-328-1808. *E-mail:* dcrowder@sbuniv.edu.

Stephens College

Columbia, Missouri

http://www.stephens.edu/

- **Independent** comprehensive, founded 1833
- **Urban** 48-acre campus
- **Endowment** $46.8 million
- **Women only** 668 undergraduate students, 83% full-time
- **Moderately difficult** entrance level, 54% of applicants were admitted

UNDERGRAD STUDENTS

556 full-time, 112 part-time. Students come from 32 states and territories; 2 other countries; 36% are from out of state; 16% Black or African American, non-Hispanic/Latino; 5% Hispanic/Latino; 2% Asian, non-Hispanic/Latino; 0.6% Native Hawaiian or other Pacific Islander, non-Hispanic/Latino; 0.4% American Indian or Alaska Native, non-Hispanic/Latino; 6% Two or more races, non-Hispanic/Latino; 2% Race/ethnicity unknown; 10% transferred in; 71% live on campus.

Freshmen

Admission: 1,153 applied, 618 admitted, 184 enrolled. ***Average high school GPA:*** 3.22. ***Test scores:*** ACT scores over 18: 100%; ACT scores over 24: 83%.

Retention: 61% of full-time freshmen returned.

FACULTY

Total: 117, 46% full-time, 38% with terminal degrees.

Student/faculty ratio: 8:1.

ACADEMICS

Calendar: semesters. *Degrees:* certificates, associate, bachelor's, master's, post-master's, and postbachelor's certificates.

Special study options: academic remediation for entering students, accelerated degree program, adult/continuing education programs, advanced placement credit, cooperative education, distance learning, double majors, external degree program, freshman honors college, honors programs, independent study, internships, off-campus study, part-time degree program, services for LD students, student-designed majors, study abroad, summer session for credit. ***ROTC:*** Army (c), Navy (c), Air Force (c).

Unusual degree programs: 3-2 occupational therapy with Washington University in St. Louis.

Computers: 130 computers/terminals are available on campus for general student use. Students can access the following: campus intranet, computer help desk, free student e-mail accounts, online (class) grades, online (class) registration, online (class) schedules. Campuswide network is available. Wireless service is available via entire campus.

STUDENT LIFE

Housing options: on-campus residence required through senior year; women-only. Campus housing is university owned and is provided by a third party. Freshman campus housing is guaranteed.

Activities and organizations: drama/theater group, student-run newspaper, radio and television station, choral group, IFA, Warehouse Theatre, student government, American Marketing Association (AMA), national sororities.

Athletics Member NAIA. ***Intercollegiate sports:*** basketball W(s), cross-country running W(s), golf W(s), soccer W(s), softball W(s), tennis W(s), volleyball W(s). ***Intramural sports:*** equestrian sports W(c).

Campus security: 24-hour emergency response devices and patrols, student patrols, late-night transport/escort service, controlled dormitory access.

Student services: health clinic, personal/psychological counseling.

COSTS & FINANCIAL AID

Costs (2014–15) ***Comprehensive fee:*** $38,042 includes full-time tuition ($28,310), mandatory fees ($200), and room and board ($9532). Full-time tuition and fees vary according to course load, degree level, program, and reciprocity agreements. Part-time tuition: $700 per credit hour. Part-time tuition and fees vary according to course load, degree level, and program. ***College room only:*** $6065. Room and board charges vary according to board plan and housing facility. ***Payment plan:*** installment. ***Waivers:*** employees or children of employees.

Financial Aid Of all full-time matriculated undergraduates who enrolled in 2014, 447 applied for aid, 434 were judged to have need, 52 had their need fully met. 54 Federal Work-Study jobs (averaging $1546). 150 state and other part-time jobs (averaging $1475). In 2014, 41 non-need-based awards were made. ***Average percent of need met:*** 70. ***Average financial aid package:*** $24,002. ***Average need-based loan:*** $4360. ***Average need-based gift aid:*** $9175. ***Average non-need-based aid:*** $7264. ***Average indebtedness upon graduation:*** $26,824.

APPLYING

Standardized Tests *Required:* SAT or ACT (for admission).

Options: electronic application, deferred entrance.

Application fee: $25.

Required: essay or personal statement, high school transcript, minimum 2.0 GPA. ***Required for some:*** 1 letter of recommendation, audition mandatory for dance, recommended for theater. ***Recommended:*** minimum 2.5 GPA, interview.

Notification: continuous until 9/15 (freshmen), continuous until 9/15 (transfers).

CONTACT

Killian Kramer, Director of Undergraduate Admissions, Stephens College, 1200 East Broadway, Box 2121, Columbia, MO 65215-0002. *Phone:* 573-876-7239. *Toll-free phone:* 800-876-7207. *Fax:* 573-876-7237. *E-mail:* apply@stephens.edu.

Stevens–The Institute of Business & Arts

St. Louis, Missouri

http://www.siba.edu/

- **Proprietary** 4-year, founded 1947
- **Urban** campus
- **Coed** 184 undergraduate students, 78% full-time, 90% women, 10% men
- **Moderately difficult** entrance level, 71% of applicants were admitted

UNDERGRAD STUDENTS

144 full-time, 40 part-time. Students come from 5 states and territories; 25% are from out of state; 59% Black or African American, non-Hispanic/Latino; 2% Hispanic/Latino; 0.5% Asian, non-Hispanic/Latino.

Freshmen

Admission: 45 applied, 32 admitted. ***Average high school GPA:*** 2.8.

Retention: 100% of full-time freshmen returned.

FACULTY

Total: 22, 32% full-time, 5% with terminal degrees.

Student/faculty ratio: 10:1.

ACADEMICS
Calendar: quarters. *Degrees:* associate and bachelor's.
Special study options: academic remediation for entering students, accelerated degree program, adult/continuing education programs, advanced placement credit, cooperative education, honors programs, independent study, internships, part-time degree program, summer session for credit.
Computers: 45 computers/terminals are available on campus for general student use. Students can access the following: campus intranet, free student e-mail accounts, online (class) schedules, wireless Internet. Campuswide network is available. Wireless service is available via entire campus.

STUDENT LIFE
Housing options: college housing not available.
Campus security: 24-hour emergency response devices, late-night transport/escort service, 24-hour controlled entrances.
Student services: personal/psychological counseling.

COSTS
Costs (2014–15) ***One-time required fee:*** $25. ***Tuition:*** $17,640 full-time, $245 per credit hour part-time. Full-time tuition and fees vary according to program. Part-time tuition and fees vary according to program. No tuition increase for student's term of enrollment. ***Payment plan:*** installment. ***Waivers:*** employees or children of employees.

APPLYING
Standardized Tests *Required for some:* SAT or ACT (for admission).
Options: electronic application.
Application fee: $25.
Required: essay or personal statement, high school transcript, interview. ***Required for some:*** minimum 2.0 GPA.
Application deadlines: rolling (freshmen), rolling (out-of-state freshmen), rolling (transfers).
Notification: continuous (freshmen), continuous (out-of-state freshmen), continuous (transfers).

CONTACT
Mr. John Willmon, Director of Admissions, Stevens–The Institute of Business & Arts, 1521 Washington Avenue, St. Louis, MO 63103. *Phone:* 314-421-0949 Ext. 1119. *Toll-free phone:* 800-871-0949. *Fax:* 314-421-0304. *E-mail:* admission@siba.edu.

★ Truman State University

Kirksville, Missouri

http://www.truman.edu/

- **State-supported** comprehensive, founded 1867
- **Small-town** 140-acre campus
- **Endowment** $38.6 million
- **Coed** 5,910 undergraduate students, 90% full-time, 59% women, 41% men
- **Moderately difficult** entrance level, 74% of applicants were admitted

UNDERGRAD STUDENTS
5,295 full-time, 615 part-time. Students come from 40 states and territories; 50 other countries; 19% are from out of state; 4% Black or African American, non-Hispanic/Latino; 3% Hispanic/Latino; 2% Asian, non-Hispanic/Latino; 0.1% Native Hawaiian or other Pacific Islander, non-Hispanic/Latino; 0.1% American Indian or Alaska Native, non-Hispanic/Latino; 3% Two or more races, non-Hispanic/Latino; 2% Race/ethnicity unknown; 7% international; 3% transferred in; 49% live on campus.

Freshmen
Admission: 4,095 applied, 3,050 admitted, 1,320 enrolled. ***Average high school GPA:*** 3.76. ***Test scores:*** SAT critical reading scores over 500: 92%; SAT math scores over 500: 90%; ACT scores over 18: 100%; SAT critical reading scores over 600: 68%; SAT math scores over 600: 56%; ACT scores over 24: 83%; SAT critical reading scores over 700: 21%; SAT math scores over 700: 22%; ACT scores over 30: 29%.
Retention: 88% of full-time freshmen returned.

FACULTY
Total: 391, 81% full-time, 78% with terminal degrees.
Student/faculty ratio: 17:1.

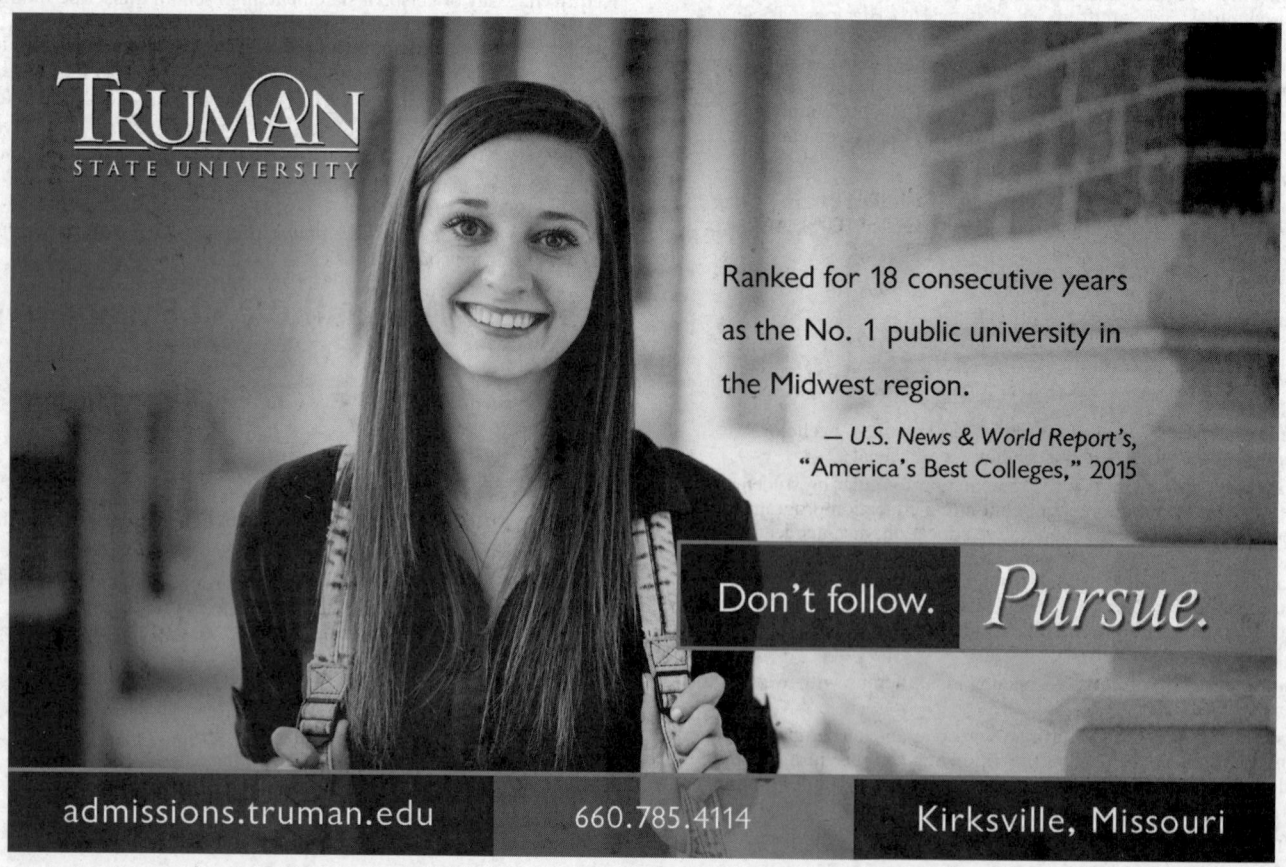

ACADEMICS

Calendar: semesters. *Degrees:* bachelor's and master's.

Special study options: accelerated degree program, advanced placement credit, cooperative education, double majors, honors programs, independent study, internships, off-campus study, part-time degree program, services for LD students, student-designed majors, study abroad, summer session for credit. ***ROTC:*** Army (b).

Unusual degree programs: 3-2 engineering with Most commonly: Missouri University of Science and Technology, University of Missouri-Columbia; Logan Chiropractic.

Computers: 1,099 computers/terminals and 3,690 ports are available on campus for general student use. Students can access the following: campus intranet, computer help desk, free student e-mail accounts, online (class) grades, online (class) registration, online (class) schedules. Campuswide network is available. 100% of college-owned or -operated housing units are wired for high-speed Internet access. Wireless service is available via entire campus.

STUDENT LIFE

Housing options: on-campus residence required for freshman year; coed, special housing for students with disabilities. Campus housing is university owned. Freshman campus housing is guaranteed.

Activities and organizations: drama/theater group, student-run newspaper, radio and television station, choral group, marching band, Alpha Phi Omega (co-ed service fraternity), American Medical Student Association, Alpha Sigma Gamma (service sorority), Nursing Students' Association, Beta Beta Beta (biology honors), national fraternities, national sororities.

Athletics Member NCAA. All Division II. ***Intercollegiate sports:*** baseball M(s), basketball M(s)/W(s), bowling M(c)/W(c), cheerleading M(c)/W(c), cross-country running M(s)/W(s), equestrian sports M(c)/W(c), football M(s), golf W(s), lacrosse W(c), riflery M(c)/W(c), rock climbing M(c)/W(c), rugby M(c)/W(c), soccer M(s)/W(s), softball W(s), swimming and diving M/W(s), tennis M(s)/W(s), track and field M(s)/W(s), ultimate Frisbee M(c)/W(c), volleyball M(c)/W(s), weight lifting M(c)/W(c), wrestling M(s). ***Intramural sports:*** badminton M/W, basketball M/W, cross-country running M/W, football M/W, skiing (cross-country) M(c)/W(c), skiing (downhill) M(c)/W(c), soccer M/W, softball M/W, swimming and diving M/W, table tennis M/W, tennis M/W, track and field M/W, ultimate Frisbee M/W, volleyball M/W.

Campus security: 24-hour emergency response devices and patrols, student patrols, late-night transport/escort service, controlled dormitory access, patrols by commissioned officers, perimeter access system, dual 911 call center for campus/community, emergency text messaging system.

Student services: health clinic, personal/psychological counseling, women's center.

COSTS & FINANCIAL AID

Costs (2014–15) ***One-time required fee:*** $315. ***Tuition:*** state resident $7096 full-time, $296 per credit hour part-time; nonresident $13,160 full-time, $548 per credit hour part-time. Full-time tuition and fees vary according to course load, degree level, and program. Part-time tuition and fees vary according to course load, degree level, and program. ***Required fees:*** $278 full-time, $278 per year part-time. ***Room and board:*** Room and board charges vary according to housing facility. ***Payment plan:*** installment. ***Waivers:*** children of alumni, senior citizens, and employees or children of employees.

Financial Aid Of all full-time matriculated undergraduates who enrolled in 2013, 3,840 applied for aid, 2,809 were judged to have need, 922 had their need fully met. 442 Federal Work-Study jobs (averaging $1673). 1,461 state and other part-time jobs (averaging $1212). In 2013, 1875 non-need-based awards were made. ***Average percent of need met:*** 81. ***Average financial aid package:*** $11,407. ***Average need-based loan:*** $4386. ***Average need-based gift aid:*** $6794. ***Average non-need-based aid:*** $5322. ***Average indebtedness upon graduation:*** $23,585.

APPLYING

Standardized Tests *Required:* SAT or ACT (for admission).

Options: electronic application, deferred entrance.

Required: essay or personal statement, high school transcript, official college entrance exam scores required, activities list/resume recommended. ***Recommended:*** minimum 3.0 GPA, interview.

Application deadlines: rolling (freshmen), rolling (out-of-state freshmen), rolling (transfers).

Notification: continuous until 9/1 (freshmen), continuous until 9/1 (out-of-state freshmen), continuous (transfers).

CONTACT

Melody Chambers, Director of Admissions, Truman State University, Ruth Towne Museum and Visitors Center, 100 East Normal Avenue, Kirksville, MO 63501-4221. *Phone:* 660-785-4114. *Toll-free phone:* 800-892-7792. *Fax:* 660-785-7456. *E-mail:* mchamber@truman.edu.

See previous page for display ad and page 1652 for the College Close-Up.

University of Central Missouri

Warrensburg, Missouri

http://www.ucmo.edu/

- **State-supported** comprehensive, founded 1871
- **Small-town** 1561-acre campus with easy access to Kansas City
- **Endowment** $37.0 million
- **Coed** 9,838 undergraduate students, 83% full-time, 55% women, 45% men
- **Moderately difficult** entrance level, 78% of applicants were admitted

UNDERGRAD STUDENTS

8,133 full-time, 1,705 part-time. Students come from 42 states and territories; 61 other countries; 10% are from out of state; 8% Black or African American, non-Hispanic/Latino; 3% Hispanic/Latino; 1% Asian, non-Hispanic/Latino; 0.1% Native Hawaiian or other Pacific Islander, non-Hispanic/Latino; 0.2% American Indian or Alaska Native, non-Hispanic/Latino; 3% Two or more races, non-Hispanic/Latino; 16% Race/ethnicity unknown; 3% international; 10% transferred in; 33% live on campus.

Freshmen

Admission: 4,612 applied, 3,595 admitted, 1,710 enrolled. ***Average high school GPA:*** 3.33. ***Test scores:*** ACT scores over 18: 90%; ACT scores over 24: 30%; ACT scores over 30: 3%.

Retention: 70% of full-time freshmen returned.

FACULTY

Total: 635, 77% full-time, 57% with terminal degrees.

Student/faculty ratio: 20:1.

ACADEMICS

Calendar: semesters. *Degrees:* certificates, bachelor's, master's, post-master's, and postbachelor's certificates.

Special study options: academic remediation for entering students, accelerated degree program, adult/continuing education programs, advanced placement credit, distance learning, double majors, English as a second language, honors programs, internships, off-campus study, part-time degree program, services for LD students, student-designed majors, study abroad, summer session for credit. ***ROTC:*** Army (b), Air Force (c).

Unusual degree programs: 3-2 engineering with University of Missouri-Columbia, University of Missouri-Rolla, University of Missouri-Kansas City; law, medical.

Computers: 6,395 computers/terminals and 19,008 ports are available on campus for general student use. Students can access the following: campus intranet, computer help desk, free student e-mail accounts, online (class) grades, online (class) registration, online (class) schedules. Campuswide network is available. 100% of college-owned or -operated housing units are wired for high-speed Internet access. Wireless service is available via classrooms, computer centers, computer labs, dorm rooms, learning centers, libraries, student centers.

STUDENT LIFE

Housing options: on-campus residence required through sophomore year; coed, women-only, special housing for students with disabilities. Campus housing is university owned. Freshman campus housing is guaranteed.

Activities and organizations: drama/theater group, student-run newspaper, radio and television station, choral group, marching band, Roaring Red (Student Booster Club), Greek Organization, Campus Christian House, BSU (Baptist Student Union), International Student Organization, national fraternities, national sororities.

Athletics Member NCAA. All Division II. ***Intercollegiate sports:*** baseball M(s), basketball M(s)/W(s), bowling M(c)/W(c), cross-country running M(s)/W(s), football M(s), golf M(s), rock climbing M(c)/W(c), soccer M(c)/W(s), softball W(s), track and field M(s)/W(s), volleyball W(s), wrestling M(s). ***Intramural sports:*** archery M/W, badminton M/W, basketball M/W, bowling M/W, cheerleading M/W, cross-country running M/W, fencing M/W, football M/W, golf M/W, racquetball M/W, riflery M/W, rock climbing M/W, soccer M/W, softball M/W, swimming and diving M/W, table tennis M/W, tennis M/W, track and field M/W, ultimate Frisbee M/W, volleyball M/W, water polo M/W, weight lifting M, wrestling M.

Campus security: 24-hour emergency response devices and patrols, student patrols, late-night transport/escort service, controlled dormitory access, canine patrol.

Student services: health clinic, personal/psychological counseling, women's center.

COSTS & FINANCIAL AID

Costs (2014–15) ***Tuition:*** state resident $6395 full-time, $213 per credit hour part-time; nonresident $12,789 full-time, $426 per credit hour part-time. Full-time tuition and fees vary according to course load and location. Part-time tuition and fees vary according to location. ***Required fees:*** $870 full-time, $29 per credit hour part-time. ***Room and board:*** $7828; room only: $5034. Room and board charges vary according to board plan, housing facility, and student level. ***Payment plans:*** installment, deferred payment. ***Waivers:*** employees or children of employees.

Financial Aid Of all full-time matriculated undergraduates who enrolled in 2013, 6,950 applied for aid, 5,123 were judged to have need, 400 had their need fully met. 211 Federal Work-Study jobs (averaging $1120). 1,415 state and other part-time jobs (averaging $1930). In 2013, 1622 non-need-based awards were made. ***Average percent of need met:*** 59. ***Average financial aid package:*** $8314. ***Average need-based gift aid:*** $4212. ***Average non-need-based aid:*** $3144. ***Average indebtedness upon graduation:*** $27,424.

APPLYING

Standardized Tests *Required:* SAT or ACT (for admission).

Options: electronic application, deferred entrance.

Application fee: $30.

Required: high school transcript, rank in upper two-thirds of high school class.

Application deadlines: rolling (freshmen), rolling (transfers).

Notification: continuous (freshmen), continuous (transfers).

CONTACT

Ms. Ann Nordyke, Director of Admissions, University of Central Missouri, 1400 Ward Edwards, Warrensburg, MO 64093. *Phone:* 660-543-4170. *Toll-free phone:* 800-729-8266. *Fax:* 660-543-8517. *E-mail:* admit@ucmo.edu.

University of Missouri

Columbia, Missouri

http://www.missouri.edu/

- **State-supported** university, founded 1839, part of University of Missouri System
- **Suburban** 1262-acre campus
- **Endowment** $804.9 million
- **Coed** 27,654 undergraduate students, 94% full-time, 52% women, 48% men
- **Moderately difficult** entrance level, 78% of applicants were admitted

UNDERGRAD STUDENTS

25,859 full-time, 1,795 part-time. Students come from 48 states and territories; 67 other countries; 25% are from out of state; 8% Black or African American, non-Hispanic/Latino; 3% Hispanic/Latino; 2% Asian, non-Hispanic/Latino; 0.1% Native Hawaiian or other Pacific Islander, non-Hispanic/Latino; 0.2% American Indian or Alaska Native, non-Hispanic/Latino; 3% Two or more races, non-Hispanic/Latino; 0.6% Race/ethnicity unknown; 4% international; 5% transferred in; 25% live on campus.

Freshmen

Admission: 21,163 applied, 16,437 admitted, 6,515 enrolled. ***Test scores:*** SAT critical reading scores over 500: 82%; SAT math scores over 500: 85%; ACT scores over 18: 100%; SAT critical reading scores over 600: 44%; SAT math scores over 600: 49%; ACT scores over 24: 72%; SAT critical reading scores over 700: 12%; SAT math scores over 700: 13%; ACT scores over 30: 17%.

Retention: 86% of full-time freshmen returned.

FACULTY

Total: 1,474, 95% full-time, 90% with terminal degrees.

Student/faculty ratio: 20:1.

ACADEMICS

Calendar: semesters. *Degrees:* bachelor's, master's, doctoral, and post-master's certificates.

Special study options: accelerated degree program, adult/continuing education programs, advanced placement credit, cooperative education, distance learning, double majors, English as a second language, external degree program, freshman honors college, honors programs, independent study, internships, off-campus study, part-time degree program, services for LD students, student-designed majors, study abroad, summer session for credit. ***ROTC:*** Army (b), Navy (b), Air Force (b).

Unusual degree programs: 3-2 accountancy, physical therapy, occupational therapy.

Computers: 1,242 computers/terminals are available on campus for general student use. Students can access the following: computer help desk, free student e-mail accounts, online (class) grades, online (class) registration, online (class) schedules. Campuswide network is available. 90% of college-owned or -operated housing units are wired for high-speed Internet access. Wireless service is available via classrooms, computer centers, computer labs, dorm rooms, learning centers, libraries, student centers.

STUDENT LIFE

Housing options: on-campus residence required for freshman year; coed, men-only, women-only, special housing for students with disabilities. Campus housing is university owned. Freshman campus housing is guaranteed.

Activities and organizations: drama/theater group, student-run newspaper, radio and television station, choral group, marching band, Academic organizations, Greek organizations, Religious/Spiritual organizations, Sports clubs, Student Governance, national fraternities, national sororities.

Athletics Member NCAA. All Division I except football (Division I-A). ***Intercollegiate sports:*** baseball M(s), basketball M(s)/W(s), cheerleading M/W, cross-country running M(s)/W(s), golf M(s)/W(s), gymnastics W(s), soccer W(s), softball W(s), swimming and diving M(s)/W(s), tennis W(s), track and field M(s)/W(s), volleyball W(s), wrestling M(s). ***Intramural sports:*** archery M(c)/W(c), badminton W(c), baseball M(c), basketball M(c)/W(c), fencing M(c)/W(c), field hockey W(c), golf M(c)/W(c), ice hockey M(c), lacrosse M(c)/W(c), racquetball M(c)/W(c), rugby M(c)/W(c), soccer M(c)/W(c), softball W(c), swimming and diving M(c)/W(c), table tennis M(c)/W(c), tennis M(c)/W(c), ultimate Frisbee M(c)/W(c), volleyball M(c)/W(c), water polo M(c)/W(c), weight lifting M(c)/W(c).

Campus security: 24-hour emergency response devices and patrols, late-night transport/escort service, controlled dormitory access.

Student services: health clinic, personal/psychological counseling, women's center, legal services.

COSTS & FINANCIAL AID

Costs (2014–15) ***Tuition:*** state resident $8220 full-time; nonresident $23,247 full-time. Full-time tuition and fees vary according to course load, program, and reciprocity agreements. Part-time tuition and fees vary according to course load, program, and reciprocity agreements. ***Required fees:*** $1213 full-time. ***Room and board:*** $9386; room only: $6530. Room and board charges vary according to board plan and housing facility. ***Payment plan:*** installment. ***Waivers:*** senior citizens and employees or children of employees.

Financial Aid Of all full-time matriculated undergraduates who enrolled in 2013, 17,210 applied for aid, 12,350 were judged to have need, 1,374 had their need fully met. In 2013, 4452 non-need-based awards were made. ***Average percent of need met:*** 78. ***Average financial aid package:*** $14,050. ***Average need-based loan:*** $4497. ***Average need-based gift aid:*** $8263. ***Average non-need-based aid:*** $4575. ***Average indebtedness upon graduation:*** $24,875.

APPLYING
Standardized Tests *Required:* SAT or ACT (for admission). *Recommended:* ACT (for admission).

Options: electronic application, deferred entrance.

Application fee: $50.

Required: high school transcript, specific high school curriculum.

Application deadlines: rolling (freshmen), rolling (transfers).

Notification: continuous (freshmen), continuous (transfers).

CONTACT
Mr. Charles May, Director of Admissions, University of Missouri, 230 Jesse Hall, Columbia, MO 65211. *Phone:* 573-882-7786. *Toll-free phone:* 800-225-6075. *Fax:* 573-882-7887. *E-mail:* mu4u@missouri.edu.

University of Missouri–Kansas City

Kansas City, Missouri

http://www.umkc.edu/

- **State-supported** university, founded 1929, part of University of Missouri System
- **Urban** 191-acre campus with easy access to Kansas City
- **Endowment** $275.3 million
- **Coed** 10,462 undergraduate students, 65% full-time, 57% women, 43% men
- **Moderately difficult** entrance level, 64% of applicants were admitted

UNDERGRAD STUDENTS
6,817 full-time, 3,645 part-time. Students come from 48 states and territories; 79 other countries; 25% are from out of state; 13% Black or African American, non-Hispanic/Latino; 7% Hispanic/Latino; 5% Asian, non-Hispanic/Latino; 0.1% Native Hawaiian or other Pacific Islander, non-Hispanic/Latino; 0.3% American Indian or Alaska Native, non-Hispanic/Latino; 4% Two or more races, non-Hispanic/Latino; 5% Race/ethnicity unknown; 6% international; 12% transferred in; 25% live on campus.

Freshmen
Admission: 4,377 applied, 2,786 admitted, 1,073 enrolled. ***Average high school GPA:*** 3.32. ***Test scores:*** SAT critical reading scores over 500: 75%; SAT math scores over 500: 79%; ACT scores over 18: 96%; SAT critical reading scores over 600: 42%; SAT math scores over 600: 45%; ACT scores over 24: 54%; SAT critical reading scores over 700: 19%; SAT math scores over 700: 19%; ACT scores over 30: 16%.

Retention: 73% of full-time freshmen returned.

FACULTY
Total: 1,172, 62% full-time, 67% with terminal degrees.

Student/faculty ratio: 14:1.

ACADEMICS
Calendar: semesters. *Degrees:* bachelor's, master's, doctoral, and post-master's certificates.

Special study options: accelerated degree program, adult/continuing education programs, advanced placement credit, cooperative education, distance learning, double majors, English as a second language, freshman honors college, honors programs, independent study, internships, off-campus study, part-time degree program, services for LD students, student-designed majors, study abroad, summer session for credit. ***ROTC:*** Army (b), Air Force (c).

Computers: 400 computers/terminals are available on campus for general student use. Students can access the following: campus intranet, computer help desk, free student e-mail accounts, online (class) grades, online (class) registration, online (class) schedules. Campuswide network is available. 100% of college-owned or -operated housing units are wired for high-speed Internet access. Wireless service is available via classrooms, computer labs, dorm rooms, libraries, student centers.

STUDENT LIFE
Housing options: coed, special housing for students with disabilities. Campus housing is university owned.

Activities and organizations: drama/theater group, student-run newspaper, radio station, choral group, Union Programming Board, International Student Council, Alpha Phi Omega, Omicron Delta Kappa, Greek Organizations, national fraternities, national sororities.

Athletics Member NCAA. All Division I. ***Intercollegiate sports:*** basketball M(s)/W(s), cross-country running M(s)/W(s), golf M(s)/W(s), soccer M(s)/W(s), softball W(s), tennis M(s)/W(s), track and field M(s)/W(s), volleyball W(s). ***Intramural sports:*** badminton M/W, basketball M/W, football M/W, racquetball M/W, soccer M/W, softball M/W, swimming and diving M/W, table tennis M/W, volleyball M/W.

Campus security: 24-hour emergency response devices and patrols, late-night transport/escort service, controlled dormitory access.

Student services: health clinic, personal/psychological counseling, women's center, legal services.

COSTS & FINANCIAL AID
Costs (2014–15) ***Tuition:*** state resident $8103 full-time, $270 per credit hour part-time; nonresident $21,163 full-time, $705 per credit hour part-time. Full-time tuition and fees vary according to course load and program. Part-time tuition and fees vary according to course load and program. ***Required fees:*** $1373 full-time, $99 per credit hour part-time. ***Room and board:*** $9815; room only: $6769. Room and board charges vary according to board plan and housing facility. ***Payment plan:*** installment. ***Waivers:*** employees or children of employees.

Financial Aid Of all full-time matriculated undergraduates who enrolled in 2014, 5,198 applied for aid, 4,441 were judged to have need, 326 had their need fully met. 487 Federal Work-Study jobs (averaging $4134). In 2014, 865 non-need-based awards were made. ***Average percent of need met:*** 53. ***Average financial aid package:*** $9709. ***Average need-based loan:*** $8046. ***Average need-based gift aid:*** $7093. ***Average non-need-based aid:*** $4828. ***Average indebtedness upon graduation:*** $29,464.

APPLYING
Standardized Tests *Required:* SAT or ACT (for admission).

Options: electronic application, deferred entrance.

Application fee: $45.

Required: high school transcript. ***Required for some:*** essay or personal statement, interview.

Application deadlines: rolling (freshmen), rolling (transfers).

Notification: continuous (freshmen), continuous (transfers).

CONTACT
Ms. Tamera Byland, Director of Admissions, University of Missouri–Kansas City, Office of Admissions, 5100 Rockhill Road, Kansas City, MO 64110-2499. *Phone:* 816-235-1111. *Toll-free phone:* 800-775-8652. *Fax:* 816-235-5544. *E-mail:* admit@umkc.edu.

University of Missouri–St. Louis

St. Louis, Missouri

http://www.umsl.edu/

- **State-supported** university, founded 1963, part of University of Missouri System
- **Suburban** 350-acre campus with easy access to St. Louis
- **Endowment** $76.1 million
- **Coed** 13,887 undergraduate students, 44% full-time, 58% women, 42% men
- **Moderately difficult** entrance level, 76% of applicants were admitted

UNDERGRAD STUDENTS
6,071 full-time, 7,816 part-time. Students come from 44 states and territories; 55 other countries; 11% are from out of state; 19% Black or African American, non-Hispanic/Latino; 3% Hispanic/Latino; 5% Asian, non-Hispanic/Latino; 0.2% Native Hawaiian or other Pacific Islander, non-Hispanic/Latino; 0.4% American Indian or Alaska Native, non-Hispanic/Latino; 2% Two or more races, non-Hispanic/Latino; 6% Race/ethnicity unknown; 3% international; 11% transferred in; 9% live on campus.

Freshmen
Admission: 1,733 applied, 1,312 admitted, 513 enrolled. ***Average high school GPA:*** 3446. ***Test scores:*** SAT critical reading scores over 500: 41%; SAT math scores over 500: 70%; SAT writing scores over 500: 41%; ACT scores over 18: 98%; SAT critical reading scores over 600: 14%; SAT math scores over 600: 48%; SAT writing scores over 600: 14%; ACT scores over 24: 53%; SAT math scores over 700: 9%; ACT scores over 30: 8%.

Retention: 79% of full-time freshmen returned.

FACULTY
Total: 961, 49% full-time, 50% with terminal degrees.

Student/faculty ratio: 16:1.

ACADEMICS
Calendar: semesters. *Degrees:* bachelor's, master's, doctoral, post-master's, and postbachelor's certificates.

Special study options: accelerated degree program, adult/continuing education programs, advanced placement credit, cooperative education, distance learning, double majors, English as a second language, freshman honors college, honors programs, independent study, internships, off-campus study, part-time degree program, services for LD students, student-designed majors, study abroad, summer session for credit. ***ROTC:*** Army (b), Air Force (c).

Unusual degree programs: 3-2 engineering with Washington University; economics, history, philosophy, political science and sociology.

Computers: 1,280 computers/terminals and 1,280 ports are available on campus for general student use. Students can access the following: campus intranet, computer help desk, free student e-mail accounts, online (class) grades, online (class) registration, online (class) schedules. Campuswide network is available. 90% of college-owned or -operated housing units are wired for high-speed Internet access. Wireless service is available via classrooms, computer centers, computer labs, dorm rooms, learning centers, libraries, student centers.

STUDENT LIFE
Housing options: coed, men-only, women-only, special housing for students with disabilities. Campus housing is university owned and is provided by a third party.

Activities and organizations: drama/theater group, student-run newspaper, radio station, choral group, Student Government Association, Associated Black Collegians, Pierre laclede Honors College Student Association, Residence Hall Association, UMSL Radio Station, national fraternities, national sororities.

Athletics Member NCAA. All Division II. ***Intercollegiate sports:*** baseball M(s), basketball M(s)/W(s), cheerleading W, golf M(s)/W(s), ice hockey M(c), soccer M(s)/W(s), softball W(s), table tennis M(c)/W(c), tennis M(s)/W(s), volleyball W(s). ***Intramural sports:*** badminton M/W, basketball M/W, bowling M/W, football M/W, golf M/W, racquetball M/W, rock climbing M/W, skiing (downhill) M/W, soccer M/W, softball M/W, table tennis M/W, tennis M/W, volleyball M/W, weight lifting M/W.

Campus security: 24-hour emergency response devices and patrols, late-night transport/escort service, controlled dormitory access, Criminal Investigations.

Student services: health clinic, personal/psychological counseling, women's center.

COSTS & FINANCIAL AID
Costs (2015–16) ***Tuition:*** state resident $10,065 full-time, $336 per credit hour part-time; nonresident $25,512 full-time, $850 per credit hour part-time. Full-time tuition and fees vary according to course level, course load, program, and reciprocity agreements. Part-time tuition and fees vary according to course level, course load, program, and reciprocity agreements. ***Room and board:*** $9052; room only: $5280. Room and board charges vary according to board plan and housing facility. ***Payment plan:*** installment. ***Waivers:*** senior citizens and employees or children of employees.

Financial Aid Of all full-time matriculated undergraduates who enrolled in 2014, 4,760 applied for aid, 4,169 were judged to have need, 500 had their need fully met. 53 Federal Work-Study jobs (averaging $3333). In 2014, 507 non-need-based awards were made. ***Average percent of need met:*** 61. ***Average financial aid package:*** $10,702. ***Average need-based loan:*** $4588. ***Average need-based gift aid:*** $7462. ***Average non-need-based aid:*** $5680. ***Average indebtedness upon graduation:*** $25,208.

APPLYING
Standardized Tests *Required:* SAT or ACT (for admission).

Options: electronic application.

Application fee: $35.

Required: high school transcript, minimum 2.0 GPA, CBHE core requirements. ***Required for some:*** essay or personal statement, 2 letters of recommendation, interview.

Application deadlines: rolling (freshmen), rolling (out-of-state freshmen), rolling (transfers).

Notification: continuous (freshmen), continuous (out-of-state freshmen), continuous (transfers).

CONTACT
Mr. Andrew L. Griffin, Dean of Admissions, University of Missouri–St. Louis, 351 Millennium Student Center, One University Boulevard, St. Louis, MO 63121-4400. *Phone:* 314-516-6941. *Toll-free phone:* 888-GO2-UMSL (in-state); 888-GO2-USML (out-of-state). *Fax:* 314-516-5310. *E-mail:* askdrew@umsl.edu.

Washington University in St. Louis

St. Louis, Missouri

http://www.wustl.edu/

- **Independent** university, founded 1853
- **Suburban** 169-acre campus
- **Endowment** $6.7 billion
- **Coed** 7,401 undergraduate students, 90% full-time, 52% women, 48% men
- **Most difficult** entrance level, 17% of applicants were admitted

UNDERGRAD STUDENTS
6,686 full-time, 715 part-time. Students come from 54 states and territories; 50 other countries; 93% are from out of state; 5% Black or African American, non-Hispanic/Latino; 6% Hispanic/Latino; 18% Asian, non-Hispanic/Latino; 0.1% American Indian or Alaska Native, non-Hispanic/Latino; 4% Two or more races, non-Hispanic/Latino; 3% Race/ethnicity unknown; 8% international; 1% transferred in; 79% live on campus.

Freshmen
Admission: 29,211 applied, 5,004 admitted, 1,734 enrolled. ***Test scores:*** SAT critical reading scores over 500: 100%; SAT math scores over 500: 100%; SAT writing scores over 500: 100%; ACT scores over 18: 100%; SAT critical reading scores over 600: 99%; SAT math scores over 600: 100%; SAT writing scores over 600: 99%; ACT scores over 24: 100%; SAT critical reading scores over 700: 78%; SAT math scores over 700: 89%; SAT writing scores over 700: 78%; ACT scores over 30: 98%.

Retention: 97% of full-time freshmen returned.

FACULTY
Total: 1,270, 70% full-time, 66% with terminal degrees.

Student/faculty ratio: 8:1.

ACADEMICS
Calendar: semesters. *Degrees:* certificates, bachelor's, master's, doctoral, post-master's, and postbachelor's certificates.

Special study options: accelerated degree program, adult/continuing education programs, advanced placement credit, cooperative education, distance learning, double majors, English as a second language, independent study, internships, off-campus study, part-time degree program, services for LD students, student-designed majors, study abroad, summer session for credit. ***ROTC:*** Army (b), Air Force (c).

Unusual degree programs: 3-2 business administration; engineering; social work; art, occupational therapy, physical therapy.

Computers: 2,500 computers/terminals are available on campus for general student use. Students can access the following: campus intranet, computer help desk, free student e-mail accounts, online (class) grades, online (class) registration, online (class) schedules. Campuswide network is available. 90% of college-owned or -operated housing units are wired for high-speed Internet access. Wireless service is available via classrooms, computer centers, computer labs, dorm rooms, learning centers, libraries, student centers.

STUDENT LIFE
Housing options: on-campus residence required for freshman year; coed, men-only, women-only, cooperative. Campus housing is university owned. Freshman campus housing is guaranteed.

Activities and organizations: drama/theater group, student-run newspaper, radio and television station, choral group, national fraternities, national sororities.

Athletics Member NCAA. All Division III. ***Intercollegiate sports:*** baseball M, basketball M/W, crew M(c)/W(c), cross-country running

M/W, equestrian sports M(c)/W(c), fencing M(c)/W(c), field hockey W(c), football M, golf M(c)/W, gymnastics M(c)/W(c), ice hockey M(c), lacrosse M(c)/W(c), rugby M(c)/W(c), sailing M(c)/W(c), soccer M/W, softball W, swimming and diving M/W, table tennis M(c)/W(c), tennis M/W, track and field M/W, ultimate Frisbee M(c)/W(c), volleyball M(c)/W, water polo M(c)/W(c), wrestling M(c). ***Intramural sports:*** badminton M/W, basketball M/W, bowling M/W, cross-country running M/W, football M/W, golf M/W, racquetball M/W, soccer M(c)/W(c), softball M/W, swimming and diving M/W, table tennis M/W, tennis M/W, track and field M/W, ultimate Frisbee M/W, volleyball M/W, water polo M/W.

Campus security: 24-hour emergency response devices and patrols, student patrols, late-night transport/escort service, controlled dormitory access.

Student services: health clinic, personal/psychological counseling, women's center.

COSTS & FINANCIAL AID

Costs (2015–16) ***Comprehensive fee:*** $63,373 includes full-time tuition ($47,300), mandatory fees ($793), and room and board ($15,280). ***College room only:*** $10,486. Room and board charges vary according to board plan and housing facility. ***Payment plans:*** tuition prepayment, installment. ***Waivers:*** employees or children of employees.

Financial Aid Of all full-time matriculated undergraduates who enrolled in 2014, 3,194 applied for aid, 2,691 were judged to have need, 2,653 had their need fully met. 1,139 Federal Work-Study jobs (averaging $2204). In 2014, 833 non-need-based awards were made. ***Average percent of need met:*** 100. ***Average financial aid package:*** $37,928. ***Average need-based loan:*** $6006. ***Average need-based gift aid:*** $35,555. ***Average non-need-based aid:*** $8665. ***Average indebtedness upon graduation:*** $23,858. ***Financial aid deadline:*** 2/1.

APPLYING

Standardized Tests *Required:* SAT or ACT (for admission).

Options: electronic application, early admission, early decision, deferred entrance.

Application fee: $75.

Required: essay or personal statement, high school transcript, 2 letters of recommendation. ***Recommended:*** minimum 3.0 GPA, Portfolios are required for students applying to the College of Art. Portfolios are strongly encouraged for students applying to the College of Architecture.

Application deadlines: 1/15 (freshmen), 3/15 (transfers).

Early decision deadline: 11/15.

Notification: 4/1 (freshmen), continuous (transfers), 12/15 (early decision).

CONTACT

Ms. Julie Shimabukuro, Director of Admissions, Washington University in St. Louis, Campus Box 1089, One Brookings Drive, St. Louis, MO 63130-4899. *Phone:* 314-935-6000. *Toll-free phone:* 800-638-0700. *Fax:* 314-935-4290. *E-mail:* admissions@wustl.edu.

Webster University

St. Louis, Missouri

http://www.webster.edu/

- **Independent** comprehensive, founded 1915
- **Suburban** 47-acre campus with easy access to St. Louis
- **Endowment** $128.1 million
- **Coed** 2,928 undergraduate students, 83% full-time, 54% women, 46% men
- **Moderately difficult** entrance level, 56% of applicants were admitted

UNDERGRAD STUDENTS

2,444 full-time, 484 part-time. Students come from 44 states and territories; 39 other countries; 25% are from out of state; 13% Black or African American, non-Hispanic/Latino; 4% Hispanic/Latino; 2% Asian, non-Hispanic/Latino; 0.1% Native Hawaiian or other Pacific Islander, non-Hispanic/Latino; 0.4% American Indian or Alaska Native, non-Hispanic/Latino; 3% Two or more races, non-Hispanic/Latino; 7% Race/ethnicity unknown; 4% international; 11% transferred in; 25% live on campus.

Freshmen

Admission: 1,863 applied, 1,038 admitted, 463 enrolled. ***Average high school GPA:*** 3.22. ***Test scores:*** ACT scores over 18: 92%; ACT scores over 24: 48%; ACT scores over 30: 10%.

Retention: 77% of full-time freshmen returned.

FACULTY

Total: 878, 23% full-time, 33% with terminal degrees.

Student/faculty ratio: 9:1.

ACADEMICS

Calendar: semesters. *Degrees:* certificates, bachelor's, master's, doctoral, post-master's, and postbachelor's certificates.

Special study options: academic remediation for entering students, accelerated degree program, adult/continuing education programs, advanced placement credit, cooperative education, distance learning, double majors, English as a second language, independent study, internships, off-campus study, part-time degree program, services for LD students, student-designed majors, study abroad, summer session for credit. ***ROTC:*** Army (c), Air Force (c).

Unusual degree programs: 3-2 engineering with University of Missouri-Columbia, Washington University in St. Louis; occupational therapy with Washington University School of Medicine.

Computers: 876 computers/terminals and 340 ports are available on campus for general student use. Students can access the following: campus intranet, computer help desk, free student e-mail accounts, online (class) grades, online (class) registration, online (class) schedules. Campuswide network is available. 100% of college-owned or -operated housing units are wired for high-speed Internet access. Wireless service is available via entire campus.

STUDENT LIFE

Housing options: on-campus residence required for freshman year; coed. Campus housing is university owned. Freshman applicants given priority for college housing.

Activities and organizations: drama/theater group, student-run newspaper, radio and television station, choral group, Student Government Association, Forensics & Debate, International Student Association, Commuter Council, Residential Housing Association.

Athletics Member NCAA. All Division III. ***Intercollegiate sports:*** baseball M, basketball M/W, cross-country running M/W, golf M, soccer M/W, softball W, tennis M/W, track and field M/W, volleyball W. ***Intramural sports:*** basketball M/W, bowling M/W, cheerleading M(c)/W(c), football M/W, soccer M(c)/W(c), swimming and diving M(c)/W(c), volleyball M/W.

Campus security: 24-hour emergency response devices and patrols, student patrols, late-night transport/escort service, controlled dormitory access.

Student services: health clinic, personal/psychological counseling, women's center.

COSTS & FINANCIAL AID

Costs (2014–15) ***Comprehensive fee:*** $35,100 includes full-time tuition ($24,500) and room and board ($10,600). Full-time tuition and fees vary according to program. Part-time tuition: $630 per credit hour. ***College room only:*** $5850. Room and board charges vary according to board plan and housing facility. ***Payment plan:*** installment. ***Waivers:*** employees or children of employees.

Financial Aid Of all full-time matriculated undergraduates who enrolled in 2014, 2,180 applied for aid, 1,801 were judged to have need, 52 had their need fully met. 1,008 Federal Work-Study jobs (averaging $2186). 475 state and other part-time jobs (averaging $1571). In 2014, 283 non-need-based awards were made. ***Average percent of need met:*** 33. ***Average financial aid package:*** $25,134. ***Average need-based loan:*** $4616. ***Average need-based gift aid:*** $8640. ***Average non-need-based aid:*** $5820. ***Average indebtedness upon graduation:*** $30,413.

APPLYING

Standardized Tests *Required:* SAT or ACT (for admission).

Options: electronic application, early admission, deferred entrance.

Application fee: $35.

Required: essay or personal statement, high school transcript, minimum 2.5 GPA, 1 letter of recommendation. ***Required for some:*** minimum 3.0 GPA, audition for dance, music, theatre, and musical theatre students;

portfolio for art and film students. ***Recommended:*** minimum 3.0 GPA, interview.

Application deadlines: 8/1 (freshmen), 8/1 (out-of-state freshmen), 8/1 (transfers).

Notification: continuous (freshmen), continuous (out-of-state freshmen), continuous (transfers).

CONTACT

Mr. Andrew Laue, Director of Undergraduate Admissions, Webster University, 470 East Lockwood Avenue, St. Louis, MO 63119-3194. *Phone:* 314-246-7712. *Toll-free phone:* 800-75-ENROL. *Fax:* 314-246-7122. *E-mail:* lauear@webster.edu.

Westminster College

Fulton, Missouri

http://www.westminster-mo.edu/

- **Independent** 4-year, founded 1851, affiliated with Presbyterian Church
- **Small-town** 80-acre campus
- **Endowment** $56.3 million
- **Coed** 944 undergraduate students, 99% full-time, 43% women, 57% men
- **Moderately difficult** entrance level, 67% of applicants were admitted

UNDERGRAD STUDENTS

934 full-time, 10 part-time. Students come from 28 states and territories; 70 other countries; 20% are from out of state; 8% Black or African American, non-Hispanic/Latino; 4% Hispanic/Latino; 1% Asian, non-Hispanic/Latino; 2% American Indian or Alaska Native, non-Hispanic/Latino; 1% Two or more races, non-Hispanic/Latino; 2% Race/ethnicity unknown; 16% international; 5% transferred in; 82% live on campus.

Freshmen

Admission: 1,356 applied, 910 admitted, 212 enrolled. ***Average high school GPA:*** 3.47. ***Test scores:*** SAT critical reading scores over 500: 55%; SAT math scores over 500: 50%; ACT scores over 18: 96%; SAT critical reading scores over 600: 17%; SAT math scores over 600: 33%; ACT scores over 24: 55%; SAT critical reading scores over 700: 4%; SAT math scores over 700: 4%; ACT scores over 30: 13%.

Retention: 78% of full-time freshmen returned.

FACULTY

Total: 84, 69% full-time, 69% with terminal degrees.

Student/faculty ratio: 13:1.

ACADEMICS

Calendar: semesters. *Degree:* bachelor's.

Special study options: academic remediation for entering students, advanced placement credit, cooperative education, double majors, English as a second language, honors programs, independent study, internships, off-campus study, part-time degree program, services for LD students, student-designed majors, study abroad, summer session for credit. ***ROTC:*** Army (c), Air Force (c).

Unusual degree programs: 3-2 engineering with Washington University in St. Louis, University of Missouri-Columbia; nursing with Golfarb School of Nursing at Barnes-Jewish College in St. Louis; BA/Doctor of Chiropractic Medicine with Logan University of Chiropractic.

Computers: 188 computers/terminals are available on campus for general student use. Students can access the following: campus intranet, computer help desk, free student e-mail accounts, online (class) grades, online (class) registration, online (class) schedules. Campuswide network is available. 100% of college-owned or -operated housing units are wired for high-speed Internet access. Wireless service is available via entire campus.

STUDENT LIFE

Housing options: on-campus residence required through junior year; coed, men-only, women-only. Campus housing is university owned. Freshman campus housing is guaranteed.

Activities and organizations: drama/theater group, student-run newspaper, choral group, Student Government Association, Environmentally Concerned Students, International Student Club, Habitat for Humanity, Little Brother/Little Sister, national fraternities, national sororities.

Athletics Member NCAA. All Division III. ***Intercollegiate sports:*** baseball M, basketball M/W, cross-country running M/W, football M, golf M/W, soccer M/W, softball M/W, tennis M/W, track and field M/W, volleyball W. ***Intramural sports:*** basketball M/W, football M, table tennis M/W, volleyball M/W.

Campus security: 24-hour emergency response devices and patrols, late-night transport/escort service, controlled dormitory access, well-lit campus.

Student services: health clinic, personal/psychological counseling, women's center.

COSTS & FINANCIAL AID

Costs (2014–15) ***Comprehensive fee:*** $31,720 includes full-time tuition ($21,360), mandatory fees ($1200), and room and board ($9160). Full-time tuition and fees vary according to reciprocity agreements. Part-time tuition: $800 per credit. ***College room only:*** $4940. Room and board charges vary according to board plan and housing facility. ***Payment plan:*** installment. ***Waivers:*** children of alumni and employees or children of employees.

Financial Aid Of all full-time matriculated undergraduates who enrolled in 2014, 717 applied for aid, 554 were judged to have need, 427 had their need fully met. 443 Federal Work-Study jobs (averaging $1401). 188 state and other part-time jobs (averaging $2042). In 2014, 364 non-need-based awards were made. ***Average percent of need met:*** 91. ***Average financial aid package:*** $20,800. ***Average need-based loan:*** $3714. ***Average need-based gift aid:*** $16,309. ***Average non-need-based aid:*** $11,477. ***Average indebtedness upon graduation:*** $29,004.

APPLYING

Standardized Tests *Required:* SAT or ACT (for admission).

Options: electronic application, early admission, deferred entrance.

Required: high school transcript, 1 letter of recommendation. ***Required for some:*** interview. ***Recommended:*** essay or personal statement, minimum 2.5 GPA.

Notification: 8/1 (freshmen), continuous (transfers).

CONTACT

Dr. Stephanie Miller, Vice President and Dean of Enrollment Services, Westminster College, 501 Westminster Avenue, Fulton, MO 65251-1299. *Phone:* 573-592-5251. *Toll-free phone:* 800-475-3361. *Fax:* 573-592-5255. *E-mail:* admissions@westminster-mo.edu.

William Jewell College

Liberty, Missouri

http://www.jewell.edu/

- **Independent** comprehensive, founded 1849
- **Suburban** 200-acre campus with easy access to Kansas City
- **Endowment** $72.8 million
- **Coed** 1,043 undergraduate students, 98% full-time, 60% women, 40% men
- **Moderately difficult** entrance level, 63% of applicants were admitted

UNDERGRAD STUDENTS

1,019 full-time, 24 part-time. Students come from 32 states and territories; 33 other countries; 37% are from out of state; 6% Black or African American, non-Hispanic/Latino; 3% Hispanic/Latino; 1% Asian, non-Hispanic/Latino; 0.2% Native Hawaiian or other Pacific Islander, non-Hispanic/Latino; 0.4% American Indian or Alaska Native, non-Hispanic/Latino; 6% Two or more races, non-Hispanic/Latino; 2% Race/ethnicity unknown; 4% international; 5% transferred in; 85% live on campus.

Freshmen

Admission: 1,391 applied, 874 admitted, 265 enrolled. ***Average high school GPA:*** 3.77. ***Test scores:*** SAT critical reading scores over 500: 68%; SAT math scores over 500: 86%; ACT scores over 18: 99%; SAT critical reading scores over 600: 22%; SAT math scores over 600: 40%; ACT scores over 24: 67%; SAT critical reading scores over 700: 8%; SAT math scores over 700: 3%; ACT scores over 30: 16%.

Retention: 77% of full-time freshmen returned.

FACULTY

Total: 141, 58% full-time, 54% with terminal degrees.

Student/faculty ratio: 10:1.

ACADEMICS
Calendar: semesters. *Degrees:* bachelor's, master's, and postbachelor's certificates (also offers evening program with significant enrollment not reflected in profile).

Special study options: accelerated degree program, advanced placement credit, cooperative education, distance learning, double majors, English as a second language, honors programs, independent study, internships, off-campus study, services for LD students, student-designed majors, study abroad, summer session for credit. ***ROTC:*** Army (c).

Unusual degree programs: 3-2 engineering with Washington University in St. Louis, University of Kansas, Vanderbilt University, Columbia University, Missouri University of Science and Technology; forestry with Duke University; occupational therapy with Washington University in St. Louis.

Computers: 220 computers/terminals and 900 ports are available on campus for general student use. Students can access the following: campus intranet, computer help desk, free student e-mail accounts, online (class) grades, online (class) registration, online (class) schedules, All students provided an iPad and support service via the eHub. Campuswide network is available. 100% of college-owned or -operated housing units are wired for high-speed Internet access. Wireless service is available via entire campus.

STUDENT LIFE
Housing options: on-campus residence required through senior year; coed, men-only, women-only, special housing for students with disabilities. Campus housing is university owned. Freshman campus housing is guaranteed.

Activities and organizations: drama/theater group, student-run newspaper, choral group, College Union Activities, Intramurals, Mosaic, Student Senate, Black Student Association, national fraternities, national sororities.

Athletics Member NCAA. All Division II. ***Intercollegiate sports:*** baseball M(s), basketball M(s)/W(s), cheerleading M(s)/W(s), cross-country running M(s)/W(s), football M(s), golf M(s)/W(s), soccer M(s)/W(s), softball W(s), swimming and diving M(s)/W(s), tennis M(s)/W(s), track and field M(s)/W(s), volleyball W(s). ***Intramural sports:*** racquetball M/W, soccer M/W, softball M/W, tennis M/W, ultimate Frisbee M/W, volleyball M/W.

Campus security: 24-hour emergency response devices and patrols, late-night transport/escort service, controlled dormitory access.

Student services: health clinic, personal/psychological counseling.

COSTS & FINANCIAL AID
Costs (2015–16) ***Comprehensive fee:*** $41,210 includes full-time tuition ($31,730), mandatory fees ($600), and room and board ($8880). Full-time tuition and fees vary according to course load and program. Part-time tuition: $930 per credit. ***Room and board:*** Room and board charges vary according to board plan and housing facility. ***Payment plan:*** installment. ***Waivers:*** employees or children of employees.

Financial Aid Of all full-time matriculated undergraduates who enrolled in 2014, 845 applied for aid, 733 were judged to have need, 176 had their need fully met. 494 Federal Work-Study jobs (averaging $2429). 146 state and other part-time jobs (averaging $359). In 2014, 142 non-need-based awards were made. ***Average percent of need met:*** 79. ***Average financial aid package:*** $26,735. ***Average need-based loan:*** $5298. ***Average need-based gift aid:*** $19,646. ***Average non-need-based aid:*** $15,269. ***Average indebtedness upon graduation:*** $29,885.

APPLYING
Standardized Tests *Recommended:* SAT or ACT (for admission).

Options: electronic application, deferred entrance.

Required: high school transcript. ***Required for some:*** essay or personal statement, interview.

Application deadlines: 8/15 (freshmen), 8/15 (transfers).

Notification: continuous (freshmen), continuous (transfers).

CONTACT
Mr. Cory Scheer, Dean of Admission, William Jewell College, 500 College Hill, Liberty, MO 64068. *Phone:* 816-415-7872. *Toll-free phone:* 888-2JEWELL. *Fax:* 816-415-5040. *E-mail:* scheerc@william.jewell.edu.

William Woods University
Fulton, Missouri
http://www.williamwoods.edu/

- **Independent** comprehensive, founded 1870, affiliated with Christian Church (Disciples of Christ)
- **Small-town** 200-acre campus with easy access to St. Louis, Kansas City
- **Endowment** $15.5 million
- **Coed** 1,006 undergraduate students, 84% full-time, 74% women, 26% men
- **Moderately difficult** entrance level, 76% of applicants were admitted

UNDERGRAD STUDENTS
850 full-time, 156 part-time. Students come from 36 states and territories; 11 other countries; 34% are from out of state; 4% Black or African American, non-Hispanic/Latino; 1% Hispanic/Latino; 0.5% Asian, non-Hispanic/Latino; 0.1% Native Hawaiian or other Pacific Islander, non-Hispanic/Latino; 0.8% American Indian or Alaska Native, non-Hispanic/Latino; 2% Two or more races, non-Hispanic/Latino; 8% Race/ethnicity unknown; 0.3% international; 6% transferred in; 65% live on campus.

Freshmen
Admission: 768 applied, 586 admitted, 200 enrolled. ***Average high school GPA:*** 3.36. ***Test scores:*** SAT critical reading scores over 500: 33%; SAT math scores over 500: 53%; SAT writing scores over 500: 33%; ACT scores over 18: 92%; SAT critical reading scores over 600: 21%; SAT math scores over 600: 6%; SAT writing scores over 600: 9%; ACT scores over 24: 39%; SAT critical reading scores over 700: 6%; ACT scores over 30: 12%.

Retention: 76% of full-time freshmen returned.

FACULTY
Total: 266, 25% full-time, 41% with terminal degrees.
Student/faculty ratio: 10:1.

ACADEMICS
Calendar: semesters. *Degrees:* associate, bachelor's, master's, doctoral, and post-master's certificates.

Special study options: academic remediation for entering students, accelerated degree program, advanced placement credit, distance learning, double majors, honors programs, independent study, internships, off-campus study, part-time degree program, services for LD students, student-designed majors, study abroad, summer session for credit. ***ROTC:*** Army (c), Navy (c), Air Force (c).

Unusual degree programs: 3-2 business administration.

Computers: 152 computers/terminals and 1,339 ports are available on campus for general student use. Students can access the following: campus intranet, computer help desk, free student e-mail accounts, online (class) grades, online (class) registration, online (class) schedules. Campuswide network is available. 100% of college-owned or -operated housing units are wired for high-speed Internet access. Wireless service is available via entire campus.

STUDENT LIFE
Housing options: on-campus residence required through senior year; coed, men-only, women-only. Campus housing is university owned. Freshman campus housing is guaranteed.

Activities and organizations: drama/theater group, student-run radio station, choral group, Campus Crusade for Christ, Students of Social Work, Active Minds, International Justice Mission, Kindness Connection, national fraternities, national sororities.

Athletics Member NAIA. ***Intercollegiate sports:*** baseball M(s), basketball M(s)/W(s), cheerleading W(s), cross-country running M(s)/W(s), golf M(s)/W(s), soccer M(s)/W(s), softball W(s), track and field M(s)/W(s), volleyball W(s). ***Intramural sports:*** basketball M/W, equestrian sports M/W, tennis M/W.

Campus security: 24-hour emergency response devices and patrols, late-night transport/escort service, controlled dormitory access.

Student services: health clinic, personal/psychological counseling.

COSTS & FINANCIAL AID
Costs (2015–16) ***Comprehensive fee:*** $31,120 includes full-time tuition ($21,370), mandatory fees ($790), and room and board ($8960). Full-time tuition and fees vary according to degree level and program. Part-time

tuition: $325 per credit hour. Part-time tuition and fees vary according to course load, degree level, and program. ***Required fees:*** $35 per term part-time. ***College room only:*** $4600. Room and board charges vary according to board plan and housing facility. ***Payment plan:*** installment. ***Waivers:*** children of alumni, senior citizens, and employees or children of employees.

Financial Aid Of all full-time matriculated undergraduates who enrolled in 2014, 639 applied for aid, 539 were judged to have need, 128 had their need fully met. In 2014, 196 non-need-based awards were made. ***Average percent of need met:*** 74. ***Average financial aid package:*** $17,991. ***Average need-based loan:*** $5459. ***Average need-based gift aid:*** $13,048. ***Average non-need-based aid:*** $9375. ***Average indebtedness upon graduation:*** $21,260.

APPLYING

Standardized Tests *Required:* SAT or ACT (for admission).

Options: electronic application, deferred entrance.

Required: high school transcript, minimum 2.5 GPA, 16 hours college preparatory units.

Application deadlines: 8/15 (freshmen), rolling (transfers).

Notification: continuous (freshmen), continuous (transfers).

CONTACT

Mrs. Kerry Collins, Prospect Coordinator, William Woods University, One University Avenue, Fulton, MO 65251. *Phone:* 573-592-4221. *Toll-free phone:* 800-995-3159 Ext. 4221. *Fax:* 573-592-1146. *E-mail:* kerry.collins@williamwoods.edu.

MONTANA

★ Carroll College

Helena, Montana

http://www.carroll.edu/

- **Independent Roman Catholic** 4-year, founded 1909
- **Small-town** 61-acre campus
- **Endowment** $36.0 million
- **Coed** 1,430 undergraduate students, 97% full-time, 58% women, 42% men
- **Moderately difficult** entrance level, 58% of applicants were admitted

UNDERGRAD STUDENTS

1,386 full-time, 44 part-time. Students come from 36 states and territories; 11 other countries; 54% are from out of state; 0.7% Black or African American, non-Hispanic/Latino; 5% Hispanic/Latino; 1% Asian, non-Hispanic/Latino; 0.3% Native Hawaiian or other Pacific Islander, non-Hispanic/Latino; 1% American Indian or Alaska Native, non-Hispanic/Latino; 2% Two or more races, non-Hispanic/Latino; 9% Race/ethnicity unknown; 2% international; 4% transferred in; 57% live on campus.

Freshmen

Admission: 3,527 applied, 2,029 admitted, 354 enrolled. ***Average high school GPA:*** 3.6. ***Test scores:*** SAT critical reading scores over 500: 77%; SAT math scores over 500: 74%; SAT writing scores over 500: 71%; ACT scores over 18: 96%; SAT critical reading scores over 600: 35%; SAT math scores over 600: 35%; SAT writing scores over 600: 25%; ACT scores over 24: 63%; SAT critical reading scores over 700: 10%; SAT math scores over 700: 7%; SAT writing scores over 700: 5%; ACT scores over 30: 12%.

Retention: 80% of full-time freshmen returned.

FACULTY

Total: 165, 54% full-time.

Student/faculty ratio: 12:1.

ACADEMICS

Calendar: semesters. *Degrees:* associate and bachelor's.

Special study options: accelerated degree program, adult/continuing education programs, advanced placement credit, cooperative education, double majors, English as a second language, freshman honors college, honors programs, independent study, internships, part-time degree program, student-designed majors, study abroad, summer session for credit. ***ROTC:*** Army (b).

Unusual degree programs: 3-2 engineering with Columbia University, University of Southern California, University of Notre Dame, Montana State University, Gonzaga University, Montana College of Mineral Science and Technology, University of Minnesota.

Computers: Students can access the following: campus intranet, computer help desk, free student e-mail accounts, online (class) grades, online (class) registration, online (class) schedules, online book order. Campuswide network is available. 100% of college-owned or -operated housing units are wired for high-speed Internet access. Wireless service is available via entire campus.

STUDENT LIFE

Housing options: on-campus residence required through sophomore year; coed. Campus housing is university owned. Freshman campus housing is guaranteed.

Activities and organizations: drama/theater group, student-run newspaper, radio station, choral group, student government, Carroll Outreach Team, Carroll Adventure and Mountaineering Program, Up 'Til Dawn, Engineers Without Borders.

Athletics Member NAIA. ***Intercollegiate sports:*** basketball M(s)/W(s), cheerleading M(s)/W(s), cross-country running M(s)/W(s), football M(s), golf M(s)/W(s), soccer M(s)/W(s), softball W(s), track and field M(s)/W(s), volleyball W(s).

Campus security: 24-hour emergency response devices, late-night transport/escort service, controlled dormitory access.

Student services: health clinic, personal/psychological counseling.

COSTS & FINANCIAL AID

Costs (2014–15) ***Comprehensive fee:*** $38,230 includes full-time tuition ($28,670), mandatory fees ($610), and room and board ($8950). Full-time tuition and fees vary according to course load. Part-time tuition: $1194 per credit hour. Part-time tuition and fees vary according to course load. ***College room only:*** $4552. Room and board charges vary according to board plan and housing facility. ***Payment plan:*** installment. ***Waivers:*** senior citizens and employees or children of employees.

Financial Aid Of all full-time matriculated undergraduates who enrolled in 2013, 1,009 applied for aid, 858 were judged to have need, 145 had their need fully met. 235 Federal Work-Study jobs (averaging $2180). In 2013, 451 non-need-based awards were made. ***Average percent of need met:*** 71. ***Average financial aid package:*** $20,324. ***Average need-based loan:*** $4298. ***Average need-based gift aid:*** $15,278. ***Average non-need-based aid:*** $11,323. ***Average indebtedness upon graduation:*** $26,996.

APPLYING

Standardized Tests *Required:* SAT or ACT (for admission). *Required for some:* SAT Subject Tests (for admission).

Options: electronic application, deferred entrance.

Application fee: $35.

Required: essay or personal statement, high school transcript. ***Required for some:*** interview. ***Recommended:*** interview.

Application deadlines: 2/15 (freshmen), 2/15 (out-of-state freshmen), 6/15 (transfers).

Notification: continuous (freshmen), continuous (out-of-state freshmen), continuous (transfers).

CONTACT

Director of Admission, Carroll College, 1601 North Benton Avenue, Helena, MT 59625-0002. *Phone:* 406-447-4384. *Toll-free phone:* 800-992-3648. *E-mail:* admission@carroll.edu.

Montana Bible College

Bozeman, Montana

http://www.montanabiblecollege.edu/

- **Independent religious** 4-year
- **Urban** campus
- **Coed**

ACADEMICS

Degree: certificates and bachelor's.

APPLYING
Standardized Tests *Required:* SAT or ACT (for admission).

CONTACT
Montana Bible College, 3625 South 19th Avenue, Bozeman, MT 59718. *Toll-free phone:* 888-462-2463.

Montana State University

Bozeman, Montana

http://www.montana.edu/

- **State-supported** university, founded 1893, part of Montana University System
- **Small-town** 1850-acre campus
- **Endowment** $126.5 million
- **Coed** 13,371 undergraduate students, 84% full-time, 46% women, 54% men
- **Moderately difficult** entrance level, 84% of applicants were admitted

UNDERGRAD STUDENTS
11,236 full-time, 2,135 part-time. Students come from 50 states and territories; 72 other countries; 37% are from out of state; 0.7% Black or African American, non-Hispanic/Latino; 3% Hispanic/Latino; 0.9% Asian, non-Hispanic/Latino; 0.1% Native Hawaiian or other Pacific Islander, non-Hispanic/Latino; 1% American Indian or Alaska Native, non-Hispanic/Latino; 3% Two or more races, non-Hispanic/Latino; 3% Race/ethnicity unknown; 3% international; 6% transferred in; 25% live on campus.

Freshmen
Admission: 13,799 applied, 11,570 admitted, 2,943 enrolled. ***Average high school GPA:*** 3.33. ***Test scores:*** SAT critical reading scores over 500: 78%; SAT math scores over 500: 78%; SAT writing scores over 500: 68%; ACT scores over 18: 94%; SAT critical reading scores over 600: 39%; SAT math scores over 600: 40%; SAT writing scores over 600: 29%; ACT scores over 24: 58%; SAT critical reading scores over 700: 7%; SAT math scores over 700: 7%; SAT writing scores over 700: 4%; ACT scores over 30: 13%.
Retention: 76% of full-time freshmen returned.

FACULTY
Total: 960, 59% full-time, 55% with terminal degrees.

Student/faculty ratio: 19:1.

ACADEMICS
Calendar: semesters. *Degrees:* certificates, associate, bachelor's, master's, doctoral, post-master's, and postbachelor's certificates.

Special study options: academic remediation for entering students, adult/continuing education programs, advanced placement credit, distance learning, double majors, English as a second language, freshman honors college, honors programs, independent study, internships, off-campus study, part-time degree program, services for LD students, student-designed majors, study abroad, summer session for credit. ***ROTC:*** Army (b), Air Force (b).

Computers: 1,000 computers/terminals are available on campus for general student use. Students can access the following: computer help desk, free student e-mail accounts, online (class) grades, online (class) registration, online (class) schedules. Campuswide network is available. 100% of college-owned or -operated housing units are wired for high-speed Internet access. Wireless service is available via entire campus.

STUDENT LIFE
Housing options: on-campus residence required for freshman year; coed, men-only, women-only, special housing for students with disabilities. Campus housing is university owned. Freshman campus housing is guaranteed.

Activities and organizations: drama/theater group, student-run newspaper, radio and television station, choral group, marching band, Spurs, Inter-Varsity Christian Fellowship, Campus Crusade for Christ, Fangs, Mortar Board, national fraternities, national sororities.

Athletics Member NCAA. All Division I except football (Division I-AA). ***Intercollegiate sports:*** basketball M(s)/W(s), cheerleading M(s)/W(s), cross-country running M(s)/W(s), golf W(s), skiing (cross-country) M(s)/W(s), skiing (downhill) M(s)/W(s), tennis M(s)/W(s), track and field M(s)/W(s), volleyball W(s). ***Intramural sports:*** archery W, badminton M/W, baseball M, basketball M/W, bowling M/W, cross-country running M/W, fencing M/W, football M, golf M/W, gymnastics M/W, racquetball M/W, rugby M/W, skiing (cross-country) M/W, skiing (downhill) M/W, soccer M/W, softball M/W, swimming and diving M/W, table tennis M/W, tennis M/W, track and field M/W, ultimate Frisbee M/W, volleyball M/W, water polo M/W, weight lifting M/W, wrestling M.

Campus security: 24-hour emergency response devices and patrols, student patrols, late-night transport/escort service, 24-hour residence hall monitoring.

Student services: health clinic, personal/psychological counseling, women's center, legal services.

COSTS & FINANCIAL AID
Costs (2015–16) ***Tuition:*** state resident $5330 full-time, $222 per credit hour part-time; nonresident $19,732 full-time, $822 per credit hour part-time. Full-time tuition and fees vary according to course load, degree level, location, and program. Part-time tuition and fees vary according to course load, degree level, location, and program. ***Room and board:*** Room and board charges vary according to board plan and housing facility. ***Payment plans:*** installment, deferred payment. ***Waivers:*** minority students, senior citizens, and employees or children of employees.

Financial Aid Of all full-time matriculated undergraduates who enrolled in 2013, 7,302 applied for aid, 5,811 were judged to have need, 275 had their need fully met. In 2013, 284 non-need-based awards were made. ***Average percent of need met:*** 74. ***Average financial aid package:*** $12,022. ***Average need-based loan:*** $4200. ***Average need-based gift aid:*** $5226. ***Average non-need-based aid:*** $1641. ***Average indebtedness upon graduation:*** $27,200.

APPLYING
Standardized Tests *Required:* SAT or ACT (for admission).

Options: electronic application, early admission, deferred entrance.

Application fee: $30.

Required: high school transcript, minimum 2.5 GPA.

Application deadlines: rolling (freshmen), rolling (out-of-state freshmen), rolling (transfers).

Notification: continuous (freshmen), continuous (out-of-state freshmen), continuous (transfers).

CONTACT
Ms. Ronda Russell, Director of Admissions, Montana State University, PO Box 172190, Bozeman, MT 59717-2190. *Phone:* 406-994-2452. *Toll-free phone:* 888-MSU-CATS. *Fax:* 406-994-1923. *E-mail:* admissions@montana.edu.

Montana State University Billings

Billings, Montana

http://www.msubillings.edu/

- **State-supported** comprehensive, founded 1927, part of Montana University System
- **Urban** 92-acre campus
- **Endowment** $2.2 million
- **Coed** 4,353 undergraduate students, 70% full-time, 62% women, 38% men
- **Minimally difficult** entrance level, 100% of applicants were admitted

UNDERGRAD STUDENTS
3,044 full-time, 1,309 part-time. Students come from 42 states and territories; 20 other countries; 11% are from out of state; 1% Black or African American, non-Hispanic/Latino; 5% Hispanic/Latino; 1% Asian, non-Hispanic/Latino; 0.3% Native Hawaiian or other Pacific Islander, non-Hispanic/Latino; 4% American Indian or Alaska Native, non-Hispanic/Latino; 2% Two or more races, non-Hispanic/Latino; 1% Race/ethnicity unknown; 3% international; 9% transferred in; 12% live on campus.

Freshmen
Admission: 1,602 applied, 1,597 admitted, 782 enrolled. ***Average high school GPA:*** 3.03. ***Test scores:*** SAT math scores over 500: 35%; ACT scores over 18: 78%; SAT math scores over 600: 11%; ACT scores over 24: 24%; SAT math scores over 700: 2%; ACT scores over 30: 2%.
Retention: 57% of full-time freshmen returned.

FACULTY
Total: 342, 48% full-time.
Student/faculty ratio: 17:1.

ACADEMICS
Calendar: semesters. *Degrees:* certificates, associate, bachelor's, and master's.
Special study options: academic remediation for entering students, accelerated degree program, adult/continuing education programs, advanced placement credit, cooperative education, distance learning, double majors, English as a second language, external degree program, honors programs, independent study, internships, off-campus study, part-time degree program, services for LD students, study abroad, summer session for credit. ***ROTC:*** Army (b).
Computers: 1,500 computers/terminals and 1,500 ports are available on campus for general student use. Students can access the following: campus intranet, computer help desk, free student e-mail accounts, online (class) grades, online (class) registration, online (class) schedules, online degree programs. Campuswide network is available. 95% of college-owned or -operated housing units are wired for high-speed Internet access. Wireless service is available via classrooms, computer labs, dorm rooms, libraries, student centers.

STUDENT LIFE
Housing options: on-campus residence required for freshman year; coed, men-only, women-only, special housing for students with disabilities. Campus housing is university owned. Freshman applicants given priority for college housing.
Activities and organizations: drama/theater group, student-run newspaper, radio station, choral group, Art Student League, Band Club, Inter-Varsity Christian Fellowship, Residence Hall Association, Student Council for Exceptional Children.
Athletics Member NCAA. All Division II. ***Intercollegiate sports:*** baseball M, basketball M(s)/W(s), cross-country running M(s)/W(s), golf M/W, soccer M(s)/W(s), softball W, volleyball W(s). ***Intramural sports:*** baseball M/W, basketball M/W, bowling M/W, cheerleading M/W, cross-country running M/W, football M/W, golf M/W, racquetball M/W, skiing (cross-country) M/W, soccer M/W, softball M/W, swimming and diving M/W, table tennis M/W, track and field M/W, volleyball M/W.
Campus security: 24-hour emergency response devices and patrols, late-night transport/escort service, controlled dormitory access.
Student services: health clinic, personal/psychological counseling, women's center, legal services.

COSTS & FINANCIAL AID
Costs (2015–16) ***Tuition:*** state resident $4397 full-time, $183 per credit hour part-time; nonresident $15,959 full-time, $665 per credit hour part-time. Full-time tuition and fees vary according to course load, degree level, and location. Part-time tuition and fees vary according to course load, degree level, and location. ***Required fees:*** $1383 full-time. ***Room and board:*** $6980. Room and board charges vary according to board plan and housing facility. ***Payment plan:*** installment. ***Waivers:*** senior citizens and employees or children of employees.
Financial Aid Of all full-time matriculated undergraduates who enrolled in 2012, 2,528 applied for aid, 2,106 were judged to have need, 66 had their need fully met. 184 Federal Work-Study jobs (averaging $1254). 101 state and other part-time jobs (averaging $1561). In 2012, 101 non-need-based awards were made. ***Average percent of need met:*** 69. ***Average financial aid package:*** $10,148. ***Average need-based loan:*** $3581. ***Average need-based gift aid:*** $5270. ***Average non-need-based aid:*** $2243. ***Average indebtedness upon graduation:*** $29,684.

APPLYING
Options: electronic application, early admission, deferred entrance.
Application fee: $30.
Required: high school transcript.
Application deadlines: rolling (freshmen), rolling (transfers).
Notification: continuous (freshmen), continuous (transfers).

CONTACT
Ms. Tammi Watson, Associate Director of Admissions, Montana State University Billings, 1500 University Drive, Billings, MT 59101. *Phone:* 406-657-2158. *Toll-free phone:* 800-565-6782. *Fax:* 406-657-2302. *E-mail:* tammi.watson@msubillings.edu.

Montana Tech of The University of Montana

Butte, Montana

http://www.mtech.edu/

- **State-supported** comprehensive, founded 1895, part of Montana University System
- **Small-town** 56-acre campus
- **Endowment** $33.3 million
- **Coed** 2,751 undergraduate students, 81% full-time, 40% women, 60% men
- **Moderately difficult** entrance level, 90% of applicants were admitted

UNDERGRAD STUDENTS
2,219 full-time, 532 part-time. Students come from 39 states and territories; 20 other countries; 15% are from out of state; 0.7% Black or African American, non-Hispanic/Latino; 2% Hispanic/Latino; 0.9% Asian, non-Hispanic/Latino; 2% American Indian or Alaska Native, non-Hispanic/Latino; 6% Race/ethnicity unknown; 8% international; 8% transferred in; 12% live on campus.

Freshmen
Admission: 952 applied, 861 admitted, 436 enrolled. ***Average high school GPA:*** 3.49. ***Test scores:*** SAT critical reading scores over 500: 71%; SAT math scores over 500: 86%; SAT writing scores over 500: 53%; ACT scores over 18: 100%; SAT critical reading scores over 600: 23%; SAT math scores over 600: 44%; SAT writing scores over 600: 9%; ACT scores over 24: 63%; SAT critical reading scores over 700: 3%; SAT math scores over 700: 3%; ACT scores over 30: 7%.
Retention: 71% of full-time freshmen returned.

FACULTY
Total: 228, 65% full-time, 41% with terminal degrees.
Student/faculty ratio: 15:1.

ACADEMICS
Calendar: semesters. *Degrees:* certificates, diplomas, associate, bachelor's, master's, doctoral, and postbachelor's certificates.
Special study options: academic remediation for entering students, adult/continuing education programs, advanced placement credit, cooperative education, distance learning, double majors, external degree program, honors programs, independent study, internships, part-time degree program, services for LD students, student-designed majors, summer session for credit.
Unusual degree programs: engineering.
Computers: 660 computers/terminals are available on campus for general student use. Students can access the following: campus intranet, computer help desk, free student e-mail accounts, online (class) grades, online (class) registration, online (class) schedules. Campuswide network is available. 100% of college-owned or -operated housing units are wired for high-speed Internet access. Wireless service is available via entire campus.

STUDENT LIFE
Housing options: on-campus residence required for freshman year; coed, special housing for students with disabilities. Campus housing is university owned. Freshman campus housing is guaranteed.
Activities and organizations: student-run newspaper, radio station, choral group, Circle K, Ski/Snowboard Club, BSU, Hockey Club, Dance Club.
Athletics Member NAIA. ***Intercollegiate sports:*** basketball M(s)/W(s), football M(s), golf M(s)/W(s), volleyball W(s). ***Intramural sports:*** basketball M/W, cheerleading M(c)/W(c), football M/W, ice hockey M(c)/W(c), racquetball M/W, rugby M(c)/W(c), skiing (cross-country) M(c)/W(c), skiing (downhill) M(c)/W(c), softball M/W, volleyball M/W.
Campus security: 24-hour patrols, controlled dormitory access.
Student services: health clinic, personal/psychological counseling.

COSTS & FINANCIAL AID
Costs (2014–15) ***Tuition:*** state resident $5177 full-time, $216 per credit part-time; nonresident $18,493 full-time, $767 per credit part-time. Full-time tuition and fees vary according to course load, degree level, location, program, and student level. Part-time tuition and fees vary according to course load, degree level, location, program, and student level. ***Required***

fees: $1575 full-time, $66 per credit part-time. ***Room and board:*** $8238; room only: $3658. Room and board charges vary according to board plan. ***Payment plan:*** installment. ***Waivers:*** minority students, senior citizens, and employees or children of employees.

Financial Aid Of all full-time matriculated undergraduates who enrolled in 2013, 1,623 applied for aid, 1,311 were judged to have need, 162 had their need fully met. In 2013, 265 non-need-based awards were made. ***Average percent of need met:*** 63. ***Average financial aid package:*** $11,296. ***Average need-based loan:*** $3847. ***Average need-based gift aid:*** $5485. ***Average non-need-based aid:*** $3817. ***Average indebtedness upon graduation:*** $24,448.

APPLYING

Standardized Tests *Required:* SAT or ACT (for admission).

Options: electronic application, deferred entrance.

Application fee: $30.

Required: high school transcript, proof of immunization. ***Required for some:*** minimum 2.5 GPA.

Application deadlines: rolling (freshmen), rolling (out-of-state freshmen), rolling (transfers).

Notification: continuous (freshmen), continuous (out-of-state freshmen), continuous (transfers).

CONTACT

Stephanie Crowe, Montana Tech of The University of Montana, 1300 West Park Street, Butte, MT 59701-8997. *Phone:* 406-496-4568. *Toll-free phone:* 800-445-TECH. *Fax:* 406-496-4705. *E-mail:* scrowe@mtech.edu.

Rocky Mountain College

Billings, Montana

http://www.rocky.edu/

- **Independent interdenominational** comprehensive, founded 1878
- **Suburban** 60-acre campus
- **Endowment** $26.3 million
- **Coed** 939 undergraduate students, 94% full-time, 48% women, 52% men
- **Moderately difficult** entrance level, 65% of applicants were admitted

UNDERGRAD STUDENTS

884 full-time, 55 part-time. Students come from 42 states and territories; 18 other countries; 45% are from out of state; 3% Black or African American, non-Hispanic/Latino; 5% Hispanic/Latino; 1% Asian, non-Hispanic/Latino; 0.6% Native Hawaiian or other Pacific Islander, non-Hispanic/Latino; 2% American Indian or Alaska Native, non-Hispanic/Latino; 5% Two or more races, non-Hispanic/Latino; 2% Race/ethnicity unknown; 4% international; 6% transferred in; 47% live on campus.

Freshmen

Admission: 1,466 applied, 960 admitted, 229 enrolled. ***Average high school GPA:*** 3.44. ***Test scores:*** SAT critical reading scores over 500: 46%; SAT math scores over 500: 52%; SAT writing scores over 500: 36%; ACT scores over 18: 169%; SAT critical reading scores over 600: 14%; SAT math scores over 600: 14%; SAT writing scores over 600: 11%; ACT scores over 24: 84%; SAT critical reading scores over 700: 1%; SAT math scores over 700: 1%; SAT writing scores over 700: 1%; ACT scores over 30: 16%.

Retention: 71% of full-time freshmen returned.

FACULTY

Total: 124, 57% full-time, 47% with terminal degrees.

Student/faculty ratio: 12:1.

ACADEMICS

Calendar: semesters. *Degrees:* associate, bachelor's, and master's.

Special study options: academic remediation for entering students, accelerated degree program, adult/continuing education programs, advanced placement credit, distance learning, double majors, English as a second language, honors programs, independent study, internships, off-campus study, part-time degree program, services for LD students, student-designed majors, study abroad, summer session for credit. ***ROTC:*** Army (c).

Unusual degree programs: 3-2 athletic training with Montana State University Billings.

Computers: 129 computers/terminals are available on campus for general student use. Students can access the following: campus intranet, computer help desk, free student e-mail accounts, online (class) grades, online (class) registration, online (class) schedules. Campuswide network is available. 100% of college-owned or -operated housing units are wired for high-speed Internet access. Wireless service is available via entire campus.

STUDENT LIFE

Housing options: on-campus residence required through sophomore year; coed, special housing for students with disabilities. Campus housing is university owned. Freshman campus housing is guaranteed.

Activities and organizations: drama/theater group, student-run newspaper, choral group, Outdoor Recreation, Enactus, Flight Team/Club, Residence Hall Association, Environmental Club.

Athletics Member NAIA. ***Intercollegiate sports:*** basketball M(s)/W(s), cheerleading M(s)/W(s), cross-country running M(s)/W(s), equestrian sports M(c)/W(c), football M(s), golf M(s)/W(s), skiing (downhill) M(s)/W(s), soccer M(s)/W(s), track and field M(s)/W(s), volleyball W(s). ***Intramural sports:*** basketball M/W, football M, golf M/W, ice hockey M(c)/W(c), racquetball M/W, skiing (downhill) M/W, soccer M/W, softball M/W, swimming and diving M/W, tennis M/W, ultimate Frisbee M/W, volleyball M/W.

Campus security: 24-hour emergency response devices, student patrols, late-night transport/escort service, controlled dormitory access, security cameras.

Student services: health clinic, personal/psychological counseling.

COSTS & FINANCIAL AID

Costs (2015–16) ***Comprehensive fee:*** $33,196 includes full-time tuition ($24,762), mandatory fees ($490), and room and board ($7944). Full-time tuition and fees vary according to course load, degree level, and program. Part-time tuition: $1052 per credit. Part-time tuition and fees vary according to course load, degree level, and program. ***College room only:*** $3692. Room and board charges vary according to board plan and housing facility. ***Payment plan:*** installment. ***Waivers:*** employees or children of employees.

Financial Aid Of all full-time matriculated undergraduates who enrolled in 2014, 728 applied for aid, 648 were judged to have need, 182 had their need fully met. 345 Federal Work-Study jobs (averaging $416). 168 state and other part-time jobs (averaging $819). In 2014, 73 non-need-based awards were made. ***Average percent of need met:*** 74. ***Average financial aid package:*** $22,121. ***Average need-based loan:*** $4236. ***Average need-based gift aid:*** $16,829. ***Average non-need-based aid:*** $10,651. ***Average indebtedness upon graduation:*** $29,206.

APPLYING

Standardized Tests *Required:* SAT or ACT (for admission).

Options: electronic application, early admission, deferred entrance.

Application fee: $35.

Required: high school transcript, minimum 2.5 GPA. ***Required for some:*** essay or personal statement, 2 letters of recommendation, interview.

Application deadlines: rolling (freshmen), rolling (transfers).

Notification: continuous (freshmen), continuous (transfers).

CONTACT

Austin Mapston, Director of Admissions, Rocky Mountain College, 1511 Poly Drive, Director of Admissions, Billings, MT 59102. *Phone:* 406-657-1026. *Toll-free phone:* 800-877-6259. *Fax:* 406-259-9751. *E-mail:* admissions@rocky.edu.

University of Great Falls

Great Falls, Montana

http://www.ugf.edu/

- **Independent Roman Catholic** comprehensive, founded 1932
- **Urban** 40-acre campus
- **Coed** 1,043 undergraduate students, 60% full-time, 70% women, 30% men
- **Noncompetitive** entrance level

UNDERGRAD STUDENTS

627 full-time, 416 part-time. 62% are from out of state; 2% Black or African American, non-Hispanic/Latino; 7% Hispanic/Latino; 3% Asian,

non-Hispanic/Latino; 0.6% Native Hawaiian or other Pacific Islander, non-Hispanic/Latino; 2% American Indian or Alaska Native, non-Hispanic/Latino; 1% Two or more races, non-Hispanic/Latino; 6% Race/ethnicity unknown; 13% transferred in; 38% live on campus.

Freshmen

Admission: 152 enrolled. ***Average high school GPA:*** 3.32. ***Test scores:*** SAT critical reading scores over 500: 43%; SAT math scores over 500: 37%; SAT writing scores over 500: 32%; ACT scores over 18: 77%; SAT critical reading scores over 600: 5%; SAT math scores over 600: 9%; SAT writing scores over 600: 8%; ACT scores over 24: 20%; ACT scores over 30: 2%.

Retention: 54% of full-time freshmen returned.

FACULTY

Total: 116, 38% full-time, 41% with terminal degrees.

Student/faculty ratio: 14:1.

ACADEMICS

Calendar: semesters. *Degrees:* certificates, associate, bachelor's, and master's.

Special study options: adult/continuing education programs, part-time degree program.

Computers: Students can access the following: campus intranet, computer help desk, free student e-mail accounts, online (class) grades, online (class) registration, online (class) schedules. Campuswide network is available. Wireless service is available via classrooms, computer centers, computer labs, dorm rooms, learning centers, libraries, student centers.

STUDENT LIFE

Housing options: on-campus residence required through sophomore year; coed. Campus housing is university owned and leased by the school. Freshman campus housing is guaranteed.

Athletics Member NAIA. ***Intercollegiate sports:*** basketball M(s)/W(s), cheerleading M(s)/W(s), cross-country running M/W, equestrian sports M(s)/W(s), golf M(s)/W(s), soccer M(s)/W(s), softball W, track and field M(s)/W(s), volleyball W(s), wrestling M(s). ***Intramural sports:*** basketball M/W, equestrian sports M/W(c), football M/W, golf M/W, skiing (downhill) M/W, soccer M/W, softball W, table tennis M/W, track and field M/W, ultimate Frisbee M/W, volleyball M/W, wrestling M.

Campus security: 24-hour emergency response devices and patrols, late-night transport/escort service, controlled dormitory access.

COSTS & FINANCIAL AID

Costs (2015–16) ***Comprehensive fee:*** $28,356 includes full-time tuition ($20,456), mandatory fees ($1100), and room and board ($6800). Full-time tuition and fees vary according to course load. Part-time tuition: $647 per credit hour. Part-time tuition and fees vary according to course load, location, and program. ***College room only:*** $3900. Room and board charges vary according to housing facility. ***Payment plan:*** installment. ***Waivers:*** employees or children of employees.

Financial Aid Of all full-time matriculated undergraduates who enrolled in 2014, 531 applied for aid, 476 were judged to have need, 11 had their need fully met. In 2014, 89 non-need-based awards were made. ***Average percent of need met:*** 69. ***Average financial aid package:*** $18,476. ***Average need-based loan:*** $4400. ***Average need-based gift aid:*** $10,773. ***Average non-need-based aid:*** $7114. ***Average indebtedness upon graduation:*** $23,340.

APPLYING

Standardized Tests *Required:* SAT or ACT (for admission). *Recommended:* SAT and SAT Subject Tests or ACT (for admission), SAT Subject Tests (for admission).

Options: electronic application, early admission, deferred entrance.

Application fee: $35.

Required: high school transcript. ***Recommended:*** essay or personal statement, interview.

Notification: continuous (freshmen), continuous (transfers).

CONTACT

Kelly Braun, Assistant Director of Admissions, University of Great Falls, 1301 20th Street South, Great Falls, MT 59405. *Phone:* 406-791-5202 Ext. 5211. *Toll-free phone:* 800-856-9544. *Fax:* 406-791-5209. *E-mail:* enroll@ugf.edu.

The University of Montana

Missoula, Montana

http://www.umt.edu/

- **State-supported** university, founded 1893, part of Montana University System
- **Urban** 220-acre campus
- **Coed** 11,692 undergraduate students, 79% full-time, 53% women, 47% men
- **Moderately difficult** entrance level, 93% of applicants were admitted

UNDERGRAD STUDENTS

9,281 full-time, 2,411 part-time. Students come from 50 states and territories; 68 other countries; 27% are from out of state; 0.7% Black or African American, non-Hispanic/Latino; 4% Hispanic/Latino; 1% Asian, non-Hispanic/Latino; 0.2% Native Hawaiian or other Pacific Islander, non-Hispanic/Latino; 3% American Indian or Alaska Native, non-Hispanic/Latino; 4% Two or more races, non-Hispanic/Latino; 7% Race/ethnicity unknown; 2% international; 10% transferred in; 25% live on campus.

Freshmen

Admission: 5,345 applied, 4,956 admitted, 2,027 enrolled. ***Average high school GPA:*** 3.31. ***Test scores:*** SAT critical reading scores over 500: 74%; SAT math scores over 500: 74%; SAT writing scores over 500: 65%; ACT scores over 18: 92%; SAT critical reading scores over 600: 30%; SAT math scores over 600: 24%; SAT writing scores over 600: 20%; ACT scores over 24: 47%; SAT critical reading scores over 700: 5%; SAT math scores over 700: 3%; SAT writing scores over 700: 2%; ACT scores over 30: 7%.

Retention: 73% of full-time freshmen returned.

FACULTY

Total: 853, 66% full-time, 68% with terminal degrees.

Student/faculty ratio: 18:1.

ACADEMICS

Calendar: semesters. *Degrees:* certificates, associate, bachelor's, master's, doctoral, post-master's, and postbachelor's certificates.

Special study options: academic remediation for entering students, advanced placement credit, cooperative education, distance learning, double majors, English as a second language, external degree program, freshman honors college, honors programs, independent study, internships, off-campus study, part-time degree program, services for LD students, study abroad, summer session for credit. ***ROTC:*** Army (b).

Computers: Students can access the following: computer help desk, free student e-mail accounts, online (class) registration, online (class) schedules. Campuswide network is available. 100% of college-owned or -operated housing units are wired for high-speed Internet access. Wireless service is available via entire campus.

STUDENT LIFE

Housing options: on-campus residence required for freshman year; coed, men-only, women-only, special housing for students with disabilities. Campus housing is university owned. Freshman campus housing is guaranteed.

Activities and organizations: drama/theater group, student-run newspaper, radio station, choral group, marching band, national fraternities, national sororities.

Athletics Member NCAA. All Division I except football (Division I-AA). ***Intercollegiate sports:*** baseball M(c), basketball M(s)/W(s), crew M(c)/W(c), cross-country running M(s)/W(s), equestrian sports M(c)/W(c), fencing M(c)/W(c), field hockey W(c), golf W(s), gymnastics W(c), ice hockey M(c)/W(c), lacrosse M(c)/W(c), rugby M(c)/W(c), skiing (downhill) M(c)/W(c), soccer W(s), softball W(s), tennis M(s)/W(s), track and field M(s)/W(s), ultimate Frisbee M(c)/W(c), volleyball W(s). ***Intramural sports:*** archery M/W, badminton M/W, baseball M, basketball M/W, bowling M/W, cross-country running M/W, football M/W, ice hockey M, racquetball M/W, rugby M/W, skiing (cross-country) M/W, soccer W, softball M/W, swimming and diving M/W, table tennis M/W, tennis M/W, track and field M/W, volleyball M/W, water polo M/W, weight lifting M/W.

Campus security: 24-hour emergency response devices and patrols, student patrols, late-night transport/escort service, controlled dormitory access.

Student services: health clinic, personal/psychological counseling, women's center, legal services.

COSTS & FINANCIAL AID

Costs (2014–15) ***Tuition:*** state resident $4604 full-time, $192 per credit hour part-time; nonresident $21,420 full-time, $889 per credit hour part-time. Full-time tuition and fees vary according to degree level, location, program, reciprocity agreements, and student level. Part-time tuition and fees vary according to course load, degree level, location, and student level. ***Required fees:*** $1726 full-time. ***Room and board:*** $8006; room only: $3494. Room and board charges vary according to board plan and housing facility. ***Payment plan:*** installment. ***Waivers:*** minority students, senior citizens, and employees or children of employees.

Financial Aid Of all full-time matriculated undergraduates who enrolled in 2014, 6,740 applied for aid, 5,578 were judged to have need, 420 had their need fully met. 1,637 Federal Work-Study jobs (averaging $2922). 110 state and other part-time jobs (averaging $2941). In 2014, 593 non-need-based awards were made. ***Average percent of need met:*** 65. ***Average financial aid package:*** $10,458. ***Average need-based loan:*** $5113. ***Average need-based gift aid:*** $4914. ***Average non-need-based aid:*** $3659. ***Average indebtedness upon graduation:*** $39,002.

APPLYING

Standardized Tests *Required:* SAT or ACT (for admission).

Options: electronic application, early admission, deferred entrance.

Application fee: $36.

Required: high school transcript, minimum 2.5 GPA.

Application deadlines: rolling (freshmen), rolling (out-of-state freshmen), rolling (transfers).

CONTACT

The University of Montana, Missoula, MT 59812-0002. *Phone:* 406-243-6266. *Toll-free phone:* 800-462-8636. *Fax:* 406-243-5711. *E-mail:* admiss@umontana.edu.

The University of Montana Western

Dillon, Montana

http://www.umwestern.edu/

- **State-supported** 4-year, founded 1893, part of Montana University System
- **Small-town** 30-acre campus
- **Endowment** $4.2 million
- **Coed** 1,470 undergraduate students, 79% full-time, 59% women, 41% men
- **Minimally difficult** entrance level, 71% of applicants were admitted

UNDERGRAD STUDENTS

1,163 full-time, 307 part-time. Students come from 36 states and territories; 1 other country; 23% are from out of state; 0.9% Black or African American, non-Hispanic/Latino; 2% Hispanic/Latino; 0.9% Asian, non-Hispanic/Latino; 0.3% Native Hawaiian or other Pacific Islander, non-Hispanic/Latino; 2% American Indian or Alaska Native, non-Hispanic/Latino; 1% Two or more races, non-Hispanic/Latino; 10% Race/ethnicity unknown; 8% transferred in; 24% live on campus.

Freshmen

Admission: 569 applied, 405 admitted, 293 enrolled. ***Average high school GPA:*** 3.08. ***Test scores:*** SAT critical reading scores over 500: 30%; SAT math scores over 500: 19%; ACT scores over 18: 69%; SAT critical reading scores over 600: 11%; SAT math scores over 600: 5%; ACT scores over 24: 16%.

Retention: 67% of full-time freshmen returned.

FACULTY

Total: 94, 69% full-time, 61% with terminal degrees.

Student/faculty ratio: 17:1.

ACADEMICS

Calendar: semesters. *Degrees:* certificates, associate, bachelor's, and postbachelor's certificates.

Special study options: academic remediation for entering students, advanced placement credit, cooperative education, distance learning, double majors, honors programs, independent study, internships, off-campus study, part-time degree program, services for LD students, study abroad, summer session for credit.

Computers: 201 computers/terminals and 201 ports are available on campus for general student use. Students can access the following: campus intranet, computer help desk, free student e-mail accounts, online (class) grades, online (class) registration, online (class) schedules. Campuswide network is available. 100% of college-owned or -operated housing units are wired for high-speed Internet access. Wireless service is available via entire campus.

STUDENT LIFE

Housing options: on-campus residence required for freshman year; coed, men-only, women-only, special housing for students with disabilities. Campus housing is university owned. Freshman campus housing is guaranteed.

Activities and organizations: drama/theater group, student-run radio station, choral group, Biology Club, Drama Club, Humans in Performance, Environmental Science Club, Music Club.

Athletics Member NAIA. ***Intercollegiate sports:*** basketball M(s)/W(s), football M(s), rugby M(c)/W(c), volleyball W(s), wrestling M(c). ***Intramural sports:*** basketball M/W, cheerleading M(c)/W(c), equestrian sports M(c)/W(c), football M/W, racquetball M/W, rock climbing M(c)/W(c), skiing (downhill) M(c)/W(c), softball M/W, ultimate Frisbee M/W, volleyball M/W.

Campus security: 24-hour emergency response devices and patrols, student patrols, late-night transport/escort service.

Student services: health clinic, personal/psychological counseling.

COSTS & FINANCIAL AID

Costs (2014–15) ***Tuition:*** state resident $3699 full-time, $153 per hour part-time; nonresident $14,356 full-time, $597 per hour part-time. Full-time tuition and fees vary according to course load, location, program, reciprocity agreements, and student level. Part-time tuition and fees vary according to course load, location, program, reciprocity agreements, and student level. ***Required fees:*** $1098 full-time, $141 per credit part-time. ***Room and board:*** $6536; room only: $2404. Room and board charges vary according to housing facility. ***Payment plans:*** installment, deferred payment. ***Waivers:*** minority students, senior citizens, and employees or children of employees.

Financial Aid Of all full-time matriculated undergraduates who enrolled in 2013, 966 applied for aid, 787 were judged to have need, 1 had their need fully met. 145 Federal Work-Study jobs (averaging $2106). 131 state and other part-time jobs (averaging $2442). In 2013, 2 non-need-based awards were made. ***Average percent of need met:*** 18. ***Average financial aid package:*** $3380. ***Average need-based loan:*** $4033. ***Average need-based gift aid:*** $3502. ***Average non-need-based aid:*** $2540. ***Average indebtedness upon graduation:*** $22,304.

APPLYING

Standardized Tests *Required:* SAT or ACT (for admission).

Options: electronic application, early admission, deferred entrance.

Application fee: $30.

Required: high school transcript, MMR (2), ACT plus writing or SAT, high school self report form.

Application deadlines: rolling (freshmen), rolling (out-of-state freshmen), rolling (transfers).

Notification: continuous (freshmen), continuous (out-of-state freshmen), continuous (transfers).

CONTACT

Mrs. Janet Jones, Admissions Evaluator, The University of Montana Western, 710 South Atlantic, Dillon, MT 59725. *Phone:* 406-683-7331. *Toll-free phone:* 877-683-7331. *E-mail:* janet.jones@umwestern.edu.

NEBRASKA

College of Saint Mary

Omaha, Nebraska

http://www.csm.edu/

- **Independent Roman Catholic** comprehensive, founded 1923
- **Urban** 25-acre campus
- **Endowment** $10.7 million
- **Women only** 770 undergraduate students, 88% full-time
- **Minimally difficult** entrance level, 53% of applicants were admitted

UNDERGRAD STUDENTS
679 full-time, 91 part-time. Students come from 21 states and territories; 9 other countries; 20% are from out of state; 6% Black or African American, non-Hispanic/Latino; 11% Hispanic/Latino; 2% Asian, non-Hispanic/Latino; 0.6% American Indian or Alaska Native, non-Hispanic/Latino; 2% Two or more races, non-Hispanic/Latino; 0.6% Race/ethnicity unknown; 1% international; 19% transferred in; 34% live on campus.

Freshmen
Admission: 333 applied, 176 admitted, 71 enrolled. ***Average high school GPA:*** 3.5. ***Test scores:*** ACT scores over 18: 96%; ACT scores over 24: 39%; ACT scores over 30: 1%.
Retention: 79% of full-time freshmen returned.

FACULTY
Total: 167, 34% full-time, 45% with terminal degrees.
Student/faculty ratio: 8:1.

ACADEMICS
Calendar: semesters. *Degrees:* certificates, associate, bachelor's, master's, doctoral, and postbachelor's certificates.
Special study options: academic remediation for entering students, accelerated degree program, advanced placement credit, distance learning, double majors, honors programs, independent study, internships, part-time degree program, services for LD students, study abroad, summer session for credit. ***ROTC:*** Army (c), Air Force (c).
Computers: 190 computers/terminals and 320 ports are available on campus for general student use. Students can access the following: campus intranet, computer help desk, free student e-mail accounts, online (class) grades, online (class) registration, online (class) schedules. Campuswide network is available. 100% of college-owned or -operated housing units are wired for high-speed Internet access. Wireless service is available via entire campus.

STUDENT LIFE
Housing options: on-campus residence required through sophomore year; women-only. Campus housing is university owned. Freshman campus housing is guaranteed.
Activities and organizations: drama/theater group, choral group, Residence Hall Council, Campus Activities Board, Student Education Association of Nebraska, Student Occupational Therapy Club, Student Nurses Association.
Athletics Member NAIA. ***Intercollegiate sports:*** basketball W(s), cross-country running W(s), golf W(s), soccer W(s), softball W(s), swimming and diving W(s), tennis W(s), volleyball W(s).
Campus security: 24-hour emergency response devices and patrols, late-night transport/escort service, controlled dormitory access, surveillance cameras at residence hall entrances; CSM Alert Text Message System.
Student services: health clinic, personal/psychological counseling.

COSTS & FINANCIAL AID
Costs (2015–16) ***Comprehensive fee:*** $36,364 includes full-time tuition ($28,964) and room and board ($7400). Full-time tuition and fees vary according to program. Part-time tuition and fees vary according to course load and program. ***Payment plans:*** installment, deferred payment. ***Waivers:*** senior citizens and employees or children of employees.
Financial Aid Of all full-time matriculated undergraduates who enrolled in 2014, 588 applied for aid, 548 were judged to have need, 76 had their need fully met. 161 Federal Work-Study jobs (averaging $2846). 14 state and other part-time jobs (averaging $4279). In 2014, 36 non-need-based awards were made. ***Average percent of need met:*** 69. ***Average financial aid package:*** $20,059. ***Average need-based loan:*** $5896. ***Average need-based gift aid:*** $13,519. ***Average non-need-based aid:*** $10,375. ***Average indebtedness upon graduation:*** $29,538.

APPLYING
Standardized Tests *Required:* SAT or ACT (for admission), Students graduating high school within the past five years with less than 12 transfer credits are required to submit ACT scores. The minimum ACT score for admission is 18 (for admission).
Options: electronic application.
Application fee: $30.
Required: high school transcript, minimum 2.0 GPA. ***Required for some:*** essay or personal statement, 3 letters of recommendation, interview.
Application deadlines: rolling (freshmen), rolling (transfers).
Notification: continuous (freshmen), continuous (transfers).

CONTACT
Enrollment Services, College of Saint Mary, 7000 Mercy Road, Omaha, NE 68106. *Phone:* 402-399-2355. *Toll-free phone:* 800-926-5534. *Fax:* 402-399-2412. *E-mail:* enroll@csm.edu.

Concordia University, Nebraska

Seward, Nebraska

http://www.cune.edu/

- **Independent** comprehensive, founded 1894, affiliated with Lutheran Church–Missouri Synod
- **Small-town** 120-acre campus with easy access to Omaha
- **Endowment** $44.5 million
- **Coed** 1,607 undergraduate students, 74% full-time, 51% women, 49% men
- **Moderately difficult** entrance level, 77% of applicants were admitted

UNDERGRAD STUDENTS
1,186 full-time, 421 part-time. Students come from 39 states and territories; 10 other countries; 54% are from out of state; 4% Black or African American, non-Hispanic/Latino; 0.6% Hispanic/Latino; 0.9% Asian, non-Hispanic/Latino; 0.2% Native Hawaiian or other Pacific Islander, non-Hispanic/Latino; 0.3% American Indian or Alaska Native, non-Hispanic/Latino; 0.6% Two or more races, non-Hispanic/Latino; 11% Race/ethnicity unknown; 3% international; 4% transferred in; 70% live on campus.

Freshmen
Admission: 1,428 applied, 1,094 admitted, 326 enrolled. ***Average high school GPA:*** 3.5. ***Test scores:*** SAT critical reading scores over 500: 40%; SAT math scores over 500: 40%; ACT scores over 18: 94%; SAT critical reading scores over 600: 18%; SAT math scores over 600: 11%; ACT scores over 24: 51%; SAT critical reading scores over 700: 7%; SAT math scores over 700: 4%; ACT scores over 30: 10%.
Retention: 80% of full-time freshmen returned.

FACULTY
Total: 250, 26% full-time, 48% with terminal degrees.
Student/faculty ratio: 13:1.

ACADEMICS
Calendar: 4-4-1. *Degrees:* bachelor's, master's, and postbachelor's certificates.
Special study options: academic remediation for entering students, accelerated degree program, adult/continuing education programs, advanced placement credit, distance learning, double majors, English as a second language, independent study, internships, off-campus study, part-time degree program, services for LD students, study abroad, summer session for credit. ***ROTC:*** Army (c), Air Force (c).
Computers: 220 computers/terminals and 1,508 ports are available on campus for general student use. Students can access the following: campus intranet, computer help desk, free student e-mail accounts, online (class) grades, online (class) registration, online (class) schedules, academic plans, human resource data. Campuswide network is available. 100% of college-owned or -operated housing units are wired for high-speed Internet access. Wireless service is available via entire campus.

STUDENT LIFE
Housing options: on-campus residence required through junior year; men-only, women-only, special housing for students with disabilities. Campus housing is university owned. Freshman campus housing is guaranteed.

Activities and organizations: drama/theater group, student-run newspaper, choral group, Student Activities Council, Musical Groups, Curtain/Drama Club, Student Senate, Concordia Youth Ministry.

Athletics Member NAIA. ***Intercollegiate sports:*** baseball M(s), basketball M(s)/W(s), cheerleading W(s), cross-country running M(s)/W(s), football M(s), golf M(s)/W(s), soccer M(s)/W(s), softball W(s), tennis M(s)/W(s), track and field M(s)/W(s), volleyball W(s), wrestling M(s). ***Intramural sports:*** badminton M/W, basketball M/W, bowling M/W, cross-country running M/W, soccer M/W, softball M/W, table tennis M/W, tennis M/W, volleyball M/W.

Campus security: 24-hour emergency response devices and patrols, controlled dormitory access.

Student services: health clinic, personal/psychological counseling.

COSTS & FINANCIAL AID
Costs (2015–16) ***Comprehensive fee:*** $34,370 includes full-time tuition ($26,810), mandatory fees ($300), and room and board ($7260). Part-time tuition: $825 per credit hour. ***College room only:*** $2980. Room and board charges vary according to board plan and housing facility. ***Payment plan:*** installment. ***Waivers:*** employees or children of employees.

Financial Aid Of all full-time matriculated undergraduates who enrolled in 2014, 996 applied for aid, 871 were judged to have need, 211 had their need fully met. 80 Federal Work-Study jobs (averaging $1400). In 2014, 134 non-need-based awards were made. ***Average percent of need met:*** 78. ***Average financial aid package:*** $20,709. ***Average need-based loan:*** $4515. ***Average need-based gift aid:*** $16,212. ***Average non-need-based aid:*** $11,475. ***Average indebtedness upon graduation:*** $29,002.

APPLYING
Standardized Tests *Required:* SAT or ACT (for admission).

Options: deferred entrance.

Required: high school transcript. ***Recommended:*** interview.

Application deadlines: 8/1 (freshmen), 8/1 (transfers).

Notification: continuous (freshmen), continuous (transfers).

CONTACT
Mr. Aaron W. Roberts, Director of Undergraduate Recruitment, Concordia University, Nebraska, 800 North Columbia Avenue, Seward, NE 68434-1556. *Phone:* 800-535-5494 Ext. 7233. *Toll-free phone:* 800-535-5494. *Fax:* 402-643-4073. *E-mail:* admiss@cune.edu.

Creative Center

Omaha, Nebraska

http://www.creativecenter.edu/

- **Proprietary** 4-year, founded 1993
- **Urban** 2-acre campus with easy access to Omaha
- **Coed** 78 undergraduate students, 97% full-time, 64% women, 36% men

UNDERGRAD STUDENTS
76 full-time, 2 part-time.

FACULTY
Total: 16, 19% full-time.

Student/faculty ratio: 11:1.

ACADEMICS
Calendar: semesters. *Degrees:* associate and bachelor's.

Special study options: accelerated degree program, part-time degree program, services for LD students.

Computers: 8 computers/terminals are available on campus for general student use. Students can access the following: campus intranet, computer help desk, All students receive a laptop computer and software- included in tuition and fees. Campuswide network is available. Wireless service is available via entire campus.

STUDENT LIFE
Housing options: college housing not available.

COSTS
Costs (2015–16) ***One-time required fee:*** $2800. ***Tuition:*** $25,600 full-time, $2560 per course part-time. Full-time tuition and fees vary according to course load, degree level, and student level. Part-time tuition and fees vary according to course load, degree level, and student level. ***Required fees:*** $2055 full-time, $200 per course part-time.

APPLYING
Required: essay or personal statement, high school transcript, 1 letter of recommendation, interview, portfolio. ***Recommended:*** minimum 2.0 GPA.

CONTACT
Mr. Richard Caldwell, Director of Admissions, Creative Center, 10850 Emmet Street, Omaha, NE 68164. *Phone:* 402-898-1000 Ext. 216. *Toll-free phone:* 888-898-1789. *Fax:* 402-898-1301. *E-mail:* rich_c@creativecenter.edu.

Creighton University

Omaha, Nebraska

http://www.creighton.edu/

- **Independent Roman Catholic (Jesuit)** university, founded 1878
- **Urban** 139-acre campus with easy access to Omaha
- **Endowment** $439.8 million
- **Coed** 4,065 undergraduate students, 95% full-time, 58% women, 42% men
- **Moderately difficult** entrance level, 73% of applicants were admitted

UNDERGRAD STUDENTS
3,842 full-time, 223 part-time. Students come from 49 states and territories; 34 other countries; 72% are from out of state; 3% Black or African American, non-Hispanic/Latino; 7% Hispanic/Latino; 9% Asian, non-Hispanic/Latino; 0.4% Native Hawaiian or other Pacific Islander, non-Hispanic/Latino; 0.5% American Indian or Alaska Native, non-Hispanic/Latino; 4% Two or more races, non-Hispanic/Latino; 0.9% Race/ethnicity unknown; 3% international; 1% transferred in; 60% live on campus.

Freshmen
Admission: 8,398 applied, 6,103 admitted, 1,025 enrolled. ***Average high school GPA:*** 3.76. ***Test scores:*** SAT critical reading scores over 500: 83%; SAT math scores over 500: 92%; SAT writing scores over 500: 87%; ACT scores over 18: 100%; SAT critical reading scores over 600: 43%; SAT math scores over 600: 56%; SAT writing scores over 600: 43%; ACT scores over 24: 81%; SAT critical reading scores over 700: 4%; SAT math scores over 700: 16%; SAT writing scores over 700: 10%; ACT scores over 30: 23%.

Retention: 91% of full-time freshmen returned.

FACULTY
Total: 827, 67% full-time, 78% with terminal degrees.

Student/faculty ratio: 11:1.

ACADEMICS
Calendar: semesters. *Degrees:* certificates, associate, bachelor's, master's, doctoral, post-master's, and postbachelor's certificates.

Special study options: accelerated degree program, adult/continuing education programs, advanced placement credit, distance learning, double majors, English as a second language, freshman honors college, honors programs, independent study, internships, off-campus study, part-time degree program, services for LD students, study abroad, summer session for credit. ***ROTC:*** Army (b), Air Force (c).

Computers: 402 computers/terminals are available on campus for general student use. Students can access the following: campus intranet, computer help desk, free student e-mail accounts, online (class) grades, online (class) registration, online (class) schedules, financial aid information. Campuswide network is available. 100% of college-owned or -operated housing units are wired for high-speed Internet access. Wireless service is available via entire campus.

STUDENT LIFE
Housing options: on-campus residence required through sophomore year; coed, special housing for students with disabilities. Campus housing is university owned. Freshman campus housing is guaranteed.

Activities and organizations: drama/theater group, student-run newspaper, radio station, choral group, Birdcage, Hui O Hawaii, Pre-Med Society, Partners Against Cancer, American Pharmacists Association Academy of Student Pharmacist, national fraternities, national sororities.

Athletics Member NCAA. All Division I. ***Intercollegiate sports:*** baseball M(s), basketball M(s)/W(s), crew W(s), cross-country running M(s)/W(s), golf M(s)/W(s), soccer M(s)/W(s), softball W(s), tennis M(s)/W(s), volleyball W(s). ***Intramural sports:*** badminton M(c)/W(c), basketball M/W, crew M(c), football M/W, golf M/W, ice hockey M(c), lacrosse M(c)/W(c), racquetball M/W, rugby M(c), skiing (downhill) M(c)/W(c), soccer M/W, softball M/W, table tennis M/W, tennis M/W, ultimate Frisbee M/W, volleyball M/W.

Campus security: 24-hour emergency response devices and patrols, student patrols, late-night transport/escort service, controlled dormitory access, shuttle buses, lighted pathway/sidewalks, self-defense education, crime prevention officer, violence intervention and prevention center.

Student services: health clinic, personal/psychological counseling, women's center.

COSTS & FINANCIAL AID

Costs (2014–15) ***Comprehensive fee:*** $45,356 includes full-time tuition ($33,796), mandatory fees ($1564), and room and board ($9996). Full-time tuition and fees vary according to course load and program. Part-time tuition: $1058 per credit hour. Part-time tuition and fees vary according to course load and program. ***Room and board:*** Room and board charges vary according to board plan and housing facility. ***Payment plan:*** installment. ***Waivers:*** adult students, senior citizens, and employees or children of employees.

Financial Aid Of all full-time matriculated undergraduates who enrolled in 2014, 2,487 applied for aid, 2,044 were judged to have need, 731 had their need fully met. 735 Federal Work-Study jobs (averaging $2074). In 2014, 1373 non-need-based awards were made. ***Average percent of need met:*** 87. ***Average financial aid package:*** $28,375. ***Average need-based loan:*** $6061. ***Average need-based gift aid:*** $22,665. ***Average non-need-based aid:*** $14,200. ***Average indebtedness upon graduation:*** $33,428.

APPLYING

Standardized Tests *Required:* SAT or ACT (for admission).

Options: electronic application, deferred entrance.

Application fee: $40.

Required: essay or personal statement, high school transcript, minimum 2.8 GPA, 1 letter of recommendation.

Application deadlines: 2/15 (freshmen), 8/1 (transfers).

Notification: continuous (freshmen), continuous (transfers).

CONTACT

Ms. Sarah Richardson, Director of Admissions and Scholarships, Creighton University, 2500 California Plaza, Omaha, NE 68178-0001. *Phone:* 402-280-2703. *Toll-free phone:* 800-282-5835. *Fax:* 402-280-2685. *E-mail:* williampierce@creighton.edu.

Doane College

Crete, Nebraska

http://www.doane.edu/

- **Independent** comprehensive, founded 1872, affiliated with United Church of Christ
- **Small-town** 300-acre campus with easy access to Omaha
- **Endowment** $116.0 million
- **Coed** 1,067 undergraduate students, 99% full-time, 50% women, 50% men

UNDERGRAD STUDENTS

1,057 full-time, 10 part-time. Students come from 30 states and territories; 7 other countries; 22% are from out of state; 4% Black or African American, non-Hispanic/Latino; 6% Hispanic/Latino; 1% Asian, non-Hispanic/Latino; 0.2% Native Hawaiian or other Pacific Islander, non-Hispanic/Latino; 0.3% American Indian or Alaska Native, non-Hispanic/Latino; 2% Two or more races, non-Hispanic/Latino; 2% Race/ethnicity unknown; 1% international; 4% transferred in; 82% live on campus.

Freshmen

Admission: 268 enrolled. ***Average high school GPA:*** 3.52. ***Test scores:*** ACT scores over 18: 90%; ACT scores over 24: 39%; ACT scores over 30: 7%.

Retention: 72% of full-time freshmen returned.

FACULTY

Total: 125, 66% full-time, 66% with terminal degrees.

Student/faculty ratio: 11:1.

ACADEMICS

Calendar: 4-1-4. *Degrees:* bachelor's, master's, and post-master's certificates (non-traditional undergraduate programs and graduate programs offered at Lincoln campus).

Special study options: advanced placement credit, cooperative education, double majors, English as a second language, honors programs, independent study, internships, off-campus study, student-designed majors, study abroad, summer session for credit. ***ROTC:*** Army (c), Air Force (c).

Unusual degree programs: 3-2 engineering with Columbia University, Washington University in St. Louis; forestry with Duke University; environmental studies with Duke University.

Computers: 250 computers/terminals and 1,000 ports are available on campus for general student use. Students can access the following: campus intranet, computer help desk, free student e-mail accounts, online (class) grades, online (class) registration, online (class) schedules. Campuswide network is available. 100% of college-owned or -operated housing units are wired for high-speed Internet access. Wireless service is available via entire campus.

STUDENT LIFE

Housing options: on-campus residence required through senior year; coed, women-only. Campus housing is university owned. Freshman campus housing is guaranteed.

Activities and organizations: drama/theater group, student-run newspaper, radio and television station, choral group, marching band, Student Activities Council, Hansen Leadership Program, band/choir, Doane Ambassadors, Doane Art League.

Athletics Member NAIA. ***Intercollegiate sports:*** baseball M(s), basketball M(s)/W(s), cross-country running M(s)/W(s), football M(s), golf M(s)/W(s), soccer M(s)/W(s), softball W(s), tennis M/W, track and field M(s)/W(s), volleyball W(s). ***Intramural sports:*** baseball M(c)/W(c), basketball M/W, bowling M/W, football M/W, golf M/W, ice hockey M, racquetball M(c)/W(c), softball M/W, swimming and diving M/W, table tennis M(c)/W(c), tennis M/W, volleyball M/W, water polo M/W.

Campus security: 24-hour emergency response devices and patrols, student patrols, late-night transport/escort service, controlled dormitory access, evening patrols by trained security personnel.

Student services: health clinic, personal/psychological counseling.

COSTS & FINANCIAL AID

Costs (2015–16) ***Tuition:*** $2720 full-time. Full-time tuition and fees vary according to location. Part-time tuition and fees vary according to course load and location. ***Room only:*** Room and board charges vary according to board plan, housing facility, and location. ***Payment plan:*** installment. ***Waivers:*** senior citizens and employees or children of employees.

Financial Aid Of all full-time matriculated undergraduates who enrolled in 2014, 912 applied for aid, 807 were judged to have need, 251 had their need fully met. In 2014, 87 non-need-based awards were made. ***Average percent of need met:*** 87. ***Average financial aid package:*** $21,187. ***Average need-based loan:*** $4653. ***Average need-based gift aid:*** $17,439. ***Average non-need-based aid:*** $13,431. ***Average indebtedness upon graduation:*** $29,994.

APPLYING

Standardized Tests *Required:* SAT or ACT (for admission).

Required: high school transcript, 2 letters of recommendation. ***Required for some:*** interview. ***Recommended:*** minimum 2.0 GPA.

CONTACT

Mr. Kyle McMurray, Director of Admission, Doane College, 1014 Boswell Avenue, Crete, NE 68333. *Phone:* 402-826-8222. *Toll-free phone:* 800-333-6263. *E-mail:* kyle.mcmurray@doane.edu.

Hastings College

Hastings, Nebraska

http://www.hastings.edu/

- **Independent Presbyterian** comprehensive, founded 1882
- **Small-town** 109-acre campus
- **Endowment** $76.8 million
- **Coed** 1,183 undergraduate students, 95% full-time, 49% women, 51% men
- **Moderately difficult** entrance level, 70% of applicants were admitted

UNDERGRAD STUDENTS
1,129 full-time, 54 part-time. Students come from 21 states and territories; 8 other countries; 33% are from out of state; 3% Black or African American, non-Hispanic/Latino; 6% Hispanic/Latino; 1% Asian, non-Hispanic/Latino; 0.4% Native Hawaiian or other Pacific Islander, non-Hispanic/Latino; 0.5% American Indian or Alaska Native, non-Hispanic/Latino; 3% Two or more races, non-Hispanic/Latino; 0.6% Race/ethnicity unknown; 2% international; 5% transferred in; 63% live on campus.

Freshmen
Admission: 1,542 applied, 1,074 admitted, 345 enrolled. ***Test scores:*** SAT critical reading scores over 500: 45%; SAT math scores over 500: 68%; ACT scores over 18: 96%; SAT critical reading scores over 600: 16%; SAT math scores over 600: 16%; ACT scores over 24: 44%; SAT critical reading scores over 700: 3%; SAT math scores over 700: 3%; ACT scores over 30: 3%.

Retention: 74% of full-time freshmen returned.

FACULTY
Total: 119, 66% full-time, 56% with terminal degrees.

Student/faculty ratio: 13:1.

ACADEMICS
Calendar: 4-1-4. *Degrees:* bachelor's and master's.

Special study options: adult/continuing education programs, advanced placement credit, double majors, independent study, internships, off-campus study, part-time degree program, services for LD students, student-designed majors, study abroad, summer session for credit.

Unusual degree programs: 3-2 engineering with Columbia University, Georgia Institute of Technology, Washington University in St. Louis, University of Colorado at Boulder, Colorado State University; occupational therapy with Washington University in St. Louis, Boston University.

Computers: 240 computers/terminals are available on campus for general student use. Students can access the following: campus intranet, computer help desk, free student e-mail accounts, online (class) registration, online (class) schedules, e-mail. Campuswide network is available. 100% of college-owned or -operated housing units are wired for high-speed Internet access. Wireless service is available via entire campus.

STUDENT LIFE
Housing options: on-campus residence required through junior year; coed, men-only, women-only. Campus housing is university owned. Freshman campus housing is guaranteed.

Activities and organizations: drama/theater group, student-run newspaper, radio and television station, choral group, marching band, Student Association, Student Alumni Ambassadors, Fellowship of Christian Athletes, Phi Mu Alpha Sinfonia, Hastings College Singers.

Athletics Member NAIA. ***Intercollegiate sports:*** baseball M(s), basketball M(s)/W(s), bowling M(s)/W(s), cheerleading W(s), cross-country running M(s)/W(s), football M(s), golf M(s)/W(s), riflery M(c)/W(c), soccer M(s)/W(s), softball W(s), tennis M(s)/W(s), track and field M(s)/W(s), volleyball W(s), wrestling M(s). ***Intramural sports:*** basketball M/W, bowling M/W, football M/W, racquetball M/W, softball M/W, table tennis M/W, ultimate Frisbee M/W, volleyball M/W.

Campus security: 24-hour emergency response devices, student patrols, late-night transport/escort service, controlled dormitory access, security cameras at entrances and parking lots.

Student services: health clinic, personal/psychological counseling.

COSTS & FINANCIAL AID
Costs (2015–16) ***Comprehensive fee:*** $35,380 includes full-time tuition ($26,110), mandatory fees ($1190), and room and board ($8080). Part-time tuition: $1070 per credit hour. Part-time tuition and fees vary according to course load. ***Required fees:*** $316 per term part-time. ***Room and board:*** Room and board charges vary according to board plan and housing facility. ***Payment plan:*** installment. ***Waivers:*** adult students and employees or children of employees.

Financial Aid Of all full-time matriculated undergraduates who enrolled in 2014, 932 applied for aid, 838 were judged to have need, 228 had their need fully met. 70 Federal Work-Study jobs (averaging $1663). In 2014, 270 non-need-based awards were made. ***Average percent of need met:*** 79. ***Average financial aid package:*** $21,151. ***Average need-based loan:*** $4583. ***Average need-based gift aid:*** $17,634. ***Average non-need-based aid:*** $13,915. ***Average indebtedness upon graduation:*** $27,784. ***Financial aid deadline:*** 9/1.

APPLYING
Standardized Tests *Required:* SAT or ACT (for admission).

Options: electronic application.

Required: high school transcript, minimum 2.0 GPA, counselor's recommendation. ***Required for some:*** essay or personal statement, 2 letters of recommendation, interview.

Application deadlines: 8/1 (freshmen), 8/1 (transfers).

Notification: continuous (freshmen), continuous (transfers).

CONTACT
Ms. Traci Boeve, Director of Admissions, Hastings College, 710 North Turner Avenue, Hastings, NE 68901-7621. *Phone:* 402-461-7789. *Toll-free phone:* 800-532-7642. *Fax:* 402-461-7490. *E-mail:* tboeve@hastings.edu.

ITT Technical Institute

Omaha, Nebraska

http://www.itt-tech.edu/

- **Proprietary** primarily 2-year, founded 1991, part of ITT Educational Services, Inc.
- **Urban** campus
- **Coed**
- **Minimally difficult** entrance level

ACADEMICS
Calendar: quarters. *Degrees:* associate and bachelor's.

STUDENT LIFE
Housing options: college housing not available.

CONTACT
Director of Recruitment, ITT Technical Institute, 1120 North 103rd Plaza, Suite 200, Omaha, NE 68114. *Phone:* 402-331-2900. *Toll-free phone:* 800-677-9260.

Nebraska Christian College

Papillion, Nebraska

http://www.nechristian.edu/

- **Independent** 4-year, founded 1944, affiliated with Christian Churches and Churches of Christ
- **Small-town** 85-acre campus with easy access to Omaha
- **Endowment** $900,000
- **Coed** 138 undergraduate students, 90% full-time, 46% women, 54% men

UNDERGRAD STUDENTS
124 full-time, 14 part-time. Students come from 12 states and territories; 2 other countries; 42% are from out of state; 3% Black or African American, non-Hispanic/Latino; 4% Hispanic/Latino; 0.7% Native Hawaiian or other Pacific Islander, non-Hispanic/Latino; 7% Race/ethnicity unknown; 75% live on campus.

Freshmen
Test scores: ACT scores over 18: 90%; ACT scores over 24: 22%; ACT scores over 30: 2%.

Retention: 83% of full-time freshmen returned.

FACULTY
Total: 25, 12% with terminal degrees.

Student/faculty ratio: 6:1.

ACADEMICS
Calendar: semesters. *Degrees:* certificates, associate, and bachelor's.
Special study options: academic remediation for entering students, distance learning, double majors, independent study, internships, off-campus study, part-time degree program, study abroad.
Computers: 12 computers/terminals and 153 ports are available on campus for general student use. Students can access the following: campus intranet, free student e-mail accounts, online (class) grades, online (class) registration, online (class) schedules. Campuswide network is available. 100% of college-owned or -operated housing units are wired for high-speed Internet access. Wireless service is available via entire campus.

STUDENT LIFE
Housing options: on-campus residence required through junior year; men-only, women-only, special housing for students with disabilities. Campus housing is university owned. Freshman campus housing is guaranteed.
Activities and organizations: choral group, Global Gospel Group, Running Club, Writing Club, Spiritual Life Group.
Athletics Member NCCAA. ***Intercollegiate sports:*** basketball M. ***Intramural sports:*** basketball M/W, football M/W, table tennis M/W, ultimate Frisbee M/W.
Campus security: student patrols, controlled dormitory access.

COSTS & FINANCIAL AID
Costs (2014–15) ***One-time required fee:*** $300. ***Comprehensive fee:*** $20,900 includes full-time tuition ($13,200) and room and board ($7700). Full-time tuition and fees vary according to course load. Part-time tuition: $550 per hour. Part-time tuition and fees vary according to course load. ***Room and board:*** Room and board charges vary according to board plan and housing facility. ***Payment plans:*** installment, deferred payment. ***Waivers:*** children of alumni and employees or children of employees.
Financial Aid Of all full-time matriculated undergraduates who enrolled in 2008, 147 applied for aid, 129 were judged to have need. 13 Federal Work-Study jobs (averaging $1183). ***Average need-based loan:*** $2958. ***Average indebtedness upon graduation:*** $11,593.

APPLYING
Standardized Tests *Required:* ACT (for admission).
Required: essay or personal statement, high school transcript, 2 letters of recommendation. ***Required for some:*** interview, Minimum ACT score of 18 for recent high school graduates.

CONTACT
Mr. Sean Badeer, Associate Director of Admissions, Nebraska Christian College, 12550 S. 114th Street, Papillion, NE 68046. *Phone:* 402-935-9439. *E-mail:* sbadeer@nechristian.edu.

Nebraska Methodist College

Omaha, Nebraska

http://www.methodistcollege.edu/

- **Independent** comprehensive, founded 1891, affiliated with United Methodist Church
- **Urban** 7-acre campus
- **Coed** 747 undergraduate students, 61% full-time, 90% women, 10% men
- **Moderately difficult** entrance level, 96% of applicants were admitted

UNDERGRAD STUDENTS
453 full-time, 294 part-time. Students come from 13 states and territories; 2 other countries; 11% are from out of state; 4% Black or African American, non-Hispanic/Latino; 4% Hispanic/Latino; 1% Asian, non-Hispanic/Latino; 0.1% Native Hawaiian or other Pacific Islander, non-Hispanic/Latino; 0.5% American Indian or Alaska Native, non-Hispanic/Latino; 2% Two or more races, non-Hispanic/Latino; 1% Race/ethnicity unknown; 0.4% international; 25% transferred in; 11% live on campus.

Freshmen
Admission: 49 applied, 47 admitted, 38 enrolled. ***Average high school GPA:*** 3.44. ***Test scores:*** ACT scores over 18: 92%; ACT scores over 24: 41%; ACT scores over 30: 3%.
Retention: 64% of full-time freshmen returned.

FACULTY
Total: 68, 81% full-time, 28% with terminal degrees.
Student/faculty ratio: 12:1.

ACADEMICS
Calendar: semesters. *Degrees:* certificates, associate, bachelor's, master's, doctoral, and post-master's certificates.
Special study options: academic remediation for entering students, accelerated degree program, adult/continuing education programs, advanced placement credit, distance learning, external degree program, independent study, internships, services for LD students, summer session for credit. ***ROTC:*** Army (c), Air Force (c).
Computers: 47 computers/terminals are available on campus for general student use. Students can access the following: campus intranet, computer help desk, free student e-mail accounts, online (class) grades, online (class) registration, online (class) schedules. Campuswide network is available. 100% of college-owned or -operated housing units are wired for high-speed Internet access. Wireless service is available via entire campus.

STUDENT LIFE
Housing options: coed. Campus housing is university owned. Freshman applicants given priority for college housing.
Activities and organizations: Student Senate, Student Nurses Association, Methodist Allied Health Student Association, Student Ambassadors, Residence Hall Council.
Campus security: 24-hour emergency response devices and patrols, late-night transport/escort service, controlled dormitory access.
Student services: health clinic, personal/psychological counseling.

COSTS & FINANCIAL AID
Costs (2014–15) ***Tuition:*** $16,560 full-time, $552 per credit hour part-time. Full-time tuition and fees vary according to degree level and program. Part-time tuition and fees vary according to degree level and program. ***Required fees:*** $1549 full-time. ***Room only:*** $6460. Room and board charges vary according to housing facility. ***Payment plan:*** installment. ***Waivers:*** employees or children of employees.
Financial Aid Of all full-time matriculated undergraduates who enrolled in 2014, 27 Federal Work-Study jobs (averaging $2080). ***Average indebtedness upon graduation:*** $31,591.

APPLYING
Standardized Tests *Required:* SAT or ACT (for admission).
Options: electronic application, deferred entrance.
Application fee: $25.
Required: essay or personal statement, high school transcript, minimum 2.5 GPA.
Application deadlines: rolling (freshmen), rolling (out-of-state freshmen), rolling (transfers).

CONTACT
Ms. Megan Maryott, Director of Enrollment Services, Nebraska Methodist College, 720 North 87th Street, Omaha, NE 68114. *Phone:* 402-354-7111. *Toll-free phone:* 800-335-5510. *Fax:* 402-354-7020. *E-mail:* megan.maryott@methodistcollege.edu.

Nebraska Wesleyan University

Lincoln, Nebraska

http://www.nebrwesleyan.edu/

- **Independent United Methodist** comprehensive, founded 1887
- **Suburban** 50-acre campus with easy access to Omaha
- **Endowment** $55.8 million
- **Coed** 1,832 undergraduate students, 82% full-time, 62% women, 38% men
- **Moderately difficult** entrance level, 78% of applicants were admitted

UNDERGRAD STUDENTS
1,511 full-time, 321 part-time. Students come from 27 states and territories; 26 other countries; 14% are from out of state; 3% Black or African American, non-Hispanic/Latino; 5% Hispanic/Latino; 2% Asian, non-Hispanic/Latino; 0.1% Native Hawaiian or other Pacific Islander, non-Hispanic/Latino; 0.3% American Indian or Alaska Native, non-Hispanic/Latino; 2% Two or more races, non-Hispanic/Latino; 4%

Race/ethnicity unknown; 2% international; 3% transferred in; 63% live on campus.

Freshmen

Admission: 1,775 applied, 1,387 admitted, 368 enrolled. ***Average high school GPA:*** 3.65. ***Test scores:*** SAT critical reading scores over 500: 62%; SAT math scores over 500: 69%; ACT scores over 18: 98%; SAT critical reading scores over 600: 31%; SAT math scores over 600: 38%; ACT scores over 24: 62%; SAT critical reading scores over 700: 8%; SAT math scores over 700: 8%; ACT scores over 30: 10%.

Retention: 81% of full-time freshmen returned.

FACULTY

Total: 233, 45% full-time.

Student/faculty ratio: 12:1.

ACADEMICS

Calendar: semesters. *Degrees:* certificates, bachelor's, master's, post-master's, and postbachelor's certificates.

Special study options: accelerated degree program, adult/continuing education programs, advanced placement credit, double majors, independent study, internships, off-campus study, part-time degree program, services for LD students, student-designed majors, study abroad, summer session for credit. ***ROTC:*** Army (c), Navy (c), Air Force (c).

Unusual degree programs: 3-2 engineering with Washington University in St. Louis, Columbia University, University of Nebraska-Lincoln.

Computers: 360 computers/terminals are available on campus for general student use. Students can access the following: computer help desk, free student e-mail accounts, online (class) grades, online (class) registration, online (class) schedules. Campuswide network is available. 100% of college-owned or -operated housing units are wired for high-speed Internet access. Wireless service is available via entire campus.

STUDENT LIFE

Housing options: on-campus residence required through junior year; coed, women-only. Campus housing is university owned. Freshman campus housing is guaranteed.

Activities and organizations: drama/theater group, student-run newspaper, radio station, choral group, marching band, national fraternities, national sororities.

Athletics Member NCAA, NAIA. All NCAA Division III. ***Intercollegiate sports:*** baseball M, basketball M/W, cheerleading W, cross-country running M/W, football M, golf M/W, soccer M/W, softball W, swimming and diving M/W, tennis M/W, track and field M/W, volleyball W. ***Intramural sports:*** basketball M/W, bowling M/W, football M/W, racquetball M/W, soccer M/W, softball M/W, tennis M/W, ultimate Frisbee M/W, volleyball M/W, weight lifting M/W.

Campus security: 24-hour emergency response devices, late-night transport/escort service, controlled dormitory access.

Student services: health clinic, personal/psychological counseling, women's center.

COSTS & FINANCIAL AID

Costs (2014–15) ***Comprehensive fee:*** $36,450 includes full-time tuition ($27,950), mandatory fees ($550), and room and board ($7950). Part-time tuition: $1045 per credit hour. Part-time tuition and fees vary according to class time and location. ***Room and board:*** Room and board charges vary according to board plan and housing facility. ***Payment plan:*** installment. ***Waivers:*** senior citizens and employees or children of employees.

Financial Aid Of all full-time matriculated undergraduates who enrolled in 2012, 1,172 applied for aid, 1,008 were judged to have need, 178 had their need fully met. In 2012, 415 non-need-based awards were made. ***Average percent of need met:*** 69. ***Average financial aid package:*** $17,992. ***Average need-based loan:*** $4729. ***Average need-based gift aid:*** $13,077. ***Average non-need-based aid:*** $8867. ***Average indebtedness upon graduation:*** $28,077.

APPLYING

Standardized Tests *Required:* SAT or ACT (for admission).

Options: electronic application, early decision, deferred entrance.

Required: high school transcript. ***Required for some:*** essay or personal statement.

Application deadlines: 8/15 (freshmen), 8/15 (transfers).

Early decision deadline: 12/1.

Notification: continuous (freshmen), continuous (transfers).

CONTACT

Mr. Gordie Coffin, Director of Admissions, Nebraska Wesleyan University, 5000 Saint Paul Avenue, Lincoln, NE 68504. *Phone:* 402-465-2218. *Toll-free phone:* 800-541-3818. *Fax:* 402-465-2177. *E-mail:* admissions@nebrwesleyan.edu.

Peru State College

Peru, Nebraska

http://www.peru.edu/

- **State-supported** comprehensive, founded 1867, part of Nebraska State College System
- **Rural** 104-acre campus
- **Coed** 2,094 undergraduate students, 57% full-time, 59% women, 41% men
- **Noncompetitive** entrance level, 49% of applicants were admitted

UNDERGRAD STUDENTS

1,192 full-time, 902 part-time. 5% Black or African American, non-Hispanic/Latino; 4% Hispanic/Latino; 1% Asian, non-Hispanic/Latino; 0.1% Native Hawaiian or other Pacific Islander, non-Hispanic/Latino; 1% American Indian or Alaska Native, non-Hispanic/Latino; 1% Two or more races, non-Hispanic/Latino; 3% Race/ethnicity unknown; 9% transferred in; 33% live on campus.

Freshmen

Admission: 869 applied, 422 admitted, 174 enrolled. ***Test scores:*** ACT scores over 18: 74%; ACT scores over 24: 16%; ACT scores over 30: 1%.

FACULTY

Total: 109, 43% full-time.

Student/faculty ratio: 24:1.

ACADEMICS

Calendar: semesters. *Degrees:* bachelor's and master's.

Special study options: academic remediation for entering students, accelerated degree program, adult/continuing education programs, advanced placement credit, cooperative education, distance learning, double majors, external degree program, freshman honors college, honors programs, internships, off-campus study, part-time degree program, services for LD students, summer session for credit. ***ROTC:*** Army (c), Air Force (c).

Computers: 125 computers/terminals are available on campus for general student use. Students can access the following: campus intranet, free student e-mail accounts, online (class) grades, online (class) registration, online (class) schedules. Campuswide network is available. 100% of college-owned or -operated housing units are wired for high-speed Internet access. Wireless service is available via entire campus.

STUDENT LIFE

Housing options: on-campus residence required through sophomore year; coed, men-only, women-only. Campus housing is university owned. Freshman campus housing is guaranteed.

Activities and organizations: drama/theater group, student-run newspaper, choral group, marching band, Campus Activities Board, Black Student Union, Peru Student Education Association (PSEA), Phi Beta Lambda (PBL), Pilot Club.

Athletics Member NAIA. ***Intercollegiate sports:*** baseball M(s), basketball M(s)/W(s), cheerleading W(s), cross-country running W(s), football M(s), golf W(s), softball W(s), volleyball W(s). ***Intramural sports:*** basketball M/W, football M/W, softball M/W, volleyball M/W.

Campus security: 24-hour emergency response devices and patrols, late-night transport/escort service.

Student services: health clinic.

COSTS

Costs (2014–15) ***Tuition:*** state resident $4200 full-time, $140 per credit hour part-time; nonresident $4200 full-time, $141 per credit hour part-time. Full-time tuition and fees vary according to course level, course load, and location. Part-time tuition and fees vary according to course level, course load, and location. ***Required fees:*** $1722 full-time. ***Room and board:*** $6492; room only: $3580. Room and board charges vary according to board plan and housing facility. ***Payment plan:*** deferred payment. ***Waivers:*** employees or children of employees.

APPLYING
Standardized Tests *Required for some:* SAT or ACT (for admission).
Options: electronic application.
Required: high school transcript.
Application deadlines: rolling (freshmen), rolling (out-of-state freshmen), rolling (transfers).
Notification: continuous (freshmen), continuous (out-of-state freshmen), continuous (transfers).

CONTACT
Ms. Micki Willis, Vice President for Enrollment Management and Student Affairs, Peru State College, PO Box 10, Peru, NE 68421. *Phone:* 402-872-2221. *Toll-free phone:* 800-742-4412 (in-state); 800-741-4412 (out-of-state). *Fax:* 402-872-2296. *E-mail:* mwillis@peru.edu.

St. Gregory the Great Seminary
Seward, Nebraska
http://www.stgregoryseminary.edu/

- **Independent Roman Catholic** 4-year
- **Small-town** 60-acre campus
- **Men only**
- 100% of applicants were admitted

FACULTY
Student/faculty ratio: 5:1.

ACADEMICS
Degrees: bachelor's and postbachelor's certificates.

STUDENT LIFE
Housing options: on-campus residence required through senior yearCampus housing is university owned. Freshman campus housing is guaranteed.

APPLYING
Standardized Tests *Required:* SAT or ACT (for admission).
Required: essay or personal statement, high school transcript, 3 letters of recommendation, interview, Church documents, letter of sponsorship from diocese.

CONTACT
Rev. Peter M. Mitchell, Dean of Men, St. Gregory the Great Seminary, 800 Fletcher Road, Seward, NE 68434. *Phone:* 402-643-4052. *Fax:* 402-643-6964. *E-mail:* sggs@stgregoryseminary.edu.

Union College
Lincoln, Nebraska
http://www.ucollege.edu/

- **Independent Seventh-day Adventist** comprehensive, founded 1891
- **Suburban** 26-acre campus with easy access to Omaha
- **Coed** 797 undergraduate students, 89% full-time, 59% women, 41% men
- **Moderately difficult** entrance level, 52% of applicants were admitted

UNDERGRAD STUDENTS
712 full-time, 85 part-time. 71% are from out of state; 7% Black or African American, non-Hispanic/Latino; 16% Hispanic/Latino; 3% Asian, non-Hispanic/Latino; 0.7% Native Hawaiian or other Pacific Islander, non-Hispanic/Latino; 0.8% American Indian or Alaska Native, non-Hispanic/Latino; 5% Two or more races, non-Hispanic/Latino; 0.9% Race/ethnicity unknown; 7% international; 12% transferred in; 73% live on campus.

Freshmen
Admission: 1,260 applied, 657 admitted, 156 enrolled. ***Average high school GPA:*** 3.24. ***Test scores:*** SAT math scores over 500: 49%; SAT writing scores over 500: 38%; ACT scores over 18: 87%; SAT math scores over 600: 13%; SAT writing scores over 600: 11%; ACT scores over 24: 41%; SAT math scores over 700: 2%; SAT writing scores over 700: 2%; ACT scores over 30: 3%.
Retention: 75% of full-time freshmen returned.

FACULTY
Total: 122, 50% full-time, 31% with terminal degrees.
Student/faculty ratio: 10:1.

ACADEMICS
Calendar: semesters. *Degrees:* associate, bachelor's, and master's.
Special study options: accelerated degree program, adult/continuing education programs, advanced placement credit, cooperative education, double majors, honors programs, independent study, internships, off-campus study, part-time degree program, services for LD students, student-designed majors, study abroad, summer session for credit.
Computers: Students can access the following: free student e-mail accounts, online (class) grades, online (class) registration, online (class) schedules. Campuswide network is available. 100% of college-owned or -operated housing units are wired for high-speed Internet access. Wireless service is available via entire campus.

STUDENT LIFE
Housing options: on-campus residence required through junior year; men-only, women-only, special housing for students with disabilities. Campus housing is university owned. Freshman campus housing is guaranteed.
Activities and organizations: drama/theater group, student-run newspaper, choral group, Business and Computer Science Club, Math and Science Club, Nursing Club, Amnesty International, International Club.
Athletics ***Intercollegiate sports:*** basketball M/W, golf M, volleyball W. ***Intramural sports:*** basketball M/W, football M/W, gymnastics M(c)/W(c), soccer M(c), softball M/W, ultimate Frisbee M/W, volleyball M/W.
Campus security: 24-hour emergency response devices, student patrols, late-night transport/escort service.
Student services: health clinic, personal/psychological counseling.

COSTS & FINANCIAL AID
Costs (2015–16) ***Comprehensive fee:*** $28,700 includes full-time tuition ($20,928), mandatory fees ($1042), and room and board ($6730). Full-time tuition and fees vary according to course load, degree level, and program. Part-time tuition: $872 per credit hour. Part-time tuition and fees vary according to program. ***College room only:*** $3800. Room and board charges vary according to housing facility. ***Payment plan:*** installment. ***Waivers:*** employees or children of employees.
Financial Aid Of all full-time matriculated undergraduates who enrolled in 2014, 581 applied for aid, 514 were judged to have need, 70 had their need fully met. In 2014, 187 non-need-based awards were made. ***Average percent of need met:*** 62. ***Average financial aid package:*** $15,499. ***Average need-based loan:*** $4867. ***Average need-based gift aid:*** $11,502. ***Average non-need-based aid:*** $6294. ***Average indebtedness upon graduation:*** $29,020.

APPLYING
Standardized Tests *Required:* SAT or ACT (for admission).
Options: electronic application.
Required: high school transcript, minimum 2.5 GPA, 3 letters of recommendation. ***Required for some:*** essay or personal statement, interview.

CONTACT
Michael Steingas, Assistant Director of Admissions, Union College, 3800 South 48th Street, Lincoln, NE 68506. *Phone:* 402-486-2969 Ext. 2052. *Toll-free phone:* 800-228-4600. *Fax:* 402-486-2895. *E-mail:* enroll@ucollege.edu.

University of Nebraska at Kearney
Kearney, Nebraska
http://www.unk.edu/

- **State-supported** comprehensive, founded 1903, part of University of Nebraska System
- **Small-town** 235-acre campus
- **Coed** 5,274 undergraduate students, 89% full-time, 57% women, 43% men
- **Moderately difficult** entrance level, 84% of applicants were admitted

UNDERGRAD STUDENTS
4,668 full-time, 606 part-time. Students come from 49 states and territories; 55 other countries; 8% are from out of state; 2% Black or African American, non-Hispanic/Latino; 10% Hispanic/Latino; 0.9% Asian, non-Hispanic/Latino; 0.1% Native Hawaiian or other Pacific Islander, non-Hispanic/Latino; 0.2% American Indian or Alaska Native, non-Hispanic/Latino; 1% Two or more races, non-Hispanic/Latino; 0.7% Race/ethnicity unknown; 8% international; 6% transferred in; 92% live on campus.

Freshmen
Admission: 2,706 applied, 2,276 admitted, 990 enrolled. ***Average high school GPA:*** 3.48. ***Test scores:*** SAT critical reading scores over 500: 43%; SAT math scores over 500: 57%; ACT scores over 18: 92%; SAT critical reading scores over 600: 10%; SAT math scores over 600: 14%; ACT scores over 24: 39%; SAT critical reading scores over 700: 10%; SAT math scores over 700: 5%; ACT scores over 30: 6%.

Retention: 80% of full-time freshmen returned.

FACULTY
Total: 442, 75% full-time, 62% with terminal degrees.

Student/faculty ratio: 15:1.

ACADEMICS
Calendar: semesters. *Degrees:* bachelor's, master's, and post-master's certificates.

Special study options: distance learning, double majors, honors programs, independent study, internships, part-time degree program, services for LD students, study abroad. ***ROTC:*** Army (b).

Computers: 600 computers/terminals and 8,500 ports are available on campus for general student use. Students can access the following: computer help desk, free student e-mail accounts, online (class) grades, online (class) registration, online (class) schedules, online degree audit, online personal information update, online bill viewing and payment, online financial aid awards and acceptance. Campuswide network is available. Wireless service is available via entire campus.

STUDENT LIFE
Housing options: on-campus residence required for freshman year; coed. Campus housing is university owned. Freshman campus housing is guaranteed.

Activities and organizations: drama/theater group, student-run newspaper, radio and television station, marching band, national fraternities, national sororities.

Athletics Member NCAA. All Division II. ***Intercollegiate sports:*** baseball M(s), basketball M(s)/W(s), cross-country running M(s)/W(s), football M(s), golf M(s)/W(s), soccer W, softball W(s), swimming and diving W(s), tennis M(s)/W(s), track and field M(s)/W(s), volleyball W(s), wrestling M(s). ***Intramural sports:*** badminton M/W, basketball M/W, cross-country running M/W, football M/W, golf M/W, racquetball M/W, soccer M/W, softball M/W, tennis M/W, volleyball M/W, water polo M/W, wrestling M/W.

Campus security: 24-hour emergency response devices and patrols, late-night transport/escort service.

Student services: health clinic.

COSTS & FINANCIAL AID
Costs (2014–15) ***Tuition:*** state resident $5235 full-time, $175 per credit hour part-time; nonresident $11,393 full-time, $380 per credit hour part-time. Full-time tuition and fees vary according to course level, course load, degree level, location, and program. Part-time tuition and fees vary according to course level, course load, degree level, location, and program. ***Required fees:*** $1349 full-time, $25 per credit hour part-time, $300 per term part-time. ***Room and board:*** $8850; room only: $4524. Room and board charges vary according to board plan and housing facility. ***Payment plan:*** installment. ***Waivers:*** employees or children of employees.

Financial Aid Of all full-time matriculated undergraduates who enrolled in 2013, 3,639 applied for aid, 3,013 were judged to have need, 160 had their need fully met. In 2013, 162 non-need-based awards were made. ***Average percent of need met:*** 63. ***Average financial aid package:*** $10,376. ***Average need-based loan:*** $4172. ***Average need-based gift aid:*** $6300. ***Average non-need-based aid:*** $2066. ***Average indebtedness upon graduation:*** $23,229.

APPLYING
Standardized Tests *Required:* SAT and SAT Subject Tests or ACT (for admission).

Options: electronic application.

Application fee: $45.

Required: high school transcript, rank in upper 50% of high school class.

Application deadlines: 9/1 (freshmen), rolling (transfers).

Notification: continuous (freshmen), continuous (transfers).

CONTACT
Mr. Dusty Newton, Director of Admissions, University of Nebraska at Kearney, 905 West 25th Street, Kearney, NE 68849-0001. *Phone:* 308-865-8702. *Toll-free phone:* 800-532-7639. *Fax:* 308-865-8987. *E-mail:* admissionsug@unk.edu.

University of Nebraska at Omaha

Omaha, Nebraska

http://www.unomaha.edu/

- **State-supported** university, founded 1908, part of University of Nebraska System
- **Urban** 503-acre campus
- **Coed**
- **Minimally difficult** entrance level

FACULTY
Student/faculty ratio: 17:1.

ACADEMICS
Calendar: semesters. *Degrees:* bachelor's, master's, doctoral, post-master's, and postbachelor's certificates.

STUDENT LIFE
Housing options: coed. Campus housing is university owned and leased by the school.

Activities and organizations: drama/theater group, student-run newspaper, radio and television station, choral group, marching band, Student Programming Board-Maverick Productions, student government, Greek Life, Emerging Leaders, PRSSA - Public Relations student society of America, national fraternities, national sororities.

Athletics Member NCAA. All Division I.

Campus security: 24-hour emergency response devices and patrols, late-night transport/escort service, controlled dormitory access.

Student services: health clinic, personal/psychological counseling, women's center, legal services.

COSTS & FINANCIAL AID
Costs (2014–15) ***Tuition:*** state resident $5312 full-time, $197 per credit hour part-time; nonresident $16,632 full-time, $598 per credit hour part-time. ***Required fees:*** $1438 full-time. ***Room and board:*** $8408. Room and board charges vary according to board plan and housing facility.

Financial Aid Of all full-time matriculated undergraduates who enrolled in 2012, 6,648 applied for aid, 5,593 were judged to have need, 1,389 had their need fully met. In 2012, 317 non-need-based awards were made. ***Average percent of need met:*** 67. ***Average financial aid package:*** $9038. ***Average need-based loan:*** $3883. ***Average need-based gift aid:*** $5335. ***Average non-need-based aid:*** $2082. ***Average indebtedness upon graduation:*** $26,212.

APPLYING
Standardized Tests *Required:* SAT or ACT (for admission).

Options: electronic application, deferred entrance.

Application fee: $45.

Required: high school transcript.

CONTACT
University of Nebraska at Omaha, 6001 Dodge Street, Omaha, NE 68182. *Phone:* 402-554-3520. *Toll-free phone:* 800-858-8648.

University of Nebraska–Lincoln

Lincoln, Nebraska

http://www.unl.edu/

- **State-supported** university, founded 1869, part of University of Nebraska System
- **Urban** 622-acre campus with easy access to Omaha
- **Endowment** $1.5 billion
- **Coed** 19,979 undergraduate students, 93% full-time, 47% women, 53% men
- **Moderately difficult** entrance level, 70% of applicants were admitted

UNDERGRAD STUDENTS

18,660 full-time, 1,319 part-time. Students come from 51 states and territories; 107 other countries; 21% are from out of state; 3% Black or African American, non-Hispanic/Latino; 5% Hispanic/Latino; 2% Asian, non-Hispanic/Latino; 0.1% Native Hawaiian or other Pacific Islander, non-Hispanic/Latino; 0.2% American Indian or Alaska Native, non-Hispanic/Latino; 3% Two or more races, non-Hispanic/Latino; 2% Race/ethnicity unknown; 8% international; 5% transferred in; 43% live on campus.

Freshmen

Admission: 11,865 applied, 8,293 admitted, 4,652 enrolled. ***Average high school GPA:*** 3.52. ***Test scores:*** SAT critical reading scores over 500: 75%; SAT math scores over 500: 80%; ACT scores over 18: 98%; SAT critical reading scores over 600: 41%; SAT math scores over 600: 49%; ACT scores over 24: 64%; SAT critical reading scores over 700: 12%; SAT math scores over 700: 18%; ACT scores over 30: 19%.

Retention: 84% of full-time freshmen returned.

FACULTY

Total: 1,101, 98% full-time, 94% with terminal degrees.

Student/faculty ratio: 21:1.

ACADEMICS

Calendar: semesters. *Degrees:* bachelor's, master's, doctoral, post-master's, and postbachelor's certificates.

Special study options: accelerated degree program, adult/continuing education programs, advanced placement credit, cooperative education, distance learning, double majors, English as a second language, honors programs, independent study, internships, off-campus study, part-time degree program, services for LD students, student-designed majors, study abroad, summer session for credit. ***ROTC:*** Army (b), Navy (b), Air Force (b).

Unusual degree programs: BS in Design/ Master of Architecture.

Computers: 650 computers/terminals are available on campus for general student use. Students can access the following: campus intranet, computer help desk, free student e-mail accounts, online (class) grades, online (class) registration, online (class) schedules. Campuswide network is available. 100% of college-owned or -operated housing units are wired for high-speed Internet access. Wireless service is available via entire campus.

STUDENT LIFE

Housing options: on-campus residence required for freshman year; coed, women-only, cooperative, special housing for students with disabilities. Campus housing is university owned. Freshman campus housing is guaranteed.

Activities and organizations: drama/theater group, student-run newspaper, radio station, choral group, marching band, Student Alumni Association, University Ambassadors, University Program Council, Golden Key Honor Society, ASUN (Association of Students of the University of Nebraska, student body government), national fraternities, national sororities.

Athletics Member NCAA. All Division I except football (Division I-A). ***Intercollegiate sports:*** baseball M(s), basketball M(s)/W(s), bowling W(s), cross-country running M(s)/W(s), golf M(s)/W(s), gymnastics M(s)/W(s), riflery W(s), soccer W(s), softball W(s), swimming and diving W(s), tennis M(s)/W(s), track and field M(s)/W(s), volleyball W(s), wrestling M(s). ***Intramural sports:*** badminton M/W, baseball M(c)/W(c), basketball M/W, bowling M(c)/W, crew M(c)/W(c), cross-country running M(c)/W(c), golf M/W, ice hockey M(c)/W(c), lacrosse M(c)/W(c), racquetball M/W, riflery M(c)/W(c), rock climbing M(c)/W(c), rugby M(c)/W(c), soccer M(c)/W(c), softball M(c)/W(c), swimming and diving M(c)/W(c), table tennis M(c)/W(c), tennis M(c)/W(c), ultimate Frisbee M(c)/W(c), volleyball M(c)/W(c), water polo M(c)/W(c), weight lifting M/W, wrestling M/W.

Campus security: 24-hour emergency response devices and patrols, controlled dormitory access.

Student services: health clinic, personal/psychological counseling, women's center, legal services.

COSTS & FINANCIAL AID

Costs (2014–15) ***Tuition:*** state resident $6480 full-time, $216 per credit hour part-time; nonresident $20,400 full-time, $680 per credit hour part-time. Full-time tuition and fees vary according to course load, program, and reciprocity agreements. Part-time tuition and fees vary according to course load, program, and reciprocity agreements. ***Required fees:*** $1590 full-time, $13 per credit hour part-time, $340 per term part-time. ***Room and board:*** $9961. Room and board charges vary according to board plan and housing facility. ***Payment plan:*** installment. ***Waivers:*** employees or children of employees.

Financial Aid Of all full-time matriculated undergraduates who enrolled in 2013, 11,180 applied for aid, 8,511 were judged to have need, 1,330 had their need fully met. 1,481 Federal Work-Study jobs (averaging $2234). In 2013, 1107 non-need-based awards were made. ***Average percent of need met:*** 77. ***Average financial aid package:*** $12,825. ***Average need-based loan:*** $4196. ***Average need-based gift aid:*** $7097. ***Average non-need-based aid:*** $6399. ***Average indebtedness upon graduation:*** $23,395.

APPLYING

Standardized Tests *Required:* SAT or ACT (for admission). *Recommended:* ACT (for admission).

Options: electronic application.

Application fee: $45.

Required: high school transcript. ***Required for some:*** 20 or higher on ACT or 950 or higher on SAT reading and math or rank in upper 50% of high school class.

Application deadlines: 5/1 (freshmen), 5/1 (out-of-state freshmen), 5/1 (transfers).

Notification: continuous (freshmen), continuous (out-of-state freshmen), continuous (transfers).

CONTACT

Ms. Amber Hunter, Associate Dean - Enrollment Management, University of Nebraska–Lincoln, 1410 Q Street, Lincoln, NE 68588-0417. *Phone:* 402-472-2023. *Toll-free phone:* 800-742-8800. *Fax:* 402-472-0670. *E-mail:* admissions@unl.edu.

Wayne State College

Wayne, Nebraska

http://www.wsc.edu/

- **State-supported** comprehensive, founded 1910, part of Nebraska State College System
- **Small-town** 128-acre campus
- **Endowment** $17.3 million
- **Coed** 2,969 undergraduate students, 91% full-time, 57% women, 43% men
- **Noncompetitive** entrance level, 100% of applicants were admitted

UNDERGRAD STUDENTS

2,693 full-time, 276 part-time. Students come from 22 states and territories; 15 other countries; 12% are from out of state; 3% Black or African American, non-Hispanic/Latino; 7% Hispanic/Latino; 0.6% Asian, non-Hispanic/Latino; 0.1% Native Hawaiian or other Pacific Islander, non-Hispanic/Latino; 0.8% American Indian or Alaska Native, non-Hispanic/Latino; 2% Two or more races, non-Hispanic/Latino; 5% Race/ethnicity unknown; 0.4% international; 8% transferred in; 47% live on campus.

Freshmen

Admission: 2,060 applied, 2,060 admitted, 685 enrolled. ***Average high school GPA:*** 3.24. ***Test scores:*** ACT scores over 18: 81%; ACT scores over 24: 32%; ACT scores over 30: 3%.

Retention: 68% of full-time freshmen returned.

FACULTY
Total: 220, 57% full-time, 53% with terminal degrees.
Student/faculty ratio: 19:1.

ACADEMICS
Calendar: semesters. *Degrees:* bachelor's, master's, and post-master's certificates.
Special study options: adult/continuing education programs, advanced placement credit, cooperative education, distance learning, double majors, honors programs, independent study, internships, off-campus study, part-time degree program, services for LD students, student-designed majors, study abroad, summer session for credit. ***ROTC:*** Army (b).
Computers: 365 computers/terminals are available on campus for general student use. Students can access the following: campus intranet, computer help desk, free student e-mail accounts, online (class) grades, online (class) registration, online (class) schedules. Campuswide network is available. 100% of college-owned or -operated housing units are wired for high-speed Internet access. Wireless service is available via classrooms, computer centers, computer labs, learning centers, libraries, student centers.

STUDENT LIFE
Housing options: on-campus residence required for freshman year; coed. Campus housing is university owned. Freshman campus housing is guaranteed.
Activities and organizations: drama/theater group, student-run newspaper, radio and television station, choral group, marching band, national fraternities, national sororities.
Athletics Member NCAA. All Division II. ***Intercollegiate sports:*** baseball M(s), basketball M(s)/W(s), cheerleading M(c)/W(c), cross-country running M(s)/W(s), football M(s), golf M(s)/W(s), rugby M(c)/W(c), soccer M(c)/W(s), softball W(s), track and field M(s)/W(s), volleyball W(s), wrestling M(c). ***Intramural sports:*** archery M/W, badminton M/W, basketball M/W, bowling M/W, football M/W, golf M/W, racquetball M/W, softball M/W, swimming and diving M/W, table tennis M/W, tennis M/W, track and field M/W, volleyball M/W, weight lifting M/W, wrestling M.
Campus security: 24-hour emergency response devices and patrols, student patrols, late-night transport/escort service, controlled dormitory access.
Student services: health clinic, personal/psychological counseling.

COSTS & FINANCIAL AID
Costs (2014–15) ***Tuition:*** state resident $4200 full-time, $140 per credit hour part-time; nonresident $8400 full-time, $280 per credit hour part-time. Full-time tuition and fees vary according to course level and course load. Part-time tuition and fees vary according to course level and course load. ***Required fees:*** $1404 full-time, $56 per credit hour part-time. ***Room and board:*** $6420; room only: $3120. Room and board charges vary according to board plan and housing facility. ***Payment plan:*** installment. ***Waivers:*** employees or children of employees.
Financial Aid Of all full-time matriculated undergraduates who enrolled in 2014, 2,346 applied for aid, 1,826 were judged to have need, 722 had their need fully met. In 2014, 183 non-need-based awards were made. ***Average percent of need met:*** 56. ***Average financial aid package:*** $8034. ***Average need-based loan:*** $3892. ***Average need-based gift aid:*** $4381. ***Average non-need-based aid:*** $2768.

APPLYING
Standardized Tests *Recommended:* SAT or ACT (for admission).
Options: electronic application, deferred entrance.
Required: high school transcript.
Application deadlines: rolling (freshmen), rolling (out-of-state freshmen), rolling (transfers).
Notification: continuous (freshmen), continuous (out-of-state freshmen), continuous (transfers).

CONTACT
Mr. Kevin Halle, Director of Admissions, Wayne State College, 1111 Main Street, Wayne, NE 68787. *Phone:* 402-375-7234. *Toll-free phone:* 866-WSC-CATS. *Fax:* 402-375-7204. *E-mail:* admit1@wsc.edu.

Wright Career College
Omaha, Nebraska
http://www.wrightcc.edu/

- **Proprietary** primarily 2-year, founded 2011
- **Suburban** campus with easy access to Omaha
- **Coed**
- **Noncompetitive** entrance level

ACADEMICS
Degrees: diplomas, associate, and bachelor's.

STUDENT LIFE
Housing options: college housing not available.

CONTACT
Wright Career College, 3000 S. 84th Street, Omaha, NE 68124. *Phone:* 402-514-2500. *Toll-free phone:* 800-555-4003. *E-mail:* info@wrightcc.edu.

NEVADA

The Art Institute of Las Vegas
Henderson, Nevada
http://www.artinstitutes.edu/lasvegas/

- **Proprietary** 4-year, founded 2002, part of Education Management Corporation
- **Suburban** campus
- **Coed**

ACADEMICS
Calendar: quarters. *Degrees:* diplomas, associate, and bachelor's.

CONTACT
The Art Institute of Las Vegas, 2350 Corporate Circle Drive, Henderson, NV 89074. *Phone:* 702-369-9944. *Toll-free phone:* 800-833-2678.

DeVry University
Henderson, Nevada
http://www.devry.edu/

- **Proprietary** comprehensive
- **Coed**

ACADEMICS
Calendar: semesters. *Degrees:* associate, bachelor's, and master's.

STUDENT LIFE
Housing options: college housing not available.

COSTS & FINANCIAL AID
Costs (2014–15) ***Tuition:*** $17,052 full-time, $609 per credit hour part-time. ***Required fees:*** $80 full-time.
Financial Aid Of all full-time matriculated undergraduates who enrolled in 2007, 32 applied for aid, 32 were judged to have need, 1 had their need fully met. ***Average percent of need met:*** 36. ***Average financial aid package:*** $10,877. ***Average need-based loan:*** $8938. ***Average need-based gift aid:*** $5641. ***Average indebtedness upon graduation:*** $62,400.

CONTACT
Admissions Office, DeVry University, 2490 Paseo Verde Parkway, Suite 150, Henderson, NV 89074-7120. *Phone:* 702-933-9700. *Toll-free phone:* 866-338-7941.

Great Basin College

Elko, Nevada

http://www.gbcnv.edu/

- **State-supported** primarily 2-year, founded 1967, part of Nevada System of Higher Education
- **Small-town** 45-acre campus
- **Endowment** $246,000
- **Coed** 3,128 undergraduate students, 31% full-time, 65% women, 35% men
- **Noncompetitive** entrance level

UNDERGRAD STUDENTS

976 full-time, 2,152 part-time. 6% are from out of state; 2% Black or African American, non-Hispanic/Latino; 16% Hispanic/Latino; 2% Asian, non-Hispanic/Latino; 0.8% Native Hawaiian or other Pacific Islander, non-Hispanic/Latino; 3% American Indian or Alaska Native, non-Hispanic/Latino; 2% Two or more races, non-Hispanic/Latino; 5% Race/ethnicity unknown; 0.1% international; 5% transferred in; 4% live on campus.

Freshmen

Admission: 436 enrolled.

Retention: 62% of full-time freshmen returned.

FACULTY

Total: 183, 34% full-time.

Student/faculty ratio: 24:1.

ACADEMICS

Calendar: semesters. *Degrees:* certificates, associate, bachelor's, and postbachelor's certificates.

Special study options: academic remediation for entering students, accelerated degree program, adult/continuing education programs, cooperative education, distance learning, double majors, English as a second language, external degree program, independent study, off-campus study, part-time degree program, services for LD students, summer session for credit.

Computers: 95 computers/terminals are available on campus for general student use. Students can access the following: computer help desk, free student e-mail accounts, online (class) grades, online (class) registration. Campuswide network is available. 100% of college-owned or -operated housing units are wired for high-speed Internet access. Wireless service is available via classrooms, computer centers, computer labs, learning centers, libraries, student centers.

STUDENT LIFE

Housing options: coed, special housing for students with disabilities. Campus housing is university owned.

Activities and organizations: Student Nurses Organization, Housing Central, Skills USA, Agriculture Student Organization, Colleges Against Cancer.

Athletics ***Intramural sports:*** rock climbing M/W, volleyball M/W, weight lifting M/W.

Campus security: late-night transport/escort service, evening patrols by trained security personnel.

Student services: personal/psychological counseling.

COSTS & FINANCIAL AID

Costs (2015–16) ***Tuition:*** state resident $2640 full-time, $88 per credit part-time; nonresident $9285 full-time. Full-time tuition and fees vary according to course level, degree level, and reciprocity agreements. Part-time tuition and fees vary according to course level, degree level, and reciprocity agreements. ***Required fees:*** $165 full-time, $6 per credit part-time. ***Payment plan:*** deferred payment. ***Waivers:*** employees or children of employees.

Financial Aid Of all full-time matriculated undergraduates who enrolled in 2013, 35 Federal Work-Study jobs (averaging $1000). 50 state and other part-time jobs (averaging $1800).

APPLYING

Options: electronic application, early admission, deferred entrance.

Application fee: $10.

Application deadlines: rolling (freshmen), rolling (out-of-state freshmen), rolling (transfers).

Notification: continuous (freshmen), continuous (out-of-state freshmen), continuous (transfers).

CONTACT

Ms. Jan King, Director of Admissions and Registrar, Great Basin College, 1500 College Parkway, Elko, NV 89801. *Phone:* 775-753-2102.

ITT Technical Institute

Henderson, Nevada

http://www.itt-tech.edu/

- **Proprietary** primarily 2-year, founded 1997, part of ITT Educational Services, Inc.
- **Coed**
- **Minimally difficult** entrance level

ACADEMICS

Degrees: associate and bachelor's.

STUDENT LIFE

Housing options: college housing not available.

FINANCIAL AID

Financial Aid Of all full-time matriculated undergraduates who enrolled in 2013, 6 Federal Work-Study jobs (averaging $5000).

CONTACT

Director of Recruitment, ITT Technical Institute, 2300 Corporate Circle, Suite 150, Henderson, NV 89074. *Phone:* 702-558-5404. *Toll-free phone:* 800-488-8459.

ITT Technical Institute

North Las Vegas, Nevada

http://www.itt-tech.edu/

- **Proprietary** primarily 2-year, part of ITT Educational Services, Inc.
- **Coed**

ACADEMICS

Calendar: quarters. *Degrees:* associate and bachelor's.

CONTACT

Director of Recruitment, ITT Technical Institute, 3825 W. Cheyenne Avenue, Suite 600, North Las Vegas, NV 89032. *Phone:* 702-240-0967. *Toll-free phone:* 877-832-8442.

Sierra Nevada College

Incline Village, Nevada

http://www.sierranevada.edu/

- **Independent** comprehensive, founded 1969
- **Small-town** 20-acre campus with easy access to Reno
- **Coed**
- **Moderately difficult** entrance level

FACULTY

Student/faculty ratio: 11:1.

ACADEMICS

Calendar: semesters. *Degrees:* certificates, diplomas, bachelor's, and master's.

STUDENT LIFE

Housing options: on-campus residence required through sophomore year; coed, special housing for students with disabilities. Campus housing is university owned. Freshman campus housing is guaranteed.

Activities and organizations: choral group, Film Club, International Club, Sustainability Club, Rock Climbing Club, First Generation Club.

Campus security: 24-hour emergency response devices and patrols, student patrols, controlled dormitory access.

COSTS

Costs (2014–15) ***Comprehensive fee:*** $41,215 includes full-time tuition ($28,170), mandatory fees ($979), and room and board ($12,066). Full-time tuition and fees vary according to course load and program. Part-time tuition: $1198 per credit hour. Part-time tuition and fees vary according to course load and program. ***College room only:*** $5900. Room and board charges vary according to board plan.

APPLYING
Standardized Tests *Required:* SAT or ACT (for admission).
Options: electronic application, early action, deferred entrance.
Required: high school transcript, minimum 2.6 GPA. ***Required for some:*** 1 letter of recommendation. ***Recommended:*** essay or personal statement, interview.

CONTACT
Ms. Julie Hernandez, Sierra Nevada College, 999 Tahoe Boulevard, Incline Village, NV 89451. *Phone:* 866-412-4636. *Fax:* 775-831-6223. *E-mail:* admissions@sierranevada.edu.

University of Nevada, Las Vegas

Las Vegas, Nevada

http://www.unlv.edu/

- **State-supported** university, founded 1957, part of Nevada System of Higher Education
- **Urban** 358-acre campus with easy access to Las Vegas
- **Endowment** $214.7 million
- **Coed** 23,813 undergraduate students, 73% full-time, 55% women, 45% men
- **Moderately difficult** entrance level, 87% of applicants were admitted

UNDERGRAD STUDENTS
17,444 full-time, 6,369 part-time. Students come from 59 other countries; 13% are from out of state; 8% Black or African American, non-Hispanic/Latino; 25% Hispanic/Latino; 15% Asian, non-Hispanic/Latino; 1% Native Hawaiian or other Pacific Islander, non-Hispanic/Latino; 0.3% American Indian or Alaska Native, non-Hispanic/Latino; 9% Two or more races, non-Hispanic/Latino; 1% Race/ethnicity unknown; 4% international; 10% transferred in; 7% live on campus.

Freshmen
Admission: 7,408 applied, 6,437 admitted, 3,865 enrolled. ***Average high school GPA:*** 3.24. ***Test scores:*** SAT critical reading scores over 500: 51%; SAT math scores over 500: 52%; SAT writing scores over 500: 38%; ACT scores over 18: 84%; SAT critical reading scores over 600: 12%; SAT math scores over 600: 15%; SAT writing scores over 600: 8%; ACT scores over 24: 32%; SAT critical reading scores over 700: 1%; SAT math scores over 700: 2%; SAT writing scores over 700: 1%; ACT scores over 30: 4%.
Retention: 77% of full-time freshmen returned.

FACULTY
Total: 1,444, 64% full-time.
Student/faculty ratio: 22:1.

ACADEMICS
Calendar: semesters. *Degrees:* certificates, bachelor's, master's, doctoral, post-master's, and postbachelor's certificates.
Special study options: academic remediation for entering students, adult/continuing education programs, advanced placement credit, cooperative education, distance learning, double majors, English as a second language, honors programs, independent study, internships, part-time degree program, services for LD students, study abroad, summer session for credit. ***ROTC:*** Army (b), Air Force (b).
Computers: Students can access the following: computer help desk, free student e-mail accounts, online (class) grades, online (class) registration, online (class) schedules. Campuswide network is available. 100% of college-owned or -operated housing units are wired for high-speed Internet access. Wireless service is available via entire campus.

STUDENT LIFE
Housing options: coed, special housing for students with disabilities. Campus housing is university owned. Freshman applicants given priority for college housing.
Activities and organizations: drama/theater group, student-run newspaper, radio and television station, choral group, marching band, national fraternities, national sororities.
Athletics Member NCAA. All Division I except football (Division I-A). ***Intercollegiate sports:*** baseball M(s), basketball M(s)/W(s), cheerleading M(s)/W(s), cross-country running W(s), golf M(s), soccer M(s)/W(s), softball W(s), swimming and diving M(s)/W(s), tennis M(s)/W(s), track and field W(s), volleyball W(s). ***Intramural sports:*** badminton M/W, basketball M/W, bowling M/W, football M/W, golf M/W, racquetball M/W, soccer M/W, softball M/W, swimming and diving M/W, tennis M/W, volleyball M/W.
Campus security: 24-hour emergency response devices and patrols, late-night transport/escort service, controlled dormitory access.
Student services: health clinic, personal/psychological counseling, women's center, legal services.

COSTS & FINANCIAL AID
Costs (2014–15) ***One-time required fee:*** $120. ***Tuition:*** state resident $6044 full-time, $192 per credit hour part-time; nonresident $19,954 full-time, $402 per credit hour part-time. Full-time tuition and fees vary according to course level, program, and reciprocity agreements. Part-time tuition and fees vary according to course level, program, and reciprocity agreements. ***Required fees:*** $546 full-time, $10 per credit hour part-time, $273 per term part-time. ***Room and board:*** $10,730; room only: $5880. Room and board charges vary according to board plan. ***Payment plan:*** deferred payment. ***Waivers:*** employees or children of employees.
Financial Aid Of all full-time matriculated undergraduates who enrolled in 2012, 11,049 applied for aid, 9,773 were judged to have need, 1,085 had their need fully met. In 2012, 789 non-need-based awards were made. ***Average percent of need met:*** 59. ***Average financial aid package:*** $9320. ***Average need-based loan:*** $4216. ***Average need-based gift aid:*** $4735. ***Average non-need-based aid:*** $3103. ***Average indebtedness upon graduation:*** $21,126.

APPLYING
Standardized Tests *Required:* SAT or ACT (for admission).
Options: electronic application, early admission, deferred entrance.
Application fee: $60.
Required: high school transcript, minimum 3.0 GPA. ***Required for some:*** 2 letters of recommendation.
Application deadlines: 7/1 (freshmen), 7/1 (transfers).
Notification: continuous (freshmen), continuous (transfers).

CONTACT
Director of Admissions, University of Nevada, Las Vegas, 4505 Maryland Parkway, Box 451021, Las Vegas, NV 89154-1021. *Phone:* 702-774-8658. *Fax:* 702-774-8008. *E-mail:* admissions@unlv.edu.

University of Nevada, Reno

Reno, Nevada

http://www.unr.edu/

- **State-supported** university, founded 1874, part of Nevada System of Higher Education
- **Urban** 200-acre campus
- **Endowment** $277.6 million
- **Coed** 16,839 undergraduate students, 83% full-time, 52% women, 48% men
- **Moderately difficult** entrance level, 84% of applicants were admitted

UNDERGRAD STUDENTS
13,999 full-time, 2,840 part-time. Students come from 48 states and territories; 50 other countries; 27% are from out of state; 4% Black or African American, non-Hispanic/Latino; 18% Hispanic/Latino; 7% Asian, non-Hispanic/Latino; 0.5% Native Hawaiian or other Pacific Islander, non-Hispanic/Latino; 0.7% American Indian or Alaska Native, non-Hispanic/Latino; 6% Two or more races, non-Hispanic/Latino; 0.4% Race/ethnicity unknown; 1% international; 8% transferred in; 17% live on campus.

Freshmen
Admission: 8,832 applied, 7,408 admitted, 3,283 enrolled. ***Average high school GPA:*** 3.37. ***Test scores:*** SAT critical reading scores over 500: 68%; SAT math scores over 500: 72%; SAT writing scores over 500: 58%; ACT scores over 18: 93%; SAT critical reading scores over 600: 23%; SAT math scores over 600: 27%; SAT writing scores over 600: 16%; ACT scores over 24: 45%; SAT critical reading scores over 700: 3%; SAT math scores over 700: 4%; SAT writing scores over 700: 2%; ACT scores over 30: 7%.
Retention: 82% of full-time freshmen returned.

FACULTY
Total: 1,041, 56% full-time, 63% with terminal degrees.
Student/faculty ratio: 22:1.

ACADEMICS
Calendar: semesters. *Degrees:* certificates, bachelor's, master's, doctoral, and postbachelor's certificates.
Special study options: academic remediation for entering students, adult/continuing education programs, advanced placement credit, distance learning, double majors, English as a second language, honors programs, independent study, internships, off-campus study, part-time degree program, services for LD students, study abroad, summer session for credit. ***ROTC:*** Army (b).
Unusual degree programs: 3-2 biotechnology.
Computers: Students can access the following: computer help desk, free student e-mail accounts, online (class) grades, online (class) registration, online (class) schedules. Campuswide network is available. 100% of college-owned or -operated housing units are wired for high-speed Internet access. Wireless service is available via entire campus.

STUDENT LIFE
Housing options: coed, men-only, women-only, special housing for students with disabilities. Campus housing is university owned. Freshman applicants given priority for college housing.
Activities and organizations: drama/theater group, student-run newspaper, radio station, choral group, marching band, Intervarsity Christian Fellowship, Student Ambassadors, Young Democrats, Asian American Association, Blue Crew, national fraternities, national sororities.
Athletics Member NCAA. All Division I except football (Division I-A). ***Intercollegiate sports:*** baseball M(s), basketball M(s)/W(s), cheerleading M(c)/W(c), cross-country running W(s), golf M(s)/W(s), riflery M(s)/W(s), soccer W(s), softball W(s), swimming and diving W(s), tennis M(s)/W(s), track and field W(s), volleyball W(s). ***Intramural sports:*** basketball M/W, bowling M/W, cross-country running M/W, equestrian sports M/W, football M, golf M/W, racquetball M/W, rock climbing M/W, rugby M/W, skiing (cross-country) M/W, skiing (downhill) M/W, soccer M/W, softball M/W, swimming and diving M/W, table tennis M/W, tennis M/W, track and field M/W, ultimate Frisbee M/W, volleyball M/W, water polo M/W.
Campus security: 24-hour emergency response devices and patrols, late-night transport/escort service, controlled dormitory access.
Student services: health clinic, personal/psychological counseling, women's center, legal services.

COSTS & FINANCIAL AID
Costs (2015–16) ***Tuition:*** $211 per credit hour part-time; state resident $6338 full-time; nonresident $20,248 full-time. Full-time tuition and fees vary according to course level, course load, degree level, and program. Part-time tuition and fees vary according to course level, course load, degree level, and program. ***Required fees:*** $534 full-time. ***Room and board:*** $10,868; room only: $6100. Room and board charges vary according to board plan and housing facility. ***Waivers:*** senior citizens and employees or children of employees.
Financial Aid Of all full-time matriculated undergraduates who enrolled in 2013, 8,524 applied for aid, 6,915 were judged to have need, 742 had their need fully met. In 2013, 3086 non-need-based awards were made. ***Average percent of need met:*** 62. ***Average financial aid package:*** $9160. ***Average need-based loan:*** $4435. ***Average need-based gift aid:*** $5127. ***Average non-need-based aid:*** $2569. ***Average indebtedness upon graduation:*** $22,500.

APPLYING
Standardized Tests *Required:* SAT or ACT (for admission).
Options: electronic application, early admission, deferred entrance.
Application fee: $60.
Required: high school transcript, minimum 3.0 GPA.
Application deadlines: 5/1 (freshmen), 5/1 (out-of-state freshmen), 7/1 (transfers).
Notification: continuous (freshmen), continuous (out-of-state freshmen), continuous (transfers).

CONTACT
Dr. Steve Maples, Director of Undergraduate Admissions, University of Nevada, Reno, Mail Stop 120, Reno, NV 89557. *Phone:* 775-784-4700. *Toll-free phone:* 866-263-8232. *Fax:* 775-784-4283. *E-mail:* asknevada@unr.edu.

Western Nevada College
Carson City, Nevada
http://www.wnc.edu/

- **State-supported** primarily 2-year, founded 1971, part of Nevada System of Higher Education
- **Small-town** 200-acre campus
- **Endowment** $257,000
- **Coed** 4,032 undergraduate students, 35% full-time, 59% women, 41% men
- **Noncompetitive** entrance level

UNDERGRAD STUDENTS
1,429 full-time, 2,603 part-time. 3% are from out of state; 1% Black or African American, non-Hispanic/Latino; 18% Hispanic/Latino; 2% Asian, non-Hispanic/Latino; 0.7% Native Hawaiian or other Pacific Islander, non-Hispanic/Latino; 3% American Indian or Alaska Native, non-Hispanic/Latino; 3% Two or more races, non-Hispanic/Latino; 4% Race/ethnicity unknown.

Freshmen
Admission: 855 enrolled.
Retention: 62% of full-time freshmen returned.

FACULTY
Total: 270, 16% full-time, 13% with terminal degrees.
Student/faculty ratio: 29:1.

ACADEMICS
Calendar: semesters. *Degrees:* certificates, associate, and bachelor's.
Special study options: academic remediation for entering students, adult/continuing education programs, advanced placement credit, cooperative education, distance learning, double majors, English as a second language, honors programs, independent study, internships, part-time degree program, services for LD students, summer session for credit.
Computers: 568 computers/terminals are available on campus for general student use. Students can access the following: computer help desk, free student e-mail accounts, online (class) grades, online (class) registration, online (class) schedules. Campuswide network is available. Wireless service is available via entire campus.

STUDENT LIFE
Housing options: college housing not available.
Activities and organizations: drama/theater group, choral group, Wildcat Productions, Lone Mountain Writers, Art Club, ASL Club, Latino Student Club.
Athletics Member NJCAA. ***Intercollegiate sports:*** baseball M, softball W.
Campus security: late-night transport/escort service.
Student services: personal/psychological counseling.

COSTS & FINANCIAL AID
Costs (2015–16) ***Tuition:*** state resident $2640 full-time, $88 per credit part-time; nonresident $9285 full-time. Full-time tuition and fees vary according to course level, degree level, and reciprocity agreements. Part-time tuition and fees vary according to course level, degree level, and reciprocity agreements. ***Required fees:*** $165 full-time, $6 per credit part-time. ***Payment plan:*** deferred payment. ***Waivers:*** employees or children of employees.
Financial Aid Of all full-time matriculated undergraduates who enrolled in 2012, 922 applied for aid, 835 were judged to have need, 70 had their need fully met. In 2012, 11 non-need-based awards were made. ***Average percent of need met:*** 44. ***Average financial aid package:*** $6417. ***Average need-based loan:*** $3749. ***Average need-based gift aid:*** $1043. ***Average non-need-based aid:*** $1043.

APPLYING
Standardized Tests *Recommended:* SAT or ACT (for admission).
Options: early admission.

Application fee: $15.

Required for some: high school transcript.

Application deadlines: rolling (freshmen), rolling (transfers).

CONTACT

Admissions and Records, Western Nevada College, 2201 West College Parkway, Carson City, NV 89703. *Phone:* 775-445-2377. *Fax:* 775-445-3147. *E-mail:* wncc_aro@wncc.edu.

NEW HAMPSHIRE

★ Colby-Sawyer College

New London, New Hampshire

http://www.colby-sawyer.edu/

- **Independent** 4-year, founded 1837
- **Small-town** 200-acre campus
- **Endowment** $39.7 million
- **Coed** 1,369 undergraduate students, 96% full-time, 69% women, 31% men
- **Moderately difficult** entrance level, 91% of applicants were admitted

UNDERGRAD STUDENTS

1,316 full-time, 53 part-time. Students come from 28 states and territories; 38 other countries; 66% are from out of state; 6% Black or African American, non-Hispanic/Latino; 3% Hispanic/Latino; 2% Asian, non-Hispanic/Latino; 0.1% Native Hawaiian or other Pacific Islander, non-Hispanic/Latino; 0.2% American Indian or Alaska Native, non-Hispanic/Latino; 0.5% Two or more races, non-Hispanic/Latino; 8% Race/ethnicity unknown; 10% international; 3% transferred in; 90% live on campus.

Freshmen

Admission: 2,933 applied, 2,656 admitted, 331 enrolled. ***Average high school GPA:*** 3.21.

Retention: 76% of full-time freshmen returned.

FACULTY

Total: 137, 59% full-time, 56% with terminal degrees.

Student/faculty ratio: 14:1.

ACADEMICS

Calendar: semesters. *Degrees:* certificates, associate, and bachelor's.

Special study options: accelerated degree program, advanced placement credit, distance learning, double majors, honors programs, independent study, internships, off-campus study, part-time degree program, services for LD students, student-designed majors, study abroad. ***ROTC:*** Army (c).

Computers: 180 computers/terminals and 1,200 ports are available on campus for general student use. Students can access the following: campus intranet, computer help desk, free student e-mail accounts, online (class) grades, online (class) registration, online (class) schedules, online bill payment, SmartCard (for use on campus and with selected local vendors) Learning Management Systems (Moodle), tutoring, reference librarians via chat, HelpDesk Ticket submission, e-databases/e-journals, disk storage space (Office365). Campuswide network is available. 100% of college-owned or -operated housing units are wired for high-speed Internet access. Wireless service is available via entire campus.

STUDENT LIFE

Housing options: on-campus residence required for freshman year; coed, women-only, special housing for students with disabilities. Campus housing is university owned and leased by the school. Freshman campus housing is guaranteed.

Activities and organizations: drama/theater group, student-run newspaper, choral group, Student Government Association, Dance Club, Campus Activities Board, Cross Cultural Club, Community Service Club.

Athletics Member NCAA. All Division III. ***Intercollegiate sports:*** baseball M, basketball M/W, cross-country running M/W, equestrian sports M/W, field hockey W, golf M(c)/W(c), ice hockey M(c)/W(c), lacrosse W, rugby M(c)/W(c), skiing (downhill) M/W, soccer M/W, softball W(c), swimming and diving M/W, tennis M/W, track and field M/W, volleyball W. ***Intramural sports:*** basketball M/W, cheerleading W(c), football M/W, golf M/W, lacrosse M(c), racquetball M/W, volleyball M/W.

Campus security: 24-hour emergency response devices and patrols, late-night transport/escort service, controlled dormitory access, Awareness seminars.

Student services: health clinic, personal/psychological counseling.

COSTS & FINANCIAL AID

Costs (2015–16) ***Tuition:*** $38,610 full-time, $1287 per credit part-time. Part-time tuition and fees vary according to course load. ***Room only:*** Room and board charges vary according to housing facility. ***Payment plan:*** installment. ***Waivers:*** employees or children of employees.

Financial Aid ***Financial aid deadline:*** 3/1.

APPLYING

Options: electronic application, early admission, early action, deferred entrance.

Application fee: $45.

Required: essay or personal statement, high school transcript, 1 letter of recommendation, Required college preparatory courses: 4 years of English, 3 years of math, 3 years of lab science, 3 years of social science and 2 years of the same language. ***Recommended:*** interview.

Application deadlines: 4/1 (freshmen), 8/1 (transfers), 12/1 (early action).

Notification: continuous until 1/1 (freshmen), continuous until 1/1 (transfers).

CONTACT

Mrs. Jaimee Hofstetter, Director of Enrollment Operations, Colby-Sawyer College, 541 Main Street, New London, NH 03257-4648. *Phone:* 603-526-3887. *Toll-free phone:* 800-272-1015. *Fax:* 603-526-3452. *E-mail:* admissions@colby-sawyer.edu.

Daniel Webster College

Nashua, New Hampshire

http://www.dwc.edu/

- **Independent** comprehensive, founded 1965
- **Suburban** 59-acre campus with easy access to Boston
- **Coed** 644 undergraduate students, 87% full-time, 18% women, 82% men
- **Moderately difficult** entrance level, 63% of applicants were admitted

UNDERGRAD STUDENTS

561 full-time, 83 part-time. Students come from 26 states and territories; 22 other countries; 55% are from out of state; 8% Black or African American, non-Hispanic/Latino; 6% Hispanic/Latino; 4% Asian, non-Hispanic/Latino; 0.2% Native Hawaiian or other Pacific Islander, non-Hispanic/Latino; 0.6% American Indian or Alaska Native, non-Hispanic/Latino; 4% Two or more races, non-Hispanic/Latino; 6% Race/ethnicity unknown; 0.2% international; 9% transferred in; 51% live on campus.

Freshmen

Admission: 698 applied, 439 admitted, 162 enrolled. ***Average high school GPA:*** 2.85.

Retention: 61% of full-time freshmen returned.

FACULTY

Total: 80, 25% full-time, 36% with terminal degrees.

Student/faculty ratio: 15:1.

ACADEMICS

Calendar: semesters. *Degrees:* bachelor's and master's.

Special study options: academic remediation for entering students, advanced placement credit, distance learning, double majors, independent study, internships, off-campus study, part-time degree program, summer session for credit. ***ROTC:*** Army (c), Navy (c), Air Force (b).

Computers: 50 computers/terminals and 535 ports are available on campus for general student use. Students can access the following: campus intranet, computer help desk, free student e-mail accounts, online (class) grades, online (class) registration, online (class) schedules. Campuswide network is available. 100% of college-owned or -operated housing units are wired for high-speed Internet access. Wireless service is available via entire campus.

A ★ indicates that the school has detailed information with a Premium Profile on Petersons.com.

STUDENT LIFE

Housing options: on-campus residence required through sophomore year; coed, men-only, women-only, special housing for students with disabilities. Campus housing is university owned. Freshman campus housing is guaranteed.

Activities and organizations: drama/theater group, choral group, Student Activity Board, Gaming Guild, SATCA (Student Air Traffic Controllers Association), AIAA (American Institute of Aeronautics and Astronautics), Culinary Club.

Athletics Member NCAA. All Division III. ***Intercollegiate sports:*** baseball M, basketball M/W, cross-country running M/W, field hockey W, golf M, ice hockey M/W, lacrosse M/W, soccer M/W, softball W, volleyball M/W, wrestling M. ***Intramural sports:*** basketball M/W, football M/W, ultimate Frisbee M/W, volleyball M/W.

Campus security: 24-hour emergency response devices and patrols, controlled dormitory access.

Student services: health clinic, personal/psychological counseling, legal services.

COSTS & FINANCIAL AID

Costs (2014–15) ***Comprehensive fee:*** $26,280 includes full-time tuition ($15,630) and room and board ($10,650). Part-time tuition: $521 per credit. ***College room only:*** $5226. Room and board charges vary according to board plan and housing facility. ***Payment plan:*** installment. ***Waivers:*** employees or children of employees.

Financial Aid Of all full-time matriculated undergraduates who enrolled in 2012, 464 applied for aid, 397 were judged to have need, 12 had their need fully met. In 2012, 6 non-need-based awards were made. ***Average percent of need met:*** 60. ***Average financial aid package:*** $9044. ***Average need-based loan:*** $4257. ***Average need-based gift aid:*** $4300. ***Average non-need-based aid:*** $8229. ***Average indebtedness upon graduation:*** $45,665.

APPLYING

Options: electronic application, early admission, deferred entrance.

Required: high school transcript. ***Required for some:*** appropriate math and science preparation for engineering and computer science majors. ***Recommended:*** minimum 2.5 GPA, interview.

Application deadlines: rolling (freshmen), rolling (out-of-state freshmen), rolling (transfers).

Notification: continuous (freshmen), continuous (out-of-state freshmen), continuous (transfers).

CONTACT

Mrs. Jennifer O'Neill, Manager of Recruitment, Daniel Webster College, 20 University Drive, Nashua, NH 03063-1300. *Phone:* 800-325-6876. *Toll-free phone:* 800-325-6876. *E-mail:* oneill@dwc.edu.

Dartmouth College

Hanover, New Hampshire

http://www.dartmouth.edu/

- **Independent** university, founded 1769
- **Small-town** 269-acre campus
- **Endowment** $4.5 billion
- **Coed** 4,289 undergraduate students, 99% full-time, 49% women, 51% men
- **Most difficult** entrance level, 12% of applicants were admitted

UNDERGRAD STUDENTS

4,228 full-time, 61 part-time. Students come from 52 states and territories; 69 other countries; 96% are from out of state; 7% Black or African American, non-Hispanic/Latino; 8% Hispanic/Latino; 14% Asian, non-Hispanic/Latino; 0.1% Native Hawaiian or other Pacific Islander, non-Hispanic/Latino; 2% American Indian or Alaska Native, non-Hispanic/Latino; 5% Two or more races, non-Hispanic/Latino; 9% Race/ethnicity unknown; 9% international; 0.3% transferred in; 88% live on campus.

Freshmen

Admission: 19,296 applied, 2,220 admitted, 1,152 enrolled. ***Test scores:*** SAT critical reading scores over 500: 99%; SAT math scores over 500: 100%; SAT writing scores over 500: 99%; SAT critical reading scores over 600: 93%; SAT math scores over 600: 95%; SAT writing scores over 600: 94%; SAT critical reading scores over 700: 70%; SAT math scores over 700: 71%; SAT writing scores over 700: 73%.

Retention: 99% of full-time freshmen returned.

FACULTY

Total: 748, 77% full-time, 87% with terminal degrees.

Student/faculty ratio: 8:1.

ACADEMICS

Calendar: quarters. *Degrees:* bachelor's, master's, and doctoral.

Special study options: advanced placement credit, double majors, honors programs, independent study, internships, off-campus study, services for LD students, student-designed majors, study abroad, summer session for credit. ***ROTC:*** Army (c).

Computers: 200 computers/terminals are available on campus for general student use. Students can access the following: campus intranet, computer help desk, free student e-mail accounts, online (class) grades, online (class) registration, online (class) schedules. Campuswide network is available. 100% of college-owned or -operated housing units are wired for high-speed Internet access. Wireless service is available via entire campus.

STUDENT LIFE

Housing options: on-campus residence required for freshman year; coed, cooperative. Campus housing is university owned. Freshman campus housing is guaranteed.

Activities and organizations: drama/theater group, student-run newspaper, radio and television station, choral group, marching band, Dartmouth Student Assembly, Dartmouth Outing Club, national fraternities, national sororities.

Athletics Member NCAA. All Division I except football (Division I-AA). ***Intercollegiate sports:*** badminton M(c)/W(c), baseball M, basketball M/W, cheerleading M(c)/W(c), crew M/W, cross-country running M/W, equestrian sports M/W, fencing M(c)/W(c), field hockey W, golf M/W, gymnastics M(c)/W(c), ice hockey M/W, lacrosse M/W, rugby M(c)/W(c), sailing M/W, skiing (cross-country) M/W, skiing (downhill) M/W, soccer M/W, softball W, squash M/W, swimming and diving M/W, table tennis M(c)/W(c), tennis M/W, track and field M/W, ultimate Frisbee M(c)/W(c), volleyball M(c)/W, water polo M(c)/W(c), wrestling M(c). ***Intramural sports:*** baseball M, basketball M/W, cross-country running M/W, football M/W, golf M/W, ice hockey M/W, lacrosse M/W, rugby M/W, skiing (cross-country) M/W, skiing (downhill) M/W, soccer M/W, softball M/W, squash M/W, swimming and diving M/W, table tennis M/W, tennis M/W, track and field M/W, volleyball M/W, water polo M/W, weight lifting M/W, wrestling M.

Campus security: 24-hour emergency response devices and patrols, student patrols, late-night transport/escort service, controlled dormitory access.

Student services: health clinic, personal/psychological counseling, women's center.

COSTS & FINANCIAL AID

Costs (2014–15) ***One-time required fee:*** $170. ***Comprehensive fee:*** $61,947 includes full-time tuition ($46,764), mandatory fees ($1344), and room and board ($13,839). ***College room only:*** $8286. Room and board charges vary according to board plan. ***Payment plans:*** tuition prepayment, installment.

Financial Aid Of all full-time matriculated undergraduates who enrolled in 2014, 2,379 applied for aid, 2,129 were judged to have need, 2,129 had their need fully met. 1,247 Federal Work-Study jobs (averaging $2136). 579 state and other part-time jobs (averaging $2178). ***Average percent of need met:*** 100. ***Average financial aid package:*** $45,359. ***Average need-based loan:*** $3951. ***Average need-based gift aid:*** $42,299. ***Average indebtedness upon graduation:*** $17,171. ***Financial aid deadline:*** 2/1.

APPLYING

Standardized Tests *Required:* SAT or ACT (for admission), SAT Subject Tests (for admission).

Options: electronic application, early admission, early decision, deferred entrance.

Application fee: $80.

Required: essay or personal statement, high school transcript, 2 letters of recommendation, peer evaluation. ***Recommended:*** interview.

Application deadlines: 1/1 (freshmen), 3/1 (transfers).

Early decision deadline: 11/1.

Notification: 4/1 (freshmen), 5/15 (transfers), 12/15 (early decision).

CONTACT
Maria Laskaris, Dean of Admissions and Financial Aid, Dartmouth College, 6016 McNutt Hall, Hanover, NH 03755. *Phone:* 603-646-2875. *E-mail:* admissions.reply@dartmouth.edu.

Franklin Pierce University

Rindge, New Hampshire

http://www.franklinpierce.edu/

- **Independent** university, founded 1962
- **Rural** 1000-acre campus
- **Endowment** $5.5 million
- **Coed** 1,671 undergraduate students, 88% full-time, 56% women, 44% men
- **Minimally difficult** entrance level, 84% of applicants were admitted

UNDERGRAD STUDENTS
1,465 full-time, 206 part-time. Students come from 40 states and territories; 7 other countries; 81% are from out of state; 4% Black or African American, non-Hispanic/Latino; 5% Hispanic/Latino; 0.9% Asian, non-Hispanic/Latino; 0.1% Native Hawaiian or other Pacific Islander, non-Hispanic/Latino; 0.2% American Indian or Alaska Native, non-Hispanic/Latino; 2% Two or more races, non-Hispanic/Latino; 12% Race/ethnicity unknown; 1% international; 2% transferred in; 85% live on campus.

Freshmen
Admission: 3,604 applied, 3,038 admitted, 450 enrolled. ***Average high school GPA:*** 2.8. ***Test scores:*** SAT critical reading scores over 500: 42%; SAT math scores over 500: 45%; SAT writing scores over 500: 41%; ACT scores over 18: 91%; SAT critical reading scores over 600: 6%; SAT math scores over 600: 8%; SAT writing scores over 600: 6%; ACT scores over 24: 19%; SAT math scores over 700: 1%; SAT writing scores over 700: 1%.
Retention: 67% of full-time freshmen returned.

FACULTY
Total: 334, 28% full-time.
Student/faculty ratio: 12:1.

ACADEMICS
Calendar: differs by branch and program. *Degrees:* certificates, associate, bachelor's, master's, doctoral, and postbachelor's certificates (profile does not reflect significant enrollment at 6 continuing education sites; master's degree is only offered at these sites).
Special study options: academic remediation for entering students, accelerated degree program, adult/continuing education programs, advanced placement credit, distance learning, double majors, English as a second language, external degree program, freshman honors college, honors programs, independent study, internships, off-campus study, part-time degree program, services for LD students, student-designed majors, study abroad, summer session for credit. ***ROTC:*** Army (c), Air Force (c).
Computers: Students can access the following: campus intranet, computer help desk, free student e-mail accounts, online (class) grades, online (class) registration, online (class) schedules. Campuswide network is available. 100% of college-owned or -operated housing units are wired for high-speed Internet access. Wireless service is available via classrooms, computer labs, libraries, student centers.

STUDENT LIFE
Housing options: on-campus residence required through senior year; coed. Campus housing is university owned. Freshman campus housing is guaranteed.
Activities and organizations: drama/theater group, student-run newspaper, radio and television station, choral group, Outing Club, WFPR Radio, Student Senate, Law Club, Business Club.
Athletics Member NCAA. All Division II. ***Intercollegiate sports:*** baseball M(s), basketball M(s)/W(s), crew M/W, cross-country running M/W, field hockey W(s), golf M, ice hockey M, lacrosse M/W, soccer M(s)/W(s), softball W(s), tennis M(s)/W(s), volleyball W(s). ***Intramural sports:*** baseball M, basketball M/W, cheerleading W(c), cross-country running M/W, fencing M(c)/W(c), field hockey W, football M, golf M, ice hockey M, lacrosse M/W, rugby M/W, soccer M/W, softball W, tennis M/W, volleyball M/W.
Campus security: 24-hour emergency response devices and patrols, student patrols, late-night transport/escort service, controlled dormitory access.
Student services: health clinic, personal/psychological counseling.

COSTS & FINANCIAL AID
Costs (2014–15) ***Comprehensive fee:*** $43,842 includes full-time tuition ($29,682), mandatory fees ($2100), and room and board ($12,060). Full-time tuition and fees vary according to course load, degree level, location, and program. Part-time tuition: $990 per credit hour. Part-time tuition and fees vary according to course load, degree level, location, and program. ***College room only:*** $7040. Room and board charges vary according to board plan, housing facility, and student level. ***Payment plan:*** installment. ***Waivers:*** senior citizens and employees or children of employees.
Financial Aid Of all full-time matriculated undergraduates who enrolled in 2013, 1,235 applied for aid, 1,139 were judged to have need, 232 had their need fully met. In 2013, 212 non-need-based awards were made. ***Average percent of need met:*** 73. ***Average financial aid package:*** $23,887. ***Average need-based loan:*** $4974. ***Average need-based gift aid:*** $19,445. ***Average non-need-based aid:*** $13,304. ***Average indebtedness upon graduation:*** $38,546.

APPLYING
Standardized Tests *Required:* SAT or ACT (for admission).
Options: electronic application, early admission, deferred entrance.
Application fee: $40.
Required: essay or personal statement, high school transcript, 1 letter of recommendation. ***Required for some:*** minimum 2.0 GPA. ***Recommended:*** minimum 2.2 GPA, interview.
Application deadlines: rolling (freshmen), rolling (out-of-state freshmen), rolling (transfers).
Notification: continuous (freshmen), continuous (out-of-state freshmen), continuous (transfers).

CONTACT
Office of Admissions, Franklin Pierce University, 40 University Drive, Rindge, NH 03461. *Phone:* 603-899-4050. *Toll-free phone:* 800-437-0048. *Fax:* 603-899-4394. *E-mail:* admissions@franklinpierce.edu.

Granite State College

Concord, New Hampshire

http://www.granite.edu/

- **State and locally supported** comprehensive, founded 1972, part of University System of New Hampshire
- **Suburban** campus
- **Endowment** $4.2 million
- **Coed** 1,870 undergraduate students, 56% full-time, 74% women, 26% men
- **Noncompetitive** entrance level, 100% of applicants were admitted

UNDERGRAD STUDENTS
1,046 full-time, 824 part-time. Students come from 35 states and territories; 11% are from out of state; 1% Black or African American, non-Hispanic/Latino; 2% Hispanic/Latino; 1% Asian, non-Hispanic/Latino; 0.1% Native Hawaiian or other Pacific Islander, non-Hispanic/Latino; 0.5% American Indian or Alaska Native, non-Hispanic/Latino; 2% Two or more races, non-Hispanic/Latino; 9% Race/ethnicity unknown; 0.1% international; 20% transferred in.

Freshmen
Admission: 253 applied, 253 admitted, 112 enrolled.
Retention: 74% of full-time freshmen returned.

FACULTY
Total: 202, 2% full-time, 37% with terminal degrees.
Student/faculty ratio: 13:1.

ACADEMICS
Calendar: trimesters. *Degrees:* associate, bachelor's, master's, and postbachelor's certificates (offers primarily part-time degree programs; courses offered at 50 locations in New Hampshire).

Special study options: academic remediation for entering students, accelerated degree program, adult/continuing education programs, advanced placement credit, cooperative education, distance learning, double majors, independent study, internships, off-campus study, part-time degree program, services for LD students, student-designed majors, summer session for credit. ***ROTC:*** Army (c), Air Force (c).

Computers: 139 computers/terminals are available on campus for general student use. Students can access the following: campus intranet, computer help desk, free student e-mail accounts, online (class) grades, online (class) registration, online (class) schedules. Campuswide network is available. Wireless service is available via entire campus.

STUDENT LIFE

Housing options: college housing not available.

Activities and organizations: Alumni Learner Association, Green Team.

Campus security: UNH Alert, a system that provides emergency notifications via text and voice messages.

COSTS

Costs (2014–15) ***Tuition:*** state resident $6840 full-time, $285 per credit part-time; nonresident $7560 full-time, $315 per credit part-time. ***Required fees:*** $225 full-time, $75 per term part-time. ***Payment plan:*** deferred payment. ***Waivers:*** senior citizens and employees or children of employees.

APPLYING

Options: electronic application.

Required for some: high school transcript, self-certify high school graduate or GED.

Application deadlines: rolling (freshmen), rolling (out-of-state freshmen), rolling (transfers).

Notification: continuous (freshmen), continuous (out-of-state freshmen), continuous (transfers).

CONTACT

Ms. Cortney Vachon, Associate Registrar, Granite State College, 25 Hall Street, Concord, NH 03301. *Phone:* 603-228-3000. *Toll-free phone:* 888-228-3000. *Fax:* 603-513-1386. *E-mail:* gsc.admissions@granite.edu.

Keene State College

Keene, New Hampshire

http://www.keene.edu/

- **State-supported** comprehensive, founded 1909, part of University System of New Hampshire
- **Small-town** 160-acre campus
- **Endowment** $29.4 million
- **Coed** 4,841 undergraduate students, 94% full-time, 57% women, 43% men
- **Moderately difficult** entrance level, 79% of applicants were admitted

UNDERGRAD STUDENTS

4,569 full-time, 272 part-time. Students come from 30 states and territories; 9 other countries; 54% are from out of state; 1% Black or African American, non-Hispanic/Latino; 3% Hispanic/Latino; 1% Asian, non-Hispanic/Latino; 0.2% American Indian or Alaska Native, non-Hispanic/Latino; 2% Two or more races, non-Hispanic/Latino; 9% Race/ethnicity unknown; 3% transferred in; 57% live on campus.

Freshmen

Admission: 6,484 applied, 5,096 admitted, 1,267 enrolled. ***Average high school GPA:*** 2.95. ***Test scores:*** SAT critical reading scores over 500: 43%; SAT math scores over 500: 44%; SAT writing scores over 500: 43%; SAT critical reading scores over 600: 8%; SAT math scores over 600: 7%; SAT writing scores over 600: 6%.

Retention: 77% of full-time freshmen returned.

ACADEMICS

Calendar: semesters. *Degrees:* certificates, bachelor's, master's, post-master's, and postbachelor's certificates.

Special study options: advanced placement credit, cooperative education, double majors, English as a second language, freshman honors college, honors programs, independent study, internships, off-campus study, part-time degree program, services for LD students, student-designed majors, study abroad, summer session for credit. ***ROTC:*** Army (c), Air Force (c).

Unusual degree programs: 3-2 engineering with Clarkson University, University of New Hampshire.

Computers: 600 computers/terminals are available on campus for general student use. Students can access the following: campus intranet, computer help desk, free student e-mail accounts, online (class) grades, online (class) registration, online (class) schedules. Campuswide network is available. 100% of college-owned or -operated housing units are wired for high-speed Internet access. Wireless service is available via entire campus.

STUDENT LIFE

Housing options: on-campus residence required through sophomore year; coed, women-only. Campus housing is university owned. Freshman campus housing is guaranteed.

Activities and organizations: drama/theater group, student-run newspaper, radio and television station, choral group, Social Activities Council, Ski & Snowboard Club, student government, Phi Sigma Sigma Sorority, Delta Phi Epsilon Sorority, national fraternities, national sororities.

Athletics Member NCAA. All Division III. ***Intercollegiate sports:*** baseball M, basketball M/W, cheerleading W, cross-country running M/W, field hockey W, ice hockey M(c)/W(c), lacrosse M/W, rugby M(c)/W(c), soccer M/W, softball W, swimming and diving M/W, track and field M/W, ultimate Frisbee M(c)/W(c), volleyball W. ***Intramural sports:*** badminton M/W, basketball M/W, bowling M/W, fencing M(c)/W(c), football M/W, racquetball M/W, skiing (downhill) M(c)/W(c), soccer M/W, softball M/W, table tennis M/W, tennis M/W, ultimate Frisbee M/W, volleyball M/W, water polo M/W, weight lifting M(c)/W(c).

Campus security: 24-hour emergency response devices and patrols, late-night transport/escort service, controlled dormitory access.

Student services: health clinic, personal/psychological counseling, women's center.

COSTS & FINANCIAL AID

Costs (2015–16) ***Tuition:*** state resident $10,410 full-time, $440 per credit hour part-time; nonresident $18,880 full-time, $790 per credit hour part-time. Part-time tuition and fees vary according to course load. ***Required fees:*** $2528 full-time, $101 per credit hour part-time. ***Room only:*** $9712. Room and board charges vary according to board plan and housing facility. ***Payment plan:*** installment. ***Waivers:*** senior citizens and employees or children of employees.

Financial Aid Of all full-time matriculated undergraduates who enrolled in 2013, 3,807 applied for aid, 3,015 were judged to have need, 337 had their need fully met. 1,324 Federal Work-Study jobs (averaging $2299). 721 state and other part-time jobs (averaging $1454). In 2013, 459 non-need-based awards were made. ***Average percent of need met:*** 61. ***Average financial aid package:*** $10,785. ***Average need-based loan:*** $4295. ***Average need-based gift aid:*** $6459. ***Average non-need-based aid:*** $3224. ***Average indebtedness upon graduation:*** $33,796. ***Financial aid deadline:*** 3/1.

APPLYING

Standardized Tests *Required:* SAT or ACT (for admission).

Options: electronic application, deferred entrance.

Application fee: $50.

Required: essay or personal statement, high school transcript, 1 letter of recommendation.

Application deadlines: 4/1 (freshmen), rolling (transfers).

Notification: continuous (freshmen), continuous (transfers).

CONTACT

Ms. Margaret Richmond, Director of Admissions, Keene State College, 229 Main Street, Keene, NH 03435-2604. *Phone:* 603-358-2273. *Toll-free phone:* 800-KSC-1909. *Fax:* 603-358-2767. *E-mail:* mrichmon@keene.edu.

New England College

Henniker, New Hampshire

http://www.nec.edu/

- **Independent** comprehensive, founded 1946
- **Small-town** 225-acre campus with easy access to Boston
- **Endowment** $11.9 million
- **Coed** 1,729 undergraduate students, 98% full-time, 57% women, 43% men
- **Minimally difficult** entrance level, 96% of applicants were admitted

UNDERGRAD STUDENTS
1,690 full-time, 39 part-time. Students come from 53 states and territories; 17 other countries; 80% are from out of state; 22% Black or African American, non-Hispanic/Latino; 8% Hispanic/Latino; 2% Asian, non-Hispanic/Latino; 0.1% Native Hawaiian or other Pacific Islander, non-Hispanic/Latino; 0.5% American Indian or Alaska Native, non-Hispanic/Latino; 1% Two or more races, non-Hispanic/Latino; 7% Race/ethnicity unknown; 3% international; 10% transferred in; 31% live on campus.

Freshmen
Admission: 5,563 applied, 5,337 admitted, 420 enrolled. ***Average high school GPA:*** 2.6. ***Test scores:*** SAT critical reading scores over 500: 29%; SAT math scores over 500: 29%; SAT writing scores over 500: 22%; SAT critical reading scores over 600: 4%; SAT math scores over 600: 6%; SAT writing scores over 600: 4%; SAT critical reading scores over 700: 1%; SAT math scores over 700: 1%.

Retention: 60% of full-time freshmen returned.

FACULTY
Total: 225, 16% full-time, 44% with terminal degrees.

Student/faculty ratio: 19:1.

ACADEMICS
Calendar: semesters. *Degrees:* associate, bachelor's, master's, and doctoral.

Special study options: academic remediation for entering students, accelerated degree program, adult/continuing education programs, advanced placement credit, distance learning, double majors, English as a second language, external degree program, freshman honors college, honors programs, independent study, internships, off-campus study, part-time degree program, services for LD students, student-designed majors, study abroad, summer session for credit. ***ROTC:*** Army (c), Air Force (c).

Unusual degree programs: 3-2 business administration; nursing with Massachusetts College of Pharmacy and Health Sciences; education BA/MED; political science BA/MA; Law (New York Law).

Computers: 191 computers/terminals and 350 ports are available on campus for general student use. Students can access the following: campus intranet, computer help desk, free student e-mail accounts, online (class) grades, online (class) registration, online (class) schedules. Campuswide network is available. 100% of college-owned or -operated housing units are wired for high-speed Internet access. Wireless service is available via entire campus.

STUDENT LIFE
Housing options: on-campus residence required through junior year; coed. Campus housing is university owned. Freshman campus housing is guaranteed.

Activities and organizations: drama/theater group, student-run newspaper, radio station, Student Senate, Campus Activities Board, Role Playing Association, International Student Association, Political Science Club, national fraternities, national sororities.

Athletics Member NCAA. All Division III. ***Intercollegiate sports:*** baseball M, basketball M/W, cross-country running M/W, field hockey W, ice hockey M/W, lacrosse M/W, soccer M/W, softball W. ***Intramural sports:*** basketball M/W, cheerleading W, golf M/W, ice hockey M/W, lacrosse M/W, rugby M/W, soccer M/W, softball W, table tennis M/W, tennis M/W, ultimate Frisbee M/W, volleyball M/W.

Campus security: 24-hour emergency response devices and patrols, student patrols, late-night transport/escort service, controlled dormitory access, Emergency Text System.

Student services: health clinic, personal/psychological counseling, women's center.

COSTS & FINANCIAL AID
Costs (2015–16) ***Comprehensive fee:*** $47,954 includes full-time tuition ($33,966), mandatory fees ($600), and room and board ($13,388). Full-time tuition and fees vary according to class time, course load, degree level, location, program, and reciprocity agreements. Part-time tuition: $416 per credit. Part-time tuition and fees vary according to class time, course load, degree level, location, and program. ***College room only:*** $6120. Room and board charges vary according to board plan and housing facility. ***Payment plan:*** installment. ***Waivers:*** children of alumni, adult students, senior citizens, and employees or children of employees.

Financial Aid Of all full-time matriculated undergraduates who enrolled in 2014, 1,377 applied for aid, 1,318 were judged to have need, 166 had their need fully met. 369 Federal Work-Study jobs (averaging $1892). 23 state and other part-time jobs (averaging $1147). In 2014, 94 non-need-based awards were made. ***Average percent of need met:*** 68. ***Average financial aid package:*** $22,768. ***Average need-based loan:*** $4572. ***Average need-based gift aid:*** $14,500. ***Average non-need-based aid:*** $15,742. ***Average indebtedness upon graduation:*** $31,073.

APPLYING
Options: electronic application, deferred entrance.

Application fee: $35.

Required: essay or personal statement, high school transcript, 3 letters of recommendation. ***Recommended:*** interview.

Application deadlines: 9/5 (freshmen), 9/5 (out-of-state freshmen), 9/5 (transfers).

Notification: continuous (freshmen), continuous (out-of-state freshmen), continuous (transfers).

CONTACT
Katie Lucier, Associate Director of Undergraduate Admissions, New England College, 102 Bridge Street, Henniker, NH 03242. *Phone:* 603-428 2341. *Toll-free phone:* 800-521-7642. *Fax:* 603-428 3155. *E-mail:* klucier@nec.edu.

New Hampshire Institute of Art

Manchester, New Hampshire

http://www.nhia.edu/

- **Proprietary** comprehensive, founded 1898
- **Urban** campus with easy access to Boston
- **Endowment** $25.3 million
- **Coed**
- **Moderately difficult** entrance level

ACADEMICS
Calendar: semesters. *Degrees:* certificates, bachelor's, master's, and postbachelor's certificates.

STUDENT LIFE
Housing options: coed. Campus housing is university owned and leased by the school.

Activities and organizations: drama/theater group, choral group, Student Council, Comic Club, Neo-Victorian Club, Crit Club, Gay/Straight Alliance.

Campus security: late-night transport/escort service, controlled dormitory access.

Student services: health clinic, personal/psychological counseling.

COSTS
Costs (2014–15) ***Comprehensive fee:*** $33,890 includes full-time tuition ($21,500), mandatory fees ($1910), and room and board ($10,480). Part-time tuition: $2150 per course. Part-time tuition and fees vary according to course load. ***Required fees:*** $455 per course part-time. ***Room and board:*** Room and board charges vary according to board plan and housing facility.

APPLYING
Standardized Tests *Recommended:* SAT or ACT (for admission).

Options: electronic application, early action, deferred entrance.

Application fee: $25.

Required: high school transcript, portfolio review. ***Required for some:*** essay or personal statement. ***Recommended:*** 2 letters of recommendation, interview.

CONTACT
Ms. Amanda Abbott, Associate Director of Admission, New Hampshire Institute of Art, 148 Concord Street, Manchester, NH 03104-4158. *Phone:* 603-836-2576. *Toll-free phone:* 866-241-4918. *E-mail:* aabbott@nhia.edu.

Plymouth State University
Plymouth, New Hampshire
http://www.plymouth.edu/

- **State-supported** comprehensive, founded 1871, part of University System of New Hampshire
- **Small-town** 170-acre campus with easy access to Manchester
- **Endowment** $18.0 million
- **Coed** 3,787 undergraduate students, 93% full-time, 47% women, 53% men
- **Moderately difficult** entrance level, 75% of applicants were admitted

UNDERGRAD STUDENTS
3,508 full-time, 279 part-time. Students come from 29 states and territories; 17 other countries; 40% are from out of state; 2% Black or African American, non-Hispanic/Latino; 3% Hispanic/Latino; 2% Asian, non-Hispanic/Latino; 0.3% American Indian or Alaska Native, non-Hispanic/Latino; 2% Two or more races, non-Hispanic/Latino; 11% Race/ethnicity unknown; 2% international; 6% transferred in; 48% live on campus.

Freshmen
Admission: 4,783 applied, 3,597 admitted, 751 enrolled. ***Average high school GPA:*** 2.91.

Retention: 74% of full-time freshmen returned.

FACULTY
Total: 413, 46% full-time, 50% with terminal degrees.

Student/faculty ratio: 16:1.

ACADEMICS
Calendar: semesters. *Degrees:* certificates, bachelor's, master's, doctoral, post-master's, and postbachelor's certificates.

Special study options: adult/continuing education programs, advanced placement credit, distance learning, double majors, honors programs, independent study, internships, off-campus study, part-time degree program, services for LD students, student-designed majors, study abroad, summer session for credit. ***ROTC:*** Army (c), Air Force (c).

Computers: 600 computers/terminals are available on campus for general student use. Students can access the following: campus intranet, computer help desk, free student e-mail accounts, online (class) grades, online (class) registration, online (class) schedules, degree audit, academic history, account status. Campuswide network is available. 100% of college-owned or -operated housing units are wired for high-speed Internet access. Wireless service is available via entire campus.

STUDENT LIFE
Housing options: on-campus residence required through sophomore year; coed. Campus housing is university owned. Freshman campus housing is guaranteed.

Activities and organizations: drama/theater group, student-run newspaper, radio station, choral group, Programming Activities in College Environment, Student Senate, Marketing Association of Plymouth State, CommonGround - Environmental and Social Justice Organization, PSU Pep Band.

Athletics Member NCAA. All Division III. ***Intercollegiate sports:*** baseball M, basketball M/W, cross-country running M/W, field hockey W, football M, ice hockey M/W, lacrosse M/W, skiing (downhill) M/W, soccer M/W, softball W, swimming and diving W, tennis W, track and field M/W, volleyball W, wrestling M. ***Intramural sports:*** basketball M(c)/W(c), golf M(c)/W(c), racquetball M(c)/W(c), rugby M(c)/W(c), sailing M(c)/W(c), table tennis M(c)/W(c), tennis M(c)/W(c), ultimate Frisbee M(c)/W(c), volleyball M(c)/W(c).

Campus security: 24-hour emergency response devices and patrols, student patrols, late-night transport/escort service, controlled dormitory access, shuttle bus service, crime prevention programs, self-defense education.

Student services: health clinic, personal/psychological counseling, women's center.

COSTS & FINANCIAL AID
Costs (2014–15) ***Tuition:*** state resident $10,410 full-time, $435 per credit hour part-time; nonresident $18,320 full-time, $763 per credit hour part-time. Full-time tuition and fees vary according to reciprocity agreements. Part-time tuition and fees vary according to reciprocity agreements. ***Required fees:*** $2267 full-time, $96 per credit hour part-time. ***Room and board:*** $10,728; room only: $6750. Room and board charges vary according to board plan and housing facility. ***Payment plan:*** installment. ***Waivers:*** senior citizens and employees or children of employees.

Financial Aid Of all full-time matriculated undergraduates who enrolled in 2013, 3,249 applied for aid, 2,606 were judged to have need, 362 had their need fully met. In 2013, 317 non-need-based awards were made. ***Average percent of need met:*** 57. ***Average financial aid package:*** $10,571. ***Average need-based loan:*** $4239. ***Average need-based gift aid:*** $6126. ***Average non-need-based aid:*** $3930. ***Average indebtedness upon graduation:*** $32,327.

APPLYING
Options: electronic application, deferred entrance.

Application fee: $50.

Required: essay or personal statement, high school transcript, 1 letter of recommendation. ***Required for some:*** interview.

Application deadlines: 4/1 (freshmen), 4/1 (transfers).

Notification: continuous until 11/15 (freshmen), continuous until 11/15 (transfers).

CONTACT
Mr. Andrew B Palumbo, AVP of Enrollment Management/Director of Admissions, Plymouth State University, 17 High Street, MSC #52, Plymouth, NH 03264-1595. *Phone:* 603-535-2237. *Toll-free phone:* 800-842-6900. *Fax:* 603-535-2714. *E-mail:* plymouthadmit@plymouth.edu.

★ Rivier University
Nashua, New Hampshire
http://www.rivier.edu/

- **Independent Roman Catholic** comprehensive, founded 1933
- **Suburban** 68-acre campus with easy access to Boston
- **Coed** 1,526 undergraduate students, 52% full-time, 81% women, 19% men
- **Moderately difficult** entrance level, 10% of applicants were admitted

UNDERGRAD STUDENTS
788 full-time, 738 part-time. Students come from 18 states and territories; 38% are from out of state; 8% transferred in; 48% live on campus.

Freshmen
Admission: 1,688 applied, 173 admitted, 176 enrolled. ***Test scores:*** SAT critical reading scores over 500: 43%; SAT math scores over 500: 52%; SAT writing scores over 500: 42%; ACT scores over 18: 81%; SAT critical reading scores over 600: 4%; SAT math scores over 600: 8%; SAT writing scores over 600: 5%; ACT scores over 24: 19%.

Retention: 74% of full-time freshmen returned.

FACULTY
Total: 193, 35% full-time, 40% with terminal degrees.

Student/faculty ratio: 14:1.

ACADEMICS
Calendar: semesters. *Degrees:* certificates, associate, bachelor's, master's, doctoral, post-master's, and postbachelor's certificates.

Special study options: advanced placement credit, distance learning, double majors, independent study, internships, off-campus study, part-time degree program, services for LD students, study abroad, summer session for credit. ***ROTC:*** Air Force (c).

Computers: 175 computers/terminals and 200 ports are available on campus for general student use. Students can access the following: campus intranet, computer help desk, free student e-mail accounts, online (class) grades, online (class) registration, online (class) schedules. Campuswide network is available. 100% of college-owned or -operated housing units are wired for high-speed Internet access. Wireless service is available via entire campus.

STUDENT LIFE

Housing options: coed. Campus housing is university owned. Freshman campus housing is guaranteed.

Activities and organizations: drama/theater group, choral group, Student Government Association, Student Program Board, Outdoor Club, Student Nurses Association, Habitat for Humanity.

Athletics Member NCAA. All Division III. ***Intercollegiate sports:*** baseball M, basketball M/W, cross-country running M/W, field hockey W, lacrosse M/W, soccer M/W, softball W, volleyball M/W. ***Intramural sports:*** basketball M/W, volleyball M/W.

Campus security: 24-hour emergency response devices and patrols, late-night transport/escort service, controlled dormitory access.

Student services: health clinic, personal/psychological counseling.

FINANCIAL AID

Financial Aid Of all full-time matriculated undergraduates who enrolled in 2010, 888 applied for aid, 822 were judged to have need, 70 had their need fully met. In 2010, 105 non-need-based awards were made. ***Average percent of need met:*** 59. ***Average financial aid package:*** $14,850. ***Average need-based loan:*** $4378. ***Average need-based gift aid:*** $10,806. ***Average non-need-based aid:*** $5066. ***Average indebtedness upon graduation:*** $43,189.

APPLYING

Standardized Tests *Required:* SAT or ACT (for admission). *Required for some:* nursing exam.

Options: electronic application, deferred entrance.

Application fee: $25.

Required: essay or personal statement, high school transcript, 1 letter of recommendation. ***Required for some:*** interview. ***Recommended:*** minimum 2.3 GPA, interview.

Application deadlines: rolling (freshmen), rolling (transfers).

Notification: continuous (freshmen), continuous (transfers).

CONTACT

Karen Schedin, Vice President for Enrollment Management, Rivier University, 420 South Main Street, Nashua, NH 03060. *Phone:* 603-897-8507. *Toll-free phone:* 800-44RIVIER. *Fax:* 603-891-1799. *E-mail:* rivadmit@rivier.edu.

See this page for display ad and page 1582 for the College Close-Up.

★ Saint Anselm College
Manchester, New Hampshire
http://www.anselm.edu/

- **Independent Roman Catholic** 4-year, founded 1889
- **Suburban** 380-acre campus with easy access to Boston
- **Endowment** $85.3 million
- **Coed** 1,968 undergraduate students, 97% full-time, 60% women, 40% men
- **Moderately difficult** entrance level, 76% of applicants were admitted

UNDERGRAD STUDENTS

1,915 full-time, 53 part-time. Students come from 24 states and territories; 5 other countries; 76% are from out of state; 2% Black or African American, non-Hispanic/Latino; 3% Hispanic/Latino; 0.6% Asian, non-Hispanic/Latino; 0.1% Native Hawaiian or other Pacific Islander, non-Hispanic/Latino; 0.2% American Indian or Alaska Native, non-Hispanic/Latino; 2% Two or more races, non-Hispanic/Latino; 12% Race/ethnicity unknown; 0.6% international; 1% transferred in; 90% live on campus.

Freshmen

Admission: 3,568 applied, 2,715 admitted, 523 enrolled. ***Average high school GPA:*** 3.24. ***Test scores:*** SAT critical reading scores over 500: 87%; SAT math scores over 500: 88%; SAT writing scores over 500: 84%; ACT scores over 18: 96%; SAT critical reading scores over 600: 32%; SAT math scores over 600: 36%; SAT writing scores over 600: 33%; ACT scores over 24: 65%; SAT critical reading scores over 700: 5%; SAT math scores over 700: 3%; SAT writing scores over 700: 6%; ACT scores over 30: 9%.

Retention: 90% of full-time freshmen returned.

FACULTY
Total: 209, 71% full-time, 67% with terminal degrees.
Student/faculty ratio: 11:1.

ACADEMICS
Calendar: semesters. *Degree:* bachelor's.
Special study options: accelerated degree program, advanced placement credit, double majors, honors programs, independent study, internships, off-campus study, part-time degree program, services for LD students, study abroad, summer session for credit. ***ROTC:*** Army (c).
Unusual degree programs: 3-2 engineering with University of Massachusetts Lowell, Catholic University of America, University of Notre Dame, Manhattan College; qualified Saint Anselm College graduates will have a seat in one of the following Massachusetts College of Pharmacy and Health Sciences programs: Doctor of Pharmacy, Doctor of Optometry, Doctor of Physical Therapy, Master of P.A. Studies.
Computers: 400 computers/terminals are available on campus for general student use. Students can access the following: campus intranet, computer help desk, free student e-mail accounts, online (class) registration, online (class) schedules. Campuswide network is available. 100% of college-owned or -operated housing units are wired for high-speed Internet access. Wireless service is available via classrooms, computer centers, computer labs, dorm rooms, learning centers, libraries, student centers.

STUDENT LIFE
Housing options: coed, men-only, women-only, special housing for students with disabilities. Campus housing is university owned. Freshman campus housing is guaranteed.
Activities and organizations: drama/theater group, student-run newspaper, choral group, Meelia Center for Community Engagement, Anselmian Abbey Players, Club Sports, Service & Solidarity Mission Trips, Saint Anselm College Crier (School Newspaper).
Athletics Member NCAA. All Division II. ***Intercollegiate sports:*** baseball M(s), basketball M(s)/W(s), cross-country running M(s)/W(s), field hockey W(s), football M(s), golf M(s), ice hockey M/W, lacrosse M(s)/W(s), rugby M(c)/W(c), skiing (downhill) M(s)/W(s), soccer M(s)/W(s), softball W(s), tennis M(s)/W(s), volleyball W(s). ***Intramural sports:*** basketball M/W, football M/W, ice hockey M/W, racquetball M/W, skiing (cross-country) M/W, soccer M/W, softball M/W, swimming and diving M(c)/W(c), tennis M/W, track and field M(c)/W(c), ultimate Frisbee M/W, volleyball M/W, weight lifting M/W.
Campus security: 24-hour emergency response devices and patrols, student patrols, late-night transport/escort service, controlled dormitory access.
Student services: health clinic, personal/psychological counseling.

FINANCIAL AID
Financial Aid Of all full-time matriculated undergraduates who enrolled in 2014, 1,614 applied for aid, 1,387 were judged to have need, 311 had their need fully met. 1,116 Federal Work-Study jobs (averaging $1481). 9 state and other part-time jobs (averaging $2000). In 2014, 417 non-need-based awards were made. ***Average percent of need met:*** 83. ***Average financial aid package:*** $27,727. ***Average need-based loan:*** $6326. ***Average need-based gift aid:*** $21,255. ***Average non-need-based aid:*** $11,563. ***Average indebtedness upon graduation:*** $35,601. ***Financial aid deadline:*** 3/15.

APPLYING
Standardized Tests *Required for some:* SAT or ACT (for admission).
Options: electronic application, early admission, early action, deferred entrance.
Application fee: $50.
Required: essay or personal statement, high school transcript, 2 letters of recommendation. ***Recommended:*** interview.
Application deadlines: 2/1 (freshmen), rolling (transfers), 11/15 (early action).
Notification: continuous until 3/15 (freshmen), continuous (transfers), 1/15 (early action).

CONTACT
Saint Anselm College, 100 Saint Anselm Drive, Manchester, NH 03102. *Phone:* 603-641-7500. *Toll-free phone:* 888-4ANSELM. *Fax:* 603-641-7550. *E-mail:* admission@anselm.edu.

See below for display ad and page 1588 for the College Close-Up.

★ Southern New Hampshire University

Manchester, New Hampshire

http://www.snhu.edu/

- **Independent** university, founded 1932
- **Suburban** 317-acre campus with easy access to Boston
- **Coed** 3,123 undergraduate students, 99% full-time, 52% women, 48% men
- **Moderately difficult** entrance level, 84% of applicants were admitted

UNDERGRAD STUDENTS

3,092 full-time, 31 part-time. Students come from 42 states and territories; 31 other countries; 41% are from out of state; 2% Black or African American, non-Hispanic/Latino; 3% Hispanic/Latino; 1% Asian, non-Hispanic/Latino; 0.1% Native Hawaiian or other Pacific Islander, non-Hispanic/Latino; 0.3% American Indian or Alaska Native, non-Hispanic/Latino; 1% Two or more races, non-Hispanic/Latino; 24% Race/ethnicity unknown; 9% international; 7% transferred in; 67% live on campus.

Freshmen

Admission: 4,199 applied, 3,536 admitted, 760 enrolled. ***Average high school GPA:*** 3.1. ***Test scores:*** SAT critical reading scores over 500: 48%; SAT math scores over 500: 54%; SAT writing scores over 500: 43%; ACT scores over 18: 87%; SAT critical reading scores over 600: 9%; SAT math scores over 600: 13%; SAT writing scores over 600: 8%; ACT scores over 24: 37%; SAT math scores over 700: 1%; SAT writing scores over 700: 1%; ACT scores over 30: 3%.

Retention: 78% of full-time freshmen returned.

FACULTY

Total: 565, 22% full-time, 22% with terminal degrees.

Student/faculty ratio: 12:1.

ACADEMICS

Calendar: semesters. *Degrees:* certificates, associate, bachelor's, master's, doctoral, post-master's, and postbachelor's certificates.

Special study options: academic remediation for entering students, accelerated degree program, adult/continuing education programs, advanced placement credit, cooperative education, distance learning, double majors, English as a second language, honors programs, independent study, internships, off-campus study, part-time degree program, services for LD students, study abroad, summer session for credit. ***ROTC:*** Army (c), Air Force (c).

Unusual degree programs: 3-2 business administration with SNHU offers a 3 year Business Bachelor's Degree with an optional additional 1year MBA.

Computers: 589 computers/terminals and 1,500 ports are available on campus for general student use. Students can access the following: campus intranet, computer help desk, free student e-mail accounts, online (class) grades, online (class) registration, online (class) schedules. Campuswide network is available. 100% of college-owned or -operated housing units are wired for high-speed Internet access. Wireless service is available via entire campus.

STUDENT LIFE

Housing options: coed, special housing for students with disabilities. Campus housing is university owned.

Activities and organizations: drama/theater group, student-run newspaper, radio and television station, choral group, Coordinators of Activities and Programming Events (CAPE), Soccer Club, Outing Club, Gaming Club, Game Design Club, national fraternities, national sororities.

Athletics Member NCAA. All Division II. ***Intercollegiate sports:*** baseball M(s), basketball M(s)/W(s), cheerleading M/W, cross-country running M(s)/W(s), field hockey W, golf M, ice hockey M, lacrosse M(s)/W(s), soccer M(s)/W(s), softball W(s), tennis M(s)/W(s), volleyball W(s). ***Intramural sports:*** badminton M/W, basketball M/W, crew M(c)/W(c), field hockey M(c)/W(c), football M/W, ice hockey M(c), racquetball M/W, soccer M/W, softball M/W, table tennis M/W, tennis M/W, track and field M(c)/W(c), ultimate Frisbee M/W, volleyball M/W.

Campus security: 24-hour emergency response devices and patrols, student patrols, late-night transport/escort service, controlled dormitory access.

Student services: health clinic, personal/psychological counseling, women's center.

COSTS & FINANCIAL AID

Costs (2015–16) ***Tuition:*** $3752 per course part-time. Full-time tuition and fees vary according to course load. ***Room only:*** Room and board charges vary according to board plan and housing facility. ***Payment plan:*** installment. ***Waivers:*** senior citizens and employees or children of employees.

Financial Aid Of all full-time matriculated undergraduates who enrolled in 2007, 1,560 applied for aid, 1,392 were judged to have need, 173 had their need fully met. In 2007, 330 non-need-based awards were made. ***Average percent of need met:*** 69. ***Average financial aid package:*** $15,514. ***Average need-based loan:*** $5174. ***Average need-based gift aid:*** $10,223. ***Average non-need-based aid:*** $3599.

APPLYING

Options: electronic application, early action, deferred entrance.

Application fee: $40.

Required: essay or personal statement, high school transcript, minimum 2.0 GPA, 1 letter of recommendation, In addition, BA in Creative Writing applicants are required to include a writing sample. BA in Music Education applicants are required to audition. ***Recommended:*** interview.

Application deadlines: rolling (freshmen), rolling (transfers), 11/15 (early action).

Notification: continuous (freshmen), continuous (transfers), 12/15 (early action).

CONTACT

Ms. Bethany Perkins, Director Freshman Admission, Southern New Hampshire University, 2500 North River Road, Manchester, NH 03106-1045. *Phone:* 603-645-9611. *Toll-free phone:* 888-327-7648. *Fax:* 603-645-9693. *E-mail:* b.perkins@snhu.edu.

See previous page for display ad and page 1626 for the College Close-Up.

University of New Hampshire

Durham, New Hampshire

http://www.unh.edu/

- **State-supported** university, founded 1866, part of University System of New Hampshire
- **Small-town** 2600-acre campus with easy access to Boston
- **Endowment** $336.4 million
- **Coed** 12,840 undergraduate students, 96% full-time, 54% women, 46% men
- **Moderately difficult** entrance level, 80% of applicants were admitted

UNDERGRAD STUDENTS

12,377 full-time, 463 part-time. Students come from 44 states and territories; 34 other countries; 50% are from out of state; 1% Black or African American, non-Hispanic/Latino; 3% Hispanic/Latino; 2% Asian, non-Hispanic/Latino; 0.2% American Indian or Alaska Native, non-Hispanic/Latino; 1% Two or more races, non-Hispanic/Latino; 9% Race/ethnicity unknown; 2% international; 4% transferred in; 56% live on campus.

Freshmen

Admission: 18,420 applied, 14,740 admitted, 3,227 enrolled. ***Test scores:*** SAT critical reading scores over 500: 70%; SAT math scores over 500: 79%; SAT writing scores over 500: 71%; ACT scores over 18: 98%; SAT critical reading scores over 600: 21%; SAT math scores over 600: 29%; SAT writing scores over 600: 22%; ACT scores over 24: 57%; SAT critical reading scores over 700: 2%; SAT math scores over 700: 3%; SAT writing scores over 700: 2%; ACT scores over 30: 8%.

Retention: 86% of full-time freshmen returned.

FACULTY

Total: 1,032, 59% full-time, 67% with terminal degrees.

Student/faculty ratio: 19:1.

ACADEMICS

Calendar: semesters. *Degrees:* associate, bachelor's, master's, doctoral, post-master's, and postbachelor's certificates.

Special study options: accelerated degree program, advanced placement credit, distance learning, double majors, English as a second language, honors programs, independent study, internships, off-campus study, part-time degree program, services for LD students, student-designed majors, study abroad, summer session for credit. ***ROTC:*** Army (b), Air Force (b).

Unusual degree programs: 3-2 business administration; engineering; social work; accounting, biochemistry, occupational therapy, education.

Computers: 360 computers/terminals are available on campus for general student use. Students can access the following: campus intranet, computer help desk, free student e-mail accounts, online (class) grades, online (class) registration, online (class) schedules. Campuswide network is available. 100% of college-owned or -operated housing units are wired for high-speed Internet access. Wireless service is available via classrooms, computer centers, computer labs, dorm rooms, libraries, student centers.

STUDENT LIFE

Housing options: coed, special housing for students with disabilities. Campus housing is university owned. Freshman campus housing is guaranteed.

Activities and organizations: drama/theater group, student-run newspaper, radio station, choral group, marching band, Campus Activity Board, The Outing Club, Resident Hall Association, Student Senate, Memorial Union Student Organization, national fraternities, national sororities.

Athletics Member NCAA. All Division I except football (Division I-AA). ***Intercollegiate sports:*** archery M(c)/W(c), baseball M(c), basketball M(s)/W(s), crew M(c)/W(c), cross-country running M(s)/W(s), fencing M(c)/W(c), field hockey W(s), golf M(c)/W(c), gymnastics W(s), ice hockey M(s)/W(s), lacrosse M(c)/W(s), riflery M(c)/W(c), rock climbing M(c)/W(c), rugby M(c)/W(c), sailing M(c)/W(c), skiing (cross-country) M(s)/W(s), skiing (downhill) M(s)/W(s), soccer M(s)/W(s), softball W(c), swimming and diving W(s), tennis M(c)/W(c), track and field M(s)/W(s), ultimate Frisbee M(c)/W(c), volleyball M(c)/W(s), wrestling M(c)/W(c). ***Intramural sports:*** basketball M/W, field hockey W, football M/W, ice hockey M/W, racquetball M/W, soccer M/W, softball M/W, table tennis M/W, tennis M/W, volleyball M/W, water polo M/W.

Campus security: 24-hour emergency response devices and patrols, student patrols, late-night transport/escort service, controlled dormitory access, lighted pathways and sidewalks.

Student services: health clinic, personal/psychological counseling, women's center, legal services.

COSTS & FINANCIAL AID

Costs (2014–15) ***Tuition:*** state resident $13,670 full-time, $570 per credit hour part-time; nonresident $26,650 full-time, $1110 per credit hour part-time. Full-time tuition and fees vary according to program. Part-time tuition and fees vary according to course load and program. ***Required fees:*** $2882 full-time, $1441 per year part-time. ***Room and board:*** $10,360; room only: $6460. Room and board charges vary according to board plan and housing facility. ***Payment plan:*** installment. ***Waivers:*** employees or children of employees.

Financial Aid Of all full-time matriculated undergraduates who enrolled in 2013, 9,477 applied for aid, 7,945 were judged to have need, 1,271 had their need fully met. 5,596 Federal Work-Study jobs (averaging $2507). 3,926 state and other part-time jobs (averaging $1634). In 2013, 1855 non-need-based awards were made. ***Average percent of need met:*** 77. ***Average financial aid package:*** $22,877. ***Average need-based loan:*** $3318. ***Average need-based gift aid:*** $4643. ***Average non-need-based aid:*** $9467. ***Average indebtedness upon graduation:*** $36,965.

APPLYING

Standardized Tests *Required:* SAT or ACT (for admission).

Options: electronic application, early action, deferred entrance.

Application fee: $50.

Required: essay or personal statement, high school transcript, 1 letter of recommendation. ***Recommended:*** minimum 3.0 GPA.

Application deadlines: 2/1 (freshmen), 2/1 (out-of-state freshmen), 4/1 (transfers), 11/15 (early action).

Notification: 4/15 (freshmen), 4/15 (out-of-state freshmen), 4/15 (transfers), 1/15 (early action).

CONTACT

Admissions Office, University of New Hampshire, 3 Garrison Avenue, Durham, NH 03824. *Phone:* 603-862-1360. *Fax:* 603-862-0077. *E-mail:* admissions@unh.edu.

See next page for display ad and page 1688 for the College Close-Up.

University of New Hampshire at Manchester

Manchester, New Hampshire

http://www.manchester.unh.edu/

- **State-supported** comprehensive, founded 1967, part of University System of New Hampshire
- **Urban** campus with easy access to Boston
- **Coed** 719 undergraduate students, 78% full-time, 50% women, 50% men
- **Moderately difficult** entrance level, 70% of applicants were admitted

UNDERGRAD STUDENTS

562 full-time, 157 part-time. 2% Black or African American, non-Hispanic/Latino; 4% Hispanic/Latino; 3% Asian, non-Hispanic/Latino; 0.1% American Indian or Alaska Native, non-Hispanic/Latino; 2% Two or more races, non-Hispanic/Latino; 14% Race/ethnicity unknown; 0.1% international.

Freshmen

Admission: 254 applied, 178 admitted, 81 enrolled. ***Test scores:*** SAT math scores over 500: 49%; ACT scores over 18: 8%; SAT math scores over 600: 16%; ACT scores over 24: 5%; SAT math scores over 700: 1%; ACT scores over 30: 2%.

FACULTY

Total: 124, 31% full-time.

Student/faculty ratio: 12:1.

ACADEMICS

Calendar: semesters. *Degrees:* associate, bachelor's, and master's.

Special study options: academic remediation for entering students, adult/continuing education programs, advanced placement credit, double majors, English as a second language, independent study, internships, off-campus study, part-time degree program, services for LD students, student-designed majors, study abroad, summer session for credit. ***ROTC:*** Army (c), Air Force (c).

Unusual degree programs: 3-2 Pharmacy program with Massachusetts College of Pharmacy and Health Sciences.

Computers: 108 computers/terminals are available on campus for general student use. Students can access the following: online (class) registration. Campuswide network is available. Wireless service is available via entire campus.

STUDENT LIFE

Housing options: college housing not available.

Activities and organizations: drama/theater group, student-run radio station, choral group, Student Council.

Campus security: 24-hour emergency response devices, late-night transport/escort service.

COSTS & FINANCIAL AID

Costs (2014–15) ***Tuition:*** state resident $13,350 full-time; nonresident $26,330 full-time. Full-time tuition and fees vary according to course load and program. Part-time tuition and fees vary according to course load and program. ***Required fees:*** $407 full-time. ***Payment plan:*** installment. ***Waivers:*** senior citizens and employees or children of employees.

Financial Aid Of all full-time matriculated undergraduates who enrolled in 2013, 616 applied for aid, 515 were judged to have need, 38 had their need fully met. 163 Federal Work-Study jobs (averaging $2450). In 2013, 18 non-need-based awards were made. ***Average percent of need met:*** 58. ***Average financial aid package:*** $12,837. ***Average need-based loan:*** $3797. ***Average need-based gift aid:*** $853. ***Average non-need-based aid:*** $1946. ***Average indebtedness upon graduation:*** $29,393.

APPLYING

Standardized Tests *Required:* SAT or ACT (for admission).

Options: electronic application, deferred entrance.

Application fee: $60.

Required: essay or personal statement, high school transcript, 1 letter of recommendation. ***Recommended:*** interview.

Application deadlines: 4/1 (freshmen), 4/1 (transfers).

Notification: continuous (freshmen), continuous (transfers).

CONTACT
Ms. Donna Lukasiak, Senior Assistant Director Admissions, University of New Hampshire at Manchester, 400 Commercial Street, Manchester, NH 03101. *Phone:* 603-641-4150. *Fax:* 603-641-4342.

NEW JERSEY

Berkeley College
Woodland Park, New Jersey
http://www.berkeleycollege.edu/

- **Proprietary** comprehensive, founded 1931
- **Suburban** 25-acre campus with easy access to New York City
- **Coed** 3,659 undergraduate students, 84% full-time, 72% women, 28% men
- **Minimally difficult** entrance level

UNDERGRAD STUDENTS
3,066 full-time, 593 part-time. 2% are from out of state; 21% Black or African American, non-Hispanic/Latino; 34% Hispanic/Latino; 2% Asian, non-Hispanic/Latino; 0.2% Native Hawaiian or other Pacific Islander, non-Hispanic/Latino; 0.2% American Indian or Alaska Native, non-Hispanic/Latino; 24% Race/ethnicity unknown; 0.6% international; 8% transferred in.

Freshmen
Admission: 796 enrolled.
Retention: 64% of full-time freshmen returned.

FACULTY
Total: 429, 28% full-time.
Student/faculty ratio: 15:1.

ACADEMICS
Calendar: quarters. *Degrees:* certificates, associate, bachelor's, and master's.
Special study options: academic remediation for entering students, accelerated degree program, adult/continuing education programs, advanced placement credit, cooperative education, distance learning, honors programs, independent study, internships, off-campus study, part-time degree program, summer session for credit. ***ROTC:*** Army (c).
Computers: 955 computers/terminals are available on campus for general student use. Students can access the following: computer help desk, free student e-mail accounts, online (class) grades, online (class) registration, online (class) schedules. Campuswide network is available. Wireless service is available via entire campus.

STUDENT LIFE
Activities and organizations: student-run newspaper.
Athletics Member USCAA. ***Intercollegiate sports:*** basketball M, cross-country running M/W, soccer M, volleyball M.
Campus security: 24-hour emergency response devices.
Student services: personal/psychological counseling.

COSTS
Costs (2014–15) ***Tuition:*** $23,100 full-time, $525 per quarter hour part-time. Full-time tuition and fees vary according to course load. Part-time tuition and fees vary according to course load. No tuition increase for student's term of enrollment. ***Required fees:*** $1200 full-time, $275 per term part-time. ***Payment plan:*** installment. ***Waivers:*** employees or children of employees.

APPLYING
Options: electronic application, deferred entrance.
Application fee: $50.
Required: high school transcript. ***Recommended:*** interview.
Application deadlines: rolling (freshmen), rolling (out-of-state freshmen), rolling (transfers).

CONTACT
Carol J Covino, Associate Vice President, High School Admissions, Berkeley College, 44 Rifle Camp Road, Woodland Park, NJ 07424. *Phone:* 973-278-5400. *Toll-free phone:* 800-446-5400. *E-mail:* info@berkeleycollege.edu.

Bloomfield College
Bloomfield, New Jersey
http://www.bloomfield.edu/

- **Independent** comprehensive, founded 1868, affiliated with Presbyterian Church (U.S.A.)
- **Suburban** 12-acre campus with easy access to New York City
- **Endowment** $12.4 million
- **Coed** 2,007 undergraduate students, 87% full-time, 64% women, 36% men
- **Moderately difficult** entrance level, 63% of applicants were admitted

UNDERGRAD STUDENTS
1,755 full-time, 252 part-time. Students come from 20 states and territories; 18 other countries; 5% are from out of state; 52% Black or African American, non-Hispanic/Latino; 25% Hispanic/Latino; 3% Asian, non-Hispanic/Latino; 0.6% American Indian or Alaska Native, non-Hispanic/Latino; 0.5% Two or more races, non-Hispanic/Latino; 5% Race/ethnicity unknown; 3% international; 10% transferred in; 28% live on campus.

Freshmen
Admission: 3,079 applied, 1,952 admitted, 447 enrolled. ***Average high school GPA:*** 2.58. ***Test scores:*** SAT critical reading scores over 500: 8%; SAT math scores over 500: 13%; ACT scores over 18: 23%; SAT critical reading scores over 600: 1%; SAT math scores over 600: 1%; ACT scores over 24: 2%.
Retention: 73% of full-time freshmen returned.

FACULTY
Total: 217, 32% full-time, 32% with terminal degrees.
Student/faculty ratio: 16:1.

ACADEMICS
Calendar: semesters. *Degrees:* certificates, bachelor's, master's, and postbachelor's certificates.
Special study options: academic remediation for entering students, accelerated degree program, advanced placement credit, distance learning, double majors, English as a second language, honors programs, independent study, internships, off-campus study, part-time degree program, services for LD students, student-designed majors, study abroad, summer session for credit. ***ROTC:*** Army (c).
Computers: 375 computers/terminals are available on campus for general student use. Students can access the following: campus intranet, computer help desk, free student e-mail accounts, online (class) grades, online (class) registration, online (class) schedules. Campuswide network is available. 100% of college-owned or -operated housing units are wired for high-speed Internet access. Wireless service is available via classrooms, computer centers, computer labs, dorm rooms, learning centers, libraries, student centers.

STUDENT LIFE
Housing options: coed. Campus housing is university owned and is provided by a third party.
Activities and organizations: drama/theater group, student-run radio station, First Ladies, Green Hearts Environmental Club, Black Student Union, Team Infinite, CARIBSO (Caribbean Student Association), national fraternities, national sororities.
Athletics Member NCAA. All Division II. ***Intercollegiate sports:*** baseball M(s), basketball M(s)/W(s), cross-country running M(s)/W(s), soccer M(s)/W(s), softball W(s), tennis M(s), volleyball W(s). ***Intramural sports:*** basketball M/W, volleyball M/W.
Campus security: 24-hour emergency response devices and patrols, late-night transport/escort service, controlled dormitory access, There are security cameras in high-traffic areas. The Franklin Street dorm has electronic access; all other dorms have key access.
Student services: health clinic, personal/psychological counseling.

COSTS & FINANCIAL AID
Costs (2015–16) ***Comprehensive fee:*** $39,100 includes full-time tuition ($27,800) and room and board ($11,300). Full-time tuition and fees vary according to degree level. Part-time tuition: $3475 per course. Part-time

tuition and fees vary according to course load and degree level. ***College room only:*** $5650. Room and board charges vary according to housing facility. ***Payment plans:*** installment, deferred payment. ***Waivers:*** senior citizens and employees or children of employees.

Financial Aid Of all full-time matriculated undergraduates who enrolled in 2014, 1,658 applied for aid, 1,543 were judged to have need, 140 had their need fully met. 365 Federal Work-Study jobs (averaging $2193). In 2014, 104 non-need-based awards were made. ***Average percent of need met:*** 25. ***Average financial aid package:*** $20,634. ***Average need-based loan:*** $4056. ***Average need-based gift aid:*** $17,229. ***Average non-need-based aid:*** $18,601. ***Average indebtedness upon graduation:*** $33,443. ***Financial aid deadline:*** 6/1.

APPLYING

Standardized Tests *Required:* SAT or ACT (for admission).

Options: electronic application, early action, deferred entrance.

Application fee: $40.

Required: essay or personal statement, high school transcript, minimum 2.5 GPA, 2 letters of recommendation, graded essay/term paper or personal essay. ***Recommended:*** interview.

Application deadlines: 8/1 (freshmen), 8/1 (out-of-state freshmen), 8/1 (transfers), 12/1 (early action).

Notification: continuous until 10/1 (freshmen), continuous until 10/1 (out-of-state freshmen), 12/23 (early action).

CONTACT

Ms. Nicole Cibelli, Director of Admissions, Bloomfield College, Office of Enrollment Management and Admission, Bloomfield, NJ 07003-9981. *Phone:* 973-748-9000 Ext. 1390. *Toll-free phone:* 800-848-4555 Ext. 230. *Fax:* 973-748-0916. *E-mail:* nicole_cibelli@bloomfield.edu.

Caldwell University

Caldwell, New Jersey

http://www.caldwell.edu/

- **Independent Roman Catholic** comprehensive, founded 1939
- **Suburban** 70-acre campus with easy access to New York City
- **Endowment** $6.1 million
- **Coed** 1,595 undergraduate students, 85% full-time, 70% women, 30% men
- **Moderately difficult** entrance level, 64% of applicants were admitted

UNDERGRAD STUDENTS

1,352 full-time, 243 part-time. Students come from 21 states and territories; 16 other countries; 8% are from out of state; 15% Black or African American, non-Hispanic/Latino; 16% Hispanic/Latino; 5% Asian, non-Hispanic/Latino; 0.3% Native Hawaiian or other Pacific Islander, non-Hispanic/Latino; 0.1% American Indian or Alaska Native, non-Hispanic/Latino; 2% Two or more races, non-Hispanic/Latino; 16% Race/ethnicity unknown; 4% international; 2% transferred in; 37% live on campus.

Freshmen

Admission: 3,132 applied, 2,008 admitted, 371 enrolled. ***Average high school GPA:*** 3.44. ***Test scores:*** SAT critical reading scores over 500: 32%; SAT math scores over 500: 43%; SAT writing scores over 500: 38%; ACT scores over 18: 71%; SAT critical reading scores over 600: 7%; SAT math scores over 600: 11%; SAT writing scores over 600: 8%; ACT scores over 24: 17%; SAT math scores over 700: 3%; SAT writing scores over 700: 1%.

Retention: 82% of full-time freshmen returned.

FACULTY

Total: 278, 32% full-time.

Student/faculty ratio: 13:1.

ACADEMICS

Calendar: semesters. *Degrees:* bachelor's, master's, doctoral, post-master's, and postbachelor's certificates.

Special study options: academic remediation for entering students, accelerated degree program, adult/continuing education programs, advanced placement credit, cooperative education, distance learning, double majors, English as a second language, external degree program, honors programs, independent study, internships, off-campus study, part-time degree program, services for LD students, student-designed majors, study abroad, summer session for credit. ***ROTC:*** Army (c).

Unusual degree programs: 3-2 business administration; social work with Rutgers University; BA Psychology/MA Counseling Psychology, BA Psychology/MA ABA, BA Education/MA Curriculum and Instruction, BA Biology or BA Psychology/MS in Occupational Therapy (Columbia University), BA Biology/MS in Athletic Training (Seton Hall University).

Computers: 286 computers/terminals and 796 ports are available on campus for general student use. Students can access the following: campus intranet, computer help desk, free student e-mail accounts, online (class) grades, online (class) registration, online (class) schedules. Campuswide network is available. 100% of college-owned or -operated housing units are wired for high-speed Internet access. Wireless service is available via classrooms, dorm rooms, learning centers, libraries.

STUDENT LIFE

Housing options: coed. Campus housing is university owned. Freshman applicants given priority for college housing.

Activities and organizations: drama/theater group, student-run newspaper, choral group, Black Student Union, Latino American Student Organization, Autism Awareness Club, Martial Arts Club, Marketing Club, national fraternities, national sororities.

Athletics Member NCAA. All Division II except bowling (Division I). ***Intercollegiate sports:*** baseball M(s), basketball M(s)/W(s), bowling W(s), cross-country running M(s)/W(s), lacrosse W(s), soccer M(s)/W(s), softball W(s), tennis M(s)/W(s), track and field M(s)/W(s), volleyball W(s). ***Intramural sports:*** basketball M/W, football M/W, soccer M/W, tennis M/W, ultimate Frisbee M/W, volleyball M/W.

Campus security: 24-hour patrols, late-night transport/escort service, controlled dormitory access, dusk-to-dawn patrols by trained security personnel.

Student services: health clinic, personal/psychological counseling.

COSTS & FINANCIAL AID

Costs (2014–15) ***Tuition:*** $28,900 full-time, $802 per credit hour part-time. Full-time tuition and fees vary according to course load and location. Part-time tuition and fees vary according to course load and location. ***Required fees:*** $1150 full-time, $200 per term part-time. ***Room only:*** Room and board charges vary according to housing facility. ***Payment plan:*** installment. ***Waivers:*** children of alumni, adult students, senior citizens, and employees or children of employees.

Financial Aid Of all full-time matriculated undergraduates who enrolled in 2014, 1,236 applied for aid, 1,066 were judged to have need, 20 had their need fully met. 92 Federal Work-Study jobs (averaging $1200). 263 state and other part-time jobs (averaging $2714). In 2014, 57 non-need-based awards were made. ***Average percent of need met:*** 73. ***Average financial aid package:*** $22,000. ***Average need-based loan:*** $4297. ***Average need-based gift aid:*** $15,485. ***Average non-need-based aid:*** $16,246. ***Average indebtedness upon graduation:*** $28,000.

APPLYING

Standardized Tests *Required:* SAT or ACT (for admission).

Options: electronic application, early admission, early action, deferred entrance.

Application fee: $40.

Required: essay or personal statement, high school transcript, 2 letters of recommendation, SAT or ACT scores. ***Required for some:*** interview. ***Recommended:*** minimum 3.0 GPA, interview.

Application deadlines: rolling (freshmen), rolling (out-of-state freshmen), rolling (transfers), 12/1 (early action).

Notification: continuous (freshmen), continuous (out-of-state freshmen), continuous (transfers), 12/31 (early action).

CONTACT

Mr. Stephen Quinn, Assistant Vice President, Enrollment Management, Caldwell University, 120 Bloomfield Avenue, Caldwell, NJ 07006. *Phone:* 973-618-3320. *Fax:* 973-618-3600. *E-mail:* squinn@caldwell.edu.

Centenary College

Hackettstown, New Jersey

http://www.centenarycollege.edu/

- **Independent** comprehensive, founded 1867, affiliated with United Methodist Church
- **Suburban** campus
- **Endowment** $3.3 million
- **Coed**
- **Moderately difficult** entrance level

FACULTY

Student/faculty ratio: 17:1.

ACADEMICS

Calendar: semesters. *Degrees:* certificates, associate, bachelor's, master's, and postbachelor's certificates.

STUDENT LIFE

Housing options: coed, women-only. Campus housing is university owned. Freshman applicants given priority for college housing.

Activities and organizations: drama/theater group, student-run newspaper, First Year Leaders, Student Government, Becca's Closet, ENACTUS, EVERGREEN.

Athletics Member NCAA. All Division III.

Campus security: 24-hour emergency response devices and patrols, late-night transport/escort service, controlled dormitory access.

Student services: health clinic, personal/psychological counseling.

COSTS & FINANCIAL AID

Costs (2014–15) ***Tuition:*** $29,360 full-time, $565 per credit part-time. Full-time tuition and fees vary according to program. Part-time tuition and fees vary according to program. ***Required fees:*** $1582 full-time. ***Room only:*** $10,420. Room and board charges vary according to board plan.

Financial Aid Of all full-time matriculated undergraduates who enrolled in 2010, 1,219 applied for aid, 1,094 were judged to have need, 121 had their need fully met. In 2010, 303 non-need-based awards were made. ***Average percent of need met:*** 72. ***Average financial aid package:*** $19,967. ***Average need-based loan:*** $5414. ***Average need-based gift aid:*** $15,457. ***Average non-need-based aid:*** $9157. ***Average indebtedness upon graduation:*** $40,588.

APPLYING

Standardized Tests *Required:* SAT or ACT (for admission).

Options: electronic application, deferred entrance.

Application fee: $30.

Required: essay or personal statement, high school transcript. ***Required for some:*** interview. ***Recommended:*** interview.

CONTACT

Centenary College, 400 Jefferson Street, Hackettstown, NJ 07840-2100. *Phone:* 908-852-1400. *Toll-free phone:* 800-236-8679.

★ The College of New Jersey

Ewing, New Jersey

http://www.tcnj.edu/

- **State-supported** comprehensive, founded 1855
- **Suburban** 255-acre campus with easy access to Philadelphia
- **Coed** 6,743 undergraduate students, 96% full-time, 57% women, 43% men
- **Very difficult** entrance level, 49% of applicants were admitted

UNDERGRAD STUDENTS

6,482 full-time, 261 part-time. Students come from 19 states and territories; 9 other countries; 7% are from out of state; 5% Black or African American, non-Hispanic/Latino; 13% Hispanic/Latino; 10% Asian, non-Hispanic/Latino; 0.3% Native Hawaiian or other Pacific Islander, non-Hispanic/Latino; 0.2% American Indian or Alaska Native, non-Hispanic/Latino; 0.7% Two or more races, non-Hispanic/Latino; 6% Race/ethnicity unknown; 0.2% international; 4% transferred in; 62% live on campus.

Freshmen

Admission: 10,937 applied, 5,356 admitted, 1,417 enrolled. ***Test scores:*** SAT critical reading scores over 500: 93%; SAT math scores over 500: 96%; SAT writing scores over 500: 92%; ACT scores over 18: 98%; SAT critical reading scores over 600: 55%; SAT math scores over 600: 69%; SAT writing scores over 600: 60%; ACT scores over 24: 81%; SAT critical reading scores over 700: 12%; SAT math scores over 700: 18%; SAT writing scores over 700: 16%; ACT scores over 30: 19%.

Retention: 93% of full-time freshmen returned.

FACULTY

Total: 820, 43% full-time, 54% with terminal degrees.

Student/faculty ratio: 13:1.

ACADEMICS

Calendar: semesters. *Degrees:* bachelor's, master's, post-master's, and postbachelor's certificates.

Special study options: academic remediation for entering students, accelerated degree program, advanced placement credit, double majors, honors programs, independent study, internships, off-campus study, part-time degree program, services for LD students, student-designed majors, study abroad, summer session for credit. ***ROTC:*** Army (c), Air Force (c).

Unusual degree programs: 3-2 education of the deaf and hard of hearing, elementary education; special education and liberal arts.

Computers: 631 computers/terminals are available on campus for general student use. Students can access the following: campus intranet, computer help desk, free student e-mail accounts, online (class) grades, online (class) registration, online (class) schedules. Campuswide network is available. 100% of college-owned or -operated housing units are wired for high-speed Internet access. Wireless service is available via classrooms, computer labs, learning centers, libraries, student centers.

STUDENT LIFE

Housing options: on-campus residence required for freshman year; coed, special housing for students with disabilities. Campus housing is university owned. Freshman campus housing is guaranteed.

Activities and organizations: drama/theater group, student-run newspaper, radio and television station, choral group, Student Government Association, College Union Board, Inter-Greek Council, The Signal, national fraternities, national sororities.

Athletics Member NCAA. All Division III. ***Intercollegiate sports:*** baseball M, basketball M/W, cross-country running M/W, field hockey W, football M, lacrosse W, soccer M/W, softball W, swimming and diving M/W, tennis M/W, track and field M/W, wrestling M. ***Intramural sports:*** baseball M(c), basketball M(c)/W, bowling M(c)/W(c), cheerleading M(c)/W(c), crew M(c)/W(c), fencing M(c)/W(c), field hockey M/W, football M/W, golf M(c)/W(c), ice hockey M(c), lacrosse M(c)/W(c), racquetball M/W, rugby M(c)/W(c), skiing (cross-country) M(c)/W(c), skiing (downhill) M(c)/W(c), soccer M(c)/W(c), softball M/W(c), swimming and diving M(c)/W(c), table tennis M(c)/W(c), tennis M(c)/W(c), ultimate Frisbee M(c)/W(c), volleyball M(c)/W(c), water polo M(c)/W(c).

Campus security: 24-hour emergency response devices and patrols, student patrols, late-night transport/escort service, controlled dormitory access.

Student services: health clinic, personal/psychological counseling, women's center, legal services.

COSTS & FINANCIAL AID

Costs (2014–15) ***Tuition:*** state resident $10,562 full-time, $374 per credit hour part-time; nonresident $21,175 full-time, $749 per credit hour part-time. Part-time tuition and fees vary according to course load. ***Required fees:*** $4462 full-time, $178 per credit hour part-time. ***Room and board:*** $11,677; room only: $8411. Room and board charges vary according to board plan. ***Payment plan:*** installment. ***Waivers:*** senior citizens and employees or children of employees.

Financial Aid Of all full-time matriculated undergraduates who enrolled in 2014, 4,664 applied for aid, 3,365 were judged to have need, 381 had their need fully met. In 2014, 517 non-need-based awards were made. ***Average percent of need met:*** 46. ***Average financial aid package:*** $11,106. ***Average need-based loan:*** $4695. ***Average need-based gift aid:*** $12,074. ***Average non-need-based aid:*** $5330. ***Average indebtedness upon graduation:*** $33,635.

APPLYING

Standardized Tests *Required:* SAT or ACT (for admission).

Options: electronic application, early decision, deferred entrance.

Application fee: $75.

Required: essay or personal statement, high school transcript. ***Required for some:*** interview, art portfolio or music audition. ***Recommended:*** minimum 2.5 GPA, 3 letters of recommendation.

Application deadlines: 1/15 (freshmen), 1/15 (transfers).

Early decision deadline: 11/15.

Notification: continuous until 1/15 (freshmen), continuous until 1/15 (transfers), 12/15 (early decision).

CONTACT

Ms. Grecia Montero, Director of Admissions, The College of New Jersey, PO Box 7718, Ewing, NJ 08628. *Phone:* 609-771-2131. *Fax:* 609-637-5174. *E-mail:* admiss@tcnj.edu.

See below for display ad and page 1402 for the College Close-Up.

College of Saint Elizabeth

Morristown, New Jersey

http://www.cse.edu/

- **Independent Roman Catholic** comprehensive, founded 1899
- **Suburban** 200-acre campus with easy access to New York City (1 hour train ride)
- **Endowment** $19.5 million
- **Coed, primarily women** 895 undergraduate students, 63% full-time, 94% women, 6% men
- **Moderately difficult** entrance level, 58% of applicants were admitted

UNDERGRAD STUDENTS

560 full-time, 335 part-time. Students come from 15 states and territories; 7 other countries; 6% are from out of state; 27% Black or African American, non-Hispanic/Latino; 17% Hispanic/Latino; 3% Asian, non-Hispanic/Latino; 0.1% Native Hawaiian or other Pacific Islander, non-Hispanic/Latino; 0.3% American Indian or Alaska Native, non-Hispanic/Latino; 1% Two or more races, non-Hispanic/Latino; 11% Race/ethnicity unknown; 4% international; 2% transferred in; 75% live on campus.

Freshmen

Admission: 2,959 applied, 1,704 admitted, 141 enrolled. ***Test scores:*** SAT writing scores over 500: 16%; SAT writing scores over 600: 3%; SAT writing scores over 700: 1%.

Retention: 69% of full-time freshmen returned.

FACULTY

Total: 158, 33% full-time.

Student/faculty ratio: 12:1.

ACADEMICS

Calendar: semesters. *Degrees:* certificates, bachelor's, master's, doctoral, and postbachelor's certificates (also offers coed adult undergraduate degree program and coed graduate programs).

Special study options: academic remediation for entering students, accelerated degree program, adult/continuing education programs, advanced placement credit, distance learning, double majors, English as a second language, external degree program, honors programs, independent study, internships, off-campus study, part-time degree program, services for LD students, student-designed majors, study abroad, summer session for credit.

Unusual degree programs: 3-2 nursing; Biology: 3 years of course work at CSE could lead to a Med.Tech, Podiatric Med. or BS/Pharma.D. degree.

Computers: 138 computers/terminals and 668 ports are available on campus for general student use. Students can access the following: campus intranet, computer help desk, free student e-mail accounts, online (class) grades, online (class) registration, online (class) schedules. Campuswide network is available. 100% of college-owned or -operated housing units are wired for high-speed Internet access. Wireless service is available via entire campus.

STUDENT LIFE

Housing options: women-only. Campus housing is university owned. Freshman campus housing is guaranteed.

Activities and organizations: drama/theater group, student-run newspaper, choral group, Student Government Association, Students Take

Action Committee, International/Intercultural Club, College Activities Board, Campus Ministry.

Athletics Member NCAA. All Division III. ***Intercollegiate sports:*** basketball W, equestrian sports W, soccer W, softball W, swimming and diving W, tennis W, volleyball W. ***Intramural sports:*** volleyball W.

Campus security: 24-hour emergency response devices and patrols, late-night transport/escort service, controlled dormitory access.

Student services: health clinic, personal/psychological counseling.

COSTS & FINANCIAL AID

Costs (2014–15) ***Comprehensive fee:*** $43,839 includes full-time tuition ($29,148), mandatory fees ($1947), and room and board ($12,744). Part-time tuition: $911 per credit hour. Part-time tuition and fees vary according to course load and location. ***Room and board:*** Room and board charges vary according to board plan. ***Payment plan:*** installment. ***Waivers:*** children of alumni, senior citizens, and employees or children of employees.

Financial Aid Of all full-time matriculated undergraduates who enrolled in 2013, 541 applied for aid, 490 were judged to have need, 47 had their need fully met. In 2013, 1 non-need-based awards were made. ***Average percent of need met:*** 98. ***Average financial aid package:*** $23,749. ***Average need-based gift aid:*** $14,708. ***Average non-need-based aid:*** $29,070.

APPLYING

Standardized Tests *Required:* SAT (for admission).

Options: electronic application, deferred entrance.

Application fee: $35.

Required: essay or personal statement, high school transcript, minimum 2.0 GPA, 2 letters of recommendation. ***Recommended:*** interview.

Application deadlines: rolling (freshmen), rolling (out-of-state freshmen), rolling (transfers).

Notification: continuous (freshmen), continuous (out-of-state freshmen), continuous (transfers).

CONTACT

Ms. Donna Tatarka, Dean of Admissions, College of Saint Elizabeth, 2 Convent Road, Morristown, NJ 07960-6989. *Phone:* 973-290-4700. *Toll-free phone:* 800-210-7900. *Fax:* 973-290-4710. *E-mail:* apply@cse.edu.

DeVry University

North Brunswick, New Jersey

http://www.devry.edu/

- **Proprietary** comprehensive, founded 1969, part of DeVry University
- **Urban** campus
- **Coed** 930 undergraduate students, 50% full-time, 30% women, 70% men
- **Minimally difficult** entrance level

UNDERGRAD STUDENTS

467 full-time, 463 part-time. 5% are from out of state; 23% Black or African American, non-Hispanic/Latino; 26% Hispanic/Latino; 8% Asian, non-Hispanic/Latino; 1% Native Hawaiian or other Pacific Islander, non-Hispanic/Latino; 0.4% American Indian or Alaska Native, non-Hispanic/Latino; 0.4% Two or more races, non-Hispanic/Latino; 3% Race/ethnicity unknown; 1% international; 25% transferred in.

Freshmen

Admission: 107 enrolled.

FACULTY

Total: 146, 17% full-time.

Student/faculty ratio: 11:1.

ACADEMICS

Calendar: semesters. *Degrees:* associate, bachelor's, master's, and postbachelor's certificates.

Special study options: adult/continuing education programs, part-time degree program.

Computers: Students can access the following: online (class) registration.

STUDENT LIFE

Housing options: college housing not available.

COSTS

Costs (2014–15) ***Tuition:*** $17,052 full-time, $609 per credit hour part-time. ***Required fees:*** $80 full-time.

APPLYING

Application fee: $40.

Required: high school transcript, interview.

CONTACT

DeVry University, 630 US Highway 1, North Brunswick, NJ 08902-3362. *Phone:* 732-729-3532. *Toll-free phone:* 866-338-7941.

DeVry University

Paramus, New Jersey

http://www.devry.edu/

- **Proprietary** comprehensive
- **Suburban** campus
- **Coed**

ACADEMICS

Degrees: associate, bachelor's, and master's.

COSTS

Costs (2014–15) ***Tuition:*** $17,052 full-time, $609 per credit hour part-time. ***Required fees:*** $80 full-time.

CONTACT

Admissions Office, DeVry University, 35 Plaza, 81 East State Route 4, Suite 102, Paramus, NJ 07652. *Phone:* 201-556-2840. *Toll-free phone:* 866-338-7941.

★ Drew University

Madison, New Jersey

http://www.drew.edu/

- **Independent** university, founded 1867, affiliated with United Methodist Church
- **Suburban** 186-acre campus with easy access to New York City
- **Endowment** $186.9 million
- **Coed** 1,417 undergraduate students, 96% full-time, 62% women, 38% men
- **Moderately difficult** entrance level, 70% of applicants were admitted

UNDERGRAD STUDENTS

1,357 full-time, 60 part-time. Students come from 39 states and territories; 25 other countries; 31% are from out of state; 10% Black or African American, non-Hispanic/Latino; 12% Hispanic/Latino; 6% Asian, non-Hispanic/Latino; 0.1% Native Hawaiian or other Pacific Islander, non-Hispanic/Latino; 0.2% American Indian or Alaska Native, non-Hispanic/Latino; 4% Two or more races, non-Hispanic/Latino; 8% Race/ethnicity unknown; 5% international; 4% transferred in; 82% live on campus.

Freshmen

Admission: 3,413 applied, 2,395 admitted, 302 enrolled. ***Average high school GPA:*** 3.43. ***Test scores:*** SAT critical reading scores over 500: 75%; SAT math scores over 500: 79%; SAT writing scores over 500: 75%; ACT scores over 18: 96%; SAT critical reading scores over 600: 34%; SAT math scores over 600: 30%; SAT writing scores over 600: 32%; ACT scores over 24: 62%; SAT critical reading scores over 700: 5%; SAT math scores over 700: 3%; SAT writing scores over 700: 5%; ACT scores over 30: 14%.

Retention: 84% of full-time freshmen returned.

FACULTY

Total: 268, 54% full-time.

Student/faculty ratio: 9:1.

ACADEMICS

Calendar: semesters. *Degrees:* bachelor's, master's, doctoral, post-master's, and postbachelor's certificates.

Special study options: accelerated degree program, adult/continuing education programs, advanced placement credit, double majors, freshman honors college, honors programs, independent study, internships, off-campus study, part-time degree program, services for LD students, student-designed majors, study abroad, summer session for credit.

Unusual degree programs: 3-2 engineering with Columbia University; BA/MA in teaching.

Computers: Students can access the following: campus intranet, computer help desk, free student e-mail accounts, online (class) grades, online (class) registration, online (class) schedules. Campuswide network is available. 100% of college-owned or -operated housing units are wired for high-speed Internet access. Wireless service is available via entire campus.

STUDENT LIFE
Housing options: coed, special housing for students with disabilities. Campus housing is university owned. Freshman campus housing is guaranteed.

Activities and organizations: drama/theater group, student-run newspaper, radio and television station, choral group, Colleges Against Cancer, Drew Organization of Gaming, Drew Health Organization, Drew First Responders, BOAS (anthropology club).

Athletics Member NCAA. All Division III. ***Intercollegiate sports:*** baseball M, basketball M/W, cross-country running M/W, equestrian sports W, fencing M/W, field hockey W, lacrosse M/W, rugby M(c)/W(c), soccer M/W, softball W, swimming and diving M/W, tennis M/W, track and field M/W. ***Intramural sports:*** basketball M/W, football M/W, racquetball M/W, soccer M/W, softball M/W, squash M/W, table tennis M/W, ultimate Frisbee M/W, volleyball M/W.

Campus security: 24-hour emergency response devices and patrols, late-night transport/escort service, controlled dormitory access.

Student services: health clinic, personal/psychological counseling.

COSTS & FINANCIAL AID
Costs (2014–15) ***Comprehensive fee:*** $57,516 includes full-time tuition ($44,232), mandatory fees ($982), and room and board ($12,302). Part-time tuition: $1843 per credit hour. Part-time tuition and fees vary according to course load. ***College room only:*** $7914. Room and board charges vary according to board plan and housing facility. ***Payment plans:*** tuition prepayment, installment, deferred payment. ***Waivers:*** employees or children of employees.

Financial Aid Of all full-time matriculated undergraduates who enrolled in 2013, 1,110 applied for aid, 1,021 were judged to have need, 144 had their need fully met. In 2013, 329 non-need-based awards were made. ***Average percent of need met:*** 77. ***Average financial aid package:*** $35,607. ***Average need-based loan:*** $4495. ***Average need-based gift aid:*** $35,607. ***Average non-need-based aid:*** $14,991. ***Average indebtedness upon graduation:*** $24,778. ***Financial aid deadline:*** 2/15.

APPLYING
Standardized Tests *Required:* SAT or ACT (for admission).

Options: electronic application, early admission, early decision, deferred entrance.

Application fee: $60.

Required: essay or personal statement, high school transcript, 1 letter of recommendation, SAT and/or ACT. ***Recommended:*** interview.

Early decision deadline: 12/1 (for plan 1), 2/2 (for plan 2).

CONTACT
Drew University, 36 Madison Avenue, Madison, NJ 07940-1493. *Phone:* 973-408-DREW.

Fairleigh Dickinson University, College at Florham

Madison, New Jersey

http://www.fdu.edu/

- **Independent** comprehensive, founded 1942
- **Suburban** 178-acre campus with easy access to New York City
- **Coed** 2,402 undergraduate students, 93% full-time, 54% women, 46% men
- **Moderately difficult** entrance level, 81% of applicants were admitted

UNDERGRAD STUDENTS
2,236 full-time, 166 part-time. 16% are from out of state; 11% Black or African American, non-Hispanic/Latino; 15% Hispanic/Latino; 4% Asian, non-Hispanic/Latino; 0.2% Native Hawaiian or other Pacific Islander, non-Hispanic/Latino; 0.6% American Indian or Alaska Native, non-Hispanic/Latino; 2% Two or more races, non-Hispanic/Latino; 7% Race/ethnicity unknown; 0.6% international; 4% transferred in; 62% live on campus.

Freshmen
Admission: 3,828 applied, 3,091 admitted, 703 enrolled. ***Average high school GPA:*** 3.07. ***Test scores:*** SAT critical reading scores over 500: 53%; SAT math scores over 500: 62%; SAT writing scores over 500: 54%; SAT critical reading scores over 600: 16%; SAT math scores over 600: 20%; SAT writing scores over 600: 15%; SAT critical reading scores over 700: 1%; SAT math scores over 700: 2%; SAT writing scores over 700: 3%.

Retention: 82% of full-time freshmen returned.

ACADEMICS
Calendar: semesters. *Degrees:* bachelor's, master's, doctoral, post-master's, and postbachelor's certificates.

Special study options: academic remediation for entering students, accelerated degree program, adult/continuing education programs, advanced placement credit, cooperative education, distance learning, double majors, honors programs, independent study, internships, off-campus study, part-time degree program, services for LD students, student-designed majors, study abroad, summer session for credit. ***ROTC:*** Army (c), Air Force (c).

Computers: Students can access the following: computer help desk, free student e-mail accounts, online (class) grades, online (class) registration, online (class) schedules. Campuswide network is available. 100% of college-owned or -operated housing units are wired for high-speed Internet access. Wireless service is available via entire campus.

STUDENT LIFE
Housing options: coed, special housing for students with disabilities. Campus housing is university owned. Freshman applicants given priority for college housing.

Activities and organizations: drama/theater group, student-run newspaper, choral group, College Panhellenic Council, Association of Black Collegians, Latin American Student Organization, Florham Programming Committee, InterFraternity Council, national fraternities, national sororities.

Athletics Member NCAA. All Division III. ***Intercollegiate sports:*** baseball M, basketball M/W, cross-country running M/W, field hockey W, football M, golf M/W, lacrosse M/W, soccer M/W, softball W, swimming and diving M/W, tennis M/W, volleyball W. ***Intramural sports:*** basketball M/W, football M/W, soccer M/W, softball M/W, volleyball M/W, weight lifting M/W.

Campus security: 24-hour emergency response devices and patrols, late-night transport/escort service, controlled dormitory access, trained law enforcement personnel on staff.

Student services: health clinic, personal/psychological counseling.

FINANCIAL AID
Financial Aid Of all full-time matriculated undergraduates who enrolled in 2007, 1,788 applied for aid, 1,568 were judged to have need. In 2007, 213 non-need-based awards were made. ***Average financial aid package:*** $17,400. ***Average need-based loan:*** $4001. ***Average need-based gift aid:*** $9956. ***Average non-need-based aid:*** $6501.

APPLYING
Standardized Tests *Required:* SAT or ACT (for admission).

Options: electronic application.

Application fee: $40.

Required: high school transcript, 2 letters of recommendation.

CONTACT
Fairleigh Dickinson University, College at Florham, 285 Madison Avenue, Madison, NJ 07940-1099. *Toll-free phone:* 800-338-8803.

Fairleigh Dickinson University, Metropolitan Campus

Teaneck, New Jersey

http://www.fdu.edu/

- **Independent** comprehensive, founded 1942
- **Suburban** 88-acre campus with easy access to New York City
- **Coed** 6,048 undergraduate students, 44% full-time, 58% women, 42% men
- **Moderately difficult** entrance level, 80% of applicants were admitted

UNDERGRAD STUDENTS

2,691 full-time, 3,357 part-time. 14% are from out of state; 14% Black or African American, non-Hispanic/Latino; 35% Hispanic/Latino; 5% Asian, non-Hispanic/Latino; 0.2% Native Hawaiian or other Pacific Islander, non-Hispanic/Latino; 0.1% American Indian or Alaska Native, non-Hispanic/Latino; 1% Two or more races, non-Hispanic/Latino; 12% Race/ethnicity unknown; 8% international; 6% transferred in; 19% live on campus.

Freshmen

Admission: 4,258 applied, 3,411 admitted, 650 enrolled. ***Average high school GPA:*** 3.08. ***Test scores:*** SAT critical reading scores over 500: 44%; SAT math scores over 500: 52%; SAT writing scores over 500: 38%; SAT critical reading scores over 600: 8%; SAT math scores over 600: 11%; SAT writing scores over 600: 9%; SAT critical reading scores over 700: 1%; SAT math scores over 700: 1%; SAT writing scores over 700: 1%.

Retention: 67% of full-time freshmen returned.

ACADEMICS

Calendar: semesters. *Degrees:* certificates, associate, bachelor's, master's, doctoral, post-master's, and postbachelor's certificates.

Special study options: academic remediation for entering students, accelerated degree program, adult/continuing education programs, advanced placement credit, cooperative education, distance learning, double majors, English as a second language, honors programs, independent study, internships, off-campus study, part-time degree program, services for LD students, student-designed majors, study abroad, summer session for credit. ***ROTC:*** Army (c), Air Force (c).

Computers: Students can access the following: computer help desk, free student e-mail accounts, online (class) grades, online (class) registration, online (class) schedules. Campuswide network is available. 100% of college-owned or -operated housing units are wired for high-speed Internet access. Wireless service is available via entire campus.

STUDENT LIFE

Housing options: coed, men-only, women-only. Campus housing is university owned.

Activities and organizations: drama/theater group, student-run newspaper, radio station, choral group, Student Programming Board, Student Government Association, Greek Life, Residence Hall Association, Spectrum (LGBT), national fraternities, national sororities.

Athletics Member NCAA. All Division I. ***Intercollegiate sports:*** baseball M(s), basketball M(s)/W(s), bowling W(s), cross-country running M(s)/W(s), fencing W(s), golf M(s)/W(s), soccer M(s)/W(s), softball W(s), tennis M(s)/W(s), track and field M(s)/W(s), volleyball W(s). ***Intramural sports:*** badminton M/W, basketball M/W, football M/W, rugby M(c)/W(c), soccer M/W, table tennis M/W, tennis M/W, volleyball M/W.

Campus security: 24-hour emergency response devices and patrols, late-night transport/escort service, controlled dormitory access, trained law enforcement personnel on staff.

Student services: health clinic, personal/psychological counseling, women's center.

COSTS & FINANCIAL AID

Costs (2014–15) ***One-time required fee:*** $795. ***Comprehensive fee:*** $48,370 includes full-time tuition ($34,904), mandatory fees ($836), and room and board ($12,630). Part-time tuition: $946 per credit. ***College room only:*** $8424. Room and board charges vary according to board plan and housing facility. ***Payment plans:*** installment, deferred payment. ***Waivers:*** senior citizens and employees or children of employees.

Financial Aid Of all full-time matriculated undergraduates who enrolled in 2007, 1,671 applied for aid, 1,549 were judged to have need. In 2007, 117 non-need-based awards were made. ***Average financial aid package:*** $18,283. ***Average need-based loan:*** $3808. ***Average need-based gift aid:*** $8702. ***Average non-need-based aid:*** $6403.

APPLYING

Standardized Tests *Required:* SAT or ACT (for admission).

Options: electronic application, early admission.

Application fee: $40.

Required: high school transcript, 2 letters of recommendation. ***Required for some:*** interview.

CONTACT

Fairleigh Dickinson University, Metropolitan Campus, 1000 River Road, Teaneck, NJ 07666-1914. *Toll-free phone:* 800-338-8803.

Felician College

Lodi, New Jersey

http://www.felician.edu/

- **Independent Roman Catholic** comprehensive, founded 1942
- **Suburban** 37-acre campus with easy access to New York City
- **Endowment** $4.8 million
- **Coed**
- **Moderately difficult** entrance level

FACULTY

Student/faculty ratio: 12:1.

ACADEMICS

Calendar: semesters. *Degrees:* certificates, associate, bachelor's, master's, doctoral, post-master's, and postbachelor's certificates.

STUDENT LIFE

Housing options: coed, men-only, women-only, special housing for students with disabilities. Campus housing is university owned. Freshman applicants given priority for college housing.

Activities and organizations: drama/theater group, student-run radio station, choral group, Student Nurses Association, Zeta Alpha Zeta teaching sorority, Campus Activity Board, Students in Free Enterprise (SIFE), Student Government Association.

Athletics Member NCAA, NAIA. All NCAA Division II.

Campus security: 24-hour patrols, student patrols, late-night transport/escort service.

Student services: health clinic, personal/psychological counseling.

COSTS & FINANCIAL AID

Costs (2014–15) ***Comprehensive fee:*** $42,255 includes full-time tuition ($28,950), mandatory fees ($1655), and room and board ($11,650). Full-time tuition and fees vary according to program. Part-time tuition: $955 per credit hour. Part-time tuition and fees vary according to course load and program. ***Room and board:*** Room and board charges vary according to housing facility.

Financial Aid Of all full-time matriculated undergraduates who enrolled in 2014, 1,267 applied for aid, 1,222 were judged to have need, 123 had their need fully met. In 2014, 99 non-need-based awards were made. ***Average percent of need met:*** 70. ***Average financial aid package:*** $26,716. ***Average need-based loan:*** $4324. ***Average need-based gift aid:*** $12,562. ***Average non-need-based aid:*** $15,428.

APPLYING

Standardized Tests *Required:* SAT or ACT (for admission). ***Required for some:*** ACT (for admission), SAT Subject Tests (for admission).

Options: deferred entrance.

Application fee: $30.

Required: high school transcript, minimum 2.0 GPA. ***Required for some:*** essay or personal statement, interview.

CONTACT

College Admissions Office, Felician College, 262 South Main Street, Lodi, NJ 07644-2117. *Phone:* 201-559-6131. *Fax:* 201-559-6138. *E-mail:* admissions@felician.edu.

Georgian Court University
Lakewood, New Jersey
http://www.georgian.edu/

- **Independent Roman Catholic** comprehensive, founded 1908
- **Suburban** 156-acre campus with easy access to New York City, Philadelphia
- **Endowment** $52.5 million
- **Coed** 1,621 undergraduate students, 80% full-time, 76% women, 24% men
- **Moderately difficult** entrance level, 68% of applicants were admitted

UNDERGRAD STUDENTS
1,299 full-time, 322 part-time. Students come from 19 states and territories; 12 other countries; 10% are from out of state; 13% Black or African American, non-Hispanic/Latino; 10% Hispanic/Latino; 2% Asian, non-Hispanic/Latino; 0.1% Native Hawaiian or other Pacific Islander, non-Hispanic/Latino; 0.3% American Indian or Alaska Native, non-Hispanic/Latino; 2% Two or more races, non-Hispanic/Latino; 22% Race/ethnicity unknown; 1% international; 14% transferred in; 28% live on campus.

Freshmen
Admission: 1,290 applied, 878 admitted, 230 enrolled. ***Average high school GPA:*** 3.21. ***Test scores:*** SAT critical reading scores over 500: 31%; SAT math scores over 500: 42%; SAT writing scores over 500: 29%; SAT critical reading scores over 600: 6%; SAT math scores over 600: 10%; SAT writing scores over 600: 6%.
Retention: 70% of full-time freshmen returned.

FACULTY
Total: 236, 41% full-time, 50% with terminal degrees.
Student/faculty ratio: 12:1.

ACADEMICS
Calendar: semesters. *Degrees:* certificates, bachelor's, master's, post-master's, and postbachelor's certificates.
Special study options: academic remediation for entering students, adult/continuing education programs, advanced placement credit, distance learning, double majors, honors programs, independent study, internships, part-time degree program, services for LD students, student-designed majors, study abroad, summer session for credit.
Computers: 198 computers/terminals are available on campus for general student use. Students can access the following: campus intranet, computer help desk, free student e-mail accounts, online (class) grades, online (class) registration, online (class) schedules. Campuswide network is available. 100% of college-owned or -operated housing units are wired for high-speed Internet access. Wireless service is available via classrooms, computer centers, computer labs, dorm rooms, learning centers, libraries, student centers.

STUDENT LIFE
Housing options: coed. Campus housing is university owned. Freshman campus housing is guaranteed.
Activities and organizations: student-run newspaper, Basketball Club, Black Student Union, Math Club, Dance Theatre Club, History Club.
Athletics Member NCAA. All Division II. ***Intercollegiate sports:*** basketball M(s)/W(s), cross-country running M(s)/W(s), lacrosse W(s), soccer M(s)/W(s), softball W(s), tennis W(s), track and field M(s)/W(s), volleyball W(s).
Campus security: 24-hour emergency response devices and patrols, late-night transport/escort service, controlled dormitory access.
Student services: health clinic, personal/psychological counseling.

COSTS & FINANCIAL AID
Costs (2014–15) ***Comprehensive fee:*** $41,594 includes full-time tuition ($29,566), mandatory fees ($1432), and room and board ($10,596). Part-time tuition: $676 per credit hour. Part-time tuition and fees vary according to location. ***Required fees:*** $358 per term part-time. ***Payment plan:*** installment. ***Waivers:*** employees or children of employees.
Financial Aid Of all full-time matriculated undergraduates who enrolled in 2014, 1,162 applied for aid, 1,081 were judged to have need, 335 had their need fully met. In 2014, 148 non-need-based awards were made. ***Average percent of need met:*** 84. ***Average financial aid package:*** $26,664. ***Average need-based loan:*** $6829. ***Average need-based gift aid:*** $17,870. ***Average non-need-based aid:*** $13,076. ***Average indebtedness upon graduation:*** $40,551. ***Financial aid deadline:*** 7/1.

APPLYING
Standardized Tests *Required:* SAT or ACT (for admission).
Options: electronic application, early action, deferred entrance.
Application fee: $40.
Required: high school transcript, minimum 2.5 GPA, 2 letters of recommendation. ***Recommended:*** essay or personal statement, interview.
Application deadlines: 8/1 (freshmen), 8/1 (transfers), 11/15 (early action).
Notification: continuous (transfers), 12/30 (early action).

CONTACT
Ms. Tracey Howard-Ubelhoer, Director of Undergraduate Admissions, Georgian Court University, 900 Lakewood Avenue, Lakewood, NH 08701-2697. *Phone:* 732-987-2765. *Toll-free phone:* 800-458-8422. *Fax:* 732-987-2000. *E-mail:* admissions@georgian.edu.

Kean University
Union, New Jersey
http://www.kean.edu/

- **State-supported** comprehensive, founded 1855, part of New Jersey State College System
- **Suburban** 185-acre campus with easy access to New York City
- **Endowment** $13.9 million
- **Coed** 11,987 undergraduate students, 77% full-time, 60% women, 40% men
- **Moderately difficult** entrance level, 70% of applicants were admitted

UNDERGRAD STUDENTS
9,283 full-time, 2,704 part-time. Students come from 20 states and territories; 49 other countries; 2% are from out of state; 20% Black or African American, non-Hispanic/Latino; 25% Hispanic/Latino; 6% Asian, non-Hispanic/Latino; 0.4% Native Hawaiian or other Pacific Islander, non-Hispanic/Latino; 0.2% American Indian or Alaska Native, non-Hispanic/Latino; 2% Two or more races, non-Hispanic/Latino; 7% Race/ethnicity unknown; 1% international; 14% transferred in; 14% live on campus.

Freshmen
Admission: 5,718 applied, 4,023 admitted, 1,502 enrolled. ***Average high school GPA:*** 3. ***Test scores:*** SAT critical reading scores over 500: 22%; SAT math scores over 500: 34%; ACT scores over 18: 57%; SAT critical reading scores over 600: 3%; SAT math scores over 600: 6%; ACT scores over 24: 13%; SAT math scores over 700: 1%; ACT scores over 30: 2%.
Retention: 75% of full-time freshmen returned.

FACULTY
Total: 1,371, 26% full-time.
Student/faculty ratio: 17:1.

ACADEMICS
Calendar: semesters. *Degrees:* bachelor's, master's, doctoral, and post-master's certificates.
Special study options: academic remediation for entering students, adult/continuing education programs, advanced placement credit, cooperative education, distance learning, double majors, English as a second language, honors programs, independent study, internships, off-campus study, part-time degree program, services for LD students, study abroad, summer session for credit. ***ROTC:*** Army (c), Air Force (c).
Computers: 1,700 computers/terminals and 2,000 ports are available on campus for general student use. Students can access the following: free student e-mail accounts, online (class) grades, online (class) registration, online (class) schedules. Campuswide network is available. 100% of college-owned or -operated housing units are wired for high-speed Internet access. Wireless service is available via entire campus.

STUDENT LIFE
Housing options: coed, special housing for students with disabilities. Campus housing is university owned. Freshman applicants given priority for college housing.
Activities and organizations: drama/theater group, student-run newspaper, radio station, choral group, American Sign Language Club,

Biology Club, Operation Smile, Thrift Nation, African Students Association, national fraternities, national sororities.

Athletics Member NCAA. All Division III. ***Intercollegiate sports:*** baseball M, basketball M/W, field hockey W, football M, lacrosse M/W, soccer M/W, softball W, tennis W, volleyball M/W. ***Intramural sports:*** basketball M/W, soccer M/W, softball M/W, tennis M/W, ultimate Frisbee M/W, volleyball M/W, weight lifting M/W.

Campus security: 24-hour emergency response devices and patrols, student patrols, late-night transport/escort service, controlled dormitory access, 24-hour patrols by campus police.

Student services: health clinic, personal/psychological counseling.

COSTS & FINANCIAL AID

Costs (2014–15) ***Tuition:*** state resident $7345 full-time, $286 per credit part-time; nonresident $13,754 full-time, $485 per credit part-time. Part-time tuition and fees vary according to course load. ***Required fees:*** $3899 full-time, $143 per credit part-time. ***Room and board:*** $12,200; room only: $9378. Room and board charges vary according to board plan, housing facility, and student level. ***Payment plan:*** installment. ***Waivers:*** senior citizens and employees or children of employees.

Financial Aid Of all full-time matriculated undergraduates who enrolled in 2014, 7,780 applied for aid, 6,671 were judged to have need, 858 had their need fully met. In 2014, 92 non-need-based awards were made. ***Average percent of need met:*** 81. ***Average financial aid package:*** $10,300. ***Average need-based loan:*** $4369. ***Average need-based gift aid:*** $7935. ***Average non-need-based aid:*** $4222. ***Average indebtedness upon graduation:*** $32,886.

APPLYING

Standardized Tests *Required:* SAT or ACT (for admission).

Options: electronic application, deferred entrance.

Application fee: $75.

Required: essay or personal statement, high school transcript, 2 letters of recommendation, SAT or ACT. ***Required for some:*** interview.

Application deadlines: 5/31 (freshmen), 7/28 (transfers).

Notification: continuous (freshmen), continuous (transfers).

CONTACT

Ms. Marsha McCarthy, Acting Associate Vice President for Enrollment Management, Kean University, 1000 Morris Avenue, Union, NJ 07083. *Phone:* 908-737-7100. *Fax:* 908-737-7105. *E-mail:* admitme@kean.edu.

★ Monmouth University

West Long Branch, New Jersey

http://www.monmouth.edu/

- **Independent** comprehensive, founded 1933
- **Suburban** 159-acre campus with easy access to New York City, Philadelphia
- **Endowment** $76.4 million
- **Coed** 4,634 undergraduate students, 94% full-time, 59% women, 41% men
- **Moderately difficult** entrance level, 74% of applicants were admitted

UNDERGRAD STUDENTS

4,370 full-time, 264 part-time. Students come from 30 states and territories; 24 other countries; 13% are from out of state; 5% Black or African American, non-Hispanic/Latino; 10% Hispanic/Latino; 3% Asian, non-Hispanic/Latino; 0.1% American Indian or Alaska Native, non-Hispanic/Latino; 2% Two or more races, non-Hispanic/Latino; 3% Race/ethnicity unknown; 0.8% international; 6% transferred in; 42% live on campus.

Freshmen

Admission: 7,691 applied, 5,706 admitted, 1,056 enrolled. ***Average high school GPA:*** 3.37. ***Test scores:*** SAT critical reading scores over 500: 61%; SAT math scores over 500: 72%; SAT writing scores over 500: 68%; ACT scores over 18: 98%; SAT critical reading scores over 600: 14%; SAT math scores over 600: 19%; SAT writing scores over 600: 18%; ACT scores over 24: 44%; SAT critical reading scores over 700: 1%; SAT math scores over 700: 2%; SAT writing scores over 700: 1%; ACT scores over 30: 1%.

Retention: 83% of full-time freshmen returned.

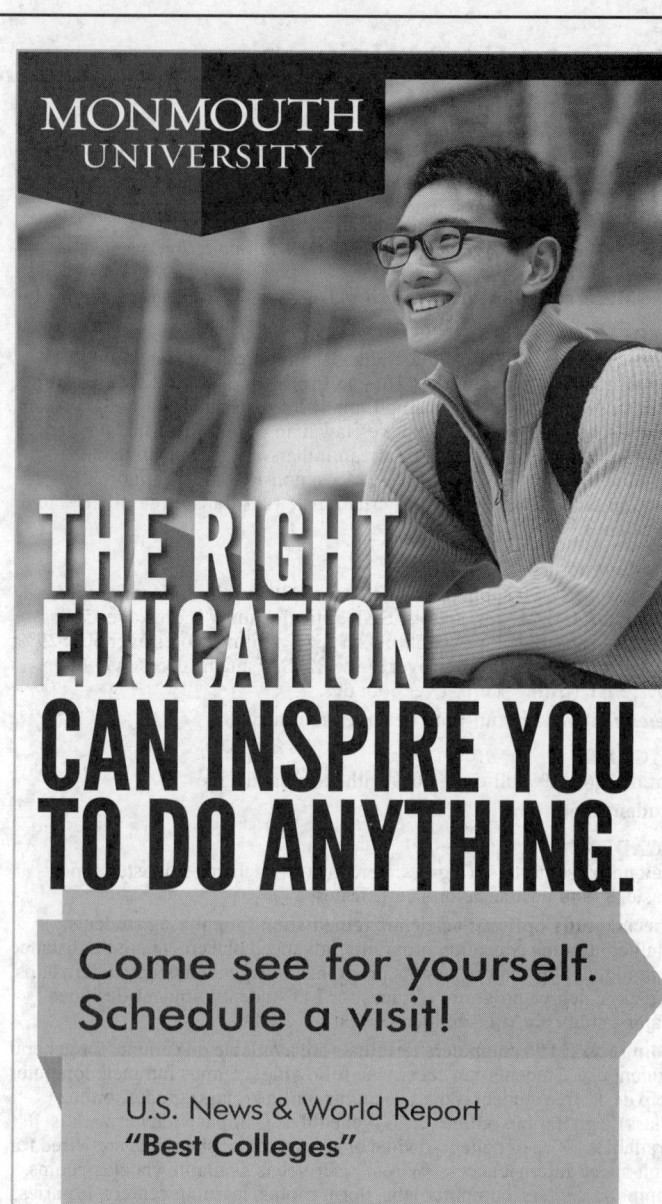

FACULTY
Total: 633, 44% full-time, 47% with terminal degrees.

Student/faculty ratio: 14:1.

ACADEMICS
Calendar: semesters. *Degrees:* certificates, associate, bachelor's, master's, doctoral, post-master's, and postbachelor's certificates.

Special study options: academic remediation for entering students, accelerated degree program, advanced placement credit, cooperative education, distance learning, double majors, honors programs, independent study, internships, part-time degree program, services for LD students, student-designed majors, study abroad, summer session for credit. ***ROTC:*** Army (c), Air Force (c).

Computers: 1,000 computers/terminals are available on campus for general student use. Students can access the following: campus intranet, computer help desk, free student e-mail accounts, online (class) grades, online (class) registration, online (class) schedules. Campuswide network is available. 100% of college-owned or -operated housing units are wired for high-speed Internet access. Wireless service is available via classrooms, computer centers, computer labs, dorm rooms, learning centers, libraries, student centers.

STUDENT LIFE
Housing options: coed. Campus housing is university owned and leased by the school. Freshman campus housing is guaranteed.

Activities and organizations: drama/theater group, student-run newspaper, radio and television station, choral group, radio station WMCX 88.9 FM, Student Government Association, student newspaper (Outlook), Student Activities Board, Shadows (yearbook), national fraternities, national sororities.

Athletics Member NCAA. All Division I except football (Division I-AA). ***Intercollegiate sports:*** baseball M(s), basketball M(s)/W(s), bowling W(s), cheerleading M(c)/W(c), cross-country running M(s)/W(s), field hockey W(s), golf M(s)/W(s), ice hockey M(c), lacrosse M(s)/W(s), sailing M(c)/W(c), soccer M(s)/W(s), softball W(s), tennis M(s)/W(s), track and field M(s)/W(s). ***Intramural sports:*** baseball M(c), basketball M/W, football M/W, lacrosse M(c)/W(c), soccer M/W, softball M/W, volleyball M/W.

Campus security: 24-hour emergency response devices and patrols, late-night transport/escort service, controlled dormitory access.

Student services: health clinic, personal/psychological counseling, women's center, legal services.

COSTS & FINANCIAL AID
Costs (2014–15) ***One-time required fee:*** $200. ***Comprehensive fee:*** $44,108 includes full-time tuition ($31,682), mandatory fees ($628), and room and board ($11,798). Part-time tuition: $917 per credit hour. Part-time tuition and fees vary according to course load. ***Required fees:*** $157 per term part-time. ***College room only:*** $6776. Room and board charges vary according to board plan and housing facility. ***Payment plan:*** installment. ***Waivers:*** senior citizens and employees or children of employees.

Financial Aid Of all full-time matriculated undergraduates who enrolled in 2014, 3,573 applied for aid, 3,101 were judged to have need, 445 had their need fully met. 930 Federal Work-Study jobs (averaging $2003). In 2014, 1270 non-need-based awards were made. ***Average percent of need met:*** 69. ***Average financial aid package:*** $24,858. ***Average need-based loan:*** $4751. ***Average need-based gift aid:*** $12,089. ***Average non-need-based aid:*** $7856. ***Average indebtedness upon graduation:*** $30,678.

APPLYING
Standardized Tests *Required:* SAT or ACT (for admission).

Options: electronic application, early action, deferred entrance.

Application fee: $50.

Required: essay or personal statement, high school transcript, 1 letter of recommendation. ***Required for some:*** interview. ***Recommended:*** resume of activities including community involvement and leadership positions.

Application deadlines: 3/1 (freshmen), 7/15 (transfers), 12/1 (early action).

Notification: 4/1 (freshmen), continuous (transfers), 1/15 (early action).

CONTACT
Ms. Victoria Bobik, Director of Undergraduate Admission, Monmouth University, 400 Cedar Avenue, West Long Branch, NJ 07764-1898. *Phone:* 732-571-3456. *Toll-free phone:* 800-543-9671. *Fax:* 732-263-5166. *E-mail:* admission@monmouth.edu.

See previous page for display ad and page 1532 for the College Close-Up.

Montclair State University
Montclair, New Jersey
http://www.montclair.edu/

- **State-supported** comprehensive, founded 1908
- **Suburban** 275-acre campus with easy access to New York City
- **Endowment** $58.8 million
- **Coed** 15,885 undergraduate students, 87% full-time, 61% women, 39% men
- **Moderately difficult** entrance level, 67% of applicants were admitted

UNDERGRAD STUDENTS
13,879 full-time, 2,006 part-time. 10% Black or African American, non-Hispanic/Latino; 24% Hispanic/Latino; 5% Asian, non-Hispanic/Latino; 0.2% Native Hawaiian or other Pacific Islander, non-Hispanic/Latino; 0.1% American Indian or Alaska Native, non-Hispanic/Latino; 4% Two or more races, non-Hispanic/Latino; 10% Race/ethnicity unknown; 2% international; 10% transferred in; 32% live on campus.

Freshmen
Admission: 12,462 applied, 8,328 admitted, 2,902 enrolled. ***Average high school GPA:*** 3.2. ***Test scores:*** SAT critical reading scores over 500: 42%; SAT math scores over 500: 51%; SAT writing scores over 500: 44%; SAT critical reading scores over 600: 7%; SAT math scores over 600: 10%; SAT writing scores over 600: 9%; SAT critical reading scores over 700: 1%; SAT math scores over 700: 1%; SAT writing scores over 700: 1%.

Retention: 81% of full-time freshmen returned.

FACULTY
Total: 1,738, 35% full-time, 35% with terminal degrees.

Student/faculty ratio: 17:1.

ACADEMICS
Calendar: semesters. *Degrees:* bachelor's, master's, doctoral, and postbachelor's certificates.

Special study options: academic remediation for entering students, accelerated degree program, adult/continuing education programs, advanced placement credit, cooperative education, double majors, English as a second language, freshman honors college, honors programs, independent study, internships, off-campus study, part-time degree program, services for LD students, study abroad, summer session for credit. ***ROTC:*** Army (b), Navy (b), Air Force (b).

Unusual degree programs: BA/MAT, BMus/MAT, BS/MS Aquatic and Coastal Science, Chemistry, Mathematics, Statistics.

Computers: 1,400 computers/terminals and 25,000 ports are available on campus for general student use. Students can access the following: campus intranet, computer help desk, free student e-mail accounts, online (class) grades, online (class) registration, online (class) schedules, online storage, Online course delivery, online computing lab. Campuswide network is available. 100% of college-owned or -operated housing units are wired for high-speed Internet access. Wireless service is available via entire campus.

STUDENT LIFE
Housing options: coed. Campus housing is university owned and is provided by a third party. Freshman campus housing is guaranteed.

Activities and organizations: drama/theater group, student-run newspaper, radio station, choral group, Latin American Student Organization, Campus Recreation, MSU Gamers, Unified Asian American Student Organization, SLAM (Student Life At Montclair), national fraternities, national sororities.

Athletics Member NCAA. All Division III. ***Intercollegiate sports:*** baseball M, basketball M/W, field hockey W, football M, lacrosse M/W, soccer M/W, softball W, swimming and diving M/W, track and field M/W, volleyball W. ***Intramural sports:*** baseball M(c), basketball M(c)/W(c), cheerleading W(c), football M, golf M(c)/W(c), ice hockey M(c)/W(c), lacrosse M(c)/W(c), racquetball W, rugby M(c)/W(c), soccer M(c)/W(c), softball M(c)/W(c), table tennis M/W, track and field M(c)/W(c), volleyball M/W, wrestling M(c)/W(c).

Campus security: 24-hour emergency response devices and patrols, late-night transport/escort service, controlled dormitory access, video surveillance, student escorts.

Student services: health clinic, personal/psychological counseling, women's center.

COSTS & FINANCIAL AID

Costs (2014–15) ***Tuition:*** state resident $8346 full-time, $278 per credit part-time; nonresident $17,060 full-time, $569 per credit part-time. ***Required fees:*** $3194 full-time, $106 per credit part-time. ***Room and board:*** $14,010. Room and board charges vary according to board plan and housing facility. ***Payment plan:*** installment. ***Waivers:*** senior citizens and employees or children of employees.

Financial Aid Of all full-time matriculated undergraduates who enrolled in 2013, 10,959 applied for aid, 9,350 were judged to have need, 183 had their need fully met. 531 Federal Work-Study jobs (averaging $1226). In 2013, 589 non-need-based awards were made. ***Average percent of need met:*** 66. ***Average financial aid package:*** $9444. ***Average need-based loan:*** $3935. ***Average need-based gift aid:*** $8541. ***Average non-need-based aid:*** $6439. ***Average indebtedness upon graduation:*** $28,070.

APPLYING

Standardized Tests *Required:* SAT or ACT (for admission).

Options: electronic application, deferred entrance.

Application fee: $65.

Required: essay or personal statement, high school transcript. ***Required for some:*** interview.

Application deadlines: 3/1 (freshmen), 6/15 (transfers).

Notification: continuous (freshmen), continuous (transfers).

CONTACT

Jeff Indiveri-Gant, Director of Admissions, Montclair State University, One Normal Avenue, Montclair, NJ 07043-1624. *Phone:* 973-655-3316. *Fax:* 973-655-7700. *E-mail:* undergraduate.admissions@montclair.edu.

New Jersey City University

Jersey City, New Jersey

http://www.njcu.edu/

- **State-supported** comprehensive, founded 1927
- **Urban** 51-acre campus with easy access to New York City
- **Endowment** $5.0 million
- **Coed** 6,229 undergraduate students, 75% full-time, 61% women, 39% men
- **Moderately difficult** entrance level, 77% of applicants were admitted

UNDERGRAD STUDENTS

4,689 full-time, 1,540 part-time. Students come from 15 states and territories; 17 other countries; 1% are from out of state; 21% Black or African American, non-Hispanic/Latino; 35% Hispanic/Latino; 9% Asian, non-Hispanic/Latino; 0.2% American Indian or Alaska Native, non-Hispanic/Latino; 1% Two or more races, non-Hispanic/Latino; 8% Race/ethnicity unknown; 1% international; 15% transferred in; 4% live on campus.

Freshmen

Admission: 2,618 applied, 2,005 admitted, 691 enrolled. ***Average high school GPA:*** 2.9. ***Test scores:*** SAT critical reading scores over 500: 18%; SAT math scores over 500: 26%; SAT critical reading scores over 600: 4%; SAT math scores over 600: 4%; SAT critical reading scores over 700: 1%.

Retention: 74% of full-time freshmen returned.

FACULTY

Total: 780, 33% full-time.

Student/faculty ratio: 14:1.

ACADEMICS

Calendar: semesters. *Degrees:* certificates, bachelor's, master's, doctoral, post-master's, and postbachelor's certificates.

Special study options: academic remediation for entering students, accelerated degree program, adult/continuing education programs, advanced placement credit, cooperative education, distance learning, double majors, English as a second language, honors programs, independent study, internships, off-campus study, part-time degree program, services for LD students, study abroad, summer session for credit. ***ROTC:*** Army (c), Air Force (c).

Computers: 704 computers/terminals are available on campus for general student use. Students can access the following: free student e-mail accounts, online (class) grades, online (class) registration, online (class) schedules. Campuswide network is available. 100% of college-owned or -operated housing units are wired for high-speed Internet access. Wireless service is available via classrooms, computer centers, computer labs, dorm rooms, learning centers, libraries, student centers.

STUDENT LIFE

Housing options: coed. Campus housing is university owned.

Activities and organizations: drama/theater group, student-run newspaper, radio station, choral group, national fraternities, national sororities.

Athletics Member NCAA. All Division III. ***Intercollegiate sports:*** baseball M, basketball M/W, bowling W, cross-country running M/W, golf M, soccer M/W, softball W, volleyball M/W. ***Intramural sports:*** bowling W, cheerleading M/W, cross-country running M/W, golf M, soccer M/W, softball W, tennis W, volleyball M/W.

Campus security: 24-hour emergency response devices and patrols, late-night transport/escort service.

Student services: health clinic, personal/psychological counseling, women's center, legal services.

COSTS & FINANCIAL AID

Costs (2014–15) ***Tuition:*** state resident $7704 full-time, $257 per credit hour part-time; nonresident $16,276 full-time, $543 per credit hour part-time. Part-time tuition and fees vary according to course load. ***Required fees:*** $3148 full-time. ***Room and board:*** $10,604; room only: $6816. ***Payment plan:*** deferred payment. ***Waivers:*** senior citizens and employees or children of employees.

Financial Aid Of all full-time matriculated undergraduates who enrolled in 2013, 4,355 applied for aid, 4,122 were judged to have need, 3,665 had their need fully met. In 2013, 56 non-need-based awards were made. ***Average percent of need met:*** 68. ***Average financial aid package:*** $15,970. ***Average need-based loan:*** $4080. ***Average need-based gift aid:*** $8065. ***Average non-need-based aid:*** $6884. ***Average indebtedness upon graduation:*** $20,763.

APPLYING

Standardized Tests *Required:* SAT (for admission).

Options: electronic application, deferred entrance.

Application fee: $50.

Required: essay or personal statement, high school transcript, minimum 2.0 GPA. ***Required for some:*** interview. ***Recommended:*** 1 letter of recommendation.

Application deadlines: 4/15 (freshmen), rolling (transfers).

Notification: continuous (freshmen).

CONTACT

Mr. Jose Balda, Director of Admissions, New Jersey City University, 2039 Kennedy Boulevard, Jersey City, NJ 07305. *Phone:* 201-200-3234. *Toll-free phone:* 888-441-NJCU. *E-mail:* admissions@nicu.edu.

★ New Jersey Institute of Technology

Newark, New Jersey

http://www.njit.edu/

- **State-supported** university, founded 1881
- **Urban** 48-acre campus with easy access to New York City
- **Endowment** $102.0 million
- **Coed** 7,550 undergraduate students, 78% full-time, 24% women, 76% men
- **Moderately difficult** entrance level, 63% of applicants were admitted

UNDERGRAD STUDENTS

5,923 full-time, 1,627 part-time. Students come from 23 states and territories; 100 other countries; 6% are from out of state; 9% Black or African American, non-Hispanic/Latino; 19% Hispanic/Latino; 21% Asian, non-Hispanic/Latino; 3% Two or more races, non-Hispanic/Latino;

11% Race/ethnicity unknown; 4% international; 9% transferred in; 23% live on campus.

Freshmen
Admission: 4,765 applied, 3,025 admitted, 1,053 enrolled. ***Average high school GPA:*** 3.49. ***Test scores:*** SAT critical reading scores over 500: 79%; SAT math scores over 500: 99%; SAT writing scores over 500: 73%; SAT critical reading scores over 600: 34%; SAT math scores over 600: 64%; SAT writing scores over 600: 33%; SAT critical reading scores over 700: 5%; SAT math scores over 700: 18%; SAT writing scores over 700: 8%.
Retention: 84% of full-time freshmen returned.

FACULTY
Total: 678, 60% full-time, 60% with terminal degrees.
Student/faculty ratio: 18:1.

ACADEMICS
Calendar: semesters. *Degrees:* bachelor's, master's, doctoral, and postbachelor's certificates.
Special study options: academic remediation for entering students, accelerated degree program, adult/continuing education programs, advanced placement credit, cooperative education, distance learning, double majors, English as a second language, freshman honors college, honors programs, independent study, internships, off-campus study, part-time degree program, services for LD students, study abroad, summer session for credit. ***ROTC:*** Army (c), Air Force (b).
Unusual degree programs: 3-2 business administration; engineering.
Computers: 1,938 computers/terminals are available on campus for general student use. Students can access the following: campus intranet, computer help desk, free student e-mail accounts, online (class) grades, online (class) registration, online (class) schedules. Campuswide network is available. 100% of college-owned or -operated housing units are wired for high-speed Internet access. Wireless service is available via entire campus.

STUDENT LIFE
Housing options: coed. Campus housing is university owned.
Activities and organizations: drama/theater group, student-run newspaper, radio station, Student Senate, Student Activities Council, Vector, Institute of Industrial Engineers, WJTB Geek Radio, national fraternities, national sororities.
Athletics Member NCAA. All Division I. ***Intercollegiate sports:*** baseball M(s), basketball M(s)/W(s), bowling M(c), cross-country running M(s)/W(s), fencing M(s)/W(s), ice hockey M(c), soccer M(s)/W(s), swimming and diving M(s)/W(s), tennis M(s)/W(s), track and field M/W, volleyball M(s)/W(s). ***Intramural sports:*** basketball M/W, bowling M/W, cheerleading M/W, ice hockey M, racquetball M/W, soccer M/W, softball M, swimming and diving M/W, tennis M/W, track and field M/W, ultimate Frisbee M/W, volleyball M/W, water polo M/W.
Campus security: 24-hour emergency response devices and patrols, late-night transport/escort service, controlled dormitory access, bicycle patrols.
Student services: health clinic, personal/psychological counseling, women's center.

COSTS & FINANCIAL AID
Costs (2014–15) ***Tuition:*** state resident $13,120 full-time, $499 per credit part-time; nonresident $26,760 full-time, $1144 per credit part-time. Full-time tuition and fees vary according to course load and degree level. Part-time tuition and fees vary according to course load and degree level. ***Required fees:*** $2528 full-time, $148 per credit part-time. ***Room and board:*** $13,280. Room and board charges vary according to board plan and housing facility. ***Payment plans:*** installment, deferred payment. ***Waivers:*** employees or children of employees.
Financial Aid Of all full-time matriculated undergraduates who enrolled in 2013, 4,419 applied for aid, 3,987 were judged to have need, 379 had their need fully met. 239 Federal Work-Study jobs (averaging $1363). 813 state and other part-time jobs (averaging $2203). In 2013, 523 non-need-based awards were made. ***Average percent of need met:*** 60. ***Average financial aid package:*** $14,123. ***Average need-based loan:*** $4586. ***Average need-based gift aid:*** $11,799. ***Average non-need-based aid:*** $12,290.

APPLYING
Standardized Tests *Required:* SAT or ACT (for admission).
Options: electronic application, early admission, deferred entrance.
Application fee: $70.
Required: high school transcript. ***Required for some:*** essay or personal statement, interview. ***Recommended:*** 1 letter of recommendation, standardized test scores recommended for some.
Application deadlines: 3/1 (freshmen), 6/1 (transfers).
Notification: continuous (freshmen), continuous (transfers).

CONTACT
Mr. Stephen M. Eck, Director of University Admissions, New Jersey Institute of Technology, University Heights, Newark, NJ 07102. *Phone:* 973-596-3306. *Toll-free phone:* 800-925-NJIT. *Fax:* 973-596-3461. *E-mail:* admissions@njit.edu.

Pillar College
Newark, New Jersey
http://www.pillar.edu/

CONTACT
Ms. Linda Aarni, Senior Admissions Counselor, Pillar College, 60 Park Place, Suite 701, Newark, NJ 07102. *Phone:* 973-803-5000. *Toll-free phone:* 800-234-9305. *Fax:* 732-356-4846. *E-mail:* info@pillar.edu.

See next page for display ad and page 1568 for the College Close-Up.

★ Princeton University
Princeton, New Jersey
http://www.princeton.edu/

- **Independent** university, founded 1746
- **Suburban** 600-acre campus with easy access to New York City, Philadelphia
- **Endowment** $20.6 billion
- **Coed** 5,391 undergraduate students, 98% full-time, 49% women, 51% men
- **Most difficult** entrance level, 7% of applicants were admitted

UNDERGRAD STUDENTS
5,275 full-time, 116 part-time. Students come from 52 states and territories; 92 other countries; 82% are from out of state; 8% Black or African American, non-Hispanic/Latino; 8% Hispanic/Latino; 21% Asian, non-Hispanic/Latino; 0.1% Native Hawaiian or other Pacific Islander, non-Hispanic/Latino; 0.1% American Indian or Alaska Native, non-Hispanic/Latino; 4% Two or more races, non-Hispanic/Latino; 2% Race/ethnicity unknown; 11% international; 98% live on campus.

Freshmen
Admission: 26,641 applied, 1,983 admitted, 1,310 enrolled. ***Average high school GPA:*** 3.91. ***Test scores:*** SAT critical reading scores over 500: 100%; SAT math scores over 500: 100%; SAT writing scores over 500: 100%; ACT scores over 18: 100%; SAT critical reading scores over 600: 96%; SAT math scores over 600: 98%; SAT writing scores over 600: 98%; ACT scores over 24: 100%; SAT critical reading scores over 700: 74%; SAT math scores over 700: 79%; SAT writing scores over 700: 76%; ACT scores over 30: 86%.
Retention: 98% of full-time freshmen returned.

FACULTY
Total: 1,103, 82% full-time, 87% with terminal degrees.
Student/faculty ratio: 6:1.

ACADEMICS
Calendar: semesters. *Degrees:* bachelor's, master's, and doctoral.
Special study options: advanced placement credit, independent study, off-campus study, services for LD students, student-designed majors, study abroad. ***ROTC:*** Army (b), Navy (c), Air Force (c).
Computers: 500 computers/terminals and 17,000 ports are available on campus for general student use. Students can access the following: campus intranet, computer help desk, free student e-mail accounts, online (class) grades, online (class) registration, online (class) schedules, academic applications and courseware, printing, network file space, Web site hosting, media lab, broadcast center. Campuswide network is

available. 100% of college-owned or -operated housing units are wired for high-speed Internet access. Wireless service is available via entire campus.

STUDENT LIFE

Housing options: on-campus residence required through sophomore year; coed, men-only, women-only, special housing for students with disabilities. Campus housing is university owned. Freshman campus housing is guaranteed.

Activities and organizations: drama/theater group, student-run newspaper, radio station, choral group, marching band.

Athletics Member NCAA. All Division I except football (Division I-AA). ***Intercollegiate sports:*** baseball M, basketball M/W, crew M/W, cross-country running M/W, fencing M/W, field hockey W, golf M/W, ice hockey M/W, lacrosse M/W, soccer M/W, softball W, squash M/W, swimming and diving M/W, tennis M/W, track and field M/W, volleyball M/W, water polo M/W, wrestling M. ***Intramural sports:*** badminton M(c)/W(c), baseball M(c), basketball M(c)/W(c), cheerleading M(c)/W(c), cross-country running M(c)/W(c), equestrian sports M(c)/W(c), fencing M(c)/W(c), field hockey W(c), ice hockey M(c)/W(c), lacrosse M(c)/W(c), rugby M(c)/W(c), sailing M(c)/W(c), skiing (downhill) M(c)/W(c), soccer M(c)/W(c), softball W(c), squash M(c)/W(c), swimming and diving M(c)/W(c), table tennis M(c)/W(c), tennis M(c)/W(c), ultimate Frisbee M(c)/W(c), volleyball M(c)/W(c).

Campus security: 24-hour emergency response devices and patrols, student patrols, late-night transport/escort service, controlled dormitory access.

Student services: health clinic, personal/psychological counseling, women's center, legal services.

COSTS & FINANCIAL AID

Costs (2015–16) ***Comprehensive fee:*** $57,610 includes full-time tuition ($43,450) and room and board ($14,160). ***College room only:*** $7920. Room and board charges vary according to board plan. ***Payment plans:*** installment, deferred payment. ***Waivers:*** employees or children of employees.

Financial Aid Of all full-time matriculated undergraduates who enrolled in 2014, 3,312 applied for aid, 3,100 were judged to have need, 3,100 had their need fully met. 688 Federal Work-Study jobs (averaging $1017). 1,366 state and other part-time jobs (averaging $1464). ***Average percent of need met:*** 100. ***Average financial aid package:*** $44,047. ***Average need-based gift aid:*** $42,097. ***Average indebtedness upon graduation:*** $6600.

APPLYING

Standardized Tests *Required:* SAT or ACT (for admission).

Options: electronic application, early action, deferred entrance.

Application fee: $65.

Required: essay or personal statement, high school transcript, 3 letters of recommendation. ***Recommended:*** interview.

Application deadlines: 1/1 (freshmen), 11/1 (early action).

Notification: 3/31 (freshmen).

CONTACT

Ms. Janet Rapelye, Dean of Admission, Princeton University, PO Box 430, Princeton, NJ 08542-0430. *Phone:* 609-258-3060. *Fax:* 609-258-6743. *E-mail:* uaoffice@princeton.edu.

Ramapo College of New Jersey

Mahwah, New Jersey

http://www.ramapo.edu/

- **State-supported** comprehensive, founded 1969, part of New Jersey State College System
- **Suburban** 300-acre campus with easy access to New York City
- **Coed** 5,710 undergraduate students, 88% full-time, 55% women, 45% men
- **Moderately difficult** entrance level, 53% of applicants were admitted

UNDERGRAD STUDENTS

5,044 full-time, 666 part-time. 5% are from out of state; 6% Black or African American, non-Hispanic/Latino; 14% Hispanic/Latino; 6% Asian, non-Hispanic/Latino; 0.2% Native Hawaiian or other Pacific Islander, non-Hispanic/Latino; 0.3% American Indian or Alaska Native, non-Hispanic/Latino; 1% Two or more races, non-Hispanic/Latino; 8%

Race/ethnicity unknown; 1% international; 11% transferred in; 48% live on campus.

Freshmen

Admission: 6,699 applied, 3,572 admitted, 965 enrolled. ***Average high school GPA:*** 3.21. ***Test scores:*** SAT critical reading scores over 500: 70%; SAT math scores over 500: 79%; SAT writing scores over 500: 70%; ACT scores over 18: 86%; SAT critical reading scores over 600: 22%; SAT math scores over 600: 30%; SAT writing scores over 600: 24%; ACT scores over 24: 43%; SAT critical reading scores over 700: 2%; SAT math scores over 700: 4%; SAT writing scores over 700: 3%; ACT scores over 30: 3%.

Retention: 88% of full-time freshmen returned.

FACULTY

Total: 465, 47% full-time.

Student/faculty ratio: 18:1.

ACADEMICS

Calendar: semesters. *Degrees:* certificates, bachelor's, master's, post-master's, and postbachelor's certificates.

Special study options: academic remediation for entering students, accelerated degree program, adult/continuing education programs, advanced placement credit, cooperative education, distance learning, double majors, external degree program, freshman honors college, honors programs, independent study, internships, off-campus study, part-time degree program, services for LD students, student-designed majors, study abroad, summer session for credit. ***ROTC:*** Army (c), Air Force (c).

Unusual degree programs: 3-2 biology, and chemistry with Rutgers, The State University of New Jersey; NY University College of Dentistry; SUNY State College of Optometry. RCNJ confers BSN, MSN degrees here on campus (with clinical internships at Valley Hospital, Englewood Hospital and Medical Center, and other state hospitals).

Computers: Students can access the following: campus intranet, computer help desk, free student e-mail accounts, online (class) grades, online (class) registration, online (class) schedules. Campuswide network is available. 100% of college-owned or -operated housing units are wired for high-speed Internet access. Wireless service is available via classrooms, computer centers, computer labs, learning centers, libraries, student centers.

STUDENT LIFE

Housing options: coed. Campus housing is university owned. Freshman campus housing is guaranteed.

Activities and organizations: drama/theater group, student-run newspaper, radio and television station, choral group, NORML, 1 Step, Biology & Biochemistry Club, Campus Crusade for Christ, Culture Club, national fraternities, national sororities.

Athletics Member NCAA. All Division III. ***Intercollegiate sports:*** baseball M, basketball M/W, cross-country running M/W, field hockey W, lacrosse W, soccer M/W, softball W, swimming and diving M/W, tennis M/W, track and field M/W, volleyball M/W. ***Intramural sports:*** basketball M/W, bowling M/W, football M/W, rock climbing M/W, soccer M/W, softball M/W, table tennis M/W, ultimate Frisbee M/W, volleyball M/W.

Campus security: 24-hour emergency response devices and patrols, late-night transport/escort service, controlled dormitory access, surveillance cameras, patrols by trained security personnel.

Student services: health clinic, personal/psychological counseling, women's center.

COSTS & FINANCIAL AID

Costs (2015–16) ***Tuition:*** state resident $8650 full-time; nonresident $17,300 full-time. ***Room and board:*** $11,550; room only: $8020. Room and board charges vary according to board plan and housing facility. ***Payment plan:*** installment. ***Waivers:*** senior citizens and employees or children of employees.

Financial Aid Of all full-time matriculated undergraduates who enrolled in 2013, 3,888 applied for aid, 3,019 were judged to have need, 432 had their need fully met. 131 Federal Work-Study jobs (averaging $1577). 764 state and other part-time jobs (averaging $1950). In 2013, 382 non-need-based awards were made. ***Average percent of need met:*** 58. ***Average financial aid package:*** $11,087. ***Average need-based loan:*** $4341. ***Average need-based gift aid:*** $8846. ***Average non-need-based aid:*** $10,586. ***Average indebtedness upon graduation:*** $30,768.

APPLYING

Standardized Tests *Required:* SAT or ACT (for admission).

Options: electronic application, early admission, early decision, deferred entrance.

Application fee: $60.

Required: essay or personal statement, high school transcript. ***Recommended:*** minimum 3.0 GPA.

CONTACT

Michael DiBartolomeo, Associate Director for Freshmen Admissions, Ramapo College of New Jersey, Office of Admissions, 505 Ramapo Valley Road, Mahwah, NJ 07430-1680. *Phone:* 201-684-7300. *Toll-free phone:* 800-9RAMAPO. *Fax:* 201-684-7964. *E-mail:* admissions@ramapo.edu.

Rider University

Lawrenceville, New Jersey

http://www.rider.edu/

- **Independent** comprehensive, founded 1865
- **Suburban** 280-acre campus with easy access to New York City, Philadelphia
- **Endowment** $65.2 million
- **Coed** 4,324 undergraduate students, 88% full-time, 59% women, 41% men
- **Moderately difficult** entrance level, 71% of applicants were admitted

UNDERGRAD STUDENTS

3,822 full-time, 502 part-time. Students come from 38 states and territories; 74 other countries; 23% are from out of state; 10% Black or African American, non-Hispanic/Latino; 11% Hispanic/Latino; 5% Asian, non-Hispanic/Latino; 0.2% Native Hawaiian or other Pacific Islander, non-Hispanic/Latino; 0.1% American Indian or Alaska Native, non-Hispanic/Latino; 3% Two or more races, non-Hispanic/Latino; 4% Race/ethnicity unknown; 4% international; 5% transferred in; 57% live on campus.

Freshmen

Admission: 9,366 applied, 6,641 admitted, 1,000 enrolled. ***Average high school GPA:*** 3.29. ***Test scores:*** SAT critical reading scores over 500: 52%; SAT math scores over 500: 61%; SAT writing scores over 500: 52%; ACT scores over 18: 88%; SAT critical reading scores over 600: 13%; SAT math scores over 600: 15%; SAT writing scores over 600: 15%; ACT scores over 24: 37%; SAT critical reading scores over 700: 1%; SAT math scores over 700: 2%; SAT writing scores over 700: 1%; ACT scores over 30: 6%.

Retention: 81% of full-time freshmen returned.

FACULTY

Total: 592, 42% full-time, 69% with terminal degrees.

Student/faculty ratio: 12:1.

ACADEMICS

Calendar: semesters. *Degrees:* certificates, associate, bachelor's, master's, post-master's, and postbachelor's certificates.

Special study options: academic remediation for entering students, adult/continuing education programs, advanced placement credit, cooperative education, distance learning, double majors, English as a second language, honors programs, independent study, internships, part-time degree program, services for LD students, study abroad, summer session for credit. ***ROTC:*** Army (c).

Computers: 300 computers/terminals are available on campus for general student use. Students can access the following: computer help desk, free student e-mail accounts, online (class) grades, online (class) registration, online (class) schedules. Campuswide network is available. 100% of college-owned or -operated housing units are wired for high-speed Internet access. Wireless service is available via entire campus.

STUDENT LIFE

Housing options: coed, women-only, special housing for students with disabilities. Campus housing is university owned. Freshman applicants given priority for college housing.

Activities and organizations: drama/theater group, student-run newspaper, radio and television station, choral group, Student Government Association, Greek Council, Association of Commuter

Students, Black Student Union, Residence Hall Association, national fraternities, national sororities.

Athletics Member NCAA. All Division I. ***Intercollegiate sports:*** baseball M(s), basketball M(s)/W(s), cheerleading M/W, cross-country running M(s)/W(s), field hockey W(s), golf M(s), soccer M(s)/W(s), softball W(s), swimming and diving M(s)/W(s), tennis M(s)/W(s), track and field M(s)/W(s), volleyball W(s), wrestling M(s). ***Intramural sports:*** basketball M/W, cheerleading M/W, equestrian sports W(c), golf M, ice hockey M(c), lacrosse M(c)/W, soccer M/W, softball M/W, track and field M/W, volleyball M/W, water polo M/W.

Campus security: 24-hour emergency response devices and patrols, student patrols, late-night transport/escort service, controlled dormitory access.

Student services: health clinic, personal/psychological counseling.

COSTS & FINANCIAL AID

Costs (2014–15) ***Comprehensive fee:*** $50,160 includes full-time tuition ($36,120), mandatory fees ($710), and room and board ($13,330). Part-time tuition: $1060 per credit. Part-time tuition and fees vary according to program. ***Required fees:*** $13 per credit part-time. ***College room only:*** $8570. Room and board charges vary according to board plan and housing facility.

Financial Aid Of all full-time matriculated undergraduates who enrolled in 2014, 3,080 applied for aid, 2,772 were judged to have need, 406 had their need fully met. In 2014, 838 non-need-based awards were made. ***Average percent of need met:*** 72. ***Average financial aid package:*** $25,946. ***Average need-based loan:*** $3701. ***Average need-based gift aid:*** $21,742. ***Average non-need-based aid:*** $14,955. ***Average indebtedness upon graduation:*** $28,080.

APPLYING

Standardized Tests *Required:* SAT or ACT (for admission).

Options: electronic application, early admission, early action, deferred entrance.

Application fee: $50.

Required: essay or personal statement, high school transcript, 2 letters of recommendation. ***Required for some:*** interview.

Application deadlines: rolling (freshmen), rolling (transfers), 11/15 (early action).

Notification: continuous (freshmen), continuous (transfers), 12/15 (early action).

CONTACT

Mr. William Larrousse, Director of Admissions, Rider University, 2083 Lawrenceville Road, Lawrenceville, NJ 08648. *Phone:* 609-896-5177. *Toll-free phone:* 800-257-9026. *Fax:* 609-895-6645. *E-mail:* wlarrousse@rider.edu.

Rowan University

Glassboro, New Jersey

http://www.rowan.edu/

- **State-supported** comprehensive, founded 1923, part of New Jersey State College System
- **Suburban** 921-acre campus with easy access to Philadelphia
- **Endowment** $189.3 million
- **Coed** 12,022 undergraduate students, 87% full-time, 47% women, 53% men
- **Moderately difficult** entrance level, 66% of applicants were admitted

UNDERGRAD STUDENTS

10,499 full-time, 1,523 part-time. Students come from 22 states and territories; 44 other countries; 5% are from out of state; 9% Black or African American, non-Hispanic/Latino; 9% Hispanic/Latino; 6% Asian, non-Hispanic/Latino; 0.1% Native Hawaiian or other Pacific Islander, non-Hispanic/Latino; 0.3% American Indian or Alaska Native, non-Hispanic/Latino; 3% Two or more races, non-Hispanic/Latino; 3% Race/ethnicity unknown; 0.9% international; 12% transferred in; 36% live on campus.

Freshmen

Admission: 10,074 applied, 6,600 admitted, 1,920 enrolled. ***Average high school GPA:*** 3.46. ***Test scores:*** SAT critical reading scores over 500: 70%; SAT math scores over 500: 80%; SAT writing scores over 500: 65%; SAT critical reading scores over 600: 21%; SAT math scores over 600: 38%; SAT writing scores over 600: 18%; SAT critical reading scores over 700: 3%; SAT math scores over 700: 7%; SAT writing scores over 700: 2%.

Retention: 86% of full-time freshmen returned.

FACULTY

Total: 1,312, 30% full-time, 33% with terminal degrees.

Student/faculty ratio: 17:1.

ACADEMICS

Calendar: semesters. *Degrees:* certificates, bachelor's, master's, doctoral, post-master's, and postbachelor's certificates.

Special study options: academic remediation for entering students, accelerated degree program, adult/continuing education programs, advanced placement credit, cooperative education, distance learning, double majors, English as a second language, freshman honors college, honors programs, independent study, internships, off-campus study, part-time degree program, services for LD students, study abroad, summer session for credit. ***ROTC:*** Army (c).

Unusual degree programs: 3-2 mathematics and computer science.

Computers: 882 computers/terminals and 2,500 ports are available on campus for general student use. Students can access the following: campus intranet, computer help desk, free student e-mail accounts, online (class) grades, online (class) registration, online (class) schedules, online library. Campuswide network is available. 100% of college-owned or -operated housing units are wired for high-speed Internet access. Wireless service is available via entire campus.

STUDENT LIFE

Housing options: on-campus residence required through sophomore year; coed, special housing for students with disabilities. Campus housing is university owned and leased by the school. Freshman campus housing is guaranteed.

Activities and organizations: drama/theater group, student-run newspaper, radio and television station, choral group, Kappa Delta Pi, Public Relations Student Society of America, Student University Programmes, Rowan Television Network, Elementary Education Club, national fraternities, national sororities.

Athletics Member NCAA. All Division III. ***Intercollegiate sports:*** baseball M, basketball M/W, cross-country running M/W, field hockey W, football M, lacrosse W, soccer M/W, softball W, swimming and diving M/W, track and field M/W, volleyball W. ***Intramural sports:*** basketball M/W, bowling M/W, cheerleading W(c), field hockey W(c), football M/W, golf M/W, ice hockey M(c), lacrosse M(c)/W, racquetball M/W, rock climbing M(c), rugby M, skiing (downhill) M(c)/W(c), soccer M/W, softball M/W, table tennis M/W, tennis M(c)/W(c), ultimate Frisbee M(c)/W(c), volleyball M/W, water polo M/W, wrestling M(c).

Campus security: 24-hour emergency response devices and patrols, student patrols, late-night transport/escort service, controlled dormitory access, EMS Service including 2 ambulances, Security and Campus Police trained as Police Officers in NJ.

Student services: health clinic, personal/psychological counseling, legal services.

COSTS & FINANCIAL AID

Costs (2015–16) ***Tuition:*** state resident $9076 full-time, $348 per credit hour part-time; nonresident $17,030 full-time, $656 per credit hour part-time. Full-time tuition and fees vary according to course load, degree level, location, and program. Part-time tuition and fees vary according to course load, degree level, location, and program. ***Required fees:*** $3540 full-time, $151 per credit hour part-time. ***Room and board:*** $11,406; room only: $7206. Room and board charges vary according to board plan and housing facility. ***Payment plans:*** installment, deferred payment. ***Waivers:*** employees or children of employees.

Financial Aid Of all full-time matriculated undergraduates who enrolled in 2013, 7,627 applied for aid, 6,088 were judged to have need, 1,704 had their need fully met. 426 Federal Work-Study jobs (averaging $1267). In 2013, 765 non-need-based awards were made. ***Average percent of need met:*** 79. ***Average financial aid package:*** $9086. ***Average need-based loan:*** $4328. ***Average need-based gift aid:*** $8551. ***Average non-need-based aid:*** $7811. ***Average indebtedness upon graduation:*** $31,759.

APPLYING

Standardized Tests *Required:* SAT or ACT (for admission).

Options: electronic application, early admission, deferred entrance.

Application fee: $65.

Required: high school transcript, minimum 2.0 GPA. ***Required for some:*** interview.

Application deadlines: 3/1 (freshmen), 3/1 (transfers).

Notification: continuous (freshmen), continuous (transfers).

CONTACT

Mr. Albert Betts, Director of Admissions, Rowan University, 201 Mullica Hill Road, Glassboro, NJ 08028. *Phone:* 856-256-4200. *Toll-free phone:* 800-447-1165 (in-state); 800-447-1165N (out-of-state). *Fax:* 856-256-4430. *E-mail:* admissions@rowan.edu.

Rutgers, The State University of New Jersey, Camden

Camden, New Jersey

http://www.camden.rutgers.edu/

- **State-supported** university, founded 1927, part of Rutgers, The State University of New Jersey
- **Urban** 32-acre campus with easy access to Philadelphia
- **Coed** 4,857 undergraduate students, 82% full-time, 56% women, 44% men
- **Moderately difficult** entrance level, 60% of applicants were admitted

UNDERGRAD STUDENTS

3,990 full-time, 867 part-time. Students come from 23 states and territories; 18 other countries; 2% are from out of state; 17% Black or African American, non-Hispanic/Latino; 12% Hispanic/Latino; 9% Asian, non-Hispanic/Latino; 0.2% Native Hawaiian or other Pacific Islander, non-Hispanic/Latino; 0.1% American Indian or Alaska Native, non-Hispanic/Latino; 4% Two or more races, non-Hispanic/Latino; 3% Race/ethnicity unknown; 1% international; 19% transferred in; 9% live on campus.

Freshmen

Admission: 6,550 applied, 3,955 admitted, 431 enrolled. ***Test scores:*** SAT critical reading scores over 500: 55%; SAT math scores over 500: 62%; SAT writing scores over 500: 53%; SAT critical reading scores over 600: 14%; SAT math scores over 600: 17%; SAT writing scores over 600: 14%; SAT critical reading scores over 700: 2%; SAT math scores over 700: 2%; SAT writing scores over 700: 2%.

Retention: 82% of full-time freshmen returned.

FACULTY

Total: 614, 50% full-time, 98% with terminal degrees.

Student/faculty ratio: 10:1.

ACADEMICS

Calendar: semesters. *Degrees:* bachelor's, master's, and doctoral.

Special study options: academic remediation for entering students, accelerated degree program, advanced placement credit, cooperative education, distance learning, double majors, English as a second language, freshman honors college, honors programs, independent study, internships, part-time degree program, services for LD students, student-designed majors, study abroad, summer session for credit. ***ROTC:*** Army (c), Air Force (c).

Unusual degree programs: 3-2 business administration; engineering; medical technology with approved hospital; African-American studies, general science, childhood studies, English, history, liberal studies, psychology; biology, chemistry and mathematics with the Graduate School-Camden.

Computers: 184 computers/terminals are available on campus for general student use. Students can access the following: campus intranet, computer help desk, free student e-mail accounts, online (class) grades, online (class) registration, online (class) schedules, online grade reports. Campuswide network is available. 100% of college-owned or -operated housing units are wired for high-speed Internet access. Wireless service is available via classrooms, computer centers, computer labs, dorm rooms, learning centers, libraries, student centers.

STUDENT LIFE

Housing options: coed, special housing for students with disabilities. Campus housing is university owned.

Activities and organizations: drama/theater group, student-run radio station.

Athletics Member NCAA. All Division III. ***Intercollegiate sports:*** baseball M, basketball M/W, crew M/W, cross-country running W, golf M, lacrosse W, soccer M/W, softball W, track and field M/W, volleyball W. ***Intramural sports:*** baseball M, basketball M/W, cheerleading W, crew M, golf M, ice hockey M, lacrosse M, racquetball M, soccer M, tennis M, track and field M, ultimate Frisbee M/W, volleyball M/W.

Campus security: 24-hour emergency response devices and patrols, student patrols, late-night transport/escort service, controlled dormitory access.

COSTS & FINANCIAL AID

Costs (2014–15) ***Tuition:*** state resident $10,954 full-time, $353 per credit part-time; nonresident $25,249 full-time, $835 per credit part-time. Part-time tuition and fees vary according to course load. ***Required fees:*** $2729 full-time, $459 per term part-time. ***Room and board:*** $11,438; room only: $7938. Room and board charges vary according to board plan and housing facility. ***Payment plan:*** installment. ***Waivers:*** employees or children of employees.

Financial Aid Of all full-time matriculated undergraduates who enrolled in 2014, 3,457 applied for aid, 3,119 were judged to have need, 72 had their need fully met. 279 Federal Work-Study jobs (averaging $1876). 452 state and other part-time jobs (averaging $1567). In 2014, 128 non-need-based awards were made. ***Average percent of need met:*** 54. ***Average financial aid package:*** $12,618. ***Average need-based loan:*** $4741. ***Average need-based gift aid:*** $10,275. ***Average non-need-based aid:*** $3185. ***Average indebtedness upon graduation:*** $28,651.

APPLYING

Standardized Tests *Required:* SAT or ACT (for admission).

Options: electronic application.

Application fee: $65.

Required: high school transcript.

Application deadlines: 12/1 (freshmen), 1/15 (transfers).

Notification: 2/28 (freshmen), 5/15 (transfers).

CONTACT

Rutgers, The State University of New Jersey, Camden, 406 Penn Street, Camden, NJ 08102-1401. *Phone:* 856-225-6104.

Rutgers, The State University of New Jersey, Newark

Newark, New Jersey

http://www.newark.rutgers.edu/

- **State-supported** university, founded 1892, part of Rutgers, The State University of New Jersey
- **Urban** 106-acre campus
- **Coed** 7,408 undergraduate students, 80% full-time, 51% women, 49% men
- **Moderately difficult** entrance level, 63% of applicants were admitted

UNDERGRAD STUDENTS

5,943 full-time, 1,465 part-time. Students come from 26 states and territories; 40 other countries; 3% are from out of state; 19% Black or African American, non-Hispanic/Latino; 26% Hispanic/Latino; 21% Asian, non-Hispanic/Latino; 0.4% Native Hawaiian or other Pacific Islander, non-Hispanic/Latino; 0.1% American Indian or Alaska Native, non-Hispanic/Latino; 3% Two or more races, non-Hispanic/Latino; 2% Race/ethnicity unknown; 3% international; 12% transferred in; 9% live on campus.

Freshmen

Admission: 10,332 applied, 6,483 admitted, 1,017 enrolled. ***Test scores:*** SAT critical reading scores over 500: 48%; SAT math scores over 500: 73%; SAT writing scores over 500: 56%; SAT critical reading scores over 600: 9%; SAT math scores over 600: 23%; SAT writing scores over 600: 12%; SAT critical reading scores over 700: 1%; SAT math scores over 700: 3%; SAT writing scores over 700: 2%.

Retention: 86% of full-time freshmen returned.

FACULTY
Total: 875, 59% full-time, 98% with terminal degrees.

Student/faculty ratio: 10:1.

ACADEMICS
Calendar: semesters. *Degrees:* associate, bachelor's, master's, and doctoral.

Special study options: academic remediation for entering students, accelerated degree program, adult/continuing education programs, advanced placement credit, cooperative education, distance learning, double majors, English as a second language, freshman honors college, honors programs, independent study, internships, off-campus study, part-time degree program, services for LD students, student-designed majors, study abroad, summer session for credit. ***ROTC:*** Army (b), Navy (b), Air Force (b).

Unusual degree programs: 3-2 business administration; engineering; nursing.

Computers: 708 computers/terminals are available on campus for general student use. Students can access the following: computer help desk, free student e-mail accounts, online (class) grades, online (class) schedules, online grade reports. Campuswide network is available. Wireless service is available via classrooms, computer centers, computer labs, dorm rooms, learning centers, libraries, student centers.

STUDENT LIFE
Housing options: coed. Campus housing is university owned.

Activities and organizations: drama/theater group, student-run newspaper, radio station, choral group.

Athletics Member NCAA. All Division III except volleyball (Division I). ***Intercollegiate sports:*** baseball M, basketball M/W, cross-country running M/W, soccer M/W, tennis M/W, track and field M, volleyball M/W. ***Intramural sports:*** baseball M/W, basketball M/W, racquetball M/W, rock climbing M/W, soccer M/W, swimming and diving M/W, weight lifting M/W.

Campus security: 24-hour emergency response devices and patrols, student patrols, late-night transport/escort service, controlled dormitory access.

COSTS & FINANCIAL AID
Costs (2014–15) ***Tuition:*** state resident $10,954 full-time, $353 per credit part-time; nonresident $25,732 full-time, $835 per credit part-time. Part-time tuition and fees vary according to course load. ***Required fees:*** $2343 full-time, $441 per term part-time. ***Room and board:*** $12,509; room only: $7743. Room and board charges vary according to board plan and housing facility. ***Payment plan:*** installment. ***Waivers:*** employees or children of employees.

Financial Aid Of all full-time matriculated undergraduates who enrolled in 2014, 5,238 applied for aid, 4,928 were judged to have need, 80 had their need fully met. 655 Federal Work-Study jobs (averaging $1650). 710 state and other part-time jobs (averaging $1210). In 2014, 35 non-need-based awards were made. ***Average percent of need met:*** 57. ***Average financial aid package:*** $13,705. ***Average need-based loan:*** $4811. ***Average need-based gift aid:*** $10,938. ***Average non-need-based aid:*** $7255. ***Average indebtedness upon graduation:*** $26,993.

APPLYING
Standardized Tests *Required:* SAT or ACT (for admission).

Options: electronic application.

Application fee: $65.

Required: high school transcript.

Application deadlines: 12/1 (freshmen), 1/15 (transfers).

Notification: 2/28 (freshmen), 5/15 (transfers).

CONTACT
Christina M. Chiaravalloti, Assistant Director of Admissions, Rutgers, The State University of New Jersey, Newark, 249 University Avenue, Newark, NJ 07102. *Phone:* 973-353-5205 Ext. 0012. *Fax:* 973-353-1440. *E-mail:* chiaravalloti@ugadm.rutgers.edu.

Rutgers, The State University of New Jersey, New Brunswick

Piscataway, New Jersey

http://newbrunswick.rutgers.edu/

- **State-supported** university, founded 1766, part of Rutgers, The State University of New Jersey
- **Urban** 2688-acre campus with easy access to New York City
- **Coed** 34,544 undergraduate students, 94% full-time, 50% women, 50% men
- **Moderately difficult** entrance level, 60% of applicants were admitted

UNDERGRAD STUDENTS
32,411 full-time, 2,133 part-time. Students come from 52 states and territories; 72 other countries; 6% are from out of state; 7% Black or African American, non-Hispanic/Latino; 13% Hispanic/Latino; 26% Asian, non-Hispanic/Latino; 0.3% Native Hawaiian or other Pacific Islander, non-Hispanic/Latino; 0.1% American Indian or Alaska Native, non-Hispanic/Latino; 3% Two or more races, non-Hispanic/Latino; 2% Race/ethnicity unknown; 6% international; 7% transferred in; 48% live on campus.

Freshmen
Admission: 31,941 applied, 19,324 admitted, 6,412 enrolled. ***Test scores:*** SAT critical reading scores over 500: 83%; SAT math scores over 500: 95%; SAT writing scores over 500: 90%; SAT critical reading scores over 600: 42%; SAT math scores over 600: 67%; SAT writing scores over 600: 50%; SAT critical reading scores over 700: 10%; SAT math scores over 700: 27%; SAT writing scores over 700: 15%.

Retention: 92% of full-time freshmen returned.

FACULTY
Total: 4,875, 40% full-time, 99% with terminal degrees.

Student/faculty ratio: 11:1.

ACADEMICS
Calendar: semesters. *Degrees:* associate, bachelor's, master's, doctoral, post-master's, and postbachelor's certificates.

Special study options: academic remediation for entering students, accelerated degree program, advanced placement credit, cooperative education, distance learning, double majors, English as a second language, honors programs, independent study, internships, part-time degree program, student-designed majors, study abroad. ***ROTC:*** Army (b), Navy (b), Air Force (b).

Unusual degree programs: 3-2 business administration; engineering; nursing; Rutgers-Robert Wood Johnson Medical School, Rutgers-New Jersey Medical School.

Computers: 1,450 computers/terminals are available on campus for general student use. Students can access the following: campus intranet, computer help desk, free student e-mail accounts, online (class) grades, online (class) registration, online (class) schedules, online grade reports. Campuswide network is available. Wireless service is available via entire campus.

STUDENT LIFE
Housing options: coed, men-only, women-only, cooperative. Campus housing is university owned.

Activities and organizations: drama/theater group, student-run newspaper, radio and television station, choral group, marching band, national fraternities, national sororities.

Athletics Member NCAA. All Division I except football (Division I-A). ***Intercollegiate sports:*** baseball M, basketball M/W, crew M/W, cross-country running M/W, fencing M/W, golf M/W, gymnastics W, lacrosse M/W, soccer M/W, softball W, swimming and diving M/W, tennis M/W, track and field M/W, volleyball W, wrestling M. ***Intramural sports:*** badminton M/W, baseball M(c), basketball M/W, bowling M/W, cross-country running M/W, equestrian sports M(c)/W(c), field hockey W(c), football M, golf M/W, ice hockey M(c), lacrosse M/W, racquetball M/W, rugby M(c)/W(c), sailing M(c)/W(c), skiing (cross-country) M(c)/W(c), skiing (downhill) M(c)/W(c), soccer M/W, softball M/W, squash M(c)/W(c), swimming and diving M/W, table tennis M(c)/W(c), tennis M/W, track and field M/W, volleyball M/W, water polo M/W, wrestling M.

Campus security: 24-hour emergency response devices and patrols, student patrols, late-night transport/escort service, controlled dormitory access.

Student services: health clinic, personal/psychological counseling, women's center.

COSTS & FINANCIAL AID

Costs (2014–15) ***Tuition:*** state resident $10,954 full-time, $353 per credit part-time; nonresident $25,732 full-time, $835 per credit part-time. Part-time tuition and fees vary according to course load. ***Required fees:*** $2859 full-time, $299 per term part-time. ***Room and board:*** $11,749; room only: $7163. Room and board charges vary according to board plan and housing facility. ***Payment plan:*** installment. ***Waivers:*** employees or children of employees.

Financial Aid Of all full-time matriculated undergraduates who enrolled in 2014, 20,843 applied for aid, 17,623 were judged to have need, 630 had their need fully met. 2,954 Federal Work-Study jobs (averaging $1952). 5,610 state and other part-time jobs (averaging $1177). In 2014, 726 non-need-based awards were made. ***Average percent of need met:*** 53. ***Average financial aid package:*** $13,491. ***Average need-based loan:*** $4690. ***Average need-based gift aid:*** $11,051. ***Average non-need-based aid:*** $8461. ***Average indebtedness upon graduation:*** $18,505.

APPLYING

Standardized Tests *Required:* SAT or ACT (for admission).

Options: electronic application.

Application fee: $65.

Required: high school transcript. ***Required for some:*** interview. ***Recommended:*** essay or personal statement.

Application deadlines: 12/1 (freshmen), 1/15 (transfers).

Notification: 2/28 (freshmen), 5/15 (transfers).

CONTACT

Rutgers, The State University of New Jersey, New Brunswick, 65 Davidson Road, Room 202, Piscataway, NJ 08854-8097. *Phone:* 732-445-4636.

Saint Peter's University

Jersey City, New Jersey

http://www.saintpeters.edu/

- **Independent Roman Catholic (Jesuit)** comprehensive, founded 1872
- **Urban** 15-acre campus with easy access to New York City
- **Endowment** $34.1 million
- **Coed** 2,506 undergraduate students, 86% full-time, 62% women, 38% men
- **Moderately difficult** entrance level, 57% of applicants were admitted

UNDERGRAD STUDENTS

2,165 full-time, 341 part-time. Students come from 27 states and territories; 66 other countries; 12% are from out of state; 30% Black or African American, non-Hispanic/Latino; 34% Hispanic/Latino; 8% Asian, non-Hispanic/Latino; 0.7% Native Hawaiian or other Pacific Islander, non-Hispanic/Latino; 0.2% American Indian or Alaska Native, non-Hispanic/Latino; 1% Two or more races, non-Hispanic/Latino; 3% Race/ethnicity unknown; 2% international; 6% transferred in; 31% live on campus.

Freshmen

Admission: 5,993 applied, 3,410 admitted, 584 enrolled. ***Average high school GPA:*** 3.15. ***Test scores:*** SAT critical reading scores over 500: 23%; SAT math scores over 500: 31%; SAT writing scores over 500: 22%; ACT scores over 18: 58%; SAT critical reading scores over 600: 3%; SAT math scores over 600: 5%; SAT writing scores over 600: 3%; ACT scores over 24: 13%; SAT writing scores over 700: 1%; ACT scores over 30: 4%.

Retention: 82% of full-time freshmen returned.

FACULTY

Total: 323, 35% full-time, 57% with terminal degrees.

Student/faculty ratio: 13:1.

ACADEMICS

Calendar: semesters. *Degrees:* certificates, associate, bachelor's, master's, doctoral, post-master's, and postbachelor's certificates.

Special study options: academic remediation for entering students, accelerated degree program, adult/continuing education programs, advanced placement credit, cooperative education, distance learning, double majors, English as a second language, honors programs, independent study, internships, off-campus study, part-time degree program, services for LD students, student-designed majors, study abroad, summer session for credit. ***ROTC:*** Army (c), Air Force (c).

Unusual degree programs: 3-2 with Rutgers University: Pharmacy and Clinical and Laboratory Sciences with emphasis on Cytotechnology or Medical Laboratory Science; With Seton Hall University: Physician's Assistant and Physical Therapy.

Computers: 415 computers/terminals and 415 ports are available on campus for general student use. Students can access the following: computer help desk, free student e-mail accounts, online (class) grades, online (class) registration, online (class) schedules. Campuswide network is available. Wireless service is available via entire campus.

STUDENT LIFE

Housing options: coed, special housing for students with disabilities. Campus housing is university owned. Freshman campus housing is guaranteed.

Activities and organizations: drama/theater group, student-run newspaper, radio station, choral group, Caribbean Culture Club, Black Action Committee, Asian American Student Union, Indian and Pakistani Culture Club, Latin American Student Organization.

Athletics Member NCAA. All Division I. ***Intercollegiate sports:*** baseball M(s), basketball M(s)/W(s), bowling M/W, cross-country running M(s)/W(s), golf M(s), soccer M(s)/W(s), softball W(s), swimming and diving M(s)/W(s), tennis M(s)/W(s), track and field M(s)/W(s), volleyball W(s). ***Intramural sports:*** badminton M/W, basketball M/W, bowling M/W, football M/W, golf M/W, racquetball M/W, soccer M/W, softball M/W, squash M/W, swimming and diving M/W, table tennis M/W, tennis M/W, track and field M/W, volleyball M/W, water polo M/W, weight lifting M/W.

Campus security: 24-hour emergency response devices and patrols, late-night transport/escort service, controlled dormitory access, ID checks at residence halls and library.

Student services: health clinic, personal/psychological counseling.

FINANCIAL AID

Financial Aid Of all full-time matriculated undergraduates who enrolled in 2012, 1,873 applied for aid, 1,658 were judged to have need, 180 had their need fully met. In 2012, 197 non-need-based awards were made. ***Average percent of need met:*** 73. ***Average financial aid package:*** $25,359. ***Average need-based loan:*** $3815. ***Average need-based gift aid:*** $20,088. ***Average non-need-based aid:*** $15,134. ***Average indebtedness upon graduation:*** $32,218.

APPLYING

Standardized Tests *Required:* SAT or ACT (for admission).

Options: early admission, early action, deferred entrance.

Required: essay or personal statement, high school transcript, minimum 2.0 GPA, 2 letters of recommendation. ***Required for some:*** interview. ***Recommended:*** interview.

CONTACT

Miss Kacey Tillotson, Director of Undergraduate Admissions, Saint Peter's University, Office of Admission - Lee House, Jersey City 07306. *Phone:* 201-761-7100. *Toll-free phone:* 888-SPC-9933. *E-mail:* ktillotson@saintpeters.edu.

★ Seton Hall University

South Orange, New Jersey

http://www.shu.edu/

- **Independent Roman Catholic** university, founded 1856
- **Suburban** 58-acre campus with easy access to New York City
- **Coed**
- **Moderately difficult** entrance level

FACULTY

Student/faculty ratio: 14:1.

ACADEMICS
Calendar: semesters. *Degrees:* bachelor's, master's, doctoral, and post-master's certificates.

STUDENT LIFE
Housing options: coed, special housing for students with disabilities. Campus housing is university owned.

Activities and organizations: drama/theater group, student-run newspaper, radio and television station, choral group, Martin Luther King Jr. Scholars Association, Adelante/Caribe, Black Student Union, National Council of Negro Women, national fraternities, national sororities.

Athletics Member NCAA. All Division I.

Campus security: 24-hour emergency response devices and patrols, late-night transport/escort service, controlled dormitory access.

Student services: health clinic, personal/psychological counseling, women's center.

COSTS & FINANCIAL AID
Costs (2014–15) ***Comprehensive fee:*** $50,618 includes full-time tuition ($34,820), mandatory fees ($2106), and room and board ($13,692). Full-time tuition and fees vary according to course load. Part-time tuition: $1061 per credit hour. Part-time tuition and fees vary according to course load. ***Required fees:*** $219 per term part-time. ***Room and board:*** Room and board charges vary according to board plan and housing facility. ***Payment plans:*** installment, deferred payment.

Financial Aid Of all full-time matriculated undergraduates who enrolled in 2004, 3,604 applied for aid, 3,103 were judged to have need, 591 had their need fully met. 807 Federal Work-Study jobs (averaging $1930). 1,116 state and other part-time jobs (averaging $1289). In 2004, 751 non-need-based awards were made. ***Average percent of need met:*** 68. ***Average financial aid package:*** $14,664. ***Average need-based loan:*** $3198. ***Average need-based gift aid:*** $4651. ***Average non-need-based aid:*** $11,243. ***Average indebtedness upon graduation:*** $29,108.

APPLYING
Standardized Tests *Required:* SAT or ACT (for admission).

Options: electronic application, early action, deferred entrance.

Application fee: $55.

Required: essay or personal statement, high school transcript, counselor report. ***Required for some:*** minimum 3.0 GPA, interview. ***Recommended:*** minimum 3.0 GPA, interview.

CONTACT
Mary Clare Cullum, Director of Undergraduate Admissions, Seton Hall University, Enrollment Management Office, 400 South Orange Ave, South Orange, NJ 07079-2697. *Phone:* 973-275-2589. *Toll-free phone:* 800-THE HALL. *Fax:* 973-275-2321. *E-mail:* maryclare.cullum@shu.edu.

See below for display ad and page 1618 for the College Close-Up.

★ Stockton University
Galloway, New Jersey
http://www.stockton.edu/

- **State-supported** comprehensive, founded 1969, part of New Jersey State College System
- **Suburban** 2000-acre campus with easy access to Philadelphia
- **Endowment** $21.5 million
- **Coed** 7,714 undergraduate students, 93% full-time, 59% women, 41% men
- **Very difficult** entrance level, 65% of applicants were admitted

UNDERGRAD STUDENTS
7,170 full-time, 544 part-time. Students come from 14 states and territories; 13 other countries; 1% are from out of state; 6% Black or African American, non-Hispanic/Latino; 10% Hispanic/Latino; 5% Asian, non-Hispanic/Latino; 0.2% Native Hawaiian or other Pacific Islander, non-Hispanic/Latino; 0.1% American Indian or Alaska Native, non-Hispanic/Latino; 3% Two or more races, non-Hispanic/Latino; 1% Race/ethnicity unknown; 0.2% international; 14% transferred in; 38% live on campus.

Freshmen
Admission: 5,229 applied, 3,386 admitted, 1,186 enrolled. ***Test scores:*** SAT critical reading scores over 500: 67%; SAT math scores over 500: 78%; SAT writing scores over 500: 52%; ACT scores over 18: 81%; SAT critical reading scores over 600: 19%; SAT math scores over 600: 26%;

SAT writing scores over 600: 19%; ACT scores over 24: 33%; SAT critical reading scores over 700: 1%; SAT math scores over 700: 3%; SAT writing scores over 700: 1%; ACT scores over 30: 1%.

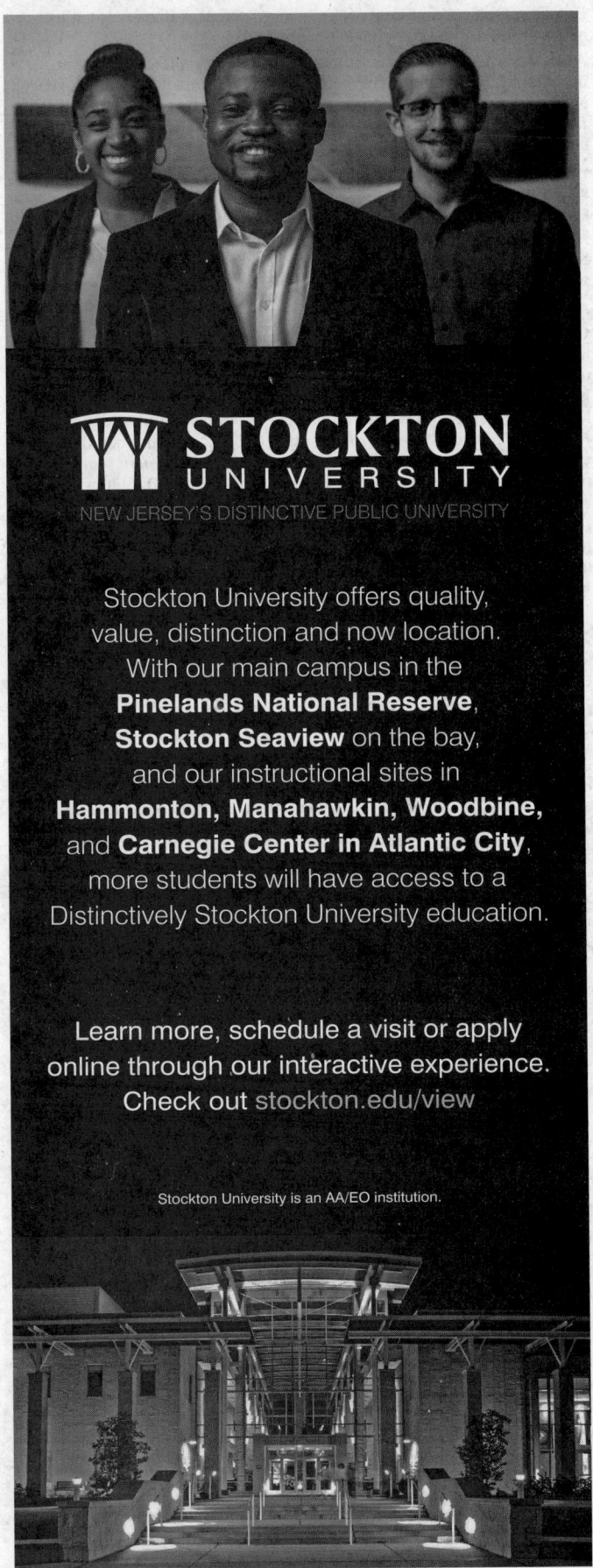

Retention: 87% of full-time freshmen returned.

FACULTY

Total: 660, 46% full-time, 63% with terminal degrees.

Student/faculty ratio: 17:1.

ACADEMICS

Calendar: semesters. *Degrees:* bachelor's, master's, doctoral, and postbachelor's certificates.

Special study options: academic remediation for entering students, accelerated degree program, adult/continuing education programs, advanced placement credit, distance learning, honors programs, independent study, internships, off-campus study, part-time degree program, services for LD students, student-designed majors, study abroad, summer session for credit. ***ROTC:*** Army (c).

Unusual degree programs: 3-2 business administration; engineering with New Jersey Institute of Technology; Rutgers, The State University of New Jersey; Rowan University; criminal justice/public health with University of Medicine and Dentistry of NJ; medical technology with University of Delaware.

Computers: 930 computers/terminals and 2,400 ports are available on campus for general student use. Students can access the following: campus intranet, computer help desk, free student e-mail accounts, online (class) grades, online (class) registration, online (class) schedules. Campuswide network is available. 100% of college-owned or -operated housing units are wired for high-speed Internet access. Wireless service is available via entire campus.

STUDENT LIFE

Housing options: coed, special housing for students with disabilities. Campus housing is university owned. Freshman campus housing is guaranteed.

Activities and organizations: drama/theater group, student-run newspaper, radio and television station, choral group, Multi-Cultural Connection, Stockton Entertainment Team, Los Latinos Unidos, Unified Black Student Society, Stockton Action Volunteers for the Environment, national fraternities, national sororities.

Athletics Member NCAA. All Division III. ***Intercollegiate sports:*** baseball M, basketball M/W, cheerleading M/W, crew W, cross-country running M/W, field hockey W, lacrosse M, soccer M/W, softball W, tennis W, track and field M/W, volleyball W. ***Intramural sports:*** basketball M/W, bowling M(c)/W(c), crew M(c), fencing M(c)/W(c), golf M(c)/W(c), ice hockey M(c), lacrosse W, soccer M/W, softball M/W, table tennis M/W, ultimate Frisbee M(c)/W(c), volleyball M(c)/W(c).

Campus security: 24-hour emergency response devices and patrols, late-night transport/escort service, controlled dormitory access, on-campus sworn/commissioned police force.

Student services: health clinic, personal/psychological counseling, women's center.

COSTS & FINANCIAL AID

Costs (2014–15) ***Tuition:*** state resident $8107 full-time, $312 per credit part-time; nonresident $14,628 full-time, $563 per credit part-time. Part-time tuition and fees vary according to course load. ***Required fees:*** $4461 full-time, $172 per credit part-time, $80 per credit part-time. ***Room and board:*** $11,164; room only: $7604. Room and board charges vary according to board plan and housing facility. ***Payment plans:*** installment, deferred payment. ***Waivers:*** senior citizens and employees or children of employees.

Financial Aid Of all full-time matriculated undergraduates who enrolled in 2014, 6,087 applied for aid, 5,100 were judged to have need, 1,496 had their need fully met. 199 Federal Work-Study jobs (averaging $2022). 885 state and other part-time jobs (averaging $1.6 million). In 2014, 504 non-need-based awards were made. ***Average percent of need met:*** 68. ***Average financial aid package:*** $15,871. ***Average need-based loan:*** $4525. ***Average need-based gift aid:*** $8507. ***Average non-need-based aid:*** $6265. ***Average indebtedness upon graduation:*** $33,543.

APPLYING

Standardized Tests *Required:* SAT or ACT (for admission).

Options: electronic application, early admission.

Application fee: $50.

Required: high school transcript, minimum 2.0 GPA. ***Recommended:*** essay or personal statement, minimum 3.0 GPA, 3 letters of recommendation.

Application deadlines: 5/1 (freshmen), 6/1 (transfers).

Notification: 5/15 (freshmen), continuous until 6/15 (transfers).

CONTACT

Stockton University, 101 Vera King Farris Drive, Galloway, NJ 08205-9441. *Phone:* 609-652-4261.

See previous page for display ad and page 1638 for the College Close-Up.

William Paterson University of New Jersey

Wayne, New Jersey

http://www.wpunj.edu/

- **State-supported** comprehensive, founded 1855
- **Suburban** 370-acre campus with easy access to New York City
- **Coed** 9,619 undergraduate students, 82% full-time, 55% women, 45% men
- **Moderately difficult** entrance level, 75% of applicants were admitted

UNDERGRAD STUDENTS

7,883 full-time, 1,736 part-time. Students come from 36 states and territories; 38 other countries; 2% are from out of state; 15% Black or African American, non-Hispanic/Latino; 27% Hispanic/Latino; 7% Asian, non-Hispanic/Latino; 0.1% American Indian or Alaska Native, non-Hispanic/Latino; 3% Two or more races, non-Hispanic/Latino; 3% Race/ethnicity unknown; 0.9% international; 13% transferred in; 23% live on campus.

Freshmen

Admission: 9,638 applied, 7,188 admitted, 1,171 enrolled. ***Average high school GPA:*** 3.09. ***Test scores:*** SAT critical reading scores over 500: 42%; SAT math scores over 500: 52%; SAT critical reading scores over 600: 8%; SAT math scores over 600: 9%; SAT critical reading scores over 700: 1%; SAT math scores over 700: 1%.

Retention: 77% of full-time freshmen returned.

FACULTY

Total: 1,148, 35% full-time.

Student/faculty ratio: 14:1.

ACADEMICS

Calendar: semesters. *Degrees:* bachelor's, master's, doctoral, post-master's, and postbachelor's certificates.

Special study options: academic remediation for entering students, accelerated degree program, adult/continuing education programs, advanced placement credit, distance learning, double majors, English as a second language, freshman honors college, honors programs, independent study, internships, off-campus study, part-time degree program, services for LD students, study abroad, summer session for credit. ***ROTC:*** Air Force (c).

Computers: 1,271 computers/terminals and 3,000 ports are available on campus for general student use. Students can access the following: campus intranet, computer help desk, free student e-mail accounts, online (class) grades, online (class) registration, online (class) schedules. Campuswide network is available. 100% of college-owned or -operated housing units are wired for high-speed Internet access. Wireless service is available via entire campus.

STUDENT LIFE

Housing options: coed, special housing for students with disabilities. Campus housing is university owned.

Activities and organizations: drama/theater group, student-run newspaper, radio and television station, choral group, Student Activities Programming Board (SAPB), Students for Awareness Black Leadership and Equality (SABLE), Student Government Association (SGA), The B.A.B.Y. Dolls (Community Service org.), Pioneer Players (drama), national fraternities, national sororities.

Athletics Member NCAA. All Division III. ***Intercollegiate sports:*** baseball M, basketball M/W, field hockey W, football M, golf M, soccer M/W, softball W, swimming and diving M/W, tennis W, volleyball W. ***Intramural sports:*** basketball M, bowling M(c), cheerleading M(c)/W(c), equestrian sports M(c)/W(c), ice hockey M(c), racquetball M/W, rugby M(c), softball M/W, volleyball M/W, wrestling M.

Campus security: 24-hour emergency response devices and patrols, student patrols, late-night transport/escort service, controlled dormitory access.

Student services: health clinic, personal/psychological counseling, women's center, legal services.

COSTS & FINANCIAL AID

Costs (2014–15) ***Tuition:*** state resident $7622 full-time, $244 per credit hour part-time; nonresident $15,298 full-time, $496 per credit hour part-time. Full-time tuition and fees vary according to course load and location. Part-time tuition and fees vary according to course load and location. ***Required fees:*** $4622 full-time, $145 per credit hour part-time. ***Room and board:*** $10,670; room only: $6700. Room and board charges vary according to board plan and housing facility. ***Payment plan:*** installment. ***Waivers:*** senior citizens and employees or children of employees.

Financial Aid Of all full-time matriculated undergraduates who enrolled in 2013, 6,972 applied for aid, 5,843 were judged to have need, 1,929 had their need fully met. In 2013, 440 non-need-based awards were made. ***Average financial aid package:*** $10,356. ***Average need-based loan:*** $4461. ***Average need-based gift aid:*** $7877. ***Average non-need-based aid:*** $5192. ***Average indebtedness upon graduation:*** $25,062.

APPLYING

Standardized Tests *Required:* SAT or ACT (for admission).

Options: electronic application, early admission, early action, deferred entrance.

Application fee: $50.

Required: high school transcript, minimum 3.0 GPA, 1 letter of recommendation. ***Required for some:*** interview, portfolio for art, audition for music. ***Recommended:*** essay or personal statement.

Application deadlines: 6/1 (freshmen), 6/1 (transfers), 12/1 (early action).

Notification: continuous (freshmen), continuous (transfers), 1/15 (early action).

CONTACT

Mr. Anthony Leckey, Senior Associate Director of Admissions, William Paterson University of New Jersey, Undergraduate Admissions, 300 Pompton Rd, Wayne, NJ 07470. *Phone:* 973-720-2900. *Toll-free phone:* 877-WPU-EXCEL. *Fax:* 973-720-2910. *E-mail:* leckeya@wpunj.edu.

NEW MEXICO

Brown Mackie College–Albuquerque

Albuquerque, New Mexico

http://www.brownmackie.edu/albuquerque/

- **Proprietary** primarily 2-year, part of Education Management Corporation
- **Coed**

ACADEMICS

Degrees: diplomas, associate, and bachelor's.

CONTACT

Brown Mackie College–Albuquerque, 10500 Copper Avenue NE, Albuquerque, NM 87123. *Phone:* 505-559-5200. *Toll-free phone:* 877-271-3488.

Eastern New Mexico University

Portales, New Mexico

http://www.enmu.edu/

- **State-supported** comprehensive, founded 1934
- **Rural** 400-acre campus
- **Endowment** $9.8 million
- **Coed** 4,600 undergraduate students, 60% full-time, 56% women, 44% men
- **Noncompetitive** entrance level, 63% of applicants were admitted

UNDERGRAD STUDENTS

2,775 full-time, 1,825 part-time. Students come from 52 states and territories; 20 other countries; 40% are from out of state; 4% Black or African American, non-Hispanic/Latino; 35% Hispanic/Latino; 0.9% Asian, non-Hispanic/Latino; 0.4% Native Hawaiian or other Pacific Islander, non-Hispanic/Latino; 3% American Indian or Alaska Native, non-Hispanic/Latino; 3% Two or more races, non-Hispanic/Latino; 8% Race/ethnicity unknown; 2% international; 10% transferred in; 16% live on campus.

Freshmen

Admission: 2,217 applied, 1,398 admitted, 639 enrolled. ***Average high school GPA:*** 3.19. ***Test scores:*** SAT critical reading scores over 500: 42%; SAT math scores over 500: 44%; ACT scores over 18: 69%; SAT critical reading scores over 600: 7%; SAT math scores over 600: 9%; ACT scores over 24: 16%; SAT critical reading scores over 700: 1%; ACT scores over 30: 1%.

Retention: 59% of full-time freshmen returned.

FACULTY

Total: 330, 47% full-time, 44% with terminal degrees.

Student/faculty ratio: 19:1.

ACADEMICS

Calendar: semesters. *Degrees:* certificates, associate, bachelor's, and master's.

Special study options: academic remediation for entering students, accelerated degree program, adult/continuing education programs, advanced placement credit, cooperative education, distance learning, double majors, English as a second language, independent study, internships, part-time degree program, services for LD students, student-designed majors, summer session for credit.

Unusual degree programs: 3-2 chemistry (qualified undergraduate students entering the chemistry program will be allowed to apply to the Graduate School during the last semester of the junior year to take a limited number of graduate courses for credit at the 500 level leading to a B.S. and an M.S. in 5-5.5 years total).

Computers: 453 computers/terminals are available on campus for general student use. Students can access the following: campus intranet, computer help desk, free student e-mail accounts, online (class) grades, online (class) registration, online (class) schedules, Wi-Fi in most buildings. Campuswide network is available. 100% of college-owned or -operated housing units are wired for high-speed Internet access. Wireless service is available via entire campus.

STUDENT LIFE

Housing options: on-campus residence required for freshman year; coed, women-only, special housing for students with disabilities. Campus housing is university owned. Freshman campus housing is guaranteed.

Activities and organizations: drama/theater group, student-run newspaper, radio and television station, choral group, marching band, student government, Student Activities Board, Residence Hall Association, IFC (Inter-Fraternity Council)Panhellenic Council, national fraternities, national sororities.

Athletics Member NCAA. All Division II. ***Intercollegiate sports:*** baseball M(s), basketball M(s)/W(s), cross-country running M(s)/W(s), football M(s), soccer M(s)/W(s), softball W(s), track and field M(s)/W(s), volleyball W(s). ***Intramural sports:*** badminton M/W, basketball M/W, cross-country running M/W, football M/W, racquetball M/W, soccer M/W, softball M/W, tennis M/W, volleyball M/W, water polo M/W.

Campus security: 24-hour emergency response devices and patrols, late-night transport/escort service, controlled dormitory access, University Emergency Notification System; security cameras; security lights.

Student services: health clinic, personal/psychological counseling.

COSTS & FINANCIAL AID

Costs (2014–15) ***Tuition:*** state resident $3064 full-time, $128 per credit hour part-time; nonresident $8838 full-time, $368 per credit hour part-time. Full-time tuition and fees vary according to course load and reciprocity agreements. Part-time tuition and fees vary according to course load. ***Required fees:*** $1792 full-time, $75 per credit hour part-time. ***Room and board:*** $6452; room only: $3108. Room and board charges vary according to board plan and housing facility. ***Payment plan:*** installment. ***Waivers:*** senior citizens and employees or children of employees.

Financial Aid Of all full-time matriculated undergraduates who enrolled in 2011, 1,635 applied for aid, 1,634 were judged to have need, 1,619 had their need fully met. In 2011, 219 non-need-based awards were made. ***Average percent of need met:*** 44. ***Average financial aid package:*** $11,015. ***Average need-based loan:*** $4130. ***Average need-based gift aid:*** $4575. ***Average non-need-based aid:*** $4213. ***Average indebtedness upon graduation:*** $14,821.

APPLYING

Standardized Tests *Required for some:* SAT (for admission), ACT (for admission).

Options: electronic application.

Required: official transcripts from any post-secondary institution attended - must be in good standing with all institutions. ***Required for some:*** high school transcript, minimum 2.5 GPA.

Application deadlines: 8/24 (freshmen), 8/24 (out-of-state freshmen), 8/24 (transfers).

Notification: continuous until 8/1 (freshmen), continuous until 8/1 (out-of-state freshmen), continuous until 8/1 (transfers).

CONTACT

Mr. Cody Spitz, Director, Enrollment Services, Eastern New Mexico University, Station #7 ENMU, Portales, NM 88130. *Phone:* 575-562-2178. *Toll-free phone:* 800-367-3668. *Fax:* 575-562-2118. *E-mail:* cody.spitz@enmu.edu.

Institute of American Indian Arts

Santa Fe, New Mexico

http://www.iaia.edu/

- **Federally supported** comprehensive, founded 1962
- **Suburban** 140-acre campus with easy access to Albuquerque, New Mexico
- **Coed** 470 undergraduate students, 46% full-time, 57% women, 43% men

UNDERGRAD STUDENTS

217 full-time, 253 part-time. 0.4% Black or African American, non-Hispanic/Latino; 4% Hispanic/Latino; 0.4% Asian, non-Hispanic/Latino; 0.4% Native Hawaiian or other Pacific Islander, non-Hispanic/Latino; 87% American Indian or Alaska Native, non-Hispanic/Latino; 0.4% Two or more races, non-Hispanic/Latino; 0.8% Race/ethnicity unknown; 2% international.

Freshmen

Admission: 49 enrolled.

ACADEMICS

Calendar: semesters. *Degrees:* certificates, associate, bachelor's, and master's.

Special study options: academic remediation for entering students, advanced placement credit, distance learning, double majors, independent study, internships, off-campus study, services for LD students, study abroad, summer session for credit.

Computers: 50 computers/terminals are available on campus for general student use. Students can access the following: campus intranet, computer help desk, free student e-mail accounts, online (class) grades, online (class) registration, online (class) schedules. Campuswide network is available. 100% of college-owned or -operated housing units are wired for high-speed Internet access. Wireless service is available via entire campus.

STUDENT LIFE
Housing options: on-campus residence required for freshman year; coed. Campus housing is university owned. Freshman campus housing is guaranteed.
Activities and organizations: drama/theater group, student-run newspaper, television station.
Athletics ***Intramural sports:*** archery M/W.
Campus security: 24-hour patrols, late-night transport/escort service, controlled dormitory access.
Student services: health clinic, personal/psychological counseling.

COSTS & FINANCIAL AID
Costs (2014–15) ***Tuition:*** state resident $3600 full-time, $150 per semester hour part-time; nonresident $3600 full-time, $150 per semester hour part-time. ***Required fees:*** $200 full-time, $100 per term part-time. ***Room and board:*** $7258; room only: $3282. Room and board charges vary according to board plan and housing facility. ***Payment plan:*** installment. ***Waivers:*** employees or children of employees.
Financial Aid Of all full-time matriculated undergraduates who enrolled in 2011, 263 applied for aid, 261 were judged to have need, 201 had their need fully met. 2 Federal Work-Study jobs (averaging $2300). 3 state and other part-time jobs (averaging $2300). In 2011, 58 non-need-based awards were made. ***Average percent of need met:*** 71. ***Average financial aid package:*** $5005. ***Average need-based gift aid:*** $2500. ***Average non-need-based aid:*** $2500.

APPLYING
Standardized Tests *Required:* ACCUPLACER, Compass, ASSET (for admission). *Recommended:* SAT or ACT (for admission).
Required: high school transcript. ***Required for some:*** essay or personal statement, 2 letters of recommendation, interview. ***Recommended:*** 2 letters of recommendation, interview.

CONTACT
Ms. Mary Curley, Director, Admissions and Recruitment, Institute of American Indian Arts, 83 Avan Nu Po Road, Santa Fe, NY 87508. *Phone:* 505-424-2307. *Fax:* 505-424-0909. *E-mail:* mary.curley@iaia.edu.

ITT Technical Institute
Albuquerque, New Mexico
http://www.itt-tech.edu/

- **Proprietary** primarily 2-year, founded 1989, part of ITT Educational Services, Inc.
- **Coed**
- **Minimally difficult** entrance level

ACADEMICS
Calendar: quarters. *Degrees:* associate and bachelor's.

STUDENT LIFE
Housing options: college housing not available.

CONTACT
Director of Recruitment, ITT Technical Institute, 5100 Masthead Street, NE, Albuquerque, NM 87109-4366. *Phone:* 505-828-1114. *Toll-free phone:* 800-636-1114.

New Mexico Highlands University
Las Vegas, New Mexico
http://www.nmhu.edu/

- **State-supported** comprehensive, founded 1893
- **Small-town** campus
- **Coed** 2,275 undergraduate students, 66% full-time, 46% women, 54% men
- **Minimally difficult** entrance level, 100% of applicants were admitted

UNDERGRAD STUDENTS
1,510 full-time, 765 part-time. 15% are from out of state; 5% Black or African American, non-Hispanic/Latino; 58% Hispanic/Latino; 0.7% Asian, non-Hispanic/Latino; 0.7% Native Hawaiian or other Pacific Islander, non-Hispanic/Latino; 7% American Indian or Alaska Native, non-Hispanic/Latino; 1% Two or more races, non-Hispanic/Latino; 1% Race/ethnicity unknown; 5% international; 16% transferred in; 24% live on campus.

Freshmen
Admission: 1,389 applied, 1,389 admitted, 281 enrolled. ***Average high school GPA:*** 2.96. ***Test scores:*** SAT critical reading scores over 500: 23%; SAT math scores over 500: 20%; SAT writing scores over 500: 15%; ACT scores over 18: 51%; SAT critical reading scores over 600: 5%; SAT math scores over 600: 5%; SAT writing scores over 600: 5%; ACT scores over 24: 7%.
Retention: 48% of full-time freshmen returned.

FACULTY
Total: 291, 49% full-time, 41% with terminal degrees.
Student/faculty ratio: 13:1.

ACADEMICS
Calendar: semesters. *Degrees:* certificates, associate, bachelor's, master's, and postbachelor's certificates.
Special study options: academic remediation for entering students, accelerated degree program, advanced placement credit, cooperative education, distance learning, double majors, honors programs, independent study, internships, off-campus study, part-time degree program, services for LD students, summer session for credit.
Computers: 500 computers/terminals are available on campus for general student use. Students can access the following: online (class) registration. Campuswide network is available.

STUDENT LIFE
Housing options: coed, special housing for students with disabilities. Campus housing is university owned.
Activities and organizations: drama/theater group, student-run radio station, choral group, marching band, Vatos Rugby, Fire Escape Club, MeChA, NMHU Cheerleaders, NMHU Student Ambassadors, national fraternities, national sororities.
Athletics Member NCAA. All Division II. ***Intercollegiate sports:*** baseball M(s), basketball M(s)/W(s), cross-country running M(s)/W(s), football M(s), soccer W(s), softball W(s), track and field M/W, volleyball W(s). ***Intramural sports:*** badminton M/W, basketball M/W, football M, golf M/W, racquetball M/W, rugby M, skiing (cross-country) M/W, skiing (downhill) M/W, softball W, swimming and diving M/W, table tennis M/W, tennis M/W, volleyball M/W, weight lifting M/W.
Campus security: 24-hour emergency response devices and patrols, late-night transport/escort service, controlled dormitory access.
Student services: health clinic, personal/psychological counseling, women's center.

COSTS & FINANCIAL AID
Costs (2014–15) ***One-time required fee:*** $20. ***Tuition:*** state resident $3192 full-time, $133 per credit hour part-time; nonresident $5796 full-time, $242 per credit hour part-time. Full-time tuition and fees vary according to course load and location. Part-time tuition and fees vary according to course load and location. ***Required fees:*** $1308 full-time, $55 per credit hour part-time. ***Room and board:*** $7404. Room and board charges vary according to board plan and housing facility. ***Payment plan:*** installment. ***Waivers:*** senior citizens and employees or children of employees.
Financial Aid Of all full-time matriculated undergraduates who enrolled in 2013, 1,433 applied for aid, 1,263 were judged to have need, 91 had their need fully met. In 2013, 635 non-need-based awards were made. ***Average financial aid package:*** $1847. ***Average need-based loan:*** $2489. ***Average need-based gift aid:*** $1792. ***Average non-need-based aid:*** $3953. ***Average indebtedness upon graduation:*** $14,106.

APPLYING
Options: electronic application, early admission, deferred entrance.
Required: high school transcript, minimum 2.0 GPA. ***Required for some:*** 2 letters of recommendation, interview.

CONTACT
Ms. Fidel Trujillo, Vice President for Student Affairs, New Mexico Highlands University, Box 9000, Las Vegas, NM 87701. *Phone:* 505-454-3566. *Toll-free phone:* 800-338-6648. *E-mail:* judycordova@nmhu.edu.

New Mexico Institute of Mining and Technology

Socorro, New Mexico

http://www.nmt.edu/

- **State-supported** university, founded 1889
- **Small-town** 320-acre campus with easy access to Albuquerque
- **Endowment** $28.3 million
- **Coed** 1,633 undergraduate students, 88% full-time, 30% women, 70% men
- **Moderately difficult** entrance level, 36% of applicants were admitted

UNDERGRAD STUDENTS
1,443 full-time, 190 part-time. 16% are from out of state; 2% Black or African American, non-Hispanic/Latino; 28% Hispanic/Latino; 3% Asian, non-Hispanic/Latino; 0.1% Native Hawaiian or other Pacific Islander, non-Hispanic/Latino; 3% American Indian or Alaska Native, non-Hispanic/Latino; 4% Two or more races, non-Hispanic/Latino; 0.9% Race/ethnicity unknown; 4% international; 7% transferred in; 50% live on campus.

Freshmen
Admission: 1,003 applied, 365 admitted, 290 enrolled. ***Average high school GPA:*** 3.64. ***Test scores:*** SAT critical reading scores over 500: 94%; SAT math scores over 500: 96%; ACT scores over 18: 100%; SAT critical reading scores over 600: 54%; SAT math scores over 600: 68%; ACT scores over 24: 75%; SAT critical reading scores over 700: 15%; SAT math scores over 700: 23%; ACT scores over 30: 23%.
Retention: 79% of full-time freshmen returned.

FACULTY
Total: 148, 78% full-time, 85% with terminal degrees.
Student/faculty ratio: 14:1.

ACADEMICS
Calendar: semesters. *Degrees:* associate, bachelor's, master's, and doctoral.
Special study options: accelerated degree program, advanced placement credit, cooperative education, distance learning, double majors, independent study, internships, services for LD students, student-designed majors, summer session for credit.
Unusual degree programs: 3-2 earth sciences.
Computers: 225 computers/terminals are available on campus for general student use. Students can access the following: computer help desk, free student e-mail accounts, online (class) registration, online (class) schedules. Campuswide network is available. Wireless service is available via computer centers, learning centers, student centers.

STUDENT LIFE
Housing options: coed, men-only, women-only. Campus housing is university owned.
Activities and organizations: drama/theater group, student-run newspaper, radio station, choral group.
Athletics ***Intercollegiate sports:*** golf M(c)/W(c), rugby M(c)/W(c), soccer M(c)/W(c). ***Intramural sports:*** badminton M/W, basketball M/W, soccer M/W, softball M/W, volleyball M/W.
Campus security: 24-hour emergency response devices and patrols, late-night transport/escort service.
Student services: health clinic, personal/psychological counseling.

COSTS & FINANCIAL AID
Costs (2014–15) ***Tuition:*** state resident $5298 full-time, $221 per credit hour part-time; nonresident $17,226 full-time, $718 per credit hour part-time. Full-time tuition and fees vary according to reciprocity agreements. Part-time tuition and fees vary according to course load. ***Required fees:*** $958 full-time, $18 per credit hour part-time, $258 per term part-time. ***Room and board:*** $6740. Room and board charges vary according to board plan and housing facility. ***Waivers:*** senior citizens and employees or children of employees.
Financial Aid Of all full-time matriculated undergraduates who enrolled in 2013, 1,286 applied for aid, 770 were judged to have need, 149 had their need fully met. In 2013, 477 non-need-based awards were made. ***Average percent of need met:*** 74. ***Average financial aid package:*** $10,821. ***Average need-based loan:*** $4151. ***Average need-based gift aid:*** $5509. ***Average non-need-based aid:*** $6651. ***Average indebtedness upon graduation:*** $20,944.

APPLYING
Standardized Tests *Required:* SAT or ACT (for admission). *Recommended:* ACT (for admission).
Options: electronic application, deferred entrance.
Application fee: $15.
Required: high school transcript, minimum 2.5 GPA. ***Required for some:*** 2 letters of recommendation. ***Recommended:*** interview.
Application deadlines: 8/1 (freshmen), 8/1 (transfers).
Notification: continuous (freshmen), continuous (transfers).

CONTACT
Mr. Tony Ortiz, Director of Admissions, New Mexico Institute of Mining and Technology, 801 Leroy Place, Socorro, NM 87801. *Phone:* 575-835-5424. *Toll-free phone:* 800-428-TECH. *Fax:* 575-835-5989. *E-mail:* admission@admin.nmt.edu.

New Mexico State University

Las Cruces, New Mexico

http://www.nmsu.edu/

- **State-supported** university, founded 1888, part of New Mexico State University System
- **Suburban** 900-acre campus with easy access to El Paso
- **Endowment** $197.0 million
- **Coed** 12,784 undergraduate students, 83% full-time, 53% women, 47% men
- **Moderately difficult** entrance level, 70% of applicants were admitted

UNDERGRAD STUDENTS
10,668 full-time, 2,116 part-time. Students come from 48 states and territories; 44 other countries; 25% are from out of state; 3% Black or African American, non-Hispanic/Latino; 53% Hispanic/Latino; 1% Asian, non-Hispanic/Latino; 0.2% Native Hawaiian or other Pacific Islander, non-Hispanic/Latino; 2% American Indian or Alaska Native, non-Hispanic/Latino; 2% Two or more races, non-Hispanic/Latino; 3% Race/ethnicity unknown; 5% international; 5% transferred in; 19% live on campus.

Freshmen
Admission: 7,101 applied, 4,942 admitted, 1,862 enrolled. ***Average high school GPA:*** 3.39. ***Test scores:*** SAT critical reading scores over 500: 39%; SAT math scores over 500: 45%; SAT writing scores over 500: 35%; ACT scores over 18: 80%; SAT critical reading scores over 600: 10%; SAT math scores over 600: 12%; SAT writing scores over 600: 8%; ACT scores over 24: 26%; SAT critical reading scores over 700: 1%; ACT scores over 30: 2%.
Retention: 74% of full-time freshmen returned.

FACULTY
Total: 1,097, 58% full-time, 68% with terminal degrees.
Student/faculty ratio: 16:1.

ACADEMICS
Calendar: semesters. *Degrees:* associate, bachelor's, master's, doctoral, post-master's, and postbachelor's certificates.
Special study options: academic remediation for entering students, accelerated degree program, adult/continuing education programs, advanced placement credit, cooperative education, distance learning, double majors, English as a second language, honors programs, independent study, internships, off-campus study, part-time degree program, services for LD students, student-designed majors, study abroad, summer session for credit. ***ROTC:*** Army (b), Air Force (b).
Unusual degree programs: 3-2 engineering with NMSU has dual bachelor's and master's degree programs in Civil Engineering, Electrical Engineering, Industrial Engineering, and Mechanical Engineering; Accountancy and Physics are dual bachelor's and master's degree programs at NMSU. Cooperative Pharmacy Program is completed at University of New Mexico.
Computers: 371 computers/terminals and 600 ports are available on campus for general student use. Students can access the following: campus intranet, computer help desk, free student e-mail accounts, online

(class) grades, online (class) registration, online (class) schedules, dialup internet, antivirus software, student portal online (Microsoft products, file share/storage space, student employee clock-in, payments system, emergency notification signup) PC/laptop/equipment rentals, short-term iPad checkout, software discounts. Campuswide network is available. 100% of college-owned or -operated housing units are wired for high-speed Internet access. Wireless service is available via entire campus.

STUDENT LIFE

Housing options: coed. Campus housing is university owned.

Activities and organizations: drama/theater group, student-run newspaper, radio and television station, choral group, marching band, Pride of New Mexico Marching Band, Delta Gamma (Social Fraternity), Chi Omega (Social Sorority), Lambda Chi Alpha (Social Fraternity), International Club of NMSU, national fraternities, national sororities.

Athletics Member NCAA. All Division I except football (Division I-A). ***Intercollegiate sports:*** baseball M(s), basketball M(s)/W(s), cross-country running M(s)/W(s), equestrian sports W(s), golf M(s)/W(s), soccer W(s), softball W(s), swimming and diving W(s), tennis M(s)/W(s), track and field W(s), volleyball W(s). ***Intramural sports:*** badminton M(c)/W(c), basketball M/W, fencing M(c)/W(c), football M/W, golf M/W, racquetball M/W, rugby M(c)/W(c), soccer M/W, softball M/W, table tennis M/W, tennis M/W, ultimate Frisbee M/W, volleyball M/W, water polo M/W.

Campus security: 24-hour emergency response devices and patrols, late-night transport/escort service, controlled dormitory access.

Student services: health clinic, personal/psychological counseling, legal services.

COSTS & FINANCIAL AID

Costs (2014–15) ***One-time required fee:*** $40. ***Tuition:*** state resident $4812 full-time, $201 per credit hour part-time; nonresident $17,974 full-time, $749 per credit hour part-time. Full-time tuition and fees vary according to course load. Part-time tuition and fees vary according to course load. ***Required fees:*** $1138 full-time, $47 per credit hour part-time. ***Room and board:*** $8100; room only: $4752. Room and board charges vary according to board plan and housing facility. ***Payment plans:*** installment, deferred payment. ***Waivers:*** senior citizens and employees or children of employees.

Financial Aid Of all full-time matriculated undergraduates who enrolled in 2013, 8,367 applied for aid, 7,102 were judged to have need, 623 had their need fully met. 341 Federal Work-Study jobs (averaging $2718). 357 state and other part-time jobs (averaging $5642). In 2013, 1214 non-need-based awards were made. ***Average percent of need met:*** 65. ***Average financial aid package:*** $9089. ***Average need-based loan:*** $3704. ***Average need-based gift aid:*** $8714. ***Average non-need-based aid:*** $2348. ***Average indebtedness upon graduation:*** $18,628. ***Financial aid deadline:*** 3/1.

APPLYING

Standardized Tests *Required:* SAT or ACT (for admission).

Options: electronic application.

Application fee: $20.

Required: high school transcript, minimum 2.0 GPA, Applicants must have minimum cumulative HS GPA of 2.5, or ACT composite of 21 (SAT of 990), or 2.0 HS GPA and 20 ACT composite (950 SAT). GED is accepted. Minimum high school participation includes 4 units of English, 3 of math, 3 of science beyond general science, and 1 foreign language/fine art.

Application deadlines: rolling (freshmen), rolling (transfers).

Notification: continuous (freshmen), continuous (transfers).

CONTACT

Delia DeLeon, Interim Director of Admissions, New Mexico State University, Box 30001, MSC 3A, Las Cruces, NM 88003-8001. *Phone:* 575-646-3121. *Toll-free phone:* 800-662-6678. *Fax:* 575-646-6330. *E-mail:* admssions@nmsu.edu.

★ St. John's College

Santa Fe, New Mexico

http://www.stjohnscollege.edu/

- **Independent** comprehensive, founded 1964
- **Suburban** 250-acre campus with easy access to Albuquerque
- **Endowment** $48.7 million
- **Coed** 342 undergraduate students, 99% full-time, 43% women, 57% men
- **Very difficult** entrance level, 81% of applicants were admitted

UNDERGRAD STUDENTS

337 full-time, 5 part-time. Students come from 44 states and territories; 16 other countries; 91% are from out of state; 0.9% Black or African American, non-Hispanic/Latino; 10% Hispanic/Latino; 2% Asian, non-Hispanic/Latino; 7% Two or more races, non-Hispanic/Latino; 3% Race/ethnicity unknown; 16% international; 4% transferred in; 84% live on campus.

Freshmen

Admission: 227 applied, 185 admitted, 76 enrolled. ***Test scores:*** SAT critical reading scores over 500: 94%; SAT math scores over 500: 94%; SAT writing scores over 500: 85%; ACT scores over 18: 100%; SAT critical reading scores over 600: 83%; SAT math scores over 600: 71%; SAT writing scores over 600: 65%; ACT scores over 24: 74%; SAT critical reading scores over 700: 57%; SAT math scores over 700: 34%; SAT writing scores over 700: 27%; ACT scores over 30: 35%.

Retention: 90% of full-time freshmen returned.

FACULTY

Total: 59, 100% full-time, 80% with terminal degrees.

Student/faculty ratio: 9:1.

ACADEMICS

Calendar: semesters. *Degrees:* bachelor's and master's.

Special study options: internships, off-campus study, summer session for credit.

Computers: 16 computers/terminals and 425 ports are available on campus for general student use. Students can access the following: campus intranet, computer help desk, free student e-mail accounts. Campuswide network is available. 100% of college-owned or -operated housing units are wired for high-speed Internet access. Wireless service is available via entire campus.

STUDENT LIFE

Housing options: on-campus residence required through senior year; coed, men-only, women-only, special housing for students with disabilities. Campus housing is university owned. Freshman campus housing is guaranteed.

Activities and organizations: drama/theater group, student-run newspaper, Iron Bookworm Workout, Chrysostomos (Theater), Jazz Dance, Student Government/Student Committee on Instruction, intramural sports.

Athletics ***Intercollegiate sports:*** fencing M/W. ***Intramural sports:*** archery M(c)/W(c), badminton M/W, basketball M/W, cross-country running M/W, fencing M/W, ice hockey M/W, racquetball M/W, rock climbing M/W, skiing (cross-country) M/W, skiing (downhill) M/W, soccer M/W, softball M/W, squash M/W, swimming and diving M/W, table tennis M/W, tennis M/W, ultimate Frisbee M/W, volleyball M/W.

Campus security: 24-hour emergency response devices and patrols, late-night transport/escort service, controlled dormitory access.

Student services: health clinic, personal/psychological counseling.

COSTS & FINANCIAL AID

Costs (2015–16) ***Comprehensive fee:*** $59,884 includes full-time tuition ($48,544), mandatory fees ($450), and room and board ($10,890). Part-time tuition: $1428 per credit. ***Room and board:*** Room and board charges vary according to board plan. ***Payment plan:*** installment. ***Waivers:*** employees or children of employees.

Financial Aid Of all full-time matriculated undergraduates who enrolled in 2013, 285 applied for aid, 275 were judged to have need, 214 had their need fully met. In 2013, 15 non-need-based awards were made. ***Average percent of need met:*** 94. ***Average financial aid package:*** $36,918. ***Average need-based loan:*** $4750. ***Average need-based gift aid:*** $30,215. ***Average non-need-based aid:*** $13,500. ***Average indebtedness upon graduation:*** $25,256.

APPLYING
Standardized Tests *Required for some:* SAT or ACT (for admission), IELTS or TOEFL required for some.

Options: electronic application, early action, deferred entrance.

Required: essay or personal statement, high school transcript, 2 letters of recommendation. ***Required for some:*** interview. ***Recommended:*** 3 letters of recommendation, interview.

Application deadlines: rolling (freshmen), rolling (out-of-state freshmen), rolling (transfers), 11/15 (early action).

Notification: continuous (freshmen), continuous (out-of-state freshmen), continuous (transfers), 12/15 (early action).

CONTACT
Ms. Yvette Sobky Shaffer, Director of Admissions, St. John's College, 1160 Camino Cruz Blanca, Santa Fe, NM 87505. *Phone:* 505-984-6060. *Toll-free phone:* 800-331-5232. *Fax:* 505-984-6162. *E-mail:* SantaFe.Admissions@sjc.edu.

Santa Fe University of Art and Design

Santa Fe, New Mexico

http://www.santafeuniversity.edu/

- **Independent** 4-year, founded 1947
- **Suburban** 100-acre campus with easy access to Albuquerque
- **Coed** 950 undergraduate students, 97% full-time, 54% women, 46% men
- **Moderately difficult** entrance level, 100% of applicants were admitted

UNDERGRAD STUDENTS
918 full-time, 32 part-time. Students come from 44 states and territories; 20 other countries; 78% are from out of state; 6% Black or African American, non-Hispanic/Latino; 25% Hispanic/Latino; 2% Asian, non-Hispanic/Latino; 2% Native Hawaiian or other Pacific Islander, non-Hispanic/Latino; 2% American Indian or Alaska Native, non-Hispanic/Latino; 7% Two or more races, non-Hispanic/Latino; 1% Race/ethnicity unknown; 16% international.

Freshmen
Admission: 608 applied, 608 admitted, 251 enrolled.

Retention: 64% of full-time freshmen returned.

FACULTY
Student/faculty ratio: 15:1.

ACADEMICS
Calendar: semesters. *Degree:* certificates and bachelor's.

Special study options: advanced placement credit, distance learning, double majors, honors programs, independent study, internships, off-campus study, services for LD students, student-designed majors, study abroad, summer session for credit.

Computers: 120 computers/terminals are available on campus for general student use. Students can access the following: campus intranet, free student e-mail accounts, online (class) grades, online (class) registration, online (class) schedules. Campuswide network is available. 100% of college-owned or -operated housing units are wired for high-speed Internet access. Wireless service is available via entire campus.

STUDENT LIFE
Housing options: on-campus residence required through sophomore year; coed, special housing for students with disabilities. Campus housing is university owned.

Activities and organizations: drama/theater group, student-run newspaper, choral group, Student Writer's Association, Performing Arts Collective, Colors: Queer Identity Group, Cluster, Film Clubs.

Athletics *Intramural sports:* basketball M/W, racquetball M/W, skiing (downhill) M/W, soccer M/W, softball M/W, table tennis M/W, tennis M/W, ultimate Frisbee M/W, volleyball M/W, weight lifting M/W.

Campus security: 24-hour patrols, late-night transport/escort service, controlled dormitory access.

Student services: health clinic, personal/psychological counseling.

FINANCIAL AID
Financial Aid Of all full-time matriculated undergraduates who enrolled in 2013, 561 applied for aid, 495 were judged to have need, 52 had their need fully met. 285,455 Federal Work-Study jobs (averaging $1471). In 2013, 122 non-need-based awards were made. ***Average percent of need met:*** 66. ***Average financial aid package:*** $22,375. ***Average need-based loan:*** $4187. ***Average need-based gift aid:*** $18,023. ***Average non-need-based aid:*** $12,987.

APPLYING
Options: electronic application, deferred entrance.

Application fee: $50.

Required: high school transcript. ***Required for some:*** portfolio or audition for visual and performing arts programs. ***Recommended:*** minimum 2.0 GPA.

Application deadlines: rolling (freshmen), rolling (out-of-state freshmen), rolling (transfers).

Notification: continuous (freshmen), continuous (out-of-state freshmen), continuous (transfers).

CONTACT
Ms. Melissa Lewis, Director of Student Services, Santa Fe University of Art and Design, 1600 Saint Michael's Drive, Santa Fe, NM 87505-7634. *Phone:* 505-473-6937. *Toll-free phone:* 800-456-2673. *Fax:* 505-473-6127. *E-mail:* admissions@santafeuniversity.edu.

University of New Mexico

Albuquerque, New Mexico

http://www.unm.edu/

- **State-supported** university, founded 1889
- **Urban** 769-acre campus with easy access to Albuquerque
- **Endowment** $358.4 million
- **Coed** 20,859 undergraduate students, 79% full-time, 55% women, 45% men
- **Moderately difficult** entrance level, 45% of applicants were admitted

UNDERGRAD STUDENTS
16,385 full-time, 4,474 part-time. 13% are from out of state; 3% Black or African American, non-Hispanic/Latino; 46% Hispanic/Latino; 3% Asian, non-Hispanic/Latino; 0.2% Native Hawaiian or other Pacific Islander, non-Hispanic/Latino; 6% American Indian or Alaska Native, non-Hispanic/Latino; 3% Two or more races, non-Hispanic/Latino; 2% Race/ethnicity unknown; 1% international; 6% transferred in; 8% live on campus.

Freshmen
Admission: 12,574 applied, 5,706 admitted, 3,134 enrolled. ***Average high school GPA:*** 3.4. ***Test scores:*** SAT critical reading scores over 500: 70%; SAT math scores over 500: 70%; ACT scores over 18: 91%; SAT critical reading scores over 600: 35%; SAT math scores over 600: 31%; ACT scores over 24: 38%; SAT critical reading scores over 700: 9%; SAT math scores over 700: 7%; ACT scores over 30: 6%.

Retention: 79% of full-time freshmen returned.

FACULTY
Total: 1,624, 67% full-time, 71% with terminal degrees.

Student/faculty ratio: 21:1.

ACADEMICS
Calendar: semesters. *Degrees:* certificates, associate, bachelor's, master's, doctoral, and post-master's certificates.

Special study options: academic remediation for entering students, accelerated degree program, adult/continuing education programs, advanced placement credit, cooperative education, distance learning, double majors, English as a second language, freshman honors college, honors programs, independent study, internships, off-campus study, part-time degree program, services for LD students, student-designed majors, study abroad, summer session for credit. ***ROTC:*** Army (b), Navy (b), Air Force (b).

Unusual degree programs: 3-2 business administration; engineering; Latin American studies, business.

Computers: 990 computers/terminals and 56,000 ports are available on campus for general student use. Students can access the following: campus intranet, computer help desk, free student e-mail accounts, online (class) grades, online (class) registration, online (class) schedules. Campuswide network is available. 100% of college-owned or -operated housing units are wired for high-speed Internet access. Wireless service is available via entire campus.

STUDENT LIFE

Housing options: coed, special housing for students with disabilities. Campus housing is university owned and is provided by a third party.

Activities and organizations: drama/theater group, student-run newspaper, radio and television station, choral group, marching band, Associated Students of UNM, Graduate and Professional Students Association, Golden Key National Honor Society, national fraternities, national sororities.

Athletics Member NCAA. All Division I except football (Division I-A). ***Intercollegiate sports:*** baseball M(s), basketball M(s)/W(s), cross-country running M(s)/W(s), golf M(s)/W(s), skiing (cross-country) M(s)/W(s), skiing (downhill) M(s)/W(s), soccer M(s)/W(s), softball W(s), swimming and diving M/W(s), tennis M(s)/W(s), track and field M(s)/W(s), volleyball W(s). ***Intramural sports:*** archery M/W, badminton M/W, basketball M/W, bowling M(c)/W(c), cheerleading M(c)/W(c), fencing M/W, football M, golf M/W, ice hockey M(c)/W(c), lacrosse M(c)/W(c), racquetball M/W, rugby M(c)/W(c), skiing (cross-country) M/W, skiing (downhill) M/W, soccer M/W, softball M/W, swimming and diving W, table tennis M/W, tennis M/W, ultimate Frisbee M(c)/W(c), volleyball M/W, water polo M/W, wrestling M(c).

Campus security: 24-hour emergency response devices and patrols, student patrols, late-night transport/escort service, controlled dormitory access.

Student services: health clinic, personal/psychological counseling, women's center.

COSTS

Costs (2014–15) ***Tuition:*** state resident $6447 full-time, $215 per hour part-time; nonresident $20,644 full-time, $861 per hour part-time. Full-time tuition and fees vary according to program. Part-time tuition and fees vary according to course load and program. ***Room and board:*** $8580. Room and board charges vary according to board plan and housing facility. ***Payment plan:*** installment. ***Waivers:*** senior citizens and employees or children of employees.

APPLYING

Standardized Tests *Required:* SAT or ACT (for admission).

Options: electronic application, early admission, deferred entrance.

Application fee: $20.

Required: high school transcript, minimum 2.5 GPA. ***Required for some:*** essay or personal statement, interview.

Application deadlines: rolling (freshmen), rolling (out-of-state freshmen), rolling (transfers).

Notification: continuous (freshmen), continuous (out-of-state freshmen), continuous (transfers).

CONTACT

Mr. Matthew Hulett, Director of Admissions and Recruitment Services, University of New Mexico, Office of Admissions, PO Box 4895, Albuquerque, NM 87196-4895. *Phone:* 505-277-8900. *Toll-free phone:* 800-CALL-UNM. *Fax:* 505-277-6686. *E-mail:* apply@unm.edu.

NEW YORK

★ Adelphi University

Garden City, New York

http://www.adelphi.edu/

- **Independent** university, founded 1896
- **Suburban** 75-acre campus with easy access to New York City
- **Endowment** $172.9 million
- **Coed** 5,071 undergraduate students, 90% full-time, 70% women, 30% men
- **Moderately difficult** entrance level, 72% of applicants were admitted

UNDERGRAD STUDENTS

4,589 full-time, 482 part-time. Students come from 35 states and territories; 42 other countries; 7% are from out of state; 10% Black or African American, non-Hispanic/Latino; 14% Hispanic/Latino; 8% Asian, non-Hispanic/Latino; 0.1% Native Hawaiian or other Pacific Islander, non-Hispanic/Latino; 0.1% American Indian or Alaska Native, non-

Hispanic/Latino; 2% Two or more races, non-Hispanic/Latino; 7% Race/ethnicity unknown; 4% international; 10% transferred in; 23% live on campus.

Freshmen
Admission: 8,806 applied, 6,377 admitted, 975 enrolled. ***Average high school GPA:*** 3.45. ***Test scores:*** SAT critical reading scores over 500: 77%; SAT math scores over 500: 82%; SAT writing scores over 500: 80%; ACT scores over 18: 95%; SAT critical reading scores over 600: 30%; SAT math scores over 600: 35%; SAT writing scores over 600: 34%; ACT scores over 24: 27%; SAT critical reading scores over 700: 5%; SAT math scores over 700: 6%; SAT writing scores over 700: 6%; ACT scores over 30: 1%.
Retention: 83% of full-time freshmen returned.

FACULTY
Total: 1,017, 31% full-time, 45% with terminal degrees.
Student/faculty ratio: 12:1.

ACADEMICS
Calendar: semesters. *Degrees:* associate, bachelor's, master's, doctoral, post-master's, and postbachelor's certificates.
Special study options: accelerated degree program, advanced placement credit, cooperative education, distance learning, double majors, English as a second language, freshman honors college, honors programs, independent study, internships, part-time degree program, services for LD students, student-designed majors, study abroad, summer session for credit. ***ROTC:*** Army (c), Air Force (c).
Unusual degree programs: 3-2 engineering with Columbia University; Physical Therapy: New York Medical Coll, New York Institute of Tech; Dentistry: NYU Coll of Dentistry; Environmental Studies: Columbia University; Medicine: Philadelphia Coll of Osteopathic Medicine, Lake Erie Coll of Osteopathic Medicine; Optometry: SUNY State Coll of Optometry; Podiatry: NYCPM.
Computers: 880 computers/terminals are available on campus for general student use. Students can access the following: computer help desk, free student e-mail accounts, online (class) grades, online (class) registration, online (class) schedules, payment, drop/add classes, check application status. Campuswide network is available. 100% of college-owned or -operated housing units are wired for high-speed Internet access. Wireless service is available via entire campus.

STUDENT LIFE
Housing options: coed, special housing for students with disabilities. Campus housing is university owned. Freshman applicants given priority for college housing.
Activities and organizations: student-run newspaper, radio station, choral group, Student Activities Board, C. A. L. I. B. E. R. (Cause to Achieve Leadership, Intelligence, Brotherhood, Excellence, and Respect), Commuter Student Organization, Christian Fellowship, Circle K International, national fraternities, national sororities.
Athletics Member NCAA. All Division II. ***Intercollegiate sports:*** baseball M(s), basketball M(s)/W(s), bowling W(s), cross-country running M(s)/W(s), field hockey W(s), golf M(s)/W(s), lacrosse M(s)/W(s), soccer M(s)/W(s), softball W(s), swimming and diving M(s)/W(s), tennis M(s)/W(s), track and field M(s)/W(s), volleyball W(s). ***Intramural sports:*** badminton M/W, baseball M(c)/W(c), basketball M/W, cheerleading W, equestrian sports M(c)/W(c), fencing M(c)/W(c), football M/W, soccer M/W, ultimate Frisbee M(c)/W(c), volleyball M/W.
Campus security: 24-hour emergency response devices and patrols, late-night transport/escort service, controlled dormitory access.
Student services: health clinic, personal/psychological counseling.

COSTS & FINANCIAL AID
Costs (2014–15) ***Comprehensive fee:*** $45,960 includes full-time tuition ($30,840), mandatory fees ($1500), and room and board ($13,620). Full-time tuition and fees vary according to course level, course load, location, program, and student level. Part-time tuition: $945 per credit hour. Part-time tuition and fees vary according to course level, course load, location, program, and student level. ***College room only:*** $7110. Room and board charges vary according to board plan and housing facility. ***Payment plans:*** tuition prepayment, installment, deferred payment. ***Waivers:*** children of alumni, senior citizens, and employees or children of employees.

Financial Aid Of all full-time matriculated undergraduates who enrolled in 2014, 3,696 applied for aid, 3,310 were judged to have need, 10 had their need fully met. 407 Federal Work-Study jobs (averaging $1508). 1,160 state and other part-time jobs (averaging $1920). In 2014, 965 non-need-based awards were made. ***Average percent of need met:*** 19. ***Average financial aid package:*** $20,900. ***Average need-based loan:*** $4240. ***Average need-based gift aid:*** $7015. ***Average non-need-based aid:*** $12,698. ***Average indebtedness upon graduation:*** $32,328.

APPLYING
Standardized Tests *Required for some:* SAT or ACT (for admission).
Options: electronic application, early action, deferred entrance.
Application fee: $40.
Required: essay or personal statement, high school transcript. ***Required for some:*** 2 letters of recommendation, interview, auditions/portfolios for performing and fine arts. ***Recommended:*** minimum 3.4 GPA.
Application deadlines: rolling (freshmen), rolling (transfers), 12/1 (early action).
Notification: continuous (freshmen), continuous (transfers), 12/31 (early action).

CONTACT
Ms. Kristen Collins, Director of Undergraduate Admissions, Adelphi University, Levermore Hall 110, 1 South Avenue, PO Box 701, Garden City, NY 11530-0701. *Phone:* 516-877-3050. *Toll-free phone:* 800-ADELPHI. *Fax:* 516-877-3039. *E-mail:* admissions@adelphi.edu.

See previous page for display ad and page 1338 for the College Close-Up.

Albany College of Pharmacy and Health Sciences

Albany, New York

http://www.acphs.edu/

- **Independent** comprehensive, founded 1881
- **Urban** 35-acre campus
- **Coed** 1,078 undergraduate students, 98% full-time, 60% women, 40% men
- **Moderately difficult** entrance level, 67% of applicants were admitted

UNDERGRAD STUDENTS
1,055 full-time, 23 part-time. Students come from 30 states and territories; 35 other countries; 23% are from out of state; 3% Black or African American, non-Hispanic/Latino; 5% Hispanic/Latino; 14% Asian, non-Hispanic/Latino; 0.1% Native Hawaiian or other Pacific Islander, non-Hispanic/Latino; 0.4% American Indian or Alaska Native, non-Hispanic/Latino; 0.8% Two or more races, non-Hispanic/Latino; 6% Race/ethnicity unknown; 7% international; 6% transferred in; 58% live on campus.

Freshmen
Admission: 1,583 applied, 1,067 admitted, 213 enrolled. ***Average high school GPA:*** 3.6. ***Test scores:*** SAT critical reading scores over 500: 82%; SAT math scores over 500: 97%; SAT writing scores over 500: 78%; ACT scores over 18: 100%; SAT critical reading scores over 600: 31%; SAT math scores over 600: 57%; SAT writing scores over 600: 27%; ACT scores over 24: 70%; SAT critical reading scores over 700: 6%; SAT math scores over 700: 6%; SAT writing scores over 700: 5%; ACT scores over 30: 11%.
Retention: 80% of full-time freshmen returned.

FACULTY
Total: 132, 77% full-time, 77% with terminal degrees.
Student/faculty ratio: 14:1.

ACADEMICS
Calendar: semesters. *Degrees:* bachelor's, master's, and doctoral.
Special study options: advanced placement credit, double majors, off-campus study, services for LD students, summer session for credit.
Computers: Students can access the following: campus intranet, computer help desk, free student e-mail accounts, online (class) grades, online (class) registration, online (class) schedules. Campuswide network is available. 100% of college-owned or -operated housing units are wired for high-speed Internet access. Wireless service is available via entire campus.

STUDENT LIFE

Housing options: on-campus residence required through sophomore year; coed. Campus housing is university owned and is provided by a third party. Freshman campus housing is guaranteed.

Activities and organizations: choral group, American Pharmacists Association Academy of Students Pharmacists (APhA-ASP), Outdoors Club, Ski Club, Colleges Against Cancer, Dance Club, national fraternities.

Athletics Member USCAA. ***Intercollegiate sports:*** basketball M/W, cross-country running M/W, soccer M/W, track and field M/W. ***Intramural sports:*** basketball M/W, football M/W, golf M(c)/W(c), ice hockey M(c), lacrosse M(c), skiing (downhill) M(c)/W(c), tennis M(c)/W(c), ultimate Frisbee M/W, volleyball M/W.

Campus security: 24-hour emergency response devices and patrols, controlled dormitory access.

Student services: health clinic, personal/psychological counseling.

COSTS & FINANCIAL AID

Costs (2014–15) ***Comprehensive fee:*** $40,371 includes full-time tuition ($29,400), mandatory fees ($731), and room and board ($10,240). Full-time tuition and fees vary according to degree level, program, and student level. Part-time tuition: $980 per credit hour. Part-time tuition and fees vary according to degree level, program, and student level. ***College room only:*** $6600. Room and board charges vary according to board plan, housing facility, and location. ***Payment plan:*** installment. ***Waivers:*** employees or children of employees.

Financial Aid Of all full-time matriculated undergraduates who enrolled in 2013, 1,005 applied for aid, 906 were judged to have need, 76 had their need fully met. In 2013, 119 non-need-based awards were made. ***Average percent of need met:*** 39. ***Average financial aid package:*** $12,329. ***Average need-based loan:*** $4529. ***Average need-based gift aid:*** $9515. ***Average non-need-based aid:*** $8114. ***Financial aid deadline:*** 5/1.

APPLYING

Standardized Tests *Required:* SAT or ACT (for admission).

Options: electronic application, early admission, early decision.

Application fee: $75.

Required: essay or personal statement, high school transcript, 2 letters of recommendation. ***Required for some:*** interview. ***Recommended:*** minimum 3.0 GPA.

Application deadlines: 2/1 (freshmen), 5/1 (transfers).

Early decision deadline: 11/15.

Notification: 2/1 (freshmen), 5/15 (transfers), 12/1 (early decision).

CONTACT

Mr. Matthew Stever, Director of Admissions, Albany College of Pharmacy and Health Sciences, 106 New Scotland Avenue, Albany, NY 12208. *Phone:* 518-694-7221. *Toll-free phone:* 888-203-8010. *Fax:* 518-694-7322. *E-mail:* admissions@acphs.edu.

Bard College

Annandale-on-Hudson, New York

http://www.bard.edu/

- **Independent** comprehensive, founded 1860
- **Rural** 600-acre campus
- **Coed** 2,059 undergraduate students, 97% full-time, 55% women, 45% men
- **Very difficult** entrance level, 45% of applicants were admitted

UNDERGRAD STUDENTS

1,987 full-time, 72 part-time. Students come from 50 states and territories; 54 other countries; 67% are from out of state; 7% Black or African American, non-Hispanic/Latino; 1% Hispanic/Latino; 5% Asian, non-Hispanic/Latino; 0.6% American Indian or Alaska Native, non-Hispanic/Latino; 12% Race/ethnicity unknown; 12% international; 3% transferred in; 73% live on campus.

Freshmen

Admission: 6,960 applied, 3,105 admitted, 560 enrolled. ***Average high school GPA:*** 3.5.

Retention: 88% of full-time freshmen returned.

FACULTY

Total: 278, 55% full-time, 91% with terminal degrees.

Student/faculty ratio: 10:1.

ACADEMICS

Calendar: semesters. *Degrees:* bachelor's, master's, and doctoral.

Special study options: adult/continuing education programs, advanced placement credit, double majors, independent study, internships, off-campus study, part-time degree program, services for LD students, student-designed majors, study abroad.

Unusual degree programs: 3-2 business administration; engineering with Columbia University, Washington University in St. Louis, Dartmouth College; forestry with Duke University; social work; teaching.

Computers: 425 computers/terminals are available on campus for general student use. Students can access the following: campus intranet, computer help desk, free student e-mail accounts, online (class) grades, online (class) registration, online (class) schedules. Campuswide network is available. 100% of college-owned or -operated housing units are wired for high-speed Internet access. Wireless service is available via classrooms, computer centers, computer labs, dorm rooms, learning centers, libraries, student centers.

STUDENT LIFE

Housing options: on-campus residence required through sophomore year; coed, women-only, cooperative. Campus housing is university owned. Freshman campus housing is guaranteed.

Activities and organizations: drama/theater group, student-run newspaper, radio station, choral group, Student government, Debate Team, Queer-Straight Alliance, International Student Organization / Black Student Organization, Free Press (student newspaper).

Athletics Member NCAA, NAIA. All NCAA Division III. ***Intercollegiate sports:*** baseball M, basketball M/W, cross-country running M/W, lacrosse M/W, soccer M/W, squash M, swimming and diving M/W, tennis M/W, track and field M/W, volleyball M/W. ***Intramural sports:*** badminton M/W, basketball M/W, bowling M/W, equestrian sports M(c)/W(c), fencing M(c)/W(c), golf M/W, rugby M(c)/W(c), softball M/W, squash M, table tennis M/W, tennis M/W, ultimate Frisbee M(c)/W(c), volleyball M/W.

Campus security: 24-hour emergency response devices and patrols, student patrols, late-night transport/escort service, controlled dormitory access.

Student services: health clinic, personal/psychological counseling, legal services.

COSTS & FINANCIAL AID

Costs (2014–15) ***One-time required fee:*** $1614. ***Comprehensive fee:*** $62,012 includes full-time tuition ($47,560), mandatory fees ($680), and room and board ($13,772). Full-time tuition and fees vary according to degree level and location. Part-time tuition: $1486 per credit hour. Part-time tuition and fees vary according to degree level and location. ***Room and board:*** Room and board charges vary according to location. ***Payment plans:*** tuition prepayment, installment. ***Waivers:*** employees or children of employees.

Financial Aid Of all full-time matriculated undergraduates who enrolled in 2014, 1,418 applied for aid, 1,375 were judged to have need, 390 had their need fully met. 818 Federal Work-Study jobs (averaging $1500). In 2014, 35 non-need-based awards were made. ***Average percent of need met:*** 81. ***Average financial aid package:*** $40,938. ***Average need-based loan:*** $6100. ***Average need-based gift aid:*** $36,796. ***Average non-need-based aid:*** $20,154. ***Average indebtedness upon graduation:*** $26,599. ***Financial aid deadline:*** 2/15.

APPLYING

Options: electronic application, early admission, early action, deferred entrance.

Application fee: $50.

Required: essay or personal statement, high school transcript, minimum 3.0 GPA, 3 letters of recommendation.

Application deadlines: 1/1 (freshmen), 3/15 (transfers), 11/1 (early action).

Notification: 4/1 (freshmen), 5/15 (transfers), 1/1 (early action).

CONTACT
Ms. Mary Inga Backlund, Director of Admissions, Bard College, PO Box 5000 / 30 Campus Road, Annandale-on-Hudson, NY 12504-5000. *Phone:* 845-758-7472. *Fax:* 845-758-5208. *E-mail:* admission@bard.edu.

★ Barnard College

New York, New York

http://www.barnard.edu/

- **Independent** 4-year, founded 1889, part of Columbia University
- **Urban** 4-acre campus
- **Endowment** $276.5 million
- **Women only** 2,577 undergraduate students, 99% full-time
- **Most difficult** entrance level, 24% of applicants were admitted

UNDERGRAD STUDENTS
2,544 full-time, 33 part-time. Students come from 41 states and territories; 46 other countries; 63% are from out of state; 6% Black or African American, non-Hispanic/Latino; 11% Hispanic/Latino; 14% Asian, non-Hispanic/Latino; 6% Two or more races, non-Hispanic/Latino; 0.2% Race/ethnicity unknown; 7% international; 2% transferred in; 91% live on campus.

Freshmen
Admission: 5,676 applied, 1,349 admitted, 619 enrolled. ***Average high school GPA:*** 3.9. ***Test scores:*** SAT critical reading scores over 500: 98%; SAT math scores over 500: 99%; SAT writing scores over 500: 98%; ACT scores over 18: 100%; SAT critical reading scores over 600: 85%; SAT math scores over 600: 84%; SAT writing scores over 600: 91%; ACT scores over 24: 94%; SAT critical reading scores over 700: 41%; SAT math scores over 700: 32%; SAT writing scores over 700: 48%; ACT scores over 30: 59%.
Retention: 97% of full-time freshmen returned.

FACULTY
Total: 334, 63% full-time, 83% with terminal degrees.
Student/faculty ratio: 10:1.

ACADEMICS
Calendar: semesters. *Degree:* bachelor's.

Special study options: accelerated degree program, advanced placement credit, double majors, independent study, internships, off-campus study, services for LD students, student-designed majors, study abroad. ***ROTC:*** Army (c), Navy (c), Air Force (c).

Unusual degree programs: 3-2 engineering with Columbia University, The Fu Foundation School of Engineering and Applied Science; joint degrees with Columbia University, School of International and Public Affairs; School of Law; School of Dentistry; double degree programs with The Juilliard School; double degree and exchange program with the Jewish Theological Seminar; exchange program with the Manhattan School of Music.

Computers: 165 computers/terminals are available on campus for general student use. Students can access the following: campus intranet, computer help desk, free student e-mail accounts, online (class) grades, online (class) registration, online (class) schedules. Campuswide network is available. 100% of college-owned or -operated housing units are wired for high-speed Internet access. Wireless service is available via entire campus.

STUDENT LIFE
Housing options: women-only, special housing for students with disabilities. Campus housing is university owned and leased by the school. Freshman campus housing is guaranteed.

Activities and organizations: drama/theater group, student-run newspaper, radio and television station, choral group, marching band, Community Impact (community Service), Student Government Association, Take Back the Night, Student Activities Council, College Democrats.

Athletics Member NCAA. All Division I. ***Intercollegiate sports:*** archery W, basketball W, crew W, cross-country running W, equestrian sports W(c), fencing W, field hockey W, golf W, ice hockey W(c), lacrosse W, rugby W(c), sailing W(c), skiing (downhill) W(c), soccer W, softball W, squash W(c), swimming and diving W, tennis W, track and field W, volleyball W. ***Intramural sports:*** archery W, badminton W, basketball W, equestrian sports W, ice hockey W, rugby W, sailing W, soccer W, squash W, tennis W, volleyball W, water polo W.

Campus security: 24-hour emergency response devices and patrols, late-night transport/escort service, controlled dormitory access, gated campus with permanent security posts.

Student services: health clinic, personal/psychological counseling, women's center.

COSTS & FINANCIAL AID
Costs (2014–15) ***Comprehensive fee:*** $60,700 includes full-time tuition ($44,300), mandatory fees ($1740), and room and board ($14,660). ***Required fees:*** $1480 per credit hour part-time. ***Room and board:*** Room and board charges vary according to board plan and housing facility. ***Payment plans:*** tuition prepayment, installment, deferred payment. ***Waivers:*** employees or children of employees.

Financial Aid Of all full-time matriculated undergraduates who enrolled in 2014, 1,186 applied for aid, 1,031 were judged to have need, 1,008 had their need fully met. 273 Federal Work-Study jobs (averaging $2116). 554 state and other part-time jobs (averaging $2096). ***Average percent of need met:*** 100. ***Average financial aid package:*** $44,040. ***Average need-based loan:*** $4477. ***Average need-based gift aid:*** $38,842. ***Average indebtedness upon graduation:*** $17,660. ***Financial aid deadline:*** 2/15.

APPLYING
Standardized Tests *Required:* SAT with writing and two subject tests or ACT with writing (for admission).

Options: early admission, early decision, deferred entrance.

Application fee: $65.

Required: essay or personal statement, high school transcript, 3 letters of recommendation, Common Application with Barnard supplement. ***Recommended:*** interview.

Application deadlines: 1/1 (freshmen), 3/15 (transfers).

Early decision deadline: 11/1.

Notification: 4/1 (freshmen), 5/15 (transfers), 12/15 (early decision).

CONTACT
Ms. Jennifer Gill Fondiller, Dean of Enrollment Management, Barnard College, Barnard College, 3009 Broadway, New York, NY 10027. *Phone:* 212-854-2014. *Fax:* 212-854-6220. *E-mail:* admissions@barnard.edu.

See previous page for display ad and page 1356 for the College Close-Up.

★ Baruch College of the City University of New York

New York, New York

http://www.baruch.cuny.edu/

- **State and locally supported** comprehensive, founded 1919, part of City University of New York System
- **Urban** 4-acre campus
- **Coed** 14,857 undergraduate students, 73% full-time, 49% women, 51% men
- **Very difficult** entrance level, 28% of applicants were admitted

UNDERGRAD STUDENTS
10,865 full-time, 3,992 part-time. Students come from 2 states and territories; 168 other countries; 4% are from out of state; 9% Black or African American, non-Hispanic/Latino; 19% Hispanic/Latino; 33% Asian, non-Hispanic/Latino; 0.4% Native Hawaiian or other Pacific Islander, non-Hispanic/Latino; 0.2% American Indian or Alaska Native, non-Hispanic/Latino; 1% Two or more races, non-Hispanic/Latino; 12% international; 14% transferred in; 2% live on campus.

Freshmen
Admission: 19,768 applied, 5,516 admitted, 1,282 enrolled. ***Average high school GPA:*** 3.3. ***Test scores:*** SAT critical reading scores over 500: 86%; SAT math scores over 500: 98%; SAT critical reading scores over 600: 43%; SAT math scores over 600: 72%; SAT critical reading scores over 700: 8%; SAT math scores over 700: 22%.

Retention: 90% of full-time freshmen returned.

FACULTY
Total: 1,173, 45% full-time, 84% with terminal degrees.

Student/faculty ratio: 16:1.

ACADEMICS
Calendar: semesters. *Degrees:* bachelor's, master's, and post-master's certificates.

Special study options: accelerated degree program, adult/continuing education programs, advanced placement credit, distance learning, double majors, English as a second language, freshman honors college, honors programs, independent study, internships, part-time degree program, services for LD students, student-designed majors, study abroad, summer session for credit. ***ROTC:*** Army (c).

Computers: 1,300 computers/terminals are available on campus for general student use. Students can access the following: campus intranet, computer help desk, free student e-mail accounts, online (class) grades, online (class) registration, online (class) schedules. Campuswide network is available. Wireless service is available via classrooms, computer centers, computer labs, learning centers, libraries, student centers.

STUDENT LIFE
Housing options: coed. Campus housing is provided by a third party.

Activities and organizations: drama/theater group, student-run newspaper, radio station, choral group, Accounting Society, Caribbean Students Association, Association of Latino Professionals in Finance and Accounting, Golden Key International Honor Society, Helpline, national fraternities, national sororities.

Athletics Member NCAA. All Division III. ***Intercollegiate sports:*** baseball M, basketball M/W, cheerleading M/W, cross-country running M/W, soccer M, softball W, swimming and diving M/W, tennis M/W, volleyball M/W. ***Intramural sports:*** archery M(c)/W(c), badminton M/W, basketball M/W, cross-country running M/W, racquetball M/W, swimming and diving M/W, table tennis M/W, volleyball M/W.

Campus security: 24-hour emergency response devices and patrols, late-night transport/escort service, controlled access by ID card.

Student services: health clinic, personal/psychological counseling, legal services.

COSTS & FINANCIAL AID
Costs (2015–16) ***Tuition:*** state resident $6330 full-time, $275 per credit part-time; nonresident $16,800 full-time, $560 per credit part-time. Full-time tuition and fees vary according to course load. Part-time tuition and fees vary according to course load. ***Required fees:*** $531 full-time. ***Room and board:*** Room and board charges vary according to housing facility. ***Payment plans:*** installment, deferred payment. ***Waivers:*** senior citizens and employees or children of employees.

Financial Aid Of all full-time matriculated undergraduates who enrolled in 2014, 7,011 applied for aid, 6,539 were judged to have need, 984 had their need fully met. 1,898 Federal Work-Study jobs (averaging $1432). 40 state and other part-time jobs (averaging $1726). In 2014, 918 non-need-based awards were made. ***Average percent of need met:*** 18. ***Average financial aid package:*** $4882. ***Average need-based loan:*** $4195. ***Average need-based gift aid:*** $4898. ***Average non-need-based aid:*** $4264. ***Average indebtedness upon graduation:*** $5511.

APPLYING
Standardized Tests *Required:* SAT or ACT (for admission).

Options: electronic application, early admission, early decision, deferred entrance.

Application fee: $65.

Required: high school transcript, minimum 2.5 GPA, 16 academic units. ***Required for some:*** interview.

Application deadlines: 2/1 (freshmen), 2/1 (transfers).

Notification: 5/15 (freshmen), continuous until 5/1 (transfers).

CONTACT
Baruch College of the City University of New York, 1 Bernard Baruch Way, New York, NY 10010-5585. *Phone:* 646-312-1383.

Berkeley College–New York City Campus

New York, New York

http://www.berkeleycollege.edu/

- **Proprietary** 4-year, founded 1936
- **Urban** campus
- **Coed** 4,029 undergraduate students, 88% full-time, 64% women, 36% men
- **Minimally difficult** entrance level

UNDERGRAD STUDENTS

3,534 full-time, 495 part-time. Students come from 26 states and territories; 10% are from out of state; 27% Black or African American, non-Hispanic/Latino; 20% Hispanic/Latino; 3% Asian, non-Hispanic/Latino; 0.3% Native Hawaiian or other Pacific Islander, non-Hispanic/Latino; 0.4% American Indian or Alaska Native, non-Hispanic/Latino; 24% Race/ethnicity unknown; 18% international; 14% transferred in.

Freshmen

Admission: 570 enrolled.

Retention: 61% of full-time freshmen returned.

FACULTY

Student/faculty ratio: 22:1.

ACADEMICS

Calendar: quarters. *Degrees:* certificates, associate, and bachelor's.

Special study options: academic remediation for entering students, accelerated degree program, adult/continuing education programs, advanced placement credit, cooperative education, distance learning, English as a second language, honors programs, independent study, internships, off-campus study, part-time degree program, student-designed majors, study abroad, summer session for credit.

Computers: 500 computers/terminals are available on campus for general student use. Students can access the following: computer help desk, free student e-mail accounts, online (class) grades, online (class) registration, online (class) schedules. Campuswide network is available. Wireless service is available via entire campus.

STUDENT LIFE

Housing options: college housing not available.

Activities and organizations: student-run newspaper.

Athletics Member USCAA. ***Intercollegiate sports:*** basketball M/W, cross-country running M/W, soccer M/W.

Campus security: 24-hour emergency response devices.

Student services: personal/psychological counseling.

COSTS

Costs (2014–15) ***Tuition:*** $23,100 full-time, $525 per quarter hour part-time. Full-time tuition and fees vary according to course load. Part-time tuition and fees vary according to course load. No tuition increase for student's term of enrollment. ***Required fees:*** $1200 full-time, $275 per term part-time. ***Payment plan:*** installment. ***Waivers:*** employees or children of employees.

APPLYING

Options: electronic application, deferred entrance.

Application fee: $50.

Required: high school transcript. ***Recommended:*** interview.

Application deadlines: rolling (freshmen), rolling (out-of-state freshmen), rolling (transfers).

CONTACT

Michelle Gomez, Director, High School Admissions, Berkeley College–New York City Campus, 3 East 43 Street, New York, NY 1007. *Phone:* 212-986-4343. *Toll-free phone:* 800-446-5400. *E-mail:* info@berkeleycollege.edu.

Berkeley College–Westchester Campus

White Plains, New York

http://www.berkeleycollege.edu/

- **Proprietary** primarily 2-year, founded 1945
- **Suburban** campus with easy access to New York City
- **Coed** 450 undergraduate students, 92% full-time, 63% women, 37% men
- **Minimally difficult** entrance level

UNDERGRAD STUDENTS

412 full-time, 38 part-time. Students come from 22 states and territories; 24% are from out of state; 29% Black or African American, non-Hispanic/Latino; 26% Hispanic/Latino; 2% Asian, non-Hispanic/Latino; 0.4% Native Hawaiian or other Pacific Islander, non-Hispanic/Latino; 0.7% American Indian or Alaska Native, non-Hispanic/Latino; 22% Race/ethnicity unknown; 8% international; 11% transferred in.

Freshmen

Admission: 104 enrolled.

Retention: 61% of full-time freshmen returned.

FACULTY

Student/faculty ratio: 22:1.

ACADEMICS

Calendar: quarters. *Degrees:* associate and bachelor's.

Special study options: academic remediation for entering students, accelerated degree program, adult/continuing education programs, advanced placement credit, cooperative education, distance learning, honors programs, independent study, internships, off-campus study, part-time degree program, study abroad, summer session for credit.

Computers: 158 computers/terminals are available on campus for general student use. Campuswide network is available. Wireless service is available via entire campus.

STUDENT LIFE

Housing options: coed. Campus housing is university owned.

Activities and organizations: student-run newspaper.

Athletics Member USCAA. ***Intercollegiate sports:*** basketball M/W, cross-country running M/W, soccer M/W.

Campus security: 24-hour emergency response devices, controlled dormitory access, monitored entrance with front desk security guard.

Student services: personal/psychological counseling.

COSTS

Costs (2014–15) ***Tuition:*** $23,100 full-time, $525 per quarter hour part-time. Full-time tuition and fees vary according to course load. Part-time tuition and fees vary according to course load. No tuition increase for student's term of enrollment. ***Required fees:*** $1200 full-time, $275 per term part-time. ***Room only:*** $9000. ***Payment plan:*** installment. ***Waivers:*** employees or children of employees.

APPLYING

Options: electronic application, deferred entrance.

Application fee: $50.

Required: high school transcript. ***Recommended:*** interview.

Application deadlines: rolling (freshmen), rolling (out-of-state freshmen), rolling (transfers).

CONTACT

Lynn Ovimeleh, Director of High School Admissions, Berkeley College–Westchester Campus, 99 Church Street, White Plains, NY 10601. *Phone:* 914-694-1122. *Toll-free phone:* 800-446-5400. *E-mail:* info@berkeleycollege.edu.

Binghamton University, State University of New York

Vestal, New York

http://www.binghamton.edu/

- **State-supported** university, founded 1946, part of State University of New York System
- **Suburban** 930-acre campus
- **Endowment** $84.2 million
- **Coed** 13,412 undergraduate students, 96% full-time, 48% women, 52% men
- **Very difficult** entrance level, 44% of applicants were admitted

UNDERGRAD STUDENTS

12,908 full-time, 504 part-time. Students come from 44 states and territories; 96 other countries; 10% are from out of state; 5% Black or African American, non-Hispanic/Latino; 10% Hispanic/Latino; 14% Asian, non-Hispanic/Latino; 0.1% Native Hawaiian or other Pacific Islander, non-Hispanic/Latino; 0.1% American Indian or Alaska Native, non-Hispanic/Latino; 2% Two or more races, non-Hispanic/Latino; 2% Race/ethnicity unknown; 10% international; 9% transferred in; 52% live on campus.

Freshmen

Admission: 28,518 applied, 12,564 admitted, 2,602 enrolled. ***Average high school GPA:*** 3.6. ***Test scores:*** SAT critical reading scores over 500: 96%; SAT math scores over 500: 99%; SAT writing scores over 500: 98%; ACT scores over 18: 100%; SAT critical reading scores over 600: 72%; SAT math scores over 600: 85%; SAT writing scores over 600: 78%; ACT scores over 24: 95%; SAT critical reading scores over 700: 15%; SAT math scores over 700: 28%; SAT writing scores over 700: 21%; ACT scores over 30: 38%.

Retention: 89% of full-time freshmen returned.

FACULTY

Total: 944, 70% full-time, 80% with terminal degrees.

Student/faculty ratio: 20:1.

ACADEMICS

Calendar: semesters. *Degrees:* bachelor's, master's, doctoral, and post-master's certificates.

Special study options: accelerated degree program, adult/continuing education programs, advanced placement credit, distance learning, double majors, English as a second language, honors programs, independent study, internships, off-campus study, part-time degree program, services for LD students, student-designed majors, study abroad, summer session for credit. ***ROTC:*** Army (c), Air Force (c).

Unusual degree programs: 3-2 business administration; engineering; anthropology; art history; Asian/AsianAmerican studies; biology; chemistry; computer science; economics; education; French; geography; geology; Italian; math; material science; philosophy, politics & law; physics; political science; public administration; sociology; Spanish; systems science; theatre.

Computers: 1,589 computers/terminals and 45,000 ports are available on campus for general student use. Students can access the following: campus intranet, computer help desk, free student e-mail accounts, online (class) grades, online (class) registration, online (class) schedules, course management system, personal Web space, wiki, virtual desktop. Campuswide network is available. 100% of college-owned or -operated housing units are wired for high-speed Internet access. Wireless service is available via entire campus.

STUDENT LIFE

Housing options: on-campus residence required for freshman year; coed, special housing for students with disabilities. Campus housing is university owned and is provided by a third party. Freshman campus housing is guaranteed.

Activities and organizations: drama/theater group, student-run newspaper, radio and television station, choral group, intramurals, club sports, Student Association, cultural organizations, Peer Counseling/Mentoring/Volunteering Program, national fraternities, national sororities.

Athletics Member NCAA. All Division I. ***Intercollegiate sports:*** baseball M(s), basketball M(s)/W(s), cross-country running M(s)/W(s), golf M(s), lacrosse M(s)/W(s), soccer M(s)/W(s), softball W(s), swimming and diving M(s)/W(s), tennis M(s)/W(s), track and field M(s)/W(s), volleyball W(s), wrestling M(s). ***Intramural sports:*** badminton M(c)/W(c), baseball M(c), basketball M/W, bowling M/W, cheerleading M/W, crew M(c)/W(c), cross-country running M(c)/W(c), equestrian sports M(c)/W(c), fencing M(c)/W(c), field hockey M(c)/W(c), golf M(c)/W(c), gymnastics M(c)/W(c), ice hockey M(c)/W(c), lacrosse M(c)/W(c), racquetball M/W, rugby M(c)/W(c), skiing (downhill) M(c)/W(c), soccer M/W, softball M/W, swimming and diving M(c)/W(c), table tennis M(c)/W(c), tennis M/W, ultimate Frisbee M(c)/W(c), volleyball M/W, water polo M(c)/W(c).

Campus security: 24-hour emergency response devices and patrols, student patrols, late-night transport/escort service, controlled dormitory access, well-lit campus, self-defense/safety programs, secured entrances 12 am-5 pm, emergency texts, Incident Mgmt & Critical Response Teams.

Student services: health clinic, personal/psychological counseling, women's center, legal services.

COSTS & FINANCIAL AID

Costs (2014–15) ***Tuition:*** state resident $6170 full-time, $257 per credit hour part-time; nonresident $17,810 full-time, $742 per credit hour part-time. Full-time tuition and fees vary according to program. Part-time tuition and fees vary according to course load and program. ***Required fees:*** $2450 full-time, $101 per credit hour part-time, $25 per term part-time. ***Room and board:*** $13,028. Room and board charges vary according to board plan and housing facility. ***Payment plan:*** installment.

Financial Aid Of all full-time matriculated undergraduates who enrolled in 2014, 8,776 applied for aid, 6,336 were judged to have need, 954 had their need fully met. 302 Federal Work-Study jobs (averaging $1450). In 2014, 340 non-need-based awards were made. ***Average percent of need met:*** 72. ***Average financial aid package:*** $12,449. ***Average need-based loan:*** $4971. ***Average need-based gift aid:*** $8065. ***Average non-need-based aid:*** $7237. ***Average indebtedness upon graduation:*** $25,727.

APPLYING

Standardized Tests *Required:* SAT or ACT (for admission).

Options: electronic application, early admission, early action, deferred entrance.

Application fee: $50.

Required: essay or personal statement, high school transcript, 1 letter of recommendation. ***Required for some:*** portfolio, audition.

Application deadlines: rolling (freshmen), rolling (out-of-state freshmen), rolling (transfers), 11/15 (early action).

Notification: 4/1 (freshmen), 4/1 (out-of-state freshmen), continuous (transfers), 1/15 (early action).

CONTACT

Randall Edouard, Assistant Provost for Undergraduate Admissions, Binghamton University, State University of New York, PO Box 6001, Binghamton, NY 13902-6001. *Phone:* 607-777-2171. *Fax:* 607-777-4445. *E-mail:* admit@binghamton.edu.

Buffalo State College, State University of New York

Buffalo, New York

http://www.buffalostate.edu/

- **State-supported** comprehensive, founded 1867, part of State University of New York System
- **Urban** 115-acre campus
- **Endowment** $36.0 million
- **Coed** 9,475 undergraduate students, 88% full-time, 57% women, 43% men
- **Moderately difficult** entrance level, 62% of applicants were admitted

UNDERGRAD STUDENTS

8,327 full-time, 1,148 part-time. Students come from 26 states and territories; 83 other countries; 1% are from out of state; 25% Black or African American, non-Hispanic/Latino; 11% Hispanic/Latino; 2% Asian, non-Hispanic/Latino; 0.2% Native Hawaiian or other Pacific Islander, non-Hispanic/Latino; 0.4% American Indian or Alaska Native, non-Hispanic/Latino; 3% Two or more races, non-Hispanic/Latino; 0.2% Race/ethnicity unknown; 1% international; 10% transferred in; 29% live on campus.

Freshmen
Admission: 12,637 applied, 7,787 admitted, 1,869 enrolled. ***Average high school GPA:*** 3.15. ***Test scores:*** SAT critical reading scores over 500: 25%; SAT math scores over 500: 28%; SAT writing scores over 500: 19%; SAT critical reading scores over 600: 3%; SAT math scores over 600: 4%; SAT writing scores over 600: 2%.
Retention: 73% of full-time freshmen returned.

FACULTY
Total: 839, 46% full-time, 52% with terminal degrees.
Student/faculty ratio: 19:1.

ACADEMICS
Calendar: semesters. *Degrees:* bachelor's, master's, and post-master's certificates.
Special study options: academic remediation for entering students, adult/continuing education programs, advanced placement credit, cooperative education, distance learning, double majors, English as a second language, freshman honors college, honors programs, independent study, internships, off-campus study, part-time degree program, services for LD students, study abroad, summer session for credit. ***ROTC:*** Army (c).
Unusual degree programs: 3-2 engineering with State University of New York at Binghamton, Clarkson University, State University of New York at Buffalo.
Computers: 1,700 computers/terminals are available on campus for general student use. Students can access the following: computer help desk, free student e-mail accounts, online (class) registration, online (class) schedules. Campuswide network is available. 100% of college-owned or -operated housing units are wired for high-speed Internet access. Wireless service is available via classrooms, libraries, student centers.

STUDENT LIFE
Housing options: on-campus residence required through sophomore year; coed. Campus housing is university owned. Freshman campus housing is guaranteed.
Activities and organizations: drama/theater group, student-run newspaper, radio station, choral group, United Student Government, African-American Student Organization, Caribbean Student Organization, The Record, WBNY radio, national fraternities, national sororities.
Athletics Member NCAA. All Division III. ***Intercollegiate sports:*** baseball M(c), basketball M/W, bowling M(c)/W(c), cheerleading W(c), cross-country running M/W, fencing M(c), football M, ice hockey M/W, lacrosse M(c)/W, rugby M(c)/W(c), skiing (cross-country) M(c)/W(c), skiing (downhill) M(c)/W(c), soccer M/W, softball W, swimming and diving M/W, tennis W, track and field M/W, volleyball M(c)/W. ***Intramural sports:*** basketball M, football M, racquetball M/W, softball M/W, volleyball M/W, water polo M(c)/W(c).
Campus security: 24-hour emergency response devices and patrols, student patrols, late-night transport/escort service, controlled dormitory access.
Student services: health clinic, personal/psychological counseling, women's center, legal services.

COSTS & FINANCIAL AID
Costs (2014–15) ***Tuition:*** state resident $6170 full-time, $257 per credit hour part-time; nonresident $15,820 full-time, $659 per credit hour part-time. Part-time tuition and fees vary according to course load. ***Required fees:*** $1177 full-time. ***Room and board:*** $11,964; room only: $7060. Room and board charges vary according to board plan, housing facility, and student level. ***Payment plan:*** installment. ***Waivers:*** employees or children of employees.
Financial Aid Of all full-time matriculated undergraduates who enrolled in 2014, 7,902 applied for aid, 7,717 were judged to have need, 1,264 had their need fully met. 372 Federal Work-Study jobs (averaging $2593). 400 state and other part-time jobs (averaging $3317). In 2014, 560 non-need-based awards were made. ***Average percent of need met:*** 20. ***Average financial aid package:*** $12,749. ***Average need-based loan:*** $418. ***Average need-based gift aid:*** $6850. ***Average non-need-based aid:*** $1959. ***Average indebtedness upon graduation:*** $24,290.

APPLYING
Standardized Tests *Required:* SAT or ACT (for admission), SAT and SAT Subject Tests or ACT (for admission). *Recommended:* SAT (for admission).
Options: electronic application, early admission, deferred entrance.
Application fee: $50.
Required: high school transcript, minimum 3.0 GPA. ***Required for some:*** essay or personal statement, interview.
Application deadlines: rolling (freshmen), rolling (transfers).
Early decision deadline: 11/15.
Notification: continuous (freshmen), continuous (transfers), 12/15 (early decision).

CONTACT
Ms. Carmella Thompson, Director of Admissions, Buffalo State College, State University of New York, 110 Moot Hall, Buffalo, NY 14222. *Phone:* 716-878-4017. *Fax:* 716-878-6100. *E-mail:* admissions@buffalostate.edu.

Canisius College

Buffalo, New York

http://www.canisius.edu/

- **Independent Roman Catholic (Jesuit)** comprehensive, founded 1870
- **Urban** 72-acre campus
- **Endowment** $104.6 million
- **Coed** 2,868 undergraduate students, 95% full-time, 53% women, 47% men
- **Moderately difficult** entrance level, 80% of applicants were admitted

UNDERGRAD STUDENTS
2,725 full-time, 143 part-time. Students come from 31 states and territories; 32 other countries; 9% are from out of state; 7% Black or African American, non-Hispanic/Latino; 5% Hispanic/Latino; 2% Asian, non-Hispanic/Latino; 0.1% Native Hawaiian or other Pacific Islander, non-Hispanic/Latino; 0.2% American Indian or Alaska Native, non-Hispanic/Latino; 2% Two or more races, non-Hispanic/Latino; 5% Race/ethnicity unknown; 4% international; 3% transferred in; 46% live on campus.

Freshmen
Admission: 3,667 applied, 2,942 admitted, 613 enrolled. ***Average high school GPA:*** 3.5. ***Test scores:*** SAT critical reading scores over 500: 67%; SAT math scores over 500: 73%; ACT scores over 18: 97%; SAT critical reading scores over 600: 19%; SAT math scores over 600: 27%; ACT scores over 24: 53%; SAT critical reading scores over 700: 2%; SAT math scores over 700: 3%; ACT scores over 30: 10%.
Retention: 86% of full-time freshmen returned.

FACULTY
Total: 406, 48% full-time, 60% with terminal degrees.
Student/faculty ratio: 12:1.

ACADEMICS
Calendar: semesters. *Degrees:* associate, bachelor's, master's, and post-master's certificates.
Special study options: academic remediation for entering students, adult/continuing education programs, advanced placement credit, cooperative education, distance learning, double majors, English as a second language, honors programs, independent study, internships, off-campus study, part-time degree program, services for LD students, study abroad, summer session for credit. ***ROTC:*** Army (b).
Unusual degree programs: 3-2 business administration with BA/BS MBA program enables a qualified student in most majors to earn an undergraduate degree and an MBA within a five-year period; engineering with Physics Engineering with SUNY Buffalo (UB).
Computers: 700 computers/terminals are available on campus for general student use. Students can access the following: computer help desk, free student e-mail accounts, online (class) grades, online (class) registration, online (class) schedules, online accounts. Campuswide network is available. 100% of college-owned or -operated housing units are wired for high-speed Internet access. Wireless service is available via entire campus.

STUDENT LIFE

Housing options: on-campus residence required through sophomore year; coed, special housing for students with disabilities. Campus housing is university owned. Freshman applicants given priority for college housing.

Activities and organizations: drama/theater group, student-run newspaper, radio and television station, choral group, Campus Programming Board, Undergraduate Student Association, Afro-American Society, Residence Hall Association, Student Association, national fraternities, national sororities.

Athletics Member NCAA. All Division I. ***Intercollegiate sports:*** baseball M(s), basketball M(s)/W(s), cross-country running M(s)/W(s), equestrian sports W(c), golf M(s), ice hockey M(s), lacrosse M(s)/W(s), rugby M(c)/W(c), soccer M(s)/W(s), softball W(s), swimming and diving M(s)/W(s), volleyball M(c)/W(s). ***Intramural sports:*** basketball M/W, bowling M(c)/W(c), cheerleading M(c)/W(c), crew M(c)/W(c), fencing M(c)/W(c), field hockey W(c), ice hockey M(c)/W(c), lacrosse M(c), racquetball M/W, riflery M(c)/W(c), skiing (downhill) M(c)/W(c), soccer M/W, softball M/W, tennis M/W, track and field M(c)/W(c), ultimate Frisbee M(c)/W(c), volleyball M/W, wrestling M(c).

Campus security: 24-hour emergency response devices and patrols, late-night transport/escort service, controlled dormitory access, crime prevention programs, closed-circuit television monitors, emergency call boxes across campus.

Student services: health clinic, personal/psychological counseling.

COSTS & FINANCIAL AID

Costs (2014–15) ***Comprehensive fee:*** $46,516 includes full-time tuition ($32,630), mandatory fees ($1370), and room and board ($12,516). Part-time tuition: $932 per credit hour. ***College room only:*** $7354. Room and board charges vary according to board plan and housing facility. ***Payment plans:*** installment, deferred payment. ***Waivers:*** employees or children of employees.

Financial Aid Of all full-time matriculated undergraduates who enrolled in 2014, 2,281 applied for aid, 2,083 were judged to have need, 466 had their need fully met. 429 Federal Work-Study jobs (averaging $1728). In 2014, 554 non-need-based awards were made. ***Average percent of need met:*** 80. ***Average financial aid package:*** $29,284. ***Average need-based loan:*** $4515. ***Average need-based gift aid:*** $22,616. ***Average non-need-based aid:*** $15,623. ***Average indebtedness upon graduation:*** $40,913.

APPLYING

Standardized Tests *Required:* SAT or ACT (for admission).

Options: electronic application, early admission, deferred entrance.

Application fee: $40.

Required: high school transcript, minimum 2.0 GPA. ***Required for some:*** interview. ***Recommended:*** essay or personal statement, 1 letter of recommendation, interview.

Application deadlines: 5/1 (freshmen), rolling (transfers).

Notification: continuous (freshmen), continuous (transfers).

CONTACT

Ms. Molly Ballaro, Director of Admissions, Canisius College, 2001 Main Street, Buffalo, NY 14208-1098. *Phone:* 716-888-2200. *Toll-free phone:* 800-843-1517. *Fax:* 716-888-3230. *E-mail:* admissions@canisius.edu.

Cazenovia College

Cazenovia, New York

http://www.cazenovia.edu/

- **Independent** 4-year, founded 1824
- **Small-town** 40-acre campus with easy access to Syracuse
- **Coed** 1,091 undergraduate students, 88% full-time, 72% women, 28% men
- **Minimally difficult** entrance level, 76% of applicants were admitted

UNDERGRAD STUDENTS

963 full-time, 128 part-time. 15% are from out of state; 7% Black or African American, non-Hispanic/Latino; 6% Hispanic/Latino; 0.7% Asian, non-Hispanic/Latino; 0.3% Native Hawaiian or other Pacific Islander, non-Hispanic/Latino; 0.9% American Indian or Alaska Native, non-Hispanic/Latino; 4% Two or more races, non-Hispanic/Latino; 14% Race/ethnicity unknown; 4% transferred in; 94% live on campus.

Freshmen

Admission: 2,382 applied, 1,815 admitted, 265 enrolled. ***Average high school GPA:*** 3.2. ***Test scores:*** SAT critical reading scores over 500: 41%; SAT math scores over 500: 38%; SAT critical reading scores over 600: 7%; SAT math scores over 600: 6%; SAT critical reading scores over 700: 1%.

Retention: 73% of full-time freshmen returned.

FACULTY

Total: 129, 44% full-time, 47% with terminal degrees.

Student/faculty ratio: 12:1.

ACADEMICS

Calendar: semesters. *Degrees:* certificates, associate, and bachelor's.

Special study options: academic remediation for entering students, accelerated degree program, adult/continuing education programs, advanced placement credit, distance learning, double majors, freshman honors college, honors programs, independent study, internships, off-campus study, part-time degree program, services for LD students, study abroad, summer session for credit. ***ROTC:*** Army (c), Air Force (c).

Computers: Students can access the following: campus intranet, computer help desk, free student e-mail accounts, online (class) grades, online (class) schedules. Campuswide network is available. 100% of college-owned or -operated housing units are wired for high-speed Internet access. Wireless service is available via classrooms, computer centers, computer labs, dorm rooms, learning centers, libraries, student centers.

STUDENT LIFE

Housing options: on-campus residence required through junior year; coed, men-only, women-only, special housing for students with disabilities. Campus housing is university owned and leased by the school. Freshman campus housing is guaranteed.

Activities and organizations: drama/theater group, student-run newspaper, radio station, choral group, Activities Board, Multicultural Student Group, performing arts, student radio station, yearbook.

Athletics Member NCAA. All Division III. ***Intercollegiate sports:*** baseball M, basketball M/W, cheerleading M/W, crew M/W, cross-country running M/W, equestrian sports M/W, golf M, lacrosse M/W, soccer M/W, softball W, swimming and diving M/W, tennis M/W, volleyball M/W. ***Intramural sports:*** archery M, basketball M/W, bowling M/W, football M/W, ice hockey M(c), skiing (downhill) M/W, soccer M/W, softball W, volleyball M/W.

Campus security: 24-hour emergency response devices and patrols, late-night transport/escort service, controlled dormitory access.

Student services: health clinic, personal/psychological counseling.

COSTS & FINANCIAL AID

Costs (2014–15) ***Comprehensive fee:*** $42,904 includes full-time tuition ($30,028), mandatory fees ($532), and room and board ($12,344). Full-time tuition and fees vary according to class time, course load, and program. Part-time tuition: $640 per credit hour. Part-time tuition and fees vary according to class time and course load. ***College room only:*** $6920. Room and board charges vary according to board plan and housing facility. ***Payment plan:*** installment. ***Waivers:*** employees or children of employees.

Financial Aid Of all full-time matriculated undergraduates who enrolled in 2014, 923 applied for aid, 874 were judged to have need, 87 had their need fully met. In 2014, 89 non-need-based awards were made. ***Average percent of need met:*** 80. ***Average financial aid package:*** $29,600. ***Average need-based loan:*** $4300. ***Average need-based gift aid:*** $16,011. ***Average non-need-based aid:*** $14,600. ***Average indebtedness upon graduation:*** $29,998.

APPLYING

Standardized Tests *Recommended:* SAT or ACT (for admission).

Options: electronic application, deferred entrance.

Application fee: $30.

Required: high school transcript, 1 letter of recommendation. ***Recommended:*** essay or personal statement, minimum 2.0 GPA, interview, portfolio for art and design students.

CONTACT
Office of Admission and Enrollment Services, Cazenovia College, 3 Sullivan Street, Cazenovia, NY 13035. *Phone:* 315-655-7208. *Toll-free phone:* 800-654-3210. *Fax:* 315-655-4860. *E-mail:* admission@cazenovia.edu.

City College of the City University of New York

New York, New York

http://www.ccny.cuny.edu/

- **State and locally supported** comprehensive, founded 1847, part of City University of New York
- **Urban** 35-acre campus with easy access to New York City
- **Coed** 16,463 undergraduate students, 77% full-time, 51% women, 49% men
- **Moderately difficult** entrance level, 38% of applicants were admitted

UNDERGRAD STUDENTS
12,724 full-time, 3,739 part-time. Students come from 140 other countries; 4% are from out of state; 19% Black or African American, non-Hispanic/Latino; 32% Hispanic/Latino; 24% Asian, non-Hispanic/Latino; 0.1% American Indian or Alaska Native, non-Hispanic/Latino; 6% international; 9% transferred in; 1% live on campus.

Freshmen
Admission: 25,445 applied, 9,694 admitted, 1,444 enrolled. ***Test scores:*** SAT critical reading scores over 500: 56%; SAT math scores over 500: 86%; SAT writing scores over 500: 57%; SAT critical reading scores over 600: 22%; SAT math scores over 600: 41%; SAT writing scores over 600: 22%; SAT critical reading scores over 700: 6%; SAT math scores over 700: 12%; SAT writing scores over 700: 6%.

Retention: 86% of full-time freshmen returned.

FACULTY
Total: 1,611, 33% full-time, 39% with terminal degrees.

Student/faculty ratio: 14:1.

ACADEMICS
Calendar: semesters. *Degrees:* bachelor's, master's, doctoral, and post-master's certificates.

Special study options: accelerated degree program, adult/continuing education programs, advanced placement credit, English as a second language, freshman honors college, honors programs, independent study, internships, off-campus study, part-time degree program, services for LD students, student-designed majors, study abroad, summer session for credit. ***ROTC:*** Army (b).

Computers: 3,000 computers/terminals are available on campus for general student use. Students can access the following: campus intranet, computer help desk, free student e-mail accounts, online (class) grades, online (class) registration, online (class) schedules. Campuswide network is available. 100% of college-owned or -operated housing units are wired for high-speed Internet access. Wireless service is available via entire campus.

STUDENT LIFE
Housing options: coed. Campus housing is provided by a third party.

Activities and organizations: drama/theater group, student-run newspaper, radio station, choral group, Latin American Engineering Student Assoc./Society of Hispanic Professional Engineers, National Society of Black Engineers, Bangladesh Student Association, Salsa-Mambo, InterVarsity Christian Fellowship, national fraternities.

Athletics Member NCAA. All Division III. ***Intercollegiate sports:*** baseball M, basketball M/W, cross-country running M/W, fencing W, lacrosse M, soccer M/W, softball W, tennis M/W, track and field M/W, volleyball W. ***Intramural sports:*** basketball M/W, fencing W, soccer M, softball W, tennis M/W, track and field M/W, volleyball W.

Campus security: 24-hour patrols, late-night transport/escort service, controlled dormitory access.

Student services: health clinic, personal/psychological counseling.

COSTS & FINANCIAL AID
Costs (2015–16) ***Tuition:*** state resident $6330 full-time; nonresident $16,800 full-time. Full-time tuition and fees vary according to course load and program. Part-time tuition and fees vary according to course load and program. ***Room and board:*** Room and board charges vary according to housing facility. ***Payment plan:*** deferred payment. ***Waivers:*** senior citizens.

Financial Aid Of all full-time matriculated undergraduates who enrolled in 2014, 8,866 applied for aid, 8,458 were judged to have need, 6,912 had their need fully met. In 2014, 605 non-need-based awards were made. ***Average percent of need met:*** 82. ***Average financial aid package:*** $8878. ***Average need-based loan:*** $4024. ***Average need-based gift aid:*** $7910. ***Average non-need-based aid:*** $4120. ***Average indebtedness upon graduation:*** $16,942.

APPLYING
Standardized Tests *Required:* SAT or ACT (for admission).

Options: early admission, deferred entrance.

Application fee: $65.

Required: high school transcript. ***Required for some:*** essay or personal statement, creative challenge for Architecture, supplemental application for Engineering.

Application deadlines: 2/1 (freshmen), 2/1 (transfers).

Notification: continuous until 2/1 (freshmen), continuous until 3/1 (transfers).

CONTACT
City College of the City University of New York, 160 Convent Avenue, New York, NY 10031-9198. *Phone:* 212-650-6977.

Clarkson University

Potsdam, New York

http://www.clarkson.edu/

- **Independent** university, founded 1896
- **Small-town** 640-acre campus
- **Endowment** $192.9 million
- **Coed** 3,247 undergraduate students, 98% full-time, 30% women, 70% men
- **Very difficult** entrance level, 62% of applicants were admitted

UNDERGRAD STUDENTS
3,166 full-time, 81 part-time. Students come from 40 states and territories; 30 other countries; 25% are from out of state; 2% Black or African American, non-Hispanic/Latino; 5% Hispanic/Latino; 3% Asian, non-Hispanic/Latino; 0.3% American Indian or Alaska Native, non-Hispanic/Latino; 2% Two or more races, non-Hispanic/Latino; 2% Race/ethnicity unknown; 2% international; 3% transferred in; 83% live on campus.

Freshmen
Admission: 7,401 applied, 4,599 admitted, 767 enrolled. ***Average high school GPA:*** 3.7. ***Test scores:*** SAT critical reading scores over 500: 85%; SAT math scores over 500: 96%; SAT writing scores over 500: 76%; ACT scores over 18: 100%; SAT critical reading scores over 600: 37%; SAT math scores over 600: 62%; SAT writing scores over 600: 27%; ACT scores over 24: 80%; SAT critical reading scores over 700: 4%; SAT math scores over 700: 16%; SAT writing scores over 700: 3%; ACT scores over 30: 22%.

Retention: 92% of full-time freshmen returned.

FACULTY
Total: 300, 79% full-time, 79% with terminal degrees.

Student/faculty ratio: 14:1.

ACADEMICS
Calendar: semesters. *Degrees:* bachelor's, master's, doctoral, and postbachelor's certificates.

Special study options: accelerated degree program, advanced placement credit, cooperative education, distance learning, double majors, English as a second language, honors programs, independent study, internships, off-campus study, part-time degree program, services for LD students, student-designed majors, study abroad, summer session for credit. ***ROTC:*** Army (b), Air Force (b).

Unusual degree programs: 3-2 engineering.

Computers: 350 computers/terminals and 6,000 ports are available on campus for general student use. Students can access the following:

campus intranet, computer help desk, free student e-mail accounts, online (class) grades, online (class) registration, online (class) schedules. Campuswide network is available. 100% of college-owned or -operated housing units are wired for high-speed Internet access. Wireless service is available via classrooms, computer centers, computer labs, dorm rooms, learning centers, libraries, student centers.

STUDENT LIFE
Housing options: on-campus residence required through senior year; coed, men-only, women-only, special housing for students with disabilities. Campus housing is university owned. Freshman campus housing is guaranteed.

Activities and organizations: drama/theater group, student-run newspaper, radio and television station, choral group, Ski Club, Outing Club, Men's Rugby, Men's Hockey Club, Crew Club, national fraternities, national sororities.

Athletics Member NCAA. All Division III except men's and women's ice hockey (Division I). ***Intercollegiate sports:*** baseball M, basketball M/W, cross-country running M/W, golf M, ice hockey M(s)/W(s), lacrosse M/W, skiing (cross-country) M/W, skiing (downhill) M/W, soccer M/W, softball W, swimming and diving M/W, volleyball W. ***Intramural sports:*** baseball M(c), basketball M/W, bowling M(c)/W(c), crew M(c)/W(c), football M/W, golf M(c), ice hockey M/W, lacrosse M(c)/W(c), racquetball M(c)/W(c), rugby M(c)/W(c), skiing (cross-country) M(c)/W(c), skiing (downhill) M(c)/W(c), soccer M/W, softball M/W, tennis M(c)/W(c), ultimate Frisbee M(c)/W(c), volleyball M/W, wrestling M(c).

Campus security: 24-hour emergency response devices and patrols, late-night transport/escort service, controlled dormitory access.

Student services: health clinic, personal/psychological counseling, legal services.

COSTS & FINANCIAL AID
Costs (2015–16) ***Comprehensive fee:*** $58,474 includes full-time tuition ($43,690), mandatory fees ($940), and room and board ($13,844). Full-time tuition and fees vary according to course load. Part-time tuition: $1457 per credit hour. Part-time tuition and fees vary according to course load. ***College room only:*** $7334. Room and board charges vary according to board plan and housing facility. ***Payment plan:*** installment. ***Waivers:*** employees or children of employees.

Financial Aid Of all full-time matriculated undergraduates who enrolled in 2014, 2,815 applied for aid, 2,637 were judged to have need, 495 had their need fully met. 1,760 Federal Work-Study jobs (averaging $1600). 74 state and other part-time jobs (averaging $9230). In 2014, 453 non-need-based awards were made. ***Average percent of need met:*** 90. ***Average financial aid package:*** $40,409. ***Average need-based loan:*** $5533. ***Average need-based gift aid:*** $29,179. ***Average non-need-based aid:*** $19,191. ***Average indebtedness upon graduation:*** $28,000. ***Financial aid deadline:*** 3/1.

APPLYING
Standardized Tests *Required:* SAT or ACT (for admission). *Recommended:* SAT Subject Tests (for admission).

Options: electronic application, early admission, early decision, deferred entrance.

Application fee: $50.

Required: essay or personal statement, high school transcript, 2 letters of recommendation, SAT or ACT. ***Recommended:*** interview.

Early decision deadline: 12/1.

Notification: continuous (freshmen), continuous (transfers), 1/1 (early decision).

CONTACT
Mr. Brian T. Grant, Dean of Admissions, Clarkson University, 8 Clarkson Ave, Box 5605, CU Box 5605, Potsdam, NY 13699. *Phone:* 315-268-6480. *Toll-free phone:* 800-527-6577. *Fax:* 315-268-7647. *E-mail:* admission@clarkson.edu.

Colgate University
Hamilton, New York
http://www.colgate.edu/

- **Independent** comprehensive, founded 1819
- **Rural** 515-acre campus with easy access to Syracuse, Utica
- **Endowment** $760.6 million
- **Coed**
- **Most difficult** entrance level

FACULTY
Student/faculty ratio: 9:1.

ACADEMICS
Calendar: semesters. *Degrees:* bachelor's and master's.

STUDENT LIFE
Housing options: on-campus residence required through junior year; coed, cooperative, special housing for students with disabilities. Campus housing is university owned. Freshman campus housing is guaranteed.

Activities and organizations: drama/theater group, student-run newspaper, radio and television station, choral group, COVE, student government, cultural/ethnic interest groups, student publications, Outdoor Education, national fraternities, national sororities.

Athletics Member NCAA. All Division I except football (Division I-AA).

Campus security: 24-hour emergency response devices and patrols, student patrols, late-night transport/escort service, controlled dormitory access.

Student services: health clinic, personal/psychological counseling, women's center, legal services.

COSTS & FINANCIAL AID
Costs (2014–15) ***One-time required fee:*** $50. ***Comprehensive fee:*** $60,145 includes full-time tuition ($47,855), mandatory fees ($320), and room and board ($11,970). Full-time tuition and fees vary according to course load. Part-time tuition: $5982 per course. Part-time tuition and fees vary according to course load. ***College room only:*** $5775. Room and board charges vary according to board plan and housing facility. ***Payment plans:*** tuition prepayment, installment, deferred payment.

Financial Aid Of all full-time matriculated undergraduates who enrolled in 2014, 1,086 applied for aid, 997 were judged to have need, 997 had their need fully met. 583 Federal Work-Study jobs (averaging $2241). 277 state and other part-time jobs (averaging $2039). ***Average percent of need met:*** 100. ***Average financial aid package:*** $45,594. ***Average need-based loan:*** $3612. ***Average need-based gift aid:*** $41,428. ***Average indebtedness upon graduation:*** $21,405. ***Financial aid deadline:*** 1/15.

APPLYING
Standardized Tests *Required:* SAT or ACT (for admission).

Options: electronic application, early decision, deferred entrance.

Application fee: $60.

Required: essay or personal statement, high school transcript, 3 letters of recommendation, Colgate supplement.

CONTACT
Mr. Gary L. Ross, Dean of Admission, Colgate University, Colgate Office of Admission, 13 Oak Drive, Hamilton, NY 13346-1383. *Phone:* 315-228-7401. *Fax:* 315-228-7544. *E-mail:* admission@colgate.edu.

The College at Brockport, State University of New York
Brockport, New York
http://www.brockport.edu/

- **State-supported** comprehensive, founded 1867, part of State University of New York System
- **Small-town** 464-acre campus with easy access to Rochester
- **Coed** 7,040 undergraduate students, 90% full-time, 55% women, 45% men
- **Moderately difficult** entrance level, 49% of applicants were admitted

UNDERGRAD STUDENTS
6,304 full-time, 736 part-time. Students come from 22 states and territories; 15 other countries; 1% are from out of state; 9% Black or African American, non-Hispanic/Latino; 5% Hispanic/Latino; 2% Asian,

non-Hispanic/Latino; 0.2% American Indian or Alaska Native, non-Hispanic/Latino; 2% Two or more races, non-Hispanic/Latino; 7% Race/ethnicity unknown; 2% international; 14% transferred in; 38% live on campus.

Freshmen

Admission: 9,769 applied, 4,782 admitted, 1,090 enrolled. ***Average high school GPA:*** 3.1. ***Test scores:*** SAT critical reading scores over 500: 61%; SAT math scores over 500: 69%; SAT writing scores over 500: 51%; ACT scores over 18: 96%; SAT critical reading scores over 600: 15%; SAT math scores over 600: 18%; SAT writing scores over 600: 11%; ACT scores over 24: 44%; SAT critical reading scores over 700: 1%; SAT math scores over 700: 1%; SAT writing scores over 700: 1%; ACT scores over 30: 4%.

Retention: 82% of full-time freshmen returned.

FACULTY

Total: 596, 56% full-time, 58% with terminal degrees.

Student/faculty ratio: 17:1.

ACADEMICS

Calendar: semesters. *Degrees:* bachelor's, master's, post-master's, and postbachelor's certificates.

Special study options: accelerated degree program, advanced placement credit, cooperative education, distance learning, double majors, English as a second language, freshman honors college, honors programs, independent study, internships, off-campus study, part-time degree program, services for LD students, student-designed majors, study abroad, summer session for credit. ***ROTC:*** Army (b), Navy (c), Air Force (c).

Unusual degree programs: 3-2 BS/Masters in Biology, BS/Masters in Environmental Science and Biology, BS/Masters in History, BS/Masters in Mathematics, BS in Sociology/Masters of Public Administration and BS Political Science/Masters of Public Administration.

Computers: 1,000 computers/terminals are available on campus for general student use. Students can access the following: campus intranet, computer help desk, free student e-mail accounts, online (class) grades, online (class) registration, online (class) schedules. Campuswide network is available. 100% of college-owned or -operated housing units are wired for high-speed Internet access. Wireless service is available via entire campus.

STUDENT LIFE

Housing options: on-campus residence required through sophomore year; coed, special housing for students with disabilities. Campus housing is university owned. Freshman campus housing is guaranteed.

Activities and organizations: drama/theater group, student-run newspaper, radio and television station, choral group, Habitat for Humanity, Organization for Students of African Descent, Caribbean Student Association, Autism Speaks U: The College at Brockport, Sexual Orientations United for Liberation, national fraternities, national sororities.

Athletics Member NCAA. All Division III. ***Intercollegiate sports:*** baseball M, basketball M/W, cross-country running M/W, field hockey W, football M, gymnastics W, ice hockey M, lacrosse M/W, soccer M/W, softball W, swimming and diving M/W, tennis W, track and field M/W, volleyball W, wrestling M. ***Intramural sports:*** badminton M/W, baseball M(c), basketball M/W, bowling M/W, cheerleading M(c)/W(c), equestrian sports M(c)/W(c), football M/W, golf M(c)/W(c), gymnastics M(c)/W(c), ice hockey M(c)/W(c), lacrosse M(c), racquetball M/W, rugby M(c)/W(c), soccer M/W, softball M/W, table tennis M/W, tennis M(c)/W(c), ultimate Frisbee M(c)/W(c), volleyball M/W.

Campus security: 24-hour emergency response devices and patrols, student patrols, late-night transport/escort service, controlled dormitory access, Emergency Notification System.

Student services: health clinic, personal/psychological counseling, women's center, legal services.

COSTS & FINANCIAL AID

Costs (2014–15) ***Tuition:*** state resident $6170 full-time, $257 per credit part-time; nonresident $15,820 full-time, $659 per credit part-time. Part-time tuition and fees vary according to course load. ***Required fees:*** $1392 full-time. ***Room and board:*** $11,440; room only: $7130. Room and board charges vary according to board plan and housing facility. ***Payment plans:*** installment, deferred payment. ***Waivers:*** senior citizens and employees or children of employees.

Financial Aid Of all full-time matriculated undergraduates who enrolled in 2014, 4,584 applied for aid, 3,663 were judged to have need, 589 had their need fully met. 572 Federal Work-Study jobs (averaging $2033). 1,683 state and other part-time jobs (averaging $1440). In 2014, 138 non-need-based awards were made. ***Average percent of need met:*** 75. ***Average financial aid package:*** $10,374. ***Average need-based loan:*** $4760. ***Average need-based gift aid:*** $6361. ***Average non-need-based aid:*** $4627. ***Average indebtedness upon graduation:*** $27,666.

APPLYING

Standardized Tests *Required:* SAT or ACT (for admission).

Options: electronic application, deferred entrance.

Application fee: $50.

Required: essay or personal statement, high school transcript, 1 letter of recommendation, SAT or ACT. ***Required for some:*** interview. ***Recommended:*** minimum 3.0 GPA.

Application deadlines: rolling (freshmen), rolling (out-of-state freshmen), 8/1 (transfers).

Notification: continuous (freshmen), continuous (out-of-state freshmen), continuous (transfers).

CONTACT

The College at Brockport, State University of New York, 350 New Campus Drive, Brockport, NY 14420-2997. *Phone:* 585-395-2137.

★ College of Mount Saint Vincent

Riverdale, New York

http://www.mountsaintvincent.edu/

- **Independent** comprehensive, founded 1911
- **Suburban** 70-acre campus with easy access to New York City
- **Coed**
- **Moderately difficult** entrance level

FACULTY

Student/faculty ratio: 12:1.

ACADEMICS

Calendar: semesters. *Degrees:* associate, bachelor's, master's, and post-master's certificates.

STUDENT LIFE

Housing options: coed, special housing for students with disabilities. Campus housing is university owned. Freshman campus housing is guaranteed.

Activities and organizations: drama/theater group, student-run newspaper, radio and television station, choral group, Casa Latina, Players, Dance Club, Student Nurse Association.

Athletics Member NCAA. All Division III.

Campus security: 24-hour emergency response devices and patrols, late-night transport/escort service, controlled dormitory access, emergency call boxes.

Student services: health clinic, personal/psychological counseling.

FINANCIAL AID

Financial Aid Of all full-time matriculated undergraduates who enrolled in 2013, 1,362 applied for aid, 1,250 were judged to have need, 169 had their need fully met. In 2013, 112 non-need-based awards were made. ***Average percent of need met:*** 68. ***Average financial aid package:*** $19,829. ***Average need-based loan:*** $4333. ***Average need-based gift aid:*** $10,243. ***Average non-need-based aid:*** $12,904.

APPLYING

Standardized Tests *Required:* SAT or ACT (for admission).

Options: electronic application, early admission, early action, deferred entrance.

Application fee: $35.

Required: essay or personal statement, high school transcript, minimum 2.0 GPA. ***Required for some:*** interview. ***Recommended:*** 2 letters of recommendation, interview.

CONTACT

Jackie Williams, Director of Admissions, College of Mount Saint Vincent, 6301 Riverdale Avenue, Riverdale, NY 10471-1093. *Phone:*

718-405-3223. *Toll-free phone:* 800-665-CMSV. *Fax:* 718-549-7945.
E-mail: jackie.williams@mountsaintvincent.edu.

See below for display ad and page 1400 for the College Close-Up.

The College of New Rochelle

New Rochelle, New York

http://www.cnr.edu/

- **Independent** comprehensive, founded 1904
- **Suburban** 20-acre campus with easy access to New York City
- **Endowment** $36.5 million
- **Coed, primarily women** 820 undergraduate students, 71% full-time, 92% women, 8% men
- **Moderately difficult** entrance level, 29% of applicants were admitted

UNDERGRAD STUDENTS

581 full-time, 239 part-time. Students come from 17 states and territories; 7% are from out of state; 37% Black or African American, non-Hispanic/Latino; 23% Hispanic/Latino; 5% Asian, non-Hispanic/Latino; 0.9% Native Hawaiian or other Pacific Islander, non-Hispanic/Latino; 0.7% American Indian or Alaska Native, non-Hispanic/Latino; 0.7% Two or more races, non-Hispanic/Latino; 15% Race/ethnicity unknown; 1% international; 7% transferred in; 29% live on campus.

Freshmen

Admission: 2,321 applied, 662 admitted, 92 enrolled. ***Average high school GPA:*** 3.2.

Retention: 71% of full-time freshmen returned.

FACULTY

Total: 202, 37% full-time.

Student/faculty ratio: 10:1.

ACADEMICS

Calendar: semesters. *Degrees:* bachelor's, master's, post-master's, and postbachelor's certificates (also offers a non-traditional adult program with significant enrollment not reflected in profile).

Special study options: academic remediation for entering students, accelerated degree program, adult/continuing education programs, advanced placement credit, cooperative education, double majors, honors programs, independent study, internships, off-campus study, part-time degree program, services for LD students, student-designed majors, study abroad, summer session for credit.

Computers: 120 computers/terminals are available on campus for general student use. Students can access the following: campus intranet, computer help desk, free student e-mail accounts, online (class) registration, online (class) schedules. Campuswide network is available. 100% of college-owned or -operated housing units are wired for high-speed Internet access. Wireless service is available via entire campus.

STUDENT LIFE

Housing options: women-only. Campus housing is university owned. Freshman campus housing is guaranteed.

Activities and organizations: drama/theater group, student-run newspaper, choral group, Drama Club, CNR Model United Nations, Student Nurses Association, Music Ensembles, Student Government.

Athletics Member NCAA. All Division III. ***Intercollegiate sports:*** basketball W, cross-country running W, softball W, swimming and diving W, tennis W, volleyball W. ***Intramural sports:*** badminton M/W, basketball M/W, cheerleading W(c), cross-country running M/W(c), table tennis M/W, ultimate Frisbee M/W, volleyball M/W.

Campus security: 24-hour emergency response devices and patrols, late-night transport/escort service, controlled dormitory access, 24-hour monitored security cameras at residence hall entrances.

Student services: health clinic, personal/psychological counseling, women's center.

COSTS & FINANCIAL AID

Costs (2014–15) ***Comprehensive fee:*** $44,500 includes full-time tuition ($31,200), mandatory fees ($1100), and room and board ($12,200). Full-time tuition and fees vary according to course load, location, and program. Part-time tuition: $896 per credit. Part-time tuition and fees vary according to course load, location, and program. ***Required fees:*** $400 per term part-time. ***Room and board:*** Room and board charges vary according to housing facility. ***Payment plan:*** installment. ***Waivers:*** employees or children of employees.

Financial Aid Of all full-time matriculated undergraduates who enrolled in 2013, 532 applied for aid, 509 were judged to have need, 23 had their need fully met. 365 Federal Work-Study jobs (averaging $2500). In 2013, 23 non-need-based awards were made. ***Average percent of need met:*** 59. ***Average financial aid package:*** $22,358. ***Average need-based loan:*** $5522. ***Average need-based gift aid:*** $9146. ***Average non-need-based aid:*** $13,843. ***Average indebtedness upon graduation:*** $37,437.

APPLYING

Standardized Tests *Required:* SAT or ACT (for admission).

Options: electronic application, early admission, early decision, deferred entrance.

Application fee: $35.

Required: high school transcript. ***Recommended:*** essay or personal statement, 1 letter of recommendation, interview.

Application deadlines: rolling (freshmen), rolling (transfers).

Early decision deadline: 11/1.

Notification: continuous (freshmen), continuous (transfers), 12/15 (early decision).

CONTACT

Ms. Danielle Robinson, Associate Director, Undergraduate Admission SAS/SON, The College of New Rochelle, 29 Castle Place, New Rochelle, NY 10805-2339. *Phone:* 914-654-5452. *Toll-free phone:* 800-933-5923. *Fax:* 914-654-5464. *E-mail:* admission@cnr.edu.

The College of Saint Rose

Albany, New York

http://www.strose.edu/

- **Independent** comprehensive, founded 1920
- **Urban** 49-acre campus
- **Endowment** $36.2 million
- **Coed** 2,773 undergraduate students, 91% full-time, 66% women, 34% men
- **Moderately difficult** entrance level, 76% of applicants were admitted

UNDERGRAD STUDENTS

2,533 full-time, 240 part-time. Students come from 32 states and territories; 37 other countries; 12% are from out of state; 7% Black or African American, non-Hispanic/Latino; 6% Hispanic/Latino; 2% Asian, non-Hispanic/Latino; 0.1% Native Hawaiian or other Pacific Islander, non-Hispanic/Latino; 0.3% American Indian or Alaska Native, non-Hispanic/Latino; 6% Two or more races, non-Hispanic/Latino; 8% Race/ethnicity unknown; 2% international; 8% transferred in; 46% live on campus.

Freshmen

Admission: 5,525 applied, 4,215 admitted, 534 enrolled. ***Average high school GPA:*** 3.39. ***Test scores:*** SAT critical reading scores over 500: 62%; SAT math scores over 500: 60%; ACT scores over 18: 94%; SAT critical reading scores over 600: 18%; SAT math scores over 600: 18%; ACT scores over 24: 46%; SAT critical reading scores over 700: 1%; ACT scores over 30: 9%.

Retention: 78% of full-time freshmen returned.

FACULTY

Total: 355, 58% full-time.

Student/faculty ratio: 14:1.

ACADEMICS

Calendar: semesters. *Degrees:* certificates, bachelor's, master's, post-master's, and postbachelor's certificates.

Special study options: academic remediation for entering students, accelerated degree program, advanced placement credit, double majors, external degree program, independent study, internships, off-campus study, part-time degree program, services for LD students, student-designed majors, study abroad, summer session for credit. ***ROTC:*** Army (c), Navy (c), Air Force (c).

Unusual degree programs: 3-2 engineering with Alfred University, Clarkson University, Union College (NY), Rensselaer Polytechnic Institute.

Computers: 823 computers/terminals and 4,636 ports are available on campus for general student use. Students can access the following: computer help desk, free student e-mail accounts, online (class) grades, online (class) registration, online (class) schedules. Campuswide network is available. 100% of college-owned or -operated housing units are wired for high-speed Internet access. Wireless service is available via entire campus.

STUDENT LIFE

Housing options: coed, men-only, women-only, special housing for students with disabilities. Campus housing is university owned and leased by the school. Freshman applicants given priority for college housing.

Activities and organizations: drama/theater group, student-run newspaper, radio and television station, choral group, Student Association, Student Events Board, Spectrum-ALANA Student Union, Colleges Against Cancer, Music & Entertainment Industry Student Association.

Athletics Member NCAA. All Division II. ***Intercollegiate sports:*** baseball M(s), basketball M(s)/W(s), cross-country running M/W, golf M/W, lacrosse M(s), soccer M(s)/W(s), softball W(s), swimming and diving M(s)/W(s), tennis W, track and field M(s)/W(s), volleyball W(s). ***Intramural sports:*** basketball M/W, cheerleading M(c)/W(c), soccer M/W, ultimate Frisbee M/W, volleyball M/W.

Campus security: 24-hour emergency response devices and patrols, late-night transport/escort service, controlled dormitory access.

Student services: health clinic, personal/psychological counseling.

COSTS & FINANCIAL AID

Costs (2014–15) ***Comprehensive fee:*** $40,548 includes full-time tuition ($28,036), mandatory fees ($980), and room and board ($11,532). Full-time tuition and fees vary according to class time and course load. Part-time tuition: $932 per credit hour. Part-time tuition and fees vary according to class time and course load. ***Required fees:*** $31 per credit hour part-time, $85 per semester part-time. ***College room only:*** $5800. Room and board charges vary according to board plan and housing facility. ***Payment plan:*** installment. ***Waivers:*** employees or children of employees.

Financial Aid Of all full-time matriculated undergraduates who enrolled in 2014, 2,443 applied for aid, 2,236 were judged to have need, 366 had their need fully met. In 2014, 264 non-need-based awards were made. ***Average percent of need met:*** 75. ***Average financial aid package:*** $18,419. ***Average need-based loan:*** $4400. ***Average need-based gift aid:*** $9611. ***Average non-need-based aid:*** $11,508. ***Average indebtedness upon graduation:*** $34,482. ***Financial aid deadline:*** 4/1.

APPLYING

Standardized Tests *Required for some:* SAT or ACT (for admission).

Options: electronic application, early admission, early action, deferred entrance.

Application fee: $40.

Required: essay or personal statement, high school transcript, 1 letter of recommendation. ***Required for some:*** interview. ***Recommended:*** minimum 3.0 GPA.

Application deadlines: 5/1 (freshmen), 5/1 (transfers), 12/1 (early action).

Notification: continuous (freshmen), continuous (transfers), 12/15 (early action).

CONTACT

Mr. Jeremy Bogan, Assistant Vice President of Undergraduate Admissions, The College of Saint Rose, 1001 Madison Avenue, Albany, NY 12203. *Phone:* 518-454-5154. *Toll-free phone:* 800-637-8556. *Fax:* 518-454-2013. *E-mail:* admit@strose.edu.

★ College of Staten Island of the City University of New York

Staten Island, New York

http://www.csi.cuny.edu/

- **State and locally supported** comprehensive, founded 1955, part of City University of New York
- **Urban** 204-acre campus with easy access to New York City
- **Endowment** $4.9 million
- **Coed** 13,343 undergraduate students, 75% full-time, 55% women, 45% men

UNDERGRAD STUDENTS

10,043 full-time, 3,300 part-time. Students come from 13 states and territories; 99 other countries; 0.7% are from out of state; 14% Black or African American, non-Hispanic/Latino; 17% Hispanic/Latino; 12% Asian, non-Hispanic/Latino; 0.2% American Indian or Alaska Native, non-Hispanic/Latino; 0.3% Race/ethnicity unknown; 2% international; 5% transferred in; 11% live on campus.

Freshmen

Admission: 2,492 enrolled. ***Average high school GPA:*** 3.02. ***Test scores:*** SAT critical reading scores over 500: 40%; SAT math scores over 500: 62%; SAT writing scores over 500: 39%; SAT critical reading scores over 600: 10%; SAT math scores over 600: 16%; SAT writing scores over 600: 8%; SAT critical reading scores over 700: 2%; SAT math scores over 700: 2%; SAT writing scores over 700: 2%.

Retention: 80% of full-time freshmen returned.

FACULTY

Total: 1,251, 28% full-time, 49% with terminal degrees.

Student/faculty ratio: 18:1.

ACADEMICS

Calendar: semesters. *Degrees:* certificates, associate, bachelor's, master's, doctoral, post-master's, and postbachelor's certificates.

Special study options: academic remediation for entering students, accelerated degree program, adult/continuing education programs, double majors, English as a second language, honors programs, independent study, internships, off-campus study, services for LD students, student-designed majors, study abroad, summer session for credit.

Computers: 1,600 computers/terminals and 1,000 ports are available on campus for general student use. Students can access the following: computer help desk, free student e-mail accounts, online (class) grades, online (class) registration, online (class) schedules. Campuswide network is available. 100% of college-owned or -operated housing units are wired for high-speed Internet access. Wireless service is available via entire campus.

STUDENT LIFE

Housing options: coed, special housing for students with disabilities. Campus housing is university owned.

Activities and organizations: drama/theater group, student-run newspaper, radio station, choral group, Japanese Visual Culture Club, Accounting Club, Nursing Club, Computer Club, Muslim Student Association.

Athletics Member NCAA. All Division III. ***Intercollegiate sports:*** baseball M, basketball M/W, cheerleading M(c)/W(c), cross-country running M/W, riflery M/W, soccer M/W, softball W, swimming and diving M/W, tennis M/W, volleyball M/W. ***Intramural sports:*** badminton M/W, basketball M/W, racquetball M/W, riflery M/W, soccer M/W, softball W, swimming and diving M/W, table tennis M/W, tennis M/W, track and field M(c)/W(c), ultimate Frisbee M/W, volleyball M/W.

Campus security: 24-hour emergency response devices and patrols, student patrols, late-night transport/escort service, controlled dormitory access, radar controlled traffic monitoring vehicle and bicycle patrols.

Student services: health clinic, personal/psychological counseling, women's center.

COSTS & FINANCIAL AID

Costs (2014–15) ***Tuition:*** area resident $0 full-time; state resident $6030 full-time, $260 per credit hour part-time; nonresident $16,050 full-time, $535 per credit hour part-time. ***Required fees:*** $479 full-time, $141 per term part-time. ***Room only:*** $12,364. Room and board charges vary according to board plan and housing facility. ***Waivers:*** senior citizens and employees or children of employees.

Financial Aid Of all full-time matriculated undergraduates who enrolled in 2013, 7,738 applied for aid, 6,671 were judged to have need, 158 had their need fully met. In 2013, 361 non-need-based awards were made. ***Average percent of need met:*** 60. ***Average financial aid package:*** $8200. ***Average need-based loan:*** $4980. ***Average need-based gift aid:*** $6577. ***Average non-need-based aid:*** $2697.

APPLYING

Standardized Tests *Required:* SAT or ACT (for admission).

Required: high school transcript. ***Required for some:*** essay or personal statement, interview.

CONTACT
College of Staten Island of the City University of New York, 2800 Victory Boulevard, 2A-103, Staten Island, NY 10314. *Phone:* 718-982-2010. *Fax:* 718-982-2500. *E-mail:* admissions@csi.cuny.edu.

See previous page for display ad and page 1406 for the College Close-Up.

The College of Westchester

White Plains, New York

http://www.cw.edu/

- **Proprietary** primarily 2-year, founded 1915
- **Suburban** campus with easy access to New York City
- **Coed** 1,125 undergraduate students, 79% full-time, 64% women, 36% men
- **Minimally difficult** entrance level, 79% of applicants were admitted

UNDERGRAD STUDENTS
892 full-time, 233 part-time. Students come from 4 states and territories; 4% are from out of state; 35% Black or African American, non-Hispanic/Latino; 43% Hispanic/Latino; 2% Asian, non-Hispanic/Latino; 0.4% American Indian or Alaska Native, non-Hispanic/Latino; 2% Two or more races, non-Hispanic/Latino; 3% Race/ethnicity unknown.

Freshmen
Admission: 741 applied, 588 admitted, 186 enrolled.
Retention: 72% of full-time freshmen returned.

FACULTY
Total: 83, 46% full-time.
Student/faculty ratio: 18:1.

ACADEMICS
Calendar: semesters. *Degrees:* certificates, associate, and bachelor's.
Special study options: academic remediation for entering students, accelerated degree program, adult/continuing education programs, cooperative education, distance learning, double majors, honors programs, internships, part-time degree program, summer session for credit.
Computers: 282 computers/terminals are available on campus for general student use. Students can access the following: campus intranet, computer help desk, free student e-mail accounts, online (class) grades, online (class) schedules. Campuswide network is available.

STUDENT LIFE
Housing options: college housing not available.
Activities and organizations: student-run newspaper.
Student services: personal/psychological counseling.

APPLYING
Standardized Tests *Recommended:* SAT (for admission).
Options: electronic application, deferred entrance.
Application fee: $40.
Required: high school transcript, interview. ***Required for some:*** essay or personal statement.
Application deadlines: rolling (freshmen), rolling (out-of-state freshmen), rolling (transfers).

CONTACT
Mr. Dale T. Smith, Vice President, The College of Westchester, 325 Central Avenue, PO Box 710, White Plains, NY 10602. *Phone:* 914-948-4442 Ext. 311. *Toll-free phone:* 800-660-7093. *Fax:* 914-948-5441. *E-mail:* admissions@cw.edu.

Columbia University

New York, New York

http://www.columbia.edu/

- **Independent** university, founded 1754
- **Urban** 36-acre campus
- **Endowment** $9.2 billion
- **Coed** 6,170 undergraduate students, 100% full-time, 48% women, 52% men
- **Most difficult** entrance level, 7% of applicants were admitted

UNDERGRAD STUDENTS
6,170 full-time. 76% are from out of state; 12% Black or African American, non-Hispanic/Latino; 12% Hispanic/Latino; 22% Asian, non-Hispanic/Latino; 2% American Indian or Alaska Native, non-Hispanic/Latino; 4% Race/ethnicity unknown; 13% international; 2% transferred in; 94% live on campus.

Freshmen
Admission: 32,967 applied, 2,291 admitted, 1,424 enrolled. ***Test scores:*** SAT critical reading scores over 500: 100%; SAT math scores over 500: 100%; SAT writing scores over 500: 100%; SAT critical reading scores over 600: 96%; SAT math scores over 600: 98%; SAT writing scores over 600: 96%; ACT scores over 24: 100%; SAT critical reading scores over 700: 74%; SAT math scores over 700: 78%; SAT writing scores over 700: 74%; ACT scores over 30: 90%.
Retention: 99% of full-time freshmen returned.

ACADEMICS
Calendar: semesters. *Degrees:* bachelor's, master's, and doctoral.

Special study options: accelerated degree program, advanced placement credit, double majors, independent study, internships, off-campus study, services for LD students, student-designed majors, study abroad, summer session for credit. ***ROTC:*** Army (c), Navy (b), Air Force (c).

Unusual degree programs: 3-2 engineering with Combined Plan Program with over 100 liberal arts colleges.

Computers: 400 computers/terminals are available on campus for general student use. Students can access the following: campus intranet, computer help desk, free student e-mail accounts, online (class) grades, online (class) registration, online (class) schedules. Campuswide network is available. Wireless service is available via entire campus.

STUDENT LIFE
Housing options: on-campus residence required for freshman year; coed, men-only, women-only, special housing for students with disabilities. Campus housing is university owned. Freshman campus housing is guaranteed.

Activities and organizations: drama/theater group, student-run newspaper, radio and television station, choral group, marching band, community service, cultural organizations, performing arts, athletics, publications, national fraternities, national sororities.

Athletics Member NCAA. All Division I except football (Division I-AA). ***Intercollegiate sports:*** archery M(c)/W, badminton M(c)/W(c), baseball M, basketball M/W, crew M/W, cross-country running M/W, fencing M/W, field hockey W, golf M, ice hockey W(c), lacrosse M(c)/W, racquetball M(c)/W(c), riflery M(c)/W(c), rugby M(c)/W(c), skiing (cross-country) M(c)/W(c), skiing (downhill) M(c)/W(c), soccer M(c)/W(c), softball W, squash M(c)/W(c), swimming and diving M/W, table tennis M(c)/W(c), tennis M(c)/W(c), track and field M/W, ultimate Frisbee M(c)/W(c), volleyball M(c)/W(c), water polo M(c)/W(c), wrestling M. ***Intramural sports:*** archery W(c), badminton M/W, basketball M(c)/W(c), cross-country running M(c)/W(c), field hockey W, lacrosse W(c), racquetball M/W, soccer M/W, softball M/W, squash M/W, swimming and diving M/W, tennis M/W, volleyball M/W, water polo W.

Campus security: 24-hour emergency response devices and patrols, late-night transport/escort service, controlled dormitory access.

Student services: health clinic, personal/psychological counseling, women's center.

COSTS & FINANCIAL AID
Costs (2014–15) ***Comprehensive fee:*** $63,440 includes full-time tuition ($48,646), mandatory fees ($2362), and room and board ($12,432). ***Payment plan:*** installment. ***Waivers:*** employees or children of employees.

Financial Aid Of all full-time matriculated undergraduates who enrolled in 2014, 3,352 applied for aid, 3,051 were judged to have need, 3,051 had their need fully met. ***Average percent of need met:*** 100. ***Average financial aid package:*** $46,516. ***Average need-based loan:*** $3919. ***Average need-based gift aid:*** $44,887. ***Financial aid deadline:*** 3/1.

APPLYING
Standardized Tests *Required:* SAT and SAT Subject Tests or ACT (for admission).

Options: electronic application, early admission, early decision, deferred entrance.

Application fee: $80.

Required: essay or personal statement, high school transcript, 3 letters of recommendation, SAT and 2 SAT Subject Tests or ACT.

Application deadlines: 1/1 (freshmen), 3/1 (transfers).

Early decision deadline: 11/1.

Notification: 4/1 (freshmen), 5/15 (transfers), 12/15 (early decision).

CONTACT
Columbia University, 116th Street and Broadway, New York, NY 10027.
Phone: 212-854-1222.

See previous page for display ad and page 1408 for the College Close-Up.

★ Columbia University, School of General Studies

New York, New York

http://www.gs.columbia.edu/

- **Independent** 4-year, founded 1754, part of Columbia University
- **Urban** 36-acre campus with easy access to New York City
- **Endowment** $9.2 billion
- **Coed** 1,898 undergraduate students, 71% full-time, 42% women, 58% men
- **Most difficult** entrance level, 34% of applicants were admitted

UNDERGRAD STUDENTS
1,349 full-time, 549 part-time. 55% are from out of state; 5% Black or African American, non-Hispanic/Latino; 10% Hispanic/Latino; 7% Asian, non-Hispanic/Latino; 0.4% Native Hawaiian or other Pacific Islander, non-Hispanic/Latino; 0.3% American Indian or Alaska Native, non-Hispanic/Latino; 0.6% Two or more races, non-Hispanic/Latino; 14% Race/ethnicity unknown; 14% international; 19% transferred in; 28% live on campus.

Freshmen
Admission: 602 applied, 206 admitted, 121 enrolled. ***Average high school GPA:*** 3.89. ***Test scores:*** SAT critical reading scores over 500: 96%; SAT math scores over 500: 98%; SAT writing scores over 500: 96%; ACT scores over 18: 100%; SAT critical reading scores over 600: 90%; SAT math scores over 600: 94%; SAT writing scores over 600: 90%; ACT scores over 24: 100%; SAT critical reading scores over 700: 53%; SAT math scores over 700: 63%; SAT writing scores over 700: 58%; ACT scores over 30: 74%.

ACADEMICS
Calendar: semesters. *Degrees:* bachelor's and postbachelor's certificates.

Special study options: accelerated degree program, adult/continuing education programs, advanced placement credit, double majors, independent study, internships, off-campus study, part-time degree program, services for LD students, student-designed majors, study abroad, summer session for credit. ***ROTC:*** Army (c), Navy (b), Air Force (c).

Unusual degree programs: 3-2 business administration with Columbia Business School; engineering with Columbia University Fu Foundation School of Engineering and Applied Science; social work with Columbia University School of Social Work; International Affairs OR Public Policy (Columbia School of International and Public Affairs); Public Health (Mailman School of Public Health); Law (Columbia Law School); Dental Medicine (Columbia College of Dental Medicine); Occupational Therapy (Columbia Program in Occupational Therapy).

Computers: Students can access the following: campus intranet, computer help desk, free student e-mail accounts, online (class) grades, online (class) registration, online (class) schedules. Campuswide network is available. 100% of college-owned or -operated housing units are wired for high-speed Internet access. Wireless service is available via entire campus.

STUDENT LIFE
Housing options: coed, cooperative, special housing for students with disabilities. Campus housing is university owned, leased by the school and is provided by a third party.

Activities and organizations: drama/theater group, student-run newspaper, radio and television station, choral group, marching band, General Studies Student Council, national fraternities, national sororities.

Athletics Member NCAA. All Division I except football (Division I-AA). ***Intercollegiate sports:*** archery W, badminton M(c)/W(c), baseball M, basketball M/W, crew M/W, cross-country running M/W, equestrian sports M(c)/W(c), fencing M/W, field hockey W, golf M/W, ice hockey M(c)/W(c), lacrosse M(c)/W, racquetball M(c)/W(c), rugby M(c)/W(c), sailing M(c)/W(c), skiing (downhill) M(c)/W(c), soccer M/W, softball W, squash M/W, swimming and diving M/W, table tennis M(c)/W(c), tennis M/W, track and field M/W, ultimate Frisbee M(c)/W(c), volleyball W, water polo M(c)/W(c), wrestling M. ***Intramural sports:*** archery M(c)/W(c), badminton M(c)/W(c), basketball M/W, bowling M(c)/W(c), equestrian sports M/W, football M/W, racquetball M/W, rock climbing M(c)/W(c), soccer M/W, table tennis M/W, volleyball M/W, weight lifting M/W.

Campus security: 24-hour emergency response devices and patrols, late-night transport/escort service.

Student services: health clinic, personal/psychological counseling, women's center.

COSTS & FINANCIAL AID

Costs (2014–15) ***Comprehensive fee:*** $60,906 includes full-time tuition ($47,100), mandatory fees ($2376), and room and board ($11,430). Full-time tuition and fees vary according to course load and program. Part-time tuition: $1570 per credit hour. Part-time tuition and fees vary according to course load and program. ***College room only:*** $7020. Room and board charges vary according to board plan and housing facility. ***Payment plans:*** tuition prepayment, installment. ***Waivers:*** employees or children of employees.

Financial Aid ***Financial aid deadline:*** 6/1.

APPLYING

Standardized Tests *Required:* SAT or ACT (for admission).

Options: electronic application, early action, deferred entrance.

Application fee: $80.

Required: essay or personal statement, high school transcript, 2 letters of recommendation. ***Required for some:*** interview.

Application deadlines: 6/1 (freshmen), 6/1 (transfers), 3/1 (early action).

Notification: continuous (freshmen), continuous (transfers), 5/1 (early action).

CONTACT

Mr. Curtis M. Rodgers, Vice Dean, Columbia University, School of General Studies, 2970 Broadway, 408 Lewisohn Hall, MC 4101, New York, NY 10027. *Phone:* 212-854-2772. *Toll-free phone:* 800-895-1169. *Fax:* 212-854-6316. *E-mail:* gsdegree@columbia.edu.

See below for display ad and page 1410 for the College Close-Up.

Concordia College–New York

Bronxville, New York

http://www.concordia-ny.edu/

- **Independent Lutheran** comprehensive, founded 1881, part of Concordia University System
- **Suburban** 33-acre campus with easy access to New York City
- **Endowment** $6.4 million
- **Coed** 887 undergraduate students, 92% full-time, 67% women, 33% men
- **Moderately difficult** entrance level, 68% of applicants were admitted

UNDERGRAD STUDENTS

814 full-time, 73 part-time. Students come from 46 states and territories; 35 other countries; 29% are from out of state; 16% Black or African American, non-Hispanic/Latino; 16% Hispanic/Latino; 1% Asian, non-Hispanic/Latino; 0.4% Native Hawaiian or other Pacific Islander, non-Hispanic/Latino; 1% American Indian or Alaska Native, non-Hispanic/Latino; 3% Two or more races, non-Hispanic/Latino; 5% Race/ethnicity unknown; 11% international; 5% transferred in; 70% live on campus.

Freshmen

Admission: 1,189 applied, 809 admitted, 213 enrolled. ***Average high school GPA:*** 2.96. ***Test scores:*** SAT critical reading scores over 500: 27%; SAT math scores over 500: 27%; SAT writing scores over 500: 22%; ACT scores over 18: 59%; SAT critical reading scores over 600: 4%; SAT math scores over 600: 2%; SAT writing scores over 600: 5%; ACT scores over 24: 15%; SAT writing scores over 700: 1%; ACT scores over 30: 4%.

Retention: 73% of full-time freshmen returned.

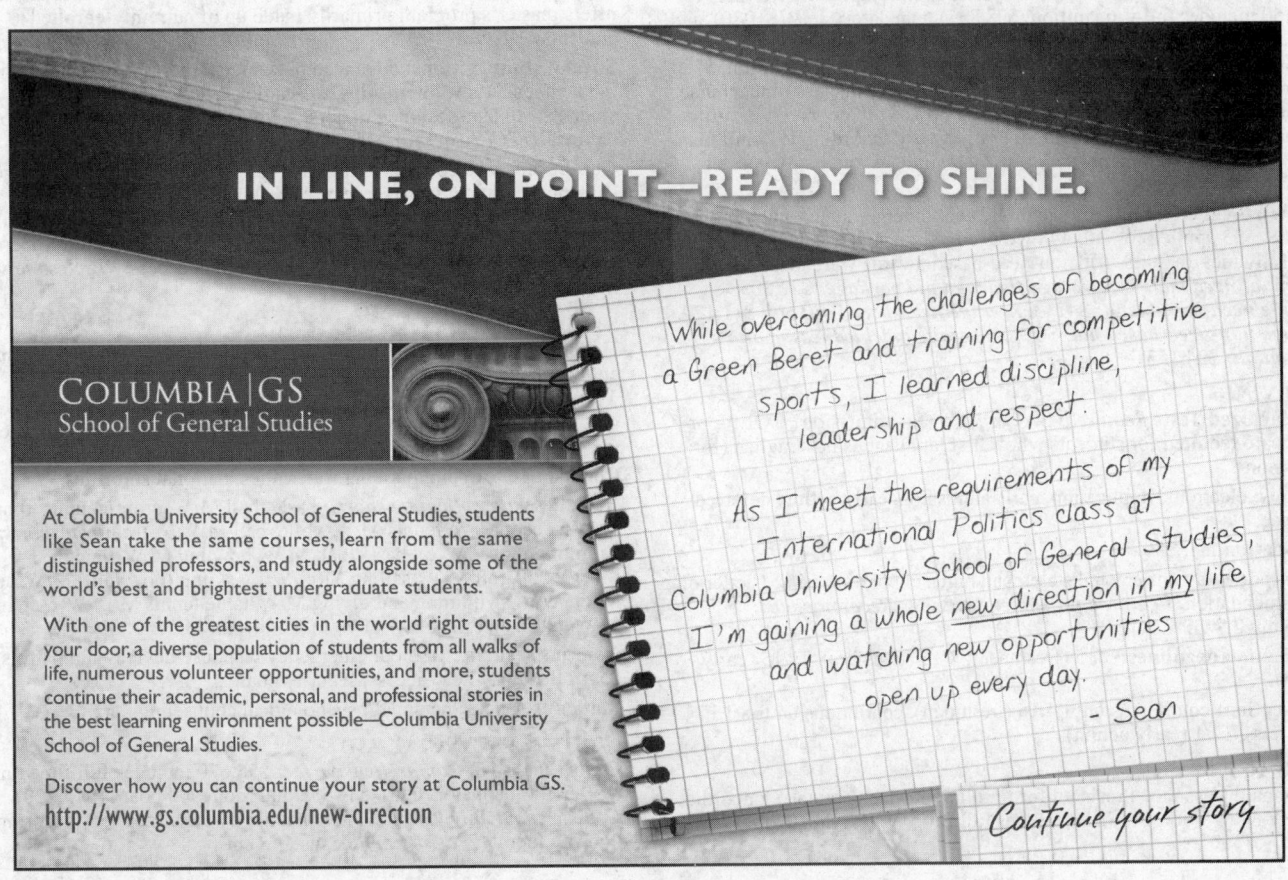

FACULTY
Total: 77, 43% full-time, 79% with terminal degrees.

Student/faculty ratio: 12:1.

ACADEMICS
Calendar: semesters. *Degrees:* associate, bachelor's, and master's.

Special study options: academic remediation for entering students, accelerated degree program, adult/continuing education programs, advanced placement credit, distance learning, double majors, English as a second language, honors programs, independent study, internships, off-campus study, part-time degree program, services for LD students, student-designed majors, study abroad.

Computers: 50 computers/terminals are available on campus for general student use. Students can access the following: campus intranet, computer help desk, free student e-mail accounts, online (class) grades, online (class) registration, online (class) schedules. Campuswide network is available. 100% of college-owned or -operated housing units are wired for high-speed Internet access. Wireless service is available via entire campus.

STUDENT LIFE
Housing options: men-only, women-only, cooperative. Campus housing is university owned. Freshman campus housing is guaranteed.

Activities and organizations: student-run newspaper, television station, choral group, Campus Christian Ministries, Choral Groups, Student Government Association, International and Afro/Latin American Club, Yearbook and newspaper.

Athletics Member NCAA. All Division II. ***Intercollegiate sports:*** baseball M(s), basketball M(s)/W(s), cross-country running M(s)/W(s), golf M, soccer M(s)/W(s), softball W(s), tennis M(s)/W(s), volleyball W(s). ***Intramural sports:*** basketball M/W, cheerleading W, football M/W, racquetball M/W, softball W, squash M/W, table tennis M/W, tennis M/W, ultimate Frisbee M/W.

Campus security: 24-hour emergency response devices and patrols, controlled dormitory access.

Student services: health clinic, personal/psychological counseling.

COSTS & FINANCIAL AID
Costs (2015–16) ***One-time required fee:*** $100. ***Comprehensive fee:*** $40,150 includes full-time tuition ($28,855), mandatory fees ($1030), and room and board ($10,265). Full-time tuition and fees vary according to class time, course load, degree level, and program. Part-time tuition: $780 per credit. Part-time tuition and fees vary according to class time, course load, degree level, and program. ***Required fees:*** $780 per credit part-time. ***Room and board:*** Room and board charges vary according to board plan. ***Payment plan:*** installment. ***Waivers:*** adult students and employees or children of employees.

Financial Aid Of all full-time matriculated undergraduates who enrolled in 2008, 533 applied for aid, 448 were judged to have need, 89 had their need fully met. In 2008, 100 non-need-based awards were made. ***Average percent of need met:*** 71. ***Average financial aid package:*** $22,309. ***Average need-based loan:*** $4133. ***Average need-based gift aid:*** $11,129. ***Average non-need-based aid:*** $6170. ***Average indebtedness upon graduation:*** $24,153.

APPLYING
Standardized Tests *Required:* SAT or ACT (for admission), TOEFL or IELTS are required for students who's first language is not English (for admission).

Options: electronic application, early admission, early action, deferred entrance.

Application fee: $50.

Required: essay or personal statement, high school transcript, 1 letter of recommendation. ***Required for some:*** interview. ***Recommended:*** minimum 2.7 GPA.

Application deadlines: 3/15 (freshmen), 7/15 (transfers), 11/15 (early action).

Notification: continuous until 4/15 (freshmen), continuous until 8/15 (transfers), 12/1 (early action).

CONTACT
Mr. Donald Vos, Vice President for Enrollment Management, Concordia College–New York, 171 White Plains Rd, Bronxville, NY 10708. *Phone:* 914-337-9300 Ext. 2155. *Toll-free phone:* 800-YES-COLLEGE. *Fax:* 914-395-4636. *E-mail:* admission@concordia-ny.edu.

Cooper Union for the Advancement of Science and Art

New York, New York

http://www.cooper.edu/

- **Independent** comprehensive, founded 1859
- **Urban** campus with easy access to New York City
- **Endowment** $722.8 million
- **Coed** 876 undergraduate students, 99% full-time, 34% women, 66% men

UNDERGRAD STUDENTS
866 full-time, 10 part-time. Students come from 39 states and territories; 22 other countries; 39% are from out of state; 5% Black or African American, non-Hispanic/Latino; 10% Hispanic/Latino; 20% Asian, non-Hispanic/Latino; 0.1% Native Hawaiian or other Pacific Islander, non-Hispanic/Latino; 1% American Indian or Alaska Native, non-Hispanic/Latino; 2% Two or more races, non-Hispanic/Latino; 13% Race/ethnicity unknown; 16% international; 2% transferred in; 20% live on campus.

Freshmen
Admission: 220 enrolled. ***Average high school GPA:*** 3.5. ***Test scores:*** SAT critical reading scores over 500: 95%; SAT math scores over 500: 93%; SAT writing scores over 500: 94%; ACT scores over 18: 100%; SAT critical reading scores over 600: 76%; SAT math scores over 600: 82%; SAT writing scores over 600: 78%; ACT scores over 24: 95%; SAT critical reading scores over 700: 33%; SAT math scores over 700: 66%; SAT writing scores over 700: 32%; ACT scores over 30: 75%.
Retention: 97% of full-time freshmen returned.

FACULTY
Total: 213, 24% full-time, 48% with terminal degrees.

Student/faculty ratio: 9:1.

ACADEMICS
Calendar: semesters. *Degrees:* certificates, bachelor's, and master's (also offers master's program primarily made up of currently-enrolled students).

Special study options: advanced placement credit, honors programs, independent study, internships, off-campus study, services for LD students, student-designed majors, study abroad, summer session for credit. ***ROTC:*** Army (c).

Computers: 100 computers/terminals are available on campus for general student use. Students can access the following: computer help desk, free student e-mail accounts, online (class) grades, online (class) schedules. Campuswide network is available. 100% of college-owned or -operated housing units are wired for high-speed Internet access. Wireless service is available via entire campus.

STUDENT LIFE
Housing options: coed. Campus housing is university owned. Freshman applicants given priority for college housing.

Activities and organizations: drama/theater group, student-run newspaper, choral group, South Asian Society, Pro Musica, Chinese Student Association, Drama Society, Outdoors Club; Intervarsity Christian Fellowship, national fraternities, national sororities.

Athletics ***Intercollegiate sports:*** basketball M/W, cross-country running M/W, soccer M/W, tennis M/W, volleyball M/W. ***Intramural sports:*** badminton M(c)/W(c), basketball M/W, bowling M/W, fencing M(c)/W(c), golf M/W, sailing M(c)/W(c), skiing (downhill) M/W, soccer M(c)/W(c), swimming and diving M/W, table tennis M(c)/W(c), tennis M/W, ultimate Frisbee M(c)/W(c), volleyball M/W.

Campus security: 24-hour emergency response devices and patrols, controlled dormitory access, security guards.

Student services: personal/psychological counseling.

COSTS & FINANCIAL AID
Costs (2014–15) ***Comprehensive fee:*** $56,670 includes full-time tuition ($39,600), mandatory fees ($1850), and room and board ($15,220). ***College room only:*** $11,220. Room and board charges vary according to housing facility. ***Payment plan:*** installment.

Financial Aid Of all full-time matriculated undergraduates who enrolled in 2013, 409 applied for aid, 272 were judged to have need, 131 had their need fully met. 47 Federal Work-Study jobs (averaging $846). 355 state and other part-time jobs (averaging $1034). In 2013, 579 non-need-based awards were made. ***Average percent of need met:*** 91. ***Average financial aid package:*** $39,600. ***Average need-based loan:*** $3723. ***Average need-based gift aid:*** $45,915. ***Average non-need-based aid:*** $39,600. ***Average indebtedness upon graduation:*** $19,072. ***Financial aid deadline:*** 5/1.

APPLYING
Standardized Tests *Required:* SAT or ACT (for admission). *Required for some:* SAT Subject Tests (for admission).

Required: essay or personal statement, high school transcript, minimum 2.0 GPA. ***Required for some:*** minimum 3.5 GPA, 3 letters of recommendation, interview, SAT Subject Tests in Math and either Chemistry or Physics for engineering applicants, portfolio, and home test for art applicants and studio test for architecture applicants. ***Recommended:*** minimum 3.0 GPA.

CONTACT
Mr. John Falls, Associate Dean of Admissions, Cooper Union for the Advancement of Science and Art, 30 Cooper Square, New York, NY 10003. *Phone:* 212-353-4192. *Fax:* 212-353-4342. *E-mail:* admissions@cooper.edu.

Cornell University
Ithaca, New York
http://www.cornell.edu/

- **Independent** university, founded 1865, part of Cornell's Colleges of Agriculture and Life Sciences, Human Ecology, Industrial and Labor Relations, and the School of Veterinary Medicine are part of the State University of New York (SUNY) System
- **Small-town** 745-acre campus with easy access to Syracuse
- **Endowment** $5.9 million
- **Coed** 14,453 undergraduate students, 100% full-time, 51% women, 49% men
- **Most difficult** entrance level, 14% of applicants were admitted

UNDERGRAD STUDENTS
14,453 full-time. Students come from 54 states and territories; 85 other countries; 64% are from out of state; 6% Black or African American, non-Hispanic/Latino; 12% Hispanic/Latino; 17% Asian, non-Hispanic/Latino; 0.1% Native Hawaiian or other Pacific Islander, non-Hispanic/Latino; 0.3% American Indian or Alaska Native, non-Hispanic/Latino; 4% Two or more races, non-Hispanic/Latino; 9% Race/ethnicity unknown; 10% international; 4% transferred in; 55% live on campus.

Freshmen
Admission: 43,037 applied, 6,105 admitted, 3,225 enrolled. ***Test scores:*** SAT critical reading scores over 500: 100%; SAT math scores over 500: 100%; ACT scores over 18: 100%; SAT critical reading scores over 600: 91%; SAT math scores over 600: 96%; ACT scores over 24: 99%; SAT critical reading scores over 700: 51%; SAT math scores over 700: 69%; ACT scores over 30: 83%.

Retention: 96% of full-time freshmen returned.

FACULTY
Total: 2,086, 82% full-time, 88% with terminal degrees.

Student/faculty ratio: 9:1.

ACADEMICS
Calendar: semesters. *Degrees:* bachelor's, master's, and doctoral.

Special study options: academic remediation for entering students, accelerated degree program, advanced placement credit, cooperative education, distance learning, double majors, English as a second language, honors programs, independent study, internships, off-campus study, services for LD students, student-designed majors, study abroad, summer session for credit. ***ROTC:*** Army (b), Navy (b), Air Force (b).

Computers: 2,650 computers/terminals and 2,500 ports are available on campus for general student use. Students can access the following: campus intranet, computer help desk, free student e-mail accounts, online (class) grades, online (class) registration. Campuswide network is available. 100% of college-owned or -operated housing units are wired for high-speed Internet access. Wireless service is available via entire campus.

STUDENT LIFE
Housing options: coed, women-only, cooperative, special housing for students with disabilities. Campus housing is university owned. Freshman campus housing is guaranteed.

Activities and organizations: drama/theater group, student-run newspaper, radio and television station, choral group, marching band, Student Assembly, Class Councils, Cornell Concert Commission, Interfraternity Council, Panhellenic Association, national fraternities, national sororities.

Athletics Member NCAA. All Division I except football (Division I-AA). ***Intercollegiate sports:*** baseball M, basketball M/W, crew M/W, cross-country running M/W, equestrian sports W, fencing W, field hockey W, golf M, gymnastics W, ice hockey M/W, lacrosse M/W, sailing W, soccer M/W, softball W, squash M/W, swimming and diving M/W, table tennis M(c)/W(c), tennis M/W, track and field M/W, ultimate Frisbee M(c)/W(c), volleyball M(c)/W, water polo M(c)/W(c), wrestling M. ***Intramural sports:*** archery M(c)/W(c), badminton M/W, baseball M(c), basketball M/W, bowling M/W, cheerleading M(c)/W(c), cross-country running M(c)/W(c), equestrian sports M(c)/W(c), fencing M(c)/W(c), field hockey W(c), football M/W, golf M/W, gymnastics M(c)/W(c), lacrosse W(c), rugby M(c)/W(c), sailing M(c)/W(c), skiing (cross-country) M(c)/W(c), skiing (downhill) M(c)/W(c), soccer M/W, softball M/W, squash M/W, table tennis M/W, tennis M/W, ultimate Frisbee M/W, volleyball M/W, water polo M(c)/W(c), wrestling M(c)/W(c).

Campus security: 24-hour emergency response devices and patrols, late-night transport/escort service, controlled dormitory access, indoor and outdoor emergency phones, lighted pathways /sidewalks, shuttle buses (6:00 PM- 2:30 AM), student escorts.

Student services: health clinic, personal/psychological counseling, women's center.

COSTS & FINANCIAL AID
Costs (2014–15) ***Comprehensive fee:*** $60,964 includes full-time tuition ($47,050), mandatory fees ($236), and room and board ($13,678). Full-time tuition and fees vary according to degree level. ***College room only:*** $8112. Room and board charges vary according to board plan and housing facility. ***Payment plan:*** installment. ***Waivers:*** employees or children of employees.

Financial Aid Of all full-time matriculated undergraduates who enrolled in 2014, 7,671 applied for aid, 6,808 were judged to have need, 6,808 had their need fully met. 4,950 Federal Work-Study jobs (averaging $2110). 1,100 state and other part-time jobs (averaging $2000). ***Average percent of need met:*** 100. ***Average financial aid package:*** $43,416. ***Average need-based loan:*** $4802. ***Average need-based gift aid:*** $37,559. ***Average indebtedness upon graduation:*** $21,411. ***Financial aid deadline:*** 2/15.

APPLYING
Standardized Tests *Required:* SAT or ACT (for admission). *Required for some:* SAT Subject Tests (for admission).

Options: electronic application, early decision, deferred entrance.

Application fee: $75.

Required: essay or personal statement, high school transcript, 2 letters of recommendation. ***Required for some:*** interview.

Application deadlines: 1/2 (freshmen), 3/15 (transfers).

Early decision deadline: 11/1.

Notification: 3/31 (freshmen), 6/15 (transfers), 12/15 (early decision).

CONTACT
Director of Undergraduate Admissions, Cornell University, Ithaca, NY 14853-0001. *Phone:* 607-255-5241. *Fax:* 607-255-0659. *E-mail:* admissions@cornell.edu.

★ The Culinary Institute of America
Hyde Park, New York
http://www.ciachef.edu/

- **Independent** 4-year, founded 1946
- **Suburban** 170-acre campus
- **Endowment** $128.4 million
- **Coed** 2,778 undergraduate students, 100% full-time, 48% women, 52% men
- **Moderately difficult** entrance level, 64% of applicants were admitted

UNDERGRAD STUDENTS
2,778 full-time. Students come from 53 states and territories; 39 other countries; 71% are from out of state; 5% Black or African American, non-Hispanic/Latino; 14% Hispanic/Latino; 6% Asian, non-Hispanic/Latino; 0.4% Native Hawaiian or other Pacific Islander, non-Hispanic/Latino; 0.3% American Indian or Alaska Native, non-Hispanic/Latino; 3% Two or more races, non-Hispanic/Latino; 6% Race/ethnicity unknown; 10% international; 9% transferred in; 80% live on campus.

Freshmen
Admission: 1,735 applied, 1,105 admitted, 511 enrolled. ***Average high school GPA:*** 3.1. ***Test scores:*** SAT critical reading scores over 500: 62%; ACT scores over 18: 92%; SAT critical reading scores over 600: 21%; ACT scores over 24: 51%; SAT critical reading scores over 700: 2%; ACT scores over 30: 3%.

FACULTY
Total: 222, 73% full-time.
Student/faculty ratio: 15:1.

ACADEMICS
Calendar: semesters plus 18 or 21 week externship program. *Degrees:* certificates, associate, and bachelor's.
Special study options: academic remediation for entering students, honors programs, internships, off-campus study, services for LD students.
Computers: 218 computers/terminals are available on campus for general student use. Students can access the following: campus intranet, computer help desk, free student e-mail accounts, online (class) grades, online (class) registration, online (class) schedules, online course guides. Campuswide network is available. 100% of college-owned or -operated housing units are wired for high-speed Internet access. Wireless service is available via entire campus.

STUDENT LIFE
Housing options: coed. Campus housing is university owned. Freshman campus housing is guaranteed.
Activities and organizations: student-run newspaper, choral group, Alliance, Baking and Pastry Society, Global Culinary Society, Eta Sigma Delta Honor Society, Chips Supporting Agriculture.
Athletics ***Intercollegiate sports:*** basketball M/W, cross-country running M/W, soccer M/W, tennis M/W, volleyball M/W. ***Intramural sports:*** basketball M/W, cross-country running M/W, football M/W, soccer M/W, softball M/W, swimming and diving M/W, tennis M/W, volleyball M/W.
Campus security: 24-hour emergency response devices and patrols, late-night transport/escort service, controlled dormitory access.
Student services: health clinic, personal/psychological counseling.

COSTS & FINANCIAL AID
Costs (2014–15) ***Comprehensive fee:*** $37,892 includes full-time tuition ($26,950), mandatory fees ($1290), and room and board ($9652). Full-time tuition and fees vary according to degree level. ***College room only:*** $6880. Room and board charges vary according to board plan and housing facility.
Financial Aid Of all full-time matriculated undergraduates who enrolled in 2014, 1,999 applied for aid, 1,821 were judged to have need, 587 had their need fully met. 808 Federal Work-Study jobs (averaging $2227). In 2014, 472 non-need-based awards were made. ***Average percent of need met:*** 70. ***Average financial aid package:*** $14,037. ***Average need-based loan:*** $4017. ***Average need-based gift aid:*** $9569. ***Average non-need-based aid:*** $3783. ***Average indebtedness upon graduation:*** $35,617.

APPLYING
Standardized Tests *Recommended:* SAT or ACT (for admission).
Options: electronic application, deferred entrance.
Application fee: $50.
Required: essay or personal statement, high school transcript, 1 letter of recommendation. ***Required for some:*** Affidavit of Support.
Notification: continuous (transfers).

CONTACT
Ms. Rachel Birchwood, Director of Admissions, The Culinary Institute of America, 1946 Campus Drive, Hyde Park, NY 12538. *Phone:* 845-451-

1459. *Toll-free phone:* 800-CULINARY. *Fax:* 845-451-1068. *E-mail:* admissions@culinary.edu.

See previous page for display ad and page 1412 for the College Close-Up.

★ Daemen College

Amherst, New York

http://www.daemen.edu/

- **Independent** comprehensive, founded 1947
- **Suburban** 35-acre campus with easy access to Buffalo
- **Endowment** $10.0 million
- **Coed** 2,058 undergraduate students, 81% full-time, 72% women, 28% men
- **Moderately difficult** entrance level, 54% of applicants were admitted

UNDERGRAD STUDENTS

1,677 full-time, 381 part-time. Students come from 9 other countries; 12% Black or African American, non-Hispanic/Latino; 6% Hispanic/Latino; 2% Asian, non-Hispanic/Latino; 0.3% Native Hawaiian or other Pacific Islander, non-Hispanic/Latino; 0.4% American Indian or Alaska Native, non-Hispanic/Latino; 0.7% Two or more races, non-Hispanic/Latino; 5% Race/ethnicity unknown; 0.8% international; 13% transferred in; 36% live on campus.

Freshmen

Admission: 2,902 applied, 1,571 admitted, 420 enrolled. ***Average high school GPA:*** 3.61. ***Test scores:*** SAT critical reading scores over 500: 57%; SAT math scores over 500: 64%; SAT writing scores over 500: 49%; ACT scores over 18: 87%; SAT critical reading scores over 600: 12%; SAT math scores over 600: 16%; SAT writing scores over 600: 12%; ACT scores over 24: 42%; SAT critical reading scores over 700: 1%; SAT math scores over 700: 1%; ACT scores over 30: 1%.

Retention: 81% of full-time freshmen returned.

FACULTY

Total: 289, 47% full-time, 44% with terminal degrees.

Student/faculty ratio: 13:1.

ACADEMICS

Calendar: semesters. *Degrees:* certificates, bachelor's, master's, doctoral, and post-master's certificates.

Special study options: academic remediation for entering students, accelerated degree program, adult/continuing education programs, advanced placement credit, double majors, honors programs, independent study, internships, off-campus study, part-time degree program, services for LD students, student-designed majors, study abroad, summer session for credit. ***ROTC:*** Army (c).

Unusual degree programs: 3-2 business administration with Business Administration/Global Business (BS/MS dual degree); physician assistant studies; professional accountancy (BS/MS dual degree).

Computers: 156 computers/terminals are available on campus for general student use. Students can access the following: campus intranet, computer help desk, free student e-mail accounts, online (class) grades, online (class) registration, online (class) schedules. Campuswide network is available. 100% of college-owned or -operated housing units are wired for high-speed Internet access. Wireless service is available via classrooms, dorm rooms, learning centers, libraries, student centers.

STUDENT LIFE

Housing options: on-campus residence required for freshman year; coed. Campus housing is university owned. Freshman campus housing is guaranteed.

Activities and organizations: student-run newspaper, Students Without Borders, Dance Club, Anime, Cynergy, Voices of Zion.

Athletics Member USCAA. ***Intercollegiate sports:*** basketball M(s)/W(s), cross-country running M(s)/W(s), golf M(s), soccer M(s)/W(s), tennis M(s)/W(s), track and field M(s)/W(s), volleyball W(s). ***Intramural sports:*** basketball M/W, cheerleading M(c)/W(c), softball M/W, ultimate Frisbee M/W, volleyball M(c)/W.

Campus security: 24-hour emergency response devices and patrols, late-night transport/escort service, 24-hour security cameras.

Student services: personal/psychological counseling.

COSTS & FINANCIAL AID
Costs (2014–15) ***Comprehensive fee:*** $36,790 includes full-time tuition ($24,480), mandatory fees ($510), and room and board ($11,800). Full-time tuition and fees vary according to location and reciprocity agreements. Part-time tuition: $815 per credit hour. Part-time tuition and fees vary according to course load, location, and reciprocity agreements. ***Required fees:*** $6 per credit hour part-time, $80 per term part-time. ***Room and board:*** Room and board charges vary according to board plan and housing facility. ***Payment plans:*** installment, deferred payment. ***Waivers:*** senior citizens and employees or children of employees.

Financial Aid Of all full-time matriculated undergraduates who enrolled in 2013, 1,666 applied for aid, 1,326 were judged to have need, 62 had their need fully met. 755 Federal Work-Study jobs (averaging $2161). 58 state and other part-time jobs (averaging $5028). In 2013, 245 non-need-based awards were made. ***Average percent of need met:*** 69. ***Average financial aid package:*** $18,236. ***Average need-based loan:*** $4607. ***Average need-based gift aid:*** $9978. ***Average non-need-based aid:*** $8962. ***Average indebtedness upon graduation:*** $30,079.

APPLYING
Standardized Tests *Recommended:* SAT or ACT (for admission).

Options: electronic application, early admission, deferred entrance.

Application fee: $25.

Required: essay or personal statement, high school transcript, minimum 2.0 GPA, 1 letter of recommendation. ***Required for some:*** 3 letters of recommendation, interview, class rank, writing sample-test optional.

Application deadlines: rolling (freshmen), rolling (out-of-state freshmen), rolling (transfers).

Notification: continuous (freshmen), continuous (out-of-state freshmen), continuous (transfers).

CONTACT
Daemen College, 4380 Main Street, Amherst, NY 14226-3592. *Phone:* 716-839-8225. *Toll-free phone:* 800-462-7652. *Fax:* 716-839-8229. *E-mail:* admissions@daemen.edu.

See previous page for display ad and page 1416 for the College Close-Up.

Davis College

Johnson City, New York

http://www.davisny.edu/

- **Independent nondenominational** 4-year, founded 1900
- **Suburban** 22-acre campus with easy access to Syracuse
- **Coed** 517 undergraduate students, 77% full-time, 50% women, 50% men
- **Minimally difficult** entrance level, 53% of applicants were admitted

UNDERGRAD STUDENTS
396 full-time, 121 part-time. Students come from 15 states and territories; 5 other countries; 50% are from out of state; 7% transferred in; 61% live on campus.

Freshmen
Admission: 215 applied, 114 admitted, 136 enrolled. ***Average high school GPA:*** 3.18. ***Test scores:*** ACT scores over 18: 62%; ACT scores over 24: 26%; ACT scores over 30: 5%.

Retention: 84% of full-time freshmen returned.

FACULTY
Total: 31, 45% full-time, 52% with terminal degrees.

Student/faculty ratio: 14:1.

ACADEMICS
Calendar: semesters. *Degrees:* certificates, diplomas, associate, and bachelor's.

Special study options: academic remediation for entering students, adult/continuing education programs, advanced placement credit, cooperative education, English as a second language, independent study, internships, part-time degree program, services for LD students, summer session for credit.

Computers: 12 computers/terminals are available on campus for general student use. Campuswide network is available. 100% of college-owned or -operated housing units are wired for high-speed Internet access. Wireless service is available via entire campus.

STUDENT LIFE
Housing options: men-only, women-only. Campus housing is university owned.

Activities and organizations: drama/theater group, student-run newspaper, choral group, Student Missionary Fellowship, Student Wives Fellowship, Student Life Committee, Married Couples Fellowship.

Athletics Member NCCAA, USCAA. ***Intercollegiate sports:*** basketball M/W, soccer M, volleyball W. ***Intramural sports:*** soccer M/W, volleyball M/W.

Campus security: 24-hour emergency response devices and patrols, student patrols, late-night transport/escort service, controlled dormitory access.

Student services: health clinic, personal/psychological counseling.

FINANCIAL AID
Financial Aid Of all full-time matriculated undergraduates who enrolled in 2007, 182 applied for aid, 175 were judged to have need, 27 had their need fully met. 77 Federal Work-Study jobs (averaging $898). In 2007, 10 non-need-based awards were made. ***Average percent of need met:*** 37. ***Average financial aid package:*** $5120. ***Average need-based loan:*** $4893. ***Average need-based gift aid:*** $4360. ***Average non-need-based aid:*** $610. ***Average indebtedness upon graduation:*** $5360.

APPLYING
Standardized Tests *Recommended:* SAT or ACT (for admission).

Options: electronic application, deferred entrance.

Application fee: $45.

Required: essay or personal statement, high school transcript, 1 letter of recommendation. ***Recommended:*** minimum 2.0 GPA, interview.

Application deadlines: rolling (freshmen), rolling (out-of-state freshmen), rolling (transfers).

Notification: continuous (freshmen), continuous (out-of-state freshmen), continuous (transfers).

CONTACT
Elizabeth A. VanTol, Admissions Coordinator, Davis College, 400 Riverside Drive, Johnson City, NY 13790. *Phone:* 607-729-1581 Ext. 406. *Toll-free phone:* 877-949-3248. *Fax:* 607-798-7754. *E-mail:* evantol@davisny.edu.

DeVry College of New York

New York, New York

http://www.devry.edu/

- **Proprietary** comprehensive, founded 1998, part of DeVry University
- **Urban** campus
- **Coed** 936 undergraduate students, 69% full-time, 30% women, 70% men
- **Minimally difficult** entrance level

UNDERGRAD STUDENTS
646 full-time, 290 part-time. 13% are from out of state; 33% Black or African American, non-Hispanic/Latino; 33% Hispanic/Latino; 6% Asian, non-Hispanic/Latino; 0.7% Native Hawaiian or other Pacific Islander, non-Hispanic/Latino; 0.4% American Indian or Alaska Native, non-Hispanic/Latino; 0.9% Two or more races, non-Hispanic/Latino; 11% Race/ethnicity unknown; 3% international; 44% transferred in.

Freshmen
Admission: 41 enrolled.

FACULTY
Total: 98, 24% full-time.

Student/faculty ratio: 22:1.

ACADEMICS
Calendar: semesters. *Degrees:* associate, bachelor's, master's, and postbachelor's certificates.

Special study options: adult/continuing education programs, part-time degree program.

STUDENT LIFE
Housing options: college housing not available.

COSTS & FINANCIAL AID
Costs (2014–15) ***Tuition:*** $17,052 full-time, $609 per credit hour part-time. ***Required fees:*** $80 full-time.

Financial Aid Of all full-time matriculated undergraduates who enrolled in 2007, 387 applied for aid, 371 were judged to have need, 8 had their need fully met. In 2007, 19 non-need-based awards were made. ***Average percent of need met:*** 5. ***Average financial aid package:*** $15,942. ***Average need-based loan:*** $8712. ***Average need-based gift aid:*** $7343. ***Average non-need-based aid:*** $11,806. ***Average indebtedness upon graduation:*** $29,136.

APPLYING

Application fee: $40.

Required: high school transcript, interview.

CONTACT

DeVry College of New York, 180 Madison Avenue, Suite 900, New York, NY 10016-5267. *Phone:* 212-312-4300. *Toll-free phone:* 866-338-7941.

Dominican College

Orangeburg, New York

http://www.dc.edu/

- **Independent** comprehensive, founded 1952
- **Suburban** 70-acre campus with easy access to New York City
- **Endowment** $4.0 million
- **Coed** 1,483 undergraduate students, 86% full-time, 64% women, 36% men
- **Noncompetitive** entrance level, 63% of applicants were admitted

UNDERGRAD STUDENTS

1,269 full-time, 214 part-time. Students come from 27 states and territories; 16 other countries; 25% are from out of state; 16% Black or African American, non-Hispanic/Latino; 27% Hispanic/Latino; 8% Asian, non-Hispanic/Latino; 0.1% American Indian or Alaska Native, non-Hispanic/Latino; 2% Two or more races, non-Hispanic/Latino; 12% Race/ethnicity unknown; 14% transferred in; 51% live on campus.

Freshmen

Admission: 2,385 applied, 1,498 admitted, 290 enrolled. ***Average high school GPA:*** 2.92.

Retention: 72% of full-time freshmen returned.

FACULTY

Total: 236, 32% full-time, 32% with terminal degrees.

Student/faculty ratio: 15:1.

ACADEMICS

Calendar: semesters. *Degrees:* certificates, associate, bachelor's, master's, and doctoral.

Special study options: academic remediation for entering students, accelerated degree program, adult/continuing education programs, advanced placement credit, cooperative education, distance learning, double majors, freshman honors college, honors programs, independent study, internships, off-campus study, part-time degree program, services for LD students, study abroad, summer session for credit.

Unusual degree programs: 3-2 engineering with Manhattan College; occupational therapy.

Computers: 150 computers/terminals are available on campus for general student use. Students can access the following: campus intranet, free student e-mail accounts, online (class) registration, online (class) schedules, Web portal, Black Board. Campuswide network is available. 100% of college-owned or -operated housing units are wired for high-speed Internet access. Wireless service is available via entire campus.

STUDENT LIFE

Housing options: coed. Campus housing is university owned. Freshman campus housing is guaranteed.

Activities and organizations: drama/theater group, student-run newspaper, radio station, choral group, Student Government Association, Business Club, Aquin Players, school newspaper, Nursing Association.

Athletics Member NCAA, NAIA. All NCAA Division II. ***Intercollegiate sports:*** baseball M(s), basketball M(s)/W(s), cross-country running M(s)/W(s), golf M(s), lacrosse M(s)/W(s), soccer M(s)/W(s), softball W(s), track and field M(s)/W(s), volleyball W(s). ***Intramural sports:*** basketball M/W, crew M(c)/W(c), volleyball M/W.

Campus security: 24-hour emergency response devices and patrols, student patrols, late-night transport/escort service, controlled dormitory access.

Student services: health clinic, personal/psychological counseling.

COSTS & FINANCIAL AID

Costs (2015–16) ***Comprehensive fee:*** $38,650 includes full-time tuition ($25,680), mandatory fees ($770), and room and board ($12,200). Full-time tuition and fees vary according to degree level. Part-time tuition: $776 per credit hour. Part-time tuition and fees vary according to degree level and program. ***Required fees:*** $180 per term part-time. ***Room and board:*** Room and board charges vary according to board plan and housing facility. ***Payment plans:*** installment, deferred payment. ***Waivers:*** senior citizens and employees or children of employees.

Financial Aid Of all full-time matriculated undergraduates who enrolled in 2014, 1,074 applied for aid, 982 were judged to have need, 114 had their need fully met. 343 Federal Work-Study jobs (averaging $1500). In 2014, 83 non-need-based awards were made. ***Average percent of need met:*** 64. ***Average financial aid package:*** $19,805. ***Average need-based loan:*** $4803. ***Average need-based gift aid:*** $15,410. ***Average non-need-based aid:*** $9170. ***Average indebtedness upon graduation:*** $22,640.

APPLYING

Standardized Tests *Required:* SAT or ACT (for admission).

Options: electronic application, deferred entrance.

Application fee: $35.

Required: high school transcript. ***Required for some:*** essay or personal statement, interview. ***Recommended:*** interview.

Application deadlines: rolling (freshmen), rolling (transfers).

Notification: continuous (freshmen), continuous (transfers).

CONTACT

Mr. Daniel Mendoza, Director of Admissions, Dominican College, 470 Western Highway, Orangeburg, NY 10962-1210. *Phone:* 845-359-7901. *Toll-free phone:* 866-432-4636. *Fax:* 845-365-3150. *E-mail:* admissions@dc.edu.

★ Dowling College

Oakdale, New York

http://www.dowling.edu/

- **Independent** comprehensive, founded 1955
- **Suburban** 157-acre campus with easy access to New York City
- **Coed** 1,783 undergraduate students, 61% full-time, 53% women, 47% men
- **Moderately difficult** entrance level, 78% of applicants were admitted

UNDERGRAD STUDENTS

1,087 full-time, 696 part-time. Students come from 28 states and territories; 26 other countries; 6% are from out of state; 10% Black or African American, non-Hispanic/Latino; 7% Hispanic/Latino; 0.4% Asian, non-Hispanic/Latino; 0.3% Native Hawaiian or other Pacific Islander, non-Hispanic/Latino; 0.2% American Indian or Alaska Native, non-Hispanic/Latino; 38% Race/ethnicity unknown; 4% international; 7% transferred in; 15% live on campus.

Freshmen

Admission: 1,885 applied, 1,477 admitted, 188 enrolled. ***Average high school GPA:*** 3.

Retention: 69% of full-time freshmen returned.

FACULTY

Total: 241, 31% full-time, 46% with terminal degrees.

Student/faculty ratio: 13:1.

ACADEMICS

Calendar: semesters. *Degrees:* bachelor's, master's, doctoral, post-master's, and postbachelor's certificates.

Special study options: academic remediation for entering students, accelerated degree program, advanced placement credit, distance learning, double majors, English as a second language, honors programs, independent study, internships, off-campus study, part-time degree program, services for LD students, student-designed majors, study abroad, summer session for credit. ***ROTC:*** Army (c), Air Force (c).

Computers: 289 computers/terminals and 89 ports are available on campus for general student use. Students can access the following: campus intranet, computer help desk, free student e-mail accounts, online (class) grades, online (class) registration, online (class) schedules. Campuswide network is available. 100% of college-owned or -operated housing units are wired for high-speed Internet access. Wireless service is available via entire campus.

STUDENT LIFE

Housing options: coed. Campus housing is university owned.

Activities and organizations: drama/theater group, student-run newspaper, radio station, choral group, Student Government Association, Dormitory Councils, Aviation Organization, student newspaper.

Athletics Member NCAA. All Division II. ***Intercollegiate sports:*** baseball M(s), basketball M(s)/W(s), cheerleading W(c), crew M(c)/W(c), cross-country running M(s)/W(s), equestrian sports W(c), field hockey W, golf M(s), lacrosse M(s)/W(s), soccer M(s)/W(s), softball W(s), tennis M(s)/W(s), volleyball W(s).

Campus security: 24-hour emergency response devices and patrols, late-night transport/escort service, controlled dormitory access.

Student services: health clinic, personal/psychological counseling.

COSTS & FINANCIAL AID

Costs (2015–16) ***Comprehensive fee:*** $39,870 includes full-time tuition ($27,300), mandatory fees ($1800), and room and board ($10,770). ***Payment plan:*** installment. ***Waivers:*** employees or children of employees.

Financial Aid Of all full-time matriculated undergraduates who enrolled in 2013, 1,065 applied for aid, 1,050 were judged to have need, 66 had their need fully met. 660 Federal Work-Study jobs (averaging $3023). 34 state and other part-time jobs (averaging $1846). In 2013, 548 non-need-based awards were made. ***Average percent of need met:*** 58. ***Average financial aid package:*** $19,348. ***Average need-based loan:*** $4484. ***Average need-based gift aid:*** $10,084. ***Average non-need-based aid:*** $6906. ***Average indebtedness upon graduation:*** $39,116.

APPLYING

Standardized Tests *Recommended:* SAT or ACT (for admission).

Options: electronic application, deferred entrance.

Application fee: $35.

Required: essay or personal statement, high school transcript, minimum 2.0 GPA, 1 letter of recommendation. ***Recommended:*** minimum 2.5 GPA.

Application deadlines: rolling (freshmen), rolling (out-of-state freshmen), rolling (transfers).

Notification: continuous (freshmen), continuous (out-of-state freshmen), continuous (transfers).

CONTACT

Mr. Jonathan White, Director of Admissions, Dowling College, 150 Idle Hour Boulevard, Oakdale, NY 11769. *Phone:* 631-244-2009. *Toll-free phone:* 800-DOWLING. *Fax:* 631-244-1059.

See below for display ad and page 1422 for the College Close-Up.

★ D'Youville College

Buffalo, New York

http://www.dyc.edu/

- **Independent** comprehensive, founded 1908
- **Urban** 11-acre campus
- **Coed**
- **Moderately difficult** entrance level

FACULTY

Student/faculty ratio: 11:1.

ACADEMICS

Calendar: semesters plus summer session. *Degrees:* bachelor's, master's, doctoral, post-master's, and postbachelor's certificates.

STUDENT LIFE

Housing options: coed, men-only, women-only, special housing for students with disabilities. Campus housing is university owned. Freshman campus housing is guaranteed.

Activities and organizations: drama/theater group, student-run newspaper, choral group, Student Association, Occupational Therapy

Student Association, Physical Therapy Student Association, Student Nurses Association, Black Student Union.

Athletics Member NCAA. All Division III.

Campus security: 24-hour emergency response devices and patrols, late-night transport/escort service, controlled dormitory access.

Student services: health clinic, personal/psychological counseling.

COSTS & FINANCIAL AID

Costs (2014–15) ***Comprehensive fee:*** $34,262 includes full-time tuition ($23,092), mandatory fees ($370), and room and board ($10,800). Full-time tuition and fees vary according to course load, degree level, and program. Part-time tuition: $720 per credit hour. Part-time tuition and fees vary according to course load, degree level, and program. No tuition increase for student's term of enrollment. ***Required fees:*** $3 per credit part-time, $55 per term part-time. ***Room and board:*** Room and board charges vary according to board plan and housing facility. ***Payment plans:*** installment, deferred payment.

Financial Aid Of all full-time matriculated undergraduates who enrolled in 2014, 758 applied for aid, 678 were judged to have need, 175 had their need fully met. 250 Federal Work-Study jobs (averaging $1500). 400 state and other part-time jobs (averaging $1000). In 2014, 94 non-need-based awards were made. ***Average percent of need met:*** 70. ***Average financial aid package:*** $17,951. ***Average need-based loan:*** $4370. ***Average need-based gift aid:*** $14,161. ***Average non-need-based aid:*** $9848. ***Average indebtedness upon graduation:*** $33,169.

APPLYING

Standardized Tests *Required:* SAT or ACT (for admission).

Options: electronic application, deferred entrance.

Required: high school transcript, minimum 2.0 GPA. ***Required for some:*** essay or personal statement, minimum 3.0 GPA, interview.

CONTACT

D'Youville College, 320 Porter Avenue, Buffalo, NY 14201-1084.
Phone: 716-829-7600. *Toll-free phone:* 800-777-3921.

See this page for display ad and page 1426 for the College Close-Up.

★ Elmira College

Elmira, New York

http://www.elmira.edu/

- **Independent** comprehensive, founded 1855
- **Suburban** 55-acre campus
- **Endowment** $43.0 million
- **Coed** 1,365 undergraduate students, 86% full-time, 70% women, 30% men
- **Moderately difficult** entrance level, 82% of applicants were admitted

UNDERGRAD STUDENTS

1,177 full-time, 188 part-time. Students come from 40 states and territories; 15 other countries; 36% are from out of state; 4% Black or African American, non-Hispanic/Latino; 3% Hispanic/Latino; 2% Asian, non-Hispanic/Latino; 0.6% American Indian or Alaska Native, non-Hispanic/Latino; 3% Two or more races, non-Hispanic/Latino; 16% Race/ethnicity unknown; 5% international; 4% transferred in; 90% live on campus.

Freshmen

Admission: 2,310 applied, 1,899 admitted, 331 enrolled. ***Average high school GPA:*** 3.21. ***Test scores:*** SAT critical reading scores over 500: 67%; SAT math scores over 500: 66%; ACT scores over 18: 96%; SAT critical reading scores over 600: 22%; SAT math scores over 600: 22%; ACT scores over 24: 52%; SAT critical reading scores over 700: 5%; SAT math scores over 700: 3%; ACT scores over 30: 6%.

Retention: 82% of full-time freshmen returned.

FACULTY

Total: 156, 46% full-time, 47% with terminal degrees.

Student/faculty ratio: 13:1.

ACADEMICS

Calendar: 4-4-1. *Degrees:* associate, bachelor's, master's, and post-master's certificates.

Special study options: accelerated degree program, adult/continuing education programs, advanced placement credit, distance learning, double

majors, English as a second language, honors programs, independent study, internships, off-campus study, part-time degree program, services for LD students, student-designed majors, study abroad, summer session for credit. ***ROTC:*** Army (b), Air Force (c).

Unusual degree programs: 3-2 Chemistry - Chemical Engineering with Clarkson University.

Computers: 327 computers/terminals and 123 ports are available on campus for general student use. Students can access the following: campus intranet, computer help desk, free student e-mail accounts, online (class) grades, online (class) registration, online (class) schedules. Campuswide network is available. 100% of college-owned or -operated housing units are wired for high-speed Internet access. Wireless service is available via entire campus.

STUDENT LIFE

Housing options: on-campus residence required through senior year; coed, women-only, cooperative, special housing for students with disabilities. Campus housing is university owned. Freshman campus housing is guaranteed.

Activities and organizations: drama/theater group, student-run newspaper, radio station, choral group, SAB (Student Activities Board), Enactus, Colleges Against Cancer (Relay for Life), Orchesis, Habitat for Humanity.

Athletics Member NCAA. All Division III. ***Intercollegiate sports:*** baseball M, basketball M/W, cheerleading W, cross-country running M/W, field hockey W, golf M/W, ice hockey M/W, lacrosse M/W, soccer M/W, softball W, tennis M/W, volleyball M/W. ***Intramural sports:*** badminton M/W, basketball M/W, bowling M/W, equestrian sports M/W, football M/W, ice hockey M/W, lacrosse M/W, racquetball M/W, skiing (cross-country) M/W, skiing (downhill) M/W, soccer M/W, softball M/W, tennis M/W, ultimate Frisbee M/W, volleyball M/W.

Campus security: 24-hour patrols, late-night transport/escort service, controlled dormitory access, 24-hour locked residence hall entrances.

Student services: health clinic, personal/psychological counseling.

COSTS & FINANCIAL AID

Costs (2015–16) ***Comprehensive fee:*** $51,950 includes full-time tuition ($38,300), mandatory fees ($1650), and room and board ($12,000). Part-time tuition and fees vary according to course load and degree level. ***Required fees:*** $55 per year part-time. ***College room only:*** $6400. Room and board charges vary according to board plan and housing facility. ***Payment plans:*** tuition prepayment, installment. ***Waivers:*** adult students and employees or children of employees.

Financial Aid Of all full-time matriculated undergraduates who enrolled in 2014, 1,032 applied for aid, 965 were judged to have need, 200 had their need fully met. 191 Federal Work-Study jobs (averaging $1600). 340 state and other part-time jobs (averaging $1300). In 2014, 204 non-need-based awards were made. ***Average percent of need met:*** 79. ***Average financial aid package:*** $30,559. ***Average need-based loan:*** $4635. ***Average need-based gift aid:*** $26,624. ***Average non-need-based aid:*** $23,065. ***Average indebtedness upon graduation:*** $26,471.

APPLYING

Standardized Tests *Required:* SAT or ACT (for admission).

Options: electronic application, early decision, deferred entrance.

Application fee: $50.

Required: essay or personal statement, high school transcript, minimum 2.0 GPA, 1 letter of recommendation. ***Required for some:*** interview. ***Recommended:*** interview.

Application deadlines: 3/31 (freshmen), rolling (transfers).

Early decision deadline: 11/15 (for plan 1), 1/15 (for plan 2).

Notification: continuous until 4/30 (freshmen), continuous (transfers), 12/15 (early decision plan 1), 1/31 (early decision plan 2).

CONTACT

Mr. Brett Moore, Dean of Admissions, Elmira College, One Park Place, Elmira, NY 14901. *Phone:* 607-735-1724. *Toll-free phone:* 800-935-6472. *Fax:* 607-735-1718. *E-mail:* admissions@elmira.edu.

See below for display ad and page 1430 for the College Close-Up.

★ Eugene Lang College The New School for Liberal Arts

New York, New York

http://www.newschool.edu/lang

- **Independent** 4-year, founded 1978, part of The New School
- **Urban** 5-acre campus with easy access to New York City
- **Endowment** $214.0 million
- **Coed**

FACULTY
Student/faculty ratio: 15:1.

ACADEMICS
Calendar: semesters. *Degree:* bachelor's.

STUDENT LIFE
Housing options: coed, special housing for students with disabilities. Campus housing is university owned and leased by the school. Freshman applicants given priority for college housing.

Activities and organizations: drama/theater group, student-run newspaper, radio station, choral group, ReNew School, Active Minds, Students for Social Justice, Slow Food TNS, DREAM:IN NY.

Campus security: 24-hour emergency response devices, controlled dormitory access, 24-hour desk attendants in residence halls.

Student services: health clinic, personal/psychological counseling.

FINANCIAL AID
Financial Aid Of all full-time matriculated undergraduates who enrolled in 2012, 1,016 applied for aid, 915 were judged to have need, 163 had their need fully met. In 2012, 87 non-need-based awards were made. ***Average percent of need met:*** 74. ***Average financial aid package:*** $24,491. ***Average need-based loan:*** $6181. ***Average need-based gift aid:*** $23,110. ***Average non-need-based aid:*** $8365. ***Average indebtedness upon graduation:*** $30,021. ***Financial aid deadline:*** 3/1.

APPLYING
Standardized Tests *Recommended:* SAT (for admission), ACT (for admission), SAT or ACT (for admission), SAT and SAT Subject Tests or ACT (for admission).

Required: essay or personal statement, high school transcript, interview, online application, 2 supplemental essays, counselor evaluation, teacher evaluation, academic paper (grade preferred), TOEFL, IELTS and PTE may be required for applicants whose first language is not English. ***Recommended:*** minimum 3.0 GPA.

CONTACT
Mr. Daniel Conforti, Admissions Coordinator, Eugene Lang College The New School for Liberal Arts, 79 Fifth Avenue, New York, NY 10003. *Phone:* 212-229-5150 Ext. 2301. *Toll-free phone:* 800-292-3040. *E-mail:* lang@newschool.edu.

See this page for display ad and page 1546 for the College Close-Up.

Excelsior College

Albany, New York

http://www.excelsior.edu/

- **Independent** comprehensive, founded 1970
- **Suburban** campus with easy access to Albany, NY
- **Coed** 35,901 undergraduate students, 55% women, 45% men

UNDERGRAD STUDENTS
35,901 part-time. Students come from 54 states and territories; 40 other countries; 87% are from out of state; 22% Black or African American, non-Hispanic/Latino; 9% Hispanic/Latino; 3% Asian, non-Hispanic/Latino; 0.6% Native Hawaiian or other Pacific Islander, non-Hispanic/Latino; 0.6% American Indian or Alaska Native, non-Hispanic/Latino; 3% Two or more races, non-Hispanic/Latino; 2% Race/ethnicity unknown; 0.6% international; 12% transferred in.

FACULTY
Student/faculty ratio: 9:1.

ACADEMICS
Calendar: continuous. *Degrees:* certificates, associate, bachelor's, master's, post-master's, and postbachelor's certificates (offers only external degree programs).

Special study options: accelerated degree program, adult/continuing education programs, advanced placement credit, distance learning, English as a second language, external degree program, honors programs, independent study, part-time degree program, services for LD students, student-designed majors.

Unusual degree programs: 3-2 business administration; nursing; BS in Nuclear Engineering Technology/Master of Business Administration (MBA), BS in Health Care Management/MBA, BS in Business/MBA, BS in Nursing/MS in Nursing, BS in Information Technology/MS in Cybersecurity, BS in Information Technology/MBA.

Computers: Students can access the following: computer help desk, online (class) grades, online (class) registration, online (class) schedules. Campuswide network is available.

STUDENT LIFE
Housing options: college housing not available.

COSTS
Costs (2014–15) ***Tuition:*** $465 per credit hour part-time. Part-time tuition and fees vary according to reciprocity agreements. ***Payment plan:*** installment. ***Waivers:*** employees or children of employees.

APPLYING
Options: electronic application.

Application fee: $100.

Required for some: college transcripts.

Application deadlines: rolling (freshmen), rolling (transfers).

Notification: continuous (freshmen), continuous (transfers).

CONTACT
Admissions, Excelsior College, 7 Columbia Circle, Albany, NY 12203-5159. *Phone:* 518-464-8500. *Toll-free phone:* 888-647-2388. *Fax:* 518-464-8777. *E-mail:* admissions@excelsior.edu.

★ Farmingdale State College
Farmingdale, New York
http://www.farmingdale.edu/

- **State-supported** 4-year, founded 1912, part of State University of New York System
- **Small-town** 380-acre campus with easy access to New York City
- **Endowment** $6.5 million
- **Coed** 8,394 undergraduate students, 75% full-time, 43% women, 57% men
- **Moderately difficult** entrance level, 47% of applicants were admitted

UNDERGRAD STUDENTS
6,287 full-time, 2,107 part-time. Students come from 12 states and territories; 79 other countries; 0.3% are from out of state; 10% Black or African American, non-Hispanic/Latino; 16% Hispanic/Latino; 7% Asian, non-Hispanic/Latino; 0.5% Native Hawaiian or other Pacific Islander, non-Hispanic/Latino; 0.2% American Indian or Alaska Native, non-Hispanic/Latino; 2% Two or more races, non-Hispanic/Latino; 0.4% Race/ethnicity unknown; 3% international; 11% transferred in; 8% live on campus.

Freshmen
Admission: 5,183 applied, 2,418 admitted, 1,068 enrolled. ***Average high school GPA:*** 3.2. ***Test scores:*** SAT critical reading scores over 500: 40%; SAT math scores over 500: 55%; ACT scores over 18: 89%; SAT critical reading scores over 600: 5%; SAT math scores over 600: 9%; ACT scores over 24: 17%; ACT scores over 30: 1%.

Retention: 80% of full-time freshmen returned.

FACULTY
Total: 658, 32% full-time.

Student/faculty ratio: 19:1.

ACADEMICS
Calendar: semesters. *Degrees:* certificates, associate, and bachelor's.

Special study options: academic remediation for entering students, accelerated degree program, advanced placement credit, cooperative education, distance learning, double majors, English as a second language, independent study, internships, part-time degree program, services for LD students, study abroad, summer session for credit. ***ROTC:*** Army (c), Navy (c), Air Force (c).

Computers: 926 computers/terminals are available on campus for general student use. Students can access the following: free student e-mail accounts, online (class) registration, online (class) schedules. Campuswide network is available. 100% of college-owned or -operated housing units are wired for high-speed Internet access. Wireless service is available via entire campus.

STUDENT LIFE

Housing options: coed. Campus housing is university owned.

Activities and organizations: drama/theater group, student-run newspaper, radio station, Campus Activities Board, Farmingdale Student Government, Ram Nation Radio, Rambler Newspaper, national fraternities, national sororities.

Athletics Member NCAA. All Division III. ***Intercollegiate sports:*** baseball M, basketball M/W, cross-country running M/W, golf M, ice hockey M(c), lacrosse M/W, soccer M/W, softball W, tennis M/W, track and field M/W, volleyball W. ***Intramural sports:*** basketball M/W, football M, golf M/W, racquetball M/W, soccer M/W, softball M/W, squash M/W, swimming and diving M/W, table tennis M(c)/W(c), tennis M/W, ultimate Frisbee M(c)/W(c), volleyball M/W, weight lifting M(c)/W(c).

Campus security: 24-hour emergency response devices and patrols, controlled dormitory access.

Student services: health clinic, personal/psychological counseling.

COSTS & FINANCIAL AID

Costs (2014–15) ***Tuition:*** state resident $6170 full-time, $257 per credit part-time; nonresident $15,820 full-time, $659 per credit part-time. Full-time tuition and fees vary according to program. Part-time tuition and fees vary according to course load and program. ***Required fees:*** $1313 full-time, $53 per credit part-time, $10 per term part-time. ***Room and board:*** $12,190; room only: $7440. Room and board charges vary according to board plan and housing facility. ***Payment plan:*** installment.

Financial Aid Of all full-time matriculated undergraduates who enrolled in 2013, 4,167 applied for aid, 3,224 were judged to have need, 255 had their need fully met. In 2013, 58 non-need-based awards were made. ***Average percent of need met:*** 57. ***Average financial aid package:*** $7717. ***Average need-based loan:*** $4282. ***Average need-based gift aid:*** $6038. ***Average non-need-based aid:*** $1624.

APPLYING

Standardized Tests *Required:* SAT or ACT (for admission).

Options: electronic application, deferred entrance.

Application fee: $50.

Required: high school transcript, minimum 3.0 GPA. ***Required for some:*** interview.

Application deadlines: 6/1 (freshmen), 6/1 (out-of-state freshmen), 6/30 (transfers).

Notification: continuous (freshmen), continuous (out-of-state freshmen), continuous (transfers).

CONTACT

Farmingdale State College, 2350 Broadhollow Road, Farmingdale, NY 11735. *Phone:* 631-420-2200.

See previous page for display ad and page 1438 for the College Close-Up.

★ Fashion Institute of Technology

New York, New York

http://www.fitnyc.edu/

- **State and locally supported** comprehensive, founded 1944, part of State University of New York System
- **Urban** 5-acre campus with easy access to New York City
- **Coed, primarily women** 9,567 undergraduate students, 78% full-time, 85% women, 15% men
- **Moderately difficult** entrance level, 44% of applicants were admitted

UNDERGRAD STUDENTS

7,454 full-time, 2,113 part-time. 32% are from out of state; 9% Black or African American, non-Hispanic/Latino; 17% Hispanic/Latino; 9% Asian, non-Hispanic/Latino; 0.3% Native Hawaiian or other Pacific Islander, non-Hispanic/Latino; 0.1% American Indian or Alaska Native, non-Hispanic/Latino; 4% Two or more races, non-Hispanic/Latino; 0.4%

Race/ethnicity unknown; 14% international; 10% transferred in; 22% live on campus.

Freshmen

Admission: 4,729 applied, 2,094 admitted, 1,322 enrolled. ***Average high school GPA:*** 3.6.

Retention: 89% of full-time freshmen returned.

FACULTY

Total: 944, 25% full-time.

Student/faculty ratio: 17:1.

ACADEMICS

Calendar: semesters. *Degrees:* certificates, associate, bachelor's, and master's.

Special study options: academic remediation for entering students, adult/continuing education programs, advanced placement credit, distance learning, English as a second language, honors programs, independent study, internships, part-time degree program, services for LD students, study abroad, summer session for credit.

Computers: 1,700 computers/terminals are available on campus for general student use. Students can access the following: campus intranet, computer help desk, free student e-mail accounts, online (class) grades, online (class) registration, online (class) schedules. Campuswide network is available. 100% of college-owned or -operated housing units are wired for high-speed Internet access. Wireless service is available via classrooms, computer centers, computer labs, dorm rooms, learning centers, libraries, student centers.

STUDENT LIFE

Housing options: coed, women-only, special housing for students with disabilities. Campus housing is university owned. Freshman applicants given priority for college housing.

Activities and organizations: drama/theater group, student-run newspaper, radio and television station, choral group.

Athletics Member NJCAA. ***Intercollegiate sports:*** cross-country running M/W, soccer W, swimming and diving M/W, table tennis M/W, tennis W, track and field M/W, volleyball W. ***Intramural sports:*** archery M(c)/W(c).

Campus security: 24-hour emergency response devices and patrols, late-night transport/escort service, controlled dormitory access.

Student services: health clinic, personal/psychological counseling.

COSTS & FINANCIAL AID

Costs (2014–15) ***Tuition:*** state resident $4500 full-time, $257 per credit hour part-time; nonresident $13,500 full-time, $742 per credit hour part-time. Full-time tuition and fees vary according to degree level. Part-time tuition and fees vary according to degree level. ***Required fees:*** $700 full-time. ***Room and board:*** $13,162. Room and board charges vary according to board plan and housing facility. ***Payment plan:*** installment. ***Waivers:*** senior citizens and employees or children of employees.

Financial Aid Of all full-time matriculated undergraduates who enrolled in 2013, 4,713 applied for aid, 3,789 were judged to have need, 1,339 had their need fully met. In 2013, 99 non-need-based awards were made. ***Average percent of need met:*** 72. ***Average financial aid package:*** $11,882. ***Average need-based loan:*** $3500. ***Average need-based gift aid:*** $5751. ***Average non-need-based aid:*** $955. ***Average indebtedness upon graduation:*** $27,303.

APPLYING

Standardized Tests *Recommended:* SAT or ACT (for admission).

Options: electronic application.

Application fee: $50.

Required: essay or personal statement, high school transcript. ***Required for some:*** portfolio for art and design programs.

Application deadlines: 1/1 (freshmen), 1/1 (transfers).

Notification: 4/1 (freshmen), 4/1 (transfers).

CONTACT

Ms. Laura Arbogast, Director of Admissions and Strategic Recruitment, Fashion Institute of Technology, Seventh Avenue at 27th Street, New York, NY 10001-5992. *E-mail:* fitinfo@fitnyc.edu.

See below for display ad and page 1440 for the College Close-Up.

★ Five Towns College

Dix Hills, New York

http://www.ftc.edu/

- **Independent** comprehensive, founded 1972
- **Suburban** 35-acre campus with easy access to New York City
- **Coed** 649 undergraduate students, 95% full-time, 34% women, 66% men
- **Moderately difficult** entrance level, 56% of applicants were admitted

UNDERGRAD STUDENTS

618 full-time, 31 part-time. Students come from 10 states and territories; 1 other country; 7% are from out of state; 20% Black or African American, non-Hispanic/Latino; 15% Hispanic/Latino; 4% Asian, non-Hispanic/Latino; 0.3% American Indian or Alaska Native, non-Hispanic/Latino; 6% Two or more races, non-Hispanic/Latino; 6% Race/ethnicity unknown; 9% transferred in; 20% live on campus.

Freshmen

Admission: 335 applied, 188 admitted, 118 enrolled. ***Average high school GPA:*** 2.6. ***Test scores:*** SAT critical reading scores over 500: 30%; SAT math scores over 500: 28%; SAT writing scores over 500: 17%; SAT critical reading scores over 600: 2%; SAT math scores over 600: 2%; SAT writing scores over 600: 2%.

Retention: 60% of full-time freshmen returned.

FACULTY

Total: 90, 24% full-time, 37% with terminal degrees.

Student/faculty ratio: 15:1.

ACADEMICS

Calendar: semesters. *Degrees:* associate, bachelor's, master's, and doctoral.

Special study options: adult/continuing education programs, advanced placement credit, distance learning, independent study, internships, off-campus study, part-time degree program, services for LD students, summer session for credit.

Computers: 110 computers/terminals are available on campus for general student use. Students can access the following: campus intranet, free student e-mail accounts, online (class) grades, online (class) schedules. Campuswide network is available. 100% of college-owned or -operated housing units are wired for high-speed Internet access. Wireless service is available via entire campus.

STUDENT LIFE

Housing options: coed. Campus housing is university owned.

Activities and organizations: drama/theater group, student-run newspaper, radio station, choral group, Film Video Club, Audio Club, Music Business Club, Jazz Club, yearbook.

Campus security: 24-hour emergency response devices and patrols, late-night transport/escort service, controlled dormitory access.

Student services: personal/psychological counseling.

COSTS & FINANCIAL AID

Costs (2015–16) ***Tuition:*** $21,000 full-time, $875 per credit part-time. Full-time tuition and fees vary according to course level, course load, degree level, program, and student level. Part-time tuition and fees vary according to course level, course load, degree level, program, and student level. ***Payment plan:*** installment. ***Waivers:*** employees or children of employees.

Financial Aid Of all full-time matriculated undergraduates who enrolled in 2014, 550 applied for aid, 528 were judged to have need, 38 had their need fully met. 113 Federal Work-Study jobs (averaging $1276). In 2014, 37 non-need-based awards were made. ***Average percent of need met:*** 51. ***Average financial aid package:*** $14,472. ***Average need-based loan:*** $4371. ***Average need-based gift aid:*** $3102. ***Average non-need-based aid:*** $4015. ***Average indebtedness upon graduation:*** $26,993.

APPLYING

Standardized Tests *Required:* SAT or ACT (for admission).

Options: electronic application, early decision, deferred entrance.

Application fee: $35.

Required: essay or personal statement, high school transcript, minimum 2.3 GPA, 2 letters of recommendation, Immunization records and an audition for Music or Theatre students. ***Required for some:*** interview.

Application deadlines: rolling (freshmen), rolling (out-of-state freshmen), rolling (transfers).

Early decision deadline: 12/1.

Notification: continuous (freshmen), continuous (out-of-state freshmen), continuous (transfers), 12/15 (early decision).

CONTACT
Ms. Cynthia Catalano, Admissions, Five Towns College, 305 North Service Road, Dix Hills, NY 11746-6055. *Phone:* 631-424-7000 Ext. 2107. *Fax:* 631-656-2107. *E-mail:* cynthia.catalano@ftc.edu.

★ Fordham University
New York, New York
http://www.fordham.edu/

- **Independent Roman Catholic (Jesuit)** university, founded 1841
- **Urban** 93-acre campus with easy access to New York City
- **Endowment** $592.5 million
- **Coed** 8,633 undergraduate students, 93% full-time, 55% women, 45% men
- **Very difficult** entrance level, 48% of applicants were admitted

UNDERGRAD STUDENTS
8,058 full-time, 575 part-time. Students come from 52 states and territories; 66 other countries; 53% are from out of state; 5% Black or African American, non-Hispanic/Latino; 14% Hispanic/Latino; 9% Asian, non-Hispanic/Latino; 0.1% Native Hawaiian or other Pacific Islander, non-Hispanic/Latino; 0.1% American Indian or Alaska Native, non-Hispanic/Latino; 3% Two or more races, non-Hispanic/Latino; 2% Race/ethnicity unknown; 6% international; 4% transferred in; 55% live on campus.

Freshmen
Admission: 40,912 applied, 19,685 admitted, 2,258 enrolled. ***Average high school GPA:*** 3.6. ***Test scores:*** SAT critical reading scores over 500: 95%; SAT math scores over 500: 97%; SAT writing scores over 500: 95%; ACT scores over 18: 100%; SAT critical reading scores over 600: 61%; SAT math scores over 600: 70%; SAT writing scores over 600: 68%; ACT scores over 24: 92%; SAT critical reading scores over 700: 16%; SAT math scores over 700: 19%; SAT writing scores over 700: 18%; ACT scores over 30: 32%.

Retention: 89% of full-time freshmen returned.

FACULTY
Total: 1,635, 46% full-time, 66% with terminal degrees.

Student/faculty ratio: 13:1.

ACADEMICS
Calendar: semesters. *Degrees:* bachelor's, master's, doctoral, post-master's, and postbachelor's certificates (branch locations at Rose Hill and Lincoln Center).

Special study options: accelerated degree program, adult/continuing education programs, advanced placement credit, cooperative education, double majors, English as a second language, honors programs, independent study, internships, off-campus study, part-time degree program, services for LD students, student-designed majors, study abroad, summer session for credit. ***ROTC:*** Army (b), Navy (c), Air Force (c).

Unusual degree programs: 3-2 engineering with Columbia University, Case Western Reserve University.

Computers: 1,400 computers/terminals are available on campus for general student use. Students can access the following: computer help desk, free student e-mail accounts, online (class) grades, online (class) registration, online (class) schedules. Campuswide network is available. 100% of college-owned or -operated housing units are wired for high-speed Internet access. Wireless service is available via entire campus.

STUDENT LIFE
Housing options: coed, special housing for students with disabilities. Campus housing is university owned.

Activities and organizations: drama/theater group, student-run newspaper, radio and television station, choral group, marching band, United Student Government, Commuting Student Association, Residence Hall Association, Ambassador Program (Admission Department Student Tour Guides), Campus Activities Board.

Athletics Member NCAA. All Division I except football (Division I-AA). ***Intercollegiate sports:*** baseball M(s), basketball M(s)/W(s), cheerleading W, crew W(s), cross-country running M(s)/W(s), golf M(s), ice hockey M(c), sailing M(c)/W(c), soccer M(s)/W(s), softball W(s), squash M(s), swimming and diving M(s)/W(s), tennis M(s)/W(s), track and field M(s)/W(s), volleyball W(s), water polo M(s). ***Intramural sports:*** baseball M(c), basketball M(c)/W(c), crew M(c), lacrosse M(c)/W(c), rugby M(c)/W(c), soccer M/W, ultimate Frisbee M(c)/W(c).

Campus security: 24-hour emergency response devices and patrols, student patrols, late-night transport/escort service, controlled dormitory access, security at each campus entrance and at residence halls.

Student services: health clinic, personal/psychological counseling.

COSTS & FINANCIAL AID
Costs (2014–15) ***Comprehensive fee:*** $61,588 includes full-time tuition ($44,450), mandatory fees ($1173), and room and board ($15,965). Part-time tuition: $1482 per credit hour. Part-time tuition and fees vary according to class time and course load. ***Room and board:*** Room and board charges vary according to board plan, housing facility, and location. ***Payment plan:*** installment. ***Waivers:*** employees or children of employees.

Financial Aid Of all full-time matriculated undergraduates who enrolled in 2013, 6,422 applied for aid, 4,925 were judged to have need, 1,269 had their need fully met. In 2013, 1392 non-need-based awards were made. ***Average percent of need met:*** 75. ***Average financial aid package:*** $30,051. ***Average need-based loan:*** $6507. ***Average need-based gift aid:*** $22,251. ***Average non-need-based aid:*** $13,165. ***Average indebtedness upon graduation:*** $37,607. ***Financial aid deadline:*** 2/1.

APPLYING
Standardized Tests *Required:* SAT or ACT (for admission).

Options: electronic application, early admission, early action, deferred entrance.

Application fee: $70.

Required: essay or personal statement, high school transcript, 1 letter of recommendation, Common Application or Fordham Application, SAT and/or ACT scores.

Application deadlines: 1/1 (freshmen), 6/1 (transfers), 11/1 (early action).

Notification: 4/1 (freshmen), continuous (transfers), 12/20 (early action).

CONTACT
Patricia Peek PhD, Director of Undergraduate Admission, Fordham University, Office of Undergraduate Admission, Duane Library, 441 East Fordham Road, Bronx, NY 10458. *Phone:* 718-817-3706. *Toll-free phone:* 800-FORDHAM. *Fax:* 718-367-9404. *E-mail:* peek@fordham.edu.

Hamilton College
Clinton, New York
http://www.hamilton.edu/

- **Independent** 4-year, founded 1812
- **Small-town** 1300-acre campus
- **Endowment** $858.9 million
- **Coed** 1,900 undergraduate students, 100% full-time, 52% women, 48% men
- **Very difficult** entrance level, 26% of applicants were admitted

UNDERGRAD STUDENTS
1,894 full-time, 6 part-time. Students come from 46 states and territories; 45 other countries; 70% are from out of state; 4% Black or African American, non-Hispanic/Latino; 8% Hispanic/Latino; 7% Asian, non-Hispanic/Latino; 0.1% American Indian or Alaska Native, non-Hispanic/Latino; 3% Two or more races, non-Hispanic/Latino; 9% Race/ethnicity unknown; 5% international; 0.5% transferred in; 97% live on campus.

Freshmen
Admission: 5,071 applied, 1,336 admitted, 469 enrolled. ***Test scores:*** SAT critical reading scores over 500: 100%; SAT math scores over 500: 100%; SAT writing scores over 500: 100%; ACT scores over 18: 100%; SAT critical reading scores over 600: 91%; SAT math scores over 600: 94%; SAT writing scores over 600: 89%; ACT scores over 24: 100%; SAT

critical reading scores over 700: 49%; SAT math scores over 700: 53%; SAT writing scores over 700: 54%; ACT scores over 30: 84%.

Retention: 96% of full-time freshmen returned.

FACULTY

Total: 230, 83% full-time, 87% with terminal degrees.

Student/faculty ratio: 9:1.

ACADEMICS

Calendar: semesters. *Degree:* bachelor's.

Special study options: accelerated degree program, adult/continuing education programs, advanced placement credit, double majors, English as a second language, independent study, internships, off-campus study, part-time degree program, services for LD students, student-designed majors, study abroad. ***ROTC:*** Army (c), Air Force (c).

Unusual degree programs: 3-2 engineering with Columbia University, Dartmouth College, Rensselaer Polytechnic Institute, Washington University in St. Louis.

Computers: 840 computers/terminals and 10,100 ports are available on campus for general student use. Students can access the following: campus intranet, computer help desk, free student e-mail accounts, online (class) grades, online (class) registration, online (class) schedules. Campuswide network is available. 100% of college-owned or -operated housing units are wired for high-speed Internet access. Wireless service is available via entire campus.

STUDENT LIFE

Housing options: on-campus residence required through senior year; coed, cooperative, special housing for students with disabilities. Campus housing is university owned. Freshman campus housing is guaranteed.

Activities and organizations: drama/theater group, student-run newspaper, radio and television station, choral group, WHCL (Hamilton College Radio), Slow Food/Real Food, GNAR Club, Culinary Society, Hamilton Space Society, national fraternities, national sororities.

Athletics Member NCAA. All Division III. ***Intercollegiate sports:*** baseball M, basketball M/W, crew M/W, cross-country running M/W, equestrian sports M(c)/W(c), fencing M(c)/W(c), field hockey W, football M, golf M/W, ice hockey M/W, lacrosse M/W, rugby M(c)/W(c), sailing M(c)/W(c), skiing (cross-country) M(c)/W(c), skiing (downhill) M(c)/W(c), soccer M/W, softball W, squash M/W, swimming and diving M/W, tennis M/W, track and field M/W, ultimate Frisbee M(c)/W(c), volleyball M(c)/W, water polo M(c). ***Intramural sports:*** badminton M/W, basketball M/W, football M/W, golf M/W, ice hockey M/W, racquetball M/W, skiing (cross-country) M/W, soccer M/W, softball M/W, squash M/W, tennis M/W, volleyball M/W, water polo M/W.

Campus security: 24-hour emergency response devices and patrols, late-night transport/escort service, controlled dormitory access, student safety program.

Student services: health clinic, personal/psychological counseling, women's center.

COSTS & FINANCIAL AID

Costs (2014–15) ***Comprehensive fee:*** $59,970 includes full-time tuition ($47,350), mandatory fees ($470), and room and board ($12,150). Part-time tuition: $5919 per course. ***College room only:*** $6640. Room and board charges vary according to board plan. ***Payment plan:*** installment. ***Waivers:*** employees or children of employees.

Financial Aid Of all full-time matriculated undergraduates who enrolled in 2014, 920 applied for aid, 880 were judged to have need, 880 had their need fully met. 576 Federal Work-Study jobs (averaging $1821). 49 state and other part-time jobs (averaging $1920). ***Average percent of need met:*** 100. ***Average financial aid package:*** $43,256. ***Average need-based loan:*** $4268. ***Average need-based gift aid:*** $38,762. ***Average indebtedness upon graduation:*** $18,941. ***Financial aid deadline:*** 2/15.

APPLYING

Standardized Tests *Required:* SAT and SAT Subject Tests or ACT (for admission).

Options: electronic application, early decision, deferred entrance.

Application fee: $70.

Required: essay or personal statement, high school transcript, 1 letter of recommendation. ***Recommended:*** interview.

Application deadlines: 1/1 (freshmen), 4/15 (transfers).

Early decision deadline: 11/15 (for plan 1), 1/1 (for plan 2).

Notification: 4/1 (freshmen), 5/15 (transfers), 12/15 (early decision plan 1), 2/15 (early decision plan 2).

CONTACT

Ms. Monica Inzer, Vice President and Dean of Admission and Financial Aid, Hamilton College, 198 College Hill Road, Clinton, NY 13323. *Phone:* 800-843-2655. *Toll-free phone:* 800-843-2655. *Fax:* 315-859-4457. *E-mail:* admission@hamilton.edu.

Hartwick College

Oneonta, New York

http://www.hartwick.edu/

- **Independent** 4-year, founded 1797
- **Small-town** 425-acre campus
- **Endowment** $70.8 million
- **Coed** 1,540 undergraduate students, 98% full-time, 61% women, 39% men
- **Moderately difficult** entrance level, 90% of applicants were admitted

UNDERGRAD STUDENTS

1,507 full-time, 33 part-time. Students come from 27 states and territories; 26 other countries; 28% are from out of state; 8% Black or African American, non-Hispanic/Latino; 7% Hispanic/Latino; 2% Asian, non-Hispanic/Latino; 0.4% American Indian or Alaska Native, non-Hispanic/Latino; 12% Race/ethnicity unknown; 3% international; 2% transferred in; 81% live on campus.

Freshmen

Admission: 5,036 applied, 4,510 admitted, 419 enrolled. ***Average high school GPA:*** 3.13. ***Test scores:*** SAT critical reading scores over 500: 77%; SAT math scores over 500: 80%; SAT writing scores over 500: 67%; ACT scores over 18: 93%; SAT critical reading scores over 600: 31%; SAT math scores over 600: 25%; SAT writing scores over 600: 28%; ACT scores over 24: 51%; SAT critical reading scores over 700: 4%; SAT math scores over 700: 1%; SAT writing scores over 700: 5%; ACT scores over 30: 6%.

Retention: 78% of full-time freshmen returned.

FACULTY

Total: 200, 56% full-time, 59% with terminal degrees.

Student/faculty ratio: 11:1.

ACADEMICS

Calendar: 4-1-4. *Degree:* bachelor's.

Special study options: accelerated degree program, advanced placement credit, distance learning, double majors, honors programs, independent study, internships, off-campus study, part-time degree program, services for LD students, student-designed majors, study abroad, summer session for credit.

Unusual degree programs: 3-2 engineering with Clarkson University, Columbia University.

Computers: 80 computers/terminals are available on campus for general student use. Students can access the following: computer help desk, free student e-mail accounts, online (class) grades, online (class) registration, online (class) schedules. Campuswide network is available. 100% of college-owned or -operated housing units are wired for high-speed Internet access. Wireless service is available via entire campus.

STUDENT LIFE

Housing options: on-campus residence required through junior year; coed. Campus housing is university owned. Freshman campus housing is guaranteed.

Activities and organizations: drama/theater group, student-run newspaper, radio station, choral group, Student Union, student radio station, Student Senate, Hilltops campus newspaper, Cardboard Alley Players (theater), national fraternities, national sororities.

Athletics Member NCAA. All Division III except soccer (Division I), water polo (Division I). ***Intercollegiate sports:*** basketball M/W, cheerleading W(c), cross-country running M/W, equestrian sports W, field hockey W, football M, lacrosse M/W, soccer M(s)/W, swimming and diving M/W, tennis M/W, volleyball W, water polo M(c)/W(s). ***Intramural sports:*** basketball M/W, football M, riflery M(c)/W(c), rugby

M(c), skiing (downhill) M(c)/W(c), soccer M/W, softball W(c), volleyball M/W, water polo M/W.

Campus security: 24-hour emergency response devices and patrols, late-night transport/escort service, controlled dormitory access.

Student services: health clinic, personal/psychological counseling.

COSTS & FINANCIAL AID

Costs (2014–15) ***One-time required fee:*** $400. ***Comprehensive fee:*** $50,870 includes full-time tuition ($39,260), mandatory fees ($810), and room and board ($10,800). Full-time tuition and fees vary according to course load. Part-time tuition: $1260 per credit hour. Part-time tuition and fees vary according to course load. ***College room only:*** $5120. Room and board charges vary according to board plan and housing facility. ***Payment plan:*** installment. ***Waivers:*** employees or children of employees.

Financial Aid Of all full-time matriculated undergraduates who enrolled in 2014, 1,331 applied for aid, 1,243 were judged to have need, 165 had their need fully met. 938 Federal Work-Study jobs (averaging $1795). In 2014, 249 non-need-based awards were made. ***Average percent of need met:*** 79. ***Average financial aid package:*** $32,197. ***Average need-based loan:*** $4273. ***Average need-based gift aid:*** $26,491. ***Average non-need-based aid:*** $19,257. ***Average indebtedness upon graduation:*** $26,708.

APPLYING

Standardized Tests *Required for some:* SAT or ACT (for admission).

Options: electronic application, early admission, early decision, deferred entrance.

Required: high school transcript. ***Required for some:*** audition for music program; portfolio for Art majors; SAT scores for Nursing majors. ***Recommended:*** minimum 2.5 GPA.

Application deadlines: rolling (freshmen), 8/1 (transfers).

Early decision deadline: 11/1.

Notification: continuous (freshmen), continuous until 8/15 (transfers), 12/1 (early decision plan 1), rolling (early decision plan 2).

CONTACT

Ms. Lisa Starkey-Wood, Director of Admissions, Hartwick College, PO Box 4022, Oneonta, NY 13820-4022. *Phone:* 607-431-4150. *Toll-free phone:* 888-HARTWICK. *Fax:* 607-431-4102. *E-mail:* admissions@hartwick.edu.

Hilbert College

Hamburg, New York

http://www.hilbert.edu/

- **Independent** comprehensive, founded 1957
- **Suburban** 40-acre campus with easy access to Buffalo
- **Endowment** $5.8 million
- **Coed** 960 undergraduate students, 88% full-time, 56% women, 44% men
- **Minimally difficult** entrance level, 75% of applicants were admitted

UNDERGRAD STUDENTS

842 full-time, 118 part-time. Students come from 12 states and territories; 2 other countries; 3% are from out of state; 8% Black or African American, non-Hispanic/Latino; 2% Hispanic/Latino; 0.2% Asian, non-Hispanic/Latino; 0.1% Native Hawaiian or other Pacific Islander, non-Hispanic/Latino; 2% American Indian or Alaska Native, non-Hispanic/Latino; 4% Two or more races, non-Hispanic/Latino; 8% Race/ethnicity unknown; 0.8% international; 9% transferred in; 28% live on campus.

Freshmen

Admission: 893 applied, 670 admitted, 168 enrolled. ***Average high school GPA:*** 3.18. ***Test scores:*** SAT critical reading scores over 500: 26%; SAT math scores over 500: 41%; SAT writing scores over 500: 19%; ACT scores over 18: 77%; SAT critical reading scores over 600: 2%; SAT math scores over 600: 5%; SAT writing scores over 600: 1%; ACT scores over 24: 13%; ACT scores over 30: 2%.

Retention: 74% of full-time freshmen returned.

FACULTY

Total: 124, 35% full-time, 40% with terminal degrees.

Student/faculty ratio: 13:1.

ACADEMICS

Calendar: semesters. *Degrees:* associate, bachelor's, and master's.

Special study options: academic remediation for entering students, advanced placement credit, cooperative education, distance learning, honors programs, independent study, internships, part-time degree program, services for LD students, study abroad, summer session for credit. ***ROTC:*** Army (c).

Computers: 146 computers/terminals are available on campus for general student use. Students can access the following: campus intranet, computer help desk, free student e-mail accounts, online (class) grades, online (class) registration, online (class) schedules. Campuswide network is available. 100% of college-owned or -operated housing units are wired for high-speed Internet access. Wireless service is available via entire campus.

STUDENT LIFE

Housing options: coed. Campus housing is university owned and leased by the school. Freshman applicants given priority for college housing.

Activities and organizations: drama/theater group, student-run radio station, Student Government Association, Student Business and Accounting Association, SADD, Students in Free Enterprise (SIFE), Criminal Justice Association.

Athletics Member NCAA. All Division III. ***Intercollegiate sports:*** baseball M, basketball M/W, cross-country running M/W, golf M, lacrosse M/W, soccer M/W, softball W, volleyball M/W. ***Intramural sports:*** baseball M, basketball M/W, bowling M/W, cheerleading W, football M/W, golf M, ice hockey M(c), lacrosse W(c), skiing (downhill) M(c)/W(c), soccer M/W, softball W, table tennis M/W, ultimate Frisbee M/W, volleyball M/W.

Campus security: 24-hour emergency response devices and patrols, student patrols, late-night transport/escort service, controlled dormitory access.

Student services: health clinic, personal/psychological counseling.

COSTS & FINANCIAL AID

Costs (2015–16) ***Comprehensive fee:*** $29,510 includes full-time tuition ($20,050), mandatory fees ($300), and room and board ($9160). Part-time tuition: $505 per credit. ***Required fees:*** $300 per term part-time. ***College room only:*** $4730. Room and board charges vary according to board plan and housing facility. ***Payment plan:*** installment. ***Waivers:*** minority students, children of alumni, adult students, senior citizens, and employees or children of employees.

Financial Aid Of all full-time matriculated undergraduates who enrolled in 2014, 761 applied for aid, 688 were judged to have need, 127 had their need fully met. 49 Federal Work-Study jobs (averaging $1852). In 2014, 76 non-need-based awards were made. ***Average percent of need met:*** 71. ***Average financial aid package:*** $14,073. ***Average need-based loan:*** $4925. ***Average need-based gift aid:*** $9696. ***Average non-need-based aid:*** $4284. ***Average indebtedness upon graduation:*** $20,139.

APPLYING

Standardized Tests *Recommended:* SAT or ACT (for admission).

Options: electronic application, deferred entrance.

Application fee: $25.

Required: high school transcript. ***Required for some:*** interview. ***Recommended:*** essay or personal statement, interview.

Application deadlines: rolling (freshmen), rolling (transfers).

Notification: continuous (freshmen), continuous (transfers).

CONTACT

Mr. Justin Rogers, Director of Admissions, Hilbert College, 5200 South Park Avenue, Hamburg, NY 14075-1597. *Phone:* 716-649-7900. *Toll-free phone:* 800-649-8003. *Fax:* 716-649-0702. *E-mail:* jrogers@hilbert.edu.

Hobart and William Smith Colleges

Geneva, New York

http://www.hws.edu/

- **Independent** comprehensive, founded 1822
- **Small-town** 200-acre campus with easy access to Rochester, Syracuse
- **Endowment** $202.4 million
- **Coed** 2,421 undergraduate students, 98% full-time, 52% women, 48% men
- **Very difficult** entrance level, 50% of applicants were admitted

UNDERGRAD STUDENTS
2,362 full-time, 59 part-time. Students come from 43 states and territories; 24 other countries; 58% are from out of state; 5% Black or African American, non-Hispanic/Latino; 6% Hispanic/Latino; 3% Asian, non-Hispanic/Latino; 0.1% Native Hawaiian or other Pacific Islander, non-Hispanic/Latino; 0.6% American Indian or Alaska Native, non-Hispanic/Latino; 10% Race/ethnicity unknown; 5% international; 0.4% transferred in; 90% live on campus.

Freshmen
Admission: 5,093 applied, 2,528 admitted, 643 enrolled. ***Average high school GPA:*** 3.41. ***Test scores:*** SAT critical reading scores over 500: 96%; SAT math scores over 500: 96%; ACT scores over 18: 100%; SAT critical reading scores over 600: 59%; SAT math scores over 600: 65%; ACT scores over 24: 91%; SAT critical reading scores over 700: 11%; SAT math scores over 700: 12%; ACT scores over 30: 39%.
Retention: 88% of full-time freshmen returned.

FACULTY
Total: 234, 95% full-time, 97% with terminal degrees.
Student/faculty ratio: 11:1.

ACADEMICS
Calendar: semesters. *Degrees:* bachelor's, master's, and postbachelor's certificates.
Special study options: accelerated degree program, adult/continuing education programs, advanced placement credit, double majors, English as a second language, honors programs, independent study, internships, off-campus study, services for LD students, student-designed majors, study abroad. ***ROTC:*** Army (c), Air Force (c).
Unusual degree programs: 3-2 business administration with Clarkson University, Rochester Institute of Technology; engineering with Columbia University, Rensselaer Polytechnic Institute, Dartmouth College; architecture with Washington University in St. Louis.
Computers: 241 computers/terminals and 9,727 ports are available on campus for general student use. Students can access the following: campus intranet, computer help desk, free student e-mail accounts, online (class) grades, online (class) registration, online (class) schedules. Campuswide network is available. 100% of college-owned or -operated housing units are wired for high-speed Internet access. Wireless service is available via entire campus.

STUDENT LIFE
Housing options: on-campus residence required through junior year; coed, men-only, women-only, cooperative. Campus housing is university owned. Freshman campus housing is guaranteed.
Activities and organizations: drama/theater group, student-run newspaper, radio station, choral group, Student Life and Leadership, student government, campus publications, Service Network, sports clubs, national fraternities, national sororities.
Athletics Member NCAA. All Division III except lacrosse (Division I). ***Intercollegiate sports:*** basketball M/W, crew M/W, cross-country running M/W, equestrian sports M(c)/W(c), field hockey W, football M, golf M/W, ice hockey M/W, lacrosse M/W, rock climbing M(c)/W(c), rugby M(c)/W(c), sailing M/W, skiing (downhill) M(c)/W(c), soccer M/W, squash M/W, swimming and diving W, tennis M/W, ultimate Frisbee M(c)/W(c). ***Intramural sports:*** badminton M/W, baseball M, basketball M/W, fencing M/W, football M, golf M/W, ice hockey M/W, lacrosse M/W, racquetball M/W, skiing (cross-country) M/W, skiing (downhill) M/W, soccer M/W, softball M/W, squash M/W, swimming and diving M/W, table tennis M/W, tennis M/W, track and field M/W, ultimate Frisbee M/W, volleyball M/W, water polo M/W, weight lifting M/W.
Campus security: 24-hour emergency response devices and patrols, late-night transport/escort service, controlled dormitory access.
Student services: health clinic, personal/psychological counseling, women's center.

COSTS & FINANCIAL AID
Costs (2014–15) ***Comprehensive fee:*** $60,034 includes full-time tuition ($46,852), mandatory fees ($1056), and room and board ($12,126). ***Room and board:*** Room and board charges vary according to board plan. ***Payment plans:*** tuition prepayment, installment. ***Waivers:*** employees or children of employees.
Financial Aid Of all full-time matriculated undergraduates who enrolled in 2014, 1,589 applied for aid, 1,346 were judged to have need, 812 had their need fully met. 887 Federal Work-Study jobs (averaging $1814). 518 state and other part-time jobs (averaging $1830). In 2014, 646 non-need-based awards were made. ***Average percent of need met:*** 78. ***Average financial aid package:*** $33,069. ***Average need-based loan:*** $4145. ***Average need-based gift aid:*** $29,012. ***Average non-need-based aid:*** $15,377. ***Average indebtedness upon graduation:*** $34,330. ***Financial aid deadline:*** 2/15.

APPLYING
Standardized Tests *Required for some:* SAT or ACT (for admission).
Options: electronic application, early admission, early decision, deferred entrance.
Application fee: $45.
Required: essay or personal statement, high school transcript, 1 letter of recommendation. ***Recommended:*** interview.
Application deadlines: 2/1 (freshmen), 7/1 (transfers).
Early decision deadline: 11/15 (for plan 1), 1/1 (for plan 2).
Notification: 4/1 (freshmen), continuous (transfers), 12/15 (early decision plan 1), 2/1 (early decision plan 2).

CONTACT
Hobart and William Smith Colleges, Geneva, NY 14456-3397. *Phone:* 315-781-3622. *Toll-free phone:* 800-852-2256.

★ Hofstra University
Hempstead, New York
http://www.hofstra.edu/

- **Independent** university, founded 1935
- **Suburban** 240-acre campus with easy access to New York City
- **Endowment** $402.7 million
- **Coed** 6,904 undergraduate students, 94% full-time, 54% women, 46% men
- **Moderately difficult** entrance level, 62% of applicants were admitted

UNDERGRAD STUDENTS
6,474 full-time, 430 part-time. Students come from 46 states and territories; 51 other countries; 35% are from out of state; 9% Black or African American, non-Hispanic/Latino; 14% Hispanic/Latino; 9% Asian, non-Hispanic/Latino; 1% Native Hawaiian or other Pacific Islander, non-Hispanic/Latino; 0.3% American Indian or Alaska Native, non-Hispanic/Latino; 2% Two or more races, non-Hispanic/Latino; 4% Race/ethnicity unknown; 4% international; 6% transferred in; 47% live on campus.

Freshmen
Admission: 26,388 applied, 16,258 admitted, 1,714 enrolled. ***Average high school GPA:*** 3.55. ***Test scores:*** SAT critical reading scores over 500: 88%; SAT math scores over 500: 91%; ACT scores over 18: 101%; SAT critical reading scores over 600: 32%; SAT math scores over 600: 40%; ACT scores over 24: 69%; SAT critical reading scores over 700: 5%; SAT math scores over 700: 6%; ACT scores over 30: 13%.
Retention: 80% of full-time freshmen returned.

FACULTY
Total: 1,157, 43% full-time, 65% with terminal degrees.
Student/faculty ratio: 14:1.

ACADEMICS
Calendar: 4-1-4. *Degrees:* certificates, bachelor's, master's, doctoral, post-master's, and postbachelor's certificates.
Special study options: accelerated degree program, advanced placement credit, cooperative education, distance learning, double majors, English as a second language, external degree program, freshman honors college, honors programs, independent study, internships, off-campus study, part-time degree program, services for LD students, student-designed majors, study abroad, summer session for credit. ***ROTC:*** Army (b).
Unusual degree programs: 3-2 business administration; MS in physician assistant studies; BA/MS and BS/MS in computer science; BA/JD LEAP Program.
Computers: 1,419 computers/terminals and 1,900 ports are available on campus for general student use. Students can access the following:

campus intranet, computer help desk, free student e-mail accounts, online (class) grades, online (class) registration, online (class) schedules, Gmail/Google Apps, online course mgmt system, online card services balance update, online e-portfolio, software tutoring, support for specific tech-enhanced assignments, repair and rebuilding-after-virus services, printing services. Campuswide network is available. 100% of college-owned or -operated housing units are wired for high-speed Internet access. Wireless service is available via entire campus.

STUDENT LIFE

Housing options: coed, special housing for students with disabilities. Campus housing is university owned. Freshman applicants given priority for college housing.

Activities and organizations: drama/theater group, student-run newspaper, radio and television station, choral group, Inter Fraternity Sorority Council, Hofstra vs. Zombies, Hofstra's Habitat for Humanity, Masquerade, ALPFA, national fraternities, national sororities.

Athletics Member NCAA. All Division I. ***Intercollegiate sports:*** baseball M(s), basketball M(s)/W(s), cross-country running M(s)/W(s), field hockey W(s), golf M(s)/W(s), lacrosse M(s)/W(s), soccer M(s)/W(s), softball W(s), tennis M(s)/W(s), volleyball W(s), wrestling M(s). ***Intramural sports:*** baseball M(c), basketball M/W, bowling M(c)/W(c), cheerleading M(c)/W(c), crew M(c)/W(c), cross-country running M(c)/W(c), equestrian sports M(c)/W(c), field hockey W(c), golf M(c)/W(c), ice hockey M(c), lacrosse M/W, riflery M(c)/W(c), rock climbing M(c)/W(c), rugby M(c)/W(c), skiing (downhill) M(c)/W(c), soccer M/W, softball M/W, table tennis M(c)/W(c), tennis M(c)/W(c), ultimate Frisbee M(c)/W(c), volleyball M/W, weight lifting M(c)/W(c).

Campus security: 24-hour emergency response devices and patrols, student patrols, late-night transport/escort service, controlled dormitory access, residence halls - security cameras/card access to entry (monitored 24/7); bike patrol; and motorist assistance program.

Student services: health clinic, personal/psychological counseling.

COSTS & FINANCIAL AID

Costs (2014–15) ***Comprehensive fee:*** $52,410 includes full-time tuition ($37,850), mandatory fees ($1050), and room and board ($13,510). Full-time tuition and fees vary according to course load. Part-time tuition: $1275 per credit hour. Part-time tuition and fees vary according to course load. No tuition increase for student's term of enrollment. ***Required fees:*** $155 per term part-time. ***College room only:*** $9050. Room and board charges vary according to board plan and housing facility. ***Payment plan:*** installment. ***Waivers:*** senior citizens and employees or children of employees.

Financial Aid Of all full-time matriculated undergraduates who enrolled in 2013, 5,099 applied for aid, 4,296 were judged to have need, 907 had their need fully met. 1,642 Federal Work-Study jobs (averaging $2937). 1,515 state and other part-time jobs (averaging $3050). In 2013, 1339 non-need-based awards were made. ***Average percent of need met:*** 62. ***Average financial aid package:*** $25,000. ***Average need-based loan:*** $5000. ***Average need-based gift aid:*** $16,000. ***Average non-need-based aid:*** $13,000.

APPLYING

Options: electronic application, early admission, early action, deferred entrance.

Application fee: $70.

Required: essay or personal statement, high school transcript, minimum 2.5 GPA, 2 letters of recommendation, Proof of degree required for all; TOEFL required for international students. ***Required for some:*** interview.

Application deadlines: rolling (freshmen), 12/15 (early action).

Notification: 2/1 (freshmen), continuous (transfers), 1/15 (early action).

CONTACT

Sunil A. Samuel, Assistant Vice President of Admission, Hofstra University, 100 Hofstra University, Hempstead, NY 11549. *Phone:* 516-463-6700. *Toll-free phone:* 800-HOFSTRA. *Fax:* 516-463-5100. *E-mail:* admission@hofstra.edu.

See below for display ad and page 1474 for the College Close-Up.

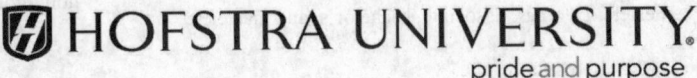

Holy Trinity Orthodox Seminary
Jordanville, New York
http://www.hts.edu/

- **Independent Russian Orthodox** 5-year, founded 1948
- **Rural** 900-acre campus
- **Men only**
- **Noncompetitive** entrance level

FACULTY
Student/faculty ratio: 2:1.

ACADEMICS
Calendar: semesters. *Degree:* certificates and bachelor's.

STUDENT LIFE
Housing options: men-only. Campus housing is university owned.

Activities and organizations: student-run newspaper, choral group, Student Union.

Campus security: 24-hour emergency response devices.

Student services: health clinic, personal/psychological counseling.

COSTS
Costs (2014–15) ***Comprehensive fee:*** $8000 includes full-time tuition ($5500) and room and board ($2500).

APPLYING
Options: deferred entrance.

Required: essay or personal statement, high school transcript, 1 letter of recommendation, interview, Orthodoxy/Orthodox baptism, entrance exam required. Recommendation from spiritual father or parish priest necessary.

CONTACT
Ephraim Willmarth, Administrative Assistant, Holy Trinity Orthodox Seminary, PO Box 36, Jordanville, NY 13361. *Phone:* 315-858-0945. *Fax:* 315-858-0945. *E-mail:* ejwillmarth@hts.edu.

Houghton College
Houghton, New York
http://www.houghton.edu/

- **Independent Wesleyan** comprehensive, founded 1883
- **Rural** 1300-acre campus with easy access to Buffalo, Rochester
- **Endowment** $42.5 million
- **Coed** 1,048 undergraduate students, 95% full-time, 65% women, 35% men
- **Moderately difficult** entrance level, 85% of applicants were admitted

UNDERGRAD STUDENTS
994 full-time, 54 part-time. Students come from 34 states and territories; 29 other countries; 38% are from out of state; 2% Black or African American, non-Hispanic/Latino; 2% Hispanic/Latino; 2% Asian, non-Hispanic/Latino; 0.2% American Indian or Alaska Native, non-Hispanic/Latino; 4% Two or more races, non-Hispanic/Latino; 3% Race/ethnicity unknown; 9% international; 5% transferred in; 87% live on campus.

Freshmen
Admission: 954 applied, 807 admitted, 237 enrolled. ***Average high school GPA:*** 3.51. ***Test scores:*** SAT critical reading scores over 500: 74%; SAT math scores over 500: 72%; SAT writing scores over 500: 67%; ACT scores over 18: 93%; SAT critical reading scores over 600: 35%; SAT math scores over 600: 29%; SAT writing scores over 600: 31%; ACT scores over 24: 60%; SAT critical reading scores over 700: 8%; SAT math scores over 700: 3%; SAT writing scores over 700: 4%; ACT scores over 30: 13%.

Retention: 87% of full-time freshmen returned.

FACULTY
Total: 128, 57% full-time, 68% with terminal degrees.

Student/faculty ratio: 12:1.

ACADEMICS
Calendar: semesters. *Degrees:* associate, bachelor's, and master's.

Special study options: accelerated degree program, adult/continuing education programs, advanced placement credit, cooperative education, distance learning, double majors, freshman honors college, honors programs, independent study, internships, off-campus study, services for LD students, student-designed majors, study abroad, summer session for credit. ***ROTC:*** Army (c).

Unusual degree programs: 3-2 engineering with Clarkson University.

Computers: 30 computers/terminals and 820 ports are available on campus for general student use. Students can access the following: campus intranet, computer help desk, free student e-mail accounts, online (class) grades, online (class) registration, online (class) schedules. Campuswide network is available. 100% of college-owned or -operated housing units are wired for high-speed Internet access. Wireless service is available via entire campus.

STUDENT LIFE
Housing options: on-campus residence required through junior year; men-only, women-only, cooperative. Campus housing is university owned. Freshman campus housing is guaranteed.

Activities and organizations: drama/theater group, student-run newspaper, choral group, Student Government Association, Global Christian Fellowship, Allegany County Outreach, Drama Clubs, Intercultural Student Association.

Athletics Member NCAA, NCCAA. All NCAA Division III. ***Intercollegiate sports:*** baseball M, basketball M/W, cross-country running M/W, field hockey W, lacrosse M/W, soccer M/W, softball W, tennis M/W, track and field M/W, volleyball W. ***Intramural sports:*** baseball M, basketball M/W, equestrian sports M(c)/W(c), football M, racquetball M/W, rock climbing M(c)/W(c), skiing (cross-country) M(c)/W(c), skiing (downhill) M(c)/W(c), soccer M/W, swimming and diving M(c)/W(c), table tennis M/W, ultimate Frisbee M(c)/W(c), volleyball M/W, water polo M/W.

Campus security: 24-hour emergency response devices and patrols, late-night transport/escort service, controlled dormitory access, emergency phone number rings directly to cell phone carried by officer on duty 24/7, automatic fire alarms throughout campus.

Student services: health clinic, personal/psychological counseling.

COSTS & FINANCIAL AID
Costs (2014–15) ***Comprehensive fee:*** $36,808 includes full-time tuition ($28,406), mandatory fees ($150), and room and board ($8252). Full-time tuition and fees vary according to location. Part-time tuition: $1194 per credit hour. Part-time tuition and fees vary according to location. ***College room only:*** $4426. Room and board charges vary according to board plan and housing facility. ***Payment plan:*** installment. ***Waivers:*** employees or children of employees.

Financial Aid Of all full-time matriculated undergraduates who enrolled in 2014, 855 applied for aid, 805 were judged to have need, 81 had their need fully met. 543 Federal Work-Study jobs (averaging $1972). 25 state and other part-time jobs (averaging $2100). In 2014, 40 non-need-based awards were made. ***Average percent of need met:*** 52. ***Average financial aid package:*** $19,967. ***Average need-based loan:*** $4558. ***Average need-based gift aid:*** $11,583. ***Average non-need-based aid:*** $9046. ***Average indebtedness upon graduation:*** $26,550.

APPLYING
Standardized Tests *Required:* SAT or ACT (for admission).

Options: electronic application, deferred entrance.

Application fee: $40.

Required: high school transcript, 1 letter of recommendation. ***Required for some:*** essay or personal statement. ***Recommended:*** essay or personal statement, minimum 3.0 GPA, interview.

Application deadlines: rolling (freshmen), rolling (transfers).

Notification: continuous (freshmen), continuous (transfers).

CONTACT
Mr. Ryan Spear, Associate Director of Admission Operations, Houghton College, PO Box 128, Houghton, NY 14744. *Phone:* 585-567-9353. *Toll-free phone:* 800-777-2556. *Fax:* 585-567-9522. *E-mail:* admission@houghton.edu.

Hunter College of the City University of New York

New York, New York

http://www.hunter.cuny.edu/

- **State and locally supported** comprehensive, founded 1870, part of City University of New York System
- **Urban** campus
- **Endowment** $63.1 million
- **Coed** 16,879 undergraduate students, 72% full-time, 64% women, 36% men
- **Moderately difficult** entrance level, 35% of applicants were admitted

UNDERGRAD STUDENTS

12,142 full-time, 4,737 part-time. Students come from 41 states and territories; 153 other countries; 4% are from out of state; 11% Black or African American, non-Hispanic/Latino; 20% Hispanic/Latino; 26% Asian, non-Hispanic/Latino; 0.2% American Indian or Alaska Native, non-Hispanic/Latino; 6% international; 11% transferred in; 1% live on campus.

Freshmen

Admission: 31,100 applied, 10,836 admitted, 2,080 enrolled. ***Average high school GPA:*** 3.2. ***Test scores:*** SAT critical reading scores over 500: 89%; SAT math scores over 500: 97%; SAT critical reading scores over 600: 33%; SAT math scores over 600: 47%; SAT critical reading scores over 700: 7%; SAT math scores over 700: 11%.

Retention: 86% of full-time freshmen returned.

FACULTY

Total: 2,218, 33% full-time, 39% with terminal degrees.

Student/faculty ratio: 14:1.

ACADEMICS

Calendar: semesters. *Degrees:* bachelor's, master's, doctoral, post-master's, and postbachelor's certificates.

Special study options: advanced placement credit, distance learning, double majors, English as a second language, freshman honors college, honors programs, independent study, internships, off-campus study, part-time degree program, services for LD students, student-designed majors, study abroad, summer session for credit.

Unusual degree programs: 3-2 anthropology, economics, English, history, mathematics, music, physics, sociology.

Computers: 600 computers/terminals are available on campus for general student use. Students can access the following: computer help desk, free student e-mail accounts, online (class) registration, online (class) schedules. Campuswide network is available.

STUDENT LIFE

Housing options: coed.

Activities and organizations: drama/theater group, student-run newspaper, radio and television station, choral group.

Athletics Member NCAA. All Division III. ***Intercollegiate sports:*** basketball M/W, cross-country running M/W, fencing M/W, gymnastics W, soccer M, swimming and diving W, tennis M/W, track and field M/W, volleyball M/W, wrestling M. ***Intramural sports:*** basketball M/W, cross-country running M/W, gymnastics M/W, racquetball M/W, rugby M, soccer M/W, swimming and diving M/W, tennis M/W, volleyball M/W.

Campus security: 24-hour emergency response devices and patrols.

Student services: personal/psychological counseling, women's center.

COSTS & FINANCIAL AID

Costs (2015–16) ***Tuition:*** state resident $275 per credit part-time; nonresident $560 per credit part-time. Full-time tuition and fees vary according to degree level and program. Part-time tuition and fees vary according to degree level and program. ***Required fees:*** $133 per term part-time. ***Payment plan:*** installment.

Financial Aid Of all full-time matriculated undergraduates who enrolled in 2013, 11,095 applied for aid, 9,732 were judged to have need, 1,260 had their need fully met. In 2013, 540 non-need-based awards were made. ***Average percent of need met:*** 72. ***Average financial aid package:*** $7641. ***Average need-based loan:*** $3003. ***Average need-based gift aid:*** $6547.

Average non-need-based aid: $3152. ***Average indebtedness upon graduation:*** $13,000.

APPLYING

Standardized Tests *Required:* SAT or ACT (for admission).

Options: early admission, early decision.

Application fee: $65.

Required: high school transcript.

Application deadlines: 3/15 (freshmen), 3/15 (transfers).

Notification: continuous (freshmen), continuous (transfers).

CONTACT

Ms. Lori Janowski, Associate Director of Undergraduate Admissions, Hunter College of the City University of New York, 695 Park Avenue, New York, NY 10065-5085. *Phone:* 212-772-4490. *Fax:* 212-650-3472. *E-mail:* lori.janowski@hunter.cuny.edu.

See previous page for display ad and page 1476 for the College Close-Up.

Iona College

New Rochelle, New York

http://www.iona.edu/

- **Independent** comprehensive, founded 1940, affiliated with Roman Catholic Church
- **Suburban** 35-acre campus with easy access to New York City
- **Endowment** $100.3 million
- **Coed** 3,301 undergraduate students, 91% full-time, 53% women, 47% men
- **Moderately difficult** entrance level, 87% of applicants were admitted

UNDERGRAD STUDENTS

2,994 full-time, 307 part-time. Students come from 39 states and territories; 19 other countries; 25% are from out of state; 8% Black or African American, non-Hispanic/Latino; 20% Hispanic/Latino; 2% Asian, non-Hispanic/Latino; 0.2% Native Hawaiian or other Pacific Islander, non-Hispanic/Latino; 0.2% American Indian or Alaska Native, non-Hispanic/Latino; 2% Two or more races, non-Hispanic/Latino; 7% Race/ethnicity unknown; 2% international; 3% transferred in; 43% live on campus.

Freshmen

Admission: 7,818 applied, 6,778 admitted, 802 enrolled. ***Test scores:*** SAT critical reading scores over 500: 55%; SAT math scores over 500: 55%; ACT scores over 18: 95%; SAT critical reading scores over 600: 10%; SAT math scores over 600: 12%; ACT scores over 24: 42%; SAT critical reading scores over 700: 1%; SAT math scores over 700: 1%; ACT scores over 30: 3%.

Retention: 83% of full-time freshmen returned.

FACULTY

Total: 352, 48% full-time.

Student/faculty ratio: 15:1.

ACADEMICS

Calendar: semesters. *Degrees:* certificates, bachelor's, master's, post-master's, and postbachelor's certificates.

Special study options: accelerated degree program, adult/continuing education programs, advanced placement credit, distance learning, double majors, English as a second language, external degree program, honors programs, independent study, internships, off-campus study, part-time degree program, services for LD students, study abroad, summer session for credit. ***ROTC:*** Army (c), Air Force (c).

Computers: 738 computers/terminals and 10,000 ports are available on campus for general student use. Students can access the following: campus intranet, computer help desk, free student e-mail accounts, online (class) grades, online (class) registration, online (class) schedules, bill payment. Campuswide network is available. 100% of college-owned or -operated housing units are wired for high-speed Internet access. Wireless service is available via entire campus.

STUDENT LIFE

Housing options: coed, special housing for students with disabilities. Campus housing is university owned and leased by the school. Freshman applicants given priority for college housing.

Activities and organizations: drama/theater group, student-run newspaper, radio and television station, choral group, marching band, Student Government Association, Gales Activities Board, Council for Greek Governance, Council of Multicultural Leaders, The Ionian - Student Newspaper, national fraternities, national sororities.

Athletics Member NCAA. All Division I. ***Intercollegiate sports:*** baseball M(s), basketball M(s)/W(s), crew M/W, cross-country running M(s)/W(s), golf M(s), lacrosse W(s), soccer M(s)/W(s), softball W(s), swimming and diving M(s)/W(s), track and field M(s)/W(s), volleyball W(s), water polo M/W(s). ***Intramural sports:*** basketball M/W, cheerleading M(c)/W(c), football M/W, rugby M(c), soccer M/W, table tennis M/W, volleyball M/W.

Campus security: 24-hour emergency response devices and patrols, controlled dormitory access.

Student services: health clinic, personal/psychological counseling.

COSTS & FINANCIAL AID

Costs (2014–15) ***Comprehensive fee:*** $47,600 includes full-time tuition ($31,880), mandatory fees ($2150), and room and board ($13,570). Part-time tuition: $1060 per credit. Part-time tuition and fees vary according to course load. ***Required fees:*** $540 per term part-time. ***Room and board:*** Room and board charges vary according to housing facility. ***Payment plan:*** installment. ***Waivers:*** children of alumni and employees or children of employees.

Financial Aid Of all full-time matriculated undergraduates who enrolled in 2014, 2,920 applied for aid, 2,425 were judged to have need, 487 had their need fully met. 359 Federal Work-Study jobs (averaging $1333). In 2014, 473 non-need-based awards were made. ***Average percent of need met:*** 20. ***Average financial aid package:*** $21,845. ***Average need-based loan:*** $4030. ***Average need-based gift aid:*** $5654. ***Average non-need-based aid:*** $15,493. ***Average indebtedness upon graduation:*** $30,885. ***Financial aid deadline:*** 4/15.

APPLYING

Standardized Tests *Required:* SAT or ACT (for admission).

Options: electronic application, early action, deferred entrance.

Application fee: $50.

Required: essay or personal statement, high school transcript, 2 letters of recommendation, SAT or ACT scores. ***Required for some:*** interview.

Application deadlines: 2/15 (freshmen), 8/15 (transfers), 12/1 (early action).

Notification: continuous (freshmen), continuous (transfers), 12/19 (early action).

CONTACT

Mr. Patrick St. Cin, Associate Director of Admissions, Iona College, Admissions, 715 North Avenue, New Rochelle, NY 10801. *Phone:* 914-633-2502. *Toll-free phone:* 800-231-IONA. *Fax:* 914-633-2778. *E-mail:* admissions@iona.edu.

Ithaca College

Ithaca, New York

http://www.ithaca.edu/

- **Independent** comprehensive, founded 1892
- **Small-town** 669-acre campus with easy access to Syracuse
- **Endowment** $270.9 million
- **Coed** 6,124 undergraduate students, 98% full-time, 57% women, 43% men
- **Moderately difficult** entrance level, 59% of applicants were admitted

UNDERGRAD STUDENTS

6,012 full-time, 112 part-time. Students come from 53 states and territories; 47 other countries; 55% are from out of state; 5% Black or African American, non-Hispanic/Latino; 8% Hispanic/Latino; 4% Asian, non-Hispanic/Latino; 0.1% American Indian or Alaska Native, non-Hispanic/Latino; 3% Two or more races, non-Hispanic/Latino; 8% Race/ethnicity unknown; 2% international; 2% transferred in; 70% live on campus.

Freshmen

Admission: 18,207 applied, 10,763 admitted, 1,560 enrolled.

Retention: 85% of full-time freshmen returned.

FACULTY
Total: 778, 64% full-time, 72% with terminal degrees.

Student/faculty ratio: 11:1.

ACADEMICS
Calendar: semesters. *Degrees:* certificates, bachelor's, master's, and doctoral.

Special study options: accelerated degree program, adult/continuing education programs, advanced placement credit, distance learning, double majors, freshman honors college, honors programs, independent study, internships, off-campus study, part-time degree program, services for LD students, student-designed majors, study abroad, summer session for credit. ***ROTC:*** Army (c), Air Force (c).

Unusual degree programs: 3-2 engineering with Cornell University, Rensselaer Polytechnic Institute, Clarkson University, State University of New York at Binghamton.

Computers: 640 computers/terminals and 20 ports are available on campus for general student use. Students can access the following: campus intranet, computer help desk, free student e-mail accounts, online (class) grades, online (class) registration, online (class) schedules. Campuswide network is available. 100% of college-owned or -operated housing units are wired for high-speed Internet access. Wireless service is available via entire campus.

STUDENT LIFE
Housing options: on-campus residence required through junior year; coed, women-only, special housing for students with disabilities. Campus housing is university owned. Freshman campus housing is guaranteed.

Activities and organizations: drama/theater group, student-run newspaper, radio and television station, choral group, Student Government Association, African-Latino Society, Residence Hall Association, Habitat for Humanity, Senior Class, national fraternities, national sororities.

Athletics Member NCAA. All Division III. ***Intercollegiate sports:*** baseball M, basketball M/W, crew M/W, cross-country running M/W, field hockey W, football M, golf W, gymnastics W, lacrosse M/W, soccer M/W, softball W, swimming and diving M/W, tennis M/W, track and field M/W, volleyball W, wrestling M. ***Intramural sports:*** basketball M/W, crew M(c)/W(c), equestrian sports M(c)/W(c), football M, golf M/W, ice hockey M(c), lacrosse M(c)/W(c), rugby W(c), skiing (downhill) M(c)/W(c), soccer M/W, softball M/W, squash M(c)/W(c), tennis M/W, ultimate Frisbee M(c)/W(c), volleyball M/W.

Campus security: 24-hour emergency response devices and patrols, student patrols, late-night transport/escort service, controlled dormitory access.

Student services: health clinic, personal/psychological counseling.

COSTS & FINANCIAL AID
Costs (2014–15) ***Comprehensive fee:*** $53,864 includes full-time tuition ($39,532) and room and board ($14,332). Part-time tuition: $1318 per credit hour. ***College room only:*** $7752. Room and board charges vary according to board plan and housing facility. ***Payment plan:*** installment. ***Waivers:*** children of alumni and employees or children of employees.

Financial Aid Of all full-time matriculated undergraduates who enrolled in 2014, 4,674 applied for aid, 4,056 were judged to have need, 1,813 had their need fully met. 3,035 Federal Work-Study jobs (averaging $2344). 1,624 state and other part-time jobs (averaging $2402). In 2014, 1332 non-need-based awards were made. ***Average percent of need met:*** 86. ***Average financial aid package:*** $33,300. ***Average need-based loan:*** $6434. ***Average need-based gift aid:*** $23,640. ***Average non-need-based aid:*** $13,029.

APPLYING
Standardized Tests *Required for some:* SAT or ACT (for admission).

Options: electronic application, early admission, early decision, early action, deferred entrance.

Application fee: $60.

Required: essay or personal statement, high school transcript, 1 letter of recommendation. ***Required for some:*** audition for some programs. ***Recommended:*** minimum 3.0 GPA.

Application deadlines: 2/1 (freshmen), 3/1 (transfers), 12/1 (early action).

Early decision deadline: 11/1.

Notification: 4/15 (freshmen), continuous (transfers), 12/15 (early decision), 2/1 (early action).

CONTACT
Mr. Gerard Turbide, Director of Admission, Ithaca College, 953 Danby Road, Ithaca, NY 14850-7002. *Phone:* 607-274-3124. *Toll-free phone:* 800-429-4274. *Fax:* 607-274-1900. *E-mail:* admission@ithaca.edu.

Jamestown Business College

Jamestown, New York

http://www.jamestownbusinesscollege.edu/

- **Proprietary** primarily 2-year, founded 1886
- **Small-town** 1-acre campus
- **Coed** 318 undergraduate students, 99% full-time, 71% women, 29% men
- **Minimally difficult** entrance level, 93% of applicants were admitted

UNDERGRAD STUDENTS
314 full-time, 4 part-time. Students come from 2 states and territories; 7% are from out of state; 2% Black or African American, non-Hispanic/Latino; 16% Hispanic/Latino; 0.6% Native Hawaiian or other Pacific Islander, non-Hispanic/Latino; 6% American Indian or Alaska Native, non-Hispanic/Latino; 4% Two or more races, non-Hispanic/Latino; 0.9% Race/ethnicity unknown; 10% transferred in.

Freshmen
Admission: 98 applied, 91 admitted, 114 enrolled.

Retention: 68% of full-time freshmen returned.

FACULTY
Total: 25, 24% full-time, 8% with terminal degrees.

Student/faculty ratio: 23:1.

ACADEMICS
Calendar: quarters. *Degrees:* certificates, associate, and bachelor's.

Special study options: advanced placement credit, double majors, off-campus study, part-time degree program, summer session for credit.

Computers: 100 computers/terminals are available on campus for general student use. Students can access the following: campus intranet, free student e-mail accounts, online (class) grades, online (class) schedules. Campuswide network is available. Wireless service is available via entire campus.

STUDENT LIFE
Housing options: college housing not available.

Athletics ***Intramural sports:*** basketball M(c)/W(c), racquetball M(c)/W(c), softball M(c)/W(c), swimming and diving M(c)/W(c), table tennis M(c)/W(c), tennis M(c)/W(c), volleyball M(c)/W(c), weight lifting M(c)/W(c).

Campus security: 24-hour emergency response devices.

COSTS & FINANCIAL AID
Costs (2014–15) ***One-time required fee:*** $25. ***Tuition:*** $11,100 full-time, $308 per credit hour part-time. Full-time tuition and fees vary according to course load. Part-time tuition and fees vary according to course load. ***Required fees:*** $900 full-time, $150 per quarter part-time. ***Waivers:*** employees or children of employees.

Financial Aid Of all full-time matriculated undergraduates who enrolled in 2013, 268 applied for aid, 268 were judged to have need. ***Average need-based loan:*** $3864. ***Average need-based gift aid:*** $7417.

APPLYING
Application fee: $25.

Required: essay or personal statement, high school transcript, interview.

Application deadlines: rolling (freshmen), rolling (transfers).

CONTACT
Mrs. Brenda Salemme, Director of Admissions and Placement, Jamestown Business College, 7 Fairmount Avenue, Box 429, Jamestown, NY 14702-0429. *Phone:* 716-664-5100. *Fax:* 716-664-3144. *E-mail:* brendasalemme@jamestownbusinesscollege.edu.

John Jay College of Criminal Justice of the City University of New York

New York, New York

http://www.jjay.cuny.edu/

- **State and locally supported** comprehensive, founded 1964, part of City University of New York System
- **Urban** campus with easy access to New York City
- **Coed**
- **Moderately difficult** entrance level

ACADEMICS
Calendar: semesters. *Degrees:* certificates, bachelor's, and master's.

STUDENT LIFE
Housing options: college housing not available.

Activities and organizations: drama/theater group, student-run newspaper, radio station, choral group, JJC Debate Team, Universal Image Dance Group, Environmental Club, Justice in Action Club, Artist United.

Athletics Member NCAA. All Division III.

Campus security: 24-hour emergency response devices and patrols.

Student services: health clinic, personal/psychological counseling, women's center, legal services.

COSTS & FINANCIAL AID
Costs (2014–15) ***Tuition:*** state resident $5730 full-time; nonresident $15,300 full-time, $485 per credit part-time. ***Required fees:*** $329 full-time.

Financial Aid Of all full-time matriculated undergraduates who enrolled in 2013, 9,641 applied for aid, 8,876 were judged to have need. ***Average percent of need met:*** 85. ***Average financial aid package:*** $9445. ***Average need-based loan:*** $4245. ***Average need-based gift aid:*** $2954. ***Average indebtedness upon graduation:*** $11,246.

APPLYING
Standardized Tests *Required:* SAT or ACT (for admission).

Options: deferred entrance.

Application fee: $65.

Required: high school transcript, minimum 2.0 GPA, high school diploma and minimum SAT score of 1100.

CONTACT
Stephanie Autenrieth, Director of Admissions, John Jay College of Criminal Justice of the City University of New York, 524 West 59th Street, L.62.20NB, New York, NY 10019. *Phone:* 212-237-8864. *Toll-free phone:* 877-JOHNJAY. *E-mail:* sautenrieth@jjay.cuny.edu.

The Juilliard School

New York, New York

http://www.juilliard.edu/

- **Independent** comprehensive, founded 1905
- **Urban** campus
- **Coed** 570 undergraduate students, 89% full-time, 44% women, 56% men
- **Most difficult** entrance level, 8% of applicants were admitted

UNDERGRAD STUDENTS
509 full-time, 61 part-time. 32% are from out of state; 4% Black or African American, non-Hispanic/Latino; 19% Hispanic/Latino; 10% Asian, non-Hispanic/Latino; 0.1% Native Hawaiian or other Pacific Islander, non-Hispanic/Latino; 5% Two or more races, non-Hispanic/Latino; 9% Race/ethnicity unknown; 20% international; 3% transferred in; 61% live on campus.

Freshmen
Admission: 2,385 applied, 201 admitted, 129 enrolled.

FACULTY
Total: 312, 42% full-time.

Student/faculty ratio: 5:1.

ACADEMICS
Calendar: semesters. *Degrees:* diplomas, bachelor's, master's, doctoral, post-master's, and postbachelor's certificates.

Special study options: adult/continuing education programs.

Computers: Campuswide network is available.

STUDENT LIFE
Housing options: on-campus residence required for freshman year; coed. Campus housing is university owned. Freshman campus housing is guaranteed.

Campus security: 24-hour emergency response devices and patrols, controlled dormitory access, electronically operated main building entrances.

COSTS & FINANCIAL AID
Costs (2014–15) ***One-time required fee:*** $250. ***Comprehensive fee:*** $52,780 includes full-time tuition ($38,190), mandatory fees ($300), and room and board ($14,290). ***Payment plan:*** installment. ***Waivers:*** employees or children of employees.

Financial Aid Of all full-time matriculated undergraduates who enrolled in 2014, 459 applied for aid, 392 were judged to have need, 120 had their need fully met. 211 Federal Work-Study jobs (averaging $2010). 231 state and other part-time jobs (averaging $1936). In 2014, 48 non-need-based awards were made. ***Average percent of need met:*** 79. ***Average financial aid package:*** $34,916. ***Average need-based loan:*** $5001. ***Average need-based gift aid:*** $28,381. ***Average non-need-based aid:*** $21,983. ***Average indebtedness upon graduation:*** $26,712. ***Financial aid deadline:*** 3/1.

APPLYING
Standardized Tests *Required for some:* SAT or ACT (for admission).

Options: electronic application.

Application fee: $110.

Required: essay or personal statement, high school transcript, audition.

Application deadlines: 12/1 (freshmen), 12/1 (transfers).

Notification: 4/1 (freshmen), 4/1 (transfers).

CONTACT
Ms. Lee Cioppa, Associate Dean for Admissions, The Juilliard School, 60 Lincoln Center Plaza, New York, NY 10023-6588. *Phone:* 212-799-5000. *Fax:* 212-724-0263. *E-mail:* admissions@juilliard.edu.

Keuka College

Keuka Park, New York

http://www.keuka.edu/

- **Independent** comprehensive, founded 1890, affiliated with American Baptist Churches in the U.S.A.
- **Rural** 173-acre campus with easy access to Rochester
- **Endowment** $10.3 million
- **Coed** 1,803 undergraduate students, 75% full-time, 75% women, 25% men
- **Moderately difficult** entrance level, 88% of applicants were admitted

UNDERGRAD STUDENTS
1,355 full-time, 448 part-time. Students come from 22 states and territories; 4 other countries; 6% are from out of state; 8% Black or African American, non-Hispanic/Latino; 3% Hispanic/Latino; 3% Asian, non-Hispanic/Latino; 0.3% Native Hawaiian or other Pacific Islander, non-Hispanic/Latino; 0.6% American Indian or Alaska Native, non-Hispanic/Latino; 1% Two or more races, non-Hispanic/Latino; 7% Race/ethnicity unknown; 4% transferred in; 81% live on campus.

Freshmen
Admission: 1,375 applied, 1,207 admitted, 220 enrolled. ***Average high school GPA:*** 3.1. ***Test scores:*** SAT critical reading scores over 500: 41%; SAT math scores over 500: 39%; SAT writing scores over 500: 27%; ACT scores over 18: 76%; SAT critical reading scores over 600: 5%; SAT math scores over 600: 8%; SAT writing scores over 600: 1%; ACT scores over 24: 21%; ACT scores over 30: 2%.

Retention: 70% of full-time freshmen returned.

FACULTY
Total: 477, 19% full-time, 25% with terminal degrees.

Student/faculty ratio: 14:1.

ACADEMICS
Calendar: 4-1-4. *Degrees:* bachelor's and master's.

Special study options: academic remediation for entering students, accelerated degree program, adult/continuing education programs, advanced placement credit, cooperative education, double majors, independent study, internships, off-campus study, part-time degree program, services for LD students, student-designed majors, study abroad, summer session for credit.

Unusual degree programs: 3-2 occupational therapy.

Computers: 256 computers/terminals are available on campus for general student use. Campuswide network is available.

STUDENT LIFE

Housing options: coed, women-only, cooperative. Campus housing is university owned. Freshman campus housing is guaranteed.

Activities and organizations: drama/theater group, student-run newspaper, radio station, choral group, Student Senate, Campus Activities Board, OTTERS (occupational therapy club), Education Club, BAKU.

Athletics Member NCAA. All Division III. ***Intercollegiate sports:*** baseball M, basketball M/W, cross-country running M/W, golf W, lacrosse M, soccer M/W, softball W, swimming and diving W, track and field M, volleyball W. ***Intramural sports:*** badminton M/W, basketball M/W, cheerleading M/W, crew M/W, lacrosse W, skiing (cross-country) M/W, skiing (downhill) M/W, soccer M/W, softball M/W, table tennis M/W, tennis M/W, volleyball W, water polo M/W.

Campus security: 24-hour emergency response devices and patrols, late-night transport/escort service.

Student services: health clinic, personal/psychological counseling.

COSTS & FINANCIAL AID

Costs (2014–15) ***Comprehensive fee:*** $39,035 includes full-time tuition ($27,260), mandatory fees ($975), and room and board ($10,800). Full-time tuition and fees vary according to degree level and program. Part-time tuition: $910 per credit hour. Part-time tuition and fees vary according to program. ***College room only:*** $5130. Room and board charges vary according to board plan and housing facility. ***Payment plan:*** installment. ***Waivers:*** employees or children of employees.

Financial Aid Of all full-time matriculated undergraduates who enrolled in 2012, 1,301 applied for aid, 1,297 were judged to have need, 45 had their need fully met. In 2012, 49 non-need-based awards were made. ***Average percent of need met:*** 65. ***Average financial aid package:*** $17,472. ***Average need-based loan:*** $4818. ***Average need-based gift aid:*** $8906. ***Average non-need-based aid:*** $9576.

APPLYING

Standardized Tests *Required:* SAT or ACT (for admission).

Options: electronic application, early admission, deferred entrance.

Application fee: $30.

Required: essay or personal statement, high school transcript, 1 letter of recommendation. ***Required for some:*** interview. ***Recommended:*** minimum 2.8 GPA, interview.

Application deadlines: rolling (freshmen), rolling (transfers).

CONTACT

Megan Ryan, Director of Admissions, Keuka College, Wagner House, Keuka Park, NY 14478. *Phone:* 315-279-5254. *Toll-free phone:* 800-33-KEUKA. *Fax:* 315-279-5386. *E-mail:* admissions@mail.keuka.edu.

★ The King's College
New York, New York
http://www.tkc.edu/

- **Independent nondenominational** 4-year, founded 1939
- **Urban** campus with easy access to New York City
- **Endowment** $488,024
- **Coed** 487 undergraduate students, 97% full-time, 61% women, 39% men
- **Moderately difficult** entrance level, 70% of applicants were admitted

UNDERGRAD STUDENTS

474 full-time, 13 part-time. Students come from 43 states and territories; 10 other countries; 91% are from out of state; 4% Black or African American, non-Hispanic/Latino; 11% Hispanic/Latino; 3% Asian, non-Hispanic/Latino; 0.6% American Indian or Alaska Native, non-Hispanic/Latino; 4% Two or more races, non-Hispanic/Latino; 0.8% Race/ethnicity unknown; 4% international; 4% transferred in; 90% live on campus.

Freshmen
Admission: 4,589 applied, 3,230 admitted, 144 enrolled. ***Average high school GPA:*** 3.5. ***Test scores:*** SAT critical reading scores over 500: 84%; SAT math scores over 500: 72%; SAT writing scores over 500: 85%; ACT scores over 18: 100%; SAT critical reading scores over 600: 40%; SAT math scores over 600: 21%; SAT writing scores over 600: 36%; ACT scores over 24: 69%; SAT critical reading scores over 700: 10%; SAT math scores over 700: 5%; SAT writing scores over 700: 5%; ACT scores over 30: 5%.

Retention: 60% of full-time freshmen returned.

FACULTY
Total: 50, 54% full-time, 82% with terminal degrees.

Student/faculty ratio: 14:1.

ACADEMICS
Calendar: semesters. *Degree:* bachelor's.

Special study options: advanced placement credit, distance learning, double majors, independent study, internships, services for LD students, study abroad, summer session for credit. ***ROTC:*** Army (c).

Computers: 28 computers/terminals are available on campus for general student use. Students can access the following: computer help desk, free student e-mail accounts, online (class) grades, online (class) registration, online (class) schedules. Campuswide network is available. 100% of college-owned or -operated housing units are wired for high-speed Internet access. Wireless service is available via entire campus.

STUDENT LIFE
Housing options: men-only, women-only. Campus housing is leased by the school. Freshman campus housing is guaranteed.

Activities and organizations: drama/theater group, student-run newspaper, choral group, The King's Players, King's Debate Society, Refuge, Empire State Tribune, The King's College Republicans.

Athletics Member NCCAA, USCAA. ***Intercollegiate sports:*** baseball M, basketball M/W, golf M/W, soccer M/W, volleyball W. ***Intramural sports:*** basketball M(c)/W(c), cheerleading W(c), fencing M(c)/W(c), football M(c), rugby M(c), ultimate Frisbee M(c)/W(c).

Campus security: 24-hour emergency response devices.

Student services: personal/psychological counseling.

COSTS & FINANCIAL AID
Costs (2015–16) ***Tuition:*** $32,870 full-time, $1370 per credit part-time. Full-time tuition and fees vary according to course load. Part-time tuition and fees vary according to course load. ***Required fees:*** $400 full-time, $200 per term part-time. ***Room only:*** Room and board charges vary according to location. ***Payment plans:*** installment, deferred payment. ***Waivers:*** employees or children of employees.

Financial Aid Of all full-time matriculated undergraduates who enrolled in 2013, 393 applied for aid, 365 were judged to have need, 61 had their need fully met. In 2013, 123 non-need-based awards were made. ***Average percent of need met:*** 71. ***Average financial aid package:*** $23,549. ***Average need-based loan:*** $7276. ***Average need-based gift aid:*** $20,667. ***Average non-need-based aid:*** $15,994. ***Average indebtedness upon graduation:*** $28,117.

APPLYING
Standardized Tests *Required:* SAT or ACT (for admission).

Options: electronic application, early action, deferred entrance.

Application fee: $30.

Required: high school transcript. ***Recommended:*** high school transcript, minimum 3.0 GPA, interview.

Application deadlines: rolling (freshmen), rolling (out-of-state freshmen), rolling (transfers), 11/15 (early action).

Notification: continuous (freshmen), continuous (out-of-state freshmen), continuous (transfers), 12/15 (early action).

CONTACT
Mr. Luke Smith, Director of Admissions, The King's College, 56 Broadway, New York, NY 10004. *Phone:* 212-659-3615. *Toll-free phone:* 888-969-7200 Ext. 3610. *Fax:* 212-659-3611. *E-mail:* lsmith@tkc.edu.

See previous page for display ad and page 1488 for the College Close-Up.

Lehman College of the City University of New York

Bronx, New York

http://www.lehman.cuny.edu/

- **State and locally supported** comprehensive, founded 1931, part of City University of New York System
- **Urban** 37-acre campus
- **Endowment** $7.1 million
- **Coed** 10,021 undergraduate students, 56% full-time, 68% women, 32% men
- **Moderately difficult** entrance level, 23% of applicants were admitted

UNDERGRAD STUDENTS
5,646 full-time, 4,375 part-time. Students come from 15 states and territories; 99 other countries; 1% are from out of state; 31% Black or African American, non-Hispanic/Latino; 50% Hispanic/Latino; 6% Asian, non-Hispanic/Latino; 0.1% American Indian or Alaska Native, non-Hispanic/Latino; 4% international; 13% transferred in.

Freshmen
Admission: 15,518 applied, 3,612 admitted, 588 enrolled. ***Test scores:*** SAT critical reading scores over 500: 33%; SAT math scores over 500: 49%; SAT writing scores over 500: 30%; SAT critical reading scores over 600: 7%; SAT math scores over 600: 11%; SAT writing scores over 600: 7%; SAT critical reading scores over 700: 2%; SAT math scores over 700: 2%; SAT writing scores over 700: 2%.

Retention: 82% of full-time freshmen returned.

FACULTY
Total: 912, 40% full-time, 42% with terminal degrees.

Student/faculty ratio: 13:1.

ACADEMICS
Calendar: semesters. *Degrees:* certificates, bachelor's, master's, and post-master's certificates.

Special study options: adult/continuing education programs, advanced placement credit, cooperative education, distance learning, double majors, English as a second language, freshman honors college, honors programs, independent study, internships, off-campus study, part-time degree program, services for LD students, student-designed majors, study abroad, summer session for credit. ***ROTC:*** Army (c).

Unusual degree programs: 3-2 mathematics.

Computers: 800 computers/terminals are available on campus for general student use. Students can access the following: campus intranet, computer help desk, free student e-mail accounts, online (class) grades, online (class) registration, online (class) schedules. Campuswide network is available. Wireless service is available via entire campus.

STUDENT LIFE
Housing options: Campus housing is university owned.

Activities and organizations: drama/theater group, student-run newspaper, radio and television station, choral group, Club Mac, African Students Association, Dominican Student Association, The Sociology Club, Club Live.

Athletics Member NCAA. All Division III. ***Intercollegiate sports:*** baseball M, basketball M/W, cross-country running M/W, racquetball M/W, soccer M/W, softball M/W, swimming and diving M/W, table tennis M/W, tennis M/W, track and field M/W, volleyball M/W, water polo M, wrestling M. ***Intramural sports:*** badminton M/W, baseball M/W, basketball M/W, cross-country running M/W, racquetball M/W, soccer M, softball M/W, swimming and diving M/W, tennis M/W, volleyball M/W, wrestling M.

Campus security: 24-hour emergency response devices and patrols, student patrols, late-night transport/escort service.

Student services: health clinic, personal/psychological counseling, women's center.

COSTS & FINANCIAL AID
Costs (2014–15) ***Tuition:*** state resident $6030 full-time, $260 per credit hour part-time; nonresident $12,840 full-time, $535 per credit hour part-time. Full-time tuition and fees vary according to course load. Part-time tuition and fees vary according to course load. ***Required fees:*** $399 full-time, $117 per degree program part-time. ***Room and board:*** Room and

board charges vary according to housing facility. ***Payment plan:*** installment.

Financial Aid Of all full-time matriculated undergraduates who enrolled in 2012, 4,454 applied for aid, 4,301 were judged to have need. ***Average percent of need met:*** 67. ***Average financial aid package:*** $4264. ***Average need-based loan:*** $1160. ***Average need-based gift aid:*** $2130. ***Average indebtedness upon graduation:*** $8525.

APPLYING

Standardized Tests *Required:* SAT or ACT (for admission).

Options: deferred entrance.

Application fee: $65.

Required: high school transcript, minimum 3.0 GPA. ***Required for some:*** essay or personal statement, interview.

Application deadlines: rolling (freshmen), rolling (transfers).

Notification: continuous (freshmen), continuous (transfers).

CONTACT

Ms. Laurie Austin, Director of Admissions, Lehman College of the City University of New York, 250 Bedford Park Boulevard West, Bronx, NY 10468. *Phone:* 718-960-8706. *Toll-free phone:* 877-LEHMAN1. *Fax:* 718-960-8712. *E-mail:* enroll@lehman.cuny.edu.

★ Le Moyne College

Syracuse, New York

http://www.lemoyne.edu/

- **Independent Roman Catholic (Jesuit)** comprehensive, founded 1946
- **Suburban** 161-acre campus
- **Endowment** $144.8 million
- **Coed** 2,849 undergraduate students, 88% full-time, 58% women, 42% men
- **Moderately difficult** entrance level, 66% of applicants were admitted

UNDERGRAD STUDENTS

2,500 full-time, 349 part-time. Students come from 26 states and territories; 37 other countries; 6% are from out of state; 6% Black or African American, non-Hispanic/Latino; 5% Hispanic/Latino; 3% Asian, non-Hispanic/Latino; 0.1% Native Hawaiian or other Pacific Islander, non-Hispanic/Latino; 0.4% American Indian or Alaska Native, non-Hispanic/Latino; 2% Two or more races, non-Hispanic/Latino; 4% Race/ethnicity unknown; 0.7% international; 7% transferred in; 61% live on campus.

Freshmen

Admission: 6,253 applied, 4,124 admitted, 678 enrolled. ***Average high school GPA:*** 3.43. ***Test scores:*** SAT critical reading scores over 500: 65%; SAT math scores over 500: 68%; ACT scores over 18: 96%; SAT critical reading scores over 600: 19%; SAT math scores over 600: 24%; ACT scores over 24: 49%; SAT critical reading scores over 700: 2%; SAT math scores over 700: 3%; ACT scores over 30: 9%.

Retention: 86% of full-time freshmen returned.

FACULTY

Total: 337, 44% full-time, 58% with terminal degrees.

Student/faculty ratio: 13:1.

ACADEMICS

Calendar: semesters. *Degrees:* bachelor's, master's, post-master's, and postbachelor's certificates.

Special study options: academic remediation for entering students, accelerated degree program, adult/continuing education programs, advanced placement credit, distance learning, double majors, honors programs, independent study, internships, off-campus study, part-time degree program, services for LD students, study abroad, summer session for credit. ***ROTC:*** Army (c), Air Force (c).

Unusual degree programs: 3-2 engineering with Manhattan College, Clarkson University, University of Detroit Mercy, Syracuse University.

Computers: 330 computers/terminals and 330 ports are available on campus for general student use. Students can access the following: campus intranet, computer help desk, free student e-mail accounts, online (class) grades, online (class) registration, online (class) schedules, ECHO (campus-wide portal), some virtual access from off campus. Campuswide network is available. 100% of college-owned or -operated housing units are wired for high-speed Internet access. Wireless service is available via entire campus.

STUDENT LIFE

Housing options: on-campus residence required through senior year; coed, special housing for students with disabilities. Campus housing is university owned. Freshman campus housing is guaranteed.

Activities and organizations: drama/theater group, student-run newspaper, radio and television station, choral group, Student Programming Board, Outing Club, performing arts groups, Cultural Groups, New Student Orientation Committee.

Athletics Member NCAA. All Division II. ***Intercollegiate sports:*** baseball M(s), basketball M(s)/W(s), cross-country running M(s)/W(s), golf M(s)/W(s), lacrosse M(s)/W(s), soccer M(s)/W(s), softball W(s), swimming and diving M(s)/W(s), tennis M(s)/W(s), track and field M(s)/W(s), volleyball W(s). ***Intramural sports:*** basketball M/W, bowling M(c)/W(c), crew M(c)/W(c), equestrian sports M(c)/W(c), fencing M(c)/W(c), field hockey W(c), football M/W, ice hockey M(c), lacrosse M(c)/W(c), racquetball M/W, rugby M(c)/W(c), sailing M(c)/W(c), soccer M/W, softball M/W, ultimate Frisbee M(c)/W(c), volleyball M/W.

Campus security: 24-hour emergency response devices and patrols, late-night transport/escort service, controlled dormitory access, lighted pathways, closed-circuit security cameras, and emergency code blue phones.

Student services: health clinic, personal/psychological counseling.

COSTS & FINANCIAL AID

Costs (2014–15) ***Comprehensive fee:*** $43,470 includes full-time tuition ($30,350), mandatory fees ($990), and room and board ($12,130). Part-time tuition: $637 per credit hour. Part-time tuition and fees vary according to class time and course load. ***College room only:*** $7650. Room and board charges vary according to board plan and housing facility. ***Payment plans:*** installment, deferred payment. ***Waivers:*** employees or children of employees.

Financial Aid Of all full-time matriculated undergraduates who enrolled in 2013, 2,166 applied for aid, 1,983 were judged to have need, 429 had their need fully met. 428 Federal Work-Study jobs (averaging $862). 472 state and other part-time jobs (averaging $1556). In 2013, 167 non-need-based awards were made. ***Average percent of need met:*** 75. ***Average financial aid package:*** $23,164. ***Average need-based loan:*** $4586. ***Average need-based gift aid:*** $18,568. ***Average non-need-based aid:*** $6733. ***Average indebtedness upon graduation:*** $34,500.

APPLYING

Standardized Tests *Required:* SAT or ACT (for admission).

Options: electronic application, early admission, early action, deferred entrance.

Application fee: $35.

Required: essay or personal statement, high school transcript, 3 letters of recommendation. ***Recommended:*** interview.

Application deadlines: 2/1 (freshmen), 8/1 (transfers), 11/15 (early action).

Notification: continuous until 1/1 (freshmen), continuous (transfers), 12/15 (early action).

CONTACT

Mrs. Mary M. Chandler, Sr. Director of Admission, Le Moyne College, 1419 Salt Springs Road, Syracuse, NY 13214-1301. *Phone:* 315-445-4300. *Toll-free phone:* 800-333-4733. *Fax:* 315-445-4711. *E-mail:* admission@lemoyne.edu.

See previous page for display ad and page 1496 for the College Close-Up.

★ LIM College
New York, New York
http://www.limcollege.edu/

- **Proprietary** comprehensive, founded 1939
- **Urban** campus with easy access to New York City
- **Coed, primarily women** 1,552 undergraduate students, 92% full-time, 92% women, 8% men
- **Moderately difficult** entrance level, 74% of applicants were admitted

UNDERGRAD STUDENTS

1,424 full-time, 128 part-time. Students come from 45 states and territories; 25 other countries; 60% are from out of state; 15% Black or African American, non-Hispanic/Latino; 17% Hispanic/Latino; 5% Asian,

★ Manhattan College
Riverdale, New York
http://www.manhattan.edu/

- **Independent** comprehensive, founded 1853, affiliated with Roman Catholic Church
- **Urban** 31-acre campus with easy access to New York City
- **Endowment** $71.8 million
- **Coed** 3,471 undergraduate students, 94% full-time, 44% women, 56% men
- **Moderately difficult** entrance level, 67% of applicants were admitted

UNDERGRAD STUDENTS
3,276 full-time, 195 part-time. Students come from 33 states and territories; 37 other countries; 29% are from out of state; 4% Black or African American, non-Hispanic/Latino; 19% Hispanic/Latino; 4% Asian, non-Hispanic/Latino; 0.2% American Indian or Alaska Native, non-Hispanic/Latino; 2% Two or more races, non-Hispanic/Latino; 12% Race/ethnicity unknown; 3% international; 5% transferred in; 67% live on campus.

Freshmen
Admission: 8,199 applied, 5,456 admitted, 747 enrolled. ***Average high school GPA:*** 3.4. ***Test scores:*** SAT critical reading scores over 500: 70%; SAT math scores over 500: 79%; SAT writing scores over 500: 67%; ACT scores over 18: 100%; SAT critical reading scores over 600: 20%; SAT math scores over 600: 31%; SAT writing scores over 600: 21%; ACT scores over 24: 62%; SAT critical reading scores over 700: 2%; SAT math scores over 700: 4%; SAT writing scores over 700: 2%; ACT scores over 30: 8%.
Retention: 84% of full-time freshmen returned.

FACULTY
Total: 460, 49% full-time, 72% with terminal degrees.
Student/faculty ratio: 12:1.

ACADEMICS
Calendar: semesters. *Degrees:* bachelor's, master's, and post-master's certificates.
Special study options: accelerated degree program, adult/continuing education programs, advanced placement credit, cooperative education, distance learning, double majors, English as a second language, honors programs, independent study, internships, off-campus study, part-time degree program, services for LD students, student-designed majors, study abroad, summer session for credit. ***ROTC:*** Army (c), Air Force (b).
Unusual degree programs: business administration; engineering; education.
Computers: 410 computers/terminals and 600 ports are available on campus for general student use. Students can access the following: campus intranet, computer help desk, free student e-mail accounts, online (class) grades, online (class) registration, online (class) schedules, course management system. Campuswide network is available. 100% of college-owned or -operated housing units are wired for high-speed Internet access. Wireless service is available via entire campus.

STUDENT LIFE
Housing options: coed, special housing for students with disabilities. Campus housing is university owned. Freshman campus housing is guaranteed.
Activities and organizations: drama/theater group, student-run newspaper, radio and television station, choral group, Society of Hispanic Professional Engineers, Gaelic Society, student government, Social Life Commission, Manhattan College Players (Theater/Drama group), national fraternities, national sororities.
Athletics Member NCAA. All Division I. ***Intercollegiate sports:*** baseball M(s), basketball M(s)/W(s), cheerleading M/W, crew M(c)/W(c), cross-country running M(s)/W(s), golf M(s), lacrosse M(s)/W(s), rugby M(c), soccer M(s)/W(s), softball W(s), swimming and diving M(s)/W(s), tennis W(s), track and field M(s)/W(s), volleyball W(s). ***Intramural sports:*** baseball M, basketball M/W, cross-country running M/W, equestrian sports M/W, soccer M/W, softball M/W, swimming and diving W, track and field M/W, volleyball M/W.

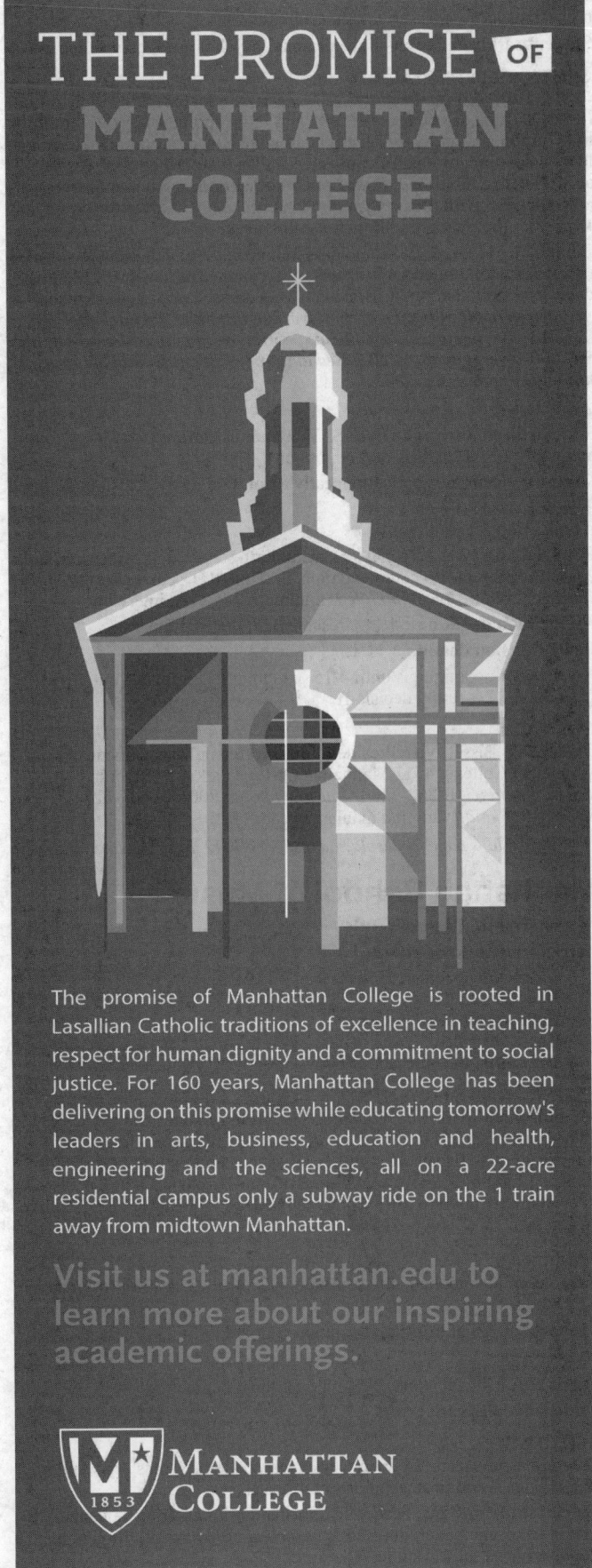

Campus security: 24-hour emergency response devices and patrols, late-night transport/escort service, controlled dormitory access.

Student services: health clinic, personal/psychological counseling.

COSTS & FINANCIAL AID

Costs (2014–15) ***Comprehensive fee:*** $51,238 includes full-time tuition ($34,300), mandatory fees ($3198), and room and board ($13,740). Full-time tuition and fees vary according to course load, program, and student level. Part-time tuition: $875 per credit. Part-time tuition and fees vary according to course load. ***Room and board:*** Room and board charges vary according to board plan. ***Payment plans:*** installment, deferred payment. ***Waivers:*** employees or children of employees.

Financial Aid Of all full-time matriculated undergraduates who enrolled in 2014, 2,725 applied for aid, 2,411 were judged to have need, 340 had their need fully met. In 2014, 844 non-need-based awards were made. ***Average percent of need met:*** 67. ***Average financial aid package:*** $23,513. ***Average need-based loan:*** $4504. ***Average need-based gift aid:*** $19,090. ***Average non-need-based aid:*** $6827. ***Average indebtedness upon graduation:*** $37,449.

APPLYING

Standardized Tests *Required:* SAT (for admission), ACT (for admission), SAT or ACT (for admission).

Options: electronic application, early admission, early decision, deferred entrance.

Application fee: $60.

Required: essay or personal statement, high school transcript, minimum 2.5 GPA, 1 letter of recommendation, SAT or ACT scores. ***Required for some:*** interview. ***Recommended:*** minimum 3.0 GPA, interview.

Application deadlines: 4/15 (freshmen), 7/1 (transfers).

Early decision deadline: 11/15.

Notification: continuous until 4/15 (freshmen), continuous until 8/15 (transfers), 12/1 (early decision).

CONTACT

Dr. William Bisset, Vice President for Enrollment Management, Manhattan College, 4513 Manhattan College Parkway, Riverdale, NY 10471. *Phone:* 718-862-7200. *Toll-free phone:* 800-622-9235. *Fax:* 718-862-8019. *E-mail:* admit@manhattan.edu.

See previous page for display ad and page 1512 for the College Close-Up.

Manhattan School of Music

New York, New York

http://www.msmnyc.edu/

- **Independent** comprehensive, founded 1917
- **Urban** 1-acre campus
- **Endowment** $19.2 million
- **Coed** 389 undergraduate students, 99% full-time, 55% women, 45% men
- **Very difficult** entrance level, 45% of applicants were admitted

UNDERGRAD STUDENTS

385 full-time, 4 part-time. Students come from 32 states and territories; 20 other countries; 61% are from out of state; 2% Black or African American, non-Hispanic/Latino; 7% Hispanic/Latino; 7% Asian, non-Hispanic/Latino; 5% Two or more races, non-Hispanic/Latino; 4% Race/ethnicity unknown; 43% international; 5% transferred in; 67% live on campus.

Freshmen

Admission: 897 applied, 402 admitted, 113 enrolled. ***Average high school GPA:*** 3.55.

Retention: 81% of full-time freshmen returned.

FACULTY

Total: 251, 27% full-time, 20% with terminal degrees.

Student/faculty ratio: 6:1.

ACADEMICS

Calendar: semesters. *Degrees:* diplomas, bachelor's, master's, doctoral, post-master's, and postbachelor's certificates.

Special study options: academic remediation for entering students, advanced placement credit, English as a second language, off-campus study, services for LD students.

Computers: 20 computers/terminals and 20 ports are available on campus for general student use. Students can access the following: campus intranet, computer help desk, free student e-mail accounts, online (class) grades, online (class) registration, online (class) schedules. Campuswide network is available. 100% of college-owned or -operated housing units are wired for high-speed Internet access. Wireless service is available via computer labs, dorm rooms, libraries, student centers.

STUDENT LIFE

Housing options: on-campus residence required through sophomore year; coed. Campus housing is university owned. Freshman campus housing is guaranteed.

Activities and organizations: Student Council, Asian Student Association, Resident Community Council.

Campus security: 24-hour patrols, student patrols, controlled dormitory access.

Student services: health clinic, personal/psychological counseling.

COSTS & FINANCIAL AID

Costs (2015–16) ***Comprehensive fee:*** $56,724 includes full-time tuition ($42,000), mandatory fees ($500), and room and board ($14,224). Part-time tuition: $1750 per credit. Part-time tuition and fees vary according to course load. ***College room only:*** $9725. Room and board charges vary according to board plan and housing facility. ***Payment plans:*** installment, deferred payment. ***Waivers:*** employees or children of employees.

Financial Aid Of all full-time matriculated undergraduates who enrolled in 2012, 262 applied for aid, 230 were judged to have need. In 2012, 21 non-need-based awards were made. ***Average percent of need met:*** 10. ***Average financial aid package:*** $20,044. ***Average need-based loan:*** $5285. ***Average need-based gift aid:*** $5519. ***Average non-need-based aid:*** $12,569. ***Average indebtedness upon graduation:*** $4699. ***Financial aid deadline:*** 3/1.

APPLYING

Standardized Tests *Recommended:* SAT or ACT (for admission).

Options: electronic application, deferred entrance.

Application fee: $125.

Required: essay or personal statement, high school transcript, minimum 2.8 GPA, 2 letters of recommendation, prescreening, audition. ***Required for some:*** interview. ***Recommended:*** minimum 3.0 GPA.

Application deadlines: 12/1 (freshmen), 12/1 (transfers).

Notification: 4/1 (freshmen), 4/1 (transfers).

CONTACT

Ms. Amy Anderson, Dean of Enrollment Management, Manhattan School of Music, 120 Claremont Avenue, New York, NY 10027-4698. *Phone:* 917-493-4501. *Fax:* 212-749-3025. *E-mail:* aanderson@msmnyc.edu.

Manhattanville College

Purchase, New York

http://www.mville.edu/

- **Independent** comprehensive, founded 1841
- **Suburban** 100-acre campus with easy access to New York City
- **Endowment** $31.1 million
- **Coed** 1,798 undergraduate students, 95% full-time, 64% women, 36% men
- **Moderately difficult** entrance level, 74% of applicants were admitted

UNDERGRAD STUDENTS

1,708 full-time, 90 part-time. Students come from 43 states and territories; 47 other countries; 36% are from out of state; 8% Black or African American, non-Hispanic/Latino; 13% Hispanic/Latino; 1% Asian, non-Hispanic/Latino; 0.1% Native Hawaiian or other Pacific Islander, non-Hispanic/Latino; 0.1% American Indian or Alaska Native, non-Hispanic/Latino; 2% Two or more races, non-Hispanic/Latino; 39% Race/ethnicity unknown; 9% international; 4% transferred in; 64% live on campus.

Freshmen

Admission: 3,929 applied, 2,902 admitted, 459 enrolled. ***Average high school GPA:*** 3.13. ***Test scores:*** SAT critical reading scores over 500: 74%; SAT math scores over 500: 68%; SAT writing scores over 500: 71%; ACT scores over 18: 94%; SAT critical reading scores over 600: 17%; SAT math scores over 600: 20%; SAT writing scores over 600: 23%; ACT

scores over 24: 64%; SAT critical reading scores over 700: 2%; SAT math scores over 700: 3%; SAT writing scores over 700: 2%; ACT scores over 30: 6%.

Retention: 79% of full-time freshmen returned.

FACULTY

Total: 310, 34% full-time, 40% with terminal degrees.

Student/faculty ratio: 12:1.

ACADEMICS

Calendar: semesters. *Degrees:* bachelor's, master's, doctoral, and post-master's certificates.

Special study options: academic remediation for entering students, accelerated degree program, adult/continuing education programs, advanced placement credit, double majors, honors programs, independent study, internships, off-campus study, part-time degree program, services for LD students, student-designed majors, study abroad, summer session for credit.

Unusual degree programs: 3-2 business administration; Education.

Computers: 240 computers/terminals are available on campus for general student use. Students can access the following: campus intranet, computer help desk, free student e-mail accounts, online (class) grades, online (class) registration, online (class) schedules. Campuswide network is available. 100% of college-owned or -operated housing units are wired for high-speed Internet access. Wireless service is available via classrooms, computer centers, computer labs, dorm rooms, learning centers, libraries, student centers.

STUDENT LIFE

Housing options: coed, special housing for students with disabilities. Campus housing is university owned. Freshman campus housing is guaranteed.

Activities and organizations: drama/theater group, student-run newspaper, radio station, choral group, Campus Activity Board, Breaking The Silence, Hillel, Student of Caribbean Ancestry, Latin American Student Organization.

Athletics Member NCAA. All Division III. ***Intercollegiate sports:*** baseball M, basketball M/W, cross-country running M/W, field hockey W, golf M/W, ice hockey M/W, lacrosse M/W, soccer M/W, softball W, track and field M/W, volleyball W.

Campus security: 24-hour emergency response devices and patrols, late-night transport/escort service, controlled dormitory access.

Student services: health clinic, personal/psychological counseling.

COSTS & FINANCIAL AID

Costs (2015–16) ***Comprehensive fee:*** $50,740 includes full-time tuition ($34,870), mandatory fees ($1350), and room and board ($14,520). Full-time tuition and fees vary according to course load. Part-time tuition: $810 per credit. Part-time tuition and fees vary according to course load and program. ***Required fees:*** $60 per term part-time. ***College room only:*** $8680. Room and board charges vary according to board plan. ***Payment plans:*** installment, deferred payment. ***Waivers:*** employees or children of employees.

Financial Aid Of all full-time matriculated undergraduates who enrolled in 2014, 1,424 applied for aid, 1,213 were judged to have need, 195 had their need fully met. In 2014, 358 non-need-based awards were made. ***Average percent of need met:*** 75. ***Average financial aid package:*** $29,347. ***Average need-based loan:*** $4553. ***Average need-based gift aid:*** $7686. ***Average non-need-based aid:*** $16,638. ***Average indebtedness upon graduation:*** $33,444.

APPLYING

Standardized Tests *Required for some:* SAT and SAT Subject Tests or ACT (for admission). *Recommended:* SAT (for admission), ACT (for admission), SAT or ACT (for admission).

Options: electronic application, early admission, early action, deferred entrance.

Application fee: $50.

Required: essay or personal statement, high school transcript, minimum 2.5 GPA, 2 letters of recommendation. ***Recommended:*** interview.

Application deadlines: 3/1 (freshmen), 3/1 (transfers).

Notification: continuous (freshmen), continuous (transfers).

CONTACT

Mr. Joseph Cosentino, Director of Admissions, Manhattanville College, 2900 Purchase Street, Purchase, NY 10577. *Phone:* 914-323-5125. *Toll-*

free phone: 800-328-4553. *Fax:* 914-694-1732. *E-mail:* Joseph.Cosentino@mville.edu.

See previous page for display ad and page 1514 for the College Close-Up.

★ Mannes College The New School for Music

New York, New York

http://www.mannes.edu/

- **Independent** comprehensive, founded 1916, part of The New School
- **Urban** campus with easy access to Manhattan
- **Endowment** $214.0 million
- **Coed**

FACULTY
Student/faculty ratio: 2:1.

ACADEMICS
Calendar: semesters. *Degrees:* diplomas, bachelor's, master's, post-master's, and postbachelor's certificates.

STUDENT LIFE
Housing options: coed, special housing for students with disabilities. Campus housing is university owned and leased by the school. Freshman applicants given priority for college housing.

Activities and organizations: drama/theater group, student-run newspaper, radio station, choral group, Musical Theatre Organization, New Light Opera, Dream:In NY, Theatre Collective, BriCollab Art Initiative.

Campus security: 24-hour emergency response devices, controlled dormitory access, 24-hour desk attendants in residence halls.

Student services: health clinic, personal/psychological counseling.

FINANCIAL AID
Financial Aid Of all full-time matriculated undergraduates who enrolled in 2012, 67 applied for aid, 57 were judged to have need, 8 had their need fully met. In 2012, 8 non-need-based awards were made. ***Average percent of need met:*** 51. ***Average financial aid package:*** $13,847. ***Average need-based loan:*** $5511. ***Average need-based gift aid:*** $15,312. ***Average non-need-based aid:*** $11,710. ***Average indebtedness upon graduation:*** $25,509. ***Financial aid deadline:*** 3/1.

APPLYING
Required: essay or personal statement, high school transcript, 2 letters of recommendation, interview, online application, pre-screening (if applicable); live auditions; English placement exam; TOEFL, IELTS or PTE scores may be required for applicants whose first language is not English.

CONTACT
Mr. Jonathan Engle, Associate Director, Mannes College The New School for Music, 150 West 85th Street, Floor 1 Room 104, New York, NY 10024. *Phone:* 212-580-0210 Ext. 4886. *Toll-free phone:* 800-292-3040. *E-mail:* mannesadmissions@newschool.edu.

See page 715 for display ad and page 1546 for the College Close-Up.

Maria College

Albany, New York

http://www.mariacollege.edu/

- **Independent** 4-year, founded 1958
- **Urban** 9-acre campus
- **Coed** 866 undergraduate students, 28% full-time, 88% women, 12% men
- **Minimally difficult** entrance level, 32% of applicants were admitted

UNDERGRAD STUDENTS
242 full-time, 624 part-time. Students come from 6 states and territories; 3% are from out of state; 13% Black or African American, non-Hispanic/Latino; 3% Hispanic/Latino; 2% Asian, non-Hispanic/Latino; 0.3% American Indian or Alaska Native, non-Hispanic/Latino; 2% Two or more races, non-Hispanic/Latino; 14% Race/ethnicity unknown; 35% transferred in.

Freshmen
Admission: 380 applied, 121 admitted, 52 enrolled. ***Test scores:*** SAT critical reading scores over 500: 26%; SAT math scores over 500: 26%; SAT writing scores over 500: 26%; ACT scores over 18: 83%; SAT math scores over 600: 5%; ACT scores over 24: 33%.

Retention: 100% of full-time freshmen returned.

FACULTY
Total: 108, 29% full-time, 11% with terminal degrees.
Student/faculty ratio: 8:1.

ACADEMICS
Calendar: semesters. *Degrees:* certificates, associate, and bachelor's.

Special study options: academic remediation for entering students, adult/continuing education programs, advanced placement credit, distance learning, independent study, off-campus study, part-time degree program, services for LD students, summer session for credit. ***ROTC:*** Air Force (c).

Computers: 78 computers/terminals are available on campus for general student use. Students can access the following: campus intranet, computer help desk, free student e-mail accounts, online (class) grades, online (class) registration, online (class) schedules. Campuswide network is available. Wireless service is available via entire campus.

STUDENT LIFE
Housing options: college housing not availableCampus housing is provided by a third party.

Activities and organizations: choral group.

Campus security: late-night transport/escort service.

Student services: personal/psychological counseling.

COSTS & FINANCIAL AID
Costs (2014–15) ***Tuition:*** $11,730 full-time, $500 per credit hour part-time. Full-time tuition and fees vary according to course load and program. Part-time tuition and fees vary according to course load and program. ***Required fees:*** $200 full-time, $50 per term part-time. ***Payment plan:*** installment. ***Waivers:*** employees or children of employees.

Financial Aid Of all full-time matriculated undergraduates who enrolled in 2013, 25 Federal Work-Study jobs (averaging $1000).

APPLYING
Standardized Tests *Required for some:* SAT or ACT (for admission), Test of Essential Academic Skills (TEAS) is required for admission to our AAS in Nursing and Practical Nursing Certificate Programs. *Recommended:* SAT or ACT (for admission).

Options: electronic application, early admission, early decision, deferred entrance.

Application fee: $35.

Required: high school transcript. ***Required for some:*** The TEAS is required of all AAS Nursing applicants and Practical Nursing Certificate applicants. ***Recommended:*** essay or personal statement, minimum 2.5 GPA, 1 letter of recommendation, interview.

Application deadlines: 3/1 (freshmen), 3/1 (out-of-state freshmen), 8/23 (transfers).

Early decision deadline: 12/1.

Notification: continuous (freshmen), continuous (out-of-state freshmen), continuous (transfers), 1/15 (early decision).

CONTACT
Mr. John Ramoska, Director of Admissions, Maria College, 700 New Scotland Ave, Albany, NV 12065. *Phone:* 518-861-2519. *Fax:* 518-453-1366. *E-mail:* admissions@mariacollege.edu.

Marist College

Poughkeepsie, New York

http://www.marist.edu/

- **Independent** comprehensive, founded 1929
- **Suburban** 210-acre campus with easy access to Albany, New York City
- **Endowment** $220.9 million
- **Coed** 5,516 undergraduate students, 88% full-time, 59% women, 41% men
- **Very difficult** entrance level, 39% of applicants were admitted

UNDERGRAD STUDENTS
4,876 full-time, 640 part-time. 43% are from out of state; 4% Black or African American, non-Hispanic/Latino; 9% Hispanic/Latino; 3% Asian, non-Hispanic/Latino; 0.1% Native Hawaiian or other Pacific Islander, non-Hispanic/Latino; 0.2% American Indian or Alaska Native, non-Hispanic/Latino; 2% Two or more races, non-Hispanic/Latino; 2% Race/ethnicity unknown; 2% international; 6% transferred in; 73% live on campus.

Freshmen
Admission: 9,751 applied, 3,755 admitted, 1,127 enrolled. ***Average high school GPA:*** 3.3. ***Test scores:*** SAT critical reading scores over 500: 91%; SAT math scores over 500: 93%; SAT writing scores over 500: 90%; ACT scores over 18: 100%; SAT critical reading scores over 600: 39%; SAT math scores over 600: 54%; SAT writing scores over 600: 48%; ACT scores over 24: 86%; SAT critical reading scores over 700: 4%; SAT math scores over 700: 8%; SAT writing scores over 700: 6%; ACT scores over 30: 15%.

Retention: 91% of full-time freshmen returned.

FACULTY
Total: 601, 39% full-time, 44% with terminal degrees.

Student/faculty ratio: 16:1.

ACADEMICS
Calendar: semesters. *Degrees:* certificates, bachelor's, master's, and postbachelor's certificates.

Special study options: academic remediation for entering students, accelerated degree program, adult/continuing education programs, advanced placement credit, cooperative education, distance learning, double majors, English as a second language, honors programs, independent study, internships, off-campus study, part-time degree program, services for LD students, study abroad, summer session for credit. ***ROTC:*** Army (b).

Computers: 810 computers/terminals and 650 ports are available on campus for general student use. Students can access the following: campus intranet, computer help desk, free student e-mail accounts, online (class) grades, online (class) registration, online (class) schedules, Adm., Billing, Transcript, Degree Audit, Financial Aid Application, Financial Aid Award Review, Student Account Summary, Payment, Library Database Search, Campus OneCard Account, Parking registration, Cap and Gown order, and all areas of campus. Campuswide network is available. 100% of college-owned or -operated housing units are wired for high-speed Internet access. Wireless service is available via entire campus.

STUDENT LIFE
Housing options: coed, special housing for students with disabilities. Campus housing is university owned and is provided by a third party. Freshman campus housing is guaranteed.

Activities and organizations: drama/theater group, student-run newspaper, radio and television station, choral group, marching band, Marist Singers, Dance Club, student government, Theater Club, Community Service and Campus Ministry, national fraternities, national sororities.

Athletics Member NCAA. All Division I except football (Division I-AA). ***Intercollegiate sports:*** baseball M(s), basketball M(s)/W(s), bowling M(c)/W(c), cheerleading M(c)/W(c), crew M/W(s), cross-country running M(s)/W(s), equestrian sports M(c)/W(c), fencing M(c)/W(c), ice hockey M(c), lacrosse M(s)/W(s), rugby M(c)/W(c), skiing (downhill) M(c)/W(c), soccer M(s)/W(s), softball W(s), swimming and diving M(s)/W(s), tennis M(s)/W(s), track and field M(s)/W(s), volleyball M(c)/W(s), water polo W(s). ***Intramural sports:*** basketball M/W, soccer M/W, softball M/W, ultimate Frisbee M(c)/W(c), volleyball M/W.

Campus security: 24-hour emergency response devices and patrols, student patrols, late-night transport/escort service, controlled dormitory access, night residence hall monitors.

Student services: health clinic, personal/psychological counseling.

COSTS & FINANCIAL AID
Costs (2014–15) ***One-time required fee:*** $90. ***Comprehensive fee:*** $46,100 includes full-time tuition ($32,000), mandatory fees ($500), and room and board ($13,600). Full-time tuition and fees vary according to course load and location. Part-time tuition: $634 per credit hour. Part-time tuition and fees vary according to course load. ***Required fees:*** $40 per term part-time. ***College room only:*** $8700. Room and board charges vary according to board plan, housing facility, and location. ***Payment plan:*** installment. ***Waivers:*** adult students and employees or children of employees.

Financial Aid Of all full-time matriculated undergraduates who enrolled in 2014, 3,482 applied for aid, 2,803 were judged to have need, 436 had their need fully met. 1,390 Federal Work-Study jobs (averaging $2479). 583 state and other part-time jobs (averaging $1781). In 2014, 1244 non-need-based awards were made. ***Average percent of need met:*** 64. ***Average financial aid package:*** $18,969. ***Average need-based loan:*** $4953. ***Average need-based gift aid:*** $15,447. ***Average non-need-based aid:*** $7619. ***Average indebtedness upon graduation:*** $34,801. ***Financial aid deadline:*** 5/1.

APPLYING
Options: electronic application, early admission, early decision, early action, deferred entrance.

Application fee: $50.

Required: essay or personal statement, high school transcript, 2 letters of recommendation.

Application deadlines: 2/1 (freshmen), 6/1 (transfers), 11/15 (early action).

Early decision deadline: 11/1.

Notification: 3/30 (freshmen), continuous (transfers), 12/15 (early decision), 1/30 (early action).

CONTACT
Mr. Kenton Rinehart, Dean of Undergraduate Admissions, Marist College, 3399 North Road, Poughkeepsie, NY 12601. *Phone:* 845-575-3226. *Toll-free phone:* 800-436-5483. *Fax:* 845-575-3215. *E-mail:* admission@marist.edu.

Marymount Manhattan College
New York, New York
http://www.mmm.edu/

- **Independent** 4-year, founded 1936
- **Urban** campus
- **Endowment** $17.9 million
- **Coed** 1,858 undergraduate students, 88% full-time, 77% women, 23% men
- **Moderately difficult** entrance level, 74% of applicants were admitted

UNDERGRAD STUDENTS
1,640 full-time, 218 part-time. Students come from 49 states and territories; 55 other countries; 60% are from out of state; 10% Black or African American, non-Hispanic/Latino; 17% Hispanic/Latino; 3% Asian, non-Hispanic/Latino; 0.2% Native Hawaiian or other Pacific Islander, non-Hispanic/Latino; 0.9% American Indian or Alaska Native, non-Hispanic/Latino; 1% Two or more races, non-Hispanic/Latino; 5% Race/ethnicity unknown; 5% international; 6% transferred in; 36% live on campus.

Freshmen
Admission: 4,385 applied, 3,226 admitted, 514 enrolled. ***Average high school GPA:*** 3.27. ***Test scores:*** SAT critical reading scores over 500: 74%; SAT math scores over 500: 60%; SAT writing scores over 500: 71%; ACT scores over 18: 95%; SAT critical reading scores over 600: 29%; SAT math scores over 600: 16%; SAT writing scores over 600: 25%; ACT scores over 24: 52%; SAT critical reading scores over 700: 3%; SAT math scores over 700: 1%; SAT writing scores over 700: 3%; ACT scores over 30: 5%.

Retention: 74% of full-time freshmen returned.

FACULTY
Total: 302, 30% full-time.

Student/faculty ratio: 11:1.

ACADEMICS
Calendar: semesters plus summer and January mini-semesters. *Degrees:* associate and bachelor's.

Special study options: academic remediation for entering students, accelerated degree program, adult/continuing education programs, advanced placement credit, distance learning, double majors, honors programs, independent study, internships, off-campus study, part-time degree program, services for LD students, student-designed majors, study abroad, summer session for credit.

Computers: 120 computers/terminals are available on campus for general student use. Students can access the following: campus intranet, computer help desk, free student e-mail accounts, online (class) grades, online (class) registration, online (class) schedules, online payments, direct deposits. Campuswide network is available. 100% of college-owned or -operated housing units are wired for high-speed Internet access. Wireless service is available via entire campus.

STUDENT LIFE

Housing options: coed, men-only, women-only. Campus housing is university owned and leased by the school. Freshman applicants given priority for college housing.

Activities and organizations: drama/theater group, student-run newspaper, radio station, choral group, Student Government Association (SGA), Black and Latino Student Association (BLSA), The Monitor-Student Newspaper, Musical Theater Association (MTA), Club Mosaic-UACT (United Artists of Color Theater).

Athletics ***Intramural sports:*** soccer M(c)/W(c).

Campus security: 24-hour emergency response devices and patrols, student patrols, 24-hour security in residence halls.

Student services: health clinic, personal/psychological counseling.

COSTS & FINANCIAL AID

Costs (2014–15) ***Comprehensive fee:*** $42,636 includes full-time tuition ($26,352), mandatory fees ($1284), and room and board ($15,000). Full-time tuition and fees vary according to course load and program. Part-time tuition: $880 per credit hour. Part-time tuition and fees vary according to course load and program. ***Required fees:*** $467 per term part-time. ***College room only:*** $13,000. Room and board charges vary according to board plan. ***Payment plan:*** installment. ***Waivers:*** senior citizens and employees or children of employees.

Financial Aid Of all full-time matriculated undergraduates who enrolled in 2013, 1,230 applied for aid, 1,088 were judged to have need, 56 had their need fully met. 134 Federal Work-Study jobs (averaging $3124). In 2013, 109 non-need-based awards were made. ***Average percent of need met:*** 44. ***Average financial aid package:*** $14,624. ***Average need-based loan:*** $4224. ***Average need-based gift aid:*** $10,840. ***Average non-need-based aid:*** $7665. ***Average indebtedness upon graduation:*** $29,419.

APPLYING

Standardized Tests *Required:* SAT or ACT (for admission).

Options: electronic application, deferred entrance.

Application fee: $60.

Required: essay or personal statement, high school transcript, 2 letters of recommendation. ***Recommended:*** interview.

Application deadlines: rolling (freshmen), rolling (out-of-state freshmen), rolling (transfers).

Notification: continuous (freshmen), continuous (out-of-state freshmen), continuous (transfers).

CONTACT

Jim Rogers, Dean of Admissions, Marymount Manhattan College, 221 East 71st Street, New York, NY 10021. *Phone:* 212-517-0430. *Toll-free phone:* 800-627-9668. *E-mail:* jrogers@mmm.edu.

Medaille College

Buffalo, New York

http://www.medaille.edu/

- **Independent** comprehensive, founded 1875
- **Urban** 13-acre campus with easy access to Buffalo/Niagara
- **Endowment** $1.2 million
- **Coed** 1,803 undergraduate students, 91% full-time, 68% women, 32% men
- **Moderately difficult** entrance level, 54% of applicants were admitted

UNDERGRAD STUDENTS

1,637 full-time, 166 part-time. Students come from 5 states and territories; 3 other countries; 1% are from out of state; 21% Black or African American, non-Hispanic/Latino; 7% Hispanic/Latino; 2% Asian, non-Hispanic/Latino; 0.2% Native Hawaiian or other Pacific Islander, non-Hispanic/Latino; 0.7% American Indian or Alaska Native, non-Hispanic/Latino; 3% Two or more races, non-Hispanic/Latino; 6% Race/ethnicity unknown; 29% transferred in; 22% live on campus.

Freshmen

Admission: 1,505 applied, 817 admitted, 438 enrolled. ***Test scores:*** SAT critical reading scores over 500: 19%; SAT math scores over 500: 24%; SAT critical reading scores over 600: 3%; SAT math scores over 600: 6%; SAT critical reading scores over 700: 1%; SAT math scores over 700: 1%.

Retention: 64% of full-time freshmen returned.

FACULTY

Total: 294, 30% full-time.

Student/faculty ratio: 14:1.

ACADEMICS

Calendar: semesters (modular courses available for evening studies and weekend college program). *Degrees:* certificates, associate, bachelor's, master's, doctoral, and post-master's certificates.

Special study options: academic remediation for entering students, accelerated degree program, adult/continuing education programs, advanced placement credit, distance learning, double majors, honors programs, independent study, internships, off-campus study, part-time degree program, services for LD students, student-designed majors, study abroad, summer session for credit. ***ROTC:*** Army (c).

Unusual degree programs: 3-2 business administration; sport management.

Computers: 120 computers/terminals are available on campus for general student use. Students can access the following: campus intranet, computer help desk, free student e-mail accounts, online (class) grades, online (class) registration, online (class) schedules. Campuswide network is available. 100% of college-owned or -operated housing units are wired for high-speed Internet access. Wireless service is available via entire campus.

STUDENT LIFE

Housing options: coed, men-only, women-only, special housing for students with disabilities. Campus housing is university owned.

Activities and organizations: drama/theater group, student-run newspaper, radio and television station, student government, Club Green, Dance Team, WMCB The Lizard (college radio station), ice hockey club.

Athletics Member NCAA. All Division III. ***Intercollegiate sports:*** baseball M, basketball M/W, bowling W, cross-country running M/W, golf M, lacrosse M/W, soccer M/W, softball W, volleyball M/W. ***Intramural sports:*** basketball M/W, soccer M/W, softball M/W, table tennis M/W, tennis M/W, volleyball M/W, weight lifting M/W.

Campus security: 24-hour emergency response devices and patrols, late-night transport/escort service, controlled dormitory access.

Student services: health clinic, personal/psychological counseling.

COSTS & FINANCIAL AID

Costs (2014–15) ***Comprehensive fee:*** $34,502 includes full-time tuition ($25,002) and room and board ($9500). Full-time tuition and fees vary according to location. Part-time tuition: $881 per credit hour. Part-time tuition and fees vary according to course load. ***Room and board:*** Room and board charges vary according to board plan and housing facility. ***Payment plan:*** installment. ***Waivers:*** adult students, senior citizens, and employees or children of employees.

Financial Aid Of all full-time matriculated undergraduates who enrolled in 2012, 1,551 applied for aid, 1,496 were judged to have need, 425 had their need fully met. In 2012, 46 non-need-based awards were made. ***Average percent of need met:*** 38. ***Average financial aid package:*** $11,000. ***Average need-based loan:*** $9129. ***Average need-based gift aid:*** $10,908. ***Average non-need-based aid:*** $7622.

APPLYING

Standardized Tests *Required:* SAT or ACT (for admission). *Recommended:* SAT (for admission).

Options: electronic application, early admission, deferred entrance.

Application fee: $25.

Required: high school transcript, interview. ***Required for some:*** essay or personal statement, 2.5 high school GPA for veterinary technology and elementary teacher education majors. ***Recommended:*** essay or personal statement, minimum 2.0 GPA, 1 letter of recommendation.

Application deadlines: 8/1 (freshmen), rolling (transfers).

Notification: continuous (freshmen), continuous (transfers).

CONTACT

Karen McGrath, Vice President for Enrollment Management and Undergraduate Admissions, Medaille College, Office of Admissions, Buffalo, NY 14214. *Phone:* 716-880-2200. *Toll-free phone:* 800-292-1582. *Fax:* 716-880-2007. *E-mail:* admissionsug@medaille.edu.

Medgar Evers College of the City University of New York

Brooklyn, New York

http://www.mec.cuny.edu/

- **State and locally supported** 4-year, founded 1969, part of City University of New York System
- **Urban** 8-acre campus
- **Endowment** $515,142
- **Coed** 6,701 undergraduate students, 65% full-time, 71% women, 29% men
- **Noncompetitive** entrance level, 91% of applicants were admitted

UNDERGRAD STUDENTS

4,324 full-time, 2,377 part-time. Students come from 7 states and territories; 77 other countries; 1% are from out of state; 85% Black or African American, non-Hispanic/Latino; 11% Hispanic/Latino; 2% Asian, non-Hispanic/Latino; 0.8% American Indian or Alaska Native, non-Hispanic/Latino; 0.5% international; 8% transferred in.

Freshmen

Admission: 9,573 applied, 8,737 admitted, 1,100 enrolled. ***Test scores:*** SAT critical reading scores over 500: 8%; SAT math scores over 500: 7%; SAT writing scores over 500: 5%.

FACULTY

Total: 490, 37% full-time, 42% with terminal degrees.

Student/faculty ratio: 17:1.

ACADEMICS

Calendar: semesters. *Degrees:* certificates, associate, and bachelor's.

Special study options: academic remediation for entering students, adult/continuing education programs, advanced placement credit, cooperative education, double majors, English as a second language, external degree program, honors programs, independent study, internships, off-campus study, part-time degree program, services for LD students, study abroad, summer session for credit.

Computers: 120 computers/terminals are available on campus for general student use. Students can access the following: free student e-mail accounts, online (class) grades, online (class) registration, online (class) schedules. Campuswide network is available. Wireless service is available via entire campus.

STUDENT LIFE

Housing options: college housing not available.

Activities and organizations: drama/theater group, student-run newspaper, radio and television station, choral group, American Marketing Association, Drama Students Association, Rising Stars, Medgar Evers College Society of Public Administrators, National Society of Black Accountants.

Athletics Member NCAA. All Division III. ***Intercollegiate sports:*** basketball M/W, cross-country running M/W, soccer M/W, tennis W, track and field M/W, volleyball M/W. ***Intramural sports:*** basketball M/W, tennis W.

Campus security: 24-hour patrols.

Student services: women's center, legal services.

COSTS & FINANCIAL AID

Costs (2015–16) ***Tuition:*** state resident $6030 full-time, $260 per credit part-time; nonresident $16,050 full-time, $535 per credit part-time. Full-time tuition and fees vary according to course load. Part-time tuition and fees vary according to course load. ***Required fees:*** $302 full-time, $101 per term part-time. ***Payment plans:*** installment, deferred payment.

Financial Aid Of all full-time matriculated undergraduates who enrolled in 2013, 3,741 were judged to have need. ***Average need-based loan:*** $3378. ***Average need-based gift aid:*** $8333.

APPLYING

Standardized Tests *Recommended:* SAT and SAT Subject Tests or ACT (for admission).

Options: electronic application, deferred entrance.

Application fee: $65.

Required: high school transcript.

Application deadlines: rolling (freshmen), rolling (transfers).

Notification: continuous (freshmen), continuous (transfers).

CONTACT

Dr. Shannon Clarke-Anderson, Director of Admissions, Medgar Evers College of the City University of New York, 1650 Bedford Avenue, Brooklyn, NY 11225. *Phone:* 718-270-5143. *Fax:* 718-270-6411. *E-mail:* shannon@mec.cuny.edu.

★ Mercy College

Dobbs Ferry, New York

http://www.mercy.edu/

- **Independent** comprehensive, founded 1951
- **Suburban** 66-acre campus with easy access to New York City
- **Endowment** $147.8 million
- **Coed** 7,939 undergraduate students, 67% full-time, 69% women, 31% men
- **Moderately difficult** entrance level, 72% of applicants were admitted

UNDERGRAD STUDENTS

5,289 full-time, 2,650 part-time. Students come from 36 states and territories; 37 other countries; 7% are from out of state; 24% Black or African American, non-Hispanic/Latino; 32% Hispanic/Latino; 4% Asian, non-Hispanic/Latino; 0.2% Native Hawaiian or other Pacific Islander, non-Hispanic/Latino; 0.3% American Indian or Alaska Native, non-Hispanic/Latino; 2% Two or more races, non-Hispanic/Latino; 5% Race/ethnicity unknown; 1% international; 11% transferred in; 8% live on campus.

Freshmen

Admission: 5,728 applied, 4,118 admitted, 747 enrolled. ***Average high school GPA:*** 2.99.

Retention: 66% of full-time freshmen returned.

FACULTY

Total: 1,037, 19% full-time, 16% with terminal degrees.

Student/faculty ratio: 19:1.

ACADEMICS

Calendar: semesters. *Degrees:* certificates, associate, bachelor's, master's, doctoral, and postbachelor's certificates.

Special study options: accelerated degree program, adult/continuing education programs, advanced placement credit, cooperative education, distance learning, double majors, honors programs, independent study, internships, off-campus study, part-time degree program, services for LD students, study abroad, summer session for credit. ***ROTC:*** Army (c), Air Force (c).

Unusual degree programs: 3-2 business administration with BS/MS Dual Degree in Public Accounting; BS/MBA Dual Degree in Business Administration; Several B.S./M.S. Dual Degrees available in Education programs; B.S./M.S. Dual Degree in Cybersecurity.

Computers: 972 computers/terminals and 300 ports are available on campus for general student use. Students can access the following: campus intranet, computer help desk, free student e-mail accounts, online (class) grades, online (class) registration, online (class) schedules. Campuswide network is available. 100% of college-owned or -operated housing units are wired for high-speed Internet access. Wireless service is available via entire campus.

STUDENT LIFE

Housing options: coed, special housing for students with disabilities. Campus housing is university owned and leased by the school. Freshman applicants given priority for college housing.

A ★ indicates that the school has detailed information with a Premium Profile on Petersons.com.

Activities and organizations: student-run newspaper, Model United Nations, Honors Club and 17 National Honor Societies, Mercy Gives Back, Maverick Society, ROTARACT Club for Community Volunteer Service.

Athletics Member NCAA. All Division II. ***Intercollegiate sports:*** baseball M(s), basketball M(s)/W(s), field hockey W(s), lacrosse M(s)/W(s), soccer M(s)/W(s), softball W(s), volleyball W(s). ***Intramural sports:*** baseball M, basketball M/W, softball W.

Campus security: 24-hour emergency response devices and patrols, late-night transport/escort service, controlled dormitory access.

Student services: health clinic, personal/psychological counseling.

COSTS & FINANCIAL AID

Costs (2014–15) ***Comprehensive fee:*** $30,456 includes full-time tuition ($17,166), mandatory fees ($600), and room and board ($12,690). Full-time tuition and fees vary according to course load. Part-time tuition: $722 per credit. Part-time tuition and fees vary according to course load. ***Required fees:*** $150 per term part-time. ***College room only:*** $8590. Room and board charges vary according to board plan. ***Payment plan:*** installment. ***Waivers:*** employees or children of employees.

Financial Aid Of all full-time matriculated undergraduates who enrolled in 2013, 5,094 applied for aid, 4,856 were judged to have need, 116 had their need fully met. 216 Federal Work-Study jobs (averaging $2025). In 2013, 91 non-need-based awards were made. ***Average percent of need met:*** 55. ***Average financial aid package:*** $13,096. ***Average need-based loan:*** $4062. ***Average need-based gift aid:*** $9212. ***Average non-need-based aid:*** $3889. ***Average indebtedness upon graduation:*** $17,399.

APPLYING

Options: electronic application, early action, deferred entrance.

Application fee: $40.

Required: high school transcript, minimum 3.0 GPA, 1 letter of recommendation. ***Required for some:*** essay or personal statement, interview. ***Recommended:*** interview.

Application deadlines: rolling (freshmen), rolling (out-of-state freshmen), rolling (transfers), 12/1 (early action).

Notification: continuous (freshmen), continuous (out-of-state freshmen), continuous (transfers), 1/2 (early action).

CONTACT

Mrs. Tara Fay-Reilly, Senior Director of Admissions, Mercy College, 555 Broadway, Dobbs Ferry, NY 10522-1189. *Phone:* 877-637-2946. *Toll-free phone:* 877-637-2946 (in-state); 877-MERCY-GO (out-of-state). *Fax:* 914-674-7382. *E-mail:* admissions@mercy.edu.

Mesivta of Eastern Parkway–Yeshiva Zichron Meilech

Brooklyn, New York

- **Independent Jewish** comprehensive, founded 1947
- **Urban** 1-acre campus with easy access to New York City
- **Men only**
- **Moderately difficult** entrance level

ACADEMICS

Calendar: semesters. *Degrees:* bachelor's and master's.

APPLYING

Required: high school transcript, 1 letter of recommendation, interview, Orthodox Jewish commitment.

CONTACT

Mesivta of Eastern Parkway–Yeshiva Zichron Meilech, 510 Dahill Road, Brooklyn, NY 11218-5559. *Phone:* 718-438-1002.

Metropolitan College of New York

New York, New York

http://www.metropolitan.edu/

- **Independent** comprehensive, founded 1964
- **Urban** campus
- **Coed** 897 undergraduate students, 90% full-time, 72% women, 28% men
- **Moderately difficult** entrance level, 53% of applicants were admitted

UNDERGRAD STUDENTS

806 full-time, 91 part-time. 3% are from out of state; 60% Black or African American, non-Hispanic/Latino; 20% Hispanic/Latino; 2% Asian, non-Hispanic/Latino; 0.2% Native Hawaiian or other Pacific Islander, non-Hispanic/Latino; 1% American Indian or Alaska Native, non-Hispanic/Latino; 1% Two or more races, non-Hispanic/Latino; 8% Race/ethnicity unknown; 2% international; 15% transferred in.

Freshmen

Admission: 251 applied, 132 admitted, 109 enrolled.

Retention: 52% of full-time freshmen returned.

ACADEMICS

Calendar: 3 15-week semesters. *Degrees:* certificates, associate, bachelor's, and master's.

Special study options: academic remediation for entering students, accelerated degree program, adult/continuing education programs, cooperative education, distance learning, English as a second language, honors programs, independent study, internships, part-time degree program, services for LD students, study abroad, summer session for credit.

Computers: 150 computers/terminals are available on campus for general student use. Students can access the following: free student e-mail accounts, online (class) grades, online (class) registration, online (class) schedules. Campuswide network is available. Wireless service is available via entire campus.

STUDENT LIFE

Housing options: college housing not available.

Activities and organizations: student-run newspaper, student government, student newsletter, Networking Club, yearbook committee.

Campus security: 24-hour patrols.

Student services: personal/psychological counseling.

COSTS & FINANCIAL AID

Costs (2015–16) ***Tuition:*** $17,490 full-time, $583 per credit part-time. Full-time tuition and fees vary according to degree level and program. Part-time tuition and fees vary according to degree level and program. No tuition increase for student's term of enrollment. ***Required fees:*** $270 full-time. ***Payment plans:*** installment, deferred payment. ***Waivers:*** employees or children of employees.

Financial Aid Of all full-time matriculated undergraduates who enrolled in 2000, 1,066 applied for aid, 1,062 were judged to have need. 52 Federal Work-Study jobs (averaging $1969). 30 state and other part-time jobs (averaging $1920). ***Average financial aid package:*** $6337. ***Average need-based loan:*** $3377. ***Average need-based gift aid:*** $3650. ***Average indebtedness upon graduation:*** $20,130.

APPLYING

Standardized Tests *Required for some:* ACCUPLACER. *Recommended:* SAT or ACT (for admission).

Options: electronic application, deferred entrance.

Application fee: $30.

Required: high school transcript, 2 letters of recommendation, interview. ***Recommended:*** essay or personal statement, minimum 3.0 GPA.

Application deadlines: 9/9 (freshmen), rolling (transfers).

Notification: continuous (freshmen), continuous (transfers).

CONTACT

Metropolitan College of New York, 431 Canal Street, New York, NY 10013. *Phone:* 212-343-1234 Ext. 2700. *Toll-free phone:* 800-33-THINK Ext. 5001. *Fax:* 212-343-8470.

★ Molloy College

Rockville Centre, New York

http://www.molloy.edu/

- **Independent** comprehensive, founded 1955
- **Suburban** 30-acre campus with easy access to New York City
- **Endowment** $33.2 million
- **Coed** 3,336 undergraduate students, 80% full-time, 75% women, 25% men
- **Moderately difficult** entrance level, 75% of applicants were admitted

UNDERGRAD STUDENTS
2,679 full-time, 657 part-time. Students come from 20 states and territories; 9 other countries; 2% are from out of state; 12% Black or African American, non-Hispanic/Latino; 14% Hispanic/Latino; 7% Asian, non-Hispanic/Latino; 0.5% Native Hawaiian or other Pacific Islander, non-Hispanic/Latino; 0.3% American Indian or Alaska Native, non-Hispanic/Latino; 0.9% Two or more races, non-Hispanic/Latino; 1% Race/ethnicity unknown; 0.2% international; 12% transferred in; 8% live on campus.

Freshmen
Admission: 3,277 applied, 2,471 admitted, 492 enrolled. ***Average high school GPA:*** 3. ***Test scores:*** SAT critical reading scores over 500: 71%; SAT math scores over 500: 74%; SAT writing scores over 500: 61%; ACT scores over 18: 98%; SAT critical reading scores over 600: 13%; SAT math scores over 600: 21%; SAT writing scores over 600: 16%; ACT scores over 24: 52%; SAT critical reading scores over 700: 2%; SAT math scores over 700: 2%; SAT writing scores over 700: 1%; ACT scores over 30: 4%.

Retention: 90% of full-time freshmen returned.

FACULTY
Total: 686, 27% full-time, 33% with terminal degrees.

Student/faculty ratio: 10:1.

ACADEMICS
Calendar: 4-1-4. *Degrees:* certificates, associate, bachelor's, master's, doctoral, and post-master's certificates.

Special study options: academic remediation for entering students, accelerated degree program, adult/continuing education programs, advanced placement credit, double majors, English as a second language, honors programs, independent study, internships, part-time degree program, services for LD students, student-designed majors, study abroad, summer session for credit. ***ROTC:*** Army (c), Navy (c).

Computers: 691 computers/terminals are available on campus for general student use. Students can access the following: computer help desk, free student e-mail accounts, online (class) grades, online (class) registration, online (class) schedules. Campuswide network is available. 100% of college-owned or -operated housing units are wired for high-speed Internet access. Wireless service is available via entire campus.

STUDENT LIFE
Housing options: coed. Campus housing is university owned. Freshman applicants given priority for college housing.

Activities and organizations: drama/theater group, student-run newspaper, choral group, Molloy Nursing Student Association, Men's Rugby, Women's Rugby, National Student Speech Language and Hearing Association, Molloy Performing Arts Club.

Athletics Member NCAA. All Division II. ***Intercollegiate sports:*** baseball M(s), basketball M(s)/W(s), cross-country running M(s)/W(s), lacrosse M(s)/W(s), soccer M(s)/W(s), softball W(s), tennis W(s), track and field M(s)/W(s), volleyball W(s). ***Intramural sports:*** cheerleading M(c)/W(c), equestrian sports W(c), rugby M(c)/W(c), ultimate Frisbee M(c)/W(c).

Campus security: 24-hour emergency response devices and patrols, late-night transport/escort service, controlled dormitory access.

Student services: health clinic, personal/psychological counseling, women's center, legal services.

COSTS & FINANCIAL AID
Costs (2014–15) ***Comprehensive fee:*** $40,440 includes full-time tuition ($25,800), mandatory fees ($1050), and room and board ($13,590). Full-time tuition and fees vary according to degree level. Part-time tuition: $850 per credit hour. Part-time tuition and fees vary according to degree level. ***Room and board:*** Room and board charges vary according to board plan. ***Payment plans:*** installment, deferred payment. ***Waivers:*** senior citizens and employees or children of employees.

Financial Aid Of all full-time matriculated undergraduates who enrolled in 2013, 2,473 applied for aid, 2,255 were judged to have need, 181 had their need fully met. 174 Federal Work-Study jobs (averaging $1638). In 2013, 160 non-need-based awards were made. ***Average percent of need met:*** 45. ***Average financial aid package:*** $14,394. ***Average need-based loan:*** $4288. ***Average need-based gift aid:*** $11,180. ***Average non-need-based aid:*** $8947. ***Financial aid deadline:*** 5/1.

APPLYING
Standardized Tests *Required:* SAT or ACT (for admission).

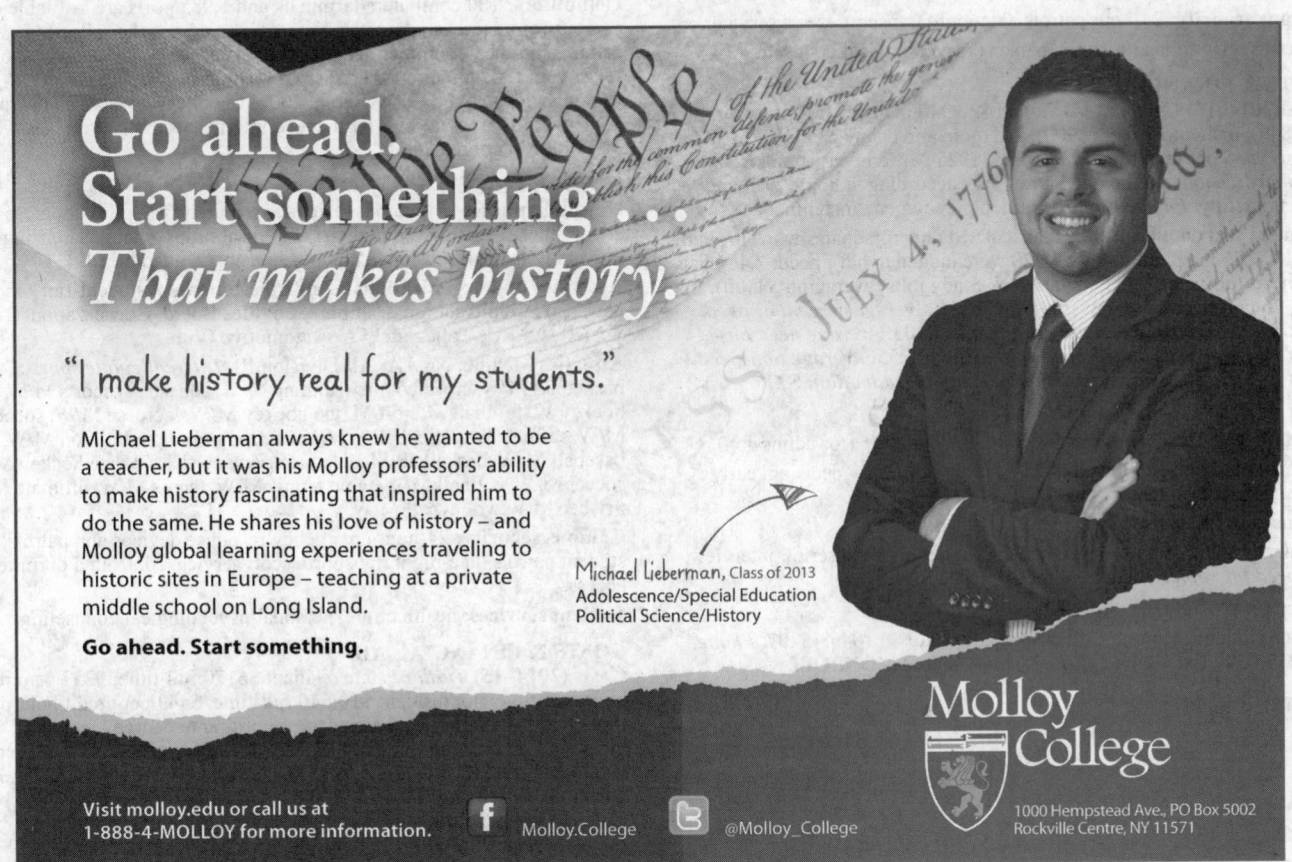

Options: electronic application, early action, deferred entrance.

Application fee: $40.

Required for some: essay or personal statement, high school transcript, 1 letter of recommendation. ***Recommended:*** interview.

Application deadlines: rolling (freshmen), rolling (transfers), 12/1 (early action).

Notification: continuous (freshmen), continuous (transfers), 12/15 (early action).

CONTACT

Ms. Marguerite Lane, Dean of Admissions, Molloy College, 1000 Hempstead Avenue, PO Box 5002, Rockville Centre, NY 11571-5002. *Phone:* 516-323-4000. *Toll-free phone:* 888-4MOLLOY. *E-mail:* admissions@molloy.edu.

See previous page for display ad and page 1530 for the College Close-Up.

Monroe College

Bronx, New York

http://www.monroecollege.edu/

- **Proprietary** comprehensive, founded 1933
- **Urban** campus
- **Coed**
- **Moderately difficult** entrance level

FACULTY

Student/faculty ratio: 15:1.

ACADEMICS

Calendar: trimesters. *Degrees:* certificates, associate, bachelor's, and master's.

STUDENT LIFE

Housing options: coed. Campus housing is university owned and leased by the school. Freshman applicants given priority for college housing.

Activities and organizations: drama/theater group, choral group, Students in Free Enterprise (SIFE), Creative Campus Club, Multicultural Student Association, Criminal Justice Club, Poetry is Truth.

Athletics Member NJCAA.

Campus security: 24-hour patrols, late-night transport/escort service.

Student services: health clinic, personal/psychological counseling.

COSTS & FINANCIAL AID

Costs (2014–15) ***Comprehensive fee:*** $22,940 includes full-time tuition ($12,840), mandatory fees ($900), and room and board ($9200). Part-time tuition: $535 per credit. ***Required fees:*** $225 per term part-time. ***Room and board:*** Room and board charges vary according to board plan and housing facility. ***Payment plans:*** tuition prepayment, installment.

Financial Aid Of all full-time matriculated undergraduates who enrolled in 2013, 4,756 applied for aid, 4,620 were judged to have need, 2,464 had their need fully met. 200 Federal Work-Study jobs (averaging $3500). In 2013, 26 non-need-based awards were made. ***Average percent of need met:*** 53. ***Average financial aid package:*** $14,103. ***Average need-based loan:*** $4713. ***Average need-based gift aid:*** $10,255. ***Average non-need-based aid:*** $3858. ***Average indebtedness upon graduation:*** $27,655.

APPLYING

Standardized Tests *Required for some:* SAT or ACT (for admission).

Options: electronic application, early admission, early decision, early action, deferred entrance.

Application fee: $35.

Required: essay or personal statement, high school transcript, interview. ***Required for some:*** 2 letters of recommendation.

CONTACT

Monroe College, Monroe College Way, Bronx, NY 10468-5407. *Phone:* 718-933-6700 Ext. 8246. *Toll-free phone:* 800-55MONROE.

Morrisville State College

Morrisville, New York

http://www.morrisville.edu/

- **State-supported** 4-year, founded 1908, part of State University of New York System
- **Rural** 185-acre campus with easy access to Syracuse
- **Coed** 2,911 undergraduate students, 86% full-time, 48% women, 52% men
- **Moderately difficult** entrance level, 56% of applicants were admitted

UNDERGRAD STUDENTS

2,505 full-time, 406 part-time. Students come from 22 states and territories; 11 other countries; 5% are from out of state; 18% Black or African American, non-Hispanic/Latino; 7% Hispanic/Latino; 0.8% Asian, non-Hispanic/Latino; 0.7% American Indian or Alaska Native, non-Hispanic/Latino; 2% Two or more races, non-Hispanic/Latino; 2% Race/ethnicity unknown; 0.8% international; 7% transferred in; 53% live on campus.

Freshmen

Admission: 4,088 applied, 2,297 admitted, 779 enrolled. ***Test scores:*** SAT critical reading scores over 500: 29%; SAT math scores over 500: 34%; ACT scores over 18: 89%; SAT critical reading scores over 600: 5%; SAT math scores over 600: 2%; ACT scores over 24: 27%; SAT math scores over 700: 1%.

Retention: 79% of full-time freshmen returned.

FACULTY

Total: 261, 55% full-time, 23% with terminal degrees.

Student/faculty ratio: 11:1.

ACADEMICS

Calendar: semesters. *Degrees:* certificates, associate, and bachelor's.

Special study options: academic remediation for entering students, advanced placement credit, cooperative education, distance learning, double majors, independent study, internships, off-campus study, part-time degree program, services for LD students, student-designed majors, study abroad, summer session for credit. ***ROTC:*** Army (c), Air Force (c).

Computers: 100 computers/terminals and 1,985 ports are available on campus for general student use. Students can access the following: campus intranet, computer help desk, free student e-mail accounts, online (class) grades, online (class) registration, online (class) schedules. Campuswide network is available. 100% of college-owned or -operated housing units are wired for high-speed Internet access. Wireless service is available via entire campus.

STUDENT LIFE

Housing options: on-campus residence required through sophomore year; coed, special housing for students with disabilities. Campus housing is university owned. Freshman campus housing is guaranteed.

Activities and organizations: drama/theater group, student-run newspaper, radio station, Campus Activities Board, Conservation Tri Society, CASU, CollegiateFFA, Automotive Club.

Athletics Member NCAA. All Division III. ***Intercollegiate sports:*** basketball M/W, cross-country running M/W, equestrian sports M/W, field hockey W, football M, golf M, ice hockey M/W, lacrosse M/W, soccer M/W, softball W, volleyball W. ***Intramural sports:*** badminton M/W, baseball M/W, basketball M/W, equestrian sports M/W, ice hockey M/W, soccer M/W, softball M/W, table tennis M/W, tennis M/W, ultimate Frisbee M/W, volleyball M/W.

Campus security: 24-hour emergency response devices and patrols, student patrols, late-night transport/escort service, controlled dormitory access.

Student services: health clinic, personal/psychological counseling.

COSTS & FINANCIAL AID

Costs (2014–15) ***Tuition:*** state resident $6170 full-time, $257 per credit hour part-time; nonresident $10,640 full-time, $443 per credit hour part-time. Full-time tuition and fees vary according to degree level and location. Part-time tuition and fees vary according to course load, degree level, and location. ***Required fees:*** $1472 full-time, $61 per credit hour part-time. ***Room and board:*** $12,858; room only: $7868. Room and board charges vary according to board plan, housing facility, and location. ***Payment plans:*** installment, deferred payment. ***Waivers:*** minority students, children of alumni, senior citizens, and employees or children of employees.

Financial Aid Of all full-time matriculated undergraduates who enrolled in 2014, 2,532 applied for aid, 2,311 were judged to have need, 8 had their need fully met. In 2014, 172 non-need-based awards were made. ***Average percent of need met:*** 52. ***Average financial aid package:*** $9641. ***Average need-based loan:*** $3935. ***Average need-based gift aid:*** $6683. ***Average non-need-based aid:*** $1531. ***Average indebtedness upon graduation:*** $29,023.

APPLYING

Standardized Tests *Required for some:* SAT or ACT (for admission). *Recommended:* SAT or ACT (for admission).

Options: electronic application, deferred entrance.

Application fee: $50.

Required: essay or personal statement, high school transcript. ***Recommended:*** interview.

Application deadlines: rolling (freshmen), rolling (out-of-state freshmen), rolling (transfers).

Notification: continuous (freshmen), continuous (out-of-state freshmen), continuous (transfers).

CONTACT

Ms. Lindsey Graham, Senior Admissions Advisor, Morrisville State College, PO Box 901, Morrisville, NY 13408. *Phone:* 315-684-6046. *Toll-free phone:* 800-258-0111. *Fax:* 315-684-6427.

Mount Saint Mary College

Newburgh, New York

http://www.msmc.edu/

- **Independent** comprehensive, founded 1960
- **Suburban** 86-acre campus with easy access to New York City
- **Endowment** $66.1 million
- **Coed** 2,123 undergraduate students, 81% full-time, 71% women, 29% men
- **Moderately difficult** entrance level, 89% of applicants were admitted

UNDERGRAD STUDENTS

1,712 full-time, 411 part-time. Students come from 17 states and territories; 11% are from out of state; 8% Black or African American, non-Hispanic/Latino; 13% Hispanic/Latino; 2% Asian, non-Hispanic/Latino; 0.3% Native Hawaiian or other Pacific Islander, non-Hispanic/Latino; 0.8% American Indian or Alaska Native, non-Hispanic/Latino; 1% Two or more races, non-Hispanic/Latino; 12% Race/ethnicity unknown; 9% transferred in; 46% live on campus.

Freshmen

Admission: 3,742 applied, 3,316 admitted, 413 enrolled. ***Average high school GPA:*** 3.2. ***Test scores:*** SAT critical reading scores over 500: 46%; SAT math scores over 500: 58%; SAT writing scores over 500: 48%; ACT scores over 18: 93%; SAT critical reading scores over 600: 9%; SAT math scores over 600: 15%; SAT writing scores over 600: 9%; ACT scores over 24: 26%; SAT critical reading scores over 700: 1%; SAT writing scores over 700: 1%; ACT scores over 30: 1%.

Retention: 74% of full-time freshmen returned.

FACULTY

Total: 258, 32% full-time, 40% with terminal degrees.

Student/faculty ratio: 14:1.

ACADEMICS

Calendar: semesters. *Degrees:* certificates, bachelor's, master's, and post-master's certificates.

Special study options: academic remediation for entering students, accelerated degree program, adult/continuing education programs, advanced placement credit, cooperative education, distance learning, double majors, freshman honors college, honors programs, independent study, internships, off-campus study, part-time degree program, services for LD students, student-designed majors, study abroad, summer session for credit. ***ROTC:*** Army (c).

Unusual degree programs: 3-2 business administration with Bachelor of Science in Accounting/Master of Business Administration; social work with Fordham University; Publishing, Counseling with Pace University.

Computers: 470 computers/terminals are available on campus for general student use. Students can access the following: campus intranet, computer help desk, free student e-mail accounts, online (class) grades, online (class) registration, online (class) schedules, Intranet. Campuswide network is available. 100% of college-owned or -operated housing units are wired for high-speed Internet access. Wireless service is available via entire campus.

STUDENT LIFE

Housing options: on-campus residence required through junior year; coed, men-only, women-only, special housing for students with disabilities. Campus housing is university owned. Freshman campus housing is guaranteed.

Activities and organizations: drama/theater group, student-run newspaper, radio station, choral group, Nursing Student Union, Colleges Against Cancer, Big Brothers/Big Sisters, Dance Team, Habitat for Humanity.

Athletics Member NCAA. All Division III. ***Intercollegiate sports:*** baseball M, basketball M/W, cheerleading W, cross-country running M/W, golf M, lacrosse M/W, soccer M/W, softball W, swimming and diving M/W, tennis M/W, track and field M/W, volleyball W. ***Intramural sports:*** basketball M/W, bowling M/W, football M, soccer M/W, softball M/W, swimming and diving M/W, table tennis M/W, volleyball M/W.

Campus security: 24-hour emergency response devices and patrols, student patrols, late-night transport/escort service, controlled dormitory access, monitored surveillance cameras in all residence halls.

Student services: health clinic, personal/psychological counseling.

COSTS & FINANCIAL AID

Costs (2014–15) ***Comprehensive fee:*** $40,868 includes full-time tuition ($26,312), mandatory fees ($1000), and room and board ($13,556). Full-time tuition and fees vary according to class time, location, and program. Part-time tuition: $877 per credit. Part-time tuition and fees vary according to class time, location, and program. ***Required fees:*** $80 per term part-time. ***College room only:*** $7852. Room and board charges vary according to board plan and housing facility. ***Payment plan:*** installment. ***Waivers:*** employees or children of employees.

Financial Aid Of all full-time matriculated undergraduates who enrolled in 2014, 1,577 applied for aid, 1,375 were judged to have need, 246 had their need fully met. 316 Federal Work-Study jobs (averaging $1434). In 2014, 207 non-need-based awards were made. ***Average percent of need met:*** 60. ***Average financial aid package:*** $17,529. ***Average need-based loan:*** $4388. ***Average need-based gift aid:*** $13,517. ***Average non-need-based aid:*** $9423. ***Average indebtedness upon graduation:*** $31,764. ***Financial aid deadline:*** 3/1.

APPLYING

Standardized Tests *Required:* SAT or ACT (for admission).

Options: electronic application, early admission, deferred entrance.

Application fee: $45.

Required: essay or personal statement, high school transcript. ***Required for some:*** 2 letters of recommendation, interview. ***Recommended:*** minimum 3.0 GPA, 2 letters of recommendation.

Notification: continuous (freshmen).

CONTACT

Ms. Nancy Scaffidi-Clark, Director of Admissions, Mount Saint Mary College, 330 Powell Avenue, Newburgh, NY 12550-3494. *Phone:* 845-569-3254. *Toll-free phone:* 888-937-6762. *Fax:* 845-562-6762. *E-mail:* admissions@msmc.edu.

Nazareth College of Rochester

Rochester, New York

http://www.naz.edu/

- **Independent** comprehensive, founded 1924
- **Suburban** 150-acre campus
- **Endowment** $67.8 million
- **Coed** 2,057 undergraduate students, 94% full-time, 71% women, 29% men
- **Moderately difficult** entrance level, 70% of applicants were admitted

UNDERGRAD STUDENTS
1,931 full-time, 126 part-time. Students come from 28 states and territories; 21 other countries; 8% are from out of state; 7% Black or African American, non-Hispanic/Latino; 4% Hispanic/Latino; 3% Asian, non-Hispanic/Latino; 0.4% American Indian or Alaska Native, non-Hispanic/Latino; 2% Two or more races, non-Hispanic/Latino; 9% Race/ethnicity unknown; 3% international; 7% transferred in; 53% live on campus.

Freshmen
Admission: 4,185 applied, 2,950 admitted, 476 enrolled. ***Average high school GPA:*** 3.4. ***Test scores:*** SAT critical reading scores over 500: 72%; SAT math scores over 500: 74%; SAT writing scores over 500: 60%; ACT scores over 18: 95%; SAT critical reading scores over 600: 23%; SAT math scores over 600: 26%; SAT writing scores over 600: 19%; ACT scores over 24: 62%; SAT critical reading scores over 700: 2%; SAT math scores over 700: 2%; SAT writing scores over 700: 2%; ACT scores over 30: 3%.

Retention: 84% of full-time freshmen returned.

FACULTY
Total: 475, 38% full-time, 47% with terminal degrees.

Student/faculty ratio: 9:1.

ACADEMICS
Calendar: semesters. *Degrees:* bachelor's, master's, doctoral, post-master's, and postbachelor's certificates.

Special study options: academic remediation for entering students, adult/continuing education programs, advanced placement credit, cooperative education, double majors, English as a second language, honors programs, independent study, internships, off-campus study, part-time degree program, services for LD students, study abroad, summer session for credit. ***ROTC:*** Army (c), Air Force (c).

Computers: 240 computers/terminals are available on campus for general student use. Students can access the following: computer help desk, free student e-mail accounts, online (class) grades, online (class) registration, online (class) schedules. Campuswide network is available. 100% of college-owned or -operated housing units are wired for high-speed Internet access. Wireless service is available via classrooms, computer centers, dorm rooms, libraries, student centers.

STUDENT LIFE
Housing options: on-campus residence required through sophomore year; coed, special housing for students with disabilities. Campus housing is university owned. Freshman campus housing is guaranteed.

Activities and organizations: drama/theater group, student-run newspaper, radio station, choral group, Student Activities Council, intramurals and recreation, Theater League, Center for Spirituality Council, NAZ Ultimate Frisbee.

Athletics Member NCAA. All Division III. ***Intercollegiate sports:*** basketball M/W, cross-country running M/W, equestrian sports M/W, field hockey W, golf M/W, ice hockey M, lacrosse M/W, soccer M/W, softball W, swimming and diving M/W, tennis M/W, track and field M/W, volleyball M/W. ***Intramural sports:*** basketball M/W, racquetball M/W, soccer M/W, ultimate Frisbee M/W, volleyball M/W.

Campus security: 24-hour emergency response devices and patrols, late-night transport/escort service, controlled dormitory access, alarm system, security beeper, lighted pathways.

Student services: health clinic, personal/psychological counseling, women's center.

COSTS & FINANCIAL AID
Costs (2014–15) ***Comprehensive fee:*** $43,160 includes full-time tuition ($29,244), mandatory fees ($1318), and room and board ($12,598). Full-time tuition and fees vary according to course load and program. Part-time tuition: $697 per credit. ***Required fees:*** $100 per term part-time. ***College room only:*** $6918. Room and board charges vary according to board plan and housing facility. ***Payment plan:*** installment. ***Waivers:*** minority students, children of alumni, and employees or children of employees.

Financial Aid Of all full-time matriculated undergraduates who enrolled in 2014, 1,726 applied for aid, 1,565 were judged to have need, 380 had their need fully met. 1,050 Federal Work-Study jobs (averaging $2123). In 2014, 344 non-need-based awards were made. ***Average percent of need met:*** 77. ***Average financial aid package:*** $24,940. ***Average need-based loan:*** $4640. ***Average need-based gift aid:*** $15,327. ***Average non-need-based aid:*** $15,594. ***Average indebtedness upon graduation:*** $35,396.

APPLYING
Standardized Tests *Required for some:* SAT or ACT (for admission).

Options: electronic application, early admission, early decision, deferred entrance.

Application fee: $45.

Required: essay or personal statement, high school transcript, 1 letter of recommendation. ***Required for some:*** audition/portfolio review. ***Recommended:*** interview.

Application deadlines: 2/1 (freshmen), rolling (transfers).

Early decision deadline: 11/15 (for plan 1), 1/15 (for plan 2).

Notification: continuous until 3/1 (freshmen), continuous (transfers), 12/15 (early decision plan 1), 2/1 (early decision plan 2).

CONTACT
Mr. Ian Mortimer, Vice President for Enrollment Management, Nazareth College of Rochester, 4245 East Avenue, Rochester, NY 14618-3790. *Phone:* 585-389-2830. *Toll-free phone:* 800-462-3944. *Fax:* 585-389-2826. *E-mail:* admissions@naz.edu.

★ The New School for Drama
New York, New York
http://www.newschool.edu/drama/

- **Independent** comprehensive, founded 2005, part of The New School
- **Urban** campus with easy access to Manhattan
- **Endowment** $214.0 million
- **Coed**

FACULTY
Student/faculty ratio: 10:1.

ACADEMICS
Degrees: bachelor's and master's.

STUDENT LIFE
Housing options: coed, special housing for students with disabilities. Campus housing is university owned and leased by the school.

Activities and organizations: drama/theater group, student-run newspaper, radio station, choral group, Film-makers United, Theatre Collective, New School Improv, Musical Theatre Organization, Collective Arts Club.

Campus security: 24-hour emergency response devices, controlled dormitory access, 24-hour security desk personnel.

Student services: health clinic, personal/psychological counseling.

FINANCIAL AID
Financial Aid ***Financial aid deadline:*** 3/1.

APPLYING
Standardized Tests *Required for some:* SAT or ACT (for admission).

Required: essay or personal statement, high school transcript, 2 letters of recommendation, interview, photograph, portfolio; short essay to be submitted via short essay to be submitted via Acceptd; audition; TOEFL, IELTS or PTE may be required for students whose first language is not English.

CONTACT
Ms. Sherri Barber, Admission Counselor, The New School for Drama, 151 Bank Street, Floor 1, Room 103, New York, NY 10014. *Phone:* 212-229-5859 Ext. 2613. *E-mail:* DramaBFA@NewSchool.edu.

See page 715 for display ad and page 1546 for the College Close-Up.

★ The New School for Jazz and Contemporary Music
New York, New York
http://www.newschool.edu/jazz/

- **Independent** 4-year, founded 1986, part of The New School
- **Urban** campus with easy access to Manhattan
- **Endowment** $214.0 million
- **Coed**

FACULTY
Student/faculty ratio: 1:1.

ACADEMICS
Calendar: semesters. *Degree:* bachelor's.

STUDENT LIFE
Housing options: coed, special housing for students with disabilities. Campus housing is university owned and leased by the school.

Activities and organizations: drama/theater group, student-run newspaper, radio station, choral group, Musical Theatre Organization, New Light Opera, Dream:In NY, Theatre Collective, BriCollab Art Initiative.

Campus security: 24-hour emergency response devices, controlled dormitory access, 24-hour desk attendants in residence halls.

Student services: health clinic, personal/psychological counseling.

FINANCIAL AID
Financial Aid Of all full-time matriculated undergraduates who enrolled in 2012, 124 applied for aid, 111 were judged to have need, 23 had their need fully met. In 2012, 7 non-need-based awards were made. ***Average percent of need met:*** 68. ***Average financial aid package:*** $18,138. ***Average need-based loan:*** $6971. ***Average need-based gift aid:*** $18,151. ***Average non-need-based aid:*** $17,985. ***Average indebtedness upon graduation:*** $15,680. ***Financial aid deadline:*** 3/1.

APPLYING
Required: essay or personal statement, high school transcript, 2 letters of recommendation, online application, $50 fee, official secondary school transcript, pre-screening recording with $25 submission fee (if applicable), audition.

CONTACT
Ms. Ashley Leach, Jazz Admission Counselor, The New School for Jazz and Contemporary Music, 55 West 13th Street, 5th Floor, New York, NY 10011. *Phone:* 212-229-5155 Ext. 4575. *Toll-free phone:* 800-292-3040. *Fax:* 212-229-8936. *E-mail:* jazzadm@newschool.edu.

See page 715 for display ad and page 1546 for the College Close-Up.

The New School for Public Engagement

New York, New York

http://www.newschool.edu/public-engagement/

- **Independent** comprehensive, founded 1919, part of The New School
- **Urban** campus with easy access to Manhattan
- **Endowment** $214.0 million
- **Coed**

FACULTY
Student/faculty ratio: 7:1.

ACADEMICS
Calendar: semesters. *Degrees:* certificates, bachelor's, master's, doctoral, and postbachelor's certificates.

STUDENT LIFE
Housing options: coed, special housing for students with disabilities. Campus housing is university owned and leased by the school.

Activities and organizations: drama/theater group, student-run newspaper, radio station, choral group, Sustainable Cities Club, Slow Food TNS, Students for Social Justice, Students of the African Diaspora, Active Minds.

Campus security: 24-hour emergency response devices, controlled dormitory access, trained security personnel in central buildings and 24-hour desk attendants in residence halls.

Student services: health clinic, personal/psychological counseling.

FINANCIAL AID
Financial Aid Of all full-time matriculated undergraduates who enrolled in 2012, 213 applied for aid, 202 were judged to have need, 16 had their need fully met. In 2012, 5 non-need-based awards were made. ***Average percent of need met:*** 62. ***Average financial aid package:*** $14,021. ***Average need-based loan:*** $8941. ***Average need-based gift aid:*** $12,074. ***Average non-need-based aid:*** $2490. ***Average indebtedness upon graduation:*** $13,526. ***Financial aid deadline:*** 3/1.

APPLYING
Standardized Tests *Required for some:* SAT or ACT (for admission).

Required: essay or personal statement, high school transcript, interview, online application; if fewer than 24 credits earned, high school transcript or GED required; 3 short essays discussing personal, academic and life experiences and goals; current resume; TOEFL, IELTS or PTE scores may be required for applicants whose first language is not English. ***Required for some:*** high school transcript, interview.

CONTACT
Mr. Matt Morgan, Assistant Director of Undergraduate Admissions, The New School for Public Engagement, 72 Fifth Avenue, Floor 2 Room 206A, New York, NY 10011. *Phone:* 212-229-5710 Ext. 2320. *Toll-free phone:* 800-292-3040. *Fax:* 212-627-2695. *E-mail:* nspeundergrad@newschool.edu.

See page 715 for display ad and page 1546 for the College Close-Up.

New York City College of Technology of the City University of New York

Brooklyn, New York

http://www.citytech.cuny.edu/

- **State and locally supported** 4-year, founded 1946, part of City University of New York System
- **Urban** campus with easy access to New York City
- **Endowment** $16.5 million
- **Coed** 17,374 undergraduate students, 61% full-time, 44% women, 56% men
- **Noncompetitive** entrance level

UNDERGRAD STUDENTS
10,587 full-time, 6,787 part-time. 3% are from out of state; 33% Black or African American, non-Hispanic/Latino; 28% Hispanic/Latino; 20% Asian, non-Hispanic/Latino; 0.4% American Indian or Alaska Native, non-Hispanic/Latino; 4% international.

Freshmen
Admission: 3,325 enrolled. ***Test scores:*** SAT critical reading scores over 500: 12%; SAT math scores over 500: 7%; SAT critical reading scores over 600: 1%.

Retention: 75% of full-time freshmen returned.

FACULTY
Total: 1,493, 29% full-time, 39% with terminal degrees.
Student/faculty ratio: 16:1.

ACADEMICS
Calendar: semesters. *Degrees:* certificates, associate, and bachelor's.

Special study options: academic remediation for entering students, accelerated degree program, adult/continuing education programs, advanced placement credit, distance learning, English as a second language, freshman honors college, honors programs, independent study, internships, off-campus study, part-time degree program, services for LD students, student-designed majors, study abroad, summer session for credit.

Computers: Students can access the following: campus intranet, computer help desk, free student e-mail accounts, online (class) grades, online (class) registration, online (class) schedules. Campuswide network is available. Wireless service is available via entire campus.

STUDENT LIFE
Housing options: college housing not available.

Activities and organizations: drama/theater group, student-run newspaper, International Business Organization (IBO), NYCCT - Mock Trial Club, Chess Club, Women in Islam, ASCE-Student Chapter of American Society of Civil Engineering.

Campus security: 24-hour emergency response devices and patrols.

Student services: health clinic, personal/psychological counseling, women's center.

COSTS & FINANCIAL AID
Costs (2015–16) ***Tuition:*** state resident $6330 full-time, $275 per credit part-time; nonresident $16,800 full-time, $560 per credit part-time. Full-time tuition and fees vary according to course load and program. Part-time

tuition and fees vary according to course load and program. ***Required fees:*** $360 full-time. ***Payment plan:*** installment. ***Waivers:*** employees or children of employees.

Financial Aid Of all full-time matriculated undergraduates who enrolled in 2012, 8,718 applied for aid, 8,272 were judged to have need, 350 had their need fully met. In 2012, 128 non-need-based awards were made. ***Average percent of need met:*** 57. ***Average financial aid package:*** $8867. ***Average need-based loan:*** $4267. ***Average need-based gift aid:*** $8356. ***Average non-need-based aid:*** $233.

APPLYING

Standardized Tests *Required for some:* SAT or ACT (for admission).

Options: electronic application, deferred entrance.

Application fee: $65.

Required: high school transcript.

Application deadlines: 2/1 (freshmen), 2/1 (transfers).

Notification: continuous until 2/1 (freshmen), 4/1 (transfers).

CONTACT

Alexis Chaconis, Director of Admissions, New York City College of Technology of the City University of New York, 300 Jay Street, Brooklyn, NY 11201-2983. *Phone:* 718-260-5500. *E-mail:* achaconis@citytech.cuny.edu.

New York Institute of Technology

Old Westbury, New York

http://www.nyit.edu/

- **Independent** university, founded 1955
- **Suburban** 215-acre campus with easy access to New York City
- **Endowment** $113.3 million
- **Coed** 4,303 undergraduate students, 87% full-time, 37% women, 63% men
- **Moderately difficult** entrance level, 64% of applicants were admitted

UNDERGRAD STUDENTS

3,727 full-time, 576 part-time. Students come from 32 states and territories; 83 other countries; 10% are from out of state; 7% Black or African American, non-Hispanic/Latino; 12% Hispanic/Latino; 13% Asian, non-Hispanic/Latino; 0.1% Native Hawaiian or other Pacific Islander, non-Hispanic/Latino; 0.3% American Indian or Alaska Native, non-Hispanic/Latino; 1% Two or more races, non-Hispanic/Latino; 28% Race/ethnicity unknown; 20% international; 9% transferred in; 21% live on campus.

Freshmen

Admission: 8,394 applied, 5,375 admitted, 712 enrolled. ***Average high school GPA:*** 3.3. ***Test scores:*** SAT critical reading scores over 500: 56%; SAT math scores over 500: 74%; ACT scores over 18: 95%; SAT critical reading scores over 600: 17%; SAT math scores over 600: 31%; ACT scores over 24: 48%; SAT critical reading scores over 700: 2%; SAT math scores over 700: 7%; ACT scores over 30: 7%.

Retention: 72% of full-time freshmen returned.

FACULTY

Total: 830, 35% full-time, 32% with terminal degrees.

Student/faculty ratio: 11:1.

ACADEMICS

Calendar: semesters. *Degrees:* certificates, associate, bachelor's, master's, doctoral, post-master's, and postbachelor's certificates.

Special study options: academic remediation for entering students, accelerated degree program, adult/continuing education programs, advanced placement credit, cooperative education, distance learning, double majors, English as a second language, honors programs, internships, off-campus study, part-time degree program, services for LD students, study abroad, summer session for credit. ***ROTC:*** Army (c), Air Force (c).

Unusual degree programs: 3-2 BS Life Sciences/DO Doctor of Osteopathic Medicine; BS Life Sciences/MS Occupational Therapy; BS Life Sciences/DPT Physical Therapy; BS Life Sciences/MS Physician Assistant Studies.

Computers: 1,250 computers/terminals are available on campus for general student use. Students can access the following: computer help desk, free student e-mail accounts, online (class) grades, online (class) registration, online (class) schedules. Campuswide network is available. 100% of college-owned or -operated housing units are wired for high-speed Internet access. Wireless service is available via entire campus.

STUDENT LIFE

Housing options: coed. Campus housing is university owned and leased by the school. Freshman campus housing is guaranteed.

Activities and organizations: drama/theater group, student-run newspaper, radio and television station, choral group, national fraternities, national sororities.

Athletics Member NCAA. All Division II except baseball (Division I). ***Intercollegiate sports:*** baseball M(s), basketball M(s)/W(s), cross-country running M(s)/W(s), lacrosse M(s), soccer M(s)/W(s), softball W(s), tennis M(s)/W(s), volleyball W(s). ***Intramural sports:*** basketball M/W, cheerleading M(c)/W(c), soccer M/W, softball W, tennis M/W, volleyball W.

Campus security: 24-hour emergency response devices and patrols, late-night transport/escort service, controlled dormitory access.

Student services: health clinic, personal/psychological counseling, women's center.

COSTS & FINANCIAL AID

Costs (2014–15) ***Comprehensive fee:*** $45,010 includes full-time tuition ($31,050), mandatory fees ($1130), and room and board ($12,830). Full-time tuition and fees vary according to program. Part-time tuition: $1050 per credit. Part-time tuition and fees vary according to course load and program. ***Required fees:*** $470 per term part-time. ***College room only:*** $8280. Room and board charges vary according to location. ***Payment plan:*** installment. ***Waivers:*** senior citizens and employees or children of employees.

Financial Aid Of all full-time matriculated undergraduates who enrolled in 2013, 3,363 applied for aid, 2,726 were judged to have need. In 2013, 438 non-need-based awards were made. ***Average financial aid package:*** $18,348. ***Average need-based loan:*** $4689. ***Average need-based gift aid:*** $6752. ***Average non-need-based aid:*** $11,290.

APPLYING

Standardized Tests *Required:* SAT or ACT (for admission).

Options: electronic application, early admission, early action, deferred entrance.

Application fee: $50.

Required: essay or personal statement, high school transcript, 2 letters of recommendation. ***Required for some:*** interview, Special program requirements apply for admission to programs in the School of Architecture and Design, School of Engineering and Computing Sciences, and School of Health Professions. ***Recommended:*** minimum 3.0 GPA.

Application deadlines: rolling (freshmen), rolling (out-of-state freshmen), rolling (transfers), 12/17 (early action).

Notification: continuous (freshmen), continuous (out-of-state freshmen), continuous (transfers), 1/17 (early action).

CONTACT

Ms. Karen Vahey, Dean, Admissions and Financial Aid, New York Institute of Technology, PO Box 8000, Northern Boulevard, Old Westbury, NY 11568. *Phone:* 516-686-7742. *Toll-free phone:* 800-345-NYIT. *Fax:* 516-686-7613. *E-mail:* admissions@nyit.edu.

New York School of Interior Design

New York, New York

http://www.nysid.edu/

- **Independent** comprehensive, founded 1916
- **Urban** 1-acre campus
- **Endowment** $3.1 million
- **Coed, primarily women** 415 undergraduate students, 35% full-time, 88% women, 12% men
- **Moderately difficult** entrance level, 46% of applicants were admitted

UNDERGRAD STUDENTS

145 full-time, 270 part-time. Students come from 24 states and territories; 28 other countries; 3% Black or African American, non-Hispanic/Latino; 8% Hispanic/Latino; 5% Asian, non-Hispanic/Latino; 2% Two or more

races, non-Hispanic/Latino; 25% Race/ethnicity unknown; 13% international; 4% live on campus.

Freshmen
Admission: 178 applied, 81 admitted, 21 enrolled.

FACULTY
Total: 109, 7% full-time, 61% with terminal degrees.

Student/faculty ratio: 5:1.

ACADEMICS
Calendar: semesters. *Degrees:* certificates, associate, bachelor's, and master's.

Special study options: adult/continuing education programs, advanced placement credit, English as a second language, external degree program, independent study, internships, part-time degree program, services for LD students, summer session for credit.

Computers: 135 computers/terminals are available on campus for general student use. Students can access the following: free student e-mail accounts, online (class) grades, online (class) registration, online (class) schedules. Campuswide network is available. Wireless service is available via classrooms, libraries.

STUDENT LIFE
Housing options: coed. Campus housing is leased by the school and is provided by a third party.

Activities and organizations: American Society of Interior Designers, Contract Club, Student Council.

Campus security: security during school hours.

COSTS & FINANCIAL AID
Costs (2015–16) ***Tuition:*** $30,195 full-time, $915 per credit part-time. Full-time tuition and fees vary according to course load. Part-time tuition and fees vary according to course load. ***Required fees:*** $595 full-time. ***Room only:*** $15,610. ***Payment plan:*** installment. ***Waivers:*** employees or children of employees.

Financial Aid Of all full-time matriculated undergraduates who enrolled in 2013, 92 applied for aid, 87 were judged to have need, 3 had their need fully met. 17 Federal Work-Study jobs (averaging $2444). In 2013, 8 non-need-based awards were made. ***Average percent of need met:*** 29. ***Average financial aid package:*** $10,155. ***Average need-based loan:*** $3970. ***Average need-based gift aid:*** $8332. ***Average non-need-based aid:*** $8000. ***Average indebtedness upon graduation:*** $33,146.

APPLYING
Standardized Tests *Required for some:* SAT or ACT (for admission).

Options: electronic application, deferred entrance.

Application fee: $60.

Required: essay or personal statement, high school transcript, minimum 2.8 GPA, 2 letters of recommendation, portfolio.

Application deadlines: 2/1 (freshmen), 2/1 (transfers).

Notification: 4/1 (freshmen), 4/1 (transfers).

CONTACT
Audrey Zahor, Admissions Associate, New York School of Interior Design, 170 East 70th Street, New York, NY 10021-5110. *Phone:* 212-472-1500 Ext. 204. *Toll-free phone:* 800-336-9743 Ext. 204. *Fax:* 212-472-1867. *E-mail:* admissions@nysid.edu.

New York University

New York, New York

http://www.nyu.edu/

- **Independent** university, founded 1831
- **Urban** campus with easy access to New York City
- **Endowment** $2.8 billion
- **Coed** 24,985 undergraduate students, 95% full-time, 57% women, 43% men
- **Very difficult** entrance level, 35% of applicants were admitted

UNDERGRAD STUDENTS
23,715 full-time, 1,270 part-time. Students come from 58 states and territories; 107 other countries; 64% are from out of state; 5% Black or African American, non-Hispanic/Latino; 11% Hispanic/Latino; 19% Asian, non-Hispanic/Latino; 0.1% Native Hawaiian or other Pacific Islander, non-Hispanic/Latino; 0.2% American Indian or Alaska Native, non-Hispanic/Latino; 4% Two or more races, non-Hispanic/Latino; 9% Race/ethnicity unknown; 15% international; 3% transferred in; 47% live on campus.

Freshmen
Admission: 50,804 applied, 18,010 admitted, 5,913 enrolled. ***Average high school GPA:*** 3.7. ***Test scores:*** SAT critical reading scores over 500: 99%; SAT math scores over 500: 99%; SAT writing scores over 500: 99%; ACT scores over 18: 100%; SAT critical reading scores over 600: 83%; SAT math scores over 600: 87%; SAT writing scores over 600: 86%; ACT scores over 24: 99%; SAT critical reading scores over 700: 30%; SAT math scores over 700: 45%; SAT writing scores over 700: 40%; ACT scores over 30: 60%.

Retention: 92% of full-time freshmen returned.

FACULTY
Total: 6,843, 42% full-time, 41% with terminal degrees.

Student/faculty ratio: 10:1.

ACADEMICS
Calendar: semesters. *Degrees:* certificates, associate, bachelor's, master's, doctoral, post-master's, and postbachelor's certificates.

Special study options: accelerated degree program, adult/continuing education programs, advanced placement credit, cooperative education, distance learning, double majors, English as a second language, honors programs, independent study, internships, off-campus study, part-time degree program, services for LD students, student-designed majors, study abroad, summer session for credit. ***ROTC:*** Army (c), Air Force (c).

Unusual degree programs: 3-2 engineering with School of Engineering and College of Arts and Science; nursing with College of Nursing.

Computers: 595 computers/terminals are available on campus for general student use. Students can access the following: computer help desk, free student e-mail accounts, online (class) grades, online (class) registration, online (class) schedules. Campuswide network is available. 100% of college-owned or -operated housing units are wired for high-speed Internet access. Wireless service is available via entire campus.

STUDENT LIFE
Housing options: coed, special housing for students with disabilities. Campus housing is university owned and leased by the school. Freshman campus housing is guaranteed.

Activities and organizations: drama/theater group, student-run newspaper, radio and television station, choral group, national fraternities, national sororities.

Athletics Member NCAA. All Division III. ***Intercollegiate sports:*** baseball M, basketball M/W, cross-country running M/W, fencing M/W, golf M/W, soccer M/W, softball W, swimming and diving M/W, tennis M/W, track and field M/W, volleyball M/W, wrestling M. ***Intramural sports:*** badminton M(c)/W(c), baseball M(c), basketball M/W, bowling M/W, cheerleading M(c)/W(c), crew M(c)/W(c), equestrian sports M(c)/W(c), football M/W, ice hockey M(c), lacrosse M(c)/W(c), racquetball M(c)/W(c), soccer M/W, softball M/W, squash M(c)/W(c), table tennis M(c)/W(c), tennis M/W, ultimate Frisbee M(c)/W(c), volleyball M(c)/W(c), water polo M/W(c).

Campus security: 24-hour emergency response devices and patrols, student patrols, late-night transport/escort service, controlled dormitory access, 24-hour security in residence halls.

Student services: health clinic, personal/psychological counseling, women's center.

COSTS & FINANCIAL AID
Costs (2014–15) ***Comprehensive fee:*** $62,952 includes full-time tuition ($43,746), mandatory fees ($2424), and room and board ($16,782). Full-time tuition and fees vary according to course load and program. Part-time tuition: $1289 per credit hour. Part-time tuition and fees vary according to program. ***Required fees:*** $65 per credit part-time, $461 per term part-time. ***College room only:*** $12,006. Room and board charges vary according to board plan and housing facility. ***Payment plans:*** tuition prepayment, installment, deferred payment. ***Waivers:*** employees or children of employees.

Financial Aid Of all full-time matriculated undergraduates who enrolled in 2012, 12,820 applied for aid, 11,124 were judged to have need, 950 had their need fully met. 7,965 Federal Work-Study jobs (averaging $2853).

In 2012, 1067 non-need-based awards were made. ***Average percent of need met:*** 60. ***Average financial aid package:*** $27,544. ***Average need-based loan:*** $5579. ***Average need-based gift aid:*** $21,738. ***Average non-need-based aid:*** $8787. ***Average indebtedness upon graduation:*** $30,688. ***Financial aid deadline:*** 2/15.

APPLYING

Standardized Tests *Required:* SAT and SAT Subject Tests or ACT (for admission), A national examination for every freshman applicant is required but we are flexible about which exams must be submitted for eligibility (for admission).

Options: electronic application, early decision, deferred entrance.

Application fee: $70.

Required: essay or personal statement, high school transcript, 1 letter of recommendation. ***Required for some:*** audition or a portfolio for some specific programs.

Application deadlines: 1/1 (freshmen), 1/1 (out-of-state freshmen), 4/1 (transfers).

Early decision deadline: 11/1 (for plan 1), 1/1 (for plan 2).

Notification: 4/1 (freshmen), 4/1 (out-of-state freshmen), 5/15 (transfers), 12/15 (early decision plan 1), 2/15 (early decision plan 2).

CONTACT

Kristy Materasso, Undergraduate Admissions Processing Center, New York University, 665 Broadway, 11th Floor, New York, NY 10011. *Phone:* 212-998-4500. *Fax:* 212-995-4902. *E-mail:* admissions@nyu.edu.

★ Niagara University
Niagara Falls, New York
http://www.niagara.edu/

- **Independent** comprehensive, founded 1856, affiliated with Roman Catholic Church
- **Suburban** 160-acre campus with easy access to Buffalo, NY and Toronto, Ontario (Canada)
- **Endowment** $80.9 million
- **Coed** 3,176 undergraduate students, 89% full-time, 61% women, 39% men
- **Moderately difficult** entrance level, 66% of applicants were admitted

UNDERGRAD STUDENTS

2,833 full-time, 343 part-time. Students come from 38 states and territories; 27 other countries; 9% are from out of state; 6% Black or African American, non-Hispanic/Latino; 4% Hispanic/Latino; 2% Asian, non-Hispanic/Latino; 0.7% American Indian or Alaska Native, non-Hispanic/Latino; 2% Two or more races, non-Hispanic/Latino; 6% Race/ethnicity unknown; 10% international; 5% transferred in; 52% live on campus.

Freshmen

Admission: 3,565 applied, 2,348 admitted, 618 enrolled. ***Average high school GPA:*** 3.4. ***Test scores:*** SAT critical reading scores over 500: 58%; SAT math scores over 500: 66%; ACT scores over 18: 89%; SAT critical reading scores over 600: 11%; SAT math scores over 600: 17%; ACT scores over 24: 41%; SAT critical reading scores over 700: 1%; SAT math scores over 700: 1%.

Retention: 84% of full-time freshmen returned.

FACULTY

Total: 384, 41% full-time, 47% with terminal degrees.

Student/faculty ratio: 13:1.

ACADEMICS

Calendar: semesters. *Degrees:* associate, bachelor's, master's, doctoral, post-master's, and postbachelor's certificates.

Special study options: academic remediation for entering students, accelerated degree program, advanced placement credit, cooperative education, distance learning, double majors, English as a second language, freshman honors college, honors programs, independent study, internships, off-campus study, part-time degree program, services for LD students, student-designed majors, study abroad, summer session for credit. ***ROTC:*** Army (b).

Computers: 175 computers/terminals are available on campus for general student use. Students can access the following: campus intranet, computer help desk, free student e-mail accounts, online (class) grades, online (class) registration, online (class) schedules. Campuswide network is available. 100% of college-owned or -operated housing units are wired for high-speed Internet access. Wireless service is available via entire campus.

STUDENT LIFE
Housing options: on-campus residence required through sophomore year; coed. Campus housing is university owned. Freshman campus housing is guaranteed.

Activities and organizations: drama/theater group, student-run newspaper, radio station, choral group, Niagara University Community Action Program, student government, Programming Board, national fraternities, national sororities.

Athletics Member NCAA. All Division I. ***Intercollegiate sports:*** baseball M(s), basketball M(s)/W(s), cross-country running M(s)/W(s), golf M(s)/W(s), ice hockey M(s), lacrosse M/W(s), soccer M(s)/W(s), softball W(s), swimming and diving M(s)/W(s), tennis M(s)/W(s), track and field W(s), volleyball W(s). ***Intramural sports:*** badminton M/W, baseball M(c), basketball M/W, field hockey W(c), golf M(c), ice hockey M(c)/W, lacrosse M(c)/W(c), racquetball M/W, rugby M(c)/W(c), skiing (downhill) M(c)/W(c), soccer M(c)/W(c), softball W(c), tennis M(c)/W(c), volleyball M(c)/W(c), wrestling M(c).

Campus security: 24-hour emergency response devices and patrols, late-night transport/escort service, controlled dormitory access, 24-hour escort service.

Student services: health clinic, personal/psychological counseling.

COSTS & FINANCIAL AID
Costs (2014–15) ***Comprehensive fee:*** $41,010 includes full-time tuition ($27,700), mandatory fees ($1360), and room and board ($11,950). Part-time tuition: $925 per credit hour. ***Room and board:*** Room and board charges vary according to housing facility. ***Payment plans:*** installment, deferred payment. ***Waivers:*** senior citizens and employees or children of employees.

Financial Aid Of all full-time matriculated undergraduates who enrolled in 2014, 2,326 applied for aid, 2,150 were judged to have need, 1,093 had their need fully met. 408 Federal Work-Study jobs (averaging $3096). 61 state and other part-time jobs (averaging $4618). In 2014, 458 non-need-based awards were made. ***Average percent of need met:*** 82. ***Average financial aid package:*** $23,602. ***Average need-based loan:*** $4846. ***Average need-based gift aid:*** $19,245. ***Average non-need-based aid:*** $13,104. ***Average indebtedness upon graduation:*** $30,289.

APPLYING
Standardized Tests *Required:* SAT or ACT (for admission).

Options: electronic application, early admission, deferred entrance.

Required: high school transcript. ***Recommended:*** minimum 3.0 GPA, 3 letters of recommendation, interview.

Application deadlines: 8/1 (freshmen), 8/15 (transfers).

Notification: continuous (freshmen), continuous (transfers).

CONTACT
Mr. Mark Wojnowski, Director of Undergraduate Admissions, Niagara University, Niagara University, NY 14109. *Phone:* 716-286-8700 Ext. 8715. *Toll-free phone:* 800-462-2111. *Fax:* 716-286-8733. *E-mail:* admissions@niagara.edu.

See previous page for display ad and page 1548 for the College Close-Up.

Nyack College

Nyack, New York

http://www.nyack.edu/

- **Independent** comprehensive, founded 1882, affiliated with The Christian and Missionary Alliance
- **Suburban** 125-acre campus with easy access to New York City
- **Coed** 1,705 undergraduate students, 83% full-time, 62% women, 38% men
- **Minimally difficult** entrance level, 99% of applicants were admitted

UNDERGRAD STUDENTS
1,416 full-time, 289 part-time. Students come from 38 states and territories; 44 other countries; 30% are from out of state; 30% Black or African American, non-Hispanic/Latino; 29% Hispanic/Latino; 8% Asian, non-Hispanic/Latino; 0.3% Native Hawaiian or other Pacific Islander, non-Hispanic/Latino; 0.4% American Indian or Alaska Native, non-Hispanic/Latino; 2% Two or more races, non-Hispanic/Latino; 3% Race/ethnicity unknown; 6% international; 14% transferred in.

Freshmen
Admission: 625 applied, 621 admitted, 250 enrolled. ***Average high school GPA:*** 2.76. ***Test scores:*** SAT critical reading scores over 500: 30%; SAT math scores over 500: 26%; ACT scores over 18: 83%; SAT critical reading scores over 600: 3%; SAT math scores over 600: 5%; ACT scores over 24: 37%; SAT critical reading scores over 700: 1%; SAT math scores over 700: 1%; ACT scores over 30: 10%.

Retention: 64% of full-time freshmen returned.

FACULTY
Total: 282, 38% full-time, 43% with terminal degrees.
Student/faculty ratio: 12:1.

ACADEMICS
Calendar: semesters. *Degrees:* associate, bachelor's, master's, and doctoral.

Special study options: academic remediation for entering students, adult/continuing education programs, advanced placement credit, distance learning, double majors, honors programs, independent study, internships, off-campus study, part-time degree program, services for LD students, student-designed majors, study abroad, summer session for credit.

Unusual degree programs: 3-2 education (BS/MS childhood special education).

Computers: 165 computers/terminals are available on campus for general student use. Students can access the following: campus intranet, computer help desk, free student e-mail accounts, online (class) grades, online (class) registration, online (class) schedules. Campuswide network is available. 95% of college-owned or -operated housing units are wired for high-speed Internet access. Wireless service is available via classrooms, computer labs, dorm rooms, libraries, student centers.

STUDENT LIFE
Housing options: on-campus residence required through sophomore year; men-only, women-only. Campus housing is university owned. Freshman campus housing is guaranteed.

Activities and organizations: drama/theater group, student-run newspaper, radio station, choral group, Student leadership, Choral groups, Lost & Found, Small group ministries, Intramurals.

Athletics Member NCAA. All Division II. ***Intercollegiate sports:*** baseball M(s), basketball M(s)/W(s), cross-country running M(s)/W(s), golf M(s), lacrosse W(s), soccer M(s)/W(s), softball W(s), volleyball W(s). ***Intramural sports:*** baseball M, basketball M/W, skiing (downhill) M/W, soccer M/W, softball W, ultimate Frisbee M/W, volleyball M/W.

Campus security: 24-hour emergency response devices and patrols.

Student services: health clinic, personal/psychological counseling.

COSTS & FINANCIAL AID
Costs (2015–16) ***One-time required fee:*** $100. ***Comprehensive fee:*** $33,250 includes full-time tuition ($24,000), mandatory fees ($300), and room and board ($8950). Part-time tuition: $1000 per credit hour. Part-time tuition and fees vary according to course load. ***Required fees:*** $75 per term part-time. ***Room and board:*** Room and board charges vary according to board plan and housing facility. ***Payment plan:*** installment. ***Waivers:*** employees or children of employees.

Financial Aid Of all full-time matriculated undergraduates who enrolled in 2013, 1,399 applied for aid, 1,325 were judged to have need, 122 had their need fully met. 163 Federal Work-Study jobs (averaging $1137). 60 state and other part-time jobs (averaging $1875). In 2013, 63 non-need-based awards were made. ***Average percent of need met:*** 62. ***Average financial aid package:*** $19,219. ***Average need-based loan:*** $3984. ***Average need-based gift aid:*** $9220. ***Average non-need-based aid:*** $9779. ***Average indebtedness upon graduation:*** $37,577.

APPLYING

Standardized Tests *Required for some:* SAT or ACT (for admission).

Options: electronic application, deferred entrance.

Application fee: $25.

Required: essay or personal statement, high school transcript, minimum 2.0 GPA, 1 letter of recommendation, Signed statement of faith and community life form. ***Required for some:*** interview.

Application deadlines: rolling (freshmen), rolling (out-of-state freshmen), rolling (transfers).

Notification: continuous (freshmen), continuous (out-of-state freshmen), continuous (transfers).

CONTACT

Mr. Dan Bailey, Director of Admissions, Nyack College, 1 South Boulevard, Nyack, NY 10960-3698. *Phone:* 845-675-4401. *Toll-free phone:* 800-33-NYACK. *Fax:* 845-358-3047. *E-mail:* admissions@nyack.edu.

Ohr Somayach/Joseph Tanenbaum Educational Center

Monsey, New York

http://ohr.edu/

- **Independent Jewish** comprehensive, founded 1979
- **Small-town** 7-acre campus with easy access to New York City
- **Men only**
- **Moderately difficult** entrance level

ACADEMICS

Calendar: semesters. *Degree:* bachelor's and doctoral.

STUDENT LIFE

Housing options: on-campus residence required through senior year; men-only. Campus housing is university owned.

Campus security: 24-hour emergency response devices and patrols, controlled dormitory access.

Student services: personal/psychological counseling.

APPLYING

Options: early admission.

Required: interview. ***Required for some:*** essay or personal statement. ***Recommended:*** high school transcript.

CONTACT

Ohr Somayach/Joseph Tanenbaum Educational Center, PO Box 334, 244 Route 306, Monsey, NY 10952-0334. *Phone:* 845-425-1370 Ext. 22.

★ Pace University

New York, New York

http://www.pace.edu/

- **Independent** university, founded 1906
- **Urban** campus with easy access to New York City
- **Endowment** $157.3 million
- **Coed** 8,694 undergraduate students, 84% full-time, 59% women, 41% men
- **Moderately difficult** entrance level, 85% of applicants were admitted

UNDERGRAD STUDENTS

7,262 full-time, 1,432 part-time. Students come from 49 states and territories; 104 other countries; 41% are from out of state; 11% Black or African American, non-Hispanic/Latino; 15% Hispanic/Latino; 9% Asian, non-Hispanic/Latino; 0.1% Native Hawaiian or other Pacific Islander, non-Hispanic/Latino; 0.2% American Indian or Alaska Native, non-Hispanic/Latino; 4% Two or more races, non-Hispanic/Latino; 3% Race/ethnicity unknown; 9% international; 7% transferred in; 40% live on campus.

Freshmen
Admission: 15,722 applied, 13,362 admitted, 2,033 enrolled. ***Average high school GPA:*** 3.22. ***Test scores:*** SAT critical reading scores over 500: 64%; SAT math scores over 500: 67%; ACT scores over 18: 97%; SAT critical reading scores over 600: 18%; SAT math scores over 600: 21%; ACT scores over 24: 44%; SAT critical reading scores over 700: 2%; SAT math scores over 700: 3%; ACT scores over 30: 4%.

Retention: 76% of full-time freshmen returned.

FACULTY
Total: 1,339, 35% full-time, 54% with terminal degrees.

Student/faculty ratio: 14:1.

ACADEMICS
Calendar: semesters. *Degrees:* certificates, associate, bachelor's, master's, doctoral, post-master's, and postbachelor's certificates.

Special study options: accelerated degree program, adult/continuing education programs, advanced placement credit, cooperative education, distance learning, double majors, English as a second language, freshman honors college, honors programs, independent study, internships, part-time degree program, services for LD students, study abroad, summer session for credit. ***ROTC:*** Army (c), Air Force (c).

Unusual degree programs: 3-2 business administration; engineering with Manhattan College, Rensselaer Polytechnic Institute; Occupational Therapy with Columbia University College of Physicians and Surgeons, Optometry with SUNY College of Optometry, Physical Therapy with New York Medical College, Podiatry with the New York College of Podiatric Medicine.

Computers: 1,144 computers/terminals are available on campus for general student use. Students can access the following: computer help desk, free student e-mail accounts, online (class) grades, online (class) registration, online (class) schedules, administrative functions - pay tuition, view student records, update personal information, view financial aid and complete health insurance waiver. Campuswide network is available. 100% of college-owned or -operated housing units are wired for high-speed Internet access. Wireless service is available via classrooms, computer centers, computer labs, libraries, student centers.

STUDENT LIFE
Housing options: coed. Campus housing is university owned and leased by the school.

Activities and organizations: drama/theater group, student-run newspaper, radio and television station, choral group, Black Student Union, Beta Alpha Psi, OLAS (Organization of Latin American Students), Pace Board, Lubin Business Association, national fraternities, national sororities.

Athletics Member NCAA. All Division II. ***Intercollegiate sports:*** baseball M(s), basketball M(s)/W(s), cross-country running M(s)/W(s), field hockey W(s), football M(s), lacrosse M(s)/W(s), soccer W(s), softball W(s), swimming and diving M(s)/W(s), volleyball W(s). ***Intramural sports:*** badminton M/W, basketball M/W, soccer M/W, ultimate Frisbee M/W, volleyball M/W.

Campus security: 24-hour emergency response devices and patrols, late-night transport/escort service, controlled dormitory access.

Student services: health clinic, personal/psychological counseling.

COSTS & FINANCIAL AID
Costs (2014–15) ***Comprehensive fee:*** $55,471 includes full-time tuition ($38,200), mandatory fees ($1497), and room and board ($15,774). Full-time tuition and fees vary according to location. Part-time tuition: $1096 per credit. Part-time tuition and fees vary according to course load and location. ***Room and board:*** Room and board charges vary according to board plan, housing facility, location, and student level. ***Payment plan:*** installment. ***Waivers:*** senior citizens and employees or children of employees.

Financial Aid Of all full-time matriculated undergraduates who enrolled in 2014, 5,656 applied for aid, 5,240 were judged to have need, 583 had their need fully met. 1,123 Federal Work-Study jobs (averaging $2241). In 2014, 1533 non-need-based awards were made. ***Average percent of need met:*** 70. ***Average financial aid package:*** $29,194. ***Average need-based loan:*** $4582. ***Average need-based gift aid:*** $24,743. ***Average non-need-based aid:*** $15,903. ***Average indebtedness upon graduation:*** $35,442.

APPLYING
Standardized Tests *Required:* SAT or ACT (for admission).

Options: electronic application, early action, deferred entrance.

Application fee: $50.

Required: essay or personal statement, high school transcript, 2 letters of recommendation. ***Recommended:*** interview.

Application deadlines: 2/15 (freshmen), rolling (transfers), 12/1 (early action).

Notification: continuous (freshmen), continuous (transfers), 1/1 (early action).

CONTACT
Ms. Donna J. Grand Pre, Dean of Admissions, Pace University, One Pace Plaza, 163 William Street, New York, NY 10038. *Phone:* 212-346-1794. *Toll-free phone:* 800-874-7223. *Fax:* 212-346-1821. *E-mail:* dgrandpre@pace.edu.

See previous page for display ad and page 1562 for the College Close-Up.

★ Parsons The New School for Design

New York, New York

http://www.newschool.edu/parsons/

- **Independent** comprehensive, founded 1896, part of The New School
- **Urban** 2-acre campus with easy access to Manhattan
- **Endowment** $214.0 million
- **Coed**

FACULTY
Student/faculty ratio: 9:1.

ACADEMICS
Calendar: semesters. *Degrees:* associate, bachelor's, master's, and postbachelor's certificates.

STUDENT LIFE
Housing options: coed, special housing for students with disabilities. Campus housing is university owned and leased by the school. Freshman applicants given priority for college housing.

Activities and organizations: drama/theater group, student-run newspaper, radio station, choral group, Fashion Design and Textiles Group, Sisters on the Runway at The New School, DREAM:IN NY, Sustainable Cities Club, BriCollab Art Initiative.

Campus security: 24-hour emergency response devices, controlled dormitory access, 24-hour security desk personnel.

Student services: health clinic, personal/psychological counseling.

FINANCIAL AID
Financial Aid Of all full-time matriculated undergraduates who enrolled in 2012, 1,901 applied for aid, 1,728 were judged to have need, 253 had their need fully met. In 2012, 163 non-need-based awards were made. ***Average percent of need met:*** 67. ***Average financial aid package:*** $20,318. ***Average need-based loan:*** $6682. ***Average need-based gift aid:*** $19,631. ***Average non-need-based aid:*** $7936. ***Average indebtedness upon graduation:*** $34,040. ***Financial aid deadline:*** 3/1.

APPLYING
Standardized Tests *Required:* SAT or ACT (for admission).

Required: essay or personal statement, high school transcript, online application, SAT or ACT (if applicable), Parson's Challenge, portfolio, TOEFL/IELTS /PTE scores may be required for applicants whose first language is not English, artist statement. ***Required for some:*** essay or personal statement, interview. ***Recommended:*** minimum 3.0 GPA.

CONTACT
Ms. Tomiko Pilson, Assistant Director of Admissions, Parsons The New School for Design, Fanton Hall/Welcome Center, 72 Fifth Avenue, Floor 2, Room 200, New York, NY 10011. *Phone:* 212-229-5665 Ext. 2305. *Toll-free phone:* 800-292-3040. *Fax:* 212-229-5665. *E-mail:* thinkparsons@newschool.edu.

See page 715 for display ad and page 1546 for the College Close-Up.

Plaza College

Forest Hills, New York

http://www.plazacollege.edu/

- **Proprietary** primarily 2-year, founded 1916
- **Urban** campus with easy access to New York City
- **Coed** 726 undergraduate students
- **Moderately difficult** entrance level

ACADEMICS

Calendar: semesters. *Degrees:* certificates, associate, and bachelor's.

Special study options: academic remediation for entering students, English as a second language, internships, services for LD students, summer session for credit.

STUDENT LIFE

Housing options: college housing not available.

Activities and organizations: drama/theater group, Ambassadors Club, VDAY, Performing Arts Society, Plaza College Psychology Society, Plaza College Social Media Society.

Campus security: 24-hour emergency response devices.

COSTS

Costs (2014–15) ***Tuition:*** $9900 full-time. Full-time tuition and fees vary according to program. Part-time tuition and fees vary according to program. ***Required fees:*** $1720 full-time, $440 per credit hour part-time, $860 per term part-time.

APPLYING

Standardized Tests *Required:* ACT Compass (for admission).

Application fee: $100.

Required: essay or personal statement, interview, placement test. ***Required for some:*** 2 letters of recommendation.

Application deadlines: rolling (freshmen), rolling (transfers).

CONTACT

Dean Vanessa Lopez, Dean of Admissions, Plaza College, 118-33 Queens Boulevard, Forest Hills, NY 11375. *Phone:* 718-779-1430. *E-mail:* info@plazacollege.edu.

★ Pratt Institute

Brooklyn, New York

http://www.pratt.edu/

- **Independent** comprehensive, founded 1887
- **Urban** 25-acre campus
- **Coed** 3,145 undergraduate students, 96% full-time, 68% women, 32% men
- **Very difficult** entrance level, 63% of applicants were admitted

UNDERGRAD STUDENTS

3,034 full-time, 111 part-time. 70% are from out of state; 4% Black or African American, non-Hispanic/Latino; 10% Hispanic/Latino; 17% Asian, non-Hispanic/Latino; 0.3% Native Hawaiian or other Pacific Islander, non-Hispanic/Latino; 0.3% American Indian or Alaska Native, non-Hispanic/Latino; 1% Two or more races, non-Hispanic/Latino; 0.9% Race/ethnicity unknown; 25% international; 5% transferred in; 52% live on campus.

Freshmen

Admission: 4,679 applied, 2,964 admitted, 640 enrolled. ***Average high school GPA:*** 3.64. ***Test scores:*** SAT critical reading scores over 500: 90%; SAT math scores over 500: 89%; SAT writing scores over 500: 89%; ACT scores over 18: 99%; SAT critical reading scores over 600: 41%; SAT math scores over 600: 50%; SAT writing scores over 600: 44%; ACT scores over 24: 76%; SAT critical reading scores over 700: 6%; SAT math scores over 700: 14%; SAT writing scores over 700: 7%; ACT scores over 30: 16%.

Retention: 85% of full-time freshmen returned.

FACULTY

Total: 1,068, 14% full-time, 11% with terminal degrees.

Student/faculty ratio: 10:1.

ACADEMICS
Calendar: semesters plus optional May term and summer session. *Degrees:* associate, bachelor's, master's, and post-master's certificates.

Special study options: part-time degree program. ***ROTC:*** Army (c).

Computers: Students can access the following: online (class) registration. Campuswide network is available.

STUDENT LIFE
Housing options: coed, special housing for students with disabilities. Campus housing is university owned. Freshman campus housing is guaranteed.

Athletics Member NCAA. All Division III. ***Intercollegiate sports:*** basketball M, cross-country running M/W, soccer M/W, tennis M/W, track and field M/W, volleyball W. ***Intramural sports:*** badminton M/W, basketball M, field hockey M, football M, golf M, lacrosse M/W, volleyball M, weight lifting M/W.

Campus security: 24-hour emergency response devices and patrols, late-night transport/escort service.

COSTS & FINANCIAL AID
Costs (2015–16) ***Comprehensive fee:*** $58,082 includes full-time tuition ($44,580), mandatory fees ($2006), and room and board ($11,496). Full-time tuition and fees vary according to program. Part-time tuition: $1438 per credit hour. Part-time tuition and fees vary according to program. ***College room only:*** $7430. Room and board charges vary according to board plan and housing facility.

Financial Aid Of all full-time matriculated undergraduates who enrolled in 2014, 2,713 applied for aid, 2,401 were judged to have need. In 2014, 593 non-need-based awards were made. ***Average percent of need met:*** 49. ***Average financial aid package:*** $23,884. ***Average need-based gift aid:*** $12,550. ***Average non-need-based aid:*** $13,000. ***Average indebtedness upon graduation:*** $34,877. ***Financial aid deadline:*** 3/1.

APPLYING
Standardized Tests *Required:* SAT or ACT (for admission). *Required for some:* SAT Subject Tests (for admission).

Options: electronic application, early action, deferred entrance.

Application fee: $50.

Required: essay or personal statement, high school transcript, 1 letter of recommendation. ***Required for some:*** portfolio. ***Recommended:*** minimum 3.0 GPA.

CONTACT
Ms. Olga Burger, Visit Coordinator, Pratt Institute, 200 Willoughby Avenue, DeKalb Hall, Brooklyn, NY 11205. *Phone:* 718-636-3779. *Toll-free phone:* 800-331-0834. *Fax:* 718-636-3670. *E-mail:* visit@pratt.edu.

See previous page for display ad and page 1570 for the College Close-Up.

Purchase College, State University of New York

Purchase, New York

http://www.purchase.edu/

- **State-supported** comprehensive, founded 1967, part of State University of New York System
- **Small-town** 500-acre campus with easy access to New York City
- **Coed** 4,188 undergraduate students, 92% full-time, 55% women, 45% men
- **Moderately difficult** entrance level, 41% of applicants were admitted

UNDERGRAD STUDENTS
3,838 full-time, 350 part-time. Students come from 43 states and territories; 31 other countries; 15% are from out of state; 9% Black or African American, non-Hispanic/Latino; 17% Hispanic/Latino; 3% Asian, non-Hispanic/Latino; 5% Two or more races, non-Hispanic/Latino; 7% Race/ethnicity unknown; 2% international; 10% transferred in; 67% live on campus.

Freshmen
Admission: 6,955 applied, 2,839 admitted, 758 enrolled. ***Average high school GPA:*** 3.24. ***Test scores:*** SAT critical reading scores over 500: 78%; SAT math scores over 500: 71%; ACT scores over 18: 86%; SAT critical reading scores over 600: 34%; SAT math scores over 600: 22%; ACT scores over 24: 50%; SAT critical reading scores over 700: 4%; SAT math scores over 700: 1%; ACT scores over 30: 5%.

Retention: 80% of full-time freshmen returned.

FACULTY
Total: 463, 37% full-time, 33% with terminal degrees.

Student/faculty ratio: 15:1.

ACADEMICS
Calendar: semesters. *Degrees:* certificates, bachelor's, master's, and post-master's certificates.

Special study options: academic remediation for entering students, adult/continuing education programs, advanced placement credit, double majors, English as a second language, independent study, internships, off-campus study, part-time degree program, services for LD students, student-designed majors, study abroad, summer session for credit.

Computers: 600 computers/terminals and 3,500 ports are available on campus for general student use. Students can access the following: campus intranet, computer help desk, free student e-mail accounts, online (class) grades, online (class) registration, online (class) schedules. Campuswide network is available. 100% of college-owned or -operated housing units are wired for high-speed Internet access. Wireless service is available via classrooms, computer centers, computer labs, learning centers, libraries, student centers.

STUDENT LIFE
Housing options: coed. Campus housing is university owned. Freshman applicants given priority for college housing.

Activities and organizations: drama/theater group, student-run newspaper, radio and television station, choral group, Student Union, WPUR radio station, Latinos Unidos, Gay/Lesbian/Bisexual/Transgender Union, Organization of African People in America.

Athletics Member NCAA. All Division III. ***Intercollegiate sports:*** baseball M, basketball M/W, cross-country running M/W, golf M, lacrosse W, soccer M/W, softball W, swimming and diving M/W, tennis M/W, volleyball M/W. ***Intramural sports:*** badminton M/W, basketball M/W, bowling M/W, cross-country running M/W, fencing M/W, football M/W, golf M/W, racquetball M/W, skiing (cross-country) M/W, skiing (downhill) M/W, soccer M/W, softball M/W, squash M/W, swimming and diving M/W, table tennis M/W, tennis M/W, volleyball M/W, water polo M/W, weight lifting M/W.

Campus security: 24-hour emergency response devices and patrols, late-night transport/escort service, controlled dormitory access, 24-hour patrols by police officers.

Student services: health clinic, personal/psychological counseling, women's center, legal services.

COSTS & FINANCIAL AID
Costs (2015–16) ***One-time required fee:*** $210. ***Tuition:*** state resident $6170 full-time, $257 per credit part-time; nonresident $15,820 full-time. Full-time tuition and fees vary according to program. Part-time tuition and fees vary according to course load and program. ***Required fees:*** $1763 full-time, $68 per credit part-time. ***Room and board:*** $12,232; room only: $7960. Room and board charges vary according to board plan and housing facility. ***Payment plan:*** installment. ***Waivers:*** employees or children of employees.

Financial Aid Of all full-time matriculated undergraduates who enrolled in 2013, 2,897 applied for aid, 2,348 were judged to have need, 97 had their need fully met. In 2013, 232 non-need-based awards were made. ***Average percent of need met:*** 48. ***Average financial aid package:*** $10,456. ***Average need-based loan:*** $4843. ***Average need-based gift aid:*** $6735. ***Average non-need-based aid:*** $2136. ***Average indebtedness upon graduation:*** $25,159.

APPLYING
Standardized Tests *Required:* SAT or ACT (for admission). *Recommended:* SAT (for admission).

Options: electronic application, early admission, early action, deferred entrance.

Application fee: $50.

Required: high school transcript, minimum 3.0 GPA. ***Required for some:*** essay or personal statement, 1 letter of recommendation, interview, audition, portfolio.

Application deadlines: 7/15 (freshmen), rolling (transfers), 11/15 (early action).

Notification: continuous until 5/1 (freshmen), continuous (transfers), 12/15 (early action).

CONTACT
Stephanie McCaine, Director of Admissions, Purchase College, State University of New York, 735 Anderson Hill Road, Purchase, NY 10577-1400. *Phone:* 914-251-6300. *Fax:* 914-251-6314. *E-mail:* admission@purchase.edu.

★ Queens College of the City University of New York

Flushing, New York

http://www.qc.cuny.edu/

- **State and locally supported** comprehensive, founded 1937, part of City University of New York System
- **Urban** 85-acre campus with easy access to New York City
- **Endowment** $43.6 million
- **Coed** 15,773 undergraduate students, 70% full-time, 56% women, 44% men
- **Very difficult** entrance level, 40% of applicants were admitted

UNDERGRAD STUDENTS
11,079 full-time, 4,694 part-time. Students come from 15 states and territories; 170 other countries; 1% are from out of state; 9% Black or African American, non-Hispanic/Latino; 20% Hispanic/Latino; 28% Asian, non-Hispanic/Latino; 0.3% American Indian or Alaska Native, non-Hispanic/Latino; 5% international; 14% transferred in; 3% live on campus.

Freshmen
Admission: 18,289 applied, 7,283 admitted, 1,544 enrolled. ***Average high school GPA:*** 3.4. ***Test scores:*** SAT critical reading scores over 500: 65%; SAT math scores over 500: 94%; SAT writing scores over 500: 62%; SAT critical reading scores over 600: 18%; SAT math scores over 600: 34%; SAT writing scores over 600: 17%; SAT critical reading scores over 700: 5%; SAT math scores over 700: 6%; SAT writing scores over 700: 4%. ***Retention:*** 87% of full-time freshmen returned.

FACULTY
Total: 1,464, 41% full-time, 54% with terminal degrees.

Student/faculty ratio: 15:1.

ACADEMICS
Calendar: semesters. *Degrees:* bachelor's, master's, post-master's, and postbachelor's certificates.

Special study options: accelerated degree program, adult/continuing education programs, advanced placement credit, double majors, English as a second language, honors programs, independent study, internships, off-campus study, part-time degree program, services for LD students, study abroad, summer session for credit. ***ROTC:*** Army (c), Navy (c).

Unusual degree programs: chemistry, biochemistry, computer science, physics, political science, music, philosophy.

Computers: 2,500 computers/terminals are available on campus for general student use. Students can access the following: campus intranet, computer help desk, free student e-mail accounts, online (class) grades, online (class) registration, online (class) schedules. Campuswide network is available. 100% of college-owned or -operated housing units are wired for high-speed Internet access. Wireless service is available via entire campus.

STUDENT LIFE
Housing options: coed. Campus housing is university owned.

Activities and organizations: drama/theater group, student-run newspaper, radio station, choral group, Science Fiction and Animation, Chabad of QC, La Tertulia, PRISM: The Sexuality and Gender Alliance of QC, Muslim Students Association, national fraternities, national sororities.

Athletics Member NCAA. All Division II. ***Intercollegiate sports:*** baseball M(s), basketball M(s)/W(s), cross-country running M(s)/W(s), fencing W(s), lacrosse W(s), soccer M(s)/W(s), softball W(s), swimming and diving M(s)/W(s), tennis M(s)/W(s), track and field M(s)/W(s), volleyball W(s). ***Intramural sports:*** basketball M/W, cross-country running M/W, football M/W, soccer M/W, softball M/W, tennis M/W, track and field M/W, volleyball M/W.

Campus security: 24-hour emergency response devices and patrols, controlled dormitory access.

Student services: health clinic, personal/psychological counseling.

COSTS & FINANCIAL AID
Costs (2014–15) ***Tuition:*** state resident $6030 full-time, $260 per credit part-time; nonresident $16,050 full-time, $535 per credit part-time. Part-time tuition and fees vary according to course load. ***Required fees:*** $608 full-time, $260 per credit part-time, $209 per term part-time. ***Room only:*** $11,000. Room and board charges vary according to board plan and housing facility. ***Payment plan:*** installment. ***Waivers:*** senior citizens.

Financial Aid Of all full-time matriculated undergraduates who enrolled in 2013, 11,176 applied for aid, 8,623 were judged to have need, 6,788 had their need fully met. 456 Federal Work-Study jobs (averaging $1033). In 2013, 209 non-need-based awards were made. ***Average percent of need met:*** 95. ***Average financial aid package:*** $6450. ***Average need-based loan:*** $5000. ***Average need-based gift aid:*** $6000. ***Average non-need-based aid:*** $7800.

APPLYING
Standardized Tests *Required:* SAT or ACT (for admission). *Required for some:* SAT Subject Tests (for admission). *Recommended:* SAT Subject Tests (for admission).

Options: electronic application, deferred entrance.

Application fee: $65.

Required: high school transcript, minimum 3.0 GPA.

Notification: 2/15 (freshmen).

CONTACT
Mr. Vincent Angrisani, Executive Director of Enrollment Management and Admissions, Queens College of the City University of New York, 65-30 Kissena Boulevard, Flushing, NY 11367-1597. *Phone:* 718-997-5600. *Fax:* 718-997-5617.

Rensselaer Polytechnic Institute

Troy, New York

http://www.rpi.edu/

- **Independent** university, founded 1824
- **Suburban** 284-acre campus with easy access to Albany, NY
- **Endowment** $611.8 million
- **Coed** 5,618 undergraduate students, 100% full-time, 31% women, 69% men
- **Very difficult** entrance level, 38% of applicants were admitted

UNDERGRAD STUDENTS
5,598 full-time, 20 part-time. Students come from 48 states and territories; 32 other countries; 67% are from out of state; 3% Black or African American, non-Hispanic/Latino; 7% Hispanic/Latino; 10% Asian, non-Hispanic/Latino; 0.1% Native Hawaiian or other Pacific Islander, non-Hispanic/Latino; 0.1% American Indian or Alaska Native, non-Hispanic/Latino; 7% Two or more races, non-Hispanic/Latino; 2% Race/ethnicity unknown; 9% international; 2% transferred in; 57% live on campus.

Freshmen
Admission: 18,602 applied, 6,976 admitted, 1,331 enrolled. ***Average high school GPA:*** 3.77. ***Test scores:*** SAT critical reading scores over 500: 99%; SAT math scores over 500: 100%; ACT scores over 18: 100%; SAT critical reading scores over 600: 83%; SAT math scores over 600: 96%; ACT scores over 24: 94%; SAT critical reading scores over 700: 33%; SAT math scores over 700: 65%; ACT scores over 30: 50%. ***Retention:*** 93% of full-time freshmen returned.

FACULTY
Total: 497, 83% full-time, 88% with terminal degrees.

Student/faculty ratio: 15:1.

ACADEMICS
Calendar: semesters. *Degrees:* bachelor's, master's, and doctoral.

Special study options: accelerated degree program, adult/continuing education programs, advanced placement credit, cooperative education, double majors, English as a second language, honors programs, independent study, internships, off-campus study, part-time degree program, services for LD students, student-designed majors, study abroad, summer session for credit. ***ROTC:*** Army (b), Navy (b), Air Force (b).

Unusual degree programs: 3-2 engineering.

Computers: Students can access the following: campus intranet, computer help desk, free student e-mail accounts, online (class) grades, online (class) registration, online (class) schedules, billing, downloadable software, web pages. Campuswide network is available. 100% of college-owned or -operated housing units are wired for high-speed Internet access. Wireless service is available via entire campus.

STUDENT LIFE

Housing options: on-campus residence required through sophomore year; coed, special housing for students with disabilities. Campus housing is university owned. Freshman campus housing is guaranteed.

Activities and organizations: drama/theater group, student-run newspaper, radio and television station, choral group, Red Army Spirit Club, Outing Club, Indian Student Association, Chinese American Student Association, pep band, national fraternities, national sororities.

Athletics Member NCAA. All Division III except men's and women's ice hockey (Division I). ***Intercollegiate sports:*** archery M(c)/W(c), badminton M(c)/W(c), baseball M/W(c), basketball M/W, crew M(c)/W(c), cross-country running M/W, equestrian sports M(c)/W(c), fencing M(c)/W(c), field hockey W, football M, golf M, ice hockey M(s)/W(s), lacrosse M/W, racquetball M(c)/W(c), riflery M(c)/W(c), rugby M(c)/W(c), sailing M(c)/W(c), skiing (cross-country) M(c)/W(c), soccer M/W, softball W, squash M(c)/W(c), swimming and diving M/W, table tennis M(c)/W(c), tennis M/W, track and field M/W, ultimate Frisbee M(c)/W(c), volleyball M(c)/W(c), water polo M(c)/W(c), weight lifting M(c)/W(c). ***Intramural sports:*** basketball M/W, bowling M(c)/W(c), cheerleading W, ice hockey M/W, lacrosse M(c), racquetball M/W, rock climbing M(c)/W(c), skiing (downhill) M/W, soccer M/W, softball M/W, swimming and diving M(c)/W(c), table tennis M/W, tennis M(c)/W(c), ultimate Frisbee M/W, volleyball M/W, wrestling M.

Campus security: 24-hour emergency response devices and patrols, late-night transport/escort service, controlled dormitory access, campus foot patrols at night.

Student services: health clinic, personal/psychological counseling, women's center, legal services.

COSTS & FINANCIAL AID

Costs (2014–15) ***Comprehensive fee:*** $61,528 includes full-time tuition ($46,700), mandatory fees ($1208), and room and board ($13,620). Part-time tuition: $1945 per credit hour. ***College room only:*** $7740. Room and board charges vary according to board plan and location. ***Payment plan:*** installment. ***Waivers:*** employees or children of employees.

Financial Aid Of all full-time matriculated undergraduates who enrolled in 2014, 3,893 applied for aid, 3,486 were judged to have need, 716 had their need fully met. 809 Federal Work-Study jobs (averaging $1854). In 2014, 1485 non-need-based awards were made. ***Average percent of need met:*** 77. ***Average financial aid package:*** $34,359. ***Average need-based loan:*** $5610. ***Average need-based gift aid:*** $28,527. ***Average non-need-based aid:*** $15,860. ***Average indebtedness upon graduation:*** $41,814.

APPLYING

Standardized Tests *Required:* SAT or ACT (for admission). *Required for some:* SAT and SAT Subject Tests or ACT (for admission).

Options: electronic application, early admission, early decision, deferred entrance.

Application fee: $70.

Required: high school transcript. ***Required for some:*** essay or personal statement, portfolio for Electronic Arts. ***Recommended:*** 1 letter of recommendation.

Early decision deadline: 11/1 (for plan 1), 12/15 (for plan 2).

Notification: 3/14 (freshmen), continuous (transfers), 12/13 (early decision plan 1), 1/17 (early decision plan 2).

CONTACT

Ms. Karen Long, Acting Vice President for Enrollment, Rensselaer Polytechnic Institute, 110 8th Street, Troy, NY 12180. *Phone:* 518-276-6216. *Fax:* 518-276-4072. *E-mail:* admissions@rpi.edu.

Roberts Wesleyan College

Rochester, New York

http://www.roberts.edu/

- **Independent** comprehensive, founded 1866, affiliated with Free Methodist Church of North America
- **Suburban** 188-acre campus with easy access to Rochester
- **Endowment** $23.0 million
- **Coed** 1,336 undergraduate students, 91% full-time, 68% women, 32% men
- **Moderately difficult** entrance level, 69% of applicants were admitted

UNDERGRAD STUDENTS

1,220 full-time, 116 part-time. Students come from 27 states and territories; 20 other countries; 8% are from out of state; 11% Black or African American, non-Hispanic/Latino; 6% Hispanic/Latino; 1% Asian, non-Hispanic/Latino; 0.1% Native Hawaiian or other Pacific Islander, non-Hispanic/Latino; 0.5% American Indian or Alaska Native, non-Hispanic/Latino; 3% Two or more races, non-Hispanic/Latino; 2% Race/ethnicity unknown; 4% international; 6% transferred in; 65% live on campus.

Freshmen

Admission: 915 applied, 631 admitted, 256 enrolled. ***Average high school GPA:*** 3.35. ***Test scores:*** SAT critical reading scores over 500: 62%; SAT math scores over 500: 59%; SAT writing scores over 500: 46%; ACT scores over 18: 89%; SAT critical reading scores over 600: 16%; SAT math scores over 600: 23%; SAT writing scores over 600: 11%; ACT scores over 24: 44%; SAT critical reading scores over 700: 4%; SAT math scores over 700: 2%; SAT writing scores over 700: 2%; ACT scores over 30: 8%.

Retention: 79% of full-time freshmen returned.

FACULTY

Total: 263, 34% full-time, 35% with terminal degrees.

Student/faculty ratio: 11:1.

ACADEMICS

Calendar: semesters. *Degrees:* bachelor's and master's.

Special study options: academic remediation for entering students, accelerated degree program, adult/continuing education programs, advanced placement credit, cooperative education, distance learning, double majors, English as a second language, honors programs, independent study, internships, off-campus study, services for LD students, student-designed majors, study abroad, summer session for credit. ***ROTC:*** Army (c), Air Force (c).

Unusual degree programs: 3-2 engineering with Clarkson University, Rensselaer Polytechnic Institute, Rochester Institute of Technology.

Computers: 140 computers/terminals are available on campus for general student use. Students can access the following: campus intranet, computer help desk, free student e-mail accounts, online (class) grades, online (class) registration, online (class) schedules. Campuswide network is available. 100% of college-owned or -operated housing units are wired for high-speed Internet access. Wireless service is available via entire campus.

STUDENT LIFE

Housing options: on-campus residence required through senior year; men-only, women-only. Campus housing is university owned. Freshman campus housing is guaranteed.

Activities and organizations: drama/theater group, student-run newspaper, choral group, Intramurals, Foot of the Cross, Fellowship of Christian Athletes, Nursing Club, Drama Club.

Athletics Member NCAA, NCCAA. All NCAA Division II. ***Intercollegiate sports:*** basketball M(s)/W(s), cheerleading M(c)/W(c), cross-country running M(s)/W(s), golf M(s), lacrosse M(s)/W(s), soccer M(s)/W(s), tennis M(s)/W(s), track and field M(s)/W(s), volleyball W(s). ***Intramural sports:*** basketball M/W, field hockey M/W, football M/W, racquetball M/W, skiing (downhill) M/W, soccer M/W, softball M/W, table tennis M/W, tennis M/W, ultimate Frisbee M/W, volleyball M/W, water polo M/W.

Campus security: 24-hour emergency response devices and patrols, student patrols, late-night transport/escort service, controlled dormitory access, 24-hour Resident Life staff on-call.

Student services: health clinic, personal/psychological counseling.

COSTS & FINANCIAL AID

Costs (2014–15) ***One-time required fee:*** $398. ***Comprehensive fee:*** $37,908 includes full-time tuition ($27,036), mandatory fees ($1032), and room and board ($9840). Part-time tuition and fees vary according to course load. ***College room only:*** $6290. Room and board charges vary according to board plan and housing facility. ***Payment plan:*** installment. ***Waivers:*** senior citizens and employees or children of employees.

Financial Aid Of all full-time matriculated undergraduates who enrolled in 2014, 1,008 applied for aid, 954 were judged to have need, 122 had their need fully met. 723 Federal Work-Study jobs (averaging $390). 36 state and other part-time jobs (averaging $1944). In 2014, 151 non-need-based awards were made. ***Average percent of need met:*** 71. ***Average financial aid package:*** $21,535. ***Average need-based loan:*** $5435. ***Average need-based gift aid:*** $16,339. ***Average non-need-based aid:*** $9673. ***Average indebtedness upon graduation:*** $35,461.

APPLYING

Standardized Tests *Required:* SAT or ACT (for admission).

Options: electronic application, early admission, deferred entrance.

Required: essay or personal statement, high school transcript, 1 letter of recommendation. ***Recommended:*** minimum 2.7 GPA, 2 letters of recommendation, interview.

Application deadlines: rolling (freshmen), rolling (out-of-state freshmen), rolling (transfers).

Notification: continuous (freshmen), continuous (out-of-state freshmen), continuous (transfers).

CONTACT

Mr. JP Anderson, Associate Vice President of Undergraduate Admissions, Roberts Wesleyan College, 2301 Westside Drive, Rochester, NY 14624-1997. *Phone:* 585-594-6400. *Toll-free phone:* 800-777-4RWC. *Fax:* 585-594-6371. *E-mail:* admissions@roberts.edu.

Rochester Institute of Technology

Rochester, New York

http://www.rit.edu/

- **Independent** comprehensive, founded 1829
- **Suburban** 1300-acre campus with easy access to Rochester
- **Endowment** $754.0 million
- **Coed** 13,460 undergraduate students, 91% full-time, 32% women, 68% men
- **Moderately difficult** entrance level, 57% of applicants were admitted

UNDERGRAD STUDENTS

12,211 full-time, 1,249 part-time. Students come from 52 states and territories; 102 other countries; 45% are from out of state; 5% Black or African American, non-Hispanic/Latino; 6% Hispanic/Latino; 6% Asian, non-Hispanic/Latino; 0.2% American Indian or Alaska Native, non-Hispanic/Latino; 3% Two or more races, non-Hispanic/Latino; 13% Race/ethnicity unknown; 6% international; 5% transferred in; 68% live on campus.

Freshmen

Admission: 17,936 applied, 10,307 admitted, 2,678 enrolled. ***Average high school GPA:*** 3.7. ***Test scores:*** SAT critical reading scores over 500: 90%; SAT math scores over 500: 96%; SAT writing scores over 500: 84%; ACT scores over 18: 100%; SAT critical reading scores over 600: 49%; SAT math scores over 600: 67%; SAT writing scores over 600: 42%; ACT scores over 24: 91%; SAT critical reading scores over 700: 10%; SAT math scores over 700: 20%; SAT writing scores over 700: 7%; ACT scores over 30: 40%.

Retention: 86% of full-time freshmen returned.

FACULTY

Total: 1,499, 66% full-time, 45% with terminal degrees.

Student/faculty ratio: 12:1.

ACADEMICS

Calendar: quarters. *Degrees:* certificates, associate, bachelor's, master's, doctoral, and postbachelor's certificates.

Special study options: accelerated degree program, adult/continuing education programs, advanced placement credit, cooperative education, distance learning, double majors, English as a second language, freshman honors college, honors programs, independent study, internships, off-campus study, part-time degree program, services for LD students, student-designed majors, study abroad, summer session for credit. ***ROTC:*** Army (b), Navy (c), Air Force (b).

Computers: 2,500 computers/terminals are available on campus for general student use. Students can access the following: campus intranet, computer help desk, free student e-mail accounts, online (class) grades, online (class) registration, student account information. Campuswide network is available. 100% of college-owned or -operated housing units are wired for high-speed Internet access. Wireless service is available via classrooms, computer centers, computer labs, learning centers, libraries, student centers.

STUDENT LIFE

Housing options: on-campus residence required for freshman year; coed, men-only, women-only, special housing for students with disabilities. Campus housing is university owned. Freshman campus housing is guaranteed.

Activities and organizations: drama/theater group, student-run newspaper, radio station, choral group, national fraternities, national sororities.

Athletics Member NCAA. All Division III except men's and women's ice hockey (Division I). ***Intercollegiate sports:*** baseball M, basketball M/W, bowling M(c)/W(c), cheerleading M(c)/W(c), crew M/W, cross-country running M/W, equestrian sports M(c)/W(c), fencing M(c)/W(c), field hockey W(c), ice hockey M/W, lacrosse M/W, skiing (downhill) M(c)/W(c), soccer M/W, softball W, swimming and diving M/W, tennis M/W, track and field M/W, ultimate Frisbee M(c)/W(c), volleyball M(c)/W, water polo M(c)/W(c), wrestling M. ***Intramural sports:*** badminton M/W, basketball M/W, bowling M/W, football M, golf M/W, ice hockey M/W, lacrosse M(c), racquetball M/W, rock climbing M(c)/W(c), soccer M/W, softball M/W, table tennis M/W, tennis M/W, volleyball M/W.

Campus security: 24-hour emergency response devices and patrols, student patrols, late-night transport/escort service, controlled dormitory access.

Student services: health clinic, personal/psychological counseling, women's center, legal services.

COSTS & FINANCIAL AID

Costs (2014–15) ***Comprehensive fee:*** $47,606 includes full-time tuition ($35,526), mandatory fees ($512), and room and board ($11,568). Full-time tuition and fees vary according to course load. Part-time tuition: $1259 per credit hour. Part-time tuition and fees vary according to class time and course load. ***Required fees:*** $65 per term part-time. ***College room only:*** $6758. Room and board charges vary according to board plan and housing facility. ***Payment plans:*** tuition prepayment, installment, deferred payment. ***Waivers:*** employees or children of employees.

Financial Aid Of all full-time matriculated undergraduates who enrolled in 2013, 10,068 applied for aid, 9,138 were judged to have need, 7,500 had their need fully met. 1,800 Federal Work-Study jobs (averaging $2600). In 2013, 1600 non-need-based awards were made. ***Average percent of need met:*** 87. ***Average financial aid package:*** $24,000. ***Average need-based loan:*** $5500. ***Average need-based gift aid:*** $19,000. ***Average non-need-based aid:*** $10,000. ***Average indebtedness upon graduation:*** $26,000.

APPLYING

Standardized Tests *Required:* SAT or ACT (for admission).

Options: electronic application, early admission, early decision, deferred entrance.

Application fee: $60.

Required: essay or personal statement, high school transcript. ***Required for some:*** Portfolio of original artwork for applicants to the School of Art, Design and Crafts. Interview required for applicants to the BS/MS physician assistant program. ***Recommended:*** minimum 3.4 GPA, 1 letter of recommendation, interview.

Early decision deadline: 12/1.

Notification: 3/15 (freshmen), continuous (transfers), 1/15 (early decision).

CONTACT

Dr. Daniel Shelley, Associate Vice President, Rochester Institute of Technology, 60 Lomb Memorial Drive, Rochester, NY 14623-5604. *Phone:* 585-475-6631. *Fax:* 585-475-7424. *E-mail:* admissions@rit.edu.

See previous page for display ad and page 1586 for the College Close-Up.

The Sage Colleges

Troy, New York

http://www.sage.edu/

- **Independent** comprehensive
- **Urban** 23-acre campus
- **Endowment** $30.3 million
- **Coed** 1,704 undergraduate students, 86% full-time, 78% women, 22% men
- **Moderately difficult** entrance level, 55% of applicants were admitted

UNDERGRAD STUDENTS

1,463 full-time, 241 part-time. Students come from 25 states and territories; 3 other countries; 7% are from out of state; 13% Black or African American, non-Hispanic/Latino; 10% Hispanic/Latino; 3% Asian, non-Hispanic/Latino; 0.1% Native Hawaiian or other Pacific Islander, non-Hispanic/Latino; 0.3% American Indian or Alaska Native, non-Hispanic/Latino; 2% Two or more races, non-Hispanic/Latino; 9% Race/ethnicity unknown; 0.3% international; 13% transferred in; 55% live on campus.

Freshmen

Admission: 2,307 applied, 1,265 admitted, 283 enrolled. ***Average high school GPA:*** 3.2. ***Test scores:*** SAT critical reading scores over 500: 45%; SAT math scores over 500: 40%; ACT scores over 18: 85%; SAT critical reading scores over 600: 15%; SAT math scores over 600: 7%; ACT scores over 24: 44%; SAT critical reading scores over 700: 1%.

Retention: 81% of full-time freshmen returned.

FACULTY

Total: 271, 55% full-time, 69% with terminal degrees.

Student/faculty ratio: 13:1.

ACADEMICS

Degrees: bachelor's, master's, doctoral, post-master's, and postbachelor's certificates.

Special study options: academic remediation for entering students, accelerated degree program, adult/continuing education programs, advanced placement credit, cooperative education, distance learning, double majors, honors programs, independent study, internships, off-campus study, part-time degree program, services for LD students, student-designed majors, study abroad, summer session for credit. ***ROTC:*** Army (b), Air Force (b).

Unusual degree programs: 3-2 business administration with Sage Graduate school; engineering with Rensselaer Polytechnic Institute; nursing with Sage Graduate School; Occupational Therapy and Physical Therapy with Sage Graduate School; Clinical Biology with Albany College of Pharmacy.

Computers: 391 computers/terminals are available on campus for general student use. Students can access the following: campus intranet, computer help desk, free student e-mail accounts, online (class) grades, online (class) registration, online (class) schedules. Campuswide network is available. 100% of college-owned or -operated housing units are wired for high-speed Internet access. Wireless service is available via classrooms, computer labs, learning centers, libraries, student centers.

STUDENT LIFE

Housing options: coed, women-only. Campus housing is university owned and leased by the school. Freshman campus housing is guaranteed.

Activities and organizations: drama/theater group, student-run newspaper, choral group, Student Government, Association of Campus Events (A.C.E), College Republicans, Crew Club, Black & Latin Student Alliance.

Athletics Member NCAA. All Division III. ***Intercollegiate sports:*** basketball M/W, cross-country running M/W, golf M, lacrosse W, soccer M/W, softball W, tennis M/W, track and field M/W, volleyball M/W. ***Intramural sports:*** badminton M/W, cheerleading W(c), crew W(c), football M/W, ice hockey M(c)/W(c), lacrosse W(c), skiing (downhill) M(c)/W(c), ultimate Frisbee M(c)/W(c).

Campus security: 24-hour emergency response devices and patrols, late-night transport/escort service, controlled dormitory access.

Student services: health clinic, personal/psychological counseling, women's center.

COSTS & FINANCIAL AID

Costs (2014–15) ***Comprehensive fee:*** $40,030 includes full-time tuition ($27,000), mandatory fees ($1200), and room and board ($11,830). Part-time tuition: $900 per credit hour. ***College room only:*** $6200. Room and board charges vary according to board plan. ***Payment plan:*** installment. ***Waivers:*** employees or children of employees.

Financial Aid Of all full-time matriculated undergraduates who enrolled in 2014, 1,407 applied for aid, 1,339 were judged to have need. 500 Federal Work-Study jobs (averaging $1951). 30 state and other part-time jobs (averaging $5585). In 2014, 55 non-need-based awards were made. ***Average need-based loan:*** $3366. ***Average need-based gift aid:*** $14,404. ***Average non-need-based aid:*** $11,790. ***Average indebtedness upon graduation:*** $26,534.

APPLYING

Standardized Tests *Required for some:* SAT or ACT (for admission).

Options: electronic application, early admission, early action, deferred entrance.

Application fee: $30.

Required: essay or personal statement, high school transcript, minimum 2.5 GPA, 2 letters of recommendation, portfolio for art and design programs. ***Recommended:*** interview.

Application deadlines: rolling (freshmen), rolling (transfers).

Notification: continuous (freshmen), continuous (transfers).

CONTACT

Mr. Thomas Breen, Senior Director of Undergraduate Admission, TSC, The Sage Colleges, 140 New Scotland Avenue, Albany, NY 12208. *Phone:* 518-292-1926. *Fax:* 518-292-1912. *E-mail:* breent@sage.edu.

St. Bonaventure University

St. Bonaventure, New York

http://www.sbu.edu/

- **Independent** comprehensive, founded 1858, affiliated with Roman Catholic Church
- **Small-town** 500-acre campus
- **Coed** 1,771 undergraduate students, 97% full-time, 50% women, 50% men
- **Moderately difficult** entrance level, 70% of applicants were admitted

UNDERGRAD STUDENTS

1,725 full-time, 46 part-time. Students come from 33 states and territories; 26 other countries; 25% are from out of state; 5% Black or African American, non-Hispanic/Latino; 7% Hispanic/Latino; 4% Asian, non-Hispanic/Latino; 0.3% Native Hawaiian or other Pacific Islander, non-Hispanic/Latino; 0.4% American Indian or Alaska Native, non-Hispanic/Latino; 2% Two or more races, non-Hispanic/Latino; 10% Race/ethnicity unknown; 2% international; 3% transferred in; 76% live on campus.

Freshmen

Admission: 2,682 applied, 1,889 admitted, 435 enrolled. ***Average high school GPA:*** 3.4. ***Test scores:*** SAT critical reading scores over 500: 65%; SAT math scores over 500: 64%; SAT writing scores over 500: 58%; ACT scores over 18: 93%; SAT critical reading scores over 600: 21%; SAT math scores over 600: 21%; SAT writing scores over 600: 18%; ACT scores over 24: 50%; SAT critical reading scores over 700: 3%; SAT math scores over 700: 4%; SAT writing scores over 700: 3%; ACT scores over 30: 14%.

Retention: 84% of full-time freshmen returned.

FACULTY

Total: 222, 65% full-time, 55% with terminal degrees.

Student/faculty ratio: 11:1.

ACADEMICS

Calendar: semesters. *Degrees:* bachelor's, master's, post-master's, and postbachelor's certificates.

Special study options: accelerated degree program, advanced placement credit, distance learning, double majors, honors programs, independent study, internships, off-campus study, part-time degree program, services for LD students, student-designed majors, study abroad, summer session for credit. ***ROTC:*** Army (b).

Unusual degree programs: 3-2 business administration.

Computers: 320 computers/terminals and 2,500 ports are available on campus for general student use. Students can access the following: campus intranet, computer help desk, free student e-mail accounts, online (class) grades, online (class) registration, online (class) schedules. Campuswide network is available. 100% of college-owned or -operated housing units are wired for high-speed Internet access. Wireless service is available via entire campus.

STUDENT LIFE

Housing options: on-campus residence required through sophomore year; coed, special housing for students with disabilities. Campus housing is university owned. Freshman campus housing is guaranteed.

Activities and organizations: drama/theater group, student-run newspaper, radio and television station, choral group, Student Government Association, Bona Responds, BV newspaper, Students for the Mountain, Student Ambassadors.

Athletics Member NCAA. All Division I. ***Intercollegiate sports:*** baseball M(s), basketball M(s)/W(s), cross-country running M(s)/W(s), field hockey W(c), golf M(s), gymnastics W(c), ice hockey M(c), lacrosse M(c)/W(s), rugby M(c)/W(c), soccer M(s)/W(s), softball W(s), swimming and diving M(s)/W(s), tennis M(s)/W(s). ***Intramural sports:*** basketball M/W, football M/W, golf M/W, soccer M(c)/W(c), softball M/W, tennis M/W, ultimate Frisbee M/W, volleyball M/W.

Campus security: 24-hour emergency response devices and patrols, late-night transport/escort service, controlled dormitory access.

Student services: health clinic, personal/psychological counseling.

COSTS & FINANCIAL AID

Costs (2014–15) ***One-time required fee:*** $100. ***Comprehensive fee:*** $41,575 includes full-time tuition ($29,510), mandatory fees ($965), and room and board ($11,100). Part-time tuition: $880 per credit hour. Part-time tuition and fees vary according to course load. ***College room only:*** $5400. Room and board charges vary according to board plan and housing facility. ***Waivers:*** senior citizens and employees or children of employees.

Financial Aid Of all full-time matriculated undergraduates who enrolled in 2013, 1,511 applied for aid, 1,371 were judged to have need, 257 had their need fully met. 335 Federal Work-Study jobs (averaging $894). 398 state and other part-time jobs (averaging $665). In 2013, 362 non-need-based awards were made. ***Average percent of need met:*** 86. ***Average financial aid package:*** $26,368. ***Average need-based loan:*** $4660. ***Average need-based gift aid:*** $18,899. ***Average non-need-based aid:*** $12,572. ***Average indebtedness upon graduation:*** $35,627.

APPLYING

Standardized Tests *Required:* SAT or ACT (for admission). *Required for some:* SAT Subject Tests (for admission).

Options: electronic application, deferred entrance.

Required: high school transcript, 1 letter of recommendation. ***Required for some:*** essay or personal statement. ***Recommended:*** essay or personal statement, minimum 3.0 GPA, 3 letters of recommendation, interview.

Application deadlines: 7/1 (freshmen), 8/15 (transfers).

Notification: continuous until 10/15 (freshmen), continuous until 10/1 (transfers).

CONTACT

Monica Emery, Director of Recruitment, St. Bonaventure University, 3261 West State Road, St. Bonaventure, NY 14778. *Phone:* 716-375-2400. *Toll-free phone:* 800-462-5050. *Fax:* 716-375-4005. *E-mail:* memery@sbu.edu.

See previous page for display ad and page 1590 for the College Close-Up.

St. Francis College
Brooklyn Heights, New York
http://www.sfc.edu/

- **Independent Roman Catholic** comprehensive, founded 1884
- **Urban** 1-acre campus with easy access to New York City
- **Coed** 2,671 undergraduate students, 90% full-time, 56% women, 44% men

UNDERGRAD STUDENTS
2,414 full-time, 257 part-time. Students come from 21 states and territories; 67 other countries; 2% are from out of state; 20% Black or African American, non-Hispanic/Latino; 20% Hispanic/Latino; 4% Asian, non-Hispanic/Latino; 1% Native Hawaiian or other Pacific Islander, non-Hispanic/Latino; ####% American Indian or Alaska Native, non-Hispanic/Latino; 2% Two or more races, non-Hispanic/Latino; 9% Race/ethnicity unknown; 5% international; 6% transferred in; 6% live on campus.

Freshmen
Admission: 516 enrolled. ***Test scores:*** SAT critical reading scores over 500: 27%; SAT math scores over 500: 37%; SAT writing scores over 500: 29%; SAT critical reading scores over 600: 3%; SAT math scores over 600: 6%; SAT writing scores over 600: 4%; SAT math scores over 700: 1%.
Retention: 81% of full-time freshmen returned.

FACULTY
Total: 301, 29% full-time, 47% with terminal degrees.
Student/faculty ratio: 17:1.

ACADEMICS
Calendar: semesters. *Degrees:* associate, bachelor's, master's, and postbachelor's certificates.
Special study options: academic remediation for entering students, accelerated degree program, advanced placement credit, cooperative education, double majors, English as a second language, honors programs, independent study, internships, part-time degree program, student-designed majors, study abroad, summer session for credit. ***ROTC:*** Army (c), Air Force (c).
Unusual degree programs: business administration with Dual-degree BS and MS in Accounting; BA and MA in Psychology.
Computers: 412 computers/terminals are available on campus for general student use. Students can access the following: campus intranet, computer help desk, free student e-mail accounts, online (class) grades, online (class) registration. Campuswide network is available. 100% of college-owned or -operated housing units are wired for high-speed Internet access. Wireless service is available via entire campus.

STUDENT LIFE
Housing options: cooperative. Campus housing is provided by a third party.
Activities and organizations: drama/theater group, student-run newspaper, radio station, choral group, Latin American Society, Fine Arts Society, Power Lifting Club, Games Club, Haitian American Students Alliance, national fraternities, national sororities.
Athletics Member NCAA. All Division I. ***Intercollegiate sports:*** basketball M(s)/W(s), cross-country running M(s)/W(s), golf M(s)/W(s), soccer M(s), swimming and diving M(s)/W(s), tennis M(s)/W(s), track and field M(s)/W(s), volleyball W(s), water polo M(s)/W(s). ***Intramural sports:*** basketball M/W, football M, soccer M/W, table tennis M/W, volleyball M/W.
Campus security: ID checks, crime awareness workshops, pamphlets, posters, films, emergency notification system.
Student services: personal/psychological counseling.

COSTS & FINANCIAL AID
Costs (2014–15) ***Tuition:*** $21,400 full-time, $10,700 per term part-time. Full-time tuition and fees vary according to course load and degree level. Part-time tuition and fees vary according to course load and degree level. ***Required fees:*** $900 full-time, $725 per credit hour part-time, $275 per term part-time. ***Room only:*** $12,000.
Financial Aid Of all full-time matriculated undergraduates who enrolled in 2006, 1,747 applied for aid, 1,683 were judged to have need, 443 had their need fully met. 161 Federal Work-Study jobs (averaging $2200). ***Average percent of need met:*** 64. ***Average financial aid package:*** $9300. ***Average need-based loan:*** $7700. ***Average need-based gift aid:*** $6640.

APPLYING
Standardized Tests *Required:* SAT (for admission).
Required: essay or personal statement, high school transcript, minimum 2.0 GPA, 1 letter of recommendation. ***Recommended:*** interview.

CONTACT
Mrs. Lisa Randazzo, Associate Director of Admissions, St. Francis College, 180 Remsen Street, Brooklyn Heights, NY 11201-4398. *Phone:* 718-489-5336. *Fax:* 718-802-0453. *E-mail:* lrandazzo@sfc.edu.

See previous page for display ad and page 1592 for the College Close-Up.

St. John Fisher College

Rochester, New York

http://www.sjfc.edu/

- **Independent** comprehensive, founded 1948, affiliated with Roman Catholic Church
- **Suburban** 154-acre campus
- **Endowment** $69.4 million
- **Coed** 2,857 undergraduate students, 93% full-time, 60% women, 40% men
- **Moderately difficult** entrance level, 68% of applicants were admitted

UNDERGRAD STUDENTS
2,661 full-time, 196 part-time. Students come from 21 states and territories; 8 other countries; 3% are from out of state; 4% Black or African American, non-Hispanic/Latino; 4% Hispanic/Latino; 3% Asian, non-Hispanic/Latino; 0.1% Native Hawaiian or other Pacific Islander, non-Hispanic/Latino; 0.2% American Indian or Alaska Native, non-Hispanic/Latino; 2% Two or more races, non-Hispanic/Latino; 3% Race/ethnicity unknown; 0.4% international; 9% transferred in; 50% live on campus.

Freshmen
Admission: 3,836 applied, 2,605 admitted, 597 enrolled. ***Average high school GPA:*** 3.5. ***Test scores:*** SAT critical reading scores over 500: 62%; SAT math scores over 500: 79%; SAT writing scores over 500: 61%; ACT scores over 18: 99%; SAT critical reading scores over 600: 16%; SAT math scores over 600: 28%; SAT writing scores over 600: 21%; ACT scores over 24: 59%; SAT math scores over 700: 2%; ACT scores over 30: 6%.
Retention: 88% of full-time freshmen returned.

FACULTY
Total: 458, 49% full-time, 44% with terminal degrees.
Student/faculty ratio: 12:1.

ACADEMICS
Calendar: semesters. *Degrees:* certificates, bachelor's, master's, doctoral, post-master's, and postbachelor's certificates.
Special study options: academic remediation for entering students, accelerated degree program, adult/continuing education programs, advanced placement credit, distance learning, double majors, honors programs, independent study, internships, off-campus study, part-time degree program, services for LD students, student-designed majors, study abroad, summer session for credit. ***ROTC:*** Army (c), Navy (c), Air Force (c).
Unusual degree programs: 3-2 engineering with 3+2 pre-engineering program with affiliated engineering schools; Columbia University, Rensselaer Polytechnic Institute, University of Rochester.
Computers: 550 computers/terminals and 1,875 ports are available on campus for general student use. Students can access the following: campus intranet, computer help desk, free student e-mail accounts, online (class) grades, online (class) registration, online (class) schedules. Campuswide network is available. 100% of college-owned or -operated housing units are wired for high-speed Internet access. Wireless service is available via entire campus.

STUDENT LIFE
Housing options: coed, women-only, special housing for students with disabilities. Campus housing is university owned. Freshman campus housing is guaranteed.
Activities and organizations: drama/theater group, student-run newspaper, television station, choral group, student government, Student Activities Board, Commuter Council, Resident Student Association, Teddi Dance for Love.
Athletics Member NCAA. All Division III. ***Intercollegiate sports:*** baseball M, basketball M/W, crew W, cross-country running M/W, field hockey W, football M, golf M/W, lacrosse M/W, soccer M/W, softball W,

tennis M/W, track and field M/W, volleyball W. ***Intramural sports:*** basketball M/W, cheerleading W(c), crew M(c), equestrian sports M(c)/W(c), ice hockey M(c)/W(c), rugby M(c)/W(c), soccer M/W, volleyball M.

Campus security: 24-hour emergency response devices and patrols, late-night transport/escort service, controlled dormitory access.

Student services: health clinic, personal/psychological counseling.

COSTS & FINANCIAL AID

Costs (2014–15) ***Comprehensive fee:*** $40,708 includes full-time tuition ($28,970), mandatory fees ($580), and room and board ($11,158). Full-time tuition and fees vary according to program. Part-time tuition: $790 per credit hour. Part-time tuition and fees vary according to course load and program. ***Required fees:*** $10 per credit hour part-time. ***College room only:*** $7230. Room and board charges vary according to board plan. ***Payment plans:*** installment, deferred payment. ***Waivers:*** employees or children of employees.

Financial Aid Of all full-time matriculated undergraduates who enrolled in 2014, 2,368 applied for aid, 2,174 were judged to have need, 763 had their need fully met. 1,280 Federal Work-Study jobs (averaging $1494). In 2014, 466 non-need-based awards were made. ***Average percent of need met:*** 71. ***Average financial aid package:*** $20,935. ***Average need-based loan:*** $4745. ***Average need-based gift aid:*** $16,063. ***Average non-need-based aid:*** $10,658. ***Average indebtedness upon graduation:*** $32,982.

APPLYING

Standardized Tests *Required:* SAT or ACT (for admission).

Options: electronic application, early decision, deferred entrance.

Required: essay or personal statement, high school transcript, minimum 3.0 GPA, 1 letter of recommendation. ***Recommended:*** interview.

Application deadlines: rolling (freshmen), rolling (transfers).

Early decision deadline: 12/1.

Notification: continuous until 12/1 (freshmen), continuous until 9/1 (transfers), 12/15 (early decision).

CONTACT

Mrs. Stacy A. Ledermann, Director of Freshmen Admissions, St. John Fisher College, 3690 East Avenue, Rochester, NY 14618. *Phone:* 585-385-8064. *Toll-free phone:* 800-444-4640. *Fax:* 585-385-8386. *E-mail:* admissions@sjfc.edu.

St. John's University

Queens, New York

http://www.stjohns.edu/

- **Independent** university, founded 1870, affiliated with Roman Catholic Church
- **Urban** 105-acre campus with easy access to New York City
- **Endowment** $644.6 million
- **Coed** 15,765 undergraduate students, 68% full-time, 55% women, 45% men
- **Moderately difficult** entrance level, 63% of applicants were admitted

UNDERGRAD STUDENTS

10,720 full-time, 5,045 part-time. Students come from 49 states and territories; 81 other countries; 30% are from out of state; 19% Black or African American, non-Hispanic/Latino; 15% Hispanic/Latino; 18% Asian, non-Hispanic/Latino; 0.3% Native Hawaiian or other Pacific Islander, non-Hispanic/Latino; 0.2% American Indian or Alaska Native, non-Hispanic/Latino; 4% Two or more races, non-Hispanic/Latino; 4% Race/ethnicity unknown; 5% international; 3% transferred in; 29% live on campus.

Freshmen

Admission: 44,597 applied, 27,883 admitted, 2,795 enrolled. ***Average high school GPA:*** 3.4. ***Test scores:*** SAT critical reading scores over 500: 73%; SAT math scores over 500: 77%; ACT scores over 18: 99%; SAT critical reading scores over 600: 25%; SAT math scores over 600: 34%; ACT scores over 24: 66%; SAT critical reading scores over 700: 4%; SAT math scores over 700: 9%; ACT scores over 30: 17%.

Retention: 79% of full-time freshmen returned.

FACULTY

Total: 1,452, 42% full-time, 55% with terminal degrees.

Student/faculty ratio: 17:1.

ACADEMICS

Calendar: semesters. *Degrees:* certificates, associate, bachelor's, master's, doctoral, post-master's, and postbachelor's certificates.

Special study options: accelerated degree program, adult/continuing education programs, advanced placement credit, distance learning, double majors, English as a second language, honors programs, independent study, internships, off-campus study, part-time degree program, services for LD students, study abroad, summer session for credit. ***ROTC:*** Army (b).

Unusual degree programs: 3-2 engineering with Manhattan College.

Computers: 12,124 computers/terminals and 400 ports are available on campus for general student use. Students can access the following: campus intranet, computer help desk, free student e-mail accounts, online (class) grades, online (class) registration, online (class) schedules. Campuswide network is available. 100% of college-owned or -operated housing units are wired for high-speed Internet access. Wireless service is available via entire campus.

STUDENT LIFE

Housing options: coed. Campus housing is university owned and leased by the school. Freshman applicants given priority for college housing.

Activities and organizations: drama/theater group, student-run newspaper, radio and television station, choral group, Student Government, Incorporated, Student Programming Board, Haraya (Pan-African Students Coalition), American Pharmaceutical Association, Muslim Student Organization, national fraternities, national sororities.

Athletics Member NCAA. All Division I. ***Intercollegiate sports:*** baseball M(s), basketball M(s)/W(s), cross-country running W(s), fencing M(s)/W(s), golf M(s)/W(s), lacrosse M(s), soccer M(s)/W(s), softball W(s), tennis M(s)/W(s), track and field W(s), volleyball W(s). ***Intramural sports:*** badminton M/W, basketball M/W, bowling M(c)/W(c), cheerleading M/W, cross-country running M(c)/W(c), fencing M/W, football M/W, soccer M/W, softball M/W, table tennis M/W, tennis M(c)/W(c), ultimate Frisbee M(c)/W(c), volleyball M/W.

Campus security: 24-hour emergency response devices and patrols, late-night transport/escort service, controlled dormitory access, Emergency Notification System.

Student services: health clinic, personal/psychological counseling.

COSTS & FINANCIAL AID

Costs (2014–15) ***Comprehensive fee:*** $55,070 includes full-time tuition ($37,870), mandatory fees ($810), and room and board ($16,390). Full-time tuition and fees vary according to course load, program, and student level. Part-time tuition: $1262 per credit. Part-time tuition and fees vary according to course load, program, and student level. ***Required fees:*** $303 per term part-time. ***College room only:*** $10,260. Room and board charges vary according to board plan, housing facility, and location. ***Payment plan:*** installment. ***Waivers:*** adult students, senior citizens, and employees or children of employees.

Financial Aid Of all full-time matriculated undergraduates who enrolled in 2013, 9,391 applied for aid, 8,863 were judged to have need, 968 had their need fully met. 850 Federal Work-Study jobs (averaging $2415). In 2013, 245 non-need-based awards were made. ***Average percent of need met:*** 80. ***Average financial aid package:*** $27,001. ***Average need-based loan:*** $4718. ***Average need-based gift aid:*** $12,101. ***Average non-need-based aid:*** $16,330. ***Average indebtedness upon graduation:*** $32,950.

APPLYING

Standardized Tests *Required:* SAT or ACT (for admission).

Options: electronic application, early admission, deferred entrance.

Application fee: $50.

Required: high school transcript. ***Required for some:*** essay or personal statement, 2 letters of recommendation, interview. ***Recommended:*** essay or personal statement, minimum 3.0 GPA.

Application deadlines: rolling (freshmen), rolling (out-of-state freshmen), rolling (transfers).

Notification: continuous (freshmen), continuous (out-of-state freshmen), continuous (transfers).

CONTACT
Ms. Beth M. Evans, Vice President for Enrollment Management, St. John's University, 8000 Utopia Parkway, Queens, NY 11439. *Phone:* 718-990-2000. *Toll-free phone:* 888-9STJOHNS. *Fax:* 718-990-2096. *E-mail:* admission@stjohns.edu.

St. Joseph's College, Long Island Campus

Patchogue, New York

http://www.sjcny.edu/

- **Independent** comprehensive, founded 1916
- **Suburban** 56-acre campus with easy access to New York City
- **Endowment** $26.7 million
- **Coed** 3,023 undergraduate students, 80% full-time, 66% women, 34% men
- **Moderately difficult** entrance level, 77% of applicants were admitted

UNDERGRAD STUDENTS
2,417 full-time, 606 part-time. Students come from 13 states and territories; 22 other countries; 1% are from out of state; 5% Black or African American, non-Hispanic/Latino; 10% Hispanic/Latino; 2% Asian, non-Hispanic/Latino; 0.2% Native Hawaiian or other Pacific Islander, non-Hispanic/Latino; 0.7% American Indian or Alaska Native, non-Hispanic/Latino; 0.9% Two or more races, non-Hispanic/Latino; 11% Race/ethnicity unknown; 13% transferred in.

Freshmen
Admission: 1,451 applied, 1,114 admitted, 321 enrolled. ***Average high school GPA:*** 3.1. ***Test scores:*** SAT critical reading scores over 500: 70%; SAT math scores over 500: 71%; SAT writing scores over 500: 55%; ACT scores over 18: 95%; SAT critical reading scores over 600: 14%; SAT math scores over 600: 19%; SAT writing scores over 600: 12%; ACT scores over 24: 42%; SAT critical reading scores over 700: 1%; SAT math scores over 700: 1%; SAT writing scores over 700: 1%; ACT scores over 30: 3%.
Retention: 85% of full-time freshmen returned.

FACULTY
Total: 402, 30% full-time, 39% with terminal degrees.
Student/faculty ratio: 13:1.

ACADEMICS
Calendar: 4-1-4. *Degrees:* certificates, bachelor's, master's, and postbachelor's certificates.
Special study options: accelerated degree program, adult/continuing education programs, advanced placement credit, distance learning, double majors, English as a second language, honors programs, independent study, internships, off-campus study, part-time degree program, services for LD students, study abroad, summer session for credit.
Computers: 260 computers/terminals are available on campus for general student use. Students can access the following: campus intranet, computer help desk, free student e-mail accounts, online (class) grades, online (class) registration, online (class) schedules, Microsoft Office suite applications are offered free for students through our Microsoft Student Advantage program. Campuswide network is available. Wireless service is available via entire campus.

STUDENT LIFE
Housing options: college housing not available.
Activities and organizations: drama/theater group, student-run newspaper, radio station, choral group, Student Leadership Experience, Biology Club, Diversity Union, Child Study Club, Stars, national fraternities, national sororities.
Athletics Member NCAA. All Division III. ***Intercollegiate sports:*** baseball M, basketball M/W, cross-country running M/W, equestrian sports W(c), golf M, lacrosse W, soccer M/W, softball W, swimming and diving W, tennis M/W, track and field M/W, volleyball W.
Campus security: 24-hour emergency response devices and patrols, late-night transport/escort service, Emergency Notification System via cell phones.
Student services: health clinic, personal/psychological counseling.

COSTS & FINANCIAL AID
Costs (2015–16) ***Tuition:*** $23,500 full-time, $760 per credit part-time. Full-time tuition and fees vary according to course load and program.

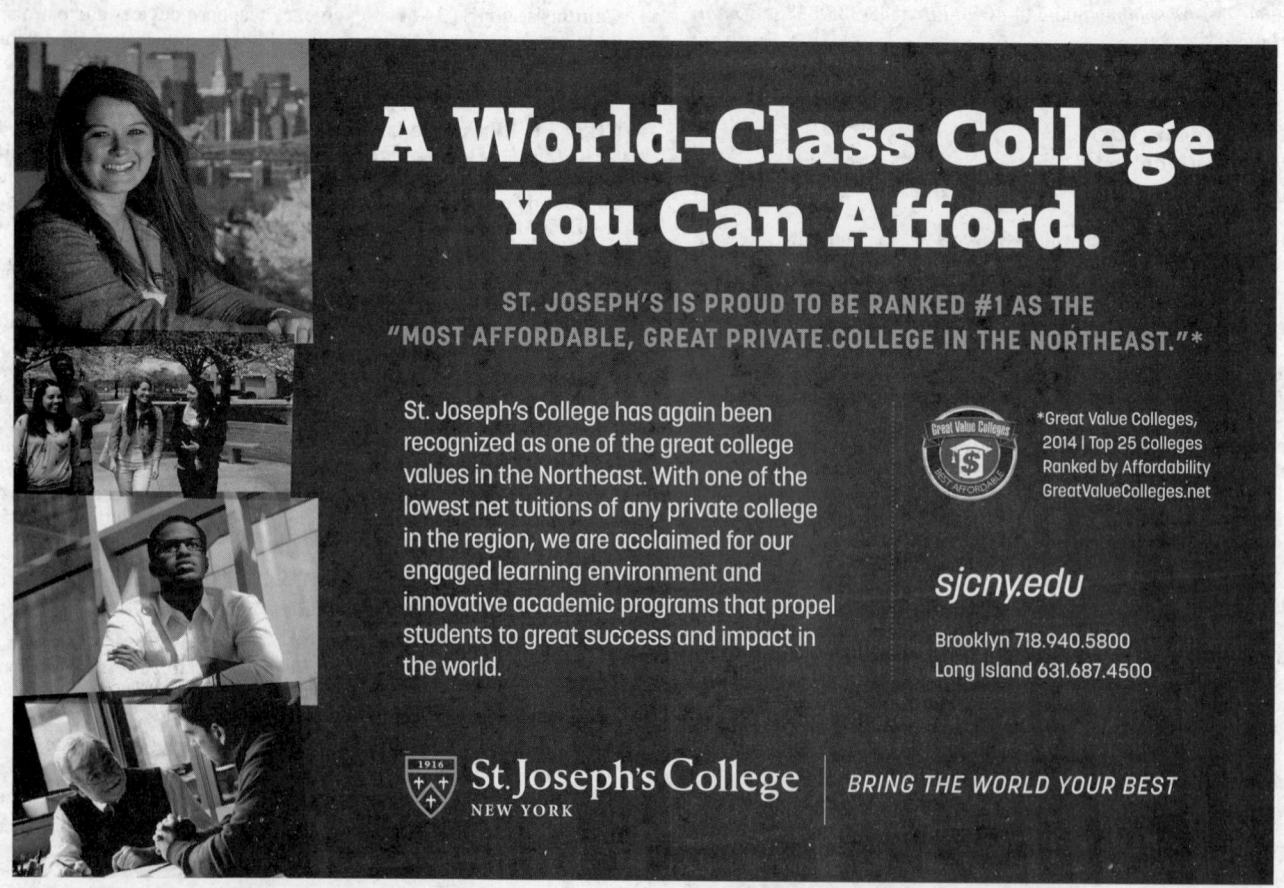

Part-time tuition and fees vary according to course load and program. ***Required fees:*** $630 full-time. ***Payment plans:*** installment, deferred payment. ***Waivers:*** senior citizens and employees or children of employees.

Financial Aid Of all full-time matriculated undergraduates who enrolled in 2013, 2,558 applied for aid, 2,044 were judged to have need, 692 had their need fully met. 85 Federal Work-Study jobs (averaging $2467). 89 state and other part-time jobs (averaging $3001). In 2013, 413 non-need-based awards were made. ***Average percent of need met:*** 61. ***Average financial aid package:*** $12,522. ***Average need-based loan:*** $4333. ***Average need-based gift aid:*** $10,256. ***Average non-need-based aid:*** $8684. ***Average indebtedness upon graduation:*** $23,603.

APPLYING

Standardized Tests *Required:* SAT or ACT (for admission).

Options: electronic application, early admission, deferred entrance.

Application fee: $25.

Required: essay or personal statement, high school transcript, minimum 3.0 GPA, 2 letters of recommendation, Completed application. ***Recommended:*** interview.

Application deadlines: rolling (freshmen), rolling (transfers).

Notification: continuous until 11/1 (freshmen), continuous until 11/1 (transfers).

CONTACT

Ms. Gigi Lamens, Associate Vice President for Enrollment Management, St. Joseph's College, Long Island Campus, 155 West Roe Boulevard, Patchogue, NY 11772. *Phone:* 631-687-4500. *E-mail:* glamens@sjcny.edu.

See previous page for display ad and page 1596 for the College Close-Up.

St. Joseph's College, New York

Brooklyn, New York

http://www.sjcny.edu/

- **Independent** comprehensive, founded 1916
- **Urban** 5-acre campus
- **Endowment** $8.0 million
- **Coed** 1,115 undergraduate students, 76% full-time, 66% women, 34% men
- **Moderately difficult** entrance level, 65% of applicants were admitted

UNDERGRAD STUDENTS

843 full-time, 272 part-time. Students come from 20 states and territories; 22 other countries; 4% are from out of state; 24% Black or African American, non-Hispanic/Latino; 20% Hispanic/Latino; 7% Asian, non-Hispanic/Latino; 0.2% Native Hawaiian or other Pacific Islander, non-Hispanic/Latino; 0.2% American Indian or Alaska Native, non-Hispanic/Latino; 0.9% Two or more races, non-Hispanic/Latino; 6% Race/ethnicity unknown; 0.1% international; 7% transferred in; 1% live on campus.

Freshmen

Admission: 1,573 applied, 1,025 admitted, 190 enrolled. ***Average high school GPA:*** 2.9. ***Test scores:*** SAT writing scores over 500: 40%; ACT scores over 18: 92%; SAT writing scores over 600: 12%; ACT scores over 24: 25%; SAT writing scores over 700: 1%; ACT scores over 30: 4%.

Retention: 78% of full-time freshmen returned.

FACULTY

Total: 190, 31% full-time, 38% with terminal degrees.

Student/faculty ratio: 10:1.

ACADEMICS

Calendar: semesters. *Degrees:* certificates, bachelor's, master's, and postbachelor's certificates.

Special study options: accelerated degree program, adult/continuing education programs, advanced placement credit, distance learning, double majors, English as a second language, honors programs, independent study, internships, part-time degree program, services for LD students, study abroad, summer session for credit.

Computers: 210 computers/terminals are available on campus for general student use. Students can access the following: campus intranet, computer help desk, free student e-mail accounts, online (class) grades, online (class) registration, online (class) schedules, Microsoft Office suite applications are offered free for students through our Microsoft Student Advantage program. Campuswide network is available. Wireless service is available via entire campus.

STUDENT LIFE

Housing options: coed. Campus housing is leased by the school.

Activities and organizations: drama/theater group, student-run newspaper, Black Student Association, Student Leadership Experience, Chapel Players, Child Study Club, Dance Team, national fraternities, national sororities.

Athletics Member NCAA, USCAA. All Division III. ***Intercollegiate sports:*** baseball M, basketball M/W, cross-country running M/W, soccer M/W, softball W, swimming and diving W, tennis M/W, volleyball M/W. ***Intramural sports:*** basketball M/W, bowling M, wrestling M(c).

Campus security: 24-hour emergency response devices and patrols, late-night transport/escort service, Emergency Notification System via cell phones.

Student services: health clinic, personal/psychological counseling.

COSTS & FINANCIAL AID

Costs (2015–16) ***Tuition:*** $23,500 full-time, $760 per credit part-time. Full-time tuition and fees vary according to course load and program. Part-time tuition and fees vary according to course load and program. ***Required fees:*** $630 full-time. ***Payment plans:*** installment, deferred payment. ***Waivers:*** senior citizens and employees or children of employees.

Financial Aid Of all full-time matriculated undergraduates who enrolled in 2013, 883 applied for aid, 715 were judged to have need, 165 had their need fully met. 88 Federal Work-Study jobs (averaging $1692). 14 state and other part-time jobs (averaging $1544). In 2013, 159 non-need-based awards were made. ***Average percent of need met:*** 63. ***Average financial aid package:*** $14,871. ***Average need-based loan:*** $4341. ***Average need-based gift aid:*** $13,287. ***Average non-need-based aid:*** $11,389. ***Average indebtedness upon graduation:*** $23,772.

APPLYING

Standardized Tests *Required:* SAT or ACT (for admission).

Options: electronic application, early admission, deferred entrance.

Application fee: $25.

Required: high school transcript, minimum 2.7 GPA. ***Recommended:*** essay or personal statement, 2 letters of recommendation, interview.

Application deadlines: 8/31 (freshmen), rolling (transfers).

Notification: continuous until 10/1 (freshmen), continuous (transfers).

CONTACT

Mr. Russell L. Watjen, Interim Vice President for Enrollment Management, St. Joseph's College, New York, 245 Clinton Avenue, Brooklyn, NY 11205. *Phone:* 718-940-5820. *E-mail:* rwatjen@sjcny.edu.

See previous page for display ad and page 1598 for the College Close-Up.

★ St. Lawrence University

Canton, New York

http://www.stlawu.edu/

- **Independent** comprehensive, founded 1856
- **Small-town** 1100-acre campus
- **Endowment** $283.9 million
- **Coed** 3,017 undergraduate students, 99% full-time, 54% women, 46% men
- **Very difficult** entrance level, 48% of applicants were admitted

UNDERGRAD STUDENTS

2,980 full-time, 37 part-time. Students come from 45 states and territories; 47 other countries; 58% are from out of state; 3% Black or African American, non-Hispanic/Latino; 4% Hispanic/Latino; 2% Asian, non-Hispanic/Latino; 0.1% Native Hawaiian or other Pacific Islander, non-Hispanic/Latino; 0.3% American Indian or Alaska Native, non-Hispanic/Latino; 3% Two or more races, non-Hispanic/Latino; 0.2%

Race/ethnicity unknown; 8% international; 0.9% transferred in; 98% live on campus.

Freshmen

Admission: 4,328 applied, 2,062 admitted, 596 enrolled. ***Average high school GPA:*** 3.5. ***Test scores:*** SAT critical reading scores over 500: 89%; SAT math scores over 500: 94%; SAT writing scores over 500: 87%; ACT scores over 18: 99%; SAT critical reading scores over 600: 48%; SAT math scores over 600: 59%; SAT writing scores over 600: 47%; ACT scores over 24: 87%; SAT critical reading scores over 700: 6%; SAT math scores over 700: 10%; SAT writing scores over 700: 7%; ACT scores over 30: 23%.

Retention: 90% of full-time freshmen returned.

FACULTY

Total: 211, 85% full-time, 89% with terminal degrees.

Student/faculty ratio: 11:1.

ACADEMICS

Calendar: semesters. *Degrees:* bachelor's, master's, and post-master's certificates.

Special study options: advanced placement credit, double majors, English as a second language, independent study, internships, off-campus study, part-time degree program, services for LD students, student-designed majors, study abroad, summer session for credit. ***ROTC:*** Army (c), Air Force (c).

Unusual degree programs: 3-2 engineering with Columbia University, Clarkson University, Rensselaer Polytechnic Institute, University of Rochester, Dartmouth College.

Computers: 758 computers/terminals are available on campus for general student use. Students can access the following: computer help desk, free student e-mail accounts, online (class) grades, online (class) registration, online (class) schedules. Campuswide network is available. 100% of college-owned or -operated housing units are wired for high-speed Internet access. Wireless service is available via entire campus.

STUDENT LIFE

Housing options: on-campus residence required through senior year; coed, women-only, cooperative. Campus housing is university owned. Freshman campus housing is guaranteed.

Activities and organizations: drama/theater group, student-run newspaper, radio station, choral group, The Thelomathesian Society - student government, Outing Club, Environmental Action Organization, Association for Campus Entertainment, Center for Civic Engagement, national fraternities, national sororities.

Athletics Member NCAA. All Division III except equestrian sports (Division II), men's and women's ice hockey (Division I). ***Intercollegiate sports:*** baseball M, basketball M/W, crew M/W, cross-country running M/W, equestrian sports W, field hockey W, football M, golf M/W, ice hockey M(s)/W(s), lacrosse M/W, skiing (downhill) M/W, soccer M/W, softball W, squash M/W, swimming and diving M/W, tennis M/W, track and field M/W, volleyball W. ***Intramural sports:*** basketball M/W, soccer M(c)/W(c).

Campus security: 24-hour emergency response devices and patrols, student patrols, late-night transport/escort service, controlled dormitory access.

Student services: health clinic, personal/psychological counseling.

COSTS & FINANCIAL AID

Costs (2014–15) ***Comprehensive fee:*** $59,972 includes full-time tuition ($47,350), mandatory fees ($336), and room and board ($12,286). ***College room only:*** $6166. Room and board charges vary according to board plan. ***Payment plans:*** tuition prepayment, installment. ***Waivers:*** employees or children of employees.

Financial Aid Of all full-time matriculated undergraduates who enrolled in 2014, 1,508 applied for aid, 1,313 were judged to have need, 338 had their need fully met. 842 Federal Work-Study jobs (averaging $1597). 319 state and other part-time jobs (averaging $1640). In 2014, 828 non-need-based awards were made. ***Average percent of need met:*** 84. ***Average financial aid package:*** $38,322. ***Average need-based loan:*** $4535. ***Average need-based gift aid:*** $31,636. ***Average non-need-based aid:*** $20,225. ***Average indebtedness upon graduation:*** $26,792. ***Financial aid deadline:*** 2/1.

APPLYING

Standardized Tests *Recommended:* SAT or ACT (for admission).

Options: electronic application, early admission, early decision, deferred entrance.

Application fee: $60.

Required: high school transcript, 2 letters of recommendation, interview.

Application deadlines: 2/1 (freshmen), 2/1 (out-of-state freshmen), 3/1 (transfers).

Early decision deadline: 11/1.

Notification: 3/31 (freshmen), 3/31 (out-of-state freshmen), continuous (transfers), rolling (early decision).

CONTACT

Jeremy Freeman, Director of Admissions, St. Lawrence University, 23 Romoda Drive, Canton, NY 13617-1455. *Phone:* 315-229-5261. *Toll-free phone:* 800-285-1856. *Fax:* 315-229-5818. *E-mail:* jfreeman@stlawu.edu.

See previous page for display ad and page 1600 for the College Close-Up.

★ St. Thomas Aquinas College

Sparkill, New York

http://www.stac.edu/

- **Independent** comprehensive, founded 1952
- **Suburban** 46-acre campus with easy access to New York City
- **Endowment** $30.6 million
- **Coed** 1,780 undergraduate students, 64% full-time, 55% women, 45% men
- **Moderately difficult** entrance level, 81% of applicants were admitted

UNDERGRAD STUDENTS

1,147 full-time, 633 part-time. Students come from 13 states and territories; 10 other countries; 21% are from out of state; 8% Black or African American, non-Hispanic/Latino; 20% Hispanic/Latino; 3% Asian, non-Hispanic/Latino; 0.1% Native Hawaiian or other Pacific Islander, non-Hispanic/Latino; 0.2% American Indian or Alaska Native, non-Hispanic/Latino; 2% Two or more races, non-Hispanic/Latino; 9% Race/ethnicity unknown; 2% international; 4% transferred in.

Freshmen

Admission: 1,423 applied, 1,150 admitted, 209 enrolled. ***Average high school GPA:*** 3.05. ***Test scores:*** SAT critical reading scores over 500: 34%; SAT math scores over 500: 42%; SAT writing scores over 500: 38%; ACT scores over 18: 78%; SAT critical reading scores over 600: 10%; SAT math scores over 600: 15%; SAT writing scores over 600: 12%; ACT scores over 24: 22%; SAT critical reading scores over 700: 2%; SAT writing scores over 700: 2%; ACT scores over 30: 7%.

Retention: 77% of full-time freshmen returned.

FACULTY

Total: 176, 33% full-time, 40% with terminal degrees.

Student/faculty ratio: 14:1.

ACADEMICS

Calendar: semesters. *Degrees:* associate, bachelor's, master's, post-master's, and postbachelor's certificates.

Special study options: academic remediation for entering students, accelerated degree program, adult/continuing education programs, advanced placement credit, double majors, freshman honors college, honors programs, independent study, internships, off-campus study, part-time degree program, services for LD students, study abroad, summer session for credit. ***ROTC:*** Air Force (c).

Unusual degree programs: 3-2 engineering with George Washington University, Manhattan College; social work with New York University School of Social Work; physical therapy with New York Medical College.

Computers: 200 computers/terminals are available on campus for general student use. Students can access the following: campus intranet, computer help desk, free student e-mail accounts, online (class) grades, online (class) registration, online (class) schedules. Campuswide network is available. 100% of college-owned or -operated housing units are wired for high-speed Internet access. Wireless service is available via entire campus.

STUDENT LIFE

Housing options: men-only, women-only, special housing for students with disabilities. Campus housing is university owned. Freshman campus housing is guaranteed.

Activities and organizations: drama/theater group, student-run newspaper, radio station, choral group, Spartan Volunteers, Campus Activities Board, WSTK campus radio, Bowling Club, Laetare Players, national fraternities.

Athletics Member NCAA, NAIA. All NCAA Division II. ***Intercollegiate sports:*** baseball M(s), basketball M(s)/W(s), cross-country running M(s)/W(s), golf M/W, lacrosse W, soccer M(s)/W(s), softball W(s), tennis M/W, volleyball W(s). ***Intramural sports:*** basketball M/W, volleyball M/W.

Campus security: 24-hour emergency response devices and patrols, student patrols, late-night transport/escort service, controlled dormitory access.

Student services: health clinic, personal/psychological counseling.

COSTS & FINANCIAL AID

Costs (2014–15) ***Comprehensive fee:*** $39,810 includes full-time tuition ($27,130), mandatory fees ($1000), and room and board ($11,680). Part-time tuition: $865 per credit. ***College room only:*** $6300. Room and board charges vary according to board plan and housing facility. ***Payment plan:*** installment. ***Waivers:*** employees or children of employees.

Financial Aid Of all full-time matriculated undergraduates who enrolled in 2013, 1,063 applied for aid, 872 were judged to have need, 152 had their need fully met. 119 Federal Work-Study jobs (averaging $1142). In 2013, 201 non-need-based awards were made. ***Average percent of need met:*** 37. ***Average financial aid package:*** $15,315. ***Average need-based loan:*** $4800. ***Average need-based gift aid:*** $10,315. ***Average non-need-based aid:*** $10,195. ***Average indebtedness upon graduation:*** $28,750.

APPLYING

Standardized Tests *Required:* SAT or ACT (for admission).

Options: electronic application, deferred entrance.

Application fee: $30.

Required: high school transcript, minimum 2.0 GPA. ***Required for some:*** 3 letters of recommendation. ***Recommended:*** essay or personal statement, 2 letters of recommendation, interview.

Application deadlines: rolling (freshmen), rolling (transfers), 12/15 (early action).

Early decision deadline: 12/1.

Notification: 10/1 (freshmen), continuous (transfers), 1/15 (early decision), 1/15 (early action).

CONTACT

Mr. Bartholomew Grachan, Director of Admissions, St. Thomas Aquinas College, 125 Route 340, Sparkill, NY 10976. *Phone:* 845-398-4102. *Toll-free phone:* 800-999-STAC. *Fax:* 845-398-4114. *E-mail:* bgrachan@stac.edu.

See below for display ad and page 1612 for the College Close-Up.

Sarah Lawrence College

Bronxville, New York

http://www.sarahlawrence.edu/

- **Independent** comprehensive, founded 1926
- **Suburban** 44-acre campus with easy access to New York City
- **Endowment** $88.5 million
- **Coed** 1,437 undergraduate students, 98% full-time, 71% women, 29% men
- **Very difficult** entrance level, 53% of applicants were admitted

UNDERGRAD STUDENTS

1,415 full-time, 22 part-time. Students come from 45 states and territories; 52 other countries; 79% are from out of state; 4% Black or African American, non-Hispanic/Latino; 9% Hispanic/Latino; 4% Asian, non-Hispanic/Latino; 0.1% Native Hawaiian or other Pacific Islander, non-Hispanic/Latino; 0.1% American Indian or Alaska Native, non-Hispanic/Latino; 6% Two or more races, non-Hispanic/Latino; 7% Race/ethnicity unknown; 13% international; 2% transferred in; 82% live on campus.

Freshmen
Admission: 2,392 applied, 1,271 admitted, 356 enrolled. ***Average high school GPA:*** 3.67. ***Test scores:*** SAT critical reading scores over 500: 97%; SAT math scores over 500: 92%; SAT writing scores over 500: 97%; ACT scores over 18: 100%; SAT critical reading scores over 600: 81%; SAT math scores over 600: 56%; SAT writing scores over 600: 77%; ACT scores over 24: 96%; SAT critical reading scores over 700: 34%; SAT math scores over 700: 12%; SAT writing scores over 700: 24%; ACT scores over 30: 52%.

Retention: 85% of full-time freshmen returned.

FACULTY
Total: 304, 35% full-time, 69% with terminal degrees.

Student/faculty ratio: 10:1.

ACADEMICS
Calendar: semesters. *Degrees:* bachelor's and master's.

Special study options: accelerated degree program, adult/continuing education programs, advanced placement credit, double majors, independent study, internships, off-campus study, part-time degree program, services for LD students, student-designed majors, study abroad, summer session for credit.

Unusual degree programs: 3-2 engineering with Engineering with Columbia University; 3-2 Art of Teaching; 3-2 Child Development; 3-2 Women's History;3-2 Health Advocacy.

Computers: 143 computers/terminals are available on campus for general student use. Students can access the following: campus intranet, computer help desk, free student e-mail accounts, online (class) grades, online (class) schedules. Campuswide network is available. 100% of college-owned or -operated housing units are wired for high-speed Internet access. Wireless service is available via entire campus.

STUDENT LIFE
Housing options: on-campus residence required for freshman year; coed, men-only, women-only, cooperative, special housing for students with disabilities. Campus housing is university owned. Freshman campus housing is guaranteed.

Activities and organizations: drama/theater group, student-run newspaper, radio station, choral group, Sarah Lawrence Activities Council, Hillel, Queer Voice Coalition, SLC Phoenix Newspaper, The Rocky Horror Picture Show Shadow Cast Production.

Athletics Member NCAA. All Division III. ***Intercollegiate sports:*** basketball M/W, crew M/W, cross-country running M/W, equestrian sports M/W, golf W, soccer M/W, softball W, swimming and diving M/W, tennis M/W, volleyball M/W. ***Intramural sports:*** fencing M/W, golf M, soccer M/W, softball M/W, squash M/W, ultimate Frisbee M/W, volleyball M/W, water polo M/W.

Campus security: 24-hour emergency response devices and patrols, late-night transport/escort service, controlled dormitory access.

Student services: health clinic, personal/psychological counseling.

COSTS & FINANCIAL AID
Costs (2014–15) ***Comprehensive fee:*** $65,240 includes full-time tuition ($49,680), mandatory fees ($1056), and room and board ($14,504). Full-time tuition and fees vary according to course load. Part-time tuition: $1656 per credit. Part-time tuition and fees vary according to course load. ***Required fees:*** $275 per term part-time. ***College room only:*** $9314. Room and board charges vary according to board plan. ***Payment plan:*** installment. ***Waivers:*** employees or children of employees.

Financial Aid Of all full-time matriculated undergraduates who enrolled in 2014, 1,127 applied for aid, 991 were judged to have need, 746 had their need fully met. 616 Federal Work-Study jobs (averaging $1617). 53 state and other part-time jobs (averaging $1638). In 2014, 283 non-need-based awards were made. ***Average percent of need met:*** 89. ***Average financial aid package:*** $35,368. ***Average need-based loan:*** $3241. ***Average need-based gift aid:*** $34,650. ***Average non-need-based aid:*** $16,582. ***Average indebtedness upon graduation:*** $18,483. ***Financial aid deadline:*** 2/1.

APPLYING
Standardized Tests *Recommended:* SAT or ACT (for admission).

Options: electronic application, early admission, early decision, deferred entrance.

Application fee: $60.

Required: essay or personal statement, high school transcript, 2 letters of recommendation. ***Recommended:*** minimum 3.0 GPA, interview.

Application deadlines: 1/15 (freshmen), 4/1 (transfers).

Early decision deadline: 11/1 (for plan 1), 1/1 (for plan 2).

Notification: 4/1 (freshmen), 5/1 (transfers), 12/15 (early decision plan 1), 2/15 (early decision plan 2).

CONTACT
Ms. Jennifer Gayles, Director of Admission and Multicultural Recruitment, Sarah Lawrence College, 1 Mead Way, Bronxville, NY 10708-5999. *Phone:* 914-395-2510. *Toll-free phone:* 800-888-2858. *Fax:* 914-395-2515. *E-mail:* slcadmit@sarahlawrence.edu.

★ School of Visual Arts
New York, New York
http://www.sva.edu/

CONTACT
Admissions Office, School of Visual Arts, 209 East 23rd Street, New York, NY 10010. *Phone:* 212-592-2100. *Toll-free phone:* 800-436-4204. *Fax:* 212-592-2116. *E-mail:* admissions@sva.edu.

Siena College
Loudonville, New York
http://www.siena.edu/

- **Independent Roman Catholic** comprehensive, founded 1937
- **Suburban** 175-acre campus with easy access to Albany NY
- **Endowment** $138.8 million
- **Coed** 3,139 undergraduate students, 95% full-time, 52% women, 48% men
- **Moderately difficult** entrance level, 58% of applicants were admitted

UNDERGRAD STUDENTS
2,990 full-time, 149 part-time. Students come from 32 states and territories; 17 other countries; 19% are from out of state; 3% Black or African American, non-Hispanic/Latino; 7% Hispanic/Latino; 4% Asian, non-Hispanic/Latino; 0.1% Native Hawaiian or other Pacific Islander, non-Hispanic/Latino; 0.1% American Indian or Alaska Native, non-Hispanic/Latino; 2% Two or more races, non-Hispanic/Latino; 1% Race/ethnicity unknown; 2% international; 4% transferred in; 78% live on campus.

Freshmen
Admission: 8,647 applied, 5,013 admitted, 709 enrolled. ***Average high school GPA:*** 3.49. ***Test scores:*** SAT critical reading scores over 500: 78%; SAT math scores over 500: 84%; SAT writing scores over 500: 72%; ACT scores over 18: 99%; SAT critical reading scores over 600: 29%; SAT math scores over 600: 38%; SAT writing scores over 600: 23%; ACT scores over 24: 64%; SAT critical reading scores over 700: 3%; SAT math scores over 700: 6%; SAT writing scores over 700: 4%; ACT scores over 30: 11%.

Retention: 89% of full-time freshmen returned.

FACULTY
Total: 350, 66% full-time, 72% with terminal degrees.

Student/faculty ratio: 11:1.

ACADEMICS
Calendar: semesters. *Degrees:* certificates, bachelor's, and master's.

Special study options: accelerated degree program, advanced placement credit, double majors, English as a second language, honors programs, independent study, internships, off-campus study, part-time degree program, services for LD students, student-designed majors, study abroad, summer session for credit. ***ROTC:*** Army (b), Air Force (c).

Unusual degree programs: 3-2 engineering with Binghamton University, Catholic University, Clarkson University, Manhattan College, Rensselaer Polytechnic Institute, Western New England College, Union Graduate College.

Computers: 402 computers/terminals and 5,341 ports are available on campus for general student use. Students can access the following: campus intranet, computer help desk, free student e-mail accounts, online (class) grades, online (class) registration, online (class) schedules. Campuswide network is available. 100% of college-owned or -operated housing units are wired for high-speed Internet access. Wireless service is available via classrooms, computer centers, computer labs, dorm rooms, learning centers, libraries, student centers.

STUDENT LIFE

Housing options: on-campus residence required through senior year; coed, special housing for students with disabilities. Campus housing is university owned. Freshman applicants given priority for college housing.

Activities and organizations: drama/theater group, student-run newspaper, radio and television station, choral group, Habitat for Humanity, Psychology Club, Outing Club, Biology Club, LUNA (Latinos Unificando Nuestra America), national fraternities.

Athletics Member NCAA. All Division I. ***Intercollegiate sports:*** baseball M(s), basketball M(s)/W(s), cheerleading W(c), cross-country running M(s)/W(s), equestrian sports M(c)/W(c), field hockey W(s), golf M(s)/W(s), ice hockey M(c), lacrosse M(s)/W(s), rugby M(c)/W(c), soccer M(s)/W(s), softball W(s), squash M(c)/W(c), swimming and diving W(s), tennis M(s)/W(s), ultimate Frisbee M(c)/W(c), volleyball M(c)/W(s), water polo W(s). ***Intramural sports:*** basketball M/W, football M, racquetball M/W, soccer M/W, softball M/W, volleyball M/W.

Campus security: 24-hour emergency response devices and patrols, late-night transport/escort service, controlled dormitory access, call boxes in parking lots and on roadways.

Student services: health clinic, personal/psychological counseling, women's center.

COSTS & FINANCIAL AID

Costs (2015–16) ***Comprehensive fee:*** $47,010 includes full-time tuition ($33,165), mandatory fees ($250), and room and board ($13,595). Full-time tuition and fees vary according to course load, program, and student level. Part-time tuition: $600 per credit. Part-time tuition and fees vary according to course load, program, and student level. ***College room only:*** $8015. Room and board charges vary according to board plan and housing facility. ***Payment plan:*** installment. ***Waivers:*** employees or children of employees.

Financial Aid Of all full-time matriculated undergraduates who enrolled in 2012, 2,541 applied for aid, 2,219 were judged to have need, 483 had their need fully met. In 2012, 593 non-need-based awards were made. ***Average percent of need met:*** 71. ***Average financial aid package:*** $21,758. ***Average need-based loan:*** $4415. ***Average need-based gift aid:*** $15,414. ***Average non-need-based aid:*** $6198. ***Average indebtedness upon graduation:*** $35,569. ***Financial aid deadline:*** 5/1.

APPLYING

Standardized Tests *Recommended:* SAT or ACT (for admission).

Options: electronic application, early admission, early decision, early action, deferred entrance.

Application fee: $50.

Required: essay or personal statement, high school transcript, 1 letter of recommendation. ***Required for some:*** interview. ***Recommended:*** interview.

Application deadlines: 2/15 (freshmen), 8/15 (transfers), 12/1 (early action).

Early decision deadline: 12/1.

Notification: 3/15 (freshmen), continuous (transfers), 12/15 (early decision), 1/1 (early action).

CONTACT

Ms. Mary Lawyer, Associate Vice President for Enrollment Management, Siena College, 515 Loudon Road, Loudonville, NY 12211-1462. *Phone:* 518-783-2427. *Toll-free phone:* 888-AT-SIENA. *Fax:* 518-783-2436. *E-mail:* admissions@siena.edu.

★ Skidmore College

Saratoga Springs, New York

http://www.skidmore.edu/

- **Independent** comprehensive, founded 1903
- **Small-town** 800-acre campus with easy access to Albany, NY
- **Endowment** $334.2 million
- **Coed** 2,632 undergraduate students, 99% full-time, 59% women, 41% men
- **Very difficult** entrance level, 37% of applicants were admitted

UNDERGRAD STUDENTS
2,609 full-time, 23 part-time. Students come from 44 states and territories; 58 other countries; 67% are from out of state; 4% Black or African American, non-Hispanic/Latino; 8% Hispanic/Latino; 6% Asian, non-Hispanic/Latino; 0.1% Native Hawaiian or other Pacific Islander, non-Hispanic/Latino; 4% Two or more races, non-Hispanic/Latino; 7% Race/ethnicity unknown; 8% international; 0.7% transferred in; 89% live on campus.

Freshmen
Admission: 8,669 applied, 3,237 admitted, 724 enrolled. ***Test scores:*** SAT critical reading scores over 500: 93%; SAT math scores over 500: 95%; SAT writing scores over 500: 93%; ACT scores over 18: 100%; SAT critical reading scores over 600: 61%; SAT math scores over 600: 64%; SAT writing scores over 600: 60%; ACT scores over 24: 89%; SAT critical reading scores over 700: 17%; SAT math scores over 700: 19%; SAT writing scores over 700: 18%; ACT scores over 30: 33%.

Retention: 95% of full-time freshmen returned.

FACULTY
Total: 368, 70% full-time, 71% with terminal degrees.

Student/faculty ratio: 8:1.

ACADEMICS
Calendar: semesters plus optional 6-week internship period. *Degrees:* bachelor's and master's.

Special study options: accelerated degree program, adult/continuing education programs, advanced placement credit, double majors, honors programs, independent study, internships, off-campus study, services for LD students, student-designed majors, study abroad, summer session for credit. ***ROTC:*** Army (c), Air Force (c).

Unusual degree programs: 3-2 business administration with Clarkson University, Union College, Rochester Institute of Technology, Syracuse University; engineering with Dartmouth College, Clarkson University, Rensselaer Polytechnic Institute; nursing with New York University; MALS at Skidmore College, MSF with Syracuse University, MSA with Syracuse University, DPT and MS in occupational therapy with Sage Graduate School.

Computers: 600 computers/terminals are available on campus for general student use. Students can access the following: campus intranet, computer help desk, free student e-mail accounts, online (class) grades, online (class) registration, online (class) schedules. Campuswide network is available. 100% of college-owned or -operated housing units are wired for high-speed Internet access. Wireless service is available via classrooms, computer centers, computer labs, dorm rooms, learning centers, libraries, student centers.

STUDENT LIFE
Housing options: on-campus residence required through sophomore year; coed, women-only, special housing for students with disabilities. Campus housing is university owned. Freshman campus housing is guaranteed.

Activities and organizations: drama/theater group, student-run newspaper, radio and television station, choral group, Student Government Association, Student radio station (WSPN), Benefaction (Student Volunteer), Outing Club, UJIMA.

Athletics Member NCAA. All Division III. ***Intercollegiate sports:*** baseball M, basketball M/W, crew M/W, equestrian sports W, field hockey W, golf M, ice hockey M, lacrosse M/W, soccer M/W, softball W, swimming and diving M/W, tennis M/W, volleyball W. ***Intramural sports:*** basketball M/W, football M/W, racquetball M/W, soccer M/W, softball M/W, tennis M/W, volleyball M/W.

Campus security: 24-hour emergency response devices and patrols, late-night transport/escort service, controlled dormitory access, well-lit campus.

Student services: health clinic, personal/psychological counseling.

COSTS & FINANCIAL AID
Costs (2014–15) ***One-time required fee:*** $150. ***Comprehensive fee:*** $59,942 includes full-time tuition ($46,390), mandatory fees ($924), and room and board ($12,628). Full-time tuition and fees vary according to course load. Part-time tuition: $1546 per credit. Part-time tuition and fees vary according to course load. ***Required fees:*** $25 per term part-time. ***College room only:*** $7466. Room and board charges vary according to board plan and housing facility. ***Payment plans:*** tuition prepayment, installment. ***Waivers:*** senior citizens and employees or children of employees.

Financial Aid Of all full-time matriculated undergraduates who enrolled in 2014, 1,350 applied for aid, 1,159 were judged to have need, 1,054 had their need fully met. In 2014, 11 non-need-based awards were made. ***Average percent of need met:*** 94. ***Average financial aid package:*** $41,800. ***Average need-based loan:*** $4100. ***Average need-based gift aid:*** $38,400. ***Average non-need-based aid:*** $12,000. ***Average indebtedness upon graduation:*** $22,887. ***Financial aid deadline:*** 2/1.

APPLYING
Standardized Tests *Required:* SAT or ACT (for admission). *Recommended:* SAT Subject Tests (for admission).

Options: electronic application, early admission, early decision, deferred entrance.

Application fee: $65.

Required: essay or personal statement, high school transcript, 2 letters of recommendation. ***Recommended:*** interview.

Application deadlines: 1/15 (freshmen), 4/1 (transfers).

Early decision deadline: 11/15 (for plan 1), 1/15 (for plan 2).

Notification: 4/1 (freshmen), 12/15 (early decision plan 1), 2/15 (early decision plan 2).

CONTACT
Ms. Mary Lou Bates, Dean of Admissions and Financial Aid, Skidmore College, 815 North Broadway, Saratoga Springs, NY 12866-1632. *Phone:* 518-580-5570. *Toll-free phone:* 800-867-6007. *Fax:* 518-580-5584. *E-mail:* admissions@skidmore.edu.

See previous page for display ad and page 1622 for the College Close-Up.

★ State University of New York at Fredonia

Fredonia, New York

http://www.fredonia.edu/

- **State-supported** comprehensive, founded 1826, part of State University of New York System
- **Small-town** 249-acre campus with easy access to Buffalo
- **Endowment** $29.0 million
- **Coed** 4,941 undergraduate students, 98% full-time, 54% women, 46% men
- **Moderately difficult** entrance level, 53% of applicants were admitted

UNDERGRAD STUDENTS
4,821 full-time, 120 part-time. Students come from 25 states and territories; 12 other countries; 2% are from out of state; 6% Black or African American, non-Hispanic/Latino; 6% Hispanic/Latino; 1% Asian, non-Hispanic/Latino; 0.1% Native Hawaiian or other Pacific Islander, non-Hispanic/Latino; 0.4% American Indian or Alaska Native, non-Hispanic/Latino; 2% Two or more races, non-Hispanic/Latino; 3% Race/ethnicity unknown; 3% international; 7% transferred in; 53% live on campus.

Freshmen
Admission: 6,095 applied, 3,244 admitted, 1,072 enrolled. ***Average high school GPA:*** 3.25. ***Test scores:*** SAT critical reading scores over 500: 61%; SAT math scores over 500: 67%; ACT scores over 18: 98%; SAT critical reading scores over 600: 16%; SAT math scores over 600: 19%; ACT scores over 24: 53%; SAT critical reading scores over 700: 1%; SAT math scores over 700: 2%; ACT scores over 30: 6%.

Retention: 79% of full-time freshmen returned.

FACULTY
Total: 488, 52% full-time, 54% with terminal degrees.

Student/faculty ratio: 16:1.

ACADEMICS
Calendar: semesters. *Degrees:* bachelor's, master's, and post-master's certificates.

Special study options: accelerated degree program, adult/continuing education programs, advanced placement credit, distance learning, double majors, English as a second language, honors programs, independent study, internships, off-campus study, part-time degree program, services for LD students, student-designed majors, study abroad, summer session for credit.

Unusual degree programs: 3-2 engineering with Clarkson University, State University of New York at Buffalo, Case Western Reserve, Columbia University, Cornell University, Louisiana Technical University, New York State College of Ceramics at Alfred, Ohio State University.

Computers: 500 computers/terminals are available on campus for general student use. Students can access the following: campus intranet, computer help desk, free student e-mail accounts, online (class) grades, online (class) registration, online (class) schedules. Campuswide network is available. 100% of college-owned or -operated housing units are wired for high-speed Internet access. Wireless service is available via entire campus.

STUDENT LIFE

Housing options: on-campus residence required through sophomore year; coed, men-only, women-only. Campus housing is university owned. Freshman campus housing is guaranteed.

Activities and organizations: drama/theater group, student-run newspaper, radio and television station, choral group, Student Association, Undergraduate Alumni Council, Communication Club, ethnic organizations, spectrum entertainment board, national fraternities, national sororities.

Athletics Member NCAA. All Division III. ***Intercollegiate sports:*** baseball M, basketball M/W, cheerleading M/W, cross-country running M/W, field hockey M(c)/W(c), ice hockey M, lacrosse M(c)/W, rugby M(c)/W(c), soccer M/W, softball W, swimming and diving M/W, tennis M/W, track and field M/W, volleyball M/W. ***Intramural sports:*** basketball M/W, cross-country running M/W, fencing M(c)/W(c), ice hockey M(c), racquetball M/W, rock climbing M/W, skiing (cross-country) M/W, skiing (downhill) M/W, soccer M/W, softball M/W, squash M/W, tennis M/W, ultimate Frisbee M/W, volleyball M(c)/W, water polo M/W.

Campus security: 24-hour emergency response devices and patrols, late-night transport/escort service, controlled dormitory access.

Student services: health clinic, personal/psychological counseling, legal services.

COSTS & FINANCIAL AID

Costs (2014–15) ***Tuition:*** state resident $6170 full-time, $257 per credit hour part-time; nonresident $15,820 full-time, $659 per credit hour part-time. ***Required fees:*** $1570 full-time, $65 per credit hour part-time. ***Room and board:*** $12,100; room only: $7200. Room and board charges vary according to board plan and housing facility. ***Payment plan:*** installment.

Financial Aid Of all full-time matriculated undergraduates who enrolled in 2014, 4,062 applied for aid, 3,256 were judged to have need, 403 had their need fully met. 220 Federal Work-Study jobs (averaging $1900). In 2014, 361 non-need-based awards were made. ***Average percent of need met:*** 62. ***Average financial aid package:*** $10,689. ***Average need-based loan:*** $5404. ***Average need-based gift aid:*** $5489. ***Average non-need-based aid:*** $3292. ***Average indebtedness upon graduation:*** $28,900.

APPLYING

Standardized Tests *Required:* SAT or ACT (for admission).

Options: electronic application, early admission, early decision, deferred entrance.

Application fee: $50.

Required: essay or personal statement, high school transcript, 1 letter of recommendation. ***Required for some:*** interview, audition for music, dance and theater programs: portfolio for visual arts and technical theatre programs.

Application deadlines: rolling (freshmen), rolling (transfers).

Early decision deadline: 11/1.

Notification: continuous (freshmen), continuous (transfers), 12/1 (early decision).

CONTACT

Office of Admissions, State University of New York at Fredonia, 178 Central Avenue, Fredonia, NY 14063. *Phone:* 716-673-3251. *Toll-free phone:* 800-252-1212. *Fax:* 716-673-3249. *E-mail:* admissions@fredonia.edu.

State University of New York at New Paltz

New Paltz, New York

http://www.newpaltz.edu/

- **State-supported** comprehensive, founded 1828, part of State University of New York System
- **Small-town** 216-acre campus
- **Endowment** $17.6 million
- **Coed** 6,642 undergraduate students, 92% full-time, 62% women, 38% men
- **Very difficult** entrance level, 42% of applicants were admitted

UNDERGRAD STUDENTS

6,097 full-time, 545 part-time. Students come from 20 states and territories; 50 other countries; 3% are from out of state; 6% Black or African American, non-Hispanic/Latino; 16% Hispanic/Latino; 5% Asian, non-Hispanic/Latino; 0.1% Native Hawaiian or other Pacific Islander, non-Hispanic/Latino; 0.2% American Indian or Alaska Native, non-Hispanic/Latino; 2% Two or more races, non-Hispanic/Latino; 5% Race/ethnicity unknown; 2% international; 10% transferred in; 43% live on campus.

Freshmen

Admission: 13,726 applied, 5,755 admitted, 1,079 enrolled. ***Average high school GPA:*** 3.6. ***Test scores:*** SAT critical reading scores over 500: 80%; SAT math scores over 500: 84%; SAT writing scores over 500: 79%; ACT scores over 18: 97%; SAT critical reading scores over 600: 29%; SAT math scores over 600: 29%; SAT writing scores over 600: 28%; ACT scores over 24: 65%; SAT critical reading scores over 700: 3%; SAT math scores over 700: 3%; SAT writing scores over 700: 3%; ACT scores over 30: 8%.

Retention: 90% of full-time freshmen returned.

FACULTY

Total: 658, 54% full-time, 55% with terminal degrees.

Student/faculty ratio: 15:1.

ACADEMICS

Calendar: semesters. *Degrees:* bachelor's, master's, post-master's, and postbachelor's certificates.

Special study options: academic remediation for entering students, advanced placement credit, cooperative education, distance learning, double majors, English as a second language, external degree program, honors programs, independent study, internships, off-campus study, part-time degree program, services for LD students, student-designed majors, study abroad, summer session for credit.

Unusual degree programs: 3-2 business administration; engineering.

Computers: 800 computers/terminals are available on campus for general student use. Students can access the following: campus intranet, computer help desk, free student e-mail accounts, online (class) grades, online (class) registration, online (class) schedules. Campuswide network is available. 100% of college-owned or -operated housing units are wired for high-speed Internet access. Wireless service is available via entire campus.

STUDENT LIFE

Housing options: on-campus residence required for freshman year; coed, special housing for students with disabilities. Campus housing is university owned. Freshman campus housing is guaranteed.

Activities and organizations: drama/theater group, student-run newspaper, radio and television station, choral group, Student Association, Residence Hall Student Association, Outing Club, The Oracle Newspaper, United Greek Association, national fraternities, national sororities.

Athletics Member NCAA. All Division III. ***Intercollegiate sports:*** baseball M, basketball M/W, cross-country running M/W, field hockey W, lacrosse W, soccer M/W, swimming and diving M/W, tennis W, volleyball M/W. ***Intramural sports:*** basketball M/W, cheerleading M(c)/W(c), equestrian sports M(c)/W(c), lacrosse M(c)/W(c), racquetball M/W, rugby M(c)/W(c), soccer M/W, swimming and diving M(c)/W(c), table tennis M(c)/W(c), tennis M/W, track and field M(c)/W(c), ultimate Frisbee M(c)/W(c), volleyball M/W, water polo M/W, wrestling M(c).

Campus security: 24-hour emergency response devices and patrols, late-night transport/escort service, controlled dormitory access, safety seminars, RAD Women's Self Defense.

Student services: health clinic, personal/psychological counseling, legal services.

COSTS & FINANCIAL AID

Costs (2014–15) ***Tuition:*** state resident $6170 full-time, $257 per credit hour part-time; nonresident $15,820 full-time, $659 per credit hour part-time. ***Required fees:*** $1248 full-time, $36 per credit hour part-time, $193 per term part-time. ***Room and board:*** $10,896; room only: $7220. Room and board charges vary according to board plan. ***Payment plan:*** installment.

Financial Aid Of all full-time matriculated undergraduates who enrolled in 2013, 4,607 applied for aid, 3,365 were judged to have need, 209 had their need fully met. 1,071 state and other part-time jobs (averaging $1240). In 2013, 35 non-need-based awards were made. ***Average percent of need met:*** 57. ***Average financial aid package:*** $9904. ***Average need-based loan:*** $4395. ***Average need-based gift aid:*** $4746. ***Average non-need-based aid:*** $2165. ***Average indebtedness upon graduation:*** $25,741.

APPLYING

Standardized Tests *Required:* SAT or ACT (for admission).

Options: electronic application, early admission, early action.

Application fee: $50.

Required: essay or personal statement, high school transcript, 1 letter of recommendation. ***Required for some:*** portfolio for art program, audition for music and theater programs.

Application deadlines: 4/1 (freshmen), 4/1 (transfers), 11/15 (early action).

Notification: continuous (freshmen), continuous (transfers), 12/15 (early action).

CONTACT

Ms. Kimberly A. Strano, Director of Freshman Admissions, State University of New York at New Paltz, 1 Hawk Drive, New Paltz, NY 12561-2499. *Phone:* 845-257-3200. *Toll-free phone:* 877-MY-NP-411. *Fax:* 845-257-3209. *E-mail:* admissions@newpaltz.edu.

★ State University of New York at Oswego

Oswego, New York

http://www.oswego.edu/

- **State-supported** comprehensive, founded 1861, part of State University of New York System
- **Small-town** 696-acre campus with easy access to Syracuse
- **Endowment** $18.6 million
- **Coed** 7,193 undergraduate students, 96% full-time, 51% women, 49% men
- **Moderately difficult** entrance level, 48% of applicants were admitted

UNDERGRAD STUDENTS

6,880 full-time, 313 part-time. Students come from 32 states and territories; 16 other countries; 2% are from out of state; 7% Black or African American, non-Hispanic/Latino; 9% Hispanic/Latino; 2% Asian, non-Hispanic/Latino; 0.1% Native Hawaiian or other Pacific Islander, non-Hispanic/Latino; 0.1% American Indian or Alaska Native, non-Hispanic/Latino; 2% Two or more races, non-Hispanic/Latino; 0.1% Race/ethnicity unknown; 2% international; 10% transferred in; 60% live on campus.

Freshmen

Admission: 11,022 applied, 5,331 admitted, 1,417 enrolled. ***Average high school GPA:*** 3.5. ***Test scores:*** SAT critical reading scores over 500: 78%; SAT math scores over 500: 83%; ACT scores over 18: 100%; SAT critical reading scores over 600: 20%; SAT math scores over 600: 25%; ACT scores over 24: 52%; SAT critical reading scores over 700: 2%; SAT math scores over 700: 2%; ACT scores over 30: 4%.

Retention: 80% of full-time freshmen returned.

FACULTY

Total: 570, 60% full-time, 61% with terminal degrees.

Student/faculty ratio: 18:1.

ACADEMICS
Calendar: semesters. *Degrees:* bachelor's, master's, post-master's, and postbachelor's certificates.

Special study options: accelerated degree program, adult/continuing education programs, advanced placement credit, cooperative education, distance learning, double majors, English as a second language, freshman honors college, honors programs, independent study, internships, off-campus study, part-time degree program, services for LD students, study abroad, summer session for credit. ***ROTC:*** Army (c), Air Force (c).

Unusual degree programs: 3-2 engineering with Clarkson University, Case Western Reserve University, State University of New York at Binghamton.

Computers: 1,250 computers/terminals are available on campus for general student use. Students can access the following: campus intranet, computer help desk, free student e-mail accounts, online (class) grades, online (class) registration, online (class) schedules. Campuswide network is available. 100% of college-owned or -operated housing units are wired for high-speed Internet access. Wireless service is available via entire campus.

STUDENT LIFE
Housing options: on-campus residence required through sophomore year; coed, special housing for students with disabilities. Campus housing is university owned. Freshman campus housing is guaranteed.

Activities and organizations: drama/theater group, student-run newspaper, radio and television station, choral group, club/intramural sports, student radio/television stations (WNYO and WTOP), Outdoor Club, Dance Organization (Del Sarte), Accounting Society, national fraternities, national sororities.

Athletics Member NCAA. All Division III. ***Intercollegiate sports:*** baseball M, basketball M/W, crew M(c)/W(c), cross-country running M/W, field hockey W, golf M, ice hockey M/W, lacrosse M/W, soccer M/W, softball W, swimming and diving M/W, tennis M/W, track and field M/W, volleyball W, wrestling M. ***Intramural sports:*** badminton M/W, basketball M/W, cheerleading W(c), equestrian sports M(c)/W(c), fencing M(c)/W(c), field hockey W(c), football M/W, golf M/W, gymnastics M(c)/W(c), ice hockey M(c)/W(c), lacrosse M(c), racquetball M/W, rock climbing M(c)/W(c), rugby M(c)/W(c), skiing (cross-country) M(c)/W(c), skiing (downhill) M(c)/W(c), soccer M/W, softball M/W, swimming and diving M/W, table tennis M/W, tennis M/W, ultimate Frisbee M(c)/W(c), volleyball M(c)/W, water polo M/W.

Campus security: 24-hour emergency response devices and patrols, controlled dormitory access.

Student services: health clinic, personal/psychological counseling, women's center, legal services.

COSTS & FINANCIAL AID
Costs (2014–15) ***Tuition:*** state resident $6170 full-time, $257 per credit hour part-time; nonresident $15,820 full-time, $659 per credit hour part-time. Part-time tuition and fees vary according to course load. ***Required fees:*** $1411 full-time, $44 per credit hour part-time. ***Room and board:*** $12,690. Room and board charges vary according to board plan and housing facility. ***Payment plan:*** installment.

Financial Aid Of all full-time matriculated undergraduates who enrolled in 2014, 5,651 applied for aid, 4,487 were judged to have need, 500 had their need fully met. 510 Federal Work-Study jobs (averaging $1156). 1,586 state and other part-time jobs (averaging $1959). In 2014, 796 non-need-based awards were made. ***Average percent of need met:*** 84. ***Average financial aid package:*** $10,616. ***Average need-based loan:*** $4495. ***Average need-based gift aid:*** $6966. ***Average non-need-based aid:*** $2371. ***Average indebtedness upon graduation:*** $28,362.

APPLYING
Standardized Tests *Required:* SAT or ACT (for admission).

Options: electronic application, early admission, early decision, deferred entrance.

Application fee: $50.

Required: essay or personal statement, high school transcript, 1 letter of recommendation. ***Recommended:*** minimum 2.7 GPA, interview.

Application deadlines: rolling (freshmen), rolling (transfers).

Early decision deadline: 11/15.

Notification: 1/15 (freshmen), 1/15 (transfers), 12/15 (early decision).

CONTACT
Mr. Daniel Griffin, Director of Admissions, State University of New York at Oswego, 7060 State Route 104, Oswego, NY 13126. *Phone:* 315-312-2250. *Fax:* 315-312-3260. *E-mail:* admiss@oswego.edu.

See previous page for display ad and page 1630 for the College Close-Up.

State University of New York at Plattsburgh

Plattsburgh, New York

http://www.plattsburgh.edu/

- **State-supported** comprehensive, founded 1889, part of State University of New York System
- **Small-town** 265-acre campus with easy access to Montreal
- **Endowment** $18.0 million
- **Coed** 5,565 undergraduate students, 92% full-time, 56% women, 44% men
- **Moderately difficult** entrance level, 48% of applicants were admitted

UNDERGRAD STUDENTS
5,143 full-time, 422 part-time. Students come from 30 states and territories; 64 other countries; 3% are from out of state; 7% Black or African American, non-Hispanic/Latino; 9% Hispanic/Latino; 2% Asian, non-Hispanic/Latino; 0.1% Native Hawaiian or other Pacific Islander, non-Hispanic/Latino; 0.3% American Indian or Alaska Native, non-Hispanic/Latino; 2% Two or more races, non-Hispanic/Latino; 4% Race/ethnicity unknown; 7% international; 10% transferred in; 46% live on campus.

Freshmen
Admission: 8,452 applied, 4,045 admitted, 1,036 enrolled. ***Average high school GPA:*** 3.2. ***Test scores:*** SAT critical reading scores over 500: 69%; SAT math scores over 500: 74%; ACT scores over 18: 98%; SAT critical reading scores over 600: 18%; SAT math scores over 600: 20%; ACT scores over 24: 36%; SAT critical reading scores over 700: 1%; SAT math scores over 700: 2%; ACT scores over 30: 3%.

Retention: 84% of full-time freshmen returned.

FACULTY
Total: 499, 59% full-time, 57% with terminal degrees.

Student/faculty ratio: 15:1.

ACADEMICS
Calendar: semesters plus 2 5-week summer sessions and 1 winter session. *Degrees:* certificates, bachelor's, master's, and post-master's certificates.

Special study options: academic remediation for entering students, accelerated degree program, adult/continuing education programs, advanced placement credit, cooperative education, distance learning, double majors, English as a second language, honors programs, independent study, internships, off-campus study, part-time degree program, services for LD students, student-designed majors, study abroad, summer session for credit.

Computers: 450 computers/terminals are available on campus for general student use. Students can access the following: campus intranet, computer help desk, free student e-mail accounts, online (class) grades, online (class) registration, online (class) schedules. Campuswide network is available. 100% of college-owned or -operated housing units are wired for high-speed Internet access. Wireless service is available via entire campus.

STUDENT LIFE
Housing options: on-campus residence required through sophomore year; coed, special housing for students with disabilities. Campus housing is university owned. Freshman campus housing is guaranteed.

Activities and organizations: drama/theater group, student-run newspaper, radio and television station, choral group, Student Association, Honor Societies, Student Media Organizations, service/leadership organizations, intramural and recreational sports, national fraternities, national sororities.

Athletics Member NCAA. All Division III. ***Intercollegiate sports:*** baseball M, basketball M/W, cross-country running M/W, ice hockey M/W, lacrosse M, soccer M/W, softball W, tennis W, track and field M/W, volleyball W. ***Intramural sports:*** basketball M/W, cheerleading

M(c)/W(c), field hockey M/W, football M, ice hockey M(c)/W(c), racquetball M/W, rock climbing M(c)/W(c), rugby M(c)/W(c), soccer M/W, softball M/W, tennis M/W, ultimate Frisbee M/W, volleyball M/W.

Campus security: 24-hour emergency response devices and patrols, late-night transport/escort service, controlled dormitory access.

Student services: health clinic, personal/psychological counseling, women's center, legal services.

COSTS & FINANCIAL AID

Costs (2014–15) ***Tuition:*** state resident $6170 full-time, $257 per credit hour part-time; nonresident $15,820 full-time, $659 per credit hour part-time. Full-time tuition and fees vary according to course load and location. Part-time tuition and fees vary according to course load and location. ***Required fees:*** $1327 full-time, $56 per credit hour part-time. ***Room and board:*** $11,304; room only: $7158. Room and board charges vary according to board plan and housing facility. ***Payment plans:*** installment, deferred payment. ***Waivers:*** employees or children of employees.

Financial Aid Of all full-time matriculated undergraduates who enrolled in 2014, 4,168 applied for aid, 3,290 were judged to have need, 627 had their need fully met. 303 Federal Work-Study jobs (averaging $2165). In 2014, 744 non-need-based awards were made. ***Average percent of need met:*** 78. ***Average financial aid package:*** $12,581. ***Average need-based loan:*** $7712. ***Average need-based gift aid:*** $7067. ***Average non-need-based aid:*** $3643. ***Average indebtedness upon graduation:*** $28,125.

APPLYING

Standardized Tests *Required:* SAT or ACT (for admission).

Options: electronic application, early admission, deferred entrance.

Application fee: $50.

Required: essay or personal statement, high school transcript, minimum 2.5 GPA, 1 letter of recommendation. ***Required for some:*** minimum 3.4 GPA. ***Recommended:*** minimum 3.0 GPA, interview.

Application deadlines: rolling (freshmen), rolling (transfers).

Notification: continuous (freshmen), continuous (transfers).

CONTACT

Mrs. Carrie Woodward, Assistant Director for Freshman Admissions, State University of New York at Plattsburgh, 101 Broad Street, Plattsburgh, NY 12901. *Phone:* 888-673-0012. *Toll-free phone:* 888-673-0012. *Fax:* 518-564-2045. *E-mail:* carrie.woodward@plattsburgh.edu.

State University of New York College at Cortland

Cortland, New York

http://www.cortland.edu/

- **State-supported** comprehensive, founded 1868, part of State University of New York System
- **Small-town** 191-acre campus with easy access to Syracuse
- **Coed** 6,317 undergraduate students, 98% full-time, 57% women, 43% men
- **Moderately difficult** entrance level, 48% of applicants were admitted

UNDERGRAD STUDENTS

6,203 full-time, 114 part-time. 4% are from out of state; 5% Black or African American, non-Hispanic/Latino; 11% Hispanic/Latino; 1% Asian, non-Hispanic/Latino; 0.1% Native Hawaiian or other Pacific Islander, non-Hispanic/Latino; 0.2% American Indian or Alaska Native, non-Hispanic/Latino; 2% Two or more races, non-Hispanic/Latino; 7% Race/ethnicity unknown; 0.6% international; 10% transferred in.

Freshmen

Admission: 11,221 applied, 5,394 admitted, 1,196 enrolled. ***Test scores:*** SAT critical reading scores over 500: 63%; SAT math scores over 500: 77%; ACT scores over 18: 99%; SAT critical reading scores over 600: 10%; SAT math scores over 600: 17%; ACT scores over 24: 48%; ACT scores over 30: 4%.

Retention: 81% of full-time freshmen returned.

FACULTY

Total: 649, 44% full-time, 45% with terminal degrees.

Student/faculty ratio: 17:1.

ACADEMICS

Calendar: semesters. *Degrees:* bachelor's, master's, post-master's, and postbachelor's certificates.

Special study options: adult/continuing education programs, off-campus study. ***ROTC:*** Army (c), Air Force (c).

Unusual degree programs: 3-2 engineering with State University of New York at Buffalo, State University of New York at Stony Brook, Alfred University, Clarkson University, State University of New York at Binghamton, Case Western Reserve University; forestry with Duke University, State University of New York College of Environmental Science and Forestry.

Computers: Campuswide network is available.

STUDENT LIFE

Housing options: coed, cooperative, special housing for students with disabilities. Campus housing is university owned.

Athletics Member NCAA. All Division III. ***Intercollegiate sports:*** baseball M, basketball M/W, cross-country running M/W, field hockey W, football M/W(c), golf W, gymnastics W, ice hockey M/W(c), lacrosse M/W, racquetball M(c)/W(c), rugby M(c)/W(c), soccer M/W, softball W, swimming and diving M/W, tennis W, track and field M/W, volleyball M(c)/W, wrestling M. ***Intramural sports:*** archery M/W, badminton M/W, baseball M, basketball M/W, bowling M/W, cross-country running M/W, fencing M/W, field hockey W, football M/W, golf M/W, gymnastics W, ice hockey M, lacrosse M/W, racquetball M/W, rugby M/W, skiing (cross-country) M/W, skiing (downhill) M/W, soccer M/W, softball M/W, squash M/W, swimming and diving M/W, table tennis M/W, tennis M/W, track and field M/W, volleyball M/W, weight lifting M/W, wrestling M.

Campus security: 24-hour emergency response devices and patrols, late-night transport/escort service.

COSTS & FINANCIAL AID

Costs (2015–16) ***Tuition:*** state resident $6170 full-time, $258 per credit hour part-time; nonresident $15,820 full-time, $660 per credit hour part-time. Full-time tuition and fees vary according to degree level. Part-time tuition and fees vary according to degree level. ***Required fees:*** $1549 full-time. ***Room and board:*** $12,040; room only: $7660. Room and board charges vary according to board plan and housing facility. ***Payment plan:*** installment.

Financial Aid Of all full-time matriculated undergraduates who enrolled in 2013, 5,192 applied for aid, 3,947 were judged to have need, 309 had their need fully met. In 2013, 188 non-need-based awards were made. ***Average percent of need met:*** 68. ***Average financial aid package:*** $13,587. ***Average need-based loan:*** $4335. ***Average need-based gift aid:*** $5825. ***Average non-need-based aid:*** $3947. ***Average indebtedness upon graduation:*** $27,472.

APPLYING

Standardized Tests *Required for some:* SAT or ACT (for admission).

Options: early admission, early action, deferred entrance.

Application fee: $50.

Required: essay or personal statement, high school transcript, minimum 2.3 GPA, 1 letter of recommendation. ***Recommended:*** minimum 3.0 GPA, 3 letters of recommendation, interview.

CONTACT

Director of Admission, State University of New York College at Cortland, PO Box 2000, Cortland, NY 13045. *Phone:* 607-753-4711. *Fax:* 607-753-5998. *E-mail:* admissions@cortland.edu.

State University of New York College at Geneseo

Geneseo, New York

http://www.geneseo.edu/

- **State-supported** comprehensive, founded 1871, part of State University of New York System
- **Small-town** 220-acre campus with easy access to Rochester
- **Endowment** $26.0 million
- **Coed** 5,553 undergraduate students, 98% full-time, 58% women, 42% men
- **Very difficult** entrance level, 59% of applicants were admitted

UNDERGRAD STUDENTS
5,455 full-time, 98 part-time. Students come from 26 states and territories; 26 other countries; 2% are from out of state; 3% Black or African American, non-Hispanic/Latino; 7% Hispanic/Latino; 6% Asian, non-Hispanic/Latino; 0.1% Native Hawaiian or other Pacific Islander, non-Hispanic/Latino; 0.2% American Indian or Alaska Native, non-Hispanic/Latino; 3% Two or more races, non-Hispanic/Latino; 3% Race/ethnicity unknown; 2% international; 6% transferred in; 56% live on campus.

Freshmen
Admission: 9,305 applied, 5,502 admitted, 1,236 enrolled. ***Average high school GPA:*** 3.67. ***Test scores:*** SAT critical reading scores over 500: 90%; SAT math scores over 500: 93%; ACT scores over 18: 98%; SAT critical reading scores over 600: 56%; SAT math scores over 600: 63%; ACT scores over 24: 92%; SAT critical reading scores over 700: 13%; SAT math scores over 700: 13%; ACT scores over 30: 17%.
Retention: 90% of full-time freshmen returned.

FACULTY
Total: 349, 72% full-time, 69% with terminal degrees.

ACADEMICS
Calendar: semesters. *Degrees:* bachelor's and master's.
Special study options: advanced placement credit, distance learning, double majors, English as a second language, honors programs, independent study, internships, off-campus study, part-time degree program, services for LD students, study abroad, summer session for credit. ***ROTC:*** Army (c), Air Force (c).
Unusual degree programs: 3-2 business administration with Syracuse University, State University of New York at Buffalo, State University of New York at Binghamton, Rochester Institute of Technology, Clarkson University, Alfred University, Union College; engineering with Columbia University, Case Western Reserve University, Alfred University, Clarkson University, Syracuse University, The Penn State University, University of Rochester, SUNY Binghamton, SUNY Buffalo, Rochester Institute of Technology; nursing with Johns Hopkins University School of Nursing; optometry with State University of New York College of Optometry; dental with State University of New York at Buffalo, physical therapy degree with SUNY Upstate Medical University, osteopathy program with New York Institute of Technology College of Osteopathic Medicine.
Computers: 361 computers/terminals and 72 ports are available on campus for general student use. Students can access the following: campus intranet, computer help desk, free student e-mail accounts, online (class) grades, online (class) registration, online (class) schedules. Campuswide network is available. 100% of college-owned or -operated housing units are wired for high-speed Internet access. Wireless service is available via entire campus.

STUDENT LIFE
Housing options: on-campus residence required through sophomore year; coed, special housing for students with disabilities. Campus housing is university owned. Freshman campus housing is guaranteed.
Activities and organizations: drama/theater group, student-run newspaper, radio and television station, choral group, Alpha Phi Omega, Inter-Varsity Christian Fellowship, Inter-Residence Council, Colleges Against Cancer, Geneseo Area Gaming Group, national fraternities, national sororities.
Athletics Member NCAA. All Division III. ***Intercollegiate sports:*** badminton M(c)/W(c), baseball M(c)/W(c), basketball M/W, cheerleading M(c)/W(c), crew M(c)/W(c), cross-country running M/W, equestrian sports W, fencing M(c)/W(c), field hockey W, ice hockey M/W(c), lacrosse M/W, rugby M(c)/W(c), skiing (downhill) M(c)/W(c), soccer M/W, softball W, swimming and diving M/W, tennis M(c)/W, track and field M/W, ultimate Frisbee M(c)/W(c), volleyball M(c)/W. ***Intramural sports:*** basketball M/W.
Campus security: 24-hour emergency response devices and patrols, student patrols, late-night transport/escort service, controlled dormitory access.
Student services: health clinic, personal/psychological counseling, legal services.

COSTS & FINANCIAL AID
Costs (2014–15) ***Tuition:*** state resident $6170 full-time, $257 per credit hour part-time; nonresident $15,820 full-time, $659 per credit hour part-time. Part-time tuition and fees vary according to course load. ***Required fees:*** $1604 full-time, $67 per credit hour part-time. ***Room and board:*** $11,518; room only: $7220. Room and board charges vary according to board plan and housing facility. ***Payment plans:*** installment, deferred payment.
Financial Aid Of all full-time matriculated undergraduates who enrolled in 2014, 3,921 applied for aid, 2,704 were judged to have need, 1,622 had their need fully met. In 2014, 579 non-need-based awards were made. ***Average percent of need met:*** 60. ***Average financial aid package:*** $10,672. ***Average need-based loan:*** $4844. ***Average need-based gift aid:*** $5718. ***Average non-need-based aid:*** $2790. ***Average indebtedness upon graduation:*** $23,308.

APPLYING
Standardized Tests *Required:* SAT or ACT (for admission).
Options: electronic application, early admission, early decision, deferred entrance.
Application fee: $50.
Required: essay or personal statement, high school transcript. ***Recommended:*** 1 letter of recommendation.

CONTACT
Mr. Kevin J. Reed, Interim Director of Admissions, State University of New York College at Geneseo, Doty Hall 200, Geneseo, NY 14454-1401. *Phone:* 585-245-5571. *Toll-free phone:* 866-245-5211. *Fax:* 585-245-5550. *E-mail:* admissions@geneseo.edu.

State University of New York College at Old Westbury

Old Westbury, New York

http://www.oldwestbury.edu/

- **State-supported** comprehensive, founded 1965, part of State University of New York System
- **Suburban** 604-acre campus with easy access to New York City
- **Coed** 4,317 undergraduate students, 85% full-time, 58% women, 42% men
- **Moderately difficult** entrance level, 62% of applicants were admitted

UNDERGRAD STUDENTS
3,670 full-time, 647 part-time. Students come from 14 states and territories; 49 other countries; 1% are from out of state; 30% Black or African American, non-Hispanic/Latino; 21% Hispanic/Latino; 10% Asian, non-Hispanic/Latino; 0.5% Native Hawaiian or other Pacific Islander, non-Hispanic/Latino; 0.3% American Indian or Alaska Native, non-Hispanic/Latino; 3% Two or more races, non-Hispanic/Latino; 2% Race/ethnicity unknown; 1% international; 16% transferred in; 21% live on campus.

Freshmen
Admission: 3,490 applied, 2,176 admitted, 457 enrolled. ***Average high school GPA:*** 3.2. ***Test scores:*** SAT critical reading scores over 500: 44%; SAT math scores over 500: 50%; SAT writing scores over 500: 41%; ACT scores over 18: 79%; SAT critical reading scores over 600: 5%; SAT math scores over 600: 8%; SAT writing scores over 600: 5%; ACT scores over 24: 8%.
Retention: 84% of full-time freshmen returned.

FACULTY
Total: 337, 45% full-time, 54% with terminal degrees.
Student/faculty ratio: 19:1.

ACADEMICS
Calendar: semesters. *Degrees:* certificates, bachelor's, master's, and post-master's certificates.
Special study options: academic remediation for entering students, advanced placement credit, distance learning, double majors, freshman honors college, honors programs, independent study, internships, off-campus study, part-time degree program, services for LD students, study abroad, summer session for credit. ***ROTC:*** Army (c), Air Force (c).
Unusual degree programs: 3-2 engineering with State University of New York at Stony Brook; Biological Sciences/Doctor of Osteopathic Medicine with NY College of Osteopathic Medicine.

Computers: 640 computers/terminals and 700 ports are available on campus for general student use. Students can access the following: campus intranet, free student e-mail accounts, online (class) grades, online (class) registration, financial aid, billing information, grades. Campuswide network is available. 100% of college-owned or -operated housing units are wired for high-speed Internet access. Wireless service is available via entire campus.

STUDENT LIFE
Housing options: coed. Campus housing is university owned. Freshman campus housing is guaranteed.

Activities and organizations: drama/theater group, student-run newspaper, radio station, choral group, Student Government Association, Alianza Latina, PRIDE, Step Tunes, Anime Magna Games Club, national fraternities, national sororities.

Athletics Member NCAA. All Division III. ***Intercollegiate sports:*** baseball M, basketball M/W, cross-country running M/W, golf M, lacrosse W, soccer M/W, softball W, swimming and diving M/W, volleyball W. ***Intramural sports:*** badminton M/W, basketball M/W, cheerleading M(c)/W(c), equestrian sports M(c)/W(c), football M/W, racquetball M/W, soccer M/W, softball W, squash M/W, ultimate Frisbee M/W, weight lifting M/W.

Campus security: 24-hour emergency response devices and patrols, student patrols, late-night transport/escort service, controlled dormitory access.

Student services: health clinic, personal/psychological counseling, women's center.

COSTS & FINANCIAL AID
Costs (2014–15) ***Tuition:*** state resident $6190 full-time, $257 per credit hour part-time; nonresident $15,820 full-time, $659 per credit hour part-time. Part-time tuition and fees vary according to course load. ***Required fees:*** $1133 full-time, $22 per credit hour part-time, $158 per term part-time. ***Room and board:*** $10,390; room only: $7000. Room and board charges vary according to board plan. ***Payment plan:*** installment. ***Waivers:*** senior citizens.

Financial Aid Of all full-time matriculated undergraduates who enrolled in 2013, 2,893 applied for aid, 2,882 were judged to have need, 2,457 had their need fully met. ***Average percent of need met:*** 54. ***Average financial aid package:*** $9420. ***Average need-based loan:*** $4572. ***Average need-based gift aid:*** $6405. ***Average indebtedness upon graduation:*** $16,653.

APPLYING
Standardized Tests *Required:* SAT or ACT (for admission).

Options: electronic application, early admission, early decision, deferred entrance.

Application fee: $50.

Required: essay or personal statement, high school transcript, 2 letters of recommendation. ***Required for some:*** interview.

Application deadlines: rolling (freshmen), 12/15 (transfers).

Early decision deadline: 11/1.

Notification: continuous (freshmen), continuous (transfers), 12/15 (early decision).

CONTACT
State University of New York College at Old Westbury, PO Box 307, Old Westbury, NY 11568. *Phone:* 516-876-3073. *Fax:* 516-876-3307. *E-mail:* enroll@oldwestbury.edu.

State University of New York College at Potsdam

Potsdam, New York

http://www.potsdam.edu/

- **State-supported** comprehensive, founded 1816, part of State University of New York System
- **Small-town** 240-acre campus
- **Endowment** $25.9 million
- **Coed** 3,681 undergraduate students, 97% full-time, 56% women, 44% men
- **Moderately difficult** entrance level, 68% of applicants were admitted

UNDERGRAD STUDENTS
3,573 full-time, 108 part-time. Students come from 27 states and territories; 40 other countries; 3% are from out of state; 8% Black or African American, non-Hispanic/Latino; 10% Hispanic/Latino; 2% Asian, non-Hispanic/Latino; 0.1% Native Hawaiian or other Pacific Islander, non-Hispanic/Latino; 2% American Indian or Alaska Native, non-Hispanic/Latino; 3% Two or more races, non-Hispanic/Latino; 6% Race/ethnicity unknown; 0.9% international; 7% transferred in; 61% live on campus.

Freshmen
Admission: 5,155 applied, 3,484 admitted, 830 enrolled. ***Test scores:*** SAT critical reading scores over 500: 57%; SAT math scores over 500: 57%; ACT scores over 18: 92%; SAT critical reading scores over 600: 17%; SAT math scores over 600: 17%; ACT scores over 24: 47%; SAT critical reading scores over 700: 1%; SAT math scores over 700: 3%; ACT scores over 30: 10%.

Retention: 80% of full-time freshmen returned.

FACULTY
Total: 357, 70% full-time, 66% with terminal degrees.

Student/faculty ratio: 13:1.

ACADEMICS
Calendar: semesters. *Degrees:* bachelor's and master's.

Special study options: advanced placement credit, distance learning, double majors, honors programs, independent study, internships, off-campus study, part-time degree program, services for LD students, student-designed majors, study abroad, summer session for credit. ***ROTC:*** Army (c), Air Force (c).

Unusual degree programs: 3-2 engineering with Clarkson University (civil and environmental), SUNY IT; geology, physics, computer science, chemistry and mathematics with Clarkson University.

Computers: 608 computers/terminals and 80 ports are available on campus for general student use. Students can access the following: campus intranet, computer help desk, free student e-mail accounts, online (class) grades, online (class) registration, online (class) schedules, online access to financial aid status, unofficial transcripts, billing, meal plan and housing sign ups, 225 wireless hot spots with 95 on campus and 130 in the residence halls. Campuswide network is available. 100% of college-owned or -operated housing units are wired for high-speed Internet access. Wireless service is available via classrooms, computer centers, computer labs, dorm rooms, learning centers, libraries, student centers.

STUDENT LIFE
Housing options: on-campus residence required through sophomore year; coed, special housing for students with disabilities. Campus housing is university owned. Freshman campus housing is guaranteed.

Activities and organizations: drama/theater group, student-run newspaper, radio station, choral group, Student Government Association, Crane Student Association, Student Entertainment Services (Programming Board), WALH Radio, Emerging Leaders, national fraternities, national sororities.

Athletics Member NCAA. All Division III. ***Intercollegiate sports:*** basketball M/W, cross-country running M/W, equestrian sports W, golf M, ice hockey M/W, lacrosse M/W, soccer M/W, swimming and diving M/W, volleyball W. ***Intramural sports:*** archery M(c)/W(c), basketball M/W, bowling M(c)/W(c), cheerleading M(c)/W(c), football M/W, ice hockey M(c), racquetball M/W, rugby W(c), soccer M/W, softball M/W, volleyball M/W.

Campus security: 24-hour emergency response devices and patrols, late-night transport/escort service, controlled dormitory access, educational programs, campus rescue squad, portable jump start packets, vehicle lock outs and parking management.

Student services: health clinic, personal/psychological counseling, women's center, legal services.

COSTS & FINANCIAL AID
Costs (2014–15) ***Tuition:*** state resident $6170 full-time, $257 per credit hour part-time; nonresident $15,820 full-time, $659 per credit hour part-time. ***Required fees:*** $1383 full-time. ***Room and board:*** $10,920; room only: $6420. Room and board charges vary according to board plan and housing facility. ***Payment plan:*** installment. ***Waivers:*** employees or children of employees.

Financial Aid Of all full-time matriculated undergraduates who enrolled in 2014, 3,297 applied for aid, 2,637 were judged to have need, 1,208 had their need fully met. 260 Federal Work-Study jobs (averaging $1091). In 2014, 284 non-need-based awards were made. ***Average percent of need met:*** 88. ***Average financial aid package:*** $14,253. ***Average need-based loan:*** $4653. ***Average need-based gift aid:*** $7614. ***Average non-need-based aid:*** $2591. ***Average indebtedness upon graduation:*** $21,531. ***Financial aid deadline:*** 5/1.

APPLYING

Standardized Tests *Required for some:* SAT or ACT (for admission).

Options: electronic application, early admission, deferred entrance.

Application fee: $50.

Required: high school transcript, minimum 2.5 GPA, 1 letter of recommendation, music students must submit DVD audition. ***Required for some:*** essay or personal statement, minimum 2.0 GPA, interview.

Application deadlines: rolling (freshmen), rolling (transfers).

Notification: continuous (freshmen), continuous (transfers).

CONTACT

Mr. Thomas Nesbitt, Director of Admissions, State University of New York College at Potsdam, 44 Pierrepont Avenue, Potsdam, NY 13676. *Phone:* 315-267-2180. *Toll-free phone:* 877-POTSDAM. *Fax:* 315-267-2163. *E-mail:* admissions@potsdam.edu.

State University of New York College of Agriculture and Technology at Cobleskill

Cobleskill, New York

http://www.cobleskill.edu/

- **State-supported** 4-year, founded 1916, part of State University of New York System
- **Rural** 75,775-acre campus with easy access to Albany, NY
- **Endowment** $2.4 million
- **Coed** 2,532 undergraduate students, 95% full-time, 52% women, 48% men
- **Minimally difficult** entrance level, 73% of applicants were admitted

UNDERGRAD STUDENTS

2,413 full-time, 119 part-time. Students come from 15 states and territories; 12 other countries; 8% are from out of state; 11% Black or African American, non-Hispanic/Latino; 7% Hispanic/Latino; 1% Asian, non-Hispanic/Latino; 0.2% American Indian or Alaska Native, non-Hispanic/Latino; 5% Race/ethnicity unknown; 2% international; 9% transferred in; 59% live on campus.

Freshmen

Admission: 3,139 applied, 2,294 admitted, 779 enrolled. ***Test scores:*** SAT critical reading scores over 500: 24%; SAT math scores over 500: 28%; ACT scores over 18: 66%; SAT critical reading scores over 600: 4%; SAT math scores over 600: 3%; ACT scores over 24: 16%; ACT scores over 30: 1%.

Retention: 76% of full-time freshmen returned.

FACULTY

Total: 173, 58% full-time, 29% with terminal degrees.

Student/faculty ratio: 15:1.

ACADEMICS

Calendar: semesters. *Degrees:* certificates, associate, and bachelor's.

Special study options: academic remediation for entering students, advanced placement credit, cooperative education, distance learning, honors programs, independent study, internships, off-campus study, part-time degree program, services for LD students, study abroad, summer session for credit.

Computers: 504 computers/terminals and 455 ports are available on campus for general student use. Students can access the following: campus intranet, computer help desk, free student e-mail accounts, online (class) grades, online (class) registration, online (class) schedules. Campuswide network is available. 100% of college-owned or -operated housing units are wired for high-speed Internet access. Wireless service is available via entire campus.

STUDENT LIFE

Housing options: on-campus residence required through sophomore year; coed, men-only, women-only, special housing for students with disabilities. Campus housing is university owned. Freshman campus housing is guaranteed.

Activities and organizations: drama/theater group, student-run newspaper, choral group, Wildlife Society, AAPC (American Animal Producers Club), Post-Secondary Agricultural Students, Society for Agricultural Engineers, Ducks Unlimited.

Athletics Member NCAA. All Division III. ***Intercollegiate sports:*** basketball M/W, cheerleading M/W, cross-country running M/W, golf M/W, lacrosse M, soccer M/W, softball W, swimming and diving M/W, tennis M/W, track and field M/W, volleyball W. ***Intramural sports:*** baseball M(c), bowling M/W, football M/W, soccer M/W, softball M/W.

Campus security: 24-hour emergency response devices and patrols, student patrols, late-night transport/escort service, controlled dormitory access, bicycle patrols, horse-mounted patrols.

Student services: health clinic, personal/psychological counseling.

COSTS & FINANCIAL AID

Costs (2015–16) ***Tuition:*** state resident $6170 full-time, $257 per credit hour part-time; nonresident $15,820 full-time, $638 per credit hour part-time. Full-time tuition and fees vary according to degree level. Part-time tuition and fees vary according to degree level. ***Required fees:*** $1439 full-time, $57 per credit hour part-time. ***Room and board:*** $12,140; room only: $7280. Room and board charges vary according to board plan. ***Payment plans:*** installment, deferred payment. ***Waivers:*** senior citizens and employees or children of employees.

Financial Aid Of all full-time matriculated undergraduates who enrolled in 2013, 2,223 applied for aid, 1,961 were judged to have need, 50 had their need fully met. In 2013, 262 non-need-based awards were made. ***Average percent of need met:*** 63. ***Average financial aid package:*** $8250. ***Average need-based loan:*** $3705. ***Average need-based gift aid:*** $5231. ***Average non-need-based aid:*** $410. ***Average indebtedness upon graduation:*** $24,952.

APPLYING

Standardized Tests *Required:* SAT or ACT (for admission).

Options: electronic application, early admission, deferred entrance.

Application fee: $50.

Required: high school transcript. ***Required for some:*** essay or personal statement, minimum 2.0 GPA, 3 letters of recommendation, interview. ***Recommended:*** minimum 1.8 GPA.

Application deadlines: rolling (freshmen), rolling (transfers).

Notification: continuous (freshmen), continuous (transfers).

CONTACT

Annie Breglia, Keyboard Specialist 1, State University of New York College of Agriculture and Technology at Cobleskill, 213 Knapp Hall, Cobleskill, NY 12043. *Phone:* 518-255-5525. *Toll-free phone:* 800-295-8988. *Fax:* 518-255-6769. *E-mail:* admissions@cobleskill.edu.

★ State University of New York College of Environmental Science and Forestry

Syracuse, New York

http://www.esf.edu/

- **State-supported** university, founded 1911, part of State University of New York System
- **Urban** 17-acre campus
- **Endowment** $26.4 million
- **Coed** 1,856 undergraduate students, 90% full-time, 45% women, 55% men
- **Very difficult** entrance level, 51% of applicants were admitted

UNDERGRAD STUDENTS

1,677 full-time, 179 part-time. Students come from 34 states and territories; 12 other countries; 19% are from out of state; 2% Black or African American, non-Hispanic/Latino; 4% Hispanic/Latino; 3% Asian, non-Hispanic/Latino; 0.3% American Indian or Alaska Native, non-Hispanic/Latino; 3% Two or more races, non-Hispanic/Latino; 3%

Race/ethnicity unknown; 2% international; 13% transferred in; 35% live on campus.

Freshmen
Admission: 1,596 applied, 816 admitted, 331 enrolled. ***Average high school GPA:*** 3.87. ***Test scores:*** SAT critical reading scores over 500: 92%; SAT math scores over 500: 97%; ACT scores over 18: 100%; SAT critical reading scores over 600: 42%; SAT math scores over 600: 54%; ACT scores over 24: 78%; SAT critical reading scores over 700: 8%; SAT math scores over 700: 9%; ACT scores over 30: 19%.

Retention: 85% of full-time freshmen returned.

FACULTY
Total: 184, 78% full-time, 82% with terminal degrees.
Student/faculty ratio: 13:1.

ACADEMICS
Calendar: semesters. *Degrees:* associate, bachelor's, master's, doctoral, and postbachelor's certificates.

Special study options: accelerated degree program, advanced placement credit, cooperative education, distance learning, double majors, English as a second language, freshman honors college, honors programs, independent study, internships, off-campus study, part-time degree program, services for LD students, study abroad, summer session for credit. ***ROTC:*** Army (c), Air Force (c).

Computers: 350 computers/terminals and 2,250 ports are available on campus for general student use. Students can access the following: campus intranet, computer help desk, free student e-mail accounts, online (class) grades, online (class) registration, online (class) schedules. Campuswide network is available. 100% of college-owned or -operated housing units are wired for high-speed Internet access. Wireless service is available via classrooms, computer centers, computer labs, dorm rooms, libraries, student centers.

STUDENT LIFE
Housing options: on-campus residence required for freshman year; coed, special housing for students with disabilities. Campus housing is university owned and is provided by a third party. Freshman campus housing is guaranteed.

Activities and organizations: drama/theater group, student-run newspaper, choral group, marching band, Bob Marshall/Outing Club, Forestry Club, Student Environmental Action Coalition, Student Green Campus Initiative, Alpha Phi Omega (Service), national fraternities, national sororities.

Athletics Member USCAA. ***Intercollegiate sports:*** basketball M, cross-country running M/W, golf M/W, soccer M/W, track and field M/W. ***Intramural sports:*** archery M/W, badminton M/W, baseball M, basketball M/W, bowling M/W, cheerleading M/W, crew M/W, cross-country running M/W, equestrian sports M/W, fencing M/W, field hockey W, football M, gymnastics M/W, ice hockey M/W, lacrosse M/W, racquetball M/W, riflery M, rugby M/W, sailing M/W, skiing (downhill) M/W, soccer M/W, softball M/W, squash M/W, swimming and diving M/W, table tennis M/W, tennis M/W, track and field M/W, ultimate Frisbee M/W, volleyball M/W.

Campus security: 24-hour emergency response devices and patrols, late-night transport/escort service, controlled dormitory access.

Student services: health clinic, personal/psychological counseling, women's center, legal services.

COSTS & FINANCIAL AID
Costs (2015–16) ***Tuition:*** state resident $6170 full-time, $270 per credit hour part-time; nonresident $15,820 full-time, $680 per credit hour part-time. Full-time tuition and fees vary according to location. Part-time tuition and fees vary according to course load and location. ***Required fees:*** $1228 full-time, $60 per term part-time. ***Room and board:*** $15,120. Room and board charges vary according to board plan, housing facility, and location. ***Payment plans:*** installment, deferred payment.

Financial Aid Of all full-time matriculated undergraduates who enrolled in 2014, 1,348 applied for aid, 1,167 were judged to have need, 800 had their need fully met. 192 Federal Work-Study jobs (averaging $1622). 336 state and other part-time jobs (averaging $1054). In 2014, 140 non-need-based awards were made. ***Average percent of need met:*** 86. ***Average financial aid package:*** $15,000. ***Average need-based loan:*** $4400. ***Average need-based gift aid:*** $4720. ***Average non-need-based aid:*** $3158. ***Average indebtedness upon graduation:*** $25,399.

APPLYING
Standardized Tests *Required:* SAT or ACT (for admission). *Recommended:* SAT Subject Tests (for admission).

Options: electronic application, early admission, early decision, deferred entrance.

Application fee: $50.

Required: essay or personal statement, high school transcript, minimum 3.0 GPA, supplemental application. ***Recommended:*** 1 letter of recommendation, interview.

Application deadlines: 2/1 (freshmen), 2/1 (out-of-state freshmen), 3/1 (transfers).

Early decision deadline: 12/1.

Notification: continuous (freshmen), continuous (out-of-state freshmen), continuous (transfers), rolling (early decision).

CONTACT
Ms. Susan Sanford, Director of Admissions, State University of New York College of Environmental Science and Forestry, Office of Undergraduate Admissions, Gateway Center 1 Forestry Drive, Syracuse, NY 13210-2779. *Phone:* 315-470-6600. *Fax:* 315-470-6933. *E-mail:* esfinfo@esf.edu.

See previous page for display ad and page 1632 for the College Close-Up.

State University of New York College of Technology at Alfred

Alfred, New York

http://www.alfredstate.edu/

- **State-supported** primarily 2-year, founded 1908, part of State University of New York System
- **Rural** 1084-acre campus with easy access to Rochester, Buffalo
- **Endowment** $4.5 million
- **Coed** 3,661 undergraduate students, 91% full-time, 39% women, 61% men
- **Moderately difficult** entrance level, 54% of applicants were admitted

UNDERGRAD STUDENTS
3,329 full-time, 332 part-time. Students come from 7 other countries; 6% are from out of state; 8% Black or African American, non-Hispanic/Latino; 6% Hispanic/Latino; 2% Asian, non-Hispanic/Latino; 0.1% Native Hawaiian or other Pacific Islander, non-Hispanic/Latino; 0.3% American Indian or Alaska Native, non-Hispanic/Latino; 2% Two or more races, non-Hispanic/Latino; 3% Race/ethnicity unknown; 9% transferred in; 66% live on campus.

Freshmen
Admission: 6,034 applied, 3,273 admitted, 1,085 enrolled. ***Average high school GPA:*** 3.

Retention: 86% of full-time freshmen returned.

FACULTY
Total: 233, 72% full-time, 17% with terminal degrees.

Student/faculty ratio: 19:1.

ACADEMICS
Calendar: semesters. *Degrees:* certificates, associate, and bachelor's.

Special study options: academic remediation for entering students, adult/continuing education programs, advanced placement credit, cooperative education, distance learning, double majors, English as a second language, honors programs, independent study, internships, off-campus study, part-time degree program, services for LD students, student-designed majors, study abroad, summer session for credit. ***ROTC:*** Army (c).

Computers: 100 computers/terminals are available on campus for general student use. Students can access the following: campus intranet, computer help desk, free student e-mail accounts, online (class) grades, online (class) registration, online (class) schedules. Campuswide network is available. 100% of college-owned or -operated housing units are wired for high-speed Internet access. Wireless service is available via entire campus.

STUDENT LIFE
Housing options: coed, men-only, women-only, special housing for students with disabilities. Campus housing is university owned. Freshman campus housing is guaranteed.

Activities and organizations: drama/theater group, student-run newspaper, radio station, choral group, Outdoor Recreation Club, Caribbean Student Association, Alfred Programming Board, Pioneer Woodsmen, Disaster Relief Team.

Athletics Member NCAA, USCAA. All Division III. ***Intercollegiate sports:*** baseball M, basketball M/W, cross-country running M/W, equestrian sports M/W, football M, lacrosse M, soccer M/W, softball W, swimming and diving M/W, track and field M/W, volleyball W, wrestling M. ***Intramural sports:*** basketball M/W, football M(c), golf M/W, ice hockey M(c)/W(c), lacrosse M(c)/W(c), rock climbing M/W, soccer M/W, softball M/W, swimming and diving M(c)/W(c), tennis M/W, ultimate Frisbee M/W, volleyball M/W.

Campus security: 24-hour emergency response devices and patrols, late-night transport/escort service, controlled dormitory access, residence hall entrance guards.

Student services: health clinic, personal/psychological counseling.

COSTS & FINANCIAL AID
Costs (2014–15) ***One-time required fee:*** $100. ***Tuition:*** state resident $6170 full-time, $257 per credit hour part-time; nonresident $9740 full-time, $406 per credit hour part-time. Full-time tuition and fees vary according to course load and degree level. Part-time tuition and fees vary according to course load and degree level. ***Required fees:*** $1476 full-time, $58 per credit hour part-time, $10 per credit hour part-time. ***Room and board:*** $11,910; room only: $7080. Room and board charges vary according to board plan and housing facility. ***Payment plan:*** installment. ***Waivers:*** employees or children of employees.

Financial Aid Of all full-time matriculated undergraduates who enrolled in 2013, 2,971 applied for aid, 2,652 were judged to have need, 219 had their need fully met. 238 Federal Work-Study jobs (averaging $1119). In 2013, 117 non-need-based awards were made. ***Average percent of need met:*** 60. ***Average financial aid package:*** $10,914. ***Average need-based loan:*** $4266. ***Average need-based gift aid:*** $6616. ***Average non-need-based aid:*** $5275. ***Average indebtedness upon graduation:*** $27,970.

APPLYING
Standardized Tests *Required for some:* SAT or ACT (for admission). *Recommended:* SAT or ACT (for admission).

Options: electronic application.

Application fee: $50.

Required: high school transcript, minimum 2.0 GPA. ***Recommended:*** essay or personal statement, interview.

Application deadlines: rolling (freshmen), rolling (out-of-state freshmen), rolling (transfers).

Notification: continuous (freshmen), continuous (out-of-state freshmen), continuous (transfers).

CONTACT
Mrs. Goodrich Deborah, Associate Vice President for Enrollment Management, State University of New York College of Technology at Alfred, Huntington Administration Building, 10 Upper College Drive, Alfred, NY 14802. *Phone:* 607-587-3945. *Toll-free phone:* 800-4-ALFRED. *Fax:* 607-587-4299. *E-mail:* admissions@alfredstate.edu.

State University of New York College of Technology at Canton

Canton, New York

http://www.canton.edu/

- **State-supported** 4-year, founded 1906, part of State University of New York System
- **Small-town** 555-acre campus
- **Endowment** $10.7 million
- **Coed** 3,278 undergraduate students, 85% full-time, 55% women, 45% men
- **Minimally difficult** entrance level, 81% of applicants were admitted

UNDERGRAD STUDENTS

2,793 full-time, 485 part-time. Students come from 26 states and territories; 14 other countries; 3% are from out of state; 14% Black or African American, non-Hispanic/Latino; 9% Hispanic/Latino; 1% Asian, non-Hispanic/Latino; 0.1% Native Hawaiian or other Pacific Islander, non-Hispanic/Latino; 2% American Indian or Alaska Native, non-Hispanic/Latino; 2% Two or more races, non-Hispanic/Latino; 3% Race/ethnicity unknown; 1% international; 9% transferred in; 40% live on campus.

Freshmen

Admission: 3,119 applied, 2,516 admitted, 733 enrolled. ***Average high school GPA:*** 2.8. ***Test scores:*** SAT critical reading scores over 500: 25%; SAT math scores over 500: 33%; SAT writing scores over 500: 16%; ACT scores over 18: 68%; SAT critical reading scores over 600: 4%; SAT math scores over 600: 5%; SAT writing scores over 600: 2%; ACT scores over 24: 20%; ACT scores over 30: 1%.

Retention: 76% of full-time freshmen returned.

FACULTY

Total: 265, 46% full-time, 28% with terminal degrees.

Student/faculty ratio: 17:1.

ACADEMICS

Calendar: semesters. *Degrees:* certificates, associate, and bachelor's.

Special study options: academic remediation for entering students, advanced placement credit, distance learning, honors programs, independent study, internships, off-campus study, services for LD students, student-designed majors, study abroad, summer session for credit. ***ROTC:*** Army (c), Air Force (c).

Computers: 1,044 computers/terminals are available on campus for general student use. Students can access the following: campus intranet, computer help desk, free student e-mail accounts, online (class) grades, online (class) registration, online (class) schedules, bill payment. Campuswide network is available. 100% of college-owned or -operated housing units are wired for high-speed Internet access. Wireless service is available via classrooms, computer centers, computer labs, dorm rooms, learning centers, libraries, student centers.

STUDENT LIFE

Housing options: on-campus residence required through sophomore year; coed, special housing for students with disabilities. Campus housing is university owned. Freshman applicants given priority for college housing.

Activities and organizations: drama/theater group, choral group, Student Government Alliance, College Activities Board, Criminal Justice Student Association.

Athletics Member NCAA, USCAA. All Division III. ***Intercollegiate sports:*** baseball M, basketball M/W, cross-country running M/W, golf M, ice hockey M/W, lacrosse M/W, soccer M/W, softball W, volleyball W. ***Intramural sports:*** basketball M/W, cheerleading M(c)/W(c), football M/W, ice hockey M(c)/W(c), soccer M/W, softball M/W, ultimate Frisbee M(c)/W(c), volleyball M/W.

Campus security: 24-hour emergency response devices and patrols, late-night transport/escort service, controlled dormitory access.

Student services: health clinic, personal/psychological counseling.

COSTS & FINANCIAL AID

Costs (2014–15) ***One-time required fee:*** $60. ***Tuition:*** state resident $6170 full-time, $257 per credit hour part-time; nonresident $10,340 full-time, $431 per credit hour part-time. Full-time tuition and fees vary according to degree level. Part-time tuition and fees vary according to degree level. ***Required fees:*** $1339 full-time, $59 per credit hour part-time, $5 per term part-time. ***Room and board:*** $11,300; room only: $6700. Room and board charges vary according to board plan and housing facility. ***Payment plans:*** installment, deferred payment. ***Waivers:*** employees or children of employees.

Financial Aid Of all full-time matriculated undergraduates who enrolled in 2014, 2,627 applied for aid, 2,374 were judged to have need, 383 had their need fully met. 145 Federal Work-Study jobs (averaging $1199). 5 state and other part-time jobs (averaging $1194). In 2014, 57 non-need-based awards were made. ***Average percent of need met:*** 16. ***Average financial aid package:*** $10,516. ***Average need-based loan:*** $3953. ***Average need-based gift aid:*** $7648. ***Average non-need-based aid:*** $1254. ***Average indebtedness upon graduation:*** $30,905.

APPLYING

Standardized Tests *Required for some:* SAT or ACT (for admission).

Options: electronic application, deferred entrance.

Application fee: $50.

Required: high school transcript. ***Required for some:*** essay or personal statement, interview. ***Recommended:*** minimum 2.0 GPA.

Application deadlines: 7/1 (freshmen), 7/1 (out-of-state freshmen), 7/1 (transfers).

Notification: continuous (freshmen), continuous (out-of-state freshmen), continuous (transfers).

CONTACT

Melissa Evans, Director of Admissions, State University of New York College of Technology at Canton, Cornell Drive, Canton, NY 13617. *Phone:* 315-386-7123. *Toll-free phone:* 800-388-7123. *Fax:* 315-386-7929. *E-mail:* admissions@canton.edu.

State University of New York College of Technology at Delhi

Delhi, New York

http://www.delhi.edu/

- **State-supported** comprehensive, founded 1913, part of State University of New York System
- **Rural** 405-acre campus
- **Endowment** $3.7 million
- **Coed** 3,614 undergraduate students, 74% full-time, 55% women, 45% men
- **Moderately difficult** entrance level, 68% of applicants were admitted

UNDERGRAD STUDENTS

2,691 full-time, 923 part-time. Students come from 28 states and territories; 5 other countries; 4% are from out of state; 17% Black or African American, non-Hispanic/Latino; 14% Hispanic/Latino; 3% Asian, non-Hispanic/Latino; 0.6% American Indian or Alaska Native, non-Hispanic/Latino; 4% Race/ethnicity unknown; 11% transferred in; 48% live on campus.

Freshmen

Admission: 5,134 applied, 3,490 admitted, 965 enrolled. ***Test scores:*** SAT math scores over 500: 30%; SAT writing scores over 500: 23%; ACT scores over 18: 78%; SAT math scores over 600: 4%; SAT writing scores over 600: 3%; ACT scores over 24: 12%.

Retention: 66% of full-time freshmen returned.

FACULTY

Total: 245, 56% full-time, 18% with terminal degrees.

Student/faculty ratio: 15:1.

ACADEMICS

Calendar: semesters. *Degrees:* certificates, associate, bachelor's, and master's.

Special study options: academic remediation for entering students, advanced placement credit, distance learning, double majors, English as a second language, honors programs, independent study, internships, off-campus study, part-time degree program, services for LD students, study abroad, summer session for credit.

Computers: 350 computers/terminals are available on campus for general student use. Students can access the following: campus intranet, computer help desk, free student e-mail accounts, online (class) grades, online (class) registration, online (class) schedules. Campuswide network is available. 100% of college-owned or -operated housing units are wired for high-speed Internet access. Wireless service is available via entire campus.

STUDENT LIFE

Housing options: on-campus residence required through sophomore year; coed, women-only. Campus housing is university owned and is provided by a third party.

Activities and organizations: drama/theater group, student-run newspaper, radio and television station, Latin American Student Organization, Hotel Sales Management Association, student radio station, Phi Theta Kappa, Student Programming Board, national fraternities.

Athletics Member NAIA, NJCAA. ***Intercollegiate sports:*** basketball M/W, cross-country running M/W, golf M/W, lacrosse M, soccer M/W, softball W, swimming and diving M/W, tennis M/W, track and field M/W, volleyball W. ***Intramural sports:*** badminton M/W(c), basketball M, bowling M(c)/W(c), equestrian sports M(c)/W(c), football M, racquetball M/W, skiing (downhill) M(c)/W(c), softball M/W, ultimate Frisbee M/W, volleyball M/W.

Campus security: 24-hour emergency response devices and patrols, late-night transport/escort service, controlled dormitory access.

Student services: health clinic, personal/psychological counseling.

COSTS & FINANCIAL AID

Costs (2015–16) ***Tuition:*** state resident $6170 full-time, $257 per credit hour part-time; nonresident $10,340 full-time, $431 per credit hour part-time. Full-time tuition and fees vary according to degree level. Part-time tuition and fees vary according to degree level. ***Required fees:*** $1360 full-time, $66 per credit hour part-time, $66 per credit hour part-time. ***Room and board:*** $10,970; room only: $6310. Room and board charges vary according to board plan and housing facility. ***Payment plan:*** installment.

Financial Aid Of all full-time matriculated undergraduates who enrolled in 2013, 2,550 were judged to have need.

APPLYING

Standardized Tests *Recommended:* SAT or ACT (for admission).

Options: electronic application, early admission, deferred entrance.

Application fee: $50.

Required: high school transcript. ***Required for some:*** minimum 2.0 GPA, some Bachelor degree programs require Associate degree for admission; BSN program requires RN license. ***Recommended:*** interview.

Application deadlines: rolling (freshmen), rolling (transfers).

Notification: continuous (freshmen), continuous (transfers).

CONTACT

State University of New York College of Technology at Delhi, 2 Main St - Stop 2, Delhi, NY 13753. *Phone:* 607-746-4550. *Toll-free phone:* 800-96-DELHI. *Fax:* 607-746-4104. *E-mail:* enroll@delhi.edu.

State University of New York Empire State College

Saratoga Springs, New York

http://www.esc.edu/

- **State-supported** comprehensive, founded 1971, part of State University of New York System
- **Small-town** campus
- **Coed** 10,878 undergraduate students, 39% full-time, 61% women, 39% men
- **Minimally difficult** entrance level, 81% of applicants were admitted

UNDERGRAD STUDENTS

4,249 full-time, 6,629 part-time. 6% are from out of state; 15% Black or African American, non-Hispanic/Latino; 11% Hispanic/Latino; 2% Asian, non-Hispanic/Latino; 0.3% Native Hawaiian or other Pacific Islander, non-Hispanic/Latino; 0.5% American Indian or Alaska Native, non-Hispanic/Latino; 2% Two or more races, non-Hispanic/Latino; 3% Race/ethnicity unknown; 3% international; 21% transferred in.

Freshmen

Admission: 1,308 applied, 1,061 admitted, 349 enrolled.

FACULTY

Total: 1,077, 18% full-time, 38% with terminal degrees.

Student/faculty ratio: 15:1.

ACADEMICS

Calendar: continuous. *Degrees:* certificates, associate, bachelor's, master's, and postbachelor's certificates (branch locations at 7 regional centers with 35 auxiliary units).

Special study options: adult/continuing education programs, advanced placement credit, cooperative education, distance learning, external degree program, independent study, off-campus study, part-time degree program, services for LD students, student-designed majors, summer session for credit.

Computers: Students can access the following: online (class) registration. Campuswide network is available.

STUDENT LIFE

Housing options: college housing not available.

COSTS

Costs (2014–15) ***Tuition:*** $257 per credit part-time; state resident $6170 full-time; nonresident $15,820 full-time, $659 per credit part-time. Full-time tuition and fees vary according to course level, course load, location, and program. Part-time tuition and fees vary according to course level, location, and program. ***Required fees:*** $495 full-time. ***Payment plan:*** installment.

APPLYING

Options: electronic application, early admission.

Application fee: $50.

Required: essay or personal statement, high school transcript. ***Required for some:*** interview.

CONTACT

Ms. Jennifer D'Agostino, Director of Admissions, State University of New York Empire State College, Two Union Avenue, Saratoga Springs, NY 12866. *Phone:* 518-587-2100 Ext. 2214. *Toll-free phone:* 800-847-3000. *E-mail:* admissions@esc.edu.

State University of New York Maritime College

Throggs Neck, New York

http://www.sunymaritime.edu/

- **State-supported** comprehensive, founded 1874, part of State University of New York System
- **Urban** 55-acre campus with easy access to New York City
- **Endowment** $6.8 million
- **Coed** 1,641 undergraduate students, 97% full-time, 10% women, 90% men
- **Very difficult** entrance level, 53% of applicants were admitted

UNDERGRAD STUDENTS

1,591 full-time, 50 part-time. Students come from 32 states and territories; 26 other countries; 26% are from out of state; 4% Black or African American, non-Hispanic/Latino; 10% Hispanic/Latino; 4% Asian, non-Hispanic/Latino; 0.1% Native Hawaiian or other Pacific Islander, non-Hispanic/Latino; 0.1% American Indian or Alaska Native, non-Hispanic/Latino; 1% Two or more races, non-Hispanic/Latino; 7% Race/ethnicity unknown; 3% international; 6% transferred in; 84% live on campus.

Freshmen

Admission: 1,795 applied, 945 admitted, 349 enrolled. ***Test scores:*** SAT critical reading scores over 500: 74%; SAT math scores over 500: 89%; SAT writing scores over 500: 60%; ACT scores over 18: 99%; SAT critical reading scores over 600: 19%; SAT math scores over 600: 34%; SAT writing scores over 600: 12%; ACT scores over 24: 53%; SAT critical reading scores over 700: 2%; SAT math scores over 700: 2%; SAT writing scores over 700: 1%; ACT scores over 30: 4%.

Retention: 85% of full-time freshmen returned.

FACULTY

Total: 142, 63% full-time, 34% with terminal degrees.

Student/faculty ratio: 15:1.

ACADEMICS

Calendar: semesters plus 2-month summer sea term. *Degrees:* associate, bachelor's, and master's.

Special study options: academic remediation for entering students, advanced placement credit, distance learning, double majors, independent study, internships, off-campus study, part-time degree program, services for LD students, study abroad, summer session for credit. ***ROTC:*** Army (c), Navy (b).

Computers: 160 computers/terminals are available on campus for general student use. Students can access the following: computer help desk, free student e-mail accounts, online (class) grades, online (class) registration, online (class) schedules. Campuswide network is available. 100% of college-owned or -operated housing units are wired for high-speed

Internet access. Wireless service is available via classrooms, computer centers, computer labs, dorm rooms, learning centers, libraries, student centers.

STUDENT LIFE

Housing options: on-campus residence required through senior year; coed. Campus housing is university owned.

Activities and organizations: choral group, marching band, Student Government, Maritime Activities and Programs, Campus Crusade for Christ, The Propeller Club, Chorale.

Athletics Member NCAA. All Division III. ***Intercollegiate sports:*** baseball M, basketball M, crew M/W, cross-country running M/W, football M, lacrosse M/W, soccer M/W, swimming and diving M/W, volleyball W. ***Intramural sports:*** basketball M/W, football M/W, ice hockey M(c), racquetball M/W, riflery M(c)/W(c), sailing M(c)/W(c), soccer M/W, softball M/W.

Campus security: 24-hour emergency response devices and patrols, student patrols, late-night transport/escort service, controlled dormitory access.

Student services: health clinic, personal/psychological counseling.

COSTS & FINANCIAL AID

Costs (2014–15) ***Tuition:*** state resident $6170 full-time, $257 per credit hour part-time; nonresident $15,820 full-time, $659 per credit hour part-time. Full-time tuition and fees vary according to course load. Part-time tuition and fees vary according to course load. ***Required fees:*** $1276 full-time. ***Room and board:*** $11,040; room only: $7132. Room and board charges vary according to board plan and housing facility. ***Payment plan:*** installment.

Financial Aid Of all full-time matriculated undergraduates who enrolled in 2013, 826 applied for aid, 792 were judged to have need, 16 had their need fully met. 33 Federal Work-Study jobs (averaging $420). In 2013, 44 non-need-based awards were made. ***Average percent of need met:*** 44. ***Average financial aid package:*** $7520. ***Average need-based loan:*** $4282. ***Average need-based gift aid:*** $5232. ***Average non-need-based aid:*** $2255. ***Financial aid deadline:*** 7/15.

APPLYING

Standardized Tests *Required:* SAT or ACT (for admission).

Options: electronic application, early decision, deferred entrance.

Application fee: $50.

Required: essay or personal statement. ***Recommended:*** high school transcript, interview.

Application deadlines: 1/31 (freshmen), 1/31 (out-of-state freshmen), rolling (transfers).

Early decision deadline: 11/1.

Notification: 3/1 (freshmen), 3/1 (out-of-state freshmen), continuous (transfers), 12/15 (early decision).

CONTACT

Ms. Yamiley Saintvil, Dean of Admissions, State University of New York Maritime College, 6 Pennyfield Avenue, Throggs Neck, NY 10465. *Phone:* 718-409-2220. *Fax:* 718-409-7465. *E-mail:* ysaintvil@sunymaritime.edu.

★ State University of New York Polytechnic Institute

Utica, New York

http://www.sunyit.edu/

- **State-supported** comprehensive, founded 1966, part of State University of New York System
- **Suburban** 850-acre campus
- **Endowment** $27.9 million
- **Coed** 2,034 undergraduate students, 81% full-time, 40% women, 60% men
- **Moderately difficult** entrance level, 57% of applicants were admitted

UNDERGRAD STUDENTS

1,646 full-time, 388 part-time. Students come from 6 states and territories; 11 other countries; 2% are from out of state; 7% Black or African American, non-Hispanic/Latino; 7% Hispanic/Latino; 3% Asian, non-Hispanic/Latino; 0.1% Native Hawaiian or other Pacific Islander, non-Hispanic/Latino; 0.2% American Indian or Alaska Native, non-Hispanic/Latino; 2% Two or more races, non-Hispanic/Latino; 0.1%

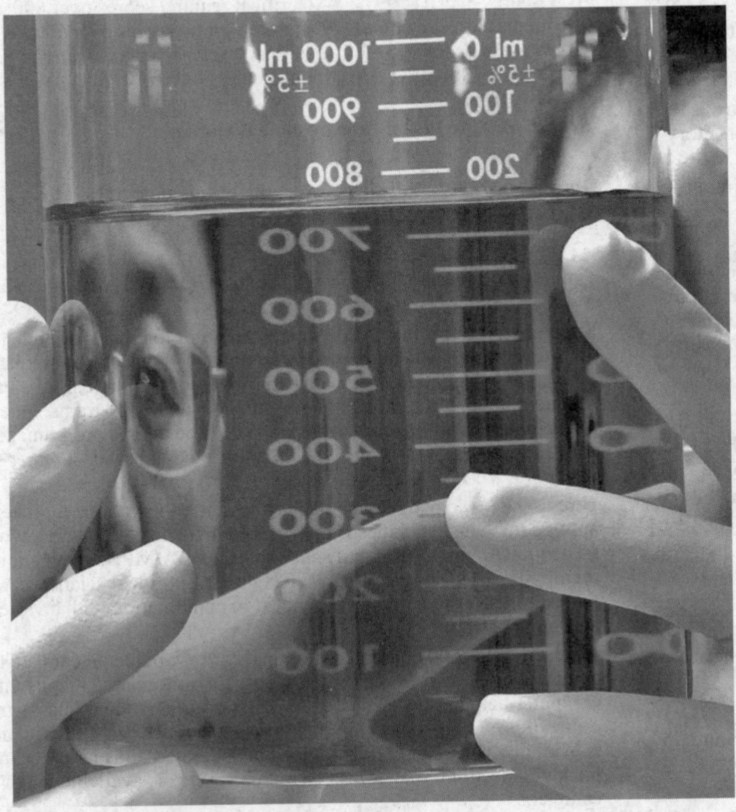

Race/ethnicity unknown; 1% international; 19% transferred in; 28% live on campus.

Freshmen

Admission: 2,233 applied, 1,263 admitted, 347 enrolled. ***Average high school GPA:*** 3.4. ***Test scores:*** SAT critical reading scores over 500: 57%; SAT math scores over 500: 77%; ACT scores over 18: 98%; SAT critical reading scores over 600: 14%; SAT math scores over 600: 28%; ACT scores over 24: 41%; SAT critical reading scores over 700: 2%; SAT math scores over 700: 3%; ACT scores over 30: 4%.

Retention: 75% of full-time freshmen returned.

FACULTY

Total: 250, 52% full-time, 56% with terminal degrees.

Student/faculty ratio: 18:1.

ACADEMICS

Calendar: semesters. *Degrees:* bachelor's, master's, post-master's, and postbachelor's certificates.

Special study options: accelerated degree program, advanced placement credit, cooperative education, distance learning, double majors, English as a second language, independent study, internships, off-campus study, part-time degree program, services for LD students, study abroad, summer session for credit. ***ROTC:*** Army (c), Air Force (c).

Computers: 380 computers/terminals and 144 ports are available on campus for general student use. Students can access the following: campus intranet, computer help desk, free student e-mail accounts, online (class) grades, online (class) registration, online (class) schedules. Campuswide network is available. 100% of college-owned or -operated housing units are wired for high-speed Internet access. Wireless service is available via entire campus.

STUDENT LIFE

Housing options: on-campus residence required through sophomore year; coed, special housing for students with disabilities. Campus housing is university owned. Freshman campus housing is guaranteed.

Activities and organizations: student-run newspaper, radio and television station, International Student Association, SUNY Tech Gamers Club, Black and Latino American Student Union, Magic the Gathering, BAJA SAE (Society of Automotive Engineers).

Athletics Member NCAA. All Division III. ***Intercollegiate sports:*** baseball M, basketball M/W, cross-country running M/W, lacrosse M/W, soccer M/W, softball W, volleyball M/W. ***Intramural sports:*** badminton M/W, basketball M/W, bowling M/W, cross-country running M/W, football M, racquetball M/W, soccer M/W, softball M/W, volleyball M/W.

Campus security: 24-hour emergency response devices and patrols, student patrols, late-night transport/escort service, controlled dormitory access, closed-circuit TV monitors, 24 hour police department.

Student services: health clinic, personal/psychological counseling, legal services.

COSTS & FINANCIAL AID

Costs (2014–15) ***Tuition:*** state resident $6170 full-time, $257 per credit hour part-time; nonresident $15,820 full-time, $659 per credit hour part-time. Part-time tuition and fees vary according to course load. ***Required fees:*** $1270 full-time, $53 per credit hour part-time. ***Room and board:*** $11,236. Room and board charges vary according to board plan. ***Payment plan:*** installment.

Financial Aid Of all full-time matriculated undergraduates who enrolled in 2014, 1,468 applied for aid, 1,163 were judged to have need, 1,151 had their need fully met. In 2014, 51 non-need-based awards were made. ***Average percent of need met:*** 99. ***Average financial aid package:*** $9820. ***Average need-based loan:*** $3731. ***Average need-based gift aid:*** $6910. ***Average non-need-based aid:*** $2308.

APPLYING

Standardized Tests *Required:* SAT or ACT (for admission). *Recommended:* SAT Subject Tests (for admission).

Options: electronic application, early admission, early action, deferred entrance.

Application fee: $50.

Required: essay or personal statement, high school transcript, minimum 3.0 GPA, 2 letters of recommendation. ***Recommended:*** interview.

Application deadlines: rolling (freshmen), rolling (out-of-state freshmen), 8/1 (transfers), 11/15 (early action).

Notification: continuous until 1/15 (freshmen), continuous until 1/15 (out-of-state freshmen), continuous until 12/1 (transfers), 12/15 (early action).

CONTACT

Ms. Gina Liscio, Director of Admissions, State University of New York Polytechnic Institute, 100 Seymour Road, Utica, NY 13502. *Phone:* 315-792-7500. *Toll-free phone:* 866-278-6948. *Fax:* 315-792-7837. *E-mail:* admissions@sunyit.edu.

See previous page for display ad and page 1642 for the College Close-Up.

Stony Brook University, State University of New York

Stony Brook, New York

http://www.stonybrook.edu/

- **State-supported** university, founded 1957, part of State University of New York System
- **Suburban** 1450-acre campus with easy access to New York City
- **Endowment** $196.4 million
- **Coed** 16,480 undergraduate students, 93% full-time, 46% women, 54% men
- **Very difficult** entrance level, 41% of applicants were admitted

UNDERGRAD STUDENTS

15,385 full-time, 1,095 part-time. Students come from 47 states and territories; 125 other countries; 8% are from out of state; 6% Black or African American, non-Hispanic/Latino; 11% Hispanic/Latino; 24% Asian, non-Hispanic/Latino; 0.1% Native Hawaiian or other Pacific Islander, non-Hispanic/Latino; 0.1% American Indian or Alaska Native, non-Hispanic/Latino; 2% Two or more races, non-Hispanic/Latino; 7% Race/ethnicity unknown; 11% international; 10% transferred in; 60% live on campus.

Freshmen

Admission: 33,714 applied, 13,938 admitted, 2,855 enrolled. ***Average high school GPA:*** 3.78. ***Test scores:*** SAT critical reading scores over 500: 87%; SAT math scores over 500: 97%; SAT writing scores over 500: 88%; ACT scores over 18: 99%; SAT critical reading scores over 600: 50%; SAT math scores over 600: 79%; SAT writing scores over 600: 49%; ACT scores over 24: 91%; SAT critical reading scores over 700: 9%; SAT math scores over 700: 30%; SAT writing scores over 700: 11%; ACT scores over 30: 29%.

Retention: 89% of full-time freshmen returned.

FACULTY

Total: 1,627, 70% full-time, 78% with terminal degrees.

Student/faculty ratio: 16:1.

ACADEMICS

Calendar: semesters. *Degrees:* bachelor's, master's, doctoral, post-master's, and postbachelor's certificates.

Special study options: academic remediation for entering students, adult/continuing education programs, advanced placement credit, cooperative education, distance learning, double majors, English as a second language, freshman honors college, honors programs, independent study, internships, off-campus study, part-time degree program, services for LD students, student-designed majors, study abroad, summer session for credit. ***ROTC:*** Army (b), Navy (c), Air Force (c).

Unusual degree programs: 3-2 business administration; engineering; applied math and statistics BS/MPH, pharmacology BS/MPH, women's students BA/MPH, earth and space sciences BA/MPH, occupational therapy BS/MS, linguistics BA/TESOL MA, political science BA/public policy MA, Masters in Adolescent Ed in combination with a variety of academic programs.

Computers: 1,500 computers/terminals are available on campus for general student use. Students can access the following: campus intranet, computer help desk, free student e-mail accounts, online (class) grades, online (class) registration, online (class) schedules. Campuswide network is available. 100% of college-owned or -operated housing units are wired for high-speed Internet access. Wireless service is available via entire campus.

STUDENT LIFE
Housing options: coed. Campus housing is university owned. Freshman campus housing is guaranteed.

Activities and organizations: drama/theater group, student-run newspaper, radio and television station, choral group, marching band, Community Service Organization, Residence Hall Association, Commuter Student Association, Asian Students Alliance, Chinese Association at Stony Brook, national fraternities, national sororities.

Athletics Member NCAA. All Division I. ***Intercollegiate sports:*** baseball M(s), basketball M(s)/W(s), cross-country running M(s)/W(s), football M(s), lacrosse M(s)/W(s), soccer M(s)/W(s), softball W(s), swimming and diving M/W(s), tennis M(s)/W(s), track and field M(s)/W(s), volleyball W(s). ***Intramural sports:*** archery M(c)/W(c), badminton M(c)/W(c), baseball W(c), basketball M/W, bowling M(c)/W(c), cheerleading M(c)/W, crew M(c)/W(c), equestrian sports M(c)/W(c), fencing M(c)/W(c), field hockey W(c), golf M(c)/W(c), ice hockey M(c), lacrosse M(c)/W(c), rugby M(c)/W(c), sailing M(c)/W(c), soccer M/W, softball W, squash M(c)/W(c), table tennis M(c)/W(c), tennis M(c)/W(c), ultimate Frisbee M(c)/W(c), volleyball M/W, weight lifting M(c), wrestling M(c).

Campus security: 24-hour emergency response devices and patrols, late-night transport/escort service, controlled dormitory access.

Student services: health clinic, personal/psychological counseling, women's center, legal services.

COSTS & FINANCIAL AID
Costs (2014–15) ***Tuition:*** state resident $6170 full-time, $257 per credit hour part-time; nonresident $19,590 full-time, $816 per credit hour part-time. Full-time tuition and fees vary according to course load. Part-time tuition and fees vary according to course load. ***Required fees:*** $2260 full-time, $113 per credit hour part-time. ***Room and board:*** $11,648; room only: $7552. Room and board charges vary according to board plan and housing facility. ***Payment plan:*** installment.

Financial Aid Of all full-time matriculated undergraduates who enrolled in 2013, 10,486 applied for aid, 8,655 were judged to have need, 1,644 had their need fully met. 491 Federal Work-Study jobs (averaging $1951). 2,276 state and other part-time jobs (averaging $3548). In 2013, 664 non-need-based awards were made. ***Average percent of need met:*** 70. ***Average financial aid package:*** $12,087. ***Average need-based loan:*** $4936. ***Average need-based gift aid:*** $7261. ***Average non-need-based aid:*** $4230. ***Average indebtedness upon graduation:*** $24,884.

APPLYING
Standardized Tests *Required:* SAT or ACT (for admission).

Options: electronic application, deferred entrance.

Application fee: $50.

Required: essay or personal statement, high school transcript, 1 letter of recommendation. ***Required for some:*** interview, audition, SAT or ACT. ***Recommended:*** minimum 3.5 GPA.

Application deadlines: 1/15 (freshmen), 3/1 (transfers).

Notification: 4/1 (freshmen), continuous until 4/1 (transfers).

CONTACT
Ms. Judith Burke-Berhanan, Dean of Undergraduate Admissions, Stony Brook University, State University of New York, Admissions Office, 118 Administration Building, Stony Brook, NY 11794-1901. *Phone:* 631-632-6868. *Fax:* 631-632-9898. *E-mail:* enroll@stonybrook.edu.

Syracuse University

Syracuse, New York

http://www.syr.edu/

- **Independent** university, founded 1870
- **Urban** 708-acre campus with easy access to Syracuse
- **Endowment** $1.2 billion
- **Coed** 15,224 undergraduate students, 95% full-time, 55% women, 45% men
- **Very difficult** entrance level, 53% of applicants were admitted

UNDERGRAD STUDENTS
14,532 full-time, 692 part-time. Students come from 49 states and territories; 84 other countries; 57% are from out of state; 9% Black or African American, non-Hispanic/Latino; 11% Hispanic/Latino; 8% Asian, non-Hispanic/Latino; 0.1% Native Hawaiian or other Pacific Islander, non-Hispanic/Latino; 0.8% American Indian or Alaska Native, non-Hispanic/Latino; 3% Two or more races, non-Hispanic/Latino; 3% Race/ethnicity unknown; 11% international; 3% transferred in; 75% live on campus.

Freshmen
Admission: 26,790 applied, 14,260 admitted, 3,470 enrolled. ***Average high school GPA:*** 3.6. ***Test scores:*** SAT critical reading scores over 500: 83%; SAT math scores over 500: 91%; SAT writing scores over 500: 86%; ACT scores over 18: 99%; SAT critical reading scores over 600: 37%; SAT math scores over 600: 56%; SAT writing scores over 600: 43%; ACT scores over 24: 79%; SAT critical reading scores over 700: 6%; SAT math scores over 700: 13%; SAT writing scores over 700: 6%; ACT scores over 30: 19%.

Retention: 92% of full-time freshmen returned.

FACULTY
Total: 1,597, 66% full-time, 64% with terminal degrees.

Student/faculty ratio: 16:1.

ACADEMICS
Calendar: semesters. *Degrees:* certificates, bachelor's, master's, doctoral, post-master's, and postbachelor's certificates.

Special study options: academic remediation for entering students, accelerated degree program, adult/continuing education programs, advanced placement credit, cooperative education, distance learning, double majors, English as a second language, freshman honors college, honors programs, independent study, internships, off-campus study, part-time degree program, services for LD students, student-designed majors, study abroad, summer session for credit. ***ROTC:*** Army (b), Air Force (b).

Computers: 3,500 computers/terminals and 678 ports are available on campus for general student use. Students can access the following: campus intranet, computer help desk, free student e-mail accounts, online (class) grades, online (class) registration, online (class) schedules, Library; web conferencing; learning management system (Blackboard); blogging service; personal websites; "View My Advising Report"; digital asset management system (Collage); Microsoft Office 365. Campuswide network is available. 100% of college-owned or -operated housing units are wired for high-speed Internet access. Wireless service is available via classrooms, computer centers, computer labs, dorm rooms, learning centers, libraries, student centers.

STUDENT LIFE
Housing options: on-campus residence required through sophomore year; coed, special housing for students with disabilities. Campus housing is university owned. Freshman campus housing is guaranteed.

Activities and organizations: drama/theater group, student-run newspaper, radio and television station, choral group, marching band, University Union, Student Association, Caribbean Student Association, Otto, Habitat for Humanity, national fraternities, national sororities.

Athletics Member NCAA. All Division I except football (Division I-A). ***Intercollegiate sports:*** badminton M(c)/W(c), baseball M(c), basketball M(s)/W(s), bowling M(c)/W(c), cheerleading M/W, crew M(s)/W(s), cross-country running M(s)/W(s), equestrian sports M(c)/W(c), fencing M(c)/W(c), field hockey W(s), gymnastics M(c)/W(c), ice hockey M(c)/W(s), lacrosse M(s)/W(s), rugby M(c)/W(c), sailing M(c)/W(c), skiing (downhill) M(c)/W(c), soccer M(s)/W(s), softball W(s), tennis M(c)/W(s), track and field M(s)/W(s), volleyball M(c)/W(s), water polo M(c)/W(c), wrestling M(c). ***Intramural sports:*** basketball M/W, field hockey W(c), golf M(c)/W(c), ice hockey M/W, lacrosse M(c)/W(c), racquetball M/W, soccer M/W, softball M/W, swimming and diving M(c)/W(c), table tennis M(c)/W(c), tennis M/W, ultimate Frisbee M(c)/W(c), volleyball M/W.

Campus security: 24-hour emergency response devices and patrols, student patrols, late-night transport/escort service, controlled dormitory access, crisis alert notification system, "Blue Light" emergency telephone system, off-campus patrols in student rental neighborhoods.

Student services: health clinic, personal/psychological counseling, women's center, legal services.

COSTS & FINANCIAL AID
Costs (2014–15) ***Comprehensive fee:*** $56,346 includes full-time tuition ($40,380), mandatory fees ($1506), and room and board ($14,460). Full-time tuition and fees vary according to course load. Part-time tuition: $1757 per credit hour. Part-time tuition and fees vary according to course load. ***College room only:*** $7640. Room and board charges vary according

to board plan and housing facility. ***Payment plans:*** tuition prepayment, installment. ***Waivers:*** employees or children of employees.

Financial Aid Of all full-time matriculated undergraduates who enrolled in 2014, 9,518 applied for aid, 8,069 were judged to have need, 2,820 had their need fully met. 5,011 Federal Work-Study jobs (averaging $2600). In 2014, 1512 non-need-based awards were made. ***Average percent of need met:*** 90. ***Average financial aid package:*** $34,620. ***Average need-based loan:*** $5400. ***Average need-based gift aid:*** $26,770. ***Average non-need-based aid:*** $10,290. ***Average indebtedness upon graduation:*** $34,584. ***Financial aid deadline:*** 2/1.

APPLYING

Standardized Tests *Required:* SAT or ACT (for admission).

Options: electronic application, early admission, early decision, deferred entrance.

Application fee: $75.

Required: essay or personal statement, high school transcript, 2 letters of recommendation.

Early decision deadline: 11/15.

CONTACT

Office of Admissions, Syracuse University, 100 Crouse-Hinds Hall, 900 South Crouse Avenue, Syracuse, NY 13244-2130. *Phone:* 315-443-3611. *Fax:* 315-443-4226. *E-mail:* orange@syr.edu.

Trocaire College

Buffalo, New York

http://www.trocaire.edu/

- **Independent** primarily 2-year, founded 1958
- **Urban** 1-acre campus
- **Endowment** $10.8 million
- **Coed, primarily women** 1,467 undergraduate students, 46% full-time, 87% women, 13% men
- **Minimally difficult** entrance level, 58% of applicants were admitted

UNDERGRAD STUDENTS

671 full-time, 796 part-time. Students come from 4 states and territories; 1 other country; 0.2% are from out of state; 14% Black or African American, non-Hispanic/Latino; 3% Hispanic/Latino; 2% Asian, non-Hispanic/Latino; 0.1% Native Hawaiian or other Pacific Islander, non-Hispanic/Latino; 1% American Indian or Alaska Native, non-Hispanic/Latino; 0.7% Two or more races, non-Hispanic/Latino; 9% Race/ethnicity unknown; 0.1% international; 17% transferred in.

Freshmen

Admission: 730 applied, 423 admitted, 137 enrolled. ***Average high school GPA:*** 83.6.

Retention: 63% of full-time freshmen returned.

FACULTY

Total: 169, 30% full-time.

Student/faculty ratio: 11:1.

ACADEMICS

Calendar: semesters. *Degrees:* certificates, associate, and bachelor's.

Special study options: academic remediation for entering students, adult/continuing education programs, advanced placement credit, cooperative education, distance learning, double majors, external degree program, independent study, internships, off-campus study, part-time degree program, services for LD students, study abroad, summer session for credit.

Computers: 122 computers/terminals are available on campus for general student use. Students can access the following: computer help desk, free student e-mail accounts, online (class) grades, online (class) registration, online (class) schedules. Campuswide network is available. Wireless service is available via entire campus.

STUDENT LIFE

Housing options: college housing not available.

Activities and organizations: student-run newspaper, Student Governance Association, TroGreen, Diversity Club.

Campus security: 24-hour emergency response devices and patrols, late-night transport/escort service.

Student services: personal/psychological counseling.

COSTS

Costs (2015–16) ***Tuition:*** $15,970 full-time, $660 per hour part-time. Full-time tuition and fees vary according to course load. Part-time tuition and fees vary according to course load. ***Required fees:*** $320 full-time, $27 per credit hour part-time. ***Payment plan:*** installment. ***Waivers:*** employees or children of employees.

APPLYING

Options: electronic application, deferred entrance.

Required: high school transcript. ***Required for some:*** essay or personal statement, letters of recommendation. ***Recommended:*** minimum 1.9 GPA, interview.

Application deadlines: rolling (freshmen), rolling (transfers).

CONTACT

Mrs. Sharon Kempton, Director of Admissions, Trocaire College, 360 Choate Avenue, Buffalo, NY 14220-2094. *Phone:* 716-827-2459. *Fax:* 716-828-6107. *E-mail:* info@trocaire.edu.

Union College

Schenectady, New York

http://www.union.edu/

- **Independent** 4-year, founded 1795
- **Urban** 100-acre campus
- **Endowment** $415.8 million
- **Coed** 2,242 undergraduate students, 99% full-time, 46% women, 54% men
- **Very difficult** entrance level, 41% of applicants were admitted

UNDERGRAD STUDENTS

2,228 full-time, 14 part-time. Students come from 41 states and territories; 35 other countries; 70% are from out of state; 4% Black or African American, non-Hispanic/Latino; 7% Hispanic/Latino; 6% Asian, non-Hispanic/Latino; 2% Two or more races, non-Hispanic/Latino; 7% international; 1% transferred in; 87% live on campus.

Freshmen

Admission: 5,406 applied, 2,223 admitted, 570 enrolled. ***Average high school GPA:*** 3.41. ***Test scores:*** SAT critical reading scores over 500: 97%; SAT math scores over 500: 100%; SAT writing scores over 500: 96%; ACT scores over 18: 100%; SAT critical reading scores over 600: 72%; SAT math scores over 600: 86%; SAT writing scores over 600: 72%; ACT scores over 24: 97%; SAT critical reading scores over 700: 18%; SAT math scores over 700: 34%; SAT writing scores over 700: 16%; ACT scores over 30: 49%.

Retention: 90% of full-time freshmen returned.

FACULTY

Total: 239, 86% full-time, 93% with terminal degrees.

Student/faculty ratio: 10:1.

ACADEMICS

Calendar: trimesters. *Degree:* bachelor's.

Special study options: accelerated degree program, advanced placement credit, double majors, honors programs, independent study, internships, off-campus study, student-designed majors, study abroad, summer session for credit. ***ROTC:*** Army (c), Navy (c), Air Force (c).

Computers: 554 computers/terminals and 3,032 ports are available on campus for general student use. Students can access the following: campus intranet, computer help desk, free student e-mail accounts, online (class) grades, online (class) registration, online (class) schedules, Digital Studio and Learning Commons. Campuswide network is available. 100% of college-owned or -operated housing units are wired for high-speed Internet access. Wireless service is available via classrooms, computer centers, computer labs, dorm rooms, learning centers, libraries, student centers.

STUDENT LIFE

Housing options: on-campus residence required through senior year; coed. Campus housing is university owned. Freshman campus housing is guaranteed.

Activities and organizations: drama/theater group, student-run newspaper, radio and television station, choral group, U-Program (Programming Board), speaker's forum, student newspaper, Concert Committee, ski club, national fraternities, national sororities.

Athletics Member NCAA. All Division III except men's and women's ice hockey (Division I). ***Intercollegiate sports:*** baseball M, basketball M/W, cheerleading M(c)/W(c), crew M/W, cross-country running M/W, equestrian sports W, field hockey W, football M, golf W, ice hockey M/W, lacrosse M/W, rugby M(c)/W(c), soccer M/W, softball W, swimming and diving M/W, tennis M/W, track and field M/W, ultimate Frisbee M(c)/W(c), volleyball W. ***Intramural sports:*** badminton M(c)/W(c), basketball M/W, bowling M(c)/W(c), equestrian sports M(c)/W(c), fencing M(c)/W(c), football M/W, golf M(c)/W(c), ice hockey M(c)/W(c), lacrosse M(c)/W, racquetball M/W, rock climbing M(c)/W(c), skiing (downhill) M(c)/W(c), soccer M/W, softball M/W, squash M/W, tennis M/W, volleyball M/W, water polo M/W.

Campus security: 24-hour emergency response devices and patrols, late-night transport/escort service, controlled dormitory access, awareness programs, bicycle patrol, shuttle service.

Student services: health clinic, personal/psychological counseling, women's center.

COSTS & FINANCIAL AID

Costs (2014–15) ***Comprehensive fee:*** $60,240 includes full-time tuition ($47,913), mandatory fees ($471), and room and board ($11,856). ***College room only:*** $6501. ***Payment plan:*** installment. ***Waivers:*** senior citizens and employees or children of employees.

Financial Aid Of all full-time matriculated undergraduates who enrolled in 2013, 1,188 applied for aid, 1,027 were judged to have need, 1,008 had their need fully met. In 2013, 498 non-need-based awards were made. ***Average percent of need met:*** 98. ***Average financial aid package:*** $36,845. ***Average need-based loan:*** $5063. ***Average need-based gift aid:*** $31,080. ***Average non-need-based aid:*** $9250. ***Average indebtedness upon graduation:*** $27,911. ***Financial aid deadline:*** 2/1.

APPLYING

Standardized Tests *Required for some:* SAT or ACT (for admission), SAT and SAT Subject Tests or ACT (for admission), Testing is optional except for combined programs. Leadership in Medicine program applicants must submit the SAT I and two SAT II's or the ACT; Law and Public Policy program applicants must submit the SAT I or the ACT. It is recommended that international applicants submit the SAT or ACT.

Options: electronic application, early admission, early decision, deferred entrance.

Required: essay or personal statement, high school transcript, 2 letters of recommendation. ***Recommended:*** interview.

Application deadlines: 1/15 (freshmen), 5/1 (transfers).

Early decision deadline: 11/15 (for plan 1), 1/15 (for plan 2).

Notification: 4/1 (freshmen), continuous (transfers), 12/15 (early decision plan 1), 2/1 (early decision plan 2).

CONTACT

Union College, Grant Hall, 807 Union Street, Schenectady, NY 12308. *Phone:* 518-388-6112. *Toll-free phone:* 888-843-6688. *Fax:* 518-388-6986. *E-mail:* admissions@union.edu.

United States Merchant Marine Academy

Kings Point, New York

http://www.usmma.edu/

- **Federally supported** comprehensive, founded 1943
- **Suburban** 82-acre campus with easy access to New York City
- **Coed** 958 undergraduate students, 100% full-time, 15% women, 85% men
- **Very difficult** entrance level, 18% of applicants were admitted

UNDERGRAD STUDENTS

958 full-time. Students come from 54 states and territories; 2 other countries; 89% are from out of state; 3% Black or African American, non-Hispanic/Latino; 9% Hispanic/Latino; 6% Asian, non-Hispanic/Latino; 0.8% American Indian or Alaska Native, non-Hispanic/Latino; 1% Race/ethnicity unknown; 1% international; 2% transferred in; 100% live on campus.

Freshmen
Admission: 2,252 applied, 409 admitted, 218 enrolled. ***Average high school GPA:*** 3.6. ***Test scores:*** SAT critical reading scores over 500: 96%; SAT math scores over 500: 100%; ACT scores over 18: 100%; SAT critical reading scores over 600: 56%; SAT math scores over 600: 85%; ACT scores over 24: 98%; SAT critical reading scores over 700: 11%; SAT math scores over 700: 19%; ACT scores over 30: 24%.
Retention: 97% of full-time freshmen returned.

FACULTY
Total: 145, 83% full-time, 29% with terminal degrees.
Student/faculty ratio: 12:1.

ACADEMICS
Calendar: trimesters. *Degrees:* bachelor's and master's.
Special study options: academic remediation for entering students, advanced placement credit, distance learning, honors programs, independent study, internships, off-campus study, study abroad.
Computers: Students can access the following: campus intranet, computer help desk, free student e-mail accounts, engineering and economics software. Campuswide network is available.

STUDENT LIFE
Housing options: on-campus residence required through senior year; coed. Campus housing is university owned. Freshman campus housing is guaranteed.
Activities and organizations: drama/theater group, student-run newspaper, choral group, marching band, Regimental Band, CFC, Neuman Club, Honor Guard.
Athletics Member NCAA. All Division III. ***Intercollegiate sports:*** baseball M, basketball M/W, crew M/W, cross-country running M/W, football M, lacrosse M/W, sailing M/W, soccer M, swimming and diving M/W, tennis M, track and field M/W, volleyball W, wrestling M. ***Intramural sports:*** basketball M/W, golf M(c), ice hockey M(c), racquetball M/W, riflery M(c)/W(c), rugby M(c), soccer W(c), ultimate Frisbee M(c), volleyball M(c), water polo M(c), weight lifting M(c)/W(c).
Campus security: 24-hour emergency response devices and patrols, controlled dormitory access.
Student services: health clinic, personal/psychological counseling.

COSTS
Costs (2014–15) ***Comprehensive fee:*** includes mandatory fees ($1032). Full-time tuition and fees vary according to student level. Midshipmen at the United States Merchant Marine Academy receive from the Federal Government their education, room and board, uniforms, and books. However, midshipmen are responsible for the payment of fees for mandatory educational supplies not provided by the government.

APPLYING
Standardized Tests *Required:* SAT or ACT (for admission).
Options: electronic application.
Required: essay or personal statement, high school transcript, 3 letters of recommendation, SAT or ACT. ***Recommended:*** interview.
Application deadlines: 3/1 (freshmen), 3/1 (transfers).
Notification: continuous until 4/1 (freshmen), continuous until 4/1 (transfers).

CONTACT
Lt. Kelly Gualtieri, Commandant, United States Merchant Marine Academy, 300 Steamboat Road, Kings Point, NY 11024-1699. *Phone:* 516-726-5646. *Toll-free phone:* 866-546-4778. *Fax:* 516-726-5390. *E-mail:* admissions@usmma.edu.

See previous page for display ad and page 1654 for the College Close-Up.

★ United States Military Academy
West Point, New York
http://www.usma.edu/

- **Federally supported** 4-year, founded 1802
- **Small-town** 16,080-acre campus with easy access to New York City
- **Endowment** $283.9 million
- **Coed, primarily men** 4,414 undergraduate students, 100% full-time, 17% women, 83% men
- **Most difficult** entrance level, 9% of applicants were admitted

UNDERGRAD STUDENTS
4,414 full-time. Students come from 55 states and territories; 32 other countries; 93% are from out of state; 9% Black or African American, non-Hispanic/Latino; 11% Hispanic/Latino; 6% Asian, non-Hispanic/Latino; 0.4% Native Hawaiian or other Pacific Islander, non-Hispanic/Latino; 1% American Indian or Alaska Native, non-Hispanic/Latino; 3% Two or more races, non-Hispanic/Latino; 2% Race/ethnicity unknown; 1% international; 100% live on campus.

Freshmen
Admission: 14,977 applied, 1,418 admitted, 1,200 enrolled. ***Test scores:*** SAT critical reading scores over 500: 96%; SAT math scores over 500: 99%; SAT writing scores over 500: 94%; ACT scores over 18: 102%; SAT critical reading scores over 600: 64%; SAT math scores over 600: 72%; SAT writing scores over 600: 57%; ACT scores over 24: 93%; SAT critical reading scores over 700: 23%; SAT math scores over 700: 29%; SAT writing scores over 700: 16%; ACT scores over 30: 46%.
Retention: 94% of full-time freshmen returned.

FACULTY
Total: 612, 100% full-time, 46% with terminal degrees.
Student/faculty ratio: 7:1.

ACADEMICS
Calendar: semesters. *Degree:* bachelor's.
Special study options: academic remediation for entering students, advanced placement credit, double majors, honors programs, independent study, off-campus study, study abroad, summer session for credit.
Computers: Students can access the following: computer help desk, free student e-mail accounts, online (class) grades, online (class) registration, online (class) schedules, All cadets will receive a laptop, printer, PDA, and portable memory device. All courses have a Blackboard presence so that once cadets log into Blackboard, they can access all their academic courses from a single interface. Campuswide network is available. 100% of college-owned or -operated housing units are wired for high-speed Internet access. Wireless service is available via entire campus.

STUDENT LIFE
Housing options: on-campus residence required through senior year; coed. Campus housing is university owned. Freshman campus housing is guaranteed.
Activities and organizations: drama/theater group, student-run radio station, choral group, Asian-Pacific Club, Big Brothers and Big Sisters, Spirit Support Group, Film Forum, Philosophy Forum.
Athletics Member NCAA. All Division I except football (Division I-A). ***Intercollegiate sports:*** baseball M, basketball M/W, cheerleading M/W, crew M(c)/W(c), cross-country running M/W, equestrian sports M(c)/W(c), fencing M(c)/W(c), golf M, gymnastics M, ice hockey M, lacrosse M/W(c), riflery M/W, rugby M/W, skiing (cross-country) M(c)/W(c), skiing (downhill) M(c)/W(c), soccer M/W, softball W, swimming and diving M/W, tennis M/W, track and field M/W, volleyball M(c)/W, water polo M(c), weight lifting M(c)/W(c), wrestling M. ***Intramural sports:*** basketball M/W, bowling M(c)/W(c), racquetball M(c)/W(c), sailing M(c)/W(c), skiing (downhill) M(c)/W(c), soccer M/W, swimming and diving M/W, ultimate Frisbee M/W, wrestling M.
Campus security: 24-hour emergency response devices and patrols, late-night transport/escort service.
Student services: health clinic, personal/psychological counseling, legal services.

COSTS
Costs (2015–16) ***Comprehensive fee:*** Cadets receive a full scholarship and an annual salary. There is no tuition charge, but there is a requirement for an initial deposit. Room, board, and medical and dental care are provided by the US Government. A portion of the cadet pay is deposited to a "Cadet Account" to help pay for uniforms, books, a laptop computer, and incidentals. The only cost is a one-time deposit upon admission to defray the initial issue of uniforms, books, supplies, and equipment. If needed, loans of $100 to $2,000 are available for the deposit. Upon graduation, cadets incur a 5-year Active Duty service obligation and 3 years of reserve duty in the US Army.

APPLYING
Standardized Tests *Required:* SAT or ACT (for admission).
Options: electronic application.

Required: essay or personal statement, high school transcript, 4 letters of recommendation, You must obtain nominations from an approved source, pass a Department of Defense qualifying medical examination, must be at least 17 but not yet 23 years of age by July 1 of year of entry, and be an unmarried U.S. citizen (foreign nationals with approval) with no parental obligations. ***Recommended:*** interview.

Notification: 5/1 (freshmen).

CONTACT
Col. Deborah J. McDonald, Director of Admissions, United States Military Academy, 600 Thayer Road, West Point, NY 10996. *Phone:* 845-938-4041. *E-mail:* admissions@usma.edu.

University at Albany, State University of New York

Albany, New York

http://www.albany.edu/

- **State-supported** university, founded 1844, part of State University of New York System
- **Suburban** 560-acre campus
- **Endowment** $50.9 million
- **Coed** 12,929 undergraduate students, 94% full-time, 48% women, 52% men
- **Very difficult** entrance level, 56% of applicants were admitted

UNDERGRAD STUDENTS
12,191 full-time, 738 part-time. Students come from 28 states and territories; 23 other countries; 6% are from out of state; 15% Black or African American, non-Hispanic/Latino; 14% Hispanic/Latino; 8% Asian, non-Hispanic/Latino; 0.1% Native Hawaiian or other Pacific Islander, non-Hispanic/Latino; 0.2% American Indian or Alaska Native, non-Hispanic/Latino; 3% Two or more races, non-Hispanic/Latino; 3% Race/ethnicity unknown; 6% international; 10% transferred in; 58% live on campus.

Freshmen
Admission: 21,755 applied, 12,148 admitted, 2,548 enrolled. ***Average high school GPA:*** 3.5. ***Test scores:*** SAT critical reading scores over 500: 71%; SAT math scores over 500: 84%; ACT scores over 18: 98%; SAT critical reading scores over 600: 18%; SAT math scores over 600: 30%; ACT scores over 24: 52%; SAT critical reading scores over 700: 2%; SAT math scores over 700: 4%; ACT scores over 30: 9%.

Retention: 82% of full-time freshmen returned.

FACULTY
Total: 1,319, 46% full-time, 65% with terminal degrees.

Student/faculty ratio: 18:1.

ACADEMICS
Calendar: semesters. *Degrees:* bachelor's, master's, doctoral, post-master's, and postbachelor's certificates.

Special study options: accelerated degree program, advanced placement credit, distance learning, double majors, English as a second language, freshman honors college, honors programs, independent study, internships, off-campus study, part-time degree program, services for LD students, student-designed majors, study abroad, summer session for credit. ***ROTC:*** Army (b), Air Force (c).

Unusual degree programs: 3-2 business administration; engineering with Rensselaer Polytechnic Institute, State University of New York at Binghamton, State University of New York at New Paltz, Clarkson University.

Computers: 500 computers/terminals are available on campus for general student use. Students can access the following: campus intranet, computer help desk, free student e-mail accounts, online (class) grades, online (class) registration, online (class) schedules. Campuswide network is available. 100% of college-owned or -operated housing units are wired for high-speed Internet access. Wireless service is available via classrooms, computer centers, computer labs, dorm rooms, libraries, student centers.

STUDENT LIFE
Housing options: on-campus residence required through sophomore year; coed. Campus housing is university owned. Freshman campus housing is guaranteed.

Activities and organizations: drama/theater group, student-run newspaper, radio and television station, choral group, intramural athletics, cultural organizations, political organizations, community service, honor societies, national fraternities, national sororities.

Athletics Member NCAA. All Division I. ***Intercollegiate sports:*** baseball M(s), basketball M(s)/W(s), crew M/W, cross-country running M(s)/W(s), field hockey W(s), football M(s), golf W(s), lacrosse M(s)/W(s), rock climbing M/W, soccer M(s)/W(s), softball W(s), tennis W(s), track and field M(s)/W(s), volleyball W(s). ***Intramural sports:*** badminton M/W, baseball M, basketball M/W, equestrian sports W, fencing M/W, football M(c), ice hockey M, lacrosse M, racquetball M/W, rugby M/W, skiing (cross-country) M/W, skiing (downhill) M/W, soccer M/W, softball W, tennis M/W, track and field M/W, ultimate Frisbee M/W, volleyball M/W, wrestling M.

Campus security: 24-hour emergency response devices and patrols, late-night transport/escort service, controlled dormitory access, Five Quad Ambulance Service; On-Campus Dead Car Battery Assistance.

Student services: health clinic, personal/psychological counseling, legal services.

COSTS & FINANCIAL AID
Costs (2015–16) ***Tuition:*** state resident $6170 full-time, $257 per credit hour part-time; nonresident $17,810 full-time, $742 per credit hour part-time. Part-time tuition and fees vary according to course load. ***Required fees:*** $2357 full-time, $61 per credit hour part-time, $243 per term part-time. ***Room and board:*** $11,986; room only: $7436. Room and board charges vary according to board plan and housing facility.

Financial Aid Of all full-time matriculated undergraduates who enrolled in 2013, 9,553 applied for aid, 7,666 were judged to have need, 477 had their need fully met. 701 Federal Work-Study jobs (averaging $1578). 247 state and other part-time jobs (averaging $6447). In 2013, 562 non-need-based awards were made. ***Average percent of need met:*** 63. ***Average financial aid package:*** $10,279. ***Average need-based loan:*** $4564. ***Average need-based gift aid:*** $6995. ***Average non-need-based aid:*** $3326. ***Average indebtedness upon graduation:*** $25,729.

APPLYING
Standardized Tests *Required:* SAT or ACT (for admission).

Options: electronic application, early admission, early action, deferred entrance.

Application fee: $50.

Required: essay or personal statement, high school transcript, 1 letter of recommendation. ***Required for some:*** portfolio, audition.

Application deadlines: 3/1 (freshmen), 3/1 (out-of-state freshmen), 7/1 (transfers), 11/15 (early action).

Notification: continuous (freshmen), continuous (transfers), 1/15 (early action).

CONTACT
University at Albany, State University of New York, Office of Undergraduate Admissions, 1400 Washington Avenue, Albany, NY 12222. *Phone:* 518-442-5435. *Fax:* 518-442-5383. *E-mail:* ugadmissions@albany.edu.

★ University at Buffalo, the State University of New York

Buffalo, New York

http://www.buffalo.edu/

- **State-supported** university, founded 1846, part of State University of New York System
- **Suburban** 1350-acre campus
- **Endowment** $624.8 million
- **Coed** 19,829 undergraduate students, 92% full-time, 46% women, 54% men
- **Moderately difficult** entrance level, 58% of applicants were admitted

UNDERGRAD STUDENTS
18,164 full-time, 1,665 part-time. Students come from 41 states and territories; 87 other countries; 3% are from out of state; 7% Black or African American, non-Hispanic/Latino; 6% Hispanic/Latino; 14% Asian, non-Hispanic/Latino; 0.1% Native Hawaiian or other Pacific Islander, non-Hispanic/Latino; 0.2% American Indian or Alaska Native, non-

Hispanic/Latino; 2% Two or more races, non-Hispanic/Latino; 6% Race/ethnicity unknown; 17% international; 10% transferred in; 35% live on campus.

Freshmen

Admission: 24,444 applied, 14,128 admitted, 3,517 enrolled. ***Average high school GPA:*** 3.2. ***Test scores:*** SAT critical reading scores over 500: 80%; SAT math scores over 500: 92%; ACT scores over 18: 100%; SAT critical reading scores over 600: 28%; SAT math scores over 600: 53%; ACT scores over 24: 80%; SAT critical reading scores over 700: 4%; SAT math scores over 700: 10%; ACT scores over 30: 20%.

Retention: 88% of full-time freshmen returned.

FACULTY

Total: 1,797, 69% full-time, 86% with terminal degrees.

Student/faculty ratio: 13:1.

ACADEMICS

Calendar: semesters. *Degrees:* certificates, bachelor's, master's, doctoral, and post-master's certificates.

Special study options: academic remediation for entering students, accelerated degree program, advanced placement credit, cooperative education, distance learning, double majors, English as a second language, freshman honors college, honors programs, independent study, internships, off-campus study, part-time degree program, services for LD students, student-designed majors, study abroad, summer session for credit. ***ROTC:*** Army (c).

Unusual degree programs: 3-2 business administration; engineering; nursing; social work; law.

Computers: 3,167 computers/terminals are available on campus for general student use. Students can access the following: campus intranet, computer help desk, free student e-mail accounts, online (class) grades, online (class) registration, online (class) schedules. Campuswide network is available. 100% of college-owned or -operated housing units are wired for high-speed Internet access. Wireless service is available via entire campus.

STUDENT LIFE

Housing options: coed, special housing for students with disabilities. Campus housing is university owned. Freshman campus housing is guaranteed.

Activities and organizations: drama/theater group, student-run newspaper, radio and television station, choral group, marching band, national fraternities, national sororities.

Athletics Member NCAA. All Division I except football (Division I-A). ***Intercollegiate sports:*** baseball M(s), basketball M(s)/W(s), crew W(s), cross-country running M(s)/W(s), soccer M(s)/W(s), softball W(s), swimming and diving M(s)/W(s), tennis M(s)/W(s), track and field M(s)/W(s), volleyball W(s), wrestling M(s). ***Intramural sports:*** badminton M(c)/W(c), baseball M(c), basketball M/W, crew M(c), cross-country running M(c)/W(c), equestrian sports M(c)/W(c), field hockey M(c)/W(c), gymnastics M(c)/W(c), ice hockey M(c)/W(c), lacrosse M(c)/W(c), rock climbing M(c)/W(c), rugby M(c)/W(c), skiing (downhill) M(c)/W(c), soccer M(c)/W(c), softball M/W, swimming and diving M(c)/W(c), track and field M(c)/W(c), ultimate Frisbee M(c)/W(c), volleyball M(c)/W(c), wrestling M(c).

Campus security: 24-hour emergency response devices and patrols, student patrols, late-night transport/escort service, controlled dormitory access, self-defense and awareness programs, security cameras.

Student services: health clinic, personal/psychological counseling, women's center, legal services.

COSTS & FINANCIAL AID

Costs (2014–15) ***Tuition:*** state resident $6170 full-time, $257 per credit hour part-time; nonresident $19,590 full-time, $816 per credit hour part-time. Part-time tuition and fees vary according to course load. ***Required fees:*** $2701 full-time, $224 per credit hour part-time. ***Room and board:*** $12,400; room only: $7210. Room and board charges vary according to board plan and housing facility. ***Payment plan:*** installment. ***Waivers:*** minority students.

Financial Aid Of all full-time matriculated undergraduates who enrolled in 2013, 15,950 applied for aid, 13,646 were judged to have need, 4,906 had their need fully met. 1,451 Federal Work-Study jobs (averaging $1189). 962 state and other part-time jobs (averaging $3889). In 2013, 174 non-need-based awards were made. ***Average percent of need met:*** 64. ***Average financial aid package:*** $9494. ***Average need-based loan:*** $4478. ***Average need-based gift aid:*** $5427. ***Average non-need-based aid:*** $6158.

APPLYING

Standardized Tests *Required:* SAT or ACT (for admission).

Options: electronic application, early admission, early decision.

Application fee: $50.

Required: essay or personal statement, high school transcript, 1 letter of recommendation. ***Required for some:*** Architecture requires a portfolio and Dance, Music Theatre, Theatre and Music require an audition.

Early decision deadline: 11/1.

Notification: continuous (freshmen), continuous (transfers), 12/15 (early decision).

CONTACT

Jose Aviles, Director of Admissions, University at Buffalo, the State University of New York, 12 Capen Hall, North Campus, Buffalo, NY 14260-1660. *Phone:* 716-645-6900. *Toll-free phone:* 888-UB-ADMIT. *E-mail:* ub-admissions@buffalo.edu.

University of Rochester

Rochester, New York

http://www.rochester.edu/

- **Independent** university, founded 1850
- **Suburban** 655-acre campus
- **Endowment** $2.0 billion
- **Coed** 6,266 undergraduate students, 95% full-time, 51% women, 49% men
- **Very difficult** entrance level, 36% of applicants were admitted

UNDERGRAD STUDENTS

5,942 full-time, 324 part-time. Students come from 52 states and territories; 97 other countries; 59% are from out of state; 5% Black or African American, non-Hispanic/Latino; 6% Hispanic/Latino; 10% Asian, non-Hispanic/Latino; 0.1% Native Hawaiian or other Pacific Islander, non-Hispanic/Latino; 0.3% American Indian or Alaska Native, non-Hispanic/Latino; 3% Two or more races, non-Hispanic/Latino; 7% Race/ethnicity unknown; 17% international; 2% transferred in; 82% live on campus.

Freshmen

Admission: 17,410 applied, 6,341 admitted, 1,436 enrolled. ***Average high school GPA:*** 3.8. ***Test scores:*** SAT critical reading scores over 500: 98%; SAT math scores over 500: 100%; SAT writing scores over 500: 99%; ACT scores over 18: 100%; SAT critical reading scores over 600: 76%; SAT math scores over 600: 90%; SAT writing scores over 600: 81%; ACT scores over 24: 100%; SAT critical reading scores over 700: 25%; SAT math scores over 700: 51%; SAT writing scores over 700: 30%; ACT scores over 30: 70%.

Retention: 97% of full-time freshmen returned.

FACULTY

Total: 793, 74% full-time, 82% with terminal degrees.

Student/faculty ratio: 10:1.

ACADEMICS

Calendar: semesters plus optional summer term. *Degrees:* bachelor's, master's, doctoral, post-master's, and postbachelor's certificates.

Special study options: accelerated degree program, advanced placement credit, cooperative education, double majors, English as a second language, honors programs, independent study, internships, off-campus study, part-time degree program, services for LD students, student-designed majors, study abroad, summer session for credit. ***ROTC:*** Army (c), Navy (b), Air Force (c).

Unusual degree programs: 3-2 business administration; nursing; Business; Computer Science; Engineering; Neuroscience; Physics; Physics and Astronomy; Public Health.

Computers: 700 computers/terminals and 4,000 ports are available on campus for general student use. Students can access the following: computer help desk, free student e-mail accounts, online (class) grades, online (class) registration, online (class) schedules. Campuswide network

is available. 100% of college-owned or -operated housing units are wired for high-speed Internet access. Wireless service is available via entire campus.

STUDENT LIFE

Housing options: on-campus residence required through sophomore year; coed. Campus housing is university owned and leased by the school. Freshman campus housing is guaranteed.

Activities and organizations: drama/theater group, student-run newspaper, radio and television station, choral group, marching band, Campus Activities Board, Black Students' Union, Grassroots (environmental group), Women's Caucus, American Sign Language Club, national fraternities, national sororities.

Athletics Member NCAA. All Division III except squash (Division I). ***Intercollegiate sports:*** archery M(c)/W(c), badminton M(c)/W(c), baseball M, basketball M/W, bowling M(c)/W(c), cheerleading M(c)/W(c), crew M(c)/W, cross-country running M/W, equestrian sports M(c)/W(c), fencing M(c)/W(c), field hockey W, football M, golf M, ice hockey M(c)/W(c), lacrosse M(c)/W, rugby M(c)/W(c), sailing M(c)/W(c), skiing (downhill) M(c)/W(c), soccer M/W, softball W, squash M(s), swimming and diving M/W, tennis M/W, track and field M/W, ultimate Frisbee M(c)/W(c), volleyball M(c)/W, water polo M(c)/W(c). ***Intramural sports:*** basketball M/W, football M/W, soccer M/W, tennis M(c)/W(c), ultimate Frisbee M/W, volleyball M/W.

Campus security: 24-hour emergency response devices and patrols, student patrols, late-night transport/escort service, controlled dormitory access.

Student services: health clinic, personal/psychological counseling, women's center, legal services.

COSTS & FINANCIAL AID

Costs (2014–15) ***Comprehensive fee:*** $60,668 includes full-time tuition ($46,150), mandatory fees ($810), and room and board ($13,708). Full-time tuition and fees vary according to student level. Part-time tuition: $1442 per credit hour. Part-time tuition and fees vary according to course load. ***College room only:*** $8416. Room and board charges vary according to board plan. ***Payment plans:*** tuition prepayment, installment. ***Waivers:*** employees or children of employees.

Financial Aid Of all full-time matriculated undergraduates who enrolled in 2014, 3,569 applied for aid, 2,966 were judged to have need, 2,671 had their need fully met. 2,099 Federal Work-Study jobs (averaging $2730). In 2014, 1747 non-need-based awards were made. ***Average percent of need met:*** 95. ***Average financial aid package:*** $40,149. ***Average need-based loan:*** $4990. ***Average need-based gift aid:*** $35,076. ***Average non-need-based aid:*** $13,617. ***Average indebtedness upon graduation:*** $30,604.

APPLYING

Standardized Tests *Required for some:* SAT and SAT Subject Tests or ACT (for admission). *Recommended:* SAT or ACT (for admission), SAT Subject Tests (for admission).

Options: electronic application, early decision, deferred entrance.

Application fee: $50.

Required: essay or personal statement, high school transcript. ***Required for some:*** Audition required for music programs at Eastman School of Music. ***Recommended:*** 2 letters of recommendation, interview.

Application deadlines: 1/5 (freshmen), 1/5 (out-of-state freshmen), 3/15 (transfers).

Early decision deadline: 11/1.

Notification: 4/1 (freshmen), 4/1 (out-of-state freshmen), 3/1 (transfers), 12/15 (early decision).

CONTACT

Office of Admissions, University of Rochester, PO Box 270251, 300 Wilson Boulevard, Rochester, NY 14627-0251. *Phone:* 585-275-3221. *Toll-free phone:* 888-822-2256. *Fax:* 585-461-4595. *E-mail:* admit@admissions.rochester.edu.

Utica College

Utica, New York

http://www.utica.edu/

- **Independent** comprehensive, founded 1946
- **Suburban** 128-acre campus
- **Endowment** $24.3 million
- **Coed** 2,921 undergraduate students, 76% full-time, 60% women, 40% men
- **Moderately difficult** entrance level, 82% of applicants were admitted

UNDERGRAD STUDENTS

2,216 full-time, 705 part-time. Students come from 48 states and territories; 28 other countries; 10% are from out of state; 11% Black or African American, non-Hispanic/Latino; 8% Hispanic/Latino; 3% Asian, non-Hispanic/Latino; 0.1% Native Hawaiian or other Pacific Islander, non-Hispanic/Latino; 0.6% American Indian or Alaska Native, non-Hispanic/Latino; 3% Two or more races, non-Hispanic/Latino; 6% Race/ethnicity unknown; 4% international; 6% transferred in; 44% live on campus.

Freshmen

Admission: 3,677 applied, 2,998 admitted, 472 enrolled. ***Average high school GPA:*** 2.86. ***Test scores:*** SAT critical reading scores over 500: 41%; SAT math scores over 500: 48%; SAT writing scores over 500: 30%; ACT scores over 18: 82%; SAT critical reading scores over 600: 7%; SAT math scores over 600: 10%; SAT writing scores over 600: 6%; ACT scores over 24: 31%; SAT math scores over 700: 1%; ACT scores over 30: 4%.

Retention: 72% of full-time freshmen returned.

FACULTY

Total: 412, 34% full-time.

Student/faculty ratio: 11:1.

ACADEMICS

Calendar: semesters. *Degrees:* certificates, bachelor's, master's, doctoral, and postbachelor's certificates.

Special study options: academic remediation for entering students, accelerated degree program, adult/continuing education programs, advanced placement credit, distance learning, double majors, English as a second language, honors programs, independent study, internships, off-campus study, part-time degree program, services for LD students, study abroad, summer session for credit. ***ROTC:*** Army (b), Air Force (c).

Unusual degree programs: 3-2 engineering with Syracuse University.

Computers: 430 computers/terminals are available on campus for general student use. Students can access the following: computer help desk, free student e-mail accounts, online (class) grades, online (class) registration, online (class) schedules. Campuswide network is available. 100% of college-owned or -operated housing units are wired for high-speed Internet access. Wireless service is available via entire campus.

STUDENT LIFE

Housing options: on-campus residence required through sophomore year; coed, special housing for students with disabilities. Campus housing is university owned. Freshman campus housing is guaranteed.

Activities and organizations: drama/theater group, student-run newspaper, radio station, choral group, Physical Therapy Society, Student Nurses Association, Kappa Delta Pi, Student Senate, Utica College Honor Association, national fraternities, national sororities.

Athletics Member NCAA. All Division III. ***Intercollegiate sports:*** baseball M, basketball M/W, cross-country running M/W, field hockey W, football M, golf M/W, ice hockey M/W, lacrosse M/W, soccer M/W, softball W, swimming and diving M/W, tennis M/W, track and field M/W, volleyball W, water polo W. ***Intramural sports:*** basketball M/W, bowling M/W, cheerleading M(c)/W(c), fencing M(c)/W(c), racquetball M/W, soccer M/W, softball M/W, tennis M/W, volleyball M/W, water polo M/W.

Campus security: 24-hour emergency response devices and patrols, late-night transport/escort service, controlled dormitory access.

Student services: health clinic, personal/psychological counseling, women's center.

COSTS & FINANCIAL AID

Costs (2014–15) ***Comprehensive fee:*** $45,670 includes full-time tuition ($33,216), mandatory fees ($520), and room and board ($11,934). Part-time tuition: $1107 per credit hour. ***Required fees:*** $50 per term part-time. ***Room and board:*** Room and board charges vary according to board plan. ***Waivers:*** employees or children of employees.

Financial Aid Of all full-time matriculated undergraduates who enrolled in 2014, 2,034 applied for aid, 1,924 were judged to have need, 178 had their need fully met. In 2014, 191 non-need-based awards were made. ***Average percent of need met:*** 68. ***Average financial aid package:*** $25,627. ***Average need-based loan:*** $4434. ***Average need-based gift aid:*** $7481. ***Average non-need-based aid:*** $17,168. ***Average indebtedness upon graduation:*** $42,083.

APPLYING

Standardized Tests *Required for some:* SAT or ACT (for admission).

Options: electronic application, deferred entrance.

Application fee: $40.

Required: essay or personal statement, high school transcript, minimum 2.0 GPA, 1 letter of recommendation. ***Required for some:*** minimum 3.0 GPA. ***Recommended:*** interview.

Application deadlines: rolling (freshmen), rolling (transfers).

Notification: 9/1 (freshmen), continuous (transfers).

CONTACT

Utica College, 1600 Burrstone Road, Utica, NY 13502-4892. *Phone:* 315-792-3006. *Toll-free phone:* 800-782-8884.

Vassar College

Poughkeepsie, New York

http://www.vassar.edu/

- **Independent** 4-year, founded 1861
- **Suburban** 1000-acre campus with easy access to New York City
- **Endowment** $914.2 million
- **Coed** 2,418 undergraduate students, 99% full-time, 56% women, 44% men
- **Very difficult** entrance level, 24% of applicants were admitted

UNDERGRAD STUDENTS

2,394 full-time, 24 part-time. Students come from 52 states and territories; 44 other countries; 73% are from out of state; 6% Black or African American, non-Hispanic/Latino; 11% Hispanic/Latino; 11% Asian, non-Hispanic/Latino; 6% Two or more races, non-Hispanic/Latino; 0.1% Race/ethnicity unknown; 7% international; 0.5% transferred in; 96% live on campus.

Freshmen

Admission: 7,784 applied, 1,832 admitted, 663 enrolled. ***Test scores:*** SAT critical reading scores over 500: 100%; SAT math scores over 500: 100%; SAT writing scores over 500: 100%; ACT scores over 18: 100%; SAT critical reading scores over 600: 96%; SAT math scores over 600: 95%; SAT writing scores over 600: 94%; ACT scores over 24: 100%; SAT critical reading scores over 700: 58%; SAT math scores over 700: 47%; SAT writing scores over 700: 56%; ACT scores over 30: 23%.

Retention: 94% of full-time freshmen returned.

FACULTY

Total: 333, 83% full-time, 81% with terminal degrees.

Student/faculty ratio: 8:1.

ACADEMICS

Calendar: semesters. *Degrees:* bachelor's and master's.

Special study options: advanced placement credit, cooperative education, double majors, independent study, internships, off-campus study, part-time degree program, services for LD students, student-designed majors, study abroad.

Unusual degree programs: 3-2 engineering with Dartmouth College.

Computers: 145 computers/terminals and 5,113 ports are available on campus for general student use. Students can access the following: campus intranet, computer help desk, free student e-mail accounts, online (class) grades, online (class) registration, online (class) schedules, Ethernet. Campuswide network is available. 100% of college-owned or -operated housing units are wired for high-speed Internet access. Wireless service is available via entire campus.

STUDENT LIFE

Housing options: on-campus residence required through senior year; coed, women-only, cooperative, special housing for students with disabilities. Campus housing is university owned. Freshman campus housing is guaranteed.

Activities and organizations: drama/theater group, student-run newspaper, radio station, choral group, Student Association, WVKR radio station, VICE (programming social events), Vassar Greens, Ultimate Frisbee.

Athletics Member NCAA. All Division III. ***Intercollegiate sports:*** baseball M, basketball M/W, crew M(c)/W(c), cross-country running M/W, fencing M/W, field hockey W, golf W, lacrosse M/W, rugby M(c)/W(c), soccer M/W, squash M(c)/W(c), swimming and diving M/W, tennis M/W, track and field M/W, volleyball M/W. ***Intramural sports:*** badminton M(c)/W(c), equestrian sports M(c)/W(c), sailing M(c)/W(c), skiing (cross-country) M(c)/W(c), skiing (downhill) M(c)/W(c), ultimate Frisbee M(c)/W(c).

Campus security: 24-hour emergency response devices and patrols, student patrols, late-night transport/escort service, controlled dormitory access.

Student services: health clinic, personal/psychological counseling, women's center.

COSTS & FINANCIAL AID

Costs (2014–15) ***One-time required fee:*** $80. ***Comprehensive fee:*** $61,140 includes full-time tuition ($48,840), mandatory fees ($730), and room and board ($11,570). Part-time tuition: $5800 per unit. ***College room only:*** $6280. Room and board charges vary according to board plan and housing facility. ***Payment plan:*** installment. ***Waivers:*** employees or children of employees.

Financial Aid Of all full-time matriculated undergraduates who enrolled in 2014, 1,581 applied for aid, 1,424 were judged to have need, 1,424 had their need fully met. 1,033 Federal Work-Study jobs (averaging $2297). 366 state and other part-time jobs (averaging $2262). ***Average percent of need met:*** 100. ***Average financial aid package:*** $47,836. ***Average need-based loan:*** $3479. ***Average need-based gift aid:*** $43,094. ***Average indebtedness upon graduation:*** $17,476. ***Financial aid deadline:*** 2/15.

APPLYING

Standardized Tests *Required:* SAT and SAT Subject Tests or ACT (for admission).

Options: electronic application, early decision, deferred entrance.

Application fee: $70.

Required: essay or personal statement, high school transcript, 2 letters of recommendation.

Application deadlines: 1/1 (freshmen), 3/15 (transfers).

Early decision deadline: 11/15.

Notification: 4/1 (freshmen), 5/10 (transfers), 12/15 (early decision).

CONTACT

Dean Art D. Rodriguez, Dean of Admission and Financial Aid, Vassar College, 124 Raymond Avenue, Poughkeepsie, NY 12604. *Phone:* 845-437-7300. *Toll-free phone:* 800-827-7270. *Fax:* 845-437-7063. *E-mail:* admissions@vassar.edu.

Vaughn College of Aeronautics and Technology

Flushing, New York

http://www.vaughn.edu/

- **Independent** comprehensive, founded 1932
- **Urban** 6-acre campus with easy access to New York City
- **Endowment** $21.9 million
- **Coed, primarily men** 1,605 undergraduate students, 79% full-time, 13% women, 87% men
- **Moderately difficult** entrance level, 75% of applicants were admitted

UNDERGRAD STUDENTS

1,261 full-time, 344 part-time. Students come from 27 states and territories; 16 other countries; 11% are from out of state; 22% Black or African American, non-Hispanic/Latino; 38% Hispanic/Latino; 12% Asian, non-Hispanic/Latino; 3% Native Hawaiian or other Pacific Islander, non-Hispanic/Latino; 0.5% American Indian or Alaska Native, non-Hispanic/Latino; 5% Two or more races, non-Hispanic/Latino; 5% Race/ethnicity unknown; 2% international; 11% transferred in; 10% live on campus.

Freshmen
Admission: 813 applied, 608 admitted, 312 enrolled. ***Test scores:*** SAT critical reading scores over 500: 58%; SAT math scores over 500: 76%; ACT scores over 18: 100%; SAT critical reading scores over 600: 12%; SAT math scores over 600: 13%; ACT scores over 24: 42%; SAT math scores over 700: 1%; ACT scores over 30: 9%.

Retention: 66% of full-time freshmen returned.

FACULTY
Total: 203, 20% full-time, 18% with terminal degrees.

Student/faculty ratio: 15:1.

ACADEMICS
Calendar: semesters. *Degrees:* certificates, associate, bachelor's, and master's.

Special study options: academic remediation for entering students, advanced placement credit, cooperative education, distance learning, double majors, English as a second language, independent study, internships, part-time degree program, services for LD students, summer session for credit. ***ROTC:*** Army (c), Air Force (c).

Computers: 60 computers/terminals are available on campus for general student use. Students can access the following: campus intranet, computer help desk, free student e-mail accounts, online (class) grades, online (class) registration, online (class) schedules, Vaughn Student Portal. Campuswide network is available. 100% of college-owned or -operated housing units are wired for high-speed Internet access. Wireless service is available via entire campus.

STUDENT LIFE
Housing options: coed, special housing for students with disabilities. Campus housing is university owned. Freshman applicants given priority for college housing.

Activities and organizations: American Association of Airport Executives, Women in Aviation-International, Veterans Club, Robotics Club, Hispanic Society of Aeronautical Engineers.

Athletics Member USCAA. ***Intercollegiate sports:*** basketball M/W, cross-country running M/W, soccer M, tennis M/W. ***Intramural sports:*** basketball M/W, cross-country running M/W, soccer M, tennis M/W.

Campus security: 24-hour emergency response devices and patrols, controlled dormitory access.

Student services: personal/psychological counseling.

COSTS & FINANCIAL AID
Costs (2014–15) ***One-time required fee:*** $160. ***Comprehensive fee:*** $34,195 includes full-time tuition ($20,840), mandatory fees ($990), and room and board ($12,365). Full-time tuition and fees vary according to course load and program. Part-time tuition: $700 per credit. Part-time tuition and fees vary according to course load and program. ***College room only:*** $9965. Room and board charges vary according to board plan. ***Payment plan:*** installment. ***Waivers:*** employees or children of employees.

Financial Aid Of all full-time matriculated undergraduates who enrolled in 2008, 704 applied for aid, 704 were judged to have need, 476 had their need fully met. 25 Federal Work-Study jobs (averaging $3000). In 2008, 145 non-need-based awards were made. ***Average percent of need met:*** 82. ***Average financial aid package:*** $18,030. ***Average need-based loan:*** $1770. ***Average need-based gift aid:*** $2950. ***Average non-need-based aid:*** $2000. ***Average indebtedness upon graduation:*** $17,125.

APPLYING
Standardized Tests *Required for some:* SAT or ACT (for admission).

Options: electronic application.

Application fee: $40.

Required: high school transcript. ***Recommended:*** essay or personal statement, 2 letters of recommendation, interview.

Application deadlines: rolling (freshmen), rolling (out-of-state freshmen), rolling (transfers).

Notification: continuous (freshmen), continuous (out-of-state freshmen), continuous (transfers).

CONTACT
Mr. David Griffey, Director of Admissions, Vaughn College of Aeronautics and Technology, 8601 23rd Avenue, Flushing, NY 11369. *Phone:* 718-429.6600 Ext. 117. *Toll-free phone:* 866-6VAUGHN. *Fax:* 718-779.2231. *E-mail:* David.griffey@vaughn.edu.

Villa Maria College

Buffalo, New York

http://www.villa.edu/

- **Independent** 4-year, founded 1960, affiliated with Roman Catholic Church
- **Suburban** 9-acre campus with easy access to Buffalo-Niagara
- **Endowment** $1.4 million
- **Coed** 524 undergraduate students, 77% full-time, 67% women, 33% men

UNDERGRAD STUDENTS
401 full-time, 123 part-time. Students come from 12 states and territories; 1 other country; 2% are from out of state; 23% Black or African American, non-Hispanic/Latino; 5% Hispanic/Latino; 0.2% Asian, non-Hispanic/Latino; 1% American Indian or Alaska Native, non-Hispanic/Latino; 5% Two or more races, non-Hispanic/Latino; 0.9% Race/ethnicity unknown; 15% transferred in; 7% live on campus.

Freshmen
Admission: 124 enrolled. ***Average high school GPA:*** 2.96.

Retention: 59% of full-time freshmen returned.

FACULTY
Total: 71, 41% full-time, 39% with terminal degrees.

Student/faculty ratio: 9:1.

ACADEMICS
Calendar: semesters. *Degrees:* certificates, associate, and bachelor's.

Special study options: academic remediation for entering students, advanced placement credit, cooperative education, independent study, internships, off-campus study, part-time degree program, services for LD students, summer session for credit.

Computers: 250 computers/terminals are available on campus for general student use. Students can access the following: computer help desk, free student e-mail accounts, online (class) grades, online (class) registration, online (class) schedules. Campuswide network is available. Wireless service is available via entire campus.

STUDENT LIFE
Housing options: college housing not availableCampus housing is provided by a third party.

Activities and organizations: choral group, Design and Beyond, Teachers Love Children, Multicultural Club, Phi Theta Kappa, Helping Adults New Dreams Succeed.

Campus security: late-night transport/escort service, security guard during hours of operation.

Student services: health clinic, personal/psychological counseling.

COSTS & FINANCIAL AID
Costs (2014–15) ***Tuition:*** $18,520 full-time, $620 per credit hour part-time. Full-time tuition and fees vary according to program. Part-time tuition and fees vary according to course load and program. ***Required fees:*** $650 full-time, $230 per term part-time. ***Payment plan:*** installment. ***Waivers:*** employees or children of employees.

Financial Aid Of all full-time matriculated undergraduates who enrolled in 2013, 321 applied for aid, 318 were judged to have need, 50 had their need fully met. In 2013, 163 non-need-based awards were made. ***Average percent of need met:*** 50. ***Average financial aid package:*** $8012. ***Average need-based loan:*** $3756. ***Average need-based gift aid:*** $5662. ***Average non-need-based aid:*** $1902. ***Average indebtedness upon graduation:*** $22,658.

APPLYING
Required: high school transcript, interview, Essay, portfolio, interview required for all BFA programs and associate level interior design assistant. Interview required for Animation program. Interview and audition required for music programs. ***Required for some:*** essay or personal statement, Essay, portfolio, interview required for all BFA programs and

associate level interior design assistant. Interview required for Animation program. Interview and audition required for music programs.

CONTACT

Mr. Kevin Donovan, Director of Admissions, Villa Maria College, Buffalo, NY 14211. *Phone:* 716-896-0700 Ext. 1802. *Fax:* 716-896-0705. *E-mail:* admissions@villa.edu.

Wagner College

Staten Island, New York

http://www.wagner.edu/

- **Independent** comprehensive, founded 1883
- **Urban** 105-acre campus with easy access to New York City
- **Endowment** $84.5 million
- **Coed** 1,809 undergraduate students, 97% full-time, 63% women, 37% men

UNDERGRAD STUDENTS

1,751 full-time, 58 part-time. Students come from 43 states and territories; 31 other countries; 52% are from out of state; 7% Black or African American, non-Hispanic/Latino; 10% Hispanic/Latino; 3% Asian, non-Hispanic/Latino; 0.1% Native Hawaiian or other Pacific Islander, non-Hispanic/Latino; 0.1% American Indian or Alaska Native, non-Hispanic/Latino; 2% Two or more races, non-Hispanic/Latino; 9% Race/ethnicity unknown; 2% international; 7% transferred in; 76% live on campus.

Freshmen

Admission: 443 enrolled. ***Test scores:*** SAT critical reading scores over 500: 90%; SAT math scores over 500: 90%; SAT writing scores over 500: 90%; ACT scores over 18: 99%; SAT critical reading scores over 600: 49%; SAT math scores over 600: 50%; SAT writing scores over 600: 48%; ACT scores over 24: 86%; SAT critical reading scores over 700: 7%; SAT math scores over 700: 6%; SAT writing scores over 700: 6%; ACT scores over 30: 6%.

Retention: 87% of full-time freshmen returned.

FACULTY

Total: 221, 44% full-time, 42% with terminal degrees.

Student/faculty ratio: 15:1.

ACADEMICS

Calendar: semesters. *Degrees:* bachelor's, master's, doctoral, and post-master's certificates.

Special study options: adult/continuing education programs, advanced placement credit, double majors, honors programs, independent study, internships, off-campus study, part-time degree program, services for LD students, student-designed majors, study abroad, summer session for credit. ***ROTC:*** Army (c).

Unusual degree programs: 3-2 business administration with accounting; Microbiology.

Computers: 230 computers/terminals are available on campus for general student use. Students can access the following: campus intranet, computer help desk, free student e-mail accounts, online (class) grades, online (class) registration, online (class) schedules. Campuswide network is available. 100% of college-owned or -operated housing units are wired for high-speed Internet access. Wireless service is available via entire campus.

STUDENT LIFE

Housing options: coed. Campus housing is university owned and leased by the school. Freshman campus housing is guaranteed.

Activities and organizations: drama/theater group, student-run newspaper, radio station, choral group, marching band, Student Government Association, Student Activities Board, Wagner College Theatre, Wagner College Choir, student newspaper, national fraternities, national sororities.

Athletics Member NCAA. All Division I except football (Division I-AA). ***Intercollegiate sports:*** baseball M(s), basketball M(s)/W(s), cheerleading W(c), cross-country running M(s)/W(s), golf M(s)/W(s), ice hockey M(c), lacrosse M(s)/W(s), soccer W(s), softball W(s), swimming and diving W(s), tennis M(s)/W(s), track and field M(s)/W(s), water polo W(s). ***Intramural sports:*** basketball M/W, bowling M/W, football M, rugby M(c), soccer M/W, softball M/W.

Campus security: 24-hour emergency response devices and patrols, late-night transport/escort service, controlled dormitory access.

Student services: health clinic, personal/psychological counseling.

COSTS & FINANCIAL AID

Costs (2014–15) ***Comprehensive fee:*** $53,200 includes full-time tuition ($40,450), mandatory fees ($300), and room and board ($12,450). Part-time tuition: $5056 per unit. ***Payment plan:*** installment. ***Waivers:*** employees or children of employees.

Financial Aid Of all full-time matriculated undergraduates who enrolled in 2014, 1,342 applied for aid, 1,131 were judged to have need, 289 had their need fully met. In 2014, 444 non-need-based awards were made. ***Average percent of need met:*** 70. ***Average financial aid package:*** $27,083. ***Average need-based loan:*** $4488. ***Average need-based gift aid:*** $21,020. ***Average non-need-based aid:*** $15,248.

APPLYING

Standardized Tests *Required for some:* SAT or ACT (for admission).

Required: essay or personal statement, high school transcript, minimum 2.5 GPA, 2 letters of recommendation. ***Required for some:*** interview. ***Recommended:*** minimum 3.0 GPA, interview.

CONTACT

Mr. James Gibbons, Director of Admissions, Wagner College, One Campus Road, Pape Admissions Building, Staten Island, NY 10301. *Phone:* 718-390-3180. *Toll-free phone:* 800-221-1010. *Fax:* 718-390-3105. *E-mail:* jgibbons@wagner.edu.

Webb Institute

Glen Cove, New York

http://www.webb.edu/

- **Independent** 4-year, founded 1889
- **Suburban** 26-acre campus with easy access to New York City
- **Endowment** $58.0 million
- **Coed** 90 undergraduate students, 100% full-time, 13% women, 87% men
- **Most difficult** entrance level, 33% of applicants were admitted

UNDERGRAD STUDENTS

90 full-time. Students come from 24 states and territories; 3 other countries; 72% are from out of state; 9% Asian, non-Hispanic/Latino; 4% Two or more races, non-Hispanic/Latino; 1% Race/ethnicity unknown; 1% international; 4% transferred in; 100% live on campus.

Freshmen

Admission: 97 applied, 32 admitted, 24 enrolled. ***Average high school GPA:*** 4.1. ***Test scores:*** SAT critical reading scores over 500: 100%; SAT math scores over 500: 100%; SAT writing scores over 500: 100%; SAT critical reading scores over 600: 93%; SAT math scores over 600: 100%; SAT writing scores over 600: 100%; ACT scores over 24: 100%; SAT critical reading scores over 700: 36%; SAT math scores over 700: 62%; SAT writing scores over 700: 33%; ACT scores over 30: 92%.

Retention: 85% of full-time freshmen returned.

FACULTY

Total: 13, 77% full-time, 62% with terminal degrees.

Student/faculty ratio: 8:1.

ACADEMICS

Calendar: semesters. *Degree:* bachelor's.

Special study options: double majors, independent study, internships, services for LD students, study abroad.

Computers: 25 computers/terminals are available on campus for general student use. Students can access the following: campus intranet, computer help desk, free student e-mail accounts. Campuswide network is available. 100% of college-owned or -operated housing units are wired for high-speed Internet access. Wireless service is available via entire campus.

STUDENT LIFE

Housing options: on-campus residence required through senior year; coed, men-only, women-only. Campus housing is university owned. Freshman campus housing is guaranteed.

Activities and organizations: choral group, Student Organization, Society of Naval Architects and Marine Engineers, American Society of Naval Engineers, Society of Women Engineers, Marine Technology Society.

Athletics ***Intercollegiate sports:*** basketball M/W, cross-country running M(c)/W(c), sailing M/W, soccer M/W, tennis M/W, volleyball M/W. ***Intramural sports:*** cross-country running M/W, ultimate Frisbee M/W.

Campus security: 24-hour emergency response devices and patrols, controlled dormitory access.

Student services: personal/psychological counseling.

COSTS & FINANCIAL AID

Costs (2015–16) ***One-time required fee:*** $2850. ***Comprehensive fee:*** $60,050 includes full-time tuition ($45,500), mandatory fees ($500), and room and board ($14,050). Webb provides scholarships that will fully cover the tuition expenses of U.S. citizens and permanent residents. One-time required fee is for a laptop charged in the first year only. ***Payment plan:*** installment.

Financial Aid Of all full-time matriculated undergraduates who enrolled in 2013, 15 applied for aid, 15 were judged to have need. In 2013, 64 non-need-based awards were made. ***Average percent of need met:*** 79. ***Average financial aid package:*** $47,255. ***Average need-based loan:*** $4505. ***Average need-based gift aid:*** $2000. ***Average non-need-based aid:*** $43,740. ***Average indebtedness upon graduation:*** $10,000.

APPLYING

Standardized Tests *Required:* SAT (for admission), SAT Subject Tests (for admission). *Recommended:* ACT (for admission).

Options: electronic application, early decision.

Application fee: $25.

Required: high school transcript, minimum 3.5 GPA, 2 letters of recommendation, interview, proof of U.S. citizenship or permanent residency status.

Application deadlines: 2/15 (freshmen), 2/15 (transfers).

Early decision deadline: 10/15.

Notification: 4/30 (freshmen), 4/30 (transfers), 12/15 (early decision).

CONTACT

Webb Institute, Crescent Beach Road, Glen Cove, NY 11542-1398. *Phone:* 516-671-8355. *Fax:* 516-674-9838. *E-mail:* admissions@webb.edu.

See below for display ad and page 1722 for the College Close-Up.

★ Wells College

Aurora, New York

http://www.wells.edu/

- **Independent** 4-year, founded 1868
- **Rural** 365-acre campus with easy access to Syracuse
- **Endowment** $23.5 million
- **Coed** 552 undergraduate students, 95% full-time, 66% women, 34% men
- **Moderately difficult** entrance level, 58% of applicants were admitted

UNDERGRAD STUDENTS

525 full-time, 27 part-time. Students come from 25 states and territories; 5 other countries; 26% are from out of state; 12% Black or African American, non-Hispanic/Latino; 9% Hispanic/Latino; 3% Asian, non-Hispanic/Latino; 0.4% Native Hawaiian or other Pacific Islander, non-Hispanic/Latino; 0.7% American Indian or Alaska Native, non-Hispanic/Latino; 2% Two or more races, non-Hispanic/Latino; 5% Race/ethnicity unknown; 1% international; 3% transferred in; 92% live on campus.

Freshmen

Admission: 2,222 applied, 1,295 admitted, 163 enrolled. ***Average high school GPA:*** 3.33. ***Test scores:*** SAT critical reading scores over 500: 62%; SAT math scores over 500: 60%; SAT writing scores over 500: 55%; ACT scores over 18: 97%; SAT critical reading scores over 600: 24%; SAT math scores over 600: 22%; SAT writing scores over 600: 16%; ACT scores over 24: 43%; SAT critical reading scores over 700: 3%; SAT math scores over 700: 1%; SAT writing scores over 700: 1%; ACT scores over 30: 4%.

Retention: 69% of full-time freshmen returned.

FACULTY
Total: 67, 57% full-time, 57% with terminal degrees.
Student/faculty ratio: 11:1.

ACADEMICS
Calendar: semesters. *Degree:* bachelor's.
Special study options: accelerated degree program, adult/continuing education programs, advanced placement credit, double majors, English as a second language, independent study, internships, off-campus study, part-time degree program, services for LD students, student-designed majors, study abroad.
Unusual degree programs: 3-2 business administration with Clarkson University; engineering with Columbia University, Clarkson University, and Cornell University; Education with University of Rochester.
Computers: 96 computers/terminals and 1,224 ports are available on campus for general student use. Students can access the following: campus intranet, computer help desk, free student e-mail accounts, online (class) grades, online (class) registration, online (class) schedules. Campuswide network is available. 100% of college-owned or -operated housing units are wired for high-speed Internet access. Wireless service is available via classrooms, dorm rooms, learning centers, libraries, student centers.

STUDENT LIFE
Housing options: on-campus residence required through junior year; coed, women-only. Campus housing is university owned. Freshman campus housing is guaranteed.
Activities and organizations: drama/theater group, student-run newspaper, choral group, Collegiate 4-H, Programming Board, Rugby Club, Campus Greens, Spanish Club.
Athletics Member NCAA. All Division III. ***Intercollegiate sports:*** basketball M/W, cross-country running M/W, field hockey W, lacrosse M/W, soccer M/W, swimming and diving M/W, tennis W, volleyball M/W. ***Intramural sports:*** rugby M(c)/W(c).
Campus security: 24-hour emergency response devices and patrols, late-night transport/escort service, controlled dormitory access.
Student services: health clinic, personal/psychological counseling, women's center.

COSTS & FINANCIAL AID
Costs (2015–16) ***Comprehensive fee:*** $50,500 includes full-time tuition ($36,000), mandatory fees ($1500), and room and board ($13,000). ***Room and board:*** Room and board charges vary according to housing facility. ***Payment plan:*** installment. ***Waivers:*** senior citizens and employees or children of employees.
Financial Aid Of all full-time matriculated undergraduates who enrolled in 2014, 515 applied for aid, 490 were judged to have need, 47 had their need fully met. 55 Federal Work-Study jobs (averaging $1850). 240 state and other part-time jobs (averaging $1850). In 2014, 35 non-need-based awards were made. ***Average percent of need met:*** 77. ***Average financial aid package:*** $31,365. ***Average need-based loan:*** $3912. ***Average need-based gift aid:*** $31,797. ***Average non-need-based aid:*** $19,183. ***Average indebtedness upon graduation:*** $36,498.

APPLYING
Standardized Tests *Required:* SAT or ACT (for admission).
Options: electronic application, early admission, early decision, early action, deferred entrance.
Application fee: $40.
Required: essay or personal statement, high school transcript, 2 letters of recommendation. ***Recommended:*** minimum 3.0 GPA, interview.
Application deadlines: 3/1 (freshmen), rolling (transfers), 12/15 (early action).
Early decision deadline: 12/15.
Notification: 4/1 (freshmen), continuous (transfers), 1/15 (early decision), 2/1 (early action).

CONTACT
Ms. Susan Raith Sloan, Director of Admissions and Financial Aid, Wells College, 170 Main Street, Aurora, NY 13026. *Phone:* 315-364-3264. *Toll-free phone:* 800-952-9355. *Fax:* 315-364-3227. *E-mail:* admissions@wells.edu.

See below for display ad and page 1724 for the College Close-Up.

Yeshiva University

New York, New York

http://www.yu.edu/

- **Independent** university, founded 1886
- **Urban** campus
- **Coed** 2,817 undergraduate students, 98% full-time, 46% women, 54% men
- **Moderately difficult** entrance level, 48% of applicants were admitted

UNDERGRAD STUDENTS
2,767 full-time, 50 part-time. 66% are from out of state; 0.2% Hispanic/Latino; 0.2% Two or more races, non-Hispanic/Latino; 1% Race/ethnicity unknown; 5% international; 1% transferred in; 78% live on campus.

Freshmen
Admission: 1,703 applied, 809 admitted, 828 enrolled. ***Average high school GPA:*** 3.48. ***Test scores:*** SAT critical reading scores over 500: 94%; SAT math scores over 500: 96%; SAT writing scores over 500: 92%; ACT scores over 18: 99%; SAT critical reading scores over 600: 61%; SAT math scores over 600: 59%; SAT writing scores over 600: 55%; ACT scores over 24: 77%; SAT critical reading scores over 700: 21%; SAT math scores over 700: 23%; SAT writing scores over 700: 17%; ACT scores over 30: 31%.

Retention: 91% of full-time freshmen returned.

FACULTY
Total: 1,298, 72% full-time.

Student/faculty ratio: 7:1.

ACADEMICS
Calendar: semesters. *Degrees:* associate, bachelor's, master's, doctoral, post-master's, and postbachelor's certificates (Yeshiva College and Stern College for Women are coordinate undergraduate colleges of arts and sciences for men and women, respectively. Sy Syms School of Business offers programs at both campuses).

Special study options: advanced placement credit, double majors, honors programs, independent study, internships, off-campus study, student-designed majors, study abroad, summer session for credit.

STUDENT LIFE
Housing options: men-only, women-only.

Activities and organizations: drama/theater group, student-run newspaper, radio station, choral group.

Athletics Member NCAA. All Division III. ***Intercollegiate sports:*** baseball M, basketball M/W, cross-country running M/W, fencing M/W, golf M, soccer M/W, tennis M/W, volleyball M, wrestling M. ***Intramural sports:*** basketball M/W, fencing M/W, swimming and diving M/W, table tennis M, volleyball M/W.

Campus security: 24-hour emergency response devices and patrols, late-night transport/escort service.

COSTS & FINANCIAL AID
Costs (2014–15) ***Comprehensive fee:*** $49,980 includes full-time tuition ($37,730), mandatory fees ($1000), and room and board ($11,250). Full-time tuition and fees vary according to student level. Part-time tuition: $1320 per credit hour. ***Payment plan:*** installment. ***Waivers:*** employees or children of employees.

Financial Aid Of all full-time matriculated undergraduates who enrolled in 2012, 2,001 applied for aid, 1,657 were judged to have need, 438 had their need fully met. In 2012, 481 non-need-based awards were made. ***Average percent of need met:*** 88. ***Average financial aid package:*** $31,293. ***Average need-based loan:*** $6229. ***Average need-based gift aid:*** $25,388. ***Average non-need-based aid:*** $21,793. ***Average indebtedness upon graduation:*** $22,718.

APPLYING
Standardized Tests *Required:* SAT or ACT (for admission).

Options: early admission, deferred entrance.

Application fee: $65.

Required: essay or personal statement, high school transcript, 2 letters of recommendation, interview.

Application deadlines: 2/1 (freshmen), rolling (transfers).

Notification: 4/1 (freshmen).

CONTACT
Yeshiva University, 500 West 185th Street, New York, NY 10033-3201. *Phone:* 212-960-5277.

York College of the City University of New York

Jamaica, New York

http://www.york.cuny.edu/

- **State and locally supported** comprehensive, founded 1967, part of City University of New York System
- **Urban** 50-acre campus with easy access to New York City
- **Coed** 8,438 undergraduate students, 61% full-time, 65% women, 35% men
- **Moderately difficult** entrance level, 61% of applicants were admitted

UNDERGRAD STUDENTS
5,121 full-time, 3,317 part-time. Students come from 4 states and territories; 131 other countries; 1% are from out of state; 43% Black or African American, non-Hispanic/Latino; 20% Hispanic/Latino; 25% Asian, non-Hispanic/Latino; 0.8% American Indian or Alaska Native, non-Hispanic/Latino; 4% international; 10% transferred in.

Freshmen
Admission: 13,726 applied, 8,334 admitted, 994 enrolled. ***Test scores:*** SAT critical reading scores over 500: 14%; SAT math scores over 500: 27%; SAT writing scores over 500: 14%; SAT critical reading scores over 600: 1%; SAT math scores over 600: 4%; SAT writing scores over 600: 1%.

Retention: 77% of full-time freshmen returned.

FACULTY
Total: 501, 39% full-time, 42% with terminal degrees.

Student/faculty ratio: 21:1.

ACADEMICS
Calendar: semesters. *Degrees:* bachelor's and master's.

Special study options: adult/continuing education programs, advanced placement credit, cooperative education, double majors, English as a second language, honors programs, independent study, internships, off-campus study, part-time degree program, services for LD students, study abroad, summer session for credit. ***ROTC:*** Army (b).

Unusual degree programs: 3-2 Occupational Therapy.

Computers: 650 computers/terminals and 844 ports are available on campus for general student use. Students can access the following: computer help desk, free student e-mail accounts, online (class) registration, online (class) schedules. Campuswide network is available. Wireless service is available via entire campus.

STUDENT LIFE
Housing options: college housing not available.

Activities and organizations: drama/theater group, student-run newspaper, television station, choral group, Haitian Students Association, Caribbean Students Association, Haitian Cultural Association, Latin Caucus, Muslim Student Association.

Athletics Member NCAA. All Division III. ***Intercollegiate sports:*** baseball M/W, basketball M/W, cross-country running M/W, soccer M, softball W, swimming and diving M/W, tennis M, track and field M/W, volleyball M/W. ***Intramural sports:*** basketball M/W, cross-country running M/W, soccer M, softball W, swimming and diving M/W, table tennis M/W, tennis M, track and field M/W, volleyball M/W.

Campus security: 24-hour emergency response devices and patrols, late-night transport/escort service.

Student services: health clinic, personal/psychological counseling, women's center.

COSTS & FINANCIAL AID
Costs (2015–16) ***Tuition:*** state resident $6030 full-time, $260 per credit part-time; nonresident $12,840 full-time, $535 per credit part-time. Full-time tuition and fees vary according to degree level and student level. Part-time tuition and fees vary according to degree level and student level. ***Required fees:*** $417 full-time, $208 per term part-time. ***Payment plan:*** installment. ***Waivers:*** senior citizens and employees or children of employees.

Financial Aid Of all full-time matriculated undergraduates who enrolled in 2014, 4,033 applied for aid, 3,720 were judged to have need, 3,372 had their need fully met. In 2014, 4 non-need-based awards were made. ***Average percent of need met:*** 84. ***Average financial aid package:*** $7436. ***Average need-based loan:*** $3169. ***Average need-based gift aid:*** $7219. ***Average non-need-based aid:*** $831. ***Average indebtedness upon graduation:*** $4745. ***Financial aid deadline:*** 6/30.

APPLYING
Standardized Tests *Required:* SAT (for admission).

Options: electronic application, early admission, deferred entrance.

Application fee: $65.

Required: high school transcript, minimum 2.8 GPA. ***Required for some:*** minimum 2.5 GPA. ***Recommended:*** minimum 3.0 GPA.

Application deadlines: rolling (freshmen), rolling (out-of-state freshmen), rolling (transfers).

Notification: continuous (freshmen), continuous (out-of-state freshmen), continuous (transfers).

CONTACT
Dr. La Toro Yates, Director of Admissions, York College of the City University of New York, 94-20 Guy R. Brewer Boulevard, Jamaica, NY 11451. *Phone:* 718-262-2165. *Fax:* 718-262-2601. *E-mail:* LYates@york.cuny.edu.

NORTH CAROLINA

Appalachian State University

Boone, North Carolina

http://www.appstate.edu/

- **State-supported** comprehensive, founded 1899, part of University of North Carolina System
- **Small-town** 411-acre campus
- **Endowment** $96.2 million
- **Coed** 16,255 undergraduate students, 94% full-time, 54% women, 46% men
- **Moderately difficult** entrance level, 63% of applicants were admitted

UNDERGRAD STUDENTS
15,312 full-time, 943 part-time. Students come from 44 states and territories; 73 other countries; 8% are from out of state; 3% Black or African American, non-Hispanic/Latino; 4% Hispanic/Latino; 2% Asian, non-Hispanic/Latino; 0.1% Native Hawaiian or other Pacific Islander, non-Hispanic/Latino; 0.2% American Indian or Alaska Native, non-Hispanic/Latino; 3% Two or more races, non-Hispanic/Latino; 2% Race/ethnicity unknown; 1% international; 8% transferred in; 34% live on campus.

Freshmen
Admission: 13,506 applied, 8,463 admitted, 3,033 enrolled. ***Average high school GPA:*** 4.06. ***Test scores:*** SAT critical reading scores over 500: 89%; SAT math scores over 500: 91%; SAT writing scores over 500: 78%; ACT scores over 18: 99%; SAT critical reading scores over 600: 38%; SAT math scores over 600: 41%; SAT writing scores over 600: 27%; ACT scores over 24: 74%; SAT critical reading scores over 700: 5%; SAT math scores over 700: 3%; SAT writing scores over 700: 3%; ACT scores over 30: 9%.

Retention: 88% of full-time freshmen returned.

FACULTY
Total: 1,277, 72% full-time, 94% with terminal degrees.

Student/faculty ratio: 16:1.

ACADEMICS
Calendar: semesters. *Degrees:* bachelor's, master's, doctoral, post-master's, and postbachelor's certificates.

Special study options: academic remediation for entering students, accelerated degree program, adult/continuing education programs, advanced placement credit, distance learning, double majors, English as a second language, honors programs, independent study, internships, off-campus study, part-time degree program, services for LD students, student-designed majors, study abroad, summer session for credit. ***ROTC:*** Army (b).

Unusual degree programs: 3-2 engineering with Auburn University, Clemson University.

Computers: 2,422 computers/terminals are available on campus for general student use. Students can access the following: campus intranet, computer help desk, free student e-mail accounts, online (class) grades, online (class) registration, online (class) schedules. Campuswide network is available. 100% of college-owned or -operated housing units are wired for high-speed Internet access. Wireless service is available via entire campus.

STUDENT LIFE
Housing options: on-campus residence required for freshman year; coed, women-only, special housing for students with disabilities. Campus housing is university owned. Freshman campus housing is guaranteed.

Activities and organizations: drama/theater group, student-run newspaper, radio station, choral group, marching band, Health Professions Club, Exercise Science Club, Appalachian Educators, Gamma Beta Phi, Appalachian Popular Programming Society, national fraternities, national sororities.

Athletics Member NCAA, NAIA. All NCAA Division I except football (Division I-AA). ***Intercollegiate sports:*** baseball M(s), basketball M(s)/W(s), cross-country running M(s)/W(s), equestrian sports M(c)/W(c), fencing M(c)/W(c), field hockey W(s), golf M(s)/W(s), ice hockey M(c)/W(c), lacrosse M(c)/W(c), racquetball M(c)/W(c), rugby M(c)/W(c), skiing (downhill) M(c)/W(c), soccer M(s)/W(s), softball W(s), swimming and diving M(c)/W(c), tennis M(s)/W(s), track and field M(s)/W(s), ultimate Frisbee M(c)/W(c), volleyball W(s), wrestling M(s). ***Intramural sports:*** badminton M/W, basketball M/W, bowling M/W, cross-country running M/W, golf M/W, racquetball M/W, soccer M/W, softball M/W, table tennis M/W, tennis M/W, ultimate Frisbee M/W, volleyball M/W.

Campus security: 24-hour emergency response devices and patrols, late-night transport/escort service, controlled dormitory access.

Student services: health clinic, personal/psychological counseling, women's center, legal services.

COSTS & FINANCIAL AID
Costs (2014–15) ***Tuition:*** state resident $3772 full-time, $128 per credit hour part-time; nonresident $16,939 full-time, $573 per credit hour part-time. Part-time tuition and fees vary according to course load. ***Required fees:*** $2781 full-time, $17 per credit hour part-time. ***Room and board:*** $7675; room only: $4125. Room and board charges vary according to board plan and housing facility. ***Payment plan:*** installment. ***Waivers:*** employees or children of employees.

Financial Aid Of all full-time matriculated undergraduates who enrolled in 2014, 7,948 applied for aid, 7,713 were judged to have need, 1,904 had their need fully met. 309 Federal Work-Study jobs (averaging $1669). In 2014, 480 non-need-based awards were made. ***Average percent of need met:*** 67. ***Average financial aid package:*** $9551. ***Average need-based loan:*** $4318. ***Average need-based gift aid:*** $8057. ***Average non-need-based aid:*** $2768. ***Average indebtedness upon graduation:*** $21,693.

APPLYING
Standardized Tests *Required:* SAT or ACT (for admission).

Options: electronic application, deferred entrance.

Application fee: $55.

Required: high school transcript.

Application deadlines: 11/15 (freshmen), 11/15 (out-of-state freshmen), rolling (transfers).

Notification: 3/15 (freshmen), 3/15 (out-of-state freshmen), continuous (transfers).

CONTACT
Mr. Lloyd M Scott, Director of Admissions, Appalachian State University, ASU Box 32004, Boone, NC 28608. *Phone:* 828-262-2120. *Fax:* 828-262-3296. *E-mail:* admissions@appstate.edu.

The Art Institute of Charlotte, a campus of South University

Charlotte, North Carolina

http://www.artinstitutes.edu/charlotte/

- **Proprietary** 4-year, founded 1973, part of Education Management Corporation
- **Suburban** campus
- **Coed**

ACADEMICS
Calendar: quarters. *Degrees:* certificates, associate, and bachelor's.

CONTACT
The Art Institute of Charlotte, a campus of South University, Three LakePointe Plaza, 2110 Water Ridge Parkway, Charlotte, NC 28217. *Phone:* 704-357-8020. *Toll-free phone:* 800-872-4417.

The Art Institute of Raleigh-Durham, a campus of South University

Durham, North Carolina

http://www.artinstitutes.edu/raleigh-durham

- **Proprietary** 4-year, founded 2008, part of Education Management Corporation
- **Coed**

ACADEMICS
Degrees: certificates, associate, and bachelor's.

CONTACT
The Art Institute of Raleigh-Durham, a campus of South University, 410 Blackwell Street, Suite 200, Durham, NC 27701. *Phone:* 919-317-3050. *Toll-free phone:* 888-245-9593.

Barton College

Wilson, North Carolina

http://www.barton.edu/

- **Independent** comprehensive, founded 1902, affiliated with Christian Church (Disciples of Christ)
- **Small-town** 76-acre campus with easy access to Raleigh-Durham
- **Endowment** $25.5 million
- **Coed**
- **Minimally difficult** entrance level

FACULTY
Student/faculty ratio: 12:1.

ACADEMICS
Calendar: 4-1-4. *Degrees:* bachelor's and master's.

STUDENT LIFE
Housing options: on-campus residence required through sophomore year; coed, women-only. Campus housing is university owned. Freshman campus housing is guaranteed.

Activities and organizations: drama/theater group, student-run newspaper, television station, choral group, Panhellenic Council, Students of the N.C. Association of Educators, Barton College Nursing Association, Inter-Fraternity Council, Delta Zeta Sorority, national fraternities, national sororities.

Athletics Member NCAA. All Division II.

Campus security: 24-hour emergency response devices and patrols, late-night transport/escort service, controlled dormitory access, city police substation on campus.

Student services: health clinic, personal/psychological counseling.

COSTS & FINANCIAL AID
Costs (2014–15) ***Comprehensive fee:*** $35,570 includes full-time tuition ($24,468), mandatory fees ($2196), and room and board ($8906). Full-time tuition and fees vary according to class time, course load, and program. Part-time tuition: $1034 per credit hour. Part-time tuition and fees vary according to class time, course load, and program. ***Required fees:*** $273 per credit hour part-time. ***College room only:*** $3894. Room and board charges vary according to board plan and housing facility.

Financial Aid Of all full-time matriculated undergraduates who enrolled in 2013, 981 applied for aid, 938 were judged to have need, 109 had their need fully met. In 2013, 80 non-need-based awards were made. ***Average percent of need met:*** 59. ***Average financial aid package:*** $17,377. ***Average need-based loan:*** $4201. ***Average need-based gift aid:*** $14,158. ***Average non-need-based aid:*** $8498.

APPLYING
Standardized Tests *Required:* SAT or ACT (for admission).

Options: electronic application, deferred entrance.

Required: high school transcript. ***Recommended:*** minimum 2.3 GPA, interview.

CONTACT
Barton College, PO Box 5000, Wilson, NC 27893-7000. *Phone:* 800-345-4973. *Toll-free phone:* 800-345-4973.

Belmont Abbey College

Belmont, North Carolina

http://www.belmontabbeycollege.edu/

- **Independent Roman Catholic** 4-year, founded 1876
- **Small-town** 650-acre campus with easy access to Charlotte
- **Endowment** $8.5 million
- **Coed** 1,560 undergraduate students, 93% full-time, 57% women, 43% men
- **Moderately difficult** entrance level, 69% of applicants were admitted

UNDERGRAD STUDENTS
1,452 full-time, 108 part-time. Students come from 40 states and territories; 18 other countries; 28% are from out of state; 25% Black or African American, non-Hispanic/Latino; 1% Hispanic/Latino; 1% Asian, non-Hispanic/Latino; 0.3% American Indian or Alaska Native, non-Hispanic/Latino; 0.3% Two or more races, non-Hispanic/Latino; 30% Race/ethnicity unknown; 1% international; 8% transferred in; 42% live on campus.

Freshmen
Admission: 1,950 applied, 1,350 admitted, 293 enrolled. ***Average high school GPA:*** 3.09. ***Test scores:*** SAT critical reading scores over 500: 49%; SAT math scores over 500: 53%; ACT scores over 18: 82%; SAT critical reading scores over 600: 17%; SAT math scores over 600: 17%; ACT scores over 24: 31%; SAT critical reading scores over 700: 6%; ACT scores over 30: 4%.

Retention: 63% of full-time freshmen returned.

FACULTY
Total: 132, 55% full-time, 45% with terminal degrees.

Student/faculty ratio: 16:1.

ACADEMICS
Calendar: semesters. *Degree:* bachelor's.

Special study options: accelerated degree program, adult/continuing education programs, advanced placement credit, cooperative education, double majors, external degree program, freshman honors college, honors programs, independent study, internships, off-campus study, part-time degree program, services for LD students, study abroad, summer session for credit. ***ROTC:*** Army (c), Air Force (c).

Computers: 92 computers/terminals are available on campus for general student use. Students can access the following: computer help desk, free student e-mail accounts, online (class) grades, online (class) schedules. Campuswide network is available. 100% of college-owned or -operated housing units are wired for high-speed Internet access. Wireless service is available via classrooms, computer labs, dorm rooms, libraries, student centers.

STUDENT LIFE
Housing options: men-only, women-only. Campus housing is university owned. Freshman campus housing is guaranteed.

Activities and organizations: drama/theater group, student-run newspaper, choral group, Crusaders for Life, Improv Troupe, Abbey Volunteers, International Club, Green Team, national fraternities, national sororities.

Athletics Member NCAA. All Division II. ***Intercollegiate sports:*** baseball M(s), basketball M(s)/W(s), cheerleading W, cross-country running M(s)/W(s), golf M(s)/W(s), lacrosse M(s)/W(s), soccer M(s)/W(s), softball W(s), tennis M(s)/W(s), track and field M(s)/W(s), volleyball M(s)/W(s), wrestling M(s). ***Intramural sports:*** bowling M/W, cheerleading W, cross-country running M/W, football M/W, soccer M/W, ultimate Frisbee M/W.

Campus security: 24-hour emergency response devices and patrols.

Student services: health clinic, personal/psychological counseling.

COSTS & FINANCIAL AID

Costs (2014–15) ***One-time required fee:*** $400. ***Comprehensive fee:*** $28,594 includes full-time tuition ($18,500) and room and board ($10,094). Full-time tuition and fees vary according to course load and reciprocity agreements. Part-time tuition: $617 per credit hour. Part-time tuition and fees vary according to course load and reciprocity agreements. ***College room only:*** $5828. Room and board charges vary according to board plan and housing facility. ***Payment plans:*** installment, deferred payment. ***Waivers:*** employees or children of employees.

Financial Aid Of all full-time matriculated undergraduates who enrolled in 2014, 1,222 applied for aid, 1,089 were judged to have need, 104 had their need fully met. In 2014, 275 non-need-based awards were made. ***Average percent of need met:*** 51. ***Average financial aid package:*** $12,140. ***Average need-based loan:*** $4538. ***Average need-based gift aid:*** $7815. ***Average non-need-based aid:*** $5645. ***Average indebtedness upon graduation:*** $27,341.

APPLYING

Standardized Tests *Required for some:* SAT or ACT (for admission).

Options: electronic application, deferred entrance.

Application fee: $35.

Required: high school transcript, minimum 2.3 GPA. ***Required for some:*** essay or personal statement, . ***Recommended:*** interview.

Application deadlines: 8/1 (freshmen), 8/15 (transfers).

Notification: continuous (freshmen), continuous (transfers).

CONTACT

Ms. Nicole Focareto, Executive Director of Admissions, Belmont Abbey College, 100 Belmont-Mt. Holly Road, Belmont, NC 28012. *Phone:* 704-461-6214. *Toll-free phone:* 888-BAC-0110. *Fax:* 704-461-6220. *E-mail:* nicolefocareto@bac.edu.

Bennett College

Greensboro, North Carolina

http://www.bennett.edu/

- **Independent United Methodist** 4-year, founded 1873
- **Urban** 55-acre campus
- **Endowment** $11.8 million
- **Women only** 633 undergraduate students, 86% full-time
- **Minimally difficult** entrance level, 92% of applicants were admitted

UNDERGRAD STUDENTS

545 full-time, 88 part-time. Students come from 29 states and territories; 1 other country; 56% are from out of state; 89% Black or African American, non-Hispanic/Latino; 3% Hispanic/Latino; 0.4% American Indian or Alaska Native, non-Hispanic/Latino; 2% Two or more races, non-Hispanic/Latino; 5% Race/ethnicity unknown; 0.2% international; 3% transferred in; 59% live on campus.

Freshmen

Admission: 1,560 applied, 1,432 admitted, 164 enrolled.

Retention: 52% of full-time freshmen returned.

FACULTY

Total: 72, 81% full-time, 63% with terminal degrees.

Student/faculty ratio: 9:1.

ACADEMICS

Calendar: semesters. *Degree:* bachelor's.

Special study options: academic remediation for entering students, advanced placement credit, double majors, honors programs, independent study, internships, off-campus study, services for LD students, student-designed majors, study abroad, summer session for credit. ***ROTC:*** Army (c), Air Force (c).

Unusual degree programs: engineering with North Carolina Agricultural and Technical State University.

Computers: 203 computers/terminals are available on campus for general student use. Students can access the following: computer help desk, free student e-mail accounts, online (class) grades, online (class) registration, online (class) schedules, Wireless capability is in all buildings except Steele and Shell halls. Campuswide network is available. 100% of college-owned or -operated housing units are wired for high-speed Internet access. Wireless service is available via entire campus.

STUDENT LIFE

Housing options: women-only. Campus housing is university owned. Freshman campus housing is guaranteed.

Activities and organizations: drama/theater group, choral group, Student Government Association, Pre-Alumnae Council, Senior Class, Junior Class, Sophomore Class, national sororities.

Athletics ***Intramural sports:*** soccer W(c), volleyball W(c).

Campus security: 24-hour emergency response devices and patrols, late-night transport/escort service, controlled dormitory access, alerts and educational programs are offered.

Student services: health clinic, personal/psychological counseling.

COSTS & FINANCIAL AID

Costs (2014–15) ***One-time required fee:*** $225. ***Comprehensive fee:*** $24,706 includes full-time tuition ($14,906), mandatory fees ($2224), and room and board ($7576). Full-time tuition and fees vary according to course load. Part-time tuition: $621 per credit hour. Part-time tuition and fees vary according to course load. ***Required fees:*** $918 per term part-time. ***College room only:*** $3772. Room and board charges vary according to board plan. ***Payment plan:*** installment. ***Waivers:*** employees or children of employees.

Financial Aid Of all full-time matriculated undergraduates who enrolled in 2011, 664 applied for aid, 643 were judged to have need, 22 had their need fully met. In 2011, 7 non-need-based awards were made. ***Average percent of need met:*** 47. ***Average financial aid package:*** $13,092. ***Average need-based loan:*** $4170. ***Average need-based gift aid:*** $9402. ***Average non-need-based aid:*** $4714. ***Financial aid deadline:*** 3/15.

APPLYING

Standardized Tests *Required:* SAT or ACT (for admission).

Options: electronic application, deferred entrance.

Application fee: $35.

Required: essay or personal statement, high school transcript, minimum 2.0 GPA. ***Required for some:*** interview.

Application deadlines: 8/1 (freshmen), rolling (out-of-state freshmen), 8/1 (transfers), rolling (early action).

CONTACT

Ms. Benita Corbin, Director of Admissions, Bennett College, 900 East Washington Street, Enrollment Management Center, Greensboro, NC 27401. *Phone:* 336-517-1818. *Toll-free phone:* 800-413-5323. *E-mail:* bcorbin@bennett.edu.

Brevard College

Brevard, North Carolina

http://www.brevard.edu/

- **Independent United Methodist** 4-year, founded 1853
- **Small-town** 120-acre campus
- **Endowment** $24.2 million
- **Coed** 705 undergraduate students, 99% full-time, 42% women, 58% men
- **Minimally difficult** entrance level, 43% of applicants were admitted

UNDERGRAD STUDENTS

697 full-time, 8 part-time. Students come from 35 states and territories; 29 other countries; 42% are from out of state; 10% Black or African American, non-Hispanic/Latino; 2% Hispanic/Latino; 0.9% Asian, non-Hispanic/Latino; 0.3% Native Hawaiian or other Pacific Islander, non-Hispanic/Latino; 0.6% American Indian or Alaska Native, non-Hispanic/Latino; 3% Two or more races, non-Hispanic/Latino; 6% Race/ethnicity unknown; 6% international; 9% transferred in; 76% live on campus.

Freshmen
Admission: 2,858 applied, 1,235 admitted, 218 enrolled. ***Average high school GPA:*** 3.07. ***Test scores:*** SAT critical reading scores over 500: 34%; SAT math scores over 500: 41%; ACT scores over 18: 72%; SAT critical reading scores over 600: 5%; SAT math scores over 600: 7%; ACT scores over 24: 18%.

Retention: 59% of full-time freshmen returned.

FACULTY
Total: 95, 54% full-time, 61% with terminal degrees.

Student/faculty ratio: 11:1.

ACADEMICS
Calendar: semesters. *Degree:* bachelor's.

Special study options: academic remediation for entering students, advanced placement credit, double majors, honors programs, independent study, internships, part-time degree program, services for LD students, student-designed majors, study abroad.

Computers: 100 computers/terminals are available on campus for general student use. Students can access the following: campus intranet, computer help desk, free student e-mail accounts, online (class) grades, online (class) schedules. Campuswide network is available. 100% of college-owned or -operated housing units are wired for high-speed Internet access. Wireless service is available via entire campus.

STUDENT LIFE
Housing options: on-campus residence required through senior year; coed, men-only, women-only, special housing for students with disabilities. Campus housing is university owned. Freshman campus housing is guaranteed.

Activities and organizations: drama/theater group, student-run newspaper, choral group, Fine Arts organizations, Omicron Delta Kappa, Fellowship of Christian Athletes, BC Greens, Business Club.

Athletics Member NCAA. All Division II. ***Intercollegiate sports:*** baseball M(s), basketball M(s)/W(s), cheerleading W(s), cross-country running M(s)/W(s), football M(s), golf M(s)/W(s), lacrosse M(s)/W(s), soccer M(s)/W(s), softball W(s), tennis M(s)/W(s), track and field M(s)/W(s), volleyball W(s). ***Intramural sports:*** badminton M/W, basketball M/W, bowling M/W, fencing M(c)/W(c), football M/W, soccer M/W, softball M/W, tennis M/W, track and field M/W, ultimate Frisbee M/W, volleyball M/W, weight lifting M/W.

Campus security: 24-hour emergency response devices and patrols, controlled dormitory access.

Student services: health clinic, personal/psychological counseling, women's center.

COSTS & FINANCIAL AID
Costs (2014–15) ***Comprehensive fee:*** $35,545 includes full-time tuition ($25,950), mandatory fees ($220), and room and board ($9375). Full-time tuition and fees vary according to course load. Part-time tuition: $510 per credit hour. Part-time tuition and fees vary according to course load. ***Room and board:*** Room and board charges vary according to board plan and housing facility. ***Payment plan:*** installment. ***Waivers:*** senior citizens and employees or children of employees.

Financial Aid Of all full-time matriculated undergraduates who enrolled in 2014, 578 applied for aid, 523 were judged to have need, 83 had their need fully met. In 2014, 112 non-need-based awards were made. ***Average percent of need met:*** 59. ***Average financial aid package:*** $10,851. ***Average need-based loan:*** $3748. ***Average need-based gift aid:*** $8154. ***Average non-need-based aid:*** $8703. ***Average indebtedness upon graduation:*** $35,211.

APPLYING
Standardized Tests *Required for some:* SAT or ACT (for admission).

Options: electronic application, deferred entrance.

Required: essay or personal statement, high school transcript, minimum 2.0 GPA. ***Required for some:*** interview, students in music require auditions, music tests; students in art require portfolio.

Application deadlines: rolling (freshmen), rolling (out-of-state freshmen), rolling (transfers).

Notification: continuous (freshmen), continuous (out-of-state freshmen), continuous (transfers).

CONTACT
Mr. David Volrath, Admissions, Brevard College, One Brevard College Drive, Brevard, NC 28712. *Phone:* 828-884-8367. *Toll-free phone:* 800-527-9090. *Fax:* 828-884-3790. *E-mail:* admissions@brevard.edu.

Cabarrus College of Health Sciences

Concord, North Carolina

http://www.cabarruscollege.edu/

- **Independent** comprehensive, founded 1942
- **Suburban** 5-acre campus with easy access to Charlotte
- **Endowment** $2.0 million
- **Coed, primarily women** 438 undergraduate students, 39% full-time, 91% women, 9% men
- **Moderately difficult** entrance level, 89% of applicants were admitted

UNDERGRAD STUDENTS
173 full-time, 265 part-time. Students come from 5 states and territories; 1% are from out of state; 9% Black or African American, non-Hispanic/Latino; 3% Hispanic/Latino; 1% Asian, non-Hispanic/Latino; 2% Two or more races, non-Hispanic/Latino; 25% transferred in.

Freshmen
Admission: 46 applied, 41 admitted, 31 enrolled. ***Average high school GPA:*** 3.6. ***Test scores:*** SAT critical reading scores over 500: 40%; SAT math scores over 500: 47%; ACT scores over 18: 100%; SAT critical reading scores over 600: 9%; SAT math scores over 600: 6%; ACT scores over 24: 15%; SAT critical reading scores over 700: 1%.

Retention: 83% of full-time freshmen returned.

FACULTY
Total: 68, 43% full-time, 38% with terminal degrees.

Student/faculty ratio: 9:1.

ACADEMICS
Calendar: semesters. *Degrees:* certificates, diplomas, associate, bachelor's, and master's.

Special study options: academic remediation for entering students, accelerated degree program, advanced placement credit, cooperative education, distance learning, independent study, part-time degree program, services for LD students.

Computers: 23 computers/terminals are available on campus for general student use. Students can access the following: free student e-mail accounts, online (class) grades, online (class) registration, online (class) schedules, degree audits. Campuswide network is available. Wireless service is available via entire campus.

STUDENT LIFE
Housing options: college housing not available.

Activities and organizations: Rotaract Service Club, Cabarrus College Association of Nursing Students, Student Government Association, Honor Society, Christian Student Union.

Campus security: 24-hour emergency response devices and patrols.

Student services: health clinic, personal/psychological counseling.

COSTS & FINANCIAL AID
Costs (2015–16) ***Tuition:*** $11,650 full-time. Full-time tuition and fees vary according to course load. Part-time tuition and fees vary according to course load. ***Required fees:*** $320 full-time. ***Payment plan:*** installment.

Financial Aid Of all full-time matriculated undergraduates who enrolled in 2013, 12 Federal Work-Study jobs (averaging $1062).

APPLYING
Standardized Tests *Required:* SAT or ACT (for admission). *Required for some:* SAT or ACT (for admission).

Options: electronic application.

Application fee: $50.

Required: essay or personal statement, high school transcript, minimum 2.0 GPA, 2 letters of recommendation. ***Required for some:*** interview. ***Recommended:*** minimum 3.0 GPA.

Application deadlines: 2/1 (freshmen), 2/1 (transfers).

Notification: 3/15 (freshmen), 3/15 (transfers).

CONTACT
Tanisha Orr, Admissions Representative, Cabarrus College of Health Sciences, 401 Medical Park Drive, Concord, NC 28025-2077. *Phone:* 704-403-2589. *Fax:* 704-403-2077. *E-mail:* tanisha.orr@cabarruscollege.edu.

Carolina Christian College

Winston-Salem, North Carolina

http://www.carolina.edu/

- **Independent nondenominational** comprehensive, founded 1949
- **Small-town** 2-acre campus
- **Endowment** $250,000
- **Coed**
- **Noncompetitive** entrance level

FACULTY
Student/faculty ratio: 9:1.

ACADEMICS
Calendar: semesters. *Degrees:* associate, bachelor's, and master's.

STUDENT LIFE
Housing options: college housing not available.
Campus security: 24-hour emergency response devices.
Student services: personal/psychological counseling.

COSTS
Costs (2014–15) ***One-time required fee:*** $100. ***Tuition:*** $7900 full-time, $325 per credit part-time. Full-time tuition and fees vary according to class time. Part-time tuition and fees vary according to class time. ***Required fees:*** $1050 full-time, $525 per term part-time.

APPLYING
Options: electronic application.
Application fee: $50.
Required: essay or personal statement, high school transcript, 2 letters of recommendation, interview.

CONTACT
Carolina Christian College, 4209 Indiana Avenue, PO Box 777, Winston-Salem, NC 27102-0777. *Phone:* 336-744-0900 Ext. 106.

Catawba College

Salisbury, North Carolina

http://www.catawba.edu/

- **Independent** comprehensive, founded 1851, affiliated with United Church of Christ
- **Small-town** 276-acre campus with easy access to Charlotte
- **Endowment** $54.9 million
- **Coed** 1,309 undergraduate students, 94% full-time, 53% women, 47% men
- **Moderately difficult** entrance level, 36% of applicants were admitted

UNDERGRAD STUDENTS
1,231 full-time, 78 part-time. Students come from 33 states and territories; 16 other countries; 20% are from out of state; 20% Black or African American, non-Hispanic/Latino; 4% Hispanic/Latino; 1% Asian, non-Hispanic/Latino; 0.9% American Indian or Alaska Native, non-Hispanic/Latino; 2% Two or more races, non-Hispanic/Latino; 0.2% Race/ethnicity unknown; 3% international; 7% transferred in; 71% live on campus.

Freshmen
Admission: 3,694 applied, 1,326 admitted, 345 enrolled. ***Average high school GPA:*** 2.82. ***Test scores:*** SAT critical reading scores over 500: 42%; SAT math scores over 500: 44%; ACT scores over 18: 79%; SAT critical reading scores over 600: 8%; SAT math scores over 600: 9%; ACT scores over 24: 30%; ACT scores over 30: 2%.
Retention: 73% of full-time freshmen returned.

FACULTY
Total: 143, 50% full-time, 58% with terminal degrees.
Student/faculty ratio: 13:1.

ACADEMICS
Calendar: semesters. *Degrees:* bachelor's and master's.
Special study options: advanced placement credit, double majors, honors programs, independent study, internships, part-time degree program, services for LD students, student-designed majors, study abroad, summer session for credit. ***ROTC:*** Army (c), Air Force (c).
Computers: 151 computers/terminals are available on campus for general student use. Students can access the following: campus intranet, computer help desk, free student e-mail accounts, online (class) grades, online (class) registration, online (class) schedules. Campuswide network is available. 100% of college-owned or -operated housing units are wired for high-speed Internet access. Wireless service is available via entire campus.

STUDENT LIFE
Housing options: on-campus residence required through senior year; coed, men-only, women-only. Campus housing is university owned. Freshman campus housing is guaranteed.
Activities and organizations: drama/theater group, student-run newspaper, choral group, marching band, Volunteer Catawba, Catawba Ambassadors (admissions guides), Blue Masque (drama), Fellowship of Christian Athletes, Wigwam Productions (student activities board).
Athletics Member NCAA. All Division II. ***Intercollegiate sports:*** baseball M(s), basketball M(s)/W(s), cheerleading M(c)/W(c), cross-country running M(s)/W(s), football M(s), golf M(s)/W(s), lacrosse M(s)/W(s), soccer M(s)/W(s), softball W(s), swimming and diving M(s)/W(s), tennis M(s)/W(s), volleyball W(s). ***Intramural sports:*** badminton M/W, basketball M/W, bowling M/W, football M, racquetball M/W, soccer M/W, softball M, table tennis M/W, tennis M/W, ultimate Frisbee M/W, volleyball M/W.
Campus security: 24-hour emergency response devices and patrols, late-night transport/escort service, controlled dormitory access.
Student services: health clinic, personal/psychological counseling.

COSTS & FINANCIAL AID
Costs (2015–16) ***Comprehensive fee:*** $39,090 includes full-time tuition ($28,730) and room and board ($10,360). Full-time tuition and fees vary according to class time, course load, and degree level. Part-time tuition: $750 per credit hour. Part-time tuition and fees vary according to class time, course load, and degree level. ***Payment plan:*** installment. ***Waivers:*** employees or children of employees.
Financial Aid Of all full-time matriculated undergraduates who enrolled in 2013, 1,086 applied for aid, 1,014 were judged to have need, 167 had their need fully met. In 2013, 155 non-need-based awards were made. ***Average percent of need met:*** 74. ***Average financial aid package:*** $21,440. ***Average need-based loan:*** $4679. ***Average need-based gift aid:*** $7175. ***Average non-need-based aid:*** $11,081. ***Average indebtedness upon graduation:*** $28,132.

APPLYING
Standardized Tests *Recommended:* SAT or ACT (for admission).
Options: electronic application, early admission, deferred entrance.
Required: essay or personal statement, high school transcript, minimum 2.0 GPA, 2 letters of recommendation. ***Recommended:*** interview.
Application deadlines: rolling (freshmen), rolling (transfers).
Notification: continuous (freshmen), continuous (transfers).

CONTACT
Catawba College, 2300 West Innes Street, Salisbury, NC 28144-2488. *Phone:* 704-645-4584. *Toll-free phone:* 800-CATAWBA.

Chowan University

Murfreesboro, North Carolina

http://www.chowan.edu/

- **Independent Baptist** comprehensive, founded 1848
- **Small-town** 300-acre campus with easy access to Norfolk
- **Coed** 1,478 undergraduate students, 95% full-time, 51% women, 49% men
- **Minimally difficult** entrance level, 60% of applicants were admitted

UNDERGRAD STUDENTS
1,408 full-time, 70 part-time. Students come from 31 states and territories; 23 other countries; 46% are from out of state; 71% Black or African

American, non-Hispanic/Latino; 3% Hispanic/Latino; 0.2% Asian, non-Hispanic/Latino; 0.5% American Indian or Alaska Native, non-Hispanic/Latino; 3% Two or more races, non-Hispanic/Latino; 2% Race/ethnicity unknown; 2% international; 6% transferred in; 83% live on campus.

Freshmen
Admission: 4,225 applied, 2,527 admitted, 531 enrolled. ***Average high school GPA:*** 2.67. ***Test scores:*** SAT critical reading scores over 500: 10%; SAT math scores over 500: 12%; ACT scores over 18: 24%; SAT critical reading scores over 600: 2%; SAT math scores over 600: 2%; ACT scores over 24: 1%; SAT critical reading scores over 700: 1%; SAT math scores over 700: 1%.

Retention: 52% of full-time freshmen returned.

FACULTY
Total: 105, 60% full-time, 42% with terminal degrees.

Student/faculty ratio: 16:1.

ACADEMICS
Calendar: semesters. *Degrees:* associate, bachelor's, and master's.

Special study options: academic remediation for entering students, advanced placement credit, cooperative education, double majors, freshman honors college, honors programs, independent study, internships, part-time degree program, services for LD students, student-designed majors, study abroad, summer session for credit.

Computers: 215 computers/terminals are available on campus for general student use. Students can access the following: campus intranet, computer help desk, free student e-mail accounts, online (class) grades, online (class) registration, online (class) schedules. Campuswide network is available. 100% of college-owned or -operated housing units are wired for high-speed Internet access. Wireless service is available via entire campus.

STUDENT LIFE
Housing options: on-campus residence required through sophomore year; men-only, women-only. Campus housing is university owned. Freshman campus housing is guaranteed.

Activities and organizations: drama/theater group, student-run newspaper, choral group, national fraternities, national sororities.

Athletics Member NCAA, NCCAA. All NCAA Division II. ***Intercollegiate sports:*** baseball M(s), basketball M(s)/W(s), bowling W(s), cheerleading M/W, cross-country running M(s)/W(s), football M(s), golf M(s)/W(s), lacrosse W(s), soccer M(s)/W(s), softball W(s), tennis M(s)/W(s), volleyball W(s). ***Intramural sports:*** basketball M/W, football M/W, racquetball M/W, soccer M/W, softball M/W, table tennis M/W, tennis M/W, volleyball M/W.

Campus security: 24-hour emergency response devices and patrols, late-night transport/escort service, controlled dormitory access.

Student services: health clinic, personal/psychological counseling.

COSTS & FINANCIAL AID
Costs (2015–16) ***Comprehensive fee:*** $32,080 includes full-time tuition ($23,400) and room and board ($8680). Full-time tuition and fees vary according to class time, course load, and program. Part-time tuition: $385 per credit. Part-time tuition and fees vary according to class time and program. ***Room and board:*** Room and board charges vary according to board plan and housing facility. ***Payment plan:*** installment. ***Waivers:*** senior citizens and employees or children of employees.

Financial Aid Of all full-time matriculated undergraduates who enrolled in 2014, 1,422 applied for aid, 1,393 were judged to have need, 27 had their need fully met. 360 Federal Work-Study jobs (averaging $1443). 162 state and other part-time jobs (averaging $1381). In 2014, 29 non-need-based awards were made. ***Average percent of need met:*** 72. ***Average financial aid package:*** $28,876. ***Average need-based loan:*** $3979. ***Average need-based gift aid:*** $16,904. ***Average non-need-based aid:*** $5998. ***Average indebtedness upon graduation:*** $33,992.

APPLYING
Standardized Tests *Required:* SAT or ACT (for admission).

Options: electronic application.

Application fee: $20.

Required: high school transcript. ***Required for some:*** essay or personal statement, interview. ***Recommended:*** minimum 2.0 GPA, 2 letters of recommendation.

Application deadlines: rolling (freshmen), rolling (out-of-state freshmen), rolling (transfers).

Notification: continuous (freshmen), continuous (out-of-state freshmen), continuous (transfers).

CONTACT
Mr. Scott Parker Esq., Director of Admissions Information, Chowan University, One University Place, Murfreesboro, NC 27855. *Phone:* 252-398-6314. *Toll-free phone:* 888-4-CHOWAN. *Fax:* 252-398-1190. *E-mail:* parkes@chowan.edu.

Davidson College
Davidson, North Carolina
http://www.davidson.edu/

- **Independent Presbyterian** 4-year, founded 1837
- **Small-town** 665-acre campus with easy access to Charlotte
- **Endowment** $647.9 million
- **Coed** 1,770 undergraduate students, 100% full-time, 51% women, 49% men
- **Very difficult** entrance level, 22% of applicants were admitted

UNDERGRAD STUDENTS
1,770 full-time. Students come from 48 states and territories; 38 other countries; 77% are from out of state; 6% Black or African American, non-Hispanic/Latino; 7% Hispanic/Latino; 6% Asian, non-Hispanic/Latino; 0.6% American Indian or Alaska Native, non-Hispanic/Latino; 4% Two or more races, non-Hispanic/Latino; 2% Race/ethnicity unknown; 6% international; 0.6% transferred in; 93% live on campus.

Freshmen
Admission: 5,560 applied, 1,205 admitted, 502 enrolled. ***Average high school GPA:*** 3.9. ***Test scores:*** SAT critical reading scores over 500: 98%; SAT math scores over 500: 100%; SAT writing scores over 500: 98%; ACT scores over 18: 100%; SAT critical reading scores over 600: 82%; SAT math scores over 600: 86%; SAT writing scores over 600: 84%; ACT scores over 24: 99%; SAT critical reading scores over 700: 33%; SAT math scores over 700: 36%; SAT writing scores over 700: 35%; ACT scores over 30: 63%.

Retention: 95% of full-time freshmen returned.

FACULTY
Total: 186, 96% full-time, 95% with terminal degrees.

Student/faculty ratio: 10:1.

ACADEMICS
Calendar: semesters. *Degree:* bachelor's.

Special study options: advanced placement credit, double majors, honors programs, independent study, internships, off-campus study, services for LD students, student-designed majors, study abroad. ***ROTC:*** Army (b), Air Force (c).

Unusual degree programs: 3-2 engineering with Columbia University, Washington University in St. Louis.

Computers: 180 computers/terminals are available on campus for general student use. Students can access the following: campus intranet, computer help desk, free student e-mail accounts, online (class) grades, online (class) registration, online (class) schedules. Campuswide network is available. 100% of college-owned or -operated housing units are wired for high-speed Internet access. Wireless service is available via entire campus.

STUDENT LIFE
Housing options: on-campus residence required through senior year; coed, cooperative. Campus housing is university owned. Freshman campus housing is guaranteed.

Activities and organizations: drama/theater group, student-run newspaper, radio station, choral group, Inter-Varsity Christian Fellowship, Dean Rusk Program Student Advisory Council, music organizations, Community Service Council, Student Government Association, national fraternities, national sororities.

Athletics Member NCAA. All Division I except football (Division I-AA). ***Intercollegiate sports:*** baseball M(s), basketball M(s)/W(s), crew

M(c)/W(c), cross-country running M(s)/W(s), fencing M(c)/W(c), field hockey W(s), golf M(s), lacrosse W(s), rugby M(c), sailing M(c)/W(c), soccer M(s)/W(s), swimming and diving M(s)/W(s), tennis M(s)/W(s), track and field M(s)/W(s), ultimate Frisbee M(c)/W(c), volleyball W(s), weight lifting M(c)/W(c), wrestling M(s). ***Intramural sports:*** basketball M/W, equestrian sports W(c), field hockey M(c)/W(c), football M/W, lacrosse M(c)/W(c), soccer M(c)/W(c), softball M/W, swimming and diving M(c)/W(c), tennis M(c)/W(c), volleyball M/W(c), water polo M(c).

Campus security: 24-hour emergency response devices and patrols, late-night transport/escort service, controlled dormitory access.

Student services: health clinic, personal/psychological counseling, women's center.

COSTS & FINANCIAL AID

Costs (2014–15) ***Comprehensive fee:*** $58,146 includes full-time tuition ($44,928), mandatory fees ($449), and room and board ($12,769). ***College room only:*** $6499. Room and board charges vary according to board plan. ***Waivers:*** employees or children of employees.

Financial Aid Of all full-time matriculated undergraduates who enrolled in 2013, 949 applied for aid, 862 were judged to have need, 862 had their need fully met. 334 Federal Work-Study jobs (averaging $1517). 129 state and other part-time jobs (averaging $1631). In 2013, 127 non-need-based awards were made. ***Average percent of need met:*** 100. ***Average financial aid package:*** $37,228. ***Average need-based loan:*** $3405. ***Average need-based gift aid:*** $35,836. ***Average non-need-based aid:*** $21,269. ***Average indebtedness upon graduation:*** $21,365. ***Financial aid deadline:*** 2/15.

APPLYING

Standardized Tests *Required:* SAT or ACT (for admission). *Recommended:* SAT and SAT Subject Tests or ACT (for admission).

Options: electronic application, early admission, early decision, deferred entrance.

Application fee: $50.

Required: essay or personal statement, high school transcript, 3 letters of recommendation. ***Recommended:*** interview.

Application deadlines: 1/2 (freshmen), 3/15 (transfers).

Early decision deadline: 11/15 (for plan 1), 1/2 (for plan 2).

Notification: 4/1 (freshmen), 5/15 (transfers), 12/15 (early decision plan 1), 2/1 (early decision plan 2).

CONTACT

Mr. Christopher J. Gruber, Vice President and Dean of Admission and Financial Aid, Davidson College, Box 7156, Davidson, NC 28035-7156. *Phone:* 704-894-2230. *Toll-free phone:* 800-768-0380. *Fax:* 704-894-2016. *E-mail:* admission@davidson.edu.

DeVry University

Charlotte, North Carolina

http://www.devry.edu/

- **Proprietary** comprehensive, part of DeVry University
- **Coed**

ACADEMICS

Calendar: semesters. *Degrees:* associate, bachelor's, and master's.

COSTS & FINANCIAL AID

Costs (2014–15) ***Tuition:*** $17,052 full-time, $609 per credit hour part-time. ***Required fees:*** $80 full-time.

Financial Aid Of all full-time matriculated undergraduates who enrolled in 2007, 34 applied for aid, 33 were judged to have need, 1 had their need fully met. In 2007, 2 non-need-based awards were made. ***Average percent of need met:*** 41. ***Average financial aid package:*** $12,613. ***Average need-based loan:*** $9286. ***Average need-based gift aid:*** $8335. ***Average non-need-based aid:*** $7635.

CONTACT

Admissions Office, DeVry University, 2015 Ayrsley Town Boulevard, Suite 109, Charlotte, NC 28273-4068. *Phone:* 704-362-2345. *Toll-free phone:* 866-338-7941.

East Carolina University

Greenville, North Carolina

http://www.ecu.edu/

- **State-supported** university, founded 1907, part of University of North Carolina System
- **Urban** 1400-acre campus
- **Endowment** $165.7 million
- **Coed** 22,252 undergraduate students, 85% full-time, 59% women, 41% men
- **Moderately difficult** entrance level, 77% of applicants were admitted

UNDERGRAD STUDENTS

18,903 full-time, 3,349 part-time. Students come from 47 states and territories; 33 other countries; 12% are from out of state; 16% Black or African American, non-Hispanic/Latino; 6% Hispanic/Latino; 3% Asian, non-Hispanic/Latino; 0.1% Native Hawaiian or other Pacific Islander, non-Hispanic/Latino; 0.6% American Indian or Alaska Native, non-Hispanic/Latino; 3% Two or more races, non-Hispanic/Latino; 2% Race/ethnicity unknown; 0.4% international; 8% transferred in; 25% live on campus.

Freshmen

Admission: 14,223 applied, 10,992 admitted, 4,226 enrolled. ***Average high school GPA:*** 3.67. ***Test scores:*** SAT critical reading scores over 500: 48%; SAT math scores over 500: 56%; SAT writing scores over 500: 39%; ACT scores over 18: 92%; SAT critical reading scores over 600: 7%; SAT math scores over 600: 11%; SAT writing scores over 600: 6%; ACT scores over 24: 24%; SAT math scores over 700: 1%; ACT scores over 30: 2%.

Retention: 81% of full-time freshmen returned.

FACULTY

Total: 1,484, 81% full-time, 73% with terminal degrees.

Student/faculty ratio: 18:1.

ACADEMICS

Calendar: semesters. *Degrees:* certificates, bachelor's, master's, doctoral, post-master's, and postbachelor's certificates.

Special study options: accelerated degree program, adult/continuing education programs, advanced placement credit, cooperative education, distance learning, double majors, English as a second language, freshman honors college, honors programs, independent study, internships, off-campus study, part-time degree program, services for LD students, student-designed majors, study abroad, summer session for credit. ***ROTC:*** Army (b), Air Force (b).

Unusual degree programs: 3-2 business administration.

Computers: 546 computers/terminals and 546 ports are available on campus for general student use. Students can access the following: campus intranet, computer help desk, free student e-mail accounts, online (class) grades, online (class) registration, online (class) schedules. Campuswide network is available. 100% of college-owned or -operated housing units are wired for high-speed Internet access. Wireless service is available via entire campus.

STUDENT LIFE

Housing options: on-campus residence required for freshman year; coed, women-only, special housing for students with disabilities. Campus housing is university owned. Freshman campus housing is guaranteed.

Activities and organizations: drama/theater group, student-run newspaper, radio and television station, choral group, marching band, Student Government Association, Student Activities Board, Residence Hall Association, Student Pirate Club, Black Student Union, national fraternities, national sororities.

Athletics Member NCAA. All Division I except football (Division I-A). ***Intercollegiate sports:*** baseball M(s), basketball M(s)/W(s), cross-country running M(s)/W(s), golf M(s)/W(s), soccer M/W(s), softball W(s), swimming and diving M(s)/W(s), tennis M(s)/W(s), track and field M(s)/W(s), volleyball W(s). ***Intramural sports:*** badminton M(c)/W(c), baseball M(c), basketball M/W, bowling M/W, cheerleading W(c), equestrian sports M(c)/W(c), fencing M(c)/W(c), field hockey M(c)/W(c), football M/W, golf M(c)/W(c), ice hockey M(c), lacrosse M(c)/W(c), racquetball M/W, rock climbing M(c)/W(c), rugby M(c)/W(c), skiing (downhill) M(c)/W(c), soccer M/W, softball M/W, swimming and diving

M(c)/W(c), table tennis M/W, tennis M/W, ultimate Frisbee M/W, volleyball M/W, wrestling M(c)/W(c).

Campus security: 24-hour emergency response devices and patrols, student patrols, late-night transport/escort service, controlled dormitory access, Operation ID, Staff and Faculty Eyes, ECU Alert.

Student services: health clinic, personal/psychological counseling, legal services.

COSTS & FINANCIAL AID

Costs (2014–15) ***Tuition:*** state resident $3959 full-time, $165 per credit hour part-time; nonresident $19,156 full-time, $798 per credit hour part-time. Full-time tuition and fees vary according to location. Part-time tuition and fees vary according to course load and location. ***Required fees:*** $2184 full-time. ***Room and board:*** $8833; room only: $4910. Room and board charges vary according to board plan and housing facility. ***Payment plans:*** installment, deferred payment. ***Waivers:*** senior citizens and employees or children of employees.

Financial Aid Of all full-time matriculated undergraduates who enrolled in 2014, 14,301 applied for aid, 11,820 were judged to have need, 1,060 had their need fully met. 406 Federal Work-Study jobs (averaging $2741). 1,992 state and other part-time jobs (averaging $2026). In 2014, 203 non-need-based awards were made. ***Average percent of need met:*** 64. ***Average financial aid package:*** $10,661. ***Average need-based loan:*** $7066. ***Average need-based gift aid:*** $7771. ***Average non-need-based aid:*** $3756. ***Average indebtedness upon graduation:*** $29,699.

APPLYING

Standardized Tests *Required:* SAT or ACT (for admission).

Options: electronic application, early admission, deferred entrance.

Application fee: $70.

Required: high school transcript, minimum 2.5 GPA.

Application deadlines: 3/15 (freshmen), 3/15 (out-of-state freshmen), 5/1 (transfers).

Notification: continuous (freshmen), continuous (out-of-state freshmen), continuous (transfers).

CONTACT

Undergraduate Admission, East Carolina University, Whichard Building 106, East Fifth St., Greenville, NC 27858-4353. *Phone:* 252-328-6640. *E-mail:* admis@ecu.edu.

Elizabeth City State University

Elizabeth City, North Carolina

http://www.ecsu.edu/

- **State-supported** comprehensive, founded 1891, part of University of North Carolina System
- **Small-town** 200-acre campus with easy access to Norfolk
- **Coed**
- **Moderately difficult** entrance level

FACULTY

Student/faculty ratio: 16:1.

ACADEMICS

Calendar: semesters. *Degrees:* bachelor's and master's.

STUDENT LIFE

Housing options: coed, men-only, women-only. Campus housing is university owned and leased by the school. Freshman campus housing is guaranteed.

Activities and organizations: drama/theater group, student-run newspaper, choral group, marching band, Vans (Vikings Assisting New Students), Student Activities Committee, Vike Nu' Fashion Troupe, Pep Squad, Essence of Praise, national fraternities, national sororities.

Athletics Member NCAA. All Division II.

Campus security: 24-hour emergency response devices and patrols.

Student services: health clinic, personal/psychological counseling.

COSTS & FINANCIAL AID

Costs (2014–15) ***Tuition:*** state resident $2776 full-time, $347 per credit hour part-time; nonresident $13,639 full-time, $1704 per credit hour part-time. ***Required fees:*** $1652 full-time. ***Room and board:*** $7213. Room and board charges vary according to housing facility.

Financial Aid Of all full-time matriculated undergraduates who enrolled in 2013, 2,248 applied for aid, 2,248 were judged to have need. ***Financial aid deadline:*** 6/1.

APPLYING

Standardized Tests *Required:* SAT or ACT (for admission).

Options: electronic application, deferred entrance.

Application fee: $30.

Required: high school transcript, minimum 2.3 GPA.

CONTACT

Elizabeth City State University, 1704 Weeksville Road, Elizabeth City, NC 27909-7806. *Toll-free phone:* 800-347-3278.

Elon University

Elon, North Carolina

http://www.elon.edu/

- **Independent** comprehensive, founded 1889, affiliated with United Church of Christ
- **Suburban** 620-acre campus with easy access to Raleigh
- **Endowment** $189.3 million
- **Coed** 5,782 undergraduate students, 98% full-time, 59% women, 41% men
- **Moderately difficult** entrance level, 54% of applicants were admitted

UNDERGRAD STUDENTS

5,638 full-time, 144 part-time. Students come from 51 states and territories; 47 other countries; 80% are from out of state; 6% Black or African American, non-Hispanic/Latino; 5% Hispanic/Latino; 2% Asian, non-Hispanic/Latino; 0.1% Native Hawaiian or other Pacific Islander, non-Hispanic/Latino; 0.3% American Indian or Alaska Native, non-Hispanic/Latino; 2% Two or more races, non-Hispanic/Latino; 0.7% Race/ethnicity unknown; 2% international; 2% transferred in; 62% live on campus.

Freshmen

Admission: 10,443 applied, 5,632 admitted, 1,497 enrolled. ***Average high school GPA:*** 3.98. ***Test scores:*** SAT critical reading scores over 500: 95%; SAT math scores over 500: 95%; SAT writing scores over 500: 96%; ACT scores over 18: 100%; SAT critical reading scores over 600: 60%; SAT math scores over 600: 62%; SAT writing scores over 600: 62%; ACT scores over 24: 84%; SAT critical reading scores over 700: 11%; SAT math scores over 700: 10%; SAT writing scores over 700: 12%; ACT scores over 30: 19%.

Retention: 91% of full-time freshmen returned.

FACULTY

Total: 558, 72% full-time, 79% with terminal degrees.

Student/faculty ratio: 12:1.

ACADEMICS

Calendar: semesters 3-week winter term. *Degrees:* bachelor's, master's, and doctoral.

Special study options: accelerated degree program, advanced placement credit, distance learning, double majors, English as a second language, honors programs, independent study, internships, off-campus study, part-time degree program, services for LD students, student-designed majors, study abroad, summer session for credit. ***ROTC:*** Army (b), Air Force (c).

Unusual degree programs: 3-2 engineering with North Carolina State University, Georgia Tech, Penn State, Virginia Tech, University of Notre Dame, Columbia University, Washington University in St. Louis, North Carolina A&T State University, University of South Carolina.

Computers: 1,200 computers/terminals and 10,000 ports are available on campus for general student use. Students can access the following: computer help desk, free student e-mail accounts, online (class) grades, online (class) registration, online (class) schedules. Campuswide network is available. 100% of college-owned or -operated housing units are wired for high-speed Internet access. Wireless service is available via entire campus.

STUDENT LIFE

Housing options: on-campus residence required through sophomore year; coed, men-only, women-only. Campus housing is university owned and leased by the school. Freshman campus housing is guaranteed.

Activities and organizations: drama/theater group, student-run newspaper, radio and television station, choral group, marching band, Elon Volunteers, Student Media, Intramural Athletics, Religious Life, Habitat for Humanity, national fraternities, national sororities.

Athletics Member NCAA. All Division I except football (Division I-AA). ***Intercollegiate sports:*** baseball M(s), basketball M(s)/W(s), cheerleading M/W, cross-country running M(s)/W(s), equestrian sports M(c)/W(c), field hockey W(c), golf M(s)/W(s), lacrosse M(c)/W(s), rugby M(c)/W(c), soccer M(s)/W(s), softball W(s), swimming and diving M(c)/W(c), tennis M(s)/W(s), track and field W(s), ultimate Frisbee M(c)/W(c), volleyball M(s)(c)/W(s). ***Intramural sports:*** basketball M/W, football M/W, golf M/W, racquetball M/W, soccer M/W, softball M/W, table tennis M/W, volleyball M/W.

Campus security: 24-hour emergency response devices and patrols, late-night transport/escort service, controlled dormitory access.

Student services: health clinic, personal/psychological counseling, women's center.

COSTS & FINANCIAL AID

Costs (2014–15) ***Comprehensive fee:*** $41,914 includes full-time tuition ($30,848), mandatory fees ($399), and room and board ($10,667). Part-time tuition: $983 per semester hour. Part-time tuition and fees vary according to course load. ***College room only:*** $5231. Room and board charges vary according to board plan and housing facility. ***Payment plan:*** installment. ***Waivers:*** employees or children of employees.

Financial Aid Of all full-time matriculated undergraduates who enrolled in 2014, 2,647 applied for aid, 1,893 were judged to have need, 333 had their need fully met. 1,418 Federal Work-Study jobs (averaging $2309). In 2014, 1095 non-need-based awards were made. ***Average percent of need met:*** 60. ***Average financial aid package:*** $17,306. ***Average need-based loan:*** $4514. ***Average need-based gift aid:*** $13,722. ***Average non-need-based aid:*** $6603. ***Average indebtedness upon graduation:*** $27,176.

APPLYING

Standardized Tests *Required:* SAT or ACT (for admission).

Options: electronic application, early admission, early decision, early action, deferred entrance.

Application fee: $50.

Required: high school transcript, standardized test scores, counselor evaluation form. ***Required for some:*** interview. ***Recommended:*** essay or personal statement.

Application deadlines: 1/10 (freshmen), rolling (transfers), 11/10 (early action).

Early decision deadline: 11/1.

Notification: 3/15 (freshmen), continuous (transfers), 12/1 (early decision), 12/20 (early action).

CONTACT

Ms. Melinda Wood, Senior Associate Dean of Admissions, Elon University, 2700 Campus Box, Elon, NC 27244. *Phone:* 336-278-3566. *Toll-free phone:* 800-334-8448. *Fax:* 336-278-7699. *E-mail:* admissions@elon.edu.

Fayetteville State University

Fayetteville, North Carolina

http://www.uncfsu.edu/

- **State-supported** comprehensive, founded 1867, part of University of North Carolina System
- **Urban** 156-acre campus with easy access to Raleigh
- **Endowment** $17.9 million
- **Coed** 5,247 undergraduate students, 75% full-time, 69% women, 31% men
- **Minimally difficult** entrance level, 50% of applicants were admitted

UNDERGRAD STUDENTS

3,935 full-time, 1,312 part-time. Students come from 28 states and territories; 16 other countries; 4% are from out of state; 66% Black or African American, non-Hispanic/Latino; 6% Hispanic/Latino; 1% Asian, non-Hispanic/Latino; 0.2% Native Hawaiian or other Pacific Islander, non-Hispanic/Latino; 3% American Indian or Alaska Native, non-Hispanic/Latino; 0.4% Two or more races, non-Hispanic/Latino; 5% Race/ethnicity unknown; 0.3% international; 15% transferred in; 28% live on campus.

Freshmen

Admission: 4,110 applied, 2,068 admitted, 476 enrolled. ***Average high school GPA:*** 3.25. ***Test scores:*** SAT critical reading scores over 500: 17%; SAT math scores over 500: 23%; SAT writing scores over 500: 13%; SAT critical reading scores over 600: 4%; SAT math scores over 600: 2%; SAT writing scores over 600: 2%.

Retention: 75% of full-time freshmen returned.

FACULTY

Total: 320, 76% full-time, 78% with terminal degrees.

Student/faculty ratio: 18:1.

ACADEMICS

Calendar: semesters. *Degrees:* bachelor's, master's, and doctoral.

Special study options: academic remediation for entering students, accelerated degree program, adult/continuing education programs, advanced placement credit, cooperative education, distance learning, double majors, honors programs, independent study, internships, part-time degree program, services for LD students, study abroad, summer session for credit. ***ROTC:*** Army (c), Air Force (b).

Unusual degree programs: 3-2 engineering with North Carolina State University.

Computers: 600 computers/terminals and 2,400 ports are available on campus for general student use. Students can access the following: campus intranet, computer help desk, free student e-mail accounts, online (class) grades, online (class) registration, online (class) schedules. Campuswide network is available. 100% of college-owned or -operated housing units are wired for high-speed Internet access. Wireless service is available via classrooms, computer centers, computer labs, learning centers, libraries, student centers.

STUDENT LIFE

Housing options: coed, men-only, women-only, special housing for students with disabilities. Campus housing is university owned. Freshman applicants given priority for college housing.

Activities and organizations: drama/theater group, student-run newspaper, radio station, choral group, marching band, Student Government Association, Student Activities Council, Pan-Hellenic Council, Residence Hall Association, Illusions and Black Millennium Modeling Clubs, national fraternities, national sororities.

Athletics Member NCAA. All Division II. ***Intercollegiate sports:*** basketball M(s)/W(s), bowling W, cross-country running M(s)/W(s), football M(s), golf M(s)/W, softball W(s), tennis M/W(s), track and field M/W(s), volleyball W(s). ***Intramural sports:*** baseball M, basketball M/W, bowling M/W, football M, golf M/W, gymnastics M/W, swimming and diving M/W, tennis M, volleyball M/W.

Campus security: 24-hour emergency response devices and patrols, late-night transport/escort service, controlled dormitory access.

Student services: health clinic, personal/psychological counseling.

COSTS & FINANCIAL AID

Costs (2014–15) ***Tuition:*** state resident $2743 full-time; nonresident $14,351 full-time. Full-time tuition and fees vary according to course level, course load, degree level, location, and program. Part-time tuition and fees vary according to course level, course load, degree level, location, and program. ***Room and board:*** $6445; room only: $3529. Room and board charges vary according to board plan and housing facility. ***Payment plan:*** installment. ***Waivers:*** senior citizens and employees or children of employees.

Financial Aid Of all full-time matriculated undergraduates who enrolled in 2014, 3,740 applied for aid, 3,570 were judged to have need, 418 had their need fully met. ***Average percent of need met:*** 73. ***Average financial aid package:*** $10,666. ***Average need-based loan:*** $4325. ***Average need-based gift aid:*** $6987. ***Average indebtedness upon graduation:*** $24,029. ***Financial aid deadline:*** 3/1.

APPLYING

Standardized Tests *Required:* SAT or ACT (for admission).

Options: electronic application, early admission, early decision, early action, deferred entrance.

Application fee: $40.

Required: high school transcript, minimum 2.5 GPA. ***Recommended:*** essay or personal statement.

Application deadlines: 6/30 (freshmen), 6/30 (transfers).

Notification: continuous (freshmen), continuous (transfers).

CONTACT
Fayetteville State University, 1200 Murchison Road, Fayetteville, NC 28301-4298. *Phone:* 910-672-1371. *Toll-free phone:* 800-222-2594. *Fax:* 910-672-1414.

Gardner-Webb University

Boiling Springs, North Carolina

http://www.gardner-webb.edu/

- **Independent Baptist** university, founded 1905
- **Small-town** 250-acre campus with easy access to Charlotte
- **Endowment** $51.1 million
- **Coed**
- **Moderately difficult** entrance level

FACULTY
Student/faculty ratio: 13:1.

ACADEMICS
Calendar: semesters. *Degrees:* certificates, associate, bachelor's, master's, and doctoral.

STUDENT LIFE
Housing options: on-campus residence required through junior year; men-only, women-only, special housing for students with disabilities. Campus housing is university owned. Freshman campus housing is guaranteed.

Activities and organizations: drama/theater group, student-run newspaper, radio station, choral group, marching band, Campus Ministries United, Student Government Association, Dawg Pound, Honors Student Association, International Club.

Athletics Member NCAA. All Division I except football (Division I-AA).

Campus security: 24-hour emergency response devices and patrols, student patrols, late-night transport/escort service, controlled dormitory access.

Student services: personal/psychological counseling.

COSTS & FINANCIAL AID
Costs (2014–15) ***Comprehensive fee:*** $35,665 includes full-time tuition ($26,690), mandatory fees ($195), and room and board ($8780). Full-time tuition and fees vary according to degree level. Part-time tuition: $426 per credit hour. Part-time tuition and fees vary according to course load. ***College room only:*** $4490. Room and board charges vary according to board plan and housing facility.

Financial Aid Of all full-time matriculated undergraduates who enrolled in 2014, 1,409 applied for aid, 1,268 were judged to have need, 254 had their need fully met. 261 Federal Work-Study jobs (averaging $1386). 38 state and other part-time jobs (averaging $1377). In 2014, 268 non-need-based awards were made. ***Average percent of need met:*** 69. ***Average financial aid package:*** $21,535. ***Average need-based loan:*** $4612. ***Average need-based gift aid:*** $7102. ***Average non-need-based aid:*** $10,506. ***Average indebtedness upon graduation:*** $29,543.

APPLYING
Standardized Tests *Required:* SAT or ACT (for admission).

Options: electronic application.

Application fee: $40.

Required: high school transcript, minimum 2.5 GPA, SAT or ACT. ***Required for some:*** 2 letters of recommendation, interview. ***Recommended:*** essay or personal statement, 2 letters of recommendation.

CONTACT
Mrs. Angie Sundell, Associate Vice President of Undergraduate Admissions, Gardner-Webb University, PO Box 817, 110 South Main Street, Boiling Springs, NC 28017. *Phone:* 704-406-4491. *Toll-free phone:* 800-253-6472. *Fax:* 704-406-4488. *E-mail:* admissions@gardner-webb.edu.

Greensboro College

Greensboro, North Carolina

http://www.greensboro.edu/

- **Independent United Methodist** comprehensive, founded 1838
- **Urban** 75-acre campus with easy access to Charlotte
- **Endowment** $20.5 million
- **Coed** 1,117 undergraduate students, 78% full-time, 53% women, 47% men
- **Moderately difficult** entrance level, 41% of applicants were admitted

UNDERGRAD STUDENTS
867 full-time, 250 part-time. Students come from 31 states and territories; 28 other countries; 25% are from out of state; 22% Black or African American, non-Hispanic/Latino; 3% Hispanic/Latino; 0.6% Asian, non-Hispanic/Latino; 0.3% American Indian or Alaska Native, non-Hispanic/Latino; 1% Two or more races, non-Hispanic/Latino; 17% Race/ethnicity unknown; 0.3% international; 10% transferred in; 73% live on campus.

Freshmen
Admission: 2,346 applied, 954 admitted, 192 enrolled. ***Average high school GPA:*** 3.27. ***Test scores:*** SAT critical reading scores over 500: 38%; SAT math scores over 500: 43%; SAT writing scores over 500: 31%; SAT critical reading scores over 600: 10%; SAT math scores over 600: 12%; SAT writing scores over 600: 9%; SAT critical reading scores over 700: 1%; SAT math scores over 700: 3%; SAT writing scores over 700: 2%.

Retention: 62% of full-time freshmen returned.

FACULTY
Total: 96, 65% full-time.

Student/faculty ratio: 13:1.

ACADEMICS
Calendar: semesters. *Degrees:* certificates, bachelor's, master's, and postbachelor's certificates.

Special study options: academic remediation for entering students, accelerated degree program, adult/continuing education programs, advanced placement credit, double majors, English as a second language, freshman honors college, honors programs, independent study, internships, off-campus study, part-time degree program, services for LD students, student-designed majors, study abroad, summer session for credit. ***ROTC:*** Army (c), Air Force (c).

Computers: 180 computers/terminals and 325 ports are available on campus for general student use. Students can access the following: campus intranet, computer help desk, free student e-mail accounts, online (class) grades, online (class) schedules. Campuswide network is available. 100% of college-owned or -operated housing units are wired for high-speed Internet access. Wireless service is available via entire campus.

STUDENT LIFE
Housing options: on-campus residence required through sophomore year; coed, men-only, women-only. Campus housing is university owned. Freshman campus housing is guaranteed.

Activities and organizations: drama/theater group, student-run newspaper, choral group, marching band, Pheta VI, Alpha Z Delta, Student Athletic Advisor Counsel, Pride Productions, United African American Society, national fraternities, national sororities.

Athletics Member NCAA. All Division III. ***Intercollegiate sports:*** baseball M, basketball M/W, cheerleading M/W, football M, golf M/W, lacrosse M/W, soccer M/W, softball W, swimming and diving M/W, tennis M/W, volleyball W, wrestling M. ***Intramural sports:*** basketball M/W, bowling M/W, football M/W, racquetball M/W, skiing (downhill) M/W, ultimate Frisbee M/W.

Campus security: 24-hour patrols, late-night transport/escort service, controlled dormitory access.

Student services: health clinic, personal/psychological counseling.

COSTS
Costs (2015–16) ***Comprehensive fee:*** $37,000 includes full-time tuition ($26,300), mandatory fees ($600), and room and board ($10,100). Full-time tuition and fees vary according to course load and program. Part-time tuition: $725 per credit hour. Part-time tuition and fees vary according to program. ***College room only:*** $5000. Room and board charges vary

according to housing facility. ***Payment plan:*** installment. ***Waivers:*** adult students, senior citizens, and employees or children of employees.

APPLYING
Standardized Tests *Required:* SAT or ACT (for admission).

Options: electronic application, early admission, early action, deferred entrance.

Application fee: $35.

Required: high school transcript. ***Required for some:*** 2 letters of recommendation, interview. ***Recommended:*** essay or personal statement, interview.

Application deadlines: rolling (freshmen), rolling (transfers), 12/15 (early action).

Notification: continuous (freshmen), continuous (transfers), 1/15 (early action).

CONTACT
Ms. Colleen Murphy, Vice President for Enrollment Management and Marketing, Greensboro College, 815 West Market Street, Greensboro, NC 27401-1875. *Phone:* 336-272-7102. *Toll-free phone:* 800-346-8226. *Fax:* 336-378-0154. *E-mail:* admissions@greensborocollege.edu.

Guilford College

Greensboro, North Carolina

http://www.guilford.edu/

- **Independent** 4-year, founded 1837, affiliated with Society of Friends
- **Suburban** 351-acre campus with easy access to Winston Salem, Raleigh
- **Endowment** $72.7 million
- **Coed** 2,137 undergraduate students, 83% full-time, 53% women, 47% men
- **Moderately difficult** entrance level, 62% of applicants were admitted

UNDERGRAD STUDENTS
1,778 full-time, 359 part-time. Students come from 38 states and territories; 35 other countries; 45% are from out of state; 23% Black or African American, non-Hispanic/Latino; 6% Hispanic/Latino; 2% Asian, non-Hispanic/Latino; 0.2% Native Hawaiian or other Pacific Islander, non-Hispanic/Latino; 0.5% American Indian or Alaska Native, non-Hispanic/Latino; 3% Two or more races, non-Hispanic/Latino; 0.9% Race/ethnicity unknown; 2% international; 2% transferred in; 72% live on campus.

Freshmen
Admission: 3,001 applied, 1,866 admitted, 351 enrolled. ***Average high school GPA:*** 3.13. ***Test scores:*** SAT critical reading scores over 500: 58%; SAT math scores over 500: 63%; SAT writing scores over 500: 49%; ACT scores over 18: 83%; SAT critical reading scores over 600: 25%; SAT math scores over 600: 22%; SAT writing scores over 600: 18%; ACT scores over 24: 40%; SAT critical reading scores over 700: 3%; SAT math scores over 700: 4%; SAT writing scores over 700: 2%; ACT scores over 30: 8%.

Retention: 74% of full-time freshmen returned.

FACULTY
Total: 181, 64% full-time, 76% with terminal degrees.

Student/faculty ratio: 14:1.

ACADEMICS
Calendar: semesters. *Degree:* certificates and bachelor's.

Special study options: academic remediation for entering students, accelerated degree program, adult/continuing education programs, advanced placement credit, cooperative education, double majors, English as a second language, honors programs, independent study, internships, off-campus study, part-time degree program, services for LD students, student-designed majors, study abroad, summer session for credit.

Unusual degree programs: 3-2 engineering with Engineering; forestry with Environmental Management and Forestry; Pre-Professional options in Pre-Medicine, Pre-Dentistry, Pre-Veterinary, Pre-Law, and Pre-Ministerial.

Computers: 275 computers/terminals are available on campus for general student use. Students can access the following: computer help desk, free student e-mail accounts, online (class) grades, online (class) registration, online (class) schedules, network storage. Campuswide network is available. 100% of college-owned or -operated housing units are wired for high-speed Internet access. Wireless service is available via entire campus.

STUDENT LIFE
Housing options: on-campus residence required through junior year; coed, women-only, cooperative, special housing for students with disabilities. Campus housing is university owned. Freshman campus housing is guaranteed.

Activities and organizations: drama/theater group, student-run newspaper, radio station, choral group, student government, student radio station, student newspaper, Project Community, African-American Cultural Society.

Athletics Member NCAA. All Division III. ***Intercollegiate sports:*** baseball M, basketball M/W, cross-country running M/W, football M, golf M, lacrosse M/W, soccer M/W, softball W, swimming and diving W, tennis M/W, volleyball W. ***Intramural sports:*** archery M(c)/W(c), badminton M(c)/W(c), basketball M(c), bowling M(c)/W(c), cheerleading M(c)/W(c), fencing M(c)/W(c), football M(c), rugby M(c)/W(c), soccer M(c)/W(c), table tennis M(c)/W(c), tennis M(c)/W(c), ultimate Frisbee M(c)/W(c), volleyball M(c)/W(c).

Campus security: 24-hour emergency response devices and patrols, student patrols, late-night transport/escort service, controlled dormitory access.

Student services: health clinic, personal/psychological counseling, women's center.

COSTS & FINANCIAL AID
Costs (2014–15) ***Comprehensive fee:*** $42,800 includes full-time tuition ($33,050), mandatory fees ($380), and room and board ($9370). Part-time tuition: $1012 per credit hour. Part-time tuition and fees vary according to course load. ***Room and board:*** Room and board charges vary according to board plan and housing facility. ***Payment plan:*** installment. ***Waivers:*** employees or children of employees.

Financial Aid Of all full-time matriculated undergraduates who enrolled in 2013, 1,752 applied for aid, 1,670 were judged to have need, 81 had their need fully met. 192 Federal Work-Study jobs (averaging $1532). 195 state and other part-time jobs (averaging $1379). In 2013, 134 non-need-based awards were made. ***Average percent of need met:*** 83. ***Average financial aid package:*** $20,980. ***Average need-based loan:*** $9703. ***Average need-based gift aid:*** $18,353. ***Average non-need-based aid:*** $14,129. ***Average indebtedness upon graduation:*** $24,255.

APPLYING
Standardized Tests *Recommended:* SAT or ACT (for admission).

Options: electronic application, early admission, early decision, early action, deferred entrance.

Required: essay or personal statement, high school transcript, minimum 2.0 GPA. ***Recommended:*** minimum 3.0 GPA, 2 letters of recommendation, interview.

Application deadlines: 2/15 (freshmen), 6/1 (transfers), 1/15 (early action).

Early decision deadline: 11/15.

Notification: 4/1 (freshmen), continuous (transfers), 2/15 (early action).

CONTACT
Mr. Andrew Strickler, Director of Admission, Guilford College, 5800 West Friendly Avenue, Greensboro, NC 27410. *Phone:* 336-316-2220. *Toll-free phone:* 800-992-7759. *Fax:* 336-316-2954. *E-mail:* admission@guilford.edu.

Heritage Bible College

Dunn, North Carolina

http://www.heritagebiblecollege.edu/

- **Independent Pentecostal Free Will Baptist** 4-year, founded 1971
- **Small-town** 82-acre campus with easy access to Raleigh-Durham
- **Endowment** $53,446
- **Coed**
- **Minimally difficult** entrance level

FACULTY
Student/faculty ratio: 20:1.

ACADEMICS
Calendar: semesters. *Degrees:* associate and bachelor's.

STUDENT LIFE
Housing options: coed. Campus housing is university owned.

Activities and organizations: choral group.

Campus security: controlled dormitory access.

COSTS & FINANCIAL AID
Costs (2014–15) ***Comprehensive fee:*** $12,570 includes full-time tuition ($7200), mandatory fees ($770), and room and board ($4600). Part-time tuition: $300 per credit hour. ***Required fees:*** $32 per credit hour part-time. ***College room only:*** $3100.

Financial Aid Of all full-time matriculated undergraduates who enrolled in 2013, 66 applied for aid, 64 were judged to have need, 64 had their need fully met. 5 Federal Work-Study jobs (averaging $5268). In 2013, 3 non-need-based awards were made. ***Average percent of need met:*** 90. ***Average financial aid package:*** $3645. ***Average need-based loan:*** $2500. ***Average need-based gift aid:*** $250. ***Average non-need-based aid:*** $200. ***Average indebtedness upon graduation:*** $14,774. ***Financial aid deadline:*** 7/1.

APPLYING
Application fee: $25.

Required: essay or personal statement, high school transcript, medical history required for all, immunization record required for some. ***Required for some:*** interview.

CONTACT
Mrs. Peggy Parker, Admissions Director, Heritage Bible College, PO Box 1628, Dunn, NC 28335-1628. *Phone:* 910-892-3178 Ext. 239. *Toll-free phone:* 800-297-6351. *Fax:* 910-891-1660. *E-mail:* pparker@heritagebiblecollege.edu.

★ High Point University
High Point, North Carolina
http://www.highpoint.edu/

- **Independent United Methodist** comprehensive, founded 1924
- **Suburban** 360-acre campus with easy access to Charlotte
- **Endowment** $48.0 million
- **Coed** 4,208 undergraduate students, 99% full-time, 60% women, 40% men
- **Moderately difficult** entrance level, 80% of applicants were admitted

UNDERGRAD STUDENTS
4,164 full-time, 44 part-time. Students come from 48 states and territories; 28 other countries; 78% are from out of state; 5% Black or African American, non-Hispanic/Latino; 4% Hispanic/Latino; 1% Asian, non-Hispanic/Latino; 0.4% American Indian or Alaska Native, non-Hispanic/Latino; 4% Two or more races, non-Hispanic/Latino; 2% Race/ethnicity unknown; 2% international; 1% transferred in; 92% live on campus.

Freshmen
Admission: 7,410 applied, 5,942 admitted, 1,386 enrolled. ***Average high school GPA:*** 3.23. ***Test scores:*** SAT critical reading scores over 500: 73%; SAT math scores over 500: 76%; SAT writing scores over 500: 68%; ACT scores over 18: 95%; SAT critical reading scores over 600: 24%; SAT math scores over 600: 28%; SAT writing scores over 600: 22%; ACT scores over 24: 47%; SAT critical reading scores over 700: 3%; SAT math scores over 700: 2%; SAT writing scores over 700: 2%; ACT scores over 30: 6%.

Retention: 77% of full-time freshmen returned.

FACULTY
Total: 381, 66% full-time, 58% with terminal degrees.

Student/faculty ratio: 15:1.

ACADEMICS
Calendar: semesters. *Degrees:* bachelor's, master's, doctoral, and postbachelor's certificates.

Special study options: academic remediation for entering students, accelerated degree program, advanced placement credit, cooperative education, double majors, English as a second language, honors programs, independent study, internships, off-campus study, services for LD students, student-designed majors, study abroad, summer session for credit. ***ROTC:*** Army (c), Air Force (c).

Unusual degree programs: 3-2 elementary education, strategic communication.

Computers: 1,500 computers/terminals are available on campus for general student use. Students can access the following: campus intranet, computer help desk, free student e-mail accounts, online (class) grades, online (class) registration, online (class) schedules. Campuswide network is available. 100% of college-owned or -operated housing units are wired for high-speed Internet access. Wireless service is available via entire campus.

STUDENT LIFE
Housing options: on-campus residence required through sophomore year; coed, men-only, women-only, cooperative, special housing for students with disabilities. Campus housing is university owned and leased by the school. Freshman campus housing is guaranteed.

Activities and organizations: drama/theater group, student-run newspaper, radio and television station, choral group, Big Brothers/Big Sisters, Campus Civitan, College Life, Psi Chi, Habitat for Humanity, national fraternities, national sororities.

Athletics Member NCAA. All Division I. ***Intercollegiate sports:*** baseball M(s), basketball M(s)/W(s), cheerleading W(s), cross-country running M(s)/W(s), golf M(s)/W(s), lacrosse M/W, soccer M(s)/W(s), track and field M(s)/W(s), volleyball W(s). ***Intramural sports:*** basketball M/W, crew M/W, cross-country running M/W, equestrian sports M/W, field hockey W, golf M/W, lacrosse M/W, soccer M/W, swimming and diving M/W, tennis M/W, volleyball M/W.

Campus security: 24-hour emergency response devices and patrols, student patrols, late-night transport/escort service, controlled dormitory access.

Student services: health clinic, personal/psychological counseling.

COSTS
Costs (2015–16) ***Comprehensive fee:*** $44,430 includes full-time tuition ($28,600), mandatory fees ($3830), and room and board ($12,000). Full-time tuition and fees vary according to course load and reciprocity agreements. Part-time tuition: $900 per credit hour. Part-time tuition and fees vary according to course load and reciprocity agreements. ***Room and board:*** Room and board charges vary according to board plan and housing facility. ***Payment plan:*** installment. ***Waivers:*** employees or children of employees.

APPLYING
Standardized Tests *Required:* SAT or ACT (for admission).

Options: electronic application, early decision, early action, deferred entrance.

Application fee: $50.

Required: high school transcript, minimum 2.0 GPA, 2 letters of recommendation. ***Recommended:*** essay or personal statement, minimum 3.0 GPA, interview.

Application deadlines: 8/15 (freshmen), 8/15 (transfers), 11/8 (early action).

Early decision deadline: 11/1.

Notification: continuous until 8/15 (freshmen), continuous (transfers), 11/23 (early decision), 12/12 (early action).

CONTACT
Mr. Kerr Ramsay, Associate Vice President of Admissions, High Point University, University Station, 833 Montlieu Avenue, High Point, NC 27268. *Phone:* 336-841-9176. *Toll-free phone:* 800-345-6993. *Fax:* 336-888-6382. *E-mail:* kramsay@highpoint.edu.

ITT Technical Institute
Cary, North Carolina
http://www.itt-tech.edu/

- **Proprietary** primarily 2-year, part of ITT Educational Services, Inc.
- **Coed**
- **Minimally difficult** entrance level

ACADEMICS
Degrees: associate and bachelor's.

STUDENT LIFE
Housing options: college housing not available.

CONTACT
Director of Recruitment, ITT Technical Institute, 5520 Dillard Drive, Suite 100, Cary, NC 27518. *Phone:* 919-233-2520. *Toll-free phone:* 877-203-5533.

ITT Technical Institute
Charlotte, North Carolina
http://www.itt-tech.edu/

- **Proprietary** 4-year, part of ITT Educational Services, Inc.
- **Coed**
- **Minimally difficult** entrance level

ACADEMICS
Calendar: quarters. *Degrees:* associate and bachelor's.

CONTACT
Director of Recruitment, ITT Technical Institute, 10926 David Taylor Drive, Suite 100, Charlotte, NC 28262. *Phone:* 704-548-2300. *Toll-free phone:* 877-243-7685.

ITT Technical Institute
Charlotte, North Carolina
http://www.itt-tech.edu/

- **Proprietary** primarily 2-year
- **Coed**
- **Minimally difficult** entrance level

ACADEMICS
Degrees: associate and bachelor's.

STUDENT LIFE
Housing options: college housing not available.

CONTACT
Director of Recruitment, ITT Technical Institute, 4135 Southstream Boulevard, Suite 200, Charlotte, NC 28217. *Phone:* 704-423-3100. *Toll-free phone:* 800-488-0173.

ITT Technical Institute
Durham, North Carolina
http://www.itt-tech.edu/

- **Proprietary** 4-year
- **Coed**
- **Minimally difficult** entrance level

ACADEMICS
Degrees: associate and bachelor's.

CONTACT
Director of Recruitment, ITT Technical Institute, 3518 Westgate Drive, Suite 150, Durham, NC 27707. *Phone:* 919-401-1400. *Toll-free phone:* 877-452-8662.

ITT Technical Institute
High Point, North Carolina
http://www.itt-tech.edu/

- **Proprietary** primarily 2-year, founded 2007, part of ITT Educational Services, Inc.
- **Coed**
- **Minimally difficult** entrance level

ACADEMICS
Calendar: quarters. *Degrees:* associate and bachelor's.

STUDENT LIFE
Housing options: college housing not available.

CONTACT
Director of Recruitment, ITT Technical Institute, 4050 Piedmont Parkway, Suite 110, High Point, NC 27265. *Phone:* 336-819-5900. *Toll-free phone:* 877-536-5231.

Johnson & Wales University - Charlotte Campus
Charlotte, North Carolina
http://www.jwu.edu/charlotte/

- **Independent** 4-year, founded 2004
- **Coed** 2,255 undergraduate students, 98% full-time, 65% women, 35% men
- **Moderately difficult** entrance level, 69% of applicants were admitted

UNDERGRAD STUDENTS
2,207 full-time, 48 part-time. 64% are from out of state; 34% Black or African American, non-Hispanic/Latino; 6% Hispanic/Latino; 0.8% Asian, non-Hispanic/Latino; 0.2% American Indian or Alaska Native, non-Hispanic/Latino; 5% Two or more races, non-Hispanic/Latino; 7% Race/ethnicity unknown; 0.8% international; 8% transferred in; 56% live on campus.

Freshmen
Admission: 4,685 applied, 3,222 admitted, 610 enrolled. ***Average high school GPA:*** 3.19. ***Test scores:*** SAT critical reading scores over 500: 44%; SAT math scores over 500: 42%; SAT writing scores over 500: 31%; SAT critical reading scores over 600: 8%; SAT math scores over 600: 5%; SAT writing scores over 600: 6%.
Retention: 74% of full-time freshmen returned.

FACULTY
Total: 120, 75% full-time.
Student/faculty ratio: 22:1.

ACADEMICS
Calendar: quarters. *Degrees:* associate and bachelor's.
Special study options: accelerated degree program, advanced placement credit, cooperative education, English as a second language, honors programs, independent study, internships, part-time degree program, services for LD students, study abroad. ***ROTC:*** Army (b).
Computers: Students can access the following: computer help desk, free student e-mail accounts, online (class) grades, online (class) registration, online (class) schedules. Campuswide network is available.

STUDENT LIFE
Housing options: on-campus residence required for freshman year; coed, special housing for students with disabilities. Campus housing is university owned. Freshman applicants given priority for college housing.
Activities and organizations: student-run newspaper.
Campus security: 24-hour emergency response devices and patrols, late-night transport/escort service, controlled dormitory access.
Student services: health clinic, personal/psychological counseling.

COSTS & FINANCIAL AID
Costs (2015–16) ***Tuition:*** $29,226 full-time, $196 per credit hour part-time. ***Required fees:*** $350 full-time.
Financial Aid Of all full-time matriculated undergraduates who enrolled in 2010, 2,294 applied for aid, 2,107 were judged to have need, 332 had their need fully met. In 2010, 299 non-need-based awards were made. ***Average percent of need met:*** 72. ***Average financial aid package:*** $18,403. ***Average need-based loan:*** $5089. ***Average need-based gift aid:*** $8161. ***Average non-need-based aid:*** $5457.

APPLYING
Standardized Tests *Required for some:* SAT or ACT (for admission).
Options: electronic application, early admission, deferred entrance.
Required: high school transcript. ***Required for some:*** interview. ***Recommended:*** minimum 2.0 GPA.

CONTACT
Joseph Campos, Director of Admissions, Johnson & Wales University - Charlotte Campus, 801 West Trade Street, Charlotte, NC 28202. *Phone:* 980-598-1100. *Toll-free phone:* 866-598-2427. *Fax:* 980-598-1111. *E-mail:* clt@admissions.jwu.edu.

Johnson C. Smith University
Charlotte, North Carolina
http://www.jcsu.edu/

- **Independent** comprehensive, founded 1867
- **Urban** 100-acre campus with easy access to Atlanta
- **Endowment** $60.2 million
- **Coed** 1,375 undergraduate students, 96% full-time, 61% women, 39% men
- **Moderately difficult** entrance level, 42% of applicants were admitted

UNDERGRAD STUDENTS
1,318 full-time, 57 part-time. Students come from 35 states and territories; 8 other countries; 40% are from out of state; 73% Black or African American, non-Hispanic/Latino; 6% Hispanic/Latino; 0.1% Asian, non-Hispanic/Latino; 0.3% Native Hawaiian or other Pacific Islander, non-Hispanic/Latino; 0.1% American Indian or Alaska Native, non-Hispanic/Latino; 2% Two or more races, non-Hispanic/Latino; 14% Race/ethnicity unknown; 3% international; 6% transferred in; 62% live on campus.

Freshmen
Admission: 3,801 applied, 1,606 admitted, 268 enrolled. ***Average high school GPA:*** 2.7. ***Test scores:*** SAT critical reading scores over 500: 13%; SAT math scores over 500: 12%; ACT scores over 18: 37%; SAT critical reading scores over 600: 2%; SAT math scores over 600: 1%; ACT scores over 24: 1%.

Retention: 66% of full-time freshmen returned.

FACULTY
Total: 173, 63% full-time, 60% with terminal degrees.

Student/faculty ratio: 11:1.

ACADEMICS
Calendar: semesters. *Degrees:* bachelor's and master's.

Special study options: adult/continuing education programs, advanced placement credit, cooperative education, double majors, independent study, internships, off-campus study, part-time degree program, services for LD students, student-designed majors, study abroad, summer session for credit. ***ROTC:*** Army (b), Air Force (c).

Computers: 50 computers/terminals are available on campus for general student use. Students can access the following: campus intranet, computer help desk, free student e-mail accounts, online (class) grades, online (class) registration, online (class) schedules. Campuswide network is available. 100% of college-owned or -operated housing units are wired for high-speed Internet access. Wireless service is available via entire campus.

STUDENT LIFE
Housing options: on-campus residence required for freshman year; coed, men-only, women-only. Campus housing is university owned and leased by the school. Freshman campus housing is guaranteed.

Activities and organizations: drama/theater group, student-run newspaper, choral group, marching band, International Club, Math Club, Karibbean Vybz, Student Orientation Leaders, Unparalleled Production Evolution, national fraternities, national sororities.

Athletics Member NCAA. All Division II. ***Intercollegiate sports:*** basketball M(s)/W(s), bowling W(s), cheerleading W(c), cross-country running M(s)/W(s), football M(s), golf M(s), softball W(s), tennis M(s)/W(s), track and field M(s)/W(s), volleyball W(s).

Campus security: 24-hour emergency response devices and patrols, late-night transport/escort service, controlled dormitory access.

Student services: health clinic, personal/psychological counseling.

COSTS & FINANCIAL AID
Costs (2014–15) ***Comprehensive fee:*** $25,336 includes full-time tuition ($18,236) and room and board ($7100). Full-time tuition and fees vary according to course load. Part-time tuition: $418 per credit hour. Part-time tuition and fees vary according to course load. ***College room only:*** $4086. Room and board charges vary according to board plan and housing facility. ***Payment plan:*** installment. ***Waivers:*** children of alumni and employees or children of employees.

Financial Aid Of all full-time matriculated undergraduates who enrolled in 2014, 1,199 applied for aid, 1,163 were judged to have need, 93 had their need fully met. 217 Federal Work-Study jobs (averaging $2008). In 2014, 120 non-need-based awards were made. ***Average percent of need met:*** 57. ***Average financial aid package:*** $15,885. ***Average need-based loan:*** $4400. ***Average need-based gift aid:*** $11,579. ***Average non-need-based aid:*** $19,057. ***Average indebtedness upon graduation:*** $33,377.

APPLYING
Standardized Tests *Required:* SAT or ACT (for admission).

Options: electronic application, early admission, deferred entrance.

Application fee: $25.

Required: high school transcript. ***Recommended:*** essay or personal statement, 2 letters of recommendation.

Notification: continuous (freshmen), continuous (out-of-state freshmen), continuous (transfers).

CONTACT
Mr. James Burrell, Director of Admissions, Johnson C. Smith University, 100 Beatties Ford Road, Charlotte, NC 28216. *Phone:* 704-378-1181. *Toll-free phone:* 800-782-7303. *Fax:* 704-378-1242. *E-mail:* jburrell@jcsu.edu.

Laurel University
High Point, North Carolina
http://www.laureluniversity.edu/

- **Independent interdenominational** comprehensive, founded 1932
- **Urban** 24-acre campus
- **Coed** 148 undergraduate students, 86% full-time, 34% women, 66% men
- **Moderately difficult** entrance level, 35% of applicants were admitted

UNDERGRAD STUDENTS
128 full-time, 20 part-time. Students come from 15 states and territories; 11% are from out of state; 36% Black or African American, non-Hispanic/Latino; 3% Hispanic/Latino; 0.5% Asian, non-Hispanic/Latino; 9% American Indian or Alaska Native, non-Hispanic/Latino; 2% Two or more races, non-Hispanic/Latino; 2% Race/ethnicity unknown; 15% transferred in; 25% live on campus.

Freshmen
Admission: 130 applied, 46 admitted, 46 enrolled. ***Average high school GPA:*** 3.3.

Retention: 83% of full-time freshmen returned.

FACULTY
Total: 37, 8% full-time, 49% with terminal degrees.

Student/faculty ratio: 4:1.

ACADEMICS
Calendar: semesters. *Degrees:* certificates, associate, bachelor's, master's, and doctoral.

Special study options: academic remediation for entering students, adult/continuing education programs, advanced placement credit, distance learning, double majors, independent study, internships, off-campus study, part-time degree program, summer session for credit.

Computers: 7 computers/terminals and 7 ports are available on campus for general student use. Students can access the following: free student e-mail accounts, online (class) grades, online (class) registration, online (class) schedules. 100% of college-owned or -operated housing units are wired for high-speed Internet access. Wireless service is available via classrooms, computer labs, libraries, student centers.

STUDENT LIFE
Housing options: men-only, women-only. Campus housing is university owned.

Activities and organizations: choral group, Student Government, Choir, Praise Band.

Athletics Member NCCAA. ***Intercollegiate sports:*** lacrosse M(s)/W(s), soccer M(s)/W(s), volleyball M(s)/W(s).

COSTS & FINANCIAL AID
Costs (2014–15) ***Tuition:*** $8890 full-time, $6 per credit hour part-time. Full-time tuition and fees vary according to program. Part-time tuition and fees vary according to program. ***Required fees:*** $1200 full-time. ***Room only:*** $2800. Room and board charges vary according to housing facility.

Financial Aid Of all full-time matriculated undergraduates who enrolled in 2011, 3 Federal Work-Study jobs (averaging $2500).

APPLYING
Standardized Tests *Required for some:* College Board ACCUPLACER Test for English.
Options: electronic application, early admission, deferred entrance.
Application fee: $20.
Required: high school transcript, 2 letters of recommendation, interview. *Recommended:* minimum 2.0 GPA.
Application deadlines: 8/1 (freshmen), 8/1 (transfers).
Notification: 8/10 (freshmen), continuous until 8/10 (transfers).

CONTACT
Mary Kate Hancock, Admissions Officer, Laurel University, 1215 Eastchester Drive, High Point, NC 27265-3197. *Phone:* 336-887-3000 Ext. 127. *E-mail:* emurray@laureluniversity.edu.

Lees-McRae College
Banner Elk, North Carolina
http://www.lmc.edu/

- **Independent** 4-year, founded 1900, affiliated with Presbyterian Church (U.S.A.)
- **Rural** 460-acre campus
- **Coed** 940 undergraduate students, 99% full-time, 66% women, 34% men
- **Minimally difficult** entrance level, 62% of applicants were admitted

UNDERGRAD STUDENTS
930 full-time, 10 part-time. Students come from 31 states and territories; 9 other countries; 25% are from out of state; 7% Black or African American, non-Hispanic/Latino; 2% Hispanic/Latino; 0.3% Asian, non-Hispanic/Latino; 0.2% American Indian or Alaska Native, non-Hispanic/Latino; 0.9% Two or more races, non-Hispanic/Latino; 29% Race/ethnicity unknown; 2% international; 21% transferred in; 64% live on campus.

Freshmen
Admission: 1,514 applied, 938 admitted, 216 enrolled. ***Average high school GPA:*** 3.29. ***Test scores:*** SAT critical reading scores over 500: 43%; SAT math scores over 500: 38%; ACT scores over 18: 79%; SAT critical reading scores over 600: 12%; SAT math scores over 600: 6%; ACT scores over 24: 23%; SAT critical reading scores over 700: 1%; ACT scores over 30: 4%.
Retention: 60% of full-time freshmen returned.

FACULTY
Total: 92, 52% full-time, 46% with terminal degrees.
Student/faculty ratio: 15:1.

ACADEMICS
Calendar: semesters. *Degree:* bachelor's.
Special study options: academic remediation for entering students, accelerated degree program, adult/continuing education programs, advanced placement credit, cooperative education, double majors, honors programs, independent study, internships, off-campus study, part-time degree program, services for LD students, study abroad, summer session for credit.
Computers: Students can access the following: computer help desk, free student e-mail accounts, online (class) schedules. 100% of college-owned or -operated housing units are wired for high-speed Internet access.

STUDENT LIFE
Housing options: coed, men-only, women-only, special housing for students with disabilities. Freshman campus housing is guaranteed.
Activities and organizations: drama/theater group, choral group.
Athletics Member NCAA. All Division II. ***Intercollegiate sports:*** basketball M(s)/W(s), cross-country running M(s)/W(s), lacrosse M(s)/W(s), soccer M(s)/W(s), softball W(s), tennis M(s)/W(s), track and field M(s)/W(s), volleyball M(s)/W(s).
Campus security: 24-hour emergency response devices and patrols.
Student services: health clinic, personal/psychological counseling.

COSTS & FINANCIAL AID
Costs (2014–15) ***Comprehensive fee:*** $34,636 includes full-time tuition ($24,154), mandatory fees ($700), and room and board ($9782). Full-time tuition and fees vary according to course load, location, and reciprocity agreements. Part-time tuition and fees vary according to course load, location, and reciprocity agreements. ***College room only:*** $4896. Room and board charges vary according to housing facility. ***Payment plan:*** installment. ***Waivers:*** employees or children of employees.
Financial Aid Of all full-time matriculated undergraduates who enrolled in 2014, 781 applied for aid, 746 were judged to have need, 11 had their need fully met. In 2014, 125 non-need-based awards were made. ***Average percent of need met:*** 71. ***Average financial aid package:*** $22,736. ***Average need-based loan:*** $5000. ***Average need-based gift aid:*** $7487. ***Average non-need-based aid:*** $17,170.

APPLYING
Standardized Tests *Required for some:* SAT or ACT (for admission), Test-optional admission for majority of students. Prospective intercollegiate athletes and Honors Program students are required to submit SAT or ACT scores.
Options: electronic application, early action.
Application fee: $35.
Required: high school transcript, minimum 2.0 GPA. ***Required for some:*** essay or personal statement, interview.
Application deadlines: rolling (freshmen), rolling (out-of-state freshmen), rolling (transfers).
Notification: continuous (freshmen), continuous (out-of-state freshmen), continuous (transfers).

CONTACT
Mrs. Candace Silver, Director of Admissions, Lees-McRae College, PO Box 128, Banner Elk, NC 28604. *Phone:* 800-280-4562. *Toll-free phone:* 800-280-4562. *Fax:* 828-898-8707. *E-mail:* admissions@lmc.edu.

Lenoir-Rhyne University
Hickory, North Carolina
http://www.lr.edu/

- **Independent Lutheran** comprehensive, founded 1891
- **Small-town** 100-acre campus with easy access to Charlotte
- **Endowment** $97.6 million
- **Coed** 1,524 undergraduate students, 88% full-time, 57% women, 43% men
- **Moderately difficult** entrance level, 66% of applicants were admitted

UNDERGRAD STUDENTS
1,334 full-time, 190 part-time. Students come from 25 states and territories; 17 other countries; 21% are from out of state; 14% Black or African American, non-Hispanic/Latino; 3% Hispanic/Latino; 2% Asian, non-Hispanic/Latino; 0.1% Native Hawaiian or other Pacific Islander, non-Hispanic/Latino; 0.6% American Indian or Alaska Native, non-Hispanic/Latino; 3% Two or more races, non-Hispanic/Latino; 2% Race/ethnicity unknown; 2% international; 8% transferred in; 53% live on campus.

Freshmen
Admission: 4,488 applied, 2,953 admitted, 347 enrolled. ***Average high school GPA:*** 3.63. ***Test scores:*** SAT critical reading scores over 500: 46%; SAT math scores over 500: 50%; SAT writing scores over 500: 34%; SAT critical reading scores over 600: 10%; SAT math scores over 600: 15%; SAT writing scores over 600: 6%; SAT math scores over 700: 1%.
Retention: 76% of full-time freshmen returned.

FACULTY
Total: 231, 51% full-time, 62% with terminal degrees.
Student/faculty ratio: 12:1.

ACADEMICS
Calendar: semesters. *Degrees:* bachelor's and master's.
Special study options: academic remediation for entering students, adult/continuing education programs, advanced placement credit, distance learning, double majors, freshman honors college, honors programs, independent study, internships, off-campus study, part-time degree program, services for LD students, study abroad, summer session for credit. ***ROTC:*** Army (c), Air Force (c).
Unusual degree programs: 3-2 engineering with North Carolina Agricultural and Technical State University, North Carolina State

University, University of North Carolina at Charlotte, or Clemson University; forestry with Duke University.

Computers: 275 computers/terminals and 275 ports are available on campus for general student use. Students can access the following: campus intranet, computer help desk, free student e-mail accounts, online (class) grades, online (class) registration, online (class) schedules. Campuswide network is available. 100% of college-owned or -operated housing units are wired for high-speed Internet access. Wireless service is available via entire campus.

STUDENT LIFE

Housing options: on-campus residence required through junior year; coed. Campus housing is university owned. Freshman campus housing is guaranteed.

Activities and organizations: drama/theater group, student-run newspaper, choral group, Circle K, CAB, Nu Generation, Greek Organizations, Sign Troupe, national sororities.

Athletics Member NCAA. All Division II. ***Intercollegiate sports:*** baseball M(s), basketball M(s)/W(s), cheerleading M(s)/W(s), cross-country running M(s)/W(s), football M(s), golf M(s)/W(s), lacrosse M(s)/W(s), soccer M(s)/W(s), softball W(s), swimming and diving M(s)/W(s), tennis M(s)/W(s), track and field M(s)/W(s), volleyball W(s). ***Intramural sports:*** basketball M/W, soccer M/W, ultimate Frisbee M/W.

Campus security: 24-hour emergency response devices and patrols, late-night transport/escort service, controlled dormitory access.

Student services: health clinic, personal/psychological counseling.

COSTS & FINANCIAL AID

Costs (2015–16) ***Comprehensive fee:*** $43,200 includes full-time tuition ($32,140) and room and board ($11,060). Part-time tuition: $520 per credit. Part-time tuition and fees vary according to class time. ***Waivers:*** senior citizens and employees or children of employees.

Financial Aid Of all full-time matriculated undergraduates who enrolled in 2013, 1,031 applied for aid, 968 were judged to have need, 157 had their need fully met. In 2013, 117 non-need-based awards were made. ***Average percent of need met:*** 74. ***Average financial aid package:*** $25,242. ***Average need-based loan:*** $4316. ***Average need-based gift aid:*** $20,624. ***Average non-need-based aid:*** $12,205. ***Average indebtedness upon graduation:*** $27,814.

APPLYING

Standardized Tests *Required:* SAT or ACT (for admission).

Options: early admission, early action, deferred entrance.

Application fee: $35.

Required: high school transcript, minimum 2.5 GPA.

Application deadlines: rolling (freshmen), rolling (out-of-state freshmen), rolling (transfers).

Notification: continuous (freshmen), continuous (out-of-state freshmen), continuous (transfers).

CONTACT

Lenoir-Rhyne University, 625 7th Avenue NE, Hickory, NC 28601. *Phone:* 828-328-7392. *Toll-free phone:* 800-277-5721.

Living Arts College

Raleigh, North Carolina

http://www.living-arts-college.edu/

- **Proprietary** primarily 2-year, founded 1992
- **Suburban** campus with easy access to Raleigh
- **Coed**
- **Moderately difficult** entrance level

FACULTY

Student/faculty ratio: 10:1.

ACADEMICS

Calendar: quarters. *Degree:* certificates, diplomas, and bachelor's.

STUDENT LIFE

Housing options: Campus housing is university owned. Freshman applicants given priority for college housing.

Activities and organizations: MODIV - student council, Student Ambassadors, Firebreathers Animation Studio, NVTHS-National Vocational Technical Honor Society.

Campus security: controlled dormitory access.

APPLYING

Standardized Tests *Required:* Wonderlic aptitude test (for admission).

Options: electronic application, early admission, early decision, early action, deferred entrance.

Application fee: $25.

Required: essay or personal statement, high school transcript, interview, portfolio for selected program.

CONTACT

Julie Wenta, Director of Admissions, Living Arts College, 3000 Wakefield Crossing Drive, Raleigh, NC 27614. *Phone:* 919-488-5902. *Toll-free phone:* 800-288-7442. *Fax:* 919-488-8490. *E-mail:* jwenta@living-arts-college.edu.

Livingstone College

Salisbury, North Carolina

http://www.livingstone.edu/

- **Independent** 4-year, founded 1879, affiliated with African Methodist Episcopal Zion Church
- **Small-town** 45-acre campus
- **Endowment** $1.8 million
- **Coed**
- **Minimally difficult** entrance level

FACULTY

Student/faculty ratio: 15:1.

ACADEMICS

Calendar: semesters. *Degree:* bachelor's.

STUDENT LIFE

Housing options: on-campus residence required for freshman year; men-only, women-only. Campus housing is university owned. Freshman applicants given priority for college housing.

Activities and organizations: drama/theater group, choral group, marching band, Greek Organizations, Modeling Troups, choirs, band, Rotary and Optimist Clubs (Community), national fraternities, national sororities.

Athletics Member NCAA. All Division II.

Campus security: 24-hour emergency response devices and patrols, late-night transport/escort service, controlled dormitory access.

Student services: health clinic, personal/psychological counseling.

COSTS

Costs (2014–15) ***Comprehensive fee:*** $23,421 includes full-time tuition ($14,637), mandatory fees ($2188), and room and board ($6596). Part-time tuition: $586 per credit hour. ***Required fees:*** $120 per credit hour part-time. ***College room only:*** $3167.

APPLYING

Standardized Tests *Required:* SAT or ACT (for admission).

Options: deferred entrance.

Application fee: $25.

Required: high school transcript, minimum 2.0 GPA.

CONTACT

Mr. Tony Baldwin, Livingstone College, 701 West Monroe Street, Salifbury, NC 28144. *Phone:* 704-216-6001. *Toll-free phone:* 800-835-3435. *Fax:* 704-216-6215. *E-mail:* admissions@livingstone.edu.

Mars Hill University

Mars Hill, North Carolina

http://www.mhu.edu/

- **Independent Baptist** comprehensive, founded 1856
- **Small-town** 194-acre campus
- **Endowment** $42.0 million
- **Coed** 1,426 undergraduate students, 92% full-time, 50% women, 50% men
- **Moderately difficult** entrance level, 64% of applicants were admitted

UNDERGRAD STUDENTS

1,319 full-time, 107 part-time. Students come from 37 states and territories; 15 other countries; 29% are from out of state; 18% Black or African American, non-Hispanic/Latino; 2% Hispanic/Latino; 0.6% Asian, non-Hispanic/Latino; 0.1% Native Hawaiian or other Pacific Islander, non-Hispanic/Latino; 2% American Indian or Alaska Native, non-Hispanic/Latino; 4% Race/ethnicity unknown; 3% international; 8% transferred in; 70% live on campus.

Freshmen

Admission: 2,899 applied, 1,869 admitted, 419 enrolled. ***Average high school GPA:*** 3.21. ***Test scores:*** SAT critical reading scores over 500: 30%; SAT math scores over 500: 36%; ACT scores over 18: 71%; SAT critical reading scores over 600: 6%; SAT math scores over 600: 6%; ACT scores over 24: 23%; SAT critical reading scores over 700: 1%; ACT scores over 30: 1%.

Retention: 58% of full-time freshmen returned.

FACULTY

Total: 157, 57% full-time.

Student/faculty ratio: 12:1.

ACADEMICS

Calendar: semesters. *Degrees:* bachelor's and master's.

Special study options: academic remediation for entering students, accelerated degree program, adult/continuing education programs, advanced placement credit, cooperative education, double majors, English as a second language, honors programs, independent study, internships, part-time degree program, services for LD students, student-designed majors, study abroad, summer session for credit.

Computers: 188 computers/terminals are available on campus for general student use. Students can access the following: campus intranet, computer help desk, free student e-mail accounts, online (class) grades, online (class) registration, online (class) schedules. Campuswide network is available. 100% of college-owned or -operated housing units are wired for high-speed Internet access. Wireless service is available via entire campus.

STUDENT LIFE

Housing options: on-campus residence required through sophomore year; men-only, women-only. Campus housing is university owned. Freshman campus housing is guaranteed.

Activities and organizations: drama/theater group, choral group, marching band, Student Government Association, Fellowship of Christian Athletes, Christian Student Movement, Fraternity/Sorority, Athletic Trainers Association, national fraternities, national sororities.

Athletics Member NCAA. All Division II. ***Intercollegiate sports:*** baseball M(s), basketball M(s)/W(s), cheerleading M(s)/W(s), cross-country running M(s)/W(s), football M(s), golf M(s)/W(s), lacrosse M(s), soccer M(s)/W(s), softball W(s), swimming and diving M(s)/W(s), tennis M(s)/W(s), track and field M(s)/W(s), volleyball W(s). ***Intramural sports:*** basketball M/W, football M/W, rock climbing M/W, skiing (downhill) M(c)/W(c), soccer M/W, track and field M(c)/W(c), ultimate Frisbee M/W, volleyball M/W, water polo M/W, weight lifting M/W.

Campus security: 24-hour emergency response devices and patrols, late-night transport/escort service, controlled dormitory access.

Student services: health clinic, personal/psychological counseling.

COSTS & FINANCIAL AID

Costs (2014–15) ***Comprehensive fee:*** $38,841 includes full-time tuition ($27,590), mandatory fees ($2584), and room and board ($8667). Part-time tuition: $885 per credit hour. Part-time tuition and fees vary according to course load. ***Required fees:*** $114 per credit hour part-time. ***Room and board:*** Room and board charges vary according to board plan and housing facility. ***Waivers:*** adult students and employees or children of employees.

Financial Aid Of all full-time matriculated undergraduates who enrolled in 2010, 2,256 applied for aid, 1,007 were judged to have need, 164 had their need fully met. 252 Federal Work-Study jobs (averaging $1354). In 2010, 141 non-need-based awards were made. ***Average percent of need met:*** 73. ***Average financial aid package:*** $17,195. ***Average need-based loan:*** $3988. ***Average need-based gift aid:*** $13,790. ***Average non-need-based aid:*** $8631. ***Average indebtedness upon graduation:*** $27,775.

APPLYING

Standardized Tests *Required:* SAT or ACT (for admission).

Options: electronic application, early admission, deferred entrance.

Application fee: $25.

Required: high school transcript, minimum 2.0 GPA. ***Required for some:*** interview. ***Recommended:*** essay or personal statement, minimum 3.0 GPA.

Application deadlines: rolling (freshmen), rolling (transfers).

CONTACT

Dr. Craig Goforth, Dean of Admissions and Financial Aid, Mars Hill University, PO Box 370, Mars Hill, NC 28754. *Phone:* 828-689-1201. *Toll-free phone:* 866-648-4968. *Fax:* 828-689-1473. *E-mail:* ehoffmeyer@mhc.edu.

★ Meredith College

Raleigh, North Carolina

http://www.meredith.edu/

- **Independent** comprehensive, founded 1891
- **Urban** 225-acre campus
- **Endowment** $93.9 million
- **Undergraduate: women only; graduate: coed** 1,644 undergraduate students, 96% full-time, 100% women, 0% men
- **Moderately difficult** entrance level, 61% of applicants were admitted

UNDERGRAD STUDENTS

1,571 full-time, 73 part-time. Students come from 27 states and territories; 24 other countries; 12% are from out of state; 11% Black or African American, non-Hispanic/Latino; 3% Hispanic/Latino; 3% Asian, non-Hispanic/Latino; 0.1% Native Hawaiian or other Pacific Islander, non-Hispanic/Latino; 0.6% American Indian or Alaska Native, non-Hispanic/Latino; 3% Two or more races, non-Hispanic/Latino; 3% Race/ethnicity unknown; 4% international; 4% transferred in; 61% live on campus.

Freshmen

Admission: 1,797 applied, 1,101 admitted, 471 enrolled. ***Average high school GPA:*** 3.28. ***Test scores:*** SAT critical reading scores over 500: 60%; SAT math scores over 500: 60%; ACT scores over 18: 94%; SAT critical reading scores over 600: 20%; SAT math scores over 600: 16%; ACT scores over 24: 36%; SAT critical reading scores over 700: 2%; SAT math scores over 700: 1%; ACT scores over 30: 3%.

Retention: 79% of full-time freshmen returned.

FACULTY

Total: 216, 56% full-time, 66% with terminal degrees.

Student/faculty ratio: 12:1.

ACADEMICS

Calendar: semesters. *Degrees:* bachelor's, master's, and postbachelor's certificates.

Special study options: academic remediation for entering students, accelerated degree program, advanced placement credit, cooperative education, double majors, honors programs, independent study, internships, off-campus study, part-time degree program, services for LD students, student-designed majors, study abroad, summer session for credit. ***ROTC:*** Army (c), Air Force (c).

Unusual degree programs: engineering with North Carolina State University.

Computers: 140 computers/terminals are available on campus for general student use. Students can access the following: free student e-mail accounts, online (class) registration, laptop computers for full-time students. Campuswide network is available. 100% of college-owned or -

operated housing units are wired for high-speed Internet access. Wireless service is available via classrooms, computer centers, computer labs, dorm rooms, learning centers, libraries, student centers.

STUDENT LIFE

Housing options: on-campus residence required through sophomore year; women-only. Campus housing is university owned. Freshman campus housing is guaranteed.

Activities and organizations: drama/theater group, student-run newspaper, choral group, Student Government Association, Entertainment Association, Recreation Association, Class Organizations, choral groups.

Athletics Member NCAA. All Division III. ***Intercollegiate sports:*** basketball W, cross-country running W, lacrosse W, soccer W, softball W, tennis W, track and field W, volleyball W. ***Intramural sports:*** swimming and diving W(c).

Campus security: 24-hour emergency response devices and patrols, late-night transport/escort service, controlled dormitory access.

Student services: health clinic, personal/psychological counseling.

COSTS & FINANCIAL AID

Costs (2014–15) ***Comprehensive fee:*** $41,736 includes full-time tuition ($32,140), mandatory fees ($80), and room and board ($9516). Full-time tuition and fees vary according to course load. Part-time tuition: $795 per credit hour. Part-time tuition and fees vary according to course load. ***Required fees:*** $80 per year part-time. ***Room and board:*** Room and board charges vary according to board plan and housing facility. ***Waivers:*** employees or children of employees.

Financial Aid Of all full-time matriculated undergraduates who enrolled in 2013, 1,254 applied for aid, 1,131 were judged to have need, 168 had their need fully met. In 2013, 115 non-need-based awards were made. ***Average percent of need met:*** 72. ***Average financial aid package:*** $22,795. ***Average need-based loan:*** $4310. ***Average need-based gift aid:*** $18,741. ***Average non-need-based aid:*** $10,411. ***Average indebtedness upon graduation:*** $35,425.

APPLYING

Standardized Tests *Required:* SAT or ACT (for admission). *Required for some:* SAT Subject Tests (for admission). *Recommended:* SAT Subject Tests (for admission).

Options: electronic application, early admission, early decision, deferred entrance.

Application fee: $40.

Required: high school transcript, minimum 2.0 GPA, 2 letters of recommendation. ***Required for some:*** essay or personal statement, interview. ***Recommended:*** essay or personal statement.

Application deadlines: 2/15 (freshmen), 2/15 (transfers).

Early decision deadline: 10/15.

Notification: continuous (freshmen), continuous (transfers), 11/1 (early decision).

CONTACT

Shery Boyles, Director of Admissions, Meredith College, 3800 Hillsborough Street, Raleigh, NC 27807-5298. *Phone:* 919-760-8026. *Toll-free phone:* 800-MEREDITH. *Fax:* 919-760-2298. *E-mail:* admissions@meredith.edu.

Mid-Atlantic Christian University

Elizabeth City, North Carolina

http://www.macuniversity.edu/

- **Independent Christian** 4-year, founded 1948
- **Small-town** 19-acre campus with easy access to Norfolk
- **Endowment** $3.0 million
- **Coed** 196 undergraduate students, 74% full-time, 58% women, 42% men
- **Minimally difficult** entrance level, 38% of applicants were admitted

UNDERGRAD STUDENTS

145 full-time, 51 part-time. Students come from 20 states and territories; 3 other countries; 32% are from out of state; 27% Black or African American, non-Hispanic/Latino; 2% Hispanic/Latino; 2% Asian, non-Hispanic/Latino; 1% American Indian or Alaska Native, non-Hispanic/Latino; 1% Two or more races, non-Hispanic/Latino; 1% Race/ethnicity unknown; 11% transferred in; 60% live on campus.

Freshmen

Admission: 227 applied, 86 admitted, 48 enrolled. ***Average high school GPA:*** 3.07. ***Test scores:*** SAT critical reading scores over 500: 36%; SAT math scores over 500: 40%; ACT scores over 18: 78%; SAT critical reading scores over 600: 8%; SAT math scores over 600: 8%; ACT scores over 24: 26%; ACT scores over 30: 4%.

Retention: 57% of full-time freshmen returned.

FACULTY

Total: 31, 26% full-time, 55% with terminal degrees.

Student/faculty ratio: 12:1.

ACADEMICS

Calendar: semesters. *Degrees:* certificates, associate, and bachelor's.

Special study options: academic remediation for entering students, adult/continuing education programs, advanced placement credit, distance learning, double majors, internships, part-time degree program, summer session for credit. ***ROTC:*** Army (c).

Computers: 24 computers/terminals are available on campus for general student use. Students can access the following: free student e-mail accounts, online (class) grades, online (class) registration, online (class) schedules. Campuswide network is available. 100% of college-owned or -operated housing units are wired for high-speed Internet access. Wireless service is available via entire campus.

STUDENT LIFE

Housing options: on-campus residence required through senior year; men-only, women-only. Campus housing is university owned. Freshman campus housing is guaranteed.

Athletics Member USCAA. ***Intercollegiate sports:*** basketball M/W, golf M, soccer M, volleyball W. ***Intramural sports:*** basketball M/W, golf M/W, soccer M/W, softball M/W, table tennis M/W, tennis M/W, volleyball M/W.

Campus security: 24-hour emergency response devices, controlled dormitory access.

Student services: personal/psychological counseling.

COSTS & FINANCIAL AID

Costs (2015–16) ***Comprehensive fee:*** $21,640 includes full-time tuition ($13,440) and room and board ($8200). Full-time tuition and fees vary according to program. Part-time tuition: $420 per credit. Part-time tuition and fees vary according to program. ***Room and board:*** Room and board charges vary according to housing facility. ***Payment plan:*** deferred payment. ***Waivers:*** children of alumni, senior citizens, and employees or children of employees.

Financial Aid Of all full-time matriculated undergraduates who enrolled in 2013, 138 applied for aid, 132 were judged to have need, 5 had their need fully met. 11 Federal Work-Study jobs (averaging $674). In 2013, 6 non-need-based awards were made. ***Average percent of need met:*** 60. ***Average financial aid package:*** $12,224. ***Average need-based loan:*** $3973. ***Average need-based gift aid:*** $8832. ***Average non-need-based aid:*** $5074. ***Average indebtedness upon graduation:*** $33,980.

APPLYING

Standardized Tests *Required:* SAT or ACT (for admission).

Options: electronic application, early admission, deferred entrance.

Application fee: $50.

Required: essay or personal statement, high school transcript, minimum 2.0 GPA, 1 letter of recommendation, reference from church or character reference. ***Required for some:*** interview.

Application deadlines: 8/1 (freshmen), 8/1 (transfers).

Notification: continuous (freshmen), continuous (transfers).

CONTACT

Mr. Dan Smith, Mid-Atlantic Christian University, 715 North Poindexter Street, Elizabeth City, NC 27909-4054. *Phone:* 252-334-2058. *Toll-free phone:* 866-996-MACU. *Fax:* 252-334-2064. *E-mail:* dan.smith@macuniversity.edu.

Montreat College

Montreat, North Carolina

http://www.montreat.edu/

- **Independent** comprehensive, founded 1916, affiliated with Presbyterian Church (U.S.A.)
- **Small-town** 112-acre campus
- **Coed** 735 undergraduate students, 60% full-time, 54% women, 46% men
- **Moderately difficult** entrance level, 46% of applicants were admitted

UNDERGRAD STUDENTS

444 full-time, 291 part-time. 23% are from out of state; 21% Black or African American, non-Hispanic/Latino; 2% Hispanic/Latino; 2% Asian, non-Hispanic/Latino; 0.2% Native Hawaiian or other Pacific Islander, non-Hispanic/Latino; 2% American Indian or Alaska Native, non-Hispanic/Latino; 3% Two or more races, non-Hispanic/Latino; 7% Race/ethnicity unknown; 6% international; 6% transferred in; 80% live on campus.

Freshmen

Admission: 836 applied, 383 admitted, 109 enrolled. ***Average high school GPA:*** 3.09. ***Test scores:*** SAT critical reading scores over 500: 32%; SAT math scores over 500: 29%; ACT scores over 18: 45%; SAT critical reading scores over 600: 9%; SAT math scores over 600: 8%; ACT scores over 24: 14%; ACT scores over 30: 1%.

Retention: 61% of full-time freshmen returned.

FACULTY

Total: 110, 28% full-time, 45% with terminal degrees.

Student/faculty ratio: 12:1.

ACADEMICS

Calendar: semesters. *Degrees:* certificates, associate, bachelor's, and master's.

Special study options: accelerated degree program, adult/continuing education programs, advanced placement credit, cooperative education, distance learning, double majors, honors programs, independent study, internships, off-campus study, part-time degree program, services for LD students, student-designed majors, study abroad, summer session for credit.

Computers: Students can access the following: campus intranet, computer help desk, free student e-mail accounts, online (class) grades, online (class) schedules. Campuswide network is available. 100% of college-owned or -operated housing units are wired for high-speed Internet access. Wireless service is available via entire campus.

STUDENT LIFE

Housing options: on-campus residence required through sophomore year; men-only, women-only. Campus housing is university owned. Freshman campus housing is guaranteed.

Activities and organizations: drama/theater group, student-run newspaper, choral group.

Athletics Member NAIA. ***Intercollegiate sports:*** baseball M(s), basketball M(s)/W(s), cross-country running M(s)/W(s), golf M(s), soccer M(s)/W(s), softball W(s), tennis M(s)/W(s), track and field M(s)/W(s), volleyball W(s). ***Intramural sports:*** basketball M/W, football M, softball M/W, table tennis M/W, tennis M/W, ultimate Frisbee M/W, volleyball M/W.

Campus security: 24-hour emergency response devices and patrols, controlled dormitory access.

Student services: health clinic, personal/psychological counseling.

COSTS & FINANCIAL AID

Costs (2015–16) ***Comprehensive fee:*** $32,506 includes full-time tuition ($24,040), mandatory fees ($200), and room and board ($8266). Full-time tuition and fees vary according to course load and degree level. Part-time tuition and fees vary according to course load and degree level. ***College room only:*** $4096. Room and board charges vary according to board plan and housing facility. ***Payment plan:*** installment. ***Waivers:*** adult students and employees or children of employees.

Financial Aid Of all full-time matriculated undergraduates who enrolled in 2013, 401 applied for aid, 332 were judged to have need, 175 had their need fully met. In 2013, 26 non-need-based awards were made. ***Average percent of need met:*** 78. ***Average financial aid package:*** $21,854. ***Average need-based loan:*** $4643. ***Average need-based gift aid:*** $21,414. ***Average non-need-based aid:*** $10,261. ***Average indebtedness upon graduation:*** $27,843.

APPLYING

Standardized Tests *Required:* SAT or ACT (for admission).

Options: early admission, deferred entrance.

Required: essay or personal statement, high school transcript, minimum 2.8 GPA. ***Required for some:*** 1 letter of recommendation, interview.

CONTACT

Miss Mandi Pike, Senior Admissions Specialist, Montreat College, PO Box 1267, Montreat, NC 28757. *Phone:* 828-669-8012 Ext. 3789. *Toll-free phone:* 800-622-6968. *Fax:* 828-669-0120. *E-mail:* admissions@montreat.edu.

North Carolina Agricultural and Technical State University

Greensboro, North Carolina

http://www.ncat.edu/

- **State-supported** university, founded 1891, part of University of North Carolina System
- **Suburban** 200-acre campus with easy access to Charlotte
- **Endowment** $39.6 million
- **Coed** 9,203 undergraduate students, 92% full-time, 55% women, 45% men
- **Moderately difficult** entrance level, 58% of applicants were admitted

UNDERGRAD STUDENTS

8,423 full-time, 780 part-time. Students come from 39 states and territories; 43 other countries; 20% are from out of state; 80% Black or African American, non-Hispanic/Latino; 2% Hispanic/Latino; 0.7% Asian, non-Hispanic/Latino; 0.3% American Indian or Alaska Native, non-Hispanic/Latino; 3% Two or more races, non-Hispanic/Latino; 7% Race/ethnicity unknown; 2% international; 7% transferred in; 41% live on campus.

Freshmen

Admission: 7,491 applied, 4,314 admitted, 1,722 enrolled. ***Average high school GPA:*** 2.48. ***Test scores:*** SAT critical reading scores over 500: 24%; SAT math scores over 500: 29%; SAT writing scores over 500: 18%; ACT scores over 18: 61%; SAT critical reading scores over 600: 3%; SAT math scores over 600: 3%; SAT writing scores over 600: 2%; ACT scores over 24: 9%.

Retention: 79% of full-time freshmen returned.

FACULTY

Total: 710, 73% full-time, 67% with terminal degrees.

Student/faculty ratio: 16:1.

ACADEMICS

Calendar: semesters. *Degrees:* bachelor's, master's, and doctoral.

Special study options: academic remediation for entering students, accelerated degree program, adult/continuing education programs, advanced placement credit, cooperative education, distance learning, double majors, honors programs, internships, off-campus study, part-time degree program, study abroad, summer session for credit. ***ROTC:*** Army (b), Air Force (b).

Computers: Students can access the following: computer help desk, free student e-mail accounts, online (class) grades, online (class) registration, online (class) schedules. Campuswide network is available.

STUDENT LIFE

Housing options: coed, men-only, women-only. Campus housing is university owned and is provided by a third party. Freshman applicants given priority for college housing.

Activities and organizations: drama/theater group, student-run newspaper, radio and television station, choral group, marching band, student government, national fraternities, national sororities.

Athletics Member NCAA. All Division I. ***Intercollegiate sports:*** baseball M(s), basketball M(s)/W(s), bowling W(s), cross-country running M(s)/W(s), football M(s), softball W(s), swimming and diving W(s), tennis W(s), track and field M(s)/W(s), volleyball W(s). ***Intramural sports:*** baseball M, basketball M/W, football M, golf M/W, soccer M/W, volleyball M/W.

Campus security: 24-hour emergency response devices and patrols, late-night transport/escort service, controlled dormitory access.

Student services: health clinic, personal/psychological counseling.

COSTS & FINANCIAL AID
Costs (2015–16) ***Tuition:*** state resident $3270 full-time; nonresident $16,030 full-time. Full-time tuition and fees vary according to course load, degree level, and program. Part-time tuition and fees vary according to course load, degree level, and program. ***Required fees:*** $2265 full-time. ***Room and board:*** $6755; room only: $6755. Room and board charges vary according to board plan and housing facility.

Financial Aid Of all full-time matriculated undergraduates who enrolled in 2013, 7,723 applied for aid, 7,035 were judged to have need, 455 had their need fully met. 300 Federal Work-Study jobs (averaging $1857). In 2013, 161 non-need-based awards were made. ***Average percent of need met:*** 63. ***Average financial aid package:*** $10,846. ***Average need-based loan:*** $4111. ***Average need-based gift aid:*** $7051. ***Average non-need-based aid:*** $6967. ***Average indebtedness upon graduation:*** $28,970.

APPLYING
Standardized Tests *Required:* SAT or ACT (for admission).

Options: early admission, deferred entrance.

Application fee: $55.

Required: high school transcript, minimum 2.0 GPA.

Application deadlines: rolling (freshmen), rolling (out-of-state freshmen), rolling (transfers).

Notification: continuous (freshmen), continuous (out-of-state freshmen), continuous (transfers).

CONTACT
Ms. Cheryl Pollard-Burns, Director of Admissions, North Carolina Agricultural and Technical State University, North Carolina Agricultural & Technical State University (Webb Hall), 1601 East Market Street, Greensboro, NC 27411. *Phone:* 336-334-7946. *Toll-free phone:* 800-443-8964. *Fax:* 336-334-7478. *E-mail:* uadmit@ncat.edu.

North Carolina Central University

Durham, North Carolina

http://www.nccu.edu/

- **State-supported** comprehensive, founded 1910, part of University of North Carolina System
- **Urban** 115-acre campus with easy access to Raleigh
- **Endowment** $22.9 million
- **Coed** 5,917 undergraduate students, 85% full-time, 66% women, 34% men
- **Minimally difficult** entrance level, 43% of applicants were admitted

UNDERGRAD STUDENTS
5,035 full-time, 882 part-time. Students come from 37 states and territories; 19 other countries; 9% are from out of state; 83% Black or African American, non-Hispanic/Latino; 3% Hispanic/Latino; 1% Asian, non-Hispanic/Latino; 0.4% American Indian or Alaska Native, non-Hispanic/Latino; 4% Two or more races, non-Hispanic/Latino; 3% Race/ethnicity unknown; 0.4% international; 8% transferred in; 40% live on campus.

Freshmen
Admission: 11,246 applied, 4,860 admitted, 925 enrolled. ***Average high school GPA:*** 3.2. ***Test scores:*** SAT critical reading scores over 500: 17%; SAT math scores over 500: 19%; SAT writing scores over 500: 12%; ACT scores over 18: 50%; SAT critical reading scores over 600: 3%; SAT math scores over 600: 3%; SAT writing scores over 600: 2%; ACT scores over 24: 6%.

Retention: 77% of full-time freshmen returned.

FACULTY
Total: 557, 72% full-time, 63% with terminal degrees.

Student/faculty ratio: 15:1.

ACADEMICS
Calendar: semesters. *Degrees:* bachelor's, master's, and doctoral.

Special study options: academic remediation for entering students, accelerated degree program, adult/continuing education programs, advanced placement credit, cooperative education, distance learning, double majors, English as a second language, external degree program, honors programs, independent study, internships, off-campus study, part-time degree program, services for LD students, study abroad, summer session for credit. ***ROTC:*** Army (b), Air Force (b).

Computers: 1,262 computers/terminals and 3,700 ports are available on campus for general student use. Students can access the following: campus intranet, computer help desk, free student e-mail accounts, online (class) grades, online (class) registration, online (class) schedules. Campuswide network is available. 100% of college-owned or -operated housing units are wired for high-speed Internet access. Wireless service is available via entire campus.

STUDENT LIFE
Housing options: coed. Campus housing is university owned and leased by the school. Freshman applicants given priority for college housing.

Activities and organizations: drama/theater group, student-run newspaper, choral group, marching band, national fraternities, national sororities.

Athletics Member NCAA, NAIA. All NCAA Division I. ***Intercollegiate sports:*** baseball M(s), basketball M(s)/W(s), bowling W(s), cross-country running M(s)/W(s), football M(s), golf M(s), softball W(s), tennis M(s)/W(s), track and field M(s)/W(s), volleyball W(s). ***Intramural sports:*** basketball M/W, football M, golf M, soccer M, volleyball W.

Campus security: 24-hour emergency response devices and patrols, student patrols, late-night transport/escort service, controlled dormitory access.

Student services: health clinic, personal/psychological counseling, women's center.

COSTS & FINANCIAL AID
Costs (2014–15) ***Tuition:*** state resident $3455 full-time; nonresident $14,870 full-time. Part-time tuition and fees vary according to course load. ***Required fees:*** $2070 full-time. ***Room and board:*** $8165; room only: $4663. Room and board charges vary according to board plan, housing facility, and location. ***Payment plan:*** installment. ***Waivers:*** employees or children of employees.

Financial Aid Of all full-time matriculated undergraduates who enrolled in 2013, 4,841 applied for aid, 4,538 were judged to have need, 230 had their need fully met. In 2013, 56 non-need-based awards were made. ***Average percent of need met:*** 59. ***Average financial aid package:*** $11,764. ***Average need-based loan:*** $4132. ***Average need-based gift aid:*** $7727. ***Average non-need-based aid:*** $12,299.

APPLYING
Standardized Tests *Required:* SAT or ACT (for admission).

Options: electronic application, deferred entrance.

Application fee: $40.

Required: high school transcript, minimum 2.5 GPA, University of North Carolina System minimum course requirements.

Application deadlines: 8/1 (freshmen), 8/1 (transfers).

Notification: continuous until 10/15 (freshmen), continuous until 10/15 (transfers).

CONTACT
Mr. Anthony Brooks, Undergraduate Director of Admissions, North Carolina Central University, 1801 Fayetteville Street, McDougald House, Durham, NC 27707. *Phone:* 919-530-6298. *Toll-free phone:* 877-667-7533. *Fax:* 919-530-6326. *E-mail:* admissions@nccu.edu.

North Carolina State University

Raleigh, North Carolina

http://www.ncsu.edu/

- **State-supported** university, founded 1887, part of University of North Carolina System
- **Urban** 2090-acre campus with easy access to Raleigh-Durham
- **Endowment** $885.1 million
- **Coed** 24,473 undergraduate students, 87% full-time, 44% women, 56% men
- **Very difficult** entrance level, 51% of applicants were admitted

UNDERGRAD STUDENTS
21,402 full-time, 3,071 part-time. Students come from 52 states and territories; 117 other countries; 10% are from out of state; 7% Black or

African American, non-Hispanic/Latino; 4% Hispanic/Latino; 6% Asian, non-Hispanic/Latino; 0.1% Native Hawaiian or other Pacific Islander, non-Hispanic/Latino; 0.4% American Indian or Alaska Native, non-Hispanic/Latino; 3% Two or more races, non-Hispanic/Latino; 3% Race/ethnicity unknown; 3% international; 5% transferred in; 34% live on campus.

Freshmen

Admission: 20,208 applied, 10,390 admitted, 4,499 enrolled. ***Average high school GPA:*** 3.63. ***Test scores:*** SAT critical reading scores over 500: 96%; SAT math scores over 500: 98%; SAT writing scores over 500: 90%; ACT scores over 18: 100%; SAT critical reading scores over 600: 55%; SAT math scores over 600: 76%; SAT writing scores over 600: 44%; ACT scores over 24: 96%; SAT critical reading scores over 700: 10%; SAT math scores over 700: 21%; SAT writing scores over 700: 6%; ACT scores over 30: 36%.

Retention: 93% of full-time freshmen returned.

FACULTY

Total: 1,819, 82% full-time, 85% with terminal degrees.

Student/faculty ratio: 20:1.

ACADEMICS

Calendar: semesters. *Degrees:* certificates, associate, bachelor's, master's, doctoral, post-master's, and postbachelor's certificates.

Special study options: academic remediation for entering students, accelerated degree program, adult/continuing education programs, advanced placement credit, cooperative education, distance learning, double majors, English as a second language, honors programs, independent study, internships, off-campus study, part-time degree program, services for LD students, student-designed majors, study abroad, summer session for credit. ***ROTC:*** Army (b), Navy (b), Air Force (b).

Unusual degree programs: business administration; engineering; Agriculture, Life Sciences, Physical Sciences, Communication, Computer Science, Economics, Foreign Languages, History, Mathematics, Education, Statistics, Textiles.

Computers: 3,024 computers/terminals are available on campus for general student use. Students can access the following: campus intranet, computer help desk, free student e-mail accounts, online (class) grades, online (class) registration, online (class) schedules, course materials, online homework submission, online testing/quizzes, financial aid/cashier's office account balances, wiki space, blogging service, Web space, online storage space, on-site OS and virus removal, online/hybrid courses. Campuswide network is available. 100% of college-owned or -operated housing units are wired for high-speed Internet access. Wireless service is available via classrooms, computer centers, computer labs, dorm rooms, learning centers, libraries, student centers.

STUDENT LIFE

Housing options: coed, men-only, women-only, special housing for students with disabilities. Campus housing is university owned. Freshman applicants given priority for college housing.

Activities and organizations: drama/theater group, student-run newspaper, radio and television station, choral group, marching band, Club Sports, Pre-professional organizations, Honor Society, Cultural Organizations, Faith-based Organizations, national fraternities, national sororities.

Athletics Member NCAA. All Division I. ***Intercollegiate sports:*** baseball M(s), basketball M(s)/W(s), bowling M(c)/W(c), cheerleading M(s)/W(s), crew M(c)/W(c), cross-country running M(s)/W(s), equestrian sports M(c)/W(c), fencing M(c)/W(c), field hockey M(c)/W(c), football M(s), golf M(s)/W(s), gymnastics M(c)/W(s), ice hockey M(c), lacrosse M(c)/W(c), racquetball M(c)/W(c), riflery M(s)/W(s), rugby M(c)/W(c), sailing M(c)/W(c), skiing (downhill) M(c)/W(c), soccer M(s)/W(s), softball W(s), swimming and diving M(s)/W(s), table tennis M(c)/W(c), tennis M(s)/W(s), track and field M(s)/W(s), ultimate Frisbee M(c)/W(c), volleyball M(c)/W(s), water polo M(c)/W(c), wrestling M(s). ***Intramural sports:*** badminton M/W, basketball M/W, bowling M/W, football M/W, golf M/W, racquetball M/W, soccer M/W, softball M/W, swimming and diving M/W, table tennis M/W, tennis M/W, track and field M/W, ultimate Frisbee M/W, volleyball M/W.

Campus security: 24-hour emergency response devices and patrols, student patrols, late-night transport/escort service, controlled dormitory access.

Student services: health clinic, personal/psychological counseling, women's center, legal services.

COSTS & FINANCIAL AID

Costs (2014–15) ***Tuition:*** state resident $6038 full-time; nonresident $21,293 full-time. Full-time tuition and fees vary according to degree level, location, program, and reciprocity agreements. Part-time tuition and fees vary according to course load, degree level, location, program, and reciprocity agreements. ***Required fees:*** $2258 full-time. ***Room and board:*** $10,030; room only: $6244. Room and board charges vary according to board plan and housing facility. ***Payment plan:*** installment. ***Waivers:*** employees or children of employees.

Financial Aid Of all full-time matriculated undergraduates who enrolled in 2014, 14,123 applied for aid, 10,656 were judged to have need, 2,426 had their need fully met. In 2014, 897 non-need-based awards were made. ***Average percent of need met:*** 78. ***Average financial aid package:*** $13,174. ***Average need-based loan:*** $4089. ***Average need-based gift aid:*** $10,015. ***Average non-need-based aid:*** $6531. ***Average indebtedness upon graduation:*** $20,482.

APPLYING

Standardized Tests *Required:* SAT or ACT (for admission). *Recommended:* SAT Subject Tests (for admission).

Options: electronic application, early action, deferred entrance.

Application fee: $75.

Required: high school transcript. ***Required for some:*** interview. ***Recommended:*** essay or personal statement.

Application deadlines: 1/15 (freshmen), 4/1 (transfers).

Notification: continuous (freshmen), continuous (transfers).

CONTACT

Mr. Thomas Griffin, Director of Undergraduate Admissions, North Carolina State University, Box 7103, Raleigh, NC 27695. *Phone:* 919-515-2434. *Fax:* 919-515-5039. *E-mail:* undergrad_admissions@ncsu.edu.

North Carolina Wesleyan College

Rocky Mount, North Carolina

http://www.ncwc.edu/

- **Independent** 4-year, founded 1956, affiliated with United Methodist Church
- **Suburban** 200-acre campus
- **Endowment** $10.8 million
- **Coed** 1,872 undergraduate students, 82% full-time, 58% women, 42% men
- **Moderately difficult** entrance level, 53% of applicants were admitted

UNDERGRAD STUDENTS

1,530 full-time, 342 part-time. Students come from 23 states and territories; 26 other countries; 13% are from out of state; 48% Black or African American, non-Hispanic/Latino; 2% Hispanic/Latino; 0.6% Asian, non-Hispanic/Latino; 1% American Indian or Alaska Native, non-Hispanic/Latino; 2% Two or more races, non-Hispanic/Latino; 13% Race/ethnicity unknown; 4% international; 2% transferred in; 32% live on campus.

Freshmen

Admission: 2,683 applied, 1,429 admitted, 314 enrolled. ***Average high school GPA:*** 3.12. ***Test scores:*** SAT critical reading scores over 500: 33%; SAT math scores over 500: 30%; ACT scores over 18: 42%; SAT critical reading scores over 600: 9%; SAT math scores over 600: 8%; ACT scores over 24: 10%; SAT critical reading scores over 700: 4%; SAT math scores over 700: 2%; ACT scores over 30: 1%.

Retention: 57% of full-time freshmen returned.

FACULTY

Total: 270, 20% full-time.

Student/faculty ratio: 13:1.

ACADEMICS

Calendar: semesters. *Degrees:* bachelor's (also offers adult part-time degree program with significant enrollment not reflected in profile).

Special study options: academic remediation for entering students, accelerated degree program, adult/continuing education programs,

advanced placement credit, cooperative education, distance learning, double majors, honors programs, independent study, internships, part-time degree program, services for LD students, summer session for credit. ***ROTC:*** Army (c).

Computers: 223 computers/terminals are available on campus for general student use. Students can access the following: campus intranet, computer help desk, free student e-mail accounts, online (class) grades, online (class) schedules. Campuswide network is available.

STUDENT LIFE
Housing options: on-campus residence required through sophomore year; coed, men-only, women-only, special housing for students with disabilities. Campus housing is university owned and leased by the school. Freshman campus housing is guaranteed.

Activities and organizations: drama/theater group, student-run newspaper, choral group, marching band, Refuge Campus Ministry, NCWC Cheerleaders, Voices of Triumph, Campus Crusade for Christ, Visions of Beauty, national fraternities, national sororities.

Athletics Member NCAA. All Division III. ***Intercollegiate sports:*** baseball M, basketball M/W, cross-country running W, football M, golf M, soccer M/W, softball W, tennis M/W, volleyball W. ***Intramural sports:*** basketball M/W, football M/W, lacrosse M/W, softball M/W, table tennis M/W, tennis M/W, volleyball M/W.

Campus security: 24-hour emergency response devices and patrols, late-night transport/escort service, controlled dormitory access.

Student services: health clinic, personal/psychological counseling.

COSTS & FINANCIAL AID
Costs (2015–16) ***Comprehensive fee:*** $37,674 includes full-time tuition ($28,000), mandatory fees ($150), and room and board ($9524). Full-time tuition and fees vary according to location. Part-time tuition: $425 per semester hour. Part-time tuition and fees vary according to course load and location. ***College room only:*** $4400. Room and board charges vary according to housing facility. ***Payment plan:*** installment. ***Waivers:*** employees or children of employees.

Financial Aid Of all full-time matriculated undergraduates who enrolled in 2008, 956 applied for aid, 788 were judged to have need, 360 had their need fully met. 323 Federal Work-Study jobs (averaging $1438). 67 state and other part-time jobs (averaging $565). In 2008, 46 non-need-based awards were made. ***Average percent of need met:*** 70. ***Average financial aid package:*** $12,524. ***Average need-based loan:*** $3898. ***Average need-based gift aid:*** $6696. ***Average non-need-based aid:*** $7876. ***Average indebtedness upon graduation:*** $7269.

APPLYING
Standardized Tests *Required:* SAT or ACT (for admission).

Options: electronic application.

Required: high school transcript. ***Required for some:*** essay or personal statement, interview. ***Recommended:*** minimum 2.0 GPA, 2 letters of recommendation, interview.

Application deadlines: rolling (freshmen), 7/15 (transfers).

Notification: continuous (freshmen), continuous (transfers).

CONTACT
Mr. Ben Lilley, Assistant Director of Admissions, North Carolina Wesleyan College, 3400 North Wesleyan Boulevard, Rocky Mount, NC 27804. *Phone:* 252-985-5113. *Toll-free phone:* 800-488-6292. *Fax:* 252-985-5295. *E-mail:* blilley@ncwc.edu.

Piedmont International University

Winston-Salem, North Carolina

http://www.piedmontu.edu/

- **Independent Baptist** comprehensive, founded 1947
- **Urban** 12-acre campus
- **Coed**
- **Noncompetitive** entrance level

FACULTY
Student/faculty ratio: 10:1.

ACADEMICS
Calendar: semesters. *Degrees:* certificates, associate, bachelor's, master's, and doctoral.

STUDENT LIFE
Housing options: on-campus residence required through sophomore year; men-only, women-only. Campus housing is university owned.

Activities and organizations: drama/theater group, choral group.

Athletics Member NCCAA.

Campus security: 24-hour emergency response devices, student patrols, late-night transport/escort service, controlled dormitory access, security guards on duty from dusk until dawn.

COSTS & FINANCIAL AID
Costs (2014–15) ***Comprehensive fee:*** $16,122 includes full-time tuition ($8850), mandatory fees ($730), and room and board ($6542). Part-time tuition: $295 per credit. Part-time tuition and fees vary according to course load. ***Required fees:*** $55 per course part-time, $90 per term part-time. ***Room and board:*** Room and board charges vary according to board plan.

Financial Aid Of all full-time matriculated undergraduates who enrolled in 2012, 149 applied for aid, 147 were judged to have need, 9 had their need fully met. 4 Federal Work-Study jobs (averaging $3400). In 2012, 6 non-need-based awards were made. ***Average percent of need met:*** 79. ***Average financial aid package:*** $8496. ***Average need-based loan:*** $3772. ***Average need-based gift aid:*** $5051. ***Average non-need-based aid:*** $5305. ***Average indebtedness upon graduation:*** $17,929.

APPLYING
Standardized Tests *Required:* SAT or ACT (for admission).

Options: electronic application.

Application fee: $55.

Required: essay or personal statement, high school transcript, 2 letters of recommendation, standardized test scores, medical history, proof of immunization. ***Recommended:*** minimum 2.0 GPA, interview.

CONTACT
Mr. Joe Edgerton, Undergraduate Admissions Counselor, Piedmont International University, 420 South Broad Street, Winston-Salem, NC 27101. *Phone:* 336-714-7933. *Toll-free phone:* 800-937-5097. *Fax:* 336-725-5522. *E-mail:* stevensons@piedmontU.edu.

St. Andrews University

Laurinburg, North Carolina

http://www.sapc.edu/

- **Independent Presbyterian** comprehensive, founded 1958
- **Small-town** 600-acre campus
- **Coed** 617 undergraduate students, 92% full-time, 54% women, 46% men
- **Moderately difficult** entrance level, 57% of applicants were admitted

UNDERGRAD STUDENTS
568 full-time, 49 part-time. 59% are from out of state; 12% Black or African American, non-Hispanic/Latino; 2% Two or more races, non-Hispanic/Latino; 14% Race/ethnicity unknown; 12% international; 11% transferred in; 85% live on campus.

Freshmen
Admission: 926 applied, 529 admitted, 153 enrolled. ***Average high school GPA:*** 3.2. ***Test scores:*** SAT critical reading scores over 500: 32%; SAT math scores over 500: 35%; SAT critical reading scores over 600: 10%; SAT math scores over 600: 4%; SAT critical reading scores over 700: 2%; SAT math scores over 700: 1%.

Retention: 59% of full-time freshmen returned.

FACULTY
Total: 57, 53% full-time, 51% with terminal degrees.

Student/faculty ratio: 15:1.

ACADEMICS
Calendar: semesters. *Degrees:* diplomas, bachelor's, and master's.

Special study options: adult/continuing education programs, part-time degree program.

Unusual degree programs: 3-2 engineering with North Carolina State University and St. Andrews University.

Computers: Students can access the following: campus intranet, computer help desk, free student e-mail accounts. Campuswide network is available. Wireless service is available via classrooms, libraries, student centers.

STUDENT LIFE

Housing options: on-campus residence required through senior year; coed, men-only, women-only. Campus housing is university owned.

Athletics Member NCAA, NAIA. All NCAA Division II. ***Intercollegiate sports:*** baseball M(s), basketball M(s)/W(s), cross-country running M(s)/W(s), equestrian sports M(s)/W(s), golf M(s)/W(s), lacrosse M(s)/W(s), soccer M(s)/W(s), softball W(s), wrestling M. ***Intramural sports:*** basketball M/W, football M/W, rugby M(c)/W(c), softball M/W, table tennis M/W, volleyball M/W.

Campus security: 24-hour emergency response devices and patrols, late-night transport/escort service.

COSTS & FINANCIAL AID

Costs (2015–16) ***Comprehensive fee:*** $33,580 includes full-time tuition ($23,682) and room and board ($9898). Full-time tuition and fees vary according to course load and location. Part-time tuition: $274 per credit hour. Part-time tuition and fees vary according to location. ***Room and board:*** Room and board charges vary according to housing facility. ***Payment plan:*** installment. ***Waivers:*** adult students, senior citizens, and employees or children of employees.

Financial Aid Of all full-time matriculated undergraduates who enrolled in 2014, 456 applied for aid, 415 were judged to have need, 39 had their need fully met. 61 Federal Work-Study jobs (averaging $1800). 40 state and other part-time jobs (averaging $1200). In 2014, 100 non-need-based awards were made. ***Average percent of need met:*** 68. ***Average financial aid package:*** $20,896. ***Average need-based loan:*** $4645. ***Average need-based gift aid:*** $17,209. ***Average non-need-based aid:*** $9290. ***Average indebtedness upon graduation:*** $27,760.

APPLYING

Options: electronic application, deferred entrance.

Application fee: $35.

Required: high school transcript. ***Required for some:*** essay or personal statement, interview. ***Recommended:*** minimum 2.0 GPA.

CONTACT

Erin Balduf, Director of Admissions, St. Andrews University, 1700 Dogwood Mile, Laurinburg, NC 28352. *Phone:* 910-277-5555. *Toll-free phone:* 800-763-0198. *Fax:* 910-277-5087. *E-mail:* admission@sapc.edu.

Saint Augustine's University

Raleigh, North Carolina

http://www.st-aug.edu/

- **Independent Episcopal** 4-year, founded 1867
- **Urban** 122-acre campus
- **Endowment** $16.3 million
- **Coed** 1,016 undergraduate students, 99% full-time, 49% women, 51% men
- **Moderately difficult** entrance level, 12% of applicants were admitted

UNDERGRAD STUDENTS

1,002 full-time, 14 part-time. Students come from 36 states and territories; 8 other countries; 44% are from out of state; 95% Black or African American, non-Hispanic/Latino; 0.8% Hispanic/Latino; 0.1% Asian, non-Hispanic/Latino; 0.3% American Indian or Alaska Native, non-Hispanic/Latino; 0.6% Race/ethnicity unknown; 2% international; 3% transferred in; 75% live on campus.

Freshmen

Admission: 2,233 applied, 268 admitted, 268 enrolled. ***Average high school GPA:*** 2.42.

Retention: 41% of full-time freshmen returned.

FACULTY

Total: 100, 70% full-time, 42% with terminal degrees.

Student/faculty ratio: 13:1.

ACADEMICS

Calendar: semesters. *Degree:* bachelor's.

Special study options: accelerated degree program, adult/continuing education programs, advanced placement credit, cooperative education, double majors, freshman honors college, honors programs, independent study, internships, off-campus study, part-time degree program, services for LD students, study abroad, summer session for credit. ***ROTC:*** Army (b), Air Force (c).

Computers: 183 computers/terminals and 1,670 ports are available on campus for general student use. Students can access the following: campus intranet, computer help desk, free student e-mail accounts, online (class) grades, online (class) registration, online (class) schedules. Campuswide network is available. 100% of college-owned or -operated housing units are wired for high-speed Internet access. Wireless service is available via entire campus.

STUDENT LIFE

Housing options: on-campus residence required through sophomore year; men-only, women-only. Campus housing is university owned and leased by the school. Freshman campus housing is guaranteed.

Activities and organizations: drama/theater group, student-run newspaper, radio and television station, choral group, marching band, Campus Activity Board, Christian Fellowship Organization, Collegiate 100 Black Men of America, Student Government Association/Student Leaders, Falcon Fanatic Pep Squad, national fraternities, national sororities.

Athletics Member NCAA. All Division II. ***Intercollegiate sports:*** baseball M(s), basketball M(s)/W(s), bowling W(s), cheerleading W(s), cross-country running M(s)/W(s), football M(s), golf M(s), softball W(s), track and field M(s)/W(s), volleyball W(s).

Campus security: 24-hour emergency response devices and patrols, RAVE - Emergency Notification System.

Student services: health clinic, personal/psychological counseling, women's center.

COSTS & FINANCIAL AID

Costs (2015–16) ***Tuition:*** $537 per credit hour part-time. Full-time tuition and fees vary according to course load. Part-time tuition and fees vary according to course load. ***Required fees:*** $208 per credit hour part-time. ***Room only:*** Room and board charges vary according to housing facility. ***Payment plan:*** deferred payment. ***Waivers:*** employees or children of employees.

Financial Aid Of all full-time matriculated undergraduates who enrolled in 2014, 906 applied for aid, 831 were judged to have need, 429 had their need fully met. In 2014, 7 non-need-based awards were made. ***Average percent of need met:*** 80. ***Average financial aid package:*** $5134. ***Average need-based loan:*** $5682. ***Average need-based gift aid:*** $5190. ***Average non-need-based aid:*** $5528. ***Average indebtedness upon graduation:*** $19,500.

APPLYING

Standardized Tests *Required:* SAT or ACT (for admission).

Options: electronic application, deferred entrance.

Application fee: $50.

Required: high school transcript, minimum 2.0 GPA, 2 letters of recommendation, medical history, social security card, background check. ***Required for some:*** essay or personal statement, interview. ***Recommended:*** minimum 2.5 GPA.

Application deadlines: rolling (freshmen), rolling (out-of-state freshmen), rolling (transfers).

Notification: continuous (freshmen), continuous (out-of-state freshmen), continuous (transfers).

CONTACT

Mr. Jorge E. Sousa, Dean of Enrollment, Saint Augustine's University, 1315 Oakwood Avenue, Raleigh, NC 27610-2298. *Phone:* 919-516-4012. *Toll-free phone:* 800-948-1126. *Fax:* 919-516-5804. *E-mail:* jesousa@st-aug.edu.

Salem College

Winston-Salem, North Carolina

http://www.salem.edu/

- **Independent Moravian** comprehensive, founded 1772
- **Urban** 57-acre campus with easy access to Charlotte
- **Coed, primarily women** 945 undergraduate students, 82% full-time, 96% women, 4% men
- **Moderately difficult** entrance level, 60% of applicants were admitted

UNDERGRAD STUDENTS
773 full-time, 172 part-time. Students come from 33 states and territories; 10 other countries; 27% are from out of state; 24% Black or African American, non-Hispanic/Latino; 12% Hispanic/Latino; 3% Asian, non-Hispanic/Latino; 0.4% American Indian or Alaska Native, non-Hispanic/Latino; 3% Two or more races, non-Hispanic/Latino; 4% Race/ethnicity unknown; 1% international; 7% transferred in; 86% live on campus.

Freshmen
Admission: 929 applied, 556 admitted, 202 enrolled.

Retention: 75% of full-time freshmen returned.

ACADEMICS
Calendar: 4-1-4. *Degrees:* certificates, bachelor's, and master's (only students age 23 or over are eligible to enroll part-time).

Special study options: adult/continuing education programs, advanced placement credit, double majors, honors programs, independent study, internships, off-campus study, part-time degree program, student-designed majors, summer session for credit. ***ROTC:*** Army (c), Air Force (c).

Computers: 54 computers/terminals are available on campus for general student use. Students can access the following: campus intranet, computer help desk, free student e-mail accounts, online (class) grades, online (class) schedules. Campuswide network is available. 100% of college-owned or -operated housing units are wired for high-speed Internet access. Wireless service is available via entire campus.

STUDENT LIFE
Housing options: on-campus residence required through senior year; women-only. Campus housing is university owned.

Activities and organizations: drama/theater group, student-run newspaper, choral group, marching band.

Athletics Member NCAA. All Division III. ***Intercollegiate sports:*** basketball W, cross-country running W, field hockey W, soccer W, swimming and diving W, tennis W, volleyball W.

Campus security: 24-hour emergency response devices and patrols, late-night transport/escort service, controlled dormitory access.

Student services: health clinic, personal/psychological counseling.

COSTS & FINANCIAL AID
Costs (2014–15) ***Comprehensive fee:*** $37,120 includes full-time tuition ($24,990), mandatory fees ($366), and room and board ($11,764). Part-time tuition: $1440 per course. ***Required fees:*** $150 per year part-time. ***Room and board:*** Room and board charges vary according to housing facility. ***Payment plan:*** installment.

Financial Aid Of all full-time matriculated undergraduates who enrolled in 2010, 476 applied for aid, 438 were judged to have need, 438 had their need fully met. 98 Federal Work-Study jobs (averaging $1009). In 2010, 38 non-need-based awards were made. ***Average percent of need met:*** 100. ***Average financial aid package:*** $18,755. ***Average need-based loan:*** $4406. ***Average need-based gift aid:*** $8440. ***Average non-need-based aid:*** $13,316. ***Average indebtedness upon graduation:*** $19,000.

APPLYING
Standardized Tests *Required:* SAT or ACT (for admission).

Options: electronic application, early admission, deferred entrance.

Application fee: $30.

Required: essay or personal statement, high school transcript. ***Recommended:*** interview.

Application deadlines: rolling (freshmen), rolling (transfers).

Notification: continuous (freshmen), continuous (transfers).

CONTACT
Dean Katherine Knapp Watts, Dean of Admissions and Financial Aid, Salem College, Single Sisters House, 601 South Church Street, Winston-Salem, NC 27101. *Phone:* 336-721-2621. *Toll-free phone:* 800-327-2536. *Fax:* 336-917-5572. *E-mail:* admissions@salem.edu.

Shaw University
Raleigh, North Carolina
http://www.shawu.edu/

- **Independent Baptist** comprehensive, founded 1865
- **Urban** 30-acre campus
- **Coed** 1,664 undergraduate students, 91% full-time, 57% women, 43% men
- **Minimally difficult** entrance level, 59% of applicants were admitted

UNDERGRAD STUDENTS
1,519 full-time, 145 part-time. Students come from 28 states and territories; 18 other countries; 28% are from out of state; 71% Black or African American, non-Hispanic/Latino; 0.2% Hispanic/Latino; 0.2% Asian, non-Hispanic/Latino; 0.4% Native Hawaiian or other Pacific Islander, non-Hispanic/Latino; 0.2% American Indian or Alaska Native, non-Hispanic/Latino; 0.5% Two or more races, non-Hispanic/Latino; 24% Race/ethnicity unknown; 2% international; 6% transferred in; 47% live on campus.

Freshmen
Admission: 5,766 applied, 3,422 admitted, 469 enrolled. ***Average high school GPA:*** 2.42.

Retention: 42% of full-time freshmen returned.

FACULTY
Total: 153, 63% full-time, 61% with terminal degrees.

Student/faculty ratio: 15:1.

ACADEMICS
Calendar: semesters. *Degrees:* certificates, bachelor's, and master's.

Special study options: academic remediation for entering students, accelerated degree program, adult/continuing education programs, advanced placement credit, distance learning, double majors, honors programs, independent study, internships, off-campus study, part-time degree program, services for LD students, student-designed majors, study abroad, summer session for credit. ***ROTC:*** Army (c).

Computers: Students can access the following: computer help desk, free student e-mail accounts, online (class) grades, online (class) registration, online (class) schedules. Campuswide network is available. Wireless service is available via classrooms, computer centers, computer labs, learning centers, libraries, student centers.

STUDENT LIFE
Housing options: on-campus residence required for freshman year; men-only, women-only. Campus housing is university owned.

Activities and organizations: drama/theater group, student-run newspaper, radio station, choral group, marching band, Student Government Association, choir, University band, Shaw Players, academic clubs, national fraternities, national sororities.

Athletics Member NCAA. All Division II. ***Intercollegiate sports:*** basketball M(s)/W(s), bowling W(s), cross-country running M(s)/W(s), football M(s), softball W(s), tennis M(s)/W(s), track and field M(s)/W(s), volleyball W(s). ***Intramural sports:*** basketball M/W, football M, tennis M/W, volleyball M/W.

Campus security: 24-hour emergency response devices and patrols, late-night transport/escort service, 24-hour electronic surveillance cameras.

Student services: health clinic, personal/psychological counseling.

COSTS & FINANCIAL AID
Costs (2014–15) ***Comprehensive fee:*** $24,638 includes full-time tuition ($11,808), mandatory fees ($4672), and room and board ($8158). Part-time tuition: $492 per credit hour. ***College room only:*** $3842. ***Payment plans:*** installment, deferred payment. ***Waivers:*** employees or children of employees.

Financial Aid Of all full-time matriculated undergraduates who enrolled in 2005, 2,197 applied for aid, 2,068 were judged to have need, 201 had their need fully met. 347 Federal Work-Study jobs (averaging $1120). In 2005, 117 non-need-based awards were made. ***Average percent of need met:*** 63. ***Average financial aid package:*** $8992. ***Average need-based loan:*** $3394. ***Average need-based gift aid:*** $5898. ***Average non-need-based aid:*** $9333. ***Average indebtedness upon graduation:*** $15,982. ***Financial aid deadline:*** 6/1.

APPLYING

Standardized Tests *Recommended:* SAT or ACT (for admission).

Options: electronic application, early admission, deferred entrance.

Application fee: $25.

Required: high school transcript, minimum 2.0 GPA.

Notification: continuous (freshmen).

CONTACT

Ms. Stacey Sowell, Director of Admissions and Recruitment, Shaw University, 118 East South Street, Raleigh, NC 27601-2399. *Phone:* 919-546-8275. *Toll-free phone:* 800-214-6683. *Fax:* 919-546-8271. *E-mail:* ssowell@shawu.edu.

South University

High Point, North Carolina

http://www.southuniversity.edu/high-point.aspx

- **Proprietary** comprehensive
- **Coed**

ACADEMICS

Degrees: associate, bachelor's, and master's.

CONTACT

South University, 3975 Premier Drive, High Point, NC 27265. *Phone:* 336-812-7200. *Toll-free phone:* 855-268-2187.

University of North Carolina at Asheville

Asheville, North Carolina

http://www.unca.edu/

- **State-supported** comprehensive, founded 1927, part of University of North Carolina System
- **Urban** 325-acre campus
- **Endowment** $33.9 million
- **Coed** 3,804 undergraduate students, 84% full-time, 56% women, 44% men
- **Moderately difficult** entrance level, 73% of applicants were admitted

UNDERGRAD STUDENTS

3,183 full-time, 621 part-time. Students come from 38 states and territories; 25 other countries; 11% are from out of state; 3% Black or African American, non-Hispanic/Latino; 4% Hispanic/Latino; 2% Asian, non-Hispanic/Latino; 0.1% Native Hawaiian or other Pacific Islander, non-Hispanic/Latino; 0.3% American Indian or Alaska Native, non-Hispanic/Latino; 3% Two or more races, non-Hispanic/Latino; 4% Race/ethnicity unknown; 0.9% international; 10% transferred in; 40% live on campus.

Freshmen

Admission: 3,109 applied, 2,280 admitted, 633 enrolled. ***Average high school GPA:*** 3.4. ***Test scores:*** SAT critical reading scores over 500: 96%; SAT math scores over 500: 95%; SAT writing scores over 500: 89%; ACT scores over 18: 100%; SAT critical reading scores over 600: 54%; SAT math scores over 600: 43%; SAT writing scores over 600: 38%; ACT scores over 24: 81%; SAT critical reading scores over 700: 12%; SAT math scores over 700: 6%; SAT writing scores over 700: 5%; ACT scores over 30: 11%.

Retention: 77% of full-time freshmen returned.

FACULTY

Total: 296, 73% full-time, 76% with terminal degrees.

Student/faculty ratio: 14:1.

ACADEMICS

Calendar: semesters. *Degrees:* bachelor's, master's, and postbachelor's certificates.

Special study options: academic remediation for entering students, adult/continuing education programs, advanced placement credit, distance learning, double majors, honors programs, independent study, internships, off-campus study, part-time degree program, services for LD students, student-designed majors, study abroad, summer session for credit.

Unusual degree programs: 3-2 chemistry and textile chemistry with North Carolina State University.

Computers: 477 computers/terminals are available on campus for general student use. Students can access the following: computer help desk, free student e-mail accounts, online (class) grades, online (class) registration, online (class) schedules. Campuswide network is available. 100% of college-owned or -operated housing units are wired for high-speed Internet access. Wireless service is available via entire campus.

STUDENT LIFE

Housing options: on-campus residence required for freshman year; coed, men-only, women-only, special housing for students with disabilities. Campus housing is university owned. Freshman campus housing is guaranteed.

Activities and organizations: drama/theater group, student-run newspaper, radio station, choral group, Student Government Association, Underdog Productions, Resident Student Association, Black Student Association, Active Students for a Healthy Environment, national fraternities, national sororities.

Athletics Member NCAA. All Division I. ***Intercollegiate sports:*** baseball M(s), basketball M(s)/W(s), cheerleading M/W, cross-country running M(s)/W(s), soccer M(s)/W(s), swimming and diving W(s), tennis M(s)/W(s), track and field M(s)/W(s), volleyball W(s). ***Intramural sports:*** archery M(c)/W(c), badminton M/W, basketball M/W, equestrian sports M(c)/W(c), fencing M(c)/W(c), football M/W, racquetball M/W, rugby M(c)/W(c), soccer M/W, ultimate Frisbee M(c)/W(c), volleyball M/W, water polo M/W.

Campus security: 24-hour emergency response devices and patrols, late-night transport/escort service, controlled dormitory access.

Student services: health clinic, personal/psychological counseling.

COSTS & FINANCIAL AID

Costs (2014–15) ***Tuition:*** state resident $3817 full-time; nonresident $18,688 full-time. Full-time tuition and fees vary according to course load. Part-time tuition and fees vary according to course load. ***Required fees:*** $2575 full-time. ***Room and board:*** $8332. Room and board charges vary according to housing facility. ***Payment plan:*** installment. ***Waivers:*** employees or children of employees.

Financial Aid Of all full-time matriculated undergraduates who enrolled in 2012, 2,258 applied for aid, 1,697 were judged to have need, 496 had their need fully met. In 2012, 173 non-need-based awards were made. ***Average percent of need met:*** 77. ***Average financial aid package:*** $11,861. ***Average need-based loan:*** $4473. ***Average need-based gift aid:*** $6747. ***Average non-need-based aid:*** $3035. ***Average indebtedness upon graduation:*** $17,696.

APPLYING

Standardized Tests *Required:* SAT or ACT (for admission).

Options: electronic application, early action, deferred entrance.

Application fee: $60.

Required: essay or personal statement, high school transcript, 1 letter of recommendation, minimum course requirement.

Application deadlines: 2/15 (freshmen), 2/15 (out-of-state freshmen), 4/15 (transfers), 11/15 (early action).

Notification: continuous until 12/15 (freshmen), continuous (transfers), 12/15 (early action).

CONTACT

Ms. Shannon Earle, Director of Admissions, University of North Carolina at Asheville, Brown Hall, CPO # 1320, Asheville, NC 28804-8510. *Phone:* 828-251-6481. *Toll-free phone:* 800-531-9842. *Fax:* 828-251-6482. *E-mail:* admissions@unca.edu.

The University of North Carolina at Chapel Hill

Chapel Hill, North Carolina

http://www.unc.edu/

- **State-supported** university, founded 1789, part of University of North Carolina System
- **Suburban** 729-acre campus with easy access to Raleigh-Durham
- **Endowment** $2.7 billion
- **Coed** 18,350 undergraduate students, 96% full-time, 58% women, 42% men
- **Very difficult** entrance level, 28% of applicants were admitted

UNDERGRAD STUDENTS

17,570 full-time, 780 part-time. Students come from 51 states and territories; 90 other countries; 17% are from out of state; 8% Black or African American, non-Hispanic/Latino; 7% Hispanic/Latino; 9% Asian, non-Hispanic/Latino; 0.1% Native Hawaiian or other Pacific Islander, non-Hispanic/Latino; 0.5% American Indian or Alaska Native, non-Hispanic/Latino; 4% Two or more races, non-Hispanic/Latino; 2% Race/ethnicity unknown; 2% international; 5% transferred in; 53% live on campus.

Freshmen

Admission: 31,332 applied, 8,929 admitted, 3,976 enrolled. ***Average high school GPA:*** 4.59. ***Test scores:*** SAT critical reading scores over 500: 98%; SAT math scores over 500: 99%; SAT writing scores over 500: 96%; ACT scores over 18: 100%; SAT critical reading scores over 600: 77%; SAT math scores over 600: 82%; SAT writing scores over 600: 73%; ACT scores over 24: 93%; SAT critical reading scores over 700: 24%; SAT math scores over 700: 32%; SAT writing scores over 700: 25%; ACT scores over 30: 47%.

Retention: 97% of full-time freshmen returned.

FACULTY

Total: 2,265, 80% full-time, 82% with terminal degrees.

Student/faculty ratio: 13:1.

ACADEMICS

Calendar: semesters. *Degrees:* certificates, bachelor's, master's, doctoral, post-master's, and postbachelor's certificates.

Special study options: advanced placement credit, distance learning, double majors, English as a second language, honors programs, independent study, internships, off-campus study, part-time degree program, services for LD students, student-designed majors, study abroad, summer session for credit. ***ROTC:*** Army (b), Navy (b), Air Force (b).

Computers: 867 computers/terminals and 9,999 ports are available on campus for general student use. Students can access the following: computer help desk, free student e-mail accounts, online (class) grades, online (class) registration, online (class) schedules. Campuswide network is available. 100% of college-owned or -operated housing units are wired for high-speed Internet access. Wireless service is available via entire campus.

STUDENT LIFE

Housing options: on-campus residence required for freshman year; coed, men-only, women-only, special housing for students with disabilities. Campus housing is university owned. Freshman campus housing is guaranteed.

Activities and organizations: drama/theater group, student-run newspaper, radio and television station, choral group, marching band, Residence Hall Association, Carolina Fever, Campus Y, UNC-CH Habitat for Humanity, Carolina for the Kids Foundation (Dance Marathon), national fraternities, national sororities.

Athletics Member NCAA. All Division I except football (Division I-A). ***Intercollegiate sports:*** badminton M(c)/W(c), baseball M(s), basketball M(s)/W(s), cheerleading W(c), crew M(c)/W(s), cross-country running M(s)/W(s), equestrian sports M(c)/W(c), fencing M(s)/W(s), field hockey M(c)/W(s), golf M(s)/W(s), gymnastics M(c)/W(s), ice hockey M(c), lacrosse M(s)/W(s), racquetball M(c)/W(c), rugby M(c)/W(c), sailing M(c)/W(c), skiing (downhill) M(c)/W(c), soccer M(s)/W(s), softball W(s), swimming and diving M(s)/W(s), tennis M(s)/W(s), track and field M(s)/W(s), ultimate Frisbee M(c)/W(c), volleyball M(c)/W(s), water polo M(c)/W(c), wrestling M(s). ***Intramural sports:*** badminton M/W, baseball M(c), basketball M(c)/W(c), cross-country running M(c)/W(c), field hockey W(c), football M(c), golf M(c)/W(c), gymnastics W(c), lacrosse W(c), racquetball M/W, soccer M(c)/W(c), softball M/W(c), swimming and diving M(c)/W(c), table tennis M/W, tennis M(c)/W(c), track and field M(c)/W(c), ultimate Frisbee M/W, volleyball M/W(c), water polo M/W, wrestling M(c).

Campus security: 24-hour emergency response devices and patrols, late-night transport/escort service, controlled dormitory access, crime prevention initiatives (date rape, violence, larceny, etc.), campus-wide emergency alert system, cell phone/GPS security options.

Student services: health clinic, personal/psychological counseling, women's center, legal services.

COSTS & FINANCIAL AID

Costs (2014–15) ***Tuition:*** state resident $6423 full-time; nonresident $31,505 full-time. Full-time tuition and fees vary according to program. Part-time tuition and fees vary according to course load and program. ***Required fees:*** $1913 full-time. ***Room and board:*** $10,592; room only: $5928. Room and board charges vary according to board plan, housing facility, and location. ***Payment plan:*** installment. ***Waivers:*** employees or children of employees.

Financial Aid Of all full-time matriculated undergraduates who enrolled in 2013, 10,259 applied for aid, 7,896 were judged to have need, 6,739 had their need fully met. 1,837 Federal Work-Study jobs (averaging $1796). In 2013, 841 non-need-based awards were made. ***Average percent of need met:*** 100. ***Average financial aid package:*** $17,946. ***Average need-based loan:*** $5202. ***Average need-based gift aid:*** $14,791. ***Average non-need-based aid:*** $6784. ***Average indebtedness upon graduation:*** $18,945.

APPLYING

Standardized Tests *Required:* SAT or ACT (for admission).

Options: electronic application, early action, deferred entrance.

Application fee: $80.

Required: essay or personal statement, high school transcript, 1 letter of recommendation, counselor's statement.

Application deadlines: 1/10 (freshmen), 2/15 (transfers), 10/15 (early action).

Notification: 3/31 (freshmen), 4/15 (transfers), 1/31 (early action).

CONTACT

The University of North Carolina at Chapel Hill, Chapel Hill, NC 27599. *Phone:* 919-966-3932.

The University of North Carolina at Charlotte

Charlotte, North Carolina

http://www.uncc.edu/

- **State-supported** university, founded 1946, part of University of North Carolina System
- **Suburban** 1000-acre campus with easy access to Charlotte
- **Endowment** $66.2 million
- **Coed** 22,216 undergraduate students, 85% full-time, 48% women, 52% men
- **Moderately difficult** entrance level, 64% of applicants were admitted

UNDERGRAD STUDENTS

18,983 full-time, 3,233 part-time. Students come from 44 states and territories; 85 other countries; 6% are from out of state; 17% Black or African American, non-Hispanic/Latino; 8% Hispanic/Latino; 5% Asian, non-Hispanic/Latino; 0.1% Native Hawaiian or other Pacific Islander, non-Hispanic/Latino; 0.3% American Indian or Alaska Native, non-Hispanic/Latino; 4% Two or more races, non-Hispanic/Latino; 3% Race/ethnicity unknown; 2% international; 13% transferred in; 23% live on campus.

Freshmen

Admission: 15,610 applied, 10,004 admitted, 3,319 enrolled. ***Average high school GPA:*** 3.86. ***Test scores:*** SAT critical reading scores over 500: 74%; SAT math scores over 500: 83%; SAT writing scores over 500: 65%; ACT scores over 18: 97%; SAT critical reading scores over 600: 17%; SAT math scores over 600: 26%; SAT writing scores over 600: 13%; ACT scores over 24: 40%; SAT critical reading scores over 700: 1%; SAT math

scores over 700: 3%; SAT writing scores over 700: 1%; ACT scores over 30: 4%.

Retention: 82% of full-time freshmen returned.

FACULTY
Total: 1,494, 72% full-time, 70% with terminal degrees.

Student/faculty ratio: 19:1.

ACADEMICS
Calendar: semesters. *Degrees:* bachelor's, master's, doctoral, post-master's, and postbachelor's certificates.

Special study options: accelerated degree program, adult/continuing education programs, advanced placement credit, cooperative education, distance learning, double majors, English as a second language, freshman honors college, honors programs, independent study, internships, off-campus study, part-time degree program, services for LD students, study abroad, summer session for credit. ***ROTC:*** Army (b), Air Force (b).

Computers: 1,500 computers/terminals are available on campus for general student use. Students can access the following: computer help desk, free student e-mail accounts, online (class) grades, online (class) registration, online (class) schedules. Campuswide network is available. 100% of college-owned or -operated housing units are wired for high-speed Internet access. Wireless service is available via classrooms, computer centers, computer labs, learning centers, libraries, student centers.

STUDENT LIFE
Housing options: coed, men-only, women-only, special housing for students with disabilities. Campus housing is university owned.

Activities and organizations: drama/theater group, student-run newspaper, radio and television station, choral group, Student Government Association, Student Alumni Ambassadors, Black Student Union, 49er Social and Ballroom Dance, Niner Nation Gold, national fraternities, national sororities.

Athletics Member NCAA. All Division I. ***Intercollegiate sports:*** baseball M(s), basketball M(s)/W(s), cheerleading M/W, cross-country running M(s)/W(s), football M(s), golf M(s), soccer M(s)/W(s), softball W(s), tennis M(s)/W(s), track and field M(s)/W(s), volleyball W(s). ***Intramural sports:*** archery M(c)/W(c), badminton M/W, baseball M(c)/W(c), basketball M/W, bowling M/W, equestrian sports M(c)/W(c), fencing M(c)/W(c), football M/W, golf M/W, ice hockey M(c)/W(c), lacrosse M(c)/W(c), rock climbing M(c)/W(c), rugby M(c)/W(c), soccer M/W, softball M(c)/W(c), swimming and diving M(c)/W(c), table tennis M/W, tennis M(c)/W(c), track and field M(c)/W(c), ultimate Frisbee M(c)/W(c), volleyball M/W, wrestling M(c)/W(c).

Campus security: 24-hour emergency response devices and patrols, late-night transport/escort service, controlled dormitory access.

Student services: health clinic, personal/psychological counseling.

COSTS & FINANCIAL AID
Costs (2014–15) ***Tuition:*** state resident $3522 full-time; nonresident $16,693 full-time. Full-time tuition and fees vary according to course load and program. Part-time tuition and fees vary according to course load and program. ***Required fees:*** $2755 full-time. ***Room and board:*** $9270; room only: $5200. Room and board charges vary according to board plan and housing facility. ***Payment plan:*** installment. ***Waivers:*** senior citizens and employees or children of employees.

Financial Aid Of all full-time matriculated undergraduates who enrolled in 2014, 15,671 applied for aid, 11,103 were judged to have need, 1,416 had their need fully met. 467 Federal Work-Study jobs (averaging $2552). In 2014, 72 non-need-based awards were made. ***Average percent of need met:*** 67. ***Average financial aid package:*** $9861. ***Average need-based loan:*** $4931. ***Average need-based gift aid:*** $6416. ***Average non-need-based aid:*** $4184. ***Average indebtedness upon graduation:*** $26,488.

APPLYING
Standardized Tests *Required:* SAT or ACT (for admission).

Options: electronic application, early admission, early action.

Application fee: $60.

Required: high school transcript, minimum 2.0 GPA, medical history, no criminal record. ***Required for some:*** interview.

Application deadlines: 7/1 (freshmen), 7/1 (out-of-state freshmen), 7/1 (transfers), 11/1 (early action).

Notification: continuous (freshmen), continuous (out-of-state freshmen), continuous (transfers), 1/30 (early action).

CONTACT
Ms. Claire Kirby, Director of Admissions, The University of North Carolina at Charlotte, 9201 University City Boulevard, 1st Floor, Cato Hall, Charlotte, NC 28223-0001. *Phone:* 704-687-5507. *Fax:* 704-687-6483. *E-mail:* admissions@uncc.edu.

The University of North Carolina at Greensboro
Greensboro, North Carolina
http://www.uncg.edu/

- **State-supported** university, founded 1891, part of University of North Carolina System
- **Urban** 210-acre campus
- **Endowment** $254.5 million
- **Coed** 15,173 undergraduate students, 84% full-time, 66% women, 34% men
- **Moderately difficult** entrance level, 60% of applicants were admitted

UNDERGRAD STUDENTS
12,773 full-time, 2,400 part-time. Students come from 48 states and territories; 55 other countries; 5% are from out of state; 27% Black or African American, non-Hispanic/Latino; 7% Hispanic/Latino; 4% Asian, non-Hispanic/Latino; 0.1% Native Hawaiian or other Pacific Islander, non-Hispanic/Latino; 0.4% American Indian or Alaska Native, non-Hispanic/Latino; 4% Two or more races, non-Hispanic/Latino; 1% Race/ethnicity unknown; 3% international; 11% transferred in; 45% live on campus.

Freshmen
Admission: 9,852 applied, 5,909 admitted, 2,608 enrolled. ***Average high school GPA:*** 3.66. ***Test scores:*** SAT critical reading scores over 500: 57%; SAT math scores over 500: 57%; SAT writing scores over 500: 43%; ACT scores over 18: 93%; SAT critical reading scores over 600: 14%; SAT math scores over 600: 12%; SAT writing scores over 600: 8%; ACT scores over 24: 27%; SAT critical reading scores over 700: 2%; SAT math scores over 700: 1%; SAT writing scores over 700: 1%; ACT scores over 30: 3%.

Retention: 78% of full-time freshmen returned.

FACULTY
Total: 952, 79% full-time, 72% with terminal degrees.

Student/faculty ratio: 18:1.

ACADEMICS
Calendar: semesters. *Degrees:* bachelor's, master's, doctoral, post-master's, and postbachelor's certificates.

Special study options: academic remediation for entering students, accelerated degree program, adult/continuing education programs, advanced placement credit, distance learning, double majors, English as a second language, freshman honors college, honors programs, independent study, internships, off-campus study, part-time degree program, services for LD students, student-designed majors, study abroad, summer session for credit. ***ROTC:*** Army (c), Air Force (c).

Unusual degree programs: 3-2 BS/MS Accounting, BS Biology/MS Chemistry, BS/MS Chemistry, BS/MS Computer Science, BA Economics/MPA Public Affairs, BS Kinesiology/MS in Athletic Training (MSAT), BA Political Science/Master of Public Affairs (MPA).

Computers: 360 computers/terminals are available on campus for general student use. Students can access the following: computer help desk, free student e-mail accounts, online (class) grades, online (class) registration, online (class) schedules. Campuswide network is available. 100% of college-owned or -operated housing units are wired for high-speed Internet access. Wireless service is available via classrooms, computer centers, computer labs, dorm rooms, learning centers, libraries, student centers.

STUDENT LIFE
Housing options: coed, special housing for students with disabilities. Campus housing is university owned. Freshman campus housing is guaranteed.

Activities and organizations: drama/theater group, student-run newspaper, radio station, choral group, Campus Crusade for Christ, National Society for Collegiate Scholars, Golden Key International Honour Society, Chi Omega Sorority, Graduate Student Association, national fraternities, national sororities.

Athletics Member NCAA. All Division I. ***Intercollegiate sports:*** baseball M(s), basketball M(s)/W(s), cross-country running M(s)/W(s), golf M(s)/W(s), soccer M(s)/W(s), softball W(s), tennis M(s)/W(s), track and field M(s)/W(s), volleyball W(s). ***Intramural sports:*** basketball M(c)/W(c), cross-country running M(c)/W(c), equestrian sports M(c)/W(c), football W(c), lacrosse M(c), racquetball M(c)/W(c), rugby M(c)/W(c), soccer M(c)/W(c), swimming and diving M(c)/W(c), tennis M(c)/W(c), ultimate Frisbee M(c)/W(c), volleyball W(c).

Campus security: 24-hour emergency response devices and patrols, student patrols, late-night transport/escort service, controlled dormitory access.

Student services: health clinic, personal/psychological counseling.

COSTS & FINANCIAL AID

Costs (2014–15) ***Tuition:*** state resident $3932 full-time, $492 per credit hour part-time; nonresident $18,794 full-time, $2349 per credit hour part-time. Part-time tuition and fees vary according to course load. ***Required fees:*** $2510 full-time, $93 per credit hour part-time. ***Room and board:*** $7688; room only: $4586. Room and board charges vary according to board plan and housing facility. ***Payment plan:*** installment. ***Waivers:*** employees or children of employees.

Financial Aid Of all full-time matriculated undergraduates who enrolled in 2014, 9,462 applied for aid, 9,379 were judged to have need, 2,328 had their need fully met. In 2014, 286 non-need-based awards were made. ***Average percent of need met:*** 70. ***Average financial aid package:*** $9757. ***Average need-based loan:*** $4145. ***Average need-based gift aid:*** $7619. ***Average non-need-based aid:*** $3482. ***Average indebtedness upon graduation:*** $23,265.

APPLYING

Standardized Tests *Required:* SAT or ACT (for admission).

Options: electronic application, early admission.

Application fee: $55.

Required: high school transcript, minimum 2.0 GPA.

Application deadlines: 3/1 (freshmen), 7/15 (transfers).

Notification: continuous until 9/15 (freshmen), continuous (transfers).

CONTACT

The University of North Carolina at Greensboro, Armfield-Preyer Admissions and Visitor Center, 1400 Spring Garden Street, Greensboro, NC 27412. *Phone:* 336-334-5243. *Fax:* 336-334-4180. *E-mail:* admissions@uncg.edu.

The University of North Carolina at Pembroke

Pembroke, North Carolina

http://www.uncp.edu/

- **State-supported** comprehensive, founded 1887, part of University of North Carolina System
- **Rural** 208-acre campus
- **Endowment** $21.2 million
- **Coed** 5,511 undergraduate students, 80% full-time, 61% women, 39% men
- **Moderately difficult** entrance level, 73% of applicants were admitted

UNDERGRAD STUDENTS

4,400 full-time, 1,111 part-time. Students come from 25 states and territories; 20 other countries; 5% are from out of state; 36% Black or African American, non-Hispanic/Latino; 5% Hispanic/Latino; 2% Asian, non-Hispanic/Latino; 15% American Indian or Alaska Native, non-Hispanic/Latino; 2% Two or more races, non-Hispanic/Latino; 2% Race/ethnicity unknown; 0.8% international; 11% transferred in; 40% live on campus.

Freshmen

Admission: 4,035 applied, 2,956 admitted, 1,074 enrolled. ***Average high school GPA:*** 3.38. ***Test scores:*** SAT critical reading scores over 500: 28%; SAT math scores over 500: 30%; SAT writing scores over 500: 16%; ACT scores over 18: 81%; SAT critical reading scores over 600: 4%; SAT math scores over 600: 3%; SAT writing scores over 600: 1%; ACT scores over 24: 12%; ACT scores over 30: 1%.

Retention: 68% of full-time freshmen returned.

FACULTY

Total: 421, 76% full-time, 60% with terminal degrees.

Student/faculty ratio: 15:1.

ACADEMICS

Calendar: semesters. *Degrees:* bachelor's and master's.

Special study options: academic remediation for entering students, accelerated degree program, adult/continuing education programs, advanced placement credit, cooperative education, distance learning, double majors, English as a second language, honors programs, internships, off-campus study, part-time degree program, services for LD students, study abroad, summer session for credit. ***ROTC:*** Army (b), Air Force (b).

Computers: 875 computers/terminals are available on campus for general student use. Students can access the following: campus intranet, computer help desk, free student e-mail accounts, online (class) grades, online (class) registration, online (class) schedules, wireless network, online library, commuter/off campus connection to network, discounted computer software/ hardware. Campuswide network is available. 100% of college-owned or -operated housing units are wired for high-speed Internet access. Wireless service is available via classrooms, computer centers, computer labs, dorm rooms, learning centers, libraries, student centers.

STUDENT LIFE

Housing options: on-campus residence required for freshman year; coed, men-only, women-only. Campus housing is university owned and is provided by a third party. Freshman applicants given priority for college housing.

Activities and organizations: drama/theater group, student-run newspaper, radio and television station, choral group, marching band, Native American Student Organization, Graduate Student Organization, Association of Campus Entertainment, Campus Association of Social Workers, Health Careers Club and Student In Free Enterprise, national fraternities, national sororities.

Athletics Member NCAA. All Division II. ***Intercollegiate sports:*** baseball M(s), basketball M(s)/W(s), cheerleading M/W, cross-country running M(s)/W(s), football M(s), golf M(s)/W(s), soccer M(s)/W(s), softball W(s), tennis W(s), track and field M(s)/W(s), volleyball W(s), wrestling M(s). ***Intramural sports:*** basketball M/W, bowling M/W, football M, golf M, racquetball M/W, soccer M, softball M/W, volleyball M/W, wrestling M.

Campus security: 24-hour emergency response devices and patrols, late-night transport/escort service, controlled dormitory access.

Student services: health clinic, personal/psychological counseling.

COSTS & FINANCIAL AID

Costs (2014–15) ***Tuition:*** state resident $3211 full-time; nonresident $13,162 full-time. Full-time tuition and fees vary according to course load and location. Part-time tuition and fees vary according to course load and location. ***Required fees:*** $2076 full-time. ***Room and board:*** $8101; room only: $5620. Room and board charges vary according to board plan, housing facility, and location. ***Payment plan:*** installment. ***Waivers:*** employees or children of employees.

Financial Aid Of all full-time matriculated undergraduates who enrolled in 2014, 3,987 applied for aid, 3,612 were judged to have need, 263 had their need fully met. 108 Federal Work-Study jobs (averaging $1953). In 2014, 17 non-need-based awards were made. ***Average percent of need met:*** 66. ***Average financial aid package:*** $9948. ***Average need-based loan:*** $4237. ***Average need-based gift aid:*** $6907. ***Average non-need-based aid:*** $1090. ***Average indebtedness upon graduation:*** $24,860.

APPLYING

Standardized Tests *Required:* SAT or ACT (for admission).

Options: electronic application, deferred entrance.

Application fee: $45.

Required: high school transcript. ***Required for some:*** 1 letter of recommendation, interview. ***Recommended:*** essay or personal statement, minimum 2.0 GPA.

Application deadlines: rolling (freshmen), rolling (transfers).
Notification: continuous (freshmen), continuous (transfers).

CONTACT
The University of North Carolina at Pembroke, One University Drive, PO Box 1510, Pembroke, NC 28372-1510. *Phone:* 910-521-6262. *Toll-free phone:* 800-949-UNCP.

University of North Carolina School of the Arts

Winston-Salem, North Carolina

http://www.uncsa.edu/

- **State-supported** comprehensive, founded 1963, part of University of North Carolina System
- **Urban** 57-acre campus
- **Endowment** $47.1 million
- **Coed** 854 undergraduate students, 99% full-time, 48% women, 52% men

UNDERGRAD STUDENTS
845 full-time, 9 part-time. Students come from 47 states and territories; 11 other countries; 50% are from out of state; 8% Black or African American, non-Hispanic/Latino; 8% Hispanic/Latino; 1% Asian, non-Hispanic/Latino; 0.2% Native Hawaiian or other Pacific Islander, non-Hispanic/Latino; 0.6% American Indian or Alaska Native, non-Hispanic/Latino; 5% Two or more races, non-Hispanic/Latino; 3% Race/ethnicity unknown; 2% international; 6% transferred in; 63% live on campus.

Freshmen
Admission: 219 enrolled. ***Average high school GPA:*** 3.7. ***Test scores:*** SAT critical reading scores over 500: 79%; SAT math scores over 500: 71%; SAT writing scores over 500: 71%; ACT scores over 18: 92%; SAT critical reading scores over 600: 39%; SAT math scores over 600: 29%; SAT writing scores over 600: 31%; ACT scores over 24: 52%; SAT critical reading scores over 700: 8%; SAT math scores over 700: 4%; SAT writing scores over 700: 4%; ACT scores over 30: 9%.
Retention: 89% of full-time freshmen returned.

FACULTY
Total: 180, 76% full-time, 39% with terminal degrees.
Student/faculty ratio: 6:1.

ACADEMICS
Calendar: trimesters. *Degrees:* certificates, bachelor's, master's, and post-master's certificates.
Special study options: advanced placement credit, English as a second language, independent study, internships, services for LD students, summer session for credit.
Computers: 117 computers/terminals are available on campus for general student use. Students can access the following: campus intranet, computer help desk, free student e-mail accounts, online (class) grades, online (class) registration, online (class) schedules, All buildings on campus have wireless internet access. Campuswide network is available. 100% of college-owned or -operated housing units are wired for high-speed Internet access. Wireless service is available via entire campus.

STUDENT LIFE
Housing options: on-campus residence required through sophomore year; coed. Campus housing is university owned. Freshman campus housing is guaranteed.
Activities and organizations: drama/theater group, student-run newspaper, choral group, Outdoor Adventure Club and various sports tournaments (i.e., Ultimate Frisbee, beach volleyball, and basketball), Arts & Soul [faith based], Young Americans for Liberty (YAL) [political awareness].
Campus security: 24-hour emergency response devices and patrols, late-night transport/escort service, controlled dormitory access.
Student services: health clinic, personal/psychological counseling.

COSTS & FINANCIAL AID
Costs (2014–15) ***Tuition:*** state resident $5870 full-time, $245 per credit hour part-time; nonresident $21,240 full-time, $890 per credit hour part-time. ***Required fees:*** $2493 full-time, $98 per credit hour part-time. ***Room and board:*** $8570; room only: $4178. Room and board charges vary according to board plan and housing facility. ***Waivers:*** employees or children of employees.
Financial Aid Of all full-time matriculated undergraduates who enrolled in 2014, 658 applied for aid, 538 were judged to have need, 46 had their need fully met. In 2014, 25 non-need-based awards were made. ***Average percent of need met:*** 63. ***Average financial aid package:*** $13,157. ***Average need-based loan:*** $4459. ***Average need-based gift aid:*** $7900. ***Average non-need-based aid:*** $3739. ***Average indebtedness upon graduation:*** $22,697.

APPLYING
Standardized Tests *Required:* SAT or ACT (for admission).
Required: essay or personal statement, high school transcript, minimum 2.5 GPA, 2 letters of recommendation, audition. ***Required for some:*** interview.

CONTACT
University of North Carolina School of the Arts, 1533 South Main Street, PO Box 12189, Winston-Salem, NC 27127-2738. *Phone:* 336-770-3290.

★ The University of North Carolina Wilmington

Wilmington, North Carolina

http://www.uncw.edu/

- **State-supported** comprehensive, founded 1947, part of University of North Carolina System
- **Urban** 656-acre campus
- **Endowment** $65.9 million
- **Coed** 12,952 undergraduate students, 90% full-time, 61% women, 39% men
- **Moderately difficult** entrance level, 59% of applicants were admitted

UNDERGRAD STUDENTS
11,690 full-time, 1,262 part-time. Students come from 49 states and territories; 51 other countries; 18% are from out of state; 5% Black or African American, non-Hispanic/Latino; 7% Hispanic/Latino; 2% Asian, non-Hispanic/Latino; 0.1% Native Hawaiian or other Pacific Islander, non-Hispanic/Latino; 0.4% American Indian or Alaska Native, non-Hispanic/Latino; 3% Two or more races, non-Hispanic/Latino; 3% Race/ethnicity unknown; 0.6% international; 11% transferred in; 32% live on campus.

Freshmen
Admission: 11,523 applied, 6,747 admitted, 2,159 enrolled. ***Average high school GPA:*** 4.1. ***Test scores:*** SAT critical reading scores over 500: 95%; SAT math scores over 500: 98%; SAT writing scores over 500: 87%; ACT scores over 18: 100%; SAT critical reading scores over 600: 44%; SAT math scores over 600: 53%; SAT writing scores over 600: 34%; ACT scores over 24: 59%; SAT critical reading scores over 700: 4%; SAT math scores over 700: 5%; SAT writing scores over 700: 3%; ACT scores over 30: 7%.
Retention: 84% of full-time freshmen returned.

FACULTY
Total: 997, 64% full-time, 68% with terminal degrees.
Student/faculty ratio: 17:1.

ACADEMICS
Calendar: semesters. *Degrees:* bachelor's, master's, doctoral, post-master's, and postbachelor's certificates.
Special study options: academic remediation for entering students, accelerated degree program, advanced placement credit, cooperative education, distance learning, double majors, English as a second language, honors programs, independent study, internships, off-campus study, services for LD students, study abroad, summer session for credit.
Computers: 1,161 computers/terminals and 5,334 ports are available on campus for general student use. Students can access the following: campus intranet, computer help desk, free student e-mail accounts, online (class) grades, online (class) registration, online (class) schedules. Campuswide network is available. 100% of college-owned or -operated housing units are wired for high-speed Internet access. Wireless service is available via entire campus.

STUDENT LIFE

Housing options: coed, women-only, special housing for students with disabilities. Campus housing is university owned and is provided by a third party. Freshman applicants given priority for college housing.

Activities and organizations: drama/theater group, student-run newspaper, radio and television station, choral group, Student Government Association, Association of Campus Entertainment, Residence Hall Association, national fraternities, national sororities.

Athletics Member NCAA. All Division I. ***Intercollegiate sports:*** baseball M(s), basketball M(s)/W(s), cheerleading M/W(s), cross-country running M(s)/W(s), golf M(s)/W(s), soccer M(s)/W(s), softball W(s), swimming and diving M(s)/W(s), tennis M(s)/W(s), track and field M(s)/W(s), volleyball W(s). ***Intramural sports:*** badminton M/W, baseball M(c), basketball W, crew M(c)/W(c), equestrian sports W(c), field hockey W(c), golf M(c)/W(c), gymnastics M(c)/W(c), ice hockey M, lacrosse M(c)/W(c), racquetball M/W, rugby M(c)/W(c), sailing M(c)/W(c), soccer M/W, softball M/W, swimming and diving M(c)/W(c), tennis M/W, ultimate Frisbee M(c)/W(c), volleyball M/W, water polo M/W.

Campus security: 24-hour emergency response devices and patrols, late-night transport/escort service, controlled dormitory access.

Student services: health clinic, personal/psychological counseling, women's center, legal services.

COSTS & FINANCIAL AID

Costs (2014–15) ***Tuition:*** state resident $4026 full-time, $154 per credit hour part-time; nonresident $18,054 full-time, $691 per credit hour part-time. Full-time tuition and fees vary according to course load and location. Part-time tuition and fees vary according to course load and location. ***Required fees:*** $2366 full-time, $75 per credit hour part-time. ***Room and board:*** $9124; room only: $5594. Room and board charges vary according to board plan and housing facility. ***Payment plan:*** installment. ***Waivers:*** employees or children of employees.

Financial Aid Of all full-time matriculated undergraduates who enrolled in 2013, 8,111 applied for aid, 6,401 were judged to have need, 745 had their need fully met. In 2013, 31 non-need-based awards were made. ***Average percent of need met:*** 58. ***Average financial aid package:*** $10,163. ***Average need-based loan:*** $4276. ***Average need-based gift aid:*** $2427. ***Average non-need-based aid:*** $3853. ***Average indebtedness upon graduation:*** $6630.

APPLYING

Standardized Tests *Required:* SAT or ACT (for admission).

Options: electronic application, early admission, early action, deferred entrance.

Application fee: $75.

Required: essay or personal statement, high school transcript, 1 letter of recommendation.

Application deadlines: 2/1 (freshmen), 3/1 (transfers), 11/1 (early action).

Notification: 4/1 (freshmen), continuous (transfers), 1/20 (early action).

CONTACT

UNCW Office of Admissions, The University of North Carolina Wilmington, 601 South College Road, Wilmington, NC 28403-3297. *Phone:* 910-962-3243. *Fax:* 910-962-3038. *E-mail:* admissions@uncw.edu.

See previous page for display ad and page 1692 for the College Close-Up.

Wake Forest University

Winston-Salem, North Carolina

http://www.wfu.edu/

- **Independent** university, founded 1834
- **Suburban** 340-acre campus
- **Coed** 4,867 undergraduate students, 99% full-time, 53% women, 47% men
- **Very difficult** entrance level, 34% of applicants were admitted

UNDERGRAD STUDENTS

4,804 full-time, 63 part-time. 79% are from out of state; 6% Black or African American, non-Hispanic/Latino; 6% Hispanic/Latino; 5% Asian, non-Hispanic/Latino; 0.1% Native Hawaiian or other Pacific Islander, non-Hispanic/Latino; 0.1% American Indian or Alaska Native, non-Hispanic/Latino; 3% Two or more races, non-Hispanic/Latino; 0.2%

Race/ethnicity unknown; 6% international; 0.6% transferred in; 77% live on campus.

Freshmen
Admission: 11,119 applied, 3,826 admitted, 1,287 enrolled. ***Test scores:*** SAT critical reading scores over 500: 96%; SAT math scores over 500: 98%; SAT writing scores over 500: 95%; ACT scores over 18: 99%; SAT critical reading scores over 600: 75%; SAT math scores over 600: 87%; SAT writing scores over 600: 81%; ACT scores over 24: 93%; SAT critical reading scores over 700: 24%; SAT math scores over 700: 43%; SAT writing scores over 700: 32%; ACT scores over 30: 59%.

Retention: 94% of full-time freshmen returned.

FACULTY
Total: 732, 78% full-time.

Student/faculty ratio: 11:1.

ACADEMICS
Calendar: semesters. *Degrees:* bachelor's, master's, and doctoral.

Special study options: advanced placement credit, double majors, honors programs, independent study, internships, part-time degree program, services for LD students, study abroad, summer session for credit. ***ROTC:*** Army (b).

Unusual degree programs: 3-2 engineering.

Computers: Students can access the following: campus intranet, computer help desk, free student e-mail accounts, online (class) grades, online (class) registration, online (class) schedules, financial information online, drop-add, transcript requests. Campuswide network is available. Wireless service is available via entire campus.

STUDENT LIFE
Housing options: on-campus residence required through sophomore year; coed. Campus housing is university owned. Freshman campus housing is guaranteed.

Activities and organizations: drama/theater group, student-run newspaper, radio and television station, choral group, marching band, national fraternities, national sororities.

Athletics Member NCAA. All Division I except football (Division I-A). ***Intercollegiate sports:*** baseball M(s), basketball M(s)/W(s), cross-country running M(s)/W(s), field hockey W(s), golf M(s)/W(s), soccer M(s)/W(s), tennis M(s)/W(s), track and field M(s)/W(s), volleyball W(s). ***Intramural sports:*** archery M(c)/W(c), baseball M(c), basketball M/W, bowling M/W, cheerleading M(c)/W(c), crew M(c)/W(c), cross-country running M(c)/W(c), equestrian sports M(c)/W(c), fencing M(c)/W(c), field hockey W(c), football M, golf M(c)/W(c), ice hockey M(c)/W(c), lacrosse M(c)/W(c), racquetball M/W, rugby M(c)/W(c), skiing (cross-country) M(c)/W(c), skiing (downhill) M(c)/W(c), soccer M(c)/W(c), softball M/W(c), swimming and diving M/W, table tennis M/W, tennis M/W, ultimate Frisbee M/W, volleyball M/W, water polo M(c)/W(c), wrestling M(c).

Campus security: 24-hour emergency response devices and patrols, late-night transport/escort service, controlled dormitory access.

Student services: health clinic, personal/psychological counseling.

COSTS & FINANCIAL AID
Costs (2015–16) ***Comprehensive fee:*** $60,678 includes full-time tuition ($47,120), mandatory fees ($562), and room and board ($12,996). Part-time tuition: $1892 per credit hour. ***College room only:*** $8496.

Financial Aid Of all full-time matriculated undergraduates who enrolled in 2014, 2,027 applied for aid, 1,696 were judged to have need, 1,313 had their need fully met. In 2014, 304 non-need-based awards were made. ***Average percent of need met:*** 99. ***Average financial aid package:*** $40,534. ***Average need-based loan:*** $11,386. ***Average need-based gift aid:*** $35,551. ***Average non-need-based aid:*** $16,055. ***Average indebtedness upon graduation:*** $34,745. ***Financial aid deadline:*** 3/1.

APPLYING
Options: electronic application, early admission, early decision.

Application fee: $50.

Required: essay or personal statement, high school transcript, 1 letter of recommendation. ***Recommended:*** interview.

CONTACT
Wake Forest University, PO Box 7373 Reynolda Station, Winston-Salem, NC 27109. *Phone:* 336-758-5201.

Warren Wilson College

Swannanoa, North Carolina

http://www.warren-wilson.edu/

- **Independent** comprehensive, founded 1894, affiliated with Presbyterian Church (U.S.A.)
- **Suburban** 1135-acre campus
- **Endowment** $53.8 million
- **Coed** 824 undergraduate students, 99% full-time, 62% women, 38% men
- **Moderately difficult** entrance level, 70% of applicants were admitted

UNDERGRAD STUDENTS
817 full-time, 7 part-time. Students come from 45 states and territories; 20 other countries; 75% are from out of state; 4% Black or African American, non-Hispanic/Latino; 6% Hispanic/Latino; 1% Asian, non-Hispanic/Latino; 1% American Indian or Alaska Native, non-Hispanic/Latino; 4% Two or more races, non-Hispanic/Latino; 0.2% Race/ethnicity unknown; 2% international; 7% transferred in; 90% live on campus.

Freshmen
Admission: 1,214 applied, 845 admitted, 234 enrolled. ***Average high school GPA:*** 3.6. ***Test scores:*** SAT critical reading scores over 500: 85%; SAT math scores over 500: 68%; SAT writing scores over 500: 67%; ACT scores over 18: 99%; SAT critical reading scores over 600: 46%; SAT math scores over 600: 22%; SAT writing scores over 600: 34%; ACT scores over 24: 71%; SAT critical reading scores over 700: 11%; SAT math scores over 700: 2%; SAT writing scores over 700: 6%; ACT scores over 30: 16%.

Retention: 66% of full-time freshmen returned.

FACULTY
Total: 113, 59% full-time, 63% with terminal degrees.

Student/faculty ratio: 10:1.

ACADEMICS
Calendar: semesters. *Degrees:* bachelor's and master's.

Special study options: advanced placement credit, cooperative education, double majors, English as a second language, honors programs, independent study, internships, off-campus study, part-time degree program, services for LD students, student-designed majors, study abroad, summer session for credit.

Unusual degree programs: 3-2 Warren Wilson College participates in the Cooperative College Program with the Nicolas School of the Environment at Duke University in a combined program of liberal arts and professional education in environmental resources. Result: BA in Environmental Studies + MEM in Environmental Management.

Computers: 92 computers/terminals are available on campus for general student use. Students can access the following: campus intranet, computer help desk, free student e-mail accounts, online (class) grades, online (class) registration, online (class) schedules, Home directory and public html for each user, word processing, GIS, Statistical Analysis. Campuswide network is available. 100% of college-owned or -operated housing units are wired for high-speed Internet access. Wireless service is available via entire campus.

STUDENT LIFE
Housing options: on-campus residence required for freshman year; coed, men-only, women-only, cooperative. Campus housing is university owned. Freshman campus housing is guaranteed.

Activities and organizations: drama/theater group, student-run newspaper, choral group, Food Not Bombs, Club Sports: Paddling, Cycling, Cyclocross, Timbersports, Multicultural Student Organizations: Engage, WHOLA, Peace, Social and Environmental Justice Groups, Student Religious Groups: Christian, Jewish, Buddhist, Quaker, Pagan, and Unitarian Universalist.

Athletics Member USCAA. ***Intercollegiate sports:*** basketball M/W, cross-country running M/W, soccer M/W, swimming and diving M/W. ***Intramural sports:*** fencing M/W, golf M/W, lacrosse M/W, rock climbing M/W, skiing (downhill) M(c)/W(c), soccer M/W, softball M/W, table tennis M/W, tennis M(c)/W(c), ultimate Frisbee M/W, volleyball M/W, weight lifting M/W.

Campus security: 24-hour emergency response devices and patrols, student patrols, late-night transport/escort service, controlled dormitory access.

Student services: health clinic, personal/psychological counseling.

COSTS & FINANCIAL AID
Costs (2015–16) ***Comprehensive fee:*** $42,460 includes full-time tuition ($31,980), mandatory fees ($580), and room and board ($9900). Full-time tuition and fees vary according to course load. Part-time tuition: $1334 per credit hour. Part-time tuition and fees vary according to course load. ***Required fees:*** $100 per term part-time. ***Room and board:*** Room and board charges vary according to board plan. ***Payment plan:*** installment. ***Waivers:*** employees or children of employees.

Financial Aid Of all full-time matriculated undergraduates who enrolled in 2014, 669 applied for aid, 618 were judged to have need, 71 had their need fully met. 556 Federal Work-Study jobs (averaging $3362). 145 state and other part-time jobs (averaging $3379). In 2014, 145 non-need-based awards were made. ***Average percent of need met:*** 79. ***Average financial aid package:*** $28,482. ***Average need-based loan:*** $4581. ***Average need-based gift aid:*** $20,991. ***Average non-need-based aid:*** $7386. ***Average indebtedness upon graduation:*** $24,839.

APPLYING
Options: electronic application, early admission, early decision, deferred entrance.

Required: essay or personal statement, high school transcript, Completed Common Application and Common Application School Report Form. ***Recommended:*** minimum 2.5 GPA, 2 letters of recommendation, interview.

Application deadlines: 1/31 (freshmen), 1/31 (out-of-state freshmen), 3/15 (transfers), 11/1 (early action).

Early decision deadline: 11/15.

Notification: continuous (freshmen), continuous (out-of-state freshmen), 4/1 (transfers), 12/1 (early decision), 12/1 (early action).

CONTACT
Monique Cote, Campus Visit Coordinator, Warren Wilson College, PO Box 9000, Asheville, NC 28815-9000. *Phone:* 828-771-2073. *Toll-free phone:* 800-934-3536. *Fax:* 828-298-1440. *E-mail:* admit@warren-wilson.edu.

Western Carolina University
Cullowhee, North Carolina
http://www.wcu.edu/

- **State-supported** comprehensive, founded 1889, part of University of North Carolina System
- **Rural** 682-acre campus
- **Coed** 8,787 undergraduate students, 84% full-time, 54% women, 46% men
- **Moderately difficult** entrance level, 43% of applicants were admitted

UNDERGRAD STUDENTS
7,373 full-time, 1,414 part-time. 7% are from out of state; 6% Black or African American, non-Hispanic/Latino; 5% Hispanic/Latino; 1% Asian, non-Hispanic/Latino; 0.1% Native Hawaiian or other Pacific Islander, non-Hispanic/Latino; 0.8% American Indian or Alaska Native, non-Hispanic/Latino; 3% Two or more races, non-Hispanic/Latino; 1% Race/ethnicity unknown; 2% international; 9% transferred in; 42% live on campus.

Freshmen
Admission: 15,397 applied, 6,637 admitted, 1,756 enrolled. ***Average high school GPA:*** 3.75. ***Test scores:*** SAT critical reading scores over 500: 60%; SAT math scores over 500: 66%; SAT writing scores over 500: 41%; ACT scores over 18: 96%; SAT critical reading scores over 600: 14%; SAT math scores over 600: 14%; SAT writing scores over 600: 9%; ACT scores over 24: 34%; SAT critical reading scores over 700: 1%; SAT math scores over 700: 1%; SAT writing scores over 700: 1%; ACT scores over 30: 2%.

Retention: 78% of full-time freshmen returned.

FACULTY
Total: 676, 73% full-time, 65% with terminal degrees.

Student/faculty ratio: 16:1.

ACADEMICS
Calendar: semesters. *Degrees:* bachelor's, master's, doctoral, post-master's, and postbachelor's certificates.

Special study options: advanced placement credit, cooperative education, distance learning, double majors, English as a second language, honors programs, independent study, internships, part-time degree program, services for LD students, student-designed majors, study abroad, summer session for credit.

Computers: Students can access the following: campus intranet, computer help desk, free student e-mail accounts, online (class) grades, online (class) registration, online (class) schedules. Campuswide network is available. 100% of college-owned or -operated housing units are wired for high-speed Internet access. Wireless service is available via entire campus.

STUDENT LIFE
Housing options: on-campus residence required for freshman year; coed, men-only, women-only, special housing for students with disabilities. Campus housing is university owned, leased by the school and is provided by a third party. Freshman campus housing is guaranteed.

Activities and organizations: drama/theater group, student-run newspaper, radio and television station, choral group, marching band, national fraternities, national sororities.

Athletics Member NCAA. All Division I except football (Division I-AA). ***Intercollegiate sports:*** baseball M(s), basketball M(s)/W(s), cheerleading M/W, cross-country running M(s)/W(s), equestrian sports M(c)/W(c), fencing M(c)/W(c), golf M(s)/W(s), rock climbing M(c)/W(c), rugby M(c), soccer W(s), softball W(s), swimming and diving M(c)/W(c), tennis M(c)/W(s), track and field M(s)/W(s), ultimate Frisbee M(c)/W(c), volleyball W(s), wrestling M(c). ***Intramural sports:*** badminton M/W, basketball M/W, bowling M/W, cross-country running M/W, racquetball M/W, soccer M/W, softball M/W, swimming and diving M/W, table tennis M/W, tennis M/W, ultimate Frisbee M/W, volleyball M/W, water polo M/W, weight lifting M/W, wrestling M/W.

Campus security: 24-hour emergency response devices and patrols, late-night transport/escort service, controlled dormitory access.

Student services: health clinic, personal/psychological counseling, women's center.

COSTS & FINANCIAL AID
Costs (2014–15) ***Tuition:*** state resident $3669 full-time; nonresident $14,062 full-time. Full-time tuition and fees vary according to degree level. Part-time tuition and fees vary according to course load and degree level. ***Required fees:*** $2862 full-time. ***Room and board:*** $8016. Room and board charges vary according to board plan and housing facility.

Financial Aid Of all full-time matriculated undergraduates who enrolled in 2012, 5,863 applied for aid, 4,828 were judged to have need, 698 had their need fully met. In 2012, 204 non-need-based awards were made. ***Average percent of need met:*** 67. ***Average financial aid package:*** $9291. ***Average need-based loan:*** $3855. ***Average need-based gift aid:*** $5983. ***Average non-need-based aid:*** $2248. ***Average indebtedness upon graduation:*** $20,273.

APPLYING
Standardized Tests *Required:* SAT or ACT (for admission).

Options: electronic application, early admission, early action.

Application fee: $55.

Required: high school transcript.

CONTACT
Office of Undergraduate Admission, Western Carolina University, 102 Camp Building, Cullowhee, NC 28723. *Phone:* 828-227-7317. *Toll-free phone:* 877-WCU4YOU. *E-mail:* admiss@email.wcu.edu.

★ William Peace University
Raleigh, North Carolina
http://www.peace.edu/

- **Independent** 4-year, founded 1857, affiliated with Presbyterian Church (U.S.A.)
- **Urban** 21-acre campus with easy access to Raleigh-Cary
- **Endowment** $37.9 million
- **Coed** 1,077 undergraduate students, 82% full-time, 66% women, 34% men
- **Moderately difficult** entrance level, 63% of applicants were admitted

UNDERGRAD STUDENTS
884 full-time, 193 part-time. Students come from 18 states and territories; 4 other countries; 13% are from out of state; 32% Black or African American, non-Hispanic/Latino; 3% Hispanic/Latino; 2% Asian, non-Hispanic/Latino; 0.2% Native Hawaiian or other Pacific Islander, non-Hispanic/Latino; 0.8% American Indian or Alaska Native, non-Hispanic/Latino; 2% Two or more races, non-Hispanic/Latino; 15% Race/ethnicity unknown; 11% transferred in; 71% live on campus.

Freshmen
Admission: 1,542 applied, 970 admitted, 280 enrolled. ***Average high school GPA:*** 3.17. ***Test scores:*** SAT critical reading scores over 500: 26%; SAT math scores over 500: 24%; ACT scores over 18: 59%; SAT critical reading scores over 600: 4%; SAT math scores over 600: 3%; ACT scores over 24: 10%; ACT scores over 30: 1%.

FACULTY
Total: 153, 17% full-time, 35% with terminal degrees.
Student/faculty ratio: 13:1.

ACADEMICS
Calendar: semesters. *Degree:* bachelor's.
Special study options: academic remediation for entering students, accelerated degree program, adult/continuing education programs, advanced placement credit, cooperative education, distance learning, double majors, honors programs, independent study, internships, off-campus study, part-time degree program, services for LD students, study abroad, summer session for credit. ***ROTC:*** Army (c), Navy (c), Air Force (c).
Computers: 92 computers/terminals are available on campus for general student use. Students can access the following: campus intranet, computer help desk, free student e-mail accounts, online (class) grades, online (class) registration, online (class) schedules. Campuswide network is available. 100% of college-owned or -operated housing units are wired for high-speed Internet access. Wireless service is available via entire campus.

STUDENT LIFE
Housing options: on-campus residence required through sophomore year; coed, women-only. Campus housing is university owned, leased by the school and is provided by a third party. Freshman applicants given priority for college housing.
Activities and organizations: drama/theater group, student-run newspaper, choral group, Campus Activities Board, Phi Beta Lamda, Gamma Sigma Sigma, Ambassadors for Christ, Class Councils.
Athletics Member NCAA. All Division III. ***Intercollegiate sports:*** baseball M, basketball M/W, cross-country running M/W, golf M, soccer M/W, softball W, tennis M/W, volleyball W. ***Intramural sports:*** basketball M/W, cheerleading M(c)/W(c), football M/W, lacrosse M/W, soccer M/W, tennis M/W, ultimate Frisbee M(c)/W(c), volleyball M/W.
Campus security: 24-hour emergency response devices and patrols, late-night transport/escort service, controlled dormitory access.
Student services: health clinic, personal/psychological counseling.

COSTS & FINANCIAL AID
Costs (2015–16) ***Comprehensive fee:*** $35,750 includes full-time tuition ($25,650), mandatory fees ($200), and room and board ($9900). Full-time tuition and fees vary according to class time and course load. Part-time tuition: $855 per credit hour. Part-time tuition and fees vary according to class time and course load. ***Payment plan:*** installment. ***Waivers:*** employees or children of employees.
Financial Aid Of all full-time matriculated undergraduates who enrolled in 2013, 982 applied for aid, 911 were judged to have need, 117 had their need fully met. 128 Federal Work-Study jobs (averaging $2000). In 2013, 72 non-need-based awards were made. ***Average percent of need met:*** 52. ***Average financial aid package:*** $19,961. ***Average need-based loan:*** $3943. ***Average need-based gift aid:*** $8202. ***Average non-need-based aid:*** $10,903. ***Average indebtedness upon graduation:*** $32,000.

APPLYING
Standardized Tests *Required:* SAT or ACT (for admission).
Options: electronic application, early admission, early action, deferred entrance.
Application fee: $35.

Required: high school transcript, minimum 2.0 GPA, Dean's Evaluation (transfers). ***Recommended:*** essay or personal statement, 2 letters of recommendation, interview.

Application deadlines: rolling (freshmen), rolling (out-of-state freshmen), rolling (transfers), 11/1 (early action).

Notification: continuous (freshmen), continuous (out-of-state freshmen), continuous (transfers), rolling (early action).

CONTACT

Office of Admissions, William Peace University, 15 East Peace Street, Raleigh, NC 27604. *Phone:* 919-508-2214. *Fax:* 919-508-2326. *E-mail:* admission@peace.edu.

See previous page for display ad and page 1742 for the College Close-Up.

Wingate University

Wingate, North Carolina

http://www.wingate.edu/

- **Independent Baptist** comprehensive, founded 1896
- **Small-town** 400-acre campus with easy access to Charlotte
- **Coed** 1,952 undergraduate students, 97% full-time, 59% women, 41% men
- **Moderately difficult** entrance level, 75% of applicants were admitted

UNDERGRAD STUDENTS

1,891 full-time, 61 part-time. Students come from 33 states and territories; 17 other countries; 17% are from out of state; 15% Black or African American, non-Hispanic/Latino; 3% Hispanic/Latino; 2% Asian, non-Hispanic/Latino; 0.2% Native Hawaiian or other Pacific Islander, non-Hispanic/Latino; 0.7% American Indian or Alaska Native, non-Hispanic/Latino; 5% Two or more races, non-Hispanic/Latino; 6% Race/ethnicity unknown; 4% international; 4% transferred in; 84% live on campus.

Freshmen

Admission: 6,601 applied, 4,955 admitted, 584 enrolled. ***Average high school GPA:*** 3.34. ***Test scores:*** SAT critical reading scores over 500: 50%; SAT math scores over 500: 57%; SAT writing scores over 500: 45%; ACT scores over 18: 90%; SAT critical reading scores over 600: 8%; SAT math scores over 600: 12%; SAT writing scores over 600: 8%; ACT scores over 24: 24%; SAT critical reading scores over 700: 1%; SAT math scores over 700: 1%; SAT writing scores over 700: 1%; ACT scores over 30: 2%.

Retention: 72% of full-time freshmen returned.

FACULTY

Total: 281, 57% full-time, 63% with terminal degrees.

Student/faculty ratio: 15:1.

ACADEMICS

Calendar: semesters. *Degrees:* bachelor's, master's, doctoral, and post-master's certificates.

Special study options: advanced placement credit, double majors, honors programs, independent study, internships, off-campus study, part-time degree program, services for LD students, study abroad, summer session for credit. ***ROTC:*** Army (c), Air Force (c).

Computers: 80 computers/terminals are available on campus for general student use. Students can access the following: campus intranet, computer help desk, free student e-mail accounts, online (class) grades, online (class) registration, online (class) schedules. Campuswide network is available. 100% of college-owned or -operated housing units are wired for high-speed Internet access. Wireless service is available via classrooms, dorm rooms, learning centers, libraries, student centers.

STUDENT LIFE

Housing options: on-campus residence required through senior year; men-only, women-only. Campus housing is university owned. Freshman campus housing is guaranteed.

Activities and organizations: drama/theater group, student-run newspaper, television station, choral group, marching band, University and Community Assistance Network (UCAN), Bulldog Activities Resource Committee, Fellowship of Christian Athletes, Student Bulldog Club, Student Government Association, national fraternities, national sororities.

Athletics Member NCAA. All Division II. ***Intercollegiate sports:*** baseball M(s), basketball M(s)/W(s), cross-country running M(s)/W(s), football M(s), golf M(s)/W(s), lacrosse M(s)/W(s), soccer M(s)/W(s), softball W(s), swimming and diving M(s)/W(s), tennis M(s)/W(s), track and field M(s)/W(s), volleyball W(s). ***Intramural sports:*** basketball M/W, bowling M/W, cross-country running M/W, football M/W, golf M/W, racquetball M/W, swimming and diving M/W, table tennis M/W, tennis M/W, track and field M/W, ultimate Frisbee M/W, volleyball M/W, water polo M/W, weight lifting M/W.

Campus security: 24-hour emergency response devices and patrols, late-night transport/escort service, controlled dormitory access.

Student services: health clinic, personal/psychological counseling.

COSTS & FINANCIAL AID

Costs (2015–16) ***Comprehensive fee:*** $38,710 includes full-time tuition ($27,930), mandatory fees ($180), and room and board ($10,600). Part-time tuition: $870 per credit hour. Part-time tuition and fees vary according to course load. ***Room and board:*** Room and board charges vary according to board plan. ***Payment plan:*** installment. ***Waivers:*** employees or children of employees.

Financial Aid Of all full-time matriculated undergraduates who enrolled in 2013, 1,738 applied for aid, 1,578 were judged to have need, 496 had their need fully met. In 2013, 379 non-need-based awards were made. ***Average percent of need met:*** 79. ***Average financial aid package:*** $21,022. ***Average need-based loan:*** $3998. ***Average need-based gift aid:*** $18,013. ***Average non-need-based aid:*** $13,028. ***Average indebtedness upon graduation:*** $29,939.

APPLYING

Standardized Tests *Required:* SAT or ACT (for admission).

Options: electronic application, early admission, deferred entrance.

Application fee: $30.

Required: high school transcript, minimum 2.0 GPA. ***Recommended:*** minimum 3.0 GPA, interview.

Application deadlines: rolling (freshmen), rolling (transfers).

Notification: continuous (freshmen), continuous (transfers).

CONTACT

Mr. Gabe Hollingsworth, Director of Admissions, Wingate University, PO Box 159, Wingate, NC 28174. *Phone:* 704-233-8000. *Toll-free phone:* 800-755-5550. *Fax:* 704-233-8110. *E-mail:* admit@wingate.edu.

NORTH DAKOTA

Bismarck State College

Bismarck, North Dakota

http://www.bismarckstate.edu/

- **State-supported** primarily 2-year, founded 1939, part of North Dakota University System
- **Urban** 100-acre campus
- **Coed**
- **Noncompetitive** entrance level

FACULTY

Student/faculty ratio: 15:1.

ACADEMICS

Calendar: semesters. *Degrees:* certificates, diplomas, associate, and bachelor's.

STUDENT LIFE

Housing options: coed, men-only, women-only, special housing for students with disabilities. Campus housing is university owned.

Activities and organizations: drama/theater group, student-run newspaper, radio station, choral group.

Athletics Member NJCAA.

Campus security: late-night transport/escort service, controlled dormitory access.

Student services: health clinic.

COSTS & FINANCIAL AID

Costs (2014–15) ***Tuition:*** state resident $2808 full-time, $117 per credit hour part-time; nonresident $7488 full-time, $312 per credit hour part-time. Full-time tuition and fees vary according to course level, course load, degree level, location, program, and reciprocity agreements. Part-time tuition and fees vary according to course level, course load, degree level, location, program, and reciprocity agreements. ***Required fees:*** $712 full-time, $30 per credit hour part-time. ***Room and board:*** $6801; room only: $2401. Room and board charges vary according to board plan and housing facility.

Financial Aid Of all full-time matriculated undergraduates who enrolled in 2012, 1,806 applied for aid, 1,301 were judged to have need, 530 had their need fully met. 53 Federal Work-Study jobs (averaging $975). In 2012, 281 non-need-based awards were made. ***Average percent of need met:*** 52. ***Average financial aid package:*** $10,330. ***Average need-based loan:*** $4428. ***Average need-based gift aid:*** $4329. ***Average non-need-based aid:*** $842. ***Average indebtedness upon graduation:*** $12,377.

APPLYING

Standardized Tests *Required for some:* SAT or ACT (for admission).

Options: electronic application, early admission.

Application fee: $35.

Required: high school transcript. ***Required for some:*** interview.

CONTACT

Karen Erickson, Director of Admissions and Enrollment Services, Bismarck State College, PO Box 5587, Bismarck, ND 58506. *Phone:* 701-224-5424. *Toll-free phone:* 800-445-5073. *Fax:* 701-224-5643. *E-mail:* karen.erickson@bismarckstate.edu.

Dickinson State University

Dickinson, North Dakota

http://www.dickinsonstate.edu/

- **State-supported** 4-year, founded 1918, part of North Dakota University System
- **Small-town** 132-acre campus
- **Endowment** $10.9 million
- **Coed** 1,475 undergraduate students, 66% full-time, 60% women, 40% men
- **Minimally difficult** entrance level, 61% of applicants were admitted

UNDERGRAD STUDENTS

980 full-time, 495 part-time. Students come from 37 states and territories; 18 other countries; 28% are from out of state; 4% Black or African American, non-Hispanic/Latino; 4% Hispanic/Latino; 0.6% Asian, non-Hispanic/Latino; 0.3% Native Hawaiian or other Pacific Islander, non-Hispanic/Latino; 0.9% American Indian or Alaska Native, non-Hispanic/Latino; 3% Two or more races, non-Hispanic/Latino; 3% Race/ethnicity unknown; 5% international; 30% live on campus.

Freshmen

Admission: 467 applied, 285 admitted, 193 enrolled. ***Average high school GPA:*** 3.15. ***Test scores:*** SAT critical reading scores over 500: 27%; SAT writing scores over 500: 27%; ACT scores over 18: 78%; SAT critical reading scores over 600: 9%; ACT scores over 24: 23%.

Retention: 57% of full-time freshmen returned.

FACULTY

Total: 161, 52% full-time, 33% with terminal degrees.

Student/faculty ratio: 17:1.

ACADEMICS

Calendar: semesters. *Degrees:* certificates, associate, and bachelor's.

Special study options: academic remediation for entering students, accelerated degree program, adult/continuing education programs, advanced placement credit, cooperative education, distance learning, double majors, external degree program, honors programs, independent study, internships, off-campus study, part-time degree program, services for LD students, student-designed majors, study abroad, summer session for credit.

Computers: 216 computers/terminals and 216 ports are available on campus for general student use. Students can access the following: campus intranet, computer help desk, free student e-mail accounts, online (class) grades, online (class) registration, online (class) schedules. Campuswide network is available. 100% of college-owned or -operated housing units are wired for high-speed Internet access. Wireless service is available via entire campus.

STUDENT LIFE

Housing options: on-campus residence required through sophomore year; coed, men-only, women-only, special housing for students with disabilities. Campus housing is university owned. Freshman campus housing is guaranteed.

Activities and organizations: drama/theater group, student-run newspaper, choral group, marching band, Rodeo Club, Blue Hawk Brigade, chorale, Business Club, Navigators.

Athletics Member NAIA. ***Intercollegiate sports:*** badminton M/W, baseball M(s), basketball M(s)/W(s), cheerleading M/W, cross-country running M(s)/W(s), football M(s), golf M(s)/W(s), softball W(s), track and field M(s)/W(s), volleyball W(s), wrestling M(s). ***Intramural sports:*** badminton M/W, basketball M/W, football M/W, soccer M/W, softball W, squash M/W, table tennis M/W, tennis M/W, volleyball M/W, water polo M/W.

Campus security: 24-hour emergency response devices and patrols, late-night transport/escort service.

Student services: health clinic.

COSTS & FINANCIAL AID

Costs (2014–15) ***Tuition:*** state resident $4891 full-time, $204 per credit part-time; nonresident $7337 full-time, $306 per credit part-time. Full-time tuition and fees vary according to course load, location, program, and reciprocity agreements. Part-time tuition and fees vary according to course load, location, program, and reciprocity agreements. ***Required fees:*** $1159 full-time, $48 per credit part-time, $48 per credit part-time. ***Room and board:*** $5850; room only: $2400. Room and board charges vary according to board plan. ***Payment plan:*** installment. ***Waivers:*** minority students, children of alumni, senior citizens, and employees or children of employees.

Financial Aid Of all full-time matriculated undergraduates who enrolled in 2012, 850 applied for aid, 645 were judged to have need, 291 had their need fully met. In 2012, 345 non-need-based awards were made. ***Average percent of need met:*** 41. ***Average financial aid package:*** $11,848. ***Average need-based loan:*** $5124. ***Average need-based gift aid:*** $4110. ***Average non-need-based aid:*** $1192. ***Average indebtedness upon graduation:*** $22,853.

APPLYING

Standardized Tests *Required:* SAT or ACT (for admission).

Options: electronic application, early admission, deferred entrance.

Application fee: $35.

Required: high school transcript, medical history, proof of measles-rubella shot.

Application deadlines: rolling (freshmen), rolling (transfers).

Notification: continuous (freshmen), continuous (transfers).

CONTACT

Miss Marie Moe, Director of University Relations, Dickinson State University, Campus Box 169, Dickinson, ND 58601. *Phone:* 701-483-2175. *Toll-free phone:* 800-279-4295. *Fax:* 701-483-2409. *E-mail:* dsu.hawk@dickinsonstate.edu.

Mayville State University

Mayville, North Dakota

http://www.mayvillestate.edu/

- **State-supported** 4-year, founded 1889, part of North Dakota University System
- **Rural** 60-acre campus
- **Coed** 1,056 undergraduate students, 60% full-time, 56% women, 44% men
- **Noncompetitive** entrance level, 57% of applicants were admitted

UNDERGRAD STUDENTS

635 full-time, 421 part-time. Students come from 38 states and territories; 6 other countries; 41% are from out of state; 7% Black or African American, non-Hispanic/Latino; 5% Hispanic/Latino; 0.2% Asian, non-Hispanic/Latino; 0.5% Native Hawaiian or other Pacific Islander, non-Hispanic/Latino; 2% American Indian or Alaska Native, non-

Hispanic/Latino; 3% Two or more races, non-Hispanic/Latino; 0.6% Race/ethnicity unknown; 3% international; 10% transferred in; 41% live on campus.

Freshmen

Admission: 413 applied, 236 admitted, 174 enrolled. ***Average high school GPA:*** 2.99. ***Test scores:*** ACT scores over 18: 69%; ACT scores over 24: 17%.

Retention: 54% of full-time freshmen returned.

FACULTY

Total: 81, 57% full-time, 26% with terminal degrees.

Student/faculty ratio: 13:1.

ACADEMICS

Calendar: semesters. *Degrees:* associate and bachelor's.

Special study options: academic remediation for entering students, accelerated degree program, adult/continuing education programs, advanced placement credit, cooperative education, distance learning, double majors, internships, off-campus study, part-time degree program, services for LD students, student-designed majors, summer session for credit. ***ROTC:*** Army (c), Air Force (c).

Computers: Students can access the following: campus intranet, computer help desk, free student e-mail accounts, online (class) grades, online (class) registration, online (class) schedules. Campuswide network is available. 100% of college-owned or -operated housing units are wired for high-speed Internet access. Wireless service is available via entire campus.

STUDENT LIFE

Housing options: on-campus residence required through sophomore year; coed, men-only, women-only. Campus housing is university owned and is provided by a third party. Freshman campus housing is guaranteed.

Activities and organizations: drama/theater group, student-run newspaper, radio station, choral group, Student Activities Council, Student Education Association, Health and Physical Education Club, Campus Crusade, Student Ambassadors.

Athletics Member NAIA. ***Intercollegiate sports:*** baseball M(s), basketball M(s)/W(s), football M(s), softball W(s), volleyball W(s). ***Intramural sports:*** basketball M/W, bowling M/W, football M/W, golf M/W, ice hockey M, racquetball M/W, soccer M/W, softball M/W, table tennis M/W, tennis M/W, track and field M/W, volleyball M/W.

Campus security: controlled dormitory access.

Student services: health clinic, personal/psychological counseling.

COSTS & FINANCIAL AID

Costs (2014–15) ***One-time required fee:*** $35. ***Tuition:*** state resident $4810 full-time, $200 per credit hour part-time; nonresident $7215 full-time, $300 per credit hour part-time. Full-time tuition and fees vary according to course load and reciprocity agreements. Part-time tuition and fees vary according to course load and reciprocity agreements. ***Required fees:*** $1679 full-time, $70 per credit hour part-time. ***Room and board:*** $5430; room only: $2044. Room and board charges vary according to board plan and housing facility. ***Payment plan:*** installment. ***Waivers:*** minority students, senior citizens, and employees or children of employees.

Financial Aid Of all full-time matriculated undergraduates who enrolled in 2014, 536 applied for aid, 398 were judged to have need, 135 had their need fully met. 66 Federal Work-Study jobs (averaging $1096). In 2014, 180 non-need-based awards were made. ***Average percent of need met:*** 67. ***Average financial aid package:*** $14,270. ***Average need-based loan:*** $6324. ***Average need-based gift aid:*** $4902. ***Average non-need-based aid:*** $1057. ***Average indebtedness upon graduation:*** $31,681.

APPLYING

Standardized Tests *Required:* SAT or ACT (for admission).

Options: electronic application, deferred entrance.

Application fee: $35.

Required: high school transcript, minimum 2.0 GPA.

Application deadlines: rolling (freshmen), rolling (out-of-state freshmen), rolling (transfers).

Notification: continuous until 1/1 (freshmen), continuous until 1/1 (out-of-state freshmen), continuous until 1/1 (transfers).

CONTACT

Jim Morowski, Director of Freshmen Enrollment Services, Mayville State University, 330 3rd Street, NE, Mayville, ND 58257-1299. *Phone:* 701-788-4842. *Toll-free phone:* 800-437-4104. *Fax:* 701-788-4748. *E-mail:* james.morowski@mayvillestate.edu.

Minot State University

Minot, North Dakota

http://www.minotstateu.edu/

- **State-supported** comprehensive, founded 1913, part of North Dakota University System
- **Small-town** 103-acre campus
- **Coed** 3,116 undergraduate students, 67% full-time, 60% women, 40% men
- **Moderately difficult** entrance level, 58% of applicants were admitted

UNDERGRAD STUDENTS

2,075 full-time, 1,041 part-time. 17% are from out of state; 4% Black or African American, non-Hispanic/Latino; 5% Hispanic/Latino; 1% Asian, non-Hispanic/Latino; 0.2% Native Hawaiian or other Pacific Islander, non-Hispanic/Latino; 2% American Indian or Alaska Native, non-Hispanic/Latino; 3% Two or more races, non-Hispanic/Latino; 2% Race/ethnicity unknown; 15% international; 10% transferred in; 17% live on campus.

Freshmen

Admission: 775 applied, 447 admitted, 341 enrolled. ***Average high school GPA:*** 3.37. ***Test scores:*** ACT scores over 18: 92%; ACT scores over 24: 38%; ACT scores over 30: 2%.

Retention: 67% of full-time freshmen returned.

FACULTY

Total: 279, 60% full-time, 35% with terminal degrees.

Student/faculty ratio: 12:1.

ACADEMICS

Calendar: semesters. *Degrees:* certificates, associate, bachelor's, master's, and postbachelor's certificates.

Special study options: academic remediation for entering students, accelerated degree program, advanced placement credit, cooperative education, distance learning, double majors, English as a second language, honors programs, independent study, internships, part-time degree program, services for LD students, student-designed majors, study abroad, summer session for credit.

Computers: Students can access the following: campus intranet, computer help desk, free student e-mail accounts, online (class) grades, online (class) registration, online (class) schedules. Campuswide network is available. Wireless service is available via entire campus.

STUDENT LIFE

Housing options: on-campus residence required for freshman year; coed, men-only, women-only, special housing for students with disabilities. Campus housing is university owned. Freshman campus housing is guaranteed.

Activities and organizations: drama/theater group, student-run newspaper, radio and television station, choral group, marching band, Residence Hall Association, Student Government Association, Beavers on Business, Student Social Work Organization, National Student Speech and Hearing Association.

Athletics Member NCAA, NAIA, NCCAA. All NCAA Division II. ***Intercollegiate sports:*** baseball M(s), basketball M(s)/W(s), cheerleading W, cross-country running M(s)/W(s), football M(s), golf M/W, ice hockey M(c), soccer W, softball W(s), track and field M(s)/W(s), volleyball W(s), wrestling M. ***Intramural sports:*** basketball M/W, racquetball M/W, softball M/W, volleyball M/W.

Campus security: controlled dormitory access, patrols by trained security personnel.

Student services: health clinic, personal/psychological counseling, women's center.

COSTS & FINANCIAL AID

Costs (2014–15) ***Tuition:*** state resident $4820 full-time, $254 per credit hour part-time; nonresident $4820 full-time, $254 per credit hour part-time. Full-time tuition and fees vary according to class time, course load, degree level, location, program, and reciprocity agreements. Part-time tuition and fees vary according to class time, course load, degree level, location, program, and reciprocity agreements. ***Required fees:*** $1266 full-time. ***Room and board:*** $5550. Room and board charges vary according to board plan and housing facility. ***Payment plan:*** installment. ***Waivers:*** minority students, children of alumni, senior citizens, and employees or children of employees.

Financial Aid Of all full-time matriculated undergraduates who enrolled in 2013, 1,422 applied for aid, 1,027 were judged to have need, 338 had their need fully met. 97 Federal Work-Study jobs (averaging $1681). In 2013, 306 non-need-based awards were made. ***Average percent of need met:*** 72. ***Average financial aid package:*** $9441. ***Average need-based loan:*** $5518. ***Average need-based gift aid:*** $4593. ***Average non-need-based aid:*** $1066. ***Average indebtedness upon graduation:*** $24,856.

APPLYING

Standardized Tests *Required:* SAT or ACT (for admission).

Options: electronic application, deferred entrance.

Application fee: $35.

Required: high school transcript. ***Required for some:*** minimum 2.5 GPA.

CONTACT

Mr. Kevin Harmon, Vice President of Enrollment Management, Minot State University, 500 University Avenue West, Minot, ND 58707-0002. *Phone:* 701-858-3126. *Toll-free phone:* 800-777-0750 Ext. 3350. *Fax:* 701-858-3825. *E-mail:* askmsu@minotstateu.edu.

North Dakota State University

Fargo, North Dakota

http://www.ndsu.edu/

- **State-supported** university, founded 1890, part of North Dakota University System
- **Urban** 2100-acre campus
- **Endowment** $414,351
- **Coed** 12,124 undergraduate students, 90% full-time, 45% women, 55% men
- **Moderately difficult** entrance level, 83% of applicants were admitted

UNDERGRAD STUDENTS

10,865 full-time, 1,259 part-time. Students come from 48 states and territories; 69 other countries; 57% are from out of state; 3% Black or African American, non-Hispanic/Latino; 2% Hispanic/Latino; 1% Asian, non-Hispanic/Latino; 0.1% Native Hawaiian or other Pacific Islander, non-Hispanic/Latino; 0.7% American Indian or Alaska Native, non-Hispanic/Latino; 2% Two or more races, non-Hispanic/Latino; 2% Race/ethnicity unknown; 4% international; 6% transferred in; 26% live on campus.

Freshmen

Admission: 5,713 applied, 4,727 admitted, 2,469 enrolled. ***Average high school GPA:*** 3.43. ***Test scores:*** SAT critical reading scores over 500: 68%; SAT math scores over 500: 78%; SAT writing scores over 500: 59%; ACT scores over 18: 98%; SAT critical reading scores over 600: 35%; SAT math scores over 600: 44%; SAT writing scores over 600: 29%; ACT scores over 24: 53%; SAT critical reading scores over 700: 20%; SAT math scores over 700: 22%; SAT writing scores over 700: 4%; ACT scores over 30: 10%.

Retention: 80% of full-time freshmen returned.

FACULTY

Total: 891, 78% full-time, 73% with terminal degrees.

Student/faculty ratio: 17:1.

ACADEMICS

Calendar: semesters. *Degrees:* certificates, bachelor's, master's, doctoral, post-master's, and postbachelor's certificates.

Special study options: advanced placement credit, cooperative education, distance learning, double majors, honors programs, independent study, internships, off-campus study, part-time degree program, services for LD students, student-designed majors, study abroad, summer session for credit. ***ROTC:*** Army (b), Air Force (b).

Computers: 610 computers/terminals are available on campus for general student use. Students can access the following: campus intranet, computer help desk, free student e-mail accounts, online (class) grades, online (class) registration, online (class) schedules, online course content (e.g., learning management system, lecture capture video recordings). Campuswide network is available. 100% of college-owned or -operated housing units are wired for high-speed Internet access. Wireless service is available via entire campus.

STUDENT LIFE

Housing options: on-campus residence required for freshman year; coed, men-only, women-only, special housing for students with disabilities. Campus housing is university owned. Freshman campus housing is guaranteed.

Activities and organizations: drama/theater group, student-run newspaper, radio and television station, choral group, marching band, Saddle and Sirloin, Students Today, Leaders Forever, International Student Association, Chi Alpha Christian Organization, fraternities/sororities, national fraternities, national sororities.

Athletics Member NCAA. All Division I. ***Intercollegiate sports:*** badminton M(c)/W(c), baseball M(s), basketball M(s)/W(s), bowling M(c)/W(c), cheerleading M(c)/W(c), cross-country running M(s)/W(s), equestrian sports M(c)/W(c), football M(s), golf M/W(s), ice hockey M(c)/W(c), lacrosse M(c)/W(c), riflery M(c)/W(c), rugby M(c)/W(c), soccer M(c)/W(s), softball W(s), track and field M(s)/W(s), volleyball M(c)/W(s), wrestling M(s). ***Intramural sports:*** baseball M, basketball M/W, football M/W, soccer M/W, softball M/W, tennis M(c)/W(c), volleyball M/W.

Campus security: 24-hour emergency response devices and patrols, student patrols, late-night transport/escort service, controlled dormitory access.

Student services: health clinic, personal/psychological counseling.

COSTS & FINANCIAL AID

Costs (2014–15) ***One-time required fee:*** $120. ***Tuition:*** state resident $6604 full-time, $291 per credit hour part-time; nonresident $17,633 full-time, $776 per credit hour part-time. Full-time tuition and fees vary according to course load, program, and reciprocity agreements. Part-time tuition and fees vary according to course load, program, and reciprocity agreements. ***Required fees:*** $1216 full-time, $51 per credit hour part-time. ***Room and board:*** $7282; room only: $3372. Room and board charges vary according to board plan and housing facility. ***Waivers:*** minority students, children of alumni, senior citizens, and employees or children of employees.

Financial Aid Of all full-time matriculated undergraduates who enrolled in 2007, 7,109 applied for aid, 4,917 were judged to have need, 980 had their need fully met. In 2007, 1763 non-need-based awards were made. ***Average percent of need met:*** 3. ***Average financial aid package:*** $7030. ***Average need-based loan:*** $4378. ***Average need-based gift aid:*** $3419. ***Average non-need-based aid:*** $1533.

APPLYING

Standardized Tests *Required:* SAT or ACT (for admission).

Options: electronic application.

Application fee: $35.

Required: high school transcript, minimum 2.5 GPA.

Application deadlines: 8/15 (freshmen), 8/15 (transfers).

Notification: continuous (freshmen), continuous (transfers).

CONTACT

Ms. Merideth Sherlin, Interim Director of Admission, North Dakota State University, NDSU Department 5230, PO Box 6050, Fargo, ND 58105-5454. *Phone:* 701-231-8643. *Toll-free phone:* 800-488-NDSU. *Fax:* 701-231-8802. *E-mail:* ndsu.admission@ndsu.edu.

Rasmussen College Bismarck

Bismarck, North Dakota

http://www.rasmussen.edu/

- **Proprietary** 4-year, part of Rasmussen College System
- **Suburban** campus
- **Coed** 210 undergraduate students, 47% full-time, 68% women, 32% men
- **Minimally difficult** entrance level

UNDERGRAD STUDENTS

98 full-time, 112 part-time.

Freshmen
Admission: 20 enrolled.

FACULTY
Total: 9, 22% full-time.

Student/faculty ratio: 22:1.

ACADEMICS
Degrees: certificates, diplomas, associate, and bachelor's.

Special study options: academic remediation for entering students, accelerated degree program, adult/continuing education programs, distance learning, double majors, internships, part-time degree program, summer session for credit.

Computers: 67 computers/terminals are available on campus for general student use. Students can access the following: computer help desk, free student e-mail accounts, online (class) grades, online (class) schedules. Campuswide network is available. Wireless service is available via entire campus.

STUDENT LIFE
Housing options: college housing not available.

COSTS
Costs (2014–15) ***Tuition:*** $10,764 full-time, $350 per credit hour part-time. Full-time tuition and fees vary according to course level, course load, degree level, location, and program. Part-time tuition and fees vary according to course level, course load, degree level, location, and program. No tuition increase for student's term of enrollment. ***Required fees:*** $1350 full-time. ***Payment plans:*** installment, deferred payment. ***Waivers:*** employees or children of employees.

APPLYING
Standardized Tests *Required:* Internal Exam (for admission).

Options: electronic application, early admission, deferred entrance.

Required: high school transcript, minimum 2.0 GPA. ***Required for some:*** interview.

Application deadlines: rolling (freshmen), rolling (transfers).

CONTACT
Susan Hammerstrom, Director of Admissions, Rasmussen College Bismarck, 1701 East Century Avenue, Bismarck, ND 58503. *Phone:* 701-530-9600. *Toll-free phone:* 888-549-6755. *E-mail:* susan.hammerstrom@rasmussen.edu.

Rasmussen College Fargo

Fargo, North Dakota

http://www.rasmussen.edu/

- **Proprietary** 4-year, founded 1902, part of Rasmussen College System
- **Suburban** campus
- **Coed** 754 undergraduate students, 57% full-time, 73% women, 27% men
- **Minimally difficult** entrance level

UNDERGRAD STUDENTS
428 full-time, 326 part-time.

Freshmen
Admission: 40 enrolled.

FACULTY
Total: 10, 40% full-time.

Student/faculty ratio: 22:1.

ACADEMICS
Calendar: quarters. *Degrees:* certificates, diplomas, associate, and bachelor's.

Special study options: academic remediation for entering students, accelerated degree program, adult/continuing education programs, distance learning, double majors, internships, part-time degree program, summer session for credit.

Computers: 87 computers/terminals are available on campus for general student use. Students can access the following: computer help desk, free student e-mail accounts, online (class) grades, online (class) schedules. Campuswide network is available. Wireless service is available via entire campus.

STUDENT LIFE
Housing options: college housing not available.

COSTS
Costs (2014–15) ***Tuition:*** $10,764 full-time, $310 per credit hour part-time. Full-time tuition and fees vary according to course level, course load, degree level, location, and program. Part-time tuition and fees vary according to course level, course load, degree level, location, and program. No tuition increase for student's term of enrollment. ***Required fees:*** $1350 full-time. ***Payment plans:*** installment, deferred payment. ***Waivers:*** employees or children of employees.

APPLYING
Standardized Tests *Required:* Internal Exam (for admission).

Options: electronic application, early admission, deferred entrance.

Required: high school transcript, minimum 2.0 GPA. ***Required for some:*** interview.

Application deadlines: rolling (freshmen), rolling (transfers).

CONTACT
Susan Hammerstrom, Director of Admissions, Rasmussen College Fargo, 4012 19th Avenue SW, Fargo, ND 58103. *Phone:* 701-277-3889. *Toll-free phone:* 888-549-6755. *E-mail:* susan.hammerstrom@rasmussen.edu.

University of Jamestown

Jamestown, North Dakota

http://www.uj.edu/

- **Independent Presbyterian** comprehensive, founded 1883
- **Small-town** 110-acre campus
- **Endowment** $35.2 million
- **Coed** 892 undergraduate students, 94% full-time, 54% women, 46% men
- **Minimally difficult** entrance level, 64% of applicants were admitted

UNDERGRAD STUDENTS
839 full-time, 53 part-time. Students come from 37 states and territories; 17 other countries; 49% are from out of state; 4% Black or African American, non-Hispanic/Latino; 5% Hispanic/Latino; 0.9% Asian, non-Hispanic/Latino; 0.3% Native Hawaiian or other Pacific Islander, non-Hispanic/Latino; 1% American Indian or Alaska Native, non-Hispanic/Latino; 0.1% Race/ethnicity unknown; 7% international; 7% transferred in; 76% live on campus.

Freshmen
Admission: 839 applied, 540 admitted, 210 enrolled. ***Average high school GPA:*** 3.45. ***Test scores:*** SAT critical reading scores over 500: 43%; SAT math scores over 500: 61%; ACT scores over 18: 97%; SAT critical reading scores over 600: 14%; SAT math scores over 600: 14%; ACT scores over 24: 46%; SAT critical reading scores over 700: 2%; SAT math scores over 700: 2%; ACT scores over 30: 5%.
Retention: 66% of full-time freshmen returned.

FACULTY
Total: 92, 71% full-time, 40% with terminal degrees.

Student/faculty ratio: 13:1.

ACADEMICS
Calendar: semesters. *Degrees:* bachelor's, master's, and doctoral.

Special study options: adult/continuing education programs, advanced placement credit, cooperative education, double majors, honors programs, independent study, internships, part-time degree program, services for LD students, student-designed majors, study abroad, summer session for credit.

Unusual degree programs: 3-2 engineering with North Dakota State University, University of North Dakota, South Dakota State University, Washington University in St. Louis.

Computers: 200 computers/terminals and 570 ports are available on campus for general student use. Students can access the following: campus intranet, computer help desk, free student e-mail accounts, online (class) grades, online (class) registration, online (class) schedules. Campuswide network is available. 100% of college-owned or -operated housing units are wired for high-speed Internet access. Wireless service is available via entire campus.

STUDENT LIFE
Housing options: on-campus residence required through junior year; coed. Campus housing is university owned. Freshman campus housing is guaranteed.

Activities and organizations: drama/theater group, student-run newspaper, radio and television station, choral group, Ignition, Student Senate, Knight Society, Jimmie Janes, Fellowship of Christian Athletes.

Athletics Member NAIA. ***Intercollegiate sports:*** baseball M(s), basketball M(s)/W(s), cross-country running M(s)/W(s), football M(s), golf M(s)/W(s), soccer M(s)/W(s), softball W(s), track and field M(s)/W(s), volleyball W(s), wrestling M(s)/W(s). ***Intramural sports:*** basketball M/W, football M/W, volleyball M/W.

Campus security: late-night transport/escort service, controlled dormitory access, Campus Security Cameras.

Student services: personal/psychological counseling.

COSTS & FINANCIAL AID
Costs (2015–16) ***Comprehensive fee:*** $26,730 includes full-time tuition ($19,350), mandatory fees ($520), and room and board ($6860). Full-time tuition and fees vary according to course load, degree level, and program. Part-time tuition: $435 per credit. Part-time tuition and fees vary according to course load, degree level, and program. ***Required fees:*** $60 per term part-time. ***College room only:*** $3235. Room and board charges vary according to housing facility. ***Payment plan:*** installment. ***Waivers:*** employees or children of employees.

Financial Aid Of all full-time matriculated undergraduates who enrolled in 2013, 692 applied for aid, 580 were judged to have need, 135 had their need fully met. 259 Federal Work-Study jobs (averaging $176,187). 100 state and other part-time jobs (averaging $70,931). In 2013, 270 non-need-based awards were made. ***Average percent of need met:*** 69. ***Average financial aid package:*** $13,893. ***Average need-based loan:*** $4025. ***Average need-based gift aid:*** $10,563. ***Average non-need-based aid:*** $6797. ***Average indebtedness upon graduation:*** $26,530.

APPLYING
Standardized Tests *Required:* SAT or ACT (for admission).

Options: electronic application, deferred entrance.

Required: high school transcript, minimum 2.5 GPA. ***Required for some:*** interview.

Application deadlines: rolling (freshmen), rolling (out-of-state freshmen), rolling (transfers).

CONTACT
Mr. Scott Goplin, Dean of Enrollment Management, University of Jamestown, 6081 College Lane, Jamestown, ND 58401. *Phone:* 701-252-3467 Ext. 5512. *Toll-free phone:* 800-336-2554. *Fax:* 701-253-4318. *E-mail:* admissions@uj.edu.

University of North Dakota
Grand Forks, North Dakota
http://www.und.edu/

- **State-supported** university, founded 1883, part of North Dakota University System
- **Urban** 548-acre campus
- **Endowment** $14.6 million
- **Coed** 11,537 undergraduate students, 79% full-time, 43% women, 57% men
- **Minimally difficult** entrance level, 86% of applicants were admitted

UNDERGRAD STUDENTS
9,079 full-time, 2,458 part-time. Students come from 58 other countries; 60% are from out of state; 2% Black or African American, non-Hispanic/Latino; 3% Hispanic/Latino; 2% Asian, non-Hispanic/Latino; 0.1% Native Hawaiian or other Pacific Islander, non-Hispanic/Latino; 2% American Indian or Alaska Native, non-Hispanic/Latino; 3% Two or more races, non-Hispanic/Latino; 3% Race/ethnicity unknown; 6% international; 6% transferred in; 28% live on campus.

Freshmen
Admission: 4,642 applied, 3,992 admitted, 1,906 enrolled. ***Average high school GPA:*** 3.4. ***Test scores:*** ACT scores over 18: 97%; ACT scores over 24: 48%; ACT scores over 30: 6%.
Retention: 80% of full-time freshmen returned.

FACULTY
Total: 753, 93% full-time, 72% with terminal degrees.

Student/faculty ratio: 19:1.

ACADEMICS
Calendar: semesters. *Degrees:* certificates, bachelor's, master's, doctoral, post-master's, and postbachelor's certificates.

Special study options: accelerated degree program, adult/continuing education programs, advanced placement credit, cooperative education, distance learning, double majors, English as a second language, external degree program, honors programs, independent study, internships, off-campus study, part-time degree program, services for LD students, student-designed majors, study abroad, summer session for credit. ***ROTC:*** Army (b), Air Force (b).

Unusual degree programs: 3-2 engineering; applied economics, counseling, chemistry, public administration.

Computers: 1,500 computers/terminals and 400 ports are available on campus for general student use. Students can access the following: campus intranet, computer help desk, free student e-mail accounts, online (class) grades, online (class) registration, online (class) schedules. Campuswide network is available. 100% of college-owned or -operated housing units are wired for high-speed Internet access. Wireless service is available via classrooms, computer centers, computer labs, dorm rooms, learning centers, libraries, student centers.

STUDENT LIFE
Housing options: coed, men-only, women-only, special housing for students with disabilities. Campus housing is university owned and leased by the school.

Activities and organizations: drama/theater group, student-run newspaper, radio and television station, choral group, marching band, NoDak Nation, Cru, Chinese Students and Scholars Association, Student Occupational Therapy Association, Several Sororities, national fraternities, national sororities.

Athletics Member NCAA. All Division I. ***Intercollegiate sports:*** baseball M(s), basketball M(s)/W(s), cross-country running M(s)/W(s), football M(s), golf M(s)/W(s), ice hockey M(s)/W(s), soccer W(s), softball W(s), swimming and diving M(s)/W(s), tennis W(s), track and field M(s)/W(s), volleyball W(s). ***Intramural sports:*** basketball M/W, ice hockey M/W, soccer M/W, softball M/W, ultimate Frisbee M/W, volleyball M/W.

Campus security: 24-hour emergency response devices and patrols, student patrols, late-night transport/escort service, controlled dormitory access, emergency telephones.

Student services: health clinic, personal/psychological counseling, women's center, legal services.

COSTS & FINANCIAL AID
Costs (2014–15) ***Tuition:*** state resident $6388 full-time, $266 per credit hour part-time; nonresident $17,056 full-time, $711 per credit hour part-time. Full-time tuition and fees vary according to degree level, program, and reciprocity agreements. Part-time tuition and fees vary according to course load, degree level, program, and reciprocity agreements. ***Required fees:*** $1353 full-time. ***Room and board:*** $6810; room only: $2660. Room and board charges vary according to board plan and housing facility. ***Payment plan:*** deferred payment. ***Waivers:*** minority students, adult students, senior citizens, and employees or children of employees.

Financial Aid Of all full-time matriculated undergraduates who enrolled in 2010, 6,878 applied for aid, 5,256 were judged to have need, 5,108 had their need fully met. In 2010, 2719 non-need-based awards were made. ***Average percent of need met:*** 39. ***Average financial aid package:*** $9651. ***Average need-based loan:*** $5349. ***Average need-based gift aid:*** $4076. ***Average non-need-based aid:*** $1602. ***Average indebtedness upon graduation:*** $31,764.

APPLYING
Standardized Tests *Required:* SAT or ACT (for admission). *Recommended:* SAT and SAT Subject Tests or ACT (for admission).

Options: electronic application, deferred entrance.

Application fee: $35.

Required: high school transcript. ***Recommended:*** minimum 2.5 GPA.

Notification: continuous (transfers).

CONTACT
Jason Trainer, Director of Admissions, University of North Dakota, Gorecki Alumni Center, 3501 University Ave. Stop 8357, Grand Forks, ND 58202. *Phone:* 701-777-3000. *Toll-free phone:* 800-CALL-UND. *Fax:* 701-777-2721. *E-mail:* UND.admissions@UND.edu.

Valley City State University

Valley City, North Dakota

http://www.vcsu.edu/

- **State-supported** comprehensive, founded 1890, part of North Dakota University System
- **Small-town** 55-acre campus
- **Coed** 1,234 undergraduate students, 63% full-time, 58% women, 42% men
- **Noncompetitive** entrance level, 90% of applicants were admitted

UNDERGRAD STUDENTS
779 full-time, 455 part-time. Students come from 42 states and territories; 11 other countries; 35% are from out of state; 3% Black or African American, non-Hispanic/Latino; 4% Hispanic/Latino; 0.6% Asian, non-Hispanic/Latino; 0.1% Native Hawaiian or other Pacific Islander, non-Hispanic/Latino; 1% American Indian or Alaska Native, non-Hispanic/Latino; 3% Two or more races, non-Hispanic/Latino; 1% Race/ethnicity unknown; 3% international; 8% transferred in; 24% live on campus.

Freshmen
Admission: 370 applied, 334 admitted, 190 enrolled. ***Average high school GPA:*** 3.19. ***Test scores:*** SAT critical reading scores over 500: 13%; SAT math scores over 500: 40%; SAT writing scores over 500: 13%; ACT scores over 18: 82%; ACT scores over 24: 26%; ACT scores over 30: 2%.
Retention: 70% of full-time freshmen returned.

ACADEMICS
Calendar: semesters. *Degrees:* bachelor's and master's.
Special study options: academic remediation for entering students, cooperative education, distance learning, double majors, internships, off-campus study, part-time degree program, services for LD students, student-designed majors, study abroad, summer session for credit.
Computers: 995 computers/terminals are available on campus for general student use. Students can access the following: campus intranet, computer help desk, free student e-mail accounts, online (class) grades, online (class) registration, online (class) schedules. Campuswide network is available. 100% of college-owned or -operated housing units are wired for high-speed Internet access. Wireless service is available via entire campus.

STUDENT LIFE
Housing options: on-campus residence required for freshman year; coed, men-only, women-only. Campus housing is university owned. Freshman campus housing is guaranteed.
Activities and organizations: drama/theater group, choral group, departmental clubs, Fellowship of Christian Athletes, intramural sports, VCAB, Viking Ambassadors.
Athletics Member NAIA. ***Intercollegiate sports:*** baseball M(s), basketball M(s)/W(s), cross-country running M(s)/W(s), football M(s), golf M(s)/W(s), softball W(s), tennis M(c)/W(c), track and field M(s)/W(s), volleyball W(s). ***Intramural sports:*** basketball M/W, bowling M/W, cross-country running M/W, football M/W, golf M/W, ice hockey M/W, racquetball M/W, skiing (cross-country) M/W, soccer M/W, softball M/W, tennis M/W, track and field M/W, volleyball M/W.
Campus security: controlled dormitory access, security cameras throughout campus.
Student services: health clinic, personal/psychological counseling.

COSTS & FINANCIAL AID
Costs (2014–15) ***Tuition:*** state resident $5027 full-time, $168 per semester hour part-time; nonresident $13,423 full-time, $448 per semester hour part-time. Full-time tuition and fees vary according to course load, location, program, and reciprocity agreements. Part-time tuition and fees vary according to course load, location, program, and reciprocity agreements. ***Required fees:*** $1647 full-time, $69 per semester hour part-time. ***Room and board:*** $5938; room only: $3070. Room and board charges vary according to board plan and housing facility. ***Payment plan:*** installment. ***Waivers:*** employees or children of employees.
Financial Aid Of all full-time matriculated undergraduates who enrolled in 2014, 639 applied for aid, 481 were judged to have need, 239 had their need fully met. 42 Federal Work-Study jobs (averaging $1850). In 2014, 172 non-need-based awards were made. ***Average percent of need met:*** 70. ***Average financial aid package:*** $9366. ***Average need-based loan:*** $3702. ***Average need-based gift aid:*** $4851. ***Average non-need-based aid:*** $2920. ***Average indebtedness upon graduation:*** $27,756.

APPLYING
Standardized Tests *Required for some:* SAT or ACT (for admission).
Options: electronic application, early admission, deferred entrance.
Application fee: $35.
Required: high school transcript.
Application deadlines: rolling (freshmen), rolling (transfers).
Notification: continuous (freshmen), continuous (transfers).

CONTACT
Ms. Kaleen Peterson, Admission Counselor, Valley City State University, 101 College Street Southwest, Valley City, ND 58072. *Phone:* 701-845-7115. *Toll-free phone:* 800-532-8641 Ext. 7101. *Fax:* 701-845-7299. *E-mail:* kaleen.peterson@vcsu.edu.

OHIO

Antioch College

Yellow Springs, Ohio

http://antiochcollege.org/

- **Independent** 4-year, founded 2011
- **Rural** 1100-acre campus with easy access to Columbus
- **Endowment** $45.3 million
- **Coed** 238 undergraduate students, 100% full-time, 66% women, 34% men
- **Very difficult** entrance level, 48% of applicants were admitted

UNDERGRAD STUDENTS
238 full-time. Students come from 10 other countries; 75% are from out of state; 5% transferred in; 95% live on campus.

Freshmen
Admission: 252 applied, 121 admitted, 59 enrolled. ***Average high school GPA:*** 3.01. ***Test scores:*** SAT critical reading scores over 500: 95%; SAT math scores over 500: 75%; ACT scores over 18: 100%; SAT critical reading scores over 600: 75%; SAT math scores over 600: 35%; ACT scores over 24: 88%; SAT critical reading scores over 700: 35%; ACT scores over 30: 38%.
Retention: 91% of full-time freshmen returned.

FACULTY
Total: 35, 89% full-time, 89% with terminal degrees.
Student/faculty ratio: 7:1.

ACADEMICS
Degree: bachelor's.
Special study options: academic remediation for entering students, advanced placement credit, cooperative education, distance learning, independent study, off-campus study, services for LD students, student-designed majors, summer session for credit.
Computers: Students can access the following: campus intranet, computer help desk, free student e-mail accounts, online (class) grades, online (class) registration, online (class) schedules. Campuswide network is available. 100% of college-owned or -operated housing units are wired for high-speed Internet access. Wireless service is available via entire campus.

STUDENT LIFE
Housing options: on-campus residence required through sophomore year; coed. Campus housing is university owned.

Activities and organizations: drama/theater group, student-run newspaper, choral group, People of Color Group, Abilities Group, Queer Center, To Shin Do.

Campus security: 24-hour patrols, controlled dormitory access.

Student services: personal/psychological counseling, women's center.

COSTS

Costs (2014–15) ***Comprehensive fee:*** $40,670 includes full-time tuition ($30,250), mandatory fees ($700), and room and board ($9720). Full-time tuition and fees vary according to reciprocity agreements. Part-time tuition and fees vary according to reciprocity agreements. ***College room only:*** $6170. ***Payment plans:*** installment, deferred payment. ***Waivers:*** employees or children of employees.

APPLYING

Options: early admission, early decision, deferred entrance.

Required: essay or personal statement, 2 letters of recommendation, interview. ***Recommended:*** high school transcript.

Application deadlines: 2/15 (freshmen), 2/15 (out-of-state freshmen).

Notification: 4/1 (freshmen), 4/1 (out-of-state freshmen).

CONTACT

Antioch College, 1 Morgan Place, Yellow Springs, OH 45387. *Phone:* 937-3196236.

Antioch University Midwest

Yellow Springs, Ohio

http://midwest.antioch.edu/

- **Independent** upper-level, founded 1988, part of Antioch University
- **Small-town** 100-acre campus with easy access to Dayton
- **Coed** 81 undergraduate students, 37% full-time, 69% women, 31% men
- **Noncompetitive** entrance level

UNDERGRAD STUDENTS

30 full-time, 51 part-time. Students come from 1 other state; 20% Black or African American, non-Hispanic/Latino; 1% Asian, non-Hispanic/Latino; 2% American Indian or Alaska Native, non-Hispanic/Latino; 2% Race/ethnicity unknown; 17% transferred in.

FACULTY

Total: 43, 35% full-time.

Student/faculty ratio: 5:1.

ACADEMICS

Calendar: quarters. *Degrees:* certificates, bachelor's, master's, post-master's, and postbachelor's certificates.

Special study options: accelerated degree program, adult/continuing education programs, advanced placement credit, cooperative education, distance learning, double majors, independent study, internships, off-campus study, part-time degree program, services for LD students, student-designed majors, summer session for credit.

Computers: 10 computers/terminals are available on campus for general student use. Students can access the following: campus intranet, computer help desk, free student e-mail accounts, online (class) grades, online (class) registration, online (class) schedules, online bill pay, and online view/acceptance of financial aid award letter, view narrative evaluations. Campuswide network is available. Wireless service is available via entire campus.

STUDENT LIFE

Housing options: college housing not available.

Campus security: 24-hour emergency response devices.

Student services: personal/psychological counseling.

COSTS & FINANCIAL AID

Costs (2015–16) ***Tuition:*** $18,972 full-time, $527 per credit part-time. ***Required fees:*** $435 full-time.

Financial Aid Of all full-time matriculated undergraduates who enrolled in 2011, 35 applied for aid, 34 were judged to have need. 5 Federal Work-Study jobs (averaging $7000). ***Average percent of need met:*** 30. ***Average financial aid package:*** $8800. ***Average need-based loan:*** $7000. ***Average need-based gift aid:*** $5000. ***Average indebtedness upon graduation:*** $40,000.

APPLYING

Options: electronic application, deferred entrance.

Application fee: $45.

CONTACT

Antioch University Midwest, 900 Dayton Street, Yellow Springs, OH 45387-1609. *Phone:* 937-769-1823.

The Art Institute of Cincinnati

Cincinnati, Ohio

http://www.aic-arts.edu/

- **Independent** primarily 2-year, founded 1976
- **Urban** 3-acre campus with easy access to Cincinnati
- **Coed** 34 undergraduate students, 88% full-time, 65% women, 35% men
- **Noncompetitive** entrance level, 74% of applicants were admitted

UNDERGRAD STUDENTS

30 full-time, 4 part-time. Students come from 3 states and territories; 27% are from out of state; 18% Black or African American, non-Hispanic/Latino.

Freshmen

Admission: 46 applied, 34 admitted, 6 enrolled. ***Average high school GPA:*** 3.3.

Retention: 90% of full-time freshmen returned.

FACULTY

Total: 11, 36% full-time, 18% with terminal degrees.

Student/faculty ratio: 5:1.

ACADEMICS

Degrees: associate and bachelor's.

Special study options: academic remediation for entering students, accelerated degree program, advanced placement credit, cooperative education, part-time degree program, services for LD students.

Computers: 20 computers/terminals and 50 ports are available on campus for general student use. Students can access the following: campus intranet, free student e-mail accounts, online (class) grades, online (class) registration, online (class) schedules. Campuswide network is available. Wireless service is available via entire campus.

STUDENT LIFE

Housing options: college housing not available.

Activities and organizations: AIGA Student Chapter.

Campus security: 24-hour emergency response devices, SMS.

Student services: personal/psychological counseling.

COSTS

Costs (2015–16) ***Tuition:*** $23,001 full-time, $511 per credit hour part-time. No tuition increase for student's term of enrollment. ***Required fees:*** $1017 full-time. ***Payment plan:*** installment. ***Waivers:*** employees or children of employees.

APPLYING

Standardized Tests *Recommended:* SAT or ACT (for admission).

Options: early admission, early decision, deferred entrance.

Application fee: $100.

Required: essay or personal statement, high school transcript, interview. ***Recommended:*** minimum 2.0 GPA, ACT or SAT score submission recommended. Placement testing is offered.

Application deadlines: rolling (freshmen), rolling (out-of-state freshmen), rolling (transfers).

Early decision deadline: rolling (for plan 1), rolling (for plan 2).

Notification: continuous (freshmen), continuous (out-of-state freshmen), continuous (transfers), rolling (early decision plan 1), rolling (early decision plan 2).

CONTACT

Megan Orsburn AIA, Admissions Assistant, The Art Institute of Cincinnati, 1171 E. Kemper Road, Cincinnati, OH 45246. *Phone:* 513-751-1206.

The Art Institute of Ohio–Cincinnati

Cincinnati, Ohio

http://www.artinstitutes.edu/cincinnati/

- **Proprietary** 4-year, part of Education Management Corporation
- **Urban** campus
- **Coed**

ACADEMICS

Calendar: continuous. *Degrees:* diplomas, associate, and bachelor's.

CONTACT

The Art Institute of Ohio–Cincinnati, 8845 Governors Hill Drive, Cincinnati, OH 45249-3317. *Phone:* 513-833-2400. *Toll-free phone:* 866-613-5184.

Ashland University

Ashland, Ohio

http://www.ashland.edu/

- **Independent** comprehensive, founded 1878, affiliated with Brethren Church
- **Small-town** 135-acre campus with easy access to Cleveland, Akron
- **Endowment** $39.4 million
- **Coed** 3,198 undergraduate students, 75% full-time, 51% women, 49% men
- **Moderately difficult** entrance level, 73% of applicants were admitted

UNDERGRAD STUDENTS

2,389 full-time, 809 part-time. Students come from 31 states and territories; 19 other countries; 6% are from out of state; 5% Black or African American, non-Hispanic/Latino; 2% Hispanic/Latino; 0.2% Asian, non-Hispanic/Latino; 0.1% Native Hawaiian or other Pacific Islander, non-Hispanic/Latino; 0.3% American Indian or Alaska Native, non-Hispanic/Latino; 2% Two or more races, non-Hispanic/Latino; 4% international; 4% transferred in; 86% live on campus.

Freshmen

Admission: 3,184 applied, 2,315 admitted, 623 enrolled. ***Average high school GPA:*** 3.44. ***Test scores:*** SAT critical reading scores over 500: 59%; SAT math scores over 500: 58%; ACT scores over 18: 96%; SAT critical reading scores over 600: 18%; SAT math scores over 600: 22%; ACT scores over 24: 40%; SAT critical reading scores over 700: 1%; SAT math scores over 700: 2%; ACT scores over 30: 4%.

Retention: 78% of full-time freshmen returned.

FACULTY

Total: 627, 42% full-time, 53% with terminal degrees.

Student/faculty ratio: 10:1.

ACADEMICS

Calendar: semesters. *Degrees:* certificates, diplomas, associate, bachelor's, master's, doctoral, post-master's, and postbachelor's certificates.

Special study options: academic remediation for entering students, accelerated degree program, adult/continuing education programs, advanced placement credit, cooperative education, distance learning, double majors, English as a second language, external degree program, honors programs, independent study, internships, off-campus study, part-time degree program, services for LD students, student-designed majors, study abroad, summer session for credit. ***ROTC:*** Army (c), Air Force (c).

Unusual degree programs: 3-2 business administration.

Computers: 760 computers/terminals are available on campus for general student use. Students can access the following: campus intranet, computer help desk, free student e-mail accounts, online (class) grades, online (class) registration, online (class) schedules. Campuswide network is available. 100% of college-owned or -operated housing units are wired for high-speed Internet access. Wireless service is available via classrooms, computer centers, computer labs, learning centers, libraries, student centers.

STUDENT LIFE

Housing options: on-campus residence required through junior year; coed, men-only, women-only, special housing for students with disabilities. Campus housing is university owned. Freshman campus housing is guaranteed.

Activities and organizations: drama/theater group, student-run newspaper, radio and television station, choral group, marching band, Campus Activity Board, Fellowship of Christian Athletes, The Well Campus Ministry, intramurals, Sororities, national fraternities, national sororities.

Athletics Member NCAA. All Division II. ***Intercollegiate sports:*** baseball M(s), basketball M(s)/W(s), cross-country running M(s)/W(s), football M(s), golf M(s)/W(s), soccer W(s), softball W(s), swimming and diving M(s)/W(s), tennis W(s), track and field M(s)/W(s), volleyball W(s), wrestling M(s). ***Intramural sports:*** badminton M/W, baseball M(c), basketball M/W, bowling M/W, cross-country running M/W, field hockey M/W, football M, golf M/W, lacrosse M(c)/W(c), racquetball M/W, rock climbing M/W, rugby M(c)/W(c), skiing (downhill) M(c)/W(c), soccer M/W, softball M(c)/W(c), swimming and diving M/W, table tennis M/W, tennis M/W, track and field M/W, ultimate Frisbee M/W, volleyball M(c)/W(c), weight lifting M(c)/W(c), wrestling M.

Campus security: 24-hour emergency response devices and patrols, student patrols, late-night transport/escort service, controlled dormitory access.

Student services: health clinic, personal/psychological counseling.

COSTS & FINANCIAL AID

Costs (2015–16) ***Tuition:*** $0 full-time. Full-time tuition and fees vary according to location and program. Part-time tuition and fees vary according to course load, location, and program. ***Room only:*** Room and board charges vary according to board plan, housing facility, and location. ***Payment plan:*** installment. ***Waivers:*** children of alumni, senior citizens, and employees or children of employees.

Financial Aid Of all full-time matriculated undergraduates who enrolled in 2013, 1,947 applied for aid, 1,947 were judged to have need. 1,380 Federal Work-Study jobs (averaging $2589). In 2013, 220 non-need-based awards were made. ***Average financial aid package:*** $25,115. ***Average need-based loan:*** $4648. ***Average need-based gift aid:*** $18,414. ***Average non-need-based aid:*** $11,236. ***Average indebtedness upon graduation:*** $36,058.

APPLYING

Standardized Tests *Required:* SAT or ACT (for admission).

Options: electronic application, deferred entrance.

Required: high school transcript, minimum 2.5 GPA, standardized test score for Freshmen applicants, 18 ACT or 860 SAT (Critical Reading and Math).

Application deadlines: rolling (freshmen), rolling (out-of-state freshmen), rolling (transfers).

Notification: continuous (freshmen), continuous (out-of-state freshmen), continuous (transfers).

CONTACT

Mr. W.C. Vance, Director of Admission, Ashland University, 401 College Avenue, Ashland, OH 44805. *Phone:* 419-289-5052. *Toll-free phone:* 800-882-1548. *Fax:* 419-289-5999. *E-mail:* enrollme@ashland.edu.

★ Baldwin Wallace University

Berea, Ohio

http://www.bw.edu/

- **Independent Methodist** comprehensive, founded 1845
- **Suburban** 120-acre campus with easy access to Cleveland
- **Endowment** $141.4 million
- **Coed** 3,362 undergraduate students, 88% full-time, 56% women, 44% men
- **Moderately difficult** entrance level, 64% of applicants were admitted

UNDERGRAD STUDENTS

2,969 full-time, 393 part-time. Students come from 44 states and territories; 26 other countries; 19% are from out of state; 9% Black or African American, non-Hispanic/Latino; 5% Hispanic/Latino; 1% Asian, non-Hispanic/Latino; 0.1% Native Hawaiian or other Pacific Islander, non-Hispanic/Latino; 0.1% American Indian or Alaska Native, non-Hispanic/Latino; 4% Two or more races, non-Hispanic/Latino; 0.4% Race/ethnicity unknown; 1% international; 6% transferred in; 63% live on campus.

Freshmen
Admission: 4,224 applied, 2,702 admitted, 717 enrolled. ***Average high school GPA:*** 3.43. ***Test scores:*** SAT critical reading scores over 500: 72%; SAT math scores over 500: 73%; SAT writing scores over 500: 67%; ACT scores over 18: 88%; SAT critical reading scores over 600: 25%; SAT math scores over 600: 25%; SAT writing scores over 600: 21%; ACT scores over 24: 42%; SAT critical reading scores over 700: 5%; SAT math scores over 700: 3%; SAT writing scores over 700: 4%; ACT scores over 30: 4%.
Retention: 81% of full-time freshmen returned.

FACULTY
Total: 441, 42% full-time, 39% with terminal degrees.
Student/faculty ratio: 13:1.

ACADEMICS
Calendar: semesters. *Degrees:* certificates, bachelor's, and master's.
Special study options: academic remediation for entering students, accelerated degree program, adult/continuing education programs, advanced placement credit, distance learning, double majors, English as a second language, honors programs, independent study, internships, off-campus study, part-time degree program, services for LD students, student-designed majors, study abroad, summer session for credit. ***ROTC:*** Army (c), Air Force (c).
Unusual degree programs: 3-2 engineering with Case Western Reserve University and Columbia University; social work with Case Western Reserve University; MBA programs in accounting, computer information systems, computer science, and human resources.
Computers: 550 computers/terminals and 100 ports are available on campus for general student use. Students can access the following: campus intranet, computer help desk, free student e-mail accounts, online (class) grades, online (class) registration, online (class) schedules. Campuswide network is available. 100% of college-owned or -operated housing units are wired for high-speed Internet access. Wireless service is available via entire campus.

STUDENT LIFE
Housing options: on-campus residence required through sophomore year; coed, special housing for students with disabilities. Campus housing is university owned. Freshman applicants given priority for college housing.
Activities and organizations: drama/theater group, student-run newspaper, radio and television station, choral group, marching band, Circle K, Habitat for Humanity, Dance Marathon, Campus Crusade, Black Student Alliance, national fraternities, national sororities.
Athletics Member NCAA. All Division III. ***Intercollegiate sports:*** baseball M, basketball M/W, cross-country running M/W, football M, golf M/W, lacrosse M/W, soccer M/W, softball W, swimming and diving M/W, tennis M/W, track and field M/W, volleyball W, wrestling M. ***Intramural sports:*** archery M(c)/W(c), badminton M/W, basketball M/W, cheerleading W(c), crew M(c)/W(c), football M, golf M/W, lacrosse M/W, racquetball M/W, riflery M(c)/W(c), rugby M(c)/W(c), skiing (cross-country) M(c)/W(c), skiing (downhill) M(c)/W(c), soccer M/W, softball M/W, table tennis M(c)/W(c), tennis M/W, ultimate Frisbee M/W, volleyball M/W, wrestling M.
Campus security: 24-hour emergency response devices and patrols, student patrols, late-night transport/escort service, controlled dormitory access, Emergency Text Messaging and Emergency Classroom phones with Public Announcement Capabilities.
Student services: health clinic, personal/psychological counseling.

COSTS & FINANCIAL AID
Costs (2014–15) ***Comprehensive fee:*** $36,862 includes full-time tuition ($28,814) and room and board ($8048). Full-time tuition and fees vary according to class time, course level, course load, degree level, program, and reciprocity agreements. Part-time tuition: $895 per semester hour. Part-time tuition and fees vary according to class time, course level, course load, degree level, program, and reciprocity agreements. ***College room only:*** $4648. Room and board charges vary according to housing facility. ***Payment plans:*** installment, deferred payment. ***Waivers:*** children of alumni and employees or children of employees.
Financial Aid Of all full-time matriculated undergraduates who enrolled in 2014, 2,585 applied for aid, 2,354 were judged to have need, 839 had their need fully met. 1,017 Federal Work-Study jobs (averaging $1273). 378 state and other part-time jobs (averaging $1273). In 2014, 483 non-

need-based awards were made. ***Average percent of need met:*** 87. ***Average financial aid package:*** $21,666. ***Average need-based loan:*** $4034. ***Average need-based gift aid:*** $16,201. ***Average non-need-based aid:*** $12,080. ***Average indebtedness upon graduation:*** $32,526.

APPLYING
Standardized Tests *Required for some:* SAT or ACT (for admission).

Options: electronic application, deferred entrance.

Application fee: $25.

Required: essay or personal statement, high school transcript, 1 letter of recommendation. ***Recommended:*** minimum 3.0 GPA, interview.

Application deadlines: 5/1 (freshmen), 8/1 (transfers).

Notification: continuous (freshmen), continuous (transfers).

CONTACT
Joyce J Cendroski, Director of Undergraduate Admission Operations/Transfer Admission, Baldwin Wallace University, Durst Welcome Center, 115 Tressel Street, Berea, OH 44017. *Phone:* 440-826-2222. *Toll-free phone:* 877-BW-APPLY. *Fax:* 440-826-3830. *E-mail:* admission@bw.edu.

See previous page for display ad and page 1352 for the College Close-Up.

Bluffton University

Bluffton, Ohio

http://www.bluffton.edu/

- **Independent Mennonite** comprehensive, founded 1899
- **Small-town** 65-acre campus with easy access to Dayton
- **Endowment** $23.5 million
- **Coed** 997 undergraduate students, 80% full-time, 50% women, 50% men
- **Moderately difficult** entrance level, 56% of applicants were admitted

UNDERGRAD STUDENTS
796 full-time, 201 part-time. Students come from 23 states and territories; 6 other countries; 14% are from out of state; 6% Black or African American, non-Hispanic/Latino; 3% Hispanic/Latino; 0.6% Asian, non-Hispanic/Latino; 2% Two or more races, non-Hispanic/Latino; 2% Race/ethnicity unknown; 0.4% international; 3% transferred in; 84% live on campus.

Freshmen
Admission: 2,315 applied, 1,297 admitted, 218 enrolled. ***Average high school GPA:*** 3.26. ***Test scores:*** SAT critical reading scores over 500: 56%; SAT math scores over 500: 52%; ACT scores over 18: 93%; SAT critical reading scores over 600: 16%; SAT math scores over 600: 16%; ACT scores over 24: 40%; SAT critical reading scores over 700: 4%; SAT math scores over 700: 8%; ACT scores over 30: 2%.

Retention: 70% of full-time freshmen returned.

FACULTY
Total: 100, 55% full-time, 63% with terminal degrees.

Student/faculty ratio: 12:1.

ACADEMICS
Calendar: semesters. *Degrees:* bachelor's, master's, and postbachelor's certificates.

Special study options: academic remediation for entering students, accelerated degree program, adult/continuing education programs, advanced placement credit, distance learning, double majors, honors programs, independent study, internships, off-campus study, part-time degree program, services for LD students, student-designed majors, study abroad, summer session for credit.

Computers: 170 computers/terminals and 1,300 ports are available on campus for general student use. Students can access the following: campus intranet, computer help desk, free student e-mail accounts, online (class) grades, online (class) registration, online (class) schedules. Campuswide network is available. 100% of college-owned or -operated housing units are wired for high-speed Internet access. Wireless service is available via classrooms, computer centers, computer labs, dorm rooms, libraries, student centers.

STUDENT LIFE
Housing options: on-campus residence required through senior year; coed, men-only, women-only. Campus housing is university owned. Freshman campus housing is guaranteed.

Activities and organizations: drama/theater group, student-run newspaper, radio station, choral group, Intramurals, Student Senate, Marbeck Center Board, Music Groups/Chorale, Campus Ministries.

Athletics Member NCAA. All Division III. ***Intercollegiate sports:*** baseball M, basketball M/W, cross-country running M/W, football M, soccer M/W, softball W, track and field M/W, volleyball W. ***Intramural sports:*** basketball M/W, bowling M/W, football M/W, softball M/W, tennis M/W, ultimate Frisbee M, volleyball M/W.

Campus security: 24-hour emergency response devices, controlled dormitory access, night security guards.

Student services: health clinic, personal/psychological counseling.

COSTS & FINANCIAL AID
Costs (2014–15) ***Comprehensive fee:*** $39,148 includes full-time tuition ($28,866), mandatory fees ($450), and room and board ($9832). Full-time tuition and fees vary according to course load and reciprocity agreements. Part-time tuition: $1203 per credit hour. Part-time tuition and fees vary according to course load. ***Required fees:*** $113 per term part-time. ***Room and board:*** Room and board charges vary according to board plan and housing facility. ***Payment plan:*** installment. ***Waivers:*** employees or children of employees.

Financial Aid Of all full-time matriculated undergraduates who enrolled in 2014, 703 applied for aid, 669 were judged to have need, 318 had their need fully met. 537 Federal Work-Study jobs (averaging $2290). 200 state and other part-time jobs (averaging $2423). In 2014, 69 non-need-based awards were made. ***Average percent of need met:*** 91. ***Average financial aid package:*** $27,372. ***Average need-based loan:*** $4910. ***Average need-based gift aid:*** $20,652. ***Average non-need-based aid:*** $14,013. ***Average indebtedness upon graduation:*** $35,883. ***Financial aid deadline:*** 10/1.

APPLYING
Standardized Tests *Required:* SAT or ACT (for admission).

Options: electronic application, deferred entrance.

Application fee: $20.

Required: high school transcript, minimum 2.3 GPA, 1 letter of recommendation, rank in upper 50% of high school class or 19 on ACT. ***Required for some:*** essay or personal statement. ***Recommended:*** interview.

Application deadlines: 8/15 (freshmen), rolling (transfers).

Notification: continuous (freshmen), continuous (transfers).

CONTACT
Mr. Derek Stemen, Director of Admissions, Bluffton University, 1 University Drive, Bluffton, OH 45817. *Phone:* 419-358-336141. *Toll-free phone:* 800-488-3257. *Fax:* 419-358-3081. *E-mail:* admissions@bluffton.edu.

Bowling Green State University

Bowling Green, Ohio

http://www.bgsu.edu/

- **State-supported** university, founded 1910
- **Small-town** 1338-acre campus with easy access to Toledo
- **Endowment** $148.3 million
- **Coed** 14,099 undergraduate students, 92% full-time, 56% women, 44% men
- **Moderately difficult** entrance level, 53% of applicants were admitted

UNDERGRAD STUDENTS
12,993 full-time, 1,106 part-time. Students come from 52 states and territories; 38 other countries; 12% are from out of state; 10% Black or African American, non-Hispanic/Latino; 4% Hispanic/Latino; 0.8% Asian, non-Hispanic/Latino; 0.1% Native Hawaiian or other Pacific Islander, non-Hispanic/Latino; 0.2% American Indian or Alaska Native, non-Hispanic/Latino; 3% Two or more races, non-Hispanic/Latino; 3% Race/ethnicity unknown; 2% international; 5% transferred in; 42% live on campus.

Freshmen
Admission: 14,509 applied, 7,743 admitted, 3,030 enrolled. ***Average high school GPA:*** 3.3. ***Test scores:*** SAT critical reading scores over 500: 61%; SAT math scores over 500: 64%; SAT writing scores over 500: 47%; ACT scores over 18: 94%; SAT critical reading scores over 600: 21%; SAT math scores over 600: 21%; SAT writing scores over 600: 13%; ACT

scores over 24: 39%; SAT critical reading scores over 700: 3%; SAT math scores over 700: 3%; SAT writing scores over 700: 1%; ACT scores over 30: 5%.

Retention: 76% of full-time freshmen returned.

FACULTY

Total: 1,015, 69% full-time, 64% with terminal degrees.

Student/faculty ratio: 19:1.

ACADEMICS

Calendar: semesters. *Degrees:* bachelor's, master's, doctoral, post-master's, and postbachelor's certificates.

Special study options: academic remediation for entering students, accelerated degree program, adult/continuing education programs, advanced placement credit, cooperative education, distance learning, double majors, English as a second language, freshman honors college, independent study, internships, off-campus study, part-time degree program, services for LD students, student-designed majors, study abroad, summer session for credit. ***ROTC:*** Army (b), Air Force (b).

Computers: 1,500 computers/terminals and 500 ports are available on campus for general student use. Students can access the following: computer help desk, free student e-mail accounts, online (class) grades, online (class) registration, online (class) schedules, wireless networking, MyFiles, OneDrive, Bursar billing information and payment, online mid-term grade reporting, view and change personal information, order official and unofficial transcripts, check meal plan balance, apply for graduation. Campuswide network is available. 100% of college-owned or -operated housing units are wired for high-speed Internet access. Wireless service is available via classrooms, computer centers, computer labs, dorm rooms, learning centers, libraries, student centers.

STUDENT LIFE

Housing options: on-campus residence required through sophomore year; coed, women-only, special housing for students with disabilities. Campus housing is university owned. Freshman campus housing is guaranteed.

Activities and organizations: drama/theater group, student-run newspaper, radio and television station, choral group, marching band, Dance Marathon, University Activities Organization, BG Undead, H2O, Black Student Union, national fraternities, national sororities.

Athletics Member NCAA. All Division I. ***Intercollegiate sports:*** baseball M(s), basketball M(s)/W(s), cross-country running M(s)/W(s), football M(s), golf M(s)/W(s), gymnastics W(s), ice hockey M(s), soccer M(s)/W(s), softball W(s), swimming and diving W(s), tennis W(s), track and field W(s), volleyball W(s). ***Intramural sports:*** badminton M/W, baseball M(c), basketball M/W, bowling M(c)/W(c), cross-country running M/W, equestrian sports M(c)/W(c), football M/W, golf M/W, gymnastics M(c)/W(c), ice hockey M(c), lacrosse M(c)/W(c), rugby M(c)/W(c), sailing M(c)/W(c), skiing (downhill) M(c)/W(c), soccer M/W, softball W, swimming and diving M(c)/W(c), tennis M(c)/W, track and field M(c)/W(c), ultimate Frisbee M/W, volleyball M/W, water polo M(c)/W(c), wrestling M(c)/W(c).

Campus security: 24-hour emergency response devices and patrols, late-night transport/escort service, controlled dormitory access.

Student services: health clinic, personal/psychological counseling, women's center, legal services.

COSTS & FINANCIAL AID

Costs (2014–15) ***Tuition:*** state resident $9096 full-time, $379 per credit hour part-time; nonresident $16,404 full-time, $684 per credit hour part-time. Full-time tuition and fees vary according to course load and location. Part-time tuition and fees vary according to course load and location. ***Required fees:*** $1630 full-time, $67 per credit hour part-time. ***Room and board:*** $8244. Room and board charges vary according to board plan and housing facility. ***Payment plan:*** installment. ***Waivers:*** senior citizens and employees or children of employees.

Financial Aid Of all full-time matriculated undergraduates who enrolled in 2014, 10,391 applied for aid, 8,548 were judged to have need, 1,052 had their need fully met. 447 Federal Work-Study jobs (averaging $1264). In 2014, 2411 non-need-based awards were made. ***Average percent of need met:*** 74. ***Average financial aid package:*** $13,927. ***Average need-based loan:*** $7441. ***Average need-based gift aid:*** $6448. ***Average non-need-based aid:*** $4676. ***Average indebtedness upon graduation:*** $30,307.

APPLYING

Standardized Tests *Required:* SAT or ACT (for admission).

Options: electronic application, deferred entrance.

Application fee: $45.

Required for some: high school transcript.

Application deadlines: 7/15 (freshmen), 7/15 (out-of-state freshmen), 7/15 (transfers).

Notification: continuous until 8/1 (freshmen), continuous until 8/1 (out-of-state freshmen), continuous (transfers).

CONTACT

Bowling Green State University, Admissions Office, 110 McFall, Bowling Green State University, Bowling Green, OH 43403. *Phone:* 419-372-BGSU. *Fax:* 419-372-6955. *E-mail:* choosebgsu@bgsu.edu.

Bowling Green State University-Firelands College

Huron, Ohio

http://www.firelands.bgsu.edu/

- **State-supported** primarily 2-year, founded 1968, part of Bowling Green State University System
- **Rural** 216-acre campus with easy access to Cleveland, Toledo
- **Coed** 2,287 undergraduate students, 52% full-time, 63% women, 37% men
- **Noncompetitive** entrance level, 77% of applicants were admitted

UNDERGRAD STUDENTS

1,191 full-time, 1,096 part-time. Students come from 8 states and territories; 6% Black or African American, non-Hispanic/Latino; 5% Hispanic/Latino; 0.5% Asian, non-Hispanic/Latino; 0.2% Native Hawaiian or other Pacific Islander, non-Hispanic/Latino; 0.4% American Indian or Alaska Native, non-Hispanic/Latino; 4% Two or more races, non-Hispanic/Latino; 4% Race/ethnicity unknown; 6% transferred in.

Freshmen

Admission: 856 applied, 658 admitted, 385 enrolled. ***Average high school GPA:*** 2.8.

Retention: 52% of full-time freshmen returned.

FACULTY

Total: 141, 37% full-time, 27% with terminal degrees.

Student/faculty ratio: 19:1.

ACADEMICS

Calendar: semesters. *Degrees:* certificates, associate, and bachelor's (also offers some upper-level and graduate courses).

Special study options: academic remediation for entering students, adult/continuing education programs, advanced placement credit, cooperative education, distance learning, double majors, honors programs, independent study, internships, part-time degree program, services for LD students, student-designed majors, study abroad, summer session for credit. ***ROTC:*** Army (c), Air Force (c).

Computers: 300 computers/terminals are available on campus for general student use. Students can access the following: computer help desk, free student e-mail accounts, online (class) grades, online (class) registration, online (class) schedules. Campuswide network is available. Wireless service is available via entire campus.

STUDENT LIFE

Housing options: college housing not available.

Activities and organizations: drama/theater group, Society of Fandom and Gaming, Student Government, Student Theater Guild, Safe Space, Society of Leadership and Success.

Athletics ***Intramural sports:*** basketball M/W, bowling M/W, football M, table tennis M/W, volleyball M/W.

Campus security: 24-hour emergency response devices, late-night transport/escort service, patrols by trained security personnel.

COSTS

Costs (2015–16) ***Tuition:*** state resident $4706 full-time, $196 per credit hour part-time; nonresident $12,014 full-time, $501 per credit hour part-time. Full-time tuition and fees vary according to location. Part-time tuition and fees vary according to location. ***Required fees:*** $240 full-time,

$9 per credit hour part-time, $120 per term part-time. ***Payment plan:*** installment. ***Waivers:*** employees or children of employees.

APPLYING
Options: electronic application, early admission, deferred entrance.
Application fee: $45.
Required: high school transcript.
Application deadlines: 8/6 (freshmen), 8/6 (transfers).
Notification: continuous (freshmen), continuous (transfers).

CONTACT
Debralee Divers, Director of Admissions and Financial Aid, Bowling Green State University-Firelands College, One University Drive, Huron, OH 44839-9791. *Phone:* 419-433-5560. *Toll-free phone:* 800-322-4787. *Fax:* 419-372-0604. *E-mail:* divers@bgsu.edu.

Brown Mackie College–Akron

Akron, Ohio

http://www.brownmackie.edu/akron/

- **Proprietary** primarily 2-year, founded 1968, part of Education Management Corporation
- **Suburban** campus
- **Coed**

ACADEMICS
Calendar: quarters. *Degrees:* diplomas, associate, and bachelor's.

CONTACT
Brown Mackie College–Akron, 755 White Pond Drive, Suite 101, Akron, OH 44320. *Phone:* 330-869-3600.

Brown Mackie College–Cincinnati

Cincinnati, Ohio

http://www.brownmackie.edu/cincinnati/

- **Proprietary** primarily 2-year, founded 1927, part of Education Management Corporation
- **Suburban** campus
- **Coed**

ACADEMICS
Calendar: quarters. *Degrees:* diplomas, associate, and bachelor's.

CONTACT
Brown Mackie College–Cincinnati, 1011 Glendale-Milford Road, Cincinnati, OH 45215. *Phone:* 513-771-2424. *Toll-free phone:* 800-888-1445.

Brown Mackie College–Findlay

Findlay, Ohio

http://www.brownmackie.edu/findlay/

- **Proprietary** primarily 2-year, founded 1929, part of Education Management Corporation
- **Rural** campus
- **Coed**

ACADEMICS
Calendar: continuous. *Degrees:* diplomas, associate, and bachelor's.

CONTACT
Brown Mackie College–Findlay, 1700 Fostoria Avenue, Suite 100, Findlay, OH 45840. *Phone:* 419-423-2211. *Toll-free phone:* 800-842-3687.

Brown Mackie College–North Canton

Canton, Ohio

http://www.brownmackie.edu/northcanton/

- **Proprietary** primarily 2-year, founded 1929, part of Education Management Corporation
- **Suburban** campus
- **Coed**

ACADEMICS
Calendar: quarters. *Degrees:* diplomas, associate, and bachelor's.

CONTACT
Brown Mackie College–North Canton, 4300 Munson Street NW, Canton, OH 44718-3674. *Phone:* 330-494-1214.

Capital University

Columbus, Ohio

http://www.capital.edu/

- **Independent** comprehensive, founded 1830, affiliated with Evangelical Lutheran Church in America
- **Suburban** 48-acre campus with easy access to Columbus
- **Endowment** $74.3 million
- **Coed** 2,742 undergraduate students, 89% full-time, 58% women, 42% men
- **Moderately difficult** entrance level, 73% of applicants were admitted

UNDERGRAD STUDENTS
2,454 full-time, 288 part-time. Students come from 38 states and territories; 21 other countries; 10% are from out of state; 9% Black or African American, non-Hispanic/Latino; 4% Hispanic/Latino; 1% Asian, non-Hispanic/Latino; 4% Two or more races, non-Hispanic/Latino; 3% Race/ethnicity unknown; 2% international; 3% transferred in; 59% live on campus.

Freshmen
Admission: 3,654 applied, 2,666 admitted, 710 enrolled. ***Average high school GPA:*** 3.46. ***Test scores:*** SAT critical reading scores over 500: 68%; SAT math scores over 500: 65%; SAT writing scores over 500: 57%; ACT scores over 18: 97%; SAT critical reading scores over 600: 24%; SAT math scores over 600: 27%; SAT writing scores over 600: 17%; ACT scores over 24: 56%; SAT critical reading scores over 700: 5%; SAT math scores over 700: 2%; SAT writing scores over 700: 1%; ACT scores over 30: 10%.
Retention: 76% of full-time freshmen returned.

FACULTY
Total: 414, 41% full-time, 49% with terminal degrees.
Student/faculty ratio: 12:1.

ACADEMICS
Calendar: semesters. *Degrees:* bachelor's, master's, doctoral, and postbachelor's certificates.
Special study options: accelerated degree program, adult/continuing education programs, advanced placement credit, cooperative education, double majors, English as a second language, external degree program, freshman honors college, honors programs, independent study, internships, off-campus study, part-time degree program, services for LD students, student-designed majors, study abroad, summer session for credit. ***ROTC:*** Army (b), Air Force (c).
Unusual degree programs: 3-2 engineering with Washington University in St. Louis, Case Western Reserve University; occupational therapy with Washington University in St. Louis, University of Indianapolis.
Computers: 457 computers/terminals and 1,400 ports are available on campus for general student use. Students can access the following: campus intranet, computer help desk, free student e-mail accounts, online (class) grades, online (class) registration, online (class) schedules. Campuswide network is available. 100% of college-owned or -operated housing units are wired for high-speed Internet access. Wireless service is available via entire campus.

STUDENT LIFE
Housing options: on-campus residence required through sophomore year; coed, special housing for students with disabilities. Campus housing is university owned. Freshman campus housing is guaranteed.
Activities and organizations: drama/theater group, student-run newspaper, radio and television station, choral group, Campus Crusade for Christ, student government, University Programming, College Republicans, American Marketing Association, national fraternities, national sororities.
Athletics Member NCAA. All Division III. ***Intercollegiate sports:*** baseball M, basketball M/W, cross-country running M/W, football M, golf M/W, lacrosse M/W, soccer M/W, softball W, tennis M/W, track and field

M/W, volleyball W. ***Intramural sports:*** basketball M/W, cheerleading M(c)/W(c), fencing M(c)/W(c), football M/W, racquetball M/W, ultimate Frisbee M/W, volleyball M/W.

Campus security: 24-hour emergency response devices and patrols, late-night transport/escort service, controlled dormitory access.

Student services: health clinic, personal/psychological counseling.

COSTS & FINANCIAL AID

Costs (2014–15) ***Comprehensive fee:*** $41,050 includes full-time tuition ($31,990) and room and board ($9060). Full-time tuition and fees vary according to course load. Part-time tuition: $1066 per credit hour. Part-time tuition and fees vary according to course load. ***Room and board:*** Room and board charges vary according to board plan and housing facility. ***Payment plan:*** installment. ***Waivers:*** senior citizens and employees or children of employees.

Financial Aid Of all full-time matriculated undergraduates who enrolled in 2013, 2,153 applied for aid, 1,986 were judged to have need, 476 had their need fully met. In 2013, 384 non-need-based awards were made. ***Average percent of need met:*** 78. ***Average financial aid package:*** $25,472. ***Average need-based loan:*** $4814. ***Average need-based gift aid:*** $19,945. ***Average non-need-based aid:*** $17,689. ***Average indebtedness upon graduation:*** $33,833.

APPLYING

Standardized Tests *Required:* SAT or ACT (for admission).

Options: electronic application, deferred entrance.

Application fee: $25.

Required: high school transcript, minimum 2.6 GPA. ***Required for some:*** 1 letter of recommendation, audition for Conservatory of Music. ***Recommended:*** interview.

Application deadlines: 5/1 (freshmen), rolling (transfers).

Notification: 9/30 (freshmen), continuous (transfers).

CONTACT

Ms. Amanda Sohl, Director of Admission, Capital University, 1 College and Main, Columbus, OH 43209. *Phone:* 614-236-6574. *Toll-free phone:* 866-544-6175. *Fax:* 614-236-6926. *E-mail:* asohl@capital.edu.

Case Western Reserve University

Cleveland, Ohio

http://www.case.edu/

- **Independent** university, founded 1826
- **Urban** 178-acre campus
- **Endowment** $1.8 billion
- **Coed** 4,911 undergraduate students, 97% full-time, 46% women, 54% men
- **Very difficult** entrance level, 38% of applicants were admitted

UNDERGRAD STUDENTS

4,766 full-time, 145 part-time. Students come from 51 states and territories; 37 other countries; 66% are from out of state; 4% Black or African American, non-Hispanic/Latino; 6% Hispanic/Latino; 19% Asian, non-Hispanic/Latino; 0.1% American Indian or Alaska Native, non-Hispanic/Latino; 4% Two or more races, non-Hispanic/Latino; 4% Race/ethnicity unknown; 9% international; 0.8% transferred in; 82% live on campus.

Freshmen

Admission: 21,733 applied, 8,326 admitted, 1,282 enrolled. ***Test scores:*** SAT critical reading scores over 500: 99%; SAT math scores over 500: 100%; SAT writing scores over 500: 99%; ACT scores over 18: 100%; SAT critical reading scores over 600: 81%; SAT math scores over 600: 94%; SAT writing scores over 600: 82%; ACT scores over 24: 99%; SAT critical reading scores over 700: 29%; SAT math scores over 700: 62%; SAT writing scores over 700: 31%; ACT scores over 30: 73%.

Retention: 93% of full-time freshmen returned.

FACULTY

Total: 940, 81% full-time, 86% with terminal degrees.

Student/faculty ratio: 11:1.

ACADEMICS

Calendar: semesters. *Degrees:* bachelor's, master's, doctoral, and postbachelor's certificates.

Special study options: accelerated degree program, adult/continuing education programs, advanced placement credit, cooperative education,

double majors, English as a second language, honors programs, independent study, internships, off-campus study, part-time degree program, services for LD students, student-designed majors, study abroad, summer session for credit. ***ROTC:*** Army (b), Air Force (c).

Unusual degree programs: 3-2 engineering.

Computers: 343 computers/terminals and 48,000 ports are available on campus for general student use. Students can access the following: campus intranet, computer help desk, free student e-mail accounts, online (class) grades, online (class) registration, online (class) schedules, software library, online reference databases, electronic books and journals, research computing, training. Campuswide network is available. 100% of college-owned or -operated housing units are wired for high-speed Internet access. Wireless service is available via entire campus.

STUDENT LIFE

Housing options: on-campus residence required through sophomore year; coed. Campus housing is university owned. Freshman campus housing is guaranteed.

Activities and organizations: drama/theater group, student-run newspaper, radio station, choral group, marching band, Footlighters, Alpha Phi Omega (national service organization), international student groups, music/dance groups, Habitat for Humanity, national fraternities, national sororities.

Athletics Member NCAA. All Division III. ***Intercollegiate sports:*** baseball M, basketball M/W, cross-country running M/W, football M, soccer M/W, softball W, swimming and diving M/W, tennis M/W, track and field M/W, ultimate Frisbee M(c)/W(c), volleyball M(c)/W, wrestling M. ***Intramural sports:*** archery M(c)/W(c), badminton M/W, basketball M/W, bowling M/W, cheerleading M(c)/W(c), crew M(c)/W(c), cross-country running M/W, fencing M(c)/W(c), football M/W, golf M/W, ice hockey M(c)/W(c), racquetball M/W, soccer M/W, softball M/W, squash M/W, swimming and diving M/W, table tennis M/W, tennis M/W, track and field M/W, ultimate Frisbee M/W, volleyball M/W, water polo M/W, weight lifting M/W, wrestling M.

Campus security: 24-hour emergency response devices and patrols, student patrols, late-night transport/escort service, controlled dormitory access, crime prevention programs.

Student services: health clinic, personal/psychological counseling, women's center, legal services.

COSTS & FINANCIAL AID

Costs (2014–15) ***One-time required fee:*** $495. ***Comprehensive fee:*** $56,534 includes full-time tuition ($42,766), mandatory fees ($392), and room and board ($13,376). Part-time tuition: $1792 per credit hour. Part-time tuition and fees vary according to course load. ***College room only:*** $7730. Room and board charges vary according to board plan, housing facility, and student level. ***Payment plan:*** installment. ***Waivers:*** employees or children of employees.

Financial Aid Of all full-time matriculated undergraduates who enrolled in 2014, 3,141 applied for aid, 2,714 were judged to have need, 622 had their need fully met. 1,877 Federal Work-Study jobs (averaging $2153). In 2014, 1350 non-need-based awards were made. ***Average percent of need met:*** 84. ***Average financial aid package:*** $37,356. ***Average need-based loan:*** $5107. ***Average need-based gift aid:*** $26,983. ***Average non-need-based aid:*** $22,087. ***Average indebtedness upon graduation:*** $33,343.

APPLYING

Standardized Tests *Required:* SAT or ACT (for admission).

Options: electronic application, early admission, early decision, early action, deferred entrance.

Required: essay or personal statement, high school transcript, 1 letter of recommendation. ***Recommended:*** interview.

Application deadlines: 1/15 (freshmen), 5/1 (transfers), 11/1 (early action).

Early decision deadline: 11/1 (for plan 1), 1/15 (for plan 2).

Notification: 3/20 (freshmen), continuous until 6/1 (transfers), 12/15 (early decision plan 1), 2/1 (early decision plan 2), 12/15 (early action).

CONTACT

Robert McCullough, Director of Undergraduate Admission, Case Western Reserve University, 10900 Euclid Avenue, Cleveland, OH 44106. *Phone:* 216-368-4450. *Fax:* 216-368-5111. *E-mail:* admission@case.edu.

See previous page for display ad and page 1386 for the College Close-Up.

Cedarville University

Cedarville, Ohio

http://www.cedarville.edu/

- **Independent Baptist** comprehensive, founded 1887
- **Rural** 400-acre campus with easy access to Columbus, Dayton
- **Endowment** $27.1 million
- **Coed** 3,303 undergraduate students, 92% full-time, 52% women, 48% men
- **Moderately difficult** entrance level, 74% of applicants were admitted

UNDERGRAD STUDENTS

3,028 full-time, 275 part-time. Students come from 49 states and territories; 33 other countries; 62% are from out of state; 2% Black or African American, non-Hispanic/Latino; 2% Hispanic/Latino; 2% Asian, non-Hispanic/Latino; 0.3% American Indian or Alaska Native, non-Hispanic/Latino; 3% Two or more races, non-Hispanic/Latino; 2% Race/ethnicity unknown; 2% international; 3% transferred in; 83% live on campus.

Freshmen

Admission: 3,003 applied, 2,237 admitted, 787 enrolled. ***Average high school GPA:*** 3.65. ***Test scores:*** SAT critical reading scores over 500: 89%; SAT math scores over 500: 89%; SAT writing scores over 500: 83%; ACT scores over 18: 100%; SAT critical reading scores over 600: 48%; SAT math scores over 600: 50%; SAT writing scores over 600: 37%; ACT scores over 24: 74%; SAT critical reading scores over 700: 11%; SAT math scores over 700: 11%; SAT writing scores over 700: 7%; ACT scores over 30: 19%.

Retention: 88% of full-time freshmen returned.

FACULTY

Total: 345, 63% full-time.

Student/faculty ratio: 13:1.

ACADEMICS

Calendar: semesters. *Degrees:* certificates, bachelor's, master's, and doctoral.

Special study options: academic remediation for entering students, adult/continuing education programs, advanced placement credit, cooperative education, distance learning, double majors, honors programs, independent study, internships, off-campus study, part-time degree program, services for LD students, student-designed majors, study abroad, summer session for credit. ***ROTC:*** Army (c), Air Force (c).

Computers: 2,100 computers/terminals and 4,000 ports are available on campus for general student use. Students can access the following: campus intranet, computer help desk, free student e-mail accounts, online (class) grades, online (class) registration, online (class) schedules, over 150 software packages. Campuswide network is available. 100% of college-owned or -operated housing units are wired for high-speed Internet access. Wireless service is available via entire campus.

STUDENT LIFE

Housing options: on-campus residence required through senior year; men-only, women-only, special housing for students with disabilities. Campus housing is university owned. Freshman campus housing is guaranteed.

Activities and organizations: drama/theater group, student-run newspaper, radio station, choral group, Christian Nursing Association, SAE - Society of Automotive Engineers, Mu Kappa - Missionary kids and international students, Tau Delta Kappa - Students in the honors program, Chi Sigma Mu - Firearm safety and marksmanship.

Athletics Member NCAA. All Division II. ***Intercollegiate sports:*** baseball M(s), basketball M(s)/W(s), cheerleading M/W, cross-country running M(s)/W(s), golf M(s), soccer M(s)/W(s), softball W(s), tennis M(s)/W(s), track and field M(s)/W(s), volleyball W(s). ***Intramural sports:*** basketball M/W, cross-country running M/W, football M/W, golf M/W, racquetball M/W, rock climbing M/W, rugby M, soccer M/W, softball M/W, table tennis M/W, tennis M/W, ultimate Frisbee M/W, volleyball M/W.

Campus security: 24-hour emergency response devices and patrols, late-night transport/escort service, controlled dormitory access.

Student services: health clinic, personal/psychological counseling.

COSTS & FINANCIAL AID

Costs (2015–16) ***Comprehensive fee:*** $33,748 includes full-time tuition ($27,006), mandatory fees ($200), and room and board ($6542). Part-time tuition: $1022 per credit hour. Part-time tuition and fees vary according to course load. ***Required fees:*** $50 per term part-time. ***College room only:*** $3708. Room and board charges vary according to board plan and housing facility. ***Payment plan:*** installment. ***Waivers:*** adult students, senior citizens, and employees or children of employees.

Financial Aid Of all full-time matriculated undergraduates who enrolled in 2014, 2,388 applied for aid, 2,067 were judged to have need, 848 had their need fully met. 396 Federal Work-Study jobs (averaging $1103). 1,597 state and other part-time jobs (averaging $1094). In 2014, 759 non-need-based awards were made. ***Average percent of need met:*** 33. ***Average financial aid package:*** $17,006. ***Average need-based loan:*** $5660. ***Average need-based gift aid:*** $4289. ***Average non-need-based aid:*** $15,983. ***Average indebtedness upon graduation:*** $29,105.

APPLYING

Standardized Tests *Required:* SAT or ACT (for admission).

Options: electronic application, early admission, deferred entrance.

Application fee: $30.

Required: essay or personal statement, high school transcript, minimum 3.0 GPA, 1 letter of recommendation, Clear testimony of faith in Jesus Christ and evidence of consistent Christian lifestyle, and the ACT or SAT. ***Required for some:*** interview.

Application deadlines: rolling (freshmen), rolling (transfers).

Notification: continuous (freshmen), continuous (transfers).

CONTACT

Mr. Roscoe Smith, Director of Admissions, Cedarville University, 251 North Main Street, Cedarville, OH 45314-0601. *Phone:* 937-766-7700. *Toll-free phone:* 800-233-2784. *E-mail:* admissions@cedarville.edu.

Central State University

Wilberforce, Ohio

http://www.centralstate.edu/

- **State-supported** 4-year, founded 1887, part of Ohio Board of Regents
- **Rural** 60-acre campus with easy access to Dayton
- **Endowment** $4.4 million
- **Coed** 1,733 undergraduate students, 91% full-time, 54% women, 46% men
- **Minimally difficult** entrance level, 38% of applicants were admitted

UNDERGRAD STUDENTS

1,576 full-time, 157 part-time. Students come from 28 states and territories; 7 other countries; 42% are from out of state; 95% Black or African American, non-Hispanic/Latino; 0.7% Hispanic/Latino; 0.2% American Indian or Alaska Native, non-Hispanic/Latino; 0.9% Two or more races, non-Hispanic/Latino; 1% Race/ethnicity unknown; 0.4% international; 7% transferred in; 62% live on campus.

Freshmen

Admission: 5,944 applied, 2,242 admitted, 402 enrolled. ***Average high school GPA:*** 2.6. ***Test scores:*** SAT critical reading scores over 500: 14%; SAT math scores over 500: 10%; ACT scores over 18: 34%; ACT scores over 24: 2%.

Retention: 51% of full-time freshmen returned.

FACULTY

Total: 214, 44% full-time, 40% with terminal degrees.

Student/faculty ratio: 12:1.

ACADEMICS

Calendar: semesters. *Degree:* bachelor's.

Special study options: adult/continuing education programs, cooperative education, double majors, honors programs, independent study, internships, off-campus study, part-time degree program, services for LD students, study abroad, summer session for credit. ***ROTC:*** Army (b).

Computers: 600 computers/terminals and 1,200 ports are available on campus for general student use. Students can access the following: campus intranet, computer help desk, free student e-mail accounts, online (class) grades, online (class) registration, online (class) schedules. Campuswide network is available. 100% of college-owned or -operated housing units are wired for high-speed Internet access. Wireless service is available via classrooms, computer centers, computer labs, dorm rooms, learning centers, libraries, student centers.

STUDENT LIFE

Housing options: on-campus residence required for freshman year; coed, men-only, women-only. Campus housing is university owned. Freshman campus housing is guaranteed.

Activities and organizations: drama/theater group, student-run newspaper, radio and television station, choral group, marching band, Student Ambassadors, student government, Make it Happen (Inter-Faith), Daughters of Nia Anaya (Social Group), Evolutions (Modeling Troupe), national fraternities, national sororities.

Athletics Member NCAA. All Division II. ***Intercollegiate sports:*** basketball M(s)/W(s), cheerleading M(s)/W(s), cross-country running M(s)/W(s), golf M(s)/W(s), tennis M(s)/W(s), track and field M(s)/W(s), volleyball W(s). ***Intramural sports:*** basketball M/W, bowling M/W, softball M/W, tennis M/W.

Campus security: 24-hour emergency response devices and patrols, controlled dormitory access.

Student services: health clinic, personal/psychological counseling.

COSTS & FINANCIAL AID

Costs (2014–15) ***Tuition:*** state resident $3926 full-time, $267 per credit hour part-time; nonresident $11,608 full-time, $612 per credit hour part-time. Full-time tuition and fees vary according to reciprocity agreements. Part-time tuition and fees vary according to reciprocity agreements. ***Required fees:*** $2320 full-time. ***Room and board:*** $9318; room only: $5008. Room and board charges vary according to board plan and housing facility. ***Waivers:*** senior citizens and employees or children of employees.

Financial Aid Of all full-time matriculated undergraduates who enrolled in 2012, 1,820 applied for aid, 1,820 were judged to have need. 337 Federal Work-Study jobs (averaging $1216). ***Average financial aid package:*** $6373. ***Average need-based loan:*** $2103. ***Average need-based gift aid:*** $3269.

APPLYING

Standardized Tests *Required:* SAT or ACT (for admission). *Recommended:* ACT (for admission).

Options: electronic application.

Application fee: $20.

Required: high school transcript. ***Required for some:*** essay or personal statement, minimum 2.0 GPA, 2 letters of recommendation, 2.5 high school GPA for nonresidents. ***Recommended:*** interview.

Application deadlines: 6/15 (freshmen), 6/15 (transfers).

Notification: continuous (freshmen), continuous (transfers).

CONTACT

Mr. Steven Peterson, Interim Director, Admissions, Central State University, PO Box 1004, 1400 Blush Row Road, Wilberforce, OH 45384. *Phone:* 937-376-6218. *Toll-free phone:* 800-388-CSU1 (in-state); 800-388-2781 (out-of-state). *Fax:* 937-376-6648. *E-mail:* admissions@centralstate.edu.

Chamberlain College of Nursing

Cleveland, Ohio

http://www.chamberlain.edu/

- **Proprietary** 4-year
- **Coed**

FACULTY

Student/faculty ratio: 18:1.

ACADEMICS

Degree: bachelor's.

APPLYING

Standardized Tests *Required:* SAT or ACT (for admission).

Application fee: $95.

CONTACT
Chamberlain College of Nursing, 6700 Euclid Avenue, Suite 201, Cleveland, OH 44103.

Chamberlain College of Nursing

Columbus, Ohio

http://www.chamberlain.edu/

- **Proprietary** 4-year
- **Coed**

FACULTY
Student/faculty ratio: 10:1.

ACADEMICS
Calendar: semesters. *Degrees:* associate and bachelor's.

COSTS
Costs (2014–15) ***Tuition:*** $17,160 full-time, $665 per credit hour part-time. Full-time tuition and fees vary according to course load. Part-time tuition and fees vary according to course load. ***Required fees:*** $600 full-time.

APPLYING
Standardized Tests *Required:* SAT or ACT (for admission).

CONTACT
Admissions, Chamberlain College of Nursing, 1350 Alum Creek Drive, Columbus, OH 43209. *Phone:* 614-252-8890. *Toll-free phone:* 888-556-8CCN.

Cincinnati Christian University

Cincinnati, Ohio

http://www.ccuniversity.edu/

- **Independent** comprehensive, founded 1924, affiliated with Church of Christ
- **Urban** 40-acre campus with easy access to Cincinnati
- **Coed** 620 undergraduate students, 86% full-time, 48% women, 52% men
- **Minimally difficult** entrance level, 59% of applicants were admitted

UNDERGRAD STUDENTS
534 full-time, 86 part-time. Students come from 12 states and territories; 36% are from out of state; 18% Black or African American, non-Hispanic/Latino; 1% Hispanic/Latino; 0.6% Asian, non-Hispanic/Latino; 0.4% Native Hawaiian or other Pacific Islander, non-Hispanic/Latino; 0.4% American Indian or Alaska Native, non-Hispanic/Latino; 2% Two or more races, non-Hispanic/Latino; 3% Race/ethnicity unknown; 2% international; 4% transferred in; 45% live on campus.

Freshmen
Admission: 241 applied, 141 admitted, 100 enrolled. ***Average high school GPA:*** 3.14. ***Test scores:*** SAT critical reading scores over 500: 52%; SAT math scores over 500: 53%; SAT writing scores over 500: 44%; ACT scores over 18: 72%; SAT critical reading scores over 600: 19%; SAT math scores over 600: 19%; SAT writing scores over 600: 11%; ACT scores over 24: 28%; SAT math scores over 700: 4%; ACT scores over 30: 3%.

FACULTY
Total: 82, 41% full-time.
Student/faculty ratio: 15:1.

ACADEMICS
Calendar: semesters. *Degrees:* associate, bachelor's, and master's.
Special study options: academic remediation for entering students, accelerated degree program, adult/continuing education programs, advanced placement credit, cooperative education, distance learning, double majors, honors programs, independent study, internships, off-campus study, part-time degree program, services for LD students, study abroad, summer session for credit.
Computers: 45 computers/terminals are available on campus for general student use. Students can access the following: campus intranet, computer help desk, free student e-mail accounts, online (class) grades, online (class) registration, online (class) schedules. Campuswide network is available. 100% of college-owned or -operated housing units are wired for high-speed Internet access. Wireless service is available via entire campus.

STUDENT LIFE
Housing options: on-campus residence required through junior year; men-only, women-only. Campus housing is university owned. Freshman campus housing is guaranteed.
Activities and organizations: drama/theater group, student-run newspaper, choral group.
Athletics Member NAIA. ***Intercollegiate sports:*** basketball M(s)/W(s), cross-country running M(s)/W(s), golf M(s), soccer M(s)/W(s), volleyball M(s)/W(s). ***Intramural sports:*** basketball M/W, soccer M/W, volleyball M/W.
Campus security: 24-hour emergency response devices and patrols, student patrols, late-night transport/escort service, controlled dormitory access.
Student services: health clinic, personal/psychological counseling.

COSTS & FINANCIAL AID
Costs (2015–16) ***Comprehensive fee:*** $24,076 includes full-time tuition ($15,966), mandatory fees ($250), and room and board ($7860). Full-time tuition and fees vary according to course load and student level. Part-time tuition: $570 per semester hour. Part-time tuition and fees vary according to course load and student level. ***College room only:*** $3760. Room and board charges vary according to board plan, housing facility, and student level. ***Payment plan:*** installment. ***Waivers:*** employees or children of employees.
Financial Aid Of all full-time matriculated undergraduates who enrolled in 2013, 518 applied for aid, 480 were judged to have need, 35 had their need fully met. 228 Federal Work-Study jobs (averaging $1375). In 2013, 63 non-need-based awards were made. ***Average percent of need met:*** 55. ***Average financial aid package:*** $12,550. ***Average need-based loan:*** $3873. ***Average need-based gift aid:*** $8988. ***Average non-need-based aid:*** $6376. ***Average indebtedness upon graduation:*** $32,675.

APPLYING
Standardized Tests *Required:* SAT or ACT (for admission).
Options: electronic application, deferred entrance.
Application fee: $40.
Required: high school transcript, 2 letters of recommendation. ***Required for some:*** essay or personal statement. ***Recommended:*** minimum 2.0 GPA, interview.
Application deadlines: 7/1 (freshmen), 7/1 (transfers).
Notification: continuous (freshmen), continuous (transfers).

CONTACT
Cincinnati Christian University, 2700 Glenway Avenue, PO Box 04320, Cincinnati, OH 45204-3200. *Phone:* 513-244-8110. *Toll-free phone:* 800-949-4228 (in-state); 800-949-4CCU (out-of-state).

Cincinnati College of Mortuary Science

Cincinnati, Ohio

http://www.ccms.edu/

- **Independent** 4-year, founded 1882
- **Urban** 10-acre campus with easy access to Cincinnati
- **Coed** 165 undergraduate students, 100% full-time, 52% women, 48% men

UNDERGRAD STUDENTS
165 full-time. Students come from 13 states and territories; 14% Black or African American, non-Hispanic/Latino; 2% Hispanic/Latino; 94% transferred in.

Freshmen
Admission: 10 enrolled.
Retention: 95% of full-time freshmen returned.

FACULTY
Total: 7, 71% full-time.
Student/faculty ratio: 33:1.

ACADEMICS
Calendar: quarters. *Degrees:* associate and bachelor's.

Special study options: adult/continuing education programs, summer session for credit.

Computers: 16 computers/terminals are available on campus for general student use.

STUDENT LIFE
Housing options: college housing not available.

Athletics ***Intramural sports:*** basketball M/W, bowling M/W, football M/W, softball M/W.

COSTS
Costs (2014–15) ***Tuition:*** $23,250 full-time, $375 per semester hour part-time. Full-time tuition and fees vary according to course load, degree level, and program. Part-time tuition and fees vary according to degree level. No tuition increase for student's term of enrollment. ***Required fees:*** $1060 full-time.

APPLYING
Standardized Tests *Required:* SAT (for admission).

Options: deferred entrance.

Application fee: $40.

Required: high school transcript, minimum 2.0 GPA.

Application deadlines: rolling (freshmen), rolling (transfers).

Notification: continuous (freshmen), continuous (transfers).

CONTACT
Cincinnati College of Mortuary Science, 645 West North Bend Road, Cincinnati, OH 45224-1462. *Phone:* 513-761-2020. *Toll-free phone:* 888-377-8433. *Fax:* 513-761-3333.

Cleveland Institute of Art

Cleveland, Ohio

http://www.cia.edu/

- **Independent** 4-year, founded 1882
- **Urban** 5-acre campus
- **Endowment** $27.9 million
- **Coed** 559 undergraduate students, 99% full-time, 55% women, 45% men
- **Moderately difficult** entrance level, 67% of applicants were admitted

UNDERGRAD STUDENTS
551 full-time, 8 part-time. Students come from 28 states and territories; 9 other countries; 37% are from out of state; 10% Black or African American, non-Hispanic/Latino; 6% Hispanic/Latino; 3% Asian, non-Hispanic/Latino; 0.2% Native Hawaiian or other Pacific Islander, non-Hispanic/Latino; 0.2% American Indian or Alaska Native, non-Hispanic/Latino; 3% Two or more races, non-Hispanic/Latino; 7% international; 7% transferred in; 37% live on campus.

Freshmen
Admission: 715 applied, 479 admitted, 139 enrolled. ***Average high school GPA:*** 3.06. ***Test scores:*** SAT critical reading scores over 500: 63%; SAT math scores over 500: 61%; SAT writing scores over 500: 49%; ACT scores over 18: 86%; SAT critical reading scores over 600: 25%; SAT math scores over 600: 13%; SAT writing scores over 600: 19%; ACT scores over 24: 44%; SAT critical reading scores over 700: 5%; SAT writing scores over 700: 3%; ACT scores over 30: 5%.
Retention: 81% of full-time freshmen returned.

FACULTY
Total: 109, 41% full-time, 50% with terminal degrees.
Student/faculty ratio: 9:1.

ACADEMICS
Calendar: semesters. *Degree:* bachelor's.

Special study options: advanced placement credit, distance learning, double majors, independent study, internships, off-campus study, part-time degree program, services for LD students, study abroad.

Computers: 135 computers/terminals are available on campus for general student use. Students can access the following: campus intranet, free student e-mail accounts, online (class) grades, online (class) registration, online (class) schedules, wireless Internet access available throughout campus. Campuswide network is available. 100% of college-owned or -operated housing units are wired for high-speed Internet access. Wireless service is available via entire campus.

STUDENT LIFE
Housing options: coed. Campus housing is leased by the school. Freshman applicants given priority for college housing.

Activities and organizations: drama/theater group, choral group, marching band, Campus Activities Board, Student Independent Exhibition, International Interior Design Association, Student Leadership Council, Community Service Club, national fraternities, national sororities.

Athletics ***Intramural sports:*** basketball M/W, cross-country running M/W, football M/W, golf M/W, racquetball M/W, soccer M/W, softball M/W, swimming and diving M/W, tennis M/W, track and field M/W, ultimate Frisbee M/W, volleyball M/W.

Campus security: 24-hour emergency response devices and patrols, late-night transport/escort service, controlled dormitory access.

Student services: health clinic, personal/psychological counseling, women's center, legal services.

COSTS & FINANCIAL AID
Costs (2015–16) ***Comprehensive fee:*** $49,775 includes full-time tuition ($35,980), mandatory fees ($2340), and room and board ($11,455). Full-time tuition and fees vary according to program, reciprocity agreements, and student level. Part-time tuition: $1499 per credit. Part-time tuition and fees vary according to course load, program, reciprocity agreements, and student level. ***College room only:*** $7325. Room and board charges vary according to board plan and housing facility. ***Payment plan:*** installment. ***Waivers:*** employees or children of employees.

Financial Aid Of all full-time matriculated undergraduates who enrolled in 2014, 463 applied for aid, 447 were judged to have need, 35 had their need fully met. 150 Federal Work-Study jobs (averaging $1082). In 2014, 86 non-need-based awards were made. ***Average percent of need met:*** 62. ***Average financial aid package:*** $26,939. ***Average need-based loan:*** $4643. ***Average need-based gift aid:*** $21,514. ***Average non-need-based aid:*** $2988. ***Average indebtedness upon graduation:*** $30,681.

APPLYING
Standardized Tests *Required:* SAT or ACT (for admission).

Options: electronic application, early admission, early action.

Application fee: $30.

Required: essay or personal statement, high school transcript, minimum 2.0 GPA, 1 letter of recommendation, portfolio. ***Recommended:*** interview.

Application deadlines: 3/1 (freshmen), 6/1 (transfers).

Notification: continuous (freshmen), continuous (transfers).

CONTACT
Office of Admissions, Cleveland Institute of Art, 11141 East Boulevard, Cleveland, OH 44106. *Phone:* 216-421-7418. *Toll-free phone:* 800-223-4700. *Fax:* 216-754-3634. *E-mail:* admissions@cia.edu.

Cleveland State University

Cleveland, Ohio

http://www.csuohio.edu/

- **State-supported** university, founded 1964, part of University System of Ohio
- **Urban** 82-acre campus with easy access to Cleveland, Ohio metro area
- **Endowment** $49.6 million
- **Coed** 12,194 undergraduate students, 71% full-time, 54% women, 46% men
- **Moderately difficult** entrance level, 67% of applicants were admitted

UNDERGRAD STUDENTS
8,674 full-time, 3,520 part-time. Students come from 33 states and territories; 96 other countries; 4% are from out of state; 18% Black or African American, non-Hispanic/Latino; 5% Hispanic/Latino; 3% Asian, non-Hispanic/Latino; 0.1% Native Hawaiian or other Pacific Islander, non-Hispanic/Latino; 0.2% American Indian or Alaska Native, non-Hispanic/Latino; 3% Two or more races, non-Hispanic/Latino; 2% Race/ethnicity unknown; 5% international; 11% transferred in; 8% live on campus.

Freshmen
Admission: 6,288 applied, 4,222 admitted, 1,591 enrolled. ***Average high school GPA:*** 3.24. ***Test scores:*** SAT critical reading scores over 500: 58%; SAT math scores over 500: 58%; ACT scores over 18: 86%; SAT critical reading scores over 600: 24%; SAT math scores over 600: 22%; ACT scores over 24: 33%; SAT critical reading scores over 700: 3%; SAT math scores over 700: 5%; ACT scores over 30: 4%.

Retention: 70% of full-time freshmen returned.

FACULTY
Total: 1,070, 48% full-time.

Student/faculty ratio: 18:1.

ACADEMICS
Calendar: semesters. *Degrees:* bachelor's, master's, doctoral, post-master's, and postbachelor's certificates.

Special study options: academic remediation for entering students, accelerated degree program, adult/continuing education programs, advanced placement credit, cooperative education, distance learning, double majors, English as a second language, freshman honors college, honors programs, independent study, internships, off-campus study, part-time degree program, services for LD students, student-designed majors, study abroad, summer session for credit. ***ROTC:*** Army (c), Air Force (c).

Computers: 736 computers/terminals are available on campus for general student use. Students can access the following: campus intranet, computer help desk, free student e-mail accounts, online (class) grades, online (class) registration, online (class) schedules, each general purpose computer lab has a scanner and printer, and students are allowed free black and white printing up to 2,000 pages per semester. Campuswide network is available. 100% of college-owned or -operated housing units are wired for high-speed Internet access. Wireless service is available via entire campus.

STUDENT LIFE
Housing options: coed, special housing for students with disabilities. Campus housing is university owned. Freshman campus housing is guaranteed.

Activities and organizations: drama/theater group, student-run newspaper, radio station, choral group, Black Student Union, Chinese Students and Scholars Association, Through the Cross Campus Ministries, Student Nurses Association, Joint Engineering Council, national fraternities, national sororities.

Athletics Member NCAA. All Division I. ***Intercollegiate sports:*** basketball M(s)/W(s), cheerleading M/W, cross-country running W(s), fencing M(s)/W(s), golf M(s)/W, soccer M(s)/W, softball W(s), swimming and diving M(s)/W(s), tennis M/W(s), track and field W(s), volleyball W(s), wrestling M(s). ***Intramural sports:*** baseball M(c), basketball M/W, crew M(c)/W(c), cross-country running M/W, fencing M/W, golf M/W, ice hockey M(c), rock climbing M(c)/W(c), rugby M(c), soccer M(c)/W(c), track and field M/W, ultimate Frisbee M/W, volleyball W, wrestling M.

Campus security: 24-hour emergency response devices and patrols, late-night transport/escort service, controlled dormitory access, Campus Watch, CSU Alert Notification System, Community Emergency and Response Team (CERT).

Student services: health clinic, personal/psychological counseling, women's center.

COSTS & FINANCIAL AID
Costs (2014–15) ***Tuition:*** state resident $9636 full-time, $402 per credit hour part-time; nonresident $12,878 full-time, $537 per credit hour part-time. Full-time tuition and fees vary according to course load, degree level, and program. Part-time tuition and fees vary according to course load, degree level, and program. ***Required fees:*** $50 full-time, $25 per term part-time. ***Room and board:*** $11,858; room only: $8108. Room and board charges vary according to board plan and housing facility. ***Payment plan:*** installment. ***Waivers:*** senior citizens and employees or children of employees.

Financial Aid Of all full-time matriculated undergraduates who enrolled in 2014, 7,299 applied for aid, 6,597 were judged to have need, 476 had their need fully met. 414 Federal Work-Study jobs (averaging $3560). In 2014, 412 non-need-based awards were made. ***Average percent of need met:*** 45. ***Average financial aid package:*** $8935. ***Average need-based loan:*** $4443. ***Average need-based gift aid:*** $6397. ***Average non-need-based aid:*** $4839. ***Average indebtedness upon graduation:*** $24,856.

APPLYING
Standardized Tests *Required:* SAT or ACT (for admission).

Options: electronic application, early action, deferred entrance.

Application fee: $30.

Required: high school transcript, minimum 2.3 GPA, minimum ACT score of 16 or SAT of 770 (combined critical reading and math).

Application deadlines: 5/15 (freshmen), 5/15 (transfers), 5/1 (early action).

Notification: continuous (freshmen), continuous (transfers).

CONTACT
Undergraduate Admissions Office, Cleveland State University, 2121 Euclid Avenue, EC 100, Cleveland, OH 44115. *Phone:* 216-523-7416. *Toll-free phone:* 888-CSU-OHIO. *E-mail:* admissions@csuohio.edu.

The College of Wooster

Wooster, Ohio

http://www.wooster.edu/

- **Independent** 4-year, founded 1866, affiliated with Presbyterian Church (U.S.A.)
- **Small-town** 240-acre campus with easy access to Cleveland
- **Endowment** $278.1 million
- **Coed** 2,066 undergraduate students, 98% full-time, 55% women, 45% men
- **Moderately difficult** entrance level, 59% of applicants were admitted

UNDERGRAD STUDENTS
2,024 full-time, 42 part-time. Students come from 47 states and territories; 39 other countries; 61% are from out of state; 8% Black or African American, non-Hispanic/Latino; 5% Hispanic/Latino; 4% Asian, non-Hispanic/Latino; 1% American Indian or Alaska Native, non-Hispanic/Latino; 4% Race/ethnicity unknown; 8% international; 1% transferred in; 99% live on campus.

Freshmen
Admission: 5,497 applied, 3,248 admitted, 547 enrolled. ***Average high school GPA:*** 3.6. ***Test scores:*** SAT critical reading scores over 500: 91%; SAT math scores over 500: 93%; SAT writing scores over 500: 89%; ACT scores over 18: 100%; SAT critical reading scores over 600: 51%; SAT math scores over 600: 58%; SAT writing scores over 600: 48%; ACT scores over 24: 83%; SAT critical reading scores over 700: 11%; SAT math scores over 700: 18%; SAT writing scores over 700: 10%; ACT scores over 30: 28%.

Retention: 90% of full-time freshmen returned.

FACULTY
Total: 215, 80% full-time, 86% with terminal degrees.

Student/faculty ratio: 11:1.

ACADEMICS
Calendar: semesters. *Degree:* bachelor's.

Special study options: advanced placement credit, double majors, independent study, internships, off-campus study, services for LD students, student-designed majors, study abroad.

Unusual degree programs: 3-2 engineering with Case Western Reserve University, Washington University in St. Louis, University of Michigan; forestry with Duke University; nursing with Case Western Reserve University; social work with Case Western Reserve University; dentistry with Case Western Reserve University, architecture with Washington University in St. Louis.

Computers: 450 computers/terminals are available on campus for general student use. Students can access the following: campus intranet, computer help desk, free student e-mail accounts, online (class) grades, online (class) registration, online (class) schedules, learning management system, campus blogging site, campus wiki site. Campuswide network is available. 100% of college-owned or -operated housing units are wired for high-speed Internet access. Wireless service is available via entire campus.

STUDENT LIFE
Housing options: on-campus residence required through senior year; coed, women-only. Campus housing is university owned. Freshman campus housing is guaranteed.

Activities and organizations: drama/theater group, student-run newspaper, radio station, choral group, marching band, Volunteer Network, International Student Association, Inter-Greek Council, Wooster Activities Crew, Women's Athletic and Recreation Association.

Athletics Member NCAA. All Division III. ***Intercollegiate sports:*** baseball M, basketball M/W, cheerleading W(c), cross-country running M/W, equestrian sports M(c)/W(c), field hockey W, football M, golf M/W, lacrosse M/W, rugby M(c)/W(c), soccer M/W, softball W, swimming and diving M/W, tennis M/W, track and field M/W, ultimate Frisbee M(c)/W(c), volleyball M(c)/W. ***Intramural sports:*** badminton M/W, ice hockey M(c)/W(c), table tennis M/W.

Campus security: 24-hour emergency response devices and patrols, student patrols, late-night transport/escort service, controlled dormitory access.

Student services: health clinic, personal/psychological counseling, women's center.

COSTS & FINANCIAL AID
Costs (2014–15) ***Comprehensive fee:*** $53,600 includes full-time tuition ($42,920), mandatory fees ($430), and room and board ($10,250). Full-time tuition and fees vary according to course load. Part-time tuition: $1335 per credit. Part-time tuition and fees vary according to course load. ***College room only:*** $4950. Room and board charges vary according to board plan and housing facility. ***Payment plan:*** installment. ***Waivers:*** employees or children of employees.

Financial Aid Of all full-time matriculated undergraduates who enrolled in 2014, 1,333 applied for aid, 1,202 were judged to have need, 641 had their need fully met. 932 Federal Work-Study jobs (averaging $1968). 116 state and other part-time jobs (averaging $2754). In 2014, 767 non-need-based awards were made. ***Average percent of need met:*** 94. ***Average financial aid package:*** $39,304. ***Average need-based loan:*** $6872. ***Average need-based gift aid:*** $29,304. ***Average non-need-based aid:*** $19,329. ***Average indebtedness upon graduation:*** $24,506.

APPLYING
Standardized Tests *Required:* SAT or ACT (for admission).

Options: electronic application, early admission, early decision, early action, deferred entrance.

Application fee: $45.

Required: essay or personal statement, high school transcript, SAT or ACT. ***Recommended:*** interview.

Application deadlines: 2/15 (freshmen), 7/15 (transfers), 11/15 (early action).

Early decision deadline: 11/1 (for plan 1), 1/15 (for plan 2).

Notification: 4/1 (freshmen), continuous (transfers), 11/15 (early decision plan 1), 2/1 (early decision plan 2), 12/31 (early action).

CONTACT
Ms. Jennifer Winge, Dean of Admissions, The College of Wooster, 1189 Beall Avenue, Wooster, OH 44691-2363. *Phone:* 330-263-2270. *Toll-free phone:* 800-877-9905. *Fax:* 330-263-2621. *E-mail:* admissions@wooster.edu.

Columbus College of Art & Design

Columbus, Ohio

http://www.ccad.edu/

- **Independent** comprehensive, founded 1879
- **Urban** 17-acre campus
- **Endowment** $11.5 million
- **Coed** 1,314 undergraduate students, 87% full-time, 66% women, 34% men
- **Moderately difficult** entrance level, 88% of applicants were admitted

UNDERGRAD STUDENTS
1,141 full-time, 173 part-time. Students come from 39 states and territories; 21 other countries; 25% are from out of state; 8% Black or African American, non-Hispanic/Latino; 4% Hispanic/Latino; 4% Asian, non-Hispanic/Latino; 0.2% Native Hawaiian or other Pacific Islander, non-Hispanic/Latino; 0.3% American Indian or Alaska Native, non-Hispanic/Latino; 4% Two or more races, non-Hispanic/Latino; 5% Race/ethnicity unknown; 6% international; 0.4% transferred in; 34% live on campus.

Freshmen
Admission: 657 applied, 581 admitted, 247 enrolled. ***Average high school GPA:*** 3. ***Test scores:*** SAT critical reading scores over 500: 75%; SAT math scores over 500: 67%; SAT writing scores over 500: 65%; ACT scores over 18: 85%; SAT critical reading scores over 600: 36%; SAT math scores over 600: 23%; SAT writing scores over 600: 23%; ACT scores over 24: 35%; SAT critical reading scores over 700: 1%; SAT math scores over 700: 2%; ACT scores over 30: 3%.

Retention: 76% of full-time freshmen returned.

FACULTY
Total: 196, 34% full-time, 50% with terminal degrees.

Student/faculty ratio: 11:1.

ACADEMICS
Calendar: semesters. *Degrees:* bachelor's and master's.

Special study options: academic remediation for entering students, advanced placement credit, distance learning, double majors, English as a second language, honors programs, independent study, internships, off-campus study, services for LD students, study abroad, summer session for credit.

Computers: 485 computers/terminals are available on campus for general student use. Students can access the following: campus intranet, computer help desk, free student e-mail accounts, online (class) grades, online (class) registration, online (class) schedules, online library. Campuswide network is available. 100% of college-owned or -operated housing units are wired for high-speed Internet access. Wireless service is available via classrooms, computer centers, computer labs, dorm rooms, learning centers, libraries, student centers.

STUDENT LIFE
Housing options: on-campus residence required for freshman year; coed, special housing for students with disabilities. Campus housing is university owned. Freshman campus housing is guaranteed.

Activities and organizations: Student Government Association, Gay/Lesbian/Bisexual Group, Bible Study, Environmental Awareness Society.

Campus security: 24-hour emergency response devices and patrols, late-night transport/escort service, controlled dormitory access.

Student services: personal/psychological counseling.

COSTS & FINANCIAL AID
Costs (2014–15) ***Comprehensive fee:*** $37,872 includes full-time tuition ($28,872), mandatory fees ($1020), and room and board ($7980). Full-time tuition and fees vary according to course load. Part-time tuition: $1203 per credit hour. Part-time tuition and fees vary according to course load. ***Room and board:*** Room and board charges vary according to board plan, housing facility, location, and student level. ***Payment plans:*** installment, deferred payment. ***Waivers:*** employees or children of employees.

Financial Aid Of all full-time matriculated undergraduates who enrolled in 2014, 1,014 applied for aid, 945 were judged to have need, 63 had their need fully met. 156 Federal Work-Study jobs (averaging $3550). 283 state and other part-time jobs (averaging $3550). In 2014, 208 non-need-based awards were made. ***Average percent of need met:*** 52. ***Average financial aid package:*** $19,911. ***Average need-based loan:*** $6777. ***Average need-based gift aid:*** $13,775. ***Average non-need-based aid:*** $10,430. ***Average indebtedness upon graduation:*** $32,006.

APPLYING
Standardized Tests *Recommended:* SAT or ACT (for admission).

Options: electronic application, deferred entrance.

Application fee: $40.

Required: essay or personal statement, high school transcript, minimum 2.0 GPA, 2 letters of recommendation, portfolio. ***Recommended:*** interview.

Application deadlines: rolling (freshmen), rolling (transfers).

Notification: continuous (freshmen), continuous (transfers).

CONTACT
Columbus College of Art & Design, 60 Cleveland Avenue, Columbus, OH 43215-1758. *Phone:* 614-224-9101. *Toll-free phone:* 877-997-2223. *Fax:* 614-232-8344. *E-mail:* admissions@ccad.edu.

Defiance College

Defiance, Ohio

http://www.defiance.edu/

- **Independent** comprehensive, founded 1850, affiliated with United Church of Christ
- **Small-town** 150-acre campus with easy access to Toledo
- **Endowment** $14.7 million
- **Coed** 824 undergraduate students, 84% full-time, 48% women, 52% men
- **Moderately difficult** entrance level, 65% of applicants were admitted

UNDERGRAD STUDENTS
690 full-time, 134 part-time. Students come from 21 states and territories; 1 other country; 28% are from out of state; 12% Black or African American, non-Hispanic/Latino; 5% Hispanic/Latino; 0.7% Asian, non-Hispanic/Latino; 1% American Indian or Alaska Native, non-Hispanic/Latino; 0.7% Two or more races, non-Hispanic/Latino; 3% Race/ethnicity unknown; 2% international; 6% transferred in; 50% live on campus.

Freshmen
Admission: 1,671 applied, 1,081 admitted, 233 enrolled. ***Average high school GPA:*** 3.1. ***Test scores:*** SAT critical reading scores over 500: 28%; SAT math scores over 500: 34%; SAT writing scores over 500: 24%; ACT scores over 18: 76%; SAT critical reading scores over 600: 9%; SAT math scores over 600: 12%; SAT writing scores over 600: 3%; ACT scores over 24: 21%; ACT scores over 30: 1%.
Retention: 55% of full-time freshmen returned.

FACULTY
Total: 93, 42% full-time, 37% with terminal degrees.
Student/faculty ratio: 12:1.

ACADEMICS
Calendar: semesters. *Degrees:* associate, bachelor's, and master's.
Special study options: academic remediation for entering students, adult/continuing education programs, advanced placement credit, double majors, honors programs, independent study, internships, off-campus study, part-time degree program, services for LD students, student-designed majors, study abroad, summer session for credit.
Computers: 200 computers/terminals are available on campus for general student use. Students can access the following: campus intranet, computer help desk, free student e-mail accounts, online (class) grades, online (class) schedules. Campuswide network is available. 100% of college-owned or -operated housing units are wired for high-speed Internet access. Wireless service is available via classrooms, computer centers, computer labs, dorm rooms, learning centers, libraries, student centers.

STUDENT LIFE
Housing options: on-campus residence required through junior year; coed. Campus housing is university owned. Freshman campus housing is guaranteed.
Activities and organizations: drama/theater group, student-run newspaper, choral group, marching band, Campus Activities Board, Criminal Justice Society, Student Senate, Black Action Student Association, DC Players, national sororities.
Athletics Member NCAA. All Division III. ***Intercollegiate sports:*** baseball M, basketball M/W, cross-country running M/W, football M, golf M/W, lacrosse M/W, soccer M/W, softball W, swimming and diving M/W, tennis M/W, track and field M/W, volleyball W. ***Intramural sports:*** baseball M, basketball M/W, cheerleading M/W, football M/W, racquetball M/W, soccer M/W, softball M/W, volleyball M/W, weight lifting M, wrestling M(c).
Campus security: late-night transport/escort service, controlled dormitory access.
Student services: health clinic, personal/psychological counseling.

COSTS & FINANCIAL AID
Costs (2014–15) ***Comprehensive fee:*** $39,438 includes full-time tuition ($29,256), mandatory fees ($660), and room and board ($9522). Full-time tuition and fees vary according to course load. Part-time tuition: $467 per credit. Part-time tuition and fees vary according to course load. ***Payment plan:*** installment. ***Waivers:*** employees or children of employees.
Financial Aid Of all full-time matriculated undergraduates who enrolled in 2013, 694 applied for aid, 658 were judged to have need, 69 had their need fully met. 419 Federal Work-Study jobs (averaging $2441). 62 state and other part-time jobs (averaging $2301). In 2013, 74 non-need-based awards were made. ***Average percent of need met:*** 71. ***Average financial aid package:*** $23,246. ***Average need-based loan:*** $4658. ***Average need-based gift aid:*** $8723. ***Average non-need-based aid:*** $15,851.

APPLYING
Standardized Tests *Required:* SAT or ACT (for admission).
Options: electronic application, deferred entrance.
Application fee: $25.
Required: high school transcript, minimum 2.3 GPA. ***Required for some:*** essay or personal statement, 1 letter of recommendation, interview. ***Recommended:*** interview.
Application deadlines: 8/15 (freshmen), 8/15 (out-of-state freshmen), 8/15 (transfers).
Notification: continuous (freshmen), continuous (out-of-state freshmen), continuous (transfers).

CONTACT
Mr. Brad Harsha, Director of Admissions, Defiance College, 701 North Clinton Street, Defiance, OH 43512. *Phone:* 419-783-2365. *Toll-free phone:* 800-520-4632. *Fax:* 419-783-2468. *E-mail:* bharsha@defiance.edu.

Denison University

Granville, Ohio

http://www.denison.edu/

- **Independent** 4-year, founded 1831
- **Small-town** 800-acre campus with easy access to Columbus
- **Endowment** $771.8 million
- **Coed** 2,280 undergraduate students, 99% full-time, 58% women, 42% men
- **Very difficult** entrance level, 51% of applicants were admitted

UNDERGRAD STUDENTS
2,263 full-time, 17 part-time. Students come from 50 states and territories; 28 other countries; 76% are from out of state; 7% Black or African American, non-Hispanic/Latino; 10% Hispanic/Latino; 4% Asian, non-Hispanic/Latino; 0.1% Native Hawaiian or other Pacific Islander, non-Hispanic/Latino; 4% Two or more races, non-Hispanic/Latino; 2% Race/ethnicity unknown; 7% international; 0.7% transferred in; 99% live on campus.

Freshmen
Admission: 4,898 applied, 2,481 admitted, 611 enrolled. ***Average high school GPA:*** 3.6. ***Test scores:*** SAT critical reading scores over 500: 98%; SAT math scores over 500: 100%; ACT scores over 18: 100%; SAT critical reading scores over 600: 72%; SAT math scores over 600: 67%; ACT scores over 24: 92%; SAT critical reading scores over 700: 23%; SAT math scores over 700: 23%; ACT scores over 30: 38%.
Retention: 89% of full-time freshmen returned.

FACULTY
Total: 236, 89% full-time, 93% with terminal degrees.
Student/faculty ratio: 10:1.

ACADEMICS
Calendar: semesters plus optional May term. *Degree:* bachelor's.
Special study options: advanced placement credit, double majors, honors programs, independent study, internships, off-campus study, part-time degree program, services for LD students, student-designed majors, study abroad. ***ROTC:*** Army (c).
Unusual degree programs: 3-2 engineering with Case Western Reserve University, Columbia University, Rensselaer Polytechnic Institute, Washington University in St. Louis; forestry with Duke University; natural resources with University of Michigan; occupational therapy with Washington University in St. Louis; environmental management,

dentistry with Case Western Reserve University; medical technology with Rochester General Hospital.

Computers: Students can access the following: campus intranet, computer help desk, free student e-mail accounts, online (class) grades, online (class) registration, online (class) schedules. Campuswide network is available. Wireless service is available via entire campus.

STUDENT LIFE

Housing options: on-campus residence required through senior year; coed, men-only, women-only, cooperative. Campus housing is university owned. Freshman campus housing is guaranteed.

Activities and organizations: drama/theater group, student-run newspaper, radio and television station, choral group, Community Association, Black Student Union, International Student Association, Student Activities Committee, national fraternities, national sororities.

Athletics Member NCAA. All Division III. ***Intercollegiate sports:*** baseball M, basketball M/W, crew M(c), cross-country running M/W, equestrian sports M(c)/W(c), field hockey W, football M, golf M, ice hockey M(c), lacrosse M/W, riflery M(c)/W(c), rugby M(c)/W(c), sailing M(c)/W(c), skiing (downhill) M(c)/W(c), soccer M/W, softball W, squash M(c)/W(c), swimming and diving M/W, tennis M/W, track and field M/W, volleyball W. ***Intramural sports:*** badminton M(c)/W(c), basketball M/W, cheerleading M/W, crew W(c), fencing M(c)/W(c), football M/W, golf M/W, lacrosse M(c), racquetball M/W, soccer M/W, softball M/W, squash M/W, table tennis M/W, tennis M/W, ultimate Frisbee M/W, volleyball M(c)/W, water polo M/W, weight lifting M/W.

Campus security: 24-hour emergency response devices and patrols, student patrols, late-night transport/escort service, controlled dormitory access, security lighting, escort service.

Student services: health clinic, personal/psychological counseling, women's center.

COSTS & FINANCIAL AID

Costs (2015–16) ***Comprehensive fee:*** $58,860 includes full-time tuition ($46,250), mandatory fees ($1040), and room and board ($11,570). Part-time tuition and fees vary according to course load. ***College room only:*** $6370. Room and board charges vary according to board plan and housing facility. ***Payment plan:*** installment. ***Waivers:*** employees or children of employees.

Financial Aid Of all full-time matriculated undergraduates who enrolled in 2014, 1,384 applied for aid, 1,204 were judged to have need, 432 had their need fully met. In 2014, 992 non-need-based awards were made. ***Average percent of need met:*** 96. ***Average financial aid package:*** $40,637. ***Average need-based loan:*** $5127. ***Average need-based gift aid:*** $34,254. ***Average non-need-based aid:*** $18,537.

APPLYING

Standardized Tests *Required for some:* SAT or ACT (for admission).

Options: early admission, early decision, deferred entrance.

Required: essay or personal statement, high school transcript, 2 letters of recommendation. ***Recommended:*** interview.

Application deadlines: 1/15 (freshmen), 6/1 (transfers).

Early decision deadline: 11/15 (for plan 1), 1/15 (for plan 2).

Notification: 4/1 (freshmen), continuous (transfers), 1/1 (early decision).

CONTACT

Mr. Perry Robinson, Director of Admissions, Denison University, Granville, OH 43023. *Phone:* 740-587-6276. *Toll-free phone:* 800-DENISON. *E-mail:* admissions@denison.edu.

DeVry University

Columbus, Ohio

http://www.devry.edu/

- **Proprietary** comprehensive, founded 1952
- **Urban** campus
- **Coed** 1,676 undergraduate students, 41% full-time, 45% women, 55% men
- **Minimally difficult** entrance level

UNDERGRAD STUDENTS

686 full-time, 990 part-time. 2% are from out of state; 18% Black or African American, non-Hispanic/Latino; 2% Hispanic/Latino; 2% Asian, non-Hispanic/Latino; 0.1% Native Hawaiian or other Pacific Islander, non-Hispanic/Latino; 0.3% American Indian or Alaska Native, non-Hispanic/Latino; 1% Two or more races, non-Hispanic/Latino; 12% Race/ethnicity unknown; 0.6% international; 26% transferred in.

Freshmen

Admission: 98 enrolled.

FACULTY

Total: 65, 29% full-time.

ACADEMICS

Calendar: semesters. *Degrees:* associate, bachelor's, master's, and postbachelor's certificates.

COSTS

Costs (2014–15) ***Tuition:*** $17,052 full-time, $609 per credit hour part-time. ***Required fees:*** $80 full-time.

APPLYING

Application fee: $40.

CONTACT

Admissions Office, DeVry University, 1350 Alum Creek Drive, Columbus, OH 43209. *Phone:* 614-253-7291. *Toll-free phone:* 866-338-7941.

DeVry University

Seven Hills, Ohio

http://www.devry.edu/

- **Proprietary** comprehensive
- **Coed**

ACADEMICS

Calendar: semesters. *Degrees:* associate, bachelor's, and master's.

COSTS & FINANCIAL AID

Costs (2014–15) ***Tuition:*** $17,052 full-time, $609 per credit hour part-time. ***Required fees:*** $80 full-time.

Financial Aid Of all full-time matriculated undergraduates who enrolled in 2006, 8 applied for aid, 8 were judged to have need. ***Average percent of need met:*** 26. ***Average financial aid package:*** $6718. ***Average need-based loan:*** $550. ***Average need-based gift aid:*** $5187.

CONTACT

Admissions Office, DeVry University, 4141 Rockside Road, Suite 110, Seven Hills, OH 44131. *Phone:* 216-328-8754. *Toll-free phone:* 866-338-7941.

Franciscan University of Steubenville

Steubenville, Ohio

http://www.franciscan.edu/

- **Independent Roman Catholic** comprehensive, founded 1946
- **Suburban** 249-acre campus
- **Endowment** $52.4 million
- **Coed** 2,135 undergraduate students, 94% full-time, 62% women, 38% men
- **Moderately difficult** entrance level, 78% of applicants were admitted

UNDERGRAD STUDENTS

2,002 full-time, 133 part-time. Students come from 50 states and territories; 13 other countries; 81% are from out of state; 0.3% Black or African American, non-Hispanic/Latino; 10% Hispanic/Latino; 2% Asian, non-Hispanic/Latino; 0.1% Native Hawaiian or other Pacific Islander, non-Hispanic/Latino; 0.2% American Indian or Alaska Native, non-Hispanic/Latino; 2% Two or more races, non-Hispanic/Latino; 2% Race/ethnicity unknown; 1% international; 6% transferred in; 83% live on campus.

Freshmen

Admission: 1,816 applied, 1,418 admitted, 464 enrolled. ***Average high school GPA:*** 3.75. ***Test scores:*** SAT critical reading scores over 500: 92%; SAT math scores over 500: 90%; SAT writing scores over 500: 87%; ACT scores over 18: 100%; SAT critical reading scores over 600: 51%; SAT math scores over 600: 39%; SAT writing scores over 600: 43%; ACT scores over 24: 73%; SAT critical reading scores over 700: 14%; SAT math scores over 700: 6%; SAT writing scores over 700: 9%; ACT scores over 30: 20%.

Retention: 87% of full-time freshmen returned.

FACULTY

Total: 232, 52% full-time, 50% with terminal degrees.

Student/faculty ratio: 14:1.

ACADEMICS

Calendar: semesters. *Degrees:* associate, bachelor's, and master's.

Special study options: accelerated degree program, adult/continuing education programs, advanced placement credit, cooperative education, distance learning, double majors, honors programs, independent study, internships, part-time degree program, services for LD students, study abroad, summer session for credit. ***ROTC:*** Army (b), Air Force (c).

Computers: Students can access the following: campus intranet, computer help desk, free student e-mail accounts, online (class) grades, online (class) registration, online (class) schedules. Campuswide network is available. 100% of college-owned or -operated housing units are wired for high-speed Internet access. Wireless service is available via classrooms, computer centers, computer labs, dorm rooms, libraries, student centers.

STUDENT LIFE

Housing options: on-campus residence required through junior year; men-only, women-only. Campus housing is university owned. Freshman applicants given priority for college housing.

Activities and organizations: student-run newspaper, radio station, choral group.

Athletics Member NCAA. All Division III. ***Intercollegiate sports:*** basketball M/W, cross-country running M/W, lacrosse M/W, rugby M(c), soccer M/W, softball W, swimming and diving W, tennis M/W, track and field M/W, volleyball W. ***Intramural sports:*** basketball M/W, football M/W, racquetball M/W, soccer M/W, softball M/W, ultimate Frisbee M/W, volleyball M/W, weight lifting M/W.

Campus security: 24-hour emergency response devices and patrols, student patrols, late-night transport/escort service.

Student services: health clinic, personal/psychological counseling.

COSTS & FINANCIAL AID

Costs (2015–16) ***Comprehensive fee:*** $33,080 includes full-time tuition ($24,320), mandatory fees ($460), and room and board ($8300). Part-time tuition: $805 per credit hour. Part-time tuition and fees vary according to class time and course load. ***College room only:*** $4800. Room and board charges vary according to board plan. ***Payment plan:*** installment. ***Waivers:*** employees or children of employees.

Financial Aid Of all full-time matriculated undergraduates who enrolled in 2011, 1,601 applied for aid, 1,353 were judged to have need, 175 had their need fully met. In 2011, 370 non-need-based awards were made. ***Average percent of need met:*** 60. ***Average financial aid package:*** $13,355. ***Average need-based loan:*** $4410. ***Average need-based gift aid:*** $8931. ***Average non-need-based aid:*** $4435. ***Average indebtedness upon graduation:*** $29,354.

APPLYING

Standardized Tests *Required:* SAT or ACT (for admission).

Options: electronic application, deferred entrance.

Application fee: $20.

Required: high school transcript, minimum 2.4 GPA. ***Required for some:*** essay or personal statement, 3 letters of recommendation. ***Recommended:*** interview.

Application deadlines: rolling (freshmen), rolling (transfers).

Notification: continuous (freshmen), continuous (transfers).

CONTACT

Mrs. Margaret Weber, Director of Admissions, Franciscan University of Steubenville, 1235 University Boulevard, Steubenville, OH 43952-1763. *Phone:* 740-283-6226. *Toll-free phone:* 800-783-6220. *Fax:* 740-284-5456. *E-mail:* admissions@franciscan.edu.

Franklin University

Columbus, Ohio

http://www.franklin.edu/

- **Independent** comprehensive, founded 1902
- **Urban** 14-acre campus with easy access to Columbus
- **Endowment** $85.8 million
- **Coed** 4,676 undergraduate students, 34% full-time, 57% women, 43% men
- **Noncompetitive** entrance level

UNDERGRAD STUDENTS

1,571 full-time, 3,105 part-time. Students come from 45 states and territories; 72 other countries; 21% are from out of state; 21% Black or African American, non-Hispanic/Latino; 3% Hispanic/Latino; 3% Asian, non-Hispanic/Latino; 0.1% Native Hawaiian or other Pacific Islander, non-Hispanic/Latino; 0.2% American Indian or Alaska Native, non-Hispanic/Latino; 3% Two or more races, non-Hispanic/Latino; 2% Race/ethnicity unknown; 1% international; 20% transferred in.

Freshmen

Admission: 59 enrolled.

FACULTY

Total: 814, 7% full-time.

Student/faculty ratio: 11:1.

ACADEMICS

Calendar: trimesters. *Degrees:* associate, bachelor's, and master's.

Special study options: academic remediation for entering students, accelerated degree program, adult/continuing education programs, advanced placement credit, cooperative education, distance learning, double majors, English as a second language, independent study, internships, off-campus study, part-time degree program, services for LD students, student-designed majors, study abroad, summer session for credit. ***ROTC:*** Army (c), Air Force (c).

Computers: 500 computers/terminals are available on campus for general student use. Students can access the following: campus intranet, computer help desk, free student e-mail accounts, online (class) grades, online (class) registration, online (class) schedules. Campuswide network is available. Wireless service is available via entire campus.

STUDENT LIFE

Housing options: college housing not available.

Campus security: 24-hour emergency response devices, late-night transport/escort service, Video monitoring capabilities of all public/customer facing locations.

COSTS & FINANCIAL AID

Costs (2014–15) ***One-time required fee:*** $25. ***Tuition:*** $13,920 full-time, $464 per credit hour part-time. Full-time tuition and fees vary according to program. Part-time tuition and fees vary according to program. ***Payment plans:*** installment, deferred payment. ***Waivers:*** employees or children of employees.

Financial Aid Of all full-time matriculated undergraduates who enrolled in 2003, 1,135 applied for aid, 1,071 were judged to have need. 29 Federal Work-Study jobs (averaging $7702). In 2003, 108 non-need-based awards were made. ***Average need-based loan:*** $5091. ***Average need-based gift aid:*** $4436. ***Average non-need-based aid:*** $2211.

APPLYING

Options: electronic application, deferred entrance.

Required for some: high school transcript.

Application deadlines: rolling (freshmen), rolling (transfers).

Notification: continuous (freshmen), continuous (transfers).

CONTACT

Mrs. Lynne Hull, Director of New Student Enrollment, Franklin University, 201 South Grant Avenue, Columbus, OH 43215. *Phone:* 614-947-6046. *Toll-free phone:* 877-341-6300. *E-mail:* hulll@franklin.edu.

God's Bible School and College

Cincinnati, Ohio

http://www.gbs.edu/

- **Independent interdenominational** 4-year, founded 1900
- **Urban** 14-acre campus
- **Coed**
- 90% of applicants were admitted

FACULTY
Student/faculty ratio: 12:1.

ACADEMICS
Calendar: semesters. *Degrees:* associate and bachelor's.

STUDENT LIFE
Housing options: on-campus residence required through senior year; men-only, women-only. Campus housing is university owned.

Activities and organizations: student-run newspaper, choral group.

Campus security: 24-hour patrols.

Student services: health clinic.

APPLYING
Standardized Tests *Required:* SAT or ACT (for admission). *Recommended:* SAT (for admission).

Application fee: $25.

Required: high school transcript, 3 letters of recommendation, interview.

CONTACT
Heather Couch, Director of Financial Aid and Admissions, God's Bible School and College, 1810 Young Street, Cincinnati, OH 45202-6838. *Phone:* 513-721-7944 Ext. 1161. *Toll-free phone:* 800-486-4637. *Fax:* 513-763-6649. *E-mail:* hcouch@gbs.edu.

Good Samaritan College of Nursing and Health Science

Cincinnati, Ohio

http://www.gscollege.edu/

- **Proprietary** primarily 2-year
- **Urban** campus with easy access to Cincinnati
- **Coed** 353 undergraduate students, 36% full-time, 91% women, 9% men
- **Minimally difficult** entrance level, 79% of applicants were admitted

UNDERGRAD STUDENTS
128 full-time, 225 part-time. 14% are from out of state; 11% Black or African American, non-Hispanic/Latino; 3% Hispanic/Latino; 2% Asian, non-Hispanic/Latino; 0.8% Two or more races, non-Hispanic/Latino; 22% transferred in.

Freshmen
Admission: 52 applied, 41 admitted, 40 enrolled. ***Average high school GPA:*** 2.8. ***Test scores:*** ACT scores over 18: 88%; ACT scores over 24: 18%; ACT scores over 30: 4%.

FACULTY
Total: 41, 73% full-time, 24% with terminal degrees.
Student/faculty ratio: 7:1.

ACADEMICS
Degrees: associate and bachelor's.

Special study options: academic remediation for entering students, advanced placement credit, cooperative education, honors programs, part-time degree program, services for LD students, summer session for credit.

STUDENT LIFE
Housing options: college housing not available.

Campus security: 24-hour emergency response devices and patrols, late-night transport/escort service.

COSTS & FINANCIAL AID
Costs (2014–15) ***Tuition:*** $17,905 full-time, $499 per credit hour part-time. ***Required fees:*** $1515 full-time, $80 per credit hour part-time. ***Payment plan:*** installment. ***Waivers:*** employees or children of employees.

Financial Aid Of all full-time matriculated undergraduates who enrolled in 2010, 155 applied for aid, 149 were judged to have need. 8 state and other part-time jobs (averaging $750). In 2010, 8 non-need-based awards were made. ***Average percent of need met:*** 68. ***Average financial aid package:*** $7488. ***Average need-based loan:*** $3477. ***Average need-based gift aid:*** $4260. ***Average non-need-based aid:*** $1100.

APPLYING
Standardized Tests *Required:* SAT or ACT (for admission).

Options: electronic application.

Application fee: $40.

Required: high school transcript, minimum 2.5 GPA, average GPA 2.25 in these high school courses: English, Math (Algebra required), Science (Chemistry required), and Social Studies.

CONTACT
Admissions Office, Good Samaritan College of Nursing and Health Science, 375 Dixmyth Avenue, Cincinnati, OH 45220. *Phone:* 513-862-2743. *Fax:* 513-862-3572.

Harrison College

Grove City, Ohio

http://www.harrison.edu/

- **Proprietary** 4-year, part of Harrison College
- **Suburban** campus with easy access to Columbus
- **Coed**
- **Moderately difficult** entrance level

FACULTY
Student/faculty ratio: 10:1.

ACADEMICS
Calendar: quarters. *Degrees:* associate and bachelor's.

STUDENT LIFE
Housing options: college housing not available.

APPLYING
Standardized Tests *Required:* Wonderlic Scholastic Level Exam (SLE) (for admission).

Options: electronic application.

Required: high school transcript, interview.

CONTACT
Jason Howanec, Vice President of Enrollment, Harrison College, 500 N. Meridian St., Indianapolis, IN 46204. *Phone:* 888-544-4422. *Toll-free phone:* 888-544-4422. *E-mail:* Admissions@harrison.edu.

Heidelberg University

Tiffin, Ohio

http://www.heidelberg.edu/

- **Independent** comprehensive, founded 1850, affiliated with United Church of Christ
- **Small-town** 115-acre campus with easy access to Toledo, Cleveland, Columbus
- **Endowment** $43.2 million
- **Coed** 1,106 undergraduate students, 97% full-time, 48% women, 52% men
- **Moderately difficult** entrance level, 70% of applicants were admitted

UNDERGRAD STUDENTS
1,069 full-time, 37 part-time. Students come from 25 states and territories; 12 other countries; 19% are from out of state; 5% Black or African American, non-Hispanic/Latino; 3% Hispanic/Latino; 1% Asian, non-Hispanic/Latino; 0.2% Native Hawaiian or other Pacific Islander, non-Hispanic/Latino; 0.2% American Indian or Alaska Native, non-Hispanic/Latino; 3% Two or more races, non-Hispanic/Latino; 13% Race/ethnicity unknown; 0.3% international; 3% transferred in; 79% live on campus.

Freshmen
Admission: 1,616 applied, 1,134 admitted, 364 enrolled. ***Average high school GPA:*** 3.28. ***Test scores:*** SAT critical reading scores over 500: 65%; SAT math scores over 500: 73%; ACT scores over 18: 94%; SAT

critical reading scores over 600: 11%; SAT math scores over 600: 22%; ACT scores over 24: 32%; ACT scores over 30: 2%.

Retention: 67% of full-time freshmen returned.

FACULTY
Total: 153, 35% full-time, 52% with terminal degrees.

Student/faculty ratio: 14:1.

ACADEMICS
Calendar: semesters. *Degrees:* bachelor's and master's.

Special study options: academic remediation for entering students, accelerated degree program, adult/continuing education programs, advanced placement credit, cooperative education, double majors, English as a second language, honors programs, independent study, internships, off-campus study, part-time degree program, services for LD students, student-designed majors, study abroad, summer session for credit. ***ROTC:*** Army (c), Air Force (c).

Unusual degree programs: 3-2 nursing with Ursuline - Breen School of Nursing.

Computers: 125 computers/terminals are available on campus for general student use. Students can access the following: computer help desk, free student e-mail accounts, online (class) grades, online (class) registration, online (class) schedules. Campuswide network is available. 100% of college-owned or -operated housing units are wired for high-speed Internet access. Wireless service is available via entire campus.

STUDENT LIFE
Housing options: on-campus residence required through junior year; coed, women-only, cooperative. Campus housing is university owned and leased by the school. Freshman campus housing is guaranteed.

Activities and organizations: drama/theater group, student-run newspaper, radio and television station, choral group, Alpha Phi Omega, BERG Events Council, Student Senate, Campus Fellowship, Black Student Union/World Student Union.

Athletics Member NCAA. All Division III. ***Intercollegiate sports:*** baseball M, basketball M/W, cheerleading M/W, cross-country running M/W, football M, golf M/W, soccer M/W, softball W, tennis M/W, track and field M/W, volleyball M/W, wrestling M. ***Intramural sports:*** archery M/W, badminton M/W, football M/W, golf M/W, soccer M/W, softball M/W, table tennis M/W, volleyball M/W, weight lifting M/W.

Campus security: 24-hour emergency response devices and patrols, student patrols, late-night transport/escort service, controlled dormitory access.

Student services: health clinic, personal/psychological counseling.

COSTS & FINANCIAL AID
Costs (2014–15) ***Comprehensive fee:*** $36,706 includes full-time tuition ($26,900), mandatory fees ($580), and room and board ($9226). Full-time tuition and fees vary according to course load and degree level. Part-time tuition and fees vary according to course load and degree level. ***Required fees:*** $695 per credit part-time. ***Room and board:*** Room and board charges vary according to housing facility. ***Payment plan:*** installment. ***Waivers:*** employees or children of employees.

Financial Aid Of all full-time matriculated undergraduates who enrolled in 2014, 1,005 applied for aid, 934 were judged to have need, 150 had their need fully met. 659 Federal Work-Study jobs (averaging $2000). 61 state and other part-time jobs (averaging $1000). In 2014, 114 non-need-based awards were made. ***Average percent of need met:*** 79. ***Average financial aid package:*** $23,339. ***Average need-based loan:*** $5010. ***Average need-based gift aid:*** $17,190. ***Average non-need-based aid:*** $13,259. ***Average indebtedness upon graduation:*** $36,962.

APPLYING
Standardized Tests *Required:* SAT or ACT (for admission).

Options: electronic application, deferred entrance.

Required: essay or personal statement, high school transcript, minimum 2.5 GPA, 1 letter of recommendation.

Application deadlines: 8/15 (freshmen), 8/15 (out-of-state freshmen), 8/15 (transfers).

Notification: 10/1 (freshmen), 8/15 (transfers).

CONTACT
Mr. Jason Miller, Director of Admission, Heidelberg University, 310 East Market Street, Tiffin, OH 44883. *Phone:* 419-448-2330. *Toll-free phone:* 800-434-3352. *Fax:* 419-448-2334. *E-mail:* jmiller7@heidelberg.edu.

Hiram College
Hiram, Ohio
http://www.hiram.edu/

- **Independent** comprehensive, founded 1850, affiliated with Christian Church (Disciples of Christ)
- **Rural** 110-acre campus with easy access to Cleveland
- **Endowment** $69.4 million
- **Coed** 1,235 undergraduate students, 86% full-time, 53% women, 47% men
- **Moderately difficult** entrance level, 62% of applicants were admitted

UNDERGRAD STUDENTS
1,068 full-time, 167 part-time. Students come from 34 states and territories; 23 other countries; 16% are from out of state; 16% Black or African American, non-Hispanic/Latino; 4% Hispanic/Latino; 1% Asian, non-Hispanic/Latino; 0.2% Native Hawaiian or other Pacific Islander, non-Hispanic/Latino; 0.2% American Indian or Alaska Native, non-Hispanic/Latino; 2% Two or more races, non-Hispanic/Latino; 5% Race/ethnicity unknown; 3% international; 2% transferred in; 78% live on campus.

Freshmen
Admission: 2,136 applied, 1,326 admitted, 276 enrolled. ***Average high school GPA:*** 3.18. ***Test scores:*** SAT critical reading scores over 500: 51%; SAT math scores over 500: 47%; ACT scores over 18: 83%; SAT critical reading scores over 600: 14%; SAT math scores over 600: 21%; ACT scores over 24: 35%; SAT critical reading scores over 700: 2%; SAT math scores over 700: 2%; ACT scores over 30: 3%.

Retention: 69% of full-time freshmen returned.

FACULTY
Total: 149, 55% full-time.

Student/faculty ratio: 11:1.

ACADEMICS
Calendar: semesters. *Degrees:* bachelor's and master's.

Special study options: academic remediation for entering students, adult/continuing education programs, advanced placement credit, cooperative education, distance learning, double majors, English as a second language, freshman honors college, honors programs, independent study, internships, off-campus study, part-time degree program, services for LD students, student-designed majors, study abroad, summer session for credit. ***ROTC:*** Army (c), Air Force (c).

Unusual degree programs: 3-2 engineering with Case Western Reserve University and Washington University in St. Louis; social work with Case Western Reserve University.

Computers: 70 computers/terminals and 3,500 ports are available on campus for general student use. Students can access the following: campus intranet, computer help desk, free student e-mail accounts, online (class) grades, online (class) registration, online (class) schedules. Campuswide network is available. 100% of college-owned or -operated housing units are wired for high-speed Internet access. Wireless service is available via entire campus.

STUDENT LIFE
Housing options: on-campus residence required through junior year; coed, women-only, special housing for students with disabilities. Campus housing is university owned. Freshman campus housing is guaranteed.

Activities and organizations: drama/theater group, student-run radio station, choral group, Greek Life, Intercultural Forum, Terrier Activities Board, Student-Athlete Advisory Committee, The BARK - WHRM Radio Station.

Athletics Member NCAA. All Division III. ***Intercollegiate sports:*** baseball M, basketball M/W, cheerleading M(c)/W(c), cross-country running M/W, equestrian sports M(c)/W(c), football M, golf M/W, lacrosse M/W, rugby M(c)/W(c), sailing M(c)/W(c), soccer M/W, softball W, swimming and diving M/W, table tennis M(c)/W(c), tennis M/W, track and field M/W, ultimate Frisbee M/W, volleyball M/W. ***Intramural sports:*** basketball M/W, cheerleading M/W, football M/W, racquetball

M/W, soccer M/W, softball M/W, tennis M/W, ultimate Frisbee M/W, volleyball M/W, water polo M/W.

Campus security: 24-hour emergency response devices, student patrols, late-night transport/escort service, controlled dormitory access, Daytime services available M-F 8am-5pm and weekends 7am-5pm; Night-time services available from 5pm-3am 365 days a year.

Student services: health clinic, personal/psychological counseling.

COSTS & FINANCIAL AID

Costs (2015–16) ***Comprehensive fee:*** $41,720 includes full-time tuition ($30,230), mandatory fees ($1300), and room and board ($10,190). Part-time tuition: $435 per credit hour. No tuition increase for student's term of enrollment. ***Required fees:*** $125 part-time. ***College room only:*** $5150. Room and board charges vary according to housing facility. ***Payment plan:*** installment. ***Waivers:*** employees or children of employees.

Financial Aid Of all full-time matriculated undergraduates who enrolled in 2002, 790 applied for aid, 736 were judged to have need, 699 had their need fully met. 587 Federal Work-Study jobs (averaging $1600). 18 state and other part-time jobs (averaging $1580). In 2002, 114 non-need-based awards were made. ***Average percent of need met:*** 95. ***Average financial aid package:*** $21,218. ***Average need-based loan:*** $6960. ***Average need-based gift aid:*** $8163. ***Average non-need-based aid:*** $8635. ***Average indebtedness upon graduation:*** $17,125.

APPLYING

Standardized Tests *Required:* SAT or ACT (for admission).

Options: electronic application, deferred entrance.

Application fee: $25.

Required: essay or personal statement, high school transcript, interview. ***Recommended:*** minimum 2.8 GPA.

Application deadlines: rolling (freshmen), rolling (out-of-state freshmen), rolling (transfers).

Notification: continuous (freshmen), continuous (out-of-state freshmen), continuous (transfers).

CONTACT

Sherman C. Dean II, Associate Director of Admission, Hiram College, PO Box 96, Hiram, OH 44234. *Phone:* 330-569-5169. *Toll-free phone:* 800-362-5280. *Fax:* 330-569-5944. *E-mail:* admission@hiram.edu.

ITT Technical Institute

Akron, Ohio

http://www.itt-tech.edu/

- **Proprietary** primarily 2-year
- **Coed**
- **Minimally difficult** entrance level

ACADEMICS

Degrees: associate and bachelor's.

CONTACT

Director of Recruitment, ITT Technical Institute, 3428 West Market Street, Akron, OH 44333. *Phone:* 330-865-8600. *Toll-free phone:* 877-818-0154.

ITT Technical Institute

Columbus, Ohio

http://www.itt-tech.edu/

- **Proprietary** primarily 2-year, part of ITT Educational Services, Inc.
- **Coed**
- **Minimally difficult** entrance level

ACADEMICS

Calendar: quarters. *Degrees:* associate and bachelor's.

CONTACT

Director of Recruitment, ITT Technical Institute, 4717 Hilton Corporate Drive, Columbus, OH 43232. *Phone:* 614-868-2000. *Toll-free phone:* 877-233-8864.

ITT Technical Institute

Dayton, Ohio

http://www.itt-tech.edu/

- **Proprietary** primarily 2-year, founded 1935, part of ITT Educational Services, Inc.
- **Suburban** campus
- **Coed**
- **Minimally difficult** entrance level

ACADEMICS

Calendar: quarters. *Degrees:* associate and bachelor's.

STUDENT LIFE

Housing options: college housing not available.

CONTACT

Director of Recruitment, ITT Technical Institute, 3325 Stop 8 Road, Dayton, OH 45414-3425. *Phone:* 937-264-7700. *Toll-free phone:* 800-568-3241.

ITT Technical Institute

Hilliard, Ohio

http://www.itt-tech.edu/

- **Proprietary** primarily 2-year, founded 2003, part of ITT Educational Services, Inc.
- **Coed**
- **Minimally difficult** entrance level

ACADEMICS

Calendar: quarters. *Degrees:* associate and bachelor's.

CONTACT

Director of Recruitment, ITT Technical Institute, 3781 Park Mill Run Drive, Hilliard, OH 43026. *Phone:* 614-771-4888. *Toll-free phone:* 888-483-4888.

ITT Technical Institute

Maumee, Ohio

http://www.itt-tech.edu/

- **Proprietary** primarily 2-year
- **Coed**

ACADEMICS

Degrees: associate and bachelor's.

STUDENT LIFE

Housing options: college housing not available.

CONTACT

Director of Recruitment, ITT Technical Institute, 1656 Henthorne Drive, Suite B, Maumee, OH 43537. *Phone:* 419-861-6500. *Toll-free phone:* 877-205-4639.

ITT Technical Institute

Norwood, Ohio

http://www.itt-tech.edu/

- **Proprietary** primarily 2-year, founded 1995, part of ITT Educational Services, Inc.
- **Coed**
- **Minimally difficult** entrance level

ACADEMICS

Calendar: quarters. *Degrees:* associate and bachelor's.

STUDENT LIFE

Housing options: college housing not available.

CONTACT

Director of Recruitment, ITT Technical Institute, 4750 Wesley Avenue, Norwood, OH 45212. *Phone:* 513-531-8300. *Toll-free phone:* 800-314-8324.

ITT Technical Institute
Strongsville, Ohio
http://www.itt-tech.edu/

- **Proprietary** primarily 2-year, founded 1994, part of ITT Educational Services, Inc.
- **Coed**
- **Minimally difficult** entrance level

ACADEMICS
Calendar: quarters. *Degrees:* associate and bachelor's.

STUDENT LIFE
Housing options: college housing not available.

CONTACT
Director of Recruitment, ITT Technical Institute, 14955 Sprague Road, Strongsville, OH 44136. *Phone:* 440-234-9091. *Toll-free phone:* 800-331-1488.

ITT Technical Institute
Warrensville Heights, Ohio
http://www.itt-tech.edu/

- **Proprietary** primarily 2-year, founded 2005
- **Coed**
- **Minimally difficult** entrance level

ACADEMICS
Calendar: quarters. *Degrees:* associate and bachelor's.

STUDENT LIFE
Housing options: college housing not available.

CONTACT
Director of Recruitment, ITT Technical Institute, 24865 Emery Road, Warrensville Heights, OH 44128. *Phone:* 216-896-6500. *Toll-free phone:* 800-741-3494.

ITT Technical Institute
Youngstown, Ohio
http://www.itt-tech.edu/

- **Proprietary** primarily 2-year, founded 1967, part of ITT Educational Services, Inc.
- **Suburban** campus
- **Coed**
- **Minimally difficult** entrance level

ACADEMICS
Calendar: quarters. *Degrees:* associate and bachelor's.

STUDENT LIFE
Housing options: college housing not available.

FINANCIAL AID
Financial Aid Of all full-time matriculated undergraduates who enrolled in 2013, 5 Federal Work-Study jobs (averaging $3979).

CONTACT
Director of Recruitment, ITT Technical Institute, 1030 North Meridian Road, Youngstown, OH 44509-4098. *Phone:* 330-270-1600. *Toll-free phone:* 800-832-5001.

★ John Carroll University
University Heights, Ohio
http://www.jcu.edu/

- **Independent Roman Catholic (Jesuit)** comprehensive, founded 1886
- **Suburban** 60-acre campus with easy access to Cleveland
- **Endowment** $200.4 million
- **Coed** 3,125 undergraduate students, 97% full-time, 47% women, 53% men
- **Moderately difficult** entrance level, 83% of applicants were admitted

UNDERGRAD STUDENTS
3,022 full-time, 103 part-time. Students come from 39 states and territories; 24 other countries; 33% are from out of state; 4% Black or African American, non-Hispanic/Latino; 3% Hispanic/Latino; 2% Asian, non-Hispanic/Latino; 0.1% American Indian or Alaska Native, non-Hispanic/Latino; 2% Two or more races, non-Hispanic/Latino; 1% Race/ethnicity unknown; 2% international; 2% transferred in; 57% live on campus.

Freshmen
Admission: 3,873 applied, 3,211 admitted, 799 enrolled. ***Average high school GPA:*** 3.51. ***Test scores:*** SAT critical reading scores over 500: 78%; SAT math scores over 500: 79%; SAT writing scores over 500: 71%; ACT scores over 18: 99%; SAT critical reading scores over 600: 25%; SAT math scores over 600: 30%; SAT writing scores over 600: 24%; ACT scores over 24: 58%; SAT critical reading scores over 700: 3%; SAT math scores over 700: 3%; SAT writing scores over 700: 4%; ACT scores over 30: 9%.
Retention: 85% of full-time freshmen returned.

FACULTY
Total: 423, 45% full-time, 67% with terminal degrees.
Student/faculty ratio: 13:1.

ACADEMICS
Calendar: semesters. *Degrees:* bachelor's, master's, and post-master's certificates.
Special study options: advanced placement credit, cooperative education, double majors, honors programs, independent study, internships, off-campus study, part-time degree program, services for LD students, student-designed majors, study abroad, summer session for credit. ***ROTC:*** Army (b).
Unusual degree programs: 3-2 engineering with Case Western Reserve University; nursing with Joint BA/BSN degree program with Ursuline College.
Computers: 411 computers/terminals and 500 ports are available on campus for general student use. Students can access the following: campus intranet, computer help desk, free student e-mail accounts, online (class) grades, online (class) registration, online (class) schedules, campus student online registration, billing, advising system, JCU mobile app, course management site (BlackBoard), online financial aid and billing; online course sites; online housing selection. Campuswide network is available. 100% of college-owned or -operated housing units are wired for high-speed Internet access. Wireless service is available via entire campus.

STUDENT LIFE
Housing options: on-campus residence required through sophomore year; coed, cooperative, special housing for students with disabilities. Campus housing is university owned. Freshman campus housing is guaranteed.
Activities and organizations: drama/theater group, student-run newspaper, radio and television station, choral group, Community Outreach/Volunteer Service Organization, Student Union, Club Sports, Fraternities and Sororities, Carroll News, national fraternities, national sororities.
Athletics Member NCAA. All Division III. ***Intercollegiate sports:*** baseball M, basketball M/W, cheerleading W(c), crew M(c)/W(c), cross-country running M/W, field hockey W(c), football M, golf M/W, ice hockey M(c), lacrosse M/W, rugby M(c)/W(c), sailing M(c)/W(c), skiing (cross-country) M(c)/W(c), skiing (downhill) M(c)/W(c), soccer M/W, softball W, swimming and diving M/W, tennis M/W, track and field M/W, ultimate Frisbee M(c), volleyball M(c)/W, wrestling M. ***Intramural sports:*** basketball M/W, football M/W, golf M/W, racquetball M/W, rock climbing M/W, soccer M/W, softball M/W, swimming and diving M/W, table tennis M/W, tennis M/W, ultimate Frisbee M/W, volleyball M/W, water polo M/W.
Campus security: 24-hour emergency response devices and patrols, late-night transport/escort service, controlled dormitory access, Distinctive Student EMS program fully staffed.
Student services: health clinic, personal/psychological counseling, women's center.

COSTS & FINANCIAL AID
Costs (2015–16) ***One-time required fee:*** $325. ***Comprehensive fee:*** $48,100 includes full-time tuition ($35,930), mandatory fees ($1250), and room and board ($10,920). Part-time tuition: $1095 per credit hour. Part-time tuition and fees vary according to course load. ***Room and board:*** Room and board charges vary according to board plan and housing

facility. ***Payment plans:*** installment, deferred payment. ***Waivers:*** senior citizens and employees or children of employees.

Financial Aid Of all full-time matriculated undergraduates who enrolled in 2014, 2,595 applied for aid, 2,210 were judged to have need, 348 had their need fully met. In 2014, 527 non-need-based awards were made. ***Average percent of need met:*** 79. ***Average financial aid package:*** $28,538. ***Average need-based loan:*** $4049. ***Average need-based gift aid:*** $23,250. ***Average non-need-based aid:*** $16,297. ***Average indebtedness upon graduation:*** $30,837. ***Financial aid deadline:*** 3/15.

APPLYING

Standardized Tests *Required:* SAT or ACT (for admission).

Options: electronic application, early admission, early action, deferred entrance.

Required: essay or personal statement, high school transcript, 1 letter of recommendation. ***Required for some:*** 2 letters of recommendation, interview.

Application deadlines: 2/1 (freshmen), rolling (transfers), 12/1 (early action).

Notification: continuous (freshmen), 12/20 (early action).

CONTACT

Mr. Steven P. Vitatoe, Executive Director of Enrollment, John Carroll University, 1 John Carroll Boulevard, University Heights, OH 44118. *Phone:* 216-397-4294. *Toll-free phone:* 888-335-6800. *Fax:* 216-397-4981. *E-mail:* svitatoe@jcu.edu.

Kent State University

Kent, Ohio

http://www.kent.edu/

- **State-supported** university, founded 1910, part of Kent State University System
- **Suburban** 946-acre campus with easy access to Cleveland-Akron-Canton
- **Endowment** $110.9 million
- **Coed** 23,328 undergraduate students, 87% full-time, 59% women, 41% men
- **Moderately difficult** entrance level, 84% of applicants were admitted

UNDERGRAD STUDENTS

20,334 full-time, 2,994 part-time. Students come from 51 states and territories; 96 other countries; 13% are from out of state; 9% Black or African American, non-Hispanic/Latino; 3% Hispanic/Latino; 1% Asian, non-Hispanic/Latino; 0.1% Native Hawaiian or other Pacific Islander, non-Hispanic/Latino; 0.2% American Indian or Alaska Native, non-Hispanic/Latino; 3% Two or more races, non-Hispanic/Latino; 3% Race/ethnicity unknown; 7% international; 5% transferred in; 28% live on campus.

Freshmen

Admission: 16,125 applied, 13,607 admitted, 4,272 enrolled. ***Average high school GPA:*** 3.34. ***Test scores:*** SAT critical reading scores over 500: 64%; SAT math scores over 500: 65%; SAT writing scores over 500: 55%; ACT scores over 18: 98%; SAT critical reading scores over 600: 19%; SAT math scores over 600: 21%; SAT writing scores over 600: 16%; ACT scores over 24: 40%; SAT critical reading scores over 700: 2%; SAT math scores over 700: 3%; SAT writing scores over 700: 2%; ACT scores over 30: 5%.

Retention: 82% of full-time freshmen returned.

FACULTY

Total: 1,730, 55% full-time.

Student/faculty ratio: 21:1.

ACADEMICS

Calendar: semesters. *Degrees:* certificates, bachelor's, master's, doctoral, post-master's, and postbachelor's certificates.

Special study options: academic remediation for entering students, accelerated degree program, adult/continuing education programs, advanced placement credit, cooperative education, distance learning, double majors, English as a second language, freshman honors college, honors programs, independent study, internships, off-campus study, part-time degree program, services for LD students, student-designed majors, study abroad, summer session for credit. ***ROTC:*** Army (b), Air Force (b).

Unusual degree programs: 3-2 business administration; nursing; Speech Pathology and Audiology; International Relations and Business Administration; Fashion Merchandising and Business Administration; Human Development and Family Services with concentration in Gerontology and Nursing Home Administration and Business Administration.

Computers: 2,000 computers/terminals and 1,200 ports are available on campus for general student use. Students can access the following: computer help desk, free student e-mail accounts, online (class) grades, online (class) registration, online (class) schedules. Campuswide network is available. 100% of college-owned or -operated housing units are wired for high-speed Internet access. Wireless service is available via entire campus.

STUDENT LIFE

Housing options: on-campus residence required through sophomore year; coed, men-only, women-only, cooperative, special housing for students with disabilities. Campus housing is university owned. Freshman campus housing is guaranteed.

Activities and organizations: drama/theater group, student-run newspaper, radio and television station, choral group, marching band, Commuter & Off-Campus Student Organization (COSO), Fashion Student Organization (FSO), Public Relations Students Society of America (PRSSA), Habitat for Humanity, Relay for Life, national fraternities, national sororities.

Athletics Member NCAA. All Division I. ***Intercollegiate sports:*** baseball M(s), basketball M(s)/W(s), cheerleading W(c), cross-country running M(s)/W(s), field hockey W(s), football M(s), golf M(s)/W(s), gymnastics W(s), soccer W(s), softball W(s), track and field M(s)/W(s), volleyball W(s), wrestling M(s). ***Intramural sports:*** badminton M(c)/W(c), baseball M(c), basketball M/W, bowling M(c)/W(c), equestrian sports M(c)/W(c), fencing M(c)/W(c), field hockey W(c), football M/W, golf M(c)/W(c), gymnastics M(c)/W(c), ice hockey M(c), lacrosse M(c), racquetball M(c)/W(c), rugby M(c)/W(c), sailing M(c)/W(c), skiing (downhill) M(c)/W(c), soccer M(c)/W(c), softball M/W, swimming and diving M(c)/W(c), table tennis M/W, tennis M/W, ultimate Frisbee M(c)/W(c), volleyball M(c)/W(c), water polo M/W.

Campus security: 24-hour emergency response devices and patrols, student patrols, late-night transport/escort service, controlled dormitory access, campus police and fire department, electronic locks on computer labs, studios and laboratory research areas.

Student services: health clinic, personal/psychological counseling, women's center, legal services.

COSTS & FINANCIAL AID

Costs (2014–15) ***One-time required fee:*** $150. ***Tuition:*** state resident $10,012 full-time, $456 per credit hour part-time; nonresident $17,972 full-time, $818 per credit hour part-time. Full-time tuition and fees vary according to course load. Part-time tuition and fees vary according to course load. ***Room and board:*** $9908; room only: $6108. Room and board charges vary according to board plan and housing facility. ***Payment plan:*** installment. ***Waivers:*** senior citizens and employees or children of employees.

Financial Aid Of all full-time matriculated undergraduates who enrolled in 2014, 14,951 applied for aid, 12,779 were judged to have need, 1,014 had their need fully met. 709 Federal Work-Study jobs (averaging $2745). In 2014, 2852 non-need-based awards were made. ***Average percent of need met:*** 46. ***Average financial aid package:*** $8888. ***Average need-based loan:*** $4564. ***Average need-based gift aid:*** $5190. ***Average non-need-based aid:*** $4660. ***Average indebtedness upon graduation:*** $32,393.

APPLYING

Standardized Tests *Required:* SAT or ACT (for admission).

Options: electronic application.

Application fee: $45.

Required: high school transcript, minimum 2.5 GPA.

Application deadlines: 5/1 (freshmen), rolling (transfers).

Notification: continuous (freshmen), continuous (transfers).

CONTACT

Mr. Christopher Buttenschon, Senior Assistant Director of Admissions, Kent State University, 161 Michael Schwartz Center, Kent, OH 44242-

0001. *Phone:* 330-672-2444. *Toll-free phone:* 800-988-KENT. *Fax:* 330-672-2499. *E-mail:* admissions@kent.edu.

Kent State University at Ashtabula

Ashtabula, Ohio

http://www.ashtabula.kent.edu/

- **State-supported** primarily 2-year, founded 1958, part of Kent State University System
- **Small-town** 120-acre campus with easy access to Cleveland
- **Coed** 2,278 undergraduate students, 51% full-time, 65% women, 35% men
- **Noncompetitive** entrance level, 97% of applicants were admitted

UNDERGRAD STUDENTS

1,168 full-time, 1,110 part-time. Students come from 23 states and territories; 7 other countries; 4% are from out of state; 5% Black or African American, non-Hispanic/Latino; 3% Hispanic/Latino; 1% Asian, non-Hispanic/Latino; 0.1% Native Hawaiian or other Pacific Islander, non-Hispanic/Latino; 0.4% American Indian or Alaska Native, non-Hispanic/Latino; 2% Two or more races, non-Hispanic/Latino; 2% Race/ethnicity unknown; 0.4% international; 5% transferred in.

Freshmen

Admission: 346 applied, 337 admitted, 221 enrolled. ***Average high school GPA:*** 2.86. ***Test scores:*** SAT critical reading scores over 500: 17%; SAT math scores over 500: 17%; SAT writing scores over 500: 17%; ACT scores over 18: 73%; SAT critical reading scores over 600: 8%; SAT math scores over 600: 17%; SAT writing scores over 600: 8%; ACT scores over 24: 10%.

Retention: 60% of full-time freshmen returned.

FACULTY

Total: 107, 48% full-time.

Student/faculty ratio: 22:1.

ACADEMICS

Calendar: semesters. *Degrees:* certificates, associate, and bachelor's (also offers some upper-level and graduate courses).

Special study options: academic remediation for entering students, advanced placement credit, distance learning, double majors, independent study, internships, part-time degree program, services for LD students, student-designed majors, study abroad, summer session for credit. ***ROTC:*** Army (c), Air Force (c).

Computers: 70 computers/terminals and 175 ports are available on campus for general student use. Students can access the following: computer help desk, free student e-mail accounts, online (class) grades, online (class) registration, online (class) schedules. Campuswide network is available. Wireless service is available via entire campus.

STUDENT LIFE

Housing options: college housing not available.

Activities and organizations: student government, student veterans association, Student Nurses Association, Student Occupational Therapy Association, Media Club.

Athletics *Intramural sports:* volleyball M/W.

Campus security: 24-hour emergency response devices.

COSTS & FINANCIAL AID

Costs (2014–15) *One-time required fee:* $150. ***Tuition:*** state resident $5664 full-time, $258 per credit hour part-time; nonresident $13,624 full-time, $620 per credit hour part-time. Full-time tuition and fees vary according to course level and course load. Part-time tuition and fees vary according to course level and course load. ***Payment plan:*** installment. ***Waivers:*** senior citizens and employees or children of employees.

Financial Aid Of all full-time matriculated undergraduates who enrolled in 2014, 612 applied for aid, 568 were judged to have need, 17 had their need fully met. In 2014, 22 non-need-based awards were made. ***Average percent of need met:*** 40. ***Average financial aid package:*** $7373. ***Average need-based loan:*** $3970. ***Average need-based gift aid:*** $4761. ***Average non-need-based aid:*** $1045.

APPLYING

Standardized Tests *Required for some:* SAT or ACT (for admission). *Recommended:* SAT or ACT (for admission).

Options: electronic application, deferred entrance.

Application fee: $40.

Required: high school transcript.

Application deadlines: rolling (freshmen), rolling (transfers).

Notification: continuous (freshmen), continuous (transfers).

CONTACT

Kent State University at Ashtabula, 3300 Lake Road West, Ashtabula, OH 44004-2299. *Phone:* 440-964-4314.

Kent State University at East Liverpool

East Liverpool, Ohio

http://www.eliv.kent.edu/

- **State-supported** primarily 2-year, founded 1967, part of Kent State University System
- **Small-town** 4-acre campus with easy access to Pittsburgh
- **Coed** 1,481 undergraduate students, 55% full-time, 67% women, 33% men
- **Noncompetitive** entrance level, 96% of applicants were admitted

UNDERGRAD STUDENTS

817 full-time, 664 part-time. Students come from 5 states and territories; 1 other country; 16% are from out of state; 6% Black or African American, non-Hispanic/Latino; 3% Hispanic/Latino; 0.9% Asian, non-Hispanic/Latino; 0.1% Native Hawaiian or other Pacific Islander, non-Hispanic/Latino; 0.2% American Indian or Alaska Native, non-Hispanic/Latino; 2% Two or more races, non-Hispanic/Latino; 3% Race/ethnicity unknown; 0.3% international; 5% transferred in.

Freshmen

Admission: 121 applied, 116 admitted, 86 enrolled. ***Average high school GPA:*** 2.87. ***Test scores:*** ACT scores over 18: 83%; ACT scores over 24: 10%.

Retention: 58% of full-time freshmen returned.

FACULTY

Total: 63, 43% full-time.

Student/faculty ratio: 27:1.

ACADEMICS

Calendar: semesters. *Degrees:* certificates, associate, bachelor's, and master's (also offers some upper-level and graduate courses).

Special study options: academic remediation for entering students, accelerated degree program, advanced placement credit, distance learning, double majors, freshman honors college, honors programs, independent study, internships, part-time degree program, services for LD students, student-designed majors, summer session for credit. ***ROTC:*** Army (c), Air Force (c).

Computers: 72 computers/terminals are available on campus for general student use. Students can access the following: computer help desk, free student e-mail accounts, online (class) grades, online (class) registration, online (class) schedules. Campuswide network is available. Wireless service is available via entire campus.

STUDENT LIFE

Housing options: college housing not available.

Activities and organizations: student government, Student Nurses Association, Environmental Club, Student Occupational Therapist Assistants, Physical Therapist Assistant Club.

Campus security: 24-hour emergency response devices, student patrols, late-night transport/escort service.

Student services: personal/psychological counseling.

COSTS & FINANCIAL AID

Costs (2014–15) *One-time required fee:* $150. ***Tuition:*** state resident $5664 full-time, $258 per credit hour part-time; nonresident $13,624 full-time, $620 per credit hour part-time. Full-time tuition and fees vary according to course level and course load. Part-time tuition and fees vary according to course level and course load. ***Payment plan:*** installment. ***Waivers:*** senior citizens and employees or children of employees.

Financial Aid Of all full-time matriculated undergraduates who enrolled in 2014, 283 applied for aid, 272 were judged to have need, 8 had their need fully met. In 2014, 1 non-need-based awards were made. ***Average percent of need met:*** 41. ***Average financial aid package:*** $7450. ***Average need-based loan:*** $3983. ***Average need-based gift aid:*** $4866. ***Average non-need-based aid:*** $2116.

APPLYING

Standardized Tests *Required for some:* SAT or ACT (for admission). *Recommended:* SAT or ACT (for admission).

Options: electronic application, deferred entrance.

Application fee: $40.

Required: high school transcript.

Application deadlines: rolling (freshmen), rolling (transfers).

Notification: continuous (freshmen), continuous (transfers).

CONTACT

Kent State University at East Liverpool, OH. *Phone:* 330-385-3805.

Kent State University at Geauga

Burton, Ohio

http://www.geauga.kent.edu/

- **State-supported** 4-year, founded 1964, part of Kent State University System
- **Rural** 87-acre campus with easy access to Cleveland
- **Coed** 2,725 undergraduate students, 58% full-time, 64% women, 36% men
- **Noncompetitive** entrance level, 94% of applicants were admitted

UNDERGRAD STUDENTS

1,583 full-time, 1,142 part-time. Students come from 7 states and territories; 10 other countries; 2% are from out of state; 11% Black or African American, non-Hispanic/Latino; 3% Hispanic/Latino; 1% Asian, non-Hispanic/Latino; 0.1% Native Hawaiian or other Pacific Islander, non-Hispanic/Latino; 0.3% American Indian or Alaska Native, non-Hispanic/Latino; 3% Two or more races, non-Hispanic/Latino; 3% Race/ethnicity unknown; 0.5% international; 6% transferred in.

Freshmen

Admission: 470 applied, 442 admitted, 340 enrolled. ***Average high school GPA:*** 2.59. ***Test scores:*** SAT critical reading scores over 500: 56%; SAT math scores over 500: 68%; SAT writing scores over 500: 59%; ACT scores over 18: 68%; SAT critical reading scores over 600: 21%; SAT math scores over 600: 26%; SAT writing scores over 600: 24%; ACT scores over 24: 13%; SAT critical reading scores over 700: 3%; SAT math scores over 700: 3%; SAT writing scores over 700: 3%.

Retention: 56% of full-time freshmen returned.

FACULTY

Total: 148, 27% full-time.

Student/faculty ratio: 26:1.

ACADEMICS

Calendar: semesters. *Degrees:* associate, bachelor's, and master's.

Special study options: academic remediation for entering students, accelerated degree program, advanced placement credit, distance learning, double majors, independent study, internships, part-time degree program, services for LD students, student-designed majors, summer session for credit. ***ROTC:*** Army (c), Air Force (c).

Computers: Students can access the following: computer help desk, free student e-mail accounts, online (class) grades, online (class) registration, online (class) schedules. Campuswide network is available. Wireless service is available via entire campus.

STUDENT LIFE

Housing options: college housing not available.

Activities and organizations: Student Ambassadors, Campus Crusade for Christ, Gaia Society, NSNA@RAC, Pride.

Campus security: 24-hour emergency response devices.

COSTS & FINANCIAL AID

Costs (2014–15) ***One-time required fee:*** $150. ***Tuition:*** state resident $5664 full-time, $258 per credit hour part-time; nonresident $13,624 full-time, $620 per credit hour part-time. Full-time tuition and fees vary according to course level and course load. Part-time tuition and fees vary according to course level and course load. ***Payment plan:*** installment. ***Waivers:*** senior citizens and employees or children of employees.

Financial Aid Of all full-time matriculated undergraduates who enrolled in 2014, 650 applied for aid, 575 were judged to have need, 27 had their need fully met. In 2014, 8 non-need-based awards were made. ***Average percent of need met:*** 41. ***Average financial aid package:*** $6607. ***Average need-based loan:*** $3817. ***Average need-based gift aid:*** $4522. ***Average non-need-based aid:*** $953.

APPLYING

Standardized Tests *Required for some:* SAT or ACT (for admission). *Recommended:* SAT or ACT (for admission).

Options: electronic application, deferred entrance.

Application fee: $40.

Required: high school transcript.

Application deadlines: rolling (freshmen), rolling (transfers).

Notification: continuous (freshmen), continuous (transfers).

CONTACT

Kent State University at Geauga, 14111 Claridon-Troy Road, Burton, OH 44021. *Phone:* 440-834-4187. *Fax:* 440-834-3786. *E-mail:* geaugaadmissions@kent.edu.

Kent State University at Salem

Salem, Ohio

http://www.salem.kent.edu/

- **State-supported** primarily 2-year, founded 1966, part of Kent State University System
- **Rural** 98-acre campus
- **Coed** 1,844 undergraduate students, 67% full-time, 71% women, 29% men
- **Noncompetitive** entrance level, 97% of applicants were admitted

UNDERGRAD STUDENTS

1,228 full-time, 616 part-time. Students come from 11 states and territories; 4 other countries; 2% are from out of state; 3% Black or African American, non-Hispanic/Latino; 2% Hispanic/Latino; 0.7% Asian, non-Hispanic/Latino; 0.1% Native Hawaiian or other Pacific Islander, non-Hispanic/Latino; 0.5% American Indian or Alaska Native, non-Hispanic/Latino; 1% Two or more races, non-Hispanic/Latino; 3% Race/ethnicity unknown; 0.2% international; 7% transferred in.

Freshmen

Admission: 342 applied, 331 admitted, 205 enrolled. ***Average high school GPA:*** 3.01. ***Test scores:*** SAT critical reading scores over 500: 50%; SAT math scores over 500: 17%; SAT writing scores over 500: 33%; ACT scores over 18: 76%; SAT critical reading scores over 600: 17%; SAT math scores over 600: 17%; SAT writing scores over 600: 17%; ACT scores over 24: 19%; ACT scores over 30: 2%.

Retention: 56% of full-time freshmen returned.

FACULTY

Total: 130, 33% full-time.

Student/faculty ratio: 20:1.

ACADEMICS

Calendar: semesters. *Degrees:* certificates, associate, and bachelor's (also offers some upper-level and graduate courses).

Special study options: academic remediation for entering students, accelerated degree program, adult/continuing education programs, advanced placement credit, cooperative education, distance learning, double majors, freshman honors college, honors programs, independent study, internships, part-time degree program, services for LD students, student-designed majors, summer session for credit. ***ROTC:*** Army (c), Air Force (c).

Computers: Students can access the following: computer help desk, free student e-mail accounts, online (class) grades, online (class) registration, online (class) schedules. Campuswide network is available. Wireless service is available via entire campus.

STUDENT LIFE

Housing options: college housing not available.

Activities and organizations: Criminal Justice Club, Human Services Technology Club, Radiologic Technology Club, Student Government Association, Students for Professional Nursing.

Athletics ***Intramural sports:*** basketball M/W, skiing (downhill) M/W, table tennis M/W, tennis M/W, volleyball M/W.

Campus security: 24-hour emergency response devices, late-night transport/escort service.

Student services: personal/psychological counseling.

COSTS & FINANCIAL AID

Costs (2014–15) ***One-time required fee:*** $150. ***Tuition:*** state resident $5664 full-time, $258 per credit hour part-time; nonresident $13,624 full-time, $620 per credit hour part-time. Full-time tuition and fees vary according to course level and course load. Part-time tuition and fees vary according to course level and course load. ***Payment plan:*** installment. ***Waivers:*** senior citizens and employees or children of employees.

Financial Aid Of all full-time matriculated undergraduates who enrolled in 2014, 732 applied for aid, 673 were judged to have need, 31 had their need fully met. In 2014, 19 non-need-based awards were made. ***Average percent of need met:*** 40. ***Average financial aid package:*** $6673. ***Average need-based loan:*** $3857. ***Average need-based gift aid:*** $4620. ***Average non-need-based aid:*** $764.

APPLYING

Standardized Tests *Required for some:* SAT or ACT (for admission). *Recommended:* SAT or ACT (for admission).

Options: electronic application, deferred entrance.

Application fee: $40.

Required: high school transcript. ***Required for some:*** essay or personal statement.

Application deadlines: rolling (freshmen), rolling (out-of-state freshmen), rolling (transfers).

Notification: continuous (freshmen), continuous (out-of-state freshmen), continuous (transfers).

CONTACT

Kent State University at Salem, 2491 State Route 45 South, Salem, OH 44460-9412. *Phone:* 330-382-7415.

Kent State University at Stark

Canton, Ohio

http://www.stark.kent.edu/

- **State-supported** comprehensive, founded 1967, part of Kent State University System
- **Suburban** 200-acre campus with easy access to Cleveland-Akron-Canton
- **Coed** 4,639 undergraduate students, 66% full-time, 60% women, 40% men
- **Noncompetitive** entrance level, 94% of applicants were admitted

UNDERGRAD STUDENTS

3,058 full-time, 1,581 part-time. Students come from 7 states and territories; 24 other countries; 1% are from out of state; 8% Black or African American, non-Hispanic/Latino; 2% Hispanic/Latino; 0.8% Asian, non-Hispanic/Latino; 0.1% Native Hawaiian or other Pacific Islander, non-Hispanic/Latino; 0.4% American Indian or Alaska Native, non-Hispanic/Latino; 3% Two or more races, non-Hispanic/Latino; 3% Race/ethnicity unknown; 0.3% international; 9% transferred in.

Freshmen

Admission: 1,068 applied, 1,000 admitted, 631 enrolled. ***Average high school GPA:*** 2.9. ***Test scores:*** SAT critical reading scores over 500: 86%; SAT math scores over 500: 93%; SAT writing scores over 500: 94%; ACT scores over 18: 78%; SAT critical reading scores over 600: 61%; SAT math scores over 600: 50%; SAT writing scores over 600: 40%; ACT scores over 24: 18%; SAT critical reading scores over 700: 18%; SAT math scores over 700: 7%; SAT writing scores over 700: 11%; ACT scores over 30: 1%.

Retention: 65% of full-time freshmen returned.

FACULTY

Total: 262, 42% full-time.

Student/faculty ratio: 23:1.

ACADEMICS

Calendar: semesters. *Degrees:* associate, bachelor's, and master's.

Special study options: academic remediation for entering students, adult/continuing education programs, advanced placement credit, distance learning, double majors, honors programs, independent study, internships, off-campus study, part-time degree program, services for LD students, student-designed majors, study abroad, summer session for credit. ***ROTC:*** Army (c), Air Force (c).

Computers: 575 computers/terminals are available on campus for general student use. Students can access the following: computer help desk, free student e-mail accounts, online (class) grades, online (class) registration, online (class) schedules. Campuswide network is available. Wireless service is available via entire campus.

STUDENT LIFE

Housing options: college housing not available.

Activities and organizations: drama/theater group, SCRUBS (nursing organization), Rooted in Faith-Bible Club (non-denominational), Kent State Stark Education Association (KSSEA), Music Technology Club, Ohio Collegiate Music Education Association (OCMEA).

Campus security: 24-hour emergency response devices, late-night transport/escort service.

Student services: personal/psychological counseling.

COSTS & FINANCIAL AID

Costs (2014–15) ***One-time required fee:*** $150. ***Tuition:*** state resident $5664 full-time, $258 per credit hour part-time; nonresident $13,624 full-time, $620 per credit hour part-time. Full-time tuition and fees vary according to course level and course load. Part-time tuition and fees vary according to course level and course load. ***Payment plan:*** installment. ***Waivers:*** senior citizens and employees or children of employees.

Financial Aid Of all full-time matriculated undergraduates who enrolled in 2014, 2,002 applied for aid, 1,799 were judged to have need, 85 had their need fully met. In 2014, 99 non-need-based awards were made. ***Average percent of need met:*** 43. ***Average financial aid package:*** $6718. ***Average need-based loan:*** $3958. ***Average need-based gift aid:*** $4193. ***Average non-need-based aid:*** $1994.

APPLYING

Standardized Tests *Required for some:* SAT or ACT (for admission). *Recommended:* SAT or ACT (for admission).

Options: electronic application, deferred entrance.

Application fee: $40.

Required: high school transcript.

Application deadlines: rolling (freshmen), rolling (out-of-state freshmen), rolling (transfers).

Notification: continuous (freshmen), continuous (out-of-state freshmen), continuous (transfers).

CONTACT

Office of Admissions, Kent State University at Stark, 6000 Frank Avenue NW, North Canton, OH 44720. *Phone:* 330-244-3251. *Fax:* 330-499-0301. *E-mail:* starkadmissions@kent.edu.

Kent State University at Trumbull

Warren, Ohio

http://www.trumbull.kent.edu/

- **State-supported** primarily 2-year, founded 1954, part of Kent State University System
- **Suburban** 200-acre campus with easy access to Cleveland-Akron-Canton
- **Coed** 2,796 undergraduate students, 65% full-time, 65% women, 35% men
- **Noncompetitive** entrance level, 99% of applicants were admitted

UNDERGRAD STUDENTS

1,811 full-time, 985 part-time. Students come from 9 states and territories; 8 other countries; 2% are from out of state; 9% Black or African American, non-Hispanic/Latino; 2% Hispanic/Latino; 0.5% Asian, non-Hispanic/Latino; 2% Two or more races, non-Hispanic/Latino; 3% Race/ethnicity unknown; 0.6% international; 6% transferred in.

Freshmen
Admission: 433 applied, 428 admitted, 326 enrolled. ***Average high school GPA:*** 2.81. ***Test scores:*** SAT critical reading scores over 500: 33%; SAT math scores over 500: 33%; ACT scores over 18: 73%; ACT scores over 24: 16%.

Retention: 57% of full-time freshmen returned.

FACULTY
Total: 110, 53% full-time.
Student/faculty ratio: 28:1.

ACADEMICS
Calendar: semesters. *Degrees:* associate and bachelor's (also offers some upper-level and graduate courses).

Special study options: academic remediation for entering students, adult/continuing education programs, advanced placement credit, distance learning, double majors, freshman honors college, honors programs, independent study, internships, part-time degree program, services for LD students, student-designed majors, summer session for credit. ***ROTC:*** Army (c), Air Force (c).

Computers: 300 computers/terminals are available on campus for general student use. Students can access the following: computer help desk, free student e-mail accounts, online (class) grades, online (class) registration, online (class) schedules. Campuswide network is available. Wireless service is available via entire campus.

STUDENT LIFE
Housing options: college housing not available.

Activities and organizations: Student Nurses Association, REACH, ENACTUS, Jurisprudence, If These Hands Could Talk - ASL.

Campus security: 24-hour emergency response devices, late-night transport/escort service, patrols by trained security personnel during open hours.

Student services: personal/psychological counseling.

COSTS & FINANCIAL AID
Costs (2014–15) ***One-time required fee:*** $150. ***Tuition:*** state resident $5664 full-time, $258 per credit hour part-time; nonresident $13,624 full-time, $620 per credit hour part-time. Full-time tuition and fees vary according to course level and course load. Part-time tuition and fees vary according to course level and course load. ***Payment plan:*** installment. ***Waivers:*** senior citizens and employees or children of employees.

Financial Aid Of all full-time matriculated undergraduates who enrolled in 2014, 957 applied for aid, 890 were judged to have need, 21 had their need fully met. In 2014, 18 non-need-based awards were made. ***Average percent of need met:*** 41. ***Average financial aid package:*** $7133. ***Average need-based loan:*** $3907. ***Average need-based gift aid:*** $4749. ***Average non-need-based aid:*** $1305.

APPLYING
Standardized Tests *Required for some:* SAT or ACT (for admission). *Recommended:* SAT or ACT (for admission).

Options: electronic application, deferred entrance.

Application fee: $40.

Required: high school transcript.

Application deadlines: rolling (freshmen), rolling (out-of-state freshmen), rolling (transfers).

Notification: continuous (freshmen), continuous (out-of-state freshmen), continuous (transfers).

CONTACT
Kent State University at Trumbull, Warren, OH 44483. *Phone:* 330-675-8935.

Kent State University at Tuscarawas
New Philadelphia, Ohio
http://www.tusc.kent.edu/

- **State-supported** primarily 2-year, founded 1962, part of Kent State University System
- **Small-town** 172-acre campus with easy access to Cleveland-Akron-Canton
- **Coed** 2,266 undergraduate students, 59% full-time, 57% women, 43% men
- **Noncompetitive** entrance level, 94% of applicants were admitted

UNDERGRAD STUDENTS
1,347 full-time, 919 part-time. Students come from 4 states and territories; 3 other countries; 1% are from out of state; 3% Black or African American, non-Hispanic/Latino; 1% Hispanic/Latino; 0.6% Asian, non-Hispanic/Latino; 2% Two or more races, non-Hispanic/Latino; 3% Race/ethnicity unknown; 0.5% international; 4% transferred in.

Freshmen
Admission: 354 applied, 331 admitted, 276 enrolled. ***Average high school GPA:*** 2.97. ***Test scores:*** SAT critical reading scores over 500: 33%; SAT math scores over 500: 33%; SAT writing scores over 500: 33%; ACT scores over 18: 80%; ACT scores over 24: 18%.

Retention: 59% of full-time freshmen returned.

FACULTY
Total: 124, 44% full-time.
Student/faculty ratio: 21:1.

ACADEMICS
Calendar: semesters. *Degrees:* certificates, associate, and bachelor's (also offers some upper-level and graduate courses).

Special study options: academic remediation for entering students, accelerated degree program, adult/continuing education programs, advanced placement credit, distance learning, double majors, freshman honors college, honors programs, independent study, internships, part-time degree program, services for LD students, student-designed majors, study abroad, summer session for credit. ***ROTC:*** Army (c), Air Force (c).

Computers: 194 computers/terminals are available on campus for general student use. Students can access the following: computer help desk, free student e-mail accounts, online (class) grades, online (class) registration, online (class) schedules. Campuswide network is available. Wireless service is available via entire campus.

STUDENT LIFE
Housing options: college housing not available.

Activities and organizations: Society of Manufacturing Engineers, IEEE, Animation Imagineers, Criminology & Justice Studies Club, Student Activities Council.

Athletics ***Intramural sports:*** basketball M/W, volleyball M/W.

Campus security: 24-hour emergency response devices.

COSTS & FINANCIAL AID
Costs (2014–15) ***One-time required fee:*** $150. ***Tuition:*** state resident $5664 full-time, $258 per credit hour part-time; nonresident $13,624 full-time, $620 per credit hour part-time. Full-time tuition and fees vary according to course level and course load. Part-time tuition and fees vary according to course level and course load. ***Payment plan:*** installment. ***Waivers:*** senior citizens and employees or children of employees.

Financial Aid Of all full-time matriculated undergraduates who enrolled in 2014, 797 applied for aid, 736 were judged to have need, 31 had their need fully met. In 2014, 31 non-need-based awards were made. ***Average percent of need met:*** 43. ***Average financial aid package:*** $6761. ***Average need-based loan:*** $3940. ***Average need-based gift aid:*** $4339. ***Average non-need-based aid:*** $1344.

APPLYING
Standardized Tests *Required for some:* SAT or ACT (for admission). *Recommended:* SAT or ACT (for admission).

Options: electronic application, deferred entrance.

Application fee: $40.

Required: high school transcript.

Application deadlines: rolling (freshmen), rolling (out-of-state freshmen), rolling (transfers).

Notification: continuous (freshmen), continuous (out-of-state freshmen), continuous (transfers).

CONTACT
Kent State University at Tuscarawas, Kent State University at Tuscarawas, 330 University Drive Northeast, New Philadelphia, OH 44663-9403. *Phone:* 330-339-3391 Ext. 47425. *Fax:* 330-339-3321. *E-mail:* info@tusc.kent.edu.

Kenyon College
Gambier, Ohio
http://www.kenyon.edu/

- **Independent** 4-year, founded 1824
- **Rural** 1000-acre campus with easy access to Columbus
- **Endowment** $212.2 million
- **Coed** 1,662 undergraduate students, 99% full-time, 55% women, 45% men
- **Very difficult** entrance level, 25% of applicants were admitted

UNDERGRAD STUDENTS
1,650 full-time, 12 part-time. Students come from 50 states and territories; 41 other countries; 78% are from out of state; 4% Black or African American, non-Hispanic/Latino; 6% Hispanic/Latino; 5% Asian, non-Hispanic/Latino; 0.5% American Indian or Alaska Native, non-Hispanic/Latino; 4% Two or more races, non-Hispanic/Latino; 3% Race/ethnicity unknown; 4% international; 0.7% transferred in; 100% live on campus.

Freshmen
Admission: 6,635 applied, 1,663 admitted, 448 enrolled. ***Average high school GPA:*** 3.9. ***Test scores:*** SAT critical reading scores over 500: 100%; SAT math scores over 500: 99%; SAT writing scores over 500: 99%; ACT scores over 18: 100%; SAT critical reading scores over 600: 86%; SAT math scores over 600: 83%; SAT writing scores over 600: 84%; ACT scores over 24: 97%; SAT critical reading scores over 700: 35%; SAT math scores over 700: 24%; SAT writing scores over 700: 32%; ACT scores over 30: 60%.

Retention: 98% of full-time freshmen returned.

FACULTY
Total: 203, 78% full-time, 95% with terminal degrees.

Student/faculty ratio: 10:1.

ACADEMICS
Calendar: semesters. *Degree:* bachelor's.

Special study options: accelerated degree program, advanced placement credit, double majors, honors programs, independent study, internships, off-campus study, services for LD students, student-designed majors, study abroad.

Unusual degree programs: 3-2 engineering with Washington University in St. Louis, Case Western Reserve University, Rensselaer Polytechnic Institute; environmental science with Duke University, education with The Bank Street College of Education.

Computers: 420 computers/terminals are available on campus for general student use. Students can access the following: campus intranet, computer help desk, free student e-mail accounts, online (class) grades, online (class) registration, online (class) schedules, commercial databases. Campuswide network is available. 99% of college-owned or -operated housing units are wired for high-speed Internet access. Wireless service is available via entire campus.

STUDENT LIFE
Housing options: on-campus residence required through senior year; coed, women-only, special housing for students with disabilities. Campus housing is university owned. Freshman campus housing is guaranteed.

Activities and organizations: drama/theater group, student-run newspaper, radio station, choral group, student advisory groups, student radio station, musical groups, intramural sports and clubs, national fraternities, national sororities.

Athletics Member NCAA. All Division III. ***Intercollegiate sports:*** baseball M, basketball M/W, cross-country running M/W, equestrian sports M(c)/W(c), field hockey W, football M, golf M, lacrosse M/W, rugby M(c)/W(c), soccer M/W, softball W, squash M(c)/W(c), swimming and diving M/W, tennis M/W, track and field M/W, ultimate Frisbee M(c)/W(c), volleyball W. ***Intramural sports:*** archery M(c)/W(c), basketball M/W, fencing M(c)/W(c), racquetball M/W, soccer M(c)/W(c), tennis M(c)/W(c), volleyball M/W.

Campus security: 24-hour emergency response devices and patrols, student patrols, late-night transport/escort service, controlled dormitory access.

Student services: health clinic, personal/psychological counseling, women's center.

COSTS & FINANCIAL AID
Costs (2015–16) ***Comprehensive fee:*** $61,030 includes full-time tuition ($47,220), mandatory fees ($1920), and room and board ($11,890). Full-time tuition and fees vary according to reciprocity agreements. Part-time tuition and fees vary according to reciprocity agreements. ***College room only:*** $5170. Room and board charges vary according to housing facility and student level. ***Payment plan:*** installment. ***Waivers:*** employees or children of employees.

Financial Aid Of all full-time matriculated undergraduates who enrolled in 2014, 853 applied for aid, 729 were judged to have need, 443 had their need fully met. 277 Federal Work-Study jobs (averaging $1691). 139 state and other part-time jobs (averaging $1710). In 2014, 205 non-need-based awards were made. ***Average percent of need met:*** 95. ***Average financial aid package:*** $40,946. ***Average need-based loan:*** $3900. ***Average need-based gift aid:*** $38,039. ***Average non-need-based aid:*** $13,311. ***Average indebtedness upon graduation:*** $20,323.

APPLYING
Standardized Tests *Required:* SAT or ACT (for admission).

Options: electronic application, early admission, early decision, deferred entrance.

Required: essay or personal statement, high school transcript, counselor recommendation. ***Recommended:*** 2 letters of recommendation, interview.

Application deadlines: 1/15 (freshmen), 4/1 (transfers).

Early decision deadline: 11/15 (for plan 1), 1/15 (for plan 2).

Notification: 4/1 (freshmen), 5/15 (transfers), 12/15 (early decision plan 1), 2/1 (early decision plan 2).

CONTACT
Mr. Darryl Uy, Interim Dean of Admissions and Financial Aid, Kenyon College, Ransom Hall, Gambier, OH 43022. *Phone:* 740-427-5780. *Toll-free phone:* 800-848-2468. *Fax:* 740-427-5780. *E-mail:* admissions@kenyon.edu.

Lake Erie College
Painesville, Ohio
http://www.lec.edu/

- **Independent** comprehensive, founded 1856
- **Suburban** 46-acre campus with easy access to Cleveland
- **Endowment** $33.4 million
- **Coed** 903 undergraduate students, 89% full-time, 50% women, 50% men
- **Moderately difficult** entrance level, 69% of applicants were admitted

UNDERGRAD STUDENTS
802 full-time, 101 part-time. Students come from 27 states and territories; 13 other countries; 26% are from out of state; 15% Black or African American, non-Hispanic/Latino; 2% Hispanic/Latino; 0.3% Asian, non-Hispanic/Latino; 0.5% American Indian or Alaska Native, non-Hispanic/Latino; 3% Two or more races, non-Hispanic/Latino; 3% Race/ethnicity unknown; 3% international; 5% transferred in; 63% live on campus.

Freshmen
Admission: 891 applied, 618 admitted, 186 enrolled. ***Average high school GPA:*** 3.02. ***Test scores:*** SAT critical reading scores over 500: 37%; SAT math scores over 500: 53%; SAT writing scores over 500: 29%; ACT scores over 18: 83%; SAT critical reading scores over 600: 10%; SAT math scores over 600: 12%; SAT writing scores over 600: 10%; ACT scores over 24: 21%; SAT math scores over 700: 4%; ACT scores over 30: 2%.

Retention: 68% of full-time freshmen returned.

FACULTY
Total: 113, 39% full-time, 31% with terminal degrees.

Student/faculty ratio: 14:1.

ACADEMICS
Calendar: semesters. *Degrees:* bachelor's, master's, and postbachelor's certificates.

Special study options: accelerated degree program, advanced placement credit, double majors, honors programs, independent study, internships, off-campus study, part-time degree program, services for LD students, student-designed majors, study abroad, summer session for credit.

Computers: 78 computers/terminals are available on campus for general student use. Students can access the following: campus intranet, computer help desk, free student e-mail accounts, online (class) grades, online (class) registration, online (class) schedules. Campuswide network is available. 100% of college-owned or -operated housing units are wired for high-speed Internet access. Wireless service is available via entire campus.

STUDENT LIFE
Housing options: on-campus residence required through sophomore year; coed, men-only, women-only. Campus housing is university owned and leased by the school. Freshman applicants given priority for college housing.

Activities and organizations: drama/theater group, choral group, marching band, Student Athlete Advisory Committee, Intercollegiate Horse Show Association, Gamma Phi Beta Sorority, Spanish Club, Student Government Association, national fraternities, national sororities.

Athletics Member NCAA. All Division II. ***Intercollegiate sports:*** baseball M(s), basketball M(s)/W(s), cross-country running M(s)/W(s), football M(s), golf M(s)/W(s), lacrosse M(s)/W(s), soccer M(s)/W(s), softball W(s), swimming and diving M(s)/W(s), track and field M(s)/W(s), volleyball W(s), wrestling M(s). ***Intramural sports:*** basketball M/W, cheerleading W(c), equestrian sports M(c)/W(c), football M/W, soccer M/W, softball M/W, ultimate Frisbee M/W, volleyball M/W.

Campus security: 24-hour emergency response devices and patrols, late-night transport/escort service.

COSTS & FINANCIAL AID
Costs (2015–16) ***One-time required fee:*** $350. ***Comprehensive fee:*** $38,340 includes full-time tuition ($27,770), mandatory fees ($1392), and room and board ($9178). Full-time tuition and fees vary according to course load, degree level, and program. Part-time tuition: $736 per credit hour. Part-time tuition and fees vary according to course load, degree level, and program. ***Required fees:*** $51 per credit hour part-time. ***College room only:*** $4464. Room and board charges vary according to board plan. ***Payment plan:*** installment. ***Waivers:*** senior citizens and employees or children of employees.

Financial Aid Of all full-time matriculated undergraduates who enrolled in 2014, 650 applied for aid, 616 were judged to have need, 107 had their need fully met. In 2014, 98 non-need-based awards were made. ***Average percent of need met:*** 72. ***Average financial aid package:*** $22,717. ***Average need-based loan:*** $4352. ***Average need-based gift aid:*** $18,788. ***Average non-need-based aid:*** $12,738. ***Average indebtedness upon graduation:*** $34,114.

APPLYING
Standardized Tests *Required:* SAT or ACT (for admission). *Recommended:* AP, CLEP, Institutional Exam.

Options: electronic application, deferred entrance.

Application fee: $30.

Required: essay or personal statement, high school transcript, minimum 2.5 GPA, SAT or ACT Tests. ***Required for some:*** high school transcript. ***Recommended:*** interview.

Application deadlines: 8/1 (freshmen), 8/1 (out-of-state freshmen), rolling (transfers).

Notification: continuous (freshmen), continuous (out-of-state freshmen), continuous (transfers).

CONTACT
Mr. Will Brown, Associate Director of Recruitment, Lake Erie College, 391 West Washington Street, Painesville, OH 44077-3389. *Phone:* 800-916-0904. *Toll-free phone:* 800-916-0904. *Fax:* 440-375-7058. *E-mail:* admissions@lec.edu.

Lourdes University

Sylvania, Ohio

http://www.lourdes.edu/

- **Independent Roman Catholic** comprehensive, founded 1958
- **Suburban** 113-acre campus with easy access to Toledo
- **Endowment** $10.8 million
- **Coed** 1,482 undergraduate students, 69% full-time, 70% women, 30% men
- **Moderately difficult** entrance level, 65% of applicants were admitted

UNDERGRAD STUDENTS
1,016 full-time, 466 part-time. Students come from 25 states and territories; 4 other countries; 17% are from out of state; 14% Black or African American, non-Hispanic/Latino; 7% Hispanic/Latino; 0.7% Asian, non-Hispanic/Latino; 0.2% Native Hawaiian or other Pacific Islander, non-Hispanic/Latino; 0.6% American Indian or Alaska Native, non-Hispanic/Latino; 3% Two or more races, non-Hispanic/Latino; 3% Race/ethnicity unknown; 0.3% international; 8% transferred in; 29% live on campus.

Freshmen
Admission: 1,024 applied, 661 admitted, 162 enrolled. ***Average high school GPA:*** 3.13. ***Test scores:*** ACT scores over 18: 75%; ACT scores over 24: 15%; ACT scores over 30: 2%.

Retention: 59% of full-time freshmen returned.

FACULTY
Total: 228, 34% full-time.

Student/faculty ratio: 10:1.

ACADEMICS
Calendar: semesters. *Degrees:* certificates, associate, bachelor's, master's, and postbachelor's certificates.

Special study options: academic remediation for entering students, adult/continuing education programs, advanced placement credit, distance learning, double majors, independent study, internships, part-time degree program, services for LD students, student-designed majors, study abroad, summer session for credit. ***ROTC:*** Army (c), Air Force (c).

Computers: 264 computers/terminals are available on campus for general student use. Students can access the following: computer help desk, free student e-mail accounts, online (class) grades, online (class) registration, online (class) schedules, Sakai/eLearning, LiveText ePortfolio system, RRS news feeds, Facebook, Twitter, online polls, webcasting, panopto, ploycom. Campuswide network is available. 100% of college-owned or -operated housing units are wired for high-speed Internet access. Wireless service is available via entire campus.

STUDENT LIFE
Housing options: on-campus residence required through senior year; coed. Campus housing is university owned. Freshman applicants given priority for college housing.

Activities and organizations: drama/theater group, choral group, Student Government Association, Student Nurses Association, Orbis Ars, Future Doctors of America, Active Minds.

Athletics Member NAIA. ***Intercollegiate sports:*** baseball M(s), basketball M(s)/W(s), cheerleading M(s)/W(s), cross-country running M(s)/W(s), golf M(s)/W(s), lacrosse M(s)/W(s), softball W(s), volleyball M(s)/W(s). ***Intramural sports:*** basketball M/W, bowling M/W, football M/W, golf M/W, ice hockey M/W, soccer M/W, tennis M/W, volleyball M/W.

Campus security: 24-hour emergency response devices and patrols, late-night transport/escort service, controlled dormitory access.

Student services: health clinic, personal/psychological counseling.

COSTS & FINANCIAL AID
Costs (2015–16) ***Comprehensive fee:*** $28,320 includes full-time tuition ($18,970), mandatory fees ($250), and room and board ($9100). Full-time tuition and fees vary according to course load and location. Part-time tuition: $633 per credit. Part-time tuition and fees vary according to course load and location. ***Required fees:*** $100 per term part-time. ***College room only:*** $4900. Room and board charges vary according to board plan and housing facility. ***Payment plans:*** installment, deferred payment. ***Waivers:*** senior citizens and employees or children of employees.

Financial Aid Of all full-time matriculated undergraduates who enrolled in 2013, 1,091 applied for aid, 938 were judged to have need. 68 Federal Work-Study jobs (averaging $1872). 128 state and other part-time jobs (averaging $1500). ***Average financial aid package:*** $13,172. ***Average need-based loan:*** $3988. ***Average need-based gift aid:*** $6089.

APPLYING

Standardized Tests *Required:* SAT or ACT (for admission).

Options: electronic application, early admission, deferred entrance.

Application fee: $25.

Required: high school transcript. ***Required for some:*** ACT/SAT test scores are required for all direct-from-high-school students and transfer students entering Lourdes University with fewer than 18 hours of college credit and who are 24 years of age or younger.

Application deadlines: rolling (freshmen), rolling (out-of-state freshmen), rolling (transfers).

Notification: continuous (freshmen), continuous (out-of-state freshmen), continuous (transfers).

CONTACT

Amy Houston, Associate Director of Admissions, Lourdes University, 6832 Convent Boulevard, Sylvania, OH 43560. *Phone:* 419-885-5291. *Toll-free phone:* 800-878-3210.

Malone University

Canton, Ohio

http://www.malone.edu/

- **Independent** comprehensive, founded 1892, affiliated with Evangelical Friends Church–Eastern Region
- **Suburban** 96-acre campus with easy access to Cleveland
- **Endowment** $18.4 million
- **Coed** 1,565 undergraduate students, 85% full-time, 59% women, 41% men
- **Moderately difficult** entrance level, 72% of applicants were admitted

UNDERGRAD STUDENTS

1,332 full-time, 233 part-time. Students come from 33 states and territories; 13 other countries; 14% are from out of state; 8% Black or African American, non-Hispanic/Latino; 2% Hispanic/Latino; 0.7% Asian, non-Hispanic/Latino; 0.2% Native Hawaiian or other Pacific Islander, non-Hispanic/Latino; 0.1% American Indian or Alaska Native, non-Hispanic/Latino; 2% Two or more races, non-Hispanic/Latino; 0.1% Race/ethnicity unknown; 1% international; 4% transferred in; 56% live on campus.

Freshmen

Admission: 1,327 applied, 952 admitted, 314 enrolled. ***Average high school GPA:*** 3.31. ***Test scores:*** SAT critical reading scores over 500: 57%; SAT math scores over 500: 48%; ACT scores over 18: 96%; SAT critical reading scores over 600: 11%; SAT math scores over 600: 19%; ACT scores over 24: 42%; ACT scores over 30: 4%.

Retention: 70% of full-time freshmen returned.

FACULTY

Total: 197, 48% full-time, 47% with terminal degrees.

Student/faculty ratio: 12:1.

ACADEMICS

Calendar: semesters. *Degrees:* bachelor's, master's, and post-master's certificates.

Special study options: academic remediation for entering students, accelerated degree program, adult/continuing education programs, advanced placement credit, distance learning, double majors, honors programs, independent study, internships, off-campus study, part-time degree program, services for LD students, student-designed majors, study abroad, summer session for credit. ***ROTC:*** Army (c), Air Force (c).

Computers: 297 computers/terminals and 3,900 ports are available on campus for general student use. Students can access the following: campus intranet, computer help desk, free student e-mail accounts, online (class) grades, online (class) registration, online (class) schedules, online advising, online financial aid information, and online credit card payments. Campuswide network is available. 100% of college-owned or -operated housing units are wired for high-speed Internet access. Wireless service is available via entire campus.

STUDENT LIFE

Housing options: on-campus residence required through junior year; men-only, women-only, special housing for students with disabilities. Campus housing is university owned. Freshman applicants given priority for college housing.

Activities and organizations: drama/theater group, choral group, marching band, Celebration Worship Services (and other Spiritual Formation activities), Student Activities Council, Student Senate, MUHOP (Malone University House of Prayer), intramural athletics.

Athletics Member NCAA. All Division II. ***Intercollegiate sports:*** baseball M(s), basketball M(s)/W(s), cheerleading M/W, cross-country running M(s)/W(s), football M(s), golf M(s)/W(s), soccer M(s)/W(s), softball W(s), swimming and diving M(s)/W(s), track and field M(s)/W(s), volleyball W(s). ***Intramural sports:*** basketball M/W, football M/W, lacrosse M(c)/W(c), soccer M/W, ultimate Frisbee M(c)/W(c), volleyball M(c)/W.

Campus security: 24-hour emergency response devices and patrols, late-night transport/escort service, controlled dormitory access.

Student services: health clinic, personal/psychological counseling.

COSTS & FINANCIAL AID

Costs (2015–16) ***Comprehensive fee:*** $36,706 includes full-time tuition ($26,456), mandatory fees ($984), and room and board ($9266). Part-time tuition: $470 per credit. Part-time tuition and fees vary according to course load. ***Required fees:*** $246 per term part-time. ***College room only:*** $4640. Room and board charges vary according to board plan. ***Payment plan:*** installment. ***Waivers:*** senior citizens and employees or children of employees.

Financial Aid Of all full-time matriculated undergraduates who enrolled in 2014, 1,143 applied for aid, 1,066 were judged to have need, 202 had their need fully met. 314 Federal Work-Study jobs (averaging $1950). In 2014, 164 non-need-based awards were made. ***Average percent of need met:*** 77. ***Average financial aid package:*** $21,583. ***Average need-based loan:*** $4837. ***Average need-based gift aid:*** $17,427. ***Average non-need-based aid:*** $10,051. ***Average indebtedness upon graduation:*** $30,679. ***Financial aid deadline:*** 7/31.

APPLYING

Standardized Tests *Required:* SAT or ACT (for admission).

Options: electronic application, early admission, deferred entrance.

Application fee: $20.

Required: essay or personal statement, high school transcript, minimum 2.0 GPA. ***Recommended:*** interview.

Application deadlines: rolling (freshmen), rolling (out-of-state freshmen), rolling (transfers).

Notification: continuous (freshmen), continuous (out-of-state freshmen), continuous (transfers).

CONTACT

Mrs. Anissa D. Scott, Admissions Office Manager, Malone University, 2600 Cleveland Avenue NW, Canton, OH 44709-3897. *Phone:* 330-471-8153. *Toll-free phone:* 800-521-1146. *Fax:* 330-471-8149. *E-mail:* admissions@malone.edu.

Marietta College

Marietta, Ohio

http://www.marietta.edu/

- **Independent** comprehensive, founded 1835
- **Small-town** 90-acre campus
- **Endowment** $78.7 million
- **Coed** 1,371 undergraduate students, 94% full-time, 40% women, 60% men
- **Moderately difficult** entrance level, 69% of applicants were admitted

UNDERGRAD STUDENTS

1,283 full-time, 88 part-time. Students come from 36 states and territories; 4 other countries; 39% are from out of state; 5% Black or African American, non-Hispanic/Latino; 3% Hispanic/Latino; 1% Asian, non-Hispanic/Latino; 0.1% American Indian or Alaska Native, non-Hispanic/Latino; 2% Two or more races, non-Hispanic/Latino; 4% Race/ethnicity unknown; 12% international; 3% transferred in; 76% live on campus.

Freshmen
Admission: 3,464 applied, 2,406 admitted, 357 enrolled. ***Average high school GPA:*** 3.49. ***Test scores:*** SAT critical reading scores over 500: 66%; SAT math scores over 500: 81%; ACT scores over 18: 97%; SAT critical reading scores over 600: 26%; SAT math scores over 600: 40%; ACT scores over 24: 57%; SAT critical reading scores over 700: 1%; SAT math scores over 700: 6%; ACT scores over 30: 6%.
Retention: 74% of full-time freshmen returned.

FACULTY
Total: 180, 63% full-time, 59% with terminal degrees.
Student/faculty ratio: 10:1.

ACADEMICS
Calendar: semesters. *Degrees:* certificates, associate, bachelor's, and master's.
Special study options: academic remediation for entering students, accelerated degree program, adult/continuing education programs, advanced placement credit, double majors, English as a second language, honors programs, independent study, internships, off-campus study, part-time degree program, services for LD students, student-designed majors, study abroad, summer session for credit.
Unusual degree programs: 3-2 engineering with Columbia University, Case Western Reserve University, Ohio University.
Computers: 400 computers/terminals and 450 ports are available on campus for general student use. Students can access the following: campus intranet, computer help desk, free student e-mail accounts, online (class) grades, online (class) registration, online (class) schedules. Campuswide network is available. 100% of college-owned or -operated housing units are wired for high-speed Internet access. Wireless service is available via classrooms, computer centers, computer labs, dorm rooms, learning centers, libraries, student centers.

STUDENT LIFE
Housing options: on-campus residence required through senior year; coed, men-only, women-only, special housing for students with disabilities. Campus housing is university owned, leased by the school and is provided by a third party. Freshman campus housing is guaranteed.
Activities and organizations: drama/theater group, student-run newspaper, radio and television station, choral group, Student Programming Board, student government, Society of Petroleum Engineers, Inter-Varsity Christian Fellowship, Arts and Humanities Council, national fraternities, national sororities.
Athletics Member NCAA. All Division III. ***Intercollegiate sports:*** baseball M, basketball M/W, cheerleading M(c)/W(c), crew M/W, cross-country running M/W, football M, soccer M/W, softball W, tennis M/W, track and field M/W, volleyball W, wrestling M(c)/W(c). ***Intramural sports:*** badminton M/W, basketball M/W, bowling M/W, cross-country running M/W, football M/W, golf M/W, racquetball M/W, rock climbing M/W, soccer M/W, softball M/W, swimming and diving M/W, tennis M/W, ultimate Frisbee M/W, volleyball M/W, weight lifting M.
Campus security: 24-hour emergency response devices and patrols, student patrols, late-night transport/escort service, controlled dormitory access.
Student services: health clinic, personal/psychological counseling.

COSTS & FINANCIAL AID
Costs (2014–15) ***Comprehensive fee:*** $43,535 includes full-time tuition ($32,215), mandatory fees ($925), and room and board ($10,395). Part-time tuition: $1050 per credit. ***College room only:*** $5995. ***Payment plan:*** installment. ***Waivers:*** employees or children of employees.
Financial Aid Of all full-time matriculated undergraduates who enrolled in 2012, 1,279 applied for aid, 969 were judged to have need, 308 had their need fully met. 678 Federal Work-Study jobs (averaging $1957). In 2012, 266 non-need-based awards were made. ***Average percent of need met:*** 87. ***Average financial aid package:*** $24,569. ***Average need-based loan:*** $4673. ***Average need-based gift aid:*** $16,772. ***Average non-need-based aid:*** $10,302. ***Average indebtedness upon graduation:*** $36,241.

APPLYING
Standardized Tests *Required:* SAT or ACT (for admission). *Recommended:* SAT Subject Tests (for admission).
Options: electronic application, early admission, deferred entrance.
Application fee: $25.
Required: essay or personal statement, high school transcript, minimum 2.5 GPA, 1 letter of recommendation. ***Recommended:*** minimum 3.4 GPA, interview.
Application deadlines: 7/1 (freshmen), rolling (transfers).
Notification: continuous until 7/1 (freshmen), continuous (transfers).

CONTACT
Mr. Scott McVicar, Director of Admission, Marietta College, 215 Fifth Street, Marietta, OH 45750. *Phone:* 740-376-4606. *Toll-free phone:* 800-331-7896. *Fax:* 740-376-8888. *E-mail:* admit@marietta.edu.

Mercy College of Ohio
Toledo, Ohio
http://www.mercycollege.edu/

- **Independent** 4-year, founded 1993, affiliated with Roman Catholic Church
- **Urban** campus with easy access to Detroit
- **Endowment** $10.0 million
- **Coed, primarily women**
- **Moderately difficult** entrance level

FACULTY
Student/faculty ratio: 11:1.

ACADEMICS
Calendar: semesters. *Degrees:* certificates, associate, and bachelor's.

STUDENT LIFE
Housing options: coed. Campus housing is leased by the school.
Activities and organizations: Student Senate, intramural sports, Student Nurses Association, Phi Theta Kappa.
Campus security: 24-hour patrols, late-night transport/escort service, controlled dormitory access.
Student services: personal/psychological counseling.

FINANCIAL AID
Financial Aid Of all full-time matriculated undergraduates who enrolled in 2013, 414 applied for aid, 387 were judged to have need, 11 had their need fully met. 28 Federal Work-Study jobs (averaging $1517). In 2013, 4 non-need-based awards were made. ***Average percent of need met:*** 28. ***Average financial aid package:*** $6910. ***Average need-based loan:*** $3776. ***Average need-based gift aid:*** $3133. ***Average non-need-based aid:*** $3037. ***Average indebtedness upon graduation:*** $28,842.

APPLYING
Standardized Tests *Required for some:* SAT or ACT (for admission), SAT and SAT Subject Tests or ACT (for admission).
Options: electronic application, deferred entrance.
Application fee: $25.
Required: high school transcript, minimum 2.3 GPA.

CONTACT
Mercy College of Ohio, OH. *Toll-free phone:* 888-80-MERCY.

Miami University
Oxford, Ohio
http://miamioh.edu/

- **State-related** university, founded 1809, part of Miami University System
- **Small-town** 2100-acre campus with easy access to Cincinnati
- **Endowment** $459.6 million
- **Coed** 15,813 undergraduate students, 97% full-time, 49% women, 51% men
- **Moderately difficult** entrance level, 66% of applicants were admitted

UNDERGRAD STUDENTS
15,311 full-time, 502 part-time. Students come from 50 states and territories; 85 other countries; 34% are from out of state; 3% Black or African American, non-Hispanic/Latino; 3% Hispanic/Latino; 2% Asian, non-Hispanic/Latino; 0.2% American Indian or Alaska Native, non-Hispanic/Latino; 3% Two or more races, non-Hispanic/Latino; 0.6% Race/ethnicity unknown; 9% international; 2% transferred in; 47% live on campus.

Freshmen
Admission: 25,301 applied, 16,657 admitted, 3,644 enrolled. ***Average high school GPA:*** 3.7. ***Test scores:*** SAT critical reading scores over 500: 89%; SAT math scores over 500: 96%; ACT scores over 18: 100%; SAT critical reading scores over 600: 48%; SAT math scores over 600: 66%; ACT scores over 24: 92%; SAT critical reading scores over 700: 12%; SAT math scores over 700: 19%; ACT scores over 30: 29%.

Retention: 90% of full-time freshmen returned.

FACULTY
Total: 1,185, 77% full-time, 70% with terminal degrees.

Student/faculty ratio: 17:1.

ACADEMICS
Calendar: semesters. *Degrees:* certificates, associate, bachelor's, master's, doctoral, and post-master's certificates.

Special study options: advanced placement credit, cooperative education, distance learning, double majors, English as a second language, honors programs, independent study, internships, off-campus study, services for LD students, student-designed majors, study abroad, summer session for credit. ***ROTC:*** Army (c), Navy (b), Air Force (b).

Unusual degree programs: 3-2 engineering with Case Western Reserve University, Columbia University; forestry with Duke University.

Computers: 1,200 computers/terminals and 11,200 ports are available on campus for general student use. Students can access the following: campus intranet, computer help desk, free student e-mail accounts, online (class) grades, online (class) registration, online (class) schedules. Campuswide network is available. 100% of college-owned or -operated housing units are wired for high-speed Internet access. Wireless service is available via entire campus.

STUDENT LIFE
Housing options: on-campus residence required through sophomore year; coed, men-only, women-only, special housing for students with disabilities. Campus housing is university owned. Freshman campus housing is guaranteed.

Activities and organizations: drama/theater group, student-run newspaper, radio and television station, choral group, marching band, College Republicans, CRU (formerly Campus Crusade for Christ), Culinary Association, Pistol Club, Stage Left, national fraternities, national sororities.

Athletics Member NCAA. All Division I except football (Division I-A). ***Intercollegiate sports:*** baseball M(s)/W(c), basketball M(s)/W(s), cross-country running M(s)/W(s), equestrian sports M(c)/W(c), fencing M(c)/W(c), field hockey M(c)/W(s), golf M(s), gymnastics M(c)/W(c), ice hockey M(s)/W(c), lacrosse M(c)/W(c), rugby M(c)/W(c), sailing M(c)/W(c), soccer M(c)/W(s), softball M(c)/W(s), swimming and diving M(s)/W(s), tennis M(c)/W(s), track and field M(s)/W(s), ultimate Frisbee M(c)/W(c), volleyball M(c)/W(s), water polo M(c)/W(c), weight lifting M(c)/W(c), wrestling M(c)/W(c). ***Intramural sports:*** badminton M(c)/W(c), baseball M/W, basketball M/W, golf M(c)/W(c), ice hockey M/W, racquetball M/W, soccer M/W, softball M/W, ultimate Frisbee M/W, volleyball M/W.

Campus security: 24-hour emergency response devices and patrols, student patrols, late-night transport/escort service, controlled dormitory access.

Student services: health clinic, personal/psychological counseling, women's center.

COSTS & FINANCIAL AID
Costs (2014–15) ***Tuition:*** state resident $13,533 full-time, $564 per credit hour part-time; nonresident $29,640 full-time, $1235 per credit hour part-time. Full-time tuition and fees vary according to location and program. Part-time tuition and fees vary according to course load, location, and program. ***Required fees:*** $754 full-time. ***Room and board:*** $11,109; room only: $5459. Room and board charges vary according to board plan and housing facility. ***Payment plan:*** installment. ***Waivers:*** employees or children of employees.

Financial Aid Of all full-time matriculated undergraduates who enrolled in 2013, 8,571 applied for aid, 5,920 were judged to have need, 898 had their need fully met. 1,424 Federal Work-Study jobs (averaging $1117). In 2013, 4277 non-need-based awards were made. ***Average percent of need met:*** 56. ***Average financial aid package:*** $11,902. ***Average need-based loan:*** $4596. ***Average need-based gift aid:*** $8064. ***Average non-need-based aid:*** $6330. ***Average indebtedness upon graduation:*** $27,181.

APPLYING
Standardized Tests *Required:* SAT or ACT (for admission).

Options: electronic application, early decision, early action, deferred entrance.

Application fee: $50.

Required: essay or personal statement, high school transcript, 1 letter of recommendation.

Application deadlines: 2/1 (freshmen), 6/1 (transfers), 12/1 (early action).

Early decision deadline: 11/15.

Notification: 3/15 (freshmen), continuous (transfers), 12/15 (early decision), 2/1 (early action).

CONTACT
Office of Admissions, Miami University, 301 South Campus Avenue, Oxford, OH 45056. *Phone:* 513-529-2531. *E-mail:* admission@miamioh.edu.

Mount Carmel College of Nursing

Columbus, Ohio

http://www.mccn.edu/

- **Independent** comprehensive, founded 1903
- **Urban** campus with easy access to Columbus
- **Coed, primarily women** 927 undergraduate students, 67% full-time, 90% women, 10% men
- **Moderately difficult** entrance level, 92% of applicants were admitted

UNDERGRAD STUDENTS
622 full-time, 305 part-time. 12% are from out of state; 5% Black or African American, non-Hispanic/Latino; 2% Hispanic/Latino; 1% Asian, non-Hispanic/Latino; 0.2% Native Hawaiian or other Pacific Islander, non-Hispanic/Latino; 0.2% American Indian or Alaska Native, non-Hispanic/Latino; 2% Two or more races, non-Hispanic/Latino; 1% Race/ethnicity unknown; 8% transferred in; 8% live on campus.

Freshmen
Admission: 144 applied, 132 admitted, 83 enrolled. ***Average high school GPA:*** 3.52. ***Test scores:*** ACT scores over 18: 98%; ACT scores over 24: 33%.

Retention: 88% of full-time freshmen returned.

FACULTY
Total: 98, 54% full-time, 20% with terminal degrees.

Student/faculty ratio: 12:1.

ACADEMICS
Calendar: semesters. *Degrees:* bachelor's, master's, and post-master's certificates.

Special study options: accelerated degree program, adult/continuing education programs, advanced placement credit, distance learning, honors programs, off-campus study, summer session for credit. ***ROTC:*** Army (c), Navy (c), Air Force (c).

Computers: 80 computers/terminals are available on campus for general student use. Students can access the following: campus intranet, computer help desk, free student e-mail accounts, online (class) grades, online (class) registration, online (class) schedules. Campuswide network is available. 100% of college-owned or -operated housing units are wired for high-speed Internet access. Wireless service is available via entire campus.

STUDENT LIFE
Housing options: on-campus residence required through sophomore year; coed. Campus housing is provided by a third party. Freshman applicants given priority for college housing.

Activities and organizations: Campus Ministry, Student Nurses Association of Mount Carmel (SNAM), Mount Carmel Rho Omicron Chapter of Sigma Theta Tau International Honor Society, Student Government Association (SGA), Student Ambassador Program.

Athletics ***Intramural sports:*** basketball W(c), softball W(c), volleyball M(c)/W(c).

Campus security: 24-hour emergency response devices and patrols, late-night transport/escort service, controlled dormitory access.

Student services: health clinic, personal/psychological counseling.

COSTS & FINANCIAL AID

Costs (2014–15) ***One-time required fee:*** $225. ***Tuition:*** $11,284 full-time, $364 per semester hour part-time. Full-time tuition and fees vary according to course level, course load, program, and student level. Part-time tuition and fees vary according to course level, course load, program, and student level. ***Required fees:*** $732 full-time, $858 per year part-time. ***Room only:*** $5000. ***Payment plan:*** installment. ***Waivers:*** employees or children of employees.

Financial Aid Of all full-time matriculated undergraduates who enrolled in 2013, 554 applied for aid, 455 were judged to have need, 129 had their need fully met. ***Average percent of need met:*** 31. ***Average financial aid package:*** $7917. ***Average need-based loan:*** $4303. ***Average need-based gift aid:*** $5470. ***Average indebtedness upon graduation:*** $35,952.

APPLYING

Standardized Tests *Required for some:* ACT (for admission).

Options: electronic application.

Application fee: $30.

Required: essay or personal statement, high school transcript, activities/interests resume. ***Required for some:*** interview. ***Recommended:*** minimum 3.0 GPA.

CONTACT

Kim Campbell, Director, Admissions and Recruitment, Mount Carmel College of Nursing, 127 South Davis Avenue, Columbus, OH 43222-1504. *Phone:* 614-234-1085. *Toll-free phone:* 800-556-6942. *Fax:* 614-234-5427. *E-mail:* kcampbell@mccn.edu.

Mount St. Joseph University

Cincinnati, Ohio

http://www.msj.edu/

- **Independent Roman Catholic** comprehensive, founded 1920
- **Suburban** 92-acre campus
- **Endowment** $37.5 million
- **Coed** 1,657 undergraduate students, 69% full-time, 62% women, 38% men
- **Moderately difficult** entrance level, 88% of applicants were admitted

UNDERGRAD STUDENTS

1,142 full-time, 515 part-time. Students come from 22 states and territories; 3 other countries; 17% are from out of state; 11% Black or African American, non-Hispanic/Latino; 2% Hispanic/Latino; 0.5% Asian, non-Hispanic/Latino; 0.1% Native Hawaiian or other Pacific Islander, non-Hispanic/Latino; 0.2% American Indian or Alaska Native, non-Hispanic/Latino; 2% Two or more races, non-Hispanic/Latino; 4% Race/ethnicity unknown; 0.3% international; 4% transferred in; 24% live on campus.

Freshmen

Admission: 1,010 applied, 885 admitted, 297 enrolled. ***Average high school GPA:*** 3.31. ***Test scores:*** SAT math scores over 500: 50%; ACT scores over 18: 87%; SAT math scores over 600: 11%; ACT scores over 24: 27%; SAT math scores over 700: 3%; ACT scores over 30: 3%. ***Retention:*** 67% of full-time freshmen returned.

FACULTY

Total: 247, 44% full-time, 44% with terminal degrees.

Student/faculty ratio: 11:1.

ACADEMICS

Calendar: semesters. *Degrees:* certificates, associate, bachelor's, master's, doctoral, and postbachelor's certificates.

Special study options: academic remediation for entering students, accelerated degree program, advanced placement credit, cooperative education, distance learning, double majors, honors programs, independent study, internships, off-campus study, part-time degree program, services for LD students, study abroad, summer session for credit. ***ROTC:*** Army (c), Air Force (c).

Computers: 190 computers/terminals are available on campus for general student use. Students can access the following: computer help desk, free student e-mail accounts, online (class) grades, online (class) registration, online (class) schedules. Campuswide network is available. 100% of college-owned or -operated housing units are wired for high-speed Internet access. Wireless service is available via entire campus.

STUDENT LIFE

Housing options: on-campus residence required through sophomore year; coed, special housing for students with disabilities. Campus housing is university owned. Freshman applicants given priority for college housing.

Activities and organizations: drama/theater group, student-run newspaper, choral group, Student Government Association, Campus Activities Board, Black Student Union, Residence Hall Council, Group Fitness.

Athletics Member NCAA. All Division III. ***Intercollegiate sports:*** baseball M, basketball M/W, cheerleading W, cross-country running M/W, football M, golf M/W, lacrosse M/W, soccer M/W, softball W, tennis M/W, track and field M/W, volleyball M/W, wrestling M. ***Intramural sports:*** basketball M/W, football M/W, racquetball M/W, soccer M/W, softball M/W, tennis M/W, volleyball M/W.

Campus security: 24-hour emergency response devices and patrols, late-night transport/escort service.

Student services: health clinic, personal/psychological counseling.

COSTS & FINANCIAL AID

Costs (2014–15) ***One-time required fee:*** $200. ***Comprehensive fee:*** $35,560 includes full-time tuition ($25,850), mandatory fees ($1000), and room and board ($8710). Full-time tuition and fees vary according to course load and reciprocity agreements. Part-time tuition: $500 per credit hour. Part-time tuition and fees vary according to course load and reciprocity agreements. ***College room only:*** $4500. Room and board charges vary according to board plan and housing facility. ***Payment plans:*** installment, deferred payment. ***Waivers:*** senior citizens and employees or children of employees.

Financial Aid Of all full-time matriculated undergraduates who enrolled in 2014, 1,017 applied for aid, 907 were judged to have need, 182 had their need fully met. 45 Federal Work-Study jobs (averaging $1464). 92 state and other part-time jobs (averaging $1455). In 2014, 206 non-need-based awards were made. ***Average percent of need met:*** 75. ***Average financial aid package:*** $18,934. ***Average need-based loan:*** $4352. ***Average need-based gift aid:*** $15,588. ***Average non-need-based aid:*** $12,578.

APPLYING

Standardized Tests *Required:* SAT or ACT (for admission).

Options: electronic application, deferred entrance.

Application fee: $25.

Required: high school transcript. ***Required for some:*** essay or personal statement, 2 letters of recommendation, interview. ***Recommended:*** minimum 2.0 GPA.

Application deadlines: 8/15 (freshmen), 8/1 (transfers).

Notification: continuous (freshmen), continuous (transfers).

CONTACT

Peggy Minnich, Director of Admission, Mount St. Joseph University, 5701 Delhi Road, Cincinnati, OH 45233-1670. *Phone:* 513-244-4531. *Toll-free phone:* 800-654-9314. *Fax:* 513-244-4629. *E-mail:* admissions@msj.edu.

Mount Vernon Nazarene University

Mount Vernon, Ohio

http://www.mvnu.edu/

- **Independent Nazarene** comprehensive, founded 1964
- **Small-town** 326-acre campus with easy access to Columbus
- **Endowment** $13.9 million
- **Coed** 1,773 undergraduate students, 79% full-time, 63% women, 37% men
- **Moderately difficult** entrance level, 56% of applicants were admitted

UNDERGRAD STUDENTS

1,394 full-time, 379 part-time. Students come from 25 states and territories; 16 other countries; 13% are from out of state; 4% Black or African American, non-Hispanic/Latino; 2% Hispanic/Latino; 0.4% Asian, non-Hispanic/Latino; 0.2% Native Hawaiian or other Pacific

Islander, non-Hispanic/Latino; 0.1% American Indian or Alaska Native, non-Hispanic/Latino; 0.6% Two or more races, non-Hispanic/Latino; 8% Race/ethnicity unknown; 1% international; 3% transferred in; 80% live on campus.

Freshmen

Admission: 1,383 applied, 775 admitted, 311 enrolled. ***Average high school GPA:*** 3.38. ***Test scores:*** SAT critical reading scores over 500: 40%; SAT math scores over 500: 52%; ACT scores over 18: 93%; SAT critical reading scores over 600: 20%; SAT math scores over 600: 10%; ACT scores over 24: 43%; SAT critical reading scores over 700: 7%; ACT scores over 30: 6%.

Retention: 82% of full-time freshmen returned.

FACULTY

Total: 247, 29% full-time, 40% with terminal degrees.

Student/faculty ratio: 14:1.

ACADEMICS

Calendar: 4-1-4. *Degrees:* associate, bachelor's, and master's.

Special study options: academic remediation for entering students, adult/continuing education programs, advanced placement credit, distance learning, double majors, honors programs, independent study, internships, off-campus study, part-time degree program, services for LD students, study abroad, summer session for credit.

Unusual degree programs: 3-2 pre-occupational therapy/physician assistant with Chatham University.

Computers: 209 computers/terminals and 1,200 ports are available on campus for general student use. Students can access the following: campus intranet, computer help desk, free student e-mail accounts, online (class) grades, online (class) schedules. Campuswide network is available. 100% of college-owned or -operated housing units are wired for high-speed Internet access. Wireless service is available via entire campus.

STUDENT LIFE

Housing options: on-campus residence required through senior year; men-only, women-only, special housing for students with disabilities. Campus housing is university owned. Freshman campus housing is guaranteed.

Activities and organizations: drama/theater group, student-run newspaper, radio station, choral group, Campus Ministry Groups, Student Government Association, Student Education Association, Drama Club, Music Department Ensembles.

Athletics Member NAIA, NCCAA. ***Intercollegiate sports:*** baseball M(s), basketball M(s)/W(s), cross-country running M(s)/W(s), golf M(s)/W(s), soccer M(s)/W(s), softball W(s), track and field M/W, volleyball W(s). ***Intramural sports:*** basketball M/W, bowling M/W, cheerleading M(c)/W(c), football M/W, soccer M/W, softball M/W, table tennis M/W, ultimate Frisbee M/W, volleyball M/W.

Campus security: 24-hour emergency response devices and patrols, late-night transport/escort service, controlled dormitory access.

Student services: health clinic, personal/psychological counseling.

COSTS & FINANCIAL AID

Costs (2014–15) ***Comprehensive fee:*** $31,910 includes full-time tuition ($24,400), mandatory fees ($250), and room and board ($7260). Part-time tuition: $678 per credit hour. ***College room only:*** $4056. ***Payment plan:*** installment. ***Waivers:*** senior citizens and employees or children of employees.

Financial Aid Of all full-time matriculated undergraduates who enrolled in 2013, 1,333 applied for aid, 1,175 were judged to have need, 206 had their need fully met. 263 Federal Work-Study jobs (averaging $1714). 335 state and other part-time jobs (averaging $1686). In 2013, 51 non-need-based awards were made. ***Average percent of need met:*** 69. ***Average financial aid package:*** $20,023. ***Average need-based loan:*** $4278. ***Average need-based gift aid:*** $12,788. ***Average non-need-based aid:*** $9332. ***Average indebtedness upon graduation:*** $28,125.

APPLYING

Standardized Tests *Required:* SAT or ACT (for admission).

Options: electronic application, deferred entrance.

Application fee: $25.

Required: essay or personal statement, high school transcript, minimum 2.5 GPA, 2 letters of recommendation.

Notification: 9/1 (freshmen), continuous (transfers).

CONTACT

Mr. Tracy Waal, Director of Admissions and Student Recruitment, Mount Vernon Nazarene University, 800 Martinsburg Road, Mount Vernon, OH 43050. *Phone:* 740-392-6868 Ext. 4518. *Toll-free phone:* 866-462-6868. *Fax:* 740-393-0511. *E-mail:* admissions@mvnu.edu.

★ Notre Dame College

South Euclid, Ohio

http://www.notredamecollege.edu/

CONTACT

Mr. David Armstrong, Dean of Admissions, Notre Dame College, 4545 College Road, South Euclid, OH 44121-4293. *Phone:* 216-373-5214. *Toll-free phone:* 877-NDC-OHIO. *Fax:* 216-381-3802. *E-mail:* admissinos@ndc.edu.

See next page for display ad and page 1556 for the College Close-Up.

Oberlin College

Oberlin, Ohio

http://www.oberlin.edu/

- **Independent** comprehensive, founded 1833
- **Small-town** 440-acre campus with easy access to Cleveland
- **Endowment** $713.9 million
- **Coed** 2,961 undergraduate students, 99% full-time, 55% women, 45% men
- **Very difficult** entrance level, 33% of applicants were admitted

UNDERGRAD STUDENTS

2,920 full-time, 41 part-time. Students come from 51 states and territories; 45 other countries; 92% are from out of state; 5% Black or African American, non-Hispanic/Latino; 7% Hispanic/Latino; 4% Asian, non-Hispanic/Latino; 0.1% Native Hawaiian or other Pacific Islander, non-Hispanic/Latino; 0.1% American Indian or Alaska Native, non-Hispanic/Latino; 6% Two or more races, non-Hispanic/Latino; 0.7% Race/ethnicity unknown; 7% international; 0.9% transferred in; 77% live on campus.

Freshmen

Admission: 7,227 applied, 2,365 admitted, 797 enrolled. ***Average high school GPA:*** 3.58. ***Test scores:*** SAT critical reading scores over 500: 99%; SAT math scores over 500: 98%; SAT writing scores over 500: 99%; ACT scores over 18: 100%; SAT critical reading scores over 600: 90%; SAT math scores over 600: 85%; SAT writing scores over 600: 89%; ACT scores over 24: 98%; SAT critical reading scores over 700: 43%; SAT math scores over 700: 35%; SAT writing scores over 700: 41%; ACT scores over 30: 60%.

Retention: 94% of full-time freshmen returned.

FACULTY

Total: 218, 99% with terminal degrees.

Student/faculty ratio: 10:1.

ACADEMICS

Calendar: 4-1-4. *Degrees:* diplomas, bachelor's, master's, and postbachelor's certificates.

Special study options: advanced placement credit, double majors, English as a second language, honors programs, independent study, internships, off-campus study, part-time degree program, services for LD students, student-designed majors, study abroad.

Unusual degree programs: 3-2 engineering with Washington University in St. Louis, Case Western Reserve University, California Institute of Technology, Columbia University.

Computers: 236 computers/terminals are available on campus for general student use. Students can access the following: campus intranet, computer help desk, free student e-mail accounts, online (class) grades, online (class) registration, online (class) schedules. Campuswide network is available. 100% of college-owned or -operated housing units are wired for high-speed Internet access. Wireless service is available via entire campus.

STUDENT LIFE

Housing options: on-campus residence required through senior year; coed, women-only, cooperative, special housing for students with disabilities. Campus housing is university owned. Freshman campus housing is guaranteed.

Activities and organizations: drama/theater group, student-run newspaper, radio station, choral group, marching band, Experimental College, Community Outreach, student government, Students Cooperative Association, student radio station.

Athletics Member NCAA. All Division III. ***Intercollegiate sports:*** badminton M(c)/W(c), baseball M, basketball M/W, bowling M(c)/W(c), cross-country running M/W, equestrian sports M(c)/W(c), fencing M(c)/W(c), field hockey W, football M, golf M/W, ice hockey M(c)/W(c), lacrosse M/W, rugby M(c)/W(c), soccer M/W, softball W(c), swimming and diving M/W, tennis M/W, track and field M/W, ultimate Frisbee M(c)/W(c), volleyball M(c)/W, water polo M(c)/W(c). ***Intramural sports:*** archery M/W, baseball M, basketball M/W, cross-country running M/W, gymnastics M(c)/W(c), racquetball M/W, rock climbing M/W, soccer M/W, softball M/W, squash M/W, table tennis M(c)/W, tennis M/W, track and field M/W, volleyball M/W, water polo M/W, weight lifting M/W.

Campus security: 24-hour emergency response devices and patrols, student patrols, late-night transport/escort service, controlled dormitory access, crime prevention programs.

Student services: health clinic, personal/psychological counseling, women's center.

COSTS & FINANCIAL AID

Costs (2015–16) ***Comprehensive fee:*** $64,194 includes full-time tuition ($49,928), mandatory fees ($636), and room and board ($13,630). Part-time tuition: $2040 per credit. ***College room only:*** $7080. Room and board charges vary according to board plan and housing facility. ***Payment plan:*** installment. ***Waivers:*** employees or children of employees.

Financial Aid Of all full-time matriculated undergraduates who enrolled in 2014, 1,663 applied for aid, 1,400 were judged to have need, 1,400 had their need fully met. 1,500 Federal Work-Study jobs (averaging $2400). 600 state and other part-time jobs (averaging $2400). In 2014, 1042 non-need-based awards were made. ***Average percent of need met:*** 100. ***Average financial aid package:*** $37,294. ***Average need-based loan:*** $3861. ***Average need-based gift aid:*** $32,317. ***Average non-need-based aid:*** $13,167. ***Average indebtedness upon graduation:*** $25,018.

APPLYING

Standardized Tests *Required:* SAT or ACT (for admission). *Required for some:* SAT Subject Tests (for admission).

Options: electronic application, early admission, early decision, deferred entrance.

Required: essay or personal statement, high school transcript, 2 letters of recommendation. ***Required for some:*** interview, audition for applicants to the Conservatory of Music.

Application deadlines: 1/15 (freshmen), 3/15 (transfers).

Early decision deadline: 11/15 (for plan 1), 1/2 (for plan 2).

Notification: 4/1 (freshmen), 5/15 (transfers), 12/15 (early decision plan 1), 2/1 (early decision plan 2).

CONTACT

Debra Chermonte, Vice President and Dean of Admissions and Financial Aid, Oberlin College, Admissions Office, Carnegie Building, 101 North Professor Street, Oberlin, OH 44074-1075. *Phone:* 440-775-8411. *Toll-free phone:* 800-622-OBIE. *Fax:* 440-775-6905. *E-mail:* college.admissions@oberlin.edu.

Ohio Dominican University

Columbus, Ohio

http://www.ohiodominican.edu/

- **Independent Roman Catholic** comprehensive, founded 1911
- **Urban** 92-acre campus
- **Endowment** $27.1 million
- **Coed** 1,865 undergraduate students, 69% full-time, 54% women, 46% men
- **Minimally difficult** entrance level, 47% of applicants were admitted

UNDERGRAD STUDENTS

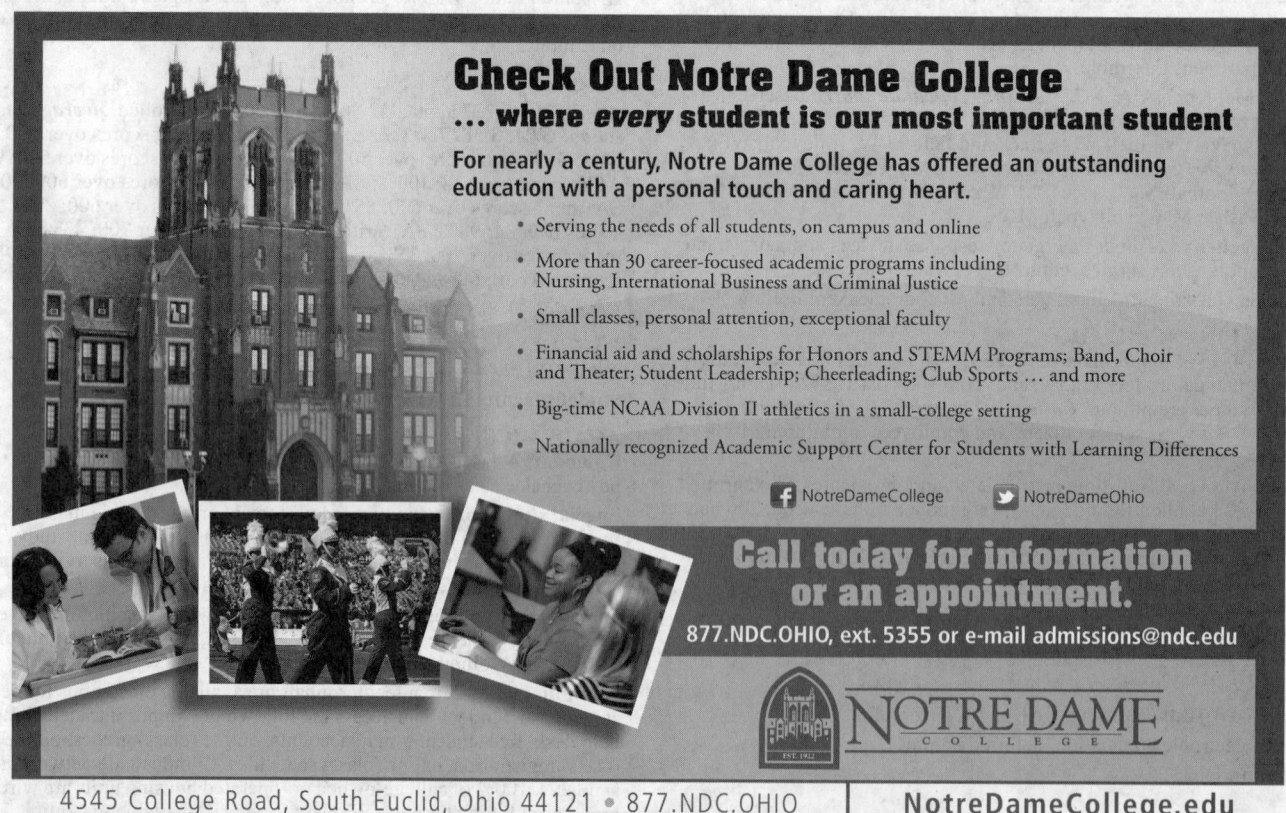

1,292 full-time, 573 part-time. Students come from 17 states and territories; 13 other countries; 3% are from out of state; 21% Black or African American, non-Hispanic/Latino; 3% Hispanic/Latino; 1% Asian,

non-Hispanic/Latino; 0.1% Native Hawaiian or other Pacific Islander, non-Hispanic/Latino; 0.3% American Indian or Alaska Native, non-Hispanic/Latino; 4% Two or more races, non-Hispanic/Latino; 6% Race/ethnicity unknown; 0.7% international; 5% transferred in; 29% live on campus.

Freshmen
Admission: 2,317 applied, 1,079 admitted, 228 enrolled. ***Average high school GPA:*** 3.3. ***Test scores:*** SAT critical reading scores over 500: 32%; SAT math scores over 500: 42%; SAT writing scores over 500: 26%; ACT scores over 18: 95%; SAT critical reading scores over 600: 11%; SAT math scores over 600: 21%; SAT writing scores over 600: 11%; ACT scores over 24: 33%; ACT scores over 30: 4%.

Retention: 70% of full-time freshmen returned.

FACULTY
Total: 264, 27% full-time, 40% with terminal degrees.

ACADEMICS
Calendar: semesters. *Degrees:* certificates, associate, bachelor's, and master's.

Special study options: academic remediation for entering students, accelerated degree program, adult/continuing education programs, advanced placement credit, distance learning, double majors, honors programs, independent study, internships, off-campus study, part-time degree program, services for LD students, student-designed majors, study abroad, summer session for credit. ***ROTC:*** Army (c).

Unusual degree programs: 3-2 business administration; Sport Management.

Computers: 198 computers/terminals and 1,900 ports are available on campus for general student use. Students can access the following: campus intranet, computer help desk, free student e-mail accounts, online (class) grades, online (class) registration, online (class) schedules. Campuswide network is available. 100% of college-owned or -operated housing units are wired for high-speed Internet access. Wireless service is available via classrooms, computer centers, computer labs, dorm rooms, learning centers, libraries, student centers.

STUDENT LIFE
Housing options: on-campus residence required through sophomore year; coed. Campus housing is university owned.

Activities and organizations: drama/theater group, student-run newspaper, radio station, choral group, marching band, Sport Management Society, Student Senate, Panther Activities Council, Student Athletic Advisory Committee, Panther Players.

Athletics Member NCAA. All Division II except golf (Division I). ***Intercollegiate sports:*** baseball M(s), basketball M(s)/W(s), cross-country running M(s)/W(s), football M(s), golf M(s)/W(s), soccer M(s)/W(s), softball W(s), tennis M(s)/W(s), track and field M/W, volleyball W(s). ***Intramural sports:*** basketball M/W, table tennis M/W, track and field M/W, ultimate Frisbee M/W, volleyball M/W.

Campus security: 24-hour emergency response devices and patrols, late-night transport/escort service, controlled dormitory access.

Student services: health clinic, personal/psychological counseling.

COSTS & FINANCIAL AID
Costs (2014–15) ***Comprehensive fee:*** $39,710 includes full-time tuition ($28,900), mandatory fees ($530), and room and board ($10,280). Part-time tuition: $585 per credit hour. ***Required fees:*** $585 per credit hour part-time. ***Room and board:*** Room and board charges vary according to board plan. ***Payment plan:*** installment. ***Waivers:*** senior citizens and employees or children of employees.

Financial Aid Of all full-time matriculated undergraduates who enrolled in 2013, 200 Federal Work-Study jobs (averaging $2000). ***Average percent of need met:*** 92. ***Average financial aid package:*** $12,467. ***Average indebtedness upon graduation:*** $13,500.

APPLYING
Standardized Tests *Required:* SAT or ACT (for admission).

Options: electronic application, deferred entrance.

Application fee: $25.

Required: high school transcript, minimum 2.3 GPA. ***Required for some:*** essay or personal statement. ***Recommended:*** interview.

Application deadlines: rolling (freshmen), rolling (transfers).

Notification: continuous (freshmen), continuous (transfers).

CONTACT
Mr. Kevin Brinkman, Director of Admissions, Ohio Dominican University, 1216 Sunbury Road, Columbus, OH 43219. *Phone:* 614-251-4500. *Toll-free phone:* 800-955-6446. *Fax:* 614-251-0156. *E-mail:* admissions@ohiodominican.edu.

Ohio Northern University
Ada, Ohio
http://www.onu.edu/

- **Independent** comprehensive, founded 1871, affiliated with United Methodist Church
- **Small-town** 340-acre campus
- **Coed** 2,854 undergraduate students, 79% full-time, 48% women, 52% men
- **Moderately difficult** entrance level, 69% of applicants were admitted

UNDERGRAD STUDENTS
2,262 full-time, 592 part-time. Students come from 34 states and territories; 25 other countries; 13% are from out of state; 3% Black or African American, non-Hispanic/Latino; 1% Hispanic/Latino; 1% Asian, non-Hispanic/Latino; 0.1% Native Hawaiian or other Pacific Islander, non-Hispanic/Latino; 0.1% American Indian or Alaska Native, non-Hispanic/Latino; 3% Two or more races, non-Hispanic/Latino; 9% Race/ethnicity unknown; 7% international; 63% live on campus.

Freshmen
Admission: 3,337 applied, 2,289 admitted, 628 enrolled. ***Average high school GPA:*** 3.7. ***Test scores:*** SAT critical reading scores over 500: 81%; SAT math scores over 500: 88%; SAT writing scores over 500: 81%; ACT scores over 18: 99%; SAT critical reading scores over 600: 34%; SAT math scores over 600: 45%; SAT writing scores over 600: 30%; ACT scores over 24: 71%; SAT critical reading scores over 700: 4%; SAT math scores over 700: 10%; SAT writing scores over 700: 5%; ACT scores over 30: 19%.

Retention: 88% of full-time freshmen returned.

FACULTY
Total: 307, 68% full-time, 67% with terminal degrees.

Student/faculty ratio: 12:1.

ACADEMICS
Calendar: quarters. *Degrees:* certificates, bachelor's, master's, doctoral, and postbachelor's certificates.

Special study options: academic remediation for entering students, advanced placement credit, cooperative education, distance learning, double majors, English as a second language, honors programs, independent study, internships, off-campus study, part-time degree program, services for LD students, study abroad, summer session for credit. ***ROTC:*** Army (c), Air Force (c).

Computers: Students can access the following: campus intranet, computer help desk, free student e-mail accounts, online (class) grades, online (class) registration, online (class) schedules. Campuswide network is available. 100% of college-owned or -operated housing units are wired for high-speed Internet access. Wireless service is available via entire campus.

STUDENT LIFE
Housing options: on-campus residence required through junior year; coed, men-only, women-only, special housing for students with disabilities. Campus housing is university owned. Freshman campus housing is guaranteed.

Activities and organizations: drama/theater group, student-run newspaper, radio and television station, choral group, marching band, Habitat for Humanity, Student Planning Committee, Student Senate, Northern Christian Fellowship, marching band, national fraternities, national sororities.

Athletics Member NCAA. All Division III. ***Intercollegiate sports:*** baseball M, basketball M/W, cross-country running M/W, football M, golf M/W, lacrosse M/W, soccer M/W, softball W, swimming and diving M/W, tennis M/W, track and field M/W, volleyball M(c)/W, wrestling M. ***Intramural sports:*** badminton M/W, basketball M/W, cheerleading

M(c)/W(c), lacrosse M(c), rugby M(c)/W(c), skiing (downhill) M(c)/W(c), soccer M/W, softball M/W, swimming and diving M/W, table tennis M/W, tennis M/W, ultimate Frisbee M(c)/W(c), volleyball M/W, water polo W(c).

Campus security: 24-hour emergency response devices and patrols, late-night transport/escort service, controlled dormitory access.

Student services: health clinic, personal/psychological counseling, legal services.

COSTS

Costs (2015–16) ***Comprehensive fee:*** $39,700 includes full-time tuition ($28,250), mandatory fees ($560), and room and board ($10,890). Full-time tuition and fees vary according to course load, degree level, and program. Part-time tuition and fees vary according to course load, degree level, and program. ***Room and board:*** Room and board charges vary according to board plan, housing facility, and student level. ***Payment plan:*** installment. ***Waivers:*** minority students, children of alumni, and employees or children of employees.

APPLYING

Standardized Tests *Required:* SAT or ACT (for admission).

Options: electronic application, deferred entrance.

Required: high school transcript. ***Recommended:*** essay or personal statement, minimum 2.5 GPA, 1 letter of recommendation, interview.

Application deadlines: 8/15 (freshmen), 8/15 (out-of-state freshmen), 8/15 (transfers).

Notification: continuous (freshmen), continuous (out-of-state freshmen), continuous (transfers).

CONTACT

Ms. Deborah Miller, Director of Admissions, Ohio Northern University, 525 South Main Street, Ada, OH 45810-1599. *Phone:* 419-772-2260 Ext. 2464. *Toll-free phone:* 888-408-4ONU. *Fax:* 419-772-2821. *E-mail:* admissions-ug@onu.edu.

See below for display ad and page 1558 for the College Close-Up.

The Ohio State University

Columbus, Ohio

http://www.osu.edu/

- **State-supported** university, founded 1870, part of The Ohio State University
- **Urban** 3996-acre campus with easy access to Columbus
- **Endowment** $3.5 billion
- **Coed** 44,741 undergraduate students, 91% full-time, 48% women, 52% men
- **Very difficult** entrance level, 53% of applicants were admitted

UNDERGRAD STUDENTS

40,613 full-time, 4,128 part-time. Students come from 58 states and territories; 71 other countries; 16% are from out of state; 6% Black or African American, non-Hispanic/Latino; 3% Hispanic/Latino; 6% Asian, non-Hispanic/Latino; 0.1% Native Hawaiian or other Pacific Islander, non-Hispanic/Latino; 0.1% American Indian or Alaska Native, non-Hispanic/Latino; 3% Two or more races, non-Hispanic/Latino; 3% Race/ethnicity unknown; 8% international; 6% transferred in; 25% live on campus.

Freshmen

Admission: 36,788 applied, 19,484 admitted, 7,079 enrolled. ***Test scores:*** SAT critical reading scores over 500: 122%; SAT math scores over 500: 98%; SAT writing scores over 500: 94%; ACT scores over 18: 100%; SAT critical reading scores over 600: 90%; SAT math scores over 600: 83%; SAT writing scores over 600: 57%; ACT scores over 24: 95%; SAT critical reading scores over 700: 47%; SAT math scores over 700: 39%; SAT writing scores over 700: 12%; ACT scores over 30: 41%.

Retention: 94% of full-time freshmen returned.

FACULTY

Total: 5,281, 70% full-time, 70% with terminal degrees.

Student/faculty ratio: 18:1.

ACADEMICS

Calendar: quarters. *Degrees:* certificates, diplomas, bachelor's, master's, doctoral, post-master's, and postbachelor's certificates.

Special study options: academic remediation for entering students, accelerated degree program, adult/continuing education programs, advanced placement credit, cooperative education, distance learning, double majors, English as a second language, freshman honors college, honors programs, independent study, internships, off-campus study, part-time degree program, services for LD students, student-designed majors, study abroad, summer session for credit. ***ROTC:*** Army (b), Navy (b), Air Force (b).

Unusual degree programs: 3-2 business administration.

Computers: Students can access the following: campus intranet, computer help desk, free student e-mail accounts, online (class) grades, online (class) registration, online (class) schedules, students can apply for admission, register, check grades, pay fees and obtain library resources, including books, online. Campuswide network is available. 100% of college-owned or -operated housing units are wired for high-speed Internet access. Wireless service is available via entire campus.

STUDENT LIFE

Housing options: on-campus residence required for freshman year; coed, women-only, cooperative, special housing for students with disabilities. Campus housing is university owned. Freshman campus housing is guaranteed.

Activities and organizations: drama/theater group, student-run newspaper, radio and television station, choral group, marching band, h2o (faith-based), Scuba Club, Jazz Club, International Friendships, Nourish International, national fraternities, national sororities.

Athletics Member NCAA. All Division I except football (Division I-A). ***Intercollegiate sports:*** baseball M(s), basketball M(s)/W(s), cheerleading M/W, cross-country running M(s)/W(s), fencing M(s)/W(s), field hockey W(s), golf M(s)/W(s), gymnastics M(s)/W(s), ice hockey M(s)/W(s), lacrosse M(s)/W(s), riflery M/W, soccer M(s)/W(s), softball W(s), swimming and diving M(s)/W(s), tennis M(s)/W(s), track and field M(s)/W(s), volleyball M(s)/W(s), wrestling M(s). ***Intramural sports:*** badminton M(c)/W(c), baseball M(c), basketball M/W, bowling M(c)/W(c), crew M(c)/W, cross-country running M/W, equestrian sports M(c)/W(c), fencing M(c)/W(c), field hockey W, football M/W, golf M/W, gymnastics M(c)/W(c), ice hockey M(c)/W(c), lacrosse M(c)/W(c), racquetball M(c)/W(c), riflery M(c)/W(c), rock climbing M/W, rugby M(c)/W(c), sailing M(c)/W(c), skiing (downhill) M(c)/W(c), soccer M(c)/W(c), softball W(c), squash M(c)/W(c), swimming and diving M(c)/W(c), table tennis M/W, tennis M/W, track and field M(c)/W(c), ultimate Frisbee M(c)/W(c), volleyball M(c)/W(c), water polo M(c)/W(c), weight lifting M(c), wrestling M/W.

Campus security: 24-hour emergency response devices and patrols, student patrols, late-night transport/escort service, controlled dormitory access, dorm entrances locked after 9 pm, lighted pathways and sidewalks, self-defense education.

Student services: health clinic, personal/psychological counseling, women's center, legal services.

COSTS & FINANCIAL AID

Costs (2014–15) ***Tuition:*** state resident $9615 full-time; nonresident $26,115 full-time. Full-time tuition and fees vary according to course load, location, program, and reciprocity agreements. Part-time tuition and fees vary according to course load, location, program, and reciprocity agreements. ***Required fees:*** $422 full-time. ***Room and board:*** $9850; room only: $6250. Room and board charges vary according to board plan, housing facility, and location. ***Payment plan:*** installment. ***Waivers:*** senior citizens and employees or children of employees.

Financial Aid Of all full-time matriculated undergraduates who enrolled in 2014, 27,308 applied for aid, 20,402 were judged to have need, 3,283 had their need fully met. 1,857 Federal Work-Study jobs (averaging $2782). 74 state and other part-time jobs (averaging $2361). In 2014, 7076 non-need-based awards were made. ***Average percent of need met:*** 65. ***Average financial aid package:*** $12,473. ***Average need-based loan:*** $4565. ***Average need-based gift aid:*** $9335. ***Average non-need-based aid:*** $6418. ***Average indebtedness upon graduation:*** $26,830.

APPLYING

Standardized Tests *Required:* SAT or ACT (for admission).

Options: electronic application, early action.

Required: essay or personal statement, high school transcript, .

Application deadlines: 2/1 (freshmen), 2/1 (out-of-state freshmen), 5/1 (transfers), 11/1 (early action).

Notification: continuous (freshmen), continuous (out-of-state freshmen), continuous (transfers), 1/15 (early action).

CONTACT

The Ohio State University, Student Academic Services Building, 281 West Lane Avenue, Columbus, OH 43210. *Phone:* 614-292-3980. *Fax:* 614-292-4818. *E-mail:* askabuckeye@osu.edu.

The Ohio State University at Lima

Lima, Ohio

http://lima.osu.edu/

- **State-supported** comprehensive, founded 1960, part of The Ohio State University
- **Suburban** 565-acre campus
- **Endowment** $6.2 million
- **Coed** 1,041 undergraduate students, 84% full-time, 55% women, 45% men
- **Noncompetitive** entrance level, 99% of applicants were admitted

UNDERGRAD STUDENTS

874 full-time, 167 part-time. Students come from 5 states and territories; 1 other country; 4% Black or African American, non-Hispanic/Latino; 2% Hispanic/Latino; 2% Asian, non-Hispanic/Latino; 0.2% American Indian or Alaska Native, non-Hispanic/Latino; 2% Two or more races, non-Hispanic/Latino; 3% Race/ethnicity unknown; 0.1% international; 4% transferred in.

Freshmen

Admission: 1,257 applied, 1,244 admitted, 432 enrolled. ***Test scores:*** SAT critical reading scores over 500: 91%; SAT math scores over 500: 68%; SAT writing scores over 500: 77%; ACT scores over 18: 87%; SAT critical reading scores over 600: 32%; SAT math scores over 600: 36%; SAT writing scores over 600: 18%; ACT scores over 24: 36%; SAT critical reading scores over 700: 5%; SAT writing scores over 700: 9%; ACT scores over 30: 3%.

Retention: 64% of full-time freshmen returned.

FACULTY

Total: 83, 42% full-time, 41% with terminal degrees.

Student/faculty ratio: 18:1.

ACADEMICS

Calendar: quarters. *Degrees:* associate, bachelor's, and master's.

Special study options: academic remediation for entering students, accelerated degree program, adult/continuing education programs, advanced placement credit, cooperative education, distance learning, double majors, English as a second language, freshman honors college, honors programs, independent study, internships, off-campus study, part-time degree program, services for LD students, student-designed majors, study abroad, summer session for credit. ***ROTC:*** Army (c), Navy (c), Air Force (c).

Computers: Students can access the following: campus intranet, computer help desk, free student e-mail accounts, online (class) grades, online (class) registration, online (class) schedules. Campuswide network is available. Wireless service is available via entire campus.

STUDENT LIFE

Housing options: college housing not available.

Activities and organizations: choral group, Student Senate, Psychology Club, Honors Club, Aggies, Newman Catholic Association.

Athletics ***Intramural sports:*** baseball M(c), basketball M(c)/W(c), football M/W, golf M(c)/W(c), soccer M/W, volleyball M(c)/W(c).

Campus security: 24-hour emergency response devices and patrols, student patrols, late-night transport/escort service, lighted pathways/sidewalks.

Student services: personal/psychological counseling.

COSTS

Costs (2014–15) ***Tuition:*** state resident $7140 full-time; nonresident $23,640 full-time. Full-time tuition and fees vary according to course load, location, program, and reciprocity agreements. Part-time tuition and fees vary according to course load, location, program, and reciprocity agreements. ***Payment plan:*** installment. ***Waivers:*** senior citizens and employees or children of employees.

APPLYING
Standardized Tests *Required for some:* SAT or ACT (for admission).
Options: electronic application.
Application fee: $60.
Required: high school transcript.
Application deadlines: 6/1 (freshmen), 6/1 (out-of-state freshmen), 6/1 (transfers).
Notification: continuous (freshmen), continuous (out-of-state freshmen), continuous (transfers).

CONTACT
The Ohio State University at Lima, OH. *Phone:* 419-995-8434. *Fax:* 419-995-8483. *E-mail:* admissions@lima.ohio-state.edu.

The Ohio State University at Marion
Marion, Ohio
http://osumarion.osu.edu/

- **State-supported** comprehensive, founded 1958, part of The Ohio State University
- **Small-town** 188-acre campus with easy access to Columbus
- **Endowment** $6.1 million
- **Coed** 1,192 undergraduate students, 80% full-time, 54% women, 46% men
- **Noncompetitive** entrance level, 99% of applicants were admitted

UNDERGRAD STUDENTS
955 full-time, 237 part-time. Students come from 5 states and territories; 1 other country; 5% Black or African American, non-Hispanic/Latino; 4% Hispanic/Latino; 4% Asian, non-Hispanic/Latino; 0.2% Native Hawaiian or other Pacific Islander, non-Hispanic/Latino; 0.3% American Indian or Alaska Native, non-Hispanic/Latino; 2% Two or more races, non-Hispanic/Latino; 2% Race/ethnicity unknown; 0.1% international; 6% transferred in.

Freshmen
Admission: 960 applied, 947 admitted, 446 enrolled. ***Test scores:*** SAT critical reading scores over 500: 53%; SAT math scores over 500: 74%; SAT writing scores over 500: 51%; ACT scores over 18: 54%; SAT critical reading scores over 600: 8%; SAT math scores over 600: 23%; SAT writing scores over 600: 15%; ACT scores over 24: 8%; SAT math scores over 700: 5%; SAT writing scores over 700: 2%.
Retention: 70% of full-time freshmen returned.

FACULTY
Total: 104, 37% full-time, 36% with terminal degrees.
Student/faculty ratio: 17:1.

ACADEMICS
Calendar: quarters. *Degrees:* associate, bachelor's, and master's.
Special study options: academic remediation for entering students, accelerated degree program, adult/continuing education programs, advanced placement credit, cooperative education, distance learning, double majors, English as a second language, freshman honors college, honors programs, independent study, internships, off-campus study, part-time degree program, services for LD students, student-designed majors, study abroad, summer session for credit. ***ROTC:*** Army (c), Navy (c), Air Force (c).
Computers: Students can access the following: campus intranet, computer help desk, free student e-mail accounts, online (class) grades, online (class) registration, online (class) schedules. Campuswide network is available. Wireless service is available via classrooms, libraries.

STUDENT LIFE
Activities and organizations: choral group.
Athletics Member USCAA. ***Intercollegiate sports:*** basketball M, golf M, volleyball W. ***Intramural sports:*** cheerleading M(c)/W(c), rugby M(c)/W(c), skiing (downhill) M(c)/W(c), soccer M(c)/W(c), softball M(c)/W(c), table tennis M/W.
Campus security: 24-hour emergency response devices.
Student services: personal/psychological counseling.

COSTS
Costs (2014–15) ***Tuition:*** state resident $7140 full-time; nonresident $23,640 full-time. Full-time tuition and fees vary according to course load, location, program, and reciprocity agreements. Part-time tuition and fees vary according to course load, location, program, and reciprocity agreements. ***Payment plan:*** installment. ***Waivers:*** senior citizens and employees or children of employees.

APPLYING
Standardized Tests *Required for some:* SAT or ACT (for admission).
Options: electronic application.
Application fee: $60.
Required: essay or personal statement, high school transcript.
Application deadlines: 6/1 (freshmen), 6/1 (out-of-state freshmen), 6/1 (transfers).
Notification: continuous (freshmen), continuous (out-of-state freshmen), continuous (transfers).

CONTACT
Mr. Matthew Moreau, Admissions and Financial Aid Coordinator, The Ohio State University at Marion, 1465 Mount Vernon Avenue, Marion, OH 43302. *Phone:* 740-725-6337. *Fax:* 740-386-2439. *E-mail:* moreau.1@osu.edu.

The Ohio State University–Mansfield Campus
Mansfield, Ohio
http://www.mansfield.osu.edu/

- **State-supported** comprehensive, founded 1958, part of The Ohio State University
- **Small-town** 640-acre campus with easy access to Columbus, Cleveland
- **Endowment** $2.3 million
- **Coed** 1,155 undergraduate students, 83% full-time, 55% women, 45% men
- **Noncompetitive** entrance level, 99% of applicants were admitted

UNDERGRAD STUDENTS
960 full-time, 195 part-time. Students come from 3 states and territories; 9% Black or African American, non-Hispanic/Latino; 3% Hispanic/Latino; 2% Asian, non-Hispanic/Latino; 0.2% American Indian or Alaska Native, non-Hispanic/Latino; 3% Two or more races, non-Hispanic/Latino; 2% Race/ethnicity unknown; 5% transferred in; 17% live on campus.

Freshmen
Admission: 1,626 applied, 1,610 admitted, 477 enrolled. ***Test scores:*** SAT critical reading scores over 500: 58%; SAT math scores over 500: 68%; SAT writing scores over 500: 46%; ACT scores over 18: 88%; SAT critical reading scores over 600: 7%; SAT math scores over 600: 28%; SAT writing scores over 600: 9%; ACT scores over 24: 40%; SAT critical reading scores over 700: 2%; SAT math scores over 700: 5%; ACT scores over 30: 4%.
Retention: 67% of full-time freshmen returned.

FACULTY
Total: 100, 39% full-time, 38% with terminal degrees.
Student/faculty ratio: 17:1.

ACADEMICS
Calendar: quarters. *Degrees:* associate, bachelor's, and master's.
Special study options: academic remediation for entering students, accelerated degree program, adult/continuing education programs, advanced placement credit, cooperative education, distance learning, double majors, English as a second language, freshman honors college, honors programs, independent study, internships, off-campus study, part-time degree program, services for LD students, student-designed majors, study abroad, summer session for credit. ***ROTC:*** Army (c), Navy (c), Air Force (c).
Computers: Students can access the following: campus intranet, computer help desk, free student e-mail accounts, online (class) grades, online (class) registration, online (class) schedules. Campuswide network is available. 100% of college-owned or -operated housing units are wired

for high-speed Internet access. Wireless service is available via computer centers, libraries, student centers.

STUDENT LIFE

Housing options: coed, special housing for students with disabilities. Campus housing is university owned.

Activities and organizations: drama/theater group, choral group, Campus Activities Board, Campus Crusader for Christ, Club Ed, Multicultural Student Association, Psychology Student Association.

Athletics *Intramural sports:* baseball M(c), basketball M(c)/W(c), bowling M/W, cheerleading M(c)/W(c), football M/W, golf M/W, soccer M(c), softball M/W, table tennis M/W, tennis M/W, volleyball M/W(c).

Campus security: 24-hour emergency response devices and patrols.

Student services: personal/psychological counseling.

COSTS

Costs (2014–15) *Tuition:* state resident $7140 full-time; nonresident $23,640 full-time. Full-time tuition and fees vary according to course load, location, program, and reciprocity agreements. Part-time tuition and fees vary according to course load, location, program, and reciprocity agreements. ***Room only:*** $5205. Room and board charges vary according to housing facility and location. ***Payment plan:*** installment. ***Waivers:*** senior citizens and employees or children of employees.

APPLYING

Standardized Tests *Required for some:* SAT or ACT (for admission).

Options: electronic application.

Application fee: $60.

Required: high school transcript.

Application deadlines: 6/1 (freshmen), 6/1 (out-of-state freshmen), 6/1 (transfers).

Notification: continuous (freshmen), continuous (out-of-state freshmen), continuous (transfers).

CONTACT

The Ohio State University–Mansfield Campus, OH. *Phone:* 419-755-4225. *Fax:* 419-755-4241. *E-mail:* admissions@mansfield.ohio-state.edu.

The Ohio State University–Newark Campus

Newark, Ohio

http://www.newark.osu.edu/

- **State-supported** comprehensive, founded 1957, part of The Ohio State University
- **Small-town** 106-acre campus with easy access to Columbus
- **Endowment** $4.1 million
- **Coed** 2,384 undergraduate students, 84% full-time, 51% women, 49% men
- **Noncompetitive** entrance level, 99% of applicants were admitted

UNDERGRAD STUDENTS

1,993 full-time, 391 part-time. Students come from 11 states and territories; 1% are from out of state; 13% Black or African American, non-Hispanic/Latino; 3% Hispanic/Latino; 4% Asian, non-Hispanic/Latino; 0.4% American Indian or Alaska Native, non-Hispanic/Latino; 4% Two or more races, non-Hispanic/Latino; 3% Race/ethnicity unknown; 5% transferred in; 8% live on campus.

Freshmen

Admission: 3,105 applied, 3,078 admitted, 1,234 enrolled. ***Test scores:*** SAT critical reading scores over 500: 61%; SAT math scores over 500: 62%; SAT writing scores over 500: 48%; ACT scores over 18: 89%; SAT critical reading scores over 600: 21%; SAT math scores over 600: 23%; SAT writing scores over 600: 11%; ACT scores over 24: 38%; SAT critical reading scores over 700: 3%; SAT math scores over 700: 2%; SAT writing scores over 700: 1%; ACT scores over 30: 2%.

Retention: 63% of full-time freshmen returned.

FACULTY

Total: 150, 35% full-time, 35% with terminal degrees.

Student/faculty ratio: 25:1.

ACADEMICS

Calendar: quarters. *Degrees:* associate, bachelor's, and master's.

Special study options: academic remediation for entering students, accelerated degree program, adult/continuing education programs, advanced placement credit, cooperative education, distance learning, double majors, English as a second language, freshman honors college, honors programs, independent study, internships, off-campus study, part-time degree program, services for LD students, student-designed majors, study abroad, summer session for credit. ***ROTC:*** Army (b), Navy (c), Air Force (c).

Computers: Students can access the following: campus intranet, computer help desk, free student e-mail accounts, online (class) grades, online (class) registration, online (class) schedules. Campuswide network is available. 100% of college-owned or -operated housing units are wired for high-speed Internet access. Wireless service is available via entire campus.

STUDENT LIFE

Housing options: coed. Campus housing is university owned.

Activities and organizations: choral group.

Athletics *Intramural sports:* baseball M(c), basketball M(c)/W(c), football M(c)/W(c), golf M(c)/W(c), soccer M(c)/W(c), softball W(c), volleyball M(c)/W(c), weight lifting M(c)/W(c).

Campus security: 24-hour emergency response devices and patrols, late-night transport/escort service, self-defense education.

Student services: personal/psychological counseling.

COSTS

Costs (2014–15) *Tuition:* state resident $7140 full-time; nonresident $23,640 full-time. Full-time tuition and fees vary according to course load, location, program, and reciprocity agreements. Part-time tuition and fees vary according to course load, location, program, and reciprocity agreements. ***Room and board:*** $7185; room only: $6075. Room and board charges vary according to board plan, housing facility, and location. ***Payment plan:*** installment. ***Waivers:*** senior citizens and employees or children of employees.

APPLYING

Standardized Tests *Required for some:* SAT or ACT (for admission).

Options: electronic application.

Application fee: $60.

Required: high school transcript.

Application deadlines: 6/1 (freshmen), 6/1 (out-of-state freshmen), 6/1 (transfers).

Notification: continuous (freshmen), continuous (out-of-state freshmen), continuous (transfers).

CONTACT

Ms. Ann Donahue, Director of Enrollment, The Ohio State University–Newark Campus, 1179 University Drive, Newark, OH 43055. *Phone:* 740-366-9333. *Fax:* 740-364-9645. *E-mail:* barclay.3@osu.edu.

Ohio University

Athens, Ohio

http://www.ohio.edu/

- **State-supported** university, founded 1804, part of Ohio Board of Regents
- **Small-town** 1774-acre campus
- **Endowment** $515.9 million
- **Coed** 23,571 undergraduate students, 72% full-time, 60% women, 40% men
- **Moderately difficult** entrance level, 74% of applicants were admitted

UNDERGRAD STUDENTS

17,019 full-time, 6,552 part-time. Students come from 49 states and territories; 64 other countries; 14% are from out of state; 5% Black or African American, non-Hispanic/Latino; 3% Hispanic/Latino; 0.9% Asian, non-Hispanic/Latino; 0.1% Native Hawaiian or other Pacific Islander, non-Hispanic/Latino; 0.1% American Indian or Alaska Native, non-Hispanic/Latino; 3% Two or more races, non-Hispanic/Latino; 1% Race/ethnicity unknown; 4% international; 2% transferred in; 40% live on campus.

Freshmen
Admission: 20,934 applied, 15,548 admitted, 4,377 enrolled. ***Average high school GPA:*** 3.43. ***Test scores:*** SAT critical reading scores over 500: 74%; SAT math scores over 500: 74%; SAT writing scores over 500: 66%; ACT scores over 18: 99%; SAT critical reading scores over 600: 25%; SAT math scores over 600: 26%; SAT writing scores over 600: 20%; ACT scores over 24: 52%; SAT critical reading scores over 700: 4%; SAT math scores over 700: 3%; SAT writing scores over 700: 3%; ACT scores over 30: 7%.
Retention: 80% of full-time freshmen returned.

FACULTY
Total: 1,301, 72% full-time, 65% with terminal degrees.
Student/faculty ratio: 18:1.

ACADEMICS
Calendar: quarters. *Degrees:* certificates, associate, bachelor's, master's, and doctoral.
Special study options: academic remediation for entering students, accelerated degree program, adult/continuing education programs, advanced placement credit, cooperative education, distance learning, double majors, English as a second language, external degree program, freshman honors college, honors programs, independent study, internships, off-campus study, part-time degree program, services for LD students, student-designed majors, study abroad, summer session for credit. ***ROTC:*** Army (b), Air Force (b).
Computers: 1,000 computers/terminals and 22,000 ports are available on campus for general student use. Students can access the following: campus intranet, computer help desk, free student e-mail accounts, online (class) grades, online (class) registration, online (class) schedules. Campuswide network is available. 100% of college-owned or -operated housing units are wired for high-speed Internet access. Wireless service is available via entire campus.

STUDENT LIFE
Housing options: on-campus residence required through sophomore year; coed, women-only, special housing for students with disabilities. Campus housing is university owned. Freshman campus housing is guaranteed.
Activities and organizations: drama/theater group, student-run newspaper, radio and television station, choral group, marching band, Alpha Phi Omega, Student Alumni Board, International Student Union, University Program Council, Cru@OU, national fraternities, national sororities.
Athletics Member NCAA. All Division I except football (Division I-A). ***Intercollegiate sports:*** baseball M(s), basketball M(s)/W(s), cross-country running M(s)/W(s), field hockey W(s), golf M(s)/W(s), ice hockey M(c), soccer W(s), softball W(s), swimming and diving W(s), track and field W(s), volleyball W(s), wrestling M(s). ***Intramural sports:*** archery M(c)/W(c), badminton M/W, basketball M/W, crew M(c)/W(c), equestrian sports M(c)/W(c), fencing M(c)/W(c), golf M(c)/W(c), gymnastics M(c)/W(c), lacrosse M(c)/W(c), rugby M(c)/W(c), soccer M(c)/W(c), softball M/W(c), swimming and diving M(c)/W(c), tennis M/W, ultimate Frisbee M(c)/W(c), volleyball M(c)/W(c), water polo M/W(c).
Campus security: 24-hour emergency response devices and patrols, student patrols, late-night transport/escort service, controlled dormitory access, electronic dormitory access is being phased in gradually as part of renovations. OU has a fully sworn, 24/7 police department.
Student services: health clinic, personal/psychological counseling, women's center, legal services.

COSTS & FINANCIAL AID
Costs (2014–15) ***Tuition:*** state resident $10,602 full-time, $502 per semester hour part-time; nonresident $19,566 full-time, $944 per semester hour part-time. Full-time tuition and fees vary according to degree level, location, program, and reciprocity agreements. Part-time tuition and fees vary according to course load, degree level, location, program, and reciprocity agreements. No tuition increase for student's term of enrollment. ***Room and board:*** $10,478; room only: $6050. Room and board charges vary according to board plan. ***Payment plan:*** installment. ***Waivers:*** senior citizens and employees or children of employees.
Financial Aid Of all full-time matriculated undergraduates who enrolled in 2014, 12,640 applied for aid, 10,181 were judged to have need, 2,342 had their need fully met. 720 Federal Work-Study jobs (averaging $1871). In 2014, 523 non-need-based awards were made. ***Average percent of need met:*** 43. ***Average financial aid package:*** $8397. ***Average need-based loan:*** $3661. ***Average need-based gift aid:*** $6184. ***Average non-need-based aid:*** $2942. ***Average indebtedness upon graduation:*** $27,645.

APPLYING
Standardized Tests *Required:* SAT or ACT (for admission).
Options: electronic application, early admission, deferred entrance.
Application fee: $45.
Required: high school transcript. ***Required for some:*** essay or personal statement, 2 letters of recommendation, interview, Auditions required for music and dance; interview and portfolio reviews for visual communication, and application supplement for Honors Tutorial College. ***Recommended:*** 2 letters of recommendation.
Application deadlines: 2/1 (freshmen), 2/1 (out-of-state freshmen), 6/15 (transfers).
Notification: continuous (freshmen), continuous (out-of-state freshmen), continuous (transfers).

CONTACT
Undergraduate Admissions, Ohio University, Athens, OH 45701-2979. *Phone:* 740-593-4100. *Fax:* 740-593-0560. *E-mail:* admissions@ohio.edu.

Ohio University–Zanesville
Zanesville, Ohio
http://www.zanesville.ohiou.edu/

- **State-supported** 4-year, founded 1946
- **Rural** 179-acre campus with easy access to Columbus
- **Coed**
- **Noncompetitive** entrance level

FACULTY
Student/faculty ratio: 23:1.

ACADEMICS
Calendar: quarters. *Degrees:* associate and bachelor's (offers first 2 years of most bachelor's degree programs available at the main campus in Athens; also offers several bachelor's degree programs that can be completed at this campus; also offers some graduate courses).

STUDENT LIFE
Activities and organizations: drama/theater group, student-run newspaper, radio station, Student Senate, Student Nurses Association, Good Intentions Group, Green Bobcats, Habitat for Humanity Club.
Campus security: student patrols, late-night transport/escort service, night security.
Student services: personal/psychological counseling.

FINANCIAL AID
Financial Aid Of all full-time matriculated undergraduates who enrolled in 2014, 812 applied for aid, 675 were judged to have need, 74 had their need fully met. 17 Federal Work-Study jobs (averaging $1226). In 2014, 10 non-need-based awards were made. ***Average percent of need met:*** 51. ***Average financial aid package:*** $6948. ***Average need-based loan:*** $2562. ***Average need-based gift aid:*** $5288. ***Average non-need-based aid:*** $3405. ***Average indebtedness upon graduation:*** $27,645.

APPLYING
Standardized Tests *Required for some:* SAT or ACT (for admission).
Options: electronic application.
Application fee: $20.
Required: high school transcript.

CONTACT
Ohio University–Zanesville, Office of Student Services, 1425 Newark Road, Zanesville, OH 43701. *Phone:* 740-588-1440. *Fax:* 740-588-1444. *E-mail:* ouzservices@ohio.edu.

Ohio Wesleyan University

Delaware, Ohio

http://www.owu.edu/

- **Independent United Methodist** 4-year, founded 1842
- **Small-town** 200-acre campus with easy access to Columbus
- **Endowment** $215,000
- **Coed** 1,734 undergraduate students, 99% full-time, 54% women, 46% men
- **Very difficult** entrance level, 74% of applicants were admitted

UNDERGRAD STUDENTS

1,717 full-time, 17 part-time. 54% are from out of state; 7% Black or African American, non-Hispanic/Latino; 4% Hispanic/Latino; 2% Asian, non-Hispanic/Latino; 0.1% American Indian or Alaska Native, non-Hispanic/Latino; 5% Two or more races, non-Hispanic/Latino; 3% Race/ethnicity unknown; 7% international; 1% transferred in; 96% live on campus.

Freshmen

Admission: 3,981 applied, 2,958 admitted, 458 enrolled. ***Average high school GPA:*** 3.46. ***Test scores:*** SAT critical reading scores over 500: 75%; SAT math scores over 500: 75%; SAT writing scores over 500: 74%; ACT scores over 18: 98%; SAT critical reading scores over 600: 31%; SAT math scores over 600: 32%; SAT writing scores over 600: 29%; ACT scores over 24: 65%; SAT critical reading scores over 700: 5%; SAT math scores over 700: 4%; SAT writing scores over 700: 6%; ACT scores over 30: 14%.

Retention: 79% of full-time freshmen returned.

FACULTY

Total: 219, 65% full-time.

Student/faculty ratio: 10:1.

ACADEMICS

Calendar: semesters. *Degree:* bachelor's.

Special study options: double majors, honors programs, internships, off-campus study, services for LD students, student-designed majors, study abroad, summer session for credit. ***ROTC:*** Army (c), Air Force (c).

Unusual degree programs: 3-2 engineering with Alfred University, California Institute of Technology, Case Western Reserve University, Polytechnic University, Rensselaer Polytechnic Institute, Washington University in St. Louis.

Computers: Students can access the following: campus intranet, computer help desk, free student e-mail accounts, online (class) grades, online (class) registration, online (class) schedules. Campuswide network is available. 100% of college-owned or -operated housing units are wired for high-speed Internet access. Wireless service is available via entire campus.

STUDENT LIFE

Housing options: on-campus residence required through senior year; coed, men-only, women-only. Campus housing is university owned. Freshman campus housing is guaranteed.

Activities and organizations: drama/theater group, student-run newspaper, radio station, choral group, national fraternities, national sororities.

Athletics Member NCAA. All Division III. ***Intercollegiate sports:*** baseball M, basketball M/W, cross-country running M/W, equestrian sports M(c)/W(c), field hockey W, football M, golf M, ice hockey M(c)/W(c), lacrosse M/W, rugby M(c)/W(c), sailing M(c)/W(c), soccer M/W, softball W, swimming and diving M/W, tennis M/W, track and field M/W, ultimate Frisbee M(c)/W(c), volleyball M(c)/W. ***Intramural sports:*** badminton M/W, basketball M/W, football M/W, golf M/W, lacrosse M/W, racquetball M/W, skiing (cross-country) M/W, skiing (downhill) M/W, soccer M/W, softball M/W, squash M/W, swimming and diving M/W, tennis M/W, track and field M/W, volleyball M/W, water polo M/W.

Campus security: 24-hour emergency response devices and patrols, late-night transport/escort service, controlled dormitory access.

Student services: health clinic, personal/psychological counseling, women's center.

COSTS & FINANCIAL AID

Costs (2014–15) ***Comprehensive fee:*** $53,130 includes full-time tuition ($41,660), mandatory fees ($260), and room and board ($11,210). Full-time tuition and fees vary according to course load. Part-time tuition: $4523 per unit. Part-time tuition and fees vary according to course load. ***College room only:*** $6050. Room and board charges vary according to board plan and housing facility. ***Payment plan:*** installment. ***Waivers:*** employees or children of employees.

Financial Aid Of all full-time matriculated undergraduates who enrolled in 2013, 1,428 applied for aid, 1,265 were judged to have need, 308 had their need fully met. In 2013, 525 non-need-based awards were made. ***Average percent of need met:*** 78. ***Average financial aid package:*** $30,917. ***Average need-based loan:*** $4582. ***Average need-based gift aid:*** $25,921. ***Average non-need-based aid:*** $21,940. ***Average indebtedness upon graduation:*** $28,516.

APPLYING

Standardized Tests *Required for some:* SAT or ACT (for admission).

Options: electronic application, early admission, early decision, early action, deferred entrance.

Required: essay or personal statement, high school transcript, minimum 2.5 GPA, 1 letter of recommendation. ***Recommended:*** 2 letters of recommendation, interview.

Application deadlines: 3/1 (freshmen), 3/1 (out-of-state freshmen), rolling (transfers), 12/15 (early action).

Early decision deadline: 11/15.

Notification: continuous (freshmen), continuous (out-of-state freshmen), continuous (transfers), 12/1 (early decision), 1/15 (early action).

CONTACT

Ms. Alisha Couch, Director of Admission, Ohio Wesleyan University, 61 South Sandusky Street, Delaware, OH 43015. *Phone:* 740-368-3099. *Toll-free phone:* 800-922-8953. *Fax:* 740-368-3314. *E-mail:* amcouch@owu.edu.

Otterbein University

Westerville, Ohio

http://www.otterbein.edu/

- **Independent United Methodist** comprehensive, founded 1847
- **Suburban** 142-acre campus with easy access to Columbus
- **Endowment** $85.6 million
- **Coed**
- **Moderately difficult** entrance level

FACULTY

Student/faculty ratio: 11:1.

ACADEMICS

Calendar: quarters. *Degrees:* bachelor's, master's, doctoral, and post-master's certificates.

STUDENT LIFE

Housing options: on-campus residence required through junior year; coed, men-only, women-only. Campus housing is university owned. Freshman campus housing is guaranteed.

Activities and organizations: drama/theater group, student-run newspaper, radio and television station, choral group, marching band, musical groups, Honoraries, academic interest clubs, Governance, national fraternities.

Athletics Member NCAA. All Division III.

Campus security: 24-hour emergency response devices and patrols, student patrols, late-night transport/escort service, controlled dormitory access, 24-hour locked residence hall entrances.

Student services: health clinic, personal/psychological counseling.

COSTS & FINANCIAL AID

Costs (2014–15) ***Comprehensive fee:*** $41,084 includes full-time tuition ($31,424), mandatory fees ($200), and room and board ($9460). Full-time tuition and fees vary according to course load and program. Part-time tuition: $564 per credit hour. Part-time tuition and fees vary according to course load and program. ***Room and board:*** Room and board charges vary according to board plan and housing facility.

Financial Aid Of all full-time matriculated undergraduates who enrolled in 2014, 1,841 applied for aid, 1,632 were judged to have need, 249 had their need fully met. 757 Federal Work-Study jobs (averaging $1616). 250 state and other part-time jobs (averaging $1500). In 2014, 460 non-need-based awards were made. ***Average percent of need met:*** 75. ***Average financial aid package:*** $23,051. ***Average need-based loan:*** $6531. ***Average need-based gift aid:*** $17,629. ***Average non-need-based aid:*** $16,204. ***Average indebtedness upon graduation:*** $37,388.

APPLYING

Standardized Tests *Required:* SAT or ACT (for admission).

Options: electronic application, deferred entrance.

Application fee: $25.

Required: high school transcript. ***Required for some:*** essay or personal statement, 1 letter of recommendation. ***Recommended:*** minimum 2.5 GPA, interview.

CONTACT

Mr. Ben Shoemaker, Director of Admissions, Otterbein University, 1 South Grove Street, Office Of Admission, Westerville, OH 43081-9924. *Phone:* 614-823-1500. *Toll-free phone:* 800-488-8144. *Fax:* 614-823-1200. *E-mail:* uotterb@otterbein.edu.

Shawnee State University

Portsmouth, Ohio

http://www.shawnee.edu/

- **State-supported** comprehensive, founded 1986
- **Small-town** 52-acre campus
- **Endowment** $18.1 million
- **Coed** 4,114 undergraduate students, 80% full-time, 57% women, 43% men
- **Noncompetitive** entrance level, 74% of applicants were admitted

UNDERGRAD STUDENTS

3,309 full-time, 805 part-time. Students come from 26 states and territories; 21 other countries; 10% are from out of state; 5% Black or African American, non-Hispanic/Latino; 0.6% Hispanic/Latino; 0.3% Asian, non-Hispanic/Latino; 0.6% American Indian or Alaska Native, non-Hispanic/Latino; 2% Two or more races, non-Hispanic/Latino; 5% Race/ethnicity unknown; 1% international; 6% transferred in; 24% live on campus.

Freshmen

Admission: 3,686 applied, 2,733 admitted, 955 enrolled. ***Test scores:*** SAT critical reading scores over 500: 56%; SAT math scores over 500: 70%; SAT writing scores over 500: 45%; ACT scores over 18: 76%; SAT critical reading scores over 600: 22%; SAT math scores over 600: 38%; SAT writing scores over 600: 9%; ACT scores over 24: 26%; SAT critical reading scores over 700: 2%; SAT math scores over 700: 4%; ACT scores over 30: 2%.

Retention: 57% of full-time freshmen returned.

FACULTY

Total: 311, 47% full-time, 28% with terminal degrees.

Student/faculty ratio: 18:1.

ACADEMICS

Calendar: semesters. *Degrees:* certificates, associate, bachelor's, and master's.

Special study options: academic remediation for entering students, accelerated degree program, adult/continuing education programs, advanced placement credit, distance learning, double majors, English as a second language, honors programs, independent study, internships, off-campus study, part-time degree program, services for LD students, student-designed majors, study abroad, summer session for credit.

Unusual degree programs: 3-2 psychology (MOT).

Computers: 620 computers/terminals are available on campus for general student use. Students can access the following: campus intranet, computer help desk, free student e-mail accounts, online (class) grades, online (class) registration, online (class) schedules, financial aid, student billing, courses, student service portal. Campuswide network is available. 100% of college-owned or -operated housing units are wired for high-speed Internet access. Wireless service is available via entire campus.

STUDENT LIFE

Housing options: on-campus residence required for freshman year; coed. Campus housing is university owned and leased by the school. Freshman applicants given priority for college housing.

Activities and organizations: drama/theater group, student-run newspaper, choral group, campus ministry, Health Executives and Administrators Learning Society, Student Programming Board, Student Government Association, national fraternities.

Athletics Member NAIA. ***Intercollegiate sports:*** baseball M(s), basketball M(s)/W(s), cross-country running M(s)/W(s), golf M(s), soccer M(s)/W(s), softball W, tennis W(s), volleyball W(s). ***Intramural sports:*** basketball M/W, bowling M/W, golf M/W, racquetball M/W, softball M, swimming and diving M/W, table tennis M/W, tennis M/W, volleyball M/W.

Campus security: 24-hour emergency response devices and patrols.

Student services: health clinic, personal/psychological counseling, women's center.

COSTS

Costs (2014–15) ***Tuition:*** state resident $6251 full-time, $260 per credit hour part-time; nonresident $11,504 full-time, $479 per credit hour part-time. Full-time tuition and fees vary according to course load and reciprocity agreements. Part-time tuition and fees vary according to course load and reciprocity agreements. ***Required fees:*** $1113 full-time, $46 per credit hour part-time. ***Room and board:*** $9552; room only: $6024. Room and board charges vary according to board plan and housing facility. ***Payment plan:*** installment. ***Waivers:*** senior citizens and employees or children of employees.

APPLYING

Standardized Tests *Required:* SAT or ACT (for admission). *Required for some:* ACT (for admission), SAT or ACT (for admission). *Recommended:* ACT (for admission), SAT or ACT (for admission).

Options: electronic application, deferred entrance.

Required: high school transcript.

Application deadlines: rolling (freshmen), rolling (out-of-state freshmen), rolling (transfers).

Notification: continuous (freshmen), continuous (out-of-state freshmen), continuous (transfers).

CONTACT

Mr. Rick Merb, Interim Director of Admissions, Shawnee State University, 940 Second St, Portsmouth, OH 45662. *Phone:* 740-351-3576. *Toll-free phone:* 800-959-2SSU. *Fax:* 740-351-3111. *E-mail:* rmerb@shawnee.edu.

South University

Cleveland, Ohio

http://www.southuniversity.edu/cleveland.aspx

- **Proprietary** comprehensive
- **Coed**

ACADEMICS

Degrees: associate, bachelor's, and master's.

CONTACT

South University, 4743 Richmond Road, Cleveland, OH 44128. *Phone:* 216-755-5000. *Toll-free phone:* 855-398-9280.

Tiffin University

Tiffin, Ohio

http://www.tiffin.edu/

- **Independent** comprehensive, founded 1888
- **Small-town** 110-acre campus with easy access to Toledo
- **Coed** 3,014 undergraduate students, 65% full-time, 54% women, 46% men
- **Moderately difficult** entrance level, 54% of applicants were admitted

UNDERGRAD STUDENTS

1,964 full-time, 1,050 part-time. Students come from 50 states and territories; 29 other countries; 34% are from out of state; 14% Black or African American, non-Hispanic/Latino; 2% Hispanic/Latino; 0.4% Asian, non-Hispanic/Latino; 0.1% American Indian or Alaska Native, non-Hispanic/Latino; 2% Two or more races, non-Hispanic/Latino; 35% Race/ethnicity unknown; 6% international; 7% transferred in; 25% live on campus.

Freshmen
Admission: 4,384 applied, 2,367 admitted, 514 enrolled. ***Average high school GPA:*** 2.99. ***Test scores:*** SAT critical reading scores over 500: 15%; SAT math scores over 500: 33%; ACT scores over 18: 78%; SAT critical reading scores over 600: 2%; SAT math scores over 600: 4%; ACT scores over 24: 19%; SAT critical reading scores over 700: 2%; SAT math scores over 700: 2%.

Retention: 62% of full-time freshmen returned.

FACULTY
Total: 306, 24% full-time, 32% with terminal degrees.

Student/faculty ratio: 15:1.

ACADEMICS
Calendar: semesters. *Degrees:* certificates, associate, bachelor's, master's, post-master's, and postbachelor's certificates.

Special study options: academic remediation for entering students, accelerated degree program, adult/continuing education programs, advanced placement credit, distance learning, double majors, English as a second language, external degree program, freshman honors college, honors programs, independent study, internships, off-campus study, services for LD students, study abroad, summer session for credit. ***ROTC:*** Army (c), Air Force (c).

Computers: 280 computers/terminals are available on campus for general student use. Students can access the following: campus intranet, computer help desk, free student e-mail accounts, online (class) grades, online (class) registration, online (class) schedules. Campuswide network is available. 100% of college-owned or -operated housing units are wired for high-speed Internet access. Wireless service is available via classrooms, computer centers, computer labs, dorm rooms, learning centers, libraries, student centers.

STUDENT LIFE
Housing options: on-campus residence required through sophomore year; coed, men-only, women-only, special housing for students with disabilities. Campus housing is university owned and leased by the school. Freshman campus housing is guaranteed.

Activities and organizations: drama/theater group, student-run newspaper, choral group, marching band, Student Government Association, H2O, International Student Association, Global Affairs Organization, Circle K, national fraternities, national sororities.

Athletics Member NCAA. All Division II. ***Intercollegiate sports:*** baseball M(s), basketball M(s)/W(s), cheerleading M(s)/W(s), cross-country running M(s)/W(s), equestrian sports M(s)/W(s), football M(s), golf M(s)/W(s), lacrosse W(s), soccer M(s)/W(s), softball W(s), swimming and diving M(s)/W(s), tennis M(s)/W(s), track and field M(s)/W(s), volleyball W(s), wrestling M(s). ***Intramural sports:*** basketball M/W, bowling M/W, equestrian sports M(c)/W(c), football M, rugby M(c), soccer M/W, softball M/W, table tennis M/W, tennis M/W, ultimate Frisbee M/W, volleyball M/W, weight lifting M/W.

Campus security: 24-hour emergency response devices, student patrols, late-night transport/escort service, controlled dormitory access.

Student services: health clinic, personal/psychological counseling, women's center.

COSTS & FINANCIAL AID
Costs (2014–15) ***Comprehensive fee:*** $31,430 includes full-time tuition ($21,510), mandatory fees ($50), and room and board ($9870). Full-time tuition and fees vary according to course load, degree level, location, and program. Part-time tuition: $717 per credit. Part-time tuition and fees vary according to course load, degree level, location, and program. ***College room only:*** $5120. Room and board charges vary according to board plan and housing facility. ***Payment plans:*** installment, deferred payment. ***Waivers:*** senior citizens and employees or children of employees.

Financial Aid Of all full-time matriculated undergraduates who enrolled in 2014, 1,690 applied for aid, 1,573 were judged to have need, 222 had their need fully met. ***Average percent of need met:*** 68. ***Average financial aid package:*** $17,005. ***Average need-based loan:*** $4133. ***Average need-based gift aid:*** $12,701. ***Average indebtedness upon graduation:*** $32,679.

APPLYING
Standardized Tests *Required for some:* SAT or ACT (for admission).

Options: electronic application.

Application fee: $20.

Required: high school transcript. ***Required for some:*** essay or personal statement, interview. ***Recommended:*** minimum 3.0 GPA.

Notification: continuous (transfers).

CONTACT
Mrs. Sarah Johnson, Director of Undergraduate Admissions, Tiffin University, 155 Miami Street, Tiffin, OH 44883. *Phone:* 419-448-3014. *Toll-free phone:* 800-968-6446. *Fax:* 419-443-5006. *E-mail:* borichj@tiffin.edu.

Union Institute & University

Cincinnati, Ohio

http://www.myunion.edu/

- **Independent** university, founded 1969
- **Urban** 5-acre campus with easy access to Cincinnati
- **Endowment** $2.3 million
- **Coed** 1,058 undergraduate students, 53% full-time, 51% women, 49% men
- **Noncompetitive** entrance level

UNDERGRAD STUDENTS
558 full-time, 500 part-time. Students come from 42 states and territories; 1 other country; 13% are from out of state; 19% Black or African American, non-Hispanic/Latino; 26% Hispanic/Latino; 1% Asian, non-Hispanic/Latino; 0.3% Native Hawaiian or other Pacific Islander, non-Hispanic/Latino; 0.4% American Indian or Alaska Native, non-Hispanic/Latino; 3% Two or more races, non-Hispanic/Latino; 7% Race/ethnicity unknown; 28% transferred in.

Freshmen
Admission: 17 enrolled.

FACULTY
Total: 298, 11% full-time, 40% with terminal degrees.

Student/faculty ratio: 9:1.

ACADEMICS
Calendar: trimesters some programs offer split (8wk) sessions. *Degrees:* bachelor's, master's, doctoral, and post-master's certificates.

Special study options: academic remediation for entering students, accelerated degree program, advanced placement credit, distance learning, double majors, external degree program, independent study, internships, off-campus study, part-time degree program, services for LD students, student-designed majors, summer session for credit.

Computers: 65 computers/terminals are available on campus for general student use. Students can access the following: computer help desk, free student e-mail accounts, online (class) grades, online (class) registration, online (class) schedules, CampusWeb-online access to basic information and grades. Campuswide network is available. 100% of college-owned or -operated housing units are wired for high-speed Internet access. Wireless service is available via classrooms, computer labs.

STUDENT LIFE
Housing options: college housing not available.

Campus security: 24-hour emergency response devices, late-night transport/escort service, security personnel on site during business and class hours.

COSTS
Costs (2014–15) ***Tuition:*** $11,760 full-time, $490 per semester hour part-time. Full-time tuition and fees vary according to course load. Part-time tuition and fees vary according to course load. ***Required fees:*** $144 full-time, $36 per term part-time. ***Payment plan:*** installment. ***Waivers:*** employees or children of employees.

APPLYING
Options: electronic application, deferred entrance.

Required: essay or personal statement, Recommendation from program faculty. ***Required for some:*** high school transcript, 1 letter of recommendation. ***Recommended:*** interview.

Application deadlines: rolling (freshmen), rolling (out-of-state freshmen), rolling (transfers).

Notification: continuous (freshmen), continuous (out-of-state freshmen), continuous (transfers).

CONTACT
Union Institute & University, 440 East McMillan Street, Cincinnati, OH 45206-1925. *Phone:* 513-487-1173. *Toll-free phone:* 800-486-3116.

The University of Akron

Akron, Ohio

http://www.uakron.edu/

- **State-supported** university, founded 1870
- **Urban** 223-acre campus with easy access to Cleveland
- **Endowment** $228.0 million
- **Coed** 19,723 undergraduate students, 79% full-time, 48% women, 52% men
- **Moderately difficult** entrance level, 96% of applicants were admitted

UNDERGRAD STUDENTS
15,512 full-time, 4,211 part-time. Students come from 39 states and territories; 60 other countries; 4% are from out of state; 13% Black or African American, non-Hispanic/Latino; 2% Hispanic/Latino; 2% Asian, non-Hispanic/Latino; 0.1% Native Hawaiian or other Pacific Islander, non-Hispanic/Latino; 0.2% American Indian or Alaska Native, non-Hispanic/Latino; 3% Two or more races, non-Hispanic/Latino; 3% Race/ethnicity unknown; 2% international; 4% transferred in; 14% live on campus.

Freshmen
Admission: 13,109 applied, 12,546 admitted, 3,780 enrolled. ***Average high school GPA:*** 3.21. ***Test scores:*** SAT critical reading scores over 500: 57%; SAT math scores over 500: 63%; ACT scores over 18: 84%; SAT critical reading scores over 600: 23%; SAT math scores over 600: 31%; ACT scores over 24: 38%; SAT critical reading scores over 700: 5%; SAT math scores over 700: 8%; ACT scores over 30: 7%.

Retention: 74% of full-time freshmen returned.

FACULTY
Total: 1,601, 49% full-time, 55% with terminal degrees.
Student/faculty ratio: 19:1.

ACADEMICS
Calendar: semesters. *Degrees:* certificates, associate, bachelor's, master's, doctoral, post-master's, and postbachelor's certificates.

Special study options: academic remediation for entering students, accelerated degree program, adult/continuing education programs, advanced placement credit, cooperative education, distance learning, double majors, English as a second language, external degree program, freshman honors college, honors programs, independent study, internships, part-time degree program, services for LD students, student-designed majors, study abroad, summer session for credit. ***ROTC:*** Army (b), Air Force (c).

Unusual degree programs: 3-2 business administration; engineering; BS/MD (NEOUCOM), BS/MS Polymer Chemistry.

Computers: 3,150 computers/terminals and 16,000 ports are available on campus for general student use. Students can access the following: campus intranet, computer help desk, free student e-mail accounts, online (class) grades, online (class) registration, online (class) schedules, library laptops for student checkout. Campuswide network is available. 100% of college-owned or -operated housing units are wired for high-speed Internet access. Wireless service is available via entire campus.

STUDENT LIFE
Housing options: on-campus residence required for freshman year; coed, men-only, women-only. Campus housing is university owned. Freshman applicants given priority for college housing.

Activities and organizations: drama/theater group, student-run newspaper, radio and television station, choral group, marching band, AK-Rowdies, Akron Animation Association, National Society of Leadership and Success, Golden Key International Honor Society, Alpha Phi Omega, national fraternities, national sororities.

Athletics Member NCAA. All Division I except football (Division I-A). ***Intercollegiate sports:*** baseball M(s), basketball M(s)/W(s), cheerleading M/W, cross-country running M(s)/W(s), golf M(s)/W(s), riflery M/W(s), soccer M(s)/W(s), softball W(s), swimming and diving W(s), tennis W(s), track and field M(s)/W(s), volleyball W(s). ***Intramural sports:*** badminton M/W, basketball M/W, bowling M/W, cross-country running M/W, golf M/W, racquetball M/W, skiing (cross-country) M/W, skiing (downhill) M/W, soccer M/W, softball M/W, swimming and diving M/W, table tennis M/W, track and field M/W, volleyball W, wrestling M.

Campus security: 24-hour emergency response devices and patrols, student patrols, late-night transport/escort service, controlled dormitory access.

Student services: health clinic, personal/psychological counseling, women's center, legal services.

COSTS & FINANCIAL AID
Costs (2014–15) ***Tuition:*** state resident $8618 full-time, $359 per credit hour part-time; nonresident $17,149 full-time, $714 per credit hour part-time. Full-time tuition and fees vary according to course load, degree level, location, and program. Part-time tuition and fees vary according to course load, degree level, location, and program. ***Required fees:*** $1642 full-time. ***Room and board:*** $10,968; room only: $7020. Room and board charges vary according to board plan and housing facility. ***Payment plan:*** installment. ***Waivers:*** senior citizens and employees or children of employees.

Financial Aid Of all full-time matriculated undergraduates who enrolled in 2013, 13,592 applied for aid, 12,085 were judged to have need, 882 had their need fully met. 540 Federal Work-Study jobs (averaging $2147). 3,563 state and other part-time jobs (averaging $2716). In 2013, 866 non-need-based awards were made. ***Average percent of need met:*** 46. ***Average financial aid package:*** $7118. ***Average need-based loan:*** $4535. ***Average need-based gift aid:*** $5711. ***Average non-need-based aid:*** $4300. ***Average indebtedness upon graduation:*** $23,124.

APPLYING
Standardized Tests *Required:* SAT or ACT (for admission).
Options: electronic application, early action, deferred entrance.
Application fee: $45.
Required: high school transcript. ***Required for some:*** essay or personal statement, 3 letters of recommendation, interview.
Application deadlines: 8/11 (freshmen), rolling (transfers), 11/1 (early action).
Notification: 9/15 (freshmen), continuous (transfers).

CONTACT
Ms. Kimberley Gentile, Senior Associate Director of Admissions Outreach, The University of Akron, Office of Admissions, Simmons Hall 109N. *Phone:* 330-972-6345. *Toll-free phone:* 800-655-4884. *E-mail:* gentile@uakron.edu.

The University of Akron Wayne College

Orrville, Ohio

http://www.wayne.uakron.edu/

- **State-supported** primarily 2-year, founded 1972, part of The University of Akron
- **Rural** 157-acre campus
- **Coed**
- **Noncompetitive** entrance level

FACULTY
Student/faculty ratio: 20:1.

ACADEMICS
Calendar: semesters. *Degrees:* certificates, associate, and bachelor's.

STUDENT LIFE
Housing options: college housing not available.

Activities and organizations: Associated Student Government (ASG), Campus Crusade for Christ (CRU), Waynessence, Nursing Club, Adult Learner Student Organization (ALSO).

Campus security: 24-hour emergency response devices, late-night transport/escort service.

Student services: personal/psychological counseling.

COSTS & FINANCIAL AID
Costs (2014–15) ***Tuition:*** state resident $5940 full-time, $248 per credit hour part-time; nonresident $14,281 full-time, $526 per credit hour part-time. Full-time tuition and fees vary according to course level, course load, location, and reciprocity agreements. Part-time tuition and fees vary

according to course level, location, and reciprocity agreements. ***Required fees:*** $176 full-time, $7 per credit hour part-time.

Financial Aid Of all full-time matriculated undergraduates who enrolled in 2013, 8 Federal Work-Study jobs (averaging $2200).

APPLYING

Standardized Tests *Required for some:* SAT or ACT (for admission), ACT Compass. *Recommended:* SAT or ACT (for admission), ACT Compass.

Options: electronic application, early admission, deferred entrance.

Application fee: $40.

Required for some: high school transcript.

CONTACT

Ms. Alicia Broadus, Student Services Counselor, The University of Akron Wayne College, Orrville, OH 44667. *Phone:* 800-221-8308 Ext. 8901. *Toll-free phone:* 800-221-8308. *Fax:* 330-684-8989. *E-mail:* wayneadmissions@uakron.edu.

University of Cincinnati

Cincinnati, Ohio

http://www.uc.edu/

- **State-supported** university, founded 1819, part of University System of Ohio
- **Urban** 137-acre campus with easy access to Cincinnati
- **Endowment** $1.0 billion
- **Coed** 24,407 undergraduate students, 85% full-time, 50% women, 50% men
- **Moderately difficult** entrance level, 76% of applicants were admitted

UNDERGRAD STUDENTS

20,788 full-time, 3,619 part-time. Students come from 55 states and territories; 92 other countries; 11% are from out of state; 7% Black or African American, non-Hispanic/Latino; 3% Hispanic/Latino; 3% Asian, non-Hispanic/Latino; 0.1% Native Hawaiian or other Pacific Islander, non-Hispanic/Latino; 0.2% American Indian or Alaska Native, non-Hispanic/Latino; 3% Two or more races, non-Hispanic/Latino; 4% Race/ethnicity unknown; 4% international; 5% transferred in; 20% live on campus.

Freshmen

Admission: 16,593 applied, 12,611 admitted, 4,618 enrolled. ***Average high school GPA:*** 3.46. ***Test scores:*** SAT critical reading scores over 500: 79%; SAT math scores over 500: 86%; SAT writing scores over 500: 74%; ACT scores over 18: 100%; SAT critical reading scores over 600: 37%; SAT math scores over 600: 49%; SAT writing scores over 600: 30%; ACT scores over 24: 70%; SAT critical reading scores over 700: 8%; SAT math scores over 700: 12%; SAT writing scores over 700: 5%; ACT scores over 30: 16%.

Retention: 86% of full-time freshmen returned.

FACULTY

Total: 1,220, 98% full-time, 75% with terminal degrees.

Student/faculty ratio: 18:1.

ACADEMICS

Calendar: quarters. *Degrees:* certificates, associate, bachelor's, master's, doctoral, post-master's, and postbachelor's certificates.

Special study options: academic remediation for entering students, accelerated degree program, adult/continuing education programs, advanced placement credit, cooperative education, distance learning, double majors, English as a second language, honors programs, independent study, internships, off-campus study, services for LD students, study abroad, summer session for credit. ***ROTC:*** Army (b), Air Force (b).

Computers: 406 computers/terminals are available on campus for general student use. Students can access the following: campus intranet, computer help desk, free student e-mail accounts, online (class) grades, online (class) registration, online (class) schedules. Campuswide network is available. 100% of college-owned or -operated housing units are wired for high-speed Internet access. Wireless service is available via entire campus.

STUDENT LIFE

Housing options: on-campus residence required for freshman year; coed, men-only, women-only, special housing for students with disabilities. Campus housing is university owned, leased by the school and is provided by a third party. Freshman campus housing is guaranteed.

Activities and organizations: drama/theater group, student-run newspaper, radio station, choral group, marching band, Navigators, Criminal Justice Society, Serve Beyond Cincinnati, United Black Student Association, Engineering Tribunal, national fraternities, national sororities.

Athletics Member NCAA. All Division I except football (Division I-A). ***Intercollegiate sports:*** baseball M(s), basketball M(s)/W(s), cheerleading M/W, cross-country running M(s)/W(s), golf M(s)/W(s), lacrosse W(s), soccer M(s)/W(s), swimming and diving M(s)/W(s), tennis W(s), track and field M(s)/W(s), volleyball W(s). ***Intramural sports:*** badminton M(c)/W(c), baseball M(c), basketball M/W, bowling M(c)/W(c), crew M(c)/W(c), cross-country running M(c)/W(c), equestrian sports M(c)/W(c), fencing M(c)/W(c), football M/W, golf M(c)/W(c), gymnastics M(c)/W(c), ice hockey M(c), lacrosse M(c)/W(c), racquetball M(c)/W(c), riflery M(c)/W(c), rugby M(c)/W(c), soccer M(c)/W(c), softball W(c), swimming and diving M(c)/W(c), table tennis M(c)/W(c), tennis M(c)/W(c), track and field W(c), ultimate Frisbee M(c)/W(c), volleyball M(c)/W(c), water polo M(c)/W(c), wrestling M(c).

Campus security: 24-hour emergency response devices and patrols, student patrols, late-night transport/escort service, controlled dormitory access.

Student services: health clinic, personal/psychological counseling, women's center.

COSTS & FINANCIAL AID

Costs (2015–16) ***Tuition:*** state resident $1100 full-time, $398 per credit hour part-time; nonresident $26,334 full-time, $1098 per credit hour part-time. Full-time tuition and fees vary according to course load, degree level, location, program, and reciprocity agreements. Part-time tuition and fees vary according to course load, degree level, location, program, and reciprocity agreements. ***Required fees:*** $2218 full-time, $70 per credit hour part-time. ***Room and board:*** $10,750; room only: $6430. Room and board charges vary according to board plan and housing facility. ***Payment plan:*** installment. ***Waivers:*** employees or children of employees.

Financial Aid Of all full-time matriculated undergraduates who enrolled in 2014, 14,579 applied for aid, 11,573 were judged to have need, 429 had their need fully met. 922 Federal Work-Study jobs (averaging $3072). In 2014, 3061 non-need-based awards were made. ***Average percent of need met:*** 43. ***Average financial aid package:*** $8470. ***Average need-based loan:*** $4588. ***Average need-based gift aid:*** $5710. ***Average non-need-based aid:*** $5026. ***Average indebtedness upon graduation:*** $28,228.

APPLYING

Standardized Tests *Required:* SAT or ACT (for admission).

Options: electronic application, early action, deferred entrance.

Application fee: $50.

Required: essay or personal statement, high school transcript, minimum 2.7 GPA. ***Required for some:*** 2 letters of recommendation, audition.

Application deadlines: 3/1 (freshmen), 7/1 (transfers), 12/1 (early action).

Notification: continuous until 5/1 (freshmen), continuous until 8/1 (transfers), rolling (early action).

CONTACT

Dr. Thomas Canepa EdD, Associate Vice President, Admissions, University of Cincinnati, Office of Admissions, PO Box210091, Cincinnati, OH 45221-0091. *Phone:* 513-556-1100. *Fax:* 513-556-1105. *E-mail:* admissions@uc.edu.

University of Dayton

Dayton, Ohio

http://www.udayton.edu/

- **Independent Roman Catholic** university, founded 1850
- **Suburban** 388-acre campus with easy access to Cincinnati
- **Endowment** $518.2 million
- **Coed** 8,529 undergraduate students, 93% full-time, 47% women, 53% men
- **Moderately difficult** entrance level, 59% of applicants were admitted

UNDERGRAD STUDENTS
7,898 full-time, 631 part-time. Students come from 50 states and territories; 39 other countries; 47% are from out of state; 3% Black or African American, non-Hispanic/Latino; 3% Hispanic/Latino; 1% Asian, non-Hispanic/Latino; 0.1% American Indian or Alaska Native, non-Hispanic/Latino; 1% Two or more races, non-Hispanic/Latino; 2% Race/ethnicity unknown; 11% international; 2% transferred in; 71% live on campus.

Freshmen
Admission: 16,974 applied, 10,016 admitted, 2,173 enrolled. ***Average high school GPA:*** 3.62. ***Test scores:*** SAT critical reading scores over 500: 81%; SAT math scores over 500: 86%; SAT writing scores over 500: 79%; ACT scores over 18: 100%; SAT critical reading scores over 600: 32%; SAT math scores over 600: 42%; SAT writing scores over 600: 29%; ACT scores over 24: 81%; SAT critical reading scores over 700: 5%; SAT math scores over 700: 9%; SAT writing scores over 700: 5%; ACT scores over 30: 22%.

Retention: 91% of full-time freshmen returned.

FACULTY
Total: 929, 55% full-time.
Student/faculty ratio: 14:1.

ACADEMICS
Calendar: semesters plus 2 6-week summer terms. *Degrees:* bachelor's, master's, doctoral, post-master's, and postbachelor's certificates.
Special study options: academic remediation for entering students, accelerated degree program, adult/continuing education programs, advanced placement credit, cooperative education, distance learning, double majors, English as a second language, honors programs, independent study, internships, off-campus study, part-time degree program, services for LD students, student-designed majors, study abroad, summer session for credit. ***ROTC:*** Army (b), Air Force (c).
Unusual degree programs: 3-2 business administration; engineering.
Computers: 7,675 computers/terminals and 19,337 ports are available on campus for general student use. Students can access the following: campus intranet, computer help desk, free student e-mail accounts, online (class) grades, online (class) registration, online (class) schedules, applications, admission/enrollment status, virtual orientation, online digital resources, online courses, assistive technology, learning management system, multimedia labs, payment, cyber cafes, centrally-licensed, downloadable software and training. Campuswide network is available. 100% of college-owned or -operated housing units are wired for high-speed Internet access. Wireless service is available via entire campus.

STUDENT LIFE
Housing options: on-campus residence required through sophomore year; coed, men-only, women-only, special housing for students with disabilities. Campus housing is university owned. Freshman campus housing is guaranteed.
Activities and organizations: drama/theater group, student-run newspaper, radio and television station, choral group, marching band, Student Government Association, marching band, Red Scare (basketball student cheering section), Campus Connection, Habitat for Humanity, national fraternities, national sororities.
Athletics Member NCAA. All Division I except football (Division I-AA). ***Intercollegiate sports:*** baseball M(s), basketball M(s)/W(s), cheerleading M/W, crew W, cross-country running M(s)/W(s), golf M(s)/W, soccer M(s)/W(s), softball W(s), tennis M(s)/W(s), track and field W(s), volleyball W(s). ***Intramural sports:*** baseball M(c), basketball M(c)/W(c), bowling M/W, crew M(c), cross-country running M(c)/W(c), field hockey M(c)/W(c), football M/W, golf M(c)/W(c), gymnastics M(c)/W(c), ice hockey M(c), lacrosse M(c)/W(c), racquetball M(c)/W(c), rugby M(c)/W(c), soccer M(c)/W(c), softball M/W(c), swimming and diving M(c)/W(c), tennis M(c)/W(c), ultimate Frisbee M(c)/W(c), volleyball M(c)/W(c), water polo M(c)/W(c), wrestling M(c)/W(c).
Campus security: 24-hour emergency response devices and patrols, student patrols, late-night transport/escort service, controlled dormitory access, approximately 1,000 recorded video cameras, automated external defibrillators in high density residential facilities and other key camp.
Student services: health clinic, personal/psychological counseling, women's center.

COSTS & FINANCIAL AID
Costs (2014–15) ***Comprehensive fee:*** $49,070 includes full-time tuition ($37,230) and room and board ($11,840). Full-time tuition and fees vary according to degree level. Part-time tuition: $1241 per credit hour. Part-time tuition and fees vary according to course load and degree level. ***College room only:*** $7100. Room and board charges vary according to board plan and housing facility. ***Payment plans:*** tuition prepayment, installment, deferred payment. ***Waivers:*** adult students, senior citizens, and employees or children of employees.
Financial Aid Of all full-time matriculated undergraduates who enrolled in 2014, 5,729 applied for aid, 4,086 were judged to have need, 1,435 had their need fully met. In 2014, 2809 non-need-based awards were made. ***Average percent of need met:*** 84. ***Average financial aid package:*** $23,498. ***Average need-based loan:*** $4895. ***Average need-based gift aid:*** $20,508. ***Average non-need-based aid:*** $12,540. ***Average indebtedness upon graduation:*** $35,278.

APPLYING
Standardized Tests *Required:* SAT or ACT (for admission).
Options: electronic application, early action, deferred entrance.
Application fee: $50.
Required: essay or personal statement, high school transcript, 1 letter of recommendation. ***Required for some:*** audition for music, music therapy, music education programs.
Application deadlines: 6/15 (transfers), 12/15 (early action).
Notification: continuous (transfers), 2/1 (early action).

CONTACT
Mr. Robert Durkle, Assistant Vice President of Enrollment Management, University of Dayton, 300 College Park, Dayton, OH 45469-1310. *Phone:* 937-229-4411. *Toll-free phone:* 800-837-7433. *Fax:* 937-229-4729. *E-mail:* admission@udayton.edu.

★ The University of Findlay

Findlay, Ohio

http://www.findlay.edu/

- **Independent** comprehensive, founded 1882, affiliated with Church of God
- **Urban** 390-acre campus with easy access to Toledo
- **Endowment** $27.6 million
- **Coed** 3,967 undergraduate students, 66% full-time, 62% women, 38% men
- **Moderately difficult** entrance level, 72% of applicants were admitted

UNDERGRAD STUDENTS
2,613 full-time, 1,354 part-time. Students come from 45 states and territories; 34 other countries; 19% are from out of state; 4% Black or African American, non-Hispanic/Latino; 1% Hispanic/Latino; 1% Asian, non-Hispanic/Latino; 0.1% American Indian or Alaska Native, non-Hispanic/Latino; 2% Two or more races, non-Hispanic/Latino; 0.7% Race/ethnicity unknown; 11% international; 5% transferred in; 40% live on campus.

Freshmen
Admission: 2,715 applied, 1,954 admitted, 619 enrolled. ***Average high school GPA:*** 3.57. ***Test scores:*** SAT critical reading scores over 500: 63%; SAT math scores over 500: 69%; SAT writing scores over 500: 64%; ACT scores over 18: 93%; SAT critical reading scores over 600: 18%; SAT math scores over 600: 23%; SAT writing scores over 600: 23%; ACT scores over 24: 43%; SAT critical reading scores over 700: 2%; SAT math

scores over 700: 2%; SAT writing scores over 700: 4%; ACT scores over 30: 5%.
Retention: 81% of full-time freshmen returned.

FACULTY
Total: 278, 75% full-time, 57% with terminal degrees.
Student/faculty ratio: 16:1.

ACADEMICS
Calendar: semesters. *Degrees:* certificates, associate, bachelor's, master's, and doctoral.
Special study options: academic remediation for entering students, accelerated degree program, adult/continuing education programs, advanced placement credit, cooperative education, distance learning, double majors, English as a second language, honors programs, independent study, internships, off-campus study, part-time degree program, services for LD students, student-designed majors, study abroad, summer session for credit. ***ROTC:*** Army (c), Air Force (c).
Unusual degree programs: 3-2 nursing with Mount Carmel College of Nursing; Master of Athletic Training, Master of Occupational Therapy, Master of Physical Therapy.
Computers: 151 computers/terminals are available on campus for general student use. Students can access the following: campus intranet, computer help desk, free student e-mail accounts, online (class) grades, online (class) registration, online (class) schedules. Campuswide network is available. 100% of college-owned or -operated housing units are wired for high-speed Internet access. Wireless service is available via entire campus.

STUDENT LIFE
Housing options: on-campus residence required through sophomore year; coed, men-only, women-only, special housing for students with disabilities. Campus housing is university owned. Freshman campus housing is guaranteed.
Activities and organizations: drama/theater group, student-run newspaper, radio and television station, choral group, marching band, Campus Program Board, Pre-Vet Club, Horse Club, Circle K, International Club, national fraternities, national sororities.
Athletics Member NCAA. All Division II. ***Intercollegiate sports:*** baseball M(s), basketball M(s)/W(s), cross-country running M(s)/W(s), equestrian sports W, football M(s), golf M(s)/W(s), lacrosse W(s), soccer M(s)/W(s), softball W(s), swimming and diving M(s)/W(s), tennis M(s)/W(s), track and field M(s)/W(s), volleyball W(s), wrestling M(s). ***Intramural sports:*** basketball M/W, bowling M/W, cheerleading M/W, equestrian sports M(c)/W(c), football M/W, golf M/W, lacrosse M, racquetball M/W, rugby W, soccer M/W, tennis M/W, volleyball M/W.
Campus security: 24-hour emergency response devices and patrols, late-night transport/escort service, controlled dormitory access, security cameras in parking lots, academic buildings, residence halls and common areas.
Student services: health clinic, personal/psychological counseling, women's center.

COSTS & FINANCIAL AID
Costs (2014–15) ***Comprehensive fee:*** $39,990 includes full-time tuition ($29,716), mandatory fees ($924), and room and board ($9350). Part-time tuition: $659 per semester hour. Part-time tuition and fees vary according to course load and program. ***Required fees:*** $397 per term part-time. ***College room only:*** $4666. Room and board charges vary according to board plan and housing facility. ***Payment plan:*** installment. ***Waivers:*** children of alumni, senior citizens, and employees or children of employees.
Financial Aid Of all full-time matriculated undergraduates who enrolled in 2013, 2,031 applied for aid, 1,734 were judged to have need, 312 had their need fully met. In 2013, 369 non-need-based awards were made. ***Average percent of need met:*** 45. ***Average financial aid package:*** $17,685. ***Average need-based loan:*** $4502. ***Average need-based gift aid:*** $14,670. ***Average non-need-based aid:*** $12,083. ***Average indebtedness upon graduation:*** $34,434. ***Financial aid deadline:*** 9/1.

APPLYING
Standardized Tests *Required:* SAT or ACT (for admission).
Options: electronic application, deferred entrance.
Required: essay or personal statement, high school transcript, minimum 2.0 GPA, . ***Required for some:*** interview.

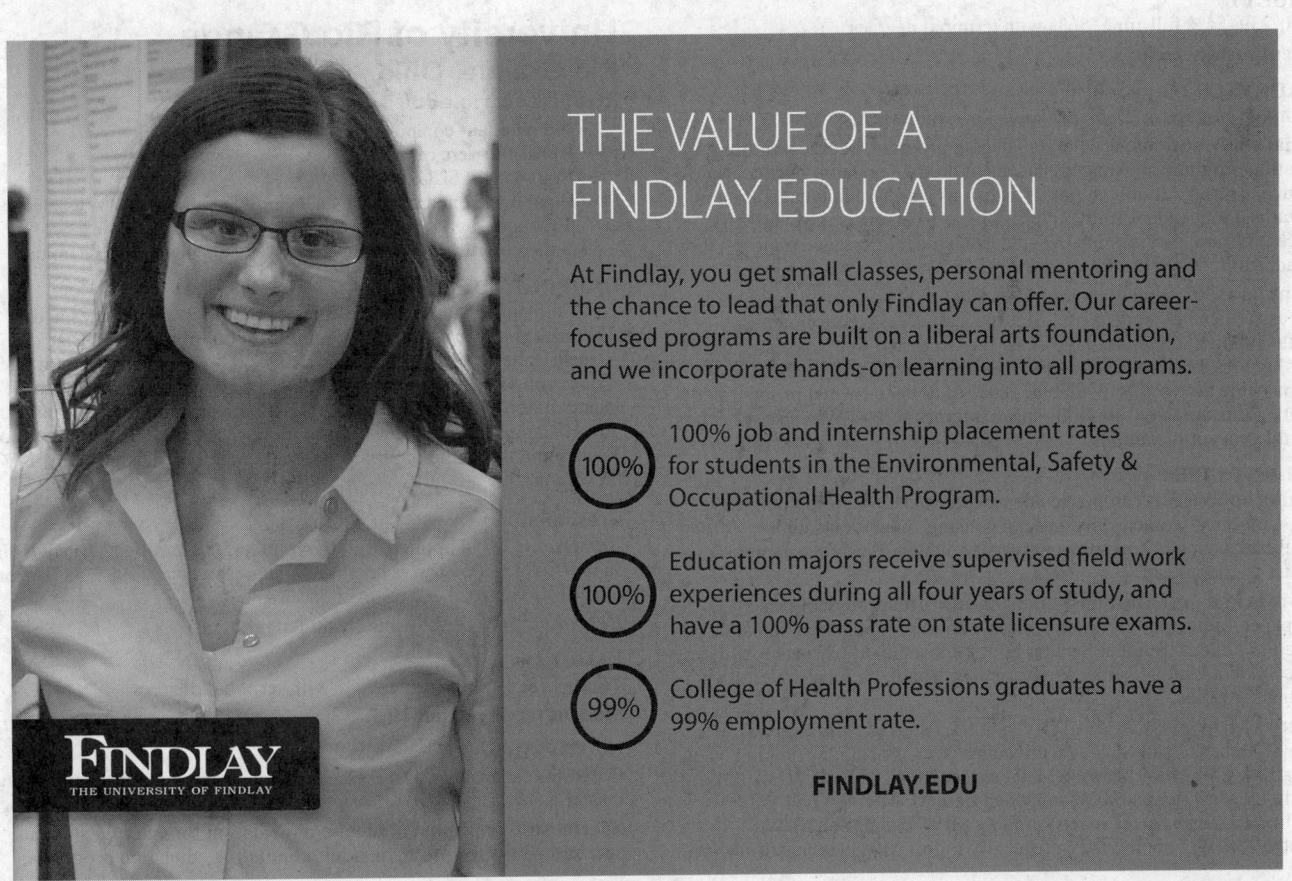

Application deadlines: rolling (freshmen), rolling (transfers).
Notification: continuous (freshmen), continuous (transfers).

CONTACT

Mr. Brandon Mooney, Assistant Director of Undergraduate Admissions, The University of Findlay, 1000 North Main Street, Findlay, OH 45840-3653. *Phone:* 419-434-4732. *Toll-free phone:* 800-548-0932. *Fax:* 419-434-4898. *E-mail:* admissions@findlay.edu.

See previous page for display ad and page 1666 for the College Close-Up.

University of Mount Union

Alliance, Ohio

http://www.mountunion.edu/

- **Independent United Methodist** comprehensive, founded 1846
- **Suburban** 122-acre campus with easy access to Cleveland
- **Endowment** $145.7 million
- **Coed** 2,174 undergraduate students, 98% full-time, 49% women, 51% men
- **Moderately difficult** entrance level, 74% of applicants were admitted

UNDERGRAD STUDENTS

2,126 full-time, 48 part-time. Students come from 33 states and territories; 19 other countries; 15% are from out of state; 6% Black or African American, non-Hispanic/Latino; 2% Hispanic/Latino; 0.6% Asian, non-Hispanic/Latino; 0.2% American Indian or Alaska Native, non-Hispanic/Latino; 4% Two or more races, non-Hispanic/Latino; 2% Race/ethnicity unknown; 3% international; 2% transferred in; 74% live on campus.

Freshmen

Admission: 2,529 applied, 1,860 admitted, 635 enrolled. ***Average high school GPA:*** 3.4. ***Test scores:*** SAT critical reading scores over 500: 40%; SAT math scores over 500: 55%; ACT scores over 18: 98%; SAT critical reading scores over 600: 5%; SAT math scores over 600: 23%; ACT scores over 24: 42%; SAT critical reading scores over 700: 1%; SAT math scores over 700: 1%; ACT scores over 30: 5%.

Retention: 78% of full-time freshmen returned.

FACULTY

Total: 239, 54% full-time, 56% with terminal degrees.

Student/faculty ratio: 13:1.

ACADEMICS

Calendar: semesters. *Degrees:* bachelor's and master's.

Special study options: accelerated degree program, adult/continuing education programs, advanced placement credit, cooperative education, distance learning, double majors, English as a second language, honors programs, independent study, internships, off-campus study, part-time degree program, services for LD students, student-designed majors, study abroad, summer session for credit. ***ROTC:*** Army (b), Air Force (c).

Computers: 265 computers/terminals and 6,000 ports are available on campus for general student use. Students can access the following: campus intranet, computer help desk, free student e-mail accounts, online (class) grades, online (class) registration, online (class) schedules. Campuswide network is available. 100% of college-owned or -operated housing units are wired for high-speed Internet access. Wireless service is available via entire campus.

STUDENT LIFE

Housing options: on-campus residence required through sophomore year; coed, men-only, women-only, special housing for students with disabilities. Campus housing is university owned. Freshman campus housing is guaranteed.

Activities and organizations: drama/theater group, student-run newspaper, radio and television station, choral group, marching band, Alpha Phi Omega, Student Senate, FCA Fellowship of Christian Athletes, Black Student Union, Raider Programming Board, national fraternities, national sororities.

Athletics Member NCAA. All Division III. ***Intercollegiate sports:*** baseball M, basketball M/W, cheerleading W, cross-country running M/W, football M, golf M/W, lacrosse M/W, soccer M/W, softball W, swimming and diving M/W, tennis M/W, track and field M/W, volleyball W, wrestling M. ***Intramural sports:*** archery M/W, badminton M/W, basketball M/W, bowling M/W, football M, golf M/W, gymnastics M/W, racquetball M/W, soccer M/W, softball M/W, swimming and diving M/W, tennis M/W, track and field M/W, volleyball M/W, weight lifting M/W.

Campus security: 24-hour emergency response devices and patrols, late-night transport/escort service, controlled dormitory access, 24-hour locked residence hall entrances, outside phones.

Student services: health clinic, personal/psychological counseling.

COSTS & FINANCIAL AID

Costs (2014–15) ***Comprehensive fee:*** $37,190 includes full-time tuition ($27,670), mandatory fees ($320), and room and board ($9200). Full-time tuition and fees vary according to course load and degree level. Part-time tuition: $1170 per credit hour. Part-time tuition and fees vary according to course load. ***Room and board:*** Room and board charges vary according to board plan and housing facility. ***Payment plans:*** tuition prepayment, installment. ***Waivers:*** children of alumni, senior citizens, and employees or children of employees.

Financial Aid Of all full-time matriculated undergraduates who enrolled in 2013, 1,811 applied for aid, 1,637 were judged to have need, 191 had their need fully met. 467 Federal Work-Study jobs (averaging $1311). 39 state and other part-time jobs (averaging $1319). In 2013, 363 non-need-based awards were made. ***Average percent of need met:*** 77. ***Average financial aid package:*** $21,420. ***Average need-based loan:*** $5733. ***Average need-based gift aid:*** $15,660. ***Average non-need-based aid:*** $10,032. ***Average indebtedness upon graduation:*** $34,586.

APPLYING

Standardized Tests *Required:* SAT or ACT (for admission).

Options: electronic application, early admission, deferred entrance.

Required: essay or personal statement, high school transcript, minimum 2.0 GPA, 1 letter of recommendation. ***Recommended:*** interview.

Application deadlines: rolling (freshmen), rolling (transfers).

Notification: continuous (freshmen), continuous (transfers).

CONTACT

Ms. Jess Canavan, Director of Admissions, University of Mount Union, 1972 Clark Avenue, Alliance, OH 44601. *Phone:* 330-823-2590. *Toll-free phone:* 800-334-6682. *Fax:* 330-823-5097. *E-mail:* admission@mountunion.edu.

University of Rio Grande

Rio Grande, Ohio

http://www.rio.edu/

- **Independent** comprehensive, founded 1876
- **Rural** 170-acre campus
- **Endowment** $23.6 million
- **Coed** 2,106 undergraduate students, 82% full-time, 64% women, 36% men
- **Noncompetitive** entrance level, 73% of applicants were admitted

UNDERGRAD STUDENTS

1,719 full-time, 387 part-time. Students come from 19 states and territories; 6 other countries; 4% are from out of state; 5% Black or African American, non-Hispanic/Latino; 0.8% Hispanic/Latino; 0.3% Asian, non-Hispanic/Latino; 0.1% Native Hawaiian or other Pacific Islander, non-Hispanic/Latino; 0.2% American Indian or Alaska Native, non-Hispanic/Latino; 0.3% Two or more races, non-Hispanic/Latino; 9% Race/ethnicity unknown; 0.8% international; 9% transferred in; 17% live on campus.

Freshmen

Admission: 1,754 applied, 1,280 admitted, 359 enrolled. ***Average high school GPA:*** 3.06. ***Test scores:*** ACT scores over 18: 70%; ACT scores over 24: 13%; ACT scores over 30: 1%.

Retention: 56% of full-time freshmen returned.

FACULTY

Total: 175, 49% full-time, 28% with terminal degrees.

Student/faculty ratio: 19:1.

ACADEMICS

Calendar: semesters. *Degrees:* certificates, associate, bachelor's, and master's.

Special study options: academic remediation for entering students, accelerated degree program, adult/continuing education programs,

advanced placement credit, cooperative education, distance learning, double majors, honors programs, independent study, internships, part-time degree program, services for LD students, student-designed majors, study abroad, summer session for credit.

Computers: 300 computers/terminals are available on campus for general student use. Students can access the following: computer help desk, free student e-mail accounts, online (class) grades, online (class) registration, online (class) schedules. Campuswide network is available. 100% of college-owned or -operated housing units are wired for high-speed Internet access. Wireless service is available via entire campus.

STUDENT LIFE
Housing options: coed, men-only, women-only. Campus housing is university owned.

Activities and organizations: drama/theater group, student-run newspaper, radio and television station, choral group, student government, Honoraries, Bible studies, ENACTA, national fraternities, national sororities.

Athletics Member NAIA. ***Intercollegiate sports:*** archery M, baseball M(s), basketball M(s)/W(s), cross-country running M(s)/W(s), soccer M(s)/W, softball W(s), track and field M(s)/W(s), volleyball W(s). ***Intramural sports:*** basketball M/W, football M, golf M, gymnastics W, racquetball M/W, soccer M/W, table tennis M/W, tennis M/W, volleyball M/W.

Campus security: 24-hour emergency response devices and patrols, late-night transport/escort service.

Student services: health clinic, personal/psychological counseling.

COSTS & FINANCIAL AID
Costs (2014–15) ***Comprehensive fee:*** $31,380 includes full-time tuition ($21,540), mandatory fees ($390), and room and board ($9450). Full-time tuition and fees vary according to course level, course load, degree level, and program. Part-time tuition: $900 per credit hour. Part-time tuition and fees vary according to course level, course load, degree level, and program. ***Waivers:*** senior citizens and employees or children of employees.

Financial Aid Of all full-time matriculated undergraduates who enrolled in 2014, 1,035 applied for aid, 1,035 were judged to have need, 736 had their need fully met. In 2014, 17 non-need-based awards were made. ***Average percent of need met:*** 87. ***Average financial aid package:*** $7030. ***Average need-based loan:*** $3191. ***Average need-based gift aid:*** $3778. ***Average non-need-based aid:*** $11,067. ***Average indebtedness upon graduation:*** $28,617.

APPLYING
Standardized Tests *Recommended:* ACT (for admission).

Options: electronic application.

Application fee: $25.

Required: high school transcript, medical history.

Application deadlines: rolling (freshmen), rolling (transfers).

Notification: continuous (freshmen), continuous (transfers).

CONTACT
Kristie Russell, Assistant Director of Admissions, University of Rio Grande, PO Box 500, Rio Grande, OH 45674. *Phone:* 740-245-7208. *Toll-free phone:* 800-282-7201. *Fax:* 740-245-7260. *E-mail:* admissions@rio.edu.

The University of Toledo

Toledo, Ohio

http://www.utoledo.edu/

- **State-supported** university, founded 1872
- **Urban** 858-acre campus with easy access to Detroit
- **Endowment** $279.9 million
- **Coed** 16,090 undergraduate students, 80% full-time, 48% women, 52% men
- **Noncompetitive** entrance level, 95% of applicants were admitted

UNDERGRAD STUDENTS
12,806 full-time, 3,284 part-time. Students come from 51 states and territories; 80 other countries; 17% are from out of state; 13% Black or African American, non-Hispanic/Latino; 5% Hispanic/Latino; 2% Asian, non-Hispanic/Latino; 0.1% Native Hawaiian or other Pacific Islander, non-Hispanic/Latino; 0.2% American Indian or Alaska Native, non-Hispanic/Latino; 3% Two or more races, non-Hispanic/Latino; 3% Race/ethnicity unknown; 5% international; 7% transferred in; 20% live on campus.

Freshmen
Admission: 10,394 applied, 9,846 admitted, 3,436 enrolled. ***Average high school GPA:*** 3.26. ***Test scores:*** ACT scores over 18: 84%; ACT scores over 24: 39%; ACT scores over 30: 6%.
Retention: 70% of full-time freshmen returned.

FACULTY
Total: 1,088, 75% full-time, 64% with terminal degrees.

Student/faculty ratio: 20:1.

ACADEMICS
Calendar: semesters. *Degrees:* certificates, associate, bachelor's, master's, doctoral, post-master's, and postbachelor's certificates.

Special study options: academic remediation for entering students, accelerated degree program, adult/continuing education programs, advanced placement credit, cooperative education, distance learning, double majors, English as a second language, freshman honors college, honors programs, independent study, internships, off-campus study, part-time degree program, services for LD students, student-designed majors, study abroad, summer session for credit. ***ROTC:*** Army (b), Air Force (c).

Unusual degree programs: 3-2 BS environmental sciences/Masters in Public Health (MPH).

Computers: 5,000 computers/terminals and 10,000 ports are available on campus for general student use. Students can access the following: campus intranet, computer help desk, free student e-mail accounts, online (class) grades, online (class) registration, online (class) schedules, online transcripts, student account. Campuswide network is available. 100% of college-owned or -operated housing units are wired for high-speed Internet access. Wireless service is available via entire campus.

STUDENT LIFE
Housing options: on-campus residence required for freshman year; coed, special housing for students with disabilities. Campus housing is university owned. Freshman campus housing is guaranteed.

Activities and organizations: drama/theater group, student-run newspaper, radio and television station, choral group, marching band, student government, University YMCA, Newman Club, International Student Association, Campus Activities and Programming, national fraternities, national sororities.

Athletics Member NCAA. All Division I except football (Division I-A). ***Intercollegiate sports:*** baseball M(s), basketball M(s)/W(s), cross-country running M(s)/W(s), golf M(s)/W(s), soccer W(s), softball W(s), swimming and diving W(s), tennis M(s)/W(s), track and field W(s), volleyball W(s). ***Intramural sports:*** badminton M/W, basketball M/W, bowling M/W, cheerleading W, crew M(c)/W(c), fencing M(c)/W(c), football M/W, golf M/W, lacrosse M/W, racquetball M/W, sailing M(c)/W(c), skiing (cross-country) M(c)/W(c), skiing (downhill) M(c)/W(c), soccer M(c)/W(c), softball M/W, swimming and diving M/W, table tennis M/W, tennis M/W, track and field M/W, volleyball M/W, water polo M/W, weight lifting M/W, wrestling M.

Campus security: 24-hour emergency response devices and patrols, student patrols, late-night transport/escort service, controlled dormitory access, bicycle patrols by security staff, crime prevention officer.

Student services: health clinic, personal/psychological counseling, women's center, legal services.

COSTS & FINANCIAL AID
Costs (2014–15) ***Tuition:*** state resident $8052 full-time, $335 per credit hour part-time; nonresident $17,390 full-time, $725 per credit hour part-time. Full-time tuition and fees vary according to course load, program, reciprocity agreements, and student level. Part-time tuition and fees vary according to course load, program, reciprocity agreements, and student level. ***Required fees:*** $1411 full-time, $58 per credit hour part-time. ***Room and board:*** $10,304; room only: $6632. Room and board charges vary according to board plan and housing facility. ***Payment plan:*** installment. ***Waivers:*** children of alumni and employees or children of employees.

Financial Aid Of all full-time matriculated undergraduates who enrolled in 2014, 10,515 applied for aid, 8,575 were judged to have need, 1,256 had their need fully met. 170 Federal Work-Study jobs (averaging $1362).

In 2014, 2899 non-need-based awards were made. ***Average percent of need met:*** 57. ***Average financial aid package:*** $11,172. ***Average need-based loan:*** $4287. ***Average need-based gift aid:*** $8683. ***Average non-need-based aid:*** $6234. ***Average indebtedness upon graduation:*** $27,928.

APPLYING

Standardized Tests *Required:* SAT or ACT (for admission).

Options: electronic application, deferred entrance.

Application fee: $40.

Required: high school transcript. ***Required for some:*** minimum 2.0 GPA, CORE high school curriculum.

CONTACT

Billy L Pierce, Director of Undergraduate Admissions, The University of Toledo, 2801 West Bancroft, Toledo, OH 43606-3390. *Phone:* 419-530-5445. *Toll-free phone:* 800-5TOLEDO. *Fax:* 419-530-5713. *E-mail:* william.pierce@utoledo.edu.

Urbana University

Urbana, Ohio

http://www.urbana.edu/

- **Independent** comprehensive, founded 1850, affiliated with Church of the New Jerusalem
- **Small-town** 128-acre campus with easy access to Columbus, Dayton
- **Endowment** $415,000
- **Coed** 1,461 undergraduate students, 62% full-time, 53% women, 47% men
- **Moderately difficult** entrance level, 65% of applicants were admitted

UNDERGRAD STUDENTS

904 full-time, 557 part-time. 4% are from out of state; 6% transferred in.

Freshmen

Admission: 495 applied, 322 admitted, 279 enrolled. ***Average high school GPA:*** 3.

Retention: 70% of full-time freshmen returned.

FACULTY

Total: 120, 46% full-time, 39% with terminal degrees.

Student/faculty ratio: 16:1.

ACADEMICS

Calendar: semesters. *Degrees:* certificates, associate, bachelor's, master's, and postbachelor's certificates.

Special study options: academic remediation for entering students, accelerated degree program, adult/continuing education programs, advanced placement credit, cooperative education, double majors, freshman honors college, honors programs, independent study, internships, off-campus study, part-time degree program, services for LD students, student-designed majors, summer session for credit.

Computers: 75 computers/terminals are available on campus for general student use. Campuswide network is available.

STUDENT LIFE

Housing options: on-campus residence required through junior year; coed, men-only, women-only. Campus housing is university owned.

Activities and organizations: drama/theater group, student-run newspaper, radio station, choral group, marching band, Student Government Association, Business Club, Education Club, Drama Club, Student Activities Planning Committee.

Athletics Member NAIA. ***Intercollegiate sports:*** baseball M(s), basketball M(s)/W(s), football M(s), golf M(s)/W(s), soccer M(s)/W(s), softball W(s), volleyball W(s). ***Intramural sports:*** basketball M/W, football M, racquetball M/W, soccer M/W, swimming and diving M/W, table tennis M/W, track and field M/W, volleyball M/W, water polo M/W, weight lifting M.

Campus security: 24-hour emergency response devices and patrols, late-night transport/escort service.

Student services: health clinic, personal/psychological counseling.

FINANCIAL AID

Financial Aid Of all full-time matriculated undergraduates who enrolled in 2006, 665 applied for aid, 614 were judged to have need, 118 had their need fully met. 124 Federal Work-Study jobs (averaging $1121). In 2006, 41 non-need-based awards were made. ***Average percent of need met:*** 71. ***Average financial aid package:*** $13,460. ***Average need-based loan:*** $4670. ***Average need-based gift aid:*** $9336. ***Average non-need-based aid:*** $11,109. ***Average indebtedness upon graduation:*** $21,322.

APPLYING

Standardized Tests *Required:* SAT or ACT (for admission).

Options: electronic application, deferred entrance.

Application fee: $25.

Required: essay or personal statement, high school transcript, minimum 2.0 GPA. ***Required for some:*** 2 letters of recommendation. ***Recommended:*** interview.

Application deadlines: rolling (freshmen), rolling (transfers).

Notification: continuous (freshmen), continuous (transfers).

CONTACT

Mr. Donnel W Wiggins, Director of Admissions, Urbana University, 579 College Way, Urbana, OH 43078. *Toll-free phone:* 800-7-URBANA. *E-mail:* admiss@urbana.edu.

Ursuline College

Pepper Pike, Ohio

http://www.ursuline.edu/

- **Independent Roman Catholic** comprehensive, founded 1871
- **Suburban** 112-acre campus with easy access to Cleveland
- **Endowment** $42.8 million
- **Coed, primarily women** 706 undergraduate students, 69% full-time, 92% women, 8% men
- **Minimally difficult** entrance level, 66% of applicants were admitted

UNDERGRAD STUDENTS

485 full-time, 221 part-time. Students come from 16 states and territories; 1 other country; 8% are from out of state; 26% Black or African American, non-Hispanic/Latino; 3% Hispanic/Latino; 1% Asian, non-Hispanic/Latino; 0.1% American Indian or Alaska Native, non-Hispanic/Latino; 3% Two or more races, non-Hispanic/Latino; 1% Race/ethnicity unknown; 1% international; 6% transferred in; 23% live on campus.

Freshmen

Admission: 374 applied, 245 admitted, 92 enrolled. ***Average high school GPA:*** 3.3. ***Test scores:*** SAT critical reading scores over 500: 52%; SAT math scores over 500: 67%; SAT writing scores over 500: 37%; ACT scores over 18: 80%; SAT critical reading scores over 600: 19%; SAT math scores over 600: 14%; SAT writing scores over 600: 14%; ACT scores over 24: 30%; SAT critical reading scores over 700: 5%.

Retention: 73% of full-time freshmen returned.

FACULTY

Total: 224, 33% full-time, 29% with terminal degrees.

Student/faculty ratio: 6:1.

ACADEMICS

Calendar: semesters. *Degrees:* certificates, bachelor's, master's, doctoral, post-master's, and postbachelor's certificates (applications from men are also accepted).

Special study options: academic remediation for entering students, accelerated degree program, adult/continuing education programs, advanced placement credit, cooperative education, distance learning, double majors, independent study, internships, off-campus study, part-time degree program, services for LD students, student-designed majors, summer session for credit. ***ROTC:*** Army (c).

Unusual degree programs: 3-2 pharmacy with University of Toledo.

Computers: 72 computers/terminals are available on campus for general student use. Students can access the following: campus intranet, computer help desk, free student e-mail accounts, online (class) grades, online (class) registration, online (class) schedules. Campuswide network is available. 100% of college-owned or -operated housing units are wired for high-speed Internet access. Wireless service is available via classrooms, computer centers, computer labs, libraries.

STUDENT LIFE
Housing options: coed, women-only. Campus housing is university owned.

Activities and organizations: drama/theater group, choral group, Student Government Association, Student Nurses of Ursuline College, Fashion Focus, Students United for Black Awareness, Drama Club.

Athletics Member NCAA. All Division II. ***Intercollegiate sports:*** basketball W(s), bowling W(s), cross-country running W(s), golf W(s), lacrosse W(s), soccer W(s), softball W(s), swimming and diving W(s), tennis W(s), track and field W(s), volleyball W(s).

Campus security: 24-hour emergency response devices and patrols, late-night transport/escort service, controlled dormitory access.

Student services: personal/psychological counseling.

COSTS & FINANCIAL AID
Costs (2015–16) ***Comprehensive fee:*** $38,010 includes full-time tuition ($28,230), mandatory fees ($290), and room and board ($9490). Full-time tuition and fees vary according to location. Part-time tuition: $565 per credit. Part-time tuition and fees vary according to location. ***Required fees:*** $100 per term part-time. ***College room only:*** $4848. Room and board charges vary according to board plan and housing facility. ***Payment plan:*** installment. ***Waivers:*** employees or children of employees.

Financial Aid Of all full-time matriculated undergraduates who enrolled in 2013, 393 applied for aid, 375 were judged to have need, 44 had their need fully met. In 2013, 39 non-need-based awards were made. ***Average percent of need met:*** 67. ***Average financial aid package:*** $20,128. ***Average need-based loan:*** $5886. ***Average need-based gift aid:*** $15,872. ***Average non-need-based aid:*** $7119. ***Average indebtedness upon graduation:*** $29,542.

APPLYING
Standardized Tests *Required:* SAT or ACT (for admission).

Options: electronic application, deferred entrance.

Application fee: $25.

Required: essay or personal statement, high school transcript, 1 letter of recommendation. ***Recommended:*** minimum 2.5 GPA, interview.

Application deadlines: 2/1 (freshmen), 2/1 (out-of-state freshmen), rolling (transfers).

Notification: continuous (freshmen), continuous (out-of-state freshmen), continuous (transfers).

CONTACT
Ursuline College, 2550 Lander Road, Pepper Pike, OH 44124-4398.
Phone: 440-449-4203. *Toll-free phone:* 888-URSULINE.

Walsh University
North Canton, Ohio
http://www.walsh.edu/

- **Independent Roman Catholic** comprehensive, founded 1958
- **Small-town** 134-acre campus with easy access to Cleveland
- **Endowment** $21.0 million
- **Coed** 2,325 undergraduate students, 82% full-time, 62% women, 38% men
- **Moderately difficult** entrance level, 81% of applicants were admitted

UNDERGRAD STUDENTS
1,895 full-time, 430 part-time. Students come from 27 states and territories; 34 other countries; 6% are from out of state; 6% Black or African American, non-Hispanic/Latino; 2% Hispanic/Latino; 0.4% Asian, non-Hispanic/Latino; 0.1% Native Hawaiian or other Pacific Islander, non-Hispanic/Latino; 0.3% American Indian or Alaska Native, non-Hispanic/Latino; 2% Two or more races, non-Hispanic/Latino; 8% Race/ethnicity unknown; 3% international; 5% transferred in; 48% live on campus.

Freshmen
Admission: 1,480 applied, 1,194 admitted, 447 enrolled. ***Average high school GPA:*** 3.37. ***Test scores:*** SAT critical reading scores over 500: 49%; SAT math scores over 500: 64%; ACT scores over 18: 95%; SAT critical reading scores over 600: 10%; SAT math scores over 600: 15%; ACT scores over 24: 37%; SAT critical reading scores over 700: 1%; SAT math scores over 700: 1%; ACT scores over 30: 4%.
Retention: 76% of full-time freshmen returned.

FACULTY
Total: 334, 40% full-time, 31% with terminal degrees.

Student/faculty ratio: 12:1.

ACADEMICS
Calendar: semesters. *Degrees:* certificates, associate, bachelor's, master's, and doctoral.

Special study options: academic remediation for entering students, accelerated degree program, adult/continuing education programs, advanced placement credit, distance learning, double majors, English as a second language, external degree program, honors programs, independent study, internships, off-campus study, part-time degree program, services for LD students, study abroad, summer session for credit.

Unusual degree programs: 3-2 behavioral science/counseling; biology/physical therapy, theology.

Computers: 336 computers/terminals and 1,622 ports are available on campus for general student use. Students can access the following: campus intranet, computer help desk, free student e-mail accounts, online (class) grades, online (class) registration, online (class) schedules. Campuswide network is available. 100% of college-owned or -operated housing units are wired for high-speed Internet access. Wireless service is available via entire campus.

STUDENT LIFE
Housing options: on-campus residence required through senior year; coed, men-only, women-only, cooperative, special housing for students with disabilities. Campus housing is university owned. Freshman campus housing is guaranteed.

Activities and organizations: drama/theater group, student-run newspaper, radio station, choral group, marching band, student government, University Programming Board, Business and Communication Club, Behavioral Science Club, Education Club.

Athletics Member NCAA. All Division II. ***Intercollegiate sports:*** baseball M(s), basketball M(s)/W(s), cheerleading W(c), cross-country running M(s)/W(s), football M(s), golf M(s)/W(s), lacrosse M(s)/W(s), soccer M(s)/W(s), softball W(s), tennis M(s)/W(s), track and field M(s)/W(s), volleyball W(s). ***Intramural sports:*** basketball M/W, bowling M/W, football M, golf M/W, skiing (downhill) M(c)/W(c), soccer M/W, table tennis M/W, tennis M/W, ultimate Frisbee M(c)/W(c), volleyball M/W.

Campus security: 24-hour emergency response devices and patrols, late-night transport/escort service, controlled dormitory access.

Student services: health clinic, personal/psychological counseling.

COSTS & FINANCIAL AID
Costs (2014–15) ***Comprehensive fee:*** $36,250 includes full-time tuition ($25,350), mandatory fees ($1320), and room and board ($9580). Full-time tuition and fees vary according to location. Part-time tuition: $845 per credit hour. Part-time tuition and fees vary according to location. ***Required fees:*** $44 per credit hour part-time. ***College room only:*** $5070. Room and board charges vary according to board plan and housing facility. ***Payment plan:*** installment. ***Waivers:*** children of alumni, senior citizens, and employees or children of employees.

Financial Aid Of all full-time matriculated undergraduates who enrolled in 2010, 1,726 applied for aid, 1,661 were judged to have need, 798 had their need fully met. In 2010, 180 non-need-based awards were made. ***Average percent of need met:*** 71. ***Average financial aid package:*** $18,133. ***Average need-based loan:*** $4850. ***Average need-based gift aid:*** $6844. ***Average non-need-based aid:*** $9372. ***Average indebtedness upon graduation:*** $24,753.

APPLYING
Standardized Tests *Required:* SAT or ACT (for admission).

Options: electronic application, early admission, deferred entrance.

Application fee: $25.

Required: high school transcript, minimum 2.4 GPA. ***Required for some:*** essay or personal statement, minimum 3.0 GPA, 2 letters of recommendation. ***Recommended:*** interview.

Application deadlines: rolling (freshmen), rolling (out-of-state freshmen), rolling (transfers).

Notification: continuous (freshmen), continuous (out-of-state freshmen), continuous (transfers).

CONTACT
Ms. Rebecca Coneglio, Director of Freshman Admission, Walsh University, 2020 East Maple, North Canton, OH 44720. *Phone:* 330-490-7190. *Toll-free phone:* 800-362-9846 (in-state); 800-362-8846 (out-of-state). *Fax:* 330-490-7165. *E-mail:* admissions@walsh.edu.

See previous page for display ad and page 1718 for the College Close-Up.

Wilberforce University

Wilberforce, Ohio

http://www.wilberforce.edu/

- **Independent** comprehensive, founded 1856, affiliated with African Methodist Episcopal Church
- **Rural** 125-acre campus with easy access to Dayton, Columbus
- **Coed** 307 undergraduate students, 94% full-time, 59% women, 41% men
- **Minimally difficult** entrance level, 38% of applicants were admitted

UNDERGRAD STUDENTS
290 full-time, 17 part-time. Students come from 8 states and territories; 40% are from out of state; 92% Black or African American, non-Hispanic/Latino; 0.9% American Indian or Alaska Native, non-Hispanic/Latino; 4% Race/ethnicity unknown; 2% international.

Freshmen
Admission: 1,243 applied, 469 admitted.

Retention: 74% of full-time freshmen returned.

FACULTY
Total: 48, 40% full-time.

Student/faculty ratio: 8:1.

ACADEMICS
Calendar: semesters. *Degrees:* bachelor's and master's.

Special study options: academic remediation for entering students, adult/continuing education programs, advanced placement credit, cooperative education, distance learning, double majors, external degree program, freshman honors college, honors programs, independent study, internships, off-campus study, study abroad. ***ROTC:*** Army (c), Air Force (c).

Computers: Students can access the following: free student e-mail accounts, online (class) grades, online (class) registration, online (class) schedules. Campuswide network is available. Wireless service is available via entire campus.

STUDENT LIFE
Housing options: on-campus residence required through junior year; coed. Campus housing is university owned. Freshman campus housing is guaranteed.

Activities and organizations: drama/theater group, student-run newspaper, radio station, choral group, national fraternities, national sororities.

Athletics Member NAIA. ***Intercollegiate sports:*** basketball M/W. ***Intramural sports:*** basketball M/W.

Campus security: 24-hour emergency response devices and patrols, controlled dormitory access.

Student services: health clinic, personal/psychological counseling.

COSTS & FINANCIAL AID
Costs (2014–15) ***Comprehensive fee:*** $20,936 includes full-time tuition ($13,250), mandatory fees ($1230), and room and board ($6456). Full-time tuition and fees vary according to course load, location, and program. Part-time tuition: $500 per credit hour. Part-time tuition and fees vary according to course load, location, and program. ***College room only:*** $3586. ***Payment plans:*** installment, deferred payment. ***Waivers:*** employees or children of employees.

Financial Aid ***Financial aid deadline:*** 6/1.

APPLYING
Standardized Tests *Required:* SAT or ACT (for admission).

Options: electronic application, early admission, early decision, deferred entrance.

Application fee: $25.

Required: essay or personal statement, high school transcript, minimum 2.5 GPA, 2 letters of recommendation.

Application deadlines: 7/1 (freshmen), 7/1 (transfers).

Notification: continuous until 8/1 (freshmen), continuous until 8/1 (transfers).

CONTACT

Ms. Dadra Driscoll, Director, Office of Admissions, Wilberforce University, 1055 N. Bickett Road, PO Box 1001, Wolfe Administration, Wilberforce, OH 45384. *Phone:* 937-708-5556. *Toll-free phone:* 800-367-8568. *E-mail:* ddriscoll@wilberforce.edu.

Wilmington College

Wilmington, Ohio

http://www.wilmington.edu/

- **Independent Friends** comprehensive, founded 1870
- **Small-town** campus
- **Coed**
- **Moderately difficult** entrance level

FACULTY

Student/faculty ratio: 14:1.

ACADEMICS

Calendar: semesters. *Degrees:* bachelor's and master's.

STUDENT LIFE

Housing options: on-campus residence required through senior year; coed, men-only, women-only. Campus housing is university owned.

Athletics Member NCAA. All Division III.

Campus security: 24-hour emergency response devices and patrols, late-night transport/escort service, controlled dormitory access.

COSTS & FINANCIAL AID

Costs (2014–15) ***Comprehensive fee:*** $38,512 includes full-time tuition ($28,420), mandatory fees ($700), and room and board ($9392). Full-time tuition and fees vary according to location. Part-time tuition: $500 per credit hour. Part-time tuition and fees vary according to course load and location. ***College room only:*** $4382. Room and board charges vary according to board plan and housing facility.

Financial Aid Of all full-time matriculated undergraduates who enrolled in 2008, 1,096 applied for aid, 1,021 were judged to have need, 306 had their need fully met. In 2008, 138 non-need-based awards were made. ***Average percent of need met:*** 81. ***Average financial aid package:*** $21,500. ***Average need-based loan:*** $6000. ***Average need-based gift aid:*** $14,300. ***Average non-need-based aid:*** $7300.

APPLYING

Standardized Tests *Recommended:* SAT or ACT (for admission).

Options: deferred entrance.

Required: high school transcript. ***Recommended:*** minimum 2.5 GPA, 1 letter of recommendation, interview.

CONTACT

Ms. Tina Garland, Director of Admission and Financial Aid, Wilmington College, 1870 Quaker Way, Wilmington, OH 45177. *Phone:* 937-382-6661 Ext. 426. *Toll-free phone:* 800-341-9318. *Fax:* 937-383-8542. *E-mail:* admissions@wilmington.edu.

★ Wittenberg University

Springfield, Ohio

http://www.wittenberg.edu/

- **Independent** comprehensive, founded 1845, affiliated with Evangelical Lutheran Church
- **Suburban** 114-acre campus with easy access to Columbus, Dayton
- **Coed** 1,948 undergraduate students, 95% full-time, 57% women, 43% men
- **Moderately difficult** entrance level, 91% of applicants were admitted

UNDERGRAD STUDENTS

1,850 full-time, 98 part-time. Students come from 37 states and territories; 25 other countries; 29% are from out of state; 7% Black or African American, non-Hispanic/Latino; 3% Hispanic/Latino; 1% Asian, non-Hispanic/Latino; 0.1% Native Hawaiian or other Pacific Islander, non-Hispanic/Latino; 0.2% American Indian or Alaska Native, non-Hispanic/Latino; 5% Two or more races, non-Hispanic/Latino; 0.9% Race/ethnicity unknown; 2% international; 2% transferred in; 86% live on campus.

Freshmen

Admission: 4,850 applied, 4,432 admitted, 516 enrolled. ***Average high school GPA:*** 3.42. ***Test scores:*** SAT critical reading scores over 500: 87%; SAT math scores over 500: 71%; SAT writing scores over 500: 95%; ACT scores over 18: 98%; SAT critical reading scores over 600: 37%; SAT math scores over 600: 28%; SAT writing scores over 600: 70%; ACT scores over 24: 64%; SAT critical reading scores over 700: 6%; SAT math scores over 700: 6%; SAT writing scores over 700: 26%; ACT scores over 30: 16%.

Retention: 80% of full-time freshmen returned.

FACULTY

Total: 185, 69% full-time, 75% with terminal degrees.

Student/faculty ratio: 13:1.

ACADEMICS

Calendar: semesters. *Degrees:* bachelor's and master's.

Special study options: academic remediation for entering students, adult/continuing education programs, advanced placement credit, cooperative education, double majors, English as a second language, freshman honors college, honors programs, independent study, internships, off-campus study, part-time degree program, student-designed majors, study abroad, summer session for credit. ***ROTC:*** Army (c), Air Force (c).

Unusual degree programs: 3-2 engineering with Georgia Institute of Technology, Washington University in St. Louis, Case Western Reserve University; forestry with Duke University; nursing with Case Western Reserve University, Johns Hopkins University; occupational therapy with Washington University in St. Louis.

Computers: 900 computers/terminals and 1,200 ports are available on campus for general student use. Students can access the following: computer help desk, free student e-mail accounts, online (class) grades, online (class) registration, online (class) schedules. Campuswide network is available. Wireless service is available via entire campus.

STUDENT LIFE

Housing options: on-campus residence required through sophomore year; coed, women-only. Campus housing is university owned, leased by the school and is provided by a third party. Freshman campus housing is guaranteed.

Activities and organizations: drama/theater group, student-run newspaper, radio station, choral group, Student Senate, Union Board, choirs, Weaver Chapel Association, national fraternities, national sororities.

Athletics Member NCAA. All Division III. ***Intercollegiate sports:*** baseball M, basketball M/W, crew M(c)/W(c), cross-country running M/W, field hockey W, football M, golf M/W, lacrosse M/W, rugby M(c)/W(c), soccer M/W, softball W, swimming and diving M/W, tennis M/W, track and field M/W, volleyball M(c)/W. ***Intramural sports:*** basketball M/W, football M, golf M/W, sailing M/W, soccer M/W, softball M/W, swimming and diving M/W, tennis M/W, track and field M/W, volleyball M/W.

Campus security: 24-hour emergency response devices and patrols, student patrols, late-night transport/escort service, controlled dormitory access, crime prevention programs.

Student services: health clinic, personal/psychological counseling, women's center.

COSTS & FINANCIAL AID

Costs (2015–16) ***Comprehensive fee:*** $48,118 includes full-time tuition ($37,230), mandatory fees ($860), and room and board ($10,028). Part-time tuition: $1241 per credit. Part-time tuition and fees vary according to course load. ***College room only:*** $5158. Room and board charges vary according to board plan and housing facility. ***Payment plan:*** installment. ***Waivers:*** minority students, children of alumni, adult students, senior citizens, and employees or children of employees.

Financial Aid Of all full-time matriculated undergraduates who enrolled in 2014, 1,623 applied for aid, 1,455 were judged to have need, 301 had their need fully met. In 2014, 373 non-need-based awards were made. ***Average percent of need met:*** 80. ***Average financial aid package:*** $31,787. ***Average need-based loan:*** $5287. ***Average need-based gift aid:***

A ★ indicates that the school has detailed information with a Premium Profile on Petersons.com.

$25,953. ***Average non-need-based aid:*** $18,495. ***Average indebtedness upon graduation:*** $30,748.

APPLYING

Standardized Tests *Recommended:* Submission of ACT/SAT test scores are optional.

Options: electronic application, early admission, early decision, early action, deferred entrance.

Application fee: $40.

Required: essay or personal statement, high school transcript, interview.

Application deadlines: rolling (transfers), 12/1 (early action).

Early decision deadline: 11/15.

Notification: continuous (freshmen), continuous (transfers), 12/15 (early decision), 1/1 (early action).

CONTACT

Ms. Karen Hunt, Director of Admission, Wittenberg University, PO Box 720, Springfield, OH 45501-0720. *Phone:* 877-206-0332 Ext. 6377. *Toll-free phone:* 800-677-7558 Ext. 6314. *Fax:* 937-327-6379. *E-mail:* admission@wittenberg.edu.

Wright State University

Dayton, Ohio

http://www.wright.edu/

- **State-supported** university, founded 1964, part of University System of Ohio
- **Suburban** 557-acre campus with easy access to Dayton, Columbus, Cincinnati
- **Endowment** $86.3 million
- **Coed** 12,682 undergraduate students, 78% full-time, 51% women, 49% men
- **Minimally difficult** entrance level, 97% of applicants were admitted

UNDERGRAD STUDENTS

9,937 full-time, 2,745 part-time. Students come from 46 states and territories; 69 other countries; 4% are from out of state; 13% Black or African American, non-Hispanic/Latino; 3% Hispanic/Latino; 2% Asian, non-Hispanic/Latino; 0.1% Native Hawaiian or other Pacific Islander, non-Hispanic/Latino; 0.3% American Indian or Alaska Native, non-Hispanic/Latino; 4% Two or more races, non-Hispanic/Latino; 0.2% Race/ethnicity unknown; 6% international; 9% transferred in; 19% live on campus.

Freshmen

Admission: 5,237 applied, 5,067 admitted, 2,284 enrolled. ***Average high school GPA:*** 3.19. ***Test scores:*** SAT critical reading scores over 500: 58%; SAT math scores over 500: 60%; SAT writing scores over 500: 45%; ACT scores over 18: 82%; SAT critical reading scores over 600: 22%; SAT math scores over 600: 20%; SAT writing scores over 600: 13%; ACT scores over 24: 33%; SAT critical reading scores over 700: 2%; SAT math scores over 700: 3%; SAT writing scores over 700: 3%; ACT scores over 30: 4%.

Retention: 66% of full-time freshmen returned.

FACULTY

Total: 654, 99% full-time.

Student/faculty ratio: 21:1.

ACADEMICS

Calendar: quarters. *Degrees:* associate, bachelor's, master's, doctoral, post-master's, and postbachelor's certificates.

Special study options: academic remediation for entering students, adult/continuing education programs, advanced placement credit, cooperative education, distance learning, double majors, English as a second language, freshman honors college, honors programs, independent study, internships, off-campus study, part-time degree program, services for LD students, student-designed majors, study abroad, summer session for credit. ***ROTC:*** Army (b), Air Force (b).

Computers: 1,700 computers/terminals are available on campus for general student use. Students can access the following: campus intranet, computer help desk, free student e-mail accounts, online (class) grades, online (class) registration, online (class) schedules, student web pages permitted; Lap tops 2 Go. Campuswide network is available. 100% of college-owned or -operated housing units are wired for high-speed Internet access. Wireless service is available via entire campus.

STUDENT LIFE

Housing options: coed, special housing for students with disabilities. Campus housing is university owned and leased by the school.

Activities and organizations: drama/theater group, student-run newspaper, radio and television station, choral group, Student Government, National Association for the Advancement of Colored People, Interfraternity Council, Panhellenic Council, Golden Key International Honor Society, national fraternities, national sororities.

Athletics Member NCAA. All Division I. ***Intercollegiate sports:*** baseball M(s), basketball M(s)/W(s), cheerleading M(s)/W(s), cross-country running M(s)/W(s), golf M(s), soccer M(s)/W(s), softball W(s), swimming and diving M(s)/W(s), tennis M(s)/W(s), track and field W(s), volleyball W(s). ***Intramural sports:*** badminton M(c)/W(c), baseball M(c), basketball M/W, bowling M(c)/W(c), cheerleading M(c)/W(c), fencing M(c)/W(c), football M, golf M(c)/W(c), gymnastics M(c)/W(c), ice hockey M(c), lacrosse M(c), racquetball M/W, rugby M(c)/W(c), skiing (downhill) M(c)/W(c), soccer M/W, softball M/W, swimming and diving M(c)/W(c), table tennis M/W, tennis M/W, ultimate Frisbee M(c)/W(c), volleyball M/W, water polo M/W, wrestling M(c).

Campus security: 24-hour emergency response devices and patrols, student patrols, late-night transport/escort service, controlled dormitory access.

Student services: health clinic, personal/psychological counseling, women's center, legal services.

COSTS & FINANCIAL AID

Costs (2014–15) ***Tuition:*** state resident $8730 full-time, $394 per credit hour part-time; nonresident $16,910 full-time, $770 per credit hour part-time. Full-time tuition and fees vary according to course load, location, and reciprocity agreements. Part-time tuition and fees vary according to course load, location, and reciprocity agreements. ***Room and board:*** $9108; room only: $5878. Room and board charges vary according to board plan, housing facility, and location. ***Payment plan:*** installment. ***Waivers:*** senior citizens and employees or children of employees.

Financial Aid Of all full-time matriculated undergraduates who enrolled in 2014, 7,645 applied for aid, 6,346 were judged to have need, 896 had their need fully met. 1,316 Federal Work-Study jobs (averaging $3206). In 2014, 1229 non-need-based awards were made. ***Average percent of need met:*** 62. ***Average financial aid package:*** $10,400. ***Average need-based loan:*** $4473. ***Average need-based gift aid:*** $6322. ***Average non-need-based aid:*** $4234. ***Average indebtedness upon graduation:*** $30,778.

APPLYING

Standardized Tests *Required:* SAT or ACT (for admission).

Options: electronic application, early admission, deferred entrance.

Application fee: $30.

Required: high school transcript. ***Recommended:*** minimum 2.0 GPA.

Application deadlines: rolling (freshmen), rolling (out-of-state freshmen), rolling (transfers).

Notification: continuous (freshmen), continuous (out-of-state freshmen), continuous (transfers).

CONTACT

Ms. Cathy Davis, Assistant Vice President for Undergraduate Admissions, Wright State University, 3640 Colonel Glenn Highway, E147 Student Union, Dayton, OH 45435. *Phone:* 937-775-5702. *Toll-free phone:* 800-247-1770. *Fax:* 937-775-5795. *E-mail:* admissions@wright.edu.

Xavier University

Cincinnati, Ohio

http://www.xavier.edu/

- **Independent Roman Catholic** university, founded 1831
- **Urban** 189-acre campus with easy access to Cincinnati-Northern Kentucky Metropolitan Area
- **Endowment** $153.5 million
- **Coed** 4,633 undergraduate students, 92% full-time, 54% women, 46% men
- **Moderately difficult** entrance level, 73% of applicants were admitted

UNDERGRAD STUDENTS
4,270 full-time, 363 part-time. Students come from 49 states and territories; 47 other countries; 49% are from out of state; 10% Black or African American, non-Hispanic/Latino; 5% Hispanic/Latino; 2% Asian, non-Hispanic/Latino; 0.2% Native Hawaiian or other Pacific Islander, non-Hispanic/Latino; 0.2% American Indian or Alaska Native, non-Hispanic/Latino; 4% Two or more races, non-Hispanic/Latino; 4% Race/ethnicity unknown; 2% international; 2% transferred in; 52% live on campus.

Freshmen
Admission: 11,605 applied, 8,489 admitted, 1,214 enrolled. ***Average high school GPA:*** 3.52. ***Test scores:*** SAT critical reading scores over 500: 73%; SAT math scores over 500: 74%; SAT writing scores over 500: 66%; ACT scores over 18: 99%; SAT critical reading scores over 600: 25%; SAT math scores over 600: 28%; SAT writing scores over 600: 23%; ACT scores over 24: 64%; SAT critical reading scores over 700: 5%; SAT math scores over 700: 4%; SAT writing scores over 700: 4%; ACT scores over 30: 11%.

Retention: 85% of full-time freshmen returned.

FACULTY
Total: 699, 50% full-time, 50% with terminal degrees.

Student/faculty ratio: 12:1.

ACADEMICS
Calendar: semesters. *Degrees:* certificates, associate, bachelor's, master's, doctoral, post-master's, and postbachelor's certificates.

Special study options: academic remediation for entering students, adult/continuing education programs, advanced placement credit, cooperative education, distance learning, double majors, English as a second language, honors programs, independent study, internships, off-campus study, part-time degree program, services for LD students, study abroad, summer session for credit. ***ROTC:*** Army (b), Air Force (c).

Unusual degree programs: 3-2 forestry with Duke University; environmental management, accounting, occupational therapy.

Computers: 450 computers/terminals and 10,128 ports are available on campus for general student use. Students can access the following: campus intranet, computer help desk, free student e-mail accounts, online (class) grades, online (class) registration, online (class) schedules. Campuswide network is available. 100% of college-owned or -operated housing units are wired for high-speed Internet access. Wireless service is available via entire campus.

STUDENT LIFE
Housing options: on-campus residence required through sophomore year; coed, special housing for students with disabilities. Campus housing is university owned. Freshman campus housing is guaranteed.

Activities and organizations: drama/theater group, student-run newspaper, television station, choral group, Student Government Association, Black Student Association, X-treme Fans, Alternative Spring Break, Club Sports.

Athletics Member NCAA. All Division I. ***Intercollegiate sports:*** baseball M(s), basketball M(s)/W(s), cheerleading M(c)/W(c), crew M(c)/W(c), cross-country running M(s)/W(s), equestrian sports M(c)/W(c), fencing M(c)/W(c), golf M(s)/W(s), gymnastics M(c)/W(c), ice hockey M(c)/W(c), lacrosse M(c)/W(c), rugby M(c), soccer M(s)/W(s), softball W(c), swimming and diving M(s)/W(s), tennis M(s)/W(s), track and field M(s)/W(s), ultimate Frisbee M(c), volleyball M(c)/W(s), water polo M(c)/W(c). ***Intramural sports:*** baseball M(c), basketball M/W, bowling M/W, football M/W, golf M(c), racquetball M/W, soccer M(c)/W(c), softball W, swimming and diving M(c)/W(c), tennis M/W, volleyball M/W.

Campus security: 24-hour emergency response devices and patrols, late-night transport/escort service, controlled dormitory access, campus-wide shuttle service.

Student services: health clinic, personal/psychological counseling, women's center.

COSTS & FINANCIAL AID
Costs (2014–15) ***Comprehensive fee:*** $44,980 includes full-time tuition ($33,030), mandatory fees ($930), and room and board ($11,020). Full-time tuition and fees vary according to class time, course load, degree level, location, and program. Part-time tuition: $635 per credit hour. Part-time tuition and fees vary according to class time, course load, degree level, location, and program. ***Required fees:*** $9 per term part-time. ***College room only:*** $6120. Room and board charges vary according to board plan and housing facility. ***Payment plans:*** installment, deferred payment. ***Waivers:*** senior citizens and employees or children of employees.

Financial Aid Of all full-time matriculated undergraduates who enrolled in 2012, 2,930 applied for aid, 2,434 were judged to have need, 472 had their need fully met. 745 Federal Work-Study jobs (averaging $2490). 26 state and other part-time jobs (averaging $2270). In 2012, 1414 non-need-based awards were made. ***Average percent of need met:*** 72. ***Average financial aid package:*** $20,431. ***Average need-based loan:*** $4572. ***Average need-based gift aid:*** $15,334. ***Average non-need-based aid:*** $12,844. ***Average indebtedness upon graduation:*** $30,540.

APPLYING
Standardized Tests *Required:* SAT or ACT (for admission).

Options: electronic application, deferred entrance.

Application fee: $35.

Required: essay or personal statement, high school transcript, 1 letter of recommendation. ***Required for some:*** minimum 3.0 GPA, interview.

Application deadlines: 2/1 (freshmen), rolling (transfers).

Notification: continuous until 10/15 (freshmen), continuous (transfers).

CONTACT
Xavier University, 3800 Victory Parkway, Cincinnati, OH 45207-5311. *Phone:* 513-745-3301. *Toll-free phone:* 877-XUADMIT. *E-mail:* xuadmit@xavier.edu.

Youngstown State University

Youngstown, Ohio

http://www.ysu.edu/

- **State-supported** comprehensive, founded 1908
- **Urban** 175-acre campus with easy access to Cleveland, Pittsburgh
- **Endowment** $236.2 million
- **Coed** 11,348 undergraduate students, 78% full-time, 53% women, 47% men
- **Minimally difficult** entrance level, 83% of applicants were admitted

UNDERGRAD STUDENTS
8,810 full-time, 2,538 part-time. Students come from 38 states and territories; 34 other countries; 12% are from out of state; 13% Black or African American, non-Hispanic/Latino; 4% Hispanic/Latino; 0.9% Asian, non-Hispanic/Latino; 0.1% Native Hawaiian or other Pacific Islander, non-Hispanic/Latino; 0.2% American Indian or Alaska Native, non-Hispanic/Latino; 2% Two or more races, non-Hispanic/Latino; 4% Race/ethnicity unknown; 1% international; 5% transferred in; 10% live on campus.

Freshmen
Admission: 3,784 applied, 3,152 admitted, 1,776 enrolled. ***Average high school GPA:*** 3.12. ***Test scores:*** SAT critical reading scores over 500: 37%; SAT math scores over 500: 46%; SAT writing scores over 500: 34%; ACT scores over 18: 80%; SAT critical reading scores over 600: 14%; SAT math scores over 600: 19%; SAT writing scores over 600: 13%; ACT scores over 24: 28%; SAT critical reading scores over 700: 3%; SAT math scores over 700: 4%; SAT writing scores over 700: 1%; ACT scores over 30: 5%.

Retention: 70% of full-time freshmen returned.

FACULTY
Total: 1,049, 41% full-time, 37% with terminal degrees.

Student/faculty ratio: 17:1.

ACADEMICS
Calendar: semesters. *Degrees:* certificates, diplomas, associate, bachelor's, master's, doctoral, post-master's, and postbachelor's certificates.

Special study options: academic remediation for entering students, accelerated degree program, adult/continuing education programs, advanced placement credit, cooperative education, distance learning, double majors, English as a second language, freshman honors college, honors programs, independent study, internships, off-campus study, part-time degree program, services for LD students, student-designed majors, study abroad, summer session for credit. ***ROTC:*** Army (b), Air Force (c).

Unusual degree programs: BS/MS chemistry; BS/MD Program.

Computers: 500 computers/terminals are available on campus for general student use. Students can access the following: campus intranet, computer help desk, free student e-mail accounts, online (class) grades, online (class) registration, online (class) schedules. Campuswide network is available. 100% of college-owned or -operated housing units are wired for high-speed Internet access. Wireless service is available via entire campus.

STUDENT LIFE

Housing options: coed, women-only. Campus housing is university owned and is provided by a third party.

Activities and organizations: drama/theater group, student-run newspaper, radio station, choral group, marching band, University Scholars, Biology Club, Golden Key Honor Society, Fraternities/Sororities (IFC, NPHC and Panhellenic Council), Catholic Student Association, national fraternities, national sororities.

Athletics Member NCAA. All Division I except football (Division I-AA). ***Intercollegiate sports:*** baseball M(s), basketball M(s)/W(s), cross-country running M(s)/W(s), golf M(s)/W(s), soccer W(s), softball W(s), swimming and diving W(s), tennis M(s)/W(s), track and field M(s)/W(s), volleyball W(s). ***Intramural sports:*** badminton M/W, basketball M/W, bowling M(c)/W(c), equestrian sports W(c), football M/W, golf M, lacrosse M(c)/W(c), racquetball M(c)/W(c), rock climbing M/W, soccer M/W, table tennis M/W, tennis M/W, ultimate Frisbee M/W, volleyball M/W, weight lifting M/W.

Campus security: 24-hour emergency response devices and patrols, student patrols, late-night transport/escort service, controlled dormitory access, residence hall patrols.

Student services: health clinic, personal/psychological counseling.

COSTS & FINANCIAL AID

Costs (2014–15) ***Tuition:*** state resident $7847 full-time, $327 per credit part-time; nonresident $13,847 full-time, $577 per credit part-time. Full-time tuition and fees vary according to course load. Part-time tuition and fees vary according to course load. ***Required fees:*** $470 full-time. ***Room and board:*** $8645. Room and board charges vary according to board plan and housing facility. ***Payment plan:*** installment. ***Waivers:*** senior citizens and employees or children of employees.

Financial Aid Of all full-time matriculated undergraduates who enrolled in 2013, 8,294 applied for aid, 7,133 were judged to have need, 534 had their need fully met. In 2013, 807 non-need-based awards were made. ***Average percent of need met:*** 32. ***Average financial aid package:*** $8724. ***Average need-based loan:*** $3849. ***Average need-based gift aid:*** $5261. ***Average non-need-based aid:*** $3358. ***Average indebtedness upon graduation:*** $30,481.

APPLYING

Standardized Tests *Required:* SAT or ACT (for admission).

Options: electronic application, early admission, deferred entrance.

Application fee: $45.

Required: high school transcript, minimum 2.0 GPA, composite score of 17 or higher on the ACT or a combined SAT critical reading and math score of 820 or higher. ***Required for some:*** interview.

Application deadlines: 8/1 (freshmen), 8/1 (out-of-state freshmen), 8/1 (transfers).

Notification: continuous (freshmen), continuous (out-of-state freshmen), continuous (transfers).

CONTACT

Ms. Sue Davis, Director of Admissions, Youngstown State University, One University Plaza, Youngstown, OH 44555-0001. *Phone:* 330-941-2000. *Toll-free phone:* 877-468-6978. *Fax:* 330-941-3674. *E-mail:* enroll@ysu.edu.

OKLAHOMA

Brown Mackie College–Oklahoma City

Oklahoma City, Oklahoma

http://www.brownmackie.edu/oklahoma-city/

- **Proprietary** primarily 2-year, part of Education Management Corporation
- **Coed**

ACADEMICS

Degrees: associate and bachelor's.

CONTACT

Brown Mackie College–Oklahoma City, 7101 Northwest Expressway, Suite 800, Oklahoma City, OK 73132. *Phone:* 405-621-8000. *Toll-free phone:* 888-229-3280.

Brown Mackie College–Tulsa

Tulsa, Oklahoma

http://www.brownmackie.edu/tulsa/

- **Proprietary** primarily 2-year, part of Education Management Corporation
- **Coed**

ACADEMICS

Degrees: diplomas, associate, and bachelor's.

CONTACT

Brown Mackie College–Tulsa, 4608 South Garnett, Suite 110, Tulsa, OK 74146. *Phone:* 918-628-3700. *Toll-free phone:* 888-794-8411.

Cameron University

Lawton, Oklahoma

http://www.cameron.edu/

- **State-supported** comprehensive, founded 1908, part of Oklahoma State Regents for Higher Education
- **Small-town** 360-acre campus
- **Endowment** $16.4 million
- **Coed** 5,056 undergraduate students, 67% full-time, 60% women, 40% men
- **Noncompetitive** entrance level, 100% of applicants were admitted

UNDERGRAD STUDENTS

3,397 full-time, 1,659 part-time. Students come from 48 states and territories; 54 other countries; 13% are from out of state; 16% Black or African American, non-Hispanic/Latino; 12% Hispanic/Latino; 2% Asian, non-Hispanic/Latino; 0.7% Native Hawaiian or other Pacific Islander, non-Hispanic/Latino; 5% American Indian or Alaska Native, non-Hispanic/Latino; 8% Two or more races, non-Hispanic/Latino; 2% Race/ethnicity unknown; 4% international; 7% transferred in; 10% live on campus.

Freshmen

Admission: 1,105 applied, 1,101 admitted, 826 enrolled. ***Average high school GPA:*** 3.11. ***Test scores:*** ACT scores over 18: 72%; ACT scores over 24: 20%; ACT scores over 30: 2%.

Retention: 62% of full-time freshmen returned.

FACULTY

Total: 312, 59% full-time, 46% with terminal degrees.

Student/faculty ratio: 19:1.

ACADEMICS

Calendar: semesters. *Degrees:* associate, bachelor's, master's, and post-master's certificates.

Special study options: academic remediation for entering students, accelerated degree program, adult/continuing education programs, advanced placement credit, distance learning, double majors, honors programs, independent study, internships, off-campus study, part-time degree program, services for LD students, student-designed majors, study abroad, summer session for credit. ***ROTC:*** Army (b).

Computers: 240 computers/terminals are available on campus for general student use. Students can access the following: computer help desk, free student e-mail accounts, online (class) grades, online (class) schedules, online courses, student information system, library, computer labs, mobile app. Campuswide network is available. 100% of college-owned or -operated housing units are wired for high-speed Internet access. Wireless service is available via classrooms, computer centers, computer labs, dorm rooms, learning centers, libraries, student centers.

STUDENT LIFE

Housing options: coed, men-only, women-only. Campus housing is university owned.

Activities and organizations: drama/theater group, student-run newspaper, television station, choral group, Student Government Association, Programming Activities Council, Nigerian Student Association, International Club, Greek Life, national fraternities, national sororities.

Athletics Member NCAA. All Division II. ***Intercollegiate sports:*** baseball M(s), basketball M(s)/W(s), cross-country running M(s), golf M(s)/W(s), softball W(s), tennis M(s)/W(s), volleyball W(s). ***Intramural sports:*** badminton M/W, basketball M/W, bowling M/W, racquetball M/W, soccer M/W, softball M/W, swimming and diving M/W, table tennis M/W, tennis M/W, volleyball M/W, weight lifting M/W.

Campus security: 24-hour emergency response devices and patrols, late-night transport/escort service, controlled dormitory access.

Student services: health clinic, personal/psychological counseling.

COSTS & FINANCIAL AID

Costs (2014–15) ***Tuition:*** state resident $3720 full-time, $124 per credit hour part-time; nonresident $11,760 full-time, $392 per credit hour part-time. Full-time tuition and fees vary according to course level, course load, and program. Part-time tuition and fees vary according to course level, course load, and program. ***Required fees:*** $1620 full-time, $54 per credit hour part-time. ***Room and board:*** $4664; room only: $1792. Room and board charges vary according to board plan and housing facility. ***Payment plan:*** installment. ***Waivers:*** senior citizens and employees or children of employees.

Financial Aid Of all full-time matriculated undergraduates who enrolled in 2013, 2,872 applied for aid, 2,547 were judged to have need, 249 had their need fully met. 64 Federal Work-Study jobs (averaging $2386). 330 state and other part-time jobs (averaging $3186). In 2013, 91 non-need-based awards were made. ***Average percent of need met:*** 52. ***Average financial aid package:*** $10,109. ***Average need-based loan:*** $3831. ***Average need-based gift aid:*** $5895. ***Average non-need-based aid:*** $1742. ***Average indebtedness upon graduation:*** $20,512.

APPLYING

Standardized Tests *Required for some:* SAT or ACT (for admission).

Options: electronic application, deferred entrance.

Application fee: $15.

Required for some: high school transcript, Baccalaureate degree: Minimum composite ACT of 20 or SAT of 890 or rank in the top 50% of high school graduation class and have a high school GPA of at least 2.7; AS degree: Meet minimum high school curricular requirements and completed the ACT or SAT; AAS degree: completed ACT or SAT.

Application deadlines: rolling (freshmen), rolling (out-of-state freshmen), rolling (transfers).

Notification: continuous (freshmen), continuous (out-of-state freshmen), continuous (transfers).

CONTACT

Ms. Ann Morris, Prospective Students Services Coordinator, Cameron University, Admissions, 2800 West Gore Boulevard, Lawton, OK 73505-6377. *Phone:* 580-581-2798. *Toll-free phone:* 888-454-7600. *Fax:* 580-581-5416. *E-mail:* admissions@cameron.edu.

DeVry University

Oklahoma City, Oklahoma

http://www.devry.edu/

- **Proprietary** comprehensive
- **Coed**

ACADEMICS

Degrees: associate, bachelor's, and master's.

COSTS & FINANCIAL AID

Costs (2014–15) ***Tuition:*** $17,052 full-time, $609 per credit hour part-time. ***Required fees:*** $80 full-time.

Financial Aid Of all full-time matriculated undergraduates who enrolled in 2007, 16 applied for aid, 15 were judged to have need. In 2007, 1 non-need-based awards were made. ***Average percent of need met:*** 39. ***Average financial aid package:*** $10,842. ***Average need-based loan:*** $4877. ***Average need-based gift aid:*** $10,483. ***Average non-need-based aid:*** $14,400.

CONTACT

Admissions Office, DeVry University, Lakepointe Towers, 4013 Northwest Expressway Street, Suite 100, Oklahoma City, OK 73116. *Phone:* 405-767-9516. *Toll-free phone:* 866-338-7941.

East Central University

Ada, Oklahoma

http://www.ecok.edu/

- **State-supported** comprehensive, founded 1909, part of Oklahoma State Regents for Higher Education
- **Small-town** 140-acre campus with easy access to Oklahoma City
- **Coed** 3,637 undergraduate students, 82% full-time, 60% women, 40% men
- **Minimally difficult** entrance level, 97% of applicants were admitted

UNDERGRAD STUDENTS

2,970 full-time, 667 part-time. Students come from 26 states and territories; 28 other countries; 7% are from out of state; 4% Black or African American, non-Hispanic/Latino; 5% Hispanic/Latino; 0.5% Asian, non-Hispanic/Latino; 0.1% Native Hawaiian or other Pacific Islander, non-Hispanic/Latino; 14% American Indian or Alaska Native, non-Hispanic/Latino; 10% Two or more races, non-Hispanic/Latino; 2% Race/ethnicity unknown; 6% international; 9% transferred in.

Freshmen

Admission: 962 applied, 935 admitted, 605 enrolled. ***Average high school GPA:*** 3.3. ***Test scores:*** SAT critical reading scores over 500: 36%; SAT math scores over 500: 58%; ACT scores over 18: 85%; SAT critical reading scores over 600: 3%; SAT math scores over 600: 20%; ACT scores over 24: 31%; ACT scores over 30: 4%.

Retention: 66% of full-time freshmen returned.

FACULTY

Total: 285, 59% full-time, 43% with terminal degrees.

Student/faculty ratio: 19:1.

ACADEMICS

Calendar: semesters. *Degrees:* certificates, bachelor's, master's, post-master's, and postbachelor's certificates.

Special study options: academic remediation for entering students, adult/continuing education programs, advanced placement credit, distance learning, double majors, English as a second language, honors programs, independent study, internships, off-campus study, part-time degree program, services for LD students, study abroad, summer session for credit.

Computers: 677 computers/terminals are available on campus for general student use. Students can access the following: campus intranet, computer help desk, free student e-mail accounts, online (class) grades, online (class) registration, online (class) schedules. Campuswide network is available. Wireless service is available via entire campus.

STUDENT LIFE

Housing options: on-campus residence required for freshman year; coed, women-only, special housing for students with disabilities. Campus housing is university owned.

Activities and organizations: drama/theater group, student-run newspaper, choral group, marching band, BACCHUS, Fellowship of Christian Athletes, Human Resources, national fraternities, national sororities.

Athletics Member NCAA, NAIA. All NCAA Division II. ***Intercollegiate sports:*** baseball M(s), basketball M(s)/W(s), cheerleading M/W, cross-country running M(s)/W(s), football M(s), golf M(s)/W, soccer W(s), softball W(s), tennis M(s)/W(s), track and field M/W, volleyball W(s). ***Intramural sports:*** basketball M/W, football M/W, racquetball M/W, soccer M/W, softball M/W, tennis M/W, volleyball M/W.

Campus security: 24-hour emergency response devices and patrols, student patrols, late-night transport/escort service, agreements with all local, state, federal, and tribal police departments for added crime and violation prevention.

Student services: health clinic, personal/psychological counseling.

COSTS & FINANCIAL AID
Costs (2014–15) ***Tuition:*** state resident $4236 full-time, $141 per semester hour part-time; nonresident $12,149 full-time, $405 per semester hour part-time. No tuition increase for student's term of enrollment. ***Required fees:*** $1363 full-time, $42 per semester hour part-time, $55 per term part-time. ***Room and board:*** $5158; room only: $2100. Room and board charges vary according to board plan and housing facility. ***Waivers:*** senior citizens and employees or children of employees.

Financial Aid Of all full-time matriculated undergraduates who enrolled in 2006, 2,396 applied for aid, 2,085 were judged to have need, 756 had their need fully met. 175 Federal Work-Study jobs (averaging $2349). 232 state and other part-time jobs (averaging $572). In 2006, 542 non-need-based awards were made. ***Average percent of need met:*** 70. ***Average financial aid package:*** $7597. ***Average need-based loan:*** $3835. ***Average need-based gift aid:*** $3420. ***Average non-need-based aid:*** $1567. ***Average indebtedness upon graduation:*** $19,190.

APPLYING
Standardized Tests *Required:* SAT or ACT (for admission). *Recommended:* ACT (for admission).

Options: electronic application, early admission.

Application fee: $20.

Required: high school transcript. ***Required for some:*** minimum 2.7 GPA, rank in upper 50% of high school class.

CONTACT
Ms. Autumn Godwin, Freshman Admissions Officer, East Central University, PMBJ8, 1100 East 14th Street, Ada, OK 74820-6999. *Phone:* 580-559-5233. *E-mail:* agodwin@ecok.edu.

Hillsdale Free Will Baptist College

Moore, Oklahoma

http://www.hc.edu/

- **Independent Free Will Baptist** comprehensive, founded 1959
- **Suburban** 41-acre campus with easy access to Oklahoma City
- **Coed** 225 undergraduate students, 83% full-time, 38% women, 62% men
- **Noncompetitive** entrance level

UNDERGRAD STUDENTS
186 full-time, 39 part-time. 10% Black or African American, non-Hispanic/Latino; 16% Hispanic/Latino; 0.4% Asian, non-Hispanic/Latino; 11% American Indian or Alaska Native, non-Hispanic/Latino; 0.4% Two or more races, non-Hispanic/Latino; 0.4% Race/ethnicity unknown; 7% international.

Freshmen
Admission: 41 enrolled.
Retention: 60% of full-time freshmen returned.

FACULTY
Total: 47, 28% full-time.

ACADEMICS
Calendar: semesters. *Degrees:* associate, bachelor's, and master's.

Special study options: academic remediation for entering students, accelerated degree program, adult/continuing education programs, advanced placement credit, English as a second language, independent study, internships, part-time degree program, summer session for credit.

Computers: 22 computers/terminals are available on campus for general student use. Students can access the following: campus intranet, free student e-mail accounts. Campuswide network is available.

STUDENT LIFE
Housing options: on-campus residence required through sophomore year; men-only, women-only. Campus housing is university owned.

Activities and organizations: drama/theater group, choral group.

Athletics Member NCCAA. ***Intercollegiate sports:*** baseball M, basketball M/W, cross-country running M/W, soccer M, softball W, volleyball W. ***Intramural sports:*** basketball M/W, volleyball M/W.

Campus security: 24-hour emergency response devices, controlled dormitory access.

Student services: personal/psychological counseling.

COSTS & FINANCIAL AID
Costs (2014–15) ***Comprehensive fee:*** $18,810 includes full-time tuition ($9300), mandatory fees ($2680), and room and board ($6830). Full-time tuition and fees vary according to course load. Part-time tuition: $388 per credit hour. Part-time tuition and fees vary according to course load. ***Required fees:*** $37 per credit hour part-time, $245 per term part-time. ***College room only:*** $2660. Room and board charges vary according to board plan and housing facility. ***Payment plan:*** installment. ***Waivers:*** children of alumni, senior citizens, and employees or children of employees.

Financial Aid Of all full-time matriculated undergraduates who enrolled in 2012, 165 applied for aid, 145 were judged to have need. 19 Federal Work-Study jobs (averaging $2500). In 2012, 39 non-need-based awards were made. ***Average percent of need met:*** 55. ***Average financial aid package:*** $10,500. ***Average need-based loan:*** $4150. ***Average need-based gift aid:*** $6900. ***Average non-need-based aid:*** $2600. ***Average indebtedness upon graduation:*** $23,500.

APPLYING
Standardized Tests *Required:* SAT or ACT (for admission).

Options: electronic application, early admission, deferred entrance.

Application fee: $20.

Required: high school transcript, 2 letters of recommendation. ***Required for some:*** interview. ***Recommended:*** minimum 2.0 GPA.

CONTACT
Hillsdale Free Will Baptist College, PO Box 7208, Moore, OK 73160. *Phone:* 405-912-9007. *Fax:* 405-912-9050. *E-mail:* recruitment@hc.edu.

ITT Technical Institute

Oklahoma City, Oklahoma

http://www.itt-tech.edu/

- **Proprietary** 4-year, founded 2006, part of ITT Educational Services, Inc.
- **Coed**
- **Minimally difficult** entrance level

ACADEMICS
Calendar: quarters. *Degrees:* associate and bachelor's.

STUDENT LIFE
Housing options: college housing not available.

CONTACT
Director of Recruitment, ITT Technical Institute, 50 Penn Place Office Tower, 1900 Northwest Expressway, Suite 305R, Oklahoma City, OK 73118. *Phone:* 405-810-4100. *Toll-free phone:* 800-518-1612.

ITT Technical Institute

Tulsa, Oklahoma

http://www.itt-tech.edu/

- **Proprietary** primarily 2-year, founded 2005
- **Coed**
- **Minimally difficult** entrance level

ACADEMICS
Calendar: quarters. *Degrees:* associate and bachelor's.

STUDENT LIFE
Housing options: college housing not available.

CONTACT
Director of Recruitment, ITT Technical Institute, 4500 South 129th East Avenue, Suite 152, Tulsa, OK 74134. *Phone:* 918-615-3900. *Toll-free phone:* 800-514-6535.

Langston University
Langston, Oklahoma
http://www.langston.edu/

- **State-supported** comprehensive, founded 1897, part of Oklahoma A & M System
- **Rural** 40-acre campus with easy access to Oklahoma City
- **Endowment** $3.7 million
- **Coed** 2,272 undergraduate students, 89% full-time, 62% women, 38% men
- **Moderately difficult** entrance level, 48% of applicants were admitted

UNDERGRAD STUDENTS
2,028 full-time, 244 part-time. Students come from 35 states and territories; 10 other countries; 40% are from out of state; 102% Black or African American, non-Hispanic/Latino; 1% Hispanic/Latino; 0.9% Asian, non-Hispanic/Latino; 0.1% Native Hawaiian or other Pacific Islander, non-Hispanic/Latino; 1% American Indian or Alaska Native, non-Hispanic/Latino; 0.7% Race/ethnicity unknown; 53% live on campus.

Freshmen
Admission: 6,638 applied, 3,165 admitted, 629 enrolled. ***Average high school GPA:*** 2.78.
Retention: 51% of full-time freshmen returned.

FACULTY
Total: 200, 76% full-time, 46% with terminal degrees.

Student/faculty ratio: 16:1.

ACADEMICS
Calendar: semesters. *Degrees:* associate, bachelor's, master's, and doctoral.

Special study options: academic remediation for entering students, accelerated degree program, adult/continuing education programs, advanced placement credit, cooperative education, distance learning, double majors, English as a second language, external degree program, honors programs, independent study, internships, part-time degree program, services for LD students, study abroad, summer session for credit. ***ROTC:*** Army (c).

Computers: 300 computers/terminals and 1,600 ports are available on campus for general student use. Students can access the following: campus intranet, computer help desk, free student e-mail accounts, online (class) grades, online (class) registration, online (class) schedules. Campuswide network is available. Wireless service is available via entire campus.

STUDENT LIFE
Housing options: on-campus residence required through sophomore year; coed, special housing for students with disabilities. Campus housing is university owned and is provided by a third party. Freshman campus housing is guaranteed.

Activities and organizations: drama/theater group, student-run newspaper, radio station, choral group, marching band, Student Government Association, Student Senate, Sorority and Fraternity (Greek Letter), NAACP, Pre- Alumni Council, national fraternities, national sororities.

Athletics Member NAIA. ***Intercollegiate sports:*** basketball M(s)/W(s), cheerleading W, cross-country running M/W, football M(s), softball W, track and field M(s)/W(s), volleyball W. ***Intramural sports:*** archery M/W, badminton M/W, basketball M/W, football M/W, golf M/W, soccer M, swimming and diving M/W, table tennis M/W, tennis M/W, track and field M/W, volleyball M/W.

Campus security: 24-hour emergency response devices and patrols, student patrols, late-night transport/escort service, controlled dormitory access.

Student services: health clinic, personal/psychological counseling, women's center.

COSTS & FINANCIAL AID
Costs (2014–15) ***Tuition:*** state resident $3305 full-time, $110 per credit hour part-time; nonresident $10,291 full-time, $343 per credit hour part-time. Full-time tuition and fees vary according to degree level and program. Part-time tuition and fees vary according to degree level and program. No tuition increase for student's term of enrollment. ***Required fees:*** $1496 full-time, $110 per credit hour part-time, $83 per credit hour part-time. ***Room and board:*** $8720; room only: $5850. Room and board charges vary according to board plan and housing facility. ***Payment plans:*** tuition prepayment, installment. ***Waivers:*** children of alumni and employees or children of employees.

Financial Aid Of all full-time matriculated undergraduates who enrolled in 2013, 2,179 applied for aid, 1,949 were judged to have need, 291 had their need fully met. In 2013, 252 non-need-based awards were made. ***Average percent of need met:*** 53. ***Average financial aid package:*** $9840. ***Average need-based loan:*** $3661. ***Average need-based gift aid:*** $5178. ***Average non-need-based aid:*** $3044.

APPLYING
Standardized Tests *Required:* SAT or ACT (for admission).

Options: electronic application, deferred entrance.

Application fee: $35.

Required: high school transcript, minimum 2.7 GPA.

Application deadlines: rolling (freshmen), rolling (transfers).

CONTACT
Mrs. Linda Williams, Director of Admissions, Langston University, Box 1550, Langston, OK 73052. *Phone:* 405-466-2050. *Fax:* 466-2915. *E-mail:* lswilliams@langston.edu.

Northeastern State University
Tahlequah, Oklahoma
http://www.nsuok.edu/

- **State-supported** comprehensive, founded 1846, part of Regional University System of Oklahoma
- **Small-town** 200-acre campus with easy access to Tulsa
- **Endowment** $4.5 million
- **Coed** 7,117 undergraduate students, 71% full-time, 61% women, 39% men
- **Moderately difficult** entrance level, 75% of applicants were admitted

UNDERGRAD STUDENTS
5,054 full-time, 2,063 part-time. Students come from 33 states and territories; 39 other countries; 5% are from out of state; 5% Black or African American, non-Hispanic/Latino; 4% Hispanic/Latino; 2% Asian, non-Hispanic/Latino; 0.1% Native Hawaiian or other Pacific Islander, non-Hispanic/Latino; 22% American Indian or Alaska Native, non-Hispanic/Latino; 14% Two or more races, non-Hispanic/Latino; 2% Race/ethnicity unknown; 1% international; 14% transferred in; 19% live on campus.

Freshmen
Admission: 1,957 applied, 1,468 admitted, 918 enrolled. ***Average high school GPA:*** 3.36. ***Test scores:*** ACT scores over 18: 85%; ACT scores over 24: 26%; ACT scores over 30: 3%.
Retention: 61% of full-time freshmen returned.

FACULTY
Total: 525, 60% full-time, 57% with terminal degrees.

Student/faculty ratio: 18:1.

ACADEMICS
Calendar: semesters. *Degrees:* bachelor's, master's, doctoral, post-master's, and postbachelor's certificates.

Special study options: academic remediation for entering students, adult/continuing education programs, advanced placement credit, cooperative education, distance learning, double majors, honors programs, independent study, internships, part-time degree program, services for LD students, student-designed majors, summer session for credit. ***ROTC:*** Army (b).

Computers: 1,169 computers/terminals and 1,200 ports are available on campus for general student use. Students can access the following: campus intranet, computer help desk, free student e-mail accounts, online (class) grades, online (class) schedules. Campuswide network is available. 100% of college-owned or -operated housing units are wired for high-speed Internet access. Wireless service is available via computer centers, computer labs, libraries, student centers.

STUDENT LIFE
Housing options: on-campus residence required for freshman year; coed, women-only, special housing for students with disabilities. Campus

housing is university owned. Freshman applicants given priority for college housing.

Activities and organizations: drama/theater group, student-run newspaper, television station, choral group, marching band, national fraternities, national sororities.

Athletics Member NCAA. All Division II. ***Intercollegiate sports:*** baseball M(s), basketball M(s)/W(s), football M(s), golf M(s)/W(s), soccer M(s)/W(s), softball W(s), tennis W(s). ***Intramural sports:*** basketball M/W, football M/W, golf M/W, racquetball M/W, soccer M/W, softball M/W, tennis M/W, volleyball M/W.

Campus security: 24-hour emergency response devices and patrols, late-night transport/escort service, controlled dormitory access.

Student services: health clinic, personal/psychological counseling.

COSTS & FINANCIAL AID

Costs (2014–15) ***Tuition:*** state resident $4163 full-time, $139 per credit hour part-time; nonresident $11,513 full-time, $384 per credit hour part-time. Full-time tuition and fees vary according to course load and program. Part-time tuition and fees vary according to course load and program. No tuition increase for student's term of enrollment. ***Required fees:*** $1122 full-time, $37 per credit hour part-time. ***Room and board:*** $6300; room only: $2700. Room and board charges vary according to board plan and housing facility. ***Waivers:*** employees or children of employees.

Financial Aid Of all full-time matriculated undergraduates who enrolled in 2013, 4,863 applied for aid, 3,660 were judged to have need, 2,758 had their need fully met. 124 Federal Work-Study jobs (averaging $1168). 494 state and other part-time jobs (averaging $2289). In 2013, 134 non-need-based awards were made. ***Average percent of need met:*** 96. ***Average financial aid package:*** $11,880. ***Average need-based loan:*** $6735. ***Average need-based gift aid:*** $6399. ***Average non-need-based aid:*** $2807. ***Average indebtedness upon graduation:*** $18,126.

APPLYING

Standardized Tests *Required:* ACT (for admission).

Options: electronic application, deferred entrance.

Application fee: $25.

Required: high school transcript, minimum 2.7 GPA, upper 50% of class or minimum ACT composite of 20. ***Required for some:*** interview.

Application deadlines: 8/1 (freshmen), 8/1 (transfers).

Notification: continuous (freshmen), continuous (transfers).

CONTACT

Mr. Jason Jesse, Director of Admissions and Recruitment, Northeastern State University, CASE 211, 600 N Grand Ave, Tahlequah, OK 74464. *Phone:* 918-444-4675. *Toll-free phone:* 800-722-9614. *E-mail:* jessiejb@nsuok.edu.

Northwestern Oklahoma State University

Alva, Oklahoma

http://www.nwosu.edu/

- **State-supported** comprehensive, founded 1897, part of Oklahoma State Regents for Higher Education
- **Rural** 70-acre campus
- **Endowment** $28.0 million
- **Coed** 1,947 undergraduate students, 73% full-time, 57% women, 43% men
- **Moderately difficult** entrance level, 67% of applicants were admitted

UNDERGRAD STUDENTS

1,412 full-time, 535 part-time. Students come from 37 states and territories; 27 other countries; 7% Black or African American, non-Hispanic/Latino; 7% Hispanic/Latino; 0.7% Asian, non-Hispanic/Latino; 0.5% Native Hawaiian or other Pacific Islander, non-Hispanic/Latino; 7% American Indian or Alaska Native, non-Hispanic/Latino; 0.5% Two or more races, non-Hispanic/Latino; 7% Race/ethnicity unknown; 7% international; 13% transferred in; 33% live on campus.

Freshmen

Admission: 1,635 applied, 1,102 admitted, 389 enrolled. ***Average high school GPA:*** 3.27. ***Test scores:*** SAT critical reading scores over 500: 4%; SAT math scores over 500: 17%; ACT scores over 18: 76%; ACT scores over 24: 17%; ACT scores over 30: 1%.

Retention: 60% of full-time freshmen returned.

FACULTY

Total: 176, 51% full-time, 38% with terminal degrees.

Student/faculty ratio: 15:1.

ACADEMICS

Calendar: semesters. *Degrees:* bachelor's and master's.

Special study options: academic remediation for entering students, adult/continuing education programs, advanced placement credit, cooperative education, distance learning, honors programs, independent study, internships, off-campus study, part-time degree program, services for LD students, study abroad, summer session for credit.

Computers: 260 computers/terminals are available on campus for general student use. Students can access the following: campus intranet, computer help desk, free student e-mail accounts, online (class) grades, online (class) registration, online (class) schedules. Campuswide network is available. 100% of college-owned or -operated housing units are wired for high-speed Internet access. Wireless service is available via classrooms, computer centers, computer labs, learning centers, libraries, student centers.

STUDENT LIFE

Housing options: on-campus residence required for freshman year; men-only, women-only. Campus housing is university owned. Freshman campus housing is guaranteed.

Activities and organizations: drama/theater group, student-run newspaper, radio and television station, choral group, marching band, Student Government Association, Aggie Club, Delta Mu Delta, Baptist Student Union, SOEA.

Athletics Member NCAA. All Division II. ***Intercollegiate sports:*** baseball M(s), basketball M(s)/W(s), cheerleading M(s)/W(s), cross-country running M(s)/W(s), football M(s), golf M(s)/W(s), soccer W(s), softball W(s), volleyball W(s). ***Intramural sports:*** basketball M/W, football M, racquetball M/W, softball M/W, ultimate Frisbee M/W, volleyball M/W.

Campus security: 24-hour emergency response devices and patrols, late-night transport/escort service.

Student services: personal/psychological counseling.

COSTS & FINANCIAL AID

Costs (2014–15) ***Tuition:*** state resident $4898 full-time; nonresident $11,348 full-time. Full-time tuition and fees vary according to course load, degree level, location, and program. Part-time tuition and fees vary according to course load, degree level, location, and program. ***Required fees:*** $945 full-time. ***Room and board:*** $4230; room only: $1600. Room and board charges vary according to board plan. ***Payment plan:*** installment. ***Waivers:*** senior citizens and employees or children of employees.

Financial Aid Of all full-time matriculated undergraduates who enrolled in 2014, 1,149 applied for aid, 950 were judged to have need. ***Average indebtedness upon graduation:*** $16,932.

APPLYING

Standardized Tests *Required:* SAT or ACT (for admission).

Options: electronic application, early admission.

Application fee: $15.

Required: high school transcript. ***Required for some:*** essay or personal statement, minimum 2.7 GPA, 3 letters of recommendation.

Application deadlines: rolling (freshmen), rolling (transfers).

Notification: continuous (freshmen), continuous (transfers).

CONTACT

Ms. Paige Fischer, Director of Recruitment, Northwestern Oklahoma State University, 709 Oklahoma Boulevard, Alva, OK 73717-2799. *Phone:* 580-327-8545. *Fax:* 580-327-8699. *E-mail:* plfischer@nwosu.edu.

Oklahoma Baptist University
Shawnee, Oklahoma
http://www.okbu.edu/

- **Independent Southern Baptist** comprehensive, founded 1910
- **Small-town** 125-acre campus with easy access to Oklahoma City
- **Endowment** $107.9 million
- **Coed** 1,921 undergraduate students, 94% full-time, 59% women, 41% men
- **Moderately difficult** entrance level, 60% of applicants were admitted

UNDERGRAD STUDENTS
1,808 full-time, 113 part-time. Students come from 42 states and territories; 30 other countries; 44% are from out of state; 6% Black or African American, non-Hispanic/Latino; 2% Hispanic/Latino; 0.9% Asian, non-Hispanic/Latino; 0.3% Native Hawaiian or other Pacific Islander, non-Hispanic/Latino; 5% American Indian or Alaska Native, non-Hispanic/Latino; 8% Two or more races, non-Hispanic/Latino; 3% Race/ethnicity unknown; 4% international; 5% transferred in; 80% live on campus.

Freshmen
Admission: 5,984 applied, 3,619 admitted, 483 enrolled. ***Average high school GPA:*** 3.66. ***Test scores:*** SAT critical reading scores over 500: 64%; SAT math scores over 500: 65%; ACT scores over 18: 98%; SAT critical reading scores over 600: 23%; SAT math scores over 600: 22%; ACT scores over 24: 52%; SAT critical reading scores over 700: 5%; SAT math scores over 700: 4%; ACT scores over 30: 10%.
Retention: 78% of full-time freshmen returned.

FACULTY
Total: 181, 67% full-time, 51% with terminal degrees.
Student/faculty ratio: 16:1.

ACADEMICS
Calendar: 4-1-4. *Degrees:* associate, bachelor's, and master's.
Special study options: academic remediation for entering students, advanced placement credit, cooperative education, double majors, honors programs, independent study, internships, off-campus study, part-time degree program, services for LD students, student-designed majors, study abroad, summer session for credit. ***ROTC:*** Air Force (c).
Unusual degree programs: 3-2 engineering; medicine.
Computers: 175 computers/terminals are available on campus for general student use. Students can access the following: campus intranet, computer help desk, free student e-mail accounts, online (class) grades, online (class) registration, online (class) schedules, campus portal, online course work. Campuswide network is available. 100% of college-owned or -operated housing units are wired for high-speed Internet access. Wireless service is available via classrooms, computer labs, dorm rooms, learning centers, libraries, student centers.

STUDENT LIFE
Housing options: on-campus residence required through junior year; men-only, women-only. Campus housing is university owned. Freshman campus housing is guaranteed.
Activities and organizations: drama/theater group, student-run newspaper, television station, choral group, Campus Activities Board, University Concert Series, Student Foundation, Blitz Week Activities, Canterbury.
Athletics Member NAIA. ***Intercollegiate sports:*** baseball M(s), basketball M(s)/W(s), cross-country running M(s)/W(s), golf M(s)/W(s), soccer M/W, softball W(s), tennis M(s)/W(s), track and field M(s)/W(s). ***Intramural sports:*** badminton M/W, basketball M/W, bowling M/W, cheerleading W, football M/W, racquetball M/W, soccer M/W, softball M/W, swimming and diving M/W, table tennis M/W, tennis M/W, volleyball M/W.
Campus security: 24-hour emergency response devices and patrols, late-night transport/escort service, controlled dormitory access.
Student services: health clinic, personal/psychological counseling.

COSTS & FINANCIAL AID
Costs (2015–16) ***Comprehensive fee:*** $30,780 includes full-time tuition ($21,630), mandatory fees ($2370), and room and board ($6780). Part-time tuition and fees vary according to course load. ***Room and board:*** Room and board charges vary according to housing facility. ***Payment plan:*** installment. ***Waivers:*** senior citizens and employees or children of employees.
Financial Aid Of all full-time matriculated undergraduates who enrolled in 2013, 1,482 applied for aid, 1,366 were judged to have need, 319 had their need fully met. 214 Federal Work-Study jobs (averaging $1231). In 2013, 470 non-need-based awards were made. ***Average percent of need met:*** 75. ***Average financial aid package:*** $19,312. ***Average need-based loan:*** $4101. ***Average need-based gift aid:*** $6907. ***Average non-need-based aid:*** $9752. ***Average indebtedness upon graduation:*** $26,557.

APPLYING
Standardized Tests *Required:* SAT or ACT (for admission).
Options: early admission, deferred entrance.
Required: high school transcript, minimum 2.5 GPA. ***Required for some:*** essay or personal statement, interview.
Application deadlines: rolling (freshmen), 8/1 (transfers).
Notification: continuous until 9/1 (freshmen), continuous until 9/1 (transfers).

CONTACT
Oklahoma Baptist University, 500 West University, Shawnee, OK 74804. *Phone:* 405-585-5000. *Toll-free phone:* 800-654-3285.

Oklahoma Christian University
Oklahoma City, Oklahoma
http://www.oc.edu/

- **Independent** comprehensive, founded 1950, affiliated with Church of Christ
- **Suburban** 200-acre campus with easy access to Oklahoma City
- **Coed** 1,973 undergraduate students, 96% full-time, 48% women, 52% men
- **Moderately difficult** entrance level, 64% of applicants were admitted

UNDERGRAD STUDENTS
1,892 full-time, 81 part-time. Students come from 42 states and territories; 38 other countries; 59% are from out of state; 5% Black or African American, non-Hispanic/Latino; 6% Hispanic/Latino; 0.8% Asian, non-Hispanic/Latino; 0.1% Native Hawaiian or other Pacific Islander, non-Hispanic/Latino; 2% American Indian or Alaska Native, non-Hispanic/Latino; 6% Two or more races, non-Hispanic/Latino; 10% international; 5% transferred in; 80% live on campus.

Freshmen
Admission: 2,159 applied, 1,382 admitted, 505 enrolled. ***Average high school GPA:*** 3.52. ***Test scores:*** SAT critical reading scores over 500: 64%; SAT math scores over 500: 69%; ACT scores over 18: 94%; SAT critical reading scores over 600: 30%; SAT math scores over 600: 32%; ACT scores over 24: 61%; SAT critical reading scores over 700: 9%; SAT math scores over 700: 7%; ACT scores over 30: 16%.
Retention: 76% of full-time freshmen returned.

FACULTY
Total: 234, 47% full-time, 44% with terminal degrees.
Student/faculty ratio: 14:1.

ACADEMICS
Calendar: semesters. *Degrees:* bachelor's and master's.
Special study options: academic remediation for entering students, accelerated degree program, advanced placement credit, distance learning, double majors, English as a second language, honors programs, independent study, internships, off-campus study, services for LD students, study abroad, summer session for credit. ***ROTC:*** Army (c), Air Force (c).
Computers: 101 computers/terminals and 450 ports are available on campus for general student use. Students can access the following: campus intranet, computer help desk, free student e-mail accounts, online (class) grades, online (class) registration, online (class) schedules. Campuswide network is available. 100% of college-owned or -operated housing units are wired for high-speed Internet access. Wireless service is available via entire campus.

STUDENT LIFE
Housing options: on-campus residence required through senior year; men-only, women-only, special housing for students with disabilities.

Campus housing is university owned. Freshman campus housing is guaranteed.

Activities and organizations: drama/theater group, student-run newspaper, radio and television station, choral group, Outreach, Wishing Well Project, Student Government Association, Young Republicans, College Democrats.

Athletics Member NCAA, NCCAA. All NCAA Division II. ***Intercollegiate sports:*** baseball M(s), basketball M(s)/W(s), cross-country running M(s)/W(s), golf M(s), soccer M(s)/W(s), softball W(s), track and field M(s)/W(s). ***Intramural sports:*** baseball M/W, basketball M/W, bowling M/W, cheerleading M/W, cross-country running M/W, football M/W, golf M/W, soccer M/W, softball M/W, swimming and diving M/W, table tennis M/W, tennis M/W, track and field M/W, volleyball M/W.

Campus security: 24-hour emergency response devices and patrols, late-night transport/escort service, controlled dormitory access.

Student services: health clinic, personal/psychological counseling.

COSTS & FINANCIAL AID

Costs (2015–16) ***Comprehensive fee:*** $26,920 includes full-time tuition ($19,890) and room and board ($7030). Full-time tuition and fees vary according to course load, program, and reciprocity agreements. Part-time tuition: $828 per credit hour. Part-time tuition and fees vary according to course load, program, and reciprocity agreements. ***College room only:*** $3870. Room and board charges vary according to board plan and housing facility. ***Payment plan:*** installment. ***Waivers:*** employees or children of employees.

Financial Aid Of all full-time matriculated undergraduates who enrolled in 2013, 1,418 applied for aid, 1,199 were judged to have need, 539 had their need fully met. 843 Federal Work-Study jobs (averaging $1627). In 2013, 471 non-need-based awards were made. ***Average percent of need met:*** 83. ***Average financial aid package:*** $21,652. ***Average need-based loan:*** $2042. ***Average need-based gift aid:*** $3078. ***Average non-need-based aid:*** $5630. ***Average indebtedness upon graduation:*** $27,065. ***Financial aid deadline:*** 8/31.

APPLYING

Standardized Tests *Required:* SAT or ACT (for admission).

Options: electronic application, early admission, deferred entrance.

Application fee: $25.

Required: high school transcript, 1 letter of recommendation, Composite ACT or SAT Score. ***Required for some:*** essay or personal statement, interview.

Application deadlines: rolling (freshmen), rolling (transfers).

Notification: continuous (freshmen), continuous (transfers).

CONTACT

Mr. Michael Mitchell, Director, Admissions, Oklahoma Christian University, Box 11000, Oklahoma City, OK 73136-1100. *Phone:* 405-425-5065. *Toll-free phone:* 800-877-5010. *Fax:* 405-425-5208. *E-mail:* info@oc.edu.

Oklahoma City University

Oklahoma City, Oklahoma

http://www.okcu.edu/

- **Independent United Methodist** comprehensive, founded 1904
- **Urban** 103-acre campus with easy access to Oklahoma City
- **Endowment** $60.6 million
- **Coed** 1,781 undergraduate students, 89% full-time, 63% women, 37% men

UNDERGRAD STUDENTS

1,578 full-time, 203 part-time. Students come from 47 states and territories; 50 other countries; 47% are from out of state; 5% Black or African American, non-Hispanic/Latino; 8% Hispanic/Latino; 2% Asian, non-Hispanic/Latino; 2% American Indian or Alaska Native, non-Hispanic/Latino; 8% Two or more races, non-Hispanic/Latino; 0.2% Race/ethnicity unknown; 13% international; 11% transferred in; 52% live on campus.

Freshmen

Admission: 297 enrolled. ***Average high school GPA:*** 3.61. ***Test scores:*** ACT scores over 18: 100%; ACT scores over 24: 70%; ACT scores over 30: 17%.

Retention: 80% of full-time freshmen returned.

FACULTY

Total: 283, 72% full-time, 49% with terminal degrees.

Student/faculty ratio: 11:1.

ACADEMICS

Calendar: semesters. *Degrees:* bachelor's, master's, and doctoral.

Special study options: accelerated degree program, adult/continuing education programs, advanced placement credit, cooperative education, distance learning, double majors, English as a second language, honors programs, independent study, internships, off-campus study, part-time degree program, services for LD students, study abroad, summer session for credit. ***ROTC:*** Army (c), Air Force (c).

Computers: 368 computers/terminals are available on campus for general student use. Students can access the following: campus intranet, computer help desk, free student e-mail accounts, online (class) grades, online (class) registration, online (class) schedules. Campuswide network is available. 100% of college-owned or -operated housing units are wired for high-speed Internet access. Wireless service is available via entire campus.

STUDENT LIFE

Housing options: coed, men-only, women-only, special housing for students with disabilities. Freshman applicants given priority for college housing.

Activities and organizations: drama/theater group, student-run newspaper, television station, choral group, Tri-Beta, Multicultural Student Association, Student Nursing Associate, Fellowship of Christian Athletes, national fraternities, national sororities.

Athletics Member NAIA. ***Intercollegiate sports:*** baseball M(s), basketball M(s)/W(s), cheerleading M(s)/W(s), crew M(s)/W(s), golf M(s)/W(s), sailing M(c)/W(c), soccer M(s)/W(s), softball W(s), track and field M(s)/W(s), volleyball W(s), wrestling M(s)/W(s). ***Intramural sports:*** basketball M/W, golf M/W, softball M/W, table tennis M/W, volleyball M/W.

Campus security: 24-hour emergency response devices and patrols, late-night transport/escort service, controlled dormitory access.

Student services: health clinic, personal/psychological counseling.

COSTS & FINANCIAL AID

Costs (2014–15) ***Comprehensive fee:*** $40,476 includes full-time tuition ($27,276), mandatory fees ($3450), and room and board ($9750). Full-time tuition and fees vary according to course level, course load, degree level, program, and student level. Part-time tuition: $925 per credit hour. Part-time tuition and fees vary according to course level, degree level, program, and student level. ***Required fees:*** $115 per credit hour part-time. ***College room only:*** $5290. Room and board charges vary according to board plan and housing facility. ***Payment plans:*** installment, deferred payment. ***Waivers:*** employees or children of employees.

Financial Aid Of all full-time matriculated undergraduates who enrolled in 2014, 1,123 applied for aid, 1,009 were judged to have need, 850 had their need fully met. 270 Federal Work-Study jobs (averaging $1458). 267 state and other part-time jobs (averaging $1383). In 2014, 335 non-need-based awards were made. ***Average percent of need met:*** 62. ***Average financial aid package:*** $20,762. ***Average need-based loan:*** $4480. ***Average need-based gift aid:*** $16,114. ***Average non-need-based aid:*** $18,945. ***Average indebtedness upon graduation:*** $27,819.

APPLYING

Standardized Tests *Required:* SAT or ACT (for admission).

Required: essay or personal statement, high school transcript. ***Required for some:*** interview.

CONTACT

Ms. Michelle cook, Senior Director of Admissions, Oklahoma City University, 2501 North Blackwelder, Oklahoma City, OK 73106. *Phone:* 405-208-5055. *Toll-free phone:* 800-633-7242. *Fax:* 405-208-5916. *E-mail:* michelle.cook@okcu.edu.

★ Oklahoma State University

Stillwater, Oklahoma

http://www.okstate.edu/

- **State-supported** university, founded 1890, part of Oklahoma State University
- **Small-town** 840-acre campus with easy access to Oklahoma City, Tulsa
- **Endowment** $754.9 million
- **Coed** 20,821 undergraduate students, 87% full-time, 49% women, 51% men
- **Moderately difficult** entrance level, 75% of applicants were admitted

UNDERGRAD STUDENTS
18,156 full-time, 2,665 part-time. Students come from 56 states and territories; 73 other countries; 27% are from out of state; 5% Black or African American, non-Hispanic/Latino; 6% Hispanic/Latino; 2% Asian, non-Hispanic/Latino; 0.1% Native Hawaiian or other Pacific Islander, non-Hispanic/Latino; 5% American Indian or Alaska Native, non-Hispanic/Latino; 8% Two or more races, non-Hispanic/Latino; 0.4% Race/ethnicity unknown; 3% international; 8% transferred in; 45% live on campus.

Freshmen
Admission: 12,259 applied, 9,188 admitted, 4,057 enrolled. ***Average high school GPA:*** 3.54. ***Test scores:*** SAT critical reading scores over 500: 71%; SAT math scores over 500: 79%; ACT scores over 18: 98%; SAT critical reading scores over 600: 27%; SAT math scores over 600: 35%; ACT scores over 24: 63%; SAT critical reading scores over 700: 4%; SAT math scores over 700: 6%; ACT scores over 30: 15%.
Retention: 81% of full-time freshmen returned.

FACULTY
Total: 1,327, 78% full-time, 74% with terminal degrees.
Student/faculty ratio: 20:1.

ACADEMICS
Calendar: semesters. *Degrees:* bachelor's, master's, doctoral, post-master's, and postbachelor's certificates.
Special study options: accelerated degree program, advanced placement credit, distance learning, double majors, English as a second language, freshman honors college, honors programs, independent study, internships, off-campus study, part-time degree program, services for LD students, student-designed majors, study abroad, summer session for credit. ***ROTC:*** Army (b), Air Force (b).
Unusual degree programs: 3-2 business administration with Accounting; Human Sciences, Education.
Computers: Students can access the following: campus intranet, computer help desk, free student e-mail accounts, online (class) grades, online (class) registration, online (class) schedules. Campuswide network is available. 97% of college-owned or -operated housing units are wired for high-speed Internet access. Wireless service is available via classrooms, computer centers, computer labs, dorm rooms, learning centers, libraries, student centers.

STUDENT LIFE
Housing options: on-campus residence required for freshman year; coed, men-only, women-only, special housing for students with disabilities. Campus housing is university owned. Freshman applicants given priority for college housing.
Activities and organizations: drama/theater group, student-run newspaper, radio and television station, choral group, marching band, national fraternities, national sororities.
Athletics Member NCAA. All Division I. ***Intercollegiate sports:*** baseball M(s), basketball M(s)/W(s), cheerleading M(s)(c)/W(s)(c), cross-country running M(s)/W(s), equestrian sports W(s), football M(s), golf M(s)/W(s), soccer W(s), softball W(s), tennis M(s)/W(s), track and field M(s)/W(s), wrestling M(s). ***Intramural sports:*** archery M/W, badminton M/W, basketball M/W, bowling M/W, football M/W, golf M/W, racquetball M/W, soccer M/W, softball M/W, swimming and diving M/W, table tennis M/W, tennis M/W, ultimate Frisbee M/W, volleyball M/W, water polo M/W, weight lifting M/W, wrestling M/W.
Campus security: 24-hour emergency response devices and patrols, student patrols, late-night transport/escort service, controlled dormitory access.
Student services: health clinic, personal/psychological counseling, legal services.

COSTS & FINANCIAL AID
Costs (2014–15) ***One-time required fee:*** $95. ***Tuition:*** state resident $4425 full-time, $148 per credit hour part-time; nonresident $17,010 full-time, $567 per credit hour part-time. Full-time tuition and fees vary according to program. Part-time tuition and fees vary according to course load and program. No tuition increase for student's term of enrollment. ***Required fees:*** $3017 full-time, $101 per credit hour part-time. ***Room and board:*** $7390; room only: $3890. Room and board charges vary according to board plan and housing facility. ***Payment plan:*** installment. ***Waivers:*** children of alumni and employees or children of employees.
Financial Aid Of all full-time matriculated undergraduates who enrolled in 2013, 11,957 applied for aid, 9,271 were judged to have need, 1,128 had their need fully met. 393 Federal Work-Study jobs (averaging $2436). 4,151 state and other part-time jobs (averaging $2790). In 2013, 4802 non-need-based awards were made. ***Average percent of need met:*** 76. ***Average financial aid package:*** $13,159. ***Average need-based loan:*** $4093. ***Average need-based gift aid:*** $6615. ***Average non-need-based aid:*** $5553. ***Average indebtedness upon graduation:*** $22,591.

APPLYING
Standardized Tests *Required:* SAT or ACT (for admission).
Options: electronic application, deferred entrance.
Application fee: $40.
Required: high school transcript, minimum 3.0 GPA, class rank. ***Required for some:*** essay or personal statement, letters of recommendation.
Application deadlines: rolling (freshmen), rolling (out-of-state freshmen), rolling (transfers).
Notification: continuous (freshmen), continuous (out-of-state freshmen), continuous (transfers).

CONTACT
Oklahoma State University, Stillwater, OK 74078. *Phone:* 405-744-3087. *Toll-free phone:* 800-233-5019.

Oklahoma State University Institute of Technology

Okmulgee, Oklahoma

http://www.osuit.edu/

- **State-supported** primarily 2-year, founded 1946, part of Oklahoma State University
- **Small-town** 160-acre campus with easy access to Tulsa
- **Endowment** $7.3 million
- **Coed** 2,624 undergraduate students, 73% full-time, 37% women, 63% men
- **Noncompetitive** entrance level, 47% of applicants were admitted

UNDERGRAD STUDENTS
1,910 full-time, 714 part-time. Students come from 30 states and territories; 13 other countries; 12% are from out of state; 5% Black or African American, non-Hispanic/Latino; 6% Hispanic/Latino; 1% Asian, non-Hispanic/Latino; 0.2% Native Hawaiian or other Pacific Islander, non-Hispanic/Latino; 18% American Indian or Alaska Native, non-Hispanic/Latino; 5% Two or more races, non-Hispanic/Latino; 4% Race/ethnicity unknown; 0.7% international; 8% transferred in; 28% live on campus.

Freshmen
Admission: 1,805 applied, 843 admitted, 490 enrolled. ***Average high school GPA:*** 2.93. ***Test scores:*** ACT scores over 18: 57%; ACT scores over 24: 9%; ACT scores over 30: 1%.
Retention: 56% of full-time freshmen returned.

FACULTY
Total: 182, 67% full-time, 5% with terminal degrees.
Student/faculty ratio: 15:1.

ACADEMICS
Calendar: trimesters. *Degrees:* associate and bachelor's.

Special study options: academic remediation for entering students, adult/continuing education programs, advanced placement credit, distance learning, double majors, independent study, internships, part-time degree program, services for LD students, summer session for credit.

Computers: 50 computers/terminals are available on campus for general student use. Students can access the following: computer help desk, free student e-mail accounts, online (class) grades, online (class) registration, online (class) schedules. Campuswide network is available. 100% of college-owned or -operated housing units are wired for high-speed Internet access. Wireless service is available via entire campus.

STUDENT LIFE

Housing options: on-campus residence required for freshman year; coed, men-only. Campus housing is university owned. Freshman applicants given priority for college housing.

Activities and organizations: Phi Theta Kappa, Future Art Directors Club, Air Conditioning and Refrigeration Club, Future Chefs Association Club, Instrumentation, Society and Automation Club.

Athletics ***Intramural sports:*** basketball M/W, football M/W, racquetball M/W, soccer M/W, softball M/W, table tennis M/W, volleyball M/W.

Campus security: 24-hour emergency response devices and patrols, late-night transport/escort service, controlled dormitory access.

Student services: health clinic, personal/psychological counseling.

COSTS

Costs (2015–16) ***Tuition:*** state resident $3465 full-time, $116 per credit hour part-time; nonresident $9075 full-time, $303 per credit hour part-time. Full-time tuition and fees vary according to course level, course load, location, program, and student level. Part-time tuition and fees vary according to course level, course load, location, program, and student level. ***Required fees:*** $1140 full-time, $38 per credit hour part-time. ***Room and board:*** $5902. Room and board charges vary according to board plan and housing facility. ***Payment plan:*** installment. ***Waivers:*** senior citizens and employees or children of employees.

APPLYING

Standardized Tests *Required for some:* SAT or ACT (for admission). *Recommended:* ACT (for admission).

Options: deferred entrance.

Required: high school transcript.

Application deadlines: rolling (freshmen), rolling (out-of-state freshmen), rolling (transfers).

CONTACT

Chenoa Worthington, Assistant Registrar, Oklahoma State University Institute of Technology, 1801 E 4th St, Okmulgee, OK 74447. *Phone:* 918-293-5274. *Toll-free phone:* 800-722-4471. *Fax:* 918-293-4643. *E-mail:* chenoa.worthington@okstate.edu.

Oklahoma State University, Oklahoma City

Oklahoma City, Oklahoma

http://www.osuokc.edu/

- **State-supported** primarily 2-year, founded 1961, part of Oklahoma State University
- **Urban** 110-acre campus
- **Coed** 6,712 undergraduate students, 32% full-time, 61% women, 39% men
- **Noncompetitive** entrance level

UNDERGRAD STUDENTS

2,175 full-time, 4,537 part-time. Students come from 25 states and territories; 3% are from out of state; 15% Black or African American, non-Hispanic/Latino; 10% Hispanic/Latino; 3% Asian, non-Hispanic/Latino; 4% American Indian or Alaska Native, non-Hispanic/Latino; 9% Two or more races, non-Hispanic/Latino; 4% Race/ethnicity unknown; 12% transferred in.

Freshmen

Admission: 952 admitted, 952 enrolled.

FACULTY

Total: 438, 20% full-time.

Student/faculty ratio: 19:1.

ACADEMICS

Calendar: semesters. *Degrees:* certificates, associate, and bachelor's.

Special study options: academic remediation for entering students, advanced placement credit, cooperative education, distance learning, double majors, honors programs, independent study, part-time degree program, services for LD students, study abroad, summer session for credit.

Computers: Campuswide network is available.

STUDENT LIFE

Housing options: college housing not available.

Activities and organizations: Student Government Association, Go Green, Wind Energy Student Association, Hispanic Student Association, OSU-OKC Chapter of the OK Student Nurse Association.

Campus security: 24-hour patrols, late-night transport/escort service.

COSTS

Costs (2015–16) ***Tuition:*** state resident $2770 full-time, $115 per credit hour part-time; nonresident $7630 full-time, $318 per credit hour part-time. Full-time tuition and fees vary according to course level, degree level, program, and student level. Part-time tuition and fees vary according to course level, degree level, program, and student level. No tuition increase for student's term of enrollment. ***Required fees:*** $89 full-time, $12 per term part-time, $65 per year part-time. ***Payment plans:*** tuition prepayment, installment. ***Waivers:*** senior citizens and employees or children of employees.

APPLYING

Options: electronic application, early admission.

Required: high school transcript.

Application deadlines: rolling (freshmen), rolling (transfers).

Notification: continuous (freshmen), continuous (transfers).

CONTACT

Mr. Kyle Williams, Director, Enrollment Management, Oklahoma State University, Oklahoma City, 900 North Portland Avenue, AD202, Oklahoma City, OK 73107. *Phone:* 405-945-9152. *Toll-free phone:* 800-560-4099. *E-mail:* wilkylw@osuokc.edu.

Oklahoma Wesleyan University

Bartlesville, Oklahoma

http://www.okwu.edu/

- **Independent** comprehensive, founded 1909, affiliated with Wesleyan Church
- **Small-town** 127-acre campus with easy access to Tulsa
- **Endowment** $3.5 million
- **Coed** 1,205 undergraduate students, 50% full-time, 63% women, 37% men
- **Minimally difficult** entrance level, 85% of applicants were admitted

UNDERGRAD STUDENTS

602 full-time, 603 part-time. Students come from 41 states and territories; 24 other countries; 44% are from out of state; 6% Black or African American, non-Hispanic/Latino; 7% Hispanic/Latino; 0.4% Asian, non-Hispanic/Latino; 0.2% Native Hawaiian or other Pacific Islander, non-Hispanic/Latino; 7% American Indian or Alaska Native, non-Hispanic/Latino; 4% Two or more races, non-Hispanic/Latino; 3% Race/ethnicity unknown; 6% international; 14% transferred in.

Freshmen

Admission: 235 applied, 200 admitted, 197 enrolled. ***Average high school GPA:*** 3.38. ***Test scores:*** SAT critical reading scores over 500: 38%; SAT math scores over 500: 45%; SAT writing scores over 500: 27%; ACT scores over 18: 78%; SAT critical reading scores over 600: 8%; SAT math scores over 600: 12%; SAT writing scores over 600: 3%; ACT scores over 24: 25%; ACT scores over 30: 2%.

Retention: 62% of full-time freshmen returned.

FACULTY
Total: 111, 32% full-time.

Student/faculty ratio: 15:1.

ACADEMICS
Calendar: semesters. *Degrees:* associate, bachelor's, and master's.

Special study options: academic remediation for entering students, accelerated degree program, adult/continuing education programs, advanced placement credit, cooperative education, distance learning, double majors, external degree program, independent study, internships, off-campus study, part-time degree program, services for LD students, student-designed majors, study abroad, summer session for credit.

Computers: 33 computers/terminals and 118 ports are available on campus for general student use. Students can access the following: campus intranet, computer help desk, free student e-mail accounts, online (class) grades, online (class) registration, online (class) schedules. Campuswide network is available. 100% of college-owned or -operated housing units are wired for high-speed Internet access. Wireless service is available via entire campus.

STUDENT LIFE
Housing options: men-only, women-only. Campus housing is university owned. Freshman campus housing is guaranteed.

Activities and organizations: drama/theater group, student-run newspaper, choral group, Operation Saturation (Community Service Opportunities), Fellowship of Christian Athletes, Missions Support Groups, intramurals, student government groups.

Athletics Member NAIA, NCCAA. ***Intercollegiate sports:*** baseball M(s), basketball M(s)/W(s), cross-country running M(s)/W(s), golf M(s)/W(s), soccer M(s)/W(s), softball W(s), tennis M(s)/W(s), track and field M(s)/W(s), volleyball W(s). ***Intramural sports:*** basketball M/W, cheerleading W, racquetball M/W, softball M/W, ultimate Frisbee M/W, volleyball M/W.

Campus security: student patrols.

Student services: health clinic, personal/psychological counseling.

COSTS & FINANCIAL AID
Costs (2015–16) ***Comprehensive fee:*** $30,668 includes full-time tuition ($21,930), mandatory fees ($1250), and room and board ($7488). Full-time tuition and fees vary according to course load. Part-time tuition: $900 per credit. ***College room only:*** $3858. Room and board charges vary according to board plan and housing facility. ***Payment plans:*** installment, deferred payment. ***Waivers:*** senior citizens and employees or children of employees.

Financial Aid Of all full-time matriculated undergraduates who enrolled in 2014, 454 applied for aid, 402 were judged to have need, 76 had their need fully met. ***Average percent of need met:*** 62. ***Average financial aid package:*** $16,533. ***Average need-based loan:*** $4694. ***Average need-based gift aid:*** $12,200. ***Average non-need-based aid:*** $5260. ***Average indebtedness upon graduation:*** $28,072.

APPLYING
Standardized Tests *Required:* SAT or ACT (for admission).

Options: electronic application.

Application fee: $25.

Required: high school transcript, ACT score 18 or higher. ***Required for some:*** interview. ***Recommended:*** minimum 2.0 GPA.

Application deadlines: rolling (freshmen), rolling (out-of-state freshmen), rolling (transfers).

CONTACT
Samantha Peterson, AVP of Enrollment, Oklahoma Wesleyan University, 2201 Silver Lake Road, Bartlesville, OK 74006. *Phone:* 866-222-8226. *Toll-free phone:* 866-222-8226. *Fax:* 918-335-6229. *E-mail:* admissions@okwu.edu.

Oral Roberts University

Tulsa, Oklahoma

http://www.oru.edu/

- **Independent interdenominational** comprehensive, founded 1963
- **Urban** 263-acre campus
- **Coed**
- **Moderately difficult** entrance level

FACULTY
Student/faculty ratio: 15:1.

ACADEMICS
Calendar: semesters. *Degrees:* certificates, diplomas, bachelor's, master's, and doctoral.

STUDENT LIFE
Housing options: on-campus residence required through senior year; men-only, women-only.

Athletics Member NCAA. All Division I.

Campus security: 24-hour emergency response devices and patrols, late-night transport/escort service.

COSTS & FINANCIAL AID
Costs (2014–15) ***Comprehensive fee:*** $33,175 includes full-time tuition ($22,564), mandatory fees ($846), and room and board ($9765). Full-time tuition and fees vary according to degree level. Part-time tuition: $943 per credit hour. Part-time tuition and fees vary according to degree level. ***College room only:*** $4775. Room and board charges vary according to board plan and housing facility.

Financial Aid Of all full-time matriculated undergraduates who enrolled in 2013, 2,050 applied for aid, 1,882 were judged to have need, 798 had their need fully met. In 2013, 611 non-need-based awards were made. ***Average percent of need met:*** 77. ***Average financial aid package:*** $22,741. ***Average need-based loan:*** $7775. ***Average need-based gift aid:*** $15,007. ***Average non-need-based aid:*** $10,903. ***Average indebtedness upon graduation:*** $33,584.

APPLYING
Options: deferred entrance.

Application fee: $35.

Required: essay or personal statement, high school transcript, minimum 2.0 GPA, 1 letter of recommendation, proof of immunization. ***Required for some:*** interview. ***Recommended:*** interview.

CONTACT
Chris Belcher, Director of Admissions, Oral Roberts University, 7777 South Lewis Avenue, Tulsa, OK 74171. *Phone:* 918-495-6529. *Toll-free phone:* 800-678-8876. *Fax:* 918-495-6222. *E-mail:* admissions@oru.edu.

Rogers State University

Claremore, Oklahoma

http://www.rsu.edu/

- **State-supported** 4-year, founded 1909, part of Oklahoma State Regents for Higher Education
- **Small-town** 40-acre campus with easy access to Tulsa
- **Endowment** $8.8 million
- **Coed**
- **Noncompetitive** entrance level

FACULTY
Student/faculty ratio: 21:1.

ACADEMICS
Calendar: semesters. *Degrees:* associate and bachelor's.

STUDENT LIFE
Housing options: coed. Campus housing is university owned.

Activities and organizations: drama/theater group, student-run newspaper, radio station, choral group, Students Veterans Association, Student Nurses Association, President's Leadership Class, Pre-Professional Health Club (Pre-SOMA), Student Athlete Advisory Committee, national sororities.

Athletics Member NAIA.

Campus security: 24-hour emergency response devices and patrols, student patrols, late-night transport/escort service, controlled dormitory access, RSU employs only State certified law enforcement officers and has a comprehensive camera surveillance system.

Student services: health clinic, personal/psychological counseling.

COSTS & FINANCIAL AID
Costs (2014–15) ***Tuition:*** state resident $3327 full-time, $111 per hour part-time; nonresident $9981 full-time, $333 per hour part-time. Full-time tuition and fees vary according to course level, course load, location,

program, and student level. Part-time tuition and fees vary according to course level, course load, location, program, and student level. ***Required fees:*** $1994 full-time, $66 per hour part-time, $15 per term part-time. ***Room and board:*** $8830. Room and board charges vary according to housing facility.

Financial Aid Of all full-time matriculated undergraduates who enrolled in 2014, 1,663 applied for aid, 1,353 were judged to have need, 101 had their need fully met. 62 Federal Work-Study jobs (averaging $1994). 258 state and other part-time jobs (averaging $1934). In 2014, 66 non-need-based awards were made. ***Average percent of need met:*** 50. ***Average financial aid package:*** $9637. ***Average need-based loan:*** $4081. ***Average need-based gift aid:*** $5914. ***Average non-need-based aid:*** $8750. ***Average indebtedness upon graduation:*** $13,403.

APPLYING

Standardized Tests *Required:* SAT or ACT (for admission). *Required for some:* ACT Compass. *Recommended:* ACT (for admission).

Options: electronic application.

Required: high school transcript. ***Required for some:*** minimum 2.8 GPA, Baccalaureate degree programs require 20 ACT composite or 2.75 GPA and top 50% rank for admission; Associate degree programs have an open admission policy.

CONTACT

Ms. Joy Lin Husted, Director of Admissions, Rogers State University, 1701 West Will Rogers Boulevard, Claremore, OK 74017. *Phone:* 918-343-7546. *Toll-free phone:* 800-256-7511. *Fax:* 918-343-7595. *E-mail:* info@rsu.edu.

St. Gregory's University

Shawnee, Oklahoma

http://www.stgregorys.edu/

- **Independent Roman Catholic** comprehensive, founded 1875
- **Small-town** 640-acre campus with easy access to Oklahoma City
- **Endowment** $9.6 million
- **Coed** 668 undergraduate students, 75% full-time, 57% women, 43% men
- **Minimally difficult** entrance level

UNDERGRAD STUDENTS

503 full-time, 165 part-time. Students come from 19 states and territories; 10 other countries; 4% are from out of state; 8% Black or African American, non-Hispanic/Latino; 12% Hispanic/Latino; 1% Asian, non-Hispanic/Latino; 0.3% Native Hawaiian or other Pacific Islander, non-Hispanic/Latino; 8% American Indian or Alaska Native, non-Hispanic/Latino; 9% Two or more races, non-Hispanic/Latino; 10% Race/ethnicity unknown; 4% international; 7% transferred in; 36% live on campus.

Freshmen

Admission: 587 applied, 108 enrolled. ***Average high school GPA:*** 3.29. ***Test scores:*** SAT math scores over 500: 41%; SAT writing scores over 500: 30%; ACT scores over 18: 88%; SAT math scores over 600: 8%; SAT writing scores over 600: 10%; ACT scores over 24: 21%; ACT scores over 30: 3%.

Retention: 60% of full-time freshmen returned.

FACULTY

Total: 206, 21% full-time.

Student/faculty ratio: 11:1.

ACADEMICS

Calendar: semesters. *Degrees:* certificates, associate, bachelor's, and master's.

Special study options: accelerated degree program, adult/continuing education programs, advanced placement credit, cooperative education, distance learning, double majors, external degree program, honors programs, independent study, internships, off-campus study, part-time degree program, services for LD students, summer session for credit.

Computers: 35 computers/terminals and 100 ports are available on campus for general student use. Students can access the following: campus intranet, computer help desk, free student e-mail accounts, online (class) grades, online (class) registration, online (class) schedules. Campuswide network is available. 100% of college-owned or -operated housing units are wired for high-speed Internet access. Wireless service is available via entire campus.

STUDENT LIFE

Housing options: on-campus residence required through senior year; men-only, women-only, special housing for students with disabilities. Campus housing is university owned. Freshman campus housing is guaranteed.

Activities and organizations: drama/theater group, choral group, Greek Life, Student Government Association, Pro-Life, Hispanic American Student Association, Campus Ministry.

Athletics Member NAIA. ***Intercollegiate sports:*** baseball M(s), basketball M(s)/W(s), cheerleading M/W, lacrosse M(s), soccer M(s)/W(s), softball W(s), track and field M(s)/W(s), volleyball W(s). ***Intramural sports:*** basketball M/W, football M/W, racquetball M/W, soccer M/W, softball M/W, swimming and diving M/W, table tennis M/W, tennis M/W, volleyball M/W.

Campus security: 24-hour emergency response devices and patrols, late-night transport/escort service, controlled dormitory access.

Student services: personal/psychological counseling.

COSTS & FINANCIAL AID

Costs (2014–15) ***Comprehensive fee:*** $27,100 includes full-time tuition ($19,320) and room and board ($7780). Part-time tuition: $644 per credit hour. Part-time tuition and fees vary according to course load. No tuition increase for student's term of enrollment. ***College room only:*** $4000. Room and board charges vary according to board plan and housing facility. ***Payment plans:*** tuition prepayment, installment, deferred payment. ***Waivers:*** adult students and employees or children of employees.

Financial Aid Of all full-time matriculated undergraduates who enrolled in 2005, 555 applied for aid, 521 were judged to have need, 60 had their need fully met. 38 Federal Work-Study jobs (averaging $867). 24 state and other part-time jobs (averaging $2551). In 2005, 61 non-need-based awards were made. ***Average percent of need met:*** 69. ***Average financial aid package:*** $10,686. ***Average need-based loan:*** $3720. ***Average need-based gift aid:*** $6883. ***Average non-need-based aid:*** $1500. ***Average indebtedness upon graduation:*** $10,160.

APPLYING

Standardized Tests *Required:* SAT or ACT (for admission).

Options: electronic application, deferred entrance.

Required: minimum 2.8 GPA. ***Required for some:*** essay or personal statement, high school transcript, interview.

Application deadlines: rolling (freshmen), rolling (transfers).

Notification: continuous (freshmen), continuous (transfers).

CONTACT

Sean Brown, Director of Admissions, St. Gregory's University, 1900 West MacArthur Drive, Shawnee, OK 74804. *Phone:* 405-878-5161. *Toll-free phone:* 888-STGREGS. *Fax:* 405-878-5198. *E-mail:* admissions@stgregorys.edu.

Southeastern Oklahoma State University

Durant, Oklahoma

http://www.se.edu/

- **State-supported** comprehensive, founded 1909, part of Oklahoma State Regents for Higher Education
- **Small-town** 276-acre campus
- **Endowment** $21.5 million
- **Coed** 3,468 undergraduate students, 78% full-time, 55% women, 45% men
- **Moderately difficult** entrance level, 79% of applicants were admitted

UNDERGRAD STUDENTS

2,703 full-time, 765 part-time. 7% Black or African American, non-Hispanic/Latino; 4% Hispanic/Latino; 1% Asian, non-Hispanic/Latino; 0.3% Native Hawaiian or other Pacific Islander, non-Hispanic/Latino; 30% American Indian or Alaska Native, non-Hispanic/Latino; 3% international; 12% transferred in; 16% live on campus.

Freshmen

Admission: 980 applied, 771 admitted, 502 enrolled. ***Average high school GPA:*** 3.28. ***Test scores:*** ACT scores over 18: 77%; ACT scores over 24: 18%; ACT scores over 30: 1%.

Retention: 68% of full-time freshmen returned.

FACULTY

Total: 271, 51% full-time, 52% with terminal degrees.

Student/faculty ratio: 17:1.

ACADEMICS

Calendar: semesters. *Degrees:* bachelor's, master's, and post-master's certificates.

Special study options: academic remediation for entering students, accelerated degree program, adult/continuing education programs, advanced placement credit, distance learning, double majors, honors programs, independent study, internships, off-campus study, part-time degree program, services for LD students, summer session for credit.

Computers: 598 computers/terminals and 598 ports are available on campus for general student use. Students can access the following: campus intranet, computer help desk, free student e-mail accounts, online (class) grades, online (class) registration, online (class) schedules, campus Blackboard classes. Campuswide network is available. 100% of college-owned or -operated housing units are wired for high-speed Internet access. Wireless service is available via classrooms, computer labs, dorm rooms, learning centers, libraries, student centers.

STUDENT LIFE

Housing options: on-campus residence required for freshman year; coed, men-only, women-only, special housing for students with disabilities. Campus housing is university owned. Freshman campus housing is guaranteed.

Activities and organizations: drama/theater group, student-run newspaper, radio station, choral group, marching band, Greek Community, Baptist Collegiate Ministries, Native American Student Association, Savage Storm Leaders (Orientation leaders), Residence Hall Association, national fraternities, national sororities.

Athletics Member NCAA. All Division II. ***Intercollegiate sports:*** baseball M(s), basketball M(s)/W(s), cross-country running W(s), football M(s), golf M(s), softball W(s), tennis M(s)/W(s), volleyball W(s). ***Intramural sports:*** basketball M/W, football M.

Campus security: 24-hour emergency response devices and patrols, late-night transport/escort service, controlled dormitory access.

Student services: health clinic, personal/psychological counseling.

COSTS & FINANCIAL AID

Costs (2014–15) ***Tuition:*** state resident $5055 full-time, $169 per credit hour part-time; nonresident $15,100 full-time, $445 per credit hour part-time. Full-time tuition and fees vary according to course level, degree level, location, and program. Part-time tuition and fees vary according to course level, course load, degree level, location, and program. No tuition increase for student's term of enrollment. ***Required fees:*** $633 full-time, $21 per credit hour part-time. ***Room and board:*** $6143; room only: $3773. Room and board charges vary according to board plan, housing facility, and student level. ***Payment plan:*** installment. ***Waivers:*** minority students, children of alumni, adult students, senior citizens, and employees or children of employees.

Financial Aid Of all full-time matriculated undergraduates who enrolled in 2013, 1,937 applied for aid, 1,771 were judged to have need, 120 had their need fully met. 736 Federal Work-Study jobs (averaging $1832). In 2013, 21 non-need-based awards were made. ***Average percent of need met:*** 13. ***Average financial aid package:*** $10,559. ***Average need-based loan:*** $1920. ***Average need-based gift aid:*** $1840. ***Average non-need-based aid:*** $646. ***Average indebtedness upon graduation:*** $19,368.

APPLYING

Standardized Tests *Required:* SAT or ACT (for admission).

Options: electronic application.

Application fee: $20.

Required: high school transcript. ***Required for some:*** interview.

Application deadlines: rolling (freshmen), rolling (transfers).

Notification: continuous (freshmen), continuous (transfers).

CONTACT

Southeastern Oklahoma State University, 1405 North 4th Avenue, Durant, OK 74701-0609. *Phone:* 580-745-2061. *Toll-free phone:* 800-435-1327.

Southern Nazarene University

Bethany, Oklahoma

http://www.snu.edu/

- **Independent Nazarene** comprehensive, founded 1899
- **Suburban** 40-acre campus with easy access to Oklahoma City
- **Endowment** $21.6 million
- **Coed**
- **Noncompetitive** entrance level

FACULTY

Student/faculty ratio: 17:1.

ACADEMICS

Calendar: semesters. *Degrees:* associate, bachelor's, and master's.

STUDENT LIFE

Housing options: on-campus residence required through senior year; men-only, women-only. Campus housing is university owned. Freshman campus housing is guaranteed.

Activities and organizations: drama/theater group, student-run newspaper, choral group, Business Gaming Team, Campus Social Life Committee, intramural sports societies, Choral Society, Inter-Club.

Athletics Member NCAA. All Division II.

Campus security: 24-hour emergency response devices, student patrols, late-night transport/escort service, controlled dormitory access.

Student services: health clinic, personal/psychological counseling.

COSTS & FINANCIAL AID

Costs (2014–15) ***Comprehensive fee:*** $30,650 includes full-time tuition ($21,990), mandatory fees ($690), and room and board ($7970). Part-time tuition: $639 per credit hour. Part-time tuition and fees vary according to course load. ***College room only:*** $4150. Room and board charges vary according to board plan and housing facility. ***Payment plans:*** tuition prepayment, installment, deferred payment.

Financial Aid Of all full-time matriculated undergraduates who enrolled in 2009, 1,485 applied for aid, 1,366 were judged to have need. 104 Federal Work-Study jobs (averaging $2125). 115 state and other part-time jobs (averaging $3000).

APPLYING

Standardized Tests *Required:* SAT or ACT (for admission). *Recommended:* ACT (for admission).

Options: electronic application, deferred entrance.

Application fee: $35.

Required: high school transcript, minimum 2.0 GPA, 2 letters of recommendation, interview.

CONTACT

Dr. Linda Cantwell, Director of Recruitment, Southern Nazarene University, 6729 Northwest 39th Expressway, Bethany, OK 73008. *Phone:* 405-491-6324. *Toll-free phone:* 800-648-9899. *Fax:* 405-491-6320. *E-mail:* admiss@snu.edu.

Southwestern Oklahoma State University

Weatherford, Oklahoma

http://www.swosu.edu/

- **State-supported** comprehensive, founded 1901
- **Small-town** campus
- **Coed**
- **Minimally difficult** entrance level

FACULTY

Student/faculty ratio: 18:1.

ACADEMICS

Calendar: semesters. *Degrees:* certificates, associate, bachelor's, master's, and doctoral.

STUDENT LIFE
Housing options: men-only, women-only. Campus housing is university owned. Freshman campus housing is guaranteed.

Athletics Member NCAA. All Division II.

Campus security: late-night transport/escort service, controlled dormitory access, 20-hour campus emergency security.

FINANCIAL AID
Financial Aid Of all full-time matriculated undergraduates who enrolled in 2013, 2,601 applied for aid, 2,162 were judged to have need, 510 had their need fully met. In 2013, 1217 non-need-based awards were made. ***Average percent of need met:*** 94. ***Average financial aid package:*** $5380. ***Average need-based loan:*** $1663. ***Average need-based gift aid:*** $1594. ***Average non-need-based aid:*** $585. ***Average indebtedness upon graduation:*** $16,833. ***Financial aid deadline:*** 3/1.

APPLYING
Standardized Tests *Required:* SAT or ACT (for admission). *Recommended:* ACT (for admission).

Options: deferred entrance.

Application fee: $15.

Required: high school transcript, minimum 2.0 GPA.

CONTACT
Ms. Connie Phillips, Admission Counselor, Southwestern Oklahoma State University, 100 Campus Drive, Weatherford, OK 73096-3098. *Phone:* 580-774-3009. *Fax:* 580-774-3795. *E-mail:* ropers@swosu.edu.

University of Central Oklahoma

Edmond, Oklahoma

http://www.uco.edu/

- **State-supported** comprehensive, founded 1890, part of Oklahoma State Regents for Higher Education
- **Suburban** 200-acre campus with easy access to Oklahoma City
- **Endowment** $19.7 million
- **Coed** 14,998 undergraduate students, 72% full-time, 58% women, 42% men
- **Minimally difficult** entrance level, 90% of applicants were admitted

UNDERGRAD STUDENTS
10,726 full-time, 4,272 part-time. Students come from 42 states and territories; 76 other countries; 3% are from out of state; 9% Black or African American, non-Hispanic/Latino; 8% Hispanic/Latino; 3% Asian, non-Hispanic/Latino; 0.2% Native Hawaiian or other Pacific Islander, non-Hispanic/Latino; 4% American Indian or Alaska Native, non-Hispanic/Latino; 8% Two or more races, non-Hispanic/Latino; 2% Race/ethnicity unknown; 8% international; 9% transferred in; 9% live on campus.

Freshmen
Admission: 4,537 applied, 4,098 admitted, 2,149 enrolled. ***Average high school GPA:*** 3.29. ***Test scores:*** ACT scores over 18: 78%; ACT scores over 24: 25%; ACT scores over 30: 3%.

Retention: 66% of full-time freshmen returned.

FACULTY
Total: 900, 51% full-time, 51% with terminal degrees.

Student/faculty ratio: 21:1.

ACADEMICS
Calendar: semesters. *Degrees:* certificates, associate, bachelor's, and master's.

Special study options: academic remediation for entering students, accelerated degree program, advanced placement credit, cooperative education, distance learning, double majors, English as a second language, independent study, internships, part-time degree program, services for LD students, summer session for credit. ***ROTC:*** Army (b).

Unusual degree programs: 3-2 engineering.

Computers: 87 computers/terminals are available on campus for general student use. Students can access the following: computer help desk, free student e-mail accounts, online (class) grades, online (class) registration, online (class) schedules. Campuswide network is available. Wireless service is available via entire campus.

STUDENT LIFE
Housing options: coed, men-only, women-only. Campus housing is university owned and leased by the school.

Activities and organizations: drama/theater group, student-run newspaper, radio and television station, choral group, marching band, Student Government Association, Student Programming Board, International Student Council, Panhellenic Council, Interfraternity Council, national fraternities, national sororities.

Athletics Member NCAA. All Division II. ***Intercollegiate sports:*** baseball M(s), basketball M(s)/W(s), cross-country running W(s), football M(s), golf M(s)/W(s), soccer W(s), softball W(s), tennis W(s), volleyball W(s), wrestling M(s). ***Intramural sports:*** badminton M/W, basketball M/W, football M/W, soccer M/W, softball M/W, table tennis M/W, tennis M/W, ultimate Frisbee M/W, volleyball M/W, water polo M/W, wrestling M.

Campus security: 24-hour emergency response devices and patrols, late-night transport/escort service.

Student services: health clinic, personal/psychological counseling.

COSTS & FINANCIAL AID
Costs (2015–16) ***Tuition:*** state resident $5807 full-time, $164 per credit hour part-time; nonresident $14,286 full-time, $447 per credit hour part-time. Full-time tuition and fees vary according to course load, degree level, and program. Part-time tuition and fees vary according to course load, degree level, and program. No tuition increase for student's term of enrollment. ***Required fees:*** $879 full-time, $181 per credit hour part-time. ***Room and board:*** $9862; room only: $6992. Room and board charges vary according to board plan and housing facility. ***Payment plan:*** deferred payment. ***Waivers:*** employees or children of employees.

Financial Aid Of all full-time matriculated undergraduates who enrolled in 2013, 7,493 applied for aid, 6,535 were judged to have need, 783 had their need fully met. 2,687 Federal Work-Study jobs (averaging $4826). 1,900 state and other part-time jobs (averaging $2158). In 2013, 140 non-need-based awards were made. ***Average percent of need met:*** 55. ***Average financial aid package:*** $9073. ***Average need-based loan:*** $3973. ***Average need-based gift aid:*** $5979. ***Average non-need-based aid:*** $1485. ***Average indebtedness upon graduation:*** $22,933.

APPLYING
Standardized Tests *Required:* SAT or ACT (for admission). *Required for some:* SAT and SAT Subject Tests or ACT (for admission). *Recommended:* ACT (for admission).

Options: electronic application, deferred entrance.

Application fee: $40.

Required: high school transcript, minimum 2.7 GPA, rank in upper 50% of high school class; composite ACT score of 20; 2.7 GPA in core curriculum classes.

Application deadlines: rolling (freshmen), rolling (out-of-state freshmen), rolling (transfers).

Notification: continuous (freshmen), continuous (out-of-state freshmen), continuous (transfers).

CONTACT
Mr. Dallas Caldwell, Director of Undergraduate Admissions, University of Central Oklahoma, Office of Enrollment Services, 100 North University Drive, Box 151, Edmond, OK 73034-5209. *Phone:* 405-974-2631. *Fax:* 405-974-3841. *E-mail:* onestop@uco.edu.

University of Oklahoma

Norman, Oklahoma

http://www.ou.edu/

- **State-supported** university, founded 1890
- **Suburban** 3304-acre campus with easy access to Oklahoma City
- **Endowment** $965.9 million
- **Coed** 21,011 undergraduate students, 86% full-time, 49% women, 51% men
- **Moderately difficult** entrance level, 81% of applicants were admitted

UNDERGRAD STUDENTS
17,985 full-time, 3,026 part-time. Students come from 52 states and territories; 122 other countries; 34% are from out of state; 5% Black or African American, non-Hispanic/Latino; 9% Hispanic/Latino; 6% Asian, non-Hispanic/Latino; 0.1% Native Hawaiian or other Pacific Islander,

non-Hispanic/Latino; 4% American Indian or Alaska Native, non-Hispanic/Latino; 7% Two or more races, non-Hispanic/Latino; 2% Race/ethnicity unknown; 6% international; 5% transferred in; 33% live on campus.

Freshmen

Admission: 11,331 applied, 9,216 admitted, 4,176 enrolled. ***Average high school GPA:*** 3.59. ***Test scores:*** SAT critical reading scores over 500: 82%; SAT math scores over 500: 89%; ACT scores over 18: 99%; SAT critical reading scores over 600: 42%; SAT math scores over 600: 53%; ACT scores over 24: 73%; SAT critical reading scores over 700: 19%; SAT math scores over 700: 19%; ACT scores over 30: 23%.

Retention: 85% of full-time freshmen returned.

FACULTY

Total: 1,409, 82% full-time, 79% with terminal degrees.

Student/faculty ratio: 18:1.

ACADEMICS

Calendar: semesters. *Degrees:* bachelor's, master's, doctoral, and postbachelor's certificates.

Special study options: academic remediation for entering students, accelerated degree program, adult/continuing education programs, advanced placement credit, cooperative education, distance learning, double majors, English as a second language, external degree program, freshman honors college, honors programs, independent study, internships, off-campus study, part-time degree program, services for LD students, student-designed majors, study abroad, summer session for credit. ***ROTC:*** Army (b), Navy (b), Air Force (b).

Unusual degree programs: 3-2 business administration; engineering; English, mathematics/biostatistics, computer science, international studies, political science/public administration.

Computers: 4,500 computers/terminals and 2,200 ports are available on campus for general student use. Students can access the following: campus intranet, computer help desk, free student e-mail accounts, online (class) grades, online (class) registration, online (class) schedules. Campuswide network is available. 100% of college-owned or -operated housing units are wired for high-speed Internet access. Wireless service is available via entire campus.

STUDENT LIFE

Housing options: on-campus residence required for freshman year; coed, men-only, women-only, special housing for students with disabilities. Campus housing is university owned. Freshman campus housing is guaranteed.

Activities and organizations: drama/theater group, student-run newspaper, radio and television station, choral group, marching band, Campus Activities Council, University of Oklahoma Student Association, OU Cousins, Fraternities/Sororities, The Big Event, national fraternities, national sororities.

Athletics Member NCAA. All Division I except football (Division I-A). ***Intercollegiate sports:*** baseball M(s), basketball M(s)/W(s), cheerleading M(s)/W(s), crew W(s), cross-country running M(s)/W(s), golf M(s)/W(s), gymnastics M(s)/W(s), soccer W(s), softball W(s), tennis M(s)/W(s), track and field M(s)/W(s), volleyball W(s), wrestling M(s). ***Intramural sports:*** badminton M(c)/W(c), basketball M/W, cross-country running M/W, equestrian sports W(c), field hockey M(c)/W(c), golf M/W, ice hockey M(c), lacrosse M(c), racquetball M/W, rugby M(c)/W(c), soccer M(c)/W, softball M/W, table tennis M/W, tennis M(c)/W(c), ultimate Frisbee M(c)/W(c), volleyball M(c)/W(c).

Campus security: 24-hour emergency response devices and patrols, student patrols, late-night transport/escort service, controlled dormitory access, crime prevention programs, police bicycle patrols, self-defense classes.

Student services: health clinic, personal/psychological counseling, women's center, legal services.

COSTS & FINANCIAL AID

Costs (2014–15) ***Tuition:*** state resident $4128 full-time, $138 per credit hour part-time; nonresident $16,902 full-time, $563 per credit hour part-time. Full-time tuition and fees vary according to course load, location, program, and reciprocity agreements. Part-time tuition and fees vary according to course load, location, program, and reciprocity agreements. No tuition increase for student's term of enrollment. ***Required fees:*** $3567 full-time, $110 per credit hour part-time, $127 per term part-time. ***Room and board:*** $9126; room only: $5022. Room and board charges vary according to board plan and housing facility. ***Payment plan:*** installment. ***Waivers:*** senior citizens and employees or children of employees.

Financial Aid Of all full-time matriculated undergraduates who enrolled in 2013, 10,801 applied for aid, 8,341 were judged to have need, 6,946 had their need fully met. 520 Federal Work-Study jobs (averaging $2598). 129 state and other part-time jobs (averaging $8535). In 2013, 1871 non-need-based awards were made. ***Average percent of need met:*** 86. ***Average financial aid package:*** $12,210. ***Average need-based loan:*** $4286. ***Average need-based gift aid:*** $5995. ***Average non-need-based aid:*** $2108. ***Average indebtedness upon graduation:*** $23,151.

APPLYING

Standardized Tests *Required:* SAT or ACT (for admission).

Options: electronic application.

Application fee: $40.

Required: essay or personal statement, high school transcript, 15 specified curricular units.

Application deadlines: 4/1 (freshmen), 4/1 (out-of-state freshmen), 4/1 (transfers).

Notification: continuous (freshmen), continuous (out-of-state freshmen), continuous (transfers).

CONTACT

Mr. Andy Roop, Executive Director of Recruitment Services, University of Oklahoma, 550 Parrington Oval, Norman, OK 73019-3032. *Phone:* 405-325-2151. *Toll-free phone:* 800-234-6868. *Fax:* 405-325-7478. *E-mail:* ou-pss@ou.edu.

University of Oklahoma Health Sciences Center

Oklahoma City, Oklahoma

http://www.ouhsc.edu/

- **State-supported** upper-level, founded 1890, part of University of Oklahoma
- **Urban** 200-acre campus with easy access to Oklahoma City
- **Endowment** $475.1 million
- **Coed** 833 undergraduate students, 94% full-time, 87% women, 13% men

UNDERGRAD STUDENTS

786 full-time, 47 part-time. Students come from 42 states and territories; 25 other countries; 16% are from out of state; 4% Black or African American, non-Hispanic/Latino; 7% Hispanic/Latino; 6% Asian, non-Hispanic/Latino; 4% American Indian or Alaska Native, non-Hispanic/Latino; 9% Two or more races, non-Hispanic/Latino; 1% Race/ethnicity unknown; 0.5% international; 37% transferred in; 16% live on campus.

FACULTY

Total: 454, 70% full-time, 70% with terminal degrees.

Student/faculty ratio: 9:1.

ACADEMICS

Calendar: semesters. *Degrees:* bachelor's, master's, doctoral, post-master's, and postbachelor's certificates.

Special study options: advanced placement credit, distance learning, honors programs, internships, part-time degree program, summer session for credit. ***ROTC:*** Army (c), Air Force (c).

Computers: 140 computers/terminals are available on campus for general student use. Students can access the following: campus intranet, computer help desk, free student e-mail accounts, online (class) grades, online (class) registration, online (class) schedules, online bursar bill and payment. Campuswide network is available. 100% of college-owned or -operated housing units are wired for high-speed Internet access. Wireless service is available via classrooms, computer centers, computer labs, learning centers, libraries, student centers.

STUDENT LIFE

Housing options: coed, special housing for students with disabilities. Campus housing is university owned.

Activities and organizations: student-run newspaper, Health Sciences Center Student Association, College of Nursing Student Association,

College of Medicine Student Association, Pharmacy Student Counsel, College of Allied Health Student Association.

Campus security: 24-hour emergency response devices and patrols, late-night transport/escort service.

Student services: health clinic, personal/psychological counseling, women's center.

COSTS

Costs (2014–15) ***Tuition:*** state resident $4128 full-time, $138 per credit hour part-time; nonresident $16,902 full-time, $563 per credit hour part-time. Full-time tuition and fees vary according to course level, course load, degree level, location, program, and student level. Part-time tuition and fees vary according to course level, course load, degree level, location, program, and student level. ***Required fees:*** $2190 full-time, $57 per credit hour part-time, $245 per term part-time. ***Room and board:*** Room and board charges vary according to location. ***Payment plan:*** installment. ***Waivers:*** employees or children of employees.

APPLYING

Options: electronic application, deferred entrance.

Notification: continuous (transfers).

CONTACT

University of Oklahoma Health Sciences Center, PO Box 26901, Oklahoma City, OK 73190. *Phone:* 405-271-2347 Ext. 48916.

★ University of Science and Arts of Oklahoma

Chickasha, Oklahoma

http://www.usao.edu/

- **State-supported** 4-year, founded 1908, part of Oklahoma State Regents for Higher Education
- **Small-town** 75-acre campus with easy access to Oklahoma City
- **Endowment** $13.1 million
- **Coed** 904 undergraduate students, 89% full-time, 64% women, 36% men
- **Moderately difficult** entrance level, 64% of applicants were admitted

UNDERGRAD STUDENTS

801 full-time, 103 part-time. Students come from 22 states and territories; 24 other countries; 9% are from out of state; 4% Black or African American, non-Hispanic/Latino; 6% Hispanic/Latino; 0.8% Asian, non-Hispanic/Latino; 11% American Indian or Alaska Native, non-Hispanic/Latino; 7% Two or more races, non-Hispanic/Latino; 0.2% Race/ethnicity unknown; 8% international; 10% transferred in; 44% live on campus.

Freshmen

Admission: 597 applied, 383 admitted, 170 enrolled. ***Average high school GPA:*** 3.41. ***Test scores:*** SAT critical reading scores over 500: 17%; SAT math scores over 500: 25%; ACT scores over 18: 88%; SAT math scores over 600: 8%; ACT scores over 24: 35%; ACT scores over 30: 6%. ***Retention:*** 76% of full-time freshmen returned.

FACULTY

Total: 83, 66% full-time, 59% with terminal degrees.

Student/faculty ratio: 12:1.

ACADEMICS

Calendar: trimesters. *Degree:* bachelor's.

Special study options: academic remediation for entering students, accelerated degree program, advanced placement credit, double majors, independent study, internships, off-campus study, part-time degree program, services for LD students, student-designed majors, summer session for credit.

Computers: 175 computers/terminals are available on campus for general student use. Students can access the following: computer help desk, free student e-mail accounts, online (class) schedules. Campuswide network is available. 100% of college-owned or -operated housing units are wired for high-speed Internet access. Wireless service is available via entire campus.

STUDENT LIFE

Housing options: on-campus residence required for freshman year; coed. Campus housing is university owned. Freshman campus housing is guaranteed.

Activities and organizations: drama/theater group, student-run newspaper, television station, choral group, Student Activities Board, Volunteer Action Council, Psychology Club, Young Democrats, Young Conservatives, national fraternities.

Athletics Member NAIA. ***Intercollegiate sports:*** baseball M(s), basketball M(s)/W(s), cheerleading M(s)/W(s), cross-country running M/W, soccer M(s)/W(s), softball W(s). ***Intramural sports:*** basketball M/W, football M/W, golf M/W, softball M/W, volleyball M/W.

Campus security: 24-hour emergency response devices and patrols, controlled dormitory access.

Student services: health clinic, personal/psychological counseling.

COSTS & FINANCIAL AID

Costs (2014–15) ***Tuition:*** state resident $5100 full-time, $170 per credit hour part-time; nonresident $14,040 full-time, $468 per credit hour part-time. Full-time tuition and fees vary according to course load. Part-time tuition and fees vary according to course load. No tuition increase for student's term of enrollment. ***Required fees:*** $1170 full-time, $39 per credit hour part-time. ***Room and board:*** $5470; room only: $2760. Room and board charges vary according to board plan and housing facility. ***Payment plan:*** installment. ***Waivers:*** senior citizens and employees or children of employees.

Financial Aid Of all full-time matriculated undergraduates who enrolled in 2014, 617 applied for aid, 526 were judged to have need, 90 had their need fully met. 171 Federal Work-Study jobs (averaging $1374). In 2014, 103 non-need-based awards were made. ***Average percent of need met:*** 62. ***Average financial aid package:*** $10,607. ***Average need-based loan:*** $3304. ***Average need-based gift aid:*** $8191. ***Average non-need-based aid:*** $2779. ***Average indebtedness upon graduation:*** $20,074.

APPLYING

Standardized Tests *Required:* SAT or ACT (for admission).

Options: electronic application, deferred entrance.

Application fee: $40.

Required for some: high school transcript, minimum 3.0 GPA, Option 1: ACT of 24 and (3.0 GPA or top 50% HS Class), Option 2: 3.0 GPA and top 25% HS Class, Option 3: 3.0 GPA in 15-unit HS core and ACT of 22. ***Recommended:*** Option 1: ACT of 24 and (3.0 GPA or top 50% HS Class), Option 2: 3.0 GPA and top 25% HS Class, Option 3: 3.0 GPA in 15-unit HS core and ACT of 22.

Application deadlines: 9/2 (freshmen), 9/2 (out-of-state freshmen), 9/2 (transfers).

Notification: continuous until 1/2 (freshmen), continuous until 1/2 (out-of-state freshmen), continuous (transfers).

CONTACT

Ms. Monica Trevino, Director of Admissions, University of Science and Arts of Oklahoma, 1727 West Alabama, Chickasha, OK 73018-5322. *Phone:* 405-574-1356. *Toll-free phone:* 800-933-8726. *Fax:* 405-574-1220. *E-mail:* usao-admissions@usao.edu.

The University of Tulsa

Tulsa, Oklahoma

http://www.utulsa.edu/

- **Independent** university, founded 1894, affiliated with Presbyterian Church (U.S.A.)
- **Urban** 209-acre campus with easy access to Tulsa
- **Endowment** $1.0 billion
- **Coed** 3,473 undergraduate students, 97% full-time, 42% women, 58% men
- **Very difficult** entrance level, 40% of applicants were admitted

UNDERGRAD STUDENTS

3,362 full-time, 111 part-time. Students come from 45 states and territories; 56 other countries; 45% are from out of state; 4% Black or African American, non-Hispanic/Latino; 4% Hispanic/Latino; 3% Asian, non-Hispanic/Latino; 0.1% Native Hawaiian or other Pacific Islander, non-Hispanic/Latino; 4% American Indian or Alaska Native, non-Hispanic/Latino; 1% Two or more races, non-Hispanic/Latino; 1%

Race/ethnicity unknown; 27% international; 4% transferred in; 73% live on campus.

Freshmen

Admission: 7,636 applied, 3,074 admitted, 764 enrolled. ***Average high school GPA:*** 3.9. ***Test scores:*** SAT critical reading scores over 500: 88%; SAT math scores over 500: 88%; ACT scores over 18: 99%; SAT critical reading scores over 600: 60%; SAT math scores over 600: 68%; ACT scores over 24: 87%; SAT critical reading scores over 700: 27%; SAT math scores over 700: 29%; ACT scores over 30: 48%.

Retention: 89% of full-time freshmen returned.

FACULTY

Total: 444, 77% full-time, 96% with terminal degrees.

Student/faculty ratio: 11:1.

ACADEMICS

Calendar: semesters. *Degrees:* bachelor's, master's, doctoral, and postbachelor's certificates.

Special study options: accelerated degree program, adult/continuing education programs, advanced placement credit, double majors, English as a second language, honors programs, independent study, internships, part-time degree program, services for LD students, student-designed majors, study abroad, summer session for credit. ***ROTC:*** Air Force (c).

Unusual degree programs: 3-2 engineering with Combined bachelor's/master's degree programs in Chemical Engineering and Engineering Physics; Combined bachelor's/master's degree programs in Accountancy, Mathematics, Biochemistry, Biology, Chemistry, Geosciences, History, Physics, Women's Studies.

Computers: 728 computers/terminals are available on campus for general student use. Students can access the following: campus intranet, computer help desk, free student e-mail accounts, online (class) grades, online (class) registration, online (class) schedules. Campuswide network is available. 100% of college-owned or -operated housing units are wired for high-speed Internet access. Wireless service is available via entire campus.

STUDENT LIFE

Housing options: on-campus residence required through sophomore year; coed, men-only, women-only, special housing for students with disabilities. Campus housing is university owned. Freshman campus housing is guaranteed.

Activities and organizations: drama/theater group, student-run newspaper, radio and television station, choral group, marching band, Student Association, Residence Hall Association, Pre-Professional organizations, intramural sports, Greek life, national fraternities, national sororities.

Athletics Member NCAA. All Division I except football (Division I-A). ***Intercollegiate sports:*** basketball M(s)/W(s), cheerleading M/W, crew W(s), cross-country running M(s)/W(s), golf M(s)/W(s), soccer M(s)/W(s), softball W(s), tennis M(s)/W(s), track and field M(s)/W(s), volleyball W(s). ***Intramural sports:*** badminton M/W, basketball M/W, bowling M/W, crew M(c), cross-country running M/W, fencing M(c)/W(c), football M/W, golf M/W, racquetball M/W, rugby M(c), soccer M/W, softball M/W, squash M/W, table tennis M/W, tennis M/W, track and field M/W, volleyball M/W, water polo M/W, weight lifting M/W.

Campus security: 24-hour emergency response devices and patrols, late-night transport/escort service, controlled dormitory access.

Student services: health clinic, personal/psychological counseling.

COSTS & FINANCIAL AID

Costs (2015–16) ***One-time required fee:*** $485. ***Comprehensive fee:*** $49,716 includes full-time tuition ($38,556), mandatory fees ($480), and room and board ($10,680). Full-time tuition and fees vary according to course load. Part-time tuition: $1384 per credit. Part-time tuition and fees vary according to course load. ***College room only:*** $6140. Room and board charges vary according to board plan and housing facility. ***Payment plan:*** installment. ***Waivers:*** employees or children of employees.

Financial Aid Of all full-time matriculated undergraduates who enrolled in 2014, 1,645 applied for aid, 1,353 were judged to have need, 683 had their need fully met. 246 Federal Work-Study jobs (averaging $2531). 2 state and other part-time jobs (averaging $4575). In 2014, 1360 non-need-based awards were made. ***Average percent of need met:*** 81. ***Average financial aid package:*** $26,493. ***Average need-based loan:*** $6003.

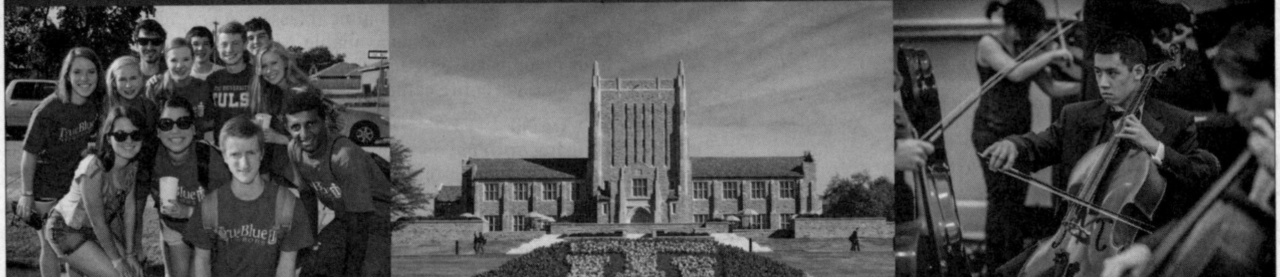

Average need-based gift aid: $5862. ***Average non-need-based aid:*** $17,829. ***Average indebtedness upon graduation:*** $29,161.

APPLYING

Standardized Tests *Required:* SAT or ACT (for admission).

Options: electronic application, early admission, early action, deferred entrance.

Application fee: $50.

Required: essay or personal statement, high school transcript, 1 letter of recommendation. ***Recommended:*** minimum 3.0 GPA, interview.

Application deadlines: rolling (freshmen), rolling (out-of-state freshmen), rolling (transfers), 11/1 (early action).

Notification: continuous (freshmen), continuous (out-of-state freshmen), continuous (transfers), 12/15 (early action).

CONTACT

Ms. Barbara Halsted Adkins, Dean of Admission, The University of Tulsa, 800 South Tucker Drive, Tulsa, OK 74104. *Phone:* 918-631-2307. *Toll-free phone:* 800-331-3050. *Fax:* 918-631-5003. *E-mail:* admission@utulsa.edu.

See previous page for display ad and page 1708 for the College Close-Up.

Wright Career College

Oklahoma City, Oklahoma

http://www.wrightcc.edu/

- **Proprietary** primarily 2-year
- **Suburban** campus with easy access to Oklahoma City
- **Coed**
- **Noncompetitive** entrance level

ACADEMICS

Degrees: diplomas, associate, and bachelor's.

STUDENT LIFE

Housing options: college housing not available.

CONTACT

Wright Career College, 2219 W I-240 Service Road, Suite #124, Oklahoma City, OK 73159. *Phone:* 405-681-2300. *Toll-free phone:* 800-555-4003. *E-mail:* info@wrightcc.edu.

Wright Career College

Tulsa, Oklahoma

http://www.wrightcc.edu/

- **Proprietary** primarily 2-year
- **Suburban** campus with easy access to Tulsa
- **Coed**
- **Noncompetitive** entrance level

ACADEMICS

Degrees: diplomas, associate, and bachelor's.

STUDENT LIFE

Housing options: college housing not available.

CONTACT

Wright Career College, 4908 S Sheridan, Tulsa, OK 74145. *Phone:* 918-628-7700. *Toll-free phone:* 800-555-4003. *E-mail:* info@wrightcc.edu.

OREGON

The Art Institute of Portland

Portland, Oregon

http://www.artinstitutes.edu/portland/

- **Proprietary** 4-year, founded 1963, part of Education Management Corporation
- **Urban** campus
- **Coed**

ACADEMICS

Calendar: quarters. *Degrees:* diplomas, associate, and bachelor's.

CONTACT

The Art Institute of Portland, 1122 NW Davis Street, Portland, OR 97209. *Phone:* 503-228-6528. *Toll-free phone:* 888-228-6528.

Corban University

Salem, Oregon

http://www.corban.edu/

- **Independent Christian** comprehensive, founded 1935
- **Suburban** 145-acre campus with easy access to Portland
- **Coed** 1,024 undergraduate students, 85% full-time, 60% women, 40% men
- **Moderately difficult** entrance level, 37% of applicants were admitted

UNDERGRAD STUDENTS

871 full-time, 153 part-time. 50% are from out of state; 1% Black or African American, non-Hispanic/Latino; 3% Hispanic/Latino; 3% Asian, non-Hispanic/Latino; 0.6% Native Hawaiian or other Pacific Islander, non-Hispanic/Latino; 1% American Indian or Alaska Native, non-Hispanic/Latino; 6% Two or more races, non-Hispanic/Latino; 6% Race/ethnicity unknown; 2% international; 4% transferred in; 63% live on campus.

Freshmen

Admission: 2,678 applied, 1,001 admitted, 220 enrolled. ***Average high school GPA:*** 3.55. ***Test scores:*** SAT critical reading scores over 500: 62%; SAT math scores over 500: 54%; SAT writing scores over 500: 52%; ACT scores over 18: 82%; SAT critical reading scores over 600: 25%; SAT math scores over 600: 16%; SAT writing scores over 600: 14%; ACT scores over 24: 39%; SAT critical reading scores over 700: 5%; SAT math scores over 700: 1%; SAT writing scores over 700: 1%; ACT scores over 30: 7%.

Retention: 77% of full-time freshmen returned.

FACULTY

Total: 104, 47% full-time, 42% with terminal degrees.

Student/faculty ratio: 14:1.

ACADEMICS

Calendar: semesters. *Degrees:* certificates, associate, bachelor's, master's, doctoral, and postbachelor's certificates.

Special study options: accelerated degree program, adult/continuing education programs, advanced placement credit, cooperative education, distance learning, double majors, freshman honors college, honors programs, independent study, internships, off-campus study, services for LD students, student-designed majors, study abroad, summer session for credit. ***ROTC:*** Army (c).

Computers: Students can access the following: computer help desk, free student e-mail accounts, online (class) grades, online (class) schedules. Campuswide network is available. 100% of college-owned or -operated housing units are wired for high-speed Internet access. Wireless service is available via entire campus.

STUDENT LIFE

Housing options: on-campus residence required through sophomore year; men-only, women-only. Campus housing is university owned. Freshman campus housing is guaranteed.

Activities and organizations: drama/theater group, student-run newspaper, choral group, Student Fellowship Groups, Poetry Club, Worship Teams, Drama Club, Westrek Hiking Club.

Athletics Member NAIA, NCCAA. ***Intercollegiate sports:*** baseball M(s), basketball M(s)/W(s), cross-country running M(s)/W(s), golf M(s)/W(s), soccer M(s)/W(s), softball W(s), track and field M(s)/W(s), volleyball W(s). ***Intramural sports:*** basketball M/W, football M, soccer M/W, table tennis M/W, volleyball M/W.

Campus security: 24-hour emergency response devices and patrols, student patrols, late-night transport/escort service, controlled dormitory access.

Student services: health clinic, personal/psychological counseling.

COSTS & FINANCIAL AID

Costs (2014–15) ***One-time required fee:*** $100. ***Comprehensive fee:*** $37,532 includes full-time tuition ($27,980), mandatory fees ($660), and room and board ($8892). Full-time tuition and fees vary according to course level, degree level, program, reciprocity agreements, and student level. Part-time tuition: $1166 per credit hour. Part-time tuition and fees vary according to course level, course load, degree level, program, reciprocity agreements, and student level. ***College room only:*** $5152. Room and board charges vary according to board plan. ***Payment plan:*** installment. ***Waivers:*** senior citizens and employees or children of employees.

Financial Aid Of all full-time matriculated undergraduates who enrolled in 2014, 733 applied for aid, 681 were judged to have need, 111 had their need fully met. In 2014, 105 non-need-based awards were made. ***Average percent of need met:*** 67. ***Average financial aid package:*** $20,591. ***Average need-based loan:*** $4532. ***Average need-based gift aid:*** $17,422. ***Average non-need-based aid:*** $8605. ***Average indebtedness upon graduation:*** $26,407.

APPLYING

Standardized Tests *Required:* SAT or ACT (for admission).

Options: electronic application.

Application fee: $40.

Required: essay or personal statement, high school transcript, minimum 2.7 GPA, 2 letters of recommendation.

CONTACT

Ms. Heidi Stowman, Director of Admissions, Corban University, 5000 Deer Park Drive, SE, Salem, OR 97301-9392. *Phone:* 503-375-7115. *Toll-free phone:* 800-845-3005. *Fax:* 503-585-4316. *E-mail:* admissions@corban.edu.

DeVry University

Portland, Oregon

http://www.devry.edu/

- **Proprietary** comprehensive
- **Coed**

ACADEMICS

Calendar: semesters. *Degrees:* associate, bachelor's, and master's.

STUDENT LIFE

Housing options: college housing not available.

COSTS & FINANCIAL AID

Costs (2014–15) ***Tuition:*** $17,052 full-time, $609 per credit hour part-time. ***Required fees:*** $80 full-time.

Financial Aid Of all full-time matriculated undergraduates who enrolled in 2007, 17 applied for aid, 17 were judged to have need. ***Average percent of need met:*** 29. ***Average financial aid package:*** $9247. ***Average need-based loan:*** $6636. ***Average need-based gift aid:*** $4932.

CONTACT

Admissions Office, DeVry University, 9755 Southwest Barnes Road, Suite 150, Portland, OR 97225-6651. *Phone:* 503-296-7468. *Toll-free phone:* 866-338-7941.

Eastern Oregon University

La Grande, Oregon

http://www.eou.edu/

- **State-supported** comprehensive, founded 1929, part of Oregon University System
- **Rural** 121-acre campus
- **Coed** 3,348 undergraduate students, 58% full-time, 63% women, 37% men
- **Moderately difficult** entrance level, 64% of applicants were admitted

UNDERGRAD STUDENTS

1,956 full-time, 1,392 part-time. Students come from 20 other countries; 28% are from out of state; 3% Black or African American, non-Hispanic/Latino; 6% Hispanic/Latino; 2% Asian, non-Hispanic/Latino; 1% Native Hawaiian or other Pacific Islander, non-Hispanic/Latino; 2% American Indian or Alaska Native, non-Hispanic/Latino; 1% Two or more races, non-Hispanic/Latino; 7% Race/ethnicity unknown; 1% international; 12% transferred in; 11% live on campus.

Freshmen

Admission: 1,530 applied, 982 admitted, 312 enrolled. ***Average high school GPA:*** 3.17. ***Test scores:*** SAT critical reading scores over 500: 37%; SAT math scores over 500: 36%; SAT writing scores over 500: 29%; ACT scores over 18: 69%; SAT critical reading scores over 600: 11%; SAT math scores over 600: 7%; SAT writing scores over 600: 6%; ACT scores over 24: 21%; SAT critical reading scores over 700: 1%; SAT math scores over 700: 1%; SAT writing scores over 700: 1%; ACT scores over 30: 3%.

Retention: 58% of full-time freshmen returned.

FACULTY

Total: 112, 95% full-time, 74% with terminal degrees.

Student/faculty ratio: 22:1.

ACADEMICS

Calendar: quarters. *Degrees:* certificates, associate, bachelor's, and master's.

Special study options: academic remediation for entering students, adult/continuing education programs, advanced placement credit, cooperative education, distance learning, double majors, external degree program, honors programs, independent study, internships, off-campus study, part-time degree program, services for LD students, student-designed majors, study abroad, summer session for credit. ***ROTC:*** Army (b).

Computers: 120 computers/terminals are available on campus for general student use. Students can access the following: free student e-mail accounts, online (class) grades, online (class) registration, online (class) schedules. Campuswide network is available. Wireless service is available via entire campus.

STUDENT LIFE

Housing options: on-campus residence required for freshman year; coed, special housing for students with disabilities. Campus housing is university owned. Freshman applicants given priority for college housing.

Activities and organizations: drama/theater group, student-run newspaper, radio station, choral group, Outdoor Club, Pre-Professional Health Club, Student Government, International Student Association, Latino Impact.

Athletics Member NAIA. ***Intercollegiate sports:*** basketball M(s)/W(s), cheerleading W(s), cross-country running M(s)/W(s), football M(s), soccer W(s), softball W(s), track and field M(s)/W(s), volleyball W(s). ***Intramural sports:*** basketball M/W, football M, rock climbing M(c)/W(c), soccer W, softball M/W, volleyball W.

Campus security: 24-hour emergency response devices, late-night transport/escort service, controlled dormitory access.

Student services: health clinic, personal/psychological counseling, women's center.

COSTS & FINANCIAL AID

Costs (2014–15) ***Tuition:*** state resident $6030 full-time, $134 per credit hour part-time; nonresident $16,110 full-time, $358 per credit hour part-time. Full-time tuition and fees vary according to course load, location, and reciprocity agreements. Part-time tuition and fees vary according to course load, location, and reciprocity agreements. ***Required fees:*** $1410 full-time. ***Room and board:*** $9642; room only: $5650. Room and board charges vary according to board plan and housing facility. ***Payment plans:*** installment, deferred payment. ***Waivers:*** senior citizens and employees or children of employees.

Financial Aid Of all full-time matriculated undergraduates who enrolled in 2012, 2,084 applied for aid, 1,880 were judged to have need, 184 had their need fully met. In 2012, 23 non-need-based awards were made. ***Average percent of need met:*** 50. ***Average financial aid package:*** $9860. ***Average need-based loan:*** $4552. ***Average need-based gift aid:*** $5495. ***Average non-need-based aid:*** $1579. ***Average indebtedness upon graduation:*** $25,109.

APPLYING

Standardized Tests *Required:* SAT or ACT (for admission).

Options: electronic application, early admission, early action, deferred entrance.

Required: high school transcript, minimum 2.8 GPA. ***Required for some:*** essay or personal statement, 2 letters of recommendation.

Application deadlines: 9/1 (freshmen), 2/1 (early action).

CONTACT
Admissions Department, Eastern Oregon University, One University Blvd., La Grande, OR. *Phone:* 800-452-8639. *Toll-free phone:* 800-452-8639. *Fax:* 541-962-3418. *E-mail:* admissions@eou.edu.

George Fox University

Newberg, Oregon

http://www.georgefox.edu/

- **Independent Friends** university, founded 1891
- **Small-town** 108-acre campus with easy access to Portland
- **Endowment** $18.0 million
- **Coed**
- **Moderately difficult** entrance level

FACULTY
Student/faculty ratio: 14:1.

ACADEMICS
Calendar: semesters. *Degrees:* bachelor's, master's, doctoral, post-master's, and postbachelor's certificates.

STUDENT LIFE
Housing options: on-campus residence required through junior year; men-only, women-only, special housing for students with disabilities. Campus housing is university owned. Freshman applicants given priority for college housing.

Activities and organizations: drama/theater group, student-run newspaper, radio station, choral group, student government, Christian Ministries, Orientation Committee, Outdoor Club and Bruin Ambassadors, Blue Zone.

Athletics Member NCAA. All Division III.

Campus security: 24-hour emergency response devices and patrols, student patrols, late-night transport/escort service, controlled dormitory access, parking lot cameras, and video surveillance of key buildings.

Student services: health clinic, personal/psychological counseling.

COSTS & FINANCIAL AID
Costs (2014–15) ***Comprehensive fee:*** $41,730 includes full-time tuition ($31,510), mandatory fees ($356), and room and board ($9864). Part-time tuition: $954 per credit hour. Part-time tuition and fees vary according to course load. ***College room only:*** $5754. Room and board charges vary according to board plan.

Financial Aid Of all full-time matriculated undergraduates who enrolled in 2013, 1,762 applied for aid, 1,597 were judged to have need, 555 had their need fully met. In 2013, 145 non-need-based awards were made. ***Average percent of need met:*** 84. ***Average financial aid package:*** $27,155. ***Average need-based loan:*** $3536. ***Average need-based gift aid:*** $9112. ***Average non-need-based aid:*** $9708. ***Average indebtedness upon graduation:*** $25,143.

APPLYING
Standardized Tests *Required:* SAT or ACT (for admission).

Options: electronic application, early action, deferred entrance.

Application fee: $40.

Required: essay or personal statement, high school transcript, 2 letters of recommendation. ***Required for some:*** interview. ***Recommended:*** minimum 2.6 GPA, interview.

CONTACT
Ms. Lindsay Knox, Director of Undergraduate Admissions, George Fox University, 414 North Meridian Street, Newberg, OR 97132. *Phone:* 503-554-2240. *Toll-free phone:* 800-765-4369. *Fax:* 503-554-3110. *E-mail:* admissions@georgefox.edu.

ITT Technical Institute

Portland, Oregon

http://www.itt-tech.edu/

- **Proprietary** primarily 2-year, founded 1971, part of ITT Educational Services, Inc.
- **Urban** campus
- **Coed**
- **Minimally difficult** entrance level

ACADEMICS
Calendar: quarters. *Degrees:* associate and bachelor's.

STUDENT LIFE
Housing options: college housing not available.

FINANCIAL AID
Financial Aid Of all full-time matriculated undergraduates who enrolled in 2013, 15 Federal Work-Study jobs (averaging $5000).

CONTACT
Director of Recruitment, ITT Technical Institute, 9500 Northeast Cascades Parkway, Portland, OR 97220. *Phone:* 503-255-6500. *Toll-free phone:* 800-234-5488.

ITT Technical Institute

Salem, Oregon

http://www.itt-tech.edu/

- **Proprietary** 4-year
- **Coed**
- **Minimally difficult** entrance level

ACADEMICS
Degrees: associate and bachelor's.

CONTACT
Director of Recruiting, ITT Technical Institute, 4825 Commercial Street SE, Suite 100, Salem, OR 97302-2177. *Phone:* 503-576-2300. *Toll-free phone:* 877-273-7397.

Lewis & Clark College

Portland, Oregon

http://www.lclark.edu/

- **Independent** comprehensive, founded 1867
- **Urban** 137-acre campus with easy access to Portland
- **Endowment** $182.3 million
- **Coed** 2,179 undergraduate students, 99% full-time, 59% women, 41% men
- **Very difficult** entrance level, 67% of applicants were admitted

UNDERGRAD STUDENTS
2,156 full-time, 23 part-time. Students come from 48 states and territories; 76 other countries; 80% are from out of state; 2% Black or African American, non-Hispanic/Latino; 9% Hispanic/Latino; 7% Asian, non-Hispanic/Latino; 0.3% Native Hawaiian or other Pacific Islander, non-Hispanic/Latino; 1% American Indian or Alaska Native, non-Hispanic/Latino; 0.7% Two or more races, non-Hispanic/Latino; 7% Race/ethnicity unknown; 9% international; 3% transferred in; 65% live on campus.

Freshmen
Admission: 6,243 applied, 4,159 admitted, 564 enrolled. ***Average high school GPA:*** 3.9. ***Test scores:*** SAT critical reading scores over 500: 99%; SAT math scores over 500: 99%; SAT writing scores over 500: 98%; ACT scores over 18: 100%; SAT critical reading scores over 600: 81%; SAT math scores over 600: 67%; SAT writing scores over 600: 75%; ACT scores over 24: 94%; SAT critical reading scores over 700: 29%; SAT math scores over 700: 15%; SAT writing scores over 700: 20%; ACT scores over 30: 45%.

Retention: 85% of full-time freshmen returned.

FACULTY
Total: 417, 57% full-time, 73% with terminal degrees.
Student/faculty ratio: 12:1.

ACADEMICS
Calendar: semesters. *Degrees:* bachelor's, master's, doctoral, and post-master's certificates.

Special study options: advanced placement credit, double majors, English as a second language, honors programs, independent study, internships, off-campus study, services for LD students, student-designed majors, study abroad, summer session for credit. ***ROTC:*** Army (c).

Unusual degree programs: 3-2 engineering with Columbia University in New York, Washington University in St. Louis, University of Southern California in Los Angeles.

Computers: 428 computers/terminals are available on campus for general student use. Students can access the following: campus intranet, computer help desk, free student e-mail accounts, online (class) grades, online (class) registration, online (class) schedules. Campuswide network is available. 100% of college-owned or -operated housing units are wired for high-speed Internet access. Wireless service is available via entire campus.

STUDENT LIFE

Housing options: on-campus residence required through sophomore year; coed, women-only. Campus housing is university owned. Freshman campus housing is guaranteed.

Activities and organizations: drama/theater group, student-run newspaper, radio and television station, choral group, International Students of Lewis & Clark, Campus Activities Board, MOSAIC (Multicultural Organizations Seeking An Inclusive Community), Bacchus Men's Ultimate Frisbee, Hillel.

Athletics Member NCAA. All Division III. ***Intercollegiate sports:*** baseball M, basketball M/W, crew M/W, cross-country running M/W, football M, golf M/W, lacrosse M(c)/W(c), soccer W, softball W, swimming and diving M/W, tennis M/W, track and field M/W, volleyball W. ***Intramural sports:*** badminton M/W, basketball M/W, cross-country running M/W, fencing M(c)/W(c), field hockey M(c)/W(c), football M/W, rock climbing M/W, rugby M(c)/W(c), sailing M(c)/W(c), skiing (cross-country) M(c)/W(c), skiing (downhill) M(c)/W(c), soccer M(c)/W(c), softball M/W, swimming and diving M(c)/W(c), table tennis M(c)/W(c), tennis M/W, ultimate Frisbee M(c)/W(c), volleyball M/W, water polo M(c)/W(c).

Campus security: 24-hour emergency response devices and patrols, late-night transport/escort service, controlled dormitory access.

Student services: health clinic, personal/psychological counseling, women's center.

COSTS & FINANCIAL AID

Costs (2014–15) ***Comprehensive fee:*** $54,382 includes full-time tuition ($43,022), mandatory fees ($360), and room and board ($11,000). Part-time tuition: $2151 per credit hour. ***College room only:*** $5894. Room and board charges vary according to board plan and housing facility. ***Payment plan:*** installment. ***Waivers:*** employees or children of employees.

Financial Aid Of all full-time matriculated undergraduates who enrolled in 2014, 1,478 applied for aid, 1,212 were judged to have need, 238 had their need fully met. 308 Federal Work-Study jobs (averaging $2465). 14 state and other part-time jobs (averaging $2107). In 2014, 525 non-need-based awards were made. ***Average percent of need met:*** 88. ***Average financial aid package:*** $36,865. ***Average need-based loan:*** $5047. ***Average need-based gift aid:*** $29,334. ***Average non-need-based aid:*** $13,832. ***Average indebtedness upon graduation:*** $27,421.

APPLYING

Standardized Tests *Required for some:* SAT or ACT (for admission).

Options: electronic application, early decision, early action, deferred entrance.

Required: essay or personal statement, high school transcript, 1 letter of recommendation, Portfolio Path (test optional) applicants are required to submit one graded writing sample, one math or science sample, and two letters of recommendation. ***Required for some:*** 2 letters of recommendation. ***Recommended:*** interview.

Application deadlines: 1/15 (freshmen), 1/15 (out-of-state freshmen), 5/1 (transfers), 11/1 (early action).

Early decision deadline: 11/1.

Notification: 4/1 (freshmen), 4/1 (out-of-state freshmen), continuous (transfers), 12/1 (early decision), 12/31 (early action).

CONTACT

Erica Johnson, Director of Admissions, Lewis & Clark College, 0615 SW Palatine Hill Road, Portland, OR 97219. *Phone:* 503-768-7040. *Toll-free phone:* 800-444-4111. *Fax:* 503-768-7055. *E-mail:* admissions@lclark.edu.

See below for display ad and page 1498 for the College Close-Up.

★ Linfield College
McMinnville, Oregon
http://www.linfield.edu/

- **Independent American Baptist Churches in the USA** 4-year, founded 1849, part of Linfield College includes the Linfield College McMinnville Campus in McMinnville, Oregon; the Linfield-Good Samaritan School of Nursing in Portland, Oregon(Portland Campus) and the Linfield College Adult Degree Program online
- **Small-town** 189-acre campus with easy access to Portland
- **Endowment** $103.5 million
- **Coed** 1,683 undergraduate students, 98% full-time, 62% women, 38% men
- **Moderately difficult** entrance level, 94% of applicants were admitted

UNDERGRAD STUDENTS

1,644 full-time, 39 part-time. Students come from 23 states and territories; 25 other countries; 50% are from out of state; 2% Black or African American, non-Hispanic/Latino; 10% Hispanic/Latino; 6% Asian, non-Hispanic/Latino; 0.6% Native Hawaiian or other Pacific Islander, non-Hispanic/Latino; 0.7% American Indian or Alaska Native, non-Hispanic/Latino; 11% Two or more races, non-Hispanic/Latino; 2% Race/ethnicity unknown; 4% international; 4% transferred in; 78% live on campus.

Freshmen

Admission: 2,054 applied, 1,926 admitted, 463 enrolled. ***Average high school GPA:*** 3.7. ***Test scores:*** SAT critical reading scores over 500: 68%; SAT math scores over 500: 70%; SAT writing scores over 500: 60%; ACT scores over 18: 97%; SAT critical reading scores over 600: 27%; SAT math scores over 600: 27%; SAT writing scores over 600: 21%; ACT scores over 24: 51%; SAT critical reading scores over 700: 4%; SAT math scores over 700: 2%; SAT writing scores over 700: 3%; ACT scores over 30: 9%.

Retention: 88% of full-time freshmen returned.

FACULTY

Total: 194, 60% full-time, 71% with terminal degrees.

Student/faculty ratio: 12:1.

ACADEMICS

Calendar: 4-1-4. *Degree:* bachelor's.

Special study options: accelerated degree program, adult/continuing education programs, advanced placement credit, distance learning, double majors, English as a second language, external degree program, independent study, internships, off-campus study, part-time degree program, services for LD students, student-designed majors, study abroad, summer session for credit. ***ROTC:*** Air Force (c).

Unusual degree programs: 3-2 engineering with Washington State University, Oregon State University, University of Southern California.

Computers: 250 computers/terminals are available on campus for general student use. Students can access the following: computer help desk, free student e-mail accounts, online (class) grades, online (class) registration, online (class) schedules. Campuswide network is available. 100% of college-owned or -operated housing units are wired for high-speed Internet access. Wireless service is available via classrooms, computer centers, computer labs, dorm rooms, learning centers, libraries, student centers.

STUDENT LIFE

Housing options: on-campus residence required through junior year; coed, men-only, women-only, special housing for students with disabilities. Campus housing is university owned. Freshman campus housing is guaranteed.

Activities and organizations: drama/theater group, student-run newspaper, radio station, choral group, Fellowship of Christian Athletes, Linfield Ultimate Players Association, Hawaiian Club, International Club, Outdoor Club, national fraternities, national sororities.

Athletics Member NCAA. All Division III. ***Intercollegiate sports:*** baseball M, basketball M/W, cross-country running M/W, football M, golf M/W, lacrosse W, soccer M/W, softball W, swimming and diving M/W, tennis M/W, track and field M/W, volleyball W. ***Intramural sports:*** basketball M/W, bowling M/W, soccer M/W, softball M/W, ultimate Frisbee M/W, volleyball M/W.

Campus security: 24-hour emergency response devices and patrols, late-night transport/escort service, controlled dormitory access.

Student services: health clinic, personal/psychological counseling.

COSTS & FINANCIAL AID

Costs (2014–15) ***Comprehensive fee:*** $47,676 includes full-time tuition ($37,000), mandatory fees ($346), and room and board ($10,330). Full-time tuition and fees vary according to course load and location. Part-time tuition: $1152 per semester hour. Part-time tuition and fees vary according to course load and location. ***Required fees:*** $202 per term part-time. ***College room only:*** $5610. Room and board charges vary according to board plan, housing facility, and location. ***Payment plan:*** installment. ***Waivers:*** senior citizens and employees or children of employees.

Financial Aid Of all full-time matriculated undergraduates who enrolled in 2014, 1,375 applied for aid, 1,211 were judged to have need, 335 had their need fully met. 522 Federal Work-Study jobs (averaging $2516). 445 state and other part-time jobs (averaging $2332). In 2014, 360 non-need-based awards were made. ***Average percent of need met:*** 81. ***Average financial aid package:*** $30,438. ***Average need-based loan:*** $4496. ***Average need-based gift aid:*** $24,216. ***Average non-need-based aid:*** $16,160. ***Average indebtedness upon graduation:*** $28,697.

APPLYING

Standardized Tests *Required:* SAT or ACT (for admission).

Options: electronic application, early action, deferred entrance.

Required: essay or personal statement, high school transcript, 1 letter of recommendation. ***Recommended:*** interview.

Application deadlines: 2/15 (freshmen), 4/15 (transfers), 11/15 (early action).

Notification: 4/1 (freshmen), 5/15 (transfers), 1/15 (early action).

CONTACT

Ms. Lisa Knodle-Bragiel, Director of Admission, Linfield College, 900 SE Baker Street, McMinnville, OR 97128. *Phone:* 503-883-2213. *Toll-free phone:* 800-640-2287. *Fax:* 503-883-2472. *E-mail:* admission@linfield.edu.

See previous page for display ad and page 1504 for the College Close-Up.

Marylhurst University

Marylhurst, Oregon

http://www.marylhurst.edu/

- **Independent Roman Catholic** comprehensive, founded 1893
- **Suburban** 63-acre campus with easy access to Portland
- **Coed** 696 undergraduate students, 24% full-time, 71% women, 29% men
- **Noncompetitive** entrance level

UNDERGRAD STUDENTS

169 full-time, 527 part-time. Students come from 42 states and territories; 12 other countries; 27% are from out of state; 3% Black or African American, non-Hispanic/Latino; 7% Hispanic/Latino; 1% Asian, non-Hispanic/Latino; 0.4% Native Hawaiian or other Pacific Islander, non-Hispanic/Latino; 0.7% American Indian or Alaska Native, non-Hispanic/Latino; 3% Two or more races, non-Hispanic/Latino; 5% Race/ethnicity unknown; 13% international.

ACADEMICS

Calendar: quarters. *Degrees:* bachelor's, master's, post-master's, and postbachelor's certificates.

Special study options: accelerated degree program, adult/continuing education programs, advanced placement credit, distance learning, double majors, English as a second language, independent study, internships, off-campus study, part-time degree program, services for LD students, student-designed majors, study abroad, summer session for credit.

Computers: Students can access the following: campus intranet, computer help desk, free student e-mail accounts, online (class) grades, online (class) registration, online (class) schedules. Campuswide network is available. Wireless service is available via entire campus.

STUDENT LIFE

Housing options: college housing not available.

Activities and organizations: student-run newspaper, choral group, Marylhurst's Writer's Club, Marylhurst Gerontology Association, Solutions: Marylhurst Mediation Resource, Marylhurst S.A.F.E. Community: Sexual Acceptance for Everyone, LABY: Labyrinth Alliance Balances You.

Campus security: security is available during campus hours.

Student services: personal/psychological counseling.

COSTS & FINANCIAL AID

Costs (2014–15) ***Tuition:*** $20,295 full-time, $451 per quarter hour part-time. ***Required fees:*** $50 full-time.

Financial Aid Of all full-time matriculated undergraduates who enrolled in 2014, 101 applied for aid, 98 were judged to have need, 5 had their need fully met. 168 Federal Work-Study jobs (averaging $4835). In 2014, 10 non-need-based awards were made. ***Average percent of need met:*** 52. ***Average financial aid package:*** $15,600. ***Average need-based loan:*** $4803. ***Average need-based gift aid:*** $9442. ***Average non-need-based aid:*** $7114. ***Average indebtedness upon graduation:*** $34,399.

APPLYING

Options: electronic application, deferred entrance.

Application fee: $50.

Required: essay or personal statement, high school transcript. ***Required for some:*** 2 letters of recommendation, interview.

Application deadlines: rolling (freshmen), rolling (transfers).

Notification: continuous (freshmen), continuous (transfers).

CONTACT

Ryan Clark, Director of Admissions, Marylhurst University, 17600 Pacific Highway, PO Box 261, Marylhurst, OR 97036-0261. *Phone:* 503-699-6268. *Toll-free phone:* 800-634-9982. *Fax:* 503-699-6320. *E-mail:* admissions@marylhurst.edu.

Multnomah University

Portland, Oregon

http://www.multnomah.edu/

- **Independent interdenominational** comprehensive, founded 1936
- **Urban** 22-acre campus
- **Endowment** $7.0 million
- **Coed** 418 undergraduate students, 85% full-time, 46% women, 54% men
- **Moderately difficult** entrance level, 55% of applicants were admitted

UNDERGRAD STUDENTS

355 full-time, 63 part-time. Students come from 13 states and territories; 2 other countries; 49% are from out of state; 3% Black or African American, non-Hispanic/Latino; 7% Hispanic/Latino; 0.9% Asian, non-Hispanic/Latino; 0.6% Native Hawaiian or other Pacific Islander, non-Hispanic/Latino; 1% American Indian or Alaska Native, non-Hispanic/Latino; 5% Two or more races, non-Hispanic/Latino; 1% Race/ethnicity unknown; 0.6% international; 15% transferred in; 59% live on campus.

Freshmen

Admission: 168 applied, 93 admitted, 48 enrolled. ***Average high school GPA:*** 3.21. ***Test scores:*** SAT critical reading scores over 500: 68%; SAT math scores over 500: 62%; SAT writing scores over 500: 60%; ACT scores over 18: 91%; SAT critical reading scores over 600: 35%; SAT math scores over 600: 19%; SAT writing scores over 600: 19%; ACT scores over 24: 27%; SAT critical reading scores over 700: 8%; SAT math scores over 700: 3%; SAT writing scores over 700: 5%; ACT scores over 30: 9%.

Retention: 75% of full-time freshmen returned.

FACULTY

Total: 87, 30% full-time, 40% with terminal degrees.

Student/faculty ratio: 14:1.

ACADEMICS

Calendar: semesters. *Degrees:* bachelor's, master's, and doctoral.

Special study options: academic remediation for entering students, adult/continuing education programs, advanced placement credit, double majors, internships, part-time degree program, services for LD students, summer session for credit.

Computers: 36 computers/terminals are available on campus for general student use. Students can access the following: campus intranet, computer help desk, free student e-mail accounts, online (class) grades, online (class) registration, online (class) schedules. Campuswide network is available. 80% of college-owned or -operated housing units are wired for high-speed Internet access. Wireless service is available via entire campus.

STUDENT LIFE

Housing options: on-campus residence required through sophomore year; men-only, women-only, special housing for students with disabilities. Campus housing is university owned. Freshman campus housing is guaranteed.

Activities and organizations: choral group, MAFIA (Missionary kids, Multicultural kids, Friends in America), SocreTea's Club, Saturday Morning Prayer, Brunch Chats, Fitness Club.

Athletics Member NCCAA. ***Intercollegiate sports:*** basketball M(s)/W(s), cross-country running M(s)/W(s), golf M(s)/W(s), soccer M(s), volleyball W(s). ***Intramural sports:*** basketball M/W, volleyball M/W.

Campus security: 24-hour emergency response devices and patrols, late-night transport/escort service, controlled dormitory access.

Student services: personal/psychological counseling.

COSTS & FINANCIAL AID

Costs (2015–16) ***Comprehensive fee:*** $30,580 includes full-time tuition ($22,230), mandatory fees ($530), and room and board ($7820). Full-time tuition and fees vary according to course load, degree level, location, and program. Part-time tuition: $700 per semester hour. Part-time tuition and fees vary according to course load, degree level, location, and program. ***Room and board:*** Room and board charges vary according to housing facility. ***Payment plan:*** installment. ***Waivers:*** employees or children of employees.

Financial Aid Of all full-time matriculated undergraduates who enrolled in 2009, 503 applied for aid, 441 were judged to have need, 11 had their need fully met. 75 Federal Work-Study jobs (averaging $1500). In 2009, 36 non-need-based awards were made. ***Average percent of need met:*** 50. ***Average financial aid package:*** $9211. ***Average need-based loan:*** $4094. ***Average need-based gift aid:*** $5846. ***Average non-need-based aid:*** $1848. ***Average indebtedness upon graduation:*** $21,020.

APPLYING

Standardized Tests *Required:* SAT or ACT (for admission).

Options: electronic application, deferred entrance.

Application fee: $40.

Required: essay or personal statement, high school transcript, minimum 2.5 GPA, 2 letters of recommendation.

Notification: continuous (freshmen), continuous (transfers).

CONTACT

Mr. Palmer Muntz, Director of Admissions, Multnomah University, 8435 Northeast Glisan Street, Portland, OR 97220-5898. *Phone:* 503-251-6483. *Toll-free phone:* 877-251-6560. *Fax:* 503-254-1268. *E-mail:* admiss@multnomah.edu.

Northwest Christian University

Eugene, Oregon

http://www.nwcu.edu/

- **Independent Christian** comprehensive, founded 1895
- **Urban** 8-acre campus with easy access to Portland
- **Endowment** $12.6 million
- **Coed** 496 undergraduate students, 80% full-time, 61% women, 39% men
- **Minimally difficult** entrance level, 72% of applicants were admitted

UNDERGRAD STUDENTS

395 full-time, 101 part-time. Students come from 13 states and territories; 3 other countries; 25% are from out of state; 2% Black or African American, non-Hispanic/Latino; 9% Hispanic/Latino; 2% Asian, non-Hispanic/Latino; 0.4% Native Hawaiian or other Pacific Islander, non-Hispanic/Latino; 3% American Indian or Alaska Native, non-Hispanic/Latino; 3% Two or more races, non-Hispanic/Latino; 1% Race/ethnicity unknown; 11% transferred in; 28% live on campus.

Freshmen

Admission: 356 applied, 256 admitted, 78 enrolled. ***Average high school GPA:*** 3.36. ***Test scores:*** ACT scores over 18: 72%; ACT scores over 24: 31%; ACT scores over 30: 3%.

Retention: 70% of full-time freshmen returned.

FACULTY

Total: 85, 29% full-time.

Student/faculty ratio: 14:1.

ACADEMICS

Calendar: quarters. *Degrees:* certificates, associate, bachelor's, master's, and postbachelor's certificates.

Special study options: academic remediation for entering students, accelerated degree program, adult/continuing education programs, advanced placement credit, cooperative education, distance learning, double majors, honors programs, independent study, internships, off-campus study, part-time degree program, services for LD students, student-designed majors, study abroad, summer session for credit.

Computers: 16 computers/terminals are available on campus for general student use. Students can access the following: campus intranet, computer help desk, free student e-mail accounts, online (class) grades, online (class) registration, online (class) schedules. Campuswide network is available. 100% of college-owned or -operated housing units are wired for high-speed Internet access. Wireless service is available via entire campus.

STUDENT LIFE

Housing options: on-campus residence required for freshman year; men-only, women-only. Campus housing is university owned and leased by the school. Freshman campus housing is guaranteed.

Activities and organizations: student-run newspaper, choral group, Community Life Groups, Kairos, Beacon Board Games, Eta Theta Xi.

Athletics Member NAIA. ***Intercollegiate sports:*** basketball M(s)/W(s), cross-country running M(s)/W(s), golf M(s)/W(s), soccer M(s)/W(s), softball W(s), track and field M(s)/W(s), volleyball W(s). ***Intramural sports:*** basketball M/W, volleyball M/W.

Campus security: 24-hour emergency response devices and patrols, late-night transport/escort service, controlled dormitory access.

Student services: personal/psychological counseling.

COSTS & FINANCIAL AID

Costs (2014–15) ***Comprehensive fee:*** $34,380 includes full-time tuition ($26,020), mandatory fees ($160), and room and board ($8200). Full-time tuition and fees vary according to course load. Part-time tuition: $865 per credit hour. Part-time tuition and fees vary according to course load. ***Required fees:*** $160 per year part-time. ***Room and board:*** Room and board charges vary according to housing facility. ***Payment plan:*** installment. ***Waivers:*** employees or children of employees.

Financial Aid Of all full-time matriculated undergraduates who enrolled in 2014, 371 applied for aid, 343 were judged to have need, 58 had their need fully met. 167 Federal Work-Study jobs (averaging $2750). 3 state and other part-time jobs (averaging $2750). In 2014, 33 non-need-based awards were made. ***Average percent of need met:*** 61. ***Average financial aid package:*** $20,379. ***Average need-based loan:*** $4269. ***Average need-based gift aid:*** $15,561. ***Average non-need-based aid:*** $9487. ***Average indebtedness upon graduation:*** $29,485.

APPLYING

Standardized Tests *Required:* SAT or ACT (for admission).

Options: electronic application, deferred entrance.

Required: essay or personal statement, minimum 2.5 GPA, Personal statement. ***Required for some:*** high school transcript. ***Recommended:*** interview.

Application deadlines: rolling (freshmen), rolling (out-of-state freshmen), rolling (transfers).

Notification: continuous (freshmen), continuous (out-of-state freshmen), continuous (transfers).

CONTACT

Kassia Galick, Admissions Counselor, Northwest Christian University, 828 E. 11th Ave., Eugene, OR 97401-3745. *Phone:* 541-684-7201. *Toll-free phone:* 877-463-6622. *Fax:* 541-684-7317. *E-mail:* admissions@nwcu.edu.

Oregon College of Art & Craft

Portland, Oregon

http://www.ocac.edu/

- **Independent** comprehensive, founded 1907
- **Urban** 10-acre campus with easy access to Portland
- **Endowment** $3.1 million
- **Coed** 147 undergraduate students, 83% full-time, 83% women, 17% men
- **Moderately difficult** entrance level, 51% of applicants were admitted

UNDERGRAD STUDENTS
122 full-time, 25 part-time. Students come from 24 states and territories; 59% are from out of state; 0.6% Black or African American, non-Hispanic/Latino; 13% Hispanic/Latino; 3% Asian, non-Hispanic/Latino; 0.6% Native Hawaiian or other Pacific Islander, non-Hispanic/Latino; 2% American Indian or Alaska Native, non-Hispanic/Latino; 11% Two or more races, non-Hispanic/Latino; 6% Race/ethnicity unknown; 0.6% international; 19% transferred in; 10% live on campus.

Freshmen
Admission: 184 applied, 93 admitted, 29 enrolled. ***Average high school GPA:*** 3.59.
Retention: 55% of full-time freshmen returned.

FACULTY
Total: 43, 23% full-time, 93% with terminal degrees.
Student/faculty ratio: 8:1.

ACADEMICS
Calendar: semesters. *Degrees:* certificates, bachelor's, master's, and postbachelor's certificates.
Special study options: adult/continuing education programs, advanced placement credit, independent study, internships, off-campus study, part-time degree program, services for LD students, study abroad.
Computers: 15 computers/terminals are available on campus for general student use. Students can access the following: free student e-mail accounts. Campuswide network is available. Wireless service is available via entire campus.

STUDENT LIFE
Housing options: coed. Campus housing is university owned. Freshman applicants given priority for college housing.
Activities and organizations: Student Commonwealth, Ceramics Club.
Campus security: 24-hour emergency response devices, late-night transport/escort service.
Student services: personal/psychological counseling.

COSTS & FINANCIAL AID
Costs (2015–16) ***One-time required fee:*** $30. ***Comprehensive fee:*** $37,530 includes full-time tuition ($28,000), mandatory fees ($1530), and room and board ($8000). Full-time tuition and fees vary according to course load and degree level. Part-time tuition: $1170 per credit. Part-time tuition and fees vary according to course load and degree level. ***Required fees:*** $60 per credit part-time, $365 per term part-time. ***College room only:*** $5000. Room and board charges vary according to board plan and housing facility. ***Payment plan:*** installment.
Financial Aid Of all full-time matriculated undergraduates who enrolled in 2012, 116 applied for aid, 112 were judged to have need, 8 had their need fully met. In 2012, 15 non-need-based awards were made. ***Average percent of need met:*** 73. ***Average financial aid package:*** $22,239. ***Average need-based loan:*** $4332. ***Average need-based gift aid:*** $6986. ***Average non-need-based aid:*** $7533. ***Average indebtedness upon graduation:*** $22,500.

APPLYING
Standardized Tests *Recommended:* SAT (for admission), ACT (for admission).
Options: electronic application, deferred entrance.
Application fee: $35.
Required: essay or personal statement, high school transcript, minimum 2.0 GPA, 2 letters of recommendation, portfolio that includes 12 to 20 pieces of studio artwork. ***Required for some:*** interview.
Application deadlines: rolling (freshmen), rolling (out-of-state freshmen), rolling (transfers).
Notification: continuous (freshmen), continuous (out-of-state freshmen), continuous (transfers).

CONTACT
Oregon College of Art & Craft, 8245 Southwest Barnes Road, Portland, OR 97225. *Phone:* 971-255-4192. *Toll-free phone:* 800-390-0632.

Oregon Health & Science University
Portland, Oregon
http://www.ohsu.edu/

- **State-related** upper-level, founded 1974
- **Urban** 120-acre campus
- **Coed** 847 undergraduate students, 24% full-time, 84% women, 16% men

UNDERGRAD STUDENTS
202 full-time, 645 part-time. 0.7% Black or African American, non-Hispanic/Latino; 7% Hispanic/Latino; 4% Asian, non-Hispanic/Latino; 0.2% Native Hawaiian or other Pacific Islander, non-Hispanic/Latino; 0.1% American Indian or Alaska Native, non-Hispanic/Latino; 5% Two or more races, non-Hispanic/Latino; 4% Race/ethnicity unknown; 0.1% international.

FACULTY
Total: 117, 80% full-time, 26% with terminal degrees.

ACADEMICS
Calendar: quarters. *Degrees:* certificates, bachelor's, master's, doctoral, post-master's, and postbachelor's certificates.
Special study options: accelerated degree program, advanced placement credit, distance learning, off-campus study, part-time degree program, summer session for credit.
Computers: Students can access the following: campus intranet, computer help desk, free student e-mail accounts, online (class) grades, online (class) registration, online (class) schedules. Campuswide network is available. Wireless service is available via entire campus.

STUDENT LIFE
Housing options: college housing not available.
Activities and organizations: student-run newspaper, choral group.
Athletics ***Intramural sports:*** basketball M/W, soccer M/W, volleyball M/W.
Campus security: 24-hour emergency response devices and patrols, late-night transport/escort service.
Student services: health clinic, personal/psychological counseling.

FINANCIAL AID
Financial Aid Of all full-time matriculated undergraduates who enrolled in 2014, 301 applied for aid, 293 were judged to have need, 14 had their need fully met. 20 Federal Work-Study jobs (averaging $1000). ***Average percent of need met:*** 34. ***Average financial aid package:*** $11,950. ***Average need-based loan:*** $6293. ***Average need-based gift aid:*** $10,184.

APPLYING
Options: electronic application.
Application fee: $120.
Notification: 6/1 (transfers).

CONTACT
Oregon Health & Science University, 3181 Southwest Sam Jackson Park Road, Portland, OR 97239-3098. *Phone:* 503-494-0954.

★ Oregon State University
Corvallis, Oregon
http://www.oregonstate.edu/

- **State-supported** university, founded 1868
- **Small-town** 422-acre campus
- **Endowment** $573.3 million
- **Coed** 23,903 undergraduate students, 77% full-time, 46% women, 54% men
- **Moderately difficult** entrance level, 78% of applicants were admitted

UNDERGRAD STUDENTS
18,477 full-time, 5,426 part-time. Students come from 52 states and territories; 71 other countries; 27% are from out of state; 1% Black or African American, non-Hispanic/Latino; 8% Hispanic/Latino; 7% Asian, non-Hispanic/Latino; 0.4% Native Hawaiian or other Pacific Islander, non-Hispanic/Latino; 0.6% American Indian or Alaska Native, non-Hispanic/Latino; 6% Two or more races, non-Hispanic/Latino; 2% Race/ethnicity unknown; 6% international; 8% transferred in; 18% live on campus.

Freshmen
Admission: 14,115 applied, 10,975 admitted, 3,718 enrolled. ***Average high school GPA:*** 3.59. ***Test scores:*** SAT critical reading scores over 500: 71%; SAT math scores over 500: 76%; SAT writing scores over 500: 63%; ACT scores over 18: 95%; SAT critical reading scores over 600: 30%; SAT math scores over 600: 37%; SAT writing scores over 600: 23%; ACT scores over 24: 56%; SAT critical reading scores over 700: 6%; SAT math scores over 700: 9%; SAT writing scores over 700: 3%; ACT scores over 30: 13%.

Retention: 84% of full-time freshmen returned.

FACULTY
Total: 1,596, 70% full-time, 76% with terminal degrees.

Student/faculty ratio: 19:1.

ACADEMICS
Calendar: quarters. *Degrees:* certificates, bachelor's, master's, doctoral, post-master's, and postbachelor's certificates.

Special study options: academic remediation for entering students, accelerated degree program, advanced placement credit, cooperative education, distance learning, double majors, English as a second language, freshman honors college, honors programs, independent study, internships, off-campus study, part-time degree program, services for LD students, student-designed majors, study abroad, summer session for credit. ***ROTC:*** Army (b), Navy (b), Air Force (b).

Computers: 2,179 computers/terminals are available on campus for general student use. Students can access the following: campus intranet, computer help desk, free student e-mail accounts, online (class) grades, online (class) registration, online (class) schedules. Campuswide network is available. 100% of college-owned or -operated housing units are wired for high-speed Internet access. Wireless service is available via entire campus.

STUDENT LIFE
Housing options: on-campus residence required for freshman year; coed, special housing for students with disabilities. Campus housing is university owned. Freshman applicants given priority for college housing.

Activities and organizations: drama/theater group, student-run newspaper, radio and television station, choral group, marching band, Ballroom Dance Club, Gaming Club, Organic Growers Club, Blood Drive Association, Residence Hall Association, national fraternities, national sororities.

Athletics Member NCAA. All Division I except football (Division I-A). ***Intercollegiate sports:*** baseball M(s), basketball M(s)/W(s), crew M/W, cross-country running W(s), golf M(s)/W(s), gymnastics W(s), soccer M(s)/W(s), softball W(s), swimming and diving W(s), track and field W(s), volleyball W(s), wrestling M(s). ***Intramural sports:*** archery M/W, badminton M/W, baseball M, basketball M/W, bowling M/W, crew M/W, cross-country running M/W, equestrian sports M(c)/W(c), fencing M(c)/W(c), football M, golf M/W, gymnastics M(c)/W(c), lacrosse M(c)/W(c), racquetball M/W, riflery M(c)/W(c), rock climbing M/W, rugby M(c)/W(c), sailing M(c)/W(c), skiing (cross-country) M(c)/W(c), skiing (downhill) M(c)/W(c), soccer M/W, softball M/W, squash M(c), swimming and diving M/W, table tennis M(c)/W(c), tennis M/W, track and field M/W, ultimate Frisbee M/W, volleyball M/W, water polo M(c)/W(c), wrestling M.

Campus security: 24-hour emergency response devices and patrols, student patrols, late-night transport/escort service, controlled dormitory access, crime prevention office.

Student services: health clinic, personal/psychological counseling, women's center, legal services.

COSTS & FINANCIAL AID
Costs (2014–15) ***One-time required fee:*** $300. ***Tuition:*** state resident $7650 full-time, $189 per credit hour part-time; nonresident $24,822 full-time, $613 per credit hour part-time. Full-time tuition and fees vary according to course load, location, and program. Part-time tuition and fees vary according to course load, location, and program. ***Required fees:*** $1472 full-time, $449 per term part-time. ***Room and board:*** $11,151; room only: $7650. Room and board charges vary according to board plan and housing facility. ***Waivers:*** employees or children of employees.

Financial Aid Of all full-time matriculated undergraduates who enrolled in 2014, 12,639 applied for aid, 10,201 were judged to have need, 776 had their need fully met. 1,422 Federal Work-Study jobs (averaging $2071). In 2014, 2290 non-need-based awards were made. ***Average percent of need met:*** 66. ***Average financial aid package:*** $12,913. ***Average need-based loan:*** $4727. ***Average need-based gift aid:*** $6966. ***Average non-need-based aid:*** $4123. ***Average indebtedness upon graduation:*** $21,955.

APPLYING
Standardized Tests *Required:* SAT or ACT (for admission). *Required for some:* SAT Subject Tests (for admission).

Options: electronic application, early action, deferred entrance.

Application fee: $60.

Required: essay or personal statement, high school transcript, minimum 3.0 GPA.

Application deadlines: 2/1 (freshmen), 6/1 (transfers), 11/1 (early action).

Notification: continuous (freshmen), continuous (transfers), 12/20 (early action).

CONTACT
Oregon State University, Corvallis, OR 97331. *Phone:* 541-737-4411. *Toll-free phone:* 800-291-4192.

Pacific Northwest College of Art

Portland, Oregon

http://www.pnca.edu/

- **Independent** comprehensive, founded 1909
- **Urban** 2-acre campus with easy access to Portland
- **Endowment** $14.8 million
- **Coed** 409 undergraduate students, 90% full-time, 70% women, 30% men
- **Minimally difficult** entrance level, 82% of applicants were admitted

UNDERGRAD STUDENTS
367 full-time, 42 part-time. Students come from 45 states and territories; 4 other countries; 78% are from out of state; 15% transferred in; 21% live on campus.

Freshmen
Admission: 238 applied, 196 admitted, 74 enrolled.

Retention: 83% of full-time freshmen returned.

FACULTY
Total: 136, 20% full-time.

Student/faculty ratio: 7:1.

ACADEMICS
Calendar: semesters. *Degrees:* bachelor's, master's, and post-master's certificates.

Special study options: advanced placement credit, cooperative education, independent study, internships, off-campus study, part-time degree program, services for LD students, student-designed majors, study abroad, summer session for credit.

Computers: 300 computers/terminals are available on campus for general student use. Students can access the following: campus intranet, computer help desk, free student e-mail accounts, online (class) grades, online (class) registration, online (class) schedules. Campuswide network is available. 100% of college-owned or -operated housing units are wired for high-speed Internet access. Wireless service is available via entire campus.

STUDENT LIFE
Housing options: on-campus residence required for freshman year; coed. Campus housing is university owned. Freshman campus housing is guaranteed.

Campus security: 24-hour emergency response devices and patrols, late-night transport/escort service, controlled dormitory access, entrance security guards during open hours.

Student services: personal/psychological counseling.

COSTS & FINANCIAL AID
Costs (2015–16) ***Tuition:*** $31,500 full-time, $1313 per credit part-time. Full-time tuition and fees vary according to degree level. Part-time tuition and fees vary according to course load and degree level. ***Required fees:*** $1570 full-time, $57 per credit part-time. ***Room only:*** $12,464. ***Payment***

plans: installment, deferred payment. ***Waivers:*** employees or children of employees.

Financial Aid Of all full-time matriculated undergraduates who enrolled in 2006, 264 applied for aid, 238 were judged to have need, 13 had their need fully met. 33 Federal Work-Study jobs (averaging $1200). 33 state and other part-time jobs (averaging $1200). In 2006, 10 non-need-based awards were made. ***Average percent of need met:*** 54. ***Average financial aid package:*** $11,845. ***Average need-based loan:*** $4040. ***Average need-based gift aid:*** $4699. ***Average non-need-based aid:*** $2442. ***Average indebtedness upon graduation:*** $22,155.

APPLYING

Options: electronic application, deferred entrance.

Required: essay or personal statement, high school transcript, portfolio of artwork. ***Recommended:*** minimum 2.0 GPA, interview.

Application deadlines: rolling (freshmen), rolling (out-of-state freshmen), rolling (transfers).

Notification: continuous (freshmen), continuous (out-of-state freshmen), continuous (transfers).

CONTACT

Pacific Northwest College of Art, 511 NW Broadway, Portland, OR 97209. *Phone:* 503-821-8926.

★ Pacific University
Forest Grove, Oregon
http://www.pacificu.edu/

- **Independent** comprehensive, founded 1849
- **Small-town** 60-acre campus with easy access to Portland
- **Coed** 1,840 undergraduate students, 98% full-time, 59% women, 41% men
- **Moderately difficult** entrance level, 80% of applicants were admitted

UNDERGRAD STUDENTS

1,797 full-time, 43 part-time. 52% are from out of state; 2% Black or African American, non-Hispanic/Latino; 11% Hispanic/Latino; 12% Asian, non-Hispanic/Latino; 2% Native Hawaiian or other Pacific Islander, non-Hispanic/Latino; 0.8% American Indian or Alaska Native, non-Hispanic/Latino; 13% Two or more races, non-Hispanic/Latino; 4% Race/ethnicity unknown; 2% international; 5% transferred in; 98% live on campus.

Freshmen

Admission: 2,665 applied, 2,144 admitted, 459 enrolled. ***Average high school GPA:*** 3.6. ***Test scores:*** SAT critical reading scores over 500: 69%; SAT math scores over 500: 80%; ACT scores over 18: 96%; SAT critical reading scores over 600: 26%; SAT math scores over 600: 26%; ACT scores over 24: 49%; SAT critical reading scores over 700: 4%; SAT math scores over 700: 3%; ACT scores over 30: 8%.

Retention: 81% of full-time freshmen returned.

FACULTY

Total: 414, 65% full-time, 63% with terminal degrees.

Student/faculty ratio: 11:1.

ACADEMICS

Calendar: semesters. *Degrees:* bachelor's, master's, doctoral, post-master's, and postbachelor's certificates.

ROTC: Army (c), Air Force (c).

Computers: Students can access the following: campus intranet, computer help desk, free student e-mail accounts, online (class) grades, online (class) schedules, Web space, printing, student and academic information, WebCT, computer peripherals. Campuswide network is available. 100% of college-owned or -operated housing units are wired for high-speed Internet access. Wireless service is available via entire campus.

STUDENT LIFE

Housing options: on-campus residence required through sophomore year; coed, special housing for students with disabilities. Campus housing is university owned. Freshman campus housing is guaranteed.

Athletics Member NCAA, NAIA. All NCAA Division III. ***Intercollegiate sports:*** baseball M, basketball M/W, cross-country running M/W, football M, golf M/W, lacrosse W, soccer M/W, softball W, swimming and diving M/W, tennis M/W, track and field M/W, volleyball W, wrestling M/W.

Intramural sports: basketball M/W, cheerleading M/W, crew M/W, football M/W, racquetball W, softball M/W, volleyball M/W.

Campus security: 24-hour emergency response devices and patrols, late-night transport/escort service, controlled dormitory access.

COSTS & FINANCIAL AID

Costs (2015–16) ***Comprehensive fee:*** $51,306 includes full-time tuition ($38,950), mandatory fees ($908), and room and board ($11,448). Part-time tuition: $1623 per credit hour. Part-time tuition and fees vary according to course load. ***College room only:*** $6154. Room and board charges vary according to board plan and housing facility. ***Payment plans:*** installment, deferred payment. ***Waivers:*** employees or children of employees.

Financial Aid Of all full-time matriculated undergraduates who enrolled in 2014, 1,558 applied for aid, 1,284 were judged to have need, 320 had their need fully met. In 2014, 302 non-need-based awards were made. ***Average percent of need met:*** 75. ***Average financial aid package:*** $32,277. ***Average need-based loan:*** $5502. ***Average need-based gift aid:*** $10,833. ***Average non-need-based aid:*** $17,030. ***Average indebtedness upon graduation:*** $25,844.

APPLYING

Standardized Tests *Required:* SAT or ACT (for admission).

Options: electronic application, deferred entrance.

Application fee: $40.

Required: essay or personal statement, high school transcript, minimum 3.0 GPA, 1 letter of recommendation. ***Recommended:*** interview.

CONTACT

Ms. Karen Dunston, Executive Director, Pacific University, 2043 College Way, Forest Grove, OR 97116-1797. *Phone:* 503-352-2218. *Toll-free phone:* 877-722-8648. *Fax:* 503-352-2975. *E-mail:* admissions@pacificu.edu.

See previous page for display ad and page 1564 for the College Close-Up.

Pioneer Pacific College

Wilsonville, Oregon

http://www.pioneerpacific.edu/

- **Proprietary** 4-year, founded 1981
- **Suburban** campus with easy access to Portland
- **Coed**
- **Noncompetitive** entrance level

ACADEMICS

Calendar: continuous. *Degrees:* diplomas, associate, and bachelor's.

STUDENT LIFE

Housing options: college housing not available.

Activities and organizations: Phi Beta Lambda.

APPLYING

Standardized Tests *Required:* ACT Compass (for admission).

Application fee: $50.

Required: high school transcript, interview. ***Required for some:*** essay or personal statement.

CONTACT

Elizabeth Cox, Director of Admissions, Pioneer Pacific College, 27501 SW Parkway Avenue, Wilsonville, OR 97070. *Phone:* 503-688-2178. *Toll-free phone:* 866-PPC-INFO. *Fax:* 503-682-1514. *E-mail:* wil-info@pioneerpacific.edu.

Portland State University

Portland, Oregon

http://www.pdx.edu/

- **State-supported** university, founded 1946, part of Oregon University System
- **Urban** 49-acre campus with easy access to Portland
- **Endowment** $84.7 million
- **Coed** 22,136 undergraduate students, 66% full-time, 52% women, 48% men
- **Moderately difficult** entrance level, 85% of applicants were admitted

UNDERGRAD STUDENTS

14,561 full-time, 7,575 part-time. Students come from 50 states and territories; 67 other countries; 14% are from out of state; 3% Black or African American, non-Hispanic/Latino; 11% Hispanic/Latino; 8% Asian, non-Hispanic/Latino; 0.7% Native Hawaiian or other Pacific Islander, non-Hispanic/Latino; 1% American Indian or Alaska Native, non-Hispanic/Latino; 5% Two or more races, non-Hispanic/Latino; 5% Race/ethnicity unknown; 7% international; 14% transferred in.

Freshmen

Admission: 4,936 applied, 4,184 admitted, 1,644 enrolled. ***Average high school GPA:*** 3.39. ***Test scores:*** SAT critical reading scores over 500: 61%; SAT math scores over 500: 58%; SAT writing scores over 500: 52%; ACT scores over 18: 82%; SAT critical reading scores over 600: 24%; SAT math scores over 600: 18%; SAT writing scores over 600: 15%; ACT scores over 24: 38%; SAT critical reading scores over 700: 4%; SAT math scores over 700: 2%; SAT writing scores over 700: 2%; ACT scores over 30: 6%.

Retention: 72% of full-time freshmen returned.

FACULTY

Total: 1,540, 55% full-time, 45% with terminal degrees.

Student/faculty ratio: 22:1.

ACADEMICS

Calendar: quarters. *Degrees:* certificates, bachelor's, master's, doctoral, and postbachelor's certificates.

Special study options: academic remediation for entering students, accelerated degree program, adult/continuing education programs, advanced placement credit, cooperative education, distance learning, double majors, English as a second language, freshman honors college, honors programs, independent study, internships, off-campus study, part-time degree program, services for LD students, study abroad, summer session for credit. ***ROTC:*** Air Force (c).

Computers: Students can access the following: campus intranet, computer help desk, free student e-mail accounts, online (class) grades, online (class) registration, online (class) schedules. Campuswide network is available. Wireless service is available via entire campus.

STUDENT LIFE

Housing options: coed, cooperative, special housing for students with disabilities. Campus housing is university owned. Freshman campus housing is guaranteed.

Activities and organizations: drama/theater group, student-run newspaper, radio station, choral group, national fraternities, national sororities.

Athletics Member NCAA. All Division I except football (Division I-AA). ***Intercollegiate sports:*** basketball M/W, cross-country running M/W, golf W, soccer W, softball W, tennis M/W, track and field M/W, volleyball W.

Campus security: 24-hour emergency response devices and patrols, late-night transport/escort service, controlled dormitory access.

Student services: health clinic, personal/psychological counseling, women's center, legal services.

COSTS & FINANCIAL AID

Costs (2014–15) ***Tuition:*** state resident $6525 full-time, $145 per credit part-time; nonresident $220,520 full-time, $490 per credit part-time. Full-time tuition and fees vary according to program and reciprocity agreements. Part-time tuition and fees vary according to program. ***Required fees:*** $1269 full-time. ***Room and board:*** $11,349. Room and board charges vary according to board plan and housing facility. ***Payment plan:*** installment. ***Waivers:*** senior citizens and employees or children of employees.

Financial Aid Of all full-time matriculated undergraduates who enrolled in 2014, 11,724 applied for aid, 9,753 were judged to have need, 432 had their need fully met. In 2014, 94 non-need-based awards were made. ***Average percent of need met:*** 65. ***Average financial aid package:*** $9509. ***Average need-based loan:*** $4395. ***Average need-based gift aid:*** $5840. ***Average non-need-based aid:*** $2785. ***Average indebtedness upon graduation:*** $28,410.

APPLYING

Standardized Tests *Required for some:* SAT or ACT (for admission).

Options: electronic application, early admission, deferred entrance.

Application fee: $50.

Required: high school transcript, minimum 3.0 GPA.

Application deadlines: rolling (freshmen), rolling (out-of-state freshmen), rolling (transfers).

Notification: continuous (freshmen), continuous (out-of-state freshmen), continuous (transfers).

CONTACT

Shannon Carr, Executive Director, Admissions and New Student Programs, Portland State University, PO Box 751, Portland, OR 97207. *Phone:* 503-725-3511. *Toll-free phone:* 800-547-8887. *Fax:* 503-725-5525. *E-mail:* shannon.carr@pdx.edu.

Reed College

Portland, Oregon

http://www.reed.edu/

- **Independent** comprehensive, founded 1908
- **Urban** 116-acre campus with easy access to Portland
- **Endowment** $494.1 million
- **Coed** 1,374 undergraduate students, 97% full-time, 53% women, 47% men
- **Most difficult** entrance level, 39% of applicants were admitted

UNDERGRAD STUDENTS

1,339 full-time, 35 part-time. Students come from 49 states and territories; 42 other countries; 86% are from out of state; 2% Black or African American, non-Hispanic/Latino; 11% Hispanic/Latino; 6% Asian, non-Hispanic/Latino; 0.2% Native Hawaiian or other Pacific Islander, non-Hispanic/Latino; 0.3% American Indian or Alaska Native, non-Hispanic/Latino; 8% Two or more races, non-Hispanic/Latino; 6% Race/ethnicity unknown; 8% international; 2% transferred in; 67% live on campus.

Freshmen

Admission: 3,956 applied, 1,532 admitted, 347 enrolled. ***Average high school GPA:*** 3.9. ***Test scores:*** SAT critical reading scores over 500: 100%; SAT math scores over 500: 99%; SAT writing scores over 500: 100%; ACT scores over 18: 100%; SAT critical reading scores over 600: 96%; SAT math scores over 600: 89%; SAT writing scores over 600: 92%; ACT scores over 24: 99%; SAT critical reading scores over 700: 58%; SAT math scores over 700: 42%; SAT writing scores over 700: 44%; ACT scores over 30: 68%.

Retention: 90% of full-time freshmen returned.

FACULTY

Total: 151, 95% full-time, 93% with terminal degrees.

Student/faculty ratio: 9:1.

ACADEMICS

Calendar: semesters. *Degrees:* bachelor's and master's.

Special study options: academic remediation for entering students, advanced placement credit, cooperative education, double majors, independent study, internships, off-campus study, services for LD students, student-designed majors, study abroad. ***ROTC:*** Air Force (c).

Unusual degree programs: 3-2 engineering with By arrangement with Caltech, the Columbia University School of Engineering and Applied Sciences, or Rensselaer Polytechnic Institute, a student may obtain a bachelor's degree in engineering and a bachelor of arts degree from Reed; forestry with By arrangement with the Nicholas School of the Environment of Duke University, a student may obtain a bachelor of arts degree at Reed and a professional master's degree from Duke (master of forestry or master of environmental management); Computer Science: a student may obtain a bachelor of arts from Reed and a bachelor of science in computer science from the University of Washington. Visual arts: a student may obtain a bachelor of arts from Reed and a bachelor of fine arts from Pacific Northwest College of Art.

Computers: 434 computers/terminals are available on campus for general student use. Students can access the following: campus intranet, computer help desk, free student e-mail accounts, online (class) grades, online (class) registration, online (class) schedules. Campuswide network is available. 100% of college-owned or -operated housing units are wired for high-speed Internet access. Wireless service is available via entire campus.

STUDENT LIFE

Housing options: coed, women-only, cooperative, special housing for students with disabilities. Campus housing is university owned. Freshman campus housing is guaranteed.

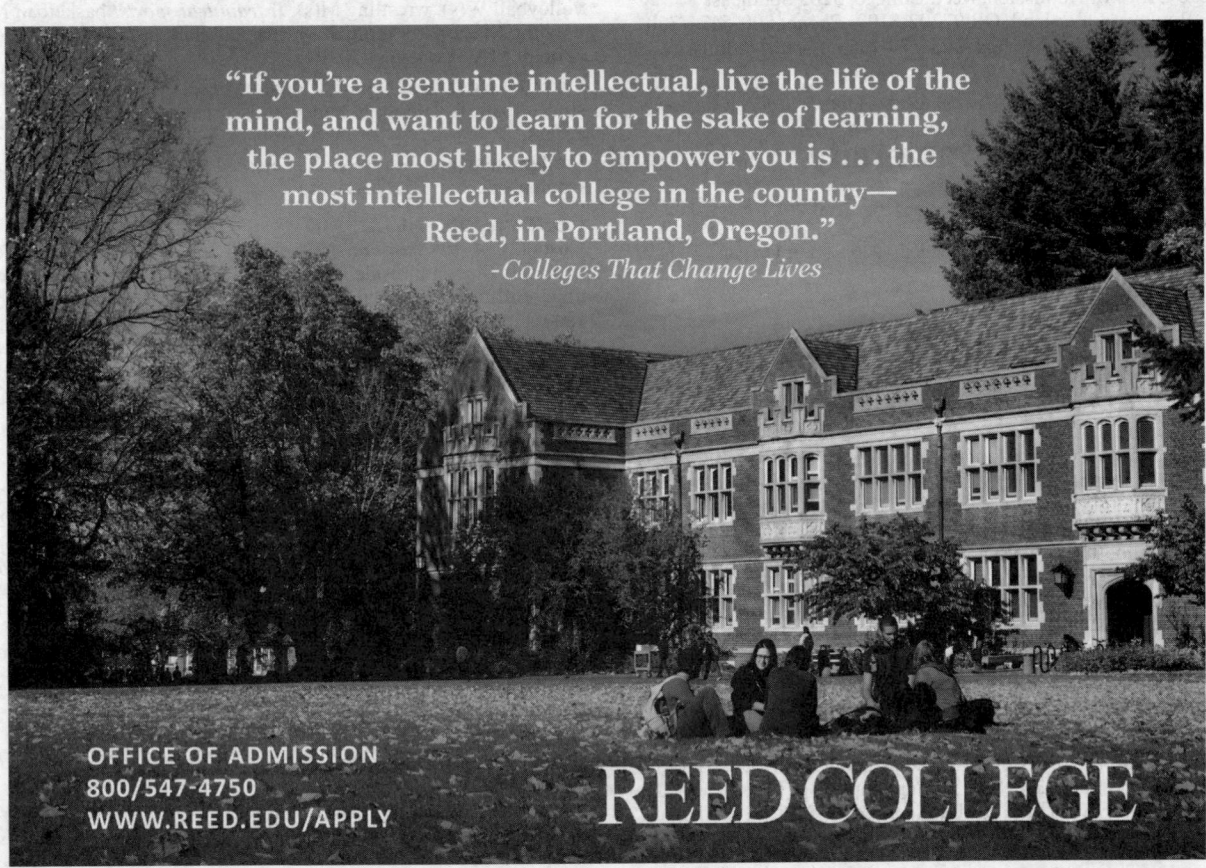

Activities and organizations: drama/theater group, student-run newspaper, radio station, choral group.

Athletics ***Intramural sports:*** basketball M/W, fencing M/W, rugby M/W, soccer M/W, squash M/W, ultimate Frisbee M/W.

Campus security: 24-hour emergency response devices and patrols, student patrols, late-night transport/escort service, controlled dormitory access.

Student services: health clinic, personal/psychological counseling, women's center, legal services.

COSTS & FINANCIAL AID

Costs (2014–15) ***Comprehensive fee:*** $59,960 includes full-time tuition ($47,500), mandatory fees ($260), and room and board ($12,200). Full-time tuition and fees vary according to degree level. Part-time tuition: $8060 per unit. Part-time tuition and fees vary according to course load and degree level. ***College room only:*** $6350. Room and board charges vary according to board plan and housing facility. ***Payment plan:*** installment. ***Waivers:*** employees or children of employees.

Financial Aid Of all full-time matriculated undergraduates who enrolled in 2013, 790 applied for aid, 660 were judged to have need, 649 had their need fully met. 385 Federal Work-Study jobs (averaging $1450). 175 state and other part-time jobs (averaging $1452). ***Average percent of need met:*** 100. ***Average financial aid package:*** $41,715. ***Average need-based loan:*** $4337. ***Average need-based gift aid:*** $37,179. ***Average indebtedness upon graduation:*** $20,079. ***Financial aid deadline:*** 2/1.

APPLYING

Standardized Tests *Required:* SAT or ACT (for admission).

Options: electronic application, early admission, early decision, deferred entrance.

Required: essay or personal statement, high school transcript, 3 letters of recommendation. ***Recommended:*** interview.

Application deadlines: 1/15 (freshmen), 3/1 (transfers).

Early decision deadline: 11/15 (for plan 1), 12/20 (for plan 2).

Notification: 4/1 (freshmen), 5/15 (transfers), 12/15 (early decision plan 1), 2/1 (early decision plan 2).

CONTACT

Reed College Office of Admission, Reed College, 3203 Southeast Woodstock Boulevard, Portland, OR 97202-8199. *Phone:* 800-547-4750. *Toll-free phone:* 800-547-4750. *Fax:* 503-777-7553. *E-mail:* admission@reed.edu.

See previous page for display ad and page 1574 for the College Close-Up.

Southern Oregon University

Ashland, Oregon

http://www.sou.edu/

- **State-supported** comprehensive, founded 1926, part of Oregon University System
- **Small-town** 175-acre campus
- **Endowment** $24.6 million
- **Coed** 5,247 undergraduate students, 70% full-time, 58% women, 42% men
- **Moderately difficult** entrance level, 93% of applicants were admitted

UNDERGRAD STUDENTS

3,678 full-time, 1,569 part-time. Students come from 41 states and territories; 15 other countries; 34% are from out of state; 2% Black or African American, non-Hispanic/Latino; 8% Hispanic/Latino; 2% Asian, non-Hispanic/Latino; 0.4% Native Hawaiian or other Pacific Islander, non-Hispanic/Latino; 0.9% American Indian or Alaska Native, non-Hispanic/Latino; 6% Two or more races, non-Hispanic/Latino; 26% Race/ethnicity unknown; 2% international; 10% transferred in; 26% live on campus.

Freshmen

Admission: 2,209 applied, 2,064 admitted, 629 enrolled. ***Average high school GPA:*** 3.31. ***Test scores:*** SAT critical reading scores over 500: 61%; SAT math scores over 500: 53%; SAT writing scores over 500: 48%; ACT scores over 18: 89%; SAT critical reading scores over 600: 23%; SAT math scores over 600: 13%; SAT writing scores over 600: 10%; ACT scores over 24: 40%; SAT critical reading scores over 700: 3%; SAT math scores over 700: 1%; SAT writing scores over 700: 1%; ACT scores over 30: 3%.

Retention: 74% of full-time freshmen returned.

FACULTY

Total: 304, 56% full-time, 55% with terminal degrees.

Student/faculty ratio: 21:1.

ACADEMICS

Calendar: quarters. *Degrees:* certificates, bachelor's, master's, and postbachelor's certificates.

Special study options: academic remediation for entering students, accelerated degree program, adult/continuing education programs, advanced placement credit, cooperative education, distance learning, double majors, English as a second language, freshman honors college, honors programs, independent study, internships, off-campus study, part-time degree program, services for LD students, student-designed majors, study abroad, summer session for credit. ***ROTC:*** Army (b).

Computers: 750 computers/terminals are available on campus for general student use. Students can access the following: campus intranet, computer help desk, free student e-mail accounts, online (class) grades, online (class) registration, online (class) schedules, online account information including bill payment, online employee records for student workers. Campuswide network is available. 100% of college-owned or -operated housing units are wired for high-speed Internet access. Wireless service is available via classrooms, computer centers, computer labs, dorm rooms, learning centers, libraries, student centers.

STUDENT LIFE

Housing options: on-campus residence required for freshman year; coed, special housing for students with disabilities. Campus housing is university owned. Freshman campus housing is guaranteed.

Activities and organizations: drama/theater group, student-run newspaper, radio and television station, choral group, Native American Student Union, International Student Association, Impact (religious club), Ho`opa`a Hawaii Club, Omicron Delta Kappa.

Athletics Member NAIA. ***Intercollegiate sports:*** basketball M(s)/W(s), cheerleading W, football M(s), lacrosse M(c), rugby M(c)/W(c), soccer M(c)/W(s), softball W(s), tennis M(c)/W(c), track and field M(s)/W(s), volleyball W(s), wrestling M(s). ***Intramural sports:*** basketball M/W, bowling M(c)/W(c), football M, rock climbing M(c)/W(c), soccer M/W, softball M/W, volleyball M/W.

Campus security: 24-hour emergency response devices and patrols, student patrols, late-night transport/escort service, controlled dormitory access.

Student services: health clinic, personal/psychological counseling, women's center, legal services.

COSTS & FINANCIAL AID

Costs (2014–15) ***Tuition:*** state resident $6307 full-time, $140 per credit hour part-time; nonresident $19,883 full-time, $442 per credit hour part-time. Full-time tuition and fees vary according to course load, program, and reciprocity agreements. Part-time tuition and fees vary according to course load, program, and reciprocity agreements. ***Required fees:*** $1413 full-time, $56 per credit hour part-time. ***Room and board:*** $11,397; room only: $6402. Room and board charges vary according to board plan and housing facility. ***Payment plans:*** installment, deferred payment. ***Waivers:*** senior citizens and employees or children of employees.

Financial Aid Of all full-time matriculated undergraduates who enrolled in 2013, 3,263 applied for aid, 2,840 were judged to have need, 200 had their need fully met. 240 Federal Work-Study jobs (averaging $2006). In 2013, 72 non-need-based awards were made. ***Average percent of need met:*** 52. ***Average financial aid package:*** $9483. ***Average need-based loan:*** $4264. ***Average need-based gift aid:*** $6262. ***Average non-need-based aid:*** $2088. ***Average indebtedness upon graduation:*** $30,936.

APPLYING

Standardized Tests *Required:* SAT or ACT (for admission). *Required for some:* SAT and SAT Subject Tests or ACT (for admission), SAT Subject Tests (for admission).

Options: electronic application, early admission, deferred entrance.

Application fee: $50.

Required: high school transcript, minimum 3.0 GPA. ***Required for some:*** essay or personal statement.

Application deadlines: rolling (freshmen), rolling (transfers).
Notification: continuous (freshmen), continuous (transfers).

CONTACT
Mr. Kelly Moutsatson, Director of Admissions, Southern Oregon University, 1250 Siskiyou Boulevard, Ashland, OR 97520. *Phone:* 541-552-6411. *Toll-free phone:* 855-470-3377. *Fax:* 541-552-6614. *E-mail:* admissions@sou.edu.

★ University of Oregon
Eugene, Oregon
http://www.uoregon.edu/

- **State-supported** university, founded 1876
- **Suburban** 295-acre campus
- **Endowment** $627.0 million
- **Coed** 20,559 undergraduate students, 91% full-time, 52% women, 48% men
- **Moderately difficult** entrance level, 75% of applicants were admitted

UNDERGRAD STUDENTS
18,673 full-time, 1,886 part-time. Students come from 55 states and territories; 74 other countries; 41% are from out of state; 2% Black or African American, non-Hispanic/Latino; 9% Hispanic/Latino; 5% Asian, non-Hispanic/Latino; 0.4% Native Hawaiian or other Pacific Islander, non-Hispanic/Latino; 0.5% American Indian or Alaska Native, non-Hispanic/Latino; 6% Two or more races, non-Hispanic/Latino; 1% Race/ethnicity unknown; 13% international; 6% transferred in; 19% live on campus.

Freshmen
Admission: 21,359 applied, 15,997 admitted, 3,961 enrolled. ***Average high school GPA:*** 3.58. ***Test scores:*** SAT critical reading scores over 500: 76%; SAT math scores over 500: 78%; SAT writing scores over 500: 72%; ACT scores over 18: 96%; SAT critical reading scores over 600: 33%; SAT math scores over 600: 33%; SAT writing scores over 600: 28%; ACT scores over 24: 62%; SAT critical reading scores over 700: 6%; SAT math scores over 700: 5%; SAT writing scores over 700: 5%; ACT scores over 30: 11%.
Retention: 87% of full-time freshmen returned.

FACULTY
Total: 1,633, 64% full-time, 94% with terminal degrees.
Student/faculty ratio: 18:1.

ACADEMICS
Calendar: quarters. *Degrees:* bachelor's, master's, doctoral, and postbachelor's certificates.
Special study options: advanced placement credit, cooperative education, distance learning, double majors, English as a second language, honors programs, independent study, internships, off-campus study, part-time degree program, services for LD students, student-designed majors, study abroad, summer session for credit. ***ROTC:*** Army (b), Air Force (c).
Unusual degree programs: 3-2 engineering with Oregon State University.
Computers: 650 computers/terminals and 650 ports are available on campus for general student use. Students can access the following: campus intranet, computer help desk, free student e-mail accounts, online (class) grades, online (class) registration, online (class) schedules. Campuswide network is available. 100% of college-owned or -operated housing units are wired for high-speed Internet access. Wireless service is available via entire campus.

STUDENT LIFE
Housing options: coed, cooperative. Campus housing is university owned. Freshman applicants given priority for college housing.
Activities and organizations: drama/theater group, student-run newspaper, radio and television station, choral group, marching band, political and environmental action, cultural organizations, major-specific organizations, community service organizations, club sports, national fraternities, national sororities.
Athletics Member NCAA. All Division I except football (Division I-A). ***Intercollegiate sports:*** baseball M(s), basketball M(s)/W(s), cross-country running M(s)/W(s), golf M(s)/W(s), lacrosse W(s), soccer W(s), softball W(s), tennis M(s)/W(s), track and field M(s)/W(s), volleyball W(s).
Intramural sports: badminton M(c)/W(c), baseball M(c), basketball M/W, crew M(c)/W(c), cross-country running M/W, equestrian sports M(c)/W(c), fencing M(c)/W(c), football M/W, ice hockey M(c)/W(c), lacrosse M(c)/W(c), racquetball M(c)/W(c), rugby M(c)/W(c), sailing M(c)/W(c), skiing (downhill) M(c)/W(c), soccer M(c)/W(c), softball M(c)/W(c), swimming and diving M/W, table tennis M(c)/W(c), tennis M/W, track and field M(c)/W(c), ultimate Frisbee M(c)/W(c), volleyball M(c)/W(c), water polo M(c)/W(c).
Campus security: 24-hour emergency response devices and patrols, late-night transport/escort service, controlled dormitory access.
Student services: health clinic, personal/psychological counseling, women's center, legal services.

COSTS & FINANCIAL AID
Costs (2014–15) ***One-time required fee:*** $375. ***Tuition:*** state resident $8190 full-time, $182 per credit hour part-time; nonresident $29,160 full-time, $648 per credit hour part-time. Full-time tuition and fees vary according to course load. Part-time tuition and fees vary according to course load. ***Required fees:*** $1728 full-time. ***Room and board:*** $11,442. Room and board charges vary according to board plan and housing facility. ***Payment plan:*** installment. ***Waivers:*** employees or children of employees.
Financial Aid Of all full-time matriculated undergraduates who enrolled in 2013, 11,336 applied for aid, 8,754 were judged to have need, 625 had their need fully met. 1,314 Federal Work-Study jobs (averaging $1474). 57 state and other part-time jobs (averaging $2294). In 2013, 2585 non-need-based awards were made. ***Average percent of need met:*** 60. ***Average financial aid package:*** $10,046. ***Average need-based loan:*** $4744. ***Average need-based gift aid:*** $7493. ***Average non-need-based aid:*** $4014. ***Average indebtedness upon graduation:*** $24,508.

APPLYING
Standardized Tests *Required:* SAT or ACT (for admission). *Required for some:* SAT and SAT Subject Tests or ACT (for admission).
Options: electronic application, early action.
Application fee: $50.
Required: essay or personal statement, high school transcript, C+ or better in 15 college preparatory units. ***Required for some:*** 2 letters of recommendation.
Application deadlines: 1/15 (freshmen), 5/15 (transfers), 11/1 (early action).
Notification: 4/1 (freshmen), 12/15 (early action).

CONTACT
University of Oregon, Eugene, OR 97403. *Phone:* 541-346-3201. *Toll-free phone:* 800-232-3825.

University of Portland
Portland, Oregon
http://www.up.edu/

- **Independent Roman Catholic** comprehensive, founded 1901
- **Urban** 125-acre campus
- **Endowment** $147.0 million
- **Coed** 3,680 undergraduate students, 98% full-time, 58% women, 42% men
- **Moderately difficult** entrance level, 63% of applicants were admitted

UNDERGRAD STUDENTS
3,609 full-time, 71 part-time. 68% are from out of state; 1% Black or African American, non-Hispanic/Latino; 11% Hispanic/Latino; 10% Asian, non-Hispanic/Latino; 2% Native Hawaiian or other Pacific Islander, non-Hispanic/Latino; 0.2% American Indian or Alaska Native, non-Hispanic/Latino; 9% Two or more races, non-Hispanic/Latino; 2% Race/ethnicity unknown; 3% international; 2% transferred in; 57% live on campus.

Freshmen
Admission: 11,099 applied, 6,986 admitted, 1,082 enrolled. ***Average high school GPA:*** 3.63. ***Test scores:*** SAT critical reading scores over 500: 91%; SAT math scores over 500: 90%; SAT critical reading scores over 600: 47%; SAT math scores over 600: 52%; SAT critical reading scores over 700: 14%; SAT math scores over 700: 10%.
Retention: 90% of full-time freshmen returned.

FACULTY
Total: 339, 62% full-time, 57% with terminal degrees.

Student/faculty ratio: 14:1.

ACADEMICS
Calendar: semesters. *Degrees:* bachelor's, master's, doctoral, and post-master's certificates.

Special study options: adult/continuing education programs, advanced placement credit, double majors, honors programs, independent study, internships, off-campus study, part-time degree program, services for LD students, study abroad, summer session for credit. ***ROTC:*** Army (b), Air Force (b).

Computers: 157 computers/terminals and 2,520 ports are available on campus for general student use. Students can access the following: campus intranet, computer help desk, free student e-mail accounts, online (class) grades, online (class) registration, online (class) schedules. Campuswide network is available. 100% of college-owned or -operated housing units are wired for high-speed Internet access. Wireless service is available via entire campus.

STUDENT LIFE
Housing options: on-campus residence required for freshman year; coed, men-only, women-only. Campus housing is university owned. Freshman campus housing is guaranteed.

Activities and organizations: drama/theater group, student-run newspaper, radio station, choral group, English Society, International Club, Hawaiian Club, rugby club, Social Science Club.

Athletics Member NCAA. All Division I. ***Intercollegiate sports:*** baseball M(s), basketball M(s)/W(s), crew W, cross-country running M(s)/W(s), rugby M(c), soccer M(s)/W(s), tennis M(s)/W(s), track and field M(s)/W(s), volleyball W(s). ***Intramural sports:*** basketball M/W, crew M/W, cross-country running M/W, football M/W, rugby M, skiing (cross-country) M/W, skiing (downhill) M/W, soccer M(c)/W, softball M/W, swimming and diving M/W, tennis M/W, track and field M/W, volleyball M/W, water polo M/W, weight lifting M/W.

Campus security: 24-hour emergency response devices and patrols, student patrols, late-night transport/escort service, controlled dormitory access.

Student services: health clinic, personal/psychological counseling.

COSTS & FINANCIAL AID
Costs (2014–15) ***Comprehensive fee:*** $49,964 includes full-time tuition ($38,350), mandatory fees ($170), and room and board ($11,444). Full-time tuition and fees vary according to program. Part-time tuition: $1200 per credit hour. Part-time tuition and fees vary according to course load and program. ***Room and board:*** Room and board charges vary according to board plan and housing facility. ***Payment plans:*** installment, deferred payment. ***Waivers:*** employees or children of employees.

Financial Aid Of all full-time matriculated undergraduates who enrolled in 2014, 2,718 applied for aid, 2,248 were judged to have need, 158 had their need fully met. 366 Federal Work-Study jobs (averaging $1474). 1,468 state and other part-time jobs (averaging $1437). In 2014, 1183 non-need-based awards were made. ***Average percent of need met:*** 71. ***Average financial aid package:*** $28,700. ***Average need-based loan:*** $5012. ***Average need-based gift aid:*** $21,981. ***Average non-need-based aid:*** $14,965. ***Average indebtedness upon graduation:*** $26,557.

APPLYING
Standardized Tests *Required:* SAT or ACT (for admission). *Recommended:* SAT (for admission), ACT (for admission).

Options: electronic application, deferred entrance.

Application fee: $50.

Required: essay or personal statement, high school transcript, 1 letter of recommendation.

Application deadlines: 6/1 (freshmen), 6/1 (transfers).

Notification: continuous (freshmen), continuous (transfers).

CONTACT
Mr. Jason McDonald, Dean of Admissions, University of Portland, 5000 North Willamette Boulevard, Portland, OR 97203-5798. *Phone:* 503-943-7147. *Toll-free phone:* 888-627-5601. *Fax:* 503-943-7315. *E-mail:* admissions@up.edu.

Warner Pacific College

Portland, Oregon

http://www.warnerpacific.edu/

- **Independent** comprehensive, founded 1937, affiliated with Church of God
- **Urban** 15-acre campus with easy access to Portland
- **Endowment** $10.2 million
- **Coed** 552 undergraduate students, 95% full-time, 56% women, 44% men
- **Moderately difficult** entrance level, 63% of applicants were admitted

UNDERGRAD STUDENTS
522 full-time, 30 part-time. Students come from 26 states and territories; 16 other countries; 32% are from out of state; 9% Black or African American, non-Hispanic/Latino; 13% Hispanic/Latino; 4% Asian, non-Hispanic/Latino; 1% Native Hawaiian or other Pacific Islander, non-Hispanic/Latino; 0.5% American Indian or Alaska Native, non-Hispanic/Latino; 4% Two or more races, non-Hispanic/Latino; 8% Race/ethnicity unknown; 2% international; 15% transferred in; 44% live on campus.

Freshmen
Admission: 476 applied, 299 admitted, 142 enrolled. ***Average high school GPA:*** 3.17. ***Test scores:*** SAT math scores over 500: 36%; SAT math scores over 600: 5%; SAT math scores over 700: 1%.

Retention: 73% of full-time freshmen returned.

FACULTY
Total: 89, 25% full-time, 28% with terminal degrees.

Student/faculty ratio: 12:1.

ACADEMICS
Calendar: semesters. *Degrees:* certificates, associate, bachelor's, and master's.

Special study options: academic remediation for entering students, accelerated degree program, adult/continuing education programs, advanced placement credit, cooperative education, double majors, honors programs, independent study, internships, off-campus study, part-time degree program, services for LD students, student-designed majors, study abroad, summer session for credit. ***ROTC:*** Air Force (c).

Computers: 90 computers/terminals are available on campus for general student use. Students can access the following: campus intranet, computer help desk, free student e-mail accounts, online (class) grades, online (class) registration, online (class) schedules. Campuswide network is available. 100% of college-owned or -operated housing units are wired for high-speed Internet access. Wireless service is available via classrooms, computer centers, computer labs, dorm rooms, learning centers, libraries, student centers.

STUDENT LIFE
Housing options: on-campus residence required through junior year; men-only, women-only, special housing for students with disabilities. Campus housing is university owned. Freshman applicants given priority for college housing.

Activities and organizations: drama/theater group, student-run newspaper, choral group, Associated Students of Warner Pacific College, yearbook, College Activities Board, Fellowship of Christian Athletes.

Athletics Member NAIA, NCCAA. ***Intercollegiate sports:*** basketball M(s)/W(s), cross-country running M(s)/W(s), golf M(s)/W(s), soccer M(s)/W(s), track and field M(s)/W(s), volleyball W(s), wrestling M/W. ***Intramural sports:*** basketball M/W, volleyball M/W.

Campus security: 24-hour emergency response devices and patrols, student patrols, late-night transport/escort service, controlled dormitory access.

Student services: health clinic, personal/psychological counseling.

COSTS & FINANCIAL AID
Costs (2014–15) ***Comprehensive fee:*** $28,530 includes full-time tuition ($19,640), mandatory fees ($660), and room and board ($8230). Part-time tuition: $900 per credit hour. Part-time tuition and fees vary according to course load. ***Required fees:*** $660 per term part-time. ***College room only:*** $3340. Room and board charges vary according to board plan and housing facility. ***Payment plans:*** installment, deferred payment. ***Waivers:*** children of alumni and employees or children of employees.

Financial Aid Of all full-time matriculated undergraduates who enrolled in 2014, 471 applied for aid, 428 were judged to have need, 58 had their need fully met. 384 Federal Work-Study jobs (averaging $1929). In 2014, 62 non-need-based awards were made. ***Average percent of need met:*** 68. ***Average financial aid package:*** $17,590. ***Average need-based loan:*** $4181. ***Average need-based gift aid:*** $6462. ***Average non-need-based aid:*** $5777. ***Average indebtedness upon graduation:*** $31,338.

APPLYING

Standardized Tests *Required:* SAT or ACT (for admission).

Options: electronic application.

Required: essay or personal statement, high school transcript, minimum 2.5 GPA. ***Required for some:*** 1 letter of recommendation, interview. ***Recommended:*** minimum 3.0 GPA, interview.

Application deadlines: rolling (freshmen), rolling (transfers).

Notification: continuous (freshmen), continuous (transfers).

CONTACT

Dale Seipp, Vice President for Enrollment Management, Warner Pacific College, 2219 Southeast 68th Avenue, Portland, OR 97215. *Phone:* 503-517-1020. *Toll-free phone:* 800-804-1510. *Fax:* 503-517-1540. *E-mail:* admiss@warnerpacific.edu.

Western Oregon University

Monmouth, Oregon

http://www.wou.edu/

- **State-supported** comprehensive, founded 1856, part of Oregon University System
- **Rural** 157-acre campus with easy access to Portland
- **Coed** 4,930 undergraduate students, 85% full-time, 58% women, 42% men
- **Moderately difficult** entrance level, 89% of applicants were admitted

UNDERGRAD STUDENTS

4,195 full-time, 735 part-time. Students come from 33 states and territories; 22 other countries; 21% are from out of state; 4% Black or African American, non-Hispanic/Latino; 8% Hispanic/Latino; 4% Asian, non-Hispanic/Latino; 3% Native Hawaiian or other Pacific Islander, non-Hispanic/Latino; 2% American Indian or Alaska Native, non-Hispanic/Latino; 0.2% Two or more races, non-Hispanic/Latino; 5% Race/ethnicity unknown; 6% international; 11% transferred in; 24% live on campus.

Freshmen

Admission: 2,887 applied, 2,562 admitted, 872 enrolled. ***Average high school GPA:*** 3.2. ***Test scores:*** SAT critical reading scores over 500: 40%; SAT math scores over 500: 38%; SAT writing scores over 500: 29%; ACT scores over 18: 63%; SAT critical reading scores over 600: 10%; SAT math scores over 600: 8%; SAT writing scores over 600: 5%; ACT scores over 24: 18%; SAT critical reading scores over 700: 1%; ACT scores over 30: 1%.

Retention: 70% of full-time freshmen returned.

FACULTY

Total: 393, 75% full-time, 47% with terminal degrees.

Student/faculty ratio: 15:1.

ACADEMICS

Calendar: quarters. *Degrees:* bachelor's, master's, and postbachelor's certificates.

Special study options: academic remediation for entering students, advanced placement credit, distance learning, double majors, English as a second language, freshman honors college, honors programs, independent study, internships, off-campus study, part-time degree program, services for LD students, student-designed majors, study abroad, summer session for credit. ***ROTC:*** Army (b), Navy (c).

Unusual degree programs: nursing.

Computers: 411 computers/terminals are available on campus for general student use. Students can access the following: computer help desk, free student e-mail accounts, online (class) grades, online (class) registration, online (class) schedules. Campuswide network is available. Wireless service is available via entire campus.

STUDENT LIFE

Housing options: on-campus residence required for freshman year; coed, men-only, women-only, special housing for students with disabilities. Campus housing is university owned. Freshman applicants given priority for college housing.

Activities and organizations: drama/theater group, student-run newspaper, television station, choral group, Model United Nations, Multicultural Student Union, Oregon Student Association, Alternative Spring Break (community service), M.E.Ch.A.

Athletics Member NCAA. All Division II. ***Intercollegiate sports:*** baseball M(s), basketball M(s)/W(s), cross-country running M(s)/W(s), football M(s), soccer W(s), softball W(s), track and field M(s)/W(s), volleyball W(s). ***Intramural sports:*** badminton M/W, basketball M/W, bowling M/W, cross-country running M(c)/W(c), football M/W, golf M/W, lacrosse M(c), racquetball M(c)/W(c), riflery M/W, rugby M(c)/W(c), skiing (downhill) M/W, soccer M(c)/W(c), softball M/W, swimming and diving M(c)/W(c), table tennis M/W, tennis M/W, track and field M/W, volleyball M(c)/W(c), water polo M(c)/W(c), weight lifting M/W, wrestling M.

Campus security: 24-hour emergency response devices and patrols, student patrols, late-night transport/escort service, controlled dormitory access.

Student services: health clinic, personal/psychological counseling, women's center.

COSTS & FINANCIAL AID

Costs (2014–15) ***Tuition:*** state resident $8723 full-time; nonresident $22,257 full-time. Full-time tuition and fees vary according to course load. Part-time tuition and fees vary according to course load. No tuition increase for student's term of enrollment. ***Room and board:*** $9416; room only: $7766. Room and board charges vary according to board plan and housing facility.

Financial Aid Of all full-time matriculated undergraduates who enrolled in 2014, 3,688 applied for aid, 3,131 were judged to have need, 267 had their need fully met. 1,044 Federal Work-Study jobs (averaging $978). In 2014, 134 non-need-based awards were made. ***Average percent of need met:*** 52. ***Average financial aid package:*** $9853. ***Average need-based loan:*** $4126. ***Average need-based gift aid:*** $7030. ***Average non-need-based aid:*** $2172. ***Average indebtedness upon graduation:*** $28,331.

APPLYING

Standardized Tests *Required:* SAT and SAT Subject Tests or ACT (for admission).

Options: electronic application, deferred entrance.

Application fee: $60.

Required: high school transcript, minimum 2.8 GPA, general college preparatory program completion.

Application deadlines: rolling (freshmen), rolling (transfers).

Notification: continuous (freshmen), continuous (transfers).

CONTACT

Mr. David Compton, Assistant Director of Admissions for Recruitment, Western Oregon University, 345 North Monmouth Avenue, Monmouth, OR 97361. *Phone:* 503-838-8211. *Toll-free phone:* 877-877-1593. *Fax:* 503-838-8067. *E-mail:* wolfgram@wou.edu.

Willamette University

Salem, Oregon

http://www.willamette.edu/

- **Independent United Methodist** comprehensive, founded 1842
- **Urban** 72-acre campus with easy access to Portland
- **Endowment** $214.3 million
- **Coed** 2,375 undergraduate students, 86% full-time, 56% women, 44% men
- **Very difficult** entrance level, 81% of applicants were admitted

UNDERGRAD STUDENTS

2,042 full-time, 333 part-time. Students come from 41 states and territories; 3 other countries; 73% are from out of state; 2% Black or African American, non-Hispanic/Latino; 11% Hispanic/Latino; 8% Asian, non-Hispanic/Latino; 0.3% Native Hawaiian or other Pacific Islander, non-Hispanic/Latino; 1% American Indian or Alaska Native, non-Hispanic/Latino; 8% Two or more races, non-Hispanic/Latino; 10%

Race/ethnicity unknown; 2% international; 2% transferred in; 66% live on campus.

Freshmen
Admission: 5,729 applied, 4,658 admitted, 553 enrolled. ***Average high school GPA:*** 3.75. ***Test scores:*** SAT critical reading scores over 500: 90%; SAT math scores over 500: 91%; SAT writing scores over 500: 89%; ACT scores over 18: 99%; SAT critical reading scores over 600: 55%; SAT math scores over 600: 52%; SAT writing scores over 600: 52%; ACT scores over 24: 83%; SAT critical reading scores over 700: 15%; SAT math scores over 700: 13%; SAT writing scores over 700: 9%; ACT scores over 30: 25%.
Retention: 83% of full-time freshmen returned.

FACULTY
Total: 271, 79% full-time, 93% with terminal degrees.
Student/faculty ratio: 11:1.

ACADEMICS
Calendar: semesters. *Degrees:* bachelor's, master's, and doctoral.
Special study options: accelerated degree program, advanced placement credit, double majors, independent study, internships, off-campus study, part-time degree program, services for LD students, student-designed majors, study abroad. ***ROTC:*** Army (c), Air Force (c).
Unusual degree programs: 3-2 engineering with University of Southern California, Washington University in St. Louis, Columbia University; forestry with Duke University.
Computers: Students can access the following: online (class) registration. Campuswide network is available. 100% of college-owned or -operated housing units are wired for high-speed Internet access.

STUDENT LIFE
Housing options: on-campus residence required through sophomore year; coed. Campus housing is university owned. Freshman campus housing is guaranteed.
Activities and organizations: drama/theater group, student-run newspaper, radio station, choral group, national fraternities, national sororities.
Athletics Member NCAA. All Division III. ***Intercollegiate sports:*** baseball M, basketball M/W, crew M/W, cross-country running M/W, football M, golf M/W, lacrosse M(c), soccer M/W, softball W, swimming and diving M/W, tennis M/W, track and field M/W, volleyball W. ***Intramural sports:*** badminton M/W, basketball M/W, bowling M/W, cross-country running M/W, football M/W, golf M/W, racquetball M/W, skiing (cross-country) M(c)/W(c), skiing (downhill) M(c)/W(c), soccer M/W, softball M/W, table tennis M/W, tennis M/W, ultimate Frisbee M/W, volleyball M/W, water polo M/W, weight lifting M/W.
Campus security: 24-hour emergency response devices and patrols, student patrols, late-night transport/escort service, controlled dormitory access.
Student services: health clinic, personal/psychological counseling, women's center.

COSTS & FINANCIAL AID
Costs (2014–15) ***Comprehensive fee:*** $54,896 includes full-time tuition ($43,760), mandatory fees ($316), and room and board ($10,820). Full-time tuition and fees vary according to course load. Part-time tuition: $5470 per course. Part-time tuition and fees vary according to course load. ***Room and board:*** Room and board charges vary according to board plan and housing facility. ***Payment plans:*** tuition prepayment, installment. ***Waivers:*** employees or children of employees.
Financial Aid Of all full-time matriculated undergraduates who enrolled in 2014, 1,444 applied for aid, 1,236 were judged to have need, 392 had their need fully met. In 2014, 710 non-need-based awards were made. ***Average percent of need met:*** 84. ***Average financial aid package:*** $33,934. ***Average need-based loan:*** $5757. ***Average need-based gift aid:*** $26,574. ***Average non-need-based aid:*** $17,896. ***Average indebtedness upon graduation:*** $26,936.

APPLYING
Standardized Tests *Required:* SAT or ACT (for admission).
Options: electronic application, early action, deferred entrance.
Application fee: $50.
Required: essay or personal statement, high school transcript, minimum 2.0 GPA, 1 letter of recommendation. ***Required for some:*** interview. ***Recommended:*** interview.
Application deadlines: 1/15 (freshmen), 2/1 (transfers), 11/15 (early action).
Notification: continuous until 4/1 (freshmen), 3/15 (transfers), 12/31 (early action).

CONTACT
Mr. Ramiro Flores, Director of Admission, Willamette University, 900 State Street, Salem, OR 97301. *Phone:* 877-542-2787. *Toll-free phone:* 877-542-2787. *Fax:* 503-375-5363. *E-mail:* libarts@williamette.edu.

PENNSYLVANIA

Albright College
Reading, Pennsylvania
http://www.albright.edu/

- **Independent** comprehensive, founded 1856, affiliated with United Methodist Church
- **Suburban** 118-acre campus with easy access to Philadelphia
- **Endowment** $64.4 million
- **Coed** 1,775 undergraduate students, 98% full-time, 57% women, 43% men
- **Moderately difficult** entrance level, 50% of applicants were admitted

UNDERGRAD STUDENTS
1,745 full-time, 30 part-time. Students come from 24 states and territories; 19 other countries; 36% are from out of state; 19% Black or African American, non-Hispanic/Latino; 10% Hispanic/Latino; 4% Asian, non-Hispanic/Latino; 0.7% American Indian or Alaska Native, non-Hispanic/Latino; 1% Two or more races, non-Hispanic/Latino; 2% Race/ethnicity unknown; 3% international; 3% transferred in; 71% live on campus.

Freshmen
Admission: 7,604 applied, 3,807 admitted, 540 enrolled. ***Average high school GPA:*** 3.4. ***Test scores:*** SAT critical reading scores over 500: 67%; SAT math scores over 500: 66%; ACT scores over 18: 97%; SAT critical reading scores over 600: 18%; SAT math scores over 600: 19%; ACT scores over 24: 37%; SAT critical reading scores over 700: 3%; SAT math scores over 700: 2%; ACT scores over 30: 1%.
Retention: 76% of full-time freshmen returned.

FACULTY
Total: 180, 61% full-time, 61% with terminal degrees.
Student/faculty ratio: 13:1.

ACADEMICS
Calendar: 4-1-4. *Degrees:* certificates, bachelor's, and master's.
Special study options: accelerated degree program, adult/continuing education programs, advanced placement credit, double majors, English as a second language, honors programs, independent study, internships, off-campus study, services for LD students, student-designed majors, study abroad, summer session for credit. ***ROTC:*** Army (c).
Computers: 450 computers/terminals are available on campus for general student use. Students can access the following: campus intranet, computer help desk, free student e-mail accounts, online (class) grades, online (class) registration, online (class) schedules, online financial statements, housing choices, course management systems. Campuswide network is available. 100% of college-owned or -operated housing units are wired for high-speed Internet access. Wireless service is available via entire campus.

STUDENT LIFE
Housing options: on-campus residence required through sophomore year; coed, men-only, women-only. Campus housing is university owned. Freshman campus housing is guaranteed.
Activities and organizations: drama/theater group, student-run newspaper, radio station, choral group, Greek Organizations (combined), Alpha Phi Omega (service organization), Student Government

Association, Albright College Activities Council, Albrightian (newspaper), national fraternities, national sororities.

Athletics Member NCAA. All Division III. ***Intercollegiate sports:*** badminton W(c), baseball M, basketball M/W, cheerleading M/W, cross-country running M/W, field hockey W, football M, golf M/W, lacrosse M/W, rugby M(c)/W(c), soccer M/W, softball W, swimming and diving M/W, tennis M/W, track and field M/W, ultimate Frisbee M(c)/W(c), volleyball W. ***Intramural sports:*** badminton W, basketball M/W, football M, racquetball M/W, soccer M/W, softball M/W, volleyball M/W.

Campus security: 24-hour emergency response devices and patrols, student patrols, late-night transport/escort service, controlled dormitory access, E2 Campus Text messaging, Rape Aggression Defense Training, Marked Patrol Cars, Partnership with Reading PD, PA State Police.

Student services: health clinic, personal/psychological counseling, women's center.

COSTS & FINANCIAL AID

Costs (2014–15) ***Comprehensive fee:*** $48,620 includes full-time tuition ($37,320), mandatory fees ($900), and room and board ($10,400). Full-time tuition and fees vary according to degree level. Part-time tuition: $4665 per course. Part-time tuition and fees vary according to degree level. ***College room only:*** $5770. Room and board charges vary according to board plan and housing facility. ***Payment plan:*** installment. ***Waivers:*** adult students, senior citizens, and employees or children of employees.

Financial Aid Of all full-time matriculated undergraduates who enrolled in 2014, 1,627 applied for aid, 1,573 were judged to have need, 159 had their need fully met. In 2014, 126 non-need-based awards were made. ***Average percent of need met:*** 78. ***Average financial aid package:*** $32,847. ***Average need-based loan:*** $5113. ***Average need-based gift aid:*** $27,027. ***Average non-need-based aid:*** $14,176. ***Average indebtedness upon graduation:*** $28,541.

APPLYING

Standardized Tests *Required:* students applying tests optional must complete an on-campus admission interview (for admission). *Recommended:* SAT (for admission), ACT (for admission), SAT or ACT (for admission).

Options: electronic application, deferred entrance.

Application fee: $25.

Required: essay or personal statement, high school transcript, 1 letter of recommendation, secondary school report (guidance department). ***Recommended:*** interview.

Application deadlines: rolling (freshmen), rolling (transfers).

Notification: continuous (freshmen), continuous (transfers).

CONTACT

Mr. Gregory Eichhorn, Vice President for Enrollment Management, Albright College, PO Box 15234, 13th and Bern Streets, Reading, PA 19612-5234. *Phone:* 610-921-7260. *Toll-free phone:* 800-252-1856. *Fax:* 610-921-7294. *E-mail:* admission@albright.edu.

Allegheny College

Meadville, Pennsylvania

http://www.allegheny.edu/

- **Independent** 4-year, founded 1815
- **Suburban** 565-acre campus
- **Endowment** $184.7 million
- **Coed** 2,023 undergraduate students, 98% full-time, 55% women, 45% men
- **Very difficult** entrance level, 72% of applicants were admitted

UNDERGRAD STUDENTS

1,979 full-time, 44 part-time. Students come from 43 states and territories; 47 other countries; 46% are from out of state; 5% Black or African American, non-Hispanic/Latino; 6% Hispanic/Latino; 2% Asian, non-Hispanic/Latino; 0.1% American Indian or Alaska Native, non-Hispanic/Latino; 4% Two or more races, non-Hispanic/Latino; 0.5% Race/ethnicity unknown; 2% international; 1% transferred in; 90% live on campus.

Freshmen

Admission: 3,857 applied, 2,768 admitted, 476 enrolled. ***Average high school GPA:*** 3.75. ***Test scores:*** SAT critical reading scores over 500: 85%; SAT math scores over 500: 85%; SAT writing scores over 500: 80%; ACT scores over 18: 98%; SAT critical reading scores over 600: 48%; SAT math scores over 600: 45%; SAT writing scores over 600: 44%; ACT scores over 24: 73%; SAT critical reading scores over 700: 10%; SAT math scores over 700: 7%; SAT writing scores over 700: 10%; ACT scores over 30: 20%.

Retention: 83% of full-time freshmen returned.

FACULTY

Total: 206, 83% full-time, 80% with terminal degrees.

Student/faculty ratio: 11:1.

ACADEMICS

Calendar: semesters. *Degree:* bachelor's.

Special study options: advanced placement credit, double majors, English as a second language, independent study, internships, off-campus study, services for LD students, student-designed majors, study abroad.

Unusual degree programs: 3-2 engineering with Columbia University, Case Western Reserve University, Duke University, Washington University, University of Pittsburgh; arts management, public policy and management, health care policy and management and information systems management at Carnegie Mellon University; physician assistant and occupational therapy at Chatham; osteopathic medicine, 3-4, at PCOM and LECOM; physical therapy 4-2 doctorate program at Chatham.

Computers: 207 computers/terminals and 200 ports are available on campus for general student use. Students can access the following: campus intranet, computer help desk, free student e-mail accounts, online (class) grades, online (class) registration, online (class) schedules, placement testing, course catalog, class lists, book buy, repair service, transcript review and ordering, billing, payroll time cards, internet kiosks, dataports for laptops, Google Apps for Education, campus organizations, financial aid. Campuswide network is available. 100% of college-owned or -operated housing units are wired for high-speed Internet access. Wireless service is available via entire campus.

STUDENT LIFE

Housing options: on-campus residence required through senior year; coed, men-only, women-only, special housing for students with disabilities. Campus housing is university owned. Freshman campus housing is guaranteed.

Activities and organizations: drama/theater group, student-run newspaper, radio and television station, choral group, student government, Gators Activity Programming, Alpha Phi Omega (service fraternity), Outing Club, Greek life, national fraternities, national sororities.

Athletics Member NCAA. All Division III. ***Intercollegiate sports:*** baseball M, basketball M/W, cheerleading M(c)/W(c), crew M(c)/W(c), cross-country running M/W, equestrian sports M(c)/W(c), fencing M(c)/W(c), football M, golf M/W, ice hockey M(c), lacrosse M(c)/W, rugby M(c)/W(c), soccer M/W, softball W, swimming and diving M/W, tennis M/W, track and field M/W, ultimate Frisbee M(c)/W(c), volleyball M(c)/W. ***Intramural sports:*** basketball M/W, soccer M/W, volleyball M/W.

Campus security: 24-hour emergency response devices and patrols, late-night transport/escort service, controlled dormitory access, local police patrol, emergency alert system, self defense education, compliance program, property engraving, CCTV system for parking.

Student services: health clinic, personal/psychological counseling.

COSTS & FINANCIAL AID

Costs (2015–16) ***Comprehensive fee:*** $53,210 includes full-time tuition ($41,970), mandatory fees ($500), and room and board ($10,740). Part-time tuition: $1749 per credit hour. Part-time tuition and fees vary according to course load. ***Required fees:*** $250 per term part-time. ***College room only:*** $5650. Room and board charges vary according to board plan and housing facility. ***Payment plan:*** installment. ***Waivers:*** employees or children of employees.

Financial Aid Of all full-time matriculated undergraduates who enrolled in 2014, 1,624 applied for aid, 1,446 were judged to have need, 496 had their need fully met. 1,139 Federal Work-Study jobs (averaging $1970). 113 state and other part-time jobs (averaging $5166). In 2014, 469 non-need-based awards were made. ***Average percent of need met:*** 90. ***Average financial aid package:*** $33,833. ***Average need-based loan:*** $5216. ***Average need-based gift aid:*** $26,535. ***Average non-need-based aid:*** $16,174.

APPLYING
Standardized Tests *Required:* SAT or ACT (for admission).

Options: electronic application, early admission, early decision, deferred entrance.

Required: essay or personal statement, high school transcript, 2 letters of recommendation, college preparatory program, standardized test scores. *Recommended:* interview.

Application deadlines: 2/15 (freshmen), 7/1 (transfers).

Early decision deadline: 11/1 (for plan 1), 1/15 (for plan 2).

Notification: 4/1 (freshmen), 8/1 (transfers), 12/15 (early decision plan 1), 2/1 (early decision plan 2).

CONTACT
Mr. Cornell LeSane II, Director of Admissions, Allegheny College, 520 North Main Street, Box 5, Meadville, PA 16335. *Phone:* 814-332-4351. *Toll-free phone:* 800-521-5293. *Fax:* 814-337-0431. *E-mail:* admissions@allegheny.edu.

Alvernia University

Reading, Pennsylvania

http://www.alvernia.edu/

- **Independent Roman Catholic** comprehensive, founded 1958
- **Suburban** 121-acre campus with easy access to Philadelphia
- **Endowment** $22.8 million
- **Coed** 2,442 undergraduate students, 74% full-time, 74% women, 26% men
- **Moderately difficult** entrance level, 75% of applicants were admitted

UNDERGRAD STUDENTS
1,798 full-time, 644 part-time. Students come from 20 states and territories; 18 other countries; 24% are from out of state; 13% Black or African American, non-Hispanic/Latino; 7% Hispanic/Latino; 1% Asian, non-Hispanic/Latino; 0.2% American Indian or Alaska Native, non-Hispanic/Latino; 1% Two or more races, non-Hispanic/Latino; 6% Race/ethnicity unknown; 0.2% international; 3% transferred in; 59% live on campus.

Freshmen
Admission: 1,747 applied, 1,305 admitted, 376 enrolled. ***Average high school GPA:*** 3.28. ***Test scores:*** SAT critical reading scores over 500: 41%; SAT math scores over 500: 48%; SAT writing scores over 500: 34%; ACT scores over 18: 74%; SAT critical reading scores over 600: 6%; SAT math scores over 600: 8%; SAT writing scores over 600: 5%; ACT scores over 24: 27%; ACT scores over 30: 1%.

Retention: 77% of full-time freshmen returned.

FACULTY
Total: 328, 32% full-time, 40% with terminal degrees.

Student/faculty ratio: 12:1.

ACADEMICS
Calendar: semesters. *Degrees:* associate, bachelor's, master's, and doctoral.

Special study options: academic remediation for entering students, accelerated degree program, adult/continuing education programs, advanced placement credit, distance learning, double majors, English as a second language, honors programs, independent study, internships, off-campus study, part-time degree program, services for LD students, student-designed majors, study abroad, summer session for credit. ***ROTC:*** Army (c).

Unusual degree programs: 3-2 occupational therapy.

Computers: 462 computers/terminals and 2,016 ports are available on campus for general student use. Students can access the following: computer help desk, free student e-mail accounts, online (class) grades, online (class) registration, online (class) schedules. Campuswide network is available. 100% of college-owned or -operated housing units are wired for high-speed Internet access. Wireless service is available via classrooms, computer centers, computer labs, dorm rooms, learning centers, libraries, student centers.

STUDENT LIFE
Housing options: on-campus residence required for freshman year; coed, special housing for students with disabilities. Campus housing is university owned. Freshman campus housing is guaranteed.

Activities and organizations: drama/theater group, student-run newspaper, choral group, Student Government Association, Student Nurses Association of Alvernia (ASNA), Criminal Justice Association (CJA), Sport Management Association (SMA), Science Association.

Athletics Member NCAA. All Division III. ***Intercollegiate sports:*** baseball M, basketball M/W, cheerleading W(c), cross-country running M/W, field hockey W, golf M/W, ice hockey M(c), lacrosse M/W, soccer M/W, softball W, tennis M/W, track and field M/W, volleyball W. ***Intramural sports:*** basketball M/W, football M/W, soccer M/W, volleyball M/W.

Campus security: 24-hour patrols, late-night transport/escort service, controlled dormitory access.

Student services: health clinic, personal/psychological counseling.

COSTS & FINANCIAL AID
Costs (2015–16) ***Comprehensive fee:*** $41,920 includes full-time tuition ($30,500), mandatory fees ($600), and room and board ($10,820). Full-time tuition and fees vary according to class time and reciprocity agreements. Part-time tuition: $810 per credit. Part-time tuition and fees vary according to class time and course load. ***College room only:*** $5380. Room and board charges vary according to board plan and housing facility. ***Payment plan:*** installment. ***Waivers:*** senior citizens and employees or children of employees.

Financial Aid Of all full-time matriculated undergraduates who enrolled in 2013, 1,612 applied for aid, 1,475 were judged to have need, 152 had their need fully met. In 2013, 184 non-need-based awards were made. ***Average percent of need met:*** 63. ***Average financial aid package:*** $18,210. ***Average need-based loan:*** $4212. ***Average need-based gift aid:*** $13,982. ***Average non-need-based aid:*** $8526. ***Average indebtedness upon graduation:*** $42,552.

APPLYING
Standardized Tests *Required:* SAT or ACT (for admission).

Options: electronic application, deferred entrance.

Application fee: $25.

Required: essay or personal statement, high school transcript. ***Required for some:*** 2 letters of recommendation, interview. ***Recommended:*** minimum 2.0 GPA, 1 letter of recommendation.

Application deadlines: rolling (freshmen), rolling (transfers).

Notification: continuous (freshmen), continuous (transfers).

CONTACT
Mr. Dan Hartzman, Director of Undergraduate Admissions, Alvernia University, 400 Saint Bernardine Street, Reading, PA 19607-1799. *Phone:* 610-568-1530. *Toll-free phone:* 888-ALVERNIA. *Fax:* 610-796-2873. *E-mail:* admissions@alvernia.edu.

★ Arcadia University

Glenside, Pennsylvania

http://www.arcadia.edu/

- **Independent** comprehensive, founded 1853, affiliated with Presbyterian Church (U.S.A.)
- **Suburban** 71-acre campus with easy access to Philadelphia
- **Endowment** $59.2 million
- **Coed** 2,594 undergraduate students, 91% full-time, 69% women, 31% men
- **Moderately difficult** entrance level, 59% of applicants were admitted

UNDERGRAD STUDENTS
2,367 full-time, 227 part-time. Students come from 42 states and territories; 19 other countries; 39% are from out of state; 9% Black or African American, non-Hispanic/Latino; 7% Hispanic/Latino; 5% Asian, non-Hispanic/Latino; 0.2% Native Hawaiian or other Pacific Islander, non-Hispanic/Latino; 0.2% American Indian or Alaska Native, non-Hispanic/Latino; 4% Two or more races, non-Hispanic/Latino; 6% Race/ethnicity unknown; 2% international; 5% transferred in; 54% live on campus.

Freshmen

Admission: 9,634 applied, 5,665 admitted, 673 enrolled. ***Average high school GPA:*** 3.65. ***Test scores:*** SAT critical reading scores over 500: 79%; SAT math scores over 500: 80%; SAT writing scores over 500: 72%; ACT scores over 18: 96%; SAT critical reading scores over 600: 30%; SAT math scores over 600: 28%; SAT writing scores over 600: 25%; ACT scores over 24: 56%; SAT critical reading scores over 700: 6%; SAT math scores over 700: 3%; SAT writing scores over 700: 4%; ACT scores over 30: 11%.

Retention: 82% of full-time freshmen returned.

FACULTY

Total: 475, 34% full-time.

Student/faculty ratio: 13:1.

ACADEMICS

Calendar: semesters. *Degrees:* bachelor's, master's, doctoral, and postbachelor's certificates.

Special study options: accelerated degree program, advanced placement credit, cooperative education, distance learning, double majors, English as a second language, honors programs, independent study, internships, off-campus study, part-time degree program, services for LD students, student-designed majors, study abroad, summer session for credit.

Unusual degree programs: 3-2 business administration with MBA with a Global Perspective; engineering with Arcadia University offers a combined five-year (3+2) Engineering Program with Columbia University in New York; Forensic Science, International Peace and Conflict Resolution.

Computers: 120 computers/terminals and 620 ports are available on campus for general student use. Students can access the following: campus intranet, computer help desk, free student e-mail accounts, online (class) grades, online (class) registration, online (class) schedules. Campuswide network is available.

STUDENT LIFE

Housing options: coed, women-only. Campus housing is university owned and leased by the school. Freshman campus housing is guaranteed.

Activities and organizations: drama/theater group, student-run newspaper, radio station, choral group, Student Program Board, Residence Hall Council, student government, Arcadia Christian Fellowship, Student Alumni Association.

Athletics Member NCAA. All Division III. ***Intercollegiate sports:*** baseball M, basketball M/W, equestrian sports M/W, field hockey W, golf M/W, lacrosse M/W, soccer M/W, softball W, swimming and diving M/W, tennis M/W, volleyball W. ***Intramural sports:*** basketball M/W, cheerleading W(c), equestrian sports M/W, field hockey W, rock climbing M/W, soccer M/W, swimming and diving M, tennis M/W, volleyball M/W, weight lifting M/W.

Campus security: 24-hour emergency response devices and patrols, student patrols, late-night transport/escort service, controlled dormitory access.

Student services: health clinic, personal/psychological counseling.

COSTS & FINANCIAL AID

Costs (2015–16) ***Comprehensive fee:*** $52,760 includes full-time tuition ($38,900), mandatory fees ($660), and room and board ($13,200). Full-time tuition and fees vary according to course load, degree level, and program. Part-time tuition: $640 per credit. ***College room only:*** $9000. Room and board charges vary according to board plan.

Financial Aid Of all full-time matriculated undergraduates who enrolled in 2013, 2,117 applied for aid, 1,976 were judged to have need, 282 had their need fully met. 1,481 Federal Work-Study jobs (averaging $1658). 209 state and other part-time jobs (averaging $1652). In 2013, 283 non-need-based awards were made. ***Average percent of need met:*** 69. ***Average financial aid package:*** $27,193. ***Average need-based loan:*** $4032. ***Average need-based gift aid:*** $22,891. ***Average non-need-based aid:*** $15,642.

APPLYING

Standardized Tests *Required:* SAT or ACT (for admission).

Options: electronic application, deferred entrance.

Application fee: $30.

Required: essay or personal statement, high school transcript, 2 letters of recommendation. ***Required for some:*** portfolio, audition. ***Recommended:*** minimum 3.0 GPA, interview.

Application deadlines: 3/1 (freshmen), 6/15 (transfers).

Notification: continuous until 9/1 (freshmen), continuous until 9/1 (transfers).

CONTACT

Colleen Pernicello, Director of Undergraduate Admissions, Arcadia University, 450 South Easton Road, Glenside, PA 19038. *Phone:* 215-572-2910. *Toll-free phone:* 877-ARCADIA. *Fax:* 215-572-4049. *E-mail:* admiss@arcadia.edu.

See previous page for display ad and page 1346 for the College Close-Up.

The Art Institute of Philadelphia

Philadelphia, Pennsylvania

http://www.artinstitutes.edu/philadelphia/

- **Proprietary** 4-year, founded 1966, part of Education Management Corporation
- **Urban** campus
- **Coed**

ACADEMICS

Calendar: quarters. *Degrees:* diplomas, associate, and bachelor's.

CONTACT

The Art Institute of Philadelphia, 1622 Chestnut Street, Philadelphia, PA 19103. *Phone:* 215-567-7080. *Toll-free phone:* 800-275-2474.

The Art Institute of Pittsburgh

Pittsburgh, Pennsylvania

http://www.artinstitutes.edu/pittsburgh/

- **Proprietary** 4-year, founded 1921, part of Education Management Corporation
- **Urban** campus
- **Coed**

ACADEMICS

Calendar: quarters. *Degrees:* certificates, diplomas, associate, and bachelor's.

CONTACT

The Art Institute of Pittsburgh, 420 Boulevard of the Allies, Pittsburgh, PA 15219. *Phone:* 412-263-6600. *Toll-free phone:* 800-275-2470.

The Art Institute of York–Pennsylvania

York, Pennsylvania

http://www.artinstitutes.edu/york/

- **Proprietary** 4-year, founded 1952, part of Education Management Corporation
- **Suburban** campus
- **Coed**

ACADEMICS

Calendar: quarters. *Degrees:* diplomas, associate, and bachelor's.

CONTACT

The Art Institute of York–Pennsylvania, 1409 Williams Road, York, PA 17402-9012. *Phone:* 717-755-2300. *Toll-free phone:* 800-864-7725.

Bloomsburg University of Pennsylvania

Bloomsburg, Pennsylvania

http://www.bloomu.edu/

- **State-supported** comprehensive, founded 1839, part of Pennsylvania State System of Higher Education
- **Rural** 366-acre campus
- **Endowment** $31.3 million
- **Coed** 9,319 undergraduate students, 93% full-time, 57% women, 43% men
- **Moderately difficult** entrance level, 88% of applicants were admitted

UNDERGRAD STUDENTS

8,630 full-time, 689 part-time. Students come from 22 states and territories; 21 other countries; 10% are from out of state; 8% Black or African American, non-Hispanic/Latino; 5% Hispanic/Latino; 1% Asian, non-Hispanic/Latino; 0.1% Native Hawaiian or other Pacific Islander, non-Hispanic/Latino; 0.1% American Indian or Alaska Native, non-Hispanic/Latino; 0.2% Two or more races, non-Hispanic/Latino; 1% Race/ethnicity unknown; 1% international; 5% transferred in; 43% live on campus.

Freshmen

Admission: 10,043 applied, 8,819 admitted, 2,171 enrolled. ***Average high school GPA:*** 3.28. ***Test scores:*** SAT critical reading scores over 500: 42%; SAT math scores over 500: 49%; SAT writing scores over 500: 34%; ACT scores over 18: 74%; SAT critical reading scores over 600: 7%; SAT math scores over 600: 8%; SAT writing scores over 600: 5%; ACT scores over 24: 17%; ACT scores over 30: 1%.

Retention: 79% of full-time freshmen returned.

FACULTY

Total: 516, 81% full-time, 72% with terminal degrees.

Student/faculty ratio: 21:1.

ACADEMICS

Calendar: semesters. *Degrees:* bachelor's, master's, doctoral, and postbachelor's certificates.

Special study options: academic remediation for entering students, advanced placement credit, cooperative education, distance learning, double majors, English as a second language, honors programs, independent study, internships, off-campus study, part-time degree program, services for LD students, student-designed majors, study abroad, summer session for credit. ***ROTC:*** Army (b), Air Force (c).

Unusual degree programs: 3-2 engineering with Penn State University (College of Engineering, College of Earth and Mineral Sciences).

Computers: 1,571 computers/terminals are available on campus for general student use. Students can access the following: computer help desk, free student e-mail accounts, online (class) grades, online (class) registration, online (class) schedules. Campuswide network is available. 100% of college-owned or -operated housing units are wired for high-speed Internet access. Wireless service is available via entire campus.

STUDENT LIFE

Housing options: on-campus residence required for freshman year; coed. Campus housing is university owned and leased by the school. Freshman campus housing is guaranteed.

Activities and organizations: drama/theater group, student-run newspaper, radio and television station, choral group, marching band, Living and Learning Communities, Band and Music Groups, Greek Organizations, Residence Hall Councils, Club Sports, national fraternities, national sororities.

Athletics Member NCAA. All Division II except wrestling (Division I). ***Intercollegiate sports:*** baseball M(s), basketball M(s)/W(s), cross-country running M(s)/W(s), field hockey W(s), football M(s), lacrosse W(s), soccer M(s)/W(s), softball W(s), swimming and diving M(s)/W(s), tennis M(s)/W(s), track and field M(s)/W(s), wrestling M(s). ***Intramural sports:*** baseball M(c), basketball M/W, equestrian sports M(c)/W(c), field hockey W, football M, ice hockey M(c), lacrosse M(c)/W(c), racquetball M/W, rugby M(c)/W(c), skiing (downhill) M(c)/W(c), soccer M(c)/W(c), softball M/W, ultimate Frisbee M(c)/W(c), volleyball M(c)/W(c), wrestling M(c).

Campus security: 24-hour emergency response devices and patrols, late-night transport/escort service, controlled dormitory access, monitored surveillance cameras.

Student services: health clinic, personal/psychological counseling, women's center, legal services.

COSTS & FINANCIAL AID

Costs (2014–15) ***Tuition:*** state resident $6820 full-time, $284 per credit part-time; nonresident $17,050 full-time, $710 per credit part-time. Full-time tuition and fees vary according to course load and location. Part-time tuition and fees vary according to course load and location. ***Required fees:*** $2094 full-time, $77 per credit part-time, $75 per term part-time. ***Room and board:*** $8168; room only: $5154. Room and board charges vary according to board plan and housing facility. ***Payment plan:*** installment. ***Waivers:*** senior citizens and employees or children of employees.

Financial Aid Of all full-time matriculated undergraduates who enrolled in 2014, 7,617 applied for aid, 5,593 were judged to have need, 600 had their need fully met. 1,042 Federal Work-Study jobs (averaging $3088). 1,371 state and other part-time jobs (averaging $3434). In 2014, 170 non-need-based awards were made. ***Average percent of need met:*** 57. ***Average financial aid package:*** $8750. ***Average need-based loan:*** $4158. ***Average need-based gift aid:*** $5835. ***Average non-need-based aid:*** $1810. ***Average indebtedness upon graduation:*** $29,661.

APPLYING
Standardized Tests *Required:* SAT or ACT (for admission).

Options: electronic application, early admission, early action, deferred entrance.

Application fee: $35.

Required: high school transcript.

Application deadlines: rolling (freshmen), rolling (out-of-state freshmen), rolling (transfers).

Notification: continuous until 9/18 (freshmen), continuous until 9/18 (out-of-state freshmen), continuous (transfers), 5/1 (early action).

CONTACT
Mr. Christopher Lapos, Interim Director of Admissions, Bloomsburg University of Pennsylvania, 104 Student Services Center, Bloomsburg, PA 17815-1905. *Phone:* 570-389-4316. *Fax:* 570-389-4741. *E-mail:* buadmiss@bloomu.edu.

Bryn Athyn College of the New Church
Bryn Athyn, Pennsylvania
http://www.brynathyn.edu/

- **Independent Christian** comprehensive, founded 1876, affiliated with Church of the New Jerusalem, part of The Academy of the New Church
- **Suburban** 130-acre campus with easy access to Philadelphia
- **Endowment** $59.3 million
- **Coed**
- **Minimally difficult** entrance level

FACULTY
Student/faculty ratio: 6:1.

ACADEMICS
Calendar: trimesters. *Degrees:* associate, bachelor's, master's, and doctoral.

STUDENT LIFE
Housing options: men-only, women-only. Campus housing is university owned. Freshman campus housing is guaranteed.

Activities and organizations: drama/theater group, student-run newspaper, choral group, C.A.R.E. (Community Service), Social council, International Student Organization, Peer Advisory Council, student government.

Campus security: 24-hour emergency response devices, controlled dormitory access, 18-hour patrols by trained personnel.

Student services: health clinic, personal/psychological counseling.

FINANCIAL AID
Financial Aid Of all full-time matriculated undergraduates who enrolled in 2008, 92 applied for aid, 66 were judged to have need, 30 had their need fully met. In 2008, 22 non-need-based awards were made. ***Average percent of need met:*** 95. ***Average financial aid package:*** $9987. ***Average need-based loan:*** $3329. ***Average need-based gift aid:*** $8358. ***Average non-need-based aid:*** $2232. ***Average indebtedness upon graduation:*** $8299. ***Financial aid deadline:*** 7/1.

APPLYING
Standardized Tests *Required:* SAT or ACT (for admission).

Options: electronic application, deferred entrance.

Required: essay or personal statement, high school transcript, minimum 2.0 GPA, 1 letter of recommendation, interest in the writings of Emanuel Swedenborg. ***Required for some:*** interview.

CONTACT
Admissions Office, Bryn Athyn College of the New Church, 2945 College Drive, Box 462, Bryn Athyn, PA 19009. *Phone:* 267-502-6000. *Toll-free phone:* 800-767-9552. *Fax:* 267-502-2593. *E-mail:* admissions@brynathyn.edu.

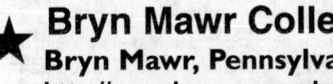

★ Bryn Mawr College
Bryn Mawr, Pennsylvania
http://www.brynmawr.edu/

- **Independent** university, founded 1885
- **Suburban** 135-acre campus with easy access to Philadelphia
- **Endowment** $854.0 million
- **Undergraduate: women only; graduate: coed** 1,308 undergraduate students, 99% full-time, 100% women
- **Most difficult** entrance level, 40% of applicants were admitted

UNDERGRAD STUDENTS
1,291 full-time, 17 part-time. Students come from 44 states and territories; 57 other countries; 81% are from out of state; 5% Black or African American, non-Hispanic/Latino; 9% Hispanic/Latino; 12% Asian, non-Hispanic/Latino; 0.1% Native Hawaiian or other Pacific Islander, non-Hispanic/Latino; 0.2% American Indian or Alaska Native, non-Hispanic/Latino; 5% Two or more races, non-Hispanic/Latino; 9% Race/ethnicity unknown; 24% international; 0.4% transferred in; 91% live on campus.

Freshmen

Admission: 2,706 applied, 1,095 admitted, 351 enrolled. ***Test scores:*** SAT critical reading scores over 500: 98%; SAT math scores over 500: 99%; SAT writing scores over 500: 98%; ACT scores over 18: 100%; SAT critical reading scores over 600: 78%; SAT math scores over 600: 75%; SAT writing scores over 600: 86%; ACT scores over 24: 91%; SAT critical reading scores over 700: 31%; SAT math scores over 700: 34%; SAT writing scores over 700: 35%; ACT scores over 30: 37%.

Retention: 91% of full-time freshmen returned.

FACULTY
Total: 212, 70% full-time, 89% with terminal degrees.

Student/faculty ratio: 8:1.

ACADEMICS
Calendar: semesters. *Degrees:* bachelor's, master's, doctoral, and postbachelor's certificates.

Special study options: academic remediation for entering students, accelerated degree program, advanced placement credit, double majors, independent study, internships, off-campus study, services for LD students, student-designed majors, study abroad, summer session for credit. ***ROTC:*** Air Force (c).

Unusual degree programs: 3-2 engineering with A student interested in engineering and recommended by Bryn Mawr may, after completing three years of work at Bryn Mawr, apply to transfer into the third year at the California Institute of Technology to complete two full years of work there.

Computers: 125 computers/terminals are available on campus for general student use. Students can access the following: computer help desk, free student e-mail accounts, online (class) grades, online (class) registration, online (class) schedules. Campuswide network is available. 100% of college-owned or -operated housing units are wired for high-speed Internet access. Wireless service is available via entire campus.

STUDENT LIFE
Housing options: on-campus residence required for freshman year; coed, women-only, cooperative. Campus housing is university owned. Freshman campus housing is guaranteed.

Activities and organizations: drama/theater group, student-run newspaper, radio station, choral group, Student Government Association.

Athletics Member NCAA. All Division III. ***Intercollegiate sports:*** badminton W, basketball W, crew W, cross-country running W, field hockey W, lacrosse W, soccer W, swimming and diving W, tennis W, track and field W, volleyball W.

Campus security: 24-hour emergency response devices and patrols, late-night transport/escort service, controlled dormitory access, shuttle bus service, awareness programs, bicycle registration, security Web site.

Student services: health clinic, personal/psychological counseling, women's center.

COSTS & FINANCIAL AID

Costs (2015–16) ***Comprehensive fee:*** $61,990 includes full-time tuition ($46,030), mandatory fees ($1110), and room and board ($14,850). Part-time tuition: $5755 per course. ***College room only:*** $8470.

Financial Aid Of all full-time matriculated undergraduates who enrolled in 2014, 778 applied for aid, 679 were judged to have need, 666 had their need fully met. In 2014, 63 non-need-based awards were made. ***Average percent of need met:*** 100. ***Average financial aid package:*** $42,369. ***Average need-based loan:*** $4821. ***Average need-based gift aid:*** $36,402. ***Average non-need-based aid:*** $10,833. ***Average indebtedness upon graduation:*** $24,466. ***Financial aid deadline:*** 3/1.

APPLYING

Standardized Tests *Required for some:* SAT and SAT Subject Tests or ACT (for admission).

Options: electronic application, early admission, early decision, deferred entrance.

Application fee: $50.

Required: essay or personal statement, high school transcript, 3 letters of recommendation. ***Recommended:*** interview.

Application deadlines: 1/15 (freshmen), 3/15 (transfers).

Early decision deadline: 11/15 (for plan 1), 1/1 (for plan 2).

Notification: 4/1 (freshmen), 6/1 (transfers), 12/15 (early decision plan 1), 2/1 (early decision plan 2).

CONTACT

Ms. Peaches Valdes, Director of Admissions, Bryn Mawr College, 101 North Merion Avenue, Bryn Mawr, PA 19010. *Phone:* 610-526-5152. *Toll-free phone:* 800-BMC-1885. *Fax:* 610-526-7471. *E-mail:* admissions@brynmawr.edu.

See below for display ad and page 1376 for the College Close-Up.

Bucknell University
Lewisburg, Pennsylvania
http://www.bucknell.edu/

- **Independent** comprehensive, founded 1846
- **Small-town** 446-acre campus
- **Endowment** $750.9 million
- **Coed** 3,565 undergraduate students, 99% full-time, 52% women, 48% men
- **Most difficult** entrance level, 31% of applicants were admitted

UNDERGRAD STUDENTS

3,538 full-time, 27 part-time. Students come from 44 states and territories; 45 other countries; 77% are from out of state; 3% Black or African American, non-Hispanic/Latino; 5% Hispanic/Latino; 4% Asian, non-Hispanic/Latino; 3% Two or more races, non-Hispanic/Latino; 0.4% Race/ethnicity unknown; 5% international; 0.8% transferred in; 86% live on campus.

Freshmen

Admission: 7,864 applied, 2,416 admitted, 939 enrolled. ***Average high school GPA:*** 3.56. ***Test scores:*** SAT critical reading scores over 500: 98%; SAT math scores over 500: 99%; SAT writing scores over 500: 97%; ACT scores over 18: 100%; SAT critical reading scores over 600: 72%; SAT math scores over 600: 88%; SAT writing scores over 600: 81%; ACT scores over 24: 97%; SAT critical reading scores over 700: 17%; SAT math scores over 700: 37%; SAT writing scores over 700: 25%; ACT scores over 30: 54%.

Retention: 93% of full-time freshmen returned.

FACULTY

Total: 419, 89% full-time, 93% with terminal degrees.

Student/faculty ratio: 9:1.

ACADEMICS

Calendar: semesters. *Degrees:* bachelor's and master's.

Special study options: advanced placement credit, double majors, honors programs, independent study, internships, off-campus study, part-time

degree program, services for LD students, student-designed majors, study abroad, summer session for credit. ***ROTC:*** Army (b).

Unusual degree programs: 3-2 engineering; biology, chemistry.

Computers: 1,020 computers/terminals and 190 ports are available on campus for general student use. Students can access the following: campus intranet, computer help desk, free student e-mail accounts, online (class) grades, online (class) registration, online (class) schedules. Campuswide network is available. 100% of college-owned or -operated housing units are wired for high-speed Internet access. Wireless service is available via entire campus.

STUDENT LIFE

Housing options: on-campus residence required through senior year; coed, men-only, cooperative, special housing for students with disabilities. Campus housing is university owned. Freshman campus housing is guaranteed.

Activities and organizations: drama/theater group, student-run newspaper, radio station, choral group, Habitat for Humanity, Outing Club, Activities and Campus Events, Catholic Campus Ministries, CALVIN and HOBBES, national fraternities, national sororities.

Athletics Member NCAA. All Division I except football (Division I-AA). ***Intercollegiate sports:*** baseball M, basketball M(s)/W(s), cheerleading M(c)/W(c), crew M(c)/W, cross-country running M/W(s), equestrian sports M(c)/W(c), field hockey W(s), golf M/W, ice hockey M(c), lacrosse M(s)/W(s), rock climbing M(c)/W(c), rugby M(c)/W(c), sailing M(c)/W(c), skiing (downhill) M(c)/W(c), soccer M(s)/W(s), softball W(s), squash M(c)/W(c), swimming and diving M(s)/W(s), tennis M/W, track and field M/W, ultimate Frisbee M(c)/W(c), volleyball M(c)/W(s), water polo M/W, weight lifting M(c)/W(c), wrestling M(s). ***Intramural sports:*** basketball M/W, cross-country running M/W, golf M/W, racquetball M/W, soccer M/W, softball M/W, squash M/W, table tennis M/W, tennis M/W, ultimate Frisbee M/W, volleyball M/W, weight lifting M, wrestling M.

Campus security: 24-hour emergency response devices and patrols, student patrols, late-night transport/escort service, controlled dormitory access, well-lit pathways, self-defense education, safety/security orientation.

Student services: health clinic, personal/psychological counseling, women's center.

COSTS & FINANCIAL AID

Costs (2015–16) ***Comprehensive fee:*** $62,368 includes full-time tuition ($49,878), mandatory fees ($274), and room and board ($12,216). Part-time tuition: $1369 per credit hour. ***College room only:*** $7450. Room and board charges vary according to board plan and housing facility. ***Payment plans:*** tuition prepayment, installment. ***Waivers:*** employees or children of employees.

Financial Aid Of all full-time matriculated undergraduates who enrolled in 2014, 1,797 applied for aid, 1,486 were judged to have need, 1,338 had their need fully met. 600 Federal Work-Study jobs (averaging $1500). 50 state and other part-time jobs (averaging $1500). In 2014, 316 non-need-based awards were made. ***Average percent of need met:*** 91. ***Average financial aid package:*** $30,000. ***Average need-based loan:*** $5500. ***Average need-based gift aid:*** $24,000. ***Average non-need-based aid:*** $13,808. ***Average indebtedness upon graduation:*** $22,500. ***Financial aid deadline:*** 1/15.

APPLYING

Standardized Tests *Required:* SAT or ACT (for admission).

Options: electronic application, early decision, deferred entrance.

Application fee: $40.

Required: essay or personal statement, high school transcript, 1 letter of recommendation.

Application deadlines: 1/15 (freshmen), 3/15 (transfers).

Early decision deadline: 11/15 (for plan 1), 1/15 (for plan 2).

Notification: 4/1 (freshmen), 5/1 (transfers), 12/15 (early decision plan 1), 2/15 (early decision plan 2).

CONTACT

Dean Robert Springall, Dean of Admissions, Bucknell University, 1 Dent Drive, Lewisburg, PA 17837. *Phone:* 570-577-3000. *Fax:* 570-577-3538. *E-mail:* admissions@bucknell.edu.

★ Cabrini College

Radnor, Pennsylvania

http://www.cabrini.edu/

- **Independent Roman Catholic** comprehensive, founded 1957
- **Suburban** 112-acre campus with easy access to Philadelphia
- **Endowment** $44.1 million
- **Coed** 1,406 undergraduate students, 91% full-time, 62% women, 38% men
- **Moderately difficult** entrance level, 75% of applicants were admitted

UNDERGRAD STUDENTS

1,283 full-time, 123 part-time. Students come from 16 states and territories; 3 other countries; 33% are from out of state; 15% Black or African American, non-Hispanic/Latino; 5% Hispanic/Latino; 0.9% Asian, non-Hispanic/Latino; 0.1% Native Hawaiian or other Pacific Islander, non-Hispanic/Latino; 0.1% American Indian or Alaska Native, non-Hispanic/Latino; 3% Two or more races, non-Hispanic/Latino; 8% Race/ethnicity unknown; 0.1% international; 4% transferred in; 66% live on campus.

Freshmen

Admission: 2,257 applied, 1,699 admitted, 393 enrolled. ***Average high school GPA:*** 3.05. ***Test scores:*** SAT critical reading scores over 500: 29%; SAT math scores over 500: 24%; SAT writing scores over 500: 24%; SAT critical reading scores over 600: 4%; SAT math scores over 600: 6%; SAT writing scores over 600: 2%.

Retention: 77% of full-time freshmen returned.

FACULTY

Total: 277, 28% full-time.

Student/faculty ratio: 11:1.

ACADEMICS

Calendar: semesters. *Degrees:* bachelor's and master's.

Special study options: academic remediation for entering students, adult/continuing education programs, advanced placement credit, cooperative education, double majors, honors programs, independent study, internships, off-campus study, part-time degree program, services for LD students, student-designed majors, study abroad, summer session for credit. ***ROTC:*** Army (c), Air Force (c).

Unusual degree programs: 3-2 physical therapy, occupational therapy with Thomas Jefferson University.

Computers: 575 computers/terminals and 2,922 ports are available on campus for general student use. Students can access the following: campus intranet, computer help desk, free student e-mail accounts, online (class) grades, online (class) registration, online (class) schedules, account balances and other services. Campuswide network is available. 100% of college-owned or -operated housing units are wired for high-speed Internet access. Wireless service is available via entire campus.

STUDENT LIFE

Housing options: coed, women-only, special housing for students with disabilities. Campus housing is university owned and leased by the school. Freshman applicants given priority for college housing.

Activities and organizations: drama/theater group, student-run newspaper, radio station, choral group, Campus Activities and Programming (CAP) Board, Student Government Association (SGA), Colleges Against Cancer, Active Minds, Power in Knowledge (P in K), national sororities.

Athletics Member NCAA. All Division III. ***Intercollegiate sports:*** basketball M/W, cross-country running M/W, field hockey W, golf M, lacrosse M/W, soccer M/W, softball W, swimming and diving M/W, tennis M/W, volleyball W. ***Intramural sports:*** basketball M/W, cheerleading M(c)/W(c), football M/W, lacrosse M(c), racquetball M(c), soccer M/W, squash M/W, ultimate Frisbee M/W, volleyball M/W.

Campus security: 24-hour emergency response devices and patrols, student patrols, late-night transport/escort service, controlled dormitory access, Resident Assistants and Directors on nightly duty.

Student services: health clinic, personal/psychological counseling.

COSTS & FINANCIAL AID

Costs (2015–16) ***Comprehensive fee:*** $42,068 includes full-time tuition ($28,932), mandatory fees ($910), and room and board ($12,226). Part-time tuition: $525 per credit hour. Part-time tuition and fees vary according to course load. ***Room and board:*** Room and board charges vary according to board plan and housing facility. ***Payment plan:*** installment. ***Waivers:*** children of alumni, senior citizens, and employees or children of employees.

Financial Aid Of all full-time matriculated undergraduates who enrolled in 2013, 1,212 applied for aid, 974 were judged to have need, 259 had their need fully met. 272 Federal Work-Study jobs (averaging $1429). In 2013, 267 non-need-based awards were made. ***Average percent of need met:*** 53. ***Average financial aid package:*** $16,687. ***Average need-based loan:*** $3777. ***Average need-based gift aid:*** $8079. ***Average non-need-based aid:*** $11,677. ***Average indebtedness upon graduation:*** $35,880.

APPLYING

Standardized Tests *Recommended:* SAT or ACT (for admission).

Options: electronic application, deferred entrance.

Application fee: $35.

Required: high school transcript, minimum 2.0 GPA. ***Recommended:*** essay or personal statement, minimum 3.0 GPA, 3 letters of recommendation, interview.

Application deadlines: rolling (freshmen), rolling (out-of-state freshmen), rolling (transfers).

CONTACT

Ms. Shannon Zottola, Director of Admissions, Cabrini College, 610 King of Prussia Road, Radnor, PA 19087-3698. *Phone:* 610-902-1027. *Toll-free phone:* 800-848-1003. *Fax:* 610-902-8508. *E-mail:* admit@cabrini.edu.

Cairn University

Langhorne, Pennsylvania

http://cairn.edu/

- **Independent nondenominational** comprehensive, founded 1913
- **Suburban** 105-acre campus with easy access to Philadelphia
- **Endowment** $11.3 million
- **Coed** 817 undergraduate students, 94% full-time, 54% women, 46% men
- **Moderately difficult** entrance level, 98% of applicants were admitted

UNDERGRAD STUDENTS

771 full-time, 46 part-time. Students come from 29 states and territories; 37 other countries; 43% are from out of state; 12% Black or African American, non-Hispanic/Latino; 7% Hispanic/Latino; 3% Asian, non-Hispanic/Latino; 0.1% Native Hawaiian or other Pacific Islander, non-Hispanic/Latino; 0.2% American Indian or Alaska Native, non-Hispanic/Latino; 2% Two or more races, non-Hispanic/Latino; 0.2% Race/ethnicity unknown; 2% international; 9% transferred in; 60% live on campus.

Freshmen

Admission: 318 applied, 311 admitted, 159 enrolled. ***Average high school GPA:*** 3.29. ***Test scores:*** SAT critical reading scores over 500: 58%; SAT math scores over 500: 43%; SAT writing scores over 500: 48%; ACT scores over 18: 80%; SAT critical reading scores over 600: 16%; SAT math scores over 600: 11%; SAT writing scores over 600: 15%; ACT scores over 24: 26%; SAT critical reading scores over 700: 4%; SAT math scores over 700: 1%; SAT writing scores over 700: 3%; ACT scores over 30: 13%.

Retention: 75% of full-time freshmen returned.

FACULTY

Total: 106, 38% full-time, 42% with terminal degrees.

Student/faculty ratio: 14:1.

ACADEMICS

Calendar: semesters. *Degrees:* bachelor's, master's, and postbachelor's certificates.

Special study options: academic remediation for entering students, accelerated degree program, adult/continuing education programs, advanced placement credit, distance learning, double majors, honors programs, independent study, internships, off-campus study, part-time degree program, services for LD students, study abroad, summer session for credit. ***ROTC:*** Air Force (c).

Computers: 68 computers/terminals are available on campus for general student use. Students can access the following: campus intranet, computer help desk, free student e-mail accounts, online (class) grades, online (class) registration, online (class) schedules. Campuswide network is available. 100% of college-owned or -operated housing units are wired for high-speed Internet access. Wireless service is available via classrooms, computer labs, dorm rooms, learning centers, libraries.

STUDENT LIFE

Housing options: on-campus residence required through senior year; men-only, women-only, special housing for students with disabilities. Campus housing is university owned and leased by the school. Freshman campus housing is guaranteed.

Activities and organizations: drama/theater group, student-run newspaper, choral group, Ascend (outdoor adventure club), Chi Beta Sigma (Social Work Club), Enactus (Business), Student Missionary Fellowship, Culture & Arts Association.

Athletics Member NCAA, NCCAA. All NCAA Division III. ***Intercollegiate sports:*** baseball M, basketball M/W, cross-country running M/W, golf M, soccer M/W, softball W, tennis W, volleyball M/W. ***Intramural sports:*** basketball M/W, soccer M/W, table tennis M/W, tennis M/W, ultimate Frisbee M/W, volleyball M/W.

Campus security: 24-hour emergency response devices and patrols, student patrols, late-night transport/escort service, controlled dormitory access.

Student services: health clinic, personal/psychological counseling.

COSTS & FINANCIAL AID

Costs (2015–16) ***Comprehensive fee:*** $33,270 includes full-time tuition ($23,710), mandatory fees ($210), and room and board ($9350). Full-time tuition and fees vary according to course load. Part-time tuition: $703 per credit. Part-time tuition and fees vary according to course load. ***College room only:*** $4895. Room and board charges vary according to board plan and location. ***Payment plan:*** installment. ***Waivers:*** employees or children of employees.

Financial Aid Of all full-time matriculated undergraduates who enrolled in 2014, 681 applied for aid, 630 were judged to have need, 88 had their need fully met. In 2014, 119 non-need-based awards were made. ***Average percent of need met:*** 73. ***Average financial aid package:*** $18,367. ***Average need-based loan:*** $4735. ***Average need-based gift aid:*** $13,987. ***Average non-need-based aid:*** $10,065. ***Average indebtedness upon graduation:*** $33,016.

APPLYING

Standardized Tests *Required:* SAT or ACT (for admission).

Options: electronic application, early admission, deferred entrance.

Application fee: $25.

Required: essay or personal statement, high school transcript, minimum 2.0 GPA, interview.

Application deadlines: rolling (freshmen), rolling (out-of-state freshmen), rolling (transfers).

Notification: continuous (freshmen), continuous (out-of-state freshmen), continuous (transfers).

CONTACT

Mr. Eric Rivera, Director of Undergraduate Admissions, Cairn University, 200 Manor Avenue, Langhorne, PA 19047. *Phone:* 215-702-4250. *Toll-free phone:* 800-366-0049. *Fax:* 215-702-4248. *E-mail:* admissions@cairn.edu.

California University of Pennsylvania

California, Pennsylvania

http://www.calu.edu/

- **State-supported** comprehensive, founded 1852, part of Pennsylvania State System of Higher Education
- **Small-town** 188-acre campus with easy access to Pittsburgh
- **Endowment** $33.3 million
- **Coed** 6,076 undergraduate students, 88% full-time, 52% women, 48% men
- **Moderately difficult** entrance level, 74% of applicants were admitted

UNDERGRAD STUDENTS

5,330 full-time, 746 part-time. 10% are from out of state; 11% Black or African American, non-Hispanic/Latino; 3% Hispanic/Latino; 0.7% Asian, non-Hispanic/Latino; 0.1% Native Hawaiian or other Pacific Islander, non-Hispanic/Latino; 0.1% American Indian or Alaska Native, non-Hispanic/Latino; 3% Two or more races, non-Hispanic/Latino; 3%

Race/ethnicity unknown; 0.8% international; 12% transferred in; 33% live on campus.

Freshmen
Admission: 3,714 applied, 2,752 admitted, 1,023 enrolled. ***Average high school GPA:*** 3.1. ***Test scores:*** SAT critical reading scores over 500: 34%; SAT math scores over 500: 33%; SAT writing scores over 500: 23%; ACT scores over 18: 66%; SAT critical reading scores over 600: 7%; SAT math scores over 600: 7%; SAT writing scores over 600: 4%; ACT scores over 24: 18%; SAT critical reading scores over 700: 1%; SAT math scores over 700: 1%; SAT writing scores over 700: 1%; ACT scores over 30: 1%.

Retention: 76% of full-time freshmen returned.

FACULTY
Total: 391, 68% full-time, 48% with terminal degrees.

Student/faculty ratio: 19:1.

ACADEMICS
Calendar: semesters. *Degrees:* certificates, associate, bachelor's, master's, post-master's, and postbachelor's certificates.

Special study options: academic remediation for entering students, adult/continuing education programs, advanced placement credit, cooperative education, distance learning, external degree program, independent study, internships, off-campus study, part-time degree program, study abroad, summer session for credit. ***ROTC:*** Army (b).

Computers: 192 computers/terminals and 172 ports are available on campus for general student use. Students can access the following: campus intranet, computer help desk, free student e-mail accounts, online (class) grades, online (class) registration, online (class) schedules. Campuswide network is available. 100% of college-owned or -operated housing units are wired for high-speed Internet access. Wireless service is available via entire campus.

STUDENT LIFE
Housing options: on-campus residence required through sophomore year; coed, men-only, women-only, cooperative, special housing for students with disabilities. Campus housing is university owned, leased by the school and is provided by a third party. Freshman campus housing is guaranteed.

Activities and organizations: drama/theater group, student-run newspaper, radio and television station, choral group, marching band, national fraternities, national sororities.

Athletics Member NCAA. All Division II. ***Intercollegiate sports:*** baseball M, basketball M/W, cross-country running M/W, football M, golf M/W, soccer M/W, softball W, swimming and diving W, tennis W, track and field M/W, volleyball W.

Campus security: 24-hour emergency response devices and patrols, student patrols, late-night transport/escort service, controlled dormitory access, residence hall entrances staffed 24/7, fire suppression and smoke detection systems, security staff are trained police officers.

Student services: health clinic, personal/psychological counseling, women's center, legal services.

COSTS & FINANCIAL AID
Costs (2014–15) ***Tuition:*** state resident $6820 full-time, $284 per credit hour part-time; nonresident $10,230 full-time, $426 per credit hour part-time. Full-time tuition and fees vary according to course load, location, and student level. Part-time tuition and fees vary according to course load, location, and student level. ***Required fees:*** $2736 full-time. ***Room and board:*** $10,086; room only: $6592. Room and board charges vary according to board plan and housing facility. ***Payment plan:*** installment. ***Waivers:*** employees or children of employees.

Financial Aid Of all full-time matriculated undergraduates who enrolled in 2013, 5,185 applied for aid, 4,367 were judged to have need, 308 had their need fully met. In 2013, 104 non-need-based awards were made. ***Average percent of need met:*** 62. ***Average financial aid package:*** $9446. ***Average need-based loan:*** $3870. ***Average need-based gift aid:*** $5688. ***Average non-need-based aid:*** $3097. ***Average indebtedness upon graduation:*** $29,105.

APPLYING
Standardized Tests *Required:* SAT or ACT (for admission).

Options: electronic application, early admission, deferred entrance.

Application fee: $25.

Required: high school transcript.

Application deadlines: rolling (freshmen), 5/1 (transfers).

Notification: continuous (freshmen), continuous (transfers).

CONTACT
Dr. William A. Edmonds, Dean of Enrollment Management and Academic Services, California University of Pennsylvania, 250 University Avenue, California, PA 15419. *Phone:* 724-938-4404. *Toll-free phone:* 888-412-0479. *Fax:* 724-938-4564.

Carlow University

Pittsburgh, Pennsylvania

http://www.carlow.edu/

- **Independent Roman Catholic** comprehensive, founded 1929
- **Urban** 13-acre campus with easy access to Pittsburgh
- **Endowment** $21.2 million
- **Coed, primarily women** 1,470 undergraduate students, 69% full-time, 89% women, 11% men
- **Minimally difficult** entrance level, 91% of applicants were admitted

UNDERGRAD STUDENTS
1,013 full-time, 457 part-time. Students come from 18 states and territories; 2 other countries; 5% are from out of state; 23% Black or African American, non-Hispanic/Latino; 2% Hispanic/Latino; 1% Asian, non-Hispanic/Latino; 0.1% Native Hawaiian or other Pacific Islander, non-Hispanic/Latino; 0.3% American Indian or Alaska Native, non-Hispanic/Latino; 4% Two or more races, non-Hispanic/Latino; 11% Race/ethnicity unknown; 0.2% international; 13% transferred in; 30% live on campus.

Freshmen
Admission: 663 applied, 601 admitted, 203 enrolled. ***Average high school GPA:*** 3.37. ***Test scores:*** SAT critical reading scores over 500: 36%; SAT math scores over 500: 36%; SAT writing scores over 500: 31%; ACT scores over 18: 73%; SAT critical reading scores over 600: 8%; SAT math scores over 600: 7%; SAT writing scores over 600: 5%; ACT scores over 24: 12%; SAT math scores over 700: 1%; SAT writing scores over 700: 1%.

Retention: 78% of full-time freshmen returned.

FACULTY
Total: 254, 40% full-time, 45% with terminal degrees.

Student/faculty ratio: 11:1.

ACADEMICS
Calendar: semesters. *Degrees:* bachelor's, master's, doctoral, post-master's, and postbachelor's certificates.

Special study options: academic remediation for entering students, accelerated degree program, advanced placement credit, cooperative education, distance learning, double majors, honors programs, independent study, internships, off-campus study, part-time degree program, services for LD students, study abroad, summer session for credit. ***ROTC:*** Army (c), Navy (c), Air Force (c).

Unusual degree programs: 3-2 Duquesne University (Biology/Environmental Science & Management).

Computers: 216 computers/terminals are available on campus for general student use. Students can access the following: campus intranet, computer help desk, free student e-mail accounts, online (class) grades, online (class) registration, online (class) schedules. Campuswide network is available. 100% of college-owned or -operated housing units are wired for high-speed Internet access. Wireless service is available via entire campus.

STUDENT LIFE
Housing options: men-only, women-only. Campus housing is university owned. Freshman applicants given priority for college housing.

Activities and organizations: drama/theater group, student-run newspaper, choral group, Student Government Association, Campus Activities Board, SPiRiT (Student Ambassadors), SNAP (Student Nursing Association), PSEA (School Education Association), national fraternities.

Athletics Member NAIA, USCAA. ***Intercollegiate sports:*** basketball M(s)/W(s), cross-country running M(s)/W(s), soccer W(s), softball W(s), tennis W(s), volleyball W(s).

Campus security: 24-hour emergency response devices and patrols, late-night transport/escort service, controlled dormitory access.

Student services: health clinic, personal/psychological counseling.

COSTS & FINANCIAL AID

Costs (2014–15) ***Comprehensive fee:*** $36,492 includes full-time tuition ($25,956), mandatory fees ($222), and room and board ($10,314). Full-time tuition and fees vary according to course load, program, and reciprocity agreements. Part-time tuition: $825 per credit hour. Part-time tuition and fees vary according to course load, program, and reciprocity agreements. ***College room only:*** $5274. Room and board charges vary according to board plan. ***Payment plan:*** installment. ***Waivers:*** children of alumni, adult students, and employees or children of employees.

Financial Aid Of all full-time matriculated undergraduates who enrolled in 2003, 431 Federal Work-Study jobs (averaging $776).

APPLYING

Standardized Tests *Required:* SAT or ACT (for admission).

Options: electronic application, deferred entrance.

Required: high school transcript. ***Recommended:*** essay or personal statement, minimum 2.5 GPA, interview.

Application deadlines: rolling (freshmen), rolling (transfers).

Notification: continuous (freshmen), continuous (transfers).

CONTACT

Ms. Wivina Chmura, Director of Undergraduate Admissions, Carlow University, 3333 Fifth Avenue, Pittsburgh, PA 15213. *Phone:* 412-578-8762. *Toll-free phone:* 800-333-CARLOW. *Fax:* 412-578-6668. *E-mail:* admissions@carlow.edu.

See below for display ad and page 1380 for the College Close-Up.

Carnegie Mellon University

Pittsburgh, Pennsylvania

http://www.cmu.edu/

- **Independent** university, founded 1900
- **Urban** 145-acre campus
- **Endowment** $1.1 billion
- **Coed**
- **Most difficult** entrance level

FACULTY

Student/faculty ratio: 13:1.

ACADEMICS

Calendar: semesters. *Degrees:* bachelor's, master's, doctoral, and post-master's certificates.

STUDENT LIFE

Housing options: on-campus residence required for freshman year; coed, men-only, women-only, special housing for students with disabilities. Campus housing is university owned and leased by the school. Freshman campus housing is guaranteed.

Activities and organizations: drama/theater group, student-run newspaper, radio and television station, choral group, marching band, Student Senate, Alpha Phi Omega, Tartan Club, Spirit Club, Greek Community, national fraternities, national sororities.

Athletics Member NCAA. All Division III.

Campus security: 24-hour emergency response devices and patrols, late-night transport/escort service, controlled dormitory access.

Student services: health clinic, personal/psychological counseling, women's center, legal services.

COSTS & FINANCIAL AID

Costs (2014–15) ***One-time required fee:*** $236. ***Comprehensive fee:*** $61,422 includes full-time tuition ($48,030), mandatory fees ($992), and room and board ($12,400). Full-time tuition and fees vary according to student level. Part-time tuition and fees vary according to student level. ***College room only:*** $7280. Room and board charges vary according to board plan and housing facility.

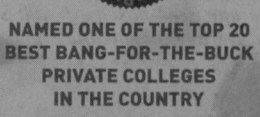

Financial Aid Of all full-time matriculated undergraduates who enrolled in 2014, 3,287 applied for aid, 2,784 were judged to have need, 691 had their need fully met. In 2014, 222 non-need-based awards were made. ***Average percent of need met:*** 83. ***Average financial aid package:*** $36,001. ***Average need-based loan:*** $5445. ***Average need-based gift aid:*** $30,068. ***Average non-need-based aid:*** $10,867. ***Average indebtedness upon graduation:*** $31,905.

APPLYING

Standardized Tests *Required:* SAT or ACT (for admission), SAT Subject Tests (for admission).

Options: electronic application, early admission, early decision, deferred entrance.

Application fee: $70.

Required: essay or personal statement, high school transcript, 2 letters of recommendation. ***Required for some:*** audition/portfolio for certain majors/BFA. ***Recommended:*** interview.

CONTACT

Mr. Michael Steidel, Director of Admissions, Carnegie Mellon University, 5000 Forbes Avenue, Pittsburgh, PA 15213. *Phone:* 412-268-2082. *Fax:* 412-268-7838. *E-mail:* undergraduate-admissions@andrew.cmu.edu.

★ Cedar Crest College

Allentown, Pennsylvania

http://www.cedarcrest.edu/

- **Independent** comprehensive, founded 1867, affiliated with United Church of Christ
- **Suburban** 84-acre campus with easy access to Philadelphia
- **Endowment** $26.0 million
- **Coed, primarily women** 1,344 undergraduate students, 53% full-time, 92% women, 8% men
- **Moderately difficult** entrance level, 52% of applicants were admitted

UNDERGRAD STUDENTS

719 full-time, 625 part-time. Students come from 23 states and territories; 19 other countries; 13% are from out of state; 10% Black or African American, non-Hispanic/Latino; 13% Hispanic/Latino; 3% Asian, non-Hispanic/Latino; 0.3% Native Hawaiian or other Pacific Islander, non-Hispanic/Latino; 0.3% American Indian or Alaska Native, non-Hispanic/Latino; 1% Two or more races, non-Hispanic/Latino; 4% Race/ethnicity unknown; 2% international; 3% transferred in; 30% live on campus.

Freshmen

Admission: 1,246 applied, 652 admitted, 170 enrolled. ***Average high school GPA:*** 3.37. ***Test scores:*** SAT critical reading scores over 500: 50%; SAT math scores over 500: 52%; SAT writing scores over 500: 47%; ACT scores over 18: 96%; SAT critical reading scores over 600: 18%; SAT math scores over 600: 15%; SAT writing scores over 600: 13%; ACT scores over 24: 25%; SAT math scores over 700: 2%; SAT writing scores over 700: 1%; ACT scores over 30: 4%.

Retention: 69% of full-time freshmen returned.

FACULTY

Total: 159, 46% full-time, 47% with terminal degrees.

Student/faculty ratio: 10:1.

ACADEMICS

Calendar: semesters. *Degrees:* certificates, bachelor's, master's, and postbachelor's certificates.

Special study options: academic remediation for entering students, advanced placement credit, double majors, honors programs, independent study, internships, off-campus study, part-time degree program, services for LD students, student-designed majors, summer session for credit. ***ROTC:*** Army (c).

Computers: 285 computers/terminals and 587 ports are available on campus for general student use. Students can access the following: campus intranet, computer help desk, free student e-mail accounts, online (class) grades, online (class) registration, online (class) schedules. Campuswide network is available. 100% of college-owned or -operated housing units are wired for high-speed Internet access. Wireless service is available via entire campus.

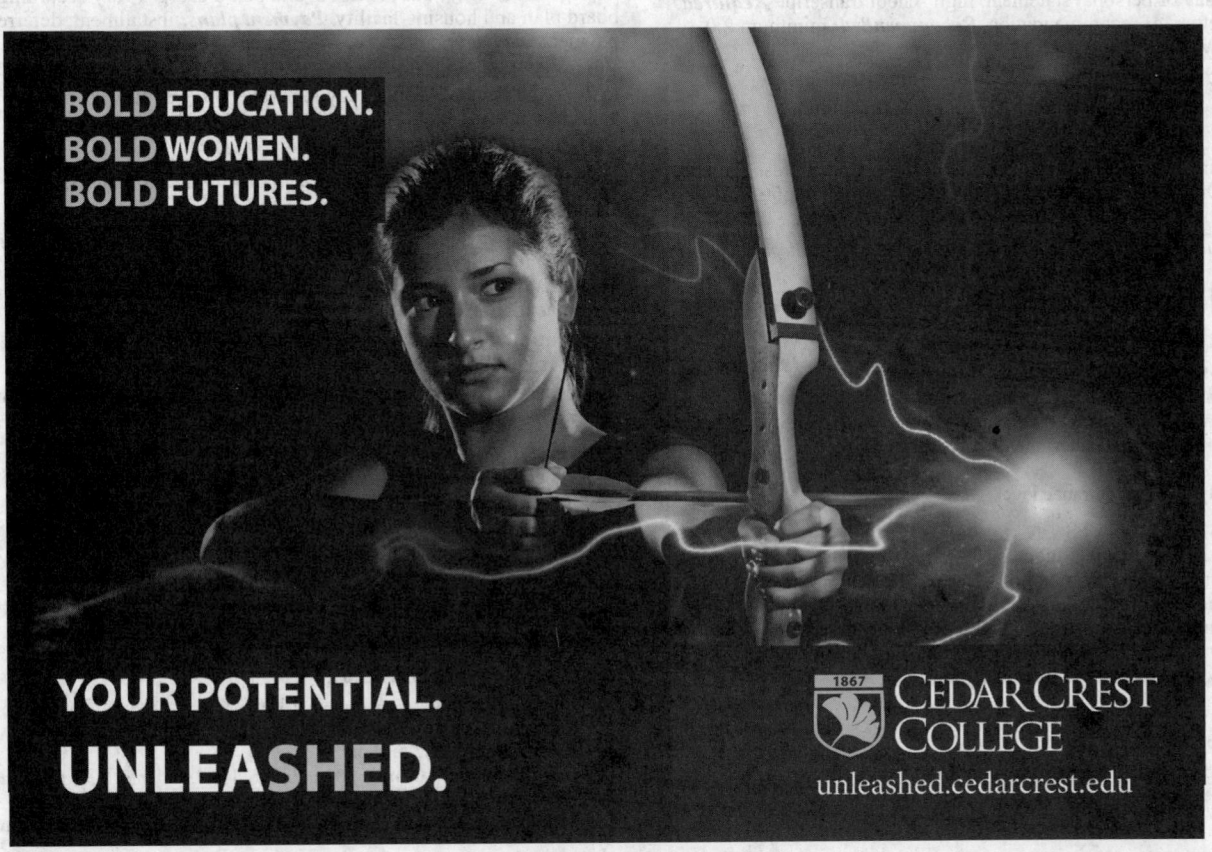

A ★ indicates that the school has detailed information with a Premium Profile on Petersons.com.

STUDENT LIFE

Housing options: women-only, special housing for students with disabilities. Campus housing is university owned. Freshman campus housing is guaranteed.

Activities and organizations: drama/theater group, student-run newspaper, radio station, choral group, Student Activities Board, Student Government Association, Commuter Awareness Board, Student Nurse Association, Forensic Student Science organization, national sororities.

Athletics Member NCAA. All Division III. ***Intercollegiate sports:*** basketball W, cross-country running W, equestrian sports W(c), field hockey W, lacrosse W, soccer W, softball W, swimming and diving W, tennis W, track and field W(c), volleyball W. ***Intramural sports:*** badminton W, basketball W, soccer W, softball W, tennis W, volleyball W.

Campus security: 24-hour emergency response devices and patrols, late-night transport/escort service, controlled dormitory access, crime prevention programs.

Student services: health clinic, personal/psychological counseling.

COSTS & FINANCIAL AID

Costs (2014–15) ***Comprehensive fee:*** $45,053 includes full-time tuition ($33,904), mandatory fees ($600), and room and board ($10,549). Full-time tuition and fees vary according to class time, course load, and program. Part-time tuition: $1130 per credit. Part-time tuition and fees vary according to class time, course load, and program. ***Required fees:*** $150 per term part-time. ***College room only:*** $5160. Room and board charges vary according to board plan and housing facility. ***Payment plans:*** installment, deferred payment. ***Waivers:*** children of alumni and employees or children of employees.

Financial Aid Of all full-time matriculated undergraduates who enrolled in 2013, 484 applied for aid, 468 were judged to have need, 44 had their need fully met. In 2013, 27 non-need-based awards were made. ***Average percent of need met:*** 73. ***Average financial aid package:*** $24,855. ***Average need-based loan:*** $4435. ***Average need-based gift aid:*** $20,700. ***Average non-need-based aid:*** $13,464. ***Average indebtedness upon graduation:*** $39,198.

APPLYING

Standardized Tests *Required:* SAT or ACT (for admission).

Options: electronic application, early admission, deferred entrance.

Required: essay or personal statement, high school transcript. ***Required for some:*** 2 letters of recommendation. ***Recommended:*** minimum 2.0 GPA, interview.

Application deadlines: rolling (freshmen), rolling (transfers).

Notification: continuous (freshmen), continuous (transfers).

CONTACT

Jonathan Squire, Associate Director of Admissions, Cedar Crest College, 100 College Drive, Allentown, PA 18104. *Phone:* 610-606-4666. *Toll-free phone:* 800-360-1222. *E-mail:* admissions@cedarcrest.edu.

See previous page for display ad and page 1390 for the College Close-Up.

Central Penn College

Summerdale, Pennsylvania

http://www.centralpenn.edu/

- **Proprietary** comprehensive, founded 1881
- **Small-town** 35-acre campus with easy access to Harrisburg
- **Coed** 1,286 undergraduate students, 56% full-time, 65% women, 35% men
- **Minimally difficult** entrance level

UNDERGRAD STUDENTS

714 full-time, 572 part-time. Students come from 18 states and territories; 2 other countries; 2% are from out of state; 22% Black or African American, non-Hispanic/Latino; 0.8% Hispanic/Latino; 2% Asian, non-Hispanic/Latino; 0.5% American Indian or Alaska Native, non-Hispanic/Latino; 0.2% Two or more races, non-Hispanic/Latino; 12% Race/ethnicity unknown; 18% live on campus.

Freshmen

Admission: 135 enrolled.

Retention: 59% of full-time freshmen returned.

FACULTY

Total: 141, 21% full-time, 38% with terminal degrees.

Student/faculty ratio: 13:1.

ACADEMICS

Calendar: quarters. *Degrees:* associate, bachelor's, and master's.

Special study options: academic remediation for entering students, adult/continuing education programs, advanced placement credit, distance learning, double majors, honors programs, independent study, internships, part-time degree program, study abroad, summer session for credit.

Computers: 100 computers/terminals are available on campus for general student use. Students can access the following: campus intranet, computer help desk, free student e-mail accounts, online (class) grades, online (class) registration, online (class) schedules. Campuswide network is available. 100% of college-owned or -operated housing units are wired for high-speed Internet access. Wireless service is available via entire campus.

STUDENT LIFE

Housing options: men-only, women-only. Campus housing is university owned. Freshman applicants given priority for college housing.

Activities and organizations: drama/theater group, student-run newspaper, choral group, International Travel Club, Student Government Association, Toastmasters, Student Ambassadors, Rainbow Society.

Athletics Member USCAA. ***Intercollegiate sports:*** baseball M, basketball M/W, cross-country running M/W, soccer M/W, volleyball W. ***Intramural sports:*** basketball M/W, football M/W, soccer M/W, tennis M/W, volleyball M/W.

Campus security: 24-hour emergency response devices and patrols, late-night transport/escort service.

Student services: personal/psychological counseling.

COSTS & FINANCIAL AID

Costs (2014–15) ***Comprehensive fee:*** $23,829 includes full-time tuition ($15,840), mandatory fees ($819), and room and board ($7170). Full-time tuition and fees vary according to course load, degree level, and program. Part-time tuition: $440 per credit hour. Part-time tuition and fees vary according to course load, degree level, and program. No tuition increase for student's term of enrollment. ***Required fees:*** $167 per term part-time. ***College room only:*** $5379. Room and board charges vary according to board plan and housing facility. ***Payment plans:*** installment, deferred payment. ***Waivers:*** employees or children of employees.

Financial Aid Of all full-time matriculated undergraduates who enrolled in 2006, 50 Federal Work-Study jobs (averaging $1500). ***Financial aid deadline:*** 5/1.

APPLYING

Standardized Tests *Recommended:* SAT or ACT (for admission).

Options: electronic application.

Required: essay or personal statement, high school transcript, minimum 2.0 GPA, interview. ***Required for some:*** 1 letter of recommendation, Some majors have special requirements. ***Recommended:*** 1 letter of recommendation.

Application deadlines: rolling (freshmen), rolling (out-of-state freshmen), rolling (transfers).

Notification: continuous (freshmen), continuous (out-of-state freshmen), continuous (transfers).

CONTACT

Ms. Rebecca Bowman, Director of Traditional Admissions, Central Penn College, College Hill and Valley Roads, Mechanicsburg, PA 17093. *Phone:* 717-728-2267. *Toll-free phone:* 800-759-2727. *Fax:* 717-728-2505. *E-mail:* rebeccabowman@centralpenn.edu.

Chatham University

Pittsburgh, Pennsylvania

http://www.chatham.edu/

- **Independent** university, founded 1869
- **Urban** 427-acre campus
- **Endowment** $84.7 million
- **Coed, primarily women** 932 undergraduate students, 60% full-time, 89% women, 11% men
- **Moderately difficult** entrance level, 53% of applicants were admitted

UNDERGRAD STUDENTS
562 full-time, 370 part-time. Students come from 28 states and territories; 31 other countries; 19% are from out of state; 8% Black or African American, non-Hispanic/Latino; 2% Hispanic/Latino; 2% Asian, non-Hispanic/Latino; 0.2% American Indian or Alaska Native, non-Hispanic/Latino; 2% Two or more races, non-Hispanic/Latino; 28% Race/ethnicity unknown; 12% international; 5% transferred in; 44% live on campus.

Freshmen
Admission: 619 applied, 330 admitted, 104 enrolled. ***Average high school GPA:*** 3.63. ***Test scores:*** SAT critical reading scores over 500: 67%; SAT math scores over 500: 51%; SAT writing scores over 500: 75%; ACT scores over 18: 97%; SAT critical reading scores over 600: 24%; SAT math scores over 600: 14%; SAT writing scores over 600: 35%; ACT scores over 24: 49%; SAT critical reading scores over 700: 6%; SAT math scores over 700: 4%; SAT writing scores over 700: 5%; ACT scores over 30: 15%.

Retention: 77% of full-time freshmen returned.

FACULTY
Total: 319, 34% full-time, 51% with terminal degrees.

Student/faculty ratio: 9:1.

ACADEMICS
Calendar: 4-4-1. *Degrees:* bachelor's, master's, doctoral, post-master's, and postbachelor's certificates.

Special study options: accelerated degree program, adult/continuing education programs, advanced placement credit, cooperative education, distance learning, double majors, English as a second language, honors programs, independent study, internships, off-campus study, part-time degree program, services for LD students, student-designed majors, study abroad, summer session for credit. ***ROTC:*** Army (c), Navy (c), Air Force (c).

Unusual degree programs: 3-2 business administration; engineering with Carnegie Mellon University, Penn State University, University of Pittsburgh; arts management with Carnegie Mellon, biology, counseling psychology, film/digital technology, leadership/organizational transformation, occupational therapy, physician assistant studies, business, teaching, writing and creative writing, architecture (landscape and interior), global/public policy.

Computers: 250 computers/terminals and 150 ports are available on campus for general student use. Students can access the following: campus intranet, computer help desk, free student e-mail accounts, online (class) grades, online (class) registration, online (class) schedules. Campuswide network is available. Wireless service is available via entire campus.

STUDENT LIFE
Housing options: on-campus residence required through sophomore year; coed, women-only. Campus housing is university owned. Freshman campus housing is guaranteed.

Activities and organizations: drama/theater group, student-run newspaper, choral group, Chatham Student Government, Residence Hall Council, Student Athletic Advisory Council (SAAC), Creative Writing Club & MFA Writing Council, Graduate Student Assembly.

Athletics Member NCAA. All Division III. ***Intercollegiate sports:*** baseball M, basketball M/W, cross-country running M/W, ice hockey W, soccer W, softball W, swimming and diving M/W, tennis W, track and field M/W, volleyball M/W, water polo W. ***Intramural sports:*** badminton W, basketball W, bowling W, cross-country running W, football W, golf W, rock climbing W, skiing (downhill) W, soccer W, softball W, squash W, swimming and diving W, volleyball W, water polo W.

Campus security: 24-hour emergency response devices and patrols, late-night transport/escort service, controlled dormitory access, self-defense education, well-lighted pathways and sidewalks.

Student services: health clinic, personal/psychological counseling, women's center.

COSTS & FINANCIAL AID
Costs (2015–16) ***Comprehensive fee:*** $45,160 includes full-time tuition ($33,200), mandatory fees ($1240), and room and board ($10,720). Part-time tuition: $805 per credit. Part-time tuition and fees vary according to course load. ***College room only:*** $5470. Room and board charges vary according to board plan and housing facility. ***Payment plan:*** installment. ***Waivers:*** employees or children of employees.

Financial Aid Of all full-time matriculated undergraduates who enrolled in 2014, 476 applied for aid, 454 were judged to have need, 42 had their need fully met. 179 Federal Work-Study jobs (averaging $2200). In 2014, 26 non-need-based awards were made. ***Average percent of need met:*** 82. ***Average financial aid package:*** $23,512. ***Average need-based loan:*** $4591. ***Average need-based gift aid:*** $8351. ***Average non-need-based aid:*** $16,007. ***Average indebtedness upon graduation:*** $32,814.

APPLYING
Standardized Tests *Recommended:* Consider SAT or ACT if submitted.

Options: electronic application, early admission, deferred entrance.

Application fee: $35.

Required: essay or personal statement, high school transcript, minimum 2.0 GPA, 1 letter of recommendation. ***Recommended:*** interview.

Application deadlines: 8/1 (freshmen), rolling (transfers).

Notification: continuous (freshmen), continuous (transfers).

CONTACT
Ms. Amy M Becher, Vice President for Enrollment Management, Chatham University, Woodland, Berry Hall, Pittsburgh, PA 15232. *Phone:* 800-837-1290. *Toll-free phone:* 800-837-1290. *Fax:* 412-365-1609. *E-mail:* admission@chatham.edu.

★ Chestnut Hill College
Philadelphia, Pennsylvania
http://www.chc.edu/

- **Independent Roman Catholic** comprehensive, founded 1924
- **Suburban** 75-acre campus with easy access to Philadelphia
- **Endowment** $8.7 million
- **Coed** 1,491 undergraduate students, 79% full-time, 67% women, 33% men
- **Moderately difficult** entrance level, 62% of applicants were admitted

UNDERGRAD STUDENTS
1,180 full-time, 311 part-time. Students come from 27 states and territories; 38 other countries; 26% are from out of state; 36% Black or African American, non-Hispanic/Latino; 9% Hispanic/Latino; 2% Asian, non-Hispanic/Latino; 0.4% Native Hawaiian or other Pacific Islander, non-Hispanic/Latino; 0.1% American Indian or Alaska Native, non-Hispanic/Latino; 3% Two or more races, non-Hispanic/Latino; 7% Race/ethnicity unknown; 2% international; 6% transferred in; 32% live on campus.

Freshmen
Admission: 1,916 applied, 1,179 admitted, 186 enrolled. ***Average high school GPA:*** 3.15. ***Test scores:*** SAT critical reading scores over 500: 42%; SAT math scores over 500: 50%; SAT writing scores over 500: 41%; ACT scores over 18: 84%; SAT critical reading scores over 600: 10%; SAT math scores over 600: 9%; SAT writing scores over 600: 9%; ACT scores over 24: 20%.

Retention: 78% of full-time freshmen returned.

FACULTY
Total: 341, 26% full-time, 41% with terminal degrees.

Student/faculty ratio: 9:1.

ACADEMICS
Calendar: semesters. *Degrees:* certificates, associate, bachelor's, master's, doctoral, post-master's, and postbachelor's certificates (profile includes figures from both traditional and accelerated (part-time) programs).

Special study options: academic remediation for entering students, adult/continuing education programs, advanced placement credit, double majors, English as a second language, honors programs, independent study, internships, off-campus study, part-time degree program, services for LD students, student-designed majors, study abroad, summer session for credit.

Unusual degree programs: 3-2 computer science/instructional technology, early education, biology/chemistry, and various medical areas of study (Thomas Jefferson University); biology/chemistry and physician assistant (Arcadia University); human services admin; counseling psychology; international business, language, and culture.

Computers: 70 computers/terminals and 150 ports are available on campus for general student use. Students can access the following: campus intranet, computer help desk, free student e-mail accounts, online (class) grades, online (class) registration, online (class) schedules. Campuswide network is available. 90% of college-owned or -operated housing units are wired for high-speed Internet access. Wireless service is available via classrooms, dorm rooms.

STUDENT LIFE

Housing options: coed. Campus housing is university owned and leased by the school.

Activities and organizations: drama/theater group, student-run newspaper, radio and television station, choral group, student government, Mask and Foil Drama Club, Association for Musical Performance, Campus Ministry Community Service Group, Business Club.

Athletics Member NCAA. All Division II. ***Intercollegiate sports:*** baseball M(s), basketball M(s)/W(s), bowling W(s), cross-country running M(s)/W(s), football M(s)(c), golf M(s)(c)/W(c), lacrosse M(s)/W(s), soccer M(s)/W(s), softball W(s), tennis M(s)/W(s), track and field M/W, volleyball W(s).

Campus security: 24-hour emergency response devices and patrols, late-night transport/escort service, controlled dormitory access.

Student services: health clinic, personal/psychological counseling.

COSTS & FINANCIAL AID

Costs (2015–16) ***One-time required fee:*** $425. ***Comprehensive fee:*** $43,320 includes full-time tuition ($32,930), mandatory fees ($190), and room and board ($10,200). Part-time tuition: $705 per credit. ***Room and board:*** Room and board charges vary according to board plan and housing facility. ***Payment plans:*** installment, deferred payment. ***Waivers:*** senior citizens and employees or children of employees.

Financial Aid Of all full-time matriculated undergraduates who enrolled in 2014, 1,082 applied for aid, 1,022 were judged to have need, 75 had their need fully met. 462 Federal Work-Study jobs (averaging $1182). In 2014, 28 non-need-based awards were made. ***Average percent of need met:*** 62. ***Average financial aid package:*** $21,138. ***Average need-based gift aid:*** $16,914. ***Average non-need-based aid:*** $9108. ***Average indebtedness upon graduation:*** $35,376.

APPLYING

Standardized Tests *Required:* SAT or ACT (for admission).

Options: electronic application, deferred entrance.

Application fee: $35.

Required: high school transcript. ***Required for some:*** interview. ***Recommended:*** essay or personal statement, minimum 2.0 GPA, 2 letters of recommendation.

Application deadlines: rolling (freshmen), rolling (out-of-state freshmen), rolling (transfers).

Notification: continuous (freshmen), continuous (out-of-state freshmen), continuous (transfers).

CONTACT

Ms. Stephanie Williams, Chestnut Hill College, 9601 Germantown Avenue, Philadelphia, PA 19118-2693. *Phone:* 215-248-7001. *Toll-free phone:* 800-248-0052. *Fax:* 215-248-7082. *E-mail:* williamss@chc.edu.

See this page for display ad and page 1396 for the College Close-Up.

★ Cheyney University of Pennsylvania

Cheyney, Pennsylvania

http://www.cheyney.edu/

- **State-supported** comprehensive, founded 1837, part of Pennsylvania State System of Higher Education
- **Suburban** 275-acre campus with easy access to Philadelphia
- **Coed** 997 undergraduate students, 94% full-time, 50% women, 50% men
- **Minimally difficult** entrance level, 85% of applicants were admitted

UNDERGRAD STUDENTS

936 full-time, 61 part-time. Students come from 20 states and territories; 30% are from out of state; 86% Black or African American, non-

Hispanic/Latino; 4% Hispanic/Latino; 0.1% Native Hawaiian or other Pacific Islander, non-Hispanic/Latino; 4% Two or more races, non-Hispanic/Latino; 6% Race/ethnicity unknown; 0.2% international; 13% transferred in; 80% live on campus.

Freshmen

Admission: 1,127 applied, 960 admitted, 231 enrolled. ***Average high school GPA:*** 2.37. ***Test scores:*** SAT critical reading scores over 500: 15%; SAT math scores over 500: 22%; SAT writing scores over 500: 12%; ACT scores over 18: 54%; SAT critical reading scores over 600: 1%; SAT math scores over 600: 2%; SAT writing scores over 600: 1%; ACT scores over 24: 7%.

Retention: 55% of full-time freshmen returned.

FACULTY

Total: 90, 50% full-time, 54% with terminal degrees.

Student/faculty ratio: 16:1.

ACADEMICS

Calendar: semesters. *Degrees:* bachelor's and master's.

Special study options: academic remediation for entering students, adult/continuing education programs, cooperative education, distance learning, double majors, honors programs, independent study, internships, off-campus study, part-time degree program, services for LD students, study abroad, summer session for credit. ***ROTC:*** Army (c).

Computers: 162 computers/terminals are available on campus for general student use. Students can access the following: campus intranet, computer help desk, free student e-mail accounts, online (class) grades, online (class) registration, online (class) schedules, online tutorials, various software packages, online payment/online Praxis study guide. Campuswide network is available. Wireless service is available via classrooms, computer centers, computer labs, learning centers, libraries, student centers.

STUDENT LIFE

Housing options: coed, men-only, women-only. Campus housing is university owned. Freshman applicants given priority for college housing.

Activities and organizations: drama/theater group, student-run radio station, choral group, marching band, National Council of Negro Women, Student Government Association, Alpha Kappa Alpha, Gospel Choir, Modern Men, national fraternities, national sororities.

Athletics Member NCAA. All Division II. ***Intercollegiate sports:*** basketball M(s)/W(s), bowling W(s), cross-country running M(s)/W(s), football M(s), track and field M(s)/W(s), volleyball W(s). ***Intramural sports:*** basketball M/W, football M.

Campus security: 24-hour emergency response devices and patrols.

Student services: health clinic, personal/psychological counseling.

COSTS & FINANCIAL AID

Costs (2014–15) ***Tuition:*** state resident $6820 full-time, $284 per credit hour part-time; nonresident $11,254 full-time, $469 per credit hour part-time. Full-time tuition and fees vary according to course load. Part-time tuition and fees vary according to course load. ***Required fees:*** $2270 full-time. ***Room and board:*** $8660; room only: $5008. Room and board charges vary according to board plan and housing facility. ***Payment plans:*** installment, deferred payment. ***Waivers:*** senior citizens and employees or children of employees.

Financial Aid Of all full-time matriculated undergraduates who enrolled in 2003, 1,030 applied for aid, 1,005 were judged to have need, 451 had their need fully met. 215 Federal Work-Study jobs (averaging $1300). 133 state and other part-time jobs (averaging $600). ***Average percent of need met:*** 87. ***Average financial aid package:*** $11,789. ***Average need-based loan:*** $3700. ***Average need-based gift aid:*** $1975. ***Average non-need-based aid:*** $10,000. ***Average indebtedness upon graduation:*** $21,000.

APPLYING

Standardized Tests *Required:* SAT (for admission), ACT (for admission), SAT and SAT Subject Tests or ACT (for admission).

Options: electronic application, deferred entrance.

Application fee: $20.

Required: essay or personal statement, high school transcript. ***Required for some:*** 3 letters of recommendation. ***Recommended:*** interview.

Notification: continuous (freshmen).

CONTACT

Shon Jeffery, Associate Director of Enrollment Management, Cheyney University of Pennsylvania, 1837 University Circle, PO Box 200, Cheyney, PA 19319. *Phone:* 610-399-2255. *Toll-free phone:* 800-CHEYNEY. *E-mail:* spjeffery@cheyney.edu.

Clarion University of Pennsylvania

Clarion, Pennsylvania

http://www.clarion.edu/

- **State-supported** comprehensive, founded 1867, part of Pennsylvania State System of Higher Education
- **Rural** 201-acre campus
- **Endowment** $30.7 million
- **Coed** 4,911 undergraduate students, 82% full-time, 63% women, 37% men

UNDERGRAD STUDENTS

4,018 full-time, 893 part-time. Students come from 12 states and territories; 1 other country; 7% are from out of state; 7% Black or African American, non-Hispanic/Latino; 2% Hispanic/Latino; 0.6% Asian, non-Hispanic/Latino; 0.1% Native Hawaiian or other Pacific Islander, non-Hispanic/Latino; 0.1% American Indian or Alaska Native, non-Hispanic/Latino; 2% Two or more races, non-Hispanic/Latino; 3% Race/ethnicity unknown; 2% international; 7% transferred in; 35% live on campus.

Freshmen

Admission: 989 enrolled. ***Average high school GPA:*** 3.21. ***Test scores:*** SAT critical reading scores over 500: 31%; SAT math scores over 500: 33%; SAT writing scores over 500: 23%; ACT scores over 18: 59%; SAT critical reading scores over 600: 6%; SAT math scores over 600: 7%; SAT writing scores over 600: 4%; ACT scores over 24: 17%; ACT scores over 30: 2%.

Retention: 74% of full-time freshmen returned.

FACULTY

Total: 294, 74% full-time, 67% with terminal degrees.

Student/faculty ratio: 19:1.

ACADEMICS

Calendar: semesters. *Degrees:* certificates, associate, bachelor's, master's, doctoral, post-master's, and postbachelor's certificates.

Special study options: academic remediation for entering students, accelerated degree program, adult/continuing education programs, advanced placement credit, cooperative education, distance learning, double majors, English as a second language, honors programs, independent study, internships, off-campus study, part-time degree program, services for LD students, study abroad, summer session for credit. ***ROTC:*** Army (c).

Unusual degree programs: 3-2 engineering with University of Pittsburgh, Case Western Reserve University.

Computers: 1,208 computers/terminals and 2,436 ports are available on campus for general student use. Students can access the following: campus intranet, computer help desk, free student e-mail accounts, online (class) grades, online (class) registration, online (class) schedules, Online Learning Management System, web-based personal disk space, other online student services (financial aid, billing etc.). Campuswide network is available. 100% of college-owned or -operated housing units are wired for high-speed Internet access. Wireless service is available via entire campus.

STUDENT LIFE

Housing options: on-campus residence required through sophomore year; coed, men-only, women-only, special housing for students with disabilities. Campus housing is university owned. Freshman campus housing is guaranteed.

Activities and organizations: drama/theater group, student-run newspaper, radio and television station, choral group, marching band, Circle K, Psychology Club, Council for Exceptional Children, Animae Club, Allies, national fraternities, national sororities.

Athletics Member NCAA. All Division II except wrestling (Division I). ***Intercollegiate sports:*** baseball M(s), basketball M(s)/W(s), cross-country running W(s), football M(s), golf M(s)/W(s), soccer W(s), softball W(s), swimming and diving M(s)/W(s), tennis W(s), track and field W(s), volleyball W(s), wrestling M(s). ***Intramural sports:*** badminton M/W, basketball M/W, cheerleading M(c)/W(c), cross-country running M/W, equestrian sports M(c)/W(c), football M/W, golf M/W, racquetball M/W, rock climbing M(c)/W(c), rugby M(c)/W(c), soccer M(c)/W(c), softball M/W, swimming and diving M/W, table tennis M/W, tennis M/W, track and field M(c)/W(c), ultimate Frisbee M(c)/W(c), volleyball M(c)/W, water polo M/W, weight lifting M/W, wrestling M/W.

Campus security: 24-hour emergency response devices and patrols, student patrols, late-night transport/escort service, controlled dormitory access.

Student services: health clinic, personal/psychological counseling, women's center.

COSTS & FINANCIAL AID

Costs (2014–15) ***One-time required fee:*** $50. ***Tuition:*** state resident $6820 full-time, $284 per credit part-time; nonresident $10,230 full-time, $426 per credit part-time. Full-time tuition and fees vary according to course load, degree level, and location. Part-time tuition and fees vary according to course load, degree level, and location. ***Required fees:*** $2968 full-time, $174 per credit hour part-time. ***Room and board:*** $8152; room only: $5138. Room and board charges vary according to board plan, housing facility, and location. ***Payment plans:*** installment, deferred payment. ***Waivers:*** senior citizens and employees or children of employees.

Financial Aid Of all full-time matriculated undergraduates who enrolled in 2013, 3,857 applied for aid, 3,398 were judged to have need, 704 had their need fully met. In 2013, 131 non-need-based awards were made. ***Average percent of need met:*** 69. ***Average financial aid package:*** $12,863. ***Average need-based loan:*** $4105. ***Average need-based gift aid:*** $5899. ***Average non-need-based aid:*** $1854. ***Average indebtedness upon graduation:*** $21,507.

APPLYING

Standardized Tests *Required:* SAT or ACT (for admission). *Required for some:* International TOEFL or TSE or IELTS students.

Required: high school transcript. ***Required for some:*** essay or personal statement, interview, NLN Test for ASN Program and SAT/ACT Scores (Required For Some). ***Recommended:*** essay or personal statement, 2 letters of recommendation, interview.

CONTACT

Clarion University of Pennsylvania, 840 Wood Street, Clarion, PA 16214. *Phone:* 814-393-2306. *Toll-free phone:* 800-672-7171.

DeSales University

Center Valley, Pennsylvania

http://www.desales.edu/

- **Independent Roman Catholic** comprehensive, founded 1964
- **Suburban** 480-acre campus
- **Endowment** $66.9 million
- **Coed** 2,381 undergraduate students, 75% full-time, 60% women, 40% men
- **Moderately difficult** entrance level, 80% of applicants were admitted

UNDERGRAD STUDENTS

1,784 full-time, 597 part-time. Students come from 17 states and territories; 5 other countries; 64% are from out of state; 4% Black or African American, non-Hispanic/Latino; 10% Hispanic/Latino; 3% Asian, non-Hispanic/Latino; 0.2% Native Hawaiian or other Pacific Islander, non-Hispanic/Latino; 0.6% American Indian or Alaska Native, non-Hispanic/Latino; 6% Race/ethnicity unknown; 4% transferred in; 67% live on campus.

Freshmen

Admission: 2,658 applied, 2,127 admitted, 408 enrolled. ***Average high school GPA:*** 3.2. ***Test scores:*** SAT critical reading scores over 500: 57%; SAT math scores over 500: 54%; ACT scores over 18: 90%; SAT critical reading scores over 600: 20%; SAT math scores over 600: 18%; ACT scores over 24: 43%; SAT critical reading scores over 700: 5%; SAT math scores over 700: 3%; ACT scores over 30: 7%.

Retention: 83% of full-time freshmen returned.

FACULTY

Total: 349, 34% full-time, 44% with terminal degrees.

Student/faculty ratio: 14:1.

ACADEMICS

Calendar: semesters. *Degrees:* certificates, bachelor's, master's, doctoral, post-master's, and postbachelor's certificates.

Special study options: academic remediation for entering students, accelerated degree program, advanced placement credit, cooperative education, distance learning, double majors, external degree program, honors programs, independent study, internships, off-campus study, part-time degree program, services for LD students, student-designed majors, study abroad, summer session for credit. ***ROTC:*** Army (c).

Unusual degree programs: 3-2 Physician Assistant Studies, MACJ, MBA/Accounting, Doctor of Physical Therapy.

Computers: 200 computers/terminals and 200 ports are available on campus for general student use. Students can access the following: computer help desk, free student e-mail accounts, online (class) grades, online (class) registration, online (class) schedules. Campuswide network is available. 100% of college-owned or -operated housing units are wired for high-speed Internet access. Wireless service is available via classrooms, computer centers, computer labs, learning centers, libraries, student centers.

STUDENT LIFE

Housing options: on-campus residence required for freshman year; men-only, women-only, special housing for students with disabilities. Campus housing is university owned. Freshman campus housing is guaranteed.

Activities and organizations: drama/theater group, student-run newspaper, radio and television station, choral group, marching band, DSU Equestrian Team, PA Student Society, Colleges Against Cancer, Colleges Against Cancer, CEO (Creative Exploration Organization), SHARE.

Athletics Member NCAA. All Division III. ***Intercollegiate sports:*** baseball M, basketball M, cross-country running M, field hockey W, golf M, lacrosse M, soccer M/W, softball W, track and field M/W, volleyball W. ***Intramural sports:*** basketball M/W, cheerleading W(c), fencing M(c), ice hockey M(c), lacrosse M/W(c), rugby M(c), soccer M/W, softball M/W, swimming and diving M(c)/W(c), tennis M(c), ultimate Frisbee M/W, volleyball M(c)/W.

Campus security: 24-hour emergency response devices and patrols, late-night transport/escort service, controlled dormitory access.

Student services: personal/psychological counseling.

COSTS & FINANCIAL AID

Costs (2014–15) ***Comprehensive fee:*** $44,110 includes full-time tuition ($31,000), mandatory fees ($1350), and room and board ($11,760). Full-time tuition and fees vary according to class time and course load. Part-time tuition: $1290 per credit hour. Part-time tuition and fees vary according to class time and course load. ***Required fees:*** $446 per credit hour part-time. ***Room and board:*** Room and board charges vary according to board plan and housing facility. ***Payment plans:*** installment, deferred payment. ***Waivers:*** adult students, senior citizens, and employees or children of employees.

Financial Aid Of all full-time matriculated undergraduates who enrolled in 2014, 1,570 applied for aid, 1,443 were judged to have need, 273 had their need fully met. 521 Federal Work-Study jobs (averaging $1951). 293 state and other part-time jobs (averaging $1948). In 2014, 254 non-need-based awards were made. ***Average percent of need met:*** 67. ***Average financial aid package:*** $23,059. ***Average need-based loan:*** $4655. ***Average need-based gift aid:*** $17,738. ***Average non-need-based aid:*** $11,076. ***Average indebtedness upon graduation:*** $36,798. ***Financial aid deadline:*** 5/1.

APPLYING

Standardized Tests *Required:* SAT or ACT (for admission).

Options: electronic application.

Application fee: $30.

Required: essay or personal statement, high school transcript, . ***Recommended:*** interview.

CONTACT

Mr. Derrick Wetzel, Director of Admissions, DeSales University, 2755 Station Avenue, Center Valley, PA 18034-9568. *Phone:* 610-282-4443.

Toll-free phone: 877-4-333725 (in-state); 877-4-33725 (out-of-state). *Fax:* 610-282-0131. *E-mail:* derrick.wetzell@desales.edu.

DeVry University

Fort Washington, Pennsylvania

http://www.devry.edu/

- **Proprietary** comprehensive, founded 2002, part of DeVry University
- **Coed** 436 undergraduate students, 38% full-time, 41% women, 59% men
- **Minimally difficult** entrance level

UNDERGRAD STUDENTS
164 full-time, 272 part-time. 7% are from out of state; 26% Black or African American, non-Hispanic/Latino; 9% Hispanic/Latino; 4% Asian, non-Hispanic/Latino; 2% Two or more races, non-Hispanic/Latino; 24% Race/ethnicity unknown; 0.7% international; 24% transferred in.

Freshmen
Admission: 38 enrolled.

FACULTY
Total: 25, 52% full-time.
Student/faculty ratio: 17:1.

ACADEMICS
Calendar: semesters. *Degrees:* associate, bachelor's, master's, and postbachelor's certificates.
Special study options: adult/continuing education programs, part-time degree program.

STUDENT LIFE
Housing options: college housing not available.

COSTS & FINANCIAL AID
Costs (2014–15) ***Tuition:*** $17,052 full-time, $609 per credit hour part-time. ***Required fees:*** $80 full-time.
Financial Aid Of all full-time matriculated undergraduates who enrolled in 2007, 254 applied for aid, 244 were judged to have need, 2 had their need fully met. In 2007, 23 non-need-based awards were made. ***Average percent of need met:*** 34. ***Average financial aid package:*** $12,114. ***Average need-based loan:*** $6836. ***Average need-based gift aid:*** $6835. ***Average non-need-based aid:*** $13,057. ***Average indebtedness upon graduation:*** $15,638.

APPLYING
Application fee: $40.
Required: high school transcript, interview.

CONTACT
DeVry University, 1140 Virginia Drive, Fort Washington, PA 19034. *Phone:* 215-591-5700. *Toll-free phone:* 866-338-7941.

DeVry University

King of Prussia, Pennsylvania

http://www.devry.edu/

- **Proprietary** comprehensive
- **Coed**

ACADEMICS
Calendar: semesters. *Degrees:* associate, bachelor's, and master's.

COSTS
Costs (2014–15) ***Tuition:*** $17,052 full-time, $609 per credit hour part-time. ***Required fees:*** $80 full-time.

CONTACT
Admissions Office, DeVry University, 150 Allendale Road, Suite 3250, King of Prussia, PA 19406-2926. *Phone:* 610-205-3130. *Toll-free phone:* 866-338-7941.

DeVry University

Philadelphia, Pennsylvania

http://www.devry.edu/

- **Proprietary** comprehensive
- **Coed**

ACADEMICS
Degrees: associate, bachelor's, and master's.

COSTS
Costs (2014–15) ***Tuition:*** $17,052 full-time, $609 per credit hour part-time. ***Required fees:*** $80 full-time.

CONTACT
Admissions Office, DeVry University, Philadelphia Downtown Center, 1800 JFK Boulevard, Suite 200, Philadelphia, PA 19103-7421. *Phone:* 215-568-2911. *Toll-free phone:* 866-338-7941.

DeVry University

Pittsburgh, Pennsylvania

http://www.devry.edu/

- **Proprietary** comprehensive
- **Coed**

ACADEMICS
Calendar: semesters. *Degrees:* bachelor's and master's.

COSTS
Costs (2014–15) ***Tuition:*** $17,052 full-time, $609 per credit hour part-time. ***Required fees:*** $80 full-time.

CONTACT
Admissions Office, DeVry University, FreeMarkets Center, 210 Sixth Avenue, Suite 200, Pittsburgh, PA 15222-2606. *Phone:* 412-642-9072. *Toll-free phone:* 866-338-7941.

Dickinson College

Carlisle, Pennsylvania

http://www.dickinson.edu/

- **Independent** 4-year, founded 1773
- **Suburban** 180-acre campus with easy access to Harrisburg
- **Endowment** $402.7 million
- **Coed** 2,364 undergraduate students, 99% full-time, 58% women, 42% men
- **Very difficult** entrance level, 48% of applicants were admitted

UNDERGRAD STUDENTS
2,332 full-time, 32 part-time. Students come from 44 states and territories; 41 other countries; 77% are from out of state; 4% Black or African American, non-Hispanic/Latino; 6% Hispanic/Latino; 2% Asian, non-Hispanic/Latino; 3% Two or more races, non-Hispanic/Latino; 2% Race/ethnicity unknown; 8% international; 0.6% transferred in; 94% live on campus.

Freshmen
Admission: 5,700 applied, 2,742 admitted, 618 enrolled. ***Test scores:*** SAT critical reading scores over 500: 98%; SAT math scores over 500: 98%; SAT writing scores over 500: 99%; ACT scores over 18: 100%; SAT critical reading scores over 600: 71%; SAT math scores over 600: 80%; SAT writing scores over 600: 75%; ACT scores over 24: 99%; SAT critical reading scores over 700: 19%; SAT math scores over 700: 23%; SAT writing scores over 700: 19%; ACT scores over 30: 46%.
Retention: 90% of full-time freshmen returned.

FACULTY
Total: 247, 91% full-time, 86% with terminal degrees.
Student/faculty ratio: 9:1.

ACADEMICS
Calendar: semesters. *Degree:* bachelor's.
Special study options: accelerated degree program, adult/continuing education programs, advanced placement credit, double majors, English as a second language, independent study, internships, off-campus study, part-time degree program, services for LD students, student-designed majors, study abroad, summer session for credit. ***ROTC:*** Army (b).
Unusual degree programs: 3-2 engineering with Case Western Reserve University; Rensselaer Polytechnic Institute, Columbia University's Fu Foundation School of Engineering and Applied Science; nursing with Johns Hopkins University School of Nursing; Johns Hopkins School of Advanced International Studies (SAIS).

Computers: 1,527 computers/terminals and 5,000 ports are available on campus for general student use. Students can access the following: campus intranet, computer help desk, free student e-mail accounts, online (class) grades, online (class) registration, online (class) schedules. Campuswide network is available. 100% of college-owned or -operated housing units are wired for high-speed Internet access. Wireless service is available via classrooms, computer centers, computer labs, dorm rooms, libraries, student centers.

STUDENT LIFE
Housing options: on-campus residence required through senior year; coed, special housing for students with disabilities. Campus housing is university owned. Freshman campus housing is guaranteed.

Activities and organizations: drama/theater group, student-run newspaper, radio station, choral group, Student Senate, CommServ, Multi-Organization Board, Hillel, Spectrum, national fraternities, national sororities.

Athletics Member NCAA. All Division III. ***Intercollegiate sports:*** baseball M, basketball M/W, cheerleading M(c)/W(c), cross-country running M/W, equestrian sports M(c)/W(c), fencing M(c)/W(c), field hockey W, football M, golf M/W, ice hockey M(c)/W(c), lacrosse M/W, skiing (downhill) M(c)/W(c), soccer M/W, softball W, squash M/W, swimming and diving M/W, tennis M/W, track and field M/W, ultimate Frisbee M(c)/W(c), volleyball M(c)/W. ***Intramural sports:*** badminton M/W, basketball M/W, field hockey W, football M, racquetball M/W, soccer M/W, softball M, tennis M/W, volleyball M/W.

Campus security: 24-hour emergency response devices and patrols, student patrols, late-night transport/escort service, controlled dormitory access.

Student services: health clinic, personal/psychological counseling, women's center.

COSTS & FINANCIAL AID
Costs (2014–15) ***One-time required fee:*** $25. ***Comprehensive fee:*** $59,664 includes full-time tuition ($47,242), mandatory fees ($450), and room and board ($11,972). Part-time tuition: $5910 per course. ***Required fees:*** $56 per course part-time. ***College room only:*** $6174. Room and board charges vary according to board plan and housing facility. ***Payment plan:*** installment. ***Waivers:*** senior citizens and employees or children of employees.

Financial Aid Of all full-time matriculated undergraduates who enrolled in 2014, 1,420 applied for aid, 1,275 were judged to have need, 733 had their need fully met. 931 Federal Work-Study jobs (averaging $2313). 152 state and other part-time jobs (averaging $3947). In 2014, 340 non-need-based awards were made. ***Average percent of need met:*** 96. ***Average financial aid package:*** $38,290. ***Average need-based loan:*** $5001. ***Average need-based gift aid:*** $32,786. ***Average non-need-based aid:*** $10,151. ***Average indebtedness upon graduation:*** $25,392. ***Financial aid deadline:*** 2/1.

APPLYING
Standardized Tests *Recommended:* SAT or ACT (for admission).

Options: electronic application, early decision, early action, deferred entrance.

Application fee: $65.

Required: essay or personal statement, high school transcript, 2 letters of recommendation. ***Recommended:*** minimum 3.0 GPA, interview.

Application deadlines: 2/1 (freshmen), 2/1 (out-of-state freshmen), 4/1 (transfers), 12/1 (early action).

Early decision deadline: 11/15 (for plan 1), 1/15 (for plan 2).

Notification: 3/20 (freshmen), 3/20 (out-of-state freshmen), continuous until 5/15 (transfers), 12/15 (early decision plan 1), 2/15 (early decision plan 2), 2/1 (early action).

CONTACT
Catherine Davenport, Dean of Admissions, Dickinson College, PO Box 1773, Admissions Office, Carlisle, PA 17013-2896. *Phone:* 717-245-1231. *Toll-free phone:* 800-644-1773. *Fax:* 717-245-1442. *E-mail:* admit@dickinson.edu.

★ Drexel University
Philadelphia, Pennsylvania
http://www.drexel.edu/

- **Independent** university, founded 1891
- **Urban** 96-acre campus with easy access to Philadelphia
- **Coed** 16,896 undergraduate students, 85% full-time, 47% women, 53% men
- **Moderately difficult** entrance level, 76% of applicants were admitted

UNDERGRAD STUDENTS
14,365 full-time, 2,531 part-time. Students come from 51 states and territories; 121 other countries; 53% are from out of state; 7% Black or African American, non-Hispanic/Latino; 6% Hispanic/Latino; 13% Asian, non-Hispanic/Latino; 0.6% Native Hawaiian or other Pacific Islander, non-Hispanic/Latino; 0.2% American Indian or Alaska Native, non-Hispanic/Latino; 3% Two or more races, non-Hispanic/Latino; 2% Race/ethnicity unknown; 13% international; 6% transferred in; 26% live on campus.

Freshmen
Admission: 47,477 applied, 36,088 admitted, 2,928 enrolled. ***Average high school GPA:*** 3.47. ***Test scores:*** SAT critical reading scores over 500: 89%; SAT math scores over 500: 95%; SAT writing scores over 500: 85%; ACT scores over 18: 99%; SAT critical reading scores over 600: 40%; SAT math scores over 600: 61%; SAT writing scores over 600: 40%; ACT scores over 24: 80%; SAT critical reading scores over 700: 8%; SAT math scores over 700: 16%; SAT writing scores over 700: 7%; ACT scores over 30: 19%.

Retention: 84% of full-time freshmen returned.

FACULTY
Total: 2,168, 54% full-time.

ACADEMICS
Calendar: quarters. *Degrees:* certificates, associate, bachelor's, master's, doctoral, post-master's, and postbachelor's certificates.

Special study options: academic remediation for entering students, accelerated degree program, adult/continuing education programs, advanced placement credit, cooperative education, distance learning, double majors, English as a second language, freshman honors college, honors programs, independent study, internships, part-time degree program, services for LD students, student-designed majors, study abroad, summer session for credit. ***ROTC:*** Army (b), Navy (c), Air Force (c).

Computers: Students can access the following: campus intranet, computer help desk, free student e-mail accounts, online (class) grades, online (class) registration, online (class) schedules. Campuswide network is available. 100% of college-owned or -operated housing units are wired for high-speed Internet access. Wireless service is available via entire campus.

STUDENT LIFE
Housing options: on-campus residence required for freshman year; coed, special housing for students with disabilities. Freshman campus housing is guaranteed.

Activities and organizations: drama/theater group, student-run newspaper, radio and television station, choral group, student government, Black Student Union, Society of Hispanic Professional Engineers, Society of Minority Engineers and Scientists, Campus Activities Board, national fraternities, national sororities.

Athletics Member NCAA. All Division I. ***Intercollegiate sports:*** basketball M(s)/W(s), crew M(s)/W(s), field hockey W(s), golf M(s), lacrosse M(s)/W(s), soccer M(s)/W(s), softball W(s), squash M(s)/W(s), swimming and diving M(s)/W(s), tennis M(s)/W(s), wrestling M(s). ***Intramural sports:*** badminton M/W, basketball M/W, fencing M/W, football M, ice hockey M, riflery M/W, sailing M/W, softball M, squash M/W, table tennis M/W, tennis M/W, volleyball M/W, water polo M/W.

Campus security: 24-hour emergency response devices and patrols, late-night transport/escort service, controlled dormitory access.

Student services: health clinic, personal/psychological counseling.

COSTS & FINANCIAL AID
Costs (2014–15) ***Comprehensive fee:*** $61,418 includes full-time tuition ($44,646), mandatory fees ($2405), and room and board ($14,367). Full-

time tuition and fees vary according to course load, location, program, and student level. Part-time tuition: $1004 per credit hour. Part-time tuition and fees vary according to course load and program. ***Room and board:*** Room and board charges vary according to board plan and housing facility. ***Payment plan:*** installment. ***Waivers:*** children of alumni and employees or children of employees.

Financial Aid Of all full-time matriculated undergraduates who enrolled in 2008, 5,878 applied for aid, 5,833 were judged to have need, 1,826 had their need fully met. In 2008, 2086 non-need-based awards were made. ***Average percent of need met:*** 56. ***Average financial aid package:*** $21,488. ***Average need-based loan:*** $12,875. ***Average need-based gift aid:*** $13,204. ***Average non-need-based aid:*** $11,641. ***Financial aid deadline:*** 3/1.

APPLYING

Standardized Tests *Required:* SAT or ACT (for admission).

Options: electronic application, early admission, deferred entrance.

Application fee: $50.

Required: essay or personal statement, high school transcript, minimum 2.0 GPA. ***Recommended:*** 2 letters of recommendation, interview.

Application deadlines: 1/13 (freshmen), rolling (transfers).

Notification: continuous (freshmen), continuous (transfers).

CONTACT

Drexel University, 3141 Chestnut Street, Philadelphia, PA 19104-2875.
Phone: 215-895-2400. *Toll-free phone:* 800-2-DREXEL.

See this page for display ad and page 1424 for the College Close-Up.

Duquesne University

Pittsburgh, Pennsylvania

http://www.duq.edu/

- **Independent Roman Catholic** university, founded 1878
- **Urban** 50-acre campus with easy access to Pittsburgh
- **Endowment** $260.6 million
- **Coed** 5,995 undergraduate students, 96% full-time, 61% women, 39% men
- **Moderately difficult** entrance level, 73% of applicants were admitted

UNDERGRAD STUDENTS

5,747 full-time, 248 part-time. Students come from 45 states and territories; 49 other countries; 26% are from out of state; 4% Black or African American, non-Hispanic/Latino; 3% Hispanic/Latino; 2% Asian, non-Hispanic/Latino; 0.1% Native Hawaiian or other Pacific Islander, non-Hispanic/Latino; 0.1% American Indian or Alaska Native, non-Hispanic/Latino; 2% Two or more races, non-Hispanic/Latino; 1% Race/ethnicity unknown; 4% international; 3% transferred in; 59% live on campus.

Freshmen

Admission: 6,534 applied, 4,774 admitted, 1,343 enrolled. ***Average high school GPA:*** 3.73. ***Test scores:*** SAT critical reading scores over 500: 87%; SAT math scores over 500: 89%; SAT writing scores over 500: 80%; ACT scores over 18: 100%; SAT critical reading scores over 600: 30%; SAT math scores over 600: 35%; SAT writing scores over 600: 30%; ACT scores over 24: 75%; SAT critical reading scores over 700: 3%; SAT math scores over 700: 4%; SAT writing scores over 700: 4%; ACT scores over 30: 11%.

Retention: 90% of full-time freshmen returned.

FACULTY

Total: 993, 48% full-time.

Student/faculty ratio: 14:1.

ACADEMICS

Calendar: semesters. *Degrees:* bachelor's, master's, doctoral, post-master's, and postbachelor's certificates.

Special study options: academic remediation for entering students, accelerated degree program, adult/continuing education programs, advanced placement credit, distance learning, double majors, English as a second language, external degree program, freshman honors college, honors programs, independent study, internships, off-campus study, part-time degree program, services for LD students, student-designed majors,

study abroad, summer session for credit. ***ROTC:*** Army (b), Navy (c), Air Force (c).

Unusual degree programs: 3-2 engineering with Case Western Reserve University, University of Pittsburgh.

Computers: 1,000 computers/terminals are available on campus for general student use. Students can access the following: campus intranet, computer help desk, free student e-mail accounts, online (class) grades, online (class) registration, online (class) schedules. Campuswide network is available. 100% of college-owned or -operated housing units are wired for high-speed Internet access. Wireless service is available via classrooms, computer centers, computer labs, dorm rooms, learning centers, libraries, student centers.

STUDENT LIFE

Housing options: on-campus residence required through sophomore year; coed, men-only, women-only, special housing for students with disabilities. Campus housing is university owned. Freshman campus housing is guaranteed.

Activities and organizations: drama/theater group, student-run newspaper, radio and television station, choral group, marching band, Duquesne University Volunteers (DUV), Red and Blue Crew, Student Government Association, Duquesne Program Council, Residence Hall Association, national fraternities, national sororities.

Athletics Member NCAA. All Division I except football (Division I-AA). ***Intercollegiate sports:*** basketball M(s)/W(s), crew W(s), cross-country running M(s)/W(s), lacrosse W(s), soccer M(s)/W(s), swimming and diving W(s), tennis M(s)/W(s), track and field M(s)/W(s), volleyball W(s). ***Intramural sports:*** baseball M(c)/W(c), basketball M/W, cheerleading W(c), crew M(c)/W(c), equestrian sports M(c)/W(c), football M/W, golf M(c)/W(c), ice hockey M(c)/W(c), lacrosse M(c)/W(c), racquetball M/W, rugby M(c)/W(c), soccer M/W, tennis M(c)/W(c), ultimate Frisbee M/W, volleyball M/W.

Campus security: 24-hour emergency response devices and patrols, late-night transport/escort service, controlled dormitory access, cameras monitor exterior 24 hours/day; card access for buildings; 8 Code Blue Emergency service stations; outside warning siren system.

Student services: health clinic, personal/psychological counseling.

COSTS & FINANCIAL AID

Costs (2014–15) ***Comprehensive fee:*** $43,720 includes full-time tuition ($30,070), mandatory fees ($2566), and room and board ($11,084). Full-time tuition and fees vary according to course load and program. Part-time tuition: $981 per credit. Part-time tuition and fees vary according to course load and program. ***Required fees:*** $100 per credit part-time. ***College room only:*** $6044. Room and board charges vary according to board plan and housing facility. ***Payment plans:*** installment, deferred payment. ***Waivers:*** senior citizens and employees or children of employees.

Financial Aid Of all full-time matriculated undergraduates who enrolled in 2013, 4,749 applied for aid, 3,981 were judged to have need, 935 had their need fully met. 3,160 Federal Work-Study jobs (averaging $2482). In 2013, 1536 non-need-based awards were made. ***Average percent of need met:*** 79. ***Average financial aid package:*** $22,848. ***Average need-based loan:*** $4675. ***Average need-based gift aid:*** $18,059. ***Average non-need-based aid:*** $10,804. ***Average indebtedness upon graduation:*** $34,522. ***Financial aid deadline:*** 5/1.

APPLYING

Standardized Tests *Required for some:* SAT or ACT (for admission).

Options: electronic application, early admission, early decision, early action, deferred entrance.

Application fee: $50.

Required: high school transcript, 1 letter of recommendation. ***Required for some:*** audition for School of Music applicants; Physical Therapy freshman-40 hours of volunteer, paid, or shadowing experience before start of freshman year. ***Recommended:*** essay or personal statement, minimum 3.0 GPA, interview.

Application deadlines: 7/1 (freshmen), 7/1 (transfers), 12/1 (early action).

Early decision deadline: 11/1.

Notification: continuous until 10/1 (freshmen), 11/15 (early decision), 1/15 (early action).

CONTACT

Ms. Debra Zugates, Director of Admissions, Duquesne University, Administration Building, 600 Forbes Avenue, Pittsburgh, PA 15282-0201. *Phone:* 412-396-5211. *Toll-free phone:* 800-456-0590. *Fax:* 412-396-5644. *E-mail:* admissions@duq.edu.

Eastern University

St. Davids, Pennsylvania

http://www.eastern.edu/

- **Independent Christian** comprehensive, founded 1952
- **Suburban** 114-acre campus with easy access to Philadelphia
- **Endowment** $290.0 million
- **Coed** 2,402 undergraduate students, 83% full-time, 71% women, 29% men
- **Moderately difficult** entrance level, 68% of applicants were admitted

UNDERGRAD STUDENTS

1,992 full-time, 410 part-time. Students come from 35 states and territories; 19 other countries; 44% are from out of state; 22% Black or African American, non-Hispanic/Latino; 16% Hispanic/Latino; 2% Asian, non-Hispanic/Latino; 0.1% Native Hawaiian or other Pacific Islander, non-Hispanic/Latino; 0.5% American Indian or Alaska Native, non-Hispanic/Latino; 0.3% Two or more races, non-Hispanic/Latino; 6% Race/ethnicity unknown; 2% international; 4% transferred in; 75% live on campus.

Freshmen

Admission: 1,711 applied, 1,156 admitted, 446 enrolled. ***Average high school GPA:*** 3.42. ***Test scores:*** SAT critical reading scores over 500: 61%; SAT math scores over 500: 54%; SAT writing scores over 500: 54%; ACT scores over 18: 86%; SAT critical reading scores over 600: 18%; SAT math scores over 600: 20%; SAT writing scores over 600: 22%; ACT scores over 24: 39%; SAT critical reading scores over 700: 4%; SAT math scores over 700: 3%; SAT writing scores over 700: 1%.

Retention: 91% of full-time freshmen returned.

FACULTY

Total: 564, 27% full-time.

Student/faculty ratio: 11:1.

ACADEMICS

Calendar: semesters. *Degrees:* certificates, diplomas, associate, bachelor's, master's, and doctoral.

Special study options: academic remediation for entering students, accelerated degree program, adult/continuing education programs, advanced placement credit, distance learning, English as a second language, external degree program, honors programs, independent study, internships, off-campus study, part-time degree program, student-designed majors, study abroad, summer session for credit. ***ROTC:*** Army (c), Air Force (c).

Computers: 98 computers/terminals and 50 ports are available on campus for general student use. Students can access the following: computer help desk, free student e-mail accounts, online (class) grades, online (class) registration, online (class) schedules. Campuswide network is available. 100% of college-owned or -operated housing units are wired for high-speed Internet access. Wireless service is available via entire campus.

STUDENT LIFE

Housing options: on-campus residence required through senior year; coed, men-only, women-only. Campus housing is university owned and leased by the school. Freshman campus housing is guaranteed.

Activities and organizations: drama/theater group, student-run newspaper, radio station, choral group, Kappa Delta Pi - Education Honor Society, ETHELS - Swing Club, Black Student League (BSL), SPSEA - Students of Pennsylvania State Education Association, Psi Chi - Psychology Honor Society.

Athletics Member NCAA. All Division III. ***Intercollegiate sports:*** baseball M, basketball M/W, cross-country running M/W, field hockey W, golf M/W, lacrosse M/W, soccer M/W, softball W, tennis M/W, volleyball W. ***Intramural sports:*** basketball M/W, cheerleading M(c)/W(c), soccer M/W, volleyball M/W.

Campus security: 24-hour emergency response devices and patrols, late-night transport/escort service, controlled dormitory access, emergency call boxes.

Student services: health clinic, personal/psychological counseling, women's center.

COSTS & FINANCIAL AID

Costs (2015–16) ***One-time required fee:*** $50. ***Comprehensive fee:*** $40,778 includes full-time tuition ($30,250), mandatory fees ($340), and room and board ($10,188). Full-time tuition and fees vary according to course load, degree level, and program. Part-time tuition: $660 per credit. Part-time tuition and fees vary according to course load, degree level, and program. ***College room only:*** $5432. Room and board charges vary according to housing facility and location. ***Payment plan:*** installment. ***Waivers:*** children of alumni and employees or children of employees.

Financial Aid Of all full-time matriculated undergraduates who enrolled in 2013, 1,974 applied for aid, 1,843 were judged to have need, 304 had their need fully met. 418 Federal Work-Study jobs (averaging $1200). In 2013, 114 non-need-based awards were made. ***Average percent of need met:*** 62. ***Average financial aid package:*** $18,517. ***Average need-based loan:*** $4281. ***Average need-based gift aid:*** $6527. ***Average non-need-based aid:*** $10,267. ***Average indebtedness upon graduation:*** $34,662.

APPLYING

Standardized Tests *Required:* SAT or ACT (for admission).

Options: electronic application, early admission, deferred entrance.

Application fee: $35.

Required: essay or personal statement, high school transcript, minimum 2.0 GPA, 1 letter of recommendation. ***Recommended:*** 2 letters of recommendation, interview.

Application deadlines: rolling (freshmen), rolling (out-of-state freshmen), rolling (transfers).

Notification: continuous (freshmen), continuous (out-of-state freshmen), continuous (transfers).

CONTACT

Mr. Michael Dziedziak, Executive Director of Enrollment, Eastern University, 1300 Eagle Road, St Davids, PA 19087-3696. *Phone:* 610-341-1376. *Toll-free phone:* 800-452-0996. *Fax:* 610-341-1723. *E-mail:* ugadm@eastern.edu.

East Stroudsburg University of Pennsylvania

East Stroudsburg, Pennsylvania

http://www.esu.edu/

- **State-supported** comprehensive, founded 1893, part of Pennsylvania State System of Higher Education
- **Suburban** 258-acre campus
- **Endowment** $16.8 million
- **Coed** 6,186 undergraduate students, 89% full-time, 55% women, 45% men
- **Moderately difficult** entrance level, 81% of applicants were admitted

UNDERGRAD STUDENTS

5,495 full-time, 691 part-time. Students come from 33 states and territories; 25 other countries; 23% are from out of state; 9% Black or African American, non-Hispanic/Latino; 10% Hispanic/Latino; 1% Asian, non-Hispanic/Latino; 0.2% Native Hawaiian or other Pacific Islander, non-Hispanic/Latino; 0.2% American Indian or Alaska Native, non-Hispanic/Latino; 2% Two or more races, non-Hispanic/Latino; 13% Race/ethnicity unknown; 0.9% international; 10% transferred in; 44% live on campus.

Freshmen

Admission: 5,584 applied, 4,549 admitted, 1,212 enrolled. ***Average high school GPA:*** 3.1. ***Test scores:*** SAT critical reading scores over 500: 32%; SAT math scores over 500: 38%; SAT writing scores over 500: 29%; ACT scores over 18: 67%; SAT critical reading scores over 600: 4%; SAT math scores over 600: 6%; SAT writing scores over 600: 3%; ACT scores over 24: 9%; SAT math scores over 700: 1%; ACT scores over 30: 1%.

Retention: 74% of full-time freshmen returned.

FACULTY

Total: 316, 80% full-time, 66% with terminal degrees.

Student/faculty ratio: 22:1.

ACADEMICS

Calendar: semesters. *Degrees:* associate, bachelor's, and master's.

Special study options: academic remediation for entering students, accelerated degree program, adult/continuing education programs, advanced placement credit, distance learning, double majors, honors programs, independent study, internships, off-campus study, part-time degree program, services for LD students, student-designed majors, study abroad, summer session for credit. ***ROTC:*** Army (b), Air Force (b).

Unusual degree programs: 3-2 engineering with Penn State University–University Park Campus.

Computers: 500 computers/terminals and 1,500 ports are available on campus for general student use. Students can access the following: campus intranet, computer help desk, free student e-mail accounts, online (class) grades, online (class) registration, online (class) schedules, Online classes. Students can connect through the wireless network. Campuswide network is available. 100% of college-owned or -operated housing units are wired for high-speed Internet access. Wireless service is available via classrooms, dorm rooms, libraries, student centers.

STUDENT LIFE

Housing options: on-campus residence required for freshman year; coed, special housing for students with disabilities. Campus housing is university owned and is provided by a third party. Freshman campus housing is guaranteed.

Activities and organizations: drama/theater group, student-run newspaper, radio station, choral group, marching band, Student Senate, Stage II, Council for Exceptional Children, United Campus Ministry/ESU Christian Fellowship, University Band/Vocal Performing Choirs, national fraternities, national sororities.

Athletics Member NCAA. All Division II. ***Intercollegiate sports:*** baseball M(s), basketball M(s)/W(s), cheerleading M/W, cross-country running M(s)/W(s), equestrian sports M(c)/W(c), field hockey W(s), football M(s), golf M(c)/W, ice hockey M(c)/W(c), lacrosse M(c)/W(s), rugby M(c)/W(c), soccer M(s)/W(s), softball W(s), swimming and diving W(s), tennis M(c)/W(s), track and field M(s)/W(s), ultimate Frisbee M(c)/W(c), volleyball M(c)/W, wrestling M(s). ***Intramural sports:*** basketball M/W, racquetball M(c)/W(c), soccer M(c)/W(c), softball M/W.

Campus security: 24-hour emergency response devices and patrols, late-night transport/escort service, controlled dormitory access.

Student services: health clinic, personal/psychological counseling, women's center, legal services.

COSTS & FINANCIAL AID

Costs (2014–15) ***Tuition:*** state resident $6820 full-time, $284 per credit part-time; nonresident $17,050 full-time, $710 per credit part-time. Full-time tuition and fees vary according to course load, location, and program. Part-time tuition and fees vary according to location and program. ***Required fees:*** $2556 full-time, $103 per credit part-time. ***Room and board:*** $7980; room only: $5372. Room and board charges vary according to board plan and housing facility. ***Payment plan:*** installment. ***Waivers:*** senior citizens and employees or children of employees.

Financial Aid Of all full-time matriculated undergraduates who enrolled in 2012, 3,689 applied for aid, 3,043 were judged to have need, 1,296 had their need fully met. In 2012, 164 non-need-based awards were made. ***Average percent of need met:*** 56. ***Average financial aid package:*** $7330. ***Average need-based loan:*** $4379. ***Average need-based gift aid:*** $4830. ***Average non-need-based aid:*** $1444. ***Average indebtedness upon graduation:*** $13,828. ***Financial aid deadline:*** 3/1.

APPLYING

Standardized Tests *Required:* SAT or ACT (for admission).

Options: electronic application.

Application fee: $25.

Required: high school transcript.

Application deadlines: 4/1 (freshmen), 5/1 (transfers).

Notification: 5/1 (freshmen), continuous (transfers).

CONTACT

Mr. Jeff Jones, Director of Admissions, East Stroudsburg University of Pennsylvania, 200 Prospect Street, East Stroudsburg, PA 18301. *Phone:* 570-422-3542. *Toll-free phone:* 877-230-5547. *Fax:* 570-422-3933. *E-mail:* undergrads@po-box.esu.edu.

Edinboro University of Pennsylvania

Edinboro, Pennsylvania

http://www.edinboro.edu/

- **State-supported** comprehensive, founded 1857, part of Pennsylvania State System of Higher Education
- **Small-town** 585-acre campus
- **Endowment** $10.5 million
- **Coed** 5,585 undergraduate students, 91% full-time, 58% women, 42% men
- **Moderately difficult** entrance level, 99% of applicants were admitted

UNDERGRAD STUDENTS

5,086 full-time, 499 part-time. 12% are from out of state; 9% Black or African American, non-Hispanic/Latino; 3% Hispanic/Latino; 0.9% Asian, non-Hispanic/Latino; 0.1% Native Hawaiian or other Pacific Islander, non-Hispanic/Latino; 0.2% American Indian or Alaska Native, non-Hispanic/Latino; 2% Two or more races, non-Hispanic/Latino; 1% Race/ethnicity unknown; 2% international; 6% transferred in; 37% live on campus.

Freshmen

Admission: 3,143 applied, 3,121 admitted, 1,239 enrolled. ***Average high school GPA:*** 3.18. ***Test scores:*** SAT critical reading scores over 500: 39%; SAT math scores over 500: 39%; SAT writing scores over 500: 26%; ACT scores over 18: 62%; SAT critical reading scores over 600: 7%; SAT math scores over 600: 6%; SAT writing scores over 600: 4%; ACT scores over 24: 16%; ACT scores over 30: 1%.

Retention: 70% of full-time freshmen returned.

FACULTY

Total: 371, 85% full-time, 75% with terminal degrees.

Student/faculty ratio: 19:1.

ACADEMICS

Calendar: semesters. *Degrees:* associate, bachelor's, master's, doctoral, post-master's, and postbachelor's certificates.

Special study options: academic remediation for entering students, adult/continuing education programs, advanced placement credit, distance learning, double majors, honors programs, independent study, internships, off-campus study, part-time degree program, services for LD students, student-designed majors, study abroad, summer session for credit. ***ROTC:*** Army (b).

Unusual degree programs: 3-2 business administration with Articulation Agreements with Graduate MBA schools: Pennsylvania State-Behrend, Rochester Institute of Technology (4+1), Clarion University of PA acceptance of Edinboro's courses; engineering with Penn State University–University Park, Penn State University–Behrend, University of Pittsburgh, Case Western Reserve University; pre-pharmacy (2+3 at Lake Erie College of Osteopathic Medicine and School of Pharmacy), MA Counseling (3-2 program for Criminal Justice Majors); 3+4 Temple School of Dentistry.

Computers: 1,157 computers/terminals and 1,157 ports are available on campus for general student use. Students can access the following: campus intranet, computer help desk, free student e-mail accounts, online (class) grades, online (class) registration, online (class) schedules, We have a staffed help desk for technology issues. New students receive technology instruction during orientation. An open 24 hour computer lab. Some software is available. Campuswide network is available. 100% of college-owned or -operated housing units are wired for high-speed Internet access. Wireless service is available via classrooms, computer centers, computer labs, dorm rooms, learning centers, libraries, student centers.

STUDENT LIFE

Housing options: on-campus residence required through sophomore year; coed, special housing for students with disabilities. Campus housing is university owned and is provided by a third party. Freshman campus housing is guaranteed.

Activities and organizations: drama/theater group, student-run newspaper, radio and television station, choral group, marching band, Student Government Association, University Programming Board, Greek Life, Recreational Sports, Student Leadership (Leadership Edinboro), national fraternities, national sororities.

Athletics Member NCAA. All Division II except wrestling (Division I). ***Intercollegiate sports:*** basketball M(s)/W(s), cross-country running M(s)/W(s), football M(s), lacrosse W(s), soccer W(s), softball W(s), swimming and diving M(s)/W(s), tennis M(s)/W(s), track and field M(s)/W(s), volleyball W(s), wrestling M(s). ***Intramural sports:*** baseball M, basketball M/W, bowling M/W, cheerleading W, equestrian sports M/W, fencing M/W, field hockey M(c)/W(c), football M(c)/W(c), golf M/W, ice hockey M/W, lacrosse M, racquetball M/W, rock climbing M/W, skiing (downhill) M/W, soccer M/W, softball M(c)/W(c), tennis M/W, ultimate Frisbee M/W, volleyball M/W.

Campus security: 24-hour emergency response devices and patrols, late-night transport/escort service, controlled dormitory access, self-defense education.

Student services: health clinic, personal/psychological counseling, women's center, legal services.

COSTS & FINANCIAL AID

Costs (2014–15) ***Tuition:*** state resident $6820 full-time, $284 per credit hour part-time; nonresident $10,230 full-time, $298 per credit hour part-time. Full-time tuition and fees vary according to degree level, location, and program. Part-time tuition and fees vary according to course load, degree level, location, program, and reciprocity agreements. ***Required fees:*** $2377 full-time. ***Room and board:*** $8612; room only: $5670. Room and board charges vary according to board plan and housing facility. ***Payment plans:*** installment, deferred payment. ***Waivers:*** senior citizens and employees or children of employees.

Financial Aid Of all full-time matriculated undergraduates who enrolled in 2012, 4,010 applied for aid, 3,570 were judged to have need, 234 had their need fully met. 422 Federal Work-Study jobs (averaging $2437). 1,410 state and other part-time jobs (averaging $3056). In 2012, 67 non-need-based awards were made. ***Average percent of need met:*** 48. ***Average financial aid package:*** $8425. ***Average need-based loan:*** $3823. ***Average need-based gift aid:*** $4066. ***Average non-need-based aid:*** $3271. ***Average indebtedness upon graduation:*** $27,774.

APPLYING

Standardized Tests *Required:* SAT or ACT (for admission).

Options: electronic application, deferred entrance.

Application fee: $30.

Required: high school transcript. ***Required for some:*** essay or personal statement, 1 letter of recommendation, interview, music auditions. ***Recommended:*** minimum 2.5 GPA.

Notification: continuous (freshmen), continuous (transfers).

CONTACT

Ms. Melissa Manning, Associate Director of Undergraduate Admissions, Edinboro University of Pennsylvania, Academy Hall, Edinboro, PA 16444. *Phone:* 814-732-2761. *Toll-free phone:* 888-846-2676. *Fax:* 814-732-2420. *E-mail:* eup_admissions@edinboro.edu.

★ Elizabethtown College

Elizabethtown, Pennsylvania

http://www.etown.edu/

- **Independent** comprehensive, founded 1899, affiliated with Church of the Brethren
- **Small-town** 201-acre campus with easy access to Philadelphia, Baltimore, Harrisburg-Carlisle
- **Endowment** $67.7 million
- **Coed** 1,788 undergraduate students, 98% full-time, 63% women, 37% men
- **Moderately difficult** entrance level, 71% of applicants were admitted

UNDERGRAD STUDENTS

1,749 full-time, 39 part-time. Students come from 27 states and territories; 23 other countries; 31% are from out of state; 3% Black or African American, non-Hispanic/Latino; 4% Hispanic/Latino; 2% Asian, non-Hispanic/Latino; 0.1% Native Hawaiian or other Pacific Islander, non-Hispanic/Latino; 0.4% American Indian or Alaska Native, non-Hispanic/Latino; 2% Two or more races, non-Hispanic/Latino; 4% international; 1% transferred in; 87% live on campus.

Freshmen

Admission: 3,468 applied, 2,456 admitted, 447 enrolled. ***Test scores:*** SAT critical reading scores over 500: 79%; SAT math scores over 500: 79%;

SAT writing scores over 500: 71%; ACT scores over 18: 95%; SAT critical reading scores over 600: 31%; SAT math scores over 600: 37%; SAT writing scores over 600: 28%; ACT scores over 24: 63%; SAT critical reading scores over 700: 5%; SAT math scores over 700: 5%; SAT writing scores over 700: 5%; ACT scores over 30: 16%.

Retention: 79% of full-time freshmen returned.

FACULTY

Total: 195, 70% full-time, 72% with terminal degrees.

Student/faculty ratio: 11:1.

ACADEMICS

Calendar: semesters. *Degrees:* bachelor's and master's.

Special study options: advanced placement credit, distance learning, double majors, English as a second language, honors programs, independent study, internships, off-campus study, services for LD students, study abroad, summer session for credit.

Unusual degree programs: 3-2 forestry with Duke University; allied health programs with Thomas Jefferson University, Widener University; MS Environmental Management with Duke University.

Computers: 200 computers/terminals and 200 ports are available on campus for general student use. Students can access the following: campus intranet, computer help desk, free student e-mail accounts, online (class) grades, online (class) registration, online (class) schedules, file space, personal web page, financial aid, student billing, residence hall selection, personal and group blogs. Campuswide network is available. 100% of college-owned or -operated housing units are wired for high-speed Internet access. Wireless service is available via classrooms, computer centers, computer labs, dorm rooms, learning centers, libraries, student centers.

STUDENT LIFE

Housing options: on-campus residence required through senior year; coed, women-only, special housing for students with disabilities. Campus housing is university owned and leased by the school. Freshman campus housing is guaranteed.

Activities and organizations: drama/theater group, student-run newspaper, radio and television station, choral group, Enactus, Emotion Dance Club, Student Senate, Acappella groups, religious groups.

Athletics Member NCAA. All Division III. ***Intercollegiate sports:*** baseball M, basketball M/W, cross-country running M/W, field hockey W, golf M, lacrosse M/W, soccer M/W, softball W, swimming and diving M/W, tennis M/W, track and field M/W, volleyball W, wrestling M. ***Intramural sports:*** badminton M/W, basketball M/W, cheerleading M(c)/W(c), equestrian sports M(c)/W(c), ice hockey M(c), racquetball M/W, soccer M/W, softball M/W, tennis M/W, volleyball M(c)/W(c), water polo M/W.

Campus security: 24-hour emergency response devices and patrols, student patrols, late-night transport/escort service, controlled dormitory access, self-defense workshops, crime prevention program.

Student services: health clinic, personal/psychological counseling.

COSTS & FINANCIAL AID

Costs (2015–16) ***Comprehensive fee:*** $51,850 includes full-time tuition ($41,710) and room and board ($10,140). Full-time tuition and fees vary according to course load. Part-time tuition and fees vary according to course load. ***College room only:*** $5020. Room and board charges vary according to board plan and housing facility. ***Payment plan:*** installment. ***Waivers:*** employees or children of employees.

Financial Aid Of all full-time matriculated undergraduates who enrolled in 2014, 1,433 applied for aid, 1,305 were judged to have need, 253 had their need fully met. 780 Federal Work-Study jobs (averaging $1319). In 2014, 405 non-need-based awards were made. ***Average percent of need met:*** 79. ***Average financial aid package:*** $27,722. ***Average need-based loan:*** $4680. ***Average need-based gift aid:*** $23,087. ***Average non-need-based aid:*** $18,489. ***Average indebtedness upon graduation:*** $30,355.

APPLYING

Standardized Tests *Required:* SAT or ACT (for admission).

Options: electronic application, deferred entrance.

Application fee: $30.

Required: essay or personal statement, high school transcript, minimum 2.0 GPA, 2 letters of recommendation. ***Required for some:*** interview. ***Recommended:*** minimum 3.0 GPA, interview.

Application deadlines: 3/1 (freshmen), 8/1 (transfers).

Notification: continuous (freshmen), continuous (transfers).

CONTACT
Ms. Debra Murray, Director of Admissions, Elizabethtown College, One Alpha Drive, Elizabethtown, PA 17022. *Phone:* 717-361-1400. *Fax:* 717-361-1365. *E-mail:* admissions@etown.edu.

See previous page for display ad and page 1428 for the College Close-Up.

Elizabethtown College School of Continuing and Professional Studies
Elizabethtown, Pennsylvania
http://www.etowndegrees.com/

- **Independent religious** comprehensive, part of Elizabethtown College
- **Small-town** campus with easy access to Philadelphia, Baltimore, Harrisburg-Carlisle
- **Endowment** $67.7 million
- **Coed** 346 undergraduate students, 69% women, 31% men

UNDERGRAD STUDENTS
346 part-time. Students come from 4 states and territories; 1 other country; 2% are from out of state; 11% Black or African American, non-Hispanic/Latino; 5% Hispanic/Latino; 0.9% Asian, non-Hispanic/Latino; 0.3% Native Hawaiian or other Pacific Islander, non-Hispanic/Latino; 0.3% American Indian or Alaska Native, non-Hispanic/Latino; 0.3% Two or more races, non-Hispanic/Latino; 0.3% international; 12% transferred in.

FACULTY
Total: 57, 5% with terminal degrees.

Student/faculty ratio: 7:1.

ACADEMICS
Degrees: diplomas, associate, bachelor's, and master's.

Special study options: academic remediation for entering students, accelerated degree program, adult/continuing education programs, advanced placement credit, distance learning, double majors, external degree program, independent study, internships, off-campus study, part-time degree program, services for LD students, summer session for credit.

Computers: 200 computers/terminals and 200 ports are available on campus for general student use. Students can access the following: campus intranet, computer help desk, free student e-mail accounts, online (class) grades, online (class) registration, online (class) schedules, file space, personal web page, financial aid, student billing. Campuswide network is available. 100% of college-owned or -operated housing units are wired for high-speed Internet access. Wireless service is available via classrooms, computer centers, computer labs, learning centers, libraries, student centers.

STUDENT LIFE
Campus security: 24-hour emergency response devices and patrols, student patrols, controlled dormitory access, self-defense workshops, crime prevention program.

COSTS
Costs (2015–16) ***Tuition:*** $525 per credit hour part-time. Full-time tuition and fees vary according to course load. Part-time tuition and fees vary according to course load. ***Payment plans:*** installment, deferred payment.

APPLYING
Options: electronic application, deferred entrance.

Required: essay or personal statement.

Application deadlines: rolling (freshmen), rolling (out-of-state freshmen), rolling (transfers).

CONTACT
Barbara A Randazzo, Assistant Dean of Enrollment Management, Elizabethtown College School of Continuing and Professional Studies, One Alpha Drive, Elizabethtown College, PA 17022. *Phone:* 717-361-3750. *Toll-free phone:* 800-877-2694. *Fax:* 717-361-1466. *E-mail:* randazzob@etown.edu.

Franklin & Marshall College
Lancaster, Pennsylvania
http://www.fandm.edu/

- **Independent** 4-year, founded 1787
- **Suburban** 209-acre campus with easy access to Philadelphia
- **Endowment** $379.0 million
- **Coed** 2,209 undergraduate students, 98% full-time, 51% women, 49% men
- **Very difficult** entrance level, 39% of applicants were admitted

UNDERGRAD STUDENTS
2,174 full-time, 35 part-time. Students come from 42 states and territories; 51 other countries; 76% are from out of state; 6% Black or African American, non-Hispanic/Latino; 8% Hispanic/Latino; 5% Asian, non-Hispanic/Latino; 0.1% American Indian or Alaska Native, non-Hispanic/Latino; 2% Two or more races, non-Hispanic/Latino; 6% Race/ethnicity unknown; 14% international; 1% transferred in; 99% live on campus.

Freshmen
Admission: 5,472 applied, 2,130 admitted, 592 enrolled. ***Average high school GPA:*** 3.8. ***Test scores:*** SAT critical reading scores over 500: 99%; SAT math scores over 500: 100%; ACT scores over 18: 100%; SAT critical reading scores over 600: 75%; SAT math scores over 600: 92%; ACT scores over 24: 98%; SAT critical reading scores over 700: 17%; SAT math scores over 700: 33%; ACT scores over 30: 39%.
Retention: 91% of full-time freshmen returned.

FACULTY
Total: 276, 82% full-time, 88% with terminal degrees.

Student/faculty ratio: 9:1.

ACADEMICS
Calendar: semesters. *Degree:* bachelor's.

Special study options: accelerated degree program, advanced placement credit, double majors, independent study, internships, off-campus study, services for LD students, student-designed majors, study abroad, summer session for credit. ***ROTC:*** Army (c).

Unusual degree programs: 3-2 engineering with Rensselaer Polytechnic Institute, Washington University in St. Louis, Columbia University, Case Western Reserve University, Penn State University College of Engineering; forestry with Duke University; environmental studies with Duke University.

Computers: 125 computers/terminals are available on campus for general student use. Students can access the following: campus intranet, computer help desk, free student e-mail accounts, online (class) grades, online (class) registration, online (class) schedules, online degree audit, unofficial transcripts, course material. Campuswide network is available. 100% of college-owned or -operated housing units are wired for high-speed Internet access. Wireless service is available via entire campus.

STUDENT LIFE
Housing options: on-campus residence required through senior year; coed, special housing for students with disabilities. Campus housing is university owned and is provided by a third party. Freshman campus housing is guaranteed.

Activities and organizations: drama/theater group, student-run newspaper, radio station, choral group, Intervarsity, Hillel, Mi Gente Latina, Cia Bella, F&M Players, national fraternities, national sororities.

Athletics Member NCAA. All Division III except wrestling (Division I). ***Intercollegiate sports:*** baseball M, basketball M/W, crew M(c)/W, cross-country running M/W, equestrian sports W(c), field hockey W, football M, golf M/W, ice hockey M(c), lacrosse M/W, rugby M(c)/W(c), soccer M/W, softball W, squash M/W, swimming and diving M/W, tennis M/W, track and field M/W, ultimate Frisbee M(c)/W(c), volleyball M(c)/W, wrestling M. ***Intramural sports:*** basketball M/W, football M, soccer M/W, softball M/W, squash M/W, tennis M/W, volleyball M/W, wrestling M.

Campus security: 24-hour emergency response devices and patrols, late-night transport/escort service, controlled dormitory access, residence hall security, campus security connected to city police and fire company.

Student services: health clinic, personal/psychological counseling, women's center.

COSTS & FINANCIAL AID

Costs (2014–15) ***One-time required fee:*** $200. ***Comprehensive fee:*** $60,799 includes full-time tuition ($48,414), mandatory fees ($100), and room and board ($12,285). Part-time tuition: $6052 per course. Part-time tuition and fees vary according to course load. ***College room only:*** $7330. Room and board charges vary according to board plan and housing facility. ***Payment plans:*** installment, deferred payment. ***Waivers:*** employees or children of employees.

Financial Aid Of all full-time matriculated undergraduates who enrolled in 2014, 1,371 applied for aid, 1,198 were judged to have need, 1,198 had their need fully met. In 2014, 32 non-need-based awards were made. ***Average percent of need met:*** 100. ***Average financial aid package:*** $43,852. ***Average need-based loan:*** $4253. ***Average need-based gift aid:*** $39,564. ***Average non-need-based aid:*** $12,636. ***Average indebtedness upon graduation:*** $27,474. ***Financial aid deadline:*** 2/15.

APPLYING

Options: electronic application, early admission, early decision, deferred entrance.

Application fee: $60.

Required: essay or personal statement, high school transcript, 2 letters of recommendation, Common Application Supplement. ***Required for some:*** interview.

Application deadlines: 1/15 (freshmen), 1/15 (out-of-state freshmen), 5/15 (transfers).

Early decision deadline: 11/15 (for plan 1), 1/15 (for plan 2).

Notification: 4/1 (freshmen), 4/1 (out-of-state freshmen), 12/15 (early decision plan 1), 2/15 (early decision plan 2).

CONTACT

Julie Kerich, Director of Admissions, Franklin & Marshall College, PO Box 3003, Lancaster, PA 17604-3003. *Phone:* 717-358-47433. *Toll-free phone:* 877-678-9111. *Fax:* 717-291-4389. *E-mail:* julie.kerich@fandm.edu.

★ Gannon University

Erie, Pennsylvania

http://www.gannon.edu/

- **Independent Roman Catholic** university, founded 1925
- **Urban** 37-acre campus with easy access to Cleveland, Buffalo, Pittsburgh
- **Endowment** $56.1 million
- **Coed** 3,205 undergraduate students, 81% full-time, 57% women, 43% men
- **Moderately difficult** entrance level, 78% of applicants were admitted

UNDERGRAD STUDENTS

2,593 full-time, 612 part-time. Students come from 39 states and territories; 27 other countries; 27% are from out of state; 5% Black or African American, non-Hispanic/Latino; 3% Hispanic/Latino; 2% Asian, non-Hispanic/Latino; 0.3% Native Hawaiian or other Pacific Islander, non-Hispanic/Latino; 0.3% American Indian or Alaska Native, non-Hispanic/Latino; 2% Two or more races, non-Hispanic/Latino; 2% Race/ethnicity unknown; 8% international; 4% transferred in; 43% live on campus.

Freshmen

Admission: 4,097 applied, 3,182 admitted, 595 enrolled. ***Average high school GPA:*** 3.52. ***Test scores:*** SAT critical reading scores over 500: 58%; SAT math scores over 500: 65%; SAT writing scores over 500: 49%; ACT scores over 18: 93%; SAT critical reading scores over 600: 13%; SAT math scores over 600: 17%; SAT writing scores over 600: 11%; ACT scores over 24: 37%; SAT math scores over 700: 2%; ACT scores over 30: 5%.

Retention: 83% of full-time freshmen returned.

FACULTY

Total: 377, 55% full-time, 54% with terminal degrees.

Student/faculty ratio: 14:1.

ACADEMICS
Calendar: semesters plus 2 summer sessions. *Degrees:* certificates, associate, bachelor's, master's, doctoral, post-master's, and postbachelor's certificates.

Special study options: academic remediation for entering students, accelerated degree program, adult/continuing education programs, advanced placement credit, cooperative education, distance learning, double majors, English as a second language, honors programs, independent study, internships, off-campus study, part-time degree program, services for LD students, study abroad, summer session for credit. ***ROTC:*** Army (b).

Unusual degree programs: 3-2 business administration; engineering with University of Pittsburgh (Chemical Engineering); occupational therapy, physician assistant.

Computers: 386 computers/terminals and 1,425 ports are available on campus for general student use. Students can access the following: campus intranet, computer help desk, free student e-mail accounts, online (class) grades, online (class) registration, online (class) schedules. Campuswide network is available. 100% of college-owned or -operated housing units are wired for high-speed Internet access. Wireless service is available via entire campus.

STUDENT LIFE
Housing options: on-campus residence required through sophomore year; coed, special housing for students with disabilities. Campus housing is university owned and leased by the school. Freshman campus housing is guaranteed.

Activities and organizations: drama/theater group, student-run newspaper, radio station, choral group, Phi Eta Sigma, GU Society of Physician Assistant Students, GU Habitat for Humanity, Activities Programming Board, Student Occupational Therapy Association, national fraternities, national sororities.

Athletics Member NCAA. All Division II. ***Intercollegiate sports:*** baseball M(s), basketball M(s)/W(s), cheerleading W(s)(c), cross-country running M(s)/W(s), football M(s), golf M(s)/W(s), gymnastics W(s)(c), ice hockey M(c), lacrosse W(s), rugby M(c), soccer M(s)/W(s), softball W(s), swimming and diving M(s)/W(s), volleyball W(s), water polo M(s)/W(s), wrestling M(s). ***Intramural sports:*** badminton M/W, basketball M/W, football M/W, racquetball M/W, soccer M/W, ultimate Frisbee M/W, volleyball M/W.

Campus security: 24-hour emergency response devices and patrols, late-night transport/escort service, controlled dormitory access, security cameras.

Student services: health clinic, personal/psychological counseling.

COSTS & FINANCIAL AID
Costs (2014–15) ***Comprehensive fee:*** $39,608 includes full-time tuition ($27,760), mandatory fees ($608), and room and board ($11,240). Full-time tuition and fees vary according to class time, course load, degree level, and program. Part-time tuition: $670 per credit hour. Part-time tuition and fees vary according to class time, course load, degree level, and program. ***Required fees:*** $18 per credit hour part-time. ***College room only:*** $5890. Room and board charges vary according to board plan and housing facility. ***Payment plans:*** installment, deferred payment. ***Waivers:*** senior citizens and employees or children of employees.

Financial Aid Of all full-time matriculated undergraduates who enrolled in 2014, 2,232 applied for aid, 2,033 were judged to have need, 427 had their need fully met. 507 Federal Work-Study jobs (averaging $2300). 169 state and other part-time jobs (averaging $2300). In 2014, 395 non-need-based awards were made. ***Average percent of need met:*** 76. ***Average financial aid package:*** $23,719. ***Average need-based loan:*** $4293. ***Average need-based gift aid:*** $19,545. ***Average non-need-based aid:*** $12,212.

APPLYING
Standardized Tests *Required:* SAT or ACT (for admission).

Options: electronic application, deferred entrance.

Application fee: $25.

Required: high school transcript, minimum 2.0 GPA, counselor's recommendation. ***Required for some:*** minimum 3.0 GPA, 3 letters of recommendation, interview. ***Recommended:*** essay or personal statement.

Application deadlines: rolling (freshmen), rolling (out-of-state freshmen), rolling (transfers).

Notification: continuous (freshmen), continuous (out-of-state freshmen), continuous (transfers).

CONTACT
Office of Admissions, Gannon University, 109 University Square, Erie, PA 16541. *Phone:* 814-871-7240. *Toll-free phone:* 800-GANNONU. *Fax:* 814-871-5803. *E-mail:* admissions@gannon.edu.

See previous page for display ad and page 1454 for the College Close-Up.

Geneva College

Beaver Falls, Pennsylvania

http://www.geneva.edu/

- **Independent** comprehensive, founded 1848, affiliated with Reformed Presbyterian Church of North America
- **Small-town** 55-acre campus with easy access to Pittsburgh
- **Endowment** $38.1 million
- **Coed** 1,267 undergraduate students, 98% full-time, 48% women, 52% men
- **Moderately difficult** entrance level, 71% of applicants were admitted

UNDERGRAD STUDENTS
1,247 full-time, 20 part-time. Students come from 36 states and territories; 10 other countries; 29% are from out of state; 3% Black or African American, non-Hispanic/Latino; 0.8% Hispanic/Latino; 0.6% Asian, non-Hispanic/Latino; 0.1% American Indian or Alaska Native, non-Hispanic/Latino; 3% Two or more races, non-Hispanic/Latino; 0.4% Race/ethnicity unknown; 0.9% international; 4% transferred in; 72% live on campus.

Freshmen
Admission: 1,537 applied, 1,091 admitted, 311 enrolled. ***Average high school GPA:*** 3.58. ***Test scores:*** SAT critical reading scores over 500: 68%; SAT math scores over 500: 63%; SAT writing scores over 500: 57%; ACT scores over 18: 90%; SAT critical reading scores over 600: 26%; SAT math scores over 600: 25%; SAT writing scores over 600: 20%; ACT scores over 24: 47%; SAT critical reading scores over 700: 6%; SAT math scores over 700: 3%; SAT writing scores over 700: 6%; ACT scores over 30: 9%.

Retention: 84% of full-time freshmen returned.

FACULTY
Total: 191, 42% full-time, 38% with terminal degrees.

Student/faculty ratio: 11:1.

ACADEMICS
Calendar: semesters. *Degrees:* associate, bachelor's, and master's (also offers non-traditional programs in Philadelphia and western Pennsylvania with significant enrollment not reflected in profile).

Special study options: academic remediation for entering students, accelerated degree program, adult/continuing education programs, advanced placement credit, cooperative education, double majors, English as a second language, honors programs, independent study, internships, off-campus study, part-time degree program, services for LD students, student-designed majors, study abroad, summer session for credit. ***ROTC:*** Army (c).

Unusual degree programs: 3-2 nursing with Roberts Wesleyan College; Master's of Divinity with Reformed Presbyterian Theological Seminary.

Computers: 150 computers/terminals and 400 ports are available on campus for general student use. Students can access the following: campus intranet, computer help desk, free student e-mail accounts, online (class) grades, online (class) registration, online (class) schedules. Campuswide network is available. 100% of college-owned or -operated housing units are wired for high-speed Internet access. Wireless service is available via entire campus.

STUDENT LIFE
Housing options: on-campus residence required through senior year; men-only, women-only. Campus housing is university owned. Freshman campus housing is guaranteed.

Activities and organizations: drama/theater group, student-run newspaper, choral group, marching band, marching band, Genevans Choir, Intramural sports, ministry groups, discipleship groups.

Athletics Member NCAA, NCCAA. All NCAA Division III. ***Intercollegiate sports:*** baseball M, basketball M/W, cross-country running M/W, football M, golf M/W, soccer M/W, softball W, tennis M/W, track and field M/W, volleyball M(c)/W. ***Intramural sports:*** basketball M/W, cheerleading W(c), football M/W, ice hockey M(c), racquetball M/W, rugby M(c)/W(c), skiing (downhill) M(c)/W(c), soccer M/W, softball M/W, table tennis M/W, ultimate Frisbee M/W, volleyball M/W.

Campus security: 24-hour emergency response devices and patrols, late-night transport/escort service, controlled dormitory access.

Student services: health clinic, personal/psychological counseling.

COSTS & FINANCIAL AID

Costs (2015–16) ***Comprehensive fee:*** $35,080 includes full-time tuition ($25,450) and room and board ($9630). Full-time tuition and fees vary according to course load. Part-time tuition: $860 per credit. Part-time tuition and fees vary according to course load. ***Room and board:*** Room and board charges vary according to board plan. ***Payment plan:*** installment. ***Waivers:*** employees or children of employees.

Financial Aid Of all full-time matriculated undergraduates who enrolled in 2014, 1,123 applied for aid, 1,021 were judged to have need, 195 had their need fully met. 250 Federal Work-Study jobs (averaging $2000). In 2014, 181 non-need-based awards were made. ***Average percent of need met:*** 77. ***Average financial aid package:*** $20,159. ***Average need-based loan:*** $4108. ***Average need-based gift aid:*** $15,958. ***Average non-need-based aid:*** $9952. ***Average indebtedness upon graduation:*** $32,673.

APPLYING

Standardized Tests *Required:* SAT or ACT (for admission).

Options: electronic application, early admission, deferred entrance.

Application fee: $40.

Required: essay or personal statement, high school transcript, minimum 2.0 GPA. ***Required for some:*** interview, Engineering students should have 1 unit of chemistry and physics and 4 units of college-prep mathematics, including trigonometry and precalculus. ***Recommended:*** minimum 3.0 GPA, 2 letters of recommendation, interview.

Application deadlines: rolling (freshmen), rolling (out-of-state freshmen), rolling (transfers).

Notification: continuous (freshmen), continuous (out-of-state freshmen), continuous (transfers).

CONTACT

Mr. David Layton, Associate Vice President for Enrollment, Geneva College, 3200 College Avenue, Beaver Falls, PA 15010-3599. *Phone:* 724-847-6500. *Toll-free phone:* 800-847-8255. *E-mail:* admissions@geneva.edu.

Gettysburg College

Gettysburg, Pennsylvania

http://www.gettysburg.edu/

- **Independent** 4-year, founded 1832, affiliated with Evangelical Lutheran Church in America
- **Suburban** 200-acre campus with easy access to Baltimore and Washington, DC
- **Endowment** $261.6 million
- **Coed** 2,451 undergraduate students, 99% full-time, 52% women, 48% men
- **Most difficult** entrance level, 45% of applicants were admitted

UNDERGRAD STUDENTS

2,429 full-time, 22 part-time. Students come from 37 states and territories; 28 other countries; 73% are from out of state; 4% Black or African American, non-Hispanic/Latino; 5% Hispanic/Latino; 2% Asian, non-Hispanic/Latino; 3% Two or more races, non-Hispanic/Latino; 3% Race/ethnicity unknown; 4% international; 0.7% transferred in; 93% live on campus.

Freshmen

Admission: 4,915 applied, 2,233 admitted, 720 enrolled. ***Test scores:*** SAT critical reading scores over 500: 100%; SAT math scores over 500: 100%; SAT critical reading scores over 600: 77%; SAT math scores over 600: 84%; SAT critical reading scores over 700: 14%; SAT math scores over 700: 16%.

Retention: 89% of full-time freshmen returned.

FACULTY

Total: 312, 72% full-time, 83% with terminal degrees.

Student/faculty ratio: 10:1.

ACADEMICS

Calendar: semesters. *Degree:* bachelor's.

Special study options: adult/continuing education programs, advanced placement credit, double majors, independent study, internships, off-campus study, student-designed majors, study abroad. ***ROTC:*** Army (c).

Unusual degree programs: 3-2 engineering with Rensselaer Polytechnic Institute, Washington University, Columbia University; forestry with Duke University; nursing with Johns Hopkins University; optometry with State University of New York College of Optometry, Pennsylvania College of Optometry; physical therapy at Drexel University.

Computers: 320 computers/terminals are available on campus for general student use. Students can access the following: campus intranet, computer help desk, free student e-mail accounts, online (class) grades, online (class) registration, online (class) schedules. Campuswide network is available. 100% of college-owned or -operated housing units are wired for high-speed Internet access. Wireless service is available via entire campus.

STUDENT LIFE

Housing options: on-campus residence required through senior year; coed, men-only, women-only. Campus housing is university owned. Freshman campus housing is guaranteed.

Activities and organizations: drama/theater group, student-run newspaper, radio and television station, choral group, marching band, community service, music, athletics, student government, national fraternities, national sororities.

Athletics Member NCAA. All Division III. ***Intercollegiate sports:*** baseball M, basketball M/W, cheerleading M/W, cross-country running M/W, equestrian sports M(c)/W(c), field hockey W, football M, golf M/W, ice hockey M(c), lacrosse M/W, rugby M(c)/W(c), soccer M/W, softball W, swimming and diving M/W, tennis M/W, track and field M/W, ultimate Frisbee M(c)/W(c), volleyball W, wrestling M. ***Intramural sports:*** basketball M/W, fencing M(c)/W(c), football M/W, soccer M/W, softball M/W, volleyball M/W, water polo M/W.

Campus security: 24-hour emergency response devices and patrols, late-night transport/escort service, controlled dormitory access.

Student services: health clinic, personal/psychological counseling, women's center.

COSTS & FINANCIAL AID

Costs (2014–15) ***Comprehensive fee:*** $58,820 includes full-time tuition ($47,480) and room and board ($11,340). ***Room and board:*** Room and board charges vary according to board plan and housing facility. ***Payment plan:*** installment. ***Waivers:*** employees or children of employees.

Financial Aid Of all full-time matriculated undergraduates who enrolled in 2014, 1,721 applied for aid, 1,484 were judged to have need, 1,300 had their need fully met. 300 Federal Work-Study jobs (averaging $264,038). 935 state and other part-time jobs (averaging $1.2 million). In 2014, 418 non-need-based awards were made. ***Average percent of need met:*** 90. ***Average financial aid package:*** $37,087. ***Average need-based loan:*** $5019. ***Average need-based gift aid:*** $32,458. ***Average non-need-based aid:*** $12,401. ***Average indebtedness upon graduation:*** $27,714. ***Financial aid deadline:*** 2/1.

APPLYING

Standardized Tests *Required:* SAT or ACT (for admission). *Recommended:* SAT Subject Tests (for admission).

Options: electronic application, early admission, early decision, deferred entrance.

Application fee: $60.

Required: essay or personal statement, high school transcript, 2 letters of recommendation. ***Recommended:*** minimum 3.0 GPA, interview, extracurricular activities.

Application deadlines: 1/15 (freshmen), 11/1 (transfers).

Early decision deadline: 11/15 (for plan 1), 1/15 (for plan 2).

Notification: 4/1 (freshmen), continuous (transfers), 12/15 (early decision plan 1), 2/15 (early decision plan 2).

CONTACT
Ms. Gail Sweezey, Director of Admissions, Gettysburg College, 300 North Washington Street, Gettysburg, PA 17325. *Phone:* 717-337-6100. *Toll-free phone:* 800-431-0803. *Fax:* 717-337-6145. *E-mail:* admiss@gettysburg.edu.

★ Grove City College
Grove City, Pennsylvania
http://www.gcc.edu/

- **Independent Presbyterian** 4-year, founded 1876
- **Small-town** 180-acre campus with easy access to Pittsburgh
- **Endowment** $111.6 million
- **Coed** 2,509 undergraduate students, 98% full-time, 51% women, 49% men
- **Moderately difficult** entrance level, 88% of applicants were admitted

UNDERGRAD STUDENTS
2,465 full-time, 44 part-time. Students come from 41 states and territories; 11 other countries; 49% are from out of state; 0.7% Black or African American, non-Hispanic/Latino; 1% Hispanic/Latino; 2% Asian, non-Hispanic/Latino; 0.2% American Indian or Alaska Native, non-Hispanic/Latino; 2% Two or more races, non-Hispanic/Latino; 0.7% international; 2% transferred in; 95% live on campus.

Freshmen
Admission: 1,492 applied, 1,306 admitted, 637 enrolled. ***Average high school GPA:*** 3.73. ***Test scores:*** SAT critical reading scores over 500: 90%; SAT math scores over 500: 91%; ACT scores over 18: 99%; SAT critical reading scores over 600: 51%; SAT math scores over 600: 53%; ACT scores over 24: 78%; SAT critical reading scores over 700: 14%; SAT math scores over 700: 12%; ACT scores over 30: 24%.
Retention: 91% of full-time freshmen returned.

FACULTY
Total: 215, 70% full-time, 63% with terminal degrees.
Student/faculty ratio: 14:1.

ACADEMICS
Calendar: semesters. *Degree:* bachelor's.
Special study options: accelerated degree program, advanced placement credit, distance learning, double majors, independent study, internships, off-campus study, services for LD students, study abroad, summer session for credit.
Computers: 50 computers/terminals and 8,000 ports are available on campus for general student use. Students can access the following: campus intranet, computer help desk, free student e-mail accounts, online (class) grades, online (class) registration, online (class) schedules. Campuswide network is available. 100% of college-owned or -operated housing units are wired for high-speed Internet access. Wireless service is available via entire campus.

STUDENT LIFE
Housing options: on-campus residence required through senior year; men-only, women-only. Campus housing is university owned. Freshman campus housing is guaranteed.
Activities and organizations: drama/theater group, student-run newspaper, radio and television station, choral group, marching band, Warriors for Christ, Orchesis, Orientation Board, Accounting Society, Association for Women Students (AWS).
Athletics Member NCAA. All Division III. ***Intercollegiate sports:*** baseball M, basketball M/W, cross-country running M/W, fencing M(c)/W(c), football M, golf M/W, lacrosse M(c)/W(c), rugby M(c)/W(c), soccer M/W, softball W, swimming and diving M/W, tennis M/W, track and field M/W, ultimate Frisbee W(c), volleyball M(c)/W, water polo M(c)/W. ***Intramural sports:*** badminton M/W, basketball M/W, bowling M/W, football M/W, racquetball M/W, soccer M/W, softball M, table tennis M/W, tennis M/W, ultimate Frisbee M/W, volleyball M/W.
Campus security: 24-hour emergency response devices and patrols, student patrols, late-night transport/escort service, controlled dormitory access, security cameras located around campus and in parking lots.
Student services: health clinic, personal/psychological counseling.

COSTS & FINANCIAL AID
Costs (2014–15) ***Comprehensive fee:*** $24,022 includes full-time tuition ($15,550) and room and board ($8472). Part-time tuition: $486 per credit

hour. ***Room and board:*** Room and board charges vary according to housing facility. ***Waivers:*** employees or children of employees.

Financial Aid Of all full-time matriculated undergraduates who enrolled in 2014, 1,304 applied for aid, 1,070 were judged to have need, 91 had their need fully met. In 2014, 395 non-need-based awards were made. ***Average percent of need met:*** 49. ***Average financial aid package:*** $6777. ***Average need-based gift aid:*** $6777. ***Average non-need-based aid:*** $1926. ***Average indebtedness upon graduation:*** $31,634. ***Financial aid deadline:*** 4/15.

APPLYING

Standardized Tests *Required:* SAT or ACT (for admission).

Options: electronic application, early admission, early decision, deferred entrance.

Application fee: $50.

Required: essay or personal statement, high school transcript, 2 letters of recommendation. ***Recommended:*** interview.

Application deadlines: 2/1 (freshmen), 8/15 (transfers), 12/1 (early action).

Early decision deadline: 11/1.

Notification: 3/15 (freshmen), continuous (transfers), 12/15 (early decision), 1/15 (early action).

CONTACT

Sarah E. Gibbs, Director of Admissions, Grove City College, 100 Campus Drive, Grove City, PA 16127-2104. *Phone:* 724-458-2100. *Fax:* 724-458-3395. *E-mail:* admissions@gcc.edu.

See previous page for display ad and page 1464 for the College Close-Up.

★ Gwynedd Mercy University

Gwynedd Valley, Pennsylvania

http://www.gmercyu.edu/

- **Independent Roman Catholic** comprehensive, founded 1948
- **Suburban** 170-acre campus with easy access to Philadelphia
- **Endowment** $21.0 million
- **Coed** 1,983 undergraduate students, 91% full-time, 75% women, 25% men
- **Moderately difficult** entrance level, 76% of applicants were admitted

UNDERGRAD STUDENTS

1,808 full-time, 175 part-time. Students come from 29 states and territories; 42 other countries; 10% are from out of state; 24% Black or African American, non-Hispanic/Latino; 5% Hispanic/Latino; 4% Asian, non-Hispanic/Latino; 0.5% American Indian or Alaska Native, non-Hispanic/Latino; 8% Race/ethnicity unknown; 0.2% international; 10% transferred in; 31% live on campus.

Freshmen

Admission: 1,016 applied, 776 admitted, 206 enrolled. ***Test scores:*** SAT critical reading scores over 500: 34%; SAT math scores over 500: 44%; SAT writing scores over 500: 36%; ACT scores over 18: 87%; SAT critical reading scores over 600: 6%; SAT math scores over 600: 8%; SAT writing scores over 600: 6%; ACT scores over 24: 26%; SAT math scores over 700: 1%; ACT scores over 30: 6%.

Retention: 73% of full-time freshmen returned.

FACULTY

Total: 316, 22% full-time, 28% with terminal degrees.

Student/faculty ratio: 13:1.

ACADEMICS

Calendar: semesters. *Degrees:* certificates, associate, bachelor's, master's, doctoral, post-master's, and postbachelor's certificates.

Special study options: academic remediation for entering students, accelerated degree program, adult/continuing education programs, advanced placement credit, cooperative education, double majors, English as a second language, freshman honors college, honors programs,

independent study, internships, part-time degree program, summer session for credit.

Computers: 218 computers/terminals are available on campus for general student use. Students can access the following: campus intranet, computer help desk, free student e-mail accounts, online (class) grades, online (class) registration, online (class) schedules. Campuswide network is available. 100% of college-owned or -operated housing units are wired for high-speed Internet access. Wireless service is available via classrooms, computer labs, libraries, student centers.

STUDENT LIFE
Housing options: coed, special housing for students with disabilities. Campus housing is university owned. Freshman applicants given priority for college housing.

Activities and organizations: student-run newspaper, choral group, Voices of Gwynedd, Athletic Association, student government, Program Board, Peer Mentors.

Athletics Member NCAA. All Division III. ***Intercollegiate sports:*** baseball M, basketball M/W, cheerleading W, cross-country running M/W, field hockey W, golf M, lacrosse M/W, soccer M/W, softball W, tennis M/W, track and field M/W, volleyball W.

Campus security: 24-hour emergency response devices and patrols, late-night transport/escort service.

Student services: health clinic, personal/psychological counseling.

COSTS & FINANCIAL AID
Costs (2015–16) ***Comprehensive fee:*** $42,370 includes full-time tuition ($30,760), mandatory fees ($600), and room and board ($11,010). Full-time tuition and fees vary according to program. Part-time tuition: $675 per contact hour. Part-time tuition and fees vary according to program. ***College room only:*** $5360. Room and board charges vary according to board plan and housing facility. ***Payment plan:*** installment. ***Waivers:*** employees or children of employees.

Financial Aid Of all full-time matriculated undergraduates who enrolled in 2014, 1,269 applied for aid, 1,096 were judged to have need, 157 had their need fully met. In 2014, 167 non-need-based awards were made. ***Average percent of need met:*** 68. ***Average financial aid package:*** $21,574. ***Average need-based loan:*** $4209. ***Average need-based gift aid:*** $17,863. ***Average non-need-based aid:*** $11,140. ***Average indebtedness upon graduation:*** $37,860. ***Financial aid deadline:*** 5/1.

APPLYING
Standardized Tests *Required:* SAT or ACT (for admission).

Options: electronic application, deferred entrance.

Application fee: $25.

Required: high school transcript. ***Required for some:*** essay or personal statement, interview.

Application deadlines: rolling (freshmen), rolling (out-of-state freshmen), 8/20 (transfers).

Notification: continuous (freshmen), continuous (out-of-state freshmen), continuous (transfers).

CONTACT
Ms. Michelle Diehl, Director of Admissions, Gwynedd Mercy University, 1325 Sumneytown Pike, Gwynedd Valley, PA 19437-0901. *Phone:* 215-646-7300. *Toll-free phone:* 800-DIAL-GMC. *Fax:* 215-641-5556. *E-mail:* admissions@gmercyu.edu.

See previous page for display ad and page 1466 for the College Close-Up.

Harrisburg University of Science and Technology
Harrisburg, Pennsylvania
http://www.HarrisburgU.edu/

- **Independent** comprehensive, founded 2005
- **Urban** campus
- **Coed**
- **Minimally difficult** entrance level

FACULTY
Student/faculty ratio: 12:1.

ACADEMICS
Calendar: semesters. *Degrees:* bachelor's and master's.

STUDENT LIFE
Housing options: on-campus residence required for freshman year; coed. Campus housing is provided by a third party. Freshman campus housing is guaranteed.

Campus security: 24-hour emergency response devices and patrols, trained security personnel during all university operating hours.

Student services: personal/psychological counseling.

FINANCIAL AID
Financial Aid Of all full-time matriculated undergraduates who enrolled in 2012, 267 applied for aid, 251 were judged to have need, 13 had their need fully met. 16 Federal Work-Study jobs (averaging $1500). In 2012, 13 non-need-based awards were made. ***Average percent of need met:*** 57. ***Average financial aid package:*** $17,502. ***Average need-based loan:*** $5075. ***Average need-based gift aid:*** $13,330. ***Average non-need-based aid:*** $10,473. ***Average indebtedness upon graduation:*** $38,779.

APPLYING
Standardized Tests *Recommended:* SAT or ACT (for admission).

Options: electronic application.

Required: high school transcript. ***Recommended:*** essay or personal statement, interview.

CONTACT
Harrisburg University of Science and Technology, 326 Market Street, Harrisburg, PA 17101. *Phone:* 717-901-5101. *Toll-free phone:* 866-HBG-UNIV.

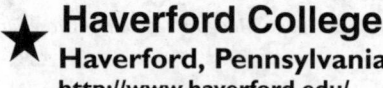

★ Haverford College
Haverford, Pennsylvania
http://www.haverford.edu/

- **Independent** 4-year, founded 1833
- **Suburban** 216-acre campus with easy access to Philadelphia
- **Endowment** $490.7 million
- **Coed** 1,194 undergraduate students, 100% full-time, 53% women, 47% men
- **Most difficult** entrance level, 25% of applicants were admitted

UNDERGRAD STUDENTS
1,189 full-time, 5 part-time. Students come from 42 states and territories; 35 other countries; 78% are from out of state; 6% Black or African American, non-Hispanic/Latino; 9% Hispanic/Latino; 9% Asian, non-Hispanic/Latino; 0.3% American Indian or Alaska Native, non-Hispanic/Latino; 6% Two or more races, non-Hispanic/Latino; 1% Race/ethnicity unknown; 6% international; 0.4% transferred in; 98% live on campus.

Freshmen
Admission: 3,496 applied, 863 admitted, 338 enrolled. ***Test scores:*** SAT critical reading scores over 500: 100%; SAT math scores over 500: 100%; SAT writing scores over 500: 100%; SAT critical reading scores over 600: 94%; SAT math scores over 600: 94%; SAT writing scores over 600: 95%; ACT scores over 24: 100%; SAT critical reading scores over 700: 57%; SAT math scores over 700: 54%; SAT writing scores over 700: 56%; ACT scores over 30: 87%.

Retention: 97% of full-time freshmen returned.

FACULTY
Total: 158, 82% full-time, 95% with terminal degrees.

Student/faculty ratio: 9:1.

ACADEMICS
Calendar: semesters. *Degree:* bachelor's.

Special study options: advanced placement credit, double majors, independent study, internships, off-campus study, services for LD students, student-designed majors, study abroad.

Unusual degree programs: 3-2 engineering with California Institute of Technology; City Planning, University of Pennsylvania.

Computers: 300 computers/terminals and 1,600 ports are available on campus for general student use. Students can access the following: campus intranet, computer help desk, free student e-mail accounts, online (class) grades, online (class) registration, online (class) schedules. Campuswide network is available. 100% of college-owned or -operated

housing units are wired for high-speed Internet access. Wireless service is available via entire campus.

STUDENT LIFE

Housing options: on-campus residence required for freshman year; coed, special housing for students with disabilities. Campus housing is university owned. Freshman campus housing is guaranteed.

Activities and organizations: drama/theater group, student-run newspaper, radio station, choral group, Volunteer Programs, Student government, Choral groups, Multicultural Groups, Orientation Team/Residential Life Leaders.

Athletics Member NCAA. All Division III. ***Intercollegiate sports:*** badminton W(c), baseball M, basketball M/W, crew M(c)/W(c), cross-country running M/W, fencing M/W, field hockey W, golf M(c)/W(c), lacrosse M/W, rugby M(c), soccer M/W, softball W, squash M/W, tennis M/W, track and field M/W, ultimate Frisbee M(c)/W(c), volleyball M(c)/W, wrestling M(c). ***Intramural sports:*** basketball M/W, ice hockey M(c)/W(c), sailing M(c)/W(c), soccer M/W, softball M/W, tennis M/W, volleyball W.

Campus security: 24-hour emergency response devices and patrols, late-night transport/escort service, controlled dormitory access.

Student services: health clinic, personal/psychological counseling, women's center.

COSTS & FINANCIAL AID

Costs (2015–16) ***One-time required fee:*** $230. ***Comprehensive fee:*** $63,986 includes full-time tuition ($48,656), mandatory fees ($442), and room and board ($14,888). ***College room only:*** $8494. ***Payment plans:*** tuition prepayment, installment. ***Waivers:*** employees or children of employees.

Financial Aid Of all full-time matriculated undergraduates who enrolled in 2014, 670 applied for aid, 599 were judged to have need, 599 had their need fully met. ***Average percent of need met:*** 100. ***Average financial aid package:*** $42,851. ***Average need-based loan:*** $844. ***Average need-based gift aid:*** $42,621. ***Average indebtedness upon graduation:*** $15,540.

APPLYING

Standardized Tests *Required:* SAT and SAT Subject Tests or ACT (for admission).

Options: electronic application, early admission, early decision, deferred entrance.

Application fee: $60.

Required: essay or personal statement, 2 letters of recommendation. ***Required for some:*** high school transcript. ***Recommended:*** interview.

Application deadlines: 1/15 (freshmen), 3/31 (transfers).

Early decision deadline: 11/15.

Notification: 4/1 (freshmen), 5/15 (transfers), 12/15 (early decision).

CONTACT

Mr. Jess Lord, Dean of Admissions and Financial Aid, Haverford College, 370 Lancaster Avenue, Haverford, PA 19041-1392. *Phone:* 610-896-1350. *Fax:* 610-896-1338. *E-mail:* admission@haverford.edu.

See below for display ad and page 1470 for the College Close-Up.

Holy Family University

Philadelphia, Pennsylvania

http://www.holyfamily.edu/

- **Independent Roman Catholic** comprehensive, founded 1954
- **Suburban** 47-acre campus with easy access to Philadelphia
- **Endowment** $15.3 million
- **Coed** 1,985 undergraduate students, 67% full-time, 73% women, 27% men
- **Minimally difficult** entrance level, 73% of applicants were admitted

UNDERGRAD STUDENTS

1,337 full-time, 648 part-time. Students come from 18 states and territories; 9 other countries; 14% are from out of state; 7% Black or African American, non-Hispanic/Latino; 6% Hispanic/Latino; 4% Asian, non-Hispanic/Latino; 0.1% Native Hawaiian or other Pacific Islander, non-Hispanic/Latino; 0.1% American Indian or Alaska Native, non-Hispanic/Latino; 24% Race/ethnicity unknown; 0.3% international; 8% transferred in; 13% live on campus.

Freshmen

Admission: 1,092 applied, 800 admitted, 252 enrolled. ***Average high school GPA:*** 3.12. ***Test scores:*** SAT critical reading scores over 500:

29%; SAT math scores over 500: 32%; SAT writing scores over 500: 27%; ACT scores over 18: 75%; SAT critical reading scores over 600: 2%; SAT math scores over 600: 6%; SAT writing scores over 600: 4%; ACT scores over 24: 17%.

Retention: 71% of full-time freshmen returned.

FACULTY

Total: 356, 21% full-time, 36% with terminal degrees.

Student/faculty ratio: 13:1.

ACADEMICS

Calendar: semesters. *Degrees:* certificates, associate, bachelor's, master's, doctoral, post-master's, and postbachelor's certificates.

Special study options: academic remediation for entering students, accelerated degree program, adult/continuing education programs, advanced placement credit, cooperative education, double majors, independent study, internships, part-time degree program, services for LD students, study abroad, summer session for credit. ***ROTC:*** Army (c).

Unusual degree programs: 3-2 Criminal Justice BA/MA Program; Psychology BA/Criminal Justice MA Program; Sociology BA/Criminal Justice Program; Business Administration BA/Human Resources Management or Information Systems Management MS.

Computers: 350 computers/terminals are available on campus for general student use. Students can access the following: campus intranet, computer help desk, free student e-mail accounts, online (class) grades, online (class) registration, online (class) schedules, online course syllabuses, online course evaluations. Campuswide network is available. 100% of college-owned or -operated housing units are wired for high-speed Internet access. Wireless service is available via entire campus.

STUDENT LIFE

Housing options: coed, special housing for students with disabilities. Campus housing is university owned. Freshman campus housing is guaranteed.

Activities and organizations: drama/theater group, student-run newspaper, television station, choral group, Students at Your Service (S.A.Y.S.), Student Government, Campus Ministry Team, Habitat for Humanity, Student Nurses Association of Holy Family.

Athletics Member NCAA. All Division II. ***Intercollegiate sports:*** basketball M(s)/W(s), cross-country running M(s)/W(s), lacrosse W(s), soccer M(s)/W(s), softball W(s), tennis W(s), track and field M(s)/W(s), volleyball W(s). ***Intramural sports:*** baseball M(c), basketball M/W, cheerleading M(c)/W(c), rugby M(c), volleyball M/W.

Campus security: 24-hour emergency response devices and patrols, late-night transport/escort service, controlled dormitory access, video surveillance.

Student services: health clinic, personal/psychological counseling.

COSTS & FINANCIAL AID

Costs (2015–16) ***Comprehensive fee:*** $42,744 includes full-time tuition ($28,198), mandatory fees ($970), and room and board ($13,576). Full-time tuition and fees vary according to class time, course level, course load, degree level, program, reciprocity agreements, and student level. Part-time tuition: $603 per credit hour. Part-time tuition and fees vary according to class time, course level, course load, degree level, program, reciprocity agreements, and student level. ***Required fees:*** $108 per term part-time. ***College room only:*** $7140. Room and board charges vary according to board plan and housing facility. ***Payment plans:*** installment, deferred payment. ***Waivers:*** senior citizens and employees or children of employees.

Financial Aid Of all full-time matriculated undergraduates who enrolled in 2014, 1,256 applied for aid, 1,170 were judged to have need, 202 had their need fully met. 332 Federal Work-Study jobs (averaging $1156). In 2014, 127 non-need-based awards were made. ***Average percent of need met:*** 71. ***Average financial aid package:*** $20,394. ***Average need-based loan:*** $4505. ***Average need-based gift aid:*** $15,358. ***Average non-need-based aid:*** $11,018. ***Average indebtedness upon graduation:*** $40,363.

APPLYING

Standardized Tests *Required:* SAT or ACT (for admission).

Options: electronic application, deferred entrance.

Application fee: $25.

Required: essay or personal statement, high school transcript, minimum 2.0 GPA, 2 letters of recommendation. ***Recommended:*** interview.

Application deadlines: rolling (freshmen), rolling (out-of-state freshmen), rolling (transfers).

Notification: continuous (freshmen), continuous (out-of-state freshmen), continuous (transfers).

CONTACT

Ms. Lauren Campbell, Director of Admissions, Holy Family University, 9801 Frankford Avenue, Philadelphia, PA 19114-2009. *Phone:* 215-637-3050. *Fax:* 215-281-1022. *E-mail:* admissions@holyfamily.edu.

Immaculata University

Immaculata, Pennsylvania

http://www.immaculata.edu/

- **Independent Roman Catholic** university, founded 1920
- **Suburban** 400-acre campus with easy access to Philadelphia
- **Coed** 2,138 undergraduate students, 52% full-time, 75% women, 25% men
- **Moderately difficult** entrance level, 76% of applicants were admitted

UNDERGRAD STUDENTS

1,107 full-time, 1,031 part-time. 26% are from out of state; 15% Black or African American, non-Hispanic/Latino; 5% Hispanic/Latino; 2% Asian, non-Hispanic/Latino; 0.1% Native Hawaiian or other Pacific Islander, non-Hispanic/Latino; 0.0% American Indian or Alaska Native, non-Hispanic/Latino; 2% Two or more races, non-Hispanic/Latino; 1% Race/ethnicity unknown; 0.7% international; 3% transferred in; 23% live on campus.

Freshmen

Admission: 1,729 applied, 1,313 admitted, 224 enrolled. ***Average high school GPA:*** 3.21. ***Test scores:*** SAT critical reading scores over 500: 43%; SAT math scores over 500: 43%; SAT writing scores over 500: 46%; ACT scores over 18: 75%; SAT critical reading scores over 600: 11%; SAT math scores over 600: 11%; SAT writing scores over 600: 13%; ACT scores over 24: 17%; SAT critical reading scores over 700: 3%; SAT math scores over 700: 1%; SAT writing scores over 700: 1%; ACT scores over 30: 2%.

Retention: 80% of full-time freshmen returned.

FACULTY

Total: 398, 25% full-time, 42% with terminal degrees.

Student/faculty ratio: 9:1.

ACADEMICS

Calendar: semesters. *Degrees:* certificates, associate, bachelor's, master's, and doctoral.

ROTC: Army (c).

Computers: Campuswide network is available.

STUDENT LIFE

Housing options: coed, men-only, women-only, special housing for students with disabilities. Campus housing is university owned. Freshman campus housing is guaranteed.

Athletics Member NCAA. All Division III. ***Intercollegiate sports:*** basketball W, cross-country running W, field hockey W, lacrosse W, soccer W, softball W, tennis W, volleyball W. ***Intramural sports:*** archery W, badminton W, cheerleading W(c), equestrian sports W(c), fencing W, swimming and diving W.

Campus security: 24-hour emergency response devices and patrols, late-night transport/escort service, controlled dormitory access.

COSTS & FINANCIAL AID

Costs (2014–15) ***Comprehensive fee:*** $44,880 includes full-time tuition ($32,000) and room and board ($12,880). Full-time tuition and fees vary according to student level. Part-time tuition: $510 per credit hour. No tuition increase for student's term of enrollment. Immaculata University has a fixed-rate tuition program. Students will pay this rate for the four years they are enrolled as undergraduates. ***College room only:*** $6890. Room and board charges vary according to board plan and housing facility. ***Payment plan:*** installment. ***Waivers:*** senior citizens and employees or children of employees.

Financial Aid Of all full-time matriculated undergraduates who enrolled in 2007, 810 applied for aid, 697 were judged to have need, 201 had their need fully met. ***Average percent of need met:*** 24. ***Average financial aid***

package: $15,657. ***Average need-based loan:*** $4132. ***Average need-based gift aid:*** $5516. ***Average non-need-based aid:*** $6508.

APPLYING

Standardized Tests *Required:* SAT or ACT (for admission).

Options: electronic application.

Required: high school transcript, minimum 2.0 GPA. ***Required for some:*** essay or personal statement. ***Recommended:*** minimum 3.0 GPA, interview.

CONTACT

Director of Admissions, Immaculata University, PO Box 642, Immaculata, PA 19345-0702. *Phone:* 610-647-4400 Ext. 3046. *Toll-free phone:* 877-428-6329. *Fax:* 610-640-0836. *E-mail:* admiss@immaculata.edu.

See below for display ad and page 1478 for the College Close-Up.

Indiana University of Pennsylvania

Indiana, Pennsylvania

http://www.iup.edu/

- **State-supported** university, founded 1875, part of Pennsylvania State System of Higher Education
- **Small-town** 374-acre campus with easy access to Pittsburgh
- **Endowment** $61.2 million
- **Coed** 12,130 undergraduate students, 93% full-time, 54% women, 46% men
- **Minimally difficult** entrance level, 95% of applicants were admitted

UNDERGRAD STUDENTS

11,288 full-time, 842 part-time. Students come from 30 states and territories; 41 other countries; 6% are from out of state; 11% Black or African American, non-Hispanic/Latino; 4% Hispanic/Latino; 1% Asian, non-Hispanic/Latino; 0.1% American Indian or Alaska Native, non-Hispanic/Latino; 3% Two or more races, non-Hispanic/Latino; 0.9% Race/ethnicity unknown; 3% international; 5% transferred in; 82% live on campus.

Freshmen

Admission: 8,754 applied, 8,293 admitted, 2,733 enrolled. ***Test scores:*** SAT critical reading scores over 500: 40%; SAT math scores over 500: 44%; SAT writing scores over 500: 31%; SAT critical reading scores over 600: 7%; SAT math scores over 600: 8%; SAT writing scores over 600: 5%; SAT critical reading scores over 700: 1%; SAT writing scores over 700: 1%.

Retention: 75% of full-time freshmen returned.

FACULTY

Total: 725, 85% full-time.

Student/faculty ratio: 17:1.

ACADEMICS

Calendar: semesters. *Degrees:* certificates, associate, bachelor's, master's, doctoral, post-master's, and postbachelor's certificates.

Special study options: academic remediation for entering students, accelerated degree program, adult/continuing education programs, advanced placement credit, cooperative education, distance learning, double majors, English as a second language, external degree program, freshman honors college, honors programs, independent study, internships, off-campus study, part-time degree program, services for LD students, study abroad, summer session for credit. ***ROTC:*** Army (b).

Unusual degree programs: 3-2 engineering with Drexel University, University of Pittsburgh; Chiropractic with Logan College of Chiropractic, New York Chiropractic College, Parker College, Sherman College of Straight Chiropractic; Dentistry with Temple University School of Dentistry; optometry with Pennsylvania College of Optometry.

Computers: 2,363 computers/terminals and 1,970 ports are available on campus for general student use. Students can access the following: computer help desk, free student e-mail accounts, online (class) grades, online (class) registration, online (class) schedules. Campuswide network is available. 100% of college-owned or -operated housing units are wired for high-speed Internet access. Wireless service is available via entire campus.

STUDENT LIFE

Housing options: on-campus residence required for freshman year; coed, women-only, special housing for students with disabilities. Campus

housing is university owned and is provided by a third party. Freshman campus housing is guaranteed.

Activities and organizations: drama/theater group, student-run newspaper, radio and television station, choral group, marching band, Student Government Association, Panhellenic Association, Interfraternity Council, The Entertainment Network, NAACP, national fraternities, national sororities.

Athletics Member NCAA. All Division II. ***Intercollegiate sports:*** baseball M(s), basketball M(s)/W(s), cross-country running M(s)/W(s), field hockey W(s), football M(s), golf M(s), lacrosse W(s), soccer W(s), softball W(s), swimming and diving M(s)/W(s), tennis W(s), track and field M(s)/W(s), volleyball W(s). ***Intramural sports:*** badminton M/W, baseball M(c), basketball M/W, equestrian sports M(c)/W(c), fencing M(c)/W(c), golf M(c)/W(c), ice hockey M(c)/W(c), lacrosse M(c)/W(c), riflery M(c)/W(c), rugby M(c)/W(c), sailing M(c)/W(c), soccer M/W, softball M/W, swimming and diving M(c)/W(c), table tennis M/W, tennis M(c)/W(c), ultimate Frisbee M(c)/W(c), volleyball M/W, wrestling M(c)/W(c).

Campus security: 24-hour emergency response devices and patrols, late-night transport/escort service, controlled dormitory access.

Student services: health clinic, personal/psychological counseling, legal services.

COSTS & FINANCIAL AID

Costs (2014–15) ***Tuition:*** state resident $6820 full-time, $284 per credit hour part-time; nonresident $17,050 full-time, $710 per credit hour part-time. Full-time tuition and fees vary according to course load and reciprocity agreements. Part-time tuition and fees vary according to course load and reciprocity agreements. ***Required fees:*** $2650 full-time, $63 per credit hour part-time, $230 per credit hour part-time. ***Room and board:*** $11,346; room only: $8290. Room and board charges vary according to board plan, housing facility, and location. ***Payment plans:*** installment, deferred payment. ***Waivers:*** senior citizens and employees or children of employees.

Financial Aid Of all full-time matriculated undergraduates who enrolled in 2013, 9,954 applied for aid, 8,291 were judged to have need, 553 had their need fully met. 930 Federal Work-Study jobs (averaging $1988). 1,663 state and other part-time jobs (averaging $2519). In 2013, 241 non-need-based awards were made. ***Average percent of need met:*** 56. ***Average financial aid package:*** $9270. ***Average need-based loan:*** $4233. ***Average need-based gift aid:*** $5913. ***Average non-need-based aid:*** $1787. ***Average indebtedness upon graduation:*** $33,807.

APPLYING

Standardized Tests *Required:* SAT or ACT (for admission). *Recommended:* SAT (for admission), ACT (for admission).

Options: electronic application, early admission, deferred entrance.

Application fee: $50.

Required: high school transcript. ***Recommended:*** essay or personal statement, 2 letters of recommendation.

Application deadlines: rolling (freshmen), rolling (transfers).

Notification: 9/1 (freshmen), continuous (transfers).

CONTACT

Office of Admissions, Indiana University of Pennsylvania, 1011 South Drive, Sutton Hall, Suite120, Indiana, PA 15705. *Phone:* 724-357-2230. *Toll-free phone:* 800-442-6830. *Fax:* 724-357-6281. *E-mail:* admissions-inquiry@iup.edu.

Juniata College

Huntingdon, Pennsylvania

http://www.juniata.edu/

- **Independent** comprehensive, founded 1876, affiliated with Church of the Brethren
- **Small-town** 110-acre campus
- **Endowment** $106.8 million
- **Coed** 1,615 undergraduate students, 96% full-time, 54% women, 46% men
- **Moderately difficult** entrance level, 74% of applicants were admitted

UNDERGRAD STUDENTS

1,547 full-time, 68 part-time. Students come from 38 states and territories; 34 other countries; 36% are from out of state; 3% Black or African American, non-Hispanic/Latino; 4% Hispanic/Latino; 3% Asian, non-Hispanic/Latino; 3% Two or more races, non-Hispanic/Latino; 6% Race/ethnicity unknown; 8% international; 1% transferred in; 82% live on campus.

Freshmen

Admission: 2,207 applied, 1,637 admitted, 423 enrolled. ***Average high school GPA:*** 3.72. ***Test scores:*** SAT critical reading scores over 500: 85%; SAT math scores over 500: 86%; SAT critical reading scores over 600: 41%; SAT math scores over 600: 38%; SAT critical reading scores over 700: 10%; SAT math scores over 700: 6%.

Retention: 88% of full-time freshmen returned.

FACULTY

Total: 149, 71% full-time, 79% with terminal degrees.

Student/faculty ratio: 13:1.

ACADEMICS

Calendar: semesters. *Degrees:* bachelor's and master's.

Special study options: advanced placement credit, double majors, English as a second language, honors programs, independent study, internships, off-campus study, part-time degree program, services for LD students, student-designed majors, study abroad, summer session for credit.

Unusual degree programs: 3-2 engineering with Columbia University, Penn State University, Washington University-St. Louis, Clarkson University; nursing with Case Western University, Johns Hopkins University.

Computers: 170 computers/terminals and 500 ports are available on campus for general student use. Students can access the following: computer help desk, free student e-mail accounts, online (class) grades, online (class) registration, online (class) schedules. Campuswide network is available. 100% of college-owned or -operated housing units are wired for high-speed Internet access. Wireless service is available via classrooms, computer centers, computer labs, dorm rooms, learning centers, libraries, student centers.

STUDENT LIFE

Housing options: on-campus residence required through senior year; coed, women-only. Campus housing is university owned. Freshman campus housing is guaranteed.

Activities and organizations: drama/theater group, student-run newspaper, radio station, choral group, Student Government Association, Juniata Activities Board (JAB), Habitat for Humanity, Colleges Against Cancer, National Society of Leadership and Success.

Athletics Member NCAA. All Division III. ***Intercollegiate sports:*** baseball M, basketball M/W, cross-country running M/W, equestrian sports M(c)/W(c), field hockey W, football M, lacrosse M(c), rugby M(c)/W(c), soccer M/W, softball W, swimming and diving W, tennis M/W, track and field M/W, ultimate Frisbee M(c)/W(c), volleyball M/W. ***Intramural sports:*** basketball M/W, bowling M/W, cheerleading W(c), field hockey M(c)/W(c), football M/W, lacrosse W(c), racquetball M(c)/W(c), skiing (downhill) M(c)/W(c), soccer M/W, swimming and diving M/W, table tennis M(c)/W(c), volleyball M(c)/W(c).

Campus security: 24-hour emergency response devices and patrols, student patrols, late-night transport/escort service, controlled dormitory access, fire safety training, adopt-an-officer program, security web site, weather/terror alerts, travel forecast, crime statistics.

Student services: health clinic, personal/psychological counseling, women's center.

COSTS & FINANCIAL AID

Costs (2015–16) ***Comprehensive fee:*** $51,740 includes full-time tuition ($39,840), mandatory fees ($760), and room and board ($11,140). Full-time tuition and fees vary according to course load and program. Part-time tuition: $1610 per credit. ***College room only:*** $5930. Room and board charges vary according to board plan. ***Payment plan:*** installment. ***Waivers:*** senior citizens and employees or children of employees.

Financial Aid Of all full-time matriculated undergraduates who enrolled in 2014, 1,222 applied for aid, 1,079 were judged to have need, 234 had their need fully met. In 2014, 441 non-need-based awards were made. ***Average percent of need met:*** 81. ***Average financial aid package:*** $30,563. ***Average need-based loan:*** $5171. ***Average need-based gift aid:***

$24,997. ***Average non-need-based aid:*** $18,054. ***Average indebtedness upon graduation:*** $33,421.

APPLYING

Standardized Tests *Recommended:* SAT or ACT (for admission).

Options: electronic application, early admission, early decision, deferred entrance.

Required: essay or personal statement, high school transcript, minimum 3.0 GPA, 1 letter of recommendation. ***Recommended:*** interview.

Application deadlines: 2/15 (freshmen), 6/15 (transfers).

Early decision deadline: 11/15 (for plan 1), 2/15 (for plan 2).

Notification: 2/1 (freshmen), continuous (transfers), 12/23 (early decision plan 1), rolling (early decision plan 2).

CONTACT

Terri Bollman-Dalansky, Senior Associate Dean of Admission, Juniata College, 1700 Moore Street, Huntingdon, PA 16652-2119. *Phone:* 814-641-3424. *Toll-free phone:* 877-JUNIATA. *Fax:* 814-641-3100. *E-mail:* admissions@juniata.edu.

★ Keystone College

La Plume, Pennsylvania

http://www.keystone.edu/

- **Independent** comprehensive, founded 1868
- **Small-town** 270-acre campus
- **Endowment** $8.1 million
- **Coed** 1,461 undergraduate students, 84% full-time, 59% women, 41% men
- **Minimally difficult** entrance level, 92% of applicants were admitted

UNDERGRAD STUDENTS

1,232 full-time, 229 part-time. Students come from 22 states and territories; 7 other countries; 14% are from out of state; 6% Black or African American, non-Hispanic/Latino; 6% Hispanic/Latino; 0.8% Asian, non-Hispanic/Latino; 0.2% Native Hawaiian or other Pacific Islander, non-Hispanic/Latino; 0.3% American Indian or Alaska Native, non-Hispanic/Latino; 1% Two or more races, non-Hispanic/Latino; 10% Race/ethnicity unknown; 0.5% international; 7% transferred in; 30% live on campus.

Freshmen

Admission: 981 applied, 903 admitted, 314 enrolled. ***Average high school GPA:*** 2.98. ***Test scores:*** SAT critical reading scores over 500: 29%; SAT math scores over 500: 29%; SAT writing scores over 500: 20%; ACT scores over 18: 67%; SAT critical reading scores over 600: 7%; SAT math scores over 600: 6%; SAT writing scores over 600: 4%; ACT scores over 24: 20%; SAT critical reading scores over 700: 1%.

Retention: 63% of full-time freshmen returned.

FACULTY

Total: 249, 26% full-time, 23% with terminal degrees.

Student/faculty ratio: 11:1.

ACADEMICS

Calendar: semesters. *Degrees:* associate, bachelor's, master's, and postbachelor's certificates.

Special study options: academic remediation for entering students, adult/continuing education programs, advanced placement credit, cooperative education, distance learning, double majors, English as a second language, honors programs, independent study, internships, part-time degree program, services for LD students, study abroad, summer session for credit. ***ROTC:*** Army (c), Air Force (c).

Computers: 100 computers/terminals are available on campus for general student use. Students can access the following: campus intranet, computer help desk, free student e-mail accounts, online (class) grades, online (class) registration, online (class) schedules. Campuswide network is available. 100% of college-owned or -operated housing units are wired for high-speed Internet access. Wireless service is available via entire campus.

STUDENT LIFE

Housing options: on-campus residence required for freshman year; coed, women-only, special housing for students with disabilities. Campus housing is university owned and leased by the school. Freshman campus housing is guaranteed.

Activities and organizations: drama/theater group, student-run newspaper, radio station, choral group, Art Society, Inter-Hall Council, O.P.E.N. (Opposing Prejudice Ending Negativity), S.M.A.R.T. (Sports Management and Recreation Team), Eco Club.

Athletics Member NCAA. All Division III. ***Intercollegiate sports:*** baseball M, basketball M/W, cross-country running M/W, field hockey W, golf M, lacrosse M/W, soccer M/W, softball W, tennis M/W, track and field M/W, volleyball W. ***Intramural sports:*** basketball M/W, cheerleading M(c)/W(c), football M/W, skiing (downhill) M/W, soccer M/W, volleyball M/W, wrestling M(c).

Campus security: 24-hour emergency response devices and patrols, student patrols, late-night transport/escort service, controlled dormitory access.

Student services: health clinic, personal/psychological counseling.

COSTS & FINANCIAL AID

Costs (2014–15) ***One-time required fee:*** $500. ***Comprehensive fee:*** $31,800 includes full-time tuition ($21,000), mandatory fees ($900), and room and board ($9900). Part-time tuition: $425 per credit. Part-time tuition and fees vary according to course load. ***Required fees:*** $275 per term part-time. ***College room only:*** $4950. Room and board charges vary according to board plan and housing facility. ***Payment plans:*** installment, deferred payment. ***Waivers:*** senior citizens and employees or children of employees.

Financial Aid Of all full-time matriculated undergraduates who enrolled in 2013, 1,301 applied for aid, 1,226 were judged to have need, 115 had their need fully met. In 2013, 34 non-need-based awards were made. ***Average percent of need met:*** 68. ***Average financial aid package:*** $17,718. ***Average need-based loan:*** $3832. ***Average need-based gift aid:*** $14,062. ***Average non-need-based aid:*** $9057. ***Average indebtedness upon graduation:*** $7801. ***Financial aid deadline:*** 5/1.

APPLYING

Standardized Tests *Required:* SAT or ACT (for admission).

Options: electronic application, early admission, deferred entrance.

Application fee: $30.

Required: essay or personal statement, high school transcript, 1 letter of recommendation. ***Required for some:*** interview, art portfolio for visual arts and art education. ***Recommended:*** interview.

Application deadlines: 6/1 (freshmen), 8/1 (transfers).

Notification: continuous (freshmen), continuous (transfers).

CONTACT

Jessica Lopez, Senior Administrative Assistant, Keystone College, One College Green, PO Box 50, La Plume, PA 18440-1099. *Phone:* 570-945-8111. *Toll-free phone:* 877-4-COLLEGE. *Fax:* 570-945-7916. *E-mail:* admissions@keystone.edu.

★ King's College

Wilkes-Barre, Pennsylvania

http://www.kings.edu/

- **Independent Roman Catholic** comprehensive, founded 1946
- **Urban** 48-acre campus
- **Endowment** $67.4 million
- **Coed** 2,002 undergraduate students, 90% full-time, 48% women, 52% men
- **Moderately difficult** entrance level, 67% of applicants were admitted

UNDERGRAD STUDENTS

1,811 full-time, 191 part-time. Students come from 20 states and territories; 5 other countries; 29% are from out of state; 3% Black or African American, non-Hispanic/Latino; 6% Hispanic/Latino; 2% Asian, non-Hispanic/Latino; 0.1% Native Hawaiian or other Pacific Islander, non-Hispanic/Latino; 0.2% American Indian or Alaska Native, non-Hispanic/Latino; 2% Two or more races, non-Hispanic/Latino; 7% Race/ethnicity unknown; 0.7% international; 3% transferred in; 51% live on campus.

Freshmen

Admission: 3,150 applied, 2,119 admitted, 487 enrolled. ***Average high school GPA:*** 3.3. ***Test scores:*** SAT critical reading scores over 500: 54%;

SAT math scores over 500: 64%; SAT writing scores over 500: 51%; SAT critical reading scores over 600: 11%; SAT math scores over 600: 22%; SAT writing scores over 600: 12%; SAT critical reading scores over 700: 1%; SAT math scores over 700: 1%.

Retention: 75% of full-time freshmen returned.

FACULTY

Total: 230, 61% full-time, 61% with terminal degrees.

Student/faculty ratio: 12:1.

ACADEMICS

Calendar: semesters. *Degrees:* certificates, associate, bachelor's, master's, and postbachelor's certificates.

Special study options: accelerated degree program, adult/continuing education programs, advanced placement credit, distance learning, double majors, English as a second language, honors programs, independent study, internships, off-campus study, part-time degree program, services for LD students, student-designed majors, study abroad, summer session for credit. ***ROTC:*** Army (b), Air Force (c).

Unusual degree programs: 3-2 engineering with The 3+2 Engineering Dual Degree Program with the University of Notre Dame will provide students with the opportunity to take math, science, and CORE courses at King's and then transfer to complete engineering courses in their chosen field.

Computers: 470 computers/terminals are available on campus for general student use. Students can access the following: computer help desk, free student e-mail accounts, online (class) grades, online (class) registration, online (class) schedules. Campuswide network is available. 100% of college-owned or -operated housing units are wired for high-speed Internet access. Wireless service is available via classrooms, computer labs, libraries, student centers.

STUDENT LIFE

Housing options: on-campus residence required through sophomore year; coed, men-only, women-only, cooperative, special housing for students with disabilities. Campus housing is university owned. Freshman campus housing is guaranteed.

Activities and organizations: drama/theater group, student-run newspaper, radio station, choral group, Association of Campus Events, Student Government Association, Accounting Association, International/Multicultural Club, Biology Club.

Athletics Member NCAA. All Division III. ***Intercollegiate sports:*** baseball M, basketball M/W, cross-country running M/W, field hockey W, football M, golf M, lacrosse M/W, soccer M/W, softball W, swimming and diving M/W, tennis M/W, volleyball W, wrestling M. ***Intramural sports:*** basketball M/W, ice hockey M(c), soccer M/W, track and field M(c)/W(c).

Campus security: 24-hour emergency response devices and patrols, late-night transport/escort service, controlled dormitory access.

Student services: health clinic, personal/psychological counseling.

COSTS & FINANCIAL AID

Costs (2014–15) ***Comprehensive fee:*** $43,502 includes full-time tuition ($31,416), mandatory fees ($400), and room and board ($11,686). Part-time tuition: $530 per credit hour. ***College room only:*** $5708. Room and board charges vary according to board plan. ***Payment plan:*** installment. ***Waivers:*** senior citizens and employees or children of employees.

Financial Aid Of all full-time matriculated undergraduates who enrolled in 2014, 1,651 applied for aid, 1,485 were judged to have need, 238 had their need fully met. 357 Federal Work-Study jobs (averaging $1008). 163 state and other part-time jobs (averaging $1687). In 2014, 291 non-need-based awards were made. ***Average percent of need met:*** 70. ***Average financial aid package:*** $22,682. ***Average need-based loan:*** $4348. ***Average need-based gift aid:*** $17,071. ***Average non-need-based aid:*** $13,452. ***Average indebtedness upon graduation:*** $29,432.

APPLYING

Standardized Tests *Recommended:* SAT or ACT (for admission).

Options: electronic application, deferred entrance.

Application fee: $30.

Required: essay or personal statement, high school transcript. ***Recommended:*** interview.

Application deadlines: rolling (freshmen), rolling (out-of-state freshmen), rolling (transfers).

Notification: continuous (freshmen), continuous (out-of-state freshmen), continuous (transfers).

CONTACT

Mr. James Anderson, Director of Admission, King's College, 133 North River Street, Wilkes-Barre, PA 18711-0801. *Phone:* 570-208-5858. *Toll-free phone:* 888-KINGSPA. *Fax:* 570-208-5971. *E-mail:* admissions@kings.edu.

See previous page for display ad and page 1486 for the College Close-Up.

★ Kutztown University of Pennsylvania

Kutztown, Pennsylvania

http://www.kutztown.edu/

- **State-supported** comprehensive, founded 1866, part of Pennsylvania State System of Higher Education
- **Rural** 289-acre campus with easy access to Philadelphia
- **Endowment** $16.4 million
- **Coed** 8,570 undergraduate students, 94% full-time, 56% women, 44% men
- **Moderately difficult** entrance level, 79% of applicants were admitted

UNDERGRAD STUDENTS

8,043 full-time, 527 part-time. Students come from 27 states and territories; 31 other countries; 11% are from out of state; 8% Black or African American, non-Hispanic/Latino; 7% Hispanic/Latino; 1% Asian, non-Hispanic/Latino; 0.2% Native Hawaiian or other Pacific Islander, non-Hispanic/Latino; 0.2% American Indian or Alaska Native, non-Hispanic/Latino; 0.2% Two or more races, non-Hispanic/Latino; 0.2% Race/ethnicity unknown; 1% international; 7% transferred in; 43% live on campus.

Freshmen

Admission: 8,061 applied, 6,388 admitted, 1,782 enrolled. ***Average high school GPA:*** 3.1. ***Test scores:*** SAT critical reading scores over 500: 41%; SAT math scores over 500: 41%; SAT writing scores over 500: 32%; ACT scores over 18: 75%; SAT critical reading scores over 600: 7%; SAT math scores over 600: 6%; SAT writing scores over 600: 4%; ACT scores over 24: 11%; SAT critical reading scores over 700: 1%.

Retention: 73% of full-time freshmen returned.

FACULTY

Total: 432, 96% full-time, 78% with terminal degrees.

Student/faculty ratio: 20:1.

ACADEMICS

Calendar: semesters. *Degrees:* bachelor's, master's, and postbachelor's certificates.

Special study options: academic remediation for entering students, accelerated degree program, adult/continuing education programs, advanced placement credit, distance learning, double majors, honors programs, independent study, internships, off-campus study, part-time degree program, services for LD students, student-designed majors, study abroad, summer session for credit. ***ROTC:*** Army (c).

Unusual degree programs: 3-2 business administration; social work.

Computers: 1,075 computers/terminals and 100 ports are available on campus for general student use. Students can access the following: computer help desk, free student e-mail accounts, online (class) grades, online (class) registration, online (class) schedules. Campuswide network is available. 100% of college-owned or -operated housing units are wired for high-speed Internet access. Wireless service is available via classrooms, computer centers, computer labs, dorm rooms, learning centers, libraries, student centers.

STUDENT LIFE

Housing options: coed, women-only, cooperative. Campus housing is university owned and leased by the school. Freshman campus housing is guaranteed.

Activities and organizations: drama/theater group, student-run newspaper, radio and television station, choral group, marching band, Student Government Board, Student Pennsylvania State Education Association, National Art Education Association, Residence Hall Association, Association of Campus Events, national fraternities, national sororities.

Athletics Member NCAA. All Division II. ***Intercollegiate sports:*** baseball M(s), basketball M(s)/W(s), bowling W(s), cheerleading W(c), cross-country running M(s)/W(s), equestrian sports M(c)/W(c), fencing M(c)/W(c), field hockey W(s), football M(s), golf W(s), ice hockey M(c), lacrosse M(c)/W(s), rugby M(c)/W(c), skiing (downhill) M(c)/W(c), soccer M(c)/W(s), softball W(s), swimming and diving W(s), tennis M(s)/W(s), track and field M(s)/W(s), ultimate Frisbee M(c)/W(c), volleyball M(c)/W(s), wrestling M(s). ***Intramural sports:*** basketball M/W, football M/W, racquetball M/W, rock climbing M/W, soccer M/W, softball M/W, table tennis M/W, tennis M/W, volleyball M/W.

Campus security: 24-hour emergency response devices and patrols, student patrols, late-night transport/escort service, secondary door electronic alarm system in residence halls, 24-hour student desk personnel at main entrance of residence halls.

Student services: health clinic, personal/psychological counseling, women's center.

COSTS & FINANCIAL AID

Costs (2014–15) ***One-time required fee:*** $238. ***Tuition:*** state resident $6820 full-time, $284 per credit hour part-time; nonresident $17,050 full-time, $710 per credit hour part-time. Full-time tuition and fees vary according to course load. Part-time tuition and fees vary according to course load. ***Required fees:*** $2013 full-time, $81 per credit hour part-time. ***Room and board:*** $8430; room only: $5552. Room and board charges vary according to board plan and housing facility. ***Payment plans:*** installment, deferred payment. ***Waivers:*** senior citizens and employees or children of employees.

Financial Aid Of all full-time matriculated undergraduates who enrolled in 2013, 6,869 applied for aid, 5,624 were judged to have need, 388 had their need fully met. 411 Federal Work-Study jobs (averaging $708). In 2013, 95 non-need-based awards were made. ***Average percent of need met:*** 50. ***Average financial aid package:*** $8197. ***Average need-based loan:*** $4175. ***Average need-based gift aid:*** $5730. ***Average non-need-based aid:*** $1240. ***Average indebtedness upon graduation:*** $33,376.

APPLYING

Standardized Tests *Required:* SAT or ACT (for admission). *Required for some:* SAT Subject Tests (for admission).

Options: electronic application, early admission, deferred entrance.

Application fee: $35.

Required: high school transcript, minimum 2.0 GPA. ***Required for some:*** audition for music; portfolio and/or art test for arts.

Application deadlines: rolling (freshmen), rolling (transfers).

Notification: continuous (freshmen), continuous (transfers).

CONTACT

Kutztown University of Pennsylvania, 15200 Kutztown Road, Kutztown, PA 19530-0730. *Phone:* 610-683-4060. *Toll-free phone:* 877-628-1915.

See previous page for display ad and page 1490 for the College Close-Up.

Lafayette College

Easton, Pennsylvania

http://www.lafayette.edu/

- **Independent** 4-year, founded 1826, affiliated with Presbyterian Church (U.S.A.)
- **Suburban** 340-acre campus with easy access to New York City, Philadelphia
- **Endowment** $832.8 million
- **Coed** 2,503 undergraduate students, 98% full-time, 47% women, 53% men

UNDERGRAD STUDENTS

2,446 full-time, 57 part-time. Students come from 45 states and territories; 47 other countries; 80% are from out of state; 5% Black or African American, non-Hispanic/Latino; 7% Hispanic/Latino; 3% Asian, non-Hispanic/Latino; 0.1% American Indian or Alaska Native, non-Hispanic/Latino; 2% Two or more races, non-Hispanic/Latino; 7% Race/ethnicity unknown; 8% international; 0.9% transferred in; 93% live on campus.

Freshmen

Admission: 648 enrolled. ***Average high school GPA:*** 3.47. ***Test scores:*** SAT critical reading scores over 500: 96%; SAT math scores over 500: 99%; SAT writing scores over 500: 96%; ACT scores over 18: 100%; SAT critical reading scores over 600: 68%; SAT math scores over 600: 83%;

SAT writing scores over 600: 75%; ACT scores over 24: 94%; SAT critical reading scores over 700: 16%; SAT math scores over 700: 32%; SAT writing scores over 700: 20%; ACT scores over 30: 43%.

Retention: 93% of full-time freshmen returned.

FACULTY

Total: 279, 80% full-time, 90% with terminal degrees.

Student/faculty ratio: 10:1.

ACADEMICS

Calendar: semesters plus interim January program. *Degree:* bachelor's.

Special study options: academic remediation for entering students, accelerated degree program, advanced placement credit, double majors, honors programs, independent study, internships, off-campus study, part-time degree program, services for LD students, student-designed majors, study abroad, summer session for credit. ***ROTC:*** Army (c).

Computers: 690 computers/terminals and 690 ports are available on campus for general student use. Students can access the following: campus intranet, computer help desk, free student e-mail accounts, online (class) grades, online (class) registration, online (class) schedules. Campuswide network is available. 100% of college-owned or -operated housing units are wired for high-speed Internet access. Wireless service is available via entire campus.

STUDENT LIFE

Housing options: on-campus residence required through senior year; coed, men-only, women-only, special housing for students with disabilities. Campus housing is university owned. Freshman campus housing is guaranteed.

Activities and organizations: drama/theater group, student-run newspaper, radio station, choral group, LAF (Lafayette Activities Forum), Student Government, Crew, International Students Association, Leopards Lair, national fraternities, national sororities.

Athletics Member NCAA. All Division I except football (Division I-AA). ***Intercollegiate sports:*** baseball M, basketball M/W, crew M(c)/W(c), cross-country running M/W, equestrian sports M(c)/W(c), fencing M/W, field hockey W, golf M, ice hockey M(c), lacrosse M/W, rugby M(c)/W(c), skiing (downhill) M(c)/W(c), soccer M/W, softball W, squash M(c), swimming and diving M/W, tennis M/W, track and field M/W, volleyball W, weight lifting M(c)/W(c), wrestling M(c). ***Intramural sports:*** badminton M/W, baseball M, basketball M/W, bowling M/W, cross-country running M/W, fencing M/W, field hockey W, football M, golf M/W, lacrosse M/W, racquetball M/W, sailing M(c)/W(c), skiing (cross-country) M(c)/W(c), soccer M/W, softball M/W, squash M/W, swimming and diving M/W, table tennis M/W, tennis M/W, track and field M/W, volleyball M/W, weight lifting M/W, wrestling M.

Campus security: 24-hour emergency response devices and patrols, student patrols, late-night transport/escort service, controlled dormitory access.

Student services: health clinic, personal/psychological counseling, women's center.

COSTS & FINANCIAL AID

Costs (2014–15) ***One-time required fee:*** $750. ***Comprehensive fee:*** $59,155 includes full-time tuition ($45,230), mandatory fees ($405), and room and board ($13,520). Full-time tuition and fees vary according to course load. Part-time tuition: $5655 per course. Part-time tuition and fees vary according to course load. ***College room only:*** $8360. Room and board charges vary according to board plan, housing facility, and student level. ***Payment plan:*** installment. ***Waivers:*** employees or children of employees.

Financial Aid Of all full-time matriculated undergraduates who enrolled in 2014, 1,344 applied for aid, 897 were judged to have need, 777 had their need fully met. 440 Federal Work-Study jobs (averaging $1379). In 2014, 210 non-need-based awards were made. ***Average percent of need met:*** 98. ***Average financial aid package:*** $41,206. ***Average need-based loan:*** $4707. ***Average need-based gift aid:*** $35,412. ***Average non-need-based aid:*** $23,469. ***Average indebtedness upon graduation:*** $27,497. ***Financial aid deadline:*** 3/1.

APPLYING

Standardized Tests *Required:* SAT or ACT (for admission). *Recommended:* SAT Subject Tests (for admission).

Required: essay or personal statement, high school transcript, 1 letter of recommendation. ***Recommended:*** interview.

CONTACT

Mr. Matthew Hyde, Director of Admissions, Lafayette College, 118 Markle Hall, 730 High Street, Easton, PA 18042-1798. *Phone:* 610-330-5100. *Fax:* 610-330-5355. *E-mail:* hydem@lafayette.edu.

See previous page for display ad and page 1492 for the College Close-Up.

La Roche College

Pittsburgh, Pennsylvania

http://www.laroche.edu/

- **Independent** comprehensive, founded 1963, affiliated with Roman Catholic Church
- **Suburban** 43-acre campus
- **Endowment** $5.3 million
- **Coed** 1,305 undergraduate students, 82% full-time, 55% women, 45% men
- **Minimally difficult** entrance level, 94% of applicants were admitted

UNDERGRAD STUDENTS

1,065 full-time, 240 part-time. Students come from 19 states and territories; 35 other countries; 6% are from out of state; 7% Black or African American, non-Hispanic/Latino; 2% Hispanic/Latino; 1% Asian, non-Hispanic/Latino; 0.1% American Indian or Alaska Native, non-Hispanic/Latino; 1% Two or more races, non-Hispanic/Latino; 14% Race/ethnicity unknown; 14% international; 12% transferred in; 39% live on campus.

Freshmen

Admission: 990 applied, 930 admitted, 223 enrolled. ***Average high school GPA:*** 3.3. ***Test scores:*** SAT critical reading scores over 500: 39%; SAT math scores over 500: 43%; SAT writing scores over 500: 34%; ACT scores over 18: 63%; SAT critical reading scores over 600: 10%; SAT math scores over 600: 6%; SAT writing scores over 600: 4%; ACT scores over 24: 24%; SAT critical reading scores over 700: 2%; SAT writing scores over 700: 1%.

Retention: 72% of full-time freshmen returned.

FACULTY

Total: 198, 31% full-time, 44% with terminal degrees.

Student/faculty ratio: 11:1.

ACADEMICS

Calendar: semesters plus summer term. *Degrees:* certificates, associate, bachelor's, master's, and postbachelor's certificates.

Special study options: academic remediation for entering students, accelerated degree program, adult/continuing education programs, advanced placement credit, distance learning, double majors, English as a second language, freshman honors college, honors programs, independent study, internships, off-campus study, part-time degree program, services for LD students, student-designed majors, study abroad, summer session for credit. ***ROTC:*** Army (c), Air Force (c).

Unusual degree programs: 3-2 engineering with University of Pittsburgh; physical therapy, physician's assistant, speech language pathologist, athletic trainer, occupational therapy with Duquesne University; pharmacy, dental and medical with LECOM; Software Engineering with Gannon University.

Computers: 200 computers/terminals are available on campus for general student use. Students can access the following: campus intranet, computer help desk, free student e-mail accounts, online (class) grades, online (class) registration, online (class) schedules. Campuswide network is available. 100% of college-owned or -operated housing units are wired for high-speed Internet access. Wireless service is available via classrooms, computer labs, learning centers, libraries, student centers.

STUDENT LIFE

Housing options: coed. Campus housing is university owned. Freshman campus housing is guaranteed.

Activities and organizations: drama/theater group, student-run newspaper, radio station, choral group, American Society of Interior Design, student government, Visions (environmental club), Helping Hands.

Athletics Member NCAA. All Division III. ***Intercollegiate sports:*** baseball M, basketball M/W, cross-country running M/W, golf M, lacrosse

M/W, soccer M/W, softball W, tennis W, volleyball W. ***Intramural sports:*** basketball M/W, weight lifting M/W.

Campus security: 24-hour emergency response devices and patrols, student patrols, late-night transport/escort service, controlled dormitory access.

Student services: health clinic, personal/psychological counseling.

COSTS & FINANCIAL AID

Costs (2014–15) ***Comprehensive fee:*** $35,824 includes full-time tuition ($24,750), mandatory fees ($750), and room and board ($10,324). Part-time tuition: $630 per credit hour. ***College room only:*** $6534. Room and board charges vary according to board plan and housing facility. ***Payment plan:*** installment. ***Waivers:*** senior citizens and employees or children of employees.

Financial Aid Of all full-time matriculated undergraduates who enrolled in 2014, 812 applied for aid, 764 were judged to have need, 266 had their need fully met. 159 Federal Work-Study jobs (averaging $1530). In 2014, 47 non-need-based awards were made. ***Average percent of need met:*** 95. ***Average financial aid package:*** $26,801. ***Average need-based loan:*** $4855. ***Average need-based gift aid:*** $8077. ***Average non-need-based aid:*** $15,680. ***Average indebtedness upon graduation:*** $26,713.

APPLYING

Standardized Tests *Required:* SAT or ACT (for admission).

Options: electronic application, early admission, deferred entrance.

Application fee: $50.

Required: high school transcript, minimum 2.0 GPA, 2 letters of recommendation. ***Recommended:*** essay or personal statement, minimum 3.0 GPA, interview.

Application deadlines: rolling (freshmen), rolling (transfers).

Notification: 9/15 (freshmen).

CONTACT

Mr. Terry Kizina, Director of Admissions, La Roche College, 9000 Babcock Boulevard, Pittsburgh, PA 15237. *Phone:* 412-536-1275. *Toll-free phone:* 800-838-4LRC. *Fax:* 412-536-1048. *E-mail:* admissions@laroche.edu.

La Salle University

Philadelphia, Pennsylvania

http://www.lasalle.edu/

- **Independent Roman Catholic** comprehensive, founded 1863
- **Urban** 133-acre campus with easy access to Philadelphia
- **Endowment** $87.4 million
- **Coed** 4,322 undergraduate students, 83% full-time, 64% women, 36% men
- **Moderately difficult** entrance level, 78% of applicants were admitted

UNDERGRAD STUDENTS

3,583 full-time, 739 part-time. Students come from 33 states and territories; 26 other countries; 33% are from out of state; 18% Black or African American, non-Hispanic/Latino; 10% Hispanic/Latino; 5% Asian, non-Hispanic/Latino; 0.1% Native Hawaiian or other Pacific Islander, non-Hispanic/Latino; 0.3% American Indian or Alaska Native, non-Hispanic/Latino; 6% Two or more races, non-Hispanic/Latino; 4% Race/ethnicity unknown; 2% international; 3% transferred in; 56% live on campus.

Freshmen

Admission: 5,778 applied, 4,520 admitted, 919 enrolled. ***Average high school GPA:*** 3.33. ***Test scores:*** SAT critical reading scores over 500: 50%; SAT math scores over 500: 48%; ACT scores over 18: 84%; SAT critical reading scores over 600: 12%; SAT math scores over 600: 13%; ACT scores over 24: 28%; SAT critical reading scores over 700: 2%; SAT math scores over 700: 2%; ACT scores over 30: 5%.

Retention: 81% of full-time freshmen returned.

FACULTY

Total: 469, 53% full-time.

Student/faculty ratio: 12:1.

ACADEMICS

Calendar: semesters. *Degrees:* associate, bachelor's, master's, doctoral, post-master's, and postbachelor's certificates.

Special study options: academic remediation for entering students, accelerated degree program, adult/continuing education programs, advanced placement credit, cooperative education, distance learning, double majors, English as a second language, freshman honors college, honors programs, independent study, internships, off-campus study, part-time degree program, services for LD students, student-designed majors, study abroad, summer session for credit. ***ROTC:*** Army (c), Air Force (c).

Unusual degree programs: 3-2 business administration; 4-year BS/MBA in Accounting, 5-year BS/MS in speech-language-hearing science, 5-year BA/BS/MS in computer information science, 5-year BA/MA in history, 5-year elementary/special education BA/MA, and an occupational therapy program with Thomas Jefferson University.

Computers: 1,100 computers/terminals are available on campus for general student use. Students can access the following: campus intranet, computer help desk, free student e-mail accounts, online (class) grades, online (class) registration, online (class) schedules, Canvas Course Management System. Campuswide network is available. 100% of college-owned or -operated housing units are wired for high-speed Internet access. Wireless service is available via classrooms, computer centers, computer labs, dorm rooms, learning centers, libraries, student centers.

STUDENT LIFE

Housing options: on-campus residence required through sophomore year; coed, men-only, women-only, special housing for students with disabilities. Campus housing is university owned. Freshman campus housing is guaranteed.

Activities and organizations: drama/theater group, student-run newspaper, radio and television station, choral group, Student Government Association, community service organization, La Salle Entertainment Organization, The Explorer (yearbook), The Masque (theater group), national fraternities, national sororities.

Athletics Member NCAA. All Division I. ***Intercollegiate sports:*** baseball M(s), basketball M(s)/W(s), cheerleading M/W, crew M(s)/W(s), cross-country running M(s)/W(s), field hockey W(s), golf M(s)/W(s), lacrosse W(s), soccer M(s)/W(s), softball W(s), swimming and diving M(s)/W(s), tennis M(s)/W(s), track and field M(s)/W(s), volleyball W(s). ***Intramural sports:*** basketball M/W, equestrian sports M(c)/W(c), ice hockey M(c), lacrosse M(c), rugby M, softball M/W, ultimate Frisbee M(c)/W(c), volleyball M/W, water polo M(c)/W(c).

Campus security: 24-hour emergency response devices and patrols, student patrols, late-night transport/escort service, controlled dormitory access.

Student services: health clinic, personal/psychological counseling, women's center.

COSTS & FINANCIAL AID

Costs (2014–15) ***One-time required fee:*** $150. ***Comprehensive fee:*** $53,740 includes full-time tuition ($39,200), mandatory fees ($600), and room and board ($13,940). Full-time tuition and fees vary according to course load and program. Part-time tuition: $540 per credit hour. Part-time tuition and fees vary according to course load and program. ***Required fees:*** $150 per term part-time. ***College room only:*** $6960. Room and board charges vary according to board plan and housing facility. ***Payment plans:*** installment, deferred payment. ***Waivers:*** employees or children of employees.

Financial Aid Of all full-time matriculated undergraduates who enrolled in 2013, 3,083 applied for aid, 2,881 were judged to have need, 414 had their need fully met. 386 Federal Work-Study jobs (averaging $1292). In 2013, 552 non-need-based awards were made. ***Average percent of need met:*** 76. ***Average financial aid package:*** $27,790. ***Average need-based loan:*** $4795. ***Average need-based gift aid:*** $22,651. ***Average non-need-based aid:*** $16,336. ***Average indebtedness upon graduation:*** $35,327.

APPLYING

Standardized Tests *Required:* SAT or ACT (for admission).

Options: electronic application, early admission, early action, deferred entrance.

Application fee: $35.

Required: essay or personal statement, high school transcript, 1 letter of recommendation, SAT or ACT. ***Recommended:*** interview.

Application deadlines: 8/15 (transfers), 11/15 (early action).

Notification: continuous (freshmen), continuous (transfers), 12/15 (early action).

CONTACT
Mr. James Plunkett, Executive Director of Undergraduate Admission, La Salle University, 1900 West Olney Avenue, Philadelphia, PA 19141-1199. *Phone:* 215-951-1500. *Toll-free phone:* 800-328-1910. *Fax:* 215-951-1656. *E-mail:* admiss@lasalle.edu.

★ Lebanon Valley College
Annville, Pennsylvania
http://www.lvc.edu/

- **Independent United Methodist** comprehensive, founded 1866
- **Small-town** 357-acre campus
- **Endowment** $55.3 million
- **Coed** 1,683 undergraduate students, 93% full-time, 54% women, 46% men
- **Moderately difficult** entrance level, 71% of applicants were admitted

UNDERGRAD STUDENTS
1,573 full-time, 110 part-time. Students come from 22 states and territories; 3 other countries; 20% are from out of state; 3% Black or African American, non-Hispanic/Latino; 5% Hispanic/Latino; 2% Asian, non-Hispanic/Latino; 0.2% Native Hawaiian or other Pacific Islander, non-Hispanic/Latino; 0.3% American Indian or Alaska Native, non-Hispanic/Latino; 2% Two or more races, non-Hispanic/Latino; 4% Race/ethnicity unknown; 0.2% international; 2% transferred in; 80% live on campus.

Freshmen
Admission: 3,643 applied, 2,570 admitted, 413 enrolled. ***Test scores:*** SAT critical reading scores over 500: 67%; SAT math scores over 500: 77%; SAT writing scores over 500: 61%; ACT scores over 18: 89%; SAT critical reading scores over 600: 22%; SAT math scores over 600: 39%; SAT writing scores over 600: 18%; ACT scores over 24: 50%; SAT critical reading scores over 700: 2%; SAT math scores over 700: 4%; SAT writing scores over 700: 2%; ACT scores over 30: 5%.

Retention: 85% of full-time freshmen returned.

FACULTY
Total: 240, 44% full-time, 56% with terminal degrees.

Student/faculty ratio: 11:1.

ACADEMICS
Calendar: semesters. *Degrees:* bachelor's, master's, doctoral, and postbachelor's certificates.

Special study options: academic remediation for entering students, adult/continuing education programs, advanced placement credit, double majors, independent study, internships, off-campus study, part-time degree program, services for LD students, student-designed majors, study abroad, summer session for credit.

Unusual degree programs: 3-2 engineering with Case Western Reserve University, The Penn State University.

Computers: 195 computers/terminals are available on campus for general student use. Students can access the following: campus intranet, computer help desk, free student e-mail accounts, online (class) grades, online (class) registration, online (class) schedules. Campuswide network is available. 100% of college-owned or -operated housing units are wired for high-speed Internet access. Wireless service is available via entire campus.

STUDENT LIFE
Housing options: on-campus residence required through senior year; coed, special housing for students with disabilities. Campus housing is university owned. Freshman campus housing is guaranteed.

Activities and organizations: drama/theater group, student-run newspaper, radio station, choral group, marching band, LVC PSEA, Cornerstone, Colleges Against Cancer, Wig and Buckle Theater Group, Habitat for Humanity, national fraternities, national sororities.

Athletics Member NCAA. All Division III. ***Intercollegiate sports:*** baseball M, basketball M/W, cross-country running M/W, field hockey W, football M, golf M/W, ice hockey M(c), lacrosse M/W, soccer M/W, softball W, swimming and diving M/W, tennis M/W, track and field M/W, volleyball W. ***Intramural sports:*** basketball M/W, cheerleading W(c), equestrian sports M(c)/W(c), football M/W, rugby W(c), ultimate Frisbee M(c)/W(c), volleyball M(c)/W.

A ★ indicates that the school has detailed information with a Premium Profile on Petersons.com.

Campus security: 24-hour emergency response devices and patrols, late-night transport/escort service, controlled dormitory access, residence hall entrances locked 24 hours a day.

Student services: health clinic, personal/psychological counseling, women's center.

COSTS & FINANCIAL AID

Costs (2014–15) ***Comprehensive fee:*** $47,570 includes full-time tuition ($36,470), mandatory fees ($1000), and room and board ($10,100). Part-time tuition: $595 per credit. Part-time tuition and fees vary according to class time and degree level. ***College room only:*** $4880. Room and board charges vary according to board plan and housing facility. ***Payment plan:*** installment. ***Waivers:*** senior citizens and employees or children of employees.

Financial Aid Of all full-time matriculated undergraduates who enrolled in 2013, 1,494 applied for aid, 1,373 were judged to have need, 254 had their need fully met. 1,032 Federal Work-Study jobs (averaging $1474). In 2013, 227 non-need-based awards were made. ***Average percent of need met:*** 74. ***Average financial aid package:*** $25,885. ***Average need-based loan:*** $4455. ***Average need-based gift aid:*** $22,115. ***Average non-need-based aid:*** $14,316. ***Average indebtedness upon graduation:*** $33,657.

APPLYING

Options: electronic application, early decision.

Required: high school transcript. ***Required for some:*** essay or personal statement, audition for music majors. ***Recommended:*** 2 letters of recommendation, interview.

Application deadlines: rolling (freshmen), rolling (transfers).

Early decision deadline: 11/1.

Notification: continuous until 12/15 (freshmen), continuous (transfers), 12/1 (early decision).

CONTACT

Ms. Susan Jones, Senior Associate Director of Admission, Lebanon Valley College, 101 North College Avenue, Annville, PA 17003. *Phone:* 717-867-6181. *Toll-free phone:* 866-LVC-4ADM. *Fax:* 717-867-6026. *E-mail:* admission@lvc.edu.

See previous page for display ad and page 1494 for the College Close-Up.

Lehigh University

Bethlehem, Pennsylvania

http://www.lehigh.edu/

- **Independent** university, founded 1865
- **Suburban** 2358-acre campus with easy access to Philadelphia
- **Endowment** $1.2 billion
- **Coed** 5,062 undergraduate students, 98% full-time, 45% women, 55% men
- **Most difficult** entrance level, 34% of applicants were admitted

UNDERGRAD STUDENTS

4,984 full-time, 78 part-time. Students come from 51 states and territories; 63 other countries; 73% are from out of state; 4% Black or African American, non-Hispanic/Latino; 8% Hispanic/Latino; 8% Asian, non-Hispanic/Latino; 0.1% American Indian or Alaska Native, non-Hispanic/Latino; 3% Two or more races, non-Hispanic/Latino; 3% Race/ethnicity unknown; 7% international; 0.6% transferred in; 67% live on campus.

Freshmen

Admission: 11,512 applied, 3,945 admitted, 1,299 enrolled. ***Test scores:*** SAT critical reading scores over 500: 97%; SAT math scores over 500: 99%; ACT scores over 18: 100%; SAT critical reading scores over 600: 70%; SAT math scores over 600: 89%; ACT scores over 24: 99%; SAT critical reading scores over 700: 14%; SAT math scores over 700: 44%; ACT scores over 30: 62%.

Retention: 96% of full-time freshmen returned.

FACULTY

Total: 697, 73% full-time, 73% with terminal degrees.

Student/faculty ratio: 10:1.

ACADEMICS

Calendar: semesters. *Degrees:* bachelor's, master's, doctoral, post-master's, and postbachelor's certificates.

Special study options: accelerated degree program, advanced placement credit, cooperative education, distance learning, double majors, English as a second language, external degree program, honors programs, independent study, internships, off-campus study, services for LD students, study abroad, summer session for credit. ***ROTC:*** Army (b).

Unusual degree programs: 3-2 engineering; education.

Computers: 573 computers/terminals are available on campus for general student use. Students can access the following: campus intranet, computer help desk, free student e-mail accounts, online (class) grades, online (class) registration, online (class) schedules. Campuswide network is available. 100% of college-owned or -operated housing units are wired for high-speed Internet access. Wireless service is available via classrooms, computer centers, computer labs, dorm rooms, learning centers, libraries, student centers.

STUDENT LIFE

Housing options: on-campus residence required through sophomore year; coed, special housing for students with disabilities. Campus housing is university owned. Freshman campus housing is guaranteed.

Activities and organizations: drama/theater group, student-run newspaper, radio station, choral group, marching band, WLVR Radio Station, Association of Student Alumni, University Productions, Accounting Club, Phi Sigma Pi, national sororities.

Athletics Member NCAA. All Division I. ***Intercollegiate sports:*** baseball M, basketball M(s)/W(s), crew M(c)/W(s), cross-country running M(s)/W(s), equestrian sports M(c)/W(c), fencing M(c)/W(c), field hockey W(s), football M(s), golf M(s)/W(s), ice hockey M(c), lacrosse M(s)/W(s), rugby M(c)/W(c), skiing (downhill) M(c)/W(c), soccer M/W, softball W(s), squash M(c)/W(c), swimming and diving M(s)/W(s), tennis M(s)/W(s), track and field M(s)/W(s), ultimate Frisbee M(c)/W(c), volleyball M(c)/W(s), water polo M(c)/W(c), wrestling M(s). ***Intramural sports:*** badminton M(c)/W(c), baseball M(c), basketball M/W, cheerleading M(c)/W(c), cross-country running M/W, field hockey W(c), football M/W, golf M(c)/W(c), gymnastics M(c)/W(c), lacrosse M(c)/W(c), skiing (downhill) M(c)/W(c), soccer M/W, softball M/W, volleyball M/W, wrestling M(c).

Campus security: 24-hour emergency response devices and patrols, student patrols, late-night transport/escort service, controlled dormitory access, self defense training.

Student services: health clinic, personal/psychological counseling, women's center.

COSTS & FINANCIAL AID

Costs (2014–15) ***Comprehensive fee:*** $56,770 includes full-time tuition ($44,520), mandatory fees ($370), and room and board ($11,880). Part-time tuition: $1860 per credit hour. ***College room only:*** $6820. Room and board charges vary according to board plan and housing facility. ***Payment plans:*** tuition prepayment, installment. ***Waivers:*** employees or children of employees.

Financial Aid Of all full-time matriculated undergraduates who enrolled in 2014, 2,738 applied for aid, 2,035 were judged to have need, 1,261 had their need fully met. 1,285 Federal Work-Study jobs (averaging $1664). 29 state and other part-time jobs (averaging $1891). In 2014, 273 non-need-based awards were made. ***Average percent of need met:*** 96. ***Average financial aid package:*** $38,996. ***Average need-based loan:*** $4714. ***Average need-based gift aid:*** $32,995. ***Average non-need-based aid:*** $12,424. ***Average indebtedness upon graduation:*** $31,877. ***Financial aid deadline:*** 2/15.

APPLYING

Standardized Tests *Required:* SAT or ACT (for admission). *Recommended:* SAT Subject Tests (for admission).

Options: electronic application, early admission, early decision, deferred entrance.

Application fee: $70.

Required: essay or personal statement, high school transcript, 2 letters of recommendation.

Application deadlines: 1/1 (freshmen), 3/1 (transfers).

Early decision deadline: 11/15 (for plan 1), 1/1 (for plan 2).

Notification: 4/1 (freshmen), 5/15 (transfers), 12/15 (early decision plan 1), 2/15 (early decision plan 2).

CONTACT

Bruce Bunnick, Director of Admissions, Lehigh University, 27 Memorial Drive West, Bethlehem, PA 18015. *Phone:* 610-758-3100. *Fax:* 610-758-4361. *E-mail:* admissions@lehigh.edu.

Lincoln University

Lincoln University, Pennsylvania

http://www.lincoln.edu/

- **State-related** comprehensive, founded 1854
- **Rural** 422-acre campus with easy access to Philadelphia
- **Endowment** $29.1 million
- **Coed** 1,589 undergraduate students, 90% full-time, 61% women, 39% men
- **Moderately difficult** entrance level, 50% of applicants were admitted

UNDERGRAD STUDENTS

1,428 full-time, 161 part-time. Students come from 33 states and territories; 27 other countries; 57% are from out of state; 80% Black or African American, non-Hispanic/Latino; 2% Hispanic/Latino; 0.3% American Indian or Alaska Native, non-Hispanic/Latino; 1% Two or more races, non-Hispanic/Latino; 10% Race/ethnicity unknown; 5% international; 6% transferred in; 99% live on campus.

Freshmen

Admission: 2,793 applied, 1,406 admitted, 318 enrolled. ***Average high school GPA:*** 2.86. ***Test scores:*** SAT critical reading scores over 500: 18%; SAT math scores over 500: 18%; SAT writing scores over 500: 13%; ACT scores over 18: 46%; SAT critical reading scores over 600: 2%; SAT math scores over 600: 2%; SAT writing scores over 600: 2%; ACT scores over 24: 2%.

Retention: 75% of full-time freshmen returned.

FACULTY

Total: 160, 57% full-time.

Student/faculty ratio: 17:1.

ACADEMICS

Calendar: semesters. *Degrees:* bachelor's and master's.

Special study options: advanced placement credit, double majors, honors programs, independent study, internships, off-campus study, part-time degree program, services for LD students, study abroad, summer session for credit. ***ROTC:*** Army (c), Air Force (c).

Computers: 1,000 computers/terminals are available on campus for general student use. Students can access the following: campus intranet, computer help desk, free student e-mail accounts, online (class) grades, online (class) registration, online (class) schedules. Campuswide network is available. 100% of college-owned or -operated housing units are wired for high-speed Internet access. Wireless service is available via entire campus.

STUDENT LIFE

Housing options: coed, men-only, women-only. Campus housing is university owned. Freshman applicants given priority for college housing.

Activities and organizations: drama/theater group, student-run newspaper, radio and television station, choral group, marching band, The Gospel Ensemble, Ziana Fashion Club, We R One, Council of Independent Organizations, national fraternities, national sororities.

Athletics Member NCAA. All Division II. ***Intercollegiate sports:*** baseball M(s), basketball M(s), cross-country running M(s)/W(s), football M(s), soccer W(s), softball W(s), track and field M(s)/W(s), volleyball W(s). ***Intramural sports:*** baseball M, cheerleading W, football M.

Campus security: 24-hour emergency response devices and patrols, late-night transport/escort service, controlled dormitory access.

Student services: health clinic, personal/psychological counseling, women's center.

COSTS & FINANCIAL AID

Costs (2014–15) ***One-time required fee:*** $202. ***Tuition:*** state resident $7160 full-time, $301 per credit part-time; nonresident $11,836 full-time, $497 per credit part-time. Full-time tuition and fees vary according to degree level, program, and student level. Part-time tuition and fees vary according to course load, degree level, program, and student level. No tuition increase for student's term of enrollment. ***Required fees:*** $3072 full-time, $127 per year part-time, $154 per year part-time. ***Room and board:*** $8686; room only: $4634. Room and board charges vary according to board plan and housing facility. ***Payment plans:*** installment, deferred payment. ***Waivers:*** children of alumni and employees or children of employees.

Financial Aid Of all full-time matriculated undergraduates who enrolled in 2013, 1,465 applied for aid, 1,446 had their need fully met. In 2013, 51 non-need-based awards were made. ***Average percent of need met:*** 99. ***Average need-based loan:*** $2120. ***Average need-based gift aid:*** $1675. ***Average indebtedness upon graduation:*** $12,082. ***Financial aid deadline:*** 5/1.

APPLYING

Standardized Tests *Required:* SAT or ACT (for admission).

Options: electronic application, deferred entrance.

Application fee: $20.

Required: essay or personal statement, high school transcript, minimum 2.0 GPA, 2 letters of recommendation. ***Recommended:*** interview.

Application deadlines: rolling (freshmen), rolling (transfers).

Notification: continuous (transfers).

CONTACT

Ms. Tiffany Harrison, Senior Assistant Director, Operations and Recruitment, Lincoln University, PO Box 179, MSC 147, Lincoln University, PA 19352. *Phone:* 484-365—7235. *Toll-free phone:* 800-790-0191. *Fax:* 484-365-8109. *E-mail:* tharrison@lincoln.edu.

Lock Haven University of Pennsylvania

Lock Haven, Pennsylvania

http://www.lhup.edu/

- **State-supported** comprehensive, founded 1870, part of Pennsylvania State System of Higher Education
- **Rural** 165-acre campus
- **Endowment** $9.8 million
- **Coed** 4,521 undergraduate students, 92% full-time, 56% women, 44% men
- **Moderately difficult** entrance level, 93% of applicants were admitted

UNDERGRAD STUDENTS

4,165 full-time, 356 part-time. Students come from 30 states and territories; 23 other countries; 7% are from out of state; 9% Black or African American, non-Hispanic/Latino; 2% Hispanic/Latino; 0.9% Asian, non-Hispanic/Latino; 0.2% American Indian or Alaska Native, non-Hispanic/Latino; 1% Two or more races, non-Hispanic/Latino; 2% Race/ethnicity unknown; 1% international; 5% transferred in; 36% live on campus.

Freshmen

Admission: 3,436 applied, 3,209 admitted, 935 enrolled. ***Average high school GPA:*** 3.23. ***Test scores:*** SAT critical reading scores over 500: 34%; SAT math scores over 500: 39%; SAT writing scores over 500: 26%; ACT scores over 18: 70%; SAT critical reading scores over 600: 7%; SAT math scores over 600: 8%; SAT writing scores over 600: 4%; ACT scores over 24: 18%; SAT critical reading scores over 700: 1%; ACT scores over 30: 1%.

Retention: 68% of full-time freshmen returned.

FACULTY

Total: 230, 91% full-time, 77% with terminal degrees.

Student/faculty ratio: 21:1.

ACADEMICS

Calendar: semesters. *Degrees:* associate, bachelor's, and master's.

Special study options: academic remediation for entering students, adult/continuing education programs, advanced placement credit, cooperative education, distance learning, double majors, English as a second language, freshman honors college, honors programs, independent study, internships, off-campus study, part-time degree program, services for LD students, student-designed majors, study abroad, summer session for credit. ***ROTC:*** Army (b).

Unusual degree programs: 3-2 engineering with Penn State University–University Park Campus; nursing with Clarion University of Pennsylvania.

Computers: 290 computers/terminals are available on campus for general student use. Students can access the following: online (class) registration. Campuswide network is available.

STUDENT LIFE
Housing options: on-campus residence required for freshman year; coed. Campus housing is university owned and is provided by a third party. Freshman applicants given priority for college housing.

Activities and organizations: drama/theater group, student-run newspaper, radio and television station, choral group, marching band, student government, Residence Hall Association, national fraternities, national sororities.

Athletics Member NCAA. All Division II except field hockey (Division I), wrestling (Division I). ***Intercollegiate sports:*** baseball M(s), basketball M(s)/W(s), cross-country running M(s)/W(s), field hockey W(s), football M(s), lacrosse W(s), soccer M(s)/W(s), softball W(s), swimming and diving W(s), track and field M(s)/W(s), volleyball W(s), wrestling M(s). ***Intramural sports:*** badminton M/W, basketball M/W, cross-country running M/W, fencing M/W, field hockey W, football M, golf M/W, ice hockey M, lacrosse M/W, racquetball M/W, rugby M/W, skiing (cross-country) M/W, skiing (downhill) M/W, soccer M/W, softball M/W, swimming and diving M/W, tennis M/W, track and field M/W, ultimate Frisbee M/W, volleyball M/W, water polo M, weight lifting M/W, wrestling M.

Campus security: 24-hour emergency response devices and patrols, late-night transport/escort service, controlled dormitory access.

Student services: health clinic, personal/psychological counseling, women's center.

COSTS & FINANCIAL AID
Costs (2014–15) ***One-time required fee:*** $30. ***Tuition:*** state resident $6820 full-time, $284 per credit hour part-time; nonresident $15,050 full-time, $284 per credit hour part-time. Full-time tuition and fees vary according to course load and location. Part-time tuition and fees vary according to course load and location. ***Required fees:*** $2456 full-time, $137 per credit hour part-time, $40 per term part-time. ***Room and board:*** $8752; room only: $5600. Room and board charges vary according to board plan and housing facility. ***Payment plan:*** installment. ***Waivers:*** minority students, senior citizens, and employees or children of employees.

Financial Aid Of all full-time matriculated undergraduates who enrolled in 2014, 2,910 applied for aid, 2,621 were judged to have need, 1,069 had their need fully met. 302 Federal Work-Study jobs (averaging $557). 431 state and other part-time jobs (averaging $1452). In 2014, 39 non-need-based awards were made. ***Average percent of need met:*** 85. ***Average financial aid package:*** $8511. ***Average need-based loan:*** $4278. ***Average need-based gift aid:*** $5445. ***Average non-need-based aid:*** $2437. ***Average indebtedness upon graduation:*** $29,353.

APPLYING
Standardized Tests *Required:* SAT or ACT (for admission).

Options: electronic application, deferred entrance.

Application fee: $25.

Required: high school transcript. ***Required for some:*** essay or personal statement. ***Recommended:*** interview.

Application deadlines: rolling (freshmen), rolling (transfers).

Notification: continuous (freshmen), continuous (transfers).

CONTACT
Ms. Robin Rockey, Associate Director of Admissions, Lock Haven University of Pennsylvania, Office of Admission, DACC, Lock Haven, PA 17745. *Phone:* 570-484-2027. *Toll-free phone:* 800-332-8900 (in-state); 800-233-8978 (out-of-state). *Fax:* 570-484-2201. *E-mail:* admissions@lhup.edu.

Lycoming College
Williamsport, Pennsylvania
http://www.lycoming.edu/

- **Independent United Methodist** 4-year, founded 1812
- **Small-town** 35-acre campus
- **Endowment** $198.1 million
- **Coed** 1,357 undergraduate students, 98% full-time, 54% women, 46% men
- **Moderately difficult** entrance level, 72% of applicants were admitted

UNDERGRAD STUDENTS
1,331 full-time, 26 part-time. Students come from 27 states and territories; 16 other countries; 34% are from out of state; 7% Black or African American, non-Hispanic/Latino; 4% Hispanic/Latino; 1% Asian, non-Hispanic/Latino; 0.1% American Indian or Alaska Native, non-Hispanic/Latino; 3% Two or more races, non-Hispanic/Latino; 5% Race/ethnicity unknown; 4% international; 2% transferred in; 87% live on campus.

Freshmen
Admission: 1,782 applied, 1,287 admitted, 394 enrolled. ***Average high school GPA:*** 3.43. ***Test scores:*** SAT critical reading scores over 500: 58%; SAT math scores over 500: 63%; SAT writing scores over 500: 47%; ACT scores over 18: 89%; SAT critical reading scores over 600: 15%; SAT math scores over 600: 23%; SAT writing scores over 600: 12%; ACT scores over 24: 34%; SAT critical reading scores over 700: 2%; SAT math scores over 700: 3%; SAT writing scores over 700: 2%; ACT scores over 30: 7%.

Retention: 82% of full-time freshmen returned.

FACULTY
Total: 119, 69% full-time, 79% with terminal degrees.

Student/faculty ratio: 14:1.

ACADEMICS
Calendar: semesters. *Degree:* bachelor's.

Special study options: accelerated degree program, advanced placement credit, double majors, honors programs, independent study, internships, off-campus study, part-time degree program, services for LD students, student-designed majors, study abroad, summer session for credit. ***ROTC:*** Army (c).

Unusual degree programs: 3-2 engineering with Watson School of Engineering at SUNY Binghamton; forestry with Duke University; environmental management with Duke University.

Computers: 193 computers/terminals and 1,848 ports are available on campus for general student use. Students can access the following: campus intranet, computer help desk, free student e-mail accounts, online (class) grades, online (class) registration, online (class) schedules, online financial aid, free printing up to a limit, password management. Campuswide network is available. 100% of college-owned or -operated housing units are wired for high-speed Internet access. Wireless service is available via entire campus.

STUDENT LIFE
Housing options: on-campus residence required through senior year; coed, women-only. Campus housing is university owned. Freshman campus housing is guaranteed.

Activities and organizations: drama/theater group, student-run newspaper, radio station, choral group, Campus Activities Board, Lycoming Dance Club, Habitat for Humanity, Circle K, United Campus Ministry, national fraternities, national sororities.

Athletics Member NCAA. All Division III. ***Intercollegiate sports:*** badminton M(c)/W(c), basketball M/W, cheerleading M(c)/W(c), crew M(c)/W(c), cross-country running M/W, equestrian sports M(c)/W(c), fencing M(c)/W(c), football M, golf M/W, lacrosse M/W, rugby M(c), soccer M/W, softball W, swimming and diving M/W, tennis M/W, ultimate Frisbee M(c)/W(c), volleyball W, water polo M(c)/W(c), wrestling M. ***Intramural sports:*** basketball M/W, football M/W, soccer M/W, softball M/W, table tennis M/W, volleyball M/W.

Campus security: 24-hour emergency response devices and patrols, student patrols, late-night transport/escort service, controlled dormitory access.

Student services: health clinic, personal/psychological counseling.

COSTS & FINANCIAL AID

Costs (2015–16) ***One-time required fee:*** $225. ***Comprehensive fee:*** $46,784 includes full-time tuition ($35,200), mandatory fees ($700), and room and board ($10,884). Part-time tuition: $1100 per credit hour. Part-time tuition and fees vary according to course load. ***Room and board:*** Room and board charges vary according to board plan and housing facility. ***Payment plan:*** installment. ***Waivers:*** employees or children of employees.

Financial Aid Of all full-time matriculated undergraduates who enrolled in 2014, 1,172 applied for aid, 1,082 were judged to have need, 321 had their need fully met. In 2014, 156 non-need-based awards were made. ***Average percent of need met:*** 81. ***Average financial aid package:*** $30,635. ***Average need-based loan:*** $4715. ***Average need-based gift aid:*** $25,355. ***Average non-need-based aid:*** $18,162.

APPLYING

Standardized Tests *Recommended:* SAT or ACT (for admission).

Options: electronic application, deferred entrance.

Application fee: $35.

Required: essay or personal statement, high school transcript, 2 letters of recommendation. ***Recommended:*** minimum 2.3 GPA, interview.

Application deadlines: 3/1 (freshmen), rolling (transfers).

Notification: continuous (freshmen), continuous (transfers).

CONTACT

Mr. Jason Moran, Director of Admissions, Lycoming College, 700 College Place, Williamsport, PA 17701. *Phone:* 570-321-4122. *Toll-free phone:* 800-345-3920 Ext. 4026. *Fax:* 570-321-4317. *E-mail:* admissions@lycoming.edu.

Mansfield University of Pennsylvania

Mansfield, Pennsylvania

http://www.mansfield.edu/

- **State-supported** comprehensive, founded 1857, part of Pennsylvania State System of Higher Education
- **Small-town** 174-acre campus
- **Coed** 2,587 undergraduate students, 90% full-time, 60% women, 40% men
- **Moderately difficult** entrance level

UNDERGRAD STUDENTS

2,341 full-time, 246 part-time. 17% are from out of state; 8% Black or African American, non-Hispanic/Latino; 3% Hispanic/Latino; 1% Asian, non-Hispanic/Latino; 0.1% Native Hawaiian or other Pacific Islander, non-Hispanic/Latino; 0.4% American Indian or Alaska Native, non-Hispanic/Latino; 2% Two or more races, non-Hispanic/Latino; 2% Race/ethnicity unknown; 0.8% international; 52% live on campus.

Freshmen

Admission: 550 enrolled. ***Test scores:*** SAT critical reading scores over 500: 38%; SAT math scores over 500: 44%; SAT writing scores over 500: 27%; SAT critical reading scores over 600: 7%; SAT math scores over 600: 10%; SAT writing scores over 600: 7%; SAT critical reading scores over 700: 1%.

Retention: 75% of full-time freshmen returned.

FACULTY

Total: 165, 71% full-time, 68% with terminal degrees.

Student/faculty ratio: 18:1.

ACADEMICS

Calendar: semesters. *Degrees:* associate, bachelor's, and master's.

Special study options: adult/continuing education programs, part-time degree program. ***ROTC:*** Army (c).

Computers: Students can access the following: campus intranet, computer help desk, free student e-mail accounts, online (class) grades, online (class) registration, online (class) schedules. Campuswide network is available. 100% of college-owned or -operated housing units are wired for high-speed Internet access. Wireless service is available via classrooms, computer centers, computer labs, dorm rooms, learning centers, libraries, student centers.

STUDENT LIFE

Housing options: on-campus residence required through sophomore year; coed. Campus housing is university owned. Freshman campus housing is guaranteed.

Activities and organizations: drama/theater group, student-run newspaper, radio and television station, choral group, marching band, national fraternities, national sororities.

Athletics Member NCAA. All Division II. ***Intercollegiate sports:*** baseball M(s), basketball M(s)/W(s), cross-country running M(s)/W(s), field hockey W(s), football M(c), soccer W(s), softball W(s), swimming and diving W, track and field M(s)/W(s). ***Intramural sports:*** badminton M/W, basketball M/W, bowling M/W, cheerleading W, cross-country running M/W, equestrian sports M/W, football M/W, golf M/W, racquetball M/W, skiing (cross-country) M/W, skiing (downhill) M/W, soccer M/W, softball M/W, swimming and diving M/W, tennis M/W, track and field M/W, volleyball M/W, water polo M/W, weight lifting M/W.

Campus security: 24-hour emergency response devices and patrols, student patrols, late-night transport/escort service, controlled dormitory access.

Student services: health clinic, personal/psychological counseling, women's center.

COSTS & FINANCIAL AID

Costs (2014–15) ***Tuition:*** state resident $6820 full-time, $284 per credit hour part-time; nonresident $17,050 full-time, $710 per credit hour part-time. Part-time tuition and fees vary according to course load. ***Required fees:*** $2706 full-time. ***Room and board:*** $10,936; room only: $7600. Room and board charges vary according to board plan and housing facility. ***Payment plans:*** installment, deferred payment. ***Waivers:*** senior citizens and employees or children of employees.

Financial Aid Of all full-time matriculated undergraduates who enrolled in 2013, 2,330 applied for aid, 2,052 were judged to have need, 213 had their need fully met. In 2013, 35 non-need-based awards were made. ***Average percent of need met:*** 74. ***Average financial aid package:*** $9650. ***Average need-based loan:*** $2708. ***Average need-based gift aid:*** $2981. ***Average non-need-based aid:*** $1404. ***Average indebtedness upon graduation:*** $33,799. ***Financial aid deadline:*** 6/30.

APPLYING

Standardized Tests *Required for some:* SAT or ACT (for admission).

Options: electronic application, early admission, deferred entrance.

Application fee: $25.

Required: high school transcript. ***Required for some:*** interview. ***Recommended:*** essay or personal statement, minimum 2.5 GPA.

CONTACT

Ms. Rachel Green, Director of Admissions, Mansfield University of Pennsylvania, Academy Street, Mansfield, PA 16933. *Phone:* 570-662-4813. *Toll-free phone:* 800-577-6826. *E-mail:* admissions@mnsfld.edu.

★ Marywood University

Scranton, Pennsylvania

http://www.marywood.edu/

- **Independent Roman Catholic** comprehensive, founded 1915
- **Suburban** 123-acre campus
- **Endowment** $40.9 million
- **Coed** 2,003 undergraduate students, 92% full-time, 66% women, 34% men
- **Moderately difficult** entrance level, 74% of applicants were admitted

UNDERGRAD STUDENTS

1,836 full-time, 167 part-time. Students come from 21 states and territories; 10 other countries; 30% are from out of state; 2% Black or African American, non-Hispanic/Latino; 6% Hispanic/Latino; 2% Asian, non-Hispanic/Latino; 0.1% Native Hawaiian or other Pacific Islander, non-Hispanic/Latino; 2% Two or more races, non-Hispanic/Latino; 11% Race/ethnicity unknown; 3% international; 7% transferred in; 43% live on campus.

Freshmen

Admission: 2,111 applied, 1,566 admitted, 373 enrolled. ***Average high school GPA:*** 3.5. ***Test scores:*** SAT critical reading scores over 500: 57%; SAT math scores over 500: 60%; SAT writing scores over 500: 57%; SAT critical reading scores over 600: 14%; SAT math scores over 600: 14%; SAT writing scores over 600: 14%; SAT critical reading scores over 700: 2%; SAT writing scores over 700: 2%.

Retention: 80% of full-time freshmen returned.

FACULTY

Total: 419, 39% full-time.

Student/faculty ratio: 11:1.

ACADEMICS

Calendar: semesters. *Degrees:* certificates, bachelor's, master's, doctoral, post-master's, and postbachelor's certificates.

Special study options: adult/continuing education programs, advanced placement credit, double majors, English as a second language, honors programs, independent study, internships, part-time degree program, services for LD students, student-designed majors, study abroad, summer session for credit. ***ROTC:*** Army (c), Air Force (c).

Unusual degree programs: 3-2 physician assistant, communication sciences disorders, criminal justice, biotechnology, health services administration.

Computers: 310 computers/terminals are available on campus for general student use. Students can access the following: computer help desk, free student e-mail accounts, online (class) grades, online (class) registration, online (class) schedules, degree audit, student account management. Campuswide network is available. 100% of college-owned or -operated housing units are wired for high-speed Internet access. Wireless service is available via entire campus.

STUDENT LIFE

Housing options: on-campus residence required through sophomore year; coed, women-only, special housing for students with disabilities. Campus housing is university owned. Freshman campus housing is guaranteed.

Activities and organizations: drama/theater group, student-run newspaper, radio and television station, choral group, Anime and Japanese Club, Diversity United, Volunteers in Action (VIA), Peers Wellness (POW), International Club.

Athletics Member NCAA. All Division III. ***Intercollegiate sports:*** baseball M, basketball M/W, cross-country running M/W, field hockey W, golf M, lacrosse M/W, soccer M/W, softball W, swimming and diving M/W, tennis M/W, track and field M/W, volleyball W. ***Intramural sports:*** badminton M/W, basketball M/W, cheerleading M(c)/W(c), golf W(c), rock climbing M(c)/W(c), soccer M/W, softball M/W, swimming and diving M/W, table tennis M/W, tennis M/W, volleyball M/W.

Campus security: 24-hour emergency response devices and patrols, late-night transport/escort service, controlled dormitory access, apartments with deadbolts, self-defense education, lighted pathways, seminars on safety.

Student services: health clinic, personal/psychological counseling.

COSTS & FINANCIAL AID

Costs (2015–16) ***Comprehensive fee:*** $46,592 includes full-time tuition ($30,942), mandatory fees ($1750), and room and board ($13,900). Full-time tuition and fees vary according to course load. Part-time tuition and fees vary according to course load. ***College room only:*** $7822. Room and board charges vary according to board plan and housing facility. ***Payment plans:*** installment, deferred payment. ***Waivers:*** senior citizens and employees or children of employees.

Financial Aid Of all full-time matriculated undergraduates who enrolled in 2014, 1,660 applied for aid, 1,529 were judged to have need, 287 had their need fully met. 665 Federal Work-Study jobs (averaging $1957). In 2014, 240 non-need-based awards were made. ***Average percent of need met:*** 73. ***Average financial aid package:*** $23,187. ***Average need-based loan:*** $4481. ***Average need-based gift aid:*** $20,072. ***Average non-need-based aid:*** $14,015. ***Average indebtedness upon graduation:*** $41,559.

APPLYING

Standardized Tests *Required:* SAT or ACT (for admission).

Options: electronic application, early admission, deferred entrance.

Application fee: $35.

Required: essay or personal statement, high school transcript, minimum 2.3 GPA, 1 letter of recommendation. ***Required for some:*** interview, art majors require portfolio, music majors require audition. ***Recommended:*** interview.

Application deadlines: rolling (freshmen), rolling (transfers).

Notification: continuous (freshmen), continuous (transfers).

CONTACT
Mr. Christian DiGregorio, Director of University Admissions, Marywood University, 2300 Adams Avenue, Scranton, PA 18509. *Phone:* 570-348-6234. *Toll-free phone:* 866-279-9663. *Fax:* 570-961-4763. *E-mail:* yourfuture@marywood.edu.

See previous page for display ad and page 1518 for the College Close-Up.

Mercyhurst University
Erie, Pennsylvania
http://www.mercyhurst.edu/

- **Independent Roman Catholic** comprehensive, founded 1926
- **Suburban** 88-acre campus with easy access to Buffalo
- **Endowment** $26.9 million
- **Coed**
- **Moderately difficult** entrance level

FACULTY
Student/faculty ratio: 14:1.

ACADEMICS
Calendar: 4-3-3. *Degrees:* bachelor's, master's, and postbachelor's certificates.

STUDENT LIFE
Housing options: on-campus residence required through sophomore year; coed, men-only, women-only. Campus housing is university owned and leased by the school. Freshman campus housing is guaranteed.

Activities and organizations: drama/theater group, student-run newspaper, radio and television station, choral group, student government, chorus, Admission Ambassadors, Amnesty International, The Merciad.

Athletics Member NCAA. All Division II except men's and women's ice hockey (Division I).

Campus security: 24-hour emergency response devices and patrols, campus-wide camera system.

Student services: health clinic, personal/psychological counseling.

COSTS & FINANCIAL AID
Costs (2014–15) ***Comprehensive fee:*** $42,285 includes full-time tuition ($29,600), mandatory fees ($1885), and room and board ($10,800). Full-time tuition and fees vary according to class time, course load, degree level, location, and program. Part-time tuition: $2960 per course. Part-time tuition and fees vary according to class time, course load, degree level, location, and program. ***Required fees:*** $65 per course part-time. ***College room only:*** $5474. Room and board charges vary according to board plan, housing facility, and location.

Financial Aid Of all full-time matriculated undergraduates who enrolled in 2013, 2,120 applied for aid, 1,922 were judged to have need, 195 had their need fully met. 536 Federal Work-Study jobs (averaging $1200). 236 state and other part-time jobs (averaging $1200). In 2013, 367 non-need-based awards were made. ***Average percent of need met:*** 57. ***Average financial aid package:*** $17,705. ***Average need-based loan:*** $4422. ***Average need-based gift aid:*** $4764. ***Average non-need-based aid:*** $11,147. ***Average indebtedness upon graduation:*** $24,881. ***Financial aid deadline:*** 5/1.

APPLYING
Standardized Tests *Required:* SAT or ACT (for admission). *Recommended:* SAT Subject Tests (for admission).

Options: electronic application, deferred entrance.

Application fee: $30.

Required: essay or personal statement, high school transcript. ***Required for some:*** 1 letter of recommendation. ***Recommended:*** interview.

CONTACT
Christopher Coons, Director of Undergraduate Admissions, Mercyhurst University, 501 East 38th Street, Erie, PA 16546-0001. *Phone:* 814-824-2202. *Toll-free phone:* 800-825-1926. *Fax:* 814-824-2071. *E-mail:* ccoons@mercyhurst.edu.

★ Messiah College
Mechanicsburg, Pennsylvania
http://www.messiah.edu/

- **Independent interdenominational** comprehensive, founded 1909
- **Small-town** 485-acre campus
- **Endowment** $136.7 million
- **Coed** 2,789 undergraduate students, 96% full-time, 60% women, 40% men
- **Moderately difficult** entrance level, 80% of applicants were admitted

UNDERGRAD STUDENTS
2,680 full-time, 109 part-time. Students come from 39 states and territories; 23 other countries; 37% are from out of state; 2% Black or African American, non-Hispanic/Latino; 4% Hispanic/Latino; 2% Asian, non-Hispanic/Latino; 3% Two or more races, non-Hispanic/Latino; 0.9% Race/ethnicity unknown; 3% international; 3% transferred in; 86% live on campus.

Freshmen
Admission: 2,472 applied, 1,977 admitted, 696 enrolled. ***Average high school GPA:*** 3.74. ***Test scores:*** SAT critical reading scores over 500: 77%; SAT math scores over 500: 80%; SAT writing scores over 500: 71%; ACT scores over 18: 96%; SAT critical reading scores over 600: 33%; SAT math scores over 600: 37%; SAT writing scores over 600: 25%; ACT scores over 24: 58%; SAT critical reading scores over 700: 6%; SAT math scores over 700: 8%; SAT writing scores over 700: 5%; ACT scores over 30: 10%.

Retention: 88% of full-time freshmen returned.

FACULTY
Total: 331, 54% full-time, 56% with terminal degrees.

Student/faculty ratio: 13:1.

ACADEMICS
Calendar: semesters. *Degrees:* bachelor's, master's, post-master's, and postbachelor's certificates.

Special study options: academic remediation for entering students, accelerated degree program, adult/continuing education programs, advanced placement credit, cooperative education, distance learning, double majors, English as a second language, freshman honors college, honors programs, independent study, internships, off-campus study, part-time degree program, services for LD students, student-designed majors, study abroad, summer session for credit.

Unusual degree programs: 3-2 Applied Health Science (BS) or Biopsychology (BS)/MSOT in Occupational Therapy with Thomas Jefferson University; Biochemistry (BA)/Doctor of Pharmacy with the University of the Sciences in Philadelphia; Politics (BA)/MS in Public Policy and Management with Carnegie Mellon University.

Computers: 571 computers/terminals are available on campus for general student use. Students can access the following: campus intranet, computer help desk, free student e-mail accounts, online (class) grades, online (class) registration, online (class) schedules, access to software. Campuswide network is available. 100% of college-owned or -operated housing units are wired for high-speed Internet access. Wireless service is available via entire campus.

STUDENT LIFE
Housing options: on-campus residence required through senior year; coed, men-only, women-only, special housing for students with disabilities. Campus housing is university owned. Freshman campus housing is guaranteed.

Activities and organizations: drama/theater group, student-run newspaper, radio station, choral group, Outreach teams, student government, choral groups and ensembles, Small Group Program, Outdoors Club.

Athletics Member NCAA. All Division III. ***Intercollegiate sports:*** baseball M, basketball M/W, cross-country running M/W, field hockey W, golf M, ice hockey M(c), lacrosse M/W, soccer M/W, softball W, swimming and diving M/W, tennis M/W, track and field M/W, ultimate Frisbee M(c)/W(c), volleyball W, wrestling M. ***Intramural sports:*** basketball M/W, field hockey W(c), football M/W, soccer M/W, softball M/W, volleyball M/W.

Campus security: 24-hour emergency response devices and patrols, student patrols, late-night transport/escort service, controlled dormitory

access, bicycle patrols, security lighting, self-defense classes, prevention/awareness programs.

Student services: health clinic, personal/psychological counseling.

COSTS & FINANCIAL AID

Costs (2015–16) ***Comprehensive fee:*** $41,870 includes full-time tuition ($31,410), mandatory fees ($830), and room and board ($9630). Part-time tuition: $1310 per credit hour. ***College room only:*** $5100. Room and board charges vary according to board plan and housing facility. ***Payment plan:*** installment. ***Waivers:*** adult students, senior citizens, and employees or children of employees.

Financial Aid Of all full-time matriculated undergraduates who enrolled in 2014, 2,165 applied for aid, 1,912 were judged to have need, 349 had their need fully met. 852 Federal Work-Study jobs (averaging $2134). 767 state and other part-time jobs (averaging $1926). In 2014, 705 non-need-based awards were made. ***Average percent of need met:*** 71. ***Average financial aid package:*** $22,327. ***Average need-based loan:*** $4883. ***Average need-based gift aid:*** $16,642. ***Average non-need-based aid:*** $12,925. ***Average indebtedness upon graduation:*** $34,301.

APPLYING

Standardized Tests *Required:* SAT or ACT (for admission).

Options: electronic application.

Application fee: $20.

Required: essay or personal statement, high school transcript. ***Required for some:*** interview.

Application deadlines: rolling (freshmen), rolling (transfers).

Notification: continuous (freshmen), continuous (transfers).

CONTACT

Mr. John Chopka, Vice President for Enrollment Management, Messiah College, One College Avenue, Suite 3005, Mechanicsburg, PA 17055. *Phone:* 717-691-6000. *Toll-free phone:* 800-233-4220. *Fax:* 717-691-2307. *E-mail:* admiss@messiah.edu.

★ Millersville University of Pennsylvania

Millersville, Pennsylvania

http://www.millersville.edu/

- **State-supported** comprehensive, founded 1855, part of Pennsylvania State System of Higher Education
- **Small-town** 250-acre campus
- **Endowment** $3.1 million
- **Coed** 7,171 undergraduate students, 89% full-time, 55% women, 45% men
- **Moderately difficult** entrance level, 69% of applicants were admitted

UNDERGRAD STUDENTS

6,358 full-time, 813 part-time. Students come from 23 states and territories; 54 other countries; 5% are from out of state; 10% Black or African American, non-Hispanic/Latino; 8% Hispanic/Latino; 2% Asian, non-Hispanic/Latino; 0.1% Native Hawaiian or other Pacific Islander, non-Hispanic/Latino; 0.2% American Indian or Alaska Native, non-Hispanic/Latino; 2% Two or more races, non-Hispanic/Latino; 0.4% Race/ethnicity unknown; 0.3% international; 8% transferred in; 33% live on campus.

Freshmen

Admission: 6,184 applied, 4,249 admitted, 1,358 enrolled. ***Test scores:*** SAT critical reading scores over 500: 53%; SAT math scores over 500: 57%; SAT writing scores over 500: 42%; ACT scores over 18: 93%; SAT critical reading scores over 600: 12%; SAT math scores over 600: 16%; SAT writing scores over 600: 9%; ACT scores over 24: 24%; SAT critical reading scores over 700: 2%; SAT math scores over 700: 1%; SAT writing scores over 700: 1%; ACT scores over 30: 3%.

Retention: 77% of full-time freshmen returned.

FACULTY

Total: 449, 64% full-time, 74% with terminal degrees.

Student/faculty ratio: 21:1.

ACADEMICS

Calendar: 4-1-4. *Degrees:* associate, bachelor's, master's, post-master's, and postbachelor's certificates.

Special study options: academic remediation for entering students, accelerated degree program, adult/continuing education programs, advanced placement credit, cooperative education, distance learning, double majors, honors programs, independent study, internships, off-campus study, part-time degree program, services for LD students, student-designed majors, study abroad, summer session for credit. ***ROTC:*** Army (b).

Unusual degree programs: 3-2 engineering with Chemistry Cooperative Engineering (BA Chemistry, BS Engineering), Physics Engineering with Penn State University (BA Physics, BS Engineering), Materials Science & Engineering with University of Delaware (BA Physics, MS Engineering).

Computers: 430 computers/terminals and 2,500 ports are available on campus for general student use. Students can access the following: campus intranet, computer help desk, free student e-mail accounts, online (class) grades, online (class) registration, online (class) schedules. Campuswide network is available. 100% of college-owned or -operated housing units are wired for high-speed Internet access. Wireless service is available via entire campus.

STUDENT LIFE

Housing options: on-campus residence required through sophomore year; coed, special housing for students with disabilities. Campus housing is university owned and leased by the school. Freshman campus housing is guaranteed.

Activities and organizations: drama/theater group, student-run newspaper, radio and television station, choral group, marching band, MUTV 99, Marching Band, University Activities Board, Student Senate, University Christian Fellowship, national fraternities, national sororities.

Athletics Member NCAA. All Division II. ***Intercollegiate sports:*** baseball M(s), basketball M(s)/W(s), cross-country running W(s), field hockey W(s), football M(s), golf M(s)/W(s), lacrosse W(s), soccer M(s)/W(s), softball W(s), swimming and diving W(s), tennis M(s)/W(s), track and field W(s), volleyball W(s), wrestling M(s). ***Intramural sports:*** badminton M(c)/W(c), basketball M/W, bowling M(c)/W(c), cheerleading W(c), cross-country running M(c)/W(c), equestrian sports M(c)/W(c), fencing M(c)/W(c), field hockey M/W, football M/W, golf M/W, ice hockey M(c)/W(c), lacrosse M(c), rugby M(c)/W(c), soccer M/W, softball M/W, table tennis M(c)/W(c), ultimate Frisbee M/W, volleyball M/W, water polo M/W.

Campus security: 24-hour emergency response devices and patrols, student patrols, late-night transport/escort service, controlled dormitory access, emergency notification system, crime awareness programs/timely warning alerts, self-defense education, shuttle buses, lighted paths.

Student services: health clinic, personal/psychological counseling, women's center.

COSTS & FINANCIAL AID

Costs (2014–15) ***Tuition:*** state resident $7920 full-time, $264 per credit part-time; nonresident $21,300 full-time, $710 per credit part-time. Full-time tuition and fees vary according to course load, location, and program. Part-time tuition and fees vary according to course load, location, and program. Mandatory fees differ for Non-Pennsylvania Residents. ***Required fees:*** $2348 full-time, $80 per credit part-time, $18 per credit part-time. ***Room and board:*** $11,380; room only: $7304. Room and board charges vary according to board plan, housing facility, and location. ***Payment plan:*** installment. ***Waivers:*** senior citizens and employees or children of employees.

Financial Aid Of all full-time matriculated undergraduates who enrolled in 2013, 5,578 applied for aid, 4,472 were judged to have need, 344 had their need fully met. 308 Federal Work-Study jobs (averaging $871). 1,942 state and other part-time jobs (averaging $1547). In 2013, 168 non-need-based awards were made. ***Average percent of need met:*** 69. ***Average financial aid package:*** $8479. ***Average need-based loan:*** $4192. ***Average need-based gift aid:*** $5891. ***Average non-need-based aid:*** $2517. ***Average indebtedness upon graduation:*** $29,791.

APPLYING

Standardized Tests *Required:* SAT or ACT (for admission).

Options: electronic application, early admission, deferred entrance.

Application fee: $50.

Required: essay or personal statement, high school transcript, minimum 2.0 GPA, SAT or ACT scores required for all applicants. Audition required for music applicants. Portfolio required for art applicants. RN required for nursing programs. ***Required for some:*** 1 letter of recommendation, interview, SAT or ACT scores required for all applicants. Audition required for music applicants. Portfolio required for art applicants. RN required for nursing programs. ***Recommended:*** minimum 3.0 GPA, 2 letters of recommendation.

Application deadlines: rolling (freshmen), rolling (out-of-state freshmen), rolling (transfers).

Notification: continuous (freshmen), continuous (out-of-state freshmen), continuous (transfers).

CONTACT

Ms. Katy A Ferrier, Director of Admissions, Millersville University of Pennsylvania, PO Box 1002, Millersville, PA 17551-0302. *Phone:* 717-871-4625. *Toll-free phone:* 800-MU-ADMIT. *Fax:* 717-871-2147. *E-mail:* admissions@millersville.edu.

See previous page for display ad and page 1522 for the College Close-Up.

★ Misericordia University
Dallas, Pennsylvania
http://www.misericordia.edu/

- **Independent Roman Catholic** comprehensive, founded 1924
- **Small-town** 120-acre campus
- **Endowment** $39.4 million
- **Coed** 2,465 undergraduate students, 72% full-time, 68% women, 32% men
- **Moderately difficult** entrance level, 71% of applicants were admitted

UNDERGRAD STUDENTS

1,773 full-time, 692 part-time. Students come from 25 states and territories; 1 other country; 24% are from out of state; 2% Black or African American, non-Hispanic/Latino; 3% Hispanic/Latino; 1% Asian, non-Hispanic/Latino; 0.1% Native Hawaiian or other Pacific Islander, non-Hispanic/Latino; 0.2% American Indian or Alaska Native, non-Hispanic/Latino; 0.8% Two or more races, non-Hispanic/Latino; 0.2% international; 4% transferred in; 43% live on campus.

Freshmen

Admission: 2,050 applied, 1,465 admitted, 438 enrolled. ***Average high school GPA:*** 3.34. ***Test scores:*** SAT critical reading scores over 500: 70%; SAT math scores over 500: 74%; ACT scores over 18: 96%; SAT critical reading scores over 600: 18%; SAT math scores over 600: 24%; ACT scores over 24: 41%; SAT critical reading scores over 700: 1%; SAT math scores over 700: 2%; ACT scores over 30: 7%.

Retention: 80% of full-time freshmen returned.

FACULTY

Total: 315, 39% full-time, 43% with terminal degrees.

Student/faculty ratio: 12:1.

ACADEMICS

Calendar: semesters. *Degrees:* certificates, bachelor's, master's, doctoral, post-master's, and postbachelor's certificates.

Special study options: accelerated degree program, adult/continuing education programs, advanced placement credit, cooperative education, distance learning, double majors, honors programs, independent study, internships, off-campus study, part-time degree program, services for LD students, student-designed majors, study abroad, summer session for credit. ***ROTC:*** Army (c), Air Force (c).

Unusual degree programs: 3-2 occupational therapy, speech-language pathology.

Computers: 150 computers/terminals and 1,000 ports are available on campus for general student use. Students can access the following: campus intranet, computer help desk, free student e-mail accounts, online (class) grades, online (class) registration, online (class) schedules. Campuswide network is available. 100% of college-owned or -operated housing units are wired for high-speed Internet access. Wireless service is available via entire campus.

STUDENT LIFE
Housing options: coed. Campus housing is university owned and is provided by a third party. Freshman applicants given priority for college housing.
Activities and organizations: drama/theater group, student-run newspaper, radio station, choral group, MSOTA, Peer Associates, Physical Therapy club, Varsity 'M' Club, Education Club.
Athletics Member NCAA. All Division III except tennis (Division II). ***Intercollegiate sports:*** baseball M, basketball M/W, cross-country running M/W, field hockey W, football M, golf M/W, lacrosse M/W, soccer M/W, softball W, swimming and diving M/W, tennis M/W, track and field M/W, volleyball W. ***Intramural sports:*** basketball M/W, football M/W, soccer M/W, softball M/W, tennis M/W, ultimate Frisbee M/W, volleyball M/W.
Campus security: 24-hour emergency response devices and patrols, late-night transport/escort service, controlled dormitory access.
Student services: health clinic, personal/psychological counseling, women's center.

COSTS & FINANCIAL AID
Costs (2014–15) ***Comprehensive fee:*** $41,060 includes full-time tuition ($27,470), mandatory fees ($1540), and room and board ($12,050). Full-time tuition and fees vary according to degree level. Part-time tuition: $535 per credit. Part-time tuition and fees vary according to class time and location. ***College room only:*** $7000. Room and board charges vary according to board plan and housing facility. ***Payment plans:*** installment, deferred payment. ***Waivers:*** employees or children of employees.
Financial Aid Of all full-time matriculated undergraduates who enrolled in 2014, 1,629 applied for aid, 1,407 were judged to have need, 294 had their need fully met. 254 Federal Work-Study jobs (averaging $1545). In 2014, 216 non-need-based awards were made. ***Average percent of need met:*** 74. ***Average financial aid package:*** $20,002. ***Average need-based loan:*** $9118. ***Average need-based gift aid:*** $14,030. ***Average non-need-based aid:*** $10,709. ***Average indebtedness upon graduation:*** $35,140.

APPLYING
Standardized Tests *Required:* SAT or ACT (for admission).
Options: electronic application, early admission, deferred entrance.
Application fee: $35.
Required: high school transcript. ***Required for some:*** essay or personal statement, minimum 2.5 GPA, 2 letters of recommendation. ***Recommended:*** interview.
Application deadlines: rolling (freshmen), rolling (out-of-state freshmen), rolling (transfers).
Notification: continuous (freshmen), continuous (out-of-state freshmen), continuous (transfers).

CONTACT
Mr. Glenn Bozinski, Director of Admissions, Misericordia University, 301 Lake Street, Dallas, PA 18612-1098. *Phone:* 570-675-6264. *Toll-free phone:* 866-262-6363. *Fax:* 570-674-6232. *E-mail:* admiss@misericordia.edu.

See below for display ad and page 1528 for the College Close-Up.

Moore College of Art & Design
Philadelphia, Pennsylvania
http://www.moore.edu/

- **Independent** comprehensive, founded 1848
- **Urban** 3-acre campus with easy access to Philadelphia
- **Endowment** $22.3 million
- **Women only** 412 undergraduate students, 95% full-time
- **Moderately difficult** entrance level, 60% of applicants were admitted

UNDERGRAD STUDENTS
393 full-time, 19 part-time. Students come from 25 states and territories; 8 other countries; 55% are from out of state; 16% Black or African American, non-Hispanic/Latino; 7% Hispanic/Latino; 3% Asian, non-Hispanic/Latino; 0.2% Native Hawaiian or other Pacific Islander, non-Hispanic/Latino; 0.2% American Indian or Alaska Native, non-Hispanic/Latino; 5% Two or more races, non-Hispanic/Latino; 3% Race/ethnicity unknown; 2% international; 30% transferred in; 35% live on campus.

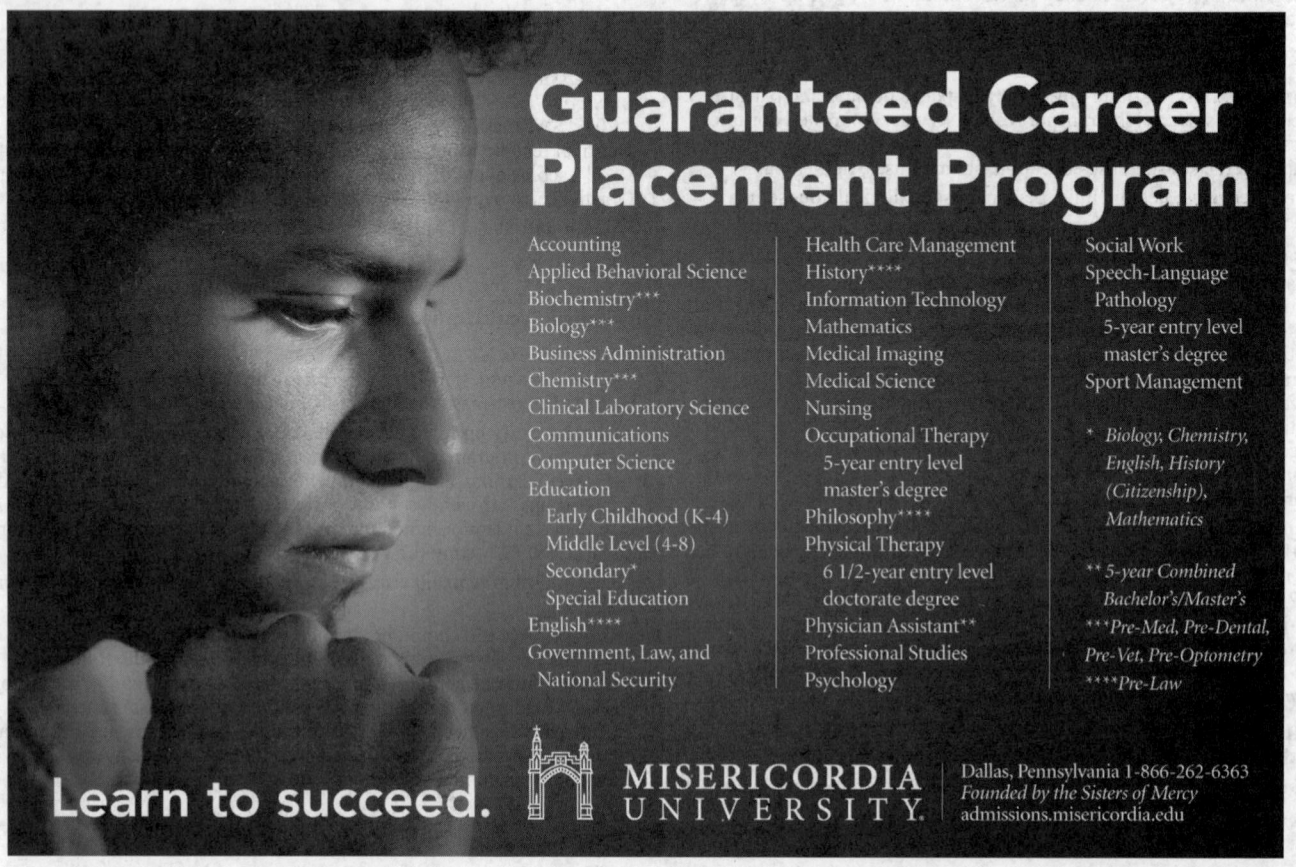

Freshmen
Admission: 612 applied, 367 admitted, 87 enrolled. ***Average high school GPA:*** 3.24.

Retention: 83% of full-time freshmen returned.

FACULTY
Total: 139, 17% full-time, 47% with terminal degrees.

Student/faculty ratio: 7:1.

ACADEMICS
Calendar: semesters. *Degrees:* certificates, bachelor's, master's, and postbachelor's certificates.

Special study options: academic remediation for entering students, advanced placement credit, cooperative education, double majors, external degree program, independent study, internships, off-campus study, part-time degree program, services for LD students, study abroad, summer session for credit.

Computers: Students can access the following: computer help desk, free student e-mail accounts, online (class) grades, online (class) registration, online (class) schedules. Campuswide network is available. Wireless service is available via entire campus.

STUDENT LIFE
Housing options: women-only. Campus housing is university owned. Freshman campus housing is guaranteed.

Activities and organizations: Student Government Association, Student Orientation Staff, Student-run Gallery, Visionary Women Honors Program, Yearbook.

Athletics ***Intramural sports:*** volleyball W.

Campus security: 24-hour patrols, late-night transport/escort service, controlled dormitory access.

Student services: health clinic, personal/psychological counseling.

COSTS
Costs (2014–15) ***One-time required fee:*** $200. ***Comprehensive fee:*** $46,838 includes full-time tuition ($32,920), mandatory fees ($1128), and room and board ($12,790). Full-time tuition and fees vary according to course load. Part-time tuition: $1374 per credit. Part-time tuition and fees vary according to course load. ***Required fees:*** $565 per year part-time. ***Room and board:*** Room and board charges vary according to board plan. ***Payment plan:*** installment. ***Waivers:*** employees or children of employees.

APPLYING
Standardized Tests *Recommended:* SAT or ACT (for admission).

Options: electronic application, deferred entrance.

Application fee: $40.

Required: high school transcript, minimum 2.5 GPA, 1 letter of recommendation, portfolio review. ***Required for some:*** minimum 3.0 GPA. ***Recommended:*** essay or personal statement, interview.

Application deadlines: 8/15 (freshmen), rolling (transfers).

Notification: continuous (freshmen), continuous (transfers).

CONTACT
Ms. Jasmine Zateeny, Assistant Director of Admissions, Recruitment Coordinator, Moore College of Art & Design, 20th and The Parkway, Philadelphia, PA 19103. *Phone:* 215-965-4015. *Toll-free phone:* 800-523-2025. *Fax:* 215-965-8544. *E-mail:* enroll@moore.edu.

★ Moravian College
Bethlehem, Pennsylvania
http://www.moravian.edu/

- **Independent** comprehensive, founded 1742, affiliated with Moravian Church
- **Suburban** 85-acre campus with easy access to Philadelphia
- **Endowment** $108.7 million
- **Coed** 1,612 undergraduate students, 92% full-time, 59% women, 41% men
- **Moderately difficult** entrance level, 86% of applicants were admitted

UNDERGRAD STUDENTS
1,481 full-time, 131 part-time. Students come from 23 states and territories; 5 other countries; 33% are from out of state; 4% Black or African American, non-Hispanic/Latino; 9% Hispanic/Latino; 2% Asian, non-Hispanic/Latino; 0.1% American Indian or Alaska Native, non-Hispanic/Latino; 2% Two or more races, non-Hispanic/Latino; 5% Race/ethnicity unknown; 3% international; 8% transferred in; 70% live on campus.

Freshmen
Admission: 1,536 applied, 1,324 admitted, 386 enrolled. ***Average high school GPA:*** 3.39. ***Test scores:*** SAT critical reading scores over 500: 55%; SAT math scores over 500: 60%; SAT writing scores over 500: 52%; ACT scores over 18: 80%; SAT critical reading scores over 600: 14%; SAT math scores over 600: 20%; SAT writing scores over 600: 14%; ACT scores over 24: 37%; SAT critical reading scores over 700: 2%; SAT math scores over 700: 1%; SAT writing scores over 700: 2%; ACT scores over 30: 6%.

Retention: 79% of full-time freshmen returned.

FACULTY
Total: 172, 56% full-time, 69% with terminal degrees.

Student/faculty ratio: 12:1.

ACADEMICS
Calendar: semesters. *Degrees:* bachelor's, master's, post-master's, and postbachelor's certificates.

Special study options: accelerated degree program, adult/continuing education programs, advanced placement credit, cooperative education, double majors, honors programs, independent study, internships, off-campus study, part-time degree program, services for LD students, student-designed majors, study abroad, summer session for credit. ***ROTC:*** Army (c).

Unusual degree programs: 3-2 engineering with Lehigh University and Washington University in St. Louis.

Computers: 263 computers/terminals and 1,500 ports are available on campus for general student use. Students can access the following: campus intranet, computer help desk, free student e-mail accounts, online (class) grades, online (class) registration, online (class) schedules. Campuswide network is available. 100% of college-owned or -operated housing units are wired for high-speed Internet access. Wireless service is available via entire campus.

STUDENT LIFE
Housing options: on-campus residence required through senior year; coed, men-only, women-only, special housing for students with disabilities. Campus housing is university owned. Freshman campus housing is guaranteed.

Activities and organizations: drama/theater group, student-run newspaper, radio station, choral group, marching band, United Student Government (USG), Moravian College Choir, Habitat for Humanity, Student Nurses Association, Moravian College Theatre Company, national fraternities, national sororities.

Athletics Member NCAA. All Division III. ***Intercollegiate sports:*** baseball M, basketball M/W, bowling M(c), cheerleading W(c), cross-country running M/W, equestrian sports W(c), field hockey W, football M, golf M/W(c), ice hockey M(c)/W(c), lacrosse M/W, rugby M(c)/W(c), soccer M/W, softball W, tennis M/W, track and field M/W, ultimate Frisbee W(c), volleyball W, wrestling M(c). ***Intramural sports:*** basketball M/W, soccer M/W, softball M/W, table tennis M/W, tennis M/W, volleyball M/W.

Campus security: 24-hour emergency response devices and patrols, late-night transport/escort service, controlled dormitory access.

Student services: health clinic, personal/psychological counseling.

COSTS & FINANCIAL AID
Costs (2014–15) ***Comprehensive fee:*** $48,654 includes full-time tuition ($35,991), mandatory fees ($1581), and room and board ($11,082). Full-time tuition and fees vary according to student level. Part-time tuition: $1000 per credit. Part-time tuition and fees vary according to class time. ***College room only:*** $6248. Room and board charges vary according to board plan and housing facility. ***Payment plan:*** installment. ***Waivers:*** employees or children of employees.

Financial Aid Of all full-time matriculated undergraduates who enrolled in 2014, 1,299 applied for aid, 1,198 were judged to have need, 150 had their need fully met. 1,032 Federal Work-Study jobs (averaging $1978). 114 state and other part-time jobs (averaging $1135). In 2014, 190 non-need-based awards were made. ***Average percent of need met:*** 73. ***Average financial aid package:*** $28,034. ***Average need-based loan:*** $4793. ***Average need-based gift aid:*** $21,958. ***Average non-need-based aid:*** $13,540.

APPLYING

Standardized Tests *Required:* SAT or ACT (for admission). *Recommended:* SAT (for admission), ACT (for admission), SAT and SAT Subject Tests or ACT (for admission).

Options: electronic application, early decision, deferred entrance.

Required: essay or personal statement, high school transcript, 1 letter of recommendation, interview, Art majors must submit a portfolio and Music majors must audition.

Application deadlines: 3/1 (freshmen), 3/1 (transfers).

Notification: continuous (freshmen), continuous (transfers).

CONTACT

Steven Soba, Vice President for Enrollment Management, Moravian College, 1200 Main Street, Bethlehem, PA 18018. *Phone:* 610-861-1320. *Toll-free phone:* 800-441-3191. *Fax:* 610-625-7930. *E-mail:* admissions@moravian.edu.

★ Mount Aloysius College

Cresson, Pennsylvania

http://www.mtaloy.edu/

- **Independent Roman Catholic** comprehensive, founded 1939
- **Small-town** 193-acre campus
- **Coed** 1,794 undergraduate students, 70% full-time, 72% women, 28% men
- **Minimally difficult** entrance level, 74% of applicants were admitted

UNDERGRAD STUDENTS

1,251 full-time, 543 part-time. 5% are from out of state; 3% Black or African American, non-Hispanic/Latino; 1% Hispanic/Latino; 0.3% Asian, non-Hispanic/Latino; 0.3% American Indian or Alaska Native, non-Hispanic/Latino; 16% Race/ethnicity unknown; 1% international; 5% transferred in; 32% live on campus.

Freshmen

Admission: 1,572 applied, 1,163 admitted, 386 enrolled. ***Average high school GPA:*** 3.2. ***Test scores:*** SAT critical reading scores over 500: 31%; SAT math scores over 500: 32%; SAT writing scores over 500: 16%; ACT scores over 18: 60%; SAT critical reading scores over 600: 3%; SAT math scores over 600: 2%; SAT writing scores over 600: 2%; ACT scores over 24: 6%.

FACULTY

Total: 204, 37% full-time.

Student/faculty ratio: 12:1.

ACADEMICS

Calendar: semesters. *Degrees:* certificates, associate, bachelor's, and master's.

Special study options: academic remediation for entering students, accelerated degree program, advanced placement credit, distance learning, double majors, external degree program, honors programs, independent study, internships, part-time degree program, student-designed majors, study abroad, summer session for credit.

Computers: Students can access the following: campus intranet, computer help desk, free student e-mail accounts, online (class) grades, online (class) registration, online (class) schedules. Campuswide network is available. 100% of college-owned or -operated housing units are wired for high-speed Internet access. Wireless service is available via entire campus.

STUDENT LIFE

Housing options: on-campus residence required through sophomore year; coed. Campus housing is university owned. Freshman campus housing is guaranteed.

Activities and organizations: drama/theater group, student-run newspaper, choral group, student government, Campus Activity Board, Student Athletic Advisory Committee, Spirit Team, Dance Team.

Athletics Member NCAA. All Division III. ***Intercollegiate sports:*** baseball M, basketball M/W, cross-country running M/W, golf M/W, soccer M/W, softball W, tennis M/W, volleyball W. ***Intramural sports:*** basketball M/W, bowling M/W, cheerleading M(c)/W(c), football M/W,

skiing (cross-country) M/W, skiing (downhill) M/W, table tennis M/W, ultimate Frisbee M/W, volleyball M/W, weight lifting M/W.

Campus security: 24-hour emergency response devices and patrols, student patrols, late-night transport/escort service, controlled dormitory access.

Student services: health clinic, personal/psychological counseling.

FINANCIAL AID

Financial Aid Of all full-time matriculated undergraduates who enrolled in 2014, 1,251 applied for aid, 1,156 were judged to have need. In 2014, 95 non-need-based awards were made. ***Average percent of need met:*** 38. ***Average financial aid package:*** $14,510. ***Average need-based loan:*** $4020. ***Average need-based gift aid:*** $4650. ***Average non-need-based aid:*** $5310.

APPLYING

Standardized Tests *Required:* SAT or ACT (for admission). *Recommended:* SAT (for admission), ACT (for admission).

Options: electronic application, early admission, deferred entrance.

Application fee: $30.

Required: high school transcript. ***Required for some:*** essay or personal statement, interview. ***Recommended:*** interview.

Application deadlines: rolling (freshmen), rolling (transfers).

Notification: continuous (freshmen), continuous (transfers).

CONTACT

Mr. Frank C. Crouse Jr., Vice President for Enrollment Management/Dean of Admissions, Mount Aloysius College, 7373 Admiral Peary Highway, Cresson, PA 16630-1999. *Phone:* 814-886-6383. *Toll-free phone:* 888-823-2220. *Fax:* 814-886-6441. *E-mail:* admissions@mtaloy.edu.

See previous page for display ad and page 1536 for the College Close-Up.

★ Muhlenberg College

Allentown, Pennsylvania

http://www.muhlenberg.edu/

- **Independent** 4-year, founded 1848, affiliated with Lutheran Church
- **Suburban** 75-acre campus with easy access to Philadelphia
- **Endowment** $247.7 million
- **Coed** 2,440 undergraduate students, 94% full-time, 60% women, 40% men
- **Very difficult** entrance level, 53% of applicants were admitted

UNDERGRAD STUDENTS

2,299 full-time, 141 part-time. Students come from 36 states and territories; 16 other countries; 72% are from out of state; 3% Black or African American, non-Hispanic/Latino; 6% Hispanic/Latino; 3% Asian, non-Hispanic/Latino; 0.2% American Indian or Alaska Native, non-Hispanic/Latino; 2% Two or more races, non-Hispanic/Latino; 8% Race/ethnicity unknown; 1% international; 0.7% transferred in; 92% live on campus.

Freshmen

Admission: 4,714 applied, 2,489 admitted, 589 enrolled. ***Average high school GPA:*** 3.28. ***Test scores:*** SAT critical reading scores over 500: 92%; SAT math scores over 500: 95%; SAT writing scores over 500: 92%; ACT scores over 18: 100%; SAT critical reading scores over 600: 57%; SAT math scores over 600: 61%; SAT writing scores over 600: 61%; ACT scores over 24: 92%; SAT critical reading scores over 700: 13%; SAT math scores over 700: 12%; SAT writing scores over 700: 15%; ACT scores over 30: 26%.

Retention: 91% of full-time freshmen returned.

FACULTY

Total: 278, 62% full-time, 62% with terminal degrees.

Student/faculty ratio: 11:1.

ACADEMICS

Calendar: semesters. *Degrees:* certificates, associate, and bachelor's.

Special study options: accelerated degree program, adult/continuing education programs, advanced placement credit, double majors, honors programs, independent study, internships, off-campus study, part-time degree program, services for LD students, student-designed majors, study abroad, summer session for credit. ***ROTC:*** Army (c).

Unusual degree programs: 3-2 engineering with Columbia University; forestry with Duke University; University of Pennsylvania School of Dental Medicine (BS and DDS); Drexel University College of Medicine and the Lehigh Valley Hospital (AB or BS and MD); State University of New York (SUNY) State College of Optometry (AB or BS and OD); OT and PT at Thomas Jefferson.

Computers: 450 computers/terminals and 100 ports are available on campus for general student use. Students can access the following: campus intranet, computer help desk, free student e-mail accounts, online (class) grades, online (class) registration, online (class) schedules. Campuswide network is available. 100% of college-owned or -operated housing units are wired for high-speed Internet access. Wireless service is available via entire campus.

STUDENT LIFE

Housing options: on-campus residence required through senior year; coed, women-only, special housing for students with disabilities. Campus housing is university owned and leased by the school. Freshman campus housing is guaranteed.

Activities and organizations: drama/theater group, student-run newspaper, radio and television station, choral group, Theater Association, Environmental Action Team, Jefferson School Partnership, Select Choir, Habitat for Humanity, national fraternities, national sororities.

Athletics Member NCAA. All Division III. ***Intercollegiate sports:*** baseball M, basketball M/W, cheerleading M/W, cross-country running M/W, field hockey W, football M, golf M/W, lacrosse M/W, soccer M/W, softball W, tennis M/W, track and field M/W, volleyball W, wrestling M. ***Intramural sports:*** basketball M/W, cross-country running M/W, football M/W, ice hockey M, racquetball M/W, rugby M/W, soccer M/W, softball M, swimming and diving M/W, tennis M/W, ultimate Frisbee M, volleyball M/W.

Campus security: 24-hour emergency response devices and patrols, late-night transport/escort service, controlled dormitory access.

Student services: health clinic, personal/psychological counseling.

COSTS & FINANCIAL AID

Costs (2014–15) ***Comprehensive fee:*** $54,595 includes full-time tuition ($43,860), mandatory fees ($285), and room and board ($10,450). Part-time tuition and fees vary according to program. ***College room only:*** $5665. Room and board charges vary according to board plan, housing facility, and location. ***Payment plan:*** installment. ***Waivers:*** employees or children of employees.

Financial Aid Of all full-time matriculated undergraduates who enrolled in 2013, 1,454 applied for aid, 1,158 were judged to have need, 1,016 had their need fully met. In 2013, 787 non-need-based awards were made. ***Average percent of need met:*** 91. ***Average financial aid package:*** $27,092. ***Average need-based loan:*** $4568. ***Average need-based gift aid:*** $23,778. ***Average non-need-based aid:*** $11,557. ***Average indebtedness upon graduation:*** $30,363. ***Financial aid deadline:*** 2/15.

APPLYING

Standardized Tests *Required for some:* SAT or ACT (for admission).

Options: electronic application, early admission, early decision, deferred entrance.

Application fee: $50.

Required: essay or personal statement, high school transcript, 2 letters of recommendation. ***Required for some:*** interview, graded paper. ***Recommended:*** interview.

Application deadlines: 2/15 (freshmen), 6/15 (transfers).

Early decision deadline: 2/15.

Notification: 3/15 (freshmen), continuous until 7/1 (transfers), rolling (early decision).

CONTACT

Mr. Christopher Hooker-Haring, Director of Undergraduate Admissions, Muhlenberg College, 2400 Chew Street, Allentown, PA 18104. *Phone:* 484-664-3245. *Fax:* 484-664-3234. *E-mail:* adm@muhlenberg.edu.

See previous page for display ad and page 1540 for the College Close-Up.

★ Neumann University
Aston, Pennsylvania
http://www.neumann.edu/

- **Independent Roman Catholic** comprehensive, founded 1965
- **Suburban** 50-acre campus with easy access to Philadelphia
- **Endowment** $27.6 million
- **Coed** 2,562 undergraduate students, 78% full-time, 65% women, 35% men
- **Minimally difficult** entrance level, 94% of applicants were admitted

UNDERGRAD STUDENTS

1,992 full-time, 570 part-time. Students come from 21 states and territories; 5 other countries; 32% are from out of state; 22% Black or African American, non-Hispanic/Latino; 3% Hispanic/Latino; 1% Asian, non-Hispanic/Latino; 0.1% American Indian or Alaska Native, non-Hispanic/Latino; 2% Two or more races, non-Hispanic/Latino; 18% Race/ethnicity unknown; 1% international; 5% transferred in; 30% live on campus.

Freshmen

Admission: 1,964 applied, 1,847 admitted, 416 enrolled. ***Average high school GPA:*** 2.92. ***Test scores:*** SAT critical reading scores over 500: 15%; SAT math scores over 500: 19%; SAT writing scores over 500: 14%; ACT scores over 18: 37%; SAT critical reading scores over 600: 2%; SAT math scores over 600: 2%; SAT writing scores over 600: 1%.

Retention: 73% of full-time freshmen returned.

FACULTY

Total: 327, 31% full-time, 45% with terminal degrees.

Student/faculty ratio: 14:1.

ACADEMICS

Calendar: semesters. *Degrees:* associate, bachelor's, master's, doctoral, and post-master's certificates.

Special study options: academic remediation for entering students, accelerated degree program, adult/continuing education programs, advanced placement credit, cooperative education, distance learning, double majors, freshman honors college, honors programs, independent study, internships, off-campus study, part-time degree program, services for LD students, study abroad, summer session for credit. ***ROTC:*** Army (c), Air Force (c).

Computers: 400 computers/terminals and 1,500 ports are available on campus for general student use. Students can access the following: campus intranet, computer help desk, free student e-mail accounts, online (class) grades, online (class) schedules. Campuswide network is available. 100% of college-owned or -operated housing units are wired for high-speed Internet access. Wireless service is available via entire campus.

STUDENT LIFE

Housing options: coed, special housing for students with disabilities. Campus housing is university owned and leased by the school. Freshman applicants given priority for college housing.

Activities and organizations: drama/theater group, student-run newspaper, radio and television station, choral group, student government, Student Activities Board, Black Student Union, Boogie Knights, Neumann Media.

Athletics Member NCAA. All Division III. ***Intercollegiate sports:*** baseball M, basketball M/W, cross-country running M/W, field hockey W, golf M, ice hockey M/W, lacrosse M/W, rugby M(c)/W(c), soccer M/W, softball W, tennis M/W, track and field M/W, volleyball W. ***Intramural sports:*** baseball M(c), basketball M/W, cheerleading W(c), ice hockey M(c), soccer M/W, softball M/W, table tennis M/W, ultimate Frisbee M/W, volleyball M/W.

Campus security: 24-hour emergency response devices and patrols, late-night transport/escort service, controlled dormitory access.

Student services: health clinic, personal/psychological counseling.

COSTS & FINANCIAL AID

Costs (2014–15) ***Comprehensive fee:*** $37,660 includes full-time tuition ($24,800), mandatory fees ($1060), and room and board ($11,800). Part-time tuition: $566 per credit hour. ***Required fees:*** $60 per term part-time. ***College room only:*** $6940. Room and board charges vary according to board plan. ***Payment plans:*** installment, deferred payment. ***Waivers:*** employees or children of employees.

Financial Aid Of all full-time matriculated undergraduates who enrolled in 2011, 1,826 applied for aid, 1,639 were judged to have need, 22 had their need fully met. In 2011, 485 non-need-based awards were made. ***Average percent of need met:*** 70. ***Average financial aid package:*** $20,250. ***Average need-based loan:*** $4500. ***Average need-based gift aid:*** $4300. ***Average non-need-based aid:*** $7400. ***Average indebtedness upon graduation:*** $27,000.

APPLYING

Standardized Tests *Required:* SAT or ACT (for admission).

Options: electronic application, deferred entrance.

Application fee: $35.

Required: high school transcript, minimum 2.0 GPA. ***Required for some:*** 1 letter of recommendation. ***Recommended:*** essay or personal statement, interview.

Application deadlines: rolling (freshmen), rolling (out-of-state freshmen), rolling (transfers).

Notification: continuous (freshmen), continuous (out-of-state freshmen), continuous (transfers).

CONTACT

Mr. Chris Mayerski, Director of Admissions, Neumann University, One Neumann Drive, Aston, PA 19014-1298. *Phone:* 610-558-5615. *Toll-free phone:* 800-963-8626. *Fax:* 610-361-2548. *E-mail:* neumann@neumann.edu.

See below for display ad and page 1542 for the College Close-Up.

Peirce College

Philadelphia, Pennsylvania

http://www.peirce.edu/

- **Independent** comprehensive, founded 1865
- **Urban** 1-acre campus
- **Coed, primarily women** 1,771 undergraduate students, 20% full-time, 72% women, 28% men
- **Noncompetitive** entrance level

UNDERGRAD STUDENTS

347 full-time, 1,424 part-time. 8% are from out of state; 69% Black or African American, non-Hispanic/Latino; 7% Hispanic/Latino; 2% Asian, non-Hispanic/Latino; 0.2% Native Hawaiian or other Pacific Islander, non-Hispanic/Latino; 0.3% American Indian or Alaska Native, non-Hispanic/Latino; 0.7% Two or more races, non-Hispanic/Latino; 1% Race/ethnicity unknown.

Freshmen

Admission: 116 enrolled.

Retention: 100% of full-time freshmen returned.

FACULTY

Student/faculty ratio: 12:1.

ACADEMICS

Calendar: semesters. *Degrees:* certificates, associate, bachelor's, and master's.

Special study options: accelerated degree program, adult/continuing education programs, advanced placement credit, cooperative education, distance learning, internships, part-time degree program, services for LD students, summer session for credit.

Computers: Students can access the following: campus intranet, computer help desk, free student e-mail accounts, online (class) grades, online (class) registration, online (class) schedules. Campuswide network is available. Wireless service is available via entire campus.

STUDENT LIFE

Housing options: college housing not available.

Campus security: 24-hour emergency response devices and patrols, late-night transport/escort service, 24-hour security cameras.

COSTS & FINANCIAL AID

Costs (2014–15) ***Tuition:*** $13,200 full-time, $550 per credit hour part-time. Full-time tuition and fees vary according to course load and reciprocity agreements. Part-time tuition and fees vary according to course load and reciprocity agreements. ***Required fees:*** $600 full-time, $600 per term part-time. ***Payment plans:*** installment, deferred payment. ***Waivers:*** children of alumni and employees or children of employees.

Financial Aid Of all full-time matriculated undergraduates who enrolled in 2012, 772 applied for aid, 750 were judged to have need, 8 had their need fully met. In 2012, 9 non-need-based awards were made. ***Average percent of need met:*** 35. ***Average financial aid package:*** $8477. ***Average need-based loan:*** $4016. ***Average need-based gift aid:*** $5089. ***Average non-need-based aid:*** $3003.

APPLYING
Options: electronic application.

Application fee: $50.

Required: high school transcript.

CONTACT
Mr. Paul Ballentine, Manager, Admissions, Peirce College, 1420 Pine Street, Philadelphia, PA 19102. *Phone:* 215-670-9214. *Toll-free phone:* 888-467-3472. *Fax:* 215-670-9366. *E-mail:* info@peirce.edu.

Penn State Abington

Abington, Pennsylvania

http://www.abington.psu.edu/

- **State-related** 4-year, founded 1950, part of Pennsylvania State University
- **Small-town** campus
- **Coed** 3,947 undergraduate students, 79% full-time, 53% women, 47% men
- **Very difficult** entrance level, 79% of applicants were admitted

UNDERGRAD STUDENTS
3,117 full-time, 830 part-time. 7% are from out of state; 13% Black or African American, non-Hispanic/Latino; 10% Hispanic/Latino; 17% Asian, non-Hispanic/Latino; 0.2% Native Hawaiian or other Pacific Islander, non-Hispanic/Latino; 0.2% American Indian or Alaska Native, non-Hispanic/Latino; 2% Two or more races, non-Hispanic/Latino; 3% Race/ethnicity unknown; 5% international; 6% transferred in.

Freshmen
Admission: 3,906 applied, 3,099 admitted, 896 enrolled. ***Average high school GPA:*** 3.18. ***Test scores:*** SAT critical reading scores over 500: 33%; SAT math scores over 500: 48%; SAT writing scores over 500: 34%; ACT scores over 18: 84%; SAT critical reading scores over 600: 8%; SAT math scores over 600: 17%; SAT writing scores over 600: 8%; ACT scores over 24: 22%; SAT math scores over 700: 4%; ACT scores over 30: 3%.

Retention: 82% of full-time freshmen returned.

FACULTY
Total: 271, 46% full-time, 46% with terminal degrees.

Student/faculty ratio: 20:1.

ACADEMICS
Calendar: semesters. *Degrees:* certificates, associate, bachelor's, and postbachelor's certificates (enrollment figures include students enrolled at The Graduate School at Penn State who are taking courses at this location).

Special study options: adult/continuing education programs, external degree program, part-time degree program. ***ROTC:*** Army (c), Air Force (c).

Computers: Students can access the following: campus intranet, computer help desk, free student e-mail accounts, online (class) grades, online (class) registration, online (class) schedules. Campuswide network is available.

STUDENT LIFE
Housing options: college housing not available.

Athletics ***Intercollegiate sports:*** baseball M, basketball M/W, golf M, soccer M/W, softball W, tennis M/W, volleyball W. ***Intramural sports:*** basketball M/W, cross-country running M/W, football M, soccer M/W, softball M, tennis M/W, volleyball M/W.

Campus security: 24-hour emergency response devices and patrols.

COSTS & FINANCIAL AID
Costs (2014–15) ***Tuition:*** state resident $13,012 full-time, $535 per credit hour part-time; nonresident $19,848 full-time, $827 per credit hour part-time. Full-time tuition and fees vary according to course level, degree level, location, program, and student level. Part-time tuition and fees vary according to course level, course load, degree level, location, program, and student level. ***Required fees:*** $930 full-time. ***Payment plans:*** installment, deferred payment. ***Waivers:*** senior citizens and employees or children of employees.

Financial Aid Of all full-time matriculated undergraduates who enrolled in 2013, 2,414 applied for aid, 2,056 were judged to have need, 61 had their need fully met. In 2013, 144 non-need-based awards were made. ***Average percent of need met:*** 60. ***Average financial aid package:*** $10,802. ***Average need-based loan:*** $4084. ***Average need-based gift aid:*** $7421. ***Average non-need-based aid:*** $3383. ***Average indebtedness upon graduation:*** $36,935.

APPLYING
Standardized Tests *Required:* SAT or ACT (for admission).

Options: electronic application, early admission, deferred entrance.

Application fee: $50.

Required: high school transcript. ***Required for some:*** interview. ***Recommended:*** essay or personal statement.

Application deadlines: rolling (freshmen), rolling (transfers).

Notification: continuous (freshmen), continuous (transfers).

CONTACT
Admissions Office, Penn State Abington, 1600 Woodland Road, Abington, PA 19001. *Phone:* 215-881-7600. *Fax:* 215-881-7655. *E-mail:* abingtonadmissions@psu.edu.

Penn State Altoona

Altoona, Pennsylvania

http://www.altoona.psu.edu/

- **State-related** 4-year, founded 1939, part of Pennsylvania State University
- **Suburban** campus
- **Coed** 3,903 undergraduate students, 95% full-time, 45% women, 55% men
- **Very difficult** entrance level, 88% of applicants were admitted

UNDERGRAD STUDENTS
3,725 full-time, 178 part-time. 19% are from out of state; 8% Black or African American, non-Hispanic/Latino; 5% Hispanic/Latino; 3% Asian, non-Hispanic/Latino; 0.1% Native Hawaiian or other Pacific Islander, non-Hispanic/Latino; 0.1% American Indian or Alaska Native, non-Hispanic/Latino; 2% Two or more races, non-Hispanic/Latino; 1% Race/ethnicity unknown; 4% international; 3% transferred in; 25% live on campus.

Freshmen
Admission: 5,630 applied, 4,974 admitted, 1,487 enrolled. ***Average high school GPA:*** 3.08. ***Test scores:*** SAT critical reading scores over 500: 45%; SAT math scores over 500: 56%; SAT writing scores over 500: 40%; ACT scores over 18: 88%; SAT critical reading scores over 600: 8%; SAT math scores over 600: 14%; SAT writing scores over 600: 6%; ACT scores over 24: 27%; SAT math scores over 700: 1%; ACT scores over 30: 1%.

Retention: 82% of full-time freshmen returned.

FACULTY
Total: 293, 65% full-time, 50% with terminal degrees.

Student/faculty ratio: 17:1.

ACADEMICS
Calendar: semesters. *Degrees:* certificates, associate, and bachelor's (enrollment figures include students enrolled at The Graduate School at Penn State who are taking courses at this location).

Special study options: independent study. ***ROTC:*** Army (b), Air Force (b).

Computers: Students can access the following: campus intranet, computer help desk, free student e-mail accounts, online (class) grades, online (class) registration, online (class) schedules.

STUDENT LIFE
Housing options: coed, special housing for students with disabilities. Campus housing is university owned.

Athletics Member NCAA. All Division III. ***Intercollegiate sports:*** baseball M, basketball M/W, cross-country running M/W, golf M/W, soccer M/W, softball W, swimming and diving M/W, tennis M/W. ***Intramural sports:*** badminton M/W, baseball M/W, basketball M/W, football M/W, golf M/W, racquetball M/W, soccer M/W, softball M/W, table tennis M/W, tennis M/W, track and field M/W, volleyball M/W, weight lifting M/W.

Campus security: 24-hour emergency response devices and patrols, late-night transport/escort service.

COSTS & FINANCIAL AID

Costs (2014–15) ***Tuition:*** state resident $13,658 full-time, $569 per credit hour part-time; nonresident $20,890 full-time, $870 per credit hour part-time. Full-time tuition and fees vary according to course level, degree level, location, program, and student level. Part-time tuition and fees vary according to course level, course load, degree level, location, program, and student level. ***Required fees:*** $930 full-time. ***Room and board:*** $10,520; room only: $5460. Room and board charges vary according to board plan, housing facility, and location. ***Payment plans:*** installment, deferred payment. ***Waivers:*** senior citizens and employees or children of employees.

Financial Aid Of all full-time matriculated undergraduates who enrolled in 2013, 2,993 applied for aid, 2,581 were judged to have need, 160 had their need fully met. In 2013, 259 non-need-based awards were made. ***Average percent of need met:*** 57. ***Average financial aid package:*** $10,438. ***Average need-based loan:*** $4061. ***Average need-based gift aid:*** $6395. ***Average non-need-based aid:*** $3639. ***Average indebtedness upon graduation:*** $36,935.

APPLYING

Standardized Tests *Required:* SAT or ACT (for admission).

Options: electronic application, early admission, deferred entrance.

Application fee: $50.

Required: high school transcript. ***Required for some:*** interview. ***Recommended:*** essay or personal statement.

Application deadlines: rolling (freshmen), rolling (transfers).

Notification: continuous (freshmen), continuous (transfers).

CONTACT

Admissions Office, Penn State Altoona, 3000 Ivyside Park, Altoona, PA 16601-3760. *Phone:* 814-949-5466. *Toll-free phone:* 800-848-9843. *Fax:* 814-949-5564. *E-mail:* aaadmit@psu.edu.

Penn State Beaver

Monaca, Pennsylvania

http://www.br.psu.edu/

- **State-related** 4-year, founded 1964, part of Pennsylvania State University
- **Small-town** campus
- **Coed** 720 undergraduate students, 90% full-time, 36% women, 64% men
- **Moderately difficult** entrance level, 81% of applicants were admitted

UNDERGRAD STUDENTS

645 full-time, 75 part-time. 9% are from out of state; 10% Black or African American, non-Hispanic/Latino; 5% Hispanic/Latino; 3% Asian, non-Hispanic/Latino; 0.2% Native Hawaiian or other Pacific Islander, non-Hispanic/Latino; 0.2% American Indian or Alaska Native, non-Hispanic/Latino; 3% Two or more races, non-Hispanic/Latino; 1% Race/ethnicity unknown; 3% international; 5% transferred in; 23% live on campus.

Freshmen

Admission: 787 applied, 638 admitted, 218 enrolled. ***Average high school GPA:*** 3.07. ***Test scores:*** SAT critical reading scores over 500: 40%; SAT math scores over 500: 45%; SAT writing scores over 500: 31%; ACT scores over 18: 68%; SAT critical reading scores over 600: 10%; SAT math scores over 600: 13%; SAT writing scores over 600: 6%; ACT scores over 24: 12%; SAT critical reading scores over 700: 2%; SAT math scores over 700: 3%.

Retention: 75% of full-time freshmen returned.

FACULTY

Total: 59, 54% full-time, 39% with terminal degrees.

Student/faculty ratio: 16:1.

ACADEMICS

Calendar: semesters. *Degree:* certificates and bachelor's.

Special study options: adult/continuing education programs.

STUDENT LIFE

Housing options: coed, special housing for students with disabilities. Campus housing is university owned. Freshman campus housing is guaranteed.

Athletics Member NJCAA. ***Intercollegiate sports:*** baseball M, basketball M, softball M/W, volleyball W. ***Intramural sports:*** basketball M/W, cheerleading M(c)/W(c), cross-country running M/W, football M, golf M/W, soccer M/W, softball M/W, table tennis M/W.

COSTS & FINANCIAL AID

Costs (2014–15) ***Tuition:*** state resident $12,718 full-time, $524 per credit hour part-time; nonresident $19,404 full-time, $809 per credit hour part-time. Full-time tuition and fees vary according to course level, degree level, location, program, and student level. Part-time tuition and fees vary according to course level, course load, degree level, location, program, and student level. ***Required fees:*** $918 full-time. ***Room and board:*** $10,520; room only: $5460. Room and board charges vary according to board plan, housing facility, and location. ***Payment plans:*** installment, deferred payment. ***Waivers:*** senior citizens and employees or children of employees.

Financial Aid Of all full-time matriculated undergraduates who enrolled in 2013, 543 applied for aid, 461 were judged to have need, 18 had their need fully met. In 2013, 65 non-need-based awards were made. ***Average percent of need met:*** 62. ***Average financial aid package:*** $11,645. ***Average need-based loan:*** $4335. ***Average need-based gift aid:*** $6916. ***Average non-need-based aid:*** $2505. ***Average indebtedness upon graduation:*** $36,935.

APPLYING

Standardized Tests *Required:* SAT or ACT (for admission).

Options: electronic application, early admission, deferred entrance.

Application fee: $50.

Required: high school transcript. ***Required for some:*** interview. ***Recommended:*** essay or personal statement.

Application deadlines: rolling (freshmen), rolling (transfers).

Notification: continuous (freshmen), continuous (transfers).

CONTACT

Admissions Office, Penn State Beaver, 100 University Drive, Monaca, PA 15061. *Phone:* 724-773-3800. *Fax:* 724-773-3658. *E-mail:* br-admissions@psu.edu.

Penn State Berks

Reading, Pennsylvania

http://www.bk.psu.edu/

- **State-related** 4-year, founded 1924, part of Pennsylvania State University
- **Suburban** campus
- **Coed** 2,828 undergraduate students, 88% full-time, 44% women, 56% men
- **Very difficult** entrance level, 89% of applicants were admitted

UNDERGRAD STUDENTS

2,480 full-time, 348 part-time. 7% are from out of state; 10% Black or African American, non-Hispanic/Latino; 11% Hispanic/Latino; 4% Asian, non-Hispanic/Latino; 0.1% American Indian or Alaska Native, non-Hispanic/Latino; 2% Two or more races, non-Hispanic/Latino; 0.9% Race/ethnicity unknown; 3% international; 5% transferred in; 30% live on campus.

Freshmen

Admission: 2,398 applied, 2,126 admitted, 855 enrolled. ***Average high school GPA:*** 3.01. ***Test scores:*** SAT critical reading scores over 500: 44%; SAT math scores over 500: 51%; SAT writing scores over 500: 35%; ACT scores over 18: 86%; SAT critical reading scores over 600: 9%; SAT math scores over 600: 16%; SAT writing scores over 600: 8%; ACT scores over 24: 32%; SAT critical reading scores over 700: 1%; SAT math scores over 700: 2%; ACT scores over 30: 1%.

Retention: 77% of full-time freshmen returned.

FACULTY
Total: 220, 56% full-time, 46% with terminal degrees.
Student/faculty ratio: 17:1.

ACADEMICS
Calendar: semesters. *Degrees:* certificates, associate, bachelor's, and postbachelor's certificates (enrollment figures include students enrolled at The Graduate School at Penn State who are taking courses at this location).
Special study options: adult/continuing education programs, part-time degree program. ***ROTC:*** Army (c).
Computers: Students can access the following: campus intranet, computer help desk, free student e-mail accounts, online (class) grades, online (class) registration, online (class) schedules. Campuswide network is available.

STUDENT LIFE
Housing options: coed, special housing for students with disabilities. Campus housing is university owned.
Athletics Member NJCAA. ***Intercollegiate sports:*** baseball M, basketball M/W, cheerleading M/W, cross-country running M/W, golf M, soccer M/W, softball W, tennis M/W, volleyball W. ***Intramural sports:*** badminton M/W, basketball M/W, football M/W, golf M/W, table tennis M/W, volleyball M/W.
Campus security: 24-hour emergency response devices and patrols, late-night transport/escort service, controlled dormitory access.

COSTS & FINANCIAL AID
Costs (2014–15) ***Tuition:*** state resident $13,658 full-time, $569 per credit hour part-time; nonresident $20,890 full-time, $870 per credit hour part-time. Full-time tuition and fees vary according to course level, degree level, location, program, and student level. Part-time tuition and fees vary according to course level, course load, degree level, location, program, and student level. ***Required fees:*** $930 full-time. ***Room and board:*** $11,500; room only: $6440. Room and board charges vary according to board plan, housing facility, and location. ***Payment plans:*** installment, deferred payment. ***Waivers:*** senior citizens and employees or children of employees.
Financial Aid Of all full-time matriculated undergraduates who enrolled in 2013, 1,987 applied for aid, 1,679 were judged to have need, 59 had their need fully met. In 2013, 114 non-need-based awards were made. ***Average percent of need met:*** 58. ***Average financial aid package:*** $10,208. ***Average need-based loan:*** $4194. ***Average need-based gift aid:*** $6815. ***Average non-need-based aid:*** $2703. ***Average indebtedness upon graduation:*** $36,935.

APPLYING
Standardized Tests *Required:* SAT or ACT (for admission).
Options: electronic application, early admission, deferred entrance.
Application fee: $50.
Required: high school transcript. ***Required for some:*** interview. ***Recommended:*** essay or personal statement.
Application deadlines: rolling (freshmen), rolling (transfers).
Notification: continuous (freshmen), continuous (transfers).

CONTACT
Admissions Office, Penn State Berks, Tulpehocken Road, PO Box 7009, Reading, PA 19610-6009. *Phone:* 610-396-6060. *Fax:* 610-396-6077. *E-mail:* admissionsbk@psu.edu.

Penn State Brandywine
Media, Pennsylvania
http://www.brandywine.psu.edu/

- **State-related** 4-year, founded 1966, part of Pennsylvania State University
- **Small-town** campus
- **Coed** 1,488 undergraduate students, 85% full-time, 41% women, 59% men
- **Moderately difficult** entrance level, 85% of applicants were admitted

UNDERGRAD STUDENTS
1,272 full-time, 216 part-time. 6% are from out of state; 15% Black or African American, non-Hispanic/Latino; 5% Hispanic/Latino; 10% Asian, non-Hispanic/Latino; 0.1% Native Hawaiian or other Pacific Islander, non-Hispanic/Latino; 2% Two or more races, non-Hispanic/Latino; 2% Race/ethnicity unknown; 1% international; 4% transferred in.

Freshmen
Admission: 1,182 applied, 1,002 admitted, 389 enrolled. ***Average high school GPA:*** 3.01. ***Test scores:*** SAT critical reading scores over 500: 37%; SAT math scores over 500: 50%; SAT writing scores over 500: 34%; ACT scores over 18: 85%; SAT critical reading scores over 600: 9%; SAT math scores over 600: 16%; SAT writing scores over 600: 6%; ACT scores over 24: 30%; SAT critical reading scores over 700: 1%; SAT math scores over 700: 2%; ACT scores over 30: 7%.
Retention: 73% of full-time freshmen returned.

FACULTY
Total: 142, 48% full-time, 48% with terminal degrees.
Student/faculty ratio: 15:1.

ACADEMICS
Calendar: semesters. *Degrees:* certificates, associate, bachelor's, and postbachelor's certificates.
Special study options: adult/continuing education programs. ***ROTC:*** Army (c), Air Force (c).
Computers: Students can access the following: online (class) registration. Campuswide network is available.

STUDENT LIFE
Housing options: college housing not available.
Athletics Member NJCAA. ***Intercollegiate sports:*** baseball M, basketball M/W, soccer M/W, tennis M/W, volleyball W. ***Intramural sports:*** basketball M/W, cheerleading M(c)/W(c), golf M/W, ice hockey M(c)/W(c), lacrosse M/W, soccer M/W, softball W(c), tennis M/W, volleyball M(c)/W.
Campus security: late-night transport/escort service, part-time trained security personnel.

COSTS & FINANCIAL AID
Costs (2014–15) ***Tuition:*** state resident $13,012 full-time, $535 per credit hour part-time; nonresident $19,848 full-time, $827 per credit hour part-time. Full-time tuition and fees vary according to course level, degree level, location, program, and student level. Part-time tuition and fees vary according to course level, course load, degree level, location, program, and student level. ***Required fees:*** $930 full-time. ***Payment plans:*** installment, deferred payment. ***Waivers:*** senior citizens and employees or children of employees.
Financial Aid Of all full-time matriculated undergraduates who enrolled in 2013, 974 applied for aid, 768 were judged to have need, 46 had their need fully met. In 2013, 125 non-need-based awards were made. ***Average percent of need met:*** 59. ***Average financial aid package:*** $9961. ***Average need-based loan:*** $4026. ***Average need-based gift aid:*** $6694. ***Average non-need-based aid:*** $3729. ***Average indebtedness upon graduation:*** $36,935.

APPLYING
Standardized Tests *Required:* SAT or ACT (for admission).
Options: electronic application, early admission, deferred entrance.
Application fee: $50.
Required: high school transcript.
Application deadlines: rolling (freshmen), rolling (transfers).
Notification: continuous (freshmen), continuous (transfers).

CONTACT
Admissions Office, Penn State Brandywine, 25 Yearsley Mill Road, Media, PA 19063-5596. *Phone:* 610-892-1200. *Fax:* 610-892-1320. *E-mail:* bwadmissions@psu.edu.

Penn State DuBois

DuBois, Pennsylvania

http://www.ds.psu.edu/

- **State-related** primarily 2-year, founded 1935, part of Pennsylvania State University
- **Small-town** campus
- **Coed** 615 undergraduate students, 76% full-time, 48% women, 52% men
- **Moderately difficult** entrance level, 89% of applicants were admitted

UNDERGRAD STUDENTS
467 full-time, 148 part-time. 3% are from out of state; 1% Black or African American, non-Hispanic/Latino; 3% Hispanic/Latino; 0.8% Asian, non-Hispanic/Latino; 0.4% Two or more races, non-Hispanic/Latino; 1% Race/ethnicity unknown; 1% international; 3% transferred in.

Freshmen
Admission: 378 applied, 335 admitted, 153 enrolled. ***Average high school GPA:*** 3.11. ***Test scores:*** SAT critical reading scores over 500: 29%; SAT math scores over 500: 36%; SAT writing scores over 500: 25%; ACT scores over 18: 50%; SAT critical reading scores over 600: 5%; SAT math scores over 600: 6%; SAT writing scores over 600: 3%; SAT math scores over 700: 1%; SAT writing scores over 700: 1%.

Retention: 77% of full-time freshmen returned.

FACULTY
Total: 60, 65% full-time, 47% with terminal degrees.

Student/faculty ratio: 11:1.

ACADEMICS
Calendar: semesters. *Degrees:* certificates, associate, and bachelor's.

Special study options: adult/continuing education programs, external degree program.

Computers: Students can access the following: online (class) registration. Campuswide network is available.

STUDENT LIFE
Housing options: college housing not available.

Athletics Member NJCAA. ***Intercollegiate sports:*** basketball M, cross-country running M/W, golf M/W, volleyball W. ***Intramural sports:*** basketball M/W, football M, soccer M/W, table tennis M/W, volleyball M/W.

COSTS & FINANCIAL AID
Costs (2014–15) ***Tuition:*** state resident $12,718 full-time, $524 per credit hour part-time; nonresident $19,404 full-time, $809 per credit hour part-time. Full-time tuition and fees vary according to course level, degree level, location, program, and student level. Part-time tuition and fees vary according to course level, course load, degree level, location, program, and student level. ***Required fees:*** $810 full-time. ***Payment plans:*** installment, deferred payment. ***Waivers:*** senior citizens and employees or children of employees.

Financial Aid Of all full-time matriculated undergraduates who enrolled in 2013, 495 applied for aid, 444 were judged to have need, 25 had their need fully met. In 2013, 23 non-need-based awards were made. ***Average percent of need met:*** 62. ***Average financial aid package:*** $11,013. ***Average need-based loan:*** $3810. ***Average need-based gift aid:*** $6293. ***Average non-need-based aid:*** $1954. ***Average indebtedness upon graduation:*** $36,935.

APPLYING
Standardized Tests *Required:* SAT or ACT (for admission).

Options: electronic application, early admission, deferred entrance.

Application fee: $50.

Required: high school transcript. ***Required for some:*** interview. ***Recommended:*** essay or personal statement.

Application deadlines: rolling (freshmen), rolling (transfers).

Notification: continuous (freshmen), continuous (transfers).

CONTACT
Admissions Office, Penn State DuBois, 1 College Place, DuBois, PA 15801. *Phone:* 814-375-4720. *Toll-free phone:* 800-346-7627. *Fax:* 814-375-4784. *E-mail:* duboisinfo@psi.edu.

Penn State Erie, The Behrend College

Erie, Pennsylvania

http://www.pserie.psu.edu/

- **State-related** comprehensive, founded 1948, part of Pennsylvania State University
- **Suburban** 725-acre campus
- **Coed** 4,001 undergraduate students, 94% full-time, 35% women, 65% men
- **Very difficult** entrance level, 87% of applicants were admitted

UNDERGRAD STUDENTS
3,773 full-time, 228 part-time. 11% are from out of state; 4% Black or African American, non-Hispanic/Latino; 3% Hispanic/Latino; 3% Asian, non-Hispanic/Latino; 1% Two or more races, non-Hispanic/Latino; 1% Race/ethnicity unknown; 7% international; 3% transferred in; 42% live on campus.

Freshmen
Admission: 4,054 applied, 3,515 admitted, 1,186 enrolled. ***Average high school GPA:*** 3.27. ***Test scores:*** SAT critical reading scores over 500: 59%; SAT math scores over 500: 70%; SAT writing scores over 500: 45%; ACT scores over 18: 86%; SAT critical reading scores over 600: 14%; SAT math scores over 600: 29%; SAT writing scores over 600: 11%; ACT scores over 24: 45%; SAT critical reading scores over 700: 1%; SAT math scores over 700: 6%; SAT writing scores over 700: 1%; ACT scores over 30: 2%.

Retention: 83% of full-time freshmen returned.

FACULTY
Total: 309, 79% full-time, 56% with terminal degrees.

Student/faculty ratio: 15:1.

ACADEMICS
Calendar: semesters. *Degrees:* certificates, associate, bachelor's, and master's.

Special study options: adult/continuing education programs, part-time degree program. ***ROTC:*** Army (b).

Computers: Students can access the following: campus intranet, computer help desk, free student e-mail accounts, online (class) grades, online (class) registration, online (class) schedules. Campuswide network is available.

STUDENT LIFE
Housing options: coed, men-only, women-only, special housing for students with disabilities. Campus housing is university owned.

Athletics Member NCAA. All Division III. ***Intercollegiate sports:*** baseball M, basketball M/W, cheerleading M/W, cross-country running M/W, golf M/W, ice hockey M(c), lacrosse M(c), skiing (downhill) M(c)/W(c), soccer M/W, softball W, swimming and diving M/W, tennis M/W, track and field M/W, volleyball M(c)/W, water polo M/W. ***Intramural sports:*** badminton M/W, basketball M/W, bowling M/W, cross-country running M/W, football M/W, golf M/W, skiing (downhill) M/W, soccer M/W, softball M/W, swimming and diving M/W, table tennis M/W, tennis M/W, volleyball M/W.

Campus security: 24-hour emergency response devices and patrols, student patrols, late-night transport/escort service, controlled dormitory access.

COSTS & FINANCIAL AID
Costs (2014–15) ***Tuition:*** state resident $13,658 full-time, $569 per credit hour part-time; nonresident $20,890 full-time, $870 per credit hour part-time. Full-time tuition and fees vary according to course level, degree level, location, program, and student level. Part-time tuition and fees vary according to course level, course load, degree level, location, program, and student level. ***Required fees:*** $930 full-time. ***Room and board:*** $10,520; room only: $5460. Room and board charges vary according to board plan, housing facility, and location. ***Payment plans:*** installment, deferred payment. ***Waivers:*** senior citizens and employees or children of employees.

Financial Aid Of all full-time matriculated undergraduates who enrolled in 2013, 3,050 applied for aid, 2,610 were judged to have need, 111 had their need fully met. In 2013, 214 non-need-based awards were made. ***Average percent of need met:*** 59. ***Average financial aid package:*** $10,689. ***Average need-based loan:*** $4342. ***Average need-based gift aid:***

$6711. ***Average non-need-based aid:*** $3236. ***Average indebtedness upon graduation:*** $36,935.

APPLYING
Standardized Tests *Required:* SAT or ACT (for admission).
Options: electronic application, early admission, deferred entrance.
Application fee: $50.
Required: high school transcript. ***Required for some:*** interview. ***Recommended:*** essay or personal statement.
Application deadlines: rolling (freshmen), rolling (transfers).
Notification: continuous (freshmen), continuous (transfers).

CONTACT
Admissions Office, Penn State Erie, The Behrend College, 4701 College Drive, Erie, PA 16563-0001. *Phone:* 814-898-6100. *Toll-free phone:* 866-374-3378. *Fax:* 814-898-6044. *E-mail:* behrend.admissions@psu.edu.

Penn State Fayette, The Eberly Campus

Lemont Furnace, Pennsylvania

http://www.fe.psu.edu/

- **State-related** primarily 2-year, founded 1934, part of Pennsylvania State University
- **Small-town** campus
- **Coed** 717 undergraduate students, 81% full-time, 58% women, 42% men
- **Moderately difficult** entrance level, 84% of applicants were admitted

UNDERGRAD STUDENTS
578 full-time, 139 part-time. 4% are from out of state; 4% Black or African American, non-Hispanic/Latino; 2% Hispanic/Latino; 0.8% Asian, non-Hispanic/Latino; 0.2% American Indian or Alaska Native, non-Hispanic/Latino; 3% Two or more races, non-Hispanic/Latino; 0.8% Race/ethnicity unknown; 2% international; 7% transferred in.

Freshmen
Admission: 579 applied, 484 admitted, 196 enrolled. ***Average high school GPA:*** 3.16. ***Test scores:*** SAT critical reading scores over 500: 34%; SAT math scores over 500: 36%; SAT writing scores over 500: 18%; ACT scores over 18: 85%; SAT critical reading scores over 600: 5%; SAT math scores over 600: 7%; SAT writing scores over 600: 3%; ACT scores over 24: 15%; SAT critical reading scores over 700: 1%; SAT math scores over 700: 1%; SAT writing scores over 700: 1%; ACT scores over 30: 8%.
Retention: 77% of full-time freshmen returned.

FACULTY
Total: 76, 59% full-time, 32% with terminal degrees.
Student/faculty ratio: 11:1.

ACADEMICS
Calendar: semesters. *Degrees:* certificates, associate, and bachelor's.
Special study options: adult/continuing education programs, external degree program. ***ROTC:*** Army (b).
Computers: Students can access the following: online (class) registration. Campuswide network is available.

STUDENT LIFE
Housing options: college housing not available.
Athletics Member NJCAA. ***Intercollegiate sports:*** baseball M, basketball M, softball W, volleyball W. ***Intramural sports:*** badminton M/W, basketball M/W, cheerleading M(c)/W(c), equestrian sports M(c)/W(c), football M/W, golf M(c)/W(c), softball M/W, tennis M/W, volleyball M/W, weight lifting M/W.
Campus security: student patrols, 8-hour patrols by trained security personnel.

COSTS & FINANCIAL AID
Costs (2014–15) ***Tuition:*** state resident $12,718 full-time, $524 per credit hour part-time; nonresident $19,404 full-time, $809 per credit hour part-time. Full-time tuition and fees vary according to course level, degree level, location, program, and student level. Part-time tuition and fees vary according to course level, course load, degree level, location, program, and student level. ***Required fees:*** $870 full-time. ***Payment plans:*** installment, deferred payment. ***Waivers:*** senior citizens and employees or children of employees.
Financial Aid Of all full-time matriculated undergraduates who enrolled in 2013, 578 applied for aid, 507 were judged to have need, 23 had their need fully met. In 2013, 57 non-need-based awards were made. ***Average percent of need met:*** 64. ***Average financial aid package:*** $11,210. ***Average need-based loan:*** $4039. ***Average need-based gift aid:*** $6644. ***Average non-need-based aid:*** $2968. ***Average indebtedness upon graduation:*** $36,935.

APPLYING
Standardized Tests *Required:* SAT or ACT (for admission).
Options: electronic application, early admission, deferred entrance.
Application fee: $50.
Required: high school transcript. ***Required for some:*** interview. ***Recommended:*** essay or personal statement.
Application deadlines: rolling (freshmen), rolling (transfers).
Notification: continuous (freshmen), continuous (transfers).

CONTACT
Admissions Office, Penn State Fayette, The Eberly Campus, 2201 University Drive, Lemont Furnace, PA 15456. *Phone:* 724-430-4130. *Toll-free phone:* 877-568-4130. *Fax:* 724-430-4175. *E-mail:* feadm@psu.edu.

Penn State Greater Allegheny

McKeesport, Pennsylvania

http://www.ga.psu.edu/

- **State-related** 4-year, founded 1947, part of Pennsylvania State University
- **Small-town** campus
- **Coed** 604 undergraduate students, 89% full-time, 44% women, 56% men
- **Moderately difficult** entrance level, 76% of applicants were admitted

UNDERGRAD STUDENTS
536 full-time, 68 part-time. 10% are from out of state; 19% Black or African American, non-Hispanic/Latino; 5% Hispanic/Latino; 2% Asian, non-Hispanic/Latino; 0.2% Native Hawaiian or other Pacific Islander, non-Hispanic/Latino; 5% Two or more races, non-Hispanic/Latino; 0.9% Race/ethnicity unknown; 7% international; 4% transferred in; 26% live on campus.

Freshmen
Admission: 741 applied, 562 admitted, 183 enrolled. ***Average high school GPA:*** 3.12. ***Test scores:*** SAT critical reading scores over 500: 36%; SAT math scores over 500: 51%; SAT writing scores over 500: 31%; ACT scores over 18: 80%; SAT critical reading scores over 600: 7%; SAT math scores over 600: 17%; SAT writing scores over 600: 5%; ACT scores over 24: 27%; SAT critical reading scores over 700: 1%; SAT math scores over 700: 3%; ACT scores over 30: 7%.
Retention: 73% of full-time freshmen returned.

FACULTY
Total: 75, 47% full-time, 44% with terminal degrees.
Student/faculty ratio: 12:1.

ACADEMICS
Calendar: semesters. *Degrees:* certificates, associate, bachelor's, and master's.
Special study options: adult/continuing education programs.
Computers: Students can access the following: online (class) registration. Campuswide network is available.

STUDENT LIFE
Housing options: coed, special housing for students with disabilities. Campus housing is university owned. Freshman campus housing is guaranteed.
Athletics Member NJCAA. ***Intercollegiate sports:*** baseball M, basketball M, softball W, volleyball W. ***Intramural sports:*** basketball M/W, cheerleading M(c)/W(c), football M/W, ice hockey M(c), racquetball M/W, skiing (cross-country) M(c)/W(c), skiing (downhill) M(c)/W(c), soccer M(c)/W(c), softball M/W, tennis M/W, volleyball M/W.
Campus security: 24-hour patrols, controlled dormitory access.

COSTS & FINANCIAL AID

Costs (2014–15) ***Tuition:*** state resident $12,718 full-time, $524 per credit hour part-time; nonresident $19,404 full-time, $809 per credit hour part-time. Full-time tuition and fees vary according to course level, degree level, location, program, and student level. Part-time tuition and fees vary according to course level, course load, degree level, location, program, and student level. ***Required fees:*** $930 full-time. ***Room and board:*** $10,520; room only: $5460. Room and board charges vary according to board plan, housing facility, and location. ***Payment plans:*** installment, deferred payment. ***Waivers:*** senior citizens and employees or children of employees.

Financial Aid Of all full-time matriculated undergraduates who enrolled in 2013, 474 applied for aid, 423 were judged to have need, 23 had their need fully met. In 2013, 48 non-need-based awards were made. ***Average percent of need met:*** 63. ***Average financial aid package:*** $12,299. ***Average need-based loan:*** $4124. ***Average need-based gift aid:*** $6998. ***Average non-need-based aid:*** $3257. ***Average indebtedness upon graduation:*** $36,935.

APPLYING

Standardized Tests *Required:* SAT or ACT (for admission).

Options: electronic application, early admission, deferred entrance.

Application fee: $50.

Required: high school transcript.

Application deadlines: rolling (freshmen), rolling (transfers).

Notification: continuous (freshmen), continuous (transfers).

CONTACT

Admissions Office, Penn State Greater Allegheny, 4000 University Drive, McKeesport, PA 15132-7698. *Phone:* 412-675-9010. *Fax:* 412-675-9046. *E-mail:* psuga@psu.edu.

Penn State Harrisburg

Middletown, Pennsylvania

http://www.hbg.psu.edu/

- **State-related** comprehensive, founded 1966, part of Pennsylvania State University
- **Small-town** campus
- **Coed** 3,691 undergraduate students, 88% full-time, 40% women, 60% men
- **Very difficult** entrance level, 82% of applicants were admitted

UNDERGRAD STUDENTS

3,250 full-time, 441 part-time. 16% are from out of state; 10% Black or African American, non-Hispanic/Latino; 7% Hispanic/Latino; 8% Asian, non-Hispanic/Latino; 0.1% Native Hawaiian or other Pacific Islander, non-Hispanic/Latino; 0.2% American Indian or Alaska Native, non-Hispanic/Latino; 3% Two or more races, non-Hispanic/Latino; 2% Race/ethnicity unknown; 10% international; 8% transferred in; 12% live on campus.

Freshmen

Admission: 3,404 applied, 2,794 admitted, 794 enrolled. ***Average high school GPA:*** 3.15. ***Test scores:*** SAT critical reading scores over 500: 51%; SAT math scores over 500: 63%; SAT writing scores over 500: 43%; ACT scores over 18: 93%; SAT critical reading scores over 600: 10%; SAT math scores over 600: 24%; SAT writing scores over 600: 8%; ACT scores over 24: 56%; SAT critical reading scores over 700: 1%; SAT math scores over 700: 5%; SAT writing scores over 700: 1%; ACT scores over 30: 6%.

Retention: 83% of full-time freshmen returned.

FACULTY

Total: 361, 63% full-time, 64% with terminal degrees.

Student/faculty ratio: 14:1.

ACADEMICS

Calendar: semesters. *Degrees:* certificates, associate, bachelor's, master's, doctoral, and postbachelor's certificates.

Special study options: adult/continuing education programs, part-time degree program. ***ROTC:*** Army (c).

Computers: Students can access the following: campus intranet, computer help desk, free student e-mail accounts, online (class) grades, online (class) registration, online (class) schedules. Campuswide network is available.

STUDENT LIFE

Housing options: special housing for students with disabilities. Campus housing is university owned.

Athletics ***Intercollegiate sports:*** baseball M, basketball M/W, cross-country running M/W, golf M/W, soccer M/W, softball W, tennis M/W, volleyball W. ***Intramural sports:*** badminton M/W, basketball M/W, racquetball M/W, tennis M/W.

Campus security: 24-hour emergency response devices and patrols, student patrols, late-night transport/escort service, controlled dormitory access.

COSTS & FINANCIAL AID

Costs (2014–15) ***Tuition:*** state resident $13,658 full-time, $569 per credit hour part-time; nonresident $20,890 full-time, $870 per credit hour part-time. Full-time tuition and fees vary according to course level, degree level, location, program, and student level. Part-time tuition and fees vary according to course level, course load, degree level, location, program, and student level. ***Required fees:*** $930 full-time. ***Room and board:*** $11,980; room only: $6920. Room and board charges vary according to board plan, housing facility, and location. ***Payment plans:*** installment, deferred payment. ***Waivers:*** senior citizens and employees or children of employees.

Financial Aid Of all full-time matriculated undergraduates who enrolled in 2013, 2,390 applied for aid, 2,071 were judged to have need, 105 had their need fully met. In 2013, 223 non-need-based awards were made. ***Average percent of need met:*** 56. ***Average financial aid package:*** $10,873. ***Average need-based loan:*** $4525. ***Average need-based gift aid:*** $6638. ***Average non-need-based aid:*** $2068. ***Average indebtedness upon graduation:*** $36,935.

APPLYING

Standardized Tests *Required:* SAT or ACT (for admission).

Options: electronic application, early admission, deferred entrance.

Application fee: $50.

Required: high school transcript. ***Required for some:*** interview. ***Recommended:*** essay or personal statement.

Application deadlines: rolling (freshmen), rolling (transfers).

Notification: continuous (freshmen), continuous (transfers).

CONTACT

Admissions Office, Penn State Harrisburg, 777 West Harrisburg Pike, Middletown, PA 17057-4898. *Phone:* 717-948-6250. *Toll-free phone:* 800-222-2056. *Fax:* 717-948-6325. *E-mail:* hbgadmit@psu.edu.

Penn State Hazleton

Hazleton, Pennsylvania

http://www.hn.psu.edu/

- **State-related** 4-year, founded 1934, part of Pennsylvania State University
- **Small-town** campus
- **Coed** 850 undergraduate students, 89% full-time, 45% women, 55% men
- **Moderately difficult** entrance level, 86% of applicants were admitted

UNDERGRAD STUDENTS

758 full-time, 92 part-time. 21% are from out of state; 14% Black or African American, non-Hispanic/Latino; 17% Hispanic/Latino; 3% Asian, non-Hispanic/Latino; 0.2% Native Hawaiian or other Pacific Islander, non-Hispanic/Latino; 0.4% American Indian or Alaska Native, non-Hispanic/Latino; 3% Two or more races, non-Hispanic/Latino; 1% Race/ethnicity unknown; 2% international; 6% transferred in; 48% live on campus.

Freshmen

Admission: 820 applied, 705 admitted, 304 enrolled. ***Average high school GPA:*** 3.06. ***Test scores:*** SAT critical reading scores over 500: 37%; SAT math scores over 500: 41%; SAT writing scores over 500: 31%; ACT scores over 18: 62%; SAT critical reading scores over 600: 11%; SAT math scores over 600: 12%; SAT writing scores over 600: 7%; ACT scores over 24: 38%; SAT critical reading scores over 700: 1%; SAT math scores over 700: 1%.

Retention: 79% of full-time freshmen returned.

FACULTY
Total: 70, 73% full-time, 54% with terminal degrees.
Student/faculty ratio: 14:1.

ACADEMICS
Calendar: semesters. *Degrees:* certificates, associate, bachelor's, and postbachelor's certificates.
Special study options: adult/continuing education programs. ***ROTC:*** Army (b), Air Force (c).
Computers: Students can access the following: online (class) registration. Campuswide network is available.

STUDENT LIFE
Housing options: coed. Campus housing is university owned. Freshman campus housing is guaranteed.
Athletics Member NJCAA. ***Intercollegiate sports:*** baseball M, basketball M/W, cheerleading M/W, soccer M, softball W(s), tennis M/W, volleyball M/W. ***Intramural sports:*** basketball M/W, skiing (downhill) M(c)/W(c), soccer M/W, volleyball M/W.
Campus security: 24-hour patrols, late-night transport/escort service, controlled dormitory access.

COSTS & FINANCIAL AID
Costs (2014–15) ***Tuition:*** state resident $13,012 full-time, $535 per credit hour part-time; nonresident $19,848 full-time, $827 per credit hour part-time. Full-time tuition and fees vary according to course level, degree level, location, program, and student level. Part-time tuition and fees vary according to course level, course load, degree level, location, program, and student level. ***Required fees:*** $870 full-time. ***Room and board:*** $10,520; room only: $5460. Room and board charges vary according to board plan, housing facility, and location. ***Payment plans:*** installment, deferred payment. ***Waivers:*** senior citizens and employees or children of employees.
Financial Aid Of all full-time matriculated undergraduates who enrolled in 2013, 799 applied for aid, 733 were judged to have need, 23 had their need fully met. In 2013, 50 non-need-based awards were made. ***Average percent of need met:*** 59. ***Average financial aid package:*** $11,189. ***Average need-based loan:*** $3964. ***Average need-based gift aid:*** $6949. ***Average non-need-based aid:*** $3375. ***Average indebtedness upon graduation:*** $36,935.

APPLYING
Standardized Tests *Required:* SAT or ACT (for admission).
Options: electronic application, early admission, deferred entrance.
Application fee: $50.
Required: high school transcript. ***Required for some:*** interview. ***Recommended:*** essay or personal statement.
Application deadlines: rolling (freshmen), rolling (transfers).
Notification: continuous (freshmen), continuous (transfers).

CONTACT
Admissions Office, Penn State Hazleton, 76 University Drive, Hazleton, PA 18202. *Phone:* 570-450-3142. *Toll-free phone:* 800-279-8495. *Fax:* 570-450-3182. *E-mail:* admissions-hn@psu.edu.

Penn State Lehigh Valley

Center Valley, Pennsylvania

http://www.lv.psu.edu/

- **State-related** 4-year, founded 1912, part of Pennsylvania State University
- **Rural** campus
- **Coed** 881 undergraduate students, 81% full-time, 46% women, 54% men
- **Moderately difficult** entrance level, 85% of applicants were admitted

UNDERGRAD STUDENTS
716 full-time, 165 part-time. 5% are from out of state; 5% Black or African American, non-Hispanic/Latino; 18% Hispanic/Latino; 8% Asian, non-Hispanic/Latino; 0.3% Native Hawaiian or other Pacific Islander, non-Hispanic/Latino; 1% Two or more races, non-Hispanic/Latino; 2% Race/ethnicity unknown; 0.5% international; 7% transferred in.

Freshmen
Admission: 887 applied, 755 admitted, 215 enrolled. ***Average high school GPA:*** 3. ***Test scores:*** SAT critical reading scores over 500: 49%; SAT math scores over 500: 54%; SAT writing scores over 500: 44%; ACT scores over 18: 87%; SAT critical reading scores over 600: 12%; SAT math scores over 600: 22%; SAT writing scores over 600: 10%; ACT scores over 24: 27%; SAT critical reading scores over 700: 2%; SAT math scores over 700: 3%.
Retention: 79% of full-time freshmen returned.

FACULTY
Total: 91, 46% full-time, 43% with terminal degrees.
Student/faculty ratio: 14:1.

ACADEMICS
Calendar: semesters. *Degrees:* certificates, associate, bachelor's, and postbachelor's certificates (enrollment figures include students enrolled at The Graduate School at Penn State who are taking courses at this location).
Special study options: adult/continuing education programs, external degree program, part-time degree program. ***ROTC:*** Army (c).
Computers: Students can access the following: online (class) registration. Campuswide network is available.

STUDENT LIFE
Housing options: college housing not available.
Athletics Member NJCAA. ***Intercollegiate sports:*** baseball M, basketball M/W, bowling M(c)/W(c), cheerleading M/W, cross-country running M/W, football M(c), golf M(c)/W(c), ice hockey M(c)/W(c), skiing (downhill) M(c)/W(c), soccer M(c)/W, tennis M/W, volleyball M(c)/W. ***Intramural sports:*** badminton M/W, basketball M/W, football M/W, golf M/W, soccer M/W, volleyball M/W.

COSTS & FINANCIAL AID
Costs (2014–15) ***Tuition:*** state resident $13,012 full-time, $535 per credit hour part-time; nonresident $19,848 full-time, $827 per credit hour part-time. Full-time tuition and fees vary according to course level, degree level, location, program, and student level. Part-time tuition and fees vary according to course level, course load, degree level, location, program, and student level. ***Required fees:*** $918 full-time. ***Payment plans:*** installment, deferred payment. ***Waivers:*** senior citizens and employees or children of employees.
Financial Aid Of all full-time matriculated undergraduates who enrolled in 2013, 594 applied for aid, 494 were judged to have need, 18 had their need fully met. In 2013, 53 non-need-based awards were made. ***Average percent of need met:*** 59. ***Average financial aid package:*** $9964. ***Average need-based loan:*** $4093. ***Average need-based gift aid:*** $6422. ***Average non-need-based aid:*** $2518. ***Average indebtedness upon graduation:*** $36,935.

APPLYING
Standardized Tests *Required:* SAT or ACT (for admission).
Options: electronic application, early admission, deferred entrance.
Application fee: $50.
Required: high school transcript.

CONTACT
Admissions Office, Penn State Lehigh Valley, 2809 Saucon Valley Road, Center Valley, PA 18034-8447. *Phone:* 610-285-5000. *Fax:* 610-285-5220. *E-mail:* admissions-lv@psu.edu.

Penn State Mont Alto

Mont Alto, Pennsylvania

http://www.ma.psu.edu/

- **State-related** primarily 2-year, founded 1929, part of Pennsylvania State University
- **Small-town** campus
- **Coed** 940 undergraduate students, 72% full-time, 57% women, 43% men
- **Moderately difficult** entrance level, 78% of applicants were admitted

UNDERGRAD STUDENTS
679 full-time, 261 part-time. 15% are from out of state; 8% Black or African American, non-Hispanic/Latino; 4% Hispanic/Latino; 1% Asian, non-Hispanic/Latino; 0.2% Native Hawaiian or other Pacific Islander, non-Hispanic/Latino; 3% Two or more races, non-Hispanic/Latino; 0.8% Race/ethnicity unknown; 0.1% international; 4% transferred in; 27% live on campus.

Freshmen
Admission: 778 applied, 607 admitted, 276 enrolled. ***Average high school GPA:*** 3.08. ***Test scores:*** SAT critical reading scores over 500: 38%; SAT math scores over 500: 40%; SAT writing scores over 500: 27%; ACT scores over 18: 100%; SAT critical reading scores over 600: 8%; SAT math scores over 600: 10%; SAT writing scores over 600: 6%; ACT scores over 24: 25%; SAT critical reading scores over 700: 1%; SAT math scores over 700: 1%; ACT scores over 30: 13%.
Retention: 75% of full-time freshmen returned.

FACULTY
Total: 95, 61% full-time, 36% with terminal degrees.
Student/faculty ratio: 11:1.

ACADEMICS
Calendar: semesters. *Degrees:* certificates, associate, and bachelor's.
Special study options: adult/continuing education programs, external degree program. ***ROTC:*** Army (c).
Computers: Students can access the following: online (class) registration. Campuswide network is available.

STUDENT LIFE
Housing options: coed, special housing for students with disabilities. Campus housing is university owned. Freshman campus housing is guaranteed.
Athletics Member NJCAA. ***Intercollegiate sports:*** basketball M/W, cheerleading M/W, cross-country running M/W, golf M/W, soccer M/W, softball W, tennis M/W, volleyball W. ***Intramural sports:*** badminton M/W, basketball M/W, cheerleading M(c)/W(c), racquetball M/W, soccer M/W, softball W, volleyball M/W.
Campus security: 24-hour patrols, controlled dormitory access.

COSTS & FINANCIAL AID
Costs (2014–15) ***Tuition:*** state resident $12,718 full-time, $524 per credit hour part-time; nonresident $19,404 full-time, $809 per credit hour part-time. Full-time tuition and fees vary according to course level, degree level, location, program, and student level. Part-time tuition and fees vary according to course level, course load, degree level, location, program, and student level. ***Required fees:*** $930 full-time. ***Room and board:*** $10,520; room only: $5460. Room and board charges vary according to board plan, housing facility, and location. ***Payment plans:*** installment, deferred payment. ***Waivers:*** senior citizens and employees or children of employees.
Financial Aid Of all full-time matriculated undergraduates who enrolled in 2013, 659 applied for aid, 581 were judged to have need, 38 had their need fully met. In 2013, 48 non-need-based awards were made. ***Average percent of need met:*** 60. ***Average financial aid package:*** $11,314. ***Average need-based loan:*** $3979. ***Average need-based gift aid:*** $6314. ***Average non-need-based aid:*** $4557. ***Average indebtedness upon graduation:*** $36,935.

APPLYING
Standardized Tests *Required:* SAT or ACT (for admission).
Options: electronic application, early admission, deferred entrance.
Application fee: $50.
Required: high school transcript. ***Required for some:*** interview. ***Recommended:*** essay or personal statement.
Application deadlines: rolling (freshmen), rolling (transfers).
Notification: continuous (freshmen), continuous (transfers).

CONTACT
Admissions Office, Penn State Mont Alto, 1 Campus Drive, Mont Alto, PA 17237-9703. *Phone:* 717-749-6130. *Toll-free phone:* 800-392-6173. *Fax:* 717-749-6132. *E-mail:* psuma@psu.edu.

Penn State New Kensington

New Kensington, Pennsylvania

http://www.nk.psu.edu/

- **State-related** 4-year, founded 1958, part of Pennsylvania State University
- **Small-town** campus
- **Coed** 665 undergraduate students, 82% full-time, 43% women, 57% men
- **Moderately difficult** entrance level, 81% of applicants were admitted

UNDERGRAD STUDENTS
548 full-time, 117 part-time. 3% are from out of state; 5% Black or African American, non-Hispanic/Latino; 2% Hispanic/Latino; 1% Asian, non-Hispanic/Latino; 1% Two or more races, non-Hispanic/Latino; 0.6% Race/ethnicity unknown; 2% international; 8% transferred in.

Freshmen
Admission: 522 applied, 424 admitted, 185 enrolled. ***Average high school GPA:*** 3.18. ***Test scores:*** SAT critical reading scores over 500: 40%; SAT math scores over 500: 49%; SAT writing scores over 500: 30%; ACT scores over 18: 100%; SAT critical reading scores over 600: 6%; SAT math scores over 600: 15%; SAT writing scores over 600: 7%; SAT critical reading scores over 700: 1%; SAT math scores over 700: 2%; SAT writing scores over 700: 1%.
Retention: 82% of full-time freshmen returned.

FACULTY
Total: 65, 55% full-time, 49% with terminal degrees.
Student/faculty ratio: 13:1.

ACADEMICS
Calendar: semesters. *Degrees:* certificates, associate, bachelor's, and master's.
Special study options: adult/continuing education programs, external degree program. ***ROTC:*** Air Force (c).
Computers: Students can access the following: online (class) registration. Campuswide network is available.

STUDENT LIFE
Athletics Member NJCAA. ***Intercollegiate sports:*** baseball M, basketball M/W, cheerleading M/W, golf M/W, softball W, volleyball W. ***Intramural sports:*** badminton M/W, basketball M/W, bowling M/W, cheerleading M(c)/W(c), football M/W, ice hockey M(c)/W(c), racquetball M/W, skiing (downhill) M(c)/W(c), soccer M/W, softball W, volleyball M/W.
Campus security: part-time trained security personnel.

COSTS & FINANCIAL AID
Costs (2014–15) ***Tuition:*** state resident $12,718 full-time, $524 per credit hour part-time; nonresident $19,404 full-time, $809 per credit hour part-time. Full-time tuition and fees vary according to course level, degree level, location, program, and student level. Part-time tuition and fees vary according to course level, course load, degree level, location, program, and student level. ***Required fees:*** $870 full-time. ***Payment plans:*** installment, deferred payment. ***Waivers:*** senior citizens and employees or children of employees.
Financial Aid Of all full-time matriculated undergraduates who enrolled in 2013, 448 applied for aid, 384 were judged to have need, 26 had their need fully met. In 2013, 42 non-need-based awards were made. ***Average percent of need met:*** 63. ***Average financial aid package:*** $9942. ***Average need-based loan:*** $4102. ***Average need-based gift aid:*** $6075. ***Average non-need-based aid:*** $2728. ***Average indebtedness upon graduation:*** $36,935.

APPLYING
Standardized Tests *Required:* SAT or ACT (for admission).
Options: electronic application, early admission, deferred entrance.
Application fee: $50.
Required: high school transcript. ***Required for some:*** interview. ***Recommended:*** essay or personal statement.
Application deadlines: rolling (freshmen), rolling (transfers).
Notification: continuous (freshmen), continuous (transfers).

CONTACT
Admissions Office, Penn State New Kensington, 3550 Seventh Street Road, New Kensington, PA 15068. *Phone:* 724-334-5466. *Toll-free phone:* 888-968-7297. *Fax:* 724-334-6111. *E-mail:* nkadmissions@psu.edu.

Penn State Schuylkill

Schuylkill Haven, Pennsylvania

http://www.sl.psu.edu/

- **State-related** 4-year, founded 1934, part of Pennsylvania State University
- **Small-town** campus
- **Coed** 796 undergraduate students, 82% full-time, 60% women, 40% men
- **Moderately difficult** entrance level, 75% of applicants were admitted

UNDERGRAD STUDENTS
653 full-time, 143 part-time. 14% are from out of state; 95% Black or African American, non-Hispanic/Latino; 28% Hispanic/Latino; 6% Asian, non-Hispanic/Latino; 1% Native Hawaiian or other Pacific Islander, non-Hispanic/Latino; 8% Two or more races, non-Hispanic/Latino; 14% Race/ethnicity unknown; 9% international; 5% transferred in; 31% live on campus.

Freshmen
Admission: 686 applied, 513 admitted, 250 enrolled. ***Average high school GPA:*** 2.83. ***Test scores:*** SAT critical reading scores over 500: 25%; SAT math scores over 500: 27%; SAT writing scores over 500: 21%; ACT scores over 18: 50%; SAT critical reading scores over 600: 3%; SAT math scores over 600: 6%; SAT writing scores over 600: 3%; ACT scores over 24: 10%; SAT math scores over 700: 1%.

Retention: 75% of full-time freshmen returned.

FACULTY
Total: 67, 63% full-time, 57% with terminal degrees.

Student/faculty ratio: 14:1.

ACADEMICS
Calendar: semesters. *Degrees:* certificates, associate, and bachelor's (bachelor's degree programs completed at the Harrisburg campus).

Special study options: adult/continuing education programs, external degree program.

Computers: Students can access the following: online (class) registration. Campuswide network is available.

STUDENT LIFE
Housing options: special housing for students with disabilities.

Athletics Member NJCAA. ***Intercollegiate sports:*** basketball M, cross-country running M/W, golf M, soccer M, softball W, volleyball W. ***Intramural sports:*** basketball M/W, football M, soccer M/W, softball M/W, table tennis M/W, volleyball M/W.

Campus security: 24-hour patrols, controlled dormitory access.

COSTS & FINANCIAL AID
Costs (2014–15) ***Tuition:*** state resident $13,012 full-time, $535 per credit hour part-time; nonresident $19,848 full-time, $827 per credit hour part-time. Full-time tuition and fees vary according to course level, degree level, location, program, and student level. Part-time tuition and fees vary according to course level, course load, degree level, location, program, and student level. ***Required fees:*** $858 full-time. ***Room and board:*** $7886; room only: $5886. Room and board charges vary according to board plan, housing facility, and location. ***Payment plans:*** installment, deferred payment. ***Waivers:*** senior citizens and employees or children of employees.

Financial Aid Of all full-time matriculated undergraduates who enrolled in 2013, 600 applied for aid, 563 were judged to have need, 29 had their need fully met. In 2013, 21 non-need-based awards were made. ***Average percent of need met:*** 62. ***Average financial aid package:*** $12,576. ***Average need-based loan:*** $4179. ***Average need-based gift aid:*** $6954. ***Average non-need-based aid:*** $2571. ***Average indebtedness upon graduation:*** $36,935.

APPLYING
Standardized Tests *Required:* SAT or ACT (for admission).

Options: electronic application, early admission, deferred entrance.

Application fee: $50.

Required: high school transcript.

Application deadlines: rolling (freshmen), rolling (transfers).

Notification: continuous (freshmen), continuous (transfers).

CONTACT
Admissions Office, Penn State Schuylkill, 200 University Drive, Schuylkill Haven, PA 17972-2208. *Phone:* 570-385-6252. *Fax:* 570-385-6272. *E-mail:* sl-admissions@psu.edu.

Penn State Shenango

Sharon, Pennsylvania

http://www.shenango.psu.edu/

- **State-related** primarily 2-year, founded 1965, part of Pennsylvania State University
- **Small-town** campus
- **Coed** 539 undergraduate students, 57% full-time, 70% women, 30% men
- **Moderately difficult** entrance level, 67% of applicants were admitted

UNDERGRAD STUDENTS
309 full-time, 230 part-time. 23% are from out of state; 9% Black or African American, non-Hispanic/Latino; 2% Hispanic/Latino; 1% Asian, non-Hispanic/Latino; 0.6% Native Hawaiian or other Pacific Islander, non-Hispanic/Latino; 3% Two or more races, non-Hispanic/Latino; 3% Race/ethnicity unknown; 9% transferred in.

Freshmen
Admission: 201 applied, 135 admitted, 79 enrolled. ***Average high school GPA:*** 2.99. ***Test scores:*** SAT critical reading scores over 500: 24%; SAT math scores over 500: 24%; SAT writing scores over 500: 9%; ACT scores over 18: 60%; SAT critical reading scores over 600: 2%; SAT writing scores over 600: 2%; ACT scores over 24: 20%.

Retention: 59% of full-time freshmen returned.

FACULTY
Total: 50, 52% full-time, 36% with terminal degrees.

Student/faculty ratio: 11:1.

ACADEMICS
Calendar: semesters. *Degrees:* certificates, associate, and bachelor's.

Special study options: adult/continuing education programs, external degree program.

Computers: Students can access the following: online (class) registration. Campuswide network is available.

STUDENT LIFE
Housing options: college housing not available.

Athletics ***Intramural sports:*** basketball M(c)/W, bowling M/W, football M(c), golf M/W, softball M/W, tennis M/W, volleyball M/W.

COSTS & FINANCIAL AID
Costs (2014–15) ***Tuition:*** state resident $12,474 full-time, $504 per credit hour part-time; nonresident $19,030 full-time, $793 per credit hour part-time. Full-time tuition and fees vary according to course level, degree level, location, program, and student level. Part-time tuition and fees vary according to course level, course load, degree level, location, program, and student level. ***Required fees:*** $858 full-time. ***Payment plans:*** installment, deferred payment. ***Waivers:*** senior citizens and employees or children of employees.

Financial Aid Of all full-time matriculated undergraduates who enrolled in 2013, 292 applied for aid, 278 were judged to have need, 16 had their need fully met. In 2013, 16 non-need-based awards were made. ***Average percent of need met:*** 61. ***Average financial aid package:*** $12,741. ***Average need-based loan:*** $4008. ***Average need-based gift aid:*** $6759. ***Average non-need-based aid:*** $4157. ***Average indebtedness upon graduation:*** $36,935.

APPLYING
Standardized Tests *Required:* SAT or ACT (for admission).

Options: electronic application, early admission, deferred entrance.

Application fee: $50.

Required: high school transcript.

Application deadlines: rolling (freshmen), rolling (transfers).

Notification: continuous (freshmen), continuous (transfers).

CONTACT
Admissions Office, Penn State Shenango, 147 Shenango Avenue, Sharon, PA 16146-1537. *Phone:* 724-983-2803. *Fax:* 724-983-2820. *E-mail:* psushenango@psu.edu.

★ Penn State University Park

State College, Pennsylvania

http://www.psu.edu/

- **State-related** university, founded 1855, part of Pennsylvania State University
- **Small-town** 8556-acre campus with easy access to Harrisburg
- **Endowment** $2.4 billion
- **Coed** 40,541 undergraduate students, 97% full-time, 46% women, 54% men
- **Very difficult** entrance level, 50% of applicants were admitted

UNDERGRAD STUDENTS
39,357 full-time, 1,184 part-time. Students come from 52 states and territories; 107 other countries; 31% are from out of state; 4% Black or African American, non-Hispanic/Latino; 5% Hispanic/Latino; 6% Asian, non-Hispanic/Latino; 0.1% Native Hawaiian or other Pacific Islander, non-Hispanic/Latino; 0.1% American Indian or Alaska Native, non-Hispanic/Latino; 2% Two or more races, non-Hispanic/Latino; 2% Race/ethnicity unknown; 10% international; 1% transferred in; 35% live on campus.

Freshmen
Admission: 50,299 applied, 25,295 admitted, 8,183 enrolled. ***Average high school GPA:*** 3.6. ***Test scores:*** SAT critical reading scores over 500: 88%; SAT math scores over 500: 95%; SAT writing scores over 500: 89%; ACT scores over 18: 100%; SAT critical reading scores over 600: 39%; SAT math scores over 600: 61%; SAT writing scores over 600: 47%; ACT scores over 24: 86%; SAT critical reading scores over 700: 6%; SAT math scores over 700: 16%; SAT writing scores over 700: 8%; ACT scores over 30: 21%.

Retention: 93% of full-time freshmen returned.

FACULTY
Total: 3,069, 87% full-time, 73% with terminal degrees.

Student/faculty ratio: 16:1.

ACADEMICS
Calendar: semesters. *Degrees:* certificates, associate, bachelor's, master's, doctoral, and postbachelor's certificates.

Special study options: academic remediation for entering students, accelerated degree program, adult/continuing education programs, advanced placement credit, cooperative education, distance learning, double majors, English as a second language, external degree program, freshman honors college, honors programs, independent study, internships, off-campus study, part-time degree program, services for LD students, student-designed majors, study abroad, summer session for credit. ***ROTC:*** Army (b), Navy (b), Air Force (b).

Unusual degree programs: 3-2 engineering; Geoscience.

Computers: 6,150 computers/terminals and 23,225 ports are available on campus for general student use. Students can access the following: campus intranet, computer help desk, free student e-mail accounts, online (class) grades, online (class) registration, online (class) schedules. Campuswide network is available. 100% of college-owned or -operated housing units are wired for high-speed Internet access. Wireless service is available via classrooms, computer centers, computer labs, dorm rooms, learning centers, libraries, student centers.

STUDENT LIFE
Housing options: on-campus residence required for freshman year; coed, women-only, special housing for students with disabilities. Campus housing is university owned. Freshman campus housing is guaranteed.

Activities and organizations: drama/theater group, student-run newspaper, radio and television station, choral group, marching band, national fraternities, national sororities.

Athletics Member NCAA, USCAA. All Division I except football (Division I-A). ***Intercollegiate sports:*** baseball M(s), basketball M(s)/W(s), cheerleading M(s)/W(s), cross-country running M(s)/W(s), fencing M(s)/W(s), field hockey W(s), golf M(s)/W(s), gymnastics M(s)/W(s), ice hockey M(s)(c)/W(s)(c), lacrosse M(s)/W(s), soccer M(s)/W(s), softball W(s), swimming and diving M(s)/W(s), tennis M(s)/W(s), track and field M(s)/W(s), volleyball M(s)/W(s), wrestling M(s). ***Intramural sports:*** archery M(c)/W(c), badminton M(c)/W, baseball M(c)/W(c), basketball M(c)/W(c), bowling M(c)/W(c), cheerleading M(c)/W(c), crew M(c)/W(c), cross-country running M/W, equestrian sports M(c)/W(c), fencing M(c)/W(c), field hockey M(c)/W(c), football M, golf M(c)/W(c), gymnastics M(c)/W(c), lacrosse M(c)/W(c), racquetball M(c)/W(c), riflery M(c)/W(c), rugby M(c)/W(c), sailing M(c)/W(c), skiing (downhill) M(c)/W(c), soccer M(c)/W(c), softball M(c)/W(c), squash M(c)/W(c), swimming and diving M(c)/W(c), table tennis M(c)/W(c), tennis M(c)/W(c), track and field M(c)/W(c), ultimate Frisbee M(c)/W(c), volleyball M(c)/W(c), water polo M(c)/W(c), weight lifting M(c)/W(c), wrestling M/W.

Campus security: 24-hour emergency response devices and patrols, student patrols, late-night transport/escort service, controlled dormitory access.

Student services: health clinic, personal/psychological counseling, women's center, legal services.

COSTS & FINANCIAL AID
Costs (2014–15) ***Tuition:*** state resident $16,572 full-time, $691 per credit hour part-time; nonresident $29,522 full-time, $1230 per credit hour part-time. Full-time tuition and fees vary according to course level, degree level, location, program, and student level. Part-time tuition and fees vary according to course level, course load, degree level, location, program, and student level. ***Required fees:*** $930 full-time. ***Room and board:*** $10,520; room only: $5460. Room and board charges vary according to board plan, housing facility, and location. ***Payment plans:*** installment, deferred payment. ***Waivers:*** senior citizens and employees or children of employees.

Financial Aid Of all full-time matriculated undergraduates who enrolled in 2013, 24,601 applied for aid, 19,348 were judged to have need, 1,357 had their need fully met. 976 Federal Work-Study jobs (averaging $1824). In 2013, 3669 non-need-based awards were made. ***Average percent of need met:*** 57. ***Average financial aid package:*** $10,875. ***Average need-based loan:*** $4681. ***Average need-based gift aid:*** $6987. ***Average non-need-based aid:*** $3757. ***Average indebtedness upon graduation:*** $36,935.

APPLYING
Standardized Tests *Required:* SAT or ACT (for admission).

Options: electronic application, early admission, deferred entrance.

Application fee: $50.

Required: high school transcript. ***Required for some:*** Honors College has additional requirements. Certain programs have special requirements such as auditions or portfolios. ***Recommended:*** essay or personal statement.

Application deadlines: rolling (freshmen), rolling (transfers).

Notification: continuous (freshmen), continuous (transfers).

CONTACT
Clark V. Brigger, Executive Director for Undergraduate Admissions, Penn State University Park, 201 Shields Building, University Park, PA 16802. *Phone:* 814-865-4700. *Fax:* 814-863-7590. *E-mail:* admissions@psu.edu.

Penn State Wilkes-Barre

Lehman, Pennsylvania

http://www.wb.psu.edu/

- **State-related** 4-year, founded 1916, part of Pennsylvania State University
- **Rural** campus
- **Coed** 536 undergraduate students, 90% full-time, 32% women, 68% men
- **Moderately difficult** entrance level, 84% of applicants were admitted

UNDERGRAD STUDENTS
485 full-time, 51 part-time. 7% are from out of state; 2% Black or African American, non-Hispanic/Latino; 6% Hispanic/Latino; 2% Asian, non-Hispanic/Latino; 2% Two or more races, non-Hispanic/Latino; 1% Race/ethnicity unknown; 0.8% international; 6% transferred in.

Freshmen
Admission: 426 applied, 357 admitted, 137 enrolled. ***Average high school GPA:*** 3.08. ***Test scores:*** SAT critical reading scores over 500: 41%; SAT math scores over 500: 50%; SAT writing scores over 500: 31%; ACT scores over 18: 33%; SAT critical reading scores over 600: 6%; SAT math scores over 600: 12%; SAT writing scores over 600: 4%.

Retention: 78% of full-time freshmen returned.

FACULTY
Total: 53, 58% full-time, 42% with terminal degrees.
Student/faculty ratio: 13:1.

ACADEMICS
Calendar: semesters. *Degrees:* certificates, associate, bachelor's, and postbachelor's certificates (enrollment figures include students enrolled at The Graduate School at Penn State who are taking courses at this location).
Special study options: adult/continuing education programs, external degree program. ***ROTC:*** Army (c), Air Force (c).
Computers: Students can access the following: online (class) registration. Campuswide network is available.

STUDENT LIFE
Housing options: college housing not available.
Athletics Member NJCAA. ***Intercollegiate sports:*** baseball M, basketball M, cross-country running M/W, golf M/W, soccer M/W, volleyball W. ***Intramural sports:*** basketball M/W, bowling M(c)/W(c), cheerleading M(c)/W(c), football M, racquetball M/W, softball W, volleyball M(c)/W.

COSTS & FINANCIAL AID
Costs (2014–15) ***Tuition:*** state resident $12,718 full-time, $524 per credit hour part-time; nonresident $19,404 full-time, $809 per credit hour part-time. Full-time tuition and fees vary according to course level, degree level, location, program, and student level. Part-time tuition and fees vary according to course level, course load, degree level, location, program, and student level. ***Required fees:*** $870 full-time. ***Payment plans:*** installment, deferred payment. ***Waivers:*** senior citizens and employees or children of employees.
Financial Aid Of all full-time matriculated undergraduates who enrolled in 2013, 457 applied for aid, 378 were judged to have need, 19 had their need fully met. In 2013, 47 non-need-based awards were made. ***Average percent of need met:*** 63. ***Average financial aid package:*** $10,174. ***Average need-based loan:*** $4196. ***Average need-based gift aid:*** $6576. ***Average non-need-based aid:*** $2405. ***Average indebtedness upon graduation:*** $36,935.

APPLYING
Standardized Tests *Required:* SAT or ACT (for admission).
Options: electronic application, early admission, deferred entrance.
Application fee: $50.
Required: high school transcript.
Application deadlines: rolling (freshmen), rolling (transfers).
Notification: continuous (freshmen), continuous (transfers).

CONTACT
Admissions Office, Penn State Wilkes-Barre, Old Route 115, PO Box PSU, Lehman, PA 18627. *Phone:* 570-675-9238. *Fax:* 570-675-9113. *E-mail:* wbadmissions@psu.edu.

Penn State Worthington Scranton

Dunmore, Pennsylvania

http://www.sn.psu.edu/

- **State-related** 4-year, founded 1923, part of Pennsylvania State University
- **Small-town** campus
- **Coed** 1,126 undergraduate students, 82% full-time, 53% women, 47% men
- **Moderately difficult** entrance level, 76% of applicants were admitted

UNDERGRAD STUDENTS
926 full-time, 200 part-time. 3% are from out of state; 3% Black or African American, non-Hispanic/Latino; 6% Hispanic/Latino; 5% Asian, non-Hispanic/Latino; 0.1% Native Hawaiian or other Pacific Islander, non-Hispanic/Latino; 2% Two or more races, non-Hispanic/Latino; 1% Race/ethnicity unknown; 0.4% international; 5% transferred in.

Freshmen
Admission: 741 applied, 564 admitted, 268 enrolled. ***Average high school GPA:*** 2.98. ***Test scores:*** SAT critical reading scores over 500: 41%; SAT math scores over 500: 43%; SAT writing scores over 500: 32%; ACT scores over 18: 58%; SAT critical reading scores over 600: 10%; SAT math scores over 600: 9%; SAT writing scores over 600: 7%; ACT scores over 24: 17%.
Retention: 70% of full-time freshmen returned.

FACULTY
Total: 95, 52% full-time, 37% with terminal degrees.
Student/faculty ratio: 16:1.

ACADEMICS
Calendar: semesters. *Degrees:* certificates, associate, and bachelor's.
Special study options: adult/continuing education programs, external degree program. ***ROTC:*** Army (c), Air Force (c).
Computers: Students can access the following: online (class) registration. Campuswide network is available.

STUDENT LIFE
Housing options: college housing not available; coed.
Athletics Member NJCAA. ***Intercollegiate sports:*** baseball M, basketball M/W, cheerleading M/W, cross-country running M/W, soccer M, softball W, volleyball W. ***Intramural sports:*** basketball M/W, bowling M(c)/W(c), skiing (downhill) M(c)/W(c), soccer M/W, softball M/W, volleyball M/W(c), weight lifting M(c)/W(c).

COSTS & FINANCIAL AID
Costs (2014–15) ***Tuition:*** state resident $13,012 full-time, $535 per credit hour part-time; nonresident $19,848 full-time, $827 per credit hour part-time. Full-time tuition and fees vary according to course level, degree level, location, program, and student level. Part-time tuition and fees vary according to course level, course load, degree level, location, program, and student level. ***Required fees:*** $870 full-time. ***Payment plans:*** installment, deferred payment. ***Waivers:*** senior citizens and employees or children of employees.
Financial Aid Of all full-time matriculated undergraduates who enrolled in 2013, 831 applied for aid, 735 were judged to have need, 30 had their need fully met. In 2013, 27 non-need-based awards were made. ***Average percent of need met:*** 59. ***Average financial aid package:*** $9902. ***Average need-based loan:*** $4100. ***Average need-based gift aid:*** $6386. ***Average non-need-based aid:*** $3410. ***Average indebtedness upon graduation:*** $36,935.

APPLYING
Standardized Tests *Required:* SAT or ACT (for admission).
Options: electronic application, early admission, deferred entrance.
Application fee: $50.
Required: high school transcript. ***Required for some:*** interview. ***Recommended:*** essay or personal statement.
Application deadlines: rolling (freshmen), rolling (transfers).
Notification: continuous (freshmen), continuous (transfers).

CONTACT
Admissions Office, Penn State Worthington Scranton, 120 Ridge View Drive, Dunmore, PA 18512-1699. *Phone:* 570-963-2500. *Fax:* 570-963-2524. *E-mail:* wsadmissions@psu.edu.

Penn State York

York, Pennsylvania

http://www.yk.psu.edu/

- **State-related** 4-year, founded 1926, part of Pennsylvania State University
- **Suburban** campus
- **Coed** 1,126 undergraduate students, 74% full-time, 43% women, 57% men
- **Moderately difficult** entrance level, 83% of applicants were admitted

UNDERGRAD STUDENTS
838 full-time, 288 part-time. 9% are from out of state; 3% Black or African American, non-Hispanic/Latino; 7% Hispanic/Latino; 5% Asian, non-Hispanic/Latino; 0.4% American Indian or Alaska Native, non-Hispanic/Latino; 2% Two or more races, non-Hispanic/Latino; 2% Race/ethnicity unknown; 11% international; 4% transferred in.

Freshmen
Admission: 1,393 applied, 1,161 admitted, 310 enrolled. ***Average high school GPA:*** 3.09. ***Test scores:*** SAT critical reading scores over 500:

50%; SAT math scores over 500: 62%; SAT writing scores over 500: 42%; ACT scores over 18: 83%; SAT critical reading scores over 600: 14%; SAT math scores over 600: 24%; SAT writing scores over 600: 11%; ACT scores over 24: 39%; SAT critical reading scores over 700: 4%; SAT math scores over 700: 9%; SAT writing scores over 700: 1%; ACT scores over 30: 4%.

Retention: 75% of full-time freshmen returned.

FACULTY

Total: 99, 51% full-time, 53% with terminal degrees.

Student/faculty ratio: 14:1.

ACADEMICS

Calendar: semesters. *Degrees:* certificates, associate, bachelor's, and master's (also offers up to 2 years of most bachelor's degree programs offered at University Park campus).

Special study options: adult/continuing education programs, external degree program.

Computers: Students can access the following: online (class) registration. Campuswide network is available.

STUDENT LIFE

Housing options: college housing not available.

Athletics Member NJCAA.

COSTS & FINANCIAL AID

Costs (2014–15) ***Tuition:*** state resident $13,012 full-time, $535 per credit hour part-time; nonresident $19,848 full-time, $827 per credit hour part-time. Full-time tuition and fees vary according to course level, degree level, location, program, and student level. Part-time tuition and fees vary according to course level, course load, degree level, location, program, and student level. ***Required fees:*** $918 full-time. ***Payment plans:*** installment, deferred payment. ***Waivers:*** senior citizens and employees or children of employees.

Financial Aid Of all full-time matriculated undergraduates who enrolled in 2013, 627 applied for aid, 521 were judged to have need, 40 had their need fully met. In 2013, 70 non-need-based awards were made. ***Average percent of need met:*** 61. ***Average financial aid package:*** $10,669. ***Average need-based loan:*** $4033. ***Average need-based gift aid:*** $6430. ***Average non-need-based aid:*** $2893. ***Average indebtedness upon graduation:*** $36,935.

APPLYING

Standardized Tests *Required:* SAT or ACT (for admission).

Options: electronic application, early admission, deferred entrance.

Application fee: $50.

Required: high school transcript.

Application deadlines: rolling (freshmen), rolling (transfers).

Notification: continuous (freshmen), continuous (transfers).

CONTACT

Admissions Office, Penn State York, 1031 Edgecomb Avenue, York, PA 17403. *Phone:* 717-771-4040. *Toll-free phone:* 800-778-6227. *Fax:* 717-771-4005. *E-mail:* ykadmission@psu.edu.

Pennsylvania College of Art & Design

Lancaster, Pennsylvania

http://www.pcad.edu/

- **Independent** 4-year, founded 1982
- **Urban** campus with easy access to Philadelphia, Baltimore
- **Coed** 206 undergraduate students, 96% full-time, 72% women, 28% men
- **Moderately difficult** entrance level, 42% of applicants were admitted

UNDERGRAD STUDENTS

198 full-time, 8 part-time. Students come from 9 states and territories; 28% are from out of state; 4% Black or African American, non-Hispanic/Latino; 4% Hispanic/Latino; 2% Asian, non-Hispanic/Latino; 0.5% American Indian or Alaska Native, non-Hispanic/Latino; 4% Two or more races, non-Hispanic/Latino; 7% Race/ethnicity unknown; 0.5% international.

Freshmen

Admission: 350 applied, 148 admitted, 58 enrolled. ***Average high school GPA:*** 3.01.

Retention: 63% of full-time freshmen returned.

FACULTY

Total: 51, 20% full-time, 35% with terminal degrees.

Student/faculty ratio: 8:1.

ACADEMICS

Calendar: semesters. *Degree:* certificates and bachelor's.

Special study options: advanced placement credit, internships.

Computers: 90 computers/terminals are available on campus for general student use. Students can access the following: campus intranet, computer help desk, free student e-mail accounts, online (class) grades, online (class) registration, online (class) schedules. Campuswide network is available. Wireless service is available via entire campus.

STUDENT LIFE

Housing options: college housing not available.

Activities and organizations: Student Council, Anime Club, Student AIGA, Society of Illustrators - Student Group.

Campus security: late-night transport/escort service, trained evening/weekend security personnel.

COSTS

Costs (2014–15) ***Tuition:*** $20,500 full-time, $854 per credit part-time. Full-time tuition and fees vary according to course load and program. Part-time tuition and fees vary according to course load and program. ***Required fees:*** $1500 full-time. ***Payment plan:*** installment. ***Waivers:*** employees or children of employees.

APPLYING

Standardized Tests *Recommended:* SAT (for admission), ACT (for admission).

Options: electronic application, deferred entrance.

Application fee: $40.

Required: essay or personal statement, high school transcript, minimum 2.5 GPA, portfolio. ***Required for some:*** 2 letters of recommendation, interview. ***Recommended:*** interview.

Application deadlines: rolling (freshmen), rolling (transfers).

Notification: continuous (freshmen), continuous (transfers).

CONTACT

Admissions Department, Pennsylvania College of Art & Design, 204 North Prince Street, PO Box 59, Lancaster, PA 17608. *Phone:* 717-396-7833. *Toll-free phone:* 800-689-0379 Ext. 1001. *Fax:* 717-396-1339. *E-mail:* admissions@pcad.edu.

★ Pennsylvania College of Health Sciences

Lancaster, Pennsylvania

http://www.pacollege.edu/

- **Independent** comprehensive, founded 1903
- **Urban** campus with easy access to Harrisburg
- **Endowment** $1.1 million
- **Coed, primarily women** 1,447 undergraduate students, 34% full-time, 86% women, 14% men
- **Moderately difficult** entrance level, 43% of applicants were admitted

UNDERGRAD STUDENTS

491 full-time, 956 part-time. Students come from 8 states and territories; 2% are from out of state; 5% Black or African American, non-Hispanic/Latino; 6% Hispanic/Latino; 3% Asian, non-Hispanic/Latino; 0.2% Native Hawaiian or other Pacific Islander, non-Hispanic/Latino; 0.2% American Indian or Alaska Native, non-Hispanic/Latino; 0.6% Two or more races, non-Hispanic/Latino; 4% Race/ethnicity unknown; 36% transferred in.

Freshmen

Admission: 663 applied, 282 admitted, 222 enrolled.

Retention: 76% of full-time freshmen returned.

FACULTY
Total: 197, 31% full-time.
Student/faculty ratio: 7:1.

ACADEMICS
Degrees: certificates, associate, bachelor's, and master's.
Special study options: accelerated degree program, adult/continuing education programs, advanced placement credit, distance learning, part-time degree program, services for LD students, summer session for credit.
Computers: 98 computers/terminals are available on campus for general student use. Students can access the following: campus intranet, free student e-mail accounts, online (class) grades, online (class) registration, online (class) schedules. Campuswide network is available. Wireless service is available via entire campus.

STUDENT LIFE
Housing options: college housing not available.
Activities and organizations: Student Government Association, Soccer Club, Distance Running.
Athletics ***Intramural sports:*** cross-country running M(c)/W(c), soccer M(c)/W(c).
Campus security: 24-hour emergency response devices and patrols, late-night transport/escort service.
Student services: health clinic, personal/psychological counseling.

COSTS
Costs (2014–15) ***Tuition:*** $14,430 full-time, $481 per credit part-time. Full-time tuition and fees vary according to program. Part-time tuition and fees vary according to program. ***Required fees:*** $825 full-time. ***Payment plans:*** installment, deferred payment. ***Waivers:*** employees or children of employees.

APPLYING
Standardized Tests *Required for some:* SAT or ACT (for admission).
Options: electronic application, deferred entrance.
Application fee: $35.
Required: minimum 3.0 GPA, 2 letters of recommendation, Official GED transcript may be substituted in lieu of high school transcript. SAT or ACT scores required if graduated from high school within last 2 years. Official transcripts of all institutions attended. ***Required for some:*** essay or personal statement, high school transcript.
Notification: continuous (freshmen).

CONTACT
Admissions Office, Pennsylvania College of Health Sciences, 410 Lime Street, Lancaster, PA 17602. *Phone:* 800-622-5443. *Toll-free phone:* 800-622-5443. *E-mail:* admission@pacollege.edu.

Pennsylvania College of Technology
Williamsport, Pennsylvania
http://www.pct.edu/

- **State-related** 4-year, founded 1965
- **Suburban** 994-acre campus
- **Coed** 5,623 undergraduate students, 85% full-time, 36% women, 64% men
- **Noncompetitive** entrance level, 88% of applicants were admitted

UNDERGRAD STUDENTS
4,772 full-time, 851 part-time. Students come from 28 states and territories; 11 other countries; 11% are from out of state; 3% Black or African American, non-Hispanic/Latino; 3% Hispanic/Latino; 0.9% Asian, non-Hispanic/Latino; 0.1% Native Hawaiian or other Pacific Islander, non-Hispanic/Latino; 0.2% American Indian or Alaska Native, non-Hispanic/Latino; 2% Two or more races, non-Hispanic/Latino; 1% international; 8% transferred in; 30% live on campus.

Freshmen
Admission: 4,640 applied, 4,091 admitted, 1,287 enrolled.
Retention: 75% of full-time freshmen returned.

FACULTY
Total: 474, 62% full-time.
Student/faculty ratio: 18:1.

ACADEMICS
Calendar: semesters. *Degrees:* certificates, associate, and bachelor's.
Special study options: academic remediation for entering students, advanced placement credit, cooperative education, distance learning, English as a second language, independent study, internships, off-campus study, part-time degree program, services for LD students, student-designed majors, study abroad, summer session for credit. ***ROTC:*** Army (b).
Computers: 1,678 computers/terminals are available on campus for general student use. Students can access the following: campus intranet, computer help desk, free student e-mail accounts, online (class) grades, online (class) registration, online (class) schedules. Campuswide network is available. 100% of college-owned or -operated housing units are wired for high-speed Internet access. Wireless service is available via entire campus.

STUDENT LIFE
Housing options: coed, special housing for students with disabilities. Campus housing is university owned.
Activities and organizations: Student Government Association, Residence Hall Association, Wildcats Event Board, Association of Computing Machinery, Campus Ministry International, national fraternities, national sororities.
Athletics Member NCAA, USCAA. All Division III. ***Intercollegiate sports:*** archery M/W, baseball M, basketball M/W, bowling M/W, cross-country running M/W, golf M/W, soccer M/W, softball W, tennis M/W, volleyball M/W, wrestling M. ***Intramural sports:*** archery M/W, badminton M/W, basketball M/W, bowling M/W, football M, golf M/W, lacrosse M, soccer M/W, softball M/W, table tennis M/W, tennis M/W, ultimate Frisbee M/W, volleyball M/W, weight lifting M/W.
Campus security: 24-hour emergency response devices and patrols, late-night transport/escort service, controlled dormitory access.
Student services: health clinic, personal/psychological counseling.

COSTS & FINANCIAL AID
Costs (2014–15) ***Tuition:*** state resident $12,960 full-time, $432 per credit hour part-time; nonresident $19,440 full-time, $648 per credit hour part-time. Full-time tuition and fees vary according to course load and program. Part-time tuition and fees vary according to course load and program. ***Required fees:*** $2490 full-time, $83 per credit hour part-time. ***Room and board:*** $10,836; room only: $6236. Room and board charges vary according to board plan and housing facility. ***Payment plan:*** deferred payment. ***Waivers:*** employees or children of employees.
Financial Aid Of all full-time matriculated undergraduates who enrolled in 2013, 4,649 applied for aid, 4,417 were judged to have need. 127 Federal Work-Study jobs (averaging $1711). ***Average financial aid package:*** $11,920. ***Average need-based loan:*** $3738. ***Average need-based gift aid:*** $7637.

APPLYING
Standardized Tests *Required for some:* SAT (for admission).
Options: electronic application, early admission, deferred entrance.
Application fee: $50.
Required for some: high school transcript, college transcripts if transfer applicant.
Application deadlines: 7/1 (freshmen), rolling (transfers).

CONTACT
Mr. Dennis L. Correll, Associate Dean for Admissions/Financial Aid, Pennsylvania College of Technology, One College Avenue, DIF #119, Williamsport, PA 17701. *Phone:* 570-327-4761 Ext. 7337. *Toll-free phone:* 800-367-9222. *Fax:* 570-321-5551. *E-mail:* admissions@pct.edu.

★ Philadelphia University
Philadelphia, Pennsylvania
http://www.philau.edu/

- **Independent** comprehensive, founded 1884
- **Suburban** 100-acre campus
- **Coed** 2,906 undergraduate students, 88% full-time, 66% women, 34% men
- **Moderately difficult** entrance level, 64% of applicants were admitted

UNDERGRAD STUDENTS
2,557 full-time, 349 part-time. 42% are from out of state; 14% Black or African American, non-Hispanic/Latino; 7% Hispanic/Latino; 5% Asian, non-Hispanic/Latino; 0.1% Native Hawaiian or other Pacific Islander, non-Hispanic/Latino; 0.1% American Indian or Alaska Native, non-Hispanic/Latino; 2% Two or more races, non-Hispanic/Latino; 8% Race/ethnicity unknown; 4% international; 7% transferred in; 50% live on campus.

Freshmen
Admission: 4,767 applied, 3,048 admitted, 661 enrolled. ***Average high school GPA:*** 3.53. ***Test scores:*** SAT critical reading scores over 500: 67%; SAT math scores over 500: 71%; SAT writing scores over 500: 63%; ACT scores over 18: 91%; SAT critical reading scores over 600: 17%; SAT math scores over 600: 27%; SAT writing scores over 600: 20%; ACT scores over 24: 52%; SAT critical reading scores over 700: 2%; SAT math scores over 700: 2%; SAT writing scores over 700: 2%; ACT scores over 30: 7%.
Retention: 79% of full-time freshmen returned.

FACULTY
Total: 531, 23% full-time.
Student/faculty ratio: 13:1.

ACADEMICS
Calendar: semesters. *Degrees:* certificates, associate, bachelor's, master's, doctoral, post-master's, and postbachelor's certificates.
Special study options: adult/continuing education programs, part-time degree program.
Computers: Students can access the following: online (class) registration. Campuswide network is available.

STUDENT LIFE
Housing options: coed, women-only, special housing for students with disabilities. Campus housing is university owned and leased by the school. Freshman campus housing is guaranteed.
Athletics Member NCAA. All Division II. ***Intercollegiate sports:*** baseball M(s), basketball M(s)/W(s), cross-country running M/W, golf M(s), lacrosse W(s), soccer M(s)/W(s), softball W(s), tennis M(s)/W(s), volleyball W(s). ***Intramural sports:*** basketball M/W, field hockey W, football M, skiing (downhill) M(c)/W(c), soccer M/W, softball M/W, swimming and diving M/W, table tennis M/W, tennis M/W, volleyball M/W, weight lifting M/W.
Campus security: 24-hour emergency response devices and patrols, late-night transport/escort service, controlled dormitory access.

COSTS & FINANCIAL AID
Costs (2014–15) ***Comprehensive fee:*** $46,690 includes full-time tuition ($34,280), mandatory fees ($800), and room and board ($11,610). Full-time tuition and fees vary according to course load, degree level, and program. Part-time tuition: $595 per credit hour. Part-time tuition and fees vary according to class time, course load, degree level, program, and reciprocity agreements. ***College room only:*** $5420. Room and board charges vary according to board plan and housing facility. ***Payment plans:*** installment, deferred payment. ***Waivers:*** employees or children of employees.
Financial Aid Of all full-time matriculated undergraduates who enrolled in 2013, 2,188 applied for aid, 2,010 were judged to have need, 240 had their need fully met. In 2013, 435 non-need-based awards were made. ***Average percent of need met:*** 67. ***Average financial aid package:*** $24,123. ***Average need-based loan:*** $4508. ***Average need-based gift aid:*** $18,837. ***Average non-need-based aid:*** $8604. ***Average indebtedness upon graduation:*** $37,423. ***Financial aid deadline:*** 4/15.

APPLYING
Standardized Tests *Required:* SAT or ACT (for admission).
Options: electronic application, deferred entrance.
Application fee: $40.
Required: high school transcript. ***Recommended:*** essay or personal statement, 2 letters of recommendation, interview.

CONTACT
Greg Potts, Director of Admissions, Philadelphia University, 4201 Henry Avenue, Philadelphia, PA 19144-5497. *Phone:* 215-951-2800. *Fax:* 215-951-2907. *E-mail:* admissions@philau.edu.

★ Point Park University
Pittsburgh, Pennsylvania
http://www.pointpark.edu/

- **Independent** comprehensive, founded 1960
- **Urban** campus
- **Endowment** $31.0 million
- **Coed**
- **Moderately difficult** entrance level

FACULTY
Student/faculty ratio: 13:1.

ACADEMICS
Calendar: semesters. *Degrees:* certificates, associate, bachelor's, master's, and postbachelor's certificates.

STUDENT LIFE
Housing options: coed, women-only, special housing for students with disabilities. Campus housing is university owned and leased by the school. Freshman campus housing is guaranteed.
Activities and organizations: drama/theater group, student-run newspaper, radio and television station, student radio station, The Body Christian Fellowship, Dance Club, Campus Activities Board, Action Sports Club.
Athletics Member NAIA.
Campus security: 24-hour emergency response devices and patrols, late-night transport/escort service, controlled dormitory access, Campus patrolled by Accredited Law Enforcement Agency (one of only 5 universities in the state),24-hour security desk, video security.
Student services: health clinic, personal/psychological counseling.

COSTS & FINANCIAL AID
Costs (2014–15) ***Comprehensive fee:*** $37,510 includes full-time tuition ($25,980), mandatory fees ($1210), and room and board ($10,320). Full-time tuition and fees vary according to program. Part-time tuition: $737 per credit. Part-time tuition and fees vary according to program. ***Required fees:*** $42 per credit part-time. ***College room only:*** $4860. Room and board charges vary according to board plan and housing facility. ***Payment plans:*** installment, deferred payment.
Financial Aid Of all full-time matriculated undergraduates who enrolled in 2013, 2,353 applied for aid, 2,149 were judged to have need, 296 had their need fully met. 286 Federal Work-Study jobs (averaging $1843). 202 state and other part-time jobs (averaging $3342). In 2013, 176 non-need-based awards were made. ***Average percent of need met:*** 68. ***Average financial aid package:*** $19,935. ***Average need-based loan:*** $5450. ***Average need-based gift aid:*** $14,427. ***Average non-need-based aid:*** $9926. ***Average indebtedness upon graduation:*** $28,725. ***Financial aid deadline:*** 3/15.

APPLYING
Standardized Tests *Required:* SAT or ACT (for admission).
Options: electronic application, deferred entrance.
Application fee: $40.
Required: high school transcript. ***Required for some:*** 2 letters of recommendation, interview, audition. ***Recommended:*** essay or personal statement, minimum 2.5 GPA.

CONTACT
Point Park University, 201 Wood Street, Pittsburgh, PA 15222-1984. *Phone:* 412-392-3430. *Toll-free phone:* 800-321-0129.

★ The Restaurant School at Walnut Hill College
Philadelphia, Pennsylvania
http://www.walnuthillcollege.edu/

CONTACT
Miss Toni Morelli, Director of Admissions, The Restaurant School at Walnut Hill College, 4207 Walnut Street, Philadelphia, PA 19104-3518. *Phone:* 267-295-2353. *Fax:* 215-222-4219. *E-mail:* tmorelli@walnuthillcollege.edu.

See next page for display ad and page 1576 for the College Close-Up.

★ Robert Morris University
Moon Township, Pennsylvania
http://www.rmu.edu/

- **Independent** university, founded 1921
- **Suburban** 230-acre campus with easy access to Pittsburgh
- **Endowment** $32.2 million
- **Coed** 4,574 undergraduate students, 87% full-time, 44% women, 56% men
- **Minimally difficult** entrance level, 76% of applicants were admitted

UNDERGRAD STUDENTS
3,968 full-time, 606 part-time. Students come from 37 states and territories; 37 other countries; 13% are from out of state; 6% Black or African American, non-Hispanic/Latino; 2% Hispanic/Latino; 1% Asian, non-Hispanic/Latino; 0.1% American Indian or Alaska Native, non-Hispanic/Latino; 2% Two or more races, non-Hispanic/Latino; 3% Race/ethnicity unknown; 10% international; 6% transferred in; 53% live on campus.

Freshmen
Admission: 6,064 applied, 4,621 admitted, 864 enrolled. ***Average high school GPA:*** 3.47. ***Test scores:*** SAT critical reading scores over 500: 67%; SAT math scores over 500: 59%; SAT writing scores over 500: 46%; ACT scores over 18: 91%; SAT critical reading scores over 600: 23%; SAT math scores over 600: 14%; SAT writing scores over 600: 11%; ACT scores over 24: 30%; SAT critical reading scores over 700: 1%; SAT math scores over 700: 1%; SAT writing scores over 700: 1%; ACT scores over 30: 1%.

Retention: 83% of full-time freshmen returned.

FACULTY
Total: 482, 44% full-time, 57% with terminal degrees.

Student/faculty ratio: 15:1.

ACADEMICS
Calendar: semesters. *Degrees:* certificates, bachelor's, master's, doctoral, and postbachelor's certificates.

Special study options: academic remediation for entering students, accelerated degree program, adult/continuing education programs, cooperative education, distance learning, double majors, honors programs, independent study, internships, off-campus study, part-time degree program, services for LD students, study abroad, summer session for credit. ***ROTC:*** Army (b), Air Force (c).

Computers: 300 computers/terminals are available on campus for general student use. Students can access the following: campus intranet, computer help desk, free student e-mail accounts, online (class) grades, online (class) registration, online (class) schedules, online payment. Campuswide network is available. 100% of college-owned or -operated housing units are wired for high-speed Internet access. Wireless service is available via classrooms, computer centers, computer labs, learning centers, libraries, student centers.

STUDENT LIFE
Housing options: on-campus residence required for freshman year; coed, men-only, women-only, special housing for students with disabilities. Campus housing is university owned. Freshman applicants given priority for college housing.

Activities and organizations: drama/theater group, student-run newspaper, radio and television station, choral group, marching band, Student Government Association, Residence Hall Association, R-MOVE, National Society of Collegiate Scholars, Black Student Union, national fraternities, national sororities.

Athletics Member NCAA. All Division I. ***Intercollegiate sports:*** baseball M(c), basketball M(s)/W(s), cheerleading M(c)/W(c), crew W(s), football M(s), ice hockey M(s)/W(s), lacrosse M(s)/W(s), soccer M(s)/W(s), softball W(s), track and field W, volleyball W(s). ***Intramural sports:*** basketball M/W, bowling M(c)/W(c), football M, ice hockey M(c), rugby M(c)/W(c), softball M/W, volleyball M(c)/W.

Campus security: 24-hour emergency response devices and patrols, late-night transport/escort service, controlled dormitory access.

Student services: health clinic, personal/psychological counseling.

COSTS & FINANCIAL AID
Costs (2014–15) ***Comprehensive fee:*** $37,864 includes full-time tuition ($25,380), mandatory fees ($674), and room and board ($11,810). Full-

time tuition and fees vary according to degree level and program. Part-time tuition: $820 per credit hour. Part-time tuition and fees vary according to course load, degree level, and program. ***Required fees:*** $40 per credit hour part-time. ***College room only:*** $5640. Room and board charges vary according to board plan and housing facility. ***Payment plans:*** installment, deferred payment. ***Waivers:*** employees or children of employees.

Financial Aid Of all full-time matriculated undergraduates who enrolled in 2014, 2,644 applied for aid, 2,403 were judged to have need, 291 had their need fully met. In 2014, 475 non-need-based awards were made. ***Average percent of need met:*** 73. ***Average financial aid package:*** $20,822. ***Average need-based loan:*** $5981. ***Average need-based gift aid:*** $14,359. ***Average non-need-based aid:*** $10,733. ***Average indebtedness upon graduation:*** $37,531.

APPLYING

Standardized Tests *Required:* SAT or ACT (for admission).

Options: electronic application, deferred entrance.

Application fee: $30.

Required: high school transcript, minimum 2.0 GPA. ***Required for some:*** interview. ***Recommended:*** essay or personal statement, minimum 3.0 GPA, interview.

Application deadlines: 4/1 (freshmen), 7/1 (transfers).

Notification: continuous until 9/1 (freshmen), continuous (transfers).

CONTACT

Enrollment Services Department, Robert Morris University, 6001 University Boulevard, Moon Township, PA 15108-1189. *Phone:* 412-397-5200. *Toll-free phone:* 800-762-0097. *Fax:* 412-397-2425. *E-mail:* admissionsoffice@rmu.edu.

See this page for display ad and page 1584 for the College Close-Up.

Rosemont College

Rosemont, Pennsylvania

http://www.rosemont.edu/

- **Independent Roman Catholic** comprehensive, founded 1921
- **Suburban** 56-acre campus with easy access to Philadelphia
- **Endowment** $16.8 million
- **Coed** 522 undergraduate students, 85% full-time, 66% women, 34% men
- **Moderately difficult** entrance level, 58% of applicants were admitted

UNDERGRAD STUDENTS

442 full-time, 80 part-time. Students come from 9 states and territories; 7 other countries; 23% are from out of state; 38% Black or African American, non-Hispanic/Latino; 6% Hispanic/Latino; 5% Asian, non-Hispanic/Latino; 0.2% American Indian or Alaska Native, non-Hispanic/Latino; 3% Two or more races, non-Hispanic/Latino; 3% Race/ethnicity unknown; 1% international; 8% transferred in; 71% live on campus.

Freshmen

Admission: 800 applied, 463 admitted, 124 enrolled. ***Average high school GPA:*** 3.07. ***Test scores:*** SAT critical reading scores over 500: 37%; SAT math scores over 500: 30%; ACT scores over 18: 61%; SAT critical reading scores over 600: 13%; SAT math scores over 600: 10%; ACT scores over 24: 23%; SAT critical reading scores over 700: 4%; SAT math scores over 700: 4%; ACT scores over 30: 11%.

Retention: 67% of full-time freshmen returned.

FACULTY

Total: 139, 20% full-time, 80% with terminal degrees.

Student/faculty ratio: 10:1.

ACADEMICS

Calendar: semesters. *Degrees:* bachelor's, master's, and postbachelor's certificates.

Special study options: academic remediation for entering students, accelerated degree program, adult/continuing education programs, advanced placement credit, double majors, English as a second language, honors programs, independent study, internships, off-campus study, part-time degree program, services for LD students, student-designed majors, study abroad, summer session for credit.

Unusual degree programs: 3-2 nursing with Drexel University; counseling psychology, dentistry, art therapy, physical therapy, creative arts in therapy, nursing with Drexel University.

Computers: 100 computers/terminals and 250 ports are available on campus for general student use. Students can access the following: campus intranet, computer help desk, free student e-mail accounts, online (class) grades, online (class) registration, online (class) schedules. Campuswide network is available. 100% of college-owned or -operated housing units are wired for high-speed Internet access. Wireless service is available via classrooms, computer centers, computer labs, dorm rooms, learning centers, libraries, student centers.

STUDENT LIFE

Housing options: on-campus residence required through junior year; coed, women-only. Campus housing is university owned. Freshman campus housing is guaranteed.

Activities and organizations: drama/theater group, student-run newspaper, choral group, student government, Triad, International Club, Best Buddies, Political Science Club.

Athletics Member NCAA. All Division III. ***Intercollegiate sports:*** basketball M/W, cross-country running M/W, golf M, lacrosse M/W, soccer M/W, softball W, tennis M/W, volleyball W.

Campus security: 24-hour emergency response devices and patrols, late-night transport/escort service, controlled dormitory access.

Student services: health clinic, personal/psychological counseling, women's center, legal services.

COSTS & FINANCIAL AID

Costs (2014–15) ***Comprehensive fee:*** $44,460 includes full-time tuition ($30,600), mandatory fees ($980), and room and board ($12,880). Full-time tuition and fees vary according to course load and program. Part-time tuition: $1165 per credit hour. Part-time tuition and fees vary according to course load and program. ***Required fees:*** $340 per term part-time. ***Room and board:*** Room and board charges vary according to board plan and housing facility. ***Payment plan:*** installment. ***Waivers:*** senior citizens and employees or children of employees.

Financial Aid Of all full-time matriculated undergraduates who enrolled in 2011, 369 applied for aid, 356 were judged to have need, 35 had their need fully met. 87 Federal Work-Study jobs (averaging $589). 65 state and other part-time jobs (averaging $190). In 2011, 27 non-need-based awards were made. ***Average percent of need met:*** 75. ***Average financial aid package:*** $27,065. ***Average need-based loan:*** $4682. ***Average need-based gift aid:*** $21,765. ***Average non-need-based aid:*** $13,203. ***Average indebtedness upon graduation:*** $22,597.

APPLYING

Standardized Tests *Required:* SAT or ACT (for admission).

Options: electronic application, early admission, deferred entrance.

Required: essay or personal statement, high school transcript, 2 letters of recommendation. ***Recommended:*** minimum 3.0 GPA, interview.

Application deadlines: rolling (freshmen), rolling (transfers).

Notification: 8/1 (freshmen), continuous until 8/1 (transfers).

CONTACT

Ms. Bettsy Thommen, Associate Director of Admissions, Rosemont College, 1400 Montgomery Avenue, Main Building, Rosemont, PA 19010. *Phone:* 610-527-0200 Ext. 2601. *Toll-free phone:* 888-2-ROSEMONT. *Fax:* 610-520-4399. *E-mail:* bettsy.thommen@rosemont.edu.

Saint Charles Borromeo Seminary, Overbrook

Wynnewood, Pennsylvania

http://www.scs.edu/

- **Independent Roman Catholic** comprehensive, founded 1832
- **Suburban** 77-acre campus with easy access to Philadelphia
- **Coed, primarily men** 98 undergraduate students, 76% full-time, 17% women, 83% men
- **Moderately difficult** entrance level, 100% of applicants were admitted

UNDERGRAD STUDENTS

74 full-time, 24 part-time. Students come from 6 states and territories; 13% are from out of state; 9% Hispanic/Latino; 2% Asian, non-Hispanic/Latino; 5% transferred in; 100% live on campus.

Freshmen

Admission: 8 applied, 8 admitted, 7 enrolled. ***Test scores:*** SAT critical reading scores over 500: 100%; SAT math scores over 500: 75%; SAT writing scores over 500: 50%; SAT critical reading scores over 600: 50%; SAT math scores over 600: 25%.

Retention: 78% of full-time freshmen returned.

FACULTY

Total: 33, 48% full-time, 48% with terminal degrees.

Student/faculty ratio: 6:1.

ACADEMICS

Calendar: semesters. *Degrees:* certificates, bachelor's, master's, and postbachelor's certificates (also offers coed part-time programs).

Special study options: academic remediation for entering students, accelerated degree program, adult/continuing education programs, advanced placement credit, English as a second language, independent study, summer session for credit.

Computers: 60 computers/terminals are available on campus for general student use. Students can access the following: campus intranet, free student e-mail accounts, online (class) grades, online (class) schedules. Campuswide network is available. Wireless service is available via classrooms, computer centers, computer labs, libraries.

STUDENT LIFE

Housing options: on-campus residence required through senior year; men-only. Campus housing is university owned. Freshman campus housing is guaranteed.

Activities and organizations: drama/theater group, student-run newspaper, choral group, Seminarians for Life, Student Council.

Athletics ***Intramural sports:*** basketball M, football M, soccer M, volleyball M.

Campus security: 24-hour emergency response devices and patrols.

Student services: health clinic, personal/psychological counseling.

FINANCIAL AID

Financial Aid Of all full-time matriculated undergraduates who enrolled in 2012, 22 applied for aid, 10 were judged to have need, 6 had their need fully met. ***Average percent of need met:*** 60. ***Average financial aid package:*** $20,000. ***Average need-based loan:*** $5500. ***Average need-based gift aid:*** $5000. ***Average indebtedness upon graduation:*** $19,000.

APPLYING

Standardized Tests *Recommended:* SAT or ACT (for admission).

Options: deferred entrance.

Required: essay or personal statement, high school transcript, minimum 2.0 GPA, 3 letters of recommendation, interview, sponsorship by diocese or religious community.

Application deadlines: 7/15 (freshmen), 7/15 (transfers).

Notification: continuous (freshmen), continuous (transfers).

CONTACT

Rev. Joseph Shenosky, Vice Rector, Saint Charles Borromeo Seminary, Overbrook, 100 East Wynnewood Road, Wynnewood, PA 19096. *Phone:* 610-785-6520. *E-mail:* jshenosky@scs.edu.

★ Saint Francis University

Loretto, Pennsylvania

http://www.francis.edu/

- **Independent Roman Catholic** comprehensive, founded 1847
- **Rural** 600-acre campus
- **Endowment** $45.1 million
- **Coed** 1,722 undergraduate students, 93% full-time, 63% women, 37% men
- **Moderately difficult** entrance level, 69% of applicants were admitted

UNDERGRAD STUDENTS

1,605 full-time, 117 part-time. Students come from 40 states and territories; 20% are from out of state; 6% Black or African American, non-Hispanic/Latino; 2% Hispanic/Latino; 0.7% Asian, non-Hispanic/Latino; 0.3% Native Hawaiian or other Pacific Islander, non-Hispanic/Latino; 0.1% American Indian or Alaska Native, non-Hispanic/Latino; 1% Two or more races, non-Hispanic/Latino; 7% Race/ethnicity unknown; 6% international; 2% transferred in; 88% live on campus.

Freshmen

Admission: 1,640 applied, 1,127 admitted, 389 enrolled. ***Average high school GPA:*** 3.5. ***Test scores:*** SAT math scores over 500: 64%; SAT writing scores over 500: 53%; ACT scores over 18: 89%; SAT math scores over 600: 18%; SAT writing scores over 600: 14%; ACT scores over 24: 40%; SAT math scores over 700: 2%; SAT writing scores over 700: 1%; ACT scores over 30: 2%.

Retention: 86% of full-time freshmen returned.

FACULTY

Total: 232, 54% full-time.

Student/faculty ratio: 13:1.

ACADEMICS

Calendar: semesters. *Degrees:* certificates, associate, bachelor's, master's, and doctoral.

Special study options: academic remediation for entering students, accelerated degree program, adult/continuing education programs, advanced placement credit, distance learning, double majors, English as a second language, external degree program, freshman honors college, honors programs, independent study, internships, off-campus study, part-time degree program, student-designed majors, study abroad, summer session for credit. ***ROTC:*** Army (b).

Unusual degree programs: 3-2 engineering with Penn State University–University Park Campus, University of Pittsburgh, Clarkson University; forestry with Duke University; Pennsylvania College of Optometry, Lake Erie College of Osteopathic Medicine (LECOM), Temple University.

Computers: 75 computers/terminals are available on campus for general student use. Students can access the following: campus intranet, computer help desk, free student e-mail accounts, online (class) grades, online (class) registration, online (class) schedules, wireless access throughout all of campus. Campuswide network is available. 95% of college-owned or -operated housing units are wired for high-speed Internet access. Wireless service is available via entire campus.

STUDENT LIFE

Housing options: on-campus residence required through junior year; men-only, women-only. Campus housing is university owned and leased by the school. Freshman campus housing is guaranteed.

Activities and organizations: drama/theater group, student-run newspaper, radio station, choral group, marching band, Student Activities Organization, Club Baseball, Student Government Association, Best Buddies, Ultimate Frisbee Club, national fraternities, national sororities.

Athletics Member NCAA. All Division I. ***Intercollegiate sports:*** basketball M(s)/W(s), bowling W, cross-country running M(s)/W(s), field hockey W(s), football M, golf M(s)/W(s), lacrosse W(s), soccer M(s)/W(s), softball W(s), swimming and diving M(s)/W(s), tennis M(s)/W(s), track and field M(s)/W(s), volleyball M(s)/W(s). ***Intramural sports:*** baseball M(c), basketball M/W, cheerleading M/W, cross-country running M/W, football M, golf M/W, ice hockey M(c), lacrosse W, racquetball M/W, skiing (cross-country) M/W, skiing (downhill) M/W, soccer M/W, softball W, swimming and diving M/W, table tennis M/W, tennis M/W, track and field M/W, ultimate Frisbee M/W, volleyball M/W.

Campus security: 24-hour emergency response devices and patrols, late-night transport/escort service, controlled dormitory access.

Student services: health clinic, personal/psychological counseling.

COSTS

Costs (2015–16) ***One-time required fee:*** $100. ***Comprehensive fee:*** $43,210 includes full-time tuition ($31,078), mandatory fees ($1050), and room and board ($11,082). Full-time tuition and fees vary according to course load, degree level, program, and student level. Part-time tuition: $971 per credit hour. Part-time tuition and fees vary according to class time, degree level, and program. ***Room and board:*** Room and board charges vary according to board plan and housing facility. ***Waivers:*** employees or children of employees.

APPLYING

Standardized Tests *Required:* SAT or ACT (for admission).

Options: electronic application, deferred entrance.

Application fee: $30.

Required: essay or personal statement, high school transcript, 1 letter of recommendation. ***Required for some:*** interview. ***Recommended:*** interview.

Application deadlines: rolling (freshmen), rolling (out-of-state freshmen), rolling (transfers).

Notification: continuous (transfers).

CONTACT

Robert Beener, Dean for Enrollment Management, Saint Francis University, 117 Evergreen Drive, PO Box 600, Loretto, PA 15940-0600. *Phone:* 814-472-3100. *Toll-free phone:* 866-DIAL-SFU. *E-mail:* rbeener@francis.edu.

See previous page for display ad and page 1594 for the College Close-Up.

★ Saint Joseph's University

Philadelphia, Pennsylvania

http://www.sju.edu/

- **Independent Roman Catholic (Jesuit)** comprehensive, founded 1851
- **Suburban** 105-acre campus
- **Endowment** $209.3 million
- **Coed** 5,512 undergraduate students, 85% full-time, 54% women, 46% men
- **Moderately difficult** entrance level, 85% of applicants were admitted

UNDERGRAD STUDENTS

4,671 full-time, 841 part-time. Students come from 44 states and territories; 35 other countries; 53% are from out of state; 7% Black or African American, non-Hispanic/Latino; 6% Hispanic/Latino; 3% Asian, non-Hispanic/Latino; 0.1% American Indian or Alaska Native, non-Hispanic/Latino; 2% Two or more races, non-Hispanic/Latino; 2% Race/ethnicity unknown; 2% international; 2% transferred in; 59% live on campus.

Freshmen

Admission: 8,462 applied, 7,160 admitted, 1,353 enrolled. ***Average high school GPA:*** 3.46. ***Test scores:*** SAT critical reading scores over 500: 84%; SAT math scores over 500: 86%; SAT writing scores over 500: 83%; ACT scores over 18: 99%; SAT critical reading scores over 600: 28%; SAT math scores over 600: 36%; SAT writing scores over 600: 32%; ACT scores over 24: 66%; SAT critical reading scores over 700: 3%; SAT math scores over 700: 4%; SAT writing scores over 700: 4%; ACT scores over 30: 14%.

Retention: 89% of full-time freshmen returned.

FACULTY

Total: 711, 42% full-time.

Student/faculty ratio: 13:1.

ACADEMICS

Calendar: semesters. *Degrees:* certificates, associate, bachelor's, master's, doctoral, post-master's, and postbachelor's certificates.

Special study options: accelerated degree program, adult/continuing education programs, advanced placement credit, cooperative education, distance learning, double majors, English as a second language, honors programs, independent study, internships, off-campus study, part-time degree program, services for LD students, student-designed majors, study abroad, summer session for credit. ***ROTC:*** Army (c), Navy (c), Air Force (b).

Computers: 829 computers/terminals are available on campus for general student use. Students can access the following: campus intranet, computer help desk, free student e-mail accounts, online (class) grades, online (class) registration, online (class) schedules. Campuswide network is available. 100% of college-owned or -operated housing units are wired for high-speed Internet access. Wireless service is available via entire campus.

STUDENT LIFE

Housing options: on-campus residence required through sophomore year; coed, men-only, women-only, special housing for students with disabilities. Campus housing is university owned, leased by the school and is provided by a third party. Freshman campus housing is guaranteed.

Activities and organizations: drama/theater group, student-run newspaper, radio station, choral group, Student Union Board, Hand-in-Hand, 54th Airborne / Booster Club, Appalachian Experience, Weekly Service, national fraternities, national sororities.

Athletics Member NCAA. All Division I. ***Intercollegiate sports:*** baseball M(s), basketball M(s)/W(s), cheerleading M(c)/W(c), crew M(s)/W(s), cross-country running M(s)/W(s), field hockey W(s), golf M(s), lacrosse M(s)/W(s), soccer M(s)/W(s), softball W(s), tennis M(s)/W(s), track and field M(s)/W(s). ***Intramural sports:*** baseball M(c), basketball M(c)/W(c), field hockey W(c), football M/W, golf M(c)/W(c), ice hockey M(c)/W(c), lacrosse M(c)/W(c), racquetball M/W, rugby M(c)/W(c), soccer M(c)/W(c), softball M/W, swimming and diving M(c)/W(c), tennis M(c)/W(c), ultimate Frisbee M(c)/W(c), volleyball M(c)/W(c), water polo M(c)/W(c).

Campus security: 24-hour emergency response devices and patrols, late-night transport/escort service, controlled dormitory access, 24-hour shuttle/escort service, bicycle patrols.

Student services: health clinic, personal/psychological counseling.

COSTS & FINANCIAL AID

Costs (2014–15) ***Comprehensive fee:*** $55,006 includes full-time tuition ($40,420), mandatory fees ($160), and room and board ($14,426). Full-time tuition and fees vary according to course load. Part-time tuition: $541 per credit. Part-time tuition and fees vary according to course load. ***College room only:*** $9397. Room and board charges vary according to board plan and housing facility. ***Payment plan:*** installment. ***Waivers:*** employees or children of employees.

Financial Aid Of all full-time matriculated undergraduates who enrolled in 2014, 3,311 applied for aid, 2,685 were judged to have need, 622 had their need fully met. In 2014, 1529 non-need-based awards were made. ***Average percent of need met:*** 73. ***Average financial aid package:*** $25,302. ***Average need-based loan:*** $4423. ***Average need-based gift aid:*** $19,065. ***Average non-need-based aid:*** $11,276.

APPLYING

Options: electronic application, early action, deferred entrance.

Application fee: $60.

Required: essay or personal statement, high school transcript, 1 letter of recommendation.

Application deadlines: 2/1 (freshmen), 3/1 (transfers), 11/15 (early action).

Notification: 3/15 (freshmen), continuous (transfers), 12/25 (early action).

CONTACT

Office of Admissions, Saint Joseph's University, 5600 City Avenue, Philadelphia, PA 19131-1395. *Phone:* 610-660-1300. *Toll-free phone:* 888-BE-A-HAWK (in-state); 800-BE-A-HAWK (out-of-state). *Fax:* 610-660-1314. *E-mail:* admit@sju.edu.

★ Saint Vincent College

Latrobe, Pennsylvania

http://www.stvincent.edu/

- **Independent Roman Catholic** comprehensive, founded 1846
- **Suburban** 200-acre campus with easy access to Pittsburgh
- **Endowment** $89.8 million
- **Coed** 1,626 undergraduate students, 96% full-time, 48% women, 52% men
- **Moderately difficult** entrance level, 72% of applicants were admitted

UNDERGRAD STUDENTS

1,560 full-time, 66 part-time. Students come from 27 states and territories; 10 other countries; 17% are from out of state; 5% Black or African American, non-Hispanic/Latino; 4% Hispanic/Latino; 2% Asian, non-Hispanic/Latino; 0.1% Native Hawaiian or other Pacific Islander, non-Hispanic/Latino; 0.3% American Indian or Alaska Native, non-Hispanic/Latino; 0.6% Two or more races, non-Hispanic/Latino; 3% Race/ethnicity unknown; 1% international; 3% transferred in; 73% live on campus.

Freshmen

Admission: 1,891 applied, 1,360 admitted, 449 enrolled. ***Average high school GPA:*** 3.56. ***Test scores:*** SAT critical reading scores over 500: 65%; SAT math scores over 500: 67%; SAT writing scores over 500: 58%; ACT scores over 18: 91%; SAT critical reading scores over 600: 19%;

SAT math scores over 600: 24%; SAT writing scores over 600: 16%; ACT scores over 24: 33%; SAT critical reading scores over 700: 3%; SAT math scores over 700: 4%; SAT writing scores over 700: 2%; ACT scores over 30: 6%.
Retention: 82% of full-time freshmen returned.

FACULTY
Total: 198, 52% full-time, 65% with terminal degrees.
Student/faculty ratio: 12:1.

ACADEMICS
Calendar: semesters. *Degrees:* certificates, bachelor's, master's, doctoral, and postbachelor's certificates.
Special study options: advanced placement credit, cooperative education, distance learning, double majors, English as a second language, external degree program, honors programs, independent study, internships, part-time degree program, services for LD students, student-designed majors, study abroad, summer session for credit. ***ROTC:*** Army (c), Air Force (c).
Unusual degree programs: engineering with University of Pittsburgh, Penn State University and Catholic University; Physical Therapy Program — Duquesne University; Physician Assistant Program — Duquesne University; Occupational Therapy — Duquesne University; Pharmacy — Duquesne University.
Computers: 281 computers/terminals are available on campus for general student use. Students can access the following: campus intranet, computer help desk, free student e-mail accounts, online (class) grades, online (class) registration, online (class) schedules, program requirement evaluation. Campuswide network is available. 100% of college-owned or -operated housing units are wired for high-speed Internet access. Wireless service is available via entire campus.

STUDENT LIFE
Housing options: coed. Campus housing is university owned. Freshman applicants given priority for college housing.
Activities and organizations: drama/theater group, student-run newspaper, choral group, marching band, Activities Programming Board, Orientation Committee, Campus Ministry, Visionaries of Hope.
Athletics Member NCAA. All Division III. ***Intercollegiate sports:*** baseball M, basketball M/W, cheerleading M(c)/W(c), cross-country running M/W, equestrian sports M(c)/W(c), fencing M(c)/W(c), golf M/W, ice hockey M(c), lacrosse M/W, soccer M/W, softball W, swimming and diving M/W, tennis M/W, track and field M/W, volleyball W. ***Intramural sports:*** basketball M/W, football M/W, ultimate Frisbee M/W, volleyball M/W.
Campus security: 24-hour emergency response devices and patrols, late-night transport/escort service, controlled dormitory access, limited access to residence halls on weekends.
Student services: health clinic, personal/psychological counseling.

COSTS & FINANCIAL AID
Costs (2014–15) ***Comprehensive fee:*** $40,244 includes full-time tuition ($29,540), mandatory fees ($1166), and room and board ($9538). Full-time tuition and fees vary according to course load and degree level. Part-time tuition and fees vary according to course load and degree level. ***Required fees:*** $955 per credit hour part-time. ***College room only:*** $4884. Room and board charges vary according to board plan and housing facility. ***Payment plan:*** installment. ***Waivers:*** employees or children of employees.
Financial Aid Of all full-time matriculated undergraduates who enrolled in 2014, 1,336 applied for aid, 1,221 were judged to have need, 222 had their need fully met. 302 Federal Work-Study jobs (averaging $1493). In 2014, 218 non-need-based awards were made. ***Average percent of need met:*** 81. ***Average financial aid package:*** $27,394. ***Average need-based loan:*** $4228. ***Average need-based gift aid:*** $6068. ***Average non-need-based aid:*** $17,680. ***Average indebtedness upon graduation:*** $29,464.

APPLYING
Standardized Tests *Required:* SAT or ACT (for admission).
Options: electronic application, early admission, deferred entrance.
Application fee: $25.
Required: essay or personal statement, high school transcript, minimum 2.5 GPA. ***Required for some:*** interview. ***Recommended:*** minimum 3.2 GPA, 3 letters of recommendation, interview.
Application deadlines: 5/1 (freshmen), 7/1 (transfers).
Notification: continuous until 10/1 (freshmen), continuous (transfers).

CONTACT
Mr. David Collins, Assistant Vice President of Admission and Financial Aid, Saint Vincent College, 300 Fraser Purchase Road, Latrobe, PA 15650-2690. *Phone:* 800-782-5549. *Toll-free phone:* 800-782-5549. *Fax:* 724-532-5069. *E-mail:* admission@stvincent.edu.

See previous page for display ad and page 1614 for the College Close-Up.

Seton Hill University
Greensburg, Pennsylvania
http://www.setonhill.edu/

- **Independent Roman Catholic** comprehensive, founded 1883
- **Small-town** 200-acre campus with easy access to Pittsburgh
- **Coed** 1,582 undergraduate students, 90% full-time, 65% women, 35% men
- **Moderately difficult** entrance level, 69% of applicants were admitted

UNDERGRAD STUDENTS
1,427 full-time, 155 part-time. Students come from 47 states and territories; 20 other countries; 23% are from out of state; 8% Black or African American, non-Hispanic/Latino; 3% Hispanic/Latino; 0.7% Asian, non-Hispanic/Latino; 0.4% American Indian or Alaska Native, non-Hispanic/Latino; 2% Two or more races, non-Hispanic/Latino; 2% Race/ethnicity unknown; 4% international; 4% transferred in; 59% live on campus.

Freshmen
Admission: 2,248 applied, 1,554 admitted, 335 enrolled. ***Average high school GPA:*** 3.61. ***Test scores:*** SAT critical reading scores over 500: 65%; SAT math scores over 500: 63%; SAT writing scores over 500: 56%; ACT scores over 18: 89%; SAT critical reading scores over 600: 17%; SAT math scores over 600: 25%; SAT writing scores over 600: 15%; ACT scores over 24: 56%; SAT critical reading scores over 700: 2%; SAT math scores over 700: 2%; SAT writing scores over 700: 1%; ACT scores over 30: 5%.

Retention: 78% of full-time freshmen returned.

FACULTY
Total: 192, 54% full-time, 59% with terminal degrees.

Student/faculty ratio: 13:1.

ACADEMICS
Calendar: semesters. *Degrees:* certificates, bachelor's, master's, post-master's, and postbachelor's certificates.

Special study options: academic remediation for entering students, adult/continuing education programs, advanced placement credit, distance learning, double majors, English as a second language, honors programs, independent study, internships, off-campus study, part-time degree program, services for LD students, student-designed majors, study abroad, summer session for credit. ***ROTC:*** Army (c).

Unusual degree programs: 3-2 engineering with University of Pittsburgh, Penn State University- University Park Campus, Georgia Institute of Technology; physician assistant with Seton Hill University, BS/DO and BS/DPharm with Lake Erie College of Osteopathic Medicine.

Computers: 66 computers/terminals and 66 ports are available on campus for general student use. Students can access the following: campus intranet, computer help desk, free student e-mail accounts, online (class) grades, online (class) registration, online (class) schedules. Campuswide network is available. 100% of college-owned or -operated housing units are wired for high-speed Internet access. Wireless service is available via entire campus.

STUDENT LIFE
Housing options: on-campus residence required for freshman year; coed. Campus housing is university owned and leased by the school. Freshman campus housing is guaranteed.

Activities and organizations: drama/theater group, student-run newspaper, choral group, marching band, Student Body Activities Council, Future Greek leaders, Peer Ministry Council, Biology Club, intramurals.

Athletics Member NCAA. All Division II. ***Intercollegiate sports:*** baseball M(s), basketball M(s)/W(s), cross-country running M(s)/W(s), equestrian sports W(s), field hockey W(s), football M(s), golf W(s), lacrosse M(s)/W(s), soccer M(s)/W(s), softball W(s), tennis W(s), track and field M(s)/W(s), volleyball W(s), wrestling M(s).

Campus security: 24-hour emergency response devices and patrols, late-night transport/escort service, controlled dormitory access, emergency phones throughout camps, campus alert system, safety committee.

Student services: health clinic, personal/psychological counseling.

COSTS & FINANCIAL AID
Costs (2015–16) ***Comprehensive fee:*** $42,776 includes full-time tuition ($31,037), mandatory fees ($1000), and room and board ($10,739). Full-time tuition and fees vary according to course load, degree level, and program. Part-time tuition: $832 per credit hour. Part-time tuition and fees vary according to course load, degree level, and program. ***Required fees:*** $25 per credit hour part-time. ***Room and board:*** Room and board charges vary according to board plan and housing facility. ***Payment plan:*** installment. ***Waivers:*** employees or children of employees.

Financial Aid Of all full-time matriculated undergraduates who enrolled in 2014, 1,155 applied for aid, 1,084 were judged to have need, 189 had their need fully met. 687 Federal Work-Study jobs (averaging $868). 93 state and other part-time jobs (averaging $351). In 2014, 174 non-need-based awards were made. ***Average percent of need met:*** 74. ***Average financial aid package:*** $24,777. ***Average need-based loan:*** $5906. ***Average need-based gift aid:*** $19,198. ***Average non-need-based aid:*** $12,333. ***Average indebtedness upon graduation:*** $36,295.

APPLYING
Standardized Tests *Recommended:* SAT or ACT (for admission).

Options: electronic application, deferred entrance.

Application fee: $35.

Required: essay or personal statement, high school transcript, 1 letter of recommendation, portfolio for art, audition for music and theatre. ***Recommended:*** interview.

Application deadlines: rolling (freshmen), rolling (out-of-state freshmen), rolling (transfers).

Notification: continuous (freshmen), continuous (out-of-state freshmen), continuous (transfers).

CONTACT
Mrs. Allison Sasso, Assistant Director of Admissions, Seton Hill University, Seton Hill Drive, Greensburg, PA 15601. *Phone:* 724-838-4255. *Toll-free phone:* 800-826-6234. *Fax:* 724-830-1294. *E-mail:* admit@setonhill.edu.

Shippensburg University of Pennsylvania
Shippensburg, Pennsylvania
http://www.ship.edu/

- **State-supported** comprehensive, founded 1871, part of Pennsylvania State System of Higher Education
- **Rural** 200-acre campus
- **Endowment** $36.5 million
- **Coed** 6,305 undergraduate students, 94% full-time, 49% women, 51% men
- **Moderately difficult** entrance level, 83% of applicants were admitted

UNDERGRAD STUDENTS
5,956 full-time, 349 part-time. Students come from 26 states and territories; 24 other countries; 7% are from out of state; 9% Black or African American, non-Hispanic/Latino; 5% Hispanic/Latino; 1% Asian, non-Hispanic/Latino; 0.1% Native Hawaiian or other Pacific Islander, non-Hispanic/Latino; 0.1% American Indian or Alaska Native, non-Hispanic/Latino; 3% Two or more races, non-Hispanic/Latino; 2% Race/ethnicity unknown; 0.4% international; 6% transferred in; 36% live on campus.

Freshmen
Admission: 6,319 applied, 5,253 admitted, 1,484 enrolled. ***Average high school GPA:*** 3.2. ***Test scores:*** SAT critical reading scores over 500: 46%; SAT math scores over 500: 50%; SAT writing scores over 500: 33%; ACT scores over 18: 74%; SAT critical reading scores over 600: 9%; SAT math scores over 600: 11%; SAT writing scores over 600: 6%; ACT scores over

24: 17%; SAT critical reading scores over 700: 1%; SAT math scores over 700: 1%.

Retention: 74% of full-time freshmen returned.

FACULTY

Total: 374, 82% full-time, 79% with terminal degrees.

Student/faculty ratio: 20:1.

ACADEMICS

Calendar: semesters. *Degrees:* certificates, bachelor's, master's, doctoral, and postbachelor's certificates.

Special study options: academic remediation for entering students, accelerated degree program, advanced placement credit, cooperative education, distance learning, double majors, honors programs, independent study, internships, off-campus study, part-time degree program, services for LD students, study abroad, summer session for credit. ***ROTC:*** Army (b).

Unusual degree programs: 3-2 engineering with Penn State University - University Park and Harrisburg Campus, University of Maryland College Park.

Computers: 1,100 computers/terminals are available on campus for general student use. Students can access the following: campus intranet, computer help desk, free student e-mail accounts, online (class) grades, online (class) registration, online (class) schedules, personal Web pages. Campuswide network is available. 100% of college-owned or -operated housing units are wired for high-speed Internet access. Wireless service is available via classrooms, computer centers, computer labs, dorm rooms, learning centers, libraries, student centers.

STUDENT LIFE

Housing options: on-campus residence required for freshman year; coed. Campus housing is university owned and leased by the school. Freshman campus housing is guaranteed.

Activities and organizations: drama/theater group, student-run newspaper, radio and television station, choral group, marching band, national fraternities, national sororities.

Athletics Member NCAA. All Division II. ***Intercollegiate sports:*** baseball M(s), basketball M(s)/W(s), cross-country running M(s)/W(s), field hockey W(s), football M(s), lacrosse W(s), soccer M(s)/W(s), softball W(s), swimming and diving M(s)/W(s), tennis W(s), track and field M(s)/W(s), volleyball W(s), wrestling M(s). ***Intramural sports:*** basketball M/W, fencing M(c), ice hockey M(c), lacrosse M(c), rugby M(c)/W(c), soccer M/W, softball M/W, ultimate Frisbee M/W, volleyball M/W.

Campus security: 24-hour emergency response devices and patrols, late-night transport/escort service, controlled dormitory access, surveillance cameras in certain parking lots and buildings, foot, vehicular and bicycle patrols by security officers.

Student services: health clinic, personal/psychological counseling, women's center.

COSTS & FINANCIAL AID

Costs (2014–15) ***Tuition:*** state resident $6820 full-time, $284 per credit hour part-time; nonresident $15,346 full-time, $639 per credit hour part-time. ***Required fees:*** $2954 full-time, $123 per credit hour part-time. ***Room and board:*** $11,160; room only: $7314. Room and board charges vary according to board plan and housing facility. ***Payment plan:*** installment. ***Waivers:*** senior citizens and employees or children of employees.

Financial Aid Of all full-time matriculated undergraduates who enrolled in 2014, 5,086 applied for aid, 4,107 were judged to have need, 402 had their need fully met. 126 Federal Work-Study jobs (averaging $1891). 595 state and other part-time jobs (averaging $2198). In 2014, 404 non-need-based awards were made. ***Average percent of need met:*** 55. ***Average financial aid package:*** $8351. ***Average need-based loan:*** $3949. ***Average need-based gift aid:*** $6151. ***Average non-need-based aid:*** $4378. ***Average indebtedness upon graduation:*** $29,988.

APPLYING

Standardized Tests *Required:* SAT or ACT (for admission).

Options: electronic application, early admission, early action, deferred entrance.

Application fee: $45.

Required: high school transcript. ***Required for some:*** interview. ***Recommended:*** essay or personal statement, class rank, letters of recommendation optional.

Application deadlines: rolling (freshmen), rolling (transfers).

Notification: continuous (freshmen), continuous (transfers).

CONTACT

Mr. William H. Washabaugh, Associate Dean of Admissions, Shippensburg University of Pennsylvania, 1871 Old Main Drive, Shippensburg, PA 17257-2299. *Phone:* 717-477-1231. *Toll-free phone:* 800-822-8028. *Fax:* 717-477-4016. *E-mail:* admiss@ship.edu.

Slippery Rock University of Pennsylvania

Slippery Rock, Pennsylvania

http://www.sru.edu/

- **State-supported** comprehensive, founded 1889, part of Pennsylvania State System of Higher Education
- **Small-town** 650-acre campus with easy access to Pittsburgh
- **Endowment** $25.1 million
- **Coed** 7,587 undergraduate students, 93% full-time, 57% women, 43% men
- **Moderately difficult** entrance level, 66% of applicants were admitted

UNDERGRAD STUDENTS

7,059 full-time, 528 part-time. Students come from 34 states and territories; 38 other countries; 10% are from out of state; 5% Black or African American, non-Hispanic/Latino; 2% Hispanic/Latino; 0.7% Asian, non-Hispanic/Latino; 0.1% Native Hawaiian or other Pacific Islander, non-Hispanic/Latino; 0.1% American Indian or Alaska Native, non-Hispanic/Latino; 3% Two or more races, non-Hispanic/Latino; 2% Race/ethnicity unknown; 1% international; 8% transferred in; 36% live on campus.

Freshmen

Admission: 5,775 applied, 3,810 admitted, 1,586 enrolled. ***Average high school GPA:*** 3.42. ***Test scores:*** SAT critical reading scores over 500: 48%; SAT math scores over 500: 53%; SAT writing scores over 500: 37%; ACT scores over 18: 88%; SAT critical reading scores over 600: 8%; SAT math scores over 600: 10%; SAT writing scores over 600: 5%; ACT scores over 24: 28%; SAT critical reading scores over 700: 1%; SAT math scores over 700: 1%; SAT writing scores over 700: 1%; ACT scores over 30: 2%.

Retention: 82% of full-time freshmen returned.

FACULTY

Total: 393, 84% full-time, 82% with terminal degrees.

Student/faculty ratio: 22:1.

ACADEMICS

Calendar: semesters. *Degrees:* certificates, bachelor's, master's, doctoral, and postbachelor's certificates.

Special study options: academic remediation for entering students, adult/continuing education programs, advanced placement credit, distance learning, double majors, honors programs, independent study, internships, off-campus study, part-time degree program, services for LD students, student-designed majors, study abroad, summer session for credit. ***ROTC:*** Army (b).

Unusual degree programs: 3-2 engineering with Penn State University–University Park Campus; Youngstown State University, West Virginia University.

Computers: 1,604 computers/terminals and 75 ports are available on campus for general student use. Students can access the following: computer help desk, free student e-mail accounts, online (class) grades, online (class) registration, online (class) schedules. Campuswide network is available. 100% of college-owned or -operated housing units are wired for high-speed Internet access. Wireless service is available via classrooms, computer labs, dorm rooms, libraries, student centers.

STUDENT LIFE

Housing options: on-campus residence required for freshman year; coed, special housing for students with disabilities. Campus housing is university owned. Freshman campus housing is guaranteed.

Activities and organizations: drama/theater group, student-run newspaper, radio and television station, choral group, marching band, SRU Pre-Physical Therapy Club, American Society of Safety Engineers, Therapeutic Recreation Club, Sport Management Alliance, University Program Board, national fraternities, national sororities.

Athletics Member NCAA. All Division II. ***Intercollegiate sports:*** baseball M(s), basketball M(s)/W(s), cheerleading M(c)/W(c), cross-country running M(s)/W(s), equestrian sports M(c)/W(c), field hockey W(s), football M(s), ice hockey M(c)/W(c), lacrosse M(c)/W(s), rugby M(c)/W(c), soccer M(s)/W(s), softball W(s), tennis M(c)/W(s), track and field M(s)/W(s), volleyball M(c)/W(s). ***Intramural sports:*** badminton M/W, baseball M(c), basketball M/W, football M/W, golf M(c)/W(c), gymnastics M(c)/W(c), soccer M/W, softball M/W, swimming and diving M(c)/W(c), ultimate Frisbee M/W, volleyball M/W, water polo M/W, wrestling M(c).

Campus security: 24-hour emergency response devices and patrols, late-night transport/escort service, controlled dormitory access.

Student services: health clinic, personal/psychological counseling, women's center, legal services.

COSTS & FINANCIAL AID

Costs (2014–15) ***Tuition:*** state resident $6820 full-time, $284 per credit hour part-time; nonresident $10,230 full-time, $426 per credit hour part-time. Full-time tuition and fees vary according to course load. Part-time tuition and fees vary according to course load. ***Required fees:*** $2489 full-time, $104 per credit hour part-time. ***Room and board:*** $9794; room only: $6490. Room and board charges vary according to board plan and housing facility. ***Payment plan:*** installment. ***Waivers:*** minority students, senior citizens, and employees or children of employees.

Financial Aid Of all full-time matriculated undergraduates who enrolled in 2014, 6,169 applied for aid, 4,952 were judged to have need, 615 had their need fully met. 556 Federal Work-Study jobs (averaging $1725). 887 state and other part-time jobs (averaging $1981). In 2014, 436 non-need-based awards were made. ***Average percent of need met:*** 60. ***Average financial aid package:*** $8831. ***Average need-based loan:*** $4354. ***Average need-based gift aid:*** $5859. ***Average non-need-based aid:*** $2734. ***Average indebtedness upon graduation:*** $30,458.

APPLYING

Standardized Tests *Required:* SAT or ACT (for admission).

Options: electronic application, deferred entrance.

Application fee: $30.

Required: high school transcript. ***Recommended:*** minimum 3.0 GPA.

Application deadlines: rolling (freshmen), rolling (out-of-state freshmen), rolling (transfers).

Notification: continuous until 6/15 (freshmen), continuous until 6/15 (out-of-state freshmen), continuous (transfers).

CONTACT

Slippery Rock University of Pennsylvania, 1 Morrow Way, Slippery Rock, PA 16057-1383. *Phone:* 724-738-2015. *Toll-free phone:* 800-SRU-9111.

Summit University

Clarks Summit, Pennsylvania

http://www.summitu.edu/

- **Independent Baptist** comprehensive, founded 1932
- **Suburban** 124-acre campus
- **Endowment** $2.1 million
- **Coed** 722 undergraduate students, 79% full-time, 50% women, 50% men
- **Minimally difficult** entrance level, 38% of applicants were admitted

UNDERGRAD STUDENTS

568 full-time, 154 part-time. Students come from 34 states and territories; 86 other countries; 51% are from out of state; 3% Black or African American, non-Hispanic/Latino; 2% Hispanic/Latino; 0.6% Asian, non-Hispanic/Latino; 0.1% Native Hawaiian or other Pacific Islander, non-Hispanic/Latino; 0.4% American Indian or Alaska Native, non-Hispanic/Latino; 1% Two or more races, non-Hispanic/Latino; 3% Race/ethnicity unknown; 0.1% international; 7% transferred in; 91% live on campus.

Freshmen

Admission: 424 applied, 159 admitted, 115 enrolled. ***Average high school GPA:*** 3.31. ***Test scores:*** SAT critical reading scores over 500: 66%; SAT math scores over 500: 46%; SAT writing scores over 500: 56%; ACT scores over 18: 85%; SAT critical reading scores over 600: 22%; SAT math scores over 600: 14%; SAT writing scores over 600: 21%; ACT scores over 24: 31%; SAT critical reading scores over 700: 6%; SAT math scores over 700: 2%; SAT writing scores over 700: 2%; ACT scores over 30: 4%.

Retention: 47% of full-time freshmen returned.

FACULTY

Total: 47, 87% full-time.

Student/faculty ratio: 11:1.

ACADEMICS

Calendar: semesters. *Degrees:* certificates, associate, bachelor's, master's, and doctoral.

Special study options: academic remediation for entering students, adult/continuing education programs, advanced placement credit, distance learning, double majors, English as a second language, external degree program, independent study, internships, part-time degree program, student-designed majors, summer session for credit. ***ROTC:*** Army (c), Navy (c), Air Force (c).

Computers: 25 computers/terminals are available on campus for general student use. Students can access the following: campus intranet, computer help desk, free student e-mail accounts, online (class) grades, online (class) registration, online (class) schedules. Campuswide network is available. 100% of college-owned or -operated housing units are wired for high-speed Internet access. Wireless service is available via entire campus.

STUDENT LIFE

Housing options: on-campus residence required through senior year; men-only, women-only. Campus housing is university owned. Freshman campus housing is guaranteed.

Activities and organizations: drama/theater group, choral group.

Athletics Member NCAA, NCCAA. All NCAA Division III. ***Intercollegiate sports:*** baseball M, basketball M/W, cheerleading W, cross-country running M/W, golf M, soccer M/W, softball W, tennis W, track and field M/W, volleyball W. ***Intramural sports:*** basketball M, golf M, soccer M/W, softball M, volleyball W.

Campus security: 24-hour patrols, student patrols, controlled dormitory access.

Student services: health clinic, personal/psychological counseling.

COSTS & FINANCIAL AID

Costs (2015–16) ***Comprehensive fee:*** $27,650 includes full-time tuition ($21,850) and room and board ($5800). Part-time tuition: $650 per credit. No tuition increase for student's term of enrollment. ***Required fees:*** $43 per credit part-time. ***College room only:*** $2200. Room and board charges vary according to board plan. ***Payment plan:*** installment. ***Waivers:*** employees or children of employees.

Financial Aid Of all full-time matriculated undergraduates who enrolled in 2013, 490 applied for aid, 447 were judged to have need, 29 had their need fully met. 63 Federal Work-Study jobs (averaging $1475). In 2013, 70 non-need-based awards were made. ***Average percent of need met:*** 60. ***Average financial aid package:*** $14,404. ***Average need-based loan:*** $4478. ***Average need-based gift aid:*** $5937. ***Average non-need-based aid:*** $4714. ***Average indebtedness upon graduation:*** $23,971.

APPLYING

Standardized Tests *Required:* SAT or ACT (for admission).

Options: electronic application, early admission, deferred entrance.

Application fee: $40.

Required: essay or personal statement, high school transcript, 2 letters of recommendation, Christian testimony. ***Required for some:*** 1 letter of recommendation, interview.

Application deadlines: 8/15 (freshmen), rolling (transfers).

Notification: continuous (freshmen).

CONTACT

Ms. Kellyn Lovell, Supervisor, Support Services, Summit University, 538 Venard Road, Clarks Summit, PA 18411-1297. *Phone:* 800-451-7664.

Toll-free phone: 800-451-7664. *Fax:* 570-585-9271. *E-mail:* admissions@bbc.edu.

Susquehanna University

Selingsgrove, Pennsylvania

http://www.susqu.edu/

- **Independent** 4-year, founded 1858, affiliated with Evangelical Lutheran Church in America
- **Small-town** 325-acre campus with easy access to Harrisburg
- **Endowment** $151.8 million
- **Coed** 2,084 undergraduate students, 96% full-time, 55% women, 45% men
- **Moderately difficult** entrance level, 78% of applicants were admitted

UNDERGRAD STUDENTS

2,008 full-time, 76 part-time. Students come from 35 states and territories; 22 other countries; 51% are from out of state; 5% Black or African American, non-Hispanic/Latino; 6% Hispanic/Latino; 2% Asian, non-Hispanic/Latino; 0.1% Native Hawaiian or other Pacific Islander, non-Hispanic/Latino; 0.1% American Indian or Alaska Native, non-Hispanic/Latino; 3% Two or more races, non-Hispanic/Latino; 2% international; 1% transferred in; 90% live on campus.

Freshmen

Admission: 4,510 applied, 3,527 admitted, 575 enrolled. ***Average high school GPA:*** 3.38. ***Test scores:*** SAT critical reading scores over 500: 78%; SAT math scores over 500: 86%; SAT writing scores over 500: 73%; ACT scores over 18: 98%; SAT critical reading scores over 600: 30%; SAT math scores over 600: 32%; SAT writing scores over 600: 27%; ACT scores over 24: 65%; SAT critical reading scores over 700: 4%; SAT math scores over 700: 2%; SAT writing scores over 700: 3%; ACT scores over 30: 9%.

Retention: 83% of full-time freshmen returned.

FACULTY

Total: 244, 57% full-time, 64% with terminal degrees.

Student/faculty ratio: 12:1.

ACADEMICS

Calendar: semesters. *Degrees:* bachelor's (also offers evening associate degree program limited to local adult students).

Special study options: accelerated degree program, advanced placement credit, distance learning, double majors, honors programs, independent study, internships, off-campus study, part-time degree program, services for LD students, student-designed majors, study abroad, summer session for credit. ***ROTC:*** Army (c).

Computers: 489 computers/terminals and 60 ports are available on campus for general student use. Students can access the following: campus intranet, computer help desk, free student e-mail accounts, online (class) grades, online (class) registration, online (class) schedules, class listings and assignments, online voting booth. Campuswide network is available. 100% of college-owned or -operated housing units are wired for high-speed Internet access. Wireless service is available via classrooms, computer centers, computer labs, dorm rooms, learning centers, libraries, student centers.

STUDENT LIFE

Housing options: on-campus residence required through senior year; coed. Campus housing is university owned. Freshman campus housing is guaranteed.

Activities and organizations: drama/theater group, student-run newspaper, radio station, choral group, Student Government Association, community service organizations, music performance groups, theater performance groups, intramurals and outdoor recreation, national fraternities, national sororities.

Athletics Member NCAA. All Division III. ***Intercollegiate sports:*** baseball M, basketball M/W, cheerleading M(c)/W(c), crew M(c)/W(c), cross-country running M/W, equestrian sports M(c)/W(c), field hockey W, football M, golf M/W, lacrosse M/W, rugby M(c)/W(c), soccer M/W, softball W, swimming and diving M/W, tennis M/W, track and field M/W, volleyball M(c)/W. ***Intramural sports:*** basketball M/W, racquetball M/W, soccer M/W, softball M/W, tennis M/W, volleyball M/W.

Campus security: 24-hour emergency response devices and patrols, late-night transport/escort service, controlled dormitory access.

Student services: health clinic, personal/psychological counseling.

COSTS & FINANCIAL AID

Costs (2014–15) ***Comprehensive fee:*** $51,150 includes full-time tuition ($39,830), mandatory fees ($520), and room and board ($10,800). Part-time tuition: $1265 per semester hour. ***College room only:*** $5650. Room and board charges vary according to board plan. ***Payment plans:*** tuition prepayment, installment. ***Waivers:*** employees or children of employees.

Financial Aid Of all full-time matriculated undergraduates who enrolled in 2014, 1,720 applied for aid, 1,555 were judged to have need, 313 had their need fully met. 1,115 Federal Work-Study jobs (averaging $2143). 93 state and other part-time jobs (averaging $6293). In 2014, 453 non-need-based awards were made. ***Average percent of need met:*** 80. ***Average financial aid package:*** $30,817. ***Average need-based loan:*** $4307. ***Average need-based gift aid:*** $26,103. ***Average non-need-based aid:*** $15,094. ***Average indebtedness upon graduation:*** $29,734.

APPLYING

Standardized Tests *Recommended:* SAT or ACT (for admission).

Options: electronic application, early admission, early decision, early action, deferred entrance.

Required: essay or personal statement, high school transcript, minimum 2.5 GPA, 1 letter of recommendation. ***Required for some:*** writing portfolio, auditions for music programs. ***Recommended:*** minimum 3.0 GPA, interview.

Application deadlines: 2/15 (freshmen), 8/15 (transfers), 11/1 (early action).

Early decision deadline: 11/15 (for plan 1), 1/15 (for plan 2).

Notification: 3/15 (freshmen), continuous until 8/1 (transfers), 12/1 (early decision plan 1), 2/15 (early decision plan 2), 12/1 (early action).

CONTACT

Mr. Scott Myers, Director of Admissions, Susquehanna University, 514 University Avenue, Selinsgrove, PA 17870. *Phone:* 570-372-4260. *Toll-free phone:* 800-326-9672. *Fax:* 570-372-2722. *E-mail:* suadmiss@susqu.edu.

See previous page for display ad and page 1644 for the College Close-Up.

Swarthmore College

Swarthmore, Pennsylvania

http://www.swarthmore.edu/

- **Independent** 4-year, founded 1864
- **Suburban** 425-acre campus with easy access to Philadelphia
- **Endowment** $1.6 billion
- **Coed**
- **Most difficult** entrance level

FACULTY

Student/faculty ratio: 8:1.

ACADEMICS

Calendar: semesters. *Degree:* bachelor's.

STUDENT LIFE

Housing options: on-campus residence required for freshman year; coed, men-only, women-only, special housing for students with disabilities. Campus housing is university owned. Freshman campus housing is guaranteed.

Activities and organizations: drama/theater group, student-run newspaper, radio station, choral group, community service and activist groups, club sports and intramurals, social/cultural clubs, music/Acappella groups, political and debate clubs, national fraternities.

Athletics Member NCAA. All Division III.

Campus security: 24-hour emergency response devices and patrols, late-night transport/escort service.

Student services: health clinic, personal/psychological counseling, women's center.

COSTS & FINANCIAL AID

Costs (2014–15) ***Comprehensive fee:*** $59,610 includes full-time tuition ($45,700), mandatory fees ($360), and room and board ($13,550). ***College room only:*** $6950. Room and board charges vary according to board plan.

Financial Aid Of all full-time matriculated undergraduates who enrolled in 2014, 891 applied for aid, 777 were judged to have need, 777 had their need fully met. 713 Federal Work-Study jobs (averaging $1826). In 2014, 16 non-need-based awards were made. ***Average percent of need met:*** 100. ***Average financial aid package:*** $41,989. ***Average need-based gift aid:*** $40,314. ***Average non-need-based aid:*** $37,474. ***Average indebtedness upon graduation:*** $21,866. ***Financial aid deadline:*** 2/15.

APPLYING

Standardized Tests *Required:* SAT and SAT Subject Tests or ACT (for admission).

Options: electronic application, early decision, deferred entrance.

Application fee: $60.

Required: essay or personal statement, high school transcript, 3 letters of recommendation. ***Required for some:*** Statement of good standing from prior institution(s) for transfer applicants.

CONTACT

Mr. James L. Bock, Vice President and Dean of Admissions, Swarthmore College, 500 College Avenue, Swarthmore, PA 19081. *Phone:* 610-328-8300. *Toll-free phone:* 800-667-3110. *Fax:* 610-328-8580. *E-mail:* admissions@swarthmore.edu.

Talmudical Yeshiva of Philadelphia

Philadelphia, Pennsylvania

- **Independent Jewish** 4-year, founded 1953
- **Urban** 3-acre campus
- **Men only**
- **Moderately difficult** entrance level

ACADEMICS

Calendar: trimesters. *Degrees:* bachelor's (also offers some graduate courses).

STUDENT LIFE

Housing options: on-campus residence required through senior year; men-only. Campus housing is university owned. Freshman campus housing is guaranteed.

Campus security: controlled dormitory access, night security patrol.

Student services: health clinic, personal/psychological counseling.

FINANCIAL AID

Financial Aid Of all full-time matriculated undergraduates who enrolled in 1998, 71 applied for aid, 71 were judged to have need, 71 had their need fully met. 28 Federal Work-Study jobs (averaging $1000). ***Average percent of need met:*** 100. ***Average financial aid package:*** $4870.

APPLYING

Options: early admission, deferred entrance.

Required: high school transcript, 1 letter of recommendation, interview, oral examination.

CONTACT

Rabbi Shmuel Kamenetsky, Co-Dean, Talmudical Yeshiva of Philadelphia, 6063 Drexel Road, Philadelphia, PA 19131-1296. *Phone:* 215-473-1212.

★ Temple University

Philadelphia, Pennsylvania

http://www.temple.edu/

- **State-related** university, founded 1884, part of Commonwealth System of Higher Education
- **Urban** 382-acre campus with easy access to Philadelphia
- **Endowment** $374.8 million
- **Coed** 28,408 undergraduate students, 88% full-time, 51% women, 49% men
- **Moderately difficult** entrance level, 62% of applicants were admitted

UNDERGRAD STUDENTS

25,110 full-time, 3,298 part-time. Students come from 52 states and territories; 92 other countries; 22% are from out of state; 13% Black or African American, non-Hispanic/Latino; 6% Hispanic/Latino; 10% Asian, non-Hispanic/Latino; 0.1% Native Hawaiian or other Pacific Islander, non-Hispanic/Latino; 0.2% American Indian or Alaska Native, non-Hispanic/Latino; 3% Two or more races, non-Hispanic/Latino; 5%

Race/ethnicity unknown; 6% international; 9% transferred in; 19% live on campus.

Freshmen

Admission: 26,495 applied, 16,356 admitted, 4,485 enrolled. ***Average high school GPA:*** 3.47. ***Test scores:*** SAT critical reading scores over 500: 77%; SAT math scores over 500: 81%; SAT writing scores over 500: 72%; ACT scores over 18: 97%; SAT critical reading scores over 600: 30%; SAT math scores over 600: 36%; SAT writing scores over 600: 28%; ACT scores over 24: 61%; SAT critical reading scores over 700: 6%; SAT math scores over 700: 7%; SAT writing scores over 700: 5%; ACT scores over 30: 19%.

Retention: 89% of full-time freshmen returned.

FACULTY

Total: 2,820, 50% full-time.

Student/faculty ratio: 14:1.

ACADEMICS

Calendar: semesters. *Degrees:* certificates, diplomas, associate, bachelor's, master's, doctoral, post-master's, and postbachelor's certificates.

Special study options: academic remediation for entering students, accelerated degree program, adult/continuing education programs, advanced placement credit, cooperative education, distance learning, double majors, English as a second language, external degree program, honors programs, independent study, internships, off-campus study, part-time degree program, services for LD students, study abroad, summer session for credit. ***ROTC:*** Army (b), Navy (c), Air Force (c).

Computers: 3,760 computers/terminals are available on campus for general student use. Students can access the following: computer help desk, free student e-mail accounts, online (class) grades, online (class) registration, online (class) schedules, student accounts, Web hosting. Campuswide network is available. 100% of college-owned or -operated housing units are wired for high-speed Internet access. Wireless service is available via entire campus.

STUDENT LIFE

Housing options: coed. Campus housing is university owned, leased by the school and is provided by a third party.

Activities and organizations: drama/theater group, student-run newspaper, radio and television station, choral group, marching band, Temple Slavic Association, Alpha Epsilon Delta (Pre-professional students with interests in pursuing careers in healthcare), Habitat for Humanity, National Student Speech Language and Hearing Association, Queer Student Union, national fraternities, national sororities.

Athletics Member NCAA. All Division I except football (Division I-A). ***Intercollegiate sports:*** basketball M(s)/W(s), cheerleading M(s)/W(s), crew M(s)/W(s), cross-country running M(s)/W(s), fencing W(s), field hockey W(s), golf M(s), gymnastics W(s), lacrosse W(s), soccer M(s)/W(s), tennis M(s)/W(s), track and field W(s), volleyball W(s). ***Intramural sports:*** badminton M/W, baseball M(c), basketball M/W, bowling M(c)/W(c), equestrian sports M(c)/W(c), gymnastics M(c)/W(c), ice hockey M(c), racquetball M/W, rugby M(c)/W(c), soccer M/W, softball M/W(c), swimming and diving M(c)/W(c), tennis M/W, track and field M(c), ultimate Frisbee M(c)/W(c), volleyball M/W, weight lifting M(c)/W(c), wrestling M(c).

Campus security: 24-hour emergency response devices and patrols, late-night transport/escort service, controlled dormitory access.

Student services: health clinic, personal/psychological counseling, legal services.

COSTS & FINANCIAL AID

Costs (2014–15) ***Tuition:*** state resident $14,406 full-time, $554 per credit hour part-time; nonresident $24,432 full-time, $834 per credit hour part-time. Full-time tuition and fees vary according to course load, degree level, location, program, reciprocity agreements, and student level. Part-time tuition and fees vary according to course load, degree level, location, program, reciprocity agreements, and student level. ***Required fees:*** $690 full-time. ***Room and board:*** $10,738; room only: $7150. Room and board charges vary according to board plan and housing facility. ***Payment plan:*** installment. ***Waivers:*** employees or children of employees.

Financial Aid Of all full-time matriculated undergraduates who enrolled in 2013, 20,373 applied for aid, 17,609 were judged to have need, 4,355 had their need fully met. 2,419 Federal Work-Study jobs (averaging

$1130). In 2013, 2467 non-need-based awards were made. ***Average percent of need met:*** 66. ***Average financial aid package:*** $16,385. ***Average need-based loan:*** $4580. ***Average need-based gift aid:*** $6335. ***Average non-need-based aid:*** $5871. ***Average indebtedness upon graduation:*** $35,760.

APPLYING

Standardized Tests *Required:* SAT or ACT (for admission).

Options: electronic application, early action, deferred entrance.

Application fee: $55.

Required: essay or personal statement, high school transcript, 1 letter of recommendation. ***Recommended:*** minimum 3.0 GPA.

Application deadlines: 3/1 (freshmen), 6/1 (transfers).

Notification: continuous (freshmen), continuous (transfers).

CONTACT

Temple University, 1801 North Broad Street, Philadelphia, PA 19122-6096. *Phone:* 215-204-7200. *Toll-free phone:* 888-340-2222.

See previous page for display ad and page 1646 for the College Close-Up.

Thiel College

Greenville, Pennsylvania

http://www.thiel.edu/

- **Independent** 4-year, founded 1866, affiliated with Evangelical Lutheran Church in America
- **Rural** 135-acre campus with easy access to Cleveland, Pittsburgh
- **Endowment** $31.1 million
- **Coed** 1,074 undergraduate students, 97% full-time, 47% women, 53% men
- **Moderately difficult** entrance level, 69% of applicants were admitted

UNDERGRAD STUDENTS

1,039 full-time, 35 part-time. Students come from 23 states and territories; 6 other countries; 32% are from out of state; 9% Black or African American, non-Hispanic/Latino; 2% Hispanic/Latino; 0.1% Native Hawaiian or other Pacific Islander, non-Hispanic/Latino; 0.2% American Indian or Alaska Native, non-Hispanic/Latino; 2% Two or more races, non-Hispanic/Latino; 7% Race/ethnicity unknown; 4% international; 1% transferred in; 89% live on campus.

Freshmen

Admission: 2,465 applied, 1,713 admitted, 280 enrolled. ***Average high school GPA:*** 3.21. ***Test scores:*** SAT critical reading scores over 500: 37%; SAT math scores over 500: 45%; ACT scores over 18: 85%; SAT critical reading scores over 600: 9%; SAT math scores over 600: 6%; ACT scores over 24: 22%; SAT critical reading scores over 700: 1%; ACT scores over 30: 3%.

Retention: 66% of full-time freshmen returned.

FACULTY

Total: 101, 62% full-time, 49% with terminal degrees.

Student/faculty ratio: 14:1.

ACADEMICS

Calendar: semesters. *Degrees:* associate and bachelor's.

Special study options: academic remediation for entering students, adult/continuing education programs, advanced placement credit, cooperative education, distance learning, double majors, honors programs, independent study, internships, off-campus study, part-time degree program, services for LD students, study abroad, summer session for credit.

Unusual degree programs: 3-2 engineering with Case Western Reserve University, University of Pittsburgh; forestry with Duke University; physician assistant with Chatham University.

Computers: 147 computers/terminals and 1,705 ports are available on campus for general student use. Students can access the following: campus intranet, computer help desk, free student e-mail accounts, online (class) grades, online (class) registration, online (class) schedules. Campuswide network is available. 100% of college-owned or -operated housing units are wired for high-speed Internet access. Wireless service is available via entire campus.

STUDENT LIFE

Housing options: on-campus residence required through senior year; coed. Campus housing is university owned. Freshman campus housing is guaranteed.

Activities and organizations: drama/theater group, student-run newspaper, radio and television station, choral group, marching band, Thiel Players Theatre Group, student government, Thiel Choir, Ski Club, Thiel Christian Fellowship, national fraternities, national sororities.

Athletics Member NCAA. All Division III. ***Intercollegiate sports:*** baseball M, basketball M/W, cheerleading W, cross-country running M/W, football M, golf M/W, lacrosse M/W, soccer M/W, softball W, tennis M/W, track and field M/W, volleyball M/W, wrestling M. ***Intramural sports:*** basketball M/W, bowling W, football M/W, riflery M/W, rugby M, soccer M/W, softball M/W, volleyball M/W.

Campus security: 24-hour emergency response devices and patrols, late-night transport/escort service, controlled dormitory access.

Student services: health clinic, personal/psychological counseling.

COSTS & FINANCIAL AID

Costs (2014–15) ***Comprehensive fee:*** $38,728 includes full-time tuition ($25,998), mandatory fees ($1830), and room and board ($10,900). Full-time tuition and fees vary according to course load. Part-time tuition: $850 per credit hour. Part-time tuition and fees vary according to course load. ***Required fees:*** $915 per term part-time. ***College room only:*** $5450. Room and board charges vary according to housing facility. ***Payment plan:*** installment. ***Waivers:*** employees or children of employees.

Financial Aid Of all full-time matriculated undergraduates who enrolled in 2014, 913 applied for aid, 867 were judged to have need, 92 had their need fully met. 60 Federal Work-Study jobs (averaging $1475). 300 state and other part-time jobs (averaging $2063). In 2014, 82 non-need-based awards were made. ***Average percent of need met:*** 70. ***Average financial aid package:*** $23,041. ***Average need-based loan:*** $4654. ***Average need-based gift aid:*** $18,846. ***Average non-need-based aid:*** $11,816. ***Average indebtedness upon graduation:*** $37,932.

APPLYING

Standardized Tests *Required:* SAT or ACT (for admission).

Options: electronic application, deferred entrance.

Required: essay or personal statement, high school transcript, minimum 2.0 GPA, 1 letter of recommendation. ***Required for some:*** interview.

Application deadlines: rolling (freshmen), rolling (out-of-state freshmen), rolling (transfers).

Notification: continuous (freshmen), continuous (out-of-state freshmen), continuous (transfers).

CONTACT

Mr. Larry Vallar, Vice President for Enrollment Management, Thiel College, 75 College Avenue, Greenville, PA 16125. *Phone:* 724-589-2182. *Toll-free phone:* 800-248-4435. *Fax:* 724-589-2013. *E-mail:* admissions@thiel.edu.

University of Pennsylvania

Philadelphia, Pennsylvania

http://www.upenn.edu/

- **Independent** university, founded 1740
- **Urban** 299-acre campus
- **Endowment** $9.6 billion
- **Coed** 9,746 undergraduate students, 97% full-time, 50% women, 50% men
- **Most difficult** entrance level, 10% of applicants were admitted

UNDERGRAD STUDENTS

9,437 full-time, 309 part-time. Students come from 54 states and territories; 102 other countries; 81% are from out of state; 7% Black or African American, non-Hispanic/Latino; 10% Hispanic/Latino; 20% Asian, non-Hispanic/Latino; 0.1% American Indian or Alaska Native, non-Hispanic/Latino; 4% Two or more races, non-Hispanic/Latino; 3% Race/ethnicity unknown; 11% international; 2% transferred in; 54% live on campus.

Freshmen

Admission: 35,866 applied, 3,718 admitted, 2,350 enrolled. ***Average high school GPA:*** 3.94. ***Test scores:*** SAT critical reading scores over 500:

100%; SAT math scores over 500: 100%; SAT writing scores over 500: 100%; ACT scores over 18: 100%; SAT critical reading scores over 600: 95%; SAT math scores over 600: 98%; SAT writing scores over 600: 97%; ACT scores over 24: 100%; SAT critical reading scores over 700: 64%; SAT math scores over 700: 74%; SAT writing scores over 700: 75%; ACT scores over 30: 88%.

Retention: 97% of full-time freshmen returned.

FACULTY
Total: 2,048, 71% full-time, 100% with terminal degrees.

Student/faculty ratio: 6:1.

ACADEMICS
Calendar: semesters plus 2 5-week summer sessions. *Degrees:* certificates, associate, bachelor's, master's, doctoral, post-master's, and postbachelor's certificates (also offers evening program with significant enrollment not reflected in profile).

Special study options: academic remediation for entering students, accelerated degree program, adult/continuing education programs, advanced placement credit, cooperative education, distance learning, double majors, English as a second language, honors programs, independent study, internships, off-campus study, part-time degree program, services for LD students, student-designed majors, study abroad, summer session for credit. ***ROTC:*** Army (c), Navy (b), Air Force (c).

Computers: Students can access the following: campus intranet, computer help desk, free student e-mail accounts, online (class) grades, online (class) registration, online (class) schedules, billing information, financial aid application, status, academic records, student services. Campuswide network is available. 100% of college-owned or -operated housing units are wired for high-speed Internet access. Wireless service is available via entire campus.

STUDENT LIFE
Housing options: coed, special housing for students with disabilities. Campus housing is university owned. Freshman campus housing is guaranteed.

Activities and organizations: drama/theater group, student-run newspaper, radio and television station, choral group, marching band, Kite and Key Society, Social Planning and Events Committee, Hillel at Penn, Sports Club Council, Interfraternity Council, national fraternities, national sororities.

Athletics Member NCAA. All Division I except football (Division I-AA). ***Intercollegiate sports:*** baseball M, basketball M/W, crew M/W, cross-country running M/W, fencing M/W, field hockey W, golf M/W, gymnastics W, lacrosse M/W, soccer M/W, softball W, squash M/W, swimming and diving M/W, tennis M/W, track and field M/W, volleyball W, wrestling M. ***Intramural sports:*** badminton M(c)/W(c), baseball M(c)/W(c), basketball M(c)/W(c), cheerleading M/W, equestrian sports M(c)/W(c), field hockey M(c)/W(c), golf M(c)/W(c), gymnastics M(c)/W(c), ice hockey M(c)/W(c), lacrosse M/W, rugby M(c)/W(c), sailing M(c)/W(c), skiing (downhill) M(c)/W(c), soccer M/W, softball M/W, squash M/W, swimming and diving M/W, table tennis M/W, tennis M/W, ultimate Frisbee M(c)/W(c), volleyball M/W, water polo M(c)/W(c).

Campus security: 24-hour emergency response devices and patrols, late-night transport/escort service, controlled dormitory access.

Student services: health clinic, personal/psychological counseling, women's center, legal services.

COSTS & FINANCIAL AID
Costs (2014–15) ***Comprehensive fee:*** $61,132 includes full-time tuition ($42,176), mandatory fees ($5492), and room and board ($13,464). Part-time tuition: $1346 per credit hour. Part-time tuition and fees vary according to course load. ***College room only:*** $8688. Room and board charges vary according to board plan and housing facility. ***Payment plans:*** tuition prepayment, installment. ***Waivers:*** employees or children of employees.

Financial Aid Of all full-time matriculated undergraduates who enrolled in 2012, 4,900 applied for aid, 4,451 were judged to have need, 4,451 had their need fully met. 3,697 Federal Work-Study jobs (averaging $3163). 936 state and other part-time jobs (averaging $2473). ***Average percent of need met:*** 100. ***Average financial aid package:*** $41,961. ***Average need-based loan:*** $366. ***Average need-based gift aid:*** $38,258. ***Average indebtedness upon graduation:*** $19,798.

APPLYING
Standardized Tests *Required:* SAT and SAT Subject Tests or ACT (for admission).

Options: electronic application, early admission, early decision, deferred entrance.

Application fee: $75.

Required: essay or personal statement, high school transcript, 2 letters of recommendation.

Application deadlines: 1/1 (freshmen), 3/15 (transfers).

Early decision deadline: 11/1.

Notification: 4/1 (freshmen), 5/15 (transfers), 12/15 (early decision).

CONTACT
Office of Undergraduate Admissions, University of Pennsylvania, 1 College Hall, Room 1, Philadelphia, PA 19104. *Phone:* 215-898-7507.

University of Pittsburgh
Pittsburgh, Pennsylvania
http://www.pitt.edu/

- **State-related** university, founded 1787, part of Commonwealth System of Higher Education
- **Urban** 145-acre campus with easy access to Pittsburgh
- **Endowment** $3.5 billion
- **Coed** 18,757 undergraduate students, 94% full-time, 51% women, 49% men
- **Very difficult** entrance level, 53% of applicants were admitted

UNDERGRAD STUDENTS
17,694 full-time, 1,063 part-time. Students come from 52 states and territories; 45 other countries; 11% are from out of state; 5% Black or African American, non-Hispanic/Latino; 3% Hispanic/Latino; 8% Asian, non-Hispanic/Latino; 0.1% Native Hawaiian or other Pacific Islander, non-Hispanic/Latino; 0.1% American Indian or Alaska Native, non-Hispanic/Latino; 3% Two or more races, non-Hispanic/Latino; 1% Race/ethnicity unknown; 4% international; 4% transferred in; 43% live on campus.

Freshmen
Admission: 30,629 applied, 16,271 admitted, 3,847 enrolled. ***Average high school GPA:*** 3.99. ***Test scores:*** SAT critical reading scores over 500: 98%; SAT math scores over 500: 99%; SAT writing scores over 500: 98%; ACT scores over 18: 99%; SAT critical reading scores over 600: 68%; SAT math scores over 600: 80%; SAT writing scores over 600: 64%; ACT scores over 24: 95%; SAT critical reading scores over 700: 15%; SAT math scores over 700: 23%; SAT writing scores over 700: 16%; ACT scores over 30: 40%.

Retention: 93% of full-time freshmen returned.

ACADEMICS
Calendar: semesters plus summer term. *Degrees:* certificates, bachelor's, master's, doctoral, post-master's, and postbachelor's certificates.

Special study options: academic remediation for entering students, accelerated degree program, adult/continuing education programs, advanced placement credit, cooperative education, distance learning, double majors, English as a second language, external degree program, freshman honors college, honors programs, independent study, internships, off-campus study, part-time degree program, services for LD students, student-designed majors, study abroad, summer session for credit. ***ROTC:*** Army (b), Navy (c), Air Force (b).

Unusual degree programs: 3-2 engineering; statistics with graduate school of public and international affairs.

Computers: 2,000 computers/terminals and 2,000 ports are available on campus for general student use. Students can access the following: campus intranet, computer help desk, free student e-mail accounts, online (class) grades, online (class) registration, online (class) schedules, online class listings, online tuition payment. Campuswide network is available. 100% of college-owned or -operated housing units are wired for high-speed Internet access. Wireless service is available via entire campus.

STUDENT LIFE
Housing options: coed, women-only, special housing for students with disabilities. Campus housing is university owned. Freshman campus housing is guaranteed.

Activities and organizations: drama/theater group, student-run newspaper, radio and television station, choral group, marching band, Resident Student Association, Black Action Society, Engineering Student Council, Interfraternity Council, Panhellenic Association, national fraternities, national sororities.

Athletics Member NCAA. All Division I except football (Division I-A). ***Intercollegiate sports:*** baseball M(s), basketball M(s)/W(s), cross-country running M(s)/W(s), gymnastics W(s), soccer M(s)/W(s), softball W(s), swimming and diving M(s)/W(s), tennis W(s), track and field M(s)/W(s), volleyball W(s), wrestling M(s). ***Intramural sports:*** badminton M/W, basketball M/W, crew M(c)/W(c), cross-country running M(c)/W(c), equestrian sports M(c)/W(c), fencing M(c)/W(c), field hockey M(c)/W(c), football M, golf M(c)/W(c), gymnastics W(c), ice hockey M(c)/W(c), lacrosse M(c)/W(c), racquetball M/W, rugby M(c)/W(c), skiing (downhill) M/W, soccer M/W, softball W(c), squash M/W, swimming and diving M(c)/W(c), table tennis M/W, tennis M(c)/W(c), ultimate Frisbee M/W, volleyball M/W, water polo M(c)/W(c), wrestling M(c).

Campus security: 24-hour emergency response devices and patrols, late-night transport/escort service, controlled dormitory access, on-call van transportation.

Student services: health clinic, personal/psychological counseling.

COSTS & FINANCIAL AID

Costs (2014–15) ***Tuition:*** state resident $16,872 full-time, $703 per credit hour part-time; nonresident $27,268 full-time, $1136 per credit hour part-time. Full-time tuition and fees vary according to location and program. Part-time tuition and fees vary according to location and program. ***Required fees:*** $900 full-time, $214 per term part-time. ***Room and board:*** $10,800; room only: $6200. Room and board charges vary according to board plan, housing facility, and location. ***Payment plans:*** installment, deferred payment. ***Waivers:*** employees or children of employees.

Financial Aid Of all full-time matriculated undergraduates who enrolled in 2013, 12,348 applied for aid, 9,737 were judged to have need, 825 had their need fully met. In 2013, 450 non-need-based awards were made. ***Average percent of need met:*** 54. ***Average financial aid package:*** $12,394. ***Average need-based loan:*** $5182. ***Average need-based gift aid:*** $8085. ***Average non-need-based aid:*** $11,460. ***Average indebtedness upon graduation:*** $36,466.

APPLYING

Standardized Tests *Required:* SAT or ACT (for admission).

Options: electronic application.

Application fee: $45.

Required: high school transcript. ***Recommended:*** essay or personal statement, interview.

Application deadlines: rolling (freshmen), rolling (transfers).

Notification: continuous (freshmen), continuous (transfers).

CONTACT

Marc L. Harding, Chief Enrollment Officer, University of Pittsburgh, 4227 Fifth Avenue, First Floor, Alumni Hall, Pittsburgh, PA 15260. *Phone:* 412-624-7488. *Fax:* 412-648-8815. *E-mail:* oafa@pitt.edu.

★ University of Pittsburgh at Bradford

Bradford, Pennsylvania

http://www.upb.pitt.edu/

- **State-related** 4-year, founded 1963
- **Small-town** 317-acre campus with easy access to Buffalo
- **Endowment** $23.3 million
- **Coed** 1,499 undergraduate students, 92% full-time, 54% women, 46% men
- **Minimally difficult** entrance level, 62% of applicants were admitted

UNDERGRAD STUDENTS

1,384 full-time, 115 part-time. Students come from 26 states and territories; 11 other countries; 16% are from out of state; 10% Black or African American, non-Hispanic/Latino; 5% Hispanic/Latino; 2% Asian, non-Hispanic/Latino; 0.1% Native Hawaiian or other Pacific Islander, non-Hispanic/Latino; 0.3% American Indian or Alaska Native, non-Hispanic/Latino; 2% Two or more races, non-Hispanic/Latino; 4%

Race/ethnicity unknown; 4% international; 7% transferred in; 67% live on campus.

Freshmen
Admission: 1,720 applied, 1,066 admitted, 398 enrolled. ***Average high school GPA:*** 3.24. ***Test scores:*** SAT critical reading scores over 500: 44%; SAT math scores over 500: 51%; SAT writing scores over 500: 30%; ACT scores over 18: 86%; SAT critical reading scores over 600: 8%; SAT math scores over 600: 15%; SAT writing scores over 600: 4%; ACT scores over 24: 33%; SAT critical reading scores over 700: 1%; SAT math scores over 700: 3%; ACT scores over 30: 3%.

Retention: 72% of full-time freshmen returned.

FACULTY
Total: 165, 42% full-time, 39% with terminal degrees.

Student/faculty ratio: 17:1.

ACADEMICS
Calendar: semesters. *Degrees:* associate and bachelor's.

Special study options: academic remediation for entering students, accelerated degree program, adult/continuing education programs, advanced placement credit, distance learning, double majors, independent study, internships, off-campus study, part-time degree program, services for LD students, study abroad, summer session for credit. ***ROTC:*** Army (c).

Computers: 134 computers/terminals and 1,200 ports are available on campus for general student use. Students can access the following: computer help desk, free student e-mail accounts, online (class) grades, online (class) registration, online (class) schedules, online bills. Campuswide network is available. 100% of college-owned or -operated housing units are wired for high-speed Internet access. Wireless service is available via entire campus.

STUDENT LIFE
Housing options: on-campus residence required for freshman year; coed, special housing for students with disabilities. Campus housing is university owned. Freshman campus housing is guaranteed.

Activities and organizations: drama/theater group, student-run newspaper, radio station, choral group, Student Government Association, Student Activities Board, The Source (student newspaper), Alpha Phi Omega, WDRQ (student radio station), national fraternities, national sororities.

Athletics Member NCAA. All Division III. ***Intercollegiate sports:*** baseball M, basketball M/W, cross-country running M/W, golf M, soccer M/W, softball W, swimming and diving M/W, tennis M/W, volleyball W. ***Intramural sports:*** basketball M/W, bowling W, cheerleading W(c), football M/W, golf M/W, ice hockey M/W, rock climbing M/W, skiing (cross-country) M/W, soccer M/W, softball M/W, swimming and diving M/W, table tennis M/W, ultimate Frisbee M/W, volleyball M/W, water polo M/W.

Campus security: 24-hour emergency response devices and patrols, late-night transport/escort service, controlled dormitory access.

Student services: health clinic, personal/psychological counseling.

COSTS & FINANCIAL AID
Costs (2014–15) ***One-time required fee:*** $90. ***Tuition:*** state resident $12,452 full-time, $518 per credit hour part-time; nonresident $23,268 full-time, $969 per credit hour part-time. Full-time tuition and fees vary according to course load and program. Part-time tuition and fees vary according to course load and program. ***Required fees:*** $870 full-time, $155 per term part-time. ***Room and board:*** $8480; room only: $5160. Room and board charges vary according to board plan and housing facility. ***Payment plan:*** installment. ***Waivers:*** employees or children of employees.

Financial Aid Of all full-time matriculated undergraduates who enrolled in 2013, 1,238 applied for aid, 1,143 were judged to have need, 142 had their need fully met. 201 Federal Work-Study jobs (averaging $1740). 2 state and other part-time jobs (averaging $1740). In 2013, 59 non-need-based awards were made. ***Average percent of need met:*** 66. ***Average financial aid package:*** $14,244. ***Average need-based loan:*** $4691. ***Average need-based gift aid:*** $8559. ***Average non-need-based aid:*** $5504. ***Average indebtedness upon graduation:*** $37,157.

APPLYING
Standardized Tests *Required:* SAT or ACT (for admission).

Options: electronic application, deferred entrance.

Application fee: $45.

Required: high school transcript, minimum 2.0 GPA. ***Required for some:*** minimum 3.0 GPA. ***Recommended:*** essay or personal statement, 2 letters of recommendation, interview.

Application deadlines: rolling (freshmen), rolling (out-of-state freshmen), rolling (transfers).

Notification: continuous (freshmen), continuous (out-of-state freshmen), continuous (transfers).

CONTACT
Ms. Vicky Pingie, Associate Director of Admissions, University of Pittsburgh at Bradford, 300 Campus Drive, Bradford, PA 16701. *Phone:* 814-362-7552. *Toll-free phone:* 800-872-1787. *Fax:* 814-362-5150. *E-mail:* monti@pitt.edu.

See previous page for display ad and page 1694 for the College Close-Up.

University of Pittsburgh at Greensburg

Greensburg, Pennsylvania

http://www.greensburg.pitt.edu/

- **State-related** 4-year, founded 1963, part of University of Pittsburgh System
- **Small-town** 219-acre campus with easy access to Pittsburgh
- **Coed** 1,578 undergraduate students, 94% full-time, 52% women, 48% men
- **Moderately difficult** entrance level, 84% of applicants were admitted

UNDERGRAD STUDENTS
1,477 full-time, 101 part-time. Students come from 15 states and territories; 6 other countries; 2% are from out of state; 6% Black or African American, non-Hispanic/Latino; 4% Hispanic/Latino; 4% Asian, non-Hispanic/Latino; 0.1% Native Hawaiian or other Pacific Islander, non-Hispanic/Latino; 0.1% American Indian or Alaska Native, non-Hispanic/Latino; 3% Two or more races, non-Hispanic/Latino; 3% Race/ethnicity unknown; 1% international; 6% transferred in; 40% live on campus.

Freshmen
Admission: 3,021 applied, 2,533 admitted, 423 enrolled. ***Average high school GPA:*** 3.51. ***Test scores:*** SAT critical reading scores over 500: 55%; SAT writing scores over 500: 45%; ACT scores over 18: 88%; SAT critical reading scores over 600: 13%; SAT writing scores over 600: 7%; ACT scores over 24: 47%; SAT critical reading scores over 700: 2%; ACT scores over 30: 2%.

Retention: 76% of full-time freshmen returned.

FACULTY
Total: 100, 80% full-time.

Student/faculty ratio: 16:1.

ACADEMICS
Calendar: semesters. *Degree:* certificates and bachelor's.

Special study options: academic remediation for entering students, accelerated degree program, adult/continuing education programs, advanced placement credit, distance learning, double majors, independent study, internships, off-campus study, part-time degree program, services for LD students, student-designed majors, study abroad, summer session for credit. ***ROTC:*** Army (c), Air Force (c).

Computers: 216 computers/terminals and 201 ports are available on campus for general student use. Students can access the following: campus intranet, computer help desk, free student e-mail accounts, online (class) grades, online (class) registration, online (class) schedules. Campuswide network is available. 100% of college-owned or -operated housing units are wired for high-speed Internet access. Wireless service is available via classrooms, computer centers, computer labs, dorm rooms, learning centers, libraries, student centers.

STUDENT LIFE
Housing options: coed. Campus housing is university owned.

Activities and organizations: drama/theater group, student-run newspaper, choral group, Habitat for Humanity, Student Government

Association, Student Activities Board, Outdoor Adventure and Community Service, Freshmen Honor Society - Phi Eta Sigma.

Athletics Member NCAA. All Division III. ***Intercollegiate sports:*** baseball M, basketball M/W, cross-country running M/W, golf M, soccer M/W, softball W, tennis M/W, volleyball W. ***Intramural sports:*** baseball M, basketball M/W, bowling M/W, football M/W, golf M/W, racquetball M/W, skiing (cross-country) M/W, skiing (downhill) M/W, soccer M/W, softball M/W, table tennis M/W, tennis M/W, volleyball M/W, weight lifting M/W.

Campus security: 24-hour emergency response devices and patrols, late-night transport/escort service, controlled dormitory access.

Student services: health clinic, personal/psychological counseling.

COSTS & FINANCIAL AID

Costs (2014–15) ***Tuition:*** state resident $12,452 full-time, $518 per credit hour part-time; nonresident $23,268 full-time, $969 per credit hour part-time. ***Required fees:*** $920 full-time. ***Room and board:*** $9490; room only: $5860. Room and board charges vary according to board plan and housing facility. ***Payment plan:*** installment. ***Waivers:*** senior citizens and employees or children of employees.

Financial Aid Of all full-time matriculated undergraduates who enrolled in 2013, 1,339 applied for aid, 1,175 were judged to have need, 146 had their need fully met. In 2013, 48 non-need-based awards were made. ***Average percent of need met:*** 61. ***Average financial aid package:*** $10,936. ***Average need-based loan:*** $4638. ***Average need-based gift aid:*** $6822. ***Average non-need-based aid:*** $4939. ***Average indebtedness upon graduation:*** $34,451.

APPLYING

Standardized Tests *Required:* SAT or ACT (for admission).

Options: electronic application, early admission, deferred entrance.

Application fee: $45.

Required: high school transcript, minimum 2.5 GPA. ***Recommended:*** essay or personal statement, interview.

Application deadlines: rolling (freshmen), rolling (out-of-state freshmen), rolling (transfers).

Notification: continuous (freshmen), continuous (transfers).

CONTACT

Ms. Heather Kabala, Director of Admissions, University of Pittsburgh at Greensburg, 150 Finoli Drive, Greensburg, PA 15601. *Phone:* 724-836-9880. *Fax:* 724-836-7471. *E-mail:* upgadmit@pitt.edu.

The University of Scranton

Scranton, Pennsylvania

http://www.scranton.edu/

- **Independent Roman Catholic (Jesuit)** comprehensive, founded 1888
- **Urban** 50-acre campus
- **Endowment** $162.5 million
- **Coed** 3,998 undergraduate students, 96% full-time, 57% women, 43% men
- **Moderately difficult** entrance level, 77% of applicants were admitted

UNDERGRAD STUDENTS

3,844 full-time, 154 part-time. Students come from 23 states and territories; 15 other countries; 60% are from out of state; 2% Black or African American, non-Hispanic/Latino; 8% Hispanic/Latino; 2% Asian, non-Hispanic/Latino; 0.1% American Indian or Alaska Native, non-Hispanic/Latino; 3% Two or more races, non-Hispanic/Latino; 3% Race/ethnicity unknown; 0.4% international; 2% transferred in; 64% live on campus.

Freshmen

Admission: 9,404 applied, 7,266 admitted, 1,067 enrolled. ***Average high school GPA:*** 3.38. ***Test scores:*** SAT critical reading scores over 500: 83%; SAT math scores over 500: 86%; ACT scores over 18: 98%; SAT critical reading scores over 600: 27%; SAT math scores over 600: 32%; ACT scores over 24: 61%; SAT critical reading scores over 700: 4%; SAT math scores over 700: 4%; ACT scores over 30: 9%.

Retention: 89% of full-time freshmen returned.

FACULTY

Total: 525, 55% full-time, 54% with terminal degrees.

Student/faculty ratio: 11:1.

ACADEMICS

Calendar: 4-1-4. *Degrees:* certificates, bachelor's, master's, doctoral, post-master's, and postbachelor's certificates.

Special study options: academic remediation for entering students, accelerated degree program, adult/continuing education programs, advanced placement credit, distance learning, double majors, honors programs, independent study, internships, off-campus study, part-time degree program, services for LD students, student-designed majors, study abroad, summer session for credit. ***ROTC:*** Army (b), Air Force (c).

Computers: 862 computers/terminals are available on campus for general student use. Students can access the following: computer help desk, free student e-mail accounts, online (class) grades, online (class) registration, online (class) schedules. Campuswide network is available. 100% of college-owned or -operated housing units are wired for high-speed Internet access. Wireless service is available via classrooms, computer centers, computer labs, dorm rooms, learning centers, libraries, student centers.

STUDENT LIFE

Housing options: on-campus residence required through sophomore year; coed, men-only, women-only, special housing for students with disabilities. Campus housing is university owned. Freshman campus housing is guaranteed.

Activities and organizations: drama/theater group, student-run newspaper, radio and television station, choral group, Service-oriented student clubs, United Colors, Retreat Programs, Biology/Pre-Medicine clubs, Pre-Law Society.

Athletics Member NCAA. All Division III. ***Intercollegiate sports:*** baseball M, basketball M/W, crew M(c)/W(c), cross-country running M/W, equestrian sports M(c)/W(c), fencing M(c)/W(c), field hockey W, golf M, ice hockey M(c), lacrosse M/W, rugby M(c)/W(c), soccer M/W, softball W, swimming and diving M/W, tennis M/W, ultimate Frisbee M(c)/W(c), volleyball M(c)/W, wrestling M. ***Intramural sports:*** badminton M/W, basketball M/W, cheerleading M(c)/W(c), field hockey W, football M/W, racquetball M/W, skiing (downhill) M(c)/W(c), soccer M/W, softball M/W, table tennis M/W, tennis M/W, ultimate Frisbee M/W, volleyball M/W.

Campus security: 24-hour emergency response devices and patrols, student patrols, late-night transport/escort service, controlled dormitory access, sprinkler systems in all University-owned housing.

Student services: health clinic, personal/psychological counseling, women's center.

COSTS & FINANCIAL AID

Costs (2014–15) ***Comprehensive fee:*** $53,522 includes full-time tuition ($39,556), mandatory fees ($400), and room and board ($13,566). ***College room only:*** $7954. Room and board charges vary according to board plan and housing facility. ***Payment plan:*** installment. ***Waivers:*** senior citizens and employees or children of employees.

Financial Aid Of all full-time matriculated undergraduates who enrolled in 2013, 3,104 applied for aid, 2,750 were judged to have need, 281 had their need fully met. In 2013, 627 non-need-based awards were made. ***Average percent of need met:*** 67. ***Average financial aid package:*** $24,187. ***Average need-based loan:*** $8310. ***Average need-based gift aid:*** $20,140. ***Average non-need-based aid:*** $12,620. ***Average indebtedness upon graduation:*** $38,640.

APPLYING

Standardized Tests *Required:* SAT or ACT (for admission).

Options: electronic application, early admission, early action, deferred entrance.

Required: essay or personal statement, high school transcript, 1 letter of recommendation. ***Required for some:*** interview.

Application deadlines: 3/1 (freshmen), rolling (transfers), 11/15 (early action).

Notification: continuous until 1/15 (freshmen), continuous (transfers), 12/15 (early action).

CONTACT
Mr. Joseph Roback, Associate Vice Provost, Admissions and Enrollment, The University of Scranton, The Estate Room 208, The University of Scranton, Scranton, PA 18510-4501. *Phone:* 570-941-7540. *Toll-free phone:* 888-SCRANTON. *Fax:* 570-941-5928. *E-mail:* admissions@scranton.edu.

The University of the Arts
Philadelphia, Pennsylvania
http://www.uarts.edu/

- **Independent** comprehensive, founded 1870
- **Urban** 21-acre campus
- **Coed** 1,754 undergraduate students, 98% full-time, 59% women, 41% men
- **Moderately difficult** entrance level, 70% of applicants were admitted

UNDERGRAD STUDENTS
1,711 full-time, 43 part-time. Students come from 41 states and territories; 26 other countries; 60% are from out of state; 12% Black or African American, non-Hispanic/Latino; 10% Hispanic/Latino; 3% Asian, non-Hispanic/Latino; 0.5% Native Hawaiian or other Pacific Islander, non-Hispanic/Latino; 0.4% American Indian or Alaska Native, non-Hispanic/Latino; 4% Two or more races, non-Hispanic/Latino; 4% Race/ethnicity unknown; 6% international; 3% transferred in; 34% live on campus.

Freshmen
Admission: 1,494 applied, 1,039 admitted, 374 enrolled.
Retention: 81% of full-time freshmen returned.

FACULTY
Total: 470, 22% full-time.
Student/faculty ratio: 8:1.

ACADEMICS
Calendar: semesters. *Degrees:* diplomas, bachelor's, master's, and postbachelor's certificates.
Special study options: academic remediation for entering students, advanced placement credit, double majors, English as a second language, honors programs, independent study, internships, off-campus study, part-time degree program, services for LD students, study abroad, summer session for credit.
Computers: 368 computers/terminals are available on campus for general student use. Students can access the following: campus intranet, computer help desk, free student e-mail accounts, online (class) grades, online (class) registration, online (class) schedules. Campuswide network is available. 100% of college-owned or -operated housing units are wired for high-speed Internet access. Wireless service is available via entire campus.

STUDENT LIFE
Housing options: coed. Campus housing is university owned and leased by the school. Freshman applicants given priority for college housing.
Activities and organizations: drama/theater group, choral group, National Society of College Scholars, Salsa Club, African Diaspora Collective, Blurring Edges, Ladies of Service.
Athletics ***Intramural sports:*** fencing M/W.
Campus security: 24-hour emergency response devices and patrols, crime prevention workshops and seminars.
Student services: health clinic, personal/psychological counseling.

COSTS & FINANCIAL AID
Costs (2014–15) ***Comprehensive fee:*** $52,414 includes full-time tuition ($38,410) and room and board ($14,004). Part-time tuition: $1601 per credit hour. Part-time tuition and fees vary according to course load. ***College room only:*** $9042. Room and board charges vary according to board plan and housing facility. ***Payment plan:*** installment. ***Waivers:*** children of alumni and employees or children of employees.
Financial Aid In 2002, 561 non-need-based awards were made. ***Average percent of need met:*** 65. ***Average financial aid package:*** $16,500. ***Average indebtedness upon graduation:*** $17,000.

APPLYING
Standardized Tests *Required:* SAT or ACT (for admission).
Options: electronic application, deferred entrance.
Application fee: $60.
Required: essay or personal statement, high school transcript, 1 letter of recommendation, Interview recommended for all; audition or portfolio required for performing arts programs; portfolio required for design, visual arts, film programs, essay required for all programs. ***Required for some:*** interview. ***Recommended:*** minimum 2.0 GPA, interview.
Application deadlines: rolling (freshmen), rolling (out-of-state freshmen), rolling (transfers).
Notification: continuous (freshmen), continuous (out-of-state freshmen), continuous (transfers).

CONTACT
Ms. Liz Boyd, Assistant Director, Admissions, The University of the Arts, 320 South Broad Street, Philadelphia, PA 19102-4944. *Phone:* 215-717-6041. *Toll-free phone:* 800-616-ARTS. *Fax:* 215-717-6045. *E-mail:* admissions@uarts.edu.

University of the Sciences
Philadelphia, Pennsylvania
http://www.usciences.edu/

- **Independent** university, founded 1821
- **Urban** 35-acre campus
- **Coed** 2,339 undergraduate students, 99% full-time, 61% women, 39% men
- **Moderately difficult** entrance level, 58% of applicants were admitted

UNDERGRAD STUDENTS
2,312 full-time, 27 part-time. 56% are from out of state; 6% Black or African American, non-Hispanic/Latino; 4% Hispanic/Latino; 38% Asian, non-Hispanic/Latino; 0.3% Native Hawaiian or other Pacific Islander, non-Hispanic/Latino; 0.1% American Indian or Alaska Native, non-Hispanic/Latino; 3% Two or more races, non-Hispanic/Latino; 7% Race/ethnicity unknown; 1% international; 0.6% transferred in.

Freshmen
Admission: 4,281 applied, 2,478 admitted, 360 enrolled. ***Average high school GPA:*** 3.77. ***Test scores:*** SAT critical reading scores over 500: 88%; SAT math scores over 500: 98%; SAT writing scores over 500: 87%; ACT scores over 18: 100%; SAT critical reading scores over 600: 30%; SAT math scores over 600: 54%; SAT writing scores over 600: 36%; ACT scores over 24: 80%; SAT critical reading scores over 700: 3%; SAT math scores over 700: 10%; SAT writing scores over 700: 5%; ACT scores over 30: 12%.
Retention: 88% of full-time freshmen returned.

FACULTY
Total: 365, 55% full-time.
Student/faculty ratio: 10:1.

ACADEMICS
Calendar: semesters. *Degrees:* bachelor's, master's, doctoral, and postbachelor's certificates.
Special study options: academic remediation for entering students, adult/continuing education programs, advanced placement credit, cooperative education, distance learning, double majors, honors programs, internships, off-campus study, part-time degree program, services for LD students, study abroad, summer session for credit. ***ROTC:*** Army (c), Air Force (c).
Computers: Students can access the following: campus intranet, computer help desk, free student e-mail accounts, online (class) grades, online (class) registration, online (class) schedules. Campuswide network is available. 100% of college-owned or -operated housing units are wired for high-speed Internet access. Wireless service is available via classrooms, computer centers, computer labs, dorm rooms, learning centers, libraries, student centers.

STUDENT LIFE
Housing options: on-campus residence required through sophomore year; coed. Campus housing is university owned and leased by the school. Freshman campus housing is guaranteed.
Activities and organizations: drama/theater group, student-run newspaper, choral group, Student Government Association, Hillel: Jewish

Student Association, Pre-Medical Society, Society of Physics Students, American Chemical Society, national fraternities, national sororities.

Athletics Member NCAA, NAIA. All NCAA Division II. ***Intercollegiate sports:*** baseball M(s), basketball M(s)/W(s), cross-country running M/W, golf M/W, riflery M/W, softball W(s), tennis M/W, volleyball W(s). ***Intramural sports:*** archery M/W, basketball M/W, bowling M/W, riflery M/W, softball M/W, table tennis M/W, volleyball M/W.

Campus security: 24-hour emergency response devices and patrols, late-night transport/escort service, controlled dormitory access.

Student services: health clinic, personal/psychological counseling.

COSTS & FINANCIAL AID

Costs (2015–16) ***Comprehensive fee:*** $50,204 includes full-time tuition ($34,336), mandatory fees ($1760), and room and board ($14,108). ***College room only:*** $8620. ***Waivers:*** employees or children of employees.

Financial Aid Of all full-time matriculated undergraduates who enrolled in 2013, 1,552 applied for aid, 1,456 were judged to have need, 527 had their need fully met. In 2013, 96 non-need-based awards were made. ***Average percent of need met:*** 32. ***Average financial aid package:*** $22,967. ***Average need-based loan:*** $4820. ***Average need-based gift aid:*** $13,322. ***Average non-need-based aid:*** $14,035. ***Financial aid deadline:*** 3/15.

APPLYING

Standardized Tests *Required:* SAT or ACT (for admission).

Options: electronic application, deferred entrance.

Application fee: $45.

Required: high school transcript. ***Recommended:*** minimum 3.0 GPA.

CONTACT

Ms. Dianna Collins, Executive Director of Admission and Enrollment Services, University of the Sciences, 600 South 43rd Street, Philadelphia, PA 19104-4495. *Phone:* 888-996-8747. *Toll-free phone:* 888-996-8747. *Fax:* 215-596-8821. *E-mail:* admit@usciences.edu.

University of Valley Forge

Phoenixville, Pennsylvania

http://www.valleyforge.edu/

- **Independent Assemblies of God** comprehensive, founded 1938
- **Small-town** 150-acre campus with easy access to Philadelphia
- **Endowment** $2.6 million
- **Coed** 895 undergraduate students, 72% full-time, 51% women, 49% men
- **Minimally difficult** entrance level, 95% of applicants were admitted

UNDERGRAD STUDENTS

644 full-time, 251 part-time. Students come from 32 states and territories; 2 other countries; 53% are from out of state; 15% Black or African American, non-Hispanic/Latino; 13% Hispanic/Latino; 0.7% Asian, non-Hispanic/Latino; 0.3% Native Hawaiian or other Pacific Islander, non-Hispanic/Latino; 0.4% American Indian or Alaska Native, non-Hispanic/Latino; 3% Two or more races, non-Hispanic/Latino; 10% Race/ethnicity unknown; 0.4% international; 5% transferred in; 81% live on campus.

Freshmen

Admission: 450 applied, 428 admitted, 149 enrolled. ***Average high school GPA:*** 3.07. ***Test scores:*** SAT critical reading scores over 500: 34%; SAT math scores over 500: 31%; SAT writing scores over 500: 26%; ACT scores over 18: 60%; SAT critical reading scores over 600: 9%; SAT math scores over 600: 8%; SAT writing scores over 600: 6%; ACT scores over 24: 30%; SAT math scores over 700: 1%; ACT scores over 30: 3%.

Retention: 62% of full-time freshmen returned.

FACULTY

Total: 92, 38% full-time, 35% with terminal degrees.

Student/faculty ratio: 12:1.

ACADEMICS

Calendar: semesters. *Degrees:* associate, bachelor's, and master's.

Special study options: academic remediation for entering students, accelerated degree program, adult/continuing education programs, advanced placement credit, distance learning, double majors, external degree program, honors programs, independent study, internships, part-time degree program, services for LD students, study abroad, summer session for credit.

Computers: 86 computers/terminals and 3,000 ports are available on campus for general student use. Students can access the following: campus intranet, computer help desk, free student e-mail accounts, online (class) grades, online (class) registration, online (class) schedules. Campuswide network is available. 100% of college-owned or -operated housing units are wired for high-speed Internet access. Wireless service is available via entire campus.

STUDENT LIFE

Housing options: on-campus residence required through senior year; men-only, women-only. Campus housing is university owned. Freshman campus housing is guaranteed.

Activities and organizations: drama/theater group, choral group, Homeless Ministry, The Art Of, Noteworthy, Inspire India, Audience of One.

Athletics Member NCAA, NCCAA. All NCAA Division III. ***Intercollegiate sports:*** baseball M, basketball M/W, cross-country running M/W, golf M, soccer M/W, softball W, volleyball W. ***Intramural sports:*** basketball M/W, soccer M/W, softball M/W, ultimate Frisbee M/W.

Campus security: 24-hour emergency response devices and patrols, student patrols, late-night transport/escort service, controlled dormitory access.

Student services: health clinic, personal/psychological counseling.

COSTS & FINANCIAL AID

Costs (2015–16) ***Comprehensive fee:*** $28,480 includes full-time tuition ($18,644), mandatory fees ($1720), and room and board ($8116). Full-time tuition and fees vary according to course load and location. Part-time tuition and fees vary according to course load and location. ***Room and board:*** Room and board charges vary according to board plan and housing facility. ***Payment plan:*** installment. ***Waivers:*** employees or children of employees.

Financial Aid Of all full-time matriculated undergraduates who enrolled in 2014, 510 applied for aid, 468 were judged to have need, 53 had their need fully met. 33 Federal Work-Study jobs (averaging $1326). In 2014, 61 non-need-based awards were made. ***Average percent of need met:*** 55. ***Average financial aid package:*** $13,598. ***Average need-based loan:*** $4286. ***Average need-based gift aid:*** $10,123. ***Average non-need-based aid:*** $5757. ***Average indebtedness upon graduation:*** $31,570.

APPLYING

Standardized Tests *Required:* SAT or ACT (for admission).

Options: electronic application, early admission, deferred entrance.

Application fee: $25.

Required: essay or personal statement, high school transcript. ***Required for some:*** interview. ***Recommended:*** minimum 2.0 GPA.

Application deadlines: 8/1 (freshmen), 8/1 (transfers).

Notification: continuous (freshmen), continuous (transfers).

CONTACT

Rev. Joseph Ocasio, Director of Admissions, University of Valley Forge, 1401 Charlestown Road, Phoenixville, PA 19460. *Phone:* 610-935-0450 Ext. 1430. *Toll-free phone:* 800-432-8322. *Fax:* 610-917-2069. *E-mail:* admissions@valleyforge.edu.

Ursinus College

Collegeville, Pennsylvania

http://www.ursinus.edu/

- **Independent** 4-year, founded 1869
- **Suburban** 170-acre campus with easy access to Philadelphia
- **Endowment** $146.6 million
- **Coed** 1,681 undergraduate students, 99% full-time, 52% women, 48% men
- **Moderately difficult** entrance level, 83% of applicants were admitted

UNDERGRAD STUDENTS

1,662 full-time, 19 part-time. Students come from 31 states and territories; 16 other countries; 46% are from out of state; 6% Black or African American, non-Hispanic/Latino; 6% Hispanic/Latino; 5% Asian, non-Hispanic/Latino; 0.2% American Indian or Alaska Native, non-

Hispanic/Latino; 4% Two or more races, non-Hispanic/Latino; 2% Race/ethnicity unknown; 2% international; 0.7% transferred in; 96% live on campus.

Freshmen

Admission: 2,672 applied, 2,222 admitted, 497 enrolled. ***Test scores:*** SAT critical reading scores over 500: 81%; SAT math scores over 500: 85%; SAT writing scores over 500: 81%; ACT scores over 18: 100%; SAT critical reading scores over 600: 40%; SAT math scores over 600: 41%; SAT writing scores over 600: 36%; ACT scores over 24: 73%; SAT critical reading scores over 700: 7%; SAT math scores over 700: 8%; SAT writing scores over 700: 8%; ACT scores over 30: 16%.

Retention: 92% of full-time freshmen returned.

FACULTY

Total: 172, 72% full-time, 78% with terminal degrees.

Student/faculty ratio: 12:1.

ACADEMICS

Calendar: semesters. *Degree:* bachelor's.

Special study options: advanced placement credit, cooperative education, double majors, English as a second language, honors programs, independent study, internships, off-campus study, services for LD students, student-designed majors, study abroad.

Unusual degree programs: 3-2 engineering with Ursinus is an affiliate institution of the Combined Plan Program in Engineering at Columbia University. Students may apply for transfer to Columbia after completing three years of prescribed work toward a BA at Ursinus.

Computers: Students can access the following: campus intranet, computer help desk, free student e-mail accounts, online (class) grades, online (class) registration, online (class) schedules. Campuswide network is available. 100% of college-owned or -operated housing units are wired for high-speed Internet access. Wireless service is available via entire campus.

STUDENT LIFE

Housing options: coed, men-only, women-only, special housing for students with disabilities. Campus housing is university owned. Freshman campus housing is guaranteed.

Activities and organizations: drama/theater group, student-run newspaper, radio and television station, choral group, Environmental Action Committee, Habitat for Humanity, Campus Activities Board, Relay for Life, Multicultural Student Union, national fraternities, national sororities.

Athletics Member NCAA. All Division III. ***Intercollegiate sports:*** baseball M, basketball M/W, cheerleading W, cross-country running M/W, field hockey W, football M, golf M/W, gymnastics W, lacrosse M/W, rugby M(c)/W(c), soccer M/W, softball W, swimming and diving M/W, tennis M/W, track and field M/W, volleyball W, wrestling M. ***Intramural sports:*** badminton M/W, basketball M/W, cross-country running M(c)/W(c), fencing M(c)/W(c), field hockey M/W, football M/W, ice hockey M(c)/W(c), soccer M/W, table tennis M(c)/W(c), ultimate Frisbee M(c)/W(c), volleyball M(c)/W(c).

Campus security: 24-hour emergency response devices and patrols, student patrols, late-night transport/escort service, student EMT Corps for first aid/emergency first response.

Student services: health clinic, personal/psychological counseling.

COSTS & FINANCIAL AID

Costs (2014–15) ***Comprehensive fee:*** $57,580 includes full-time tuition ($45,890), mandatory fees ($190), and room and board ($11,500). Part-time tuition: $1434 per credit hour. ***Waivers:*** employees or children of employees.

Financial Aid Of all full-time matriculated undergraduates who enrolled in 2014, 1,367 applied for aid, 1,195 were judged to have need, 235 had their need fully met. 773 Federal Work-Study jobs (averaging $1834). 2 state and other part-time jobs (averaging $5322). In 2014, 429 non-need-based awards were made. ***Average percent of need met:*** 79. ***Average financial aid package:*** $34,458. ***Average need-based loan:*** $4558. ***Average need-based gift aid:*** $29,968. ***Average non-need-based aid:*** $17,949. ***Average indebtedness upon graduation:*** $35,360.

APPLYING

Standardized Tests *Recommended:* SAT or ACT (for admission).

Options: electronic application, early decision, early action, deferred entrance.

Required: essay or personal statement, high school transcript, letters of recommendation.

Application deadlines: 2/15 (freshmen), 8/1 (transfers), 12/15 (early action).

Early decision deadline: 1/15.

Notification: continuous until 11/1 (freshmen), 8/15 (transfers), 2/1 (early decision), 1/15 (early action).

CONTACT

Ms. Dana Matassino, Director of Admission, Ursinus College, 601 E Main Street, Collegeville, PA 19426. *Phone:* 610-409-3200. *Fax:* 610-409-3197. *E-mail:* admissions@ursinus.edu.

Villanova University

Villanova, Pennsylvania

http://www.villanova.edu/

- **Independent Roman Catholic** comprehensive, founded 1842
- **Suburban** 254-acre campus with easy access to Philadelphia
- **Endowment** $511.0 million
- **Coed** 7,118 undergraduate students, 92% full-time, 52% women, 48% men
- **Very difficult** entrance level, 49% of applicants were admitted

UNDERGRAD STUDENTS

6,553 full-time, 565 part-time. 81% are from out of state; 5% Black or African American, non-Hispanic/Latino; 7% Hispanic/Latino; 7% Asian, non-Hispanic/Latino; 0.1% American Indian or Alaska Native, non-Hispanic/Latino; 2% Two or more races, non-Hispanic/Latino; 2% Race/ethnicity unknown; 2% international; 0.8% transferred in; 70% live on campus.

Freshmen

Admission: 15,705 applied, 7,748 admitted, 1,669 enrolled. ***Average high school GPA:*** 3.87. ***Test scores:*** SAT critical reading scores over 500: 97%; SAT math scores over 500: 99%; SAT writing scores over 500: 97%; ACT scores over 18: 100%; SAT critical reading scores over 600: 75%; SAT math scores over 600: 85%; SAT writing scores over 600: 77%; ACT scores over 24: 96%; SAT critical reading scores over 700: 20%; SAT math scores over 700: 33%; SAT writing scores over 700: 26%; ACT scores over 30: 60%.

Retention: 94% of full-time freshmen returned.

FACULTY

Total: 1,011, 61% full-time, 67% with terminal degrees.

Student/faculty ratio: 12:1.

ACADEMICS

Calendar: semesters. *Degrees:* bachelor's, master's, doctoral, post-master's, and postbachelor's certificates.

Special study options: accelerated degree program, adult/continuing education programs, advanced placement credit, cooperative education, distance learning, double majors, English as a second language, external degree program, honors programs, independent study, internships, off-campus study, part-time degree program, services for LD students, study abroad, summer session for credit. ***ROTC:*** Army (b), Navy (b), Air Force (c).

Unusual degree programs: 3-2 engineering with Civil Engineering, Chemical Engineering, Computer Engineering, Electrical Engineering, and Mechanical Engineering; arts/liberal studies; classical studies; communication; criminal justice; political science; psychology; Spanish; religious studies; computer science; biology; chemistry; mathematics; mathematics/applied statistics; human resources development; business information systems/software engineering.

Computers: 700 computers/terminals and 15,000 ports are available on campus for general student use. Students can access the following: campus intranet, computer help desk, free student e-mail accounts, online (class) grades, online (class) registration, online (class) schedules, learning management system with anti-plagiarism software, testing software, online faculty hours, videoconferencing; electronic portfolios; data vaulting/backup service; emergency notification system; Citrix-based library of advanced software. Campuswide network is available. 100% of college-owned or -operated housing units are wired for high-speed Internet access. Wireless service is available via classrooms, computer centers, computer labs, dorm rooms, learning centers, libraries, student centers.

STUDENT LIFE

Housing options: coed, women-only, special housing for students with disabilities. Campus housing is university owned. Freshman campus housing is guaranteed.

Activities and organizations: drama/theater group, student-run newspaper, radio and television station, choral group, marching band, Blue Key Society, New Student Orientation Counselor Program, Special Olympics, Campus Activities Team, Student Government Association, national fraternities, national sororities.

Athletics Member NCAA. All Division I except football (Division I-AA). ***Intercollegiate sports:*** baseball M(s), basketball M(s)/W(s), cheerleading M/W, crew M(c)/W, cross-country running M(s)/W(s), equestrian sports W(c), field hockey W(s), golf M, ice hockey M(c)/W(c), lacrosse M(s)/W(s), sailing M(c)/W(c), skiing (downhill) M(c)/W(c), soccer M(s)/W(s), softball W(s), swimming and diving M/W(s), tennis M/W, track and field M(s)/W(s), volleyball M(c)/W(s), water polo M(c)/W. ***Intramural sports:*** badminton M(c)/W(c), baseball M(c), basketball M(c)/W(c), crew M(c), cross-country running M(c)/W(c), equestrian sports W(c), field hockey W(c), football M/W, golf M(c)/W(c), ice hockey M(c)/W(c), lacrosse M(c)/W(c), rugby M(c), sailing M(c)/W(c), skiing (downhill) M(c)/W(c), soccer M(c)/W(c), softball M/W, swimming and diving M(c)/W(c), tennis M(c)/W(c), ultimate Frisbee M(c)/W(c), volleyball M(c)/W(c), water polo M(c).

Campus security: 24-hour emergency response devices and patrols, late-night transport/escort service, controlled dormitory access, Nova Alert - email, text messaging re: emergency situations.

Student services: health clinic, personal/psychological counseling.

COSTS & FINANCIAL AID

Costs (2014–15) ***One-time required fee:*** $150. ***Comprehensive fee:*** $58,244 includes full-time tuition ($45,376), mandatory fees ($590), and room and board ($12,278). Part-time tuition: $1894 per credit hour. Part-time tuition and fees vary according to class time, course load, and program. ***Required fees:*** $845 per credit hour part-time. ***College room only:*** $6508. Room and board charges vary according to board plan and housing facility. ***Payment plan:*** installment. ***Waivers:*** senior citizens and employees or children of employees.

Financial Aid Of all full-time matriculated undergraduates who enrolled in 2014, 3,805 applied for aid, 3,162 were judged to have need, 510 had their need fully met. 2,344 Federal Work-Study jobs (averaging $2837). 31 state and other part-time jobs (averaging $3000). In 2014, 438 non-need-based awards were made. ***Average percent of need met:*** 80. ***Average financial aid package:*** $33,845. ***Average need-based loan:*** $4965. ***Average need-based gift aid:*** $29,629. ***Average non-need-based aid:*** $4965. ***Average indebtedness upon graduation:*** $35,122. ***Financial aid deadline:*** 2/7.

APPLYING

Standardized Tests *Required:* SAT or ACT (for admission).

Options: electronic application, early admission, early action, deferred entrance.

Application fee: $80.

Required: essay or personal statement, high school transcript, 1 letter of recommendation, test scores (SAT or ACT).

Application deadlines: 1/15 (freshmen), 1/15 (out-of-state freshmen), 6/1 (transfers), 11/1 (early action).

Notification: 4/1 (freshmen), 4/1 (out-of-state freshmen), continuous (transfers), 12/20 (early action).

CONTACT

Mr. Michael Gaynor, Director of University Admission, Villanova University, 800 Lancaster Avenue, Villanova, PA 19085-1672. *Phone:* 610-519-4000. *Fax:* 610-519-6450. *E-mail:* gotovu@villanova.edu.

See below for display ad and page 1716 for the College Close-Up.

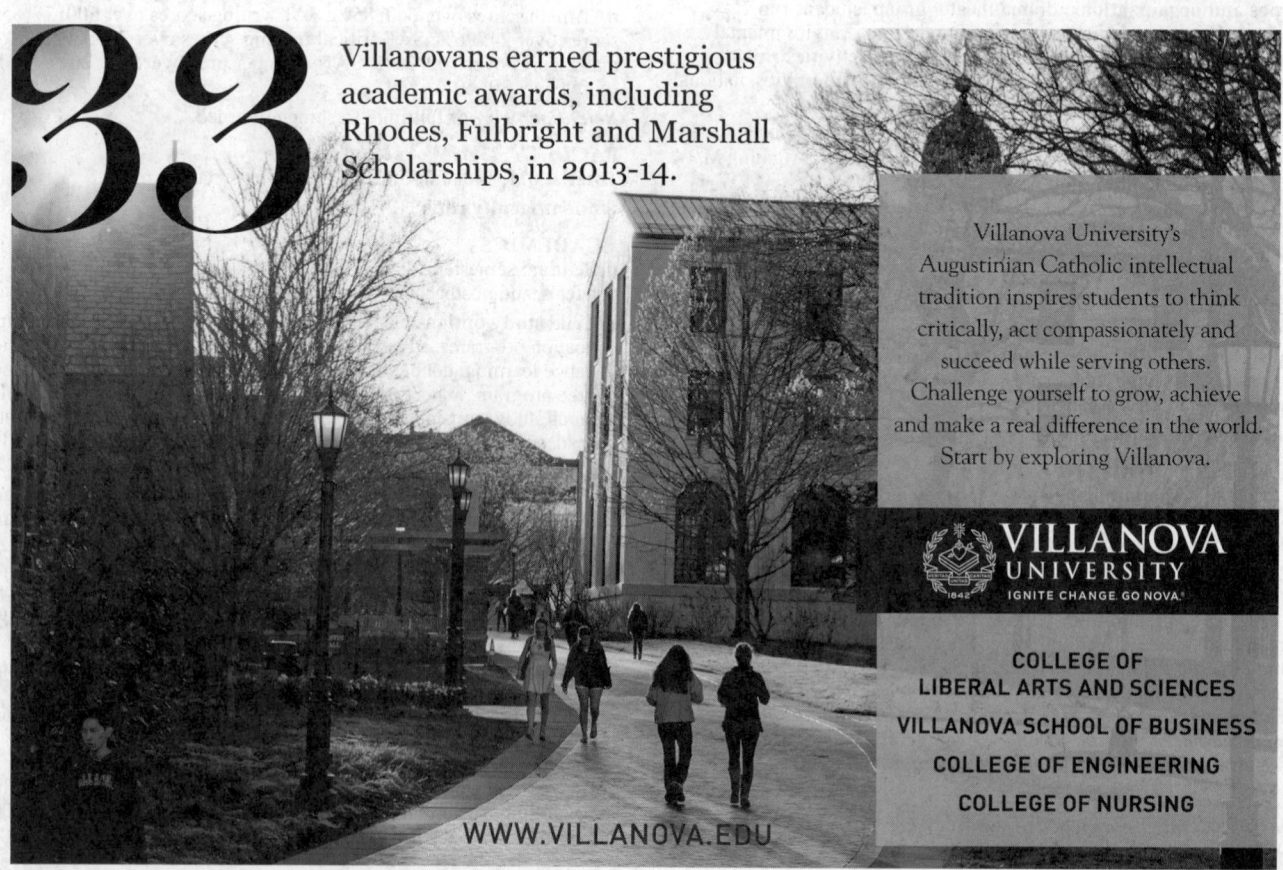

Washington & Jefferson College

Washington, Pennsylvania

http://www.washjeff.edu/

- **Independent** 4-year, founded 1781
- **Suburban** 60-acre campus with easy access to Pittsburgh
- **Endowment** $135.7 million
- **Coed** 1,362 undergraduate students, 99% full-time, 49% women, 51% men
- **Very difficult** entrance level, 42% of applicants were admitted

UNDERGRAD STUDENTS

1,354 full-time, 8 part-time. Students come from 33 states and territories; 20 other countries; 23% are from out of state; 3% Black or African American, non-Hispanic/Latino; 3% Hispanic/Latino; 2% Asian, non-Hispanic/Latino; 0.1% Native Hawaiian or other Pacific Islander, non-Hispanic/Latino; 0.4% American Indian or Alaska Native, non-Hispanic/Latino; 3% Two or more races, non-Hispanic/Latino; 3% Race/ethnicity unknown; 4% international; 1% transferred in; 94% live on campus.

Freshmen

Admission: 7,094 applied, 2,955 admitted, 399 enrolled. ***Average high school GPA:*** 3.35. ***Test scores:*** SAT critical reading scores over 500: 84%; SAT math scores over 500: 86%; ACT scores over 18: 99%; SAT critical reading scores over 600: 30%; SAT math scores over 600: 38%; ACT scores over 24: 67%; SAT critical reading scores over 700: 3%; SAT math scores over 700: 5%; ACT scores over 30: 15%.

FACULTY

Total: 154, 71% full-time, 75% with terminal degrees.

Student/faculty ratio: 11:1.

ACADEMICS

Calendar: 4-1-4. *Degree:* bachelor's.

Special study options: academic remediation for entering students, accelerated degree program, advanced placement credit, double majors, English as a second language, freshman honors college, honors programs, independent study, internships, off-campus study, part-time degree program, services for LD students, student-designed majors, study abroad, summer session for credit. ***ROTC:*** Army (b), Air Force (c).

Unusual degree programs: 3-2 engineering with Columbia University in New York City; Case Western Reserve University in Ohio, Washington University in St. Louis.

Computers: 450 computers/terminals and 2,000 ports are available on campus for general student use. Students can access the following: campus intranet, computer help desk, free student e-mail accounts, online (class) grades, online (class) registration, online (class) schedules. Campuswide network is available. 100% of college-owned or -operated housing units are wired for high-speed Internet access. Wireless service is available via entire campus.

STUDENT LIFE

Housing options: on-campus residence required through senior year; coed, men-only, women-only, special housing for students with disabilities. Campus housing is university owned. Freshman campus housing is guaranteed.

Activities and organizations: drama/theater group, student-run newspaper, radio station, choral group, Student Government Association, Student Activities Board, Black Student Union, Student Athlete Advisory Council, Zumba Club, national fraternities, national sororities.

Athletics Member NCAA. All Division III. ***Intercollegiate sports:*** baseball M, basketball M/W, cheerleading M(c)/W(c), cross-country running M/W, equestrian sports M(c)/W(c), field hockey W, football M, golf M/W, ice hockey M(c), lacrosse M/W, rugby M(c)/W(c), soccer M/W, softball W, swimming and diving M/W, tennis M/W, track and field M/W, ultimate Frisbee M(c)/W(c), volleyball W, water polo M/W, wrestling M. ***Intramural sports:*** basketball M/W, bowling M/W, soccer M/W, softball M/W, tennis M/W, ultimate Frisbee M/W, volleyball M/W.

Campus security: 24-hour emergency response devices and patrols, late-night transport/escort service, controlled dormitory access, blue light emergency phones, security cameras monitored 24/7 throughout campus.

Student services: health clinic, personal/psychological counseling, women's center.

COSTS & FINANCIAL AID

Costs (2014–15) ***Comprehensive fee:*** $52,166 includes full-time tuition ($40,722), mandatory fees ($560), and room and board ($10,884). Full-time tuition and fees vary according to reciprocity agreements. Part-time tuition: $1023 per credit hour. Part-time tuition and fees vary according to course load. ***College room only:*** $6390. Room and board charges vary according to board plan and housing facility. ***Payment plans:*** tuition prepayment, installment, deferred payment. ***Waivers:*** employees or children of employees.

Financial Aid Of all full-time matriculated undergraduates who enrolled in 2014, 1,145 applied for aid, 1,033 were judged to have need, 179 had their need fully met. 519 Federal Work-Study jobs (averaging $1570). 180 state and other part-time jobs (averaging $1000). In 2014, 259 non-need-based awards were made. ***Average percent of need met:*** 79. ***Average financial aid package:*** $31,274. ***Average need-based loan:*** $4440. ***Average need-based gift aid:*** $13,270. ***Average non-need-based aid:*** $15,129.

APPLYING

Standardized Tests *Recommended:* SAT or ACT (for admission), SAT Subject Tests (for admission).

Options: electronic application, early admission, early decision, early action, deferred entrance.

Application fee: $25.

Required: essay or personal statement, high school transcript, 1 letter of recommendation. ***Required for some:*** interview. ***Recommended:*** interview.

Application deadlines: 3/1 (freshmen), rolling (transfers), 1/15 (early action).

Early decision deadline: 12/1.

Notification: 3/15 (freshmen), 12/15 (early decision), 2/15 (early action).

CONTACT

Mr. Robert J. Gould, Vice President for Enrollment, Washington & Jefferson College, 60 South Lincoln Street, Washington, PA 15301. *Phone:* 724-223-6025. *Toll-free phone:* 888-WANDJAY. *Fax:* 724-223-6534. *E-mail:* admission@washjeff.edu.

Waynesburg University

Waynesburg, Pennsylvania

http://www.waynesburg.edu/

- **Independent** comprehensive, founded 1849, affiliated with Presbyterian Church (U.S.A.)
- **Small-town** 30-acre campus with easy access to Pittsburgh
- **Coed** 1,528 undergraduate students, 93% full-time, 61% women, 39% men
- **Moderately difficult** entrance level, 84% of applicants were admitted

UNDERGRAD STUDENTS

1,414 full-time, 114 part-time. Students come from 31 states and territories; 3 other countries; 20% are from out of state; 4% Black or African American, non-Hispanic/Latino; 1% Hispanic/Latino; 0.5% Asian, non-Hispanic/Latino; 0.3% Native Hawaiian or other Pacific Islander, non-Hispanic/Latino; 0.4% American Indian or Alaska Native, non-Hispanic/Latino; 1% Two or more races, non-Hispanic/Latino; 1% Race/ethnicity unknown; 0.3% international; 2% transferred in; 77% live on campus.

Freshmen

Admission: 1,448 applied, 1,210 admitted, 335 enrolled. ***Average high school GPA:*** 3.6.

Retention: 81% of full-time freshmen returned.

FACULTY

Total: 263, 29% full-time, 33% with terminal degrees.

Student/faculty ratio: 13:1.

ACADEMICS

Calendar: semesters. *Degrees:* bachelor's, master's, and doctoral.

Special study options: accelerated degree program, adult/continuing education programs, advanced placement credit, distance learning, double majors, honors programs, independent study, internships, part-time degree program, services for LD students, study abroad, summer session for credit. ***ROTC:*** Army (c).

Unusual degree programs: 3-2 engineering with Washington University in St. Louis, MO, Penn State University in State College, PA.

Computers: 150 computers/terminals are available on campus for general student use. Students can access the following: campus intranet, computer help desk, free student e-mail accounts, online (class) grades, online (class) registration, online (class) schedules. Campuswide network is available. 100% of college-owned or -operated housing units are wired for high-speed Internet access. Wireless service is available via classrooms, computer labs, libraries.

STUDENT LIFE

Housing options: on-campus residence required through junior year; coed, men-only, women-only, special housing for students with disabilities. Campus housing is university owned. Freshman campus housing is guaranteed.

Activities and organizations: drama/theater group, student-run newspaper, radio and television station, choral group, Student-Pennsylvania State Education Association, Lamplighter Choir, Student Nurses Association, Christian Fellowship.

Athletics Member NCAA. All Division III. ***Intercollegiate sports:*** baseball M, basketball M/W, cross-country running M/W, football M, golf M/W, lacrosse W, soccer M/W, softball W, tennis M/W, track and field M/W, volleyball W, wrestling M. ***Intramural sports:*** basketball M/W, bowling M/W, racquetball M/W, softball M/W, table tennis M/W, volleyball M/W.

Campus security: 24-hour emergency response devices and patrols, late-night transport/escort service, controlled dormitory access.

Student services: health clinic, personal/psychological counseling.

COSTS & FINANCIAL AID

Costs (2014–15) ***Comprehensive fee:*** $30,150 includes full-time tuition ($20,890), mandatory fees ($400), and room and board ($8860). Full-time tuition and fees vary according to class time. Part-time tuition: $870 per credit hour. Part-time tuition and fees vary according to class time, course load, and location. ***Required fees:*** $16 per credit hour part-time. ***College room only:*** $4480. Room and board charges vary according to board plan and housing facility. ***Payment plan:*** installment. ***Waivers:*** employees or children of employees.

Financial Aid Of all full-time matriculated undergraduates who enrolled in 2014, 1,316 applied for aid, 1,177 were judged to have need, 327 had their need fully met. 200 Federal Work-Study jobs (averaging $1500). In 2014, 179 non-need-based awards were made. ***Average percent of need met:*** 76. ***Average financial aid package:*** $16,597. ***Average need-based loan:*** $4875. ***Average need-based gift aid:*** $12,596. ***Average non-need-based aid:*** $8743. ***Average indebtedness upon graduation:*** $30,250.

APPLYING

Standardized Tests *Required:* SAT or ACT (for admission).

Options: electronic application, early admission.

Application fee: $20.

Required: high school transcript, minimum 2.8 GPA. ***Required for some:*** essay or personal statement, 2 letters of recommendation. ***Recommended:*** minimum 3.0 GPA, interview.

Application deadlines: rolling (freshmen), rolling (transfers).

Notification: continuous (freshmen), continuous (transfers).

CONTACT

Ms. Robin L. King, Senior Vice President for Enrollment and University Relations, Waynesburg University, 51 West College Street, Waynesburg, PA 15370. *Phone:* 724-852-3333. *Toll-free phone:* 800-225-7393. *Fax:* 724-627-8124. *E-mail:* admissions@waynesburg.edu.

West Chester University of Pennsylvania

West Chester, Pennsylvania

http://www.wcupa.edu/

- **State-supported** comprehensive, founded 1871, part of Pennsylvania State System of Higher Education
- **Suburban** 409-acre campus with easy access to Philadelphia
- **Endowment** $21.2 million
- **Coed** 13,844 undergraduate students, 91% full-time, 60% women, 40% men
- **Moderately difficult** entrance level, 53% of applicants were admitted

UNDERGRAD STUDENTS

12,582 full-time, 1,262 part-time. Students come from 26 states and territories; 75 other countries; 12% are from out of state; 10% Black or African American, non-Hispanic/Latino; 5% Hispanic/Latino; 2% Asian, non-Hispanic/Latino; 0.1% Native Hawaiian or other Pacific Islander, non-Hispanic/Latino; 0.1% American Indian or Alaska Native, non-Hispanic/Latino; 3% Two or more races, non-Hispanic/Latino; 0.4% Race/ethnicity unknown; 0.3% international; 10% transferred in; 36% live on campus.

Freshmen

Admission: 13,291 applied, 7,108 admitted, 2,351 enrolled. ***Average high school GPA:*** 3.51. ***Test scores:*** SAT critical reading scores over 500: 73%; SAT math scores over 500: 78%; SAT writing scores over 500: 69%; SAT critical reading scores over 600: 17%; SAT math scores over 600: 21%; SAT writing scores over 600: 15%; SAT critical reading scores over 700: 1%; SAT math scores over 700: 1%; SAT writing scores over 700: 1%.

Retention: 88% of full-time freshmen returned.

FACULTY

Total: 913, 72% full-time, 69% with terminal degrees.

ACADEMICS

Calendar: semesters. *Degrees:* bachelor's, master's, doctoral, and postbachelor's certificates.

Special study options: academic remediation for entering students, accelerated degree program, adult/continuing education programs, advanced placement credit, distance learning, double majors, English as a second language, freshman honors college, honors programs, independent study, internships, off-campus study, part-time degree program, services for LD students, student-designed majors, study abroad, summer session for credit. ***ROTC:*** Army (b), Air Force (c).

Unusual degree programs: 3-2 engineering with Dual-degree program where the student spends three years at WCU and two years at one of our partner institutions, after which a student holds a BS in Physics from WCU and BS in engineering from either Penn State University or Philadelphia University.

Computers: 2,000 computers/terminals are available on campus for general student use. Students can access the following: campus intranet, computer help desk, free student e-mail accounts, online (class) grades, online (class) registration, online (class) schedules. Campuswide network is available. 100% of college-owned or -operated housing units are wired for high-speed Internet access. Wireless service is available via entire campus.

STUDENT LIFE

Housing options: coed, special housing for students with disabilities. Campus housing is university owned and is provided by a third party. Freshman applicants given priority for college housing.

Activities and organizations: drama/theater group, student-run newspaper, radio and television station, choral group, marching band, Student Government Association, Residence Hall Association, Inter-Greek Council, Sports Club Council, Campus Crusade for Christ, national fraternities, national sororities.

Athletics Member NCAA. All Division II. ***Intercollegiate sports:*** baseball M(s), basketball M(s)/W(s), bowling M(c)/W(c), cheerleading W, cross-country running M(s)/W(s), equestrian sports M(c)/W(c), fencing M(c)/W(c), field hockey W(s), football M(s), golf M(s)/W(s), gymnastics W(s), ice hockey M(c)/W(c), lacrosse M(c)/W(s), rugby M(c)/W(s), skiing (downhill) M(c)/W(c), soccer M(s)/W(s), softball W(s), swimming and diving M(s)/W(s), tennis M(s)/W(s), track and field M(s)/W(s), volleyball M(c)/W(s), water polo W(c), wrestling M(c). ***Intramural sports:*** badminton M/W, basketball M/W, football M/W, racquetball M/W, rock climbing M/W, soccer M/W, softball M/W, squash M/W, tennis M/W, volleyball M/W.

Campus security: 24-hour emergency response devices and patrols, late-night transport/escort service, controlled dormitory access, officers are on site 24/7, 365. Camera systems in campus residence halls, recreational and classroom facilities and outdoor areas.

Student services: health clinic, personal/psychological counseling, women's center, legal services.

COSTS & FINANCIAL AID

Costs (2014–15) ***Tuition:*** state resident $6820 full-time, $284 per credit part-time; nonresident $17,050 full-time, $710 per credit part-time. Full-time tuition and fees vary according to course load. Part-time tuition and fees vary according to course load. ***Required fees:*** $2234 full-time, $97 per credit part-time. ***Room and board:*** $8042; room only: $4848. Room and board charges vary according to board plan and housing facility. ***Payment plan:*** installment. ***Waivers:*** senior citizens and employees or children of employees.

Financial Aid Of all full-time matriculated undergraduates who enrolled in 2013, 9,750 applied for aid, 7,585 were judged to have need, 667 had their need fully met. In 2013, 161 non-need-based awards were made. ***Average percent of need met:*** 50. ***Average financial aid package:*** $7619. ***Average need-based loan:*** $4408. ***Average need-based gift aid:*** $5543. ***Average non-need-based aid:*** $4242. ***Average indebtedness upon graduation:*** $30,366.

APPLYING

Standardized Tests *Required:* SAT or ACT (for admission).

Options: electronic application.

Application fee: $45.

Required: essay or personal statement, high school transcript, SAT or ACT. ***Required for some:*** interview. ***Recommended:*** minimum 3.0 GPA.

Application deadlines: rolling (freshmen), rolling (transfers).

Notification: continuous (freshmen), continuous (transfers).

CONTACT

West Chester University of Pennsylvania, University Avenue and High Street, West Chester, PA 19383. *Phone:* 610-436-3414. *Toll-free phone:* 877-315-2165.

See below for display ad and page 1728 for the College Close-Up.

Widener University

Chester, Pennsylvania

http://www.widener.edu/

- **Independent** comprehensive, founded 1821
- **Suburban** 110-acre campus with easy access to Philadelphia
- **Coed** 3,437 undergraduate students, 84% full-time, 56% women, 44% men
- **Moderately difficult** entrance level, 65% of applicants were admitted

UNDERGRAD STUDENTS

2,883 full-time, 554 part-time. 40% are from out of state; 13% Black or African American, non-Hispanic/Latino; 5% Hispanic/Latino; 4% Asian, non-Hispanic/Latino; 0.1% Native Hawaiian or other Pacific Islander, non-Hispanic/Latino; 0.3% American Indian or Alaska Native, non-Hispanic/Latino; 3% Two or more races, non-Hispanic/Latino; 1% Race/ethnicity unknown; 4% international; 3% transferred in; 47% live on campus.

Freshmen

Admission: 5,501 applied, 3,576 admitted, 739 enrolled. ***Average high school GPA:*** 3.46. ***Test scores:*** SAT critical reading scores over 500: 52%; SAT math scores over 500: 61%; ACT scores over 18: 92%; SAT critical reading scores over 600: 10%; SAT math scores over 600: 21%; ACT scores over 24: 35%; SAT critical reading scores over 700: 2%; SAT math scores over 700: 3%; ACT scores over 30: 5%.

Retention: 76% of full-time freshmen returned.

FACULTY

Total: 625, 46% full-time, 64% with terminal degrees.

Student/faculty ratio: 12:1.

ACADEMICS
Calendar: semesters. *Degrees:* associate, bachelor's, master's, and doctoral.

Special study options: academic remediation for entering students, accelerated degree program, adult/continuing education programs, advanced placement credit, cooperative education, distance learning, double majors, English as a second language, honors programs, independent study, internships, off-campus study, part-time degree program, services for LD students, student-designed majors, study abroad, summer session for credit. ***ROTC:*** Army (b), Navy (c), Air Force (c).

Unusual degree programs: 3-2 business administration; engineering; social work; physical therapy, education.

Computers: 710 computers/terminals are available on campus for general student use. Students can access the following: campus intranet, computer help desk, free student e-mail accounts, online (class) grades, online (class) registration, online (class) schedules. Campuswide network is available. 100% of college-owned or -operated housing units are wired for high-speed Internet access. Wireless service is available via classrooms, computer centers, computer labs, dorm rooms, learning centers, libraries, student centers.

STUDENT LIFE
Housing options: on-campus residence required through sophomore year; coed, men-only, women-only, cooperative. Campus housing is university owned. Freshman campus housing is guaranteed.

Activities and organizations: drama/theater group, student-run newspaper, radio and television station, choral group, WDNR Radio, Black Student Union, volunteer services, rugby club, Theatre Widener, national fraternities, national sororities.

Athletics Member NCAA. All Division III. ***Intercollegiate sports:*** baseball M, basketball M/W, cheerleading W, cross-country running M/W, field hockey W, football M, golf M, lacrosse M/W, soccer M/W, softball W, swimming and diving M/W, track and field M/W, volleyball W. ***Intramural sports:*** crew M, ice hockey M(c), rock climbing M(c)/W(c), rugby M(c), skiing (downhill) M(c)/W(c), soccer M, volleyball M(c).

Campus security: 24-hour emergency response devices and patrols, late-night transport/escort service, controlled dormitory access, blue light emergency phones located throughout campus.

Student services: health clinic, personal/psychological counseling.

COSTS & FINANCIAL AID
Costs (2014–15) ***Comprehensive fee:*** $52,418 includes full-time tuition ($39,052), mandatory fees ($778), and room and board ($12,588). Full-time tuition and fees vary according to class time, course load, and program. Part-time tuition: $1300 per credit hour. ***College room only:*** $6552. Room and board charges vary according to board plan and housing facility. ***Payment plan:*** installment. ***Waivers:*** senior citizens and employees or children of employees.

Financial Aid Of all full-time matriculated undergraduates who enrolled in 2014, 2,506 applied for aid, 2,311 were judged to have need, 464 had their need fully met. 1,634 Federal Work-Study jobs (averaging $1400). In 2014, 1887 non-need-based awards were made. ***Average percent of need met:*** 77. ***Average financial aid package:*** $29,545. ***Average need-based loan:*** $4600. ***Average need-based gift aid:*** $23,917. ***Average non-need-based aid:*** $20,604.

APPLYING
Standardized Tests *Required:* SAT or ACT (for admission).

Options: electronic application, deferred entrance.

Application fee: $35.

Required: essay or personal statement, high school transcript. ***Required for some:*** minimum 2.9 GPA. ***Recommended:*** interview.

Application deadlines: rolling (freshmen), rolling (transfers).

Notification: continuous (freshmen), continuous (transfers).

CONTACT
Office of Admissions, Widener University, One University Place, Chester, PA 19013. *Phone:* 610-499-4126. *Toll-free phone:* 888-WIDENER. *Fax:* 610-499-4676. *E-mail:* admissions.office@widener.edu.

Wilkes University
Wilkes-Barre, Pennsylvania
http://www.wilkes.edu/

- **Independent** comprehensive, founded 1933
- **Urban** 25-acre campus
- **Endowment** $43.7 million
- **Coed** 2,360 undergraduate students, 94% full-time, 47% women, 53% men
- **Moderately difficult** entrance level, 79% of applicants were admitted

UNDERGRAD STUDENTS
2,217 full-time, 143 part-time. Students come from 21 states and territories; 11 other countries; 16% are from out of state; 3% Black or African American, non-Hispanic/Latino; 6% Hispanic/Latino; 2% Asian, non-Hispanic/Latino; 0.1% Native Hawaiian or other Pacific Islander, non-Hispanic/Latino; 0.1% American Indian or Alaska Native, non-Hispanic/Latino; 4% Two or more races, non-Hispanic/Latino; 2% Race/ethnicity unknown; 9% international; 7% transferred in; 41% live on campus.

Freshmen
Admission: 2,812 applied, 2,211 admitted, 559 enrolled. ***Test scores:*** SAT critical reading scores over 500: 58%; SAT math scores over 500: 67%; SAT writing scores over 500: 50%; SAT critical reading scores over 600: 15%; SAT math scores over 600: 24%; SAT writing scores over 600: 13%; SAT critical reading scores over 700: 1%; SAT math scores over 700: 2%; SAT writing scores over 700: 1%.

Retention: 79% of full-time freshmen returned.

FACULTY
Total: 314, 55% full-time.

Student/faculty ratio: 15:1.

ACADEMICS
Calendar: semesters. *Degrees:* bachelor's, master's, and doctoral.

Special study options: academic remediation for entering students, accelerated degree program, adult/continuing education programs, advanced placement credit, cooperative education, distance learning, double majors, English as a second language, honors programs, independent study, internships, off-campus study, part-time degree program, services for LD students, student-designed majors, study abroad, summer session for credit. ***ROTC:*** Army (c), Air Force (b).

Computers: 790 computers/terminals are available on campus for general student use. Students can access the following: campus intranet, computer help desk, free student e-mail accounts, online (class) grades, online (class) registration, online (class) schedules. Campuswide network is available. Wireless service is available via libraries, student centers.

STUDENT LIFE
Housing options: on-campus residence required through sophomore year; coed, men-only, women-only. Campus housing is university owned. Freshman campus housing is guaranteed.

Activities and organizations: drama/theater group, student-run newspaper, radio and television station, choral group, marching band.

Athletics Member NCAA. All Division III. ***Intercollegiate sports:*** baseball M, basketball M/W, cross-country running M/W, field hockey W, football M, golf M/W, lacrosse M/W, soccer M/W, softball W, swimming and diving M/W, tennis M/W, volleyball W, wrestling M. ***Intramural sports:*** basketball M/W, bowling M/W, cheerleading W(c), crew M(c)/W(c), cross-country running M(c)/W(c), fencing M(c)/W(c), football M, ice hockey M(c)/W(c), lacrosse M(c), racquetball M(c)/W(c), rock climbing M(c)/W(c), skiing (downhill) M(c)/W(c), soccer M/W, softball M/W, swimming and diving M(c)/W(c), ultimate Frisbee M(c)/W(c), volleyball M/W.

Campus security: 24-hour emergency response devices and patrols, late-night transport/escort service, controlled dormitory access.

Student services: health clinic, personal/psychological counseling.

COSTS & FINANCIAL AID
Costs (2014–15) ***Comprehensive fee:*** $44,070 includes full-time tuition ($29,750), mandatory fees ($1512), and room and board ($12,808). Part-time tuition: $826 per credit hour. ***Required fees:*** $68 per credit hour part-time. ***College room only:*** $7704. Room and board charges vary according

to board plan and housing facility. ***Payment plans:*** installment, deferred payment. ***Waivers:*** employees or children of employees.

Financial Aid Of all full-time matriculated undergraduates who enrolled in 2014, 1,908 applied for aid, 1,802 were judged to have need, 182 had their need fully met. In 2014, 91 non-need-based awards were made. ***Average percent of need met:*** 73. ***Average financial aid package:*** $24,265. ***Average need-based loan:*** $4743. ***Average need-based gift aid:*** $18,937. ***Average non-need-based aid:*** $11,645. ***Average indebtedness upon graduation:*** $38,082.

APPLYING

Standardized Tests *Required:* SAT or ACT (for admission).

Options: electronic application, early admission, deferred entrance.

Application fee: $40.

Required: high school transcript. ***Recommended:*** interview.

Application deadlines: rolling (freshmen), rolling (transfers).

Notification: 8/30 (freshmen), continuous until 8/30 (transfers).

CONTACT

Ms. Melanie Wade, Vice President of Enrollment Services, Wilkes University, 84 West South Street, Wilkes-Barre, PA 18766. *Phone:* 570-408-4400. *Toll-free phone:* 800-945-5378 Ext. 4400. *Fax:* 570-408-4904. *E-mail:* admissions@wilkes.edu.

See below for display ad and page 1740 for the College Close-Up.

★ Wilson College

Chambersburg, Pennsylvania

http://www.wilson.edu/

- **Independent** comprehensive, founded 1869, affiliated with Presbyterian Church (U.S.A.)
- **Small-town** 300-acre campus
- **Endowment** $70.7 million
- **Coed, primarily women**
- **Moderately difficult** entrance level

FACULTY

Student/faculty ratio: 8:1.

ACADEMICS

Calendar: 4-1-4. *Degrees:* associate, bachelor's, and master's.

STUDENT LIFE

Housing options: on-campus residence required through junior year; women-only. Campus housing is university owned. Freshman campus housing is guaranteed.

Activities and organizations: drama/theater group, student-run newspaper, choral group, Muhibbah Club, Orchesis Club, student newspaper, student government, Campus Activity Board.

Athletics Member NCAA. All Division III.

Campus security: 24-hour emergency response devices and patrols, late-night transport/escort service, controlled dormitory access.

Student services: health clinic, personal/psychological counseling, women's center.

COSTS

Costs (2014–15) ***Comprehensive fee:*** $35,080 includes full-time tuition ($23,745), mandatory fees ($635), and room and board ($10,700). Full-time tuition and fees vary according to program. Part-time tuition: $2375 per course. Part-time tuition and fees vary according to course load and program. ***Required fees:*** $55 per course part-time, $56 per term part-time. ***College room only:*** $5390. Room and board charges vary according to board plan and housing facility.

APPLYING

Standardized Tests *Required for some:* SAT or ACT (for admission), SAT/ACT optional for students with high school GPA of 3.0 and specified college prep curriculum from regionally accredited schools; TOEFL/IELTS/STEP for international students.

Options: electronic application, early admission, deferred entrance.

Required: essay or personal statement, high school transcript, 1 letter of recommendation, college preparatory program that includes 4 units of English, 4 units of History/Civics, 3 units of Mathematics (preferably Algebra I, II or Geometry), 2 units of same Foreign Language, and 2 units of Natural Sciences with lab. ***Recommended:*** minimum 2.8 GPA, interview.

CONTACT
Ms. Patricia Beidel, Director of Admissions, Wilson College, 1015 Philadelphia Avenue, Chambersburg, PA 17201. *Phone:* 717-262-2002. *Toll-free phone:* 800-421-8402. *Fax:* 717-262-2546. *E-mail:* admissions@wilson.edu.

York College of Pennsylvania

York, Pennsylvania

http://www.ycp.edu/

- **Independent** comprehensive, founded 1787
- **Suburban** 190-acre campus with easy access to Baltimore
- **Coed** 4,853 undergraduate students, 89% full-time, 56% women, 44% men
- **Moderately difficult** entrance level, 45% of applicants were admitted

UNDERGRAD STUDENTS
4,340 full-time, 513 part-time. 46% are from out of state; 6% Black or African American, non-Hispanic/Latino; 6% Hispanic/Latino; 2% Asian, non-Hispanic/Latino; 0.1% American Indian or Alaska Native, non-Hispanic/Latino; 3% Two or more races, non-Hispanic/Latino; 1% Race/ethnicity unknown; 0.3% international; 4% transferred in; 52% live on campus.

Freshmen
Admission: 15,270 applied, 6,946 admitted, 1,091 enrolled. ***Average high school GPA:*** 3.5. ***Test scores:*** SAT critical reading scores over 500: 65%; SAT math scores over 500: 69%; SAT writing scores over 500: 53%; ACT scores over 18: 95%; SAT critical reading scores over 600: 13%; SAT math scores over 600: 21%; SAT writing scores over 600: 11%; ACT scores over 24: 32%; SAT critical reading scores over 700: 1%; SAT math scores over 700: 1%; ACT scores over 30: 2%.

Retention: 79% of full-time freshmen returned.

FACULTY
Total: 519, 33% full-time, 40% with terminal degrees.

Student/faculty ratio: 16:1.

ACADEMICS
Calendar: semesters. *Degrees:* associate, bachelor's, master's, doctoral, and post-master's certificates.

Special study options: academic remediation for entering students, advanced placement credit, cooperative education, double majors, independent study, internships, part-time degree program, services for LD students, student-designed majors, study abroad, summer session for credit.

Unusual degree programs: 3-2 business administration.

Computers: Students can access the following: campus intranet, computer help desk, free student e-mail accounts, online (class) grades, online (class) registration, online (class) schedules. Campuswide network is available. 100% of college-owned or -operated housing units are wired for high-speed Internet access. Wireless service is available via entire campus.

STUDENT LIFE
Housing options: on-campus residence required through senior year; coed, special housing for students with disabilities. Campus housing is university owned. Freshman campus housing is guaranteed.

Activities and organizations: drama/theater group, student-run newspaper, radio and television station, choral group, Pre-Med Society, Ski and Outdoor Club, Habitat for Humanity, Students in Free Enterprise (SIFE), WVYC Radio Station, national fraternities, national sororities.

Athletics Member NCAA. All Division III. ***Intercollegiate sports:*** baseball M, basketball M/W, cheerleading M/W, cross-country running M/W, field hockey W, golf M, lacrosse M/W, soccer M/W, softball W, swimming and diving M/W, tennis M/W, track and field M/W, volleyball W, wrestling M. ***Intramural sports:*** badminton M/W, basketball M/W, equestrian sports M(c)/W(c), football M/W, lacrosse M(c)/W(c), racquetball M/W, rugby M(c)/W(c), soccer M/W, softball M/W, table tennis M/W, tennis M/W, ultimate Frisbee M(c)/W(c), volleyball M/W.

Campus security: 24-hour emergency response devices and patrols, student patrols, late-night transport/escort service, controlled dormitory access.

Student services: health clinic, personal/psychological counseling.

COSTS & FINANCIAL AID
Costs (2015–16) ***Comprehensive fee:*** $28,400 includes full-time tuition ($16,480), mandatory fees ($1760), and room and board ($10,160). Full-time tuition and fees vary according to program. Part-time tuition: $510 per credit hour. ***Room and board:*** Room and board charges vary according to board plan and housing facility. ***Payment plan:*** installment. ***Waivers:*** employees or children of employees.

Financial Aid Of all full-time matriculated undergraduates who enrolled in 2014, 3,651 applied for aid, 2,967 were judged to have need, 710 had their need fully met. 311 Federal Work-Study jobs (averaging $2090). 8 state and other part-time jobs (averaging $2200). In 2014, 1078 non-need-based awards were made. ***Average percent of need met:*** 67. ***Average financial aid package:*** $13,707. ***Average need-based loan:*** $7258. ***Average need-based gift aid:*** $5302. ***Average non-need-based aid:*** $4377. ***Average indebtedness upon graduation:*** $35,669.

APPLYING
Standardized Tests *Required:* SAT or ACT (for admission).

Options: electronic application, deferred entrance.

Required: high school transcript, minimum 2.0 GPA. ***Required for some:*** interview. ***Recommended:*** essay or personal statement, 1 letter of recommendation.

CONTACT
York College of Pennsylvania, York, PA 17405-7199. *Phone:* 717-849-1600. *Toll-free phone:* 800-455-8018.

RHODE ISLAND

Brown University

Providence, Rhode Island

http://www.brown.edu/

- **Independent** university, founded 1764
- **Urban** 140-acre campus with easy access to Boston
- **Endowment** $3.0 million
- **Coed** 6,548 undergraduate students, 96% full-time, 52% women, 48% men
- **Most difficult** entrance level, 9% of applicants were admitted

UNDERGRAD STUDENTS
6,255 full-time, 293 part-time. Students come from 52 states and territories; 104 other countries; 95% are from out of state; 7% Black or African American, non-Hispanic/Latino; 11% Hispanic/Latino; 13% Asian, non-Hispanic/Latino; 0.2% Native Hawaiian or other Pacific Islander, non-Hispanic/Latino; 0.4% American Indian or Alaska Native, non-Hispanic/Latino; 5% Two or more races, non-Hispanic/Latino; 8% Race/ethnicity unknown; 12% international; 0.8% transferred in; 79% live on campus.

Freshmen
Admission: 30,431 applied, 2,661 admitted, 1,559 enrolled. ***Test scores:*** SAT critical reading scores over 500: 100%; SAT math scores over 500: 100%; SAT writing scores over 500: 100%; ACT scores over 18: 100%; SAT critical reading scores over 600: 93%; SAT math scores over 600: 95%; SAT writing scores over 600: 95%; ACT scores over 24: 99%; SAT critical reading scores over 700: 62%; SAT math scores over 700: 68%; SAT writing scores over 700: 66%; ACT scores over 30: 77%.

Retention: 97% of full-time freshmen returned.

ACADEMICS
Calendar: semesters. *Degrees:* bachelor's, master's, and doctoral.

Special study options: adult/continuing education programs, advanced placement credit, double majors, honors programs, independent study, internships, off-campus study, services for LD students, student-designed majors, study abroad, summer session for credit. ***ROTC:*** Army (c).

Computers: Students can access the following: campus intranet, computer help desk, free student e-mail accounts, online (class) grades, online (class) registration, online (class) schedules. Campuswide network is available. 100% of college-owned or -operated housing units are wired for high-speed Internet access. Wireless service is available via entire campus.

STUDENT LIFE

Housing options: on-campus residence required through junior year; coed, cooperative, special housing for students with disabilities. Campus housing is university owned. Freshman campus housing is guaranteed.

Activities and organizations: drama/theater group, student-run newspaper, radio and television station, choral group, marching band, national fraternities, national sororities.

Athletics Member NCAA. All Division I except football (Division I-AA). ***Intercollegiate sports:*** baseball M, basketball M/W, crew M/W, cross-country running M/W, equestrian sports W, fencing M/W, field hockey W, golf M/W, gymnastics W, ice hockey M/W, lacrosse M/W, rugby M(c)/W(c), sailing M(c)/W(c), skiing (downhill) M(c)/W, soccer M/W, softball W, squash M/W, swimming and diving M/W, tennis M/W, track and field M/W, volleyball M(c)/W, water polo M/W, wrestling M. ***Intramural sports:*** badminton M(c)/W(c), basketball M/W, cheerleading M/W, fencing M/W, field hockey W, football M, ice hockey M/W, lacrosse M/W, racquetball M(c)/W(c), rugby M/W, skiing (downhill) M/W, soccer M/W, softball M/W, squash M/W, swimming and diving M/W, table tennis M(c)/W(c), tennis M/W, ultimate Frisbee M(c)/W(c), volleyball M/W, water polo M/W.

Campus security: 24-hour emergency response devices and patrols, late-night transport/escort service, controlled dormitory access.

Student services: health clinic, personal/psychological counseling, women's center.

COSTS & FINANCIAL AID

Costs (2014–15) ***Comprehensive fee:*** $59,428 includes full-time tuition ($46,408), mandatory fees ($1026), and room and board ($11,994). ***College room only:*** $7416. Room and board charges vary according to board plan. ***Payment plan:*** installment. ***Waivers:*** employees or children of employees.

Financial Aid Of all full-time matriculated undergraduates who enrolled in 2014, 3,088 applied for aid, 2,820 were judged to have need, 2,791 had their need fully met. 1,537 Federal Work-Study jobs (averaging $2472). 369 state and other part-time jobs (averaging $2513). In 2014, 12 non-need-based awards were made. ***Average percent of need met:*** 100. ***Average financial aid package:*** $42,468. ***Average need-based loan:*** $5628. ***Average need-based gift aid:*** $40,917. ***Average non-need-based aid:*** $9452. ***Average indebtedness upon graduation:*** $24,300. ***Financial aid deadline:*** 2/1.

APPLYING

Standardized Tests *Required:* SAT and SAT Subject Tests or ACT (for admission).

Options: electronic application, early decision, deferred entrance.

Application fee: $75.

Required: essay or personal statement, high school transcript, 2 letters of recommendation, Common Application; Brown University Supplement. ***Recommended:*** interview.

Application deadlines: 1/1 (freshmen), 3/1 (transfers).

Early decision deadline: 11/1.

Notification: 4/1 (freshmen), 5/15 (transfers), 12/15 (early decision).

CONTACT

Mr. James Miller, Dean of Admission, Brown University, Box 1876, Providence, RI 02912. *Phone:* 401-863-2378. *Fax:* 401-863-9300. *E-mail:* admission_undergraduate@brown.edu.

★ Bryant University

Smithfield, Rhode Island

http://www.bryant.edu/

- **Independent** comprehensive, founded 1863
- **Suburban** 435-acre campus with easy access to Boston, Providence
- **Endowment** $172.8 million
- **Coed** 3,320 undergraduate students, 97% full-time, 42% women, 58% men
- **Moderately difficult** entrance level, 75% of applicants were admitted

UNDERGRAD STUDENTS

3,232 full-time, 88 part-time. Students come from 32 states and territories; 62 other countries; 87% are from out of state; 4% Black or African American, non-Hispanic/Latino; 7% Hispanic/Latino; 4% Asian, non-Hispanic/Latino; 0.2% Native Hawaiian or other Pacific Islander, non-Hispanic/Latino; 0.4% American Indian or Alaska Native, non-Hispanic/Latino; 1% Two or more races, non-Hispanic/Latino; 2% Race/ethnicity unknown; 8% international; 3% transferred in; 82% live on campus.

Freshmen

Admission: 6,227 applied, 4,675 admitted, 826 enrolled. ***Average high school GPA:*** 3.36. ***Test scores:*** SAT critical reading scores over 500: 82%; SAT math scores over 500: 95%; SAT writing scores over 500: 78%; ACT scores over 18: 99%; SAT critical reading scores over 600: 25%; SAT math scores over 600: 48%; SAT writing scores over 600: 24%; ACT scores over 24: 74%; SAT critical reading scores over 700: 3%; SAT math scores over 700: 6%; SAT writing scores over 700: 3%; ACT scores over 30: 11%.

Retention: 87% of full-time freshmen returned.

FACULTY

Total: 275, 60% full-time, 57% with terminal degrees.

Student/faculty ratio: 14:1.

ACADEMICS

Calendar: semesters. *Degrees:* bachelor's and master's.

Special study options: adult/continuing education programs, advanced placement credit, double majors, English as a second language, honors programs, independent study, internships, off-campus study, part-time degree program, services for LD students, study abroad, summer session for credit. ***ROTC:*** Army (c).

Unusual degree programs: 3-2 business administration.

Computers: 574 computers/terminals and 3,585 ports are available on campus for general student use. Students can access the following: campus intranet, computer help desk, free student e-mail accounts, online (class) grades, online (class) registration, online (class) schedules, e-mail, online library, wireless network, student Web hosts. Campuswide network is available. 100% of college-owned or -operated housing units are wired for high-speed Internet access. Wireless service is available via entire campus.

STUDENT LIFE

Housing options: coed, special housing for students with disabilities. Campus housing is university owned. Freshman campus housing is guaranteed.

Activities and organizations: drama/theater group, student-run newspaper, radio and television station, choral group, Ski & Snowboard Club, Bryant Outdoor Adventures Club, Collegiate Entrepreneurs Organization, The Podium (public speaking), Student Programming Board, national fraternities, national sororities.

Athletics Member NCAA. All Division I except football (Division I-AA). ***Intercollegiate sports:*** baseball M(s), basketball M(s)/W(s), bowling M(c)/W(c), cheerleading W(c), crew W(c), cross-country running M(s)/W(s), field hockey W(s), golf M(s), ice hockey M(c), lacrosse M(s)/W(s), racquetball M(c)/W(c), rugby M(c)/W(c), soccer M(s)/W(s), softball W(s), squash M(c)/W(c), swimming and diving M(s)/W(s), tennis M(s)/W(s), track and field M(s)/W(s), ultimate Frisbee M(c)/W(c), volleyball M(c)/W(s). ***Intramural sports:*** basketball M/W, soccer M/W, softball M/W, table tennis M/W, volleyball M/W, wrestling M.

Campus security: 24-hour emergency response devices and patrols, late-night transport/escort service, controlled dormitory access, 24 full-time staff; 20 patrol officers on foot, bike, golf cart, and car; Entry Control Station staffed 24/7 at only campus entry point.

Student services: health clinic, personal/psychological counseling, women's center.

COSTS & FINANCIAL AID

Costs (2015–16) ***Comprehensive fee:*** $54,361 includes full-time tuition ($39,421), mandatory fees ($387), and room and board ($14,553). Part-time tuition: $977 per credit hour. Part-time tuition and fees vary according to course load. ***College room only:*** $8542. Room and board charges vary according to board plan and housing facility. ***Payment plan:*** installment. ***Waivers:*** employees or children of employees.

Financial Aid Of all full-time matriculated undergraduates who enrolled in 2014, 2,310 applied for aid, 2,038 were judged to have need, 1,016 had their need fully met. In 2014, 682 non-need-based awards were made. ***Average percent of need met:*** 52. ***Average financial aid package:*** $21,753. ***Average need-based loan:*** $5115. ***Average need-based gift aid:***

$10,320. ***Average non-need-based aid:*** $13,406. ***Average indebtedness upon graduation:*** $39,283.

APPLYING

Standardized Tests *Recommended:* Standardized tests are optional.

Options: electronic application, early decision, early action, deferred entrance.

Application fee: $50.

Required: essay or personal statement, high school transcript, 1 letter of recommendation, senior year first-quarter grades; SAT or ACT optional. ***Recommended:*** minimum 3.3 GPA, 2 letters of recommendation, interview.

Application deadlines: 2/3 (freshmen), 2/3 (out-of-state freshmen), 5/1 (transfers), 12/2 (early action).

Early decision deadline: 11/15 (for plan 1), 1/15 (for plan 2).

Notification: 3/23 (freshmen), 3/23 (out-of-state freshmen), continuous (transfers), 12/16 (early decision plan 1), 2/17 (early decision plan 2), 1/15 (early action).

CONTACT

Ms. Michelle Cloutier, Executive Director of Admission, Bryant University, 1150 Douglas Pike, Smithfield, RI 02917. *Phone:* 401-232-6100. *Toll-free phone:* 800-622-7001. *Fax:* 401-232-6741. *E-mail:* admission@bryant.edu.

Johnson & Wales University

Providence, Rhode Island

http://www.jwu.edu/providence/

- **Independent** comprehensive, founded 1914
- **Urban** 47-acre campus with easy access to Boston
- **Coed** 9,173 undergraduate students, 93% full-time, 59% women, 41% men
- **Moderately difficult** entrance level, 81% of applicants were admitted

UNDERGRAD STUDENTS

8,529 full-time, 644 part-time. 81% are from out of state; 11% Black or African American, non-Hispanic/Latino; 11% Hispanic/Latino; 1% Asian, non-Hispanic/Latino; 0.1% Native Hawaiian or other Pacific Islander, non-Hispanic/Latino; 0.2% American Indian or Alaska Native, non-Hispanic/Latino; 6% Two or more races, non-Hispanic/Latino; 7% Race/ethnicity unknown; 8% international; 44% live on campus.

Freshmen

Admission: 11,899 applied, 9,656 admitted, 1,898 enrolled. ***Average high school GPA:*** 3.16. ***Test scores:*** SAT critical reading scores over 500: 42%; SAT math scores over 500: 45%; SAT writing scores over 500: 40%; SAT critical reading scores over 600: 8%; SAT math scores over 600: 9%; SAT writing scores over 600: 6%; SAT critical reading scores over 700: 1%; SAT math scores over 700: 1%; SAT writing scores over 700: 1%.

Retention: 79% of full-time freshmen returned.

FACULTY

Total: 604, 48% full-time.

Student/faculty ratio: 15:1.

ACADEMICS

Calendar: quarters. *Degrees:* certificates, diplomas, associate, bachelor's, master's, and doctoral (branch locations in Charlotte, NC; Denver, CO; North Miami, FL).

Special study options: academic remediation for entering students, accelerated degree program, adult/continuing education programs, advanced placement credit, cooperative education, English as a second language, freshman honors college, honors programs, independent study, internships, part-time degree program, services for LD students, study abroad, summer session for credit. ***ROTC:*** Army (b).

Computers: Students can access the following: computer help desk, free student e-mail accounts, online (class) grades, online (class) registration, online (class) schedules. Campuswide network is available.

STUDENT LIFE

Housing options: on-campus residence required for freshman year; coed, special housing for students with disabilities. Campus housing is university owned. Freshman campus housing is guaranteed.

Activities and organizations: student-run newspaper, national fraternities, national sororities.

Athletics Member NCAA. All Division III. ***Intercollegiate sports:*** baseball M(c), basketball M/W, cross-country running M/W, equestrian sports M(c)/W(c), golf M/W, ice hockey M(c), sailing M/W, soccer M/W, softball W, tennis M/W, volleyball M/W, wrestling M. ***Intramural sports:*** badminton M/W, basketball M/W, bowling M(c)/W(c), cheerleading M/W, football M/W, skiing (downhill) M(c)/W(c), soccer M/W, softball M/W, table tennis M/W, tennis M(c)/W(c), volleyball M/W.

Campus security: 24-hour emergency response devices and patrols, student patrols, late-night transport/escort service.

Student services: health clinic, personal/psychological counseling, women's center.

COSTS & FINANCIAL AID

Costs (2015–16) ***Tuition:*** $29,226 full-time, $196 per credit hour part-time. ***Required fees:*** $350 full-time.

Financial Aid Of all full-time matriculated undergraduates who enrolled in 2010, 6,987 applied for aid, 6,254 were judged to have need, 833 had their need fully met. In 2010, 1517 non-need-based awards were made. ***Average percent of need met:*** 69. ***Average financial aid package:*** $16,400. ***Average need-based loan:*** $5096. ***Average need-based gift aid:*** $7514. ***Average non-need-based aid:*** $4962.

APPLYING

Standardized Tests *Required for some:* SAT or ACT (for admission).

Options: electronic application, early admission, deferred entrance.

Required: high school transcript. ***Required for some:*** essay or personal statement, minimum 2.8 GPA, interview. ***Recommended:*** minimum 2.0 GPA.

CONTACT

Amy Podbelski, Dean of Undergraduate Admissions, Johnson & Wales University, 8 Abbott Park Place, Providence, RI 02903-3703. *Phone:* 401-598-2310. *Toll-free phone:* 800-342-5598. *Fax:* 401-598-2948. *E-mail:* pvd@admissions.jwu.edu.

New England Institute of Technology

East Greenwich, Rhode Island

http://www.neit.edu/

- **Independent** comprehensive, founded 1940
- **Suburban** 225-acre campus with easy access to Boston
- **Coed** 2,841 undergraduate students, 85% full-time, 32% women, 68% men
- **Noncompetitive** entrance level

UNDERGRAD STUDENTS

2,417 full-time, 424 part-time. Students come from 17 states and territories; 18 other countries; 5% Black or African American, non-Hispanic/Latino; 10% Hispanic/Latino; 2% Asian, non-Hispanic/Latino; 0.6% American Indian or Alaska Native, non-Hispanic/Latino; 1% Two or more races, non-Hispanic/Latino; 11% Race/ethnicity unknown; 4% international.

Freshmen

Admission: 490 enrolled.

FACULTY

Total: 341, 38% full-time, 9% with terminal degrees.

ACADEMICS

Calendar: quarters. *Degrees:* associate, bachelor's, and master's.

Special study options: academic remediation for entering students, accelerated degree program, adult/continuing education programs, advanced placement credit, cooperative education, distance learning, double majors, internships, part-time degree program, services for LD students, student-designed majors, summer session for credit.

Computers: 1,000 computers/terminals are available on campus for general student use. Students can access the following: computer help desk, free student e-mail accounts, online (class) grades, online (class) registration, online (class) schedules. Campuswide network is available. Wireless service is available via entire campus.

STUDENT LIFE

Housing options: college housing not available.

Activities and organizations: Skills USA, Rotaract Club, Student Nurses Association, Student Occupational Therapy Association, Phi Theta Kappa (International Honor Society).

Athletics ***Intramural sports:*** golf M(c)/W(c), soccer M(c)/W(c).

Campus security: security personnel during open hours.

Student services: personal/psychological counseling.

COSTS & FINANCIAL AID

Costs (2014–15) ***Tuition:*** $20,775 full-time. Full-time tuition and fees vary according to degree level and program. Part-time tuition and fees vary according to degree level and program. No tuition increase for student's term of enrollment. ***Required fees:*** $1455 full-time. ***Payment plans:*** tuition prepayment, installment. ***Waivers:*** employees or children of employees.

Financial Aid Of all full-time matriculated undergraduates who enrolled in 2013, 250 Federal Work-Study jobs (averaging $2290).

APPLYING

Options: electronic application, early admission, deferred entrance.

Application fee: $25.

Required: high school transcript, interview, Basic skills testing is used for academic placement. Portfolios required for advanced standing.

Application deadlines: rolling (freshmen), rolling (transfers).

CONTACT

Mr. James Jessup, Director of Admissions, New England Institute of Technology, One New England Tech Blvd., East Greenwich, RI 02818. *Phone:* 401-739-5000 Ext. 3339. *Toll-free phone:* 800-736-7744. *Fax:* 401-886-0868. *E-mail:* jjessup@neit.edu.

Providence College

Providence, Rhode Island

http://www.providence.edu/

- **Independent Roman Catholic** comprehensive, founded 1917
- **Urban** 105-acre campus with easy access to Boston
- **Endowment** $213.8 million
- **Coed** 4,176 undergraduate students, 93% full-time, 57% women, 43% men

UNDERGRAD STUDENTS

3,866 full-time, 310 part-time. Students come from 44 states and territories; 27 other countries; 87% are from out of state; 4% Black or African American, non-Hispanic/Latino; 7% Hispanic/Latino; 1% Asian, non-Hispanic/Latino; 0.2% Native Hawaiian or other Pacific Islander, non-Hispanic/Latino; 0.2% American Indian or Alaska Native, non-Hispanic/Latino; 2% Two or more races, non-Hispanic/Latino; 6% Race/ethnicity unknown; 2% international; 2% transferred in; 72% live on campus.

Freshmen

Admission: 1,032 enrolled. ***Average high school GPA:*** 3.38. ***Test scores:*** SAT critical reading scores over 500: 83%; SAT math scores over 500: 84%; SAT writing scores over 500: 85%; ACT scores over 18: 98%; SAT critical reading scores over 600: 33%; SAT math scores over 600: 44%; SAT writing scores over 600: 44%; ACT scores over 24: 70%; SAT critical reading scores over 700: 5%; SAT math scores over 700: 6%; SAT writing scores over 700: 8%; ACT scores over 30: 14%.

Retention: 92% of full-time freshmen returned.

FACULTY

Total: 482, 61% full-time, 66% with terminal degrees.

Student/faculty ratio: 12:1.

ACADEMICS

Calendar: semesters. *Degrees:* certificates, associate, bachelor's, and master's.

Special study options: adult/continuing education programs, advanced placement credit, double majors, honors programs, independent study, internships, part-time degree program, services for LD students, student-designed majors, study abroad, summer session for credit. ***ROTC:*** Army (b).

Unusual degree programs: 3-2 engineering with Columbia University, Washington University in St. Louis; Biology/Optometry, New England School of Optometry.

Computers: 376 computers/terminals and 5,000 ports are available on campus for general student use. Students can access the following: campus intranet, computer help desk, free student e-mail accounts, online (class) grades, online (class) registration, online (class) schedules. Campuswide network is available. 100% of college-owned or -operated housing units are wired for high-speed Internet access. Wireless service is available via entire campus.

STUDENT LIFE

Housing options: on-campus residence required through sophomore year; coed, men-only, women-only, special housing for students with disabilities. Campus housing is university owned. Freshman campus housing is guaranteed.

Activities and organizations: drama/theater group, student-run newspaper, radio and television station, choral group, Student Congress, Board of Multicultural Student Affairs, Dance Club, Friars Club, Board of Programmers.

Athletics Member NCAA. All Division I. ***Intercollegiate sports:*** basketball M(s)/W(s), cheerleading M/W, cross-country running M(s)/W(s), field hockey W(s), ice hockey M(s)/W(s), lacrosse M(s), racquetball M(c)/W(c), soccer M(s)/W(s), softball W(s), swimming and diving M/W, tennis W, track and field M(s)/W(s), volleyball W(s). ***Intramural sports:*** badminton M/W, basketball M/W, cheerleading M(c)/W(c), crew M(c)/W(c), cross-country running M/W, field hockey W, football M/W, ice hockey M/W, lacrosse M, racquetball M(c)/W(c), rugby M(c)/W(c), sailing M(c)/W(c), skiing (downhill) M(c)/W(c), soccer M/W, softball W, swimming and diving M/W, tennis W, track and field M/W, ultimate Frisbee M(c)/W(c), volleyball W, water polo M/W, weight lifting M/W, wrestling M(c).

Campus security: 24-hour emergency response devices and patrols, student patrols, late-night transport/escort service, controlled dormitory access.

Student services: health clinic, personal/psychological counseling.

COSTS & FINANCIAL AID

Costs (2014–15) ***Comprehensive fee:*** $57,383 includes full-time tuition ($43,443), mandatory fees ($880), and room and board ($13,060). Full-time tuition and fees vary according to class time and degree level. Part-time tuition: $1551 per credit hour. Part-time tuition and fees vary according to class time and degree level. ***College room only:*** $7530. Room and board charges vary according to board plan and housing facility. ***Payment plan:*** installment. ***Waivers:*** employees or children of employees.

Financial Aid Of all full-time matriculated undergraduates who enrolled in 2014, 2,595 applied for aid, 2,118 were judged to have need, 476 had their need fully met. 1,250 Federal Work-Study jobs (averaging $1750). In 2014, 642 non-need-based awards were made. ***Average percent of need met:*** 84. ***Average financial aid package:*** $27,800. ***Average need-based loan:*** $5143. ***Average need-based gift aid:*** $22,860. ***Average non-need-based aid:*** $20,050. ***Average indebtedness upon graduation:*** $32,475. ***Financial aid deadline:*** 2/1.

APPLYING

Standardized Tests *Recommended:* Test scores are considered if submitted.

Required: essay or personal statement, high school transcript, 2 letters of recommendation.

CONTACT

Providence College, 1 Cunningham Square, Providence, RI 02918. *Phone:* 401-865-2535. *Toll-free phone:* 800-721-6444.

★ Rhode Island College

Providence, Rhode Island

http://www.ric.edu/

- **State-supported** comprehensive, founded 1854
- **Suburban** 180-acre campus with easy access to Boston
- **Endowment** $16.1 million
- **Coed** 7,518 undergraduate students, 75% full-time, 67% women, 33% men
- **Moderately difficult** entrance level, 65% of applicants were admitted

UNDERGRAD STUDENTS

5,616 full-time, 1,902 part-time. Students come from 21 states and territories; 15% are from out of state; 8% Black or African American, non-Hispanic/Latino; 14% Hispanic/Latino; 3% Asian, non-Hispanic/Latino; 0.1% Native Hawaiian or other Pacific Islander, non-Hispanic/Latino; 0.4% American Indian or Alaska Native, non-Hispanic/Latino; 2% Two or more races, non-Hispanic/Latino; 9% Race/ethnicity unknown; 0.2% international; 9% transferred in; 13% live on campus.

Freshmen

Admission: 4,837 applied, 3,166 admitted, 1,094 enrolled. ***Test scores:*** SAT critical reading scores over 500: 37%; SAT math scores over 500: 32%; SAT writing scores over 500: 31%; ACT scores over 18: 59%; SAT critical reading scores over 600: 6%; SAT math scores over 600: 5%; SAT writing scores over 600: 5%; ACT scores over 24: 17%; SAT critical reading scores over 700: 1%; ACT scores over 30: 1%.

Retention: 79% of full-time freshmen returned.

FACULTY

Total: 746, 44% full-time.

Student/faculty ratio: 15:1.

ACADEMICS

Calendar: semesters. *Degrees:* certificates, bachelor's, master's, doctoral, post-master's, and postbachelor's certificates.

Special study options: academic remediation for entering students, adult/continuing education programs, advanced placement credit, double majors, honors programs, independent study, internships, off-campus study, part-time degree program, services for LD students, student-designed majors, study abroad, summer session for credit. ***ROTC:*** Army (c).

Unusual degree programs: 3-2 public administration with University of Rhode Island.

Computers: 220 computers/terminals are available on campus for general student use. Students can access the following: campus intranet, computer help desk, free student e-mail accounts, online (class) grades, online (class) registration, online (class) schedules. Campuswide network is available. 100% of college-owned or -operated housing units are wired for high-speed Internet access. Wireless service is available via classrooms, computer centers, computer labs, dorm rooms, learning centers, libraries, student centers.

STUDENT LIFE

Housing options: coed, women-only, special housing for students with disabilities. Campus housing is university owned. Freshman applicants given priority for college housing.

Activities and organizations: drama/theater group, student-run newspaper, radio and television station, choral group, student government, newspaper (The Anchor), campus radio station (WXIN), Programming Board, Resident Student Association, national fraternities, national sororities.

Athletics Member NCAA. All Division III. ***Intercollegiate sports:*** baseball M, basketball M/W, cross-country running M/W, golf M/W, gymnastics W, lacrosse W, soccer M/W, softball W, swimming and diving W, tennis M/W, track and field M/W, volleyball W, wrestling M. ***Intramural sports:*** badminton M/W, basketball M/W, football M, soccer M/W, softball M/W, swimming and diving M/W, tennis M/W, volleyball M/W, water polo M/W.

Campus security: 24-hour emergency response devices and patrols, late-night transport/escort service, controlled dormitory access.

Student services: health clinic, personal/psychological counseling, women's center.

COSTS & FINANCIAL AID

Costs (2014–15) ***Tuition:*** state resident $6530 full-time, $272 per credit part-time; nonresident $17,228 full-time, $670 per credit part-time. Part-time tuition and fees vary according to course load. ***Required fees:*** $1072 full-time, $32 per credit part-time, $72 per term part-time. ***Room and board:*** $10,094; room only: $5744. Room and board charges vary according to housing facility. ***Payment plan:*** installment. ***Waivers:*** employees or children of employees.

Financial Aid Of all full-time matriculated undergraduates who enrolled in 2014, 4,682 applied for aid, 3,839 were judged to have need, 557 had their need fully met. In 2014, 135 non-need-based awards were made. ***Average percent of need met:*** 70. ***Average financial aid package:*** $8999. ***Average need-based loan:*** $4000. ***Average need-based gift aid:*** $5731. ***Average non-need-based aid:*** $2572. ***Average indebtedness upon graduation:*** $25,567.

APPLYING

Standardized Tests *Required:* SAT or ACT (for admission).

Options: electronic application, early admission.

Application fee: $50.

Required: essay or personal statement, high school transcript, 1 letter of recommendation, one letter from guidance counselor. ***Required for some:*** interview. ***Recommended:*** minimum 3.0 GPA.

Application deadlines: 3/15 (freshmen), 3/15 (out-of-state freshmen), 6/1 (transfers).

Notification: continuous (freshmen), continuous (out-of-state freshmen), continuous (transfers).

CONTACT

John McLaughlin, Director of Admissions, Rhode Island College, 600 Mount Pleasant Avenue, Providence, RI 02908-1927. *Phone:* 401-456-8234. *Toll-free phone:* 800-669-5760. *Fax:* 401-456-8817. *E-mail:* admissions@ric.edu.

Rhode Island School of Design

Providence, Rhode Island

http://www.risd.edu/

- **Independent** comprehensive, founded 1877
- **Urban** 19-acre campus with easy access to Boston
- **Endowment** $321.6 million
- **Coed** 2,014 undergraduate students, 100% full-time, 67% women, 33% men
- **Very difficult** entrance level, 41% of applicants were admitted

UNDERGRAD STUDENTS

2,014 full-time. Students come from 45 states and territories; 47 other countries; 94% are from out of state; 2% Black or African American, non-Hispanic/Latino; 8% Hispanic/Latino; 18% Asian, non-Hispanic/Latino; 0.1% Native Hawaiian or other Pacific Islander, non-Hispanic/Latino; 0.1% American Indian or Alaska Native, non-Hispanic/Latino; 4% Two or more races, non-Hispanic/Latino; 10% Race/ethnicity unknown; 26% international; 3% transferred in; 60% live on campus.

Freshmen

Admission: 2,408 applied, 993 admitted, 462 enrolled. ***Average high school GPA:*** 3.4. ***Test scores:*** SAT critical reading scores over 500: 87%; SAT math scores over 500: 94%; SAT writing scores over 500: 92%; ACT scores over 18: 100%; SAT critical reading scores over 600: 58%; SAT math scores over 600: 68%; SAT writing scores over 600: 65%; ACT scores over 24: 98%; SAT critical reading scores over 700: 17%; SAT math scores over 700: 31%; SAT writing scores over 700: 20%; ACT scores over 30: 46%.

Retention: 95% of full-time freshmen returned.

FACULTY

Total: 463, 33% full-time, 57% with terminal degrees.

Student/faculty ratio: 10:1.

ACADEMICS

Calendar: 4-1-4. *Degrees:* bachelor's and master's.

Special study options: advanced placement credit, cooperative education, double majors, honors programs, independent study, internships, off-campus study, services for LD students, study abroad. ***ROTC:*** Army (c).

Computers: 400 computers/terminals are available on campus for general student use. Students can access the following: campus intranet, computer help desk, free student e-mail accounts, online (class) grades, online (class) registration, online (class) schedules. Campuswide network is available. 100% of college-owned or -operated housing units are wired for high-speed Internet access. Wireless service is available via entire campus.

STUDENT LIFE
Housing options: on-campus residence required through sophomore year; coed. Campus housing is university owned. Freshman campus housing is guaranteed.

Activities and organizations: drama/theater group, student-run newspaper, choral group, athletic clubs, Religious clubs, South Asian Student Association, RISD Global Initiative, Community Service Club.

Athletics ***Intramural sports:*** basketball M/W, fencing M(c)/W(c), football M(c)/W(c), ice hockey M/W, skiing (downhill) M(c)/W(c), soccer M/W, volleyball M/W.

Campus security: 24-hour emergency response devices and patrols, late-night transport/escort service, controlled dormitory access.

Student services: health clinic, personal/psychological counseling, legal services.

COSTS & FINANCIAL AID
Costs (2014–15) ***Comprehensive fee:*** $57,234 includes full-time tuition ($44,284), mandatory fees ($310), and room and board ($12,640). ***College room only:*** $7167. Room and board charges vary according to board plan and housing facility. ***Payment plan:*** installment. ***Waivers:*** employees or children of employees.

Financial Aid Of all full-time matriculated undergraduates who enrolled in 2013, 919 applied for aid, 780 were judged to have need, 20 had their need fully met. In 2013, 20 non-need-based awards were made. ***Average percent of need met:*** 62. ***Average financial aid package:*** $28,778. ***Average need-based loan:*** $5500. ***Average need-based gift aid:*** $24,337. ***Average non-need-based aid:*** $10,000. ***Average indebtedness upon graduation:*** $30,376.

APPLYING
Standardized Tests *Required:* SAT or ACT (for admission).

Options: electronic application, early admission, early decision, deferred entrance.

Application fee: $60.

Required: essay or personal statement, high school transcript, portfolio, drawing assignments. ***Recommended:*** 3 letters of recommendation.

Application deadlines: 2/1 (freshmen), 2/1 (transfers).

Early decision deadline: 11/1.

CONTACT
Mr. Edward Newhall, Associate Vice President for Enrollment, Rhode Island School of Design, 2 College Street, Providence, RI 02903-2784. *Phone:* 401-454-6300. *Toll-free phone:* 800-364-7473. *Fax:* 401-454-6309. *E-mail:* admissions@risd.edu.

★ Roger Williams University
Bristol, Rhode Island
http://www.rwu.edu/

- **Independent** comprehensive, founded 1956
- **Small-town** 140-acre campus with easy access to Boston
- **Endowment** $90.2 million
- **Coed** 4,610 undergraduate students, 87% full-time, 50% women, 50% men
- **Moderately difficult** entrance level, 78% of applicants were admitted

UNDERGRAD STUDENTS
4,030 full-time, 580 part-time. Students come from 44 states and territories; 62 other countries; 91% are from out of state; 2% Black or African American, non-Hispanic/Latino; 5% Hispanic/Latino; 2% Asian, non-Hispanic/Latino; 0.9% American Indian or Alaska Native, non-Hispanic/Latino; 11% Race/ethnicity unknown; 5% international; 2% transferred in; 77% live on campus.

Freshmen
Admission: 9,913 applied, 7,726 admitted, 1,152 enrolled. ***Average high school GPA:*** 3.3. ***Test scores:*** SAT critical reading scores over 500: 82%; SAT math scores over 500: 88%; SAT writing scores over 500: 81%; ACT scores over 18: 98%; SAT critical reading scores over 600: 25%; SAT math scores over 600: 31%; SAT writing scores over 600: 28%; ACT scores over 24: 70%; SAT critical reading scores over 700: 2%; SAT math scores over 700: 2%; SAT writing scores over 700: 3%; ACT scores over 30: 9%.

Retention: 79% of full-time freshmen returned.

FACULTY
Total: 410, 50% full-time, 49% with terminal degrees.

Student/faculty ratio: 15:1.

ACADEMICS
Calendar: semesters. *Degrees:* certificates, associate, bachelor's, master's, doctoral, and postbachelor's certificates.

Special study options: accelerated degree program, adult/continuing education programs, advanced placement credit, cooperative education, distance learning, double majors, English as a second language, external degree program, freshman honors college, honors programs, independent study, internships, part-time degree program, services for LD students, student-designed majors, study abroad, summer session for credit. ***ROTC:*** Army (c).

Computers: 270 computers/terminals are available on campus for general student use. Students can access the following: campus intranet, computer help desk, free student e-mail accounts, online (class) registration, online (class) schedules. Campuswide network is available. 100% of college-owned or -operated housing units are wired for high-speed Internet access. Wireless service is available via classrooms, computer centers, computer labs, dorm rooms, learning centers, libraries, student centers.

STUDENT LIFE
Housing options: on-campus residence required through sophomore year; coed, special housing for students with disabilities. Campus housing is university owned and leased by the school. Freshman campus housing is guaranteed.

Activities and organizations: drama/theater group, student-run newspaper, radio station, choral group, Campus Entertainment Network, Dance Club, Inter Residence Hall Association, WQRI 88.3 radio station, Inter Class Council.

Athletics Member NCAA. All Division III. ***Intercollegiate sports:*** baseball M, basketball M/W, cheerleading M(c)/W(c), crew M(c)/W(c), cross-country running M/W, equestrian sports M/W, field hockey W, golf M, lacrosse M/W, rugby M(c)/W(c), sailing M/W, soccer M/W, softball W, swimming and diving M/W, tennis M/W, track and field M/W, volleyball M(c)/W, wrestling M. ***Intramural sports:*** basketball M/W, football M/W, ice hockey M(c), racquetball M/W, skiing (downhill) M/W, soccer M/W, softball M/W, squash M(c)/W(c), tennis M/W, track and field M/W(c), ultimate Frisbee M/W, volleyball M/W, water polo M(c)/W(c).

Campus security: 24-hour emergency response devices and patrols, student patrols, late-night transport/escort service, controlled dormitory access.

Student services: health clinic, personal/psychological counseling, women's center.

COSTS & FINANCIAL AID
Costs (2014–15) ***Comprehensive fee:*** $46,296 includes full-time tuition ($29,976), mandatory fees ($1774), and room and board ($14,546). Full-time tuition and fees vary according to class time, course load, and program. Part-time tuition: $966 per course. Part-time tuition and fees vary according to class time. No tuition increase for student's term of enrollment. ***Room and board:*** Room and board charges vary according to board plan and housing facility. ***Payment plans:*** installment, deferred payment. ***Waivers:*** employees or children of employees.

Financial Aid Of all full-time matriculated undergraduates who enrolled in 2014, 2,990 applied for aid, 2,440 were judged to have need, 234 had their need fully met. 1,554 Federal Work-Study jobs (averaging $2104). In 2014, 484 non-need-based awards were made. ***Average percent of need met:*** 89. ***Average financial aid package:*** $20,466. ***Average need-based loan:*** $4752. ***Average need-based gift aid:*** $13,501. ***Average non-need-based aid:*** $11,527. ***Average indebtedness upon graduation:*** $40,612. ***Financial aid deadline:*** 2/1.

APPLYING
Standardized Tests *Required for some:* SAT or ACT (for admission).

Options: electronic application, early action, deferred entrance.

Application fee: $50.

Required: essay or personal statement, high school transcript, 1 letter of recommendation. ***Required for some:*** Programs that require portfolio reviews, auditions, specific preparatory courses for admission include visual arts studies, graphic design communications, architecture, creative writing, dance and theater.

A ★ indicates that the school has detailed information with a Premium Profile on Petersons.com.

Application deadlines: 2/1 (freshmen), 2/1 (out-of-state freshmen), rolling (transfers), 11/1 (early action).

Notification: continuous until 2/15 (freshmen), continuous until 2/15 (out-of-state freshmen), continuous (transfers), 12/5 (early action).

CONTACT

Admissions Office (Undergraduate), Roger Williams University, 1 Old Ferry Road, Bristol, RI 02809. *Phone:* 401-254-3500. *Toll-free phone:* 800-458-7144. *Fax:* 401-254-3557. *E-mail:* admit@rwu.edu.

Salve Regina University

Newport, Rhode Island

http://www.salve.edu/

- **Independent Roman Catholic** comprehensive, founded 1934
- **Suburban** 80-acre campus with easy access to Boston, Providence
- **Endowment** $58.6 million
- **Coed** 2,121 undergraduate students, 92% full-time, 70% women, 30% men
- **Moderately difficult** entrance level, 71% of applicants were admitted

UNDERGRAD STUDENTS

1,959 full-time, 162 part-time. Students come from 34 states and territories; 18 other countries; 78% are from out of state; 2% Black or African American, non-Hispanic/Latino; 7% Hispanic/Latino; 1% Asian, non-Hispanic/Latino; 0.2% American Indian or Alaska Native, non-Hispanic/Latino; 2% Two or more races, non-Hispanic/Latino; 8% Race/ethnicity unknown; 2% international; 2% transferred in; 58% live on campus.

Freshmen

Admission: 4,810 applied, 3,412 admitted, 623 enrolled. ***Average high school GPA:*** 3.2. ***Test scores:*** SAT critical reading scores over 500: 83%; SAT math scores over 500: 84%; SAT writing scores over 500: 79%; ACT scores over 18: 100%; SAT critical reading scores over 600: 24%; SAT math scores over 600: 26%; SAT writing scores over 600: 26%; ACT scores over 24: 53%; SAT critical reading scores over 700: 2%; SAT math scores over 700: 2%; SAT writing scores over 700: 1%; ACT scores over 30: 4%.

Retention: 84% of full-time freshmen returned.

FACULTY

Total: 277, 43% full-time, 44% with terminal degrees.

Student/faculty ratio: 13:1.

ACADEMICS

Calendar: semesters. *Degrees:* certificates, associate, bachelor's, master's, doctoral, post-master's, and postbachelor's certificates.

Special study options: accelerated degree program, adult/continuing education programs, advanced placement credit, double majors, English as a second language, honors programs, independent study, internships, off-campus study, part-time degree program, services for LD students, study abroad, summer session for credit. ***ROTC:*** Army (c).

Unusual degree programs: 3-2 business administration; administration of justice, business administration, holistic counseling, international relations, management, rehabilitation counseling.

Computers: 163 computers/terminals are available on campus for general student use. Students can access the following: campus intranet, computer help desk, free student e-mail accounts, online (class) grades, online (class) registration, online (class) schedules. Campuswide network is available. 95% of college-owned or -operated housing units are wired for high-speed Internet access. Wireless service is available via entire campus.

STUDENT LIFE

Housing options: on-campus residence required through sophomore year; coed, men-only, women-only, special housing for students with disabilities. Campus housing is university owned and leased by the school. Freshman campus housing is guaranteed.

Activities and organizations: drama/theater group, student-run newspaper, radio station, choral group, Orpheus Musical Society, Student Government Association, Student Outdoor Adventures, Student Nurse Organization, Stagefright Theatre Company.

Athletics Member NCAA. All Division III. ***Intercollegiate sports:*** baseball M, basketball M/W, cross-country running M/W, field hockey W, football M, ice hockey M/W, lacrosse M/W, rugby M(c)/W(c), sailing M/W, soccer M/W, softball W, tennis M/W, track and field W, volleyball W. ***Intramural sports:*** baseball M, basketball M/W, cheerleading W(c), field hockey W, football M/W, soccer M/W, softball M/W, tennis M/W, track and field W, volleyball M/W, weight lifting M/W.

Campus security: 24-hour emergency response devices and patrols, late-night transport/escort service, controlled dormitory access.

Student services: health clinic, personal/psychological counseling.

COSTS & FINANCIAL AID

Costs (2014–15) ***Comprehensive fee:*** $48,550 includes full-time tuition ($35,140), mandatory fees ($550), and room and board ($12,860). Full-time tuition and fees vary according to location. Part-time tuition: $1171 per credit. Part-time tuition and fees vary according to course load and location. ***Required fees:*** $50 per term part-time. ***Room and board:*** Room and board charges vary according to board plan and housing facility. ***Payment plan:*** installment. ***Waivers:*** employees or children of employees.

Financial Aid Of all full-time matriculated undergraduates who enrolled in 2013, 1,606 applied for aid, 1,442 were judged to have need, 153 had their need fully met. 474 Federal Work-Study jobs (averaging $537). 110 state and other part-time jobs (averaging $1190). In 2013, 276 non-need-based awards were made. ***Average percent of need met:*** 68. ***Average financial aid package:*** $23,472. ***Average need-based loan:*** $4611. ***Average need-based gift aid:*** $18,602. ***Average non-need-based aid:*** $11,111. ***Average indebtedness upon graduation:*** $38,885.

APPLYING

Standardized Tests *Required for some:* SAT (for admission), SAT or ACT (for admission).

Options: electronic application, early action, deferred entrance.

Application fee: $50.

Required: essay or personal statement, high school transcript, 2 letters of recommendation. ***Recommended:*** minimum 2.7 GPA.

Application deadlines: 2/1 (freshmen), rolling (transfers), 11/1 (early action).

Notification: 12/25 (freshmen), continuous (transfers), 12/25 (early action).

CONTACT

Dean Colleen Emerson, Dean of Undergraduate Admissions, Salve Regina University, 100 Ochre Point Avenue, Newport, RI 02840-4192. *Phone:* 401-341-2908. *Toll-free phone:* 888-GO SALVE. *Fax:* 401-848-2823. *E-mail:* sruadmis@salve.edu.

★ University of Rhode Island

Kingston, Rhode Island

http://www.uri.edu/

- **State-supported** university, founded 1892
- **Small-town** 1200-acre campus
- **Coed** 13,589 undergraduate students, 89% full-time, 54% women, 46% men
- **Moderately difficult** entrance level, 76% of applicants were admitted

UNDERGRAD STUDENTS

12,139 full-time, 1,450 part-time. Students come from 44 states and territories; 49 other countries; 44% are from out of state; 5% Black or African American, non-Hispanic/Latino; 9% Hispanic/Latino; 3% Asian, non-Hispanic/Latino; 0.2% American Indian or Alaska Native, non-Hispanic/Latino; 3% Two or more races, non-Hispanic/Latino; 9% Race/ethnicity unknown; 2% international; 4% transferred in; 45% live on campus.

Freshmen

Admission: 20,928 applied, 15,846 admitted, 3,145 enrolled. ***Average high school GPA:*** 3.4. ***Test scores:*** SAT critical reading scores over 500: 76%; SAT math scores over 500: 80%; SAT writing scores over 500: 72%; ACT scores over 18: 96%; SAT critical reading scores over 600: 23%; SAT math scores over 600: 29%; SAT writing scores over 600: 20%; ACT scores over 24: 55%; SAT critical reading scores over 700: 2%; SAT math scores over 700: 3%; SAT writing scores over 700: 2%; ACT scores over 30: 7%.

Retention: 82% of full-time freshmen returned.

FACULTY
Total: 1,123, 63% full-time, 56% with terminal degrees.
Student/faculty ratio: 16:1.

ACADEMICS
Calendar: semesters. *Degrees:* bachelor's, master's, doctoral, and postbachelor's certificates.
Special study options: academic remediation for entering students, accelerated degree program, adult/continuing education programs, advanced placement credit, cooperative education, distance learning, double majors, English as a second language, honors programs, independent study, internships, off-campus study, part-time degree program, services for LD students, study abroad, summer session for credit. ***ROTC:*** Army (b).
Unusual degree programs: 3-2 engineering; nursing; accounting, pharmacy, chemistry, education, psychology.
Computers: 2,500 computers/terminals are available on campus for general student use. Students can access the following: campus intranet, computer help desk, free student e-mail accounts, online (class) grades, online (class) registration, online (class) schedules. Campuswide network is available. 100% of college-owned or -operated housing units are wired for high-speed Internet access. Wireless service is available via entire campus.

STUDENT LIFE
Housing options: coed, cooperative, special housing for students with disabilities. Campus housing is university owned and leased by the school. Freshman campus housing is guaranteed.
Activities and organizations: drama/theater group, student-run newspaper, radio and television station, choral group, marching band, Student Entertainment Committee, student radio station, Intramural sport clubs, Student Alumni Association, student newspaper, national fraternities, national sororities.
Athletics Member NCAA. All Division I. ***Intercollegiate sports:*** baseball M(s), basketball M(s), crew M(s), cross-country running M(s)/W(s), football M(s), golf M(s), soccer M(s)/W(s), softball W(s), swimming and diving W(s), tennis W(s), track and field M(s)/W(s), volleyball W(s). ***Intramural sports:*** equestrian sports M(c)/W(c), gymnastics W(c), ice hockey M(c)/W(c), lacrosse M(c)/W(c), rugby M(c)/W(c), sailing M(c)/W(c), skiing (downhill) M(c)/W(c), swimming and diving M(c), ultimate Frisbee M(c)/W(c), volleyball M(c), wrestling M(c).
Campus security: 24-hour emergency response devices and patrols, student patrols, late-night transport/escort service, controlled dormitory access.
Student services: health clinic, personal/psychological counseling, women's center.

COSTS & FINANCIAL AID
Costs (2014–15) ***Tuition:*** state resident $10,878 full-time, $453 per credit hour part-time; nonresident $26,444 full-time, $1102 per credit hour part-time. Full-time tuition and fees vary according to course load, location, and reciprocity agreements. Part-time tuition and fees vary according to course load, location, and reciprocity agreements. ***Required fees:*** $1628 full-time, $3 per credit hour part-time, $58 per term part-time. ***Room and board:*** $7256; room only: $4240. Room and board charges vary according to board plan and housing facility. ***Payment plan:*** installment. ***Waivers:*** minority students, senior citizens, and employees or children of employees.
Financial Aid Of all full-time matriculated undergraduates who enrolled in 2014, 11,732 applied for aid, 10,009 were judged to have need, 8,409 had their need fully met. In 2014, 828 non-need-based awards were made. ***Average percent of need met:*** 59. ***Average financial aid package:*** $15,819. ***Average need-based loan:*** $5636. ***Average need-based gift aid:*** $9713. ***Average non-need-based aid:*** $6564. ***Average indebtedness upon graduation:*** $30,731.

APPLYING
Standardized Tests *Required:* SAT or ACT (for admission).
Options: electronic application, early admission, early action, deferred entrance.
Application fee: $65.
Required: essay or personal statement, high school transcript, 1 letter of recommendation, List of senior courses (admission is contingent upon successful completion of all your current coursework); Official SAT* or ACT Scores (MUST be sent electronically by the testing service: the URI ID code is 3919 for SAT and 3818 for ACT); pharmacy applicants are required to provide two letters of. ***Required for some:*** 2 letters of recommendation, List of senior courses (admission is contingent upon successful completion of all your current coursework); Official SAT* or ACT Scores (MUST be sent electronically by the testing service: the URI ID code is 3919 for SAT and 3818 for ACT); pharmacy applicants are required to provide two letters of.
Application deadlines: 2/1 (freshmen), 2/1 (out-of-state freshmen), 6/1 (transfers), 12/1 (early action).
Notification: 3/31 (freshmen), 3/31 (out-of-state freshmen), continuous (transfers), 1/31 (early action).

CONTACT
Ms. Joanne Lynch, Assistant Dean of Admissions, University of Rhode Island, Undergraduate Admission Office, Newman Hall, 14 Upper College Road, Kingston, RI 02881. *Phone:* 401-874-7110. *Fax:* 401-874-5523. *E-mail:* lynch@uri.edu.

SOUTH CAROLINA

Anderson University
Anderson, South Carolina
http://www.andersonuniversity.edu/

- **Independent Baptist** comprehensive, founded 1911
- **Suburban** 271-acre campus with easy access to Greenville
- **Endowment** $32.2 million
- **Coed** 2,630 undergraduate students, 82% full-time, 65% women, 35% men
- **Minimally difficult** entrance level, 65% of applicants were admitted

UNDERGRAD STUDENTS
2,152 full-time, 478 part-time. Students come from 35 states and territories; 22 other countries; 18% are from out of state; 11% Black or African American, non-Hispanic/Latino; 3% Hispanic/Latino; 0.9% Asian, non-Hispanic/Latino; 0.9% Native Hawaiian or other Pacific Islander, non-Hispanic/Latino; 0.7% American Indian or Alaska Native, non-Hispanic/Latino; 1% international; 4% transferred in; 47% live on campus.

Freshmen
Admission: 2,190 applied, 1,424 admitted, 538 enrolled. ***Average high school GPA:*** 3.54. ***Test scores:*** SAT critical reading scores over 500: 67%; SAT math scores over 500: 68%; SAT writing scores over 500: 62%; ACT scores over 18: 93%; SAT critical reading scores over 600: 26%; SAT math scores over 600: 21%; SAT writing scores over 600: 21%; ACT scores over 24: 39%; SAT critical reading scores over 700: 4%; SAT math scores over 700: 3%; SAT writing scores over 700: 2%; ACT scores over 30: 4%.
Retention: 77% of full-time freshmen returned.

FACULTY
Total: 259, 38% full-time, 56% with terminal degrees.
Student/faculty ratio: 16:1.

ACADEMICS
Calendar: semesters. *Degrees:* bachelor's, master's, and doctoral.
Special study options: academic remediation for entering students, accelerated degree program, adult/continuing education programs, advanced placement credit, cooperative education, distance learning, double majors, honors programs, independent study, internships, part-time degree program, services for LD students, study abroad, summer session for credit. ***ROTC:*** Army (c), Air Force (c).
Computers: 192 computers/terminals are available on campus for general student use. Students can access the following: campus intranet, computer help desk, free student e-mail accounts, online (class) grades, online (class) registration, online (class) schedules. Campuswide network is available. 100% of college-owned or -operated housing units are wired for high-speed Internet access. Wireless service is available via entire campus.

STUDENT LIFE

Housing options: on-campus residence required through sophomore year; men-only, women-only. Campus housing is university owned. Freshman campus housing is guaranteed.

Activities and organizations: drama/theater group, student-run newspaper, choral group, Baptist Campus Ministries, Fellowship of Christian Athletes, Student Government Association, Gamma Beta Phi, Student Alumni Council.

Athletics Member NCAA. All Division II. ***Intercollegiate sports:*** baseball M(s), basketball M(s)/W(s), cheerleading W(s), cross-country running M(s)/W(s), golf M(s)/W(s), soccer M(s)/W(s), softball W(s), tennis M(s)/W(s), track and field M(s)/W(s), volleyball W(s), wrestling M(s). ***Intramural sports:*** basketball M/W, football M/W, racquetball M/W, softball M/W, table tennis M/W, ultimate Frisbee M/W, volleyball M/W, weight lifting M.

Campus security: 24-hour emergency response devices and patrols, late-night transport/escort service, controlled dormitory access.

Student services: health clinic, personal/psychological counseling.

COSTS & FINANCIAL AID

Costs (2014–15) ***Comprehensive fee:*** $32,424 includes full-time tuition ($21,660), mandatory fees ($2090), and room and board ($8674). Full-time tuition and fees vary according to course load and program. Part-time tuition and fees vary according to program. ***College room only:*** $4490. Room and board charges vary according to board plan and housing facility. ***Payment plan:*** installment. ***Waivers:*** employees or children of employees.

Financial Aid Of all full-time matriculated undergraduates who enrolled in 2013, 2,048 applied for aid, 1,808 were judged to have need, 443 had their need fully met. 100 Federal Work-Study jobs (averaging $1427). 167 state and other part-time jobs (averaging $1020). In 2013, 301 non-need-based awards were made. ***Average percent of need met:*** 68. ***Average financial aid package:*** $17,688. ***Average need-based loan:*** $5145. ***Average need-based gift aid:*** $14,556. ***Average non-need-based aid:*** $10,764. ***Average indebtedness upon graduation:*** $27,711. ***Financial aid deadline:*** 7/30.

APPLYING

Standardized Tests *Required:* SAT or ACT (for admission).

Options: electronic application, deferred entrance.

Application fee: $25.

Required: high school transcript. ***Required for some:*** essay or personal statement, 2 letters of recommendation, interview. ***Recommended:*** minimum 2.9 GPA.

Notification: continuous (freshmen), continuous (transfers).

CONTACT

Mrs. Pam Bryant-Ross, Anderson University, 316 Boulevard, Anderson, SC 29621-4035. *Phone:* 864-231-2030. *Toll-free phone:* 800-542-3594.

The Art Institute of Charleston, a branch of The Art Institute of Atlanta

Charleston, South Carolina

http://www.artinstitutes.edu/charleston/

- **Proprietary** 4-year, founded 2007, part of Education Management Corporation
- **Urban** campus
- **Coed**

ACADEMICS

Calendar: quarters. *Degrees:* certificates, associate, and bachelor's.

CONTACT

The Art Institute of Charleston, a branch of The Art Institute of Atlanta, 24 North Market Street, Charleston, SC 29401. *Phone:* 843-727-3500. *Toll-free phone:* 866-211-0107.

Bob Jones University

Greenville, South Carolina

http://www.bju.edu/

- **Independent Christian** university, founded 1927
- **Urban** 225-acre campus
- **Coed** 2,721 undergraduate students, 92% full-time, 56% women, 44% men
- **Minimally difficult** entrance level, 81% of applicants were admitted

UNDERGRAD STUDENTS

2,496 full-time, 225 part-time. Students come from 54 states and territories; 40 other countries; 73% are from out of state; 1% Black or African American, non-Hispanic/Latino; 6% Hispanic/Latino; 2% Asian, non-Hispanic/Latino; 0.4% Native Hawaiian or other Pacific Islander, non-Hispanic/Latino; 0.3% American Indian or Alaska Native, non-Hispanic/Latino; 3% Two or more races, non-Hispanic/Latino; 7% Race/ethnicity unknown; 5% international; 3% transferred in; 74% live on campus.

Freshmen

Admission: 1,049 applied, 849 admitted, 610 enrolled. ***Average high school GPA:*** 3.13. ***Test scores:*** ACT scores over 18: 87%; ACT scores over 24: 50%; ACT scores over 30: 7%.

Retention: 79% of full-time freshmen returned.

FACULTY

Total: 220, 86% full-time, 61% with terminal degrees.

Student/faculty ratio: 14:1.

ACADEMICS

Calendar: semesters. *Degrees:* associate, bachelor's, master's, doctoral, and post-master's certificates.

Special study options: accelerated degree program, adult/continuing education programs, advanced placement credit, distance learning, English as a second language, internships, off-campus study, part-time degree program, services for LD students, summer session for credit.

Computers: 450 computers/terminals and 500 ports are available on campus for general student use. Students can access the following: campus intranet, computer help desk, free student e-mail accounts, online (class) grades, online (class) registration, online (class) schedules. Campuswide network is available. 100% of college-owned or -operated housing units are wired for high-speed Internet access. Wireless service is available via classrooms, computer labs, dorm rooms, learning centers, libraries, student centers.

STUDENT LIFE

Housing options: on-campus residence required through senior year; men-only, women-only, special housing for students with disabilities. Campus housing is university owned. Freshman campus housing is guaranteed.

Activities and organizations: drama/theater group, student-run newspaper, radio and television station, choral group, Community Service Council, Missions Advance, Societies, Mission Prayer Band, University Business Association.

Athletics Member NCCAA. ***Intercollegiate sports:*** basketball M/W, cross-country running M/W, golf M/W, soccer M/W. ***Intramural sports:*** badminton M/W, basketball M/W, cheerleading W, racquetball M, soccer M/W, softball M/W, table tennis M/W, tennis M/W, volleyball M/W, water polo W.

Campus security: 24-hour patrols, student patrols, late-night transport/escort service, controlled dormitory access, 24/7 emergency dispatcher.

Student services: health clinic, personal/psychological counseling.

COSTS & FINANCIAL AID

Costs (2014–15) ***Comprehensive fee:*** $20,310 includes full-time tuition ($13,570), mandatory fees ($650), and room and board ($6090). Full-time tuition and fees vary according to course load and program. Part-time tuition: $680 per credit hour. Part-time tuition and fees vary according to course load and program. ***Payment plan:*** installment. ***Waivers:*** senior citizens and employees or children of employees.

Financial Aid Of all full-time matriculated undergraduates who enrolled in 2013, 1,502 applied for aid, 1,502 were judged to have need, 543 had their need fully met. ***Average percent of need met:*** 24.

APPLYING
Standardized Tests *Required:* ACT (for admission).

Options: electronic application.

Required: essay or personal statement, high school transcript, 3 letters of recommendation.

Application deadlines: 8/1 (freshmen), 8/1 (transfers).

Notification: continuous (freshmen), continuous (transfers).

CONTACT
Mr. Gary Deedrick, Director of Admission, Bob Jones University, 1700 Wade Hampton Boulevard, Greenville, SC 29614. *Phone:* 864-242-5100. *Toll-free phone:* 800-252-6363. *Fax:* 800-232-9258. *E-mail:* admission@bju.edu.

Brown Mackie College–Greenville

Greenville, South Carolina

http://www.brownmackie.edu/greenville/

- **Proprietary** primarily 2-year, part of Education Management Corporation
- **Coed**

ACADEMICS
Degrees: certificates, associate, and bachelor's.

CONTACT
Brown Mackie College–Greenville, Two Liberty Square, 75 Beattie Place, Suite 100, Greenville, SC 29601. *Phone:* 864-239-5300. *Toll-free phone:* 877-479-8465.

Charleston Southern University

Charleston, South Carolina

http://www.charlestonsouthern.edu/

- **Independent Baptist** comprehensive, founded 1964
- **Suburban** 500-acre campus
- **Endowment** $16.9 million
- **Coed** 2,967 undergraduate students, 89% full-time, 63% women, 37% men
- **Moderately difficult** entrance level, 59% of applicants were admitted

UNDERGRAD STUDENTS
2,638 full-time, 329 part-time. Students come from 38 states and territories; 17 other countries; 15% are from out of state; 28% Black or African American, non-Hispanic/Latino; 3% Hispanic/Latino; 1% Asian, non-Hispanic/Latino; 0.1% Native Hawaiian or other Pacific Islander, non-Hispanic/Latino; 0.5% American Indian or Alaska Native, non-Hispanic/Latino; 3% Two or more races, non-Hispanic/Latino; 4% Race/ethnicity unknown; 0.8% international; 11% transferred in; 49% live on campus.

Freshmen
Admission: 4,197 applied, 2,463 admitted, 652 enrolled. ***Average high school GPA:*** 3.63.

Retention: 65% of full-time freshmen returned.

FACULTY
Total: 275, 63% full-time.

Student/faculty ratio: 15:1.

ACADEMICS
Calendar: 4-4-1. *Degrees:* bachelor's, master's, and post-master's certificates.

Special study options: academic remediation for entering students, accelerated degree program, advanced placement credit, double majors, honors programs, internships, off-campus study, part-time degree program, services for LD students, summer session for credit. ***ROTC:*** Army (b), Air Force (b).

Unusual degree programs: 3-2 engineering with University of South Carolina.

Computers: 250 computers/terminals are available on campus for general student use. Students can access the following: computer help desk, free student e-mail accounts, online (class) grades, online (class) registration, online (class) schedules, online course work. Campuswide network is available. 100% of college-owned or -operated housing units are wired for high-speed Internet access. Wireless service is available via entire campus.

STUDENT LIFE
Housing options: on-campus residence required for freshman year; men-only, women-only. Campus housing is university owned. Freshman applicants given priority for college housing.

Activities and organizations: drama/theater group, student-run newspaper, choral group, marching band, student government, Baptist Student Union, Fellowship of Christian Athletes, national fraternities, national sororities.

Athletics Member NCAA. All Division I except football (Division I-AA). ***Intercollegiate sports:*** baseball M(s), basketball M(s)/W(s), cheerleading M/W, cross-country running M(s)/W(s), golf M(s)/W(s), soccer W(s), softball W(s), tennis W(s), track and field M(s)/W(s), volleyball W(s). ***Intramural sports:*** basketball M/W, football M/W, soccer M/W, softball M/W, volleyball M/W.

Campus security: 24-hour emergency response devices and patrols, late-night transport/escort service, controlled dormitory access.

Student services: personal/psychological counseling.

COSTS & FINANCIAL AID
Costs (2014–15) ***Comprehensive fee:*** $31,840 includes full-time tuition ($22,800), mandatory fees ($40), and room and board ($9000). Full-time tuition and fees vary according to program. Part-time tuition: $470 per credit hour. Part-time tuition and fees vary according to program. ***Required fees:*** $40 per term part-time. ***Room and board:*** Room and board charges vary according to board plan. ***Waivers:*** employees or children of employees.

Financial Aid Of all full-time matriculated undergraduates who enrolled in 2007, 1,968 applied for aid, 1,749 were judged to have need, 421 had their need fully met. 614 Federal Work-Study jobs (averaging $1406). In 2007, 306 non-need-based awards were made. ***Average percent of need met:*** 73. ***Average financial aid package:*** $15,036. ***Average need-based loan:*** $4804. ***Average need-based gift aid:*** $11,008. ***Average non-need-based aid:*** $10,832. ***Average indebtedness upon graduation:*** $20,252.

APPLYING
Standardized Tests *Required:* SAT or ACT (for admission).

Options: electronic application.

Application fee: $40.

Required: high school transcript, minimum 2.0 GPA. ***Required for some:*** essay or personal statement, 1 letter of recommendation, interview.

Application deadlines: rolling (freshmen), rolling (transfers).

Notification: continuous (freshmen), continuous (transfers).

CONTACT
Mr. Jim Rhoden, Director of Enrollment Management, Charleston Southern University, Charleston, SC 29423-8087. *Phone:* 843-863-7050. *Toll-free phone:* 800-947-7474. *E-mail:* enroll@csuniv.edu.

The Citadel, The Military College of South Carolina

Charleston, South Carolina

http://www.citadel.edu/

- **State-supported** comprehensive, founded 1842
- **Suburban** 300-acre campus
- **Endowment** $70.2 million
- **Coed, primarily men** 2,763 undergraduate students, 92% full-time, 10% women, 90% men
- **Moderately difficult** entrance level, 76% of applicants were admitted

UNDERGRAD STUDENTS
2,531 full-time, 232 part-time. 42% are from out of state; 8% Black or African American, non-Hispanic/Latino; 7% Hispanic/Latino; 2% Asian, non-Hispanic/Latino; 0.3% Native Hawaiian or other Pacific Islander, non-Hispanic/Latino; 1% American Indian or Alaska Native, non-Hispanic/Latino; 3% Two or more races, non-Hispanic/Latino; 0.3% Race/ethnicity unknown; 1% international; 3% transferred in; 100% live on campus.

Freshmen
Admission: 2,625 applied, 1,983 admitted, 618 enrolled. ***Average high school GPA:*** 3.59. ***Test scores:*** SAT critical reading scores over 500: 72%; SAT math scores over 500: 78%; ACT scores over 18: 99%; SAT critical reading scores over 600: 24%; SAT math scores over 600: 26%; ACT scores over 24: 41%; SAT critical reading scores over 700: 3%; SAT math scores over 700: 2%; ACT scores over 30: 4%.

Retention: 86% of full-time freshmen returned.

FACULTY
Total: 289, 65% full-time, 74% with terminal degrees.

Student/faculty ratio: 13:1.

ACADEMICS
Calendar: semesters. *Degrees:* bachelor's, master's, and post-master's certificates.

Special study options: advanced placement credit, cooperative education, distance learning, double majors, English as a second language, honors programs, independent study, internships, off-campus study, part-time degree program, services for LD students, study abroad, summer session for credit. ***ROTC:*** Army (b), Navy (b), Air Force (b).

Computers: 350 computers/terminals are available on campus for general student use. Students can access the following: campus intranet, computer help desk, free student e-mail accounts, online (class) grades, online (class) registration, online (class) schedules. Campuswide network is available. Wireless service is available via classrooms, dorm rooms, libraries, student centers.

STUDENT LIFE
Housing options: on-campus residence required through senior year; coed. Campus housing is university owned. Freshman campus housing is guaranteed.

Activities and organizations: student-run newspaper, choral group, marching band, The Republican Society, Semper Fi Society, HESS Majors, Rod & Gun Club, Cordell Airborne Rangers.

Athletics Member NCAA. All Division I except football (Division I-AA). ***Intercollegiate sports:*** baseball M(s), basketball M(s), cross-country running M(s)/W(s), golf W(s), ice hockey M(c), lacrosse M(c), riflery M(s)/W(s), rugby M(c)/W(c), soccer M(c)/W(s), tennis M(s), track and field M(s)/W(s), volleyball W(s), wrestling M(s). ***Intramural sports:*** badminton M/W, basketball M/W, football M, golf M/W, racquetball M/W, soccer M/W, softball M/W, swimming and diving M/W, table tennis M/W, tennis M/W, track and field M/W, ultimate Frisbee M/W, volleyball M/W, weight lifting M/W, wrestling M/W.

Campus security: 24-hour patrols.

Student services: health clinic, personal/psychological counseling.

COSTS & FINANCIAL AID
Costs (2014–15) ***Tuition:*** state resident $11,098 full-time, $432 per credit part-time; nonresident $30,706 full-time, $792 per credit part-time. ***Required fees:*** $1470 full-time. ***Room and board:*** $6381. ***Waivers:*** senior citizens and employees or children of employees.

Financial Aid Of all full-time matriculated undergraduates who enrolled in 2014, 1,890 applied for aid, 1,457 were judged to have need, 337 had their need fully met. 82 Federal Work-Study jobs (averaging $2500). In 2014, 499 non-need-based awards were made. ***Average percent of need met:*** 58. ***Average financial aid package:*** $14,819. ***Average need-based loan:*** $4404. ***Average need-based gift aid:*** $14,451. ***Average non-need-based aid:*** $15,380. ***Average indebtedness upon graduation:*** $29,701.

APPLYING
Standardized Tests *Required:* SAT or ACT (for admission).

Options: electronic application.

Application fee: $40.

Required: high school transcript. ***Recommended:*** interview.

Application deadlines: rolling (freshmen), rolling (transfers).

Notification: continuous (freshmen), continuous (transfers).

CONTACT
Lt. Col. John W. Powell Jr., Director of Admissions, The Citadel, The Military College of South Carolina, 171 Moultrie Street, Charleston, SC 29409. *Phone:* 843-953-5230. *Toll-free phone:* 800-868-1842. *Fax:* 843-953-7036. *E-mail:* john.powell@citadel.edu.

Claflin University
Orangeburg, South Carolina
http://www.claflin.edu/

- **Independent United Methodist** comprehensive, founded 1869
- **Small-town** 46-acre campus with easy access to Columbia
- **Endowment** $21.7 million
- **Coed** 1,836 undergraduate students, 96% full-time, 64% women, 36% men
- **Minimally difficult** entrance level, 60% of applicants were admitted

UNDERGRAD STUDENTS
1,769 full-time, 67 part-time. Students come from 27 states and territories; 18 other countries; 19% are from out of state; 91% Black or African American, non-Hispanic/Latino; 2% Hispanic/Latino; 0.4% Asian, non-Hispanic/Latino; 0.8% American Indian or Alaska Native, non-Hispanic/Latino; 0.5% Two or more races, non-Hispanic/Latino; 4% international; 5% transferred in; 70% live on campus.

Freshmen
Admission: 4,073 applied, 2,437 admitted, 387 enrolled. ***Average high school GPA:*** 3.28. ***Test scores:*** SAT critical reading scores over 500: 21%; SAT math scores over 500: 20%; ACT scores over 18: 39%; SAT critical reading scores over 600: 3%; SAT math scores over 600: 8%; ACT scores over 24: 7%; SAT math scores over 700: 2%.

Retention: 70% of full-time freshmen returned.

FACULTY
Total: 162, 70% full-time, 64% with terminal degrees.

Student/faculty ratio: 14:1.

ACADEMICS
Calendar: semesters. *Degrees:* bachelor's and master's.

Special study options: academic remediation for entering students, accelerated degree program, adult/continuing education programs, advanced placement credit, cooperative education, distance learning, double majors, freshman honors college, honors programs, independent study, internships, off-campus study, part-time degree program, study abroad, summer session for credit. ***ROTC:*** Army (c).

Unusual degree programs: 3-2 engineering with Clemson University, South Carolina State University.

Computers: 530 computers/terminals are available on campus for general student use. Students can access the following: computer help desk, free student e-mail accounts, online (class) grades, online (class) registration, online (class) schedules. Campuswide network is available. 100% of college-owned or -operated housing units are wired for high-speed Internet access. Wireless service is available via entire campus.

STUDENT LIFE
Housing options: men-only, women-only. Campus housing is university owned and leased by the school. Freshman applicants given priority for college housing.

Activities and organizations: drama/theater group, student-run newspaper, television station, choral group, Gospel Choir, NAACP, American Chemical Society, Sisters of Service, International Student Association, national fraternities, national sororities.

Athletics Member NCAA. All Division II. ***Intercollegiate sports:*** baseball M(s), basketball M(s)/W(s), cheerleading M(s)/W(s), cross-country running M(s)/W(s), softball W(s), track and field M(s)/W(s), volleyball W(s). ***Intramural sports:*** basketball M/W.

Campus security: 24-hour emergency response devices and patrols, student patrols, controlled dormitory access.

Student services: health clinic, personal/psychological counseling.

COSTS & FINANCIAL AID
Costs (2014–15) ***Comprehensive fee:*** $23,430 includes full-time tuition ($14,640), mandatory fees ($370), and room and board ($8420). Full-time tuition and fees vary according to class time. Part-time tuition: $610 per credit hour. Part-time tuition and fees vary according to class time. ***College room only:*** $3580. Room and board charges vary according to housing facility. ***Payment plans:*** installment, deferred payment. ***Waivers:*** employees or children of employees.

Financial Aid Of all full-time matriculated undergraduates who enrolled in 2006, 1,517 applied for aid, 1,475 were judged to have need, 144 had their need fully met. In 2006, 300 non-need-based awards were made.

Average percent of need met: 56. ***Average financial aid package:*** $10,917. ***Average need-based loan:*** $3734. ***Average need-based gift aid:*** $8220. ***Average non-need-based aid:*** $17,712. ***Average indebtedness upon graduation:*** $19,993.

APPLYING
Standardized Tests *Required:* SAT or ACT (for admission).
Options: electronic application, deferred entrance.
Application fee: $30.
Required: essay or personal statement, high school transcript, minimum 2.0 GPA.
Application deadlines: rolling (freshmen), rolling (transfers).
Notification: continuous (freshmen), continuous (transfers).

CONTACT
Claflin University, 400 Magnolia Street, Orangeburg, SC 29115. *Phone:* 803-535-5340. *Toll-free phone:* 800-922-1276.

★ Clemson University
Clemson, South Carolina
http://www.clemson.edu/

- **State-supported** university, founded 1889
- **Small-town** 1400-acre campus
- **Endowment** $518.6 million
- **Coed**
- **Moderately difficult** entrance level

FACULTY
Student/faculty ratio: 17:1.

ACADEMICS
Calendar: semesters. *Degrees:* bachelor's, master's, doctoral, and post-master's certificates.

STUDENT LIFE
Housing options: on-campus residence required for freshman year; coed, men-only, women-only. Campus housing is university owned. Freshman campus housing is guaranteed.
Activities and organizations: drama/theater group, student-run newspaper, radio and television station, choral group, marching band, student government, Fellowship of Christian Athletes, Tiger Band, national fraternities, national sororities.
Athletics Member NCAA. All Division I except football (Division I-A).
Campus security: 24-hour emergency response devices and patrols, late-night transport/escort service, controlled dormitory access.
Student services: health clinic, personal/psychological counseling, legal services.

COSTS & FINANCIAL AID
Costs (2014–15) ***Tuition:*** state resident $13,808 full-time, $562 per credit hour part-time; nonresident $31,824 full-time, $1345 per credit hour part-time. Full-time tuition and fees vary according to course load, location, and program. Part-time tuition and fees vary according to program. ***Room and board:*** $8358. Room and board charges vary according to board plan, housing facility, and location.
Financial Aid Of all full-time matriculated undergraduates who enrolled in 2014, 10,892 applied for aid, 7,926 were judged to have need, 1,348 had their need fully met. 939 Federal Work-Study jobs (averaging $2362). In 2014, 4191 non-need-based awards were made. ***Average percent of need met:*** 52. ***Average financial aid package:*** $10,812. ***Average need-based loan:*** $4413. ***Average need-based gift aid:*** $8590. ***Average non-need-based aid:*** $5280. ***Average indebtedness upon graduation:*** $30,213.

APPLYING
Standardized Tests *Required:* SAT or ACT (for admission).
Options: electronic application.
Application fee: $100.
Required: high school transcript. ***Recommended:*** essay or personal statement.

CONTACT
Ms. Audrey R. Bodell, Associate Director of Admissions, Clemson University, PO Box 345124, 105 Sikes Hall, Clemson, SC 29634. *Phone:* 864-656-2287. *Fax:* 864-656-2464. *E-mail:* cuadmissions@clemson.edu.

See below for display ad and page 1398 for the College Close-Up.

Coastal Carolina University

Conway, South Carolina

http://www.coastal.edu/

- **State-supported** comprehensive, founded 1954
- **Suburban** 620-acre campus
- **Endowment** $32.2 million
- **Coed** 9,364 undergraduate students, 91% full-time, 54% women, 46% men
- **Moderately difficult** entrance level, 64% of applicants were admitted

UNDERGRAD STUDENTS

8,502 full-time, 862 part-time. Students come from 46 states and territories; 55 other countries; 50% are from out of state; 20% Black or African American, non-Hispanic/Latino; 4% Hispanic/Latino; 0.8% Asian, non-Hispanic/Latino; 0.1% Native Hawaiian or other Pacific Islander, non-Hispanic/Latino; 0.4% American Indian or Alaska Native, non-Hispanic/Latino; 4% Two or more races, non-Hispanic/Latino; 0.5% Race/ethnicity unknown; 1% international; 9% transferred in; 39% live on campus.

Freshmen

Admission: 14,799 applied, 9,412 admitted, 2,375 enrolled. ***Average high school GPA:*** 3.4. ***Test scores:*** SAT critical reading scores over 500: 48%; SAT math scores over 500: 52%; ACT scores over 18: 90%; SAT critical reading scores over 600: 8%; SAT math scores over 600: 10%; ACT scores over 24: 25%; SAT critical reading scores over 700: 1%; SAT math scores over 700: 1%; ACT scores over 30: 2%.

Retention: 67% of full-time freshmen returned.

FACULTY

Total: 704, 59% full-time, 56% with terminal degrees.

Student/faculty ratio: 17:1.

ACADEMICS

Calendar: semesters. *Degrees:* certificates, bachelor's, master's, doctoral, post-master's, and postbachelor's certificates.

Special study options: accelerated degree program, adult/continuing education programs, advanced placement credit, cooperative education, distance learning, double majors, honors programs, independent study, internships, part-time degree program, services for LD students, student-designed majors, study abroad, summer session for credit. ***ROTC:*** Army (b).

Computers: 1,100 computers/terminals are available on campus for general student use. Students can access the following: computer help desk, free student e-mail accounts, online (class) grades, online (class) registration, online (class) schedules. Campuswide network is available. Wireless service is available via classrooms, computer centers, computer labs, dorm rooms, learning centers, libraries, student centers.

STUDENT LIFE

Housing options: on-campus residence required through sophomore year; coed, men-only, women-only, special housing for students with disabilities. Campus housing is university owned. Freshman campus housing is guaranteed.

Activities and organizations: drama/theater group, student-run newspaper, radio station, choral group, marching band, National Society of Leadership and Success, Leadership Challenge, Alpha Delta Pi, Salt Water Anglers, Aqua League (Scuba Club), national fraternities, national sororities.

Athletics Member NCAA. All Division I. ***Intercollegiate sports:*** baseball M(s), basketball M(s)/W(s), bowling M(c)/W(c), cheerleading M(c)/W(c), cross-country running M(s)/W(s), equestrian sports M(c)/W(c), field hockey M(c)/W(c), football M(s), golf M(s)/W(s), lacrosse M(c)/W(s), rugby M(c)/W(c), soccer M(s)/W(s), softball W(s), swimming and diving M(c)/W(c), tennis M(s)/W(s), track and field M(s)/W(s), volleyball M(c)/W(s), weight lifting M(c)/W(c), wrestling M(c). ***Intramural sports:*** badminton M/W, basketball M/W, soccer M/W, softball M/W, table tennis M/W, tennis M/W, volleyball M/W, water polo M/W.

Campus security: 24-hour emergency response devices and patrols, late-night transport/escort service.

Student services: health clinic, personal/psychological counseling, women's center.

COSTS & FINANCIAL AID

Costs (2014–15) ***Tuition:*** state resident $9960 full-time, $425 per credit hour part-time; nonresident $23,300 full-time, $975 per credit hour part-time. Full-time tuition and fees vary according to course load and degree level. Part-time tuition and fees vary according to course load and degree level. ***Required fees:*** $180 full-time. ***Room and board:*** $8440; room only: $5440. Room and board charges vary according to board plan and housing facility. ***Payment plan:*** installment. ***Waivers:*** senior citizens and employees or children of employees.

Financial Aid Of all full-time matriculated undergraduates who enrolled in 2013, 6,839 applied for aid, 5,799 were judged to have need, 487 had their need fully met. 122 Federal Work-Study jobs (averaging $2446). 1,035 state and other part-time jobs (averaging $2459). In 2013, 1279 non-need-based awards were made. ***Average percent of need met:*** 48. ***Average financial aid package:*** $9855. ***Average need-based loan:*** $8846. ***Average need-based gift aid:*** $4798. ***Average non-need-based aid:*** $12,574. ***Average indebtedness upon graduation:*** $35,207.

APPLYING

Standardized Tests *Required:* SAT or ACT (for admission).

Options: electronic application, deferred entrance.

Application fee: $45.

Required: high school transcript, minimum 2.0 GPA. ***Recommended:*** essay or personal statement, 1 letter of recommendation, interview.

Application deadlines: rolling (freshmen), rolling (transfers).

Notification: continuous until 10/1 (freshmen), continuous until 10/1 (transfers).

CONTACT

Coastal Carolina University, PO Box 261954, Conway, SC 29528-6054. *Phone:* 843-349-2037. *Toll-free phone:* 800-277-7000.

Coker College

Hartsville, South Carolina

http://www.coker.edu/

- **Independent** comprehensive, founded 1908
- **Small-town** 37-acre campus with easy access to Charlotte
- **Endowment** $28.4 million
- **Coed** 1,165 undergraduate students, 83% full-time, 62% women, 38% men
- **Moderately difficult** entrance level, 51% of applicants were admitted

UNDERGRAD STUDENTS

967 full-time, 198 part-time. Students come from 33 states and territories; 19 other countries; 23% are from out of state; 35% Black or African American, non-Hispanic/Latino; 3% Hispanic/Latino; 0.3% Asian, non-Hispanic/Latino; 0.6% American Indian or Alaska Native, non-Hispanic/Latino; 8% Race/ethnicity unknown; 1% international; 11% transferred in; 48% live on campus.

Freshmen

Admission: 1,393 applied, 709 admitted, 239 enrolled. ***Average high school GPA:*** 3.52. ***Test scores:*** SAT critical reading scores over 500: 43%; SAT math scores over 500: 52%; ACT scores over 18: 80%; SAT critical reading scores over 600: 12%; SAT math scores over 600: 6%; ACT scores over 24: 19%; SAT math scores over 700: 1%; ACT scores over 30: 1%.

Retention: 64% of full-time freshmen returned.

FACULTY

Total: 105, 61% full-time, 61% with terminal degrees.

Student/faculty ratio: 13:1.

ACADEMICS

Calendar: semesters. *Degrees:* bachelor's and master's (also offers evening program with significant enrollment not reflected in profile).

Special study options: adult/continuing education programs, advanced placement credit, distance learning, double majors, honors programs, independent study, internships, off-campus study, part-time degree program, services for LD students, student-designed majors, study abroad, summer session for credit.

Computers: 116 computers/terminals and 400 ports are available on campus for general student use. Students can access the following:

campus intranet, computer help desk, free student e-mail accounts, online (class) grades, online (class) registration, online (class) schedules. Campuswide network is available. 100% of college-owned or -operated housing units are wired for high-speed Internet access. Wireless service is available via entire campus.

STUDENT LIFE

Housing options: coed, special housing for students with disabilities. Campus housing is university owned. Freshman campus housing is guaranteed.

Activities and organizations: drama/theater group, choral group, Student Government Association.

Athletics Member NCAA. All Division II except lacrosse (Division I). ***Intercollegiate sports:*** baseball M(s), basketball M(s)/W(s), cross-country running M(s)/W(s), golf M(s)/W(s), lacrosse M(s)/W(s), soccer M(s)/W(s), softball W(s), tennis M(s)/W(s), track and field M(s)/W(s), volleyball M(s)/W(s), wrestling M(s). ***Intramural sports:*** basketball M/W, football M/W, table tennis M/W, track and field M/W, volleyball M/W, weight lifting M/W.

Campus security: 24-hour patrols, late-night transport/escort service, controlled dormitory access.

Student services: health clinic, personal/psychological counseling.

COSTS & FINANCIAL AID

Costs (2014–15) ***Comprehensive fee:*** $33,366 includes full-time tuition ($25,536) and room and board ($7830). Full-time tuition and fees vary according to course load, degree level, location, and program. Part-time tuition: $1064 per credit hour. Part-time tuition and fees vary according to course load, degree level, location, and program. ***Room and board:*** Room and board charges vary according to board plan and housing facility. ***Payment plan:*** installment. ***Waivers:*** employees or children of employees.

Financial Aid Of all full-time matriculated undergraduates who enrolled in 2012, 921 applied for aid, 854 were judged to have need, 284 had their need fully met. 82 Federal Work-Study jobs (averaging $839). 16 state and other part-time jobs (averaging $809). In 2012, 97 non-need-based awards were made. ***Average percent of need met:*** 93. ***Average financial aid package:*** $22,922. ***Average need-based loan:*** $4405. ***Average need-based gift aid:*** $6567. ***Average non-need-based aid:*** $7522. ***Average indebtedness upon graduation:*** $33,648. ***Financial aid deadline:*** 6/1.

APPLYING

Standardized Tests *Required:* SAT or ACT (for admission).

Options: electronic application, deferred entrance.

Application fee: $25.

Required: high school transcript. ***Required for some:*** interview, Auditions or portfolios may be required for certain programs.

Application deadlines: 8/1 (freshmen), 8/1 (out-of-state freshmen), rolling (transfers).

Notification: continuous (freshmen), continuous (out-of-state freshmen), continuous (transfers).

CONTACT

Mr. Adam Connolly, Associate Vice President Enrollment Management, Coker College, 300 E. College Avenue, Hartsville, SC 29550. *Phone:* 843-383-8050. *Toll-free phone:* 800-950-1908. *Fax:* 843-383-8056. *E-mail:* admissions@coker.edu.

College of Charleston

Charleston, South Carolina

http://www.cofc.edu/

- **State-supported** comprehensive, founded 1770
- **Urban** 52-acre campus
- **Endowment** $67.4 million
- **Coed** 10,440 undergraduate students, 92% full-time, 63% women, 37% men
- **Moderately difficult** entrance level, 78% of applicants were admitted

UNDERGRAD STUDENTS

9,608 full-time, 832 part-time. Students come from 49 states and territories; 55 other countries; 36% are from out of state; 7% Black or African American, non-Hispanic/Latino; 4% Hispanic/Latino; 2% Asian, non-Hispanic/Latino; 0.1% Native Hawaiian or other Pacific Islander, non-Hispanic/Latino; 0.2% American Indian or Alaska Native, non-Hispanic/Latino; 4% Two or more races, non-Hispanic/Latino; 0.9% Race/ethnicity unknown; 0.7% international; 7% transferred in; 31% live on campus.

Freshmen

Admission: 11,179 applied, 8,722 admitted, 2,166 enrolled. ***Average high school GPA:*** 3.86. ***Test scores:*** SAT critical reading scores over 500: 84%; SAT math scores over 500: 85%; ACT scores over 18: 100%; SAT critical reading scores over 600: 34%; SAT math scores over 600: 31%; ACT scores over 24: 66%; SAT critical reading scores over 700: 5%; SAT math scores over 700: 3%; ACT scores over 30: 12%.

Retention: 79% of full-time freshmen returned.

FACULTY

Total: 979, 58% full-time, 68% with terminal degrees.

Student/faculty ratio: 15:1.

ACADEMICS

Calendar: semesters. *Degrees:* bachelor's, master's, post-master's, and postbachelor's certificates (also offers graduate degree programs through University of Charleston, South Carolina).

Special study options: accelerated degree program, adult/continuing education programs, advanced placement credit, cooperative education, distance learning, double majors, English as a second language, honors programs, independent study, internships, off-campus study, part-time degree program, services for LD students, study abroad, summer session for credit. ***ROTC:*** Air Force (c).

Unusual degree programs: 3-2 BS-MS Computer Science and BS-MS Mathematics.

Computers: 750 computers/terminals and 1,200 ports are available on campus for general student use. Students can access the following: campus intranet, computer help desk, free student e-mail accounts, online (class) grades, online (class) registration, online (class) schedules. Campuswide network is available. 100% of college-owned or -operated housing units are wired for high-speed Internet access. Wireless service is available via entire campus.

STUDENT LIFE

Housing options: coed, men-only, women-only, special housing for students with disabilities. Campus housing is university owned. Freshman campus housing is guaranteed.

Activities and organizations: drama/theater group, student-run newspaper, radio station, choral group, Student Government Association, Cougar Activities Board, Intramural basketball, Black Student Union, Committed to Charleston Society, national fraternities, national sororities.

Athletics Member NCAA. All Division I. ***Intercollegiate sports:*** baseball M(s), basketball M(s)/W(s), cheerleading W, cross-country running M(s)/W(s), equestrian sports W, golf M(s)/W(s), sailing M/W, soccer M(s)/W(s), softball W(s), swimming and diving M(s)/W(s), tennis M(s)/W(s), volleyball W(s). ***Intramural sports:*** badminton M/W, basketball M/W, crew M(c)/W(c), golf M(c)/W(c), gymnastics M(c)/W(c), ice hockey M(c)/W(c), lacrosse M(c)/W(c), racquetball M/W, rugby M(c)/W(c), soccer M/W, softball M/W, squash M(c)/W(c), swimming and diving M(c)/W(c), table tennis M/W, tennis M(c)/W(c), ultimate Frisbee M(c)/W(c), volleyball M/W, weight lifting M/W.

Campus security: 24-hour emergency response devices and patrols, student patrols, late-night transport/escort service, controlled dormitory access, shuttle service.

Student services: health clinic, personal/psychological counseling, women's center, legal services.

FINANCIAL AID

Financial Aid Of all full-time matriculated undergraduates who enrolled in 2014, 5,948 applied for aid, 4,555 were judged to have need, 833 had their need fully met. In 2014, 1814 non-need-based awards were made. ***Average percent of need met:*** 57. ***Average financial aid package:*** $13,248. ***Average need-based loan:*** $3597. ***Average need-based gift aid:*** $3176. ***Average non-need-based aid:*** $11,255. ***Average indebtedness upon graduation:*** $25,644.

APPLYING

Standardized Tests *Required:* SAT or ACT (for admission).

Options: electronic application, early action, deferred entrance.

Application fee: $50.

Required: essay or personal statement, high school transcript, SAT or ACT.

Application deadlines: 2/1 (freshmen), 5/1 (transfers), 11/1 (early action).

Notification: 4/1 (freshmen), continuous until 6/1 (transfers), 1/1 (early action).

CONTACT

Ms. Suzette Stille, Executive Director of Admissions, College of Charleston, 66 George Street, Charleston, SC 29424-0001. *Phone:* 843-953-5670. *Fax:* 843-953-6322. *E-mail:* admissions@cofc.edu.

Columbia College

Columbia, South Carolina

http://www.columbiasc.edu/

- **Independent United Methodist** comprehensive, founded 1854
- **Suburban** campus
- **Endowment** $22.9 million
- **Coed, primarily women** 1,126 undergraduate students, 71% full-time, 86% women, 14% men
- **Moderately difficult** entrance level, 79% of applicants were admitted

UNDERGRAD STUDENTS

800 full-time, 326 part-time. Students come from 22 states and territories; 5 other countries; 8% are from out of state; 34% Black or African American, non-Hispanic/Latino; 2% Hispanic/Latino; 2% Asian, non-Hispanic/Latino; 1% American Indian or Alaska Native, non-Hispanic/Latino; 14% Race/ethnicity unknown; 0.3% international; 12% transferred in; 47% live on campus.

Freshmen

Admission: 413 applied, 326 admitted, 137 enrolled. ***Average high school GPA:*** 3.68. ***Test scores:*** SAT critical reading scores over 500: 60%; SAT math scores over 500: 53%; SAT writing scores over 500: 52%; ACT scores over 18: 91%; SAT critical reading scores over 600: 24%; SAT math scores over 600: 15%; SAT writing scores over 600: 18%; ACT scores over 24: 35%; SAT critical reading scores over 700: 3%; SAT math scores over 700: 1%; SAT writing scores over 700: 1%; ACT scores over 30: 9%.

Retention: 68% of full-time freshmen returned.

FACULTY

Total: 151, 46% full-time, 42% with terminal degrees.

Student/faculty ratio: 10:1.

ACADEMICS

Calendar: semesters. *Degrees:* bachelor's, master's, and doctoral.

Special study options: academic remediation for entering students, adult/continuing education programs, advanced placement credit, distance learning, double majors, honors programs, independent study, internships, off-campus study, part-time degree program, student-designed majors, study abroad, summer session for credit. ***ROTC:*** Army (c), Navy (c), Air Force (c).

Computers: Students can access the following: campus intranet, computer help desk, free student e-mail accounts, online (class) grades, online (class) registration, online (class) schedules. Campuswide network is available. Wireless service is available via student centers.

STUDENT LIFE

Housing options: on-campus residence required through sophomore year; women-only. Campus housing is university owned. Freshman campus housing is guaranteed.

Activities and organizations: drama/theater group, student-run newspaper, choral group.

Athletics Member NAIA. ***Intercollegiate sports:*** basketball W(s), cross-country running W(s), golf W(s), lacrosse W(s), soccer W(s), softball W(s), swimming and diving W(s), tennis W(s), track and field W(s), volleyball W(s).

Campus security: 24-hour emergency response devices and patrols, late-night transport/escort service, controlled dormitory access.

Student services: health clinic, personal/psychological counseling, women's center.

COSTS & FINANCIAL AID

Costs (2015–16) ***Comprehensive fee:*** $35,500 includes full-time tuition ($28,100) and room and board ($7400). Full-time tuition and fees vary according to class time. Part-time tuition: $725 per credit hour. Part-time tuition and fees vary according to course load. ***College room only:*** $3700. Room and board charges vary according to board plan and housing facility. ***Payment plan:*** installment. ***Waivers:*** employees or children of employees.

Financial Aid Of all full-time matriculated undergraduates who enrolled in 2005, 794 applied for aid, 698 were judged to have need, 310 had their need fully met. 200 Federal Work-Study jobs (averaging $1000). In 2005, 152 non-need-based awards were made. ***Average percent of need met:*** 70. ***Average financial aid package:*** $20,052. ***Average need-based loan:*** $3810. ***Average need-based gift aid:*** $8495. ***Average non-need-based aid:*** $7775. ***Average indebtedness upon graduation:*** $25,333.

APPLYING

Standardized Tests *Required:* SAT or ACT (for admission).

Options: electronic application.

Required: high school transcript. ***Required for some:*** interview. ***Recommended:*** essay or personal statement.

Application deadlines: 8/1 (freshmen), 8/1 (transfers).

CONTACT

Ms. Julie King, Director of Admissions, Columbia College, 1301 Columbia College Drive, Columbia, SC 29203. *Phone:* 803-786-3871. *Toll-free phone:* 800-277-1301. *E-mail:* juking@columbiasc.edu.

Columbia International University

Columbia, South Carolina

http://www.ciu.edu/

- **Independent nondenominational** university, founded 1923
- **Suburban** 400-acre campus
- **Endowment** $15.1 million
- **Coed** 560 undergraduate students, 89% full-time, 51% women, 49% men
- **Moderately difficult** entrance level, 33% of applicants were admitted

UNDERGRAD STUDENTS

497 full-time, 63 part-time. Students come from 23 states and territories; 14 other countries; 41% are from out of state; 13% Black or African American, non-Hispanic/Latino; 4% Hispanic/Latino; 2% Asian, non-Hispanic/Latino; 0.4% American Indian or Alaska Native, non-Hispanic/Latino; 2% Two or more races, non-Hispanic/Latino; 4% Race/ethnicity unknown; 3% international; 12% transferred in; 60% live on campus.

Freshmen

Admission: 569 applied, 189 admitted, 101 enrolled. ***Average high school GPA:*** 3.67. ***Test scores:*** SAT critical reading scores over 500: 78%; SAT math scores over 500: 62%; SAT writing scores over 500: 60%; ACT scores over 18: 82%; SAT critical reading scores over 600: 26%; SAT math scores over 600: 19%; SAT writing scores over 600: 18%; ACT scores over 24: 23%; SAT critical reading scores over 700: 5%; SAT writing scores over 700: 5%; ACT scores over 30: 7%.

Retention: 69% of full-time freshmen returned.

FACULTY

Total: 92, 52% full-time, 66% with terminal degrees.

Student/faculty ratio: 14:1.

ACADEMICS

Calendar: semesters. *Degrees:* certificates, associate, bachelor's, master's, doctoral, and postbachelor's certificates.

Special study options: academic remediation for entering students, advanced placement credit, cooperative education, distance learning, double majors, honors programs, independent study, internships, off-campus study, services for LD students, study abroad, summer session for credit.

Computers: 106 computers/terminals and 374 ports are available on campus for general student use. Students can access the following: campus intranet, computer help desk, free student e-mail accounts, online (class) grades, online (class) registration, online (class) schedules. Campuswide network is available. 100% of college-owned or -operated housing units are wired for high-speed Internet access. Wireless service is available via classrooms, computer centers, computer labs, dorm rooms, learning centers, libraries, student centers.

STUDENT LIFE

Housing options: on-campus residence required through senior year; men-only, women-only. Campus housing is university owned. Freshman campus housing is guaranteed.

Activities and organizations: drama/theater group, student-run newspaper, choral group, Student Union, Mu Kappa, Student Missions Connection, GradLife, African American Fellowship Ministries.

Athletics Member NCCAA. ***Intercollegiate sports:*** basketball M(s)/W(s), cross-country running M(s)/W(s), golf M(s), soccer M(s)/W(s). ***Intramural sports:*** basketball M, football M/W, soccer M/W, ultimate Frisbee M/W, volleyball M/W.

Campus security: 24-hour emergency response devices and patrols, late-night transport/escort service.

Student services: health clinic, personal/psychological counseling.

COSTS & FINANCIAL AID

Costs (2015–16) ***Comprehensive fee:*** $27,960 includes full-time tuition ($19,890), mandatory fees ($540), and room and board ($7530). Full-time tuition and fees vary according to course load, program, and reciprocity agreements. Part-time tuition: $795 per credit hour. Part-time tuition and fees vary according to course load, program, and reciprocity agreements. ***Required fees:*** $10 per credit hour part-time, $120 per term part-time. ***Room and board:*** Room and board charges vary according to board plan and housing facility. ***Payment plan:*** installment. ***Waivers:*** employees or children of employees.

Financial Aid Of all full-time matriculated undergraduates who enrolled in 2013, 434 applied for aid, 392 were judged to have need, 65 had their need fully met. 106 Federal Work-Study jobs (averaging $1424). 248 state and other part-time jobs (averaging $1899). In 2013, 100 non-need-based awards were made. ***Average percent of need met:*** 61. ***Average financial aid package:*** $15,803. ***Average need-based loan:*** $3676. ***Average need-based gift aid:*** $12,843. ***Average non-need-based aid:*** $5082. ***Average indebtedness upon graduation:*** $24,428.

APPLYING

Standardized Tests *Required:* SAT or ACT (for admission).

Options: electronic application, deferred entrance.

Required: essay or personal statement, minimum 2.0 GPA, 1 letter of recommendation. ***Required for some:*** high school transcript, interview, SAT or ACT scores. SAT/ACT is not necessary if applicant is 24 years of age or older or if applicant is transferring in 24 or more hours.

Application deadlines: 8/1 (freshmen), 8/1 (out-of-state freshmen), 8/1 (transfers).

Notification: continuous (freshmen), continuous (out-of-state freshmen), continuous (transfers).

CONTACT

Undergraduate Admissions Office, Columbia International University, Columbia, SC 29230-3122. *Phone:* 803-777-2227. *Toll-free phone:* 800-777-2227 Ext. 5024. *Fax:* 803-786-4041. *E-mail:* yesciu@ciu.edu.

Converse College

Spartanburg, South Carolina

http://www.converse.edu/

- **Independent** comprehensive, founded 1889
- **Urban** 70-acre campus
- **Endowment** $78.2 million
- **Undergraduate: women only; graduate: coed**
- **Moderately difficult** entrance level

FACULTY

Student/faculty ratio: 11:1.

ACADEMICS

Calendar: 4-2-4. *Degrees:* bachelor's, master's, and post-master's certificates.

STUDENT LIFE

Housing options: on-campus residence required through senior year; women-only. Campus housing is university owned. Freshman campus housing is guaranteed.

Activities and organizations: drama/theater group, student-run newspaper, choral group, student government, student volunteer services, Student Christian Organization, Student Activities Committee, Athletic Association.

Athletics Member NCAA. All Division II.

Campus security: 24-hour emergency response devices and patrols, late-night transport/escort service, controlled dormitory access.

Student services: health clinic, personal/psychological counseling, women's center.

COSTS & FINANCIAL AID

Costs (2014–15) ***Comprehensive fee:*** $26,000 includes full-time tuition ($15,500), mandatory fees ($1000), and room and board ($9500). Full-time tuition and fees vary according to course load and program. Part-time tuition and fees vary according to course load and program. ***Room and board:*** Room and board charges vary according to board plan.

Financial Aid Of all full-time matriculated undergraduates who enrolled in 2013, 613 applied for aid, 561 were judged to have need, 122 had their need fully met. 90 Federal Work-Study jobs (averaging $1594). 60 state and other part-time jobs (averaging $1200). In 2013, 104 non-need-based awards were made. ***Average percent of need met:*** 78. ***Average financial aid package:*** $24,613. ***Average need-based loan:*** $4869. ***Average need-based gift aid:*** $20,888. ***Average non-need-based aid:*** $16,032. ***Average indebtedness upon graduation:*** $27,826.

APPLYING

Standardized Tests *Required:* SAT or ACT (for admission).

Options: electronic application, deferred entrance.

Required: high school transcript, SAT or ACT. Essay section not required for either. ***Recommended:*** essay or personal statement, minimum 3.0 GPA.

CONTACT

Ms. April Lewis, Director of Admissions, Converse College, 580 East Main Street, Spartanburg, SC 29302. *Phone:* 864-596-9040 Ext. 9746. *Toll-free phone:* 800-766-1125. *Fax:* 864-596-9225. *E-mail:* admissions@converse.edu.

★ Erskine College

Due West, South Carolina

http://www.erskine.edu/

- **Independent** comprehensive, founded 1839, affiliated with Associate Reformed Presbyterian Church
- **Rural** 90-acre campus
- **Endowment** $39.6 million
- **Coed** 599 undergraduate students, 99% full-time, 49% women, 51% men
- **Moderately difficult** entrance level, 41% of applicants were admitted

UNDERGRAD STUDENTS

591 full-time, 8 part-time. Students come from 19 states and territories; 8 other countries; 24% are from out of state; 11% Black or African American, non-Hispanic/Latino; 3% Hispanic/Latino; 1% Asian, non-Hispanic/Latino; 1% Two or more races, non-Hispanic/Latino; 18% Race/ethnicity unknown; 2% transferred in; 89% live on campus.

Freshmen

Admission: 913 applied, 373 admitted, 187 enrolled. ***Test scores:*** SAT critical reading scores over 500: 60%; SAT math scores over 500: 63%; ACT scores over 18: 95%; SAT critical reading scores over 600: 24%; SAT math scores over 600: 28%; ACT scores over 24: 45%; SAT critical reading scores over 700: 5%; SAT math scores over 700: 5%; ACT scores over 30: 8%.

Retention: 68% of full-time freshmen returned.

FACULTY

Total: 79, 75% full-time, 62% with terminal degrees.

Student/faculty ratio: 11:1.

ACADEMICS

Calendar: 4-1-4. *Degrees:* certificates, bachelor's, master's, and doctoral.

Special study options: advanced placement credit, double majors, independent study, internships, off-campus study, part-time degree program, study abroad, summer session for credit.

Unusual degree programs: 3-2 engineering with Clemson University, University of Tennessee, Knoxville; allied health programs with Medical University of South Carolina.

Computers: Students can access the following: free student e-mail accounts. Campuswide network is available. Wireless service is available via classrooms, dorm rooms, libraries, student centers.

STUDENT LIFE

Housing options: on-campus residence required through senior year; men-only, women-only. Campus housing is university owned. Freshman campus housing is guaranteed.

Activities and organizations: drama/theater group, student-run newspaper, radio station, choral group, literary societies, religious organizations, Student Government Organization, publications, honor societies.

Athletics Member NCAA. All Division II. ***Intercollegiate sports:*** baseball M(s), basketball M(s)/W(s), cross-country running M(s)/W(s), equestrian sports W(c), golf M(s)/W(s), lacrosse W(s), soccer M(s)/W(s), softball W(s), tennis M(s)/W(s), volleyball W(s). ***Intramural sports:*** basketball M/W, football M/W, soccer M/W, softball M/W, tennis M/W, volleyball M/W.

Campus security: 24-hour patrols, late-night transport/escort service, controlled dormitory access.

Student services: health clinic, personal/psychological counseling.

COSTS & FINANCIAL AID

Costs (2015–16) ***Comprehensive fee:*** $41,825 includes full-time tuition ($29,310), mandatory fees ($2365), and room and board ($10,150). ***College room only:*** $5250.

Financial Aid Of all full-time matriculated undergraduates who enrolled in 2009, 498 applied for aid, 400 were judged to have need, 156 had their need fully met. In 2009, 121 non-need-based awards were made. ***Average percent of need met:*** 86. ***Average financial aid package:*** $21,093. ***Average need-based loan:*** $4750. ***Average need-based gift aid:*** $16,222. ***Average non-need-based aid:*** $10,725. ***Average indebtedness upon graduation:*** $24,450.

APPLYING

Standardized Tests *Required:* SAT or ACT (for admission).

Options: electronic application, early admission, early action, deferred entrance.

Application fee: $25.

Required: essay or personal statement, high school transcript, 1 letter of recommendation. ***Recommended:*** interview.

Application deadlines: rolling (freshmen), rolling (transfers), 11/1 (early action).

Notification: continuous (freshmen), continuous (transfers), 11/15 (early action).

CONTACT

Erskine College, 2 Washington Street, PO Box 338, Due West, SC 29639. *Phone:* 864-379-8838. *Toll-free phone:* 800-241-8721.

Francis Marion University

Florence, South Carolina

http://www.fmarion.edu/

- **State-supported** comprehensive, founded 1970
- **Rural** 400-acre campus
- **Endowment** $27.1 million
- **Coed** 3,605 undergraduate students, 88% full-time, 69% women, 31% men
- **Moderately difficult** entrance level, 59% of applicants were admitted

UNDERGRAD STUDENTS

3,168 full-time, 437 part-time. Students come from 29 states and territories; 22 other countries; 4% are from out of state; 48% Black or African American, non-Hispanic/Latino; 1% Hispanic/Latino; 1% Asian, non-Hispanic/Latino; 0.1% Native Hawaiian or other Pacific Islander, non-Hispanic/Latino; 0.3% American Indian or Alaska Native, non-Hispanic/Latino; 0.9% Two or more races, non-Hispanic/Latino; 0.8% Race/ethnicity unknown; 2% international; 6% transferred in; 39% live on campus.

Freshmen

Admission: 3,759 applied, 2,222 admitted, 757 enrolled. ***Average high school GPA:*** 3.69. ***Test scores:*** SAT critical reading scores over 500: 38%; SAT math scores over 500: 37%; SAT writing scores over 500: 29%; ACT scores over 18: 67%; SAT critical reading scores over 600: 9%; SAT math scores over 600: 8%; SAT writing scores over 600: 4%; ACT scores over 24: 14%; SAT critical reading scores over 700: 1%; SAT math scores over 700: 1%; SAT writing scores over 700: 1%; ACT scores over 30: 1%. ***Retention:*** 68% of full-time freshmen returned.

FACULTY

Total: 292, 73% full-time, 66% with terminal degrees.

Student/faculty ratio: 15:1.

ACADEMICS

Calendar: semesters. *Degrees:* bachelor's, master's, and post-master's certificates.

Special study options: accelerated degree program, adult/continuing education programs, advanced placement credit, distance learning, double majors, honors programs, independent study, internships, off-campus study, part-time degree program, services for LD students, study abroad, summer session for credit. ***ROTC:*** Army (b).

Unusual degree programs: 3-2 engineering with Clemson University; forestry with Clemson University; Wildlife & Fisheries (Clemson University).

Computers: 634 computers/terminals are available on campus for general student use. Students can access the following: computer help desk, free student e-mail accounts, online (class) grades, online (class) registration, online (class) schedules, Blackboard. Campuswide network is available. 100% of college-owned or -operated housing units are wired for high-speed Internet access. Wireless service is available via entire campus.

STUDENT LIFE

Housing options: men-only, women-only, special housing for students with disabilities. Campus housing is university owned and is provided by a third party. Freshman applicants given priority for college housing.

Activities and organizations: drama/theater group, student-run newspaper, choral group, Baptist Collegiate Ministries, University Programming Board, Psychology Club, Student Alumni Association, Young Gifted and Blessed Chorus, national fraternities, national sororities.

Athletics Member NCAA. All Division II except golf (Division I), soccer (Division I). ***Intercollegiate sports:*** baseball M(s), basketball M(s)/W(s), cross-country running M(s)/W(s), golf M(s), soccer M(s)/W(s), softball W(s), tennis M(s)/W(s), track and field M/W, volleyball W(s). ***Intramural sports:*** basketball M/W, cheerleading M(c)/W(c), football M/W, racquetball M/W, soccer M/W, softball M/W, table tennis M/W, tennis M/W, ultimate Frisbee M/W, volleyball M/W.

Campus security: 24-hour emergency response devices and patrols, late-night transport/escort service, controlled dormitory access.

Student services: health clinic, personal/psychological counseling.

COSTS & FINANCIAL AID

Costs (2014–15) ***Tuition:*** state resident $9266 full-time, $463 per credit hour part-time; nonresident $18,532 full-time, $927 per credit hour part-time. Full-time tuition and fees vary according to degree level and program. Part-time tuition and fees vary according to course load, degree level, and program. ***Required fees:*** $472 full-time, $14 per credit hour part-time, $57 per term part-time. ***Room and board:*** $7256; room only: $4088. Room and board charges vary according to board plan and housing facility. ***Payment plan:*** installment. ***Waivers:*** senior citizens and employees or children of employees.

Financial Aid Of all full-time matriculated undergraduates who enrolled in 2013, 3,188 applied for aid, 2,662 were judged to have need, 633 had their need fully met. In 2013, 79 non-need-based awards were made. ***Average percent of need met:*** 77. ***Average financial aid package:*** $13,514. ***Average need-based loan:*** $7292. ***Average need-based gift aid:*** $4205. ***Average non-need-based aid:*** $2422. ***Average indebtedness upon graduation:*** $32,118. ***Financial aid deadline:*** 6/30.

APPLYING

Standardized Tests *Required:* SAT or ACT (for admission).

Options: electronic application, early admission, deferred entrance.

Application fee: $35.

Required: minimum 2.0 GPA. ***Required for some:*** essay or personal statement, high school transcript.

Application deadlines: 8/15 (freshmen), 8/15 (out-of-state freshmen), rolling (transfers).

Notification: 9/1 (freshmen), 9/1 (out-of-state freshmen).

CONTACT
Mrs. Perry Wilson, Director of Admissions, Francis Marion University, PO Box 100547, Florence, SC 29502-0547. *Phone:* 843-661-1231. *Toll-free phone:* 800-368-7551. *Fax:* 843-661-4635. *E-mail:* admissions@fmarion.edu.

Furman University

Greenville, South Carolina

http://www.furman.edu/

- **Independent** comprehensive, founded 1826
- **Suburban** 800-acre campus
- **Endowment** $650.0 million
- **Coed** 2,810 undergraduate students, 96% full-time, 57% women, 43% men
- **Moderately difficult** entrance level, 69% of applicants were admitted

UNDERGRAD STUDENTS
2,698 full-time, 112 part-time. Students come from 47 states and territories; 55 other countries; 72% are from out of state; 5% Black or African American, non-Hispanic/Latino; 4% Hispanic/Latino; 2% Asian, non-Hispanic/Latino; 0.1% American Indian or Alaska Native, non-Hispanic/Latino; 3% Two or more races, non-Hispanic/Latino; 2% Race/ethnicity unknown; 5% international; 1% transferred in; 96% live on campus.

Freshmen
Admission: 4,583 applied, 3,149 admitted, 725 enrolled. ***Test scores:*** SAT critical reading scores over 500: 92%; SAT math scores over 500: 94%; SAT writing scores over 500: 90%; ACT scores over 18: 99%; SAT critical reading scores over 600: 60%; SAT math scores over 600: 64%; SAT writing scores over 600: 61%; ACT scores over 24: 87%; SAT critical reading scores over 700: 15%; SAT math scores over 700: 18%; SAT writing scores over 700: 15%; ACT scores over 30: 34%.

Retention: 89% of full-time freshmen returned.

FACULTY
Total: 259, 90% full-time, 92% with terminal degrees.

Student/faculty ratio: 11:1.

ACADEMICS
Calendar: 3-2-3. *Degrees:* bachelor's, master's, and post-master's certificates.

Special study options: accelerated degree program, adult/continuing education programs, advanced placement credit, double majors, independent study, internships, part-time degree program, services for LD students, student-designed majors, study abroad, summer session for credit. ***ROTC:*** Army (b).

Unusual degree programs: 3-2 engineering with Georgia Institute of Technology, Clemson University, Auburn University, North Carolina State University, Washington University in St. Louis; forestry with Duke University.

Computers: 425 computers/terminals and 3,500 ports are available on campus for general student use. Students can access the following: campus intranet, computer help desk, free student e-mail accounts, online (class) grades, online (class) registration, online (class) schedules. Campuswide network is available. 100% of college-owned or -operated housing units are wired for high-speed Internet access. Wireless service is available via entire campus.

STUDENT LIFE
Housing options: on-campus residence required through senior year; coed, men-only, women-only. Campus housing is university owned. Freshman campus housing is guaranteed.

Activities and organizations: drama/theater group, student-run newspaper, radio and television station, choral group, marching band, Collegiate Educational Service Corps, Fellowship of Christian Athletes, Baptist Student Union, Student Activities Board, Furman Singers, national fraternities, national sororities.

Athletics Member NCAA. All Division I except football (Division I-AA). ***Intercollegiate sports:*** baseball M(s), basketball M(s)/W(s), cheerleading M/W, crew M(c)/W(c), cross-country running M(s)/W(s), equestrian sports W(c), fencing M(c)/W(c), golf M(c)/W(s), ice hockey M(c), lacrosse M/W, rugby M(c)/W(c), soccer M(s)/W(s), softball W(s), swimming and diving M(c)/W(c), tennis M(s)/W(s), track and field M(s)/W(s), ultimate Frisbee M(c)/W(c), volleyball W(s), weight lifting M(c)/W(c), wrestling M(c). ***Intramural sports:*** basketball M/W, bowling M/W, cross-country running M/W, football M/W, golf M/W, racquetball M/W, soccer M/W, softball M/W, swimming and diving M/W, tennis M/W, track and field M/W, volleyball M/W.

Campus security: 24-hour emergency response devices and patrols, student patrols, late-night transport/escort service, controlled dormitory access.

Student services: health clinic, personal/psychological counseling, women's center.

COSTS & FINANCIAL AID
Costs (2014–15) ***Comprehensive fee:*** $55,872 includes full-time tuition ($44,288), mandatory fees ($380), and room and board ($11,204). Part-time tuition: $1384 per credit. Part-time tuition and fees vary according to course load. ***College room only:*** $6022. Room and board charges vary according to board plan and housing facility. ***Payment plan:*** installment. ***Waivers:*** employees or children of employees.

Financial Aid Of all full-time matriculated undergraduates who enrolled in 2014, 1,398 applied for aid, 1,160 were judged to have need, 387 had their need fully met. 583 Federal Work-Study jobs (averaging $1552). In 2014, 1118 non-need-based awards were made. ***Average percent of need met:*** 77. ***Average financial aid package:*** $35,321. ***Average need-based loan:*** $5130. ***Average need-based gift aid:*** $31,665. ***Average non-need-based aid:*** $17,166. ***Average indebtedness upon graduation:*** $25,903. ***Financial aid deadline:*** 1/15.

APPLYING
Standardized Tests *Recommended:* SAT or ACT (for admission).

Options: electronic application, early decision, early action.

Application fee: $50.

Required: essay or personal statement, high school transcript. ***Recommended:*** interview.

Application deadlines: 1/15 (freshmen), 1/15 (transfers), 11/15 (early action).

Early decision deadline: 11/1.

Notification: 4/1 (freshmen), 4/1 (transfers), 12/1 (early decision), 2/1 (early action).

CONTACT
Mr. Brad Pochard, Associate Vice President of Admission, Furman University, 3300 Poinsett Highway, Greenville, SC 29613. *Phone:* 864-294-2034. *Fax:* 864-294-2018. *E-mail:* admissions@furman.edu.

ITT Technical Institute

Columbia, South Carolina

http://www.itt-tech.edu/

- **Proprietary** primarily 2-year, part of ITT Educational Services, Inc.
- **Coed**

ACADEMICS
Degrees: associate and bachelor's.

STUDENT LIFE
Housing options: college housing not available.

CONTACT
Director of Recruitment, ITT Technical Institute, 1628 Browning Road, Suite 180, Columbia, SC 29210. *Phone:* 803-216-6000. *Toll-free phone:* 800-242-5158.

ITT Technical Institute
Greenville, South Carolina
http://www.itt-tech.edu/

- **Proprietary** primarily 2-year, founded 1992, part of ITT Educational Services, Inc.
- **Coed**
- **Minimally difficult** entrance level

ACADEMICS
Calendar: quarters. *Degrees:* associate and bachelor's.

STUDENT LIFE
Housing options: college housing not available.

FINANCIAL AID
Financial Aid Of all full-time matriculated undergraduates who enrolled in 2013, 3 Federal Work-Study jobs.

CONTACT
Director of Recruitment, ITT Technical Institute, 6 Independence Pointe, Greenville, SC 29615. *Phone:* 864-288-0777. *Toll-free phone:* 800-932-4488.

ITT Technical Institute
Myrtle Beach, South Carolina
http://www.itt-tech.edu/

- **Proprietary** primarily 2-year, part of ITT Educational Services, Inc.
- **Coed**

ACADEMICS
Calendar: quarters. *Degrees:* associate and bachelor's.

CONTACT
Director of Recruitment, ITT Technical Institute, 9654 N. Kings Highway, Suite 101, Myrtle Beach, SC 29572. *Phone:* 843-497-7820. *Toll-free phone:* 877-316-7054.

ITT Technical Institute
North Charleston, South Carolina
http://www.itt-tech.edu/

- **Proprietary** primarily 2-year, part of ITT Educational Services, Inc.
- **Coed**

ACADEMICS
Calendar: quarters. *Degrees:* associate and bachelor's.

CONTACT
Director of Recruitment, ITT Technical Institute, 2431 W. Aviation Avenue, North Charleston, SC 29406. *Phone:* 843-745-5700. *Toll-free phone:* 877-291-0900.

Limestone College
Gaffney, South Carolina
http://www.limestone.edu/

- **Independent** comprehensive, founded 1845
- **Suburban** 123-acre campus with easy access to Charlotte
- **Endowment** $16.1 million
- **Coed** 1,188 undergraduate students, 99% full-time, 39% women, 61% men
- **Minimally difficult** entrance level, 52% of applicants were admitted

UNDERGRAD STUDENTS
1,171 full-time, 17 part-time. Students come from 32 states and territories; 19 other countries; 38% are from out of state; 32% Black or African American, non-Hispanic/Latino; 4% Hispanic/Latino; 3% Two or more races, non-Hispanic/Latino; 10% Race/ethnicity unknown; 6% transferred in; 62% live on campus.

Freshmen
Admission: 3,154 applied, 1,640 admitted, 512 enrolled. ***Average high school GPA:*** 3.24. ***Test scores:*** SAT math scores over 500: 69%; ACT scores over 18: 99%; SAT math scores over 600: 15%; ACT scores over 24: 20%; ACT scores over 30: 5%.
Retention: 62% of full-time freshmen returned.

FACULTY
Total: 106, 76% full-time, 64% with terminal degrees.
Student/faculty ratio: 11:1.

ACADEMICS
Calendar: semesters. *Degrees:* associate, bachelor's, and master's.
Special study options: academic remediation for entering students, accelerated degree program, adult/continuing education programs, advanced placement credit, distance learning, double majors, honors programs, independent study, internships, part-time degree program, services for LD students, student-designed majors, summer session for credit. ***ROTC:*** Army (c).
Computers: 137 computers/terminals are available on campus for general student use. Students can access the following: campus intranet, computer help desk, free student e-mail accounts, online (class) grades, online (class) registration, online (class) schedules. Campuswide network is available. 100% of college-owned or -operated housing units are wired for high-speed Internet access. Wireless service is available via classrooms, dorm rooms, learning centers, libraries, student centers.

STUDENT LIFE
Housing options: on-campus residence required through junior year; men-only, women-only. Campus housing is university owned. Freshman applicants given priority for college housing.
Activities and organizations: drama/theater group, choral group, marching band, Fellowship of Christian Athletes, Student Government Association, Student Alumni Leadership Council, Campus Crusade (CRU), Limestone Activities Board (LAB), national fraternities.
Athletics Member NCAA. All Division II. ***Intercollegiate sports:*** baseball M(s), basketball M(s)/W(s), cheerleading M(s)/W(s), cross-country running M(s)/W(s), field hockey W(s), football M(s), golf M(s)/W(s), lacrosse M(s)/W(s), soccer M(s)/W(s), softball W(s), swimming and diving M(s)/W(s), tennis M(s)/W(s), track and field M(s)/W(s), volleyball M(s)/W(s), wrestling M(s). ***Intramural sports:*** badminton M/W, basketball M/W, bowling M/W, racquetball M/W, soccer M/W, table tennis M/W, ultimate Frisbee M/W, volleyball M/W, weight lifting M/W.
Campus security: 24-hour emergency response devices and patrols, late-night transport/escort service, controlled dormitory access.
Student services: health clinic, personal/psychological counseling.

COSTS & FINANCIAL AID
Costs (2015–16) ***Comprehensive fee:*** $32,100 includes full-time tuition ($23,900) and room and board ($8200). Full-time tuition and fees vary according to class time and course load. Part-time tuition: $996 per semester hour. Part-time tuition and fees vary according to class time. ***College room only:*** $4150. Room and board charges vary according to board plan and housing facility. ***Payment plan:*** installment. ***Waivers:*** employees or children of employees.
Financial Aid Of all full-time matriculated undergraduates who enrolled in 2013, 972 applied for aid, 883 were judged to have need, 101 had their need fully met. 112 Federal Work-Study jobs (averaging $1360). 121 state and other part-time jobs (averaging $768). In 2013, 198 non-need-based awards were made. ***Average percent of need met:*** 61. ***Average financial aid package:*** $17,351. ***Average need-based loan:*** $3755. ***Average need-based gift aid:*** $13,939. ***Average non-need-based aid:*** $6242. ***Average indebtedness upon graduation:*** $30,856.

APPLYING
Standardized Tests *Required:* SAT or ACT (for admission). *Required for some:* Students whose native language is not English are required to submit a score of 500 or above on the TOEFL test or have proof they have successfully completed an ESL program and/or have a satisfactory score on the SAT or ACT.
Options: electronic application.
Application fee: $25.
Required: high school transcript, minimum 2.0 GPA. ***Recommended:*** 2 letters of recommendation, interview.
Application deadlines: rolling (freshmen), rolling (out-of-state freshmen), rolling (transfers).

Notification: continuous (freshmen), continuous (out-of-state freshmen), continuous (transfers).

CONTACT
Ms. Lisa Hobbs, Admissions Office Manager, Limestone College, 1115 College Drive, Gaffney, SC 29340-3799. *Phone:* 864-488-4554. *Toll-free phone:* 800-795-7151. *Fax:* 864-487-8706. *E-mail:* lhobbs@limestone.edu.

Medical University of South Carolina
Charleston, South Carolina
http://www.musc.edu/

- **State-supported** upper-level, founded 1824
- **Urban** 82-acre campus
- **Endowment** $230.3 million
- **Coed**
- **Very difficult** entrance level

FACULTY
Student/faculty ratio: 2:1.

ACADEMICS
Calendar: semesters. *Degrees:* bachelor's, master's, doctoral, post-master's, and postbachelor's certificates.

STUDENT LIFE
Housing options: college housing not available.

Activities and organizations: choral group, MUSC Student Government Association, Multicultural Group Advisory Board, Public Health Interest Group, International Association, Crisis Ministries.

Campus security: 24-hour emergency response devices and patrols, late-night transport/escort service.

Student services: health clinic, personal/psychological counseling, legal services.

FINANCIAL AID
Financial Aid Of all full-time matriculated undergraduates who enrolled in 2014, 169 applied for aid, 156 were judged to have need, 1 had their need fully met. ***Average percent of need met:*** 24. ***Average financial aid package:*** $8164. ***Average need-based loan:*** $5397. ***Average need-based gift aid:*** $5067.

APPLYING
Options: electronic application, deferred entrance.

Application fee: $95.

CONTACT
Lyla E. Hudson, Director of Admissions, Medical University of South Carolina, 41 Bee Street MSC203, Charleston, SC 29425-2030. *Phone:* 843-792-7408. *E-mail:* hudsonly@musc.edu.

Morris College
Sumter, South Carolina
http://www.morris.edu/

- **Independent** 4-year, founded 1908, affiliated with Baptist Educational and Missionary Convention of South Carolina
- **Small-town** 41-acre campus with easy access to Columbia, SC
- **Endowment** $14.0 million
- **Coed** 780 undergraduate students, 99% full-time, 57% women, 43% men
- **Noncompetitive** entrance level, 62% of applicants were admitted

UNDERGRAD STUDENTS
770 full-time, 10 part-time. Students come from 20 states and territories; 20% are from out of state; 98% Black or African American, non-Hispanic/Latino; 0.8% Hispanic/Latino; 0.1% Asian, non-Hispanic/Latino; 0.1% American Indian or Alaska Native, non-Hispanic/Latino; 1% Two or more races, non-Hispanic/Latino; 6% transferred in; 80% live on campus.

Freshmen
Admission: 2,031 applied, 1,268 admitted, 225 enrolled. ***Average high school GPA:*** 2.68.

Retention: 52% of full-time freshmen returned.

FACULTY
Total: 59, 80% full-time, 63% with terminal degrees.

Student/faculty ratio: 13:1.

ACADEMICS
Calendar: semesters. *Degree:* bachelor's.

Special study options: academic remediation for entering students, accelerated degree program, adult/continuing education programs, advanced placement credit, cooperative education, double majors, honors programs, internships, study abroad, summer session for credit. ***ROTC:*** Army (b).

Unusual degree programs: 3-2 engineering with North Carolina Agricultural and Technical State University.

Computers: 281 computers/terminals and 688 ports are available on campus for general student use. Students can access the following: campus intranet, free student e-mail accounts, online (class) grades, online (class) registration, online (class) schedules, online financial aid Information. Campuswide network is available. 100% of college-owned or -operated housing units are wired for high-speed Internet access. Wireless service is available via entire campus.

STUDENT LIFE
Housing options: men-only, women-only. Campus housing is university owned. Freshman applicants given priority for college housing.

Activities and organizations: drama/theater group, student-run newspaper, radio station, choral group, Student Government Association, New Emphasis on Nontraditional Students (NEONS), Block M Club, Pre Alumni Council, Baptist Student Union, national fraternities, national sororities.

Athletics Member NAIA. ***Intercollegiate sports:*** baseball M(s), basketball M(s)/W(s), cheerleading M(s)/W(s), cross-country running M(s)/W(s), softball W(s), track and field M(s)/W(s), volleyball W(s). ***Intramural sports:*** basketball M/W, table tennis M/W.

Campus security: 24-hour patrols, controlled dormitory access, cameras in select locations.

Student services: health clinic, personal/psychological counseling.

COSTS & FINANCIAL AID
Costs (2014–15) ***Comprehensive fee:*** $17,345 includes full-time tuition ($10,962), mandatory fees ($1355), and room and board ($5028). Part-time tuition: $457 per credit hour. ***Required fees:*** $160 per year part-time. ***College room only:*** $2138. ***Payment plan:*** installment.

Financial Aid Of all full-time matriculated undergraduates who enrolled in 2013, 887 applied for aid, 859 were judged to have need, 10 had their need fully met. 300 Federal Work-Study jobs (averaging $818). ***Average percent of need met:*** 85. ***Average financial aid package:*** $12,100. ***Average need-based loan:*** $3900. ***Average need-based gift aid:*** $7400. ***Average indebtedness upon graduation:*** $17,125.

APPLYING
Options: electronic application, deferred entrance.

Application fee: $20.

Required: high school transcript, minimum 2.0 GPA, Medical Examination Form completed by licensed medical personnel. ***Required for some:*** interview.

Application deadlines: rolling (freshmen), rolling (out-of-state freshmen), rolling (transfers).

Notification: continuous (freshmen), continuous (out-of-state freshmen), continuous (transfers).

CONTACT
Ms. Deborah C. Calhoun, Director of Admissions and Records, Morris College, 100 West College Street, Sumter, SC 29150-3599. *Phone:* 803-934-3225. *Toll-free phone:* 866-853-1345. *Fax:* 803-773-8241. *E-mail:* gscriven@morris.edu.

Newberry College
Newberry, South Carolina
http://www.newberry.edu/

- **Independent Evangelical Lutheran** 4-year, founded 1856
- **Small-town** 90-acre campus with easy access to Columbia, SC and Greenville, SC
- **Endowment** $20.9 million
- **Coed** 1,093 undergraduate students, 96% full-time, 47% women, 53% men
- **Moderately difficult** entrance level, 57% of applicants were admitted

UNDERGRAD STUDENTS
1,049 full-time, 44 part-time. Students come from 31 states and territories; 18 other countries; 23% are from out of state; 26% Black or African American, non-Hispanic/Latino; 4% Hispanic/Latino; 0.6% Asian, non-Hispanic/Latino; 0.1% Native Hawaiian or other Pacific Islander, non-Hispanic/Latino; 0.4% American Indian or Alaska Native, non-Hispanic/Latino; 3% Two or more races, non-Hispanic/Latino; 2% Race/ethnicity unknown; 4% international; 8% transferred in; 77% live on campus.

Freshmen
Admission: 1,045 applied, 593 admitted, 277 enrolled. ***Average high school GPA:*** 3.4. ***Test scores:*** SAT critical reading scores over 500: 37%; SAT math scores over 500: 41%; SAT writing scores over 500: 23%; ACT scores over 18: 70%; SAT critical reading scores over 600: 5%; SAT math scores over 600: 9%; SAT writing scores over 600: 3%; ACT scores over 24: 23%; SAT critical reading scores over 700: 1%; SAT math scores over 700: 1%; ACT scores over 30: 3%.

Retention: 72% of full-time freshmen returned.

FACULTY
Total: 131, 53% full-time, 47% with terminal degrees.

Student/faculty ratio: 12:1.

ACADEMICS
Calendar: semesters. *Degree:* bachelor's.

Special study options: academic remediation for entering students, adult/continuing education programs, advanced placement credit, double majors, honors programs, independent study, internships, part-time degree program, services for LD students, student-designed majors, study abroad, summer session for credit. ***ROTC:*** Army (b).

Unusual degree programs: 3-2 forestry with Forestry and Environmental Management Dual-Degree Program with Duke University. Students may earn the Bachelor's and Master's degrees in 5 years, spending 3 years at Newberry and 2 years at Duke University.

Computers: 22 computers/terminals are available on campus for general student use. Students can access the following: campus intranet, computer help desk, free student e-mail accounts, online (class) grades, online (class) registration, online (class) schedules. Campuswide network is available. 100% of college-owned or -operated housing units are wired for high-speed Internet access. Wireless service is available via entire campus.

STUDENT LIFE
Housing options: on-campus residence required through senior year; coed, men-only, women-only. Campus housing is university owned and is provided by a third party. Freshman applicants given priority for college housing.

Activities and organizations: drama/theater group, student-run radio station, choral group, marching band, Future Educators Association, Multi Cultural Student Association, American Chemistry Society, Blue Key Honor Club, Baptist Collegiate Ministry, national fraternities, national sororities.

Athletics Member NCAA. All Division II. ***Intercollegiate sports:*** baseball M(s), basketball M(s)/W(s), cheerleading M(s)/W(s), cross-country running M(s)/W(s), field hockey W(s), football M(s), golf M(s)/W(s), lacrosse W(s), soccer M(s)/W(s), softball W(s), tennis M(s)/W(s), volleyball W(s), wrestling M(s). ***Intramural sports:*** basketball M/W, soccer M/W, volleyball M/W.

Campus security: 24-hour emergency response devices and patrols, late-night transport/escort service, controlled dormitory access.

Student services: health clinic, personal/psychological counseling.

COSTS & FINANCIAL AID
Costs (2014–15) ***Comprehensive fee:*** $33,600 includes full-time tuition ($22,500), mandatory fees ($1800), and room and board ($9300). Full-time tuition and fees vary according to course load and student level. Part-time tuition: $525 per hour. Part-time tuition and fees vary according to course load and student level. No tuition increase for student's term of enrollment. ***Required fees:*** $125 per term part-time. ***College room only:*** $4700. Room and board charges vary according to board plan and housing facility. ***Payment plan:*** installment. ***Waivers:*** employees or children of employees.

Financial Aid Of all full-time matriculated undergraduates who enrolled in 2013, 903 applied for aid, 839 were judged to have need, 139 had their need fully met. 93 Federal Work-Study jobs (averaging $1100). In 2013, 101 non-need-based awards were made. ***Average percent of need met:*** 70. ***Average financial aid package:*** $21,948. ***Average need-based loan:*** $4577. ***Average need-based gift aid:*** $18,487. ***Average non-need-based aid:*** $10,784. ***Average indebtedness upon graduation:*** $26,908.

APPLYING
Standardized Tests *Required:* SAT or ACT (for admission).

Options: electronic application, deferred entrance.

Application fee: $30.

Required: essay or personal statement, high school transcript, minimum 2.0 GPA, 1 letter of recommendation. ***Recommended:*** interview.

Application deadlines: rolling (freshmen), rolling (out-of-state freshmen), rolling (transfers).

Notification: continuous (freshmen), continuous (out-of-state freshmen), continuous (transfers).

CONTACT
Mr. Joel Vander Horst, Director of Admissions, Newberry College, 2100 College Street, Newberry, SC 29108. *Phone:* 803-947-2110. *Toll-free phone:* 800-845-4955. *Fax:* 803-321-5138. *E-mail:* admissions@newberry.edu.

North Greenville University
Tigerville, South Carolina
http://www.ngu.edu/

- **Independent Southern Baptist** comprehensive, founded 1892
- **Rural** 380-acre campus with easy access to Greenville
- **Endowment** $20.9 million
- **Coed** 2,320 undergraduate students, 89% full-time, 49% women, 51% men
- **Minimally difficult** entrance level, 59% of applicants were admitted

UNDERGRAD STUDENTS
2,063 full-time, 257 part-time. Students come from 33 states and territories; 22 other countries; 23% are from out of state; 7% Black or African American, non-Hispanic/Latino; 3% Hispanic/Latino; 0.5% Asian, non-Hispanic/Latino; 0.2% Native Hawaiian or other Pacific Islander, non-Hispanic/Latino; 0.3% American Indian or Alaska Native, non-Hispanic/Latino; 2% Two or more races, non-Hispanic/Latino; 8% Race/ethnicity unknown; 0.3% international; 5% transferred in; 65% live on campus.

Freshmen
Admission: 1,776 applied, 1,056 admitted, 575 enrolled. ***Average high school GPA:*** 3.5. ***Test scores:*** SAT critical reading scores over 500: 71%; SAT math scores over 500: 66%; SAT writing scores over 500: 56%; ACT scores over 18: 97%; SAT critical reading scores over 600: 25%; SAT math scores over 600: 22%; SAT writing scores over 600: 16%; ACT scores over 24: 51%; SAT critical reading scores over 700: 5%; SAT math scores over 700: 2%; SAT writing scores over 700: 4%; ACT scores over 30: 6%.

Retention: 77% of full-time freshmen returned.

FACULTY
Total: 210, 65% full-time, 45% with terminal degrees.

Student/faculty ratio: 14:1.

ACADEMICS
Calendar: semesters. *Degrees:* bachelor's, master's, and doctoral.

Special study options: academic remediation for entering students, accelerated degree program, advanced placement credit, cooperative education, distance learning, double majors, English as a second language, freshman honors college, honors programs, independent study, internships, part-time degree program, services for LD students, student-designed majors, study abroad, summer session for credit. ***ROTC:*** Army (c).

Unusual degree programs: 3-2 engineering with Dual degree in Mathematics and Engineering with Clemson University.

Computers: 95 computers/terminals and 6 ports are available on campus for general student use. Students can access the following: campus intranet, computer help desk, free student e-mail accounts, online (class) grades, online (class) registration, online (class) schedules. Campuswide network is available. 100% of college-owned or -operated housing units are wired for high-speed Internet access. Wireless service is available via entire campus.

STUDENT LIFE

Housing options: on-campus residence required through sophomore year; men-only, women-only. Campus housing is university owned. Freshman campus housing is guaranteed.

Activities and organizations: drama/theater group, student-run newspaper, radio station, choral group, marching band, Baptist Student Union, Fellowship of Christians in Service, Fellowship of Christian Athletes, Black Student Fellowship, Education Club.

Athletics Member NCAA, NCCAA. All NCAA Division II. ***Intercollegiate sports:*** baseball M(s), basketball M(s)/W(s), cheerleading M(s)/W(s), cross-country running M(s)/W(s), football M(s), golf M(s)/W(s), lacrosse M(s)/W(s), soccer M(s)/W(s), softball W(s), tennis M(s)/W(s), track and field M(s)/W(s), volleyball M(s)/W(s). ***Intramural sports:*** basketball M/W, bowling M/W, football M, golf M/W, softball M/W, table tennis M/W, tennis M/W, ultimate Frisbee M/W, volleyball W, weight lifting M/W.

Campus security: 24-hour emergency response devices and patrols, late-night transport/escort service, controlled dormitory access.

Student services: health clinic, personal/psychological counseling.

COSTS & FINANCIAL AID

Costs (2015–16) ***Comprehensive fee:*** $25,930 includes full-time tuition ($16,290) and room and board ($9640). Full-time tuition and fees vary according to course load. Part-time tuition: $3900 per credit. ***Room and board:*** Room and board charges vary according to housing facility. ***Payment plan:*** installment. ***Waivers:*** employees or children of employees.

Financial Aid Of all full-time matriculated undergraduates who enrolled in 2013, 1,144 applied for aid, 1,144 were judged to have need, 1,144 had their need fully met. ***Average percent of need met:*** 25. ***Average financial aid package:*** $13,469. ***Average need-based gift aid:*** $3367.

APPLYING

Standardized Tests *Required:* SAT or ACT (for admission). *Required for some:* CPT. *Recommended:* CPT.

Options: electronic application, early admission, deferred entrance.

Application fee: $25.

Required: high school transcript. ***Required for some:*** interview. ***Recommended:*** minimum 2.0 GPA.

Application deadlines: 8/22 (freshmen), 8/26 (transfers).

Notification: continuous (freshmen), continuous (transfers).

CONTACT

North Greenville University, PO Box 1892, Tigerville, SC 29688-1892. *Phone:* 864-977-7052. *Toll-free phone:* 800-468-6642 Ext. 7001.

Presbyterian College

Clinton, South Carolina

http://www.presby.edu/

- **Independent** comprehensive, founded 1880, affiliated with Presbyterian Church (U.S.A.)
- **Small-town** 240-acre campus with easy access to Greenville, Spartanburg
- **Endowment** $92.0 million
- **Coed** 1,146 undergraduate students, 94% full-time, 55% women, 45% men
- **Very difficult** entrance level, 54% of applicants were admitted

UNDERGRAD STUDENTS

1,078 full-time, 68 part-time. Students come from 30 states and territories; 23 other countries; 38% are from out of state; 12% Black or African American, non-Hispanic/Latino; 2% Hispanic/Latino; 1% Asian, non-Hispanic/Latino; 0.2% American Indian or Alaska Native, non-Hispanic/Latino; 2% Two or more races, non-Hispanic/Latino; 0.6% Race/ethnicity unknown; 1% international; 2% transferred in.

Freshmen

Admission: 1,506 applied, 809 admitted, 275 enrolled. ***Average high school GPA:*** 3.49. ***Test scores:*** SAT critical reading scores over 500: 63%; SAT math scores over 500: 72%; ACT scores over 18: 99%; SAT critical reading scores over 600: 27%; SAT math scores over 600: 31%; ACT scores over 24: 54%; SAT critical reading scores over 700: 4%; SAT math scores over 700: 3%; ACT scores over 30: 6%.

Retention: 84% of full-time freshmen returned.

FACULTY

Total: 135, 73% full-time, 81% with terminal degrees.

Student/faculty ratio: 12:1.

ACADEMICS

Calendar: semesters. *Degrees:* bachelor's and doctoral.

Special study options: advanced placement credit, distance learning, double majors, honors programs, independent study, internships, off-campus study, services for LD students, study abroad, summer session for credit. ***ROTC:*** Army (b).

Unusual degree programs: 3-2 engineering with Auburn University, Clemson University, Vanderbilt University, University of South Carolina.

Computers: 100 computers/terminals and 275 ports are available on campus for general student use. Students can access the following: campus intranet, free student e-mail accounts, online (class) grades, online (class) registration, online (class) schedules. Campuswide network is available. 100% of college-owned or -operated housing units are wired for high-speed Internet access. Wireless service is available via entire campus.

STUDENT LIFE

Housing options: on-campus residence required through senior year; coed, men-only, women-only, special housing for students with disabilities. Campus housing is university owned. Freshman campus housing is guaranteed.

Activities and organizations: drama/theater group, student-run newspaper, choral group, Student Volunteer Services, Intramural sports, Student Union Board, Fellowship of Christian Athletes, Student Government Association, national fraternities, national sororities.

Athletics Member NCAA. All Division I. ***Intercollegiate sports:*** baseball M(s), basketball M(s)/W(s), cheerleading M(s)/W(s), cross-country running M(s)/W(s), football M(s), golf M(s)/W(s), lacrosse W(s), soccer M(s)/W(s), softball W(s), tennis M(s)/W(s), volleyball W(s). ***Intramural sports:*** basketball M/W, football M/W, golf M/W, rock climbing M/W, skiing (cross-country) M/W, soccer M/W, softball M/W, table tennis M/W, tennis M/W, ultimate Frisbee M/W, volleyball M/W.

Campus security: 24-hour emergency response devices and patrols, late-night transport/escort service, controlled dormitory access.

Student services: health clinic, personal/psychological counseling.

COSTS & FINANCIAL AID

Costs (2014–15) ***Comprehensive fee:*** $44,172 includes full-time tuition ($32,076), mandatory fees ($2752), and room and board ($9344). Full-time tuition and fees vary according to course load and reciprocity agreements. Part-time tuition: $1337 per credit hour. Part-time tuition and fees vary according to course load and program. ***Required fees:*** $52 per term part-time. ***College room only:*** $4542. Room and board charges vary according to board plan and housing facility. ***Payment plan:*** installment. ***Waivers:*** senior citizens and employees or children of employees.

Financial Aid Of all full-time matriculated undergraduates who enrolled in 2014, 916 applied for aid, 812 were judged to have need, 355 had their need fully met. In 2014, 186 non-need-based awards were made. ***Average percent of need met:*** 88. ***Average financial aid package:*** $33,373. ***Average need-based loan:*** $4299. ***Average need-based gift aid:*** $30,703. ***Average non-need-based aid:*** $15,692. ***Average indebtedness upon graduation:*** $30,835. ***Financial aid deadline:*** 6/30.

APPLYING
Standardized Tests *Required for some:* SAT or ACT (for admission).

Options: electronic application, early admission, early decision, early action, deferred entrance.

Required: essay or personal statement, high school transcript, minimum 2.0 GPA, 1 letter of recommendation. ***Recommended:*** interview.

Application deadlines: 6/30 (freshmen), 6/30 (out-of-state freshmen), 7/1 (transfers), 11/15 (early action).

Early decision deadline: 11/1.

Notification: 3/15 (freshmen), 3/15 (out-of-state freshmen), 7/15 (transfers), 12/1 (early decision), 12/15 (early action).

CONTACT
Mr. Brian J. Fortman, Dean for Enrollment Management, Presbyterian College, 503 South Broad Street, Clinton, SC 29325. *Phone:* 864-833-8258. *Toll-free phone:* 800-960-7583. *Fax:* 864-833-8481. *E-mail:* bjfortman@presby.edu.

South Carolina State University

Orangeburg, South Carolina

http://www.scsu.edu/

- **State-supported** comprehensive, founded 1896, part of South Carolina Commission on Higher Education
- **Small-town** 160-acre campus
- **Coed** 2,791 undergraduate students, 92% full-time, 51% women, 49% men
- **Minimally difficult** entrance level, 85% of applicants were admitted

UNDERGRAD STUDENTS
2,581 full-time, 210 part-time. Students come from 34 states and territories; 23 other countries; 18% are from out of state; 95% Black or African American, non-Hispanic/Latino; 0.6% Hispanic/Latino; 0.6% Asian, non-Hispanic/Latino; 0.1% American Indian or Alaska Native, non-Hispanic/Latino; 0.8% Race/ethnicity unknown; 0.1% international; 5% transferred in; 54% live on campus.

Freshmen
Admission: 2,911 applied, 2,461 admitted, 641 enrolled. ***Average high school GPA:*** 2.97. ***Test scores:*** SAT critical reading scores over 500: 13%; SAT math scores over 500: 13%; ACT scores over 18: 27%; SAT critical reading scores over 600: 2%; SAT math scores over 600: 4%; ACT scores over 24: 1%; SAT math scores over 700: 1%.
Retention: 63% of full-time freshmen returned.

FACULTY
Total: 234, 75% full-time, 64% with terminal degrees.
Student/faculty ratio: 15:1.

ACADEMICS
Calendar: semesters. *Degrees:* bachelor's, master's, doctoral, and postbachelor's certificates.

Special study options: adult/continuing education programs, advanced placement credit, cooperative education, distance learning, honors programs, independent study, internships, off-campus study, part-time degree program, study abroad, summer session for credit. ***ROTC:*** Army (b), Air Force (c).

Computers: 400 computers/terminals and 250 ports are available on campus for general student use. Students can access the following: computer help desk, free student e-mail accounts, online (class) grades, online (class) registration, online (class) schedules. Campuswide network is available. 100% of college-owned or -operated housing units are wired for high-speed Internet access. Wireless service is available via entire campus.

STUDENT LIFE
Housing options: coed, men-only, women-only, special housing for students with disabilities. Campus housing is university owned, leased by the school and is provided by a third party. Freshman applicants given priority for college housing.

Activities and organizations: drama/theater group, student-run newspaper, choral group, marching band, Student Government Association, Campus Activity Board, NAACP, United Voices of Christ, Student Media, national fraternities, national sororities.

Athletics Member NCAA. All Division I except football (Division I-AA). ***Intercollegiate sports:*** basketball M(s)/W(s), cross-country running M(s)/W(s), soccer W(s), softball W(s), tennis M(s)/W(s), track and field M(s)/W(s), volleyball W(s). ***Intramural sports:*** basketball M/W, softball M/W.

Campus security: 24-hour emergency response devices and patrols, late-night transport/escort service, controlled dormitory access.

Student services: health clinic, personal/psychological counseling.

COSTS & FINANCIAL AID
Costs (2014–15) ***Tuition:*** state resident $7290 full-time, $420 per credit hour part-time; nonresident $17,058 full-time, $811 per credit hour part-time. Full-time tuition and fees vary according to course load, program, and reciprocity agreements. Part-time tuition and fees vary according to course load, program, and reciprocity agreements. ***Required fees:*** $2798 full-time. ***Room and board:*** $9402; room only: $6300. Room and board charges vary according to board plan and housing facility. ***Payment plan:*** installment. ***Waivers:*** senior citizens and employees or children of employees.

Financial Aid Of all full-time matriculated undergraduates who enrolled in 2007, 343 Federal Work-Study jobs (averaging $1048). 360 state and other part-time jobs (averaging $2050). ***Average indebtedness upon graduation:*** $26,678.

APPLYING
Standardized Tests *Required:* SAT or ACT (for admission). *Recommended:* SAT Subject Tests (for admission).

Options: electronic application, deferred entrance.

Application fee: $25.

Required: high school transcript, minimum 2.0 GPA.

Application deadlines: 7/31 (freshmen), 7/31 (transfers).

Notification: continuous (freshmen), continuous (transfers).

CONTACT
Mr. Justin Pearson, Director of Admissions, South Carolina State University, 300 College Street Northeast, Orangeburg, SC 29117-0001. *Phone:* 803-536-7186. *Toll-free phone:* 800-260-5956. *Fax:* 803-536-8990. *E-mail:* admissions@scsu.edu.

South University

Columbia, South Carolina

http://www.southuniversity.edu/columbia/

- **Proprietary** comprehensive, founded 1935, part of Education Management Corporation
- **Coed**

ACADEMICS
Calendar: quarters. *Degrees:* associate, bachelor's, master's, and doctoral.

CONTACT
South University, 9 Science Court, Columbia, SC 29203. *Phone:* 803-799-9082. *Toll-free phone:* 866-629-3031.

University of South Carolina

Columbia, South Carolina

http://www.sc.edu/

- **State-supported** university, founded 1801, part of University of South Carolina System
- **Urban** 444-acre campus
- **Coed**
- **Moderately difficult** entrance level

ACADEMICS
Calendar: semesters. *Degrees:* associate, bachelor's, master's, doctoral, post-master's, and postbachelor's certificates.

STUDENT LIFE
Housing options: on-campus residence required for freshman year; coed, men-only, women-only, special housing for students with disabilities. Campus housing is university owned. Freshman campus housing is guaranteed.

Activities and organizations: drama/theater group, student-run newspaper, radio and television station, choral group, marching band, Social Work Student Association, Friendship Association of Chinese Students and Scholars, Alpha Lambda Delta, Residence Hall Association, Student Bar Association, national fraternities, national sororities.

Athletics Member NCAA. All Division I except football (Division I-A).

Campus security: 24-hour emergency response devices and patrols, student patrols, late-night transport/escort service, controlled dormitory access.

Student services: health clinic, personal/psychological counseling, women's center.

COSTS & FINANCIAL AID

Costs (2014–15) ***Tuition:*** state resident $10,758 full-time, $448 per credit hour part-time; nonresident $29,040 full-time, $1210 per credit hour part-time. Full-time tuition and fees vary according to program and reciprocity agreements. Part-time tuition and fees vary according to course load. ***Required fees:*** $400 full-time. ***Room and board:*** $9248; room only: $6216. Room and board charges vary according to board plan, housing facility, and location.

Financial Aid Of all full-time matriculated undergraduates who enrolled in 2013, 14,979 applied for aid, 11,120 were judged to have need, 2,813 had their need fully met. 591 Federal Work-Study jobs (averaging $3110). 3,195 state and other part-time jobs (averaging $1760). In 2013, 6650 non-need-based awards were made. ***Average percent of need met:*** 73. ***Average financial aid package:*** $13,332. ***Average need-based loan:*** $3453. ***Average need-based gift aid:*** $4973. ***Average non-need-based aid:*** $6224. ***Average indebtedness upon graduation:*** $25,711.

APPLYING

Standardized Tests *Required:* SAT or ACT (for admission).

Options: electronic application, early action.

Application fee: $50.

Required: high school transcript, minimum 2.0 GPA.

CONTACT

Dr. Mary Wagner, Senior Associate Director, Undergraduate Admissions, University of South Carolina, Columbia, SC 29208. *Phone:* 803-777-7700. *Toll-free phone:* 800-868-5872. *Fax:* 803-777-0101. *E-mail:* admissions-ugrad@sc.edu.

University of South Carolina Aiken

Aiken, South Carolina

http://www.usca.edu/

- **State-supported** comprehensive, founded 1961, part of University of South Carolina System
- **Suburban** 453-acre campus with easy access to Columbia
- **Endowment** $23.6 million
- **Coed** 3,256 undergraduate students, 82% full-time, 62% women, 38% men
- **Moderately difficult** entrance level, 66% of applicants were admitted

UNDERGRAD STUDENTS

2,663 full-time, 593 part-time. Students come from 29 states and territories; 23 other countries; 12% are from out of state; 26% Black or African American, non-Hispanic/Latino; 4% Hispanic/Latino; 1% Asian, non-Hispanic/Latino; 0.4% American Indian or Alaska Native, non-Hispanic/Latino; 4% Two or more races, non-Hispanic/Latino; 2% Race/ethnicity unknown; 3% international; 10% transferred in; 30% live on campus.

Freshmen

Admission: 2,091 applied, 1,373 admitted, 643 enrolled. ***Average high school GPA:*** 3.66. ***Test scores:*** SAT critical reading scores over 500: 42%; SAT math scores over 500: 44%; SAT writing scores over 500: 32%; ACT scores over 18: 77%; SAT critical reading scores over 600: 10%; SAT math scores over 600: 11%; SAT writing scores over 600: 5%; ACT scores over 24: 20%; ACT scores over 30: 1%.

Retention: 67% of full-time freshmen returned.

FACULTY

Total: 265, 56% full-time, 52% with terminal degrees.

Student/faculty ratio: 15:1.

ACADEMICS

Calendar: semesters. *Degrees:* bachelor's and master's.

Special study options: adult/continuing education programs, advanced placement credit, cooperative education, distance learning, double majors, English as a second language, honors programs, independent study, internships, off-campus study, part-time degree program, services for LD students, student-designed majors, study abroad, summer session for credit.

Computers: 550 computers/terminals and 1,400 ports are available on campus for general student use. Students can access the following: computer help desk, free student e-mail accounts, online (class) grades, online (class) registration, online (class) schedules. Campuswide network is available. 100% of college-owned or -operated housing units are wired for high-speed Internet access. Wireless service is available via entire campus.

STUDENT LIFE

Housing options: coed, special housing for students with disabilities. Campus housing is university owned. Freshman applicants given priority for college housing.

Activities and organizations: drama/theater group, student-run newspaper, choral group, National Society of Leadership and Success, Pacer Fanatics, Circle K, Alpha Omicron Pi, Pacesetters, national fraternities, national sororities.

Athletics Member NCAA. All Division II. ***Intercollegiate sports:*** baseball M(s), basketball M(s)/W(s), cross-country running W(s), golf M(s), soccer M(s)/W(s), softball W(s), tennis M(s)/W(s), volleyball W(s). ***Intramural sports:*** basketball M/W, cheerleading M(c)/W(c), equestrian sports M(c)/W(c), soccer M/W, ultimate Frisbee M/W, volleyball M/W.

Campus security: 24-hour emergency response devices and patrols, late-night transport/escort service, controlled dormitory access.

Student services: health clinic, personal/psychological counseling.

COSTS & FINANCIAL AID

Costs (2014–15) ***Tuition:*** state resident $9312 full-time, $388 per credit hour part-time; nonresident $18,636 full-time, $777 per credit hour part-time. Full-time tuition and fees vary according to reciprocity agreements. Part-time tuition and fees vary according to course load and reciprocity agreements. ***Required fees:*** $290 full-time, $9 per credit hour part-time, $25 per term part-time. ***Room and board:*** $7110. Room and board charges vary according to board plan and housing facility. ***Payment plan:*** deferred payment. ***Waivers:*** senior citizens and employees or children of employees.

Financial Aid Of all full-time matriculated undergraduates who enrolled in 2013, 2,267 applied for aid, 1,463 were judged to have need, 188 had their need fully met. 54 Federal Work-Study jobs (averaging $1655). 351 state and other part-time jobs (averaging $1806). In 2013, 246 non-need-based awards were made. ***Average percent of need met:*** 62. ***Average financial aid package:*** $10,374. ***Average need-based loan:*** $4267. ***Average need-based gift aid:*** $6547. ***Average non-need-based aid:*** $2213. ***Average indebtedness upon graduation:*** $28,104.

APPLYING

Standardized Tests *Required:* SAT or ACT (for admission).

Options: electronic application, early admission, deferred entrance.

Application fee: $45.

Required: high school transcript.

Application deadlines: 8/1 (freshmen), 8/1 (out-of-state freshmen), 8/1 (transfers).

Notification: continuous (freshmen), continuous (out-of-state freshmen), continuous (transfers).

CONTACT

Mr. Andrew Hendrix, Director of Admissions, University of South Carolina Aiken, 471 University Parkway, Aiken, SC 29801-6309. *Phone:* 803-641-3366. *Toll-free phone:* 888-WOW-USCA. *Fax:* 803-641-3727. *E-mail:* admit@usca.edu.

University of South Carolina Beaufort

Bluffton, South Carolina

http://www.uscb.edu/

- **State-supported** 4-year, founded 1959, part of University of South Carolina system
- **Suburban** 200-acre campus
- **Coed** 1,794 undergraduate students, 80% full-time, 62% women, 38% men
- **Minimally difficult** entrance level

UNDERGRAD STUDENTS

1,435 full-time, 359 part-time. Students come from 31 states and territories; 7 other countries; 14% are from out of state; 20% Black or African American, non-Hispanic/Latino; 6% Hispanic/Latino; 2% Asian, non-Hispanic/Latino; 0.1% Native Hawaiian or other Pacific Islander, non-Hispanic/Latino; 0.3% American Indian or Alaska Native, non-Hispanic/Latino; 3% Two or more races, non-Hispanic/Latino; 8% Race/ethnicity unknown; 1% international; 14% transferred in; 20% live on campus.

Freshmen

Admission: 402 enrolled. ***Average high school GPA:*** 3.61.

FACULTY

Total: 141, 42% full-time.

Student/faculty ratio: 18:1.

ACADEMICS

Calendar: semesters. *Degrees:* associate and bachelor's.

Special study options: adult/continuing education programs, advanced placement credit, distance learning, double majors, independent study, internships, part-time degree program, services for LD students, study abroad, summer session for credit.

Computers: Students can access the following: computer help desk, free student e-mail accounts, online (class) grades, online (class) registration, online (class) schedules, wireless computing. Campuswide network is available. 100% of college-owned or -operated housing units are wired for high-speed Internet access. Wireless service is available via entire campus.

STUDENT LIFE

Housing options: on-campus residence required for freshman yearCampus housing is university owned and leased by the school.

Activities and organizations: drama/theater group, student-run newspaper, Student Government Association, Gamma Beta Phi, Black Student Organization, Business Club, Environmental Awareness Club, national fraternities, national sororities.

Athletics Member NAIA. ***Intercollegiate sports:*** baseball M(s), cross-country running M(s)/W(s), golf M(s)/W(s), soccer W(s), softball W, track and field M(s)/W(s).

Campus security: 24-hour emergency response devices, evening security service.

Student services: personal/psychological counseling.

COSTS & FINANCIAL AID

Costs (2014–15) ***One-time required fee:*** $175. ***Tuition:*** state resident $9018 full-time, $376 per credit hour part-time; nonresident $19,038 full-time, $793 per credit hour part-time. Full-time tuition and fees vary according to course load, program, and reciprocity agreements. Part-time tuition and fees vary according to course load, program, and reciprocity agreements. ***Required fees:*** $386 full-time, $14 per credit hour part-time, $25 per term part-time. ***Room and board:*** $7310; room only: $5050. Room and board charges vary according to board plan, housing facility, and location. ***Payment plan:*** deferred payment. ***Waivers:*** senior citizens and employees or children of employees.

Financial Aid Of all full-time matriculated undergraduates who enrolled in 2011, 23 Federal Work-Study jobs (averaging $2800).

APPLYING

Standardized Tests *Required:* SAT or ACT (for admission).

Options: electronic application, deferred entrance.

Application fee: $40.

Required: high school transcript, specific college prep classes required from high school. ***Recommended:*** minimum 2.0 GPA.

Application deadlines: rolling (freshmen), rolling (transfers).

Notification: continuous (freshmen), continuous (transfers).

CONTACT

Ms. Monica Williams, University of South Carolina Beaufort, 1 University Boulevard, Bluffton, SC 29909. *Phone:* 843-208-8112. *Fax:* 843-208-8015. *E-mail:* monicaw@sc.edu.

University of South Carolina Union

Union, South Carolina

http://uscunion.sc.edu/

- **State-supported** primarily 2-year, founded 1965, part of University of South Carolina System
- **Small-town** campus with easy access to Charlotte
- **Coed** 500 undergraduate students, 50% full-time, 60% women, 40% men
- **Minimally difficult** entrance level

UNDERGRAD STUDENTS

250 full-time, 250 part-time.

Freshmen

Admission: 400 enrolled. ***Average high school GPA:*** 3.

FACULTY

Total: 38, 26% full-time.

Student/faculty ratio: 18:1.

ACADEMICS

Calendar: semesters. *Degrees:* associate and bachelor's.

Special study options: cooperative education, part-time degree program.

Computers: 60 computers/terminals are available on campus for general student use. Students can access the following: campus intranet, computer help desk, free student e-mail accounts, online (class) grades, online (class) registration, online (class) schedules. Campuswide network is available. Wireless service is available via entire campus.

STUDENT LIFE

Housing options: college housing not available.

Activities and organizations: drama/theater group, student-run newspaper, choral group.

Athletics ***Intramural sports:*** baseball M(c).

COSTS & FINANCIAL AID

Costs (2015–16) ***Tuition:*** state resident $3147 full-time, $262 per credit hour part-time; nonresident $7869 full-time, $656 per credit hour part-time. Full-time tuition and fees vary according to course load, degree level, and student level. Part-time tuition and fees vary according to student level. ***Required fees:*** $361 full-time, $180 per term part-time. ***Payment plan:*** deferred payment. ***Waivers:*** senior citizens.

Financial Aid Of all full-time matriculated undergraduates who enrolled in 2013, 16 Federal Work-Study jobs (averaging $3400).

APPLYING

Standardized Tests *Required:* SAT or ACT (for admission).

Options: electronic application.

Application fee: $40.

Required: high school transcript.

CONTACT

Mr. Michael B. Greer, Director of Enrollment Services, University of South Carolina Union, PO Drawer 729, Union, SC 29379-0729. *Phone:* 864-429-8728. *E-mail:* tyoung@gwm.sc.edu.

University of South Carolina Upstate

Spartanburg, South Carolina

http://www.uscupstate.edu/

- **State-supported** comprehensive, founded 1967, part of University of South Carolina System
- **Urban** 330-acre campus with easy access to Charlotte
- **Endowment** $7.7 million
- **Coed** 5,334 undergraduate students, 79% full-time, 65% women, 35% men
- **Moderately difficult** entrance level, 53% of applicants were admitted

UNDERGRAD STUDENTS
4,232 full-time, 1,102 part-time. Students come from 35 states and territories; 20 other countries; 5% are from out of state; 28% Black or African American, non-Hispanic/Latino; 5% Hispanic/Latino; 3% Asian, non-Hispanic/Latino; 0.1% Native Hawaiian or other Pacific Islander, non-Hispanic/Latino; 0.3% American Indian or Alaska Native, non-Hispanic/Latino; 3% Two or more races, non-Hispanic/Latino; 5% Race/ethnicity unknown; 1% international; 15% transferred in; 19% live on campus.

Freshmen
Admission: 3,995 applied, 2,098 admitted, 791 enrolled. ***Average high school GPA:*** 2.53. ***Test scores:*** SAT critical reading scores over 500: 35%; SAT math scores over 500: 37%; SAT writing scores over 500: 27%; ACT scores over 18: 80%; SAT critical reading scores over 600: 6%; SAT math scores over 600: 6%; SAT writing scores over 600: 4%; ACT scores over 24: 16%; SAT critical reading scores over 700: 1%; ACT scores over 30: 1%.
Retention: 73% of full-time freshmen returned.

FACULTY
Total: 429, 49% full-time, 45% with terminal degrees.
Student/faculty ratio: 16:1.

ACADEMICS
Calendar: semesters. *Degrees:* bachelor's, master's, and postbachelor's certificates.
Special study options: academic remediation for entering students, accelerated degree program, adult/continuing education programs, advanced placement credit, cooperative education, distance learning, double majors, English as a second language, honors programs, independent study, internships, off-campus study, part-time degree program, services for LD students, student-designed majors, study abroad, summer session for credit. ***ROTC:*** Army (c).
Computers: 450 computers/terminals are available on campus for general student use. Students can access the following: campus intranet, computer help desk, free student e-mail accounts, online (class) grades, online (class) registration, online (class) schedules. Campuswide network is available. Wireless service is available via classrooms, computer centers, computer labs, dorm rooms, libraries, student centers.

STUDENT LIFE
Housing options: coed, special housing for students with disabilities. Campus housing is university owned. Freshman applicants given priority for college housing.
Activities and organizations: drama/theater group, student-run newspaper, choral group, African-American Association, Campus Activity Board, Student Nurses Association, Student Government Association, Impact, national fraternities, national sororities.
Athletics Member NCAA. All Division I. ***Intercollegiate sports:*** baseball M(s), basketball M(s)/W(s), cheerleading M(s)/W(s), cross-country running M(s)/W(s), golf M(s)/W(s), soccer M(s)/W(s), softball W(s), tennis M(s)/W(s), track and field M(s)/W(s), volleyball W(s). ***Intramural sports:*** badminton M/W, baseball M, basketball M/W, bowling M/W, football M/W, golf M/W, racquetball M/W, soccer M/W, softball M/W, table tennis M/W, tennis M/W, track and field M/W, volleyball M/W.
Campus security: 24-hour emergency response devices and patrols, late-night transport/escort service, campus security cameras.
Student services: health clinic, personal/psychological counseling, women's center.

COSTS & FINANCIAL AID
Costs (2014–15) ***One-time required fee:*** $75. ***Tuition:*** state resident $10,068 full-time, $420 per semester hour part-time; nonresident $20,418 full-time, $851 per semester hour part-time. Full-time tuition and fees vary according to course load and program. Part-time tuition and fees vary according to course load and program. ***Required fees:*** $450 full-time. ***Room and board:*** $7682; room only: $4732. Room and board charges vary according to board plan and housing facility. ***Payment plan:*** deferred payment. ***Waivers:*** senior citizens.
Financial Aid Of all full-time matriculated undergraduates who enrolled in 2013, 3,484 applied for aid, 2,931 were judged to have need, 312 had their need fully met. 60 Federal Work-Study jobs (averaging $1987). 482 state and other part-time jobs (averaging $1795). In 2013, 148 non-need-based awards were made. ***Average percent of need met:*** 52. ***Average financial aid package:*** $9953. ***Average need-based loan:*** $4299. ***Average need-based gift aid:*** $4774. ***Average non-need-based aid:*** $7688. ***Average indebtedness upon graduation:*** $26,566.

APPLYING
Standardized Tests *Required:* SAT or ACT (for admission).
Options: electronic application, deferred entrance.
Application fee: $40.
Required: high school transcript, minimum 2.0 GPA, college preparatory courses.
Notification: continuous (freshmen), continuous (transfers).

CONTACT
Ms. Donette Stewart, Associate Vice Chancellor for Enrollment Services, University of South Carolina Upstate, 800 University Way, Spartanburg, SC 29303. *Phone:* 864-503-5280. *Toll-free phone:* 800-277-8727. *Fax:* 864-503-5727. *E-mail:* dstewart@uscupstate.edu.

Voorhees College
Denmark, South Carolina
http://www.voorhees.edu/

- **Independent Episcopal** 4-year, founded 1897
- **Rural** 350-acre campus
- **Endowment** $5.9 million
- **Coed** 468 undergraduate students, 97% full-time, 54% women, 46% men
- **Moderately difficult** entrance level, 50% of applicants were admitted

UNDERGRAD STUDENTS
452 full-time, 16 part-time. 5% transferred in; 70% live on campus.

Freshmen
Admission: 2,776 applied, 1,389 admitted, 138 enrolled. ***Average high school GPA:*** 2.

FACULTY
Total: 44, 89% full-time.

ACADEMICS
Calendar: semesters. *Degree:* bachelor's.
Special study options: academic remediation for entering students, adult/continuing education programs, advanced placement credit, cooperative education, double majors, honors programs, internships, part-time degree program, services for LD students, summer session for credit. ***ROTC:*** Army (c).
Computers: 300 computers/terminals and 300 ports are available on campus for general student use. Students can access the following: campus intranet, computer help desk, free student e-mail accounts, online (class) grades, online (class) registration, online (class) schedules. Campuswide network is available. 100% of college-owned or -operated housing units are wired for high-speed Internet access. Wireless service is available via entire campus.

STUDENT LIFE
Housing options: coed, men-only, women-only. Campus housing is university owned. Freshman campus housing is guaranteed.
Activities and organizations: drama/theater group, student-run newspaper, radio station, choral group, national fraternities, national sororities.
Athletics Member NAIA. ***Intercollegiate sports:*** baseball M(s), basketball M(s)/W(s), cheerleading W, cross-country running M(s)/W(s), softball W(s), track and field M(s)/W(s). ***Intramural sports:*** basketball M/W.
Campus security: 24-hour emergency response devices and patrols, student patrols, late-night transport/escort service, controlled dormitory access.
Student services: health clinic, personal/psychological counseling.

COSTS & FINANCIAL AID
Costs (2015–16) ***Comprehensive fee:*** $19,976 includes full-time tuition ($11,630), mandatory fees ($1000), and room and board ($7346). Part-time tuition: $484 per hour. ***College room only:*** $3676.
Financial Aid Of all full-time matriculated undergraduates who enrolled in 2004, 813 applied for aid, 791 were judged to have need, 61 had their need fully met. 223 Federal Work-Study jobs (averaging $2000). In 2004,

65 non-need-based awards were made. ***Average percent of need met:*** 51. ***Average financial aid package:*** $7449. ***Average need-based loan:*** $2840. ***Average need-based gift aid:*** $4805. ***Average non-need-based aid:*** $9582. ***Average indebtedness upon graduation:*** $13,383.

APPLYING

Standardized Tests *Recommended:* SAT or ACT (for admission).

Options: electronic application, deferred entrance.

Application fee: $25.

Required: high school transcript, minimum 2.0 GPA, secondary school GPA. ***Required for some:*** interview.

Application deadlines: rolling (freshmen), rolling (transfers).

CONTACT

Adrain West, Dean of Enrollment Management, Voorhees College, PO Box 678, Denmark, SC 29042. *Phone:* 803-780-1269. *Toll-free phone:* 866-237-4570. *E-mail:* west@voorhees.edu.

Winthrop University

Rock Hill, South Carolina

http://www.winthrop.edu/

- **State-supported** comprehensive, founded 1886, part of South Carolina Commission on Higher Education
- **Suburban** 456-acre campus with easy access to Charlotte
- **Coed** 4,974 undergraduate students, 89% full-time, 68% women, 32% men
- **Moderately difficult** entrance level, 72% of applicants were admitted

UNDERGRAD STUDENTS

4,421 full-time, 553 part-time. Students come from 38 states and territories; 37 other countries; 9% are from out of state; 29% Black or African American, non-Hispanic/Latino; 4% Hispanic/Latino; 1% Asian, non-Hispanic/Latino; 0.1% Native Hawaiian or other Pacific Islander, non-Hispanic/Latino; 0.4% American Indian or Alaska Native, non-Hispanic/Latino; 3% Two or more races, non-Hispanic/Latino; 0.4% Race/ethnicity unknown; 3% international; 7% transferred in; 47% live on campus.

Freshmen

Admission: 4,285 applied, 3,096 admitted, 1,019 enrolled. ***Average high school GPA:*** 3.91. ***Test scores:*** SAT critical reading scores over 500: 60%; SAT math scores over 500: 60%; ACT scores over 18: 96%; SAT critical reading scores over 600: 23%; SAT math scores over 600: 20%; ACT scores over 24: 38%; SAT critical reading scores over 700: 4%; SAT math scores over 700: 2%; ACT scores over 30: 5%.

Retention: 77% of full-time freshmen returned.

FACULTY

Total: 561, 51% full-time, 60% with terminal degrees.

Student/faculty ratio: 14:1.

ACADEMICS

Calendar: semesters. *Degrees:* certificates, bachelor's, master's, post-master's, and postbachelor's certificates.

Special study options: adult/continuing education programs, advanced placement credit, cooperative education, distance learning, double majors, honors programs, independent study, internships, off-campus study, part-time degree program, services for LD students, student-designed majors, study abroad, summer session for credit. ***ROTC:*** Army (c), Air Force (c).

Computers: 620 computers/terminals are available on campus for general student use. Students can access the following: campus intranet, computer help desk, free student e-mail accounts, online (class) grades, online (class) registration, online (class) schedules, vast majority of university services are available online. Campuswide network is available. 100% of college-owned or -operated housing units are wired for high-speed Internet access. Wireless service is available via entire campus.

STUDENT LIFE

Housing options: on-campus residence required for freshman year; coed, men-only, women-only, special housing for students with disabilities. Campus housing is university owned. Freshman campus housing is guaranteed.

Activities and organizations: drama/theater group, student-run newspaper, radio station, choral group, Association of Ebonites, WU Crew, Greek Life, DiGiorgio Student Union, Campus Ministries, national fraternities, national sororities.

Athletics Member NCAA. All Division I. ***Intercollegiate sports:*** baseball M(s), basketball M(s)/W(s), cheerleading M(c)/W(c), cross-country running M(s)/W(s), fencing M(c)/W(c), golf M(s)/W(s), lacrosse M(c)/W, rugby M(c), soccer M(s)/W(s), softball W(s), tennis M(s)/W(s), track and field M(s)/W(s), volleyball W(s). ***Intramural sports:*** badminton M/W, basketball M/W, cross-country running M/W, equestrian sports M(c)/W(c), football M/W, golf M/W, racquetball M/W, soccer M/W, softball M/W, swimming and diving M/W, table tennis M/W, tennis M/W, ultimate Frisbee M/W, volleyball M/W, water polo M/W, weight lifting M/W.

Campus security: 24-hour emergency response devices and patrols, late-night transport/escort service, controlled dormitory access.

Student services: health clinic, personal/psychological counseling.

COSTS & FINANCIAL AID

Costs (2014–15) ***Tuition:*** state resident $13,812 full-time, $576 per credit hour part-time; nonresident $26,738 full-time, $1115 per credit hour part-time. Full-time tuition and fees vary according to degree level, reciprocity agreements, and student level. Part-time tuition and fees vary according to degree level and student level. ***Room and board:*** $8182; room only: $5135. Room and board charges vary according to board plan and housing facility. ***Payment plan:*** installment. ***Waivers:*** senior citizens and employees or children of employees.

Financial Aid Of all full-time matriculated undergraduates who enrolled in 2014, 3,735 applied for aid, 3,249 were judged to have need, 414 had their need fully met. 171 Federal Work-Study jobs (averaging $1427). In 2014, 490 non-need-based awards were made. ***Average percent of need met:*** 57. ***Average financial aid package:*** $12,387. ***Average need-based loan:*** $4357. ***Average need-based gift aid:*** $8324. ***Average non-need-based aid:*** $4976. ***Average indebtedness upon graduation:*** $32,165.

APPLYING

Standardized Tests *Required:* SAT or ACT (for admission).

Options: electronic application, deferred entrance.

Application fee: $40.

Required: high school transcript, minimum 3.0 GPA. ***Required for some:*** essay or personal statement.

Application deadlines: 5/1 (freshmen), 5/1 (out-of-state freshmen), 5/1 (transfers).

Notification: continuous (freshmen), continuous (transfers).

CONTACT

Winthrop University, 701 Oakland Avenue, Rock Hill, SC 29733. *Phone:* 803-323-2191. *Toll-free phone:* 800-763-0230.

Wofford College

Spartanburg, South Carolina

http://www.wofford.edu/

- **Independent** 4-year, founded 1854, affiliated with United Methodist Church
- **Urban** 170-acre campus with easy access to Charlotte
- **Endowment** $192.2 million
- **Coed** 1,608 undergraduate students, 98% full-time, 50% women, 50% men
- **Very difficult** entrance level, 77% of applicants were admitted

UNDERGRAD STUDENTS

1,578 full-time, 30 part-time. Students come from 28 states and territories; 7 other countries; 45% are from out of state; 0.7% Black or African American, non-Hispanic/Latino; 3% Hispanic/Latino; 2% Asian, non-Hispanic/Latino; 0.2% Native Hawaiian or other Pacific Islander, non-Hispanic/Latino; 0.2% American Indian or Alaska Native, non-Hispanic/Latino; 3% Two or more races, non-Hispanic/Latino; 0.9% Race/ethnicity unknown; 2% international; 0.5% transferred in; 94% live on campus.

Freshmen

Admission: 2,556 applied, 1,978 admitted, 487 enrolled. ***Average high school GPA:*** 3.54. ***Test scores:*** SAT critical reading scores over 500: 87%; SAT math scores over 500: 91%; SAT writing scores over 500: 81%; ACT scores over 18: 99%; SAT critical reading scores over 600: 44%;

SAT math scores over 600: 48%; SAT writing scores over 600: 34%; ACT scores over 24: 72%; SAT critical reading scores over 700: 6%; SAT math scores over 700: 7%; SAT writing scores over 700: 4%; ACT scores over 30: 20%.

Retention: 90% of full-time freshmen returned.

FACULTY

Total: 158, 83% full-time, 84% with terminal degrees.

Student/faculty ratio: 11:1.

ACADEMICS

Calendar: 4-1-4. *Degree:* bachelor's.

Special study options: accelerated degree program, advanced placement credit, double majors, independent study, internships, off-campus study, part-time degree program, student-designed majors, study abroad, summer session for credit. ***ROTC:*** Army (b).

Unusual degree programs: 3-2 engineering with Clemson University.

Computers: 200 computers/terminals are available on campus for general student use. Students can access the following: campus intranet, computer help desk, free student e-mail accounts, online (class) grades, online (class) registration, online (class) schedules. Campuswide network is available. 100% of college-owned or -operated housing units are wired for high-speed Internet access. Wireless service is available via entire campus.

STUDENT LIFE

Housing options: on-campus residence required through senior year; coed. Campus housing is university owned. Freshman applicants given priority for college housing.

Activities and organizations: drama/theater group, student-run newspaper, choral group, W.A.C. (Wofford Activities Council), Twin Towers (Service), Psychology Kingdom, Beta Beta Beta (Biology), national fraternities, national sororities.

Athletics Member NCAA. All Division I except football (Division I-AA). ***Intercollegiate sports:*** baseball M(s), basketball M(s)/W(s), cheerleading W, cross-country running M(s)/W(s), golf M(s)/W(s), riflery M/W, soccer M(s)/W(s), tennis M(s)/W(s), track and field M(s)/W(s), volleyball W(s). ***Intramural sports:*** basketball M/W, bowling M/W, equestrian sports M/W, football M/W, lacrosse M(c)/W(c), racquetball M/W, riflery M/W, skiing (downhill) M/W, soccer M/W, softball M/W, swimming and diving M/W, table tennis M/W, tennis M/W, ultimate Frisbee M/W, volleyball M/W, weight lifting M/W.

Campus security: 24-hour emergency response devices and patrols, late-night transport/escort service, controlled dormitory access.

Student services: health clinic, personal/psychological counseling.

COSTS & FINANCIAL AID

Costs (2014–15) ***Comprehensive fee:*** $47,850 includes full-time tuition ($37,120) and room and board ($10,730). Part-time tuition: $1475 per semester hour. ***Payment plan:*** installment. ***Waivers:*** employees or children of employees.

Financial Aid Of all full-time matriculated undergraduates who enrolled in 2014, 1,187 applied for aid, 982 were judged to have need, 381 had their need fully met. 146 Federal Work-Study jobs (averaging $843). In 2014, 410 non-need-based awards were made. ***Average percent of need met:*** 86. ***Average financial aid package:*** $33,209. ***Average need-based loan:*** $4242. ***Average need-based gift aid:*** $29,598. ***Average non-need-based aid:*** $15,057. ***Average indebtedness upon graduation:*** $24,999.

APPLYING

Standardized Tests *Required:* SAT or ACT (for admission).

Options: electronic application, early admission, early decision, early action, deferred entrance.

Application fee: $35.

Required: essay or personal statement, high school transcript. ***Recommended:*** 2 letters of recommendation, interview.

Application deadlines: 2/1 (freshmen), rolling (transfers), 11/15 (early action).

Early decision deadline: 11/1.

Notification: 3/15 (freshmen), continuous (transfers), 12/3 (early decision), 2/1 (early action).

CONTACT

Ms. Ashley S. Hill, Student Experience Coordinator, Wofford College, 429 N. Church St., Spartanburg, SC 29303. *Phone:* 864-597-4132. *Fax:* 864-597-4147. *E-mail:* admission@wofford.edu.

SOUTH DAKOTA

Augustana College

Sioux Falls, South Dakota

http://www.augie.edu/

- **Independent** comprehensive, founded 1860, affiliated with Evangelical Lutheran Church in America
- **Urban** 100-acre campus
- **Endowment** $66.5 million
- **Coed** 1,671 undergraduate students, 95% full-time, 59% women, 41% men
- **Moderately difficult** entrance level, 61% of applicants were admitted

UNDERGRAD STUDENTS

1,592 full-time, 79 part-time. Students come from 30 states and territories; 43 other countries; 54% are from out of state; 2% Black or African American, non-Hispanic/Latino; 2% Hispanic/Latino; 1% Asian, non-Hispanic/Latino; 0.1% Native Hawaiian or other Pacific Islander, non-Hispanic/Latino; 0.2% American Indian or Alaska Native, non-Hispanic/Latino; 1% Two or more races, non-Hispanic/Latino; 8% international; 3% transferred in; 71% live on campus.

Freshmen

Admission: 1,545 applied, 947 admitted, 396 enrolled. ***Average high school GPA:*** 3.7. ***Test scores:*** ACT scores over 18: 99%; ACT scores over 24: 71%; ACT scores over 30: 17%.

Retention: 81% of full-time freshmen returned.

FACULTY

Total: 171, 74% full-time, 67% with terminal degrees.

Student/faculty ratio: 12:1.

ACADEMICS

Calendar: 4-1-4. *Degrees:* bachelor's and master's.

Special study options: academic remediation for entering students, accelerated degree program, advanced placement credit, cooperative education, distance learning, double majors, honors programs, independent study, internships, off-campus study, part-time degree program, services for LD students, student-designed majors, study abroad, summer session for credit. ***ROTC:*** Army (c), Air Force (c).

Unusual degree programs: 3-2 engineering with Columbia University, University of Minnesota, Washington University in St. Louis; Medical Laboratory Scientist programs with Sanford Heath in Sioux Falls and St. Luke in Sioux City.

Computers: 290 computers/terminals and 1,900 ports are available on campus for general student use. Students can access the following: campus intranet, computer help desk, free student e-mail accounts, online (class) grades, online (class) registration, online (class) schedules. Campuswide network is available. 100% of college-owned or -operated housing units are wired for high-speed Internet access. Wireless service is available via entire campus.

STUDENT LIFE

Housing options: on-campus residence required through junior year; coed, special housing for students with disabilities. Campus housing is university owned. Freshman campus housing is guaranteed.

Activities and organizations: drama/theater group, student-run newspaper, choral group, Augieholics (student athletics support organization), intramurals, Union Board of Governors (student union), Augie Green, Campus Ministries.

Athletics Member NCAA. All Division II. ***Intercollegiate sports:*** baseball M(s), basketball M(s)/W(s), cheerleading M/W, cross-country running M(s)/W(s), football M(s), golf M(s)/W(s), rugby W(c), soccer M(c)/W(s), softball W(s), tennis M(s)/W(s), track and field M(s)/W(s), ultimate Frisbee M(c)/W(c), volleyball W(s), wrestling M(s). ***Intramural sports:*** basketball M/W, bowling M/W, cross-country running M/W, football M/W, golf M/W, racquetball M/W, rock climbing M/W, skiing (cross-country) M/W, soccer M/W, softball M/W, swimming and diving M/W, table tennis M/W, tennis M/W, ultimate Frisbee M/W, volleyball M(c)/W(c), weight lifting M/W.

Campus security: 24-hour emergency response devices and patrols, late-night transport/escort service, controlled dormitory access, special 'day lighting' night lights throughout the campus grounds.

Student services: health clinic, personal/psychological counseling.

COSTS & FINANCIAL AID

Costs (2014–15) ***Comprehensive fee:*** $36,242 includes full-time tuition ($28,764), mandatory fees ($450), and room and board ($7028). Full-time tuition and fees vary according to course load and degree level. Part-time tuition: $450 per credit hour. Part-time tuition and fees vary according to course load and degree level. ***College room only:*** $3360. Room and board charges vary according to board plan and housing facility. ***Payment plan:*** installment. ***Waivers:*** employees or children of employees.

Financial Aid Of all full-time matriculated undergraduates who enrolled in 2014, 1,177 applied for aid, 987 were judged to have need, 269 had their need fully met. 357 Federal Work-Study jobs (averaging $1806). 120 state and other part-time jobs (averaging $950). In 2014, 586 non-need-based awards were made. ***Average percent of need met:*** 91. ***Average financial aid package:*** $23,975. ***Average need-based loan:*** $5037. ***Average need-based gift aid:*** $19,796. ***Average non-need-based aid:*** $14,322. ***Average indebtedness upon graduation:*** $35,385.

APPLYING

Standardized Tests *Required:* SAT or ACT (for admission), minimum ACT score of 20 (for admission).

Options: electronic application, deferred entrance.

Required: essay or personal statement, high school transcript, minimum 2.7 GPA, 1 letter of recommendation. ***Recommended:*** interview.

Application deadlines: rolling (freshmen), rolling (out-of-state freshmen), rolling (transfers).

Notification: continuous until 10/1 (freshmen), continuous until 10/1 (out-of-state freshmen), continuous (transfers).

CONTACT

Nancy Davidson, Vice President for Enrollment, Augustana College, 2001 South Summit Avenue, Sioux Falls, SD 57197. *Phone:* 605-274-5516. *Toll-free phone:* 800-727-2844. *Fax:* 605-274-5518. *E-mail:* admission@augie.edu.

Black Hills State University

Spearfish, South Dakota

http://www.bhsu.edu/

- **State-supported** comprehensive, founded 1883, part of South Dakota Board of Regents for Public Universities and Special Schools
- **Small-town** 123-acre campus
- **Coed** 4,020 undergraduate students, 57% full-time, 64% women, 36% men

UNDERGRAD STUDENTS

2,279 full-time, 1,741 part-time. Students come from 44 states and territories; 22 other countries; 28% are from out of state; 1% Black or African American, non-Hispanic/Latino; 5% Hispanic/Latino; 0.4% Asian, non-Hispanic/Latino; 0.2% Native Hawaiian or other Pacific Islander, non-Hispanic/Latino; 4% American Indian or Alaska Native, non-Hispanic/Latino; 4% Two or more races, non-Hispanic/Latino; 0.8% Race/ethnicity unknown; 1% international; 8% transferred in.

Freshmen

Admission: 507 enrolled. ***Average high school GPA:*** 3.09. ***Test scores:*** ACT scores over 18: 83%; ACT scores over 24: 23%; ACT scores over 30: 1%.

Retention: 63% of full-time freshmen returned.

FACULTY

Total: 235, 37% with terminal degrees.

Student/faculty ratio: 19:1.

ACADEMICS

Calendar: semesters. *Degrees:* associate, bachelor's, master's, post-master's, and postbachelor's certificates.

Special study options: academic remediation for entering students, accelerated degree program, advanced placement credit, cooperative education, distance learning, double majors, English as a second language, honors programs, independent study, internships, off-campus study, part-time degree program, services for LD students, study abroad, summer session for credit. ***ROTC:*** Army (b).

Computers: Students can access the following: campus intranet, computer help desk, free student e-mail accounts, online (class) grades, online (class) registration, online (class) schedules, Wi-Fi. Campuswide network is available. 100% of college-owned or -operated housing units are wired for high-speed Internet access. Wireless service is available via classrooms, computer centers, computer labs, dorm rooms, learning centers, libraries, student centers.

STUDENT LIFE

Housing options: on-campus residence required through sophomore year; coed, men-only, women-only, special housing for students with disabilities. Campus housing is university owned. Freshman applicants given priority for college housing.

Activities and organizations: drama/theater group, student-run newspaper, radio and television station, choral group, Student Activities Committee, Student Government, national fraternities, national sororities.

Athletics Member NCAA. All Division II. ***Intercollegiate sports:*** basketball M(s)/W(s), cross-country running M(s)/W(s), football M(s), golf W, track and field M(s)/W(s), volleyball W(s). ***Intramural sports:*** archery M/W, badminton M/W, basketball M/W, bowling M/W, football M, golf M/W, racquetball M/W, skiing (cross-country) M/W, skiing (downhill) M/W, soccer M/W, softball M/W, tennis M/W, volleyball M/W, weight lifting M/W.

Campus security: 24-hour patrols, late-night transport/escort service, controlled dormitory access.

Student services: health clinic, personal/psychological counseling.

COSTS & FINANCIAL AID

Costs (2014–15) ***Tuition:*** state resident $7617 full-time; nonresident $10,097 full-time. Full-time tuition and fees vary according to course load, location, program, and reciprocity agreements. Part-time tuition and fees vary according to course load, location, program, and reciprocity agreements. ***Room and board:*** $6330; room only: $3310. Room and board charges vary according to board plan and housing facility. ***Payment plan:*** installment. ***Waivers:*** senior citizens and employees or children of employees.

Financial Aid Of all full-time matriculated undergraduates who enrolled in 2010, 239 Federal Work-Study jobs (averaging $1714). 414 state and other part-time jobs (averaging $4217). ***Average indebtedness upon graduation:*** $25,628.

APPLYING

Standardized Tests *Required:* SAT or ACT (for admission).

Required: high school transcript, minimum 2.0 high school GPA in core curriculum.

CONTACT

Mrs. Beth Oaks, Director of Admissions, Black Hills State University, 1200 University Station, Unit 9502, Spearfish, SD 57799-9502. *Phone:* 605-642-6343. *Toll-free phone:* 800-255-2478. *Fax:* 605-642-6254. *E-mail:* Admissions@BHSU.edu.

Dakota State University

Madison, South Dakota

http://www.dsu.edu/

- **State-supported** comprehensive, founded 1881, part of South Dakota Board of Regents
- **Small-town** 56-acre campus with easy access to Sioux Falls
- **Endowment** $9.8 million
- **Coed** 2,736 undergraduate students, 42% full-time, 46% women, 54% men
- **Minimally difficult** entrance level, 84% of applicants were admitted

UNDERGRAD STUDENTS

1,154 full-time, 1,582 part-time. Students come from 48 states and territories; 12 other countries; 31% are from out of state; 4% Black or African American, non-Hispanic/Latino; 4% Hispanic/Latino; 1% Asian, non-Hispanic/Latino; 0.2% Native Hawaiian or other Pacific Islander, non-Hispanic/Latino; 1% American Indian or Alaska Native, non-Hispanic/Latino; 2% Two or more races, non-Hispanic/Latino; 1% Race/ethnicity unknown; 1% international; 9% transferred in; 32% live on campus.

Freshmen

Admission: 772 applied, 650 admitted, 291 enrolled. ***Average high school GPA:*** 3.1. ***Test scores:*** SAT critical reading scores over 500: 50%; SAT math scores over 500: 50%; ACT scores over 18: 87%; SAT critical reading scores over 600: 14%; SAT math scores over 600: 14%; ACT scores over 24: 38%; SAT critical reading scores over 700: 4%; ACT scores over 30: 4%.

Retention: 65% of full-time freshmen returned.

FACULTY

Total: 133, 73% full-time, 59% with terminal degrees.

Student/faculty ratio: 16:1.

ACADEMICS

Calendar: semesters. *Degrees:* certificates, associate, bachelor's, master's, doctoral, and postbachelor's certificates.

Special study options: academic remediation for entering students, adult/continuing education programs, advanced placement credit, cooperative education, distance learning, double majors, honors programs, independent study, internships, off-campus study, part-time degree program, services for LD students, study abroad, summer session for credit. ***ROTC:*** Air Force (c).

Computers: 165 computers/terminals and 356 ports are available on campus for general student use. Students can access the following: campus intranet, computer help desk, free student e-mail accounts, online (class) grades, online (class) registration, online (class) schedules, wireless computing initiative requires full-time students to have a tablet computer. Campuswide network is available. 100% of college-owned or -operated housing units are wired for high-speed Internet access. Wireless service is available via entire campus.

STUDENT LIFE

Housing options: on-campus residence required through sophomore year; coed, men-only. Campus housing is university owned and leased by the school. Freshman campus housing is guaranteed.

Activities and organizations: drama/theater group, student-run newspaper, radio station, choral group, Gaming Club, Student Senate, Student Activities Board, Campus Crusade for Christ, Phi Beta Lambda Business Club.

Athletics Member NAIA. ***Intercollegiate sports:*** baseball M(s), basketball M(s)/W(s), cheerleading M/W, cross-country running M(s)/W(s), football M(s), softball W(s), track and field M(s)/W(s), volleyball W(s). ***Intramural sports:*** basketball M/W, softball M/W, volleyball M/W.

Campus security: late-night transport/escort service, controlled dormitory access, night watchman.

Student services: health clinic, personal/psychological counseling.

COSTS & FINANCIAL AID

Costs (2014–15) ***Tuition:*** state resident $3993 full-time, $133 per credit hour part-time; nonresident $5993 full-time, $200 per credit hour part-time. Full-time tuition and fees vary according to location and reciprocity agreements. Part-time tuition and fees vary according to location and reciprocity agreements. ***Required fees:*** $4293 full-time. ***Room and board:*** $5941; room only: $3231. Room and board charges vary according to board plan and housing facility. ***Payment plans:*** installment, deferred payment. ***Waivers:*** senior citizens and employees or children of employees.

Financial Aid Of all full-time matriculated undergraduates who enrolled in 2013, 995 applied for aid, 810 were judged to have need, 75 had their need fully met. 151 Federal Work-Study jobs (averaging $1676). 20 state and other part-time jobs (averaging $5640). In 2013, 91 non-need-based awards were made. ***Average percent of need met:*** 73. ***Average financial aid package:*** $7997. ***Average need-based loan:*** $4203. ***Average need-based gift aid:*** $4424. ***Average non-need-based aid:*** $3980. ***Average indebtedness upon graduation:*** $24,728.

APPLYING

Standardized Tests *Required:* SAT or ACT (for admission).

Options: electronic application, deferred entrance.

Application fee: $20.

Required: high school transcript, minimum 2.6 GPA, Students must meet one of these three requirements: GPA of 2.6 or rank in top 60% of high school class or receive an 18 or higher on ACT / Receive an 870 or higher on SAT (Combined Math and Critical Reading).

Application deadlines: rolling (freshmen), rolling (out-of-state freshmen), rolling (transfers).

Notification: continuous (freshmen), continuous (out-of-state freshmen), continuous (transfers).

CONTACT

Ms. Tory Bickett, Admissions Secretary, Dakota State University, 820 North Washington, Madison, SD 57042-1799. *Phone:* 605-256-5139. *Toll-free phone:* 888-DSU-9988. *Fax:* 605-256-5020. *E-mail:* admissions@dsu.edu.

Globe University–Sioux Falls

Sioux Falls, South Dakota

http://www.globeuniversity.edu/

- **Proprietary** 4-year, part of Globe Education Network (GEN) which is composed of Globe University, Minnesota School of Business, Broadview University, The Institute of Production and Recording and Minnesota School of Cosmetology
- **Small-town** 3-acre campus
- **Coed**

ACADEMICS

Degrees: certificates, diplomas, associate, and bachelor's.

STUDENT LIFE

Campus security: 24-hour emergency response devices.

APPLYING

Standardized Tests *Required:* ACCUPLACER is required of most applicants unless documentation of a minimum ACT composite score of 21 or documentation of a minimum composite score of 1485 on the SAT is presented (for admission).

Options: electronic application.

Application fee: $50.

Required: interview. ***Required for some:*** Certification of high school graduation or GED.

CONTACT

Globe University–Sioux Falls, 5101 South Broadband Lane, Sioux Falls, SD 57108-2208. *Toll-free phone:* 866-437-0705.

Mount Marty College

Yankton, South Dakota

http://www.mtmc.edu/

- **Independent Roman Catholic** comprehensive, founded 1936
- **Small-town** 80-acre campus
- **Endowment** $19.7 million
- **Coed** 1,108 undergraduate students, 48% full-time, 58% women, 42% men
- **Minimally difficult** entrance level, 72% of applicants were admitted

UNDERGRAD STUDENTS

530 full-time, 578 part-time. Students come from 21 states and territories; 2 other countries; 39% are from out of state; 3% Black or African American, non-Hispanic/Latino; 6% Hispanic/Latino; 1% Asian, non-Hispanic/Latino; 0.5% Native Hawaiian or other Pacific Islander, non-Hispanic/Latino; 3% American Indian or Alaska Native, non-Hispanic/Latino; 0.2% Race/ethnicity unknown; 9% transferred in; 66% live on campus.

Freshmen

Admission: 416 applied, 301 admitted, 122 enrolled. ***Average high school GPA:*** 3.4. ***Test scores:*** ACT scores over 18: 91%; ACT scores over 24: 42%; ACT scores over 30: 3%.

Retention: 70% of full-time freshmen returned.

FACULTY
Total: 61, 79% full-time, 57% with terminal degrees.
Student/faculty ratio: 10:1.

ACADEMICS
Calendar: semesters. *Degrees:* certificates, associate, bachelor's, master's, and post-master's certificates.
Special study options: academic remediation for entering students, accelerated degree program, adult/continuing education programs, advanced placement credit, cooperative education, distance learning, double majors, honors programs, independent study, internships, off-campus study, part-time degree program, services for LD students, student-designed majors, summer session for credit. ***ROTC:*** Army (c).
Computers: 12 computers/terminals are available on campus for general student use. Students can access the following: campus intranet, computer help desk, free student e-mail accounts, online (class) grades, online (class) registration, online (class) schedules. Campuswide network is available. 100% of college-owned or -operated housing units are wired for high-speed Internet access. Wireless service is available via entire campus.

STUDENT LIFE
Housing options: on-campus residence required through senior year; men-only, women-only. Campus housing is university owned. Freshman campus housing is guaranteed.
Activities and organizations: drama/theater group, student-run newspaper, choral group, Campus Ministry, Student Government Association, Nursing Club, Education Club, Theater Club.
Athletics Member NAIA. ***Intercollegiate sports:*** archery M(c)/W(c), baseball M(s), basketball M(s)/W(s), cross-country running M(s)/W(s), golf M(s)/W(s), riflery M(c)/W(c), soccer M(s)/W(s), softball W(s), tennis W(s), track and field M(s)/W(s), volleyball W(s). ***Intramural sports:*** archery M/W, basketball M/W, soccer M/W, softball W, volleyball M/W.
Campus security: 24-hour emergency response devices and patrols, late-night transport/escort service.
Student services: health clinic, personal/psychological counseling.

COSTS & FINANCIAL AID
Costs (2014–15) ***Comprehensive fee:*** $29,870 includes full-time tuition ($21,062), mandatory fees ($1830), and room and board ($6978). Full-time tuition and fees vary according to degree level, location, and program. Part-time tuition and fees vary according to course load, degree level, location, and program. ***Room and board:*** Room and board charges vary according to board plan. ***Payment plan:*** installment. ***Waivers:*** employees or children of employees.
Financial Aid Of all full-time matriculated undergraduates who enrolled in 2014, 482 applied for aid, 413 were judged to have need, 221 had their need fully met. 170 Federal Work-Study jobs (averaging $1774). 55 state and other part-time jobs (averaging $1800). In 2014, 58 non-need-based awards were made. ***Average percent of need met:*** 89. ***Average financial aid package:*** $23,212. ***Average need-based loan:*** $4992. ***Average need-based gift aid:*** $12,798. ***Average non-need-based aid:*** $9295. ***Average indebtedness upon graduation:*** $33,945.

APPLYING
Standardized Tests *Required:* SAT or ACT (for admission).
Options: electronic application, early admission, deferred entrance.
Application fee: $35.
Required: high school transcript, minimum 2.0 GPA. ***Recommended:*** interview.
Application deadlines: rolling (freshmen), rolling (transfers).
Notification: continuous (freshmen), continuous (transfers).

CONTACT
Paula Tacke, Vice President for Marketing and Admissions, Mount Marty College, 1105 West 8th Street, Yankton, SD 57078. *Phone:* 605-668-1545. *Toll-free phone:* 800-658-4552. *E-mail:* paula.tacke@mtmc.edu.

Northern State University
Aberdeen, South Dakota
http://www.northern.edu/

- **State-supported** comprehensive, founded 1901, part of South Dakota Board of Regents
- **Small-town** 72-acre campus
- **Endowment** $25.1 million
- **Coed** 3,001 undergraduate students, 49% full-time, 58% women, 42% men
- **Minimally difficult** entrance level, 83% of applicants were admitted

UNDERGRAD STUDENTS
1,477 full-time, 1,524 part-time. Students come from 41 states and territories; 35 other countries; 18% are from out of state; 1% Black or African American, non-Hispanic/Latino; 2% Hispanic/Latino; 0.9% Asian, non-Hispanic/Latino; 0.2% Native Hawaiian or other Pacific Islander, non-Hispanic/Latino; 2% American Indian or Alaska Native, non-Hispanic/Latino; 1% Two or more races, non-Hispanic/Latino; 1% Race/ethnicity unknown; 5% international; 4% transferred in; 41% live on campus.

Freshmen
Admission: 1,379 applied, 1,143 admitted, 363 enrolled. ***Average high school GPA:*** 3.25. ***Test scores:*** SAT critical reading scores over 500: 42%; SAT math scores over 500: 52%; ACT scores over 18: 83%; SAT critical reading scores over 600: 12%; SAT math scores over 600: 14%; ACT scores over 24: 31%; SAT critical reading scores over 700: 4%; SAT math scores over 700: 3%; ACT scores over 30: 2%.
Retention: 67% of full-time freshmen returned.

FACULTY
Total: 169, 53% full-time, 46% with terminal degrees.
Student/faculty ratio: 21:1.

ACADEMICS
Calendar: semesters. *Degrees:* certificates, associate, bachelor's, master's, and postbachelor's certificates.
Special study options: academic remediation for entering students, accelerated degree program, adult/continuing education programs, advanced placement credit, cooperative education, distance learning, double majors, English as a second language, freshman honors college, honors programs, independent study, internships, off-campus study, part-time degree program, services for LD students, student-designed majors, study abroad, summer session for credit.
Computers: 135 computers/terminals are available on campus for general student use. Students can access the following: campus intranet, computer help desk, free student e-mail accounts, online (class) grades, online (class) registration, online (class) schedules. Campuswide network is available. 100% of college-owned or -operated housing units are wired for high-speed Internet access. Wireless service is available via entire campus.

STUDENT LIFE
Housing options: on-campus residence required through sophomore year; coed, special housing for students with disabilities. Campus housing is university owned.
Activities and organizations: drama/theater group, student-run newspaper, television station, choral group, marching band, Student Ambassadors, Choices, honor society, Native American Student Association, International Student Association.
Athletics Member NCAA. All Division II. ***Intercollegiate sports:*** baseball M(s), basketball M(s)/W(s), cross-country running M(s)/W(s), football M(s), soccer W(s), softball W(s), swimming and diving W(s), track and field M(s)/W(s), volleyball W(s), wrestling M(s). ***Intramural sports:*** badminton M(c)/W(c), basketball M/W, football M/W, racquetball M/W, rugby M(c)/W(c), soccer M/W, softball M/W, table tennis M/W, ultimate Frisbee M/W, volleyball M/W.
Campus security: 24-hour emergency response devices, controlled dormitory access, evening patrols.
Student services: health clinic, personal/psychological counseling, women's center, legal services.

COSTS & FINANCIAL AID

Costs (2015–16) ***Tuition:*** state resident $3993 full-time, $133 per credit hour part-time; nonresident $5992 full-time, $200 per credit hour part-time. Full-time tuition and fees vary according to course level, course load, location, and reciprocity agreements. Part-time tuition and fees vary according to course level, course load, location, and reciprocity agreements. ***Required fees:*** $4050 full-time. ***Room and board:*** $6942; room only: $3155. Room and board charges vary according to board plan. ***Payment plan:*** installment. ***Waivers:*** senior citizens.

Financial Aid Of all full-time matriculated undergraduates who enrolled in 2013, 1,201 applied for aid, 941 were judged to have need, 286 had their need fully met. 396 Federal Work-Study jobs (averaging $2182). 361 state and other part-time jobs (averaging $1474). In 2013, 141 non-need-based awards were made. ***Average percent of need met:*** 69. ***Average financial aid package:*** $10,097. ***Average need-based loan:*** $5439. ***Average need-based gift aid:*** $4216. ***Average non-need-based aid:*** $1443. ***Average indebtedness upon graduation:*** $29,288.

APPLYING

Standardized Tests *Required:* SAT or ACT (for admission).

Options: electronic application, early admission, deferred entrance.

Application fee: $20.

Required: high school transcript, minimum 2.6 GPA.

Notification: continuous (freshmen), continuous (transfers).

CONTACT

Ms. Joellen Lindner, Vice President for Student Affairs and Enrollment Management, Northern State University, 1200 South Jay Street, Aberdeen, SD 57401. *Phone:* 605-626-2530. *Toll-free phone:* 800-678-5330. *Fax:* 605-626-2531. *E-mail:* admission2@northern.edu.

South Dakota School of Mines and Technology

Rapid City, South Dakota

http://www.sdsmt.edu/

- **State-supported** university, founded 1885, part of South Dakota State Board of Regents University System
- **Suburban** 120-acre campus
- **Coed** 2,471 undergraduate students, 84% full-time, 22% women, 78% men
- **Moderately difficult** entrance level, 88% of applicants were admitted

UNDERGRAD STUDENTS

2,079 full-time, 392 part-time. Students come from 38 states and territories; 39 other countries; 50% are from out of state; 2% Black or African American, non-Hispanic/Latino; 4% Hispanic/Latino; 2% Asian, non-Hispanic/Latino; 0.2% Native Hawaiian or other Pacific Islander, non-Hispanic/Latino; 2% American Indian or Alaska Native, non-Hispanic/Latino; 4% Two or more races, non-Hispanic/Latino; 0.6% Race/ethnicity unknown; 3% international; 5% transferred in; 63% live on campus.

Freshmen

Admission: 1,549 applied, 1,360 admitted, 599 enrolled. ***Average high school GPA:*** 3.51. ***Test scores:*** SAT critical reading scores over 500: 80%; SAT math scores over 500: 95%; SAT writing scores over 500: 64%; ACT scores over 18: 100%; SAT critical reading scores over 600: 44%; SAT math scores over 600: 61%; SAT writing scores over 600: 32%; ACT scores over 24: 78%; SAT critical reading scores over 700: 11%; SAT math scores over 700: 11%; SAT writing scores over 700: 2%; ACT scores over 30: 20%.

Retention: 77% of full-time freshmen returned.

FACULTY

Total: 178, 85% full-time, 80% with terminal degrees.

Student/faculty ratio: 15:1.

ACADEMICS

Calendar: semesters. *Degrees:* certificates, associate, bachelor's, master's, doctoral, and postbachelor's certificates.

Special study options: academic remediation for entering students, adult/continuing education programs, advanced placement credit, cooperative education, distance learning, English as a second language, independent study, internships, off-campus study, part-time degree program, services for LD students, study abroad, summer session for credit. ***ROTC:*** Army (b).

Computers: 105 computers/terminals and 662 ports are available on campus for general student use. Students can access the following: campus intranet, computer help desk, free student e-mail accounts, online (class) grades, online (class) registration, online (class) schedules, laptop rental, our whole campus has wireless connections. Campuswide network is available. 100% of college-owned or -operated housing units are wired for high-speed Internet access. Wireless service is available via entire campus.

STUDENT LIFE

Housing options: on-campus residence required through sophomore year; coed, men-only, women-only, special housing for students with disabilities. Campus housing is university owned and leased by the school. Freshman campus housing is guaranteed.

Activities and organizations: drama/theater group, student-run newspaper, radio station, choral group, ASCE (American Society of Civil Engineers), ASME (American Society of Mechanical Engineers), Drill and Crucible Club, Tau Beta Pi, Formula SAE (Mini Indy race car team), national fraternities, national sororities.

Athletics Member NCAA. All Division II. ***Intercollegiate sports:*** basketball M(s)/W(s), cross-country running M(s)/W(s), football M(s), golf M(s)/W(s), soccer M, track and field M(s)/W(s), volleyball W(s). ***Intramural sports:*** badminton M(c)/W(c), cheerleading M(c)/W(c), racquetball M/W, riflery M(c)/W(c), rock climbing M(c)/W(c), skiing (downhill) M(c)/W(c), soccer M(c)/W(c), squash M(c), tennis M(c)/W(c), ultimate Frisbee M(c)/W(c), volleyball M/W, water polo M/W.

Campus security: 24-hour emergency response devices and patrols, student patrols, late-night transport/escort service, controlled dormitory access.

Student services: health clinic, personal/psychological counseling.

COSTS & FINANCIAL AID

Costs (2014–15) ***Tuition:*** state resident $4170 full-time, $139 per credit hour part-time; nonresident $7000 full-time, $233 per credit hour part-time. Full-time tuition and fees vary according to course load, program, and reciprocity agreements. Part-time tuition and fees vary according to course load, program, and reciprocity agreements. ***Required fees:*** $5870 full-time, $202 per credit hour part-time. ***Room and board:*** $6370; room only: $3350. Room and board charges vary according to board plan and housing facility. ***Payment plan:*** installment. ***Waivers:*** senior citizens and employees or children of employees.

Financial Aid Of all full-time matriculated undergraduates who enrolled in 2013, 1,767 applied for aid, 1,086 were judged to have need, 412 had their need fully met. 127 Federal Work-Study jobs (averaging $1899). In 2013, 384 non-need-based awards were made. ***Average percent of need met:*** 76. ***Average financial aid package:*** $13,722. ***Average need-based loan:*** $4300. ***Average need-based gift aid:*** $4482. ***Average non-need-based aid:*** $2829. ***Average indebtedness upon graduation:*** $22,810.

APPLYING

Standardized Tests *Required:* SAT or ACT (for admission). *Required for some:* SAT or ACT (for admission). *Recommended:* SAT or ACT (for admission).

Options: electronic application.

Application fee: $20.

Required: high school transcript. ***Recommended:*** minimum 2.8 GPA.

Application deadlines: rolling (freshmen), rolling (out-of-state freshmen), rolling (transfers).

Notification: continuous (freshmen), continuous (out-of-state freshmen), continuous (transfers).

CONTACT

Genene Sigler, Applications Processor, South Dakota School of Mines and Technology, 501 East Saint Joseph Street, Rapid City, SD 57701-3995. *Phone:* 605-394-2414 Ext. 5209. *Toll-free phone:* 800-544-8162. *Fax:* 605-394-1979. *E-mail:* admissions@sdsmt.edu.

South Dakota State University

Brookings, South Dakota

http://www.sdstate.edu/

- **State-supported** university, founded 1881, part of South Dakota Board of Regents
- **Small-town** 275-acre campus
- **Coed** 10,951 undergraduate students, 79% full-time, 53% women, 47% men
- **Minimally difficult** entrance level, 92% of applicants were admitted

UNDERGRAD STUDENTS

8,621 full-time, 2,330 part-time. 37% are from out of state; 2% Black or African American, non-Hispanic/Latino; 2% Hispanic/Latino; 1% Asian, non-Hispanic/Latino; 0.1% Native Hawaiian or other Pacific Islander, non-Hispanic/Latino; 0.9% American Indian or Alaska Native, non-Hispanic/Latino; 2% Two or more races, non-Hispanic/Latino; 0.4% Race/ethnicity unknown; 3% international; 6% transferred in; 42% live on campus.

Freshmen

Admission: 5,133 applied, 4,723 admitted, 2,283 enrolled. ***Average high school GPA:*** 3.36. ***Test scores:*** SAT critical reading scores over 500: 45%; SAT math scores over 500: 66%; ACT scores over 18: 94%; SAT critical reading scores over 600: 9%; SAT math scores over 600: 26%; ACT scores over 24: 45%; SAT critical reading scores over 700: 1%; SAT math scores over 700: 3%; ACT scores over 30: 6%.

Retention: 77% of full-time freshmen returned.

FACULTY

Student/faculty ratio: 19:1.

ACADEMICS

Calendar: semesters. *Degrees:* certificates, associate, bachelor's, master's, doctoral, post-master's, and postbachelor's certificates.

Special study options: academic remediation for entering students, accelerated degree program, adult/continuing education programs, advanced placement credit, cooperative education, distance learning, double majors, English as a second language, freshman honors college, honors programs, independent study, internships, off-campus study, part-time degree program, services for LD students, study abroad, summer session for credit. ***ROTC:*** Army (b), Air Force (b).

Unusual degree programs: 3-2 Economics.

Computers: 125 computers/terminals and 100 ports are available on campus for general student use. Students can access the following: campus intranet, computer help desk, free student e-mail accounts, online (class) grades, online (class) registration, online (class) schedules. Campuswide network is available. 100% of college-owned or -operated housing units are wired for high-speed Internet access. Wireless service is available via entire campus.

STUDENT LIFE

Housing options: on-campus residence required through sophomore year; coed, special housing for students with disabilities. Campus housing is university owned. Freshman campus housing is guaranteed.

Activities and organizations: drama/theater group, student-run newspaper, radio station, choral group, marching band, national fraternities, national sororities.

Athletics Member NCAA. All Division I. ***Intercollegiate sports:*** baseball M(s), basketball M(s)/W(s), bowling M(c)/W(c), cheerleading M(c)/W(c), cross-country running M(s)/W(s), equestrian sports W(s), football M(s), golf M(s)/W(s), ice hockey M(c)/W(c), soccer W(s), softball W(s), swimming and diving M(s)/W(s), tennis M(s)/W(s), track and field M(s)/W(s), volleyball W(s), wrestling M(s). ***Intramural sports:*** badminton M/W, baseball M, basketball M/W, cross-country running M/W, football M/W, golf M/W, rock climbing M/W, rugby M(c)/W(c), soccer W, softball M/W, swimming and diving M/W, table tennis M/W, tennis M/W, track and field M/W, ultimate Frisbee M/W, volleyball M/W, wrestling M.

Campus security: 24-hour emergency response devices and patrols, student patrols, late-night transport/escort service, controlled dormitory access.

Student services: health clinic, personal/psychological counseling, legal services.

COSTS & FINANCIAL AID

Costs (2014–15) ***Tuition:*** state resident $4164 full-time, $139 per credit hour part-time; nonresident $6246 full-time, $208 per credit hour part-time. Full-time tuition and fees vary according to course level, course load, degree level, location, program, and reciprocity agreements. Part-time tuition and fees vary according to course level, course load, degree level, location, program, and reciprocity agreements. ***Required fees:*** $3549 full-time. ***Room and board:*** $6985; room only: $3214. Room and board charges vary according to board plan and housing facility. ***Payment plans:*** installment, deferred payment. ***Waivers:*** senior citizens and employees or children of employees.

Financial Aid Of all full-time matriculated undergraduates who enrolled in 2013, 6,787 applied for aid, 5,093 were judged to have need, 1,614 had their need fully met. In 2013, 1395 non-need-based awards were made. ***Average percent of need met:*** 68. ***Average financial aid package:*** $12,474. ***Average need-based loan:*** $4384. ***Average need-based gift aid:*** $4031. ***Average non-need-based aid:*** $1904. ***Average indebtedness upon graduation:*** $23,183.

APPLYING

Standardized Tests *Required:* SAT or ACT (for admission).

Options: electronic application.

Application fee: $20.

Required: high school transcript, minimum 2.6 GPA.

Application deadlines: rolling (freshmen), rolling (transfers).

Notification: continuous (freshmen), continuous (transfers).

CONTACT

Ms. Michelle Kuebler, Assistant Director of Admissions, South Dakota State University, PO Box 2201, Brookings, SD 57007. *Phone:* 605-688-4121. *Toll-free phone:* 800-952-3541. *Fax:* 605-688-6891. *E-mail:* sdsu.admissions@sdstate.edu.

The University of South Dakota

Vermillion, South Dakota

http://www.usd.edu/

- **State-supported** university, founded 1862, part of South Dakota Board of Regents
- **Small-town** 275-acre campus
- **Endowment** $178.5 million
- **Coed** 7,541 undergraduate students, 65% full-time, 63% women, 37% men
- **Moderately difficult** entrance level, 89% of applicants were admitted

UNDERGRAD STUDENTS

4,876 full-time, 2,665 part-time. Students come from 46 states and territories; 29 other countries; 33% are from out of state; 2% Black or African American, non-Hispanic/Latino; 3% Hispanic/Latino; 1% Asian, non-Hispanic/Latino; 0.1% Native Hawaiian or other Pacific Islander, non-Hispanic/Latino; 2% American Indian or Alaska Native, non-Hispanic/Latino; 3% Two or more races, non-Hispanic/Latino; 0.4% Race/ethnicity unknown; 2% international; 8% transferred in; 28% live on campus.

Freshmen

Admission: 3,542 applied, 3,146 admitted, 1,247 enrolled. ***Average high school GPA:*** 3.37. ***Test scores:*** SAT critical reading scores over 500: 64%; SAT math scores over 500: 63%; SAT writing scores over 500: 40%; ACT scores over 18: 95%; SAT critical reading scores over 600: 27%; SAT math scores over 600: 36%; SAT writing scores over 600: 10%; ACT scores over 24: 44%; SAT critical reading scores over 700: 8%; SAT math scores over 700: 5%; ACT scores over 30: 5%.

Retention: 75% of full-time freshmen returned.

FACULTY

Total: 595, 76% full-time, 65% with terminal degrees.

Student/faculty ratio: 17:1.

ACADEMICS

Calendar: semesters. *Degrees:* certificates, associate, bachelor's, master's, doctoral, post-master's, and postbachelor's certificates.

Special study options: academic remediation for entering students, accelerated degree program, adult/continuing education programs, advanced placement credit, cooperative education, distance learning,

double majors, English as a second language, external degree program, honors programs, independent study, internships, off-campus study, part-time degree program, services for LD students, student-designed majors, study abroad, summer session for credit. ***ROTC:*** Army (b).

Unusual degree programs: 3-2 business administration; social work; accounting, political science, public administration.

Computers: 975 computers/terminals are available on campus for general student use. Students can access the following: campus intranet, computer help desk, free student e-mail accounts, online (class) registration. Campuswide network is available. Wireless service is available via computer centers, computer labs, learning centers, libraries, student centers.

STUDENT LIFE

Housing options: on-campus residence required through sophomore year; coed, men-only, women-only, special housing for students with disabilities. Campus housing is university owned. Freshman campus housing is guaranteed.

Activities and organizations: drama/theater group, student-run newspaper, radio station, choral group, marching band, Program Council, Residence Hall Association, Student Ambassadors, Delta Sigma Pi, national fraternities, national sororities.

Athletics Member NCAA. All Division I. ***Intercollegiate sports:*** basketball M(s)/W(s), cross-country running M(s)/W(s), football M(s), golf M/W(s), soccer W(s), softball W(s), swimming and diving M(s)/W(s), tennis W(s), track and field M(s)/W(s), volleyball W(s). ***Intramural sports:*** baseball M(c), basketball M/W, bowling M/W, crew M(c)/W(c), fencing M(c)/W(c), football M, ice hockey M(c), lacrosse M(c)/W(c), rock climbing M(c)/W(c), rugby M(c)/W(c), soccer M(c)/W(c), softball M(c)/W(c), tennis M/W.

Campus security: 24-hour emergency response devices and patrols, student patrols, late-night transport/escort service, controlled dormitory access.

Student services: health clinic, personal/psychological counseling, legal services.

COSTS & FINANCIAL AID

Costs (2014–15) ***Tuition:*** state resident $4164 full-time, $139 per credit hour part-time; nonresident $6246 full-time, $208 per credit hour part-time. Full-time tuition and fees vary according to course load. Part-time tuition and fees vary according to course load. ***Required fees:*** $3858 full-time, $129 per credit hour part-time. ***Room and board:*** $7089; room only: $3785. Room and board charges vary according to board plan and housing facility. ***Payment plan:*** deferred payment. ***Waivers:*** children of alumni, senior citizens, and employees or children of employees.

Financial Aid Of all full-time matriculated undergraduates who enrolled in 2013, 4,413 applied for aid, 3,423 were judged to have need, 2,025 had their need fully met. In 2013, 1065 non-need-based awards were made. ***Average percent of need met:*** 77. ***Average financial aid package:*** $6507. ***Average need-based loan:*** $4234. ***Average need-based gift aid:*** $4192. ***Average non-need-based aid:*** $4513. ***Average indebtedness upon graduation:*** $25,554.

APPLYING

Standardized Tests *Required:* SAT or ACT (for admission).

Options: electronic application, early admission, deferred entrance.

Application fee: $20.

Required: high school transcript. ***Recommended:*** minimum 2.0 GPA.

Application deadlines: rolling (freshmen), rolling (transfers).

Notification: continuous (freshmen), continuous (transfers).

CONTACT

Mr. Travis Vlasman, Director of Enrollment Services, The University of South Dakota, 414 East Clark Street, Vermillion, SD 57069-2390. *Phone:* 605-677-5434. *Toll-free phone:* 877-269-6837. *Fax:* 605-677-6753. *E-mail:* admiss@usd.edu.

TENNESSEE

American Baptist College of American Baptist Theological Seminary

Nashville, Tennessee

http://www.abcnash.edu/

- **Independent Baptist** 4-year, founded 1924
- **Urban** 52-acre campus with easy access to Nashville
- **Endowment** $622,546
- **Coed** 157 undergraduate students, 70% full-time, 36% women, 64% men
- **Noncompetitive** entrance level, 51% of applicants were admitted

UNDERGRAD STUDENTS

110 full-time, 47 part-time. Students come from 12 states and territories; 1 other country; 8% transferred in; 63% live on campus.

Freshmen

Admission: 55 applied, 28 admitted, 14 enrolled.

Retention: 6% of full-time freshmen returned.

FACULTY

Total: 19, 21% full-time, 21% with terminal degrees.

Student/faculty ratio: 12:1.

ACADEMICS

Calendar: semesters. *Degrees:* diplomas, associate, and bachelor's.

Special study options: academic remediation for entering students, adult/continuing education programs, double majors, off-campus study, part-time degree program, summer session for credit.

Computers: 22 computers/terminals and 32 ports are available on campus for general student use. Students can access the following: campus intranet, free student e-mail accounts, online (class) grades, online (class) registration, online (class) schedules, IT support person on campus during regular campus hours. Campuswide network is available. 100% of college-owned or -operated housing units are wired for high-speed Internet access. Wireless service is available via entire campus.

STUDENT LIFE

Housing options: coed, men-only, women-only. Campus housing is university owned.

Activities and organizations: choral group, Student Government Association, Vespers Service, Baptist Student Union, Choir, Greek Letter Fraternity and Hoi Adelphoi Fraternity, national fraternities.

Campus security: 24-hour emergency response devices.

COSTS & FINANCIAL AID

Costs (2014–15) ***Comprehensive fee:*** $15,462 includes full-time tuition ($8688), mandatory fees ($934), and room and board ($5840). Part-time tuition: $362 per credit. ***College room only:*** $3840. Room and board charges vary according to housing facility. ***Payment plan:*** deferred payment.

Financial Aid Of all full-time matriculated undergraduates who enrolled in 2014, 128 applied for aid, 128 were judged to have need. 5 Federal Work-Study jobs (averaging $7452). ***Average percent of need met:*** 40. ***Average financial aid package:*** $10,412. ***Average need-based loan:*** $3823. ***Average need-based gift aid:*** $8263. ***Average indebtedness upon graduation:*** $9743. ***Financial aid deadline:*** 7/23.

APPLYING

Standardized Tests *Required:* (for admission).

Options: electronic application, deferred entrance.

Application fee: $30.

Required: essay or personal statement, high school transcript, minimum 2.0 GPA, 2 letters of recommendation, official transcript(s) from any and all Institution(s) student attended prior to enrollment at American Baptist College. ***Required for some:*** interview.

Application deadlines: rolling (freshmen), rolling (out-of-state freshmen), rolling (transfers).

Notification: continuous (freshmen), continuous (out-of-state freshmen), continuous (transfers).

CONTACT
Recruiter, American Baptist College of American Baptist Theological Seminary, 1800 Baptist World Center Drive, Nashville, TN 37207. *Phone:* 615-687-6907. *Fax:* 615-226-7855. *E-mail:* admissions@abcnash.edu.

Aquinas College

Nashville, Tennessee

http://www.aquinascollege.edu/

- **Independent Roman Catholic** comprehensive, founded 1961
- **Urban** 83-acre campus
- **Endowment** $16.1 million
- **Coed** 415 undergraduate students, 46% full-time, 79% women, 21% men
- **Minimally difficult** entrance level, 61% of applicants were admitted

UNDERGRAD STUDENTS
191 full-time, 224 part-time. Students come from 24 states and territories; 4 other countries; 16% are from out of state; 5% Black or African American, non-Hispanic/Latino; 3% Hispanic/Latino; 4% Asian, non-Hispanic/Latino; 1% Native Hawaiian or other Pacific Islander, non-Hispanic/Latino; 2% Two or more races, non-Hispanic/Latino; 8% Race/ethnicity unknown; 2% international; 23% transferred in; 13% live on campus.

Freshmen
Admission: 154 applied, 94 admitted, 30 enrolled. ***Average high school GPA:*** 3.63. ***Test scores:*** SAT critical reading scores over 500: 91%; SAT math scores over 500: 36%; ACT scores over 18: 90%; SAT critical reading scores over 600: 64%; SAT math scores over 600: 18%; ACT scores over 24: 55%; SAT critical reading scores over 700: 27%; SAT math scores over 700: 9%; ACT scores over 30: 15%.

Retention: 74% of full-time freshmen returned.

FACULTY
Total: 87, 34% full-time, 32% with terminal degrees.

Student/faculty ratio: 8:1.

ACADEMICS
Calendar: semesters. *Degrees:* associate, bachelor's, master's, and post-master's certificates.

Special study options: academic remediation for entering students, accelerated degree program, advanced placement credit, cooperative education, double majors, independent study, internships, part-time degree program, study abroad, summer session for credit.

Computers: 59 computers/terminals are available on campus for general student use. Students can access the following: computer help desk, free student e-mail accounts, online (class) grades, online (class) registration, online (class) schedules. Campuswide network is available. Wireless service is available via dorm rooms, libraries, student centers.

STUDENT LIFE
Housing options: men-only, women-only. Campus housing is leased by the school. Freshman applicants given priority for college housing.

Activities and organizations: choral group, Campus Ministry, Student Activities Board, Association for Supervision and Curriculum Development, Association of Student Nurses, Socratic Club.

Athletics ***Intramural sports:*** table tennis M/W.

Campus security: 24-hour emergency response devices and patrols.

Student services: personal/psychological counseling.

COSTS
Costs (2014–15) ***Comprehensive fee:*** $29,250 includes full-time tuition ($19,950), mandatory fees ($600), and room and board ($8700). Full-time tuition and fees vary according to course load and program. Part-time tuition: $680 per credit hour. Part-time tuition and fees vary according to course load and program. ***College room only:*** $5500. ***Payment plan:*** installment. ***Waivers:*** employees or children of employees.

APPLYING
Standardized Tests *Required:* SAT or ACT (for admission).

Options: electronic application, deferred entrance.

Application fee: $25.

Required: high school transcript, minimum 2.4 GPA. ***Required for some:*** essay or personal statement.

Application deadlines: rolling (freshmen), rolling (out-of-state freshmen), rolling (transfers).

Notification: continuous (freshmen), continuous (out-of-state freshmen), continuous (transfers).

CONTACT
Ms. Connie Hansom, Director of Admissions, Aquinas College, 4210 Harding Pike, Nashville, TN 37205-2005. *Phone:* 615-297-7545 Ext. 411. *Toll-free phone:* 800-649-9956. *Fax:* 615-279-3893. *E-mail:* hansomc@aquinascollege.edu.

Argosy University, Nashville

Nashville, Tennessee

http://www.argosy.edu/locations/nashville/

- **Proprietary** university, founded 2001
- **Coed**

ACADEMICS
Calendar: semesters. *Degrees:* associate, bachelor's, master's, and doctoral.

CONTACT
Argosy University, Nashville, 100 Centerview Drive, Suite 225, Nashville, TN 37214. *Phone:* 615-525-2800. *Toll-free phone:* 866-833-6598.

The Art Institute of Tennessee–Nashville, a branch of The Art Institute of Atlanta

Nashville, Tennessee

http://www.artinstitutes.edu/nashville/

- **Proprietary** 4-year, founded 2006, part of Education Management Corporation
- **Urban** campus
- **Coed**

ACADEMICS
Degrees: diplomas, associate, and bachelor's.

CONTACT
The Art Institute of Tennessee–Nashville, a branch of The Art Institute of Atlanta, 100 Centerview Drive, Suite 250, Nashville, TN 37214. *Phone:* 615-874-1067. *Toll-free phone:* 866-747-5770.

Austin Peay State University

Clarksville, Tennessee

http://www.apsu.edu/

- **State-supported** comprehensive, founded 1927, part of Tennessee Board of Regents
- **Suburban** 169-acre campus with easy access to Nashville
- **Endowment** $8.9 million
- **Coed** 9,246 undergraduate students, 74% full-time, 59% women, 41% men
- **Moderately difficult** entrance level, 89% of applicants were admitted

UNDERGRAD STUDENTS
6,798 full-time, 2,448 part-time. Students come from 48 states and territories; 22 other countries; 11% are from out of state; 20% Black or African American, non-Hispanic/Latino; 6% Hispanic/Latino; 2% Asian, non-Hispanic/Latino; 0.2% Native Hawaiian or other Pacific Islander, non-Hispanic/Latino; 0.4% American Indian or Alaska Native, non-Hispanic/Latino; 5% Two or more races, non-Hispanic/Latino; 2% Race/ethnicity unknown; 0.4% international; 9% transferred in; 15% live on campus.

Freshmen
Admission: 3,307 applied, 2,952 admitted, 1,494 enrolled. ***Average high school GPA:*** 3.2. ***Test scores:*** SAT critical reading scores over 500: 43%; SAT math scores over 500: 57%; ACT scores over 18: 91%; SAT critical reading scores over 600: 14%; SAT math scores over 600: 28%; ACT

scores over 24: 30%; SAT math scores over 700: 14%; ACT scores over 30: 3%.

Retention: 72% of full-time freshmen returned.

FACULTY

Total: 604, 59% full-time.

Student/faculty ratio: 19:1.

ACADEMICS

Calendar: semesters. *Degrees:* certificates, associate, bachelor's, master's, post-master's, and postbachelor's certificates.

Special study options: academic remediation for entering students, accelerated degree program, adult/continuing education programs, advanced placement credit, cooperative education, distance learning, double majors, English as a second language, honors programs, independent study, internships, part-time degree program, services for LD students, study abroad, summer session for credit. ***ROTC:*** Army (b), Air Force (c).

Computers: 950 computers/terminals are available on campus for general student use. Students can access the following: campus intranet, computer help desk, free student e-mail accounts, online (class) grades, online (class) registration, online (class) schedules. Campuswide network is available. Wireless service is available via entire campus.

STUDENT LIFE

Housing options: on-campus residence required for freshman year; coed, men-only, women-only, special housing for students with disabilities. Campus housing is university owned. Freshman campus housing is guaranteed.

Activities and organizations: drama/theater group, student-run newspaper, radio and television station, choral group, marching band, national fraternities, national sororities.

Athletics Member NCAA. All Division I except football (Division I-AA). ***Intercollegiate sports:*** baseball M(s), basketball M(s)/W(s), cheerleading M(s)/W(s), cross-country running M(s)/W(s), golf M(s)/W(s), soccer W(s), softball W(s), tennis M(s)/W(s), track and field W(s), volleyball W(s). ***Intramural sports:*** badminton M/W, basketball M/W, football M/W, golf M/W, ice hockey M/W, racquetball M/W, soccer M/W, softball M/W, table tennis M/W, ultimate Frisbee M/W, volleyball M/W.

Campus security: 24-hour emergency response devices and patrols, student patrols, late-night transport/escort service, controlled dormitory access.

Student services: health clinic, personal/psychological counseling.

COSTS & FINANCIAL AID

Costs (2015–16) ***Tuition:*** state resident $246 per credit hour part-time; nonresident $850 per credit hour part-time. Full-time tuition and fees vary according to location and program. Part-time tuition and fees vary according to location and program. ***Room and board:*** Room and board charges vary according to board plan and housing facility. ***Payment plan:*** installment. ***Waivers:*** senior citizens and employees or children of employees.

Financial Aid Of all full-time matriculated undergraduates who enrolled in 2013, 6,311 applied for aid, 5,547 were judged to have need. 127 Federal Work-Study jobs (averaging $2199). 422 state and other part-time jobs (averaging $1511). In 2013, 543 non-need-based awards were made. ***Average financial aid package:*** $9972. ***Average need-based loan:*** $3895. ***Average need-based gift aid:*** $7376. ***Average non-need-based aid:*** $4313. ***Average indebtedness upon graduation:*** $28,820.

APPLYING

Standardized Tests *Required for some:* SAT or ACT (for admission).

Options: electronic application, early admission, deferred entrance.

Application fee: $15.

Required: high school transcript. ***Required for some:*** minimum 2.8 GPA.

Application deadlines: 8/5 (freshmen), rolling (transfers).

Notification: continuous (freshmen), continuous (transfers).

CONTACT

Ms. Amy Deaton, Director of Admissions, Austin Peay State University, 601 College Street, Clarksville, TN 37044. *Phone:* 931-221-7661. *Toll-free phone:* 800-844-2778. *Fax:* 931-221-6168. *E-mail:* admissions@apsu.edu.

★ Belmont University
Nashville, Tennessee
http://www.belmont.edu/

- **Independent Christian** university, founded 1951
- **Urban** 77-acre campus
- **Endowment** $73.8 million
- **Coed** 5,837 undergraduate students, 93% full-time, 61% women, 39% men
- **Moderately difficult** entrance level, 83% of applicants were admitted

UNDERGRAD STUDENTS

5,440 full-time, 397 part-time. Students come from 51 states and territories; 33 other countries; 63% are from out of state; 4% Black or African American, non-Hispanic/Latino; 5% Hispanic/Latino; 2% Asian, non-Hispanic/Latino; 0.1% Native Hawaiian or other Pacific Islander, non-Hispanic/Latino; 0.3% American Indian or Alaska Native, non-Hispanic/Latino; 3% Two or more races, non-Hispanic/Latino; 4% Race/ethnicity unknown; 1% international; 8% transferred in; 50% live on campus.

Freshmen

Admission: 5,665 applied, 4,686 admitted, 1,392 enrolled. ***Average high school GPA:*** 3.5. ***Test scores:*** SAT critical reading scores over 500: 90%; SAT math scores over 500: 87%; ACT scores over 18: 100%; SAT critical reading scores over 600: 40%; SAT math scores over 600: 40%; ACT scores over 24: 74%; SAT critical reading scores over 700: 6%; SAT math scores over 700: 6%; ACT scores over 30: 19%.

Retention: 83% of full-time freshmen returned.

FACULTY

Total: 745, 45% full-time.

Student/faculty ratio: 13:1.

ACADEMICS

Calendar: semesters. *Degrees:* bachelor's, master's, doctoral, and post-master's certificates.

Special study options: accelerated degree program, adult/continuing education programs, advanced placement credit, cooperative education, distance learning, double majors, English as a second language, honors programs, independent study, internships, off-campus study, part-time degree program, student-designed majors, study abroad, summer session for credit. ***ROTC:*** Army (c), Navy (c), Air Force (c).

Unusual degree programs: 3-2 engineering with Auburn University, Georgia Institute of Technology, University of Tennessee.

Computers: 500 computers/terminals are available on campus for general student use. Students can access the following: campus intranet, free student e-mail accounts, online (class) grades, online (class) registration, online (class) schedules, individual student information via BANNER Web. Campuswide network is available. 100% of college-owned or -operated housing units are wired for high-speed Internet access. Wireless service is available via entire campus.

STUDENT LIFE

Housing options: on-campus residence required through sophomore year; men-only, women-only. Campus housing is university owned. Freshman campus housing is guaranteed.

Activities and organizations: drama/theater group, student-run newspaper, radio and television station, choral group, marching band, Service Corp, Alpha Sigma Tau, Phi Mu, Phi Kappa Tau, MOB, national fraternities, national sororities.

Athletics Member NCAA. All Division I. ***Intercollegiate sports:*** baseball M(s), basketball M(s)/W(s), cross-country running M(s)/W(s), golf M(s)/W(s), soccer M(s)/W(s), softball W(s), tennis M(s)/W(s), track and field M(s)/W(s), volleyball W(s). ***Intramural sports:*** baseball M, basketball M/W, bowling M/W, cheerleading M/W, football M, golf M, ice hockey M/W, racquetball M/W, soccer M/W, softball M/W, table tennis M/W, tennis M/W, volleyball M/W.

Campus security: 24-hour emergency response devices and patrols, late-night transport/escort service, controlled dormitory access, bicycle patrol.

Student services: health clinic, personal/psychological counseling, women's center.

COSTS & FINANCIAL AID
Costs (2014–15) ***Comprehensive fee:*** $39,190 includes full-time tuition ($27,320), mandatory fees ($1340), and room and board ($10,530). Full-time tuition and fees vary according to course load. Part-time tuition: $1040 per credit hour. Part-time tuition and fees vary according to course load. ***College room only:*** $5850. Room and board charges vary according to board plan and housing facility. ***Payment plans:*** installment, deferred payment. ***Waivers:*** senior citizens and employees or children of employees.

Financial Aid Of all full-time matriculated undergraduates who enrolled in 2013, 3,585 applied for aid, 2,785 were judged to have need, 235 had their need fully met. In 2013, 972 non-need-based awards were made. ***Average percent of need met:*** 49. ***Average financial aid package:*** $14,105. ***Average need-based loan:*** $4420. ***Average need-based gift aid:*** $12,096. ***Average non-need-based aid:*** $7438. ***Average indebtedness upon graduation:*** $28,306.

APPLYING
Standardized Tests *Required:* SAT or ACT (for admission).

Options: electronic application, early admission, deferred entrance.

Application fee: $50.

Required: essay or personal statement, high school transcript, minimum 3.0 GPA, 2 letters of recommendation, resume of activities. ***Required for some:*** interview.

Application deadlines: 8/1 (freshmen), 8/1 (transfers).

Notification: continuous (freshmen), continuous (transfers).

CONTACT
Mr. David Mee, Associate Provost and Dean of Enrollment, Belmont University, 1900 Belmont Boulevard, Nashville, TN 37212-3757. *Phone:* 615-460-5479. *Fax:* 615-460-5434. *E-mail:* david.mee@belmont.edu.

Bethel University

McKenzie, Tennessee

http://www.bethelu.edu/

- **Independent Cumberland Presbyterian** comprehensive, founded 1842
- **Small-town** 100-acre campus
- **Endowment** $2.9 million
- **Coed**
- **Minimally difficult** entrance level

FACULTY
Student/faculty ratio: 13:1.

ACADEMICS
Calendar: semesters. *Degrees:* associate, bachelor's, and master's.

STUDENT LIFE
Housing options: on-campus residence required through junior year; coed, men-only, women-only, special housing for students with disabilities. Campus housing is university owned and leased by the school. Freshman applicants given priority for college housing.

Activities and organizations: drama/theater group, choral group, marching band, Campus Crusade for Christ, STEA (Education), Student Government Association, Students in Free Enterprise (SIFE), Arete.

Athletics Member NAIA.

Campus security: night patrols by trained security personnel.

Student services: personal/psychological counseling.

COSTS
Costs (2014–15) ***Comprehensive fee:*** $42,430 includes full-time tuition ($32,840), mandatory fees ($150), and room and board ($9440). Part-time tuition: $1370 per credit. ***College room only:*** $5400.

APPLYING
Standardized Tests *Recommended:* SAT or ACT (for admission).

Options: electronic application, early admission, deferred entrance.

Application fee: $30.

Required: high school transcript, minimum 2.0 GPA. ***Required for some:*** essay or personal statement, interview.

CONTACT
Tina Hodges, Enrollment Director of Admissions and Financial Aid, Bethel University, 325 Cherry Avenue, McKenzie, TN 38201. *Phone:* 731-352-4030. *Fax:* 731-352-4069. *E-mail:* hodgest@bethelu.edu.

Bryan College

Dayton, Tennessee

http://www.bryan.edu/

- **Independent interdenominational** comprehensive, founded 1930
- **Small-town** 130-acre campus
- **Coed** 1,512 undergraduate students, 65% full-time, 55% women, 45% men
- **Moderately difficult** entrance level, 48% of applicants were admitted

UNDERGRAD STUDENTS
976 full-time, 536 part-time. Students come from 44 states and territories; 21 other countries; 66% are from out of state; 3% Black or African American, non-Hispanic/Latino; 2% Hispanic/Latino; 0.4% Asian, non-Hispanic/Latino; 2% Two or more races, non-Hispanic/Latino; 8% Race/ethnicity unknown; 3% international; 2% transferred in; 77% live on campus.

Freshmen
Admission: 759 applied, 367 admitted, 173 enrolled. ***Average high school GPA:*** 3.55. ***Test scores:*** SAT critical reading scores over 500: 66%; SAT math scores over 500: 57%; SAT writing scores over 500: 54%; ACT scores over 18: 93%; SAT critical reading scores over 600: 26%; SAT math scores over 600: 17%; SAT writing scores over 600: 20%; ACT scores over 24: 38%; SAT critical reading scores over 700: 9%; SAT math scores over 700: 3%; SAT writing scores over 700: 9%; ACT scores over 30: 9%.

Retention: 60% of full-time freshmen returned.

FACULTY
Total: 121, 35% full-time, 37% with terminal degrees.

Student/faculty ratio: 15:1.

ACADEMICS
Calendar: semesters. *Degrees:* certificates, diplomas, associate, bachelor's, and master's.

Special study options: academic remediation for entering students, adult/continuing education programs, advanced placement credit, distance learning, double majors, honors programs, independent study, internships, off-campus study, part-time degree program, services for LD students, study abroad, summer session for credit.

Unusual degree programs: 3-2 nursing with Vanderbilt University; Psychology: Richmont Graduate University.

Computers: 84 computers/terminals are available on campus for general student use. Students can access the following: campus intranet, computer help desk, free student e-mail accounts, online (class) grades, online (class) registration, online (class) schedules. Campuswide network is available. Wireless service is available via entire campus.

STUDENT LIFE
Housing options: on-campus residence required through senior year; men-only, women-only. Campus housing is university owned. Freshman campus housing is guaranteed.

Activities and organizations: drama/theater group, student-run newspaper, choral group, Practical Christian Involvement (PCI), International Students Association, Rugby club, Nutella Club, Navigators.

Athletics Member NAIA. ***Intercollegiate sports:*** baseball M(s), basketball M(s)/W(s), cross-country running M(s)/W(s), golf M(s)/W(s), soccer M(s)/W(s), softball W(s), track and field M(s)/W(s), volleyball M(s)/W(s). ***Intramural sports:*** basketball M/W, cheerleading M(c)/W(c), football M, rugby M(c), soccer M/W, softball M/W, table tennis M/W, ultimate Frisbee M/W, volleyball M/W.

Campus security: controlled dormitory access, police patrols; night watch.

Student services: health clinic, personal/psychological counseling.

COSTS & FINANCIAL AID
Costs (2015–16) ***Comprehensive fee:*** $29,990 includes full-time tuition ($23,300) and room and board ($6690). Part-time tuition: $990 per credit hour. ***College room only:*** $4190. Room and board charges vary according

to housing facility. ***Payment plan:*** installment. ***Waivers:*** employees or children of employees.

Financial Aid Of all full-time matriculated undergraduates who enrolled in 2010, 918 applied for aid, 786 were judged to have need, 769 had their need fully met. In 2010, 105 non-need-based awards were made. ***Average percent of need met:*** 92. ***Average financial aid package:*** $31,573. ***Average need-based loan:*** $7073. ***Average need-based gift aid:*** $18,160. ***Average non-need-based aid:*** $8448. ***Average indebtedness upon graduation:*** $15,637.

APPLYING

Standardized Tests *Required:* SAT or ACT (for admission).

Options: electronic application, early action, deferred entrance.

Application fee: $35.

Required: essay or personal statement, high school transcript, minimum 2.0 GPA, 3 letters of recommendation, ACT 18 or SAT 860. ***Required for some:*** interview.

Application deadlines: rolling (freshmen), rolling (out-of-state freshmen), rolling (transfers), 5/1 (early action).

Notification: continuous (freshmen), continuous (out-of-state freshmen), rolling (early action).

CONTACT

Mr. Andrew Smith, Senior Enrollment Counselor, Bryan College, 721 Bryan Drive, Dayton, TN 37321-7000. *Phone:* 423-775-2041 Ext. 218. *Toll-free phone:* 800-277-9522. *Fax:* 423-775-7199. *E-mail:* admissions@bryan.edu.

★ Carson-Newman University

Jefferson City, Tennessee

http://www.cn.edu/

- **Independent Southern Baptist** comprehensive, founded 1851
- **Small-town** 90-acre campus with easy access to Knoxville
- **Endowment** $50.4 million
- **Coed** 1,757 undergraduate students, 96% full-time, 57% women, 43% men
- **Moderately difficult** entrance level, 62% of applicants were admitted

UNDERGRAD STUDENTS

1,682 full-time, 75 part-time. Students come from 31 states and territories; 20 other countries; 24% are from out of state; 8% Black or African American, non-Hispanic/Latino; 2% Hispanic/Latino; 0.6% Asian, non-Hispanic/Latino; 0.2% American Indian or Alaska Native, non-Hispanic/Latino; 3% Race/ethnicity unknown; 2% international; 6% transferred in; 59% live on campus.

Freshmen

Admission: 4,880 applied, 3,045 admitted, 491 enrolled. ***Average high school GPA:*** 3.51. ***Test scores:*** SAT critical reading scores over 500: 60%; SAT math scores over 500: 51%; ACT scores over 18: 98%; SAT critical reading scores over 600: 18%; SAT math scores over 600: 21%; ACT scores over 24: 48%; SAT critical reading scores over 700: 4%; SAT math scores over 700: 1%; ACT scores over 30: 8%.

Retention: 71% of full-time freshmen returned.

FACULTY

Total: 209, 62% full-time, 57% with terminal degrees.

Student/faculty ratio: 11:1.

ACADEMICS

Calendar: semesters. *Degrees:* associate, bachelor's, master's, doctoral, and postbachelor's certificates.

Special study options: academic remediation for entering students, accelerated degree program, adult/continuing education programs, advanced placement credit, English as a second language, honors programs, internships, off-campus study, part-time degree program, services for LD students, student-designed majors, study abroad, summer session for credit. ***ROTC:*** Army (b).

Unusual degree programs: 3-2 engineering with Georgia Institute of Technology, University of Tennessee, Tennessee Technological University; pharmacy with Campbell University, Mercer University, University of Georgia.

Computers: 200 computers/terminals are available on campus for general student use. Campuswide network is available.

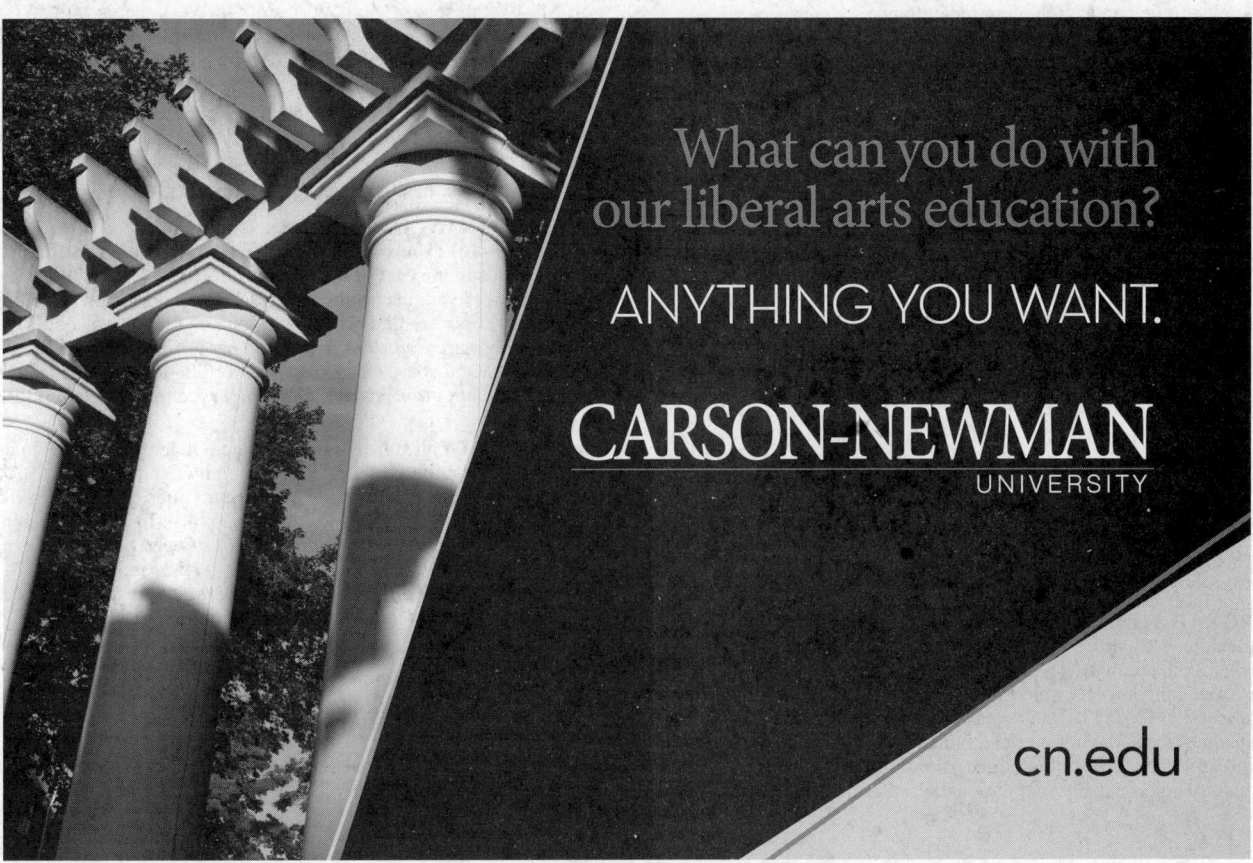

STUDENT LIFE
Housing options: on-campus residence required through junior year; men-only, women-only, special housing for students with disabilities. Freshman campus housing is guaranteed.

Activities and organizations: drama/theater group, student-run newspaper, choral group, marching band, Baptist Student Union, Fellowship of Christian Athletes, Student Government Association, Student Ambassadors Association, Columbians, national fraternities, national sororities.

Athletics Member NCAA. All Division II. ***Intercollegiate sports:*** baseball M(s), basketball M(s)/W(s), cross-country running M(s)/W(s), football M(s), golf M(s), soccer M(s)/W(s), softball W(s), swimming and diving M(s)/W(s), tennis M(s)/W(s), track and field M(s)/W(s), volleyball W(s), wrestling M(s). ***Intramural sports:*** badminton M/W, baseball M/W, basketball M/W, football M/W, golf M/W, racquetball M/W, skiing (downhill) M/W, soccer M/W, softball M/W, swimming and diving M/W, table tennis M/W, tennis M/W, volleyball M/W.

Campus security: 24-hour emergency response devices and patrols, late-night transport/escort service, controlled dormitory access.

Student services: health clinic, personal/psychological counseling.

COSTS & FINANCIAL AID
Costs (2015–16) ***Comprehensive fee:*** $33,630 includes full-time tuition ($24,200), mandatory fees ($1160), and room and board ($8270). Full-time tuition and fees vary according to class time and course load. Part-time tuition: $1010 per credit hour. ***College room only:*** $3930. Room and board charges vary according to board plan, gender, and housing facility. ***Payment plans:*** installment, deferred payment. ***Waivers:*** senior citizens and employees or children of employees.

Financial Aid Of all full-time matriculated undergraduates who enrolled in 2013, 1,320 applied for aid, 1,320 were judged to have need, 291 had their need fully met. In 2013, 225 non-need-based awards were made. ***Average percent of need met:*** 82. ***Average financial aid package:*** $21,549. ***Average need-based loan:*** $3840. ***Average need-based gift aid:*** $16,082. ***Average non-need-based aid:*** $7554. ***Average indebtedness upon graduation:*** $25,555.

APPLYING
Standardized Tests *Required:* SAT or ACT (for admission).

Options: electronic application, deferred entrance.

Required: high school transcript, minimum 2.3 GPA, medical history. ***Required for some:*** essay or personal statement, interview. ***Recommended:*** interview.

Application deadlines: 8/1 (freshmen), 8/1 (transfers).

Notification: continuous (freshmen), continuous (transfers).

CONTACT
Melanie Redding, Director of Admissions, Carson-Newman University, 1646 Russell Avenue, PO Box 557, Jefferson City, TN 37760. *Phone:* 865-471-3223. *Toll-free phone:* 800-678-9061. *Fax:* 865-471-3502. *E-mail:* cnadmiss@cn.edu.

See previous page for display ad and page 1384 for the College Close-Up.

Christian Brothers University

Memphis, Tennessee

http://www.cbu.edu/

- **Independent Roman Catholic** comprehensive, founded 1871
- **Urban** 75-acre campus with easy access to Memphis
- **Endowment** $31.7 million
- **Coed** 1,299 undergraduate students, 91% full-time, 55% women, 45% men
- **Moderately difficult** entrance level, 50% of applicants were admitted

UNDERGRAD STUDENTS
1,186 full-time, 113 part-time. Students come from 27 states and territories; 22 other countries; 20% are from out of state; 32% Black or African American, non-Hispanic/Latino; 7% Hispanic/Latino; 5% Asian, non-Hispanic/Latino; 0.1% Native Hawaiian or other Pacific Islander, non-Hispanic/Latino; 0.4% American Indian or Alaska Native, non-Hispanic/Latino; 2% Two or more races, non-Hispanic/Latino; 5% Race/ethnicity unknown; 3% international; 9% transferred in; 40% live on campus.

Freshmen
Admission: 2,229 applied, 1,108 admitted, 354 enrolled. ***Average high school GPA:*** 3.73. ***Test scores:*** ACT scores over 18: 100%; ACT scores over 24: 54%; ACT scores over 30: 10%.

Retention: 83% of full-time freshmen returned.

FACULTY
Total: 179, 58% full-time, 65% with terminal degrees.

Student/faculty ratio: 10:1.

ACADEMICS
Calendar: semesters. *Degrees:* associate, bachelor's, master's, and postbachelor's certificates.

Special study options: accelerated degree program, adult/continuing education programs, advanced placement credit, cooperative education, distance learning, double majors, honors programs, independent study, internships, off-campus study, part-time degree program, services for LD students, study abroad, summer session for credit. ***ROTC:*** Army (c), Navy (c), Air Force (c).

Unusual degree programs: 3-2 engineering with Three years at Rhodes College and two years at CBU in engineering.

Computers: 310 computers/terminals are available on campus for general student use. Students can access the following: campus intranet, computer help desk, free student e-mail accounts, online (class) grades, online (class) registration, online (class) schedules. Campuswide network is available. 100% of college-owned or -operated housing units are wired for high-speed Internet access. Wireless service is available via entire campus.

STUDENT LIFE
Housing options: on-campus residence required through sophomore year; coed, men-only, women-only. Campus housing is university owned. Freshman campus housing is guaranteed.

Activities and organizations: drama/theater group, choral group, Black Student Association, BACCHUS Alcohol Awareness Group, Intercultural Club, The Chosen Generation, Lasallian Collegians, national fraternities, national sororities.

Athletics Member NCAA. All Division II. ***Intercollegiate sports:*** baseball M(s), basketball M(s)/W(s), cross-country running M(s)/W(s), golf M(s)/W(s), soccer M(s)/W(s), softball W(s), tennis M(s)/W(s), track and field M(s)/W(s), volleyball W(s). ***Intramural sports:*** basketball M/W, lacrosse W(c), soccer M/W, softball M/W, ultimate Frisbee M(c)/W(c), volleyball M/W.

Campus security: 24-hour emergency response devices and patrols, student patrols, late-night transport/escort service, controlled dormitory access.

Student services: health clinic, personal/psychological counseling.

COSTS & FINANCIAL AID
Costs (2015–16) ***Comprehensive fee:*** $37,106 includes full-time tuition ($29,316), mandatory fees ($790), and room and board ($7000). Full-time tuition and fees vary according to class time and program. Part-time tuition: $1051 per credit. Part-time tuition and fees vary according to class time and program. ***Required fees:*** $225 per term part-time. ***Room and board:*** Room and board charges vary according to board plan and housing facility. ***Payment plan:*** installment. ***Waivers:*** employees or children of employees.

Financial Aid Of all full-time matriculated undergraduates who enrolled in 2013, 1,013 applied for aid, 808 were judged to have need, 157 had their need fully met. 224 Federal Work-Study jobs (averaging $980). 116 state and other part-time jobs (averaging $1140). In 2013, 205 non-need-based awards were made. ***Average percent of need met:*** 76. ***Average financial aid package:*** $23,390. ***Average need-based loan:*** $4431. ***Average need-based gift aid:*** $17,557. ***Average non-need-based aid:*** $13,031. ***Average indebtedness upon graduation:*** $22,759.

APPLYING
Standardized Tests *Required:* SAT or ACT (for admission).

Options: electronic application, deferred entrance.

Application fee: $25.

Required: essay or personal statement, high school transcript, minimum 2.0 GPA. ***Required for some:*** 2 letters of recommendation. ***Recommended:*** interview.

Application deadlines: 8/1 (freshmen), 8/23 (transfers).

Notification: 12/1 (freshmen), continuous (transfers).

CONTACT
Ms. Kristi Forman, Director of Admissions, Christian Brothers University, 650 East Parkway South, Memphis, TN 38104. *Phone:* 901-321-3205. *Toll-free phone:* 877-321-4CBU. *Fax:* 901-321-3202. *E-mail:* admissions@cbu.edu.

Cumberland University

Lebanon, Tennessee

http://www.cumberland.edu/

- **Independent** comprehensive, founded 1842
- **Small-town** 44-acre campus with easy access to Nashville
- **Endowment** $11.5 million
- **Coed** 1,254 undergraduate students, 78% full-time, 58% women, 42% men
- **Moderately difficult** entrance level, 46% of applicants were admitted

UNDERGRAD STUDENTS
984 full-time, 270 part-time. Students come from 31 states and territories; 19 other countries; 83% are from out of state; 12% Black or African American, non-Hispanic/Latino; 3% Hispanic/Latino; 0.9% Asian, non-Hispanic/Latino; 0.3% American Indian or Alaska Native, non-Hispanic/Latino; 15% Race/ethnicity unknown; 3% international; 18% transferred in; 30% live on campus.

Freshmen
Admission: 713 applied, 331 admitted, 178 enrolled. ***Average high school GPA:*** 3.3. ***Test scores:*** SAT critical reading scores over 500: 36%; SAT math scores over 500: 43%; SAT writing scores over 500: 14%; ACT scores over 18: 92%; SAT critical reading scores over 600: 7%; SAT math scores over 600: 7%; ACT scores over 24: 39%; ACT scores over 30: 4%.

Retention: 62% of full-time freshmen returned.

FACULTY
Total: 159, 35% full-time, 40% with terminal degrees.

Student/faculty ratio: 14:1.

ACADEMICS
Calendar: semesters. *Degrees:* associate, bachelor's, and master's.

Special study options: academic remediation for entering students, accelerated degree program, adult/continuing education programs, advanced placement credit, cooperative education, double majors, freshman honors college, honors programs, internships, part-time degree program, services for LD students, summer session for credit. ***ROTC:*** Army (b).

Computers: 150 computers/terminals are available on campus for general student use. Students can access the following: campus intranet, computer help desk, free student e-mail accounts, online (class) grades, online (class) schedules. Campuswide network is available. 100% of college-owned or -operated housing units are wired for high-speed Internet access. Wireless service is available via entire campus.

STUDENT LIFE
Housing options: on-campus residence required for freshman year; men-only, women-only, special housing for students with disabilities. Campus housing is university owned.

Activities and organizations: drama/theater group, student-run newspaper, radio station, choral group, marching band, African-American Student Association, Baptist Collegiate Ministry, Law and Government Club, Student Government Association, Student Nurses' Association, national fraternities, national sororities.

Athletics Member NAIA. ***Intercollegiate sports:*** baseball M(s), basketball M(s)/W(s), bowling M(s)/W(s), cheerleading M(s)/W(s), cross-country running M(s)/W(s), football M(s), golf M(s)/W(s), soccer M(s)/W(s), softball W(s), tennis M(s)/W(s), volleyball W(s), wrestling M(s). ***Intramural sports:*** basketball M/W, bowling M/W, softball W, table tennis M/W, volleyball M/W.

Campus security: 24-hour emergency response devices and patrols, late-night transport/escort service.

Student services: personal/psychological counseling.

COSTS & FINANCIAL AID
Costs (2015–16) ***One-time required fee:*** $100. ***Comprehensive fee:*** $28,760 includes full-time tuition ($20,160), mandatory fees ($1050), and room and board ($7550). Full-time tuition and fees vary according to degree level. Part-time tuition: $840 per credit hour. Part-time tuition and fees vary according to course load and degree level. ***Room and board:*** Room and board charges vary according to housing facility. ***Payment plan:*** installment. ***Waivers:*** employees or children of employees.

Financial Aid Of all full-time matriculated undergraduates who enrolled in 2013, 983 applied for aid, 911 were judged to have need, 136 had their need fully met. 120 Federal Work-Study jobs (averaging $750). 15 state and other part-time jobs (averaging $750). In 2013, 67 non-need-based awards were made. ***Average percent of need met:*** 69. ***Average financial aid package:*** $16,665. ***Average need-based loan:*** $4065. ***Average need-based gift aid:*** $5590. ***Average non-need-based aid:*** $4096. ***Average indebtedness upon graduation:*** $25,827.

APPLYING
Standardized Tests *Required:* SAT or ACT (for admission). *Recommended:* SAT (for admission).

Options: electronic application, deferred entrance.

Application fee: $25.

Required: high school transcript. ***Required for some:*** 3 letters of recommendation. ***Recommended:*** essay or personal statement, minimum 3.0 GPA.

Application deadlines: rolling (freshmen), rolling (transfers).

Notification: continuous (freshmen), continuous (transfers).

CONTACT
Ms. Beatrice LaChance, Director of Enrollment Services, Cumberland University, One Cumberland Square, Lebanon, TN 37087. *Phone:* 615-547-1244. *Toll-free phone:* 800-467-0562. *Fax:* 615-444-2569. *E-mail:* admissions@cumberland.edu.

DeVry University

Memphis, Tennessee

http://www.devry.edu/

- **Proprietary** comprehensive, founded 2007
- **Coed**

ACADEMICS
Degrees: associate, bachelor's, and master's.

COSTS & FINANCIAL AID
Costs (2014–15) ***Tuition:*** $17,052 full-time, $609 per credit hour part-time. ***Required fees:*** $80 full-time.

Financial Aid Of all full-time matriculated undergraduates who enrolled in 2007, 6 applied for aid, 6 were judged to have need, 1 had their need fully met. ***Average percent of need met:*** 42. ***Average financial aid package:*** $11,341. ***Average need-based loan:*** $7566. ***Average need-based gift aid:*** $4530.

CONTACT
Admissions Office, DeVry University, 6401 Poplar Avenue, Suite 600, Memphis, TN 38119. *Phone:* 901-537-2560. *Toll-free phone:* 866-338-7941.

DeVry University

Nashville, Tennessee

http://www.devry.edu/

- **Proprietary** comprehensive
- **Coed**

ACADEMICS
Degrees: associate, bachelor's, and master's.

COSTS
Costs (2014–15) ***Tuition:*** $17,052 full-time, $609 per credit hour part-time. ***Required fees:*** $80 full-time.

CONTACT
Admissions Office, DeVry University, 3343 Perimeter Hill Drive, Suite 200, Nashville, TN 37211-4147. *Phone:* 615-445-3456. *Toll-free phone:* 866-338-7941.

East Tennessee State University

Johnson City, Tennessee

http://www.etsu.edu/

- **State-supported** university, founded 1911, part of State University and Community College System of Tennessee; Tennessee Board of Regents
- **Small-town** 366-acre campus
- **Endowment** $2.2 million
- **Coed** 11,550 undergraduate students, 83% full-time, 57% women, 43% men
- **Moderately difficult** entrance level, 92% of applicants were admitted

UNDERGRAD STUDENTS

9,574 full-time, 1,976 part-time. Students come from 44 states and territories; 58 other countries; 13% are from out of state; 6% Black or African American, non-Hispanic/Latino; 2% Hispanic/Latino; 1% Asian, non-Hispanic/Latino; 0.1% Native Hawaiian or other Pacific Islander, non-Hispanic/Latino; 0.3% American Indian or Alaska Native, non-Hispanic/Latino; 2% Two or more races, non-Hispanic/Latino; 1% Race/ethnicity unknown; 3% international; 9% transferred in; 20% live on campus.

Freshmen

Admission: 5,252 applied, 4,818 admitted, 2,055 enrolled. ***Average high school GPA:*** 3.4. ***Test scores:*** SAT critical reading scores over 500: 59%; SAT math scores over 500: 44%; ACT scores over 18: 87%; SAT critical reading scores over 600: 26%; SAT math scores over 600: 26%; ACT scores over 24: 38%; SAT critical reading scores over 700: 6%; SAT math scores over 700: 6%; ACT scores over 30: 5%.

Retention: 69% of full-time freshmen returned.

FACULTY

Total: 897, 66% full-time.

Student/faculty ratio: 17:1.

ACADEMICS

Calendar: semesters. *Degrees:* certificates, bachelor's, master's, doctoral, post-master's, and postbachelor's certificates.

Special study options: adult/continuing education programs, advanced placement credit, cooperative education, distance learning, double majors, English as a second language, external degree program, freshman honors college, honors programs, independent study, internships, off-campus study, part-time degree program, services for LD students, student-designed majors, study abroad, summer session for credit. ***ROTC:*** Army (b).

Computers: 1,400 computers/terminals are available on campus for general student use. Students can access the following: computer help desk, free student e-mail accounts, online (class) grades, online (class) registration, online (class) schedules. Campuswide network is available. Wireless service is available via entire campus.

STUDENT LIFE

Housing options: coed, men-only, women-only, special housing for students with disabilities. Campus housing is university owned.

Activities and organizations: drama/theater group, student-run newspaper, radio and television station, choral group, marching band, honor societies, Volunteer ETSU, religious groups, residence hall councils, national fraternities, national sororities.

Athletics Member NCAA. All Division I except football (Division I-AA). ***Intercollegiate sports:*** baseball M(s), basketball M(s)/W(s), cross-country running M(s)/W(s), golf M(s)/W(s), soccer M(s)/W(s), softball W(s), tennis M(s)/W(s), track and field M(s)/W(s), volleyball W(s). ***Intramural sports:*** basketball M/W, cross-country running M/W, football M/W, golf M/W, racquetball M/W, softball M/W, tennis M/W, volleyball W, weight lifting M.

Campus security: 24-hour emergency response devices and patrols, student patrols, late-night transport/escort service, controlled dormitory access.

Student services: health clinic, personal/psychological counseling, women's center.

COSTS & FINANCIAL AID

Costs (2014–15) ***Tuition:*** state resident $6630 full-time, $263 per credit hour part-time; nonresident $23,796 full-time, $944 per credit hour part-time. Full-time tuition and fees vary according to course load and program. Part-time tuition and fees vary according to course load and program. ***Required fees:*** $1355 full-time, $85 per credit hour part-time. ***Room and board:*** $7822; room only: $4602. Room and board charges vary according to board plan and housing facility. ***Payment plans:*** tuition prepayment, installment. ***Waivers:*** senior citizens and employees or children of employees.

Financial Aid Of all full-time matriculated undergraduates who enrolled in 2012, 9,608 applied for aid, 8,531 were judged to have need, 422 had their need fully met. In 2012, 827 non-need-based awards were made. ***Average percent of need met:*** 49. ***Average financial aid package:*** $9319. ***Average need-based loan:*** $4222. ***Average need-based gift aid:*** $5790. ***Average non-need-based aid:*** $16,782. ***Average indebtedness upon graduation:*** $27,007.

APPLYING

Standardized Tests *Required:* SAT or ACT (for admission).

Options: electronic application, early admission.

Application fee: $25.

Required: high school transcript, minimum 2.3 GPA, 2.3 high school GPA or 19 ACT.

Application deadlines: rolling (freshmen), rolling (out-of-state freshmen), rolling (transfers).

Notification: continuous (freshmen), continuous (out-of-state freshmen), continuous (transfers).

CONTACT

Mr. Brian Henley, Director of Admissions, East Tennessee State University, PO Box 70731, Johnson City, TN 37614-0734. *Phone:* 423-439-4213. *Toll-free phone:* 800-462-3878. *Fax:* 423-439-4630. *E-mail:* go2etsu@etsu.edu.

Fisk University

Nashville, Tennessee

http://www.fisk.edu/

- **Independent** comprehensive, founded 1866, affiliated with United Church of Christ
- **Urban** 40-acre campus
- **Endowment** $12.5 million
- **Coed**
- **Moderately difficult** entrance level

FACULTY

Student/faculty ratio: 11:1.

ACADEMICS

Calendar: semesters. *Degrees:* certificates, bachelor's, master's, and postbachelor's certificates.

STUDENT LIFE

Housing options: coed, men-only, women-only, special housing for students with disabilities. Campus housing is university owned. Freshman applicants given priority for college housing.

Activities and organizations: drama/theater group, student-run newspaper, choral group, Student Government Association, State Clubs, Class organizations, Greek Fraternities and Sororities, University Choir, national fraternities, national sororities.

Athletics Member NAIA.

Campus security: 24-hour emergency response devices and patrols, late-night transport/escort service, controlled dormitory access.

Student services: health clinic, personal/psychological counseling.

COSTS & FINANCIAL AID

Costs (2014–15) ***One-time required fee:*** $535. ***Comprehensive fee:*** $31,018 includes full-time tuition ($19,240), mandatory fees ($1618), and room and board ($10,160). Full-time tuition and fees vary according to course load and degree level. Part-time tuition: $801 per credit hour. ***Required fees:*** $801 per credit hour part-time. ***College room only:*** $5752.

Financial Aid Of all full-time matriculated undergraduates who enrolled in 2011, 554 applied for aid, 499 were judged to have need, 160 had their need fully met. ***Average percent of need met:*** 75. ***Average financial aid package:*** $12,920. ***Average need-based loan:*** $3780. ***Average need-based gift aid:*** $10,417. ***Average indebtedness upon graduation:*** $6147. ***Financial aid deadline:*** 6/1.

APPLYING
Standardized Tests *Required:* SAT or ACT (for admission).

Options: electronic application, early admission, early decision.

Application fee: $25.

Required: essay or personal statement, high school transcript, 2 letters of recommendation, FAFSA after January 1st, SAT or ACT Score.

CONTACT
Ms. Loretta McDonald, Interim Director of the Office of Recruitment and Admission, Fisk University, 1000 17th Avenue North, Nashville, TN 37208-3051. *Phone:* 615-329-8503. *Toll-free phone:* 888-702-0022. *Fax:* 615-329-8774. *E-mail:* lmcdonald@fisk.edu.

Freed-Hardeman University

Henderson, Tennessee

http://www.fhu.edu/

- **Independent** comprehensive, founded 1869, affiliated with Church of Christ
- **Small-town** 120-acre campus
- **Endowment** $35.4 million
- **Coed**
- **Moderately difficult** entrance level

FACULTY
Student/faculty ratio: 13:1.

ACADEMICS
Calendar: semesters. *Degrees:* associate, bachelor's, master's, doctoral, post-master's, and postbachelor's certificates.

STUDENT LIFE
Housing options: on-campus residence required through senior year; men-only, women-only, special housing for students with disabilities. Campus housing is university owned. Freshman campus housing is guaranteed.

Activities and organizations: drama/theater group, student-run newspaper, radio and television station, choral group, Student Government Association, University Program Council, Campus Delegate Team, Student Alumni Association, College Republicans.

Athletics Member NAIA.

Campus security: 24-hour patrols, controlled dormitory access.

Student services: health clinic, personal/psychological counseling.

COSTS & FINANCIAL AID
Costs (2014–15) ***Comprehensive fee:*** $27,858 includes full-time tuition ($20,468) and room and board ($7390). Part-time tuition: $650 per credit hour. ***College room only:*** $3980. Room and board charges vary according to board plan and housing facility.

Financial Aid Of all full-time matriculated undergraduates who enrolled in 2012, 1,221 applied for aid, 1,070 were judged to have need, 244 had their need fully met. In 2012, 177 non-need-based awards were made. ***Average percent of need met:*** 65. ***Average financial aid package:*** $16,249. ***Average need-based loan:*** $3730. ***Average need-based gift aid:*** $12,433. ***Average non-need-based aid:*** $8625. ***Average indebtedness upon graduation:*** $41,086.

APPLYING
Standardized Tests *Required:* SAT or ACT (for admission).

Options: electronic application, deferred entrance.

Required: high school transcript, minimum 2.3 GPA, ACT and/or SAT scores. ***Required for some:*** interview. ***Recommended:*** essay or personal statement.

CONTACT
Freed-Hardeman University, 158 East Main Street, Henderson, TN 38340-2399. *Phone:* 731-989-6557. *Toll-free phone:* 800-FHU-FHU-1.

Huntington College of Health Sciences

Knoxville, Tennessee

http://www.hchs.edu/

- **Proprietary** comprehensive, founded 1984
- **Suburban** campus
- **Coed**
- **Noncompetitive** entrance level

FACULTY
Student/faculty ratio: 11:1.

ACADEMICS
Calendar: continuous. *Degrees:* certificates, diplomas, associate, bachelor's, master's, doctoral, and postbachelor's certificates (offers only external degree programs conducted through home study).

COSTS
Costs (2014–15) ***One-time required fee:*** $275. ***Tuition:*** $5880 full-time, $2940 per year part-time. ***Required fees:*** $120 full-time, $60 per course part-time.

APPLYING
Options: deferred entrance.

Application fee: $75.

Required for some: high school transcript, interview. ***Recommended:*** minimum 2.0 GPA.

CONTACT
Kim Galyon, Director of Admissions, Huntington College of Health Sciences, 1204 Kenesaw Avenue, Suite D, Knoxville, TN 37919. *Phone:* 800-290-4226 Ext. 1. *Toll-free phone:* 800-290-4226. *Fax:* 865-524-8339. *E-mail:* studentservices@hchs.edu.

ITT Technical Institute

Chattanooga, Tennessee

http://www.itt-tech.edu/

- **Proprietary** primarily 2-year, part of ITT Educational Services, Inc.
- **Coed**
- **Minimally difficult** entrance level

ACADEMICS
Degrees: associate and bachelor's.

STUDENT LIFE
Housing options: college housing not available.

CONTACT
Director of Recruitment, ITT Technical Institute, 5600 Brainerd Road, Suite G-1, Chattanooga, TN 37411. *Phone:* 423-510-6800. *Toll-free phone:* 877-474-8312.

ITT Technical Institute

Cordova, Tennessee

http://www.itt-tech.edu/

- **Proprietary** primarily 2-year, founded 1994, part of ITT Educational Services, Inc.
- **Suburban** campus
- **Coed**
- **Minimally difficult** entrance level

ACADEMICS
Calendar: quarters. *Degrees:* associate and bachelor's.

STUDENT LIFE
Housing options: college housing not available.

CONTACT
Director of Recruitment, ITT Technical Institute, 7260 Goodlett Farms Parkway, Cordova, TN 38016. *Phone:* 901-381-0200. *Toll-free phone:* 866-444-5141.

ITT Technical Institute

Johnson City, Tennessee

http://www.itt-tech.edu/

- **Proprietary** primarily 2-year
- **Coed**
- **Minimally difficult** entrance level

ACADEMICS
Degrees: associate and bachelor's.

CONTACT
Director of Recruitment, ITT Technical Institute, 4721 Lake Park Drive, Suite 100, Johnson City, TN 37615. *Phone:* 423-952-4400. *Toll-free phone:* 877-301-9691.

ITT Technical Institute

Knoxville, Tennessee

http://www.itt-tech.edu/

- **Proprietary** primarily 2-year, founded 1988, part of ITT Educational Services, Inc.
- **Suburban** campus
- **Coed**
- **Minimally difficult** entrance level

ACADEMICS
Calendar: quarters. *Degrees:* associate and bachelor's.

STUDENT LIFE
Housing options: college housing not available.

CONTACT
Director of Recruitment, ITT Technical Institute, 9123 Executive Park Drive, Knoxville, TN 37923. *Phone:* 865-342-2300. *Toll-free phone:* 800-671-2801.

ITT Technical Institute

Nashville, Tennessee

http://www.itt-tech.edu/

- **Proprietary** primarily 2-year, founded 1984, part of ITT Educational Services, Inc.
- **Urban** campus
- **Coed**
- **Minimally difficult** entrance level

ACADEMICS
Calendar: quarters. *Degrees:* associate and bachelor's.

STUDENT LIFE
Housing options: college housing not available.

CONTACT
Director of Recruitment, ITT Technical Institute, 2845 Elm Hill Pike, Nashville, TN 37214. *Phone:* 615-889-8700. *Toll-free phone:* 800-331-8386.

Johnson University

Knoxville, Tennessee

http://www.johnsonu.edu/

- **Independent** comprehensive, founded 1893, affiliated with Christian Churches and Churches of Christ
- **Rural** 175-acre campus with easy access to Knoxville
- **Endowment** $99.9 million
- **Coed**
- **Moderately difficult** entrance level

FACULTY
Student/faculty ratio: 17:1.

ACADEMICS
Calendar: semesters. *Degrees:* certificates, associate, bachelor's, master's, and doctoral.

STUDENT LIFE
Housing options: on-campus residence required through senior year; men-only, women-only. Campus housing is university owned.

Activities and organizations: student-run radio station, choral group, Quest, Timothy Club, International Harvesters.

Athletics Member NCCAA.

Campus security: 24-hour emergency response devices and patrols, student patrols, controlled dormitory access.

Student services: health clinic, personal/psychological counseling.

COSTS & FINANCIAL AID
Costs (2014–15) ***Comprehensive fee:*** $17,400 includes full-time tuition ($11,000), mandatory fees ($850), and room and board ($5550). Part-time tuition: $415 per credit hour. ***Room and board:*** Room and board charges vary according to board plan, housing facility, and location.

Financial Aid Of all full-time matriculated undergraduates who enrolled in 2010, 649 applied for aid, 543 were judged to have need, 51 had their need fully met. 64 Federal Work-Study jobs (averaging $1602). 335 state and other part-time jobs (averaging $1611). ***Average percent of need met:*** 63. ***Average financial aid package:*** $11,642. ***Average need-based loan:*** $3414. ***Average need-based gift aid:*** $6471. ***Average indebtedness upon graduation:*** $18,494.

APPLYING
Standardized Tests *Required:* SAT or ACT (for admission). *Required for some:* ACT (for admission).

Options: electronic application, deferred entrance.

Application fee: $35.

Required: essay or personal statement, high school transcript, 3 letters of recommendation. ***Required for some:*** interview.

CONTACT
Mr. Tim Wingfield, Director of Admissions, Johnson University, 7900 Johnson Drive, Knoxville, TN 37998-1001. *Phone:* 865-251-2346. *Toll-free phone:* 800-827-2122. *Fax:* 865-251-2336. *E-mail:* twingfield@jbc.edu.

King University

Bristol, Tennessee

http://www.king.edu/

- **Independent** comprehensive, founded 1867, affiliated with Presbyterian Church (U.S.A.)
- **Suburban** 135-acre campus
- **Endowment** $36.2 million
- **Coed** 2,431 undergraduate students, 94% full-time, 67% women, 33% men
- **Moderately difficult** entrance level, 57% of applicants were admitted

UNDERGRAD STUDENTS
2,273 full-time, 158 part-time. Students come from 41 states and territories; 21 other countries; 36% are from out of state; 6% Black or African American, non-Hispanic/Latino; 2% Hispanic/Latino; 0.4% Asian, non-Hispanic/Latino; 0.1% Native Hawaiian or other Pacific Islander, non-Hispanic/Latino; 0.2% American Indian or Alaska Native, non-Hispanic/Latino; 2% Two or more races, non-Hispanic/Latino; 7% Race/ethnicity unknown; 3% international; 23% transferred in; 42% live on campus.

Freshmen
Admission: 927 applied, 526 admitted, 185 enrolled. ***Average high school GPA:*** 3.52. ***Test scores:*** SAT critical reading scores over 500: 55%; SAT math scores over 500: 55%; ACT scores over 18: 88%; SAT critical reading scores over 600: 11%; SAT math scores over 600: 15%; ACT scores over 24: 43%; ACT scores over 30: 7%.
Retention: 71% of full-time freshmen returned.

FACULTY
Total: 505, 26% full-time, 15% with terminal degrees.

Student/faculty ratio: 11:1.

ACADEMICS
Calendar: semesters. *Degrees:* associate, bachelor's, master's, doctoral, and post-master's certificates.

Special study options: academic remediation for entering students, accelerated degree program, adult/continuing education programs, advanced placement credit, cooperative education, distance learning, double majors, honors programs, independent study, internships, off-campus study, part-time degree program, services for LD students, student-designed majors, study abroad, summer session for credit.

Unusual degree programs: 3-2 Pharmacy-Campbell University.

Computers: 90 computers/terminals and 500 ports are available on campus for general student use. Students can access the following: campus intranet, computer help desk, free student e-mail accounts, online (class) grades, online (class) registration, online (class) schedules, student portal. Campuswide network is available. 100% of college-owned or -operated housing units are wired for high-speed Internet access. Wireless service is available via classrooms, computer centers, computer labs, dorm rooms, learning centers, libraries, student centers.

STUDENT LIFE

Housing options: on-campus residence required through junior year; men-only, women-only. Campus housing is university owned. Freshman campus housing is guaranteed.

Activities and organizations: drama/theater group, student-run newspaper, choral group, Student Government Association, Fellowship of Christian Athletes, King Security and Intelligence Studies Student Group, Enactus (formerly Students in Free Enterprise), Alpha Phi Omega (service organization).

Athletics Member NCAA. All Division II. ***Intercollegiate sports:*** baseball M(s), basketball M(s)/W(s), cheerleading M(s)/W(s), cross-country running M(s)/W(s), golf M(s)/W(s), soccer M(s)/W(s), softball W(s), swimming and diving M(s)/W(s), tennis M(s)/W(s), track and field M(s)/W(s), volleyball M(s)/W(s), wrestling M(s)/W(s). ***Intramural sports:*** badminton M/W, basketball M/W, gymnastics M(c)/W(c), soccer M/W, softball M/W, table tennis M/W, tennis M/W, ultimate Frisbee M/W, volleyball M/W, weight lifting M.

Campus security: 24-hour emergency response devices and patrols, late-night transport/escort service, controlled dormitory access, Emergency Notification System.

Student services: personal/psychological counseling.

COSTS & FINANCIAL AID

Costs (2014–15) ***One-time required fee:*** $125. ***Comprehensive fee:*** $33,888 includes full-time tuition ($24,316), mandatory fees ($1392), and room and board ($8180). Full-time tuition and fees vary according to course load, degree level, and program. Part-time tuition: $600 per credit hour. Part-time tuition and fees vary according to course load, degree level, and program. ***Required fees:*** $100 per credit hour part-time. ***College room only:*** $4108. Room and board charges vary according to board plan and housing facility. ***Payment plan:*** installment. ***Waivers:*** senior citizens and employees or children of employees.

Financial Aid Of all full-time matriculated undergraduates who enrolled in 2014, 1,915 applied for aid, 1,754 were judged to have need, 245 had their need fully met. 83 Federal Work-Study jobs (averaging $1610). 131 state and other part-time jobs (averaging $1401). In 2014, 130 non-need-based awards were made. ***Average percent of need met:*** 65. ***Average financial aid package:*** $14,128. ***Average need-based loan:*** $4789. ***Average need-based gift aid:*** $11,789. ***Average non-need-based aid:*** $9648. ***Average indebtedness upon graduation:*** $21,091.

APPLYING

Standardized Tests *Required:* SAT or ACT (for admission).

Options: electronic application, deferred entrance.

Required: high school transcript. ***Required for some:*** essay or personal statement. ***Recommended:*** minimum 3.0 GPA.

Application deadlines: rolling (freshmen), rolling (out-of-state freshmen), rolling (transfers).

Notification: continuous (freshmen), continuous (out-of-state freshmen), continuous (transfers).

CONTACT

Mrs. Nicole Martin, Director of Undergraduate Recruitment, King University, 1350 King College Road, Bristol, TN 37620. *Phone:* 423-652-4769. *Toll-free phone:* 800-362-0014. *Fax:* 423-652-4727. *E-mail:* admissions@king.edu.

Lane College

Jackson, Tennessee

http://www.lanecollege.edu/

- **Independent** 4-year, founded 1882, affiliated with Christian Methodist Episcopal Church
- **Suburban** 55-acre campus with easy access to Memphis
- **Endowment** $4.9 million
- **Coed** 1,262 undergraduate students, 99% full-time, 48% women, 52% men
- **Minimally difficult** entrance level, 43% of applicants were admitted

UNDERGRAD STUDENTS

1,249 full-time, 13 part-time. Students come from 28 states and territories; 45% are from out of state; 100% Black or African American, non-Hispanic/Latino; 7% transferred in; 61% live on campus.

Freshmen

Admission: 5,842 applied, 2,528 admitted, 312 enrolled. ***Average high school GPA:*** 2.3. ***Test scores:*** ACT scores over 18: 11%; ACT scores over 24: 1%.

Retention: 50% of full-time freshmen returned.

FACULTY

Total: 87, 93% full-time, 59% with terminal degrees.

Student/faculty ratio: 15:1.

ACADEMICS

Calendar: semesters. *Degree:* bachelor's.

Special study options: academic remediation for entering students, accelerated degree program, adult/continuing education programs, advanced placement credit, cooperative education, honors programs, independent study, internships, off-campus study, part-time degree program, services for LD students, study abroad, summer session for credit. ***ROTC:*** Army (b).

Computers: 258 computers/terminals and 258 ports are available on campus for general student use. Students can access the following: campus intranet, computer help desk, free student e-mail accounts, online (class) grades, online (class) schedules, online admissions and advising. Campuswide network is available. 100% of college-owned or -operated housing units are wired for high-speed Internet access. Wireless service is available via classrooms, computer centers, computer labs, dorm rooms, learning centers, libraries, student centers.

STUDENT LIFE

Housing options: on-campus residence required for freshman year; men-only, women-only. Campus housing is university owned. Freshman applicants given priority for college housing.

Activities and organizations: drama/theater group, choral group, marching band, Student Government Association, Pre-Law Club, Student Christian Association, Drama Club, Sociology Club, national fraternities, national sororities.

Athletics Member NCAA. All Division II. ***Intercollegiate sports:*** baseball M(s), basketball M(s)/W(s), cheerleading W, cross-country running M(s)/W(s), football M(s), softball W(s), tennis M(s)/W(s), track and field M(s)/W(s), volleyball W(s).

Campus security: 24-hour emergency response devices and patrols, late-night transport/escort service, surveillance cameras, lighted parking areas.

Student services: health clinic, personal/psychological counseling, legal services.

COSTS & FINANCIAL AID

Costs (2014–15) ***Comprehensive fee:*** $16,400 includes full-time tuition ($8980), mandatory fees ($800), and room and board ($6620). Full-time tuition and fees vary according to course load. Part-time tuition: $375 per credit hour. Part-time tuition and fees vary according to course load. ***Required fees:*** $400 per semester hour part-time, $400 per semester part-time. ***Payment plans:*** installment, deferred payment. ***Waivers:*** adult students and employees or children of employees.

Financial Aid Of all full-time matriculated undergraduates who enrolled in 2012, 1,470 applied for aid, 1,440 were judged to have need, 24 had their need fully met. In 2012, 11 non-need-based awards were made. ***Average percent of need met:*** 55. ***Average financial aid package:*** $4422. ***Average need-based loan:*** $2049. ***Average need-based gift aid:*** $3677.

Average non-need-based aid: $1773. ***Average indebtedness upon graduation:*** $12,348.

APPLYING

Standardized Tests *Required:* SAT or ACT (for admission).

Options: electronic application, deferred entrance.

Required: high school transcript, 2 letters of recommendation.

Application deadlines: rolling (freshmen), rolling (out-of-state freshmen), rolling (transfers).

Notification: continuous (freshmen), continuous (transfers).

CONTACT

Dr. Monica C. Scott, Director of Enrollment Management, Lane College, 545 Lane Avenue, Jackson, TN 38301. *Phone:* 731-426-7533. *Toll-free phone:* 800-960-7533. *Fax:* 731-426-7559. *E-mail:* mclayborne@lanecollege.edu.

Lee University

Cleveland, Tennessee

http://www.leeuniversity.edu/

- **Independent** comprehensive, founded 1918, affiliated with Church of God
- **Small-town** 107-acre campus with easy access to Chattanooga
- **Endowment** $17.1 million
- **Coed** 4,575 undergraduate students, 82% full-time, 58% women, 42% men

UNDERGRAD STUDENTS

3,770 full-time, 805 part-time. Students come from 53 states and territories; 50 other countries; 57% are from out of state; 5% Black or African American, non-Hispanic/Latino; 4% Hispanic/Latino; 1% Asian, non-Hispanic/Latino; 0.1% Native Hawaiian or other Pacific Islander, non-Hispanic/Latino; 0.4% American Indian or Alaska Native, non-Hispanic/Latino; 0.5% Two or more races, non-Hispanic/Latino; 8% Race/ethnicity unknown; 4% international; 5% transferred in; 47% live on campus.

Freshmen

Admission: 757 enrolled. ***Average high school GPA:*** 3.56. ***Test scores:*** SAT critical reading scores over 500: 61%; SAT math scores over 500: 54%; ACT scores over 18: 90%; SAT critical reading scores over 600: 23%; SAT math scores over 600: 13%; ACT scores over 24: 58%; SAT critical reading scores over 700: 2%; SAT math scores over 700: 2%; ACT scores over 30: 10%.

Retention: 79% of full-time freshmen returned.

FACULTY

Total: 409, 41% full-time, 51% with terminal degrees.

Student/faculty ratio: 17:1.

ACADEMICS

Calendar: semesters. *Degrees:* bachelor's, master's, and post-master's certificates.

Special study options: academic remediation for entering students, adult/continuing education programs, advanced placement credit, cooperative education, distance learning, double majors, English as a second language, external degree program, honors programs, independent study, internships, off-campus study, part-time degree program, services for LD students, student-designed majors, study abroad, summer session for credit.

Computers: 410 computers/terminals and 410 ports are available on campus for general student use. Students can access the following: campus intranet, computer help desk, free student e-mail accounts, online (class) grades, online (class) registration, online (class) schedules. Campuswide network is available. 95% of college-owned or -operated housing units are wired for high-speed Internet access. Wireless service is available via entire campus.

STUDENT LIFE

Housing options: on-campus residence required through sophomore year; men-only, women-only. Campus housing is university owned and leased by the school. Freshman campus housing is guaranteed.

Activities and organizations: drama/theater group, student-run newspaper, choral group, Student Leadership Council, Pioneers for Christ, International Student Fellowship, Big Pal Little Pal, Back Yard Ministries.

Athletics Member NCAA, NCCAA. All NCAA Division II. ***Intercollegiate sports:*** baseball M(s), basketball M(s)/W(s), cross-country running M(s)/W(s), golf M(s)/W(s), soccer M(s)/W(s), softball W(s), tennis M(s)/W(s), track and field M(s)/W(s), volleyball W(s). ***Intramural sports:*** basketball M/W, bowling M/W, football M/W, golf M/W, racquetball M/W, rugby M(c)/W(c), soccer M/W, softball M/W, table tennis M/W, tennis M/W, ultimate Frisbee M/W, volleyball M/W.

Campus security: 24-hour emergency response devices and patrols, late-night transport/escort service, controlled dormitory access.

Student services: health clinic, personal/psychological counseling.

COSTS & FINANCIAL AID

Costs (2015–16) ***Comprehensive fee:*** $22,045 includes full-time tuition ($14,400), mandatory fees ($600), and room and board ($7045). Full-time tuition and fees vary according to course load, location, and program. Part-time tuition: $600 per credit hour. Part-time tuition and fees vary according to course load, location, and program. ***Required fees:*** $60 per term part-time. ***College room only:*** $3595. Room and board charges vary according to board plan and housing facility. ***Payment plan:*** deferred payment. ***Waivers:*** senior citizens and employees or children of employees.

Financial Aid Of all full-time matriculated undergraduates who enrolled in 2014, 3,193 applied for aid, 2,729 were judged to have need, 336 had their need fully met. 251 Federal Work-Study jobs (averaging $1632). 577 state and other part-time jobs (averaging $1358). In 2014, 526 non-need-based awards were made. ***Average percent of need met:*** 47. ***Average financial aid package:*** $11,183. ***Average need-based loan:*** $4247. ***Average need-based gift aid:*** $8449. ***Average non-need-based aid:*** $6898. ***Average indebtedness upon graduation:*** $32,163.

APPLYING

Standardized Tests *Required:* SAT or ACT (for admission).

Required: high school transcript, minimum 2.0 GPA, MMR immunization record. ***Required for some:*** 3 letters of recommendation.

CONTACT

Mr. Phillip Cook, Vice President for Enrollment, Lee University, 1120 N. Ocoee Street, Cleveland, TN 37311. *Phone:* 423-614-8500. *Toll-free phone:* 800-533-9930. *Fax:* 423-614-8533. *E-mail:* admissions@leeuniversity.edu.

LeMoyne-Owen College

Memphis, Tennessee

http://www.loc.edu/

- **Independent** 4-year, founded 1862, affiliated with United Church of Christ
- **Urban** 15-acre campus
- **Endowment** $15.1 million
- **Coed** 1,023 undergraduate students, 87% full-time, 64% women, 36% men
- **Minimally difficult** entrance level, 49% of applicants were admitted

UNDERGRAD STUDENTS

891 full-time, 132 part-time. Students come from 12 states and territories; 4 other countries; 12% are from out of state; 13% transferred in; 25% live on campus.

Freshmen

Admission: 1,247 applied, 607 admitted, 161 enrolled. ***Average high school GPA:*** 2.5. ***Test scores:*** ACT scores over 18: 15%; ACT scores over 24: 3%.

Retention: 43% of full-time freshmen returned.

FACULTY

Total: 88, 63% full-time, 42% with terminal degrees.

Student/faculty ratio: 14:1.

ACADEMICS

Calendar: semesters. *Degrees:* bachelor's and postbachelor's certificates.

Special study options: academic remediation for entering students, accelerated degree program, advanced placement credit, cooperative education, double majors, honors programs, independent study, internships, off-campus study, part-time degree program, services for LD students, study abroad, summer session for credit. ***ROTC:*** Army (c), Air Force (c).

Computers: 239 computers/terminals are available on campus for general student use. Students can access the following: computer help desk, free student e-mail accounts, online (class) grades, online (class) registration, online (class) schedules. Campuswide network is available. 90% of college-owned or -operated housing units are wired for high-speed Internet access. Wireless service is available via computer centers, dorm rooms, learning centers, student centers.

STUDENT LIFE

Housing options: men-only, women-only. Campus housing is university owned.

Activities and organizations: drama/theater group, student-run newspaper, choral group, Greek Fraternities and Sororities, Black Business Students Association, National Black Student Accountant Club, Gospel Choir, Pre-Alumni organization, national fraternities, national sororities.

Athletics Member NCAA, NAIA. All NCAA Division I except baseball (Division II), men's and women's basketball (Division II), men's and women's cross-country running (Division II), men's and women's golf (Division II), softball (Division II), men's and women's tennis (Division II). ***Intercollegiate sports:*** baseball M(s), basketball M(s)/W(s), cross-country running M(s)/W(s), golf M(s)/W(s), softball W(s), tennis M(s)/W(s), volleyball W(s).

Campus security: 24-hour patrols, late-night transport/escort service, controlled dormitory access.

Student services: health clinic, personal/psychological counseling.

COSTS & FINANCIAL AID

Costs (2014–15) ***Comprehensive fee:*** $16,810 includes full-time tuition ($10,680), mandatory fees ($220), and room and board ($5910). Part-time tuition: $436 per credit hour. ***College room only:*** $3600. Room and board charges vary according to housing facility. ***Payment plan:*** installment. ***Waivers:*** employees or children of employees.

Financial Aid Of all full-time matriculated undergraduates who enrolled in 2013, 773 applied for aid, 762 were judged to have need, 17 had their need fully met. 145 Federal Work-Study jobs (averaging $1670). In 2013, 9 non-need-based awards were made. ***Average percent of need met:*** 47. ***Average financial aid package:*** $10,423. ***Average need-based loan:*** $3603. ***Average need-based gift aid:*** $7384. ***Average non-need-based aid:*** $11,002. ***Average indebtedness upon graduation:*** $27,441.

APPLYING

Standardized Tests *Required:* SAT or ACT (for admission).

Options: electronic application, early decision, early action.

Application fee: $25.

Required: essay or personal statement, high school transcript, minimum 2.0 GPA, 2 letters of recommendation, interview.

Application deadlines: 4/1 (freshmen), rolling (transfers).

CONTACT

LeMoyne-Owen College, 807 Walker Avenue, Memphis, TN 38126-6595. *Phone:* 901-435-1500. *Toll-free phone:* 800-737-7778.

Lincoln Memorial University

Harrogate, Tennessee

http://www.lmunet.edu/

- **Independent** comprehensive, founded 1897
- **Small-town** 1000-acre campus
- **Endowment** $34.2 million
- **Coed** 1,699 undergraduate students, 76% full-time, 70% women, 30% men
- **Moderately difficult** entrance level, 74% of applicants were admitted

UNDERGRAD STUDENTS

1,298 full-time, 401 part-time. Students come from 46 states and territories; 25 other countries; 36% are from out of state; 4% Black or African American, non-Hispanic/Latino; 2% Hispanic/Latino; 0.8% Asian, non-Hispanic/Latino; 0.1% American Indian or Alaska Native, non-Hispanic/Latino; 2% Two or more races, non-Hispanic/Latino; 2% Race/ethnicity unknown; 3% international; 15% transferred in; 36% live on campus.

Freshmen

Admission: 2,306 applied, 1,715 admitted, 260 enrolled. ***Average high school GPA:*** 3.41. ***Test scores:*** SAT critical reading scores over 500: 60%; SAT math scores over 500: 49%; ACT scores over 18: 92%; SAT critical reading scores over 600: 20%; SAT math scores over 600: 23%; ACT scores over 24: 34%; ACT scores over 30: 5%.

Retention: 69% of full-time freshmen returned.

FACULTY

Total: 290, 71% full-time, 72% with terminal degrees.

Student/faculty ratio: 13:1.

ACADEMICS

Calendar: semesters. *Degrees:* associate, bachelor's, master's, doctoral, and post-master's certificates.

Special study options: academic remediation for entering students, accelerated degree program, adult/continuing education programs, advanced placement credit, distance learning, double majors, English as a second language, honors programs, independent study, internships, part-time degree program, summer session for credit.

Computers: Students can access the following: campus intranet, computer help desk, free student e-mail accounts, online (class) grades, online (class) registration, online (class) schedules. Campuswide network is available. 100% of college-owned or -operated housing units are wired for high-speed Internet access.

STUDENT LIFE

Housing options: coed, men-only, women-only, special housing for students with disabilities. Campus housing is university owned.

Activities and organizations: drama/theater group, student-run radio and television station, choral group, Enactus, Baptist Campus Ministries, Pre-Med Club, Fishing Club, Earth Club.

Athletics Member NCAA. All Division II. ***Intercollegiate sports:*** baseball M(s), basketball M(s)/W(s), cross-country running M(s)/W(s), golf M(s)/W(s), lacrosse M(s)/W(s), soccer M(s)/W(s), softball W(s), tennis M(s)/W(s), volleyball W(s). ***Intramural sports:*** basketball M/W, football M/W, soccer M/W, softball M/W, swimming and diving M/W, table tennis M/W, tennis M/W, ultimate Frisbee M/W, volleyball M/W.

Campus security: 24-hour emergency response devices and patrols.

Student services: health clinic, personal/psychological counseling.

COSTS & FINANCIAL AID

Costs (2015–16) ***Comprehensive fee:*** $27,846 includes full-time tuition ($20,016), mandatory fees ($530), and room and board ($7300). Part-time tuition: $834 per credit hour. Part-time tuition and fees vary according to course load. ***Room and board:*** Room and board charges vary according to board plan and housing facility. ***Payment plan:*** installment. ***Waivers:*** children of alumni, senior citizens, and employees or children of employees.

Financial Aid Of all full-time matriculated undergraduates who enrolled in 2013, 1,182 applied for aid, 1,083 were judged to have need, 200 had their need fully met. In 2013, 145 non-need-based awards were made. ***Average percent of need met:*** 77. ***Average financial aid package:*** $17,135. ***Average need-based loan:*** $4105. ***Average need-based gift aid:*** $8992. ***Average non-need-based aid:*** $9718. ***Average indebtedness upon graduation:*** $19,987.

APPLYING

Standardized Tests *Required:* SAT or ACT (for admission).

Options: electronic application.

Application fee: $25.

Required: high school transcript, minimum 3.0 GPA, immunization records, financial aid application.

Application deadlines: rolling (freshmen), rolling (transfers).

Notification: continuous (freshmen), continuous (transfers).

CONTACT

Lincoln Memorial University, 6965 Cumberland Gap Parkway, Harrogate, TN 37752-1901. *Phone:* 423-869-6280. *Toll-free phone:* 800-325-0900.

★ Lipscomb University
Nashville, Tennessee
http://www.lipscomb.edu/

- **Independent** comprehensive, founded 1891, affiliated with Church of Christ
- **Suburban** 75-acre campus
- **Endowment** $69.8 million
- **Coed** 2,883 undergraduate students, 90% full-time, 61% women, 39% men
- **Moderately difficult** entrance level, 56% of applicants were admitted

UNDERGRAD STUDENTS
2,583 full-time, 300 part-time. Students come from 40 states and territories; 38 other countries; 34% are from out of state; 7% Black or African American, non-Hispanic/Latino; 6% Hispanic/Latino; 3% Asian, non-Hispanic/Latino; 2% Two or more races, non-Hispanic/Latino; 5% Race/ethnicity unknown; 2% international; 5% transferred in; 50% live on campus.

Freshmen
Admission: 3,699 applied, 2,056 admitted, 630 enrolled. ***Average high school GPA:*** 3.55. ***Test scores:*** SAT critical reading scores over 500: 78%; SAT math scores over 500: 81%; ACT scores over 18: 99%; SAT critical reading scores over 600: 41%; SAT math scores over 600: 39%; ACT scores over 24: 68%; SAT critical reading scores over 700: 9%; SAT math scores over 700: 9%; ACT scores over 30: 21%.

Retention: 80% of full-time freshmen returned.

FACULTY
Total: 558, 35% full-time, 54% with terminal degrees.

Student/faculty ratio: 12:1.

ACADEMICS
Calendar: semesters. *Degrees:* associate, bachelor's, master's, doctoral, and postbachelor's certificates.

Special study options: academic remediation for entering students, accelerated degree program, adult/continuing education programs, advanced placement credit, distance learning, double majors, English as a second language, honors programs, independent study, internships, services for LD students, student-designed majors, study abroad, summer session for credit. ***ROTC:*** Army (c), Air Force (c).

Computers: 150 computers/terminals are available on campus for general student use. Students can access the following: campus intranet, computer help desk, free student e-mail accounts, online (class) grades, online (class) registration, online (class) schedules. Campuswide network is available. 100% of college-owned or -operated housing units are wired for high-speed Internet access. Wireless service is available via entire campus.

STUDENT LIFE
Housing options: on-campus residence required through junior year; men-only, women-only. Campus housing is university owned. Freshman applicants given priority for college housing.

Activities and organizations: drama/theater group, student-run newspaper, radio and television station, choral group, Sigma Pi Beta, business fraternities, Multicultural Association, Alpha Phi Chi men's service club, Pi Kappa Sigma women's service club.

Athletics Member NCAA. All Division I. ***Intercollegiate sports:*** baseball M(s), basketball M(s)/W(s), cross-country running M(s)/W(s), golf M(s)/W(s), soccer M(s)/W(s), softball W(s), tennis M(s)/W(s), track and field M(s)/W(s), volleyball W(s). ***Intramural sports:*** badminton M/W, basketball M/W, football M/W, racquetball M/W, soccer M/W, softball M/W, table tennis M/W, ultimate Frisbee M/W, volleyball M/W.

Campus security: 24-hour emergency response devices and patrols, late-night transport/escort service, controlled dormitory access.

Student services: health clinic, personal/psychological counseling.

COSTS & FINANCIAL AID
Costs (2014–15) ***Comprehensive fee:*** $37,740 includes full-time tuition ($25,290), mandatory fees ($2100), and room and board ($10,350). Full-time tuition and fees vary according to course load. Part-time tuition: $1055 per credit hour. Part-time tuition and fees vary according to course load. ***College room only:*** $5730. Room and board charges vary according to board plan and housing facility. ***Payment plan:*** installment. ***Waivers:*** adult students and employees or children of employees.

Financial Aid Of all full-time matriculated undergraduates who enrolled in 2014, 2,499 applied for aid, 1,681 were judged to have need, 464 had their need fully met. 133 Federal Work-Study jobs. In 2014, 738 non-need-based awards were made. ***Average percent of need met:*** 56. ***Average financial aid package:*** $21,630. ***Average need-based loan:*** $5097. ***Average need-based gift aid:*** $3799. ***Average non-need-based aid:*** $13,435. ***Average indebtedness upon graduation:*** $30,480.

APPLYING
Standardized Tests *Required:* SAT or ACT (for admission).

Options: electronic application, early admission, deferred entrance.

Application fee: $50.

Required: high school transcript, minimum 2.3 GPA, 1 letter of recommendation, interview. ***Recommended:*** essay or personal statement.

Application deadlines: rolling (freshmen), rolling (transfers).

Notification: continuous (freshmen), continuous (transfers).

CONTACT
Office of Admissions, Lipscomb University, One University Park Drive, Nashville, TN 37204-3951. *Phone:* 615-966-1776. *Toll-free phone:* 877-582-4766. *Fax:* 615-966-1804. *E-mail:* admissions@lipscomb.edu.

Maryville College
Maryville, Tennessee
http://www.maryvillecollege.edu/

- **Independent Presbyterian** 4-year, founded 1819
- **Suburban** 350-acre campus
- **Endowment** $68.2 million
- **Coed** 1,213 undergraduate students, 96% full-time, 54% women, 46% men
- **Moderately difficult** entrance level, 71% of applicants were admitted

UNDERGRAD STUDENTS
1,166 full-time, 47 part-time. Students come from 36 states and territories; 24 other countries; 28% are from out of state; 11% Black or African American, non-Hispanic/Latino; 3% Hispanic/Latino; 1% Asian, non-Hispanic/Latino; 0.2% Native Hawaiian or other Pacific Islander, non-Hispanic/Latino; 0.7% American Indian or Alaska Native, non-Hispanic/Latino; 3% Two or more races, non-Hispanic/Latino; 0.5% Race/ethnicity unknown; 2% international; 4% transferred in; 68% live on campus.

Freshmen
Admission: 2,036 applied, 1,442 admitted, 334 enrolled. ***Average high school GPA:*** 3.41. ***Test scores:*** SAT critical reading scores over 500: 48%; SAT math scores over 500: 47%; ACT scores over 18: 94%; SAT critical reading scores over 600: 14%; SAT math scores over 600: 12%; ACT scores over 24: 49%; SAT critical reading scores over 700: 1%; SAT math scores over 700: 3%; ACT scores over 30: 9%.

Retention: 71% of full-time freshmen returned.

FACULTY
Total: 108, 60% full-time, 76% with terminal degrees.

Student/faculty ratio: 15:1.

ACADEMICS
Calendar: 4-1-4. *Degree:* bachelor's.

Special study options: academic remediation for entering students, advanced placement credit, double majors, English as a second language, honors programs, independent study, internships, off-campus study, part-time degree program, services for LD students, student-designed majors, study abroad, summer session for credit.

Unusual degree programs: 3-2 engineering with Vanderbilt University, Washington University in St. Louis, Auburn University, Tennessee Technological University; nursing with Vanderbilt University.

Computers: 290 computers/terminals are available on campus for general student use. Students can access the following: campus intranet, computer help desk, free student e-mail accounts, online (class) grades, online (class) registration, online (class) schedules. Campuswide network is available. 100% of college-owned or -operated housing units are wired for

high-speed Internet access. Wireless service is available via entire campus.

STUDENT LIFE
Housing options: on-campus residence required through senior year; coed, men-only, women-only, special housing for students with disabilities. Campus housing is university owned. Freshman campus housing is guaranteed.

Activities and organizations: drama/theater group, student-run newspaper, choral group, Voices of Praise, student government, Student Programming Board, Global Citizenship, Peer Mentors.

Athletics Member NCAA. All Division III. ***Intercollegiate sports:*** baseball M, basketball M/W, cheerleading M/W, cross-country running M/W, equestrian sports M(s)(c)/W(s)(c), football M, golf M/W, soccer M/W, softball W, swimming and diving M/W, tennis M/W, ultimate Frisbee M(c)/W(c), volleyball W. ***Intramural sports:*** archery M/W, badminton M/W, basketball M/W, bowling M/W, football M/W, racquetball M/W, rugby M/W, skiing (downhill) M/W, soccer M/W, softball M/W, table tennis M/W, tennis M/W, track and field M/W, ultimate Frisbee M/W, volleyball M/W, water polo M/W.

Campus security: 24-hour emergency response devices and patrols, late-night transport/escort service, controlled dormitory access, campus-wide emergency alert system via cell phones, home phones, and email.

Student services: health clinic, personal/psychological counseling.

COSTS & FINANCIAL AID
Costs (2015–16) ***Comprehensive fee:*** $43,308 includes full-time tuition ($32,104), mandatory fees ($762), and room and board ($10,442). Full-time tuition and fees vary according to course load. Part-time tuition: $825 per credit hour. Part-time tuition and fees vary according to course load. ***College room only:*** $5182. Room and board charges vary according to board plan and housing facility. ***Payment plan:*** installment. ***Waivers:*** employees or children of employees.

Financial Aid Of all full-time matriculated undergraduates who enrolled in 2013, 1,132 applied for aid, 957 were judged to have need, 186 had their need fully met. 614 Federal Work-Study jobs (averaging $1698). 29 state and other part-time jobs (averaging $1324). In 2013, 180 non-need-based awards were made. ***Average percent of need met:*** 85. ***Average financial aid package:*** $30,274. ***Average need-based loan:*** $4823. ***Average need-based gift aid:*** $24,493. ***Average non-need-based aid:*** $15,436.

APPLYING
Standardized Tests *Required:* SAT or ACT (for admission).

Options: electronic application, early admission, deferred entrance.

Required: high school transcript, minimum 2.5 GPA, 1 letter of recommendation. ***Required for some:*** essay or personal statement, interview. ***Recommended:*** minimum 3.0 GPA.

Application deadlines: 3/1 (freshmen), rolling (transfers).

Notification: continuous until 4/1 (freshmen).

CONTACT
Ms. Linda L. Moore, Administrative Assistant of Admissions, Maryville College, 502 East Lamar Alexander Parkway, Maryville, TN 37804-5907. *Phone:* 865-981-8096. *Toll-free phone:* 800-597-2687. *Fax:* 865-981-8005. *E-mail:* admissions@maryvillecollege.edu.

★ Memphis College of Art
Memphis, Tennessee
http://www.mca.edu/

- **Independent** comprehensive, founded 1936
- **Urban** 200-acre campus
- **Coed**
- **Moderately difficult** entrance level

FACULTY
Student/faculty ratio: 10:1.

ACADEMICS
Calendar: semesters. *Degrees:* bachelor's and master's.

STUDENT LIFE
Housing options: on-campus residence required for freshman year; coed. Campus housing is university owned. Freshman campus housing is guaranteed.

Activities and organizations: student-run newspaper, Student Alliance, Photo Club, Design Club-AIGA, Clay Club, Swiftness (Running Club).

Campus security: 24-hour emergency response devices and patrols, late-night transport/escort service, controlled dormitory access.

Student services: personal/psychological counseling.

COSTS & FINANCIAL AID
Costs (2014–15) ***Comprehensive fee:*** $37,320 includes full-time tuition ($28,170), mandatory fees ($650), and room and board ($8500). Full-time tuition and fees vary according to degree level and program. Part-time tuition and fees vary according to course load and program. ***College room only:*** $6500. Room and board charges vary according to housing facility.

Financial Aid Of all full-time matriculated undergraduates who enrolled in 2013, 309 applied for aid, 287 were judged to have need, 30 had their need fully met. 117 Federal Work-Study jobs (averaging $500). 32 state and other part-time jobs (averaging $500). In 2013, 37 non-need-based awards were made. ***Average percent of need met:*** 63. ***Average financial aid package:*** $21,314. ***Average need-based loan:*** $4133. ***Average need-based gift aid:*** $17,588. ***Average non-need-based aid:*** $12,536. ***Average indebtedness upon graduation:*** $34,207.

APPLYING
Standardized Tests *Required:* SAT or ACT (for admission).

Options: electronic application, deferred entrance.

Application fee: $25.

Required: high school transcript, minimum 2.0 GPA, portfolio. ***Recommended:*** essay or personal statement, interview.

CONTACT
Memphis College of Art, Overton Park, 1930 Poplar Avenue, Memphis, TN 38104-2764. *Phone:* 901-272-5153. *Toll-free phone:* 800-727-1088.

Middle Tennessee State University
Murfreesboro, Tennessee
http://www.mtsu.edu/

- **State-supported** university, founded 1911, part of Tennessee Board of Regents
- **Urban** 500-acre campus with easy access to Nashville
- **Coed** 20,262 undergraduate students, 82% full-time, 53% women, 47% men
- **Moderately difficult** entrance level, 72% of applicants were admitted

UNDERGRAD STUDENTS
16,627 full-time, 3,635 part-time. 4% are from out of state; 19% Black or African American, non-Hispanic/Latino; 4% Hispanic/Latino; 3% Asian, non-Hispanic/Latino; 0.1% Native Hawaiian or other Pacific Islander, non-Hispanic/Latino; 0.3% American Indian or Alaska Native, non-Hispanic/Latino; 3% Two or more races, non-Hispanic/Latino; 1% Race/ethnicity unknown; 2% international; 9% transferred in; 27% live on campus.

Freshmen
Admission: 9,353 applied, 6,740 admitted, 2,932 enrolled. ***Average high school GPA:*** 3.39. ***Test scores:*** SAT critical reading scores over 500: 65%; SAT math scores over 500: 64%; ACT scores over 18: 91%; SAT critical reading scores over 600: 26%; SAT math scores over 600: 24%; ACT scores over 24: 34%; SAT critical reading scores over 700: 3%; SAT math scores over 700: 4%; ACT scores over 30: 4%.

Retention: 71% of full-time freshmen returned.

FACULTY
Total: 1,256, 73% full-time, 67% with terminal degrees.

Student/faculty ratio: 19:1.

ACADEMICS
Calendar: semesters. *Degrees:* bachelor's, master's, doctoral, post-master's, and postbachelor's certificates.

Special study options: adult/continuing education programs, part-time degree program. ***ROTC:*** Army (b), Air Force (c).

Unusual degree programs: 3-2 engineering with University of Tennessee, Knoxville; Georgia Institute of Technology; Tennessee Technological University; The University of Memphis; Tennessee State University; Vanderbilt University.

Computers: Students can access the following: online (class) registration. Campuswide network is available.

STUDENT LIFE

Housing options: coed, men-only, women-only, special housing for students with disabilities. Campus housing is university owned.

Activities and organizations: drama/theater group, student-run newspaper, radio and television station, choral group, marching band, national fraternities, national sororities.

Athletics Member NCAA. All Division I except football (Division I-A). ***Intercollegiate sports:*** baseball M(s), basketball M(s)/W(s), cheerleading M(s)/W(s), cross-country running M(s)/W(s), equestrian sports M/W, golf M(s), soccer W(s), softball W(s), tennis M(s)/W(s), track and field M(s)/W(s), volleyball W(s). ***Intramural sports:*** badminton M/W, basketball M/W, bowling M(c)/W(c), fencing M(c)/W(c), field hockey M(c)/W(c), football M, ice hockey M(c), lacrosse M(c)/W(c), racquetball M(c)/W(c), riflery M, rugby M(c)/W(c), soccer M(c)/W, softball M/W, swimming and diving M/W, tennis M/W, ultimate Frisbee M(c)/W(c), volleyball M(c)/W(c), wrestling M(c)/W(c).

Campus security: 24-hour emergency response devices and patrols, student patrols, late-night transport/escort service, controlled dormitory access.

Student services: health clinic, personal/psychological counseling, women's center, legal services.

COSTS & FINANCIAL AID

Costs (2014–15) ***Tuition:*** state resident $6240 full-time, $260 per credit hour part-time; nonresident $22,488 full-time, $937 per credit hour part-time. Full-time tuition and fees vary according to course load. Part-time tuition and fees vary according to course load. ***Required fees:*** $1636 full-time, $69 per credit hour part-time. ***Room and board:*** $8302. Room and board charges vary according to board plan and housing facility. ***Payment plan:*** installment. ***Waivers:*** employees or children of employees.

Financial Aid Of all full-time matriculated undergraduates who enrolled in 2014, 15,942 applied for aid, 12,900 were judged to have need, 1,201 had their need fully met. 280 Federal Work-Study jobs (averaging $2304). In 2014, 2165 non-need-based awards were made. ***Average percent of need met:*** 61. ***Average financial aid package:*** $9059. ***Average need-based loan:*** $4050. ***Average need-based gift aid:*** $5017. ***Average non-need-based aid:*** $7444. ***Average indebtedness upon graduation:*** $24,834.

APPLYING

Standardized Tests *Required:* SAT or ACT (for admission).

Application fee: $25.

Required: high school transcript, minimum 3.0 GPA. ***Required for some:*** essay or personal statement.

CONTACT

Director of Admissions, Middle Tennessee State University, 1301 East Main Street, Murfreesboro, TN 37132. *Phone:* 615-898-2111. *Toll-free phone:* 800-331-MTSU. *Fax:* 615-898-5478. *E-mail:* admissions@mtsu.edu.

Milligan College

Milligan College, Tennessee

http://www.milligan.edu/

- **Independent Christian** comprehensive, founded 1866
- **Suburban** 181-acre campus
- **Endowment** $23.4 million
- **Coed** 979 undergraduate students, 87% full-time, 65% women, 35% men
- **Moderately difficult** entrance level, 62% of applicants were admitted

UNDERGRAD STUDENTS

854 full-time, 125 part-time. Students come from 36 states and territories; 17 other countries; 30% are from out of state; 4% Black or African American, non-Hispanic/Latino; 5% Hispanic/Latino; 1% Asian, non-Hispanic/Latino; 0.2% Native Hawaiian or other Pacific Islander, non-Hispanic/Latino; 0.3% American Indian or Alaska Native, non-Hispanic/Latino; 2% Two or more races, non-Hispanic/Latino; 0.8%

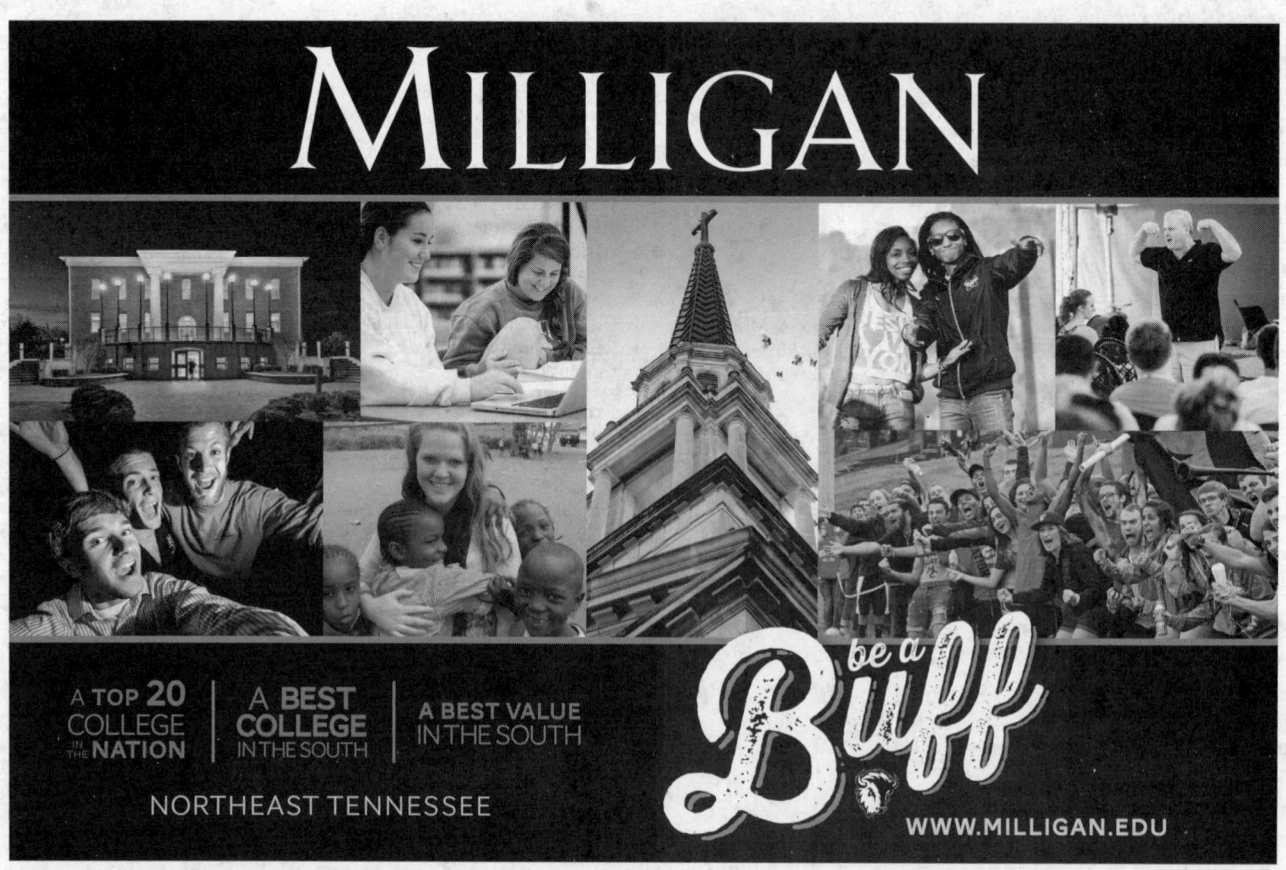

Race/ethnicity unknown; 3% international; 8% transferred in; 74% live on campus.

Freshmen

Admission: 580 applied, 362 admitted, 189 enrolled. ***Average high school GPA:*** 3.6. ***Test scores:*** SAT critical reading scores over 500: 74%; SAT math scores over 500: 70%; SAT writing scores over 500: 71%; ACT scores over 18: 97%; SAT critical reading scores over 600: 23%; SAT math scores over 600: 21%; SAT writing scores over 600: 16%; ACT scores over 24: 52%; SAT critical reading scores over 700: 3%; ACT scores over 30: 8%.

Retention: 80% of full-time freshmen returned.

FACULTY

Total: 134, 53% full-time, 56% with terminal degrees.

Student/faculty ratio: 12:1.

ACADEMICS

Calendar: semesters. *Degrees:* bachelor's and master's.

Special study options: academic remediation for entering students, adult/continuing education programs, advanced placement credit, cooperative education, distance learning, double majors, independent study, internships, off-campus study, part-time degree program, study abroad, summer session for credit.

Unusual degree programs: 3-2 pharmacy with Gatton College of Pharmacy at East Tennessee State University.

Computers: 97 computers/terminals are available on campus for general student use. Students can access the following: campus intranet, computer help desk, free student e-mail accounts, online (class) grades, online (class) registration, online (class) schedules. Campuswide network is available. 100% of college-owned or -operated housing units are wired for high-speed Internet access. Wireless service is available via classrooms, computer centers, computer labs, dorm rooms, libraries, student centers.

STUDENT LIFE

Housing options: on-campus residence required through senior year; men-only, women-only. Campus housing is university owned. Freshman campus housing is guaranteed.

Activities and organizations: drama/theater group, student-run newspaper, radio station, choral group, Social Affairs Committee, Buffalo Ramblers, Concert Council, Volunteer Milligan, Students for Life.

Athletics Member NAIA. ***Intercollegiate sports:*** baseball M(s), basketball M(s)/W(s), cross-country running M(s)/W(s), golf M(s)/W(s), soccer M(s)/W(s), softball W(s), swimming and diving M(s)/W(s), tennis M(s)/W(s), track and field M(s)/W(s), volleyball W(s). ***Intramural sports:*** basketball M/W, cheerleading W, football M/W, softball M/W, swimming and diving M/W, table tennis M/W, tennis M/W, ultimate Frisbee M/W, volleyball M/W, weight lifting M/W.

Campus security: 24-hour emergency response devices and patrols, late-night transport/escort service.

Student services: health clinic, personal/psychological counseling.

COSTS & FINANCIAL AID

Costs (2015–16) ***One-time required fee:*** $75. ***Comprehensive fee:*** $36,330 includes full-time tuition ($28,800), mandatory fees ($1030), and room and board ($6500). Full-time tuition and fees vary according to course load and degree level. Part-time tuition: $800 per credit hour. Part-time tuition and fees vary according to course load and degree level. ***Room and board:*** Room and board charges vary according to housing facility. ***Payment plan:*** installment. ***Waivers:*** employees or children of employees.

Financial Aid Of all full-time matriculated undergraduates who enrolled in 2014, 752 applied for aid, 644 were judged to have need, 178 had their need fully met. 105 Federal Work-Study jobs (averaging $1200). 211 state and other part-time jobs (averaging $1494). In 2014, 124 non-need-based awards were made. ***Average percent of need met:*** 77. ***Average financial aid package:*** $21,490. ***Average need-based loan:*** $4896. ***Average need-based gift aid:*** $18,088. ***Average non-need-based aid:*** $9036. ***Average indebtedness upon graduation:*** $25,626.

APPLYING

Standardized Tests *Required:* SAT or ACT (for admission).

Options: electronic application, deferred entrance.

Application fee: $30.

Required: essay or personal statement, high school transcript, minimum 2.0 GPA, 2 letters of recommendation. ***Required for some:*** interview. ***Recommended:*** minimum 3.0 GPA.

Application deadlines: 8/1 (freshmen), rolling (transfers).

Notification: continuous (freshmen), continuous (transfers).

CONTACT

Mr. Jason Makowsky, Director of Enrollment Management, Milligan College, PO Box 210, Milligan College, TN 37682. *Phone:* 423-461-8730. *Toll-free phone:* 800-262-8337. *Fax:* 423-461-8982. *E-mail:* admissions@milligan.edu.

See previous page for display ad and page 1524 for the College Close-Up.

Nossi College of Art

Nashville, Tennessee

http://www.nossi.edu/

- **Independent** 4-year
- **Urban** 10-acre campus with easy access to Nashville
- **Coed** 275 undergraduate students, 100% full-time, 56% women, 44% men

UNDERGRAD STUDENTS

275 full-time. 11% are from out of state; 20% Black or African American, non-Hispanic/Latino; 2% Hispanic/Latino; 1% Asian, non-Hispanic/Latino; 0.4% Native Hawaiian or other Pacific Islander, non-Hispanic/Latino; 1% Two or more races, non-Hispanic/Latino; 0.4% Race/ethnicity unknown; 17% transferred in.

Freshmen

Admission: 77 enrolled.

Retention: 82% of full-time freshmen returned.

FACULTY

Total: 30, 17% full-time.

Student/faculty ratio: 9:1.

ACADEMICS

Calendar: semesters. *Degrees:* associate and bachelor's.

Special study options: independent study, internships, off-campus study, part-time degree program.

Computers: 39 computers/terminals are available on campus for general student use. Students can access the following: campus intranet, free student e-mail accounts, online (class) grades, online (class) schedules. Wireless service is available via entire campus.

STUDENT LIFE

Housing options: college housing not available.

Activities and organizations: Kappa Pi, CMA.EDU, national fraternities, national sororities.

Campus security: campus has a gated entrance, all doors are kept locked.

COSTS

Costs (2014–15) ***One-time required fee:*** $200. ***Tuition:*** $0 full-time. Full-time tuition and fees vary according to degree level. Part-time tuition and fees vary according to degree level. No tuition increase for student's term of enrollment. ***Payment plan:*** installment.

APPLYING

Options: electronic application, early admission.

Application fee: $100.

Required: essay or personal statement, high school transcript, interview, portfolio of work for Associate or Bachelor of Graphic Art and Design program and the Bachelor of Illustration program.

Application deadlines: rolling (freshmen), rolling (out-of-state freshmen).

Notification: continuous (freshmen), continuous (out-of-state freshmen).

CONTACT

Ms. Mary Alexander, Admissions Director, Nossi College of Art, 590 Cheron Road, Madison, TN 37115. *Phone:* 615-514-2787 (ARTS). *Toll-free phone:* 888-986-ARTS. *Fax:* 615-514-2788. *E-mail:* admissions@nossi.edu.

Rhodes College

Memphis, Tennessee

http://www.rhodes.edu/

- **Independent** comprehensive, founded 1848
- **Urban** 100-acre campus with easy access to Memphis
- **Endowment** $335.1 million
- **Coed** 2,031 undergraduate students, 99% full-time, 58% women, 42% men
- **Very difficult** entrance level, 60% of applicants were admitted

UNDERGRAD STUDENTS
2,016 full-time, 15 part-time. Students come from 49 states and territories; 15 other countries; 74% are from out of state; 6% Black or African American, non-Hispanic/Latino; 4% Hispanic/Latino; 6% Asian, non-Hispanic/Latino; 0.3% American Indian or Alaska Native, non-Hispanic/Latino; 3% Two or more races, non-Hispanic/Latino; 2% Race/ethnicity unknown; 3% international; 0.8% transferred in; 71% live on campus.

Freshmen
Admission: 3,382 applied, 2,029 admitted, 507 enrolled. ***Average high school GPA:*** 3.73. ***Test scores:*** SAT critical reading scores over 500: 97%; SAT math scores over 500: 98%; ACT scores over 18: 100%; SAT critical reading scores over 600: 77%; SAT math scores over 600: 76%; ACT scores over 24: 97%; SAT critical reading scores over 700: 24%; SAT math scores over 700: 20%; ACT scores over 30: 46%.
Retention: 88% of full-time freshmen returned.

FACULTY
Total: 210, 83% full-time, 92% with terminal degrees.
Student/faculty ratio: 11:1.

ACADEMICS
Calendar: semesters. *Degrees:* bachelor's and master's (master's degree in accounting only).
Special study options: advanced placement credit, cooperative education, double majors, honors programs, independent study, internships, off-campus study, part-time degree program, services for LD students, student-designed majors, study abroad, summer session for credit. ***ROTC:*** Army (c), Air Force (c).
Unusual degree programs: 3-2 engineering with Washington University in St. Louis, Christian Brothers University (Memphis), University of Memphis/University of Tennessee.
Computers: 220 computers/terminals are available on campus for general student use. Students can access the following: campus intranet, computer help desk, free student e-mail accounts, online (class) grades, online (class) registration, online (class) schedules. Campuswide network is available. Wireless service is available via entire campus.

STUDENT LIFE
Housing options: on-campus residence required through sophomore year; coed, men-only, women-only. Campus housing is university owned. Freshman campus housing is guaranteed.
Activities and organizations: drama/theater group, student-run newspaper, radio and television station, choral group, Health Professions Society, Rhodes Outdoors Club, Kinney, RhodeKill (ultimate Frisbee), Reformed University Fellowship, national fraternities, national sororities.
Athletics Member NCAA. All Division III. ***Intercollegiate sports:*** badminton M(c)/W(c), baseball M, basketball M/W, cheerleading W(c), crew M(c)/W(c), cross-country running M/W, fencing M(c)/W(c), field hockey W, football M, golf M/W, lacrosse M(c)/W(c), rugby M(c), soccer M/W, softball W, swimming and diving M/W, tennis M/W, track and field M/W, ultimate Frisbee M(c)/W(c), volleyball W. ***Intramural sports:*** basketball M/W, racquetball M/W, soccer M/W, squash M, volleyball M/W.
Campus security: 24-hour emergency response devices and patrols, student patrols, late-night transport/escort service, 24-hour monitored security cameras in parking areas, fenced campus with monitored access at night.
Student services: health clinic, personal/psychological counseling, women's center.

COSTS & FINANCIAL AID
Costs (2015–16) ***Comprehensive fee:*** $53,970 includes full-time tuition ($42,914), mandatory fees ($310), and room and board ($10,746). Part-time tuition: $1800 per credit hour. ***College room only:*** $5373. Room and board charges vary according to board plan and housing facility. ***Payment plan:*** installment. ***Waivers:*** employees or children of employees.
Financial Aid Of all full-time matriculated undergraduates who enrolled in 2014, 1,351 applied for aid, 827 were judged to have need, 390 had their need fully met. In 2014, 1012 non-need-based awards were made. ***Average percent of need met:*** 90. ***Average financial aid package:*** $34,455. ***Average need-based loan:*** $5056. ***Average need-based gift aid:*** $26,183. ***Average non-need-based aid:*** $18,642. ***Average indebtedness upon graduation:*** $27,077. ***Financial aid deadline:*** 3/1.

APPLYING
Standardized Tests *Required:* SAT or ACT (for admission).
Options: electronic application, early admission, early decision, early action, deferred entrance.
Required: essay or personal statement, high school transcript, 2 letters of recommendation. ***Recommended:*** interview.
Application deadlines: 1/15 (freshmen), 1/15 (out-of-state freshmen), 1/15 (transfers), 11/15 (early action).
Early decision deadline: 11/1 (for plan 1), 1/1 (for plan 2).
Notification: 4/1 (freshmen), 4/1 (out-of-state freshmen), 4/1 (transfers), 12/1 (early decision plan 1), 2/1 (early decision plan 2), 1/15 (early action).

CONTACT
Mr. Carey Thompson, Vice President of Enrollment and Communications, Dean of Admissions, Rhodes College, 2000 N Parkway, Memphis, TN 38112. *Phone:* 901-843-3700. *Toll-free phone:* 800-844-5969. *Fax:* 901-843-3631. *E-mail:* adminfo@rhodes.edu.

Sewanee: The University of the South

Sewanee, Tennessee

http://www.sewanee.edu/

- **Independent Episcopal** comprehensive, founded 1857
- **Rural** 13,000-acre campus
- **Endowment** $374.3 million
- **Coed** 1,631 undergraduate students, 99% full-time, 52% women, 48% men
- **Very difficult** entrance level, 65% of applicants were admitted

UNDERGRAD STUDENTS
1,620 full-time, 11 part-time. Students come from 46 states and territories; 24 other countries; 74% are from out of state; 5% Black or African American, non-Hispanic/Latino; 5% Hispanic/Latino; 2% Asian, non-Hispanic/Latino; 0.1% Native Hawaiian or other Pacific Islander, non-Hispanic/Latino; 4% Two or more races, non-Hispanic/Latino; 3% international; 1% transferred in; 98% live on campus.

Freshmen
Admission: 2,977 applied, 1,926 admitted, 466 enrolled. ***Average high school GPA:*** 3.69. ***Test scores:*** SAT critical reading scores over 500: 95%; SAT math scores over 500: 95%; SAT writing scores over 500: 94%; ACT scores over 18: 100%; SAT critical reading scores over 600: 65%; SAT math scores over 600: 63%; SAT writing scores over 600: 65%; ACT scores over 24: 93%; SAT critical reading scores over 700: 24%; SAT math scores over 700: 15%; SAT writing scores over 700: 15%; ACT scores over 30: 33%.
Retention: 88% of full-time freshmen returned.

FACULTY
Total: 220, 67% full-time, 86% with terminal degrees.
Student/faculty ratio: 10:1.

ACADEMICS
Calendar: semesters. *Degrees:* bachelor's, master's, doctoral, post-master's, and postbachelor's certificates.
Special study options: advanced placement credit, double majors, independent study, internships, off-campus study, services for LD students, student-designed majors, study abroad, summer session for credit.

Unusual degree programs: 3-2 engineering with Washington University in St. Louis, Vanderbilt University, Rensselaer Polytechnic Institute, Columbia University; forestry with Duke University.

Computers: 267 computers/terminals are available on campus for general student use. Students can access the following: computer help desk, free student e-mail accounts, online (class) grades, online (class) registration, online (class) schedules. Campuswide network is available. 100% of college-owned or -operated housing units are wired for high-speed Internet access. Wireless service is available via entire campus.

STUDENT LIFE

Housing options: on-campus residence required through senior year; coed, men-only, women-only, special housing for students with disabilities. Campus housing is university owned. Freshman campus housing is guaranteed.

Activities and organizations: drama/theater group, student-run newspaper, radio station, choral group, Sewanee Outing Program, Sewanee Outreach, Organization for Cross Cultural Understanding, Alpha Phi Omega (APO) National Service Fraternity, African American Alliance, national fraternities, national sororities.

Athletics Member NCAA. All Division III. ***Intercollegiate sports:*** baseball M, basketball M/W, cheerleading W, crew M(c)/W(c), cross-country running M/W, equestrian sports M/W, fencing M(c)/W(c), field hockey W, football M, golf M/W, lacrosse M/W, rugby M(c)/W(c), soccer M/W, softball W, swimming and diving M/W, tennis M/W, track and field M/W, volleyball W. ***Intramural sports:*** badminton M/W, basketball M/W, cross-country running M/W, football M, golf M/W, racquetball M/W, soccer M/W, softball M/W, swimming and diving M/W, table tennis M/W, tennis M/W, track and field M/W, volleyball M/W.

Campus security: 24-hour emergency response devices and patrols, late-night transport/escort service, controlled dormitory access, security lighting.

Student services: health clinic, personal/psychological counseling, women's center.

COSTS & FINANCIAL AID

Costs (2015–16) ***Comprehensive fee:*** $49,750 includes full-time tuition ($38,428), mandatory fees ($272), and room and board ($11,050). Full-time tuition and fees vary according to student level. Part-time tuition: $1350 per credit hour. Part-time tuition and fees vary according to student level. No tuition increase for student's term of enrollment. ***College room only:*** $5730. Room and board charges vary according to student level. ***Payment plan:*** installment. ***Waivers:*** employees or children of employees.

Financial Aid Of all full-time matriculated undergraduates who enrolled in 2014, 1,013 applied for aid, 783 were judged to have need, 319 had their need fully met. In 2014, 411 non-need-based awards were made. ***Average percent of need met:*** 96. ***Average financial aid package:*** $31,602. ***Average need-based loan:*** $4062. ***Average need-based gift aid:*** $26,247. ***Average non-need-based aid:*** $10,883. ***Average indebtedness upon graduation:*** $21,277. ***Financial aid deadline:*** 2/1.

APPLYING

Standardized Tests *Required for some:* SAT or ACT (for admission), TEOFL for International Students. *Recommended:* SAT or ACT (for admission).

Options: electronic application, early admission, early decision, early action, deferred entrance.

Required: essay or personal statement, high school transcript, 2 letters of recommendation. ***Recommended:*** interview.

Application deadlines: 2/1 (freshmen), 4/1 (transfers).

Early decision deadline: 11/15 (for plan 1), 1/15 (for plan 2).

Notification: 3/17 (freshmen), continuous (transfers), 12/15 (early decision plan 1), 2/15 (early decision plan 2).

CONTACT

Ms. Lisa Burns, Associate Dean of Admission, Sewanee: The University of the South, 735 University Avenue, Sewanee, TN 37383-1000. *Phone:* 931-598-1238. *Toll-free phone:* 800-522-2234. *Fax:* 931-598-3248. *E-mail:* admiss@sewanee.edu.

Southern Adventist University

Collegedale, Tennessee

http://www.southern.edu/

- **Independent Seventh-day Adventist** comprehensive, founded 1892
- **Small-town** 1000-acre campus with easy access to Chattanooga
- **Endowment** $21.1 million
- **Coed** 2,728 undergraduate students, 83% full-time, 56% women, 44% men
- **Moderately difficult** entrance level, 57% of applicants were admitted

UNDERGRAD STUDENTS

2,252 full-time, 476 part-time. Students come from 49 states and territories; 118 other countries; 66% are from out of state; 11% Black or African American, non-Hispanic/Latino; 21% Hispanic/Latino; 8% Asian, non-Hispanic/Latino; 0.7% Native Hawaiian or other Pacific Islander, non-Hispanic/Latino; 0.4% American Indian or Alaska Native, non-Hispanic/Latino; 4% Two or more races, non-Hispanic/Latino; 5% international; 5% transferred in; 61% live on campus.

Freshmen

Admission: 2,332 applied, 1,340 admitted, 559 enrolled. ***Average high school GPA:*** 3.36. ***Test scores:*** SAT critical reading scores over 500: 70%; SAT math scores over 500: 62%; SAT writing scores over 500: 62%; ACT scores over 18: 93%; SAT critical reading scores over 600: 31%; SAT math scores over 600: 23%; SAT writing scores over 600: 26%; ACT scores over 24: 43%; SAT critical reading scores over 700: 7%; SAT math scores over 700: 5%; SAT writing scores over 700: 3%; ACT scores over 30: 10%.

Retention: 76% of full-time freshmen returned.

FACULTY

Total: 174, 99% full-time, 54% with terminal degrees.

Student/faculty ratio: 15:1.

ACADEMICS

Calendar: semesters. *Degrees:* certificates, associate, bachelor's, master's, doctoral, and post-master's certificates.

Special study options: advanced placement credit, distance learning, double majors, English as a second language, honors programs, independent study, internships, off-campus study, services for LD students, student-designed majors, study abroad, summer session for credit.

Computers: 350 computers/terminals and 2,000 ports are available on campus for general student use. Students can access the following: campus intranet, computer help desk, free student e-mail accounts, online (class) grades, online (class) registration, online (class) schedules. Campuswide network is available. 95% of college-owned or -operated housing units are wired for high-speed Internet access. Wireless service is available via entire campus.

STUDENT LIFE

Housing options: on-campus residence required through junior year; men-only, women-only. Campus housing is university owned. Freshman campus housing is guaranteed.

Activities and organizations: drama/theater group, student-run newspaper, radio and television station, choral group, Men's Club, Women's Club, Asian Club, Black Christian Union, Latin American Club.

Athletics ***Intramural sports:*** basketball M/W, football M/W, soccer M/W, softball M/W, volleyball M/W.

Campus security: 24-hour emergency response devices and patrols, student patrols, late-night transport/escort service, controlled dormitory access.

Student services: health clinic, personal/psychological counseling.

COSTS & FINANCIAL AID

Costs (2015–16) ***Comprehensive fee:*** $26,550 includes full-time tuition ($19,850), mandatory fees ($800), and room and board ($5900). Full-time tuition and fees vary according to course load. Part-time tuition: $840 per credit hour. Part-time tuition and fees vary according to course load. ***Required fees:*** $400 per term part-time. ***College room only:*** $3700. Room and board charges vary according to board plan. ***Payment plan:*** installment. ***Waivers:*** senior citizens.

Financial Aid Of all full-time matriculated undergraduates who enrolled in 2012, 1,668 applied for aid, 1,207 were judged to have need, 1,015 had their need fully met. In 2012, 453 non-need-based awards were made. ***Average percent of need met:*** 83. ***Average financial aid package:*** $17,378. ***Average need-based loan:*** $4739. ***Average need-based gift aid:*** $11,536. ***Average non-need-based aid:*** $7161. ***Average indebtedness upon graduation:*** $34,114.

APPLYING

Standardized Tests *Required:* SAT or ACT (for admission).

Options: electronic application, deferred entrance.

Application fee: $25.

Required: high school transcript, minimum 2.5 GPA. ***Required for some:*** essay or personal statement, minimum 2.3 GPA.

Application deadlines: rolling (freshmen), rolling (transfers).

Notification: continuous (freshmen), continuous (transfers).

CONTACT

Mr. Marc Grundy, Associate Vice President, Marketing and Enrollment Services, Southern Adventist University, PO Box 370, Collegedale, TN 37315-0370. *Phone:* 423-236-2844. *Toll-free phone:* 800-768-8437. *Fax:* 423-236-1844. *E-mail:* admissions@southern.edu.

Tennessee State University

Nashville, Tennessee

http://www.tnstate.edu/

- **State-supported** comprehensive, founded 1912, part of Tennessee Board of Regents
- **Urban** 450-acre campus with easy access to Nashville
- **Coed** 7,073 undergraduate students, 80% full-time, 59% women, 41% men
- **Minimally difficult** entrance level, 53% of applicants were admitted

UNDERGRAD STUDENTS

5,677 full-time, 1,396 part-time. Students come from 42 states and territories; 15 other countries; 21% are from out of state; 72% Black or African American, non-Hispanic/Latino; 1% Hispanic/Latino; 1% Asian, non-Hispanic/Latino; 0.2% American Indian or Alaska Native, non-Hispanic/Latino; 0.8% Race/ethnicity unknown; 9% international; 9% transferred in.

Freshmen

Admission: 3,934 applied, 2,085 admitted, 1,377 enrolled. ***Average high school GPA:*** 2.89. ***Test scores:*** ACT scores over 18: 50%; ACT scores over 24: 8%.

Retention: 60% of full-time freshmen returned.

FACULTY

Total: 575, 70% full-time.

Student/faculty ratio: 17:1.

ACADEMICS

Calendar: semesters. *Degrees:* associate, bachelor's, master's, doctoral, post-master's, and postbachelor's certificates.

Special study options: academic remediation for entering students, accelerated degree program, adult/continuing education programs, cooperative education, external degree program, freshman honors college, honors programs, independent study, internships, off-campus study, part-time degree program, services for LD students, summer session for credit. ***ROTC:*** Army (c), Navy (c), Air Force (b).

Computers: 1,025 computers/terminals are available on campus for general student use. Students can access the following: campus intranet, computer help desk, free student e-mail accounts, online (class) grades, online (class) registration, online (class) schedules. Campuswide network is available. Wireless service is available via entire campus.

STUDENT LIFE

Housing options: coed, men-only, women-only. Campus housing is university owned. Freshman applicants given priority for college housing.

Activities and organizations: drama/theater group, student-run newspaper, radio and television station, choral group, marching band, national fraternities, national sororities.

Athletics Member NCAA. All Division I except football (Division I-AA). ***Intercollegiate sports:*** basketball M(s)/W(s), cross-country running M(s)/W(s), golf M(s), softball W, tennis M(s)/W(s), track and field M(s)/W(s), volleyball W. ***Intramural sports:*** baseball M, basketball M/W, cheerleading M/W, football M, softball W, track and field M/W, volleyball M/W.

Campus security: 24-hour patrols, controlled dormitory access.

Student services: health clinic, personal/psychological counseling, women's center.

COSTS & FINANCIAL AID

Costs (2014–15) ***Tuition:*** state resident $6930 full-time, $310 per hour part-time; nonresident $19,650 full-time, $840 per hour part-time. ***Room and board:*** $6240; room only: $3560.

Financial Aid Of all full-time matriculated undergraduates who enrolled in 2014, 5,529 applied for aid, 5,209 were judged to have need, 355 had their need fully met. 781 Federal Work-Study jobs (averaging $1926). In 2014, 167 non-need-based awards were made. ***Average percent of need met:*** 57. ***Average financial aid package:*** $10,704. ***Average need-based loan:*** $4030. ***Average need-based gift aid:*** $5376. ***Average non-need-based aid:*** $13,455. ***Average indebtedness upon graduation:*** $35,645.

APPLYING

Standardized Tests *Required:* SAT or ACT (for admission).

Options: electronic application.

Application fee: $25.

Required: high school transcript, minimum 2.3 GPA. ***Required for some:*** 3 letters of recommendation.

Application deadlines: 8/1 (freshmen), 8/1 (transfers).

Notification: continuous until 8/15 (freshmen), continuous until 8/15 (transfers).

CONTACT

Dr. Sedric Griffin, Director of Admissions and Recruitment, Tennessee State University, 3500 John A. Merritt Blvd, Nashville, TN 37209. *Phone:* 615-963-5101. *E-mail:* sgriffin01@tnstate.edu.

Tennessee Technological University

Cookeville, Tennessee

http://www.tntech.edu/

- **State-supported** university, founded 1915, part of Tennessee Board of Regents
- **Small-town** campus
- **Endowment** $65.9 million
- **Coed**
- **Moderately difficult** entrance level

FACULTY

Student/faculty ratio: 22:1.

ACADEMICS

Calendar: semesters. *Degrees:* bachelor's, master's, doctoral, post-master's, and postbachelor's certificates.

STUDENT LIFE

Housing options: on-campus residence required through sophomore year; coed, men-only, women-only. Campus housing is university owned. Freshman campus housing is guaranteed.

Activities and organizations: drama/theater group, student-run newspaper, radio station, choral group, marching band, Baptist Collegiate Center, Fellowship of Christian Athletes, University Christian Student Center, Residence Hall Association, national fraternities, national sororities.

Athletics Member NCAA. All Division I except football (Division I-AA).

Campus security: 24-hour emergency response devices and patrols, late-night transport/escort service, student safety organization, lighted pathways.

Student services: health clinic, personal/psychological counseling, women's center.

COSTS & FINANCIAL AID

Costs (2014–15) ***Tuition:*** state resident $7317 full-time, $352 per credit hour part-time; nonresident $22,317 full-time, $976 per credit hour part-time. Full-time tuition and fees vary according to course load and program. Part-time tuition and fees vary according to course load and program. ***Required fees:*** $181 full-time. ***Room and board:*** $8296; room only: $4370. Room and board charges vary according to board plan and housing facility.

Financial Aid Of all full-time matriculated undergraduates who enrolled in 2013, 8,180 applied for aid, 6,609 were judged to have need, 522 had their need fully met. 1,315 Federal Work-Study jobs (averaging $1401). In 2013, 2182 non-need-based awards were made. ***Average percent of need met:*** 60. ***Average financial aid package:*** $9271. ***Average need-based loan:*** $3836. ***Average need-based gift aid:*** $5163. ***Average non-need-based aid:*** $12,252. ***Average indebtedness upon graduation:*** $18,467.

APPLYING

Standardized Tests *Required:* SAT or ACT (for admission). *Recommended:* ACT (for admission).

Options: electronic application, early admission, deferred entrance.

Application fee: $25.

Required: high school transcript, minimum 2.5 GPA. ***Recommended:*** interview.

CONTACT

Mr. Alexis Pope, Director of Admissions, Tennessee Technological University, PO Box 5006, Cookeville, TN 38505. *Phone:* 931-372-3888. *Toll-free phone:* 800-255-8881. *Fax:* 931-372-6250. *E-mail:* admissions@tntech.edu.

Tennessee Wesleyan College

Athens, Tennessee

http://www.twcnet.edu/

- **Independent United Methodist** comprehensive, founded 1857
- **Small-town** 40-acre campus with easy access to Knoxville, Chattanooga
- **Endowment** $9.7 million
- **Coed** 1,019 undergraduate students, 92% full-time, 63% women, 37% men
- **Minimally difficult** entrance level, 67% of applicants were admitted

UNDERGRAD STUDENTS

940 full-time, 79 part-time. Students come from 28 states and territories; 21 other countries; 10% are from out of state; 5% Black or African American, non-Hispanic/Latino; 1% Hispanic/Latino; 0.9% Asian, non-Hispanic/Latino; 0.4% Native Hawaiian or other Pacific Islander, non-Hispanic/Latino; 0.1% American Indian or Alaska Native, non-Hispanic/Latino; 2% Two or more races, non-Hispanic/Latino; 7% Race/ethnicity unknown; 5% international; 17% transferred in; 32% live on campus.

Freshmen

Admission: 1,023 applied, 682 admitted, 192 enrolled. ***Average high school GPA:*** 3.41. ***Test scores:*** SAT critical reading scores over 500: 40%; SAT math scores over 500: 37%; ACT scores over 18: 84%; SAT critical reading scores over 600: 3%; SAT math scores over 600: 7%; ACT scores over 24: 31%; SAT critical reading scores over 700: 3%; ACT scores over 30: 4%.

Retention: 63% of full-time freshmen returned.

FACULTY

Total: 141, 44% full-time, 43% with terminal degrees.

Student/faculty ratio: 12:1.

ACADEMICS

Calendar: semesters. *Degrees:* bachelor's and master's (profile includes information for both the main and branch campuses).

Special study options: academic remediation for entering students, accelerated degree program, adult/continuing education programs, advanced placement credit, distance learning, double majors, honors programs, independent study, internships, off-campus study, part-time degree program, services for LD students, student-designed majors, study abroad, summer session for credit.

Computers: 170 computers/terminals and 350 ports are available on campus for general student use. Students can access the following: campus intranet, computer help desk, free student e-mail accounts, online (class) grades, online (class) registration, online (class) schedules. Campuswide network is available. 100% of college-owned or -operated housing units are wired for high-speed Internet access. Wireless service is available via entire campus.

STUDENT LIFE

Housing options: on-campus residence required through senior year; men-only, women-only. Campus housing is university owned. Freshman campus housing is guaranteed.

Activities and organizations: drama/theater group, student-run newspaper, choral group, Student Government Association, national sororities.

Athletics Member NAIA. ***Intercollegiate sports:*** baseball M(s), basketball M(s)/W(s), cheerleading M(s)/W(s), cross-country running M(s)/W(s), golf M(s)/W(s), lacrosse M(s)/W(s), soccer M(s)/W(s), softball W(s), tennis M(s)/W(s), track and field M(s)/W(s), volleyball W(s).

Campus security: 24-hour patrols, late-night transport/escort service, controlled dormitory access, night patrols by trained security personnel.

COSTS & FINANCIAL AID

Costs (2015–16) ***Comprehensive fee:*** $30,210 includes full-time tuition ($22,000), mandatory fees ($900), and room and board ($7310). Full-time tuition and fees vary according to class time and degree level. Part-time tuition: $570 per credit. Part-time tuition and fees vary according to class time, course load, degree level, location, and program. ***Room and board:*** Room and board charges vary according to board plan and housing facility. ***Payment plan:*** installment. ***Waivers:*** employees or children of employees.

Financial Aid Of all full-time matriculated undergraduates who enrolled in 2013, 903 applied for aid, 803 were judged to have need, 124 had their need fully met. In 2013, 68 non-need-based awards were made. ***Average percent of need met:*** 60. ***Average financial aid package:*** $16,283. ***Average need-based loan:*** $3899. ***Average need-based gift aid:*** $13,930. ***Average non-need-based aid:*** $9675. ***Average indebtedness upon graduation:*** $21,280.

APPLYING

Standardized Tests *Required:* SAT or ACT (for admission).

Options: electronic application, deferred entrance.

Application fee: $30.

Required: high school transcript, minimum 2.3 GPA, 1 letter of recommendation. ***Required for some:*** essay or personal statement, interview. ***Recommended:*** essay or personal statement.

Application deadlines: rolling (freshmen), rolling (out-of-state freshmen), rolling (transfers).

Notification: continuous (freshmen), continuous (out-of-state freshmen), continuous (transfers).

CONTACT

Jessica Edwards, Assistant Vice President of Enrollment and Communications, Tennessee Wesleyan College, 204 East College Street, Athens, TN 37303. *Phone:* 423-746-5285. *Toll-free phone:* 800-PICK-TWC. *Fax:* 423-745-9335. *E-mail:* admissions@twcnet.edu.

Trevecca Nazarene University

Nashville, Tennessee

http://www.trevecca.edu/

- **Independent Nazarene** comprehensive, founded 1901
- **Urban** 65-acre campus
- **Endowment** $26.3 million
- **Coed** 1,677 undergraduate students, 70% full-time, 56% women, 44% men
- **Moderately difficult** entrance level, 73% of applicants were admitted

UNDERGRAD STUDENTS

1,176 full-time, 501 part-time. Students come from 42 states and territories; 11 other countries; 38% are from out of state; 9% Black or African American, non-Hispanic/Latino; 4% Hispanic/Latino; 1% Asian, non-Hispanic/Latino; 0.1% Native Hawaiian or other Pacific Islander, non-Hispanic/Latino; 0.5% American Indian or Alaska Native, non-Hispanic/Latino; 3% Two or more races, non-Hispanic/Latino; 11% Race/ethnicity unknown; 1% international; 5% transferred in; 48% live on campus.

Freshmen

Admission: 1,029 applied, 752 admitted, 320 enrolled. ***Average high school GPA:*** 3.41. ***Test scores:*** SAT critical reading scores over 500:

68%; SAT math scores over 500: 63%; ACT scores over 18: 91%; SAT critical reading scores over 600: 25%; SAT math scores over 600: 22%; ACT scores over 24: 43%; SAT critical reading scores over 700: 10%; SAT math scores over 700: 4%; ACT scores over 30: 9%.

Retention: 79% of full-time freshmen returned.

FACULTY

Total: 188, 43% full-time, 68% with terminal degrees.

Student/faculty ratio: 18:1.

ACADEMICS

Calendar: semesters. *Degrees:* certificates, associate, bachelor's, master's, and doctoral.

Special study options: academic remediation for entering students, adult/continuing education programs, advanced placement credit, distance learning, double majors, internships, services for LD students, study abroad, summer session for credit. ***ROTC:*** Army (c).

Computers: 200 computers/terminals and 1,460 ports are available on campus for general student use. Students can access the following: campus intranet, computer help desk, free student e-mail accounts, online (class) grades, online (class) registration, online (class) schedules, Non-traditional and graduate student registered through Academic Records. Campuswide network is available. 100% of college-owned or -operated housing units are wired for high-speed Internet access. Wireless service is available via entire campus.

STUDENT LIFE

Housing options: on-campus residence required through senior year; men-only, women-only. Campus housing is university owned.

Activities and organizations: drama/theater group, student-run newspaper, choral group, marching band.

Athletics Member NCAA. All Division II. ***Intercollegiate sports:*** baseball M(s), basketball M(s)/W(s), cross-country running M/W, golf M(s)/W(s), soccer M(s)/W(s), softball W(s), track and field M(s)/W(s), volleyball W(s). ***Intramural sports:*** badminton M/W, basketball M/W, football M/W, golf M/W, racquetball M/W, softball M/W, table tennis M/W, track and field M/W, volleyball M/W.

Campus security: 24-hour patrols, late-night transport/escort service, weather alert warning system (phone, email, siren).

Student services: health clinic, personal/psychological counseling.

COSTS & FINANCIAL AID

Costs (2014–15) ***Comprehensive fee:*** $31,186 includes full-time tuition ($22,626), mandatory fees ($500), and room and board ($8060). Full-time tuition and fees vary according to course load and program. Part-time tuition: $874 per credit hour. Part-time tuition and fees vary according to course load and program. ***College room only:*** $4030. Room and board charges vary according to board plan. ***Payment plans:*** tuition prepayment, installment. ***Waivers:*** senior citizens and employees or children of employees.

Financial Aid ***Average indebtedness upon graduation:*** $28,430.

APPLYING

Standardized Tests *Required:* SAT or ACT (for admission).

Options: electronic application, early admission, deferred entrance.

Application fee: $25.

Required: high school transcript, minimum 2.5 GPA, ACT composite score of 18 or above, or SAT Critical Reading + Math score of 860 or above; enrollment fee; medical history and immunization records.

Application deadlines: 8/1 (freshmen), rolling (transfers).

Notification: continuous (freshmen), continuous (transfers).

CONTACT

Ms. Melinda Miller, Director of Undergraduate Admissions, Trevecca Nazarene University, 333 Murfreesboro Road, Nashville, TN 37210-2834. *Phone:* 615-248-1320. *Toll-free phone:* 888-210-4TNU. *Fax:* 615-248-7406. *E-mail:* admissions_und@trevecca.edu.

Tusculum College

Greeneville, Tennessee

http://www.tusculum.edu/

- **Independent Presbyterian** comprehensive, founded 1794
- **Small-town** 140-acre campus
- **Endowment** $17.6 million
- **Coed** 1,746 undergraduate students, 92% full-time, 54% women, 46% men
- **Moderately difficult** entrance level, 72% of applicants were admitted

UNDERGRAD STUDENTS

1,608 full-time, 138 part-time. Students come from 37 states and territories; 15 other countries; 24% are from out of state; 12% Black or African American, non-Hispanic/Latino; 2% Hispanic/Latino; 0.4% Asian, non-Hispanic/Latino; 0.1% Native Hawaiian or other Pacific Islander, non-Hispanic/Latino; 0.7% American Indian or Alaska Native, non-Hispanic/Latino; 0.6% Two or more races, non-Hispanic/Latino; 11% Race/ethnicity unknown; 2% international; 4% transferred in; 65% live on campus.

Freshmen

Admission: 2,537 applied, 1,825 admitted, 287 enrolled. ***Average high school GPA:*** 3. ***Test scores:*** SAT critical reading scores over 500: 28%; SAT math scores over 500: 39%; ACT scores over 18: 79%; SAT critical reading scores over 600: 9%; SAT math scores over 600: 7%; ACT scores over 24: 25%; SAT critical reading scores over 700: 1%; ACT scores over 30: 3%.

Retention: 62% of full-time freshmen returned.

FACULTY

Total: 189, 47% full-time.

Student/faculty ratio: 15:1.

ACADEMICS

Calendar: semesters. *Degrees:* bachelor's and master's.

Special study options: academic remediation for entering students, adult/continuing education programs, advanced placement credit, double majors, honors programs, independent study, internships, part-time degree program, services for LD students, student-designed majors, study abroad, summer session for credit.

Computers: 200 computers/terminals are available on campus for general student use. Students can access the following: campus intranet, computer help desk, free student e-mail accounts, online (class) grades, online (class) registration, online (class) schedules. Campuswide network is available. 100% of college-owned or -operated housing units are wired for high-speed Internet access. Wireless service is available via entire campus.

STUDENT LIFE

Housing options: on-campus residence required through senior year; coed, men-only, women-only, special housing for students with disabilities. Campus housing is university owned. Freshman campus housing is guaranteed.

Activities and organizations: drama/theater group, student-run newspaper, radio and television station, choral group, marching band, Pioneer Newspaper, Bonwondi, Campus Activities Board, Fellowship of Christian Athletes, Tusculana (yearbook).

Athletics Member NCAA. All Division II. ***Intercollegiate sports:*** baseball M(s), basketball M(s)/W(s), cheerleading W(s), cross-country running M(s)/W(s), football M(s), golf M(s)/W(s), lacrosse M(s)/W(s), soccer M(s)/W(s), softball W(s), tennis M(s)/W(s), volleyball W(s). ***Intramural sports:*** baseball M, basketball M/W, football M, softball M, tennis M/W, volleyball M/W.

Campus security: 24-hour emergency response devices and patrols, student patrols, late-night transport/escort service, controlled dormitory access, trained security personnel on duty.

Student services: health clinic, personal/psychological counseling, women's center.

COSTS & FINANCIAL AID

Costs (2014–15) ***Comprehensive fee:*** $31,170 includes full-time tuition ($22,670) and room and board ($8500). Part-time tuition: $704 per credit hour. ***College room only:*** $5610.

Financial Aid Of all full-time matriculated undergraduates who enrolled in 2013, 1,596 applied for aid, 1,520 were judged to have need, 126 had their need fully met. ***Average percent of need met:*** 61. ***Average financial aid package:*** $16,213. ***Average need-based loan:*** $4368. ***Average need-based gift aid:*** $7572. ***Average indebtedness upon graduation:*** $28,687.

APPLYING
Standardized Tests *Required:* SAT or ACT (for admission).

Options: electronic application, early admission, deferred entrance.

Required: essay or personal statement, high school transcript, minimum 2.0 GPA. ***Required for some:*** 3 letters of recommendation. ***Recommended:*** interview.

Application deadlines: rolling (freshmen), rolling (transfers).

CONTACT
Ms. Melissa Ripley, Director of Operations, Tusculum College, PO Box 5047, Greeneville, TN 37743-9997. *Phone:* 423-636-7300 Ext. 5374. *Toll-free phone:* 800-729-0256. *Fax:* 423-798-1622. *E-mail:* admissions@tusculum.edu.

Union University

Jackson, Tennessee

http://www.uu.edu/

- **Independent Southern Baptist** comprehensive, founded 1823
- **Small-town** 360-acre campus with easy access to Memphis
- **Coed** 2,717 undergraduate students, 73% full-time, 61% women, 39% men
- **Moderately difficult** entrance level, 69% of applicants were admitted

UNDERGRAD STUDENTS
1,976 full-time, 741 part-time. 23% are from out of state; 19% Black or African American, non-Hispanic/Latino; 3% Hispanic/Latino; 1% Asian, non-Hispanic/Latino; 0.1% Native Hawaiian or other Pacific Islander, non-Hispanic/Latino; 0.2% American Indian or Alaska Native, non-Hispanic/Latino; 2% Two or more races, non-Hispanic/Latino; 4% Race/ethnicity unknown; 1% international; 3% transferred in.

Freshmen
Admission: 1,983 applied, 1,360 admitted, 387 enrolled. ***Average high school GPA:*** 3.68. ***Test scores:*** SAT critical reading scores over 500: 86%; SAT math scores over 500: 81%; ACT scores over 18: 97%; SAT critical reading scores over 600: 48%; SAT math scores over 600: 46%; ACT scores over 24: 64%; SAT critical reading scores over 700: 16%; SAT math scores over 700: 8%; ACT scores over 30: 21%.

Retention: 88% of full-time freshmen returned.

FACULTY
Total: 244, 99% full-time, 79% with terminal degrees.

Student/faculty ratio: 11:1.

ACADEMICS
Calendar: 4-1-4. *Degrees:* certificates, diplomas, associate, bachelor's, master's, doctoral, and post-master's certificates.

Special study options: academic remediation for entering students, accelerated degree program, adult/continuing education programs, advanced placement credit, cooperative education, distance learning, double majors, English as a second language, honors programs, independent study, internships, off-campus study, part-time degree program, services for LD students, study abroad, summer session for credit. ***ROTC:*** Army (c).

Computers: Students can access the following: campus intranet, computer help desk, free student e-mail accounts, online (class) grades, online (class) registration, online (class) schedules. Campuswide network is available. 100% of college-owned or -operated housing units are wired for high-speed Internet access. Wireless service is available via entire campus.

STUDENT LIFE
Housing options: on-campus residence required through junior year; men-only, women-only, special housing for students with disabilities. Campus housing is university owned. Freshman applicants given priority for college housing.

Activities and organizations: drama/theater group, student-run newspaper, choral group, Campus Ministries, Student Government Association, Student Activities Council, Students in Free Enterprise (SIFE), national fraternities, national sororities.

Athletics Member NCAA, NCCAA. All NCAA Division II. ***Intercollegiate sports:*** baseball M(s), basketball M(s)/W(s), cheerleading W(s), cross-country running M/W(s), golf M(s), soccer M(s)/W(s), softball W(s), track and field M/W, volleyball W(s). ***Intramural sports:*** basketball M/W, bowling M/W, cross-country running M/W, football M/W, golf M/W, racquetball M/W, soccer W, softball M/W, swimming and diving M/W, table tennis M/W, track and field M/W, ultimate Frisbee M/W, volleyball M/W.

Campus security: 24-hour emergency response devices and patrols, student patrols, late-night transport/escort service.

Student services: health clinic, personal/psychological counseling.

COSTS & FINANCIAL AID
Costs (2014–15) ***Comprehensive fee:*** $36,620 includes full-time tuition ($27,470), mandatory fees ($720), and room and board ($8430). Full-time tuition and fees vary according to class time, course load, degree level, location, and program. Part-time tuition: $915 per credit hour. Part-time tuition and fees vary according to class time, course load, degree level, location, and program. ***Required fees:*** $295 per term part-time. ***Room and board:*** Room and board charges vary according to board plan and housing facility. ***Payment plans:*** installment, deferred payment. ***Waivers:*** children of alumni and employees or children of employees.

Financial Aid Of all full-time matriculated undergraduates who enrolled in 2014, 1,768 applied for aid, 1,575 were judged to have need, 239 had their need fully met. 98 Federal Work-Study jobs (averaging $1827). 191 state and other part-time jobs (averaging $1744). In 2014, 371 non-need-based awards were made. ***Average percent of need met:*** 59. ***Average financial aid package:*** $18,840. ***Average need-based loan:*** $4434. ***Average need-based gift aid:*** $5886. ***Average non-need-based aid:*** $12,889. ***Average indebtedness upon graduation:*** $29,187.

APPLYING
Standardized Tests *Required:* SAT or ACT (for admission).

Options: electronic application, early admission, deferred entrance.

Application fee: $35.

Required: high school transcript, minimum 2.5 GPA. ***Required for some:*** 3 letters of recommendation. ***Recommended:*** essay or personal statement, interview.

CONTACT
Mr. Robbie Graves, Director of Enrollment Services, Union University, 1050 Union University Drive, Jackson, TN 38305-3697. *Phone:* 731-661-5590. *Toll-free phone:* 800-33-UNION. *Fax:* 731-661-5017. *E-mail:* rgraves@uu.edu.

University of Memphis

Memphis, Tennessee

http://www.memphis.edu/

- **State-supported** university, founded 1912, part of Tennessee Board of Regents
- **Urban** 1160-acre campus with easy access to Memphis
- **Endowment** $200.8 million
- **Coed** 17,068 undergraduate students, 72% full-time, 60% women, 40% men
- **Moderately difficult** entrance level, 47% of applicants were admitted

UNDERGRAD STUDENTS
12,372 full-time, 4,696 part-time. Students come from 52 states and territories; 82 other countries; 11% are from out of state; 38% Black or African American, non-Hispanic/Latino; 4% Hispanic/Latino; 3% Asian, non-Hispanic/Latino; 0.1% Native Hawaiian or other Pacific Islander, non-Hispanic/Latino; 0.2% American Indian or Alaska Native, non-Hispanic/Latino; 3% Two or more races, non-Hispanic/Latino; 0.2% Race/ethnicity unknown; 0.9% international; 9% transferred in; 13% live on campus.

Freshmen
Admission: 11,311 applied, 5,361 admitted, 2,365 enrolled. ***Average high school GPA:*** 3.38. ***Test scores:*** SAT critical reading scores over 500: 62%; SAT math scores over 500: 62%; SAT writing scores over 500: 48%; ACT scores over 18: 96%; SAT critical reading scores over 600: 17%; SAT math scores over 600: 17%; SAT writing scores over 600: 17%; ACT

scores over 24: 40%; SAT critical reading scores over 700: 6%; SAT math scores over 700: 4%; SAT writing scores over 700: 4%; ACT scores over 30: 7%.

Retention: 79% of full-time freshmen returned.

FACULTY

Total: 1,425, 61% full-time, 62% with terminal degrees.

Student/faculty ratio: 16:1.

ACADEMICS

Calendar: semesters. *Degrees:* bachelor's, master's, doctoral, post-master's, and postbachelor's certificates.

Special study options: academic remediation for entering students, accelerated degree program, adult/continuing education programs, advanced placement credit, cooperative education, distance learning, double majors, English as a second language, external degree program, honors programs, independent study, internships, off-campus study, part-time degree program, services for LD students, student-designed majors, study abroad, summer session for credit. ***ROTC:*** Army (b), Navy (b), Air Force (b).

Computers: 1,600 computers/terminals and 35 ports are available on campus for general student use. Students can access the following: campus intranet, computer help desk, free student e-mail accounts, online (class) grades, online (class) registration, online (class) schedules. Campuswide network is available. 100% of college-owned or -operated housing units are wired for high-speed Internet access. Wireless service is available via entire campus.

STUDENT LIFE

Housing options: coed, men-only, women-only, cooperative, special housing for students with disabilities. Campus housing is university owned.

Activities and organizations: drama/theater group, student-run newspaper, radio station, choral group, marching band, Student Activities Council, Fraternity and Sorority Life, Black Student Association, Student Government Association, Up 'til Dawn- St. Jude Philanthropy, national fraternities, national sororities.

Athletics Member NCAA. All Division I except football (Division I-A). ***Intercollegiate sports:*** baseball M(s), basketball M(s)/W(s), cheerleading M(s)/W(s), cross-country running M(s)/W(s), golf M(s)/W(s), racquetball M(c)/W(c), riflery M(s)/W(s), soccer M(s)/W(s), softball W, swimming and diving M(c)/W(c), tennis M(s)/W(s), track and field M(s)/W(s), volleyball W(s). ***Intramural sports:*** basketball M/W, bowling M/W, golf M/W, racquetball M/W, soccer M/W, softball M/W, table tennis M/W, tennis M/W, track and field M/W, ultimate Frisbee M/W, volleyball M/W, water polo M/W.

Campus security: 24-hour emergency response devices and patrols, student patrols, late-night transport/escort service, controlled dormitory access.

Student services: health clinic, personal/psychological counseling, women's center.

COSTS & FINANCIAL AID

Costs (2014–15) ***Tuition:*** state resident $7410 full-time, $294 per credit hour part-time; nonresident $19,122 full-time, $488 per credit hour part-time. Full-time tuition and fees vary according to course load, degree level, program, and reciprocity agreements. Part-time tuition and fees vary according to course load, degree level, and program. ***Required fees:*** $1563 full-time, $94 per credit hour part-time. ***Room and board:*** $8976; room only: $5386. Room and board charges vary according to board plan, housing facility, and location. ***Payment plan:*** installment. ***Waivers:*** senior citizens and employees or children of employees.

Financial Aid Of all full-time matriculated undergraduates who enrolled in 2014, 11,446 applied for aid, 9,691 were judged to have need, 1,280 had their need fully met. 152 Federal Work-Study jobs (averaging $2318). In 2014, 1273 non-need-based awards were made. ***Average percent of need met:*** 72. ***Average financial aid package:*** $9087. ***Average need-based loan:*** $3187. ***Average need-based gift aid:*** $5647. ***Average non-need-based aid:*** $6410. ***Average indebtedness upon graduation:*** $25,244.

APPLYING

Standardized Tests *Required:* SAT or ACT (for admission).

Options: electronic application, early admission.

Application fee: $25.

Required: high school transcript. ***Required for some:*** minimum 2.0 GPA, 2 letters of recommendation, interview.

Application deadlines: 7/1 (freshmen), 7/1 (transfers).

Notification: continuous (freshmen), continuous (transfers).

CONTACT

Gloria W Moore, Associate Director of Admissions, University of Memphis, Office of Admissions, 101 Wilder Tower, Memphis, TN 38152. *Phone:* 901-678-2111. *Toll-free phone:* 800-669-2678. *Fax:* 901-678-5318. *E-mail:* admissions@memphis.edu.

See previous page for display ad and page 1684 for the College Close-Up.

The University of Tennessee

Knoxville, Tennessee

http://www.utk.edu/

- **State-supported** university, founded 1794, part of University of Tennessee System
- **Urban** 560-acre campus
- **Endowment** $680.7 million
- **Coed** 21,664 undergraduate students, 94% full-time, 50% women, 50% men
- **Moderately difficult** entrance level, 75% of applicants were admitted

UNDERGRAD STUDENTS

20,337 full-time, 1,327 part-time. Students come from 51 states and territories; 72 other countries; 10% are from out of state; 7% Black or African American, non-Hispanic/Latino; 3% Hispanic/Latino; 3% Asian, non-Hispanic/Latino; 0.2% American Indian or Alaska Native, non-Hispanic/Latino; 3% Two or more races, non-Hispanic/Latino; 2% Race/ethnicity unknown; 1% international; 6% transferred in; 37% live on campus.

Freshmen

Admission: 15,442 applied, 11,555 admitted, 4,701 enrolled. ***Average high school GPA:*** 3.79. ***Test scores:*** SAT critical reading scores over 500: 85%; SAT math scores over 500: 86%; ACT scores over 18: 100%; SAT critical reading scores over 600: 39%; SAT math scores over 600: 42%; ACT scores over 24: 82%; SAT critical reading scores over 700: 10%; SAT math scores over 700: 10%; ACT scores over 30: 25%.

Retention: 87% of full-time freshmen returned.

FACULTY

Total: 2,090, 85% full-time, 83% with terminal degrees.

Student/faculty ratio: 17:1.

ACADEMICS

Calendar: semesters. *Degrees:* bachelor's, master's, doctoral, and postbachelor's certificates.

Special study options: accelerated degree program, advanced placement credit, cooperative education, distance learning, double majors, English as a second language, external degree program, freshman honors college, honors programs, independent study, internships, off-campus study, part-time degree program, services for LD students, student-designed majors, study abroad, summer session for credit. ***ROTC:*** Army (b), Air Force (b).

Computers: 727 computers/terminals are available on campus for general student use. Students can access the following: campus intranet, computer help desk, free student e-mail accounts, online (class) grades, online (class) registration, online (class) schedules, Blackboard Course Management System. Campuswide network is available. 100% of college-owned or -operated housing units are wired for high-speed Internet access. Wireless service is available via entire campus.

STUDENT LIFE

Housing options: on-campus residence required for freshman year; coed, men-only, women-only, special housing for students with disabilities. Campus housing is university owned. Freshman campus housing is guaranteed.

Activities and organizations: drama/theater group, student-run newspaper, radio and television station, choral group, marching band, Fraternities/Sororities, Religious organizations, Central Program Council, Black Cultural Programming Committee, Student Government Association, national fraternities, national sororities.

Athletics Member NCAA. All Division I. ***Intercollegiate sports:*** baseball M(s), basketball M(s)/W(s), crew W(s), cross-country running M/W, football M(s), golf M(s)/W(s), soccer W(s), softball W(s), swimming and diving M(s)/W(s), tennis M(s)/W(s), track and field M(s)/W(s), volleyball W(s). ***Intramural sports:*** badminton M/W, basketball M/W, bowling M/W, field hockey M/W, football M/W, racquetball M/W, soccer M/W, softball M/W, table tennis M/W, tennis M/W, ultimate Frisbee M/W, volleyball M/W, water polo M/W, weight lifting M/W.

Campus security: 24-hour emergency response devices and patrols, late-night transport/escort service, controlled dormitory access, security cameras on all building entrances; card entry into the living sections of residence hall buildings.

Student services: health clinic, personal/psychological counseling, women's center.

COSTS & FINANCIAL AID

Costs (2014–15) ***Tuition:*** state resident $10,366 full-time, $346 per hour part-time; nonresident $28,556 full-time, $1105 per hour part-time. Full-time tuition and fees vary according to course level, location, program, and reciprocity agreements. Part-time tuition and fees vary according to course level, location, program, and reciprocity agreements. ***Required fees:*** $1510 full-time, $71 per hour part-time. ***Room and board:*** $10,296. Room and board charges vary according to board plan and housing facility. ***Payment plan:*** installment. ***Waivers:*** senior citizens and employees or children of employees.

Financial Aid Of all full-time matriculated undergraduates who enrolled in 2014, 17,831 applied for aid, 12,057 were judged to have need, 2,467 had their need fully met. 657 Federal Work-Study jobs (averaging $2294). In 2014, 2323 non-need-based awards were made. ***Average percent of need met:*** 57. ***Average financial aid package:*** $12,313. ***Average need-based loan:*** $6414. ***Average need-based gift aid:*** $8961. ***Average non-need-based aid:*** $3685. ***Average indebtedness upon graduation:*** $23,870.

APPLYING

Standardized Tests *Required:* SAT or ACT (for admission).

Options: electronic application, early admission.

Application fee: $40.

Required: essay or personal statement, high school transcript, minimum 2.0 GPA, 1 letter of recommendation. ***Required for some:*** Specific high school units, audition for music, essay for nursing, essay for pre-pharmacy.

Application deadlines: 6/1 (freshmen), 7/1 (transfers).

Notification: 8/15 (freshmen), continuous (transfers).

CONTACT

Ms. Norma Harrington, Senior Associate Director, The University of Tennessee, 320 Student Services Building, Knoxville, TN 37996-0230. *Phone:* 865-974-2184. *Fax:* 865-974-4689. *E-mail:* admissions@utk.edu.

The University of Tennessee at Chattanooga

Chattanooga, Tennessee

http://www.utc.edu/

- **State-supported** comprehensive, founded 1886, part of University of Tennessee System
- **Urban** 133-acre campus with easy access to Atlanta
- **Coed** 10,315 undergraduate students, 87% full-time, 55% women, 45% men
- **Moderately difficult** entrance level, 77% of applicants were admitted

UNDERGRAD STUDENTS

8,985 full-time, 1,330 part-time. 6% are from out of state; 11% Black or African American, non-Hispanic/Latino; 3% Hispanic/Latino; 2% Asian, non-Hispanic/Latino; 0.1% Native Hawaiian or other Pacific Islander, non-Hispanic/Latino; 0.3% American Indian or Alaska Native, non-Hispanic/Latino; 8% Two or more races, non-Hispanic/Latino; 1% Race/ethnicity unknown; 0.7% international; 8% transferred in; 31% live on campus.

Freshmen

Admission: 7,399 applied, 5,718 admitted, 2,160 enrolled. ***Average high school GPA:*** 3.4. ***Test scores:*** SAT critical reading scores over 500: 61%; SAT math scores over 500: 58%; ACT scores over 18: 99%; SAT critical reading scores over 600: 25%; SAT math scores over 600: 21%; ACT scores over 24: 44%; SAT critical reading scores over 700: 2%; SAT math scores over 700: 5%; ACT scores over 30: 6%.

Retention: 70% of full-time freshmen returned.

FACULTY
Total: 766, 61% full-time, 55% with terminal degrees.

Student/faculty ratio: 18:1.

ACADEMICS
Calendar: semesters. *Degrees:* certificates, bachelor's, master's, doctoral, post-master's, and postbachelor's certificates.

Special study options: academic remediation for entering students, accelerated degree program, adult/continuing education programs, advanced placement credit, cooperative education, distance learning, double majors, English as a second language, freshman honors college, honors programs, independent study, internships, off-campus study, part-time degree program, services for LD students, student-designed majors, study abroad, summer session for credit. ***ROTC:*** Army (b).

Computers: 965 computers/terminals are available on campus for general student use. Students can access the following: campus intranet, computer help desk, free student e-mail accounts, online (class) grades, online (class) registration, online (class) schedules, pay fees. Campuswide network is available. 100% of college-owned or -operated housing units are wired for high-speed Internet access. Wireless service is available via entire campus.

STUDENT LIFE
Housing options: on-campus residence required for freshman yearCampus housing is university owned. Freshman applicants given priority for college housing.

Activities and organizations: drama/theater group, student-run newspaper, radio station, choral group, marching band, Student Government Association, Association for Campus Entertainment, national fraternities, national sororities.

Athletics Member NCAA. All Division I except football (Division I-AA). ***Intercollegiate sports:*** basketball M(s)/W(s), cross-country running M(s)/W(s), golf M(s)/W(s), soccer W(s), softball W(s), tennis M(s)/W(s), track and field M(s)/W(s), volleyball W(s), wrestling M(s). ***Intramural sports:*** badminton M/W, baseball M(c), basketball M/W, crew M(c)/W(c), cross-country running M/W, fencing M(c)/W(c), golf M/W, racquetball M/W, soccer M/W, swimming and diving M/W, tennis M/W, ultimate Frisbee M(c)/W(c), volleyball W, wrestling M.

Campus security: 24-hour emergency response devices and patrols, late-night transport/escort service, controlled dormitory access.

Student services: health clinic, personal/psychological counseling.

COSTS & FINANCIAL AID
Costs (2014–15) ***Tuition:*** state resident $6430 full-time, $268 per credit hour part-time; nonresident $22,548 full-time, $940 per credit hour part-time. Full-time tuition and fees vary according to degree level. Part-time tuition and fees vary according to course load and degree level. ***Required fees:*** $1708 full-time, $252 per credit hour part-time. ***Room and board:*** $8110; room only: $4910. Room and board charges vary according to board plan and housing facility. ***Payment plan:*** installment. ***Waivers:*** senior citizens and employees or children of employees.

Financial Aid Of all full-time matriculated undergraduates who enrolled in 2014, 8,096 applied for aid, 5,646 were judged to have need, 785 had their need fully met. In 2014, 801 non-need-based awards were made. ***Average percent of need met:*** 66. ***Average financial aid package:*** $9765. ***Average need-based loan:*** $3967. ***Average need-based gift aid:*** $7720. ***Average non-need-based aid:*** $3094. ***Average indebtedness upon graduation:*** $21,420. ***Financial aid deadline:*** 5/1.

APPLYING
Standardized Tests *Required:* SAT or ACT (for admission).

Options: electronic application, deferred entrance.

Application fee: $30.

Required: high school transcript. ***Recommended:*** essay or personal statement.

Application deadlines: 5/1 (freshmen), 5/1 (out-of-state freshmen), 7/1 (transfers).

Notification: continuous (freshmen), continuous (out-of-state freshmen), continuous (transfers).

CONTACT
Ms. Lee Pierce, Director, Admissions and Recruitment, The University of Tennessee at Chattanooga, 615 McCallie Ave, University Center, Room 101, Dept. 5105, Chattanooga, TN 37403. *Phone:* 423-425-4662. *Toll-free phone:* 800-UTC-MOCS (in-state); 800-UTC.MOCS (out-of-state). *Fax:* 423-425-4157. *E-mail:* lee-pierce@utc.edu.

The University of Tennessee at Martin

Martin, Tennessee

http://www.utm.edu/

- **State-supported** comprehensive, founded 1900, part of University of Tennessee System
- **Small-town** 250-acre campus
- **Endowment** $32.4 million
- **Coed** 6,677 undergraduate students, 86% full-time, 58% women, 42% men
- **Moderately difficult** entrance level, 73% of applicants were admitted

UNDERGRAD STUDENTS
5,738 full-time, 939 part-time. Students come from 40 states and territories; 19 other countries; 5% are from out of state; 15% Black or African American, non-Hispanic/Latino; 2% Hispanic/Latino; 0.6% Asian, non-Hispanic/Latino; 0.1% American Indian or Alaska Native, non-Hispanic/Latino; 2% Two or more races, non-Hispanic/Latino; 3% international; 7% transferred in; 28% live on campus.

Freshmen
Admission: 3,526 applied, 2,586 admitted, 1,181 enrolled. ***Average high school GPA:*** 3.52. ***Test scores:*** ACT scores over 18: 96%; ACT scores over 24: 39%; ACT scores over 30: 4%.

Retention: 71% of full-time freshmen returned.

FACULTY
Total: 523, 56% full-time, 51% with terminal degrees.

Student/faculty ratio: 17:1.

ACADEMICS
Calendar: semesters. *Degrees:* bachelor's and master's.

Special study options: accelerated degree program, adult/continuing education programs, advanced placement credit, cooperative education, distance learning, double majors, English as a second language, honors programs, independent study, internships, off-campus study, part-time degree program, services for LD students, student-designed majors, study abroad, summer session for credit. ***ROTC:*** Army (b).

Unusual degree programs: veterinary medicine, dentistry, medicine, and pharmacy.

Computers: 831 computers/terminals and 7,150 ports are available on campus for general student use. Students can access the following: campus intranet, computer help desk, free student e-mail accounts, online (class) grades, online (class) registration, online (class) schedules, online fee payments, degree progress, financial aid data, housing applications, transcripts. Campuswide network is available. 100% of college-owned or -operated housing units are wired for high-speed Internet access. Wireless service is available via entire campus.

STUDENT LIFE
Housing options: on-campus residence required for freshman year; men-only, women-only, special housing for students with disabilities. Campus housing is university owned. Freshman applicants given priority for college housing.

Activities and organizations: drama/theater group, student-run newspaper, radio and television station, choral group, marching band, Student Government Association, Student Activities Council, Sigma Theta Tau, Gamma Beta Phi, Student Tennessee Education Association, national fraternities, national sororities.

Athletics Member NCAA. All Division I except football (Division I-AA). ***Intercollegiate sports:*** baseball M(s), basketball M(s)/W(s), cheerleading W(s), cross-country running M(s)/W(s), equestrian sports W(s), golf M(s), riflery M(s)/W(s), soccer W(s), softball W(s), tennis W(s), volleyball W(s). ***Intramural sports:*** basketball M/W, football M/W, golf M/W, racquetball M/W, soccer M/W, softball M/W, tennis M/W, ultimate Frisbee M/W, volleyball M/W, water polo M/W.

Campus security: 24-hour emergency response devices and patrols, student patrols, controlled dormitory access.

Student services: health clinic, personal/psychological counseling, women's center.

COSTS & FINANCIAL AID

Costs (2014–15) ***Tuition:*** state resident $6716 full-time, $280 per credit hour part-time; nonresident $20,660 full-time, $861 per credit hour part-time. Part-time tuition and fees vary according to course load. ***Required fees:*** $1308 full-time, $54 per credit hour part-time. ***Room and board:*** $5786; room only: $2780. Room and board charges vary according to board plan and housing facility. ***Payment plans:*** installment, deferred payment. ***Waivers:*** senior citizens and employees or children of employees.

Financial Aid Of all full-time matriculated undergraduates who enrolled in 2014, 5,463 applied for aid, 4,416 were judged to have need, 898 had their need fully met. 252 Federal Work-Study jobs (averaging $2269). In 2014, 824 non-need-based awards were made. ***Average percent of need met:*** 73. ***Average financial aid package:*** $13,437. ***Average need-based loan:*** $4342. ***Average need-based gift aid:*** $6029. ***Average non-need-based aid:*** $6787. ***Average indebtedness upon graduation:*** $28,701.

APPLYING

Standardized Tests *Required:* SAT or ACT (for admission).

Options: electronic application, early admission, deferred entrance.

Application fee: $30.

Required: high school transcript, minimum 2.7 GPA.

Application deadlines: rolling (freshmen), rolling (out-of-state freshmen), rolling (transfers).

Notification: continuous until 8/1 (freshmen), continuous until 8/1 (out-of-state freshmen), continuous until 8/1 (transfers).

CONTACT

Dr. Brandy Cartmell, Interim Executive Director for Student Engagement, The University of Tennessee at Martin, 200 Hall-Moody Administration Building, Martin, TN 38238. *Phone:* 731-881-7032. *Toll-free phone:* 800-829-8861. *Fax:* 731-881-7029. *E-mail:* bcartmel@utm.edu.

★ Vanderbilt University

Nashville, Tennessee

http://www.vanderbilt.edu/

- **Independent** university, founded 1873
- **Urban** 330-acre campus
- **Endowment** $4.0 billion
- **Coed** 6,851 undergraduate students, 99% full-time, 50% women, 50% men
- **Most difficult** entrance level, 13% of applicants were admitted

UNDERGRAD STUDENTS

6,778 full-time, 73 part-time. Students come from 55 states and territories; 49 other countries; 89% are from out of state; 8% Black or African American, non-Hispanic/Latino; 8% Hispanic/Latino; 10% Asian, non-Hispanic/Latino; 0.1% Native Hawaiian or other Pacific Islander, non-Hispanic/Latino; 0.3% American Indian or Alaska Native, non-Hispanic/Latino; 5% Two or more races, non-Hispanic/Latino; 4% Race/ethnicity unknown; 6% international; 3% transferred in; 95% live on campus.

Freshmen

Admission: 29,518 applied, 3,865 admitted, 1,605 enrolled. ***Average high school GPA:*** 3.78. ***Test scores:*** SAT critical reading scores over 500: 99%; SAT math scores over 500: 99%; SAT writing scores over 500: 98%; ACT scores over 18: 100%; SAT critical reading scores over 600: 94%; SAT math scores over 600: 96%; SAT writing scores over 600: 95%; ACT scores over 24: 98%; SAT critical reading scores over 700: 78%; SAT math scores over 700: 82%; SAT writing scores over 700: 69%; ACT scores over 30: 90%.

Retention: 97% of full-time freshmen returned.

FACULTY

Total: 1,194, 76% full-time.

Student/faculty ratio: 8:1.

ACADEMICS

Calendar: semesters. *Degrees:* bachelor's, master's, and doctoral.

Special study options: accelerated degree program, advanced placement credit, cooperative education, double majors, English as a second language, honors programs, independent study, internships, off-campus study, services for LD students, student-designed majors, study abroad, summer session for credit. ***ROTC:*** Army (b), Navy (b), Air Force (c).

Unusual degree programs: 3-2 business administration with Joint Five-Year Baccalaureate MBA Program. (one and one-half years of study in the Vanderbilt Owen Graduate School of Management, three and one-half years in Vanderbilt's College of Arts and Science); engineering with BE/MS Biomedical Engineering, Chemical Engineering, Civil Engineering, Electrical Engineering, and Mechanical Engineering; BS/MS Computer Science; BS/MBA Engineering Science Management; nursing with Baccalaureate from College of Arts and Science/MSN or BS at Peabody (human and organizational development or child development)/MSN through a senior-in-absentia program in the School of Nursing; BA/MA English, French, German, History, Latin American Studies, Mathematics, Philosophy, Political Science, Psychology, and Medicine, Health and Society. BMUS/MBA Blair-to-Owen Program.

Computers: Students can access the following: campus intranet, computer help desk, free student e-mail accounts, online (class) grades, online (class) registration, online (class) schedules, productivity and educational software. Campuswide network is available. Wireless service is available via entire campus.

STUDENT LIFE

Housing options: on-campus residence required for freshman year; coed, men-only, women-only, special housing for students with disabilities. Campus housing is university owned. Freshman campus housing is guaranteed.

Activities and organizations: drama/theater group, student-run newspaper, radio and television station, choral group, marching band, national sororities.

Athletics Member NCAA. All Division I except football (Division I-A). ***Intercollegiate sports:*** baseball M(s), basketball M(s)/W(s), bowling W(s), cross-country running M(s)/W(s), golf M(s)/W(s), lacrosse W(s), soccer W(s), swimming and diving W(s), tennis M(s)/W(s), track and field W(s). ***Intramural sports:*** badminton M(c)/W(c), baseball M(c), basketball M(c)/W(c), bowling M(c)/W(c), crew M(c)/W(c), cross-country running M(c)/W(c), equestrian sports M(c)/W(c), fencing M(c)/W(c), field hockey M(c)/W(c), golf M(c)/W(c), ice hockey M(c), lacrosse M(c)/W(c), racquetball M(c)/W(c), rugby M(c), sailing M(c)/W(c), soccer M(c)/W(c), softball M(c)/W(c), squash M(c)/W(c), swimming and diving M(c)/W(c), table tennis M(c)/W(c), tennis M(c)/W(c), track and field M(c)/W(c), ultimate Frisbee M(c)/W(c), volleyball M(c)/W(c), water polo M(c)/W(c), weight lifting M(c)/W(c), wrestling M(c).

Campus security: 24-hour emergency response devices and patrols, student patrols, late-night transport/escort service, controlled dormitory access.

Student services: health clinic, personal/psychological counseling, women's center.

COSTS & FINANCIAL AID

Costs (2014–15) ***Comprehensive fee:*** $58,220 includes full-time tuition ($42,768), mandatory fees ($1070), and room and board ($14,382). Part-time tuition: $1782 per credit hour. ***College room only:*** $9392. Room and board charges vary according to board plan. ***Payment plans:*** tuition prepayment, installment. ***Waivers:*** employees or children of employees.

Financial Aid Of all full-time matriculated undergraduates who enrolled in 2014, 3,764 applied for aid, 3,329 were judged to have need, 3,301 had their need fully met. 1,407 Federal Work-Study jobs (averaging $2319). In 2014, 702 non-need-based awards were made. ***Average percent of need met:*** 100. ***Average financial aid package:*** $45,477. ***Average need-based loan:*** $3520. ***Average need-based gift aid:*** $39,953. ***Average non-need-based aid:*** $22,372. ***Average indebtedness upon graduation:*** $20,790.

APPLYING

Standardized Tests *Required:* SAT or ACT (for admission).

Options: electronic application, early admission, early decision, deferred entrance.

Application fee: $50.

Required: essay or personal statement, high school transcript, 3 letters of recommendation, 3 letters of recommendation (two from teachers in core subject areas and one from counselor).

Application deadlines: 1/5 (freshmen), 3/15 (transfers).

Early decision deadline: 11/1 (for plan 1), 1/5 (for plan 2).

Notification: 4/1 (freshmen), 4/15 (transfers), 12/15 (early decision plan 1), 2/15 (early decision plan 2).

CONTACT

Mr. John O. Gaines, Director of Undergraduate Admissions, Vanderbilt University, 2305 West End Avenue, Nashville, TN 37203. *Phone:* 615-936-2811. *Toll-free phone:* 800-288-0432. *Fax:* 615-343-8326. *E-mail:* admissions@vanderbilt.edu.

See page 1714 for the College Close-Up.

Watkins College of Art, Design, & Film

Nashville, Tennessee

http://www.watkins.edu/

- **Independent** 4-year, founded 1885
- **Urban** 13-acre campus
- **Endowment** $1.8 million
- **Coed** 362 undergraduate students, 69% full-time, 54% women, 46% men
- **Moderately difficult** entrance level, 94% of applicants were admitted

UNDERGRAD STUDENTS

251 full-time, 111 part-time. Students come from 25 states and territories; 4 other countries; 27% are from out of state; 12% Black or African American, non-Hispanic/Latino; 5% Hispanic/Latino; 0.8% Asian, non-Hispanic/Latino; 0.3% Native Hawaiian or other Pacific Islander, non-Hispanic/Latino; 0.3% American Indian or Alaska Native, non-Hispanic/Latino; 6% Two or more races, non-Hispanic/Latino; 2% Race/ethnicity unknown; 1% international; 24% live on campus.

Freshmen

Admission: 89 applied, 84 admitted. ***Average high school GPA:*** 3. ***Test scores:*** SAT writing scores over 500: 50%; ACT scores over 18: 79%; SAT writing scores over 600: 10%; ACT scores over 24: 20%.

Retention: 70% of full-time freshmen returned.

FACULTY

Total: 56, 36% full-time, 64% with terminal degrees.

Student/faculty ratio: 13:1.

ACADEMICS

Calendar: semesters. *Degree:* certificates and bachelor's.

Special study options: advanced placement credit, cooperative education, independent study, internships, part-time degree program, services for LD students, summer session for credit.

Computers: 200 computers/terminals and 175 ports are available on campus for general student use. Students can access the following: campus intranet, computer help desk, free student e-mail accounts, online (class) grades, online (class) registration, online (class) schedules. Campuswide network is available. 100% of college-owned or -operated housing units are wired for high-speed Internet access. Wireless service is available via entire campus.

STUDENT LIFE

Housing options: on-campus residence required for freshman year; men-only, women-only, special housing for students with disabilities. Campus housing is university owned. Freshman applicants given priority for college housing.

Activities and organizations: Company Q (art society), Film club, sports club, student government.

Campus security: 24-hour emergency response devices and patrols, late-night transport/escort service, controlled dormitory access, monitored 24 hour camera security.

Student services: health clinic, personal/psychological counseling.

COSTS & FINANCIAL AID

Costs (2014–15) ***Tuition:*** $20,850 full-time, $695 per credit part-time. ***Required fees:*** $1650 full-time, $55 per credit part-time. ***Room only:*** $6380. ***Payment plan:*** installment. ***Waivers:*** employees or children of employees.

Financial Aid Of all full-time matriculated undergraduates who enrolled in 2008, 174 applied for aid, 174 were judged to have need, 30 had their need fully met. 17 Federal Work-Study jobs (averaging $1300). 25 state and other part-time jobs (averaging $2000). In 2008, 30 non-need-based awards were made. ***Average percent of need met:*** 45. ***Average financial aid package:*** $11,150. ***Average need-based loan:*** $4750. ***Average need-based gift aid:*** $4000. ***Average non-need-based aid:*** $4000. ***Average indebtedness upon graduation:*** $15,000.

APPLYING

Standardized Tests *Required:* SAT or ACT (for admission).

Options: electronic application, early admission, deferred entrance.

Application fee: $50.

Required: essay or personal statement, high school transcript, minimum 2.6 GPA, 1 letter of recommendation. ***Required for some:*** high school transcript, artistic exercises, optional portfolio. ***Recommended:*** interview.

Application deadlines: 7/15 (freshmen), 7/15 (transfers).

Notification: 8/1 (freshmen), 8/1 (transfers).

CONTACT

Ms. Linda E. Schwab, Director of Admissions, Watkins College of Art, Design, & Film, 2298 Rosa L. Parks Boulevard, Nashville, TN 37228. *Phone:* 615-383-4848 Ext. 7458. *Fax:* 615-383-4849. *E-mail:* admissions@watkins.edu.

Welch College

Nashville, Tennessee

http://www.welch.edu/

- **Independent Free Will Baptist** 4-year, founded 1942
- **Urban** 8-acre campus with easy access to Nashville
- **Endowment** $1.5 million
- **Coed** 328 undergraduate students, 73% full-time, 45% women, 55% men
- **Noncompetitive** entrance level, 100% of applicants were admitted

UNDERGRAD STUDENTS

241 full-time, 87 part-time. Students come from 24 states and territories; 3 other countries; 53% are from out of state; 10% Black or African American, non-Hispanic/Latino; 3% Hispanic/Latino; 0.7% Asian, non-Hispanic/Latino; 0.4% American Indian or Alaska Native, non-Hispanic/Latino; 2% Two or more races, non-Hispanic/Latino; 3% Race/ethnicity unknown; 10% transferred in; 59% live on campus.

Freshmen

Admission: 66 applied, 66 admitted, 56 enrolled. ***Average high school GPA:*** 3.34. ***Test scores:*** SAT critical reading scores over 500: 71%; SAT math scores over 500: 78%; SAT writing scores over 500: 80%; ACT scores over 18: 74%; SAT critical reading scores over 600: 43%; SAT math scores over 600: 31%; SAT writing scores over 600: 40%; ACT scores over 24: 36%; SAT critical reading scores over 700: 11%; SAT writing scores over 700: 20%; ACT scores over 30: 3%.

Retention: 66% of full-time freshmen returned.

FACULTY

Total: 47, 49% full-time, 45% with terminal degrees.

Student/faculty ratio: 9:1.

ACADEMICS

Calendar: semesters. *Degrees:* associate and bachelor's.

Special study options: academic remediation for entering students, advanced placement credit, distance learning, double majors, internships, part-time degree program, student-designed majors, summer session for credit. ***ROTC:*** Army (c), Air Force (c).

Unusual degree programs: nursing.

Computers: 41 computers/terminals are available on campus for general student use. Students can access the following: campus intranet, computer help desk, free student e-mail accounts, online (class) grades, online (class) schedules. Campuswide network is available. Wireless service is available via computer centers, computer labs, dorm rooms, libraries, student centers.

STUDENT LIFE

Housing options: on-campus residence required through senior year; men-only, women-only. Campus housing is university owned. Freshman campus housing is guaranteed.

Activities and organizations: drama/theater group, choral group, GMF-Global Missions Fellowship, Four Women's Societies, Four Men's Societies.

Athletics Member NCCAA. ***Intercollegiate sports:*** basketball M/W, golf M/W, volleyball W. ***Intramural sports:*** basketball M/W, tennis M/W, ultimate Frisbee M/W, volleyball M/W.

Campus security: 24-hour emergency response devices, student patrols, late-night transport/escort service, controlled dormitory access.

Student services: personal/psychological counseling.

COSTS & FINANCIAL AID

Costs (2014–15) ***Comprehensive fee:*** $23,733 includes full-time tuition ($16,891) and room and board ($6842). Part-time tuition: $578 per credit hour. ***Room and board:*** Room and board charges vary according to board plan. ***Payment plans:*** installment, deferred payment. ***Waivers:*** employees or children of employees.

Financial Aid Of all full-time matriculated undergraduates who enrolled in 2011, 178 applied for aid, 172 were judged to have need. 7 Federal Work-Study jobs (averaging $1871). 101 state and other part-time jobs (averaging $1960). ***Average percent of need met:*** 71. ***Average financial aid package:*** $5331. ***Average need-based loan:*** $2195. ***Average need-based gift aid:*** $4214. ***Average indebtedness upon graduation:*** $19,688.

APPLYING

Standardized Tests *Required:* SAT or ACT (for admission).

Options: electronic application, early admission, deferred entrance.

Application fee: $35.

Required: essay or personal statement, high school transcript, 3 letters of recommendation, medical history.

Application deadlines: rolling (freshmen), rolling (out-of-state freshmen), rolling (transfers).

Notification: continuous (freshmen), continuous (out-of-state freshmen), continuous (transfers).

CONTACT

Mrs. Debbie Mouser, Director of Enrollment Services, Welch College, 3606 West End Avenue, Nashville, TN 37205. *Phone:* 615-844-5222. *Toll-free phone:* 800-763-9222. *Fax:* 615-269-6028. *E-mail:* dmouser@welch.edu.

Williamson Christian College

Franklin, Tennessee

http://www.williamsoncc.edu/

- **Independent interdenominational** comprehensive, founded 1997
- **Suburban** 1-acre campus with easy access to Nashville
- **Coed** 62 undergraduate students, 98% full-time, 53% women, 47% men
- **Noncompetitive** entrance level

UNDERGRAD STUDENTS

61 full-time, 1 part-time. Students come from 2 states and territories; 4 other countries; 5% Black or African American, non-Hispanic/Latino; 5% Hispanic/Latino; 15% Asian, non-Hispanic/Latino; 2% American Indian or Alaska Native, non-Hispanic/Latino; 11% transferred in.

Freshmen

Admission: 4 enrolled. ***Average high school GPA:*** 3.25.

Retention: 73% of full-time freshmen returned.

FACULTY

Total: 17, 29% full-time.

Student/faculty ratio: 5:1.

ACADEMICS

Calendar: semesters. *Degrees:* associate, bachelor's, and master's.

Special study options: accelerated degree program, adult/continuing education programs, advanced placement credit, distance learning, double majors, external degree program, independent study, internships, part-time degree program.

Computers: 3 computers/terminals are available on campus for general student use. Wireless service is available via entire campus.

STUDENT LIFE

Housing options: college housing not available.

Student services: health clinic, personal/psychological counseling.

COSTS & FINANCIAL AID

Costs (2014–15) ***Tuition:*** $10,125 full-time, $400 per credit hour part-time. Full-time tuition and fees vary according to course load. ***Required fees:*** $260 full-time, $260 per year part-time. ***Payment plan:*** installment.

Financial Aid Of all full-time matriculated undergraduates who enrolled in 2003, 11 applied for aid, 10 were judged to have need, 1 had their need fully met. 2 Federal Work-Study jobs (averaging $2000). ***Average percent of need met:*** 50. ***Average financial aid package:*** $4858. ***Average need-based gift aid:*** $2556.

APPLYING

Standardized Tests *Required for some:* SAT or ACT (for admission).

Options: early admission, deferred entrance.

Application fee: $25.

Required: essay or personal statement, high school transcript, minimum 2.0 GPA. ***Required for some:*** interview.

Application deadlines: 9/1 (freshmen), 9/1 (transfers).

Notification: continuous until 10/1 (freshmen), continuous until 10/1 (transfers).

CONTACT

Ms. Laura Flowers, Recruiter, Williamson Christian College, 274 Mallory Station Road, Franklin, TN 37067. *Phone:* 615-771-7821. *Fax:* 615-771-7810. *E-mail:* laura@williamsoncc.edu.

TEXAS

Abilene Christian University

Abilene, Texas

http://www.acu.edu/

- **Independent** university, founded 1906, affiliated with Church of Christ
- **Urban** 208-acre campus
- **Endowment** $370.4 million
- **Coed** 3,650 undergraduate students, 94% full-time, 57% women, 43% men
- **Moderately difficult** entrance level, 50% of applicants were admitted

UNDERGRAD STUDENTS

3,417 full-time, 233 part-time. Students come from 48 states and territories; 37 other countries; 14% are from out of state; 8% Black or African American, non-Hispanic/Latino; 14% Hispanic/Latino; 0.8% Asian, non-Hispanic/Latino; 0.4% American Indian or Alaska Native, non-Hispanic/Latino; 5% Two or more races, non-Hispanic/Latino; 2% Race/ethnicity unknown; 4% international; 3% transferred in; 47% live on campus.

Freshmen

Admission: 9,384 applied, 4,736 admitted, 974 enrolled. ***Average high school GPA:*** 3.7. ***Test scores:*** SAT critical reading scores over 500: 67%; SAT math scores over 500: 72%; SAT writing scores over 500: 86%; ACT scores over 18: 98%; SAT critical reading scores over 600: 22%; SAT math scores over 600: 27%; SAT writing scores over 600: 34%; ACT scores over 24: 57%; SAT critical reading scores over 700: 5%; SAT math scores over 700: 4%; SAT writing scores over 700: 5%; ACT scores over 30: 13%.

Retention: 75% of full-time freshmen returned.

FACULTY

Total: 382, 66% full-time, 59% with terminal degrees.

Student/faculty ratio: 14:1.

ACADEMICS

Calendar: semesters. *Degrees:* certificates, associate, bachelor's, master's, doctoral, post-master's, and postbachelor's certificates.

Special study options: advanced placement credit, distance learning, double majors, English as a second language, honors programs, independent study, internships, off-campus study, part-time degree program, services for LD students, student-designed majors, study abroad, summer session for credit.

Computers: 430 computers/terminals and 3,900 ports are available on campus for general student use. Students can access the following: campus intranet, computer help desk, free student e-mail accounts, online (class) grades, online (class) registration, online (class) schedules. Campuswide network is available. 100% of college-owned or -operated housing units are wired for high-speed Internet access. Wireless service is available via entire campus.

STUDENT LIFE

Housing options: on-campus residence required through sophomore year; men-only, women-only. Campus housing is university owned. Freshman campus housing is guaranteed.

Activities and organizations: drama/theater group, student-run newspaper, radio and television station, choral group, marching band, Student Association, Graduate Students Association, Spring Break Campaigns, International Students Association, LYNAY.

Athletics Member NCAA. All Division I. ***Intercollegiate sports:*** baseball M(s), basketball M(s)/W(s), cross-country running M(s)/W(s), football M(s), golf M(s), soccer W(s), softball W(s), tennis M(s)/W(s), track and field M(s)/W(s), volleyball W(s). ***Intramural sports:*** basketball M/W, bowling M/W, football M/W, golf M/W, racquetball M/W, soccer M/W, softball M/W, tennis M/W, volleyball M/W, water polo M/W.

Campus security: 24-hour emergency response devices and patrols, student patrols, late-night transport/escort service, controlled dormitory access.

Student services: health clinic, personal/psychological counseling.

COSTS & FINANCIAL AID

Costs (2014–15) ***Comprehensive fee:*** $38,450 includes full-time tuition ($29,450) and room and board ($9000). Full-time tuition and fees vary according to course load. Part-time tuition: $1090 per credit hour. Part-time tuition and fees vary according to course load. ***College room only:*** $4180. Room and board charges vary according to board plan and housing facility. ***Payment plans:*** tuition prepayment, installment. ***Waivers:*** employees or children of employees.

Financial Aid Of all full-time matriculated undergraduates who enrolled in 2014, 2,696 applied for aid, 2,272 were judged to have need, 608 had their need fully met. In 2014, 1136 non-need-based awards were made. ***Average percent of need met:*** 69. ***Average financial aid package:*** $20,931. ***Average need-based loan:*** $4424. ***Average need-based gift aid:*** $18,066. ***Average non-need-based aid:*** $10,590. ***Average indebtedness upon graduation:*** $43,841.

APPLYING

Standardized Tests *Required:* SAT or ACT (for admission).

Options: electronic application, early admission, early action.

Application fee: $50.

Required: high school transcript. ***Required for some:*** essay or personal statement.

Application deadlines: 2/15 (freshmen), rolling (transfers).

Notification: 3/15 (freshmen), continuous until 9/1 (transfers).

CONTACT

Admissions, Abilene Christian University, ACU Box 29000, Abilene, TX 79699-9000. *Phone:* 325-674-2650. *Toll-free phone:* 800-460-6228. *Fax:* 325-674-2130. *E-mail:* info@admissions.acu.edu.

Angelo State University

San Angelo, Texas

http://www.angelo.edu/

- **State-supported** comprehensive, founded 1928, part of Texas Tech University System
- **Urban** 268-acre campus
- **Endowment** $130.8 million
- **Coed** 5,425 undergraduate students, 86% full-time, 54% women, 46% men
- **Moderately difficult** entrance level, 89% of applicants were admitted

UNDERGRAD STUDENTS

4,646 full-time, 779 part-time. Students come from 47 states and territories; 29 other countries; 3% are from out of state; 8% Black or African American, non-Hispanic/Latino; 31% Hispanic/Latino; 0.9% Asian, non-Hispanic/Latino; 0.2% Native Hawaiian or other Pacific Islander, non-Hispanic/Latino; 0.4% American Indian or Alaska Native, non-Hispanic/Latino; 3% Two or more races, non-Hispanic/Latino; 1% Race/ethnicity unknown; 3% international; 6% transferred in; 32% live on campus.

Freshmen

Admission: 3,291 applied, 2,944 admitted, 1,316 enrolled. ***Test scores:*** SAT critical reading scores over 500: 38%; SAT math scores over 500: 41%; SAT writing scores over 500: 27%; ACT scores over 18: 72%; SAT critical reading scores over 600: 9%; SAT math scores over 600: 11%; SAT writing scores over 600: 5%; ACT scores over 24: 35%; SAT critical reading scores over 700: 1%; SAT math scores over 700: 1%; SAT writing scores over 700: 1%; ACT scores over 30: 3%.

Retention: 62% of full-time freshmen returned.

FACULTY

Total: 351, 80% full-time, 67% with terminal degrees.

Student/faculty ratio: 18:1.

ACADEMICS

Calendar: semesters. *Degrees:* bachelor's, master's, and doctoral.

Special study options: academic remediation for entering students, advanced placement credit, distance learning, double majors, English as a second language, honors programs, independent study, internships, part-time degree program, study abroad, summer session for credit. ***ROTC:*** Air Force (b).

Unusual degree programs: 3-2 business administration with accounting.

Computers: 640 computers/terminals and 3,900 ports are available on campus for general student use. Students can access the following: campus intranet, computer help desk, free student e-mail accounts, online (class) grades, online (class) registration, online (class) schedules, online courses, tuition payments, purchase books, purchase parking permits, university calendar, library card catalog and library resources. Discounted hardware and software programs for personally owned computers. Campuswide network is available. 100% of college-owned or -operated housing units are wired for high-speed Internet access. Wireless service is available via entire campus.

STUDENT LIFE

Housing options: on-campus residence required through sophomore year; coed, special housing for students with disabilities. Campus housing is university owned.

Activities and organizations: drama/theater group, student-run newspaper, radio and television station, choral group, marching band, Association of Mexican-American Students, Block and Bridle Club, Air force ROTC, University Center Program Council, Baptist Student Union, national fraternities, national sororities.

Athletics Member NCAA. All Division II. ***Intercollegiate sports:*** baseball M(s), basketball M(s)/W(s), cross-country running M(s)/W(s), football M(s), golf W(s), soccer W(s), softball W(s), track and field M(s)/W(s), volleyball W(s). ***Intramural sports:*** badminton M/W, basketball M/W, bowling M/W, football M/W, golf M/W, racquetball M/W, soccer M/W, softball M/W, swimming and diving M/W, table tennis M/W, tennis M/W, ultimate Frisbee M/W, volleyball M/W, weight lifting M/W.

Campus security: 24-hour emergency response devices and patrols, student patrols, late-night transport/escort service, controlled dormitory access.

Student services: health clinic, personal/psychological counseling.

COSTS & FINANCIAL AID

Costs (2014–15) ***Tuition:*** state resident $4700 full-time, $157 per credit hour part-time; nonresident $15,560 full-time, $519 per credit hour part-time. ***Required fees:*** $2942 full-time. ***Room and board:*** $7602.

Financial Aid Of all full-time matriculated undergraduates who enrolled in 2013, 4,169 applied for aid, 3,512 were judged to have need, 455 had their need fully met. In 2013, 627 non-need-based awards were made. ***Average percent of need met:*** 65. ***Average financial aid package:*** $10,579. ***Average need-based loan:*** $4024. ***Average need-based gift aid:*** $3315. ***Average non-need-based aid:*** $3210. ***Average indebtedness upon graduation:*** $25,728.

APPLYING

Standardized Tests *Required:* SAT or ACT (for admission).

Options: electronic application, early admission, deferred entrance.

Application fee: $35.

Required: high school transcript, high school class rank.

Application deadlines: rolling (freshmen), rolling (out-of-state freshmen), rolling (transfers).

Notification: continuous (freshmen), continuous (out-of-state freshmen), continuous (transfers).

CONTACT

Ms. Sharla Adam, Director of Admissions, Angelo State University, 2601 West Avenue N, San Angelo, TX 76909. *Phone:* 325-942-2185. *Toll-free phone:* 800-946-8627. *Fax:* 325-942-2078. *E-mail:* admissions@angelo.edu.

Argosy University, Dallas

Farmers Branch, Texas

http://www.argosy.edu/dallas-texas/default.aspx

- **Proprietary** university, founded 2002, part of Education Management Corporation
- **Urban** campus
- **Coed**

ACADEMICS

Calendar: semesters. *Degrees:* certificates, associate, bachelor's, master's, and doctoral.

CONTACT

Argosy University, Dallas, 5001 Lyndon B. Johnson Freeway, Heritage Square, Farmers Branch, TX 75244. *Phone:* 214-890-9900. *Toll-free phone:* 866-954-9900.

The Art Institute of Austin, a branch of The Art Institute of Houston

Austin, Texas

http://www.artinstitutes.edu/austin

- **Proprietary** 4-year, part of Education Management Corporation
- **Coed**

ACADEMICS

Degrees: diplomas, associate, and bachelor's.

CONTACT

The Art Institute of Austin, a branch of The Art Institute of Houston, 101 W. Louis Henna Boulevard, Suite 100, Austin, TX 78728. *Phone:* 512-691-1707. *Toll-free phone:* 866-583-7952.

The Art Institute of Dallas, a campus of South University

Dallas, Texas

http://www.artinstitutes.edu/dallas/

- **Proprietary** comprehensive, founded 1978, part of Education Management Corporation
- **Urban** 2-acre campus
- **Coed**

ACADEMICS

Calendar: quarters. *Degrees:* certificates, associate, bachelor's, and master's.

CONTACT

The Art Institute of Dallas, a campus of South University, 8080 Park Lane, Suite 100, Dallas, TX 75231-5993. *Phone:* 214-692-8080. *Toll-free phone:* 800-275-4243.

The Art Institute of Fort Worth, a campus of South University

Fort Worth, Texas

http://www.artinstitutes.edu/fort-worth/

- **Proprietary** 4-year
- **Coed**

ACADEMICS

Degrees: certificates, associate, and bachelor's.

CONTACT

The Art Institute of Fort Worth, a campus of South University, 7000 Calmont Avenue, Suite 150, Fort Worth, TX 76116. *Phone:* 817-210-0808. *Toll-free phone:* 888-422-9686.

The Art Institute of Houston

Houston, Texas

http://www.artinstitutes.edu/houston/

- **Proprietary** 4-year, founded 1978, part of Education Management Corporation
- **Urban** campus
- **Coed**

ACADEMICS

Calendar: quarters. *Degrees:* diplomas, associate, and bachelor's.

CONTACT

The Art Institute of Houston, 4140 Southwest Freeway, Houston, TX 77027. *Phone:* 713-623-2040. *Toll-free phone:* 800-275-4244.

The Art Institute of Houston–North, a branch of The Art Institute of Houston

Houston, Texas

http://www.artinstitutes.edu/houston-north

- **Proprietary** 4-year
- **Coed**

ACADEMICS

Degrees: diplomas, associate, and bachelor's.

CONTACT

The Art Institute of Houston–North, a branch of The Art Institute of Houston, 10740 North Gessner Drive, Suite 190, Houston, TX 77064. *Phone:* 281-671-3381. *Toll-free phone:* 866-830-4450.

The Art Institute of San Antonio, a branch of The Art Institute of Houston

San Antonio, Texas

http://www.artinstitutes.edu/san-antonio/

- **Proprietary** 4-year
- **Coed**

ACADEMICS

Degrees: diplomas, associate, and bachelor's.

CONTACT

The Art Institute of San Antonio, a branch of The Art Institute of Houston, 1000 IH-10 West, Suite 200, San Antonio, TX 78230. *Phone:* 210-338-7320. *Toll-free phone:* 888-222-0040.

Austin College

Sherman, Texas

http://www.austincollege.edu/

- **Independent Presbyterian** comprehensive, founded 1849
- **Small-town** 60-acre campus with easy access to Dallas-Fort Worth
- **Endowment** $135.8 million
- **Coed** 1,278 undergraduate students, 99% full-time, 52% women, 48% men
- **Very difficult** entrance level, 54% of applicants were admitted

UNDERGRAD STUDENTS

1,271 full-time, 7 part-time. Students come from 32 states and territories; 15 other countries; 10% are from out of state; 7% Black or African American, non-Hispanic/Latino; 19% Hispanic/Latino; 14% Asian, non-Hispanic/Latino; 0.1% Native Hawaiian or other Pacific Islander, non-Hispanic/Latino; 1% American Indian or Alaska Native, non-Hispanic/Latino; 0.3% Two or more races, non-Hispanic/Latino; 0.3%

Race/ethnicity unknown; 3% international; 4% transferred in; 77% live on campus.

Freshmen

Admission: 3,038 applied, 1,652 admitted, 357 enrolled. ***Average high school GPA:*** 3.45. ***Test scores:*** SAT critical reading scores over 500: 90%; SAT math scores over 500: 90%; SAT writing scores over 500: 84%; ACT scores over 18: 99%; SAT critical reading scores over 600: 50%; SAT math scores over 600: 53%; SAT writing scores over 600: 44%; ACT scores over 24: 61%; SAT critical reading scores over 700: 17%; SAT math scores over 700: 11%; SAT writing scores over 700: 9%; ACT scores over 30: 9%.

Retention: 86% of full-time freshmen returned.

FACULTY

Total: 107, 85% full-time, 93% with terminal degrees.

Student/faculty ratio: 12:1.

ACADEMICS

Calendar: 4-1-4. *Degrees:* bachelor's and master's.

Special study options: adult/continuing education programs, advanced placement credit, double majors, honors programs, independent study, internships, off-campus study, part-time degree program, services for LD students, student-designed majors, study abroad, summer session for credit.

Unusual degree programs: 3-2 engineering with University of Texas at Dallas, Texas A&M University, Washington University in St. Louis, Columbia University.

Computers: 160 computers/terminals are available on campus for general student use. Students can access the following: campus intranet, computer help desk, free student e-mail accounts, online (class) grades, online (class) registration, online (class) schedules. Campuswide network is available. 100% of college-owned or -operated housing units are wired for high-speed Internet access. Wireless service is available via entire campus.

STUDENT LIFE

Housing options: on-campus residence required through junior year; coed, men-only, women-only, special housing for students with disabilities. Campus housing is university owned. Freshman campus housing is guaranteed.

Activities and organizations: drama/theater group, student-run newspaper, choral group, Inter-Varsity Christian Fellowship (IVCF), Campus Activity Board (CAB), Indian Cultural Association, Students Today Alumni Tomorrow (STAT), ACtivators.

Athletics Member NCAA. All Division III. ***Intercollegiate sports:*** baseball M, basketball M/W, cheerleading M(c)/W(c), cross-country running M/W, football M, soccer M/W, softball W, swimming and diving M/W, tennis M/W, volleyball W. ***Intramural sports:*** basketball M/W, football M/W, golf M(c)/W(c), soccer M/W, softball M/W, swimming and diving M/W, table tennis M/W, tennis M/W, ultimate Frisbee M/W, volleyball W.

Campus security: 24-hour emergency response devices and patrols, late-night transport/escort service, controlled dormitory access.

Student services: health clinic, personal/psychological counseling.

COSTS & FINANCIAL AID

Costs (2014–15) ***One-time required fee:*** $25. ***Comprehensive fee:*** $46,343 includes full-time tuition ($34,655), mandatory fees ($185), and room and board ($11,503). Full-time tuition and fees vary according to student level. Part-time tuition: $5025 per course. ***College room only:*** $5360. Room and board charges vary according to board plan. ***Payment plan:*** installment. ***Waivers:*** employees or children of employees.

Financial Aid Of all full-time matriculated undergraduates who enrolled in 2013, 933 applied for aid, 809 were judged to have need, 175 had their need fully met. 326 Federal Work-Study jobs (averaging $1847). 117 state and other part-time jobs (averaging $1448). In 2013, 124 non-need-based awards were made. ***Average percent of need met:*** 77. ***Average financial aid package:*** $28,827. ***Average need-based loan:*** $5027. ***Average need-based gift aid:*** $23,329. ***Average non-need-based aid:*** $17,460.

APPLYING

Standardized Tests *Required:* SAT or ACT (for admission).

Options: electronic application, early action, deferred entrance.

Required: essay or personal statement, high school transcript, 2 letters of recommendation. ***Recommended:*** minimum 3.0 GPA, interview.

Application deadlines: 5/1 (freshmen), 5/1 (transfers).

CONTACT

Mrs. Nan Davis, Vice President for Institutional Enrollment, Austin College, 900 North Grand Avenue, Suite 6N, Sherman, TX 75090-4400. *Phone:* 903-813-3000. *Toll-free phone:* 800-596-4276 (in-state); 800-526.4276 (out-of-state). *Fax:* 903-813-3198. *E-mail:* admission@austincollege.edu.

Baptist University of the Americas

San Antonio, Texas

http://www.bua.edu/

- **Independent Baptist** 4-year, founded 1947
- **Urban** 90-acre campus with easy access to San Antonio
- **Endowment** $2.9 million
- **Coed** 168 undergraduate students, 70% full-time, 46% women, 54% men

UNDERGRAD STUDENTS

118 full-time, 50 part-time. Students come from 12 states and territories; 14 other countries; 5% are from out of state; 2% Black or African American, non-Hispanic/Latino; 67% Hispanic/Latino; 0.6% Asian, non-Hispanic/Latino; 24% international; 7% transferred in; 46% live on campus.

Freshmen

Admission: 22 enrolled.

Retention: 80% of full-time freshmen returned.

FACULTY

Total: 8, 100% full-time, 38% with terminal degrees.

Student/faculty ratio: 11:1.

ACADEMICS

Calendar: semesters. *Degrees:* certificates, diplomas, associate, bachelor's, and postbachelor's certificates (associate degree in Cross-Cultural Studies).

Special study options: academic remediation for entering students, advanced placement credit, double majors, English as a second language, honors programs, independent study, internships, part-time degree program, services for LD students.

Computers: 56 computers/terminals and 42 ports are available on campus for general student use. Students can access the following: campus intranet, computer help desk, free student e-mail accounts, online (class) grades, online (class) registration, online (class) schedules. Campuswide network is available. 100% of college-owned or -operated housing units are wired for high-speed Internet access. Wireless service is available via entire campus.

STUDENT LIFE

Housing options: coed, men-only, women-only, special housing for students with disabilities. Campus housing is university owned. Freshman campus housing is guaranteed.

Activities and organizations: choral group, Communities In Schools, Missions Society, Navigators, Student Council/Embajadores, BSM.

Athletics ***Intramural sports:*** soccer M(c).

Campus security: 24-hour emergency response devices, student patrols, late-night transport/escort service, Gate code is required to enter the residence area.

Student services: personal/psychological counseling.

COSTS & FINANCIAL AID

Costs (2015–16) ***Tuition:*** $5040 full-time, $210 per credit part-time. ***Required fees:*** $720 full-time. ***Room only:*** $2500. Room and board charges vary according to housing facility. ***Payment plan:*** installment. ***Waivers:*** employees or children of employees.

Financial Aid Of all full-time matriculated undergraduates who enrolled in 2013, 1 Federal Work-Study job (averaging $600). 67 state and other part-time jobs (averaging $3826).

APPLYING

Standardized Tests *Required:* SAT and SAT Subject Tests or ACT (for admission), ACCUPLACER, THEA (Texas Higher Education

Assessment), CPT (Computer Proficiency Test) (for admission). *Required for some:* ACCUPLACER, THEA (Texas Higher Education Assessment), CPT (Computer Proficiency Test). *Recommended:* SAT and SAT Subject Tests or ACT (for admission), ACCUPLACER, THEA (Texas Higher Education Assessment), CPT (Computer Proficiency Test).

Required: essay or personal statement, high school transcript, 3 letters of recommendation, Meningitis Vaccine for students under 30 years; Application Fee and 1 year prepaid tuition for international students. ***Required for some:*** interview.

CONTACT

Mrs. Alejandra Pichola, Admissions Counselor, Baptist University of the Americas, 8019 Pan Am Expressway, San Antonio, TX 78224. *Phone:* 210-924-4338 Ext. 229. *Toll-free phone:* 800-721-1396. *Fax:* 210-924-2701. *E-mail:* admissions@bua.edu.

Baylor University

Waco, Texas

http://www.baylor.edu/

- **Independent Baptist** university, founded 1845
- **Urban** 1000-acre campus with easy access to Dallas-Fort Worth
- **Endowment** $1.2 billion
- **Coed** 13,859 undergraduate students, 98% full-time, 58% women, 42% men
- **Moderately difficult** entrance level, 55% of applicants were admitted

UNDERGRAD STUDENTS

13,613 full-time, 246 part-time. Students come from 51 states and territories; 73 other countries; 26% are from out of state; 7% Black or African American, non-Hispanic/Latino; 14% Hispanic/Latino; 6% Asian, non-Hispanic/Latino; 0.1% Native Hawaiian or other Pacific Islander, non-Hispanic/Latino; 0.4% American Indian or Alaska Native, non-Hispanic/Latino; 5% Two or more races, non-Hispanic/Latino; 0.2% Race/ethnicity unknown; 3% international; 3% transferred in; 38% live on campus.

Freshmen

Admission: 33,898 applied, 18,766 admitted, 3,625 enrolled. ***Test scores:*** SAT critical reading scores over 500: 95%; SAT math scores over 500: 97%; SAT writing scores over 500: 89%; ACT scores over 18: 100%; SAT critical reading scores over 600: 53%; SAT math scores over 600: 64%; SAT writing scores over 600: 45%; ACT scores over 24: 84%; SAT critical reading scores over 700: 14%; SAT math scores over 700: 17%; SAT writing scores over 700: 10%; ACT scores over 30: 26%.

Retention: 89% of full-time freshmen returned.

FACULTY

Total: 1,185, 81% full-time.

Student/faculty ratio: 15:1.

ACADEMICS

Calendar: semesters. *Degrees:* certificates, bachelor's, master's, doctoral, and post-master's certificates.

Special study options: accelerated degree program, advanced placement credit, double majors, honors programs, internships, part-time degree program, services for LD students, student-designed majors, study abroad, summer session for credit. ***ROTC:*** Army (b), Air Force (b).

Unusual degree programs: 3-2 clinical laboratory science.

Computers: Students can access the following: campus intranet, computer help desk, free student e-mail accounts, online (class) grades, online (class) registration, online (class) schedules. Campuswide network is available. 99% of college-owned or -operated housing units are wired for high-speed Internet access. Wireless service is available via entire campus.

STUDENT LIFE

Housing options: on-campus residence required for freshman year; coed, men-only, women-only, special housing for students with disabilities. Campus housing is university owned. Freshman campus housing is guaranteed.

Activities and organizations: drama/theater group, student-run newspaper, radio and television station, choral group, marching band, The Bear Pit, Alpha Lambda Delta, Delta Epsilon Iota, National Society of Collegiate Scholars, American Medical Student Association, national fraternities, national sororities.

Athletics Member NCAA. All Division I except football (Division I-A). ***Intercollegiate sports:*** baseball M(s), basketball M(s)/W(s), cheerleading M(s)/W(s), crew M(c)/W(c), cross-country running M(s)/W(s), equestrian sports W(s), fencing M(c)/W(c), golf M(s)/W(s), gymnastics M(c)/W(c), ice hockey M(c), lacrosse M(c)/W(c), rock climbing M(c)/W(c), rugby M(c), sailing M(c)/W(c), skiing (downhill) M(c)/W(c), soccer M(c)/W(s), softball W(s), tennis M(s)/W(s), track and field M(s)/W(s), ultimate Frisbee M(c), volleyball M(c)/W(s), water polo M(c)/W(c). ***Intramural sports:*** basketball M/W, cross-country running M/W, football M/W, racquetball M/W, soccer M/W, softball M/W, table tennis M/W, tennis M/W, ultimate Frisbee M/W, volleyball M/W.

Campus security: 24-hour emergency response devices and patrols, late-night transport/escort service, controlled dormitory access, bicycle patrols.

Student services: health clinic, personal/psychological counseling, legal services.

COSTS & FINANCIAL AID

Costs (2015–16) ***Comprehensive fee:*** $51,558 includes full-time tuition ($36,360), mandatory fees ($3838), and room and board ($11,360). Part-time tuition: $1515 per semester hour. ***Required fees:*** $160 per semester hour part-time. ***College room only:*** $6160. Room and board charges vary according to board plan and housing facility. ***Payment plan:*** installment. ***Waivers:*** employees or children of employees.

Financial Aid Of all full-time matriculated undergraduates who enrolled in 2014, 9,114 applied for aid, 7,694 were judged to have need, 1,226 had their need fully met. 5,367 Federal Work-Study jobs (averaging $2879). In 2014, 4682 non-need-based awards were made. ***Average percent of need met:*** 65. ***Average financial aid package:*** $26,017. ***Average need-based loan:*** $3782. ***Average need-based gift aid:*** $20,015. ***Average non-need-based aid:*** $13,131.

APPLYING

Standardized Tests *Required:* SAT or ACT (for admission).

Options: electronic application, early admission, early action.

Application fee: $50.

Required: high school transcript. ***Required for some:*** essay or personal statement, minimum 2.5 GPA, 2 letters of recommendation. ***Recommended:*** interview.

Application deadlines: 2/1 (freshmen), rolling (transfers), 11/1 (early action).

Notification: 3/15 (freshmen), continuous (transfers), 1/15 (early action).

CONTACT

Ms. Jessica King Gereghty, Director of Admissions, Baylor University, PO Box 97056, Waco, TX 76798. *Phone:* 254-710-3435. *Toll-free phone:* 800-BAYLORU. *Fax:* 254-710-3436. *E-mail:* admissions@baylor.edu.

Brown Mackie College–Dallas/Ft. Worth

Bedford, Texas

http://www.brownmackie.edu/dallas/

- **Proprietary** 4-year
- **Coed**

ACADEMICS

Degrees: diplomas, associate, and bachelor's.

CONTACT

Brown Mackie College–Dallas/Ft. Worth, 2200 Hwy 121, Suite 270, Bedford, TX 76021. *Phone:* 817-799-0500.

Brown Mackie College–San Antonio

San Antonio, Texas

http://www.brownmackie.edu/san-antonio

- **Proprietary** 4-year, part of Education Management Corporation
- **Coed**

ACADEMICS

Degrees: diplomas, associate, and bachelor's.

CONTACT
Brown Mackie College–San Antonio, 4715 Fredericksburg Road, Suite 100, San Antonio, TX 78229. *Phone:* 210-428-2210. *Toll-free phone:* 877-460-1714.

Chamberlain College of Nursing

Houston, Texas

http://www.chamberlain.edu/

- **Proprietary** 4-year
- **Coed**
- **Moderately difficult** entrance level

FACULTY
Student/faculty ratio: 9:1.

ACADEMICS
Degree: bachelor's.

STUDENT LIFE
Housing options: college housing not available.

COSTS
Costs (2014–15) ***Tuition:*** $17,160 full-time, $665 per credit hour part-time. Full-time tuition and fees vary according to course load. Part-time tuition and fees vary according to course load. ***Required fees:*** $600 full-time.

APPLYING
Standardized Tests *Required:* SAT or ACT (for admission).
Application fee: $95.

CONTACT
Director of Recruitment, Chamberlain College of Nursing, 11025 Equity Drive, Houston, TX 77041. *Phone:* 713-277-9800.

College of Biblical Studies–Houston

Houston, Texas

http://www.cbshouston.edu/

- **Independent nondenominational** 4-year, founded 1979
- **Urban** 12-acre campus with easy access to Houston
- **Endowment** $1.4 million
- **Coed** 496 undergraduate students, 11% full-time, 45% women, 55% men
- **Noncompetitive** entrance level, 47% of applicants were admitted

UNDERGRAD STUDENTS
57 full-time, 439 part-time. Students come from 1 other state; 48% Black or African American, non-Hispanic/Latino; 30% Hispanic/Latino; 1% Asian, non-Hispanic/Latino; 3% Two or more races, non-Hispanic/Latino; 1% Race/ethnicity unknown; 10% transferred in.

Freshmen
Admission: 130 applied, 61 admitted, 42 enrolled.
Retention: 29% of full-time freshmen returned.

ACADEMICS
Calendar: trimesters. *Degrees:* certificates, associate, and bachelor's.
Special study options: academic remediation for entering students, accelerated degree program, adult/continuing education programs, cooperative education, distance learning, double majors, English as a second language, independent study, off-campus study, part-time degree program, services for LD students, summer session for credit.
Computers: 50 computers/terminals and 24 ports are available on campus for general student use. Students can access the following: computer help desk, free student e-mail accounts, online (class) grades, online (class) registration, online (class) schedules. Campuswide network is available. Wireless service is available via entire campus.

STUDENT LIFE
Housing options: college housing not available.
Activities and organizations: Student Ministries.
Campus security: 24-hour emergency response devices, late-night transport/escort service, hourly patrols by trained security guards and police.

COSTS & FINANCIAL AID
Costs (2014–15) ***Tuition:*** $6946 full-time, $274 per credit hour part-time. Full-time tuition and fees vary according to program. Part-time tuition and fees vary according to program. ***Required fees:*** $370 full-time, $185 per term part-time. ***Payment plans:*** installment, deferred payment. ***Waivers:*** employees or children of employees.
Financial Aid Of all full-time matriculated undergraduates who enrolled in 2013, 81 applied for aid, 81 were judged to have need, 32 had their need fully met. ***Average financial aid package:*** $10,902. ***Average need-based gift aid:*** $10,977. ***Average indebtedness upon graduation:*** $22,607. ***Financial aid deadline:*** 8/5.

APPLYING
Options: electronic application.
Application fee: $40.
Required: essay or personal statement, high school transcript. ***Required for some:*** interview.
Application deadlines: rolling (freshmen), rolling (out-of-state freshmen), rolling (transfers).

CONTACT
Admissions, College of Biblical Studies–Houston, 7000 Regency Square Boulevard, Houston, TX 77036. *Phone:* 832-252-3377. *Toll-free phone:* 844-227-9673. *Fax:* 713-532-8150. *E-mail:* admissions@cbshouston.edu.

Concordia University Texas

Austin, Texas

http://www.concordia.edu/

- **Independent** comprehensive, founded 1926, affiliated with Lutheran Church–Missouri Synod, part of Concordia University System
- **Urban** 385-acre campus with easy access to Austin
- **Coed** 1,567 undergraduate students, 76% full-time, 64% women, 36% men
- **Moderately difficult** entrance level, 83% of applicants were admitted

UNDERGRAD STUDENTS
1,192 full-time, 375 part-time. Students come from 29 states and territories; 2 other countries; 6% are from out of state; 12% Black or African American, non-Hispanic/Latino; 22% Hispanic/Latino; 3% Asian, non-Hispanic/Latino; 0.6% American Indian or Alaska Native, non-Hispanic/Latino; 13% Race/ethnicity unknown; 0.5% international; 5% transferred in; 13% live on campus.

Freshmen
Admission: 853 applied, 712 admitted, 242 enrolled. ***Average high school GPA:*** 3.3. ***Test scores:*** SAT critical reading scores over 500: 51%; SAT math scores over 500: 64%; SAT writing scores over 500: 43%; ACT scores over 18: 90%; SAT critical reading scores over 600: 14%; SAT math scores over 600: 14%; SAT writing scores over 600: 10%; ACT scores over 24: 30%; SAT critical reading scores over 700: 2%; SAT writing scores over 700: 2%; ACT scores over 30: 5%.
Retention: 61% of full-time freshmen returned.

FACULTY
Total: 302, 24% full-time, 60% with terminal degrees.
Student/faculty ratio: 11:1.

ACADEMICS
Calendar: semesters. *Degrees:* associate, bachelor's, and master's.
Special study options: academic remediation for entering students, accelerated degree program, adult/continuing education programs, advanced placement credit, honors programs, independent study, internships, part-time degree program, services for LD students, study abroad, summer session for credit. ***ROTC:*** Army (c), Air Force (c).
Computers: 25 computers/terminals and 50 ports are available on campus for general student use. Students can access the following: computer help desk, free student e-mail accounts, online (class) grades, online (class) registration, online (class) schedules. Campuswide network is available. 100% of college-owned or -operated housing units are wired for high-speed Internet access. Wireless service is available via entire campus.

STUDENT LIFE
Housing options: on-campus residence required for freshman year; coed. Campus housing is university owned. Freshman campus housing is guaranteed.

Activities and organizations: drama/theater group, student-run newspaper, radio station, choral group, student government, Business Club (The Executives), Education Club, Student Nursing Association, Student Athlete Advisory Committee.

Athletics Member NCAA. All Division III. ***Intercollegiate sports:*** baseball M, basketball M/W, cross-country running M/W, golf M/W, soccer M/W, softball W, track and field M/W, volleyball W. ***Intramural sports:*** badminton M/W, basketball M/W, football M/W, golf M/W, racquetball M/W, softball M/W, table tennis M/W, tennis M/W, volleyball M/W.

Campus security: student patrols, late-night transport/escort service, controlled dormitory access.

Student services: personal/psychological counseling.

COSTS & FINANCIAL AID
Costs (2015–16) ***Comprehensive fee:*** $37,444 includes full-time tuition ($27,600), mandatory fees ($560), and room and board ($9284). Full-time tuition and fees vary according to course load, degree level, and program. Part-time tuition: $905 per credit hour. Part-time tuition and fees vary according to course load, degree level, and program. ***College room only:*** $4954. Room and board charges vary according to board plan. ***Payment plan:*** installment. ***Waivers:*** employees or children of employees.

Financial Aid Of all full-time matriculated undergraduates who enrolled in 2014, 872 applied for aid, 763 were judged to have need, 124 had their need fully met. In 2014, 179 non-need-based awards were made. ***Average percent of need met:*** 74. ***Average financial aid package:*** $20,814. ***Average need-based loan:*** $5486. ***Average need-based gift aid:*** $15,528. ***Average non-need-based aid:*** $12,008. ***Average indebtedness upon graduation:*** $24,882.

APPLYING
Standardized Tests *Required:* SAT or ACT (for admission).

Options: electronic application, early admission, deferred entrance.

Application fee: $25.

Required: high school transcript, minimum 2.5 GPA. ***Required for some:*** essay or personal statement, interview.

Application deadlines: rolling (freshmen), rolling (transfers).

Notification: continuous (freshmen), continuous (transfers).

CONTACT
Ms. Kristin Coulter, Director of Admissions, Concordia University Texas, 11400 Concordia University Drive, Austin, TX 78726. *Phone:* 800-865-4282. *Toll-free phone:* 800-865-4282. *Fax:* 512-313-3999. *E-mail:* admissions@concordia.edu.

Dallas Baptist University

Dallas, Texas

http://www.dbu.edu/

- **Independent** comprehensive, founded 1965, affiliated with Baptist General Convention of Texas
- **Suburban** 293-acre campus with easy access to Dallas-Fort Worth
- **Endowment** $40.1 million
- **Coed** 3,457 undergraduate students, 69% full-time, 58% women, 42% men
- **Moderately difficult** entrance level, 46% of applicants were admitted

UNDERGRAD STUDENTS
2,397 full-time, 1,060 part-time. Students come from 41 states and territories; 42 other countries; 7% are from out of state; 15% Black or African American, non-Hispanic/Latino; 14% Hispanic/Latino; 2% Asian, non-Hispanic/Latino; 0.2% Native Hawaiian or other Pacific Islander, non-Hispanic/Latino; 0.7% American Indian or Alaska Native, non-Hispanic/Latino; 6% international; 8% transferred in; 55% live on campus.

Freshmen
Admission: 2,787 applied, 1,288 admitted, 494 enrolled. ***Average high school GPA:*** 3.5. ***Test scores:*** SAT critical reading scores over 500: 86%; SAT math scores over 500: 83%; ACT scores over 18: 93%; SAT critical reading scores over 600: 31%; SAT math scores over 600: 30%; ACT scores over 24: 29%; SAT critical reading scores over 700: 4%; SAT math scores over 700: 2%; ACT scores over 30: 3%.

Retention: 72% of full-time freshmen returned.

FACULTY
Total: 618, 21% full-time, 48% with terminal degrees.

Student/faculty ratio: 13:1.

ACADEMICS
Calendar: 4-1-4. *Degrees:* certificates, associate, bachelor's, master's, doctoral, post-master's, and postbachelor's certificates.

Special study options: academic remediation for entering students, accelerated degree program, adult/continuing education programs, advanced placement credit, distance learning, double majors, English as a second language, honors programs, independent study, internships, off-campus study, part-time degree program, services for LD students, study abroad, summer session for credit. ***ROTC:*** Army (c), Air Force (c).

Computers: 296 computers/terminals are available on campus for general student use. Students can access the following: computer help desk, free student e-mail accounts, online (class) grades, online (class) registration, online (class) schedules. Campuswide network is available. 100% of college-owned or -operated housing units are wired for high-speed Internet access. Wireless service is available via entire campus.

STUDENT LIFE
Housing options: on-campus residence required through senior year; men-only, women-only, special housing for students with disabilities. Campus housing is university owned and leased by the school. Freshman applicants given priority for college housing.

Activities and organizations: drama/theater group, choral group, Ministry Fellowship, Baptist Student Ministry, Student Government Association, Student Education Association, International Student Organization.

Athletics Member NCAA, NCCAA. All NCAA Division II except baseball (Division I). ***Intercollegiate sports:*** baseball M(s), basketball M(s), cheerleading W(c), cross-country running M/W(s), golf M/W(s), ice hockey M(c), lacrosse M(c), soccer M/W(s), swimming and diving M(c)/W(c), tennis M/W(s), track and field M/W(s), volleyball W(s). ***Intramural sports:*** badminton M/W, basketball M/W, football M/W, golf M/W, soccer M/W, softball M/W, table tennis M/W, tennis M/W, ultimate Frisbee M/W, volleyball M/W.

Campus security: 24-hour emergency response devices and patrols, late-night transport/escort service, controlled dormitory access.

Student services: health clinic, personal/psychological counseling.

COSTS & FINANCIAL AID
Costs (2014–15) ***Comprehensive fee:*** $30,580 includes full-time tuition ($23,250), mandatory fees ($400), and room and board ($6930). Part-time tuition: $775 per credit hour. ***Required fees:*** $200 per term part-time. ***College room only:*** $3313. Room and board charges vary according to board plan and housing facility. ***Payment plans:*** installment, deferred payment. ***Waivers:*** employees or children of employees.

Financial Aid Of all full-time matriculated undergraduates who enrolled in 2014, 1,965 applied for aid, 1,568 were judged to have need, 550 had their need fully met. 168 Federal Work-Study jobs (averaging $2279). 25 state and other part-time jobs (averaging $1324). In 2014, 429 non-need-based awards were made. ***Average percent of need met:*** 59. ***Average financial aid package:*** $15,583. ***Average need-based loan:*** $4146. ***Average need-based gift aid:*** $3987. ***Average non-need-based aid:*** $8219. ***Average indebtedness upon graduation:*** $28,279.

APPLYING
Standardized Tests *Required:* SAT or ACT (for admission).

Options: electronic application, early admission, deferred entrance.

Application fee: $25.

Required: essay or personal statement, high school transcript, minimum 2.5 GPA, rank in upper 50% of high school class. ***Recommended:*** interview.

Application deadlines: rolling (freshmen), rolling (out-of-state freshmen), rolling (transfers).

Notification: continuous (freshmen), continuous (out-of-state freshmen), continuous (transfers).

CONTACT
Mr. Bobby Soto, Director of Undergraduate Admissions, Dallas Baptist University, 3000 Mountain Creek Parkway, Dallas, TX 75211-9299. *Phone:* 214-333-5360. *Toll-free phone:* 800-460-1328. *Fax:* 214-333-5447. *E-mail:* admiss@dbu.edu.

Dallas Christian College
Dallas, Texas
http://www.dallas.edu/

- **Independent** 4-year, founded 1950, affiliated with Christian Churches and Churches of Christ
- **Urban** 22-acre campus with easy access to Dallas-Fort Worth
- **Endowment** $169,907
- **Coed**
- **Minimally difficult** entrance level

FACULTY
Student/faculty ratio: 16:1.

ACADEMICS
Calendar: semesters. *Degrees:* associate and bachelor's.

STUDENT LIFE
Housing options: on-campus residence required through sophomore year; men-only, women-only. Campus housing is university owned.

Activities and organizations: drama/theater group, student-run newspaper, choral group.

Athletics Member NCCAA.

Campus security: controlled dormitory access.

Student services: personal/psychological counseling.

COSTS & FINANCIAL AID
Costs (2014–15) ***Comprehensive fee:*** $19,244 includes full-time tuition ($10,944), mandatory fees ($900), and room and board ($7400). Full-time tuition and fees vary according to program. Part-time tuition: $456 per credit hour. Part-time tuition and fees vary according to program. ***Required fees:*** $500 per term part-time.

Financial Aid Of all full-time matriculated undergraduates who enrolled in 2005, 189 applied for aid, 132 were judged to have need. 36 Federal Work-Study jobs (averaging $1404). In 2005, 26 non-need-based awards were made. ***Average percent of need met:*** 43. ***Average financial aid package:*** $3940. ***Average need-based loan:*** $3589. ***Average need-based gift aid:*** $1282. ***Average non-need-based aid:*** $3664. ***Average indebtedness upon graduation:*** $15,000.

APPLYING
Standardized Tests *Required:* SAT or ACT (for admission).

Options: electronic application, deferred entrance.

Application fee: $25.

Required: essay or personal statement, high school transcript, minimum 2.0 GPA, 2 letters of recommendation. ***Required for some:*** interview.

CONTACT
Mr. Brian Condra, Admissions Counselor, Dallas Christian College, 2700 Christian Parkway, Dallas, TX 75234-7299. *Phone:* 972-241-3371 Ext. 104. *Toll-free phone:* 800-688-1029. *Fax:* 972-241-8021. *E-mail:* bcondra@dallas.edu.

DeVry University
Houston, Texas
http://www.devry.edu/

- **Proprietary** comprehensive
- **Coed** 640 undergraduate students, 41% full-time, 48% women, 52% men
- **Minimally difficult** entrance level

UNDERGRAD STUDENTS
264 full-time, 376 part-time. 4% are from out of state; 36% Black or African American, non-Hispanic/Latino; 29% Hispanic/Latino; 5% Asian, non-Hispanic/Latino; 1% Native Hawaiian or other Pacific Islander, non-Hispanic/Latino; 0.3% American Indian or Alaska Native, non-Hispanic/Latino; 0.6% Two or more races, non-Hispanic/Latino; 4% Race/ethnicity unknown; 3% international; 37% transferred in.

Freshmen
Admission: 20 enrolled.

FACULTY
Total: 126, 20% full-time.
Student/faculty ratio: 9:1.

ACADEMICS
Calendar: semesters. *Degrees:* associate, bachelor's, master's, and postbachelor's certificates.

COSTS & FINANCIAL AID
Costs (2014–15) ***Tuition:*** $17,052 full-time, $609 per credit hour part-time. ***Required fees:*** $80 full-time.

Financial Aid Of all full-time matriculated undergraduates who enrolled in 2007, 306 applied for aid, 299 were judged to have need, 3 had their need fully met. In 2007, 20 non-need-based awards were made. ***Average percent of need met:*** 39. ***Average financial aid package:*** $12,662. ***Average need-based loan:*** $7855. ***Average need-based gift aid:*** $5374. ***Average non-need-based aid:*** $14,939. ***Average indebtedness upon graduation:*** $30,068.

APPLYING
Application fee: $40.

CONTACT
DeVry University, 11125 Equity Drive, Houston, TX 77041. *Phone:* 713-973-3100. *Toll-free phone:* 866-338-7941.

DeVry University
Irving, Texas
http://www.devry.edu/

- **Proprietary** comprehensive, founded 1969, part of DeVry University
- **Suburban** campus
- **Coed** 578 undergraduate students, 35% full-time, 38% women, 62% men
- **Minimally difficult** entrance level

UNDERGRAD STUDENTS
204 full-time, 374 part-time. 5% are from out of state; 27% Black or African American, non-Hispanic/Latino; 19% Hispanic/Latino; 5% Asian, non-Hispanic/Latino; 0.5% Native Hawaiian or other Pacific Islander, non-Hispanic/Latino; 0.7% American Indian or Alaska Native, non-Hispanic/Latino; 0.5% Two or more races, non-Hispanic/Latino; 16% Race/ethnicity unknown; 2% international; 34% transferred in.

Freshmen
Admission: 27 enrolled.

FACULTY
Total: 96, 22% full-time.
Student/faculty ratio: 10:1.

ACADEMICS
Calendar: semesters. *Degrees:* associate, bachelor's, master's, and postbachelor's certificates.

Special study options: adult/continuing education programs, part-time degree program.

STUDENT LIFE
Housing options: college housing not available.

COSTS
Costs (2014–15) ***Tuition:*** $17,052 full-time, $609 per credit hour part-time. ***Required fees:*** $80 full-time.

APPLYING
Application fee: $40.

Required: high school transcript, interview.

CONTACT
DeVry University, 4800 Regent Boulevard, Irving, TX 75063-2439. *Phone:* 972-929-6777. *Toll-free phone:* 866-338-7941.

East Texas Baptist University

Marshall, Texas

http://www.etbu.edu/

- **Independent Baptist** comprehensive, founded 1912
- **Small-town** 250-acre campus
- **Endowment** $72.9 million
- **Coed** 1,231 undergraduate students, 90% full-time, 52% women, 48% men
- **Moderately difficult** entrance level, 58% of applicants were admitted

UNDERGRAD STUDENTS
1,113 full-time, 118 part-time. Students come from 19 states and territories; 13 other countries; 7% are from out of state; 19% Black or African American, non-Hispanic/Latino; 10% Hispanic/Latino; 0.3% Asian, non-Hispanic/Latino; 0.2% Native Hawaiian or other Pacific Islander, non-Hispanic/Latino; 0.6% American Indian or Alaska Native, non-Hispanic/Latino; 3% Two or more races, non-Hispanic/Latino; 2% international; 8% transferred in; 84% live on campus.

Freshmen
Admission: 941 applied, 545 admitted, 363 enrolled. ***Average high school GPA:*** 3.36. ***Test scores:*** SAT critical reading scores over 500: 34%; SAT math scores over 500: 45%; ACT scores over 18: 89%; SAT critical reading scores over 600: 4%; SAT math scores over 600: 9%; ACT scores over 24: 14%; SAT math scores over 700: 1%.

Retention: 61% of full-time freshmen returned.

FACULTY
Total: 118, 60% full-time, 63% with terminal degrees.

Student/faculty ratio: 14:1.

ACADEMICS
Calendar: semesters 4-4-1. *Degrees:* certificates, bachelor's, and master's.

Special study options: accelerated degree program, adult/continuing education programs, advanced placement credit, distance learning, double majors, English as a second language, honors programs, independent study, internships, off-campus study, part-time degree program, services for LD students, student-designed majors, study abroad, summer session for credit.

Computers: 200 computers/terminals and 720 ports are available on campus for general student use. Students can access the following: campus intranet, computer help desk, free student e-mail accounts, online (class) grades, online (class) registration, online (class) schedules. Campuswide network is available. 100% of college-owned or -operated housing units are wired for high-speed Internet access. Wireless service is available via entire campus.

STUDENT LIFE
Housing options: on-campus residence required through senior year; men-only, women-only. Campus housing is university owned. Freshman campus housing is guaranteed.

Activities and organizations: drama/theater group, student-run newspaper, radio station, choral group, marching band, Baptist Student Ministry, Student Foundation, Student Government Association, Spirit Program, Freshman Class Council.

Athletics Member NCAA. All Division III. ***Intercollegiate sports:*** baseball M, basketball M/W, cross-country running M/W, football M, soccer M/W, softball W, tennis M/W, track and field M/W, volleyball W. ***Intramural sports:*** basketball M/W, football M/W, racquetball M/W, soccer M/W, softball M/W, ultimate Frisbee M/W, volleyball M/W.

Campus security: 24-hour emergency response devices and patrols, controlled dormitory access.

Student services: personal/psychological counseling.

COSTS & FINANCIAL AID
Costs (2014–15) ***Comprehensive fee:*** $31,577 includes full-time tuition ($22,350), mandatory fees ($930), and room and board ($8297). Part-time tuition: $745 per credit hour. ***Required fees:*** $39 per credit hour part-time. ***College room only:*** $4400. Room and board charges vary according to board plan and housing facility. ***Payment plan:*** installment. ***Waivers:*** employees or children of employees.

Financial Aid Of all full-time matriculated undergraduates who enrolled in 2013, 1,016 applied for aid, 921 were judged to have need, 109 had their need fully met. 143 Federal Work-Study jobs (averaging $1409). 186 state and other part-time jobs (averaging $1364). In 2013, 143 non-need-based awards were made. ***Average percent of need met:*** 34. ***Average financial aid package:*** $16,873. ***Average need-based loan:*** $4129. ***Average need-based gift aid:*** $5989. ***Average non-need-based aid:*** $8974. ***Average indebtedness upon graduation:*** $30,718.

APPLYING
Standardized Tests *Required:* SAT or ACT (for admission).

Options: electronic application.

Application fee: $25.

Required: high school transcript. ***Required for some:*** interview.

Application deadlines: 8/15 (freshmen), 8/15 (out-of-state freshmen), 8/15 (transfers).

Notification: continuous (freshmen), continuous (out-of-state freshmen), continuous (transfers).

CONTACT
Mr. Jason Soles, Director of Admissions, East Texas Baptist University, One Tiger Drive, Marshall, TX 75670. *Phone:* 903-923-2000. *Toll-free phone:* 800-804-ETBU. *Fax:* 903-923-2001. *E-mail:* admissions@etbu.edu.

★ Hallmark University

San Antonio, Texas

http://www.hallmarkuniversity.edu/

- **Independent** comprehensive, founded 1969
- **Suburban** 2-acre campus with easy access to San Antonio
- **Coed** 729 undergraduate students, 100% full-time, 38% women, 62% men
- **Moderately difficult** entrance level, 100% of applicants were admitted

UNDERGRAD STUDENTS
729 full-time. Students come from 1 other state; 10% Black or African American, non-Hispanic/Latino; 51% Hispanic/Latino; 3% Asian, non-Hispanic/Latino; 1% American Indian or Alaska Native, non-Hispanic/Latino; 5% Two or more races, non-Hispanic/Latino; 131% transferred in.

Freshmen
Admission: 81 applied, 81 admitted, 81 enrolled.

Retention: 35% of full-time freshmen returned.

FACULTY
Total: 60, 52% full-time, 13% with terminal degrees.

Student/faculty ratio: 18:1.

ACADEMICS
Calendar: continuous. *Degrees:* diplomas, associate, bachelor's, and master's.

Special study options: academic remediation for entering students, accelerated degree program, advanced placement credit, distance learning, internships.

Computers: 250 computers/terminals and 250 ports are available on campus for general student use. Students can access the following: campus intranet, computer help desk, free student e-mail accounts, online (class) grades, online (class) schedules, Online class admissions is in progress for this year. Campuswide network is available. Wireless service is available via entire campus.

STUDENT LIFE
Housing options: college housing not available.

Activities and organizations: Alpha Beta Kappa Honor Society.

Campus security: 24-hour emergency response devices and patrols, Security Guard on duty generally during hours when students are on campus.

COSTS
Costs (2014–15) ***Tuition:*** Tuition is charged by program: AAS Medical Assistant students are charged $330 per credit. The following programs are charged $440 per credit: AS Business Administration, AAS IT Cisco, AAS IT Microsoft, AAS Nursing, BS Aviation Maintenance Management, BS Business Administration, BS Business Management and BS Information Systems. Registration fee is $60 for all programs except

$25 for AAS Nursing. Technology fee varies by program ranging between $60 and $150 per term except AAS Medical Assistant, AAS Nursing. Lab fee but no Technology fee for AAS Medical Assistant, AAS Nursing.

APPLYING

Standardized Tests *Required:* Wonderlic aptitude test for the Main Campus and Aviation Assessment for the Satellite Campus, SAT/ACT is used for entrance to some degree programs (for admission).

Options: electronic application.

Required: high school transcript, interview, Tour, completed hybrid readiness test (main campus only), passed the entrance exam/assessment and approved by the Acceptance Committee. Registration Fee: Main, $60 except nursing $25, Satellite, $110 plus Security Fee $150. ***Required for some:*** essay or personal statement, .

Application deadlines: rolling (freshmen), rolling (transfers).

Notification: continuous (freshmen), continuous (out-of-state freshmen), continuous (transfers).

CONTACT

Sal Ross, Vice President of Admissions, Hallmark University, 10401 IH-10 West, San Antonio, TX 78230. *Phone:* 210-690-9000 Ext. 214. *Toll-free phone:* 800-880-6600. *Fax:* 210-697-8225. *E-mail:* slross@hallmarkuniversity.edu.

Hardin-Simmons University

Abilene, Texas

http://www.hsutx.edu/

- **Independent Baptist** comprehensive, founded 1891
- **Urban** 220-acre campus
- **Endowment** $160.7 million
- **Coed** 1,640 undergraduate students, 90% full-time, 52% women, 48% men
- **Moderately difficult** entrance level, 57% of applicants were admitted

UNDERGRAD STUDENTS

1,469 full-time, 171 part-time. Students come from 29 states and territories; 18 other countries; 4% are from out of state; 7% Black or African American, non-Hispanic/Latino; 15% Hispanic/Latino; 1% Asian, non-Hispanic/Latino; 0.1% Native Hawaiian or other Pacific Islander, non-Hispanic/Latino; 0.2% American Indian or Alaska Native, non-Hispanic/Latino; 3% Two or more races, non-Hispanic/Latino; 0.9% Race/ethnicity unknown; 2% international; 8% transferred in; 48% live on campus.

Freshmen

Admission: 1,456 applied, 827 admitted, 339 enrolled. ***Average high school GPA:*** 3.59. ***Test scores:*** SAT critical reading scores over 500: 53%; SAT math scores over 500: 62%; SAT writing scores over 500: 47%; ACT scores over 18: 91%; SAT critical reading scores over 600: 17%; SAT math scores over 600: 17%; SAT writing scores over 600: 12%; ACT scores over 24: 35%; SAT critical reading scores over 700: 5%; SAT writing scores over 700: 3%; ACT scores over 30: 2%.

Retention: 64% of full-time freshmen returned.

FACULTY

Total: 201, 70% full-time, 79% with terminal degrees.

Student/faculty ratio: 12:1.

ACADEMICS

Calendar: semesters. *Degrees:* bachelor's, master's, doctoral, post-master's, and postbachelor's certificates.

Special study options: academic remediation for entering students, accelerated degree program, adult/continuing education programs, advanced placement credit, distance learning, double majors, honors programs, independent study, internships, off-campus study, part-time degree program, services for LD students, study abroad, summer session for credit.

Computers: 258 computers/terminals and 1,100 ports are available on campus for general student use. Students can access the following: campus intranet, computer help desk, free student e-mail accounts, online (class) grades, online (class) registration, online (class) schedules. Campuswide network is available. 100% of college-owned or -operated housing units are wired for high-speed Internet access. Wireless service is available via entire campus.

STUDENT LIFE

Housing options: on-campus residence required through sophomore year; men-only, women-only, special housing for students with disabilities. Campus housing is university owned. Freshman campus housing is guaranteed.

Activities and organizations: drama/theater group, student-run newspaper, choral group, marching band, Baptist Student Ministries, Student Government, Alpha Phi Omega, Student Activities Board, Fellowship of Christian Athletes.

Athletics Member NCAA. All Division III. ***Intercollegiate sports:*** baseball M, basketball M/W, cheerleading M(c)/W(c), cross-country running M/W, football M, golf M/W, soccer M/W, softball W, tennis M/W, track and field M/W, volleyball W. ***Intramural sports:*** badminton M/W, basketball M/W, bowling M/W, football M/W, golf M/W, racquetball M/W, rock climbing M(c)/W(c), soccer M/W, softball M/W, table tennis M(c)/W(c), tennis M(c)/W(c), ultimate Frisbee M/W, volleyball M/W.

Campus security: 24-hour emergency response devices and patrols, late-night transport/escort service, controlled dormitory access.

Student services: health clinic, personal/psychological counseling.

COSTS & FINANCIAL AID

Costs (2014–15) ***Comprehensive fee:*** $32,240 includes full-time tuition ($24,500) and room and board ($7740). Full-time tuition and fees vary according to program. Part-time tuition: $750 per credit hour. Part-time tuition and fees vary according to course load and program. No tuition increase for student's term of enrollment. ***Required fees:*** $525 per term part-time. ***College room only:*** $3600. Room and board charges vary according to board plan and housing facility. ***Payment plan:*** installment. ***Waivers:*** employees or children of employees.

Financial Aid Of all full-time matriculated undergraduates who enrolled in 2013, 1,494 applied for aid, 1,127 were judged to have need, 247 had their need fully met. In 2013, 344 non-need-based awards were made. ***Average percent of need met:*** 69. ***Average financial aid package:*** $20,386. ***Average need-based loan:*** $4158. ***Average need-based gift aid:*** $6638. ***Average non-need-based aid:*** $10,174. ***Average indebtedness upon graduation:*** $38,032.

APPLYING

Standardized Tests *Required:* SAT or ACT (for admission).

Options: electronic application, deferred entrance.

Required: high school transcript, minimum 2.0 GPA. ***Required for some:*** 3 letters of recommendation.

Application deadlines: rolling (freshmen), rolling (transfers).

Notification: continuous (freshmen), continuous (transfers).

CONTACT

Ms. Brynn Reynolds, Campus Guest Coordinator, Hardin-Simmons University, Box 16050, Abilene, TX 79698-0001. *Phone:* 325-670-5890. *Toll-free phone:* 877-464-7889. *Fax:* 325-671-2115. *E-mail:* breynolds@hsutx.edu.

Houston Baptist University

Houston, Texas

http://www.hbu.edu/

- **Independent Baptist** comprehensive, founded 1960
- **Urban** 150-acre campus with easy access to Houston
- **Endowment** $90.6 million
- **Coed** 2,288 undergraduate students, 93% full-time, 61% women, 39% men
- **Moderately difficult** entrance level, 36% of applicants were admitted

UNDERGRAD STUDENTS

2,137 full-time, 151 part-time. 4% are from out of state; 20% Black or African American, non-Hispanic/Latino; 27% Hispanic/Latino; 13% Asian, non-Hispanic/Latino; 0.3% Native Hawaiian or other Pacific Islander, non-Hispanic/Latino; 0.4% American Indian or Alaska Native, non-Hispanic/Latino; 5% Two or more races, non-Hispanic/Latino; 2% Race/ethnicity unknown; 4% international; 9% transferred in; 41% live on campus.

Freshmen

Admission: 12,769 applied, 4,562 admitted, 615 enrolled. ***Test scores:*** SAT critical reading scores over 500: 60%; SAT math scores over 500:

71%; SAT writing scores over 500: 53%; ACT scores over 18: 98%; SAT critical reading scores over 600: 20%; SAT math scores over 600: 20%; SAT writing scores over 600: 15%; ACT scores over 24: 36%; SAT critical reading scores over 700: 4%; SAT math scores over 700: 2%; SAT writing scores over 700: 2%; ACT scores over 30: 10%.

Retention: 66% of full-time freshmen returned.

FACULTY

Total: 240, 56% full-time, 65% with terminal degrees.

Student/faculty ratio: 16:1.

ACADEMICS

Calendar: semesters. *Degrees:* bachelor's and master's.

Special study options: academic remediation for entering students, accelerated degree program, adult/continuing education programs, distance learning, double majors, freshman honors college, honors programs, independent study, internships, off-campus study, part-time degree program, services for LD students, study abroad, summer session for credit. ***ROTC:*** Army (c), Navy (c), Air Force (c).

Unusual degree programs: 3-2 business administration with accounting.

Computers: Students can access the following: campus intranet, computer help desk, free student e-mail accounts, online (class) grades, online (class) registration, online (class) schedules. Campuswide network is available. 100% of college-owned or -operated housing units are wired for high-speed Internet access. Wireless service is available via entire campus.

STUDENT LIFE

Housing options: on-campus residence required through sophomore year; coed, men-only, women-only. Campus housing is university owned. Freshman campus housing is guaranteed.

Activities and organizations: drama/theater group, student-run newspaper, choral group, Alpha Epsilon Delta, Alpha Phi Omega, Association of Student Educators, Alpha Kappa Psi, Phi Mu, national fraternities, national sororities.

Athletics Member NCAA. All Division I. ***Intercollegiate sports:*** baseball M(s), basketball M(s)/W(s), cheerleading M(s)/W(s), cross-country running M(s)/W(s), football M(s), golf M(s)/W(s), soccer M(s)/W(s), softball W(s), track and field M(s)/W(s), volleyball W(s). ***Intramural sports:*** basketball M/W, golf M/W, soccer M/W, softball M/W, tennis M/W, ultimate Frisbee M/W, volleyball M/W.

Campus security: 24-hour emergency response devices and patrols, late-night transport/escort service, controlled dormitory access.

Student services: health clinic, personal/psychological counseling.

COSTS & FINANCIAL AID

Costs (2015–16) ***Comprehensive fee:*** $37,515 includes full-time tuition ($27,950), mandatory fees ($1850), and room and board ($7715). Part-time tuition and fees vary according to course load. ***College room only:*** $4500. Room and board charges vary according to board plan and housing facility. ***Payment plan:*** installment. ***Waivers:*** employees or children of employees.

Financial Aid Of all full-time matriculated undergraduates who enrolled in 2014, 1,656 applied for aid, 1,555 were judged to have need, 274 had their need fully met. 1,064 Federal Work-Study jobs (averaging $1893). In 2014, 495 non-need-based awards were made. ***Average percent of need met:*** 70. ***Average financial aid package:*** $25,617. ***Average need-based loan:*** $5233. ***Average need-based gift aid:*** $17,558. ***Average non-need-based aid:*** $13,153. ***Financial aid deadline:*** 4/15.

APPLYING

Standardized Tests *Required:* SAT or ACT (for admission).

Options: electronic application, early admission.

Required: high school transcript. ***Required for some:*** essay or personal statement, interview.

Application deadlines: rolling (freshmen), rolling (transfers).

Notification: continuous (freshmen), continuous (transfers).

CONTACT

Mr. Eduardo Borges, Director of Admissions, Houston Baptist University, 7502 Fondren Road, Houston, TX 77074-3298. *Phone:* 281-649-3299. *Toll-free phone:* 800-696-3210. *Fax:* 281-649-3217. *E-mail:* eborges@hbu.edu.

Howard Payne University

Brownwood, Texas

http://www.hputx.edu/

- **Independent** comprehensive, founded 1889, affiliated with Baptist General Convention of Texas
- **Small-town** 80-acre campus
- **Endowment** $63.1 million
- **Coed** 1,073 undergraduate students, 88% full-time, 50% women, 50% men
- **Moderately difficult** entrance level, 82% of applicants were admitted

UNDERGRAD STUDENTS

945 full-time, 128 part-time. Students come from 15 states and territories; 3% are from out of state; 8% Black or African American, non-Hispanic/Latino; 22% Hispanic/Latino; 0.4% Asian, non-Hispanic/Latino; 0.1% Native Hawaiian or other Pacific Islander, non-Hispanic/Latino; 0.3% American Indian or Alaska Native, non-Hispanic/Latino; 3% Two or more races, non-Hispanic/Latino; 3% Race/ethnicity unknown; 7% transferred in; 63% live on campus.

Freshmen

Admission: 1,057 applied, 868 admitted, 302 enrolled. ***Average high school GPA:*** 3.32. ***Test scores:*** SAT critical reading scores over 500: 38%; SAT math scores over 500: 45%; ACT scores over 18: 87%; SAT critical reading scores over 600: 11%; SAT math scores over 600: 10%; ACT scores over 24: 24%; ACT scores over 30: 3%.

Retention: 54% of full-time freshmen returned.

FACULTY

Total: 147, 60% full-time, 52% with terminal degrees.

Student/faculty ratio: 9:1.

ACADEMICS

Calendar: semesters. *Degrees:* certificates, bachelor's, and master's.

Special study options: academic remediation for entering students, accelerated degree program, advanced placement credit, distance learning, double majors, honors programs, independent study, internships, off-campus study, part-time degree program, services for LD students, study abroad, summer session for credit.

Computers: 260 computers/terminals and 200 ports are available on campus for general student use. Students can access the following: campus intranet, computer help desk, free student e-mail accounts, online (class) grades, online (class) schedules. Campuswide network is available. 100% of college-owned or -operated housing units are wired for high-speed Internet access. Wireless service is available via entire campus.

STUDENT LIFE

Housing options: on-campus residence required through sophomore year; men-only, women-only. Campus housing is university owned. Freshman campus housing is guaranteed.

Activities and organizations: drama/theater group, student-run newspaper, choral group, marching band, Baptist Student Ministry, Archery Club, New Age Disciples, Student Activities Council, Student Government Association, national fraternities, national sororities.

Athletics Member NCAA. All Division III. ***Intercollegiate sports:*** baseball M, basketball M/W, football M, soccer M/W, softball W, tennis M/W, volleyball W. ***Intramural sports:*** basketball M/W, football M/W, soccer M/W, softball M/W, table tennis M/W, tennis M/W, ultimate Frisbee M/W, volleyball M/W.

Campus security: 24-hour emergency response devices and patrols, late-night transport/escort service, controlled dormitory access.

Student services: health clinic, personal/psychological counseling.

COSTS & FINANCIAL AID

Costs (2015–16) ***Comprehensive fee:*** $33,089 includes full-time tuition ($23,600), mandatory fees ($2000), and room and board ($7489). Full-time tuition and fees vary according to course load, location, and program. Part-time tuition: $760 per credit. Part-time tuition and fees vary according to location and program. ***Room and board:*** Room and board charges vary according to board plan and housing facility. ***Payment plan:*** installment. ***Waivers:*** employees or children of employees.

Financial Aid Of all full-time matriculated undergraduates who enrolled in 2013, 890 applied for aid, 832 were judged to have need, 183 had their need fully met. In 2013, 139 non-need-based awards were made. ***Average***

percent of need met: 73. ***Average financial aid package:*** $17,043. ***Average need-based loan:*** $3865. ***Average need-based gift aid:*** $14,066. ***Average non-need-based aid:*** $10,722. ***Average indebtedness upon graduation:*** $27,018.

APPLYING
Standardized Tests *Required:* SAT or ACT (for admission). *Required for some:* ACCUPLACER.

Options: electronic application, early admission.

Required: high school transcript. ***Required for some:*** 3 letters of recommendation, interview. ***Recommended:*** essay or personal statement, minimum 3.0 GPA.

Application deadlines: rolling (freshmen), rolling (out-of-state freshmen), rolling (transfers).

Notification: continuous (freshmen), continuous (out-of-state freshmen), continuous (transfers).

CONTACT
Mrs. PJ Gramling, Director of Admission, Howard Payne University, 1000 Fisk Street, Brownwood, TX 76801. *Phone:* 325-649-8406. *Toll-free phone:* 800-880-4478. *Fax:* 325-649-8901. *E-mail:* enroll@hputx.edu.

Huston-Tillotson University

Austin, Texas

http://www.htu.edu/

- **Independent interdenominational** comprehensive, founded 1875
- **Urban** 23-acre campus
- **Endowment** $11.7 million
- **Coed** 975 undergraduate students, 95% full-time, 55% women, 45% men
- **Moderately difficult** entrance level, 60% of applicants were admitted

UNDERGRAD STUDENTS
927 full-time, 48 part-time. Students come from 21 states and territories; 19 other countries; 6% are from out of state; 70% Black or African American, non-Hispanic/Latino; 19% Hispanic/Latino; 0.5% Asian, non-Hispanic/Latino; 0.1% American Indian or Alaska Native, non-Hispanic/Latino; 0.8% Two or more races, non-Hispanic/Latino; 1% Race/ethnicity unknown; 5% international; 8% transferred in; 37% live on campus.

Freshmen
Admission: 2,042 applied, 1,219 admitted, 206 enrolled. ***Average high school GPA:*** 2.91. ***Test scores:*** SAT critical reading scores over 500: 12%; SAT math scores over 500: 16%; ACT scores over 18: 42%; SAT critical reading scores over 600: 3%; SAT math scores over 600: 2%; ACT scores over 24: 7%; SAT math scores over 700: 1%; ACT scores over 30: 2%.
Retention: 57% of full-time freshmen returned.

FACULTY
Total: 87, 56% full-time, 56% with terminal degrees.
Student/faculty ratio: 16:1.

ACADEMICS
Calendar: semesters. *Degrees:* bachelor's, master's, and postbachelor's certificates.

Special study options: academic remediation for entering students, advanced placement credit, cooperative education, distance learning, double majors, honors programs, independent study, internships, part-time degree program, services for LD students, study abroad, summer session for credit. ***ROTC:*** Army (c), Navy (c), Air Force (c).

Unusual degree programs: 3-2 engineering with Prairie View A&M University.

Computers: Students can access the following: campus intranet, computer help desk, free student e-mail accounts, online (class) grades, online (class) registration, online (class) schedules. Campuswide network is available. Wireless service is available via entire campus.

STUDENT LIFE
Housing options: on-campus residence required for freshman year; men-only, women-only. Campus housing is university owned. Freshman campus housing is guaranteed.

Activities and organizations: drama/theater group, choral group, Campus Ministries, Zeta Phi Beta Sorority, Inc, Alpha Phi Alpha Fraternity, Inc, The Gentlemen's Club, Pre-Alumni Council, national fraternities, national sororities.

Athletics Member NAIA. ***Intercollegiate sports:*** baseball M(s), basketball M(s)/W(s), cross-country running M(s), soccer M(s)/W(s), softball W(s), track and field M(s)/W(s), volleyball W(s). ***Intramural sports:*** cheerleading W.

Campus security: 24-hour emergency response devices and patrols, late-night transport/escort service, controlled dormitory access.

Student services: health clinic, personal/psychological counseling.

COSTS & FINANCIAL AID
Costs (2014–15) ***Comprehensive fee:*** $21,112 includes full-time tuition ($11,460), mandatory fees ($2084), and room and board ($7568). Full-time tuition and fees vary according to course load. Part-time tuition: $383 per credit hour. Part-time tuition and fees vary according to course load. ***Required fees:*** $457 per term part-time. ***College room only:*** $3642. Room and board charges vary according to housing facility. ***Payment plans:*** installment, deferred payment. ***Waivers:*** employees or children of employees.

Financial Aid ***Average financial aid package:*** $113,980. ***Average need-based loan:*** $3747. ***Average need-based gift aid:*** $7860.

APPLYING
Standardized Tests *Required:* SAT or ACT (for admission). *Recommended:* SAT (for admission), ACT (for admission), SAT and SAT Subject Tests or ACT (for admission).

Options: electronic application, deferred entrance.

Application fee: $25.

Required: high school transcript, minimum 2.5 GPA, university admission application. ***Required for some:*** interview.

CONTACT
Ms. Shakitha Stinson, Director of Admission, Huston-Tillotson University, 900 Chicon Street, Austin, TX 78702. *Phone:* 512-505-3029. *Fax:* 512-505-3192. *E-mail:* slstinson@htu.edu.

ITT Technical Institute

Arlington, Texas

http://www.itt-tech.edu/

- **Proprietary** primarily 2-year, founded 1982, part of ITT Educational Services, Inc.
- **Suburban** campus
- **Coed**
- **Minimally difficult** entrance level

ACADEMICS
Calendar: quarters. *Degrees:* associate and bachelor's.

STUDENT LIFE
Housing options: college housing not available.

CONTACT
Director of Recruitment, ITT Technical Institute, 551 Ryan Plaza Drive, Arlington, TX 76011. *Phone:* 817-794-5100. *Toll-free phone:* 888-288-4950.

ITT Technical Institute

Austin, Texas

http://www.itt-tech.edu/

- **Proprietary** primarily 2-year, founded 1985, part of ITT Educational Services, Inc.
- **Urban** campus
- **Coed**
- **Minimally difficult** entrance level

ACADEMICS
Calendar: quarters. *Degrees:* associate and bachelor's.

STUDENT LIFE
Housing options: college housing not available.

FINANCIAL AID

Financial Aid Of all full-time matriculated undergraduates who enrolled in 2013, 1 Federal Work-Study job.

CONTACT

Director of Recruitment, ITT Technical Institute, 6330 East Highway 290, Suite 150, Austin, TX 78723-1061. *Phone:* 512-467-6800. *Toll-free phone:* 800-431-0677.

ITT Technical Institute

DeSoto, Texas

http://www.itt-tech.edu/

- **Proprietary** primarily 2-year
- **Coed**
- **Minimally difficult** entrance level

ACADEMICS

Degrees: associate and bachelor's.

CONTACT

Director of Recruitment, ITT Technical Institute, 921 West Belt Line Road, Suite 181, DeSoto, TX 75115. *Phone:* 972-274-8600. *Toll-free phone:* 877-854-5728.

ITT Technical Institute

Houston, Texas

http://www.itt-tech.edu/

- **Proprietary** primarily 2-year, founded 1985, part of ITT Educational Services, Inc.
- **Suburban** campus
- **Coed**
- **Minimally difficult** entrance level

ACADEMICS

Calendar: quarters. *Degrees:* associate and bachelor's.

STUDENT LIFE

Housing options: college housing not available.

CONTACT

Director of Recruitment, ITT Technical Institute, 15651 North Freeway, Houston, TX 77090. *Phone:* 281-873-0512. *Toll-free phone:* 800-879-6486.

ITT Technical Institute

Houston, Texas

http://www.itt-tech.edu/

- **Proprietary** primarily 2-year, founded 1983, part of ITT Educational Services, Inc.
- **Urban** campus
- **Coed**
- **Minimally difficult** entrance level

ACADEMICS

Calendar: quarters. *Degrees:* associate and bachelor's.

STUDENT LIFE

Housing options: college housing not available.

CONTACT

Director of Recruitment, ITT Technical Institute, 2950 South Gessner, Houston, TX 77063-3751. *Phone:* 713-952-2294. *Toll-free phone:* 800-235-4787.

ITT Technical Institute

Richardson, Texas

http://www.itt-tech.edu/

- **Proprietary** primarily 2-year, founded 1989, part of ITT Educational Services, Inc.
- **Suburban** campus
- **Coed**
- **Minimally difficult** entrance level

ACADEMICS

Calendar: quarters. *Degrees:* associate and bachelor's.

STUDENT LIFE

Housing options: college housing not available.

FINANCIAL AID

Financial Aid Of all full-time matriculated undergraduates who enrolled in 2013, 5 Federal Work-Study jobs (averaging $5000).

CONTACT

Director of Recruitment, ITT Technical Institute, 2101 Waterview Parkway, Richardson, TX 75080. *Phone:* 972-690-9100. *Toll-free phone:* 888-488-5761.

ITT Technical Institute

San Antonio, Texas

http://www.itt-tech.edu/

- **Proprietary** primarily 2-year
- **Coed**

ACADEMICS

Degrees: associate and bachelor's.

CONTACT

Director of Recruiting, ITT Technical Institute, 2895 NE Loop 410, San Antonio, TX 78218. *Phone:* 210-651-8500. *Toll-free phone:* 877-400-8894.

ITT Technical Institute

San Antonio, Texas

http://www.itt-tech.edu/

- **Proprietary** primarily 2-year, founded 1988, part of ITT Educational Services, Inc.
- **Urban** campus
- **Coed**
- **Minimally difficult** entrance level

ACADEMICS

Calendar: quarters. *Degrees:* associate and bachelor's.

STUDENT LIFE

Housing options: college housing not available.

CONTACT

Director of Recruitment, ITT Technical Institute, 5700 Northwest Parkway, San Antonio, TX 78249-3303. *Phone:* 210-694-4612. *Toll-free phone:* 800-880-0570.

ITT Technical Institute

Waco, Texas

http://www.itt-tech.edu/

- **Proprietary** primarily 2-year, part of ITT Educational Services, Inc.
- **Coed**

ACADEMICS

Calendar: quarters. *Degrees:* associate and bachelor's.

CONTACT

Director of Recruitment, ITT Technical Institute, 3700 S. Jack Kultgen Expressway, Suite 100, Waco, TX 76706. *Phone:* 254-523-3940. *Toll-free phone:* 877-201-7143.

ITT Technical Institute

Webster, Texas

http://www.itt-tech.edu/

- **Proprietary** primarily 2-year, founded 1995, part of ITT Educational Services, Inc.
- **Coed**
- **Minimally difficult** entrance level

ACADEMICS

Calendar: quarters. *Degrees:* associate and bachelor's.

STUDENT LIFE
Housing options: college housing not available.

CONTACT
Director of Recruitment, ITT Technical Institute, 1001 Magnolia Avenue, Webster, TX 77598. *Phone:* 281-316-4700. *Toll-free phone:* 888-488-9347.

Jarvis Christian College

Hawkins, Texas

http://www.jarvis.edu/

- **Independent** 4-year, founded 1912, affiliated with Christian Church (Disciples of Christ)
- **Rural** 465-acre campus
- **Endowment** $11.5 million
- **Coed** 763 undergraduate students, 89% full-time, 48% women, 52% men
- **Minimally difficult** entrance level, 42% of applicants were admitted

UNDERGRAD STUDENTS
680 full-time, 83 part-time. Students come from 25 states and territories; 1 other country; 17% are from out of state; 81% Black or African American, non-Hispanic/Latino; 11% Hispanic/Latino; 0.4% Native Hawaiian or other Pacific Islander, non-Hispanic/Latino; 0.4% American Indian or Alaska Native, non-Hispanic/Latino; 0.9% Race/ethnicity unknown; 0.1% international; 19% transferred in; 73% live on campus.

Freshmen
Admission: 1,419 applied, 591 admitted, 190 enrolled. ***Average high school GPA:*** 2.75. ***Test scores:*** SAT critical reading scores over 500: 7%; SAT math scores over 500: 14%; SAT writing scores over 500: 3%; ACT scores over 18: 27%; SAT critical reading scores over 600: 1%; SAT math scores over 600: 1%; SAT critical reading scores over 700: 1%.

Retention: 56% of full-time freshmen returned.

FACULTY
Total: 32, 100% full-time, 72% with terminal degrees.

Student/faculty ratio: 22:1.

ACADEMICS
Calendar: semesters. *Degree:* bachelor's.

Special study options: academic remediation for entering students, adult/continuing education programs, advanced placement credit, cooperative education, double majors, English as a second language, honors programs, internships, off-campus study, part-time degree program, student-designed majors, summer session for credit.

Unusual degree programs: 3-2 engineering with University of Texas at Arlington; nursing with University of Texas at Tyler.

Computers: 100 computers/terminals and 200 ports are available on campus for general student use. Students can access the following: campus intranet, computer help desk, free student e-mail accounts, online (class) grades, online (class) registration, online (class) schedules. Campuswide network is available. 100% of college-owned or -operated housing units are wired for high-speed Internet access. Wireless service is available via entire campus.

STUDENT LIFE
Housing options: men-only, women-only. Campus housing is university owned.

Activities and organizations: drama/theater group, choral group, Student Government Association, Pre-Alumni Club, Student Ministers' Association, Women 2 Women, Panhellenic Council, national fraternities, national sororities.

Athletics Member NAIA. ***Intercollegiate sports:*** baseball M(s), basketball M(s)/W(s), cross-country running M(s)/W(s), soccer M(s)/W(s). ***Intramural sports:*** baseball M, basketball M/W, volleyball W.

Campus security: 24-hour emergency response devices and patrols.

Student services: health clinic.

COSTS & FINANCIAL AID
Costs (2015–16) ***Comprehensive fee:*** $19,552 includes full-time tuition ($10,090), mandatory fees ($1279), and room and board ($8183). Part-time tuition: $420 per semester hour. ***College room only:*** $3996. Room and board charges vary according to housing facility. ***Payment plan:*** installment. ***Waivers:*** employees or children of employees.

Financial Aid Of all full-time matriculated undergraduates who enrolled in 2011, 476 applied for aid, 476 were judged to have need, 30 had their need fully met. 149 Federal Work-Study jobs (averaging $1538). 2 state and other part-time jobs (averaging $2315). In 2011, 5 non-need-based awards were made. ***Average percent of need met:*** 80. ***Average financial aid package:*** $12,115. ***Average need-based loan:*** $5392. ***Average need-based gift aid:*** $8062. ***Average non-need-based aid:*** $17,192. ***Average indebtedness upon graduation:*** $29,296.

APPLYING
Standardized Tests *Required:* SAT or ACT (for admission).

Options: electronic application.

Application fee: $50.

Required: high school transcript. ***Recommended:*** minimum 2.0 GPA.

Application deadlines: 8/1 (freshmen), 8/1 (out-of-state freshmen), rolling (transfers).

Notification: 8/15 (freshmen), 8/15 (out-of-state freshmen).

CONTACT
Director of Admissions and Enrollment, Jarvis Christian College, PO Box 1470, Hawkins, TX 75765-9989. *Phone:* 903-730-4890 Ext. 2201. *Fax:* 903-769-4842.

King's University

Southlake, Texas

http://tku.edu/

- **Independent** comprehensive, affiliated with International Church of the Foursquare Gospel
- **Suburban** campus with easy access to Dallas-Ft. Worth Metroplex
- **Coed** 704 students

ACADEMICS
Calendar: quarters. *Degrees:* certificates, associate, bachelor's, master's, and postbachelor's certificates.

STUDENT LIFE
Housing options: college housing not available.

APPLYING
Application fee: $45.

CONTACT
Tyler Maxey, Director of Admissions, King's University, 2121 E. Southlake Blvd., Southlake, TX 76092. *Phone:* 817-552-7570. *Toll-free phone:* 888-779-8040. *E-mail:* tyler.maxey@tku.edu.

Lamar University

Beaumont, Texas

http://www.lamar.edu/

- **State-supported** university, founded 1923, part of Texas State University System
- **Suburban** 270-acre campus with easy access to Houston
- **Endowment** $89.3 million
- **Coed** 9,279 undergraduate students, 70% full-time, 58% women, 42% men
- **Minimally difficult** entrance level, 79% of applicants were admitted

UNDERGRAD STUDENTS
6,460 full-time, 2,819 part-time. Students come from 39 states and territories; 45 other countries; 3% are from out of state; 28% Black or African American, non-Hispanic/Latino; 14% Hispanic/Latino; 4% Asian, non-Hispanic/Latino; 0.1% Native Hawaiian or other Pacific Islander, non-Hispanic/Latino; 0.4% American Indian or Alaska Native, non-Hispanic/Latino; 2% Two or more races, non-Hispanic/Latino; 1% Race/ethnicity unknown; 2% international; 7% transferred in; 17% live on campus.

Freshmen
Admission: 4,572 applied, 3,603 admitted, 1,290 enrolled. ***Test scores:*** SAT critical reading scores over 500: 35%; SAT math scores over 500: 40%; SAT writing scores over 500: 24%; ACT scores over 18: 76%; SAT critical reading scores over 600: 9%; SAT math scores over 600: 10%; SAT writing scores over 600: 3%; ACT scores over 24: 23%; SAT critical

reading scores over 700: 1%; SAT math scores over 700: 1%; ACT scores over 30: 2%.

Retention: 61% of full-time freshmen returned.

FACULTY

Total: 589, 71% full-time, 58% with terminal degrees.

Student/faculty ratio: 21:1.

ACADEMICS

Calendar: semesters. *Degrees:* bachelor's, master's, doctoral, post-master's, and postbachelor's certificates.

Special study options: academic remediation for entering students, accelerated degree program, advanced placement credit, cooperative education, distance learning, double majors, English as a second language, honors programs, independent study, internships, off-campus study, part-time degree program, services for LD students, student-designed majors, study abroad, summer session for credit. ***ROTC:*** Air Force (c).

Computers: 644 computers/terminals and 50 ports are available on campus for general student use. Students can access the following: campus intranet, computer help desk, free student e-mail accounts, online (class) grades, online (class) registration, online (class) schedules. Campuswide network is available. 100% of college-owned or -operated housing units are wired for high-speed Internet access. Wireless service is available via entire campus.

STUDENT LIFE

Housing options: on-campus residence required for freshman year; coed, special housing for students with disabilities. Campus housing is university owned. Freshman campus housing is guaranteed.

Activities and organizations: drama/theater group, student-run newspaper, television station, choral group, marching band, national fraternities, national sororities.

Athletics Member NCAA. All Division I except football (Division I-AA). ***Intercollegiate sports:*** baseball M(s), basketball M(s)/W(s), cheerleading M/W, cross-country running M(s)/W(s), golf M(s)/W(s), soccer W(s), softball W, tennis M(s)/W(s), track and field M(s)/W(s), volleyball W(s). ***Intramural sports:*** badminton M/W, basketball M/W, cross-country running M/W, football M, golf M/W, racquetball M/W, rugby M/W, sailing M/W, soccer M/W, softball M/W, swimming and diving M/W, table tennis M/W, tennis M/W, track and field M/W, volleyball M/W, weight lifting M/W.

Campus security: 24-hour emergency response devices and patrols, student patrols, late-night transport/escort service, controlled dormitory access.

Student services: health clinic, personal/psychological counseling.

COSTS & FINANCIAL AID

Costs (2015–16) ***One-time required fee:*** $10. ***Tuition:*** state resident $6450 full-time, $218 per credit hour part-time; nonresident $17,400 full-time, $580 per credit hour part-time. Full-time tuition and fees vary according to course load, location, and program. Part-time tuition and fees vary according to course load, location, and program. No tuition increase for student's term of enrollment. ***Required fees:*** $2801 full-time, $382 per credit hour part-time, $784 per credit hour part-time. ***Room and board:*** $8302; room only: $5252. Room and board charges vary according to board plan. ***Payment plan:*** installment. ***Waivers:*** senior citizens and employees or children of employees.

Financial Aid Of all full-time matriculated undergraduates who enrolled in 2012, 5,784 applied for aid, 4,905 were judged to have need, 206 had their need fully met. 192 Federal Work-Study jobs (averaging $2263). 58 state and other part-time jobs (averaging $1266). In 2012, 1250 non-need-based awards were made. ***Average percent of need met:*** 68. ***Average financial aid package:*** $6782. ***Average need-based loan:*** $3830. ***Average need-based gift aid:*** $4778. ***Average non-need-based aid:*** $2649. ***Average indebtedness upon graduation:*** $28,380.

APPLYING

Standardized Tests *Required:* SAT or ACT (for admission).

Options: electronic application, early admission.

Required: high school transcript. ***Required for some:*** essay or personal statement.

Application deadlines: 8/11 (freshmen), 8/11 (transfers).

Notification: continuous (freshmen).

CONTACT

Ms. Melissa Gallien, Director of Admissions, Lamar University, PO Box 10009, Beaumont, TX 77710. *Phone:* 409-880-8888. *Fax:* 409-880-8463. *E-mail:* admissions@lamar.edu.

LeTourneau University

Longview, Texas

http://www.letu.edu/

- **Independent nondenominational** comprehensive, founded 1946
- **Suburban** 162-acre campus
- **Coed** 2,250 undergraduate students, 60% full-time, 47% women, 53% men
- **Moderately difficult** entrance level, 49% of applicants were admitted

UNDERGRAD STUDENTS

1,341 full-time, 909 part-time. 43% are from out of state; 10% Black or African American, non-Hispanic/Latino; 9% Hispanic/Latino; 1% Asian, non-Hispanic/Latino; 0.1% Native Hawaiian or other Pacific Islander, non-Hispanic/Latino; 0.4% American Indian or Alaska Native, non-Hispanic/Latino; 4% Two or more races, non-Hispanic/Latino; 5% Race/ethnicity unknown; 4% international; 6% transferred in; 75% live on campus.

Freshmen

Admission: 1,761 applied, 870 admitted, 367 enrolled. ***Average high school GPA:*** 3.59. ***Test scores:*** SAT critical reading scores over 500: 78%; SAT math scores over 500: 85%; SAT writing scores over 500: 68%; ACT scores over 18: 97%; SAT critical reading scores over 600: 42%; SAT math scores over 600: 49%; SAT writing scores over 600: 31%; ACT scores over 24: 66%; SAT critical reading scores over 700: 12%; SAT math scores over 700: 14%; SAT writing scores over 700: 7%; ACT scores over 30: 26%.

Retention: 83% of full-time freshmen returned.

FACULTY

Total: 202, 45% full-time, 58% with terminal degrees.

Student/faculty ratio: 14:1.

ACADEMICS

Calendar: semesters. *Degrees:* associate, bachelor's, and master's.

Special study options: part-time degree program.

Computers: Students can access the following: campus intranet, computer help desk, free student e-mail accounts, online (class) grades, online (class) registration, online (class) schedules. Campuswide network is available. 100% of college-owned or -operated housing units are wired for high-speed Internet access. Wireless service is available via entire campus.

STUDENT LIFE

Housing options: on-campus residence required through junior year; men-only, women-only, special housing for students with disabilities. Campus housing is university owned. Freshman campus housing is guaranteed.

Activities and organizations: drama/theater group, choral group.

Athletics Member NCAA, NCCAA. All NCAA Division III. ***Intercollegiate sports:*** baseball M, basketball M/W, cross-country running M/W, golf M/W, soccer M/W, softball W, tennis M/W, volleyball W. ***Intramural sports:*** badminton M/W, basketball M/W, bowling M/W, cross-country running M/W, football M/W, golf M/W, racquetball M/W, rugby M, soccer M/W, softball M/W, swimming and diving M/W, table tennis M/W, tennis M/W, volleyball M/W.

Campus security: 24-hour emergency response devices and patrols, student patrols, late-night transport/escort service, controlled dormitory access, University police department.

Student services: personal/psychological counseling.

COSTS & FINANCIAL AID

Costs (2014–15) ***Comprehensive fee:*** $36,210 includes full-time tuition ($26,390), mandatory fees ($520), and room and board ($9300). Full-time tuition and fees vary according to course level, course load, location, and program. Part-time tuition: $1053 per credit hour. Part-time tuition and fees vary according to course level, course load, location, and program. ***Room and board:*** Room and board charges vary according to board plan.

Payment plan: installment. ***Waivers:*** employees or children of employees.

Financial Aid Of all full-time matriculated undergraduates who enrolled in 2014, 1,243 applied for aid, 1,146 were judged to have need, 124 had their need fully met. In 2014, 166 non-need-based awards were made. ***Average percent of need met:*** 61. ***Average financial aid package:*** $19,491. ***Average need-based loan:*** $5016. ***Average need-based gift aid:*** $15,122. ***Average non-need-based aid:*** $8037. ***Average indebtedness upon graduation:*** $38,211.

APPLYING

Standardized Tests *Required for some:* SAT or ACT (for admission).

Options: electronic application, deferred entrance.

Application deadlines: rolling (freshmen), rolling (out-of-state freshmen), rolling (transfers).

Notification: continuous (freshmen), continuous (transfers).

CONTACT

LeTourneau University, TX. *Toll-free phone:* 800-759-8811.

Lubbock Christian University

Lubbock, Texas

http://www.lcu.edu/

- **Independent** comprehensive, founded 1957, affiliated with Church of Christ
- **Suburban** 120-acre campus
- **Endowment** $17.1 million
- **Coed** 1,439 undergraduate students, 85% full-time, 61% women, 39% men
- **Moderately difficult** entrance level, 94% of applicants were admitted

UNDERGRAD STUDENTS

1,222 full-time, 217 part-time. Students come from 39 states and territories; 16 other countries; 13% are from out of state; 6% Black or African American, non-Hispanic/Latino; 23% Hispanic/Latino; 0.6% Asian, non-Hispanic/Latino; 0.1% Native Hawaiian or other Pacific Islander, non-Hispanic/Latino; 0.6% American Indian or Alaska Native, non-Hispanic/Latino; 2% international; 13% transferred in; 36% live on campus.

Freshmen

Admission: 828 applied, 781 admitted, 264 enrolled. ***Average high school GPA:*** 3.5. ***Test scores:*** SAT critical reading scores over 500: 53%; SAT math scores over 500: 51%; SAT writing scores over 500: 39%; ACT scores over 18: 92%; SAT critical reading scores over 600: 18%; SAT math scores over 600: 22%; SAT writing scores over 600: 8%; ACT scores over 24: 37%; SAT critical reading scores over 700: 2%; SAT math scores over 700: 3%; ACT scores over 30: 4%.

Retention: 72% of full-time freshmen returned.

FACULTY

Total: 180, 53% full-time, 52% with terminal degrees.

Student/faculty ratio: 12:1.

ACADEMICS

Calendar: semesters. *Degrees:* bachelor's and master's.

Special study options: academic remediation for entering students, adult/continuing education programs, advanced placement credit, distance learning, double majors, English as a second language, honors programs, internships, part-time degree program, services for LD students, study abroad, summer session for credit. ***ROTC:*** Army (c), Air Force (c).

Unusual degree programs: 3-2 engineering with Texas Tech University.

Computers: 169 computers/terminals are available on campus for general student use. Students can access the following: campus intranet, computer help desk, free student e-mail accounts, online (class) grades, online (class) registration, online (class) schedules. Campuswide network is available. 100% of college-owned or -operated housing units are wired for high-speed Internet access. Wireless service is available via entire campus.

STUDENT LIFE

Housing options: on-campus residence required through sophomore year; men-only, women-only. Campus housing is university owned. Freshman campus housing is guaranteed.

Activities and organizations: drama/theater group, student-run newspaper, radio station, choral group, Flight Plan/TRIO Program, College Republicans, Aggie Club, International Justice Mission, Enactus.

Athletics Member NCAA. All Division II. ***Intercollegiate sports:*** baseball M(s), basketball M(s)/W(s), cheerleading M/W, cross-country running M(s)/W(s), golf M(s)/W(s), soccer M(s)/W(s), softball W(s), track and field M/W, volleyball W(s). ***Intramural sports:*** badminton M/W, basketball M/W, cross-country running M/W, football M/W, golf M/W, racquetball M/W, rock climbing M/W, soccer M/W, softball M/W, table tennis M/W, tennis M/W, track and field M/W, ultimate Frisbee M/W, volleyball M/W.

Campus security: 24-hour patrols, controlled dormitory access.

Student services: health clinic, personal/psychological counseling.

COSTS & FINANCIAL AID

Costs (2014–15) ***Comprehensive fee:*** $26,308 includes full-time tuition ($19,400) and room and board ($6908). Full-time tuition and fees vary according to degree level and program. Part-time tuition: $621 per credit hour. Part-time tuition and fees vary according to course load, degree level, and program. ***Required fees:*** $60 per term part-time. ***Room and board:*** Room and board charges vary according to board plan and housing facility. ***Payment plan:*** installment. ***Waivers:*** employees or children of employees.

Financial Aid Of all full-time matriculated undergraduates who enrolled in 2014, 872 applied for aid, 740 were judged to have need, 79 had their need fully met. 567 Federal Work-Study jobs (averaging $1686). 70 state and other part-time jobs (averaging $304). In 2014, 181 non-need-based awards were made. ***Average percent of need met:*** 69. ***Average financial aid package:*** $15,287. ***Average need-based loan:*** $4740. ***Average need-based gift aid:*** $10,534. ***Average non-need-based aid:*** $5278. ***Average indebtedness upon graduation:*** $27,949.

APPLYING

Standardized Tests *Required:* SAT or ACT (for admission).

Options: electronic application.

Application fee: $25.

Required: high school transcript.

Application deadlines: 8/1 (freshmen), rolling (transfers).

Notification: continuous (freshmen), continuous (transfers).

CONTACT

Mr. Chris Hayes, Director of Admissions, Lubbock Christian University, 5601 19th Street, Lubbock, TX 79407. *Phone:* 806-720-7156. *Toll-free phone:* 800-933-7601. *Fax:* 806-720-7162. *E-mail:* admissions@lcu.edu.

McMurry University

Abilene, Texas

http://www.mcm.edu/

- **Independent United Methodist** comprehensive, founded 1923
- **Suburban** 43-acre campus
- **Endowment** $76.3 million
- **Coed** 1,003 undergraduate students, 85% full-time, 48% women, 52% men
- **Moderately difficult** entrance level, 61% of applicants were admitted

UNDERGRAD STUDENTS

848 full-time, 155 part-time. Students come from 21 states and territories; 3 other countries; 5% are from out of state; 18% Black or African American, non-Hispanic/Latino; 22% Hispanic/Latino; 1% Asian, non-Hispanic/Latino; 0.4% Native Hawaiian or other Pacific Islander, non-Hispanic/Latino; 1% American Indian or Alaska Native, non-Hispanic/Latino; 1% Two or more races, non-Hispanic/Latino; 0.1% Race/ethnicity unknown; 0.4% international; 7% transferred in; 45% live on campus.

Freshmen

Admission: 1,031 applied, 633 admitted, 208 enrolled. ***Average high school GPA:*** 3.4. ***Test scores:*** SAT critical reading scores over 500: 30%; SAT math scores over 500: 29%; SAT writing scores over 500: 14%; ACT scores over 18: 64%; SAT critical reading scores over 600: 6%; SAT math scores over 600: 6%; SAT writing scores over 600: 1%; ACT scores over

24: 11%; SAT critical reading scores over 700: 1%; SAT math scores over 700: 1%.

Retention: 52% of full-time freshmen returned.

FACULTY

Total: 111, 71% full-time, 64% with terminal degrees.

Student/faculty ratio: 10:1.

ACADEMICS

Calendar: semesters plus May term. *Degrees:* bachelor's and master's.

Special study options: academic remediation for entering students, accelerated degree program, adult/continuing education programs, advanced placement credit, double majors, honors programs, independent study, internships, part-time degree program, services for LD students, student-designed majors, study abroad, summer session for credit.

Computers: 50 computers/terminals and 705 ports are available on campus for general student use. Students can access the following: campus intranet, computer help desk, free student e-mail accounts, online (class) grades, online (class) registration, online (class) schedules, Moodle. Campuswide network is available. 100% of college-owned or -operated housing units are wired for high-speed Internet access. Wireless service is available via entire campus.

STUDENT LIFE

Housing options: on-campus residence required through junior year; coed, men-only, women-only. Campus housing is university owned and is provided by a third party. Freshman campus housing is guaranteed.

Activities and organizations: drama/theater group, student-run newspaper, choral group, marching band, Alpha Phi Omega, Religious Life Council, McMurry Student Government, Campus Activity Board, Servant Leadership.

Athletics Member NCAA, NCCAA. All NCAA Division III. ***Intercollegiate sports:*** baseball M, basketball M/W, cross-country running M/W, football M, golf M/W, soccer M/W, swimming and diving M/W, tennis M/W, track and field M/W, volleyball W. ***Intramural sports:*** basketball M/W, football M/W, golf M/W, racquetball M/W, soccer M/W, softball M/W, tennis M/W, ultimate Frisbee M/W, volleyball M/W.

Campus security: 24-hour emergency response devices and patrols, late-night transport/escort service, controlled dormitory access.

Student services: health clinic, personal/psychological counseling.

COSTS & FINANCIAL AID

Costs (2014–15) ***One-time required fee:*** $175. ***Comprehensive fee:*** $32,832 includes full-time tuition ($24,844) and room and board ($7988). Full-time tuition and fees vary according to course load. Part-time tuition: $776 per credit hour. Part-time tuition and fees vary according to course load. ***College room only:*** $3886. Room and board charges vary according to board plan and housing facility. ***Payment plan:*** installment. ***Waivers:*** employees or children of employees.

Financial Aid Of all full-time matriculated undergraduates who enrolled in 2013, 982 applied for aid, 900 were judged to have need, 137 had their need fully met. 147 Federal Work-Study jobs (averaging $1635). 56 state and other part-time jobs (averaging $1670). In 2013, 125 non-need-based awards were made. ***Average percent of need met:*** 64. ***Average financial aid package:*** $19,729. ***Average need-based loan:*** $4660. ***Average need-based gift aid:*** $14,809. ***Average non-need-based aid:*** $8503. ***Average indebtedness upon graduation:*** $34,742.

APPLYING

Standardized Tests *Required:* SAT or ACT (for admission).

Options: electronic application, deferred entrance.

Application fee: $25.

Required: essay or personal statement, high school transcript, minimum 2.0 GPA, official ACT or SAT score report. ***Required for some:*** 3 letters of recommendation, interview.

Application deadlines: 8/15 (freshmen), 8/5 (out-of-state freshmen), 8/15 (transfers).

Notification: continuous (freshmen), continuous (out-of-state freshmen), continuous (transfers).

CONTACT

Ms. Kim Tate, Admission and Recruitment Coordinator, McMurry University, 1 McMurry University, #278, Abilene, TX 79697. *Phone:* 325-793-4700. *Toll-free phone:* 800-460-2392. *Fax:* 325-793-4701. *E-mail:* admissions@mcm.edu.

Midland College

Midland, Texas

http://www.midland.edu/

- **State and locally supported** 4-year, founded 1969
- **Suburban** 163-acre campus
- **Endowment** $34.7 million
- **Coed** 5,233 undergraduate students, 29% full-time, 59% women, 41% men
- **Noncompetitive** entrance level

UNDERGRAD STUDENTS

1,537 full-time, 3,696 part-time. Students come from 34 states and territories; 2 other countries; 2% are from out of state; 6% Black or African American, non-Hispanic/Latino; 42% Hispanic/Latino; 2% Asian, non-Hispanic/Latino; 0.1% Native Hawaiian or other Pacific Islander, non-Hispanic/Latino; 0.3% American Indian or Alaska Native, non-Hispanic/Latino; 1% Two or more races, non-Hispanic/Latino; 3% Race/ethnicity unknown; 0.2% international; 5% transferred in.

Freshmen

Admission: 758 enrolled.

FACULTY

Total: 271, 50% full-time, 13% with terminal degrees.

Student/faculty ratio: 16:1.

ACADEMICS

Calendar: semesters. *Degrees:* certificates, associate, and bachelor's.

Special study options: academic remediation for entering students, adult/continuing education programs, advanced placement credit, distance learning, honors programs, services for LD students, summer session for credit.

Computers: 950 computers/terminals are available on campus for general student use. Students can access the following: computer help desk, free student e-mail accounts, online (class) grades, online (class) registration, online (class) schedules. Campuswide network is available. 100% of college-owned or -operated housing units are wired for high-speed Internet access. Wireless service is available via entire campus.

STUDENT LIFE

Housing options: coed, men-only, women-only. Campus housing is university owned.

Activities and organizations: drama/theater group, student-run newspaper, choral group, OIKOS, Midland College Latin American Student Society, Student Government Association, Student Nurses Association, Baptist Student Ministries.

Athletics Member NJCAA. ***Intercollegiate sports:*** baseball M(s), basketball M(s)/W(s), cheerleading W, golf M(s), softball W(s), volleyball W(s). ***Intramural sports:*** basketball M/W, cheerleading W, volleyball M/W.

Campus security: 24-hour patrols, controlled dormitory access.

Student services: personal/psychological counseling.

COSTS

Costs (2015–16) ***Tuition:*** area resident $2340 full-time; state resident $3750 full-time; nonresident $4920 full-time. Full-time tuition and fees vary according to course level, course load, degree level, program, reciprocity agreements, and student level. Part-time tuition and fees vary according to student level. ***Room and board:*** Room and board charges vary according to board plan and housing facility. ***Payment plans:*** installment, deferred payment. ***Waivers:*** senior citizens and employees or children of employees.

APPLYING

Required: high school transcript.

Application deadlines: rolling (freshmen), rolling (out-of-state freshmen), rolling (transfers).

Notification: continuous (freshmen), continuous (out-of-state freshmen), continuous (transfers).

CONTACT
Mr. Jeremy Martinez, Director of Admissions, Midland College, 3600 North Garfield, Midland, TX 79705-6399. *Phone:* 432-685-5523. *Fax:* 432-685-6887. *E-mail:* jmartinez@midland.edu.

Midwestern State University

Wichita Falls, Texas

http://www.mwsu.edu/

- **State-supported** comprehensive, founded 1922
- **Urban** 255-acre campus
- **Endowment** $20.9 million
- **Coed** 5,144 undergraduate students, 75% full-time, 58% women, 42% men
- **Moderately difficult** entrance level, 26% of applicants were admitted

UNDERGRAD STUDENTS
3,864 full-time, 1,280 part-time. Students come from 50 states and territories; 53 other countries; 8% are from out of state; 14% Black or African American, non-Hispanic/Latino; 16% Hispanic/Latino; 3% Asian, non-Hispanic/Latino; 0.3% Native Hawaiian or other Pacific Islander, non-Hispanic/Latino; 0.8% American Indian or Alaska Native, non-Hispanic/Latino; 3% Two or more races, non-Hispanic/Latino; 0.8% Race/ethnicity unknown; 8% international; 10% transferred in; 28% live on campus.

Freshmen
Admission: 3,259 applied, 843 admitted, 843 enrolled. ***Average high school GPA:*** 3.44. ***Test scores:*** SAT critical reading scores over 500: 47%; SAT math scores over 500: 54%; SAT writing scores over 500: 34%; ACT scores over 18: 93%; SAT critical reading scores over 600: 9%; SAT math scores over 600: 11%; SAT writing scores over 600: 6%; ACT scores over 24: 25%; ACT scores over 30: 1%.
Retention: 72% of full-time freshmen returned.

FACULTY
Total: 332, 71% full-time, 65% with terminal degrees.
Student/faculty ratio: 17:1.

ACADEMICS
Calendar: semesters. *Degrees:* associate, bachelor's, master's, and postbachelor's certificates.
Special study options: academic remediation for entering students, adult/continuing education programs, advanced placement credit, distance learning, double majors, English as a second language, honors programs, independent study, internships, part-time degree program, services for LD students, study abroad, summer session for credit. ***ROTC:*** Air Force (c).
Unusual degree programs: 3-2 business administration.
Computers: 405 computers/terminals are available on campus for general student use. Students can access the following: campus intranet, computer help desk, free student e-mail accounts, online (class) grades, online (class) registration, online (class) schedules. Campuswide network is available. 100% of college-owned or -operated housing units are wired for high-speed Internet access. Wireless service is available via entire campus.

STUDENT LIFE
Housing options: on-campus residence required through sophomore year; coed, men-only, women-only, special housing for students with disabilities. Campus housing is university owned. Freshman applicants given priority for college housing.
Activities and organizations: drama/theater group, student-run newspaper, television station, choral group, marching band, Caribbean Students Organization, Baptist Student Ministry, Catholic Campus Ministry, African Students Organization, University Programming Board, national fraternities, national sororities.
Athletics Member NCAA. All Division II. ***Intercollegiate sports:*** basketball M(s)/W(s), cheerleading M(s)(c)/W(s)(c), cross-country running W(s), fencing M(c)/W(c), football M(s), golf M(s)/W(s), soccer M(s)/W(s), softball W(s), tennis M(s)/W(s), volleyball W(s). ***Intramural sports:*** archery M/W, badminton M/W, basketball M/W, bowling M/W, football M/W, golf M/W, rugby M(c), soccer M/W, softball M/W, table tennis M/W, tennis M/W, ultimate Frisbee M/W, volleyball M/W, weight lifting M/W.
Campus security: 24-hour emergency response devices and patrols, controlled dormitory access.
Student services: health clinic, personal/psychological counseling, legal services.

COSTS & FINANCIAL AID
Costs (2014–15) ***Tuition:*** state resident $5070 full-time, $169 per credit hour part-time; nonresident $7020 full-time, $234 per credit hour part-time. Full-time tuition and fees vary according to course load, location, and program. Part-time tuition and fees vary according to course load, location, and program. ***Required fees:*** $2683 full-time, $80 per credit hour part-time, $185 per credit hour part-time. ***Room and board:*** $6810. Room and board charges vary according to board plan and housing facility. ***Payment plan:*** installment. ***Waivers:*** senior citizens and employees or children of employees.
Financial Aid Of all full-time matriculated undergraduates who enrolled in 2014, 3,341 applied for aid, 2,426 were judged to have need, 317 had their need fully met. 45 Federal Work-Study jobs (averaging $2203). 23 state and other part-time jobs (averaging $1585). In 2014, 564 non-need-based awards were made. ***Average percent of need met:*** 64. ***Average financial aid package:*** $9339. ***Average need-based loan:*** $6533. ***Average need-based gift aid:*** $6478. ***Average non-need-based aid:*** $1885. ***Average indebtedness upon graduation:*** $25,550.

APPLYING
Standardized Tests *Required:* SAT or ACT (for admission).
Options: electronic application.
Application fee: $25.
Required: high school transcript.
Application deadlines: 8/7 (freshmen), 8/7 (transfers).
Notification: continuous (freshmen), continuous (transfers).

CONTACT
Ms. Leah Vineyard, Interim Director of Admissions, Midwestern State University, 3410 Taft Boulevard, Wichita Falls, TX 76308. *Phone:* 940-397-4343. *Toll-free phone:* 800-842-1922. *Fax:* 940-397-4672. *E-mail:* leah.vineyard@mwsu.edu.

Northwood University, Texas Campus

Cedar Hill, Texas

http://www.northwood.edu/

- **Independent** comprehensive, founded 1966
- **Small-town** 360-acre campus with easy access to Dallas-Fort Worth
- **Coed** 278 undergraduate students, 57% full-time, 61% women, 39% men
- **Moderately difficult** entrance level

UNDERGRAD STUDENTS
159 full-time, 119 part-time. 40% Black or African American, non-Hispanic/Latino; 19% Hispanic/Latino; 0.4% Asian, non-Hispanic/Latino; 0.7% American Indian or Alaska Native, non-Hispanic/Latino; 0.7% Two or more races, non-Hispanic/Latino; 18% Race/ethnicity unknown; 1% international; 13% transferred in.

Freshmen
Admission: 3 admitted, 3 enrolled.
Retention: 7% of full-time freshmen returned.

FACULTY
Total: 29, 17% full-time, 21% with terminal degrees.
Student/faculty ratio: 17:1.

ACADEMICS
Calendar: quarters. *Degrees:* bachelor's and master's.
Special study options: academic remediation for entering students, accelerated degree program, adult/continuing education programs, advanced placement credit, distance learning, double majors, external degree program, internships, off-campus study, part-time degree program, summer session for credit.
Computers: 73 computers/terminals are available on campus for general student use. Students can access the following: campus intranet, computer help desk, free student e-mail accounts, online (class) grades, online (class) registration, online (class) schedules. Campuswide network is available. 100% of college-owned or -operated housing units are wired for

high-speed Internet access. Wireless service is available via entire campus.

STUDENT LIFE
Housing options: college housing not available.

Athletics ***Intercollegiate sports:*** baseball M(s), cross-country running M(s)/W(s), golf M(s)/W(s), soccer M(s)/W(s), softball W(s), track and field M(s)/W(s). ***Intramural sports:*** basketball M/W, soccer M/W, volleyball M/W.

Campus security: 24-hour patrols, late-night transport/escort service.

COSTS & FINANCIAL AID
Costs (2014–15) ***Tuition:*** $21,950 full-time. Part-time tuition and fees vary according to course load. ***Required fees:*** $1182 full-time. ***Payment plan:*** installment. ***Waivers:*** employees or children of employees.

Financial Aid Of all full-time matriculated undergraduates who enrolled in 2013, 360 applied for aid, 334 were judged to have need, 41 had their need fully met. 21 Federal Work-Study jobs (averaging $1857). In 2013, 31 non-need-based awards were made. ***Average percent of need met:*** 60. ***Average financial aid package:*** $20,560. ***Average need-based loan:*** $4339. ***Average need-based gift aid:*** $6498. ***Average non-need-based aid:*** $9072. ***Average indebtedness upon graduation:*** $24,633.

APPLYING
Standardized Tests *Required:* SAT or ACT (for admission).

Options: electronic application, early admission, deferred entrance.

Application fee: $30.

Required: essay or personal statement, high school transcript, minimum 2.0 GPA. ***Recommended:*** 1 letter of recommendation, interview.

Application deadlines: 8/1 (freshmen), 8/1 (out-of-state freshmen), rolling (transfers).

Notification: continuous (freshmen), continuous (out-of-state freshmen), continuous (transfers).

CONTACT
Dr. Terry Silva, Director of Admissions, Northwood University, Texas Campus, 1114 West FM 1382, Cedar Hill, TX 75104. *Phone:* 972-293-5400. *Toll-free phone:* 800-927-9663. *Fax:* 972-291-3824. *E-mail:* txadmit@northwood.edu.

Our Lady of the Lake University of San Antonio

San Antonio, Texas

http://www.ollusa.edu/

- **Independent Roman Catholic** comprehensive, founded 1895
- **Urban** 75-acre campus
- **Endowment** $23.5 million
- **Coed** 1,595 undergraduate students, 85% full-time, 70% women, 30% men

UNDERGRAD STUDENTS
1,359 full-time, 236 part-time. Students come from 20 states and territories; 10 other countries; 3% are from out of state; 9% Black or African American, non-Hispanic/Latino; 71% Hispanic/Latino; 0.9% Asian, non-Hispanic/Latino; 0.1% Native Hawaiian or other Pacific Islander, non-Hispanic/Latino; 0.5% American Indian or Alaska Native, non-Hispanic/Latino; 1% Two or more races, non-Hispanic/Latino; 3% Race/ethnicity unknown; 0.9% international; 40% transferred in; 38% live on campus.

Freshmen
Admission: 357 enrolled. ***Average high school GPA:*** 3.35. ***Test scores:*** SAT critical reading scores over 500: 31%; SAT math scores over 500: 39%; ACT scores over 18: 82%; SAT critical reading scores over 600: 6%; SAT math scores over 600: 4%; ACT scores over 24: 11%; ACT scores over 30: 1%.
Retention: 63% of full-time freshmen returned.

FACULTY
Total: 320, 31% full-time, 63% with terminal degrees.
Student/faculty ratio: 16:1.

ACADEMICS
Calendar: semesters plus 2 summer sessions. *Degrees:* bachelor's, master's, and doctoral.

Special study options: accelerated degree program, adult/continuing education programs, advanced placement credit, cooperative education, distance learning, double majors, honors programs, independent study, internships, off-campus study, part-time degree program, services for LD students, study abroad, summer session for credit. ***ROTC:*** Army (c).

Computers: 230 computers/terminals are available on campus for general student use. Students can access the following: computer help desk, free student e-mail accounts, online (class) grades, online (class) registration, online (class) schedules. Campuswide network is available. 100% of college-owned or -operated housing units are wired for high-speed Internet access. Wireless service is available via entire campus.

STUDENT LIFE
Housing options: coed, women-only, special housing for students with disabilities. Campus housing is university owned.

Activities and organizations: drama/theater group, student-run newspaper, television station, choral group, First Year Connection, Kappa Delta Chi, Epsilon Sigma Alpha, Social Justice Organization, Higher Achievement Through Leadership Opportunities, national sororities.

Athletics Member NAIA. ***Intercollegiate sports:*** baseball M(s), basketball M(s)/W(s), cross-country running M(s)/W(s), golf M(s), soccer M(s)/W(s), softball W(s), tennis M(s)/W(s), track and field M(s)/W(s), volleyball W(s). ***Intramural sports:*** cheerleading W, football M/W, volleyball M.

Campus security: 24-hour emergency response devices and patrols, late-night transport/escort service, controlled dormitory access.

Student services: health clinic, personal/psychological counseling, women's center.

COSTS & FINANCIAL AID
Costs (2014–15) ***Comprehensive fee:*** $32,032 includes full-time tuition ($23,868), mandatory fees ($728), and room and board ($7436). Full-time tuition and fees vary according to course load and location. Part-time tuition: $765 per credit hour. Part-time tuition and fees vary according to course load and location. ***Required fees:*** $208 per term part-time. ***College room only:*** $4138. Room and board charges vary according to board plan and housing facility. ***Payment plans:*** installment, deferred payment. ***Waivers:*** employees or children of employees.

Financial Aid Of all full-time matriculated undergraduates who enrolled in 2013, 1,231 applied for aid, 1,158 were judged to have need, 326 had their need fully met. In 2013, 90 non-need-based awards were made. ***Average percent of need met:*** 77. ***Average financial aid package:*** $19,688. ***Average need-based loan:*** $4423. ***Average need-based gift aid:*** $9091. ***Average non-need-based aid:*** $9182. ***Average indebtedness upon graduation:*** $28,362.

APPLYING
Standardized Tests *Required:* SAT or ACT (for admission).

Required: high school transcript, minimum 2.0 GPA.

CONTACT
Shannon Tijerina, Assistant Director of Traditional Admissions, Our Lady of the Lake University of San Antonio, 411 Southwest 24th Street, San Antonio, TX 78207-4689. *Phone:* 210-434-6711 Ext. 4133. *Toll-free phone:* 800-436-6558. *Fax:* 210-431-4036. *E-mail:* sytijeria@lake.ollusa.edu.

Paul Quinn College

Dallas, Texas

http://www.pqc.edu/

- **Independent African Methodist Episcopal** 4-year, founded 1872
- **Suburban** 132-acre campus
- **Endowment** $5.3 million
- **Coed**
- **Moderately difficult** entrance level

FACULTY
Student/faculty ratio: 11:1.

ACADEMICS
Calendar: semesters. *Degree:* bachelor's.

STUDENT LIFE
Housing options: on-campus residence required through sophomore year; coed. Campus housing is university owned. Freshman applicants given priority for college housing.

Activities and organizations: drama/theater group, choral group, marching band, Student Ambassadors, NAACP, Student Government Association, intramurals, Honda Campus All Star Challenge (academic quiz bowl), national fraternities, national sororities.

Athletics Member NAIA.

Campus security: 24-hour patrols.

Student services: health clinic, personal/psychological counseling.

COSTS & FINANCIAL AID
Costs (2014–15) ***Comprehensive fee:*** $22,850 includes full-time tuition ($9300), mandatory fees ($4375), and room and board ($9175). Full-time tuition and fees vary according to course load. Part-time tuition: $388 per semester hour. Part-time tuition and fees vary according to course load. ***College room only:*** $5325. Room and board charges vary according to board plan and housing facility.

Financial Aid Of all full-time matriculated undergraduates who enrolled in 2003, 743 applied for aid, 735 were judged to have need, 611 had their need fully met. 149 Federal Work-Study jobs (averaging $826). 16 state and other part-time jobs (averaging $607). ***Average percent of need met:*** 83. ***Average financial aid package:*** $9900. ***Average need-based loan:*** $3875. ***Average need-based gift aid:*** $2954. ***Average indebtedness upon graduation:*** $2375.

APPLYING
Standardized Tests *Required:* SAT or ACT (for admission).

Options: electronic application.

Application fee: $25.

Required: essay or personal statement, high school transcript, minimum 2.5 GPA, interview, meningitis shot, SAT or ACT scores, college placement exam scores.

CONTACT
Paul Quinn College, 3837 Simpson-Stuart Road, Dallas, TX 75241-4331. *Phone:* 214-379-5494. *Toll-free phone:* 877-346-1063.

Prairie View A&M University

Prairie View, Texas

http://www.pvamu.edu/

- **State-supported** university, founded 1878, part of Texas A&M University System
- **Small-town** 1502-acre campus with easy access to Houston
- **Endowment** $71.1 million
- **Coed** 6,905 undergraduate students, 91% full-time, 59% women, 41% men
- **Moderately difficult** entrance level, 39% of applicants were admitted

UNDERGRAD STUDENTS
6,313 full-time, 592 part-time. Students come from 42 states and territories; 39 other countries; 8% are from out of state; 86% Black or African American, non-Hispanic/Latino; 3% Hispanic/Latino; 2% Asian, non-Hispanic/Latino; 0.1% Native Hawaiian or other Pacific Islander, non-Hispanic/Latino; 0.3% American Indian or Alaska Native, non-Hispanic/Latino; 0.7% Two or more races, non-Hispanic/Latino; 2% Race/ethnicity unknown; 1% international; 32% transferred in; 53% live on campus.

Freshmen
Admission: 9,850 applied, 3,854 admitted, 1,609 enrolled. ***Average high school GPA:*** 3.02. ***Test scores:*** SAT critical reading scores over 500: 12%; SAT math scores over 500: 19%; SAT writing scores over 500: 10%; ACT scores over 18: 47%; SAT critical reading scores over 600: 2%; SAT math scores over 600: 3%; SAT writing scores over 600: 1%; ACT scores over 24: 5%.

Retention: 66% of full-time freshmen returned.

FACULTY
Total: 461, 82% full-time, 56% with terminal degrees.

Student/faculty ratio: 18:1.

ACADEMICS
Calendar: semesters. *Degrees:* bachelor's, master's, doctoral, post-master's, and postbachelor's certificates.

Special study options: academic remediation for entering students, accelerated degree program, advanced placement credit, cooperative education, distance learning, double majors, honors programs, independent study, internships, off-campus study, part-time degree program, services for LD students, study abroad, summer session for credit. ***ROTC:*** Army (b), Navy (b).

Computers: 341 computers/terminals and 1,000 ports are available on campus for general student use. Students can access the following: campus intranet, computer help desk, free student e-mail accounts, online (class) grades, online (class) registration, online (class) schedules. Campuswide network is available. 100% of college-owned or -operated housing units are wired for high-speed Internet access. Wireless service is available via entire campus.

STUDENT LIFE
Housing options: men-only, women-only, special housing for students with disabilities. Campus housing is provided by a third party. Freshman applicants given priority for college housing.

Activities and organizations: drama/theater group, student-run newspaper, radio station, choral group, marching band, National Society of Black Engineers, National Association of Black Accountants, National Organization of Black Chemists and Chemical Engineers, Toastmasters International, Baptist Student Movement, national fraternities, national sororities.

Athletics Member NCAA, NAIA. All NCAA Division I except football (Division I-AA). ***Intercollegiate sports:*** baseball M(s), basketball M(s)/W(s), cross-country running M(s)/W(s), golf M(s)/W(s), soccer W(s), softball W(s), tennis M(s)/W(s), track and field M(s)/W(s), volleyball W(s). ***Intramural sports:*** baseball M, basketball M/W, bowling W, cross-country running M/W, golf M/W, soccer W, softball W, tennis M/W, track and field M/W, volleyball M/W.

Campus security: 24-hour emergency response devices and patrols, late-night transport/escort service, controlled dormitory access.

Student services: health clinic, personal/psychological counseling.

COSTS & FINANCIAL AID
Costs (2014–15) ***Tuition:*** state resident $5393 full-time, $217 per credit hour part-time; nonresident $16,013 full-time, $599 per credit hour part-time. Full-time tuition and fees vary according to course load, degree level, program, and reciprocity agreements. Part-time tuition and fees vary according to course load, degree level, program, and reciprocity agreements. No tuition increase for student's term of enrollment. ***Required fees:*** $2705 full-time. ***Room and board:*** $7467; room only: $5144. Room and board charges vary according to board plan, housing facility, and student level. ***Payment plan:*** installment. ***Waivers:*** senior citizens.

Financial Aid Of all full-time matriculated undergraduates who enrolled in 2012, 5,939 applied for aid, 4,463 were judged to have need, 19 had their need fully met. In 2012, 509 non-need-based awards were made. ***Average percent of need met:*** 84. ***Average financial aid package:*** $13,345. ***Average need-based loan:*** $3745. ***Average need-based gift aid:*** $4052. ***Average non-need-based aid:*** $2578. ***Average indebtedness upon graduation:*** $26,500.

APPLYING
Standardized Tests *Required:* SAT or ACT (for admission).

Options: electronic application, deferred entrance.

Application fee: $25.

Required: high school transcript, minimum 2.5 GPA.

Application deadlines: 6/1 (freshmen), 6/1 (out-of-state freshmen).

CONTACT
Ms. Lenice D. Brown, Interim Director of Admissions, Prairie View A&M University, PO Box 519, MS #1009, Prairie View, TX 77446-0188. *Phone:* 936-261-1068. *E-mail:* ldbrown@pvamu.edu.

Rice University

Houston, Texas

http://www.rice.edu/

- **Independent** university, founded 1912
- **Urban** 300-acre campus with easy access to Houston
- **Endowment** $5.5 billion
- **Coed** 3,926 undergraduate students, 99% full-time, 48% women, 52% men
- **Most difficult** entrance level, 15% of applicants were admitted

UNDERGRAD STUDENTS
3,872 full-time, 54 part-time. Students come from 53 states and territories; 44 other countries; 7% Black or African American, non-Hispanic/Latino; 15% Hispanic/Latino; 22% Asian, non-Hispanic/Latino; 0.1% American Indian or Alaska Native, non-Hispanic/Latino; 4% Two or more races, non-Hispanic/Latino; 1% Race/ethnicity unknown; 12% international; 0.8% transferred in; 70% live on campus.

Freshmen
Admission: 17,728 applied, 2,677 admitted, 949 enrolled. ***Test scores:*** SAT critical reading scores over 500: 98%; SAT math scores over 500: 99%; SAT writing scores over 500: 98%; ACT scores over 18: 99%; SAT critical reading scores over 600: 93%; SAT math scores over 600: 96%; SAT writing scores over 600: 91%; ACT scores over 24: 96%; SAT critical reading scores over 700: 66%; SAT math scores over 700: 80%; SAT writing scores over 700: 64%; ACT scores over 30: 84%.

Retention: 96% of full-time freshmen returned.

FACULTY
Total: 849, 76% full-time, 91% with terminal degrees.

Student/faculty ratio: 6:1.

ACADEMICS
Calendar: semesters. *Degrees:* bachelor's, master's, and doctoral.

Special study options: accelerated degree program, advanced placement credit, double majors, English as a second language, honors programs, independent study, internships, off-campus study, services for LD students, student-designed majors, study abroad, summer session for credit. ***ROTC:*** Army (c), Navy (b), Air Force (c).

Computers: 495 computers/terminals are available on campus for general student use. Students can access the following: campus intranet, computer help desk, free student e-mail accounts, online (class) grades, online (class) registration, online (class) schedules. Campuswide network is available. 100% of college-owned or -operated housing units are wired for high-speed Internet access. Wireless service is available via entire campus.

STUDENT LIFE
Housing options: coed. Campus housing is university owned. Freshman applicants given priority for college housing.

Activities and organizations: drama/theater group, student-run newspaper, radio and television station, choral group, marching band, Drama Club, Community service/volunteer program, intramural sports, College government, Marching Owl Band.

Athletics Member NCAA. All Division I except football (Division I-A). ***Intercollegiate sports:*** badminton M(c)/W(c), baseball M(s), basketball M(s)/W(s), cheerleading M(c)/W(c), crew M(c)/W(c), cross-country running M(s)/W(s), equestrian sports M(c)/W(c), fencing M(c)/W(c), field hockey W(c), golf M(s), lacrosse M(c)/W(c), riflery M(c)/W(c), rugby M(c)/W(c), sailing M(c)/W(c), soccer M(c)/W(s), softball W(c), swimming and diving W(s), tennis M(s)/W(s), track and field M(s)/W(s), ultimate Frisbee M(c)/W(c), volleyball M(c)/W(s), water polo M(c)/W(c). ***Intramural sports:*** badminton M/W, basketball M/W, cross-country running M/W, football M/W, racquetball M/W, soccer M/W, softball M/W, swimming and diving M/W, table tennis M/W, tennis M/W, track and field M/W, ultimate Frisbee M/W, volleyball M/W.

Campus security: 24-hour emergency response devices and patrols, late-night transport/escort service, controlled dormitory access.

Student services: health clinic, personal/psychological counseling, women's center.

COSTS & FINANCIAL AID
Costs (2014–15) ***One-time required fee:*** $575. ***Comprehensive fee:*** $53,966 includes full-time tuition ($39,880), mandatory fees ($686), and room and board ($13,400). Part-time tuition: $1662 per credit hour. ***College room only:*** $9100. ***Payment plan:*** installment. ***Waivers:*** employees or children of employees.

Financial Aid Of all full-time matriculated undergraduates who enrolled in 2013, 2,076 applied for aid, 1,626 were judged to have need, 1,625 had their need fully met. In 2013, 575 non-need-based awards were made. ***Average percent of need met:*** 100. ***Average financial aid package:*** $36,556. ***Average need-based loan:*** $3308. ***Average need-based gift aid:*** $34,565. ***Average non-need-based aid:*** $11,833. ***Average indebtedness upon graduation:*** $17,856.

APPLYING
Standardized Tests *Required:* SAT and 2 SAT Subject Tests OR ACT Plus Writing (for admission).

Options: electronic application, early decision, deferred entrance.

Application fee: $75.

Required: essay or personal statement, high school transcript, 2 letters of recommendation. ***Required for some:*** portfolio for architecture; audition for music. ***Recommended:*** interview.

Application deadlines: 1/1 (freshmen), 3/15 (transfers).

Early decision deadline: 11/1.

Notification: 4/1 (freshmen), continuous until 5/15 (transfers), 12/15 (early decision).

CONTACT
Office of Admission, Rice University, Office of Admission, PO Box 1892, MS 17, Houston, TX 77251-1892. *Phone:* 713-348-RICE. *E-mail:* admi@rice.edu.

St. Edward's University

Austin, Texas

http://www.stedwards.edu/

- **Independent Roman Catholic** comprehensive, founded 1885
- **Urban** 160-acre campus
- **Endowment** $94.6 million
- **Coed** 4,003 undergraduate students, 86% full-time, 61% women, 39% men
- **Moderately difficult** entrance level, 78% of applicants were admitted

UNDERGRAD STUDENTS
3,436 full-time, 567 part-time. Students come from 44 states and territories; 54 other countries; 12% are from out of state; 4% Black or African American, non-Hispanic/Latino; 40% Hispanic/Latino; 3% Asian, non-Hispanic/Latino; 0.2% Native Hawaiian or other Pacific Islander, non-Hispanic/Latino; 0.4% American Indian or Alaska Native, non-Hispanic/Latino; 3% Two or more races, non-Hispanic/Latino; 2% Race/ethnicity unknown; 9% international; 6% transferred in; 39% live on campus.

Freshmen
Admission: 4,423 applied, 3,466 admitted, 811 enrolled. ***Test scores:*** SAT critical reading scores over 500: 85%; SAT math scores over 500: 81%; SAT writing scores over 500: 73%; ACT scores over 18: 99%; SAT critical reading scores over 600: 35%; SAT math scores over 600: 24%; SAT writing scores over 600: 26%; ACT scores over 24: 58%; SAT critical reading scores over 700: 4%; SAT math scores over 700: 2%; SAT writing scores over 700: 1%; ACT scores over 30: 9%.

Retention: 83% of full-time freshmen returned.

FACULTY
Total: 495, 41% full-time, 65% with terminal degrees.

Student/faculty ratio: 13:1.

ACADEMICS
Calendar: semesters. *Degrees:* bachelor's, master's, and postbachelor's certificates.

Special study options: academic remediation for entering students, adult/continuing education programs, advanced placement credit, double majors, honors programs, independent study, internships, part-time degree program, services for LD students, study abroad, summer session for credit. ***ROTC:*** Army (c), Air Force (c).

Computers: 967 computers/terminals and 7,200 ports are available on campus for general student use. Students can access the following:

computer help desk, free student e-mail accounts, online (class) grades, online (class) registration, online (class) schedules, online library, ability to change address and biographical data, look at transcripts, pull up statements of account, grades, online progress reports and degree audit, campus job postings, student timesheets, financial aid information. Campuswide network is available. 100% of college-owned or -operated housing units are wired for high-speed Internet access. Wireless service is available via classrooms, computer centers, computer labs, dorm rooms, learning centers, libraries, student centers.

STUDENT LIFE

Housing options: on-campus residence required for freshman year; coed, special housing for students with disabilities. Campus housing is university owned. Freshman campus housing is guaranteed.

Activities and organizations: drama/theater group, student-run newspaper, radio and television station, choral group, Academy of Science, Outdoor Adventure Club, American Medical Student Association, PRIDE, Asian Student Association.

Athletics Member NCAA. All Division II. ***Intercollegiate sports:*** baseball M(s), basketball M(s)/W(s), cheerleading M/W, cross-country running M/W, golf M(s)/W(s), soccer M(s)/W(s), softball W(s), tennis M(s)/W(s), volleyball W(s). ***Intramural sports:*** archery M(c)/W(c), basketball M(c)/W, bowling M/W, crew M(c)/W(c), golf M/W, lacrosse M(c)/W(c), racquetball M/W, rugby M(c), soccer M(c)/W(c), swimming and diving M(c)/W(c), tennis M(c)/W(c), ultimate Frisbee M(c)/W(c), volleyball M(c)/W(c).

Campus security: 24-hour emergency response devices and patrols, late-night transport/escort service, controlled dormitory access, self-defense education, informal discussions, pamphlets, posters, alcohol awareness meetings, lighted pathways and sidewalks.

Student services: health clinic, personal/psychological counseling.

COSTS & FINANCIAL AID

Costs (2015–16) ***Comprehensive fee:*** $50,384 includes full-time tuition ($38,320), mandatory fees ($400), and room and board ($11,664). Full-time tuition and fees vary according to course load and degree level. Part-time tuition: $1278 per credit hour. Part-time tuition and fees vary according to course load and degree level. ***College room only:*** $6734. Room and board charges vary according to board plan and housing facility. ***Payment plan:*** installment. ***Waivers:*** employees or children of employees.

Financial Aid Of all full-time matriculated undergraduates who enrolled in 2014, 2,508 applied for aid, 2,237 were judged to have need, 213 had their need fully met. 217 Federal Work-Study jobs (averaging $1984). 16 state and other part-time jobs (averaging $2063). In 2014, 152 non-need-based awards were made. ***Average percent of need met:*** 67. ***Average financial aid package:*** $28,906. ***Average need-based loan:*** $4523. ***Average need-based gift aid:*** $18,539. ***Average non-need-based aid:*** $11,337. ***Average indebtedness upon graduation:*** $34,444.

APPLYING

Standardized Tests *Required:* SAT or ACT (for admission).

Options: electronic application, deferred entrance.

Application fee: $50.

Required: essay or personal statement, high school transcript, 1 letter of recommendation. ***Recommended:*** interview.

Application deadlines: 5/1 (freshmen), 5/1 (out-of-state freshmen), 7/1 (transfers).

Notification: continuous (freshmen), continuous (out-of-state freshmen), continuous (transfers).

CONTACT

Ms. Stacy Knighton, Office Specialist, St. Edward's University, 3001 South Congress Avenue, Austin, TX 78704. *Phone:* 512-448-8500. *Toll-free phone:* 800-555-0164. *Fax:* 512-464-8877. *E-mail:* seu.admit@stedwards.edu.

★ St. Mary's University

San Antonio, Texas

http://www.stmarytx.edu/

- **Independent Roman Catholic** comprehensive, founded 1852
- **Urban** 135-acre campus with easy access to San Antonio
- **Endowment** $175.0 million
- **Coed** 2,322 undergraduate students, 95% full-time, 56% women, 44% men
- **Moderately difficult** entrance level, 59% of applicants were admitted

UNDERGRAD STUDENTS

2,211 full-time, 111 part-time. Students come from 31 states and territories; 30 other countries; 8% are from out of state; 4% Black or African American, non-Hispanic/Latino; 69% Hispanic/Latino; 2% Asian, non-Hispanic/Latino; 0.3% Native Hawaiian or other Pacific Islander, non-Hispanic/Latino; 0.4% American Indian or Alaska Native, non-Hispanic/Latino; 0.3% Two or more races, non-Hispanic/Latino; 3% Race/ethnicity unknown; 6% international; 6% transferred in; 59% live on campus.

Freshmen

Admission: 4,282 applied, 2,546 admitted, 469 enrolled. ***Test scores:*** SAT critical reading scores over 500: 58%; SAT math scores over 500: 66%; SAT writing scores over 500: 51%; ACT scores over 18: 97%; SAT critical reading scores over 600: 15%; SAT math scores over 600: 17%; SAT writing scores over 600: 12%; ACT scores over 24: 31%; SAT critical reading scores over 700: 1%; SAT math scores over 700: 2%; SAT writing scores over 700: 1%; ACT scores over 30: 4%.

Retention: 77% of full-time freshmen returned.

FACULTY

Total: 384, 53% full-time, 80% with terminal degrees.

Student/faculty ratio: 12:1.

ACADEMICS

Calendar: semesters. *Degrees:* bachelor's, master's, and doctoral.

Special study options: academic remediation for entering students, adult/continuing education programs, advanced placement credit, cooperative education, distance learning, double majors, English as a second language, honors programs, independent study, internships, off-campus study, part-time degree program, services for LD students, study abroad, summer session for credit. ***ROTC:*** Army (b), Air Force (c).

Computers: 200 computers/terminals and 125 ports are available on campus for general student use. Students can access the following: campus intranet, computer help desk, free student e-mail accounts, online (class) grades, online (class) registration, online (class) schedules. Campuswide network is available. 100% of college-owned or -operated housing units are wired for high-speed Internet access. Wireless service is available via entire campus.

STUDENT LIFE

Housing options: on-campus residence required for freshman year; coed, special housing for students with disabilities. Campus housing is university owned. Freshman applicants given priority for college housing.

Activities and organizations: drama/theater group, student-run newspaper, choral group, National Society of Leadership and Success, Beta Beta Beta Biological Honor Society, Habitat for Humanity, American Red Cross Campus Club, Student Government Association, national fraternities, national sororities.

Athletics Member NCAA. All Division II. ***Intercollegiate sports:*** baseball M(s), basketball M(s)/W(s), cheerleading M/W, golf M(s)/W, soccer M(s)/W(s), softball W, tennis M(s)/W(s), volleyball W(s). ***Intramural sports:*** basketball M/W, football M/W, racquetball M/W, soccer M/W, softball M/W, table tennis M/W, tennis M/W, volleyball M/W.

Campus security: 24-hour emergency response devices and patrols, late-night transport/escort service, controlled dormitory access.

Student services: health clinic, personal/psychological counseling.

COSTS & FINANCIAL AID

Costs (2014–15) ***Comprehensive fee:*** $35,786 includes full-time tuition ($26,186), mandatory fees ($706), and room and board ($8894). Full-time tuition and fees vary according to course level, course load, degree level, and program. Part-time tuition: $785 per credit hour. Part-time tuition and fees vary according to course level, course load, degree level, and program. ***Room and board:*** Room and board charges vary according to board plan, housing facility, and student level. ***Payment plan:*** installment. ***Waivers:*** employees or children of employees.

Financial Aid Of all full-time matriculated undergraduates who enrolled in 2009, 1,747 applied for aid, 1,633 were judged to have need, 406 had their need fully met. In 2009, 509 non-need-based awards were made. ***Average percent of need met:*** 76. ***Average financial aid package:*** $20,138. ***Average need-based loan:*** $6124. ***Average need-based gift aid:*** $14,206. ***Average non-need-based aid:*** $7292. ***Average indebtedness upon graduation:*** $22,592.

APPLYING

Standardized Tests *Required:* SAT or ACT (for admission).

Options: electronic application, deferred entrance.

Application fee: $30.

Required: high school transcript. ***Recommended:*** essay or personal statement, minimum 2.0 GPA, interview.

Application deadlines: rolling (freshmen), rolling (transfers).

Notification: continuous (freshmen), continuous (transfers).

CONTACT

Mr. Nelson Delgado, Dean of Admission, St. Mary's University, One Camino Santa Maria, Box #3, San Antonio, TX 78228. *Phone:* 210-436-3126. *Toll-free phone:* 800-FOR-STMU. *Fax:* 210-431-6742. *E-mail:* uadm@stmarytx.edu.

Sam Houston State University

Huntsville, Texas

http://www.shsu.edu/

- **State-supported** university, founded 1879, part of Texas State University System
- **Small-town** 2750-acre campus with easy access to Houston
- **Endowment** $75.8 million
- **Coed** 16,819 undergraduate students, 81% full-time, 60% women, 40% men
- **Moderately difficult** entrance level, 74% of applicants were admitted

UNDERGRAD STUDENTS

13,553 full-time, 3,266 part-time. Students come from 41 states and territories; 49 other countries; 2% are from out of state; 19% Black or African American, non-Hispanic/Latino; 19% Hispanic/Latino; 1% Asian, non-Hispanic/Latino; 0.2% Native Hawaiian or other Pacific Islander, non-Hispanic/Latino; 0.5% American Indian or Alaska Native, non-Hispanic/Latino; 3% Two or more races, non-Hispanic/Latino; 2% Race/ethnicity unknown; 1% international; 15% transferred in; 20% live on campus.

Freshmen

Admission: 9,175 applied, 6,759 admitted, 2,542 enrolled. ***Test scores:*** SAT critical reading scores over 500: 43%; SAT math scores over 500: 50%; ACT scores over 18: 85%; SAT critical reading scores over 600: 7%; SAT math scores over 600: 9%; ACT scores over 24: 19%; SAT critical reading scores over 700: 1%; ACT scores over 30: 1%.

Retention: 78% of full-time freshmen returned.

FACULTY

Total: 973, 70% full-time, 68% with terminal degrees.

Student/faculty ratio: 21:1.

ACADEMICS

Calendar: semesters. *Degrees:* bachelor's, master's, doctoral, and postbachelor's certificates.

Special study options: academic remediation for entering students, advanced placement credit, distance learning, double majors, English as a second language, honors programs, independent study, internships, off-campus study, part-time degree program, services for LD students, study abroad, summer session for credit. ***ROTC:*** Army (b).

Computers: 1,613 computers/terminals are available on campus for general student use. Students can access the following: campus intranet, computer help desk, free student e-mail accounts, online (class) grades, online (class) registration, online (class) schedules. Campuswide network is available. 100% of college-owned or -operated housing units are wired for high-speed Internet access. Wireless service is available via entire campus.

STUDENT LIFE

Housing options: on-campus residence required for freshman year; coed, men-only, women-only, special housing for students with disabilities. Campus housing is university owned and is provided by a third party. Freshman campus housing is guaranteed.

Activities and organizations: drama/theater group, student-run newspaper, radio and television station, choral group, marching band, Chi Alpha Christian Fellowship, Non-Traditional Student Organization, Sigma Alpha Pi Leadership Society, Baptist Student Ministry, Bearkats for Life, national fraternities, national sororities.

Athletics Member NCAA. All Division I except football (Division I-AA). ***Intercollegiate sports:*** baseball M(s), basketball M(s)/W(s), bowling W(s), cheerleading M(s)/W(s), cross-country running M(s)/W(s), equestrian sports M/W, golf M(s)/W(s), lacrosse M(c)/W(c), soccer W(s), softball W(s), tennis W(s), track and field M(s)/W(s), ultimate Frisbee M(c)/W(c), volleyball W(s). ***Intramural sports:*** basketball M/W, football M/W, racquetball M/W, riflery M(c), rugby M(c)/W(c), soccer M/W, softball M/W, tennis M(c)/W(c), volleyball M/W.

Campus security: 24-hour emergency response devices and patrols, student patrols, late-night transport/escort service, controlled dormitory access.

Student services: health clinic, personal/psychological counseling, legal services.

COSTS & FINANCIAL AID

Costs (2014–15) ***Tuition:*** state resident $6120 full-time; nonresident $16,980 full-time. Full-time tuition and fees vary according to course load and location. Part-time tuition and fees vary according to course load and location. No tuition increase for student's term of enrollment. ***Required fees:*** $2812 full-time. ***Room and board:*** $8324. Room and board charges vary according to board plan and housing facility. ***Payment plan:*** installment. ***Waivers:*** employees or children of employees.

Financial Aid Of all full-time matriculated undergraduates who enrolled in 2012, 9,793 applied for aid, 8,292 were judged to have need, 753 had their need fully met. In 2012, 1059 non-need-based awards were made. ***Average percent of need met:*** 56. ***Average financial aid package:*** $10,827. ***Average need-based loan:*** $4233. ***Average need-based gift aid:*** $6276. ***Average non-need-based aid:*** $2371. ***Average indebtedness upon graduation:*** $27,689.

APPLYING

Standardized Tests *Required:* SAT or ACT (for admission).

Options: electronic application, early admission.

Application fee: $45.

Required: high school transcript.

Application deadlines: 8/1 (freshmen), 8/1 (out-of-state freshmen), 8/1 (transfers).

Notification: continuous (freshmen), continuous (out-of-state freshmen), continuous (transfers).

CONTACT

Mr. Trevor B. Thorn, Director of Admissions and Recruitment, Sam Houston State University, Box 2418, Huntsville, TX 77341. *Phone:* 936-294-1828. *Toll-free phone:* 866-232-7528 Ext. 1828. *Fax:* 936-294-3758. *E-mail:* admissions@shsu.edu.

Schreiner University

Kerrville, Texas

http://www.schreiner.edu/

- **Independent Presbyterian** comprehensive, founded 1923
- **Small-town** 205-acre campus with easy access to San Antonio, Austin
- **Endowment** $55.6 million
- **Coed**
- **Moderately difficult** entrance level

FACULTY

Student/faculty ratio: 14:1.

ACADEMICS

Calendar: semesters. *Degrees:* certificates, associate, bachelor's, and master's.

STUDENT LIFE

Housing options: on-campus residence required through junior year; coed, special housing for students with disabilities. Campus housing is university owned. Freshman campus housing is guaranteed.

Activities and organizations: drama/theater group, student-run newspaper, choral group, Student Senate, Greek Life, Campus Ministry, honor societies, Hall Councils, national fraternities, national sororities.

Athletics Member NCAA. All Division III.

Campus security: 24-hour emergency response devices and patrols, late-night transport/escort service.

Student services: health clinic, personal/psychological counseling.

COSTS & FINANCIAL AID

Costs (2014–15) ***Comprehensive fee:*** $34,970 includes full-time tuition ($22,760), mandatory fees ($1600), and room and board ($10,610). Part-time tuition: $972 per credit hour. ***Room and board:*** Room and board charges vary according to board plan and housing facility.

Financial Aid Of all full-time matriculated undergraduates who enrolled in 2012, 939 applied for aid, 854 were judged to have need, 112 had their need fully met. 51 Federal Work-Study jobs (averaging $1447). 227 state and other part-time jobs (averaging $1068). In 2012, 76 non-need-based awards were made. ***Average percent of need met:*** 67. ***Average financial aid package:*** $16,983. ***Average need-based loan:*** $3671. ***Average need-based gift aid:*** $13,872. ***Average non-need-based aid:*** $7666. ***Average indebtedness upon graduation:*** $31,189.

APPLYING

Standardized Tests *Required:* SAT or ACT (for admission).

Options: electronic application, deferred entrance.

Application fee: $25.

Required: high school transcript.

CONTACT

Caroline Randall, Director of Admissions, Schreiner University, 2100 Memorial Boulevard, Kerrville, TX 78028. *Phone:* 800-343-4919. *Toll-free phone:* 800-343-4919. *E-mail:* admissions@schreiner.edu.

★ Southern Methodist University

Dallas, Texas

http://www.smu.edu/

- **Independent** university, founded 1911, affiliated with United Methodist Church
- **Urban** 234-acre campus with easy access to Dallas-Fort Worth
- **Endowment** $1.5 billion
- **Coed** 6,391 undergraduate students, 97% full-time, 50% women, 50% men
- **Moderately difficult** entrance level, 52% of applicants were admitted

UNDERGRAD STUDENTS

6,193 full-time, 198 part-time. Students come from 51 states and territories; 62 other countries; 51% are from out of state; 5% Black or African American, non-Hispanic/Latino; 12% Hispanic/Latino; 7% Asian, non-Hispanic/Latino; 0.2% Native Hawaiian or other Pacific Islander, non-Hispanic/Latino; 0.3% American Indian or Alaska Native, non-Hispanic/Latino; 3% Two or more races, non-Hispanic/Latino; 0.2% Race/ethnicity unknown; 7% international; 4% transferred in; 38% live on campus.

Freshmen

Admission: 11,817 applied, 6,192 admitted, 1,459 enrolled. ***Average high school GPA:*** 3.67. ***Test scores:*** SAT critical reading scores over 500: 97%; SAT math scores over 500: 98%; SAT writing scores over 500: 97%; ACT scores over 18: 100%; SAT critical reading scores over 600: 77%; SAT math scores over 600: 85%; SAT writing scores over 600: 76%; ACT scores over 24: 97%; SAT critical reading scores over 700: 22%; SAT math scores over 700: 32%; SAT writing scores over 700: 25%; ACT scores over 30: 51%.

Retention: 89% of full-time freshmen returned.

FACULTY

Total: 1,125, 65% full-time, 66% with terminal degrees.

Student/faculty ratio: 11:1.

ACADEMICS

Calendar: semesters. *Degrees:* bachelor's, master's, doctoral, and postbachelor's certificates.

Special study options: academic remediation for entering students, accelerated degree program, adult/continuing education programs, advanced placement credit, cooperative education, distance learning, double majors, English as a second language, honors programs, independent study, internships, part-time degree program, services for LD students, student-designed majors, study abroad, summer session for credit. ***ROTC:*** Army (b), Air Force (c).

Computers: 758 computers/terminals are available on campus for general student use. Students can access the following: campus intranet, computer help desk, free student e-mail accounts, online (class) grades, online (class) registration, online (class) schedules, online billing/payment processing. Campuswide network is available. Wireless service is available via classrooms, computer centers, computer labs, dorm rooms, learning centers, libraries, student centers.

STUDENT LIFE

Housing options: on-campus residence required for freshman year; coed, special housing for students with disabilities. Campus housing is university owned. Freshman campus housing is guaranteed.

Activities and organizations: drama/theater group, student-run newspaper, radio and television station, choral group, marching band, Program Council, Student Senate, Student Foundation, Residence Hall Association, SPARC (Students Promoting Awareness, Responsibility, and Citizenship), national fraternities, national sororities.

Athletics Member NCAA. All Division I except football (Division I-A). ***Intercollegiate sports:*** baseball M(c), basketball M(s)/W(s), cheerleading M(s)(c)/W(s)(c), crew W(s), cross-country running W(s), equestrian sports W(s), fencing M(c)/W(c), golf M(s)/W(s), ice hockey M(c), lacrosse M(c), rugby M(c)/W(c), soccer M(s)/W(s), swimming and diving M(s)/W(s), tennis M(s)/W(s), track and field W, volleyball W(s), wrestling M(c). ***Intramural sports:*** basketball M/W, bowling M/W, football M, golf M/W, racquetball M/W, rock climbing M(c)/W(c), soccer M/W, softball M/W, swimming and diving M/W, table tennis M(c)/W(c), tennis M/W, ultimate Frisbee M/W, volleyball M/W, water polo M/W, weight lifting M(c)/W(c).

Campus security: 24-hour emergency response devices and patrols, late-night transport/escort service, controlled dormitory access.

Student services: health clinic, personal/psychological counseling, women's center.

COSTS & FINANCIAL AID

Costs (2015–16) ***Comprehensive fee:*** $63,765 includes full-time tuition ($42,770), mandatory fees ($5420), and room and board ($15,575). Part-time tuition: $1787 per credit hour. Part-time tuition and fees vary according to course load. ***Room and board:*** Room and board charges vary according to board plan and housing facility. ***Payment plans:*** tuition prepayment, installment. ***Waivers:*** employees or children of employees.

Financial Aid Of all full-time matriculated undergraduates who enrolled in 2014, 2,659 applied for aid, 2,242 were judged to have need, 699 had their need fully met. In 2014, 2044 non-need-based awards were made. ***Average percent of need met:*** 86. ***Average financial aid package:*** $37,976. ***Average need-based loan:*** $4373. ***Average need-based gift aid:*** $19,674. ***Average non-need-based aid:*** $20,479. ***Average indebtedness upon graduation:*** $34,671.

APPLYING

Standardized Tests *Required:* SAT or ACT (for admission). *Required for some:* SAT Subject Tests (for admission).

Options: electronic application, early decision, early action, deferred entrance.

Application fee: $60.

Required: high school transcript, minimum 2.0 GPA, 1 letter of recommendation, statement of good standing from prior institution(s). ***Recommended:*** essay or personal statement, minimum 2.7 GPA.

Application deadlines: 1/15 (freshmen), 4/1 (transfers), 11/1 (early action).

Early decision deadline: 11/1 (for plan 1), 1/15 (for plan 2).

Notification: continuous (freshmen), 12/31 (early decision plan 1), 4/1 (early decision plan 2), 12/31 (early action).

CONTACT
Mr. Wes Waggoner, Dean of Undergraduate Admission and Executive Director of Enrollment Services, Southern Methodist University, PO Box 750181, Dallas, TX 75275-0181. *Phone:* 214-768-3417. *Toll-free phone:* 800-323-0672. *Fax:* 214-768-1083. *E-mail:* ugadmission@smu.edu.

South University

Austin, Texas

http://www.southuniversity.edu/austin.aspx

- **Proprietary** comprehensive
- **Coed**

ACADEMICS
Degrees: associate, bachelor's, and master's.

CONTACT
Director of Admissions, South University, 7700 West Parmer Lane, Building A, Suite A100, Austin, TX 78729. *Phone:* 512-516-8800. *Toll-free phone:* 877-659-5706. *Fax:* 512-516-8680.

Southwestern Adventist University

Keene, Texas

http://www.swau.edu/

- **Independent Seventh-day Adventist** comprehensive, founded 1894
- **Small-town** 150-acre campus with easy access to Dallas-Fort Worth
- **Endowment** $7.6 million
- **Coed** 787 undergraduate students, 86% full-time, 57% women, 43% men
- **Minimally difficult** entrance level, 50% of applicants were admitted

UNDERGRAD STUDENTS
677 full-time, 110 part-time. Students come from 31 states and territories; 34 other countries; 11% are from out of state; 17% Black or African American, non-Hispanic/Latino; 44% Hispanic/Latino; 5% Asian, non-Hispanic/Latino; 2% Native Hawaiian or other Pacific Islander, non-Hispanic/Latino; 0.1% American Indian or Alaska Native, non-Hispanic/Latino; 4% Two or more races, non-Hispanic/Latino; 1% Race/ethnicity unknown; 3% international; 9% transferred in; 45% live on campus.

Freshmen
Admission: 1,424 applied, 707 admitted, 165 enrolled. *Average high school GPA:* 3.2. *Test scores:* SAT critical reading scores over 500: 31%; SAT math scores over 500: 30%; ACT scores over 18: 58%; SAT critical reading scores over 600: 9%; SAT math scores over 600: 4%; ACT scores over 24: 12%.
Retention: 69% of full-time freshmen returned.

FACULTY
Total: 83, 55% full-time, 48% with terminal degrees.
Student/faculty ratio: 12:1.

ACADEMICS
Calendar: semesters. *Degrees:* associate, bachelor's, and master's.
Special study options: academic remediation for entering students, accelerated degree program, adult/continuing education programs, advanced placement credit, double majors, English as a second language, external degree program, honors programs, independent study, internships, off-campus study, part-time degree program, services for LD students, student-designed majors, study abroad, summer session for credit.
Computers: 100 computers/terminals are available on campus for general student use. Students can access the following: campus intranet, computer help desk, free student e-mail accounts, online (class) grades, online (class) registration, online (class) schedules. Campuswide network is available. 100% of college-owned or -operated housing units are wired for high-speed Internet access. Wireless service is available via entire campus.

STUDENT LIFE
Housing options: on-campus residence required through sophomore year; men-only, women-only, cooperative. Campus housing is university owned. Freshman campus housing is guaranteed.
Activities and organizations: drama/theater group, student-run newspaper, radio and television station, choral group, Student Association, Enactus (to enable progress through entrepreneurial action), Education/Psychology Club, Theology Club, Nursing Club.
Athletics *Intercollegiate sports:* basketball M/W, soccer M/W, volleyball W. *Intramural sports:* basketball M/W, football M/W, racquetball M/W, soccer M/W, softball M/W, table tennis M/W, tennis M/W, volleyball M/W(c).
Campus security: 24-hour emergency response devices, student patrols, controlled dormitory access.
Student services: health clinic, personal/psychological counseling.

COSTS
Costs (2014–15) *Comprehensive fee:* $26,860 includes full-time tuition ($18,840), mandatory fees ($620), and room and board ($7400). Full-time tuition and fees vary according to course load and program. Part-time tuition: $785 per semester hour. Part-time tuition and fees vary according to course load and program. *Required fees:* $310 per term part-time. *Room and board:* Room and board charges vary according to board plan. *Payment plans:* installment, deferred payment. *Waivers:* senior citizens and employees or children of employees.

APPLYING
Standardized Tests *Required:* SAT or ACT (for admission).
Options: electronic application, deferred entrance.
Application fee: $25.
Required: high school transcript, minimum 2.0 GPA. *Required for some:* essay or personal statement, 1 letter of recommendation, interview. *Recommended:* minimum 2.5 GPA.
Application deadlines: 8/31 (freshmen), 8/31 (transfers).
Notification: 9/1 (freshmen), 9/1 (transfers).

CONTACT
Ms. Rahneeka Hazelton, Director of Admissions, Southwestern Adventist University, 100 West Hillcrest, Keene, TX 76059. *Phone:* 817-202-6733. *Toll-free phone:* 800-433-2240. *E-mail:* rahneeka@swau.edu.

Southwestern Assemblies of God University

Waxahachie, Texas

http://www.sagu.edu/

- **Independent** comprehensive, founded 1927, affiliated with Assemblies of God
- **Small-town** 70-acre campus with easy access to Dallas-Fort Worth
- **Endowment** $4.0 million
- **Coed** 1,666 undergraduate students, 87% full-time, 52% women, 48% men
- **Noncompetitive** entrance level, 33% of applicants were admitted

UNDERGRAD STUDENTS
1,445 full-time, 221 part-time. Students come from 50 states and territories; 11 other countries; 37% are from out of state; 12% Black or African American, non-Hispanic/Latino; 22% Hispanic/Latino; 1% Asian, non-Hispanic/Latino; 0.2% Native Hawaiian or other Pacific Islander, non-Hispanic/Latino; 1% American Indian or Alaska Native, non-Hispanic/Latino; 1% Two or more races, non-Hispanic/Latino; 0.9% Race/ethnicity unknown; 0.6% international; 13% transferred in; 85% live on campus.

Freshmen
Admission: 1,327 applied, 444 admitted, 319 enrolled. *Test scores:* SAT critical reading scores over 500: 40%; SAT writing scores over 500: 31%; ACT scores over 18: 82%; SAT critical reading scores over 600: 7%; SAT writing scores over 600: 4%; ACT scores over 24: 28%; SAT critical reading scores over 700: 1%; ACT scores over 30: 3%.
Retention: 61% of full-time freshmen returned.

FACULTY
Total: 161, 47% full-time, 38% with terminal degrees.
Student/faculty ratio: 15:1.

ACADEMICS
Calendar: semesters. *Degrees:* associate, bachelor's, and master's.
Special study options: academic remediation for entering students, adult/continuing education programs, advanced placement credit, distance

learning, double majors, external degree program, independent study, internships, part-time degree program, services for LD students, summer session for credit. ***ROTC:*** Air Force (c).

Computers: 96 computers/terminals and 1,000 ports are available on campus for general student use. Students can access the following: computer help desk, free student e-mail accounts, online (class) grades, online (class) registration, online (class) schedules. Campuswide network is available. 95% of college-owned or -operated housing units are wired for high-speed Internet access. Wireless service is available via entire campus.

STUDENT LIFE

Housing options: on-campus residence required through senior year; coed. Campus housing is university owned. Freshman campus housing is guaranteed.

Activities and organizations: drama/theater group, student-run newspaper, choral group, Student Congress, Southwestern Missions Association, Street Hope, Gold Jackets, Women in Ministry.

Athletics Member NAIA, NCCAA. ***Intercollegiate sports:*** baseball M(s), basketball M(s)/W(s), football M(s), soccer M(s)/W(s), softball W(s), volleyball W(s). ***Intramural sports:*** basketball M/W, cheerleading W, football M/W, soccer M(c)/W, softball M/W, table tennis M/W, tennis M/W, ultimate Frisbee M/W, volleyball M/W.

Campus security: 24-hour patrols, late-night transport/escort service, controlled dormitory access, 2 dorms electronic access; 4 dorms key access to rooms, camera surveillance, 24 hour dispatch monitored fire alarm systems (offsite).

Student services: health clinic, personal/psychological counseling.

COSTS & FINANCIAL AID

Costs (2014–15) ***Comprehensive fee:*** $25,790 includes full-time tuition ($18,570), mandatory fees ($880), and room and board ($6340). Part-time tuition: $619 per credit hour. ***College room only:*** $3140. Room and board charges vary according to board plan and housing facility. ***Payment plan:*** deferred payment.

Financial Aid Of all full-time matriculated undergraduates who enrolled in 2000, 1,116 applied for aid, 1,002 were judged to have need, 110 had their need fully met. 178 Federal Work-Study jobs, 7 state and other part-time jobs (averaging $890). In 2000, 316 non-need-based awards were made. ***Average percent of need met:*** 64. ***Average financial aid package:*** $6728. ***Average need-based loan:*** $3177. ***Average need-based gift aid:*** $3511. ***Average indebtedness upon graduation:*** $13,938. ***Financial aid deadline:*** 7/1.

APPLYING

Standardized Tests *Required:* SAT or ACT (for admission).

Options: early admission, deferred entrance.

Application fee: $35.

Required: essay or personal statement, high school transcript, minimum 2.0 GPA, 1 letter of recommendation, medical history, evidence of approved Christian character.

Application deadlines: rolling (freshmen), rolling (transfers).

CONTACT

Mr. Bryan Brooks, Assistant Dean of Admissions, Southwestern Assemblies of God University, 1200 Sycamore Street, Waxahachie, TX 75165. *Phone:* 972-825-4821. *Toll-free phone:* 888-937-7248. *Fax:* 972-923-8131. *E-mail:* bbrooks@sagu.edu.

Southwestern University

Georgetown, Texas

http://www.southwestern.edu/

- **Independent Methodist** 4-year, founded 1840
- **Suburban** 700-acre campus with easy access to Austin
- **Endowment** $265.6 million
- **Coed** 1,538 undergraduate students, 99% full-time, 58% women, 42% men
- **Very difficult** entrance level, 49% of applicants were admitted

UNDERGRAD STUDENTS

1,517 full-time, 21 part-time. Students come from 36 states and territories; 9 other countries; 88% are from out of state; 5% Black or African American, non-Hispanic/Latino; 19% Hispanic/Latino; 5% Asian, non-Hispanic/Latino; 0.2% Native Hawaiian or other Pacific Islander, non-Hispanic/Latino; 0.4% American Indian or Alaska Native, non-Hispanic/Latino; 3% Two or more races, non-Hispanic/Latino; 1% Race/ethnicity unknown; 3% international; 4% transferred in; 21% live on campus.

Freshmen

Admission: 3,487 applied, 1,692 admitted, 382 enrolled. ***Test scores:*** SAT critical reading scores over 500: 82%; SAT math scores over 500: 85%; ACT scores over 18: 99%; SAT critical reading scores over 600: 42%; SAT math scores over 600: 41%; ACT scores over 24: 68%; SAT critical reading scores over 700: 9%; SAT math scores over 700: 8%; ACT scores over 30: 17%.

Retention: 82% of full-time freshmen returned.

FACULTY

Total: 165, 68% full-time, 88% with terminal degrees.

Student/faculty ratio: 12:1.

ACADEMICS

Calendar: semesters. *Degree:* bachelor's.

Special study options: advanced placement credit, double majors, honors programs, independent study, internships, off-campus study, services for LD students, student-designed majors, study abroad, summer session for credit.

Computers: 410 computers/terminals are available on campus for general student use. Students can access the following: campus intranet, computer help desk, free student e-mail accounts, online (class) grades, online (class) registration, online (class) schedules, transcripts. Campuswide network is available. 100% of college-owned or -operated housing units are wired for high-speed Internet access. Wireless service is available via entire campus.

STUDENT LIFE

Housing options: on-campus residence required through sophomore year; coed, men-only, women-only, special housing for students with disabilities. Campus housing is university owned. Freshman campus housing is guaranteed.

Activities and organizations: drama/theater group, student-run newspaper, radio station, choral group, Student Peace Alliance (SPA), Students for Environmental Activism & Knowledge (SEAK), Alpha Phi Omega, Men's IFC, Women's Panhellenic, national fraternities, national sororities.

Athletics Member NCAA. All Division III. ***Intercollegiate sports:*** baseball M, basketball M/W, cross-country running M/W, football M, golf M/W, lacrosse M/W, soccer M/W, softball W, swimming and diving M/W, tennis M/W, track and field M/W, volleyball W. ***Intramural sports:*** basketball M/W, cheerleading M/W, football W, racquetball M/W, rock climbing M/W, soccer M/W, table tennis M/W, tennis M/W, ultimate Frisbee M/W, volleyball M/W.

Campus security: 24-hour emergency response devices and patrols, late-night transport/escort service, controlled dormitory access.

Student services: health clinic, personal/psychological counseling, women's center.

COSTS & FINANCIAL AID

Costs (2015–16) ***Comprehensive fee:*** $49,668 includes full-time tuition ($37,560) and room and board ($12,108). Part-time tuition: $1565 per credit hour. Part-time tuition and fees vary according to course load. ***College room only:*** $5960. Room and board charges vary according to board plan and housing facility. ***Payment plan:*** installment. ***Waivers:*** employees or children of employees.

Financial Aid Of all full-time matriculated undergraduates who enrolled in 2014, 1,093 applied for aid, 954 were judged to have need, 259 had their need fully met. 233 Federal Work-Study jobs (averaging $1996). 569 state and other part-time jobs (averaging $2396). In 2014, 534 non-need-based awards were made. ***Average percent of need met:*** 88. ***Average financial aid package:*** $31,865. ***Average need-based loan:*** $5018. ***Average need-based gift aid:*** $26,126. ***Average non-need-based aid:*** $18,514. ***Average indebtedness upon graduation:*** $30,935.

APPLYING

Standardized Tests *Required:* SAT or ACT (for admission).

Options: electronic application, early admission, early action, deferred entrance.

Required: essay or personal statement, high school transcript, 1 letter of recommendation, Counselor recommendation; teacher and parent recommendation optional. ***Required for some:*** interview. ***Recommended:*** interview.

Application deadlines: rolling (freshmen), rolling (out-of-state freshmen), 4/1 (transfers), 11/15 (early action).

Notification: continuous (freshmen), continuous (out-of-state freshmen), 8/1 (transfers), 2/15 (early action).

CONTACT

Ms. Christine Bowman, Director of Admissions, Southwestern University, 1001 East University Avenue, Georgetown, TX 78626. *Phone:* 512-863-1200. *Toll-free phone:* 800-252-3166. *Fax:* 512-863-9601. *E-mail:* admission@southwestern.edu.

★ Stephen F. Austin State University

Nacogdoches, Texas

http://www.sfasu.edu/

- **State-supported** comprehensive, founded 1923
- **Small-town** 418-acre campus
- **Endowment** $71.0 million
- **Coed** 11,024 undergraduate students, 85% full-time, 63% women, 37% men
- **Moderately difficult** entrance level, 59% of applicants were admitted

UNDERGRAD STUDENTS

9,335 full-time, 1,689 part-time. Students come from 41 states and territories; 34 other countries; 2% are from out of state; 21% Black or African American, non-Hispanic/Latino; 15% Hispanic/Latino; 1% Asian, non-Hispanic/Latino; 0.1% Native Hawaiian or other Pacific Islander, non-Hispanic/Latino; 0.5% American Indian or Alaska Native, non-Hispanic/Latino; 3% Two or more races, non-Hispanic/Latino; 2% Race/ethnicity unknown; 0.7% international; 8% transferred in; 42% live on campus.

Freshmen

Admission: 10,631 applied, 6,220 admitted, 2,013 enrolled. ***Test scores:*** SAT critical reading scores over 500: 47%; SAT math scores over 500: 53%; SAT writing scores over 500: 35%; ACT scores over 18: 84%; SAT critical reading scores over 600: 9%; SAT math scores over 600: 10%; SAT writing scores over 600: 6%; ACT scores over 24: 26%; SAT critical reading scores over 700: 1%; ACT scores over 30: 1%.

Retention: 70% of full-time freshmen returned.

FACULTY

Total: 685, 74% full-time, 66% with terminal degrees.

Student/faculty ratio: 20:1.

ACADEMICS

Calendar: semesters. *Degrees:* bachelor's, master's, and doctoral.

Special study options: academic remediation for entering students, accelerated degree program, adult/continuing education programs, advanced placement credit, cooperative education, distance learning, double majors, freshman honors college, honors programs, independent study, internships, off-campus study, part-time degree program, services for LD students, student-designed majors, study abroad, summer session for credit. ***ROTC:*** Army (b).

Unusual degree programs: 3-2 professional accountancy.

Computers: 1,000 computers/terminals are available on campus for general student use. Students can access the following: campus intranet, computer help desk, free student e-mail accounts, online (class) grades, online (class) registration, online (class) schedules. Campuswide network is available. 100% of college-owned or -operated housing units are wired for high-speed Internet access. Wireless service is available via classrooms, computer centers, computer labs, dorm rooms, learning centers, libraries, student centers.

STUDENT LIFE

Housing options: on-campus residence required through sophomore year; coed, men-only, women-only, special housing for students with disabilities. Campus housing is university owned. Freshman campus housing is guaranteed.

Activities and organizations: drama/theater group, student-run newspaper, radio and television station, choral group, marching band, Residence Hall Association, Baptist Student Ministries, Greek Life, Student Activities Association, Student Government Association, national fraternities, national sororities.

Athletics Member NCAA. All Division I except football (Division I-AA). ***Intercollegiate sports:*** baseball M(s), basketball M(s)/W(s), bowling W(s), cheerleading M(s)/W(s), cross-country running M(s)/W(s), golf M(s)/W(s), lacrosse M(c), rugby M(c), soccer M(c)/W(s), softball W(s), tennis M(c)/W(s), track and field M(s)/W(s), volleyball W(s). ***Intramural sports:*** badminton M/W, baseball M(c), basketball M(c)/W(c), football M/W, golf M/W, racquetball M/W, rock climbing M/W, soccer M/W, softball M/W, swimming and diving M(c)/W(c), table tennis M/W, tennis M/W, ultimate Frisbee M/W, volleyball M/W, water polo M/W.

Campus security: 24-hour emergency response devices and patrols, student patrols, late-night transport/escort service, controlled dormitory access.

Student services: health clinic, personal/psychological counseling.

COSTS & FINANCIAL AID

Costs (2014–15) ***Tuition:*** state resident $6630 full-time, $221 per credit hour part-time; nonresident $17,490 full-time, $583 per credit hour part-time. Full-time tuition and fees vary according to course load, degree level, and location. Part-time tuition and fees vary according to course load, degree level, and location. No tuition increase for student's term of enrollment. ***Required fees:*** $2262 full-time, $157 per credit hour part-time. ***Room and board:*** $8868. Room and board charges vary according to board plan and housing facility. ***Payment plan:*** installment. ***Waivers:*** senior citizens and employees or children of employees.

Financial Aid Of all full-time matriculated undergraduates who enrolled in 2013, 7,974 applied for aid, 6,737 were judged to have need, 928 had their need fully met. In 2013, 723 non-need-based awards were made. ***Average percent of need met:*** 58. ***Average financial aid package:*** $11,487. ***Average need-based loan:*** $4798. ***Average need-based gift aid:*** $6537. ***Average non-need-based aid:*** $2795. ***Average indebtedness upon graduation:*** $24,818.

APPLYING

Standardized Tests *Required:* SAT or ACT (for admission).

Options: electronic application.

Application fee: $45.

Required: high school transcript.

Application deadlines: rolling (freshmen), rolling (out-of-state freshmen), rolling (transfers).

Notification: continuous (freshmen), continuous (out-of-state freshmen), continuous (transfers).

CONTACT

Mr. Kevin Davis, Associate Director of Admissions, Stephen F. Austin State University, PO Box 13051, SFA Station, Nacogdoches, TX 75962. *Phone:* 936-468-2504. *Toll-free phone:* 800-731-2902. *Fax:* 936-468-3849. *E-mail:* admissions@sfasu.edu.

Sul Ross State University

Alpine, Texas

http://www.sulross.edu/

- **State-supported** comprehensive, founded 1920, part of Texas State University System
- **Rural** 640-acre campus
- **Endowment** $18.4 million
- **Coed** 2,031 undergraduate students, 61% full-time, 57% women, 43% men
- **Noncompetitive** entrance level, 95% of applicants were admitted

UNDERGRAD STUDENTS

1,238 full-time, 793 part-time. Students come from 19 states and territories; 2 other countries; 2% are from out of state; 7% Black or African American, non-Hispanic/Latino; 65% Hispanic/Latino; 0.3% Asian, non-Hispanic/Latino; 0.0% Native Hawaiian or other Pacific Islander, non-Hispanic/Latino; 0.3% American Indian or Alaska Native, non-Hispanic/Latino; 1% Two or more races, non-Hispanic/Latino; 1% Race/ethnicity unknown; 0.4% international; 15% transferred in; 48% live on campus.

Freshmen
Admission: 1,256 applied, 1,190 admitted, 332 enrolled. ***Average high school GPA:*** 30.3. ***Test scores:*** SAT math scores over 500: 19%; SAT writing scores over 500: 17%; ACT scores over 18: 14%; SAT math scores over 600: 1%; SAT writing scores over 600: 2%; ACT scores over 24: 2%.

Retention: 52% of full-time freshmen returned.

FACULTY
Total: 173, 64% full-time.

Student/faculty ratio: 15:1.

ACADEMICS
Calendar: semesters. *Degrees:* certificates, associate, bachelor's, master's, and postbachelor's certificates.

Special study options: distance learning, double majors, honors programs, independent study, internships, part-time degree program, student-designed majors, study abroad, summer session for credit.

Computers: Students can access the following: campus intranet, computer help desk, free student e-mail accounts, online (class) grades. Campuswide network is available.

STUDENT LIFE
Housing options: on-campus residence required through sophomore year; coed. Campus housing is university owned. Freshman campus housing is guaranteed.

Activities and organizations: drama/theater group, student-run newspaper, marching band.

Athletics Member NCAA. All Division III. ***Intercollegiate sports:*** baseball M, basketball M/W, cheerleading M/W, cross-country running W, football M, softball W, tennis M/W, track and field M/W, volleyball W. ***Intramural sports:*** basketball M/W, cheerleading M/W, equestrian sports M/W, football M/W, racquetball M/W, soccer M/W, softball M, tennis M/W, ultimate Frisbee M/W, volleyball M/W, water polo M/W, weight lifting M/W.

Campus security: 24-hour patrols, late-night transport/escort service.

Student services: health clinic, personal/psychological counseling.

COSTS & FINANCIAL AID
Costs (2014–15) ***Tuition:*** state resident $4980 full-time, $166 per credit hour part-time; nonresident $15,840 full-time, $528 per credit hour part-time. ***Required fees:*** $1920 full-time, $167 per credit hour part-time. ***Room and board:*** $7416. Room and board charges vary according to board plan and housing facility. ***Payment plan:*** installment. ***Waivers:*** employees or children of employees.

Financial Aid Of all full-time matriculated undergraduates who enrolled in 2013, 1,060 applied for aid, 921 were judged to have need. 126 Federal Work-Study jobs (averaging $204,909). 156 state and other part-time jobs (averaging $253,036). ***Financial aid deadline:*** 4/1.

APPLYING
Standardized Tests *Required:* SAT or ACT (for admission).

Options: early decision, deferred entrance.

Application fee: $25.

Required: high school transcript. ***Recommended:*** interview.

Application deadlines: rolling (freshmen), rolling (transfers).

Notification: continuous (freshmen), continuous (transfers).

CONTACT
Sul Ross State University, PO Box C - 114, Alpine, TX 79832. *Phone:* 432-837-8050. *Toll-free phone:* 888-722-7778.

Tarleton State University
Stephenville, Texas
http://www.tarleton.edu/

- **State-supported** comprehensive, founded 1899, part of Texas A&M University System
- **Small-town** 175-acre campus with easy access to Fort Worth
- **Endowment** $57.0 million
- **Coed** 10,277 undergraduate students, 78% full-time, 61% women, 39% men
- **Moderately difficult** entrance level, 74% of applicants were admitted

UNDERGRAD STUDENTS
8,055 full-time, 2,222 part-time. Students come from 45 states and territories; 25 other countries; 2% are from out of state; 8% Black or African American, non-Hispanic/Latino; 16% Hispanic/Latino; 1% Asian, non-Hispanic/Latino; 0.1% Native Hawaiian or other Pacific Islander, non-Hispanic/Latino; 0.6% American Indian or Alaska Native, non-Hispanic/Latino; 3% Two or more races, non-Hispanic/Latino; 0.7% Race/ethnicity unknown; 0.4% international; 13% transferred in; 35% live on campus.

Freshmen
Admission: 6,590 applied, 4,889 admitted, 1,971 enrolled. ***Test scores:*** SAT critical reading scores over 500: 37%; SAT math scores over 500: 47%; SAT writing scores over 500: 27%; ACT scores over 18: 79%; SAT critical reading scores over 600: 6%; SAT math scores over 600: 8%; SAT writing scores over 600: 2%; ACT scores over 24: 20%; ACT scores over 30: 1%.

Retention: 69% of full-time freshmen returned.

FACULTY
Total: 672, 56% full-time.

Student/faculty ratio: 19:1.

ACADEMICS
Calendar: semesters. *Degrees:* associate, bachelor's, master's, and doctoral.

Special study options: academic remediation for entering students, accelerated degree program, adult/continuing education programs, advanced placement credit, cooperative education, distance learning, double majors, honors programs, independent study, internships, off-campus study, part-time degree program, services for LD students, study abroad, summer session for credit. ***ROTC:*** Army (b).

Computers: 1,200 computers/terminals are available on campus for general student use. Students can access the following: campus intranet, computer help desk, free student e-mail accounts, online (class) grades, online (class) registration, online (class) schedules. Campuswide network is available. 100% of college-owned or -operated housing units are wired for high-speed Internet access. Wireless service is available via entire campus.

STUDENT LIFE
Housing options: on-campus residence required through sophomore year; coed, men-only, women-only. Campus housing is university owned and leased by the school. Freshman campus housing is guaranteed.

Activities and organizations: drama/theater group, student-run newspaper, radio station, choral group, marching band, Student Government Association, Student Programming Association, Kappa Delta Rho, Delta Zeta, Chi Alpha, national fraternities, national sororities.

Athletics Member NCAA. All Division II. ***Intercollegiate sports:*** baseball M(s), basketball M(s)/W(s), cheerleading M(s)/W(s), cross-country running M(s)/W(s), football M(s), golf W(s), softball W(s), tennis W(s), track and field M(s)/W(s), volleyball W(s). ***Intramural sports:*** archery M/W, basketball M/W, football M/W, golf M/W, racquetball M/W, soccer M/W, softball M/W, table tennis M/W, tennis M/W, volleyball M/W.

Campus security: 24-hour emergency response devices and patrols, student patrols, late-night transport/escort service, controlled dormitory access.

Student services: health clinic, personal/psychological counseling, legal services.

COSTS & FINANCIAL AID
Costs (2014–15) ***Tuition:*** state resident $4922 full-time, $154 per credit part-time; nonresident $15,782 full-time, $516 per hour part-time. Full-time tuition and fees vary according to course load and degree level. Part-time tuition and fees vary according to course load and degree level. No tuition increase for student's term of enrollment. ***Required fees:*** $3324 full-time. ***Room and board:*** $9042; room only: $5400. Room and board charges vary according to board plan and housing facility. ***Payment plan:*** installment.

Financial Aid Of all full-time matriculated undergraduates who enrolled in 2013, 5,763 applied for aid, 4,850 were judged to have need, 159 had their need fully met. ***Average percent of need met:*** 51. ***Average financial aid package:*** $8940. ***Average need-based loan:*** $4173. ***Average need-***

based gift aid: $6305. ***Average indebtedness upon graduation:*** $26,267. ***Financial aid deadline:*** 11/1.

APPLYING

Standardized Tests *Required:* SAT or ACT (for admission).

Options: electronic application, early action.

Application fee: $30.

Required: high school transcript.

Application deadlines: 7/21 (freshmen), 7/21 (transfers), 3/1 (early action).

CONTACT

Ms. Cindy Hess, Director of Undergraduate Admissions, Tarleton State University, Box T-0030, Tarleton Station, Stephenville, TX 76402. *Phone:* 254-968-9123. *Toll-free phone:* 800-687-8236. *Fax:* 254-968-9951. *E-mail:* uadm@tarleton.edu.

Texas A&M International University

Laredo, Texas

http://www.tamiu.edu/

- **State-supported** comprehensive, founded 1969, part of Texas A&M University System
- **Urban** 300-acre campus
- **Endowment** $44.6 million
- **Coed** 6,741 undergraduate students, 63% full-time, 59% women, 41% men
- **Moderately difficult** entrance level, 48% of applicants were admitted

UNDERGRAD STUDENTS

4,279 full-time, 2,462 part-time. Students come from 21 states and territories; 23 other countries; 1% are from out of state; 0.5% Black or African American, non-Hispanic/Latino; 95% Hispanic/Latino; 0.6% Asian, non-Hispanic/Latino; 0.1% American Indian or Alaska Native, non-Hispanic/Latino; 0.3% Two or more races, non-Hispanic/Latino; 0.2% Race/ethnicity unknown; 2% international; 7% transferred in; 11% live on campus.

Freshmen

Admission: 6,184 applied, 2,961 admitted, 903 enrolled. ***Average high school GPA:*** 3.6. ***Test scores:*** SAT critical reading scores over 500: 24%; SAT math scores over 500: 37%; SAT writing scores over 500: 18%; ACT scores over 18: 56%; SAT critical reading scores over 600: 3%; SAT math scores over 600: 5%; SAT writing scores over 600: 1%; ACT scores over 24: 6%.

Retention: 76% of full-time freshmen returned.

FACULTY

Total: 360, 53% full-time, 50% with terminal degrees.

Student/faculty ratio: 20:1.

ACADEMICS

Calendar: semesters. *Degrees:* bachelor's, master's, and doctoral.

Special study options: academic remediation for entering students, advanced placement credit, distance learning, double majors, English as a second language, honors programs, independent study, internships, part-time degree program, services for LD students, study abroad, summer session for credit. ***ROTC:*** Army (b).

Computers: 970 computers/terminals are available on campus for general student use. Students can access the following: campus intranet, computer help desk, free student e-mail accounts, online (class) grades, online (class) registration, online (class) schedules. Campuswide network is available. 100% of college-owned or -operated housing units are wired for high-speed Internet access. Wireless service is available via classrooms, computer centers, computer labs, learning centers, libraries, student centers.

STUDENT LIFE

Housing options: coed. Campus housing is university owned and is provided by a third party.

Activities and organizations: student-run newspaper, choral group, marching band, Psychology Club, National Student Speech Language Hearing Association (NSSLHA), Association of International Students (AIS), Tri-Beta Biological Honor Society, Kappa Delta Chi, national sororities.

Athletics Member NCAA. All Division II. ***Intercollegiate sports:*** baseball M(s), basketball M(s)/W(s), cross-country running M(s)/W(s), golf M(s)/W(s), soccer M(s)/W(s), softball W(s), volleyball W(s). ***Intramural sports:*** badminton M/W, basketball M/W, soccer M/W, softball M/W, table tennis M/W, ultimate Frisbee M/W, volleyball M/W.

Campus security: 24-hour emergency response devices and patrols, late-night transport/escort service, controlled dormitory access, provide training to faculty, staff, a new students on active shooter. Timely On-going Threat Information Dissemination.

Student services: health clinic, personal/psychological counseling, women's center.

COSTS & FINANCIAL AID

Costs (2014–15) ***Tuition:*** state resident $7558 full-time; nonresident $18,652 full-time. Full-time tuition and fees vary according to course load. Part-time tuition and fees vary according to course load and reciprocity agreements. ***Room and board:*** $8028. Room and board charges vary according to board plan and housing facility. ***Payment plan:*** installment. ***Waivers:*** senior citizens.

Financial Aid Of all full-time matriculated undergraduates who enrolled in 2013, 3,964 applied for aid, 3,578 were judged to have need, 230 had their need fully met. 91 Federal Work-Study jobs (averaging $2232). 33 state and other part-time jobs (averaging $1924). In 2013, 201 non-need-based awards were made. ***Average percent of need met:*** 51. ***Average financial aid package:*** $8502. ***Average need-based loan:*** $3758. ***Average need-based gift aid:*** $6343. ***Average non-need-based aid:*** $3413. ***Average indebtedness upon graduation:*** $17,394. ***Financial aid deadline:*** 7/30.

APPLYING

Standardized Tests *Required:* SAT or ACT (for admission).

Options: electronic application, early admission, deferred entrance.

Required: high school transcript.

Application deadlines: 7/1 (freshmen), 7/1 (transfers).

Notification: 7/15 (freshmen), 7/15 (transfers).

CONTACT

Ms. Rosa Dickinson, Director of Admissions, Texas A&M International University, 5201 University Boulevard, Laredo, TX 78041-1900. *Phone:* 956-326-2200. *Toll-free phone:* 888-489-2648. *E-mail:* adms@tamiu.edu.

Texas A&M University

College Station, Texas

http://www.tamu.edu/

- **State-supported** university, founded 1876, part of Texas A&M University System
- **Suburban** 5200-acre campus with easy access to Houston
- **Endowment** $11.1 billion
- **Coed** 47,093 undergraduate students, 89% full-time, 49% women, 51% men
- **Moderately difficult** entrance level, 71% of applicants were admitted

UNDERGRAD STUDENTS

42,129 full-time, 4,964 part-time. Students come from 53 states and territories; 86 other countries; 4% are from out of state; 3% Black or African American, non-Hispanic/Latino; 21% Hispanic/Latino; 5% Asian, non-Hispanic/Latino; 0.1% Native Hawaiian or other Pacific Islander, non-Hispanic/Latino; 0.3% American Indian or Alaska Native, non-Hispanic/Latino; 3% Two or more races, non-Hispanic/Latino; 0.2% Race/ethnicity unknown; 2% international; 5% transferred in; 25% live on campus.

Freshmen

Admission: 32,190 applied, 22,863 admitted, 10,835 enrolled. ***Test scores:*** SAT critical reading scores over 500: 83%; SAT math scores over 500: 92%; SAT writing scores over 500: 74%; ACT scores over 18: 99%; SAT critical reading scores over 600: 44%; SAT math scores over 600: 58%; SAT writing scores over 600: 32%; ACT scores over 24: 81%; SAT critical reading scores over 700: 9%; SAT math scores over 700: 15%; SAT writing scores over 700: 5%; ACT scores over 30: 30%.

Retention: 90% of full-time freshmen returned.

FACULTY
Total: 3,762, 72% full-time, 85% with terminal degrees.
Student/faculty ratio: 21:1.

ACADEMICS
Calendar: semesters. *Degrees:* bachelor's, master's, doctoral, post-master's, and postbachelor's certificates.
Special study options: academic remediation for entering students, accelerated degree program, advanced placement credit, cooperative education, distance learning, double majors, English as a second language, honors programs, independent study, internships, off-campus study, part-time degree program, services for LD students, study abroad, summer session for credit. ***ROTC:*** Army (b), Navy (b), Air Force (b).
Computers: 2,282 computers/terminals and 5,500 ports are available on campus for general student use. Students can access the following: campus intranet, computer help desk, free student e-mail accounts, online (class) grades, online (class) registration, online (class) schedules. Campuswide network is available. 100% of college-owned or -operated housing units are wired for high-speed Internet access. Wireless service is available via entire campus.

STUDENT LIFE
Housing options: coed, men-only, women-only, special housing for students with disabilities. Campus housing is university owned and leased by the school.
Activities and organizations: drama/theater group, student-run newspaper, radio and television station, choral group, marching band, Memorial Student Center, Corps of Cadets, Fish Camp, student government, national fraternities, national sororities.
Athletics Member NCAA. All Division I except football (Division I-A). ***Intercollegiate sports:*** archery W(s), baseball M(s), basketball M(s)/W(s), cross-country running M(s)/W(s), equestrian sports W(s), golf M(s)/W(s), soccer W(s), softball W(s), swimming and diving M(s)/W(s), tennis M(s)/W(s), track and field M(s)/W(s), volleyball W(s). ***Intramural sports:*** archery M/W, badminton M/W, basketball M/W, bowling M/W, cross-country running M/W, fencing M(c)/W(c), field hockey M(c)/W(c), football M/W, golf M/W, gymnastics M(c)/W(c), lacrosse M(c)/W(c), racquetball M(c)/W(c), riflery M/W, rugby M(c)/W(c), sailing M(c)/W(c), soccer M/W, softball M/W, squash M/W, swimming and diving M/W, table tennis M/W, tennis M/W, track and field M/W, ultimate Frisbee M(c)/W(c), volleyball M/W, water polo M/W, weight lifting M(c)/W(c), wrestling M(c).
Campus security: 24-hour emergency response devices and patrols, late-night transport/escort service, controlled dormitory access, student escorts.
Student services: health clinic, personal/psychological counseling, women's center, legal services.

COSTS & FINANCIAL AID
Costs (2014–15) ***Tuition:*** state resident $5971 full-time, $199 per credit hour part-time; nonresident $23,147 full-time, $772 per credit hour part-time. Full-time tuition and fees vary according to program. Part-time tuition and fees vary according to program. No tuition increase for student's term of enrollment. ***Required fees:*** $3209 full-time. ***Room and board:*** $9522. Room and board charges vary according to board plan, housing facility, and location. ***Payment plan:*** installment.
Financial Aid Of all full-time matriculated undergraduates who enrolled in 2013, 24,520 applied for aid, 17,183 were judged to have need, 6,853 had their need fully met. 748 Federal Work-Study jobs (averaging $2967). 189 state and other part-time jobs (averaging $2385). In 2013, 2664 non-need-based awards were made. ***Average percent of need met:*** 69. ***Average financial aid package:*** $15,337. ***Average need-based loan:*** $6671. ***Average need-based gift aid:*** $9572. ***Average non-need-based aid:*** $3502. ***Average indebtedness upon graduation:*** $23,703.

APPLYING
Standardized Tests *Required:* SAT or ACT (for admission).
Options: electronic application.
Application fee: $75.
Required: essay or personal statement, high school transcript. ***Required for some:*** Apply Texas Application. Applicants applying to the Dwight Look College of Engineering are required to meet a minimum math score of 550 on the SAT or a minimum math score or 24 on the ACT.
Application deadlines: 12/1 (freshmen), 12/1 (out-of-state freshmen), 3/15 (transfers).
Notification: continuous (freshmen), continuous (transfers).

CONTACT
Office of Admissions, Texas A&M University, Admissions Processing-GSC, 750 Agronomy 0200 TAMU, College Station, TX 77843-1265.
Phone: 979-845-1060. *Fax:* 979-845-1808.

Texas A&M University–Commerce

Commerce, Texas

http://www.tamuc.edu/

- **State-supported** university, founded 1889, part of Texas A&M University System
- **Small-town** 1883-acre campus with easy access to Dallas-Fort Worth
- **Coed** 7,148 undergraduate students, 73% full-time, 60% women, 40% men
- **Moderately difficult** entrance level, 48% of applicants were admitted

UNDERGRAD STUDENTS
5,250 full-time, 1,898 part-time. 2% are from out of state; 22% Black or African American, non-Hispanic/Latino; 16% Hispanic/Latino; 2% Asian, non-Hispanic/Latino; 0.2% Native Hawaiian or other Pacific Islander, non-Hispanic/Latino; 0.6% American Indian or Alaska Native, non-Hispanic/Latino; 4% Two or more races, non-Hispanic/Latino; 1% Race/ethnicity unknown; 3% international; 17% transferred in; 31% live on campus.

Freshmen
Admission: 6,614 applied, 3,164 admitted, 960 enrolled. ***Average high school GPA:*** 2.94. ***Test scores:*** SAT critical reading scores over 500: 42%; SAT math scores over 500: 47%; ACT scores over 18: 62%; SAT critical reading scores over 600: 10%; SAT math scores over 600: 10%; ACT scores over 24: 22%; SAT critical reading scores over 700: 1%; SAT math scores over 700: 1%; ACT scores over 30: 5%.
Retention: 68% of full-time freshmen returned.

FACULTY
Total: 679, 53% full-time, 56% with terminal degrees.
Student/faculty ratio: 17:1.

ACADEMICS
Calendar: semesters. *Degrees:* bachelor's, master's, and doctoral.
Special study options: academic remediation for entering students, accelerated degree program, adult/continuing education programs, advanced placement credit, cooperative education, distance learning, double majors, English as a second language, freshman honors college, honors programs, independent study, internships, off-campus study, part-time degree program, services for LD students, student-designed majors, study abroad, summer session for credit. ***ROTC:*** Air Force (c).
Computers: Students can access the following: campus intranet, computer help desk, free student e-mail accounts, online (class) grades, online (class) registration, online (class) schedules. Campuswide network is available. 100% of college-owned or -operated housing units are wired for high-speed Internet access. Wireless service is available via entire campus.

STUDENT LIFE
Housing options: on-campus residence required for freshman year; coed, women-only, special housing for students with disabilities. Campus housing is university owned. Freshman campus housing is guaranteed.
Activities and organizations: drama/theater group, student-run newspaper, radio and television station, choral group, marching band, National Society for Leadership and Success, Residence Hall Association, Indian Students Association, The Pride Alliance, National Association of Colored Women's Club, Inc, national fraternities, national sororities.
Athletics Member NCAA. All Division II. ***Intercollegiate sports:*** basketball M(s)/W(s), cheerleading M(s)/W(s), cross-country running M(s)/W(s), football M(s), golf M(s)/W(s), soccer W(s), softball W, track and field M(s)/W(s), volleyball W(s). ***Intramural sports:*** archery M/W, badminton M/W, basketball M/W, bowling M/W, cross-country running M/W, equestrian sports M/W, football M/W, golf M/W, racquetball M/W, soccer M, softball M/W, swimming and diving M/W, table tennis M/W, tennis M/W, track and field M/W, volleyball W.

Campus security: 24-hour emergency response devices and patrols, controlled dormitory access.

Student services: health clinic, personal/psychological counseling, legal services.

COSTS & FINANCIAL AID

Costs (2015–16) ***Tuition:*** state resident $4790 full-time, $160 per credit hour part-time; nonresident $15,650 full-time, $522 per credit hour part-time. Full-time tuition and fees vary according to course load, location, program, and reciprocity agreements. Part-time tuition and fees vary according to course load, location, program, and reciprocity agreements. No tuition increase for student's term of enrollment. ***Required fees:*** $2306 full-time. ***Room and board:*** $8106. Room and board charges vary according to board plan and housing facility. ***Payment plan:*** installment. ***Waivers:*** senior citizens and employees or children of employees.

Financial Aid Of all full-time matriculated undergraduates who enrolled in 2014, 4,533 applied for aid, 4,066 were judged to have need, 250 had their need fully met. In 2014, 179 non-need-based awards were made. ***Average percent of need met:*** 61. ***Average financial aid package:*** $10,814. ***Average need-based loan:*** $4057. ***Average need-based gift aid:*** $7885. ***Average non-need-based aid:*** $1814.

APPLYING

Standardized Tests *Required:* SAT or ACT (for admission).

Options: electronic application, deferred entrance.

Required: high school transcript. ***Required for some:*** Honors College requires an interview.

CONTACT

Mr. Jody Todhunter, Director of Admissions, Texas A&M University–Commerce, PO Box 3011, Commerce, TX 75429. *Phone:* 903-886-5072. *Toll-free phone:* 888-868-2682. *Fax:* 903-468-8698. *E-mail:* admissions@tamu-commerce.edu.

Texas A&M University–Corpus Christi

Corpus Christi, Texas

http://www.tamucc.edu/

- **State-supported** university, founded 1947, part of Texas A&M University System
- **Suburban** 317-acre campus
- **Endowment** $13.7 million
- **Coed** 9,058 undergraduate students, 79% full-time, 59% women, 41% men
- **Moderately difficult** entrance level, 61% of applicants were admitted

UNDERGRAD STUDENTS

7,114 full-time, 1,944 part-time. Students come from 24 states and territories; 22 other countries; 2% are from out of state; 6% Black or African American, non-Hispanic/Latino; 48% Hispanic/Latino; 2% Asian, non-Hispanic/Latino; 0.3% American Indian or Alaska Native, non-Hispanic/Latino; 2% Two or more races, non-Hispanic/Latino; 1% Race/ethnicity unknown; 3% international; 9% transferred in.

Freshmen

Admission: 11,034 applied, 6,687 admitted, 1,948 enrolled. ***Average high school GPA:*** 3.12. ***Test scores:*** SAT critical reading scores over 500: 41%; SAT math scores over 500: 48%; SAT writing scores over 500: 30%; ACT scores over 18: 77%; SAT critical reading scores over 600: 8%; SAT math scores over 600: 10%; SAT writing scores over 600: 4%; ACT scores over 24: 18%; SAT critical reading scores over 700: 1%; SAT math scores over 700: 1%; ACT scores over 30: 1%.

Retention: 53% of full-time freshmen returned.

FACULTY

Total: 599, 67% full-time.

ACADEMICS

Calendar: semesters. *Degrees:* bachelor's, master's, and doctoral.

Special study options: academic remediation for entering students, advanced placement credit, cooperative education, distance learning, double majors, English as a second language, honors programs, independent study, internships, off-campus study, part-time degree program, services for LD students, study abroad, summer session for credit. ***ROTC:*** Army (b).

Unusual degree programs: business administration with accounting; engineering; nursing.

Computers: Students can access the following: campus intranet, computer help desk, free student e-mail accounts, online (class) grades, online (class) registration, online (class) schedules. Campuswide network is available. 100% of college-owned or -operated housing units are wired for high-speed Internet access. Wireless service is available via entire campus.

STUDENT LIFE

Housing options: college housing not available; coed. Campus housing is provided by a third party.

Activities and organizations: drama/theater group, student-run newspaper, choral group, Student Accounting Society: Alpha Epsilon Delta, Student Art Association: Golden Key, Islander Cultural Alliance: Kinesiology Club, Graduate Student Association: Sea Turtle Club, Student Nurses Association, national fraternities, national sororities.

Athletics Member NCAA. All Division I. ***Intercollegiate sports:*** baseball M(s), basketball M(s)/W(s), cross-country running M(s)/W(s), golf W(s), soccer W(s), softball W(s), tennis M(s)/W(s), track and field M/W, volleyball W(s). ***Intramural sports:*** badminton M/W, fencing M/W, football M/W, lacrosse M/W, riflery M/W, rock climbing M/W, rugby M/W, soccer M, softball M/W, table tennis M/W, volleyball M/W, weight lifting M/W.

Campus security: 24-hour emergency response devices and patrols, late-night transport/escort service, controlled dormitory access.

Student services: health clinic, personal/psychological counseling.

COSTS & FINANCIAL AID

Costs (2014–15) ***Tuition:*** state resident $4623 full-time, $174 per credit hour part-time; nonresident $13,255 full-time, $532 per credit hour part-time. Full-time tuition and fees vary according to course load, degree level, location, program, and student level. Part-time tuition and fees vary according to course load, degree level, location, program, and student level. No tuition increase for student's term of enrollment. ***Required fees:*** $2968 full-time. ***Room and board:*** $8583; room only: $5283. Room and board charges vary according to board plan and housing facility. ***Payment plan:*** installment. ***Waivers:*** senior citizens.

Financial Aid Of all full-time matriculated undergraduates who enrolled in 2013, 4,746 applied for aid, 4,153 were judged to have need, 530 had their need fully met. 131 Federal Work-Study jobs (averaging $3665). 156 state and other part-time jobs (averaging $3474). In 2013, 429 non-need-based awards were made. ***Average percent of need met:*** 45. ***Average financial aid package:*** $8708. ***Average need-based loan:*** $4022. ***Average need-based gift aid:*** $5969. ***Average non-need-based aid:*** $2082. ***Average indebtedness upon graduation:*** $24,513.

APPLYING

Standardized Tests *Required:* SAT or ACT (for admission).

Options: electronic application.

Application fee: $50.

Required: high school transcript, minimum 2.0 GPA.

Application deadlines: 7/1 (freshmen), 7/1 (out-of-state freshmen), 7/1 (transfers).

Notification: continuous (freshmen), continuous (out-of-state freshmen), continuous (transfers).

CONTACT

Mrs. Monica Martinez, Assistant Director of Admissions, Texas A&M University–Corpus Christi, SSC 107, 6300 Ocean Drive, Unit 5774, Corpus Christi, TX 78412-5774. *Phone:* 361-825-2624. *Toll-free phone:* 800-482-6822. *Fax:* 361-825-5887. *E-mail:* monica.martinez@tamucc.edu.

Texas A&M University–Kingsville

Kingsville, Texas

http://www.tamuk.edu/

- **State-supported** university, founded 1925, part of Texas A&M University System
- **Small-town** 255-acre campus
- **Endowment** $71.8 million
- **Coed** 6,302 undergraduate students, 77% full-time, 48% women, 52% men
- **Moderately difficult** entrance level, 84% of applicants were admitted

UNDERGRAD STUDENTS
4,828 full-time, 1,474 part-time. Students come from 33 states and territories; 28 other countries; 1% are from out of state; 6% Black or African American, non-Hispanic/Latino; 70% Hispanic/Latino; 0.9% Asian, non-Hispanic/Latino; 0.1% Native Hawaiian or other Pacific Islander, non-Hispanic/Latino; 0.1% American Indian or Alaska Native, non-Hispanic/Latino; 0.5% Two or more races, non-Hispanic/Latino; 1% Race/ethnicity unknown; 2% international; 7% transferred in; 64% live on campus.

Freshmen
Admission: 6,504 applied, 5,432 admitted, 1,026 enrolled. ***Average high school GPA:*** 3.28. ***Test scores:*** SAT critical reading scores over 500: 26%; SAT math scores over 500: 40%; SAT writing scores over 500: 16%; ACT scores over 18: 61%; SAT critical reading scores over 600: 5%; SAT math scores over 600: 6%; SAT writing scores over 600: 1%; ACT scores over 24: 11%.

Retention: 64% of full-time freshmen returned.

FACULTY
Total: 460, 69% full-time, 67% with terminal degrees.

Student/faculty ratio: 20:1.

ACADEMICS
Calendar: semesters. *Degrees:* bachelor's, master's, and doctoral.

Special study options: academic remediation for entering students, advanced placement credit, cooperative education, distance learning, double majors, English as a second language, honors programs, internships, off-campus study, part-time degree program, services for LD students, study abroad, summer session for credit. ***ROTC:*** Army (b).

Computers: 250 computers/terminals are available on campus for general student use. Students can access the following: campus intranet, computer help desk, free student e-mail accounts, online (class) grades, online (class) registration, online (class) schedules, Blackboard. Campuswide network is available. 100% of college-owned or -operated housing units are wired for high-speed Internet access. Wireless service is available via classrooms, computer centers, computer labs, dorm rooms, learning centers, libraries, student centers.

STUDENT LIFE
Housing options: on-campus residence required for freshman year; coed, men-only, women-only. Campus housing is university owned. Freshman campus housing is guaranteed.

Activities and organizations: drama/theater group, student-run newspaper, radio and television station, choral group, marching band, Catholic Student Organization, Baptist Student Ministry, Gamerz Elite, Javelina Students for Sustainability, Aggie Club, national fraternities, national sororities.

Athletics Member NCAA. All Division II. ***Intercollegiate sports:*** baseball M(s), basketball M(s)/W(s), cross-country running M/W, football M(s), golf W(s), softball W(s), tennis M(s)/W(s), track and field M(s)/W(s), volleyball W(s). ***Intramural sports:*** archery M/W, bowling M/W, equestrian sports M/W, golf M/W, racquetball M/W, soccer M/W, softball M/W, volleyball M/W.

Campus security: 24-hour emergency response devices and patrols, late-night transport/escort service, controlled dormitory access.

Student services: health clinic, personal/psychological counseling, women's center.

COSTS & FINANCIAL AID
Costs (2014–15) ***Tuition:*** state resident $7554 full-time; nonresident $18,414 full-time. Full-time tuition and fees vary according to course load and degree level. Part-time tuition and fees vary according to course load and degree level. ***Room and board:*** $7554; room only: $3858. Room and board charges vary according to board plan and housing facility. ***Payment plans:*** tuition prepayment, installment, deferred payment. ***Waivers:*** senior citizens and employees or children of employees.

Financial Aid Of all full-time matriculated undergraduates who enrolled in 2005, 4,449 applied for aid, 4,214 were judged to have need, 2,899 had their need fully met. ***Average financial aid package:*** $6500. ***Average need-based loan:*** $3875. ***Average need-based gift aid:*** $6500. ***Average indebtedness upon graduation:*** $2867.

APPLYING
Standardized Tests *Required:* SAT or ACT (for admission).

Options: electronic application.

Application fee: $25.

Required: high school transcript. ***Required for some:*** interview. ***Recommended:*** minimum 2.0 GPA.

Application deadlines: 8/1 (freshmen), 8/1 (out-of-state freshmen), rolling (transfers).

Notification: continuous (freshmen), continuous (out-of-state freshmen), continuous (transfers).

CONTACT
Laura Knippers, Associate Director of Admissions and Enrollment Management, Texas A&M University–Kingsville, MSC 116, 700 University Boulevard, Kingsville, TX 78363. *Phone:* 361-593-3907. *Toll-free phone:* 800-687-6000. *Fax:* 361-593-2991. *E-mail:* laura.knippers@tamuk.edu.

Texas Christian University

Fort Worth, Texas

http://www.tcu.edu/

- **Independent** university, founded 1873, affiliated with Christian Church (Disciples of Christ)
- **Suburban** 278-acre campus with easy access to Dallas-Fort Worth
- **Endowment** $1.4 billion
- **Coed** 8,647 undergraduate students, 96% full-time, 60% women, 40% men
- **Very difficult** entrance level, 49% of applicants were admitted

UNDERGRAD STUDENTS
8,338 full-time, 309 part-time. Students come from 52 states and territories; 70 other countries; 43% are from out of state; 5% Black or African American, non-Hispanic/Latino; 11% Hispanic/Latino; 3% Asian, non-Hispanic/Latino; 0.3% Native Hawaiian or other Pacific Islander, non-Hispanic/Latino; 0.9% American Indian or Alaska Native, non-Hispanic/Latino; 0.5% Two or more races, non-Hispanic/Latino; 1% Race/ethnicity unknown; 5% international; 4% transferred in; 48% live on campus.

Freshmen
Admission: 17,029 applied, 8,322 admitted, 1,891 enrolled.

Retention: 90% of full-time freshmen returned.

FACULTY
Total: 958, 64% full-time, 66% with terminal degrees.

Student/faculty ratio: 13:1.

ACADEMICS
Calendar: semesters. *Degrees:* certificates, diplomas, bachelor's, master's, doctoral, post-master's, and postbachelor's certificates.

Special study options: accelerated degree program, advanced placement credit, distance learning, double majors, English as a second language, honors programs, independent study, internships, part-time degree program, services for LD students, study abroad, summer session for credit. ***ROTC:*** Army (b), Air Force (b).

Computers: 1,400 computers/terminals and 10,000 ports are available on campus for general student use. Students can access the following: campus intranet, computer help desk, free student e-mail accounts, online (class) grades, online (class) registration, online (class) schedules. Campuswide network is available. 100% of college-owned or -operated housing units are wired for high-speed Internet access. Wireless service is available via entire campus.

STUDENT LIFE

Housing options: on-campus residence required through sophomore year; coed, women-only, special housing for students with disabilities. Campus housing is university owned and leased by the school. Freshman campus housing is guaranteed.

Activities and organizations: drama/theater group, student-run newspaper, radio and television station, choral group, marching band, Entrepreneurship Club, LEAPS, Honors College Community Service, Catholic Community, Ignite, national fraternities, national sororities.

Athletics Member NCAA. All Division I. ***Intercollegiate sports:*** baseball M(s), basketball M(s)/W(s), cross-country running M(s)/W(s), equestrian sports W(s), football M(s), golf M(s)/W(s), gymnastics M(c)/W(c), ice hockey M(c), lacrosse M(c), riflery W(s), rugby M(c)/W(c), soccer M(c)/W(s), swimming and diving M(s)/W(s), tennis M(s)/W(s), track and field M(s)/W(s), ultimate Frisbee M(c)/W(c), volleyball M(c)/W(s), water polo M(c)/W(c), wrestling M(c)/W(c). ***Intramural sports:*** baseball M(c), basketball M/W, bowling M/W, golf M(c)/W(c), racquetball M/W, soccer W(c), table tennis M/W, tennis M(c)/W(c), volleyball W(c).

Campus security: 24-hour emergency response devices and patrols, late-night transport/escort service, controlled dormitory access, emergency call boxes, video surveillance in parking lots, self-defense education, lighted sidewalks, Emergency Mass Notification System.

Student services: health clinic, personal/psychological counseling, women's center.

COSTS & FINANCIAL AID

Costs (2014–15) ***Comprehensive fee:*** $49,980 includes full-time tuition ($38,510), mandatory fees ($90), and room and board ($11,380). Part-time tuition: $1625 per credit hour. Part-time tuition and fees vary according to course load. ***Required fees:*** $45 per term part-time. ***College room only:*** $6900. Room and board charges vary according to board plan and housing facility. ***Payment plan:*** installment. ***Waivers:*** employees or children of employees.

Financial Aid Of all full-time matriculated undergraduates who enrolled in 2014, 4,218 applied for aid, 3,217 were judged to have need, 741 had their need fully met. 1,246 Federal Work-Study jobs (averaging $1900). 30 state and other part-time jobs (averaging $1583). In 2014, 2106 non-need-based awards were made. ***Average percent of need met:*** 63. ***Average financial aid package:*** $24,785. ***Average need-based loan:*** $4691. ***Average need-based gift aid:*** $21,732. ***Average non-need-based aid:*** $14,330. ***Average indebtedness upon graduation:*** $39,584. ***Financial aid deadline:*** 5/1.

APPLYING

Standardized Tests *Required:* SAT or ACT (for admission).

Options: electronic application, early decision, early action, deferred entrance.

Application fee: $40.

Required: essay or personal statement, high school transcript, 2 letters of recommendation, interview.

Application deadlines: 2/15 (freshmen), 8/1 (transfers), 11/1 (early action).

Early decision deadline: 11/1.

Notification: 4/1 (freshmen), continuous (transfers), 1/1 (early decision), 1/1 (early action).

CONTACT

Mr. Heath Einstein, Director of Freshman Admission, Texas Christian University, TCU Office of Admission, TCU Box 297013, Fort Worth, TX 76129. *Phone:* 817-257-7490. *Toll-free phone:* 800-828-3764. *Fax:* 817-257-7268. *E-mail:* frogmail@tcu.edu.

Texas Lutheran University

Seguin, Texas

http://www.tlu.edu/

- **Independent** comprehensive, founded 1891, affiliated with Evangelical Lutheran Church
- **Suburban** 196-acre campus with easy access to San Antonio, Austin
- **Endowment** $92.6 million
- **Coed** 1,306 undergraduate students, 94% full-time, 52% women, 48% men

UNDERGRAD STUDENTS

1,229 full-time, 77 part-time. Students come from 21 states and territories; 7 other countries; 3% are from out of state; 8% Black or African American, non-Hispanic/Latino; 31% Hispanic/Latino; 1% Asian, non-Hispanic/Latino; 0.5% American Indian or Alaska Native, non-Hispanic/Latino; 1% Two or more races, non-Hispanic/Latino; 4% Race/ethnicity unknown; 0.1% international; 4% transferred in; 59% live on campus.

Freshmen

Admission: 309 enrolled. ***Average high school GPA:*** 3.65. ***Test scores:*** SAT critical reading scores over 500: 50%; SAT math scores over 500: 62%; SAT writing scores over 500: 39%; ACT scores over 18: 88%; SAT critical reading scores over 600: 13%; SAT math scores over 600: 18%; SAT writing scores over 600: 6%; ACT scores over 24: 30%; SAT critical reading scores over 700: 2%; SAT math scores over 700: 2%; SAT writing scores over 700: 1%; ACT scores over 30: 1%.

Retention: 70% of full-time freshmen returned.

FACULTY

Total: 125, 65% full-time, 66% with terminal degrees.

Student/faculty ratio: 13:1.

ACADEMICS

Calendar: semesters. *Degrees:* bachelor's and master's.

Special study options: advanced placement credit, double majors, honors programs, independent study, internships, part-time degree program, services for LD students, study abroad, summer session for credit. ***ROTC:*** Army (c), Air Force (c).

Unusual degree programs: 3-2 engineering with Texas A&M University, Texas Tech University, Texas State University.

Computers: 266 computers/terminals and 374 ports are available on campus for general student use. Students can access the following: campus intranet, computer help desk, free student e-mail accounts, online (class) grades, online (class) registration, online (class) schedules, free printing. Campuswide network is available. 100% of college-owned or -operated housing units are wired for high-speed Internet access. Wireless service is available via entire campus.

STUDENT LIFE

Housing options: on-campus residence required through senior year; coed. Campus housing is university owned. Freshman campus housing is guaranteed.

Activities and organizations: drama/theater group, student-run newspaper, choral group, Campus Ministry, Mexican American Student Association, Student Government Association, Black Student Union.

Athletics Member NCAA. All Division III. ***Intercollegiate sports:*** baseball M, basketball M/W, cross-country running M/W, football M, golf M/W, soccer M/W, softball W, tennis M/W, track and field M/W, volleyball W. ***Intramural sports:*** basketball M/W, bowling M/W, football M, racquetball M/W, softball M/W, tennis M/W, volleyball M/W.

Campus security: 24-hour emergency response devices and patrols, late-night transport/escort service, controlled dormitory access.

Student services: health clinic, personal/psychological counseling, women's center.

COSTS & FINANCIAL AID

Costs (2014–15) ***Comprehensive fee:*** $36,040 includes full-time tuition ($26,670), mandatory fees ($130), and room and board ($9240). Full-time tuition and fees vary according to course load. Part-time tuition: $885 per semester hour. ***College room only:*** $5400. Room and board charges vary according to board plan and housing facility. ***Payment plan:*** installment. ***Waivers:*** children of alumni and employees or children of employees.

Financial Aid Of all full-time matriculated undergraduates who enrolled in 2014, 1,108 applied for aid, 1,006 were judged to have need, 259 had their need fully met. 145 Federal Work-Study jobs (averaging $2063). 9 state and other part-time jobs (averaging $1344). In 2014, 203 non-need-based awards were made. ***Average percent of need met:*** 80. ***Average financial aid package:*** $22,525. ***Average need-based loan:*** $5056. ***Average need-based gift aid:*** $17,431. ***Average non-need-based aid:*** $12,993. ***Average indebtedness upon graduation:*** $31,576.

APPLYING

Standardized Tests *Required:* SAT or ACT (for admission).

Required: high school transcript, 2 letters of recommendation. ***Required for some:*** minimum 2.0 GPA. ***Recommended:*** essay or personal statement, interview.

CONTACT

Mr. Tom Oliver, Vice President for Enrollment Services, Texas Lutheran University, 1000 West Court Street, Seguin, TX 78155-5999. *Phone:* 830-372-8053. *Toll-free phone:* 800-771-8521. *Fax:* 830-372-8096. *E-mail:* toliver@tlu.edu.

Texas Southern University

Houston, Texas

http://www.tsu.edu/

- **State-supported** university, founded 1947
- **Urban** 147-acre campus
- **Endowment** $43.5 million
- **Coed** 6,915 undergraduate students, 84% full-time, 57% women, 43% men
- **Noncompetitive** entrance level, 51% of applicants were admitted

UNDERGRAD STUDENTS

5,842 full-time, 1,073 part-time. Students come from 40 states and territories; 35 other countries; 10% are from out of state; 82% Black or African American, non-Hispanic/Latino; 7% Hispanic/Latino; 2% Asian, non-Hispanic/Latino; 0.1% Native Hawaiian or other Pacific Islander, non-Hispanic/Latino; 0.5% American Indian or Alaska Native, non-Hispanic/Latino; 0.4% Race/ethnicity unknown; 6% international; 14% transferred in; 22% live on campus.

Freshmen

Admission: 10,239 applied, 5,253 admitted, 1,532 enrolled. ***Average high school GPA:*** 2.84.

Retention: 53% of full-time freshmen returned.

FACULTY

Total: 605, 57% full-time.

Student/faculty ratio: 18:1.

ACADEMICS

Calendar: semesters. *Degrees:* certificates, bachelor's, master's, doctoral, and postbachelor's certificates.

Special study options: academic remediation for entering students, accelerated degree program, adult/continuing education programs, advanced placement credit, cooperative education, distance learning, double majors, English as a second language, external degree program, honors programs, independent study, internships, off-campus study, part-time degree program, services for LD students, study abroad, summer session for credit. ***ROTC:*** Army (b), Navy (c), Air Force (c).

Computers: Students can access the following: computer help desk, free student e-mail accounts, online (class) grades, online (class) registration, online (class) schedules, Blackboard Learning and Community Portal System (E-education). Campuswide network is available. Wireless service is available via entire campus.

STUDENT LIFE

Housing options: on-campus residence required for freshman year; coed, women-only. Campus housing is university owned, leased by the school and is provided by a third party. Freshman campus housing is guaranteed.

Activities and organizations: drama/theater group, student-run newspaper, radio station, choral group, marching band, Debate Team, University Program Council, Student Government Association, Band, Greek Letter Organizations, national fraternities, national sororities.

Athletics Member NCAA. All Division I except football (Division I-AA). ***Intercollegiate sports:*** baseball M(s), basketball M(s)/W(s), bowling W(s), cross-country running M(s)/W(s), golf M(s), soccer M/W(s), softball W(s), tennis M(s)/W(s), track and field M(s)/W(s), volleyball M/W(s). ***Intramural sports:*** softball M/W, swimming and diving M/W, tennis M/W, volleyball M/W.

Campus security: 24-hour emergency response devices and patrols, student patrols, late-night transport/escort service.

Student services: health clinic, personal/psychological counseling, women's center, legal services.

COSTS & FINANCIAL AID

Costs (2014–15) ***Tuition:*** state resident $8126 full-time, $263 per credit hour part-time; nonresident $18,986 full-time, $362 per credit hour part-time. Full-time tuition and fees vary according to course level, course load, degree level, and program. Part-time tuition and fees vary according to course level, course load, degree level, and program. No tuition increase for student's term of enrollment. ***Room and board:*** $9438. Room and board charges vary according to board plan, housing facility, and location. ***Payment plans:*** installment, deferred payment. ***Waivers:*** minority students and senior citizens.

Financial Aid Of all full-time matriculated undergraduates who enrolled in 2014, 5,338 applied for aid, 4,318 were judged to have need, 3,980 had their need fully met. 303 Federal Work-Study jobs (averaging $4000). 20 state and other part-time jobs (averaging $4000). ***Average percent of need met:*** 92. ***Average financial aid package:*** $18,986. ***Average need-based loan:*** $4133. ***Average need-based gift aid:*** $6262. ***Average indebtedness upon graduation:*** $43,600.

APPLYING

Standardized Tests *Required for some:* SAT or ACT (for admission).

Options: electronic application, early admission, early decision.

Application fee: $42.

Required: high school transcript, minimum 2.5 GPA. ***Required for some:*** TSI (Texas Success Initiative) Assessment, ACT 17/SAT 820.

Application deadlines: 8/15 (freshmen), 8/15 (transfers).

Notification: 8/28 (freshmen), continuous until 8/28 (transfers).

CONTACT

Enrollment Services Customer Service Center, Texas Southern University, 3100 Cleburne Street, Houston, TX 77004-4598. *Phone:* 713-313-7071. *Fax:* 713-313-7851. *E-mail:* eservices@em.tsu.edu.

Texas State University

San Marcos, Texas

http://www.txstate.edu/

- **State-supported** university, founded 1899, part of Texas State University System
- **Suburban** 423-acre campus with easy access to San Antonio, Austin
- **Endowment** $139.5 million
- **Coed** 32,177 undergraduate students, 82% full-time, 56% women, 44% men
- **Moderately difficult** entrance level, 73% of applicants were admitted

UNDERGRAD STUDENTS

26,234 full-time, 5,943 part-time. Students come from 52 states and territories; 40 other countries; 2% are from out of state; 8% Black or African American, non-Hispanic/Latino; 33% Hispanic/Latino; 2% Asian, non-Hispanic/Latino; 0.2% Native Hawaiian or other Pacific Islander, non-Hispanic/Latino; 0.3% American Indian or Alaska Native, non-Hispanic/Latino; 3% Two or more races, non-Hispanic/Latino; 1% Race/ethnicity unknown; 0.5% international; 12% transferred in; 21% live on campus.

Freshmen

Admission: 18,413 applied, 13,423 admitted, 5,357 enrolled. ***Test scores:*** SAT critical reading scores over 500: 55%; SAT math scores over 500: 63%; SAT writing scores over 500: 46%; ACT scores over 18: 97%; SAT critical reading scores over 600: 13%; SAT math scores over 600: 15%; SAT writing scores over 600: 8%; ACT scores over 24: 37%; SAT critical reading scores over 700: 1%; SAT math scores over 700: 1%; SAT writing scores over 700: 1%; ACT scores over 30: 3%.

Retention: 76% of full-time freshmen returned.

FACULTY

Total: 1,780, 69% full-time, 64% with terminal degrees.

Student/faculty ratio: 20:1.

ACADEMICS

Calendar: semesters. *Degrees:* bachelor's, master's, doctoral, and postbachelor's certificates.

Special study options: academic remediation for entering students, accelerated degree program, adult/continuing education programs, advanced placement credit, distance learning, double majors, English as a second language, freshman honors college, honors programs, independent study, internships, off-campus study, part-time degree program, services for LD students, study abroad, summer session for credit. ***ROTC:*** Army (b), Air Force (b).

Unusual degree programs: 3-2 engineering with University of Texas at Austin, Texas A&M University, Texas Tech University, University of Texas at San Antonio.

Computers: 1,792 computers/terminals are available on campus for general student use. Students can access the following: computer help desk, free student e-mail accounts, online (class) grades, online (class) registration, online (class) schedules. Campuswide network is available. 100% of college-owned or -operated housing units are wired for high-speed Internet access. Wireless service is available via entire campus.

STUDENT LIFE

Housing options: on-campus residence required through sophomore year; coed, men-only, women-only. Campus housing is university owned. Freshman campus housing is guaranteed.

Activities and organizations: drama/theater group, student-run newspaper, radio station, choral group, marching band, Non-traditional Students Association, Student Association for Campus Activities, Association Student Government, Annual Martin Luther King Jr. Commemoration, national fraternities, national sororities.

Athletics Member NCAA. All Division I except football (Division I-AA). ***Intercollegiate sports:*** baseball M(s), basketball M(s)/W(s), cheerleading M/W, cross-country running M(s)/W(s), equestrian sports M(c)/W(c), fencing M(c)/W(c), golf M(s)/W(s), gymnastics M(c)/W(c), lacrosse M(c)/W(c), rugby M(c)/W(c), soccer M(c)/W(s), softball M(c)/W(s), tennis M(c)/W(s), track and field M(s)/W(s), ultimate Frisbee M(c)/W(c), volleyball W(s), water polo M(c)/W(c), weight lifting M(c)/W(c), wrestling M(c)/W(c). ***Intramural sports:*** basketball M/W, bowling M/W, cross-country running M/W, football M/W, golf M/W, racquetball M/W, rock climbing M/W, soccer M/W, softball M/W, tennis M/W, ultimate Frisbee M/W, volleyball M/W.

Campus security: 24-hour emergency response devices and patrols, late-night transport/escort service, controlled dormitory access, Emergency Notification System (electronic signs) within classrooms and offices delivering notices of what to do and where to go.

Student services: health clinic, personal/psychological counseling, legal services.

COSTS & FINANCIAL AID

Costs (2014–15) ***Tuition:*** state resident $7160 full-time, $239 per credit hour part-time; nonresident $18,020 full-time, $601 per credit hour part-time. Full-time tuition and fees vary according to course load and degree level. Part-time tuition and fees vary according to course load and degree level. No tuition increase for student's term of enrollment. ***Required fees:*** $2356 full-time, $54 per credit hour part-time, $413 per term part-time. ***Room and board:*** $7612; room only: $5050. Room and board charges vary according to board plan and housing facility. ***Payment plan:*** installment. ***Waivers:*** employees or children of employees.

Financial Aid Of all full-time matriculated undergraduates who enrolled in 2014, 21,651 applied for aid, 15,256 were judged to have need, 1,044 had their need fully met. 1,437 Federal Work-Study jobs (averaging $3219). 171 state and other part-time jobs (averaging $2130). In 2014, 469 non-need-based awards were made. ***Average percent of need met:*** 73. ***Average financial aid package:*** $11,301. ***Average need-based loan:*** $4963. ***Average need-based gift aid:*** $6867. ***Average non-need-based aid:*** $3305. ***Average indebtedness upon graduation:*** $26,031.

APPLYING

Standardized Tests *Required:* SAT or ACT (for admission). *Recommended:* SAT (for admission), ACT (for admission).

Options: electronic application, early admission, deferred entrance.

Application fee: $75.

Required: essay or personal statement, high school transcript.

Application deadlines: 5/1 (freshmen), 5/1 (out-of-state freshmen), 7/1 (transfers).

Notification: continuous (freshmen), continuous (transfers).

CONTACT

Texas State University, 601 University Drive, San Marcos, TX 78666. *Phone:* 512-245-2364 Ext. 2803.

Texas Tech University

Lubbock, Texas

http://www.ttu.edu/

- **State-supported** university, founded 1923, part of Texas Tech University System
- **Urban** 1839-acre campus
- **Endowment** $674.3 million
- **Coed** 28,632 undergraduate students, 89% full-time, 45% women, 55% men
- **Moderately difficult** entrance level, 66% of applicants were admitted

UNDERGRAD STUDENTS

25,589 full-time, 3,043 part-time. Students come from 53 states and territories; 72 other countries; 6% are from out of state; 6% Black or African American, non-Hispanic/Latino; 22% Hispanic/Latino; 3% Asian, non-Hispanic/Latino; 0.1% Native Hawaiian or other Pacific Islander, non-Hispanic/Latino; 0.3% American Indian or Alaska Native, non-Hispanic/Latino; 3% Two or more races, non-Hispanic/Latino; 0.5% Race/ethnicity unknown; 4% international; 10% transferred in; 27% live on campus.

Freshmen

Admission: 21,873 applied, 14,464 admitted, 5,619 enrolled. ***Test scores:*** SAT critical reading scores over 500: 73%; SAT math scores over 500: 84%; SAT writing scores over 500: 60%; ACT scores over 18: 99%; SAT critical reading scores over 600: 21%; SAT math scores over 600: 33%; SAT writing scores over 600: 13%; ACT scores over 24: 58%; SAT critical reading scores over 700: 2%; SAT math scores over 700: 4%; SAT writing scores over 700: 1%; ACT scores over 30: 8%.

Retention: 83% of full-time freshmen returned.

FACULTY

Total: 1,636, 86% full-time.

Student/faculty ratio: 22:1.

ACADEMICS

Calendar: semesters. *Degrees:* bachelor's, master's, doctoral, and postbachelor's certificates.

Special study options: academic remediation for entering students, accelerated degree program, advanced placement credit, cooperative education, distance learning, double majors, English as a second language, external degree program, freshman honors college, honors programs, independent study, internships, off-campus study, part-time degree program, services for LD students, student-designed majors, study abroad, summer session for credit. ***ROTC:*** Army (b), Air Force (b).

Unusual degree programs: 3-2 business administration with accounting, management information systems; engineering with chemical, computer, electrical, environmental, industrial, mechanical, petroleum, and software engineering; computer science; agribusiness, agriculture and applied economics, architecture, classics, environmental design, French, German, interior design, mathematics, music education, personal and financial planning, political science, psychology, romance languages, and Spanish.

Computers: 1,830 computers/terminals and 3,000 ports are available on campus for general student use. Students can access the following: campus intranet, computer help desk, free student e-mail accounts, online (class) grades, online (class) registration, online (class) schedules, online degree plans, accounts, transcripts, schedules, financial aid, course and instructor evaluations. Campuswide network is available. 100% of college-owned or -operated housing units are wired for high-speed Internet access. Wireless service is available via classrooms, computer centers, computer labs, dorm rooms, learning centers, libraries, student centers.

STUDENT LIFE

Housing options: on-campus residence required for freshman year; coed, men-only, women-only, special housing for students with disabilities. Campus housing is university owned. Freshman campus housing is guaranteed.

Activities and organizations: drama/theater group, student-run newspaper, radio station, choral group, marching band, Health Occupation Students of America, Dr. Bernard Harris Pre-Medical Society, Gamma Beta Phi, Epsilon Omicron Nu, Society of Petroleum Engineers, national fraternities, national sororities.

Athletics Member NCAA. All Division I except football (Division I-A). ***Intercollegiate sports:*** baseball M(s), basketball M(s)/W(s), cross-country running M(s)/W(s), golf M(s)/W(s), soccer W(s), softball W(s), tennis M(s)/W(s), track and field M(s)/W(s), volleyball W(s). ***Intramural sports:*** badminton M(c)/W(c), baseball M/W, basketball M/W, bowling M/W, equestrian sports M(c)/W(c), fencing M(c)/W(c), golf M/W, gymnastics M(c)/W(c), ice hockey M(c), lacrosse M(c)/W(c), racquetball M/W, rock climbing M(c)/W(c), rugby M(c)/W(c), soccer M/W, softball M/W, swimming and diving M/W, table tennis M/W, tennis M/W, ultimate Frisbee M(c)/W(c), volleyball M/W, water polo M(c)/W(c), weight lifting M, wrestling M(c)/W(c).

Campus security: 24-hour emergency response devices and patrols, late-night transport/escort service, controlled dormitory access.

Student services: health clinic, personal/psychological counseling, legal services.

COSTS & FINANCIAL AID

Costs (2014–15) ***Tuition:*** state resident $6388 full-time, $213 per credit hour part-time; nonresident $17,248 full-time, $575 per credit hour part-time. Full-time tuition and fees vary according to course level, course load, degree level, location, program, reciprocity agreements, and student level. Part-time tuition and fees vary according to course level, course load, degree level, location, program, reciprocity agreements, and student level. ***Required fees:*** $2920 full-time, $37 per credit hour part-time, $909 per term part-time. ***Room and board:*** $8405; room only: $4510. Room and board charges vary according to board plan and housing facility. ***Payment plan:*** installment. ***Waivers:*** senior citizens and employees or children of employees.

Financial Aid Of all full-time matriculated undergraduates who enrolled in 2013, 14,923 applied for aid, 12,264 were judged to have need, 1,073 had their need fully met. In 2013, 2349 non-need-based awards were made. ***Average percent of need met:*** 71. ***Average financial aid package:*** $14,063. ***Average need-based loan:*** $4781. ***Average need-based gift aid:*** $7187. ***Average non-need-based aid:*** $3289. ***Average indebtedness upon graduation:*** $27,879.

APPLYING

Standardized Tests *Required:* SAT or ACT (for admission).

Options: electronic application.

Application fee: $60.

Required: high school transcript. ***Recommended:*** essay or personal statement, .

Application deadlines: 8/1 (freshmen), rolling (transfers).

Notification: 10/1 (freshmen), continuous (transfers).

CONTACT

Texas Tech University, Lubbock, TX 79409. *Phone:* 806-742-1480.

Texas Wesleyan University

Fort Worth, Texas

http://www.txwes.edu/

- **Independent United Methodist** comprehensive, founded 1890
- **Urban** 74-acre campus with easy access to Dallas-Fort Worth
- **Coed** 1,917 undergraduate students, 74% full-time, 50% women, 50% men
- **Moderately difficult** entrance level, 38% of applicants were admitted

UNDERGRAD STUDENTS

1,424 full-time, 493 part-time. Students come from 26 states and territories; 45 other countries; 4% are from out of state; 13% Black or African American, non-Hispanic/Latino; 21% Hispanic/Latino; 2% Asian, non-Hispanic/Latino; 0.1% Native Hawaiian or other Pacific Islander, non-Hispanic/Latino; 0.6% American Indian or Alaska Native, non-Hispanic/Latino; 3% Two or more races, non-Hispanic/Latino; 7% Race/ethnicity unknown; 22% international; 15% transferred in; 21% live on campus.

Freshmen

Admission: 1,855 applied, 706 admitted, 313 enrolled. ***Average high school GPA:*** 3.41. ***Test scores:*** SAT critical reading scores over 500: 43%; SAT math scores over 500: 60%; SAT writing scores over 500: 41%; ACT scores over 18: 90%; SAT critical reading scores over 600: 6%; SAT math scores over 600: 8%; SAT writing scores over 600: 7%; ACT scores over 24: 20%; SAT math scores over 700: 1%; SAT writing scores over 700: 1%.

Retention: 51% of full-time freshmen returned.

FACULTY

Total: 229, 61% full-time, 52% with terminal degrees.

Student/faculty ratio: 16:1.

ACADEMICS

Calendar: semesters. *Degrees:* bachelor's, master's, and doctoral.

Special study options: academic remediation for entering students, accelerated degree program, advanced placement credit, distance learning, double majors, honors programs, independent study, internships, off-campus study, part-time degree program, services for LD students, study abroad, summer session for credit. ***ROTC:*** Army (c), Air Force (c).

Unusual degree programs: 3-2 business administration; Education.

Computers: 605 computers/terminals and 487 ports are available on campus for general student use. Students can access the following: campus intranet, computer help desk, free student e-mail accounts, online (class) grades, online (class) registration, online (class) schedules. Campuswide network is available. 100% of college-owned or -operated housing units are wired for high-speed Internet access. Wireless service is available via entire campus.

STUDENT LIFE

Housing options: coed, special housing for students with disabilities. Campus housing is university owned.

Activities and organizations: drama/theater group, student-run newspaper, radio and television station, choral group, Kappa Alpha Order, Alpha Xi Delta, Gay-Straight Alliance, Lambda Kappa Kappa, Burleson BLUE, national fraternities, national sororities.

Athletics Member NAIA. ***Intercollegiate sports:*** baseball M(s), basketball M(s)/W(s), cheerleading M(s)/W(s), cross-country running M(s)/W(s), golf M(s)/W(s), soccer M(s)/W(s), softball W(s), table tennis M(s)/W(s), tennis W, track and field M(s)/W(s), volleyball W(s). ***Intramural sports:*** badminton M/W, basketball M/W, football M/W, golf M/W, soccer M/W, volleyball M/W.

Campus security: 24-hour emergency response devices and patrols, student patrols, late-night transport/escort service, controlled dormitory access.

Student services: health clinic, personal/psychological counseling.

COSTS & FINANCIAL AID

Costs (2014–15) ***Comprehensive fee:*** $31,382 includes full-time tuition ($20,642), mandatory fees ($2502), and room and board ($8238). Full-time tuition and fees vary according to course level, course load, degree level, program, and student level. Part-time tuition: $700 per credit hour. Part-time tuition and fees vary according to course level, course load, degree level, program, and student level. ***College room only:*** $4830. Room and board charges vary according to housing facility. ***Payment plans:*** installment, deferred payment. ***Waivers:*** employees or children of employees.

Financial Aid Of all full-time matriculated undergraduates who enrolled in 2013, 972 applied for aid, 865 were judged to have need, 140 had their need fully met. 125 Federal Work-Study jobs (averaging $4000). 12 state and other part-time jobs (averaging $4000). In 2013, 241 non-need-based awards were made. ***Average percent of need met:*** 67. ***Average financial aid package:*** $20,304. ***Average need-based loan:*** $4145. ***Average need-based gift aid:*** $13,732. ***Average non-need-based aid:*** $8623. ***Average indebtedness upon graduation:*** $37,014.

APPLYING

Standardized Tests *Required:* SAT or ACT (for admission).

Options: electronic application, deferred entrance.

Required: minimum 2.0 GPA. ***Required for some:*** essay or personal statement, high school transcript.

Application deadlines: rolling (freshmen), rolling (out-of-state freshmen), rolling (transfers).

Notification: continuous (freshmen), continuous (out-of-state freshmen), continuous (transfers).

CONTACT

Mrs. Denelle Rodriguez, Asst. Director of Freshman Admissions, Texas Wesleyan University, 1201 Wesleyan Street, Fort Worth, TX 76105-1536.

Phone: 817-531-7529. *Toll-free phone:* 800-580-8980. *Fax:* 817-531-7515. *E-mail:* admissions@txwes.edu.

Texas Woman's University

Denton, Texas

http://www.twu.edu/

- **State-supported** university, founded 1901
- **Suburban** 270-acre campus with easy access to Dallas-Fort Worth
- **Coed, primarily women** 9,679 undergraduate students, 70% full-time, 89% women, 11% men
- **Minimally difficult** entrance level, 85% of applicants were admitted

UNDERGRAD STUDENTS

6,798 full-time, 2,881 part-time. 21% Black or African American, non-Hispanic/Latino; 25% Hispanic/Latino; 8% Asian, non-Hispanic/Latino; 0.1% Native Hawaiian or other Pacific Islander, non-Hispanic/Latino; 0.5% American Indian or Alaska Native, non-Hispanic/Latino; 4% Two or more races, non-Hispanic/Latino; 0.6% Race/ethnicity unknown; 1% international; 14% transferred in; 24% live on campus.

Freshmen

Admission: 4,582 applied, 3,909 admitted, 1,134 enrolled. ***Average high school GPA:*** 3.07. ***Test scores:*** SAT critical reading scores over 500: 37%; SAT math scores over 500: 43%; ACT scores over 18: 100%; SAT critical reading scores over 600: 9%; SAT math scores over 600: 11%; ACT scores over 24: 40%; SAT critical reading scores over 700: 1%; SAT math scores over 700: 1%.

Retention: 73% of full-time freshmen returned.

FACULTY

Total: 791, 52% full-time.

Student/faculty ratio: 14:1.

ACADEMICS

Calendar: semesters. *Degrees:* bachelor's, master's, doctoral, post-master's, and postbachelor's certificates.

Special study options: academic remediation for entering students, accelerated degree program, adult/continuing education programs, advanced placement credit, cooperative education, distance learning, double majors, honors programs, independent study, internships, off-campus study, part-time degree program, services for LD students, study abroad, summer session for credit. ***ROTC:*** Army (c), Air Force (c).

Computers: Students can access the following: campus intranet, computer help desk, free student e-mail accounts, online (class) grades, online (class) registration, online (class) schedules. Campuswide network is available. Wireless service is available via classrooms, computer centers, computer labs, learning centers, libraries, student centers.

STUDENT LIFE

Housing options: on-campus residence required through sophomore year; coed, men-only, women-only, special housing for students with disabilities. Campus housing is university owned and leased by the school. Freshman campus housing is guaranteed.

Activities and organizations: drama/theater group, student-run newspaper, choral group, Helping Hands, Athenian Honor Society, Campus Activities Board, Nursing Student Organization, Graduate Library and Information Studies Association, national fraternities, national sororities.

Athletics Member NCAA. All Division II. ***Intercollegiate sports:*** basketball W(s), gymnastics W(s), soccer W(s), softball W(s), volleyball W(s). ***Intramural sports:*** badminton M/W, basketball M(c)/W(c), football M/W, golf M(c)/W(c), soccer M(c)/W(c), softball M(c)/W(c), tennis M/W, track and field M(c)/W(c), volleyball M/W, weight lifting M(c)/W(c), wrestling M(c)/W(c).

Campus security: 24-hour emergency response devices and patrols, late-night transport/escort service, controlled dormitory access.

Student services: health clinic, personal/psychological counseling.

COSTS & FINANCIAL AID

Costs (2015–16) ***Tuition:*** state resident $5650 full-time, $188 per credit hour part-time; nonresident $16,510 full-time, $550 per credit hour part-time. Full-time tuition and fees vary according to course load, program, and reciprocity agreements. Part-time tuition and fees vary according to course load, program, and reciprocity agreements. ***Required fees:*** $2345 full-time. ***Room and board:*** $6780; room only: $3690. Room and board charges vary according to board plan and housing facility. ***Payment plan:*** installment. ***Waivers:*** senior citizens.

Financial Aid Of all full-time matriculated undergraduates who enrolled in 2013, 5,567 applied for aid, 4,893 were judged to have need, 1,382 had their need fully met. In 2013, 78 non-need-based awards were made. ***Average percent of need met:*** 82. ***Average financial aid package:*** $8249. ***Average need-based loan:*** $3843. ***Average need-based gift aid:*** $6466. ***Average non-need-based aid:*** $2287.

APPLYING

Standardized Tests *Required for some:* SAT or ACT (for admission).

Options: electronic application, early admission, deferred entrance.

Application fee: $50.

Required: high school transcript, minimum 2.0 GPA.

CONTACT

Ms. Erma Nieto-Brecht, Director of Admissions, Texas Woman's University, 304 Administration Drive, Denton, TX 76201. *Phone:* 940-898-3188. *Toll-free phone:* 866-809-6130. *Fax:* 940-898-3081. *E-mail:* admissions@twu.edu.

Trinity University

San Antonio, Texas

http://www.trinity.edu/

- **Independent** comprehensive, founded 1869, affiliated with Presbyterian Church
- **Urban** 117-acre campus
- **Endowment** $1.2 billion
- **Coed** 2,297 undergraduate students, 98% full-time, 52% women, 48% men
- **Very difficult** entrance level, 48% of applicants were admitted

UNDERGRAD STUDENTS

2,259 full-time, 38 part-time. Students come from 45 states and territories; 72 other countries; 25% are from out of state; 4% Black or African American, non-Hispanic/Latino; 18% Hispanic/Latino; 6% Asian, non-Hispanic/Latino; 0.2% American Indian or Alaska Native, non-Hispanic/Latino; 5% Two or more races, non-Hispanic/Latino; 4% Race/ethnicity unknown; 7% international; 1% transferred in; 75% live on campus.

Freshmen

Admission: 5,502 applied, 2,664 admitted, 655 enrolled. ***Average high school GPA:*** 3.48. ***Test scores:*** SAT critical reading scores over 500: 97%; SAT math scores over 500: 99%; SAT writing scores over 500: 92%; ACT scores over 18: 100%; SAT critical reading scores over 600: 68%; SAT math scores over 600: 75%; SAT writing scores over 600: 59%; ACT scores over 24: 98%; SAT critical reading scores over 700: 20%; SAT math scores over 700: 22%; SAT writing scores over 700: 11%; ACT scores over 30: 41%.

Retention: 88% of full-time freshmen returned.

FACULTY

Total: 307, 74% full-time, 83% with terminal degrees.

Student/faculty ratio: 9:1.

ACADEMICS

Calendar: semesters. *Degrees:* bachelor's and master's.

Special study options: accelerated degree program, advanced placement credit, double majors, honors programs, independent study, internships, off-campus study, part-time degree program, services for LD students, student-designed majors, study abroad, summer session for credit. ***ROTC:*** Army (c), Air Force (c).

Computers: 500 computers/terminals and 2,000 ports are available on campus for general student use. Students can access the following: campus intranet, computer help desk, free student e-mail accounts, online (class) grades, online (class) registration, online (class) schedules. Campuswide network is available. 100% of college-owned or -operated housing units are wired for high-speed Internet access. Wireless service is available via entire campus.

STUDENT LIFE

Housing options: on-campus residence required through junior year; coed. Campus housing is university owned. Freshman campus housing is guaranteed.

Activities and organizations: drama/theater group, student-run newspaper, radio and television station, choral group, Tiger Stand Band, Alpha Phi Omega, Association of Student Representatives, Acabellas/Trinitones, Multicultural Network, national fraternities.

Athletics Member NCAA. All Division III. ***Intercollegiate sports:*** baseball M, basketball M/W, cross-country running M/W, fencing M(c)/W(c), football M, golf M/W, lacrosse M(c)/W(c), riflery M(c)/W(c), soccer M/W, softball W, swimming and diving M/W, tennis M/W, track and field M/W, volleyball M(c)/W, water polo M(c)/W(c). ***Intramural sports:*** basketball M/W, cross-country running M/W, equestrian sports M(c)/W(c), football M, racquetball M/W, soccer M/W, softball M/W, swimming and diving M/W, table tennis M/W, tennis M/W, ultimate Frisbee M/W, volleyball M/W, wrestling M/W.

Campus security: 24-hour emergency response devices and patrols, late-night transport/escort service, controlled dormitory access.

Student services: health clinic, personal/psychological counseling.

COSTS & FINANCIAL AID

Costs (2014–15) ***Comprehensive fee:*** $48,150 includes full-time tuition ($35,688), mandatory fees ($526), and room and board ($11,936). Full-time tuition and fees vary according to course load. Part-time tuition: $1487 per credit hour. Part-time tuition and fees vary according to course load. ***College room only:*** $7714. Room and board charges vary according to board plan. ***Payment plan:*** installment. ***Waivers:*** employees or children of employees.

Financial Aid Of all full-time matriculated undergraduates who enrolled in 2014, 1,235 applied for aid, 1,004 were judged to have need, 561 had their need fully met. 687 Federal Work-Study jobs (averaging $2245). In 2014, 1052 non-need-based awards were made. ***Average percent of need met:*** 93. ***Average financial aid package:*** $34,073. ***Average need-based loan:*** $5577. ***Average need-based gift aid:*** $25,809. ***Average non-need-based aid:*** $16,583. ***Average indebtedness upon graduation:*** $35,318.

APPLYING

Standardized Tests *Required:* SAT or ACT (for admission).

Options: electronic application, early decision, early action, deferred entrance.

Required: essay or personal statement, high school transcript, 2 letters of recommendation, Official SAT or ACT Test Scores. ***Recommended:*** interview.

Application deadlines: 2/1 (freshmen), 3/1 (transfers), 11/1 (early action).

Early decision deadline: 11/1 (for plan 1), 1/1 (for plan 2).

Notification: 4/1 (freshmen), 5/1 (transfers), 12/15 (early decision plan 1), 2/15 (early decision plan 2), 12/15 (early action).

CONTACT

Office of Admissions, Trinity University, One Trinity Place, Northrup Hall 140, San Antonio, TX 78212-7200. *Phone:* 210-999-7207. *Toll-free phone:* 800-TRINITY. *Fax:* 210-999-8164. *E-mail:* admissions@trinity.edu.

University of Dallas

Irving, Texas

http://www.udallas.edu/

- **Independent Roman Catholic** university, founded 1955
- **Suburban** 215-acre campus with easy access to Dallas-Fort Worth
- **Endowment** $54.9 million
- **Coed** 1,327 undergraduate students, 99% full-time, 55% women, 45% men
- **Moderately difficult** entrance level, 85% of applicants were admitted

UNDERGRAD STUDENTS

1,313 full-time, 14 part-time. Students come from 48 states and territories; 19 other countries; 55% are from out of state; 2% Black or African American, non-Hispanic/Latino; 19% Hispanic/Latino; 4% Asian, non-Hispanic/Latino; 0.2% Native Hawaiian or other Pacific Islander, non-Hispanic/Latino; 0.4% American Indian or Alaska Native, non-Hispanic/Latino; 3% Two or more races, non-Hispanic/Latino; 2%

Race/ethnicity unknown; 3% international; 3% transferred in; 63% live on campus.

Freshmen

Admission: 1,432 applied, 1,219 admitted, 342 enrolled. ***Average high school GPA:*** 3.81. ***Test scores:*** SAT critical reading scores over 500: 91%; SAT math scores over 500: 90%; SAT writing scores over 500: 86%; ACT scores over 18: 99%; SAT critical reading scores over 600: 60%; SAT math scores over 600: 46%; SAT writing scores over 600: 46%; ACT scores over 24: 81%; SAT critical reading scores over 700: 18%; SAT math scores over 700: 11%; SAT writing scores over 700: 11%; ACT scores over 30: 31%.

Retention: 80% of full-time freshmen returned.

FACULTY

Total: 234, 60% full-time.

Student/faculty ratio: 11:1.

ACADEMICS

Calendar: semesters. *Degrees:* bachelor's, master's, doctoral, post-master's, and postbachelor's certificates.

Special study options: advanced placement credit, double majors, independent study, internships, off-campus study, part-time degree program, services for LD students, student-designed majors, study abroad, summer session for credit. ***ROTC:*** Army (c), Air Force (c).

Unusual degree programs: 3-2 engineering with University of Texas at Arlington - College of Engineering; nursing with Texas Woman's University-College of Nursing.

Computers: 125 computers/terminals are available on campus for general student use. Students can access the following: campus intranet, computer help desk, free student e-mail accounts, online (class) grades, online (class) registration, online (class) schedules. Campuswide network is available. 100% of college-owned or -operated housing units are wired for high-speed Internet access. Wireless service is available via entire campus.

STUDENT LIFE

Housing options: on-campus residence required through junior year; men-only, women-only. Campus housing is university owned. Freshman campus housing is guaranteed.

Activities and organizations: drama/theater group, student-run newspaper, choral group, SPUD (Programming Board), Residence Hall Association, student government, Best Buddies, Alpha Phi Omega.

Athletics Member NCAA. All Division III. ***Intercollegiate sports:*** baseball M, basketball M/W, cross-country running M/W, golf M, lacrosse M/W, soccer M/W, softball W, track and field M/W, volleyball W. ***Intramural sports:*** basketball M, equestrian sports M(c)/W(c), football M/W, rugby M(c)/W(c), sailing M(c)/W(c), soccer M/W, softball M/W, tennis M(c)/W(c), ultimate Frisbee M(c)/W(c), volleyball M/W.

Campus security: 24-hour emergency response devices and patrols, late-night transport/escort service, controlled dormitory access.

Student services: health clinic, personal/psychological counseling.

COSTS & FINANCIAL AID

Costs (2015–16) ***Comprehensive fee:*** $47,100 includes full-time tuition ($33,360), mandatory fees ($2440), and room and board ($11,300). Full-time tuition and fees vary according to course load. Part-time tuition: $1330 per credit. Part-time tuition and fees vary according to course load. ***Required fees:*** $2440 per year part-time. ***College room only:*** $6450. Room and board charges vary according to board plan and housing facility. ***Payment plan:*** installment. ***Waivers:*** employees or children of employees.

Financial Aid Of all full-time matriculated undergraduates who enrolled in 2014, 906 applied for aid, 802 were judged to have need, 177 had their need fully met. 274 Federal Work-Study jobs (averaging $1522). 73 state and other part-time jobs (averaging $1587). In 2014, 646 non-need-based awards were made. ***Average percent of need met:*** 79. ***Average financial aid package:*** $28,690. ***Average need-based loan:*** $5929. ***Average need-based gift aid:*** $23,392. ***Average non-need-based aid:*** $16,730. ***Average indebtedness upon graduation:*** $36,561. ***Financial aid deadline:*** 11/15.

APPLYING

Standardized Tests *Required:* SAT or ACT (for admission).

Options: electronic application, early action, deferred entrance.

Application fee: $50.

Required: essay or personal statement, high school transcript, 2 letters of recommendation. ***Required for some:*** interview.

Application deadlines: 3/1 (freshmen), 3/1 (out-of-state freshmen), 8/1 (transfers), 12/1 (early action).

Notification: continuous (freshmen), continuous (transfers), 1/15 (early action).

CONTACT

Elizabeth Griffin-Smith, Director of Admissions, University of Dallas, 1845 East Northgate Drive, Irving, TX 75062-4736. *Phone:* 800-628-6999. *Toll-free phone:* 800-628-6999. *Fax:* 972-721-5017. *E-mail:* ugadmis@udallas.edu.

See previous page for display ad and page 1660 for the College Close-Up.

University of Houston

Houston, Texas

http://www.uh.edu/

- **State-supported** university, founded 1927, part of University of Houston System
- **Urban** 594-acre campus with easy access to Houston
- **Endowment** $413.5 million
- **Coed** 32,915 undergraduate students, 73% full-time, 49% women, 51% men
- **Moderately difficult** entrance level, 63% of applicants were admitted

UNDERGRAD STUDENTS

23,973 full-time, 8,942 part-time. Students come from 48 states and territories; 105 other countries; 2% are from out of state; 11% Black or African American, non-Hispanic/Latino; 31% Hispanic/Latino; 22% Asian, non-Hispanic/Latino; 0.3% Native Hawaiian or other Pacific Islander, non-Hispanic/Latino; 0.1% American Indian or Alaska Native, non-Hispanic/Latino; 3% Two or more races, non-Hispanic/Latino; 0.8% Race/ethnicity unknown; 5% international; 14% transferred in; 19% live on campus.

Freshmen

Admission: 17,328 applied, 10,915 admitted, 4,048 enrolled. ***Test scores:*** SAT critical reading scores over 500: 78%; SAT math scores over 500: 90%; ACT scores over 18: 97%; SAT critical reading scores over 600: 30%; SAT math scores over 600: 46%; ACT scores over 24: 62%; SAT critical reading scores over 700: 4%; SAT math scores over 700: 8%; ACT scores over 30: 11%.

Retention: 86% of full-time freshmen returned.

FACULTY

Total: 2,018, 72% full-time, 74% with terminal degrees.

Student/faculty ratio: 22:1.

ACADEMICS

Calendar: semesters. *Degrees:* bachelor's, master's, and doctoral.

Special study options: academic remediation for entering students, adult/continuing education programs, advanced placement credit, cooperative education, distance learning, double majors, freshman honors college, honors programs, independent study, internships, off-campus study, part-time degree program, services for LD students, study abroad, summer session for credit. ***ROTC:*** Army (b), Navy (c), Air Force (b).

Unusual degree programs: 3-2 business administration with BBA/MS in Accountancy.

Computers: 1,032 computers/terminals and 40,000 ports are available on campus for general student use. Students can access the following: campus intranet, computer help desk, free student e-mail accounts, online (class) grades, online (class) registration, online (class) schedules, online Bus Loop schedule. Campuswide network is available. 100% of college-owned or -operated housing units are wired for high-speed Internet access. Wireless service is available via entire campus.

STUDENT LIFE

Housing options: coed, special housing for students with disabilities. Campus housing is university owned and is provided by a third party.

Activities and organizations: drama/theater group, student-run newspaper, radio and television station, choral group, marching band, Student Government Association, Residence Hall Association,

Metropolitan Volunteer Program, Student Governing Board- Honors College, Student Alumni Connection, national fraternities, national sororities.

Athletics Member NCAA. All Division I except football (Division I-A). ***Intercollegiate sports:*** baseball M(s), basketball M(s)/W(s), cross-country running M(s)/W(s), golf M(s)/W(s), soccer W(s), softball W(s), swimming and diving W(s), tennis W(s), track and field M(s)/W(s), volleyball W(s). ***Intramural sports:*** badminton M/W, basketball M/W, bowling M(c)/W, fencing M(c)/W(c), golf M/W, racquetball M/W, rock climbing M/W, soccer M/W, softball M/W, swimming and diving M/W, table tennis M/W, tennis M/W, track and field M/W, ultimate Frisbee M(c)/W(c), volleyball M/W(c), water polo M(c)/W(c), weight lifting M/W.

Campus security: 24-hour emergency response devices and patrols, student patrols, late-night transport/escort service, controlled dormitory access, vehicle assistance.

Student services: health clinic, personal/psychological counseling, women's center, legal services.

COSTS & FINANCIAL AID

Costs (2014–15) ***Tuition:*** state resident $9564 full-time, $319 per credit hour part-time; nonresident $23,424 full-time, $781 per credit hour part-time. Full-time tuition and fees vary according to course level, course load, degree level, program, and student level. Part-time tuition and fees vary according to course level, course load, degree level, program, and student level. No tuition increase for student's term of enrollment. ***Required fees:*** $954 full-time. ***Room and board:*** $9278. Room and board charges vary according to board plan and housing facility. ***Payment plans:*** installment, deferred payment.

Financial Aid Of all full-time matriculated undergraduates who enrolled in 2014, 16,692 applied for aid, 14,908 were judged to have need, 1,865 had their need fully met. 515 Federal Work-Study jobs (averaging $3909). In 2014, 749 non-need-based awards were made. ***Average percent of need met:*** 60. ***Average financial aid package:*** $12,119. ***Average need-based loan:*** $7429. ***Average need-based gift aid:*** $8089. ***Average non-need-based aid:*** $5075. ***Average indebtedness upon graduation:*** $18,453.

APPLYING

Standardized Tests *Required:* SAT or ACT (for admission).

Options: electronic application.

Application fee: $50.

Required: high school transcript, SAT or ACT scores.

Application deadlines: 8/1 (freshmen), 6/1 (transfers).

Notification: continuous (freshmen), continuous (transfers).

CONTACT

Jeff Fuller, Director, Student Recruitment, University of Houston, Welcome Center, 4400 University Boulevard, Houston, TX 77204-2023. *Phone:* 713-743-1010. *Fax:* 713-743-9633. *E-mail:* jdfuller@central.uh.edu.

University of Houston–Clear Lake

Houston, Texas

http://www.uhcl.edu/

- **State-supported** comprehensive, founded 1971, part of University of Houston System
- **Suburban** 524-acre campus with easy access to Houston
- **Endowment** $27.6 million
- **Coed** 5,077 undergraduate students, 47% full-time, 67% women, 33% men
- **Minimally difficult** entrance level, 35% of applicants were admitted

UNDERGRAD STUDENTS

2,374 full-time, 2,703 part-time. Students come from 47 other countries; 0.1% are from out of state; 9% Black or African American, non-Hispanic/Latino; 35% Hispanic/Latino; 6% Asian, non-Hispanic/Latino; 0.1% Native Hawaiian or other Pacific Islander, non-Hispanic/Latino; 0.2% American Indian or Alaska Native, non-Hispanic/Latino; 3% Two or more races, non-Hispanic/Latino; 2% Race/ethnicity unknown; 2% international; 27% transferred in; 3% live on campus.

Freshmen

Admission: 1,698 applied, 601 admitted, 201 enrolled. ***Average high school GPA:*** 3.47. ***Test scores:*** SAT critical reading scores over 500: 63%; SAT math scores over 500: 73%; SAT writing scores over 500: 47%; ACT scores over 18: 95%; SAT critical reading scores over 600: 19%; SAT math scores over 600: 18%; SAT writing scores over 600: 12%; ACT scores over 24: 46%; SAT critical reading scores over 700: 4%; SAT math scores over 700: 2%; SAT writing scores over 700: 3%; ACT scores over 30: 8%.

FACULTY

Total: 529, 51% full-time.

Student/faculty ratio: 16:1.

ACADEMICS

Calendar: semesters. *Degrees:* certificates, bachelor's, master's, doctoral, post-master's, and postbachelor's certificates.

Special study options: academic remediation for entering students, advanced placement credit, cooperative education, distance learning, double majors, English as a second language, independent study, internships, off-campus study, part-time degree program, services for LD students, study abroad, summer session for credit.

Computers: 693 computers/terminals are available on campus for general student use. Students can access the following: campus intranet, computer help desk, free student e-mail accounts, online (class) grades, online (class) registration, online (class) schedules. Campuswide network is available. Wireless service is available via entire campus.

STUDENT LIFE

Housing options: coed, special housing for students with disabilities. Campus housing is provided by a third party. Freshman applicants given priority for college housing.

Activities and organizations: student-run newspaper, National Society of Leadership and Success, Student Government Association, Texas State Student Association, Indian Students Association, Communication and Digital Media Association.

Athletics ***Intramural sports:*** weight lifting M(c).

Campus security: 24-hour emergency response devices and patrols, student patrols, late-night transport/escort service.

Student services: health clinic, personal/psychological counseling, women's center.

COSTS

Costs (2014–15) ***Tuition:*** state resident $5670 full-time, $189 per credit hour part-time; nonresident $18,630 full-time, $621 per credit hour part-time. Full-time tuition and fees vary according to course load, degree level, and program. Part-time tuition and fees vary according to course load, degree level, and program. ***Required fees:*** $1266 full-time, $462 per term part-time. ***Room only:*** $9682. Room and board charges vary according to housing facility. ***Payment plans:*** installment, deferred payment. ***Waivers:*** senior citizens.

APPLYING

Standardized Tests *Required:* SAT or ACT (for admission).

Options: electronic application, early admission, deferred entrance.

Application fee: $45.

Required: high school transcript, All students must meet the Texas Education Code (TEC) 51.803-51.809 (State of Texas Uniform Admission Policy - SAT or ACT scores) to be eligible for admission. ***Required for some:*** essay or personal statement, 2 letters of recommendation.

Application deadlines: 6/1 (freshmen), 6/1 (out-of-state freshmen), 8/24 (transfers).

Notification: continuous (transfers).

CONTACT

Ms. Rauchelle Jones, Executive Director of Admissions, University of Houston–Clear Lake, 2700 Bay Area Boulevard, Box 13, Houston, TX 77058-1002. *Phone:* 281-283-2518. *Fax:* 281-283-2530. *E-mail:* admissions@uhcl.edu.

University of Houston–Downtown

Houston, Texas

http://www.uhd.edu/

- **State-supported** comprehensive, founded 1974, part of University of Houston System
- **Urban** 24-acre campus
- **Coed** 13,830 undergraduate students, 51% full-time, 60% women, 40% men
- **Noncompetitive** entrance level, 84% of applicants were admitted

UNDERGRAD STUDENTS

7,069 full-time, 6,761 part-time. 1% are from out of state; 24% Black or African American, non-Hispanic/Latino; 41% Hispanic/Latino; 9% Asian, non-Hispanic/Latino; 0.3% Native Hawaiian or other Pacific Islander, non-Hispanic/Latino; 0.4% American Indian or Alaska Native, non-Hispanic/Latino; 1% Two or more races, non-Hispanic/Latino; 1% Race/ethnicity unknown; 5% international; 17% transferred in.

Freshmen

Admission: 3,235 applied, 2,723 admitted, 993 enrolled. ***Test scores:*** SAT critical reading scores over 500: 17%; SAT math scores over 500: 34%; SAT writing scores over 500: 19%; ACT scores over 18: 51%; SAT critical reading scores over 600: 2%; SAT math scores over 600: 4%; SAT writing scores over 600: 2%; ACT scores over 24: 4%.

Retention: 66% of full-time freshmen returned.

FACULTY

Total: 668, 50% full-time, 63% with terminal degrees.

Student/faculty ratio: 22:1.

ACADEMICS

Calendar: semesters. *Degrees:* bachelor's, master's, and postbachelor's certificates.

Special study options: academic remediation for entering students, advanced placement credit, distance learning, double majors, English as a second language, independent study, internships, off-campus study, part-time degree program, services for LD students, study abroad, summer session for credit. ***ROTC:*** Army (c), Air Force (c).

Computers: Students can access the following: computer help desk, free student e-mail accounts, online (class) grades, online (class) registration, online (class) schedules. Campuswide network is available. Wireless service is available via entire campus.

STUDENT LIFE

Housing options: college housing not available.

Activities and organizations: drama/theater group, student-run newspaper, national fraternities, national sororities.

Athletics ***Intramural sports:*** badminton M/W, baseball M(c), basketball M(c)/W(c), bowling M/W, cheerleading M(c)/W(c), soccer M(c)/W(c), tennis M/W, volleyball M(c)/W(c), weight lifting M(c)/W(c).

Campus security: 24-hour emergency response devices and patrols, late-night transport/escort service.

Student services: health clinic, personal/psychological counseling, legal services.

COSTS & FINANCIAL AID

Costs (2014–15) ***Tuition:*** state resident $5490 full-time, $183 per credit hour part-time; nonresident $16,350 full-time, $545 per credit hour part-time. Full-time tuition and fees vary according to course load and program. Part-time tuition and fees vary according to course load and program. ***Required fees:*** $1124 full-time, $456 per term part-time. ***Payment plan:*** installment. ***Waivers:*** senior citizens.

Financial Aid Of all full-time matriculated undergraduates who enrolled in 2014, 5,621 applied for aid, 5,188 were judged to have need, 4,593 had their need fully met. In 2014, 107 non-need-based awards were made. ***Average percent of need met:*** 57. ***Average financial aid package:*** $10,289. ***Average need-based loan:*** $8156. ***Average need-based gift aid:*** $5573. ***Average non-need-based aid:*** $2705. ***Average indebtedness upon graduation:*** $23,249.

APPLYING

Standardized Tests *Required:* SAT or ACT (for admission).

Options: electronic application.

Application fee: $35.

Required: high school transcript.

CONTACT

Ms. Kecia Osbourne, Assistant Director of Admissions-Outreach Services, University of Houston–Downtown, One Main Street, Suite 350-S, Houston, TX 77002. *Phone:* 713-221-8522. *Fax:* 713-221-8157. *E-mail:* uhdadmit@uhd.edu.

University of Houston–Victoria

Victoria, Texas

http://www.uhv.edu/

- **State-supported** upper-level, founded 1973, part of University of Houston System
- **Small-town** 20-acre campus
- **Endowment** $7.5 million
- **Coed** 3,012 undergraduate students, 51% full-time, 66% women, 34% men
- **Minimally difficult** entrance level, 56% of applicants were admitted

UNDERGRAD STUDENTS

1,541 full-time, 1,471 part-time. 16% Black or African American, non-Hispanic/Latino; 34% Hispanic/Latino; 8% Asian, non-Hispanic/Latino; 0.2% Native Hawaiian or other Pacific Islander, non-Hispanic/Latino; 0.2% American Indian or Alaska Native, non-Hispanic/Latino; 2% Two or more races, non-Hispanic/Latino; 0.9% Race/ethnicity unknown; 2% international; 16% transferred in.

Freshmen

Admission: 3,950 applied, 2,197 admitted.

FACULTY

Total: 239, 57% full-time, 67% with terminal degrees.

Student/faculty ratio: 18:1.

ACADEMICS

Calendar: semesters. *Degrees:* bachelor's, master's, post-master's, and postbachelor's certificates.

Special study options: accelerated degree program, adult/continuing education programs, distance learning, double majors, honors programs, independent study, internships, part-time degree program, study abroad. ***ROTC:*** Air Force (c).

Computers: Students can access the following: campus intranet, computer help desk, free student e-mail accounts, online (class) grades, online (class) registration, online (class) schedules. Campuswide network is available. 100% of college-owned or -operated housing units are wired for high-speed Internet access. Wireless service is available via entire campus.

STUDENT LIFE

Housing options: coed. Campus housing is university owned. Freshman applicants given priority for college housing.

Athletics Member NAIA. ***Intercollegiate sports:*** baseball M, golf M/W, soccer M/W, softball W.

Campus security: 24-hour emergency response devices and patrols, controlled dormitory access.

Student services: personal/psychological counseling.

COSTS & FINANCIAL AID

Costs (2014–15) ***Tuition:*** state resident $5189 full-time, $173 per credit hour part-time; nonresident $16,049 full-time, $535 per credit hour part-time. Full-time tuition and fees vary according to course level and course load. Part-time tuition and fees vary according to course level and course load. ***Required fees:*** $1560 full-time, $78 per credit hour part-time. ***Room and board:*** $7108. Room and board charges vary according to board plan and housing facility. ***Payment plan:*** installment. ***Waivers:*** senior citizens and employees or children of employees.

Financial Aid Of all full-time matriculated undergraduates who enrolled in 2010, 804 applied for aid, 740 were judged to have need. In 2010, 29 non-need-based awards were made. ***Average financial aid package:*** $8649. ***Average need-based loan:*** $4082. ***Average need-based gift aid:*** $5557. ***Average non-need-based aid:*** $1574.

APPLYING

Standardized Tests *Required for some:* SAT or ACT (for admission).

Options: electronic application, deferred entrance.

Application deadlines: rolling (transfers), rolling (early action).

Early decision deadline: rolling (for plan 1), rolling (for plan 2).

Notification: continuous (transfers), rolling (early decision plan 1), rolling (early decision plan 2), rolling (early action).

CONTACT

Mrs. Trudy Wortham, Registrar, University of Houston–Victoria, 3007 North Ben Wilson, Victoria, TX 77901. *Phone:* 361-485-4521 Ext. 4184. *Toll-free phone:* 877-970-4848 Ext. 110. *E-mail:* worthamt@uhv.edu.

University of Mary Hardin-Baylor

Belton, Texas

http://www.umhb.edu/

- **Independent Southern Baptist** comprehensive, founded 1845
- **Small-town** 330-acre campus with easy access to Austin
- **Endowment** $78.8 million
- **Coed** 3,110 undergraduate students, 91% full-time, 61% women, 39% men
- **Moderately difficult** entrance level, 80% of applicants were admitted

UNDERGRAD STUDENTS

2,840 full-time, 270 part-time. Students come from 29 states and territories; 14 other countries; 2% are from out of state; 14% Black or African American, non-Hispanic/Latino; 18% Hispanic/Latino; 2% Asian, non-Hispanic/Latino; 0.3% Native Hawaiian or other Pacific Islander, non-Hispanic/Latino; 0.5% American Indian or Alaska Native, non-Hispanic/Latino; 3% Two or more races, non-Hispanic/Latino; 1% Race/ethnicity unknown; 2% international; 10% transferred in; 50% live on campus.

Freshmen

Admission: 7,037 applied, 5,623 admitted, 711 enrolled. ***Average high school GPA:*** 3.49. ***Test scores:*** SAT critical reading scores over 500: 62%; SAT math scores over 500: 69%; SAT writing scores over 500: 41%; ACT scores over 18: 96%; SAT critical reading scores over 600: 15%; SAT math scores over 600: 17%; SAT writing scores over 600: 11%; ACT scores over 24: 46%; SAT critical reading scores over 700: 2%; SAT math scores over 700: 1%; SAT writing scores over 700: 1%; ACT scores over 30: 7%.

Retention: 68% of full-time freshmen returned.

FACULTY

Total: 294, 53% full-time, 56% with terminal degrees.

Student/faculty ratio: 17:1.

ACADEMICS

Calendar: semesters. *Degrees:* bachelor's, master's, doctoral, and post-master's certificates.

Special study options: academic remediation for entering students, accelerated degree program, advanced placement credit, distance learning, double majors, English as a second language, honors programs, independent study, internships, part-time degree program, services for LD students, study abroad, summer session for credit. ***ROTC:*** Army (b), Air Force (c).

Unusual degree programs: 3-2 business administration; engineering with Baylor University.

Computers: 275 computers/terminals and 1,000 ports are available on campus for general student use. Students can access the following: campus intranet, computer help desk, free student e-mail accounts, online (class) grades, online (class) registration, online (class) schedules. Campuswide network is available. Wireless service is available via entire campus.

STUDENT LIFE

Housing options: on-campus residence required through sophomore year; men-only, women-only, special housing for students with disabilities. Campus housing is university owned. Freshman applicants given priority for college housing.

Activities and organizations: drama/theater group, student-run newspaper, choral group, marching band, Baptist Student Ministry, Student Government Association, Residence Hall Association, Campus Activities Board, Focus.

Athletics Member NCAA. All Division III. ***Intercollegiate sports:*** baseball M, basketball M/W, football M, golf M/W, soccer M/W, softball W, tennis M/W, volleyball W. ***Intramural sports:*** basketball M/W, football M/W, golf M/W, soccer M/W, softball M/W, table tennis M/W, tennis M/W, ultimate Frisbee M/W, volleyball M/W.

Campus security: 24-hour emergency response devices and patrols, late-night transport/escort service, controlled dormitory access, campus police force, lighted pathways and sidewalks.

Student services: health clinic, personal/psychological counseling.

COSTS & FINANCIAL AID

Costs (2015–16) ***Comprehensive fee:*** $31,480 includes full-time tuition ($22,260), mandatory fees ($2200), and room and board ($7020). Full-time tuition and fees vary according to course load and degree level. Part-time tuition: $795 per credit hour. Part-time tuition and fees vary according to course load and degree level. ***Room and board:*** Room and board charges vary according to housing facility. ***Payment plan:*** installment. ***Waivers:*** employees or children of employees.

Financial Aid Of all full-time matriculated undergraduates who enrolled in 2014, 2,643 applied for aid, 2,228 were judged to have need, 183 had their need fully met. In 2014, 352 non-need-based awards were made. ***Average percent of need met:*** 56. ***Average financial aid package:*** $15,833. ***Average need-based loan:*** $4602. ***Average need-based gift aid:*** $11,562. ***Average non-need-based aid:*** $5823. ***Average indebtedness upon graduation:*** $37,048.

APPLYING

Standardized Tests *Required:* SAT or ACT (for admission).

Options: electronic application, early admission, deferred entrance.

Application fee: $35.

Required: high school transcript. ***Required for some:*** essay or personal statement, interview.

Application deadlines: rolling (freshmen), rolling (out-of-state freshmen), rolling (transfers).

Notification: continuous (freshmen), continuous (out-of-state freshmen), continuous (transfers).

CONTACT

Dr. Brent Burks, Director of Admissions, University of Mary Hardin-Baylor, UMHB Station Box 8004, 900 College Street, Belton, TX 76513-2599. *Phone:* 254-295-4520. *Toll-free phone:* 800-727-8642. *Fax:* 254-295-5049. *E-mail:* admission@umhb.edu.

University of North Texas

Denton, Texas

http://www.unt.edu/

- **State-supported** university, founded 1890, part of University of North Texas System
- **Suburban** 875-acre campus with easy access to Dallas-Fort Worth
- **Endowment** $145.8 million
- **Coed** 29,724 undergraduate students, 81% full-time, 52% women, 48% men
- **Moderately difficult** entrance level, 61% of applicants were admitted

UNDERGRAD STUDENTS

24,180 full-time, 5,544 part-time. Students come from 49 states and territories; 164 other countries; 3% are from out of state; 13% Black or African American, non-Hispanic/Latino; 21% Hispanic/Latino; 6% Asian, non-Hispanic/Latino; 0.1% Native Hawaiian or other Pacific Islander, non-Hispanic/Latino; 0.5% American Indian or Alaska Native, non-Hispanic/Latino; 4% Two or more races, non-Hispanic/Latino; 1% Race/ethnicity unknown; 3% international; 13% transferred in; 19% live on campus.

Freshmen

Admission: 16,361 applied, 9,982 admitted, 4,373 enrolled. ***Test scores:*** SAT critical reading scores over 500: 74%; SAT math scores over 500: 80%; SAT writing scores over 500: 59%; ACT scores over 18: 96%; SAT critical reading scores over 600: 28%; SAT math scores over 600: 29%; SAT writing scores over 600: 17%; ACT scores over 24: 44%; SAT critical reading scores over 700: 4%; SAT math scores over 700: 6%; SAT writing scores over 700: 2%; ACT scores over 30: 4%.

Retention: 76% of full-time freshmen returned.

FACULTY
Total: 1,438, 70% full-time, 56% with terminal degrees.

Student/faculty ratio: 24:1.

ACADEMICS
Calendar: semesters. *Degrees:* bachelor's, master's, doctoral, and postbachelor's certificates.

Special study options: academic remediation for entering students, accelerated degree program, advanced placement credit, cooperative education, distance learning, double majors, English as a second language, freshman honors college, honors programs, independent study, internships, off-campus study, part-time degree program, services for LD students, study abroad, summer session for credit. ***ROTC:*** Army (b), Air Force (b).

Computers: 977 computers/terminals are available on campus for general student use. Students can access the following: campus intranet, computer help desk, free student e-mail accounts, online (class) grades, online (class) registration, online (class) schedules. Campuswide network is available. 100% of college-owned or -operated housing units are wired for high-speed Internet access. Wireless service is available via entire campus.

STUDENT LIFE
Housing options: on-campus residence required for freshman year; coed, women-only, special housing for students with disabilities. Campus housing is university owned. Freshman applicants given priority for college housing.

Activities and organizations: drama/theater group, student-run newspaper, radio and television station, choral group, marching band, Student Government Association, Residence Hall Association, Panhellenic Association, Interfraternity Council, College Life, national fraternities, national sororities.

Athletics Member NCAA. All Division I except football (Division I-A). ***Intercollegiate sports:*** archery M(c)/W(c), badminton M(c)/W(c), baseball M(c), basketball M(s)/W(s), bowling M(c)/W(c), cross-country running M(s)/W(s), equestrian sports M(c)/W(c), fencing M(c)/W(c), golf M(s)/W(s), ice hockey M(c)/W(c), lacrosse M(c)/W(c), racquetball M(c)/W(c), rugby M(c), sailing M(c)/W(c), soccer M(c)/W(s), softball M/W(s), swimming and diving W(s), table tennis M(c)/W(c), tennis M(c)/W, track and field M(s)/W(s), ultimate Frisbee M(c)/W(c), volleyball M(c)/W(s), wrestling M(c)/W(c). ***Intramural sports:*** basketball M/W, football M, racquetball M/W, soccer M/W, softball M/W, table tennis M/W, tennis M/W, ultimate Frisbee M/W, volleyball M/W.

Campus security: 24-hour emergency response devices and patrols, late-night transport/escort service, controlled dormitory access.

Student services: health clinic, personal/psychological counseling, women's center, legal services.

COSTS & FINANCIAL AID
Costs (2015–16) ***Tuition:*** state resident $7204 full-time, $240 per credit hour part-time; nonresident $18,064 full-time, $602 per credit hour part-time. No tuition increase for student's term of enrollment. ***Required fees:*** $2502 full-time. ***Room and board:*** $7760. Room and board charges vary according to board plan and housing facility. ***Payment plan:*** installment. ***Waivers:*** senior citizens and employees or children of employees.

Financial Aid Of all full-time matriculated undergraduates who enrolled in 2014, 17,584 applied for aid, 14,526 were judged to have need, 1,876 had their need fully met. In 2014, 2622 non-need-based awards were made. ***Average percent of need met:*** 58. ***Average financial aid package:*** $11,039. ***Average need-based loan:*** $4447. ***Average need-based gift aid:*** $7619. ***Average non-need-based aid:*** $5289.

APPLYING
Standardized Tests *Required:* SAT or ACT (for admission).

Options: electronic application, early admission, deferred entrance.

Application fee: $75.

Required: high school transcript. ***Required for some:*** essay or personal statement.

Application deadlines: 8/1 (freshmen), rolling (transfers).

Notification: continuous (freshmen), continuous (transfers).

CONTACT
Mr. Randall Nunn, Associate Director of Admissions, University of North Texas, Denton, TX 76203. *Phone:* 940-565-3920. *Toll-free phone:* 800-868-8211. *E-mail:* Randall.Nunn@unt.edu.

University of St. Thomas

Houston, Texas

http://www.stthom.edu/

- **Independent Roman Catholic** comprehensive, founded 1947
- **Urban** 23-acre campus
- **Endowment** $91.4 million
- **Coed** 1,645 undergraduate students, 77% full-time, 61% women, 39% men
- **Moderately difficult** entrance level, 79% of applicants were admitted

UNDERGRAD STUDENTS
1,274 full-time, 371 part-time. Students come from 28 states and territories; 38 other countries; 4% are from out of state; 7% Black or African American, non-Hispanic/Latino; 38% Hispanic/Latino; 12% Asian, non-Hispanic/Latino; 0.3% Native Hawaiian or other Pacific Islander, non-Hispanic/Latino; 0.3% American Indian or Alaska Native, non-Hispanic/Latino; 3% Two or more races, non-Hispanic/Latino; 2% Race/ethnicity unknown; 10% international; 10% transferred in; 18% live on campus.

Freshmen
Admission: 795 applied, 628 admitted, 227 enrolled. ***Average high school GPA:*** 3.54. ***Test scores:*** SAT critical reading scores over 500: 73%; SAT math scores over 500: 78%; SAT writing scores over 500: 67%; ACT scores over 18: 100%; SAT critical reading scores over 600: 27%; SAT math scores over 600: 34%; SAT writing scores over 600: 17%; ACT scores over 24: 58%; SAT critical reading scores over 700: 7%; SAT math scores over 700: 6%; SAT writing scores over 700: 4%; ACT scores over 30: 15%.

Retention: 88% of full-time freshmen returned.

FACULTY
Total: 356, 50% full-time, 76% with terminal degrees.

Student/faculty ratio: 9:1.

ACADEMICS
Calendar: semesters. *Degrees:* diplomas, bachelor's, master's, and doctoral.

Special study options: accelerated degree program, adult/continuing education programs, advanced placement credit, distance learning, double majors, honors programs, independent study, internships, off-campus study, part-time degree program, services for LD students, student-designed majors, study abroad, summer session for credit. ***ROTC:*** Army (c), Air Force (c).

Unusual degree programs: 3-2 business administration; engineering with University of Notre Dame, University of Houston, Texas A&M University.

Computers: 312 computers/terminals and 400 ports are available on campus for general student use. Students can access the following: campus intranet, computer help desk, free student e-mail accounts, online (class) grades, online (class) registration, online (class) schedules. Campuswide network is available. 95% of college-owned or -operated housing units are wired for high-speed Internet access. Wireless service is available via entire campus.

STUDENT LIFE
Housing options: coed, special housing for students with disabilities. Campus housing is university owned. Freshman applicants given priority for college housing.

Activities and organizations: drama/theater group, student-run newspaper, choral group, Health Occupations Students of America (HOSA), Nursing Student Association, Student Activities Board (SAB), American Chemical Society, Soccer.

Athletics Member NAIA. ***Intercollegiate sports:*** basketball M(s)/W(s), cheerleading M(c)/W(c), fencing M(c)/W(c), golf M(s)/W(s), rugby M(c), soccer M(s)/W(s), table tennis M(c)/W(c), tennis M(c)/W(c), ultimate Frisbee M(c)/W(c), volleyball W(s). ***Intramural sports:*** basketball M/W, bowling M/W, racquetball M/W, rock climbing M/W, soccer M(c)/W(c), table tennis M/W, tennis M/W, ultimate Frisbee M/W, volleyball M/W.

Campus security: 24-hour emergency response devices and patrols, late-night transport/escort service, controlled dormitory access.

Student services: personal/psychological counseling.

COSTS & FINANCIAL AID

Costs (2014–15) ***Comprehensive fee:*** $37,690 includes full-time tuition ($29,100), mandatory fees ($340), and room and board ($8250). Full-time tuition and fees vary according to course load. Part-time tuition: $970 per credit hour. Part-time tuition and fees vary according to course load. ***College room only:*** $5000. Room and board charges vary according to board plan and housing facility. ***Payment plans:*** installment, deferred payment. ***Waivers:*** senior citizens and employees or children of employees.

Financial Aid Of all full-time matriculated undergraduates who enrolled in 2014, 816 applied for aid, 755 were judged to have need, 64 had their need fully met. 79 Federal Work-Study jobs (averaging $3880). 2 state and other part-time jobs (averaging $4000). In 2014, 339 non-need-based awards were made. ***Average percent of need met:*** 59. ***Average financial aid package:*** $21,618. ***Average need-based loan:*** $5085. ***Average need-based gift aid:*** $17,466. ***Average non-need-based aid:*** $10,520. ***Average indebtedness upon graduation:*** $36,497.

APPLYING

Standardized Tests *Required:* SAT or ACT (for admission).

Options: electronic application, early action, deferred entrance.

Required: essay or personal statement, high school transcript, minimum 2.8 GPA, 1070 SAT (Critical Reading and Math) or 23 ACT.

Application deadlines: 5/1 (freshmen), 5/1 (out-of-state freshmen), rolling (transfers), 12/1 (early action).

Notification: continuous until 11/1 (freshmen), continuous until 11/1 (out-of-state freshmen), continuous (transfers), 12/15 (early action).

CONTACT

Mr. Arthur Ortiz, Assistant Vice President of Enrollment, University of St. Thomas, 3800 Montrose Boulevard, Houston, TX 77006-4696. *Phone:* 713-525-3848. *Toll-free phone:* 800-856-8565. *Fax:* 713-525-3558. *E-mail:* admissions@stthom.edu.

The University of Texas at Arlington

Arlington, Texas

http://www.uta.edu/

- **State-supported** university, founded 1895, part of University of Texas System
- **Urban** 420-acre campus with easy access to Dallas-Fort Worth
- **Endowment** $115.3 million
- **Coed** 29,883 undergraduate students, 53% full-time, 60% women, 40% men
- **Moderately difficult** entrance level, 61% of applicants were admitted

UNDERGRAD STUDENTS

15,957 full-time, 13,926 part-time. Students come from 55 states and territories; 91 other countries; 11% are from out of state; 15% Black or African American, non-Hispanic/Latino; 24% Hispanic/Latino; 11% Asian, non-Hispanic/Latino; 0.3% Native Hawaiian or other Pacific Islander, non-Hispanic/Latino; 0.3% American Indian or Alaska Native, non-Hispanic/Latino; 3% Two or more races, non-Hispanic/Latino; 0.6% Race/ethnicity unknown; 5% international; 19% transferred in; 13% live on campus.

Freshmen

Admission: 10,245 applied, 6,290 admitted, 2,736 enrolled. ***Test scores:*** SAT critical reading scores over 500: 50%; SAT math scores over 500: 75%; SAT writing scores over 500: 47%; ACT scores over 18: 89%; SAT critical reading scores over 600: 22%; SAT math scores over 600: 30%; SAT writing scores over 600: 11%; ACT scores over 24: 44%; SAT math scores over 700: 4%; SAT writing scores over 700: 1%; ACT scores over 30: 7%.

Retention: 69% of full-time freshmen returned.

ACADEMICS

Calendar: semesters. *Degrees:* bachelor's, master's, doctoral, post-master's, and postbachelor's certificates.

Special study options: academic remediation for entering students, adult/continuing education programs, advanced placement credit, cooperative education, distance learning, double majors, English as a second language, freshman honors college, honors programs, independent study, internships, off-campus study, part-time degree program, services for LD students, student-designed majors, study abroad, summer session for credit. ***ROTC:*** Army (b), Air Force (c).

Unusual degree programs: 3-2 business administration; psychology, health care administration.

Computers: 500 computers/terminals and 6,000 ports are available on campus for general student use. Students can access the following: campus intranet, computer help desk, free student e-mail accounts, online (class) grades, online (class) registration. Campuswide network is available. 90% of college-owned or -operated housing units are wired for high-speed Internet access. Wireless service is available via classrooms, computer centers, computer labs, dorm rooms, learning centers, libraries, student centers.

STUDENT LIFE

Housing options: coed, men-only, women-only. Campus housing is university owned and leased by the school.

Activities and organizations: drama/theater group, student-run newspaper, radio station, choral group, marching band, Delta Delta Delta Sorority, EXCEL Campus Activities, Baptist Student Ministry, Honors College Council, Beta Alpha Psi - Accounting, national fraternities, national sororities.

Athletics Member NCAA. All Division I. ***Intercollegiate sports:*** baseball M(s), basketball M(s)/W(s), cross-country running M(s)/W(s), golf M(s), softball W(s), tennis M(s)/W(s), track and field M(s)/W(s), volleyball W(s). ***Intramural sports:*** badminton M/W, basketball M/W, bowling M/W, racquetball M/W, soccer M/W, softball M/W, table tennis M/W, tennis M/W, volleyball M/W.

Campus security: 24-hour emergency response devices and patrols, late-night transport/escort service, controlled dormitory access, remote emergency telephones, bicycle patrols, crime prevention program, student shuttle service.

Student services: health clinic, personal/psychological counseling, legal services.

COSTS & FINANCIAL AID

Costs (2014–15) ***Tuition:*** state resident $8878 full-time; nonresident $20,274 full-time. No tuition increase for student's term of enrollment. ***Room and board:*** $8156; room only: $4408. Room and board charges vary according to board plan and housing facility. ***Payment plan:*** installment. ***Waivers:*** employees or children of employees.

Financial Aid Of all full-time matriculated undergraduates who enrolled in 2014, 12,273 applied for aid, 11,747 were judged to have need, 1,259 had their need fully met. 1,822 Federal Work-Study jobs (averaging $3178). 20 state and other part-time jobs (averaging $560). In 2014, 213 non-need-based awards were made. ***Average percent of need met:*** 68. ***Average financial aid package:*** $12,559. ***Average need-based loan:*** $4235. ***Average need-based gift aid:*** $7033. ***Average non-need-based aid:*** $4819. ***Average indebtedness upon graduation:*** $23,210.

APPLYING

Standardized Tests *Required:* SAT or ACT (for admission).

Options: electronic application, deferred entrance.

Application fee: $60.

Required: high school transcript, class rank.

Application deadlines: 6/1 (freshmen), 6/1 (transfers).

Notification: continuous (freshmen), continuous (transfers).

CONTACT

Dr. Hans Gatterdam, Executive Director of Admissions, Records and Registration, The University of Texas at Arlington, UTA Box 19088, 701 South Nedderman Drive, Arlington, TX 76019-0088. *Phone:* 817-272-3275. *Fax:* 817-272-5114.

The University of Texas at Austin

Austin, Texas

http://www.utexas.edu/

- **State-supported** university, founded 1883, part of University of Texas System
- **Urban** 434-acre campus with easy access to Austin
- **Endowment** $3.4 billion
- **Coed** 39,523 undergraduate students, 92% full-time, 52% women, 48% men

UNDERGRAD STUDENTS

36,309 full-time, 3,214 part-time. Students come from 54 states and territories; 103 other countries; 5% are from out of state; 4% Black or African American, non-Hispanic/Latino; 22% Hispanic/Latino; 19% Asian, non-Hispanic/Latino; 0.1% Native Hawaiian or other Pacific Islander, non-Hispanic/Latino; 0.2% American Indian or Alaska Native, non-Hispanic/Latino; 3% Two or more races, non-Hispanic/Latino; 0.5% Race/ethnicity unknown; 5% international; 6% transferred in; 18% live on campus.

Freshmen

Admission: 7,285 enrolled. ***Test scores:*** SAT critical reading scores over 500: 93%; SAT math scores over 500: 97%; SAT writing scores over 500: 92%; ACT scores over 18: 99%; SAT critical reading scores over 600: 66%; SAT math scores over 600: 77%; SAT writing scores over 600: 65%; ACT scores over 24: 90%; SAT critical reading scores over 700: 23%; SAT math scores over 700: 37%; SAT writing scores over 700: 25%; ACT scores over 30: 50%.

Retention: 95% of full-time freshmen returned.

FACULTY

Total: 3,026, 91% full-time, 88% with terminal degrees.

Student/faculty ratio: 18:1.

ACADEMICS

Calendar: semesters. *Degrees:* certificates, bachelor's, master's, doctoral, and postbachelor's certificates.

Special study options: academic remediation for entering students, accelerated degree program, advanced placement credit, cooperative education, distance learning, double majors, English as a second language, honors programs, independent study, internships, off-campus study, part-time degree program, services for LD students, student-designed majors, study abroad, summer session for credit. ***ROTC:*** Army (b), Navy (b), Air Force (b).

Unusual degree programs: 3-2 business administration; engineering; computer science.

Computers: 275 computers/terminals are available on campus for general student use. Students can access the following: campus intranet, computer help desk, free student e-mail accounts, online (class) grades, online (class) registration, online (class) schedules. Campuswide network is available. 100% of college-owned or -operated housing units are wired for high-speed Internet access. Wireless service is available via entire campus.

STUDENT LIFE

Housing options: coed, men-only, women-only, special housing for students with disabilities. Campus housing is university owned. Freshman applicants given priority for college housing.

Activities and organizations: drama/theater group, student-run newspaper, radio and television station, choral group, marching band, Alpha Phi Omega, Student Events Center, Texas Exes-Student Chapter, Longhorn Band Student Organization, Student Volunteer Board, national fraternities, national sororities.

Athletics Member NCAA. All Division I except football (Division I-A). ***Intercollegiate sports:*** archery M(c)/W(c), badminton M(c)/W(c), baseball M(s)/W(c), basketball M(s)/W(s), crew M(c)/W(s), cross-country running M(s)/W(s), fencing M(c)/W(c), golf M(s)/W(s), gymnastics M(c)/W(c), ice hockey M(c)/W(c), lacrosse M(c)/W(c), racquetball M(c)/W(c), rock climbing M(c)/W(c), rugby M(c)/W(c), sailing M(c)/W(c), soccer M(c)/W(s), softball W(s), swimming and diving M(s)/W(s), table tennis M(c)/W(c), tennis M(s)/W(s), track and field M(s)/W(s), ultimate Frisbee M(c)/W(c), volleyball M(c)/W(s), water polo M(c)/W(c), weight lifting M(c)/W(c), wrestling M(c)/W(c). ***Intramural sports:*** basketball M/W, football M/W, golf M/W, racquetball M/W, rock climbing M/W, soccer M/W, softball M/W, swimming and diving M/W, table tennis M/W, tennis M/W, track and field M/W, ultimate Frisbee M/W, volleyball M/W.

Campus security: 24-hour emergency response devices and patrols, late-night transport/escort service, controlled dormitory access.

Student services: health clinic, personal/psychological counseling, women's center, legal services.

COSTS & FINANCIAL AID

Costs (2014–15) ***Tuition:*** state resident $9830 full-time; nonresident $34,836 full-time. Full-time tuition and fees vary according to course load, degree level, and program. Part-time tuition and fees vary according to course load, degree level, and program. No tuition increase for student's term of enrollment. ***Room and board:*** $11,456. Room and board charges vary according to housing facility. ***Payment plan:*** installment. ***Waivers:*** senior citizens and employees or children of employees.

Financial Aid Of all full-time matriculated undergraduates who enrolled in 2014, 21,734 applied for aid, 15,482 were judged to have need, 2,566 had their need fully met. In 2014, 404 non-need-based awards were made. ***Average percent of need met:*** 67. ***Average financial aid package:*** $12,935. ***Average need-based loan:*** $4987. ***Average need-based gift aid:*** $9118. ***Average non-need-based aid:*** $6047. ***Average indebtedness upon graduation:*** $27,207.

APPLYING

Standardized Tests *Required:* SAT or ACT (for admission).

Required: essay or personal statement, high school transcript.

CONTACT

Dr. Kedra B. Ishop, Vice Provost and Director of Admissions, The University of Texas at Austin, Office of Admissions, Freshman Admissions Center, PO Box 8058, Austin, TX 78713-8058. *Phone:* 512-475-7440. *Fax:* 512-475-7475. *E-mail:* kedra.ishop@austin.utexas.edu.

The University of Texas at Brownsville

Brownsville, Texas

http://www.utb.edu/

- **State-supported** comprehensive, founded 1973, part of University of Texas System
- **Urban** 199-acre campus
- **Endowment** $9.1 million
- **Coed**
- **Noncompetitive** entrance level

ACADEMICS

Calendar: semesters. *Degrees:* bachelor's, master's, doctoral, and postbachelor's certificates.

STUDENT LIFE

Housing options: coed. Campus housing is university owned.

Activities and organizations: student-run newspaper, radio station, choral group, Alpha Chi, Anime Viewing Club, Counseling and Guidance Student Association, Gorgas Science, Alpha Chi Psi.

Athletics Member NAIA.

Campus security: 24-hour emergency response devices and patrols, late-night transport/escort service.

Student services: health clinic, personal/psychological counseling, legal services.

FINANCIAL AID

Financial Aid Of all full-time matriculated undergraduates who enrolled in 2013, 3,342 applied for aid, 3,147 were judged to have need. In 2013, 53 non-need-based awards were made. ***Average percent of need met:*** 49. ***Average financial aid package:*** $9352. ***Average need-based loan:*** $3906. ***Average need-based gift aid:*** $6757. ***Average non-need-based aid:*** $7458. ***Financial aid deadline:*** 7/1.

APPLYING

Standardized Tests *Required:* SAT or ACT (for admission).

Options: electronic application, early admission.

Required: high school transcript, minimum 2.0 GPA.

CONTACT
Mr. Carlo Tamayo, Director of Admissions and Recruitment, The University of Texas at Brownsville, 80 Fort Brown, Tandy 115, Brownsville, TX 78520-4991. *Phone:* 956-882-8295. *Toll-free phone:* 877-UTBTSC1. *Fax:* 956-882-7810. *E-mail:* admissions@utb.edu.

The University of Texas at Dallas

Richardson, Texas

http://www.utdallas.edu/

- **State-supported** university, founded 1969, part of University of Texas System
- **Suburban** 500-acre campus with easy access to Dallas-Fort Worth
- **Endowment** $387.4 million
- **Coed** 14,300 undergraduate students, 81% full-time, 43% women, 57% men
- **Very difficult** entrance level, 62% of applicants were admitted

UNDERGRAD STUDENTS
11,630 full-time, 2,670 part-time. Students come from 50 states and territories; 76 other countries; 4% are from out of state; 6% Black or African American, non-Hispanic/Latino; 18% Hispanic/Latino; 28% Asian, non-Hispanic/Latino; 0.2% Native Hawaiian or other Pacific Islander, non-Hispanic/Latino; 0.2% American Indian or Alaska Native, non-Hispanic/Latino; 4% Two or more races, non-Hispanic/Latino; 1% Race/ethnicity unknown; 4% international; 14% transferred in; 29% live on campus.

Freshmen
Admission: 9,587 applied, 5,938 admitted, 2,520 enrolled. ***Test scores:*** SAT critical reading scores over 500: 90%; SAT math scores over 500: 97%; SAT writing scores over 500: 86%; ACT scores over 18: 99%; SAT critical reading scores over 600: 57%; SAT math scores over 600: 75%; SAT writing scores over 600: 48%; ACT scores over 24: 86%; SAT critical reading scores over 700: 16%; SAT math scores over 700: 29%; SAT writing scores over 700: 14%; ACT scores over 30: 38%.
Retention: 87% of full-time freshmen returned.

FACULTY
Total: 1,110, 71% full-time, 85% with terminal degrees.
Student/faculty ratio: 22:1.

ACADEMICS
Calendar: semesters. *Degrees:* bachelor's, master's, doctoral, and postbachelor's certificates.
Special study options: academic remediation for entering students, accelerated degree program, adult/continuing education programs, advanced placement credit, cooperative education, distance learning, double majors, freshman honors college, honors programs, independent study, internships, part-time degree program, services for LD students, student-designed majors, study abroad, summer session for credit. ***ROTC:*** Army (c), Air Force (c).
Unusual degree programs: 3-2 engineering with Abilene Christian University, Austin College, Paul Quinn College, Texas Woman's University.
Computers: 170 computers/terminals are available on campus for general student use. Students can access the following: computer help desk, free student e-mail accounts, online (class) grades, online (class) registration, online (class) schedules. Campuswide network is available. 100% of college-owned or -operated housing units are wired for high-speed Internet access. Wireless service is available via classrooms, computer centers, dorm rooms, libraries, student centers.

STUDENT LIFE
Housing options: coed. Campus housing is university owned and is provided by a third party. Freshman applicants given priority for college housing.
Activities and organizations: drama/theater group, student-run newspaper, radio and television station, choral group, Student Government Association, Golden Key National Honor Society, Muslim Students Association, Indian Student Association, Friendship Association of Chinese Students and Scholars, national fraternities, national sororities.
Athletics Member NCAA. All Division III. ***Intercollegiate sports:*** baseball M, basketball M/W, cross-country running M/W, golf M/W, soccer M/W, softball W, tennis M/W, volleyball W. ***Intramural sports:*** archery M(c)/W(c), badminton M(c)/W(c), basketball M(c)/W(c), bowling M(c)/W(c), cheerleading M/W, cross-country running M(c)/W(c), fencing M(c)/W(c), football M(c)/W(c), gymnastics M(c)/W(c), lacrosse M(c), racquetball M(c)/W(c), rock climbing M(c)/W(c), rugby M(c)/W(c), soccer M(c)/W(c), softball M(c)/W(c), squash M(c)/W(c), swimming and diving M(c)/W(c), table tennis M(c)/W(c), tennis M(c)/W(c), ultimate Frisbee M(c)/W(c), volleyball M(c)/W(c).
Campus security: 24-hour emergency response devices and patrols, student patrols, late-night transport/escort service, controlled dormitory access.
Student services: health clinic, personal/psychological counseling, women's center, legal services.

COSTS & FINANCIAL AID
Costs (2014–15) ***Tuition:*** state resident $11,806 full-time, $394 per credit hour part-time; nonresident $31,328 full-time, $1044 per credit hour part-time. Full-time tuition and fees vary according to course load and degree level. Part-time tuition and fees vary according to course load and degree level. No tuition increase for student's term of enrollment. ***Room and board:*** $9542. Room and board charges vary according to board plan and housing facility. ***Payment plan:*** installment. ***Waivers:*** senior citizens and employees or children of employees.
Financial Aid Of all full-time matriculated undergraduates who enrolled in 2013, 6,810 applied for aid, 5,826 were judged to have need, 989 had their need fully met. 203 Federal Work-Study jobs (averaging $2702). 32 state and other part-time jobs (averaging $3127). In 2013, 2303 non-need-based awards were made. ***Average percent of need met:*** 64. ***Average financial aid package:*** $12,488. ***Average need-based loan:*** $4395. ***Average need-based gift aid:*** $8592. ***Average non-need-based aid:*** $11,813. ***Average indebtedness upon graduation:*** $19,613.

APPLYING
Standardized Tests *Required:* SAT or ACT (for admission). *Required for some:* THEA.
Options: electronic application, deferred entrance.
Application fee: $50.
Required: essay or personal statement, high school transcript. ***Required for some:*** interview. ***Recommended:*** 3 letters of recommendation.
Notification: continuous (freshmen), continuous (transfers).

CONTACT
Enrollment Services, The University of Texas at Dallas, 800 West Campbell Road, Mail Station ROC12, Richardson, TX 75083-0688. *Phone:* 972-883-2270. *Toll-free phone:* 800-889-2443. *Fax:* 972-883-2599. *E-mail:* interest@utdallas.edu.

The University of Texas at El Paso

El Paso, Texas

http://www.utep.edu/

- **State-supported** university, founded 1913, part of University of Texas System
- **Urban** 360-acre campus
- **Coed** 5,849 undergraduate students, 73% full-time, 57% women, 43% men
- **Minimally difficult** entrance level, 84% of applicants were admitted

UNDERGRAD STUDENTS
4,282 full-time, 1,567 part-time. 1% are from out of state; 9% Black or African American, non-Hispanic/Latino; 16% Hispanic/Latino; 3% Asian, non-Hispanic/Latino; 0.1% Native Hawaiian or other Pacific Islander, non-Hispanic/Latino; 0.3% American Indian or Alaska Native, non-Hispanic/Latino; 8% Two or more races, non-Hispanic/Latino; 2% Race/ethnicity unknown; 2% international; 16% transferred in.

Freshmen
Admission: 2,156 applied, 1,802 admitted, 692 enrolled. ***Average high school GPA:*** 3.4. ***Test scores:*** SAT critical reading scores over 500: 64%; SAT math scores over 500: 71%; SAT writing scores over 500: 50%; ACT scores over 18: 96%; SAT critical reading scores over 600: 14%; SAT math scores over 600: 23%; SAT writing scores over 600: 9%; ACT scores over 24: 36%; SAT critical reading scores over 700: 2%; SAT math scores over 700: 4%; SAT writing scores over 700: 1%; ACT scores over 30: 4%.

ACADEMICS

Calendar: semesters. *Degrees:* certificates, bachelor's, master's, doctoral, and post-master's certificates.

Special study options: academic remediation for entering students, accelerated degree program, adult/continuing education programs, advanced placement credit, cooperative education, distance learning, double majors, English as a second language, honors programs, independent study, internships, off-campus study, part-time degree program, services for LD students, study abroad, summer session for credit.

Computers: Students can access the following: computer help desk, free student e-mail accounts, online (class) grades, online (class) registration, online (class) schedules. Campuswide network is available.

STUDENT LIFE

Housing options: coed. Campus housing is university owned.

Activities and organizations: drama/theater group, student-run newspaper, radio station, choral group, marching band, national fraternities, national sororities.

Athletics Member NCAA. All Division I except football (Division I-A). ***Intercollegiate sports:*** basketball M(s)/W(s), cross-country running M(s)/W(s), golf M(s), riflery M/W, tennis W(s), track and field M(s)/W(s), volleyball W(s). ***Intramural sports:*** archery M/W, badminton M/W, basketball M/W, bowling M/W, fencing M/W, field hockey M, golf M/W, gymnastics M/W, racquetball M/W, skiing (downhill) M, soccer M/W, squash M/W, swimming and diving M/W, tennis M/W, track and field M/W, volleyball M/W, water polo M/W, weight lifting M, wrestling M/W.

Campus security: 24-hour emergency response devices and patrols, late-night transport/escort service.

Student services: health clinic, personal/psychological counseling, women's center, legal services.

COSTS & FINANCIAL AID

Costs (2014–15) ***Tuition:*** state resident $5606 full-time, $187 per credit hour part-time; nonresident $17,456 full-time, $582 per credit hour part-time. ***Required fees:*** $1649 full-time. ***Room and board:*** $9180.

Financial Aid Of all full-time matriculated undergraduates who enrolled in 2013, 11,653 applied for aid, 10,222 were judged to have need, 1,119 had their need fully met. 287 Federal Work-Study jobs (averaging $3321). 100 state and other part-time jobs (averaging $2053). In 2013, 549 non-need-based awards were made. ***Average percent of need met:*** 64. ***Average financial aid package:*** $11,957. ***Average need-based loan:*** $6171. ***Average need-based gift aid:*** $7569. ***Average non-need-based aid:*** $4654. ***Average indebtedness upon graduation:*** $24,000.

APPLYING

Standardized Tests *Required:* SAT or ACT (for admission).

Options: deferred entrance.

Application fee: $40.

Required: high school transcript.

CONTACT

Dr. Luisa S. Havens, Executive Director of Admissions, The University of Texas at El Paso, Academic Services Building, Room 102, El Paso, TX 779968. *Phone:* 915-747-5890. *Toll-free phone:* 877-74MINER. *Fax:* 915-747-5890. *E-mail:* futureminer@utep.edu.

The University of Texas at San Antonio

San Antonio, Texas

http://www.utsa.edu/

- **State-supported** university, founded 1969, part of University of Texas System
- **Suburban** 725-acre campus with easy access to San Antonio
- **Endowment** $113.9 million
- **Coed** 24,492 undergraduate students, 83% full-time, 49% women, 51% men
- **Moderately difficult** entrance level, 76% of applicants were admitted

UNDERGRAD STUDENTS

20,248 full-time, 4,244 part-time. Students come from 50 states and territories; 73 other countries; 3% are from out of state; 9% Black or African American, non-Hispanic/Latino; 51% Hispanic/Latino; 5% Asian, non-Hispanic/Latino; 0.2% Native Hawaiian or other Pacific Islander, non-Hispanic/Latino; 0.2% American Indian or Alaska Native, non-Hispanic/Latino; 3% Two or more races, non-Hispanic/Latino; 0.9% Race/ethnicity unknown; 4% international; 8% transferred in; 21% live on campus.

Freshmen

Admission: 14,933 applied, 11,336 admitted, 4,983 enrolled. ***Test scores:*** SAT critical reading scores over 500: 56%; SAT math scores over 500: 68%; SAT writing scores over 500: 45%; ACT scores over 18: 91%; SAT critical reading scores over 600: 15%; SAT math scores over 600: 23%; SAT writing scores over 600: 10%; ACT scores over 24: 33%; SAT critical reading scores over 700: 2%; SAT math scores over 700: 3%; SAT writing scores over 700: 1%; ACT scores over 30: 4%.

Retention: 64% of full-time freshmen returned.

ACADEMICS

Calendar: semesters. *Degrees:* bachelor's, master's, and doctoral.

Special study options: academic remediation for entering students, adult/continuing education programs, advanced placement credit, cooperative education, distance learning, double majors, English as a second language, honors programs, independent study, internships, off-campus study, part-time degree program, services for LD students, student-designed majors, study abroad, summer session for credit. ***ROTC:*** Army (b), Air Force (b).

Computers: 400 computers/terminals and 1,000 ports are available on campus for general student use. Students can access the following: campus intranet, computer help desk, free student e-mail accounts, online (class) grades, online (class) registration, online (class) schedules. Campuswide network is available. 100% of college-owned or -operated housing units are wired for high-speed Internet access. Wireless service is available via entire campus.

STUDENT LIFE

Housing options: coed, special housing for students with disabilities. Campus housing is university owned and is provided by a third party.

Activities and organizations: student-run newspaper, radio station, choral group, marching band, Student Government, VOICES, Chi Alpha Christian Fellowship, Hispanic Student Association, Panhellenic Council, national fraternities, national sororities.

Athletics Member NCAA. All Division I. ***Intercollegiate sports:*** badminton M(c)/W(c), baseball M(s), basketball M(s)/W(s), cross-country running M(s)/W(s), fencing M(c)/W(c), football M(s), golf M(s)/W(s), ice hockey M(c), lacrosse M(c)/W(c), racquetball M(c)/W(c), rock climbing M(c)/W(c), rugby M(c)/W(c), soccer M(c)/W(s), softball W(s), swimming and diving M(c)/W(c), table tennis M(c)/W(c), tennis M(s)/W(s), track and field M(s)/W(s), ultimate Frisbee M(c)/W(c), volleyball M(c)/W(s), weight lifting M(c)/W(c). ***Intramural sports:*** badminton M/W, baseball M(c), basketball M/W, cross-country running M/W, football M/W, golf M/W, racquetball M/W, soccer M/W, softball M/W, table tennis M/W, tennis M/W, track and field M/W, ultimate Frisbee M/W, volleyball M/W.

Campus security: 24-hour emergency response devices and patrols, late-night transport/escort service, controlled dormitory access, close to 1,000 security cameras, Reverse 911 emergency telephone notification system, and Giant Voice speaker arrays.

Student services: health clinic, personal/psychological counseling, women's center.

COSTS & FINANCIAL AID

Costs (2014–15) ***Tuition:*** state resident $5982 full-time, $199 per credit hour part-time; nonresident $17,295 full-time, $577 per credit hour part-time. Full-time tuition and fees vary according to course load and degree level. Part-time tuition and fees vary according to course load and degree level. ***Required fees:*** $2755 full-time. ***Room and board:*** $7624; room only: $4690. Room and board charges vary according to board plan and housing facility. ***Payment plans:*** installment, deferred payment. ***Waivers:*** employees or children of employees.

Financial Aid Of all full-time matriculated undergraduates who enrolled in 2013, 15,178 applied for aid, 13,089 were judged to have need, 1,547 had their need fully met. 304 Federal Work-Study jobs (averaging $2831). 797 state and other part-time jobs (averaging $2481). In 2013, 421 non-need-based awards were made. ***Average percent of need met:*** 51. ***Average***

financial aid package: $9553. ***Average need-based loan:*** $4167. ***Average need-based gift aid:*** $6263. ***Average non-need-based aid:*** $3300. ***Average indebtedness upon graduation:*** $27,337.

APPLYING

Standardized Tests *Required:* SAT or ACT (for admission).

Options: electronic application.

Application fee: $60.

Required: high school transcript. ***Required for some:*** Transfer applicants with less than 30 hours must meet freshman requirements and have a 2.25 GPA on a 4.0 scale and submit all college transcripts; transfer applicants with 30 or more completed hours must have a 2.25 GPA on a 4.0 scale and submit all college transcripts. ***Recommended:*** essay or personal statement, 1 letter of recommendation.

Application deadlines: 6/1 (freshmen), 6/1 (out-of-state freshmen), 6/1 (transfers).

Notification: continuous (freshmen), continuous (out-of-state freshmen), continuous (transfers).

CONTACT

Mrs. Beverly Woodson Day, Director of Admissions, The University of Texas at San Antonio, One UTSA Circle, San Antonio, TX 78249. *Phone:* 210-458-4536. *Toll-free phone:* 800-669-0919. *Fax:* 210-458-2001. *E-mail:* prospects@utsa.edu.

The University of Texas at Tyler

Tyler, Texas

http://www.uttyler.edu/

- **State-supported** comprehensive, founded 1971, part of University of Texas System
- **Urban** 200-acre campus
- **Coed** 5,849 undergraduate students, 73% full-time, 57% women, 43% men
- **Moderately difficult** entrance level, 84% of applicants were admitted

UNDERGRAD STUDENTS

4,282 full-time, 1,567 part-time. 1% are from out of state; 9% Black or African American, non-Hispanic/Latino; 16% Hispanic/Latino; 3% Asian, non-Hispanic/Latino; 0.1% Native Hawaiian or other Pacific Islander, non-Hispanic/Latino; 0.3% American Indian or Alaska Native, non-Hispanic/Latino; 8% Two or more races, non-Hispanic/Latino; 2% Race/ethnicity unknown; 2% international; 16% transferred in.

Freshmen

Admission: 2,156 applied, 1,802 admitted, 692 enrolled. ***Average high school GPA:*** 3.4. ***Test scores:*** SAT critical reading scores over 500: 64%; SAT math scores over 500: 71%; SAT writing scores over 500: 50%; ACT scores over 18: 96%; SAT critical reading scores over 600: 14%; SAT math scores over 600: 23%; SAT writing scores over 600: 9%; ACT scores over 24: 36%; SAT critical reading scores over 700: 2%; SAT math scores over 700: 4%; SAT writing scores over 700: 1%; ACT scores over 30: 4%.

FACULTY

Total: 512, 62% full-time, 46% with terminal degrees.

Student/faculty ratio: 16:1.

ACADEMICS

Calendar: semesters. *Degrees:* bachelor's, master's, doctoral, and post-master's certificates.

Special study options: adult/continuing education programs, advanced placement credit, distance learning, double majors, honors programs, independent study, internships, part-time degree program, services for LD students, study abroad.

Computers: Students can access the following: computer help desk, free student e-mail accounts, online (class) grades, online (class) registration, online (class) schedules. Campuswide network is available. 100% of college-owned or -operated housing units are wired for high-speed Internet access. Wireless service is available via classrooms, computer centers, computer labs, learning centers, libraries, student centers.

STUDENT LIFE

Housing options: on-campus residence required for freshman year; coed. Campus housing is university owned and is provided by a third party. Freshman applicants given priority for college housing.

Activities and organizations: student-run newspaper, choral group, national fraternities, national sororities.

Athletics Member NCAA. All Division III. ***Intercollegiate sports:*** baseball M, basketball M/W, cheerleading M/W, cross-country running M/W, golf M/W, soccer M/W, tennis M/W, track and field M/W, volleyball W. ***Intramural sports:*** baseball M, basketball M/W, bowling M/W, football M/W, golf M/W, racquetball M/W, soccer M/W, softball M/W, swimming and diving M/W, table tennis M/W, tennis M/W, ultimate Frisbee M/W, volleyball W, wrestling M.

Campus security: 24-hour emergency response devices and patrols, late-night transport/escort service, controlled dormitory access.

COSTS & FINANCIAL AID

Costs (2014–15) ***Tuition:*** state resident $5370 full-time, $50 per semester hour part-time; nonresident $16,230 full-time, $412 per semester hour part-time. Full-time tuition and fees vary according to course load. Part-time tuition and fees vary according to course load. ***Required fees:*** $1942 full-time. ***Room and board:*** $8979; room only: $5679. Room and board charges vary according to board plan and housing facility. ***Payment plan:*** installment. ***Waivers:*** senior citizens and employees or children of employees.

Financial Aid Of all full-time matriculated undergraduates who enrolled in 2012, 3,220 applied for aid, 3,098 were judged to have need, 90 had their need fully met. In 2012, 8 non-need-based awards were made. ***Average percent of need met:*** 41. ***Average financial aid package:*** $7962. ***Average need-based loan:*** $3654. ***Average need-based gift aid:*** $6395. ***Average non-need-based aid:*** $2563. ***Average indebtedness upon graduation:*** $20,151.

APPLYING

Standardized Tests *Required:* SAT or ACT (for admission).

Options: electronic application, deferred entrance.

Application fee: $40.

Required: high school transcript.

CONTACT

Ms. Sarah Bowdin, Interim Assistant Vice President for Enrollment Management, The University of Texas at Tyler, 3900 University Boulevard, Tyler, TX 75799-0001. *Phone:* 903-566-7057. *Toll-free phone:* 800-UTTYLER. *Fax:* 903-566-7068. *E-mail:* admissions@uttyler.edu.

The University of Texas Health Science Center at Houston

Houston, Texas

http://www.uthouston.edu/

- **State-supported** upper-level, founded 1972, part of University of Texas System
- **Urban** campus with easy access to Houston
- **Endowment** $217.5 million
- **Coed** 657 undergraduate students, 82% full-time, 85% women, 15% men
- **Moderately difficult** entrance level

UNDERGRAD STUDENTS

539 full-time, 118 part-time. Students come from 6 states and territories; 3 other countries; 1% are from out of state; 9% Black or African American, non-Hispanic/Latino; 24% Hispanic/Latino; 18% Asian, non-Hispanic/Latino; 0.9% Native Hawaiian or other Pacific Islander, non-Hispanic/Latino; 0.3% American Indian or Alaska Native, non-Hispanic/Latino; 3% Two or more races, non-Hispanic/Latino; 2% Race/ethnicity unknown; 0.9% international.

FACULTY

Total: 128, 66% full-time, 70% with terminal degrees.

Student/faculty ratio: 9:1.

ACADEMICS

Calendar: semesters. *Degrees:* certificates, bachelor's, master's, doctoral, post-master's, and postbachelor's certificates.

Special study options: accelerated degree program, distance learning, independent study, internships, part-time degree program, summer session for credit. ***ROTC:*** Army (c).

Computers: Students can access the following: online (class) registration. Campuswide network is available.

STUDENT LIFE
Housing options: college housing not available.

Activities and organizations: student-run newspaper, Student Inter-council (SIC), School of Nursing Student Government Organization (School of Nursing), Student Council (Dental Branch), Student Senate (Medical School), SPH Student Association (School of Public Health).

Campus security: 24-hour emergency response devices and patrols, late-night transport/escort service, controlled access to all buildings.

Student services: health clinic, personal/psychological counseling.

COSTS & FINANCIAL AID
Costs (2014–15) ***Tuition:*** state resident $5520 full-time; nonresident $24,180 full-time. Full-time tuition and fees vary according to course load. Part-time tuition and fees vary according to course load. ***Required fees:*** $987 full-time. ***Payment plan:*** installment.

Financial Aid Of all full-time matriculated undergraduates who enrolled in 2014, 636 applied for aid, 591 were judged to have need, 219 had their need fully met. In 2014, 2 non-need-based awards were made. ***Average percent of need met:*** 36. ***Average financial aid package:*** $8299. ***Average need-based loan:*** $5966. ***Average need-based gift aid:*** $4762. ***Average non-need-based aid:*** $1000.

APPLYING
Standardized Tests *Required:* HESI A2-Nursing Entrance Test for BSN programs (for admission).

Options: electronic application.

Application fee: $60.

CONTACT
The University of Texas Health Science Center at Houston, PO Box 20036, Houston, TX 77225-0036. *Phone:* 713-500-3388.

The University of Texas of the Permian Basin

Odessa, Texas

http://www.utpb.edu/

- **State-supported** comprehensive, founded 1969, part of University of Texas System
- **Urban** 600-acre campus
- **Endowment** $40.6 million
- **Coed** 4,661 undergraduate students, 43% full-time, 58% women, 42% men
- **Moderately difficult** entrance level, 87% of applicants were admitted

UNDERGRAD STUDENTS
2,023 full-time, 2,638 part-time. Students come from 25 states and territories; 26 other countries; 4% are from out of state; 6% Black or African American, non-Hispanic/Latino; 43% Hispanic/Latino; 3% Asian, non-Hispanic/Latino; 0.2% Native Hawaiian or other Pacific Islander, non-Hispanic/Latino; 0.9% American Indian or Alaska Native, non-Hispanic/Latino; 0.6% Two or more races, non-Hispanic/Latino; 4% Race/ethnicity unknown; 1% international; 19% transferred in; 22% live on campus.

Freshmen
Admission: 1,169 applied, 1,017 admitted, 405 enrolled. ***Test scores:*** SAT critical reading scores over 500: 42%; SAT math scores over 500: 53%; ACT scores over 18: 77%; SAT critical reading scores over 600: 10%; SAT math scores over 600: 13%; ACT scores over 24: 20%; SAT math scores over 700: 2%; ACT scores over 30: 1%.

Retention: 69% of full-time freshmen returned.

FACULTY
Total: 237, 53% full-time, 57% with terminal degrees.

Student/faculty ratio: 21:1.

ACADEMICS
Calendar: semesters. *Degrees:* bachelor's, master's, and postbachelor's certificates.

Special study options: academic remediation for entering students, accelerated degree program, advanced placement credit, cooperative education, distance learning, double majors, English as a second language, honors programs, independent study, internships, part-time degree program, services for LD students, study abroad, summer session for credit.

Unusual degree programs: 3-2 business administration with Accountancy (BBA and MPA).

Computers: 517 computers/terminals are available on campus for general student use. Students can access the following: campus intranet, computer help desk, free student e-mail accounts, online (class) grades, online (class) registration, online (class) schedules. Campuswide network is available. 100% of college-owned or -operated housing units are wired for high-speed Internet access. Wireless service is available via entire campus.

STUDENT LIFE
Housing options: coed. Campus housing is university owned.

Activities and organizations: drama/theater group, student-run newspaper, choral group, The American Society for Mechanical Engineers, The Student Veteran Association, Marketing Experiences, The National Society for Leadership and Success, Students in Free Enterprise, national fraternities.

Athletics Member NCAA. All Division II. ***Intercollegiate sports:*** baseball M(s), basketball M(s)/W(s), cheerleading M(s)/W(s), cross-country running M(s)/W(s), soccer M(s)/W(s), softball W(s), swimming and diving M(s)/W(s), tennis M(s)/W(s), volleyball W(s). ***Intramural sports:*** basketball M/W, soccer M/W, softball W, volleyball M/W.

Campus security: 24-hour emergency response devices and patrols, late-night transport/escort service.

Student services: health clinic, personal/psychological counseling.

COSTS & FINANCIAL AID
Costs (2014–15) ***Tuition:*** state resident $5036 full-time, $168 per credit hour part-time; nonresident $15,896 full-time, $530 per credit hour part-time. Full-time tuition and fees vary according to course load, degree level, and location. Part-time tuition and fees vary according to course load, degree level, and location. No tuition increase for student's term of enrollment. ***Required fees:*** $1422 full-time, $68 per credit hour part-time. ***Room and board:*** $7978; room only: $4894. Room and board charges vary according to board plan and housing facility. ***Payment plan:*** installment.

Financial Aid Of all full-time matriculated undergraduates who enrolled in 2013, 1,481 applied for aid, 1,289 were judged to have need, 896 had their need fully met. In 2013, 258 non-need-based awards were made. ***Average percent of need met:*** 66. ***Average financial aid package:*** $9532. ***Average need-based loan:*** $3889. ***Average need-based gift aid:*** $6011. ***Average non-need-based aid:*** $3008. ***Average indebtedness upon graduation:*** $10,972.

APPLYING
Standardized Tests *Required:* SAT or ACT (for admission).

Options: electronic application.

Required: high school transcript.

Application deadlines: 8/26 (freshmen), 8/26 (transfers).

Notification: continuous (freshmen), continuous (transfers).

CONTACT
The University of Texas of the Permian Basin, 4901 East University Boulevard, Odessa, TX 79762-0001. *Phone:* 432-552-2605. *Toll-free phone:* 866-552-UTPB.

The University of Texas–Pan American

Edinburg, Texas

http://www.utpa.edu/

- **State-supported** comprehensive, founded 1927, part of University of Texas System
- **Small-town** 331-acre campus with easy access to McAllen-Edinburg-Mission
- **Endowment** $72.0 million
- **Coed** 18,200 undergraduate students, 74% full-time, 56% women, 44% men
- **Noncompetitive** entrance level, 63% of applicants were admitted

UNDERGRAD STUDENTS

13,551 full-time, 4,649 part-time. Students come from 31 states and territories; 25 other countries; 0.5% are from out of state; 0.6% Black or African American, non-Hispanic/Latino; 91% Hispanic/Latino; 1% Asian, non-Hispanic/Latino; 0.1% Native Hawaiian or other Pacific Islander, non-Hispanic/Latino; 0.0% American Indian or Alaska Native, non-Hispanic/Latino; 0.3% Two or more races, non-Hispanic/Latino; 2% Race/ethnicity unknown; 2% international; 7% transferred in; 4% live on campus.

Freshmen

Admission: 10,679 applied, 6,706 admitted, 3,483 enrolled. ***Test scores:*** SAT critical reading scores over 500: 34%; SAT math scores over 500: 47%; SAT writing scores over 500: 29%; ACT scores over 18: 82%; SAT critical reading scores over 600: 8%; SAT math scores over 600: 12%; SAT writing scores over 600: 6%; ACT scores over 24: 12%; SAT critical reading scores over 700: 1%; SAT math scores over 700: 2%; SAT writing scores over 700: 1%; ACT scores over 30: 1%.

Retention: 76% of full-time freshmen returned.

FACULTY

Total: 865, 82% full-time, 69% with terminal degrees.

Student/faculty ratio: 22:1.

ACADEMICS

Calendar: semesters. *Degrees:* bachelor's, master's, doctoral, and postbachelor's certificates.

Special study options: academic remediation for entering students, accelerated degree program, adult/continuing education programs, advanced placement credit, cooperative education, distance learning, double majors, English as a second language, honors programs, independent study, internships, part-time degree program, services for LD students, study abroad, summer session for credit. ***ROTC:*** Army (b).

Unusual degree programs: business administration with accounting.

Computers: Students can access the following: campus intranet, computer help desk, free student e-mail accounts, online (class) grades, online (class) registration, online (class) schedules. Campuswide network is available. Wireless service is available via entire campus.

STUDENT LIFE

Housing options: coed, men-only, women-only. Campus housing is university owned.

Activities and organizations: drama/theater group, student-run newspaper, choral group, Alpha Lambda Delta National Honor Society for First-Year Students, The National Society of Collegiate Scholars, Golden Key International Honor Society, Pre-Medical Bio-Medical Society, Environmental Awareness Club, national fraternities, national sororities.

Athletics Member NCAA. All Division I. ***Intercollegiate sports:*** baseball M(s), basketball M(s)/W(s), cross-country running M(s)/W(s), golf M(s)/W(s), tennis M(s)/W(s), track and field M(s)/W(s), volleyball W(s). ***Intramural sports:*** badminton M/W, basketball M/W, bowling M/W, cheerleading M/W, football M/W, racquetball M/W, soccer M/W, softball M/W, table tennis M/W, tennis M/W, ultimate Frisbee M/W, volleyball M/W.

Campus security: 24-hour emergency response devices and patrols, late-night transport/escort service.

Student services: health clinic, personal/psychological counseling.

COSTS & FINANCIAL AID

Costs (2014–15) ***Tuition:*** state resident $4176 full-time, $174 per credit hour part-time; nonresident $13,026 full-time, $543 per credit hour part-time. Full-time tuition and fees vary according to course load and degree level. Part-time tuition and fees vary according to course load and degree level. ***Required fees:*** $997 full-time. ***Room and board:*** $5952; room only: $3580. Room and board charges vary according to board plan and housing facility. ***Payment plan:*** installment.

Financial Aid Of all full-time matriculated undergraduates who enrolled in 2013, 11,358 applied for aid, 10,937 were judged to have need, 295 had their need fully met. 644 Federal Work-Study jobs (averaging $2529). 149 state and other part-time jobs (averaging $2474). In 2013, 300 non-need-based awards were made. ***Average percent of need met:*** 63. ***Average financial aid package:*** $9468. ***Average need-based loan:*** $4830. ***Average need-based gift aid:*** $10,224. ***Average non-need-based aid:*** $3385. ***Average indebtedness upon graduation:*** $14,900.

APPLYING

Standardized Tests *Required:* SAT or ACT (for admission).

Options: electronic application.

Required: high school transcript, minimum 2.0 GPA. ***Required for some:*** interview.

Application deadlines: 8/14 (freshmen), 8/14 (transfers).

Notification: continuous (freshmen), continuous (transfers).

CONTACT

Dr. Magdalena Hinojosa, Sr. Associate Vice President for Enrollment Services, The University of Texas–Pan American, Office of Enrollment Services, 1201 West University Drive, Edinburg, TX 78539. *Phone:* 956-665-2999. *Toll-free phone:* 866-441-8872. *Fax:* 956-665-2212. *E-mail:* admissions@utpa.edu.

★ University of the Incarnate Word

San Antonio, Texas

http://www.uiw.edu/

- **Independent Roman Catholic** comprehensive, founded 1881
- **Urban** 200-acre campus with easy access to San Antonio
- **Endowment** $122.6 million
- **Coed** 6,496 undergraduate students, 67% full-time, 61% women, 39% men
- **Moderately difficult** entrance level, 93% of applicants were admitted

UNDERGRAD STUDENTS

4,324 full-time, 2,172 part-time. Students come from 46 states and territories; 44 other countries; 6% are from out of state; 7% Black or African American, non-Hispanic/Latino; 59% Hispanic/Latino; 2% Asian, non-Hispanic/Latino; 0.2% Native Hawaiian or other Pacific Islander, non-Hispanic/Latino; 0.3% American Indian or Alaska Native, non-Hispanic/Latino; 1% Two or more races, non-Hispanic/Latino; 6% Race/ethnicity unknown; 5% international; 12% transferred in; 18% live on campus.

Freshmen

Admission: 4,257 applied, 3,968 admitted, 946 enrolled. ***Average high school GPA:*** 3.47. ***Test scores:*** SAT critical reading scores over 500: 39%; SAT math scores over 500: 47%; SAT writing scores over 500: 33%; ACT scores over 18: 79%; SAT critical reading scores over 600: 7%; SAT math scores over 600: 10%; SAT writing scores over 600: 6%; ACT scores over 24: 19%; SAT critical reading scores over 700: 1%; SAT math scores over 700: 1%; SAT writing scores over 700: 1%; ACT scores over 30: 1%.

Retention: 74% of full-time freshmen returned.

FACULTY

Total: 577, 48% full-time, 39% with terminal degrees.

Student/faculty ratio: 14:1.

ACADEMICS

Calendar: semesters. *Degrees:* diplomas, associate, bachelor's, master's, and doctoral.

Special study options: academic remediation for entering students, accelerated degree program, adult/continuing education programs, advanced placement credit, cooperative education, distance learning,

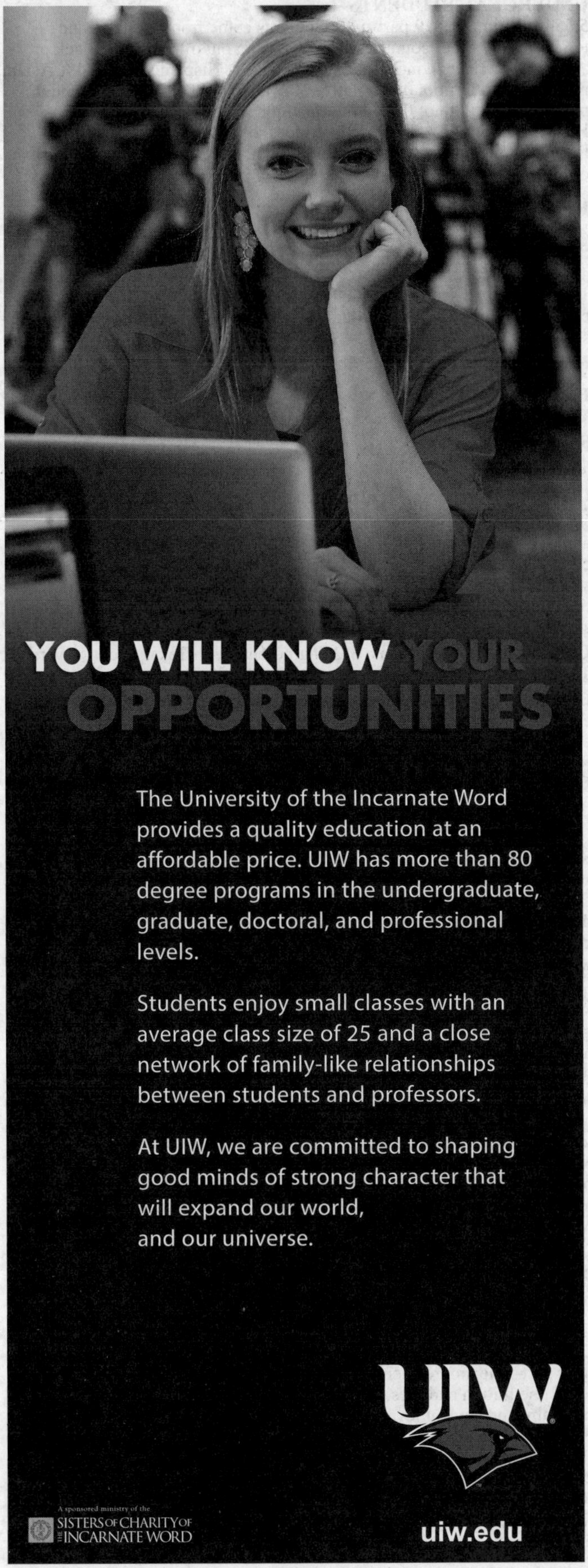
YOU WILL KNOW YOUR
OPPORTUNITIES
The University of the Incarnate Word provides a quality education at an affordable price. UIW has more than 80 degree programs in the undergraduate, graduate, doctoral, and professional levels.
Students enjoy small classes with an average class size of 25 and a close network of family-like relationships between students and professors.
At UIW, we are committed to shaping good minds of strong character that will expand our world, and our universe.
UIW
A sponsored ministry of the
SISTERS OF CHARITY OF THE INCARNATE WORD
uiw.edu

double majors, English as a second language, freshman honors college, honors programs, independent study, internships, off-campus study, part-time degree program, services for LD students, study abroad, summer session for credit. ***ROTC:*** Army (c), Air Force (c).

Unusual degree programs: 3-2 business administration; communications, accounting.

Computers: 185 computers/terminals are available on campus for general student use. Students can access the following: computer help desk, free student e-mail accounts, online (class) grades, online (class) registration, online (class) schedules, Ports available in general use area and other locations. Also dedicated computers for graduate/doctoral students. Campuswide network is available. 100% of college-owned or -operated housing units are wired for high-speed Internet access. Wireless service is available via entire campus.

STUDENT LIFE

Housing options: coed, men-only, women-only, special housing for students with disabilities. Campus housing is university owned. Freshman campus housing is guaranteed.

Activities and organizations: drama/theater group, student-run newspaper, radio and television station, choral group, marching band, Society of Leadership and Success, Pre-Pharmacy Association, Alpha Sigma Alpha, Lambda Chi Alpha, Student Government Association, national fraternities, national sororities.

Athletics Member NCAA. All Division I except football (Division I-AA), softball (Division II). ***Intercollegiate sports:*** baseball M(s), basketball M(s)/W(s), cross-country running M(s)/W(s), golf M(s)/W(s), soccer M(s)/W(s), softball W(s), swimming and diving M(s)/W(s), tennis M(s)/W(s), track and field M(s)/W(s), volleyball W(s). ***Intramural sports:*** basketball M/W, cheerleading M/W, football M/W, racquetball M/W, soccer M/W, softball M/W, tennis M/W, ultimate Frisbee M/W, volleyball M/W, water polo M/W.

Campus security: 24-hour emergency response devices and patrols, late-night transport/escort service, controlled dormitory access.

Student services: health clinic, personal/psychological counseling.

COSTS & FINANCIAL AID

Costs (2015–16) ***Comprehensive fee:*** $39,162 includes full-time tuition ($25,900), mandatory fees ($1898), and room and board ($11,364). Full-time tuition and fees vary according to course load, degree level, location, program, and reciprocity agreements. Part-time tuition: $850 per credit hour. Part-time tuition and fees vary according to course load, degree level, location, program, and reciprocity agreements. ***College room only:*** $6600. Room and board charges vary according to board plan and housing facility. ***Payment plan:*** installment. ***Waivers:*** senior citizens and employees or children of employees.

Financial Aid Of all full-time matriculated undergraduates who enrolled in 2013, 3,459 applied for aid, 3,254 were judged to have need, 863 had their need fully met. In 2013, 782 non-need-based awards were made. ***Average percent of need met:*** 80. ***Average financial aid package:*** $20,598. ***Average need-based loan:*** $4509. ***Average need-based gift aid:*** $15,277. ***Average non-need-based aid:*** $7720. ***Average indebtedness upon graduation:*** $29,744.

APPLYING

Standardized Tests *Required:* SAT or ACT (for admission).

Options: electronic application, deferred entrance.

Application fee: $20.

Required: high school transcript. ***Required for some:*** essay or personal statement, interview. ***Recommended:*** minimum 2.0 GPA, letter(s) of recommendation recommended for all, required for some.

Application deadlines: rolling (freshmen), rolling (out-of-state freshmen), rolling (transfers).

Notification: continuous (freshmen), continuous (out-of-state freshmen), continuous (transfers).

CONTACT

Ms. Andrea Cyterski-Acosta, Dean of Enrollment, University of the Incarnate Word, 4301 Broadway Avenue, University of the Incarnate Word, San Antonio, TN 78209. *Phone:* 210-829-6005. *Toll-free phone:* 800-749-WORD. *Fax:* 210-829-3921. *E-mail:* admis@uiwtx.edu.

See this page for display ad and page 1706 for the College Close-Up.

Wayland Baptist University

Plainview, Texas

http://www.wbu.edu/

- **Independent Baptist** comprehensive, founded 1908
- **Small-town** 80-acre campus
- **Endowment** $71.5 million
- **Coed**
- **Minimally difficult** entrance level

FACULTY

Student/faculty ratio: 9:1.

ACADEMICS

Calendar: semesters. *Degrees:* associate, bachelor's, and master's (branch locations in Anchorage, AK; Amarillo, TX; Luke Air Force Base, AZ; Glorieta, NM; Aiea, HI; Lubbock, TX; San Antonio, TX; Wichita Falls, TX).

STUDENT LIFE

Housing options: on-campus residence required through junior year; men-only, women-only. Campus housing is university owned. Freshman campus housing is guaranteed.

Activities and organizations: drama/theater group, student-run newspaper, radio and television station, choral group, marching band, student government, Wayland Singers, Baptist Student Ministries, International Choir, President's Ambassadors, national fraternities, national sororities.

Athletics Member NAIA.

Campus security: 24-hour emergency response devices and patrols, security lighting, campus police department.

Student services: health clinic, personal/psychological counseling.

COSTS & FINANCIAL AID

Costs (2014–15) ***Comprehensive fee:*** $21,882 includes full-time tuition ($14,850), mandatory fees ($1080), and room and board ($5952). Full-time tuition and fees vary according to course load and location. Part-time tuition: $495 per credit hour. Part-time tuition and fees vary according to course load and location. ***Required fees:*** $110 per term part-time. ***College room only:*** $2000. Room and board charges vary according to board plan and housing facility.

Financial Aid Of all full-time matriculated undergraduates who enrolled in 2014, 821 applied for aid, 726 were judged to have need, 90 had their need fully met. 138 Federal Work-Study jobs (averaging $1374). 138 state and other part-time jobs (averaging $1775). In 2014, 145 non-need-based awards were made. ***Average percent of need met:*** 65. ***Average financial aid package:*** $13,512. ***Average need-based loan:*** $4410. ***Average need-based gift aid:*** $10,113. ***Average non-need-based aid:*** $5469. ***Average indebtedness upon graduation:*** $25,725.

APPLYING

Standardized Tests *Required:* SAT or ACT (for admission).

Options: electronic application.

Application fee: $35.

Required: high school transcript. ***Required for some:*** interview.

CONTACT

Ms. Debbie Stennett, Director of Student Admissions, Wayland Baptist University, 1900 West 7th Street, CMB 1294, Plainview, TX 79072. *Phone:* 806-291-3500. *Toll-free phone:* 800-588-1928. *Fax:* 806-291-1973. *E-mail:* admityou@wbu.edu.

West Texas A&M University

Canyon, Texas

http://www.wtamu.edu/

- **State-supported** comprehensive, founded 1909, part of Texas A&M University System
- **Small-town** 128-acre campus
- **Endowment** $71.8 million
- **Coed** 7,133 undergraduate students, 79% full-time, 54% women, 46% men
- **Moderately difficult** entrance level, 67% of applicants were admitted

UNDERGRAD STUDENTS

5,654 full-time, 1,479 part-time. Students come from 44 states and territories; 47 other countries; 12% are from out of state; 6% Black or African American, non-Hispanic/Latino; 25% Hispanic/Latino; 1% Asian, non-Hispanic/Latino; 0.1% Native Hawaiian or other Pacific Islander, non-Hispanic/Latino; 0.5% American Indian or Alaska Native, non-Hispanic/Latino; 2% Two or more races, non-Hispanic/Latino; 2% Race/ethnicity unknown; 2% international; 14% transferred in; 26% live on campus.

Freshmen

Admission: 5,234 applied, 3,529 admitted, 1,279 enrolled. ***Test scores:*** SAT critical reading scores over 500: 41%; SAT math scores over 500: 48%; ACT scores over 18: 80%; SAT critical reading scores over 600: 11%; SAT math scores over 600: 12%; ACT scores over 24: 23%; SAT critical reading scores over 700: 1%; SAT math scores over 700: 1%; ACT scores over 30: 2%.

Retention: 67% of full-time freshmen returned.

FACULTY

Total: 445, 72% full-time, 53% with terminal degrees.

Student/faculty ratio: 20:1.

ACADEMICS

Calendar: semesters. *Degrees:* bachelor's, master's, and doctoral.

Special study options: academic remediation for entering students, adult/continuing education programs, advanced placement credit, cooperative education, distance learning, double majors, English as a second language, honors programs, independent study, internships, part-time degree program, services for LD students, study abroad, summer session for credit.

Unusual degree programs: 3-2 engineering with Texas Tech University, Texas A&M University.

Computers: 1,200 computers/terminals and 1,200 ports are available on campus for general student use. Students can access the following: campus intranet, computer help desk, free student e-mail accounts, online (class) grades, online (class) registration, online (class) schedules. Campuswide network is available. 100% of college-owned or -operated housing units are wired for high-speed Internet access. Wireless service is available via entire campus.

STUDENT LIFE

Housing options: on-campus residence required through sophomore year; coed, men-only, women-only, special housing for students with disabilities. Campus housing is university owned. Freshman campus housing is guaranteed.

Activities and organizations: drama/theater group, student-run newspaper, radio station, choral group, marching band, Residence Hall Association, National Society for Leadership and Success, student government, Students in Free Enterprise (SIFE), Baptist Student Ministries, national fraternities, national sororities.

Athletics Member NCAA. All Division II. ***Intercollegiate sports:*** baseball M(s), basketball M(s)/W(s), bowling M(s)(c)/W(s)(c), cross-country running M(s)/W(s), equestrian sports M(c)/W(s), football M(s), golf M(s)/W(s), soccer M(s)/W(s), softball W(s), track and field M(s)/W(s), volleyball W(s). ***Intramural sports:*** badminton M/W, basketball M/W, bowling M/W, football M/W, golf M/W, racquetball M/W, soccer M/W, softball M/W, swimming and diving M/W, table tennis M/W, tennis M/W, volleyball M/W, wrestling M.

Campus security: 24-hour emergency response devices and patrols, late-night transport/escort service, controlled dormitory access.

Student services: health clinic, personal/psychological counseling.

COSTS & FINANCIAL AID

Costs (2014–15) ***Tuition:*** state resident $4863 full-time, $50 per credit hour part-time; nonresident $6124 full-time, $80 per credit hour part-time. Full-time tuition and fees vary according to course load, degree level, program, and student level. Part-time tuition and fees vary according to course load, degree level, program, and student level. No tuition increase for student's term of enrollment. ***Required fees:*** $1242 full-time, $74 per credit hour part-time, $232 per term part-time. ***Room and board:*** $7196. Room and board charges vary according to board plan and housing facility. ***Payment plan:*** installment. ***Waivers:*** employees or children of employees.

Financial Aid Of all full-time matriculated undergraduates who enrolled in 2012, 3,978 applied for aid, 3,271 were judged to have need, 507 had their need fully met. In 2012, 278 non-need-based awards were made. ***Average percent of need met:*** 65. ***Average financial aid package:*** $10,245. ***Average need-based loan:*** $4693. ***Average need-based gift aid:*** $5129. ***Average non-need-based aid:*** $1599. ***Average indebtedness upon graduation:*** $19,774.

APPLYING
Standardized Tests *Required:* SAT or ACT (for admission).

Options: electronic application, deferred entrance.

Application fee: $40.

Required: high school transcript, class rank and Texas high school curriculum or equivalent.

Application deadlines: rolling (freshmen), rolling (transfers).

Notification: continuous (freshmen), continuous (transfers).

CONTACT
Mr. Kyle Moore, Director of Admissions, West Texas A&M University, WT Box 60907, Canyon, TX 79016-0001. *Phone:* 806-651-5288. *Toll-free phone:* 800-99-WTAMU. *Fax:* 806-651-5285. *E-mail:* kmoore@mail.wtamu.edu.

UTAH

Argosy University, Salt Lake City

Draper, Utah

http://www.argosy.edu/locations/salt-lake-city/

- **Proprietary** university, founded 2008
- **Coed**

ACADEMICS
Degrees: associate, bachelor's, master's, and doctoral.

CONTACT
Argosy University, Salt Lake City, 121 Election Road, Suite 300, Draper, UT 84020. *Phone:* 801-601-5000. *Toll-free phone:* 888-639-4756.

The Art Institute of Salt Lake City

Draper, Utah

http://www.artinstitutes.edu/SaltLakeCity/

- **Proprietary** 4-year, part of Education Management Corporation
- **Coed**

ACADEMICS
Degrees: diplomas, associate, and bachelor's.

CONTACT
The Art Institute of Salt Lake City, 121 West Election Road, Suite 100, Draper, UT 84020-9492. *Phone:* 801-601-4700. *Toll-free phone:* 800-978-0096.

Brigham Young University

Provo, Utah

http://www.byu.edu/

- **Independent** university, founded 1875, affiliated with The Church of Jesus Christ of Latter-day Saints, part of Church Education System (CES) of The Church of Jesus Christ of Latter-day Saints
- **Suburban** 557-acre campus with easy access to Salt Lake City
- **Coed** 27,163 undergraduate students, 90% full-time, 45% women, 55% men
- **Moderately difficult** entrance level, 47% of applicants were admitted

UNDERGRAD STUDENTS
24,499 full-time, 2,664 part-time. 67% are from out of state; 0.5% Black or African American, non-Hispanic/Latino; 6% Hispanic/Latino; 2% Asian, non-Hispanic/Latino; 0.6% Native Hawaiian or other Pacific Islander, non-Hispanic/Latino; 0.4% American Indian or Alaska Native, non-Hispanic/Latino; 3% Two or more races, non-Hispanic/Latino; 1% Race/ethnicity unknown; 3% international; 3% transferred in; 19% live on campus.

Freshmen
Admission: 11,078 applied, 5,207 admitted, 4,060 enrolled. ***Average high school GPA:*** 3.81. ***Test scores:*** SAT critical reading scores over 500: 94%; SAT math scores over 500: 96%; SAT writing scores over 500: 93%; ACT scores over 18: 100%; SAT critical reading scores over 600: 65%; SAT math scores over 600: 68%; SAT writing scores over 600: 59%; ACT scores over 24: 92%; SAT critical reading scores over 700: 21%; SAT math scores over 700: 20%; SAT writing scores over 700: 15%; ACT scores over 30: 40%.

Retention: 87% of full-time freshmen returned.

FACULTY
Total: 1,741, 72% full-time, 76% with terminal degrees.

Student/faculty ratio: 18:1.

ACADEMICS
Calendar: semesters. *Degrees:* bachelor's, master's, doctoral, post-master's, and postbachelor's certificates.

Special study options: adult/continuing education programs, external degree program, off-campus study, part-time degree program. ***ROTC:*** Army (b), Air Force (b).

Computers: Students can access the following: campus intranet, computer help desk, online (class) grades, online (class) registration, online (class) schedules. Campuswide network is available.

STUDENT LIFE
Housing options: men-only, women-only, special housing for students with disabilities. Campus housing is university owned.

Athletics Member NCAA. All Division I except football (Division I-A). ***Intercollegiate sports:*** baseball M(s), basketball M(s)/W(s), cheerleading M(s)/W(s), cross-country running M(s)/W(s), golf M(s)/W(s), gymnastics W(s), lacrosse M(c), racquetball M/W, rugby M(c), soccer M(c)/W(s), softball W(s), swimming and diving M(s)/W(s), tennis M(s)/W(s), track and field M(s)/W(s), volleyball M(s)/W(s). ***Intramural sports:*** badminton W, basketball M/W, field hockey M, football M/W, golf M/W, racquetball M/W, soccer M/W, softball M/W, table tennis M/W, tennis M/W, ultimate Frisbee M/W, volleyball M/W, water polo M/W, wrestling M.

Campus security: 24-hour emergency response devices and patrols, late-night transport/escort service, controlled dormitory access.

COSTS & FINANCIAL AID
Costs (2014–15) ***Comprehensive fee:*** $12,330 includes full-time tuition ($5000) and room and board ($7330). Part-time tuition: $257 per credit hour. Part-time tuition and fees vary according to course load. Latter Day Saints full-time student $5,000 per year, non-LDS full-time student $10,000. ***Room and board:*** Room and board charges vary according to board plan, housing facility, and location. ***Waivers:*** employees or children of employees.

Financial Aid Of all full-time matriculated undergraduates who enrolled in 2013, 14,722 applied for aid, 12,559 were judged to have need, 5,311 had their need fully met. In 2013, 5655 non-need-based awards were made. ***Average percent of need met:*** 34. ***Average financial aid package:*** $7258. ***Average need-based loan:*** $4215. ***Average need-based gift aid:*** $4897. ***Average non-need-based aid:*** $3944. ***Average indebtedness upon graduation:*** $14,021.

APPLYING
Standardized Tests *Required:* SAT or ACT (for admission).

Options: electronic application, early admission, deferred entrance.

Application fee: $35.

Required: essay or personal statement, high school transcript, 1 letter of recommendation, interview.

CONTACT
Mr. Tom Gourley, Dean of Admissions and Records, Brigham Young University, A-153 Abraham Smoot Building, Provo, UT 84602. *Phone:* 801-422-2507. *Fax:* 801-422-0005. *E-mail:* admissions@byu.edu.

Broadview Entertainment Arts University

Salt Lake City, Utah

http://www.broadviewuniversity.edu/

- **Proprietary** 4-year, part of Globe Education Network (GEN) which is composed of Globe University, Minnesota School of Business, Broadview University, The Institute of Production and Recording and Minnesota School of Cosmetology
- **Urban** 3-acre campus
- **Coed**

ACADEMICS
Degrees: associate and bachelor's.

STUDENT LIFE
Campus security: 24-hour emergency response devices, late-night transport/escort service.

APPLYING
Standardized Tests *Required:* ACCUPLACER is required of all applicants unless documentation of a minimum ACT composite score of 21 or documentation of a minimum composite score of 1485 on the SAT is presented (for admission).

Options: electronic application.

Application fee: $50.

Required: interview. ***Required for some:*** 2 letters of recommendation, Certification of high school graduation or GE.

CONTACT
Broadview Entertainment Arts University, 240 East Morris Avenue, Salt Lake City, UT 84115. *Toll-free phone:* 877-801-8889.

Broadview University–Layton

Layton, Utah

http://www.broadviewuniversity.edu/

- **Proprietary** 4-year, part of Globe Education Network (GEN) which is composed of Globe University, Minnesota School of Business, Broadview University, The Institute of Production and Recording and Minnesota School of Cosmetology
- **Suburban** campus
- **Coed**

ACADEMICS
Degrees: certificates, diplomas, associate, and bachelor's.

STUDENT LIFE
Housing options: college housing not available.

Campus security: 24-hour emergency response devices, late-night transport/escort service.

APPLYING
Standardized Tests *Required:* ACCUPLACER is required of most applicants unless documentation of a minimum ACT composite score of 21 or documentation of a minimum composite score of 1485 on the SAT is presented (for admission).

Options: electronic application.

Application fee: $50.

Required: interview, Certification of high school graduation or GED.

CONTACT
Broadview University–Layton, 869 West Hill Field Road, Layton, UT 84041. *Toll-free phone:* 866-253-7744.

Broadview University–Orem

Orem, Utah

http://www.broadviewuniversity.edu/

- **Proprietary** 4-year, part of Globe Education Network (GEN) which is composed of Globe University, Minnesota School of Business, Broadview University, The Institute of Production and Recording and Minnesota School of Cosmetology
- **Small-town** 3-acre campus
- **Coed**

ACADEMICS
Degrees: certificates, diplomas, associate, and bachelor's.

STUDENT LIFE
Campus security: 24-hour emergency response devices.

APPLYING
Standardized Tests *Required:* ACCUPLACER is required of most applicants unless documentation of a minimum ACT composite score of 21 or documentation of a minimum composite score of 1485 on the SAT is presented (for admission).

Options: electronic application.

Application fee: $50.

Required: interview, Certification of high school graduation or GED.

CONTACT
Broadview University–Orem, 898 North 1200 West, Orem, UT 84057. *Toll-free phone:* 877-822-5838.

Broadview University–West Jordan

West Jordan, Utah

http://www.broadviewuniversity.edu/

- **Proprietary** comprehensive, part of Globe Education Network (GEN) which is composed of Globe University, Minnesota School of Business, Broadview University, The Institute of Production and Recording and Minnesota School of Cosmetology
- **Urban** 4-acre campus
- **Coed**

ACADEMICS
Calendar: quarters. *Degrees:* certificates, diplomas, associate, bachelor's, and master's.

STUDENT LIFE
Housing options: college housing not available.

Campus security: 24-hour emergency response devices, late-night transport/escort service.

APPLYING
Standardized Tests *Required:* ACCUPLACER is required of most applicants unless documentation of a minimum ACT composite score of 21 or documentation of a minimum composite score of 1485 on the SAT is presented (for admission).

Options: electronic application.

Application fee: $50.

Required: interview, Certification of high school graduation or GED. ***Required for some:*** essay or personal statement.

CONTACT
Broadview University–West Jordan, 1902 West 7800 South, West Jordan, UT 84088. *Toll-free phone:* 866-304-4224.

DeVry University

Sandy, Utah

http://www.devry.edu/

- **Proprietary** comprehensive
- **Coed**

ACADEMICS
Degrees: associate, bachelor's, and master's.

COSTS & FINANCIAL AID
Costs (2014–15) ***Tuition:*** $17,052 full-time, $609 per credit hour part-time. ***Required fees:*** $80 full-time.

Financial Aid Of all full-time matriculated undergraduates who enrolled in 2007, 9 applied for aid, 8 were judged to have need, 1 had their need fully met. In 2007, 1 non-need-based awards were made. ***Average percent of need met:*** 34. ***Average financial aid package:*** $11,508. ***Average need-based loan:*** $9109. ***Average need-based gift aid:*** $4798. ***Average non-need-based aid:*** $6900.

CONTACT
Admissions Office, DeVry University, 9350 South 150 E, Suite 420, Sandy, UT 84070. *Phone:* 801-565-5110. *Toll-free phone:* 866-338-7941.

Dixie State University

St. George, Utah

http://www.dixie.edu/

- **State-supported** 4-year, founded 1911, part of Utah System of Higher Education
- **Small-town** 117-acre campus
- **Endowment** $33.0 million
- **Coed** 8,570 undergraduate students, 62% full-time, 53% women, 47% men
- **Noncompetitive** entrance level, 100% of applicants were admitted

UNDERGRAD STUDENTS
5,299 full-time, 3,271 part-time. Students come from 44 states and territories; 32 other countries; 19% are from out of state; 2% Black or African American, non-Hispanic/Latino; 10% Hispanic/Latino; 0.8% Asian, non-Hispanic/Latino; 1% Native Hawaiian or other Pacific Islander, non-Hispanic/Latino; 1% American Indian or Alaska Native, non-Hispanic/Latino; 3% Two or more races, non-Hispanic/Latino; 1% Race/ethnicity unknown; 3% international; 6% transferred in; 4% live on campus.

Freshmen
Admission: 4,038 applied, 4,038 admitted, 1,925 enrolled. ***Average high school GPA:*** 3.22. ***Test scores:*** SAT critical reading scores over 500: 27%; SAT math scores over 500: 28%; SAT writing scores over 500: 17%; ACT scores over 18: 75%; SAT critical reading scores over 600: 3%; SAT math scores over 600: 3%; SAT writing scores over 600: 3%; ACT scores over 24: 24%; ACT scores over 30: 1%.
Retention: 55% of full-time freshmen returned.

FACULTY
Total: 550, 36% full-time, 31% with terminal degrees.
Student/faculty ratio: 20:1.

ACADEMICS
Calendar: semesters. *Degrees:* certificates, diplomas, associate, and bachelor's.
Special study options: academic remediation for entering students, accelerated degree program, adult/continuing education programs, advanced placement credit, cooperative education, distance learning, double majors, English as a second language, honors programs, independent study, internships, off-campus study, part-time degree program, services for LD students, student-designed majors, study abroad, summer session for credit. ***ROTC:*** Army (b).
Computers: 400 computers/terminals and 350 ports are available on campus for general student use. Students can access the following: computer help desk, free student e-mail accounts, online (class) grades, online (class) registration, online (class) schedules. Campuswide network is available. 100% of college-owned or -operated housing units are wired for high-speed Internet access. Wireless service is available via entire campus.

STUDENT LIFE
Housing options: coed, men-only. Campus housing is university owned.
Activities and organizations: drama/theater group, student-run newspaper, radio and television station, choral group, marching band, Dixie Spirit, Outdoor Club, Association of Women Students, intramurals, Futbol Club.
Athletics Member NCAA. except baseball (Division II), men's and women's basketball (Division II), men's and women's cross-country running (Division II), football (Division II), men's and women's golf (Division II), men's and women's soccer (Division II), softball (Division II), tennis (Division II), volleyball (Division II)***Intercollegiate sports:*** baseball M(s), basketball M(s)/W(s), cross-country running M(s)/W(s), football M(s), golf M(s)/W(s), soccer M(s)/W(s), softball W(s), tennis W(s), volleyball W(s). ***Intramural sports:*** basketball M/W, football M, soccer M/W, table tennis M/W, tennis M/W, volleyball M/W.
Campus security: 24-hour emergency response devices and patrols.
Student services: health clinic, personal/psychological counseling, women's center.

COSTS & FINANCIAL AID
Costs (2014–15) ***Tuition:*** state resident $3792 full-time, $158 per credit hour part-time; nonresident $12,120 full-time, $505 per credit hour part-time. Full-time tuition and fees vary according to course load. Part-time tuition and fees vary according to course load. ***Required fees:*** $662 full-time, $158 per credit hour part-time. ***Room and board:*** $5918; room only: $3260. Room and board charges vary according to board plan, housing facility, and location. ***Payment plan:*** installment. ***Waivers:*** senior citizens and employees or children of employees.
Financial Aid Of all full-time matriculated undergraduates who enrolled in 2013, 3,962 applied for aid, 3,879 were judged to have need, 118 had their need fully met. 116 Federal Work-Study jobs (averaging $3558). 51 state and other part-time jobs (averaging $3790). In 2013, 18 non-need-based awards were made. ***Average percent of need met:*** 57. ***Average financial aid package:*** $9835. ***Average need-based loan:*** $4248. ***Average need-based gift aid:*** $4892. ***Average non-need-based aid:*** $13,294. ***Average indebtedness upon graduation:*** $24,441. ***Financial aid deadline:*** 6/30.

APPLYING
Standardized Tests *Recommended:* SAT or ACT (for admission).
Options: electronic application, early admission, deferred entrance.
Application fee: $35.
Required: high school transcript.
Application deadlines: 8/15 (freshmen), 8/15 (out-of-state freshmen), 8/15 (transfers).
Notification: continuous (freshmen), continuous (out-of-state freshmen), continuous (transfers).

CONTACT
Dixie State University, 225 South 700 East, St. George, UT 84770-3876. *Phone:* 435-652-7698.

Eagle Gate College

Layton, Utah

http://eaglegatecollege.edu/

- **Proprietary** 4-year, part of Eagle Gate College Group includes the Murray campus, the Layton campus and our partner school, Provo College in Provo, UT
- **Suburban** campus with easy access to Salt Lake City
- **Coed**

ACADEMICS
Degrees: certificates, diplomas, associate, and bachelor's.

CONTACT
Eagle Gate College, 915 North 400 West, Layton, UT 84041. *Phone:* 801-546-7500. *Toll-free phone:* 866-29-EAGLE.

Eagle Gate College

Murray, Utah

http://eaglegatecollege.edu/

- **Proprietary** 4-year, part of Eagle Gate College Group includes the Murray campus, the Layton campus and our partner school, Provo College in Provo, UT
- **Suburban** campus with easy access to Salt Lake City
- **Coed**

ACADEMICS
Degrees: certificates, diplomas, associate, and bachelor's.

CONTACT
Eagle Gate College, 5588 South Green Street, Murray, UT 84123. *Phone:* 801-333-8100. *Toll-free phone:* 866-29-EAGLE.

ITT Technical Institute

Murray, Utah

http://www.itt-tech.edu/

- **Proprietary** primarily 2-year, founded 1984, part of ITT Educational Services, Inc.
- **Suburban** campus
- **Coed**
- **Minimally difficult** entrance level

ACADEMICS
Calendar: quarters. *Degrees:* associate and bachelor's.

STUDENT LIFE
Housing options: college housing not available.

CONTACT
Director of Recruitment, ITT Technical Institute, 920 West Levoy Drive, Murray, UT 84123-2500. *Phone:* 801-263-3313. *Toll-free phone:* 800-365-2136.

★ Neumont University
Salt Lake City, Utah
http://www.neumont.edu/

- **Proprietary** comprehensive, founded 2002
- **Urban** campus with easy access to Salt Lake City
- **Coed** 397 undergraduate students, 100% full-time, 7% women, 93% men
- **Moderately difficult** entrance level, 84% of applicants were admitted

UNDERGRAD STUDENTS
397 full-time. 82% are from out of state; 5% Black or African American, non-Hispanic/Latino; 11% Hispanic/Latino; 3% Asian, non-Hispanic/Latino; 0.3% Native Hawaiian or other Pacific Islander, non-Hispanic/Latino; 0.3% American Indian or Alaska Native, non-Hispanic/Latino; 6% Two or more races, non-Hispanic/Latino; 19% Race/ethnicity unknown; 80% live on campus.

Freshmen
Admission: 605 applied, 507 admitted, 136 enrolled. ***Average high school GPA:*** 3.1. ***Test scores:*** SAT critical reading scores over 500: 74%; SAT math scores over 500: 80%; SAT writing scores over 500: 42%; ACT scores over 18: 94%; SAT critical reading scores over 600: 28%; SAT math scores over 600: 33%; SAT writing scores over 600: 13%; ACT scores over 24: 52%; SAT critical reading scores over 700: 7%; SAT math scores over 700: 12%; SAT writing scores over 700: 3%; ACT scores over 30: 14%.
Retention: 81% of full-time freshmen returned.

FACULTY
Total: 26, 58% full-time, 4% with terminal degrees.
Student/faculty ratio: 21:1.

ACADEMICS
Calendar: quarters. *Degrees:* bachelor's and master's.
Special study options: accelerated degree program, internships, services for LD students.
Computers: Students can access the following: campus intranet, computer help desk, free student e-mail accounts, online (class) grades, online (class) registration, online (class) schedules. Campuswide network is available. 100% of college-owned or -operated housing units are wired for high-speed Internet access. Wireless service is available via entire campus.

STUDENT LIFE
Housing options: men-only, women-only, special housing for students with disabilities. Campus housing is university owned and leased by the school. Freshman campus housing is guaranteed.
Activities and organizations: choral group, Neumont Tactical Federation, Epically Good Gamer's Group, Beyond The Screen Order, Rhythm Rockers Gaming Association, Unified Student Government.
Athletics ***Intramural sports:*** basketball M(c), soccer M(c), table tennis M(c)/W(c).
Student services: health clinic, personal/psychological counseling.

COSTS
Costs (2015–16) ***Tuition:*** $22,500 full-time, $495 per credit hour part-time. ***Required fees:*** $1500 full-time. ***Room only:*** $5400. Room and board charges vary according to housing facility. ***Payment plan:*** installment. ***Waivers:*** employees or children of employees.

APPLYING
Standardized Tests *Required:* SAT or ACT (for admission).
Options: electronic application.
Application fee: $35.
Required: essay or personal statement, high school transcript. ***Recommended:*** 2 letters of recommendation, interview.
Application deadlines: rolling (freshmen), rolling (transfers).

CONTACT
Karick Heaton, Director of Admissions, Neumont University, 143 South Main Street, Salt Lake City, UT 84111. *Phone:* 801-302-2879. *Toll-free phone:* 888-NEUMONT. *Fax:* 801-302-2811. *E-mail:* karick.heaton@neumont.edu.

Nightingale College
Ogden, Utah
http://www.nightingale.edu/

- **Proprietary** primarily 2-year
- **Suburban** campus with easy access to Salt Lake City
- **Coed**

ACADEMICS
Degree: diplomas and bachelor's.

APPLYING
Standardized Tests *Required:* Nightingale Entrance Exam (for admission).
Options: early admission.
Required: essay or personal statement, high school transcript, interview.

CONTACT
Nightingale College, 4155 Harrison Boulevard #100, Ogden, UT 84403.

Southern Utah University
Cedar City, Utah
http://www.suu.edu/

- **State-supported** comprehensive, founded 1897, part of Utah System of Higher Education
- **Small-town** 130-acre campus
- **Coed** 6,953 undergraduate students, 74% full-time, 55% women, 45% men
- **Moderately difficult** entrance level, 61% of applicants were admitted

UNDERGRAD STUDENTS
5,131 full-time, 1,822 part-time. Students come from 48 states and territories; 26 other countries; 20% are from out of state; 1% Black or African American, non-Hispanic/Latino; 5% Hispanic/Latino; 0.8% Asian, non-Hispanic/Latino; 1% Native Hawaiian or other Pacific Islander, non-Hispanic/Latino; 1% American Indian or Alaska Native, non-Hispanic/Latino; 0.8% Two or more races, non-Hispanic/Latino; 5% Race/ethnicity unknown; 5% international; 4% transferred in.

Freshmen
Admission: 8,268 applied, 5,046 admitted, 1,198 enrolled. ***Average high school GPA:*** 3.4. ***Test scores:*** SAT math scores over 500: 56%; SAT writing scores over 500: 50%; ACT scores over 18: 94%; SAT math scores over 600: 14%; SAT writing scores over 600: 14%; ACT scores over 24: 43%; SAT math scores over 700: 3%; SAT writing scores over 700: 2%; ACT scores over 30: 5%.
Retention: 66% of full-time freshmen returned.

FACULTY
Total: 281.

ACADEMICS
Calendar: semesters. *Degrees:* certificates, diplomas, associate, bachelor's, and master's.
Special study options: academic remediation for entering students, adult/continuing education programs, advanced placement credit, cooperative education, distance learning, double majors, English as a second language, honors programs, independent study, internships, part-time degree program, services for LD students, study abroad, summer session for credit. ***ROTC:*** Army (b).
Computers: Students can access the following: campus intranet, computer help desk, free student e-mail accounts, online (class) grades, online (class) registration, online (class) schedules. Campuswide network is available. 100% of college-owned or -operated housing units are wired

for high-speed Internet access. Wireless service is available via entire campus.

STUDENT LIFE

Housing options: coed, special housing for students with disabilities. Campus housing is university owned.

Activities and organizations: drama/theater group, student-run newspaper, radio and television station, choral group, national fraternities, national sororities.

Athletics Member NCAA. All Division I. ***Intercollegiate sports:*** basketball M(s)/W(s), cross-country running M(s)/W(s), football M(s), golf M(s)/W(s), gymnastics W(s), soccer W(s), softball W(s), tennis M(s)/W(s), track and field M(s)/W(s), volleyball W(s). ***Intramural sports:*** basketball M/W, cheerleading M(c)/W(c), golf M/W, soccer M/W, tennis M/W, volleyball M/W.

Campus security: 24-hour emergency response devices, student patrols, late-night transport/escort service, controlled dormitory access.

Student services: health clinic, personal/psychological counseling, women's center.

COSTS & FINANCIAL AID

Costs (2014–15) ***Tuition:*** state resident $5416 full-time, $254 per credit hour part-time; nonresident $17,874 full-time, $842 per credit hour part-time. Full-time tuition and fees vary according to program. Part-time tuition and fees vary according to course load and program. ***Required fees:*** $722 full-time, $361 per term part-time. ***Room only:*** $3100. Room and board charges vary according to board plan and housing facility. ***Payment plan:*** installment. ***Waivers:*** children of alumni, senior citizens, and employees or children of employees.

Financial Aid Of all full-time matriculated undergraduates who enrolled in 2013, 3,667 applied for aid, 3,302 were judged to have need, 161 had their need fully met. In 2013, 814 non-need-based awards were made. ***Average percent of need met:*** 45. ***Average financial aid package:*** $8272. ***Average need-based loan:*** $3843. ***Average need-based gift aid:*** $6413. ***Average non-need-based aid:*** $4704. ***Average indebtedness upon graduation:*** $14,978.

APPLYING

Standardized Tests *Required:* SAT or ACT (for admission).

Options: electronic application, deferred entrance.

Application fee: $50.

Required: high school transcript.

Application deadlines: 5/1 (freshmen), 5/1 (out-of-state freshmen).

Notification: continuous (freshmen), continuous (out-of-state freshmen).

CONTACT

Southern Utah University, 351 West University Boulevard, Cedar City, UT 84720-2498. *Phone:* 435-586-7740.

University of Utah

Salt Lake City, Utah

http://www.utah.edu/

- **State-supported** university, founded 1850, part of Utah System of Higher Education
- **Urban** 1535-acre campus with easy access to Salt Lake City
- **Endowment** $644.7 million
- **Coed** 23,907 undergraduate students, 72% full-time, 45% women, 55% men
- **Moderately difficult** entrance level, 81% of applicants were admitted

UNDERGRAD STUDENTS

17,137 full-time, 6,770 part-time. Students come from 52 states and territories; 120 other countries; 20% are from out of state; 1% Black or African American, non-Hispanic/Latino; 10% Hispanic/Latino; 5% Asian, non-Hispanic/Latino; 0.6% Native Hawaiian or other Pacific Islander, non-Hispanic/Latino; 0.5% American Indian or Alaska Native, non-Hispanic/Latino; 4% Two or more races, non-Hispanic/Latino; 3% Race/ethnicity unknown; 7% international; 7% transferred in; 13% live on campus.

Freshmen

Admission: 10,991 applied, 8,949 admitted, 3,151 enrolled. ***Average high school GPA:*** 3.57. ***Test scores:*** SAT critical reading scores over 500: 77%; SAT math scores over 500: 81%; SAT writing scores over 500: 73%; ACT scores over 18: 96%; SAT critical reading scores over 600: 39%; SAT math scores over 600: 45%; SAT writing scores over 600: 32%; ACT scores over 24: 59%; SAT critical reading scores over 700: 9%; SAT math scores over 700: 11%; SAT writing scores over 700: 5%; ACT scores over 30: 17%.

Retention: 89% of full-time freshmen returned.

FACULTY

Total: 1,865, 76% full-time, 77% with terminal degrees.

Student/faculty ratio: 17:1.

ACADEMICS

Calendar: semesters. *Degrees:* bachelor's, master's, doctoral, post-master's, and postbachelor's certificates.

Special study options: academic remediation for entering students, accelerated degree program, advanced placement credit, cooperative education, distance learning, double majors, English as a second language, freshman honors college, honors programs, independent study, internships, off-campus study, part-time degree program, services for LD students, student-designed majors, study abroad, summer session for credit. ***ROTC:*** Army (b), Navy (b), Air Force (b).

Unusual degree programs: 3-2 engineering; computer science, math, public policy.

Computers: 3,000 computers/terminals are available on campus for general student use. Students can access the following: campus intranet, computer help desk, free student e-mail accounts, online (class) grades, online (class) registration, online (class) schedules, online classes. Campuswide network is available. 100% of college-owned or -operated housing units are wired for high-speed Internet access. Wireless service is available via entire campus.

STUDENT LIFE

Housing options: coed, men-only, women-only, special housing for students with disabilities. Campus housing is university owned.

Activities and organizations: drama/theater group, student-run newspaper, radio and television station, choral group, marching band, Latter-Day Saints Student Association, Lowell Bennion Community Service Center, Newman Center, Center for Ethnic Student Affairs, national fraternities, national sororities.

Athletics Member NCAA. All Division I. ***Intercollegiate sports:*** baseball M(s), basketball M(s)/W(s), cheerleading M(s)/W(s), cross-country running W(s), fencing M(c)/W(c), football M(s), golf M(s), gymnastics W(s), ice hockey M(c), lacrosse M(c)/W(c), racquetball M(c)/W(c), riflery M(c)/W(c), rugby M(c), skiing (cross-country) M(s)/W(s), skiing (downhill) M(s)/W(s), soccer M(c)/W(s), softball W(s), swimming and diving M(s)/W(s), table tennis M(c)/W(c), tennis M(s)/W(s), track and field W(s), ultimate Frisbee M(c)/W(c), volleyball M(c)/W(s), water polo M(c)/W(c), wrestling M(c). ***Intramural sports:*** basketball M/W, fencing M/W, football M, racquetball M/W, soccer M/W, softball M/W, tennis M/W, ultimate Frisbee M/W, volleyball M/W, water polo M/W.

Campus security: 24-hour emergency response devices and patrols, student patrols, late-night transport/escort service, controlled dormitory access.

Student services: health clinic, personal/psychological counseling, women's center, legal services.

COSTS & FINANCIAL AID

Costs (2014–15) ***Tuition:*** state resident $6889 full-time, $194 per credit hour part-time; nonresident $24,111 full-time, $665 per credit hour part-time. Full-time tuition and fees vary according to course level, course load, degree level, program, and student level. Part-time tuition and fees vary according to course level, course load, degree level, program, and student level. ***Required fees:*** $946 full-time. ***Room and board:*** $8528; room only: $4338. Room and board charges vary according to board plan, housing facility, and location. ***Payment plans:*** installment, deferred payment. ***Waivers:*** senior citizens and employees or children of employees.

Financial Aid Of all full-time matriculated undergraduates who enrolled in 2014, 9,297 applied for aid, 7,730 were judged to have need, 648 had their need fully met. 357 Federal Work-Study jobs (averaging $4662). In 2014, 1907 non-need-based awards were made. ***Average percent of need met:*** 61. ***Average financial aid package:*** $18,259. ***Average need-based***

loan: $4322. ***Average need-based gift aid:*** $4618. ***Average non-need-based aid:*** $4661. ***Average indebtedness upon graduation:*** $20,019.

APPLYING

Standardized Tests *Required:* SAT or ACT (for admission). *Recommended:* ACT (for admission).

Options: electronic application, early admission, deferred entrance.

Application fee: $45.

Required: high school transcript, minimum 2.6 GPA. ***Required for some:*** essay or personal statement. ***Recommended:*** minimum 3.0 GPA.

Application deadlines: 4/1 (freshmen), 4/1 (out-of-state freshmen), 4/1 (transfers).

Notification: continuous (freshmen), continuous (out-of-state freshmen), continuous (transfers).

CONTACT

Mateo Remsburg, Associate Director, Office of Admissions, University of Utah, 201 S. 1460 E. Room 250 S, Salt Lake City, UT 84112. *Phone:* 801-581-8761. *Toll-free phone:* 800-685-8856. *Fax:* 801-585-3257. *E-mail:* mremsburg@sa.utah.edu.

Utah State University

Logan, Utah

http://www.usu.edu/

- **State-supported** university, founded 1888, part of Utah System of Higher Education
- **Urban** 456-acre campus
- **Endowment** $283.1 million
- **Coed** 24,271 undergraduate students, 65% full-time, 54% women, 46% men
- **Moderately difficult** entrance level, 98% of applicants were admitted

UNDERGRAD STUDENTS

15,823 full-time, 8,448 part-time. Students come from 53 states and territories; 46 other countries; 25% are from out of state; 0.9% Black or African American, non-Hispanic/Latino; 6% Hispanic/Latino; 1% Asian, non-Hispanic/Latino; 0.3% Native Hawaiian or other Pacific Islander, non-Hispanic/Latino; 2% American Indian or Alaska Native, non-Hispanic/Latino; 2% Two or more races, non-Hispanic/Latino; 5% Race/ethnicity unknown; 2% international; 7% transferred in.

Freshmen

Admission: 12,835 applied, 12,557 admitted, 4,071 enrolled. ***Average high school GPA:*** 3.45. ***Test scores:*** SAT critical reading scores over 500: 61%; SAT math scores over 500: 58%; ACT scores over 18: 90%; SAT critical reading scores over 600: 24%; SAT math scores over 600: 23%; ACT scores over 24: 46%; SAT critical reading scores over 700: 4%; SAT math scores over 700: 4%; ACT scores over 30: 9%.

Retention: 71% of full-time freshmen returned.

FACULTY

Total: 1,107, 79% full-time, 71% with terminal degrees.

Student/faculty ratio: 22:1.

ACADEMICS

Calendar: semesters. *Degrees:* certificates, associate, bachelor's, master's, doctoral, and postbachelor's certificates.

Special study options: academic remediation for entering students, accelerated degree program, adult/continuing education programs, advanced placement credit, cooperative education, distance learning, double majors, English as a second language, freshman honors college, honors programs, independent study, internships, off-campus study, part-time degree program, services for LD students, student-designed majors, study abroad, summer session for credit. ***ROTC:*** Army (b), Air Force (b).

Computers: 1,000 computers/terminals are available on campus for general student use. Students can access the following: computer help desk, free student e-mail accounts, online (class) grades, online (class) registration, online (class) schedules. Campuswide network is available. 100% of college-owned or -operated housing units are wired for high-speed Internet access. Wireless service is available via classrooms, computer centers, computer labs, dorm rooms, learning centers, libraries, student centers.

STUDENT LIFE

Housing options: coed, men-only, women-only, special housing for students with disabilities. Campus housing is university owned.

Activities and organizations: drama/theater group, student-run newspaper, radio station, choral group, marching band, Latter-Day Saints Student Association, multicultural clubs, volunteer groups, college councils, national fraternities, national sororities.

Athletics Member NCAA. All Division I except football (Division I-A). ***Intercollegiate sports:*** baseball M(c), basketball M(s)/W(s), cross-country running M(s)/W(s), equestrian sports M(c)/W(c), golf M(s), gymnastics W(s), ice hockey M(c), racquetball M(c)/W(c), rugby M(c)/W(c), soccer M(c)/W(s), softball W(s), tennis M(s)/W(s), track and field M(s)/W(s), volleyball M(c)/W(s). ***Intramural sports:*** badminton M/W, basketball M/W, football M/W, ice hockey W(c), lacrosse M(c)/W(c), racquetball M/W, soccer M/W, softball M/W, swimming and diving M(c)/W(c), table tennis M/W, tennis M/W, ultimate Frisbee M(c)/W(c), volleyball M/W.

Campus security: 24-hour emergency response devices and patrols, student patrols, late-night transport/escort service, video monitors in pedestrian tunnels.

Student services: health clinic, personal/psychological counseling, women's center, legal services.

COSTS & FINANCIAL AID

Costs (2014–15) ***Tuition:*** state resident $5454 full-time; nonresident $17,561 full-time. Full-time tuition and fees vary according to course level, course load, program, and reciprocity agreements. Part-time tuition and fees vary according to course level, course load, program, and reciprocity agreements. ***Required fees:*** $930 full-time. ***Room and board:*** $5680; room only: $1980. Room and board charges vary according to board plan and housing facility. ***Payment plan:*** deferred payment. ***Waivers:*** minority students, children of alumni, adult students, senior citizens, and employees or children of employees.

Financial Aid Of all full-time matriculated undergraduates who enrolled in 2013, 9,952 applied for aid, 8,678 were judged to have need, 814 had their need fully met. In 2013, 1152 non-need-based awards were made. ***Average percent of need met:*** 57. ***Average financial aid package:*** $8800. ***Average need-based loan:*** $4100. ***Average need-based gift aid:*** $6749. ***Average non-need-based aid:*** $4438. ***Average indebtedness upon graduation:*** $19,100.

APPLYING

Standardized Tests *Required:* SAT or ACT (for admission).

Options: electronic application, deferred entrance.

Application fee: $40.

Required: high school transcript. ***Recommended:*** minimum 2.8 GPA.

Application deadlines: rolling (freshmen), rolling (transfers).

Notification: continuous (freshmen), continuous (transfers).

CONTACT

Mr. Jeff Sorenson, Assistant Director, Admissions Office, Utah State University, 0160 Old Main Hill, Logan, UT 84322-0160. *Phone:* 435-797-1079. *Toll-free phone:* 800-488-8108. *Fax:* 435-797-3708. *E-mail:* admit@usu.edu.

Utah Valley University

Orem, Utah

http://www.uvu.edu/

- **State-supported** comprehensive, founded 1941, affiliated with Advent Christian Church, part of Utah System of Higher Education
- **Suburban** 537-acre campus with easy access to Salt Lake City
- **Coed** 31,163 undergraduate students, 52% full-time, 45% women, 55% men
- **Noncompetitive** entrance level, 100% of applicants were admitted

UNDERGRAD STUDENTS

16,259 full-time, 14,904 part-time. Students come from 50 states and territories; 72 other countries; 15% are from out of state; 0.9% Black or African American, non-Hispanic/Latino; 10% Hispanic/Latino; 1% Asian, non-Hispanic/Latino; 0.9% Native Hawaiian or other Pacific Islander, non-Hispanic/Latino; 0.7% American Indian or Alaska Native, non-Hispanic/Latino; 2% Two or more races, non-Hispanic/Latino; 2% Race/ethnicity unknown; 2% international; 7% transferred in.

Freshmen
Admission: 7,132 applied, 7,126 admitted, 3,528 enrolled. ***Average high school GPA:*** 3.27. ***Test scores:*** ACT scores over 18: 80%; ACT scores over 24: 33%; ACT scores over 30: 3%.

Retention: 60% of full-time freshmen returned.

FACULTY
Total: 1,708, 35% full-time, 27% with terminal degrees.

Student/faculty ratio: 22:1.

ACADEMICS
Calendar: semesters. *Degrees:* certificates, diplomas, associate, bachelor's, master's, and postbachelor's certificates.

Special study options: academic remediation for entering students, advanced placement credit, cooperative education, distance learning, double majors, English as a second language, honors programs, independent study, internships, off-campus study, part-time degree program, services for LD students, student-designed majors, study abroad, summer session for credit. ***ROTC:*** Army (b), Air Force (c).

Computers: 1,000 computers/terminals are available on campus for general student use. Students can access the following: campus intranet, computer help desk, free student e-mail accounts, online (class) grades, online (class) registration, online (class) schedules. Campuswide network is available. Wireless service is available via entire campus.

STUDENT LIFE
Housing options: college housing not available.

Activities and organizations: drama/theater group, student-run newspaper, television station, choral group, LDSSA Orem Institute, Center for the Advancement of Leadership.

Athletics Member NCAA. All Division I. ***Intercollegiate sports:*** baseball M(s), basketball M(s)/W(s), cross-country running M(s)/W(s), golf M(s)/W(s), soccer W(s), softball W(s), track and field M(s)/W(s), volleyball W(s), wrestling M(s).

Campus security: 24-hour patrols.

Student services: health clinic, personal/psychological counseling, women's center, legal services.

COSTS & FINANCIAL AID
Costs (2014–15) ***Tuition:*** state resident $4542 full-time, $189 per credit part-time; nonresident $14,074 full-time, $586 per credit part-time. Full-time tuition and fees vary according to course load and degree level. Part-time tuition and fees vary according to course load and degree level. ***Required fees:*** $728 full-time, $364 per term part-time, $364 per term part-time. ***Payment plans:*** installment, deferred payment. ***Waivers:*** employees or children of employees.

Financial Aid Of all full-time matriculated undergraduates who enrolled in 2014, 11,104 applied for aid, 10,116 were judged to have need, 724 had their need fully met. In 2014, 169 non-need-based awards were made. ***Average percent of need met:*** 63. ***Average financial aid package:*** $7777. ***Average need-based loan:*** $3087. ***Average need-based gift aid:*** $4814. ***Average non-need-based aid:*** $1841. ***Average indebtedness upon graduation:*** $16,784.

APPLYING
Standardized Tests *Required:* SAT or ACT (for admission).

Options: electronic application, deferred entrance.

Application fee: $35.

Required: high school transcript, ACT or SAT, or Accuplacer.

Application deadlines: 8/1 (freshmen), 8/1 (out-of-state freshmen), 8/1 (transfers).

Notification: continuous (freshmen), continuous (out-of-state freshmen), continuous (transfers).

CONTACT
Mrs. Liz Childs, Senior Director of Admissions, Utah Valley University, 800 West University Parkway, Orem, UT 84058-5999. *Phone:* 801-863-8460. *Fax:* 801-225-4677. *E-mail:* info@uvsc.edu.

Weber State University

Ogden, Utah

http://www.weber.edu/

- **State-supported** comprehensive, founded 1889, part of Utah System of Higher Education
- **Urban** 526-acre campus with easy access to Salt Lake City
- **Endowment** $119.9 million
- **Coed** 25,335 undergraduate students, 44% full-time, 54% women, 46% men
- **Noncompetitive** entrance level, 100% of applicants were admitted

UNDERGRAD STUDENTS
11,084 full-time, 14,251 part-time. Students come from 55 states and territories; 47 other countries; 10% are from out of state; 2% Black or African American, non-Hispanic/Latino; 10% Hispanic/Latino; 2% Asian, non-Hispanic/Latino; 0.5% Native Hawaiian or other Pacific Islander, non-Hispanic/Latino; 0.5% American Indian or Alaska Native, non-Hispanic/Latino; 2% Two or more races, non-Hispanic/Latino; 12% Race/ethnicity unknown; 2% international; 3% transferred in; 4% live on campus.

Freshmen
Admission: 5,188 applied, 5,188 admitted, 2,865 enrolled. ***Average high school GPA:*** 3.25. ***Test scores:*** ACT scores over 18: 77%; ACT scores over 24: 27%; ACT scores over 30: 3%.

Retention: 72% of full-time freshmen returned.

FACULTY
Total: 1,280, 38% full-time, 39% with terminal degrees.

Student/faculty ratio: 20:1.

ACADEMICS
Calendar: semesters. *Degrees:* certificates, associate, bachelor's, master's, and postbachelor's certificates.

Special study options: academic remediation for entering students, accelerated degree program, adult/continuing education programs, advanced placement credit, cooperative education, distance learning, double majors, English as a second language, external degree program, freshman honors college, honors programs, independent study, internships, off-campus study, part-time degree program, services for LD students, student-designed majors, study abroad, summer session for credit. ***ROTC:*** Army (b), Navy (c), Air Force (c).

Computers: 1,000 computers/terminals are available on campus for general student use. Students can access the following: campus intranet, computer help desk, free student e-mail accounts, online (class) grades, online (class) registration, online (class) schedules. Campuswide network is available. 100% of college-owned or -operated housing units are wired for high-speed Internet access. Wireless service is available via entire campus.

STUDENT LIFE
Housing options: men-only, women-only, cooperative, special housing for students with disabilities. Campus housing is university owned and is provided by a third party.

Activities and organizations: drama/theater group, student-run newspaper, radio and television station, choral group, marching band, LDSSA (Latter-day Saint Student Association), SAA (Student Alumni Association), GSA (Gay-Straight Alliance), Chinese Club, Golden Key Honor Society, national fraternities, national sororities.

Athletics Member NCAA. All Division I. ***Intercollegiate sports:*** archery M(c)/W(c), baseball M(c), basketball M(s)/W(s), bowling M(c)/W(c), cheerleading M(s)/W(s), cross-country running M/W, fencing M(c)/W(c), football M(s), golf M(s)/W(s), ice hockey M(c), lacrosse M(c)/W(c), racquetball M(c)/W(c), rock climbing M(c)/W(c), rugby M(c)/W(c), skiing (downhill) M(c)/W(c), soccer M(c)/W(s), softball W(s), swimming and diving M(c)/W(c), tennis M(s)/W(s), track and field M(s)/W(s), volleyball M(c)/W(s), weight lifting M(c)/W(c), wrestling M(c). ***Intramural sports:*** basketball M/W, racquetball M(c)/W(c), riflery M(c)/W(c), soccer M(c)/W, tennis M/W, ultimate Frisbee M(c)/W(c), volleyball M(c)/W(c).

Campus security: 24-hour emergency response devices and patrols, student patrols, late-night transport/escort service, controlled dormitory access.

Student services: health clinic, personal/psychological counseling, women's center, legal services.

COSTS & FINANCIAL AID

Costs (2014–15) ***Tuition:*** state resident $4326 full-time, $180 per credit hour part-time; nonresident $12,980 full-time, $540 per credit hour part-time. Full-time tuition and fees vary according to course level and course load. Part-time tuition and fees vary according to course level and course load. ***Required fees:*** $858 full-time, $36 per credit hour part-time. ***Room and board:*** $8400. Room and board charges vary according to board plan and housing facility. ***Payment plan:*** installment. ***Waivers:*** senior citizens and employees or children of employees.

Financial Aid Of all full-time matriculated undergraduates who enrolled in 2014, 7,573 applied for aid, 6,676 were judged to have need, 2,194 had their need fully met. ***Average financial aid package:*** $3282. ***Average need-based loan:*** $1934. ***Average need-based gift aid:*** $2347.

APPLYING

Standardized Tests *Required for some:* ACCUPLACER. *Recommended:* SAT or ACT (for admission).

Options: electronic application, early admission, deferred entrance.

Application fee: $30.

Required: high school transcript.

Application deadlines: 8/21 (freshmen), 8/21 (out-of-state freshmen), rolling (transfers).

Notification: continuous (freshmen), continuous (out-of-state freshmen), continuous (transfers).

CONTACT

Patrick Moody, Student Recruitment, Weber State University, 1137 University Circle, Ogden, UT 84408-1137. *Phone:* 801-626-8775. *Toll-free phone:* 800-848-7700 (in-state); 800-848-7770 (out-of-state). *Fax:* 801-626-6744. *E-mail:* admissions@weber.edu.

Western Governors University

Salt Lake City, Utah

http://www.wgu.edu/

- **Independent** comprehensive, founded 1998
- **Urban** campus
- **Coed** 44,499 undergraduate students, 100% full-time, 60% women, 40% men
- **Minimally difficult** entrance level

UNDERGRAD STUDENTS

44,499 full-time. Students come from 58 states and territories; 9% Black or African American, non-Hispanic/Latino; 8% Hispanic/Latino; 4% Asian, non-Hispanic/Latino; 0.5% Native Hawaiian or other Pacific Islander, non-Hispanic/Latino; 0.6% American Indian or Alaska Native, non-Hispanic/Latino; 3% Two or more races, non-Hispanic/Latino; 3% Race/ethnicity unknown; 0.1% international; 97% transferred in.

Freshmen

Admission: 92 enrolled.

Retention: 73% of full-time freshmen returned.

FACULTY

Total: 1,654, 66% full-time.

Student/faculty ratio: 41:1.

ACADEMICS

Calendar: continuous. *Degrees:* bachelor's, master's, and postbachelor's certificates.

Special study options: accelerated degree program, adult/continuing education programs, distance learning, double majors, external degree program, independent study, part-time degree program, services for LD students.

Computers: Students can access the following: online (class) grades, online (class) registration, online (class) schedules. Campuswide network is available.

STUDENT LIFE

Housing options: college housing not available.

COSTS & FINANCIAL AID

Costs (2014–15) ***One-time required fee:*** $65. ***Tuition:*** $5780 full-time. Full-time tuition and fees vary according to program. ***Required fees:*** $290 full-time.

Financial Aid Of all full-time matriculated undergraduates who enrolled in 2013, 23,111 applied for aid, 19,331 were judged to have need, 223 had their need fully met. ***Average percent of need met:*** 55. ***Average financial aid package:*** $5127. ***Average need-based loan:*** $5471. ***Average need-based gift aid:*** $3673. ***Average indebtedness upon graduation:*** $19,880.

APPLYING

Options: electronic application.

Application fee: $65.

Required for some: high school transcript.

CONTACT

Western Governors University, 4001 South 700 East, Suite 700, Salt Lake City, UT 84107. *Phone:* 801-274-3280 Ext. 336. *Toll-free phone:* 866-225-5948.

Westminster College

Salt Lake City, Utah

http://www.westminstercollege.edu/

- **Independent** comprehensive, founded 1875
- **Suburban** 27-acre campus
- **Endowment** $72.5 million
- **Coed** 2,233 undergraduate students, 93% full-time, 54% women, 46% men
- **Moderately difficult** entrance level, 97% of applicants were admitted

UNDERGRAD STUDENTS

2,075 full-time, 158 part-time. Students come from 48 states and territories; 23 other countries; 40% are from out of state; 1% Black or African American, non-Hispanic/Latino; 9% Hispanic/Latino; 2% Asian, non-Hispanic/Latino; 0.2% Native Hawaiian or other Pacific Islander, non-Hispanic/Latino; 0.4% American Indian or Alaska Native, non-Hispanic/Latino; 3% Two or more races, non-Hispanic/Latino; 7% Race/ethnicity unknown; 5% international; 9% transferred in; 32% live on campus.

Freshmen

Admission: 1,784 applied, 1,737 admitted, 485 enrolled. ***Average high school GPA:*** 3.57. ***Test scores:*** SAT critical reading scores over 500: 75%; SAT math scores over 500: 76%; ACT scores over 18: 97%; SAT critical reading scores over 600: 34%; SAT math scores over 600: 35%; ACT scores over 24: 59%; SAT critical reading scores over 700: 4%; SAT math scores over 700: 5%; ACT scores over 30: 11%.

Retention: 72% of full-time freshmen returned.

FACULTY

Total: 387, 42% full-time, 53% with terminal degrees.

Student/faculty ratio: 9:1.

ACADEMICS

Calendar: 4-4-1. *Degrees:* bachelor's, master's, and postbachelor's certificates.

Special study options: academic remediation for entering students, accelerated degree program, advanced placement credit, cooperative education, distance learning, double majors, English as a second language, external degree program, freshman honors college, honors programs, independent study, internships, off-campus study, part-time degree program, services for LD students, student-designed majors, study abroad, summer session for credit. ***ROTC:*** Army (c), Navy (c), Air Force (c).

Unusual degree programs: 3-2 engineering with University of Southern California, Washington University in St. Louis.

Computers: 244 computers/terminals and 457 ports are available on campus for general student use. Students can access the following: campus intranet, computer help desk, free student e-mail accounts, online (class) grades, online (class) registration, online (class) schedules. Campuswide network is available. 100% of college-owned or -operated housing units are wired for high-speed Internet access. Wireless service is available via entire campus.

STUDENT LIFE
Housing options: on-campus residence required through sophomore year; coed, special housing for students with disabilities. Campus housing is university owned and leased by the school. Freshman campus housing is guaranteed.

Activities and organizations: drama/theater group, student-run newspaper, choral group, Associated Students of Westminster College (Student Government), Associated Residents of Westminster College (Residential Government), Westminster Ski and Snowboard Club (WSSC), V-Day, Westminster Entrepreneurship Club.

Athletics Member NAIA. ***Intercollegiate sports:*** basketball M(s)/W(s), cross-country running M(s)/W(s), golf M(s)/W(s), lacrosse M(s)/W(s), skiing (downhill) M(s)/W(s), soccer M(s)/W(s), track and field M(s)/W(s), volleyball W(s). ***Intramural sports:*** basketball M/W, skiing (cross-country) M/W, soccer M/W, volleyball M/W.

Campus security: 24-hour emergency response devices and patrols, student patrols, late-night transport/escort service, controlled dormitory access.

Student services: health clinic, personal/psychological counseling.

COSTS & FINANCIAL AID
Costs (2014–15) ***Comprehensive fee:*** $38,820 includes full-time tuition ($29,856), mandatory fees ($508), and room and board ($8456). Full-time tuition and fees vary according to course load and program. Part-time tuition: $1244 per credit hour. Part-time tuition and fees vary according to course load and program. ***Room and board:*** Room and board charges vary according to board plan. ***Payment plans:*** installment, deferred payment. ***Waivers:*** employees or children of employees.

Financial Aid Of all full-time matriculated undergraduates who enrolled in 2014, 1,417 applied for aid, 1,222 were judged to have need, 261 had their need fully met. 410 Federal Work-Study jobs (averaging $2514). In 2014, 635 non-need-based awards were made. ***Average percent of need met:*** 76. ***Average financial aid package:*** $23,513. ***Average need-based loan:*** $4833. ***Average need-based gift aid:*** $18,811. ***Average non-need-based aid:*** $13,176. ***Average indebtedness upon graduation:*** $27,523.

APPLYING
Standardized Tests *Required:* SAT or ACT (for admission).

Options: electronic application, deferred entrance.

Application fee: $50.

Required: essay or personal statement, high school transcript, minimum 2.5 GPA, 1 letter of recommendation. ***Recommended:*** interview.

Application deadlines: rolling (freshmen), rolling (out-of-state freshmen), rolling (transfers).

Notification: continuous (freshmen), continuous (out-of-state freshmen), continuous (transfers).

CONTACT
Elizabeth Key, Associate Vice President for Enrollment Management, Westminster College, 1840 South 1300 East, Salt Lake City, UT 84105-3697. *Phone:* 801-832-2200. *Toll-free phone:* 800-748-4753. *Fax:* 801-832-3101. *E-mail:* admission@westminstercollege.edu.

VERMONT

Bennington College

Bennington, Vermont

http://www.bennington.edu/

- **Independent** comprehensive, founded 1932
- **Small-town** 440-acre campus with easy access to Albany, NY
- **Endowment** $15.6 million
- **Coed** 660 undergraduate students, 95% full-time, 66% women, 34% men
- **Very difficult** entrance level, 67% of applicants were admitted

UNDERGRAD STUDENTS
629 full-time, 31 part-time. Students come from 41 states and territories; 44 other countries; 97% are from out of state; 1% Black or African American, non-Hispanic/Latino; 5% Hispanic/Latino; 3% Asian, non-Hispanic/Latino; 2% American Indian or Alaska Native, non-Hispanic/Latino; 3% Two or more races, non-Hispanic/Latino; 4% Race/ethnicity unknown; 13% international; 1% transferred in; 95% live on campus.

Freshmen
Admission: 1,101 applied, 740 admitted, 192 enrolled. ***Test scores:*** SAT critical reading scores over 500: 97%; SAT math scores over 500: 96%; SAT writing scores over 500: 98%; ACT scores over 18: 101%; SAT critical reading scores over 600: 80%; SAT math scores over 600: 58%; SAT writing scores over 600: 75%; ACT scores over 24: 97%; SAT critical reading scores over 700: 32%; SAT math scores over 700: 17%; SAT writing scores over 700: 25%; ACT scores over 30: 43%.

Retention: 84% of full-time freshmen returned.

FACULTY
Total: 107, 53% full-time, 67% with terminal degrees.

Student/faculty ratio: 9:1.

ACADEMICS
Calendar: semesters plus winter work term in January and February. *Degrees:* bachelor's, master's, and postbachelor's certificates.

Special study options: double majors, independent study, internships, off-campus study, services for LD students, student-designed majors, study abroad.

Computers: 40 computers/terminals are available on campus for general student use. Students can access the following: campus intranet, computer help desk, free student e-mail accounts, online (class) schedules. Campuswide network is available. 100% of college-owned or -operated housing units are wired for high-speed Internet access. Wireless service is available via entire campus.

STUDENT LIFE
Housing options: on-campus residence required through senior year; coed. Campus housing is university owned. Freshman campus housing is guaranteed.

Activities and organizations: drama/theater group, student-run newspaper, choral group, Program Activity Council, Bennington Free Press, Student Endowment for the Arts, SILO: Student Journal of Arts and Letters, Bennington Zombie Defense: Humans vs. Zombies Game.

Athletics ***Intercollegiate sports:*** basketball M(c)/W(c), fencing M(c)/W(c), soccer M(c)/W(c), ultimate Frisbee M(c)/W(c), volleyball M(c)/W(c). ***Intramural sports:*** archery M/W, badminton M/W, basketball M/W, bowling M/W, cheerleading M/W, cross-country running M/W, equestrian sports M/W, golf M/W, skiing (cross-country) M/W, skiing (downhill) M/W, softball M/W, table tennis M/W, tennis M/W, volleyball M/W, weight lifting M/W.

Campus security: 24-hour emergency response devices and patrols, late-night transport/escort service, prevention/awareness program.

Student services: health clinic, personal/psychological counseling.

COSTS & FINANCIAL AID
Costs (2014–15) ***Comprehensive fee:*** $60,310 includes full-time tuition ($46,048), mandatory fees ($610), and room and board ($13,652). Part-time tuition: $1535 per credit hour. ***College room only:*** $7328. Room and board charges vary according to board plan. ***Payment plan:*** installment. ***Waivers:*** employees or children of employees.

Financial Aid Of all full-time matriculated undergraduates who enrolled in 2014, 448 applied for aid, 448 were judged to have need, 44 had their need fully met. In 2014, 142 non-need-based awards were made. ***Average percent of need met:*** 58. ***Average financial aid package:*** $42,405. ***Average need-based loan:*** $3891. ***Average need-based gift aid:*** $24,475. ***Average non-need-based aid:*** $13,181. ***Average indebtedness upon graduation:*** $26,073. ***Financial aid deadline:*** 2/15.

APPLYING
Options: electronic application, early admission, early decision, early action, deferred entrance.

Application fee: $60.

Required: essay or personal statement, high school transcript, 2 letters of recommendation, graded analytic paper. ***Recommended:*** interview.

Application deadlines: 1/15 (freshmen), 1/15 (out-of-state freshmen), 3/15 (transfers), 12/1 (early action).

Early decision deadline: 11/15 (for plan 1), 1/15 (for plan 2).

CONTACT
Ms. Lauren Magrath, Director of Admissions, Bennington College, One College Drive, Bennington, VT 05201-6003. *Phone:* 802-440-4312. *Toll-free phone:* 800-833-6845. *Fax:* 802-440-4320. *E-mail:* admissions@bennington.edu.

Castleton State College

Castleton, Vermont

http://www.castleton.edu/

- **State-supported** comprehensive, founded 1787, part of Vermont State Colleges System
- **Rural** 165-acre campus
- **Endowment** $7.5 million
- **Coed** 1,985 undergraduate students, 87% full-time, 52% women, 48% men
- **Moderately difficult** entrance level, 78% of applicants were admitted

UNDERGRAD STUDENTS
1,720 full-time, 265 part-time. Students come from 26 states and territories; 17 other countries; 30% are from out of state; 2% Black or African American, non-Hispanic/Latino; 2% Hispanic/Latino; 0.7% Asian, non-Hispanic/Latino; 0.5% American Indian or Alaska Native, non-Hispanic/Latino; 2% Two or more races, non-Hispanic/Latino; 6% Race/ethnicity unknown; 2% international; 9% transferred in; 54% live on campus.

Freshmen
Admission: 2,397 applied, 1,868 admitted, 369 enrolled. ***Average high school GPA:*** 3. ***Test scores:*** SAT critical reading scores over 500: 40%; SAT math scores over 500: 44%; SAT writing scores over 500: 36%; ACT scores over 18: 82%; SAT critical reading scores over 600: 9%; SAT math scores over 600: 10%; SAT writing scores over 600: 8%; ACT scores over 24: 13%; SAT critical reading scores over 700: 1%; SAT math scores over 700: 1%; SAT writing scores over 700: 1%.
Retention: 70% of full-time freshmen returned.

FACULTY
Total: 228, 45% full-time, 58% with terminal degrees.
Student/faculty ratio: 13:1.

ACADEMICS
Calendar: semesters. *Degrees:* associate, bachelor's, master's, post-master's, and postbachelor's certificates.
Special study options: academic remediation for entering students, advanced placement credit, cooperative education, double majors, honors programs, independent study, internships, off-campus study, part-time degree program, services for LD students, student-designed majors, study abroad, summer session for credit. ***ROTC:*** Army (b).
Unusual degree programs: business administration.
Computers: 250 computers/terminals are available on campus for general student use. Students can access the following: campus intranet, computer help desk, free student e-mail accounts, online (class) grades, online (class) registration, online (class) schedules, Castleton app for smartphones/tablets. Campuswide network is available. 100% of college-owned or -operated housing units are wired for high-speed Internet access. Wireless service is available via entire campus.

STUDENT LIFE
Housing options: on-campus residence required for freshman year; coed. Campus housing is university owned. Freshman campus housing is guaranteed.
Activities and organizations: drama/theater group, student-run newspaper, radio station, choral group, marching band, community service, clubs in the academic majors, Women's issues organization, Spanish and International, Skiing/Snowboarding.
Athletics Member NCAA. All Division III. ***Intercollegiate sports:*** baseball M, basketball M/W, cheerleading M(c)/W(c), cross-country running M/W, equestrian sports W(c), field hockey W, football M, golf M, ice hockey M/W, lacrosse M/W, rugby M(c)/W(c), skiing (downhill) M/W, soccer M/W, softball W, tennis M/W, volleyball W. ***Intramural sports:*** basketball M/W, racquetball M/W, rock climbing M/W, soccer M/W, softball M/W, table tennis M/W, tennis M/W, track and field M(c)/W(c), volleyball M/W, water polo M/W.

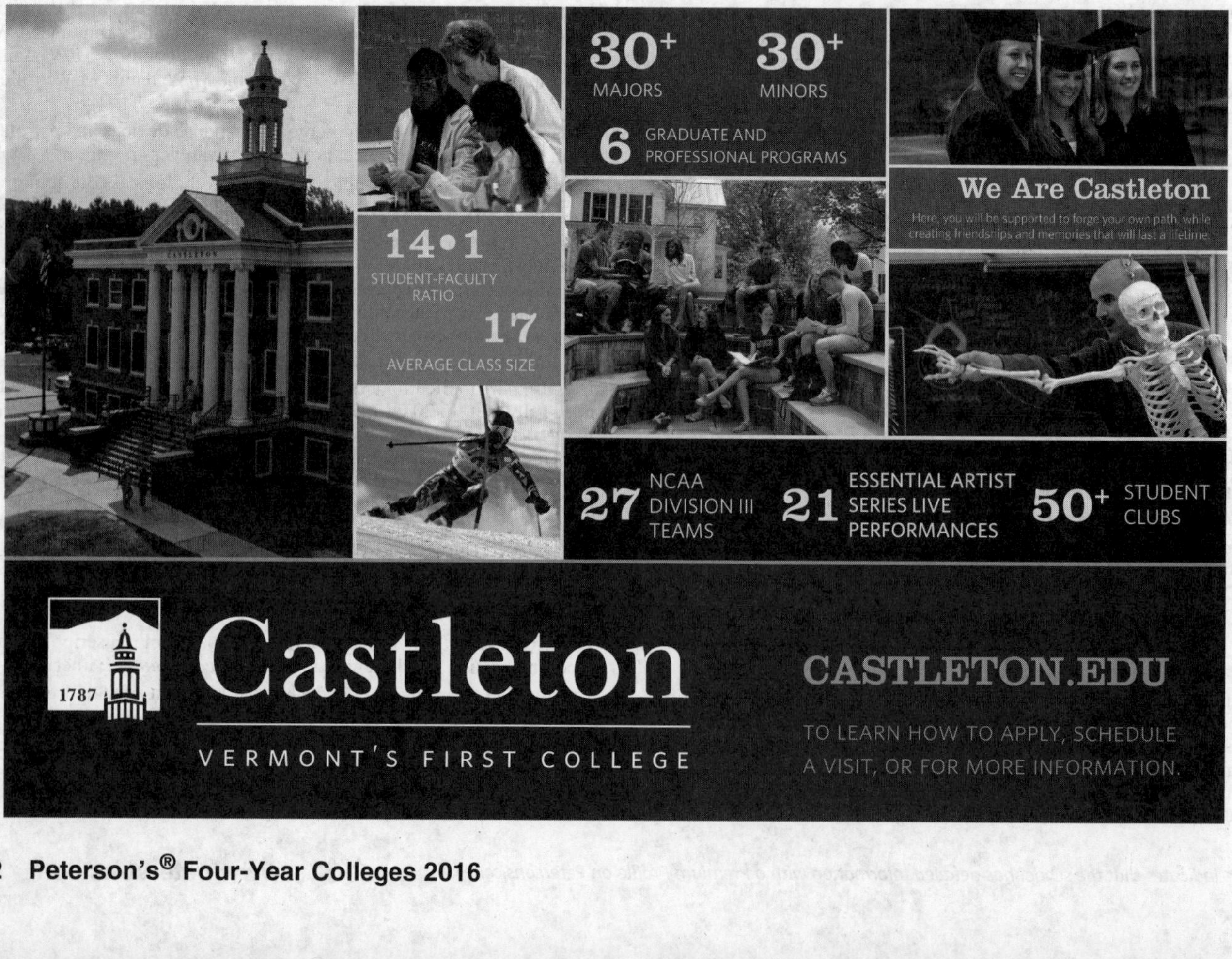

30+ MAJORS
30+ MINORS
6 GRADUATE AND PROFESSIONAL PROGRAMS
We Are Castleton
Here, you will be supported to forge your own path, while creating friendships and memories that will last a lifetime.
14•1 STUDENT-FACULTY RATIO
17 AVERAGE CLASS SIZE
27 NCAA DIVISION III TEAMS
21 ESSENTIAL ARTIST SERIES LIVE PERFORMANCES
50+ STUDENT CLUBS
1787
Castleton
VERMONT'S FIRST COLLEGE
CASTLETON.EDU
TO LEARN HOW TO APPLY, SCHEDULE A VISIT, OR FOR MORE INFORMATION.

Campus security: 24-hour emergency response devices and patrols, student patrols, late-night transport/escort service, controlled dormitory access.

Student services: health clinic, personal/psychological counseling.

COSTS & FINANCIAL AID

Costs (2014–15) ***One-time required fee:*** $200. ***Tuition:*** state resident $9768 full-time, $407 per credit part-time; nonresident $24,432 full-time, $1018 per credit part-time. Full-time tuition and fees vary according to course load and program. Part-time tuition and fees vary according to course load and program. ***Required fees:*** $1004 full-time, $42 per credit part-time, $502 per term part-time. ***Room and board:*** $9414; room only: $5606. Room and board charges vary according to board plan. ***Payment plan:*** installment. ***Waivers:*** senior citizens and employees or children of employees.

Financial Aid Of all full-time matriculated undergraduates who enrolled in 2012, 349 Federal Work-Study jobs (averaging $1150).

APPLYING

Standardized Tests *Required:* SAT or ACT (for admission).

Options: electronic application, deferred entrance.

Application fee: $40.

Required: essay or personal statement, high school transcript, minimum 3.0 GPA, 2 letters of recommendation. ***Recommended:*** Visits to campus, though not required, are highly recommended.

Application deadlines: rolling (freshmen), rolling (out-of-state freshmen), rolling (transfers).

Notification: continuous (freshmen), continuous (out-of-state freshmen), continuous (transfers).

CONTACT

Mr. Maurice Ouimet Jr., Dean of Enrollment, Castleton State College, 62 Alumni Drive, Woodruff Hall, Castleton, VT 05735. *Phone:* 802-468-1213. *Toll-free phone:* 800-639-8521. *Fax:* 802-468-1476. *E-mail:* info@castleton.edu.

See previous page for display ad and page 1388 for the College Close-Up.

Champlain College

Burlington, Vermont

http://www.champlain.edu/

- **Independent** comprehensive, founded 1878
- **Urban** 22-acre campus with easy access to Montreal
- **Endowment** $14.6 million
- **Coed** 3,124 undergraduate students, 74% full-time, 40% women, 60% men
- **Moderately difficult** entrance level, 64% of applicants were admitted

UNDERGRAD STUDENTS

2,309 full-time, 815 part-time. Students come from 52 states and territories; 25 other countries; 69% are from out of state; 3% Black or African American, non-Hispanic/Latino; 4% Hispanic/Latino; 2% Asian, non-Hispanic/Latino; 0.1% Native Hawaiian or other Pacific Islander, non-Hispanic/Latino; 0.5% American Indian or Alaska Native, non-Hispanic/Latino; 2% Two or more races, non-Hispanic/Latino; 16% Race/ethnicity unknown; 1% international; 2% transferred in; 62% live on campus.

Freshmen

Admission: 5,600 applied, 3,596 admitted, 637 enrolled. ***Average high school GPA:*** 3.15. ***Test scores:*** SAT critical reading scores over 500: 85%; SAT math scores over 500: 80%; SAT writing scores over 500: 74%; ACT scores over 18: 98%; SAT critical reading scores over 600: 41%; SAT math scores over 600: 37%; SAT writing scores over 600: 27%; ACT scores over 24: 69%; SAT critical reading scores over 700: 8%; SAT math scores over 700: 6%; SAT writing scores over 700: 3%; ACT scores over 30: 20%.

Retention: 81% of full-time freshmen returned.

FACULTY

Total: 408, 26% full-time, 32% with terminal degrees.

Student/faculty ratio: 14:1.

ACADEMICS

Calendar: semesters. *Degrees:* certificates, associate, bachelor's, master's, and postbachelor's certificates.

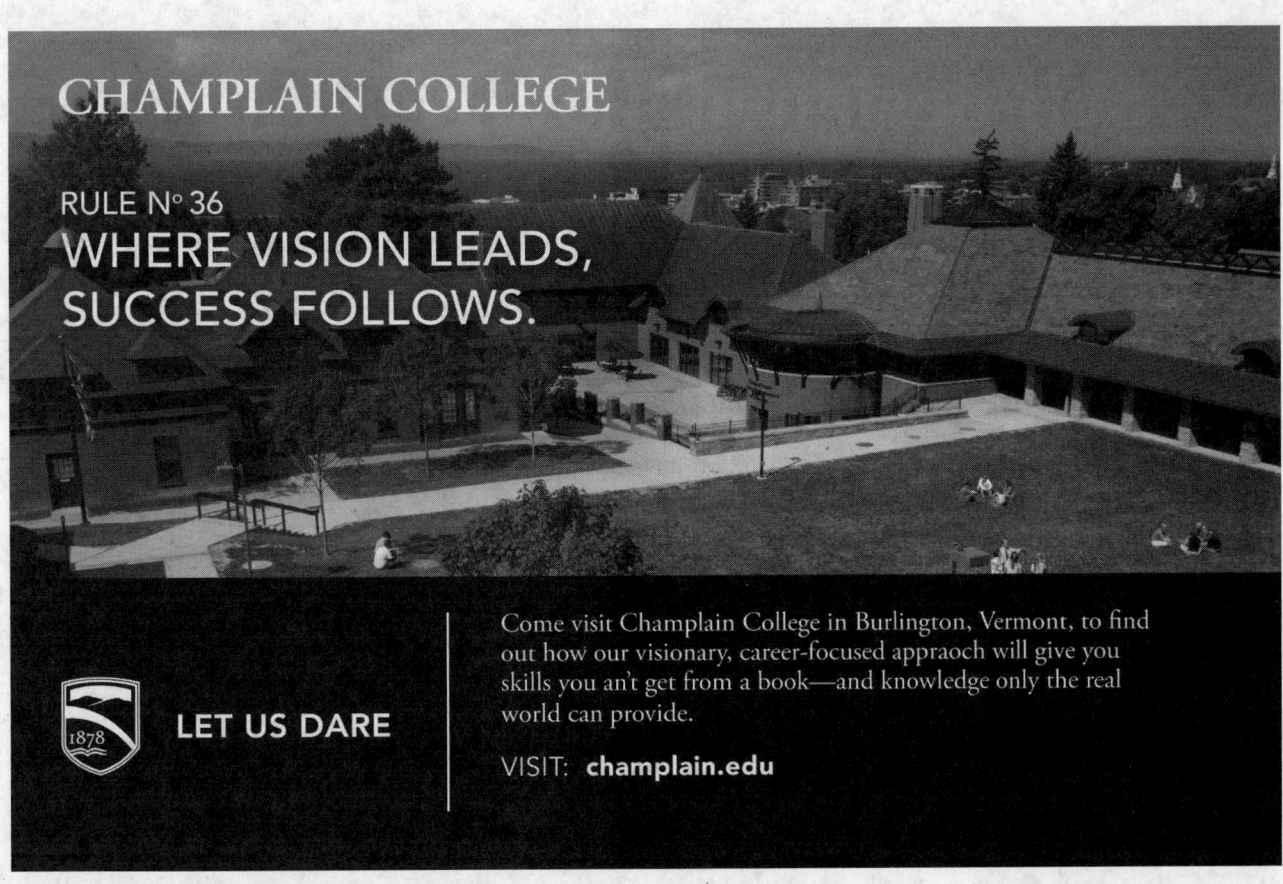

Special study options: adult/continuing education programs, advanced placement credit, cooperative education, distance learning, double majors, independent study, internships, off-campus study, part-time degree program, services for LD students, study abroad, summer session for credit. ***ROTC:*** Army (c).

Computers: 640 computers/terminals are available on campus for general student use. Students can access the following: campus intranet, computer help desk, free student e-mail accounts, online (class) grades, online (class) registration, online (class) schedules. Campuswide network is available. 100% of college-owned or -operated housing units are wired for high-speed Internet access. Wireless service is available via entire campus.

STUDENT LIFE

Housing options: coed, women-only. Campus housing is university owned and leased by the school. Freshman campus housing is guaranteed.

Activities and organizations: drama/theater group, student-run newspaper, choral group, Diversity Champlain, International Club, community service organization, Champlain Players (theater group), Outing Club/Skiing Snowboarding Club.

Athletics ***Intramural sports:*** basketball M/W, cross-country running M/W, golf M/W, ice hockey M/W, rock climbing M/W, rugby M/W, sailing M/W, skiing (cross-country) M/W, skiing (downhill) M(c)/W(c), soccer M/W, softball M/W, ultimate Frisbee M/W, volleyball M/W.

Campus security: 24-hour emergency response devices and patrols, late-night transport/escort service, controlled dormitory access.

Student services: health clinic, personal/psychological counseling.

COSTS & FINANCIAL AID

Costs (2014–15) ***Comprehensive fee:*** $46,650 includes full-time tuition ($32,800), mandatory fees ($100), and room and board ($13,750). Part-time tuition: $1367 per credit hour. ***Payment plans:*** tuition prepayment, installment. ***Waivers:*** employees or children of employees.

Financial Aid Of all full-time matriculated undergraduates who enrolled in 2014, 1,852 applied for aid, 1,620 were judged to have need, 207 had their need fully met. In 2014, 457 non-need-based awards were made. ***Average percent of need met:*** 66. ***Average financial aid package:*** $21,773. ***Average need-based loan:*** $4650. ***Average need-based gift aid:*** $15,566. ***Average non-need-based aid:*** $8144. ***Average indebtedness upon graduation:*** $35,444. ***Financial aid deadline:*** 2/15.

APPLYING

Standardized Tests *Required:* SAT or ACT (for admission). *Required for some:* SAT Subject Tests (for admission).

Options: electronic application, early decision.

Required: essay or personal statement, high school transcript. ***Recommended:*** 2 letters of recommendation, interview.

Application deadlines: 2/1 (freshmen), rolling (transfers).

Early decision deadline: 11/15 (for plan 1), 1/15 (for plan 2).

Notification: 3/25 (freshmen), continuous (transfers), 12/15 (early decision plan 1), 2/15 (early decision plan 2).

CONTACT

Sarah Andriano, Director of Admissions, Champlain College, PO Box 670, Burlington, VT 05401. *Phone:* 802-860-2727. *Toll-free phone:* 800-570-5858. *Fax:* 802-860-2767. *E-mail:* admission@champlain.edu.

See previous page for display ad and page 1392 for the College Close-Up.

★ Goddard College
Plainfield, Vermont
http://www.goddard.edu/

- **Independent** comprehensive, founded 1938
- **Rural** 200-acre campus
- **Endowment** $1.1 million
- **Coed** 191 undergraduate students, 100% full-time, 63% women, 37% men
- **Minimally difficult** entrance level, 83% of applicants were admitted

UNDERGRAD STUDENTS

191 full-time. Students come from 25 states and territories; 89% are from out of state; 6% Black or African American, non-Hispanic/Latino; 5% Hispanic/Latino; 2% Asian, non-Hispanic/Latino; 2% Two or more races, non-Hispanic/Latino; 11% Race/ethnicity unknown; 23% transferred in.

Freshmen
Admission: 6 applied, 5 admitted, 5 enrolled.
Retention: 74% of full-time freshmen returned.

FACULTY
Total: 94, 16% full-time, 82% with terminal degrees.

ACADEMICS
Calendar: semesters. *Degrees:* bachelor's and master's.

Special study options: accelerated degree program, adult/continuing education programs, advanced placement credit, distance learning, double majors, external degree program, independent study, internships, off-campus study, services for LD students, student-designed majors, study abroad.

Computers: 55 computers/terminals are available on campus for general student use. Students can access the following: campus intranet, computer help desk, free student e-mail accounts, online (class) registration, online (class) schedules, library services. Campuswide network is available. 80% of college-owned or -operated housing units are wired for high-speed Internet access. Wireless service is available via entire campus.

STUDENT LIFE
Housing options: coed, women-only, special housing for students with disabilities. Campus housing is university owned.

Activities and organizations: student-run radio station.

Campus security: 24-hour patrols, patrols by trained security personnel 9 pm to 6 am.

Student services: personal/psychological counseling.

COSTS & FINANCIAL AID
Costs (2014–15) ***Comprehensive fee:*** $16,418 includes full-time tuition ($14,738), mandatory fees ($192), and room and board ($1488). Full-time tuition and fees vary according to course load, location, program, and reciprocity agreements. Part-time tuition and fees vary according to program. ***Room and board:*** Room and board charges vary according to location. ***Payment plan:*** installment. ***Waivers:*** employees or children of employees.

Financial Aid Of all full-time matriculated undergraduates who enrolled in 2010, 315 applied for aid, 273 were judged to have need, 6 had their need fully met. ***Average percent of need met:*** 41. ***Average financial aid package:*** $7824. ***Average need-based loan:*** $4329. ***Average need-based gift aid:*** $4539. ***Average indebtedness upon graduation:*** $23,228.

APPLYING
Options: electronic application, deferred entrance.

Application fee: $40.

Required: essay or personal statement, 2 letters of recommendation, interview. ***Required for some:*** high school transcript, 3 letters of recommendation. ***Recommended:*** Four years of English, Mathematics, Social Studies, Natural Sciences; three years of lab science and two years of a foreign language. Creative portfolio for those applying in the arts.

Application deadlines: rolling (freshmen), rolling (out-of-state freshmen), rolling (transfers).

Notification: continuous (freshmen), continuous (out-of-state freshmen), continuous (transfers).

CONTACT
Jen Morin, Admissions Counselor, Goddard College, 123 Pitkin Road, Plainfield, VT 05667-9432. *Phone:* 802-322-1670. *Toll-free phone:* 800-906-8312. *Fax:* 802-454-1029. *E-mail:* admissions@goddard.edu.

See previous page for display ad and page 1458 for the College Close-Up.

Green Mountain College

Poultney, Vermont

http://www.greenmtn.edu/

- **Independent** comprehensive, founded 1834
- **Small-town** 155-acre campus
- **Endowment** $3.9 million
- **Coed** 572 undergraduate students, 97% full-time, 51% women, 49% men
- **Moderately difficult** entrance level, 68% of applicants were admitted

UNDERGRAD STUDENTS
557 full-time, 15 part-time. Students come from 39 states and territories; 15 other countries; 86% are from out of state; 5% Black or African American, non-Hispanic/Latino; 4% Hispanic/Latino; 1% Asian, non-Hispanic/Latino; 0.7% American Indian or Alaska Native, non-Hispanic/Latino; 0.9% Two or more races, non-Hispanic/Latino; 27% Race/ethnicity unknown; 3% international; 8% transferred in; 83% live on campus.

Freshmen
Admission: 973 applied, 665 admitted, 131 enrolled. ***Average high school GPA:*** 2.7.
Retention: 69% of full-time freshmen returned.

FACULTY
Total: 84, 49% full-time, 54% with terminal degrees.
Student/faculty ratio: 14:1.

ACADEMICS
Calendar: semesters. *Degrees:* certificates, bachelor's, and master's.

Special study options: accelerated degree program, adult/continuing education programs, advanced placement credit, cooperative education, distance learning, double majors, English as a second language, honors programs, independent study, internships, off-campus study, part-time degree program, services for LD students, student-designed majors, study abroad, summer session for credit.

Unusual degree programs: 3-2 Vermont Law School - Environmental Law & Policy, Juris Doctorate, Energy Regulation & Law.

Computers: 105 computers/terminals are available on campus for general student use. Students can access the following: campus intranet, computer help desk, free student e-mail accounts, online (class) grades, online (class) registration, online (class) schedules, personal network folders, electronic course folders. Campuswide network is available. 100% of college-owned or -operated housing units are wired for high-speed Internet access. Wireless service is available via computer labs, libraries, student centers.

STUDENT LIFE
Housing options: on-campus residence required through senior year; coed. Campus housing is university owned. Freshman campus housing is guaranteed.

Activities and organizations: drama/theater group, student-run newspaper, radio station, choral group, Student Government Association, Green Mountain College Ultimate Frisbee, Diversity, College Programming Board, International Awareness Club.

Athletics Member NCAA. All Division III. ***Intercollegiate sports:*** basketball M/W, cross-country running M/W, lacrosse M/W, soccer M/W, tennis M, track and field M/W, volleyball W. ***Intramural sports:*** golf M(c)/W(c), rugby M(c)/W(c), ultimate Frisbee M(c)/W(c).

Campus security: 24-hour emergency response devices and patrols, late-night transport/escort service.

Student services: personal/psychological counseling.

COSTS & FINANCIAL AID
Costs (2014–15) ***Comprehensive fee:*** $45,228 includes full-time tuition ($32,594), mandatory fees ($1142), and room and board ($11,492). ***Payment plan:*** installment.

Financial Aid Of all full-time matriculated undergraduates who enrolled in 2012, 520 applied for aid, 486 were judged to have need, 52 had their need fully met. 188 Federal Work-Study jobs (averaging $1700). 122 state and other part-time jobs (averaging $1700). In 2012, 110 non-need-based awards were made. ***Average percent of need met:*** 67. ***Average financial aid package:*** $23,458. ***Average need-based loan:*** $3753. ***Average need-based gift aid:*** $19,712. ***Average non-need-based aid:*** $13,191. ***Average indebtedness upon graduation:*** $42,269.

APPLYING
Standardized Tests *Recommended:* SAT or ACT (for admission).

Options: electronic application, deferred entrance.

Required: essay or personal statement, high school transcript, 1 letter of recommendation. ***Required for some:*** interview. ***Recommended:*** minimum 2.5 GPA, interview.

Application deadlines: rolling (freshmen), rolling (transfers).

Notification: continuous until 8/15 (freshmen), continuous until 8/15 (transfers).

CONTACT
Green Mountain College, One Brennan Circle, Poultney, VT 05764.
Phone: 802-287-2150. *Toll-free phone:* 800-776-6675.

★ Johnson State College
Johnson, Vermont
http://www.jsc.edu/

- **State-supported** comprehensive, founded 1828, part of Vermont State Colleges System
- **Rural** 350-acre campus with easy access to Montreal
- **Endowment** $2.3 million
- **Coed** 1,458 undergraduate students, 67% full-time, 64% women, 36% men
- **Moderately difficult** entrance level, 86% of applicants were admitted

UNDERGRAD STUDENTS
979 full-time, 479 part-time. Students come from 18 states and territories; 20 other countries; 19% are from out of state; 2% Black or African American, non-Hispanic/Latino; 3% Hispanic/Latino; 1% Asian, non-Hispanic/Latino; 0.3% Native Hawaiian or other Pacific Islander, non-Hispanic/Latino; 0.7% American Indian or Alaska Native, non-Hispanic/Latino; 2% Two or more races, non-Hispanic/Latino; 8% Race/ethnicity unknown; 0.3% international; 11% transferred in; 60% live on campus.

Freshmen
Admission: 1,291 applied, 1,107 admitted, 222 enrolled. ***Average high school GPA:*** 3.32. ***Test scores:*** SAT critical reading scores over 500: 45%; SAT math scores over 500: 36%; SAT critical reading scores over 600: 11%; SAT math scores over 600: 6%; SAT critical reading scores over 700: 1%.
Retention: 64% of full-time freshmen returned.

FACULTY
Total: 179, 25% full-time, 36% with terminal degrees.
Student/faculty ratio: 14:1.

ACADEMICS
Calendar: semesters. *Degrees:* certificates, associate, bachelor's, master's, and post-master's certificates.
Special study options: accelerated degree program, advanced placement credit, cooperative education, distance learning, double majors, English as a second language, external degree program, honors programs, independent study, internships, off-campus study, part-time degree program, services for LD students, study abroad, summer session for credit. ***ROTC:*** Army (c).
Computers: 160 computers/terminals are available on campus for general student use. Students can access the following: campus intranet, computer help desk, free student e-mail accounts, online (class) grades, online (class) registration, online (class) schedules. Campuswide network is available. Wireless service is available via classrooms, libraries, student centers.

STUDENT LIFE
Housing options: on-campus residence required through sophomore year; coed. Campus housing is university owned. Freshman applicants given priority for college housing.
Activities and organizations: drama/theater group, student-run newspaper, radio station, choral group, SERVE (Break Away), A Global partnership: Students for Children's Right, Ski/Snowboarding Club, Dance Club, Christian Fellowship Club.
Athletics Member NCAA. All Division III. ***Intercollegiate sports:*** basketball M/W, cross-country running M/W, golf M, lacrosse M/W, soccer M/W, softball W, tennis M/W, volleyball W. ***Intramural sports:*** badminton M/W, basketball M/W, cross-country running M/W, golf M(c)/W(c), ice hockey M(c)/W(c), lacrosse M(c)/W, racquetball M/W, rock climbing M(c)/W(c), skiing (downhill) M(c)/W(c), soccer M/W, softball M/W, swimming and diving M(c)/W(c), table tennis M/W, tennis M/W, ultimate Frisbee M(c)/W(c), volleyball M/W, water polo M/W, weight lifting M/W.
Campus security: 24-hour emergency response devices and patrols, student patrols, late-night transport/escort service, controlled dormitory access.
Student services: health clinic, personal/psychological counseling, women's center.

COSTS & FINANCIAL AID
Costs (2014–15) ***Tuition:*** state resident $9600 full-time; nonresident $21,600 full-time. ***Room and board:*** $9414; room only: $5606. Room and board charges vary according to board plan. ***Waivers:*** employees or children of employees.
Financial Aid Of all full-time matriculated undergraduates who enrolled in 2013, 901 applied for aid, 812 were judged to have need, 337 had their need fully met. In 2013, 57 non-need-based awards were made. ***Average percent of need met:*** 83. ***Average financial aid package:*** $16,372. ***Average need-based loan:*** $4273. ***Average need-based gift aid:*** $8225. ***Average non-need-based aid:*** $6379. ***Average indebtedness upon graduation:*** $31,595.

APPLYING
Standardized Tests *Recommended:* SAT or ACT (for admission).
Options: electronic application, early admission, early action, deferred entrance.
Application fee: $40.
Required: essay or personal statement, high school transcript, minimum 2.0 GPA, 1 letter of recommendation. ***Recommended:*** minimum 3.0 GPA, interview.
Application deadlines: rolling (freshmen), rolling (out-of-state freshmen), rolling (transfers).
Notification: continuous (freshmen), continuous (out-of-state freshmen), continuous (transfers).

CONTACT
Bethany Harrington, Admissions Specialist, Johnson State College, 337 College Hill, Johnson, VT 05656. *Phone:* 802-635-1219. *Toll-free phone:* 800-635-2356. *Fax:* 802-635-1230. *E-mail:* jscadmissions@jsc.edu.

Landmark College
Putney, Vermont
http://www.landmark.edu/

- **Independent** primarily 2-year, founded 1983
- **Small-town** 125-acre campus
- **Endowment** $19.1 million
- **Coed** 514 undergraduate students, 96% full-time, 27% women, 73% men
- **Moderately difficult** entrance level, 86% of applicants were admitted

UNDERGRAD STUDENTS
494 full-time, 20 part-time. Students come from 39 states and territories; 7 other countries; 93% are from out of state; 4% Black or African American, non-Hispanic/Latino; 4% Hispanic/Latino; 2% Asian, non-Hispanic/Latino; 0.2% Native Hawaiian or other Pacific Islander, non-Hispanic/Latino; 0.2% American Indian or Alaska Native, non-Hispanic/Latino; 2% Two or more races, non-Hispanic/Latino; 14% Race/ethnicity unknown; 2% international; 15% transferred in; 95% live on campus.

Freshmen
Admission: 266 applied, 230 admitted, 119 enrolled.
Retention: 66% of full-time freshmen returned.

FACULTY
Total: 78, 100% full-time, 13% with terminal degrees.
Student/faculty ratio: 6:1.

ACADEMICS
Calendar: semesters. *Degrees:* certificates, associate, and bachelor's.
Special study options: academic remediation for entering students, advanced placement credit, distance learning, internships, services for LD students, study abroad, summer session for credit.
Computers: 120 computers/terminals and 500 ports are available on campus for general student use. Students can access the following: campus intranet, computer help desk, free student e-mail accounts, online (class) grades, online (class) schedules, online access to assignment grades, attendance, and other course data, pay bills, view/print unofficial transcripts. Campuswide network is available. 100% of college-owned or -operated housing units are wired for high-speed Internet access. Wireless service is available via entire campus.

STUDENT LIFE
Housing options: on-campus residence required for freshman year; coed, special housing for students with disabilities. Campus housing is university owned. Freshman campus housing is guaranteed.

Activities and organizations: drama/theater group, student-run newspaper, radio station, choral group, Student Government Association, Campus Activities Board, Phi Theta Kappa Honor Society, Equestrian Club, PBL Business Club.

Athletics ***Intercollegiate sports:*** baseball M(c), basketball M(c)/W(c), cross-country running M(c)/W(c), equestrian sports M/W, rock climbing M(c)/W(c), soccer M/W, softball W(c). ***Intramural sports:*** badminton M(c)/W(c), basketball M(c)/W(c), fencing M(c)/W(c), skiing (cross-country) M(c)/W(c), tennis M(c)/W(c), volleyball M(c)/W(c), weight lifting M(c)/W(c).

Campus security: 24-hour emergency response devices and patrols, late-night transport/escort service, controlled dormitory access.

Student services: health clinic, personal/psychological counseling, women's center.

COSTS & FINANCIAL AID
Costs (2014–15) ***Comprehensive fee:*** $60,530 includes full-time tuition ($49,950), mandatory fees ($130), and room and board ($10,450). ***College room only:*** $5390. Room and board charges vary according to board plan and housing facility. ***Payment plan:*** installment. ***Waivers:*** employees or children of employees.

Financial Aid Of all full-time matriculated undergraduates who enrolled in 2010, 341 applied for aid, 243 were judged to have need, 3 had their need fully met. 85 Federal Work-Study jobs (averaging $1000). 3 state and other part-time jobs (averaging $1000). In 2010, 18 non-need-based awards were made. ***Average percent of need met:*** 45. ***Average financial aid package:*** $26,000. ***Average need-based loan:*** $4500. ***Average need-based gift aid:*** $21,000. ***Average non-need-based aid:*** $7800. ***Average indebtedness upon graduation:*** $6100.

APPLYING
Standardized Tests *Required:* Cognitive and achievement tests such as the Wechsler Adult Intelligence Scale III and the Nelson Denny Reading Test are required (for admission).

Options: electronic application, early action, deferred entrance.

Application fee: $75.

Required: essay or personal statement, high school transcript, diagnosis of LD and/or ADHD and cognitive testing. ***Recommended:*** 2 letters of recommendation, interview.

Application deadlines: rolling (freshmen), rolling (transfers), 12/1 (early action).

Notification: continuous (freshmen), continuous (transfers), 1/5 (early action).

CONTACT
Admissions Main Desk, Landmark College, Admissions Office, River Road South, Putney, VT 05346. *Phone:* 802-387-6718. *Fax:* 802-387-6868. *E-mail:* admissions@landmark.edu.

★ Marlboro College
Marlboro, Vermont
http://www.marlboro.edu/

CONTACT
Ms. Jessica Nelson, Assistant Director of Admissions, Marlboro College, PO Box A, 2582 South Road, Marlboro, VT 05344-0300. *Phone:* 800-343-0049. *Toll-free phone:* 800-343-0049. *Fax:* 802-451-7555. *E-mail:* admissions@marlboro.edu.

See below for display ad and page 1516 for the College Close-Up.

Middlebury College
Middlebury, Vermont
http://www.middlebury.edu/

- **Independent** comprehensive, founded 1800
- **Small-town** 350-acre campus
- **Endowment** $1.1 million
- **Coed** 2,526 undergraduate students, 99% full-time, 52% women, 48% men
- **Most difficult** entrance level, 17% of applicants were admitted

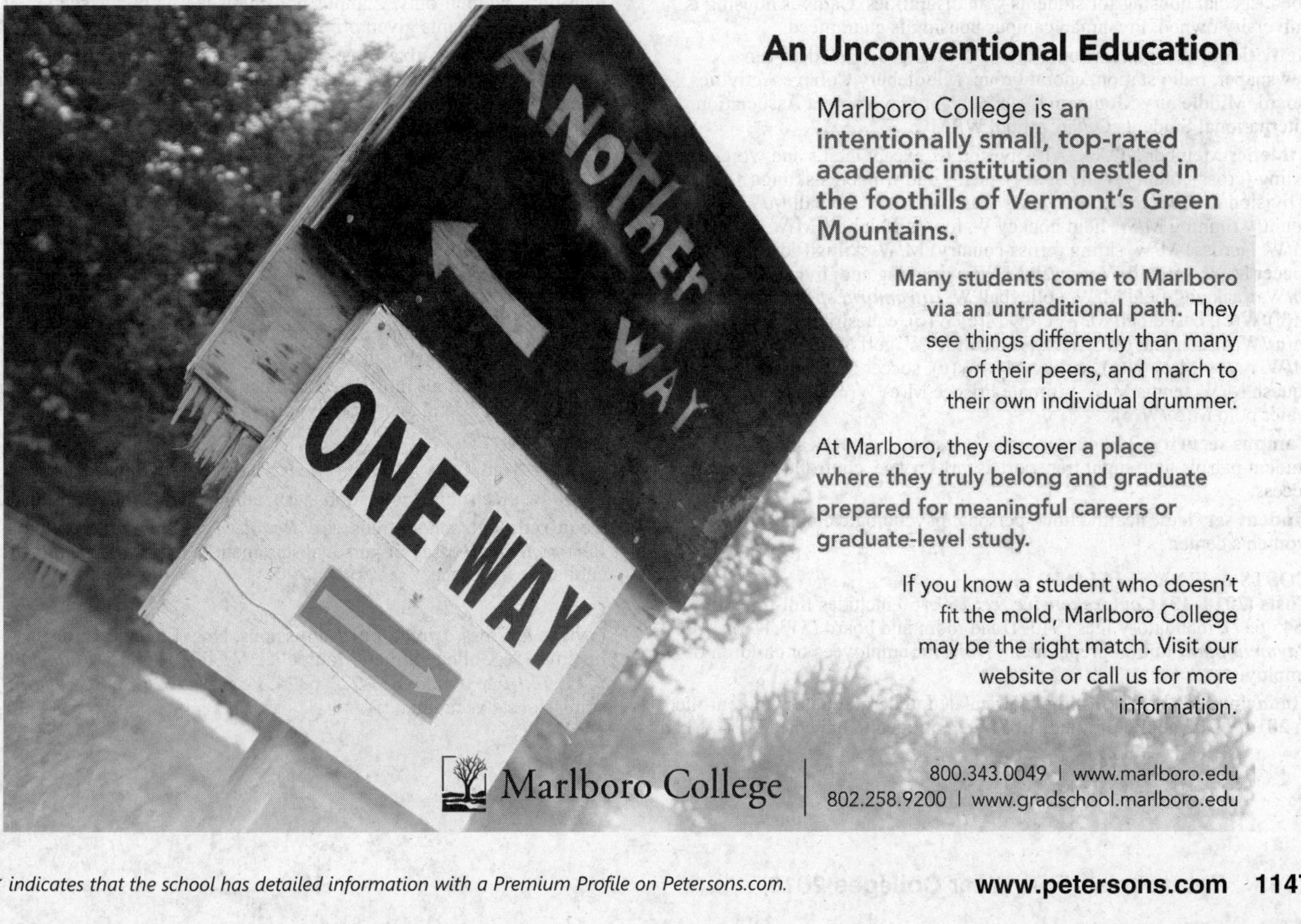

UNDERGRAD STUDENTS
2,492 full-time, 34 part-time. Students come from 52 states and territories; 74 other countries; 94% are from out of state; 3% Black or African American, non-Hispanic/Latino; 9% Hispanic/Latino; 7% Asian, non-Hispanic/Latino; 0.3% American Indian or Alaska Native, non-Hispanic/Latino; 5% Two or more races, non-Hispanic/Latino; 2% Race/ethnicity unknown; 11% international; 0.4% transferred in; 96% live on campus.

Freshmen
Admission: 8,195 applied, 1,407 admitted, 580 enrolled. ***Test scores:*** SAT critical reading scores over 500: 99%; SAT math scores over 500: 100%; SAT writing scores over 500: 99%; ACT scores over 18: 100%; SAT critical reading scores over 600: 85%; SAT math scores over 600: 88%; SAT writing scores over 600: 87%; ACT scores over 24: 99%; SAT critical reading scores over 700: 45%; SAT math scores over 700: 48%; SAT writing scores over 700: 53%; ACT scores over 30: 77%.
Retention: 96% of full-time freshmen returned.

FACULTY
Total: 331, 82% full-time, 92% with terminal degrees.
Student/faculty ratio: 9:1.

ACADEMICS
Calendar: 4-1-4. *Degrees:* bachelor's, master's, and doctoral.
Special study options: accelerated degree program, advanced placement credit, double majors, honors programs, independent study, internships, off-campus study, services for LD students, student-designed majors, study abroad, summer session for credit. ***ROTC:*** Army (c).
Unusual degree programs: 3-2 engineering with Columbia University, Dartmouth College.
Computers: 250 computers/terminals are available on campus for general student use. Students can access the following: campus intranet, computer help desk, free student e-mail accounts, online (class) grades, online (class) registration, online (class) schedules, helpdesk, personal Web pages, file servers. Campuswide network is available. Wireless service is available via entire campus.

STUDENT LIFE
Housing options: on-campus residence required through junior year; coed, special housing for students with disabilities. Campus housing is university owned. Freshman campus housing is guaranteed.
Activities and organizations: drama/theater group, student-run newspaper, radio station, choral group, Middlebury College Activities Board, Middlebury Mountain Club, Student Government Association, International Students Organization, WRMC.
Athletics Member NCAA. All Division III except men's and women's skiing (cross-country) (Division I), men's and women's skiing (downhill) (Division I). ***Intercollegiate sports:*** baseball M, basketball M/W, cross-country running M/W, field hockey W, football M, golf M/W, ice hockey M/W, lacrosse M/W, skiing (cross-country) M/W, skiing (downhill) M/W, soccer M/W, softball W, squash M/W, swimming and diving M/W, tennis M/W, track and field M/W, volleyball W. ***Intramural sports:*** badminton M(c)/W(c), basketball M/W, crew M(c)/W(c), equestrian sports M(c)/W(c), fencing M(c)/W(c), football M/W, golf M/W, ice hockey M/W, rugby M(c)/W(c), sailing M(c)/W(c), soccer M/W, softball M/W, squash M/W, tennis M/W, ultimate Frisbee M(c)/W(c), volleyball M(c), water polo M(c)/W(c).
Campus security: 24-hour emergency response devices and patrols, student patrols, late-night transport/escort service, controlled dormitory access.
Student services: health clinic, personal/psychological counseling, women's center.

COSTS & FINANCIAL AID
Costs (2014–15) ***Comprehensive fee:*** $59,160 includes full-time tuition ($45,637), mandatory fees ($407), and room and board ($13,116). ***Payment plan:*** tuition prepayment. ***Waivers:*** employees or children of employees.
Financial Aid Of all full-time matriculated undergraduates who enrolled in 2014, 1,202 applied for aid, 1,071 were judged to have need, 1,071 had their need fully met. ***Average percent of need met:*** 100. ***Average financial aid package:*** $41,870. ***Average need-based loan:*** $3923. ***Average need-based gift aid:*** $39,238. ***Average indebtedness upon graduation:*** $17,975. ***Financial aid deadline:*** 2/1.

APPLYING
Standardized Tests *Required:* SAT and SAT Subject Tests or ACT (for admission).
Options: electronic application, early admission, early decision, deferred entrance.
Application fee: $65.
Required: essay or personal statement, high school transcript, 2 letters of recommendation. ***Recommended:*** interview.
Application deadlines: 1/1 (freshmen), 3/1 (transfers).
Early decision deadline: 11/1 (for plan 1), 1/1 (for plan 2).
Notification: 3/31 (freshmen), 4/10 (transfers), 12/15 (early decision plan 1), 2/15 (early decision plan 2).

CONTACT
Mr. Greg Buckles, Dean of Admissions, Middlebury College, Emma Willard House, Middlebury, VT 05753-6002. *Phone:* 802-443-3000. *Fax:* 802-443-2056. *E-mail:* admissions@middlebury.edu.

New England Culinary Institute
Montpelier, Vermont
http://www.neci.edu/

- **Proprietary** primarily 2-year, founded 1980
- **Small-town** campus
- **Coed**
- **Moderately difficult** entrance level

FACULTY
Student/faculty ratio: 10:1.

ACADEMICS
Calendar: quarters. *Degrees:* certificates, associate, and bachelor's.

STUDENT LIFE
Housing options: on-campus residence required for freshman year; coed, men-only, women-only. Campus housing is leased by the school. Freshman applicants given priority for college housing.
Activities and organizations: American Culinary Federation, Slow Food, Student Council, Special Guest Lecture Series, Student Ambassadors (Leadership Program).
Campus security: 24-hour emergency response devices, student patrols.

COSTS & FINANCIAL AID
Costs (2014–15) ***Comprehensive fee:*** $36,990 includes full-time tuition ($26,250), mandatory fees ($2740), and room and board ($8000). Full-time tuition and fees vary according to course load, degree level, program, reciprocity agreements, and student level. Part-time tuition: $7500 per term. Part-time tuition and fees vary according to course load, degree level, program, reciprocity agreements, and student level. ***Required fees:*** $5625 per term part-time, $200 per term part-time. ***College room only:*** $5600. Room and board charges vary according to housing facility.
Financial Aid Of all full-time matriculated undergraduates who enrolled in 2013, 320 Federal Work-Study jobs (averaging $1000).

APPLYING
Standardized Tests *Recommended:* SAT or ACT (for admission).
Options: electronic application, early admission, deferred entrance.
Required: high school transcript. ***Required for some:*** interview. ***Recommended:*** essay or personal statement, 2 letters of recommendation, culinary experience.

CONTACT
Dwight A Cross, Director of Admissions, New England Culinary Institute, 56 College Street, Montpelier, VT 05602-3115. *Phone:* 802-225-3211. *Toll-free phone:* 877-223-6324. *Fax:* 802-225-3280. *E-mail:* admissions@neci.edu.

★ Norwich University
Northfield, Vermont
http://www.norwich.edu/

- **Independent** comprehensive, founded 1819
- **Small-town** 1125-acre campus with easy access to Burlington
- **Coed** 2,649 undergraduate students, 86% full-time, 23% women, 77% men
- **Moderately difficult** entrance level, 66% of applicants were admitted

UNDERGRAD STUDENTS
2,271 full-time, 378 part-time. 86% are from out of state; 4% Black or African American, non-Hispanic/Latino; 7% Hispanic/Latino; 2% Asian, non-Hispanic/Latino; 0.4% Native Hawaiian or other Pacific Islander, non-Hispanic/Latino; 0.5% American Indian or Alaska Native, non-Hispanic/Latino; 5% Two or more races, non-Hispanic/Latino; 1% Race/ethnicity unknown; 2% international; 4% transferred in; 75% live on campus.

Freshmen
Admission: 3,138 applied, 2,063 admitted, 657 enrolled. ***Average high school GPA:*** 3.07. ***Test scores:*** SAT critical reading scores over 500: 61%; SAT math scores over 500: 68%; SAT writing scores over 500: 49%; ACT scores over 18: 91%; SAT critical reading scores over 600: 20%; SAT math scores over 600: 20%; SAT writing scores over 600: 11%; ACT scores over 24: 47%; SAT critical reading scores over 700: 2%; SAT math scores over 700: 1%; ACT scores over 30: 5%.
Retention: 73% of full-time freshmen returned.

FACULTY
Total: 332, 45% full-time, 51% with terminal degrees.
Student/faculty ratio: 16:1.

ACADEMICS
Calendar: semesters. *Degrees:* bachelor's, master's, and post-master's certificates.
Special study options: academic remediation for entering students, adult/continuing education programs, advanced placement credit, cooperative education, distance learning, double majors, English as a second language, external degree program, honors programs, independent study, internships, part-time degree program, services for LD students, study abroad, summer session for credit. ***ROTC:*** Army (b), Navy (b), Air Force (b).
Computers: Students can access the following: campus intranet, computer help desk, free student e-mail accounts, online (class) grades, online (class) schedules. Campuswide network is available. 100% of college-owned or -operated housing units are wired for high-speed Internet access. Wireless service is available via entire campus.

STUDENT LIFE
Housing options: on-campus residence required through senior year; coed. Campus housing is university owned. Freshman campus housing is guaranteed.
Activities and organizations: drama/theater group, student-run newspaper, radio station, choral group, marching band, DREAM, NUEMS, IEEE, CJSA, Politeia/Model UN.
Athletics Member NCAA. All Division III. ***Intercollegiate sports:*** baseball M, basketball M/W, cross-country running M/W, fencing M(c)/W(c), football M, ice hockey M/W(c), lacrosse M, riflery M/W, rugby M(c)/W(c), sailing M(c)/W(c), skiing (cross-country) M(c)/W(c), skiing (downhill) M(c)/W(c), soccer M/W, softball W, swimming and diving M/W, tennis M/W(c), track and field M/W, volleyball M(c)/W(c), weight lifting M(c)/W(c), wrestling M. ***Intramural sports:*** basketball M/W, cross-country running M/W, football M, golf M/W, ice hockey M/W, lacrosse M/W, racquetball M/W, rugby M/W, soccer M/W, softball W, swimming and diving M/W, tennis M/W, track and field M/W, volleyball M/W, water polo M/W, weight lifting M/W, wrestling M.
Campus security: 24-hour emergency response devices and patrols, late-night transport/escort service.
Student services: health clinic, personal/psychological counseling.

COSTS & FINANCIAL AID
Costs (2015–16) ***Comprehensive fee:*** $44,796 includes full-time tuition ($32,812) and room and board ($11,984). Part-time tuition: $962 per credit hour. Part-time tuition and fees vary according to course load.
Financial Aid Of all full-time matriculated undergraduates who enrolled in 2014, 1,854 applied for aid, 1,854 were judged to have need, 389 had

their need fully met. In 2014, 459 non-need-based awards were made. ***Average percent of need met:*** 66. ***Average financial aid package:*** $29,218. ***Average need-based loan:*** $5003. ***Average need-based gift aid:*** $25,047. ***Average non-need-based aid:*** $14,966. ***Average indebtedness upon graduation:*** $32,498.

APPLYING

Standardized Tests *Required for some:* SAT (for admission), ACT (for admission), SAT or ACT (for admission).

Options: electronic application.

Application fee: $35.

Required: essay or personal statement, high school transcript. ***Required for some:*** portfolio. ***Recommended:*** minimum 2.0 GPA, 2 letters of recommendation, interview.

CONTACT

Norwich University, 158 Harmon Drive, Northfield, VT 05663. *Phone:* 802-485-2658. *Toll-free phone:* 800-468-6679.

See previous page for display ad and page 1554 for the College Close-Up.

★ Saint Michael's College

Colchester, Vermont

http://www.smcvt.edu/

- **Independent Roman Catholic** comprehensive, founded 1904
- **Suburban** 440-acre campus with easy access to Montreal
- **Endowment** $91.4 million
- **Coed** 2,123 undergraduate students, 97% full-time, 54% women, 46% men
- **Moderately difficult** entrance level, 80% of applicants were admitted

UNDERGRAD STUDENTS

2,064 full-time, 59 part-time. Students come from 35 states and territories; 22 other countries; 81% are from out of state; 2% Black or African American, non-Hispanic/Latino; 5% Hispanic/Latino; 2% Asian, non-Hispanic/Latino; 0.1% American Indian or Alaska Native, non-Hispanic/Latino; 2% Two or more races, non-Hispanic/Latino; 0.5% Race/ethnicity unknown; 3% international; 1% transferred in; 95% live on campus.

Freshmen

Admission: 4,299 applied, 3,459 admitted, 574 enrolled. ***Average high school GPA:*** 3.4. ***Test scores:*** SAT critical reading scores over 500: 90%; SAT math scores over 500: 85%; SAT writing scores over 500: 84%; ACT scores over 18: 100%; SAT critical reading scores over 600: 44%; SAT math scores over 600: 36%; SAT writing scores over 600: 37%; ACT scores over 24: 79%; SAT critical reading scores over 700: 8%; SAT math scores over 700: 4%; SAT writing scores over 700: 5%; ACT scores over 30: 12%.

Retention: 90% of full-time freshmen returned.

FACULTY

Total: 252, 58% full-time, 58% with terminal degrees.

Student/faculty ratio: 12:1.

ACADEMICS

Calendar: semesters. *Degrees:* bachelor's, master's, post-master's, and postbachelor's certificates.

Special study options: advanced placement credit, distance learning, double majors, English as a second language, honors programs, independent study, internships, off-campus study, part-time degree program, services for LD students, student-designed majors, study abroad, summer session for credit. ***ROTC:*** Army (c), Air Force (c).

Unusual degree programs: 3-2 business administration with Clarkson University, Syracuse University, Northeastern University, and Boston College; engineering with University of Vermont, and Clarkson University; Pre-pharmacy dual degree (BS/D.Pharm) with Albany College of Pharmacy and Health Sciences.

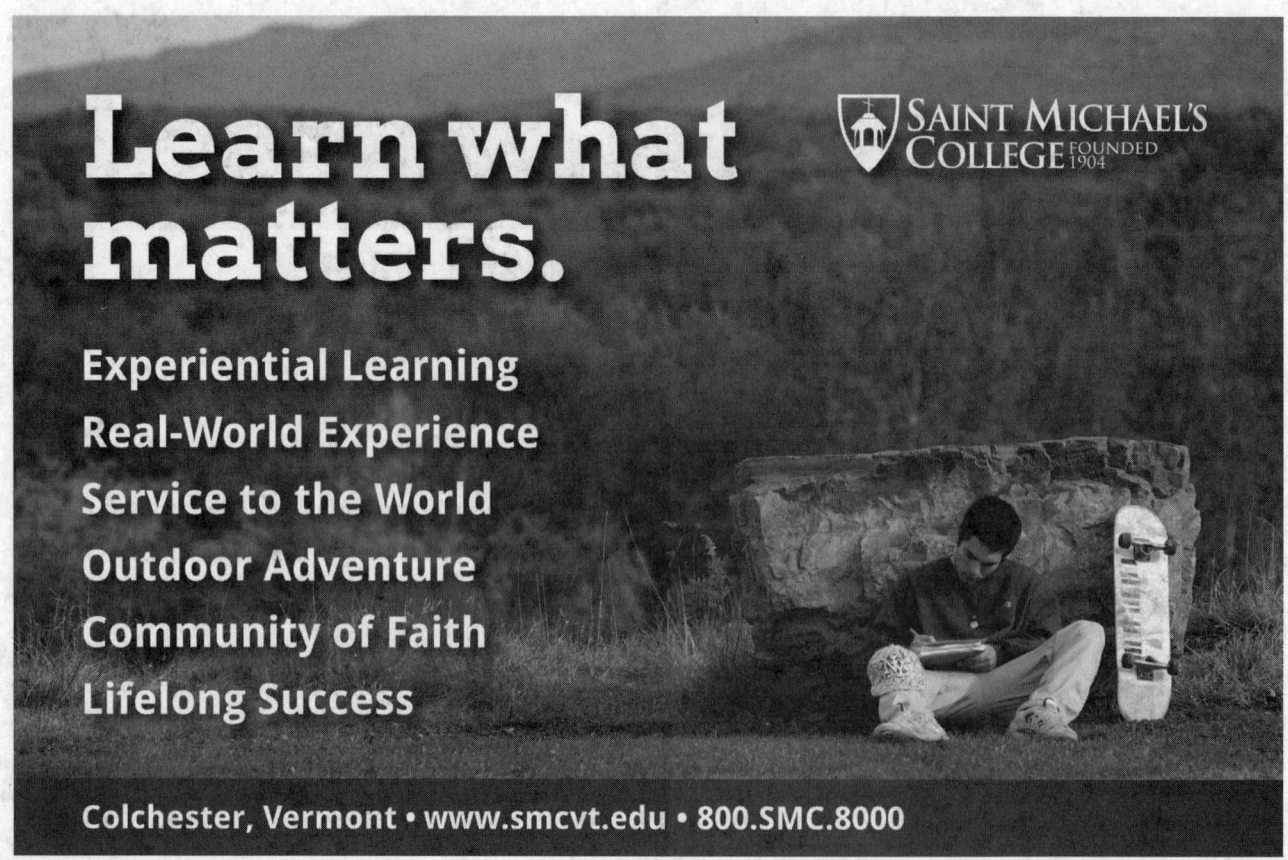

Computers: 350 computers/terminals and 5,000 ports are available on campus for general student use. Students can access the following: computer help desk, free student e-mail accounts, online (class) grades, online (class) registration, online (class) schedules. Campuswide network is available. 100% of college-owned or -operated housing units are wired for high-speed Internet access. Wireless service is available via classrooms, computer centers, computer labs, dorm rooms, learning centers, libraries, student centers.

STUDENT LIFE

Housing options: on-campus residence required through senior year; coed, men-only, women-only, special housing for students with disabilities. Campus housing is university owned. Freshman campus housing is guaranteed.

Activities and organizations: drama/theater group, student-run newspaper, radio station, choral group, Student Association (governing board), Mobilization of Volunteer Efforts (MOVE), WWPV-FM (student run radio station), Wilderness Program, student newspaper/online publication (The Defender).

Athletics Member NCAA. All Division II. ***Intercollegiate sports:*** baseball M, basketball M(s)/W(s), cross-country running M/W, field hockey W, golf M, ice hockey M/W, lacrosse M/W, rugby M(c)/W(c), skiing (cross-country) M/W, skiing (downhill) M/W, soccer M/W, softball W, swimming and diving M/W, tennis M/W, volleyball W. ***Intramural sports:*** basketball M/W, ice hockey M/W, racquetball M/W, rock climbing M/W, skiing (cross-country) M/W, skiing (downhill) M/W, soccer M/W, softball M/W, table tennis M/W, tennis M/W, track and field M(c)/W(c), ultimate Frisbee M(c)/W(c), volleyball M/W, water polo M/W.

Campus security: 24-hour emergency response devices and patrols, student patrols, late-night transport/escort service, controlled dormitory access, Bicycle patrols; Fire and Rescue Squad serving the College and surrounding community with professionals and trained student volunteers.

Student services: health clinic, personal/psychological counseling, women's center.

COSTS & FINANCIAL AID

Costs (2015–16) ***Comprehensive fee:*** $51,725 includes full-time tuition ($40,425), mandatory fees ($325), and room and board ($10,975). Full-time tuition and fees vary according to course load. Part-time tuition: $1300 per credit hour. Part-time tuition and fees vary according to course load. ***Room and board:*** Room and board charges vary according to board plan and housing facility. ***Payment plan:*** installment. ***Waivers:*** employees or children of employees.

Financial Aid Of all full-time matriculated undergraduates who enrolled in 2014, 1,447 applied for aid, 1,251 were judged to have need, 351 had their need fully met. 229 Federal Work-Study jobs (averaging $1650). 249 state and other part-time jobs (averaging $1650). In 2014, 556 non-need-based awards were made. ***Average percent of need met:*** 78. ***Average financial aid package:*** $28,612. ***Average need-based loan:*** $5334. ***Average need-based gift aid:*** $21,999. ***Average non-need-based aid:*** $14,525. ***Average indebtedness upon graduation:*** $36,967.

APPLYING

Standardized Tests *Recommended:* SAT or ACT (for admission), Saint Michael's is a test-optional institution. Therefore, you do not have to submit standardized test scores (SAT Reasoning Test or ACT with Writing) to be considered for admission. If you choose to submit scores for consideration they will be used in the decision process.

Options: electronic application, early action, deferred entrance.

Application fee: $50.

Required: essay or personal statement, high school transcript. ***Recommended:*** minimum 3.0 GPA, 3 letters of recommendation, interview.

Application deadlines: 2/1 (freshmen), 3/15 (transfers), 11/1 (early action).

Notification: 4/1 (freshmen), 4/15 (transfers), 1/1 (early action).

CONTACT

Ms. Jacqueline Murphy, Director of Admission, Saint Michael's College, One Winooski Park, Colchester, VT 05452. *Phone:* 802-654-3000. *Toll-free phone:* 800-762-8000. *Fax:* 802-654-2906. *E-mail:* admission@smcvt.edu.

See previous page for display ad and page 1608 for the College Close-Up.

Southern Vermont College

Bennington, Vermont

http://www.svc.edu/

- **Independent** 4-year, founded 1926
- **Small-town** 371-acre campus with easy access to Albany, NY
- **Endowment** $1.2 million
- **Coed** 455 undergraduate students, 94% full-time, 61% women, 39% men
- **Minimally difficult** entrance level, 94% of applicants were admitted

UNDERGRAD STUDENTS

426 full-time, 29 part-time. Students come from 22 states and territories; 1 other country; 72% are from out of state; 13% Black or African American, non-Hispanic/Latino; 9% Hispanic/Latino; 0.7% Asian, non-Hispanic/Latino; 0.2% Native Hawaiian or other Pacific Islander, non-Hispanic/Latino; 0.9% American Indian or Alaska Native, non-Hispanic/Latino; 2% Two or more races, non-Hispanic/Latino; 16% Race/ethnicity unknown; 0.2% international; 8% transferred in; 55% live on campus.

Freshmen

Admission: 303 applied, 284 admitted, 90 enrolled. ***Average high school GPA:*** 2.5. ***Test scores:*** SAT critical reading scores over 500: 24%; SAT math scores over 500: 27%; ACT scores over 18: 56%; SAT critical reading scores over 600: 7%; SAT math scores over 600: 3%; ACT scores over 24: 12%; SAT critical reading scores over 700: 1%.

Retention: 61% of full-time freshmen returned.

FACULTY

Total: 50, 44% full-time.

Student/faculty ratio: 14:1.

ACADEMICS

Calendar: semesters. *Degrees:* associate, bachelor's, and postbachelor's certificates.

Special study options: academic remediation for entering students, accelerated degree program, adult/continuing education programs, advanced placement credit, cooperative education, distance learning, double majors, external degree program, independent study, internships, off-campus study, part-time degree program, services for LD students, student-designed majors, study abroad, summer session for credit.

Computers: 50 computers/terminals are available on campus for general student use. Students can access the following: campus intranet, computer help desk, free student e-mail accounts, online (class) grades, online (class) registration, online (class) schedules. Campuswide network is available. 100% of college-owned or -operated housing units are wired for high-speed Internet access. Wireless service is available via entire campus.

STUDENT LIFE

Housing options: on-campus residence required through sophomore year; coed. Campus housing is university owned. Freshman campus housing is guaranteed.

Activities and organizations: drama/theater group, Student Government Association, Mountaineer Event Board, Japanese Culture and Anime Club, Big Brothers Big Sisters, Moosecorps.

Athletics Member NCAA. All Division III. ***Intercollegiate sports:*** baseball M, basketball M/W, cross-country running M/W, lacrosse W, soccer M/W, softball W, volleyball M/W. ***Intramural sports:*** basketball M/W, cheerleading W(c), golf M/W, rugby M(c)/W(c), skiing (cross-country) M(c)/W(c), skiing (downhill) M(c)/W(c), soccer M/W, volleyball M/W.

Campus security: 24-hour patrols, late-night transport/escort service, controlled dormitory access.

Student services: health clinic, personal/psychological counseling.

COSTS & FINANCIAL AID

Costs (2015–16) ***Comprehensive fee:*** $33,960 includes full-time tuition ($22,985), mandatory fees ($275), and room and board ($10,700). Part-time tuition: $960 per credit hour. Part-time tuition and fees vary according to course load. ***Required fees:*** $275 per year part-time. ***Room and board:*** Room and board charges vary according to board plan and housing facility. ***Payment plan:*** installment. ***Waivers:*** senior citizens and employees or children of employees.

Financial Aid Of all full-time matriculated undergraduates who enrolled in 2013, 389 applied for aid, 389 were judged to have need, 44 had their need fully met. 91 Federal Work-Study jobs (averaging $849).

APPLYING

Standardized Tests *Required:* SAT or ACT (for admission).

Options: electronic application, early admission, deferred entrance.

Application fee: $30.

Required: essay or personal statement, high school transcript, 2 letters of recommendation. ***Required for some:*** interview, Deans report and college transcripts for transfer students. ***Recommended:*** minimum 2.0 GPA, interview.

Application deadlines: rolling (freshmen), rolling (out-of-state freshmen), rolling (transfers).

Notification: continuous (freshmen), continuous (out-of-state freshmen), continuous (transfers).

CONTACT

Southern Vermont College, 982 Mansion Drive, Bennington, VT 05201. *Phone:* 802-447-6300. *Fax:* 802-681-2868. *E-mail:* admissions@svc.edu.

★ Sterling College

Craftsbury Common, Vermont

http://www.sterlingcollege.edu/

- **Independent** 4-year, founded 1958
- **Rural** 430-acre campus
- **Endowment** $1.3 million
- **Coed** 119 undergraduate students, 100% full-time, 49% women, 51% men

UNDERGRAD STUDENTS

119 full-time. Students come from 22 states and territories; 4 other countries; 82% are from out of state; 4% Black or African American, non-Hispanic/Latino; 2% Hispanic/Latino; 0.8% Asian, non-Hispanic/Latino; 2% Two or more races, non-Hispanic/Latino; 6% Race/ethnicity unknown; 3% international; 15% transferred in; 85% live on campus.

Freshmen

Admission: 20 enrolled. ***Average high school GPA:*** 3.1.

Retention: 85% of full-time freshmen returned.

FACULTY

Total: 27, 56% full-time, 44% with terminal degrees.

Student/faculty ratio: 6:1.

ACADEMICS

Calendar: semesters. *Degree:* bachelor's.

Special study options: academic remediation for entering students, advanced placement credit, cooperative education, double majors, independent study, internships, off-campus study, services for LD students, student-designed majors, study abroad, summer session for credit.

Computers: 18 computers/terminals are available on campus for general student use. Students can access the following: campus intranet, computer help desk, free student e-mail accounts. Campuswide network is available. 100% of college-owned or -operated housing units are wired for high-speed Internet access. Wireless service is available via entire campus.

STUDENT LIFE

Housing options: on-campus residence required for freshman year; coed, women-only, cooperative. Campus housing is university owned. Freshman campus housing is guaranteed.

Activities and organizations: drama/theater group, Outing Club, Timbersports Team, Student Union, Art Club, Musical Groups.

Athletics ***Intercollegiate sports:*** cross-country running M/W, skiing (cross-country) M/W.

Campus security: 24-hour pager.

Student services: personal/psychological counseling, women's center.

COSTS

Costs (2015–16) ***Comprehensive fee:*** $42,438 includes full-time tuition ($29,992), mandatory fees ($3650), and room and board ($8796). Full-time tuition and fees vary according to course load. Part-time tuition and fees vary according to course load. ***College room only:*** $4006. Room and board charges vary according to board plan. ***Waivers:*** employees or children of employees.

APPLYING

Required: essay or personal statement, high school transcript, 2 letters of recommendation. ***Recommended:*** minimum 2.0 GPA, interview.

CONTACT

Tim Patterson, Director of Admission, Sterling College, PO Box 72, Craftsbury Common, VT 05827. *Phone:* 802-586-7711 Ext. 135. *Toll-free phone:* 800-648-3591 Ext. 100. *Fax:* 802-586-2596. *E-mail:* tpatterson@sterlingcollege.edu.

See previous page for display ad and page 1634 for the College Close-Up.

University of Vermont

Burlington, Vermont

http://www.uvm.edu/

- **State-supported** university, founded 1791
- **Suburban** 459-acre campus
- **Endowment** $367.0 million
- **Coed** 10,994 undergraduate students, 90% full-time, 55% women, 45% men
- **Moderately difficult** entrance level, 73% of applicants were admitted

UNDERGRAD STUDENTS

9,898 full-time, 1,096 part-time. Students come from 48 states and territories; 50 other countries; 69% are from out of state; 1% Black or African American, non-Hispanic/Latino; 4% Hispanic/Latino; 2% Asian, non-Hispanic/Latino; 0.2% American Indian or Alaska Native, non-Hispanic/Latino; 3% Two or more races, non-Hispanic/Latino; 3% Race/ethnicity unknown; 3% international; 4% transferred in; 51% live on campus.

Freshmen

Admission: 24,231 applied, 17,796 admitted, 2,310 enrolled. ***Average high school GPA:*** 3.49. ***Test scores:*** SAT critical reading scores over 500: 89%; SAT math scores over 500: 89%; SAT writing scores over 500: 89%; ACT scores over 18: 99%; SAT critical reading scores over 600: 46%; SAT math scores over 600: 48%; SAT writing scores over 600: 48%; ACT scores over 24: 80%; SAT critical reading scores over 700: 9%; SAT math scores over 700: 7%; SAT writing scores over 700: 7%; ACT scores over 30: 23%.

Retention: 87% of full-time freshmen returned.

FACULTY

Total: 770, 79% full-time, 75% with terminal degrees.

Student/faculty ratio: 17:1.

ACADEMICS

Calendar: semesters. *Degrees:* bachelor's, master's, doctoral, post-master's, and postbachelor's certificates.

Special study options: adult/continuing education programs, advanced placement credit, cooperative education, distance learning, double majors, freshman honors college, honors programs, independent study, internships, off-campus study, part-time degree program, services for LD students, student-designed majors, study abroad, summer session for credit. ***ROTC:*** Army (b).

Unusual degree programs: 3-2 computer science.

Computers: 850 computers/terminals and 299 ports are available on campus for general student use. Students can access the following: campus intranet, computer help desk, free student e-mail accounts, online (class) grades, online (class) registration, online (class) schedules, Web pages, online course support. Campuswide network is available. 100% of college-owned or -operated housing units are wired for high-speed Internet access. Wireless service is available via entire campus.

STUDENT LIFE

Housing options: on-campus residence required through sophomore year; coed. Campus housing is university owned. Freshman campus housing is guaranteed.

Activities and organizations: drama/theater group, student-run newspaper, radio and television station, choral group, Volunteers in Action, Outing Club, Ski and Snowboard Club, national fraternities, national sororities.

Athletics Member NCAA. All Division I. ***Intercollegiate sports:*** basketball M(s)/W(s), cheerleading M(c)/W(c), crew M(c)/W(c), cross-country running M(s)/W(s), equestrian sports M(c)/W(c), fencing M(c)/W(c), field hockey W(s), gymnastics M(c)/W(c), ice hockey M(s)/W(s), lacrosse M(s)/W(s), rugby M(c)/W(c), sailing M(c)/W(c), skiing (cross-country) M(s)/W(s), skiing (downhill) M(s)/W(s), soccer M(s)/W(s), swimming and diving W(s), table tennis M(c)/W(c), track and field M(s)/W(s), ultimate Frisbee M(c)/W(c), volleyball M(c)/W(c), water polo M(c)/W(c). ***Intramural sports:*** basketball M/W, bowling M/W, football M(c)/W, ice hockey M/W, lacrosse M/W, racquetball M/W, soccer M/W, softball M/W, tennis M/W, volleyball M/W, water polo M/W.

Campus security: 24-hour emergency response devices and patrols, late-night transport/escort service, controlled dormitory access, Campus alert system (via phone, email, text).

Student services: health clinic, personal/psychological counseling, women's center, legal services.

COSTS & FINANCIAL AID

Costs (2014–15) ***Tuition:*** state resident $14,184 full-time; nonresident $35,832 full-time. Part-time tuition and fees vary according to course load. ***Required fees:*** $2042 full-time. ***Room and board:*** $10,780; room only: $7116. Room and board charges vary according to board plan and housing facility. ***Payment plan:*** installment. ***Waivers:*** employees or children of employees.

Financial Aid Of all full-time matriculated undergraduates who enrolled in 2013, 6,587 applied for aid, 5,373 were judged to have need, 552 had their need fully met. 1,527 Federal Work-Study jobs (averaging $1600). In 2013, 2451 non-need-based awards were made. ***Average percent of need met:*** 65. ***Average financial aid package:*** $21,989. ***Average need-based loan:*** $4494. ***Average need-based gift aid:*** $14,736. ***Average non-need-based aid:*** $8658. ***Average indebtedness upon graduation:*** $27,276.

APPLYING

Standardized Tests *Required:* SAT or ACT (for admission).

Options: electronic application, early action, deferred entrance.

Application fee: $55.

Required: essay or personal statement, high school transcript, 1 letter of recommendation.

Application deadlines: 1/15 (freshmen), 4/15 (transfers), 11/1 (early action).

Notification: 3/15 (freshmen), continuous (transfers), 12/15 (early action).

CONTACT

Beth A. Wiser PhD, Director of Admissions, University of Vermont, Office of Admissions, 194 South Prospect Street, Burlington, VT 05401. *Phone:* 802-656-3370. *Fax:* 802-656-8611. *E-mail:* admissions@uvm.edu.

Vermont Technical College

Randolph Center, Vermont

http://www.vtc.edu/

- **State-supported** 4-year, founded 1866, part of Vermont State Colleges System
- **Rural** 544-acre campus
- **Coed** 1,544 undergraduate students, 65% full-time, 46% women, 54% men
- **Moderately difficult** entrance level, 67% of applicants were admitted

UNDERGRAD STUDENTS

996 full-time, 548 part-time. Students come from 19 states and territories; 8 other countries; 14% are from out of state; 1% Black or African American, non-Hispanic/Latino; 2% Hispanic/Latino; 2% Asian, non-Hispanic/Latino; 1% American Indian or Alaska Native, non-Hispanic/Latino; 2% Race/ethnicity unknown; 2% international; 16% transferred in.

Freshmen

Admission: 841 applied, 560 admitted, 543 enrolled. ***Average high school GPA:*** 3.02. ***Test scores:*** SAT critical reading scores over 500: 36%; SAT math scores over 500: 47%; SAT writing scores over 500: 36%; ACT scores over 18: 65%; SAT critical reading scores over 600: 9%; SAT math scores over 600: 11%; SAT writing scores over 600: 5%; ACT scores over 24: 14%; SAT critical reading scores over 700: 2%; SAT math scores over 700: 1%; SAT writing scores over 700: 1%.

Retention: 70% of full-time freshmen returned.

FACULTY

Total: 200, 42% full-time, 16% with terminal degrees.

Student/faculty ratio: 10:1.

ACADEMICS

Calendar: semesters. *Degrees:* certificates, associate, and bachelor's.

Special study options: academic remediation for entering students, accelerated degree program, advanced placement credit, cooperative education, distance learning, double majors, English as a second language, honors programs, independent study, internships, part-time degree program, services for LD students, summer session for credit. ***ROTC:*** Army (c).

Computers: 480 computers/terminals and 600 ports are available on campus for general student use. Students can access the following: campus intranet, computer help desk, free student e-mail accounts, online (class) grades, online (class) registration, online (class) schedules, online (network) file storage, wireless network. Campuswide network is available. 98% of college-owned or -operated housing units are wired for high-speed Internet access. Wireless service is available via entire campus.

STUDENT LIFE

Housing options: on-campus residence required through sophomore year; coed. Campus housing is university owned.

Activities and organizations: student-run radio and television station, choral group, Student Council (student government), Adventurer's Guild (board and video gaming), WVTC (student radio station), Outing Club, Veterinary Technology Club.

Athletics Member USCAA. ***Intercollegiate sports:*** baseball M, basketball M/W, golf M/W, soccer M/W, softball W. ***Intramural sports:*** basketball M/W, bowling M(c)/W(c), cross-country running M/W, fencing M(c)/W(c), football M/W, golf M(c)/W(c), ice hockey M(c)/W(c), racquetball M/W, riflery M(c)/W(c), rock climbing M(c)/W(c), rugby M(c), skiing (cross-country) M(c)/W(c), skiing (downhill) M(c)/W(c), soccer M/W, softball M/W, swimming and diving M/W, table tennis M/W, tennis M/W, volleyball M/W, water polo M/W, weight lifting M(c)/W(c).

Campus security: 24-hour emergency response devices and patrols, late-night transport/escort service, controlled dormitory access.

Student services: health clinic.

COSTS & FINANCIAL AID

Costs (2014–15) ***Tuition:*** state resident $11,856 full-time, $494 per credit part-time; nonresident $22,704 full-time, $946 per credit part-time. Full-time tuition and fees vary according to course load and program. Part-time tuition and fees vary according to program. ***Required fees:*** $1344 full-time. ***Room and board:*** $9414; room only: $5606. Room and board charges vary according to board plan. ***Payment plan:*** installment. ***Waivers:*** employees or children of employees.

Financial Aid Of all full-time matriculated undergraduates who enrolled in 2014, 840 applied for aid, 768 were judged to have need, 60 had their need fully met. 154 Federal Work-Study jobs (averaging $1000). In 2014, 12 non-need-based awards were made. ***Average percent of need met:*** 50. ***Average financial aid package:*** $10,716. ***Average need-based loan:*** $3982. ***Average need-based gift aid:*** $6530. ***Average non-need-based aid:*** $4606. ***Average indebtedness upon graduation:*** $23,530.

APPLYING

Standardized Tests *Required for some:* SAT or ACT (for admission).

Options: electronic application.

Application fee: $40.

Required: high school transcript. ***Required for some:*** essay or personal statement, 2 letters of recommendation, interview. ***Recommended:*** minimum 3.0 GPA, 2 letters of recommendation, interview.

Application deadlines: rolling (freshmen), rolling (transfers).

Notification: continuous (freshmen), continuous (transfers).

CONTACT

Jessica Van Deren, Director of Admissions, Vermont Technical College, PO Box 500, Randolph Center, VT 05061. *Phone:* 802-728-1244. *Toll-free phone:* 800-442-VTC1. *Fax:* 802-728-1390. *E-mail:* admissions@vtc.edu.

VIRGINIA

Argosy University, Washington DC

Arlington, Virginia

http://www.argosy.edu/locations/washington-dc/

- **Proprietary** university, founded 1994, part of Argosy Education Group
- **Urban** campus
- **Coed**

ACADEMICS

Calendar: semesters. *Degrees:* associate, bachelor's, master's, and doctoral.

CONTACT

Argosy University, Washington DC, 1550 Wilson Boulevard, Suite 600, Arlington, VA 22209. *Phone:* 703-526-5800. *Toll-free phone:* 866-703-2777.

The Art Institute of Virginia Beach, a branch of The Art Institute of Atlanta

Virginia Beach, Virginia

http://www.artinstitutes.edu/virginia-beach/

- **Proprietary** 4-year
- **Coed**

ACADEMICS

Degrees: diplomas, associate, and bachelor's.

CONTACT

The Art Institute of Virginia Beach, a branch of The Art Institute of Atlanta, Two Columbus Center, 4500 Main Street, Suite 100, Virginia Beach, VA 23462. *Phone:* 757-493-6700. *Toll-free phone:* 877-437-4428.

The Art Institute of Washington, a branch of The Art Institute of Atlanta

Arlington, Virginia

http://www.artinstitutes.edu/arlington/

- **Proprietary** 4-year, founded 2000, part of Education Management Corporation
- **Urban** campus
- **Coed**

ACADEMICS

Calendar: quarters. *Degrees:* diplomas, associate, and bachelor's.

CONTACT

The Art Institute of Washington, a branch of The Art Institute of Atlanta, 1820 North Fort Meyer Drive, Arlington, VA 22209. *Phone:* 703-358-9550. *Toll-free phone:* 877-303-3771.

The Art Institute of Washington–Dulles, a branch of The Art Institute of Atlanta

Dulles, Virginia

http://www.artinstitutes.edu/washington-dulles/

- **Proprietary** 4-year
- **Coed**

ACADEMICS

Degrees: diplomas, associate, and bachelor's.

CONTACT

The Art Institute of Washington–Dulles, a branch of The Art Institute of Atlanta, The Corporate Office Park at Dulles Town Center, 21000 Atlantic

Boulevard, Suite 100, Dulles, VA 20166. *Phone:* 571-449-4400. *Toll-free phone:* 888-627-5008.

Averett University

Danville, Virginia

http://www.averett.edu/

- **Independent** comprehensive, founded 1859, affiliated with Baptist General Association of Virginia
- **Small-town** 252-acre campus with easy access to Greensboro, Raleigh, Durham, and Cary
- **Endowment** $27.1 million
- **Coed** 858 undergraduate students, 96% full-time, 52% women, 48% men
- **Moderately difficult** entrance level, 60% of applicants were admitted

UNDERGRAD STUDENTS

822 full-time, 36 part-time. Students come from 26 states and territories; 11 other countries; 29% are from out of state; 28% Black or African American, non-Hispanic/Latino; 4% Hispanic/Latino; 0.6% Asian, non-Hispanic/Latino; 0.7% American Indian or Alaska Native, non-Hispanic/Latino; 0.6% Race/ethnicity unknown; 5% international; 11% transferred in; 57% live on campus.

Freshmen

Admission: 1,878 applied, 1,119 admitted, 202 enrolled. ***Average high school GPA:*** 3.23. ***Test scores:*** SAT critical reading scores over 500: 33%; SAT math scores over 500: 35%; ACT scores over 18: 62%; SAT critical reading scores over 600: 6%; SAT math scores over 600: 4%; ACT scores over 24: 16%.

Retention: 54% of full-time freshmen returned.

FACULTY

Total: 114, 49% full-time, 48% with terminal degrees.

Student/faculty ratio: 11:1.

ACADEMICS

Calendar: semesters. *Degrees:* associate, bachelor's, and master's.

Special study options: academic remediation for entering students, accelerated degree program, adult/continuing education programs, advanced placement credit, cooperative education, distance learning, double majors, English as a second language, external degree program, honors programs, independent study, internships, off-campus study, part-time degree program, services for LD students, student-designed majors, study abroad, summer session for credit.

Computers: 150 computers/terminals are available on campus for general student use. Students can access the following: campus intranet, computer help desk, free student e-mail accounts, online (class) grades, online (class) registration, online (class) schedules. Campuswide network is available. 100% of college-owned or -operated housing units are wired for high-speed Internet access. Wireless service is available via entire campus.

STUDENT LIFE

Housing options: on-campus residence required through junior year; coed, men-only, women-only. Campus housing is university owned. Freshman campus housing is guaranteed.

Activities and organizations: drama/theater group, student-run newspaper, choral group, Student Government Association, Cougar Activities Board, Christian Student Union and Catholic Campus Ministries, AU Gospel Ensemble, Alpha Psi Omega (Averett Players - Theatre Group), national fraternities.

Athletics Member NCAA. All Division III. ***Intercollegiate sports:*** baseball M, basketball M/W, cheerleading M(c)/W(c), cross-country running M/W, equestrian sports M(c)/W(c), football M, golf M, soccer M/W, softball W, tennis M/W, volleyball W. ***Intramural sports:*** basketball M/W, soccer M/W, softball M/W, volleyball M/W.

Campus security: 24-hour emergency response devices and patrols, late-night transport/escort service, controlled dormitory access.

Student services: personal/psychological counseling.

COSTS & FINANCIAL AID

Costs (2015–16) ***Comprehensive fee:*** $39,600 includes full-time tuition ($30,900) and room and board ($8700). Full-time tuition and fees vary according to class time, course load, location, and program. Part-time tuition: $960 per credit. Part-time tuition and fees vary according to class time, course load, location, and program. ***College room only:*** $5870. Room and board charges vary according to board plan and housing facility. ***Payment plan:*** installment. ***Waivers:*** senior citizens and employees or children of employees.

Financial Aid Of all full-time matriculated undergraduates who enrolled in 2014, 743 applied for aid, 704 were judged to have need, 76 had their need fully met. 127 Federal Work-Study jobs (averaging $926). In 2014, 105 non-need-based awards were made. ***Average percent of need met:*** 74. ***Average financial aid package:*** $23,741. ***Average need-based loan:*** $4739. ***Average need-based gift aid:*** $19,619. ***Average non-need-based aid:*** $12,178. ***Average indebtedness upon graduation:*** $31,876.

APPLYING

Standardized Tests *Required:* SAT or ACT (for admission), TOEFL for international students (for admission).

Options: electronic application.

Required: high school transcript, minimum 2.5 GPA, High school diploma. ***Recommended:*** essay or personal statement, 1 letter of recommendation.

Application deadlines: 9/1 (freshmen), 9/1 (out-of-state freshmen), 8/15 (transfers).

Notification: continuous (freshmen), continuous (out-of-state freshmen), continuous (transfers).

CONTACT

Mr. Joel Nester, Director of Admissions and International Counselor, Averett University, 420 West Main Street, English Hall, Danville, VA 24541. *Phone:* 434-791-5663. *Toll-free phone:* 800-AVERETT. *E-mail:* joel.nester@averett.edu.

Bluefield College

Bluefield, Virginia

http://www.bluefield.edu/

- **Independent Southern Baptist** comprehensive, founded 1922
- **Small-town** 82-acre campus
- **Endowment** $6.1 million
- **Coed** 926 undergraduate students, 86% full-time, 57% women, 43% men

UNDERGRAD STUDENTS

799 full-time, 127 part-time. Students come from 26 states and territories; 17 other countries; 23% are from out of state; 22% Black or African American, non-Hispanic/Latino; 4% Hispanic/Latino; 0.9% Asian, non-Hispanic/Latino; 3% Two or more races, non-Hispanic/Latino; 1% Race/ethnicity unknown; 2% international; 23% transferred in; 65% live on campus.

Freshmen

Admission: 160 enrolled. ***Average high school GPA:*** 3.2. ***Test scores:*** SAT critical reading scores over 500: 39%; SAT math scores over 500: 33%; ACT scores over 18: 42%; SAT critical reading scores over 600: 8%; SAT math scores over 600: 3%; ACT scores over 24: 8%; ACT scores over 30: 1%.

Retention: 60% of full-time freshmen returned.

FACULTY

Total: 105, 39% full-time, 47% with terminal degrees.

Student/faculty ratio: 14:1.

ACADEMICS

Calendar: semesters. *Degrees:* bachelor's and master's.

Special study options: academic remediation for entering students, adult/continuing education programs, advanced placement credit, cooperative education, distance learning, double majors, honors programs, independent study, internships, off-campus study, services for LD students, study abroad, summer session for credit.

Computers: 110 computers/terminals are available on campus for general student use. Students can access the following: campus intranet, free student e-mail accounts, online (class) grades, online (class) registration, online (class) schedules, career assessment tests, library database. Campuswide network is available. 100% of college-owned or -operated housing units are wired for high-speed Internet access. Wireless service is available via entire campus.

STUDENT LIFE

Housing options: on-campus residence required through junior year; men-only, women-only. Campus housing is university owned. Freshman applicants given priority for college housing.

Activities and organizations: drama/theater group, student-run newspaper, choral group, Baptist Collegiate Ministries, Fellowship of Christian Athletes, Student Union Board, Student Government Association, Arts Club.

Athletics Member NAIA, NCCAA. ***Intercollegiate sports:*** baseball M(s), basketball M(s)/W(s), cross-country running M(s)/W(s), football M(s), golf M(s), soccer M(s)/W(s), softball W(s), tennis M(s)/W(s), track and field M(s)/W(s), volleyball M(s)/W(s). ***Intramural sports:*** badminton M/W, baseball M, basketball M/W, football M/W, softball M/W, table tennis M/W, tennis M/W, volleyball M/W.

Campus security: controlled dormitory access, night security patrols.

Student services: personal/psychological counseling.

COSTS & FINANCIAL AID

Costs (2015–16) ***Comprehensive fee:*** $31,823 includes full-time tuition ($23,296) and room and board ($8527). Full-time tuition and fees vary according to course load and program. Part-time tuition: $953 per credit. Part-time tuition and fees vary according to course load and program. ***College room only:*** $3672. Room and board charges vary according to housing facility. ***Payment plan:*** installment. ***Waivers:*** senior citizens and employees or children of employees.

Financial Aid Of all full-time matriculated undergraduates who enrolled in 2014, 671 applied for aid, 643 were judged to have need, 60 had their need fully met. 73 Federal Work-Study jobs (averaging $856). 16 state and other part-time jobs (averaging $469). In 2014, 63 non-need-based awards were made. ***Average percent of need met:*** 54. ***Average financial aid package:*** $15,576. ***Average need-based loan:*** $4376. ***Average need-based gift aid:*** $11,647. ***Average non-need-based aid:*** $6975. ***Average indebtedness upon graduation:*** $24,344.

APPLYING

Standardized Tests *Required:* SAT or ACT (for admission).

Required: high school transcript, minimum 2.0 GPA, SAT/ACT scores. ***Required for some:*** essay or personal statement.

CONTACT

Mr. Evan Sherman, Admissions Counselor, Bluefield College, 3000 College Drive, Bluefield, VA 24605-1799. *Phone:* 276-326-4602. *Toll-free phone:* 800-872-0175. *Fax:* 276-326-4395. *E-mail:* esherman@bluefield.edu.

Bridgewater College

Bridgewater, Virginia

http://www.bridgewater.edu/

- **Independent** 4-year, founded 1880, affiliated with Church of the Brethren
- **Small-town** 300-acre campus
- **Endowment** $85.0 million
- **Coed** 1,785 undergraduate students, 99% full-time, 54% women, 46% men
- **Moderately difficult** entrance level, 48% of applicants were admitted

UNDERGRAD STUDENTS

1,766 full-time, 19 part-time. Students come from 26 states and territories; 11 other countries; 24% are from out of state; 10% Black or African American, non-Hispanic/Latino; 4% Hispanic/Latino; 1% Asian, non-Hispanic/Latino; 0.1% Native Hawaiian or other Pacific Islander, non-Hispanic/Latino; 0.5% American Indian or Alaska Native, non-Hispanic/Latino; 5% Two or more races, non-Hispanic/Latino; 3% Race/ethnicity unknown; 0.7% international; 3% transferred in; 80% live on campus.

Freshmen

Admission: 6,169 applied, 2,950 admitted, 488 enrolled. ***Average high school GPA:*** 3.61. ***Test scores:*** SAT critical reading scores over 500: 60%; SAT math scores over 500: 63%; SAT writing scores over 500: 47%; ACT scores over 18: 98%; SAT critical reading scores over 600: 19%; SAT math scores over 600: 17%; SAT writing scores over 600: 11%; ACT scores over 24: 53%; SAT critical reading scores over 700: 3%; SAT math scores over 700: 1%; SAT writing scores over 700: 1%; ACT scores over 30: 11%.

Retention: 74% of full-time freshmen returned.

FACULTY

Total: 145, 77% full-time, 70% with terminal degrees.

Student/faculty ratio: 15:1.

ACADEMICS

Calendar: 4-1-4. *Degree:* bachelor's.

Special study options: adult/continuing education programs, advanced placement credit, distance learning, double majors, honors programs, independent study, internships, off-campus study, part-time degree program, services for LD students, study abroad, summer session for credit.

Unusual degree programs: 3-2 engineering with George Washington University (BA/BA); Virginia Tech (BA/BA); nursing with Vanderbilt University (BA/MN).

Computers: 173 computers/terminals and 700 ports are available on campus for general student use. Students can access the following: campus intranet, computer help desk, free student e-mail accounts, online (class) grades, online (class) registration, online (class) schedules, Moodle (course management system), campus bulletin board system. Campuswide network is available. 100% of college-owned or -operated housing units are wired for high-speed Internet access. Wireless service is available via entire campus.

STUDENT LIFE

Housing options: on-campus residence required through senior year; coed, men-only, women-only, special housing for students with disabilities. Campus housing is university owned. Freshman campus housing is guaranteed.

Activities and organizations: drama/theater group, student-run newspaper, radio station, choral group, Eagle Productions (program board), Student Alumni Network, Physics Club, Active Minds, BC Allies.

Athletics Member NCAA. All Division III. ***Intercollegiate sports:*** baseball M, basketball M/W, cheerleading M(c)/W(c), cross-country running M/W, equestrian sports M(c)/W(c), field hockey W, football M, golf M/W, lacrosse M/W, soccer M/W, softball W, swimming and diving W, tennis M/W, track and field M/W, volleyball W, wrestling M(c). ***Intramural sports:*** badminton M/W, basketball M/W, bowling M/W, football M/W, golf M/W, racquetball M/W, soccer M/W, softball M/W, table tennis M/W, tennis M/W, ultimate Frisbee M/W, volleyball M/W.

Campus security: 24-hour emergency response devices and patrols, controlled dormitory access, emergency alert system.

Student services: health clinic, personal/psychological counseling.

COSTS & FINANCIAL AID

Costs (2015–16) ***Comprehensive fee:*** $43,000 includes full-time tuition ($30,800), mandatory fees ($680), and room and board ($11,520). Part-time tuition: $1070 per credit hour. ***Room and board:*** Room and board charges vary according to housing facility. ***Payment plan:*** installment. ***Waivers:*** senior citizens and employees or children of employees.

Financial Aid Of all full-time matriculated undergraduates who enrolled in 2014, 1,553 applied for aid, 1,417 were judged to have need, 424 had their need fully met. 324 Federal Work-Study jobs (averaging $1226). 168 state and other part-time jobs (averaging $853). In 2014, 340 non-need-based awards were made. ***Average percent of need met:*** 86. ***Average financial aid package:*** $26,549. ***Average need-based loan:*** $5004. ***Average need-based gift aid:*** $22,846. ***Average non-need-based aid:*** $16,753. ***Average indebtedness upon graduation:*** $33,326.

APPLYING

Standardized Tests *Required:* SAT or ACT (for admission).

Options: electronic application, deferred entrance.

Required: high school transcript. ***Required for some:*** interview. ***Recommended:*** essay or personal statement, minimum 3.0 GPA, interview.

Application deadlines: 5/1 (freshmen), 5/1 (out-of-state freshmen), 5/1 (transfers).

Notification: continuous (freshmen), continuous (out-of-state freshmen), continuous (transfers).

CONTACT
Mr. Jarret L. Smith, Director of Admissions, Bridgewater College, 402 East College Street, Bridgewater, VA 22812. *Phone:* 540-828-5469. *Toll-free phone:* 800-759-8328. *Fax:* 540-828-5481. *E-mail:* admissions@bridgewater.edu.

Chamberlain College of Nursing
Arlington, Virginia
http://www.chamberlain.edu/

- **Proprietary** 4-year
- **Coed**

FACULTY
Student/faculty ratio: 15:1.

ACADEMICS
Calendar: semesters. *Degree:* bachelor's.

COSTS
Costs (2014–15) ***Tuition:*** $17,160 full-time, $665 per credit hour part-time. Full-time tuition and fees vary according to course load. Part-time tuition and fees vary according to course load. ***Required fees:*** $600 full-time.

APPLYING
Standardized Tests *Required:* SAT or ACT (for admission).

CONTACT
Admissions, Chamberlain College of Nursing, 2450 Crystal Drive, Arlington, VA 22202. *Phone:* 703-416-7300. *Toll-free phone:* 888-556-8CCN.

Christendom College
Front Royal, Virginia
http://www.christendom.edu/

- **Independent Roman Catholic** comprehensive, founded 1977
- **Rural** 120-acre campus with easy access to Washington, DC
- **Endowment** $3.1 million
- **Coed** 433 undergraduate students, 100% full-time, 59% women, 41% men
- **Moderately difficult** entrance level, 88% of applicants were admitted

UNDERGRAD STUDENTS
433 full-time. Students come from 45 states and territories; 3 other countries; 75% are from out of state; 99% Race/ethnicity unknown; 0.9% international; 2% transferred in; 90% live on campus.

Freshmen
Admission: 308 applied, 271 admitted, 122 enrolled. ***Average high school GPA:*** 3.7. ***Test scores:*** SAT critical reading scores over 500: 93%; SAT math scores over 500: 76%; SAT writing scores over 500: 94%; ACT scores over 18: 100%; SAT critical reading scores over 600: 65%; SAT math scores over 600: 36%; SAT writing scores over 600: 62%; ACT scores over 24: 73%; SAT critical reading scores over 700: 29%; SAT math scores over 700: 6%; SAT writing scores over 700: 27%; ACT scores over 30: 35%.
Retention: 80% of full-time freshmen returned.

FACULTY
Total: 44, 52% full-time, 66% with terminal degrees.
Student/faculty ratio: 14:1.

ACADEMICS
Calendar: semesters. *Degrees:* associate, bachelor's, and master's.
Special study options: academic remediation for entering students, accelerated degree program, advanced placement credit, cooperative education, double majors, independent study, internships, services for LD students, study abroad, summer session for credit.
Computers: 60 computers/terminals are available on campus for general student use. Students can access the following: campus intranet, computer help desk, free student e-mail accounts. Campuswide network is available. Wireless service is available via computer centers, computer labs, learning centers, libraries, student centers.

STUDENT LIFE
Housing options: on-campus residence required through senior year; men-only, women-only. Campus housing is university owned. Freshman campus housing is guaranteed.
Activities and organizations: drama/theater group, student-run newspaper, choral group, drama, choir, Shield of Roses, Swing Dance Club, debate team.
Athletics Member USCAA. ***Intercollegiate sports:*** basketball M/W, rugby M, soccer M/W, softball W, volleyball W. ***Intramural sports:*** basketball M/W, equestrian sports M/W, football M/W, racquetball M/W, soccer M/W, table tennis M/W, tennis M/W, volleyball M/W.
Campus security: 24-hour emergency response devices, late-night transport/escort service, night patrols by trained security personnel.
Student services: health clinic, personal/psychological counseling.

COSTS & FINANCIAL AID
Costs (2015–16) ***Comprehensive fee:*** includes mandatory fees ($790) and room and board ($8980). ***Payment plan:*** installment. ***Waivers:*** employees or children of employees.
Financial Aid Of all full-time matriculated undergraduates who enrolled in 2014, 274 applied for aid, 257 were judged to have need, 242 had their need fully met. 145 state and other part-time jobs (averaging $2100). In 2014, 81 non-need-based awards were made. ***Average percent of need met:*** 85. ***Average financial aid package:*** $19,350. ***Average need-based loan:*** $7115. ***Average need-based gift aid:*** $8260. ***Average non-need-based aid:*** $10,430. ***Average indebtedness upon graduation:*** $31,991.

APPLYING
Standardized Tests *Required:* SAT or ACT (for admission).
Options: electronic application, early admission, early action.
Application fee: $25.
Required: essay or personal statement, high school transcript, 2 letters of recommendation. ***Recommended:*** minimum 3.0 GPA, interview.
Application deadlines: 3/1 (freshmen), 3/1 (transfers), 12/1 (early action).
Notification: 4/1 (freshmen), continuous until 4/1 (transfers), 12/15 (early action).

CONTACT
Christendom College, 134 Christendom Drive, Front Royal, VA 22630-5103. *Phone:* 540-636-2900 Ext. 1290. *Toll-free phone:* 800-877-5456.

Christopher Newport University
Newport News, Virginia
http://www.cnu.edu/

- **State-supported** comprehensive, founded 1960
- **Suburban** 260-acre campus with easy access to Virginia Beach
- **Endowment** $22.2 million
- **Coed** 5,096 undergraduate students, 98% full-time, 57% women, 43% men
- **Very difficult** entrance level, 56% of applicants were admitted

UNDERGRAD STUDENTS
4,990 full-time, 106 part-time. Students come from 30 states and territories; 31 other countries; 7% are from out of state; 8% Black or African American, non-Hispanic/Latino; 5% Hispanic/Latino; 2% Asian, non-Hispanic/Latino; 0.1% Native Hawaiian or other Pacific Islander, non-Hispanic/Latino; 0.3% American Indian or Alaska Native, non-Hispanic/Latino; 5% Two or more races, non-Hispanic/Latino; 4% Race/ethnicity unknown; 0.2% international; 3% transferred in; 74% live on campus.

Freshmen
Admission: 7,366 applied, 4,116 admitted, 1,228 enrolled. ***Average high school GPA:*** 3.76. ***Test scores:*** SAT critical reading scores over 500: 90%; SAT math scores over 500: 90%; ACT scores over 18: 99%; SAT critical reading scores over 600: 39%; SAT math scores over 600: 36%; ACT scores over 24: 65%; SAT critical reading scores over 700: 6%; SAT math scores over 700: 4%; ACT scores over 30: 11%.
Retention: 87% of full-time freshmen returned.

FACULTY
Total: 448, 61% full-time, 64% with terminal degrees.
Student/faculty ratio: 15:1.

ACADEMICS
Calendar: semesters. *Degrees:* bachelor's and master's.
Special study options: advanced placement credit, double majors, honors programs, independent study, internships, off-campus study, services for LD students, student-designed majors, study abroad, summer session for credit. ***ROTC:*** Army (b).
Computers: 540 computers/terminals and 1,000 ports are available on campus for general student use. Students can access the following: campus intranet, computer help desk, free student e-mail accounts, online (class) grades, online (class) registration, online (class) schedules. Campuswide network is available. 100% of college-owned or -operated housing units are wired for high-speed Internet access. Wireless service is available via entire campus.

STUDENT LIFE
Housing options: on-campus residence required through junior year; coed. Campus housing is university owned. Freshman campus housing is guaranteed.
Activities and organizations: drama/theater group, student-run newspaper, radio and television station, choral group, marching band, Intervarsity, Alpha Delta Pi, Delta Gamma, Gamma Phi Beta, Phi Mu, national fraternities, national sororities.
Athletics Member NCAA. All Division III. ***Intercollegiate sports:*** baseball M, basketball M/W, cheerleading M/W, cross-country running M/W, field hockey W, football M, golf M, lacrosse M/W, sailing M/W, soccer M/W, softball W, tennis M/W, track and field M/W, volleyball W. ***Intramural sports:*** badminton M/W, basketball M/W, crew M(c)/W(c), equestrian sports M(c)/W(c), field hockey M(c)/W(c), football M/W, gymnastics M(c)/W(c), ice hockey M(c), lacrosse M(c)/W(c), rock climbing M(c)/W(c), rugby M(c), sailing M(c)/W(c), soccer M/W, softball M/W, swimming and diving M(c)/W(c), table tennis M(c)/W(c), tennis M/W, ultimate Frisbee M/W, volleyball M/W, wrestling M(c).
Campus security: 24-hour emergency response devices and patrols, late-night transport/escort service, controlled dormitory access, campus-based University Police; Emergency Notification System; Crime Prevention Programs.
Student services: health clinic, personal/psychological counseling.

COSTS & FINANCIAL AID
Costs (2014–15) ***Tuition:*** state resident $6928 full-time, $288 per credit hour part-time; nonresident $16,860 full-time, $702 per credit hour part-time. Full-time tuition and fees vary according to course load. Part-time tuition and fees vary according to course load. ***Required fees:*** $4718 full-time, $196 per credit hour part-time. ***Room and board:*** $10,314; room only: $6564. Room and board charges vary according to board plan and housing facility. ***Payment plan:*** installment. ***Waivers:*** senior citizens and employees or children of employees.
Financial Aid Of all full-time matriculated undergraduates who enrolled in 2014, 3,251 applied for aid, 2,227 were judged to have need, 350 had their need fully met. 90 Federal Work-Study jobs (averaging $699). 1,397 state and other part-time jobs (averaging $2133). In 2014, 574 non-need-based awards were made. ***Average percent of need met:*** 63. ***Average financial aid package:*** $8511. ***Average need-based loan:*** $4205. ***Average need-based gift aid:*** $5599. ***Average non-need-based aid:*** $2093. ***Average indebtedness upon graduation:*** $28,135.

APPLYING
Standardized Tests *Required for some:* SAT or ACT (for admission).
Options: electronic application, early admission, early decision, early action, deferred entrance.
Application fee: $50.
Required: essay or personal statement, high school transcript. ***Required for some:*** interview. ***Recommended:*** minimum 3.5 GPA, 2 letters of recommendation.
Application deadlines: 2/1 (freshmen), 3/1 (transfers), 12/1 (early action).
Early decision deadline: 11/15.
Notification: 3/15 (freshmen), 4/15 (transfers), 12/15 (early decision), 1/15 (early action).

CONTACT
Mr. Rob Lange, Dean of Admission, Christopher Newport University, Office of Admission, 1 Avenue of the Arts, Newport News, VA 23606-3072. *Phone:* 757-594-7015. *Toll-free phone:* 800-333-4268. *Fax:* 757-594-7333. *E-mail:* admit@cnu.edu.

The College of William and Mary
Williamsburg, Virginia
http://www.wm.edu/

- **State-supported** university, founded 1693
- **Small-town** 1200-acre campus with easy access to Richmond
- **Endowment** $797.6 million
- **Coed** 6,299 undergraduate students, 99% full-time, 56% women, 44% men
- **Most difficult** entrance level, 33% of applicants were admitted

UNDERGRAD STUDENTS
6,214 full-time, 85 part-time. Students come from 50 states and territories; 37 other countries; 30% are from out of state; 7% Black or African American, non-Hispanic/Latino; 9% Hispanic/Latino; 8% Asian, non-Hispanic/Latino; 0.2% American Indian or Alaska Native, non-Hispanic/Latino; 4% Two or more races, non-Hispanic/Latino; 7% Race/ethnicity unknown; 5% international; 2% transferred in; 74% live on campus.

Freshmen
Admission: 14,552 applied, 4,805 admitted, 1,511 enrolled. ***Average high school GPA:*** 4.16. ***Test scores:*** SAT critical reading scores over 500: 98%; SAT math scores over 500: 99%; SAT writing scores over 500: 97%; ACT scores over 18: 100%; SAT critical reading scores over 600: 86%; SAT math scores over 600: 86%; SAT writing scores over 600: 83%; ACT scores over 24: 97%; SAT critical reading scores over 700: 45%; SAT math scores over 700: 43%; SAT writing scores over 700: 38%; ACT scores over 30: 65%.
Retention: 95% of full-time freshmen returned.

ACADEMICS
Calendar: semesters. *Degrees:* bachelor's, master's, doctoral, and post-master's certificates.
Special study options: accelerated degree program, advanced placement credit, distance learning, double majors, honors programs, independent study, internships, off-campus study, part-time degree program, services for LD students, student-designed majors, study abroad, summer session for credit. ***ROTC:*** Army (b).
Unusual degree programs: 3-2 engineering with Columbia University; 5 Year BA to MAED Programs: Elementary Education, Secondary Education, Special Education. Accelerated Combined BS /MS Degrees in Chemistry.
Computers: 275 computers/terminals and 8,000 ports are available on campus for general student use. Students can access the following: campus intranet, computer help desk, free student e-mail accounts, online (class) grades, online (class) registration, online (class) schedules. Campuswide network is available. 100% of college-owned or -operated housing units are wired for high-speed Internet access. Wireless service is available via entire campus.

STUDENT LIFE
Housing options: on-campus residence required for freshman year; coed, special housing for students with disabilities. Campus housing is university owned and leased by the school. Freshman campus housing is guaranteed.
Activities and organizations: drama/theater group, student-run newspaper, radio and television station, choral group, Alma Mater Productions, Student Assembly, Residence Hall Association, Alpha Phi Omega, International Relations Club, national fraternities, national sororities.
Athletics Member NCAA. All Division I except football (Division I-AA). ***Intercollegiate sports:*** baseball M(s), basketball M(s)/W(s), cross-country running M(s)/W(s), field hockey W(s), golf M(s)/W(s), gymnastics M(s)/W(s), lacrosse W(s), soccer M(s)/W(s), swimming and diving M/W, tennis M(s)/W(s), track and field M(s)/W(s), volleyball W(s). ***Intramural sports:*** badminton M(c)/W(c), baseball M(c), basketball M/W, bowling M/W, cheerleading M(c)/W(c), crew M(c)/W(c), cross-country running

M(c)/W(c), equestrian sports M(c)/W(c), fencing M(c)/W(c), field hockey M(c)/W(c), football M/W, golf M(c)/W(c), gymnastics M(c)/W(c), ice hockey M(c), lacrosse M(c)/W(c), racquetball M(c)/W(c), rock climbing M(c)/W(c), rugby M(c)/W(c), sailing M(c)/W(c), soccer M/W, softball M/W, swimming and diving M(c)/W(c), table tennis M(c)/W(c), tennis M(c)/W(c), ultimate Frisbee M(c)/W(c), volleyball M/W, water polo M(c)/W(c), weight lifting M/W, wrestling M(c).

Campus security: 24-hour emergency response devices and patrols, late-night transport/escort service, controlled dormitory access, The WMPD is a State certified law enforcement agency with 37 employees, providing law enforcement services for the College.

Student services: health clinic, personal/psychological counseling, legal services.

COSTS & FINANCIAL AID

Costs (2014–15) ***Tuition:*** state resident $12,428 full-time, $350 per credit hour part-time; nonresident $34,132 full-time, $1080 per credit hour part-time. Full-time tuition and fees vary according to program. No tuition increase for student's term of enrollment. ***Required fees:*** $5228 full-time. ***Room and board:*** $10,344; room only: $6398. Room and board charges vary according to board plan and housing facility. ***Payment plan:*** installment. ***Waivers:*** senior citizens and employees or children of employees.

Financial Aid Of all full-time matriculated undergraduates who enrolled in 2013, 3,098 applied for aid, 2,133 were judged to have need, 540 had their need fully met. 120 Federal Work-Study jobs (averaging $1108). In 2013, 314 non-need-based awards were made. ***Average percent of need met:*** 76. ***Average financial aid package:*** $18,442. ***Average need-based loan:*** $4463. ***Average need-based gift aid:*** $13,914. ***Average non-need-based aid:*** $6673. ***Average indebtedness upon graduation:*** $25,733.

APPLYING

Standardized Tests *Required:* SAT or ACT (for admission).

Options: electronic application, early admission, early decision, deferred entrance.

Application fee: $70.

Required: essay or personal statement, high school transcript, 1 letter of recommendation. ***Recommended:*** 2 letters of recommendation.

Application deadlines: 1/1 (freshmen), 3/1 (transfers).

Early decision deadline: 11/1.

Notification: 4/1 (freshmen), 5/1 (transfers), 12/1 (early decision).

CONTACT

Deborah Basket, Associate Dean of Admission, The College of William and Mary, PO Box 8795, Williamsburg, VA 23187-8795. *Phone:* 757-221-4223. *Fax:* 757-221-1242. *E-mail:* admission@wm.edu.

DeVry University

Arlington, Virginia

http://www.devry.edu/

- **Proprietary** comprehensive, founded 2001, part of DeVry University
- **Coed** 424 undergraduate students, 48% full-time, 30% women, 70% men
- **Minimally difficult** entrance level

UNDERGRAD STUDENTS

202 full-time, 222 part-time. 55% are from out of state; 48% Black or African American, non-Hispanic/Latino; 13% Hispanic/Latino; 3% Asian, non-Hispanic/Latino; 0.9% American Indian or Alaska Native, non-Hispanic/Latino; 2% Two or more races, non-Hispanic/Latino; 3% Race/ethnicity unknown; 5% international; 41% transferred in.

Freshmen

Admission: 18 enrolled.

FACULTY

Total: 138, 10% full-time.

Student/faculty ratio: 7:1.

ACADEMICS

Calendar: semesters. *Degrees:* associate, bachelor's, master's, and postbachelor's certificates.

Special study options: adult/continuing education programs, part-time degree program.

Computers: Students can access the following: online (class) registration.

STUDENT LIFE

Housing options: college housing not available.

COSTS & FINANCIAL AID

Costs (2014–15) ***Tuition:*** $17,052 full-time, $609 per credit hour part-time. ***Required fees:*** $80 full-time.

Financial Aid Of all full-time matriculated undergraduates who enrolled in 2007, 175 applied for aid, 164 were judged to have need, 9 had their need fully met. In 2007, 21 non-need-based awards were made. ***Average percent of need met:*** 38. ***Average financial aid package:*** $11,581. ***Average need-based loan:*** $7979. ***Average need-based gift aid:*** $5610. ***Average non-need-based aid:*** $18,172. ***Average indebtedness upon graduation:*** $12,479.

APPLYING

Application fee: $40.

Required: high school transcript, interview.

CONTACT

DeVry University, 2450 Crystal Drive, Arlington, VA 22202. *Phone:* 703-414-4000. *Toll-free phone:* 866-338-7941.

DeVry University

Chesapeake, Virginia

http://www.devry.edu/

- **Proprietary** comprehensive
- **Coed**

ACADEMICS

Degrees: associate, bachelor's, and master's.

COSTS

Costs (2014–15) ***Tuition:*** $17,052 full-time, $609 per credit hour part-time. ***Required fees:*** $80 full-time.

CONTACT

Admissions Office, DeVry University, 1317 Executive Boulevard, Suite 100, Chesapeake, VA 23320-3671. *Phone:* 757-382-5680. *Toll-free phone:* 866-338-7941.

DeVry University

Manassas, Virginia

http://www.devry.edu/

- **Proprietary** comprehensive
- **Coed**

ACADEMICS

Calendar: semesters. *Degrees:* associate, bachelor's, and master's.

COSTS

Costs (2014–15) ***Tuition:*** $17,052 full-time, $609 per credit hour part-time. ***Required fees:*** $80 full-time.

CONTACT

Admissions Office, DeVry University, 10342 Balls Ford Road, Suite 130, Manassas, VA 20109-3173. *Phone:* 703-396-6611. *Toll-free phone:* 866-338-7941.

Eastern Mennonite University

Harrisonburg, Virginia

http://www.emu.edu/

- **Independent Mennonite** comprehensive, founded 1917
- **Small-town** 93-acre campus
- **Endowment** $21.1 million
- **Coed**
- **Moderately difficult** entrance level

FACULTY

Student/faculty ratio: 10:1.

ACADEMICS

Calendar: semesters. *Degrees:* certificates, associate, bachelor's, master's, and postbachelor's certificates.

STUDENT LIFE

Housing options: on-campus residence required through junior year; coed, cooperative, special housing for students with disabilities. Campus housing is university owned. Freshman campus housing is guaranteed.

Activities and organizations: drama/theater group, student-run newspaper, choral group, Young People's Christian Association, Student Government Association, Student Education Association, Creation Care Council, Black Student Union.

Athletics Member NCAA. All Division III.

Campus security: 24-hour emergency response devices, controlled dormitory access, night watchman.

Student services: health clinic, personal/psychological counseling.

COSTS & FINANCIAL AID

Costs (2014–15) ***Comprehensive fee:*** $40,660 includes full-time tuition ($30,660), mandatory fees ($140), and room and board ($9860). Part-time tuition: $1200 per credit hour. Part-time tuition and fees vary according to course load. ***Required fees:*** $6 per credit hour part-time. ***College room only:*** $5620. Room and board charges vary according to board plan and housing facility.

Financial Aid Of all full-time matriculated undergraduates who enrolled in 2003, 735 applied for aid, 652 were judged to have need, 246 had their need fully met. 326 Federal Work-Study jobs (averaging $1787). In 2003, 82 non-need-based awards were made. ***Average percent of need met:*** 87. ***Average financial aid package:*** $15,530. ***Average need-based loan:*** $5665. ***Average need-based gift aid:*** $5520. ***Average non-need-based aid:*** $7765. ***Average indebtedness upon graduation:*** $18,208.

APPLYING

Standardized Tests *Required:* SAT or ACT (for admission).

Options: electronic application, deferred entrance.

Application fee: $25.

Required: high school transcript, minimum 2.2 GPA, Community Lifestyle Commitment. ***Required for some:*** 2 letters of recommendation. ***Recommended:*** interview.

CONTACT

Jason Good, Director of Admissions, Eastern Mennonite University, 1200 Park Road, Harrisonburg, VA 22802. *Phone:* 540-432-4118. *Toll-free phone:* 800-368-2665. *Fax:* 540-432-4444. *E-mail:* admiss@emu.edu.

★ Emory & Henry College

Emory, Virginia

http://www.ehc.edu/

- **Independent United Methodist** comprehensive, founded 1836
- **Rural** 330-acre campus
- **Endowment** $96.6 million
- **Coed** 1,012 undergraduate students, 98% full-time, 49% women, 51% men
- 72% of applicants were admitted

UNDERGRAD STUDENTS

994 full-time, 18 part-time. Students come from 33 states and territories; 6 other countries; 37% are from out of state; 10% Black or African American, non-Hispanic/Latino; 2% Hispanic/Latino; 0.5% Asian, non-Hispanic/Latino; 0.1% Native Hawaiian or other Pacific Islander, non-Hispanic/Latino; 0.7% American Indian or Alaska Native, non-Hispanic/Latino; 2% Two or more races, non-Hispanic/Latino; 7% Race/ethnicity unknown; 1% international; 7% transferred in; 80% live on campus.

Freshmen

Admission: 1,471 applied, 1,055 admitted, 253 enrolled. ***Average high school GPA:*** 3.45. ***Test scores:*** SAT critical reading scores over 500: 53%; SAT math scores over 500: 77%; SAT writing scores over 500: 36%; ACT scores over 18: 80%; SAT critical reading scores over 600: 19%; SAT math scores over 600: 12%; SAT writing scores over 600: 8%; ACT scores over 24: 34%; SAT critical reading scores over 700: 1%; SAT math scores over 700: 2%; SAT writing scores over 700: 1%; ACT scores over 30: 8%.

Retention: 74% of full-time freshmen returned.

FACULTY

Total: 130, 60% full-time, 51% with terminal degrees.

Student/faculty ratio: 11:1.

ACADEMICS

Calendar: semesters. *Degrees:* bachelor's and master's.

Special study options: academic remediation for entering students, advanced placement credit, cooperative education, double majors, external degree program, honors programs, independent study, internships, services for LD students, student-designed majors, study abroad, summer session for credit.

Computers: 200 computers/terminals are available on campus for general student use. Students can access the following: campus intranet, computer help desk, free student e-mail accounts, online (class) grades, online (class) registration, online (class) schedules. Campuswide network is available. 100% of college-owned or -operated housing units are wired for high-speed Internet access. Wireless service is available via entire campus.

STUDENT LIFE

Housing options: on-campus residence required through junior year; coed, men-only, women-only, special housing for students with disabilities. Campus housing is university owned. Freshman campus housing is guaranteed.

Activities and organizations: drama/theater group, student-run newspaper, radio and television station, choral group, marching band, E&H Outdoor Program, Alpha Psi Omega Honors Fraternity, Alpha Phi Omega Honors Fraternity, Blue Key/ Cardinal Key Honors Society, The Emory Activities Board, national sororities.

Athletics Member NCAA. All Division III. ***Intercollegiate sports:*** baseball M, basketball M/W, cheerleading M(c)/W(c), cross-country running M/W, equestrian sports M/W, football M, soccer M/W, softball W, swimming and diving W, tennis M/W, volleyball W. ***Intramural sports:*** basketball M/W, football M/W, racquetball M/W, soccer M/W, table tennis M/W, tennis M/W, ultimate Frisbee M/W, volleyball M/W.

Campus security: 24-hour emergency response devices and patrols, late-night transport/escort service, controlled dormitory access.

Student services: health clinic, personal/psychological counseling.

COSTS & FINANCIAL AID

Costs (2015–16) ***Comprehensive fee:*** $41,410 includes full-time tuition ($30,700), mandatory fees ($200), and room and board ($10,510). Full-time tuition and fees vary according to course load, degree level, and location. Part-time tuition and fees vary according to course load, degree level, and location. ***College room only:*** $5220. Room and board charges vary according to board plan, housing facility, and location. ***Payment plans:*** installment, deferred payment. ***Waivers:*** employees or children of employees.

Financial Aid Of all full-time matriculated undergraduates who enrolled in 2014, 884 applied for aid, 799 were judged to have need, 186 had their need fully met. 177 Federal Work-Study jobs (averaging $1720). In 2014, 177 non-need-based awards were made. ***Average percent of need met:*** 82. ***Average financial aid package:*** $27,315. ***Average need-based loan:*** $4559. ***Average need-based gift aid:*** $23,496. ***Average non-need-based aid:*** $15,530. ***Average indebtedness upon graduation:*** $28,126.

APPLYING

Standardized Tests *Required:* SAT or ACT (for admission).

Options: electronic application, early decision.

Required: high school transcript. ***Recommended:*** essay or personal statement, interview.

Application deadlines: rolling (freshmen), rolling (out-of-state freshmen), rolling (transfers).

Early decision deadline: 11/15.

Notification: continuous (freshmen), continuous (out-of-state freshmen), continuous (transfers), 12/15 (early decision).

CONTACT

Mr. Matt Chrisman, Director of First-Year Admissions, Emory & Henry College, PO Box 947, Emory, VA 24327-0947. *Phone:* 276-944-4121. *Toll-free phone:* 800-848-5493. *E-mail:* mchrisman@ehc.edu.

Ferrum College

Ferrum, Virginia

http://www.ferrum.edu/

- **Independent United Methodist** 4-year, founded 1913
- **Rural** 720-acre campus
- **Coed** 1,451 undergraduate students, 99% full-time, 47% women, 53% men
- **Minimally difficult** entrance level, 73% of applicants were admitted

UNDERGRAD STUDENTS

1,432 full-time, 19 part-time. 19% are from out of state; 30% Black or African American, non-Hispanic/Latino; 5% Hispanic/Latino; 0.6% Asian, non-Hispanic/Latino; 0.2% Native Hawaiian or other Pacific Islander, non-Hispanic/Latino; 0.4% American Indian or Alaska Native, non-Hispanic/Latino; 5% Two or more races, non-Hispanic/Latino; 3% Race/ethnicity unknown; 0.8% international; 5% transferred in; 89% live on campus.

Freshmen

Admission: 3,286 applied, 2,409 admitted, 499 enrolled. ***Average high school GPA:*** 2.88. ***Test scores:*** SAT critical reading scores over 500: 22%; SAT math scores over 500: 21%; SAT writing scores over 500: 12%; ACT scores over 18: 53%; SAT critical reading scores over 600: 3%; SAT math scores over 600: 1%; SAT writing scores over 600: 1%; ACT scores over 24: 25%; ACT scores over 30: 2%.

Retention: 47% of full-time freshmen returned.

FACULTY

Total: 116, 67% full-time, 60% with terminal degrees.

Student/faculty ratio: 16:1.

ACADEMICS

Calendar: semesters. *Degree:* bachelor's.

Special study options: academic remediation for entering students, adult/continuing education programs, advanced placement credit, double majors, honors programs, independent study, internships, services for LD students, student-designed majors, study abroad, summer session for credit.

Computers: Students can access the following: campus intranet, computer help desk, free student e-mail accounts, online (class) grades, online (class) registration, online (class) schedules. Campuswide network is available. 100% of college-owned or -operated housing units are wired for high-speed Internet access. Wireless service is available via entire campus.

STUDENT LIFE

Housing options: on-campus residence required through senior year; coed, women-only, special housing for students with disabilities. Campus housing is university owned. Freshman campus housing is guaranteed.

Activities and organizations: drama/theater group, student-run newspaper, radio station, choral group, Student Government Association, Agriculture Club, BACCHUS, Panther Productions, African American Student Association, Students in Free Enterprise (SIFE), national sororities.

Athletics Member NCAA. All Division III. ***Intercollegiate sports:*** baseball M, basketball M/W, cheerleading M/W, cross-country running M/W, football M, golf M, lacrosse M/W, soccer M/W, softball W, swimming and diving M/W, tennis M/W, volleyball W. ***Intramural sports:*** basketball M/W, football M/W, racquetball M/W, softball M/W, tennis M/W, ultimate Frisbee M/W.

Campus security: 24-hour emergency response devices and patrols, student patrols, late-night transport/escort service, controlled dormitory access.

Student services: health clinic, personal/psychological counseling.

COSTS & FINANCIAL AID

Costs (2014–15) ***Comprehensive fee:*** $39,765 includes full-time tuition ($29,680), mandatory fees ($115), and room and board ($9970). Part-time tuition: $595 per credit hour.

Financial Aid Of all full-time matriculated undergraduates who enrolled in 2012, 1,475 applied for aid, 1,398 were judged to have need, 93 had their need fully met. In 2012, 126 non-need-based awards were made. ***Average percent of need met:*** 79. ***Average financial aid package:*** $26,515. ***Average need-based loan:*** $4317. ***Average need-based gift aid:*** $11,128. ***Average non-need-based aid:*** $10,564. ***Average indebtedness upon graduation:*** $33,777.

APPLYING

Standardized Tests *Required:* SAT or ACT (for admission).

Options: electronic application, early admission, deferred entrance.

Application fee: $25.

Required: high school transcript. ***Required for some:*** interview. ***Recommended:*** essay or personal statement, minimum 2.0 GPA, interview.

CONTACT

Ms. Gilda Q. Woods, Associate Vice President for Enrollment Management and Dean of Admissions, Ferrum College, Spilman-Daniel House, PO Box 1000, Ferrum, VA 24088-9001. *Phone:* 540-365-4290. *Toll-free phone:* 800-868-9797. *Fax:* 540-365-4266. *E-mail:* admissions@ferrum.edu.

George Mason University

Fairfax, Virginia

http://www.gmu.edu/

- **State-supported** university, founded 1957
- **Suburban** 817-acre campus with easy access to Washington, DC
- **Endowment** $69.6 million
- **Coed** 22,343 undergraduate students, 80% full-time, 51% women, 49% men

UNDERGRAD STUDENTS

17,812 full-time, 4,531 part-time. Students come from 50 states and territories; 97 other countries; 11% are from out of state; 10% Black or African American, non-Hispanic/Latino; 12% Hispanic/Latino; 18% Asian, non-Hispanic/Latino; 0.4% Native Hawaiian or other Pacific Islander, non-Hispanic/Latino; 0.2% American Indian or Alaska Native, non-Hispanic/Latino; 4% Two or more races, non-Hispanic/Latino; 5% Race/ethnicity unknown; 4% international; 11% transferred in; 28% live on campus.

Freshmen

Admission: 3,078 enrolled. ***Average high school GPA:*** 3.65. ***Test scores:*** SAT critical reading scores over 500: 86%; SAT math scores over 500: 89%; ACT scores over 18: 99%; SAT critical reading scores over 600: 36%; SAT math scores over 600: 40%; ACT scores over 24: 74%; SAT critical reading scores over 700: 6%; SAT math scores over 700: 7%; ACT scores over 30: 13%.

Retention: 88% of full-time freshmen returned.

FACULTY

Total: 2,546, 49% full-time.

Student/faculty ratio: 16:1.

ACADEMICS

Calendar: semesters. *Degrees:* bachelor's, master's, doctoral, post-master's, and postbachelor's certificates.

Special study options: accelerated degree program, adult/continuing education programs, advanced placement credit, cooperative education, distance learning, double majors, English as a second language, freshman honors college, honors programs, independent study, internships, off-campus study, part-time degree program, services for LD students, student-designed majors, study abroad, summer session for credit. ***ROTC:*** Army (b), Air Force (c).

Computers: 622 computers/terminals and 45,871 ports are available on campus for general student use. Students can access the following: campus intranet, computer help desk, free student e-mail accounts, online (class) grades, online (class) registration, online (class) schedules. Campuswide network is available. 100% of college-owned or -operated housing units are wired for high-speed Internet access. Wireless service is available via entire campus.

STUDENT LIFE

Housing options: coed, special housing for students with disabilities. Campus housing is university owned and leased by the school. Freshman campus housing is guaranteed.

Activities and organizations: drama/theater group, student-run newspaper, radio and television station, choral group, Catholic Campus

Ministry, Muslim Student Association, National Society of Collegiate Scholars, Campus Crusade for Christ, The Gathering, national fraternities, national sororities.

Athletics Member NCAA. All Division I. ***Intercollegiate sports:*** baseball M(s), basketball M(s)/W(s), crew W(s), cross-country running M(s)/W(s), golf M(s), lacrosse W(s), soccer M(s)/W(s), softball W(s), swimming and diving M(s)/W(s), tennis M(s)/W(s), track and field M(s)/W(s), volleyball M(s)/W(s), wrestling M(s). ***Intramural sports:*** badminton M(c)/W(c), baseball M(c), basketball M/W, bowling M(c)/W(c), crew M(c)/W(c), cross-country running M(c)/W(c), equestrian sports M(c)/W(c), fencing M(c)/W(c), field hockey M(c)/W(c), football M(c), golf M/W, ice hockey M(c), lacrosse M(c)/W(c), rugby M(c)/W(c), soccer M(c)/W(c), softball M/W(c), swimming and diving M/W, tennis M(c)/W(c), track and field M(c)/W(c), ultimate Frisbee M(c)/W(c), volleyball M(c)/W(c), water polo M/W, wrestling M(c).

Campus security: 24-hour emergency response devices and patrols, student patrols, late-night transport/escort service, controlled dormitory access.

Student services: health clinic, personal/psychological counseling, women's center.

COSTS & FINANCIAL AID

Costs (2014–15) ***Tuition:*** state resident $7562 full-time, $315 per credit hour part-time; nonresident $27,140 full-time, $1131 per credit hour part-time. Full-time tuition and fees vary according to course load. Part-time tuition and fees vary according to course load. ***Required fees:*** $2820 full-time, $118 per credit hour part-time. ***Room and board:*** $10,100; room only: $6000. Room and board charges vary according to board plan and housing facility. ***Payment plans:*** installment, deferred payment. ***Waivers:*** senior citizens and employees or children of employees.

Financial Aid Of all full-time matriculated undergraduates who enrolled in 2013, 11,714 applied for aid, 9,244 were judged to have need, 475 had their need fully met. 331 Federal Work-Study jobs (averaging $2234). In 2013, 472 non-need-based awards were made. ***Average percent of need met:*** 56. ***Average financial aid package:*** $11,955. ***Average need-based loan:*** $4591. ***Average need-based gift aid:*** $5889. ***Average non-need-based aid:*** $6936. ***Average indebtedness upon graduation:*** $27,206.

APPLYING

Standardized Tests *Required for some:* SAT or ACT (for admission). *Recommended:* SAT and SAT Subject Tests or ACT (for admission).

Required: high school transcript. ***Required for some:*** Essay or personal statement not required, but strongly preferred. Audition required for dance and music. Portfolio required for art and visual technology and computer game design. Interview and audition or portfolio required for theater. ***Recommended:*** 3 letters of recommendation.

CONTACT

Matthew Boyce, Director, Undergraduate Admissions, George Mason University, 4400 University Drive, MSN 3A4, Fairfax, VA 22030-4444. *Phone:* 703-993-5304. *Fax:* 703-993-2392. *E-mail:* mboyce3@gmu.edu.

Hampden-Sydney College

Hampden-Sydney, Virginia

http://www.hsc.edu/

- **Independent** 4-year, founded 1776, affiliated with Presbyterian Church (U.S.A.)
- **Rural** 1340-acre campus with easy access to Richmond, Lynchburg, Charlottesville
- **Endowment** $150.9 million
- **Men only** 1,105 undergraduate students, 100% full-time
- **Moderately difficult** entrance level, 47% of applicants were admitted

UNDERGRAD STUDENTS

1,105 full-time. Students come from 32 states and territories; 14 other countries; 30% are from out of state; 8% Black or African American, non-Hispanic/Latino; 2% Hispanic/Latino; 2% Asian, non-Hispanic/Latino; 0.5% American Indian or Alaska Native, non-Hispanic/Latino; 5% Two or more races, non-Hispanic/Latino; 0.8% Race/ethnicity unknown; 0.1% international; 2% transferred in; 95% live on campus.

Freshmen

Admission: 3,639 applied, 1,720 admitted, 322 enrolled. ***Average high school GPA:*** 3.38. ***Test scores:*** SAT critical reading scores over 500: 74%; SAT math scores over 500: 79%; SAT critical reading scores over 600: 26%; SAT math scores over 600: 28%; SAT critical reading scores over 700: 5%; SAT math scores over 700: 3%.

Retention: 83% of full-time freshmen returned.

FACULTY

Total: 105, 81% full-time, 84% with terminal degrees.

Student/faculty ratio: 11:1.

ACADEMICS

Calendar: semesters. *Degree:* bachelor's.

Special study options: academic remediation for entering students, advanced placement credit, double majors, honors programs, independent study, internships, off-campus study, study abroad, summer session for credit. ***ROTC:*** Army (c).

Unusual degree programs: 3-2 engineering with University of Virginia, Old Dominion University.

Computers: 200 computers/terminals are available on campus for general student use. Students can access the following: campus intranet, computer help desk, free student e-mail accounts, online (class) grades, online (class) registration, online (class) schedules. Campuswide network is available. 100% of college-owned or -operated housing units are wired for high-speed Internet access. Wireless service is available via entire campus.

STUDENT LIFE

Housing options: on-campus residence required through senior year; men-only, special housing for students with disabilities. Campus housing is university owned. Freshman campus housing is guaranteed.

Activities and organizations: drama/theater group, student-run newspaper, radio station, choral group, Republican Society, Pre-Health Society, Outdoors Club, Tiger Athletic Club, Pre-Law Society, national fraternities.

Athletics Member NCAA. All Division III. ***Intercollegiate sports:*** baseball M, basketball M, crew M(c), cross-country running M, fencing M(c), football M, golf M, lacrosse M, riflery M(c), rugby M(c), soccer M, swimming and diving M, tennis M, ultimate Frisbee M(c), wrestling M(c). ***Intramural sports:*** archery M(c), basketball M, fencing M(c), football M, lacrosse M(c), racquetball M(c), riflery M(c), soccer M, softball M, swimming and diving M(c), volleyball M, water polo M(c), wrestling M(c).

Campus security: 24-hour emergency response devices and patrols, controlled dormitory access.

Student services: health clinic, personal/psychological counseling.

COSTS & FINANCIAL AID

Costs (2014–15) ***Comprehensive fee:*** $51,916 includes full-time tuition ($38,018), mandatory fees ($1586), and room and board ($12,312). Part-time tuition: $1200 per credit hour. ***College room only:*** $5156. Room and board charges vary according to board plan and housing facility. ***Payment plan:*** installment. ***Waivers:*** employees or children of employees.

Financial Aid Of all full-time matriculated undergraduates who enrolled in 2014, 809 applied for aid, 712 were judged to have need, 148 had their need fully met. 205 Federal Work-Study jobs (averaging $1385). In 2014, 373 non-need-based awards were made. ***Average percent of need met:*** 79. ***Average financial aid package:*** $31,035. ***Average need-based loan:*** $4889. ***Average need-based gift aid:*** $26,540. ***Average non-need-based aid:*** $13,692. ***Average indebtedness upon graduation:*** $30,644.

APPLYING

Standardized Tests *Required:* SAT or ACT (for admission).

Options: electronic application, early admission, early decision, early action.

Application fee: $30.

Required: essay or personal statement, high school transcript, 2 letters of recommendation. ***Recommended:*** interview.

Application deadlines: 3/1 (freshmen), 7/1 (transfers), 1/15 (early action).

Early decision deadline: 11/15.

Notification: 4/15 (freshmen), 7/31 (transfers), 12/15 (early decision), 2/15 (early action).

CONTACT
Dean Anita Garland, Dean of Admissions, Hampden-Sydney College, PO Box 667, Hampden-Sydney, VA 23943-0667. *Phone:* 434-223-6120. *Toll-free phone:* 800-755-0733. *Fax:* 434-223-6346. *E-mail:* hsapp@hsc.edu.

Hampton University
Hampton, Virginia
http://www.hamptonu.edu/

- **Independent** comprehensive, founded 1868
- **Urban** 314-acre campus with easy access to Norfolk
- **Endowment** $288.4 million
- **Coed** 3,504 undergraduate students, 94% full-time, 65% women, 35% men
- **Moderately difficult** entrance level, 29% of applicants were admitted

UNDERGRAD STUDENTS
3,277 full-time, 227 part-time. Students come from 44 states and territories; 33 other countries; 78% are from out of state; 94% Black or African American, non-Hispanic/Latino; 1% Hispanic/Latino; 0.7% Asian, non-Hispanic/Latino; 0.1% American Indian or Alaska Native, non-Hispanic/Latino; 1% international; 4% transferred in; 75% live on campus.

Freshmen
Admission: 19,473 applied, 5,659 admitted, 882 enrolled. ***Average high school GPA:*** 3.2. ***Test scores:*** SAT critical reading scores over 500: 52%; SAT math scores over 500: 47%; ACT scores over 18: 77%; SAT critical reading scores over 600: 11%; SAT math scores over 600: 10%; ACT scores over 24: 26%; SAT critical reading scores over 700: 1%; SAT math scores over 700: 1%; ACT scores over 30: 4%.
Retention: 76% of full-time freshmen returned.

FACULTY
Student/faculty ratio: 10:1.

ACADEMICS
Calendar: semesters. *Degrees:* certificates, associate, bachelor's, master's, doctoral, and post-master's certificates.
Special study options: academic remediation for entering students, accelerated degree program, adult/continuing education programs, advanced placement credit, cooperative education, distance learning, double majors, honors programs, independent study, internships, off-campus study, part-time degree program, services for LD students, study abroad, summer session for credit. ***ROTC:*** Army (b), Navy (b).
Computers: 1,500 computers/terminals are available on campus for general student use. Students can access the following: campus intranet, computer help desk, free student e-mail accounts, online (class) grades, online (class) registration, online (class) schedules, Banner Systems. Campuswide network is available. 100% of college-owned or -operated housing units are wired for high-speed Internet access. Wireless service is available via entire campus.

STUDENT LIFE
Housing options: coed, men-only, women-only. Campus housing is university owned. Freshman applicants given priority for college housing.
Activities and organizations: drama/theater group, student-run newspaper, radio station, choral group, marching band, student government, student leaders, Student Union Board, student recruitment team, resident assistants, national fraternities, national sororities.
Athletics Member NCAA. All Division I. ***Intercollegiate sports:*** basketball M(s)/W(s), bowling W(s), cheerleading W, cross-country running M(s)/W(s), football M(s), golf M(s)/W(s), sailing M(s)/W(s), softball W(s), tennis M(s)/W(s), track and field M(s)/W(s), volleyball W(s). ***Intramural sports:*** badminton M/W, basketball M/W, bowling W, football M, lacrosse M/W, soccer M, softball W, swimming and diving M/W, table tennis M/W, volleyball W.
Campus security: 24-hour emergency response devices and patrols, controlled dormitory access, emergency call boxes.
Student services: health clinic, personal/psychological counseling, women's center.

COSTS & FINANCIAL AID
Costs (2014–15) ***Comprehensive fee:*** $31,452 includes full-time tuition ($19,548), mandatory fees ($2212), and room and board ($9692). Full-time tuition and fees vary according to course load, degree level, location, program, and reciprocity agreements. Part-time tuition: $496 per credit hour. Part-time tuition and fees vary according to class time, course load, location, and reciprocity agreements. ***College room only:*** $5040. Room and board charges vary according to board plan, housing facility, and location. ***Payment plans:*** installment, deferred payment. ***Waivers:*** employees or children of employees.
Financial Aid Of all full-time matriculated undergraduates who enrolled in 2014, 2,046 applied for aid, 1,740 were judged to have need, 546 had their need fully met. 172 Federal Work-Study jobs (averaging $655). 138 state and other part-time jobs (averaging $967). In 2014, 29 non-need-based awards were made. ***Average percent of need met:*** 52. ***Average financial aid package:*** $5789. ***Average need-based loan:*** $5502. ***Average need-based gift aid:*** $5003. ***Average non-need-based aid:*** $12,424. ***Average indebtedness upon graduation:*** $9231. ***Financial aid deadline:*** 4/15.

APPLYING
Standardized Tests *Required for some:* SAT or ACT (for admission).
Options: electronic application, early admission, early action, deferred entrance.
Application fee: $35.
Required: essay or personal statement, high school transcript, minimum 2.5 GPA, 3 letters of recommendation. ***Required for some:*** Audition required for music.
Application deadlines: 3/1 (freshmen), 11/1 (early action).
Notification: 12/15 (early action).

CONTACT
Mr. Derrick Boone, Director, Freshman Studies, Hampton University, 204 Student Center, Hampton University, Hampton, VA 23668. *Phone:* 757-727-5901. *Toll-free phone:* 800-624-3328. *Fax:* 757-727-5095. *E-mail:* derrick.boone@hamptonu.edu.

Hollins University
Roanoke, Virginia
http://www.hollins.edu/

- **Independent** comprehensive, founded 1842
- **Suburban** 475-acre campus
- **Endowment** $180.7 million
- **Undergraduate: women only; graduate: coed** 596 undergraduate students, 97% full-time, 100% women
- **Moderately difficult** entrance level, 57% of applicants were admitted

UNDERGRAD STUDENTS
580 full-time, 16 part-time. Students come from 36 states and territories; 23 other countries; 44% are from out of state; 11% Black or African American, non-Hispanic/Latino; 5% Hispanic/Latino; 3% Asian, non-Hispanic/Latino; 0.9% American Indian or Alaska Native, non-Hispanic/Latino; 2% Two or more races, non-Hispanic/Latino; 1% Race/ethnicity unknown; 6% international; 4% transferred in; 77% live on campus.

Freshmen
Admission: 1,782 applied, 1,008 admitted, 165 enrolled. ***Average high school GPA:*** 3.6. ***Test scores:*** SAT critical reading scores over 500: 76%; SAT math scores over 500: 64%; SAT writing scores over 500: 75%; ACT scores over 18: 96%; SAT critical reading scores over 600: 38%; SAT math scores over 600: 15%; SAT writing scores over 600: 25%; ACT scores over 24: 54%; SAT critical reading scores over 700: 8%; SAT math scores over 700: 2%; SAT writing scores over 700: 5%; ACT scores over 30: 14%.
Retention: 80% of full-time freshmen returned.

FACULTY
Total: 97, 73% full-time, 87% with terminal degrees.
Student/faculty ratio: 8:1.

ACADEMICS
Calendar: 4-1-4. *Degrees:* bachelor's, master's, post-master's, and postbachelor's certificates.

Special study options: accelerated degree program, adult/continuing education programs, advanced placement credit, double majors, independent study, internships, off-campus study, part-time degree program, services for LD students, student-designed majors, study abroad.

Computers: 100 computers/terminals and 3,000 ports are available on campus for general student use. Students can access the following: campus intranet, computer help desk, free student e-mail accounts, online (class) grades, online (class) registration, online (class) schedules, applications software. Campuswide network is available. 100% of college-owned or -operated housing units are wired for high-speed Internet access. Wireless service is available via entire campus.

STUDENT LIFE

Housing options: on-campus residence required through senior year; women-only, special housing for students with disabilities. Campus housing is university owned. Freshman campus housing is guaranteed.

Activities and organizations: drama/theater group, student-run radio and television station, choral group, Student Government Association, Hollins Activity Board, Hollins Repertory Dance Company, Black Student Alliance, Arts Association.

Athletics Member NCAA. All Division III. ***Intercollegiate sports:*** basketball W, equestrian sports W, fencing W(c), golf W, lacrosse W, soccer W, swimming and diving W, tennis W, volleyball W.

Campus security: 24-hour emergency response devices and patrols, late-night transport/escort service, controlled dormitory access, emergency call boxes.

Student services: health clinic, personal/psychological counseling, women's center.

COSTS & FINANCIAL AID

Costs (2015–16) ***Comprehensive fee:*** $47,935 includes full-time tuition ($35,000), mandatory fees ($635), and room and board ($12,300). Part-time tuition: $1094 per credit hour. ***Required fees:*** $323 per year part-time. ***Payment plans:*** tuition prepayment, installment. ***Waivers:*** employees or children of employees.

Financial Aid Of all full-time matriculated undergraduates who enrolled in 2014, 500 applied for aid, 462 were judged to have need, 93 had their need fully met. In 2014, 109 non-need-based awards were made. ***Average percent of need met:*** 83. ***Average financial aid package:*** $33,342. ***Average need-based loan:*** $5164. ***Average need-based gift aid:*** $28,320. ***Average non-need-based aid:*** $23,067. ***Average indebtedness upon graduation:*** $37,332.

APPLYING

Standardized Tests *Required:* SAT or ACT (for admission).

Options: electronic application, early admission, early decision, early action, deferred entrance.

Required: essay or personal statement, high school transcript, 2 letters of recommendation. ***Recommended:*** interview.

Application deadlines: rolling (freshmen), 12/1 (early action).

Early decision deadline: 11/1.

Notification: continuous (freshmen), 11/15 (early decision), 12/15 (early action).

CONTACT

Ms. Nicole Johnson Williams, Associate Dean of Admissions, Hollins University, PO Box 9707, Roanoke, VA 24020-1707. *Phone:* 540-362-6401. *Toll-free phone:* 800-456-9595. *Fax:* 540-362-6218. *E-mail:* huadm@hollins.edu.

ITT Technical Institute

Chantilly, Virginia

http://www.itt-tech.edu/

- **Proprietary** primarily 2-year, founded 2002, part of ITT Educational Services, Inc.
- **Coed**
- **Minimally difficult** entrance level

ACADEMICS

Calendar: quarters. *Degrees:* associate and bachelor's.

STUDENT LIFE

Housing options: college housing not available.

CONTACT

Director of Recruitment, ITT Technical Institute, 14420 Albemarle Point Place, Suite 100, Chantilly, VA 20151. *Phone:* 703-263-2541. *Toll-free phone:* 888-895-8324.

ITT Technical Institute

Norfolk, Virginia

http://www.itt-tech.edu/

- **Proprietary** primarily 2-year, founded 1988, part of ITT Educational Services, Inc.
- **Suburban** campus
- **Coed**
- **Minimally difficult** entrance level

ACADEMICS

Calendar: quarters. *Degrees:* associate and bachelor's.

STUDENT LIFE

Housing options: college housing not available.

FINANCIAL AID

Financial Aid Of all full-time matriculated undergraduates who enrolled in 2013, 3 Federal Work-Study jobs (averaging $5000).

CONTACT

Director of Recruitment, ITT Technical Institute, 5425 Robin Hood Road, Norfolk, VA 23513. *Phone:* 757-466-1260. *Toll-free phone:* 888-253-8324.

ITT Technical Institute

Richmond, Virginia

http://www.itt-tech.edu/

- **Proprietary** primarily 2-year, founded 1999, part of ITT Educational Services, Inc.
- **Coed**
- **Minimally difficult** entrance level

ACADEMICS

Calendar: quarters. *Degrees:* associate and bachelor's.

STUDENT LIFE

Housing options: college housing not available.

CONTACT

Director of Recruitment, ITT Technical Institute, 300 Gateway Centre Parkway, Richmond, VA 23235. *Phone:* 804-330-4992. *Toll-free phone:* 888-330-4888.

ITT Technical Institute

Salem, Virginia

http://www.itt-tech.edu/

- **Proprietary** primarily 2-year
- **Coed**
- **Minimally difficult** entrance level

ACADEMICS

Degrees: associate and bachelor's.

CONTACT

Director of Recruitment, ITT Technical Institute, 2159 Apperson Drive, Salem, VA 24153. *Phone:* 540-989-2500. *Toll-free phone:* 877-208-6132.

ITT Technical Institute

Springfield, Virginia

http://www.itt-tech.edu/

- **Proprietary** primarily 2-year, founded 2002, part of ITT Educational Services, Inc.
- **Coed**
- **Minimally difficult** entrance level

ACADEMICS

Calendar: quarters. *Degrees:* associate and bachelor's.

STUDENT LIFE
Housing options: college housing not available.

CONTACT
Director of Recruitment, ITT Technical Institute, 7300 Boston Boulevard, Springfield, VA 22153. *Phone:* 703-440-9535. *Toll-free phone:* 866-817-8324.

James Madison University

Harrisonburg, Virginia

http://www.jmu.edu/

- **State-supported** comprehensive, founded 1908
- **Small-town** 721-acre campus
- **Coed** 19,142 undergraduate students, 94% full-time, 59% women, 41% men
- **Very difficult** entrance level, 66% of applicants were admitted

UNDERGRAD STUDENTS
18,057 full-time, 1,085 part-time. 25% are from out of state; 4% Black or African American, non-Hispanic/Latino; 5% Hispanic/Latino; 4% Asian, non-Hispanic/Latino; 0.2% Native Hawaiian or other Pacific Islander, non-Hispanic/Latino; 0.2% American Indian or Alaska Native, non-Hispanic/Latino; 4% Two or more races, non-Hispanic/Latino; 3% Race/ethnicity unknown; 2% international; 4% transferred in; 32% live on campus.

Freshmen
Admission: 22,550 applied, 14,823 admitted, 4,364 enrolled. ***Test scores:*** SAT critical reading scores over 500: 82%; SAT math scores over 500: 86%; ACT scores over 18: 99%; SAT critical reading scores over 600: 27%; SAT math scores over 600: 32%; ACT scores over 24: 65%; SAT critical reading scores over 700: 3%; SAT math scores over 700: 2%; ACT scores over 30: 6%.

Retention: 92% of full-time freshmen returned.

FACULTY
Total: 1,487, 67% full-time, 57% with terminal degrees.

Student/faculty ratio: 16:1.

ACADEMICS
Calendar: semesters. *Degrees:* bachelor's, master's, and doctoral (also offers specialist in education degree).

Special study options: accelerated degree program, adult/continuing education programs, advanced placement credit, distance learning, double majors, English as a second language, freshman honors college, honors programs, independent study, internships, off-campus study, part-time degree program, services for LD students, student-designed majors, study abroad, summer session for credit. ***ROTC:*** Army (b), Air Force (c).

Unusual degree programs: 3-2 forestry with Virginia Polytechnic Institute and State University.

Computers: Students can access the following: campus intranet, computer help desk, free student e-mail accounts, online (class) grades, online (class) registration, online (class) schedules. Campuswide network is available. Wireless service is available via classrooms, dorm rooms, learning centers, libraries, student centers.

STUDENT LIFE
Housing options: on-campus residence required for freshman year; coed, special housing for students with disabilities. Campus housing is university owned and leased by the school. Freshman campus housing is guaranteed.

Activities and organizations: drama/theater group, student-run newspaper, radio station, choral group, marching band, national fraternities, national sororities.

Athletics Member NCAA. All Division I except football (Division I-AA). ***Intercollegiate sports:*** baseball M(s), basketball M(s)/W(s), cheerleading M/W, cross-country running W(s), field hockey W(s), golf M(s)/W(s), lacrosse W(s), soccer M(s)/W(s), softball W(s), swimming and diving W(s), tennis M(s)/W(s), track and field W(s), volleyball W(s). ***Intramural sports:*** archery M(c)/W(c), baseball M(c), basketball M/W, bowling M/W, cheerleading W(c), crew M(c)/W(c), cross-country running M(c)/W(c), equestrian sports M(c)/W(c), fencing M(c)/W(c), field hockey W(c), football M/W, golf M/W, gymnastics M(c)/W(c), ice hockey M(c)/W(c), lacrosse M(c)/W(c), racquetball M/W, rugby M(c)/W(c), skiing (downhill) M(c)/W(c), soccer M/W, softball M/W, squash M(c)/W(c), swimming and diving M(c)/W(c), table tennis M/W, tennis M/W, track and field M(c)/W(c), ultimate Frisbee M(c)/W(c), volleyball M/W, water polo M(c)/W(c), wrestling M(c).

Campus security: 24-hour emergency response devices and patrols, student patrols, late-night transport/escort service, controlled dormitory access, lighted pathways.

Student services: health clinic, personal/psychological counseling, women's center.

COSTS & FINANCIAL AID
Costs (2014–15) ***Tuition:*** state resident $5406 full-time, $179 per credit hour part-time; nonresident $20,266 full-time, $656 per credit hour part-time. ***Required fees:*** $4256 full-time. ***Room and board:*** $8828; room only: $4564.

Financial Aid Of all full-time matriculated undergraduates who enrolled in 2014, 10,592 applied for aid, 7,303 were judged to have need, 5,012 had their need fully met. In 2014, 144 non-need-based awards were made. ***Average percent of need met:*** 43. ***Average financial aid package:*** $10,025. ***Average need-based loan:*** $4670. ***Average need-based gift aid:*** $7613. ***Average non-need-based aid:*** $3172. ***Average indebtedness upon graduation:*** $23,732.

APPLYING
Standardized Tests *Required:* SAT or ACT (for admission).

Options: electronic application, early action, deferred entrance.

Application fee: $60.

Required: high school transcript. ***Recommended:*** minimum 3.0 GPA.

CONTACT
James Madison University, 800 South Main Street, Harrisonburg, VA 22807. *Phone:* 540-568-5681.

Jefferson College of Health Sciences

Roanoke, Virginia

http://www.jchs.edu/

- **Independent** comprehensive, founded 1982
- **Urban** 1-acre campus
- **Endowment** $2.0 million
- **Coed** 876 undergraduate students, 84% full-time, 80% women, 20% men
- **Moderately difficult** entrance level, 38% of applicants were admitted

UNDERGRAD STUDENTS
739 full-time, 137 part-time. Students come from 30 states and territories; 11% are from out of state; 8% Black or African American, non-Hispanic/Latino; 4% Hispanic/Latino; 2% Asian, non-Hispanic/Latino; 0.1% American Indian or Alaska Native, non-Hispanic/Latino; 2% Two or more races, non-Hispanic/Latino; 1% Race/ethnicity unknown; 0.1% international; 21% transferred in; 16% live on campus.

Freshmen
Admission: 540 applied, 206 admitted, 76 enrolled. ***Average high school GPA:*** 3.49. ***Test scores:*** SAT critical reading scores over 500: 46%; SAT math scores over 500: 35%; SAT writing scores over 500: 40%; SAT critical reading scores over 600: 11%; SAT math scores over 600: 3%; SAT writing scores over 600: 5%; SAT math scores over 700: 1%.

Retention: 61% of full-time freshmen returned.

FACULTY
Total: 140, 56% full-time.

Student/faculty ratio: 7:1.

ACADEMICS
Calendar: semesters. *Degrees:* certificates, associate, bachelor's, and master's.

Special study options: accelerated degree program, adult/continuing education programs, advanced placement credit, cooperative education, distance learning, double majors, English as a second language, independent study, internships, off-campus study, part-time degree program, services for LD students, summer session for credit.

Computers: 72 computers/terminals are available on campus for general student use. Students can access the following: free student e-mail accounts, online (class) grades, online (class) registration, online (class) schedules. Campuswide network is available. 100% of college-owned or -

operated housing units are wired for high-speed Internet access. Wireless service is available via classrooms, computer labs, learning centers, libraries.

STUDENT LIFE

Housing options: coed. Campus housing is university owned.

Activities and organizations: student-run newspaper, choral group, Jefferson Activities Group (JAG), Student Ambassadors, Hands of Healing, American Medical Students Association (AMSA), Student Nurses Association.

Athletics *Intercollegiate sports:* basketball M(c), cross-country running M(c)/W(c), softball M(c)/W(c), tennis M(c)/W(c), volleyball M(c)/W(c). ***Intramural sports:*** table tennis M(c)/W(c).

Campus security: 24-hour emergency response devices and patrols, late-night transport/escort service, controlled dormitory access.

Student services: personal/psychological counseling.

COSTS & FINANCIAL AID

Costs (2014–15) *Comprehensive fee:* $31,050 includes full-time tuition ($23,080), mandatory fees ($300), and room and board ($7670). Full-time tuition and fees vary according to course load. Part-time tuition: $670 per credit hour. Part-time tuition and fees vary according to course load. ***Waivers:*** employees or children of employees.

Financial Aid Of all full-time matriculated undergraduates who enrolled in 2013, 686 applied for aid, 625 were judged to have need.

APPLYING

Standardized Tests *Required:* SAT or ACT (for admission). *Recommended:* SAT (for admission).

Options: electronic application, deferred entrance.

Application fee: $35.

Required: high school transcript, minimum 2.0 GPA. ***Required for some:*** interview.

Application deadlines: rolling (freshmen), rolling (transfers).

Notification: continuous (freshmen), continuous (transfers).

CONTACT

Jefferson College of Health Sciences, 101 Elm Avenue, SE, Roanoke, VA 24013. *Phone:* 540-985-9083. *Toll-free phone:* 888-985-8483.

★ Liberty University

Lynchburg, Virginia

http://www.liberty.edu/

- **Independent nondenominational** comprehensive, founded 1971
- **Suburban** 6500-acre campus
- **Coed** 12,645 undergraduate students, 97% full-time, 52% women, 48% men
- **Minimally difficult** entrance level, 20% of applicants were admitted

UNDERGRAD STUDENTS

12,215 full-time, 430 part-time. 60% are from out of state; 6% Black or African American, non-Hispanic/Latino; 2% Hispanic/Latino; 2% Asian, non-Hispanic/Latino; 0.2% Native Hawaiian or other Pacific Islander, non-Hispanic/Latino; 0.4% American Indian or Alaska Native, non-Hispanic/Latino; 3% Two or more races, non-Hispanic/Latino; 14% Race/ethnicity unknown; 6% international; 60% live on campus.

Freshmen

Admission: 29,490 applied, 5,966 admitted, 2,719 enrolled. ***Average high school GPA:*** 3.39. ***Test scores:*** SAT critical reading scores over 500: 63%; SAT math scores over 500: 56%; SAT writing scores over 500: 53%; ACT scores over 18: 87%; SAT critical reading scores over 600: 24%; SAT math scores over 600: 19%; SAT writing scores over 600: 17%; ACT scores over 24: 44%; SAT critical reading scores over 700: 4%; SAT math scores over 700: 3%; SAT writing scores over 700: 3%; ACT scores over 30: 9%.

Retention: 78% of full-time freshmen returned.

FACULTY

Total: 2,873, 63% full-time.

Student/faculty ratio: 18:1.

ACADEMICS

Calendar: semesters. *Degrees:* certificates, associate, bachelor's, master's, doctoral, and post-master's certificates (also offers external degree program with significant enrollment not reflected in profile).

Special study options: academic remediation for entering students, accelerated degree program, advanced placement credit, cooperative education, distance learning, double majors, English as a second language, external degree program, honors programs, independent study, internships, off-campus study, part-time degree program, services for LD students, student-designed majors, study abroad, summer session for credit. ***ROTC:*** Army (b), Air Force (c).

Computers: 820 computers/terminals are available on campus for general student use. Students can access the following: computer help desk, free student e-mail accounts, online (class) grades, online (class) registration, online (class) schedules. Campuswide network is available. 100% of college-owned or -operated housing units are wired for high-speed Internet access. Wireless service is available via entire campus.

STUDENT LIFE

Housing options: on-campus residence required through senior year; men-only, women-only, special housing for students with disabilities. Campus housing is university owned. Freshman campus housing is guaranteed.

Activities and organizations: drama/theater group, student-run newspaper, radio station, choral group, marching band, Campus Serve.

Athletics Member NCAA. All Division I except football (Division I-AA). ***Intercollegiate sports:*** baseball M(s), basketball M(s)/W(s), cheerleading M(s)/W(s), crew M(c)/W(c), cross-country running M(s)/W(s), equestrian sports W(c), field hockey W(s), golf M(s), ice hockey M(c)/W(c), lacrosse W(s), soccer M(s)/W(s), softball W(s), swimming and diving W(s), tennis M(s)/W(s), track and field M(s)/W(s), volleyball M(c)/W(s). ***Intramural sports:*** archery M(c)/W(c), basketball M/W, football M/W, gymnastics M(c)/W(c), lacrosse M(c), racquetball M(c)/W(c), skiing (downhill) M(c)/W(c), soccer M/W, softball M/W, table tennis M/W, tennis M/W, ultimate Frisbee M(c)/W(c), wrestling M(c).

Campus security: 24-hour patrols, late-night transport/escort service, 24-hour emergency dispatch.

Student services: health clinic, personal/psychological counseling.

COSTS & FINANCIAL AID

Costs (2014–15) *Comprehensive fee:* $30,786 includes full-time tuition ($21,300), mandatory fees ($700), and room and board ($8786). Full-time tuition and fees vary according to course load. Part-time tuition: $730 per credit hour. Part-time tuition and fees vary according to course load. ***College room only:*** $5486. Room and board charges vary according to housing facility. ***Payment plan:*** installment. ***Waivers:*** employees or children of employees.

Financial Aid Of all full-time matriculated undergraduates who enrolled in 2014, 11,102 applied for aid, 8,918 were judged to have need, 1,014 had their need fully met. In 2014, 804 non-need-based awards were made. ***Average percent of need met:*** 59. ***Average financial aid package:*** $13,999. ***Average need-based loan:*** $4174. ***Average need-based gift aid:*** $10,006. ***Average non-need-based aid:*** $8404. ***Average indebtedness upon graduation:*** $20,451. ***Financial aid deadline:*** 3/1.

APPLYING

Standardized Tests *Required:* SAT or ACT (for admission).

Options: electronic application.

Application fee: $40.

Required: essay or personal statement, high school transcript, minimum 2.0 GPA. ***Recommended:*** minimum 2.0 GPA.

Application deadlines: rolling (freshmen), rolling (out-of-state freshmen), rolling (transfers).

Notification: continuous (freshmen), continuous (out-of-state freshmen), continuous (transfers).

CONTACT

Dr. Terry Elam, Director of Admissions, Liberty University, 1971 University Boulevard, Lynchburg, VA 24515. *Phone:* 434-592-3966. *Toll-free phone:* 800-543-5317. *Fax:* 800-542-2311. *E-mail:* admissions@liberty.edu.

Longwood University
Farmville, Virginia
http://www.longwood.edu/

- **State-supported** comprehensive, founded 1839, part of The State Council of Higher Education for Virginia
- **Small-town** 60-acre campus with easy access to Richmond
- **Endowment** $54.1 million
- **Coed** 4,574 undergraduate students, 91% full-time, 66% women, 34% men
- **Moderately difficult** entrance level, 73% of applicants were admitted

UNDERGRAD STUDENTS
4,183 full-time, 391 part-time. Students come from 35 states and territories; 18 other countries; 4% are from out of state; 8% Black or African American, non-Hispanic/Latino; 5% Hispanic/Latino; 1% Asian, non-Hispanic/Latino; 0.1% Native Hawaiian or other Pacific Islander, non-Hispanic/Latino; 0.3% American Indian or Alaska Native, non-Hispanic/Latino; 3% Two or more races, non-Hispanic/Latino; 4% Race/ethnicity unknown; 1% international; 5% transferred in; 70% live on campus.

Freshmen
Admission: 4,593 applied, 3,349 admitted, 1,097 enrolled. ***Average high school GPA:*** 3.41. ***Test scores:*** SAT critical reading scores over 500: 58%; SAT math scores over 500: 53%; ACT scores over 18: 91%; SAT critical reading scores over 600: 11%; SAT math scores over 600: 7%; ACT scores over 24: 20%.

Retention: 78% of full-time freshmen returned.

FACULTY
Total: 303, 82% full-time, 73% with terminal degrees.

Student/faculty ratio: 17:1.

ACADEMICS
Calendar: semesters. *Degrees:* bachelor's, master's, post-master's, and postbachelor's certificates.

Special study options: accelerated degree program, advanced placement credit, distance learning, double majors, English as a second language, honors programs, independent study, internships, off-campus study, part-time degree program, services for LD students, study abroad, summer session for credit. ***ROTC:*** Army (b).

Unusual degree programs: 3-2 engineering with University of Virginia, Old Dominion University, Virginia Polytechnic Institute and State University.

Computers: 315 computers/terminals and 650 ports are available on campus for general student use. Students can access the following: campus intranet, computer help desk, free student e-mail accounts, online (class) grades, online (class) registration, online (class) schedules. Campuswide network is available. 100% of college-owned or -operated housing units are wired for high-speed Internet access. Wireless service is available via entire campus.

STUDENT LIFE
Housing options: on-campus residence required through sophomore year; coed, women-only, special housing for students with disabilities. Campus housing is university owned. Freshman campus housing is guaranteed.

Activities and organizations: drama/theater group, student-run newspaper, radio station, choral group, Student Government Association, Alpha Phi Omega, Baptist Campus Ministries, Longwood Ambassadors, Chi Alpha, national fraternities, national sororities.

Athletics Member NCAA. All Division I. ***Intercollegiate sports:*** baseball M(s), basketball M(s)/W(s), cross-country running M(s)/W(s), field hockey W(s), football M(c), golf M(s)/W(s), lacrosse W(s), soccer M(s)/W(s), softball W(s), tennis M(s)/W(s), volleyball M(c)/W(c). ***Intramural sports:*** baseball M(c), basketball M(c)/W(c), cheerleading M/W, equestrian sports M(c)/W(c), field hockey W(c), football M(c)/W, golf M/W, lacrosse M(c), racquetball M/W, rock climbing M/W, rugby M(c)/W(c), soccer M(c)/W(c), softball M/W, swimming and diving M(c)/W(c), table tennis M/W, tennis M/W, ultimate Frisbee M/W, volleyball M/W, weight lifting M/W, wrestling M(c).

Campus security: 24-hour emergency response devices and patrols, late-night transport/escort service, controlled dormitory access.

Student services: health clinic, personal/psychological counseling.

COSTS & FINANCIAL AID
Costs (2015–16) ***Tuition:*** state resident $7170 full-time, $239 per credit part-time; nonresident $21,330 full-time, $688 per credit part-time. Full-time tuition and fees vary according to course load. Part-time tuition and fees vary according to course load. ***Required fees:*** $4740 full-time, $158 per credit hour part-time. ***Room and board:*** $10,272; room only: $6394. Room and board charges vary according to board plan, housing facility, and location. ***Payment plan:*** installment. ***Waivers:*** senior citizens and employees or children of employees.

Financial Aid Of all full-time matriculated undergraduates who enrolled in 2013, 3,046 applied for aid, 2,306 were judged to have need, 657 had their need fully met. In 2013, 197 non-need-based awards were made. ***Average percent of need met:*** 82. ***Average financial aid package:*** $13,743. ***Average need-based loan:*** $4369. ***Average need-based gift aid:*** $7375. ***Average non-need-based aid:*** $4270. ***Average indebtedness upon graduation:*** $27,644.

APPLYING
Standardized Tests *Required:* SAT or ACT (for admission).

Options: electronic application, early admission, early action, deferred entrance.

Application fee: $50.

Required: essay or personal statement, high school transcript.

Application deadlines: 3/1 (freshmen), 3/1 (out-of-state freshmen), 3/1 (transfers), 12/1 (early action).

Notification: 6/1 (freshmen), 6/1 (out-of-state freshmen), continuous until 6/1 (transfers), 1/15 (early action).

CONTACT
Mrs. Sallie McMullin, Dean of Admissions, Longwood University, 201 High Street, Farmville, VA 23909. *Phone:* 434-395-2060. *Toll-free phone:* 800-281-4677. *Fax:* 434-395-2332. *E-mail:* admissions@longwood.edu.

Lynchburg College
Lynchburg, Virginia
http://www.lynchburg.edu/

- **Independent** comprehensive, founded 1903, affiliated with Christian Church (Disciples of Christ)
- **Suburban** 264-acre campus
- **Endowment** $97.5 million
- **Coed** 2,161 undergraduate students, 92% full-time, 60% women, 40% men
- **Moderately difficult** entrance level, 67% of applicants were admitted

UNDERGRAD STUDENTS
1,996 full-time, 165 part-time. Students come from 36 states and territories; 13 other countries; 31% are from out of state; 11% Black or African American, non-Hispanic/Latino; 5% Hispanic/Latino; 1% Asian, non-Hispanic/Latino; 0.1% Native Hawaiian or other Pacific Islander, non-Hispanic/Latino; 0.5% American Indian or Alaska Native, non-Hispanic/Latino; 4% Two or more races, non-Hispanic/Latino; 3% Race/ethnicity unknown; 3% international; 6% transferred in; 73% live on campus.

Freshmen
Admission: 5,515 applied, 3,681 admitted, 512 enrolled. ***Average high school GPA:*** 3.27. ***Test scores:*** SAT critical reading scores over 500: 52%; SAT math scores over 500: 49%; SAT writing scores over 500: 41%; ACT scores over 18: 87%; SAT critical reading scores over 600: 11%; SAT math scores over 600: 11%; SAT writing scores over 600: 6%; ACT scores over 24: 32%; SAT critical reading scores over 700: 1%; ACT scores over 30: 2%.

Retention: 70% of full-time freshmen returned.

FACULTY
Total: 282, 61% full-time, 61% with terminal degrees.

Student/faculty ratio: 11:1.

ACADEMICS
Calendar: semesters. *Degrees:* bachelor's, master's, doctoral, post-master's, and postbachelor's certificates.

Special study options: accelerated degree program, adult/continuing education programs, advanced placement credit, distance learning, double

majors, honors programs, independent study, internships, off-campus study, part-time degree program, services for LD students, study abroad, summer session for credit.

Unusual degree programs: 3-2 engineering with Old Dominion University, University of Virginia.

Computers: 300 computers/terminals are available on campus for general student use. Students can access the following: campus intranet, computer help desk, free student e-mail accounts, online (class) grades, online (class) registration, online (class) schedules. Campuswide network is available. 100% of college-owned or -operated housing units are wired for high-speed Internet access. Wireless service is available via entire campus.

STUDENT LIFE

Housing options: on-campus residence required through junior year; coed, special housing for students with disabilities. Campus housing is university owned. Freshman campus housing is guaranteed.

Activities and organizations: drama/theater group, student-run newspaper, choral group, Student Government Association, Student Activities Board, Enrollment Student Ambassadors, Emergency Services, Greek Life, national fraternities, national sororities.

Athletics Member NCAA. All Division III. ***Intercollegiate sports:*** baseball M, basketball M/W, cheerleading M/W, cross-country running M/W, equestrian sports M/W, field hockey W, golf M, lacrosse M/W, soccer M/W, softball W, tennis M/W, track and field M/W, volleyball W. ***Intramural sports:*** basketball M(c)/W(c), equestrian sports M(c)/W(c), field hockey W(c), golf M(c)/W(c), ice hockey M(c), lacrosse M(c)/W(c), rugby M/W, soccer M(c)/W(c), softball W(c), tennis M(c)/W(c), volleyball M/W, wrestling M(c).

Campus security: 24-hour emergency response devices and patrols, late-night transport/escort service, controlled dormitory access.

Student services: health clinic, personal/psychological counseling.

COSTS & FINANCIAL AID

Costs (2014–15) ***Comprehensive fee:*** $43,875 includes full-time tuition ($33,600), mandatory fees ($945), and room and board ($9330). Part-time tuition: $460 per credit hour. Part-time tuition and fees vary according to course load. ***Required fees:*** $5 per credit hour part-time. ***College room only:*** $4720. Room and board charges vary according to board plan and housing facility. ***Payment plans:*** tuition prepayment, installment. ***Waivers:*** adult students, senior citizens, and employees or children of employees.

Financial Aid Of all full-time matriculated undergraduates who enrolled in 2014, 1,642 applied for aid, 1,505 were judged to have need, 228 had their need fully met. 445 Federal Work-Study jobs (averaging $1550). 309 state and other part-time jobs (averaging $1534). In 2014, 385 non-need-based awards were made. ***Average percent of need met:*** 78. ***Average financial aid package:*** $25,845. ***Average need-based loan:*** $3566. ***Average need-based gift aid:*** $22,164. ***Average non-need-based aid:*** $13,152. ***Average indebtedness upon graduation:*** $33,592.

APPLYING

Standardized Tests *Required:* SAT or ACT (for admission).

Options: electronic application, early admission, early decision, deferred entrance.

Application fee: $30.

Required: high school transcript. ***Recommended:*** essay or personal statement, 2 letters of recommendation, interview.

Application deadlines: rolling (freshmen), rolling (transfers).

Early decision deadline: 11/15.

Notification: continuous (freshmen), continuous (transfers), 12/15 (early decision).

CONTACT

Lynchburg College, 1501 Lakeside Drive, Lynchburg, VA 24501-3199. *Phone:* 434-544-8300. *Toll-free phone:* 800-426-8101.

See below for display ad and page 1510 for the College Close-Up.

Mary Baldwin College

Staunton, Virginia

http://www.mbc.edu/

- **Independent** comprehensive, founded 1842
- **Small-town** 54-acre campus
- **Endowment** $34.3 million
- **Coed, primarily women** 1,423 undergraduate students, 69% full-time, 93% women, 7% men
- **Moderately difficult** entrance level, 51% of applicants were admitted

UNDERGRAD STUDENTS

988 full-time, 435 part-time. Students come from 36 states and territories; 7 other countries; 31% are from out of state; 24% Black or African American, non-Hispanic/Latino; 6% Hispanic/Latino; 4% Asian, non-Hispanic/Latino; 0.1% Native Hawaiian or other Pacific Islander, non-Hispanic/Latino; 0.8% American Indian or Alaska Native, non-Hispanic/Latino; 3% Two or more races, non-Hispanic/Latino; 6% Race/ethnicity unknown; 0.3% international; 9% transferred in; 85% live on campus.

Freshmen

Admission: 5,860 applied, 2,989 admitted, 257 enrolled. ***Average high school GPA:*** 3.3. ***Test scores:*** SAT critical reading scores over 500: 53%; SAT math scores over 500: 37%; SAT writing scores over 500: 43%; ACT scores over 18: 87%; SAT critical reading scores over 600: 14%; SAT math scores over 600: 7%; SAT writing scores over 600: 13%; ACT scores over 24: 21%; SAT critical reading scores over 700: 2%; SAT math scores over 700: 1%; ACT scores over 30: 2%.

Retention: 68% of full-time freshmen returned.

FACULTY

Total: 219, 39% full-time, 84% with terminal degrees.

Student/faculty ratio: 11:1.

ACADEMICS

Calendar: 4-1-4. *Degrees:* certificates, bachelor's, master's, and doctoral.

Special study options: academic remediation for entering students, accelerated degree program, adult/continuing education programs, advanced placement credit, double majors, English as a second language, external degree program, freshman honors college, honors programs, independent study, internships, off-campus study, part-time degree program, services for LD students, student-designed majors, study abroad. ***ROTC:*** Army (b), Navy (c), Air Force (c).

Unusual degree programs: 3-2 engineering with University of Virginia; nursing with Vanderbilt University.

Computers: 244 computers/terminals are available on campus for general student use. Students can access the following: computer help desk, free student e-mail accounts, online (class) grades, online (class) registration, online (class) schedules, 100% wireless. Campuswide network is available. 100% of college-owned or -operated housing units are wired for high-speed Internet access. Wireless service is available via entire campus.

STUDENT LIFE

Housing options: on-campus residence required through senior year; women-only. Campus housing is university owned. Freshman campus housing is guaranteed.

Activities and organizations: drama/theater group, student-run newspaper, radio station, choral group, marching band, International Club council, Minority Clubs United, Student Senate, Baldwin Program Board, Resident Hall Association.

Athletics Member NCAA. All Division III. ***Intercollegiate sports:*** basketball W, cross-country running W, soccer W, softball W, swimming and diving W(c), tennis W, volleyball W. ***Intramural sports:*** basketball W, fencing W(c), racquetball W, swimming and diving W, volleyball W.

Campus security: 24-hour emergency response devices and patrols, late-night transport/escort service, controlled dormitory access.

Student services: health clinic, personal/psychological counseling.

COSTS & FINANCIAL AID

Costs (2014–15) ***Comprehensive fee:*** $38,245 includes full-time tuition ($29,210), mandatory fees ($385), and room and board ($8650). Full-time tuition and fees vary according to degree level. Part-time tuition: $219 per credit hour. Part-time tuition and fees vary according to degree level. ***College room only:*** $5521. Room and board charges vary according to housing facility. ***Payment plan:*** installment. ***Waivers:*** employees or children of employees.

Financial Aid Of all full-time matriculated undergraduates who enrolled in 2013, 904 applied for aid, 843 were judged to have need, 96 had their need fully met. 248 Federal Work-Study jobs (averaging $1312). 107 state and other part-time jobs (averaging $1293). In 2013, 99 non-need-based awards were made. ***Average percent of need met:*** 71. ***Average financial aid package:*** $21,761. ***Average need-based loan:*** $4476. ***Average need-based gift aid:*** $17,439. ***Average non-need-based aid:*** $14,800. ***Average indebtedness upon graduation:*** $31,218.

APPLYING

Standardized Tests *Required:* SAT or ACT (for admission).

Options: electronic application, early admission, deferred entrance.

Required: high school transcript, minimum 2.0 GPA, 1 letter of recommendation. ***Recommended:*** interview.

Application deadlines: rolling (freshmen), rolling (transfers).

Early decision deadline: 11/15.

Notification: continuous (freshmen), continuous (transfers), 12/1 (early decision).

CONTACT

Ms. Roberta Palmer, Director of Admissions, Mary Baldwin College, Frederick and New Streets, Staunton, VA 24401. *Phone:* 540-887-7229 Ext. 7019. *Toll-free phone:* 800-468-2262. *Fax:* 540-887-7292. *E-mail:* rpalmer@mbc.edu.

Marymount University

Arlington, Virginia

http://www.marymount.edu/

- **Independent** comprehensive, founded 1950, affiliated with Roman Catholic Church
- **Suburban** 21-acre campus with easy access to Washington, DC
- **Endowment** $37.8 million
- **Coed** 2,363 undergraduate students, 90% full-time, 65% women, 35% men
- **Moderately difficult** entrance level, 84% of applicants were admitted

UNDERGRAD STUDENTS

2,127 full-time, 236 part-time. Students come from 42 states and territories; 58 other countries; 37% are from out of state; 15% Black or African American, non-Hispanic/Latino; 16% Hispanic/Latino; 9% Asian, non-Hispanic/Latino; 0.5% Native Hawaiian or other Pacific Islander, non-Hispanic/Latino; 0.6% American Indian or Alaska Native, non-Hispanic/Latino; 4% Two or more races, non-Hispanic/Latino; 3% Race/ethnicity unknown; 10% international; 14% transferred in; 34% live on campus.

Freshmen

Admission: 1,976 applied, 1,659 admitted, 353 enrolled. ***Average high school GPA:*** 3.16. ***Test scores:*** SAT critical reading scores over 500: 53%; SAT math scores over 500: 49%; SAT writing scores over 500: 43%; ACT scores over 18: 82%; SAT critical reading scores over 600: 10%; SAT math scores over 600: 10%; SAT writing scores over 600: 9%; ACT scores over 24: 28%; SAT critical reading scores over 700: 1%; SAT writing scores over 700: 1%; ACT scores over 30: 1%.

Retention: 81% of full-time freshmen returned.

FACULTY

Total: 381, 41% full-time, 60% with terminal degrees.

Student/faculty ratio: 13:1.

ACADEMICS

Calendar: semesters plus 2 summer terms. *Degrees:* certificates, bachelor's, master's, doctoral, post-master's, and postbachelor's certificates.

Special study options: academic remediation for entering students, accelerated degree program, advanced placement credit, distance learning, double majors, honors programs, independent study, internships, off-campus study, part-time degree program, services for LD students, student-designed majors, study abroad, summer session for credit. ***ROTC:*** Army (c).

Computers: 250 computers/terminals are available on campus for general student use. Students can access the following: campus intranet, computer help desk, free student e-mail accounts, online (class) grades, online (class) registration, online (class) schedules, online drive space. Campuswide network is available. 100% of college-owned or -operated housing units are wired for high-speed Internet access. Wireless service is available via entire campus.

STUDENT LIFE

Housing options: on-campus residence required through sophomore year; coed, men-only, women-only. Campus housing is university owned and leased by the school. Freshman applicants given priority for college housing.

Activities and organizations: drama/theater group, student-run newspaper, choral group, Fashion Club, Student Nurses Association, International Club, Association for Campus Events, Blue Harmony (show choir).

Athletics Member NCAA. All Division III. ***Intercollegiate sports:*** baseball M, basketball M/W, cross-country running M/W, golf M/W, lacrosse M/W, soccer M/W, swimming and diving M/W, volleyball M/W. ***Intramural sports:*** basketball M/W, cheerleading W, football M/W, soccer M/W, ultimate Frisbee M/W, volleyball M/W, water polo M/W.

Campus security: 24-hour emergency response devices and patrols, late-night transport/escort service, controlled dormitory access.

Student services: health clinic, personal/psychological counseling.

COSTS & FINANCIAL AID

Costs (2014–15) ***One-time required fee:*** $410. ***Comprehensive fee:*** $39,480 includes full-time tuition ($27,100), mandatory fees ($370), and room and board ($12,010). Part-time tuition: $885 per credit hour. ***Room and board:*** Room and board charges vary according to housing facility. ***Payment plan:*** installment. ***Waivers:*** senior citizens and employees or children of employees.

Financial Aid Of all full-time matriculated undergraduates who enrolled in 2014, 1,515 applied for aid, 1,384 were judged to have need, 179 had their need fully met. 692 Federal Work-Study jobs (averaging $2016). In 2014, 381 non-need-based awards were made. ***Average percent of need met:*** 54. ***Average financial aid package:*** $17,828. ***Average need-based loan:*** $4557. ***Average need-based gift aid:*** $6344. ***Average non-need-based aid:*** $12,302. ***Average indebtedness upon graduation:*** $26,528.

APPLYING

Standardized Tests *Required:* SAT or ACT (for admission).

Options: electronic application, deferred entrance.

Application fee: $40.

Required: essay or personal statement, high school transcript, minimum 2.6 GPA, 1 letter of recommendation. ***Required for some:*** interview. ***Recommended:*** interview.

Application deadlines: rolling (freshmen), rolling (transfers).

Notification: continuous (freshmen), continuous (transfers).

CONTACT

Mrs. Heather Renault, Director of Undergraduate Admissions, Marymount University, 2807 North Glebe Road, Arlington, VA 22207-4299. *Phone:* 703-284-1500. *Toll-free phone:* 800-548-7638. *Fax:* 703-522-0349. *E-mail:* admissions@marymount.edu.

Norfolk State University

Norfolk, Virginia

http://www.nsu.edu/

- **State-supported** comprehensive, founded 1935, part of State Council of Higher Education for Virginia
- **Urban** 134-acre campus
- **Coed** 5,356 undergraduate students, 82% full-time, 64% women, 36% men
- **Moderately difficult** entrance level, 67% of applicants were admitted

UNDERGRAD STUDENTS

4,416 full-time, 940 part-time. 14% are from out of state; 83% Black or African American, non-Hispanic/Latino; 3% Hispanic/Latino; 0.5% Asian, non-Hispanic/Latino; 0.2% Native Hawaiian or other Pacific Islander, non-Hispanic/Latino; 0.2% American Indian or Alaska Native, non-Hispanic/Latino; 3% Two or more races, non-Hispanic/Latino; 4% Race/ethnicity unknown; 0.4% international; 8% transferred in; 38% live on campus.

Freshmen

Admission: 2,817 applied, 1,895 admitted, 572 enrolled. ***Average high school GPA:*** 2.9. ***Test scores:*** SAT critical reading scores over 500: 16%; SAT math scores over 500: 15%; SAT writing scores over 500: 9%; ACT scores over 18: 15%; SAT critical reading scores over 600: 1%; SAT math scores over 600: 1%; SAT writing scores over 600: 1%; ACT scores over 24: 1%.

ACADEMICS

Calendar: semesters. *Degrees:* associate, bachelor's, master's, and doctoral.

ROTC: Army (b), Navy (b).

Computers: Students can access the following: online (class) registration. Campuswide network is available.

STUDENT LIFE

Housing options: men-only, women-only. Campus housing is university owned.

Athletics Member NCAA. All Division I. ***Intercollegiate sports:*** baseball M(s), basketball M(s)/W(s), bowling W, football M(s), softball W, tennis M(s)/W(s), track and field M(s)/W(s), volleyball W(s).

Campus security: 24-hour emergency response devices and patrols, late-night transport/escort service.

COSTS & FINANCIAL AID

Costs (2014–15) ***Tuition:*** state resident $7552 full-time, $295 per credit hour part-time; nonresident $20,696 full-time, $718 per credit hour part-time. Full-time tuition and fees vary according to course load. Part-time tuition and fees vary according to course load. ***Required fees:*** $1508 full-time. ***Room and board:*** $8624; room only: $5574. Room and board charges vary according to board plan and housing facility.

Financial Aid ***Financial aid deadline:*** 5/31.

APPLYING

Standardized Tests *Required:* SAT or ACT (for admission).

Options: electronic application, deferred entrance.

Required: high school transcript, minimum 2.3 GPA.

CONTACT

Mr. Kevin M. Holmes, Director of Recruitment and Admissions, Norfolk State University, 700 Park Avenue, Norfolk, VA 23504. *Phone:* 757-823-9222. *Toll-free phone:* 800-274-1821. *Fax:* 757-823-2078. *E-mail:* admissions@nsu.edu.

Old Dominion University

Norfolk, Virginia

http://www.odu.edu/

- **State-supported** university, founded 1930
- **Urban** 251-acre campus with easy access to Virginia Beach
- **Endowment** $213.7 million
- **Coed** 20,115 undergraduate students, 76% full-time, 54% women, 46% men
- **Moderately difficult** entrance level, 82% of applicants were admitted

UNDERGRAD STUDENTS

15,261 full-time, 4,854 part-time. Students come from 49 states and territories; 68 other countries; 8% are from out of state; 27% Black or African American, non-Hispanic/Latino; 7% Hispanic/Latino; 4% Asian, non-Hispanic/Latino; 0.4% Native Hawaiian or other Pacific Islander, non-Hispanic/Latino; 0.4% American Indian or Alaska Native, non-Hispanic/Latino; 6% Two or more races, non-Hispanic/Latino; 4% Race/ethnicity unknown; 1% international; 12% transferred in; 23% live on campus.

Freshmen

Admission: 9,161 applied, 7,502 admitted, 2,795 enrolled. ***Average high school GPA:*** 3.29. ***Test scores:*** SAT critical reading scores over 500: 55%; SAT math scores over 500: 55%; ACT scores over 18: 80%; SAT critical reading scores over 600: 13%; SAT math scores over 600: 14%; ACT scores over 24: 24%; SAT critical reading scores over 700: 1%; SAT math scores over 700: 1%; ACT scores over 30: 2%.

Retention: 81% of full-time freshmen returned.

FACULTY
Total: 1,321, 61% full-time, 58% with terminal degrees.

Student/faculty ratio: 20:1.

ACADEMICS
Calendar: semesters. *Degrees:* bachelor's, master's, doctoral, post-master's, and postbachelor's certificates.

Special study options: accelerated degree program, adult/continuing education programs, advanced placement credit, cooperative education, distance learning, double majors, English as a second language, freshman honors college, honors programs, independent study, internships, off-campus study, part-time degree program, services for LD students, student-designed majors, study abroad, summer session for credit. ***ROTC:*** Army (b), Navy (b).

Unusual degree programs: 3-2 business administration; engineering; nursing; international studies, dental hygiene, communications/humanities, English, English/applied linguistics, history, interdisciplinary studies/humanities, computer science, women's studies/humanities, philosophy/humanities, health science/public health, environmental health/public health.

Computers: 1,817 computers/terminals and 6,303 ports are available on campus for general student use. Students can access the following: campus intranet, computer help desk, free student e-mail accounts, online (class) grades, online (class) registration, online (class) schedules, online courses. Campuswide network is available. 100% of college-owned or -operated housing units are wired for high-speed Internet access. Wireless service is available via entire campus.

STUDENT LIFE
Housing options: coed, women-only, special housing for students with disabilities. Campus housing is university owned and leased by the school. Freshman campus housing is guaranteed.

Activities and organizations: drama/theater group, student-run newspaper, radio station, choral group, marching band, Student Activities Council, Student Government Association, Veteran Student Association, Colleges Against Cancer, Ebony Impact Gospel Choir, national fraternities, national sororities.

Athletics Member NCAA. All Division I. ***Intercollegiate sports:*** baseball M(s), basketball M(s)/W(s), cheerleading M(s)/W(s), crew M(c)/W(s), cross-country running M(c)/W(c), fencing M(c)/W(c), field hockey W(s), football M(s), golf M(s)/W(s), ice hockey M(c)/W(c), lacrosse M(c)/W(s), rugby M(c)/W(c), sailing M/W, soccer M(s)/W(s), softball W(c), swimming and diving M(s)/W(s), tennis M(s)/W(s), ultimate Frisbee M(c)/W(c), volleyball M(c)/W(c), wrestling M(s). ***Intramural sports:*** badminton M/W, basketball M/W, cross-country running M/W, golf M/W, racquetball M/W, soccer M/W, softball M/W, table tennis M/W, tennis M/W, volleyball M/W.

Campus security: 24-hour emergency response devices and patrols, student patrols, late-night transport/escort service, controlled dormitory access, lighted pathways, video cameras, on-campus EMTs, emergency notification system.

Student services: health clinic, personal/psychological counseling, women's center.

COSTS & FINANCIAL AID
Costs (2014–15) ***Tuition:*** state resident $8970 full-time, $299 per credit hour part-time; nonresident $25,140 full-time, $838 per credit hour part-time. Full-time tuition and fees vary according to location. Part-time tuition and fees vary according to location. ***Required fees:*** $280 full-time, $64 per term part-time. ***Room and board:*** $10,233; room only: $5689. Room and board charges vary according to board plan and housing facility. ***Payment plans:*** installment, deferred payment. ***Waivers:*** senior citizens and employees or children of employees.

Financial Aid Of all full-time matriculated undergraduates who enrolled in 2014, 11,913 applied for aid, 9,941 were judged to have need, 1,055 had their need fully met. 200 Federal Work-Study jobs (averaging $2400). In 2014, 995 non-need-based awards were made. ***Average percent of need met:*** 47. ***Average financial aid package:*** $9681. ***Average need-based loan:*** $4348. ***Average need-based gift aid:*** $6049. ***Average non-need-based aid:*** $3902. ***Average indebtedness upon graduation:*** $29,357. ***Financial aid deadline:*** 3/15.

APPLYING
Standardized Tests *Required:* SAT or ACT (for admission).

Options: electronic application, early admission, early action, deferred entrance.

Application fee: $50.

Required: high school transcript, minimum 2.7 GPA, test scores. ***Recommended:*** essay or personal statement, 1 letter of recommendation.

Application deadlines: 2/1 (freshmen), 2/1 (out-of-state freshmen), 5/1 (transfers), 12/1 (early action).

Notification: continuous (freshmen), continuous (out-of-state freshmen), continuous (transfers), 1/15 (early action).

CONTACT
Ms. Shereen Williams, Customer Service Manager, Admissions Office, Old Dominion University, 108 Rollins Hall, 5215 Hampton Boulevard, Norfolk, VA 23529. *Phone:* 757-683-3648. *Toll-free phone:* 800-348-7926. *Fax:* 757-683-3255. *E-mail:* admissions@odu.edu.

Patrick Henry College

Purcellville, Virginia

http://www.phc.edu/

- **Independent nondenominational** 4-year, founded 1999
- **Small-town** 106-acre campus with easy access to Washington, DC
- **Endowment** $514,202
- **Coed** 338 undergraduate students, 92% full-time, 49% women, 51% men
- **Moderately difficult** entrance level, 95% of applicants were admitted

UNDERGRAD STUDENTS
312 full-time, 26 part-time. Students come from 47 states and territories; 20% are from out of state; 0.9% Black or African American, non-Hispanic/Latino; 3% Hispanic/Latino; 2% Asian, non-Hispanic/Latino; 0.6% Native Hawaiian or other Pacific Islander, non-Hispanic/Latino; 0.3% American Indian or Alaska Native, non-Hispanic/Latino; 8% Race/ethnicity unknown; 4% transferred in; 90% live on campus.

Freshmen
Admission: 227 applied, 216 admitted, 80 enrolled. ***Average high school GPA:*** 3.83. ***Test scores:*** SAT critical reading scores over 500: 98%; SAT math scores over 500: 92%; SAT writing scores over 500: 95%; ACT scores over 18: 100%; SAT critical reading scores over 600: 82%; SAT math scores over 600: 54%; SAT writing scores over 600: 71%; ACT scores over 24: 95%; SAT critical reading scores over 700: 44%; SAT math scores over 700: 14%; SAT writing scores over 700: 33%; ACT scores over 30: 28%.

Retention: 83% of full-time freshmen returned.

FACULTY
Total: 43, 47% full-time, 70% with terminal degrees.

Student/faculty ratio: 12:1.

ACADEMICS
Calendar: semesters. *Degree:* bachelor's.

Special study options: advanced placement credit, cooperative education, independent study, internships, off-campus study, summer session for credit.

Computers: 6 computers/terminals and 100 ports are available on campus for general student use. Students can access the following: campus intranet, computer help desk, free student e-mail accounts, online (class) grades, online (class) registration, online (class) schedules. Campuswide network is available. 100% of college-owned or -operated housing units are wired for high-speed Internet access. Wireless service is available via entire campus.

STUDENT LIFE
Housing options: on-campus residence required through sophomore year; men-only, women-only. Campus housing is university owned. Freshman applicants given priority for college housing.

Activities and organizations: drama/theater group, student-run newspaper, choral group, Drama Club, Eden Troupe, Student Government, Chorale, College Republicans, Debate/Moot Court.

Athletics ***Intercollegiate sports:*** basketball M/W, soccer M/W. ***Intramural sports:*** baseball M, basketball M/W, fencing M(c)/W(c), football M(c), racquetball M(c)/W(c), rugby M(c), table tennis M(c)/W(c), tennis M/W, ultimate Frisbee M/W, volleyball M/W, weight lifting M.

Campus security: 24-hour emergency response devices and patrols, student patrols, late-night transport/escort service, controlled dormitory access, after hours patrols by trained security personnel.

Student services: personal/psychological counseling.

COSTS & FINANCIAL AID

Costs (2014–15) ***Comprehensive fee:*** $37,826 includes full-time tuition ($26,848), mandatory fees ($250), and room and board ($10,728). Full-time tuition and fees vary according to course load. Part-time tuition: $1118 per credit hour. Part-time tuition and fees vary according to course level and course load. ***Room and board:*** Room and board charges vary according to board plan and housing facility. ***Payment plans:*** installment, deferred payment. ***Waivers:*** employees or children of employees.

Financial Aid Of all full-time matriculated undergraduates who enrolled in 2013, 143 applied for aid, 115 were judged to have need. In 2013, 172 non-need-based awards were made. ***Average percent of need met:*** 37. ***Average financial aid package:*** $11,200. ***Average need-based loan:*** $12,500. ***Average need-based gift aid:*** $5600. ***Average non-need-based aid:*** $10,380. ***Average indebtedness upon graduation:*** $35,400. ***Financial aid deadline:*** 6/15.

APPLYING

Standardized Tests *Required:* SAT or ACT (for admission).

Options: electronic application, early action, deferred entrance.

Application fee: $20.

Required: essay or personal statement, high school transcript, 2 letters of recommendation, interview, Official transcripts from all colleges attended, Reading list.

Application deadlines: 6/15 (freshmen), 6/15 (transfers), 11/1 (early action).

Notification: continuous (freshmen), continuous (transfers), rolling (early action).

CONTACT

Mr. William K. Kellaris, Assistant Vice President for Enrollment Management, Patrick Henry College, 10 Patrick Henry Circle, Purcellville, VA 20132. *Phone:* 540-338-1776. *Toll-free phone:* 888-338-1776. *Fax:* 540-441-8119. *E-mail:* admissions@phc.edu.

Radford University

Radford, Virginia

http://www.radford.edu/

- **State-supported** comprehensive, founded 1910
- **Small-town** 191-acre campus
- **Endowment** $47.2 million
- **Coed** 8,885 undergraduate students, 96% full-time, 56% women, 44% men
- **Minimally difficult** entrance level, 79% of applicants were admitted

UNDERGRAD STUDENTS

8,507 full-time, 378 part-time. Students come from 42 states and territories; 63 other countries; 5% are from out of state; 12% Black or African American, non-Hispanic/Latino; 5% Hispanic/Latino; 1% Asian, non-Hispanic/Latino; 0.2% Native Hawaiian or other Pacific Islander, non-Hispanic/Latino; 0.3% American Indian or Alaska Native, non-Hispanic/Latino; 5% Two or more races, non-Hispanic/Latino; 1% Race/ethnicity unknown; 0.8% international; 8% transferred in; 36% live on campus.

Freshmen

Admission: 7,737 applied, 6,105 admitted, 2,015 enrolled. ***Average high school GPA:*** 3.2. ***Test scores:*** SAT critical reading scores over 500: 48%; SAT math scores over 500: 43%; SAT writing scores over 500: 36%; ACT scores over 18: 77%; SAT critical reading scores over 600: 8%; SAT math scores over 600: 7%; SAT writing scores over 600: 4%; ACT scores over 24: 15%; ACT scores over 30: 1%.

Retention: 75% of full-time freshmen returned.

FACULTY

Total: 717, 62% full-time, 59% with terminal degrees.

Student/faculty ratio: 18:1.

ACADEMICS

Calendar: semesters. *Degrees:* certificates, bachelor's, master's, doctoral, post-master's, and postbachelor's certificates.

Special study options: accelerated degree program, adult/continuing education programs, advanced placement credit, distance learning, double majors, English as a second language, honors programs, independent study, internships, off-campus study, part-time degree program, services for LD students, student-designed majors, study abroad, summer session for credit. ***ROTC:*** Army (b).

Computers: 810 computers/terminals and 340 ports are available on campus for general student use. Students can access the following: campus intranet, computer help desk, free student e-mail accounts, online (class) grades, online (class) registration, online (class) schedules, online financial aid status and student accounts payable. Campuswide network is available. 100% of college-owned or -operated housing units are wired for high-speed Internet access. Wireless service is available via entire campus.

STUDENT LIFE

Housing options: on-campus residence required through sophomore year; coed, special housing for students with disabilities. Campus housing is university owned and leased by the school. Freshman campus housing is guaranteed.

Activities and organizations: drama/theater group, student-run newspaper, radio station, choral group, American Sign Language Club, Think in Pink, Gay-Straight Alliance, Radford Student Programming and Campus Events (R-SPaCE), Psychology Club, national fraternities, national sororities.

Athletics Member NCAA. All Division I. ***Intercollegiate sports:*** baseball M(s), basketball M(s)/W(s), cross-country running M(s)/W(s), golf M(s)/W(s), lacrosse W(s), soccer M(s)/W(s), softball W(s), tennis M(s)/W(s), track and field W(s), volleyball W(s). ***Intramural sports:*** archery M(c)/W(c), basketball M/W, bowling M(c)/W(c), cheerleading M(c)/W(c), cross-country running M/W, equestrian sports M(c)/W(c), field hockey W(c), football M/W, ice hockey M(c)/W(c), lacrosse M(c)/W(c), riflery M(c)/W(c), rugby M(c)/W(c), skiing (downhill) M(c)/W(c), soccer M(c)/W(c), softball M/W, swimming and diving M(c)/W(c), table tennis M/W, tennis M/W, ultimate Frisbee M/W, volleyball M/W, wrestling M(c)/W(c).

Campus security: 24-hour emergency response devices and patrols, late-night transport/escort service, controlled dormitory access.

Student services: health clinic, personal/psychological counseling.

COSTS & FINANCIAL AID

Costs (2014–15) ***Tuition:*** state resident $6386 full-time, $266 per credit hour part-time; nonresident $18,626 full-time, $776 per credit hour part-time. Part-time tuition and fees vary according to course load. ***Required fees:*** $2974 full-time, $125 per credit hour part-time. ***Room and board:*** $8406; room only: $4632. Room and board charges vary according to board plan and housing facility. ***Payment plan:*** installment. ***Waivers:*** senior citizens and employees or children of employees.

Financial Aid Of all full-time matriculated undergraduates who enrolled in 2014, 6,256 applied for aid, 4,785 were judged to have need, 1,288 had their need fully met. 295 Federal Work-Study jobs (averaging $2471). 544 state and other part-time jobs (averaging $2393). In 2014, 306 non-need-based awards were made. ***Average percent of need met:*** 80. ***Average financial aid package:*** $9421. ***Average need-based loan:*** $4186. ***Average need-based gift aid:*** $6998. ***Average non-need-based aid:*** $3637. ***Average indebtedness upon graduation:*** $26,333.

APPLYING

Standardized Tests *Recommended:* SAT or ACT (for admission).

Options: electronic application, early admission, early action, deferred entrance.

Application fee: $50.

Required: high school transcript. ***Recommended:*** essay or personal statement, .

Application deadlines: 2/1 (freshmen), 6/1 (transfers), 12/1 (early action).

Notification: 4/1 (freshmen), continuous (transfers), 1/15 (early action).

CONTACT
Mr. James A. Pennix, Dean of Admissions and Enrollment Management, Radford University, PO Box 6903, Radford, VA 24142. *Phone:* 540-831-5371. *Fax:* 540-831-5038. *E-mail:* admissions@radford.edu.

Randolph College

Lynchburg, Virginia

http://www.randolphcollege.edu/

- **Independent Methodist** comprehensive, founded 1891
- **Suburban** 100-acre campus
- **Coed** 675 undergraduate students, 97% full-time, 64% women, 36% men
- **Moderately difficult** entrance level, 81% of applicants were admitted

UNDERGRAD STUDENTS
657 full-time, 18 part-time. 45% are from out of state; 11% Black or African American, non-Hispanic/Latino; 5% Hispanic/Latino; 3% Asian, non-Hispanic/Latino; 0.6% American Indian or Alaska Native, non-Hispanic/Latino; 3% Two or more races, non-Hispanic/Latino; 10% international; 4% transferred in; 85% live on campus.

Freshmen
Admission: 1,353 applied, 1,096 admitted, 191 enrolled. ***Average high school GPA:*** 3.49. ***Test scores:*** SAT critical reading scores over 500: 67%; SAT math scores over 500: 63%; SAT writing scores over 500: 64%; ACT scores over 18: 92%; SAT critical reading scores over 600: 27%; SAT math scores over 600: 25%; SAT writing scores over 600: 20%; ACT scores over 24: 56%; SAT critical reading scores over 700: 7%; SAT math scores over 700: 6%; SAT writing scores over 700: 4%; ACT scores over 30: 25%.

Retention: 74% of full-time freshmen returned.

FACULTY
Total: 71, 96% full-time, 92% with terminal degrees.

Student/faculty ratio: 10:1.

ACADEMICS
Calendar: semesters. *Degrees:* bachelor's and master's.

Special study options: adult/continuing education programs, part-time degree program.

Computers: Students can access the following: campus intranet, computer help desk, free student e-mail accounts, online (class) grades, online (class) registration, online (class) schedules. Campuswide network is available. Wireless service is available via entire campus.

STUDENT LIFE
Housing options: on-campus residence required through senior year; coed. Campus housing is university owned. Freshman campus housing is guaranteed.

Athletics Member NCAA. All Division III. ***Intercollegiate sports:*** basketball M/W, cross-country running M/W, equestrian sports M/W, lacrosse M/W, soccer M/W, softball W, tennis M/W, volleyball W.

Campus security: 24-hour emergency response devices and patrols, late-night transport/escort service.

COSTS & FINANCIAL AID
Costs (2014–15) ***Comprehensive fee:*** $45,760 includes full-time tuition ($33,500), mandatory fees ($610), and room and board ($11,650). Part-time tuition: $1400 per credit hour. Part-time tuition and fees vary according to course load. ***Required fees:*** $53 per term part-time. ***Payment plan:*** installment. ***Waivers:*** adult students and employees or children of employees.

Financial Aid Of all full-time matriculated undergraduates who enrolled in 2012, 468 applied for aid, 435 were judged to have need, 8 had their need fully met. In 2012, 124 non-need-based awards were made. ***Average percent of need met:*** 33. ***Average financial aid package:*** $23,278. ***Average need-based loan:*** $6350. ***Average need-based gift aid:*** $5907. ***Average non-need-based aid:*** $14,208. ***Average indebtedness upon graduation:*** $12,454.

APPLYING
Standardized Tests *Required:* SAT or ACT (for admission).

Options: electronic application, early admission, early action, deferred entrance.

Required: essay or personal statement, high school transcript, 2 letters of recommendation. ***Recommended:*** interview.

CONTACT
Ms. Margaret Blount, Director of Admissions, Randolph College, 2500 Rivermont Avenue, Lynchburg, VA 24503-1555. *Phone:* 434-947-8100. *Toll-free phone:* 800-745-7692. *Fax:* 434-947-8996. *E-mail:* admissions@randolphcollege.edu.

Randolph-Macon College

Ashland, Virginia

http://www.rmc.edu/

- **Independent United Methodist** 4-year, founded 1830
- **Suburban** 116-acre campus with easy access to Richmond
- **Endowment** $152.1 million
- **Coed** 1,394 undergraduate students, 98% full-time, 54% women, 46% men
- **Moderately difficult** entrance level, 60% of applicants were admitted

UNDERGRAD STUDENTS
1,365 full-time, 29 part-time. Students come from 29 states and territories; 25 other countries; 26% are from out of state; 9% Black or African American, non-Hispanic/Latino; 4% Hispanic/Latino; 2% Asian, non-Hispanic/Latino; 0.3% American Indian or Alaska Native, non-Hispanic/Latino; 4% Two or more races, non-Hispanic/Latino; 2% Race/ethnicity unknown; 2% international; 2% transferred in; 84% live on campus.

Freshmen
Admission: 2,955 applied, 1,783 admitted, 427 enrolled. ***Average high school GPA:*** 3.59. ***Test scores:*** SAT critical reading scores over 500: 75%; SAT math scores over 500: 71%; SAT writing scores over 500: 65%; ACT scores over 18: 99%; SAT critical reading scores over 600: 26%; SAT math scores over 600: 23%; SAT writing scores over 600: 18%; ACT scores over 24: 49%; SAT critical reading scores over 700: 4%; SAT math scores over 700: 3%; SAT writing scores over 700: 2%; ACT scores over 30: 7%.

Retention: 77% of full-time freshmen returned.

FACULTY
Total: 148, 65% full-time, 75% with terminal degrees.

Student/faculty ratio: 12:1.

ACADEMICS
Calendar: 4-1-4. *Degree:* bachelor's.

Special study options: academic remediation for entering students, accelerated degree program, advanced placement credit, double majors, honors programs, independent study, internships, off-campus study, part-time degree program, services for LD students, study abroad, summer session for credit. ***ROTC:*** Army (c).

Unusual degree programs: 3-2 business administration with accounting with Virginia Commonwealth University; engineering with Columbia University, University of Virginia; forestry with Duke University.

Computers: 356 computers/terminals and 1,500 ports are available on campus for general student use. Students can access the following: computer help desk, free student e-mail accounts, online (class) registration, online (class) schedules. Campuswide network is available. 100% of college-owned or -operated housing units are wired for high-speed Internet access. Wireless service is available via classrooms, computer labs, dorm rooms, libraries, student centers.

STUDENT LIFE
Housing options: on-campus residence required through junior year; coed, men-only, women-only, special housing for students with disabilities. Campus housing is university owned. Freshman campus housing is guaranteed.

Activities and organizations: drama/theater group, student-run newspaper, radio and television station, choral group, Leadership Fellows, Service Fellows, Student Government Association, Habitat for Humanity, Relay for Life, national fraternities, national sororities.

Athletics Member NCAA. All Division III. ***Intercollegiate sports:*** baseball M, basketball M/W, cheerleading W(c), equestrian sports M(c)/W(c), field hockey W, football M, golf M/W, lacrosse M/W, soccer M/W, softball W, swimming and diving M/W, tennis M/W, volleyball W.

Intramural sports: badminton M/W, basketball M/W, cheerleading M(c)/W(c), cross-country running M(c)/W(c), football M/W, lacrosse M/W, racquetball M/W, rugby M/W, soccer M/W, softball M/W, table tennis M/W, tennis M/W, ultimate Frisbee M/W, volleyball M/W, water polo M/W.

Campus security: 24-hour emergency response devices and patrols, late-night transport/escort service, controlled dormitory access.

Student services: health clinic, personal/psychological counseling, women's center.

COSTS & FINANCIAL AID

Costs (2014–15) ***Comprehensive fee:*** $47,090 includes full-time tuition ($35,360), mandatory fees ($980), and room and board ($10,750). Full-time tuition and fees vary according to reciprocity agreements. Part-time tuition: $3930 per course. ***College room only:*** $6100. Room and board charges vary according to board plan and housing facility. ***Payment plan:*** installment. ***Waivers:*** employees or children of employees.

Financial Aid Of all full-time matriculated undergraduates who enrolled in 2013, 1,134 applied for aid, 964 were judged to have need, 231 had their need fully met. In 2013, 313 non-need-based awards were made. ***Average percent of need met:*** 78. ***Average financial aid package:*** $25,779. ***Average need-based loan:*** $4560. ***Average need-based gift aid:*** $21,834. ***Average non-need-based aid:*** $15,475.

APPLYING

Standardized Tests *Required:* SAT or ACT (for admission). *Recommended:* SAT Subject Tests (for admission).

Options: electronic application, early admission, early action, deferred entrance.

Application fee: $30.

Required: essay or personal statement, high school transcript, minimum 2.0 GPA, 1 letter of recommendation. ***Recommended:*** interview.

Application deadlines: 3/1 (freshmen), 4/1 (transfers), 11/15 (early action).

Notification: 4/1 (freshmen), 5/1 (transfers), 1/1 (early action).

CONTACT

Anthony Ambrogi, Director of Admissions and Enrollment Research, Randolph-Macon College, PO Box 5005, Ashland, VA 23005-5505. *Phone:* 804-752-7305. *Toll-free phone:* 800-888-1762. *Fax:* 804-752-4707. *E-mail:* admissions@rmc.edu.

Regent University

Virginia Beach, Virginia

http://www.regent.edu/

- **Independent Christian** comprehensive, founded 1977
- **Suburban** 70-acre campus
- **Endowment** $156.0 million
- **Coed** 2,410 undergraduate students, 62% full-time, 61% women, 39% men
- **Minimally difficult** entrance level, 92% of applicants were admitted

UNDERGRAD STUDENTS

1,496 full-time, 914 part-time. Students come from 50 states and territories; 29 other countries; 49% are from out of state; 20% Black or African American, non-Hispanic/Latino; 5% Hispanic/Latino; 2% Asian, non-Hispanic/Latino; 0.6% American Indian or Alaska Native, non-Hispanic/Latino; 14% Race/ethnicity unknown; 0.9% international; 19% transferred in; 22% live on campus.

Freshmen

Admission: 937 applied, 859 admitted, 223 enrolled. ***Average high school GPA:*** 3.52. ***Test scores:*** SAT critical reading scores over 500: 64%; SAT math scores over 500: 47%; SAT writing scores over 500: 52%; ACT scores over 18: 92%; SAT critical reading scores over 600: 22%; SAT math scores over 600: 12%; SAT writing scores over 600: 16%; ACT scores over 24: 39%; SAT critical reading scores over 700: 3%; SAT math scores over 700: 1%; SAT writing scores over 700: 1%; ACT scores over 30: 8%.

Retention: 78% of full-time freshmen returned.

FACULTY

Total: 609, 26% full-time, 73% with terminal degrees.

Student/faculty ratio: 18:1.

ACADEMICS

Calendar: trimesters. *Degrees:* certificates, associate, bachelor's, master's, doctoral, post-master's, and postbachelor's certificates.

Special study options: academic remediation for entering students, adult/continuing education programs, advanced placement credit, distance learning, double majors, external degree program, internships, off-campus study, part-time degree program, services for LD students, study abroad, summer session for credit. ***ROTC:*** Army (c), Navy (c).

Computers: 70 computers/terminals and 75 ports are available on campus for general student use. Students can access the following: campus intranet, computer help desk, free student e-mail accounts, online (class) grades, online (class) registration, online (class) schedules. Campuswide network is available. 100% of college-owned or -operated housing units are wired for high-speed Internet access. Wireless service is available via entire campus.

STUDENT LIFE

Housing options: on-campus residence required for freshman year; men-only, women-only, special housing for students with disabilities. Campus housing is university owned. Freshman applicants given priority for college housing.

Activities and organizations: drama/theater group, student-run newspaper, choral group, Regent Undergraduate Council, Students in Free Enterprise (SIFE), Psychology Club, Student Alumni Ambassadors, Regent Undergraduate Debate Association, national fraternities, national sororities.

Athletics ***Intramural sports:*** basketball M/W, golf M/W, soccer M/W, tennis M/W, volleyball M/W.

Campus security: 24-hour emergency response devices and patrols, student patrols, late-night transport/escort service, controlled dormitory access.

Student services: personal/psychological counseling.

COSTS & FINANCIAL AID

Costs (2015–16) ***Comprehensive fee:*** $25,400 includes full-time tuition ($16,350), mandatory fees ($800), and room and board ($8250). Full-time tuition and fees vary according to course level, course load, program, and student level. Part-time tuition: $545 per credit hour. Part-time tuition and fees vary according to course level, course load, program, and student level. ***Required fees:*** $545 per credit hour part-time, $400 per term part-time. ***College room only:*** $5730. Room and board charges vary according to board plan and housing facility. ***Payment plan:*** installment. ***Waivers:*** employees or children of employees.

Financial Aid Of all full-time matriculated undergraduates who enrolled in 2014, 1,278 applied for aid, 1,140 were judged to have need, 116 had their need fully met. In 2014, 196 non-need-based awards were made. ***Average percent of need met:*** 53. ***Average financial aid package:*** $11,678. ***Average need-based loan:*** $3841. ***Average need-based gift aid:*** $7870. ***Average non-need-based aid:*** $7508. ***Average indebtedness upon graduation:*** $36,564.

APPLYING

Standardized Tests *Required for some:* SAT or ACT (for admission).

Options: electronic application, deferred entrance.

Application fee: $50.

Required: high school transcript. ***Required for some:*** essay or personal statement, minimum 3.0 GPA.

Application deadlines: 8/1 (freshmen), 8/1 (out-of-state freshmen), 8/1 (transfers).

Notification: continuous (freshmen), continuous (out-of-state freshmen), continuous (transfers).

CONTACT

Mr. Ken Baker, Director of Admissions, Regent University, 1000 Regent University Drive, SC 218, Virginia Beach, VA 23464. *Phone:* 757-352-4845. *Toll-free phone:* 800-373-5504. *Fax:* 757-352-4509. *E-mail:* kbaker@regent.edu.

Roanoke College

Salem, Virginia

http://www.roanoke.edu/

- **Independent** 4-year, founded 1842, affiliated with Evangelical Lutheran Church in America
- **Suburban** 80-acre campus
- **Endowment** $133.0 million
- **Coed** 2,054 undergraduate students, 96% full-time, 60% women, 40% men
- **Moderately difficult** entrance level, 69% of applicants were admitted

UNDERGRAD STUDENTS

1,978 full-time, 76 part-time. Students come from 43 states and territories; 33 other countries; 47% are from out of state; 6% Black or African American, non-Hispanic/Latino; 4% Hispanic/Latino; 2% Asian, non-Hispanic/Latino; 0.1% Native Hawaiian or other Pacific Islander, non-Hispanic/Latino; 0.3% American Indian or Alaska Native, non-Hispanic/Latino; 4% Two or more races, non-Hispanic/Latino; 2% international; 4% transferred in; 75% live on campus.

Freshmen

Admission: 4,824 applied, 3,344 admitted, 562 enrolled. ***Average high school GPA:*** 3.5. ***Test scores:*** SAT critical reading scores over 500: 74%; SAT math scores over 500: 70%; SAT writing scores over 500: 69%; ACT scores over 18: 94%; SAT critical reading scores over 600: 32%; SAT math scores over 600: 26%; SAT writing scores over 600: 23%; ACT scores over 24: 47%; SAT critical reading scores over 700: 6%; SAT math scores over 700: 1%; SAT writing scores over 700: 3%; ACT scores over 30: 8%.

Retention: 80% of full-time freshmen returned.

FACULTY

Total: 224, 73% full-time, 72% with terminal degrees.

Student/faculty ratio: 11:1.

ACADEMICS

Calendar: semesters. *Degree:* bachelor's.

Special study options: accelerated degree program, adult/continuing education programs, advanced placement credit, double majors, English as a second language, honors programs, independent study, internships, off-campus study, part-time degree program, services for LD students, study abroad, summer session for credit.

Unusual degree programs: 3-2 engineering with Virginia Polytechnic Institute and State University.

Computers: 245 computers/terminals and 1,600 ports are available on campus for general student use. Students can access the following: campus intranet, computer help desk, free student e-mail accounts, online (class) grades, online (class) registration, online (class) schedules, discounts on computer hardware and software purchases, free Microsoft Office software, free security software. Campuswide network is available. 100% of college-owned or -operated housing units are wired for high-speed Internet access. Wireless service is available via entire campus.

STUDENT LIFE

Housing options: on-campus residence required through senior year; coed, women-only, special housing for students with disabilities. Campus housing is university owned. Freshman campus housing is guaranteed.

Activities and organizations: drama/theater group, student-run newspaper, radio station, choral group, Catholic Campus Ministry, Lutheran Student Movement, Habitat for Humanity, Biology Club, National Society for Leadership & Success, national fraternities, national sororities.

Athletics Member NCAA. All Division III. ***Intercollegiate sports:*** baseball M, basketball M/W, cross-country running M/W, field hockey W, golf M, lacrosse M/W, soccer M/W, softball W, tennis M/W, track and field M/W, volleyball W. ***Intramural sports:*** badminton M/W, baseball M(c), basketball M/W, cheerleading M(c)/W(c), equestrian sports M(c)/W(c), football M/W, golf M(c)/W(c), lacrosse W(c), racquetball M/W, rugby M(c), soccer M(c)/W, softball M/W, table tennis M/W, ultimate Frisbee M(c)/W(c), volleyball M/W.

Campus security: 24-hour emergency response devices and patrols, late-night transport/escort service, controlled dormitory access, Campus emergency phones, Maroon Alert system.

Student services: health clinic, personal/psychological counseling.

COSTS & FINANCIAL AID

Costs (2015–16) ***One-time required fee:*** $125. ***Comprehensive fee:*** $52,036 includes full-time tuition ($38,302), mandatory fees ($1364), and room and board ($12,370). Full-time tuition and fees vary according to reciprocity agreements. Part-time tuition: $1832 per course. Part-time tuition and fees vary according to course load and reciprocity agreements. ***Required fees:*** $38 per term part-time. ***College room only:*** $5746. Room and board charges vary according to board plan and housing facility. ***Payment plan:*** installment. ***Waivers:*** adult students, senior citizens, and employees or children of employees.

Financial Aid Of all full-time matriculated undergraduates who enrolled in 2014, 1,655 applied for aid, 1,461 were judged to have need, 289 had their need fully met. In 2014, 493 non-need-based awards were made. ***Average percent of need met:*** 79. ***Average financial aid package:*** $30,036. ***Average need-based loan:*** $4854. ***Average need-based gift aid:*** $24,298. ***Average non-need-based aid:*** $15,554. ***Average indebtedness upon graduation:*** $34,320.

APPLYING

Standardized Tests *Required:* SAT or ACT (for admission).

Options: electronic application, early admission, early decision, deferred entrance.

Required: high school transcript. ***Recommended:*** essay or personal statement, 1 letter of recommendation, interview.

Application deadlines: 3/15 (freshmen), 8/1 (transfers).

Early decision deadline: 11/1.

Notification: continuous until 4/1 (freshmen), continuous until 8/15 (transfers), 12/1 (early decision).

CONTACT

Admissions Office, Roanoke College, 221 College Lane, Salem, VA 24153. *Phone:* 540-375-2270. *Toll-free phone:* 800-388-2276. *Fax:* 540-375-2267. *E-mail:* admissions@roanoke.edu.

Sentara College of Health Sciences

Chesapeake, Virginia

http://www.sentara.edu/

- **Proprietary** 4-year
- **Urban** campus with easy access to Virginia Beach
- **Coed** 367 undergraduate students, 62% full-time, 93% women, 7% men

UNDERGRAD STUDENTS

226 full-time, 141 part-time. 11% Black or African American, non-Hispanic/Latino; 1% Hispanic/Latino; 9% Asian, non-Hispanic/Latino; 1% Native Hawaiian or other Pacific Islander, non-Hispanic/Latino; 0.3% American Indian or Alaska Native, non-Hispanic/Latino; 3% Two or more races, non-Hispanic/Latino; 1% Race/ethnicity unknown; 100% transferred in.

FACULTY

Total: 51, 57% full-time, 10% with terminal degrees.

Student/faculty ratio: 8:1.

ACADEMICS

Degrees: certificates, associate, and bachelor's.

Special study options: adult/continuing education programs, advanced placement credit, distance learning, honors programs, part-time degree program, services for LD students, summer session for credit.

Computers: Students can access the following: free student e-mail accounts, online (class) grades. Campuswide network is available. Wireless service is available via entire campus.

STUDENT LIFE

Campus security: 24-hour emergency response devices.

Student services: personal/psychological counseling.

COSTS

Costs (2014–15) ***Tuition:*** $317 per credit hour part-time. Full-time tuition and fees vary according to course load, degree level, and program. Part-time tuition and fees vary according to course load, degree level, and program.

APPLYING

Standardized Tests *Required:* TEAS test for BSN and TEAS V for Allied Health (for admission).

Required: high school transcript, minimum 3.5 GPA, Complete general education courses specified by the degree programs, maintain a cumulative GPA of 3.3 on all college transcripts, take required pre-admission test (TEAS). ***Required for some:*** interview.

CONTACT

Sentara College of Health Sciences, 1441 Crossways Boulevard, Crossways I, Suite 105, Chesapeake, VA 23320.

★ Shenandoah University

Winchester, Virginia

http://www.su.edu/

- **Independent United Methodist** comprehensive, founded 1875
- **Small-town** 315-acre campus with easy access to Washington, DC
- **Endowment** $62.7 million
- **Coed** 1,892 undergraduate students, 96% full-time, 56% women, 44% men

UNDERGRAD STUDENTS

1,823 full-time, 69 part-time. Students come from 36 states and territories; 30 other countries; 38% are from out of state; 14% Black or African American, non-Hispanic/Latino; 6% Hispanic/Latino; 3% Asian, non-Hispanic/Latino; 0.5% Native Hawaiian or other Pacific Islander, non-Hispanic/Latino; 2% American Indian or Alaska Native, non-Hispanic/Latino; 3% Race/ethnicity unknown; 5% international; 8% transferred in; 47% live on campus.

Freshmen

Admission: 417 enrolled. ***Average high school GPA:*** 3.39. ***Test scores:*** SAT critical reading scores over 500: 52%; SAT math scores over 500: 53%; SAT writing scores over 500: 45%; ACT scores over 18: 79%; SAT critical reading scores over 600: 12%; SAT math scores over 600: 16%; SAT writing scores over 600: 13%; ACT scores over 24: 33%; SAT critical reading scores over 700: 2%; SAT math scores over 700: 1%; SAT writing scores over 700: 2%; ACT scores over 30: 3%.

Retention: 76% of full-time freshmen returned.

FACULTY

Total: 427, 56% full-time, 63% with terminal degrees.

Student/faculty ratio: 9:1.

ACADEMICS

Calendar: semesters. *Degrees:* certificates, bachelor's, master's, doctoral, post-master's, and postbachelor's certificates.

Special study options: accelerated degree program, adult/continuing education programs, advanced placement credit, distance learning, double majors, English as a second language, independent study, internships, part-time degree program, services for LD students, student-designed majors, study abroad, summer session for credit.

Unusual degree programs: Athletic Training, Occupational Training.

Computers: 32 computers/terminals and 218 ports are available on campus for general student use. Students can access the following: campus intranet, computer help desk, free student e-mail accounts, online (class) grades, online (class) registration, online (class) schedules, online student account information. Campuswide network is available. 100% of college-owned or -operated housing units are wired for high-speed Internet access. Wireless service is available via entire campus.

STUDENT LIFE

Housing options: on-campus residence required through sophomore year; coed, special housing for students with disabilities. Campus housing is university owned and leased by the school. Freshman campus housing is guaranteed.

Activities and organizations: drama/theater group, student-run newspaper, radio station, choral group, Student Government Association, Graduate Student Assembly, Campus Activities Network, Colleges Against Cancer, Variety of Groups for Professional Fraternities.

Athletics Member NCAA. All Division III. ***Intercollegiate sports:*** baseball M, basketball M/W, cross-country running M/W, field hockey W, football M, golf M/W, lacrosse M/W, soccer M/W, softball W, tennis M/W, track and field M/W, volleyball W. ***Intramural sports:*** basketball M/W, football M/W, soccer M/W, softball M/W, ultimate Frisbee M/W, volleyball M/W.

Campus security: 24-hour emergency response devices and patrols, late-night transport/escort service, controlled dormitory access, LiveSafe mobile app, anonymous reporting, side-door alarms, campus shuttle, Safe in Sixty Seconds Program, Safe Walk/Safe Ride Program.

Student services: health clinic, personal/psychological counseling, women's center.

COSTS & FINANCIAL AID

Costs (2015–16) ***Comprehensive fee:*** $40,680 includes full-time tuition ($29,570), mandatory fees ($1190), and room and board ($9920). Full-time tuition and fees vary according to course load and program. Part-time tuition: $860 per credit. Part-time tuition and fees vary according to course load and program. ***Required fees:*** $515 per term part-time. ***Room and board:*** Room and board charges vary according to board plan and housing facility. ***Payment plan:*** installment. ***Waivers:*** employees or children of employees.

Financial Aid Of all full-time matriculated undergraduates who enrolled in 2014, 1,590 applied for aid, 1,356 were judged to have need, 284 had their need fully met. 883 Federal Work-Study jobs (averaging $2300). 467 state and other part-time jobs (averaging $2300). In 2014, 260 non-need-based awards were made. ***Average percent of need met:*** 30. ***Average financial aid package:*** $29,205. ***Average need-based loan:*** $4913. ***Average need-based gift aid:*** $5821. ***Average non-need-based aid:*** $9461. ***Average indebtedness upon graduation:*** $28,831.

APPLYING

Standardized Tests *Required:* SAT or ACT (for admission).

Required: high school transcript. ***Required for some:*** essay or personal statement, interview, Applicants are strongly recommended to indicate community and extra-curricular involvement. Conservatory applicants are also required to successfully complete an audition. ***Recommended:*** minimum 2.5 GPA.

CONTACT

Mr. Kevin Zimmerman, Assistant Director Transfer Students, Recruitment-Admissions, Shenandoah University, 1460 University Drive, Wilkins Building, Admissions Office, Winchester, VA 22601-5195. *Phone:* 540-665.4695. *Toll-free phone:* 800-432-2266. *Fax:* 540-665.4627. *E-mail:* admit@su.edu.

South University

Glen Allen, Virginia

http://www.southuniversity.edu/richmond

- **Proprietary** comprehensive
- **Coed**

ACADEMICS

Degrees: associate, bachelor's, master's, and post-master's certificates.

CONTACT

South University, 2151 Old Brick Road, Glen Allen, VA 23060. *Phone:* 804-727-6800. *Toll-free phone:* 888-422-5076.

South University

Virginia Beach, Virginia

http://www.southuniversity.edu/virginia-beach

- **Proprietary** comprehensive
- **Coed**

ACADEMICS

Degrees: associate, bachelor's, and master's.

CONTACT

South University, 301 Bendix Road, Suite 100, Virginia Beach, VA 23452. *Phone:* 757-493-6900. *Toll-free phone:* 877-206-1845.

★ Stratford University
Falls Church, Virginia
http://www.stratford.edu/

- **Proprietary** comprehensive, founded 1976
- **Suburban** campus with easy access to Washington, DC
- **Coed** 604 undergraduate students, 23% full-time, 55% women, 45% men
- **Noncompetitive** entrance level, 29% of applicants were admitted

UNDERGRAD STUDENTS
141 full-time, 463 part-time. 52% are from out of state; 42% Black or African American, non-Hispanic/Latino; 9% Hispanic/Latino; 4% Asian, non-Hispanic/Latino; 0.7% Native Hawaiian or other Pacific Islander, non-Hispanic/Latino; 5% Two or more races, non-Hispanic/Latino; 11% Race/ethnicity unknown; 6% international.

Freshmen
Admission: 218 applied, 64 admitted, 211 enrolled.
Retention: 52% of full-time freshmen returned.

FACULTY
Total: 110, 17% full-time, 25% with terminal degrees.
Student/faculty ratio: 88:1.

ACADEMICS
Calendar: quarters. *Degrees:* certificates, diplomas, associate, bachelor's, and master's.
Special study options: academic remediation for entering students, accelerated degree program, advanced placement credit, cooperative education, distance learning, English as a second language, internships, part-time degree program, summer session for credit.
Computers: 104 computers/terminals are available on campus for general student use. Students can access the following: campus intranet, computer help desk, free student e-mail accounts, online (class) grades, online (class) registration, online (class) schedules. Campuswide network is available. Wireless service is available via entire campus.

STUDENT LIFE
Housing options: college housing not available.
Campus security: 24-hour emergency response devices.

COSTS
Costs (2015–16) ***Tuition:*** $370 per quarter hour part-time. Full-time tuition and fees vary according to course level, degree level, and program. Part-time tuition and fees vary according to course level, degree level, and program. ***Required fees:*** $100 per degree program part-time. ***Payment plan:*** installment. ***Waivers:*** employees or children of employees.

APPLYING
Options: electronic application, deferred entrance.
Application fee: $50.
Required: essay or personal statement, proof of high school graduation or equivalent is required for all students; personal statement, transcript, and letters of recommendation are only required for the Nursing program.
Application deadlines: rolling (freshmen), rolling (out-of-state freshmen), rolling (transfers).
Notification: continuous (freshmen), continuous (out-of-state freshmen), continuous (transfers).

CONTACT
Gina Rice-Holland, Director of Admissions, Stratford University, 7777 Leesburg Pike, Falls Church, VA 22043. *Phone:* 800-444-0804. *Toll-free phone:* 800-444-0804. *E-mail:* grice-holland@stratford.edu.

Stratford University
Glen Allen, Virginia
http://www.stratford.edu/

- **Proprietary** comprehensive
- **Suburban** campus
- **Coed** 363 undergraduate students, 100% full-time, 65% women, 35% men

UNDERGRAD STUDENTS
363 full-time. 45% Black or African American, non-Hispanic/Latino; 3% Hispanic/Latino; 21% Asian, non-Hispanic/Latino; 0.2% Native Hawaiian or other Pacific Islander, non-Hispanic/Latino; 0.4% American Indian or Alaska Native, non-Hispanic/Latino; 0.2% Two or more races, non-Hispanic/Latino; 0.4% Race/ethnicity unknown.

Freshmen
Admission: 233 enrolled.
Retention: 63% of full-time freshmen returned.

FACULTY
Total: 23, 9% full-time, 48% with terminal degrees.
Student/faculty ratio: 21:1.

ACADEMICS
Degrees: certificates, diplomas, associate, bachelor's, and master's.
Special study options: academic remediation for entering students, adult/continuing education programs, cooperative education, external degree program, independent study, internships, part-time degree program.

COSTS
Costs (2015–16) ***Tuition:*** $370 per quarter hour part-time. Full-time tuition and fees vary according to course level, degree level, and program. Part-time tuition and fees vary according to course level, degree level, and program. ***Required fees:*** $100 per degree program part-time. ***Payment plan:*** installment. ***Waivers:*** employees or children of employees.

CONTACT
Stratford University, 11104 W. Broad Street, Glen Allen, VA 23060. *Toll-free phone:* 877-373-5173.

Stratford University
Newport News, Virginia
http://www.stratford.edu/

- **Proprietary** comprehensive
- **Urban** campus
- **Coed** 152 undergraduate students, 16% full-time, 64% women, 36% men

UNDERGRAD STUDENTS
24 full-time, 128 part-time. 86% Black or African American, non-Hispanic/Latino; 4% Hispanic/Latino; 4% transferred in.

Freshmen
Admission: 75 enrolled.
Retention: 83% of full-time freshmen returned.

FACULTY
Total: 19, 16% full-time, 11% with terminal degrees.
Student/faculty ratio: 4:1.

ACADEMICS
Degrees: certificates, diplomas, associate, bachelor's, and master's.
Special study options: academic remediation for entering students, accelerated degree program, cooperative education, distance learning, external degree program, part-time degree program, services for LD students, summer session for credit.
Computers: 19 computers/terminals and 6 ports are available on campus for general student use. Students can access the following: campus intranet, computer help desk, free student e-mail accounts, online (class) grades, online (class) schedules. Campuswide network is available. Wireless service is available via entire campus.

STUDENT LIFE
Housing options: college housing not available.
Campus security: 24-hour emergency response devices, security officer during evening hours / classes.

COSTS
Costs (2015–16) ***Tuition:*** $370 per credit part-time. Full-time tuition and fees vary according to course level, degree level, and program. Part-time tuition and fees vary according to course level, degree level, and program. ***Required fees:*** $100 per degree program part-time. ***Payment plan:*** installment. ***Waivers:*** employees or children of employees.

APPLYING
Required: essay or personal statement, high school transcript, interview.

CONTACT
Director of Admissions, Stratford University, 836 J. Clyde Morris Boulevard, Newport News, VA 23601. *Phone:* 757-873.4235. *Toll-free phone:* 855-873-4235.

Stratford University

Woodbridge, Virginia

http://www.stratford.edu/

- **Proprietary** comprehensive
- **Suburban** campus
- **Coed** 694 undergraduate students, 14% full-time, 73% women, 27% men

UNDERGRAD STUDENTS
96 full-time, 598 part-time.

Freshmen
Admission: 132 enrolled.

FACULTY
Total: 51, 29% full-time, 27% with terminal degrees.

ACADEMICS
Degrees: certificates, diplomas, associate, bachelor's, and master's.

Special study options: academic remediation for entering students, accelerated degree program, adult/continuing education programs, advanced placement credit, cooperative education, distance learning, double majors, independent study, internships, off-campus study, part-time degree program, summer session for credit.

Computers: 100 computers/terminals and 138 ports are available on campus for general student use. Students can access the following: campus intranet, computer help desk, free student e-mail accounts, online (class) grades, online (class) registration, online (class) schedules. Campuswide network is available. Wireless service is available via classrooms, computer centers, computer labs, learning centers, libraries, student centers.

COSTS
Costs (2015–16) ***Tuition:*** $370 per quarter hour part-time. Full-time tuition and fees vary according to course level, degree level, and program. Part-time tuition and fees vary according to course level, degree level, and program. ***Required fees:*** $100 per degree program part-time. ***Payment plan:*** installment. ***Waivers:*** employees or children of employees.

APPLYING
Options: electronic application.

Application fee: $50.

CONTACT
Director of Admissions, Stratford University, 14349 Gideon Drive, Woodbridge, VA 22192. *Phone:* 703-897-1982. *Toll-free phone:* 888-546-1250. *E-mail:* admissions@stratford.edu.

University of Mary Washington

Fredericksburg, Virginia

http://www.umw.edu/

- **State-supported** comprehensive, founded 1908
- **Small-town** 234-acre campus with easy access to Richmond, Washington DC
- **Endowment** $46.8 million
- **Coed** 4,167 undergraduate students, 88% full-time, 65% women, 35% men
- **Very difficult** entrance level, 77% of applicants were admitted

UNDERGRAD STUDENTS
3,666 full-time, 501 part-time. Students come from 35 states and territories; 27 other countries; 11% are from out of state; 6% Black or African American, non-Hispanic/Latino; 7% Hispanic/Latino; 4% Asian, non-Hispanic/Latino; 0.1% American Indian or Alaska Native, non-Hispanic/Latino; 5% Two or more races, non-Hispanic/Latino; 8% Race/ethnicity unknown; 1% international; 8% transferred in; 59% live on campus.

Freshmen
Admission: 5,336 applied, 4,094 admitted, 853 enrolled. *Average high school GPA:* 3.54. *Test scores:* SAT critical reading scores over 500: 84%; SAT math scores over 500: 77%; SAT writing scores over 500: 76%; ACT scores over 18: 99%; SAT critical reading scores over 600: 33%; SAT math scores over 600: 23%; SAT writing scores over 600: 26%; ACT scores over 24: 54%; SAT critical reading scores over 700: 5%; SAT math scores over 700: 2%; SAT writing scores over 700: 2%; ACT scores over 30: 4%.

Retention: 78% of full-time freshmen returned.

FACULTY
Total: 387, 65% full-time, 73% with terminal degrees.
Student/faculty ratio: 15:1.

ACADEMICS
Calendar: semesters. *Degrees:* certificates, bachelor's, master's, and postbachelor's certificates.

Special study options: adult/continuing education programs, advanced placement credit, distance learning, double majors, honors programs, independent study, internships, part-time degree program, services for LD students, student-designed majors, study abroad, summer session for credit. ***ROTC:*** Army (c).

Computers: 456 computers/terminals are available on campus for general student use. Students can access the following: campus intranet, computer help desk, free student e-mail accounts, online (class) grades, online (class) registration, online (class) schedules, Library resources, foreign languages resources, course management system. Campuswide network is available. 100% of college-owned or -operated housing units are wired for high-speed Internet access. Wireless service is available via entire campus.

STUDENT LIFE
Housing options: on-campus residence required through sophomore year; coed, men-only, women-only, special housing for students with disabilities. Campus housing is university owned and leased by the school. Freshman campus housing is guaranteed.

Activities and organizations: drama/theater group, student-run newspaper, radio station, choral group, Alpha Mu Sigma, Giant Productions (campus entertainment group), PRISM, College Republicans, Young Democrats.

Athletics Member NCAA. All Division III. ***Intercollegiate sports:*** baseball M, basketball M/W, cross-country running M/W, equestrian sports M/W, field hockey W, lacrosse M/W, rugby M(c)/W(c), soccer M/W, softball W, swimming and diving M/W, tennis M/W, track and field M/W, volleyball M(c)/W. ***Intramural sports:*** badminton M/W, baseball M(c), basketball M/W, cheerleading M(c)/W(c), crew M/W(c), fencing M(c)/W(c), field hockey W(c), football M/W, lacrosse M(c)/W(c), skiing (downhill) M(c)/W(c), soccer M(c)/W(c), softball W, swimming and diving M(c)/W(c), tennis M(c)/W(c), ultimate Frisbee M(c)/W(c), volleyball W.

Campus security: 24-hour emergency response devices and patrols, student patrols, late-night transport/escort service, controlled dormitory access, self-defense and safety classes.

Student services: health clinic, personal/psychological counseling.

COSTS & FINANCIAL AID
Costs (2014–15) ***One-time required fee:*** $60. ***Tuition:*** state resident $5190 full-time, $222 per credit hour part-time; nonresident $18,476 full-time, $774 per credit hour part-time. Full-time tuition and fees vary according to course load, degree level, and location. Part-time tuition and fees vary according to course load, degree level, and location. ***Required fees:*** $5062 full-time, $144 per credit hour part-time, $30 per term part-time. ***Room and board:*** $9430; room only: $5766. Room and board charges vary according to board plan and housing facility. ***Payment plan:*** installment. ***Waivers:*** senior citizens.

Financial Aid Of all full-time matriculated undergraduates who enrolled in 2014, 2,298 applied for aid, 1,506 were judged to have need, 190 had their need fully met. 37 Federal Work-Study jobs (averaging $1881). 802 state and other part-time jobs (averaging $1724). In 2014, 455 non-need-based awards were made. ***Average percent of need met:*** 50. ***Average financial aid package:*** $8575. ***Average need-based loan:*** $4255. ***Average need-based gift aid:*** $3695. ***Average non-need-based aid:*** $2803. ***Average indebtedness upon graduation:*** $17,460. ***Financial aid deadline:*** 6/1.

APPLYING
Standardized Tests *Required:* SAT or ACT (for admission). *Recommended:* SAT Subject Tests (for admission).

Options: electronic application, early admission, early action, deferred entrance.

Application fee: $50.

Required: essay or personal statement, high school transcript.

Application deadlines: 2/1 (freshmen), 4/1 (transfers), 11/15 (early action).

Notification: 4/1 (freshmen), 5/15 (transfers), 1/31 (early action).

CONTACT
Ms. Melissa Yakabouski, Director of Undergraduate Admissions, University of Mary Washington, 1301 College Avenue, Fredericksburg, VA 22401-5358. *Phone:* 540-654-2000. *Toll-free phone:* 800-468-5614. *Fax:* 540-654-1857. *E-mail:* admit@umw.edu.

University of Richmond

Richmond, Virginia

http://www.richmond.edu/

- **Independent** comprehensive, founded 1830
- **Suburban** 350-acre campus
- **Endowment** $2.3 billion
- **Coed** 2,984 undergraduate students, 98% full-time, 52% women, 48% men
- **Very difficult** entrance level, 32% of applicants were admitted

UNDERGRAD STUDENTS
2,938 full-time, 46 part-time. Students come from 48 states and territories; 69 other countries; 80% are from out of state; 6% Black or African American, non-Hispanic/Latino; 8% Hispanic/Latino; 7% Asian, non-Hispanic/Latino; 0.2% American Indian or Alaska Native, non-Hispanic/Latino; 4% Two or more races, non-Hispanic/Latino; 8% Race/ethnicity unknown; 9% international; 2% transferred in; 90% live on campus.

Freshmen
Admission: 9,921 applied, 3,155 admitted, 816 enrolled. ***Test scores:*** SAT critical reading scores over 500: 97%; SAT math scores over 500: 99%; SAT writing scores over 500: 96%; ACT scores over 18: 100%; SAT critical reading scores over 600: 79%; SAT math scores over 600: 83%; SAT writing scores over 600: 79%; ACT scores over 24: 97%; SAT critical reading scores over 700: 27%; SAT math scores over 700: 37%; SAT writing scores over 700: 29%; ACT scores over 30: 66%. ***Retention:*** 94% of full-time freshmen returned.

FACULTY
Total: 416, 78% full-time, 85% with terminal degrees.

Student/faculty ratio: 8:1.

ACADEMICS
Calendar: semesters. *Degrees:* bachelor's, master's, and doctoral.

Special study options: advanced placement credit, double majors, English as a second language, honors programs, independent study, internships, off-campus study, part-time degree program, services for LD students, student-designed majors, study abroad, summer session for credit. ***ROTC:*** Army (b).

Unusual degree programs: 3-2 engineering with Columbia University School of Engineering and Applied Science.

Computers: 1,109 computers/terminals and 3,300 ports are available on campus for general student use. Students can access the following: campus intranet, computer help desk, free student e-mail accounts, online (class) grades, online (class) registration, online (class) schedules. Campuswide network is available. 100% of college-owned or -operated housing units are wired for high-speed Internet access. Wireless service is available via entire campus.

STUDENT LIFE
Housing options: coed, men-only, women-only, special housing for students with disabilities. Campus housing is university owned. Freshman campus housing is guaranteed.

Activities and organizations: drama/theater group, student-run newspaper, radio station, choral group, Greek Life, Club Sports, Alpha Phi Omega Service Fraternity, InterVarsity Christian Fellowship, Richmond and Westhampton College Student Government Associations, national fraternities, national sororities.

Athletics Member NCAA. All Division I except football (Division I-AA). ***Intercollegiate sports:*** archery M(c)/W(c), badminton M(c)/W(c), baseball M(s), basketball M(s)/W(s), crew M(c)/W(c), cross-country running M(s)/W(s), equestrian sports M(c)/W(c), field hockey W(s), golf M(s)/W(s), ice hockey M(c), lacrosse M(s)/W(s), rugby M(c)/W(c), soccer W(s), squash M(c)/W(c), swimming and diving W(s), tennis M(s)/W(s), track and field W(s), ultimate Frisbee M(c)/W(c), volleyball M(c)/W(c), water polo M(c)/W(c). ***Intramural sports:*** baseball M(c), basketball M/W, field hockey M(c)/W(c), football M/W, golf M/W, lacrosse M(c)/W(c), racquetball M/W, soccer M/W, softball M/W, squash M/W, table tennis M/W, tennis M/W, volleyball M/W.

Campus security: 24-hour emergency response devices and patrols, late-night transport/escort service, controlled dormitory access, campus police.

Student services: health clinic, personal/psychological counseling, women's center.

COSTS & FINANCIAL AID
Costs (2014–15) ***Comprehensive fee:*** $57,470 includes full-time tuition ($46,680) and room and board ($10,790). Full-time tuition and fees vary according to course load. Part-time tuition: $2334 per credit hour. Part-time tuition and fees vary according to course load. ***College room only:*** $4870. Room and board charges vary according to board plan and housing facility. ***Payment plan:*** installment. ***Waivers:*** employees or children of employees.

Financial Aid Of all full-time matriculated undergraduates who enrolled in 2014, 1,568 applied for aid, 1,279 were judged to have need, 1,089 had their need fully met. 529 Federal Work-Study jobs (averaging $1390). In 2014, 481 non-need-based awards were made. ***Average percent of need met:*** 100. ***Average financial aid package:*** $43,016. ***Average need-based loan:*** $3656. ***Average need-based gift aid:*** $37,199. ***Average non-need-based aid:*** $23,692. ***Average indebtedness upon graduation:*** $22,550. ***Financial aid deadline:*** 2/15.

APPLYING
Standardized Tests *Required:* SAT or ACT (for admission).

Options: electronic application, early decision, deferred entrance.

Application fee: $50.

Required: essay or personal statement, high school transcript, 1 letter of recommendation.

Application deadlines: 1/15 (freshmen), 2/15 (transfers).

Early decision deadline: 11/15 (for plan 1), 1/15 (for plan 2).

Notification: 4/1 (freshmen), 4/15 (transfers), 12/15 (early decision plan 1), 2/15 (early decision plan 2).

CONTACT
Mr. Gil Villanueva, Dean of Admission, University of Richmond, Brunet Memorial Hall, 28 Westhampton Way, University of Richmond, VA 23173. *Phone:* 804-289-8640. *Toll-free phone:* 800-700-1662. *Fax:* 804-287-6003. *E-mail:* admissions@richmond.edu.

University of Valley Forge Virginia Campus

Woodbridge, Virginia

http://www.valleyforge.edu/

- **Independent Assemblies of God** 4-year
- **Suburban** campus with easy access to Washington, DC
- **Coed**
- **Minimally difficult** entrance level

FACULTY
Student/faculty ratio: 6:1.

ACADEMICS
Degrees: certificates, associate, and bachelor's.

STUDENT LIFE
Campus security: 24-hour emergency response devices.

COSTS
Costs (2014–15) ***Tuition:*** $8970 full-time, $299 per credit hour part-time. Full-time tuition and fees vary according to course load and location. Part-time tuition and fees vary according to course load and location. ***Required fees:*** $700 full-time, $350 per term part-time.

APPLYING
Options: electronic application.

Application fee: $75.

Required: essay or personal statement, high school transcript, minimum 1.5 GPA, interview, Pastor's recommendation.

CONTACT
Admissions Coordinator, University of Valley Forge Virginia Campus, 13909 Smoketown Road, Woodbridge, VA 22192. *Phone:* 703-580-4810 Ext. 210. *Toll-free phone:* 800-432-8322.

University of Virginia

Charlottesville, Virginia

http://www.virginia.edu/

- **State-supported** university, founded 1819
- **Suburban** 1167-acre campus with easy access to Richmond
- **Endowment** $5.9 billion
- **Coed** 16,483 undergraduate students, 95% full-time, 56% women, 44% men
- **Very difficult** entrance level, 29% of applicants were admitted

UNDERGRAD STUDENTS
15,632 full-time, 851 part-time. Students come from 51 states and territories; 119 other countries; 28% are from out of state; 6% Black or African American, non-Hispanic/Latino; 6% Hispanic/Latino; 12% Asian, non-Hispanic/Latino; 0.1% American Indian or Alaska Native, non-Hispanic/Latino; 5% Two or more races, non-Hispanic/Latino; 5% Race/ethnicity unknown; 5% international; 4% transferred in; 41% live on campus.

Freshmen
Admission: 31,021 applied, 8,997 admitted, 3,709 enrolled. ***Average high school GPA:*** 4.23. ***Test scores:*** SAT critical reading scores over 500: 98%; SAT math scores over 500: 98%; SAT writing scores over 500: 97%; ACT scores over 18: 100%; SAT critical reading scores over 600: 83%; SAT math scores over 600: 86%; SAT writing scores over 600: 83%; ACT scores over 24: 97%; SAT critical reading scores over 700: 35%; SAT math scores over 700: 44%; SAT writing scores over 700: 37%; ACT scores over 30: 64%.

Retention: 97% of full-time freshmen returned.

FACULTY
Total: 1,415, 94% full-time, 89% with terminal degrees.

Student/faculty ratio: 15:1.

ACADEMICS
Calendar: semesters. *Degrees:* bachelor's, master's, doctoral, and post-master's certificates.

Special study options: accelerated degree program, adult/continuing education programs, advanced placement credit, cooperative education, double majors, English as a second language, honors programs, independent study, internships, part-time degree program, services for LD students, student-designed majors, study abroad, summer session for credit. ***ROTC:*** Army (b), Navy (b), Air Force (b).

Unusual degree programs: 3-2 BA in College of Arts and Sciences/MT in Education.

Computers: 115 computers/terminals are available on campus for general student use. Students can access the following: campus intranet, computer help desk, free student e-mail accounts, online (class) grades, online (class) registration, online (class) schedules, online course management tool. Campuswide network is available. 100% of college-owned or -operated housing units are wired for high-speed Internet access. Wireless service is available via classrooms, computer centers, computer labs, dorm rooms, learning centers, libraries, student centers.

STUDENT LIFE
Housing options: on-campus residence required for freshman year; coed. Campus housing is university owned. Freshman campus housing is guaranteed.

Activities and organizations: drama/theater group, student-run newspaper, radio and television station, choral group, marching band, Madison House, student government, university guides, University Union, The Cavalier Daily, national fraternities, national sororities.

Athletics Member NCAA. All Division I except football (Division I-A). ***Intercollegiate sports:*** baseball M(s), basketball M(s)/W(s), crew W(s), cross-country running M(s)/W(s), field hockey W(s), golf M(s)/W(s), lacrosse M(s)/W(s), soccer M(s)/W(s), softball W(s), swimming and diving M(s)/W(s), tennis M(s)/W(s), track and field M(s)/W(s), volleyball W(s), wrestling M(s). ***Intramural sports:*** archery M(c)/W(c), badminton M(c)/W(c), baseball M(c), basketball M(c)/W(c), cheerleading M(c)/W(c), crew M(c)/W, cross-country running M(c)/W(c), equestrian sports M(c)/W(c), fencing M(c)/W(c), field hockey W(c), football M, golf M(c)/W(c), gymnastics M(c)/W(c), ice hockey M(c), lacrosse W(c), racquetball M(c)/W(c), riflery M(c)/W(c), rock climbing M(c)/W(c), rugby M(c)/W(c), sailing M(c)/W(c), skiing (downhill) M(c)/W(c), soccer M(c)/W(c), softball W(c), squash M(c)/W(c), swimming and diving M(c)/W(c), tennis M(c)/W(c), track and field M(c)/W(c), ultimate Frisbee M(c)/W(c), volleyball M(c)/W(c), water polo M(c)/W(c), wrestling M(c)/W(c).

Campus security: 24-hour emergency response devices and patrols, student patrols, late-night transport/escort service, controlled dormitory access.

Student services: health clinic, personal/psychological counseling, women's center, legal services.

COSTS & FINANCIAL AID
Costs (2014–15) ***Tuition:*** state resident $10,484 full-time, $349 per credit hour part-time; nonresident $38,988 full-time, $1300 per credit hour part-time. Full-time tuition and fees vary according to program and student level. ***Required fees:*** $2514 full-time, $2541 per year part-time. ***Room and board:*** $10,052; room only: $5492. Room and board charges vary according to board plan and housing facility. ***Payment plan:*** installment. ***Waivers:*** senior citizens and employees or children of employees.

Financial Aid Of all full-time matriculated undergraduates who enrolled in 2014, 8,782 applied for aid, 4,967 were judged to have need, 4,967 had their need fully met. In 2014, 407 non-need-based awards were made. ***Average percent of need met:*** 100. ***Average financial aid package:*** $24,427. ***Average need-based loan:*** $6466. ***Average need-based gift aid:*** $19,406. ***Average non-need-based aid:*** $7277. ***Average indebtedness upon graduation:*** $22,933.

APPLYING
Standardized Tests *Required:* SAT or ACT (for admission). *Recommended:* SAT Subject Tests (for admission), SAT or ACT plus optional ACT writing test (ACT alone does not satisfy requirement). At least two SAT subject tests (student's choice) are recommended.

Options: electronic application, early action, deferred entrance.

Application fee: $60.

Required: essay or personal statement, high school transcript, 2 letters of recommendation.

Application deadlines: 1/1 (freshmen), 3/1 (transfers), 11/1 (early action).

Notification: 4/1 (freshmen), 5/1 (transfers), 1/31 (early action).

CONTACT
Mr. Gregory W. Roberts, Dean of Admission, University of Virginia, PO Box 400160, Charlottesville, VA 22904-4727. *Phone:* 434-982-3200. *Fax:* 434-924-3587. *E-mail:* undergrad-admission@virginia.edu.

The University of Virginia's College at Wise

Wise, Virginia

http://www.uvawise.edu/

- **State-supported** 4-year, founded 1954, part of University of Virginia
- **Small-town** 396-acre campus
- **Endowment** $58.8 million
- **Coed** 2,183 undergraduate students, 64% full-time, 60% women, 40% men
- **Moderately difficult** entrance level, 69% of applicants were admitted

UNDERGRAD STUDENTS
1,407 full-time, 776 part-time. Students come from 17 states and territories; 10 other countries; 6% are from out of state; 10% Black or African American, non-Hispanic/Latino; 2% Hispanic/Latino; 0.9% Asian, non-Hispanic/Latino; 0.3% American Indian or Alaska Native, non-Hispanic/Latino; 0.4% Two or more races, non-Hispanic/Latino; 7% Race/ethnicity unknown; 5% transferred in; 24% live on campus.

Freshmen
Admission: 1,113 applied, 766 admitted, 309 enrolled. ***Average high school GPA:*** 3.4. ***Test scores:*** SAT critical reading scores over 500: 41%; SAT math scores over 500: 35%; SAT writing scores over 500: 26%; ACT scores over 18: 98%; SAT critical reading scores over 600: 7%; SAT math scores over 600: 4%; SAT writing scores over 600: 2%; ACT scores over 24: 47%; ACT scores over 30: 29%.
Retention: 66% of full-time freshmen returned.

FACULTY
Total: 209, 48% full-time, 39% with terminal degrees.
Student/faculty ratio: 12:1.

ACADEMICS
Calendar: semesters. *Degree:* bachelor's.
Special study options: academic remediation for entering students, accelerated degree program, adult/continuing education programs, advanced placement credit, cooperative education, distance learning, double majors, honors programs, independent study, internships, part-time degree program, services for LD students, student-designed majors, summer session for credit. ***ROTC:*** Army (b).
Computers: 300 computers/terminals are available on campus for general student use. Students can access the following: campus intranet, computer help desk, free student e-mail accounts, online (class) grades, online (class) registration, online (class) schedules. Campuswide network is available. 100% of college-owned or -operated housing units are wired for high-speed Internet access. Wireless service is available via learning centers, libraries, student centers.

STUDENT LIFE
Housing options: on-campus residence required for freshman year; coed, men-only, women-only. Campus housing is university owned.
Activities and organizations: drama/theater group, student-run newspaper, radio and television station, choral group, marching band, student government, Student Activities Board, Multicultural Association, Residence Hall Association, intramurals, national fraternities, national sororities.
Athletics Member NCAA. All Division II. ***Intercollegiate sports:*** baseball M(s), basketball M(s)/W(s), cross-country running M(s)/W(s), football M(s), golf M/W, softball W(s), tennis M(s)/W(s), track and field M/W, volleyball W(s). ***Intramural sports:*** badminton M/W, basketball M/W, football M/W, golf M/W, racquetball M/W, soccer M/W, softball M/W, table tennis M/W, tennis M/W, ultimate Frisbee M/W, volleyball M/W, water polo M/W.
Campus security: 24-hour emergency response devices and patrols, student patrols, late-night transport/escort service, self-defense, informal discussions, pamphlets/posters/films, and crime prevention office.
Student services: health clinic, personal/psychological counseling.

COSTS & FINANCIAL AID
Costs (2014–15) ***Tuition:*** state resident $4862 full-time, $208 per credit hour part-time; nonresident $19,864 full-time, $840 per credit hour part-time. Part-time tuition and fees vary according to course load. ***Required fees:*** $4006 full-time, $254 per credit hour part-time. ***Room and board:*** $10,340. Room and board charges vary according to board plan and housing facility. ***Payment plans:*** installment, deferred payment. ***Waivers:*** senior citizens and employees or children of employees.
Financial Aid Of all full-time matriculated undergraduates who enrolled in 2013, 1,209 applied for aid, 1,103 were judged to have need, 299 had their need fully met. In 2013, 149 non-need-based awards were made. ***Average percent of need met:*** 83. ***Average financial aid package:*** $13,141. ***Average need-based loan:*** $3996. ***Average need-based gift aid:*** $6898. ***Average non-need-based aid:*** $5077. ***Average indebtedness upon graduation:*** $12,662.

APPLYING
Standardized Tests *Required:* SAT or ACT (for admission).
Options: early admission, early action.
Application fee: $25.
Required: high school transcript, minimum 2.3 GPA. ***Recommended:*** 2 letters of recommendation.
Application deadlines: 8/1 (freshmen), 8/15 (transfers), 2/1 (early action).
Notification: 8/20 (freshmen), continuous until 8/20 (transfers), 2/15 (early action).

CONTACT
Mr. Russell D. Necessary, Vice Chancellor for Enrollment Management, The University of Virginia's College at Wise, 1 College Avenue, Wise, VA 24293. *Phone:* 276-328-0322. *Toll-free phone:* 888-282-9324. *Fax:* 276-328-0251. *E-mail:* admissions@uvawise.edu.

Virginia Commonwealth University

Richmond, Virginia

http://www.vcu.edu/

- **State-supported** university, founded 1838
- **Urban** 150-acre campus
- **Endowment** $50.6 million
- **Coed** 23,962 undergraduate students, 85% full-time, 57% women, 43% men
- 69% of applicants were admitted

UNDERGRAD STUDENTS
20,294 full-time, 3,668 part-time. Students come from 106 other countries; 7% are from out of state; 18% Black or African American, non-Hispanic/Latino; 8% Hispanic/Latino; 12% Asian, non-Hispanic/Latino; 0.2% Native Hawaiian or other Pacific Islander, non-Hispanic/Latino; 0.3% American Indian or Alaska Native, non-Hispanic/Latino; 5% Two or more races, non-Hispanic/Latino; 3% Race/ethnicity unknown; 3% international; 10% transferred in.

Freshmen
Admission: 15,126 applied, 10,426 admitted, 3,586 enrolled. ***Average high school GPA:*** 3.59. ***Test scores:*** SAT critical reading scores over 500: 79%; SAT math scores over 500: 77%; SAT writing scores over 500: 70%; ACT scores over 18: 97%; SAT critical reading scores over 600: 31%; SAT math scores over 600: 28%; SAT writing scores over 600: 23%; ACT scores over 24: 50%; SAT critical reading scores over 700: 5%; SAT math scores over 700: 5%; SAT writing scores over 700: 4%; ACT scores over 30: 11%.
Retention: 87% of full-time freshmen returned.

FACULTY
Total: 3,311, 67% full-time.
Student/faculty ratio: 17:1.

ACADEMICS
Calendar: semesters. *Degrees:* certificates, bachelor's, master's, doctoral, post-master's, and postbachelor's certificates.
Special study options: academic remediation for entering students, accelerated degree program, adult/continuing education programs, advanced placement credit, cooperative education, distance learning, double majors, English as a second language, freshman honors college, honors programs, independent study, internships, off-campus study, part-time degree program, services for LD students, student-designed majors, study abroad, summer session for credit. ***ROTC:*** Army (c).
Computers: 1,500 computers/terminals and ####### ports are available on campus for general student use. Students can access the following: campus intranet, computer help desk, free student e-mail accounts, online (class) grades, online (class) registration, online (class) schedules. Campuswide network is available. 100% of college-owned or -operated housing units are wired for high-speed Internet access. Wireless service is available via classrooms, computer centers, computer labs, dorm rooms, learning centers, libraries, student centers.

STUDENT LIFE
Housing options: coed. Campus housing is university owned.
Activities and organizations: drama/theater group, student-run newspaper, radio and television station, choral group, national fraternities, national sororities.

Athletics Member NCAA. All Division I. ***Intercollegiate sports:*** baseball M(s), basketball M(s)/W(s), cross-country running M(s)/W(s), field hockey W(s), golf M(s), soccer M(s)/W(s), tennis M(s)/W(s), track and field M(s)/W(s), volleyball W(s). ***Intramural sports:*** badminton M(c)/W(c), baseball M(c), basketball M(c)/W(c), bowling M(c)/W(c), crew M(c), cross-country running M(c)/W(c), equestrian sports M(c)/W(c), field hockey M(c)/W(c), ice hockey M(c)/W(c), lacrosse M(c)/W(c), rugby M(c)/W(c), skiing (downhill) M(c), soccer M(c)/W(c), softball W(c), swimming and diving M(c)/W(c), table tennis M(c)/W(c), tennis M(c)/W(c), ultimate Frisbee M(c)/W(c), volleyball M/W(c).

Campus security: 24-hour emergency response devices and patrols, student patrols, late-night transport/escort service, controlled dormitory access, security personnel in residence halls, RAD classes and special event coverage.

Student services: health clinic, personal/psychological counseling, women's center.

COSTS & FINANCIAL AID

Costs (2014–15) ***Tuition:*** state resident $12,398 full-time, $353 per credit hour part-time; nonresident $30,459 full-time, $954 per credit hour part-time. ***Required fees:*** $2175 full-time. ***Room and board:*** $9318. Room and board charges vary according to board plan and housing facility. ***Payment plan:*** installment. ***Waivers:*** employees or children of employees.

Financial Aid Of all full-time matriculated undergraduates who enrolled in 2013, 13,866 applied for aid, 11,456 were judged to have need, 812 had their need fully met. 827 Federal Work-Study jobs (averaging $1803). In 2013, 1885 non-need-based awards were made. ***Average percent of need met:*** 52. ***Average financial aid package:*** $10,527. ***Average need-based loan:*** $4444. ***Average need-based gift aid:*** $7211. ***Average non-need-based aid:*** $10,354. ***Average indebtedness upon graduation:*** $32,411.

APPLYING

Standardized Tests *Required for some:* SAT or ACT (for admission).

Options: electronic application, early admission.

Application fee: $50.

Required: high school transcript. ***Required for some:*** SAT or ACT scores.

CONTACT

Virginia Commonwealth University, 901 West Franklin Street, Richmond, VA 23284-9005. *Phone:* 804-828-6125. *Toll-free phone:* 800-841-3638.

★ Virginia Military Institute

Lexington, Virginia

http://www.vmi.edu/

- **State-supported** 4-year, founded 1839
- **Small-town** 134-acre campus
- **Endowment** $371.1 million
- **Coed, primarily men** 1,700 undergraduate students, 100% full-time, 11% women, 89% men
- **Moderately difficult** entrance level, 44% of applicants were admitted

UNDERGRAD STUDENTS

1,700 full-time. Students come from 45 states and territories; 9 other countries; 40% are from out of state; 5% Black or African American, non-Hispanic/Latino; 5% Hispanic/Latino; 4% Asian, non-Hispanic/Latino; 0.8% Native Hawaiian or other Pacific Islander, non-Hispanic/Latino; 0.4% American Indian or Alaska Native, non-Hispanic/Latino; 2% Two or more races, non-Hispanic/Latino; 0.1% Race/ethnicity unknown; 1% international; 2% transferred in; 100% live on campus.

Freshmen

Admission: 2,036 applied, 904 admitted, 452 enrolled. ***Average high school GPA:*** 3.67. ***Test scores:*** SAT critical reading scores over 500: 82%; SAT math scores over 500: 89%; SAT writing scores over 500: 71%; ACT scores over 18: 96%; SAT critical reading scores over 600: 32%; SAT math scores over 600: 38%; SAT writing scores over 600: 21%; ACT scores over 24: 61%; SAT critical reading scores over 700: 4%; SAT math scores over 700: 4%; SAT writing scores over 700: 2%; ACT scores over 30: 6%.

Retention: 89% of full-time freshmen returned.

FACULTY

Total: 188, 67% full-time, 79% with terminal degrees.

Student/faculty ratio: 12:1.

ACADEMICS

Calendar: semesters. *Degree:* bachelor's.

Special study options: advanced placement credit, double majors, honors programs, independent study, internships, services for LD students, study abroad, summer session for credit. ***ROTC:*** Army (b), Navy (b), Air Force (b).

Computers: 200 computers/terminals are available on campus for general student use. Students can access the following: computer help desk, free student e-mail accounts, online (class) registration, online (class) schedules. Campuswide network is available. 100% of college-owned or -operated housing units are wired for high-speed Internet access. Wireless service is available via classrooms, dorm rooms, libraries, student centers.

STUDENT LIFE

Housing options: on-campus residence required through senior yearCampus housing is university owned. Freshman campus housing is guaranteed.

Activities and organizations: drama/theater group, student-run newspaper, choral group, marching band, Newman Club, Officers Christian Fellowship, strength and fitness organizations, Promaji, Pre-Law Society.

Athletics Member NCAA. All Division I. ***Intercollegiate sports:*** baseball M(s), basketball M(s), cross-country running M(s)/W(s), football M(s), lacrosse M(s), riflery M(s)/W(s), soccer M(s)/W, swimming and diving M(s)/W, track and field M(s)/W(s), water polo W, wrestling M(s).

Campus security: 24-hour emergency response devices and patrols, student patrols.

Student services: health clinic, personal/psychological counseling.

COSTS & FINANCIAL AID

Costs (2014–15) ***Tuition:*** state resident $7498 full-time; nonresident $29,554 full-time. ***Required fees:*** $8020 full-time. ***Room and board:*** $8372. ***Payment plan:*** installment.

Financial Aid Of all full-time matriculated undergraduates who enrolled in 2013, 1,145 applied for aid, 858 were judged to have need, 442 had their need fully met. In 2013, 241 non-need-based awards were made. ***Average percent of need met:*** 88. ***Average financial aid package:*** $15,481. ***Average need-based loan:*** $4393. ***Average need-based gift aid:*** $14,402. ***Average non-need-based aid:*** $4195. ***Average indebtedness upon graduation:*** $26,720.

APPLYING

Standardized Tests *Required:* SAT or ACT (for admission).

Options: electronic application, early admission, early decision.

Application fee: $40.

Required: high school transcript. ***Recommended:*** essay or personal statement, 2 letters of recommendation, interview.

Early decision deadline: 11/15.

Notification: continuous (freshmen), 12/15 (early decision).

CONTACT

Lt. Col. Tom Mortenson, Associate Director of Admissions, Virginia Military Institute, Admissions Office, Lexington, VA 24450. *Phone:* 540-464-7211. *Toll-free phone:* 800-767-4207. *Fax:* 540-464-7746. *E-mail:* admissions@vmi.edu.

Virginia Polytechnic Institute and State University

Blacksburg, Virginia

http://www.vt.edu/

- **State-supported** university, founded 1872
- **Small-town** 2600-acre campus
- **Endowment** $796.4 million
- **Coed** 24,247 undergraduate students, 98% full-time, 42% women, 58% men
- **Moderately difficult** entrance level, 71% of applicants were admitted

UNDERGRAD STUDENTS
23,685 full-time, 562 part-time. Students come from 116 other countries; 4% Black or African American, non-Hispanic/Latino; 5% Hispanic/Latino; 9% Asian, non-Hispanic/Latino; 0.1% Native Hawaiian or other Pacific Islander, non-Hispanic/Latino; 0.2% American Indian or Alaska Native, non-Hispanic/Latino; 4% Two or more races, non-Hispanic/Latino; 3% Race/ethnicity unknown; 5% international; 4% transferred in; 37% live on campus.

Freshmen
Admission: 20,907 applied, 14,904 admitted, 5,494 enrolled. ***Test scores:*** SAT critical reading scores over 500: 90%; SAT math scores over 500: 96%; SAT writing scores over 500: 89%; SAT critical reading scores over 600: 47%; SAT math scores over 600: 65%; SAT writing scores over 600: 45%; SAT critical reading scores over 700: 8%; SAT math scores over 700: 19%; SAT writing scores over 700: 7%.

Retention: 93% of full-time freshmen returned.

FACULTY
Total: 1,661, 87% full-time.

Student/faculty ratio: 16:1.

ACADEMICS
Calendar: semesters. *Degrees:* associate, bachelor's, master's, doctoral, and post-master's certificates.

Special study options: accelerated degree program, adult/continuing education programs, advanced placement credit, cooperative education, distance learning, double majors, English as a second language, honors programs, independent study, internships, part-time degree program, services for LD students, study abroad, summer session for credit. ***ROTC:*** Army (b), Navy (b), Air Force (b).

Computers: 8,000 computers/terminals are available on campus for general student use. Students can access the following: campus intranet, computer help desk, free student e-mail accounts, online (class) grades, online (class) registration, online (class) schedules. Campuswide network is available. Wireless service is available via entire campus.

STUDENT LIFE
Housing options: on-campus residence required for freshman year; coed, men-only, women-only. Campus housing is university owned. Freshman campus housing is guaranteed.

Activities and organizations: drama/theater group, student-run newspaper, radio and television station, choral group, marching band, Virginia Tech Union, Student Government Association, international student organizations, national fraternities, national sororities.

Athletics Member NCAA. All Division I except football (Division I-A). ***Intercollegiate sports:*** baseball M, basketball M, cross-country running M/W, golf M(s), lacrosse W(s), soccer M(s)/W(s), swimming and diving M(s)/W(s), tennis M(s)/W(s), track and field M(s)/W(s), ultimate Frisbee M/W, volleyball W. ***Intramural sports:*** baseball M(c), basketball M, bowling M/W, crew M(c)/W(c), cross-country running M/W, equestrian sports M(c)/W(c), fencing M(c)/W(c), field hockey M(c)/W(c), football M/W, golf M/W, gymnastics M(c)/W(c), ice hockey M/W, lacrosse M(c)/W(c), racquetball M/W, riflery M(c)/W(c), rugby M(c)/W(c), soccer M/W, softball M/W, swimming and diving M/W, table tennis M/W, tennis M/W, volleyball M/W, water polo M/W.

Campus security: 24-hour emergency response devices and patrols, student patrols, late-night transport/escort service, controlled dormitory access.

Student services: health clinic, personal/psychological counseling, women's center, legal services.

FINANCIAL AID
Financial Aid Of all full-time matriculated undergraduates who enrolled in 2013, 15,673 applied for aid, 10,585 were judged to have need, 1,793 had their need fully met. In 2013, 2744 non-need-based awards were made. ***Average percent of need met:*** 64. ***Average financial aid package:*** $16,455. ***Average need-based loan:*** $4711. ***Average need-based gift aid:*** $6736. ***Average non-need-based aid:*** $3526. ***Average indebtedness upon graduation:*** $27,865.

APPLYING
Standardized Tests *Required:* SAT or ACT (for admission). *Required for some:* SAT and SAT Subject Tests or ACT (for admission).

Options: electronic application, early admission, early decision, deferred entrance.

Application fee: $60.

Required: high school transcript. ***Recommended:*** minimum 3.0 GPA.

Application deadlines: 1/15 (freshmen), 2/15 (transfers).

Early decision deadline: 11/1.

Notification: 4/1 (freshmen), 5/1 (transfers), 12/15 (early decision).

CONTACT
Virginia Polytechnic Institute and State University, Blacksburg, VA 24061. *Phone:* 540-231-6267.

Virginia State University

Petersburg, Virginia

http://www.vsu.edu/

- **State-supported** comprehensive, founded 1882, part of State Council of Higher Education for Virginia
- **Suburban** 236-acre campus with easy access to Richmond
- **Endowment** $32.2 million
- **Coed** 4,498 undergraduate students, 95% full-time, 60% women, 40% men
- **Minimally difficult** entrance level, 80% of applicants were admitted

UNDERGRAD STUDENTS
4,284 full-time, 214 part-time. Students come from 39 states and territories; 24% are from out of state; 85% Black or African American, non-Hispanic/Latino; 2% Hispanic/Latino; 0.4% Asian, non-Hispanic/Latino; 0.3% American Indian or Alaska Native, non-Hispanic/Latino; 9% Race/ethnicity unknown; 0.1% international; 7% transferred in.

Freshmen
Admission: 5,923 applied, 4,742 admitted, 907 enrolled. ***Average high school GPA:*** 2.8. ***Test scores:*** SAT critical reading scores over 500: 12%; SAT math scores over 500: 12%; SAT writing scores over 500: 7%; ACT scores over 18: 39%; SAT critical reading scores over 600: 1%; SAT math scores over 600: 1%; ACT scores over 24: 6%.

Retention: 61% of full-time freshmen returned.

FACULTY
Total: 446, 66% full-time.

Student/faculty ratio: 13:1.

ACADEMICS
Calendar: semesters. *Degrees:* associate, bachelor's, master's, doctoral, and postbachelor's certificates.

Special study options: adult/continuing education programs, advanced placement credit, cooperative education, double majors, honors programs, independent study, internships, off-campus study, part-time degree program, services for LD students, student-designed majors, study abroad, summer session for credit. ***ROTC:*** Army (b).

Computers: 2,100 computers/terminals and 1,400 ports are available on campus for general student use. Students can access the following: computer help desk, free student e-mail accounts, online (class) grades, online (class) registration, online (class) schedules. Campuswide network is available. 100% of college-owned or -operated housing units are wired for high-speed Internet access. Wireless service is available via entire campus.

STUDENT LIFE
Housing options: on-campus residence required for freshman year; coed, men-only, women-only. Campus housing is university owned. Freshman applicants given priority for college housing.

Activities and organizations: drama/theater group, student-run newspaper, choral group, marching band, AbstraKt Entertainment, Golden Key Honor Society, The Betterment of Brothers and Sisters, Diversified Virtue Entertainment, Sankofa, national fraternities, national sororities.

Athletics Member NCAA. All Division II. ***Intercollegiate sports:*** baseball M(s), basketball M(s)/W(s), bowling W(s), cheerleading M/W, cross-country running M(s)/W(s), football M(s), golf M(s)/W(s), softball W(s), tennis M(s)/W(s), track and field M(s)/W(s), volleyball W(s).

Intramural sports: basketball M/W, football M, tennis M/W, track and field M/W, volleyball W.

Campus security: 24-hour emergency response devices and patrols, late-night transport/escort service, controlled dormitory access.

Student services: health clinic, personal/psychological counseling.

COSTS & FINANCIAL AID

Costs (2014–15) ***Tuition:*** state resident $4876 full-time, $348 per credit hour part-time; nonresident $14,132 full-time, $770 per credit hour part-time. Full-time tuition and fees vary according to course load and program. Part-time tuition and fees vary according to course load and program. ***Required fees:*** $3126 full-time, $10 per credit hour part-time. ***Room and board:*** $10,128; room only: $5990. Room and board charges vary according to board plan and housing facility. ***Payment plan:*** installment. ***Waivers:*** senior citizens.

Financial Aid Of all full-time matriculated undergraduates who enrolled in 2013, 4,566 applied for aid, 4,566 were judged to have need, 685 had their need fully met. 300 Federal Work-Study jobs (averaging $2000). In 2013, 503 non-need-based awards were made. ***Average percent of need met:*** 65. ***Average financial aid package:*** $11,487. ***Average need-based loan:*** $5500. ***Average need-based gift aid:*** $6708. ***Average non-need-based aid:*** $1000. ***Average indebtedness upon graduation:*** $28,250.

APPLYING

Standardized Tests *Required:* SAT or ACT (for admission).

Options: electronic application.

Application fee: $25.

Required: high school transcript, minimum 2.2 GPA, 2 letters of recommendation. ***Recommended:*** essay or personal statement.

Application deadlines: 5/1 (freshmen), 5/1 (transfers).

Notification: continuous (freshmen), continuous (transfers).

CONTACT

Mrs. Irene Logan, Director of Admissions, Virginia State University, Office of Admissions, Petersburg, VA 23806-2096. *Phone:* 804-524-5902. *Toll-free phone:* 800-871-7611. *Fax:* 804-524-5055. *E-mail:* ilogan@vsu.edu.

Virginia Union University

Richmond, Virginia

http://www.vuu.edu/

- **Independent Baptist** comprehensive, founded 1865
- **Urban** 84-acre campus with easy access to Washington, DC
- **Endowment** $31.5 million
- **Coed** 1,323 undergraduate students, 97% full-time, 56% women, 44% men
- **Moderately difficult** entrance level, 24% of applicants were admitted

UNDERGRAD STUDENTS

1,286 full-time, 37 part-time. Students come from 29 states and territories; 12 other countries; 49% are from out of state; 96% Black or African American, non-Hispanic/Latino; 1% Hispanic/Latino; 0.2% Asian, non-Hispanic/Latino; 0.2% Native Hawaiian or other Pacific Islander, non-Hispanic/Latino; 0.4% American Indian or Alaska Native, non-Hispanic/Latino; 9% Race/ethnicity unknown; 0.1% international; 0.1% transferred in.

Freshmen

Admission: 10,021 applied, 2,394 admitted, 421 enrolled. ***Average high school GPA:*** 2.7. ***Test scores:*** SAT critical reading scores over 500: 24%; ACT scores over 18: 26%; SAT critical reading scores over 600: 2%; ACT scores over 24: 1%; SAT critical reading scores over 700: 1%; ACT scores over 30: 1%.

Retention: 50% of full-time freshmen returned.

FACULTY

Total: 120, 69% full-time.

Student/faculty ratio: 14:1.

ACADEMICS

Calendar: semesters. *Degrees:* bachelor's, master's, and doctoral.

Special study options: academic remediation for entering students, adult/continuing education programs, advanced placement credit, cooperative education, double majors, English as a second language, honors programs, internships, off-campus study, summer session for credit. ***ROTC:*** Army (c).

Unusual degree programs: 3-2 engineering with Howard University, University of Michigan, University of Iowa, Virginia Commonwealth University.

Computers: 2 computers/terminals are available on campus for general student use. Students can access the following: campus intranet, computer help desk, free student e-mail accounts, online (class) grades, online (class) registration, online (class) schedules. Campuswide network is available. Wireless service is available via entire campus.

STUDENT LIFE

Housing options: coed, men-only, women-only. Campus housing is university owned and leased by the school. Freshman applicants given priority for college housing.

Activities and organizations: drama/theater group, student-run newspaper, choral group, marching band, Student Government Association, NAACP, NPHC-VUU Chapter (National Pan-Hellenic Council), Mr. and Miss Royal Court, national fraternities, national sororities.

Athletics Member NCAA. All Division II. ***Intercollegiate sports:*** basketball M(s)/W(s), bowling M(s)/W(s), cross-country running M(s)/W(s), football M(s), golf M(s), softball W(s), tennis M(s)/W(s), track and field M(s)/W(s), volleyball W(s). ***Intramural sports:*** basketball M, softball W.

Campus security: 24-hour emergency response devices and patrols, controlled dormitory access.

Student services: health clinic, personal/psychological counseling.

COSTS & FINANCIAL AID

Costs (2014–15) ***One-time required fee:*** $200. ***Comprehensive fee:*** $23,004 includes full-time tuition ($13,614), mandatory fees ($1316), and room and board ($8074). Full-time tuition and fees vary according to course level, course load, and reciprocity agreements. Part-time tuition: $422 per credit hour. Part-time tuition and fees vary according to course level, course load, and reciprocity agreements. ***Required fees:*** $40 per credit hour part-time. ***College room only:*** $3690. Room and board charges vary according to housing facility. ***Payment plans:*** installment, deferred payment. ***Waivers:*** employees or children of employees.

Financial Aid Of all full-time matriculated undergraduates who enrolled in 2014, 1,110 applied for aid, 1,067 were judged to have need, 64 had their need fully met. 303 Federal Work-Study jobs (averaging $1912). In 2014, 37 non-need-based awards were made. ***Average percent of need met:*** 53. ***Average financial aid package:*** $13,322. ***Average need-based loan:*** $3899. ***Average need-based gift aid:*** $9590. ***Average non-need-based aid:*** $5046. ***Average indebtedness upon graduation:*** $33,286.

APPLYING

Standardized Tests *Required:* SAT or ACT (for admission).

Options: electronic application, deferred entrance.

Application fee: $25.

Required: high school transcript. ***Required for some:*** interview. ***Recommended:*** essay or personal statement.

Application deadlines: rolling (freshmen), rolling (transfers).

Notification: continuous (freshmen), continuous (transfers).

CONTACT

Ms. Sharnae Randolph, Assistant Director of Admissions, Virginia Union University, 1500 North Lombardy Street, Richmond, VA 23220-1170. *Phone:* 804-342-3571. *Toll-free phone:* 800-368-3227. *Fax:* 804-342-3511. *E-mail:* sarandolph@vuu.edu.

Virginia Wesleyan College

Norfolk, Virginia

http://www.vwc.edu/

- **Independent United Methodist** 4-year, founded 1961
- **Urban** 300-acre campus with easy access to Norfolk, Virginia Beach
- **Endowment** $57.7 million
- **Coed** 1,502 undergraduate students, 95% full-time, 62% women, 38% men
- **Moderately difficult** entrance level, 89% of applicants were admitted

UNDERGRAD STUDENTS
1,420 full-time, 82 part-time. Students come from 32 states and territories; 8 other countries; 25% are from out of state; 23% Black or African American, non-Hispanic/Latino; 8% Hispanic/Latino; 1% Asian, non-Hispanic/Latino; 0.1% Native Hawaiian or other Pacific Islander, non-Hispanic/Latino; 0.5% American Indian or Alaska Native, non-Hispanic/Latino; 6% Two or more races, non-Hispanic/Latino; 4% Race/ethnicity unknown; 0.9% international; 6% transferred in; 61% live on campus.

Freshmen
Admission: 2,072 applied, 1,845 admitted, 406 enrolled. ***Average high school GPA:*** 3.3. ***Test scores:*** SAT critical reading scores over 500: 50%; SAT math scores over 500: 50%; SAT writing scores over 500: 43%; ACT scores over 18: 80%; SAT critical reading scores over 600: 13%; SAT math scores over 600: 9%; SAT writing scores over 600: 10%; ACT scores over 24: 33%; SAT critical reading scores over 700: 1%; SAT math scores over 700: 1%; SAT writing scores over 700: 1%; ACT scores over 30: 5%.

Retention: 66% of full-time freshmen returned.

FACULTY
Total: 130, 71% full-time, 71% with terminal degrees.

Student/faculty ratio: 13:1.

ACADEMICS
Calendar: 4-1-4. *Degree:* bachelor's.

Special study options: academic remediation for entering students, adult/continuing education programs, advanced placement credit, double majors, freshman honors college, honors programs, independent study, internships, off-campus study, part-time degree program, services for LD students, student-designed majors, study abroad, summer session for credit. ***ROTC:*** Army (c).

Unusual degree programs: 3-2 engineering.

Computers: 130 computers/terminals are available on campus for general student use. Students can access the following: campus intranet, computer help desk, free student e-mail accounts, online (class) grades, online (class) registration, online (class) schedules. Campuswide network is available. 100% of college-owned or -operated housing units are wired for high-speed Internet access. Wireless service is available via entire campus.

STUDENT LIFE
Housing options: on-campus residence required through senior year; coed, women-only, special housing for students with disabilities. Campus housing is university owned. Freshman applicants given priority for college housing.

Activities and organizations: drama/theater group, student-run newspaper, radio station, choral group, Wesleyan Activities Council, community service, Student Government Association, student newspaper, Black Student Union, national fraternities, national sororities.

Athletics Member NCAA. All Division III. ***Intercollegiate sports:*** baseball M, basketball M/W, cheerleading W, cross-country running M/W, field hockey W, golf M, lacrosse M/W, soccer M/W, softball W, tennis M/W, track and field M/W, volleyball W. ***Intramural sports:*** basketball M/W, crew M(c)/W(c), fencing M(c)/W(c), field hockey W, football M/W, racquetball M/W, soccer M/W, softball M/W, table tennis M/W, ultimate Frisbee M/W, volleyball M/W.

Campus security: 24-hour emergency response devices and patrols, late-night transport/escort service, controlled dormitory access, well-lit pathways.

Student services: health clinic, personal/psychological counseling, women's center.

COSTS & FINANCIAL AID
Costs (2015–16) ***One-time required fee:*** $350. ***Comprehensive fee:*** $43,108 includes full-time tuition ($33,778), mandatory fees ($650), and room and board ($8680). Full-time tuition and fees vary according to course load. Part-time tuition: $1408 per credit hour. Part-time tuition and fees vary according to course load. ***Room and board:*** Room and board charges vary according to board plan and housing facility. ***Payment plan:*** installment. ***Waivers:*** adult students, senior citizens, and employees or children of employees.

Financial Aid Of all full-time matriculated undergraduates who enrolled in 2013, 1,394 applied for aid, 1,153 were judged to have need, 162 had their need fully met. 209 Federal Work-Study jobs (averaging $968). In 2013, 239 non-need-based awards were made. ***Average percent of need met:*** 66. ***Average financial aid package:*** $21,869. ***Average need-based loan:*** $7142. ***Average need-based gift aid:*** $18,774. ***Average non-need-based aid:*** $18,893. ***Average indebtedness upon graduation:*** $31,891.

APPLYING
Standardized Tests *Required for some:* SAT or ACT (for admission). *Recommended:* SAT or ACT (for admission).

Options: electronic application.

Application fee: $40.

Required: high school transcript, minimum 2.5 GPA. ***Required for some:*** interview. ***Recommended:*** essay or personal statement, .

Application deadlines: rolling (freshmen), rolling (transfers).

Notification: continuous (freshmen), continuous (transfers).

CONTACT
Virginia Wesleyan College, 1584 Wesleyan Drive, Norfolk, VA 23502-5599. *Phone:* 757-455-3208. *Toll-free phone:* 800-737-8684.

Washington and Lee University
Lexington, Virginia
http://www.wlu.edu/

- **Independent** comprehensive, founded 1749
- **Small-town** 430-acre campus
- **Endowment** $1.5 billion
- **Coed** 1,890 undergraduate students, 100% full-time, 50% women, 50% men
- **Most difficult** entrance level, 20% of applicants were admitted

UNDERGRAD STUDENTS
1,882 full-time, 8 part-time. Students come from 51 states and territories; 38 other countries; 86% are from out of state; 2% Black or African American, non-Hispanic/Latino; 4% Hispanic/Latino; 3% Asian, non-Hispanic/Latino; 0.1% Native Hawaiian or other Pacific Islander, non-Hispanic/Latino; 0.1% American Indian or Alaska Native, non-Hispanic/Latino; 2% Two or more races, non-Hispanic/Latino; 2% Race/ethnicity unknown; 4% international; 0.1% transferred in; 56% live on campus.

Freshmen
Admission: 5,797 applied, 1,136 admitted, 471 enrolled. ***Test scores:*** SAT critical reading scores over 500: 100%; SAT math scores over 500: 100%; SAT writing scores over 500: 100%; ACT scores over 18: 100%; SAT critical reading scores over 600: 99%; SAT math scores over 600: 95%; SAT writing scores over 600: 94%; ACT scores over 24: 100%; SAT critical reading scores over 700: 46%; SAT math scores over 700: 53%; SAT writing scores over 700: 47%; ACT scores over 30: 88%.

Retention: 97% of full-time freshmen returned.

FACULTY
Total: 361, 71% full-time, 92% with terminal degrees.

Student/faculty ratio: 8:1.

ACADEMICS
Calendar: 4-4-2. *Degrees:* bachelor's, master's, and doctoral.

Special study options: advanced placement credit, double majors, honors programs, independent study, internships, off-campus study, services for LD students, student-designed majors, study abroad. ***ROTC:*** Army (c).

Computers: 176 computers/terminals and 1,200 ports are available on campus for general student use. Students can access the following: campus intranet, computer help desk, free student e-mail accounts, online (class) grades, online (class) registration, online (class) schedules. Campuswide network is available. 100% of college-owned or -operated housing units are wired for high-speed Internet access. Wireless service is available via entire campus.

STUDENT LIFE
Housing options: on-campus residence required through sophomore year; coed, men-only, women-only, special housing for students with disabilities. Campus housing is university owned. Freshman campus housing is guaranteed.

Activities and organizations: drama/theater group, student-run newspaper, radio and television station, choral group, Mock Convention, General Activities Board, Nabors Service League, Outing Club, Sports Clubs, national fraternities, national sororities.

Athletics Member NCAA. All Division III. ***Intercollegiate sports:*** baseball M, basketball M/W, cheerleading M(c)/W(c), cross-country running M/W, equestrian sports W, fencing M(c)/W(c), field hockey W, football M, golf M/W, ice hockey M(c)/W(c), lacrosse M/W, rugby M(c), skiing (cross-country) M(c)/W(c), soccer M/W, softball W(c), swimming and diving M/W, tennis M/W, track and field M/W, ultimate Frisbee M(c)/W(c), volleyball M(c)/W, wrestling M. ***Intramural sports:*** badminton M/W, baseball M(c), basketball M/W, equestrian sports W(c), football M/W, golf M/W, lacrosse M(c)/W(c), racquetball M/W, rock climbing M(c), skiing (downhill) M(c)/W(c), soccer M/W, softball M/W, squash M(c)/W(c), swimming and diving M/W, table tennis M/W, tennis M/W, track and field M/W, ultimate Frisbee M/W, volleyball M/W, wrestling M.

Campus security: 24-hour emergency response devices and patrols, late-night transport/escort service, controlled dormitory access, Emergency Alert System.

Student services: health clinic, personal/psychological counseling.

COSTS & FINANCIAL AID

Costs (2014–15) ***Comprehensive fee:*** $56,262 includes full-time tuition ($44,660), mandatory fees ($957), and room and board ($10,645). Full-time tuition and fees vary according to degree level. Part-time tuition: $1595 per credit hour. Part-time tuition and fees vary according to degree level. ***College room only:*** $4750. Room and board charges vary according to board plan and housing facility. ***Payment plan:*** installment. ***Waivers:*** employees or children of employees.

Financial Aid Of all full-time matriculated undergraduates who enrolled in 2014, 872 applied for aid, 782 were judged to have need, 782 had their need fully met. 212 Federal Work-Study jobs (averaging $2000). 371 state and other part-time jobs (averaging $2000). In 2014, 159 non-need-based awards were made. ***Average percent of need met:*** 100. ***Average financial aid package:*** $46,604. ***Average need-based loan:*** $973. ***Average need-based gift aid:*** $41,472. ***Average non-need-based aid:*** $36,293. ***Average indebtedness upon graduation:*** $23,224. ***Financial aid deadline:*** 2/15.

APPLYING

Standardized Tests *Required:* SAT or ACT (for admission). *Recommended:* SAT Subject Tests (for admission), 2 unrelated SAT subject tests are recommended, but not required.

Options: electronic application, early decision, deferred entrance.

Application fee: $50.

Required: high school transcript, 3 letters of recommendation. ***Recommended:*** essay or personal statement, interview.

Application deadlines: 1/1 (freshmen), 4/1 (transfers).

Early decision deadline: 11/1 (for plan 1), 1/1 (for plan 2).

Notification: 4/1 (freshmen), continuous (transfers), 12/22 (early decision plan 1), 2/1 (early decision plan 2).

CONTACT

Mr. William M. Hartog, Dean of Admissions and Financial Aid, Washington and Lee University, 204 West Washington Street, Lexington, VA 24450-2116. *Phone:* 540-458-8710. *Fax:* 540-458-8062. *E-mail:* admissions@wlu.edu.

WASHINGTON

Argosy University, Seattle

Seattle, Washington

http://www.argosy.edu/locations/seattle/

- **Proprietary** university, founded 1995, part of Education Management Corporation
- **Urban** campus
- **Coed**

ACADEMICS

Calendar: semesters. *Degrees:* associate, bachelor's, master's, doctoral, and post-master's certificates.

CONTACT

Argosy University, Seattle, 2601-A Elliott Avenue, Seattle, WA 98121. *Phone:* 206-283-4500. *Toll-free phone:* 866-283-2777.

The Art Institute of Seattle

Seattle, Washington

http://www.artinstitutes.edu/seattle/

- **Proprietary** 4-year, founded 1982, part of Education Management Corporation
- **Urban** campus
- **Coed**

ACADEMICS

Calendar: quarters. *Degrees:* diplomas, associate, and bachelor's.

CONTACT

The Art Institute of Seattle, 2323 Elliott Avenue, Seattle, WA 98121-1642. *Phone:* 206-448-6600. *Toll-free phone:* 800-275-2471.

Bastyr University

Kenmore, Washington

http://www.bastyr.edu/

- **Independent** upper-level, founded 1978
- **Suburban** 51-acre campus with easy access to Seattle
- **Coed** 267 undergraduate students, 80% full-time, 84% women, 16% men

UNDERGRAD STUDENTS

214 full-time, 53 part-time. Students come from 28 states and territories; 10 other countries; 36% are from out of state; 5% Black or African American, non-Hispanic/Latino; 4% Hispanic/Latino; 8% Asian, non-Hispanic/Latino; 0.4% American Indian or Alaska Native, non-Hispanic/Latino; 4% Two or more races, non-Hispanic/Latino; 3% Race/ethnicity unknown; 4% international; 37% transferred in; 10% live on campus.

FACULTY

Total: 299, 14% full-time.

ACADEMICS

Calendar: quarters. *Degrees:* certificates, bachelor's, master's, doctoral, and post-master's certificates.

Special study options: cooperative education, double majors, independent study, internships, part-time degree program, summer session for credit.

Computers: 71 computers/terminals and 20 ports are available on campus for general student use. Students can access the following: campus intranet, computer help desk, free student e-mail accounts, online (class) grades, online (class) schedules. Campuswide network is available. 100% of college-owned or -operated housing units are wired for high-speed Internet access. Wireless service is available via entire campus.

STUDENT LIFE

Housing options: coed, special housing for students with disabilities. Campus housing is university owned.

Activities and organizations: Naturopaths Without Borders, Nature Club, Multicultural Student Association of Natural Medicine, Environmental Action Team, Venture Grant.

Athletics ***Intramural sports:*** basketball M, soccer M/W, ultimate Frisbee M/W, volleyball M/W.

Campus security: student patrols, late-night transport/escort service, controlled dormitory access.

Student services: health clinic, personal/psychological counseling.

COSTS & FINANCIAL AID

Costs (2014–15) ***Tuition:*** $23,355 full-time, $613 per credit part-time. Full-time tuition and fees vary according to course load and program. Part-time tuition and fees vary according to course load and program. ***Room only:*** $6975. Room and board charges vary according to housing facility. ***Waivers:*** employees or children of employees.

Financial Aid Of all full-time matriculated undergraduates who enrolled in 2013, 186 applied for aid, 175 were judged to have need. ***Average financial aid package:*** $18,159. ***Average need-based loan:*** $11,000. ***Average need-based gift aid:*** $10,230.

APPLYING

Options: electronic application, deferred entrance.

Application fee: $60.

CONTACT

Ms. Lauren Marani, Assistant Director of Admissions, Bastyr University, 14500 Juanita Drive NE, Kenmore, WA 98028-4966. *Phone:* 425-602-1300. *Fax:* 425-602-3090. *E-mail:* admissions@bastyr.edu.

Central Washington University

Ellensburg, Washington

http://www.cwu.edu/

- **State-supported** comprehensive, founded 1891
- **Small-town** 380-acre campus with easy access to Seattle
- **Endowment** $23.4 million
- **Coed** 10,964 undergraduate students, 80% full-time, 52% women, 48% men
- **Moderately difficult** entrance level, 87% of applicants were admitted

UNDERGRAD STUDENTS

8,753 full-time, 2,211 part-time. Students come from 41 states and territories; 17 other countries; 6% are from out of state; 3% Black or African American, non-Hispanic/Latino; 13% Hispanic/Latino; 4% Asian, non-Hispanic/Latino; 1% Native Hawaiian or other Pacific Islander, non-Hispanic/Latino; 0.5% American Indian or Alaska Native, non-Hispanic/Latino; 7% Two or more races, non-Hispanic/Latino; 9% Race/ethnicity unknown; 0.6% international; 12% transferred in; 31% live on campus.

Freshmen

Admission: 4,041 applied, 3,508 admitted, 1,362 enrolled. ***Average high school GPA:*** 3.06. ***Test scores:*** SAT critical reading scores over 500: 45%; SAT math scores over 500: 48%; SAT writing scores over 500: 32%; ACT scores over 18: 79%; SAT critical reading scores over 600: 11%; SAT math scores over 600: 11%; SAT writing scores over 600: 6%; ACT scores over 24: 25%; SAT critical reading scores over 700: 1%; SAT math scores over 700: 1%; SAT writing scores over 700: 1%; ACT scores over 30: 1%.

Retention: 79% of full-time freshmen returned.

FACULTY

Total: 687, 62% full-time.

Student/faculty ratio: 19:1.

ACADEMICS

Calendar: quarters. *Degrees:* certificates, bachelor's, master's, post-master's, and postbachelor's certificates.

Special study options: academic remediation for entering students, advanced placement credit, cooperative education, distance learning, double majors, English as a second language, freshman honors college, honors programs, independent study, internships, off-campus study, part-time degree program, services for LD students, student-designed majors, study abroad, summer session for credit. ***ROTC:*** Army (b), Air Force (b).

Computers: 700 computers/terminals and 1,500 ports are available on campus for general student use. Students can access the following: campus intranet, computer help desk, free student e-mail accounts, online (class) grades, online (class) registration, online (class) schedules. Campuswide network is available. 100% of college-owned or -operated housing units are wired for high-speed Internet access. Wireless service is available via entire campus.

STUDENT LIFE

Housing options: on-campus residence required for freshman year; coed, cooperative, special housing for students with disabilities. Campus housing is university owned. Freshman campus housing is guaranteed.

Activities and organizations: drama/theater group, student-run newspaper, radio and television station, choral group, marching band, SALT: non-denominational, religious, EMPIRE: Extraordinary Men Pursuing Intellectual Readiness Through Education, EQuAL: Equality through Queers and Allies, Swing Cats: swing dance club, participation and interaction between students and community, MeCha: promoting higher education to raza youth.

Athletics Member NCAA. All Division II. ***Intercollegiate sports:*** archery M(c)/W(c), baseball M(s), basketball M(s)/W(s), bowling M(c)/W(c), cheerleading M/W, cross-country running M(s)/W(s), equestrian sports M(c)/W(c), fencing M(c)/W(c), football M(s), golf M(c)/W(c), ice hockey M(c)/W(c), lacrosse M(c)/W(c), rock climbing M(c)/W(c), rugby M(s)/W(s), soccer M(c)/W(s), softball W(s), swimming and diving M(c)/W(c), tennis M(c)/W(c), track and field M(s)/W(s), ultimate Frisbee M(c)/W(c), volleyball W(s), water polo M(c)/W(c), wrestling M(c)/W(c). ***Intramural sports:*** badminton M/W, basketball M/W, rock climbing M/W, skiing (cross-country) M/W, soccer M/W, softball M/W, table tennis M/W, tennis M/W, volleyball M/W.

Campus security: 24-hour emergency response devices and patrols, late-night transport/escort service, controlled dormitory access, Alert Update system: emergency notification across digital platforms. Rape Aggression Defense System: realistic self-defense for women.

Student services: health clinic, personal/psychological counseling.

COSTS & FINANCIAL AID

Costs (2014–15) ***Tuition:*** state resident $7245 full-time, $265 per credit hour part-time; nonresident $20,304 full-time, $680 per credit hour part-time. Full-time tuition and fees vary according to course load, degree level, location, and reciprocity agreements. Part-time tuition and fees vary according to course load, degree level, location, and reciprocity agreements. ***Required fees:*** $1076 full-time, $16 per credit part-time, $303 per term part-time. ***Room and board:*** $9316. Room and board charges vary according to board plan and housing facility. ***Payment plan:*** installment. ***Waivers:*** senior citizens and employees or children of employees.

Financial Aid Of all full-time matriculated undergraduates who enrolled in 2012, 7,356 applied for aid, 6,016 were judged to have need, 2,647 had their need fully met. 196 Federal Work-Study jobs (averaging $2307). 173 state and other part-time jobs (averaging $2654). In 2012, 15 non-need-based awards were made. ***Average percent of need met:*** 83. ***Average financial aid package:*** $11,191. ***Average need-based loan:*** $4319. ***Average need-based gift aid:*** $8607. ***Average non-need-based aid:*** $923. ***Average indebtedness upon graduation:*** $24,098.

APPLYING

Standardized Tests *Required:* SAT or ACT (for admission).

Options: electronic application.

Application fee: $50.

Required: high school transcript, minimum 2.0 GPA. ***Required for some:*** essay or personal statement, interview.

Application deadlines: 3/1 (freshmen), 3/1 (out-of-state freshmen), 3/1 (transfers).

Notification: continuous (freshmen), continuous (out-of-state freshmen), continuous (transfers).

CONTACT

Ms. Kathy Gaer-Carlton, Director of Admissions, Central Washington University, 400 East University Way, Ellensburg, WA 98926-7463. *Phone:* 509-963.1211. *Fax:* 509-963.3065. *E-mail:* admissions@cwu.edu.

Cornish College of the Arts

Seattle, Washington

http://www.cornish.edu/

- **Independent** 4-year, founded 1914
- **Urban** 4-acre campus with easy access to Seattle
- **Coed** 765 undergraduate students, 99% full-time, 64% women, 36% men
- **Moderately difficult** entrance level, 86% of applicants were admitted

UNDERGRAD STUDENTS

758 full-time, 7 part-time. 52% are from out of state; 4% Black or African American, non-Hispanic/Latino; 9% Hispanic/Latino; 6% Asian, non-Hispanic/Latino; 0.2% Native Hawaiian or other Pacific Islander, non-Hispanic/Latino; 1% American Indian or Alaska Native, non-Hispanic/Latino; 7% Two or more races, non-Hispanic/Latino; 6% Race/ethnicity unknown; 4% international; 12% transferred in; 32% live on campus.

Freshmen
Admission: 1,134 applied, 970 admitted, 161 enrolled. *Average high school GPA:* 3.15.

ACADEMICS
Calendar: semesters. *Degrees:* bachelor's and postbachelor's certificates.

Special study options: advanced placement credit, cooperative education, independent study, internships, services for LD students, study abroad, summer session for credit.

Computers: 28 computers/terminals and 50 ports are available on campus for general student use. Students can access the following: campus intranet, computer help desk, free student e-mail accounts, online (class) grades, online (class) registration, online (class) schedules. Campuswide network is available. 100% of college-owned or -operated housing units are wired for high-speed Internet access. Wireless service is available via entire campus.

STUDENT LIFE
Housing options: on-campus residence required for freshman year; coed. Campus housing is university owned. Freshman campus housing is guaranteed.

Activities and organizations: drama/theater group, student-run radio station, choral group, Student Leadership Council, Black Student Alliance, Sigma Alpha Phi, AIGA, Cheese Tasting.

Campus security: 24-hour emergency response devices and patrols, late-night transport/escort service, controlled dormitory access.

Student services: personal/psychological counseling.

COSTS & FINANCIAL AID
Costs (2014–15) ***Comprehensive fee:*** $45,600 includes full-time tuition ($35,400), mandatory fees ($400), and room and board ($9800). Full-time tuition and fees vary according to program. Part-time tuition: $1475 per credit hour. Part-time tuition and fees vary according to program. ***College room only:*** $6900. Room and board charges vary according to board plan. ***Payment plan:*** installment. ***Waivers:*** employees or children of employees.

Financial Aid Of all full-time matriculated undergraduates who enrolled in 2012, 716 applied for aid, 617 were judged to have need, 38 had their need fully met. 272 Federal Work-Study jobs (averaging $3000). 276 state and other part-time jobs (averaging $3000). In 2012, 139 non-need-based awards were made. ***Average percent of need met:*** 52. ***Average financial aid package:*** $18,090. ***Average need-based loan:*** $4435. ***Average need-based gift aid:*** $12,538. ***Average non-need-based aid:*** $5428. ***Average indebtedness upon graduation:*** $32,430.

APPLYING
Standardized Tests *Recommended:* SAT or ACT (for admission).

Options: electronic application, deferred entrance.

Application fee: $40.

Required: essay or personal statement, high school transcript, minimum 2.5 GPA, portfolio or audition. ***Required for some:*** 2 letters of recommendation. ***Recommended:*** 2 letters of recommendation, interview.

CONTACT
Ms. Sharron Starling, Director of Admissions, Cornish College of the Arts, 1000 Lenora Street, Seattle, WA 98121. *Phone:* 206-726-5017. *Toll-free phone:* 800-726-ARTS. *Fax:* 206-720-1011. *E-mail:* admissions@cornish.edu.

DeVry University

Federal Way, Washington

http://www.devry.edu/

- **Proprietary** comprehensive, founded 2001, part of DeVry University
- **Suburban** campus
- **Coed** 311 undergraduate students, 50% full-time, 32% women, 68% men
- **Minimally difficult** entrance level

UNDERGRAD STUDENTS
154 full-time, 157 part-time. 4% are from out of state; 11% Black or African American, non-Hispanic/Latino; 7% Hispanic/Latino; 8% Asian, non-Hispanic/Latino; 3% Native Hawaiian or other Pacific Islander, non-Hispanic/Latino; 1% American Indian or Alaska Native, non-Hispanic/Latino; 3% Two or more races, non-Hispanic/Latino; 8% Race/ethnicity unknown; 0.3% international; 41% transferred in.

Freshmen
Admission: 15 enrolled.

FACULTY
Total: 35, 17% full-time.

Student/faculty ratio: 16:1.

ACADEMICS
Calendar: semesters. *Degrees:* associate, bachelor's, master's, and postbachelor's certificates.

Special study options: adult/continuing education programs, part-time degree program.

STUDENT LIFE
Housing options: college housing not available.

COSTS & FINANCIAL AID
Costs (2014–15) ***Tuition:*** $17,052 full-time, $609 per credit hour part-time. ***Required fees:*** $80 full-time.

Financial Aid Of all full-time matriculated undergraduates who enrolled in 2007, 259 applied for aid, 250 were judged to have need, 8 had their need fully met. In 2007, 15 non-need-based awards were made. ***Average percent of need met:*** 34. ***Average financial aid package:*** $10,833. ***Average need-based loan:*** $6622. ***Average need-based gift aid:*** $5975. ***Average non-need-based aid:*** $20,202. ***Average indebtedness upon graduation:*** $50,600.

APPLYING
Options: electronic application.

Application fee: $40.

Required: high school transcript, interview.

CONTACT
DeVry University, 3600 South 344th Way, Federal Way, WA 98001. *Phone:* 253-943-2800. *Toll-free phone:* 866-338-7941.

DigiPen Institute of Technology

Redmond, Washington

http://www.digipen.edu/

- **Proprietary** comprehensive, founded 1988
- **Suburban** 3-acre campus with easy access to Seattle
- **Coed** 904 undergraduate students
- **Minimally difficult** entrance level, 44% of applicants were admitted

UNDERGRAD STUDENTS
Students come from 50 states and territories; 45 other countries; 37% are from out of state; 0.5% Black or African American, non-Hispanic/Latino; 5% Hispanic/Latino; 5% Asian, non-Hispanic/Latino; 0.4% Native Hawaiian or other Pacific Islander, non-Hispanic/Latino; 6% Two or more races, non-Hispanic/Latino; 27% Race/ethnicity unknown; 14% international.

Freshmen
Admission: 691 applied, 302 admitted.

Retention: 74% of full-time freshmen returned.

FACULTY
Total: 107, 56% full-time.

Student/faculty ratio: 13:1.

ACADEMICS
Calendar: semesters. *Degrees:* bachelor's and master's.

Special study options: academic remediation for entering students, accelerated degree program, advanced placement credit, English as a second language, independent study, internships, services for LD students, study abroad, summer session for credit.

Computers: 794 computers/terminals and 500 ports are available on campus for general student use. Students can access the following: campus intranet, computer help desk, free student e-mail accounts, online (class) grades, online (class) registration, online (class) schedules. Campuswide network is available. 100% of college-owned or -operated housing units are wired for high-speed Internet access. Wireless service is available via entire campus.

STUDENT LIFE
Housing options: men-only, women-only. Campus housing is leased by the school and is provided by a third party. Freshman applicants given priority for college housing.

Activities and organizations: choral group, Game Testing Club, Student Senate, Outbreak Club, Cage of the Week, SMASH Club.

Campus security: late-night transport/escort service, controlled dormitory access, on-site security during campus hours.

Student services: personal/psychological counseling.

COSTS & FINANCIAL AID
Costs (2015–16) ***One-time required fee:*** $150. ***Tuition:*** $27,600 full-time, $890 per credit hour part-time. Full-time tuition and fees vary according to course load and program. Part-time tuition and fees vary according to course load and program. ***Required fees:*** $200 full-time. ***Room only:*** Room and board charges vary according to board plan and housing facility. ***Payment plan:*** installment. ***Waivers:*** employees or children of employees.

Financial Aid Of all full-time matriculated undergraduates who enrolled in 2011, 11 applied for aid, 10 were judged to have need. In 2011, 58 non-need-based awards were made. ***Average financial aid package:*** $7000. ***Average need-based loan:*** $3981. ***Average need-based gift aid:*** $3345. ***Average non-need-based aid:*** $2050. ***Average indebtedness upon graduation:*** $47,500.

APPLYING
Standardized Tests *Required for some:* SAT or ACT (for admission).

Options: electronic application, deferred entrance.

Application fee: $35.

Required: essay or personal statement, high school transcript, minimum 2.5 GPA. ***Required for some:*** art portfolio for BFA in Digital Art and Animation applicants; audition portfolio for BA in Music and Sound Design applicants; Precalculus for Bachelor of Science applicants. ***Recommended:*** 2 letters of recommendation.

Application deadlines: rolling (freshmen), rolling (out-of-state freshmen), rolling (transfers).

Notification: continuous (freshmen), continuous (out-of-state freshmen), continuous (transfers).

CONTACT
Ms. Danial Powers, Director of Admissions, DigiPen Institute of Technology, 9931 Willows Road NE, Redmond, WA 98052. *Phone:* 425-629-5071. *Toll-free phone:* 866-478-5236. *Fax:* 425-558-0378. *E-mail:* admissions@digipen.edu.

Eastern Washington University

Cheney, Washington

http://www.ewu.edu/

- **State-supported** comprehensive, founded 1882
- **Suburban** 335-acre campus with easy access to Spokane
- **Endowment** $23.5 million
- **Coed**

FACULTY
Student/faculty ratio: 21:1.

ACADEMICS
Calendar: quarters. *Degrees:* certificates, bachelor's, master's, doctoral, post-master's, and postbachelor's certificates.

STUDENT LIFE
Housing options: on-campus residence required for freshman year; coed, special housing for students with disabilities. Campus housing is university owned. Freshman campus housing is guaranteed.

Activities and organizations: drama/theater group, student-run newspaper, radio station, choral group, marching band, Circle K International, Saudi Club, Gamers Club, Hui O Hawaii, Sportsman's Club, national fraternities, national sororities.

Athletics Member NCAA. All Division I except football (Division I-AA).

Campus security: 24-hour emergency response devices and patrols, student patrols, late-night transport/escort service, controlled dormitory access, emergency call boxes.

Student services: health clinic, personal/psychological counseling, women's center.

COSTS & FINANCIAL AID
Costs (2014–15) ***Tuition:*** state resident $7372 full-time, $246 per credit hour part-time; nonresident $20,503 full-time, $683 per credit hour part-time. Full-time tuition and fees vary according to course level, course load, degree level, program, reciprocity agreements, and student level. Part-time tuition and fees vary according to course level, course load, degree level, program, reciprocity agreements, and student level. ***Required fees:*** $610 full-time. ***Room and board:*** $9628; room only: $5278. Room and board charges vary according to board plan and housing facility.

Financial Aid Of all full-time matriculated undergraduates who enrolled in 2013, 7,800 applied for aid, 6,613 were judged to have need, 499 had their need fully met. 185 Federal Work-Study jobs (averaging $2484). 182 state and other part-time jobs (averaging $2573). In 2013, 477 non-need-based awards were made. ***Average percent of need met:*** 55. ***Average financial aid package:*** $10,884. ***Average need-based loan:*** $4160. ***Average need-based gift aid:*** $8319. ***Average non-need-based aid:*** $3958. ***Average indebtedness upon graduation:*** $27,259.

APPLYING
Standardized Tests *Required:* SAT or ACT (for admission).

Required: high school transcript, minimum 2.0 GPA. ***Required for some:*** essay or personal statement. ***Recommended:*** minimum 3.0 GPA.

CONTACT
Ms. Shannon Carr, Director of Admissions, Eastern Washington University, 101 Sutton Hall, Cheney, WA 99004-2447. *Phone:* 509-359-6582. *Fax:* 509-359-6692. *E-mail:* admissions@ewu.edu.

The Evergreen State College

Olympia, Washington

http://www.evergreen.edu/

- **State-supported** comprehensive, founded 1967, part of Washington State Public Baccalaureate Institution
- **Rural** 1000-acre campus with easy access to Seattle
- **Endowment** $10.2 million
- **Coed** 3,878 undergraduate students, 92% full-time, 54% women, 46% men
- **Moderately difficult** entrance level, 99% of applicants were admitted

UNDERGRAD STUDENTS
3,555 full-time, 323 part-time. Students come from 49 states and territories; 23 other countries; 26% are from out of state; 6% Black or African American, non-Hispanic/Latino; 8% Hispanic/Latino; 2% Asian, non-Hispanic/Latino; 0.3% Native Hawaiian or other Pacific Islander, non-Hispanic/Latino; 2% American Indian or Alaska Native, non-Hispanic/Latino; 8% Two or more races, non-Hispanic/Latino; 9% Race/ethnicity unknown; 0.5% international; 18% transferred in; 21% live on campus.

Freshmen
Admission: 1,544 applied, 1,527 admitted, 543 enrolled. ***Average high school GPA:*** 2.95. ***Test scores:*** SAT critical reading scores over 500: 68%; SAT math scores over 500: 48%; SAT writing scores over 500: 58%; ACT scores over 18: 84%; SAT critical reading scores over 600: 37%; SAT math scores over 600: 16%; SAT writing scores over 600: 21%; ACT scores over 24: 41%; SAT critical reading scores over 700: 10%; SAT math scores over 700: 2%; SAT writing scores over 700: 3%; ACT scores over 30: 6%.

Retention: 69% of full-time freshmen returned.

FACULTY
Total: 224, 71% full-time, 79% with terminal degrees.

Student/faculty ratio: 22:1.

ACADEMICS
Calendar: quarters. *Degrees:* bachelor's and master's.

Special study options: accelerated degree program, advanced placement credit, double majors, independent study, internships, off-campus study, part-time degree program, services for LD students, student-designed majors, study abroad, summer session for credit.

Computers: 510 computers/terminals are available on campus for general student use. Students can access the following: campus intranet, computer help desk, free student e-mail accounts, online (class) grades, online (class) registration, online (class) schedules, online payment, student accounts history, financial aid records, academic history, housing application, evaluations. Campuswide network is available. 100% of college-owned or -operated housing units are wired for high-speed Internet access. Wireless service is available via entire campus.

STUDENT LIFE

Housing options: coed, special housing for students with disabilities. Campus housing is university owned. Freshman campus housing is guaranteed.

Activities and organizations: drama/theater group, student-run newspaper, radio and television station, choral group, Circus Resurgence, Womyn's Resource Center, Greeners for Christ, Common Bread, Community Gardens.

Athletics Member NAIA. ***Intercollegiate sports:*** basketball M(s)/W(s), soccer M(s)/W(s), track and field M(s)/W(s), volleyball W(s). ***Intramural sports:*** archery M(c)/W(c), basketball M/W, crew M(c)/W(c), cross-country running M(c)/W(c), fencing M(c)/W(c), rugby M(c), soccer M/W, tennis M(c)/W(c), ultimate Frisbee M(c)/W(c), volleyball M/W, wrestling M(c)/W(c).

Campus security: 24-hour emergency response devices and patrols, student patrols, late-night transport/escort service, controlled dormitory access.

Student services: health clinic, personal/psychological counseling, women's center.

COSTS & FINANCIAL AID

Costs (2014–15) ***Tuition:*** state resident $7845 full-time, $262 per credit hour part-time; nonresident $20,901 full-time, $697 per credit hour part-time. Full-time tuition and fees vary according to course load, location, and program. Part-time tuition and fees vary according to course load, location, and program. ***Required fees:*** $678 full-time, $9 per credit hour part-time, $5 per term part-time. ***Room and board:*** $9492; room only: $6270. Room and board charges vary according to board plan, housing facility, location, and student level. ***Payment plan:*** installment. ***Waivers:*** senior citizens and employees or children of employees.

Financial Aid Of all full-time matriculated undergraduates who enrolled in 2013, 2,903 applied for aid, 2,630 were judged to have need, 191 had their need fully met. In 2013, 12 non-need-based awards were made. ***Average percent of need met:*** 70. ***Average financial aid package:*** $10,111. ***Average need-based loan:*** $4233. ***Average need-based gift aid:*** $10,258. ***Average non-need-based aid:*** $4679. ***Average indebtedness upon graduation:*** $21,054.

APPLYING

Standardized Tests *Required:* SAT or ACT (for admission).

Options: electronic application, deferred entrance.

Application fee: $50.

Required: high school transcript, minimum 2.0 GPA. ***Required for some:*** essay or personal statement. ***Recommended:*** essay or personal statement.

Application deadlines: 2/1 (freshmen), 2/1 (transfers).

Notification: continuous until 11/1 (freshmen), continuous until 11/1 (transfers).

CONTACT

The Evergreen State College, 2700 Evergreen Parkway, NW, Olympia, WA 98505. *Phone:* 360-867-6170.

Gonzaga University

Spokane, Washington

http://www.gonzaga.edu/

- **Independent Roman Catholic** comprehensive, founded 1887
- **Urban** 131-acre campus
- **Endowment** $164.9 million
- **Coed** 4,837 undergraduate students, 98% full-time, 54% women, 46% men
- **Moderately difficult** entrance level, 68% of applicants were admitted

UNDERGRAD STUDENTS

4,752 full-time, 85 part-time. Students come from 48 states and territories; 23 other countries; 50% are from out of state; 1% Black or African American, non-Hispanic/Latino; 9% Hispanic/Latino; 5% Asian, non-Hispanic/Latino; 0.2% Native Hawaiian or other Pacific Islander, non-Hispanic/Latino; 0.5% American Indian or Alaska Native, non-Hispanic/Latino; 5% Two or more races, non-Hispanic/Latino; 3% Race/ethnicity unknown; 2% international; 3% transferred in; 58% live on campus.

Freshmen

Admission: 7,162 applied, 4,835 admitted, 1,048 enrolled. ***Average high school GPA:*** 3.7. ***Test scores:*** SAT critical reading scores over 500: 93%; SAT math scores over 500: 96%; ACT scores over 18: 100%; SAT critical reading scores over 600: 45%; SAT math scores over 600: 54%; ACT scores over 24: 84%; SAT critical reading scores over 700: 7%; SAT math scores over 700: 10%; ACT scores over 30: 21%.

Retention: 92% of full-time freshmen returned.

FACULTY

Total: 728, 59% full-time, 50% with terminal degrees.

Student/faculty ratio: 11:1.

ACADEMICS

Calendar: semesters. *Degrees:* bachelor's, master's, and doctoral.

Special study options: accelerated degree program, adult/continuing education programs, advanced placement credit, distance learning, double majors, English as a second language, honors programs, independent study, internships, off-campus study, part-time degree program, services for LD students, study abroad, summer session for credit. ***ROTC:*** Army (b).

Unusual degree programs: 3-2 nursing.

Computers: 271 computers/terminals and 900 ports are available on campus for general student use. Students can access the following: computer help desk, free student e-mail accounts, online (class) grades, online (class) registration, online (class) schedules. Campuswide network is available. 100% of college-owned or -operated housing units are wired for high-speed Internet access. Wireless service is available via entire campus.

STUDENT LIFE

Housing options: on-campus residence required through sophomore year; coed, men-only, women-only, special housing for students with disabilities. Campus housing is university owned and leased by the school. Freshman campus housing is guaranteed.

Activities and organizations: drama/theater group, student-run newspaper, radio and television station, choral group, Student Body Association, Kennel Club, Search, Circle K, Encore.

Athletics Member NCAA. All Division I. ***Intercollegiate sports:*** baseball M(s), basketball M(s)/W(s), crew M/W(s), cross-country running M(s)/W(s), golf M/W, ice hockey M(c), lacrosse M(c)/W(c), rugby M(c)/W(c), skiing (downhill) M(c)/W(c), soccer M(s)/W(s), tennis M(s)/W(s), track and field M(s)/W(s), ultimate Frisbee M(c)/W(c), volleyball M(c)/W(s). ***Intramural sports:*** badminton M/W, basketball M/W, football M/W, racquetball M/W, soccer M(c)/W(c), softball M/W, swimming and diving M(c)/W(c), ultimate Frisbee M/W, volleyball M/W.

Campus security: 24-hour emergency response devices and patrols, late-night transport/escort service, controlled dormitory access.

Student services: health clinic, personal/psychological counseling.

COSTS & FINANCIAL AID

Costs (2015–16) ***Comprehensive fee:*** $48,825 includes full-time tuition ($37,480), mandatory fees ($510), and room and board ($10,835). Full-time tuition and fees vary according to course load, location, program, reciprocity agreements, and student level. Part-time tuition: $1055 per credit. Part-time tuition and fees vary according to course load, location, program, reciprocity agreements, and student level. ***Required fees:*** $200 per term part-time. ***College room only:*** $5565. Room and board charges vary according to board plan, housing facility, and location. ***Payment plans:*** installment, deferred payment. ***Waivers:*** employees or children of employees.

Financial Aid Of all full-time matriculated undergraduates who enrolled in 2013, 3,443 applied for aid, 2,764 were judged to have need, 748 had their need fully met. 461 Federal Work-Study jobs (averaging $2612). 429

state and other part-time jobs (averaging $4086). In 2013, 1812 non-need-based awards were made. ***Average percent of need met:*** 80. ***Average financial aid package:*** $25,554. ***Average need-based loan:*** $5595. ***Average need-based gift aid:*** $19,305. ***Average non-need-based aid:*** $12,083. ***Average indebtedness upon graduation:*** $29,513.

APPLYING

Standardized Tests *Required:* SAT or ACT (for admission).

Options: electronic application, early action, deferred entrance.

Application fee: $50.

Required: essay or personal statement, high school transcript, minimum 3.2 GPA, 1 letter of recommendation. ***Recommended:*** interview.

Application deadlines: 2/1 (freshmen), 6/1 (transfers), 11/15 (early action).

Notification: 3/15 (freshmen), continuous (transfers), 1/15 (early action).

CONTACT

Ms. Julie McCulloh, Dean of Admission, Gonzaga University, 502 East Boone Avenue, Spokane, WA 99258-0102. *Phone:* 800-322-2584. *Toll-free phone:* 800-322-2584 Ext. 6572. *Fax:* 509-313-6572. *E-mail:* admissions@gonzaga.edu.

Heritage University
Toppenish, Washington
http://www.heritage.edu/

- **Independent** comprehensive, founded 1982
- **Rural** 48-acre campus with easy access to Tri-Cities, Washington
- **Coed** 861 undergraduate students, 84% full-time, 76% women, 24% men

UNDERGRAD STUDENTS

724 full-time, 137 part-time. Students come from 1 other state; 1% Black or African American, non-Hispanic/Latino; 62% Hispanic/Latino; 0.7% Asian, non-Hispanic/Latino; 0.7% Native Hawaiian or other Pacific Islander, non-Hispanic/Latino; 5% American Indian or Alaska Native, non-Hispanic/Latino; 5% Two or more races, non-Hispanic/Latino; 2% Race/ethnicity unknown; 1% international.

Freshmen

Admission: 122 enrolled.

Retention: 68% of full-time freshmen returned.

FACULTY

Total: 185, 40% full-time.

Student/faculty ratio: 8:1.

ACADEMICS

Calendar: semesters. *Degrees:* certificates, associate, bachelor's, master's, post-master's, and postbachelor's certificates.

Special study options: academic remediation for entering students, adult/continuing education programs, advanced placement credit, cooperative education, distance learning, double majors, English as a second language, honors programs, independent study, internships, part-time degree program, services for LD students, student-designed majors, summer session for credit.

Computers: 350 computers/terminals are available on campus for general student use. Students can access the following: campus intranet, computer help desk, free student e-mail accounts, online (class) grades, online (class) registration, online (class) schedules. Campuswide network is available. Wireless service is available via entire campus.

STUDENT LIFE

Housing options: college housing not available.

Activities and organizations: choral group, Student Government Association, ENACTUS (Business Club), MECHA (National Cultural Club), Nursing Club, Omega Delta Phi (Fraternity), national sororities.

Athletics ***Intramural sports:*** soccer M(c), softball M(c)/W(c).

Campus security: 24-hour emergency response devices, late-night transport/escort service, 24-hour camera monitoring.

Student services: personal/psychological counseling.

COSTS & FINANCIAL AID

Costs (2014–15) ***Tuition:*** $18,456 full-time. ***Required fees:*** $110 full-time. ***Payment plan:*** installment. ***Waivers:*** employees or children of employees.

Financial Aid Of all full-time matriculated undergraduates who enrolled in 2003, 342 applied for aid, 322 were judged to have need, 9 had their need fully met. 71 Federal Work-Study jobs (averaging $1885). 91 state and other part-time jobs (averaging $1895). In 2003, 7 non-need-based awards were made. ***Average percent of need met:*** 61. ***Average financial aid package:*** $9516. ***Average need-based loan:*** $3175. ***Average need-based gift aid:*** $7159. ***Average non-need-based aid:*** $6251. ***Average indebtedness upon graduation:*** $11,909.

APPLYING

Standardized Tests *Required for some:* SAT or ACT (for admission).

Required: high school transcript. ***Required for some:*** interview.

CONTACT

Olivia Gutierrez, Director of Admissions, Heritage University, 3240 Fort Road, Toppenish, WA 98948-9599. *Phone:* 509-865-8697. *Toll-free phone:* 888-272-6190. *Fax:* 509-865-4469. *E-mail:* admissions@heritage.edu.

ITT Technical Institute
Everett, Washington
http://www.itt-tech.edu/

- **Proprietary** primarily 2-year, part of ITT Educational Services, Inc.
- **Coed**
- **Minimally difficult** entrance level

ACADEMICS

Degrees: associate and bachelor's.

CONTACT

Director of Recruitment, ITT Technical Institute, 1615 75th Street SW, Everett, WA 98203. *Phone:* 425-583-0200. *Toll-free phone:* 800-272-3791.

ITT Technical Institute
Seattle, Washington
http://www.itt-tech.edu/

- **Proprietary** primarily 2-year, founded 1932, part of ITT Educational Services, Inc.
- **Urban** campus
- **Coed**
- **Minimally difficult** entrance level

ACADEMICS

Calendar: quarters. *Degrees:* associate and bachelor's.

STUDENT LIFE

Housing options: college housing not available.

CONTACT

Director of Recruitment, ITT Technical Institute, 12720 Gateway Drive, Suite 100, Seattle, WA 98168-3333. *Phone:* 206-244-3300. *Toll-free phone:* 800-422-2029.

ITT Technical Institute
Spokane Valley, Washington
http://www.itt-tech.edu/

- **Proprietary** primarily 2-year, founded 1985, part of ITT Educational Services, Inc.
- **Suburban** campus
- **Coed**
- **Minimally difficult** entrance level

ACADEMICS

Calendar: quarters. *Degrees:* associate and bachelor's.

STUDENT LIFE

Housing options: college housing not available.

CONTACT

Director of Recruitment, ITT Technical Institute, 13518 East Indiana Avenue, Spokane Valley, WA 99216. *Phone:* 509-926-2900. *Toll-free phone:* 800-777-8324.

Northwest College of Art & Design

Poulsbo, Washington

http://www.ncad.edu/

- **Proprietary** 4-year, founded 1982
- **Small-town** 26-acre campus with easy access to Seattle
- **Coed**

UNDERGRAD STUDENTS

Students come from 1 other country.

ACADEMICS

Calendar: semesters. *Degree:* bachelor's.

Special study options: double majors, internships, summer session for credit.

Computers: 76 computers/terminals are available on campus for general student use.

STUDENT LIFE

Housing options: college housing not available.

COSTS

Costs (2015–16) ***One-time required fee:*** $50. ***Tuition:*** $18,200 full-time, $800 per credit part-time. Part-time tuition and fees vary according to course load. ***Required fees:*** $850 full-time. ***Payment plans:*** installment, deferred payment.

APPLYING

Standardized Tests *Required for some:* SAT or ACT (for admission).

Required: essay or personal statement, high school transcript, 3 letters of recommendation, interview, Portfolio (5 pieces).

CONTACT

Mr. Kyle Tonahill, Admissions, Northwest College of Art & Design, 16301 Creative Drive, NE, Poulsbo, WA 98370. *Phone:* 360-779-9993. *Toll-free phone:* 800-769-ARTS. *E-mail:* ktonahill@nca.edu.

Northwest University

Kirkland, Washington

http://www.northwestu.edu/

- **Independent** comprehensive, founded 1934, affiliated with Assemblies of God
- **Suburban** 56-acre campus with easy access to Seattle
- **Endowment** $5.7 million
- **Coed** 1,376 undergraduate students, 88% full-time, 59% women, 41% men
- **Moderately difficult** entrance level, 97% of applicants were admitted

UNDERGRAD STUDENTS

1,206 full-time, 170 part-time. Students come from 34 states and territories; 23 other countries; 23% are from out of state; 3% Black or African American, non-Hispanic/Latino; 8% Hispanic/Latino; 5% Asian, non-Hispanic/Latino; 1% Native Hawaiian or other Pacific Islander, non-Hispanic/Latino; 1% American Indian or Alaska Native, non-Hispanic/Latino; 2% Two or more races, non-Hispanic/Latino; 4% Race/ethnicity unknown; 3% international; 21% transferred in; 55% live on campus.

Freshmen

Admission: 497 applied, 484 admitted, 146 enrolled. ***Average high school GPA:*** 2.86. ***Test scores:*** SAT critical reading scores over 500: 59%; SAT writing scores over 500: 49%; ACT scores over 18: 91%; SAT critical reading scores over 600: 13%; SAT writing scores over 600: 14%; ACT scores over 24: 31%; SAT critical reading scores over 700: 2%; SAT writing scores over 700: 5%; ACT scores over 30: 3%.

Retention: 78% of full-time freshmen returned.

FACULTY

Total: 252, 33% full-time, 15% with terminal degrees.

Student/faculty ratio: 13:1.

ACADEMICS

Calendar: semesters. *Degrees:* certificates, diplomas, associate, bachelor's, master's, and doctoral.

Special study options: academic remediation for entering students, accelerated degree program, adult/continuing education programs, advanced placement credit, cooperative education, double majors, English as a second language, independent study, internships, part-time degree program, study abroad, summer session for credit. ***ROTC:*** Army (c), Air Force (c).

Computers: 134 computers/terminals are available on campus for general student use. Students can access the following: campus intranet, computer help desk, free student e-mail accounts, online (class) grades, online (class) registration, online (class) schedules, online classes. Campuswide network is available. 100% of college-owned or -operated housing units are wired for high-speed Internet access. Wireless service is available via entire campus.

STUDENT LIFE

Housing options: on-campus residence required through sophomore year; men-only, women-only. Campus housing is university owned. Freshman campus housing is guaranteed.

Activities and organizations: drama/theater group, choral group, Student Ministries, Pursuit (worship service), Northwest University Business Club, Environmental Stewardship Club.

Athletics Member NAIA. ***Intercollegiate sports:*** basketball M(s)/W(s), cross-country running M(s)/W(s), soccer M(s)/W(s), softball W(s), track and field M(s)/W(s), volleyball W(s).

Campus security: 24-hour emergency response devices and patrols, late-night transport/escort service, controlled dormitory access.

Student services: health clinic, personal/psychological counseling.

COSTS & FINANCIAL AID

Costs (2015–16) ***Comprehensive fee:*** $35,490 includes full-time tuition ($27,700) and room and board ($7790). Full-time tuition and fees vary according to course load and program. Part-time tuition: $1100 per credit. Part-time tuition and fees vary according to course load. ***Required fees:*** $95 per term part-time. ***Room and board:*** Room and board charges vary according to housing facility. ***Payment plan:*** installment. ***Waivers:*** employees or children of employees.

Financial Aid Of all full-time matriculated undergraduates who enrolled in 2014, 1,014 applied for aid, 908 were judged to have need, 126 had their need fully met. In 2014, 143 non-need-based awards were made. ***Average percent of need met:*** 64. ***Average financial aid package:*** $18,121. ***Average need-based loan:*** $3933. ***Average need-based gift aid:*** $14,394. ***Average non-need-based aid:*** $9006. ***Average indebtedness upon graduation:*** $27,479. ***Financial aid deadline:*** 8/1.

APPLYING

Standardized Tests *Required:* SAT or ACT (for admission).

Options: electronic application, early action, deferred entrance.

Application fee: $30.

Required: essay or personal statement, high school transcript, minimum 2.3 GPA, 2 letters of recommendation. ***Required for some:*** interview.

Application deadlines: 8/1 (freshmen), 8/1 (transfers), 1/15 (early action).

Notification: continuous (freshmen), continuous (transfers), 2/15 (early action).

CONTACT

Anna Pflug, Northwest University, 5520 108th Avenue NE, PO Box 579, Kirkland, WA 98083-0579. *Phone:* 425-889-5212. *Toll-free phone:* 800-669-3781. *Fax:* 425-889-5224. *E-mail:* admissions@northwestu.edu.

Olympic College

Bremerton, Washington

http://www.olympic.edu/

- **State-supported** primarily 2-year, founded 1946, part of Washington State Board for Community and Technical Colleges
- **Suburban** 33-acre campus with easy access to Seattle by ferry 30 miles, Tacoma by hwy 35 miles
- **Coed**
- **Noncompetitive** entrance level

ACADEMICS

Calendar: quarters. *Degrees:* certificates, diplomas, associate, and bachelor's.

STUDENT LIFE
Housing options: coed. Campus housing is university owned.

Activities and organizations: drama/theater group, student-run newspaper, choral group, Phi Theta Kappa, International Student Club, Environmental Outreach, Armed Services, ASL.

Campus security: 24-hour emergency response devices and patrols, student patrols, late-night transport/escort service.

Student services: personal/psychological counseling.

FINANCIAL AID
Financial Aid Of all full-time matriculated undergraduates who enrolled in 2013, 105 Federal Work-Study jobs (averaging $2380). 31 state and other part-time jobs (averaging $2880).

APPLYING
Options: electronic application.

Required for some: high school transcript.

CONTACT
Ms. Jennifer Fyllingness, Director of Admissions, Outreach and International Student Services, Olympic College, 1600 Chester Avenue, Bremerton, WA 98337-1699. *Phone:* 360-475-7128. *Toll-free phone:* 800-259-6718. *Fax:* 360-475-7202. *E-mail:* jfyllingness@olympic.edu.

Pacific Lutheran University

Tacoma, Washington

http://www.plu.edu/

- **Independent** comprehensive, founded 1890, affiliated with Evangelical Lutheran Church in America
- **Suburban** 156-acre campus with easy access to Seattle
- **Endowment** $85.6 million
- **Coed** 2,959 undergraduate students, 96% full-time, 63% women, 37% men
- **Moderately difficult** entrance level, 75% of applicants were admitted

UNDERGRAD STUDENTS
2,855 full-time, 104 part-time. Students come from 37 states and territories; 24 other countries; 20% are from out of state; 3% Black or African American, non-Hispanic/Latino; 8% Hispanic/Latino; 7% Asian, non-Hispanic/Latino; 0.8% Native Hawaiian or other Pacific Islander, non-Hispanic/Latino; 0.9% American Indian or Alaska Native, non-Hispanic/Latino; 8% Two or more races, non-Hispanic/Latino; 1% Race/ethnicity unknown; 5% international; 8% transferred in; 43% live on campus.

Freshmen
Admission: 3,438 applied, 2,579 admitted, 574 enrolled. ***Average high school GPA:*** 3.66. ***Test scores:*** SAT critical reading scores over 500: 72%; SAT math scores over 500: 73%; SAT writing scores over 500: 66%; ACT scores over 18: 91%; SAT critical reading scores over 600: 30%; SAT math scores over 600: 27%; SAT writing scores over 600: 24%; ACT scores over 24: 62%; SAT critical reading scores over 700: 4%; SAT math scores over 700: 4%; SAT writing scores over 700: 3%; ACT scores over 30: 18%.

Retention: 82% of full-time freshmen returned.

FACULTY
Total: 353, 61% full-time, 70% with terminal degrees.

Student/faculty ratio: 12:1.

ACADEMICS
Calendar: 4-1-4. *Degrees:* certificates, bachelor's, master's, doctoral, and post-master's certificates.

Special study options: advanced placement credit, cooperative education, double majors, honors programs, independent study, internships, part-time degree program, services for LD students, student-designed majors, study abroad, summer session for credit. ***ROTC:*** Army (b).

Unusual degree programs: 3-2 engineering with Columbia University in New York and Washington University in Missouri.

Computers: 735 computers/terminals and 3,500 ports are available on campus for general student use. Students can access the following: campus intranet, computer help desk, free student e-mail accounts, online (class) grades, online (class) registration, online (class) schedules. Campuswide network is available. 100% of college-owned or -operated housing units are wired for high-speed Internet access. Wireless service is available via entire campus.

STUDENT LIFE
Housing options: on-campus residence required through sophomore year; coed, women-only. Campus housing is university owned. Freshman campus housing is guaranteed.

Activities and organizations: drama/theater group, student-run newspaper, radio and television station, choral group, Queer Ally Student, IGNITE Ministry, Residence Hall Government, ROTC Cadet Activities Council, Delta Iota Chi Nursing Club.

Athletics Member NCAA. All Division III. ***Intercollegiate sports:*** baseball M, basketball M/W, crew M(c)/W, cross-country running M/W, football M, golf M/W, lacrosse M(c)/W(c), soccer M/W, softball W, swimming and diving M/W, tennis M/W, track and field M/W, ultimate Frisbee M(c)/W(c), volleyball W. ***Intramural sports:*** badminton M/W, basketball M/W, football M/W, soccer M/W, softball M/W, tennis M/W, volleyball M/W.

Campus security: 24-hour emergency response devices and patrols, student patrols, late-night transport/escort service, controlled dormitory access, over 60 surveillance camera monitoring stations. Emergency notification system with indoor/outdoor speakers and text/phone/email alerts.

Student services: health clinic, personal/psychological counseling, women's center.

COSTS & FINANCIAL AID
Costs (2015–16) ***Comprehensive fee:*** $48,280 includes full-time tuition ($37,600), mandatory fees ($350), and room and board ($10,330). Full-time tuition and fees vary according to course load. Part-time tuition: $1175 per semester hour. Part-time tuition and fees vary according to course load. ***College room only:*** $4870. Room and board charges vary according to board plan and housing facility. ***Payment plan:*** installment. ***Waivers:*** children of alumni and employees or children of employees.

Financial Aid Of all full-time matriculated undergraduates who enrolled in 2014, 2,376 applied for aid, 2,124 were judged to have need, 454 had their need fully met. 624 Federal Work-Study jobs (averaging $3245). 323 state and other part-time jobs (averaging $3786). In 2014, 619 non-need-based awards were made. ***Average percent of need met:*** 82. ***Average financial aid package:*** $33,960. ***Average need-based loan:*** $4963. ***Average need-based gift aid:*** $21,449. ***Average non-need-based aid:*** $15,315. ***Average indebtedness upon graduation:*** $32,459.

APPLYING
Standardized Tests *Required:* SAT or ACT (for admission).

Options: electronic application, deferred entrance.

Application fee: $40.

Required: essay or personal statement, high school transcript, 1 letter of recommendation. ***Required for some:*** interview. ***Recommended:*** minimum 2.5 GPA.

Application deadlines: rolling (freshmen), rolling (transfers).

Notification: continuous (freshmen), continuous (transfers).

CONTACT
Melody A. Ferguson, Director of Admission, Pacific Lutheran University, Tacoma, WA 98447. *Phone:* 253-535-7151. *Toll-free phone:* 800-274-6758. *Fax:* 253-536-5136. *E-mail:* admission@plu.edu.

Renton Technical College

Renton, Washington

http://www.rtc.edu/

- **State-supported** primarily 2-year, founded 1942, part of Washington State Board for Community and Technical Colleges
- **Suburban** 30-acre campus with easy access to Seattle
- **Coed** 9,301 undergraduate students, 43% full-time, 43% women, 57% men
- **Noncompetitive** entrance level

UNDERGRAD STUDENTS
4,019 full-time, 5,282 part-time. Students come from 9 states and territories; 13 other countries.

FACULTY
Total: 282, 30% full-time.

Student/faculty ratio: 15:1.

ACADEMICS
Calendar: quarters. *Degrees:* certificates, diplomas, associate, and bachelor's.

Special study options: academic remediation for entering students, adult/continuing education programs, advanced placement credit, cooperative education, distance learning, English as a second language, internships, off-campus study, part-time degree program, services for LD students, summer session for credit.

Computers: 96 computers/terminals are available on campus for general student use. Campuswide network is available.

STUDENT LIFE
Housing options: college housing not available.

Campus security: patrols by security, security system.

Student services: personal/psychological counseling.

COSTS
Costs (2014–15) ***Tuition:*** state resident $4735 full-time, $113 per credit hour part-time; nonresident $5028 full-time, $126 per credit hour part-time. Full-time tuition and fees vary according to course load and program. Part-time tuition and fees vary according to course load and program. ***Payment plan:*** installment.

APPLYING
Standardized Tests *Required for some:* ACT ASSET, CLEP, ACT Compass.

Options: electronic application, early admission.

Application fee: $30.

Required for some: essay or personal statement, high school transcript, interview.

Application deadlines: rolling (freshmen), rolling (out-of-state freshmen), rolling (transfers).

Notification: continuous (freshmen), continuous (out-of-state freshmen), continuous (transfers).

CONTACT
Linh Bracking, Student Success Advisor, Renton Technical College, 3000 NE 4th St, Reton, WA 98056. *Phone:* 425-235-2352 Ext. 5543. *E-mail:* lbracking@rtc.edu.

Saint Martin's University

Lacey, Washington

http://www.stmartin.edu/

- **Independent Roman Catholic** comprehensive, founded 1895
- **Suburban** 300-acre campus with easy access to Seattle
- **Endowment** $16.8 million
- **Coed** 1,415 undergraduate students, 77% full-time, 48% women, 52% men
- **Moderately difficult** entrance level, 89% of applicants were admitted

UNDERGRAD STUDENTS
1,092 full-time, 323 part-time. Students come from 25 states and territories; 12 other countries; 27% are from out of state; 5% Black or African American, non-Hispanic/Latino; 12% Hispanic/Latino; 5% Asian, non-Hispanic/Latino; 2% Native Hawaiian or other Pacific Islander, non-Hispanic/Latino; 0.7% American Indian or Alaska Native, non-Hispanic/Latino; 8% Two or more races, non-Hispanic/Latino; 3% Race/ethnicity unknown; 6% international; 14% transferred in; 30% live on campus.

Freshmen
Admission: 679 applied, 603 admitted, 153 enrolled. ***Average high school GPA:*** 3.46. ***Test scores:*** SAT critical reading scores over 500: 61%; SAT math scores over 500: 64%; SAT writing scores over 500: 58%; ACT scores over 18: 91%; SAT critical reading scores over 600: 15%; SAT math scores over 600: 21%; SAT writing scores over 600: 16%; ACT scores over 24: 45%; SAT critical reading scores over 700: 4%; SAT math scores over 700: 2%; SAT writing scores over 700: 2%; ACT scores over 30: 3%.

Retention: 80% of full-time freshmen returned.

FACULTY
Total: 223, 33% full-time, 44% with terminal degrees.

Student/faculty ratio: 12:1.

ACADEMICS
Calendar: semesters. *Degrees:* bachelor's, master's, post-master's, and postbachelor's certificates.

Special study options: academic remediation for entering students, adult/continuing education programs, advanced placement credit, cooperative education, distance learning, double majors, English as a second language, independent study, internships, off-campus study, part-time degree program, services for LD students, study abroad, summer session for credit. ***ROTC:*** Army (c), Air Force (c).

Computers: 80 computers/terminals and 130 ports are available on campus for general student use. Students can access the following: campus intranet, computer help desk, free student e-mail accounts, online (class) grades, online (class) registration, online (class) schedules. Campuswide network is available. 100% of college-owned or -operated housing units are wired for high-speed Internet access. Wireless service is available via entire campus.

STUDENT LIFE
Housing options: on-campus residence required through sophomore year; coed. Campus housing is university owned. Freshman campus housing is guaranteed.

Activities and organizations: drama/theater group, student-run newspaper, choral group.

Athletics Member NCAA. All Division II. ***Intercollegiate sports:*** baseball M(s), basketball M(s)/W(s), cross-country running M(s)/W(s), golf M(s)/W(s), soccer M/W(s), softball W(s), track and field M(s)/W(s), volleyball W(s). ***Intramural sports:*** basketball M/W, bowling M/W, golf M/W, soccer M/W, softball M/W, table tennis M/W, tennis M/W, ultimate Frisbee M/W, volleyball M/W.

Campus security: 24-hour emergency response devices and patrols, student patrols, late-night transport/escort service, controlled dormitory access, CCTV cameras throughout campus, emergency Blue Light phones and WEBs, emergency text messaging/notification.

Student services: health clinic, personal/psychological counseling.

COSTS & FINANCIAL AID
Costs (2014–15) ***Comprehensive fee:*** $41,678 includes full-time tuition ($31,300), mandatory fees ($388), and room and board ($9990). Full-time tuition and fees vary according to course load, degree level, location, and program. Part-time tuition: $1045 per credit. Part-time tuition and fees vary according to degree level, location, and program. ***College room only:*** $5000. Room and board charges vary according to board plan and housing facility. ***Payment plan:*** installment. ***Waivers:*** children of alumni and employees or children of employees.

Financial Aid Of all full-time matriculated undergraduates who enrolled in 2013, 766 applied for aid, 693 were judged to have need, 152 had their need fully met. 173 Federal Work-Study jobs (averaging $2045). 59 state and other part-time jobs (averaging $5064). In 2013, 67 non-need-based awards were made. ***Average percent of need met:*** 79. ***Average financial aid package:*** $25,247. ***Average need-based loan:*** $4519. ***Average need-based gift aid:*** $20,971. ***Average non-need-based aid:*** $12,176. ***Average indebtedness upon graduation:*** $27,944.

APPLYING
Standardized Tests *Required:* SAT or ACT (for admission).

Options: electronic application, deferred entrance.

Required: essay or personal statement, high school transcript, 1 letter of recommendation, SAT or ACT. ***Required for some:*** interview.

Application deadlines: 7/31 (freshmen), 7/31 (out-of-state freshmen), 7/31 (transfers).

Notification: continuous (freshmen), continuous (out-of-state freshmen), continuous (transfers).

CONTACT
Ms. Emilie Schnabel, Admissions Counselor, Saint Martin's University, 5000 Abbey Way SE, Lacey, WA 98503-7500. *Phone:* 360-438-4596. *Toll-free phone:* 800-368-8803. *Fax:* 360-412-6189. *E-mail:* admissions@stmartin.edu.

Seattle Pacific University
Seattle, Washington
http://www.spu.edu/

- **Independent Free Methodist** comprehensive, founded 1891
- **Urban** 35-acre campus
- **Coed** 3,264 undergraduate students, 95% full-time, 67% women, 33% men
- **Moderately difficult** entrance level, 83% of applicants were admitted

UNDERGRAD STUDENTS
3,106 full-time, 158 part-time. 39% are from out of state; 4% Black or African American, non-Hispanic/Latino; 9% Hispanic/Latino; 11% Asian, non-Hispanic/Latino; 0.2% Native Hawaiian or other Pacific Islander, non-Hispanic/Latino; 0.4% American Indian or Alaska Native, non-Hispanic/Latino; 8% Two or more races, non-Hispanic/Latino; 1% Race/ethnicity unknown; 3% international; 7% transferred in; 51% live on campus.

Freshmen
Admission: 4,447 applied, 3,709 admitted, 685 enrolled. ***Average high school GPA:*** 3.55. ***Test scores:*** SAT critical reading scores over 500: 83%; SAT math scores over 500: 83%; SAT writing scores over 500: 78%; ACT scores over 18: 98%; SAT critical reading scores over 600: 36%; SAT math scores over 600: 34%; SAT writing scores over 600: 30%; ACT scores over 24: 64%; SAT critical reading scores over 700: 7%; SAT math scores over 700: 5%; SAT writing scores over 700: 3%; ACT scores over 30: 15%.
Retention: 85% of full-time freshmen returned.

FACULTY
Total: 384, 53% full-time, 48% with terminal degrees.
Student/faculty ratio: 15:1.

ACADEMICS
Calendar: quarters. *Degrees:* bachelor's, master's, doctoral, and post-master's certificates.
Special study options: academic remediation for entering students, adult/continuing education programs, advanced placement credit, distance learning, double majors, external degree program, honors programs, independent study, internships, off-campus study, part-time degree program, services for LD students, student-designed majors, study abroad, summer session for credit. ***ROTC:*** Army (c), Navy (c), Air Force (c).
Computers: 150 computers/terminals are available on campus for general student use. Students can access the following: campus intranet, computer help desk, free student e-mail accounts, online (class) grades, online (class) registration, online (class) schedules. Campuswide network is available. Wireless service is available via entire campus.

STUDENT LIFE
Housing options: on-campus residence required through sophomore year; coed, special housing for students with disabilities. Campus housing is university owned. Freshman campus housing is guaranteed.
Activities and organizations: drama/theater group, student-run newspaper, radio station, choral group, Centurions, Falconettes, forensics organization, Amnesty International, University Players.
Athletics Member NCAA. All Division II. ***Intercollegiate sports:*** basketball M(s)/W(s), crew M/W(s), cross-country running M(s)/W(s), gymnastics W(s), soccer M(s)/W(s), track and field M(s)/W(s), volleyball W(s). ***Intramural sports:*** archery M/W, basketball M/W, bowling M/W, cross-country running M/W, football M/W, soccer M/W(c), softball M/W, tennis M/W, volleyball M(c)/W(c), weight lifting M/W.
Campus security: 24-hour emergency response devices and patrols, student patrols, late-night transport/escort service, closed-circuit TV monitors.
Student services: health clinic, personal/psychological counseling.

COSTS & FINANCIAL AID
Costs (2014–15) ***Comprehensive fee:*** $45,558 includes full-time tuition ($35,100), mandatory fees ($372), and room and board ($10,086). Part-time tuition: $975 per credit hour. Part-time tuition and fees vary according to course load. ***Required fees:*** $6 per credit hour part-time. ***College room only:*** $5553. Room and board charges vary according to board plan and housing facility. ***Payment plans:*** installment, deferred payment. ***Waivers:*** senior citizens and employees or children of employees.
Financial Aid Of all full-time matriculated undergraduates who enrolled in 2014, 2,557 applied for aid, 2,206 were judged to have need, 126 had their need fully met. 299 Federal Work-Study jobs (averaging $1759). 160 state and other part-time jobs (averaging $1948). In 2014, 663 non-need-based awards were made. ***Average percent of need met:*** 80. ***Average financial aid package:*** $30,933. ***Average need-based loan:*** $5278. ***Average need-based gift aid:*** $26,101. ***Average non-need-based aid:*** $18,566. ***Average indebtedness upon graduation:*** $28,844.

APPLYING
Standardized Tests *Required:* SAT or ACT (for admission). *Required for some:* SAT and SAT Subject Tests or ACT (for admission), SAT Subject Tests (for admission).
Options: electronic application, early admission, early action.
Application fee: $50.
Required: essay or personal statement, high school transcript, minimum 2.5 GPA, 2 letters of recommendation. ***Recommended:*** interview.
Application deadlines: 2/1 (freshmen), 8/1 (transfers), 11/15 (early action).
Notification: 3/1 (freshmen), continuous (transfers), 1/5 (early action).

CONTACT
Mr. Jobe Korb-Nice, Director of Admissions, Seattle Pacific University, 3307 3rd Avenue, West, Seattle, WA 98119-1997. *Phone:* 206-281-2021. *Toll-free phone:* 800-366-3344. *Fax:* 206-281-2669. *E-mail:* admissions@spu.edu.

★ Seattle University
Seattle, Washington
http://www.seattleu.edu/

- **Independent Roman Catholic** comprehensive, founded 1891
- **Urban** 50-acre campus with easy access to Seattle
- **Coed** 4,511 undergraduate students, 95% full-time, 59% women, 41% men
- **Moderately difficult** entrance level, 73% of applicants were admitted

UNDERGRAD STUDENTS
4,286 full-time, 225 part-time. Students come from 50 states and territories; 80 other countries; 65% are from out of state; 3% Black or African American, non-Hispanic/Latino; 9% Hispanic/Latino; 16% Asian, non-Hispanic/Latino; 0.7% Native Hawaiian or other Pacific Islander, non-Hispanic/Latino; 0.5% American Indian or Alaska Native, non-Hispanic/Latino; 7% Two or more races, non-Hispanic/Latino; 9% Race/ethnicity unknown; 11% international; 10% transferred in; 47% live on campus.

Freshmen
Admission: 7,412 applied, 5,438 admitted, 927 enrolled. ***Average high school GPA:*** 3.58. ***Test scores:*** SAT critical reading scores over 500: 87%; SAT math scores over 500: 88%; SAT writing scores over 500: 89%; ACT scores over 18: 100%; SAT critical reading scores over 600: 46%; SAT math scores over 600: 45%; SAT writing scores over 600: 43%; ACT scores over 24: 79%; SAT critical reading scores over 700: 7%; SAT math scores over 700: 9%; SAT writing scores over 700: 8%; ACT scores over 30: 23%.
Retention: 87% of full-time freshmen returned.

FACULTY
Total: 748, 68% full-time, 72% with terminal degrees.
Student/faculty ratio: 12:1.

ACADEMICS
Calendar: quarters. *Degrees:* bachelor's, master's, doctoral, post-master's, and postbachelor's certificates.
Special study options: accelerated degree program, adult/continuing education programs, advanced placement credit, double majors, English as a second language, freshman honors college, honors programs, independent study, internships, off-campus study, part-time degree program, services for LD students, student-designed majors, study abroad, summer session for credit. ***ROTC:*** Army (b), Navy (c), Air Force (c).

Computers: 467 computers/terminals are available on campus for general student use. Students can access the following: campus intranet, computer help desk, free student e-mail accounts, online (class) grades, online (class) registration, online (class) schedules. Campuswide network is available. 100% of college-owned or -operated housing units are wired for high-speed Internet access. Wireless service is available via entire campus.

STUDENT LIFE

Housing options: on-campus residence required through sophomore year; coed, special housing for students with disabilities. Campus housing is university owned and leased by the school. Freshman campus housing is guaranteed.

Activities and organizations: drama/theater group, student-run newspaper, radio station, choral group, Student Government of Seattle University (SGSU), Student Events and Activities Council (SEAC), Redzone, Dance Marathon, Hui 'O Nani Hawaii Club.

Athletics Member NCAA. All Division I. ***Intercollegiate sports:*** baseball M, basketball M(s)/W(s), cheerleading M(c)/W(c), crew W(c), cross-country running M(s)/W(s), golf M(s)/W(s), soccer M(s)/W(s), softball W(s), swimming and diving M(s)/W(s), tennis M/W, track and field M(s)/W(s), volleyball W(s). ***Intramural sports:*** archery M(c)/W(c), basketball M/W, crew M(c)/W(c), field hockey M/W, football M/W, riflery M(c)/W(c), rock climbing M/W, skiing (downhill) M(c)/W(c), soccer M/W, softball M/W, tennis M/W, ultimate Frisbee M/W, volleyball M/W, water polo M/W.

Campus security: 24-hour emergency response devices and patrols, late-night transport/escort service, controlled dormitory access, bicycle patrols.

Student services: health clinic, personal/psychological counseling, women's center.

COSTS & FINANCIAL AID

Costs (2014–15) ***Comprehensive fee:*** $49,035 includes full-time tuition ($37,485), mandatory fees ($720), and room and board ($10,830). Full-time tuition and fees vary according to course load. Part-time tuition: $833 per credit hour. Part-time tuition and fees vary according to course load. ***Room and board:*** Room and board charges vary according to board plan and housing facility. ***Payment plans:*** installment, deferred payment. ***Waivers:*** employees or children of employees.

Financial Aid Of all full-time matriculated undergraduates who enrolled in 2014, 2,969 applied for aid, 2,470 were judged to have need, 300 had their need fully met. 462 Federal Work-Study jobs (averaging $3755). 237 state and other part-time jobs (averaging $6009). In 2014, 187 non-need-based awards were made. ***Average percent of need met:*** 67. ***Average financial aid package:*** $30,502. ***Average need-based loan:*** $5781. ***Average need-based gift aid:*** $20,689. ***Average non-need-based aid:*** $10,810. ***Average indebtedness upon graduation:*** $29,044.

APPLYING

Standardized Tests *Required:* SAT or ACT (for admission).

Options: electronic application, early action, deferred entrance.

Application fee: $50.

Required: essay or personal statement, high school transcript, minimum 2.5 GPA, 2 letters of recommendation.

Application deadlines: rolling (freshmen), 3/1 (transfers), 11/15 (early action).

Notification: continuous until 3/1 (freshmen), continuous (transfers), 12/23 (early action).

CONTACT

Melore Nielsen, Dean of Undergraduate Admissions, Seattle University, 901 12th Avenue, PO Box 222000, Seattle, WA 98122-1090. *Phone:* 206-296-2000. *Toll-free phone:* 800-542-0833 (in-state); 800-426-7123 (out-of-state). *Fax:* 206-296-5656. *E-mail:* admissions@seattleu.edu.

See this page for display ad and page 1616 for the College Close-Up.

University of Puget Sound
Tacoma, Washington
http://www.pugetsound.edu/

- **Independent** comprehensive, founded 1888
- **Urban** 97-acre campus with easy access to Seattle
- **Endowment** $318.5 million
- **Coed** 2,554 undergraduate students, 99% full-time, 57% women, 43% men
- **Moderately difficult** entrance level, 79% of applicants were admitted

UNDERGRAD STUDENTS
2,525 full-time, 29 part-time. Students come from 43 states and territories; 11 other countries; 76% are from out of state; 0.9% Black or African American, non-Hispanic/Latino; 7% Hispanic/Latino; 7% Asian, non-Hispanic/Latino; 0.1% American Indian or Alaska Native, non-Hispanic/Latino; 9% Two or more races, non-Hispanic/Latino; 0.7% Race/ethnicity unknown; 0.4% international; 2% transferred in; 65% live on campus.

Freshmen
Admission: 5,583 applied, 4,427 admitted, 663 enrolled. ***Average high school GPA:*** 3.51. ***Test scores:*** SAT critical reading scores over 500: 92%; SAT math scores over 500: 91%; SAT writing scores over 500: 92%; ACT scores over 18: 99%; SAT critical reading scores over 600: 61%; SAT math scores over 600: 53%; SAT writing scores over 600: 54%; ACT scores over 24: 85%; SAT critical reading scores over 700: 20%; SAT math scores over 700: 10%; SAT writing scores over 700: 11%; ACT scores over 30: 28%.

Retention: 87% of full-time freshmen returned.

FACULTY
Total: 284, 83% full-time, 83% with terminal degrees.

Student/faculty ratio: 11:1.

ACADEMICS
Calendar: semesters. *Degrees:* bachelor's, master's, and doctoral.

Special study options: advanced placement credit, cooperative education, double majors, honors programs, independent study, internships, part-time degree program, services for LD students, student-designed majors, study abroad, summer session for credit. ***ROTC:*** Army (c).

Unusual degree programs: 3-2 engineering with Washington University in St. Louis, Columbia University, and University of Southern California.

Computers: 320 computers/terminals and 6,500 ports are available on campus for general student use. Students can access the following: campus intranet, computer help desk, free student e-mail accounts, online (class) grades, online (class) registration, online (class) schedules, financial aid, admission, student employment. Campuswide network is available. 100% of college-owned or -operated housing units are wired for high-speed Internet access. Wireless service is available via entire campus.

STUDENT LIFE
Housing options: on-campus residence required through sophomore year; coed, men-only, women-only, special housing for students with disabilities. Campus housing is university owned. Freshman campus housing is guaranteed.

Activities and organizations: drama/theater group, student-run newspaper, radio station, choral group, Puget Sound Outdoors, Repertory Dance Group, Hui-O-Hawaii, Student Theatre Productions, Relay for Life, national fraternities, national sororities.

Athletics Member NCAA. All Division III. ***Intercollegiate sports:*** baseball M, basketball M/W, cheerleading M/W, crew M/W, cross-country running M/W, fencing M(c)/W(c), football M, golf M/W, lacrosse M(c)/W, rugby M(c)/W(c), sailing M(c)/W(c), skiing (downhill) M(c)/W(c), soccer M/W, softball W, swimming and diving M/W, tennis M/W, track and field M/W, ultimate Frisbee M(c)/W(c), volleyball W, water polo M(c)/W(c). ***Intramural sports:*** basketball M/W, football M/W, soccer M/W, softball M/W, volleyball M/W.

Campus security: 24-hour emergency response devices and patrols, student patrols, late-night transport/escort service, controlled dormitory access, 24-hour locked residence hall entrances, surveillance cameras, and emergency telephone towers.

Student services: health clinic, personal/psychological counseling.

COSTS & FINANCIAL AID
Costs (2014–15) ***Comprehensive fee:*** $54,608 includes full-time tuition ($43,200), mandatory fees ($228), and room and board ($11,180). Full-time tuition and fees vary according to course load. Part-time tuition: $5450 per unit. Part-time tuition and fees vary according to course load. ***College room only:*** $6150. Room and board charges vary according to board plan and housing facility. ***Payment plans:*** installment, deferred payment. ***Waivers:*** employees or children of employees.

Financial Aid Of all full-time matriculated undergraduates who enrolled in 2014, 1,641 applied for aid, 1,409 were judged to have need, 214 had their need fully met. 567 Federal Work-Study jobs (averaging $2730). 842 state and other part-time jobs (averaging $2487). In 2014, 1062 non-need-based awards were made. ***Average percent of need met:*** 73. ***Average financial aid package:*** $29,668. ***Average need-based loan:*** $6276. ***Average need-based gift aid:*** $23,410. ***Average non-need-based aid:*** $14,886. ***Average indebtedness upon graduation:*** $27,776.

APPLYING
Standardized Tests *Required:* SAT or ACT (for admission).

Options: electronic application, early admission, early decision, deferred entrance.

Application fee: $50.

Required: essay or personal statement, high school transcript, 2 letters of recommendation. ***Recommended:*** minimum 3.0 GPA, interview.

Application deadlines: 1/15 (freshmen), 3/1 (transfers).

Early decision deadline: 11/15 (for plan 1), 1/1 (for plan 2).

Notification: 4/1 (freshmen), continuous (transfers), 12/15 (early decision plan 1), 2/15 (early decision plan 2).

CONTACT
Dr. Jenny Rickard, Vice President for Enrollment, University of Puget Sound, 1500 North Warner Street, CMB 1062, Tacoma, WA 98416. *Phone:* 253-879-3211. *Toll-free phone:* 800-396-7191. *Fax:* 253-879-3993. *E-mail:* admission@pugetsound.edu.

See previous page for display ad and page 1696 for the College Close-Up.

★ University of Washington
Seattle, Washington
http://www.washington.edu/

- **State-supported** university, founded 1861, part of University of Washington
- **Urban** 703-acre campus
- **Endowment** $2.8 billion
- **Coed** 30,672 undergraduate students, 91% full-time, 52% women, 48% men
- **Very difficult** entrance level, 55% of applicants were admitted

UNDERGRAD STUDENTS
27,764 full-time, 2,908 part-time. Students come from 50 states and territories; 80 other countries; 16% are from out of state; 3% Black or African American, non-Hispanic/Latino; 6% Hispanic/Latino; 23% Asian, non-Hispanic/Latino; 0.4% Native Hawaiian or other Pacific Islander, non-Hispanic/Latino; 0.5% American Indian or Alaska Native, non-Hispanic/Latino; 7% Two or more races, non-Hispanic/Latino; 4% Race/ethnicity unknown; 14% international; 6% transferred in; 24% live on campus.

Freshmen
Admission: 31,611 applied, 17,451 admitted, 6,360 enrolled. ***Average high school GPA:*** 3.76. ***Test scores:*** SAT critical reading scores over 500: 86%; SAT math scores over 500: 95%; SAT writing scores over 500: 84%; ACT scores over 18: 99%; SAT critical reading scores over 600: 49%; SAT math scores over 600: 70%; SAT writing scores over 600: 45%; ACT scores over 24: 86%; SAT critical reading scores over 700: 12%; SAT math scores over 700: 26%; SAT writing scores over 700: 9%; ACT scores over 30: 35%.

Retention: 94% of full-time freshmen returned.

FACULTY
Total: 4,277, 77% full-time, 83% with terminal degrees.

Student/faculty ratio: 11:1.

ACADEMICS
Calendar: quarters. *Degrees:* bachelor's, master's, doctoral, and post-master's certificates.

Special study options: adult/continuing education programs, advanced placement credit, cooperative education, distance learning, double majors, English as a second language, honors programs, independent study, internships, off-campus study, part-time degree program, services for LD students, student-designed majors, study abroad, summer session for credit. ***ROTC:*** Army (b), Navy (b), Air Force (b).

Computers: 450 computers/terminals are available on campus for general student use. Students can access the following: computer help desk, free student e-mail accounts, online (class) grades, online (class) registration, online (class) schedules. Campuswide network is available. 100% of college-owned or -operated housing units are wired for high-speed Internet access. Wireless service is available via entire campus.

STUDENT LIFE
Housing options: coed, special housing for students with disabilities. Campus housing is university owned, leased by the school and is provided by a third party.

Activities and organizations: drama/theater group, student-run newspaper, radio and television station, choral group, marching band, Interfraternity Council/Pan-Hellenic Council, Taiwanese Student Association, Chinese Student Association, Yacht Club, Asian American Intervarsity Christian Fellowship/Muslim Students Association, national sororities.

Athletics Member NCAA. All Division I except football (Division I-A). ***Intercollegiate sports:*** baseball M(s), basketball M(s)/W(s), cheerleading M/W, crew M(s)/W(s), cross-country running M(s)/W(s), golf M(s)/W(s), gymnastics W(s), soccer M(s)/W(s), softball W(s), tennis M(s)/W(s), track and field M(s)/W(s), volleyball W(s). ***Intramural sports:*** archery M(c)/W(c), badminton M/W, baseball M(c)/W(c), basketball M/W, bowling M/W, crew M(c)/W(c), equestrian sports M(c)/W(c), fencing M(c)/W(c), field hockey M(c)/W(c), football M/W, golf M/W, gymnastics M(c)/W(c), ice hockey M(c)/W(c), lacrosse M(c)/W(c), racquetball M(c)/W(c), rock climbing M/W, rugby M(c)/W(c), sailing M(c)/W(c), skiing (cross-country) M(c)/W(c), skiing (downhill) M(c)/W(c), soccer M(c)/W(c), squash M(c)/W(c), table tennis M/W, tennis M/W, track and field M/W, ultimate Frisbee M(c)/W(c), volleyball M/W, water polo M(c)/W(c), wrestling M(c).

Campus security: 24-hour emergency response devices and patrols, late-night transport/escort service, controlled dormitory access.

Student services: health clinic, personal/psychological counseling, women's center, legal services.

COSTS & FINANCIAL AID
Costs (2014–15) ***Tuition:*** state resident $11,305 full-time, $377 per credit part-time; nonresident $32,424 full-time, $1081 per credit part-time. Full-time tuition and fees vary according to course load and location. Part-time tuition and fees vary according to course load and location. ***Required fees:*** $1089 full-time, $29 per credit part-time, $76 per term part-time. ***Room and board:*** $10,833. Room and board charges vary according to board plan and housing facility. ***Waivers:*** senior citizens and employees or children of employees.

Financial Aid Of all full-time matriculated undergraduates who enrolled in 2014, 17,700 applied for aid, 13,450 were judged to have need, 2,700 had their need fully met. 1,500 Federal Work-Study jobs (averaging $2800). 200 state and other part-time jobs (averaging $3200). In 2014, 1290 non-need-based awards were made. ***Average percent of need met:*** 82. ***Average financial aid package:*** $18,500. ***Average need-based loan:*** $7000. ***Average need-based gift aid:*** $15,000. ***Average non-need-based aid:*** $5500. ***Average indebtedness upon graduation:*** $21,532.

APPLYING
Standardized Tests *Required:* SAT or ACT (for admission).

Options: electronic application.

Application fee: $60.

Required: essay or personal statement, minimum 2.0 GPA, Admission is competitive. ***Required for some:*** high school transcript.

Application deadlines: 12/1 (freshmen), 2/15 (transfers).

CONTACT
Office of Admissions, University of Washington, 1410 NE Campus Parkway, Seattle, WA 98195. *Phone:* 206-543-9686. *Fax:* 206-685-3655.

University of Washington, Bothell

Bothell, Washington

http://www.uwb.edu/

- **State-supported** comprehensive, founded 1990, part of University of Washington
- **Suburban** 128-acre campus with easy access to Seattle
- **Endowment** $3.9 million
- **Coed** 4,405 undergraduate students, 85% full-time, 50% women, 50% men
- **Moderately difficult** entrance level, 79% of applicants were admitted

UNDERGRAD STUDENTS

3,742 full-time, 663 part-time. Students come from 25 states and territories; 25 other countries; 2% are from out of state; 5% Black or African American, non-Hispanic/Latino; 8% Hispanic/Latino; 26% Asian, non-Hispanic/Latino; 1% Native Hawaiian or other Pacific Islander, non-Hispanic/Latino; 0.5% American Indian or Alaska Native, non-Hispanic/Latino; 6% Two or more races, non-Hispanic/Latino; 1% Race/ethnicity unknown; 8% international; 17% transferred in; 6% live on campus.

Freshmen

Admission: 2,389 applied, 1,891 admitted, 639 enrolled. ***Average high school GPA:*** 3.27. ***Test scores:*** SAT critical reading scores over 500: 48%; SAT math scores over 500: 59%; SAT writing scores over 500: 42%; ACT scores over 18: 76%; SAT critical reading scores over 600: 13%; SAT math scores over 600: 24%; SAT writing scores over 600: 10%; ACT scores over 24: 25%; SAT critical reading scores over 700: 2%; SAT math scores over 700: 3%; SAT writing scores over 700: 1%; ACT scores over 30: 2%.
Retention: 83% of full-time freshmen returned.

FACULTY

Total: 297, 58% full-time, 75% with terminal degrees.
Student/faculty ratio: 20:1.

ACADEMICS

Degrees: bachelor's and master's.
Special study options: adult/continuing education programs, advanced placement credit, cooperative education, double majors, English as a second language, independent study, internships, off-campus study, part-time degree program, services for LD students, student-designed majors, study abroad, summer session for credit. ***ROTC:*** Army (c), Navy (c), Air Force (c).
Computers: 420 computers/terminals and 1,100 ports are available on campus for general student use. Students can access the following: campus intranet, computer help desk, free student e-mail accounts, online (class) grades, online (class) registration, online (class) schedules. Campuswide network is available. Wireless service is available via classrooms, computer centers, computer labs, learning centers, libraries, student centers.

STUDENT LIFE

Housing options: coed, special housing for students with disabilities. Campus housing is university owned and leased by the school. Freshman applicants given priority for college housing.
Activities and organizations: student-run newspaper, radio station, Campus Events Board, Social Justice Organizers, Associated Students of University of Washington Bothell (ASUWB), Recreation & Intramurals Program, Club Council.
Athletics ***Intramural sports:*** basketball M/W, rock climbing M/W, soccer M/W, softball M/W, tennis M/W, ultimate Frisbee M/W, volleyball M/W.
Campus security: 24-hour emergency response devices and patrols, late-night transport/escort service.
Student services: personal/psychological counseling.

COSTS & FINANCIAL AID

Costs (2014–15) ***Tuition:*** state resident $11,911 full-time, $377 per credit part-time; nonresident $33,030 full-time, $1081 per credit part-time. Full-time tuition and fees vary according to course load. Part-time tuition and fees vary according to course load. ***Required fees:*** $606 full-time, $20 per credit part-time. ***Room and board:*** $10,833. Room and board charges vary according to board plan, housing facility, and location. ***Waivers:*** senior citizens and employees or children of employees.
Financial Aid Of all full-time matriculated undergraduates who enrolled in 2014, 2,525 applied for aid, 2,197 were judged to have need, 250 had

their need fully met. 280 Federal Work-Study jobs (averaging $2800). 40 state and other part-time jobs (averaging $3400). In 2014, 60 non-need-based awards were made. ***Average percent of need met:*** 79. ***Average financial aid package:*** $18,500. ***Average need-based loan:*** $7000. ***Average need-based gift aid:*** $15,000. ***Average non-need-based aid:*** $5000. ***Average indebtedness upon graduation:*** $19,536.

APPLYING
Standardized Tests *Required:* SAT or ACT (for admission).
Options: electronic application, deferred entrance.
Application fee: $60.
Required: essay or personal statement, high school transcript, minimum 2.0 GPA. ***Required for some:*** letters of recommendation.
Application deadlines: 1/15 (freshmen), 1/15 (transfers).
Notification: continuous (freshmen), continuous (transfers).

CONTACT
Jill Orcutt, Assistant Vice Chancellor for Enrollment, University of Washington, Bothell, 18115 Campus Way NE, Box 358500, Bothell, WA 8011-8246. *Phone:* 425-352-5000. *Fax:* 425-352-5455. *E-mail:* freshmen@uwb.edu.

See previous page for display ad and page 1710 for the College Close-Up.

University of Washington, Tacoma
Tacoma, Washington
http://www.tacoma.washington.edu/

- **State-supported** comprehensive, founded 1990, part of University of Washington
- **Urban** 46-acre campus with easy access to Seattle
- **Endowment** $39.4 million
- **Coed** 3,809 undergraduate students, 87% full-time, 52% women, 48% men
- **Moderately difficult** entrance level, 85% of applicants were admitted

UNDERGRAD STUDENTS
3,297 full-time, 512 part-time. Students come from 28 states and territories; 18 other countries; 2% are from out of state; ####% Black or African American, non-Hispanic/Latino; ####% Hispanic/Latino; ####% Asian, non-Hispanic/Latino; ####% Native Hawaiian or other Pacific Islander, non-Hispanic/Latino; ####% American Indian or Alaska Native, non-Hispanic/Latino; ####% Two or more races, non-Hispanic/Latino; ####% Race/ethnicity unknown; ####% international; 23% transferred in; 3% live on campus.

Freshmen
Admission: 1,382 applied, 1,168 admitted, 435 enrolled. ***Average high school GPA:*** 3.26. ***Test scores:*** SAT critical reading scores over 500: 46%; SAT math scores over 500: 50%; SAT writing scores over 500: 31%; ACT scores over 18: 78%; SAT critical reading scores over 600: 12%; SAT math scores over 600: 12%; SAT writing scores over 600: 5%; ACT scores over 24: 23%; SAT critical reading scores over 700: 1%; SAT math scores over 700: 1%; ACT scores over 30: 3%.
Retention: 71% of full-time freshmen returned.

FACULTY
Total: 295, 70% full-time, 70% with terminal degrees.
Student/faculty ratio: 17:1.

ACADEMICS
Calendar: quarters. *Degrees:* bachelor's, master's, and doctoral.
Special study options: academic remediation for entering students, accelerated degree program, advanced placement credit, cooperative education, distance learning, double majors, honors programs, independent study, internships, part-time degree program, services for LD students, student-designed majors, study abroad, summer session for credit. ***ROTC:*** Army (c), Navy (c), Air Force (c).
Computers: 195 computers/terminals are available on campus for general student use. Students can access the following: campus intranet, computer help desk, free student e-mail accounts, online (class) grades, online (class) registration, online (class) schedules, online courseware-Blackboard, Canvas and Catalyst proprietary CMS. Campuswide network is available. 100% of college-owned or -operated housing units are wired for high-speed Internet access. Wireless service is available via entire campus.

STUDENT LIFE
Housing options: special housing for students with disabilities. Campus housing is leased by the school. Freshman applicants given priority for college housing.
Activities and organizations: drama/theater group, student-run newspaper, choral group, Accounting Student Association, International Student Association, Partners in Action to Transform Healthcare (PATH), Asian Pacific Islander Student Union (APISU).
Athletics ***Intramural sports:*** soccer M(c)/W(c), softball M(c).
Campus security: 24-hour emergency response devices and patrols, late-night transport/escort service, key card access to buildings after hours.
Student services: health clinic, personal/psychological counseling.

COSTS & FINANCIAL AID
Costs (2014–15) ***Tuition:*** state resident $11,305 full-time, $377 per credit part-time; nonresident $32,424 full-time, $1081 per credit part-time. Full-time tuition and fees vary according to course load. Part-time tuition and fees vary according to course load. ***Required fees:*** $957 full-time, $20 per credit part-time. ***Room and board:*** $10,833. Room and board charges vary according to housing facility and location. ***Waivers:*** senior citizens and employees or children of employees.
Financial Aid Of all full-time matriculated undergraduates who enrolled in 2014, 2,715 applied for aid, 2,491 were judged to have need, 450 had their need fully met. 360 Federal Work-Study jobs (averaging $2600). 20 state and other part-time jobs (averaging $3800). In 2014, 190 non-need-based awards were made. ***Average percent of need met:*** 79. ***Average financial aid package:*** $18,500. ***Average need-based loan:*** $7000. ***Average need-based gift aid:*** $15,000. ***Average non-need-based aid:*** $2400. ***Average indebtedness upon graduation:*** $23,396.

APPLYING
Standardized Tests *Required:* SAT or ACT (for admission).
Options: electronic application, deferred entrance.
Application fee: $60.
Required: essay or personal statement, minimum 2.0 GPA. ***Required for some:*** high school transcript, 3 letters of recommendation.
Application deadlines: 6/1 (freshmen), 3/15 (transfers).
Notification: continuous (freshmen), continuous (transfers).

CONTACT
Ms. Megan Beresford, Associate Director of University Recruitment, University of Washington, Tacoma, 1900 Commerce Street, Tacoma, WA 98402-3100. *Phone:* 253-692-4738. *Toll-free phone:* 800-736-7750. *Fax:* 253-692-4414. *E-mail:* megan61@u.washington.edu.

Walla Walla University
College Place, Washington
http://www.wallawalla.edu/

- **Independent Seventh-day Adventist** comprehensive, founded 1892
- **Small-town** 77-acre campus
- **Coed** 1,689 undergraduate students, 94% full-time, 51% women, 49% men
- **Moderately difficult** entrance level, 86% of applicants were admitted

UNDERGRAD STUDENTS
1,589 full-time, 100 part-time. 63% are from out of state; 3% Black or African American, non-Hispanic/Latino; 13% Hispanic/Latino; 7% Asian, non-Hispanic/Latino; 0.5% Native Hawaiian or other Pacific Islander, non-Hispanic/Latino; 0.9% American Indian or Alaska Native, non-Hispanic/Latino; 0.2% Two or more races, non-Hispanic/Latino; 5% Race/ethnicity unknown; 0.8% international; 5% transferred in; 64% live on campus.

Freshmen
Admission: 1,689 applied, 1,457 admitted, 364 enrolled. ***Average high school GPA:*** 3.5. ***Test scores:*** SAT critical reading scores over 500: 65%; SAT math scores over 500: 60%; SAT writing scores over 500: 61%; ACT scores over 18: 93%; SAT critical reading scores over 600: 27%; SAT math scores over 600: 22%; SAT writing scores over 600: 19%; ACT scores over 24: 50%; SAT critical reading scores over 700: 6%; SAT math

scores over 700: 4%; SAT writing scores over 700: 2%; ACT scores over 30: 9%.

Retention: 79% of full-time freshmen returned.

FACULTY

Student/faculty ratio: 14:1.

ACADEMICS

Calendar: quarters. *Degrees:* diplomas, associate, bachelor's, and master's.

Special study options: academic remediation for entering students, advanced placement credit, cooperative education, distance learning, double majors, freshman honors college, honors programs, independent study, internships, off-campus study, part-time degree program, services for LD students, study abroad, summer session for credit.

Computers: Students can access the following: campus intranet, computer help desk, free student e-mail accounts, online (class) grades, online (class) registration, online (class) schedules, online forum, online classifieds, online student directory. Campuswide network is available. 100% of college-owned or -operated housing units are wired for high-speed Internet access. Wireless service is available via entire campus.

STUDENT LIFE

Housing options: on-campus residence required through junior year; men-only, women-only, special housing for students with disabilities. Campus housing is university owned and leased by the school. Freshman campus housing is guaranteed.

Activities and organizations: drama/theater group, student-run newspaper, radio and television station, choral group, Associated Students of Walla Walla University, Campus Ministries, Village Club, OPS Club (Men's residence hall club), AGA Club (women's residence hall club).

Athletics Member NAIA. ***Intercollegiate sports:*** basketball M/W, soccer M, softball W, volleyball W. ***Intramural sports:*** basketball M/W, football M/W, ice hockey M, softball W, table tennis M/W, volleyball M/W.

Campus security: 24-hour emergency response devices and patrols, student patrols, late-night transport/escort service, controlled dormitory access.

Student services: health clinic, personal/psychological counseling.

COSTS & FINANCIAL AID

Costs (2014–15) ***Comprehensive fee:*** $32,721 includes full-time tuition ($25,296), mandatory fees ($570), and room and board ($6855). ***College room only:*** $3735. Room and board charges vary according to board plan and housing facility.

Financial Aid Of all full-time matriculated undergraduates who enrolled in 2012, 1,222 applied for aid, 1,051 were judged to have need, 240 had their need fully met. In 2012, 374 non-need-based awards were made. ***Average percent of need met:*** 90. ***Average financial aid package:*** $20,765. ***Average need-based loan:*** $4432. ***Average need-based gift aid:*** $6297. ***Average non-need-based aid:*** $6953. ***Average indebtedness upon graduation:*** $38,174.

APPLYING

Standardized Tests *Required:* SAT or ACT (for admission). *Recommended:* ACT (for admission).

Options: electronic application, early decision, deferred entrance.

Application fee: $40.

Required: high school transcript, minimum 2.5 GPA.

Application deadlines: rolling (freshmen), rolling (transfers).

Notification: continuous (freshmen), continuous (transfers).

CONTACT

Mr. Dallas Weis, Director of Admissions, Walla Walla University, Marketing and Enrollment Services, 204 S. College Avenue, College Place, WA 99324. *Phone:* 509-527-2327. *Toll-free phone:* 800-541-8900. *Fax:* 509-527-2397.

Washington State University

Pullman, Washington

http://www.wsu.edu/

- **State-supported** university, founded 1890
- **Small-town** 620-acre campus with easy access to Spokane
- **Endowment** $868.1 million
- **Coed** 23,867 undergraduate students, 87% full-time, 51% women, 49% men
- **Moderately difficult** entrance level, 80% of applicants were admitted

UNDERGRAD STUDENTS

20,843 full-time, 3,024 part-time. Students come from 50 states and territories; 96 other countries; 8% are from out of state; 3% Black or African American, non-Hispanic/Latino; 12% Hispanic/Latino; 5% Asian, non-Hispanic/Latino; 0.4% Native Hawaiian or other Pacific Islander, non-Hispanic/Latino; 0.6% American Indian or Alaska Native, non-Hispanic/Latino; 7% Two or more races, non-Hispanic/Latino; 2% Race/ethnicity unknown; 5% international; 10% transferred in; 26% live on campus.

Freshmen

Admission: 18,716 applied, 15,029 admitted, 4,457 enrolled. ***Average high school GPA:*** 3.3. ***Test scores:*** SAT critical reading scores over 500: 55%; SAT math scores over 500: 62%; SAT writing scores over 500: 48%; ACT scores over 18: 85%; SAT critical reading scores over 600: 17%; SAT math scores over 600: 20%; SAT writing scores over 600: 12%; ACT scores over 24: 38%; SAT critical reading scores over 700: 2%; SAT math scores over 700: 2%; SAT writing scores over 700: 1%; ACT scores over 30: 4%.

Retention: 80% of full-time freshmen returned.

FACULTY

Total: 1,825, 70% full-time, 77% with terminal degrees.

Student/faculty ratio: 18:1.

ACADEMICS

Calendar: semesters. *Degrees:* certificates, bachelor's, master's, doctoral, post-master's, and postbachelor's certificates.

Special study options: accelerated degree program, adult/continuing education programs, advanced placement credit, cooperative education, distance learning, double majors, English as a second language, external degree program, honors programs, independent study, internships, off-campus study, part-time degree program, services for LD students, student-designed majors, study abroad, summer session for credit. ***ROTC:*** Army (b), Navy (c), Air Force (b).

Computers: 2,500 computers/terminals and 2,500 ports are available on campus for general student use. Students can access the following: campus intranet, computer help desk, free student e-mail accounts, online (class) grades, online (class) registration, online (class) schedules. Campuswide network is available. 100% of college-owned or -operated housing units are wired for high-speed Internet access. Wireless service is available via classrooms, computer centers, computer labs, dorm rooms, learning centers, libraries, student centers.

STUDENT LIFE

Housing options: on-campus residence required for freshman year; coed, men-only, women-only, cooperative, special housing for students with disabilities. Campus housing is university owned. Freshman campus housing is guaranteed.

Activities and organizations: drama/theater group, student-run newspaper, radio and television station, choral group, marching band, Panhellenic Association - Sororities, Interfraternity Council - Fraternities, Student Entertainment Board, International Students Council, ChiLaStAl (Chicana/o Latina/o Student Alliance), national fraternities, national sororities.

Athletics Member NCAA. All Division I except football (Division I-A). ***Intercollegiate sports:*** baseball M(s), basketball M(s)/W(s), bowling M(c)/W(c), cheerleading M/W, crew M(c)/W(s), cross-country running M(s)/W(s), fencing M/W(c), golf M(s)/W(s), ice hockey M(c), lacrosse M(c)/W(c), rugby M(c)/W(c), sailing M(c)/W(c), skiing (cross-country) M(c)/W(c), skiing (downhill) M(c)/W(c), soccer M(c)/W(s), softball W(c), swimming and diving W(s), tennis M(c)/W(s), track and field M(s)/W(s), ultimate Frisbee M(c)/W(c), volleyball M(c)/W(s), water polo M(c)/W(c). ***Intramural sports:*** badminton M/W, basketball M/W, football

M/W, golf M/W, racquetball M/W, rock climbing M/W, soccer M/W, softball M/W, table tennis M/W, tennis M/W, ultimate Frisbee M/W, volleyball M/W.

Campus security: 24-hour emergency response devices and patrols, student patrols, late-night transport/escort service, controlled dormitory access.

Student services: health clinic, personal/psychological counseling, women's center, legal services.

COSTS & FINANCIAL AID

Costs (2014–15) ***Tuition:*** state resident $10,874 full-time, $571 per credit hour part-time; nonresident $23,956 full-time, $1225 per credit hour part-time. Full-time tuition and fees vary according to location and reciprocity agreements. Part-time tuition and fees vary according to course load, location, and reciprocity agreements. ***Required fees:*** $1554 full-time. ***Room and board:*** $11,276; room only: $6858. Room and board charges vary according to board plan, housing facility, and location. ***Waivers:*** senior citizens and employees or children of employees.

Financial Aid Of all full-time matriculated undergraduates who enrolled in 2013, 16,469 applied for aid, 13,859 were judged to have need, 3,192 had their need fully met. In 2013, 490 non-need-based awards were made. ***Average percent of need met:*** 71. ***Average financial aid package:*** $12,737. ***Average need-based loan:*** $4312. ***Average need-based gift aid:*** $10,397. ***Average non-need-based aid:*** $3229. ***Average indebtedness upon graduation:*** $24,298.

APPLYING

Standardized Tests *Required:* SAT or ACT (for admission).

Options: electronic application.

Application fee: $50.

Required: high school transcript, minimum 2.0 GPA. ***Recommended:*** essay or personal statement.

Application deadlines: 1/31 (freshmen), 1/7 (out-of-state freshmen), 1/31 (transfers).

Notification: continuous until 11/1 (freshmen), continuous until 11/1 (out-of-state freshmen), continuous until 11/1 (transfers).

CONTACT

Ms. Wendy Peterson, Director of Admissions, Washington State University, PO Box 641067, Pullman, WA 99164-1067. *Phone:* 888-468-6978. *Toll-free phone:* 888-468-6978. *Fax:* 509-335-4902. *E-mail:* admissions@wsu.edu.

Washington State University Spokane

Spokane, Washington

http://www.spokane.wsu.edu/

- **State-supported** upper-level, founded 1989
- **Coed**

ACADEMICS

Calendar: semesters. *Degrees:* bachelor's, master's, and doctoral.

COSTS

Costs (2014–15) ***Tuition:*** state resident $10,874 full-time, $570 per credit hour part-time; nonresident $23,956 full-time, $1224 per credit hour part-time. Full-time tuition and fees vary according to course load, location, and reciprocity agreements. Part-time tuition and fees vary according to course load, location, and reciprocity agreements. ***Required fees:*** $696 full-time. ***Waivers:*** senior citizens and employees or children of employees.

CONTACT

Washington State University Spokane, 412 East Spokane Falls Boulevard, PO Box 1495, Spokane, WA 99210-1495.

Washington State University Tri-Cities

Richland, Washington

http://www.tricity.wsu.edu/

- **State-supported** comprehensive, founded 1989
- **Urban** campus
- **Coed** 1,107 undergraduate students, 78% full-time, 54% women, 46% men
- **Moderately difficult** entrance level, 71% of applicants were admitted

UNDERGRAD STUDENTS

866 full-time, 241 part-time. 1% Black or African American, non-Hispanic/Latino; 28% Hispanic/Latino; 2% Asian, non-Hispanic/Latino; 0.3% American Indian or Alaska Native, non-Hispanic/Latino; 4% Two or more races, non-Hispanic/Latino; 3% Race/ethnicity unknown; 0.6% international.

Freshmen

Admission: 316 applied, 224 admitted, 135 enrolled. ***Average high school GPA:*** 3.23. ***Test scores:*** SAT critical reading scores over 500: 39%; SAT math scores over 500: 44%; SAT writing scores over 500: 79%; ACT scores over 18: 76%; SAT critical reading scores over 600: 11%; SAT math scores over 600: 12%; SAT writing scores over 600: 28%; ACT scores over 24: 19%; SAT critical reading scores over 700: 3%; SAT math scores over 700: 1%; SAT writing scores over 700: 6%.

Retention: 76% of full-time freshmen returned.

ACADEMICS

Calendar: semesters. *Degrees:* certificates, bachelor's, master's, doctoral, and postbachelor's certificates.

Special study options: adult/continuing education programs, external degree program, part-time degree program.

Computers: Students can access the following: campus intranet, computer help desk, free student e-mail accounts, online (class) grades, online (class) registration. Campuswide network is available.

STUDENT LIFE

Housing options: Campus housing is provided by a third party.

Campus security: 24-hour emergency response devices and patrols, student patrols.

COSTS

Costs (2014–15) ***Tuition:*** state resident $10,874 full-time, $571 per credit part-time; nonresident $23,956 full-time, $1225 per credit part-time. Full-time tuition and fees vary according to course load and location. Part-time tuition and fees vary according to course load, location, and reciprocity agreements. ***Required fees:*** $1554 full-time. ***Room and board:*** $11,276; room only: $6858. Room and board charges vary according to board plan, housing facility, and location. ***Waivers:*** senior citizens and employees or children of employees.

APPLYING

Standardized Tests *Required:* SAT or ACT (for admission).

Options: electronic application.

Application fee: $50.

Required: high school transcript, minimum 2.0 GPA. ***Recommended:*** essay or personal statement.

Application deadlines: 1/31 (freshmen), 1/7 (out-of-state freshmen), 1/31 (transfers).

Notification: continuous until 11/1 (freshmen), continuous until 11/1 (out-of-state freshmen), continuous until 11/1 (transfers).

CONTACT

Washington State University Tri-Cities, 2710 University Drive, Richland, WA 99352-1671.

Washington State University Vancouver

Vancouver, Washington

http://www.vancouver.wsu.edu/

- **State-supported** comprehensive, founded 1989
- **Urban** campus
- **Coed** 2,650 undergraduate students, 77% full-time, 53% women, 47% men
- **Moderately difficult** entrance level, 77% of applicants were admitted

UNDERGRAD STUDENTS

2,046 full-time, 604 part-time. 1% Black or African American, non-Hispanic/Latino; 7% Hispanic/Latino; 6% Asian, non-Hispanic/Latino; 0.5% Native Hawaiian or other Pacific Islander, non-Hispanic/Latino; 0.8% American Indian or Alaska Native, non-Hispanic/Latino; 6% Two or more races, non-Hispanic/Latino; 4% Race/ethnicity unknown; 0.7% international.

Freshmen

Admission: 593 applied, 454 admitted, 236 enrolled. ***Average high school GPA:*** 3.45. ***Test scores:*** SAT critical reading scores over 500: 60%; SAT math scores over 500: 70%; SAT writing scores over 500: 57%; SAT critical reading scores over 600: 24%; SAT math scores over 600: 19%; SAT writing scores over 600: 15%; SAT critical reading scores over 700: 3%; SAT math scores over 700: 2%; SAT writing scores over 700: 3%.

Retention: 78% of full-time freshmen returned.

ACADEMICS

Calendar: semesters. *Degrees:* certificates, bachelor's, and master's.

Special study options: adult/continuing education programs, external degree program, part-time degree program.

STUDENT LIFE

Campus security: 24-hour emergency response devices and patrols, student patrols.

APPLYING

Standardized Tests *Required:* SAT or ACT (for admission).

Options: electronic application.

Application fee: $50.

Required: high school transcript, minimum 2.0 GPA. ***Recommended:*** essay or personal statement.

Application deadlines: 1/31 (freshmen), 1/7 (out-of-state freshmen), 1/31 (transfers).

Notification: continuous until 11/1 (freshmen), continuous until 11/1 (out-of-state freshmen), continuous until 11/1 (transfers).

CONTACT

Washington State University Vancouver, 14204 Northeast Salmon Creek Avenue, Vancouver, WA 98686.

Western Washington University

Bellingham, Washington

http://www.wwu.edu/

- **State-supported** comprehensive, founded 1893
- **Small-town** 223-acre campus with easy access to Seattle, Vancouver
- **Endowment** $59.6 million
- **Coed** 14,152 undergraduate students, 92% full-time, 55% women, 45% men
- **Moderately difficult** entrance level, 85% of applicants were admitted

UNDERGRAD STUDENTS

13,050 full-time, 1,102 part-time. Students come from 48 states and territories; 36 other countries; 9% are from out of state; 2% Black or African American, non-Hispanic/Latino; 7% Hispanic/Latino; 7% Asian, non-Hispanic/Latino; 0.2% Native Hawaiian or other Pacific Islander, non-Hispanic/Latino; 0.4% American Indian or Alaska Native, non-Hispanic/Latino; 8% Two or more races, non-Hispanic/Latino; 0.8% Race/ethnicity unknown; 1% international; 8% transferred in; 29% live on campus.

Freshmen

Admission: 9,283 applied, 7,850 admitted, 2,786 enrolled. ***Average high school GPA:*** 3.43. ***Test scores:*** SAT critical reading scores over 500: 77%; SAT math scores over 500: 75%; SAT writing scores over 500: 66%; ACT scores over 18: 95%; SAT critical reading scores over 600: 31%; SAT math scores over 600: 29%; SAT writing scores over 600: 20%; ACT scores over 24: 58%; SAT critical reading scores over 700: 5%; SAT math scores over 700: 3%; SAT writing scores over 700: 2%; ACT scores over 30: 11%.

Retention: 83% of full-time freshmen returned.

FACULTY

Total: 898, 63% full-time, 70% with terminal degrees.

Student/faculty ratio: 19:1.

ACADEMICS

Calendar: quarters. *Degrees:* certificates, bachelor's, master's, post-master's, and postbachelor's certificates.

Special study options: accelerated degree program, advanced placement credit, cooperative education, distance learning, double majors, English as a second language, honors programs, independent study, internships, off-campus study, services for LD students, student-designed majors, study abroad, summer session for credit.

Computers: 2,708 computers/terminals are available on campus for general student use. Students can access the following: free student e-mail accounts, online (class) registration. Campuswide network is available. 99% of college-owned or -operated housing units are wired for high-speed Internet access. Wireless service is available via classrooms, computer centers, computer labs, dorm rooms, learning centers, libraries, student centers.

STUDENT LIFE

Housing options: coed, special housing for students with disabilities. Campus housing is university owned and leased by the school. Freshman campus housing is guaranteed.

Activities and organizations: drama/theater group, student-run newspaper, radio and television station, choral group, intramurals, Residence Hall Association, Associated Students, Outdoor Center, Ethnic Student Center.

Athletics Member NCAA. All Division II. ***Intercollegiate sports:*** basketball M(s)/W(s), cheerleading M/W, crew M(s)/W(s), cross-country running M(s)/W(s), golf M(s)/W(s), soccer M(s)/W(s), softball W(s), track and field M(s)/W(s), volleyball W(s). ***Intramural sports:*** badminton M/W, baseball M, basketball M/W, equestrian sports M(c)/W(c), ice hockey M, lacrosse M/W, racquetball M/W, rock climbing M/W, sailing M/W, skiing (downhill) M/W, soccer M/W, softball M/W, swimming and diving M/W, table tennis M/W, tennis M/W, volleyball M/W, water polo M/W, wrestling M.

Campus security: 24-hour emergency response devices and patrols, student patrols, late-night transport/escort service, controlled dormitory access.

Student services: health clinic, personal/psychological counseling, women's center, legal services.

COSTS & FINANCIAL AID

Costs (2014–15) ***Tuition:*** state resident $7503 full-time, $270 per credit hour part-time; nonresident $18,945 full-time, $651 per credit hour part-time. Full-time tuition and fees vary according to course load, location, and reciprocity agreements. Part-time tuition and fees vary according to course load, location, and reciprocity agreements. ***Required fees:*** $1462 full-time. ***Room and board:*** $10,042. Room and board charges vary according to board plan, housing facility, and location. ***Payment plan:*** installment. ***Waivers:*** minority students and employees or children of employees.

Financial Aid Of all full-time matriculated undergraduates who enrolled in 2014, 8,834 applied for aid, 6,587 were judged to have need, 1,205 had their need fully met. 132 Federal Work-Study jobs (averaging $3378). 624 state and other part-time jobs (averaging $3525). In 2014, 262 non-need-based awards were made. ***Average percent of need met:*** 85. ***Average financial aid package:*** $14,092. ***Average need-based loan:*** $4544. ***Average need-based gift aid:*** $9063. ***Average non-need-based aid:*** $2020. ***Average indebtedness upon graduation:*** $21,520.

APPLYING

Standardized Tests *Required:* SAT or ACT (for admission).

Options: electronic application, deferred entrance.

Application fee: $55.

Required: high school transcript. ***Recommended:*** essay or personal statement.

Application deadlines: 1/31 (freshmen), 4/1 (transfers).

Notification: 4/15 (freshmen), continuous until 6/1 (transfers).

CONTACT

Ms. Clara Capron, Assistant Vice President, Enrollment and Student Services, Western Washington University, 516 High Street, Bellingham, WA 98225-9009. *Phone:* 360-650-2422. *Fax:* 360-650-7369. *E-mail:* admit@wwu.edu.

Whitman College

Walla Walla, Washington

http://www.whitman.edu/

- **Independent** 4-year, founded 1859
- **Small-town** 117-acre campus
- **Endowment** $504.5 million
- **Coed** 1,498 undergraduate students, 98% full-time, 56% women, 44% men
- **Very difficult** entrance level, 41% of applicants were admitted

UNDERGRAD STUDENTS

1,467 full-time, 31 part-time. Students come from 42 states and territories; 26 other countries; 65% are from out of state; 0.9% Black or African American, non-Hispanic/Latino; 8% Hispanic/Latino; 5% Asian, non-Hispanic/Latino; 0.3% American Indian or Alaska Native, non-Hispanic/Latino; 6% Two or more races, non-Hispanic/Latino; 3% Race/ethnicity unknown; 4% international; 1% transferred in; 67% live on campus.

Freshmen

Admission: 3,653 applied, 1,498 admitted, 395 enrolled. ***Average high school GPA:*** 3.79. ***Test scores:*** SAT critical reading scores over 500: 96%; SAT math scores over 500: 96%; SAT writing scores over 500: 97%; ACT scores over 18: 100%; SAT critical reading scores over 600: 78%; SAT math scores over 600: 78%; SAT writing scores over 600: 77%; ACT scores over 24: 97%; SAT critical reading scores over 700: 33%; SAT math scores over 700: 29%; SAT writing scores over 700: 31%; ACT scores over 30: 62%.

Retention: 94% of full-time freshmen returned.

FACULTY

Total: 216, 71% full-time, 71% with terminal degrees.

Student/faculty ratio: 9:1.

ACADEMICS

Calendar: semesters. *Degree:* bachelor's.

Special study options: advanced placement credit, cooperative education, double majors, honors programs, independent study, internships, off-campus study, services for LD students, student-designed majors, study abroad.

Unusual degree programs: 3-2 engineering with California Institute of Technology, Columbia University, Duke University, University of Washington, Washington University in St. Louis; forestry with Duke University; international studies with Monterey Institute of International Studies; oceanography with University of Washington; teacher education with Bank Street College of Education; law with Columbia University.

Computers: 397 computers/terminals are available on campus for general student use. Students can access the following: computer help desk, free student e-mail accounts, online (class) grades, online (class) registration, online (class) schedules, course registration information. Campuswide network is available. 100% of college-owned or -operated housing units are wired for high-speed Internet access. Wireless service is available via classrooms, computer centers, computer labs, dorm rooms, learning centers, libraries, student centers.

STUDENT LIFE

Housing options: on-campus residence required through sophomore year; coed, women-only. Campus housing is university owned. Freshman campus housing is guaranteed.

Activities and organizations: drama/theater group, student-run newspaper, radio station, choral group, Associated Students, Outdoor Program, Center for Community Service, Club Sports, national fraternities, national sororities.

Athletics Member NCAA. All Division III. ***Intercollegiate sports:*** baseball M, basketball M/W, cross-country running M/W, golf M/W, lacrosse M(c)/W, rugby M(c)/W(c), skiing (cross-country) M(c)/W(c), skiing (downhill) M(c)/W(c), soccer M/W, swimming and diving M/W, tennis M/W, track and field M(c)/W(c), ultimate Frisbee M(c)/W(c), volleyball M(c)/W, water polo M(c)/W(c). ***Intramural sports:*** basketball M/W, football M/W, rock climbing M/W, soccer M/W, softball M/W, tennis M/W, ultimate Frisbee M/W, volleyball M/W.

Campus security: 24-hour emergency response devices and patrols, student patrols, late-night transport/escort service, controlled dormitory access.

Student services: health clinic, personal/psychological counseling, women's center.

COSTS & FINANCIAL AID

Costs (2014–15) ***Comprehensive fee:*** $56,028 includes full-time tuition ($44,440), mandatory fees ($360), and room and board ($11,228). Part-time tuition: $1852 per credit. ***College room only:*** $5192. Room and board charges vary according to board plan and housing facility. ***Payment plan:*** deferred payment. ***Waivers:*** employees or children of employees.

Financial Aid Of all full-time matriculated undergraduates who enrolled in 2014, 796 applied for aid, 678 were judged to have need, 274 had their need fully met. 455 Federal Work-Study jobs (averaging $1967). 143 state and other part-time jobs (averaging $1846). In 2014, 450 non-need-based awards were made. ***Average percent of need met:*** 92. ***Average financial aid package:*** $34,254. ***Average need-based loan:*** $4337. ***Average need-based gift aid:*** $28,484. ***Average non-need-based aid:*** $9104. ***Average indebtedness upon graduation:*** $19,147. ***Financial aid deadline:*** 2/1.

APPLYING

Standardized Tests *Required:* SAT or ACT (for admission).

Options: electronic application, early decision, deferred entrance.

Application fee: $50.

Required: essay or personal statement, high school transcript, 1 letter of recommendation. ***Recommended:*** interview.

Application deadlines: 1/15 (freshmen), 3/1 (transfers).

Early decision deadline: 11/15 (for plan 1), 1/1 (for plan 2).

Notification: 4/1 (freshmen), 4/20 (transfers), 12/21 (early decision plan 1), 1/25 (early decision plan 2).

CONTACT

Mr. Tony Cabasco, Dean of Admission and Financial Aid, Whitman College, 515 Boyer Avenue, Walla Walla, WA 99362-2083. *Phone:* 509-527-5176. *Toll-free phone:* 877-462-9448. *Fax:* 509-527-4967. *E-mail:* admission@whitman.edu.

See previous page for display ad and page 1738 for the College Close-Up.

Whitworth University

Spokane, Washington

http://www.whitworth.edu/

- **Independent Presbyterian** comprehensive, founded 1890
- **Suburban** 200-acre campus
- **Endowment** $107.9 million
- **Coed** 2,370 undergraduate students, 98% full-time, 59% women, 41% men
- **Moderately difficult** entrance level, 75% of applicants were admitted

UNDERGRAD STUDENTS

2,319 full-time, 51 part-time. Students come from 32 states and territories; 27 other countries; 40% are from out of state; 2% Black or African American, non-Hispanic/Latino; 9% Hispanic/Latino; 4% Asian, non-Hispanic/Latino; 0.5% Native Hawaiian or other Pacific Islander, non-Hispanic/Latino; 0.7% American Indian or Alaska Native, non-Hispanic/Latino; 5% Two or more races, non-Hispanic/Latino; 1% Race/ethnicity unknown; 2% international; 3% transferred in; 36% live on campus.

Freshmen

Admission: 4,247 applied, 3,175 admitted, 619 enrolled. ***Average high school GPA:*** 3.76. ***Test scores:*** SAT critical reading scores over 500: 84%; SAT math scores over 500: 86%; SAT writing scores over 500: 80%; ACT scores over 18: 98%; SAT critical reading scores over 600: 42%; SAT math scores over 600: 44%; SAT writing scores over 600: 38%; ACT scores over 24: 75%; SAT critical reading scores over 700: 9%; SAT math scores over 700: 10%; SAT writing scores over 700: 6%; ACT scores over 30: 22%.

Retention: 85% of full-time freshmen returned.

FACULTY

Total: 305, 58% full-time.

Student/faculty ratio: 11:1.

ACADEMICS

Calendar: 4-1-4. *Degrees:* bachelor's, master's, post-master's, and postbachelor's certificates.

Special study options: adult/continuing education programs, advanced placement credit, cooperative education, double majors, English as a second language, honors programs, independent study, internships, off-campus study, part-time degree program, services for LD students, student-designed majors, study abroad, summer session for credit. ***ROTC:*** Army (c).

Unusual degree programs: 3-2 engineering with Seattle Pacific University, University of Southern California, Washington University in St. Louis, Columbia University; nursing with Washington State University College of Nursing (WSU/CON).

Computers: 280 computers/terminals and 200 ports are available on campus for general student use. Students can access the following: campus intranet, computer help desk, free student e-mail accounts, online (class) grades, online (class) registration, online (class) schedules. Campuswide network is available. 100% of college-owned or -operated housing units are wired for high-speed Internet access. Wireless service is available via classrooms, computer centers, computer labs, dorm rooms, libraries, student centers.

STUDENT LIFE

Housing options: on-campus residence required through sophomore year; coed, men-only, women-only. Campus housing is university owned. Freshman campus housing is guaranteed.

Activities and organizations: drama/theater group, student-run newspaper, radio station, choral group, International Club, Young Life, En Christo, Hawaiian Club, intramural sports.

Athletics Member NCAA. All Division III. ***Intercollegiate sports:*** baseball M, basketball M/W, cross-country running M/W, football M, golf M/W, soccer M/W, softball W, swimming and diving M/W, tennis M/W, track and field M/W, volleyball W. ***Intramural sports:*** basketball M/W, football M/W, soccer M/W, ultimate Frisbee M/W, volleyball M/W.

Campus security: 24-hour emergency response devices and patrols, late-night transport/escort service, controlled dormitory access.

Student services: health clinic, personal/psychological counseling.

COSTS & FINANCIAL AID

Costs (2014–15) ***Comprehensive fee:*** $47,908 includes full-time tuition ($36,734), mandatory fees ($896), and room and board ($10,278). Part-time tuition: $1530 per credit hour. Part-time tuition and fees vary according to course load. ***Required fees:*** $1530 per credit hour part-time. ***Room and board:*** Room and board charges vary according to board plan and housing facility. ***Payment plan:*** installment. ***Waivers:*** senior citizens and employees or children of employees.

Financial Aid Of all full-time matriculated undergraduates who enrolled in 2014, 1,799 applied for aid, 1,605 were judged to have need, 261 had their need fully met. 863 Federal Work-Study jobs (averaging $2329). 88 state and other part-time jobs (averaging $3300). In 2014, 598 non-need-based awards were made. ***Average percent of need met:*** 80. ***Average financial aid package:*** $31,373. ***Average need-based loan:*** $4963. ***Average need-based gift aid:*** $22,974. ***Average non-need-based aid:*** $16,897. ***Average indebtedness upon graduation:*** $26,132.

APPLYING

Standardized Tests *Required for some:* SAT (for admission), ACT (for admission), SAT and SAT Subject Tests or ACT (for admission). *Recommended:* SAT or ACT (for admission).

Options: electronic application, early admission, early action, deferred entrance.

Required: essay or personal statement, high school transcript. ***Required for some:*** interview.

Application deadlines: 3/1 (freshmen), 12/1 (early action).

Notification: continuous (freshmen), 12/20 (early action).

CONTACT

Ms. Marianne Hansen, Director of Admission, Whitworth University, 300 West, Hawthorne Road, Spokane, WA 99251. *Phone:* 509-777-4347. *Toll-free phone:* 800-533-4668. *Fax:* 509-777-3758. *E-mail:* admission@whitworth.edu.

WEST VIRGINIA

Alderson Broaddus University

Philippi, West Virginia

http://www.ab.edu/

- **Independent** comprehensive, founded 1871, affiliated with American Baptist Churches in the U.S.A.
- **Rural** 170-acre campus
- **Endowment** $16.3 million
- **Coed**
- **Moderately difficult** entrance level

FACULTY

Student/faculty ratio: 15:1.

ACADEMICS

Calendar: semesters. *Degrees:* certificates, associate, bachelor's, and master's.

STUDENT LIFE

Housing options: on-campus residence required through senior year; coed, special housing for students with disabilities. Campus housing is university owned. Freshman campus housing is guaranteed.

Activities and organizations: drama/theater group, student-run newspaper, radio and television station, choral group, marching band, AAPA/Hu C. Myers Society, Alpha Beta Nu, Student Athletic Advisory Committee, Sigma Alpha Iota, Kappa Xi Omega.

Athletics Member NCAA. All Division II.

Campus security: 24-hour patrols, controlled dormitory access, emergency notification system, lighted pathways and sidewalks.

Student services: health clinic, personal/psychological counseling.

COSTS & FINANCIAL AID

Costs (2014–15) ***Comprehensive fee:*** $29,976 includes full-time tuition ($22,530), mandatory fees ($210), and room and board ($7236). Part-time tuition: $751 per credit. ***Required fees:*** $53 per term part-time. ***Room and board:*** Room and board charges vary according to housing facility.

Financial Aid Of all full-time matriculated undergraduates who enrolled in 2013, 976 applied for aid, 860 were judged to have need, 613 had their need fully met. 479 Federal Work-Study jobs (averaging $1304). 116 state and other part-time jobs (averaging $2440). In 2013, 98 non-need-based awards were made. ***Average percent of need met:*** 82. ***Average financial aid package:*** $25,574. ***Average need-based loan:*** $3719. ***Average need-based gift aid:*** $16,106. ***Average non-need-based aid:*** $10,285. ***Average indebtedness upon graduation:*** $26,765.

APPLYING

Standardized Tests *Required:* SAT and SAT Subject Tests or ACT (for admission).

Options: electronic application, deferred entrance.

Required: high school transcript, minimum 2.0 GPA. ***Required for some:*** 3 letters of recommendation, interview.

CONTACT

Mr. Zachary A Ward, Director of Admissions, Alderson Broaddus University, 101 College Hill Drive, Campus Box 2003, Philippi, WV 26416. *Phone:* 304-457-6256. *Toll-free phone:* 800-263-1549. *Fax:* 304-457-6239. *E-mail:* admissions@ab.edu.

American Public University System

Charles Town, West Virginia

http://www.apus.edu/

- **Proprietary** comprehensive, founded 1991
- **Rural** campus with easy access to Washington, DC
- **Coed** 46,997 undergraduate students, 7% full-time, 38% women, 62% men
- **Noncompetitive** entrance level

UNDERGRAD STUDENTS

3,076 full-time, 43,921 part-time. Students come from 57 states and territories; 56 other countries; 21% Black or African American, non-Hispanic/Latino; 10% Hispanic/Latino; 2% Asian, non-Hispanic/Latino; 1% Native Hawaiian or other Pacific Islander, non-Hispanic/Latino; 0.7% American Indian or Alaska Native, non-Hispanic/Latino; 4% Two or more races, non-Hispanic/Latino; 5% Race/ethnicity unknown; 0.8% international; 11% transferred in.

Freshmen

Admission: 5,387 enrolled.

FACULTY

Total: 2,290, 19% full-time, 52% with terminal degrees.

Student/faculty ratio: 22:1.

ACADEMICS

Calendar: courses start on the first Monday of each month. *Degrees:* certificates, associate, bachelor's, master's, and postbachelor's certificates (profile includes American Public University, American Military University and American Community College).

Special study options: advanced placement credit, distance learning, external degree program, independent study, internships, part-time degree program, services for LD students, summer session for credit.

Computers: Students can access the following: free student e-mail accounts, online (class) grades, online (class) registration, online (class) schedules.

STUDENT LIFE

Housing options: college housing not available.

Activities and organizations: Student Veterans of America, Saber and Scroll Historical Club, Regional-Southeast, Veterans Connect-Army, Regional-Northeast.

COSTS

Costs (2015–16) ***Tuition:*** $6000 full-time. ***Required fees:*** $400 full-time. ***Payment plan:*** installment. ***Waivers:*** employees or children of employees.

APPLYING

Options: electronic application, deferred entrance.

Required: high school transcript, orientation (no-fee).

Application deadlines: rolling (freshmen), rolling (out-of-state freshmen), rolling (transfers).

CONTACT

Ms. Terry Grant, Vice President, Enrollment Management and Student Support, American Public University System, 111 West Congress Street, Charles Town, WV 25414. *Phone:* 877-468-6268. *Toll-free phone:* 877-755-2787. *Fax:* 304-724-3788. *E-mail:* info@apus.edu.

Bethany College

Bethany, West Virginia

http://www.bethanywv.edu/

- **Independent** comprehensive, founded 1840, affiliated with Christian Church (Disciples of Christ)
- **Rural** 1300-acre campus with easy access to Pittsburgh
- **Coed** 905 undergraduate students, 79% full-time, 47% women, 53% men
- **Moderately difficult** entrance level, 62% of applicants were admitted

UNDERGRAD STUDENTS

719 full-time, 186 part-time. 68% are from out of state; 20% Black or African American, non-Hispanic/Latino; 4% Hispanic/Latino; 0.1% Asian, non-Hispanic/Latino; 0.4% Native Hawaiian or other Pacific Islander, non-Hispanic/Latino; 0.6% American Indian or Alaska Native, non-Hispanic/Latino; 3% Two or more races, non-Hispanic/Latino; 16% Race/ethnicity unknown; 2% international; 3% transferred in; 97% live on campus.

Freshmen

Admission: 1,394 applied, 865 admitted, 246 enrolled. ***Average high school GPA:*** 2.94. ***Test scores:*** SAT critical reading scores over 500: 26%; SAT math scores over 500: 24%; SAT writing scores over 500: 16%; ACT scores over 18: 70%; SAT critical reading scores over 600: 5%; SAT math scores over 600: 6%; SAT writing scores over 600: 2%; ACT scores over 24: 18%.

Retention: 70% of full-time freshmen returned.

FACULTY
Total: 98, 49% full-time, 54% with terminal degrees.

Student/faculty ratio: 12:1.

ACADEMICS
Calendar: 4-1-4. *Degrees:* bachelor's and master's.

Special study options: academic remediation for entering students, accelerated degree program, advanced placement credit, cooperative education, distance learning, double majors, English as a second language, independent study, internships, off-campus study, part-time degree program, services for LD students, student-designed majors, study abroad, summer session for credit.

Unusual degree programs: 3-2 engineering with Columbia University, Case Western Reserve University; Carnegie Mellon University (various programs), Duquesne University (Law).

Computers: 145 computers/terminals are available on campus for general student use. Students can access the following: campus intranet, computer help desk, free student e-mail accounts, online (class) grades, online (class) registration, online (class) schedules. Campuswide network is available. 100% of college-owned or -operated housing units are wired for high-speed Internet access. Wireless service is available via entire campus.

STUDENT LIFE
Housing options: on-campus residence required through senior year; coed, men-only, women-only, special housing for students with disabilities. Campus housing is university owned. Freshman campus housing is guaranteed.

Activities and organizations: drama/theater group, student-run newspaper, radio and television station, choral group, marching band, Student Government Association, Culture Clubs, Equestrian Club, Outdoors Club, Black Alliance, national fraternities, national sororities.

Athletics Member NCAA. All Division III. ***Intercollegiate sports:*** baseball M, basketball M/W, cross-country running M/W, field hockey W, football M, golf M/W, lacrosse M, soccer M/W, softball W, swimming and diving M/W, tennis M/W, track and field M/W, volleyball W. ***Intramural sports:*** baseball M(c), basketball M(c)/W(c), cheerleading M(c)/W(c), equestrian sports M/W, racquetball M(c)/W(c), skiing (downhill) M(c)/W(c), soccer M(c)/W(c), softball M(c)/W(c), tennis M(c)/W(c), ultimate Frisbee M(c)/W(c), volleyball W(c).

Campus security: 24-hour emergency response devices and patrols, late-night transport/escort service, controlled dormitory access.

Student services: health clinic, personal/psychological counseling.

COSTS
Costs (2014–15) ***Comprehensive fee:*** $35,372 includes full-time tuition ($24,836), mandatory fees ($900), and room and board ($9636). Full-time tuition and fees vary according to course load. Part-time tuition: $675 per credit hour. Part-time tuition and fees vary according to course load. ***Required fees:*** $113 per credit hour part-time. ***College room only:*** $5000. Room and board charges vary according to board plan and housing facility. ***Payment plan:*** installment. ***Waivers:*** employees or children of employees.

APPLYING
Standardized Tests *Required:* SAT or ACT (for admission).

Options: electronic application, deferred entrance.

Required: essay or personal statement, high school transcript. ***Required for some:*** SAT/ACT scores (domestic students only), TOEFL/IELTS scores (foreign students only), documentation of student involvement in extracurricular activities (recommended for all students). ***Recommended:*** minimum 2.5 GPA, 2 letters of recommendation, interview.

Application deadlines: rolling (freshmen), rolling (out-of-state freshmen), rolling (transfers).

Notification: continuous (freshmen), continuous (out-of-state freshmen), continuous (transfers).

CONTACT
Ms. Mollie Cecere, Director of Enrollment, Bethany College, Bethany College Center for Enrollment and Financial Aid, 31 E Campus Dr #4, Bethany, WV 26032. *Phone:* 304-829-7611. *Toll-free phone:* 800-922-7611. *Fax:* 304-829-7142. *E-mail:* enrollment@bethanywv.edu.

Bluefield State College

Bluefield, West Virginia

http://www.bluefieldstate.edu/

- **State-supported** 4-year, founded 1895, part of West Virginia Higher Education Policy Commission
- **Small-town** 45-acre campus
- **Coed** 1,563 undergraduate students, 80% full-time, 38% women, 62% men
- **Noncompetitive** entrance level, 38% of applicants were admitted

UNDERGRAD STUDENTS
1,251 full-time, 312 part-time. 3% are from out of state; 10% Black or African American, non-Hispanic/Latino; 0.9% Hispanic/Latino; 0.1% Asian, non-Hispanic/Latino; 0.3% American Indian or Alaska Native, non-Hispanic/Latino; 2% Two or more races, non-Hispanic/Latino; 3% international; 10% transferred in.

Freshmen
Admission: 1,046 applied, 401 admitted, 242 enrolled. ***Average high school GPA:*** 3.36. ***Test scores:*** SAT critical reading scores over 500: 24%; SAT math scores over 500: 37%; ACT scores over 18: 66%; SAT math scores over 600: 10%; ACT scores over 24: 11%; ACT scores over 30: 1%.

Retention: 60% of full-time freshmen returned.

FACULTY
Total: 130, 58% full-time, 28% with terminal degrees.

Student/faculty ratio: 15:1.

ACADEMICS
Calendar: semesters. *Degrees:* associate and bachelor's.

Special study options: adult/continuing education programs, part-time degree program.

Computers: Students can access the following: computer help desk, free student e-mail accounts, online (class) grades, online (class) registration. Campuswide network is available. Wireless service is available via entire campus.

STUDENT LIFE
Housing options: college housing not available.

Activities and organizations: drama/theater group, student-run newspaper, radio station, choral group, national fraternities, national sororities.

Athletics Member NCAA. All Division II. ***Intercollegiate sports:*** baseball M(s), basketball M(s)/W(s), cheerleading W, cross-country running M(s)/W(s), golf M(s), softball W(s), tennis M(s)/W(s). ***Intramural sports:*** badminton M/W, basketball M/W, football M, soccer M, swimming and diving M/W, table tennis M/W, volleyball M/W, water polo M/W.

Campus security: 24-hour emergency response devices and patrols, student patrols.

Student services: health clinic, personal/psychological counseling.

COSTS & FINANCIAL AID
Costs (2014–15) ***Tuition:*** state resident $5832 full-time, $243 per credit hour part-time; nonresident $11,064 full-time, $460 per credit hour part-time. ***Payment plan:*** installment. ***Waivers:*** adult students and senior citizens.

Financial Aid Of all full-time matriculated undergraduates who enrolled in 2014, 1,300 applied for aid, 1,200 were judged to have need, 150 had their need fully met. 51 Federal Work-Study jobs (averaging $2600). In 2014, 10 non-need-based awards were made. ***Average percent of need met:*** 68. ***Average financial aid package:*** $3600. ***Average need-based loan:*** $4300. ***Average need-based gift aid:*** $3800. ***Average non-need-based aid:*** $300. ***Average indebtedness upon graduation:*** $27,000.

APPLYING
Standardized Tests *Required:* SAT or ACT (for admission).

Options: early admission, deferred entrance.

Required: high school transcript, minimum 2.0 GPA.

CONTACT
Bluefield State College, 219 Rock Street, Bluefield, WV 24701-2198. *Phone:* 304-327-4067. *Toll-free phone:* 800-344-8892 Ext. 4065 (in-state); 800-654-7798 Ext. 4065 (out-of-state).

Concord University

Athens, West Virginia

http://www.concord.edu/

- **State-supported** comprehensive, founded 1872, part of State College System of West Virginia
- **Rural** 100-acre campus
- **Endowment** $22.9 million
- **Coed** 2,259 undergraduate students, 90% full-time, 55% women, 45% men
- **Minimally difficult** entrance level, 38% of applicants were admitted

UNDERGRAD STUDENTS
2,031 full-time, 228 part-time. Students come from 29 states and territories; 22 other countries; 15% are from out of state; 7% Black or African American, non-Hispanic/Latino; 1% Hispanic/Latino; 0.7% Asian, non-Hispanic/Latino; 0.4% American Indian or Alaska Native, non-Hispanic/Latino; 0.1% Two or more races, non-Hispanic/Latino; 0.4% Race/ethnicity unknown; 5% international; 6% transferred in; 36% live on campus.

Freshmen
Admission: 2,099 applied, 800 admitted, 427 enrolled. ***Average high school GPA:*** 3.31. ***Test scores:*** SAT critical reading scores over 500: 38%; SAT math scores over 500: 45%; SAT writing scores over 500: 30%; ACT scores over 18: 312%; SAT critical reading scores over 600: 8%; SAT math scores over 600: 13%; SAT writing scores over 600: 6%; ACT scores over 24: 96%; ACT scores over 30: 6%.

Retention: 67% of full-time freshmen returned.

FACULTY
Total: 212, 56% full-time, 52% with terminal degrees.

Student/faculty ratio: 15:1.

ACADEMICS
Calendar: semesters. *Degrees:* associate, bachelor's, and master's.

Special study options: academic remediation for entering students, accelerated degree program, adult/continuing education programs, advanced placement credit, cooperative education, distance learning, double majors, English as a second language, external degree program, honors programs, independent study, internships, off-campus study, part-time degree program, services for LD students, student-designed majors, study abroad, summer session for credit.

Computers: 350 computers/terminals and 1,100 ports are available on campus for general student use. Students can access the following: campus intranet, computer help desk, free student e-mail accounts, online (class) grades, online (class) registration, online (class) schedules. Campuswide network is available. 100% of college-owned or -operated housing units are wired for high-speed Internet access. Wireless service is available via classrooms, computer centers, computer labs, libraries, student centers.

STUDENT LIFE
Housing options: on-campus residence required through senior year; coed, men-only, women-only. Campus housing is university owned. Freshman campus housing is guaranteed.

Activities and organizations: drama/theater group, student-run newspaper, radio and television station, choral group, marching band, Service Groups, student government, student-run publications, intramurals, Student Activities Committee, national fraternities, national sororities.

Athletics Member NCAA. All Division II. ***Intercollegiate sports:*** baseball M(s), basketball M(s)/W(s), cheerleading M/W, cross-country running M(s)/W(s), football M(s), golf M(s)/W(s), soccer M(s)/W(s), softball W(s), tennis M(s)/W(s), track and field M(s)/W(s), volleyball W(s). ***Intramural sports:*** basketball M/W, football M, soccer M/W, tennis M/W, volleyball M/W.

Campus security: 24-hour emergency response devices and patrols, student patrols, late-night transport/escort service, controlled dormitory access.

Student services: health clinic, personal/psychological counseling.

COSTS & FINANCIAL AID
Costs (2014–15) ***Tuition:*** state resident $6422 full-time, $268 per credit hour part-time; nonresident $14,118 full-time, $588 per credit hour part-time. Full-time tuition and fees vary according to course load and program. Part-time tuition and fees vary according to course load and program. ***Required fees:*** $158 full-time. ***Room and board:*** $7818; room only: $3982. ***Payment plan:*** installment. ***Waivers:*** employees or children of employees.

Financial Aid Of all full-time matriculated undergraduates who enrolled in 2014, 1,804 applied for aid, 1,541 were judged to have need, 736 had their need fully met. 238 Federal Work-Study jobs (averaging $1352). In 2014, 204 non-need-based awards were made. ***Average percent of need met:*** 88. ***Average financial aid package:*** $8896. ***Average need-based loan:*** $3715. ***Average need-based gift aid:*** $6194. ***Average non-need-based aid:*** $3201. ***Average indebtedness upon graduation:*** $21,273. ***Financial aid deadline:*** 4/15.

APPLYING
Standardized Tests *Required:* SAT or ACT (for admission).

Options: electronic application, early admission, early decision.

Required: high school transcript, minimum 2.0 GPA. ***Required for some:*** essay or personal statement, interview. ***Recommended:*** interview.

Application deadlines: rolling (freshmen), rolling (out-of-state freshmen), rolling (transfers).

Notification: continuous (freshmen), continuous (out-of-state freshmen), continuous (transfers).

CONTACT
Mr. Kent Gamble, Director of Enrollment, Concord University, 1000 Vermillion Street, Athens, WV 24712. *Phone:* 304-384-5316. *Toll-free phone:* 888-384-5249. *Fax:* 304-384-9044. *E-mail:* admissions@concord.edu.

Fairmont State University

Fairmont, West Virginia

http://www.fairmontstate.edu/

- **State-supported** comprehensive, founded 1865, part of State College System of West Virginia
- **Small-town** 120-acre campus
- **Endowment** $22.6 million
- **Coed** 3,785 undergraduate students, 86% full-time, 55% women, 45% men
- **Minimally difficult** entrance level, 59% of applicants were admitted

UNDERGRAD STUDENTS
3,270 full-time, 515 part-time. Students come from 32 states and territories; 29 other countries; 8% are from out of state; 5% Black or African American, non-Hispanic/Latino; 2% Hispanic/Latino; 0.4% Asian, non-Hispanic/Latino; 0.1% Native Hawaiian or other Pacific Islander, non-Hispanic/Latino; 0.3% American Indian or Alaska Native, non-Hispanic/Latino; 2% Two or more races, non-Hispanic/Latino; 0.9% Race/ethnicity unknown; 3% international; 9% transferred in; 21% live on campus.

Freshmen
Admission: 3,019 applied, 1,783 admitted, 689 enrolled. ***Average high school GPA:*** 3.27. ***Test scores:*** SAT critical reading scores over 500: 35%; SAT math scores over 500: 34%; ACT scores over 18: 82%; SAT critical reading scores over 600: 9%; SAT math scores over 600: 5%; ACT scores over 24: 21%; SAT critical reading scores over 700: 3%; SAT math scores over 700: 1%; ACT scores over 30: 1%.

Retention: 63% of full-time freshmen returned.

FACULTY
Total: 325, 54% full-time, 46% with terminal degrees.

Student/faculty ratio: 15:1.

ACADEMICS
Calendar: semesters. *Degrees:* associate, bachelor's, and master's.

Special study options: academic remediation for entering students, accelerated degree program, adult/continuing education programs, advanced placement credit, cooperative education, distance learning,

double majors, English as a second language, honors programs, independent study, internships, off-campus study, part-time degree program, services for LD students, study abroad, summer session for credit. ***ROTC:*** Army (b), Air Force (c).

Computers: 1,350 computers/terminals are available on campus for general student use. Students can access the following: campus intranet, computer help desk, free student e-mail accounts, online (class) grades, online (class) registration, online (class) schedules. Campuswide network is available. Wireless service is available via entire campus.

STUDENT LIFE

Housing options: on-campus residence required through sophomore year; coed, men-only, women-only. Campus housing is university owned. Freshman campus housing is guaranteed.

Activities and organizations: drama/theater group, student-run newspaper, choral group, marching band, Alpha Phi Omega, Circle K, Society for Non-traditional Students, Criminal Justice Club, Honors Association, national fraternities, national sororities.

Athletics Member NCAA. All Division II. ***Intercollegiate sports:*** baseball M(s), basketball M(s)/W(s), cheerleading W, cross-country running M(s)/W(s), football M(s), golf M(s)/W(s), softball W(s), swimming and diving M(s)/W(s), tennis M(s)/W(s), volleyball W(s). ***Intramural sports:*** badminton M/W, basketball M/W, bowling M/W, football M, golf M/W, softball M/W, table tennis M/W, tennis M/W, volleyball M/W.

Campus security: 24-hour emergency response devices and patrols, student patrols, controlled dormitory access.

Student services: health clinic, personal/psychological counseling, legal services.

COSTS & FINANCIAL AID

Costs (2015–16) ***Tuition:*** state resident $6306 full-time, $255 per credit hour part-time; nonresident $13,306 full-time, $546 per credit hour part-time. Full-time tuition and fees vary according to location. Part-time tuition and fees vary according to course load and location. ***Room and board:*** $7800; room only: $4026. Room and board charges vary according to board plan and housing facility. ***Payment plan:*** installment. ***Waivers:*** employees or children of employees.

Financial Aid Of all full-time matriculated undergraduates who enrolled in 2013, 3,092 applied for aid, 2,561 were judged to have need, 155 had their need fully met. 143 Federal Work-Study jobs (averaging $1344). 660 state and other part-time jobs (averaging $2100). In 2013, 260 non-need-based awards were made. ***Average percent of need met:*** 65. ***Average financial aid package:*** $8643. ***Average need-based loan:*** $3791. ***Average need-based gift aid:*** $5940. ***Average non-need-based aid:*** $5299. ***Average indebtedness upon graduation:*** $26,420.

APPLYING

Standardized Tests *Required:* SAT or ACT (for admission).

Options: electronic application.

Required: high school transcript. ***Recommended:*** minimum 2.0 GPA.

Application deadlines: rolling (freshmen), rolling (transfers).

Notification: continuous (freshmen), continuous (transfers).

CONTACT

Mrs. Amie Fazalare, Director of Recruiting, Fairmont State University, 1201 Locust Avenue, Fairmont, WV 26554. *Phone:* 304-367-4892. *Toll-free phone:* 800-641-5678. *Fax:* 304-367-4789. *E-mail:* admit@fairmontstate.edu.

Glenville State College

Glenville, West Virginia

http://www.glenville.edu/

- **State-supported** 4-year, founded 1872, part of West Virginia Higher Education Policy Commission
- **Rural** 331-acre campus
- **Endowment** $13.1 million
- **Coed**
- **Noncompetitive** entrance level

FACULTY

Student/faculty ratio: 16:1.

ACADEMICS

Calendar: semesters. *Degrees:* associate and bachelor's.

STUDENT LIFE

Housing options: on-campus residence required through sophomore year; coed, men-only, women-only, special housing for students with disabilities. Campus housing is university owned. Freshman campus housing is guaranteed.

Activities and organizations: drama/theater group, student-run newspaper, choral group, marching band, Music Educators National Conference, Student Government Association, Student Support Services, Student Advisory Committee, Glenville Student Action, national fraternities.

Athletics Member NCAA. All Division II.

Campus security: 24-hour emergency response devices and patrols, student patrols, late-night transport/escort service, controlled dormitory access.

Student services: health clinic, personal/psychological counseling.

FINANCIAL AID

Financial Aid Of all full-time matriculated undergraduates who enrolled in 2014, 948 applied for aid, 847 were judged to have need, 150 had their need fully met. 134 Federal Work-Study jobs (averaging $994). 245 state and other part-time jobs (averaging $1772). In 2014, 47 non-need-based awards were made. ***Average percent of need met:*** 74. ***Average financial aid package:*** $13,554. ***Average need-based loan:*** $3753. ***Average need-based gift aid:*** $6193. ***Average non-need-based aid:*** $1967. ***Average indebtedness upon graduation:*** $27,932.

APPLYING

Standardized Tests *Required:* SAT or ACT (for admission).

Options: electronic application, deferred entrance.

Application fee: $20.

Required: high school transcript, minimum 3.0 GPA, college preparatory program. ***Required for some:*** interview.

CONTACT

Ms. Ashley Weir, Admission Counselor, Glenville State College, 200 High Street, Glenville, WV 26351-1200. *Phone:* 304-462-4128 Ext. 6133. *Toll-free phone:* 800-924-2010. *Fax:* 304-462-8619. *E-mail:* ashley.weir@glenville.edu.

Marshall University

Huntington, West Virginia

http://www.marshall.edu/

- **State-supported** university, founded 1837, part of University System of West Virginia
- **Urban** 100-acre campus
- **Coed** 9,536 undergraduate students, 85% full-time, 57% women, 43% men
- **Moderately difficult** entrance level, 77% of applicants were admitted

UNDERGRAD STUDENTS

8,142 full-time, 1,394 part-time. Students come from 43 states and territories; 38 other countries; 23% are from out of state; 6% Black or African American, non-Hispanic/Latino; 2% Hispanic/Latino; 0.7% Asian, non-Hispanic/Latino; 0.1% Native Hawaiian or other Pacific Islander, non-Hispanic/Latino; 0.4% American Indian or Alaska Native, non-Hispanic/Latino; 2% Two or more races, non-Hispanic/Latino; 3% Race/ethnicity unknown; 2% international; 7% transferred in; 21% live on campus.

Freshmen

Admission: 2,863 applied, 2,191 admitted, 1,848 enrolled. ***Average high school GPA:*** 3.4. ***Test scores:*** SAT critical reading scores over 500: 47%; SAT math scores over 500: 46%; ACT scores over 18: 89%; SAT critical reading scores over 600: 10%; SAT math scores over 600: 12%; ACT scores over 24: 33%; SAT critical reading scores over 700: 1%; SAT math scores over 700: 3%; ACT scores over 30: 4%.

Retention: 73% of full-time freshmen returned.

FACULTY

Total: 722, 68% full-time, 56% with terminal degrees.

Student/faculty ratio: 19:1.

ACADEMICS

Calendar: semesters. *Degrees:* associate, bachelor's, master's, doctoral, post-master's, and postbachelor's certificates.

Special study options: academic remediation for entering students, accelerated degree program, adult/continuing education programs, advanced placement credit, cooperative education, distance learning, double majors, English as a second language, honors programs, independent study, internships, off-campus study, part-time degree program, services for LD students, study abroad, summer session for credit. ***ROTC:*** Army (b).

Unusual degree programs: 3-2 forestry with Duke University.

Computers: 1,461 computers/terminals and 2,900 ports are available on campus for general student use. Students can access the following: campus intranet, computer help desk, free student e-mail accounts, online (class) grades, online (class) registration, online (class) schedules, Virtual Computer Lab - MU Remote and Web Conferencing. Campuswide network is available. 100% of college-owned or -operated housing units are wired for high-speed Internet access. Wireless service is available via classrooms, computer centers, computer labs, dorm rooms, learning centers, libraries, student centers.

STUDENT LIFE

Housing options: on-campus residence required through sophomore year; coed, women-only, special housing for students with disabilities. Campus housing is university owned and is provided by a third party. Freshman campus housing is guaranteed.

Activities and organizations: drama/theater group, student-run newspaper, radio and television station, choral group, marching band, Campus Crusade for Christ, Gamma Beta Phi, The International Students' Organization, Newman Association, Phi Alpha Theta, national fraternities, national sororities.

Athletics Member NCAA. All Division I except football (Division I-A). ***Intercollegiate sports:*** baseball M(s), basketball M(s)/W(s), cross-country running M(s)/W(s), golf M(s)/W(s), lacrosse M(c), rugby M(c)/W(c), soccer M(s)/W(s), softball W(s), swimming and diving W(s), tennis W(s), track and field M(s)/W(s), volleyball W(s). ***Intramural sports:*** basketball M/W, bowling M/W, football M/W, golf M/W, racquetball M/W, soccer M/W, softball M/W, swimming and diving M/W, tennis M/W, track and field M/W, volleyball M/W.

Campus security: 24-hour emergency response devices and patrols, student patrols, late-night transport/escort service, controlled dormitory access.

Student services: health clinic, personal/psychological counseling, women's center, legal services.

COSTS & FINANCIAL AID

Costs (2014–15) ***Tuition:*** state resident $5450 full-time, $227 per credit hour part-time; nonresident $13,950 full-time, $582 per credit hour part-time. Full-time tuition and fees vary according to degree level, location, program, and reciprocity agreements. Part-time tuition and fees vary according to course load, degree level, location, program, and reciprocity agreements. ***Required fees:*** $1076 full-time, $45 per credit hour part-time. ***Room and board:*** $9546; room only: $5908. Room and board charges vary according to board plan and housing facility. ***Payment plan:*** installment. ***Waivers:*** senior citizens and employees or children of employees.

Financial Aid Of all full-time matriculated undergraduates who enrolled in 2014, 7,168 applied for aid, 5,746 were judged to have need, 1,594 had their need fully met. In 2014, 785 non-need-based awards were made. ***Average percent of need met:*** 50. ***Average financial aid package:*** $10,192. ***Average need-based loan:*** $7078. ***Average need-based gift aid:*** $5984. ***Average non-need-based aid:*** $1659. ***Average indebtedness upon graduation:*** $26,625.

APPLYING

Standardized Tests *Required:* SAT or ACT (for admission).

Options: electronic application, deferred entrance.

Application fee: $30.

Required for some: high school transcript.

Application deadlines: rolling (freshmen), rolling (transfers).

Notification: continuous (freshmen), continuous (transfers).

CONTACT

Dr. Tammy Johnson, Director of Admissions, Marshall University, 1 John Marshall Drive, Huntington, WV 25755. *Phone:* 800-642-3499. *Toll-free phone:* 800-642-3499. *Fax:* 304-696-3135. *E-mail:* admissions@marshall.edu.

Ohio Valley University

Vienna, West Virginia

http://www.ovu.edu/

- **Independent** comprehensive, founded 1960, affiliated with Church of Christ
- **Small-town** 299-acre campus
- **Coed** 397 undergraduate students, 93% full-time, 45% women, 55% men
- **Minimally difficult** entrance level

UNDERGRAD STUDENTS

370 full-time, 27 part-time. 61% are from out of state; 11% Black or African American, non-Hispanic/Latino; 5% Hispanic/Latino; 0.8% Asian, non-Hispanic/Latino; 3% Two or more races, non-Hispanic/Latino; 6% Race/ethnicity unknown; 8% international; 8% transferred in; 61% live on campus.

Freshmen

Admission: 88 enrolled. ***Average high school GPA:*** 3.07. ***Test scores:*** SAT critical reading scores over 500: 30%; SAT math scores over 500: 37%; SAT writing scores over 500: 23%; ACT scores over 18: 75%; SAT critical reading scores over 600: 7%; SAT writing scores over 600: 7%; ACT scores over 24: 21%; SAT critical reading scores over 700: 3%.

Retention: 56% of full-time freshmen returned.

ACADEMICS

Calendar: semesters. *Degrees:* associate, bachelor's, master's, and postbachelor's certificates.

Special study options: academic remediation for entering students, adult/continuing education programs, advanced placement credit, cooperative education, distance learning, double majors, English as a second language, honors programs, independent study, internships, off-campus study, part-time degree program, services for LD students, student-designed majors, study abroad, summer session for credit.

Computers: Students can access the following: campus intranet, computer help desk, free student e-mail accounts, online (class) grades, online (class) registration, online (class) schedules. Campuswide network is available. Wireless service is available via entire campus.

STUDENT LIFE

Housing options: on-campus residence required through sophomore year; men-only, women-only, special housing for students with disabilities. Campus housing is university owned. Freshman campus housing is guaranteed.

Activities and organizations: drama/theater group, student-run newspaper, choral group, Social Clubs, intramural sports, Theatre Production, Acappella Choir, Ambassadors.

Athletics Member NCAA. All Division II. ***Intercollegiate sports:*** baseball M(s), basketball M(s)/W(s), cross-country running M(s)/W(s), golf M(s)/W(s), lacrosse M(s), soccer M(s)/W(s), softball W(s), volleyball W(s), wrestling M(s). ***Intramural sports:*** basketball M/W, bowling M/W, football M/W, golf M/W, soccer M/W, softball M/W, volleyball M/W.

Campus security: 24-hour emergency response devices and patrols, controlled dormitory access.

COSTS & FINANCIAL AID

Costs (2014–15) ***Comprehensive fee:*** $26,270 includes full-time tuition ($17,510), mandatory fees ($1750), and room and board ($7010). Full-time tuition and fees vary according to course load and program. Part-time tuition: $525 per credit hour. Part-time tuition and fees vary according to class time, course load, and program. ***Required fees:*** $75 per credit hour part-time. ***College room only:*** $3500. Room and board charges vary according to board plan and housing facility. ***Payment plan:*** installment. ***Waivers:*** employees or children of employees.

Financial Aid Of all full-time matriculated undergraduates who enrolled in 2012, 377 applied for aid, 324 were judged to have need, 79 had their need fully met. In 2012, 66 non-need-based awards were made. ***Average percent of need met:*** 73. ***Average financial aid package:*** $14,612. ***Average need-based loan:*** $4089. ***Average need-based gift aid:*** $11,211.

Average non-need-based aid: $5351. ***Average indebtedness upon graduation:*** $25,659.

APPLYING

Options: electronic application, early admission, early action, deferred entrance.

Required: high school transcript. ***Required for some:*** essay or personal statement, interview.

CONTACT

Mrs. Valerie Wright, Admissions Office Manager, Ohio Valley University, 1 Campus View Drive, Vienna, WV 26105. *Phone:* 304-865-6200. *Toll-free phone:* 877-446-8668. *Fax:* 304-865-6001. *E-mail:* admissions@ovu.edu.

Potomac State College of West Virginia University

Keyser, West Virginia

http://www.potomacstatecollege.edu/

- **State-supported** primarily 2-year, founded 1901, part of West Virginia Higher Education Policy Commission
- **Small-town** 18-acre campus
- **Coed**
- **Noncompetitive** entrance level

FACULTY

Student/faculty ratio: 25:1.

ACADEMICS

Calendar: semesters. *Degrees:* associate and bachelor's.

STUDENT LIFE

Housing options: on-campus residence required through sophomore year; coed. Campus housing is university owned. Freshman applicants given priority for college housing.

Activities and organizations: drama/theater group, student-run newspaper, choral group, Agriculture & Forestry Club, Black Student Alliance, Gamers & Geeks Club, Campus & Community Ministries.

Athletics Member NJCAA.

Campus security: 24-hour patrols, late-night transport/escort service, controlled dormitory access.

Student services: health clinic, personal/psychological counseling.

COSTS & FINANCIAL AID

Costs (2014–15) ***Tuition:*** state resident $3480 full-time, $145 per credit hour part-time; nonresident $9456 full-time, $394 per credit hour part-time. Full-time tuition and fees vary according to course load and degree level. Part-time tuition and fees vary according to course load and degree level. ***Room and board:*** $8230; room only: $4334. Room and board charges vary according to board plan and housing facility.

Financial Aid Of all full-time matriculated undergraduates who enrolled in 2013, 70 Federal Work-Study jobs (averaging $1300).

APPLYING

Standardized Tests *Recommended:* SAT or ACT (for admission).

Options: electronic application.

Required: high school transcript.

CONTACT

Ms. Beth Little, Director of Enrollment Services, Potomac State College of West Virginia University, 75 Arnold Street, Keyser, WV 26726. *Phone:* 304-788-6820. *Toll-free phone:* 800-262-7332 Ext. 6820. *Fax:* 304-788-6939. *E-mail:* go2psc@mail.wvu.edu.

Shepherd University

Shepherdstown, West Virginia

http://www.shepherd.edu/

- **State-supported** comprehensive, founded 1871, part of West Virginia Higher Education Policy Commission
- **Small-town** 320-acre campus with easy access to Washington, DC
- **Endowment** $24.1 million
- **Coed** 3,776 undergraduate students, 82% full-time, 59% women, 41% men
- **Moderately difficult** entrance level, 98% of applicants were admitted

UNDERGRAD STUDENTS

3,093 full-time, 683 part-time. Students come from 47 states and territories; 15 other countries; 37% are from out of state; 9% Black or African American, non-Hispanic/Latino; 3% Hispanic/Latino; 2% Asian, non-Hispanic/Latino; 0.1% Native Hawaiian or other Pacific Islander, non-Hispanic/Latino; 0.4% American Indian or Alaska Native, non-Hispanic/Latino; 0.9% Two or more races, non-Hispanic/Latino; 2% Race/ethnicity unknown; 0.4% international; 9% transferred in; 34% live on campus.

Freshmen

Admission: 1,817 applied, 1,786 admitted, 642 enrolled. ***Average high school GPA:*** 3.33. ***Test scores:*** SAT critical reading scores over 500: 53%; SAT math scores over 500: 42%; ACT scores over 18: 89%; SAT critical reading scores over 600: 12%; SAT math scores over 600: 12%; ACT scores over 24: 25%; SAT critical reading scores over 700: 1%; SAT math scores over 700: 1%; ACT scores over 30: 1%.

Retention: 68% of full-time freshmen returned.

FACULTY

Total: 363, 38% full-time, 47% with terminal degrees.

Student/faculty ratio: 16:1.

ACADEMICS

Calendar: semesters. *Degrees:* bachelor's and master's.

Special study options: academic remediation for entering students, adult/continuing education programs, advanced placement credit, cooperative education, distance learning, double majors, honors programs, independent study, internships, part-time degree program, services for LD students, study abroad, summer session for credit. ***ROTC:*** Air Force (c).

Computers: 611 computers/terminals and 150 ports are available on campus for general student use. Students can access the following: campus intranet, computer help desk, free student e-mail accounts, online (class) grades, online (class) registration, online (class) schedules, personal Web pages. Campuswide network is available. 100% of college-owned or -operated housing units are wired for high-speed Internet access. Wireless service is available via entire campus.

STUDENT LIFE

Housing options: on-campus residence required through senior year; coed, special housing for students with disabilities. Campus housing is university owned. Freshman campus housing is guaranteed.

Activities and organizations: drama/theater group, student-run newspaper, radio station, choral group, marching band, Relay for Life, Student Government Association, Ram Marching Band, Sigma Sigma Sigma, Alpha Phi Omega, national fraternities, national sororities.

Athletics Member NCAA. All Division II. ***Intercollegiate sports:*** baseball M(s), basketball M(s)/W(s), football M(s), golf M(s), lacrosse W(s), soccer M(s)/W(s), softball W(s), tennis M(s)/W(s), volleyball W(s). ***Intramural sports:*** basketball M/W, football M/W, racquetball M/W, soccer M/W, softball M/W, ultimate Frisbee M/W, volleyball M/W.

Campus security: 24-hour emergency response devices and patrols, late-night transport/escort service, controlled dormitory access, student security in academic buildings, RAVE emergency alert system.

Student services: health clinic, personal/psychological counseling.

COSTS & FINANCIAL AID

Costs (2015–16) ***Tuition:*** state resident $6830 full-time, $286 per credit hour part-time; nonresident $16,628 full-time, $693 per credit hour part-time. Full-time tuition and fees vary according to program and reciprocity agreements. Part-time tuition and fees vary according to program. ***Room and board:*** $9682. Room and board charges vary according to board plan and housing facility. ***Payment plan:*** installment. ***Waivers:*** minority students, senior citizens, and employees or children of employees.

Financial Aid Of all full-time matriculated undergraduates who enrolled in 2014, 2,861 applied for aid, 2,025 were judged to have need, 638 had their need fully met. 109 Federal Work-Study jobs (averaging $661). 535 state and other part-time jobs (averaging $2467). In 2014, 642 non-need-based awards were made. ***Average percent of need met:*** 78. ***Average financial aid package:*** $11,874. ***Average need-based loan:*** $4150. ***Average need-based gift aid:*** $5076. ***Average non-need-based aid:*** $10,377. ***Average indebtedness upon graduation:*** $27,938.

APPLYING

Standardized Tests *Required:* SAT or ACT (for admission).

Options: electronic application, early admission, early action, deferred entrance.

Application fee: $45.

Required: high school transcript, minimum 2.0 GPA. ***Recommended:*** essay or personal statement, minimum 3.0 GPA, 2 letters of recommendation.

Application deadlines: rolling (freshmen), rolling (out-of-state freshmen), rolling (transfers), 11/15 (early action).

Notification: continuous until 8/15 (freshmen), continuous until 8/15 (out-of-state freshmen), continuous until 8/15 (transfers), 12/15 (early action).

CONTACT

Ms. Kristen Lorenz, Director of Admissions, Shepherd University, PO Box 5000, Shepherdstown, WV 25443-5000. *Phone:* 304-876-5212. *Toll-free phone:* 800-344-5231. *Fax:* 304-876-5165. *E-mail:* admissions@shepherd.edu.

University of Charleston

Charleston, West Virginia

http://www.ucwv.edu/

- **Independent** comprehensive, founded 1888
- **Urban** 40-acre campus
- **Coed** 1,549 undergraduate students, 87% full-time, 57% women, 43% men
- **Moderately difficult** entrance level, 61% of applicants were admitted

UNDERGRAD STUDENTS

1,355 full-time, 194 part-time. 10% Black or African American, non-Hispanic/Latino; 3% Hispanic/Latino; 1% Asian, non-Hispanic/Latino; 0.1% Native Hawaiian or other Pacific Islander, non-Hispanic/Latino; 1% American Indian or Alaska Native, non-Hispanic/Latino; 0.7% Two or more races, non-Hispanic/Latino; 11% Race/ethnicity unknown; 7% international; 47% live on campus.

Freshmen

Admission: 1,787 applied, 1,086 admitted, 335 enrolled. ***Average high school GPA:*** 3.3. ***Test scores:*** SAT critical reading scores over 500: 39%; SAT math scores over 500: 49%; ACT scores over 18: 85%; SAT critical reading scores over 600: 8%; SAT math scores over 600: 14%; ACT scores over 24: 21%; SAT critical reading scores over 700: 1%; ACT scores over 30: 1%.

Retention: 61% of full-time freshmen returned.

FACULTY

Total: 174, 58% full-time.

Student/faculty ratio: 15:1.

ACADEMICS

Calendar: semesters. *Degrees:* associate, bachelor's, master's, and doctoral.

Special study options: academic remediation for entering students, accelerated degree program, adult/continuing education programs, advanced placement credit, cooperative education, distance learning, double majors, English as a second language, independent study, internships, part-time degree program, services for LD students, student-designed majors, study abroad, summer session for credit. ***ROTC:*** Army (b).

Computers: 200 computers/terminals are available on campus for general student use. Students can access the following: campus intranet, computer help desk, free student e-mail accounts, online (class) grades, online (class) registration, online (class) schedules. Campuswide network is available. 100% of college-owned or -operated housing units are wired for high-speed Internet access. Wireless service is available via entire campus.

STUDENT LIFE

Housing options: on-campus residence required through sophomore year; coed, special housing for students with disabilities. Campus housing is university owned. Freshman campus housing is guaranteed.

Activities and organizations: student-run newspaper, choral group, Student Activities Board, American Society of Interior Designers, Student Government Association, Capito Association of Nursing Students, International Student Organization, national fraternities, national sororities.

Athletics Member NCAA. All Division II. ***Intercollegiate sports:*** baseball M(s), basketball M(s)/W(s), cheerleading W(s), crew W(s), cross-country running W(s), football M(s), golf M(s)/W(s), soccer M(s)/W(s), softball W(s), swimming and diving M(s)/W(s), tennis M(s)/W(s), track and field M(s)/W(s), volleyball M(s)/W(s). ***Intramural sports:*** basketball M/W, bowling M/W, football M/W, tennis M/W, volleyball M/W, water polo M/W.

Campus security: 24-hour emergency response devices and patrols, student patrols, late-night transport/escort service, controlled dormitory access, radio connection to city police and ambulance.

Student services: health clinic, personal/psychological counseling.

COSTS & FINANCIAL AID

Costs (2014–15) ***Comprehensive fee:*** $33,300 includes full-time tuition ($23,000), mandatory fees ($1200), and room and board ($9100). Full-time tuition and fees vary according to location, program, and student level. Part-time tuition and fees vary according to course load, location, and program. ***Room and board:*** Room and board charges vary according to board plan, housing facility, and location. ***Payment plan:*** installment. ***Waivers:*** children of alumni, senior citizens, and employees or children of employees.

Financial Aid Of all full-time matriculated undergraduates who enrolled in 2013, 1,049 applied for aid, 1,014 were judged to have need, 219 had their need fully met. In 2013, 190 non-need-based awards were made. ***Average percent of need met:*** 74. ***Average financial aid package:*** $17,500. ***Average need-based loan:*** $4050. ***Average need-based gift aid:*** $9490. ***Average non-need-based aid:*** $10,971. ***Financial aid deadline:*** 8/15.

APPLYING

Standardized Tests *Required:* SAT or ACT (for admission).

Options: electronic application, early admission, deferred entrance.

Application fee: $25.

Required: high school transcript, minimum 2.3 GPA. ***Required for some:*** interview. ***Recommended:*** essay or personal statement.

Application deadlines: rolling (freshmen), rolling (out-of-state freshmen), rolling (transfers).

Notification: continuous (freshmen), continuous (out-of-state freshmen), continuous (transfers).

CONTACT

Sandy Dolin, Application Coordinator, University of Charleston, 2300 MacCorkle Avenue, SE, Charleston, WV 25304. *Phone:* 304-357-4752. *Toll-free phone:* 800-995-GOUC. *E-mail:* admissions@ucwv.edu.

West Liberty University

West Liberty, West Virginia

http://www.westliberty.edu/

- **State-supported** comprehensive, founded 1837, part of West Virginia Higher Education Policy Commission
- **Rural** campus
- **Coed** 2,530 undergraduate students, 83% full-time, 60% women, 40% men
- **Minimally difficult** entrance level, 72% of applicants were admitted

UNDERGRAD STUDENTS

2,099 full-time, 431 part-time. 30% are from out of state; 5% Black or African American, non-Hispanic/Latino; 0.9% Hispanic/Latino; 0.6%

Asian, non-Hispanic/Latino; 0.3% American Indian or Alaska Native, non-Hispanic/Latino; 1% Two or more races, non-Hispanic/Latino; 3% Race/ethnicity unknown; 1% international; 7% transferred in; 44% live on campus.

Freshmen
Admission: 1,896 applied, 1,372 admitted, 468 enrolled. ***Average high school GPA:*** 3.32. ***Test scores:*** SAT critical reading scores over 500: 33%; SAT math scores over 500: 43%; SAT writing scores over 500: 21%; ACT scores over 18: 78%; SAT critical reading scores over 600: 12%; SAT math scores over 600: 7%; SAT writing scores over 600: 5%; ACT scores over 24: 24%; ACT scores over 30: 3%.

Retention: 66% of full-time freshmen returned.

ACADEMICS
Calendar: semesters. *Degrees:* associate, bachelor's, and master's.

Special study options: academic remediation for entering students, accelerated degree program, adult/continuing education programs, advanced placement credit, cooperative education, distance learning, double majors, external degree program, honors programs, independent study, internships, off-campus study, part-time degree program, services for LD students, student-designed majors, study abroad, summer session for credit.

Computers: Students can access the following: campus intranet, computer help desk, free student e-mail accounts, online (class) grades, online (class) registration, online (class) schedules. Campuswide network is available. 100% of college-owned or -operated housing units are wired for high-speed Internet access. Wireless service is available via classrooms, computer labs, dorm rooms, learning centers, libraries, student centers.

STUDENT LIFE
Housing options: coed, men-only, women-only, special housing for students with disabilities. Campus housing is university owned.

Athletics Member NCAA. All Division II. ***Intercollegiate sports:*** baseball M(s), basketball M(s)/W(s), cross-country running M(s)/W(s), football M(s), golf M(s)/W(s), softball W(s), tennis M(s)/W(s), track and field M(s)/W(s), volleyball W(s), wrestling M(s). ***Intramural sports:*** basketball M/W, golf M/W, racquetball M/W, softball M/W, table tennis M/W, tennis M/W, volleyball M/W.

Campus security: 24-hour emergency response devices and patrols, controlled dormitory access.

COSTS & FINANCIAL AID
Costs (2014–15) ***One-time required fee:*** $150. ***Tuition:*** state resident $6412 full-time, $261 per semester hour part-time; nonresident $13,540 full-time, $558 per semester hour part-time. Full-time tuition and fees vary according to course load, degree level, and program. Part-time tuition and fees vary according to course load, degree level, and program. ***Room and board:*** $8550; room only: $4720. Room and board charges vary according to housing facility and location. ***Payment plans:*** installment, deferred payment. ***Waivers:*** senior citizens and employees or children of employees.

Financial Aid Of all full-time matriculated undergraduates who enrolled in 2010, 2,138 applied for aid, 1,799 were judged to have need, 391 had their need fully met. In 2010, 43 non-need-based awards were made. ***Average percent of need met:*** 70. ***Average financial aid package:*** $7990. ***Average need-based loan:*** $3974. ***Average need-based gift aid:*** $5196. ***Average non-need-based aid:*** $1507. ***Average indebtedness upon graduation:*** $25,000.

APPLYING
Standardized Tests *Required:* SAT or ACT (for admission).

Options: electronic application.

Required: high school transcript, minimum 2.0 GPA. ***Recommended:*** interview.

CONTACT
Ms. Stephanie North, Admissions Counselor, West Liberty University, 208 University Drive, West Liberty, WV 26074. *Phone:* 304-336-8078. *Toll-free phone:* 800-732-6204 (in-state); 866-WESTLIB (out-of-state). *Fax:* 304-336-8403. *E-mail:* wladmsn1@westliberty.edu.

West Virginia State University

Institute, West Virginia

http://www.wvstateu.edu/

- **State-supported** comprehensive, founded 1891, part of State College System of West Virginia
- **Suburban** 98-acre campus
- **Endowment** $4.4 million
- **Coed** 2,836 undergraduate students, 69% full-time, 55% women, 45% men
- **Minimally difficult** entrance level, 41% of applicants were admitted

UNDERGRAD STUDENTS
1,950 full-time, 886 part-time. Students come from 20 states and territories; 4 other countries; 8% are from out of state; 10% Black or African American, non-Hispanic/Latino; 0.5% Hispanic/Latino; 0.4% Asian, non-Hispanic/Latino; 0.5% American Indian or Alaska Native, non-Hispanic/Latino; 40% Race/ethnicity unknown; 0.5% international; 9% transferred in; 12% live on campus.

Freshmen
Admission: 2,587 applied, 1,068 admitted, 414 enrolled. ***Average high school GPA:*** 3.05. ***Test scores:*** ACT scores over 18: 77%; ACT scores over 24: 11%.

Retention: 58% of full-time freshmen returned.

FACULTY
Total: 195, 56% full-time.

Student/faculty ratio: 17:1.

ACADEMICS
Calendar: semesters. *Degrees:* bachelor's, master's, and postbachelor's certificates.

Special study options: academic remediation for entering students, accelerated degree program, adult/continuing education programs, advanced placement credit, cooperative education, double majors, external degree program, honors programs, internships, part-time degree program, services for LD students, summer session for credit. ***ROTC:*** Army (b).

Computers: 625 computers/terminals and 5,500 ports are available on campus for general student use. Students can access the following: campus intranet, computer help desk, free student e-mail accounts, online (class) grades, online (class) registration, online (class) schedules. Campuswide network is available. 100% of college-owned or -operated housing units are wired for high-speed Internet access. Wireless service is available via entire campus.

STUDENT LIFE
Housing options: on-campus residence required through sophomore year; coed. Campus housing is university owned.

Activities and organizations: drama/theater group, student-run newspaper, radio station, choral group, marching band, Student Social Work Organization 20, WVSU College Chapter - NAACP 17, CHOICES Peer Educators 13, WVSU International Student Services 13, C.E. Jones Historical Society 12, national fraternities, national sororities.

Athletics Member NCAA. All Division II. ***Intercollegiate sports:*** baseball M(s), basketball M(s)/W(s), cross-country running W(s), football M(s), golf M(s), softball W(s), tennis M(s)/W(s), volleyball W(s). ***Intramural sports:*** baseball M, basketball M/W, cheerleading W, cross-country running W, football M, golf M, softball W, tennis M/W, volleyball W.

Campus security: 24-hour emergency response devices and patrols, late-night transport/escort service, controlled dormitory access.

Student services: health clinic, personal/psychological counseling.

COSTS & FINANCIAL AID
Costs (2014–15) ***Tuition:*** state resident $6228 full-time, $254 per credit hour part-time; nonresident $14,558 full-time, $602 per credit hour part-time. Full-time tuition and fees vary according to course load and program. Part-time tuition and fees vary according to course load and program. ***Room and board:*** $10,356; room only: $6700. Room and board charges vary according to board plan and housing facility. ***Payment plan:*** installment.

Financial Aid ***Financial aid deadline:*** 6/15.

APPLYING
Standardized Tests *Required:* SAT or ACT (for admission). *Recommended:* SAT (for admission).
Options: electronic application.
Application fee: $20.
Required: high school transcript, minimum 2.0 GPA, 18 ACT (870 SAT) or higher composite.
Application deadlines: 8/20 (freshmen), 8/20 (out-of-state freshmen), 8/11 (transfers).
Notification: continuous (freshmen), continuous (out-of-state freshmen), continuous (transfers).

CONTACT
Ms. Amanda Anderson, Director of Admissions, West Virginia State University, Campus Box 197, PO Box 1000, Ferrell Hall, Room 106, Institute, WV 25112-1000. *Phone:* 304-766-3033. *Toll-free phone:* 800-987-2112. *Fax:* 304-766-5182.

West Virginia University

Morgantown, West Virginia

http://www.wvu.edu/

- **State-supported** university, founded 1867, part of West Virginia Higher Education Policy Commission
- **Small-town** 1884-acre campus with easy access to Pittsburgh
- **Endowment** $403.6 million
- **Coed** 22,563 undergraduate students, 92% full-time, 46% women, 54% men
- **Moderately difficult** entrance level, 86% of applicants were admitted

UNDERGRAD STUDENTS
20,863 full-time, 1,700 part-time. Students come from 53 states and territories; 83 other countries; 54% are from out of state; 4% Black or African American, non-Hispanic/Latino; 3% Hispanic/Latino; 2% Asian, non-Hispanic/Latino; 0.1% Native Hawaiian or other Pacific Islander, non-Hispanic/Latino; 0.1% American Indian or Alaska Native, non-Hispanic/Latino; 3% Two or more races, non-Hispanic/Latino; 0.3% Race/ethnicity unknown; 5% international; 4% transferred in; 15% live on campus.

Freshmen
Admission: 15,604 applied, 13,386 admitted, 4,868 enrolled. ***Average high school GPA:*** 3.42. ***Test scores:*** SAT critical reading scores over 500: 53%; SAT math scores over 500: 61%; ACT scores over 18: 92%; SAT critical reading scores over 600: 12%; SAT math scores over 600: 18%; ACT scores over 24: 41%; SAT critical reading scores over 700: 2%; SAT math scores over 700: 2%; ACT scores over 30: 5%.
Retention: 77% of full-time freshmen returned.

FACULTY
Total: 1,475, 73% full-time, 73% with terminal degrees.
Student/faculty ratio: 21:1.

ACADEMICS
Calendar: semesters. *Degrees:* bachelor's, master's, and doctoral.
Special study options: academic remediation for entering students, accelerated degree program, adult/continuing education programs, advanced placement credit, distance learning, double majors, English as a second language, external degree program, honors programs, independent study, internships, off-campus study, part-time degree program, services for LD students, student-designed majors, study abroad, summer session for credit. ***ROTC:*** Army (b), Air Force (b).
Unusual degree programs: 3-2 education, business/foreign language, occupational therapy, physical therapy, social work.
Computers: 1,810 computers/terminals and 1,810 ports are available on campus for general student use. Students can access the following: campus intranet, computer help desk, free student e-mail accounts, online (class) grades, online (class) registration, online (class) schedules. Campuswide network is available. 100% of college-owned or -operated housing units are wired for high-speed Internet access. Wireless service is available via entire campus.

STUDENT LIFE
Housing options: on-campus residence required for freshman year; coed, men-only, women-only, cooperative, special housing for students with disabilities. Campus housing is university owned and leased by the school. Freshman campus housing is guaranteed.
Activities and organizations: drama/theater group, student-run newspaper, radio station, choral group, marching band, Residential Hall Association, Alpha Phi Omega, WVU Greek System, Mountaineer Maniacs, Campus Crusade for Christ, national fraternities, national sororities.
Athletics Member NCAA. All Division I except football (Division I-A). ***Intercollegiate sports:*** baseball M(s), basketball M(s)/W(s), crew W(s), cross-country running W(s), golf M(s), gymnastics W(s), riflery M(s)/W(s), soccer M(s)/W(s), swimming and diving M(s)/W(s), tennis W(s), track and field W(s), volleyball W(s), wrestling M(s). ***Intramural sports:*** archery M(c)/W(c), baseball M(c), basketball M(c)/W(c), bowling M(c)/W(c), cheerleading M(c)/W(c), crew M(c)/W(c), cross-country running M(c)/W(c), equestrian sports M(c)/W(c), fencing M(c)/W(c), field hockey M(c)/W(c), football M, golf M(c)/W(c), ice hockey M(c), lacrosse M(c)/W(c), riflery M(c)/W(c), rock climbing M(c)/W(c), rugby M(c)/W(c), skiing (cross-country) M(c)/W(c), skiing (downhill) M(c)/W(c), soccer M(c)/W(c), softball M(c)/W(c), swimming and diving M(c)/W(c), table tennis M(c)/W(c), tennis M(c)/W(c), track and field M(c)/W(c), ultimate Frisbee M(c)/W(c), volleyball M(c)/W(c), wrestling M(c).
Campus security: 24-hour emergency response devices and patrols, student patrols, late-night transport/escort service, controlled dormitory access, patrol officers just for housing.
Student services: health clinic, personal/psychological counseling, women's center, legal services.

COSTS & FINANCIAL AID
Costs (2014–15) ***Tuition:*** state resident $6960 full-time, $290 per credit hour part-time; nonresident $20,424 full-time, $851 per credit hour part-time. Full-time tuition and fees vary according to location, program, and reciprocity agreements. Part-time tuition and fees vary according to course load, location, program, and reciprocity agreements. ***Room and board:*** $9582. Room and board charges vary according to board plan, housing facility, and location. ***Payment plan:*** installment. ***Waivers:*** senior citizens and employees or children of employees.
Financial Aid Of all full-time matriculated undergraduates who enrolled in 2014, 16,637 applied for aid, 10,511 were judged to have need, 3,852 had their need fully met. 875 Federal Work-Study jobs (averaging $1874). 1,089 state and other part-time jobs (averaging $1950). In 2014, 4325 non-need-based awards were made. ***Average percent of need met:*** 75. ***Average financial aid package:*** $9060. ***Average need-based loan:*** $5214. ***Average need-based gift aid:*** $6601. ***Average non-need-based aid:*** $2554. ***Average indebtedness upon graduation:*** $27,332. ***Financial aid deadline:*** 3/1.

APPLYING
Standardized Tests *Required:* SAT or ACT (for admission).
Application fee: $60.
Required: high school transcript, minimum 2.0 GPA. ***Required for some:*** essay or personal statement, minimum 2.3 GPA.
Application deadlines: 8/1 (freshmen), 8/1 (transfers).
Notification: continuous (transfers).

CONTACT
Ms. Marilyn Potts, Director of Admissions, West Virginia University, PO Box 6009, Morgantown, WV 26506-6009. *Phone:* 304-293-2121. *Toll-free phone:* 800-344-9881. *Fax:* 304-293-3080. *E-mail:* marilyn.potts@mail.wvu.edu.

West Virginia University Institute of Technology

Montgomery, West Virginia

http://www.wvutech.edu/

- **State-supported** 4-year, founded 1895
- **Small-town** 200-acre campus
- **Endowment** $515.0 million
- **Coed** 1,261 undergraduate students, 78% full-time, 39% women, 61% men
- **Minimally difficult** entrance level, 62% of applicants were admitted

UNDERGRAD STUDENTS
978 full-time, 283 part-time. Students come from 35 states and territories; 23 other countries; 18% are from out of state; 7% Black or African American, non-Hispanic/Latino; 4% Hispanic/Latino; 1% Asian, non-Hispanic/Latino; 0.4% American Indian or Alaska Native, non-Hispanic/Latino; 3% Two or more races, non-Hispanic/Latino; 2% Race/ethnicity unknown; 7% international; 8% transferred in; 35% live on campus.

Freshmen
Admission: 733 applied, 452 admitted, 264 enrolled. ***Average high school GPA:*** 3.21. ***Test scores:*** ACT scores over 18: 72%; ACT scores over 24: 20%; ACT scores over 30: 1%.

Retention: 53% of full-time freshmen returned.

FACULTY
Total: 102, 81% full-time, 72% with terminal degrees.

Student/faculty ratio: 12:1.

ACADEMICS
Calendar: semesters. *Degrees:* bachelor's and postbachelor's certificates.

Special study options: academic remediation for entering students, advanced placement credit, cooperative education, distance learning, double majors, independent study, internships, part-time degree program, services for LD students, student-designed majors, study abroad, summer session for credit. ***ROTC:*** Army (b).

Unusual degree programs: 3-2 teacher education with West Virginia University.

Computers: 200 computers/terminals are available on campus for general student use. Students can access the following: computer help desk, free student e-mail accounts, online (class) grades, online (class) registration, online (class) schedules, electronic course materials through eCampus. Campuswide network is available. 100% of college-owned or -operated housing units are wired for high-speed Internet access. Wireless service is available via classrooms, computer centers, computer labs, dorm rooms, learning centers, libraries, student centers.

STUDENT LIFE
Housing options: on-campus residence required through sophomore year; coed. Campus housing is university owned. Freshman campus housing is guaranteed.

Activities and organizations: drama/theater group, student-run newspaper, Christian Student Union, Student Activities Board, Alpha Phi Omega, Student Government Association, American Society of Mechanical Engineers, national fraternities, national sororities.

Athletics Member NAIA, USCAA. ***Intercollegiate sports:*** baseball M(s), basketball M(s)/W(s), cheerleading M(s)/W(s), cross-country running M(s)/W(s), golf M(s), soccer M(s)/W(s), softball W(s), swimming and diving M(s)/W(s), volleyball W(s), wrestling M(s). ***Intramural sports:*** badminton M(c)/W(c), basketball M(c)/W(c), soccer M(c)/W(c), ultimate Frisbee M(c)/W(c), volleyball M(c)/W(c).

Campus security: 24-hour emergency response devices and patrols.

Student services: health clinic, personal/psychological counseling.

COSTS & FINANCIAL AID
Costs (2014–15) ***Tuition:*** state resident $6048 full-time, $252 per credit hour part-time; nonresident $15,192 full-time, $633 per credit hour part-time. Full-time tuition and fees vary according to program. Part-time tuition and fees vary according to course load and program. ***Room and board:*** $8902; room only: $5192. Room and board charges vary according to board plan and housing facility. ***Payment plan:*** installment. ***Waivers:*** senior citizens.

Financial Aid Of all full-time matriculated undergraduates who enrolled in 2014, 973 applied for aid, 822 were judged to have need, 97 had their need fully met. 28 Federal Work-Study jobs (averaging $1521). 122 state and other part-time jobs (averaging $2023). In 2014, 128 non-need-based awards were made. ***Average percent of need met:*** 76. ***Average financial aid package:*** $7398. ***Average need-based loan:*** $3942. ***Average need-based gift aid:*** $5095. ***Average non-need-based aid:*** $2397. ***Average indebtedness upon graduation:*** $27,663.

APPLYING
Standardized Tests *Required:* SAT or ACT (for admission). *Required for some:* TOEFL or IELTS.

Options: electronic application, early admission.

Required: high school transcript, minimum 2.0 GPA, Must have minimum ACT composite score of 18 or 870 SAT math + verbal; Requirement waived for students having 3.0 HS GPA or higher.

Application deadlines: rolling (freshmen), rolling (out-of-state freshmen), rolling (transfers).

Notification: continuous until 8/15 (freshmen), continuous (out-of-state freshmen), continuous until 8/15 (transfers).

CONTACT
William Allen Jr., Dean of Enrollment Services, West Virginia University Institute of Technology, Old Main Box 80, 405 Fayette Pike, Montgomery, WV 25136. *Phone:* 304-442-3146. *Toll-free phone:* 888-554-8324. *Fax:* 304-442-3067. *E-mail:* Tech-Admissions@mail.wvu.edu.

West Virginia Wesleyan College

Buckhannon, West Virginia

http://www.wvwc.edu/

- **Independent** comprehensive, founded 1890, affiliated with United Methodist Church
- **Small-town** 180-acre campus
- **Endowment** $44.9 million
- **Coed** 1,390 undergraduate students, 98% full-time, 54% women, 46% men
- **Moderately difficult** entrance level, 78% of applicants were admitted

UNDERGRAD STUDENTS
1,357 full-time, 33 part-time. Students come from 32 states and territories; 16 other countries; 38% are from out of state; 9% Black or African American, non-Hispanic/Latino; 2% Hispanic/Latino; 0.1% Asian, non-Hispanic/Latino; 0.1% Native Hawaiian or other Pacific Islander, non-Hispanic/Latino; 0.3% American Indian or Alaska Native, non-Hispanic/Latino; 3% Two or more races, non-Hispanic/Latino; 1% Race/ethnicity unknown; 5% international; 3% transferred in; 81% live on campus.

Freshmen
Admission: 1,789 applied, 1,388 admitted, 416 enrolled. ***Average high school GPA:*** 3.49. ***Test scores:*** SAT critical reading scores over 500: 42%; SAT math scores over 500: 43%; SAT writing scores over 500: 38%; ACT scores over 18: 88%; SAT critical reading scores over 600: 9%; SAT math scores over 600: 12%; SAT writing scores over 600: 8%; ACT scores over 24: 44%; SAT critical reading scores over 700: 2%; SAT math scores over 700: 2%; SAT writing scores over 700: 1%; ACT scores over 30: 5%.

Retention: 73% of full-time freshmen returned.

FACULTY
Total: 152, 59% full-time, 52% with terminal degrees.

Student/faculty ratio: 13:1.

ACADEMICS
Calendar: semesters. *Degrees:* bachelor's and master's.

Special study options: academic remediation for entering students, advanced placement credit, double majors, English as a second language, honors programs, independent study, internships, off-campus study, part-time degree program, services for LD students, student-designed majors, study abroad, summer session for credit.

Unusual degree programs: 3-2 engineering with University of Virginia, West Virginia University, Virginia Polytechnic Institute and State University.

Computers: Students can access the following: campus intranet, computer help desk, free student e-mail accounts, online (class) grades, online (class) registration, online (class) schedules. Campuswide network is available. 100% of college-owned or -operated housing units are wired for high-speed Internet access. Wireless service is available via entire campus.

STUDENT LIFE

Housing options: on-campus residence required through senior year; coed, men-only, women-only, special housing for students with disabilities. Campus housing is university owned. Freshman campus housing is guaranteed.

Activities and organizations: drama/theater group, student-run newspaper, radio station, choral group, marching band, Campus Activities Board, Green Club, WE LEAD, Wesleyan Ambassadors, Enactus, national fraternities, national sororities.

Athletics Member NCAA. All Division II. ***Intercollegiate sports:*** baseball M(s), basketball M(s)/W(s), cheerleading M/W, cross-country running M(s)/W(s), football M(s), golf M(s)/W(s), lacrosse M(c)/W(s), skiing (downhill) M(c)/W(c), soccer M(s)/W(s), softball W(s), swimming and diving M(s)/W(s), tennis M(s)/W(s), track and field M(s)/W(s), volleyball W(s). ***Intramural sports:*** basketball M/W, bowling M/W, football M/W, golf M/W, racquetball M/W, soccer M/W, softball M/W, table tennis M/W, volleyball M/W, water polo M/W.

Campus security: 24-hour emergency response devices and patrols, student patrols, late-night transport/escort service, controlled dormitory access.

Student services: health clinic, personal/psychological counseling.

COSTS & FINANCIAL AID

Costs (2015–16) ***Comprehensive fee:*** $32,832 includes full-time tuition ($27,614), mandatory fees ($1178), and room and board ($4040). Full-time tuition and fees vary according to course load and student level. Part-time tuition and fees vary according to course load. ***College room only:*** $4026. Room and board charges vary according to housing facility. ***Payment plan:*** installment. ***Waivers:*** employees or children of employees.

Financial Aid Of all full-time matriculated undergraduates who enrolled in 2013, 1,179 applied for aid, 1,071 were judged to have need, 335 had their need fully met. In 2013, 260 non-need-based awards were made. ***Average percent of need met:*** 86. ***Average financial aid package:*** $28,234. ***Average need-based loan:*** $7376. ***Average need-based gift aid:*** $18,582. ***Average non-need-based aid:*** $14,178. ***Average indebtedness upon graduation:*** $28,232.

APPLYING

Standardized Tests *Required:* SAT or ACT (for admission). *Required for some:* SAT Subject Tests (for admission).

Options: electronic application, deferred entrance.

Application fee: $35.

Required: high school transcript. ***Recommended:*** essay or personal statement, interview.

Notification: continuous (freshmen), continuous (transfers).

CONTACT

John Waltz, Director of Admission, West Virginia Wesleyan College, 59 College Avenue, Buckhannon, WV 26201. *Phone:* 304-473-8510. *Toll-free phone:* 800-722-9933. *Fax:* 304-473-8108. *E-mail:* admission@wvwc.edu.

See below for display ad and page 1734 for the College Close-Up.

Wheeling Jesuit University

Wheeling, West Virginia

http://www.wju.edu/

- **Independent Roman Catholic (Jesuit)** comprehensive, founded 1954
- **Suburban** 65-acre campus with easy access to Pittsburgh
- **Endowment** $16.1 million
- **Coed** 1,187 undergraduate students, 81% full-time, 53% women, 47% men
- **Moderately difficult** entrance level, 63% of applicants were admitted

UNDERGRAD STUDENTS

964 full-time, 223 part-time. Students come from 33 states and territories; 21 other countries; 66% are from out of state; 6% Black or African

American, non-Hispanic/Latino; 2% Hispanic/Latino; 1% Asian, non-Hispanic/Latino; 0.2% Native Hawaiian or other Pacific Islander, non-Hispanic/Latino; 0.4% American Indian or Alaska Native, non-Hispanic/Latino; 2% Two or more races, non-Hispanic/Latino; 8% Race/ethnicity unknown; 4% international; 4% transferred in; 61% live on campus.

Freshmen
Admission: 1,445 applied, 905 admitted, 252 enrolled. ***Average high school GPA:*** 3.38. ***Test scores:*** SAT critical reading scores over 500: 44%; SAT math scores over 500: 53%; SAT writing scores over 500: 34%; ACT scores over 18: 95%; SAT critical reading scores over 600: 8%; SAT math scores over 600: 13%; SAT writing scores over 600: 9%; ACT scores over 24: 36%; SAT critical reading scores over 700: 3%; SAT math scores over 700: 4%; SAT writing scores over 700: 2%; ACT scores over 30: 4%.

Retention: 74% of full-time freshmen returned.

FACULTY
Total: 162, 54% full-time, 52% with terminal degrees.

Student/faculty ratio: 12:1.

ACADEMICS
Calendar: semesters. *Degrees:* bachelor's, master's, doctoral, post-master's, and postbachelor's certificates.

Special study options: academic remediation for entering students, accelerated degree program, adult/continuing education programs, advanced placement credit, distance learning, double majors, English as a second language, honors programs, independent study, internships, off-campus study, part-time degree program, services for LD students, student-designed majors, study abroad, summer session for credit.

Unusual degree programs: 3-2 engineering with Case Western Reserve University, West Virginia University.

Computers: 215 computers/terminals are available on campus for general student use. Students can access the following: campus intranet, computer help desk, free student e-mail accounts, online (class) grades, online (class) registration, online (class) schedules. Campuswide network is available. 100% of college-owned or -operated housing units are wired for high-speed Internet access. Wireless service is available via entire campus.

STUDENT LIFE
Housing options: on-campus residence required for freshman year; coed, men-only, women-only, special housing for students with disabilities. Campus housing is university owned and is provided by a third party. Freshman campus housing is guaranteed.

Activities and organizations: drama/theater group, student-run newspaper, choral group, Campus Activity Board (CAB), Theater Guild, Student Senate, International Student Club, Campus Ministry.

Athletics Member NCAA. All Division II except rugby (Division I). ***Intercollegiate sports:*** baseball M(s), basketball M(s)/W(s), cheerleading M(c)/W(c), cross-country running M(s)/W(s), golf M(s)/W(s), lacrosse M(s)/W(s), rugby M(s), soccer M(s)/W(s), softball W(s), swimming and diving M(s)/W(s), track and field M(s)/W(s), volleyball W(s), wrestling M(s). ***Intramural sports:*** basketball M/W, cross-country running M/W, football M, ice hockey M(c), racquetball M/W, soccer M/W, softball M/W, tennis M/W, ultimate Frisbee M/W, volleyball M/W.

Campus security: 24-hour patrols, late-night transport/escort service, controlled dormitory access.

Student services: health clinic, personal/psychological counseling.

COSTS & FINANCIAL AID
Costs (2014–15) ***Comprehensive fee:*** $33,500 includes full-time tuition ($27,000), mandatory fees ($1030), and room and board ($5470). Part-time tuition: $735 per credit hour. ***College room only:*** $3230. Room and board charges vary according to board plan, housing facility, and student level. ***Waivers:*** employees or children of employees.

Financial Aid Of all full-time matriculated undergraduates who enrolled in 2014, 833 applied for aid, 704 were judged to have need, 250 had their need fully met. 148 Federal Work-Study jobs (averaging $2200). 130 state and other part-time jobs (averaging $2200). In 2014, 247 non-need-based awards were made. ***Average percent of need met:*** 83. ***Average financial aid package:*** $24,604. ***Average need-based loan:*** $4760. ***Average need-based gift aid:*** $7422. ***Average non-need-based aid:*** $11,816. ***Average indebtedness upon graduation:*** $29,131.

APPLYING
Standardized Tests *Required:* SAT or ACT (for admission).

Options: electronic application, deferred entrance.

Application fee: $25.

Required: high school transcript. ***Required for some:*** interview. ***Recommended:*** essay or personal statement, minimum 3.0 GPA, 2 letters of recommendation, interview.

Application deadlines: rolling (freshmen), rolling (out-of-state freshmen), rolling (transfers).

Notification: continuous (freshmen), continuous (out-of-state freshmen), continuous (transfers).

CONTACT
Ms. Amber George, Coordinator for Undergraduate Student Services, Wheeling Jesuit University, 316 Washington Avenue, Wheeling, WV 26003. *Phone:* 304-243-2280. *Toll-free phone:* 800-624-6992 Ext. 2359. *Fax:* 304-243-2397. *E-mail:* ageorge@wju.edu.

WISCONSIN

Alverno College

Milwaukee, Wisconsin

http://www.alverno.edu/

- **Independent Roman Catholic** comprehensive, founded 1887
- **Urban** 46-acre campus
- **Endowment** $25.3 million
- **Undergraduate: women only; graduate: coed** 1,723 undergraduate students, 74% full-time, 100% women, 0% men
- **Moderately difficult** entrance level, 65% of applicants were admitted

UNDERGRAD STUDENTS
1,283 full-time, 440 part-time. Students come from 13 states and territories; 9 other countries; 5% are from out of state; 16% Black or African American, non-Hispanic/Latino; 21% Hispanic/Latino; 5% Asian, non-Hispanic/Latino; 0.3% Native Hawaiian or other Pacific Islander, non-Hispanic/Latino; 1% American Indian or Alaska Native, non-Hispanic/Latino; 3% Two or more races, non-Hispanic/Latino; 0.5% international; 7% transferred in; 12% live on campus.

Freshmen
Admission: 655 applied, 427 admitted, 198 enrolled. ***Average high school GPA:*** 3.03. ***Test scores:*** ACT scores over 18: 74%; ACT scores over 24: 14%; ACT scores over 30: 2%.

Retention: 74% of full-time freshmen returned.

FACULTY
Total: 269, 40% full-time, 66% with terminal degrees.

Student/faculty ratio: 10:1.

ACADEMICS
Calendar: semesters. *Degrees:* associate, bachelor's, master's, post-master's, and postbachelor's certificates (also offers weekend program with significant enrollment not reflected in profile).

Special study options: academic remediation for entering students, accelerated degree program, adult/continuing education programs, advanced placement credit, double majors, independent study, internships, part-time degree program, services for LD students, student-designed majors, study abroad, summer session for credit. ***ROTC:*** Army (c), Air Force (c).

Computers: 626 computers/terminals are available on campus for general student use. Students can access the following: campus intranet, computer help desk, free student e-mail accounts, online (class) registration, online (class) schedules. Campuswide network is available. 100% of college-owned or -operated housing units are wired for high-speed Internet access. Wireless service is available via classrooms, computer centers, computer labs, dorm rooms, libraries.

STUDENT LIFE

Housing options: women-only. Campus housing is university owned. Freshman campus housing is guaranteed.

Activities and organizations: drama/theater group, student-run newspaper, radio station, choral group, Student Nurses Association, Team Green, Alverno Student Wisconsin Education Association, Circle K, Gay-Straight Alliance.

Athletics Member NCAA. All Division III. ***Intercollegiate sports:*** basketball W, cross-country running W, golf W, soccer W, softball W, tennis W, volleyball W.

Campus security: 24-hour emergency response devices and patrols, late-night transport/escort service, controlled dormitory access, well-lit parking lots and pathways, emergency first-aid and CPR, crisis intervention team and plan in place.

Student services: health clinic, personal/psychological counseling.

COSTS & FINANCIAL AID

Costs (2014–15) ***Comprehensive fee:*** $31,934 includes full-time tuition ($23,784), mandatory fees ($650), and room and board ($7500). Full-time tuition and fees vary according to program. Part-time tuition: $991 per credit hour. Part-time tuition and fees vary according to program. ***Room and board:*** Room and board charges vary according to board plan and housing facility. ***Payment plans:*** installment, deferred payment. ***Waivers:*** employees or children of employees.

Financial Aid Of all full-time matriculated undergraduates who enrolled in 2014, 1,206 applied for aid, 1,147 were judged to have need. 111 Federal Work-Study jobs (averaging $1497). In 2014, 98 non-need-based awards were made. ***Average financial aid package:*** $18,262. ***Average need-based loan:*** $3836. ***Average need-based gift aid:*** $14,160. ***Average non-need-based aid:*** $8617. ***Average indebtedness upon graduation:*** $38,642.

APPLYING

Standardized Tests *Required:* SAT or ACT (for admission).

Options: electronic application, deferred entrance.

Required: essay or personal statement, high school transcript, 2.0 on any college work, ACT or SAT. ***Recommended:*** minimum 2.0 GPA, interview.

Application deadlines: rolling (freshmen), rolling (transfers).

Notification: continuous (freshmen), continuous (transfers).

CONTACT

Mr. Edward Minter, Director of Admissions, Alverno College, 3400 South 43 Street, PO Box 343922, Milwaukee, WI 53234-3922. *Phone:* 414-382-6108. *Toll-free phone:* 800-933-3401. *Fax:* 414-382-6055. *E-mail:* admissions@alverno.edu.

The Art Institute of Wisconsin

Milwaukee, Wisconsin

http://www.artinstitutes.edu/milwaukee

- **Proprietary** 4-year, part of Education Management Corporation
- **Coed**

ACADEMICS

Degrees: associate and bachelor's.

CONTACT

The Art Institute of Wisconsin, 320 East Buffalo Street, Suite 100, Milwaukee, WI 53202. *Phone:* 414-978-5000. *Toll-free phone:* 877-285-4234.

Beloit College

Beloit, Wisconsin

http://www.beloit.edu/

- **Independent** 4-year, founded 1846
- **Small-town** 84-acre campus with easy access to Chicago, Milwaukee
- **Endowment** $130.8 million
- **Coed** 1,303 undergraduate students, 96% full-time, 58% women, 42% men

UNDERGRAD STUDENTS

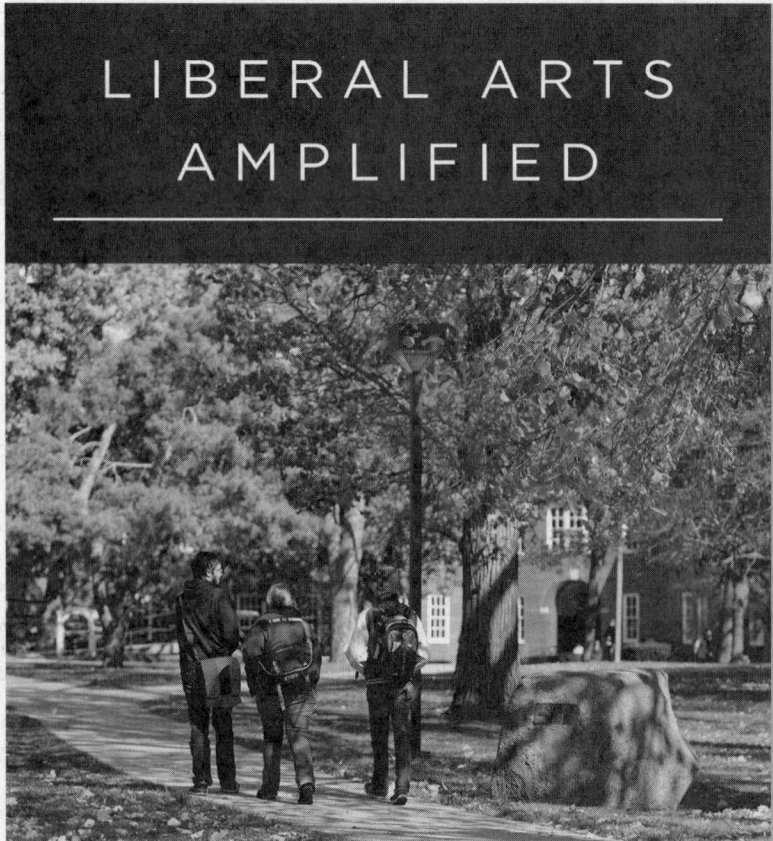

1,249 full-time, 54 part-time. Students come from 47 states and territories; 37 other countries; 81% are from out of state; 5% Black or African American, non-Hispanic/Latino; 9% Hispanic/Latino; 3% Asian, non-Hispanic/Latino; 0.2% Native Hawaiian or other Pacific Islander, non-

Hispanic/Latino; 0.4% American Indian or Alaska Native, non-Hispanic/Latino; 2% Two or more races, non-Hispanic/Latino; 2% Race/ethnicity unknown; 10% international; 2% transferred in; 87% live on campus.

Freshmen
Admission: 299 enrolled. ***Average high school GPA:*** 3.34. ***Test scores:*** SAT critical reading scores over 500: 83%; SAT math scores over 500: 93%; ACT scores over 18: 99%; SAT critical reading scores over 600: 59%; SAT math scores over 600: 59%; ACT scores over 24: 81%; SAT critical reading scores over 700: 24%; SAT math scores over 700: 16%; ACT scores over 30: 27%.

Retention: 85% of full-time freshmen returned.

FACULTY
Total: 147, 75% full-time, 86% with terminal degrees.

Student/faculty ratio: 10:1.

ACADEMICS
Calendar: semesters. *Degree:* bachelor's.

Special study options: adult/continuing education programs, advanced placement credit, double majors, English as a second language, independent study, internships, off-campus study, services for LD students, student-designed majors, study abroad, summer session for credit.

Unusual degree programs: 3-2 engineering with Students may attend any accredited engineering college. Beloit is formally affiliated with Columbia University, University of Illinois at Urbana-Champaign, University of Michigan, Rensselaer Polytechnic Institute, and Washington University-St. Louis; forestry with Beloit College offers a cooperative program with the Nicholas School of the Environment at Duke University.

Computers: 300 computers/terminals are available on campus for general student use. Students can access the following: campus intranet, computer help desk, free student e-mail accounts, online (class) grades, online (class) registration, online (class) schedules. Campuswide network is available. 100% of college-owned or -operated housing units are wired for high-speed Internet access. Wireless service is available via classrooms, computer centers, computer labs, dorm rooms, libraries, student centers.

STUDENT LIFE
Housing options: on-campus residence required through junior year; coed, women-only, cooperative. Campus housing is university owned. Freshman campus housing is guaranteed.

Activities and organizations: drama/theater group, student-run newspaper, radio and television station, choral group, BSFFA - Beloit Science Fiction and Fantasy Association, Ceramics Club, Anthropology Club, Yoga Club, Outdoor Environmental Club, national fraternities, national sororities.

Athletics Member NCAA. All Division III. ***Intercollegiate sports:*** baseball M, basketball M/W, cross-country running M/W, football M, ice hockey M(c)/W(c), lacrosse M/W, soccer M/W, softball W, swimming and diving M/W, tennis M/W, track and field M/W, ultimate Frisbee M(c)/W(c), volleyball W. ***Intramural sports:*** badminton M/W, basketball M/W, bowling M/W, football M, racquetball M/W, sailing M(c)/W(c), skiing (downhill) M(c)/W(c), soccer M/W, ultimate Frisbee M/W, volleyball M/W.

Campus security: 24-hour emergency response devices and patrols, late-night transport/escort service, controlled dormitory access.

Student services: health clinic, personal/psychological counseling.

COSTS & FINANCIAL AID
Costs (2014–15) ***Comprehensive fee:*** $49,970 includes full-time tuition ($42,220), mandatory fees ($280), and room and board ($7470). Part-time tuition: $1320 per credit hour. ***College room only:*** $4320. Room and board charges vary according to board plan. ***Payment plan:*** installment. ***Waivers:*** employees or children of employees.

Financial Aid Of all full-time matriculated undergraduates who enrolled in 2014, 950 applied for aid, 838 were judged to have need, 260 had their need fully met. 465 Federal Work-Study jobs (averaging $1891). 373 state and other part-time jobs (averaging $1176). In 2014, 340 non-need-based awards were made. ***Average percent of need met:*** 92. ***Average financial aid package:*** $33,965. ***Average need-based loan:*** $4933. ***Average need-based gift aid:*** $25,688. ***Average non-need-based aid:*** $17,256. ***Average indebtedness upon graduation:*** $28,768. ***Financial aid deadline:*** 3/1.

APPLYING
Standardized Tests *Required:* SAT or ACT (for admission).

Required: essay or personal statement, high school transcript, 1 letter of recommendation. ***Recommended:*** interview.

CONTACT
Ms. Lindsey R. Duerr, Director of Enrollment Operations, Beloit College, 700 College Street, Beloit, WI 53511-5596. *Phone:* 608-363-2500. *Toll-free phone:* 800-9-BELOIT. *Fax:* 608-363-2075. *E-mail:* admiss@beloit.edu.

See previous page for display ad and page 1362 for the College Close-Up.

Cardinal Stritch University
Milwaukee, Wisconsin
http://www.stritch.edu/

- **Independent Roman Catholic** university, founded 1937
- **Suburban** 40-acre campus with easy access to Milwaukee
- **Coed** 2,308 undergraduate students, 94% full-time, 66% women, 34% men
- **Moderately difficult** entrance level, 83% of applicants were admitted

UNDERGRAD STUDENTS
2,158 full-time, 150 part-time. Students come from 25 states and territories; 29 other countries; 13% are from out of state; 22% Black or African American, non-Hispanic/Latino; 9% Hispanic/Latino; 2% Asian, non-Hispanic/Latino; 0.2% Native Hawaiian or other Pacific Islander, non-Hispanic/Latino; 0.5% American Indian or Alaska Native, non-Hispanic/Latino; 2% Two or more races, non-Hispanic/Latino; 3% Race/ethnicity unknown; 4% international; 9% transferred in; 13% live on campus.

Freshmen
Admission: 711 applied, 590 admitted, 188 enrolled. ***Average high school GPA:*** 3.07. ***Test scores:*** SAT critical reading scores over 500: 26%; SAT math scores over 500: 26%; ACT scores over 18: 95%; ACT scores over 24: 28%; ACT scores over 30: 2%.

Retention: 72% of full-time freshmen returned.

FACULTY
Total: 461, 22% full-time.

Student/faculty ratio: 17:1.

ACADEMICS
Calendar: semesters. *Degrees:* certificates, associate, bachelor's, master's, doctoral, post-master's, and postbachelor's certificates.

Special study options: academic remediation for entering students, accelerated degree program, adult/continuing education programs, advanced placement credit, cooperative education, distance learning, double majors, English as a second language, honors programs, independent study, internships, off-campus study, part-time degree program, services for LD students, student-designed majors, study abroad, summer session for credit.

Computers: 550 computers/terminals and 1,251 ports are available on campus for general student use. Students can access the following: computer help desk, free student e-mail accounts, online (class) grades, online (class) registration, online (class) schedules. Campuswide network is available. 100% of college-owned or -operated housing units are wired for high-speed Internet access. Wireless service is available via entire campus.

STUDENT LIFE
Housing options: on-campus residence required for freshman year; coed. Campus housing is university owned and leased by the school.

Activities and organizations: drama/theater group, student-run newspaper, radio station, choral group, Student Government, Student Programming Board, Res Hall Association, Hispanic Club, University Ministry, national sororities.

Athletics Member NAIA. ***Intercollegiate sports:*** baseball M(s), basketball M(s)/W(s), bowling M(s)/W(s), cheerleading M(s)/W(s), cross-country running M(s)/W(s), golf M(s)/W(s), soccer M(s)/W(s), softball W(s), tennis M(s)/W(s), track and field M(s)/W(s), volleyball M(s)/W(s).

Campus security: 24-hour emergency response devices and patrols, controlled dormitory access.

Student services: health clinic, personal/psychological counseling.

COSTS & FINANCIAL AID

Costs (2014–15) ***Comprehensive fee:*** $34,040 includes full-time tuition ($25,920), mandatory fees ($650), and room and board ($7470). Full-time tuition and fees vary according to degree level and program. Part-time tuition: $810 per credit. Part-time tuition and fees vary according to course load, degree level, and program. ***Required fees:*** $325 per term part-time. ***Room and board:*** Room and board charges vary according to board plan and housing facility. ***Payment plan:*** installment. ***Waivers:*** employees or children of employees.

Financial Aid Of all full-time matriculated undergraduates who enrolled in 2014, 1,519 applied for aid, 1,292 were judged to have need, 120 had their need fully met. In 2014, 174 non-need-based awards were made. ***Average percent of need met:*** 52. ***Average financial aid package:*** $13,949. ***Average need-based loan:*** $3974. ***Average need-based gift aid:*** $11,704. ***Average non-need-based aid:*** $13,307. ***Average indebtedness upon graduation:*** $29,473.

APPLYING

Standardized Tests *Required for some:* SAT or ACT (for admission), TOEFL required for international students.

Options: electronic application, deferred entrance.

Required for some: high school transcript, minimum 2.0 GPA.

Application deadlines: rolling (freshmen), rolling (transfers).

Notification: continuous (freshmen), continuous (transfers).

CONTACT

Sarah C. Blake, Associate Director of Admissions, Cardinal Stritch University, 6801 N. Yates Road, Milwaukee, WI 53217. *Phone:* 414-410-4052. *Toll-free phone:* 800-347-8822 Ext. 4040. *Fax:* 414-410-4058. *E-mail:* admityou@stritch.edu.

Carroll University

Waukesha, Wisconsin

http://www.carrollu.edu/

CONTACT

Mr. James Wiseman, Vice President of Enrollment, Carroll University, 100 North East Avenue, Waukesha, WI 53186-5593. *Phone:* 262-524-7221. *Toll-free phone:* 800-CARROLL. *Fax:* 262-524-7139. *E-mail:* info@carrollu.edu.

See this page for display ad and page 1382 for the College Close-Up.

Concordia University Wisconsin

Mequon, Wisconsin

http://www.cuw.edu/

- **Independent** comprehensive, founded 1881, affiliated with Lutheran Church–Missouri Synod, part of Concordia University System
- **Suburban** 192-acre campus with easy access to Milwaukee
- **Coed** 4,377 undergraduate students, 71% full-time, 65% women, 35% men
- **Moderately difficult** entrance level, 75% of applicants were admitted

UNDERGRAD STUDENTS

3,112 full-time, 1,265 part-time. 24% are from out of state; 16% Black or African American, non-Hispanic/Latino; 3% Hispanic/Latino; 2% Asian, non-Hispanic/Latino; 0.1% Native Hawaiian or other Pacific Islander, non-Hispanic/Latino; 1% American Indian or Alaska Native, non-Hispanic/Latino; 3% Two or more races, non-Hispanic/Latino; 2% Race/ethnicity unknown; 1% international; 3% transferred in; 56% live on campus.

Freshmen

Admission: 2,582 applied, 1,947 admitted, 640 enrolled. ***Average high school GPA:*** 3.44. ***Test scores:*** SAT critical reading scores over 500: 70%; SAT math scores over 500: 60%; SAT writing scores over 500: 52%; ACT scores over 18: 96%; SAT critical reading scores over 600: 20%; SAT math scores over 600: 20%; SAT writing scores over 600: 5%; ACT scores over 24: 46%; SAT critical reading scores over 700: 10%; ACT scores over 30: 8%.

Retention: 75% of full-time freshmen returned.

FACULTY
Total: 565, 35% full-time, 39% with terminal degrees.

Student/faculty ratio: 13:1.

ACADEMICS
Calendar: 4-1-4. *Degrees:* certificates, associate, bachelor's, master's, doctoral, and post-master's certificates.

Special study options: academic remediation for entering students, accelerated degree program, adult/continuing education programs, advanced placement credit, distance learning, double majors, English as a second language, independent study, internships, off-campus study, part-time degree program, services for LD students, student-designed majors, study abroad, summer session for credit.

Computers: Students can access the following: computer help desk, free student e-mail accounts. Campuswide network is available.

STUDENT LIFE
Housing options: men-only, women-only. Campus housing is university owned. Freshman applicants given priority for college housing.

Activities and organizations: drama/theater group, student-run newspaper, radio station, choral group.

Athletics Member NCAA. All Division III. ***Intercollegiate sports:*** baseball M, basketball M/W, cross-country running M/W, football M, golf M/W, ice hockey M/W, soccer M/W, softball W, tennis M/W, track and field M/W, volleyball W, wrestling M. ***Intramural sports:*** basketball M/W, softball M/W, volleyball M/W.

Campus security: 24-hour patrols, student patrols, late-night transport/escort service, controlled dormitory access.

Student services: health clinic, personal/psychological counseling.

COSTS & FINANCIAL AID
Costs (2014–15) ***Comprehensive fee:*** $35,940 includes full-time tuition ($25,930), mandatory fees ($230), and room and board ($9780). Full-time tuition and fees vary according to program. Part-time tuition and fees vary according to program. ***Room and board:*** Room and board charges vary according to board plan.

Financial Aid Of all full-time matriculated undergraduates who enrolled in 2014, 2,645 applied for aid, 2,360 were judged to have need, 516 had their need fully met. 195 Federal Work-Study jobs (averaging $1358). In 2014, 388 non-need-based awards were made. ***Average percent of need met:*** 68. ***Average financial aid package:*** $19,601. ***Average need-based loan:*** $6659. ***Average need-based gift aid:*** $12,887. ***Average non-need-based aid:*** $10,326. ***Average indebtedness upon graduation:*** $30,880.

APPLYING
Standardized Tests *Required:* ACT (for admission).

Application fee: $35.

Required: high school transcript, minimum 2.0 GPA. ***Required for some:*** essay or personal statement, minimum 3.0 GPA, 3 letters of recommendation. ***Recommended:*** interview.

CONTACT
Ms. Julie Schroeder, Concordia University Wisconsin, Admissions Office, 12800 North Lake Drive, Mequon, WI 53097. *Phone:* 262-243-4305 Ext. 4305. *Toll-free phone:* 888-628-9472. *E-mail:* admission@cuw.edu.

DeVry University
Milwaukee, Wisconsin
http://www.devry.edu/

- **Proprietary** comprehensive, part of DeVry University
- **Coed**

ACADEMICS
Calendar: semesters. *Degrees:* associate, bachelor's, and master's.

COSTS & FINANCIAL AID
Costs (2014–15) ***Tuition:*** $17,052 full-time, $609 per credit hour part-time. ***Required fees:*** $80 full-time.

Financial Aid Of all full-time matriculated undergraduates who enrolled in 2007, 12 applied for aid, 12 were judged to have need. ***Average percent of need met:*** 35. ***Average financial aid package:*** $11,858. ***Average need-based loan:*** $7870. ***Average need-based gift aid:*** $5981.

CONTACT
Admissions Office, DeVry University, 411 East Wisconsin Avenue, Suite 300, Milwaukee, WI 53202. *Phone:* 414-278-7677. *Toll-free phone:* 866-338-7941.

Edgewood College
Madison, Wisconsin
http://www.edgewood.edu/

- **Independent Roman Catholic** comprehensive, founded 1927
- **Urban** 55-acre campus
- **Endowment** $26.1 million
- **Coed** 1,935 undergraduate students, 85% full-time, 70% women, 30% men
- **Moderately difficult** entrance level, 76% of applicants were admitted

UNDERGRAD STUDENTS
1,647 full-time, 288 part-time. Students come from 17 states and territories; 31 other countries; 7% are from out of state; 2% Black or African American, non-Hispanic/Latino; 6% Hispanic/Latino; 3% Asian, non-Hispanic/Latino; 0.1% Native Hawaiian or other Pacific Islander, non-Hispanic/Latino; 0.4% American Indian or Alaska Native, non-Hispanic/Latino; 3% Two or more races, non-Hispanic/Latino; 2% Race/ethnicity unknown; 4% international; 10% transferred in; 28% live on campus.

Freshmen
Admission: 1,253 applied, 955 admitted, 290 enrolled. ***Average high school GPA:*** 3.4. ***Test scores:*** ACT scores over 18: 97%; ACT scores over 24: 42%; ACT scores over 30: 3%.

Retention: 81% of full-time freshmen returned.

FACULTY
Total: 307, 51% full-time, 53% with terminal degrees.

Student/faculty ratio: 11:1.

ACADEMICS
Calendar: semesters. *Degrees:* certificates, bachelor's, master's, doctoral, post-master's, and postbachelor's certificates.

Special study options: academic remediation for entering students, accelerated degree program, adult/continuing education programs, advanced placement credit, cooperative education, distance learning, double majors, honors programs, independent study, internships, off-campus study, part-time degree program, services for LD students, student-designed majors, study abroad, summer session for credit. ***ROTC:*** Army (c), Navy (c), Air Force (c).

Computers: 100 computers/terminals and 200 ports are available on campus for general student use. Students can access the following: campus intranet, computer help desk, free student e-mail accounts, online (class) grades, online (class) registration, online (class) schedules, online library. Campuswide network is available. 100% of college-owned or -operated housing units are wired for high-speed Internet access. Wireless service is available via entire campus.

STUDENT LIFE
Housing options: on-campus residence required through sophomore year; coed, special housing for students with disabilities. Campus housing is university owned. Freshman campus housing is guaranteed.

Activities and organizations: drama/theater group, student-run newspaper, choral group, Circle K, Student Education Association, Student Government Association, Rotaract, Ambassadors.

Athletics Member NCAA. All Division III. ***Intercollegiate sports:*** baseball M, basketball M/W, cross-country running M/W, golf M/W, soccer M/W, softball W, tennis M/W, track and field M/W, volleyball W. ***Intramural sports:*** basketball M/W, soccer M/W, swimming and diving M/W, volleyball M/W.

Campus security: 24-hour emergency response devices and patrols, student patrols, late-night transport/escort service, controlled dormitory access, lighted pathways/sidewalks, Eagle Alert System, Public Address System, Safe Ride Shuttle, and Extensive video surveillance system.

Student services: health clinic, personal/psychological counseling.

COSTS & FINANCIAL AID
Costs (2014–15) ***Comprehensive fee:*** $34,563 includes full-time tuition ($25,590) and room and board ($8973). Full-time tuition and fees vary

according to degree level. Part-time tuition: $805 per credit. Part-time tuition and fees vary according to course load and degree level. ***Room and board:*** Room and board charges vary according to housing facility. ***Payment plan:*** installment. ***Waivers:*** employees or children of employees.

Financial Aid Of all full-time matriculated undergraduates who enrolled in 2013, 1,277 applied for aid, 1,156 were judged to have need, 131 had their need fully met. 390 Federal Work-Study jobs (averaging $2051). 807 state and other part-time jobs (averaging $1943). In 2013, 274 non-need-based awards were made. ***Average percent of need met:*** 75. ***Average financial aid package:*** $20,413. ***Average need-based loan:*** $5408. ***Average need-based gift aid:*** $14,030. ***Average non-need-based aid:*** $5020. ***Average indebtedness upon graduation:*** $31,522.

APPLYING

Standardized Tests *Required:* SAT or ACT (for admission).

Options: electronic application, deferred entrance.

Application fee: $30.

Required: high school transcript, minimum 2.5 GPA, Students must meet two of the following three requirements. Students must present a cumulative high school GPA of 2.5 on a 4.0 scale, a rank in the top 50% of their high school graduating class and/or a composite score of 18 on the ACT or an equivalent SAT score. ***Required for some:*** essay or personal statement, 2 letters of recommendation, interview.

Application deadlines: 8/1 (freshmen), 8/1 (out-of-state freshmen), 8/1 (transfers).

Notification: continuous (freshmen), continuous (transfers).

CONTACT

Ms. Christine Benedict, Vice President for Enrollment Management, Admissions Office, Edgewood College, 1000 Edgewood College Drive, Madison, WI 53711-1997. *Phone:* 608-663-2294. *Toll-free phone:* 800-444-4861 Ext. 2294. *Fax:* 608-663-2214. *E-mail:* admissions@edgewood.edu.

Globe University–Appleton

Grand Chute, Wisconsin

http://www.globeuniversity.edu/

- **Proprietary** 4-year, part of Globe Education Network (GEN) which is composed of Globe University, Minnesota School of Business, Broadview University, The Institute of Production and Recording and Minnesota School of Cosmetology
- **Small-town** 4-acre campus
- **Coed**

ACADEMICS

Degrees: diplomas, associate, and bachelor's.

STUDENT LIFE

Housing options: college housing not available.

Campus security: 24-hour emergency response devices, late-night transport/escort service.

APPLYING

Standardized Tests *Required:* ACCUPLACER is required of most applicants unless documentation of a minimum ACT composite score of 21 or documentation of a minimum composite score of 1485 on the SAT is presented (for admission).

Options: electronic application.

Application fee: $50.

Required: interview, Certification of high school graduation or GED. ***Required for some:*** 2 letters of recommendation.

CONTACT

Globe University–Appleton, 5045 West Grande Market Drive, Grand Chute, WI 54913.

Globe University–Eau Claire

Eau Claire, Wisconsin

http://www.globeuniversity.edu/

- **Proprietary** 4-year, part of Globe Education Network (GEN) which is composed of Globe University, Minnesota School of Business, Broadview University, The Institute of Production and Recording and Minnesota School of Cosmetology
- **Small-town** 5-acre campus
- **Coed**

ACADEMICS

Degrees: certificates, diplomas, associate, and bachelor's.

STUDENT LIFE

Campus security: 24-hour emergency response devices, late-night transport/escort service.

APPLYING

Standardized Tests *Required:* ACCUPLACER is required of most applicants unless documentation of a minimum ACT composite score of 21 or documentation of a minimum composite score of 1485 on the SAT is presented (for admission).

Options: electronic application.

Application fee: $50.

Required: interview. ***Required for some:*** 2 letters of recommendation, Certification of high school graduation or GED.

CONTACT

Globe University–Eau Claire, 4955 Bullis Farm Road, Eau Claire, WI 54701-5168. *Toll-free phone:* 877-303-6060 (in-state); 377-303-6060 (out-of-state).

Globe University–Green Bay

Bellevue, Wisconsin

http://www.globeuniversity.edu/

- **Proprietary** 4-year, part of Globe Education Network (GEN) which is composed of Globe University, Minnesota School of Business, Broadview University, The Institute of Production and Recording and Minnesota School of Cosmetology
- **Urban** 5-acre campus
- **Coed**

ACADEMICS

Degrees: certificates, diplomas, associate, and bachelor's.

STUDENT LIFE

Housing options: college housing not available.

Campus security: 24-hour emergency response devices.

APPLYING

Standardized Tests *Required for some:* ACCUPLACER is required of most applicants unless documentation of a minimum ACT composite score of 21 or documentation of a minimum composite score of 1485 on the SAT.

Options: electronic application.

Application fee: $50.

Required: interview. ***Required for some:*** Certification of high school graduation or GED.

CONTACT

Globe University–Green Bay, 2620 Development Drive, Bellevue, WI 54311.

Globe University–La Crosse

Onalaska, Wisconsin

http://www.globeuniversity.edu/

- **Proprietary** 4-year, part of Globe Education Network (GEN) which is composed of Globe University, Minnesota School of Business, Broadview University, The Institute of Production and Recording and Minnesota School of Cosmetology
- **Small-town** campus
- **Coed**

ACADEMICS

Degrees: certificates, diplomas, associate, and bachelor's.

STUDENT LIFE

Campus security: 24-hour emergency response devices.

APPLYING
Standardized Tests *Required:* ACCUPLACER is required of most applicants unless documentation of a minimum ACT composite score of 21 or documentation of a minimum composite score of 1485 on the SAT is presented (for admission).
Options: electronic application.
Application fee: $50.
Required: interview. ***Required for some:*** 2 letters of recommendation, Certification of high school graduation or GED.

CONTACT
Globe University–La Crosse, 2651 Midwest Drive, Onalaska, WI 54650.

Globe University–Madison East

Madison, Wisconsin

http://www.globeuniversity.edu/

- **Proprietary** 4-year, part of Globe Education Network (GEN) which is composed of Globe University, Minnesota School of Business, Broadview University, The Institute of Production and Recording and Minnesota School of Cosmetology
- **Urban** 7-acre campus
- **Coed**

ACADEMICS
Degrees: certificates, diplomas, associate, and bachelor's.

STUDENT LIFE
Housing options: college housing not available.
Campus security: 24-hour emergency response devices.

APPLYING
Standardized Tests *Required:* ACCUPLACER is required of most applicants unless documentation of a minimum ACT composite score of 21 or documentation of a minimum composite score of 1485 on the SAT is presented (for admission).
Options: electronic application.
Application fee: $50.
Required: interview, Certification of high school graduation or GED.

CONTACT
Globe University–Madison East, 4901 Eastpark Boulevard, Madison, WI 53718.

Globe University–Madison West

Middleton, Wisconsin

http://www.globeuniversity.edu/

- **Proprietary** 4-year, part of Globe Education Network (GEN) which is composed of Globe University, Minnesota School of Business, Broadview University, The Institute of Production and Recording and Minnesota School of Cosmetology
- **Small-town** campus
- **Coed**

ACADEMICS
Degrees: certificates, diplomas, associate, and bachelor's.

STUDENT LIFE
Housing options: college housing not available.
Campus security: 24-hour emergency response devices.

APPLYING
Standardized Tests *Required:* ACCUPLACER is required of most applicants unless documentation of a minimum ACT composite score of 21 or documentation of a minimum composite score of 1485 on the SAT is presented (for admission).
Options: electronic application.
Application fee: $50.
Required: interview, Certification of high school graduation or GED.

CONTACT
Globe University–Madison West, 1345 Deming Way, Middleton, WI 53562.

Globe University–Wausau

Rothschild, Wisconsin

http://www.globeuniversity.edu/

- **Proprietary** 4-year, part of Globe Education Network (GEN) which is composed of Globe University, Minnesota School of Business, Broadview University, The Institute of Production and Recording and Minnesota School of Cosmetology
- **Small-town** 5-acre campus
- **Coed**

ACADEMICS
Degrees: certificates, diplomas, associate, and bachelor's.

STUDENT LIFE
Housing options: college housing not available.
Campus security: 24-hour emergency response devices.

APPLYING
Standardized Tests *Required:* ACCUPLACER is required of most applicants unless documentation of a minimum ACT composite score of 21 or documentation of a minimum composite score of 1485 on the SAT is presented (for admission).
Options: electronic application.
Application fee: $50.
Required: interview, Certification of high school graduation or GED.

CONTACT
Globe University–Wausau, 1480 Country Road XX, Rothschild, WI 54474.

ITT Technical Institute

Green Bay, Wisconsin

http://www.itt-tech.edu/

- **Proprietary** primarily 2-year, founded 2000, part of ITT Educational Services, Inc.
- **Coed**
- **Minimally difficult** entrance level

ACADEMICS
Calendar: quarters. *Degrees:* associate and bachelor's.

STUDENT LIFE
Housing options: college housing not available.

CONTACT
Director of Recruitment, ITT Technical Institute, 470 Security Boulevard, Green Bay, WI 54313. *Phone:* 920-662-9000. *Toll-free phone:* 888-884-3626.

ITT Technical Institute

Greenfield, Wisconsin

http://www.itt-tech.edu/

- **Proprietary** primarily 2-year, founded 1968, part of ITT Educational Services, Inc.
- **Suburban** campus
- **Coed**
- **Minimally difficult** entrance level

ACADEMICS
Calendar: quarters. *Degrees:* associate and bachelor's.

STUDENT LIFE
Housing options: college housing not available.

CONTACT
Director of Recruitment, ITT Technical Institute, 6300 West Layton Avenue, Greenfield, WI 53220-4612. *Phone:* 414-282-9494.

ITT Technical Institute
Madison, Wisconsin
http://www.itt-tech.edu/

- **Proprietary** primarily 2-year, part of ITT Educational Services, Inc.
- **Coed**
- **Minimally difficult** entrance level

ACADEMICS
Degrees: associate and bachelor's.

CONTACT
Director of Recruitment, ITT Technical Institute, 2450 Rimrock Road, Suite 100, Madison, WI 53713. *Phone:* 608-288-6301. *Toll-free phone:* 877-628-5960.

★ Lawrence University
Appleton, Wisconsin
http://www.lawrence.edu/

- **Independent** 4-year, founded 1847
- **Small-town** 84-acre campus
- **Coed** 1,519 undergraduate students, 97% full-time, 54% women, 46% men
- **Very difficult** entrance level, 73% of applicants were admitted

UNDERGRAD STUDENTS
1,473 full-time, 46 part-time. 65% are from out of state; 3% Black or African American, non-Hispanic/Latino; 7% Hispanic/Latino; 4% Asian, non-Hispanic/Latino; 0.5% American Indian or Alaska Native, non-Hispanic/Latino; 4% Two or more races, non-Hispanic/Latino; 0.5% Race/ethnicity unknown; 9% international; 2% transferred in; 1% live on campus.

Freshmen
Admission: 2,747 applied, 2,004 admitted, 385 enrolled. ***Average high school GPA:*** 3.51. ***Test scores:*** SAT critical reading scores over 500: 96%; SAT math scores over 500: 95%; SAT writing scores over 500: 95%; ACT scores over 18: 99%; SAT critical reading scores over 600: 69%; SAT math scores over 600: 65%; SAT writing scores over 600: 63%; ACT scores over 24: 85%; SAT critical reading scores over 700: 23%; SAT math scores over 700: 28%; SAT writing scores over 700: 19%; ACT scores over 30: 41%.

Retention: 90% of full-time freshmen returned.

FACULTY
Total: 192, 83% full-time, 85% with terminal degrees.
Student/faculty ratio: 9:1.

ACADEMICS
Calendar: trimesters. *Degree:* bachelor's.
Special study options: advanced placement credit, double majors, independent study, internships, off-campus study, part-time degree program, services for LD students, student-designed majors, study abroad.
Unusual degree programs: 3-2 engineering with Columbia University in New York, New York, Rensselaer Polytechnic Institute in Troy, New York, Washington University in St. Louis, Missouri; forestry with Duke University; occupational therapy with Washington University in St. Louis.
Computers: Students can access the following: campus intranet, computer help desk, free student e-mail accounts, online (class) grades, online (class) registration, online (class) schedules, online transcripts, financial aid, financial account information. Campuswide network is available. 100% of college-owned or -operated housing units are wired for high-speed Internet access. Wireless service is available via classrooms, computer centers, computer labs, dorm rooms, learning centers, libraries, student centers.

STUDENT LIFE
Housing options: on-campus residence required through senior year; coed, men-only, women-only, cooperative, special housing for students with disabilities. Campus housing is university owned. Freshman campus housing is guaranteed.
Activities and organizations: drama/theater group, student-run newspaper, radio station, choral group, Lawrence Swing Dancers, Lawrence International, Outdoor Recreation Club, Sustainable Lawrence University Gardens (SLUG), Greenfire, national fraternities, national sororities.
Athletics Member NCAA. All Division III. ***Intercollegiate sports:*** baseball M, basketball M/W, crew M(c)/W(c), cross-country running M/W, fencing M/W, football M, golf M, ice hockey M/W(c), soccer M/W, softball W, swimming and diving M/W, tennis M/W, track and field M/W, ultimate Frisbee M(c)/W(c), volleyball M(c)/W. ***Intramural sports:*** badminton M/W, basketball M/W, fencing M/W, racquetball M/W, skiing (downhill) M/W, soccer M/W, softball M/W, table tennis M/W, tennis M/W, volleyball M/W, water polo M/W.
Campus security: 24-hour emergency response devices and patrols, student patrols, late-night transport/escort service, controlled dormitory access, evening patrols by trained security personnel.
Student services: health clinic, personal/psychological counseling.

COSTS & FINANCIAL AID
Costs (2014–15) ***Comprehensive fee:*** $51,465 includes full-time tuition ($42,357), mandatory fees ($300), and room and board ($8808). ***College room only:*** $4152. ***Payment plan:*** installment. ***Waivers:*** employees or children of employees.
Financial Aid Of all full-time matriculated undergraduates who enrolled in 2014, 1,079 applied for aid, 952 were judged to have need, 317 had their need fully met. 631 Federal Work-Study jobs (averaging $2105). 431 state and other part-time jobs (averaging $1937). In 2014, 451 non-need-based awards were made. ***Average percent of need met:*** 90. ***Average financial aid package:*** $35,069. ***Average need-based loan:*** $5474. ***Average need-based gift aid:*** $29,111. ***Average non-need-based aid:*** $18,007. ***Average indebtedness upon graduation:*** $33,755.

APPLYING
Options: electronic application, early admission, early decision, early action, deferred entrance.
Application fee: $40.
Required: essay or personal statement, high school transcript, 1 letter of recommendation, English Language Proficiency Exam {SAT/TOEFL/IELTS/ACT} required for some, Music majors: Music Audition. ***Recommended:*** minimum 3.0 GPA, interview.

CONTACT
Mr. Ken Anselment, Dean of Admissions and Financial Aid, Lawrence University, 711 East Boldt Way SPC 29, Appleton, WI 54911-5699. *Phone:* 920-832-6500. *Toll-free phone:* 800-227-0982. *Fax:* 920-832-6782. *E-mail:* excel@lawrence.edu.

Maranatha Baptist University
Watertown, Wisconsin
http://www.mbu.edu/

- **Independent Baptist** comprehensive, founded 1968
- **Small-town** 60-acre campus with easy access to Milwaukee
- **Coed** 942 undergraduate students, 71% full-time, 56% women, 44% men
- **Noncompetitive** entrance level, 16% of applicants were admitted

UNDERGRAD STUDENTS
670 full-time, 272 part-time. 72% are from out of state; 1% Black or African American, non-Hispanic/Latino; 3% Hispanic/Latino; 0.8% Asian, non-Hispanic/Latino; 0.3% Native Hawaiian or other Pacific Islander, non-Hispanic/Latino; 0.3% American Indian or Alaska Native, non-Hispanic/Latino; 5% Two or more races, non-Hispanic/Latino; 3% Race/ethnicity unknown; 0.9% international; 71% live on campus.

Freshmen
Admission: 1,621 applied, 262 admitted, 193 enrolled. ***Test scores:*** SAT critical reading scores over 500: 71%; SAT math scores over 500: 29%; SAT writing scores over 500: 47%; ACT scores over 18: 93%; SAT critical reading scores over 600: 18%; SAT math scores over 600: 18%; SAT writing scores over 600: 12%; ACT scores over 24: 41%; SAT critical reading scores over 700: 6%; ACT scores over 30: 5%.

Retention: 67% of full-time freshmen returned.

FACULTY
Total: 123, 32% full-time, 25% with terminal degrees.
Student/faculty ratio: 12:1.

ACADEMICS
Calendar: semesters. *Degrees:* certificates, associate, bachelor's, and master's.

Special study options: academic remediation for entering students, advanced placement credit, distance learning, double majors, independent study, internships, off-campus study, part-time degree program, study abroad, summer session for credit. ***ROTC:*** Army (b), Air Force (c).

Computers: Students can access the following: campus intranet, computer help desk, free student e-mail accounts, online (class) grades, online (class) registration, online (class) schedules. Campuswide network is available. 100% of college-owned or -operated housing units are wired for high-speed Internet access. Wireless service is available via entire campus.

STUDENT LIFE
Housing options: on-campus residence required through senior year; men-only, women-only. Campus housing is university owned. Freshman campus housing is guaranteed.

Activities and organizations: drama/theater group, choral group.

Athletics Member NCAA, NCCAA. All NCAA Division III. ***Intercollegiate sports:*** baseball M, basketball M/W, cross-country running M/W, football M, soccer M/W, softball W, volleyball W, wrestling M. ***Intramural sports:*** basketball M/W.

Campus security: student patrols, late-night transport/escort service, controlled dormitory access.

Student services: health clinic, personal/psychological counseling.

COSTS & FINANCIAL AID
Costs (2014–15) ***Comprehensive fee:*** $19,990 includes full-time tuition ($12,370), mandatory fees ($1140), and room and board ($6480). Full-time tuition and fees vary according to location and program. Part-time tuition: $515 per credit hour. Part-time tuition and fees vary according to course load. ***Required fees:*** $48 per credit hour part-time. ***Payment plan:*** installment. ***Waivers:*** employees or children of employees.

Financial Aid Of all full-time matriculated undergraduates who enrolled in 2013, 606 applied for aid, 565 were judged to have need, 55 had their need fully met. In 2013, 39 non-need-based awards were made. ***Average percent of need met:*** 53. ***Average financial aid package:*** $9867. ***Average need-based loan:*** $4559. ***Average need-based gift aid:*** $6286. ***Average non-need-based aid:*** $3076. ***Average indebtedness upon graduation:*** $11,034.

APPLYING
Standardized Tests *Required:* SAT or ACT (for admission).

Options: electronic application.

Application fee: $50.

Required: essay or personal statement, high school transcript, 4 letters of recommendation.

CONTACT
Dr. James Harrison, Director of Admissions, Maranatha Baptist University, 745 West Main Street, Watertown, WI 53094. *Phone:* 920-206-2327. *Toll-free phone:* 800-622-2947. *Fax:* 920-261-9109. *E-mail:* admissions@mbbc.edu.

★ Marian University
Fond du Lac, Wisconsin
http://www.marianuniversity.edu/

- **Independent Roman Catholic** comprehensive, founded 1936
- **Small-town** 78-acre campus with easy access to Milwaukee
- **Endowment** $12.5 million
- **Coed** 1,628 undergraduate students, 79% full-time, 71% women, 29% men
- **Moderately difficult** entrance level, 77% of applicants were admitted

UNDERGRAD STUDENTS
1,293 full-time, 335 part-time. Students come from 18 states and territories; 14 other countries; 13% are from out of state; 8% Black or African American, non-Hispanic/Latino; 7% Hispanic/Latino; 0.9% Asian, non-Hispanic/Latino; 0.2% Native Hawaiian or other Pacific Islander, non-Hispanic/Latino; 1% American Indian or Alaska Native, non-Hispanic/Latino; 0.2% Two or more races, non-Hispanic/Latino; 3% Race/ethnicity unknown; 3% international; 8% transferred in; 34% live on campus.

Freshmen
Admission: 1,178 applied, 904 admitted, 250 enrolled. ***Average high school GPA:*** 3.03. ***Test scores:*** ACT scores over 18: 67%; ACT scores over 24: 21%; ACT scores over 30: 3%.

Retention: 73% of full-time freshmen returned.

FACULTY
Total: 271, 36% full-time, 33% with terminal degrees.

Student/faculty ratio: 11:1.

ACADEMICS
Calendar: semesters. *Degrees:* certificates, bachelor's, master's, doctoral, post-master's, and postbachelor's certificates.

Special study options: academic remediation for entering students, accelerated degree program, advanced placement credit, cooperative education, distance learning, double majors, English as a second language, honors programs, independent study, internships, part-time degree program, services for LD students, student-designed majors, study abroad, summer session for credit. ***ROTC:*** Army (b).

Computers: 500 computers/terminals are available on campus for general student use. Students can access the following: campus intranet, computer help desk, free student e-mail accounts, online (class) grades, online (class) registration, online (class) schedules. Campuswide network is available. 100% of college-owned or -operated housing units are wired for high-speed Internet access. Wireless service is available via entire campus.

STUDENT LIFE
Housing options: on-campus residence required through sophomore year; coed, special housing for students with disabilities. Campus housing is university owned. Freshman campus housing is guaranteed.

Activities and organizations: student-run newspaper, choral group, Student Senate, Student Nurses Association, Student Education Association, Science and Math Association, Business Club, national sororities.

Athletics Member NCAA. All Division III. ***Intercollegiate sports:*** baseball M, basketball M/W, cross-country running M/W, golf M/W, ice hockey M/W, soccer M/W, softball W, tennis M/W, track and field M/W, volleyball W. ***Intramural sports:*** badminton M/W, basketball M/W, bowling M/W, football M, skiing (downhill) M/W, softball M, tennis M/W, volleyball M/W.

Campus security: 24-hour emergency response devices and patrols, student patrols, late-night transport/escort service, controlled dormitory access.

Student services: health clinic, personal/psychological counseling.

COSTS & FINANCIAL AID
Costs (2015–16) ***One-time required fee:*** $100. ***Comprehensive fee:*** $32,420 includes full-time tuition ($25,510), mandatory fees ($420), and room and board ($6490). Full-time tuition and fees vary according to course load and program. Part-time tuition and fees vary according to course load and program. ***College room only:*** $3900. Room and board charges vary according to board plan. ***Payment plan:*** installment. ***Waivers:*** senior citizens and employees or children of employees.

Financial Aid Of all full-time matriculated undergraduates who enrolled in 2013, 1,310 applied for aid, 1,210 were judged to have need, 153 had their need fully met. 435 Federal Work-Study jobs (averaging $67,887). 395 state and other part-time jobs (averaging $1447). In 2013, 87 non-need-based awards were made. ***Average percent of need met:*** 69. ***Average financial aid package:*** $17,414. ***Average need-based loan:*** $4374. ***Average need-based gift aid:*** $13,801. ***Average non-need-based aid:*** $9124. ***Average indebtedness upon graduation:*** $31,000.

APPLYING
Standardized Tests *Required:* SAT or ACT (for admission). *Recommended:* ACT (for admission).

Options: electronic application, deferred entrance.

Application fee: $20.

Required: high school transcript. ***Required for some:*** interview. ***Recommended:*** interview.

Application deadlines: rolling (freshmen), rolling (transfers).

Notification: 8/15 (freshmen), continuous until 8/15 (transfers).

CONTACT

Shannon LaLuzerne, Dean of Admission, Marian University, 45 S. National Avenue, Fond du Lac, WI 54935-4699. *Phone:* 920-923-7650. *Toll-free phone:* 800-2-MARIAN. *E-mail:* admission@marianuniversity.edu.

Marquette University

Milwaukee, Wisconsin

http://www.marquette.edu/

- **Independent Roman Catholic (Jesuit)** university, founded 1881
- **Urban** 100-acre campus with easy access to Milwaukee
- **Endowment** $458.0 million
- **Coed** 8,410 undergraduate students, 96% full-time, 52% women, 48% men
- **Moderately difficult** entrance level, 67% of applicants were admitted

UNDERGRAD STUDENTS

8,078 full-time, 332 part-time. Students come from 51 states and territories; 44 other countries; 66% are from out of state; 4% Black or African American, non-Hispanic/Latino; 10% Hispanic/Latino; 5% Asian, non-Hispanic/Latino; 0.1% Native Hawaiian or other Pacific Islander, non-Hispanic/Latino; 0.2% American Indian or Alaska Native, non-Hispanic/Latino; 3% Two or more races, non-Hispanic/Latino; 0.2% Race/ethnicity unknown; 4% international; 2% transferred in; 54% live on campus.

Freshmen

Admission: 21,755 applied, 14,513 admitted, 1,992 enrolled. ***Test scores:*** SAT critical reading scores over 500: 92%; SAT math scores over 500: 91%; SAT writing scores over 500: 85%; ACT scores over 18: 100%; SAT critical reading scores over 600: 46%; SAT math scores over 600: 58%; SAT writing scores over 600: 38%; ACT scores over 24: 86%; SAT critical reading scores over 700: 7%; SAT math scores over 700: 9%; SAT writing scores over 700: 6%; ACT scores over 30: 24%.

Retention: 89% of full-time freshmen returned.

FACULTY

Total: 1,168, 54% full-time, 71% with terminal degrees.

Student/faculty ratio: 14:1.

ACADEMICS

Calendar: semesters. *Degrees:* bachelor's, master's, doctoral, post-master's, and postbachelor's certificates.

Special study options: accelerated degree program, adult/continuing education programs, advanced placement credit, cooperative education, distance learning, double majors, English as a second language, honors programs, independent study, internships, off-campus study, part-time degree program, services for LD students, student-designed majors, study abroad, summer session for credit. ***ROTC:*** Army (b), Navy (b), Air Force (b).

Unusual degree programs: 3-2 business administration; engineering with Biomedical Engineering, Civil Engineering, Electrical and Computer Engineering, Mechanical Engineering are administered through the Marquette University Graduate School; exercise science/clinical and translational rehabilitation health sciences, speech and language pathology, international affairs, and physical therapy programs are administered through the Graduate School; physical therapy is administered through the College of Health Sciences.

Computers: 1,720 computers/terminals and 550 ports are available on campus for general student use. Students can access the following: campus intranet, computer help desk, free student e-mail accounts, online (class) grades, online (class) registration, online (class) schedules, AV Software, MATLAB, Printwise. Campuswide network is available. 100% of college-owned or -operated housing units are wired for high-speed Internet access. Wireless service is available via classrooms, computer centers, computer labs, dorm rooms, learning centers, libraries, student centers.

STUDENT LIFE

Housing options: on-campus residence required through sophomore year; coed, men-only, women-only, cooperative, special housing for students with disabilities. Campus housing is university owned. Freshman campus housing is guaranteed.

Activities and organizations: drama/theater group, student-run newspaper, radio and television station, choral group, student government, club sports, community service organizations, band/jazz/orchestra, Residence Hall Association, national fraternities, national sororities.

Athletics Member NCAA. All Division I. ***Intercollegiate sports:*** basketball M(s)/W(s), cheerleading M/W, cross-country running M(s)/W(s), golf M(s), lacrosse M(s)/W(s), soccer M(s)/W(s), tennis M(s)/W(s), track and field M(s)/W(s), volleyball W(s). ***Intramural sports:*** badminton M/W, baseball M(c), basketball M(c)/W(c), crew M(c)/W(c), cross-country running M(c)/W(c), equestrian sports M(c)/W(c), fencing M(c)/W(c), football M/W, golf M(c)/W(c), ice hockey M(c), lacrosse M(c)/W(c), racquetball M/W, rugby M(c)/W(c), sailing M(c)/W(c), skiing (downhill) M(c)/W(c), soccer M(c)/W(c), softball M/W(c), swimming and diving M(c)/W(c), table tennis M(c)/W(c), tennis M(c)/W(c), ultimate Frisbee M(c)/W(c), volleyball M(c)/W(c), water polo M(c)/W(c), weight lifting M/W.

Campus security: 24-hour emergency response devices and patrols, student patrols, late-night transport/escort service, 24-hour desk attendants in residence halls.

Student services: health clinic, personal/psychological counseling.

COSTS & FINANCIAL AID

Costs (2015–16) ***Tuition:*** $36,720 full-time, $995 per credit part-time. Full-time tuition and fees vary according to course load and program. Part-time tuition and fees vary according to program. ***Required fees:*** $450 full-time. ***Room only:*** Room and board charges vary according to housing facility. ***Payment plan:*** installment. ***Waivers:*** senior citizens and employees or children of employees.

Financial Aid Of all full-time matriculated undergraduates who enrolled in 2014, 5,847 applied for aid, 4,576 were judged to have need, 1,092 had their need fully met. In 2014, 3197 non-need-based awards were made. ***Average percent of need met:*** 77. ***Average financial aid package:*** $24,753. ***Average need-based loan:*** $6665. ***Average need-based gift aid:*** $17,782. ***Average non-need-based aid:*** $10,294. ***Average indebtedness upon graduation:*** $35,211.

APPLYING

Standardized Tests *Required:* SAT or ACT (for admission).

Options: electronic application, deferred entrance.

Required: essay or personal statement, high school transcript, minimum 2.5 GPA. ***Recommended:*** minimum 3.4 GPA.

Application deadlines: 12/1 (freshmen), 6/1 (transfers).

Notification: 1/31 (freshmen), continuous (transfers).

CONTACT

Ms. Jean Burke, Interim Dean of Admissions, Marquette University, PO Box 1881, Milwaukee, WI 53201-1881. *Phone:* 414-288-7004. *Toll-free phone:* 800-222-6544. *Fax:* 414-288-3764. *E-mail:* admissions@marquette.edu.

Milwaukee Institute of Art and Design

Milwaukee, Wisconsin

http://www.miad.edu/

- **Independent** 4-year, founded 1974
- **Urban** campus with easy access to Milwaukee
- **Coed**
- **Moderately difficult** entrance level

FACULTY

Student/faculty ratio: 15:1.

ACADEMICS

Calendar: semesters. *Degree:* bachelor's.

STUDENT LIFE

Housing options: on-campus residence required through sophomore year; coed. Campus housing is university owned. Freshman applicants given priority for college housing.

Activities and organizations: drama/theater group.

Campus security: 24-hour emergency response devices, late-night transport/escort service.

Student services: health clinic, personal/psychological counseling.

COSTS & FINANCIAL AID

Costs (2014–15) ***Tuition:*** $30,800 full-time. ***Required fees:*** $1600 full-time. ***Room only:*** $7500.

Financial Aid Of all full-time matriculated undergraduates who enrolled in 2008, 566 applied for aid, 530 were judged to have need, 58 had their need fully met. In 2008, 81 non-need-based awards were made. ***Average percent of need met:*** 68. ***Average financial aid package:*** $19,455. ***Average need-based loan:*** $6236. ***Average need-based gift aid:*** $12,888. ***Average non-need-based aid:*** $9611. ***Average indebtedness upon graduation:*** $24,162. ***Financial aid deadline:*** 2/15.

APPLYING

Options: electronic application, deferred entrance.

Application fee: $25.

Required: essay or personal statement, high school transcript, interview, portfolio. ***Recommended:*** minimum 2.0 GPA.

CONTACT

David Sigman, Director of Admissions, Milwaukee Institute of Art and Design, 273 East Erie Street, Milwaukee, WI 53202. *Phone:* 414-847-3200. *Toll-free phone:* 888-749-MIAD. *Fax:* 414-291-8077. *E-mail:* admissions@miad.edu.

Milwaukee School of Engineering

Milwaukee, Wisconsin

http://www.msoe.edu/

- **Independent** comprehensive, founded 1903
- **Urban** 15-acre campus
- **Endowment** $59.5 million
- **Coed, primarily men** 2,596 undergraduate students, 94% full-time, 24% women, 76% men
- **Moderately difficult** entrance level, 69% of applicants were admitted

UNDERGRAD STUDENTS

2,434 full-time, 162 part-time. Students come from 35 states and territories; 32 other countries; 33% are from out of state; 2% Black or African American, non-Hispanic/Latino; 4% Hispanic/Latino; 3% Asian, non-Hispanic/Latino; 0.5% Native Hawaiian or other Pacific Islander, non-Hispanic/Latino; 0.2% American Indian or Alaska Native, non-Hispanic/Latino; 2% Two or more races, non-Hispanic/Latino; 7% Race/ethnicity unknown; 12% international; 8% transferred in; 42% live on campus.

Freshmen

Admission: 2,574 applied, 1,767 admitted, 580 enrolled. ***Average high school GPA:*** 3.62. ***Test scores:*** SAT critical reading scores over 500: 84%; SAT math scores over 500: 97%; ACT scores over 18: 100%; SAT critical reading scores over 600: 48%; SAT math scores over 600: 74%; ACT scores over 24: 87%; SAT critical reading scores over 700: 15%; SAT math scores over 700: 23%; ACT scores over 30: 28%.

Retention: 82% of full-time freshmen returned.

FACULTY

Total: 258, 52% full-time, 57% with terminal degrees.

Student/faculty ratio: 15:1.

ACADEMICS

Calendar: quarters. *Degrees:* bachelor's and master's.

Special study options: academic remediation for entering students, adult/continuing education programs, advanced placement credit, double majors, English as a second language, honors programs, independent study, internships, part-time degree program, services for LD students, study abroad, summer session for credit. ***ROTC:*** Army (c), Navy (c), Air Force (c).

Computers: 125 computers/terminals and 2,000 ports are available on campus for general student use. Students can access the following: campus intranet, computer help desk, free student e-mail accounts, online (class) grades, online (class) registration, online (class) schedules. Campuswide network is available. 100% of college-owned or -operated housing units are wired for high-speed Internet access. Wireless service is available via entire campus.

STUDENT LIFE

Housing options: on-campus residence required through sophomore year; coed, special housing for students with disabilities. Campus housing is university owned. Freshman campus housing is guaranteed.

Activities and organizations: drama/theater group, student-run radio station, choral group, Architectural Engineering and Construction Management Societies, Student Athletic Advisory Committee, MAGE, Student Government Association, Student Union Board, national fraternities, national sororities.

Athletics Member NCAA. All Division III. ***Intercollegiate sports:*** baseball M, basketball M/W, cheerleading M/W, crew M/W, cross-country running M/W, golf M, ice hockey M, lacrosse M, soccer M/W, softball W, tennis M/W, track and field M/W, volleyball M/W, wrestling M. ***Intramural sports:*** badminton M(c)/W(c), basketball M/W, bowling M(c)/W(c), fencing M(c)/W(c), football M/W, rugby M(c), soccer M/W, softball M/W, ultimate Frisbee M(c)/W(c), volleyball M/W, weight lifting M(c)/W(c).

Campus security: 24-hour emergency response devices and patrols, late-night transport/escort service, controlled dormitory access.

Student services: health clinic, personal/psychological counseling, women's center.

COSTS & FINANCIAL AID

Costs (2015–16) ***Comprehensive fee:*** $45,153 includes full-time tuition ($34,890), mandatory fees ($1650), and room and board ($8613). Full-time tuition and fees vary according to course load. Part-time tuition: $605 per credit. Part-time tuition and fees vary according to course load. ***College room only:*** $5439. Room and board charges vary according to board plan and housing facility. ***Payment plan:*** installment. ***Waivers:*** employees or children of employees.

Financial Aid Of all full-time matriculated undergraduates who enrolled in 2013, 1,882 applied for aid, 1,727 were judged to have need, 318 had their need fully met. 253 Federal Work-Study jobs (averaging $987). In 2013, 328 non-need-based awards were made. ***Average percent of need met:*** 73. ***Average financial aid package:*** $25,083. ***Average need-based loan:*** $3692. ***Average need-based gift aid:*** $21,887. ***Average non-need-based aid:*** $14,286. ***Average indebtedness upon graduation:*** $37,243.

APPLYING

Standardized Tests *Required:* SAT or ACT (for admission).

Options: electronic application, deferred entrance.

Required: high school transcript, minimum 2.5 GPA. ***Required for some:*** essay or personal statement, minimum 3.0 GPA, interview.

Application deadlines: 1/1 (freshmen), 1/1 (transfers).

Notification: continuous until 10/1 (freshmen), continuous until 10/1 (transfers).

CONTACT

Seandra Mitchell, Director, Undergraduate Admission, Milwaukee School of Engineering, 1025 North Broadway, Milwaukee, WI 53202-3109. *Phone:* 414-277-6762. *Toll-free phone:* 800-332-6763. *Fax:* 414-277-7475. *E-mail:* mitchell@msoe.edu.

★ Mount Mary University

Milwaukee, Wisconsin

http://www.mtmary.edu/

- **Independent Roman Catholic** comprehensive, founded 1913
- **Urban** 80-acre campus
- **Endowment** $14.7 million
- **Undergraduate: women only; graduate: coed** 860 undergraduate students, 79% full-time, 99% women, 1% men
- **Moderately difficult** entrance level, 35% of applicants were admitted

UNDERGRAD STUDENTS

681 full-time, 179 part-time. Students come from 13 states and territories; 9 other countries; 5% are from out of state; 23% Black or African American, non-Hispanic/Latino; 14% Hispanic/Latino; 7% Asian, non-Hispanic/Latino; 0.1% Native Hawaiian or other Pacific Islander, non-Hispanic/Latino; 0.6% American Indian or Alaska Native, non-Hispanic/Latino; 3% Two or more races, non-Hispanic/Latino; 0.5% Race/ethnicity unknown; 0.3% international; 7% transferred in; 24% live on campus.

Freshmen
Admission: 638 applied, 225 admitted, 155 enrolled. ***Average high school GPA:*** 3.08. ***Test scores:*** ACT scores over 18: 73%; ACT scores over 24: 18%; ACT scores over 30: 1%.

Retention: 78% of full-time freshmen returned.

FACULTY
Total: 200, 33% full-time, 49% with terminal degrees.

Student/faculty ratio: 10:1.

ACADEMICS
Calendar: semesters. *Degrees:* bachelor's, master's, doctoral, post-master's, and postbachelor's certificates.

Special study options: academic remediation for entering students, accelerated degree program, advanced placement credit, double majors, honors programs, independent study, internships, part-time degree program, services for LD students, student-designed majors, study abroad, summer session for credit. ***ROTC:*** Air Force (c).

Unusual degree programs: 3-2 occupational therapy, public health.

Computers: 240 computers/terminals and 10 ports are available on campus for general student use. Students can access the following: campus intranet, computer help desk, free student e-mail accounts, online (class) grades, online (class) registration, online (class) schedules. Campuswide network is available. 100% of college-owned or -operated housing units are wired for high-speed Internet access. Wireless service is available via entire campus.

STUDENT LIFE
Housing options: on-campus residence required for freshman year; women-only. Campus housing is university owned. Freshman campus housing is guaranteed.

Activities and organizations: student-run newspaper, choral group, Programming and Activities Council, Student Government Association, International Club, Caroline Hall Council, Department Affiliated Clubs.

Athletics Member NCAA. All Division III. ***Intercollegiate sports:*** basketball W, cross-country running W, soccer W, softball W, tennis W, volleyball W.

Campus security: 24-hour patrols, late-night transport/escort service, controlled dormitory access.

Student services: personal/psychological counseling.

COSTS & FINANCIAL AID
Costs (2014–15) ***Comprehensive fee:*** $33,590 includes full-time tuition ($25,336), mandatory fees ($516), and room and board ($7738). Full-time tuition and fees vary according to degree level and program. Part-time tuition: $768 per credit. Part-time tuition and fees vary according to course load, degree level, and program. ***Required fees:*** $320 per year part-time. ***Room and board:*** Room and board charges vary according to board plan and housing facility. ***Payment plan:*** installment. ***Waivers:*** senior citizens and employees or children of employees.

Financial Aid Of all full-time matriculated undergraduates who enrolled in 2014, 604 applied for aid, 561 were judged to have need, 50 had their need fully met. 125 Federal Work-Study jobs (averaging $1337). 127 state and other part-time jobs (averaging $1302). In 2014, 72 non-need-based awards were made. ***Average percent of need met:*** 70. ***Average financial aid package:*** $22,040. ***Average need-based loan:*** $4501. ***Average need-based gift aid:*** $17,522. ***Average non-need-based aid:*** $10,803. ***Average indebtedness upon graduation:*** $29,759.

APPLYING
Standardized Tests *Required:* SAT or ACT (for admission).

Options: electronic application, deferred entrance.

Required: high school transcript, ACT or SAT scores. ***Required for some:*** essay or personal statement, 1 letter of recommendation. ***Recommended:*** minimum 2.5 GPA.

Application deadlines: rolling (freshmen), rolling (out-of-state freshmen), rolling (transfers).

Notification: continuous (freshmen), continuous (out-of-state freshmen), continuous (transfers).

CONTACT
Mary Ellen Strieter, Admission Counselor Assistant/Receptionist, Mount Mary University, 2900 North Menomonee River Parkway, Milwaukee,

WI 53222. *Phone:* 414-258-4810 Ext. 219. *Toll-free phone:* 800-321-6265. *Fax:* 414-256-0180. *E-mail:* admiss@mtmary.edu.

See previous page for display ad and page 1538 for the College Close-Up.

Northland College

Ashland, Wisconsin

http://www.northland.edu/

- **Independent** 4-year, founded 1892, affiliated with United Church of Christ
- **Small-town** 130-acre campus
- **Endowment** $20.7 million
- **Coed** 584 undergraduate students, 97% full-time, 49% women, 51% men
- **Moderately difficult** entrance level, 63% of applicants were admitted

UNDERGRAD STUDENTS
567 full-time, 17 part-time. Students come from 32 states and territories; 3 other countries; 50% are from out of state; 1% Black or African American, non-Hispanic/Latino; 5% Hispanic/Latino; 0.2% Asian, non-Hispanic/Latino; 2% American Indian or Alaska Native, non-Hispanic/Latino; 3% Two or more races, non-Hispanic/Latino; 6% Race/ethnicity unknown; 2% international; 8% transferred in; 74% live on campus.

Freshmen
Admission: 1,020 applied, 647 admitted, 150 enrolled. ***Average high school GPA:*** 3.4. ***Test scores:*** SAT critical reading scores over 500: 66%; SAT math scores over 500: 60%; SAT writing scores over 500: 50%; ACT scores over 18: 94%; SAT critical reading scores over 600: 34%; SAT math scores over 600: 25%; SAT writing scores over 600: 16%; ACT scores over 24: 50%; SAT critical reading scores over 700: 6%; SAT math scores over 700: 6%; ACT scores over 30: 7%.

Retention: 66% of full-time freshmen returned.

FACULTY
Total: 54, 87% full-time, 78% with terminal degrees.

Student/faculty ratio: 12:1.

ACADEMICS
Calendar: 4-4-1. *Degree:* bachelor's.

Special study options: advanced placement credit, cooperative education, double majors, honors programs, independent study, internships, off-campus study, part-time degree program, services for LD students, student-designed majors, study abroad, summer session for credit.

Unusual degree programs: 3-2 engineering with Michigan Technological University, Washington University in St. Louis.

Computers: 125 computers/terminals are available on campus for general student use. Students can access the following: campus intranet, computer help desk, free student e-mail accounts, online (class) grades, online (class) registration, online (class) schedules. Campuswide network is available. 100% of college-owned or -operated housing units are wired for high-speed Internet access. Wireless service is available via classrooms, computer centers, computer labs, learning centers, libraries, student centers.

STUDENT LIFE
Housing options: on-campus residence required through junior year; coed, women-only, cooperative. Campus housing is university owned. Freshman campus housing is guaranteed.

Activities and organizations: drama/theater group, student-run newspaper, radio station, choral group, Northland Volunteer Program, Northland College Student Association, Native American Student Association, Environmental Council, N Club.

Athletics Member NCAA. All Division III. ***Intercollegiate sports:*** baseball M, basketball M/W, cross-country running M/W, golf M/W, ice hockey M, skiing (cross-country) M(c)/W(c), soccer M/W, softball W, volleyball W. ***Intramural sports:*** soccer M/W, softball M/W, table tennis M/W, ultimate Frisbee M/W, volleyball M/W.

Campus security: 24-hour emergency response devices and patrols, late-night transport/escort service, controlled dormitory access.

Student services: health clinic, personal/psychological counseling.

COSTS & FINANCIAL AID
Costs (2014–15) ***Comprehensive fee:*** $39,338 includes full-time tuition ($30,450), mandatory fees ($1030), and room and board ($7858). Full-time tuition and fees vary according to course load. Part-time tuition: $600 per credit hour. Part-time tuition and fees vary according to course load. No tuition increase for student's term of enrollment. ***College room only:*** $3468. Room and board charges vary according to board plan and housing facility. ***Payment plan:*** installment. ***Waivers:*** employees or children of employees.

Financial Aid Of all full-time matriculated undergraduates who enrolled in 2014, 543 applied for aid, 502 were judged to have need, 105 had their need fully met. 292 Federal Work-Study jobs (averaging $1772). 251 state and other part-time jobs (averaging $1763). In 2014, 63 non-need-based awards were made. ***Average percent of need met:*** 82. ***Average financial aid package:*** $36,066. ***Average need-based loan:*** $4939. ***Average need-based gift aid:*** $21,714. ***Average non-need-based aid:*** $17,530. ***Average indebtedness upon graduation:*** $30,637.

APPLYING
Standardized Tests *Required:* SAT or ACT (for admission).

Options: electronic application, deferred entrance.

Required: high school transcript. ***Recommended:*** minimum 2.0 GPA.

Application deadlines: rolling (freshmen), rolling (out-of-state freshmen), rolling (transfers).

Notification: continuous (freshmen), continuous (out-of-state freshmen), continuous (transfers).

CONTACT
Teege Mettille, Director of Admissions, Northland College, 1411 Ellis Avenue, Ashland, WI 54806. *Phone:* 715-682-1224. *Toll-free phone:* 800-753-1840 (in-state); 800-753-1040 (out-of-state). *Fax:* 715-682-1258. *E-mail:* admit@northland.edu.

Rasmussen College Appleton

Appleton, Wisconsin

http://www.rasmussen.edu/

- **Proprietary** 4-year, part of Rasmussen College System
- **Suburban** campus
- **Coed** 398 undergraduate students, 53% full-time, 78% women, 22% men
- **Minimally difficult** entrance level

UNDERGRAD STUDENTS
210 full-time, 188 part-time.

Freshmen
Admission: 24 enrolled.

FACULTY
Total: 5, 60% full-time.

Student/faculty ratio: 22:1.

ACADEMICS
Degrees: certificates, diplomas, associate, and bachelor's.

Special study options: academic remediation for entering students, accelerated degree program, adult/continuing education programs, distance learning, double majors, internships, part-time degree program, summer session for credit.

Computers: 76 computers/terminals are available on campus for general student use. Students can access the following: computer help desk, free student e-mail accounts, online (class) grades, online (class) schedules. Campuswide network is available. Wireless service is available via entire campus.

STUDENT LIFE
Housing options: college housing not available.

COSTS
Costs (2014–15) ***Tuition:*** $10,764 full-time, $350 per credit hour part-time. Full-time tuition and fees vary according to course level, course load, degree level, location, and program. Part-time tuition and fees vary according to course level, course load, degree level, location, and program. No tuition increase for student's term of enrollment. ***Required fees:*** $1350 full-time. ***Payment plans:*** installment, deferred payment. ***Waivers:*** employees or children of employees.

APPLYING
Standardized Tests *Required:* Internal Exam (for admission).
Options: electronic application, early admission, deferred entrance.
Required: high school transcript, minimum 2.0 GPA. ***Required for some:*** interview.
Application deadlines: rolling (freshmen), rolling (transfers).

CONTACT
Susan Hammerstrom, Director of Admissions, Rasmussen College Appleton, 3500 E. Destination Drive, Appleton, WI 54915. *Phone:* 920-750-5900. *Toll-free phone:* 888-549-6755. *E-mail:* susan.hammerstrom@rasmussen.edu.

Rasmussen College Green Bay

Green Bay, Wisconsin

http://www.rasmussen.edu/

- **Proprietary** 4-year, part of Rasmussen College System
- **Suburban** campus
- **Coed** 564 undergraduate students, 60% full-time, 84% women, 16% men
- **Minimally difficult** entrance level

UNDERGRAD STUDENTS
336 full-time, 228 part-time.

Freshmen
Admission: 25 enrolled.

FACULTY
Total: 36, 28% full-time.
Student/faculty ratio: 22:1.

ACADEMICS
Degrees: certificates, diplomas, associate, and bachelor's.
Special study options: academic remediation for entering students, accelerated degree program, adult/continuing education programs, distance learning, double majors, internships, part-time degree program, summer session for credit.
Computers: 137 computers/terminals are available on campus for general student use. Students can access the following: computer help desk, free student e-mail accounts, online (class) grades, online (class) schedules. Campuswide network is available. Wireless service is available via entire campus.

STUDENT LIFE
Housing options: college housing not available.

COSTS
Costs (2014–15) ***Tuition:*** $10,764 full-time, $310 per credit hour part-time. Full-time tuition and fees vary according to course level, course load, degree level, location, and program. Part-time tuition and fees vary according to course level, course load, degree level, location, and program. No tuition increase for student's term of enrollment. ***Required fees:*** $1350 full-time. ***Payment plans:*** installment, deferred payment. ***Waivers:*** employees or children of employees.

APPLYING
Standardized Tests *Required:* Internal Exam (for admission).
Options: electronic application, early admission, deferred entrance.
Required: high school transcript, minimum 2.0 GPA. ***Required for some:*** interview.
Application deadlines: rolling (freshmen), rolling (transfers).

CONTACT
Susan Hammerstrom, Director of Admissions, Rasmussen College Green Bay, 940 South Taylor Street, Suite 100, Green Bay, WI 54303. *Phone:* 920-593-8400. *Toll-free phone:* 888-549-6755. *E-mail:* susan.hammerstrom@rasmussen.edu.

Rasmussen College Wausau

Wausau, Wisconsin

http://www.rasmussen.edu/

- **Proprietary** 4-year, part of Rasmussen College System
- **Suburban** campus
- **Coed** 544 undergraduate students, 53% full-time, 82% women, 18% men
- **Minimally difficult** entrance level

UNDERGRAD STUDENTS
288 full-time, 256 part-time.

Freshmen
Admission: 19 enrolled.

FACULTY
Total: 18, 50% full-time.
Student/faculty ratio: 22:1.

ACADEMICS
Degrees: certificates, diplomas, associate, and bachelor's.
Special study options: academic remediation for entering students, accelerated degree program, adult/continuing education programs, distance learning, double majors, internships, part-time degree program, summer session for credit.
Computers: 74 computers/terminals are available on campus for general student use. Students can access the following: computer help desk, free student e-mail accounts, online (class) grades, online (class) schedules. Campuswide network is available. Wireless service is available via entire campus.

STUDENT LIFE
Housing options: college housing not available.

COSTS
Costs (2014–15) ***Tuition:*** $10,764 full-time, $310 per credit hour part-time. Full-time tuition and fees vary according to course level, course load, degree level, location, and program. Part-time tuition and fees vary according to course level, course load, degree level, location, and program. No tuition increase for student's term of enrollment. ***Required fees:*** $1350 full-time. ***Payment plans:*** installment, deferred payment. ***Waivers:*** employees or children of employees.

APPLYING
Standardized Tests *Required:* Internal Exam (for admission).
Options: electronic application, early admission, deferred entrance.
Required: high school transcript, minimum 2.0 GPA. ***Required for some:*** interview.
Application deadlines: rolling (freshmen), rolling (transfers).

CONTACT
Susan Hammerstrom, Director of Admissions, Rasmussen College Wausau, 1101 Westwood Drive, Wausau, WI 54401. *Phone:* 715-841-8000. *Toll-free phone:* 888-549-6755. *E-mail:* susan.hammerstrom@rasmussen.edu.

Ripon College

Ripon, Wisconsin

http://www.ripon.edu/

- **Independent** 4-year, founded 1851
- **Small-town** 250-acre campus with easy access to Milwaukee
- **Endowment** $84.8 million
- **Coed** 840 undergraduate students, 98% full-time, 53% women, 47% men
- **Moderately difficult** entrance level, 67% of applicants were admitted

UNDERGRAD STUDENTS
820 full-time, 20 part-time. Students come from 31 states and territories; 9 other countries; 27% are from out of state; 2% Black or African American, non-Hispanic/Latino; 5% Hispanic/Latino; 1% Asian, non-Hispanic/Latino; 0.2% American Indian or Alaska Native, non-Hispanic/Latino; 2% Two or more races, non-Hispanic/Latino; 2% Race/ethnicity unknown; 3% international; 2% transferred in; 89% live on campus.

Freshmen
Admission: 1,493 applied, 1,006 admitted, 211 enrolled. ***Average high school GPA:*** 3.41. ***Test scores:*** SAT critical reading scores over 500: 76%; SAT math scores over 500: 60%; ACT scores over 18: 94%; SAT critical reading scores over 600: 35%; SAT math scores over 600: 42%; ACT scores over 24: 44%; SAT critical reading scores over 700: 12%; SAT math scores over 700: 24%; ACT scores over 30: 12%.

Retention: 85% of full-time freshmen returned.

FACULTY
Total: 94, 68% full-time, 80% with terminal degrees.

Student/faculty ratio: 11:1.

ACADEMICS
Calendar: semesters. *Degree:* bachelor's.

Special study options: accelerated degree program, advanced placement credit, double majors, internships, off-campus study, part-time degree program, services for LD students, student-designed majors, study abroad. ***ROTC:*** Army (b).

Unusual degree programs: 3-2 engineering with Rensselaer Polytechnic Institute, Washington University in St. Louis, University of Wisconsin-Madison; forestry with Duke University; nursing with Rush University; environmental studies with Duke University.

Computers: 150 computers/terminals are available on campus for general student use. Students can access the following: campus intranet, computer help desk, free student e-mail accounts, online (class) grades, online (class) schedules. Campuswide network is available. 100% of college-owned or -operated housing units are wired for high-speed Internet access. Wireless service is available via classrooms, libraries, student centers.

STUDENT LIFE
Housing options: on-campus residence required through senior year; coed, men-only, women-only. Campus housing is university owned. Freshman campus housing is guaranteed.

Activities and organizations: drama/theater group, student-run newspaper, radio and television station, choral group, Environmental Group, Student Senate, Community Service Coalition, SMAC (Student Media and Activities Committee), national fraternities, national sororities.

Athletics Member NCAA. All Division III. ***Intercollegiate sports:*** baseball M, basketball M/W, cheerleading M(c)/W, cross-country running M/W, football M, rugby M(c)/W(c), soccer M/W, softball W, swimming and diving M/W, tennis M/W, track and field M/W, volleyball W. ***Intramural sports:*** basketball M/W, bowling M/W, equestrian sports M(c)/W(c), fencing M/W, football M/W, racquetball M/W, soccer M/W, softball M/W, table tennis M/W, tennis M/W, ultimate Frisbee M/W, volleyball M/W.

Campus security: 24-hour emergency response devices and patrols, student patrols, late-night transport/escort service, controlled dormitory access.

Student services: health clinic, personal/psychological counseling.

COSTS & FINANCIAL AID
Costs (2014–15) ***Comprehensive fee:*** $42,567 includes full-time tuition ($33,207), mandatory fees ($275), and room and board ($9085). Part-time tuition: $1100 per credit. ***College room only:*** $4665. ***Payment plan:*** installment. ***Waivers:*** employees or children of employees.

Financial Aid Of all full-time matriculated undergraduates who enrolled in 2012, 840 applied for aid, 760 were judged to have need, 135 had their need fully met. 437 Federal Work-Study jobs (averaging $1777). 326 state and other part-time jobs (averaging $1727). In 2012, 124 non-need-based awards were made. ***Average percent of need met:*** 84. ***Average financial aid package:*** $25,418. ***Average need-based loan:*** $5329. ***Average need-based gift aid:*** $19,763. ***Average non-need-based aid:*** $10,803. ***Average indebtedness upon graduation:*** $31,216.

APPLYING
Standardized Tests *Required:* SAT or ACT (for admission).

Options: electronic application, deferred entrance.

Application fee: $30.

Required: essay or personal statement, high school transcript, minimum 2.0 GPA, 1 letter of recommendation. ***Required for some:*** interview. ***Recommended:*** interview.

Application deadlines: rolling (freshmen), rolling (transfers).

Notification: continuous (freshmen), continuous (transfers).

CONTACT
Office of Admission, Ripon College, 300 Seward Street, PO Box 248, Ripon, WI 54971. *Phone:* 920-748-8337. *Toll-free phone:* 800-947-4766. *Fax:* 920-748-8335. *E-mail:* adminfo@ripon.edu.

See previous page for display ad and page 1580 for the College Close-Up.

St. Norbert College
De Pere, Wisconsin
http://www.snc.edu/

- **Independent Roman Catholic** comprehensive, founded 1898
- **Suburban** 111-acre campus
- **Endowment** $97.6 million
- **Coed** 2,112 undergraduate students, 97% full-time, 57% women, 43% men
- **Moderately difficult** entrance level, 82% of applicants were admitted

UNDERGRAD STUDENTS
2,048 full-time, 64 part-time. Students come from 29 states and territories; 16 other countries; 22% are from out of state; 0.7% Black or African American, non-Hispanic/Latino; 3% Hispanic/Latino; 1% Asian, non-Hispanic/Latino; 0.8% American Indian or Alaska Native, non-Hispanic/Latino; 2% Two or more races, non-Hispanic/Latino; 0.1% Race/ethnicity unknown; 2% international; 2% transferred in; 82% live on campus.

Freshmen
Admission: 2,149 applied, 1,756 admitted, 536 enrolled. ***Average high school GPA:*** 3.48. ***Test scores:*** ACT scores over 18: 99%; ACT scores over 24: 60%; ACT scores over 30: 11%.

Retention: 84% of full-time freshmen returned.

FACULTY
Total: 202, 66% full-time, 69% with terminal degrees.

Student/faculty ratio: 14:1.

ACADEMICS
Calendar: semesters. *Degrees:* bachelor's and master's.

Special study options: academic remediation for entering students, advanced placement credit, distance learning, double majors, English as a second language, honors programs, independent study, internships, off-campus study, part-time degree program, services for LD students, student-designed majors, study abroad, summer session for credit. ***ROTC:*** Army (b).

Computers: 225 computers/terminals are available on campus for general student use. Students can access the following: campus intranet, computer help desk, free student e-mail accounts, online (class) grades, online (class) registration, online (class) schedules. Campuswide network is available. 100% of college-owned or -operated housing units are wired for high-speed Internet access. Wireless service is available via classrooms, computer centers, computer labs, dorm rooms, learning centers, libraries, student centers.

STUDENT LIFE
Housing options: on-campus residence required through senior year; coed, women-only, special housing for students with disabilities. Campus housing is university owned. Freshman campus housing is guaranteed.

Activities and organizations: drama/theater group, student-run newspaper, radio and television station, choral group, Wisconsin Student Education Association, Pre-Health Sciences Club, SNC Times, Beta Beta Beta, CC Hams, national fraternities, national sororities.

Athletics Member NCAA. All Division III. ***Intercollegiate sports:*** baseball M, basketball M/W, cross-country running M/W, football M, golf M/W, ice hockey M/W, soccer M/W, softball W, tennis M/W, track and field M/W, volleyball W. ***Intramural sports:*** basketball M/W, cheerleading W, crew M(c)/W(c), football M/W, lacrosse M(c), skiing (downhill) M(c)/W(c), soccer M/W, volleyball M/W.

Campus security: 24-hour emergency response devices and patrols, student patrols, late-night transport/escort service, controlled dormitory access, ConnectED emergency information system; crime prevention programs.

Student services: health clinic, personal/psychological counseling, women's center.

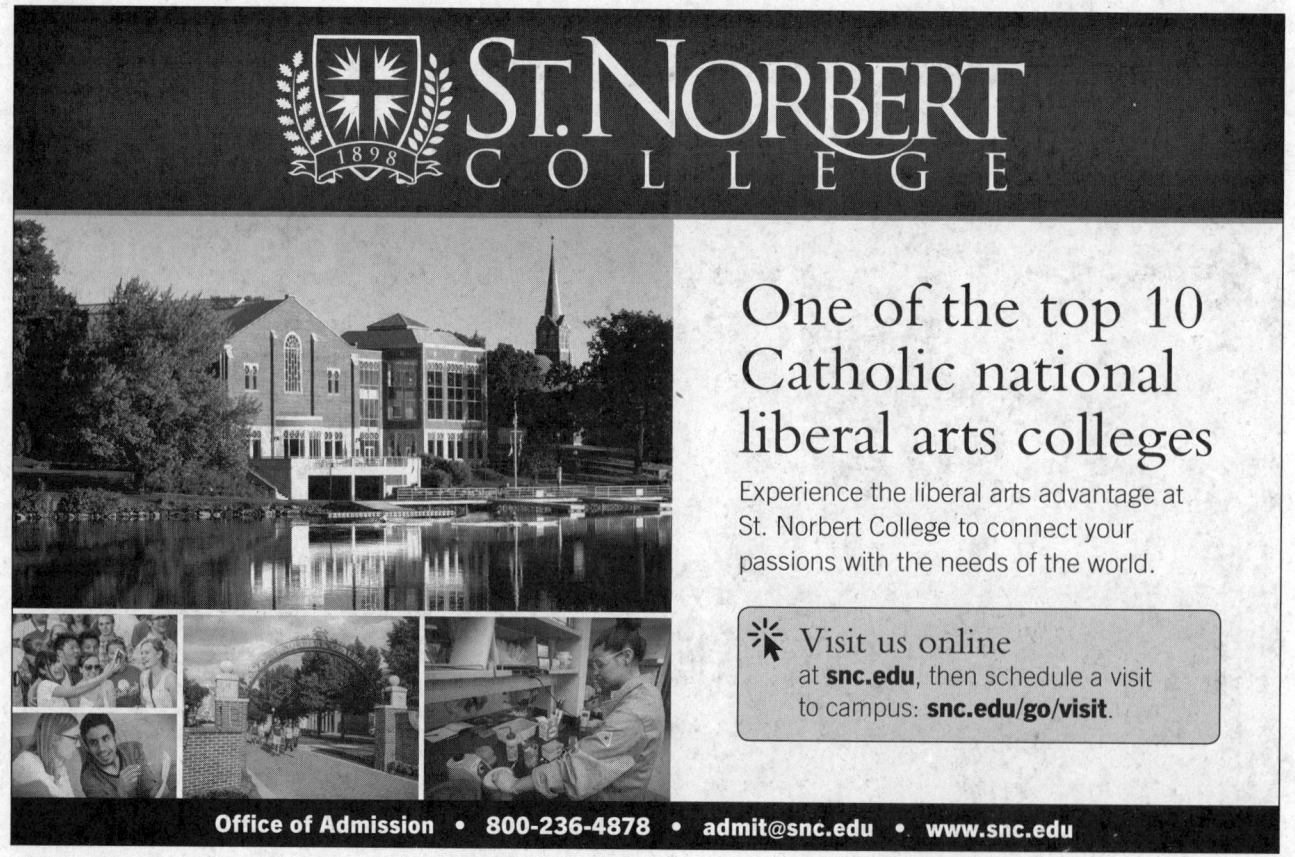

COSTS & FINANCIAL AID
Costs (2014–15) ***Comprehensive fee:*** $41,478 includes full-time tuition ($32,408), mandatory fees ($615), and room and board ($8455). Full-time tuition and fees vary according to course load. Part-time tuition: $1013 per credit. Part-time tuition and fees vary according to course load. ***College room only:*** $4514. Room and board charges vary according to board plan and housing facility. ***Payment plans:*** installment, deferred payment. ***Waivers:*** employees or children of employees.

Financial Aid Of all full-time matriculated undergraduates who enrolled in 2013, 1,725 applied for aid, 1,496 were judged to have need, 386 had their need fully met. 375 Federal Work-Study jobs (averaging $1194). In 2013, 507 non-need-based awards were made. ***Average percent of need met:*** 83. ***Average financial aid package:*** $23,755. ***Average need-based loan:*** $4661. ***Average need-based gift aid:*** $18,342. ***Average non-need-based aid:*** $11,107. ***Average indebtedness upon graduation:*** $31,438.

APPLYING
Standardized Tests *Required:* SAT or ACT (for admission).

Options: electronic application, deferred entrance.

Application fee: $10.

Required: high school transcript, 1 letter of recommendation. ***Required for some:*** interview. ***Recommended:*** essay or personal statement.

Application deadlines: rolling (freshmen), rolling (out-of-state freshmen), rolling (transfers).

Notification: continuous (freshmen), continuous (out-of-state freshmen), continuous (transfers).

CONTACT
Mr. Mark Selin, Acting Executive Director of Enrollment and Marketing, St. Norbert College, 100 Grant Street, De Pere, WI 54115-2099. *Phone:* 920-403-3005. *Toll-free phone:* 800-236-4878. *Fax:* 920-403-4072. *E-mail:* admit@snc.edu.

See previous page for display ad and page 1610 for the College Close-Up.

Silver Lake College of the Holy Family

Manitowoc, Wisconsin

http://www.sl.edu/

- **Independent Roman Catholic** comprehensive, founded 1869
- **Rural** 30-acre campus with easy access to Milwaukee
- **Endowment** $7.2 million
- **Coed** 436 undergraduate students, 50% full-time, 64% women, 36% men
- **Minimally difficult** entrance level, 83% of applicants were admitted

UNDERGRAD STUDENTS
218 full-time, 218 part-time. Students come from 15 states and territories; 4 other countries; 9% are from out of state; 15% Black or African American, non-Hispanic/Latino; 3% Hispanic/Latino; 1% Asian, non-Hispanic/Latino; 1% American Indian or Alaska Native, non-Hispanic/Latino; 3% Two or more races, non-Hispanic/Latino; 12% Race/ethnicity unknown; 2% international; 6% transferred in; 24% live on campus.

Freshmen
Admission: 221 applied, 184 admitted, 45 enrolled. ***Average high school GPA:*** 2.73. ***Test scores:*** ACT scores over 18: 37%; ACT scores over 24: 14%.

Retention: 73% of full-time freshmen returned.

FACULTY
Total: 88, 48% full-time, 36% with terminal degrees.

Student/faculty ratio: 6:1.

ACADEMICS
Calendar: semesters. *Degrees:* certificates, bachelor's, master's, and postbachelor's certificates.

Special study options: academic remediation for entering students, accelerated degree program, adult/continuing education programs, advanced placement credit, distance learning, double majors, independent study, internships, off-campus study, part-time degree program, services for LD students, student-designed majors, study abroad, summer session for credit.

Computers: 120 computers/terminals are available on campus for general student use. Students can access the following: campus intranet, computer help desk, free student e-mail accounts, online (class) grades, online (class) registration, online (class) schedules. Campuswide network is available. 100% of college-owned or -operated housing units are wired for high-speed Internet access. Wireless service is available via classrooms, computer centers, computer labs, dorm rooms, learning centers, libraries, student centers.

STUDENT LIFE
Housing options: on-campus residence required through junior year; coed, men-only, women-only, special housing for students with disabilities. Campus housing is university owned. Freshman campus housing is guaranteed.

Activities and organizations: choral group, Wellness Club, Card & Game Club, Student For Life, Campus Activity Board, Silver Lake Serves.

Athletics Member USCAA. ***Intercollegiate sports:*** basketball M(s)/W(s), cross-country running M(s)/W(s), golf M(s)/W(s), soccer M(s)/W(s), volleyball W(s). ***Intramural sports:*** bowling M/W, table tennis M/W, ultimate Frisbee M/W, volleyball M/W.

Campus security: student patrols, late-night transport/escort service, controlled dormitory access.

Student services: health clinic, personal/psychological counseling.

COSTS & FINANCIAL AID
Costs (2014–15) ***Comprehensive fee:*** $33,850 includes full-time tuition ($23,850), mandatory fees ($500), and room and board ($9500). Full-time tuition and fees vary according to program. Part-time tuition and fees vary according to course load and program. ***College room only:*** $5600. Room and board charges vary according to board plan and housing facility. ***Payment plans:*** installment, deferred payment. ***Waivers:*** senior citizens and employees or children of employees.

Financial Aid Of all full-time matriculated undergraduates who enrolled in 2011, 157 applied for aid, 149 were judged to have need, 17 had their need fully met. 97 Federal Work-Study jobs (averaging $1429). 3 state and other part-time jobs (averaging $2450). In 2011, 7 non-need-based awards were made. ***Average percent of need met:*** 77. ***Average financial aid package:*** $18,970. ***Average need-based loan:*** $4210. ***Average need-based gift aid:*** $14,197. ***Average non-need-based aid:*** $10,140. ***Average indebtedness upon graduation:*** $35,164.

APPLYING
Standardized Tests *Required:* SAT or ACT (for admission).

Options: electronic application, deferred entrance.

Application fee: $50.

Required: high school transcript, minimum 2.0 GPA, 1 letter of recommendation, ACT/SAT score. ***Required for some:*** essay or personal statement, interview.

Application deadlines: 9/1 (freshmen), 9/1 (transfers).

Notification: continuous (freshmen), continuous (transfers).

CONTACT
Jamie Grant, Executive Director of Enrollment Management, Silver Lake College of the Holy Family, 2406 South Alverno Road, Manitowoc, WI 54220-9319. *Phone:* 920-686-6206. *Toll-free phone:* 800-236-4752 Ext. 175. *Fax:* 920-686-6322. *E-mail:* jamie.grant@sl.edu.

University of Wisconsin–Eau Claire

Eau Claire, Wisconsin

http://www.uwec.edu/

- **State-supported** comprehensive, founded 1916, part of University of Wisconsin System
- **Small-town** 337-acre campus with easy access to Minneapolis-St. Paul
- **Endowment** $62.1 million
- **Coed** 10,164 undergraduate students, 91% full-time, 59% women, 41% men
- **Moderately difficult** entrance level, 84% of applicants were admitted

UNDERGRAD STUDENTS
9,204 full-time, 960 part-time. Students come from 35 states and territories; 36 other countries; 26% are from out of state; 0.7% Black or African American, non-Hispanic/Latino; 2% Hispanic/Latino; 4% Asian, non-Hispanic/Latino; 0.0% Native Hawaiian or other Pacific Islander, non-Hispanic/Latino; 0.3% American Indian or Alaska Native, non-

Hispanic/Latino; 2% Two or more races, non-Hispanic/Latino; 0.1% Race/ethnicity unknown; 3% international; 5% transferred in; 38% live on campus.

Freshmen
Admission: 5,441 applied, 4,552 admitted, 2,020 enrolled. *Test scores:* SAT critical reading scores over 500: 76%; SAT math scores over 500: 71%; ACT scores over 18: 99%; SAT critical reading scores over 600: 17%; SAT math scores over 600: 42%; ACT scores over 24: 53%; SAT math scores over 700: 6%; ACT scores over 30: 6%.
Retention: 83% of full-time freshmen returned.

FACULTY
Total: 542, 82% full-time, 72% with terminal degrees.
Student/faculty ratio: 21:1.

ACADEMICS
Calendar: semesters. *Degrees:* certificates, associate, bachelor's, master's, doctoral, post-master's, and postbachelor's certificates.
Special study options: academic remediation for entering students, accelerated degree program, adult/continuing education programs, advanced placement credit, cooperative education, distance learning, double majors, English as a second language, external degree program, honors programs, independent study, internships, off-campus study, part-time degree program, services for LD students, student-designed majors, study abroad, summer session for credit. *ROTC:* Army (b).
Unusual degree programs: 3-2 Joint degree with Professional Studies.
Computers: 900 computers/terminals are available on campus for general student use. Students can access the following: campus intranet, computer help desk, free student e-mail accounts, online (class) grades, online (class) registration, online (class) schedules, course management system, online library databases and card catalog, other online library services (e.g. Interlibrary loan), library reference staff online chat, ability to check where there are open seats in the general access computer labs, laptop check. Campuswide network is available. 100% of college-owned or -operated housing units are wired for high-speed Internet access. Wireless service is available via entire campus.

STUDENT LIFE
Housing options: on-campus residence required through sophomore year; coed, men-only. Campus housing is university owned. Freshman campus housing is guaranteed.
Activities and organizations: drama/theater group, student-run newspaper, radio and television station, choral group, marching band, American Marketing Association, Beta Upsilon Sigma (Business Fraternity), Blue Gold Marching Band, Singing Statesmen, Navigators, national fraternities, national sororities.
Athletics Member NCAA. All Division III. *Intercollegiate sports:* basketball M/W, cross-country running M/W, football M, golf M/W, gymnastics W, ice hockey M/W, soccer W, softball W, swimming and diving M/W, tennis M/W, track and field M/W, volleyball W, wrestling M. *Intramural sports:* baseball M(c)/W(c), basketball M/W, bowling M/W, cheerleading M(c)/W(c), equestrian sports M(c)/W(c), football M/W, ice hockey M(c), lacrosse M(c)/W(c), rugby M(c)/W(c), skiing (cross-country) M(c)/W(c), skiing (downhill) M(c)/W(c), soccer M/W, softball M/W, table tennis M(c)/W(c), tennis M/W, ultimate Frisbee M/W, volleyball M/W.
Campus security: 24-hour emergency response devices and patrols, student patrols, late-night transport/escort service, controlled dormitory access.
Student services: health clinic, personal/psychological counseling, women's center, legal services.

COSTS & FINANCIAL AID
Costs (2014–15) *Tuition:* state resident $7361 full-time, $307 per credit part-time; nonresident $14,934 full-time, $622 per credit part-time. Full-time tuition and fees vary according to reciprocity agreements. Part-time tuition and fees vary according to reciprocity agreements. *Required fees:* $1383 full-time, $58 per credit part-time. *Room and board:* $6986; room only: $3656. Room and board charges vary according to board plan and housing facility. *Payment plan:* installment.
Financial Aid Of all full-time matriculated undergraduates who enrolled in 2013, 7,308 applied for aid, 5,339 were judged to have need, 4,019 had their need fully met. 4,569 Federal Work-Study jobs (averaging $1517). In 2013, 436 non-need-based awards were made. *Average percent of need met:* 86. *Average financial aid package:* $9751. *Average need-based loan:* $4644. *Average need-based gift aid:* $5887. *Average non-need-based aid:* $1840. *Average indebtedness upon graduation:* $26,210.

APPLYING
Standardized Tests *Required:* SAT or ACT (for admission).
Options: electronic application, early admission.
Application fee: $44.
Required: essay or personal statement, high school transcript.
Application deadlines: rolling (freshmen), rolling (transfers).
Notification: continuous (freshmen), continuous (transfers).

CONTACT
Heather Kretz, Director of Admissions, University of Wisconsin–Eau Claire, PO Box 4004, Eau Claire, WI 54702-4004. *Phone:* 715-836-5415. *Fax:* 715-836-2409. *E-mail:* admissions@uwec.edu.

University of Wisconsin–Green Bay
Green Bay, Wisconsin
http://www.uwgb.edu/

- **State-supported** comprehensive, founded 1968, part of University of Wisconsin System
- **Suburban** 700-acre campus with easy access to Milwaukee
- **Endowment** $28.7 million
- **Coed** 6,668 undergraduate students, 63% full-time, 66% women, 34% men
- **Moderately difficult** entrance level, 68% of applicants were admitted

UNDERGRAD STUDENTS
4,207 full-time, 2,461 part-time. Students come from 38 states and territories; 31 other countries; 7% are from out of state; 1% Black or African American, non-Hispanic/Latino; 4% Hispanic/Latino; 3% Asian, non-Hispanic/Latino; 0.1% Native Hawaiian or other Pacific Islander, non-Hispanic/Latino; 1% American Indian or Alaska Native, non-Hispanic/Latino; 3% Two or more races, non-Hispanic/Latino; 0.2% Race/ethnicity unknown; 1% international; 13% transferred in; 34% live on campus.

Freshmen
Admission: 2,483 applied, 1,700 admitted, 770 enrolled. *Average high school GPA:* 3.33. *Test scores:* ACT scores over 18: 96%; ACT scores over 24: 38%; ACT scores over 30: 3%.
Retention: 77% of full-time freshmen returned.

FACULTY
Total: 317, 60% full-time, 62% with terminal degrees.
Student/faculty ratio: 21:1.

ACADEMICS
Calendar: semesters. *Degrees:* associate, bachelor's, and master's.
Special study options: academic remediation for entering students, adult/continuing education programs, advanced placement credit, distance learning, double majors, external degree program, independent study, internships, off-campus study, part-time degree program, services for LD students, student-designed majors, study abroad, summer session for credit. *ROTC:* Army (c).
Unusual degree programs: 3-2 engineering with University of Wisconsin-Milwaukee.
Computers: 550 computers/terminals are available on campus for general student use. Students can access the following: computer help desk, free student e-mail accounts, online (class) grades, online (class) registration, online (class) schedules, online degree progress, online financial records and bill paying. Campuswide network is available. 100% of college-owned or -operated housing units are wired for high-speed Internet access. Wireless service is available via entire campus.

STUDENT LIFE
Housing options: coed. Campus housing is university owned and is provided by a third party. Freshman applicants given priority for college housing.
Activities and organizations: drama/theater group, student-run newspaper, radio station, choral group, Good Times, Psychology and

Human Development Club, Student Ambassadors, Residence Hall Apartment Association, Student Government Association.

Athletics Member NCAA. All Division I. ***Intercollegiate sports:*** basketball M(s)/W(s), cross-country running M(s)/W(s), golf M(s)/W(s), skiing (cross-country) M(s)/W(s), soccer M(s)/W(s), softball W(s), swimming and diving M(s)/W(s), tennis M(s)/W(s), volleyball W(s). ***Intramural sports:*** basketball M/W, bowling M/W, cheerleading M/W, football M/W, golf M/W, racquetball M/W, sailing M/W, skiing (cross-country) M/W, soccer M/W, softball M/W, swimming and diving M/W, tennis M/W, ultimate Frisbee M/W, volleyball M/W, weight lifting M/W.

Campus security: 24-hour emergency response devices and patrols, late-night transport/escort service, controlled dormitory access.

Student services: health clinic, personal/psychological counseling.

COSTS & FINANCIAL AID

Costs (2014–15) ***One-time required fee:*** $212. ***Tuition:*** state resident $6298 full-time, $262 per credit hour part-time; nonresident $13,871 full-time, $578 per credit hour part-time. Full-time tuition and fees vary according to course load and reciprocity agreements. Part-time tuition and fees vary according to reciprocity agreements. ***Required fees:*** $1460 full-time, $57 per credit hour part-time. ***Room and board:*** $7224; room only: $4116. Room and board charges vary according to board plan and housing facility. ***Payment plan:*** installment. ***Waivers:*** senior citizens.

Financial Aid Of all full-time matriculated undergraduates who enrolled in 2014, 3,458 applied for aid, 2,888 were judged to have need, 850 had their need fully met. 219 Federal Work-Study jobs (averaging $1071). 219 state and other part-time jobs (averaging $357). In 2014, 73 non-need-based awards were made. ***Average percent of need met:*** 75. ***Average financial aid package:*** $10,258. ***Average need-based loan:*** $5878. ***Average need-based gift aid:*** $5713. ***Average non-need-based aid:*** $2177. ***Average indebtedness upon graduation:*** $27,239.

APPLYING

Standardized Tests *Required:* SAT or ACT (for admission).

Options: electronic application, deferred entrance.

Application fee: $44.

Required: essay or personal statement, high school transcript. ***Required for some:*** interview.

Application deadlines: rolling (freshmen), rolling (out-of-state freshmen), rolling (transfers).

Notification: continuous (freshmen), continuous (out-of-state freshmen), continuous (transfers).

CONTACT

Ms. Pam Harvey-Jacobs, Director of Admissions, University of Wisconsin–Green Bay, 2420 Nicolet Drive, Green Bay, WI 54311-7001. *Phone:* 920-465-2111. *Fax:* 920-465-5754. *E-mail:* uwgb@uwgb.edu.

University of Wisconsin–La Crosse

La Crosse, Wisconsin

http://www.uwlax.edu/

- **State-supported** comprehensive, founded 1909, part of University of Wisconsin System
- **Suburban** 121-acre campus
- **Endowment** $20.1 million
- **Coed** 9,755 undergraduate students, 95% full-time, 57% women, 43% men
- **Moderately difficult** entrance level, 76% of applicants were admitted

UNDERGRAD STUDENTS

9,276 full-time, 479 part-time. Students come from 31 states and territories; 26 other countries; 17% are from out of state; 0.7% Black or African American, non-Hispanic/Latino; 3% Hispanic/Latino; 2% Asian, non-Hispanic/Latino; 0.1% Native Hawaiian or other Pacific Islander, non-Hispanic/Latino; 0.2% American Indian or Alaska Native, non-Hispanic/Latino; 3% Two or more races, non-Hispanic/Latino; 0.1% Race/ethnicity unknown; 3% international; 5% transferred in; 36% live on campus.

Freshmen

Admission: 6,030 applied, 4,564 admitted, 1,980 enrolled. ***Test scores:*** SAT critical reading scores over 500: 71%; SAT math scores over 500: 71%; ACT scores over 18: 100%; SAT critical reading scores over 600: 39%; SAT math scores over 600: 43%; ACT scores over 24: 64%; ACT scores over 30: 6%.

Retention: 86% of full-time freshmen returned.

FACULTY

Total: 602, 83% full-time, 76% with terminal degrees.

Student/faculty ratio: 19:1.

ACADEMICS

Calendar: semesters. *Degrees:* certificates, associate, bachelor's, master's, doctoral, and postbachelor's certificates.

Special study options: academic remediation for entering students, adult/continuing education programs, advanced placement credit, cooperative education, distance learning, double majors, English as a second language, independent study, internships, off-campus study, part-time degree program, services for LD students, study abroad, summer session for credit. ***ROTC:*** Army (b).

Unusual degree programs: 3-2 engineering with University of Wisconsin-Madison, University of Wisconsin-Milwaukee, University of Wisconsin- Platteville, University of Minnesota; physical therapy and physics, physical therapy and biology, occupational therapy and psychology.

Computers: 200 computers/terminals are available on campus for general student use. Students can access the following: campus intranet, computer help desk, free student e-mail accounts, online (class) grades, online (class) registration, online (class) schedules. Campuswide network is available. 100% of college-owned or -operated housing units are wired for high-speed Internet access. Wireless service is available via classrooms, computer centers, computer labs, dorm rooms, learning centers, libraries, student centers.

STUDENT LIFE

Housing options: on-campus residence required for freshman year; coed, special housing for students with disabilities. Campus housing is university owned. Freshman applicants given priority for college housing.

Activities and organizations: drama/theater group, student-run newspaper, radio and television station, choral group, marching band, Sports and Activities Club, Residential Hall Council, religious/spiritual organizations, Human Diversity Organizations, departmental/professional, national fraternities, national sororities.

Athletics Member NCAA. All Division III. ***Intercollegiate sports:*** baseball M, basketball M/W, cross-country running M/W, football M, gymnastics W, soccer W, softball W, swimming and diving M/W, tennis M/W, track and field M/W, volleyball W, wrestling M. ***Intramural sports:*** archery M(c)/W(c), basketball M/W, cheerleading M/W, equestrian sports M(c)/W(c), football M/W, ice hockey M(c)/W(c), lacrosse M(c)/W(c), racquetball M/W, rugby M(c)/W(c), skiing (cross-country) M(c)/W(c), skiing (downhill) M(c)/W(c), soccer M(c)/W(c), softball M/W, table tennis M/W, tennis M/W, ultimate Frisbee M(c)/W(c), volleyball M(c)/W(c), weight lifting M(c)/W(c).

Campus security: 24-hour emergency response devices and patrols, late-night transport/escort service, controlled dormitory access.

Student services: health clinic, personal/psychological counseling, women's center, legal services.

COSTS & FINANCIAL AID

Costs (2014–15) ***Tuition:*** state resident $7585 full-time; nonresident $15,158 full-time. Full-time tuition and fees vary according to program and reciprocity agreements. Part-time tuition and fees vary according to course load, program, and reciprocity agreements. ***Required fees:*** $1210 full-time. ***Room and board:*** $5910; room only: $3500. Room and board charges vary according to board plan and housing facility. ***Payment plan:*** installment. ***Waivers:*** minority students.

Financial Aid Of all full-time matriculated undergraduates who enrolled in 2013, 6,895 applied for aid, 4,784 were judged to have need, 755 had their need fully met. In 2013, 187 non-need-based awards were made. ***Average percent of need met:*** 67. ***Average financial aid package:*** $7188. ***Average need-based loan:*** $4192. ***Average need-based gift aid:*** $5715. ***Average non-need-based aid:*** $1583. ***Average indebtedness upon graduation:*** $25,932.

APPLYING

Standardized Tests *Required:* SAT or ACT (for admission).

Options: electronic application.

Application fee: $44.

Required: essay or personal statement, high school transcript. ***Required for some:*** interview.

Application deadlines: rolling (freshmen), rolling (out-of-state freshmen), rolling (transfers).

Notification: continuous (freshmen), continuous (out-of-state freshmen), continuous (transfers).

CONTACT
Mr. Corey Sjoquist, Director of Admissions, University of Wisconsin–La Crosse, 1725 State Street, La Crosse, WI 54601. *Phone:* 608-785-8939. *Fax:* 608-785-8940. *E-mail:* admissions@uwlax.edu.

University of Wisconsin–Madison

Madison, Wisconsin

http://www.wisc.edu/

- **State-supported** university, founded 1848, part of University of Wisconsin System
- **Urban** 936-acre campus with easy access to Milwaukee
- **Endowment** $1.9 billion
- **Coed** 31,289 undergraduate students, 91% full-time, 51% women, 49% men
- **Very difficult** entrance level, 50% of applicants were admitted

UNDERGRAD STUDENTS
28,324 full-time, 2,965 part-time. Students come from 52 states and territories; 126 other countries; 33% are from out of state; 2% Black or African American, non-Hispanic/Latino; 5% Hispanic/Latino; 5% Asian, non-Hispanic/Latino; 0.1% Native Hawaiian or other Pacific Islander, non-Hispanic/Latino; 0.2% American Indian or Alaska Native, non-Hispanic/Latino; 3% Two or more races, non-Hispanic/Latino; 0.3% Race/ethnicity unknown; 7% international; 2% transferred in; 25% live on campus.

Freshmen
Admission: 30,464 applied, 15,183 admitted, 6,264 enrolled. ***Average high school GPA:*** 3.83. ***Test scores:*** SAT critical reading scores over 500: 96%; SAT math scores over 500: 98%; SAT writing scores over 500: 96%; ACT scores over 18: 100%; SAT critical reading scores over 600: 61%; SAT math scores over 600: 85%; SAT writing scores over 600: 74%; ACT scores over 24: 95%; SAT critical reading scores over 700: 14%; SAT math scores over 700: 45%; SAT writing scores over 700: 20%; ACT scores over 30: 39%.

Retention: 95% of full-time freshmen returned.

FACULTY
Total: 2,935, 83% full-time, 87% with terminal degrees.

Student/faculty ratio: 17:1.

ACADEMICS
Calendar: semesters. *Degrees:* bachelor's, master's, doctoral, and postbachelor's certificates.

Special study options: accelerated degree program, adult/continuing education programs, advanced placement credit, cooperative education, distance learning, double majors, English as a second language, honors programs, independent study, internships, part-time degree program, services for LD students, student-designed majors, study abroad, summer session for credit. ***ROTC:*** Army (b), Navy (b), Air Force (b).

Unusual degree programs: 3-2 BS/MS, BBA/MACC.

Computers: 1,000 computers/terminals are available on campus for general student use. Students can access the following: computer help desk, free student e-mail accounts, online (class) grades, online (class) registration, online (class) schedules. Campuswide network is available. 100% of college-owned or -operated housing units are wired for high-speed Internet access. Wireless service is available via entire campus.

STUDENT LIFE
Housing options: coed, men-only, women-only, cooperative. Campus housing is university owned. Freshman applicants given priority for college housing.

Activities and organizations: drama/theater group, student-run newspaper, radio station, choral group, marching band, national fraternities, national sororities.

Athletics Member NCAA. All Division I except football (Division I-A). ***Intercollegiate sports:*** basketball M(s)/W(s), cheerleading M/W, crew M/W, cross-country running M(s)/W(s), fencing M(c)/W(c), golf M(s)/W(s), ice hockey M(s)/W(s), lacrosse M(c)/W(c), racquetball M(c)/W(c), rugby M(c)/W(c), sailing M(c)/W(c), soccer M(s)/W(s), softball W(s), swimming and diving M(s)/W(s), tennis M(s)/W(s), track and field M(s)/W(s), ultimate Frisbee M(c)/W(c), volleyball M(c)/W(s), water polo M(c)/W(c), wrestling M(s). ***Intramural sports:*** badminton M(c)/W(c), basketball M/W, fencing M(c)/W(c), racquetball M/W, softball M/W, tennis M/W, ultimate Frisbee M/W, volleyball M/W.

Campus security: 24-hour emergency response devices and patrols, late-night transport/escort service, controlled dormitory access.

Student services: health clinic, personal/psychological counseling, women's center.

COSTS & FINANCIAL AID
Costs (2014–15) ***Tuition:*** state resident $9273 full-time, $386 per credit hour part-time; nonresident $25,523 full-time, $1063 per credit hour part-time. Full-time tuition and fees vary according to program and reciprocity agreements. Part-time tuition and fees vary according to course load, program, and reciprocity agreements. ***Required fees:*** $1137 full-time, $94 per credit hour part-time. ***Room and board:*** $8600. Room and board charges vary according to board plan and housing facility.

Financial Aid Of all full-time matriculated undergraduates who enrolled in 2014, 15,549 applied for aid, 10,750 were judged to have need, 4,129 had their need fully met. In 2014, 1893 non-need-based awards were made. ***Average percent of need met:*** 80. ***Average financial aid package:*** $14,015. ***Average need-based loan:*** $5995. ***Average need-based gift aid:*** $9890. ***Average non-need-based aid:*** $3876. ***Average indebtedness upon graduation:*** $26,579.

APPLYING
Standardized Tests *Required:* SAT or ACT (for admission).

Options: electronic application, deferred entrance.

Application fee: $44.

Required: essay or personal statement, high school transcript. ***Recommended:*** 2 letters of recommendation.

Application deadlines: 2/1 (freshmen), 2/1 (transfers).

Notification: continuous (freshmen), continuous (transfers).

CONTACT
Office of Admissions and Recruitment, University of Wisconsin–Madison, 702 West Johnson Street, Suite 101, Madison, WI 53706-1481. *Phone:* 608-262-3961. *Fax:* 608-262-7706. *E-mail:* onwisconsin@admissions.wisc.edu.

University of Wisconsin–Milwaukee

Milwaukee, Wisconsin

http://www.uwm.edu/

- **State-supported** university, founded 1956, part of University of Wisconsin System
- **Urban** 104-acre campus with easy access to Milwaukee
- **Endowment** $94.5 million
- **Coed** 23,079 undergraduate students, 81% full-time, 51% women, 49% men
- **Moderately difficult** entrance level, 75% of applicants were admitted

UNDERGRAD STUDENTS
18,772 full-time, 4,307 part-time. Students come from 49 states and territories; 89 other countries; 6% are from out of state; 8% Black or African American, non-Hispanic/Latino; 8% Hispanic/Latino; 6% Asian, non-Hispanic/Latino; 0.1% Native Hawaiian or other Pacific Islander, non-Hispanic/Latino; 0.5% American Indian or Alaska Native, non-Hispanic/Latino; 3% Two or more races, non-Hispanic/Latino; 0.3% Race/ethnicity unknown; 4% international; 8% transferred in; 18% live on campus.

Freshmen
Admission: 9,635 applied, 7,193 admitted, 3,453 enrolled. ***Average high school GPA:*** 3.05. ***Test scores:*** ACT scores over 18: 89%; ACT scores over 24: 32%; ACT scores over 30: 3%.

FACULTY
Total: 1,644, 68% full-time, 61% with terminal degrees.

Student/faculty ratio: 18:1.

ACADEMICS
Calendar: semesters. *Degrees:* certificates, bachelor's, master's, doctoral, post-master's, and postbachelor's certificates.

Special study options: academic remediation for entering students, accelerated degree program, adult/continuing education programs, advanced placement credit, cooperative education, distance learning, double majors, English as a second language, freshman honors college, honors programs, independent study, internships, off-campus study, part-time degree program, services for LD students, student-designed majors, study abroad, summer session for credit. ***ROTC:*** Army (c), Navy (c), Air Force (c).

Computers: 500 computers/terminals are available on campus for general student use. Students can access the following: campus intranet, computer help desk, free student e-mail accounts, online (class) grades, online (class) registration, online (class) schedules. Campuswide network is available. 100% of college-owned or -operated housing units are wired for high-speed Internet access. Wireless service is available via classrooms, computer centers, computer labs, learning centers, libraries, student centers.

STUDENT LIFE
Housing options: on-campus residence required for freshman year; coed, special housing for students with disabilities. Campus housing is university owned. Freshman applicants given priority for college housing.

Activities and organizations: drama/theater group, student-run newspaper, choral group, national fraternities, national sororities.

Athletics Member NCAA. All Division I. ***Intercollegiate sports:*** baseball M(s), basketball M(s)/W(s), bowling M(c)/W(c), cross-country running M(s)/W(s), equestrian sports M(c)/W(c), football M(c)/W(c), ice hockey M(c)/W(c), lacrosse M(c)/W(c), rugby M(c)/W(c), sailing M(c)/W(c), soccer M(s)/W(s), swimming and diving M(s)/W(s), tennis W(s), track and field M(s)/W(s), ultimate Frisbee M(c)/W(c), volleyball M(c)/W(s). ***Intramural sports:*** badminton M/W, baseball M(c)/W(c), basketball M/W, cross-country running M/W, football M/W, racquetball M/W, skiing (downhill) M(c)/W(c), soccer M/W, swimming and diving M/W, tennis M(c)/W(c), track and field M(c)/W(c), volleyball M/W.

Campus security: 24-hour emergency response devices and patrols, student patrols, late-night transport/escort service, controlled dormitory access.

Student services: health clinic, personal/psychological counseling, women's center, legal services.

COSTS & FINANCIAL AID
Costs (2015–16) ***Tuition:*** state resident $8091 full-time, $337 per credit part-time; nonresident $17,820 full-time, $742 per credit part-time. Full-time tuition and fees vary according to course load, degree level, location, program, and reciprocity agreements. Part-time tuition and fees vary according to course load, degree level, location, program, and reciprocity agreements. ***Required fees:*** $1300 full-time, $1300 per year part-time. ***Room and board:*** $9126; room only: $6126. Room and board charges vary according to board plan, housing facility, and location. ***Payment plan:*** installment. ***Waivers:*** senior citizens.

Financial Aid Of all full-time matriculated undergraduates who enrolled in 2013, 16,936 applied for aid, 14,620 were judged to have need, 2,836 had their need fully met. In 2013, 83 non-need-based awards were made. ***Average percent of need met:*** 46. ***Average financial aid package:*** $7635. ***Average need-based loan:*** $4220. ***Average need-based gift aid:*** $5890. ***Average non-need-based aid:*** $2239. ***Average indebtedness upon graduation:*** $33,234.

APPLYING
Standardized Tests *Required:* SAT or ACT (for admission). *Required for some:* Students whose native language is not English and who were not educated in an entirely English-speaking country will likely need to submit results from the Test of English as a Foreign Language (TOEFL).

Options: electronic application, deferred entrance.

Application fee: $44.

Required: high school transcript. ***Recommended:*** essay or personal statement.

Application deadlines: rolling (freshmen), 7/1 (transfers).

Notification: continuous (freshmen), continuous (transfers).

CONTACT
Brian Troyer, Director, Admissions and Recruitment, University of Wisconsin–Milwaukee, PO Box 413, Milwaukee, WI 53201-0413. *Phone:* 414-229-4445. *E-mail:* uwmlook@uwm.edu.

University of Wisconsin–Oshkosh

Oshkosh, Wisconsin

http://www.uwosh.edu/

- **State-supported** comprehensive, founded 1871, part of University of Wisconsin System
- **Suburban** 192-acre campus with easy access to Milwaukee
- **Coed** 13,194 undergraduate students, 68% full-time, 60% women, 40% men
- **Moderately difficult** entrance level, 68% of applicants were admitted

UNDERGRAD STUDENTS
9,020 full-time, 4,174 part-time. 6% are from out of state; 2% Black or African American, non-Hispanic/Latino; 3% Hispanic/Latino; 4% Asian, non-Hispanic/Latino; 0.1% Native Hawaiian or other Pacific Islander, non-Hispanic/Latino; 0.6% American Indian or Alaska Native, non-Hispanic/Latino; 2% Two or more races, non-Hispanic/Latino; 0.5% Race/ethnicity unknown; 0.8% international; 7% transferred in; 32% live on campus.

Freshmen
Admission: 5,846 applied, 3,966 admitted, 1,691 enrolled. ***Average high school GPA:*** 3.3. ***Test scores:*** ACT scores over 18: 95%; ACT scores over 24: 33%; ACT scores over 30: 2%.

Retention: 75% of full-time freshmen returned.

FACULTY
Total: 628, 69% full-time, 62% with terminal degrees.

Student/faculty ratio: 22:1.

ACADEMICS
Calendar: semesters. *Degrees:* certificates, associate, bachelor's, master's, doctoral, and postbachelor's certificates.

Special study options: academic remediation for entering students, accelerated degree program, adult/continuing education programs, advanced placement credit, cooperative education, distance learning, double majors, English as a second language, honors programs, independent study, internships, part-time degree program, services for LD students, student-designed majors, study abroad, summer session for credit. ***ROTC:*** Army (b).

Computers: Students can access the following: campus intranet, computer help desk, free student e-mail accounts, online (class) grades, online (class) registration, online (class) schedules. Campuswide network is available. 100% of college-owned or -operated housing units are wired for high-speed Internet access. Wireless service is available via entire campus.

STUDENT LIFE
Housing options: on-campus residence required through sophomore year; coed. Campus housing is university owned. Freshman campus housing is guaranteed.

Activities and organizations: drama/theater group, student-run newspaper, radio and television station, choral group, national fraternities, national sororities.

Athletics Member NCAA. All Division III. ***Intercollegiate sports:*** baseball M, basketball M/W, cross-country running M/W, football M, golf W, gymnastics W, riflery M/W, soccer M/W, softball W, swimming and diving M/W, tennis M/W, track and field M/W, volleyball W, wrestling M. ***Intramural sports:*** basketball M/W, bowling M(c)/W(c), cross-country running M/W, football M/W, golf M/W, gymnastics M(c), ice hockey M(c), lacrosse M(c)/W(c), racquetball M/W, skiing (downhill) M/W, soccer M/W, softball M/W, tennis M/W, volleyball M(c)/W, wrestling M.

Campus security: 24-hour emergency response devices and patrols, student patrols, late-night transport/escort service, controlled dormitory access.

Student services: health clinic, personal/psychological counseling, women's center, legal services.

COSTS & FINANCIAL AID
Costs (2014–15) ***Tuition:*** state resident $7437 full-time, $310 per credit part-time; nonresident $15,010 full-time, $625 per credit part-time. ***Room and board:*** $7386.

Financial Aid Of all full-time matriculated undergraduates who enrolled in 2013, 8,368 applied for aid, 6,630 were judged to have need, 2,354 had their need fully met. In 2013, 870 non-need-based awards were made. ***Average percent of need met:*** 42. ***Average financial aid package:*** $7800. ***Average need-based loan:*** $2120. ***Average need-based gift aid:*** $4747. ***Average non-need-based aid:*** $961. ***Average indebtedness upon graduation:*** $25,259.

APPLYING
Standardized Tests *Required:* ACT (for admission).

Options: electronic application, deferred entrance.

Application fee: $44.

Required: high school transcript. ***Recommended:*** essay or personal statement.

CONTACT
Associate Director of Admissions, University of Wisconsin–Oshkosh, 800 Algoma Boulevard, Oshkosh, WI 54901. *Phone:* 920-424-0202. *E-mail:* oshadmuw@uwosh.edu.

University of Wisconsin–Parkside
Kenosha, Wisconsin
http://www.uwp.edu/

- **State-supported** comprehensive, founded 1968, part of University of Wisconsin System
- **Suburban** 700-acre campus with easy access to Chicago, Milwaukee
- **Coed** 4,448 undergraduate students, 75% full-time, 52% women, 48% men
- **Moderately difficult** entrance level, 86% of applicants were admitted

UNDERGRAD STUDENTS
3,338 full-time, 1,110 part-time. 15% are from out of state; 8% Black or African American, non-Hispanic/Latino; 12% Hispanic/Latino; 3% Asian, non-Hispanic/Latino; 0.2% Native Hawaiian or other Pacific Islander, non-Hispanic/Latino; 0.2% American Indian or Alaska Native, non-Hispanic/Latino; 4% Two or more races, non-Hispanic/Latino; 0.4% Race/ethnicity unknown; 2% international; 10% transferred in; 18% live on campus.

Freshmen
Admission: 1,509 applied, 1,298 admitted, 618 enrolled. ***Average high school GPA:*** 3.05. ***Test scores:*** ACT scores over 18: 86%; ACT scores over 24: 24%; ACT scores over 30: 1%.

Retention: 74% of full-time freshmen returned.

FACULTY
Total: 231, 69% full-time, 60% with terminal degrees.

Student/faculty ratio: 21:1.

ACADEMICS
Calendar: semesters. *Degrees:* certificates, bachelor's, and master's.

Special study options: academic remediation for entering students, advanced placement credit, distance learning, double majors, external degree program, honors programs, independent study, internships, off-campus study, part-time degree program, services for LD students, study abroad, summer session for credit. ***ROTC:*** Army (c).

Unusual degree programs: 3-2 molecular biology.

Computers: 84 computers/terminals are available on campus for general student use. Students can access the following: campus intranet, computer help desk, free student e-mail accounts, online (class) grades, online (class) registration, online (class) schedules. Campuswide network is available. 100% of college-owned or -operated housing units are wired for high-speed Internet access. Wireless service is available via entire campus.

STUDENT LIFE
Housing options: on-campus residence required through sophomore year; coed, special housing for students with disabilities. Campus housing is university owned.

Activities and organizations: drama/theater group, student-run newspaper, radio station, choral group, Black Student Union, Parkside Asian Organization, Parkside Activities Board, Latinos Unidos, Men's Rugby Club, national fraternities, national sororities.

Athletics Member NCAA. All Division II. ***Intercollegiate sports:*** baseball M(s), basketball M(s)/W(s), cross-country running M(s)/W(s), golf M(s), soccer M(s)/W(s), softball W(s), track and field M(s)/W(s), volleyball W(s), wrestling M(s). ***Intramural sports:*** basketball M/W, cheerleading M(c)/W(c), football M(c), racquetball M/W, rugby M(c)/W(c), soccer M/W, softball M/W, table tennis M/W, tennis M/W, volleyball M/W.

Campus security: 24-hour emergency response devices and patrols, late-night transport/escort service, controlled dormitory access.

Student services: health clinic, personal/psychological counseling, women's center.

COSTS & FINANCIAL AID
Costs (2015–16) ***Tuition:*** state resident $7316 full-time; nonresident $14,889 full-time. Full-time tuition and fees vary according to course load and program. Part-time tuition and fees vary according to course load and program. ***Required fees:*** $1018 full-time. ***Room and board:*** $6572; room only: $4276. Room and board charges vary according to board plan.

Financial Aid Of all full-time matriculated undergraduates who enrolled in 2013, 2,624 applied for aid, 2,243 were judged to have need. ***Average need-based gift aid:*** $6264.

APPLYING
Standardized Tests *Required for some:* SAT or ACT (for admission).

Options: electronic application.

Application fee: $44.

Required: high school transcript, minimum of 17 high school units distribution.

Application deadlines: 8/1 (freshmen), 7/15 (transfers).

Notification: continuous (freshmen), continuous (transfers).

CONTACT
Mrs. DeAnn Possehl, Director, Enrollment Management, University of Wisconsin–Parkside, PO Box 2000, 900 Wood Road, Kenosha, WI 53141-2000. *Phone:* 262-595-2454. *E-mail:* possehl@uwp.edu.

University of Wisconsin–Platteville
Platteville, Wisconsin
http://www.uwplatt.edu/

- **State-supported** comprehensive, founded 1866, part of University of Wisconsin System
- **Small-town** 820-acre campus
- **Endowment** $23.4 million
- **Coed** 8,047 undergraduate students, 89% full-time, 35% women, 65% men

UNDERGRAD STUDENTS
7,147 full-time, 900 part-time. Students come from 12 states and territories; 11 other countries; 24% are from out of state; 1% Black or African American, non-Hispanic/Latino; 3% Hispanic/Latino; 1% Asian, non-Hispanic/Latino; 0.1% Native Hawaiian or other Pacific Islander, non-Hispanic/Latino; 0.2% American Indian or Alaska Native, non-Hispanic/Latino; 2% Two or more races, non-Hispanic/Latino; 0.2% Race/ethnicity unknown; 2% international; 6% transferred in; 47% live on campus.

Freshmen
Admission: 1,705 enrolled. ***Test scores:*** ACT scores over 18: 96%; ACT scores over 24: 45%; ACT scores over 30: 6%.

Retention: 78% of full-time freshmen returned.

FACULTY
Total: 424, 83% full-time, 54% with terminal degrees.

Student/faculty ratio: 21:1.

ACADEMICS
Calendar: semesters. *Degrees:* certificates, associate, bachelor's, master's, and postbachelor's certificates.

Special study options: academic remediation for entering students, adult/continuing education programs, advanced placement credit, cooperative education, distance learning, double majors, external degree program, honors programs, independent study, internships, off-campus study, part-time degree program, services for LD students, student-designed majors, study abroad, summer session for credit. ***ROTC:*** Army (c).

Computers: Students can access the following: campus intranet, computer help desk, free student e-mail accounts, online (class) grades, online (class) registration, online (class) schedules. Campuswide network is available. 100% of college-owned or -operated housing units are wired for high-speed Internet access. Wireless service is available via classrooms, libraries, student centers.

STUDENT LIFE

Housing options: on-campus residence required through sophomore year; coed, men-only, women-only, special housing for students with disabilities. Campus housing is university owned. Freshman campus housing is guaranteed.

Activities and organizations: drama/theater group, student-run newspaper, radio and television station, choral group, marching band, Criminal Justice Association, Platteville Gaming Association, Dodgeball, American Society of Mechanical Engineers, Outdoor Adventure Club, national fraternities, national sororities.

Athletics Member NCAA. All Division III. ***Intercollegiate sports:*** baseball M, basketball M/W, bowling M(c)/W(c), cheerleading M/W, cross-country running M/W, football M, golf W, ice hockey M(c)/W(c), lacrosse M(c)/W(c), rugby M(c)/W(c), soccer M/W, softball W, track and field M/W, ultimate Frisbee M(c)/W(c), volleyball M(c)/W, wrestling M. ***Intramural sports:*** badminton M/W, basketball M/W, bowling M(c)/W(c), cheerleading M(c)/W(c), football M/W, racquetball M/W, soccer M/W, softball M/W, tennis M/W, ultimate Frisbee M/W, volleyball M/W, water polo M/W.

Campus security: 24-hour emergency response devices and patrols, student patrols, late-night transport/escort service.

Student services: health clinic, personal/psychological counseling, women's center.

COSTS & FINANCIAL AID

Costs (2014–15) ***Tuition:*** state resident $6298 full-time, $262 per credit hour part-time; nonresident $13,871 full-time, $578 per credit hour part-time. ***Required fees:*** $1193 full-time. ***Room and board:*** $7080; room only: $3890. Room and board charges vary according to board plan and housing facility.

Financial Aid Of all full-time matriculated undergraduates who enrolled in 2002, 3,289 applied for aid, 2,468 were judged to have need. 382 Federal Work-Study jobs (averaging $1392). In 2002, 652 non-need-based awards were made. ***Average financial aid package:*** $6161. ***Average need-based loan:*** $3499. ***Average need-based gift aid:*** $3599. ***Average non-need-based aid:*** $1427. ***Average indebtedness upon graduation:*** $15,785.

APPLYING

Standardized Tests *Required:* SAT or ACT (for admission).

Required: high school transcript. ***Recommended:*** essay or personal statement.

CONTACT

Mrs. Angela Udelhofen, Director of Admissions and Enrollment Management, University of Wisconsin–Platteville, 1 University Plaza, 1300 Ullsvik Hall, Platteville, WI 53818-3099. *Phone:* 608-342-1125. *Toll-free phone:* 800-362-5515. *Fax:* 608-342-1122. *E-mail:* rulea@uwplatt.edu.

University of Wisconsin–River Falls

River Falls, Wisconsin

http://www.uwrf.edu/

- **State-supported** comprehensive, founded 1874, part of University of Wisconsin System
- **Suburban** 303-acre campus with easy access to Minneapolis-St. Paul
- **Endowment** $14.8 million
- **Coed** 5,721 undergraduate students, 91% full-time, 60% women, 40% men
- **Moderately difficult** entrance level, 78% of applicants were admitted

UNDERGRAD STUDENTS

5,179 full-time, 542 part-time. Students come from 30 states and territories; 21 other countries; 53% are from out of state; 2% Black or African American, non-Hispanic/Latino; 3% Hispanic/Latino; 2% Asian, non-Hispanic/Latino; 0.1% Native Hawaiian or other Pacific Islander, non-Hispanic/Latino; 0.3% American Indian or Alaska Native, non-Hispanic/Latino; 2% Two or more races, non-Hispanic/Latino; 0.3% Race/ethnicity unknown; 1% international; 8% transferred in; 40% live on campus.

Freshmen

Admission: 2,684 applied, 2,082 admitted, 978 enrolled. ***Average high school GPA:*** 3.31. ***Test scores:*** SAT critical reading scores over 500: 55%; SAT math scores over 500: 36%; SAT writing scores over 500: 55%; ACT scores over 18: 96%; SAT critical reading scores over 600: 27%; SAT math scores over 600: 9%; SAT writing scores over 600: 9%; ACT scores over 24: 38%; ACT scores over 30: 3%.

Retention: 76% of full-time freshmen returned.

FACULTY

Total: 400, 51% full-time.

Student/faculty ratio: 20:1.

ACADEMICS

Calendar: semesters. *Degrees:* certificates, bachelor's, master's, post-master's, and postbachelor's certificates.

Special study options: academic remediation for entering students, adult/continuing education programs, advanced placement credit, distance learning, double majors, English as a second language, external degree program, honors programs, independent study, internships, off-campus study, part-time degree program, services for LD students, study abroad, summer session for credit. ***ROTC:*** Army (b).

Unusual degree programs: 3-2 engineering with University of Wisconsin-Madison and University of Minnesota-Twin Cities.

Computers: 700 computers/terminals are available on campus for general student use. Students can access the following: computer help desk, free student e-mail accounts, online (class) grades, online (class) registration, online (class) schedules, 100% wireless on campus. Campuswide network is available. 100% of college-owned or -operated housing units are wired for high-speed Internet access. Wireless service is available via classrooms, computer centers, computer labs, dorm rooms, learning centers, libraries, student centers.

STUDENT LIFE

Housing options: on-campus residence required through sophomore year; coed, women-only, special housing for students with disabilities. Campus housing is university owned. Freshman campus housing is guaranteed.

Activities and organizations: drama/theater group, student-run newspaper, radio and television station, choral group, Intervarsity Christian Fellowship, Swing Dance Club, Gender and Sexuality Alliance, Dairy Club, Asian American Student Association, national fraternities, national sororities.

Athletics Member NCAA. All Division III. ***Intercollegiate sports:*** badminton M(c)/W(c), baseball M(c), basketball M/W, cross-country running M/W, equestrian sports M(c)/W(c), football M, golf W, ice hockey M/W, lacrosse M(c)/W(c), racquetball M(c)/W(c), rock climbing M(c)/W(c), rugby M(c)/W(c), skiing (cross-country) M(c)/W(c), soccer W, softball W, swimming and diving M/W, tennis W, track and field M/W, volleyball M(c)/W, wrestling M(c). ***Intramural sports:*** basketball M/W, football M/W, soccer M/W, softball M/W, tennis W, ultimate Frisbee M/W, volleyball M/W.

Campus security: 24-hour emergency response devices and patrols, student patrols, late-night transport/escort service, controlled dormitory access.

Student services: health clinic, personal/psychological counseling.

COSTS & FINANCIAL AID
Costs (2014–15) ***Tuition:*** state resident $6428 full-time, $268 per credit hour part-time; nonresident $14,001 full-time, $583 per credit hour part-time. Full-time tuition and fees vary according to course load, degree level, and reciprocity agreements. Part-time tuition and fees vary according to course load, degree level, and reciprocity agreements. ***Required fees:*** $1323 full-time. ***Room and board:*** $6435. Room and board charges vary according to board plan and housing facility.

Financial Aid Of all full-time matriculated undergraduates who enrolled in 2013, 4,096 applied for aid, 3,241 were judged to have need, 35 had their need fully met. 452 Federal Work-Study jobs (averaging $1031). In 2013, 137 non-need-based awards were made. ***Average percent of need met:*** 54. ***Average financial aid package:*** $6846. ***Average need-based loan:*** $4194. ***Average need-based gift aid:*** $4906. ***Average non-need-based aid:*** $1275. ***Average indebtedness upon graduation:*** $27,134.

APPLYING
Standardized Tests *Required:* SAT or ACT (for admission). *Recommended:* ACT (for admission).

Options: electronic application, deferred entrance.

Application fee: $44.

Required: essay or personal statement, high school transcript. ***Recommended:*** rank in upper 40% of high school class.

Application deadlines: rolling (freshmen), rolling (transfers).

Notification: continuous (freshmen), continuous (transfers).

CONTACT
Sarah Egerstrom, Director of Admissions, University of Wisconsin–River Falls, 410 South Third Street, River Falls, WI 54022. *Phone:* 715-425-3500. *Fax:* 715-425-0676. *E-mail:* admit@uwrf.edu.

University of Wisconsin–Stevens Point

Stevens Point, Wisconsin

http://www.uwsp.edu/

- **State-supported** comprehensive, founded 1894, part of University of Wisconsin System
- **Small-town** 400-acre campus
- **Endowment** $21.8 million
- **Coed** 8,975 undergraduate students, 93% full-time, 52% women, 48% men
- **Moderately difficult** entrance level, 81% of applicants were admitted

UNDERGRAD STUDENTS
8,334 full-time, 641 part-time. Students come from 36 states and territories; 29 other countries; 10% are from out of state; 2% Black or African American, non-Hispanic/Latino; 3% Hispanic/Latino; 3% Asian, non-Hispanic/Latino; 0.4% American Indian or Alaska Native, non-Hispanic/Latino; 2% Two or more races, non-Hispanic/Latino; 0.2% Race/ethnicity unknown; 2% international; 8% transferred in; 26% live on campus.

Freshmen
Admission: 4,593 applied, 3,729 admitted, 1,616 enrolled. ***Average high school GPA:*** 3.33. ***Test scores:*** SAT critical reading scores over 500: 50%; SAT math scores over 500: 36%; SAT writing scores over 500: 46%; ACT scores over 18: 99%; SAT critical reading scores over 600: 14%; SAT math scores over 600: 18%; SAT writing scores over 600: 14%; ACT scores over 24: 42%; ACT scores over 30: 4%.

Retention: 78% of full-time freshmen returned.

FACULTY
Total: 532, 75% full-time, 76% with terminal degrees.

Student/faculty ratio: 20:1.

ACADEMICS
Calendar: semesters. *Degrees:* associate, bachelor's, master's, and doctoral.

Special study options: academic remediation for entering students, accelerated degree program, advanced placement credit, cooperative education, distance learning, double majors, English as a second language, independent study, internships, off-campus study, part-time degree program, services for LD students, student-designed majors, study abroad, summer session for credit. ***ROTC:*** Army (b).

Computers: 1,233 computers/terminals and 3,963 ports are available on campus for general student use. Students can access the following: computer help desk, free student e-mail accounts, online (class) grades, online (class) registration, online (class) schedules. Campuswide network is available. 100% of college-owned or -operated housing units are wired for high-speed Internet access. Wireless service is available via entire campus.

STUDENT LIFE
Housing options: on-campus residence required through sophomore year; coed, men-only, women-only. Campus housing is university owned. Freshman applicants given priority for college housing.

Activities and organizations: drama/theater group, student-run newspaper, radio and television station, choral group, The Wildlife Society, Student Impact, WWSP 90-FM radio station, Gender and Sexuality Alliance, Student Wisconsin Education Association, national fraternities, national sororities.

Athletics Member NCAA. All Division III. ***Intercollegiate sports:*** baseball M, basketball M/W, cross-country running M/W, football M, golf W, ice hockey M/W, soccer W, softball W, swimming and diving M/W, tennis W, track and field M/W, volleyball W, wrestling M. ***Intramural sports:*** archery M(c)/W(c), badminton M/W, basketball M/W, football M, golf M/W, ice hockey M/W, lacrosse M(c), racquetball M/W, rugby M(c)/W(c), skiing (downhill) M(c)/W(c), soccer M/W, softball M/W, table tennis M/W, tennis M/W, ultimate Frisbee M/W, volleyball M/W.

Campus security: 24-hour emergency response devices and patrols, student patrols, late-night transport/escort service, controlled dormitory access.

Student services: health clinic, personal/psychological counseling, women's center.

COSTS & FINANCIAL AID
Costs (2014–15) ***Tuition:*** state resident $7669 full-time, $378 per credit part-time; nonresident $15,242 full-time, $694 per credit part-time. Full-time tuition and fees vary according to course load, program, and reciprocity agreements. Part-time tuition and fees vary according to course load, program, and reciprocity agreements. ***Room and board:*** $6786; room only: $3660. Room and board charges vary according to board plan and housing facility. ***Payment plans:*** installment, deferred payment.

Financial Aid Of all full-time matriculated undergraduates who enrolled in 2013, 7,291 applied for aid, 5,477 were judged to have need, 342 had their need fully met. In 2013, 469 non-need-based awards were made. ***Average percent of need met:*** 70. ***Average financial aid package:*** $8513. ***Average need-based loan:*** $5208. ***Average need-based gift aid:*** $5189. ***Average non-need-based aid:*** $1559. ***Average indebtedness upon graduation:*** $25,871. ***Financial aid deadline:*** 5/1.

APPLYING
Standardized Tests *Required:* SAT or ACT (for admission).

Options: electronic application, deferred entrance.

Application fee: $44.

Required: high school transcript. ***Recommended:*** essay or personal statement, 3 letters of recommendation.

Application deadlines: rolling (freshmen), rolling (transfers).

Notification: continuous (freshmen), continuous (transfers).

CONTACT
Mr. William Jordan, Director of Admissions, University of Wisconsin–Stevens Point, 102 Student Services Center, University of Wisconsin-Stevens Point, Stevens Point, WI 54481. *Phone:* 715-346-4021. *Fax:* 715-346-3296. *E-mail:* bjordan@uwsp.edu.

University of Wisconsin–Stout

Menomonie, Wisconsin

http://www.uwstout.edu/

- **State-supported** comprehensive, founded 1891, part of University of Wisconsin System
- **Small-town** 120-acre campus with easy access to Minneapolis-St. Paul
- **Coed** 8,254 undergraduate students, 83% full-time, 47% women, 53% men
- **Moderately difficult** entrance level, 82% of applicants were admitted

UNDERGRAD STUDENTS
6,890 full-time, 1,364 part-time. 32% are from out of state; 2% Black or African American, non-Hispanic/Latino; 0.7% Hispanic/Latino; 0.1% Asian, non-Hispanic/Latino; 88% Native Hawaiian or other Pacific Islander, non-Hispanic/Latino; 3% American Indian or Alaska Native, non-Hispanic/Latino; 3% Two or more races, non-Hispanic/Latino; 0.3% Race/ethnicity unknown; 3% international; 9% transferred in; 40% live on campus.

Freshmen
Admission: 3,352 applied, 2,744 admitted, 1,441 enrolled. ***Average high school GPA:*** 3.3. ***Test scores:*** ACT scores over 18: 93%; ACT scores over 24: 34%; ACT scores over 30: 3%.

Retention: 76% of full-time freshmen returned.

FACULTY
Total: 489, 83% full-time, 67% with terminal degrees.

Student/faculty ratio: 17:1.

ACADEMICS
Calendar: 4-1-4. *Degrees:* certificates, bachelor's, master's, doctoral, post-master's, and postbachelor's certificates.

Special study options: accelerated degree program, adult/continuing education programs, cooperative education, distance learning, double majors, external degree program, honors programs, independent study, internships, off-campus study, part-time degree program, services for LD students, study abroad, summer session for credit. ***ROTC:*** Army (b), Air Force (c).

Computers: Students can access the following: computer help desk, free student e-mail accounts, online (class) grades, online (class) registration, online (class) schedules, all undergraduates receive a laptop computer and have unlimited access to Internet. Campuswide network is available. 100% of college-owned or -operated housing units are wired for high-speed Internet access. Wireless service is available via entire campus.

STUDENT LIFE
Housing options: on-campus residence required through sophomore year; coed, special housing for students with disabilities. Campus housing is university owned. Freshman campus housing is guaranteed.

Activities and organizations: drama/theater group, student-run newspaper, radio and television station, choral group, marching band, national fraternities, national sororities.

Athletics Member NCAA. All Division III. ***Intercollegiate sports:*** baseball M, basketball M/W, cross-country running M/W, football M, gymnastics W, ice hockey M/W(c), soccer M(c)/W, softball W, tennis W, track and field M/W, volleyball M(c)/W. ***Intramural sports:*** baseball M, basketball M/W, bowling M(c)/W(c), football M/W, golf M/W, ice hockey M/W, racquetball M/W, rugby M(c)/W(c), skiing (cross-country) M(c)/W(c), skiing (downhill) M(c)/W(c), softball M/W, ultimate Frisbee M/W, volleyball M/W.

Campus security: 24-hour emergency response devices and patrols, student patrols, controlled dormitory access.

Student services: health clinic, personal/psychological counseling, legal services.

COSTS & FINANCIAL AID
Costs (2014–15) ***Tuition:*** state resident $7014 full-time, $234 per credit hour part-time; nonresident $14,760 full-time, $492 per credit hour part-time. Full-time tuition and fees vary according to degree level and reciprocity agreements. Part-time tuition and fees vary according to degree level and reciprocity agreements. ***Required fees:*** $2011 full-time. ***Room and board:*** $6434; room only: $3890. Room and board charges vary according to board plan and housing facility.

Financial Aid Of all full-time matriculated undergraduates who enrolled in 2014, 5,410 applied for aid, 4,045 were judged to have need, 565 had their need fully met. 1,537 Federal Work-Study jobs (averaging $1468). In 2014, 132 non-need-based awards were made. ***Average percent of need met:*** 82. ***Average financial aid package:*** $10,638. ***Average need-based loan:*** $4639. ***Average need-based gift aid:*** $5646. ***Average non-need-based aid:*** $2389. ***Average indebtedness upon graduation:*** $27,397.

APPLYING
Standardized Tests *Required:* SAT or ACT (for admission).

Options: electronic application.

Application fee: $44.

Required: high school transcript. ***Required for some:*** minimum 2.8 GPA. ***Recommended:*** minimum 2.5 GPA.

Application deadlines: rolling (freshmen), rolling (out-of-state freshmen), rolling (transfers).

Notification: continuous (freshmen), continuous (out-of-state freshmen), continuous (transfers).

CONTACT
Dr. Pamela Holsinger-Fuchs, Executive Director of Enrollment Services, University of Wisconsin–Stout, Admissions, Bowman Hall, Menomonie, WI 54751. *Phone:* 715-232-2639. *Toll-free phone:* 800-HI-STOUT. *Fax:* 715-232-1667. *E-mail:* admissions@uwstout.edu.

University of Wisconsin–Superior

Superior, Wisconsin

http://www.uwsuper.edu/

- **State-supported** comprehensive, founded 1893, part of University of Wisconsin System
- **Suburban** 230-acre campus
- **Coed** 2,455 undergraduate students, 78% full-time, 61% women, 39% men
- **Moderately difficult** entrance level, 68% of applicants were admitted

UNDERGRAD STUDENTS
1,926 full-time, 529 part-time. Students come from 34 states and territories; 43 other countries; 43% are from out of state; 2% Black or African American, non-Hispanic/Latino; 2% Hispanic/Latino; 1% Asian, non-Hispanic/Latino; 0.1% Native Hawaiian or other Pacific Islander, non-Hispanic/Latino; 2% American Indian or Alaska Native, non-Hispanic/Latino; 3% Two or more races, non-Hispanic/Latino; 0.4% Race/ethnicity unknown; 6% international; 11% transferred in; 28% live on campus.

Freshmen
Admission: 877 applied, 599 admitted, 330 enrolled. ***Average high school GPA:*** 3.17. ***Test scores:*** ACT scores over 18: 92%; ACT scores over 24: 27%; ACT scores over 30: 1%.

Retention: 72% of full-time freshmen returned.

FACULTY
Total: 218, 58% full-time, 49% with terminal degrees.

Student/faculty ratio: 14:1.

ACADEMICS
Calendar: semesters. *Degrees:* certificates, associate, bachelor's, master's, post-master's, and postbachelor's certificates.

Special study options: academic remediation for entering students, accelerated degree program, adult/continuing education programs, advanced placement credit, cooperative education, distance learning, double majors, English as a second language, external degree program, freshman honors college, independent study, internships, off-campus study, part-time degree program, services for LD students, student-designed majors, study abroad, summer session for credit. ***ROTC:*** Air Force (c).

Unusual degree programs: 3-2 engineering with Michigan Technological University, University of Wisconsin-Madison; forestry with Michigan Technological University.

Computers: 343 computers/terminals are available on campus for general student use. Students can access the following: campus intranet, computer help desk, free student e-mail accounts, online (class) grades, online (class) registration, online (class) schedules. Campuswide network is

available. 100% of college-owned or -operated housing units are wired for high-speed Internet access. Wireless service is available via entire campus.

STUDENT LIFE
Housing options: on-campus residence required through sophomore year; coed, women-only, special housing for students with disabilities. Campus housing is university owned. Freshman campus housing is guaranteed.

Activities and organizations: drama/theater group, student-run newspaper, radio station, choral group, Student Senate, Student Activities Board, Residence Hall Association, Inter-Varsity Christian Fellowship, World Student Association.

Athletics Member NCAA. All Division III. ***Intercollegiate sports:*** baseball M, basketball M/W, cross-country running M/W, ice hockey M/W, soccer M/W, softball W, track and field M/W, volleyball W. ***Intramural sports:*** badminton M/W, baseball M(c), basketball M/W, bowling M/W, football M/W, ice hockey M(c)/W(c), racquetball M/W, riflery M/W, rock climbing M/W, soccer M/W, softball M/W, swimming and diving M/W, table tennis M/W, tennis M(c)/W(c), ultimate Frisbee M(c)/W(c), volleyball M(c)/W(c).

Campus security: 24-hour emergency response devices and patrols, student patrols, late-night transport/escort service, controlled dormitory access.

Student services: health clinic, personal/psychological counseling, women's center.

COSTS & FINANCIAL AID
Costs (2014–15) ***Tuition:*** state resident $6535 full-time, $272 per credit hour part-time; nonresident $14,108 full-time, $588 per credit hour part-time. Full-time tuition and fees vary according to course load and reciprocity agreements. Part-time tuition and fees vary according to course load and reciprocity agreements. ***Required fees:*** $1459 full-time. ***Room and board:*** $6320; room only: $3400. Room and board charges vary according to board plan and housing facility. ***Payment plan:*** installment.

Financial Aid Of all full-time matriculated undergraduates who enrolled in 2014, 1,591 applied for aid, 1,344 were judged to have need, 159 had their need fully met. In 2014, 50 non-need-based awards were made. ***Average percent of need met:*** 82. ***Average financial aid package:*** $11,623. ***Average need-based loan:*** $4298. ***Average need-based gift aid:*** $5360. ***Average non-need-based aid:*** $1813. ***Average indebtedness upon graduation:*** $29,410.

APPLYING
Standardized Tests *Required:* SAT or ACT (for admission).

Options: electronic application, early admission, deferred entrance.

Application fee: $44.

Required: high school transcript. ***Required for some:*** essay or personal statement, 1 letter of recommendation. ***Recommended:*** interview.

Application deadlines: 8/1 (freshmen), 8/1 (out-of-state freshmen), rolling (transfers).

Notification: continuous until 9/16 (freshmen), continuous until 9/16 (out-of-state freshmen), continuous (transfers).

CONTACT
University of Wisconsin–Superior, Belknap and Catlin, PO Box 2000, Superior, WI 54880-4500. *Phone:* 715-394-8230. *Fax:* 715-394-8407. *E-mail:* admissions@uwsuper.edu.

University of Wisconsin–Waukesha
Waukesha, Wisconsin
http://www.waukesha.uwc.edu/

- **State-supported** primarily 2-year, founded 1966, part of University of Wisconsin System
- **Suburban** 86-acre campus with easy access to Milwaukee
- **Coed** 2,239 undergraduate students, 48% full-time, 47% women, 53% men
- **Minimally difficult** entrance level

UNDERGRAD STUDENTS
1,069 full-time, 1,170 part-time. Students come from 16 states and territories; 1 other country; 7% are from out of state; 4% Black or African American, non-Hispanic/Latino; 4% Hispanic/Latino; 3% Asian, non-Hispanic/Latino; 0.9% Native Hawaiian or other Pacific Islander, non-Hispanic/Latino; 0.1% American Indian or Alaska Native, non-Hispanic/Latino; 0.1% Race/ethnicity unknown; 0.1% international; 7% transferred in.

Freshmen
Admission: 1,418 enrolled.

FACULTY
Total: 92, 67% full-time, 93% with terminal degrees.

Student/faculty ratio: 24:1.

ACADEMICS
Calendar: semesters. *Degrees:* associate and bachelor's.

Special study options: academic remediation for entering students, accelerated degree program, advanced placement credit, distance learning, honors programs, internships, off-campus study, part-time degree program, services for LD students, study abroad, summer session for credit.

Computers: 90 computers/terminals are available on campus for general student use. Students can access the following: computer help desk, free student e-mail accounts, online (class) grades, online (class) registration, online (class) schedules. Campuswide network is available. Wireless service is available via entire campus.

STUDENT LIFE
Housing options: college housing not available.

Activities and organizations: drama/theater group, student-run newspaper, choral group, Student Government, Student Activities Committee, Campus Crusade, Phi Theta Kappa, Circle K.

Athletics Member NJCAA. ***Intercollegiate sports:*** basketball M/W, golf M/W, soccer M/W, tennis M/W, volleyball W. ***Intramural sports:*** basketball M, bowling M/W, cheerleading W, cross-country running W, football M/W, skiing (downhill) M/W, table tennis M/W, volleyball M(c).

Campus security: late-night transport/escort service, part-time patrols by trained security personnel.

Student services: personal/psychological counseling.

COSTS
Costs (2014–15) ***Tuition:*** state resident $5091 full-time, $215 per credit part-time; nonresident $12,072 full-time, $506 per credit part-time. Full-time tuition and fees vary according to course load. Part-time tuition and fees vary according to course load. ***Required fees:*** $230 full-time. ***Payment plan:*** installment.

APPLYING
Standardized Tests *Required:* SAT or ACT (for admission).

Options: electronic application, early admission, deferred entrance.

Application fee: $44.

Required: high school transcript. ***Required for some:*** interview. ***Recommended:*** essay or personal statement, Admission interview may be recommended.

Notification: continuous (freshmen).

CONTACT
Ms. Deb Kusick, Sr. Admission Specialist, University of Wisconsin–Waukesha, 1500 North University Drive, Waukesha, WI 53188-2799. *Phone:* 262-521-5040. *Fax:* 262-521-5530. *E-mail:* deborah.kusick@uwc.edu.

University of Wisconsin–Whitewater
Whitewater, Wisconsin
http://www.uww.edu/

- **State-supported** comprehensive, founded 1868, part of University of Wisconsin System
- **Small-town** 400-acre campus with easy access to Milwaukee
- **Endowment** $17.3 million
- **Coed** 10,971 undergraduate students, 91% full-time, 50% women, 50% men
- **Moderately difficult** entrance level, 70% of applicants were admitted

UNDERGRAD STUDENTS
9,979 full-time, 992 part-time. Students come from 37 states and territories; 38 other countries; 15% are from out of state; 5% Black or

African American, non-Hispanic/Latino; 5% Hispanic/Latino; 2% Asian, non-Hispanic/Latino; 0.1% Native Hawaiian or other Pacific Islander, non-Hispanic/Latino; 0.2% American Indian or Alaska Native, non-Hispanic/Latino; 4% Two or more races, non-Hispanic/Latino; 0.1% Race/ethnicity unknown; 1% international; 6% transferred in; 40% live on campus.

Freshmen
Admission: 6,833 applied, 4,810 admitted, 2,151 enrolled. ***Average high school GPA:*** 3.24. ***Test scores:*** SAT critical reading scores over 500: 55%; SAT math scores over 500: 45%; SAT writing scores over 500: 64%; ACT scores over 18: 93%; SAT critical reading scores over 600: 10%; SAT math scores over 600: 18%; SAT writing scores over 600: 9%; ACT scores over 24: 37%; ACT scores over 30: 3%.

Retention: 81% of full-time freshmen returned.

FACULTY
Total: 620, 75% full-time.

Student/faculty ratio: 21:1.

ACADEMICS
Calendar: semesters. *Degrees:* associate, bachelor's, and master's.

Special study options: academic remediation for entering students, accelerated degree program, adult/continuing education programs, advanced placement credit, cooperative education, distance learning, double majors, English as a second language, external degree program, honors programs, independent study, internships, part-time degree program, services for LD students, student-designed majors, study abroad, summer session for credit. ***ROTC:*** Army (b), Air Force (b).

Unusual degree programs: engineering with UW-Madison and UW-Milwaukee.

Computers: Students can access the following: campus intranet, computer help desk, free student e-mail accounts, online (class) grades, online (class) registration, online (class) schedules. Campuswide network is available. 100% of college-owned or -operated housing units are wired for high-speed Internet access. Wireless service is available via entire campus.

STUDENT LIFE
Housing options: on-campus residence required through sophomore year; coed, women-only. Campus housing is university owned. Freshman campus housing is guaranteed.

Activities and organizations: drama/theater group, student-run newspaper, radio and television station, choral group, marching band, Finance Association, American Marketing Association, Black Student Union, Golden Key Honor Society, Wisconsin Education Association, national fraternities, national sororities.

Athletics Member NCAA. All Division III. ***Intercollegiate sports:*** archery M(c)/W(c), baseball M, basketball M/W, bowling M(c)/W, cheerleading M(c)/W(c), cross-country running M/W, football M, golf M(c)/W, gymnastics W, ice hockey M(c)/W(c), lacrosse M(c), rugby M(c)/W(c), soccer M/W, softball W, swimming and diving M/W, tennis M/W, track and field M/W, volleyball M(c)/W, water polo M(c)/W(c), weight lifting M(c)/W(c), wrestling M. ***Intramural sports:*** basketball M/W, bowling M/W, football M/W, golf M/W, racquetball M/W, rock climbing M(c)/W(c), skiing (downhill) M(c)/W(c), soccer M, softball M/W, table tennis M/W, tennis M/W, ultimate Frisbee M(c)/W(c), volleyball M/W, water polo M/W.

Campus security: 24-hour emergency response devices, late-night transport/escort service, controlled dormitory access.

Student services: health clinic, personal/psychological counseling, women's center, legal services.

COSTS & FINANCIAL AID
Costs (2014–15) ***Tuition:*** state resident $6519 full-time; nonresident $14,092 full-time. Full-time tuition and fees vary according to degree level and reciprocity agreements. ***Required fees:*** $1081 full-time. ***Room and board:*** $6144; room only: $3744. Room and board charges vary according to board plan and housing facility. ***Payment plan:*** installment. ***Waivers:*** children of alumni and senior citizens.

Financial Aid Of all full-time matriculated undergraduates who enrolled in 2014, 8,097 applied for aid, 6,099 were judged to have need, 2,483 had their need fully met. 742 Federal Work-Study jobs (averaging $1281). 2,273 state and other part-time jobs (averaging $1910). In 2014, 419 non-need-based awards were made. ***Average percent of need met:*** 60. ***Average financial aid package:*** $8047. ***Average need-based loan:*** $4264. ***Average need-based gift aid:*** $5511. ***Average non-need-based aid:*** $1862. ***Average indebtedness upon graduation:*** $27,623.

APPLYING
Standardized Tests *Required:* SAT or ACT (for admission).

Options: electronic application, deferred entrance.

Application fee: $44.

Required: high school transcript. ***Recommended:*** essay or personal statement.

Application deadlines: 8/1 (freshmen), rolling (transfers).

Notification: continuous (transfers).

CONTACT
Mr. Nelson Edmonds, Interim Director of Admissions, University of Wisconsin–Whitewater, 800 West Main Street, Whitewater, WI 53190-1790. *Phone:* 262-472-1234. *Fax:* 262-472-1515. *E-mail:* uwwadmit@uww.edu.

Viterbo University

La Crosse, Wisconsin

http://www.viterbo.edu/

- **Independent Roman Catholic** comprehensive, founded 1890
- **Suburban** 72-acre campus
- **Coed** 2,034 undergraduate students, 76% full-time, 73% women, 27% men
- **Moderately difficult** entrance level, 69% of applicants were admitted

UNDERGRAD STUDENTS
1,539 full-time, 495 part-time. Students come from 17 states and territories; 5 other countries; 24% are from out of state; 2% Black or African American, non-Hispanic/Latino; 2% Hispanic/Latino; 2% Asian, non-Hispanic/Latino; 0.0% Native Hawaiian or other Pacific Islander, non-Hispanic/Latino; 0.4% American Indian or Alaska Native, non-Hispanic/Latino; 2% Two or more races, non-Hispanic/Latino; 0.3% Race/ethnicity unknown; 1% international; 13% transferred in; 33% live on campus.

Freshmen
Admission: 1,643 applied, 1,136 admitted, 322 enrolled. ***Average high school GPA:*** 3.53. ***Test scores:*** ACT scores over 18: 98%; ACT scores over 24: 44%; ACT scores over 30: 5%.

Retention: 71% of full-time freshmen returned.

FACULTY
Total: 320, 38% full-time, 37% with terminal degrees.

Student/faculty ratio: 12:1.

ACADEMICS
Calendar: semesters. *Degrees:* certificates, associate, bachelor's, master's, doctoral, post-master's, and postbachelor's certificates.

Special study options: accelerated degree program, adult/continuing education programs, distance learning, double majors, English as a second language, honors programs, independent study, internships, part-time degree program, student-designed majors, study abroad. ***ROTC:*** Army (c).

Computers: Students can access the following: campus intranet, computer help desk, free student e-mail accounts, online (class) grades, online (class) registration, online (class) schedules, Blackboard courses. Campuswide network is available. 100% of college-owned or -operated housing units are wired for high-speed Internet access. Wireless service is available via entire campus.

STUDENT LIFE
Housing options: on-campus residence required for freshman year; coed. Campus housing is university owned. Freshman campus housing is guaranteed.

Activities and organizations: drama/theater group, student-run newspaper, choral group, Student Activities Board (SAB), Viterbo Student Nurses Association (VSNA), Education Club, Colleges Against Cancer (CAL), Residence Hall Association.

Athletics Member NAIA. ***Intercollegiate sports:*** baseball M(s), basketball M(s)/W(s), bowling M(s)/W(s), cross-country running

M(s)/W(s), golf M(s)/W(s), soccer M(s)/W(s), softball W(s), track and field M/W, volleyball W(s). ***Intramural sports:*** basketball M/W, bowling M/W, soccer M/W, softball M/W, ultimate Frisbee M/W, volleyball M/W.

Campus security: 24-hour emergency response devices, late-night transport/escort service, controlled dormitory access, Campus Safety 24/7, 365 days a year, lighted pathways, emergency evacuation plan, self-defense education programs, security cameras.

Student services: health clinic, personal/psychological counseling.

COSTS & FINANCIAL AID

Costs (2015–16) ***Comprehensive fee:*** $33,310 includes full-time tuition ($24,360), mandatory fees ($690), and room and board ($8260). Full-time tuition and fees vary according to program. Part-time tuition and fees vary according to program. ***College room only:*** $3650. Room and board charges vary according to board plan and housing facility.

Financial Aid Of all full-time matriculated undergraduates who enrolled in 2003, 1,311 applied for aid, 1,208 were judged to have need, 309 had their need fully met. 387 Federal Work-Study jobs (averaging $1680). 19 state and other part-time jobs (averaging $1615). In 2003, 223 non-need-based awards were made. ***Average percent of need met:*** 71. ***Average financial aid package:*** $13,534. ***Average need-based loan:*** $4317. ***Average need-based gift aid:*** $8859. ***Average non-need-based aid:*** $5629. ***Average indebtedness upon graduation:*** $16,619.

APPLYING

Standardized Tests *Required:* SAT or ACT (for admission).

Options: electronic application, deferred entrance.

Application fee: $25.

Required: high school transcript, minimum 2.0 GPA. ***Required for some:*** essay or personal statement, interview, audition for theater and music, portfolio for art.

Application deadlines: 8/15 (freshmen), 8/1 (transfers).

Notification: continuous (freshmen), continuous (transfers).

CONTACT

Ms. Alexa Ferro, Freshman Admission Counselor, Viterbo University, 900 Viterbo Drive, La Crosse, WI 54601. *Phone:* 608-796-3013. *Toll-free phone:* 800-VITERBO. *E-mail:* admission@viterbo.edu.

Wisconsin Lutheran College

Milwaukee, Wisconsin

http://www.wlc.edu/

- **Independent** comprehensive, founded 1973, affiliated with Wisconsin Evangelical Lutheran Synod
- **Suburban** 54-acre campus
- **Endowment** $19.0 million
- **Coed**
- **Moderately difficult** entrance level

FACULTY

Student/faculty ratio: 11:1.

ACADEMICS

Calendar: semesters. *Degrees:* bachelor's and master's.

STUDENT LIFE

Housing options: on-campus residence required through junior year; men-only, women-only. Campus housing is university owned. Freshman campus housing is guaranteed.

Activities and organizations: student-run newspaper, choral group.

Athletics Member NCAA. All Division III.

Campus security: 24-hour emergency response devices and patrols, late-night transport/escort service, controlled dormitory access, closed-circuit TV monitors.

Student services: health clinic, personal/psychological counseling.

COSTS & FINANCIAL AID

Costs (2014–15) ***Comprehensive fee:*** $34,860 includes full-time tuition ($25,810), mandatory fees ($150), and room and board ($8900). Full-time tuition and fees vary according to program. Part-time tuition: $700 per credit. Part-time tuition and fees vary according to program. ***Room and board:*** Room and board charges vary according to housing facility.

Financial Aid Of all full-time matriculated undergraduates who enrolled in 2013, 897 applied for aid, 815 were judged to have need, 128 had their need fully met. 235 Federal Work-Study jobs (averaging $1892). 194 state and other part-time jobs (averaging $1787). In 2013, 157 non-need-based awards were made. ***Average percent of need met:*** 78. ***Average financial aid package:*** $19,114. ***Average need-based loan:*** $4155. ***Average need-based gift aid:*** $15,114. ***Average non-need-based aid:*** $8586. ***Average indebtedness upon graduation:*** $25,784.

APPLYING

Standardized Tests *Required:* SAT or ACT (for admission).

Options: electronic application, deferred entrance.

Required: high school transcript, minimum 2.7 GPA. ***Required for some:*** interview. ***Recommended:*** 1 letter of recommendation.

CONTACT

Mr. Cameron Teske, Admissions Office Coordinator, Wisconsin Lutheran College, 8800 West Bluemound Road, Milwaukee, WI 53226-9942. *Phone:* 414-443-8811. *Fax:* 414-443-8547. *E-mail:* cameron.teske@wlc.edu.

WYOMING

★ University of Wyoming

Laramie, Wyoming

http://www.uwyo.edu/

- **State-supported** university, founded 1886
- **Small-town** 785-acre campus
- **Endowment** $419.9 million
- **Coed** 10,124 undergraduate students, 82% full-time, 52% women, 48% men
- **Moderately difficult** entrance level, 98% of applicants were admitted

UNDERGRAD STUDENTS

8,272 full-time, 1,852 part-time. Students come from 48 states and territories; 68 other countries; 31% are from out of state; 1% Black or African American, non-Hispanic/Latino; 7% Hispanic/Latino; 1% Asian, non-Hispanic/Latino; 0.3% Native Hawaiian or other Pacific Islander, non-Hispanic/Latino; 0.6% American Indian or Alaska Native, non-Hispanic/Latino; 3% Two or more races, non-Hispanic/Latino; 5% Race/ethnicity unknown; 4% international; 10% transferred in; 23% live on campus.

Freshmen

Admission: 4,187 applied, 4,089 admitted, 1,567 enrolled. ***Average high school GPA:*** 3.46. ***Test scores:*** SAT critical reading scores over 500: 65%; SAT math scores over 500: 68%; ACT scores over 18: 97%; SAT critical reading scores over 600: 26%; SAT math scores over 600: 30%; ACT scores over 24: 58%; SAT critical reading scores over 700: 4%; SAT math scores over 700: 7%; ACT scores over 30: 12%.

Retention: 75% of full-time freshmen returned.

FACULTY

Total: 790, 95% full-time, 78% with terminal degrees.

Student/faculty ratio: 15:1.

ACADEMICS

Calendar: semesters. *Degrees:* certificates, bachelor's, master's, doctoral, post-master's, and postbachelor's certificates.

Special study options: accelerated degree program, advanced placement credit, distance learning, double majors, external degree program, honors programs, independent study, internships, off-campus study, part-time degree program, services for LD students, student-designed majors, study abroad, summer session for credit. ***ROTC:*** Army (b), Air Force (b).

Computers: 1,683 computers/terminals and 10 ports are available on campus for general student use. Students can access the following: campus intranet, computer help desk, free student e-mail accounts, online (class) grades, online (class) registration, online (class) schedules. Campuswide network is available. 100% of college-owned or -operated housing units are wired for high-speed Internet access. Wireless service is available via classrooms, computer centers, computer labs, dorm rooms, learning centers, libraries, student centers.

STUDENT LIFE

Housing options: on-campus residence required for freshman year; coed, men-only, women-only, special housing for students with disabilities. Campus housing is university owned. Freshman campus housing is guaranteed.

Activities and organizations: drama/theater group, student-run newspaper, television station, choral group, marching band, national fraternities, national sororities.

Athletics Member NCAA. All Division I except football (Division I-A). ***Intercollegiate sports:*** badminton M(c)/W(c), baseball M(c), basketball M(s)/W(s), cross-country running M(s)/W(s), equestrian sports M(c)/W(c), fencing M(c)/W(c), golf M(s)/W(s), ice hockey M(c)/W(c), lacrosse M(c)/W(c), racquetball M(c)/W(c), riflery M(c)/W(c), rugby M(c)/W(c), skiing (cross-country) M(c)/W(c), skiing (downhill) M(c)/W(c), soccer M(c)/W(s), softball W(c), swimming and diving M(s)/W(s), tennis M(c)/W(s), track and field M(s)/W(s), ultimate Frisbee M(c)/W(c), volleyball W(s), water polo M(c), wrestling M(s). ***Intramural sports:*** badminton M/W, basketball M/W, bowling M/W, football M/W, golf M/W, racquetball M(c)/W(c), soccer M/W, softball M/W, swimming and diving M/W, table tennis M/W, tennis M/W, track and field M/W, ultimate Frisbee M/W, volleyball M/W, water polo M/W, wrestling M/W.

Campus security: 24-hour emergency response devices and patrols, student patrols, late-night transport/escort service, controlled dormitory access, 24-hour front desk coverage at campus housing and at campus police.

Student services: health clinic, personal/psychological counseling, women's center, legal services.

COSTS & FINANCIAL AID

Costs (2014–15) ***One-time required fee:*** $40. ***Tuition:*** state resident $3390 full-time, $113 per credit hour part-time; nonresident $13,620 full-time, $454 per credit hour part-time. Full-time tuition and fees vary according to course load, location, and reciprocity agreements. Part-time tuition and fees vary according to course load, location, and reciprocity agreements. ***Required fees:*** $1256 full-time, $293 per term part-time. ***Room and board:*** $9755; room only: $4160. Room and board charges vary according to board plan and housing facility. ***Payment plan:*** installment. ***Waivers:*** children of alumni, senior citizens, and employees or children of employees.

Financial Aid Of all full-time matriculated undergraduates who enrolled in 2013, 5,423 applied for aid, 3,950 were judged to have need, 572 had their need fully met. 289 Federal Work-Study jobs (averaging $1771). In 2013, 1753 non-need-based awards were made. ***Average percent of need met:*** 60. ***Average financial aid package:*** $9422. ***Average need-based loan:*** $4518. ***Average need-based gift aid:*** $4918. ***Average non-need-based aid:*** $4815. ***Average indebtedness upon graduation:*** $23,708.

APPLYING

Standardized Tests *Required:* SAT or ACT (for admission).

Options: electronic application, deferred entrance.

Application fee: $40.

Required: high school transcript, minimum 3.0 GPA, pre-college curriculum; minimum ACT composite of 21 or SAT of 980.

Application deadlines: 8/10 (freshmen), 8/10 (out-of-state freshmen), 8/10 (transfers).

Notification: continuous (freshmen), continuous (out-of-state freshmen), continuous (transfers).

CONTACT

Ryan Goeken, Assistant Director of Admissions, University of Wyoming, 1000 E. University Avenue, Dept 3435, Laramie, WY 82071. *Phone:* 307-766-3868. *Toll-free phone:* 800-342-5996. *Fax:* 307-766-4042. *E-mail:* admissions@uwyo.edu.

See below for display ad and page 1712 for the College Close-Up.

AMERICAN SAMOA

American Samoa Community College

Pago Pago, American Samoa

http://www.amsamoa.edu/

- **Territory-supported** primarily 2-year, founded 1969
- **Rural** 20-acre campus
- **Endowment** $3.1 million
- **Coed**
- **Noncompetitive** entrance level

ACADEMICS

Calendar: semesters. *Degrees:* certificates, associate, and bachelor's.

STUDENT LIFE

Housing options: college housing not available.

Activities and organizations: student-run newspaper, Student Government Association, Phi Theta Kappa, ASCC Research Foundation Student Club, Fa'aSamoa (Samoan Culture) Club, Journalism Club.

Campus security: 24-hour patrols.

Student services: personal/psychological counseling.

COSTS & FINANCIAL AID

Costs (2014–15) ***Tuition:*** territory resident $3300 full-time, $110 per credit part-time; nonresident $3600 full-time, $120 per credit part-time. Full-time tuition and fees vary according to course load. Part-time tuition and fees vary according to course load. ***Required fees:*** $250 full-time, $125 per term part-time.

Financial Aid Of all full-time matriculated undergraduates who enrolled in 2012, 929 applied for aid, 929 were judged to have need. 125 Federal Work-Study jobs (averaging $471). ***Average percent of need met:*** 50. ***Average financial aid package:*** $5550.

APPLYING

Standardized Tests *Recommended:* SAT (for admission), ACT (for admission), SAT or ACT (for admission), SAT and SAT Subject Tests or ACT (for admission), SAT Subject Tests (for admission).

Options: early admission, deferred entrance.

CONTACT

American Samoa Community College, PO Box 2609, Pago Pago, AS 96799-2609. *Phone:* 684-699-1141.

GUAM

University of Guam

Mangilao, Guam

http://www.uog.edu/

- **Territory-supported** comprehensive, founded 1952
- **Suburban** 100-acre campus
- **Coed** 3,660 undergraduate students, 77% full-time, 58% women, 42% men
- **Noncompetitive** entrance level, 96% of applicants were admitted

UNDERGRAD STUDENTS

2,801 full-time, 859 part-time. Students come from 36 states and territories; 11 other countries; 1% are from out of state; 0.7% Black or African American, non-Hispanic/Latino; 0.6% Hispanic/Latino; 44% Asian, non-Hispanic/Latino; 49% Native Hawaiian or other Pacific Islander, non-Hispanic/Latino; 0.1% American Indian or Alaska Native, non-Hispanic/Latino; 2% Race/ethnicity unknown; 0.8% international; 3% transferred in; 5% live on campus.

Freshmen

Admission: 634 applied, 606 admitted, 602 enrolled. ***Average high school GPA:*** 3.24.

Retention: 76% of full-time freshmen returned.

ACADEMICS

Calendar: semesters. *Degrees:* certificates, bachelor's, master's, and postbachelor's certificates.

Special study options: academic remediation for entering students, accelerated degree program, advanced placement credit, cooperative education, distance learning, double majors, English as a second language, honors programs, independent study, internships, off-campus study, part-time degree program, services for LD students, study abroad, summer session for credit. ***ROTC:*** Army (b).

Computers: 187 computers/terminals are available on campus for general student use. Students can access the following: campus intranet, computer help desk, free student e-mail accounts, online (class) grades, online (class) registration, online (class) schedules, wireless internet access. Campuswide network is available. 100% of college-owned or -operated housing units are wired for high-speed Internet access. Wireless service is available via entire campus.

STUDENT LIFE

Housing options: coed. Campus housing is university owned.

Activities and organizations: drama/theater group, student-run newspaper, choral group, American Marketing Association, Student Nurses Association of Guam, Social Work Student Alliance, GO CNMI, Association of Early Childhood Education International.

Athletics ***Intramural sports:*** basketball M/W, crew M(c)/W(c), football M, softball M/W, table tennis M/W, volleyball M/W.

Campus security: 24-hour emergency response devices and patrols, late-night transport/escort service.

Student services: health clinic, personal/psychological counseling, women's center.

COSTS

Costs (2014–15) ***Tuition:*** territory resident $4560 full-time, $190 per credit part-time; nonresident $13,560 full-time, $565 per credit part-time. Part-time tuition and fees vary according to course load. ***Required fees:*** $538 full-time, $269 per term part-time. ***Room only:*** $1910. Room and board charges vary according to housing facility. ***Payment plans:*** installment, deferred payment. ***Waivers:*** senior citizens and employees or children of employees.

APPLYING

Options: electronic application, deferred entrance.

Application fee: $49.

Required: high school transcript.

Application deadlines: 6/1 (freshmen), 6/1 (out-of-state freshmen), 6/1 (transfers).

Notification: continuous (freshmen), continuous (transfers).

CONTACT

Ms. Angelica Anthonio, Admissions Supervisor, University of Guam, Admissions and Records Office, UOG Station, Mangilao, GU 96923. *Phone:* 671-735-2201. *Fax:* 671-735-2203. *E-mail:* admitme@uguam.uog.edu.

PUERTO RICO

Caribbean University

Bayamón, Puerto Rico

http://www.caribbean.edu/

- **Independent** comprehensive, founded 1969
- **Urban** 16-acre campus with easy access to San Juan
- **Endowment** $259,761
- **Coed** 3,696 undergraduate students, 74% full-time, 58% women, 42% men
- **Minimally difficult** entrance level, 60% of applicants were admitted

UNDERGRAD STUDENTS

2,732 full-time, 964 part-time. 100% Hispanic/Latino.

Freshmen

Admission: 1,169 applied, 701 admitted, 544 enrolled. ***Average high school GPA:*** 2.64.

Retention: 73% of full-time freshmen returned.

FACULTY
Total: 466, 21% full-time, 36% with terminal degrees.
Student/faculty ratio: 20:1.

ACADEMICS
Calendar: trimesters. *Degrees:* certificates, associate, bachelor's, master's, and doctoral.

Special study options: academic remediation for entering students, accelerated degree program, adult/continuing education programs, English as a second language, part-time degree program, services for LD students, summer session for credit. ***ROTC:*** Army (c).

Computers: 378 computers/terminals are available on campus for general student use. Students can access the following: campus intranet, computer help desk, free student e-mail accounts, online (class) grades, online (class) registration, online (class) schedules. Campuswide network is available. Wireless service is available via entire campus.

STUDENT LIFE
Housing options: college housing not available.

Activities and organizations: drama/theater group, choral group, Engineering Student Association, Nursing, Social Work, Speech Therapy, Criminal Justices.

Athletics ***Intercollegiate sports:*** baseball M, basketball M/W, cheerleading M/W, cross-country running M/W, soccer M/W, softball W, table tennis M, track and field M/W, volleyball M/W, wrestling M/W. ***Intramural sports:*** basketball M/W, volleyball M/W.

Campus security: 24-hour patrols.

Student services: health clinic, personal/psychological counseling.

COSTS
Costs (2015–16) ***Tuition:*** $4200 full-time. Full-time tuition and fees vary according to class time, degree level, location, and program. Part-time tuition and fees vary according to class time, degree level, location, and program. ***Required fees:*** $770 full-time. ***Payment plan:*** installment. ***Waivers:*** employees or children of employees.

APPLYING
Standardized Tests *Required for some:* Only for the engineering applicants, we request test for verbal and math attitude offer by the College Board.

Options: deferred entrance.

Application fee: $30.

Required: high school transcript. ***Required for some:*** minimum 2.0 GPA, 1 letter of recommendation, interview.

CONTACT
Caribbean University, Box 493, Bayamón, PR 00960-0493. *Phone:* 787-780-0070 Ext. 1129.

Carlos Albizu University

San Juan, Puerto Rico

http://www.albizu.edu/

- **Independent** university, founded 1966
- **Urban** campus
- **Endowment** $732,270
- **Coed**
- **Noncompetitive** entrance level

FACULTY
Student/faculty ratio: 10:1.

ACADEMICS
Calendar: semesters. *Degrees:* bachelor's, master's, and doctoral.

STUDENT LIFE
Housing options: college housing not available.

Activities and organizations: student-run newspaper, Student Council, Community Services, Gender and Sexual Diversity Organization, OASIS, Speech/Language Pathology Students Organization.

Campus security: 24-hour emergency response devices, late-night transport/escort service, security cameras.

COSTS & FINANCIAL AID
Costs (2014–15) ***Tuition:*** $5940 full-time, $165 per credit part-time. ***Required fees:*** $979 full-time, $333 per term part-time.

Financial Aid Of all full-time matriculated undergraduates who enrolled in 2013, 50 applied for aid, 50 were judged to have need. 2 Federal Work-Study jobs (averaging $1094). ***Average percent of need met:*** 47. ***Average financial aid package:*** $4630. ***Average need-based loan:*** $2750. ***Average need-based gift aid:*** $2823.

APPLYING
Standardized Tests *Required:* CEEB or SAT (for admission).

Options: early admission, deferred entrance.

Application fee: $75.

Required: minimum 2.0 GPA, 2 letters of recommendation. ***Required for some:*** health certificate, Good Conduct Crete, official university transcript.

CONTACT
Carlos Albizu University, 151 Tanca Street, San Juan, PR 00901. *Phone:* 787-725-6500 Ext. 1521.

Columbia Centro Universitario

Caguas, Puerto Rico

http://www.columbiaco.edu/

- **Proprietary** comprehensive, founded 1966
- **Urban** 6-acre campus with easy access to San Juan
- **Coed** 1,750 undergraduate students, 42% full-time, 71% women, 29% men
- **Noncompetitive** entrance level, 54% of applicants were admitted

UNDERGRAD STUDENTS
743 full-time, 1,007 part-time. 100% Hispanic/Latino.

Freshmen
Admission: 967 applied, 525 admitted, 243 enrolled.

Retention: 40% of full-time freshmen returned.

FACULTY
Total: 145, 13% full-time, 15% with terminal degrees.
Student/faculty ratio: 19:1.

ACADEMICS
Calendar: semesters. *Degrees:* certificates, associate, bachelor's, and master's.

Special study options: accelerated degree program, part-time degree program.

Computers: 147 computers/terminals are available on campus for general student use. Students can access the following: campus intranet, free student e-mail accounts, online (class) grades, online (class) registration, online (class) schedules, online courses / technical support. Campuswide network is available. Wireless service is available via entire campus.

STUDENT LIFE
Housing options: college housing not available.

Campus security: 24-hour patrols.

Student services: personal/psychological counseling.

COSTS & FINANCIAL AID
Costs (2015–16) ***Tuition:*** $9630 full-time, $1605 per semester hour part-time. Full-time tuition and fees vary according to class time, degree level, and program. Part-time tuition and fees vary according to class time, degree level, and program. ***Required fees:*** $100 full-time, $267 per credit hour part-time. ***Payment plan:*** installment. ***Waivers:*** employees or children of employees.

Financial Aid Of all full-time matriculated undergraduates who enrolled in 2008, 974 applied for aid, 818 were judged to have need. 61 Federal Work-Study jobs (averaging $982). ***Average percent of need met:*** 11. ***Average financial aid package:*** $4035.

APPLYING
Options: electronic application.

Application fee: $50.

Required: high school transcript. ***Required for some:*** essay or personal statement, minimum 2.0 GPA, 3 letters of recommendation, interview.

Notification: continuous (freshmen).

CONTACT
Mrs. Linette J. Miletti, Admission and Recruitment Coordinator, Columbia Centro Universitario, PO Box 8517, Caguas, PR 00726. *Phone:* 787-743-4041 Ext. 239. *Fax:* 787-744-7031. *E-mail:* lmiletti@columbiaco.edu.

Columbia Centro Universitario

Yauco, Puerto Rico

http://www.columbiaco.edu/

- **Proprietary** 4-year, founded 1976
- **Urban** campus
- **Coed** 407 undergraduate students, 52% full-time, 71% women, 29% men
- **Minimally difficult** entrance level

UNDERGRAD STUDENTS
212 full-time, 195 part-time. 100% Hispanic/Latino.

Freshmen
Admission: 118 admitted, 74 enrolled.

FACULTY
Total: 37, 19% full-time, 16% with terminal degrees.
Student/faculty ratio: 11:1.

ACADEMICS
Calendar: trimesters. *Degrees:* certificates, associate, and bachelor's.

Special study options: cooperative education, distance learning, independent study, part-time degree program, services for LD students.

Computers: 14 computers/terminals are available on campus for general student use. Students can access the following: computer help desk, free student e-mail accounts, online (class) grades, online (class) registration, online (class) schedules. Wireless service is available via entire campus.

STUDENT LIFE
Housing options: college housing not available.

Activities and organizations: Nursing Group, Librarian Group, Photography Club.

Athletics ***Intramural sports:*** basketball M, softball M/W, volleyball W.

Campus security: trained security personnel while branch is operating.

Student services: personal/psychological counseling.

COSTS
Costs (2015–16) ***Tuition:*** $9630 full-time. Full-time tuition and fees vary according to course load and program. Part-time tuition and fees vary according to course load and program. ***Required fees:*** $100 full-time. ***Payment plan:*** installment. ***Waivers:*** employees or children of employees.

APPLYING
Options: electronic application.

Application fee: $50.

Required: high school transcript, minimum 2.0 GPA. ***Required for some:*** interview.

Application deadlines: rolling (freshmen), rolling (transfers).

Notification: continuous (freshmen), continuous (transfers).

CONTACT
Mrs. Carmen Ivette Pabon MSC, Admissions Coordinator, Columbia Centro Universitario, PO Box 3062, Yauco, PR 00698. *Phone:* 787-856-0845 Ext. 118. *Fax:* 787-267-0994. *E-mail:* cipabon@columbiaco.edu.

EDP University of Puerto Rico

Hato Rey, Puerto Rico

http://www.edpuniversity.edu/

- **Proprietary** comprehensive, founded 1968
- **Urban** 1-acre campus with easy access to San Juan
- **Coed** 1,466 undergraduate students, 63% full-time, 68% women, 32% men
- **Noncompetitive** entrance level, 37% of applicants were admitted

UNDERGRAD STUDENTS
922 full-time, 544 part-time. Students come from 13 states and territories; 22% are from out of state; 29% transferred in.

Freshmen
Admission: 486 applied, 179 admitted, 114 enrolled. ***Average high school GPA:*** 2.93.

Retention: 89% of full-time freshmen returned.

FACULTY
Total: 156, 19% full-time, 13% with terminal degrees.
Student/faculty ratio: 21:1.

ACADEMICS
Calendar: semesters. *Degrees:* associate, bachelor's, master's, and postbachelor's certificates.

Special study options: academic remediation for entering students, accelerated degree program, adult/continuing education programs, advanced placement credit, cooperative education, distance learning, English as a second language, independent study, internships, part-time degree program, services for LD students, summer session for credit.

Computers: 314 computers/terminals and 316 ports are available on campus for general student use. Students can access the following: campus intranet, computer help desk, free student e-mail accounts, online (class) grades, online (class) registration, online (class) schedules. Campuswide network is available. Wireless service is available via entire campus.

STUDENT LIFE
Housing options: college housing not available.

Activities and organizations: Student Council, Graduate Student Association, Dance Group.

Campus security: 24-hour emergency response devices, student patrols, late-night transport/escort service, security and emergency telephones in working hours.

Student services: personal/psychological counseling.

COSTS & FINANCIAL AID
Costs (2015–16) ***Tuition:*** $5100 full-time, $170 per credit part-time. Full-time tuition and fees vary according to course load and program. Part-time tuition and fees vary according to course load and program. ***Required fees:*** $840 full-time, $170 per credit part-time, $420 per credit part-time. ***Payment plan:*** installment. ***Waivers:*** employees or children of employees.

Financial Aid Of all full-time matriculated undergraduates who enrolled in 2011, 1,028 applied for aid, 1,028 were judged to have need. 35 Federal Work-Study jobs (averaging $1972). ***Average percent of need met:*** 90. ***Average financial aid package:*** $5587. ***Average need-based loan:*** $3137. ***Average need-based gift aid:*** $5416. ***Average indebtedness upon graduation:*** $4256.

APPLYING
Standardized Tests *Required:* College Entrance Examination Board (CEEB) Test, Institutional Admission Exam (for admission).

Options: electronic application, early admission, early decision, deferred entrance.

Application fee: $15.

Required: high school transcript, minimum 1.6 GPA, placement test or College Board test, vaccination certificate, social security number. ***Required for some:*** essay or personal statement, minimum 2.5 GPA, 3 letters of recommendation, interview, placement test or College Board test, vaccination certificate, social security number. ***Recommended:*** minimum 2.0 GPA.

Application deadlines: rolling (freshmen), rolling (out-of-state freshmen), rolling (transfers).

CONTACT
Mr. Oscar Morales, Student Affairs Dean, EDP University of Puerto Rico, Avenue Ponce de Leon, #560, Hato Rey, PR 00918, Puerto Rico. *Phone:* 787-765-3560 Ext. 272. *Fax:* 787-777-0024. *E-mail:* oscarmorales@edpuniversity.edu.

EDP University of Puerto Rico–San Sebastian

San Sebastian, Puerto Rico

http://www.edpuniversity.edu/

- **Proprietary** comprehensive, founded 1976
- **Rural** campus
- **Coed** 1,168 undergraduate students, 67% full-time, 64% women, 36% men
- **Minimally difficult** entrance level, 87% of applicants were admitted

UNDERGRAD STUDENTS
785 full-time, 383 part-time. 100% Hispanic/Latino.

Freshmen
Admission: 299 applied, 260 admitted, 292 enrolled. ***Average high school GPA:*** 2.5.

Retention: 44% of full-time freshmen returned.

FACULTY
Total: 99, 21% full-time, 6% with terminal degrees.

Student/faculty ratio: 21:1.

ACADEMICS
Calendar: semesters. *Degrees:* associate, bachelor's, and master's.

Special study options: academic remediation for entering students, accelerated degree program, adult/continuing education programs, advanced placement credit, cooperative education, distance learning, independent study, internships, part-time degree program, services for LD students, summer session for credit.

Computers: 146 computers/terminals are available on campus for general student use. Students can access the following: computer help desk, free student e-mail accounts, online (class) grades, online (class) registration, online (class) schedules. Campuswide network is available. Wireless service is available via entire campus.

STUDENT LIFE
Housing options: college housing not available.

Activities and organizations: Nursing, Physical Therapy, Information Systems, Pharmacy, Digital Fashion Design.

Campus security: private security.

Student services: personal/psychological counseling.

COSTS & FINANCIAL AID
Costs (2015–16) ***Tuition:*** $5100 full-time, $170 per credit part-time. Full-time tuition and fees vary according to course load and program. Part-time tuition and fees vary according to course load and program. ***Required fees:*** $840 full-time, $170 per credit part-time, $420 per term part-time. ***Payment plan:*** installment. ***Waivers:*** employees or children of employees.

Financial Aid Of all full-time matriculated undergraduates who enrolled in 2012, 1,098 applied for aid, 1,097 were judged to have need. 32 Federal Work-Study jobs (averaging $1714). ***Average percent of need met:*** 92. ***Average financial aid package:*** $5000. ***Average need-based loan:*** $2601. ***Average need-based gift aid:*** $4545.

APPLYING
Standardized Tests *Required:* College Board or Institutional Entrance Test (for admission).

Application fee: $15.

Required: high school transcript, minimum 2.0 GPA, College Board or Institutional Entrance Test. ***Required for some:*** high school transcript, minimum 2.5 GPA, interview.

Application deadlines: rolling (freshmen), rolling (out-of-state freshmen), rolling (transfers).

CONTACT
Dr. Damarys Varela Velez, Student Affairs Dean, EDP University of Puerto Rico–San Sebastian, Avenue Betances #49, San Sebastian, PR 00685. *Phone:* 787-896-2252 Ext. 303. *Fax:* 787-896-0066. *E-mail:* dvarela@edpuniversity.edu.

Escuela de Artes Plasticas de Puerto Rico

San Juan, Puerto Rico

http://www.eap.edu/

- **Commonwealth-supported** 4-year, founded 1966
- **Urban** campus
- **Endowment** $1.3 million
- **Coed** 555 undergraduate students, 74% full-time, 63% women, 37% men
- **Moderately difficult** entrance level, 93% of applicants were admitted

UNDERGRAD STUDENTS
408 full-time, 147 part-time. Students come from 2 states and territories; 2 other countries; 0.2% are from out of state; 99% Hispanic/Latino; 0.4% international; 6% transferred in.

Freshmen
Admission: 110 applied, 102 admitted, 91 enrolled. ***Average high school GPA:*** 3.15.

Retention: 85% of full-time freshmen returned.

FACULTY
Total: 72, 21% full-time, 65% with terminal degrees.

Student/faculty ratio: 13:1.

ACADEMICS
Calendar: 3 semesters each calendar year; participant in Year Round Pell. *Degree:* bachelor's.

Special study options: adult/continuing education programs, advanced placement credit, internships, off-campus study, part-time degree program, services for LD students.

Computers: 110 computers/terminals and 110 ports are available on campus for general student use. Students can access the following: computer help desk, free student e-mail accounts, library online catalog, wireless access. Wireless service is available via entire campus.

STUDENT LIFE
Housing options: college housing not available.

Activities and organizations: Student government, Fatamorgana, CINEAP.

Campus security: 24-hour emergency response devices and patrols, security cameras and institutional police of privacy.

Student services: personal/psychological counseling.

COSTS & FINANCIAL AID
Costs (2014–15) ***Tuition:*** commonwealth resident $2997 full-time; nonresident $5157 full-time. Full-time tuition and fees vary according to course load and program. ***Required fees:*** $251 full-time. ***Payment plan:*** installment.

Financial Aid Of all full-time matriculated undergraduates who enrolled in 2007, 276 applied for aid, 276 were judged to have need. 10 Federal Work-Study jobs (averaging $1850). ***Average percent of need met:*** 82. ***Financial aid deadline:*** 5/25.

APPLYING
Standardized Tests *Recommended:* SAT (for admission).

Application fee: $25.

Required: high school transcript, minimum 2.0 GPA, The applicants must approve an evaluation regarding artistic skills through a portfolio or seminar and complete the security seminar. The portfolio evaluation fee is $30 and for seminar is $50.

Application deadlines: 3/18 (freshmen), 3/18 (out-of-state freshmen), 3/18 (transfers).

Notification: 5/1 (freshmen), 5/1 (out-of-state freshmen), 5/1 (transfers).

CONTACT
Mrs. Nitza Melendez, Officer of Admissions, Escuela de Artes Plasticas de Puerto Rico, PO Box 902112, San Juan, PR 00902-1112. *Phone:* 787-725-8120 Ext. 333. *Fax:* 787-721-3798. *E-mail:* nmelendez@eap.edu.

Inter American University of Puerto Rico, Aguadilla Campus

Aguadilla, Puerto Rico

http://www.aguadilla.inter.edu/

- **Independent** comprehensive, founded 1957, part of Inter American University of Puerto Rico
- **Small-town** 50-acre campus
- **Endowment** $1.5 million
- **Coed** 4,357 undergraduate students, 86% full-time, 55% women, 45% men
- **Moderately difficult** entrance level, 64% of applicants were admitted

UNDERGRAD STUDENTS
3,744 full-time, 613 part-time. Students come from 25 states and territories; 2% are from out of state; 100% Hispanic/Latino; 0.1% American Indian or Alaska Native, non-Hispanic/Latino; 2% transferred in.

Freshmen
Admission: 1,565 applied, 994 admitted, 963 enrolled. ***Average high school GPA:*** 2.93.
Retention: 76% of full-time freshmen returned.

FACULTY
Total: 255, 30% full-time, 100% with terminal degrees.
Student/faculty ratio: 29:1.

ACADEMICS
Calendar: semesters. *Degrees:* certificates, associate, bachelor's, master's, and postbachelor's certificates.
Special study options: academic remediation for entering students, accelerated degree program, adult/continuing education programs, advanced placement credit, cooperative education, distance learning, double majors, English as a second language, external degree program, honors programs, independent study, internships, part-time degree program, services for LD students, study abroad, summer session for credit. ***ROTC:*** Army (b), Air Force (b).
Computers: 786 computers/terminals are available on campus for general student use. Students can access the following: campus intranet, free student e-mail accounts, online (class) grades, online (class) registration, online (class) schedules. Campuswide network is available. Wireless service is available via entire campus.

STUDENT LIFE
Housing options: college housing not available.
Activities and organizations: drama/theater group, student-run newspaper, choral group, Criminal Justice Association, Microbiot Science Association, Social Workers Association, Nursing Association, Psychology Association.
Athletics *Intercollegiate sports:* baseball M(s), basketball M(s)/W(s), cheerleading M(s)/W(s), cross-country running M(s)/W(s), soccer M(s)/W(s), softball M(s)/W(s), swimming and diving M(s)/W(s), table tennis M(s)/W(s), tennis M(s)/W(s), track and field M(s)/W(s), volleyball M(s)/W(s), weight lifting M(s)/W(s), wrestling M(s)/W(s). ***Intramural sports:*** basketball M/W, cheerleading M/W, cross-country running M/W, soccer M/W, softball M/W, table tennis M/W, tennis M/W, track and field M/W, volleyball M/W, weight lifting M/W, wrestling M/W.
Campus security: 24-hour emergency response devices and patrols.
Student services: personal/psychological counseling.

COSTS
Costs (2015–16) ***Tuition:*** $4272 full-time, $178 per semester hour part-time. Full-time tuition and fees vary according to course load and program. Part-time tuition and fees vary according to course load and program. ***Required fees:*** $542 full-time, $224 per semester part-time. ***Payment plans:*** installment, deferred payment.

APPLYING
Standardized Tests *Required:* SAT or ACT (for admission), PAA (for admission).
Options: electronic application.
Required: high school transcript, minimum 2.0 GPA.
Application deadlines: rolling (freshmen), rolling (transfers).

CONTACT
Mrs. Doris Perez, Admissions Director, Inter American University of Puerto Rico, Aguadilla Campus, PO Box 20,000, Road 459 Intersection 463, Aguadilla, PR 00605. *Phone:* 787-891-0925 Ext. 2101. *Fax:* 787-882-3020.

Inter American University of Puerto Rico, Bayamón Campus

Bayamón, Puerto Rico

http://bayamon.inter.edu/

- **Independent** comprehensive, founded 1912, part of Inter American University of Puerto Rico
- **Urban** 51-acre campus with easy access to San Juan
- **Endowment** $6.0 million
- **Coed** 4,717 undergraduate students, 87% full-time, 43% women, 57% men
- 61% of applicants were admitted

UNDERGRAD STUDENTS
4,109 full-time, 608 part-time. 0.3% Black or African American, non-Hispanic/Latino; 99% Hispanic/Latino; 0.4% American Indian or Alaska Native, non-Hispanic/Latino; 3% transferred in.

Freshmen
Admission: 1,730 applied, 1,054 admitted, 1,080 enrolled. ***Average high school GPA:*** 3.
Retention: 74% of full-time freshmen returned.

FACULTY
Total: 295, 33% full-time, 27% with terminal degrees.
Student/faculty ratio: 26:1.

ACADEMICS
Calendar: semesters. *Degrees:* certificates, associate, bachelor's, and master's.
Special study options: accelerated degree program, adult/continuing education programs, advanced placement credit, cooperative education, distance learning, external degree program, honors programs, independent study, internships, part-time degree program, services for LD students, summer session for credit. ***ROTC:*** Army (c).
Computers: 660 computers/terminals are available on campus for general student use. Students can access the following: computer help desk, free student e-mail accounts, online (class) grades, online (class) registration. Campuswide network is available.

STUDENT LIFE
Housing options: Campus housing is university owned.
Activities and organizations: student-run newspaper, choral group, Asociacion de Estudiantes de Administracion de Empresas, Estudiantes Unidos por la Ciencia, Asociacion Estudiantes de Aviacion, Consejo de Estudiante, Asociacion Estudiantes de Ingenieria.
Athletics *Intercollegiate sports:* baseball M(s), basketball M(s)/W(s), cross-country running M(s)/W(s), softball M(s)/W(s), swimming and diving M(s)/W(s), table tennis M(s)/W(s), track and field M(s)/W(s), volleyball M(s)/W(s), weight lifting M(s). ***Intramural sports:*** basketball M/W, cross-country running M/W, softball M/W, swimming and diving M/W, table tennis M/W, tennis M/W, track and field M/W, volleyball M/W, weight lifting M.
Campus security: 24-hour patrols.
Student services: health clinic, personal/psychological counseling.

COSTS & FINANCIAL AID
Costs (2015–16) ***Tuition:*** $5340 full-time, $260 per semester hour part-time. Full-time tuition and fees vary according to class time, course load, and program. Part-time tuition and fees vary according to class time, course load, and program. ***Required fees:*** $520 full-time. ***Payment plan:*** deferred payment.
Financial Aid Of all full-time matriculated undergraduates who enrolled in 2014, 2,760 applied for aid, 2,727 were judged to have need, 11 had their need fully met. ***Average percent of need met:*** 11. ***Average financial aid package:*** $1458. ***Average need-based loan:*** $2375. ***Average need-based gift aid:*** $482.

APPLYING
Standardized Tests *Required:* CEEB (for admission). *Required for some:* SAT (for admission).

Options: electronic application.

Required: high school transcript, minimum 2.0 GPA, 2.5 GPA for engineering programs.

Notification: continuous (freshmen), continuous (transfers).

CONTACT
Inter American University of Puerto Rico, Bayamón Campus, Dr. John Will Harris 500, Bayamón, PR 00957. *Phone:* 787-279-1912 Ext. 2017.

Inter American University of Puerto Rico, Fajardo Campus

Fajardo, Puerto Rico

http://www.fajardo.inter.edu/

- **Independent** comprehensive, founded 1965, part of Inter American University of Puerto Rico
- **Small-town** 11-acre campus with easy access to San Juan
- **Endowment** $4.3 million
- **Coed** 2,043 undergraduate students, 75% full-time, 46% women, 54% men
- **Moderately difficult** entrance level, 76% of applicants were admitted

UNDERGRAD STUDENTS
1,533 full-time, 510 part-time. Students come from 3 states and territories; 100% Hispanic/Latino.

Freshmen
Admission: 759 applied, 580 admitted, 544 enrolled. ***Average high school GPA:*** 2.

Retention: 67% of full-time freshmen returned.

FACULTY
Total: 105, 38% full-time, 11% with terminal degrees.

Student/faculty ratio: 11:1.

ACADEMICS
Calendar: semesters. *Degrees:* certificates, associate, bachelor's, and master's.

Special study options: academic remediation for entering students, adult/continuing education programs, advanced placement credit, cooperative education, distance learning, English as a second language, external degree program, honors programs, independent study, internships, off-campus study, part-time degree program, services for LD students, summer session for credit. ***ROTC:*** Army (c).

Computers: 280 computers/terminals are available on campus for general student use. Students can access the following: free student e-mail accounts, online (class) grades, online (class) registration, online (class) schedules. Campuswide network is available. Wireless service is available via entire campus.

STUDENT LIFE
Housing options: college housing not available.

Activities and organizations: drama/theater group, Future Teachers Association, Criminal Justice Student Association, Honor Program Association, Computer Science Association, Social Work Association.

Athletics ***Intercollegiate sports:*** baseball M, basketball M(s)/W, bowling M, cheerleading W, softball W, table tennis M/W, tennis M/W, track and field M(s)/W(s), volleyball M/W.

Campus security: 24-hour patrols.

Student services: personal/psychological counseling.

COSTS
Costs (2015–16) ***Tuition:*** $178 per credit part-time. Full-time tuition and fees vary according to class time, course level, course load, degree level, location, program, and student level. Part-time tuition and fees vary according to class time, course level, course load, degree level, location, program, and student level. ***Payment plans:*** installment, deferred payment. ***Waivers:*** adult students and employees or children of employees.

APPLYING
Standardized Tests *Required:* College Board (for admission).

Options: electronic application, early admission, deferred entrance.

Required: high school transcript. ***Required for some:*** interview.

Application deadlines: 5/15 (freshmen), rolling (transfers).

CONTACT
Ms. Ghisita M. Garcia, Administrative Assistant II, Inter American University of Puerto Rico, Fajardo Campus, Call Box 70003, Fajardo, PR 00738-7003. *Phone:* 787-863-2390 Ext. 2210. *Fax:* 787-860-3470. *E-mail:* ghisita.garcia@fajardo.inter.edu.

Inter American University of Puerto Rico, Guayama Campus

Guayama, Puerto Rico

http://www.guayama.inter.edu/

- **Independent** comprehensive, founded 1958, part of Inter American University of Puerto Rico
- **Small-town** 50-acre campus
- **Endowment** $1.4 million
- **Coed** 2,069 undergraduate students, 86% full-time, 67% women, 33% men
- **Moderately difficult** entrance level, 71% of applicants were admitted

UNDERGRAD STUDENTS
1,784 full-time, 285 part-time. Students come from 7 states and territories; 0.5% are from out of state; 0.1% Black or African American, non-Hispanic/Latino; 100% Hispanic/Latino; 4% transferred in.

Freshmen
Admission: 295 applied, 208 admitted, 350 enrolled.

Retention: 72% of full-time freshmen returned.

FACULTY
Total: 183, 22% full-time, 16% with terminal degrees.

Student/faculty ratio: 12:1.

ACADEMICS
Calendar: semesters. *Degrees:* certificates, associate, bachelor's, and master's.

Special study options: academic remediation for entering students, adult/continuing education programs, cooperative education, distance learning, English as a second language, external degree program, honors programs, independent study, internships, off-campus study, part-time degree program, services for LD students, summer session for credit. ***ROTC:*** Army (c).

Computers: 261 computers/terminals are available on campus for general student use. Students can access the following: campus intranet, computer help desk, free student e-mail accounts, online (class) grades, online (class) registration, online (class) schedules. Campuswide network is available. Wireless service is available via entire campus.

STUDENT LIFE
Housing options: college housing not available.

Activities and organizations: drama/theater group, student-run radio station, Nursing Student Association, Criminal Justice, Office Professionals, Future Educators Association, Pharmacy Technician.

Athletics ***Intercollegiate sports:*** baseball M, basketball M(s)/W(s), cross-country running M(s)/W(s), swimming and diving M. ***Intramural sports:*** baseball M, basketball M/W, cross-country running M/W, soccer M, softball M/W, swimming and diving M, table tennis W, tennis W, track and field M/W.

Campus security: 24-hour emergency response devices.

Student services: health clinic, personal/psychological counseling.

COSTS & FINANCIAL AID
Costs (2015–16) ***Tuition:*** $4272 full-time. ***Required fees:*** $1262 full-time. ***Payment plan:*** deferred payment. ***Waivers:*** employees or children of employees.

Financial Aid Of all full-time matriculated undergraduates who enrolled in 2014, 1,246 applied for aid, 1,207 were judged to have need, 1 had their need fully met. ***Average percent of need met:*** 31. ***Average financial aid***

package: $1904. ***Average need-based loan:*** $1818. ***Average need-based gift aid:*** $697.

APPLYING

Standardized Tests *Required:* SAT (for admission), PAA (for admission).

Options: electronic application.

Required: high school transcript, minimum 2.0 GPA. ***Required for some:*** essay or personal statement, interview.

Application deadlines: 8/1 (freshmen), 8/1 (transfers).

CONTACT

Mrs. Laura E. Ferrer, Director of Admissions, Inter American University of Puerto Rico, Guayama Campus, Call Box 10004, Guayama, PR 00785. *Phone:* 787-864-2222 Ext. 2220. *Fax:* 787-864-8232. *E-mail:* laura.ferrer@guayama.inter.edu.

Inter American University of Puerto Rico, Metropolitan Campus

San Juan, Puerto Rico

http://metro.inter.edu/

- **Independent** comprehensive, founded 1960, part of Inter American University of Puerto Rico
- **Urban** campus
- **Endowment** $10.8 million
- **Coed**
- **Moderately difficult** entrance level

ACADEMICS

Calendar: semesters. *Degrees:* certificates, associate, bachelor's, master's, doctoral, and postbachelor's certificates.

STUDENT LIFE

Housing options: college housing not available.

Activities and organizations: drama/theater group, student-run newspaper, choral group, Intercultural Student Association, Club Rotaract, Christian University Association, Nursing Student Association, Psychology Student Graduate Association.

Campus security: 24-hour emergency response devices and patrols, Video Security System.

Student services: health clinic, personal/psychological counseling.

COSTS & FINANCIAL AID

Costs (2014–15) ***Tuition:*** $6408 full-time, $178 per credit part-time. ***Required fees:*** $603 full-time.

Financial Aid Of all full-time matriculated undergraduates who enrolled in 1999, 4,328 applied for aid, 3,935 were judged to have need, 29 had their need fully met. ***Average percent of need met:*** 11. ***Average financial aid package:*** $2144. ***Average need-based loan:*** $1149. ***Average need-based gift aid:*** $1617. ***Financial aid deadline:*** 4/30.

APPLYING

Standardized Tests *Required:* CEEB (for admission). *Required for some:* SAT (for admission).

Options: electronic application.

Required: high school transcript.

CONTACT

Ms. Ida G. Betancourt, Official Admission, Inter American University of Puerto Rico, Metropolitan Campus, PO Box 191293, San Juan, PR 00919-1293. *Phone:* 787-250-1912 Ext. 2188. *Fax:* 787-250-1025. *E-mail:* jbetancourt@metro.inter.edu.

Inter American University of Puerto Rico, Ponce Campus

Mercedita, Puerto Rico

http://www.ponce.inter.edu/

- **Independent** comprehensive, founded 1962, part of Inter American University of Puerto Rico
- **Urban** 50-acre campus with easy access to San Juan
- **Endowment** $14.5 million
- **Coed** 5,361 undergraduate students, 86% full-time, 60% women, 40% men
- **Moderately difficult** entrance level, 66% of applicants were admitted

UNDERGRAD STUDENTS

4,632 full-time, 729 part-time. Students come from 12 other countries; 1% are from out of state; 0.1% Black or African American, non-Hispanic/Latino; 99% Hispanic/Latino; 0.2% American Indian or Alaska Native, non-Hispanic/Latino; 3% transferred in.

Freshmen

Admission: 1,908 applied, 1,268 admitted, 980 enrolled. ***Average high school GPA:*** 2.75.

Retention: 76% of full-time freshmen returned.

FACULTY

Total: 295, 34% full-time, 29% with terminal degrees.

Student/faculty ratio: 32:1.

ACADEMICS

Calendar: semesters. *Degrees:* certificates, associate, bachelor's, and master's.

Special study options: academic remediation for entering students, adult/continuing education programs, cooperative education, distance learning, English as a second language, honors programs, internships, off-campus study, part-time degree program, services for LD students, study abroad, summer session for credit.

Computers: 336 computers/terminals and 447 ports are available on campus for general student use. Students can access the following: free student e-mail accounts, online (class) grades, online (class) registration. Campuswide network is available. Wireless service is available via entire campus.

STUDENT LIFE

Housing options: college housing not available.

Activities and organizations: drama/theater group, choral group, Association of Future Teachers of Special Education, Hotel Management Association, American Chemical Society (ACS), Criminal Justice Association, Students Board of Honor Program, national fraternities.

Athletics ***Intercollegiate sports:*** baseball M(s), cross-country running M(s)/W(s), soccer M(s)/W(s), softball M(s)/W(s), swimming and diving M(s)/W(s), table tennis M(s)/W(s), track and field M(s)/W(s), volleyball M(s)/W(s), weight lifting M(s)/W(s), wrestling M(s). ***Intramural sports:*** cross-country running M/W, soccer M/W, softball M/W, table tennis M/W, tennis M/W, track and field M/W, volleyball M/W, weight lifting M/W.

Campus security: 24-hour emergency response devices and patrols.

Student services: health clinic, personal/psychological counseling.

COSTS & FINANCIAL AID

Costs (2014–15) ***Tuition:*** $4272 full-time, $178 per credit part-time. Full-time tuition and fees vary according to course load and program. Part-time tuition and fees vary according to course load and program. ***Required fees:*** $594 full-time. ***Payment plan:*** deferred payment.

Financial Aid Of all full-time matriculated undergraduates who enrolled in 2012, 3,337 applied for aid, 3,323 were judged to have need, 2 had their need fully met. ***Average percent of need met:*** 8. ***Average financial aid package:*** $1160. ***Average need-based loan:*** $1476. ***Average need-based gift aid:*** $533.

APPLYING

Standardized Tests *Required:* CEEB (for admission). *Required for some:* SAT (for admission).

Options: deferred entrance.

Required: high school transcript, minimum 2.0 GPA.

Application deadlines: 5/15 (freshmen), 5/15 (transfers).

CONTACT
Mr. Franco Diaz, Admissions Officer, Inter American University of Puerto Rico, Ponce Campus, 104 Turpo Industrial Park, Road #1, Mercedita, PR 00715-1602. *Phone:* 787-284-1912 Ext. 2025. *Fax:* 787-841-0103. *E-mail:* fidiaz@ponce.inter.edu.

Inter American University of Puerto Rico, San Germán Campus

San Germán, Puerto Rico

http://www.sg.inter.edu/

- **Independent** university, founded 1912, part of Inter American University of Puerto Rico
- **Small-town** 275-acre campus with easy access to Ponce, Aguadilla, Mayaguez
- **Endowment** $37.9 million
- **Coed** 4,453 undergraduate students, 90% full-time, 52% women, 48% men
- **Moderately difficult** entrance level, 76% of applicants were admitted

UNDERGRAD STUDENTS
4,003 full-time, 450 part-time. Students come from 12 states and territories; 1 other country; 0.4% are from out of state; 0.1% Black or African American, non-Hispanic/Latino; 99% Hispanic/Latino; 0.1% Native Hawaiian or other Pacific Islander, non-Hispanic/Latino; 0.1% American Indian or Alaska Native, non-Hispanic/Latino; 2% transferred in; 5% live on campus.

Freshmen
Admission: 1,400 applied, 1,060 admitted, 1,003 enrolled.
Retention: 81% of full-time freshmen returned.

FACULTY
Total: 281, 40% full-time, 37% with terminal degrees.
Student/faculty ratio: 28:1.

ACADEMICS
Calendar: semesters. *Degrees:* certificates, associate, bachelor's, master's, doctoral, and postbachelor's certificates.
Special study options: academic remediation for entering students, accelerated degree program, adult/continuing education programs, advanced placement credit, cooperative education, distance learning, double majors, English as a second language, external degree program, honors programs, independent study, internships, off-campus study, part-time degree program, services for LD students, summer session for credit. ***ROTC:*** Army (c), Navy (c), Air Force (c).
Computers: 1,000 computers/terminals and 1,000 ports are available on campus for general student use. Students can access the following: campus intranet, computer help desk, free student e-mail accounts, online (class) grades, online (class) registration, online (class) schedules. Campuswide network is available. Wireless service is available via computer centers, computer labs, dorm rooms, learning centers, libraries, student centers.

STUDENT LIFE
Housing options: men-only, women-only. Campus housing is university owned.
Activities and organizations: drama/theater group, student-run newspaper, choral group, Asociacion de Pre-Medica-Caduceus, Business Professionals of America, Sociedad de Honor en Biologia Beta Beta Beta (TriBeta, Asociacion de Estudiantes de Futuros Exalumnos, Asociacion de Estudiantes del Programa de Honor.
Athletics *Intercollegiate sports:* baseball M(s), basketball M(s)/W(s), cross-country running M(s)/W(s), soccer M(s), softball M/W, swimming and diving M/W, table tennis M(s)/W(s), tennis M(s)/W(s), track and field M(s)/W(s), volleyball M(s)/W(s), weight lifting M(s). ***Intramural sports:*** badminton M/W, basketball M/W, cross-country running M/W, softball M/W, table tennis M/W, tennis M/W, track and field M/W, volleyball M/W.
Campus security: 24-hour emergency response devices and patrols, electronic vigilance systems with nonstop digital video cameras, access control permits, periodic surveillance.
Student services: personal/psychological counseling.

COSTS & FINANCIAL AID
Costs (2014–15) *Comprehensive fee:* $8620 includes full-time tuition ($5340), mandatory fees ($580), and room and board ($2700). Part-time tuition: $178 per credit. ***Required fees:*** $178 per credit part-time. ***College room only:*** $1200. Room and board charges vary according to board plan and housing facility. ***Payment plan:*** installment. ***Waivers:*** employees or children of employees.
Financial Aid Of all full-time matriculated undergraduates who enrolled in 2009, 2,797 applied for aid, 2,755 were judged to have need, 4 had their need fully met. ***Average percent of need met:*** 12. ***Average financial aid package:*** $2009. ***Average need-based loan:*** $3080. ***Average need-based gift aid:*** $642.

APPLYING
Standardized Tests *Required:* CEEB (for admission). *Required for some:* SAT or ACT (for admission).
Options: electronic application, early admission.
Required: high school transcript, medical history, vaccination. ***Required for some:*** 1 letter of recommendation, interview. ***Recommended:*** essay or personal statement, minimum 2.0 GPA.
Application deadlines: 5/15 (freshmen), 5/15 (transfers).
Notification: continuous (freshmen), continuous (transfers).

CONTACT
Prof. Mildred Camacho, Director of Admissions, Inter American University of Puerto Rico, San Germán Campus, PO Box 5100, San German, PR 00683-5008. *Phone:* 787-264-1912 Ext. 7283. *Toll-free phone:* 800-981-8075. *Fax:* 787-892-7020. *E-mail:* milcama@intersg.edu.

National University College

Bayamón, Puerto Rico

http://www.nuc.edu/

- **Private** comprehensive, part of EDUK Services Center
- **Urban** campus with easy access to Bayamon
- **Coed**

FACULTY
Total: 464, 18% full-time, 9% with terminal degrees.
Student/faculty ratio: 17:1.

ACADEMICS
Degrees: associate, bachelor's, and master's.
Special study options: adult/continuing education programs, advanced placement credit, distance learning, internships, part-time degree program, services for LD students.
Computers: 150 computers/terminals are available on campus for general student use. Students can access the following: campus intranet, free student e-mail accounts, online (class) grades, online (class) registration, online (class) schedules. Campuswide network is available. Wireless service is available via entire campus.

STUDENT LIFE
Housing options: college housing not available.

COSTS & FINANCIAL AID
Costs (2015–16) *One-time required fee:* $25. ***Tuition:*** $6120 full-time, $170 per credit part-time. Full-time tuition and fees vary according to course load and location. Part-time tuition and fees vary according to course load and location. ***Required fees:*** $390 full-time, $130 per term part-time. ***Payment plan:*** installment. ***Waivers:*** employees or children of employees.
Financial Aid Of all full-time matriculated undergraduates who enrolled in 2011, 5,214 applied for aid, 5,214 were judged to have need. 415 Federal Work-Study jobs (averaging $1059). ***Average percent of need met:*** 90. ***Average financial aid package:*** $4462. ***Average need-based loan:*** $4527. ***Average need-based gift aid:*** $5140. ***Average indebtedness upon graduation:*** $4633.

APPLYING
Standardized Tests *Required:* Required College Board Test; if the student doesn't have it, then the institution requires SAT, if the student

doesn't have either, it would be required the Institutional Admission Test (for admission). *Required for some:* SAT Subject Tests (for admission).

Required: high school transcript, certificate of immunization.

CONTACT

Admissions, National University College, PO Box 2036, National College Plaza Building, Bayamón, PR 00960. *Toll-free phone:* 800-780-5134.

Polytechnic University of Puerto Rico

Hato Rey, Puerto Rico

http://www.pupr.edu/

- **Independent** comprehensive, founded 1966
- **Urban** 10-acre campus with easy access to San Juan
- **Endowment** $13.7 million
- **Coed** 3,788 undergraduate students, 47% full-time, 20% women, 80% men
- **Minimally difficult** entrance level, 87% of applicants were admitted

UNDERGRAD STUDENTS

1,795 full-time, 1,993 part-time. Students come from 2 states and territories; 5 other countries; 100% Hispanic/Latino; 6% transferred in.

Freshmen

Admission: 623 applied, 543 admitted, 438 enrolled. ***Average high school GPA:*** 3.21.

Retention: 77% of full-time freshmen returned.

FACULTY

Total: 253, 56% full-time, 28% with terminal degrees.

Student/faculty ratio: 14:1.

ACADEMICS

Calendar: trimesters. *Degrees:* associate, bachelor's, master's, and doctoral.

Special study options: academic remediation for entering students, distance learning, English as a second language, honors programs, independent study, internships, part-time degree program, student-designed majors, summer session for credit. ***ROTC:*** Army (c).

Computers: 550 computers/terminals and 550 ports are available on campus for general student use. Students can access the following: campus intranet, computer help desk, free student e-mail accounts, online (class) grades, online (class) registration, online (class) schedules. Campuswide network is available. Wireless service is available via entire campus.

STUDENT LIFE

Housing options: college housing not available.

Activities and organizations: choral group, ASCE (American Society of Civil Engineering), PRWEA (Puerto Rico Water and Environment Association), ACI (American Concrete Institute), SAE PUPR AERO DESIGN TEAM, SHPE (Society of Hispanic Professional Engineers).

Athletics ***Intercollegiate sports:*** basketball M(s), cross-country running M(s)/W(s), soccer M, table tennis M(s), tennis M(s)/W(s), track and field M(s)/W(s), volleyball M(s)/W(s), wrestling M. ***Intramural sports:*** basketball M.

Campus security: 24-hour emergency response devices and patrols, over 250 security cameras on campus.

Student services: personal/psychological counseling.

COSTS & FINANCIAL AID

Costs (2015–16) ***Tuition:*** $7020 full-time, $195 per credit part-time. Full-time tuition and fees vary according to course level, course load, degree level, and program. Part-time tuition and fees vary according to course level, course load, degree level, and program. ***Required fees:*** $780 full-time. ***Payment plan:*** deferred payment. ***Waivers:*** employees or children of employees.

Financial Aid Of all full-time matriculated undergraduates who enrolled in 2013, 1,918 applied for aid, 1,865 were judged to have need, 8 had their need fully met. ***Average percent of need met:*** 45. ***Average financial aid package:*** $7698. ***Average need-based loan:*** $2665. ***Average need-based gift aid:*** $2535. ***Average non-need-based aid:*** $245. ***Financial aid deadline:*** 5/15.

APPLYING

Standardized Tests *Required for some:* SAT (for admission).

Options: electronic application.

Application fee: $30.

Required: high school transcript, minimum 2.0 GPA.

CONTACT

Ms. Teresa Cardona, Director of Admissions, Polytechnic University of Puerto Rico, PO Box 192017, San Juan, PR 00919-2017. *Phone:* 787-754-8000 Ext. 240. *Fax:* 787-764-8712. *E-mail:* tcardona@pupr.edu.

Universidad del Turabo

Gurabo, Puerto Rico

http://www.suagm.edu/ut/

- **Independent** university, founded 1972, part of Ana G. Mendez University System
- **Urban** 140-acre campus with easy access to San Juan
- **Coed** 14,596 undergraduate students, 74% full-time, 58% women, 42% men
- **Minimally difficult** entrance level, 41% of applicants were admitted

UNDERGRAD STUDENTS

10,836 full-time, 3,760 part-time. 4% transferred in.

Freshmen

Admission: 10,688 applied, 4,331 admitted, 2,553 enrolled.

Retention: 75% of full-time freshmen returned.

FACULTY

Total: 993, 22% full-time, 30% with terminal degrees.

Student/faculty ratio: 29:1.

ACADEMICS

Calendar: semesters. *Degrees:* certificates, associate, bachelor's, master's, doctoral, post-master's, and postbachelor's certificates.

Special study options: academic remediation for entering students, accelerated degree program, adult/continuing education programs, advanced placement credit, cooperative education, distance learning, double majors, English as a second language, honors programs, independent study, internships, off-campus study, part-time degree program, services for LD students, study abroad, summer session for credit. ***ROTC:*** Army (c), Air Force (c).

Computers: Campuswide network is available.

STUDENT LIFE

Housing options: college housing not available.

Activities and organizations: drama/theater group, student-run newspaper, radio station, choral group.

Campus security: 24-hour patrols.

Student services: health clinic, personal/psychological counseling.

COSTS & FINANCIAL AID

Costs (2014–15) ***Tuition:*** $4680 full-time. Full-time tuition and fees vary according to course level, course load, and program. ***Required fees:*** $900 full-time.

Financial Aid Of all full-time matriculated undergraduates who enrolled in 2013, 10,405 applied for aid, 10,405 were judged to have need. 493 Federal Work-Study jobs (averaging $634). ***Financial aid deadline:*** 6/30.

APPLYING

Standardized Tests *Required for some:* College Board Exam. *Recommended:* SAT (for admission).

Options: electronic application.

Application fee: $15.

Required: high school transcript. ***Required for some:*** essay or personal statement, interview.

Application deadlines: rolling (freshmen), rolling (transfers).

Notification: continuous (freshmen), continuous (transfers).

CONTACT

Universidad del Turabo, PO Box 3030, Gurabo, PR 00778-3030. *Phone:* 787-743-7979 Ext. 4351.

Universidad Metropolitana

San Juan, Puerto Rico

http://www.suagm.edu/umet/

- **Independent** comprehensive, founded 1980, part of Ana G. Mendez University System
- **Urban** campus with easy access to San Juan
- **Coed** 11,529 undergraduate students, 79% full-time, 64% women, 36% men
- **Moderately difficult** entrance level, 53% of applicants were admitted

UNDERGRAD STUDENTS
9,081 full-time, 2,448 part-time. 100% Hispanic/Latino; 5% transferred in.

Freshmen
Admission: 10,662 applied, 5,648 admitted, 2,228 enrolled. ***Average high school GPA:*** 2.83.

Retention: 71% of full-time freshmen returned.

FACULTY
Total: 1,149, 16% full-time, 27% with terminal degrees.
Student/faculty ratio: 23:1.

ACADEMICS
Calendar: semesters. *Degrees:* certificates, associate, bachelor's, master's, doctoral, and postbachelor's certificates.

Special study options: academic remediation for entering students, accelerated degree program, adult/continuing education programs, advanced placement credit, cooperative education, distance learning, double majors, freshman honors college, honors programs, independent study, internships, off-campus study, part-time degree program, summer session for credit.

Computers: 50 computers/terminals are available on campus for general student use. Students can access the following: campus intranet, computer help desk, free student e-mail accounts, online (class) grades, online (class) registration, online (class) schedules. Campuswide network is available. Wireless service is available via entire campus.

STUDENT LIFE
Housing options: college housing not available.

Activities and organizations: drama/theater group, student-run newspaper, radio and television station, choral group.

Athletics ***Intercollegiate sports:*** softball M/W, table tennis M/W, tennis M/W, track and field M/W, volleyball M/W, weight lifting M/W. ***Intramural sports:*** table tennis M/W, track and field M/W, volleyball M/W, weight lifting M/W.

Campus security: 24-hour patrols.

Student services: health clinic, personal/psychological counseling.

COSTS
Costs (2014–15) ***Tuition:*** $4680 full-time, $195 per credit hour part-time. Full-time tuition and fees vary according to degree level, location, and program. Part-time tuition and fees vary according to degree level, location, and program. ***Required fees:*** $900 full-time, $450 per term part-time. ***Waivers:*** employees or children of employees.

APPLYING
Standardized Tests *Required:* College Board Exam (for admission). *Recommended:* SAT (for admission).

Options: electronic application, early admission.

Application fee: $15.

Required: high school transcript. ***Required for some:*** essay or personal statement, interview.

Application deadlines: 8/15 (freshmen), 8/15 (transfers).

CONTACT
Mr. Julio Rodriguez Soiza, Director of Admissions, Universidad Metropolitana, Box 21150, San Juan, PR 00928-1150. *Phone:* 787-766-1717 Ext. 6587. *Toll-free phone:* 800-747-8362. *Fax:* 787-751-0992. *E-mail:* um_frivera@suagm1.suagm.edu.

Universidad Teológica del Caribe

St. Just, Puerto Rico

http://www.utcpr.edu/

- **Independent Pentecostal** comprehensive, founded 1956
- **Suburban** 4-acre campus with easy access to San Juan
- **Endowment** $136,730
- **Coed** 209 undergraduate students, 48% full-time, 41% women, 59% men
- 100% of applicants were admitted

UNDERGRAD STUDENTS
101 full-time, 108 part-time. Students come from 1 other state; 100% Hispanic/Latino; 3% transferred in.

Freshmen
Admission: 44 applied, 44 admitted, 10 enrolled.

Retention: 52% of full-time freshmen returned.

FACULTY
Total: 35, 14% full-time, 34% with terminal degrees.
Student/faculty ratio: 6:1.

ACADEMICS
Calendar: semesters. *Degrees:* certificates, diplomas, bachelor's, master's, and doctoral.

Special study options: honors programs, independent study, internships, off-campus study, part-time degree program, services for LD students, summer session for credit.

Computers: 8 computers/terminals and 8 ports are available on campus for general student use. Students can access the following: free student e-mail accounts, online (class) grades, online (class) registration, online (class) schedules. 90% of college-owned or -operated housing units are wired for high-speed Internet access. Wireless service is available via classrooms, computer labs, dorm rooms, libraries, student centers.

STUDENT LIFE
Housing options: coed. Campus housing is university owned.

Activities and organizations: student-run newspaper, choral group, Student Council, Missionary Evangelistic Association, Ministerial Association, FESI.

Athletics ***Intercollegiate sports:*** basketball M.

Campus security: private security personnel during Special Time.

Student services: personal/psychological counseling.

COSTS & FINANCIAL AID
Costs (2015–16) ***One-time required fee:*** $13. ***Comprehensive fee:*** $6848 includes full-time tuition ($3784), mandatory fees ($664), and room and board ($2400). Full-time tuition and fees vary according to course load. Part-time tuition: $18 per credit hour. Part-time tuition and fees vary according to course load. ***Required fees:*** $130 per credit hour part-time, $3004 per term part-time. ***College room only:*** $1200. Room and board charges vary according to board plan. ***Payment plan:*** deferred payment. ***Waivers:*** employees or children of employees.

Financial Aid Of all full-time matriculated undergraduates who enrolled in 2012, 96 applied for aid, 96 were judged to have need. ***Financial aid deadline:*** 6/30.

APPLYING
Options: early admission.

Application fee: $25.

Required: Medical Certificate, Certificate of Immunization, 1 photo 2x2 and Bible Content Exam. ***Required for some:*** high school transcript.

CONTACT
Raul McClin, Recruitment Officer, Universidad Teológica del Caribe, PO Box 901, Saint Just, PR 00978-901. *Phone:* 787-761-0640 Ext. 246. *Fax:* 787-748-9220. *E-mail:* admisiones1@utcpr.edu.

University of Puerto Rico in Bayamón
Bayamón, Puerto Rico
http://www.uprb.edu/

- **Commonwealth-supported** 4-year, founded 1971, part of University of Puerto Rico System
- **Urban** 78-acre campus with easy access to San Juan
- **Coed**
- **Very difficult** entrance level

FACULTY
Student/faculty ratio: 24:1.

ACADEMICS
Calendar: semesters. *Degrees:* associate and bachelor's.

STUDENT LIFE
Activities and organizations: drama/theater group, choral group, American Marketing Association, Collegiate International Secretaries, Electronic Association, Materials Management Association, Society for Human Resources Management.

Athletics Member NCAA.

Campus security: 24-hour patrols.

Student services: health clinic, personal/psychological counseling.

COSTS & FINANCIAL AID
Costs (2014–15) ***Tuition:*** commonwealth resident $1870 full-time, $55 per credit part-time; nonresident $3910 full-time, $115 per credit part-time. Full-time tuition and fees vary according to class time, course load, program, and student level. Part-time tuition and fees vary according to class time, course load, program, and student level. No tuition increase for student's term of enrollment. ***Required fees:*** $342 full-time.

Financial Aid Of all full-time matriculated undergraduates who enrolled in 2012, 254 Federal Work-Study jobs (averaging $1587).

APPLYING
Standardized Tests *Required:* College Board (for admission).

Options: electronic application.

Application fee: $25.

Required: high school transcript.

CONTACT
Ms. Carmen I. Montes, Admissions Director, University of Puerto Rico in Bayamón, OPEI Office, Street 174 #170 Minillas Industrial Park, Bayamon, PR 00959. *Phone:* 787-993-8952 Ext. 4015. *Fax:* 787-993-8929. *E-mail:* carmen.montes@upr.edu.

University of Puerto Rico in Ponce
Ponce, Puerto Rico
http://www.uprp.edu/

- **Commonwealth-supported** 4-year, founded 1970, part of University of Puerto Rico System
- **Urban** 86-acre campus with easy access to San Juan
- **Coed** 3,229 undergraduate students, 94% full-time, 56% women, 44% men
- **Moderately difficult** entrance level, 74% of applicants were admitted

UNDERGRAD STUDENTS
3,028 full-time, 201 part-time. Students come from 1 other state; 100% Hispanic/Latino; 10% transferred in.

Freshmen
Admission: 1,222 applied, 900 admitted, 812 enrolled. ***Average high school GPA:*** 3.64.

Retention: 84% of full-time freshmen returned.

FACULTY
Total: 188, 71% full-time, 35% with terminal degrees.

Student/faculty ratio: 17:1.

ACADEMICS
Calendar: semesters. *Degrees:* associate and bachelor's.

Special study options: academic remediation for entering students, accelerated degree program, advanced placement credit, English as a second language, freshman honors college, honors programs, internships, part-time degree program, summer session for credit. ***ROTC:*** Army (b).

Computers: 81 computers/terminals and 132 ports are available on campus for general student use. Students can access the following: campus intranet, free student e-mail accounts, online (class) registration, online (class) schedules. Campuswide network is available. Wireless service is available via computer centers, computer labs, learning centers, libraries, student centers.

STUDENT LIFE
Activities and organizations: drama/theater group, choral group.

Athletics ***Intercollegiate sports:*** baseball M, basketball M(s)/W(s), cross-country running M(s)/W(s), table tennis M/W, tennis M(s), track and field M(s)/W(s), volleyball M(s)/W(s), weight lifting M(s)/W(s). ***Intramural sports:*** basketball M/W, cross-country running M/W, racquetball M/W, softball M/W, table tennis M/W, tennis M/W, track and field M/W, volleyball M/W, weight lifting M/W.

Campus security: 24-hour patrols.

Student services: health clinic.

COSTS & FINANCIAL AID
Costs (2014–15) ***Tuition:*** commonwealth resident $1870 full-time; nonresident $3892 full-time. Full-time tuition and fees vary according to student level. Part-time tuition and fees vary according to student level. No tuition increase for student's term of enrollment. ***Required fees:*** $149 full-time. ***Room and board:*** $8280. ***Waivers:*** employees or children of employees.

Financial Aid Of all full-time matriculated undergraduates who enrolled in 1998, 3,461 applied for aid, 3,133 were judged to have need. ***Average percent of need met:*** 40. ***Financial aid deadline:*** 6/30.

APPLYING
Standardized Tests *Required:* The UPR System uses the results of First-time degree seeking student on the University Evaluation and Admissions Tests (PEAU, according to its name in Spanish) offered by the College Entrance Examination Board. For admission to the UPR System, only the Verbal and Mathematical Academic Aptitude.

Options: early admission.

Application fee: $20.

Required: high school transcript.

Application deadlines: 11/15 (freshmen), 2/23 (transfers).

Notification: 3/4 (freshmen), continuous until 5/15 (transfers).

CONTACT
University of Puerto Rico in Ponce, PO Box 7186, Ponce, PR 00732-7186. *Phone:* 787-844-8181 Ext. 2533.

VIRGIN ISLANDS

University of the Virgin Islands
Saint Thomas, Virgin Islands
http://www.uvi.edu/

- **Territory-supported** comprehensive, founded 1962
- **Small-town** 518-acre campus
- **Coed** 2,110 undergraduate students, 65% full-time, 69% women, 31% men
- **Noncompetitive** entrance level, 97% of applicants were admitted

UNDERGRAD STUDENTS
1,369 full-time, 741 part-time. Students come from 28 states and territories; 16 other countries; 3% are from out of state; 71% Black or African American, non-Hispanic/Latino; 7% Hispanic/Latino; 0.5% Asian, non-Hispanic/Latino; 0.2% American Indian or Alaska Native, non-Hispanic/Latino; 0.9% Two or more races, non-Hispanic/Latino; 9% Race/ethnicity unknown; 6% international; 4% transferred in; 15% live on campus.

Freshmen
Admission: 752 applied, 730 admitted, 393 enrolled. ***Average high school GPA:*** 2.8. ***Test scores:*** SAT critical reading scores over 500: 16%; SAT math scores over 500: 10%; SAT writing scores over 500: 12%; ACT

scores over 18: 46%; SAT critical reading scores over 600: 2%; SAT math scores over 600: 1%; SAT writing scores over 600: 2%; ACT scores over 24: 7%.

Retention: 76% of full-time freshmen returned.

FACULTY

Total: 260, 42% full-time, 33% with terminal degrees.

Student/faculty ratio: 11:1.

ACADEMICS

Calendar: semesters. *Degrees:* associate, bachelor's, master's, and post-master's certificates.

Special study options: academic remediation for entering students, adult/continuing education programs, advanced placement credit, cooperative education, distance learning, double majors, external degree program, honors programs, independent study, internships, off-campus study, part-time degree program, services for LD students, study abroad, summer session for credit. ***ROTC:*** Army (b).

Unusual degree programs: 3-2 engineering with Columbia University, University of Florida, University of South Carolina.

Computers: 500 computers/terminals are available on campus for general student use. Students can access the following: campus intranet, computer help desk, free student e-mail accounts, online (class) grades, online (class) registration, online (class) schedules. Campuswide network is available. 100% of college-owned or -operated housing units are wired for high-speed Internet access. Wireless service is available via entire campus.

STUDENT LIFE

Housing options: coed, men-only, women-only. Campus housing is university owned.

Activities and organizations: drama/theater group, student-run newspaper, radio station, choral group, The Squad, Predators, Golden Key Honor Society, National Student Exchange Club, St. Kitts and Nevis, national sororities.

Athletics Member NCAA. ***Intercollegiate sports:*** basketball M(s)/W(s), cheerleading W, cross-country running M/W, soccer M, track and field M/W. ***Intramural sports:*** archery M/W, badminton M/W, basketball M/W, fencing M/W, football M/W, golf M/W, gymnastics M/W, racquetball M/W, sailing M/W, softball M/W, table tennis M/W, tennis M/W, track and field M/W, volleyball M/W.

Campus security: 24-hour emergency response devices and patrols.

Student services: health clinic, personal/psychological counseling.

COSTS & FINANCIAL AID

Costs (2015–16) ***Tuition:*** territory resident $4190 full-time, $140 per credit part-time; nonresident $12,570 full-time, $420 per credit part-time. Full-time tuition and fees vary according to reciprocity agreements. Part-time tuition and fees vary according to course load and reciprocity agreements. ***Required fees:*** $604 full-time, $254 per term part-time. ***Room and board:*** Room and board charges vary according to board plan and housing facility. ***Payment plan:*** installment. ***Waivers:*** senior citizens and employees or children of employees.

Financial Aid Of all full-time matriculated undergraduates who enrolled in 2007, 1,202 applied for aid, 1,118 were judged to have need, 10 had their need fully met. 39 Federal Work-Study jobs (averaging $2130). 28 state and other part-time jobs (averaging $1900). In 2007, 5 non-need-based awards were made. ***Average financial aid package:*** $4450. ***Average need-based loan:*** $3240. ***Average need-based gift aid:*** $3440. ***Average non-need-based aid:*** $8500. ***Average indebtedness upon graduation:*** $9480.

APPLYING

Standardized Tests *Required:* SAT or ACT (for admission). *Required for some:* SAT or ACT (for admission).

Options: electronic application, early admission, deferred entrance.

Application fee: $25.

Recommended: high school transcript, minimum 2.0 GPA.

Application deadlines: 4/30 (freshmen), 4/30 (transfers).

Notification: continuous (freshmen), 6/15 (transfers).

CONTACT

Dr. Xuri Maurice Allen, Director of Admissions/Recruitment, University of the Virgin Islands, #2 John Brewers Bay, St. Thomas, VI 00802. *Phone:* 340-693-1224. *Fax:* 340-693-1167. *E-mail:* xallen@uvi.edu.

CANADA

Acadia University

Wolfville, Nova Scotia, Canada

http://www.acadiau.ca/

- **Province-supported** comprehensive, founded 1838
- **Small-town** 250-acre campus
- **Coed**
- **Moderately difficult** entrance level

FACULTY

Student/faculty ratio: 16:1.

ACADEMICS

Calendar: Canadian standard year. *Degrees:* bachelor's, master's, and doctoral.

STUDENT LIFE

Housing options: coed, women-only. Campus housing is university owned. Freshman campus housing is guaranteed.

Activities and organizations: drama/theater group, student-run newspaper, radio station, choral group, Dance Acadia, Power Cheerleading, Water Watch Canada, LINC, Biology.

Athletics Member CIS.

Campus security: 24-hour emergency response devices and patrols, student patrols, late-night transport/escort service, controlled dormitory access, video surveillance, emergency response, emergency notification, emergency management planning.

Student services: health clinic, personal/psychological counseling, women's center, legal services.

COSTS

Costs (2014–15) ***One-time required fee:*** $397 Canadian dollars. ***Tuition:*** province resident $7020 Canadian dollars full-time, $874 Canadian dollars per course part-time; nonresident $8042 Canadian dollars full-time, $976 Canadian dollars per course part-time; International tuition $15,805 Canadian dollars full-time. Full-time tuition and fees vary according to course level, course load, degree level, and program. Part-time tuition and fees vary according to course level, course load, degree level, and program. ***Required fees:*** $259 Canadian dollars full-time, $10 Canadian dollars per course part-time. ***Room and board:*** $9350 Canadian dollars; room only: $5240 Canadian dollars. Room and board charges vary according to board plan and housing facility.

APPLYING

Options: electronic application, deferred entrance.

Application fee: $25 Canadian dollars.

Required: high school transcript, minimum 2.5 GPA. ***Required for some:*** essay or personal statement, 1 letter of recommendation, interview.

CONTACT

Ms. Anne Scott, Manager of Admissions, Acadia University, Wolfville, NS B4P 2R6, Canada. *Phone:* 902-585-1016. *Toll-free phone:* 877-585-1121. *Fax:* 902-585-1092. *E-mail:* admissions@acadiau.ca.

Alberta College of Art & Design

Calgary, Alberta, Canada

http://www.acad.ca/

- **Province-supported** 4-year, founded 1926
- **Urban** 1-acre campus with easy access to Calgary
- **Endowment** $4.4 million
- **Coed**
- **Moderately difficult** entrance level

FACULTY
Student/faculty ratio: 16:1.

ACADEMICS
Calendar: semesters. *Degree:* bachelor's.

STUDENT LIFE
Housing options: coed, special housing for students with disabilities. Campus housing is provided by a third party.

Activities and organizations: The Rendez-Vous Collective, Conceptual Arts Club, Arts Mob, Anime and Gaming Club, ACAD Glass.

Campus security: 24-hour emergency response devices and patrols, late-night transport/escort service, controlled dormitory access.

Student services: health clinic, personal/psychological counseling.

APPLYING
Options: electronic application, early decision.

Application fee: $85 Canadian dollars.

Required: essay or personal statement, high school transcript, minimum 2.0 GPA, portfolio of artwork.

CONTACT
Ms. Katie Potapoff, Admissions Officer, Alberta College of Art & Design, 1407-14 Avenue NW, Calgary, AB T2N 4R3, Canada. *Phone:* 403-284-7617. *Toll-free phone:* 800-251-8290. *Fax:* 403-284-7644. *E-mail:* admissions@acad.ca.

Ambrose University College

Calgary, Alberta, Canada

http://www.ambrose.edu/

- **Independent** comprehensive, founded 1941, affiliated with The Christian and Missionary Alliance
- **Urban** 37-acre campus
- **Endowment** $6.0 million
- **Coed** 665 undergraduate students, 90% full-time, 57% women, 43% men

UNDERGRAD STUDENTS
601 full-time, 64 part-time. Students come from 10 provinces and territories; 6 other countries; 2% Black or African American, non-Hispanic/Latino; 1% Hispanic/Latino; 9% Asian, non-Hispanic/Latino; 2% American Indian or Alaska Native, non-Hispanic/Latino; 4% Race/ethnicity unknown; 2% international; 4% transferred in; 29% live on campus.

Freshmen
Admission: 311 enrolled.
Retention: 54% of full-time freshmen returned.

FACULTY
Total: 84, 52% full-time, 44% with terminal degrees.

Student/faculty ratio: 13:1.

ACADEMICS
Calendar: semesters. *Degrees:* certificates, diplomas, bachelor's, and master's (graduate and professional degrees are offered by Canadian Theological Seminary).

Special study options: academic remediation for entering students, accelerated degree program, adult/continuing education programs, advanced placement credit, cooperative education, distance learning, double majors, English as a second language, honors programs, independent study, internships, off-campus study, part-time degree program, services for LD students, study abroad, summer session for credit.

Computers: 20 computers/terminals are available on campus for general student use. Students can access the following: campus intranet, computer help desk, free student e-mail accounts, online (class) grades, online (class) registration, online (class) schedules. Campuswide network is available. 50% of college-owned or -operated housing units are wired for high-speed Internet access. Wireless service is available via entire campus.

STUDENT LIFE
Housing options: on-campus residence required for freshman year; men-only, women-only. Campus housing is university owned. Freshman applicants given priority for college housing.

Activities and organizations: drama/theater group, student-run newspaper, choral group.

Athletics ***Intercollegiate sports:*** basketball M(s)/W(s), soccer M(s)/W(s), volleyball M(s)/W(s). ***Intramural sports:*** ice hockey M(c).

Campus security: 24-hour emergency response devices, student patrols, controlled dormitory access.

Student services: personal/psychological counseling.

COSTS
Costs (2015–16) ***Comprehensive fee:*** $17,008 Canadian dollars includes full-time tuition ($10,050 Canadian dollars), mandatory fees ($908 Canadian dollars), and room and board ($6050 Canadian dollars). Full-time tuition and fees vary according to course load, degree level, and program. Part-time tuition: $335 Canadian dollars per credit hour. Part-time tuition and fees vary according to course load, degree level, and program. ***Required fees:*** $30 Canadian dollars per credit hour part-time. ***College room only:*** $3250 Canadian dollars. Room and board charges vary according to board plan and housing facility. ***Payment plans:*** installment, deferred payment. ***Waivers:*** employees or children of employees.

APPLYING
Standardized Tests *Required for some:* SAT or ACT (for admission).

Required: high school transcript, 1 letter of recommendation. ***Required for some:*** essay or personal statement, 3 letters of recommendation, interview, 60% overall average on 5 grade 12 level courses.

CONTACT
Kalie eeles, Enrolment Coordinator, Ambrose University College, 150 Ambrose Circle SW, Calgary, AB T3H 0L5, Canada. *Phone:* 403-410-2000 Ext. 2954. *Toll-free phone:* 800-461-1222. *Fax:* 403-571-6556. *E-mail:* enrolment@ambrose.edu.

Cape Breton University

Sydney, Nova Scotia, Canada

http://www.cbu.ca/

- **Province-supported** comprehensive, founded 1974
- **Urban** campus
- **Coed** 2,689 undergraduate students, 86% full-time, 54% women, 46% men
- **Moderately difficult** entrance level, 79% of applicants were admitted

UNDERGRAD STUDENTS
2,304 full-time, 385 part-time. 24% live on campus.

Freshmen
Admission: 972 applied, 771 admitted, 504 enrolled.
Retention: 78% of full-time freshmen returned.

FACULTY
Total: 164, 95% with terminal degrees.

ACADEMICS
Calendar: semesters. *Degrees:* certificates, diplomas, bachelor's, and master's.

Special study options: advanced placement credit, cooperative education, distance learning, double majors, honors programs, services for LD students, study abroad.

Computers: Students can access the following: computer help desk, free student e-mail accounts, online (class) grades, online (class) registration, online (class) schedules. Campuswide network is available. 100% of college-owned or -operated housing units are wired for high-speed Internet access. Wireless service is available via entire campus.

STUDENT LIFE
Housing options: coed. Campus housing is university owned.

Activities and organizations: drama/theater group, student-run newspaper, radio station.

Athletics Member CIS. ***Intercollegiate sports:*** basketball M/W, ice hockey W(c), rugby M(c), soccer M/W, volleyball W. ***Intramural sports:*** badminton M(c)/W(c), baseball M(c), basketball M/W, soccer M/W.

Campus security: 24-hour emergency response devices and patrols, student patrols, late-night transport/escort service, controlled dormitory access.

Student services: health clinic, personal/psychological counseling, women's center, legal services.

COSTS & FINANCIAL AID
Costs (2014–15) ***Tuition:*** province resident $5097 full-time, $510 per course part-time; nonresident $6119 full-time, $612 per course part-time; International tuition $12,870 full-time. Full-time tuition and fees vary according to course load, degree level, and program. Part-time tuition and fees vary according to course load, degree level, and program. ***Required fees:*** $255 full-time, $20 per course part-time, $60 per year part-time. ***Room and board:*** $8485; room only: $3960. Room and board charges vary according to board plan and housing facility. ***Payment plan:*** installment. ***Waivers:*** senior citizens and employees or children of employees.

Financial Aid Of all full-time matriculated undergraduates who enrolled in 2013, 2 applied for aid, 2 were judged to have need, 2 had their need fully met. ***Average percent of need met:*** 100. ***Average financial aid package:*** $5000. ***Average need-based loan:*** $5000.

APPLYING
Options: electronic application, early admission, deferred entrance.

Application fee: $36 Canadian dollars.

Required: high school transcript. ***Required for some:*** essay or personal statement, 3 letters of recommendation, interview.

Application deadlines: 8/1 (freshmen), rolling (transfers).

Notification: continuous (freshmen), continuous (transfers).

CONTACT
Cape Breton University, Box 5300, 1250 Grand Lake Road, Sydney, NS B1P 6L2, Canada. *Phone:* 902-563-1844. *Toll-free phone:* 888-959-9995.

Centennial College
Scarborough, Ontario, Canada
http://www.centennialcollege.ca/

- **Province-supported** 4-year, part of Ontario College Application System
- **Urban** campus with easy access to Greater Toronto Area
- **Coed**

ACADEMICS
Degrees: certificates, diplomas, bachelor's, and postbachelor's certificates.

Special study options: cooperative education, distance learning, English as a second language, internships, services for LD students, study abroad, summer session for credit.

Computers: Students can access the following: campus intranet, computer help desk, free student e-mail accounts, online (class) grades, online (class) registration, online (class) schedules. Campuswide network is available. Wireless service is available via entire campus.

STUDENT LIFE
Housing options: Campus housing is university owned. Freshman applicants given priority for college housing.

Campus security: 24-hour emergency response devices and patrols.

Student services: personal/psychological counseling.

APPLYING
Options: electronic application.

Application fee: $95 Canadian dollars.

Required: high school transcript.

CONTACT
Enrolment Services, Centennial College, PO Box 631, Station 'A', Scarborough, ON M1K 5E9, Canada. *Phone:* 416-289-5325. *Toll-free phone:* 800-268-4419. *E-mail:* success@centennialcollege.ca.

Columbia Bible College
Abbotsford, British Columbia, Canada
http://www.columbiabc.edu/

- **Independent Mennonite Brethren** 4-year, founded 1936
- **Urban** 9-acre campus with easy access to Vancouver
- **Endowment** $915,262
- **Coed** 405 undergraduate students
- **Noncompetitive** entrance level, 79% of applicants were admitted

UNDERGRAD STUDENTS
Students come from 7 provinces and territories; 8 other countries; 27% are from out of state; 45% live on campus.

Freshmen
Admission: 258 applied, 204 admitted.
Retention: 66% of full-time freshmen returned.

FACULTY
Total: 41, 34% full-time, 15% with terminal degrees.

Student/faculty ratio: 21:1.

ACADEMICS
Calendar: semesters. *Degree:* certificates, diplomas, and bachelor's.

Special study options: academic remediation for entering students, advanced placement credit, distance learning, independent study, internships, off-campus study, part-time degree program, services for LD students, study abroad.

Computers: 30 computers/terminals are available on campus for general student use. Students can access the following: campus intranet, online (class) grades, online (class) schedules. Campuswide network is available. 85% of college-owned or -operated housing units are wired for high-speed Internet access. Wireless service is available via entire campus.

STUDENT LIFE
Housing options: on-campus residence required for freshman year; men-only, women-only. Campus housing is university owned. Freshman applicants given priority for college housing.

Activities and organizations: choral group.

Athletics ***Intercollegiate sports:*** basketball M/W, volleyball M/W.

Campus security: late-night transport/escort service, controlled dormitory access, night watchman 11 pm to 6 am.

Student services: personal/psychological counseling.

COSTS & FINANCIAL AID
Costs (2015–16) ***Tuition:*** $9951 Canadian dollars full-time, $321 Canadian dollars per credit part-time. Full-time tuition and fees vary according to course load. Part-time tuition and fees vary according to course load. ***Room only:*** Room and board charges vary according to board plan. ***Payment plans:*** installment, deferred payment. ***Waivers:*** senior citizens and employees or children of employees.

Financial Aid ***Financial aid deadline:*** 5/15.

APPLYING
Options: electronic application, early admission, early decision, deferred entrance.

Application fee: $50.

Required: essay or personal statement, high school transcript, minimum 2.0 GPA, 1 letter of recommendation, must be Christian.

Application deadlines: 8/15 (freshmen), 8/15 (out-of-state freshmen), 8/15 (transfers).

Early decision deadline: 3/14 (for plan 1), 5/15 (for plan 2).

Notification: continuous (freshmen), continuous (out-of-state freshmen), continuous (transfers).

CONTACT
Nathan Martin, Admissions Coordinator, Columbia Bible College, 2940 Clearbrook Road, Abbotsford, BC V2T 2Z8, Canada. *Phone:* 604-853-

3358 Ext. 309. *Toll-free phone:* 800-283-0881. *Fax:* 604-853-3063. *E-mail:* nathan.martin@columbiabc.edu.

Concordia University

Montréal, Quebec, Canada

http://www.concordia.ca/

- **Province-supported** university, founded 1974, part of Quebec University Network
- **Urban** 52-acre campus with easy access to Montreal
- **Coed** 30,674 undergraduate students, 67% full-time, 52% women, 48% men
- **Moderately difficult** entrance level, 71% of applicants were admitted

UNDERGRAD STUDENTS
20,642 full-time, 10,032 part-time. Students come from 12 provinces and territories; 150 other countries; 9% are from out of state; 2% live on campus.

Freshmen
Admission: 14,771 applied, 10,516 admitted, 5,814 enrolled.
Retention: 85% of full-time freshmen returned.

FACULTY
Total: 1,636, 58% full-time.
Student/faculty ratio: 25:1.

ACADEMICS
Calendar: semesters. *Degrees:* certificates, diplomas, bachelor's, master's, doctoral, and postbachelor's certificates.

Special study options: academic remediation for entering students, accelerated degree program, adult/continuing education programs, advanced placement credit, cooperative education, distance learning, double majors, English as a second language, honors programs, independent study, internships, off-campus study, part-time degree program, services for LD students, student-designed majors, study abroad, summer session for credit.

Computers: 350 computers/terminals and 3,000 ports are available on campus for general student use. Students can access the following: campus intranet, computer help desk, free student e-mail accounts, online (class) grades, online (class) registration, online (class) schedules, specialized software applications. Campuswide network is available. 100% of college-owned or -operated housing units are wired for high-speed Internet access. Wireless service is available via classrooms, computer centers, computer labs, learning centers, libraries, student centers.

STUDENT LIFE
Housing options: coed, special housing for students with disabilities. Campus housing is university owned. Freshman applicants given priority for college housing.

Activities and organizations: drama/theater group, student-run newspaper, radio and television station, choral group, undergraduate student union, departmental clubs, religious clubs, ethnic clubs, social action groups, national fraternities, national sororities.

Athletics Member CIS. ***Intercollegiate sports:*** baseball M, basketball M(s)/W(s), cross-country running M(c)/W(c), football M(s), golf M(c)/W(c), ice hockey M(s)/W(s), rugby M(s)/W(s), skiing (downhill) M(c)/W(c), soccer M(s)/W(s), wrestling M(s)/W(s). ***Intramural sports:*** basketball M/W, cross-country running M/W, ice hockey M/W, soccer M/W, ultimate Frisbee M/W, volleyball M/W, wrestling M/W.

Campus security: 24-hour emergency response devices and patrols, student patrols, late-night transport/escort service, controlled dormitory access.

Student services: health clinic, personal/psychological counseling, women's center.

COSTS & FINANCIAL AID
Costs (2015–16) ***Tuition:*** province resident $2273 Canadian dollars full-time, $76 Canadian dollars per credit part-time; nonresident $6632 Canadian dollars full-time, $221 Canadian dollars per credit part-time; International tuition $17,127 Canadian dollars full-time. Full-time tuition and fees vary according to course load. Part-time tuition and fees vary according to course load. ***Required fees:*** $1390 Canadian dollars full-time, $46 Canadian dollars per credit part-time. ***Room and board:*** $8382 Canadian dollars; room only: $4392 Canadian dollars. Room and board charges vary according to housing facility and location. ***Payment plan:*** installment. ***Waivers:*** senior citizens and employees or children of employees.

Financial Aid Of all full-time matriculated undergraduates who enrolled in 2013, 349 state and other part-time jobs (averaging $1286). ***Financial aid deadline:*** 3/31.

APPLYING
Options: electronic application, deferred entrance.

Application fee: $100 Canadian dollars.

Required: high school transcript, minimum 2.5 GPA. ***Required for some:*** essay or personal statement, high school transcript, minimum 3.7 GPA, 2 letters of recommendation, interview, Portfolio and/or auditions are required for Performing and Visual Arts. Communications and Journalism require interview/essay/portfolio, and certain programs in Education require a letter of intent and interview.

Application deadlines: 3/1 (freshmen), 3/1 (out-of-state freshmen), 3/1 (transfers).

Notification: continuous (freshmen), continuous (transfers).

CONTACT
Dr. Matthew Stiegemeyer, Director, Student Recruitment (Enrolment and Student Services), Concordia University, 1455 de Maisonneuve Boulevard West, Building LB-718, Montreal, QC H3G 1M8, Canada. *Phone:* 514-848-2424 Ext. 4781. *Fax:* 514-848-2837. *E-mail:* matthew.stiegemeyer@concordia.ca.

Crandall University

Moncton, New Brunswick, Canada

http://www.crandallu.ca/

- **Independent Baptist** comprehensive, founded 1949
- **Urban** 220-acre campus
- **Coed** 515 undergraduate students, 85% full-time, 59% women, 41% men
- **Minimally difficult** entrance level, 85% of applicants were admitted

UNDERGRAD STUDENTS
440 full-time, 75 part-time. Students come from 7 provinces and territories; 7 other countries; 16% are from out of state; 7% transferred in; 29% live on campus.

Freshmen
Admission: 201 applied, 171 admitted, 66 enrolled. ***Average high school GPA:*** 3.67.
Retention: 68% of full-time freshmen returned.

FACULTY
Total: 57, 51% full-time, 42% with terminal degrees.
Student/faculty ratio: 14:1.

ACADEMICS
Calendar: semesters. *Degrees:* certificates, bachelor's, master's, and postbachelor's certificates.

Special study options: accelerated degree program, adult/continuing education programs, advanced placement credit, cooperative education, double majors, English as a second language, honors programs, independent study, internships, off-campus study, part-time degree program, services for LD students, study abroad, summer session for credit.

Computers: Students can access the following: campus intranet, computer help desk, free student e-mail accounts, online (class) grades, online (class) registration, online (class) schedules. Campuswide network is available. 100% of college-owned or -operated housing units are wired for high-speed Internet access. Wireless service is available via entire campus.

STUDENT LIFE
Housing options: men-only, women-only, special housing for students with disabilities. Campus housing is university owned.

Activities and organizations: student-run newspaper, choral group, Crandall Student Association, Worship Ministry Teams, Community Service Teams, Student Newspaper, Movie Nights.

Athletics ***Intercollegiate sports:*** baseball M, basketball M/W, cross-country running M/W, soccer M/W. ***Intramural sports:*** basketball M/W, ice hockey M, soccer M/W, softball M, volleyball M/W, weight lifting M/W.

Campus security: student patrols, controlled dormitory access, trained security personnel on campus for specific times.

Student services: personal/psychological counseling.

COSTS & FINANCIAL AID
Costs (2014–15) ***Comprehensive fee:*** $15,725 Canadian dollars includes full-time tuition ($7630 Canadian dollars), mandatory fees ($815 Canadian dollars), and room and board ($7280 Canadian dollars). Full-time tuition and fees vary according to course load, degree level, and program. Part-time tuition: $765 Canadian dollars per course. Part-time tuition and fees vary according to course load, degree level, and program. ***Required fees:*** $79 Canadian dollars per course part-time. ***College room only:*** $3780 Canadian dollars. Room and board charges vary according to board plan and housing facility. ***Payment plan:*** installment. ***Waivers:*** senior citizens and employees or children of employees.

Financial Aid ***Financial aid deadline:*** 5/15.

APPLYING
Options: electronic application, early admission, early decision, deferred entrance.

Application fee: $35 Canadian dollars.

Required: high school transcript, minimum 2.7 GPA. ***Required for some:*** essay or personal statement, minimum 3.0 GPA, 3 letters of recommendation, interview.

Application deadlines: rolling (freshmen), rolling (out-of-state freshmen), rolling (transfers).

Early decision deadline: 11/30.

Notification: continuous (freshmen), continuous (out-of-state freshmen), continuous (transfers), rolling (early decision).

CONTACT
Mrs. Lorrie Weir, Admissions Administrative Assistant, Crandall University, Box 6004, Moncton, NB E1C 9L7, Canada. *Phone:* 506-858-8970 Ext. 434. *Toll-free phone:* 888-968-6228. *Fax:* 506-863-6460. *E-mail:* lorrie.weir@crandallu.ca; admissions@crandallu.ca.

Dalhousie University
Halifax, Nova Scotia, Canada
http://www.dal.ca/

- **Province-supported** university, founded 1818
- **Urban** 80-acre campus
- **Endowment** $478.0 million
- **Coed** 14,791 undergraduate students, 90% full-time, 56% women, 44% men
- **Moderately difficult** entrance level, 66% of applicants were admitted

UNDERGRAD STUDENTS
13,275 full-time, 1,516 part-time. Students come from 13 provinces and territories; 101 other countries.

Freshmen
Admission: 10,626 applied, 6,964 admitted.

FACULTY
Student/faculty ratio: 14:1.

ACADEMICS
Calendar: semesters. *Degrees:* certificates, diplomas, bachelor's, master's, doctoral, and postbachelor's certificates.

Special study options: academic remediation for entering students, accelerated degree program, advanced placement credit, cooperative education, distance learning, double majors, English as a second language, honors programs, internships, off-campus study, part-time degree program, services for LD students, study abroad, summer session for credit.

Computers: 710 computers/terminals are available on campus for general student use. Students can access the following: campus intranet, computer help desk, free student e-mail accounts, online (class) grades, online (class) registration, online (class) schedules. Campuswide network is available. 100% of college-owned or -operated housing units are wired for high-speed Internet access. Wireless service is available via entire campus.

STUDENT LIFE
Housing options: coed, women-only, special housing for students with disabilities. Campus housing is university owned. Freshman applicants given priority for college housing.

Activities and organizations: drama/theater group, student-run newspaper, radio station, choral group, International Students Association, Arts Society, Science Society, Commerce Society, Dalhousie Outdoors Club, national fraternities, national sororities.

Athletics Member CIS. ***Intercollegiate sports:*** basketball M/W, cross-country running M/W, field hockey W(c), ice hockey M/W, soccer M/W, swimming and diving M/W, track and field M/W, volleyball M/W. ***Intramural sports:*** badminton M(c)/W(c), baseball M(c), basketball M/W, crew M(c)/W(c), cross-country running M/W, fencing M(c)/W(c), field hockey W, football M/W, golf M/W, gymnastics M/W, ice hockey M, lacrosse M, racquetball M/W, rugby M(c)/W(c), sailing M(c)/W(c), skiing (cross-country) M/W, skiing (downhill) M/W, soccer M/W, softball M/W, squash M(c)/W(c), swimming and diving M(c)/W(c), tennis M/W, track and field M/W, ultimate Frisbee M/W, volleyball M/W, water polo M/W, weight lifting M/W, wrestling M(c)/W(c).

Campus security: 24-hour emergency response devices and patrols, student patrols, late-night transport/escort service, controlled dormitory access.

Student services: health clinic, personal/psychological counseling, women's center, legal services.

APPLYING
Standardized Tests *Required:* SAT or ACT (for admission).

Options: electronic application, early admission, deferred entrance.

Application fee: $65 Canadian dollars.

Required: high school transcript, minimum 3.0 GPA. ***Required for some:*** essay or personal statement, 1 letter of recommendation, interview.

Application deadlines: 6/1 (freshmen), 6/1 (transfers).

Notification: continuous (freshmen), continuous (transfers).

CONTACT
Katie Sparks, Assistant Registrar - Admissions, Dalhousie University, Office of the Registrar, Halifax, NS B3H 4H6, Canada. *Phone:* 902-494-2148. *Fax:* 902-494-1630. *E-mail:* admissions@dal.ca.

Emily Carr University of Art + Design
Vancouver, British Columbia, Canada
http://www.ecuad.ca/

- **Province-supported** comprehensive, founded 1925
- **Urban** campus
- **Coed** 1,800 undergraduate students
- **Moderately difficult** entrance level

FACULTY
Total: 220, 25% full-time.

Student/faculty ratio: 18:1.

ACADEMICS
Degrees: bachelor's and master's.

Special study options: advanced placement credit, cooperative education, part-time degree program, services for LD students, study abroad.

Computers: Students can access the following: campus intranet, computer help desk, free student e-mail accounts, online (class) grades, online (class) registration, online (class) schedules. Campuswide network is available. Wireless service is available via entire campus.

STUDENT LIFE
Housing options: college housing not available.

Activities and organizations: student-run newspaper, radio station.

Campus security: 24-hour emergency response devices and patrols.

Student services: personal/psychological counseling.

COSTS
Costs (2015–16) ***Tuition:*** province resident $3902 full-time, $129 per credit part-time; International tuition $13,925 full-time. Full-time tuition and fees vary according to course load. Part-time tuition and fees vary according to course load. ***Required fees:*** $410 full-time. ***Payment plan:*** installment. ***Waivers:*** employees or children of employees.

APPLYING

Options: electronic application.

Application fee: $70 Canadian dollars.

Required: essay or personal statement, high school transcript, minimum 2.7 GPA, portfolio and questionnaire.

Application deadlines: 1/15 (freshmen), 1/15 (transfers).

Notification: 3/1 (freshmen), 3/1 (transfers).

CONTACT

Admissions, Emily Carr University of Art + Design, 1399 Johnston Street, Vancouver, BC V6H 3R9, Canada. *Phone:* 604-844-3800. *Toll-free phone:* 800-832-7788. *Fax:* 604-844-3801. *E-mail:* admissions@ecuad.ca.

HEC Montreal

Montréal, Quebec, Canada

http://www.hec.ca/

- **Province-supported** comprehensive, founded 1910, part of Universite de Montreal
- **Urban** 9-acre campus
- **Coed** 10,069 undergraduate students, 48% full-time, 51% women, 49% men
- **Moderately difficult** entrance level, 64% of applicants were admitted

UNDERGRAD STUDENTS

4,880 full-time, 5,189 part-time. Students come from 3 provinces and territories; 45 other countries; 0.2% are from out of state.

Freshmen

Admission: 2,873 applied, 1,825 admitted, 1,004 enrolled.

Retention: 89% of full-time freshmen returned.

FACULTY

Total: 755, 37% full-time, 36% with terminal degrees.

Student/faculty ratio: 21:1.

ACADEMICS

Calendar: trimesters. *Degrees:* certificates, bachelor's, master's, doctoral, and postbachelor's certificates.

Special study options: academic remediation for entering students, adult/continuing education programs, English as a second language, honors programs, independent study, off-campus study, student-designed majors, study abroad, summer session for credit.

Computers: 211 computers/terminals and 9,000 ports are available on campus for general student use. Students can access the following: campus intranet, computer help desk, free student e-mail accounts, online (class) grades, online (class) registration, online (class) schedules, Complete Learning Management System, corporate calendar and web sites for all the resources available for classes. Campuswide network is available. 100% of college-owned or -operated housing units are wired for high-speed Internet access. Wireless service is available via entire campus.

STUDENT LIFE

Housing options: Campus housing is provided by a third party.

Activities and organizations: student-run newspaper, radio station, AEMBA (MBA Students' Association), AEHEC (BBA Students' Association), AEPC (Certificate Students' Association), AECS (Graduate Students' Association).

Campus security: 24-hour emergency response devices and patrols.

Student services: health clinic, personal/psychological counseling.

COSTS & FINANCIAL AID

Costs (2014–15) ***Tuition:*** province resident $2273 full-time, $76 per credit part-time; nonresident $6632 full-time, $221 per credit part-time; International tuition $18,140 full-time. Full-time tuition and fees vary according to program. Part-time tuition and fees vary according to program. ***Required fees:*** $1353 full-time, $41 per credit part-time, $73 per term part-time. ***Room and board:*** $3750. Room and board charges vary according to board plan and housing facility. ***Waivers:*** employees or children of employees.

Financial Aid Of all full-time matriculated undergraduates who enrolled in 2013, 2,600 applied for aid, 2,600 were judged to have need. 14 state and other part-time jobs (averaging $2400). ***Average financial aid package:*** $7700. ***Average need-based loan:*** $3100. ***Average need-based gift aid:*** $5900. ***Average indebtedness upon graduation:*** $3100.

APPLYING

Options: electronic application, deferred entrance.

Application fee: $83 Canadian dollars.

Required: high school transcript. ***Required for some:*** "R score" collegial/College performance rating.

Application deadlines: 3/1 (freshmen), 2/1 (out-of-state freshmen).

Notification: continuous (freshmen), continuous (out-of-state freshmen).

CONTACT

Mrs. Marie-Eve Porlier, Head Admissions Officer, HEC Montreal, 3000 Chemin de la Cote-Sainte-Catherine, Montreal, QC H3T 2A7, Canada. *Phone:* 514-340-6705. *Fax:* 514-340-5640. *E-mail:* admission.info@hec.ca.

Horizon College & Seminary

Saskatoon, Saskatchewan, Canada

http://www.horizon.edu/

- **Independent** 4-year, founded 1930, affiliated with Pentecostal Assemblies of Canada
- **Urban** 5-acre campus
- **Coed**
- **Noncompetitive** entrance level

FACULTY

Student/faculty ratio: 11:1.

ACADEMICS

Calendar: semesters. *Degree:* certificates, diplomas, and bachelor's.

STUDENT LIFE

Housing options: men-only, women-only. Campus housing is university owned. Freshman campus housing is guaranteed.

Campus security: 24-hour emergency response devices, late-night transport/escort service, controlled dormitory access.

Student services: personal/psychological counseling.

APPLYING

Options: electronic application, deferred entrance.

Application fee: $50 Canadian dollars.

Required: essay or personal statement, high school transcript, 3 letters of recommendation. ***Required for some:*** interview.

CONTACT

Mrs. Jenn Lundy, Assistant Registrar, Horizon College & Seminary, 1303 Jackson Avenue, Saskatoon, SK S7H 2M9, Canada. *Phone:* 306-374-6655 Ext. 225. *Toll-free phone:* 877-374-6655. *Fax:* 306-373-6968. *E-mail:* admissions@horizon.edu.

The King's University College

Edmonton, Alberta, Canada

http://www.kingsu.ca/

- **Independent interdenominational** 4-year, founded 1979
- **Suburban** 20-acre campus
- **Endowment** $2.1 million
- **Coed** 644 undergraduate students, 93% full-time, 56% women, 44% men
- **Moderately difficult** entrance level, 89% of applicants were admitted

UNDERGRAD STUDENTS

600 full-time, 44 part-time. Students come from 7 provinces and territories; 21 other countries; 14% are from out of state; 13% transferred in; 31% live on campus.

Freshmen

Admission: 308 applied, 274 admitted, 189 enrolled. ***Average high school GPA:*** 3.

Retention: 71% of full-time freshmen returned.

FACULTY

Total: 121, 40% full-time, 79% with terminal degrees.

Student/faculty ratio: 9:1.

ACADEMICS
Calendar: Canadian standard year. *Degrees:* certificates, diplomas, bachelor's, and postbachelor's certificates.

Special study options: adult/continuing education programs, advanced placement credit, double majors, English as a second language, independent study, internships, off-campus study, part-time degree program, services for LD students, study abroad, summer session for credit.

Unusual degree programs: 3-2 elementary education, secondary education.

Computers: 70 computers/terminals are available on campus for general student use. Students can access the following: campus intranet, computer help desk, free student e-mail accounts, online (class) grades, online (class) registration, online (class) schedules. Campuswide network is available. 100% of college-owned or -operated housing units are wired for high-speed Internet access. Wireless service is available via entire campus.

STUDENT LIFE
Housing options: coed, women-only. Campus housing is university owned. Freshman applicants given priority for college housing.

Activities and organizations: drama/theater group, student-run newspaper, choral group, Micah Action and Awareness, The King's Players (drama club), Chamber and Concert Choirs, King's Science Society, The King's Commerce Association.

Athletics ***Intercollegiate sports:*** badminton M(s)/W(s), basketball M(s)/W(s), soccer M(s)/W(s), volleyball M(s)/W(s). ***Intramural sports:*** basketball M/W, ice hockey M, soccer M/W, volleyball M/W.

Campus security: 24-hour emergency response devices, student patrols, controlled dormitory access.

Student services: personal/psychological counseling.

COSTS & FINANCIAL AID
Costs (2015–16) ***Comprehensive fee:*** $18,611 includes full-time tuition ($11,408), mandatory fees ($853), and room and board ($6350). Full-time tuition and fees vary according to course load. Part-time tuition: $368 per credit. Part-time tuition and fees vary according to course load. ***College room only:*** $3460. Room and board charges vary according to board plan and housing facility. ***Payment plan:*** installment. ***Waivers:*** employees or children of employees.

Financial Aid ***Financial aid deadline:*** 3/31.

APPLYING
Options: electronic application.

Application fee: $70 Canadian dollars.

Required: high school transcript, minimum 2.0 GPA, 1 letter of recommendation. ***Required for some:*** essay or personal statement, interview.

Application deadlines: rolling (freshmen), rolling (transfers).

Notification: 8/15 (freshmen), 8/15 (transfers).

CONTACT
Ms. Hilda Buisman, Director of Admissions, The King's University College, 9125-50 Street, Edmonton, AB T6B 2H3, Canada. *Phone:* 780-465-3500 Ext. 8031. *Toll-free phone:* 800-661-8582. *Fax:* 780-465-3534. *E-mail:* admissions@kingsu.ca.

Kingswood University

Sussex, New Brunswick, Canada

http://www.kingswood.edu/

- **Independent** comprehensive, founded 1945, affiliated with Wesleyan Church
- **Small-town** 57-acre campus
- **Endowment** $324,835
- **Coed** 186 undergraduate students, 92% full-time, 52% women, 48% men
- **Moderately difficult** entrance level, 40% of applicants were admitted

UNDERGRAD STUDENTS
172 full-time, 14 part-time. Students come from 21 provinces and territories; 1 other country; 62% are from out of state; 5% transferred in; 69% live on campus.

Freshmen
Admission: 175 applied, 70 admitted, 55 enrolled.
Retention: 73% of full-time freshmen returned.

FACULTY
Total: 16, 69% full-time, 38% with terminal degrees.
Student/faculty ratio: 14:1.

ACADEMICS
Calendar: semesters. *Degrees:* associate, bachelor's, and master's.

Special study options: academic remediation for entering students, advanced placement credit, double majors, internships, part-time degree program, student-designed majors, summer session for credit.

Computers: 8 computers/terminals are available on campus for general student use. Students can access the following: campus intranet, free student e-mail accounts, online (class) grades, online (class) schedules, free Wi-Fi Internet access. Campuswide network is available. 100% of college-owned or -operated housing units are wired for high-speed Internet access. Wireless service is available via entire campus.

STUDENT LIFE
Housing options: on-campus residence required through junior year; men-only, women-only. Campus housing is university owned. Freshman campus housing is guaranteed.

Activities and organizations: drama/theater group, choral group, Outreach Association, Student Fellowship Association, Spiritual Life Association, Athletic Association, Student Global Impact Association.

Athletics ***Intercollegiate sports:*** basketball M. ***Intramural sports:*** basketball M/W, ice hockey M/W, soccer M/W, swimming and diving M/W, table tennis M/W, volleyball M/W, weight lifting M/W.

Campus security: student patrols, controlled dormitory access.

Student services: personal/psychological counseling.

COSTS & FINANCIAL AID
Costs (2015–16) ***Comprehensive fee:*** $16,850 Canadian dollars includes full-time tuition ($10,100 Canadian dollars), mandatory fees ($650 Canadian dollars), and room and board ($6100 Canadian dollars). Full-time tuition and fees vary according to program. Part-time tuition: $325 Canadian dollars per contact hour. Part-time tuition and fees vary according to program. ***College room only:*** $2650 Canadian dollars. Room and board charges vary according to board plan and housing facility. ***Payment plan:*** installment. ***Waivers:*** senior citizens and employees or children of employees.

Financial Aid ***Financial aid deadline:*** 7/15.

APPLYING
Standardized Tests *Required for some:* SAT or ACT (for admission).

Options: electronic application, early admission, deferred entrance.

Application fee: $20 Canadian dollars.

Required: essay or personal statement, high school transcript, 2 letters of recommendation, 2 English credits, 2 Math Science credits, and 2 Social Studies credits. ***Recommended:*** interview.

Application deadlines: rolling (freshmen), rolling (out-of-state freshmen), rolling (transfers).

Early decision deadline: rolling (for plan 1), rolling (for plan 2).

Notification: continuous (freshmen), continuous (out-of-state freshmen), continuous (transfers), rolling (early decision plan 1), rolling (early decision plan 2).

CONTACT
Mrs. Shelley Vail, Associate Director for Admissions and Financial Aid, Kingswood University, PO Box 5125, Sussex, NB E4E 5L2, Canada. *Phone:* 506-432.4422. *Toll-free phone:* 888-432-4422. *Fax:* 506-432.4442. *E-mail:* vails@kingswood.edu.

Master's College and Seminary

Peterborough, Ontario, Canada

http://www.mcs.edu/

- **Independent Pentecostal** 4-year, founded 1939
- **Suburban** campus with easy access to Toronto
- **Endowment** $843,855
- **Coed** 288 undergraduate students
- **Noncompetitive** entrance level, 88% of applicants were admitted

UNDERGRAD STUDENTS
Students come from 6 provinces and territories; 1 other country; 17% are from out of state; 65% live on campus.

Freshmen
Admission: 101 applied, 89 admitted.

Retention: 87% of full-time freshmen returned.

FACULTY
Total: 26, 19% full-time, 31% with terminal degrees.

Student/faculty ratio: 18:1.

ACADEMICS
Calendar: semesters. *Degree:* certificates, diplomas, and bachelor's.

Special study options: academic remediation for entering students, distance learning, independent study, internships, off-campus study, part-time degree program, services for LD students, summer session for credit.

Computers: 6 computers/terminals are available on campus for general student use. Students can access the following: computer help desk, free student e-mail accounts, online (class) registration, online (class) schedules. Campuswide network is available. Wireless service is available via entire campus.

STUDENT LIFE
Housing options: on-campus residence required for freshman year; men-only, women-only. Campus housing is leased by the school. Freshman campus housing is guaranteed.

Campus security: 24-hour emergency response devices, student patrols, controlled dormitory access.

COSTS
Costs (2015–16) ***One-time required fee:*** $280 Canadian dollars. ***Comprehensive fee:*** $14,862 Canadian dollars includes full-time tuition ($7480 Canadian dollars), mandatory fees ($782 Canadian dollars), and room and board ($6600 Canadian dollars). Full-time tuition and fees vary according to course load, location, and program. Part-time tuition: $197 Canadian dollars per credit hour. Part-time tuition and fees vary according to course load, location, and program. ***Required fees:*** $23 Canadian dollars per credit hour part-time. ***Payment plan:*** deferred payment. ***Waivers:*** adult students, senior citizens, and employees or children of employees.

APPLYING
Options: deferred entrance.

Application fee: $75 Canadian dollars.

Required: essay or personal statement, high school transcript, 3 letters of recommendation, Christian commitment. ***Required for some:*** interview. ***Recommended:*** minimum 2.0 GPA.

Application deadlines: 8/31 (freshmen), 8/31 (transfers).

CONTACT
Ms. Flora Anthony, Admissions, Master's College and Seminary, 780 Argyle Street, Peterborough, ON K9H 5T2, Canada. *Phone:* 800-295-6368. *Toll-free phone:* 800-295-6368. *Fax:* 705-749-0417. *E-mail:* flora.anthony@mcs.edu.

Mount Allison University

Sackville, New Brunswick, Canada

http://www.mta.ca/

- **Province-supported** comprehensive, founded 1839
- **Small-town** 50-acre campus
- **Endowment** $65.0 million
- **Coed** 2,517 undergraduate students, 96% full-time, 58% women, 42% men
- **Moderately difficult** entrance level, 90% of applicants were admitted

UNDERGRAD STUDENTS
2,411 full-time, 106 part-time. Students come from 22 provinces and territories; 44 other countries; 58% are from out of state; 4% transferred in; 50% live on campus.

Freshmen
Admission: 1,628 applied, 1,464 admitted, 701 enrolled. ***Average high school GPA:*** 3.31.

Retention: 80% of full-time freshmen returned.

FACULTY
Total: 187, 71% full-time, 88% with terminal degrees.

Student/faculty ratio: 16:1.

ACADEMICS
Calendar: Canadian standard year. *Degrees:* certificates, bachelor's, and master's.

Special study options: academic remediation for entering students, adult/continuing education programs, advanced placement credit, distance learning, double majors, honors programs, independent study, internships, off-campus study, part-time degree program, services for LD students, student-designed majors, study abroad, summer session for credit.

Computers: 100 computers/terminals and 240 ports are available on campus for general student use. Students can access the following: computer help desk, free student e-mail accounts, online (class) grades, online (class) registration, online (class) schedules, online student account/Websis. Campuswide network is available. 100% of college-owned or -operated housing units are wired for high-speed Internet access. Wireless service is available via entire campus.

STUDENT LIFE
Housing options: coed, women-only, cooperative. Campus housing is university owned. Freshman campus housing is guaranteed.

Activities and organizations: drama/theater group, student-run newspaper, radio station, choral group, Commerce Society, Windsor Theatre, President's Leadership Development Certificate, Leadership Mount Allison, Garnet and Gold Society.

Athletics Member CIS. ***Intercollegiate sports:*** basketball M/W, football M, ice hockey W, rugby M/W, soccer M/W, swimming and diving M/W. ***Intramural sports:*** archery M(c)/W(c), badminton M/W, baseball M/W, basketball M/W, football M/W, golf M/W, ice hockey M/W, rugby M/W, skiing (cross-country) M/W, skiing (downhill) M/W, soccer M/W, softball M/W, tennis M/W, ultimate Frisbee M/W, volleyball M/W, weight lifting M/W.

Campus security: 24-hour emergency response devices, late-night transport/escort service.

Student services: health clinic, personal/psychological counseling.

APPLYING
Options: electronic application, deferred entrance.

Application fee: $50 Canadian dollars.

Required: high school transcript, minimum 2.5 GPA. ***Required for some:*** essay or personal statement, interview. ***Recommended:*** 2 letters of recommendation.

Application deadlines: rolling (freshmen), rolling (transfers).

Notification: continuous (freshmen), continuous (transfers).

CONTACT
Mr. Joceylyn Ollerhead, Manager of Admissions, Mount Allison University, 65 York Street, Sackville, NB E4L 1E4, Canada. *Phone:* 506-364-3294. *Fax:* 506-364-2272. *E-mail:* admissions@mta.ca.

Okanagan College

Kelowna, British Columbia, Canada

http://www.okanagan.bc.ca/

- **Province-supported** 4-year, founded 2005, part of Ministry of Advanced Education, Industry Training Authority
- **Urban** 13-acre campus
- **Coed**

FACULTY
Student/faculty ratio: 12:1.

ACADEMICS
Degrees: certificates, diplomas, associate, and bachelor's.

STUDENT LIFE
Housing options: coed. Campus housing is university owned.

Activities and organizations: student-run newspaper, choral group.

Campus security: 24-hour emergency response devices and patrols, late-night transport/escort service, controlled dormitory access.

Student services: personal/psychological counseling.

COSTS
Costs (2014–15) ***Tuition:*** province resident $3267 Canadian dollars full-time, $105 Canadian dollars per credit part-time; nonresident $3267 Canadian dollars full-time, $105 Canadian dollars per credit part-time; International tuition $11,000 Canadian dollars full-time. Full-time tuition and fees vary according to course level, course load, location, and program. Part-time tuition and fees vary according to course level, course load, location, and program. ***Required fees:*** $732 Canadian dollars full-time, $41 Canadian dollars per course part-time, $126 Canadian dollars per term part-time. ***Room only:*** $3800 Canadian dollars. Room and board charges vary according to housing facility.

APPLYING
Required for some: essay or personal statement, high school transcript, minimum 2.0 GPA, interview.

CONTACT
Mr. Allan Hickey, Associate Registrar Systems, Okanagan College, 1000 K.L.O. Rd., Kelowna, BC V1Y 4X8, Canada. *Phone:* 250-762-5445 Ext. 4332. *Toll-free phone:* 877-755-2266. *E-mail:* ahickey@okanagan.bc.ca.

Queen's University at Kingston

Kingston, Ontario, Canada

http://www.queensu.ca/

- **Province-supported** university, founded 1841
- **Urban** 160-acre campus
- **Endowment** $710.3 million
- **Coed**
- **Most difficult** entrance level

FACULTY
Student/faculty ratio: 15:1.

ACADEMICS
Calendar: Canadian standard year. *Degrees:* certificates, bachelor's, master's, and doctoral.

STUDENT LIFE
Housing options: coed, men-only, women-only, cooperative, special housing for students with disabilities. Campus housing is university owned. Freshman campus housing is guaranteed.

Activities and organizations: drama/theater group, student-run newspaper, radio station, choral group, marching band, Arts and Sciences Undergraduate Society, Alma Mater Society, Engineering Society, Commerce Society, dance club.

Athletics Member CIS.

Campus security: 24-hour emergency response devices and patrols, student patrols, late-night transport/escort service, controlled dormitory access.

Student services: health clinic, personal/psychological counseling, women's center, legal services.

FINANCIAL AID
Financial Aid Of all full-time matriculated undergraduates who enrolled in 2012, 431 state and other part-time jobs (averaging $1200). ***Average financial aid package:*** $8796.

APPLYING
Standardized Tests *Required:* SAT or ACT (for admission).

Options: deferred entrance.

Application fee: $230 Canadian dollars.

Required: essay or personal statement, high school transcript, minimum 2.7 GPA. ***Required for some:*** 1 letter of recommendation.

CONTACT
Ms. Iveta Reinikovaite, Admission Coordinator, Queen's University at Kingston, Undergraduate Admissions, Gordon Hall, 74 Union Street, Kingston, ON K7L 3N6, Canada. *Phone:* 613-533-2218. *Fax:* 613-533-6810. *E-mail:* admission@queensu.ca.

Redeemer University College

Ancaster, Ontario, Canada

http://www.redeemer.ca/

- **Independent interdenominational** 4-year, founded 1980
- **Small-town** 86-acre campus with easy access to Toronto
- **Endowment** $4.0 million
- **Coed**
- **Moderately difficult** entrance level

FACULTY
Student/faculty ratio: 12:1.

ACADEMICS
Calendar: semesters. *Degree:* certificates and bachelor's.

STUDENT LIFE
Housing options: on-campus residence required through sophomore year; men-only, women-only. Campus housing is university owned. Freshman campus housing is guaranteed.

Activities and organizations: drama/theater group, student-run newspaper, choral group, Church in the Box, Service Learning Trips, Deedz, Athletics and Recreation, Concert Choir.

Campus security: 24-hour emergency response devices, student patrols, late-night transport/escort service, controlled dormitory access, path lighting.

Student services: personal/psychological counseling.

COSTS & FINANCIAL AID
Costs (2014–15) ***Comprehensive fee:*** $22,505 Canadian dollars includes full-time tuition ($15,162 Canadian dollars), mandatory fees ($535 Canadian dollars), and room and board ($6808 Canadian dollars). Full-time tuition and fees vary according to course load. Part-time tuition: $1518 Canadian dollars per course. Part-time tuition and fees vary according to course load. ***Required fees:*** $38 Canadian dollars per course part-time. ***College room only:*** $4660 Canadian dollars. Room and board charges vary according to board plan and housing facility.

Financial Aid Of all full-time matriculated undergraduates who enrolled in 2010, 640 applied for aid, 607 were judged to have need, 200 had their need fully met. 385 state and other part-time jobs (averaging $1238). In 2010, 99 non-need-based awards were made. ***Average percent of need met:*** 82. ***Average financial aid package:*** $12,582. ***Average need-based loan:*** $7464. ***Average need-based gift aid:*** $4587. ***Average non-need-based aid:*** $3061. ***Average indebtedness upon graduation:*** $23,598. ***Financial aid deadline:*** 3/31.

APPLYING
Standardized Tests *Required for some:* SAT or ACT (for admission).

Options: electronic application, deferred entrance.

Application fee: $40 Canadian dollars.

Required: essay or personal statement, high school transcript, minimum 2.0 GPA, 1 letter of recommendation, personal reference. ***Required for some:*** interview.

CONTACT
Recruitment, Redeemer University College, 777 Garner Road East, Ancaster, ON L9K 1J4, Canada. *Phone:* 905-648-2131 Ext. 4280. *Toll-free phone:* 800-263-6467. *Fax:* 905-648-9545. *E-mail:* recruitment@redeemer.ca.

Rocky Mountain College

Calgary, Alberta, Canada

http://www.rockymountaincollege.ca/

- **Independent** 4-year, founded 1992, affiliated with Missionary Church
- **Urban** 1-acre campus with easy access to Calgary
- **Endowment** $343,200
- **Coed**
- **Noncompetitive** entrance level

ACADEMICS
Calendar: semesters. *Degree:* certificates, diplomas, and bachelor's.

Special study options: academic remediation for entering students, adult/continuing education programs, advanced placement credit, distance learning, double majors, independent study, internships, off-campus study, part-time degree program, student-designed majors, study abroad, summer session for credit.

Computers: 12 computers/terminals are available on campus for general student use. Students can access the following: campus intranet, computer help desk, free student e-mail accounts, online (class) grades, online (class) registration, online (class) schedules. Campuswide network is available. 100% of college-owned or -operated housing units are wired for high-speed Internet access. Wireless service is available via entire campus.

STUDENT LIFE
Housing options: college housing not available.

Activities and organizations: drama/theater group.

Campus security: 24-hour emergency response devices.

Student services: personal/psychological counseling.

COSTS
Costs (2014–15) ***Tuition:*** $325 per credit hour part-time.

APPLYING
Options: electronic application, early decision, deferred entrance.

Application fee: $50 Canadian dollars.

Required: essay or personal statement, high school transcript, 2 letters of recommendation. ***Required for some:*** interview.

Application deadlines: rolling (freshmen), rolling (transfers).

CONTACT
Rocky Mountain College, 4039 Brentwood Road, NW, Calgary, AB T2L 1L1, Canada. *Phone:* 403-284-5100 Ext. 222. *Toll-free phone:* 877-YOUnRMC.

Royal Roads University

Victoria, British Columbia, Canada

http://www.royalroads.ca/

- **Province-supported** upper-level, founded 1996
- **Suburban** 565-acre campus
- **Coed**
- **Moderately difficult** entrance level

ACADEMICS
Calendar: continuous. *Degrees:* certificates, diplomas, bachelor's, master's, and doctoral.

STUDENT LIFE
Housing options: college housing not available.

Campus security: 24-hour emergency response devices and patrols, late-night transport/escort service.

APPLYING
Options: electronic application.

Application fee: $110 Canadian dollars.

CONTACT
Royal Roads University, 2005 Sooke Road, Victoria, BC V9B 5Y2, Canada. *Phone:* 250-391-2511. *Toll-free phone:* 800-788-8028.

St. Thomas University

Fredericton, New Brunswick, Canada

http://www.stu.ca/

- **Independent Roman Catholic** 4-year, founded 1910
- **Small-town** 16-acre campus
- **Endowment** $26.4 million
- **Coed** 2,036 undergraduate students, 91% full-time, 69% women, 31% men
- **Moderately difficult** entrance level, 90% of applicants were admitted

UNDERGRAD STUDENTS
1,854 full-time, 182 part-time. Students come from 10 provinces and territories; 46 other countries; 21% are from out of state; 94% Race/ethnicity unknown; 6% international; 5% transferred in; 27% live on campus.

Freshmen
Admission: 966 applied, 872 admitted, 511 enrolled. ***Average high school GPA:*** 3.4.

Retention: 69% of full-time freshmen returned.

FACULTY
Total: 200, 54% full-time, 68% with terminal degrees.

Student/faculty ratio: 16:1.

ACADEMICS
Calendar: semesters. *Degrees:* certificates, bachelor's, and postbachelor's certificates.

Special study options: academic remediation for entering students, accelerated degree program, advanced placement credit, double majors, English as a second language, honors programs, independent study, internships, off-campus study, part-time degree program, services for LD students, student-designed majors, study abroad, summer session for credit.

Computers: 59 computers/terminals are available on campus for general student use. Students can access the following: computer help desk, free student e-mail accounts, online (class) grades, online (class) registration, online (class) schedules, Moodle. Campuswide network is available. 100% of college-owned or -operated housing units are wired for high-speed Internet access. Wireless service is available via entire campus.

STUDENT LIFE
Housing options: coed, women-only, special housing for students with disabilities. Campus housing is university owned. Freshman campus housing is guaranteed.

Activities and organizations: drama/theater group, student-run newspaper, radio station, choral group, Theatre St. Thomas, St. Thomas Student Union, Criminology Society, Model UN, International Students' Association.

Athletics Member CIS. ***Intercollegiate sports:*** basketball M/W, cross-country running M/W, golf M/W, ice hockey M(s)/W(s), soccer M/W, volleyball M/W. ***Intramural sports:*** badminton M/W, basketball M/W, cross-country running M/W, fencing M/W, football M, ice hockey M/W, rock climbing M/W, soccer M/W, softball M/W, squash M/W, swimming and diving M/W, table tennis M/W, track and field M/W, ultimate Frisbee M/W, volleyball M/W, water polo M/W.

Campus security: 24-hour emergency response devices and patrols, student patrols, late-night transport/escort service, controlled dormitory access.

Student services: health clinic, personal/psychological counseling, women's center.

COSTS & FINANCIAL AID
Costs (2014–15) ***Comprehensive fee:*** $13,855 includes full-time tuition ($5552), mandatory fees ($398), and room and board ($7905). Full-time tuition and fees vary according to course load, degree level, and program. Part-time tuition: $600 per course. Part-time tuition and fees vary according to course load. International tuition: $13,192 full-time. ***Required fees:*** $31 per course part-time. ***Room and board:*** Room and board charges vary according to board plan, housing facility, and location. ***Payment plans:*** installment, deferred payment. ***Waivers:*** senior citizens and employees or children of employees.

Financial Aid ***Financial aid deadline:*** 3/1.

APPLYING
Standardized Tests *Recommended:* SAT (for admission).

Options: electronic application, early action.

Application fee: $40 Canadian dollars.

Required: essay or personal statement, high school transcript, minimum 3.0 GPA. ***Required for some:*** interview.

Application deadlines: 8/31 (freshmen), 8/31 (transfers), 12/7 (early action).

Notification: continuous (freshmen), continuous (transfers).

CONTACT
Ms. Kathryn Monti, Director of Admissions, St. Thomas University, Duffie Hall, St. Thomas University, Fredericton, NB E3B 5G3, Canada. *Phone:* 506-452-0532. *Fax:* 506-452-0617. *E-mail:* admissions@stu.ca.

Simon Fraser University

Burnaby, British Columbia, Canada

http://www.sfu.ca/

- **Province-supported** university, founded 1965
- **Suburban** campus with easy access to Vancouver
- **Coed** 25,215 undergraduate students, 53% full-time, 54% women, 46% men
- **Moderately difficult** entrance level, 60% of applicants were admitted

UNDERGRAD STUDENTS
13,317 full-time, 11,898 part-time. Students come from 84 other countries; 8% are from out of state; 5% transferred in; 9% live on campus.

Freshmen
Admission: 14,708 applied, 8,848 admitted, 3,319 enrolled. ***Average high school GPA:*** 3.35.
Retention: 87% of full-time freshmen returned.

FACULTY
Total: 964, 99% full-time, 89% with terminal degrees.
Student/faculty ratio: 22:1.

ACADEMICS
Calendar: trimesters. *Degrees:* certificates, diplomas, bachelor's, master's, doctoral, post-master's, and postbachelor's certificates.
Special study options: academic remediation for entering students, adult/continuing education programs, advanced placement credit, cooperative education, distance learning, double majors, English as a second language, honors programs, independent study, internships, off-campus study, part-time degree program, services for LD students, study abroad, summer session for credit.
Computers: Students can access the following: free student e-mail accounts, online (class) grades, online (class) registration, online (class) schedules. Campuswide network is available. 100% of college-owned or -operated housing units are wired for high-speed Internet access. Wireless service is available via entire campus.

STUDENT LIFE
Housing options: coed, women-only, special housing for students with disabilities. Campus housing is university owned. Freshman applicants given priority for college housing.
Activities and organizations: drama/theater group, student-run newspaper, radio station, The Peak Newspaper, orientation leaders, Crisis line, Women's Centre, Simon Fraser Public Interest Research Group.
Athletics Member NCAA. All Division II. ***Intercollegiate sports:*** basketball M(s)/W(s), cross-country running M(s)/W(s), football M(s), golf M(s)/W, gymnastics M, soccer M(s)/W(s), softball W(s), swimming and diving M(s)/W(s), track and field M(s)/W(s), volleyball W(s), wrestling M(s)/W(s). ***Intramural sports:*** archery M(c)/W(c), badminton M(c)/W(c), basketball M/W, cheerleading M(c)/W(c), crew M(c)/W(c), fencing M(c)/W(c), field hockey W(c), football M/W, golf W(c), gymnastics W(c), ice hockey M(c)/W(c), lacrosse M(c), rugby M(c)/W(c), soccer M/W, softball M/W, squash M(c)/W(c), table tennis M(c)/W(c), tennis M/W, ultimate Frisbee M(c)/W(c), volleyball M(c)/W(c), water polo M(c)/W(c).
Campus security: 24-hour emergency response devices and patrols, student patrols, late-night transport/escort service, controlled dormitory access, safe-walk stations, 24-hour safe study area.
Student services: health clinic, personal/psychological counseling, women's center.

COSTS & FINANCIAL AID
Costs (2014–15) ***Tuition:*** province resident $5217 full-time, $174 per credit hour part-time; nonresident $5217 full-time, $174 per credit hour part-time; International tuition $19,648 full-time. Full-time tuition and fees vary according to course level and program. Part-time tuition and fees vary according to course level and program. ***Required fees:*** $705 full-time, $174 per credit hour part-time, $174 per credit hour part-time. ***Room and board:*** $9036; room only: $5536. Room and board charges vary according to housing facility. ***Waivers:*** employees or children of employees.
Financial Aid ***Financial aid deadline:*** 11/15.

APPLYING
Standardized Tests *Required for some:* SAT or ACT (for admission).
Options: electronic application, early admission, early action, deferred entrance.
Application fee: $75 Canadian dollars.
Required: high school transcript, minimum 3.0 GPA. ***Required for some:*** essay or personal statement, interview.
Application deadlines: 2/28 (freshmen), rolling (transfers).
Notification: continuous until 6/30 (freshmen), continuous (transfers).

CONTACT
Ms. Louise Legris, Director of Admissions, Simon Fraser University, 8888 University Drive, Burnaby, BC V5A 1S6, Canada. *Phone:* 778-782-3498. *Fax:* 778-782-4969. *E-mail:* undergraduate-admissions@sfu.ca.

Trent University

Peterborough, Ontario, Canada

http://www.trentu.ca/

- **Province-supported** university, founded 1963
- **Suburban** 1400-acre campus with easy access to Toronto
- **Coed** 7,376 undergraduate students, 85% full-time, 66% women, 34% men
- **Moderately difficult** entrance level, 18% of applicants were admitted

UNDERGRAD STUDENTS
6,298 full-time, 1,078 part-time. Students come from 13 provinces and territories; 81 other countries; 2% are from out of state; 7% transferred in; 17% live on campus.

Freshmen
Admission: 9,300 applied, 1,700 admitted, 1,412 enrolled.
Retention: 83% of full-time freshmen returned.

FACULTY
Total: 500, 60% full-time.
Student/faculty ratio: 18:1.

ACADEMICS
Calendar: Canadian standard year. *Degrees:* diplomas, bachelor's, master's, and doctoral.
Special study options: academic remediation for entering students, accelerated degree program, advanced placement credit, cooperative education, distance learning, double majors, English as a second language, honors programs, independent study, internships, off-campus study, part-time degree program, services for LD students, student-designed majors, study abroad, summer session for credit.
Computers: Students can access the following: campus intranet, computer help desk, free student e-mail accounts, online (class) grades, online (class) registration, online (class) schedules, online tuition payment. Campuswide network is available. 100% of college-owned or -operated housing units are wired for high-speed Internet access. Wireless service is available via entire campus.

STUDENT LIFE
Housing options: coed, women-only. Campus housing is university owned. Freshman applicants given priority for college housing.
Activities and organizations: drama/theater group, student-run newspaper, radio station, choral group, Trent Radio, Trent International Program, Trent Central Student Association, Arthur (student newspaper), Excalibur (yearbook).
Athletics Member CIS. ***Intercollegiate sports:*** crew M/W, cross-country running M/W, golf M, lacrosse M/W, rugby M/W, soccer M/W, track and field M/W, volleyball M/W. ***Intramural sports:*** badminton M/W, baseball M/W, basketball M/W, cross-country running M/W, football M/W, ice hockey M/W, soccer M/W, softball M/W, squash M/W, swimming and diving M/W, tennis M/W, track and field M/W, ultimate Frisbee M/W, volleyball M/W, water polo M/W.

Campus security: 24-hour emergency response devices and patrols, student patrols, late-night transport/escort service, controlled dormitory access.

Student services: health clinic, personal/psychological counseling, women's center.

COSTS

Costs (2014–15) ***Tuition:*** province resident $6040 full-time, $1208 per course part-time; nonresident $3559 per course part-time; International tuition $17,773 full-time. Full-time tuition and fees vary according to course load, location, program, and student level. Part-time tuition and fees vary according to course load, location, program, and student level. ***Required fees:*** $1434 full-time, $110 per credit part-time. ***Room and board:*** $9236. Room and board charges vary according to board plan, housing facility, and location. ***Payment plans:*** installment, deferred payment. ***Waivers:*** employees or children of employees.

APPLYING

Options: electronic application, deferred entrance.

Application fee: $135 Canadian dollars.

Required: high school transcript, minimum 2.8 GPA. ***Required for some:*** essay or personal statement, interview.

Application deadlines: 6/1 (freshmen), 6/1 (transfers).

Notification: continuous (freshmen), continuous (transfers).

CONTACT

Mr. Kevin Whitmore, Manager, Admissions, Trent University, 1600 West Bank Drive, Peterborough, ON K9J 7B8, Canada. *Phone:* 705-748-1011 Ext. 7748. *Fax:* 705-748-1629. *E-mail:* admissions@trentu.ca.

Université de Montréal

Montréal, Quebec, Canada

http://www.umontreal.ca/

- **Independent** university, founded 1920
- **Urban** 150-acre campus
- **Endowment** $837.0 million
- **Coed** 34,143 undergraduate students, 74% full-time, 68% women, 32% men
- **Moderately difficult** entrance level

UNDERGRAD STUDENTS

25,239 full-time, 8,904 part-time. Students come from 12 provinces and territories; 128 other countries.

ACADEMICS

Calendar: trimesters. *Degrees:* certificates, bachelor's, master's, and doctoral.

Special study options: accelerated degree program, adult/continuing education programs, cooperative education, distance learning, English as a second language, honors programs, independent study, internships, off-campus study, part-time degree program, services for LD students, summer session for credit.

Computers: 1,500 computers/terminals are available on campus for general student use. Students can access the following: online (class) registration. Campuswide network is available.

STUDENT LIFE

Housing options: coed, men-only, women-only, special housing for students with disabilities. Campus housing is university owned.

Activities and organizations: drama/theater group, student-run newspaper, radio station, choral group, Federation des Associations Etudiantes du Campus.

Athletics Member CIS. ***Intercollegiate sports:*** badminton M/W, skiing (downhill) M/W, soccer M/W, swimming and diving M/W, volleyball M/W. ***Intramural sports:*** archery M/W, badminton M/W, basketball M/W, fencing M/W, golf M/W, gymnastics M/W, ice hockey M/W, racquetball M/W, soccer M/W, squash M/W, swimming and diving M/W, table tennis M/W, tennis M/W, volleyball M/W, water polo M/W.

Campus security: 24-hour emergency response devices and patrols, student patrols, late-night transport/escort service, controlled dormitory access, cameras, alarm systems, crime prevention programs.

Student services: health clinic, personal/psychological counseling, legal services.

FINANCIAL AID

Financial Aid Of all full-time matriculated undergraduates who enrolled in 2006, 400 state and other part-time jobs.

APPLYING

Options: electronic application.

Application fee: $50 Canadian dollars.

Required: Diploma of Collegiate Studies (and transcript) or equivalent. ***Required for some:*** interview.

Application deadlines: 3/1 (freshmen), 3/1 (transfers).

Notification: 5/15 (freshmen), 5/15 (transfers).

CONTACT

Mme. Marie-Claude Binette, Registrar, Université de Montréal, Bureau du registraire, CP 6128, Succursale Centre-Ville, Montreal, QC H3C 3J7, Canada. *Phone:* 514-343-2214. *Fax:* 514-343-2097. *E-mail:* marie-claude.binette@umontreal.ca.

Université de Sherbrooke

Sherbrooke, Quebec, Canada

http://www.usherbrooke.ca/

- **Independent** university, founded 1954
- **Urban** 800-acre campus with easy access to Montreal
- **Coed** 14,288 undergraduate students, 78% full-time, 56% women, 44% men
- **Moderately difficult** entrance level, 55% of applicants were admitted

UNDERGRAD STUDENTS

11,158 full-time, 3,130 part-time. Students come from 12 provinces and territories; 59 other countries; 1% are from out of state.

Freshmen

Admission: 17,772 applied, 9,697 admitted, 3,210 enrolled.

FACULTY

Total: 3,021, 40% full-time.

ACADEMICS

Calendar: Canadian standard year. *Degrees:* certificates, diplomas, bachelor's, master's, and doctoral.

Special study options: accelerated degree program, adult/continuing education programs, cooperative education, English as a second language, internships, off-campus study, part-time degree program, services for LD students, student-designed majors, study abroad, summer session for credit.

Computers: 300 computers/terminals are available on campus for general student use. Students can access the following: computer help desk, free student e-mail accounts, online (class) registration, online (class) schedules. Campuswide network is available. Wireless service is available via classrooms, computer centers, computer labs, learning centers, libraries.

STUDENT LIFE

Housing options: coed. Campus housing is university owned.

Activities and organizations: drama/theater group, student-run newspaper, radio station.

Athletics Member CIS. ***Intercollegiate sports:*** badminton M/W, cheerleading M/W, golf M/W, rugby M/W. ***Intramural sports:*** badminton M/W, basketball M/W, field hockey M/W, ice hockey M, racquetball M/W, soccer M/W, squash M/W, track and field M/W, ultimate Frisbee M/W, volleyball M/W, water polo M/W.

Campus security: 24-hour emergency response devices and patrols.

Student services: health clinic, personal/psychological counseling, legal services.

COSTS & FINANCIAL AID

Costs (2015–16) ***Tuition:*** province resident $2273 full-time, $76 per credit part-time; nonresident $6632 full-time, $221 per credit part-time; International tuition $17,127 full-time. Full-time tuition and fees vary according to course load and location. Part-time tuition and fees vary according to course load and location. ***Required fees:*** $587 full-time, $13 part-time, $86 part-time. ***Room only:*** $3360. Room and board charges vary according to location. ***Waivers:*** employees or children of employees.

Financial Aid ***Financial aid deadline:*** 3/31.

APPLYING

Options: electronic application, early admission.

Application fee: $70 Canadian dollars.

Required: high school transcript. ***Required for some:*** interview.

Notification: continuous until 5/15 (freshmen).

CONTACT

Ms. Lisa Bedard, Admissions Officer, Université de Sherbrooke, 2500 boulevard de l'Universite, Sherbrooke, QC J1K 2R1, Canada. *Phone:* 819-821-7687. *Toll-free phone:* 800-267-UDES.

Université du Québec en Outaouais

Gatineau, Quebec, Canada

http://www.uqo.ca/

- **Province-supported** university, founded 1981, part of Université du Québec
- **Small-town** campus with easy access to Ottawa
- **Coed** 5,976 undergraduate students
- **Noncompetitive** entrance level

UNDERGRAD STUDENTS

Students come from 34 other countries.

ACADEMICS

Calendar: trimesters. *Degrees:* certificates, bachelor's, master's, doctoral, post-master's, and postbachelor's certificates.

Special study options: accelerated degree program, adult/continuing education programs, cooperative education, independent study, internships, off-campus study, part-time degree program, services for LD students, study abroad, summer session for credit.

Computers: 500 computers/terminals are available on campus for general student use. Students can access the following: computer help desk, free student e-mail accounts, online (class) registration, online (class) schedules, pay tuition fees online. Campuswide network is available. Wireless service is available via entire campus.

STUDENT LIFE

Housing options: coed. Campus housing is university owned.

Activities and organizations: student-run newspaper, radio station, AGE (Association Generale des Etudiants), AIESEC (Association Internationale des Etudiants en Sciences Economiques et Commerciales, AEME (Association for Events Management Education), REMAA (Regroupement des Etudiants du Monde de l'Administration des Affaires.

Athletics ***Intercollegiate sports:*** cheerleading M/W, golf M/W, soccer M/W, swimming and diving M/W, volleyball W. ***Intramural sports:*** badminton M/W, basketball M/W, ice hockey M, rock climbing M/W, soccer M/W, swimming and diving M/W, table tennis M/W, volleyball M/W, water polo M/W, weight lifting M/W.

Campus security: 24-hour emergency response devices and patrols.

Student services: personal/psychological counseling.

COSTS

Costs (2014–15) ***Tuition:*** $431 per course part-time; province resident $867 per course part-time; nonresident $1712 per course part-time. Full-time tuition and fees vary according to class time, course load, degree level, program, and reciprocity agreements. Part-time tuition and fees vary according to class time, course load, degree level, and program. ***Room and board:*** Room and board charges vary according to housing facility. ***Payment plan:*** installment.

APPLYING

Options: electronic application.

Application fee: $60 Canadian dollars.

Required: high school transcript, birth certificate. ***Required for some:*** essay or personal statement, 3 letters of recommendation, interview.

CONTACT

Registrar Office, Université du Québec en Outaouais, CP 1250, Succursale Hull, 101 Saint-Jean-Bosco, 101 rue Saint-Jean-Bosco, Gatineau, QC J8X 3X7, Canada. *Phone:* 819-595-3900 Ext. 1850. *Toll-free phone:* 800-567-1283. *Fax:* 819-773-1835. *E-mail:* registraire@uqo.ca.

University of Alberta

Edmonton, Alberta, Canada

http://www.ualberta.ca/

- **Province-supported** university, founded 1906
- **Urban** 1200-acre campus
- **Endowment** $1.0 million
- **Coed** 31,161 undergraduate students, 93% full-time, 55% women, 45% men
- **Moderately difficult** entrance level

UNDERGRAD STUDENTS

29,098 full-time, 2,063 part-time. Students come from 13 provinces and territories; 128 other countries; 9% are from out of state.

FACULTY

Student/faculty ratio: 20:1.

ACADEMICS

Calendar: Canadian standard year. *Degrees:* certificates, diplomas, bachelor's, master's, doctoral, and postbachelor's certificates.

Special study options: academic remediation for entering students, accelerated degree program, adult/continuing education programs, advanced placement credit, cooperative education, distance learning, double majors, English as a second language, external degree program, honors programs, independent study, internships, off-campus study, part-time degree program, services for LD students, student-designed majors, study abroad, summer session for credit.

Unusual degree programs: 3-2 education.

Computers: 2,500 computers/terminals are available on campus for general student use. Students can access the following: computer help desk, free student e-mail accounts, online (class) grades, online (class) registration, online (class) schedules. Campuswide network is available. Wireless service is available via entire campus.

STUDENT LIFE

Housing options: coed, men-only, women-only, special housing for students with disabilities. Campus housing is university owned. Freshman campus housing is guaranteed.

Activities and organizations: drama/theater group, student-run newspaper, radio station, choral group, national fraternities, national sororities.

Athletics Member CIS. ***Intercollegiate sports:*** basketball M(s)/W(s), cross-country running M(s)/W(s), football M(s), golf M/W, ice hockey M(s)/W(s), rugby W(s), soccer M(s)/W(s), swimming and diving M(s)/W(s), tennis M(s)/W(s), track and field M(s)/W(s), volleyball M(s)/W(s), wrestling M(s)/W(s). ***Intramural sports:*** archery M/W, badminton M/W, basketball M/W, bowling M/W, cheerleading M(c)/W(c), fencing M(c)/W(c), golf M/W, ice hockey M/W, lacrosse M(c), racquetball M/W, rock climbing M/W, rugby M/W, skiing (downhill) M/W, soccer M/W, softball M/W, squash M/W, table tennis M/W, tennis M/W, ultimate Frisbee M(c)/W(c), volleyball M/W, water polo M(c)/W(c), weight lifting M(c)/W(c).

Campus security: 24-hour emergency response devices and patrols, student patrols, late-night transport/escort service, controlled dormitory access.

Student services: health clinic, personal/psychological counseling, women's center, legal services.

APPLYING

Standardized Tests *Recommended:* SAT (for admission), ACT (for admission), SAT or ACT (for admission), SAT and SAT Subject Tests or ACT (for admission), SAT Subject Tests (for admission), AP.

Options: electronic application, early decision, early action.

Application fee: $125 Canadian dollars.

Required for some: essay or personal statement, high school transcript, interview, portfolios/auditions. ***Recommended:*** minimum 2.0 GPA.

Application deadlines: 5/1 (freshmen), 5/1 (transfers).

CONTACT

Melissa Padfield, Deputy Registrar, University of Alberta, Administration Building, University of Alberta, Edmonton, AB T6G 2M7, Canada. *Phone:* 780-492-3113. *Fax:* 780-492-7172.

The University of British Columbia

Vancouver, British Columbia, Canada

http://www.ubc.ca/

- **Province-supported** university, founded 1915
- **Urban** 1000-acre campus with easy access to Vancouver
- **Endowment** $1.2 billion
- **Coed** 35,344 undergraduate students, 69% full-time, 55% women, 45% men
- **Very difficult** entrance level, 70% of applicants were admitted

UNDERGRAD STUDENTS
24,322 full-time, 11,022 part-time. Students come from 44 provinces and territories; 151 other countries; 82% Race/ethnicity unknown; 18% international; 5% transferred in; 25% live on campus.

Freshmen
Admission: 20,733 applied, 14,491 admitted, 5,966 enrolled.
Retention: 92% of full-time freshmen returned.

FACULTY
Total: 3,347, 83% full-time.
Student/faculty ratio: 15:1.

ACADEMICS
Calendar: Canadian standard year. *Degrees:* certificates, diplomas, bachelor's, master's, doctoral, and postbachelor's certificates.
Special study options: academic remediation for entering students, adult/continuing education programs, advanced placement credit, cooperative education, distance learning, double majors, English as a second language, freshman honors college, honors programs, internships, off-campus study, part-time degree program, services for LD students, student-designed majors, study abroad, summer session for credit.
Computers: Students can access the following: free student e-mail accounts, online (class) grades, online (class) registration, online (class) schedules. Campuswide network is available. 100% of college-owned or -operated housing units are wired for high-speed Internet access. Wireless service is available via entire campus.

STUDENT LIFE
Housing options: coed, men-only, women-only, special housing for students with disabilities. Campus housing is university owned. Freshman applicants given priority for college housing.
Activities and organizations: drama/theater group, student-run newspaper, radio station, choral group, Ski and Board Club, Dance Club, AIESEC (international leadership organization), UBC Film Society, Varsity Outdoors Club, national fraternities, national sororities.
Athletics Member NAIA, CIS. ***Intercollegiate sports:*** baseball M(s), basketball M(s)/W(s), cheerleading W(c), crew M(s)/W(s), cross-country running M(s)/W(s), equestrian sports M/W, field hockey M(s)/W(s), football M(s), golf M(s)/W(s), ice hockey M(s)/W(s), rugby M(s)/W(s), skiing (downhill) M/W, soccer M(s)/W(s), softball M/W, swimming and diving M(s)/W(s), track and field M(s)/W(s), volleyball M(s)/W(s). ***Intramural sports:*** badminton M/W, basketball M/W, cross-country running M/W, fencing M/W, football M/W, gymnastics M/W, ice hockey M/W, racquetball M/W, rock climbing M/W, rugby M/W, sailing M/W, skiing (cross-country) M/W, skiing (downhill) M/W, soccer M/W, softball M/W, squash M/W, swimming and diving M/W, table tennis M/W, tennis M/W, ultimate Frisbee M/W, volleyball M/W, water polo M/W, weight lifting M/W, wrestling M/W.
Campus security: 24-hour emergency response devices and patrols, student patrols, late-night transport/escort service, 24-hour desk attendants in residence halls.
Student services: health clinic, personal/psychological counseling, women's center, legal services.

COSTS & FINANCIAL AID
Costs (2015–16) ***Tuition:*** province resident $5037 full-time, $168 per credit part-time; nonresident $5037 full-time, $168 per credit part-time; International tuition $26,399 full-time. Full-time tuition and fees vary according to course level, course load, program, and student level. Part-time tuition and fees vary according to course level, course load, and program. ***Required fees:*** $935 full-time. ***Room and board:*** $9625. Room and board charges vary according to board plan, housing facility, and location.
Financial Aid Of all full-time matriculated undergraduates who enrolled in 2013, 13,128 were judged to have need. 1,832 state and other part-time jobs (averaging $1763). In 2013, 6107 non-need-based awards were made. ***Average financial aid package:*** $10,586. ***Average need-based loan:*** $9165. ***Average need-based gift aid:*** $2961. ***Average non-need-based aid:*** $2218. ***Financial aid deadline:*** 9/15.

APPLYING
Standardized Tests *Required for some:* SAT or ACT (for admission), SAT or ACT plus Writing required of applicants following US curriculum.
Options: electronic application, deferred entrance.
Application fee: $108 Canadian dollars.
Required: essay or personal statement, high school transcript, minimum 2.6 GPA, English Language Admission Standard.
Application deadlines: 1/31 (freshmen), 1/31 (out-of-state freshmen), 1/31 (transfers).
Notification: continuous (freshmen), continuous (out-of-state freshmen), continuous (transfers).

CONTACT
The University of British Columbia, V6T 1Z1, Canada. *Phone:* 604-822-3014.

The University of British Columbia–Okanagan Campus

Kelowna, British Columbia, Canada

http://www.ubc.ca/okanagan/welcome.html

- **Province-supported** university, founded 2005, part of University of British Columbia
- **Urban** 500-acre campus with easy access to Kelowna
- **Endowment** $1.2 billion
- **Coed** 7,308 undergraduate students, 76% full-time, 54% women, 46% men
- **Moderately difficult** entrance level, 85% of applicants were admitted

UNDERGRAD STUDENTS
5,524 full-time, 1,784 part-time. Students come from 25 provinces and territories; 79 other countries; 90% Race/ethnicity unknown; 10% international; 31% live on campus.

Freshmen
Admission: 4,477 applied, 3,798 admitted, 1,311 enrolled.
Retention: 74% of full-time freshmen returned.

FACULTY
Total: 412, 91% full-time.
Student/faculty ratio: 18:1.

ACADEMICS
Degrees: certificates, diplomas, bachelor's, master's, doctoral, and postbachelor's certificates.
Special study options: academic remediation for entering students, advanced placement credit, cooperative education, distance learning, double majors, English as a second language, freshman honors college, honors programs, internships, off-campus study, part-time degree program, services for LD students, student-designed majors, study abroad, summer session for credit.
Computers: Students can access the following: campus intranet, computer help desk, free student e-mail accounts, online (class) grades, online (class) registration, online (class) schedules. Campuswide network is available. 100% of college-owned or -operated housing units are wired for high-speed Internet access. Wireless service is available via entire campus.

STUDENT LIFE
Housing options: coed, men-only, women-only. Campus housing is university owned. Freshman campus housing is guaranteed.
Activities and organizations: drama/theater group, student-run newspaper, radio station, choral group, Film Club, International Student Club, UBCSUO Mountain Riders Ski and Snowboard Club, Engineers without Borders, Model United Nations Club, national fraternities.

Athletics Member CIS. ***Intercollegiate sports:*** basketball M(s)/W(s), cross-country running M(s)/W(s), golf M(s)/W(s), rugby M(s)/W(s), soccer M(s)/W(s), volleyball M(s)/W(s). ***Intramural sports:*** badminton M(c)/W(c), basketball M/W, field hockey M(c)/W(c), gymnastics M/W, soccer M/W, squash M(c)/W(c), tennis M(c)/W(c), volleyball M/W.

Campus security: 24-hour emergency response devices and patrols, controlled dormitory access, 24-hour desk attendants in residence halls.

Student services: health clinic, personal/psychological counseling, women's center, legal services.

COSTS & FINANCIAL AID

Costs (2015–16) ***Tuition:*** province resident $5061 full-time, $169 per credit part-time; nonresident $5061 full-time, $880 per credit part-time; International tuition $26,399 full-time. Full-time tuition and fees vary according to course load and program. Part-time tuition and fees vary according to course load and program. ***Required fees:*** $665 full-time. ***Room and board:*** $10,760. Room and board charges vary according to board plan and housing facility. ***Waivers:*** senior citizens.

Financial Aid ***Financial aid deadline:*** 12/10.

APPLYING

Standardized Tests *Required for some:* SAT or ACT (for admission).

Options: electronic application, deferred entrance.

Application fee: $108 Canadian dollars.

Required: essay or personal statement, high school transcript, minimum 2.6 GPA.

Application deadlines: 1/31 (freshmen), 1/31 (out-of-state freshmen), 1/31 (transfers).

Notification: continuous (freshmen), continuous (out-of-state freshmen), continuous (transfers).

CONTACT

International Student Recruitment, The University of British Columbia–Okanagan Campus, UC222 University Centre, 3333 University Way, Kelowna, BC V1V 1V7, Canada. *Phone:* 250-807-9447. *Fax:* 250-807-8552.

University of Guelph

Guelph, Ontario, Canada

http://www.uoguelph.ca/

- **Province-supported** university, founded 1964
- **Suburban** 1017-acre campus with easy access to Toronto
- **Endowment** $263.4 million
- **Coed** 20,205 undergraduate students, 89% full-time, 59% women, 41% men
- **Moderately difficult** entrance level, 66% of applicants were admitted

UNDERGRAD STUDENTS

17,979 full-time, 2,226 part-time. Students come from 13 provinces and territories; 100 other countries; 2% transferred in; 28% live on campus.

Freshmen

Admission: 23,750 applied, 15,564 admitted, 4,707 enrolled. ***Average high school GPA:*** 3.5.

Retention: 92% of full-time freshmen returned.

FACULTY

Total: 840, 90% full-time.

Student/faculty ratio: 23:1.

ACADEMICS

Calendar: trimesters. *Degrees:* certificates, diplomas, associate, bachelor's, master's, and doctoral.

Special study options: academic remediation for entering students, accelerated degree program, advanced placement credit, cooperative education, distance learning, double majors, English as a second language, honors programs, independent study, internships, off-campus study, part-time degree program, services for LD students, student-designed majors, study abroad, summer session for credit.

Computers: 1,500 computers/terminals and 16,000 ports are available on campus for general student use. Students can access the following: campus intranet, computer help desk, free student e-mail accounts, online (class) grades, online (class) registration, online (class) schedules. Campuswide network is available. 100% of college-owned or -operated

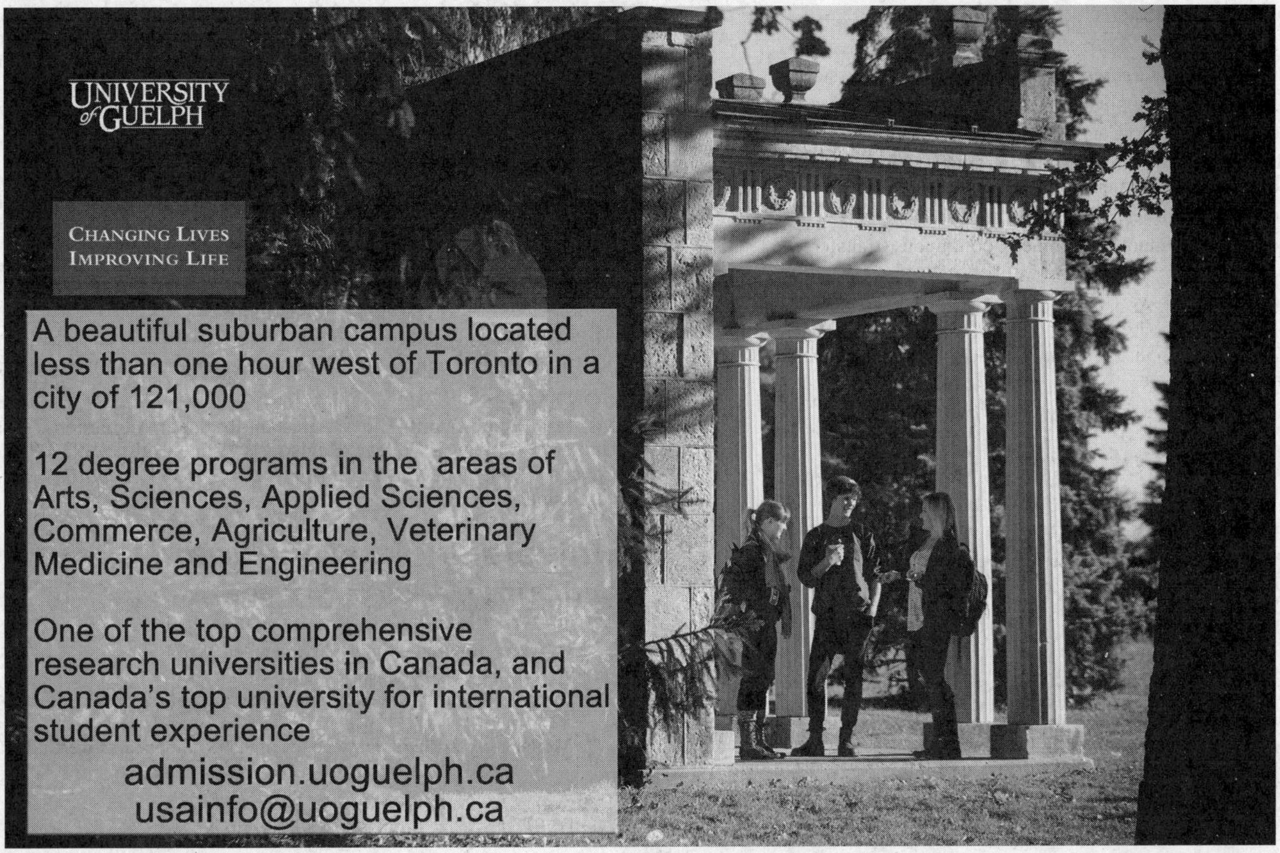
UNIVERSITY of GUELPH
CHANGING LIVES
IMPROVING LIFE
A beautiful suburban campus located less than one hour west of Toronto in a city of 121,000
12 degree programs in the areas of Arts, Sciences, Applied Sciences, Commerce, Agriculture, Veterinary Medicine and Engineering
One of the top comprehensive research universities in Canada, and Canada's top university for international student experience
admission.uoguelph.ca
usainfo@uoguelph.ca

housing units are wired for high-speed Internet access. Wireless service is available via entire campus.

STUDENT LIFE
Housing options: coed, women-only, cooperative, special housing for students with disabilities. Campus housing is university owned and is provided by a third party. Freshman campus housing is guaranteed.

Activities and organizations: drama/theater group, student-run newspaper, radio station, choral group, Guelph Gryphon Athletics, Habitat for Humanity, Curtain Call Productions, West Indian Students Association, OXFAM-Guelph Chapter.

Athletics Member CIS. ***Intercollegiate sports:*** baseball M, basketball M(s)/W(s), crew M/W, cross-country running M(s)/W(s), field hockey W(s), football M, golf M/W, ice hockey M(s)/W(s), lacrosse M/W, rugby M(s)/W(s), skiing (cross-country) M/W, soccer M(s)/W(s), swimming and diving M(s)/W(s), track and field M(s)/W(s), volleyball M(s)/W(s), wrestling M(s)/W(s). ***Intramural sports:*** badminton M(c)/W(c), basketball M/W, cheerleading M(c)/W(c), football M/W, ice hockey M/W, lacrosse M(c)/W(c), rock climbing M(c)/W(c), soccer M/W, softball M/W(c), squash M(c)/W(c), table tennis M(c)/W(c), ultimate Frisbee M(c)/W(c), volleyball M/W, water polo M(c)/W(c).

Campus security: 24-hour emergency response devices and patrols, student patrols, late-night transport/escort service, controlled dormitory access, video camera surveillance in parking lots, alarms in women's locker room.

Student services: health clinic, personal/psychological counseling, women's center, legal services.

COSTS
Costs (2014–15) ***Tuition:*** province resident $6022 Canadian dollars full-time, $602 Canadian dollars per course part-time; International tuition $18,429 Canadian dollars full-time. Full-time tuition and fees vary according to degree level and program. Part-time tuition and fees vary according to course load, degree level, and program. No tuition increase for student's term of enrollment. ***Required fees:*** $1427 Canadian dollars full-time, $22 Canadian dollars per course part-time, $459 Canadian dollars per term part-time. ***Room and board:*** $10,383 Canadian dollars; room only: $5718 Canadian dollars. Room and board charges vary according to board plan, housing facility, and location. ***Payment plan:*** installment. ***Waivers:*** senior citizens and employees or children of employees.

APPLYING
Standardized Tests *Required:* SAT or ACT (for admission).

Options: electronic application, early admission, deferred entrance.

Application fee: $135 Canadian dollars.

Required: high school transcript, minimum 3.0 GPA. ***Required for some:*** essay or personal statement.

Application deadlines: 3/1 (freshmen), 5/1 (transfers).

Notification: continuous (freshmen), continuous (transfers).

CONTACT
Ms. Janette Hogan, Assistant Registrar, Admissions, University of Guelph, L-3 University Centre, Guelph, ON N1G 2W1, Canada. *Phone:* 519-824-4120 Ext. 58529. *Fax:* 519-766-9481. *E-mail:* jhogan@registrar.uoguelph.ca.

See previous page for display ad and page 1668 for the College Close-Up.

University of King's College
Halifax, Nova Scotia, Canada
http://www.ukings.ca/

- **Province-supported** comprehensive, founded 1789
- **Urban** 4-acre campus
- **Endowment** $35.4 million
- **Coed** 1,064 undergraduate students, 94% full-time, 62% women, 38% men
- **Moderately difficult** entrance level, 83% of applicants were admitted

UNDERGRAD STUDENTS
1,000 full-time, 64 part-time. Students come from 12 provinces and territories; 17 other countries; 65% are from out of state; 6% transferred in; 23% live on campus.

Freshmen
Admission: 830 applied, 690 admitted, 264 enrolled.

FACULTY
Total: 53, 96% full-time, 72% with terminal degrees.

Student/faculty ratio: 21:1.

ACADEMICS
Calendar: Canadian standard year. *Degrees:* bachelor's and master's.

Special study options: accelerated degree program, advanced placement credit, cooperative education, double majors, honors programs, independent study, internships, off-campus study, part-time degree program, services for LD students, student-designed majors, study abroad, summer session for credit.

Computers: Students can access the following: online (class) grades, online (class) registration, online (class) schedules. Campuswide network is available. Wireless service is available via libraries, student centers.

STUDENT LIFE
Housing options: coed, men-only, women-only. Campus housing is university owned. Freshman applicants given priority for college housing.

Activities and organizations: drama/theater group, student-run newspaper, radio station, choral group, King's Theatrical Society, student newspaper, King's College Dance Collective, St. Andrew's Missionary Society, King's Independent Film-Makers Society.

Athletics ***Intercollegiate sports:*** badminton M/W, basketball M/W, rugby M/W, soccer M/W, volleyball M. ***Intramural sports:*** badminton M/W, basketball M/W, field hockey M/W, soccer M/W, softball M/W, tennis M/W, ultimate Frisbee M/W, volleyball M/W, water polo M/W.

Campus security: student patrols, late-night transport/escort service, controlled dormitory access.

Student services: health clinic, personal/psychological counseling, women's center, legal services.

COSTS
Costs (2014–15) ***Tuition:*** province resident $7000 Canadian dollars full-time, $226 Canadian dollars per credit hour part-time; nonresident $7000 Canadian dollars full-time; International tuition $16,000 Canadian dollars full-time. Full-time tuition and fees vary according to course load and program. Part-time tuition and fees vary according to course load and program. ***Required fees:*** $1600 Canadian dollars full-time, $120 Canadian dollars per term part-time, $235 Canadian dollars per term part-time. ***Room and board:*** $10,000 Canadian dollars; room only: $7000 Canadian dollars. Room and board charges vary according to board plan and housing facility. ***Waivers:*** employees or children of employees.

APPLYING
Standardized Tests *Required for some:* SAT (for admission).

Options: electronic application, early admission, early decision, deferred entrance.

Application fee: $65 Canadian dollars.

Required: high school transcript, minimum 3.0 GPA. ***Required for some:*** essay or personal statement, writing sample.

Application deadlines: 3/1 (freshmen), 6/1 (transfers).

Notification: continuous until 4/15 (freshmen), continuous (transfers).

CONTACT
Ms. Tara Wigglesworth-Hines, Assistant Registrar/Admissions, University of King's College, Registrar's Office, Halifax, NS B3H 3A1, Canada. *Phone:* 902-422-1271. *Fax:* 902-425-8183. *E-mail:* admissions@ukings.ns.ca.

University of Lethbridge
Lethbridge, Alberta, Canada
http://www.uleth.ca/

- **Province-supported** university, founded 1967
- **Urban** 576-acre campus
- **Coed** 7,498 undergraduate students, 89% full-time, 58% women, 42% men
- **Moderately difficult** entrance level, 82% of applicants were admitted

UNDERGRAD STUDENTS

6,653 full-time, 845 part-time. Students come from 13 provinces and territories; 62 other countries; 12% are from out of state; 12% live on campus.

Freshmen

Admission: 2,635 applied, 2,159 admitted.

Retention: 77% of full-time freshmen returned.

ACADEMICS

Calendar: semesters. *Degrees:* certificates, diplomas, bachelor's, master's, doctoral, post-master's, and postbachelor's certificates.

Special study options: academic remediation for entering students, accelerated degree program, advanced placement credit, cooperative education, distance learning, double majors, English as a second language, independent study, internships, off-campus study, part-time degree program, services for LD students, student-designed majors, study abroad, summer session for credit.

Unusual degree programs: 3-2 Education.

Computers: Students can access the following: computer help desk, free student e-mail accounts, online (class) grades, online (class) registration, online (class) schedules. Campuswide network is available. 100% of college-owned or -operated housing units are wired for high-speed Internet access. Wireless service is available via entire campus.

STUDENT LIFE

Housing options: coed. Campus housing is university owned.

Activities and organizations: drama/theater group, student-run newspaper, radio station, choral group, national fraternities.

Athletics Member CIS. ***Intercollegiate sports:*** basketball M(s)/W(s), ice hockey M(s)/W(s), rugby W(s), soccer M(s)/W(s), swimming and diving M(s)/W(s), track and field M(s)/W(s). ***Intramural sports:*** badminton M/W, basketball M/W, fencing M(c)/W(c), golf M/W, ice hockey M/W, rock climbing M/W, rugby M(c)/W(c), soccer M/W, softball W, tennis M(c)/W(c), volleyball M/W, water polo M/W.

Campus security: 24-hour emergency response devices and patrols, student patrols, late-night transport/escort service, controlled dormitory access, video camera monitored entrances, hallways.

Student services: health clinic, personal/psychological counseling, women's center.

COSTS

Costs (2014–15) ***Tuition:*** province resident $4974 Canadian dollars full-time; nonresident $4974 Canadian dollars full-time; International tuition $11,262 Canadian dollars full-time. Full-time tuition and fees vary according to course load. Part-time tuition and fees vary according to course load. ***Required fees:*** $1006 Canadian dollars full-time. ***Room and board:*** $6081 Canadian dollars; room only: $2520 Canadian dollars. Room and board charges vary according to board plan and housing facility.

APPLYING

Options: electronic application, deferred entrance.

Application fee: $100 Canadian dollars.

Required: high school transcript, minimum 2.0 GPA. ***Required for some:*** minimum 3.0 GPA, interview.

Application deadlines: 6/30 (freshmen), 6/30 (transfers).

Notification: continuous (freshmen), continuous (transfers).

CONTACT

Registrar's Office, University of Lethbridge, 4401 University Drive, Lethbridge, AB T1K 3M4, Canada. *Phone:* 403-320-5700. *Fax:* 403-329-5159. *E-mail:* regoffice@uleth.ca.

University of New Brunswick Fredericton

Fredericton, New Brunswick, Canada

http://www.unb.ca/

- **Province-supported** university, founded 1785
- **Urban** 7100-acre campus
- **Endowment** $188.6 million
- **Coed**

ACADEMICS

Calendar: Canadian standard year. *Degrees:* bachelor's, master's, and doctoral.

STUDENT LIFE

Housing options: coed, men-only, women-only, special housing for students with disabilities. Campus housing is university owned. Freshman campus housing is guaranteed.

Activities and organizations: drama/theater group, student-run newspaper, radio station, choral group.

Athletics Member CIS.

Campus security: 24-hour emergency response devices and patrols, student patrols, late-night transport/escort service, controlled dormitory access.

Student services: health clinic, personal/psychological counseling, women's center, legal services.

COSTS & FINANCIAL AID

Costs (2014–15) ***Tuition:*** province resident $6187 Canadian dollars full-time, $619 Canadian dollars per term part-time; International tuition $13,680 Canadian dollars full-time. Full-time tuition and fees vary according to course load, location, and program. Part-time tuition and fees vary according to course load, location, and program. ***Required fees:*** $569 Canadian dollars full-time, $35 Canadian dollars per term part-time. ***Room and board:*** $8896 Canadian dollars; room only: $5255 Canadian dollars. Room and board charges vary according to board plan and location. ***Payment plans:*** installment, deferred payment.

Financial Aid Of all full-time matriculated undergraduates who enrolled in 2007, 123 state and other part-time jobs (averaging $1264). ***Financial aid deadline:*** 5/15.

APPLYING

Standardized Tests *Required for some:* SAT (for admission).

Required: high school transcript. ***Required for some:*** essay or personal statement, interview, Several of our programs require the completion of supplementary documents for our HS/HSA application, e.g., Nursing requires supplementary form and life sketch. Renaissance College requires resume and cover letter.

CONTACT

University of New Brunswick Fredericton, PO Box 4400, Fredericton, NB E3B 5A3, Canada. *Phone:* 506-453-4865.

University of New Brunswick Saint John

Saint John, New Brunswick, Canada

http://www.unb.ca/

- **Province-supported** comprehensive, founded 1964
- **Urban** 250-acre campus
- **Coed**
- **Moderately difficult** entrance level

UNDERGRAD STUDENTS

5% live on campus.

ACADEMICS

Calendar: Canadian standard year. *Degrees:* certificates, diplomas, bachelor's, master's, doctoral, and postbachelor's certificates.

Special study options: academic remediation for entering students, accelerated degree program, adult/continuing education programs, advanced placement credit, cooperative education, distance learning, double majors, English as a second language, honors programs, independent study, internships, off-campus study, part-time degree program, services for LD students, student-designed majors, study abroad, summer session for credit.

Computers: 100 computers/terminals are available on campus for general student use. Students can access the following: campus intranet, computer help desk, free student e-mail accounts, online (class) grades, online (class) registration, online (class) schedules. Campuswide network is available. Wireless service is available via entire campus.

STUDENT LIFE

Housing options: coed. Campus housing is university owned.

Activities and organizations: drama/theater group, student-run newspaper, radio station, choral group, Business Administration Society, OPTAMUS, International Student Association, Chinese Cultural Association, Muslim Student Association.

Athletics ***Intercollegiate sports:*** badminton M/W, basketball M/W, crew M/W, cross-country running M/W, fencing M/W, ice hockey M/W, rugby M/W, soccer M/W, volleyball M/W. ***Intramural sports:*** badminton M/W, basketball M/W, fencing M/W, golf M/W, soccer M/W, table tennis M/W, tennis M/W, volleyball M/W.

Campus security: 24-hour emergency response devices and patrols, student patrols, late-night transport/escort service, controlled dormitory access.

Student services: health clinic, personal/psychological counseling, women's center.

COSTS & FINANCIAL AID

Costs (2014–15) ***Tuition:*** province resident $6187 full-time, $619 per course part-time; nonresident $6187 full-time, $619 per course part-time; International tuition $13,680 full-time. Full-time tuition and fees vary according to location and program. Part-time tuition and fees vary according to course load, location, and program. ***Required fees:*** $760 full-time, $40 per course part-time. ***Room and board:*** $6826. Room and board charges vary according to board plan, housing facility, and location. ***Payment plan:*** installment.

Financial Aid Of all full-time matriculated undergraduates who enrolled in 2013, 140 state and other part-time jobs (averaging $500).

APPLYING

Standardized Tests *Required:* SAT (for admission).

Options: electronic application, early admission, deferred entrance.

Application fee: $55 Canadian dollars.

Required: high school transcript.

Application deadlines: rolling (freshmen), 3/31 (out-of-state freshmen), rolling (transfers).

Notification: continuous until 8/31 (freshmen), continuous (out-of-state freshmen), continuous until 8/31 (transfers).

CONTACT

University of New Brunswick Saint John, PO Box 5050, Saint John, NB E2L 4L5, Canada.

University of Ottawa

Ottawa, Ontario, Canada

http://www.uottawa.ca/

- **Province-supported** university, founded 1848
- **Urban** 43-hectare campus with easy access to Ottawa-Gatineau
- **Endowment** $186.0 million
- **Coed** 31,658 undergraduate students, 84% full-time, 60% women, 40% men
- **Moderately difficult** entrance level, 55% of applicants were admitted

UNDERGRAD STUDENTS

26,563 full-time, 5,095 part-time. Students come from 13 provinces and territories; 166 other countries; 21% are from out of state; 9% live on campus.

Freshmen

Admission: 45,600 applied, 25,000 admitted. ***Average high school GPA:*** 3.34.

Retention: 87% of full-time freshmen returned.

FACULTY

Total: 2,246, 56% full-time.

Student/faculty ratio: 26:1.

ACADEMICS

Calendar: semesters. *Degrees:* certificates, diplomas, bachelor's, master's, doctoral, and postbachelor's certificates.

Special study options: academic remediation for entering students, advanced placement credit, cooperative education, distance learning, double majors, English as a second language, honors programs, internships, off-campus study, part-time degree program, services for LD students, study abroad, summer session for credit.

Unusual degree programs: 3-2 law, education.

Computers: 1,540 computers/terminals are available on campus for general student use. Students can access the following: computer help desk, free student e-mail accounts, online (class) grades, online (class) registration, online (class) schedules, wireless connection available on campus. Campuswide network is available. 100% of college-owned or -operated housing units are wired for high-speed Internet access. Wireless service is available via entire campus.

STUDENT LIFE

Housing options: coed, special housing for students with disabilities. Campus housing is university owned. Freshman campus housing is guaranteed.

Activities and organizations: drama/theater group, student-run newspaper, radio station, choral group, Student Federation of the University of Ottawa, Graduate Students Association, national fraternities, national sororities.

Athletics Member CIS. ***Intercollegiate sports:*** badminton M(c)/W(c), baseball M(c)/W(c), basketball M(s)/W(s), cheerleading M(c)/W(c), crew M(c)/W(c), cross-country running M(s)/W(s), equestrian sports M(c)/W(c), fencing M(c)/W(c), football M(s), golf M(c)/W(c), ice hockey W(s), rugby W(s), soccer M(s)(c)/W(s), swimming and diving M(s)/W(s), track and field M(s)/W(s), ultimate Frisbee M(c)/W(c), volleyball M(c)/W(s), water polo M(c)/W(c). ***Intramural sports:*** basketball M/W, football M, ice hockey M/W, soccer M/W, ultimate Frisbee M/W, volleyball M/W.

Campus security: 24-hour emergency response devices and patrols, student patrols, late-night transport/escort service, controlled dormitory access.

Student services: health clinic, personal/psychological counseling, women's center, legal services.

COSTS & FINANCIAL AID

Costs (2014–15) ***One-time required fee:*** $360. ***Tuition:*** province resident $6010 full-time, $238 per credit part-time; nonresident $842 per credit part-time; International tuition $21,711 full-time. Full-time tuition and fees vary according to course load, degree level, program, and student level. Part-time tuition and fees vary according to course load, degree level, program, and student level. ***Required fees:*** $690 full-time, $128 per term part-time. ***Room and board:*** $7108; room only: $4808. Room and board charges vary according to board plan and housing facility. ***Waivers:*** employees or children of employees.

Financial Aid ***Financial aid deadline:*** 1/31.

APPLYING

Standardized Tests *Required for some:* SAT or ACT required for American citizens.

Options: electronic application, early admission, deferred entrance.

Application fee: $167 Canadian dollars.

Required: high school transcript, minimum 3.0 GPA. ***Required for some:*** interview.

Notification: continuous (freshmen).

CONTACT

University of Ottawa, 550 Cumberland Street, Ottawa, ON K1N 6N5, Canada. *Phone:* 613-562-5800 Ext. 1594.

University of Regina

Regina, Saskatchewan, Canada

http://www.uregina.ca/

- **Province-supported** university, founded 1974
- **Urban** 76-hectare campus
- **Endowment** $36.4 million
- **Coed** 12,242 undergraduate students, 82% full-time, 63% women, 37% men
- **Minimally difficult** entrance level, 62% of applicants were admitted

UNDERGRAD STUDENTS

10,090 full-time, 2,152 part-time. Students come from 13 provinces and territories; 100 other countries; 16% are from out of state; 4% transferred in; 10% live on campus.

Freshmen
Admission: 4,944 applied, 3,059 admitted, 1,944 enrolled. ***Average high school GPA:*** 3.7.

Retention: 80% of full-time freshmen returned.

FACULTY
Total: 417, 100% full-time, 75% with terminal degrees.

Student/faculty ratio: 24:1.

ACADEMICS
Calendar: semesters. *Degrees:* certificates, diplomas, bachelor's, master's, doctoral, and postbachelor's certificates.

Special study options: academic remediation for entering students, adult/continuing education programs, advanced placement credit, cooperative education, distance learning, double majors, English as a second language, honors programs, independent study, internships, off-campus study, part-time degree program, services for LD students, student-designed majors, study abroad, summer session for credit.

Computers: 412 computers/terminals are available on campus for general student use. Students can access the following: computer help desk, free student e-mail accounts, online (class) grades, online (class) registration, online (class) schedules. Campuswide network is available. 100% of college-owned or -operated housing units are wired for high-speed Internet access. Wireless service is available via entire campus.

STUDENT LIFE
Housing options: special housing for students with disabilities. Campus housing is university owned. Freshman campus housing is guaranteed.

Activities and organizations: drama/theater group, student-run newspaper, television station, choral group.

Athletics Member CIS. ***Intercollegiate sports:*** basketball M(s)/W(s), cross-country running M(s)/W(s), football M(s), ice hockey M(s)/W(s), soccer W(s), swimming and diving M(s)/W(s), track and field M(s)/W(s), volleyball M(s)/W(s), wrestling M(s)/W(s). ***Intramural sports:*** badminton M/W, basketball M/W, bowling M/W, cheerleading M(c)/W(c), football M/W, golf M(c)/W(c), rugby M(c)/W(c), soccer M/W, softball M/W(c), tennis M/W, ultimate Frisbee M/W, volleyball M/W.

Campus security: 24-hour emergency response devices and patrols, late-night transport/escort service, controlled dormitory access, crime prevention assistance, CCTV, card access and some alarm monitoring.

Student services: health clinic, personal/psychological counseling, women's center.

COSTS
Costs (2014–15) ***Tuition:*** province resident $5753 Canadian dollars full-time, $192 Canadian dollars per credit hour part-time; International tuition $17,258 Canadian dollars full-time. Full-time tuition and fees vary according to course load and program. Part-time tuition and fees vary according to course load and program. ***Required fees:*** $604 Canadian dollars full-time, $8 Canadian dollars per credit hour part-time, $63 Canadian dollars per term part-time. ***Room and board:*** $7193 Canadian dollars; room only: $4828 Canadian dollars. Room and board charges vary according to board plan and housing facility. ***Waivers:*** senior citizens and employees or children of employees.

APPLYING
Standardized Tests *Required for some:* SAT or ACT (for admission).

Options: electronic application, early admission, early action, deferred entrance.

Application fee: $100 Canadian dollars.

Required: high school transcript, minimum 2.3 GPA. ***Required for some:*** essay or personal statement, 2 letters of recommendation, interview, portfolio, audition, some programs require a higher than 2.3 minimum GPA for admission.

Application deadlines: 8/15 (freshmen), 8/15 (out-of-state freshmen), 8/15 (transfers), 6/15 (early action).

CONTACT
University of Regina, 3737 Wascana Parkway, Regina, SK S4S 0A2, Canada. *Phone:* 306-585-5345. *Toll-free phone:* 800-644-4756.

University of Saskatchewan
Saskatoon, Saskatchewan, Canada
http://www.usask.ca/

- **Province-supported** university, founded 1907
- **Urban** 1865-acre campus
- **Coed** 16,851 undergraduate students

FACULTY
Total: 1,131.

ACADEMICS
Calendar: Canadian standard year. *Degrees:* certificates, diplomas, bachelor's, master's, doctoral, and postbachelor's certificates.

Special study options: accelerated degree program, advanced placement credit, cooperative education, distance learning, double majors, English as a second language, honors programs, independent study, internships, off-campus study, part-time degree program, services for LD students, study abroad, summer session for credit.

Computers: Students can access the following: computer help desk, free student e-mail accounts, online (class) grades, online (class) registration, online (class) schedules, student portal. 100% of college-owned or -operated housing units are wired for high-speed Internet access. Wireless service is available via entire campus.

STUDENT LIFE
Housing options: coed. Campus housing is university owned.

Activities and organizations: drama/theater group, student-run newspaper, choral group.

Athletics Member CIS. ***Intercollegiate sports:*** basketball M/W, cross-country running M/W, football M, ice hockey M/W, soccer M/W, track and field M/W, volleyball M/W, wrestling M/W(c). ***Intramural sports:*** badminton M/W, basketball M/W, football M/W, ice hockey M/W, soccer M/W, ultimate Frisbee M/W, volleyball M/W.

Campus security: 24-hour emergency response devices and patrols, student patrols, late-night transport/escort service, controlled dormitory access.

Student services: health clinic, personal/psychological counseling, women's center, legal services.

COSTS & FINANCIAL AID
Costs (2015–16) ***Tuition:*** province resident $5790 Canadian dollars full-time; nonresident $5790 Canadian dollars full-time; International tuition $15,054 Canadian dollars full-time. ***Required fees:*** $843 Canadian dollars full-time. ***Room and board:*** $7607 Canadian dollars; room only: $2737 Canadian dollars.

Financial Aid ***Financial aid deadline:*** 3/15.

APPLYING
Standardized Tests *Recommended:* scores sometimes used for home-educated students.

Options: electronic application, early admission.

Application fee: $90 Canadian dollars.

Required: high school transcript. ***Required for some:*** essay or personal statement, interview.

Application deadlines: 5/1 (freshmen), 5/1 (transfers).

Notification: continuous (freshmen), continuous (transfers).

CONTACT
University of Saskatchewan, 105 Administration Place, Saskatoon, SK S7N 5A2, Canada. *Phone:* 306-966-5788.

University of the Fraser Valley
Abbotsford, British Columbia, Canada
http://www.ufv.ca/

- **Province-supported** comprehensive, founded 1974
- **Urban** 48-acre campus with easy access to Vancouver
- **Endowment** $6.5 million
- **Coed** 8,407 undergraduate students, 73% full-time, 58% women, 42% men

UNDERGRAD STUDENTS
6,113 full-time, 2,294 part-time. Students come from 41 other countries; 5% American Indian or Alaska Native, non-Hispanic/Latino; 84% Race/ethnicity unknown; 11% international.

Freshmen
Admission: 1,498 enrolled.
Retention: 68% of full-time freshmen returned.

FACULTY
Total: 731, 47% full-time, 31% with terminal degrees.

ACADEMICS
Calendar: semesters. *Degrees:* certificates, diplomas, associate, bachelor's, master's, and postbachelor's certificates.
Special study options: academic remediation for entering students, adult/continuing education programs, advanced placement credit, cooperative education, distance learning, double majors, English as a second language, independent study, internships, off-campus study, part-time degree program, services for LD students, summer session for credit.

STUDENT LIFE
Housing options: coed. Campus housing is university owned. Freshman applicants given priority for college housing.
Activities and organizations: drama/theater group, student-run newspaper, radio station.
Athletics ***Intercollegiate sports:*** basketball M(s)/W(s), soccer M(s)/W(s). ***Intramural sports:*** badminton M/W, basketball M/W, cross-country running M(c)/W(c), soccer M/W, volleyball M/W, wrestling M(c)/W(c).
Campus security: 24-hour emergency response devices and patrols, late-night transport/escort service, controlled dormitory access.
Student services: personal/psychological counseling.

COSTS
Costs (2015–16) ***Tuition:*** province resident $4422 Canadian dollars full-time; nonresident $4422 Canadian dollars full-time; International tuition $14,700 Canadian dollars full-time. Full-time tuition and fees vary according to course load. Part-time tuition and fees vary according to course load. ***Required fees:*** $512 Canadian dollars full-time. ***Room and board:*** $7471 Canadian dollars; room only: $5471 Canadian dollars. Room and board charges vary according to board plan. ***Waivers:*** senior citizens and employees or children of employees.

APPLYING
Options: electronic application, deferred entrance.
Application fee: $45 Canadian dollars.
Required: high school transcript. ***Required for some:*** essay or personal statement, 2 letters of recommendation, interview, minimum GPA of 2.0 to 2.67 for specific undergraduate programs.
Notification: continuous (freshmen), continuous (transfers).

CONTACT
Ms. Julie Croft, Admissions Assistant, University of the Fraser Valley, 33844 King Road, Abbotsford, BC V2S 7M8, Canada. *Phone:* 604-504-7441 Ext. 4450. *Toll-free phone:* 888-504-7441. *E-mail:* Julie.Croft@ufv.ca.

University of Toronto
Toronto, Ontario, Canada
http://www.utoronto.ca/

- **Province-supported** university, founded 1827
- **Urban** 714-hectare campus
- **Endowment** $1.2 billion
- **Coed** 67,024 undergraduate students, 91% full-time, 55% women, 45% men
- **Very difficult** entrance level, 22% of applicants were admitted

UNDERGRAD STUDENTS
60,816 full-time, 6,208 part-time. Students come from 12 provinces and territories; 161 other countries; 6% are from out of state; 1% transferred in; 15% live on campus.

Freshmen
Admission: 73,691 applied, 16,505 admitted, 18,012 enrolled.
Retention: 91% of full-time freshmen returned.

FACULTY
Total: 3,175, 89% full-time.
Student/faculty ratio: 24:1.

ACADEMICS
Calendar: Canadian standard year. *Degrees:* certificates, diplomas, bachelor's, master's, and doctoral.
Special study options: adult/continuing education programs, cooperative education, double majors, English as a second language, off-campus study, part-time degree program, services for LD students, study abroad, summer session for credit.
Computers: 2,000 computers/terminals are available on campus for general student use. Students can access the following: campus intranet, computer help desk, free student e-mail accounts, online (class) registration, online (class) schedules. Campuswide network is available. Wireless service is available via classrooms, computer centers, computer labs, dorm rooms, learning centers, libraries, student centers.

STUDENT LIFE
Housing options: coed, women-only. Campus housing is university owned and leased by the school. Freshman campus housing is guaranteed.
Activities and organizations: drama/theater group, student-run newspaper, radio station, choral group, national fraternities, national sororities.
Athletics Member CIS. ***Intercollegiate sports:*** archery M/W, badminton M/W, basketball M/W, crew M, cross-country running M/W, fencing M/W, field hockey W, football M, golf M, gymnastics M/W, ice hockey M/W, rugby M, skiing (cross-country) M/W, skiing (downhill) M/W, soccer M/W, squash M/W, swimming and diving M/W, tennis M/W, track and field M/W, volleyball M/W, wrestling M. ***Intramural sports:*** archery M/W, badminton M/W, basketball M/W, crew M, fencing M/W, field hockey W, football M/W, gymnastics M/W, ice hockey M/W, lacrosse M/W, racquetball M, rugby M, skiing (downhill) M/W, soccer M/W, squash M/W, swimming and diving M/W, tennis M/W, track and field M/W, volleyball M/W, water polo M/W.
Campus security: 24-hour emergency response devices and patrols, student patrols, late-night transport/escort service.
Student services: health clinic, personal/psychological counseling, women's center, legal services.

COSTS
Costs (2014–15) ***Tuition:*** province resident $5500 full-time; nonresident $5500 full-time; International tuition $27,000 full-time. Full-time tuition and fees vary according to course level, course load, program, and student level. Part-time tuition and fees vary according to course load, program, and student level. ***Required fees:*** $1500 full-time. ***Room and board:*** $10,000; room only: $5000. Room and board charges vary according to board plan, housing facility, and location. ***Payment plan:*** installment. ***Waivers:*** senior citizens and employees or children of employees.

APPLYING
Standardized Tests *Required:* SAT and SAT Subject Tests or ACT (for admission).
Options: deferred entrance.
Application fee: $235 Canadian dollars.
Required: high school transcript. ***Required for some:*** interview.
Application deadlines: 3/1 (freshmen), 7/1 (transfers).
Notification: continuous (freshmen), continuous (transfers).

CONTACT
University of Toronto, 563 Spadina Crescent, Toronto, ON M5S 2J7, Canada. *Phone:* 416-978-2190. *Fax:* 416-978-7022. *E-mail:* admissions.help@utoronto.caadmissions.help@utoronto.caadmissions.help@utoronto.ca.

University of Waterloo
Waterloo, Ontario, Canada
http://www.uwaterloo.ca/

- **Province-supported** university, founded 1957
- **Suburban** 1000-acre campus with easy access to Toronto
- **Coed** 30,989 undergraduate students, 96% full-time, 45% women, 55% men
- **Moderately difficult** entrance level, 53% of applicants were admitted

UNDERGRAD STUDENTS
29,623 full-time, 1,366 part-time. Students come from 163 other countries; 23% live on campus.

Freshmen
Admission: 43,347 applied, 23,089 admitted.
Retention: 92% of full-time freshmen returned.

FACULTY
Total: 1,093.
Student/faculty ratio: 30:1.

ACADEMICS
Calendar: trimesters. *Degrees:* certificates, diplomas, bachelor's, master's, doctoral, and postbachelor's certificates.

Special study options: academic remediation for entering students, accelerated degree program, advanced placement credit, cooperative education, distance learning, double majors, English as a second language, honors programs, independent study, internships, off-campus study, part-time degree program, services for LD students, student-designed majors, study abroad, summer session for credit.

Computers: 6,000 computers/terminals are available on campus for general student use. Students can access the following: computer help desk, free student e-mail accounts, online (class) grades, online (class) registration, online (class) schedules. Campuswide network is available. 100% of college-owned or -operated housing units are wired for high-speed Internet access. Wireless service is available via entire campus.

STUDENT LIFE
Housing options: coed, men-only, women-only. Campus housing is university owned. Freshman campus housing is guaranteed.

Activities and organizations: drama/theater group, student-run newspaper, radio station, choral group, marching band, national fraternities, national sororities.

Athletics Member CIS. ***Intercollegiate sports:*** badminton M/W, baseball M, basketball M/W, cheerleading M/W, cross-country running M/W, field hockey W, football M, golf M/W, ice hockey M/W, rugby M/W, skiing (cross-country) M/W, soccer M/W, squash M/W, swimming and diving M/W, tennis M/W, track and field M/W, volleyball M/W. ***Intramural sports:*** archery M(c)/W(c), badminton M(c)/W(c), baseball M/W, basketball M/W, bowling M/W, crew M(c)/W(c), cross-country running M(c)/W(c), equestrian sports M(c)/W(c), fencing M(c)/W(c), football M/W, golf M(c)/W(c), ice hockey M/W, racquetball M(c)/W(c), rock climbing M(c)/W(c), sailing M(c)/W(c), skiing (cross-country) M(c)/W(c), skiing (downhill) M(c)/W(c), soccer M(c)/W(c), softball M/W, squash M(c)/W(c), swimming and diving M(c)/W(c), table tennis M(c)/W(c), tennis M/W, ultimate Frisbee M(c)/W(c), volleyball M/W, water polo M(c)/W(c), weight lifting M(c)/W(c).

Campus security: 24-hour emergency response devices and patrols, student patrols, late-night transport/escort service.

Student services: health clinic, personal/psychological counseling, women's center, legal services.

COSTS
Costs (2014–15) ***Tuition:*** Full-time tuition and fees vary according to course load and program. Part-time tuition and fees vary according to course load and program. ***Required fees:*** $9600 Canadian dollars full-time. ***Room and board:*** $9386 Canadian dollars; room only: $5812 Canadian dollars. Room and board charges vary according to housing facility.

APPLYING
Standardized Tests *Required for some:* SAT or ACT (for admission), SAT Subject Tests (for admission).

Options: electronic application, early admission, deferred entrance.

Application fee: $135 Canadian dollars.

Required: high school transcript. ***Required for some:*** essay or personal statement, minimum 3.0 GPA, interview.

Notification: continuous (transfers).

CONTACT
University of Waterloo, 200 University Avenue West, Waterloo, ON N2L 3G1, Canada. *Phone:* 519-888-4567 Ext. 32265.

The University of Western Ontario

London, Ontario, Canada

http://www.uwo.ca/

- **Province-supported** university, founded 1878
- **Suburban** 1200-acre campus
- **Coed** 32,000 undergraduate students, 91% full-time, 56% women, 44% men
- **Very difficult** entrance level, 55% of applicants were admitted

UNDERGRAD STUDENTS
29,177 full-time, 2,823 part-time. Students come from 13 provinces and territories; 114 other countries; 20% live on campus.

Freshmen
Admission: 34,286 applied, 18,875 admitted. ***Average high school GPA:*** 3.9.
Retention: 93% of full-time freshmen returned.

FACULTY
Total: 1,410, 100% full-time.
Student/faculty ratio: 19:1.

ACADEMICS
Calendar: Canadian standard year. *Degrees:* certificates, diplomas, bachelor's, master's, doctoral, and postbachelor's certificates.

Special study options: academic remediation for entering students, accelerated degree program, adult/continuing education programs, advanced placement credit, cooperative education, distance learning, double majors, English as a second language, honors programs, independent study, internships, off-campus study, part-time degree program, services for LD students, student-designed majors, study abroad, summer session for credit.

Computers: 414 computers/terminals are available on campus for general student use. Students can access the following: campus intranet, computer help desk, free student e-mail accounts, online (class) grades, online (class) registration, online (class) schedules. Campuswide network is available. 100% of college-owned or -operated housing units are wired for high-speed Internet access. Wireless service is available via classrooms, computer centers, computer labs, learning centers, libraries, student centers.

STUDENT LIFE
Housing options: coed, special housing for students with disabilities. Campus housing is university owned. Freshman campus housing is guaranteed.

Activities and organizations: drama/theater group, student-run newspaper, radio and television station, choral group, marching band, Western Investment Club, Pre-Medical Society, Pre-Law Society, Western Climbing Club, DAN Management Students' Association, national fraternities, national sororities.

Athletics Member CIS. ***Intercollegiate sports:*** badminton M/W, baseball M, basketball M(s)/W(s), cheerleading M/W, crew M/W, cross-country running M/W, equestrian sports W, fencing M/W, field hockey W, football M(s), golf M/W, ice hockey M(s)/W(s), lacrosse M/W, rugby M(s)/W, soccer M(s)/W, softball W, squash M(s)/W, swimming and diving M(s)/W(s), table tennis M/W, tennis M(s)/W(s), track and field M(s)/W(s), ultimate Frisbee M/W, volleyball M(s)/W(s), water polo M, wrestling M(s)/W(s). ***Intramural sports:*** badminton M/W, basketball M/W, equestrian sports M(c)/W(c), fencing M(c)/W(c), ice hockey M/W, rock climbing M(c)/W(c), soccer M/W, squash M(c)/W(c), table tennis M(c)/W(c), tennis M(c)/W(c), track and field M(c)/W(c), ultimate Frisbee M/W, volleyball M/W, water polo M/W.

Campus security: 24-hour emergency response devices and patrols, student patrols, late-night transport/escort service, controlled dormitory access, Campus Community Police, SERT: Student Emergency Response Team, Western Foot Patrol.

Student services: health clinic, personal/psychological counseling, legal services.

COSTS & FINANCIAL AID
Costs (2014–15) ***Tuition:*** area resident $5975 Canadian dollars full-time; province resident $1195 Canadian dollars per credit part-time; nonresident $4225 Canadian dollars per credit part-time; International tuition $21,127 Canadian dollars full-time. Full-time tuition and fees vary according to

course level, program, and student level. Part-time tuition and fees vary according to course level, course load, location, program, and student level. ***Required fees:*** $1247 Canadian dollars full-time, $159 Canadian dollars per credit part-time. ***Room and board:*** $10,740 Canadian dollars; room only: $7640 Canadian dollars. Room and board charges vary according to board plan, housing facility, and location. ***Payment plan:*** installment. ***Waivers:*** employees or children of employees.

Financial Aid Of all full-time matriculated undergraduates who enrolled in 2013, 1,547 state and other part-time jobs (averaging $2311).

APPLYING

Standardized Tests *Required:* SAT or ACT (for admission).

Options: electronic application, deferred entrance.

Application fee: $145 Canadian dollars.

Required: high school transcript, minimum 3.5 GPA. ***Required for some:*** Some programs require a supplemental profile, interview or audition.

Application deadlines: 6/1 (freshmen), 5/15 (out-of-state freshmen), 6/1 (transfers).

Early decision deadline: 3/1.

Notification: continuous (freshmen), continuous (out-of-state freshmen), rolling (early decision).

CONTACT

Undergraduate Recruitment and Admissions, The University of Western Ontario, Western University, London, ON N6A 3K7, Canada. *Phone:* 519-661-2100. *Fax:* 519-661-3710. *E-mail:* reg-admissions@uwo.ca.

University of Windsor

Windsor, Ontario, Canada

http://www.uwindsor.ca/

- **Province-supported** university, founded 1857
- **Urban** 125-acre campus with easy access to Detroit
- **Endowment** $70.9 million
- **Coed** 12,420 undergraduate students, 85% full-time, 52% women, 48% men
- **Moderately difficult** entrance level, 66% of applicants were admitted

UNDERGRAD STUDENTS

10,504 full-time, 1,916 part-time. Students come from 11 provinces and territories; 99 other countries; 1% transferred in; 10% live on campus.

Freshmen

Admission: 10,991 applied, 7,225 admitted, 2,059 enrolled.

Retention: 85% of full-time freshmen returned.

FACULTY

Total: 902, 62% full-time, 54% with terminal degrees.

Student/faculty ratio: 22:1.

ACADEMICS

Calendar: semesters. *Degrees:* certificates, bachelor's, master's, doctoral, and postbachelor's certificates.

Special study options: academic remediation for entering students, accelerated degree program, adult/continuing education programs, advanced placement credit, cooperative education, distance learning, double majors, external degree program, honors programs, internships, off-campus study, part-time degree program, services for LD students, student-designed majors, study abroad, summer session for credit.

Unusual degree programs: computer science.

Computers: 1,225 computers/terminals are available on campus for general student use. Students can access the following: campus intranet, computer help desk, free student e-mail accounts, online (class) grades, online (class) registration, online (class) schedules, online transcripts, degree audits, grades, bursaries, grants, online applications for graduation. Campuswide network is available. 100% of college-owned or -operated housing units are wired for high-speed Internet access. Wireless service is available via entire campus.

STUDENT LIFE

Housing options: coed, men-only, women-only, special housing for students with disabilities. Campus housing is university owned. Freshman campus housing is guaranteed.

Activities and organizations: drama/theater group, student-run newspaper, radio station, choral group, University of Windsor Student Alliance, Environmental Awareness Association, Social Science Society, Commerce Society, Science Society, national fraternities.

Athletics Member NAIA, CIS. ***Intercollegiate sports:*** basketball M(s)/W(s), cross-country running M(s)/W(s), football M(s), golf M/W, ice hockey M(s)/W(s), soccer M(s)/W(s), track and field M(s)/W(s), volleyball M(s)/W(s). ***Intramural sports:*** badminton M/W, baseball M/W, basketball M/W, cheerleading M(c)/W(c), football M/W, ice hockey M/W, rugby M/W, soccer M/W, softball M/W, swimming and diving M/W, table tennis M/W, ultimate Frisbee M/W, volleyball M/W, water polo M/W, weight lifting M/W.

Campus security: 24-hour emergency response devices and patrols, student patrols, late-night transport/escort service, controlled dormitory access.

Student services: health clinic, personal/psychological counseling, women's center, legal services.

FINANCIAL AID

Financial Aid Of all full-time matriculated undergraduates who enrolled in 2010, 450 state and other part-time jobs (averaging $1166). ***Financial aid deadline:*** 6/15.

APPLYING

Standardized Tests *Required for some:* SAT or ACT (for admission), SAT and SAT Subject Tests or ACT (for admission), SAT Subject Tests (for admission).

Options: electronic application, early admission.

Application fee: $120 Canadian dollars.

Required: high school transcript, minimum 3.0 GPA. ***Required for some:*** essay or personal statement, minimum 3.3 GPA, 1 letter of recommendation, interview.

Application deadlines: rolling (freshmen), 7/1 (out-of-state freshmen), rolling (transfers).

Notification: continuous until 8/30 (freshmen), continuous until 8/30 (transfers).

CONTACT

Ms. Charlene Yates, Manager of Undergraduate Admissions, University of Windsor, Office of the Registrar, 401 Sunset Avenue, Windsor, ON N9B 3P4, Canada. *Phone:* 519-253-3000 Ext. 3332. *Toll-free phone:* 800-864-2860. *Fax:* 519-971-3653. *E-mail:* registrar@uwindsor.ca.

Vancouver Island University

Nanaimo, British Columbia, Canada

http://www.viu.ca/

- **Province-supported** comprehensive, founded 1969
- **Suburban** 110-acre campus
- **Coed**

ACADEMICS

Calendar: semesters. *Degrees:* certificates, diplomas, associate, bachelor's, master's, and postbachelor's certificates.

STUDENT LIFE

Activities and organizations: student-run newspaper, radio station.

Student services: personal/psychological counseling.

APPLYING

Application fee: $30 Canadian dollars.

CONTACT

Mr. Andrew Amour, Associate Registrar, Admissions and Registration, Vancouver Island University, 900 Fifth Street, Nanaimo, BC V9R 5S5, Canada. *Phone:* 250-740-6355. *Fax:* 250-740-6479.

York University

Toronto, Ontario, Canada

http://www.yorku.ca/

- **Province-supported** university, founded 1959
- **Urban** 457-acre campus
- **Coed**
- **Moderately difficult** entrance level

ACADEMICS
Calendar: semesters. *Degrees:* certificates, diplomas, bachelor's, master's, doctoral, post-master's, and postbachelor's certificates.

STUDENT LIFE
Housing options: coed, men-only, women-only, special housing for students with disabilities. Campus housing is university owned. Freshman campus housing is guaranteed.

Activities and organizations: drama/theater group, student-run newspaper, radio station, choral group, college student councils, York Federation of Students, Jewish Student Association, First Nations and Aboriginal Student Association, International and Exchange Students Club.

Athletics Member CIS.

Campus security: 24-hour emergency response devices and patrols, student patrols, late-night transport/escort service, controlled dormitory access.

Student services: health clinic, personal/psychological counseling, women's center, legal services.

COSTS & FINANCIAL AID
Costs (2014–15) ***Tuition:*** province resident $6713 Canadian dollars full-time, $224 Canadian dollars per credit part-time; nonresident $6713 Canadian dollars full-time, $224 Canadian dollars per credit part-time; International tuition $19,576 Canadian dollars full-time. Full-time tuition and fees vary according to course load, degree level, and program. Part-time tuition and fees vary according to course load, degree level, and program. ***Room and board:*** $8202 Canadian dollars; room only: $4702 Canadian dollars. Room and board charges vary according to board plan and housing facility.

Financial Aid ***Financial aid deadline:*** 3/15.

APPLYING
Standardized Tests *Required:* SAT or ACT (for admission).

Options: electronic application, deferred entrance.

Application fee: $210 Canadian dollars.

Required: high school transcript, minimum 3.0 GPA, audition for fine arts, supplemental application for business. ***Required for some:*** essay or personal statement, interview.

CONTACT
International Recruitment, York University, N301 Bennett Centre for Student Services, 4700 Keele Street, Toronto, ON M3J 1P3, Canada. *Phone:* 416-736-5825. *Fax:* 416-736-5741. *E-mail:* intlenq@yorku.ca.

INTERNATIONAL

BULGARIA

American University in Bulgaria

Blagoevgrad, Bulgaria

http://www.aubg.bg/

- **Independent** comprehensive, founded 1991
- **Small-town** 12-acre campus with easy access to Sofia, Bulgaria
- **Endowment** $25.4 million
- **Coed** 924 undergraduate students, 100% full-time, 50% women, 50% men
- **Very difficult** entrance level, 58% of applicants were admitted

UNDERGRAD STUDENTS
924 full-time. Students come from 39 other countries; 100% Race/ethnicity unknown; 0.3% transferred in; 84% live on campus.

Freshmen
Admission: 637 applied, 368 admitted, 198 enrolled. ***Average high school GPA:*** 3.71. ***Test scores:*** SAT critical reading scores over 500: 73%; SAT math scores over 500: 97%; SAT critical reading scores over 600: 31%; SAT math scores over 600: 75%; ACT scores over 24: 100%; SAT critical reading scores over 700: 5%; SAT math scores over 700: 29%; ACT scores over 30: 67%.

Retention: 93% of full-time freshmen returned.

FACULTY
Total: 75, 68% full-time, 73% with terminal degrees.

Student/faculty ratio: 16:1.

ACADEMICS
Calendar: semesters. *Degrees:* bachelor's and master's.

Special study options: advanced placement credit, double majors, honors programs, independent study, internships, services for LD students, student-designed majors, study abroad.

Computers: 254 computers/terminals and 4 ports are available on campus for general student use. Students can access the following: computer help desk, free student e-mail accounts, online (class) grades, online (class) registration, online (class) schedules. Campuswide network is available. 100% of college-owned or -operated housing units are wired for high-speed Internet access. Wireless service is available via entire campus.

STUDENT LIFE
Housing options: on-campus residence required through senior year; coed, special housing for students with disabilities. Campus housing is university owned. Freshman campus housing is guaranteed.

Activities and organizations: drama/theater group, student-run newspaper, radio station, choral group, Computer Science Student Union, AUBG Political Science Club, Better Community Club, AUBG Broadway Performance Club, Business Club.

Athletics ***Intramural sports:*** basketball M/W, cheerleading W(c), equestrian sports M(c)/W(c), football M(c), gymnastics W, soccer M(c), softball M/W, volleyball M/W.

Campus security: 24-hour patrols.

Student services: health clinic, personal/psychological counseling.

COSTS & FINANCIAL AID
Costs (2015–16) ***Comprehensive fee:*** $13,440 includes full-time tuition ($11,300), mandatory fees ($550), and room and board ($1590). Part-time tuition: $942 per credit. ***College room only:*** $1390. Room and board charges vary according to board plan and housing facility. ***Waivers:*** employees or children of employees.

Financial Aid ***Average indebtedness upon graduation:*** $3950.

APPLYING
Standardized Tests *Required for some:* TOEFL, IELTS, or ESOL for students whose primary language is not English. *Recommended:* SAT (for admission), SAT or ACT (for admission).

Options: electronic application, early admission, deferred entrance.

Application fee: $25.

Required: essay or personal statement, high school transcript, minimum 3.0 GPA, 2 letters of recommendation.

Application deadlines: 6/1 (freshmen), 6/1 (transfers).

CONTACT
Ms. Boriana Shalyavska, Director of Admissions, American University in Bulgaria, 1 Izmirliev Square 1st floor, Blagoevgrad 2700, Bulgaria. *Phone:* 359-73 888 111. *Fax:* 359-73 883 227. *E-mail:* admissions@aubg.edu.

EGYPT

The American University in Cairo

Cairo, Egypt

http://www.aucegypt.edu/

- **Independent** comprehensive, founded 1919
- **Suburban** 260-acre campus with easy access to Cairo
- **Endowment** $595.2 million
- **Coed** 5,715 undergraduate students, 90% full-time, 53% women, 47% men
- **Very difficult** entrance level, 51% of applicants were admitted

UNDERGRAD STUDENTS
5,141 full-time, 574 part-time. Students come from 38 other countries; 0.8% transferred in; 8% live on campus.

Freshmen
Admission: 3,042 applied, 1,559 admitted, 1,139 enrolled. ***Test scores:*** SAT critical reading scores over 500: 36%; SAT math scores over 500: 93%; SAT writing scores over 500: 85%; SAT critical reading scores over 600: 8%; SAT math scores over 600: 53%; SAT writing scores over 600: 32%; SAT critical reading scores over 700: 2%; SAT math scores over 700: 14%; SAT writing scores over 700: 6%.

Retention: 94% of full-time freshmen returned.

FACULTY
Total: 747, 60% full-time, 71% with terminal degrees.

Student/faculty ratio: 12:1.

ACADEMICS
Calendar: semesters. *Degrees:* diplomas, bachelor's, master's, and doctoral (majority of students are Egyptians; enrollment open to all nationalities).

Special study options: academic remediation for entering students, cooperative education, double majors, English as a second language, honors programs, independent study, internships, services for LD students, study abroad, summer session for credit.

Computers: 120 computers/terminals are available on campus for general student use. Students can access the following: campus intranet, computer help desk, free student e-mail accounts, online (class) grades, online (class) registration, online (class) schedules, Blackboard, on-line unofficial transcripts, ID creation. Campuswide network is available. 100% of college-owned or -operated housing units are wired for high-speed Internet access. Wireless service is available via entire campus.

STUDENT LIFE
Housing options: men-only, women-only, special housing for students with disabilities. Campus housing is university owned and leased by the school. Freshman applicants given priority for college housing.

Activities and organizations: drama/theater group, student-run newspaper, choral group.

Athletics ***Intercollegiate sports:*** archery M, badminton M/W, basketball M/W, crew M/W, fencing M/W, gymnastics M/W, soccer M/W, squash M/W, swimming and diving M/W, table tennis M/W, tennis M/W, track and field M/W, volleyball M/W, water polo M. ***Intramural sports:*** basketball M/W, soccer M/W, squash M/W, table tennis M/W, tennis M/W, volleyball M/W, weight lifting M.

Campus security: 24-hour emergency response devices and patrols, controlled dormitory access.

Student services: health clinic, personal/psychological counseling.

FINANCIAL AID
Financial Aid ***Average financial aid package:*** $3615. ***Average need-based gift aid:*** $2881. ***Financial aid deadline:*** 9/15.

APPLYING
Standardized Tests *Required for some:* SAT (for admission), SAT or ACT (for admission), SAT Subject Tests (for admission).

Options: electronic application, early admission, early action, deferred entrance.

Application fee: $50.

Required: essay or personal statement, high school transcript, minimum 2.0 GPA. ***Required for some:*** TOEFL/IELTS tests are required for all students for placement.

Application deadlines: 5/15 (freshmen), 5/15 (transfers), 5/1 (early action).

Notification: continuous (freshmen), continuous (transfers), rolling (early action).

CONTACT
Ms. Randa Kamel, Executive Director of Enrollment, The American University in Cairo, AUC Avenue, PO Box 74 New Cairo 11835, Cairo, Egypt. *Phone:* 202-26154601. *E-mail:* randakamel@aucegypt.edu.

FRANCE

The American University of Paris

Paris, France

http://www.aup.edu/

- **Independent** comprehensive, founded 1962
- **Urban** campus
- **Coed** 697 undergraduate students, 90% full-time, 68% women, 32% men
- **Moderately difficult** entrance level, 81% of applicants were admitted

UNDERGRAD STUDENTS
626 full-time, 71 part-time. Students come from 34 states and territories; 93 other countries; 7% transferred in; 60% live on campus.

Freshmen
Admission: 2,294 applied, 1,862 admitted, 135 enrolled.

Retention: 76% of full-time freshmen returned.

FACULTY
Total: 144, 54% full-time, 72% with terminal degrees.

Student/faculty ratio: 10:1.

ACADEMICS
Calendar: semesters. *Degrees:* bachelor's and master's.

Special study options: advanced placement credit, double majors, English as a second language, honors programs, independent study, internships, off-campus study, part-time degree program, student-designed majors, study abroad, summer session for credit.

Computers: 172 computers/terminals are available on campus for general student use. Students can access the following: campus intranet, computer help desk, free student e-mail accounts, online (class) grades, online (class) registration, online (class) schedules. Campuswide network is available. Wireless service is available via entire campus.

STUDENT LIFE
Housing options: college housing not availableCampus housing is provided by a third party.

Activities and organizations: drama/theater group, student-run newspaper, television station, choral group, AUP Student Media (ASM) - Print, Video, Audio, White Mask (Theatre), Student Government Association, Environmental and Community Services Committee, Sports Association.

Athletics ***Intercollegiate sports:*** equestrian sports M/W, soccer M, volleyball W. ***Intramural sports:*** basketball M/W, cheerleading M/W, equestrian sports M/W, football M/W, volleyball M/W, wrestling M/W.

Campus security: 24-hour emergency response devices.

Student services: personal/psychological counseling.

COSTS & FINANCIAL AID
Costs (2015–16) ***Comprehensive fee:*** $37,985 includes full-time tuition ($27,220), mandatory fees ($1225), and room and board ($9540). Full-time tuition and fees vary according to degree level. Part-time tuition and fees vary according to course load and degree level. ***College room only:*** $7200. Room and board charges vary according to housing facility. ***Payment plan:*** installment. ***Waivers:*** children of alumni and employees or children of employees.

Financial Aid Of all full-time matriculated undergraduates who enrolled in 2014, 210 applied for aid, 200 were judged to have need, 13 had their need fully met. In 2014, 246 non-need-based awards were made. ***Average percent of need met:*** 20. ***Average financial aid package:*** $14,228. ***Average need-based gift aid:*** $7114. ***Average non-need-based aid:*** $1671.

APPLYING
Standardized Tests *Required for some:* SAT or ACT (for admission), TOEFL, TOEIC or IELTS for students whose primary language is not English.

Options: electronic application, deferred entrance.

Application fee: $70.

Required: essay or personal statement, high school transcript, 2 letters of recommendation. ***Recommended:*** minimum 3.0 GPA, interview.

Application deadlines: 3/15 (freshmen), 3/15 (transfers).

Notification: continuous (freshmen), continuous (transfers).

CONTACT
International Admissions Office Counselors, The American University of Paris, 6 rue du Colonel Combes, Paris 75007, France. *Phone:* -+33 1 40 62 07 20. *Fax:* +33 1 47 05 34 32. *E-mail:* admissions@aup.edu.

Paris College of Art

Paris, France

http://www.paris.edu/

- **Independent** comprehensive
- **Urban** 1-hectare campus with easy access to Paris - Ile de France (France)
- **Coed** 192 undergraduate students, 100% full-time, 83% women, 17% men

UNDERGRAD STUDENTS
192 full-time. Students come from 28 states and territories; 51 other countries; 100% are from out of state; 4% transferred in.

Freshmen
Admission: 34 enrolled.

Retention: 74% of full-time freshmen returned.

FACULTY
Total: 95, 24% with terminal degrees.

Student/faculty ratio: 4:1.

ACADEMICS
Degrees: certificates, bachelor's, and master's.

Special study options: academic remediation for entering students, accelerated degree program, adult/continuing education programs, cooperative education, English as a second language, independent study, internships, part-time degree program, services for LD students, study abroad, summer session for credit.

Computers: 20 computers/terminals are available on campus for general student use. Students can access the following: campus intranet, computer help desk, free student e-mail accounts, online (class) grades, online (class) schedules. Campuswide network is available. Wireless service is available via entire campus.

STUDENT LIFE
Housing options: college housing not available.

Activities and organizations: Student Council.

Campus security: electronically operated campus entrance.

Student services: personal/psychological counseling.

COSTS & FINANCIAL AID
Costs (2015–16) ***Tuition:*** 26,700 euros full-time, 1116 euros per credit hour part-time. Part-time tuition and fees vary according to course load. ***Required fees:*** 215 euros full-time, 1116 euros per credit part-time. ***Payment plan:*** installment.

Financial Aid Of all full-time matriculated undergraduates who enrolled in 2010, 46 applied for aid, 41 were judged to have need. 40 state and other part-time jobs (averaging $2300). In 2010, 14 non-need-based awards were made. ***Average percent of need met:*** 75. ***Average financial aid package:*** $11,500. ***Average need-based gift aid:*** $8600. ***Average non-need-based aid:*** $4200. ***Financial aid deadline:*** 8/1.

APPLYING
Standardized Tests *Required for some:* SAT or ACT (for admission).

Required: essay or personal statement, high school transcript, minimum 2.0 GPA, interview, portfolio / design essay / TOEFL / IELTS / SAT / ACT / university transcript. ***Required for some:*** 2 letters of recommendation.

CONTACT
Paris College of Art, 75010 Paris. *Phone:* 33-(0) 1.45.77.19.99 Ext. 1117.

Schiller International University

Paris, France

http://www.schiller.edu/

- **Independent** comprehensive, founded 1967, part of Schiller International University
- **Urban** campus
- **Coed**
- **Minimally difficult** entrance level

FACULTY
Student/faculty ratio: 4:1.

ACADEMICS
Calendar: semesters. *Degrees:* associate, bachelor's, and master's.

STUDENT LIFE
Housing options: college housing not available.

Activities and organizations: student-run newspaper, student government, student newspaper, yearbook.

Student services: personal/psychological counseling.

COSTS & FINANCIAL AID
Costs (2014–15) ***Tuition:*** 7080 euros full-time, 1770 euros per course part-time. Full-time tuition and fees vary according to degree level. Part-time tuition and fees vary according to degree level. ***Required fees:*** 14,160 euros full-time.

Financial Aid ***Financial aid deadline:*** 6/1.

APPLYING
Options: electronic application, deferred entrance.

Application fee: 65 euros.

Required: essay or personal statement, high school transcript. ***Recommended:*** minimum 2.0 GPA, interview.

CONTACT
Schiller International University, 9 rue d'Yvart, F-75015 Paris, France. *Toll-free phone:* 800-261-9571 (in-state); 800-261-9751 (out-of-state).

GREECE

American College of Thessaloniki

Pylea-Thessaloniki, Greece

http://www.act.edu/

- **Independent** comprehensive, founded 1886
- **Suburban** 40-acre campus with easy access to Thessaloniki
- **Endowment** $4.6 million
- **Coed** 503 undergraduate students, 89% full-time, 55% women, 45% men
- **Minimally difficult** entrance level, 92% of applicants were admitted

UNDERGRAD STUDENTS
449 full-time, 54 part-time. Students come from 21 other countries; 0.8% transferred in; 28% live on campus.

Freshmen
Admission: 77 applied, 71 admitted, 51 enrolled. ***Average high school GPA:*** 3.

Retention: 71% of full-time freshmen returned.

FACULTY
Total: 54, 24% full-time, 50% with terminal degrees.

Student/faculty ratio: 15:1.

ACADEMICS
Calendar: semesters. *Degrees:* certificates, bachelor's, and master's.

Special study options: academic remediation for entering students, accelerated degree program, advanced placement credit, double majors, English as a second language, honors programs, independent study, internships, part-time degree program, services for LD students, study abroad, summer session for credit.

Computers: 137 computers/terminals and 19 ports are available on campus for general student use. Students can access the following: campus intranet, computer help desk, free student e-mail accounts, online (class) grades, online (class) schedules, remote access to library resources. Campuswide network is available. 100% of college-owned or -operated housing units are wired for high-speed Internet access. Wireless service is available via classrooms, computer centers, learning centers, libraries, student centers.

STUDENT LIFE
Housing options: coed. Campus housing is university owned and leased by the school. Freshman applicants given priority for college housing.

Activities and organizations: student-run newspaper, radio station, ACT Radio Station, Newspaper Club, ACT Diplomat's Society, Tennis Club, Astronomy Club.

Athletics ***Intercollegiate sports:*** soccer M, table tennis M/W, tennis M/W, volleyball M/W. ***Intramural sports:*** basketball M/W, sailing M/W, soccer M, table tennis M/W, tennis M/W, volleyball M/W.

Campus security: 24-hour emergency response devices and patrols.

Student services: personal/psychological counseling.

COSTS
Costs (2015–16) ***Tuition:*** $8250 full-time, $275 per contact hour part-time. Part-time tuition and fees vary according to course load. US Study Abroad students (tuition: $5,340/semester; fees: $2,140/semester), plus housing. ***Required fees:*** $100 full-time. ***Room only:*** $5100. Room and board charges vary according to housing facility. ***Waivers:*** employees or children of employees.

APPLYING
Standardized Tests *Recommended:* SAT (for admission).

Options: electronic application, deferred entrance.

Application fee: 95 euros.

Required: high school transcript, proficiency in English, CV. ***Required for some:*** essay or personal statement, interview. ***Recommended:*** minimum 2.0 GPA.

Application deadlines: rolling (freshmen), rolling (transfers).

Notification: continuous (freshmen), continuous (transfers).

CONTACT
Mrs. Roula Lebetli, Director of Admissions, American College of Thessaloniki, PO Box 21021, Pylea, Thessaloniki 55510, Greece. *Phone:* +30-2310-398239. *Fax:* +30-2310-398389. *E-mail:* admissions@act.edu.

DEREE - The American College of Greece

Athens, Greece

http://www.acg.edu/

- **Independent** comprehensive, founded 1875
- **Suburban** 64-acre campus with easy access to Athens
- **Coed** 2,612 undergraduate students, 42% full-time, 51% women, 49% men
- **Moderately difficult** entrance level, 69% of applicants were admitted

UNDERGRAD STUDENTS
1,099 full-time, 1,513 part-time. Students come from 64 other countries; 4% live on campus.

Freshmen
Admission: 1,005 applied, 694 admitted. ***Average high school GPA:*** 2.8. ***Retention:*** 84% of full-time freshmen returned.

FACULTY
Total: 206, 61% full-time, 54% with terminal degrees.

Student/faculty ratio: 13:1.

ACADEMICS
Calendar: 4-1-4. *Degrees:* bachelor's, master's, and postbachelor's certificates.

Special study options: academic remediation for entering students, accelerated degree program, adult/continuing education programs, advanced placement credit, double majors, English as a second language, honors programs, independent study, internships, part-time degree program, services for LD students, student-designed majors, study abroad, summer session for credit.

Computers: 307 computers/terminals are available on campus for general student use. Students can access the following: computer help desk, free student e-mail accounts, online (class) grades, online (class) registration, online (class) schedules, Blackboard LMS. Campuswide network is available. 100% of college-owned or -operated housing units are wired for high-speed Internet access. Wireless service is available via computer centers, computer labs, dorm rooms, learning centers, libraries.

STUDENT LIFE
Housing options: coed, special housing for students with disabilities. Campus housing is university owned. Freshman applicants given priority for college housing.

Activities and organizations: drama/theater group, choral group, DEREE SAB (Student Activities Board), DEREE Orientation Leaders, DEREE Ambassadors, Debate Club, AFCEA.

Athletics ***Intercollegiate sports:*** basketball M/W(s), rugby M, soccer M/W, volleyball W(s), water polo M. ***Intramural sports:*** archery M/W, basketball M/W, rock climbing M/W, soccer M/W, swimming and diving M/W, table tennis M/W, tennis M/W, track and field M/W, volleyball M/W.

Campus security: 24-hour emergency response devices and patrols, controlled dormitory access.

Student services: health clinic, personal/psychological counseling.

COSTS & FINANCIAL AID
Costs (2014–15) ***One-time required fee:*** $125. ***Tuition:*** $9330 full-time, $320 per credit hour part-time. Full-time tuition and fees vary according to course load. Part-time tuition and fees vary according to course load. No tuition increase for student's term of enrollment. ***Room only:*** Room and board charges vary according to housing facility. ***Payment plan:*** installment. ***Waivers:*** employees or children of employees.

Financial Aid ***Financial aid deadline:*** 9/1.

APPLYING
Standardized Tests *Recommended:* SAT or ACT (for admission).

Options: electronic application, deferred entrance.

Required: essay or personal statement, high school transcript, minimum 2.0 GPA, 1 letter of recommendation, interview.

Application deadlines: rolling (freshmen), rolling (transfers).

Notification: 7/25 (freshmen), 7/25 (transfers).

CONTACT
Ms. Loukia Kanatsouli, Dean of Enrollment and International Students, DEREE - The American College of Greece, 6 Gravias Street, Aghia Paraskevi, Athens 15342, Greece. *Phone:* +30-210-600-9800 Ext. 1474. *Fax:* +30-210-608-2344. *E-mail:* lkanatsouli@acg.edu.

ITALY

The American University of Rome

Rome, Italy

http://www.aur.edu/

- **Independent** comprehensive, founded 1969
- **Urban** 1-acre campus
- **Endowment** $1.4 million
- **Coed** 441 undergraduate students, 100% full-time, 67% women, 33% men
- **Moderately difficult** entrance level, 100% of applicants were admitted

UNDERGRAD STUDENTS
441 full-time. Students come from 41 states and territories; 52 other countries; 5% transferred in; 55% live on campus.

Freshmen
Admission: 126 applied, 126 admitted, 38 enrolled. ***Average high school GPA:*** 3. ***Test scores:*** SAT critical reading scores over 500: 75%; SAT math scores over 500: 75%; SAT writing scores over 500: 50%; ACT scores over 18: 82%; SAT critical reading scores over 600: 25%; ACT scores over 24: 46%; ACT scores over 30: 28%.

Retention: 65% of full-time freshmen returned.

FACULTY
Total: 68, 15% full-time, 56% with terminal degrees.

Student/faculty ratio: 15:1.

ACADEMICS
Calendar: semesters. *Degrees:* associate, bachelor's, and master's.

Special study options: academic remediation for entering students, advanced placement credit, double majors, English as a second language, independent study, internships, off-campus study, part-time degree program, services for LD students, student-designed majors, study abroad, summer session for credit.

Computers: 68 computers/terminals and 80 ports are available on campus for general student use. Students can access the following: campus intranet, computer help desk, free student e-mail accounts, online (class) grades, online (class) registration, online (class) schedules, Learning Management System. Campuswide network is available. 100% of college-owned or -operated housing units are wired for high-speed Internet access. Wireless service is available via entire campus.

STUDENT LIFE
Housing options: men-only, women-only. Campus housing is provided by a third party. Freshman applicants given priority for college housing.

Activities and organizations: drama/theater group, student-run newspaper, choral group, student government, Community Services, Men and Female soccer teams, Business Club, International Relations Club.

Athletics ***Intercollegiate sports:*** soccer M/W, volleyball M/W. ***Intramural sports:*** basketball M, cross-country running M/W, gymnastics M/W, tennis M/W.

Campus security: 24-hour emergency response devices, security guards during opening hours and 24-hour surveillance cameras.

Student services: health clinic, personal/psychological counseling.

COSTS
Costs (2015–16) ***Comprehensive fee:*** 22,546 euros includes full-time tuition (17,500 euros), mandatory fees (394 euros), and room and board (4652 euros). Full-time tuition and fees vary according to course load and degree level. Part-time tuition: 2188 euros per course. Part-time tuition and fees vary according to course load and degree level. ***Required fees:*** 394 euros per year part-time. ***College room only:*** 3800 euros. ***Payment plan:*** installment. ***Waivers:*** employees or children of employees.

APPLYING
Standardized Tests *Recommended:* SAT or ACT (for admission).

Options: electronic application, deferred entrance.

Application fee: $75.

Required: essay or personal statement, high school transcript, minimum 2.5 GPA, 1 letter of recommendation, interview, TOEFL or IELTS for non-English high school students.

Application deadlines: rolling (freshmen), rolling (transfers).

Notification: continuous (freshmen), continuous (transfers).

CONTACT
Ms. Jessica York, Admissions Counselor, The American University of Rome, Via Pietro Roselli 4, Rome 00153, Italy. *Phone:* -+39 0658330919. *Toll-free phone:* 877-592-1287. *Fax:* +39 0658330992. *E-mail:* admissions@aur.edu.

★ John Cabot University
Rome, Italy
http://www.johncabot.edu/

- **Independent** 4-year, founded 1972
- **Urban** campus with easy access to Rome
- **Coed** 1,274 undergraduate students, 100% full-time, 66% women, 34% men

UNDERGRAD STUDENTS
1,274 full-time. Students come from 46 states and territories; 76 other countries; 0.7% transferred in; 46% live on campus.

Freshmen
Admission: 148 enrolled. ***Average high school GPA:*** 3.1.
Retention: 87% of full-time freshmen returned.

FACULTY
Total: 109, 19% full-time, 61% with terminal degrees.
Student/faculty ratio: 9:1.

ACADEMICS
Calendar: semesters. *Degrees:* associate and bachelor's.
Special study options: advanced placement credit, cooperative education, double majors, English as a second language, freshman honors college, honors programs, independent study, internships, off-campus study, part-time degree program, services for LD students, study abroad, summer session for credit.
Computers: 80 computers/terminals are available on campus for general student use. Students can access the following: campus intranet, computer help desk, free student e-mail accounts, online (class) grades, online (class) registration, online (class) schedules, wireless connection across campus. Campuswide network is available. Wireless service is available via entire campus.

STUDENT LIFE
Housing options: coed, men-only, women-only. Campus housing is leased by the school. Freshman campus housing is guaranteed.
Activities and organizations: drama/theater group, student-run newspaper, Business Club, Model United Nations, Student Government, Universities Fighting World Hunger, Stand.
Athletics *Intercollegiate sports:* basketball M/W, soccer M/W, volleyball M/W. ***Intramural sports:*** basketball M/W, cheerleading M/W, cross-country running M/W, sailing M/W, skiing (downhill) M/W, soccer M/W, swimming and diving M/W, tennis M/W, volleyball M/W, weight lifting M/W.
Campus security: 24-hour emergency response devices, controlled dormitory access.
Student services: health clinic, personal/psychological counseling.

COSTS
Costs (2015–16) *Comprehensive fee:* $33,500 includes full-time tuition ($23,900) and room and board ($9600). Full-time tuition and fees vary according to course load. Part-time tuition and fees vary according to course load. ***Room and board:*** Room and board charges vary according to board plan and housing facility. ***Payment plan:*** installment. ***Waivers:*** employees or children of employees.

APPLYING
Standardized Tests *Required for some:* SAT or ACT (for admission).
Required: essay or personal statement, high school transcript, 2 letters of recommendation, interview. ***Recommended:*** minimum 2.7 GPA, interview.

CONTACT
Ms. Nadia Spagnoli, Associate Coordinator of Admissions, John Cabot University, Via della Lungara 233, Roma 00165, Italy. *Phone:* 855-528-7662. *Toll-free phone:* 855-528-7662. *E-mail:* admissions@johncabot.edu.

See previous page for display ad and page 1480 for the College Close-Up.

LEBANON

American University of Beirut

Beirut, Lebanon

http://www.aub.edu.lb/

- **Independent** university, founded 1866
- **Urban** 61-acre campus with easy access to Beirut
- **Endowment** $549.5 million
- **Coed** 6,838 undergraduate students, 96% full-time, 50% women, 50% men
- 65% of applicants were admitted

UNDERGRAD STUDENTS
6,565 full-time, 273 part-time. Students come from 74 other countries; 0.4% transferred in; 16% live on campus.

Freshmen
Admission: 5,146 applied, 3,338 admitted, 1,769 enrolled. ***Average high school GPA:*** 2.79. ***Test scores:*** SAT critical reading scores over 500: 44%; SAT math scores over 500: 95%; SAT writing scores over 500: 58%; SAT critical reading scores over 600: 10%; SAT math scores over 600: 71%; SAT writing scores over 600: 14%; SAT critical reading scores over 700: 1%; SAT math scores over 700: 24%; SAT writing scores over 700: 1%.
Retention: 91% of full-time freshmen returned.

FACULTY
Total: 857, 65% full-time, 57% with terminal degrees.
Student/faculty ratio: 12:1.

ACADEMICS
Calendar: semesters. *Degrees:* certificates, diplomas, bachelor's, master's, doctoral, and postbachelor's certificates.
Special study options: academic remediation for entering students, advanced placement credit, double majors, English as a second language, honors programs, independent study, internships, services for LD students, study abroad, summer session for credit.
Computers: 1,863 computers/terminals and 1,320 ports are available on campus for general student use. Students can access the following: campus intranet, computer help desk, free student e-mail accounts, online (class) grades, online (class) registration, online (class) schedules. Campuswide network is available. 100% of college-owned or -operated housing units are wired for high-speed Internet access. Wireless service is available via entire campus.

STUDENT LIFE
Housing options: on-campus residence required for freshman year; men-only, women-only. Campus housing is university owned. Freshman campus housing is guaranteed.
Activities and organizations: drama/theater group, student-run newspaper, choral group, Red Cross Club, Biology Society, Business Society, Music Club, Palestinian Cultural Club.
Athletics *Intercollegiate sports:* basketball M/W, cheerleading W, cross-country running M/W, football M, gymnastics M, rugby M, skiing (downhill) M/W, soccer M/W, squash M/W, swimming and diving M/W, table tennis M/W, tennis M/W, track and field M/W, volleyball M/W, water polo M. ***Intramural sports:*** basketball M/W, cross-country running M/W, gymnastics M, lacrosse M/W, racquetball M/W, soccer M/W, squash M/W, swimming and diving M/W, table tennis M/W, tennis M/W, volleyball M/W, weight lifting M/W.
Campus security: 24-hour emergency response devices and patrols, late-night transport/escort service, staff monitors entrance 24/7.
Student services: health clinic, personal/psychological counseling, legal services.

COSTS & FINANCIAL AID
Costs (2014–15) *Tuition:* $19,680 full-time, $656 per credit part-time. Full-time tuition and fees vary according to course load, degree level, program, and student level. Part-time tuition and fees vary according to course load, degree level, program, and student level. ***Required fees:*** $692 full-time. ***Room only:*** $2652. Room and board charges vary according to housing facility and location. ***Payment plan:*** deferred payment. ***Waivers:*** employees or children of employees.
Financial Aid Of all full-time matriculated undergraduates who enrolled in 2013, 3,604 applied for aid, 2,945 were judged to have need. 32 state and other part-time jobs (averaging $1350). In 2013, 37 non-need-based awards were made. ***Average financial aid package:*** $8714. ***Average need-based loan:*** $5347. ***Average need-based gift aid:*** $8561. ***Average non-need-based aid:*** $20,894. ***Average indebtedness upon graduation:*** $4749. ***Financial aid deadline:*** 12/19.

APPLYING
Standardized Tests *Required:* SAT (for admission). *Required for some:* SAT Subject Tests (for admission).
Options: electronic application, early admission, early action, deferred entrance.
Application fee: $80.

Required: high school transcript. ***Required for some:*** 2 letters of recommendation, interview, TOEFL for international applicants. ***Recommended:*** essay or personal statement.

Application deadlines: 12/20 (freshmen), 4/30 (transfers), 11/30 (early action).

Notification: 3/30 (freshmen), continuous until 6/30 (transfers), 1/31 (early action).

CONTACT
Dr. Salim Kanaan, Director of Admissions Office, American University of Beirut, PO Box 11-0236, Riad El-Solh, 1107 2020, Lebanon. *Phone:* -961 1-374 374 Ext. 2592. *Fax:* 961 1-750 775. *E-mail:* admissions@aub.edu.lb.

Lebanese American University
Beirut, Lebanon
http://www.lau.edu.lb/

- **Private** comprehensive, founded 1835
- **Urban** 50-acre campus with easy access to Beirut Campus: Beirut/Byblos Campus:Byblos,Tripoli
- **Endowment** $401.1 million
- **Coed** 7,463 undergraduate students, 94% full-time, 49% women, 51% men
- **Moderately difficult** entrance level, 87% of applicants were admitted

UNDERGRAD STUDENTS
7,006 full-time, 457 part-time. Students come from 80 other countries; 20% are from out of state; 1% transferred in; 8% live on campus.

Freshmen
Admission: 4,074 applied, 3,548 admitted, 1,761 enrolled. ***Average high school GPA:*** 2.73. ***Test scores:*** SAT critical reading scores over 500: 17%; SAT math scores over 500: 78%; SAT writing scores over 500: 69%; SAT critical reading scores over 600: 3%; SAT math scores over 600: 38%; SAT writing scores over 600: 20%; SAT math scores over 700: 7%; SAT writing scores over 700: 1%.

Retention: 89% of full-time freshmen returned.

FACULTY
Total: 765, 38% full-time, 43% with terminal degrees.

Student/faculty ratio: 17:1.

ACADEMICS
Degrees: bachelor's, master's, doctoral, and postbachelor's certificates.

Special study options: academic remediation for entering students, English as a second language, internships, part-time degree program, services for LD students, study abroad, summer session for credit.

Computers: 1,227 computers/terminals and 2,200 ports are available on campus for general student use. Students can access the following: campus intranet, computer help desk, free student e-mail accounts, online (class) grades, online (class) registration, online (class) schedules, online library book reservation; Online forms requests (grades, diplomas, etc.); Online and Mobile course management system (Blackboard) Mobile Access to grades and schedules also available on smart devices. Campuswide network is available. 100% of college-owned or -operated housing units are wired for high-speed Internet access. Wireless service is available via entire campus.

STUDENT LIFE
Housing options: men-only, women-only, special housing for students with disabilities. Campus housing is university owned, leased by the school and is provided by a third party.

Activities and organizations: drama/theater group, student-run newspaper, choral group, Model United Nations, Safety & Awareness Club, UNESCO Club, Event Organization Club, Red Cross Club.

Athletics ***Intercollegiate sports:*** badminton M/W, basketball M(s)/W(s), rugby M(s), skiing (downhill) M/W, soccer M(s)/W(s), swimming and diving M(s)/W(s), table tennis M(s)/W(s), tennis M(s)/W(s), track and field M(s)/W(s), volleyball M(s)/W(s), water polo M. ***Intramural sports:*** basketball M/W, soccer M/W, swimming and diving M/W, table tennis M/W, tennis M/W, volleyball M/W.

Campus security: 24-hour emergency response devices and patrols, 24/7 security at Residence Halls.

Student services: health clinic, personal/psychological counseling, women's center.

COSTS
Costs (2014–15) ***Tuition:*** $15,200 full-time. Full-time tuition and fees vary according to course load, degree level, and program. Part-time tuition and fees vary according to course load, degree level, and program. ***Required fees:*** $528 full-time, $632 per credit hour part-time. ***Room only:*** $6114. Room and board charges vary according to housing facility and location. ***Payment plans:*** installment, deferred payment. ***Waivers:*** employees or children of employees.

APPLYING
Standardized Tests *Required:* SAT (for admission). *Required for some:* SAT Subject Tests (for admission), Institutional English Test (English Entrance Exam EEE) or International TOFEL.

Options: electronic application, early admission, early action, deferred entrance.

Application fee: $60.

Required: high school transcript, minimum 2.0 GPA, official high school diploma, SAT I, Institutional English Test (English Entrance Exam EEE) or International TOFEL or SAT Writing.

Application deadlines: 7/31 (freshmen), 7/31 (out-of-state freshmen), 7/31 (transfers), 12/31 (early action).

Notification: continuous until 3/1 (freshmen), continuous until 3/1 (out-of-state freshmen), continuous until 3/1 (transfers), 3/1 (early action).

CONTACT
Miss Nada Hajj, Director of Admissions, Lebanese American University, PO Box 13-5053 Chouran Beirut 1102 2801, Lebanon, Beirut, Lebanon. *Phone:* 961-1786456 Ext. 1111. *Fax:* 961-1786456. *E-mail:* nhajj@lau.edu.lb.

MEXICO

Alliant International University–México City
Mexico City, Mexico
http://www.alliantmexico.com/

- **Independent** comprehensive, founded 1970, part of Alliant International University
- **Urban** campus with easy access to Mexico City
- **Coed**
- **Moderately difficult** entrance level

FACULTY
Student/faculty ratio: 12:1.

ACADEMICS
Calendar: semesters. *Degrees:* bachelor's and master's.

STUDENT LIFE
Housing options: college housing not available.

Activities and organizations: student-run newspaper, International Business Club, German Club, Student Council.

COSTS
Costs (2014–15) ***Tuition:*** $8784 full-time, $350 per credit part-time. ***Required fees:*** $846 full-time, $180 per term part-time.

APPLYING
Standardized Tests *Recommended:* SAT or ACT (for admission).

Options: electronic application, deferred entrance.

Application fee: 500 Mexican pesos.

Required: essay or personal statement, high school transcript, minimum 2.0 GPA, 1 letter of recommendation. ***Required for some:*** interview. ***Recommended:*** minimum 3.0 GPA.

CONTACT
Alliant International University–México City, Hamburgo #115, Col. Juarez, Mexico D.F. 06600, Mexico. *Phone:* -52 5555257651. *E-mail:* mexicoadmissions@alliant.edu.

SPAIN

Saint Louis University–Madrid Campus

Madrid, Spain

http://spain.slu.edu/

- **Independent Roman Catholic (Jesuit)** comprehensive
- **Urban** 1-acre campus with easy access to Madrid, Spain
- **Coed**
- **Moderately difficult** entrance level

FACULTY
Student/faculty ratio: 7:1.

ACADEMICS
Calendar: semesters. *Degrees:* bachelor's and master's.

STUDENT LIFE
Housing options: men-only, women-only. Campus housing is provided by a third party. Freshman campus housing is guaranteed.
Activities and organizations: drama/theater group, student-run newspaper, choral group, student government, Campus Ambassadors, Student Magazine, Theatre Club, Babel Language Exchange.
Campus security: 24-hour emergency response devices.
Student services: personal/psychological counseling.

COSTS
Costs (2014–15) ***One-time required fee:*** 200 euros. ***Comprehensive fee:*** 24,840 euros includes full-time tuition (18,000 euros) and room and board (6840 euros). Part-time tuition: 775 euros per credit. Part-time tuition and fees vary according to course load and degree level. ***Room and board:*** Room and board charges vary according to board plan.

APPLYING
Standardized Tests *Required for some:* SAT or ACT (for admission), IB, A-Levels, French Baccalaureate, Selectividad, Maturita, Abitur, etc., depending on each educational system.
Options: electronic application, deferred entrance.
Required: essay or personal statement, high school transcript, Minimum English Level. ***Recommended:*** 2 letters of recommendation.

CONTACT
Ms. Maria-Jose Morell, Director of Enrollment Management, Saint Louis University–Madrid Campus, Avenida del Valle, 34, Madrid 28003, Spain. *Phone:* -34 91-554-5858. *Fax:* 34 91-554-6202. *E-mail:* mmorell@slu.edu.

SWITZERLAND

★ Franklin University Switzerland

Sorengo, Switzerland

http://www.fus.edu/

- **Independent** comprehensive, founded 1969
- **Suburban** 7-acre campus with easy access to Milan, Italy
- **Endowment** $941,230
- **Coed**
- **Moderately difficult** entrance level

FACULTY
Student/faculty ratio: 12:1.

ACADEMICS
Calendar: semesters. *Degrees:* associate, bachelor's, and master's.

STUDENT LIFE
Housing options: on-campus residence required through sophomore year; coed, women-only. Campus housing is university owned and leased by the school. Freshman campus housing is guaranteed.
Activities and organizations: drama/theater group, student-run newspaper, Student Government Association, Newspaper, Literary Society, Drama Club, Peer Educators Program.

Campus security: 24-hour emergency response devices, student patrols, late-night transport/escort service, controlled dormitory access, late night patrols by professional security service personnel.

Student services: health clinic, personal/psychological counseling.

FINANCIAL AID

Financial Aid Of all full-time matriculated undergraduates who enrolled in 2011, 192 applied for aid, 186 were judged to have need, 6 had their need fully met. In 2011, 91 non-need-based awards were made. ***Average percent of need met:*** 39. ***Average financial aid package:*** $21,653. ***Average need-based loan:*** $4125. ***Average need-based gift aid:*** $17,653. ***Average non-need-based aid:*** $9494. ***Financial aid deadline:*** 3/15.

APPLYING

Standardized Tests *Required:* SAT or ACT (for admission). *Recommended:* SAT Subject Tests (for admission).

Options: electronic application, early action, deferred entrance.

Application fee: $90.

Required: essay or personal statement, high school transcript, minimum 2.0 GPA, 3 letters of recommendation. ***Recommended:*** interview.

CONTACT

Peter Dorthe, Director of Admissions, Franklin University Switzerland, Franklin University Switzerland US Office, The Graybar Building, Suite 2746, 420 Lexington Avenue, New York, NY 10170. *Phone:* 212-922-9650. *Fax:* 212-922-9870. *E-mail:* Info@fc.edu.

See previous page for display ad and page 1452 for the College Close-Up.

UNITED ARAB EMIRATES

The American University in Dubai

Dubai, United Arab Emirates

http://www.aud.edu/

- **Proprietary** comprehensive, founded 1995
- **Urban** campus
- **Coed** 2,408 undergraduate students, 88% full-time, 50% women, 50% men
- 49% of applicants were admitted

UNDERGRAD STUDENTS

2,112 full-time, 296 part-time.

Freshmen

Admission: 1,523 applied, 746 admitted, 471 enrolled.

FACULTY

Total: 175, 61% full-time.

ACADEMICS

Calendar: semesters. *Degrees:* certificates, bachelor's, and master's.

Special study options: accelerated degree program, advanced placement credit, double majors, English as a second language, honors programs, independent study, internships, part-time degree program, services for LD students, study abroad, summer session for credit.

Computers: 864 computers/terminals are available on campus for general student use. Students can access the following: computer help desk, free student e-mail accounts, online (class) grades, online (class) registration, online (class) schedules. Campuswide network is available. 100% of college-owned or -operated housing units are wired for high-speed Internet access.

STUDENT LIFE

Housing options: men-only, women-only. Campus housing is university owned. Freshman campus housing is guaranteed.

Activities and organizations: drama/theater group, student-run newspaper, Student Government Association, Community Service Club, Drama Club, Music Club, Debate Club.

Athletics ***Intercollegiate sports:*** basketball M/W, soccer M/W, tennis M/W, volleyball M/W. ***Intramural sports:*** basketball M/W, football M/W, soccer M/W, swimming and diving M/W, table tennis M/W, tennis M/W, track and field M/W, volleyball M/W.

Campus security: 24-hour patrols.

Student services: health clinic, personal/psychological counseling.

APPLYING

Standardized Tests *Required for some:* SAT or ACT (for admission), SAT Subject Tests (for admission).

Options: early admission.

Application fee: 55 United Arab Emirates dirhams.

Required: high school transcript, minimum 2.0 GPA, 2 letters of recommendation. ***Recommended:*** essay or personal statement.

CONTACT

Mrs. Carol Maalouf, Director of Admissions, The American University in Dubai, PO Box 28282, Dubai, United Arab Emirates. *Phone:* -971 4 399 9000 Ext. 170. *Fax:* 971 4 399 8899. *E-mail:* admissions@aud.edu.

American University of Sharjah

Sharjah, United Arab Emirates

http://www.aus.edu/

- **Independent** comprehensive, founded 1997
- **Coed**
- 85% of applicants were admitted

FACULTY

Student/faculty ratio: 15:1.

ACADEMICS

Calendar: semesters. *Degrees:* bachelor's and master's.

STUDENT LIFE

Housing options: men-only, women-only. Campus housing is university owned.

Activities and organizations: drama/theater group, student-run newspaper, radio station, choral group.

Campus security: 24-hour patrols, controlled dormitory access.

Student services: health clinic, personal/psychological counseling, women's center.

COSTS

Costs (2014–15) ***Tuition:*** full-time. Full-time tuition and fees vary according to course load and program. Part-time tuition and fees vary according to course load and program. ***Required fees:*** full-time. ***Room only:*** Room and board charges vary according to gender.

APPLYING

Options: electronic application, early admission, early decision, deferred entrance.

Required: high school transcript.

CONTACT

American University of Sharjah, PO Box 26666, Sharjah, United Arab Emirates. *Phone:* -971 6 515-5555.

UNITED KINGDOM

Hult International Business School

London, United Kingdom

http://www.hult.edu/

- **Independent** comprehensive, founded 1975
- **Urban** campus with easy access to London
- **Coed** 930 undergraduate students, 100% full-time, 38% women, 62% men
- **Moderately difficult** entrance level, 43% of applicants were admitted

UNDERGRAD STUDENTS

930 full-time. Students come from 27 states and territories; 88 other countries.

Freshmen

Admission: 2,574 applied, 1,099 admitted, 467 enrolled. ***Average high school GPA:*** 3.1.

Retention: 92% of full-time freshmen returned.

FACULTY
Total: 70, 57% full-time, 26% with terminal degrees.
Student/faculty ratio: 13:1.

ACADEMICS
Calendar: semesters. *Degrees:* bachelor's and master's.
Special study options: academic remediation for entering students, accelerated degree program, advanced placement credit, English as a second language, honors programs, independent study, internships, services for LD students, study abroad, summer session for credit.
Computers: Students can access the following: campus intranet, computer help desk, free student e-mail accounts, online (class) grades, online (class) registration, online (class) schedules. Campuswide network is available. Wireless service is available via entire campus.

STUDENT LIFE
Housing options: on-campus residence required through sophomore year; coed. Freshman applicants given priority for college housing.
Activities and organizations: student-run newspaper, Language Caf, Model United Nations, International Law Society, Hult RISE (charity club), Consultancy Club.
Athletics ***Intercollegiate sports:*** basketball M/W, soccer M/W. ***Intramural sports:*** badminton M/W, cheerleading W, golf M/W, rugby M, skiing (downhill) M/W, swimming and diving M/W, table tennis M/W.
Campus security: 24-hour emergency response devices, controlled dormitory access.
Student services: personal/psychological counseling.

COSTS
Costs (2014–15) ***Tuition:*** $35,000 full-time. Full-time tuition and fees vary according to location. No tuition increase for student's term of enrollment. ***Room only:*** $11,240. Room and board charges vary according to housing facility and location. ***Payment plan:*** installment. ***Waivers:*** employees or children of employees.

APPLYING
Standardized Tests *Recommended:* SAT or ACT (for admission).
Options: electronic application.
Application fee: 75 British pounds.
Required: essay or personal statement, high school transcript, 2 letters of recommendation. ***Required for some:*** TOEFL, IELTS, or PTE for non-native English speakers. ***Recommended:*** interview.
Application deadlines: rolling (freshmen), rolling (transfers).
Notification: continuous (freshmen), continuous (transfers).

CONTACT
Mr. Niccolo Del Monte, Global Undergraduate Programs, Hult International Business School, 33-35 Commercial Rd, London E1 1LD, United Kingdom. *Phone:* -44 207 341 8555. *E-mail:* niccolo.delmonte@hult.edu.

★ Richmond, The American International University in London

Richmond, United Kingdom

http://www.richmond.ac.uk/

CONTACT
Mr. Nick Atkinson, Director of United States Admissions, Richmond, The American International University in London, 343 Congress Street, Suite 3100, Boston, MA 02210-1214. *Phone:* 617-450-5617. *Fax:* 617-450-5601. *E-mail:* us_admissions@richmond.ac.uk.
See below for display ad and page 1578 for the College Close-Up.

Other Colleges to Consider

Academy College
Bloomington, Minnesota
http://www.academycollege.edu/
Contact: Ms. Tracey Schantz, Director, Academy College, Bloomington, MN 55420. *Phone:* 952-851-0066. *Toll-free phone:* 800-292-9149. *Fax:* 952-851-0094. *E-mail:* admissions@academycollege.edu.

Alabama Agricultural and Mechanical University
Huntsville, Alabama
http://www.aamu.edu/
Contact: Dr. Evelyn Ellis, Interim Director of Admissions, Alabama Agricultural and Mechanical University, 4900 Meridian Street, Huntsville, AL 35811. *Phone:* 256-372-5245. *Toll-free phone:* 800-553-0816. *Fax:* 256-851-9747.

Alfred University
Alfred, New York
http://www.alfred.edu/
Contact: Mr. Corry D. Unis, Director of Admissions, Alfred University, Alumni Hall, Alfred, NY 14802-1205. *Phone:* 607-871-2115. *Toll-free phone:* 800-541-9229. *Fax:* 607-871-2198. *E-mail:* admissions@alfred.edu.

Allegheny Wesleyan College
Salem, Ohio
http://www.awc.edu/
Contact: Admissions Office, Allegheny Wesleyan College, 2161 Woodsdale Road, Salem, OH 44460. *Phone:* 330-337-6403. *Toll-free phone:* 800-292-3153. *E-mail:* college@awc.edu.

Allen University
Columbia, South Carolina
http://www.allenuniversity.edu/
Contact: Terri Parker, Director of Admission, Allen University, 1530 Harden Street, Columbia, SC 29204. *Phone:* 803-376-5733. *Toll-free phone:* 877-625-5368. *E-mail:* tparker@allenuniversity.edu.

Amberton University
Garland, Texas
http://www.amberton.edu/
Contact: Dr. Don Hebbard, Academic Dean, Amberton University, 1700 Eastgate Drive, Garland, TX 75041-5595. *Phone:* 972-279-6511. *E-mail:* advisor@amberton.edu.

American Indian College of the Assemblies of God, Inc.
Phoenix, Arizona
http://www.aicag.edu/
Contact: Sandra Gonzales, Director of Enrollment Management, American Indian College of the Assemblies of God, Inc., 10020 North Fifteenth Avenue, Phoenix, AZ 85021-2199. *Phone:* 602-944-3335 Ext. 226. *E-mail:* sgonzales@aicag.edu.

American InterContinental University Atlanta
Atlanta, Georgia
http://www.aiuniv.edu/
Contact: American InterContinental University Atlanta, 6600 Peachtree-Dunwoody Road, 500 Embassy Row, Atlanta, GA 30328. *Phone:* 877-564-6248. *Toll-free phone:* 800-353-1744. *Fax:* 877-564-6248.

American InterContinental University Houston
Houston, Texas
http://www.aiuniv.edu/
Contact: American InterContinental University Houston, 9999 Richmond Avenue, Houston, TX 77042. *Phone:* 877-564-6248. *Toll-free phone:* 888-607-9888.

American InterContinental University Online
Schaumburg, Illinois
http://www.aiuniv.edu/
Contact: Jennifer Ziegenmier, Senior Vice President of Admissions and Marketing, American InterContinental University Online, 231 N. Martingale Road, 6th Floor, Schaumburg, IL 60173. *Phone:* 877-564-6248. *Toll-free phone:* 877-701-3800. *E-mail:* jziegenmier@aiuonline.edu.

American National University
Danville, Virginia
http://www.national-college.edu/
Contact: Admissions Office, American National University, 336 Old Riverside Drive, Danville, VA 24541. *Phone:* 434-793-6822. *Toll-free phone:* 888-9-JOBREADY.

American National University
Harrisonburg, Virginia
http://www.national-college.edu/
Contact: Jack Evey, Campus Director, American National University, 1515 Country Club Road, Harrisonburg, VA 22802. *Phone:* 540-432-0943. *Toll-free phone:* 888-9-JOBREADY.

American National University
Lynchburg, Virginia
http://www.national-college.edu/
Contact: Admissions Representative, American National University, 104 Candlewood Court, Lynchburg, VA 24502-2653. *Phone:* 804-239-3500. *Toll-free phone:* 888-9-JOBREADY.

American National University
Salem, Virginia
http://www.national-college.edu/
Contact: Director of Admissions, American National University, 1813 East Main Street, Salem, VA 24153. *Phone:* 540-986-1800. *Toll-free phone:* 888-9-JOBREADY. *Fax:* 540-444-4198.

American University of Puerto Rico
Bayamón, Puerto Rico
http://www.aupr.edu/
Contact: Ms. Keren Llanos Figueroa, Director of Admissions, American University of Puerto Rico, P O Box 2037, Bayamon, PR 00960-2037. *Phone:* 787-620-2040 Ext. 2020. *Fax:* 787-785-7377. *E-mail:* kllanos@aupr.edu.

Antioch University Los Angeles
Culver City, California
http://www.antiochla.edu/
Contact: Admissions, Antioch University Los Angeles, 400 Corporate Pointe, Culver City, CA 90230. *Phone:* 310-578-1080 Ext. 100. *Toll-free phone:* 800-726-8462. *Fax:* 310-822-4824. *E-mail:* admissions@antiochla.edu.

Antioch University Seattle
Seattle, Washington
http://www.antiochsea.edu/
Contact: Admissions Office, Antioch University Seattle, 2326 Sixth Avenue, Seattle, WA 98121-1814. *Phone:* 206-268-4202. *Toll-free phone:* 888-268-4477. *E-mail:* admissions@antiochseattle.edu.

Apex School of Theology
Durham, North Carolina
http://www.apexsot.edu/
Contact: Dr. Henry D. Wells Jr., Registrar, Apex School of Theology, 2945 South Miami Boulevard, Suite 114, Durham, NC 27703. *Phone:* 919-572-1625. *Fax:* 919-572-1762. *E-mail:* registrar@apexsot.edu.

Appalachian Bible College
Bradley, West Virginia
http://www.abc.edu/
Contact: Miss Rachel Delevan, Admissions Assistant, Appalachian Bible College, 161 College Drive, Bradley, WV 25818. *Phone:* 304-877-6428 Ext. 3213. *Toll-free phone:* 800-678-9ABC. *Fax:* 304-877-5082. *E-mail:* admissions2@abc.edu.

Arkansas Baptist College
Little Rock, Arkansas
http://www.arkansasbaptist.edu/
Contact: Arkansas Baptist College, 1621 Dr. Martin Luther King, Jr. Drive, Little Rock, AR 72202-6067. *Phone:* 501-244-5104 Ext. 5124.

Arlington Baptist College
Arlington, Texas
http://www.arlingtonbaptistcollege.edu/
Contact: Ms. Janie Taylor, Registrar/Admissions, Arlington Baptist College, 3001 West Division, Arlington, TX 76012-3425. *Phone:* 817-461-8741 Ext. 105. *Fax:* 817-274-1138. *E-mail:* jtaylor@arlingtonbaptistcollege.edu.

Art Academy of Cincinnati
Cincinnati, Ohio
http://www.artacademy.edu/
Contact: Mr. John J. Wadell, Director of Admissions, Art Academy of Cincinnati, 1212 Jackson Street, Cincinnati, OH 45202-7106. *Phone:* 513-562-8744. *Toll-free phone:* 800-323-5692. *Fax:* 513-562-8778. *E-mail:* admissions@artacademy.edu.

Ashford University
Clinton, Iowa
http://www.ashford.edu/
Contact: Ms. Waunita M. Sullivan, Director of Enrollment, Ashford University, 400 North Bluff Boulevard, PO Box 2967, Clinton, IA 52733-2967. *Phone:* 563-242-4023 Ext. 3401. *Toll-free phone:* 866-711-1700. *E-mail:* admissns@tfu.edu.

Ashworth College
Norcross, Georgia
http://www.ashworthcollege.edu/
Contact: Eric Ryall, Registrar, Ashworth College, 6625 The Corners Parkway, Suite 500, Norcross, GA 30092. *Phone:* 770-729-8400 Ext. 5297. *Toll-free phone:* 800-957-5412.

Athabasca University
Athabasca, Alberta, Canada
http://www.athabascau.ca/
Contact: Information Centre, Athabasca University, 1 University Drive, Athabasca, AB T9S 3A3, Canada. *Phone:* 800-788-9041. *Toll-free phone:* 800-788-9041. *Fax:* 780-675-6437.

Atlantic University College
Guaynabo, Puerto Rico
http://www.atlanticu.edu/
Contact: Ms. Zaida Perez, Admission's Officer, Atlantic University College, PO Box 3918, Guaynabo, PR 00970. *Phone:* 787-720-1022 Ext. 13. *E-mail:* admisiones@atlanticcollege.edu.

Austin Graduate School of Theology
Austin, Texas
http://www.austingrad.edu/
Contact: Mrs. Celeste Scarbrough, Director of Admissions, Austin Graduate School of Theology, 7640 Guadalupe Street, Austin, TX 78752. *Phone:* 512-476-2772. *Toll-free phone:* 866-AUS-GRAD. *Fax:* 512-476-3919. *E-mail:* registrar@austingrad.edu.

Bacone College
Muskogee, Oklahoma
http://www.bacone.edu/
Contact: Bacone College, 2299 Old Bacone Road, Muskogee, OK 74403-1597. *Phone:* 918-781-7342. *Toll-free phone:* 888-682-5514 Ext. 7340.

Bais Binyomin Academy
Stamford, Connecticut
Contact: Director of Admissions, Bais Binyomin Academy, 132 Prospect Street, Stamford, CT 06901-1202. *Phone:* 203-325-4351.

Baptist Bible College
Springfield, Missouri
http://www.gobbc.edu/
Contact: Mr. Terry Allcorn, Director of Admissions, Baptist Bible College, 628 East Kearney Street, Springfield, MO 65803-3498. *Phone:* 417-268-6000. *Toll-free phone:* 800-228-5754. *Fax:* 417-268-6694.

Baptist College of Health Sciences
Memphis, Tennessee
http://www.bchs.edu/
Contact: Baptist College of Health Sciences, 1003 Monroe Avenue, Memphis, TN 38104. *Phone:* 901-572-2441. *Toll-free phone:* 866-575-2247.

Baptist Missionary Association Theological Seminary
Jacksonville, Texas
http://www.bmats.edu/
Contact: Baptist Missionary Association Theological Seminary, 1530 East Pine Street, Jacksonville, TX 75766-5407. *Phone:* 903-586-2501 Ext. 229. *Toll-free phone:* 800-259-5673.

Bayamón Central University
Bayamón, Puerto Rico
http://www.ucb.edu.pr/
Contact: Bayamón Central University, PO Box 1725, Bayamón, PR 00960-1725. *Phone:* 787-786-3030 Ext. 2102.

Beckfield College
Florence, Kentucky
http://www.beckfield.edu/
Contact: Mrs. Leah Boerger, Director of Admissions, Beckfield College, 16 Spiral Drive, Florence, KY 41042. *Phone:* 859-371-9393. *E-mail:* lboerger@beckfield.edu.

Beis Medrash Heichal Dovid
Far Rockaway, New York
Contact: Beis Medrash Heichal Dovid, 257 Beach 17th Street, Far Rockaway, NY 11691.

Bellevue College
Bellevue, Washington
http://www.bcc.ctc.edu/
Contact: Morenika Jacobs, Associate Dean of Enrollment Services, Bellevue College, 3000 Landerholm Circle, SE, Bellevue, WA 98007-6484. *Phone:* 425-564-2205. *Fax:* 425-564-4065.

Bellevue University
Bellevue, Nebraska
http://www.bellevue.edu/
Contact: Nick Baker, Director of Undergraduate Enrollment, Bellevue University, 1000 Galvin Road South, Bellevue, NE 68005-3098. *Phone:* 402-557-7250. *Toll-free phone:* 800-756-7920. *E-mail:* nick.baker@bellevue.edu.

Bellin College
Green Bay, Wisconsin
http://www.bellincollege.edu/
Contact: Dr. Penny Croghan, Admissions Director, Bellin College, 3201 Eaton Road, Green Bay, WI 54305. *Phone:* 920-433-5803. *Toll-free phone:* 800-236-8707. *Fax:* 920-433-7416. *E-mail:* admissio@bcon.edu.

Benedict College
Columbia, South Carolina
http://www.benedict.edu/
Contact: Benedict College, 1600 Harden Street, Columbia, SC 29204. *Phone:* 803-705-4491. *Toll-free phone:* 800-868-6598.

Bethany College
Hepburn, Saskatchewan, Canada
http://www.bethany.sk.ca/
Contact: Mr. Dave Carey, Admissions Director, Bethany College, Box 160, Hepburn, SK S0K 1Z0, Canada. *Phone:* 306-947-2175. *Toll-free phone:* 866-772-2175.

Bethesda University
Anaheim, California
http://www.buc.edu/
Contact: Jacquie Ha, Director of Admission, Bethesda University, 730 North Euclid Street, Anaheim, CA 92801. *Phone:* 714-517-1945. *Fax:* 714-517-1948. *E-mail:* admission@bcu.edu.

Beth HaMedrash Shaarei Yosher Institute
Brooklyn, New York
Contact: Director of Admissions, Beth HaMedrash Shaarei Yosher Institute, 4102-10 Sixteenth Avenue, Brooklyn, NY 11204. *Phone:* 718-854-2290.

Beth Hatalmud Rabbinical College
Brooklyn, New York
Contact: Rabbi Osina, Director of Admissions, Beth Hatalmud Rabbinical College, 2127 Eighty-second Street, Brooklyn, NY 11214. *Phone:* 718-259-2525.

Beth Medrash Govoha
Lakewood, New Jersey
Contact: Director of Admissions, Beth Medrash Govoha, 617 Sixth Street, Lakewood, NJ 08701-2797. *Phone:* 908-367-1060 Ext. 4224.

Bishop's University
Sherbrooke, Quebec, Canada
http://www.ubishops.ca/
Contact: Mrs. Jacqueline Belleau, Coordinator of Student Recruitment, Bishop's University, 2600 College Street, Sherbrooke, QC J1M 0C8, Canada. *Phone:* 819-822-9600 Ext. 2691. *Toll-free phone:* 877-822-8200. *Fax:* 819-822-9661. *E-mail:* recruitment@ubishops.ca.

Boise Bible College
Boise, Idaho
http://www.boisebible.edu/
Contact: Russell Grove, Director of Admissions, Boise Bible College, 8695 West Marigold Street, Boise, ID 83714-1220. *Phone:*

208-376-7731. *Toll-free phone:* 800-893-7755. *Fax:* 208-376-7743. *E-mail:* rgrove@boisebible.edu.

Booth University College

Winnipeg, Manitoba, Canada

http://www.boothuc.ca/

Contact: Chantel Burt, Director of Admission, Booth University College, 447 Webb Place, Winnipeg, MB R3B 2P2, Canada. *Phone:* 204-924-4867. *Toll-free phone:* 877-942-6684. *E-mail:* cburt@boothcollege.ca.

Boricua College

New York, New York

http://www.boricuacollege.edu/

Contact: Mrs. Miriam Pfeffer, Director of Student Services, Boricua College, 186 North 6th Street, Brooklyn, NY 11211. *Phone:* 718-782-2200. *Fax:* 718-782-2025. *E-mail:* mpfeffer@boricuacollege.edu.

Brandon University

Brandon, Manitoba, Canada

http://www.brandonu.ca/

Contact: Murray Kerr, Director of Admissions, Brandon University, 270 18th Street, Brandon, MB R7A 6A9, Canada. *Phone:* 204-727-7352. *Toll-free phone:* 800-644-7644. *Fax:* 204-728-3221. *E-mail:* kerr@brandonu.ca.

Brazosport College

Lake Jackson, Texas

http://www.brazosport.edu/

Contact: Brazosport College, 500 College Drive, Lake Jackson, TX 77566-3199. *Phone:* 979-230-3020.

Brescia University

Owensboro, Kentucky

http://www.brescia.edu/

Contact: Brescia University, 717 Frederica Street, Owensboro, KY 42301-3023. *Phone:* 270-686-4241 Ext. 241. *Toll-free phone:* 877-273-7242.

Brewton-Parker College

Mt. Vernon, Georgia

http://www.bpc.edu/

Contact: Director of Admissions, Brewton-Parker College, PO Box 197, Mount Vernon, GA 30445. *Phone:* 912-583-3247. *Toll-free phone:* 800-342-1087. *Fax:* 912-583-3598. *E-mail:* admissions@bpc.edu.

Briarcliffe College

Bethpage, New York

http://www.briarcliffe.edu/

Contact: Admissions Office, Briarcliffe College, 1055 Stewart Avenue, Bethpage, NY 11714. *Phone:* 516-918-3600. *Toll-free phone:* 888-349-4999 (in-state); 888-348-4999 (out-of-state). *Fax:* 516-470-6020.

Briercrest College

Caronport, Saskatchewan, Canada

http://www.briercrest.ca/

Contact: Mr. Ralph Troshke, Director of Enrolment, Briercrest College, 510 College Drive, Caronport, SK S0H 0S0, Canada. *Phone:* 306-756.3200. *Toll-free phone:* 800-667-5199. *Fax:* 800-667.5199. *E-mail:* admissions@briercrest.ca.

Brigham Young University–Hawaii

Laie, Hawaii

http://www.byuh.edu/

Contact: Mr. Arapata P. Meha, Brigham Young University–Hawaii, 55-220 Kulanui Street, Laie, HI 96762-1294. *Phone:* 808-675-3731. *Fax:* 808-675-3741. *E-mail:* admissions@byuh.edu.

Brigham Young University–Idaho

Rexburg, Idaho

http://www.byui.edu/

Contact: Brigham Young University–Idaho, Rexburg, ID 83460. *Phone:* 208-496-1310.

British Columbia Institute of Technology

Burnaby, British Columbia, Canada

http://www.bcit.ca/

Contact: Ms. Anna Dosen, Supervisor of Admissions, British Columbia Institute of Technology, 3700 Willingdon Avenue, Burnaby, BC V5G 3H2, Canada. *Phone:* 604-432-8496. *Toll-free phone:* 866-434-1610. *Fax:* 604-431-6917.

Brock University

St. Catharines, Ontario, Canada

http://www.brocku.ca/

Contact: Mrs. Lynn Thompson-Dovi, International Admissions Officer, Brock University, 500 Glenridge Avenue, L2S 3A1, Canada. *Phone:* 905-688-5550 Ext. 3431. *Fax:* 905-688-5488. *E-mail:* admissns@brocku.ca.

Brookline College

Phoenix, Arizona

http://brooklinecollege.edu/

Contact: Ms. Theresa Dean, Director of Admissions, Brookline College, 2445 West Dunlap Avenue, Suite 100, Phoenix, AZ 85021. *Phone:* 602-242-6265. *Toll-free phone:* 800-793-2428. *Fax:* 602-973-2572. *E-mail:* tdean@brooklinecollege.edu.

Brookline College

Tempe, Arizona

http://brooklinecollege.edu/

Contact: Ms. Cheryl Kindred, Campus Director, Brookline College, 1140-1150 South Priest Drive, Tempe, AZ 85281. *Phone:* 480-545-8755. *Toll-free phone:* 888-886-2428. *Fax:* 480-926-1371. *E-mail:* ckindred@brooklinecollege.edu.

Brookline College

Tucson, Arizona

http://brooklinecollege.edu/

Contact: Ms. Leigh Anne Pechota, Campus Director, Brookline College, 5441 East 22nd Street, Suite 125, Tucson, AZ 85711. *Phone:* 520-748-9799. *Toll-free phone:* 888-292-2428. *Fax:* 520-748-9355. *E-mail:* lpechota@brooklinecollege.edu.

Brookline College

Albuquerque, New Mexico

http://brooklinecollege.edu/

Contact: Mr. Andrew Webb, Campus Director, Brookline College, 4201 Central Avenue NW, Suite J, Albuquerque, NM 87105. *Phone:* 505-880-2877. *Toll-free phone:* 888-660-2428. *Fax:* 505-352-0199. *E-mail:* awebb@brooklinecollege.edu.

Brooklyn College of the City University of New York

Brooklyn, New York

http://www.brooklyn.cuny.edu/

Contact: Office of Admissions, Brooklyn College of the City University of New York, 2900 Bedford Avenue, West Quad Building, Room 222, Brooklyn, NY 11210-2889. *Phone:* 718-951-5001. *Fax:* 718-951-4506. *E-mail:* adminqry@brooklyn.cuny.edu.

Brooks Institute

Ventura, California

http://www.brooks.edu/

Contact: Admissions Office, Brooks Institute, 5301 North Ventura Avenue, Ventura, CA 93001. *Phone:* 805-966-3888. *Toll-free phone:* 888-276-4999. *Fax:* 805-565-1386. *E-mail:* admissions@brooks.edu.

Bryant & Stratton College–Amherst Campus

Clarence, New York

http://www.bryantstratton.edu/

Contact: Mr. Brian K. Dioguardi, Director of Admissions, Bryant & Stratton College–Amherst Campus, Audubon Business Center, 40 Hazelwood Drive, Amherst, NY 14228. *Phone:* 716-691-0012. *Fax:* 716-691-0012. *E-mail:* bkdioguardi@bryantstratton.edu.

Bryant & Stratton College–Buffalo Campus

Buffalo, New York

http://www.bryantstratton.edu/

Contact: Mr. Philip J. Struebel, Director of Admissions, Bryant & Stratton College–Buffalo Campus, 465 Main Street, Suite 400, Buffalo, NY 14203. *Phone:* 716-884-9120. *Fax:* 716-884-0091. *E-mail:* pjstruebel@bryantstratton.edu.

Bryant & Stratton College–Cleveland Campus

Cleveland, Ohio

http://www.bryantstratton.edu/

Contact: Bryant & Stratton College–Cleveland Campus, Cleveland, OH 44114-3203. *Phone:* 216-771-1700. *Fax:* 216-771-7787.

Bryant & Stratton College–Eastlake Campus

Eastlake, Ohio

http://www.bryantstratton.edu/

Contact: Ms. Melanie Pettit, Director of Admissions, Bryant & Stratton College–Eastlake Campus, 35350 Curtis Boulevard, Eastlake, OH 44095. *Phone:* 440-510-1112.

Bryant & Stratton College–Milwaukee Campus

Milwaukee, Wisconsin

http://www.bryantstratton.edu/

Contact: Mr. Dan Basile, Director of Admissions, Bryant & Stratton College–Milwaukee Campus, 310 West Wisconsin Avenue, Suite 500 East, Milwaukee, WI 53203-2214. *Phone:* 414-276-5200.

Bryant & Stratton College–Parma Campus

Parma, Ohio

http://www.bryantstratton.edu/

Contact: Bryant & Stratton College–Parma Campus, 12955 Snow Road, Parma, OH 44130-1013. *Phone:* 216-265-3151. *Toll-free phone:* 866-948-0571.

Bryant & Stratton College–Richmond Campus

Richmond, Virginia

http://www.bryantstratton.edu/

Contact: Mr. David K. Mayle, Director of Admissions, Bryant & Stratton College–Richmond Campus, 8141 Hull Street Road, Richmond, VA 23235-6411. *Phone:* 804-745-2444. *Fax:* 804-745-6884. *E-mail:* tlawson@bryanstratton.edu.

Bryant & Stratton College–Southtowns Campus

Orchard Park, New York

http://www.bryantstratton.edu/

Contact: Bryant & Stratton College–Southtowns Campus, 200 Redtail Road, Orchard Park, NY 14127. *Phone:* 716-677-9500.

Bryant & Stratton College–Virginia Beach Campus

Virginia Beach, Virginia

http://www.bryantstratton.edu/

Contact: Bryant & Stratton College–Virginia Beach Campus, 301 Centre Pointe Drive, Virginia Beach, VA 23462-4417. *Phone:* 757-499-7900 Ext. 173.

Bryant & Stratton College–Wauwatosa Campus

Wauwatosa, Wisconsin

http://www.bryantstratton.edu/

Contact: Bryant & Stratton College–Wauwatosa Campus, 10950 W. Potter Road, Wauwatosa, WI 53226. *Phone:* 414-302-7000 Ext. 502.

Burlington College

Burlington, Vermont

http://www.burlington.edu/

Contact: Ms. Gillian Homsted, Admissions Director, Burlington College, 351 North Avenue, Burlington, VT 05401-2998. *Phone:* 802-862-9616 Ext. 104. *Toll-free phone:* 800-862-9616. *Fax:* 802-660-4331. *E-mail:* admissions@burlington.edu.

California Coast University
Santa Ana, California
http://www.calcoast.edu/
Contact: California Coast University, 925 North Spurgeon Street, Santa Ana, CA 92701. *Phone:* 714-547-9625. *Toll-free phone:* 888-CCU-UNIV.

California Maritime Academy
Vallejo, California
http://www.csum.edu/
Contact: California Maritime Academy, 200 Maritime Academy Drive, Vallejo, CA 94590. *Phone:* 707-654-1330. *Toll-free phone:* 800-561-1945.

California National University for Advanced Studies
Northridge, California
http://www.cnuas.edu/
Contact: Ms. Stephanie Smith, Registrar, California National University for Advanced Studies, Admissions, 8550 Balboa Boulevard, Suite 210, Northridge, CA 91325. *Phone:* 818-830-2411. *Toll-free phone:* 800-782-2422. *Fax:* 818-830-2418. *E-mail:* cnuadms@mail.cnuas.edu.

California State University Channel Islands
Camarillo, California
http://www.csuci.edu/
Contact: Ms. Ginger Reyes, California State University Channel Islands, One University Drive, Camarillo, CA 93012. *Phone:* 805-437-8520. *Fax:* 805-437-8519. *E-mail:* prospective.student@csuci.edu.

Cambridge College
Cambridge, Massachusetts
http://www.cambridgecollege.edu/
Contact: Denise Haile, Director of Admissions, Cambridge College, 1000 Massachusetts Avenue, Cambridge, MA 02138-5304. *Phone:* 800-877-4725. *Toll-free phone:* 800-877-4723. *Fax:* 617-349-3561. *E-mail:* denise.haile@cambridgecollege.edu.

Campbell University
Buies Creek, North Carolina
http://www.campbell.edu/
Contact: Ms. Peggy Mason, Director of Admissions, Campbell University, PO Box 546, 450 Leslie Campbell Avenue, Buies Creek, NC 27506. *Phone:* 910-893-1290. *Toll-free phone:* 800-334-4111. *Fax:* 910-893-1288. *E-mail:* adm@mailcenter.campbell.edu.

Capella University
Minneapolis, Minnesota
http://www.capella.edu/
Contact: Enrollment Services, Capella University, 225 South Sixth Street, Capella Tower, 9th Floor, Minneapolis, MN 55402. *Phone:* 866-2837921. *Toll-free phone:* 866-283-7921. *Fax:* 612-977-5060. *E-mail:* info@capella.edu.

Carleton University
Ottawa, Ontario, Canada
http://www.carleton.ca/
Contact: Ms. Jean Mullan, Director, Undergraduate Recruitment Office, Carleton University, 1125 Colonel By Drive, Ottawa, ON K1S 5B6, Canada. *Phone:* 613-520-3663. *Toll-free phone:* 888-354-4414. *E-mail:* liaison@admissions.carleton.ca.

Carthage College
Kenosha, Wisconsin
http://www.carthage.edu/
Contact: Carthage College, 2001 Alford Park Drive, Kenosha, WI 53140. *Phone:* 262-551-6000. *Toll-free phone:* 800-351-4058.

Carver College
Atlanta, Georgia
http://www.carver.edu/
Contact: Bertha Mack, Admissions Officer, Carver College, 3870 Cascade Road SW, Atlanta, GA 30331. *Phone:* 404-527-4520. *Fax:* 404-527-4524. *E-mail:* info@carver.edu.

Central Baptist College
Conway, Arkansas
http://www.cbc.edu/
Contact: Mr. Thomas Mobly, Admissions Counselor, Central Baptist College, 1501 College Avenue, Conway, AR 72034. *Phone:* 501-2058875. *Toll-free phone:* 800-205-6872. *Fax:* 501-329-2941. *E-mail:* tmobly@cbc.edu.

Central Christian College of Kansas
McPherson, Kansas
http://www.centralchristian.edu/
Contact: Central Christian College of Kansas, 1200 South Main, PO Box 1403, McPherson, KS 67460-5799. *Phone:* 620-241-0723 Ext. 380. *Toll-free phone:* 800-835-0078.

Central Christian College of the Bible
Moberly, Missouri
http://www.cccb.edu/
Contact: Mr. Aaron Merritt, Director of Admissions, Central Christian College of the Bible, 911 Urbandale Drive East, Moberly, MO 65270-1997. *Phone:* 660-263-3900. *Toll-free phone:* 888-263-3900. *Fax:* 660-263-3936. *E-mail:* admissions@cccb.edu.

Central Yeshiva Tomchei Tmimim-Lubavitch
Brooklyn, New York
Contact: Director of Admissions, Central Yeshiva Tomchei Tmimim-Lubavitch, 841-853 Ocean Parkway, Brooklyn, NY 11230. *Phone:* 718-859-7600.

Centura College
Virginia Beach, Virginia
http://www.centuracollege.edu/
Contact: Admissions Office, Centura College, 2697 Dean Drive, Suite 100, Virginia Beach, VA 23452. *Phone:* 757-340-2121. *Toll-free phone:* 877-575-5627. *Fax:* 757-340-9704.

Everest College
Springfield, Missouri
http://www.everest.edu/
Contact: Admissions Office, Everest College, 1010 West Sunshine, Springfield, MO 65807-2488. *Phone:* 417-864-7220. *Toll-free phone:* 888-741-4270. *Fax:* 417-864-5697.

Everest University
Jacksonville, Florida
http://www.everest.edu/
Contact: Ted Wilkins, Admissions Director, Everest University, 8226 Phillips Highway, Jacksonville, FL 32256. *Phone:* 904-731-4949. *Toll-free phone:* 888-741-4270. *E-mail:* rmanning@cci.edu.

Everest University
Lakeland, Florida
http://www.everest.edu/
Contact: Ms. Patricia Sabol, Director of Student Services, Everest University, 995 East Memorial Boulevard, Suite 110, Lakeland, FL 33801. *Phone:* 863-686-1444 Ext. 144. *Toll-free phone:* 888-741-4270. *E-mail:* psabol@cci.edu.

Everest University
Largo, Florida
http://www.everest.edu/
Contact: Ted Wilkins, Director of Admissions, Everest University, 2471 McMullen Road, Clearwater, FL 33759. *Phone:* 727-725-2688. *Toll-free phone:* 888-741-4270. *Fax:* 727-796-3406. *E-mail:* kbuskirk@cci.edu.

Everest University
Melbourne, Florida
http://www.everest.edu/
Contact: Ted Wilkins, Director of Admissions, Everest University, 2401 North Harbor City Boulevard, Melbourne, FL 32935-6657. *Phone:* 321-253-2929 Ext. 121.

Everest University
Orange Park, Florida
http://www.everest.edu/
Contact: Admissions Office, Everest University, 805 Wells Road, Orange Park, FL 32073. *Phone:* 904-264-9122.

Everest University
Orlando, Florida
http://www.everest.edu/
Contact: Ted Wilkins, Director of Admissions, Everest University, 5421 Diplomat Circle, Orlando, FL 32810-5674. *Phone:* 407-628-5870. *Toll-free phone:* 800-628-5870. *Fax:* 407-628-1344.

Everest University
Orlando, Florida
http://www.everest.edu/
Contact: Ms. Annette Cloin, Director of Admissions, Everest University, 9200 South Park Center Loop, Orlando, FL 32819. *Phone:* 407-851-2525 Ext. 111. *Toll-free phone:* 888-741-4270 (in-state); 888-471-4270 (out-of-state). *Fax:* 407-354-7946.

Everest University
Pompano Beach, Florida
http://www.everest.edu/
Contact: Martin Levert, Director of Admissions, Everest University, 225 North Federal Highway, Pompano Beach, FL 33062. *Phone:* 954-783-7339. *Fax:* 954-943-2571.

Everest University
Tampa, Florida
http://www.everest.edu/
Contact: Everest University, 3319 West Hillsborough Avenue, Tampa, FL 33614-5899. *Phone:* 813-879-6000 Ext. 129.

Everest University
Tampa, Florida
http://www.everest.edu/
Contact: Everest University, 3924 Coconut Palm Drive, Tampa, FL 33619. *Phone:* 813-621-0041 Ext. 106. *Toll-free phone:* 888-741-4270.

Everglades University
Boca Raton, Florida
http://www.evergladesuniversity.edu/
Contact: Everglades University, 5002 T-Rex Avenue, Suite 100, Boca Raton, FL 33431. *Phone:* 561-912-1211. *Toll-free phone:* 888-772-6077.

Faith Theological Seminary
Baltimore, Maryland
http://www.faiththeological.org/
Contact: Faith Theological Seminary, 529 Walker Avenue, Baltimore, MD 21212. *Phone:* 410-323-6211.

Finlandia University
Hancock, Michigan
http://www.finlandia.edu/
Contact: Martin Kinard, Finlandia University, 601 Quincy Street, Hancock, MI 49930. *Phone:* 906-487-7352. *Toll-free phone:* 877-202-5491. *Fax:* 906-487-7383. *E-mail:* admissions@finlandia.edu.

Florida Memorial University
Miami-Dade, Florida
http://www.fmuniv.edu/
Contact: Mrs. Peggy Murray Martin, Director of Admissions and International Student Advisor, Florida Memorial University, 15800 NW 42nd Avenue, Miami-Dade, FL 33054. *Phone:* 305-626-3147. *Toll-free phone:* 800-822-1362.

Fountainhead College of Technology
Knoxville, Tennessee
http://www.fountainheadcollege.edu/
Contact: Mr. Joel B Southern, Director of Admissions, Fountainhead College of Technology, 10208 Technology Drive, Knoxville, TN 37932. *Phone:* 865-688-9422. *Toll-free phone:* 888-218-7335. *Fax:* 865-688-2419. *E-mail:* joel.southern@fountainheadcollege.edu.

Full Sail University
Winter Park, Florida
http://www.fullsail.edu/
Contact: Ms. Mary Beth Plank, Director of Admissions, Full Sail University, 3300 University Boulevard, Winter Park, FL 32792-7437. *Phone:* 407-679-6333. *Toll-free phone:* 800-226-7625. *E-mail:* admissions@fullsail.com.

Global University
Springfield, Missouri
http://www.globaluniversity.edu/
Contact: Rev. Todd Waggoner, Enrollment and International Student Services Director, Global University, 1211 South Glenstone Avenue, Springfield, MO 65804. *Phone:* 417-862-9533 Ext. 2335. *Toll-free phone:* 800-443-1083. *Fax:* 417-863-9621. *E-mail:* twaggoner@globaluniversity.edu.

Globe Institute of Technology
New York, New York
http://www.globe.edu/
Contact: Mr. Michael Scalice, Admissions Director, Globe Institute of Technology, 500 7th Avenue, New York, NY 10018. *Phone:* 212-349-4330 Ext. 1624. *Toll-free phone:* 888-51-GLOBE (in-state); 800-51-GLOBE (out-of-state). *Fax:* 212-227-5920. *E-mail:* admissions@globe.edu.

Golden Gate University
San Francisco, California
http://www.ggu.edu/
Contact: Mr. Louis D. Riccardi Jr., Director of Enrollment Services, Golden Gate University, 536 Mission Street, San Francisco, CA 94105-2968. *Phone:* 415-442-7800. *Toll-free phone:* 800-448-3381. *Fax:* 415-442-7807. *E-mail:* info@ggu.edu.

Goldey-Beacom College
Wilmington, Delaware
http://www.gbc.edu/
Contact: Mr. Larry Eby, Director of Admissions, Goldey-Beacom College, 4701 Limestone Road, Wilmington, DE 19808. *Phone:* 302-225-6289. *Toll-free phone:* 800-833-4877. *Fax:* 302-996-5408. *E-mail:* admissions@gbc.edu.

Grace Bible College
Grand Rapids, Michigan
http://www.gbcol.edu/
Contact: Mr. Kevin Gilliam, Director of Enrollment, Grace Bible College, 1101 Aldon Street, SW, PO Box 910, Grand Rapids, MI 49509. *Phone:* 616-538-2330 Ext. 239. *Toll-free phone:* 800-968-1887. *Fax:* 616-538-0599. *E-mail:* gbc@gbcol.edu.

Graceland University
Independence, Missouri
http://www.graceland.edu/
Contact: Admissions, Graceland University, 1401 West Truman Road, Independence, MO 64050-3434. *Phone:* 816-833-0524. *Toll-free phone:* 866-GRACELAND. *E-mail:* gic@graceland.edu.

Grace University
Omaha, Nebraska
http://www.graceuniversity.edu/
Contact: Angela Wayman, Director of Admissions, Grace University, 1311 South Ninth Street, Omaha, NE 68108. *Phone:* 402-449-2831. *Toll-free phone:* 800-383-1422. *Fax:* 402-341-9587. *E-mail:* admissions@graceuniversity.com.

Grand Canyon University
Phoenix, Arizona
http://www.gcu.edu/
Contact: Enrollment, Grand Canyon University, 3300 West Camelback Road, PO Box 11097, Phoenix, AZ 86017-3030. *Phone:* 800-486-7085. *Toll-free phone:* 800-800-9776. *E-mail:* admissionsonline@gcu.edu.

Grantham University
Lenexa, Kansas
http://www.grantham.edu/
Contact: Mr. Les Hyde, Vice President Admissions, Grantham University, 7200 NW 86th Street, Kansas City, MO 64153. *Phone:* 800-955-2527. *Toll-free phone:* 800-955-2527. *Fax:* 816-595-5757. *E-mail:* admissions@grantham.edu.

Gulf Coast State College
Panama City, Florida
http://www.gulfcoast.edu/
Contact: Mrs. Jackie Kuczenski, Administrative Secretary of Admissions, Gulf Coast State College, 5230 West U.S. Highway 98, Panama City, FL 32401. *Phone:* 850-769-1551 Ext. 4892. *Fax:* 850-913-3308. *E-mail:* jkuczenski@gulfcoast.edu.

Gutenberg College
Eugene, Oregon
http://www.gutenberg.edu/
Contact: Mr. Terry Stollar, Director of Admissions and Development, Gutenberg College, 1883 University Street, Eugene, OR 97403. *Phone:* 541-736-9071. *Fax:* 541-683-6997. *E-mail:* tstollar@gutenberg.edu.

Hamilton Technical College
Davenport, Iowa
http://www.hamiltontechcollege.edu/
Contact: Hamilton Technical College, 1011 East 53rd Street, Davenport, IA 52807-2653. *Phone:* 563-386-3570. *Toll-free phone:* 866-966-4825.

Haskell Indian Nations University
Lawrence, Kansas
http://www.haskell.edu/
Contact: Ms. Patty Grant, Recruitment Officer, Haskell Indian Nations University, 155 Indian Avenue, #5031, Lawrence, KS 66046-4800. *Phone:* 785-749-8437 Ext. 437.

Hebrew Theological College
Skokie, Illinois
http://www.htc.edu/
Contact: Rabbi Berish Cardash, Hebrew Theological College, 7135 North Carpenter Road, Skokie, IL 60077-3263. *Phone:* 847-982-2500.

Hellenic College
Brookline, Massachusetts
http://www.hchc.edu/
Contact: Mr. Gregory Floor, Director of Admissions, Hellenic College, 50 Goddard Avenue, Brookline, MA 02445-7496. *Phone:* 617-850-1285. *Toll-free phone:* 866-424-2338. *Fax:* 617-850-1460. *E-mail:* admissions@hchc.edu.

Heritage Christian University
Florence, Alabama
http://www.hcu.edu/
Contact: Mr. Brad McKinnon, Dean of Students, Heritage Christian University, PO Box HCU, Florence, AL 35630. *Phone:* 256-766-6610 Ext. 305. *Toll-free phone:* 800-367-3565. *Fax:* 256-766-9289. *E-mail:* bmckinnon@hcu.edu.

Heritage College and Seminary
Cambridge, Ontario, Canada
http://www.heritagecambridge.com/
Contact: Mr. Mark Walther, Assistant Dean of Students, Heritage College and Seminary, New York, NY 10023-6588. *Phone:* 519-651-2869 Ext. 251. *Toll-free phone:* 800-465-1961. *Fax:* 519-651-2870. *E-mail:* mwalther@heritagecollege.net.

Herzing University
Birmingham, Alabama
http://www.herzing.edu/birmingham/
Contact: Ms. Tess Anderson, Admissions Coordinator, Herzing University, 280 West Valley Avenue, Birmingham, AL 35209. *Phone:* 205-916-2800. *Toll-free phone:* 800-596-0724. *E-mail:* admiss@bhm.herzing.edu.

Herzing University
Winter Park, Florida
http://www.herzing.edu/
Contact: Tessie Uranga, Director of Admissions, Herzing University, 1595 South Semoran Boulevard, Winter Park, FL 32792. *Phone:* 407-478-0500. *Toll-free phone:* 800-596-0724. *Fax:* 407-380-0269.

Herzing University
Atlanta, Georgia
http://www.herzing.edu/atlanta/
Contact: Miss Anissa Elder, Director of Admissions, Herzing University, 3393 Peachtree Road, NE, Suite 1003, Atlanta, GA 30326. *Phone:* 404-816-4533. *Toll-free phone:* 800-596-0724. *Fax:* 404-816-5576. *E-mail:* aelder@atl.herzing.edu.

Herzing University
Kenner, Louisiana
http://www.herzing.edu/
Contact: Genny Bordelon, Director of Admissions, Herzing University, 2500 Williams Boulevard, Kenner, LA 70062. *Phone:* 504-733-0074. *Toll-free phone:* 800-596-0724. *Fax:* 504-733-0020.

Herzing University
Minneapolis, Minnesota
http://www.herzing.edu/minneapolis
Contact: Ms. Shelly Larson, Director of Admissions, Herzing University, 5700 West Broadway, Minneapolis, MN 55428. *Phone:* 763-231-3155. *Toll-free phone:* 800-596-0724. *Fax:* 763-535-9205. *E-mail:* info@mpls.herzing.edu.

Herzing University
Madison, Wisconsin
http://www.herzing.edu/madison/
Contact: Mr. Tom Beatty, Associate Director of Admissions, Herzing University, 5218 East Terrace Drive, Madison, WI 53718. *Phone:* 608-395-3441. *Toll-free phone:* 800-596-0724. *Fax:* 608-249-8593. *E-mail:* info@msn.herzing.edu.

Humphreys College
Stockton, California
http://www.humphreys.edu/
Contact: Director of Admission, Humphreys College, 6650 Inglewood Avenue, Stockton, CA 95207-3896. *Phone:* 209-235-2901. *E-mail:* ugadmission@humphreys.edu.

Idaho State University
Pocatello, Idaho
http://www.isu.edu/
Contact: Admissions and Registration Office, Idaho State University, 921 South 8th, Stop 8270, Pocatello, ID 83209-8270. *Phone:* 208-282-2475. *Fax:* 208-282-4511. *E-mail:* info@isu.edu.

Independence University
Salt Lake City, Utah
http://www.independence.edu/
Contact: Ms. Deborah Hopkins, Enrollment Manager, Independence University, 5295 South Commerce Drive, Salt Lake City, UT 84107. *Toll-free phone:* 800-972-5149.

Institute of Public Administration
Dublin, Ireland
http://www.ipa.ie/
Contact: Dr. Denis O'Brien, Registrar, Institute of Public Administration, 57-61 Lansdowne Road, Dublin 4, Ireland. *Phone:* 353-1-240-3600. *Fax:* 353-1-668-9135. *E-mail:* undergrad@ipa.ie.

Instituto Tecnológico y de Estudios Superiores de Monterrey, Campus Central de Veracruz
Córdoba, Mexico
http://www.ver.itesm.mx/
Contact: Ing. Luis Pablo Villareal, Registrar, Instituto Tecnológico y de Estudios Superiores de Monterrey, Campus Central de Veracruz, Avenida Eugenio Garza Sada 1, Apartado Postal 314, 94500 Córdoba, Veracruz, Mexico. *Phone:* -27-13-23-40 Ext. 123.

Instituto Tecnológico y de Estudios Superiores de Monterrey, Campus Chiapas
Tuxtla Gutiérrez, Mexico
http://www.chs.itesm.mx/
Contact: Lic. Luis Enrique Cancino, Registrar, Instituto Tecnológico y de Estudios Superiores de Monterrey, Campus Chiapas, Carretera a Tapanatepec Km 149&746, Apartado Postal 312, 29000 Tuxtla Gutiérrez, Chiapas, Mexico. *Phone:* -96-15-1723.

Instituto Tecnológico y de Estudios Superiores de Monterrey, Campus Chihuahua

Chihuahua, Mexico

http://www.chi.itesm.mx/

Contact: Ing. Juan Manuel Fernandez, Registrar, Instituto Tecnológico y de Estudios Superiores de Monterrey, Campus Chihuahua, Colegio Militar 4700, Colonia Nombre de Dios, Apartado Postal 728, 31300 Chihuahua, Chihuahua, Mexico. *Phone:* -14-17-48-58 Ext. 117.

Instituto Tecnológico y de Estudios Superiores de Monterrey, Campus Ciudad de México

Ciudad de Mexico, Mexico

http://www.ccm.itesm.mx/

Contact: Admissions Office, Instituto Tecnológico y de Estudios Superiores de Monterrey, Campus Ciudad de México, Calle del Puente #222 esquina con Periférico, 14380 Colonia Huipulco, Tlalpan, MDF, Mexico. *Phone:* -5-673-6488.

Instituto Tecnológico y de Estudios Superiores de Monterrey, Campus Ciudad Juárez

Ciudad Juárez, Mexico

http://www.cdj.itesm.mx/

Contact: Lic. Alberto Trejo, Registrar, Instituto Tecnológico y de Estudios Superiores de Monterrey, Campus Ciudad Juárez, Boulevard Tomas Fernandez y Avenida A J Bermudez, Apartado Postal 3105-J, 32320 Ciudad Juárez, Chihuahua, Mexico. *Phone:* -16-17-88-07 Ext. 113.

Instituto Tecnológico y de Estudios Superiores de Monterrey, Campus Ciudad Obregón

Ciudad Obregón, Mexico

http://www.cob.itesm.mx/

Contact: Lic. Judith Almeida, Registrar, Instituto Tecnológico y de Estudios Superiores de Monterrey, Campus Ciudad Obregón, Dr Norman E Borlaug Km 14, Apartado Postal 662, 85000 Ciudad Obregón, Sonora, Mexico. *Phone:* -64-15-03-12.

Instituto Tecnológico y de Estudios Superiores de Monterrey, Campus Colima

Colima, Mexico

http://www.itesm.edu/wps/wcm/connect/Campus/COL/colima/

Contact: Lic. Manuel Perez Rivera, Registrar, Instituto Tecnológico y de Estudios Superiores de Monterrey, Campus Colima, Prolongacion Ignacio Sandoval s/n, Fraccionamiento Jardines de Vista Hermosa, Apartado Postal 190, 28010 Colima, Colima, Mexico. *Phone:* -33-12-53-39.

Instituto Tecnológico y de Estudios Superiores de Monterrey, Campus Cuernavaca

Temixco, Mexico

http://www.cva.itesm.mx/

Contact: Lic. Miguel Angel Machua, Registrar, Instituto Tecnológico y de Estudios Superiores de Monterrey, Campus Cuernavaca, Paseo de la Reforma 182-A, Colonia Lomas de Cuernavaca, 62000 Temixco, Morelos, Mexico. *Phone:* -73 18-49-57.

Instituto Tecnológico y de Estudios Superiores de Monterrey, Campus Estado de México

Estado de Mexico, Mexico

http://www.cem.itesm.mx/

Contact: Prof. Jose de Jesus Molina, Registrar, Instituto Tecnológico y de Estudios Superiores de Monterrey, Campus Estado de México, Carretera Lago de Guadalupe Km. 3.5, Atizapan de Zaragoza, Estado de Mexico 52926, Mexico. *Phone:* -5-873-3600.

Instituto Tecnológico y de Estudios Superiores de Monterrey, Campus Guadalajara

Zapopan, Mexico

http://www.gda.itesm.mx/

Contact: Ms. Janet Martell Sotomayor, Registration Director, Instituto Tecnológico y de Estudios Superiores de Monterrey, Campus Guadalajara, Avenida General Ramón Corona 2514, Colonia Nuevo Mexico, 45140 Zapopan, Jalisco, Mexico. *Phone:* -3-669-3006.

Instituto Tecnológico y de Estudios Superiores de Monterrey, Campus Hidalgo

Pachuca, Mexico

http://www.hgo.itesm.mx/

Contact: Lic. Lizbet Melo, Registrar, Instituto Tecnológico y de Estudios Superiores de Monterrey, Campus Hidalgo, Boulevard Felipe Angeles s/n al lado de la Unidad Deportiva, Apartado Postal 337, 42090 Pachuca, Hidalgo, Mexico. *Phone:* -714-25-00 Ext. 128.

Instituto Tecnológico y de Estudios Superiores de Monterrey, Campus Irapuato

Irapuato, Mexico

http://www.ira.itesm.mx/

Contact: Ing. Marcela Beltrán, Registrar, Instituto Tecnológico y de Estudios Superiores de Monterrey, Campus Irapuato, Paseo Mirador del Valle No. 445, Col. Villas de Irapuato, Apartado Postal 568, 36660 Irapuato, Guanajuato, Mexico. *Phone:* -46-230342.

Instituto Tecnológico y de Estudios Superiores de Monterrey, Campus Laguna

Torreón, Mexico

http://www.lag.itesm.mx/

Contact: Ing. Aroldo Camargo Soto, Registrar, Instituto Tecnológico y de Estudios Superiores de Monterrey, Campus Laguna, Paseo del Tecnologico s/n Ampliacion La Rosita, Apartado Postal 506, 27250 Torreón, Coahuila, Mexico. *Phone:* -17-20-66-61 Ext. 23.

Instituto Tecnológico y de Estudios Superiores de Monterrey, Campus León

León, Mexico

http://www.leo.itesm.mx/

Contact: Lic. Eddie Villegas, Registrar, Instituto Tecnológico y de Estudios Superiores de Monterrey, Campus León, Avenida Eugenio Garza Sada s/n Colonia Cerro Gordo, Apartado Postal 872, 37120 León, Guanajuato, Mexico. *Phone:* -47-17-10-00 Ext. 131.

Instituto Tecnológico y de Estudios Superiores de Monterrey, Campus Monterrey

Monterrey, Mexico

http://www.mty.itesm.mx/

Contact: Lic. Carlos Ordoñez, International Student Advisor, Instituto Tecnológico y de Estudios Superiores de Monterrey, Campus Monterrey, Avenida Eugenio Garza Sada 2501 Sur Colonia Tecnnologico, Sucursal de Correos J, 64849 Monterrey, Nuevo León, Mexico. *Phone:* -52 81 8328 4065 Ext. 3942.

Instituto Tecnológico y de Estudios Superiores de Monterrey, Campus Querétaro

Santiago de Querétaro, Mexico

http://www.qro.itesm.mx/

Contact: Lic. Marco Vinicio Lopez, Registrar, Instituto Tecnológico y de Estudios Superiores de Monterrey, Campus Querétaro, Avenida Epigmenio González #500, Apartado Postal 37, 76130 Querétaro, Querétaro, Mexico. *Phone:* -42-17-38-25 Ext. 156.

Instituto Tecnológico y de Estudios Superiores de Monterrey, Campus Saltillo

Saltillo, Mexico

http://www.sal.itesm.mx/

Contact: Lic. Esteban Ramos, Registrar, Instituto Tecnológico y de Estudios Superiores de Monterrey, Campus Saltillo, Prolongacion Juan de la Barrera 1241 Ote, Apartado Postal 539, 25270 Saltillo, Coahuila, Mexico. *Phone:* -84-15-06-90 Ext. 12.

Instituto Tecnológico y de Estudios Superiores de Monterrey, Campus San Luis Potosí

San Luis Potosí, Mexico

http://www.slp.itesm.mx/

Contact: Ing. Consuelo Gonzalez, Registrar, Instituto Tecnológico y de Estudios Superiores de Monterrey, Campus San Luis Potosí, Avenida Robles 600, Colonia Jacarandas, Apartado Postal 1473 Suc E, 78140 San Luis Potosí, SLP, Mexico. *Phone:* -48 13-3441 Ext. 14.

Instituto Tecnológico y de Estudios Superiores de Monterrey, Campus Sinaloa

Culiacán, Mexico

http://www.sin.itesm.mx/

Contact: Lic. Hugo Guerrero, Registrar, Instituto Tecnológico y de Estudios Superiores de Monterrey, Campus Sinaloa, Boulevard Culiacán 3773, Apartado Postal 69-F, 80800 Culiacán, Sinaloa, Mexico. *Phone:* -67-14-03-69.

Instituto Tecnológico y de Estudios Superiores de Monterrey, Campus Sonora Norte

Hermosillo, Mexico

http://www.her.itesm.mx/

Contact: Ing. Victor Eduardo Perez Orozco, Library and Admissions/Registration Director, Instituto Tecnológico y de Estudios Superiores de Monterrey, Campus Sonora Norte, Carretera Hermosillo-Nogales Km 9, Apartado Postal 216, 83000 Hermosillo, Sonora, Mexico. *Phone:* -62-15-52-05 Ext. 131.

Instituto Tecnológico y de Estudios Superiores de Monterrey, Campus Tampico

Altimira, Mexico

http://www.itesm.edu/wps/portal?WCM_GLOBAL_CONTEXT=/migration/TAM2/Tampico

Contact: Ing. Javier Ponce, Registrar, Instituto Tecnológico y de Estudios Superiores de Monterrey, Campus Tampico, Boulevard Petrocel Km 1.3, Corredor Industrial, Carretera Tampico-Mante, 89120 Altimira, Tamaulipas, Mexico. *Phone:* -126-4-19-79.

Instituto Tecnológico y de Estudios Superiores de Monterrey, Campus Toluca

Toluca, Mexico

http://www.tol.itesm.mx/

Contact: Ing. Victor M. Martinez Orta, Registrar, Instituto Tecnológico y de Estudios Superiores de Monterrey, Campus Toluca, Ex-hacienda La Pila, 100 metros al norte de San Antonio Buenavista, 50252 Toluca, Estado de Mexico, Mexico. *Phone:* -72-74-11-92.

Instituto Tecnológico y de Estudios Superiores de Monterrey, Campus Zacatecas

Zacatecas, Mexico

http://www.zac.itesm.mx/

Contact: Lic. de Lourdes Zorrilla, Business Affairs Director and Registrar, Instituto Tecnológico y de Estudios Superiores de Monterrey, Campus Zacatecas, Calzada Pedro Coronel #16, Frente al Club Bernades, Municipio de Guadalupe, 98000 Zacatecas, Zacatecas, Mexico. *Phone:* -49 23-00-40.

Inter American University of Puerto Rico, Arecibo Campus

Arecibo, Puerto Rico

http://www.arecibo.inter.edu/

Contact: Ms. Provi Montalvo, Admission Director, Inter American University of Puerto Rico, Arecibo Campus, PO Box 4050, Arecibo, PR 00614-4050. *Phone:* 787-878-5475. *Fax:* 787-880-1624. *E-mail:* pmontalvo@arecibo.inter.edu.

Inter American University of Puerto Rico, Barranquitas Campus

Barranquitas, Puerto Rico

http://www.br.inter.edu/

Contact: Mrs. Aramilda Cartagena, Dean of Students, Inter American University of Puerto Rico, Barranquitas Campus, PO Box 517, Barranquitas, PR 00794. *Phone:* 787-857-3600 Ext. 2009. *Fax:* 787-857-2125. *E-mail:* acartagena@br.inter.edu.

International Baptist College and Seminary

Chandler, Arizona

http://www.ibcs.edu/

Contact: Director of Admissions, International Baptist College and Seminary, 2211 West Germann Road, Chandler, AZ 85286. *Phone:* 480-245-7970. *Toll-free phone:* 800-422-4858. *E-mail:* admissions@ibconline.edu.

International College of the Cayman Islands

Newlands, Cayman Islands

http://www.icci.edu.ky/

Contact: International College of the Cayman Islands, PO Box 136, Savannah Post Office, Newlands, Grand Cayman, Cayman Islands. *Phone:* 345-325-6454.

International University in Geneva

Geneva, Switzerland

http://www.iun.ch/

Contact: Ms. Virginie Morel, Admissions Officer, International University in Geneva, Geneva 1215, Switzerland. *Phone:* -41 22710-7110. *Toll-free phone:* -01141227107110. *Fax:* 41 22710-7111. *E-mail:* bachelor@iun.ch.

The International University of Monaco

Monte Carlo, Monaco

http://www.monaco.edu/

Contact: Dr. Gisele Dudognon, Director of Admissions, The International University of Monaco, 2, Avenue Albert II, MC-98000 Principality of Monaco, Monaco. *Phone:* -377 97986 994. *Fax:* 377 92052 830. *E-mail:* gdudognon@monaco.edu.

ITT Technical Institute

Bradenton, Florida

http://www.itt-tech.edu/

Contact: Director of Recruitment, ITT Technical Institute, 8039 Cooper Creek Boulevard, Bradenton, FL 34201. *Phone:* 941-309-9200. *Toll-free phone:* 800-342-8684.

ITT Technical Institute

Deerfield Beach, Florida

http://www.itt-tech.edu/

Contact: Director of Recruitment, ITT Technical Institute, 700 W. Hillsboro Boulevard, Suite 100, Building 1, Deerfield Beach, FL 33441. *Phone:* 954-360-4701. *Toll-free phone:* 877-243-8548.

ITT Technical Institute

Cedar Rapids, Iowa

http://www.itt-tech.edu/

Contact: Director of Recruitment, ITT Technical Institute, 3735 Queen Court SW, Cedar Rapids, IA 52404. *Phone:* 319-297-3400. *Toll-free phone:* 877-320-4625.

The Jewish Theological Seminary

New York, New York

http://www.jtsa.edu/

Contact: Mr. Sergio Lineberge, List College Admissions Coordinator, The Jewish Theological Seminary, 3080 Broadway, New York, NY 10027. *Phone:* 212-678-8820. *E-mail:* lcadmissions@jtsa.edu.

John F. Kennedy University

Pleasant Hill, California

http://www.jfku.edu/

Contact: Ms. Jen Miller-Hogg, Director of Admissions, John F. Kennedy University, 100 Ellinwood Way, Pleasant Hill, CA 94523-4817. *Phone:* 925-969-3584. *Toll-free phone:* 800-696-JFKU. *E-mail:* jmhogg@jfku.edu.

Johnson University Florida

Kissimmee, Florida

http://www.johnsonu.edu/

Contact: Johnson University Florida, 1011 Bill Beck Boulevard, Kissimmee, FL 34744-5301. *Phone:* 407-569-1172. *Toll-free phone:* 888-GO-TO-FCC.

Kaplan University, Cedar Falls

Cedar Falls, Iowa

http://www.kaplanuniversity.edu/

Contact: Kaplan University, Cedar Falls, 7009 Nordic Drive, Cedar Falls, IA 50613. *Phone:* 319-277-0220. *Toll-free phone:* 866-527-5268 (in-state); 800-527-5268 (out-of-state).

Kaplan University, Cedar Rapids

Cedar Rapids, Iowa

http://www.kaplanuniversity.edu/

Contact: Kaplan University, Cedar Rapids, 3165 Edgewood Parkway, SW, Cedar Rapids, IA 52404. *Phone:* 319-363-0481. *Toll-free phone:* 866-527-5268 (in-state); 800-527-5268 (out-of-state).

Kaplan University, Davenport Campus

Davenport, Iowa

http://www.kaplanuniversity.edu/

Contact: Kaplan University, Davenport Campus, 1801 East Kimberly Road, Suite 1, Davenport, IA 52807-2095. *Phone:* 563-355-3500. *Toll-free phone:* 866-527-5268 (in-state); 800-527-5268 (out-of-state).

Kaplan University, Des Moines

Urbandale, Iowa

http://www.kaplanuniversity.edu/

Contact: Kaplan University, Des Moines, 4655 121st Street, Urbandale, IA 50323. *Phone:* 515-727-2100. *Toll-free phone:* 866-527-5268 (in-state); 800-527-5268 (out-of-state).

Kaplan University, Hagerstown Campus

Hagerstown, Maryland

http://www.kaplanuniversity.edu/

Contact: Kaplan University, Hagerstown Campus, 18618 Crestwood Drive, Hagerstown, MD 21742-2797. *Phone:* 301-739-2680 Ext. 217. *Toll-free phone:* 866-527-5268 (in-state); 800-527-5268 (out-of-state).

Kaplan University, Lincoln

Lincoln, Nebraska

http://www.kaplanuniversity.edu/

Contact: Kaplan University, Lincoln, 1821 K Street, Lincoln, NE 68501-2826. *Phone:* 402-474-5315. *Toll-free phone:* 866-527-5268 (in-state); 800-527-5268 (out-of-state).

Kaplan University, Mason City Campus

Mason City, Iowa

http://www.kaplanuniversity.edu/

Contact: Kaplan University, Mason City Campus, 2570 4th Street, SW, Mason City, IA 50401. *Phone:* 641-423-2530. *Toll-free phone:* 866-527-5268 (in-state); 800-527-5268 (out-of-state).

Kaplan University, Omaha

Omaha, Nebraska

http://www.kaplanuniversity.edu/

Contact: Kaplan University, Omaha, 5425 North 103rd Street, Omaha, NE 68134. *Phone:* 402-572-8500. *Toll-free phone:* 866-527-5268 (in-state); 800-527-5268 (out-of-state).

Kehilath Yakov Rabbinical Seminary

Ossining, New York

http://kehilathyakov.com/

Contact: Admissions Officer, Kehilath Yakov Rabbinical Seminary, 340 Illington Road, Ossining, NY 10562. *Phone:* 718-963-1212.

Kettering College

Kettering, Ohio

http://www.kc.edu/

Contact: Mrs. Becky McDonald, Director of Enrollment Services, Kettering College, 3737 Southern Boulevard, Kettering, OH 45429-1299. *Phone:* 937-395-8628. *Toll-free phone:* 800-433-5262. *Fax:* 937-296-4238.

Lakehead University

Thunder Bay, Ontario, Canada

http://www.lakeheadu.ca/

Contact: Mr. Nicholas Chamut, Manager of Undergraduate Admissions, Lakehead University, 955 Oliver Road, Thunder Bay, ON P7B 5E1, Canada. *Phone:* 807-343-8676. *Toll-free phone:* 800-465-3959. *Fax:* 807-766-7209. *E-mail:* admissions@lakeheadu.ca.

Lakehead University–Orillia

Orillia, Ontario, Canada

http://orillia.lakeheadu.ca/

Contact: Lakehead University–Orillia, 500 University Avenue, Orillia, ON L3V 0B9, Canada.

Lakeland College

Sheboygan, Wisconsin

http://www.lakeland.edu/

Contact: Mr. Nick Spaeth, Director of Admissions, Lakeland College, PO Box 359, Nash Visitors Center, Sheboygan, WI 53082-0359. *Phone:* 920-565-1007. *Toll-free phone:* 800-569-2166. *Fax:* 920-565-1215. *E-mail:* admissions@lakeland.edu.

Lancaster Bible College

Lancaster, Pennsylvania

http://www.lbc.edu/

Contact: Mrs. Joanne M. Roper, Associate Vice President for Admissions, Lancaster Bible College, PO Box 83403, Lancaster, PA 17608. *Phone:* 717-560-8271. *Toll-free phone:* 800-544-7335. *Fax:* 717-560-8213. *E-mail:* admissions@lbc.edu.

Lander University

Greenwood, South Carolina

http://www.lander.edu/

Contact: Ms. Jennifer M. Mathis, Director of Admissions, Lander University, 320 Stanley Avenue, Greenwood, SC 29649. *Phone:* 864-388-8307. *Toll-free phone:* 888-452-6337. *Fax:* 864-388-8125. *E-mail:* admissions@lander.edu.

Laurentian University

Sudbury, Ontario, Canada

http://www.laurentian.ca/

Contact: Laurentian University, Ramsey Lake Road, P3E 2C6, Canada. *Phone:* 705-675-1151. *Toll-free phone:* 800-263-4188. *Fax:* 705-675-4891. *E-mail:* admissions@laurentian.ca.

Le Cordon Bleu College of Culinary Arts in Scottsdale

Scottsdale, Arizona

http://www.chefs.edu/Scottsdale/

Contact: Le Cordon Bleu College of Culinary Arts in Scottsdale, 8100 East Camelback Road, Suite 1001, Scottsdale, AZ 85251-3940. *Toll-free phone:* 888-557-4222.

Life Pacific College
San Dimas, California
http://www.lifepacific.edu/
Contact: Ms. Dorienne Elston, Director of Admissions, Life Pacific College, 1100 Covina Boulevard, San Dimas, CA 91773-3298. *Phone:* 909-599-5433 Ext. 314. *Toll-free phone:* 877-886-5433 Ext. 314. *Fax:* 909-706-3070. *E-mail:* adm@lifepacific.edu.

Lincoln College–Normal
Normal, Illinois
http://www.lincolncollege.edu/normal/
Contact: Mr. Steve Puck, Director of Admissions, Lincoln College–Normal, 715 West Raab Road, Normal, IL 61761. *Phone:* 309-268-4314. *Toll-free phone:* 800-569-0558. *Fax:* 309-862-3352. *E-mail:* spuck@lincolncollege.edu.

Lincoln College of Technology
West Palm Beach, Florida
http://www.lincolnedu.com/
Contact: Mr. Kevin Cassidy, Director of Admissions, Lincoln College of Technology, 2410 Metrocentre Boulevard, West Palm Beach, FL 33407. *Phone:* 561-842-8324 Ext. 117. *Fax:* 561-842-9503.

Lincoln Culinary Institute
West Palm Beach, Florida
http://www.lincolnedu.com/campus/west-palm-beach-culinary-fl
Contact: Lincoln Culinary Institute, 2410 Metrocentre Boulevard, West Palm Beach, FL 33407. *Phone:* 561-842-8324 Ext. 202.

Loma Linda University
Loma Linda, California
http://www.llu.edu/
Contact: Admissions Office, Loma Linda University, Loma Linda, CA 92350. *Phone:* 909-558-1000. *Toll-free phone:* 800-422-4558.

Louisiana State University at Alexandria
Alexandria, Louisiana
http://www.lsua.edu/
Contact: Ms. Shelly Kieffer, Director of Admissions and Recruiting, Louisiana State University at Alexandria, 8100 Highway 71 South, Alexandria, LA 71302-9121. *Phone:* 318-473-6424. *Toll-free phone:* 888-473-6417. *Fax:* 318-473-6418. *E-mail:* admissions@lsua.edu.

Luther Rice College & Seminary
Lithonia, Georgia
http://www.lutherrice.edu/
Contact: Mr. Steve Pray, Admissions Counselor, Luther Rice College & Seminary, 3038 Evans Mill Road, Lithonia, GA 30038-2454. *Phone:* 770-484-1204. *Toll-free phone:* 800-442-1577. *E-mail:* admissions@lru.edu.

Lyme Academy College of Fine Arts
Old Lyme, Connecticut
http://www.lymeacademy.edu/
Contact: Mr. Karl Holzenthal, Admissions Representative, Lyme Academy College of Fine Arts, 84 Lyme Street, Old Lyme, CT 06371. *Phone:* 860-434-3571 Ext. 127. *Fax:* 860-434-8725. *E-mail:* kholzenthal@lymeacademy.edu.

Lyndon State College
Lyndonville, Vermont
http://www.lyndonstate.edu/
Contact: Ms. Cheri Goldrick, Admissions Assistant, Lyndon State College, 1001 College Road, PO Box 919, Lyndonville, VT 05851. *Phone:* 802-626-6451. *Toll-free phone:* 800-225-1998. *Fax:* 802-626-6335. *E-mail:* admissions@lyndonstate.edu.

Machzikei Hadath Rabbinical College
Brooklyn, New York
Contact: Rabbi Abraham M. Lezerowitz, Director of Admissions, Machzikei Hadath Rabbinical College, 5407 Sixteenth Avenue, Brooklyn, NY 11204-1805. *Phone:* 718-854-8777.

MacMurray College
Jacksonville, Illinois
http://www.mac.edu/
Contact: Ms. Alicia Zeone, Assistant Director of Admission, MacMurray College, 447 East College Avenue, Jacksonville, IL 62650. *Phone:* 217-479-7059. *Toll-free phone:* 800-252-7485. *Fax:* 217-291-0702. *E-mail:* alicia.zeone@mac.edu.

Maine College of Art
Portland, Maine
http://www.meca.edu/
Contact: Maine College of Art, 522 Congress Street, Portland, ME 04101. *Phone:* 207-699-5023. *Toll-free phone:* 800-699-1509.

Maple Springs Baptist Bible College and Seminary
Capitol Heights, Maryland
http://www.msbbcs.edu/
Contact: Ms. Jeannie Bowman, Assistant Director of Admissions and Records, Maple Springs Baptist Bible College and Seminary, 4130 Belt Road, Capitol Heights, MD 20743. *Phone:* 301-736-3631. *Fax:* 301-735-6507.

Martin Methodist College
Pulaski, Tennessee
http://www.martinmethodist.edu/
Contact: Lisa Smith, Director of Admissions, Martin Methodist College, 433 West Madison Street, Pulaski, TN 38478-2716. *Phone:* 931-363-9868. *Toll-free phone:* 800-467-1273. *Fax:* 931-363-9818. *E-mail:* admit@martinmethodist.edu.

Martin University
Indianapolis, Indiana
http://www.martin.edu/
Contact: Ms. Brenda Shaheed, Director of Enrollment Management, Martin University, 2171 Avondale Place, PO Box 18567, Indianapolis, IN 46218-3867. *Phone:* 317-543-3237. *Fax:* 317-543-4790.

Marygrove College
Detroit, Michigan
http://www.marygrove.edu/
Contact: Mr. John Ambrose, Director of Undergraduate Admissions, Marygrove College, Admissions Office, Detroit, MI 48221-2599. *Phone:* 313-927-1236. *Toll-free phone:* 866-313-1297. *Fax:* 313-927-1345. *E-mail:* info@marygrove.edu.

McGill University
Montréal, Quebec, Canada
http://www.mcgill.ca/
Contact: Enrollment Services, McGill University, 845 Sherbrooke Street West, James Administration Building, Room 205, Montreal, QC H3A 2T5, Canada. *Phone:* 514-398-3910. *Fax:* 514-398-4193. *E-mail:* admissions@mcgill.ca.

McMaster University
Hamilton, Ontario, Canada
http://www.mcmaster.ca/
Contact: Olivia Demerling, Admissions Officer, McMaster University, 1280 Main Street West, Hamilton, ON L8S 4M2, Canada. *Phone:* 905-525-4600. *Fax:* 905-527-1105. *E-mail:* admitmac@mcmaster.ca.

Memorial University of Newfoundland
St. John's, Newfoundland and Labrador, Canada
http://www.mun.ca/
Contact: Ms. Marian Abbott, Admissions Office, Memorial University of Newfoundland, Elizabeth Avenue, St. John's, NL A1C 5S7, Canada. *Phone:* 709-737-3705. *E-mail:* sturecru@morgan.ucs.mun.ca.

Mesivta Torah Vodaath Rabbinical Seminary
Brooklyn, New York
http://www.torahvodaath.org/
Contact: Rabbi Issac Braun, Administrator, Mesivta Torah Vodaath Rabbinical Seminary, 425 East Ninth Street, Brooklyn, NY 11218-5299. *Phone:* 718-941-8000.

Mesivtha Tifereth Jerusalem of America
New York, New York
Contact: Rabbi Fishellis, Director of Admissions, Mesivtha Tifereth Jerusalem of America, 145 East Broadway, New York, NY 10002-6301. *Phone:* 212-964-2830.

Messenger College
Euless, Texas
http://www.messengercollege.edu/
Contact: Ron Cannon, Vice President of Academic Affairs, Messenger College, PO Box 1207, Euless, TX 76039. *Phone:* 417-624-7070 Ext. 108. *Toll-free phone:* 800-385-8940. *Fax:* 417-624-5070. *E-mail:* info@messengercollege.edu.

Methodist University
Fayetteville, North Carolina
http://www.methodist.edu/
Contact: Mr. Jamie Legg, Director of Admissions, Methodist University, 5400 Ramset Street, Fayetteville, NC 28311-1496. *Phone:* 910-630-7027. *Toll-free phone:* 800-488-7110 Ext. 7027. *Fax:* 910-630-7285. *E-mail:* admissions@methodist.edu.

Metro Business College
Cape Girardeau, Missouri
http://www.metrobusinesscollege.edu/
Contact: Ms. Kyla Evans, Admissions Director, Metro Business College, 1732 North Kingshighway Street, Cape Girardeau, MO 63701. *Phone:* 573-334-9181. *Toll-free phone:* 888-206-4545. *Fax:* 573-334-0617.

Metropolitan State University of Denver
Denver, Colorado
http://www.msudenver.edu/
Contact: Ms. Michelle Brown, Associate Director of Admissions, Metropolitan State University of Denver, PO Box 173362, Denver, CO 80217-3362. *Phone:* 303-556-2615.

Miami University Hamilton
Hamilton, Ohio
http://www.ham.muohio.edu/
Contact: Mr. Archie Nelson, Director of Admission and Financial Aid, Miami University Hamilton, 1601 Peck Boulevard, Hamilton, OH 45011-3399. *Phone:* 513-785-3111. *Fax:* 513-785-1807. *E-mail:* nelsona3@muohio.edu.

Miami University–Middletown Campus
Middletown, Ohio
http://www.mid.muohio.edu/
Contact: Diane Cantonwine, Assistant Director of Admission and Financial Aid, Miami University–Middletown Campus, 4200 East University Boulevard, Middletown, OH 45042-3497. *Phone:* 513-727-3346. *Toll-free phone:* 866-426-4643. *Fax:* 513-727-3223. *E-mail:* cantondm@muohio.edu.

Michigan Jewish Institute
West Bloomfield, Michigan
http://www.mji.edu/
Contact: Mr. Dov Stein, Michigan Jewish Institute, 6890 Maple Road, West Bloomfield, MI 48322. *Phone:* 248-414-6900 Ext. 103. *Toll-free phone:* 888-INFO-MJI. *Fax:* 248-414-6907. *E-mail:* dstein@mji.edu.

Mid-America Baptist Theological Seminary
Cordova, Tennessee
http://www.mabts.edu/
Contact: Mr. Duffy Guyton, Director of Admissions, Mid-America Baptist Theological Seminary, PO Box 2350, Cordova, TN 38016. *Phone:* 901-751-8453 Ext. 3066. *Toll-free phone:* 800-968-4508. *Fax:* 901-751-8454. *E-mail:* info@mabts.edu.

Mid-America Christian University
Oklahoma City, Oklahoma
http://www.macu.edu/
Contact: Mid-America Christian University, 3500 Southwest 119th Street, Oklahoma City, OK 73170-4504. *Phone:* 405-392-3180. *Toll-free phone:* 888-436-3035.

Mid-America College of Funeral Service

Jeffersonville, Indiana

http://www.mid-america.edu/

Contact: Mr. Richard Nelson, Dean of Students, Mid-America College of Funeral Service, 3111 Hamburg Pike, Jeffersonville, IN 47130-9630. *Phone:* 812-288-8878. *Toll-free phone:* 800-221-6158. *Fax:* 812-288-5942. *E-mail:* macfs@mindspring.com.

Middle Georgia State College

Cochran, Georgia

http://www.mga.edu/

Contact: Ms. Jennifer Brannon, Director of Admissions, Middle Georgia State College, 1100 2nd Street, Southeast, Cochran, GA 31014. *Phone:* 478-934-3103. *Fax:* 478-934-3403. *E-mail:* admissions@mgc.edu.

Midland University

Fremont, Nebraska

http://www.midlandu.edu/

Contact: Danielle Oliver, Associate Director of Admissions, Midland University, Fremont, NE 68025-4200. *Phone:* 402-941-6501. *Toll-free phone:* 800-642-8382 Ext. 6501. *E-mail:* oliver@midlandu.edu.

Midstate College

Peoria, Illinois

http://www.midstate.edu/

Contact: Ms. Jessica Hancock, Director of Admissions, Midstate College, 411 West Northmoor Road, Peoria, IL 61614. *Phone:* 309-692-4092. *Toll-free phone:* 800-251-4299. *Fax:* 309-692-3893. *E-mail:* jhancock2@midstate.edu.

Midway College

Midway, Kentucky

http://www.midway.edu/

Contact: Midway College, 512 East Stephens Street, Midway, KY 40347-1120. *Phone:* 859-846-5799. *Toll-free phone:* 800-755-0031.

Midwest University

Wentzville, Missouri

http://www.midwest.edu/

Contact: Jeoung H. Ham, Registrar/Director of Admissions, Midwest University, 851 Parr Road, Wentzville, MO 63385. *Phone:* 636-327-4645. *Fax:* 636-327-4715. *E-mail:* usa@midwest.edu.

Midwives College of Utah

Salt Lake City, Utah

http://www.midwifery.edu/

Contact: Kristi Ridd-Young, President, Midwives College of Utah, 1174 East 2700 South, Suite 2, Salt Lake City, UT 84106. *Phone:* 801-649-5230. *Toll-free phone:* 866-680-2756. *Fax:* 866-207-2024. *E-mail:* office@midwifery.edu.

Miles College

Fairfield, Alabama

http://www.miles.edu/

Contact: Mr. Christopher Robertson, Director of Admissions and Recruitment, Miles College, 5500 Myron Massey Boulevard, Bell Building, Fairfield, AL 35064. *Phone:* 205-929-1657. *Toll-free phone:* 800-445-0708. *Fax:* 205-929-1627. *E-mail:* admissions@miles.edu.

Mirrer Yeshiva

Brooklyn, New York

Contact: Director of Admissions, Mirrer Yeshiva, 1795 Ocean Parkway, Brooklyn, NY 11223-2010. *Phone:* 718-645-0536.

Mississippi College

Clinton, Mississippi

http://www.mc.edu/

Contact: Mr. William Kyle Brantley, Director of Admissions, Mississippi College, Box 4026, 200 South Capitol Street, Clinton, MS 39058-0001. *Phone:* 601-925-3800. *Toll-free phone:* 800-738-1236. *Fax:* 601-925-3804. *E-mail:* enrollment-services@mc.edu.

Missouri College

Brentwood, Missouri

http://www.missouricollege.edu/

Contact: Mr. Doug Brinker, Admissions Director, Missouri College, 1405 South Hanley Road, Brentwood, MO 63117. *Phone:* 314-821-7700. *Toll-free phone:* 800-216-6732. *Fax:* 314-821-0891.

Missouri Tech

St. Charles, Missouri

http://www.motech.edu/

Contact: Mr. Bob Honaker, Director of Admissions, Missouri Tech, 1167 Corporate Lake Drive, St. Louis, MO 63132. *Phone:* 314-569-3600. *Toll-free phone:* 800-960-TECH. *Fax:* 314-569-1167.

Montana State University–Northern

Havre, Montana

http://www.msun.edu/

Contact: Montana State University–Northern, PO Box 7751, Havre, MT 59501-7751. *Phone:* 406-265-3704. *Toll-free phone:* 800-662-6132.

Montserrat College of Art

Beverly, Massachusetts

http://www.montserrat.edu/

Contact: Mr. Jeffrey Newell, Director of Admissions, Montserrat College of Art, 23 Essex Street, Beverly, MA 01915. *Phone:* 978-921-4242 Ext. 1152. *Toll-free phone:* 800-836-0487. *Fax:* 978-921-4241. *E-mail:* jeffrey.newell@montserrat.edu.

Moody Bible Institute

Chicago, Illinois

http://www.moody.edu/

Contact: Ms. Jacqueline Holman, Admissions Office, Moody Bible Institute, 820 North LaSalle Boulevard, Chicago, IL 60610. *Phone:* 312-329-4307. *Toll-free phone:* 800-967-4MBI. *Fax:* 312-329-8987. *E-mail:* admissions@moody.edu.

Morgan State University

Baltimore, Maryland

http://www.morgan.edu/

Contact: Ms. Shonda Gray, Acting Director of Admissions and Recruitment, Morgan State University, 1700 East Cold Spring Lane, Baltimore, MD 21251. *Phone:* 443-885-3000. *Toll-free phone:* 800-332-6674. *E-mail:* shantell.saunders@morgan.edu.

Mount Angel Seminary
Saint Benedict, Oregon
http://www.mountangelabbey.org/seminary/
Contact: Registrar/Admissions Officer, Mount Angel Seminary, Saint Benedict, OR 97373. *Phone:* 503-845-3951 Ext. 14. *E-mail:* admissions@mtangel.edu.

Mount Ida College
Newton, Massachusetts
http://www.mountida.edu/
Contact: Calvin Conyers, Assistant Dean of Admissions, Mount Ida College, 777 Dedham Street, Newton, MA 02459-3310. *Phone:* 617-928-4553. *Fax:* 617-928-4507. *E-mail:* admissions@mountida.edu.

Mount Saint Vincent University
Halifax, Nova Scotia, Canada
http://www.msvu.ca/
Contact: Ms. Heidi Tattrie, Assistant Registrar/Admissions, Mount Saint Vincent University, 166 Bedford Highway, Halifax, NS B3M2J6, Canada. *Phone:* 902-457-6117. *Toll-free phone:* 877-733-6788. *Fax:* 902-457-6498. *E-mail:* admissions@msvu.ca.

Mt. Sierra College
Monrovia, California
http://www.mtsierra.edu/
Contact: Mt. Sierra College, 101 East Huntington Drive, Monrovia, CA 91016. *Phone:* 888-486-9818. *Toll-free phone:* 888-828-8000.

Mount Washington College
Manchester, New Hampshire
http://www.mountwashington.edu/
Contact: Mount Washington College, 3 Sundial Avenue, Manchester, NH 03103. *Phone:* 603-668-6660. *Toll-free phone:* 888-971-2190.

Musicians Institute
Hollywood, California
http://www.mi.edu/
Contact: Musicians Institute, 1655 North McCadden Place, Hollywood, CA 90028. *Phone:* 323-860-4345. *Toll-free phone:* 800-255-PLAY.

Muskingum University
New Concord, Ohio
http://www.muskingum.edu/
Contact: Mrs. Beth DaLonzo, Director of Admission, Muskingum University, 163 Stormont Street, New Concord, OH 43762. *Phone:* 740-826-8137. *Toll-free phone:* 800-752-6082. *Fax:* 740-826-8100. *E-mail:* adminfo@muskingum.edu.

National American University
Colorado Springs, Colorado
http://www.national.edu/
Contact: Director of Admissions, National American University, 1915 Jamboree Drive, Suite 185, Colorado Springs, CO 80918. *Phone:* 719-590-8300. *E-mail:* csadmissions@national.edu.

National American University
Denver, Colorado
http://www.national.edu/
Contact: National American University, 1325 South Colorado Boulevard, Suite 100, Denver, CO 80222. *Phone:* 303-876-7112.

National American University
Kansas City, Missouri
http://www.national.edu/
Contact: Admissions Office, National American University, 7490 Northwest 87th Street, Kansas City, MO 64153. *Phone:* 816-412-5500. *E-mail:* zradmissions@national.edu.

National American University
Albuquerque, New Mexico
http://www.national.edu/
Contact: National American University, 4775 Indian School Road, NE, Suite 200, Albuquerque, NM 87110. *Phone:* 505-265-7517. *Toll-free phone:* 800-895-9904.

National American University
Rapid City, South Dakota
http://www.national.edu/
Contact: Ms. Angela Beck, Director of Enrollment Management, National American University, 321 Kansas City Street, Rapid City, SD 57701. *Phone:* 605-394-4902. *Toll-free phone:* 800-209-0490 (in-state); 800-209-4090 (out-of-state). *Fax:* 605-394-4871. *E-mail:* abeck@national.edu.

National American University
Sioux Falls, South Dakota
http://www.national.edu/
Contact: Ms. Lisa Houtsma, Director of Admissions, National American University, 5801 S. Corporate Place, Sioux Falls, SD 57108. *Phone:* 605-336-4600. *Toll-free phone:* 800-388-5430. *Fax:* 605-336-4605. *E-mail:* lhoutsma@national.edu.

National College
Lexington, Kentucky
http://www.national-college.edu/
Contact: Kim Thomasson, Campus Director, National College, 2376 Sir Barton Way, Lexington, KY 40509. *Phone:* 859-253-0621. *Toll-free phone:* 888-9-JOBREADY.

National College
Louisville, Kentucky
http://www.national-college.edu/
Contact: Vincent C. Tinebra, Campus Director, National College, 4205 Dixie Highway, Louisville, KY 40216. *Phone:* 502-447-7634. *Toll-free phone:* 888-9-JOBREADY.

National College
Bristol, Tennessee
http://www.national-college.edu/
Contact: National College, 1328 Highway 11 West, Bristol, TN 37620. *Phone:* 423-878-4440. *Toll-free phone:* 888-9-JOBREADY.

National College of Midwifery
Taos, New Mexico
http://www.midwiferycollege.org/
Contact: Ms. Beth Enson, Dean of Students, National College of Midwifery, 209 State Road 240, Taos, NM 87571. *Phone:* 505-758-8914. *E-mail:* info@midwiferycollege.org.

National Louis University
Chicago, Illinois
http://www.nl.edu/
Contact: National Louis University, 1000 Capitol Drive, Wheeling, IL 60090. *Phone:* 888-NLU-TODAY. *Toll-free phone:* 888-658-8632.

Ner Israel Rabbinical College
Baltimore, Maryland
Contact: Ner Israel Rabbinical College, 400 Mount Wilson Lane, Baltimore, MD 21208. *Phone:* 410-484-7200.

Ner Israel Yeshiva College of Toronto
Thornhill, Ontario, Canada
Contact: Rabbi Y. Kravetz, Director of Admissions, Ner Israel Yeshiva College of Toronto, 8950 Bathurst Street, Thornhill, ON L4J 8A7, Canada. *Phone:* 905-731-1224.

Nevada State College at Henderson
Henderson, Nevada
http://www.nsc.nevada.edu/
Contact: Ms. Patricia Ring, Registrar, Nevada State College at Henderson, Office of Admissions and Records, 1125 Nevada State Drive, Henderson, NV 89002. *Phone:* 702-992-2114. *Fax:* 702-992-2111. *E-mail:* admissions@nsc.nevada.edu.

New Charter University
San Francisco, California
http://www.new.edu/
Contact: Ms. Tammy J. Kassner, Director of Admissions, New Charter University, 2919 John Hawkins Parkway, Birmingham, AL 35244. *Phone:* 205-871-9288 Ext. 107. *Toll-free phone:* 888-639-1388. *Fax:* 800-871-9294. *E-mail:* admissions@aju.edu.

New England College of Business and Finance
Boston, Massachusetts
http://necb.edu/
Contact: New England College of Business and Finance, 10 High Street, Suite 204, Boston, MA 02111-2645. *Phone:* 617-951-2350 Ext. 6912. *Toll-free phone:* 800-997-1673.

New Hope Christian College
Eugene, Oregon
http://www.newhope.edu/
Contact: Sarah Slater, Director of Admissions, New Hope Christian College, 2155 Bailey Hill Road, Eugene, OR 97405. *Phone:* 541-485-1780 Ext. 3115. *Toll-free phone:* 800-322-2638. *Fax:* 541-343-5801. *E-mail:* sarahslater@newhope.edu.

New Orleans Baptist Theological Seminary
New Orleans, Louisiana
http://www.nobts.edu/
Contact: Dr. Paul E. Gregoire Jr., Registrar/Director of Admissions, New Orleans Baptist Theological Seminary, 3939 Gentilly Boulevard, New Orleans, LA 70126-4858. *Phone:* 504-282-4455 Ext. 3337. *Toll-free phone:* 800-662-8701.

New World School of the Arts
Miami, Florida
http://www.mdc.edu/nwsa/
Contact: Recruitment and Admissions Coordinator, New World School of the Arts, 300 NE Second Avenue, Miami, FL 33132. *Phone:* 305-237-7408. *Fax:* 305-237-3794. *E-mail:* nwsaadm@mdc.edu.

New York College of Health Professions
Syosset, New York
http://www.nycollege.edu/
Contact: Ms. Mary Rodas, Associate Director of Admissions, New York College of Health Professions, 6801 Jericho Turnpike, Syosset, NY 11791-4413. *Toll-free phone:* 800-922-7337 Ext. 351. *E-mail:* rdodas@nycollege.edu.

Nipissing University
North Bay, Ontario, Canada
http://www.nipissingu.ca/
Contact: Ms. Lori-Ann Beckford, Assistant Registrar, Liaison, Nipissing University, 100 College Drive, Box 5002, North Bay, ON P1B 8L7, Canada. *Phone:* 705-474-3461 Ext. 4518. *Fax:* 705-474-1947. *E-mail:* liaison@nipissingu.ca.

Northeast Catholic College
Warner, New Hampshire
http://www.magdalen.edu/
Contact: Admissions Director, Northeast Catholic College, 511 Kearsarge Mountain Road, Warner, NH 03278. *Phone:* 603-456-2656. *Toll-free phone:* 877-498-1723. *Fax:* 603-456-2660. *E-mail:* admissions@magdalen.edu.

Northern Marianas College
Saipan, Northern Mariana Islands
http://www.marianas.edu/
Contact: Ms. Leilani M. Basa-Alam, Admission Specialist, Northern Marianas College, PO Box 501250, Saipan, MP 96950-1250. *Phone:* 670-234-3690 Ext. 1539. *Fax:* 670-235-4967. *E-mail:* leilanib@nmcnet.edu.

Northern New Mexico University
Española, New Mexico
http://www.nnmc.edu/
Contact: Mr. Mike L. Costello, Registrar, Northern New Mexico University, 921 Paseo de Oñate, Española, NM 87532. *Phone:* 505-747-2193. *Fax:* 505-747-2191. *E-mail:* dms@nnmc.edu.

Northpoint Bible College

Haverhill, Massachusetts

http://northpoint.edu/

Contact: Helen Brouillette, Admissions Director, Northpoint Bible College, 320 South Main Street, Haverhill, MA 01835. *Phone:* 800-356-4014. *Toll-free phone:* 800-356-4014. *E-mail:* admissions@zbc.edu.

Northwestern Polytechnic University

Fremont, California

http://www.npu.edu/

Contact: Mr. Michael Tang, Admission Officer, Northwestern Polytechnic University, 47671 Westinghouse Drive, Fremont, CA 94539. *Phone:* 510-592-9688 Ext. 15. *Fax:* 510-657-8975. *E-mail:* admission@npu.edu.

Northwest Indian College

Bellingham, Washington

http://www.nwic.edu/

Contact: Office of Admissions, Northwest Indian College, 2522 Kwina Road, Bellingham, WA 98226. *Phone:* 360-676-2772. *Toll-free phone:* 866-676-2772. *Fax:* 360-392-4333. *E-mail:* admissions@nwic.edu.

NSCAD University

Halifax, Nova Scotia, Canada

http://www.nscad.ca/

Contact: Mr. Terry Bailey, Director of Admissions and Enrollment Services, NSCAD University, 5163 Duke Street, Halifax, NS B3J 3J6, Canada. *Phone:* 902-494-8129. *Toll-free phone:* 888-444-5989. *Fax:* 902-425-2987. *E-mail:* admissions@nscad.ca.

Oak Hills Christian College

Bemidji, Minnesota

http://www.oakhills.edu/

Contact: Shelly Fast, Assistant Director of Admissions, Oak Hills Christian College, 1600 Oak Hills Road SW, Bemidji, MN 56601. *Phone:* 218-751-8670 Ext. 1285. *Toll-free phone:* 888-751-8670 Ext. 1285. *Fax:* 218-751-8825. *E-mail:* admissions@oakhills.edu.

Oakwood University

Huntsville, Alabama

http://www.oakwood.edu/

Contact: Mr. Jason McCracken, Director of Enrollment Management, Oakwood University, 7000 Adventist Boulevard, NW, Huntsville, AL 35896. *Phone:* 256-726-7354. *Toll-free phone:* 800-824-5312. *Fax:* 256-726-7154. *E-mail:* admission@oakwood.edu.

Oglala Lakota College

Kyle, South Dakota

http://www.olc.edu/

Contact: Director of Admissions, Oglala Lakota College, 490 Piya Wiconi Road, Kyle, SD 57752-0490. *Phone:* 605-455-2321 Ext. 236. *E-mail:* lmeseteth@olc.edu.

Ohio Christian University

Circleville, Ohio

http://www.ohiochristian.edu/

Contact: Mike Egenreider, Associate Vice President for Enrollment, Ohio Christian University, 1476 Lancaster Pike, PO Box 458, Circleville, OH 43113-9487. *Phone:* 740-477-7741. *Toll-free phone:* 877-762-8669. *E-mail:* enroll@ohiochristian.edu.

Ohio University–Chillicothe

Chillicothe, Ohio

http://www.chillicothe.ohiou.edu/

Contact: Neeley Allen, Coordinator, Recruitment, Ohio University–Chillicothe, 101 University Drive, Chillicothe, OH 45601. *Phone:* 740-774-7241. *Toll-free phone:* 877-462-6824. *Fax:* 740-774-7214. *E-mail:* evelandt@ohio.edu.

Ohio University–Eastern

St. Clairsville, Ohio

http://www.eastern.ohiou.edu/

Contact: N. Kip Howard, Assistant Vice President for Enrollment Services/Director of Admissions, Ohio University–Eastern, 45425 National Road, St. Clairsville, OH 43950-9724. *Phone:* 740-593-4120. *Toll-free phone:* 800-648-3331. *E-mail:* howardn@ohio.edu.

Ohio University–Lancaster

Lancaster, Ohio

http://www.ohiou.edu/lancaster/

Contact: Pat Fox, Enrollment Manager, Ohio University–Lancaster, 1570 Granville Pike, Lancaster, OH 43130-1097. *Phone:* 740-654-6711 Ext. 215. *Toll-free phone:* 888-446-4468. *E-mail:* fox@ohio.edu.

Ohio University–Southern Campus

Ironton, Ohio

http://www.ohiou.edu/

Contact: Linda Harlow, Admission, Registration and Records Coordinator, Ohio University–Southern Campus, 1804 Liberty Avenue, Ironton, OH 45638-2214. *Phone:* 740-533-4584. *Toll-free phone:* 800-626-0513. *E-mail:* harlow@ohio.edu.

Ohr Hameir Theological Seminary

Cortlandt Manor, New York

Contact: Director of Admissions, Ohr Hameir Theological Seminary, 141 Furnace Woods Road, Cortlandt Manor, NY 10567. *Phone:* 914-736-1500.

Oklahoma Panhandle State University

Goodwell, Oklahoma

http://www.opsu.edu/

Contact: Mr. Bobby Jenkins, Registrar and Director of Admissions, Oklahoma Panhandle State University, PO Box 430, 323 Eagle Boulevard, Goodwell, OK 73939-0430. *Phone:* 580-349-1376. *Toll-free phone:* 800-664-6778. *Fax:* 580-349-1371. *E-mail:* opsu@opsu.edu.

O'More College of Design

Franklin, Tennessee

http://www.omorecollege.edu/

Contact: Mrs. Tori Bagsby, Assistant Director of Admissions, O'More College of Design, 423 South Margin Street, Franklin, TN 37064-2816. *Phone:* 615-794-4254 Ext. 230. *Toll-free phone:* 888-662-1970. *Fax:* 615-790-1662. *E-mail:* tbagsby@omorecollege.edu.

Oregon Institute of Technology

Klamath Falls, Oregon

http://www.oit.edu/

Contact: Oregon Institute of Technology, 3201 Campus Drive, Klamath Falls, OR 97601-8801. *Phone:* 541-885-1151. *Toll-free phone:* 800-422-2017.

Oregon State University–Cascades

Bend, Oregon

http://www.osucascades.edu/

Contact: Admissions Department, Oregon State University–Cascades, 2600 Northwest College Way, Bend, OR 97701. *Phone:* 541-322-3150. *E-mail:* cascadeadmit@osucascades.edu.

Ottawa University

Ottawa, Kansas

http://www.ottawa.edu/

Contact: Ottawa University, 1001 South Cedar, Ottawa, KS 66067-3399. *Phone:* 785-229-1051. *Toll-free phone:* 800-755-5200.

Our Lady of Holy Cross College

New Orleans, Louisiana

http://www.olhcc.edu/

Contact: Donna Kennedy, Director of Admissions and Financial Aid, Our Lady of Holy Cross College, 4123 Woodland Drive, New Orleans, LA 70131-7399. *Phone:* 504-398-2175. *Toll-free phone:* 800-259-7744. *E-mail:* dkennedy@olhcc.edu.

Ozark Christian College

Joplin, Missouri

http://www.occ.edu/

Contact: Mr. Troy B. Nelson, Executive Director of Admissions, Ozark Christian College, 1111 North Main Street, Joplin, MO 64801-4804. *Phone:* 417-624-2518. *Toll-free phone:* 800-299-4622. *Fax:* 417-624-0090. *E-mail:* occadmin@occ.edu.

Pacific Islands University

Mangilao, Guam

http://www.piu.edu/

Contact: Ethel Laco, Admissions Office, Pacific Islands University, 172 Kinney's Road, Mangilao, GU 96913. *Phone:* 671-734-1812. *Fax:* 671-734-1813. *E-mail:* guamcampus@pibc.edu.

Pacific Oaks College

Pasadena, California

http://www.pacificoaks.edu/

Contact: Ms. Augusta Pickens, Office of Admissions, Pacific Oaks College, 5 Westmoreland Place, Pasadena, CA 91103. *Phone:* 626-397-1349. *Toll-free phone:* 877-314-2380. *Fax:* 626-666-1220. *E-mail:* admissions@pacificoaks.edu.

Pacific States University

Los Angeles, California

http://www.psuca.edu/

Contact: Mr. Maawiya Ayeva, Admission officer, Pacific States University, 3450 Wilshire Boulevard, #500, Los Angeles, CA 90010. *Phone:* 323-731-2383 Ext. 202. *Toll-free phone:* 888-200-0383. *Fax:* 323-731-7276. *E-mail:* admissions@psuca.edu.

Palmer College of Chiropractic

Davenport, Iowa

http://www.palmer.edu/

Contact: Ms. Lisa Gisel, Undergraduate Admissions Representative, Palmer College of Chiropractic, 1000 Brady Street, Davenport, IA 52803-5287. *Phone:* 563-884-5743. *Toll-free phone:* 800-722-3648. *Fax:* 563-884-5226. *E-mail:* lisa.gisel@palmer.edu.

Patten University

Oakland, California

http://patten.edu/

Contact: Ms. Kim Guerra, Director of Admissions, Patten University, 2433 Coolidge Avenue, Oakland, CA 94601-2699. *Phone:* 510-261-8500 Ext. 7763. *Toll-free phone:* 877-4PATTEN. *Fax:* 510-534-4344.

Paul Smith's College

Paul Smiths, New York

http://www.paulsmiths.edu/

Contact: Admissions Office, Paul Smith's College, Routes 86 and 30, PO Box 265, Paul Smiths, NY 12970. *Phone:* 518-327-6227. *Toll-free phone:* 800-421-2605. *Fax:* 518-327-6016. *E-mail:* admissions@paulsmiths.edu.

Peninsula College

Port Angeles, Washington

http://www.pc.ctc.edu/

Contact: Ms. Pauline Marvin, Peninsula College, 1502 East Lauridsen Boulevard, Port Angeles, WA 98362. *Phone:* 360-417-6596. *Toll-free phone:* 877-452-9277. *Fax:* 360-457-8100. *E-mail:* admissions@pencol.edu.

Pfeiffer University

Misenheimer, North Carolina

http://www.pfeiffer.edu/

Contact: Ms. Diane Martin, Associate Director of Admissions, Pfeiffer University, PO Box 960, Highway 52 North, Misenheimer, NC 28109. *Phone:* 704-463-3052. *Toll-free phone:* 800-338-2060. *Fax:* 704-463-1363. *E-mail:* admiss@pfeiffer.edu.

Pima Medical Institute

Mesa, Arizona

http://www.pmi.edu/

Contact: Admissions Office, Pima Medical Institute, 957 South Dobson Road, Mesa, AZ 85202. *Phone:* 480-644-0267 Ext. 225. *Toll-free phone:* 800-477-PIMA (in-state); 888-477-PIMA (out-of-state).

Pima Medical Institute

Tucson, Arizona

http://www.pmi.edu/

Contact: Admissions Office, Pima Medical Institute, 3350 East Grant Road, Tucson, AZ 85716. *Phone:* 520-326-1600 Ext. 5112. *Toll-free phone:* 800-477-PIMA (in-state); 888-477-PIMA (out-of-state).

Pima Medical Institute

Chula Vista, California

http://www.pmi.edu/

Contact: Admissions Office, Pima Medical Institute, 780 Bay Boulevard, Suite 101, Chula Vista, CA 91910. *Phone:* 619-425-3200. *Toll-free phone:* 800-477-PIMA (in-state); 888-477-PIMA (out-of-state).

Pima Medical Institute

Denver, Colorado

http://www.pmi.edu/

Contact: Admissions Office, Pima Medical Institute, 7475 Dakin Street, Denver, CO 80221. *Phone:* 303-426-1800. *Toll-free phone:* 800-477-PIMA (in-state); 888-477-PIMA (out-of-state).

Pima Medical Institute

Las Vegas, Nevada

http://www.pmi.edu/

Contact: Admissions Office, Pima Medical Institute, 3333 East Flamingo Road, Las Vegas, NV 89121. *Phone:* 702-458-9650 Ext. 202. *Toll-free phone:* 800-477-PIMA.

Pima Medical Institute

Albuquerque, New Mexico

http://www.pmi.edu/

Contact: Admissions Office, Pima Medical Institute, 4400 Cutler Avenue NE, Albuquerque, NM 87110. *Phone:* 505-881-1234. *Toll-free phone:* 800-477-PIMA (in-state); 888-477-PIMA (out-of-state). *Fax:* 505-881-5329.

Pima Medical Institute

Seattle, Washington

http://www.pmi.edu/

Contact: Admissions Office, Pima Medical Institute, 9709 Third Avenue NE, Suite 400, Seattle, WA 98115. *Phone:* 206-322-6100. *Toll-free phone:* 800-477-PIMA (in-state); 888-477-PIMA (out-of-state).

Pioneer Pacific College–Eugene/Springfield Branch

Springfield, Oregon

http://www.pioneerpacific.edu/

Contact: Admissions Office, Pioneer Pacific College–Eugene/Springfield Branch, 3800 Sports Way, Springfield, OR 97477. *Phone:* 541-684-4644. *Toll-free phone:* 866-772-4636. *E-mail:* inquiries@pioneerpacific.edu.

Platt College

Alhambra, California

http://www.plattcollege.edu/

Contact: Mr. Detroit Whiteside, Director of Admissions, Platt College, 1000 South Fremont A9W, Alhambra, CA 91803. *Phone:* 323-258-8050. *Toll-free phone:* 888-866-6697 (in-state); 888-80-PLATT (out-of-state).

Platt College

Ontario, California

http://www.plattcollege.edu/

Contact: Ms. Jennifer Abandonato, Director of Admissions, Platt College, 3700 Inland Empire Boulevard, Suite 400, Ontario, CA 91764. *Phone:* 909-941-9410. *Toll-free phone:* 888-80-PLATT.

Platt College

Aurora, Colorado

http://www.plattcolorado.edu/

Contact: Admissions Office, Platt College, 3100 South Parker Road, Suite 200, Aurora, CO 80014-3141. *Phone:* 303-369-5151.

Pontifical Catholic University of Puerto Rico

Ponce, Puerto Rico

http://www.pucpr.edu/

Contact: Sra. Ana O. Bonilla, Director of Admissions, Pontifical Catholic University of Puerto Rico, 2250 Avenida Las Americas Avenue, Suite 584, Ponce, PR 00717-9777. *Phone:* 787-841-2000 Ext. 1004. *Toll-free phone:* 800-961-7696. *Fax:* 787-840-4295. *E-mail:* admissions@email.pucpr.edu.

Pontifical College Josephinum

Columbus, Ohio

http://www.pcj.edu/

Contact: Mrs. Arminda Crawford, Secretary for Admissions, Pontifical College Josephinum, 7825 North High Street, Columbus, OH 43235. *Phone:* 614-985-2241. *Toll-free phone:* 888-252-5812. *Fax:* 614-885-2307. *E-mail:* acrawford@pcj.edu.

Prairie Bible Institute

Three Hills, Alberta, Canada

http://www.prairie.edu/

Contact: Mr. Kevin Kirk, Vice President, Marketing and Enrollment Management, Prairie Bible Institute, 330 Sixth Avenue North, PO Box 4000, Three Hills, AB T0M 2N0, Canada. *Phone:* 403-443-5511 Ext. 3007. *Toll-free phone:* 800-661-2425. *E-mail:* admissions@prairie.edu.

Presentation College

Aberdeen, South Dakota

http://www.presentation.edu/

Contact: Mr. Robert Schuchardt, Vice President for Student Services, Presentation College, 1500 North Main Street, Aberdeen, SD 57401. *Phone:* 605-229-8406. *Toll-free phone:* 800-437-6060. *Fax:* 605-229-8425. *E-mail:* admit@presentation.edu.

Providence University College & Theological Seminary

Otterburne, Manitoba, Canada

http://www.providenceuc.ca/

Contact: Mr. Adrian Enns, Director of College Enrollment, Providence University College & Theological Seminary, 10 College Crescent, Otterburne, MB R0A 1G0, Canada. *Phone:* 204-433-7488. *Toll-free phone:* 800-668-7768. *Fax:* 204-433-7158. *E-mail:* info@prov.ca.

Queens University of Charlotte

Charlotte, North Carolina

http://www.queens.edu/

Contact: Queens University of Charlotte, 1900 Selwyn Avenue, Harris Welcome Center - MSC 1428, Charlotte, NC 28274. *Phone:* 704-337-2212. *Toll-free phone:* 800-849-0202. *Fax:* 704-337-2403. *E-mail:* admissions@queens.edu.

Rabbi Jacob Joseph School

Edison, New Jersey

Contact: Rabbi Jacob Joseph School, One Plainfield Ave, Edison, NJ 08817.

Rabbinical Academy Mesivta Rabbi Chaim Berlin

Brooklyn, New York

Contact: Executive Administrator, Rabbinical Academy Mesivta Rabbi Chaim Berlin, 1605 Coney Island Avenue, Brooklyn, NY 11230-4715. *Phone:* 718-377-0777. *Fax:* 718-338-5578.

Rabbinical College Beth Shraga

Monsey, New York

Contact: Rabbi Sydney Schiff, Director of Admissions, Rabbinical College Beth Shraga, 28 Saddle River Road, Monsey, NY 10952-3035.

Rabbinical College Bobover Yeshiva B'nei Zion

Brooklyn, New York

Contact: Director of Admissions, Rabbinical College Bobover Yeshiva B'nei Zion, 1577 Forty-eighth Street, Brooklyn, NY 11219. *Phone:* 718-438-2018.

Rabbinical College Ch'san Sofer

Brooklyn, New York

Contact: Director of Admissions, Rabbinical College Ch'san Sofer, 1876 Fiftieth Street, Brooklyn, NY 11204. *Phone:* 718-236-1171.

Rabbinical College of America

Morristown, New Jersey

http://www.rca.edu/

Contact: Shoshana Solomon, Registrar, Rabbinical College of America, 226 Sussex Avenue, PO Box 1996, Morristown, NJ 07962-1996. *Phone:* 973-267-9404. *E-mail:* rca079@aol.com.

Rabbinical College of Long Island

Long Beach, New York

Contact: Director of Admissions, Rabbinical College of Long Island, 205 West Beech Street, Long Beach, NY 11561-3305. *Phone:* 516-431-7414.

Rabbinical College of Ohr Shimon Yisroel

Brooklyn, New York

Contact: Rabbinical College of Ohr Shimon Yisroel, 215-217 Hewes Street, Brooklyn, NY 11211.

Rabbinical Seminary of America

Flushing, New York

Contact: Rabbi Abraham Semmel, Director of Admissions, Rabbinical Seminary of America, 76-01 147th Street, Flushing, NY 11367. *Phone:* 718-268-4700.

Ranken Technical College

St. Louis, Missouri

http://www.ranken.edu/

Contact: Ms. Elizabeth Keserauskis, Director of Admissions, Ranken Technical College, 4431 Finney Avenue, St. Louis, MO 63113. *Phone:* 314-371-0233 Ext. 4811. *Toll-free phone:* 866-4-RANKEN.

Remington College–Honolulu Campus

Honolulu, Hawaii

http://www.remingtoncollege.edu/

Contact: Louis LaMair, Director of Recruitment, Remington College–Honolulu Campus, 1111 Bishop Street, Suite 400, Honolulu, HI 96813. *Phone:* 808-942-1000. *Fax:* 808-533-3064. *E-mail:* louis.lamair@remingtoncollege.edu.

Remington College–Memphis Campus

Memphis, Tennessee

http://www.remingtoncollege.edu/

Contact: Randal Hayes, Director of Recruitment, Remington College–Memphis Campus, 2710 Nonconnah Boulevard, Memphis, TN 38132. *Phone:* 901-345-1000. *Fax:* 901-396-8310. *E-mail:* randal.hayes@remingtoncollege.edu.

Remington College–Mobile Campus

Mobile, Alabama

http://www.remingtoncollege.edu/

Contact: Remington College–Mobile Campus, 828 Downtowner Loop West, Mobile, AL 36609-5404. *Phone:* 251-343-8200. *Toll-free phone:* 800-560-6192.

Remington College–Tampa Campus

Tampa, Florida

http://www.remingtoncollege.edu/

Contact: Remington College–Tampa Campus, 6302 E. Dr. Martin Luther King, Jr. Boulevard, Suite 400, Tampa, FL 33619. *Phone:* 813-932-0701. *Toll-free phone:* 800-560-6192.

Rochester College

Rochester Hills, Michigan

http://www.rc.edu/

Contact: Mr. Larry Norman, Dean of Admissions, Rochester College, 800 West Avon Road, Rochester Hills, MI 48307-2764. *Phone:* 248-218-2190. *Toll-free phone:* 800-521-6010. *Fax:* 248-218-2035. *E-mail:* admissions@rc.edu.

Rochester Community and Technical College

Rochester, Minnesota

http://www.rctc.edu/

Contact: Mr. Troy Tynsky, Director of Admissions, Rochester Community and Technical College, 851 30th Avenue, SE, Rochester, MN 55904-4999. *Phone:* 507-280-3509.

Royal Military College of Canada

Kingston, Ontario, Canada

http://www.rmc.ca/

Contact: Royal Military College of Canada, PO Box 17000, Station Forces, Kingston, ON K7K 7B4, Canada. *Phone:* 613-541-6000 Ext. 6579.

Rush University
Chicago, Illinois
http://www.rushu.rush.edu/
Contact: Rush University, 600 South Paulina, Chicago, IL 60612-3832. *Phone:* 312-942-7100.

Ryerson University
Toronto, Ontario, Canada
http://www.ryerson.ca/
Contact: Michelle Beaton, Manager of International Student Recruitment, Ryerson University, 350 Victoria Street, Toronto, ON M5B 2K3, Canada. *Phone:* 416-979-5080. *Fax:* 416-979-5067. *E-mail:* inquire@ryerson.ca.

Sacred Heart Major Seminary
Detroit, Michigan
http://www.shms.edu/
Contact: Fr. Michael Byrnes, Vice Rector, Sacred Heart Major Seminary, 2701 Chicago Boulevard, Detroit, MI 48206. *Phone:* 313-883-8552. *Fax:* 313-868-6400.

St. Ambrose University
Davenport, Iowa
http://www.sau.edu/
Contact: St. Ambrose University, 518 West Locust Street, Davenport, IA 52803-2898. *Phone:* 563-333-6300 Ext. 6311. *Toll-free phone:* 800-383-2627.

St. Augustine College
Chicago, Illinois
http://www.staugustine.edu/
Contact: Ms. Gloria Quiroz, Director of Admissions, St. Augustine College, 1333-1345 West Argyle, Chicago, IL 60640-3501. *Phone:* 773-878-3256. *Fax:* 773-878-0937. *E-mail:* info@staugustine.edu.

St. Francis Xavier University
Antigonish, Nova Scotia, Canada
http://www.stfx.ca/
Contact: Ms. Sarah Murray, Admissions Officer, St. Francis Xavier University, PO Box 5000, Antigonish, NS B2G 2W5, Canada. *Phone:* 902-867-2219. *Toll-free phone:* 877-867-7839 (in-state); 877-867-STFX (out-of-state). *Fax:* 902-867-2329. *E-mail:* mbarry@stfx.ca.

St. John Vianney College Seminary
Miami, Florida
http://www.sjvcs.edu/
Contact: Br. Edward Van Merrienboer, Academic Dean, St. John Vianney College Seminary, 2900 Southwest 87th Avenue, Miami, FL 33165-3244. *Phone:* 305-223-4561 Ext. 13.

Saint Joseph's College of Maine
Standish, Maine
http://www.sjcme.edu/
Contact: Kathleen Davis, Vice President for Enrollment Management, Saint Joseph's College of Maine, 278 Whites Bridge Road, Standish, ME 04084-5263. *Phone:* 207-893-7746. *Toll-free phone:* 800-338-7057. *Fax:* 207-893-7862. *E-mail:* admission@sjcme.edu.

Saint Luke's College of Health Sciences
Kansas City, Missouri
http://www.saintlukescollege.edu/
Contact: Mrs. Jennifer Wright, Student Services Associate, Saint Luke's College of Health Sciences, 8320 Ward Parkway, Suite 300, Kansas City, MO 64114. *Phone:* 816-932-8629. *Fax:* 816-932-9064.

Saint Mary's University
Halifax, Nova Scotia, Canada
http://www.smu.ca/
Contact: Mr. Greg Ferguson, Director of Admissions, Saint Mary's University, Halifax, NS B3H 3C3, Canada. *Phone:* 902-420-5415. *Fax:* 902-496-8100. *E-mail:* greg.ferguson@smu.ca.

Saint Paul University
Ottawa, Ontario, Canada
http://www.ustpaul.ca/
Contact: Admission and Recruitment Office, Saint Paul University, 223 Main Street, Ottawa, ON K1S 1C4, Canada. *Phone:* 613-236-1393 Ext. 8990. *Toll-free phone:* 800-637-6859. *Fax:* 613-782-3014. *E-mail:* admission@ustpaul.ca.

St. Petersburg College
St. Petersburg, Florida
http://www.spcollege.edu/
Contact: Ms. Susan Fell, Director of Admissions and Records, St. Petersburg College, PO Box 13489, St. Petersburg, FL 33733-3489. *Phone:* 727-341-3166. *E-mail:* information@spcollege.edu.

Saint Xavier University
Chicago, Illinois
http://www.sxu.edu/
Contact: Dr. Kathleen Carlson, Vice President, Saint Xavier University, 3700 West 103rd Street, Chicago, IL 60655-3105. *Phone:* 773-298-3305. *Toll-free phone:* 800-462-9288. *E-mail:* carlson@sxu.edu.

Salem International University
Salem, West Virginia
http://www.salemu.edu/
Contact: Mrs. Brenda Davis, Admissions Representative, Salem International University, PO Box 500, Salem, WV 26426-0500. *Phone:* 304-326-1359. *Toll-free phone:* 888-235-5024. *Fax:* 304-326-1592. *E-mail:* admissions@salemiu.edu.

Salish Kootenai College
Pablo, Montana
http://www.skc.edu/
Contact: Ms. Jackie Moran, Admissions Officer, Salish Kootenai College, PO Box 70, Pablo, MT 59855-0117. *Phone:* 406-275-4866. *Fax:* 406-275-4810. *E-mail:* jackie_moran@skc.edu.

Sanford-Brown College
Mendota Heights, Minnesota
http://www.sanfordbrown.edu/Mendota-Heights
Contact: Mr. Mark Fredrichs, Registrar, Sanford-Brown College, 1440 Northland Drive, Mendota Heights, MN 55120. *Phone:* 651-905-3400. *Toll-free phone:* 855-502-7016. *Fax:* 651-905-3550.

Schiller International University

Heidelberg, Germany

http://www.schiller.edu/

Contact: Ms. Kamala Dontamsetti, Associate Director of Admissions, Schiller International University, 300 East Bay Drive, Largo, FL 33770. *Phone:* 727-736-5082 Ext. 234. *Toll-free phone:* 800-261-9571 (in-state); 800-261-9751 (out-of-state). *Fax:* 727-734-0359. *E-mail:* kamala_dontamsetti@schiller.edu.

Schiller International University

Madrid, Spain

http://www.schiller.edu/

Contact: Ms. Kamala Dontamsetti, Associate Director of Admissions, Schiller International University, 300 East Bay Drive, Largo, FL 33700. *Phone:* 727-736-5082 Ext. 234. *Toll-free phone:* 800-261-9571 (in-state); 800-261-9751 (out-of-state). *Fax:* 727-734-0359. *E-mail:* admissions@schiller.edu.

Shorter University

Rome, Georgia

http://www.shorter.edu/

Contact: Shorter University, 315 Shorter Avenue, Rome, GA 30165. *Phone:* 706-233-7342. *Toll-free phone:* 800-868-6980.

Sh'or Yoshuv Rabbinical College

Lawrence, New York

http://www.shoryoshuv.org/

Contact: Rabbi Moshe Rubin, Registrar, Sh'or Yoshuv Rabbinical College, 1 Cedarlawn Avenue, Lawrence, NY 11559-1714. *Phone:* 516-239-9002 Ext. 124. *Fax:* 516-977-1282. *E-mail:* mrubin@shoryoshuv.org.

Sinte Gleska University

Mission, South Dakota

http://www.sintegleska.edu/

Contact: Mr. Jack Herman, Registrar and Director of Admissions, Sinte Gleska University, 101 Antelope Lake Circle, PO Box 105, Mission, SD 57555. *Phone:* 605-856-8100 Ext. 8479.

Sitting Bull College

Fort Yates, North Dakota

http://www.sittingbull.edu/

Contact: Ms. Melody Silk, Director of Registration and Admissions, Sitting Bull College, 1341 92nd Street, Fort Yates, ND 58538-9701. *Phone:* 701-854-3864. *Fax:* 701-854-3403. *E-mail:* melodys@sbcl.edu.

Skyline College

Roanoke, Virginia

http://www.skyline.edu/

Contact: Dr. Walter Merchant, Campus Provost (Interim), Skyline College, 5234 Airport Road, Roanoke, VA 24012. *Phone:* 540-563-8080. *Toll-free phone:* 866-708-6178. *Fax:* 540-362-5400. *E-mail:* wmerchant@ecpi.edu.

South College

Knoxville, Tennessee

http://www.southcollegetn.edu/

Contact: Mr. Walter Hosea, Director of Admissions, South College, 720 North Fifth Avenue, Knoxville, TN 37917. *Phone:* 865-524-3043 Ext. 1825. *E-mail:* whosea@southcollegetn.edu.

South College–Asheville

Asheville, North Carolina

http://www.southcollegenc.edu/

Contact: Director of Admissions, South College–Asheville, 1567 Patton Avenue, Asheville, NC 28806. *Phone:* 828-277-5521. *Fax:* 828-277-6151.

Southeastern Baptist College

Laurel, Mississippi

http://www.southeasternbaptist.edu/

Contact: Mrs. Emma Bond, Director of Admissions, Southeastern Baptist College, 4229 Highway 15 North, Laurel, MS 39440-1096. *Phone:* 601-426-6346.

Southeastern Baptist Theological Seminary

Wake Forest, North Carolina

http://www.sebts.edu/

Contact: Mrs. Audrey Greeson, Admissions Counselor, Southeastern Baptist Theological Seminary, PO Box 1889, Wake Forest, NC 27588-1889. *Phone:* 800-284-6317. *Toll-free phone:* 800-284-6317.

Southern Alberta Institute of Technology

Calgary, Alberta, Canada

http://www.sait.ca/

Contact: Southern Alberta Institute of Technology, 1301 16th Avenue NW, Calgary, AB T2M 0L4, Canada. *Phone:* 403-284-8857. *Toll-free phone:* 877-284-SAIT.

Southern Baptist Theological Seminary

Louisville, Kentucky

http://www.sbts.edu/

Contact: Dr. Daniel DeWitt, Southern Baptist Theological Seminary, 2825 Lexington Road, Louisville, KY 40280-0004. *Phone:* 502-897-4011 Ext. 4617.

Southern Polytechnic State University

Marietta, Georgia

http://www.spsu.edu/

Contact: Mr. Gary Bush, Director of Admissions, Southern Polytechnic State University, 1100 South Marietta Parkway, Marietta, GA 30060. *Phone:* 678-915-7468. *Toll-free phone:* 800-635-3204. *Fax:* 678-915-7496. *E-mail:* gbush@spsu.edu.

Southern Technical College

Fort Myers, Florida

http://www.southerntech.edu/locations/ft-myers/

Contact: Mr. Ken Reynolds, Director of Admissions, Southern Technical College, 1685 Medical Lane, Fort Myers, FL 33907. *Phone:* 239-939-4766. *Toll-free phone:* 877-347-5492. *Fax:* 239-936-4040. *E-mail:* kreynolds@swfc.edu.

Southern University and Agricultural and Mechanical College
Baton Rouge, Louisiana
http://www.subr.edu/
Contact: Ms. Velva Thomas, Director of Admissions, Southern University and Agricultural and Mechanical College, PO Box 9901, Baton Rouge, LA 70813. *Phone:* 225-771-2430. *Fax:* 225-771-2500. *E-mail:* velva_thomas@subr.edu.

Southern University at New Orleans
New Orleans, Louisiana
http://www.suno.edu/
Contact: Southern University at New Orleans, 6400 Press Drive, New Orleans, LA 70126-1009. *Phone:* 504-286-5033.

Southern Virginia University
Buena Vista, Virginia
http://www.svu.edu/
Contact: Mr. Tony Caputo, Dean of Admissions, Southern Virginia University, One University Hill Drive, Buena Vista, VA 24416. *Phone:* 540-261-2756. *Toll-free phone:* 800-229-8420. *Fax:* 540-261-8559. *E-mail:* admissions@southernvirginia.edu.

Southern Wesleyan University
Central, South Carolina
http://www.swu.edu/
Contact: Mrs. Beth Roe, Director of First Year Experience, Southern Wesleyan University, PO Box 1020, 907 Wesleyan Drive, Central, SC 29630-1020. *Phone:* 864-644-5149. *Toll-free phone:* 800-CU-AT-SWU. *Fax:* 864-644-5901. *E-mail:* broe@swu.edu.

South Texas College
McAllen, Texas
http://www.southtexascollege.edu/
Contact: Mr. Matthew Hebbard, Director of Enrollment Services and Registrar, South Texas College, 3201 West Pecan, McAllen, TX 78501. *Phone:* 956-872-2147. *Toll-free phone:* 800-742-7822. *E-mail:* mshebbar@southtexascollege.edu.

Southwestern Christian College
Terrell, Texas
http://www.swcc.edu/
Contact: Admissions Department, Southwestern Christian College, Box 10, 200 Bowser Street, Terrell, TX 75160. *Phone:* 214-524-3341.

Southwestern Christian University
Bethany, Oklahoma
http://www.swcu.edu/
Contact: Jessie Burpo, Admissions Counselor, Southwestern Christian University, PO Box 340, Bethany, OK 73008-0340. *Phone:* 405-789-7661 Ext. 3432. *Fax:* 405-495-0078. *E-mail:* admissions@swcu.edu.

Southwest University
Kenner, Louisiana
http://www.southwest.edu/
Contact: Admissions Office, Southwest University, 2200 Veterans Memorial Blvd., Kenner, LA 70062. *Phone:* 504-468-2900. *Toll-free phone:* 800-433-5923. *Fax:* 504-468-3213. *E-mail:* admissions@southwest.edu.

Southwest University of Visual Arts
Tucson, Arizona
http://www.suva.edu/
Contact: Sarah LaVetter, Director of Admissions, Southwest University of Visual Arts, 2525 North Country Club Road, Tucson, AZ 85716-2505. *Phone:* 520-325-0123. *Toll-free phone:* 800-825-8753. *Fax:* 520-325-5535.

Spartan College of Aeronautics and Technology
Tulsa, Oklahoma
http://www.spartan.edu/
Contact: Mr. Mark Fowler, Vice President of Student Records and Finance, Spartan College of Aeronautics and Technology, 8820 East Pine Street, PO Box 582833, Tulsa, OK 74158-2833. *Phone:* 918-836-6886. *Toll-free phone:* 800-331-1204 (in-state); 800-331-124 (out-of-state).

State University of New York College at Oneonta
Oneonta, New York
http://www.oneonta.edu/
Contact: Ms. Karen Brown, Director of Admissions, State University of New York College at Oneonta, Alumni Hall 116, Oneonta, NY 13820-4015. *Phone:* 607-436-2524. *Toll-free phone:* 800-SUNY-123. *Fax:* 607-436-3074. *E-mail:* admissions@oneonta.edu.

State University of New York Downstate Medical Center
Brooklyn, New York
http://www.downstate.edu/
Contact: Admissions Office, State University of New York Downstate Medical Center, 450 Clarkson Avenue, Brooklyn, NY 11203-2446. *Phone:* 718-270-2446. *Fax:* 718-270-7592. *E-mail:* admissions@downstate.edu.

State University of New York Upstate Medical University
Syracuse, New York
http://www.upstate.edu/
Contact: Mrs. Donna L. Vavonese, Associate Director of Admissions, State University of New York Upstate Medical University, Weiskotten Hall, 766 Irving Avenue, Syracuse, NY 13210. *Phone:* 315-464-4570. *Toll-free phone:* 800-736-2171. *Fax:* 315-464-8867. *E-mail:* admiss@upstate.edu.

Steinbach Bible College
Steinbach, Manitoba, Canada
http://www.sbcollege.ca/
Contact: Mrs. Kaylene Buhler, Admissions Counselor, Steinbach Bible College, 50 PTH 12 North, Steinbach, MB R5G 1T4, Canada. *Phone:* 204-326-6451 Ext. 232. *Toll-free phone:* 800-230-8478. *Fax:* 204-326-6908. *E-mail:* info@sbcollege.ca.

Stevens-Henager College–Ogden/West Haven
Ogden, Utah
http://www.stevenshenager.edu/
Contact: Admissions Office, Stevens-Henager College–Ogden/West Haven, 1890 South 1350 West, Ogden, UT 84401. *Phone:* 801-394-7791. *Toll-free phone:* 800-622-2640.

Stevens Institute of Technology
Hoboken, New Jersey
http://www.stevens.edu/
Contact: Mr. Daniel Gallagher, Dean of University Admissions, Stevens Institute of Technology, Castle Point on Hudson, Hoboken, NJ 07030. *Phone:* 201-216-5197. *Toll-free phone:* 800-458-5323. *E-mail:* admissions@stevens.edu.

Stillman College
Tuscaloosa, Alabama
http://www.stillman.edu/
Contact: Stillman College, PO Drawer 1430, 3600 Stillman Boulevard, Tuscaloosa, AL 35403-9990. *Phone:* 205-366-8837. *Toll-free phone:* 800-841-5722.

Strayer University–Alexandria Campus
Alexandria, Virginia
http://www.strayer.edu/virginia/alexandria/
Contact: Strayer University–Alexandria Campus, 2730 Eisenhower Avenue, Alexandria, VA 22314.

Strayer University–Allentown Campus
Center Valley, Pennsylvania
http://www.strayer.edu/pennsylvania/allentown/
Contact: Strayer University–Allentown Campus, 3800 Sierra Circle, Suite 300, Center Valley, PA 18034.

Strayer University–Anne Arundel Campus
Millersville, Maryland
http://www.strayer.edu/maryland/anne-arundel/
Contact: Strayer University–Anne Arundel Campus, 1520 Jabez Run, Millersville, MD 21108.

Strayer University–Arlington Campus
Arlington, Virginia
http://www.strayer.edu/virginia/arlington/
Contact: Strayer University–Arlington Campus, 2121 15th Street North, Arlington, VA 22201.

Strayer University–Augusta Campus
Augusta, Georgia
http://www.strayer.edu/georgia/augusta/
Contact: Strayer University–Augusta Campus, 1330 Augusta West Parkway, Augusta, GA 30909.

Strayer University–Baymeadows Campus
Jacksonville, Florida
http://www.strayer.edu/florida/baymeadows/
Contact: Strayer University–Baymeadows Campus, 8375 Dix Ellis Trail, Suite 200, Jacksonville, FL 32256.

Strayer University–Birmingham Campus
Birmingham, Alabama
http://www.strayer.edu/alabama/birmingham/
Contact: Strayer University–Birmingham Campus, 3570 Grandview Parkway, Suite 200, Birmingham, AL 35243.

Strayer University–Brickell Campus
Miami, Florida
http://www.strayer.edu/florida/brickell/
Contact: Strayer University–Brickell Campus, 1201 Brickell Avenue, Suite 700, Miami, FL 33131.

Strayer University–Cedar Hill Campus
Cedar Hill, Texas
http://www.strayer.edu/texas/cedar-hill/
Contact: Strayer University–Cedar Hill Campus, 610 Uptown Boulevard, Suite 3500, Cedar Hill, TX 75104.

Strayer University–Center City Campus
Philadelphia, Pennsylvania
http://www.strayer.edu/pennsylvania/center-city/
Contact: Strayer University–Center City Campus, 1601 Cherry Street, Suite 100, Philadelphia, PA 19102.

Strayer University–Chamblee Campus
Atlanta, Georgia
http://www.strayer.edu/georgia/chamblee/
Contact: Strayer University–Chamblee Campus, 3355 Northeast Expressway, Suite 100, Atlanta, GA 30341.

Strayer University–Charleston Campus
North Charleston, South Carolina
http://www.strayer.edu/south-carolina/charleston/
Contact: Strayer University–Charleston Campus, 5010 Wetland Crossing, North Charleston, SC 29418.

Strayer University–Cherry Hill Campus
Cherry Hill, New Jersey
http://www.strayer.edu/new-jersey/cherry-hill/
Contact: Strayer University–Cherry Hill Campus, 2201 Route 38, Suite 100, Cherry Hill, NJ 08002.

Strayer University–Chesapeake Campus
Chesapeake, Virginia
http://www.strayer.edu/virginia/chesapeake/
Contact: Strayer University–Chesapeake Campus, 676 Independence Parkway, Suite 300, Chesapeake, VA 23320.

Strayer University–Chesterfield Campus
Midlothian, Virginia
http://www.strayer.edu/virginia/chesterfield/
Contact: Strayer University–Chesterfield Campus, 2820 Waterford Lake Drive, Suite 100, Midlothian, VA 23112.

Strayer University–Christiana Campus
Newark, Delaware
http://www.strayer.edu/delaware/christiana/
Contact: Strayer University–Christiana Campus, 240 Continental Drive, Suite 108, Newark, DE 19713.

Strayer University–Cobb County Campus
Atlanta, Georgia
http://www.strayer.edu/georgia/cobb-county/
Contact: Strayer University–Cobb County Campus, 3101 Towercreek Parkway, SE, Suite 700, Atlanta, GA 30339-3256.

Strayer University–Columbia Campus
Columbia, South Carolina
http://www.strayer.edu/south-carolina/columbia/
Contact: Strayer University–Columbia Campus, 200 Center Point Circle, Suite 300, Columbia, SC 29210.

Strayer University–Columbus Campus
Columbus, Georgia
http://www.strayer.edu/georgia/columbus/
Contact: Strayer University–Columbus Campus, 6003 Veterans Parkway, Suite 100, Columbus, GA 31909.

Strayer University–Coral Springs Campus
Pompano Beach, Florida
http://www.strayer.edu/florida/coral-springs/
Contact: Strayer University–Coral Springs Campus, 5830 Coral Ridge Drive, Suite 300, Pompano Beach, FL 33076.

Strayer University–Delaware County Campus
Springfield, Pennsylvania
http://www.strayer.edu/pennsylvania/delaware-county/
Contact: Strayer University–Delaware County Campus, 760 West Sproul Road, Suite 200, Springfield, PA 19064-1215.

Strayer University–Doral Campus
Miami, Florida
http://www.strayer.edu/florida/doral/
Contact: Strayer University–Doral Campus, 11430 Northwest 20th Street, Suite 150, Miami, FL 33172.

Strayer University–Douglasville Campus
Douglasville, Georgia
http://www.strayer.edu/georgia/douglasville/
Contact: Strayer University–Douglasville Campus, 4655 Timber Ridge Drive, Douglasville, GA 30135.

Strayer University–Fort Lauderdale Campus
Fort Lauderdale, Florida
http://www.strayer.edu/florida/fort-lauderdale/
Contact: Strayer University–Fort Lauderdale Campus, 2307 West Broward Boulevard, Suite 100, Fort Lauderdale, FL 33312.

Strayer University–Fredericksburg Campus
Fredericksburg, Virginia
http://www.strayer.edu/virginia/fredericksburg/
Contact: Strayer University–Fredericksburg Campus, 150 Riverside Parkway, Suite 100, Fredericksburg, VA 22406.

Strayer University–Greensboro Campus
Greensboro, North Carolina
http://www.strayer.edu/north-carolina/greensboro/
Contact: Strayer University–Greensboro Campus, 4900 Koger Boulevard, Suite 400, Greensboro, NC 27407.

Strayer University–Greenville Campus
Greenville, South Carolina
http://www.strayer.edu/south-carolina/greenville/
Contact: Strayer University–Greenville Campus, 555 North Pleasantburg Drive, Suite 300, Greenville, SC 29607.

Strayer University–Henrico Campus
Glen Allen, Virginia
http://www.strayer.edu/virginia/henrico/
Contact: Strayer University–Henrico Campus, 11501 Nuckols Road, Glen Allen, VA 23059.

Strayer University–Huntersville Campus
Huntersville, North Carolina
http://www.strayer.edu/north-carolina/huntersville/
Contact: Strayer University–Huntersville Campus, 13620 Reese Boulevard, Suite 130, Huntersville, NC 28078.

Strayer University–Huntsville Campus
Huntsville, Alabama
http://www.strayer.edu/alabama/huntsville/
Contact: Strayer University–Huntsville Campus, 4955 Corporate Drive, NW, Suite 200, Huntsville, AL 35805.

Strayer University–Irving Campus
Irving, Texas
http://www.strayer.edu/texas/irving/
Contact: Strayer University–Irving Campus, 7701 Las Colinas Ridge, Suite 450, Irving, TX 75063.

Strayer University–Jackson Campus
Jackson, Mississippi
http://www.strayer.edu/mississippi/jackson/
Contact: Strayer University–Jackson Campus, 460 Briarwood Drive, Suite 200, Jackson, MS 39206.

Strayer University–Katy Campus
Houston, Texas
http://www.strayer.edu/texas/katy/
Contact: Strayer University–Katy Campus, 14511 Old Katy Road, Suite 200, Houston, TX 77079.

Strayer University–King of Prussia Campus
King of Prussia, Pennsylvania
http://www.strayer.edu/pennsylvania/king-prussia/
Contact: Strayer University–King of Prussia Campus, 234 Mall Boulevard, Suite G-50, King of Prussia, PA 19406.

Strayer University–Knoxville Campus
Knoxville, Tennessee
http://www.strayer.edu/tennessee/knoxville/
Contact: Strayer University–Knoxville Campus, 10118 Parkside Drive, Suite 200, Knoxville, TN 37922.

Strayer University–Lawrenceville Campus
Lawrenceville, New Jersey
http://www.strayer.edu/new-jersey/lawrenceville/
Contact: Strayer University–Lawrenceville Campus, 3150 Brunswick Pike, Suite 100, Lawrenceville, NJ 08648.

Strayer University–Lithonia Campus
Lithonia, Georgia
http://www.strayer.edu/georgia/lithonia/
Contact: Strayer University–Lithonia Campus, 3120 Stonecrest Boulevard, Suite 200, Lithonia, GA 30038.

Strayer University–Little Rock Campus
Little Rock, Arkansas
http://www.strayer.edu/arkansas/little-rock/
Contact: Strayer University–Little Rock Campus, 10825 Financial Centre Parkway, Suite 131, Little Rock, AR 72211.

Strayer University–Loudoun Campus
Ashburn, Virginia
http://www.strayer.edu/virginia/loudoun/
Contact: Strayer University–Loudoun Campus, 45150 Russell Branch Parkway, Suite 200, Ashburn, VA 20147.

Strayer University–Lower Bucks County Campus
Trevose, Pennsylvania
http://www.strayer.edu/pennsylvania/lower-bucks-county/
Contact: Strayer University–Lower Bucks County Campus, 3800 Horizon Boulevard, Suite 100, Trevose, PA 19053.

Strayer University–Maitland Campus
Maitland, Florida
http://www.strayer.edu/florida/maitland/
Contact: Strayer University–Maitland Campus, 850 Trafalgar Court, Suite 360, Maitland, FL 32751.

Strayer University–Manassas Campus
Manassas, Virginia
http://www.strayer.edu/virginia/manassas/
Contact: Strayer University–Manassas Campus, 9990 Battleview Parkway, Manassas, VA 20109.

Strayer University–Metairie Campus
Metairie, Louisiana
http://www.strayer.edu/louisiana/metairie/
Contact: Strayer University–Metairie Campus, 111 Veterans Memorial Boulevard, Suite 420, Metairie, LA 70005.

Strayer University–Miramar Campus
Miramar, Florida
http://www.strayer.edu/florida/miramar/
Contact: Strayer University–Miramar Campus, 15620 Southwest 29th Street, Miramar, FL 33027.

Strayer University–Morrow Campus
Morrow, Georgia
http://www.strayer.edu/georgia/morrow/
Contact: Strayer University–Morrow Campus, 3000 Corporate Center Drive, Suite 100, Morrow, GA 30260.

Strayer University–Nashville Campus
Nashville, Tennessee
http://www.strayer.edu/tennessee/nashville/
Contact: Strayer University–Nashville Campus, 1809 Dabbs Avenue, Nashville, TN 37210.

Strayer University–Newport News Campus
Newport News, Virginia
http://www.strayer.edu/virginia/newport-news/
Contact: Strayer University–Newport News Campus, 99 Old Oyster Point Road, Unit 1, Newport News, VA 23602.

Strayer University–North Austin Campus

Austin, Texas

http://www.strayer.edu/texas/north-austin/

Contact: Strayer University–North Austin Campus, 8501 North Mopac Expressway, Suite 100, Austin, TX 78759.

Strayer University–North Charlotte Campus

Concord, North Carolina

http://www.strayer.edu/north-carolina/north-charlotte/

Contact: Strayer University–North Charlotte Campus, 7870 Commons Park Circle NW, Concord, NC 28027.

Strayer University–North Raleigh Campus

Raleigh, North Carolina

http://www.strayer.edu/north-carolina/north-raleigh/

Contact: Strayer University–North Raleigh Campus, 8701 Wadford Drive, Raleigh, NC 27616.

Strayer University–Northwest Houston Campus

Houston, Texas

http://www.strayer.edu/texas/northwest-houston/

Contact: Strayer University–Northwest Houston Campus, 10940 W. Sam Houston Parkway N., Suite 200, Houston, TX 77064.

Strayer University–Orlando East Campus

Orlando, Florida

http://www.strayer.edu/florida/orlando-east/

Contact: Strayer University–Orlando East Campus, 2200 North Alafaya Trail, Suite 500, Orlando, FL 32826.

Strayer University–Owings Mills Campus

Owings Mills, Maryland

http://www.strayer.edu/maryland/owings-mills/

Contact: Strayer University–Owings Mills Campus, 500 Redland Court, Suite 100, Owings Mills, MD 21117.

Strayer University–Palm Beach Gardens Campus

West Palm Beach, Florida

http://www.strayer.edu/florida/palm-beach-gardens/

Contact: Strayer University–Palm Beach Gardens Campus, 11025 RCA Center Drive, Suite 200, West Palm Beach, FL 33410.

Strayer University–Piscataway Campus

Piscataway, New Jersey

http://www.strayer.edu/new-jersey/piscataway/

Contact: Strayer University–Piscataway Campus, 242 Old New Brunswick Road, Suite 220, Piscataway, NJ 08854.

Strayer University–Plano Campus

Plano, Texas

http://www.strayer.edu/texas/plano/

Contact: Strayer University–Plano Campus, 2701 North Dallas Parkway, Suite 300, Plano, TX 75093.

Strayer University–Prince George's Campus

Suitland, Maryland

http://www.strayer.edu/maryland/prince-georges/

Contact: Strayer University–Prince George's Campus, 4710 Auth Place, First Floor, Suitland, MD 20746.

Strayer University–Rockville Campus

Rockville, Maryland

http://www.strayer.edu/maryland/rockville/

Contact: Strayer University–Rockville Campus, 4 Research Place, Suite 100, Rockville, MD 20850.

Strayer University–Roswell Campus

Roswell, Georgia

http://www.strayer.edu/georgia/roswell/

Contact: Strayer University–Roswell Campus, 100 Mansell Court East, Suite 100, Roswell, GA 30076.

Strayer University–RTP Campus

Morrisville, North Carolina

http:/www.strayer.edu/north-carolina/rtp/

Contact: Strayer University–RTP Campus, 4 Copley Parkway, Morrisville, NC 27560.

Strayer University–Sand Lake Campus

Orlando, Florida

http://www.strayer.edu/florida/sand-lake/

Contact: Strayer University–Sand Lake Campus, 8541 South Park Circle, Building 900, Orlando, FL 32819.

Strayer University–Savannah Campus

Savannah, Georgia

http://www.strayer.edu/georgia/savannah/

Contact: Strayer University–Savannah Campus, 20 Martin Court, Savannah, GA 31419.

Strayer University–Shelby Campus

Memphis, Tennessee

http://www.strayer.edu/tennessee/shelby/

Contact: Strayer University–Shelby Campus, 7275 Appling Farms Parkway, Memphis, TN 38133.

Strayer University–South Charlotte Campus

Charlotte, North Carolina

http://www.strayer.edu/north-carolina/south-charlotte/

Contact: Strayer University–South Charlotte Campus, 9101 Kings Parade Boulevard, Suite 200, Charlotte, NC 28273.

Strayer University–South Raleigh Campus

Raleigh, North Carolina

http://www.strayer.edu/north-carolina/south-raleigh/

Contact: Strayer University–South Raleigh Campus, 3421 Olympia Drive, Raleigh, NC 27603.

Strayer University–Takoma Park Campus

Washington, District of Columbia

http://www.strayer.edu/district-columbia/takoma-park/

Contact: Strayer University–Takoma Park Campus, 6830 Laurel Street, NW, Washington, DC 20012.

Strayer University–Tampa East Campus

Tampa, Florida

http://www.strayer.edu/florida/tampa-east/

Contact: Strayer University–Tampa East Campus, 5650 Breckenridge Park Drive, Suite 300, Tampa, FL 33610.

Strayer University–Tampa Westshore Campus

Tampa, Florida

http://www.strayer.edu/florida/tampa-westshore/

Contact: Strayer University–Tampa Westshore Campus, 4902 Eisenhower Boulevard, Suite 100, Tampa, FL 33634.

Strayer University–Teays Valley Campus

Scott Depot, West Virginia

http://www.strayer.edu/west-virginia/teays-valley/

Contact: Strayer University–Teays Valley Campus, 100 Corporate Center Drive, Scott Depot, WV 25560.

Strayer University–Thousand Oaks Campus

Memphis, Tennessee

http://www.strayer.edu/tennessee/thousand-oaks/

Contact: Strayer University–Thousand Oaks Campus, 2620 Thousand Oaks Boulevard, Suite 1100, Memphis, TN 38118.

Strayer University–Virginia Beach Campus

Virginia Beach, Virginia

http://www.strayer.edu/virginia/virginia-beach/

Contact: Strayer University–Virginia Beach Campus, 249 Central Park Avenue, Suite 350, Virginia Beach, VA 23462.

Strayer University–Warrendale Campus

Warrendale, Pennsylvania

http://www.strayer.edu/pennsylvania/warrendale/

Contact: Strayer University–Warrendale Campus, 802 Warrendale Village Drive, Warrendale, PA 15086.

Strayer University–Washington Campus

Washington, District of Columbia

http://www.strayer.edu/district-columbia/washington/

Contact: Strayer University–Washington Campus, 1133 15th Street, NW, Washington, DC 20025.

Strayer University–White Marsh Campus

Nottingham, Maryland

http://www.strayer.edu/maryland/white-marsh/

Contact: Strayer University–White Marsh Campus, 9920 Franklin Square Drive, Suite 200, Nottingham, MD 21236.

Strayer University–Willingboro Campus

Willingboro, New Jersey

http://www.strayer.edu/new-jersey/willingboro/

Contact: Strayer University–Willingboro Campus, 300 Willingboro Parkway, Willingboro Town Center, Suite 125, Willingboro, NJ 08046.

Strayer University–Woodbridge Campus

Woodbridge, Virginia

http://www.strayer.edu/virginia/woodbridge/

Contact: Strayer University–Woodbridge Campus, 13385 Minnieville Road, Woodbridge, VA 22192.

SUM Bible College & Theological Seminary

Oakland, California

http://www.sum.edu/

Contact: Admissions, SUM Bible College & Theological Seminary, 735 105th Avenue, Oakland, CA 94603. *Phone:* 510-567-6174. *Toll-free phone:* 888-567-6174. *Fax:* 510-568-1024.

Summit Pacific College

Abbotsford, British Columbia, Canada

http://www.summitpacific.ca/

Contact: Ms. Melody Deeley, Admissions and Registration, Summit Pacific College, Box 1700, Abbotsford, BC V2S 7E7, Canada. *Phone:* 604-851-7225. *Toll-free phone:* 800-976-8388. *E-mail:* registrar@summitpacific.ca.

Swedish Institute, College of Health Sciences

New York, New York

http://www.swedishinstitute.edu/

Contact: Admissions Advisor, Swedish Institute, College of Health Sciences, 226 West 26th Street, New York, NY 10001. *Phone:* 212-914-5900 Ext. 125. *E-mail:* admissions@swedishinstitute.edu.

Talladega College

Talladega, Alabama

http://www.talladega.edu/

Contact: Talladega College, 627 West Battle Street, Talladega, AL 35160-2354. *Phone:* 256-761-6415. *Toll-free phone:* 866-540-3956.

Talmudical Academy of New Jersey

Adelphia, New Jersey

Contact: Director of Admissions, Talmudical Academy of New Jersey, 868 Route 524, Adelphia, NJ 07710. *Phone:* 201-431-1600.

Talmudical Institute of Upstate New York

Rochester, New York

http://www.tiuny.org/

Contact: Rabbi Menachem Davidowitz, Director of Admissions, Talmudical Institute of Upstate New York, 769 Park Avenue, Rochester, NY 14607-3046. *Phone:* 716-473-2810. *E-mail:* yeshiva@tiuny.org.

Talmudical Seminary Oholei Torah

Brooklyn, New York

Contact: Rabbi Yisroel Friedman, Director of Academic Affairs, Talmudical Seminary Oholei Torah, 667 Eastern Parkway, Brooklyn, NY 11213-3310. *Phone:* 718-363-2034. *E-mail:* info@oholeitorah.com.

Talmudic College of Florida

Miami Beach, Florida

http://www.talmudicu.edu/

Contact: Rabbi Yeshaya Greenberg, Dean of Students, Talmudic College of Florida, 1910 Alton Road, Miami Beach, FL 33139. *Phone:* 305-534-7050. *Fax:* 305-534-8444. *E-mail:* yandtg@gmail.com.

Télé-université

Québec, Quebec, Canada

http://www.teluq.uquebec.ca/

Contact: Ms. Louise Bertrand, Registraire, Télé-université, 455, rue de l'Église, C.P. 4800, succ. Terminus, Québec, QC G1K 9H5, Canada. *Phone:* 418-657-2262 Ext. 5307. *Toll-free phone:* 888-843-4333.

Telshe Yeshiva–Chicago

Chicago, Illinois

Contact: Rosh Hayeshiva, Telshe Yeshiva–Chicago, 3535 West Foster Avenue, Chicago, IL 60625-5598. *Phone:* 773-463-7738.

Texas A&M University–Texarkana

Texarkana, Texas

http://www.tamut.edu/

Contact: Mrs. Patricia Black, Director of Admissions and Registrar, Texas A&M University–Texarkana, PO Box 5518, Texarkana, TX 75505-5518. *Phone:* 903-223-3068. *Fax:* 903-223-3140. *E-mail:* admissions@tamut.edu.

Texas College

Tyler, Texas

http://www.texascollege.edu/

Contact: Mr. John Roberts, Interim Dean for Enrollment Services, Texas College, 2404 North Grand Avenue, Tyler, TX 75702. *Phone:* 903-593-8311 Ext. 2297. *Toll-free phone:* 800-306-6299. *Fax:* 903-363-1854. *E-mail:* jroberts@texascollege.edu.

Thomas College

Waterville, Maine

http://www.thomas.edu/

Contact: Mr. James Love, Dean of Admissions, Thomas College, 180 West River Road, Waterville, ME 04901. *Phone:* 207-859-1101. *Toll-free phone:* 800-339-7001. *Fax:* 207-859-1114. *E-mail:* admiss@thomas.edu.

Thomas Edison State College

Trenton, New Jersey

http://www.tesc.edu/

Contact: Mr. David Hoftiezer, Director of Admissions, Thomas Edison State College, 101 West State Street, Trenton, NJ 08608. *Phone:* 888-442-8372. *Toll-free phone:* 888-442-8372. *Fax:* 609-984-8447. *E-mail:* admissions@tesc.edu.

Thomas Jefferson University

Philadelphia, Pennsylvania

http://www.jefferson.edu/university.html

Contact: Ms. Karen Jacobs, Director of Admissions, Thomas Jefferson University, Edison Building, 130 South Ninth Street, Philadelphia, PA 19107. *Phone:* 215-503-8890. *Toll-free phone:* 877-533-3247. *Fax:* 215-503-7241. *E-mail:* chpadmissions@mail.tju.edu.

Thomas More College of Liberal Arts

Merrimack, New Hampshire

http://www.thomasmorecollege.edu/

Contact: Teddy Sifert, Director of Admissions, Thomas More College of Liberal Arts, 6 Manchester Street, Merrimack, NH 03054-4818. *Toll-free phone:* 800-880-8308. *Fax:* 603-880-9280. *E-mail:* admissions@thomasmorecollege.edu.

Thomas University

Thomasville, Georgia

http://www.thomasu.edu/

Contact: Mrs. Kerri Knight, Office of Admission, Thomas University, 1501 Millpond Road, Thomasville, GA 31792. *Phone:* 229-227-6942 Ext. 1074. *Toll-free phone:* 800-538-9784. *Fax:* 229-227-6919. *E-mail:* kknight@thomasu.edu.

Thompson Rivers University

Kamloops, British Columbia, Canada

http://www.tru.ca/

Contact: Mr. Josh Keller, Director, Student Recruitment and Liaison, Thompson Rivers University, 900 McGill Road, Kamloops, BC V2C 0C8, Canada. *Phone:* 250-828-5008. *Fax:* 250-828-5159. *E-mail:* jkeller@tru.ca.

Torah Temimah Talmudical Seminary

Brooklyn, New York

Contact: Principal, Torah Temimah Talmudical Seminary, 507 Ocean Parkway, Brooklyn, NY 11218-5913. *Phone:* 718-853-8500.

Touro College

New York, New York

http://www.touro.edu/

Contact: Mr. David Luk, Associate Director of Admissions, Touro College, 27-33 West 23rd Street, New York, NY 10010. *Phone:* 212-463-0400 Ext. 5644. *Fax:* 212-627-9542. *E-mail:* david.luk@touro.edu.

Trinity Baptist College
Jacksonville, Florida
http://www.tbc.edu/
Contact: Trinity Baptist College, FL. *Phone:* 904-596-2538. *Toll-free phone:* 800-786-2206. *E-mail:* trinity@tbc.edu.

Trinity Bible College
Ellendale, North Dakota
http://www.trinitybiblecollege.edu/
Contact: Rev. Steve Tvedt, Vice President of College Relations, Trinity Bible College, 50 South 6th Avenue, Ellendale, ND 58436-7150. *Phone:* 701-349-3621 Ext. 2045. *Toll-free phone:* 800-523-1603.

Trinity College of Nursing and Health Sciences
Rock Island, Illinois
http://www.trinitycollegeqc.edu/
Contact: Ms. Lori Perez, Admissions Representative, Trinity College of Nursing and Health Sciences, 2122 - 25th Avenue, Rock Island, IL 61201. *Phone:* 309-779-7700. *Fax:* 309-779-7748. *E-mail:* PerezLJ@ihs.org.

Trinity International University
Deerfield, Illinois
http://www.tiu.edu/
Contact: Mr. Aaron Mahl, Director of Undergraduate Admissions, Trinity International University, 2065 Half Day Road, Deerfield, IL 60015-1284. *Phone:* 847-317-7000. *Toll-free phone:* 800-822-3225. *Fax:* 847-317-8097. *E-mail:* tcadmissions@tiu.edu.

Trinity Lutheran College
Issaquah, Washington
http://www.tlc.edu/
Contact: Ms. Tracy Sisk, Admissions Counselor, Trinity Lutheran College, 2802 Wetmore AVE, Everett, WA 98201. *Phone:* 425-249-4755. *Toll-free phone:* 800-843-5659. *Fax:* 425-249-4801. *E-mail:* tracy.sisk@tlc.edu.

Trinity Washington University
Washington, District of Columbia
http://www.trinitydc.edu/
Contact: Director of Admissions, Trinity Washington University, 125 Michigan Avenue, NE, Washington, DC 20017-1094. *Phone:* 800-492-6882. *Toll-free phone:* 800-IWANTTC. *E-mail:* admissions@trinitydc.edu.

Trinity Western University
Langley, British Columbia, Canada
http://www.twu.ca/
Contact: Trinity Western University, 7600 Glover Road, Langley, BC V2Y 1Y1, Canada. *Toll-free phone:* 888-468-6898.

Tri-State Bible College
South Point, Ohio
http://www.tsbc.edu/
Contact: Tri-State Bible College, 506 Margaret Street, PO Box 445, South Point, OH 45680-8402. *Phone:* 740-377-2520.

Tyndale University College & Seminary
Toronto, Ontario, Canada
http://www.tyndale.ca/
Contact: Tricia McKenley, Admissions Office Coordinator, Tyndale University College & Seminary, 25 Ballyconnor Court, Toronto, ON M2M 4B3, Canada. *Phone:* 416-218-6757 Ext. 6738. *Toll-free phone:* 877-896-3253. *E-mail:* admissions@tydale.ca.

United States International University
Nairobi, Kenya
http://www.usiu.ac.ke/
Contact: United States International University, PO Box 14634, Thika Road Kasarani, Nairobi 00800, Kenya. *Phone:* 254-02-3606563.

United Talmudical Seminary
Brooklyn, New York
Contact: Director of Admissions, United Talmudical Seminary, 191 Rodney Street, Brooklyn, NY 11211. *Phone:* 718-963-9770.

Universidad Adventista de las Antillas
Mayagüez, Puerto Rico
http://www.uaa.edu/
Contact: Mrs. Yolanda Ferrer, Director of Admissions, Universidad Adventista de las Antillas, Oficina de Admisiones, PO Box 118, Mayaguez, PR 00681-0118. *Phone:* 787-834-9595 Ext. 2208. *Fax:* 787-834-9597. *E-mail:* admissions@uaa.edu.

Universidad Central del Caribe
Bayamón, Puerto Rico
http://www.uccaribe.edu/
Contact: Admissions Department, Universidad Central del Caribe, PO Box 60-327, Bayamón, PR 00960-6032. *Phone:* 787-740-1611.

Universidad de las Américas Puebla
Puebla, Mexico
http://www.udlap.mx/
Contact: Miss Madet Ruisenor-Quintero, Director of Student Enrollment Office, Universidad de las Américas Puebla, Ex-Hacienda Santa Catarina Martir S/N, Cholula, Puebla 72820, Mexico. *Phone:* -52 229-2024.

Universidad del Este
Carolina, Puerto Rico
http://www.suagm.edu/une/
Contact: Universidad del Este, PO Box 2010, Carolina, PR 00984. *Phone:* 787-257-7373 Ext. 3401.

Universidad Pentecostal Mizpa
San Juan, Puerto Rico
http://www.mizpa.edu/
Contact: Omar Alicea, Recruitment, Universidad Pentecostal Mizpa, Bo Caimito Road 199, Apartado 20966, San Juan, PR 00928-0966. *Phone:* 787-720-4476. *Fax:* 787-720-2012.

Université de Moncton

Moncton, New Brunswick, Canada

http://www.umoncton.ca/

Contact: Miss Nicole Savois, Chief Admission Officer, Université de Moncton, Moncton, NB E1A 3E9, Canada. *Phone:* 506-858-4115. *Toll-free phone:* 800-363-8336. *E-mail:* gallanrm@umoncton.ca.

Université du Québec à Chicoutimi

Chicoutimi, Quebec, Canada

http://www.uqac.ca/

Contact: Jean Wauthier, Admissions Officer, Université du Québec à Chicoutimi, 555, boulevard de L'Université, Chicoutimi, QC G7H 2B1, Canada. *Phone:* 418-545-5005. *E-mail:* czoccast@uqac.uquebec.ca.

Université du Québec à Montréal

Montréal, Quebec, Canada

http://www.uqam.ca/

Contact: Ms. Lucille Boisselle-Roy, Admissions Officer, Université du Québec à Montréal, CP 8888, Succursale Centreville, Montréal, QC H2L 4S8, Canada. *Phone:* 514-987-3132. *E-mail:* admission@uqam.ca.

Université du Québec à Rimouski

Rimouski, Quebec, Canada

http://www.uqar.ca/

Contact: Ms. Marie Saint-Laurent, Admissions Officer, Université du Québec à Rimouski, 300 Allee des Ursulines, CP3300, Rimouski QC G5L 3A1, Canada. *Phone:* 418-724-1433. *E-mail:* philippe_horth@uqar.uquebec.ca.

Université du Québec à Trois-Rivières

Trois-Rivières, Quebec, Canada

http://www.uqtr.ca/

Contact: Ms. Jean Bois, Admissions Officer, Université du Québec à Trois-Rivières, 3351 blvd des Forges, Case post 500, Trois-Rivières, QC G9A 5H7, Canada. *Phone:* 819-376-5011. *Toll-free phone:* 800-365-0922. *Fax:* 819-376-5232. *E-mail:* registraire@uqtr.ca.

Université du Québec, École de technologie supérieure

Montréal, Quebec, Canada

http://www.etsmtl.ca/

Contact: Mme. Francine Gamache, Registraire, Université du Québec, École de technologie supérieure, 1100, rue Notre Dame Ouest, Montréal, QC H3C 1K3, Canada. *Phone:* 514-396-8885. *E-mail:* admission@ets.mtl.ca.

Université du Québec en Abitibi-Témiscamingue

Rouyn-Noranda, Quebec, Canada

http://www.uqat.ca/

Contact: Mrs. Monique Fay, Admissions Officer, Université du Québec en Abitibi-Témiscamingue, 445 boulevard de l'Université, Rouyn-Noranda, QC J9X 5E4, Canada. *Phone:* 819-762-0971. *E-mail:* micheline.chevalier@uqat.uquebec.ca.

Université Laval

Québec, Quebec, Canada

http://www.ulaval.ca/

Contact: Promotion and Recruitment Division, Université Laval, Quebec, QC G1K 7P4, Canada. *Phone:* 418-656-2764. *Toll-free phone:* 877-785-2825. *Fax:* 418-656-5216. *E-mail:* info@dap.ulaval.ca.

Université Sainte-Anne

Church Point, Nova Scotia, Canada

http://www.usainteanne.ca/

Contact: Mrs. Blanche Theriault, Admissions Officer, Université Sainte-Anne, Church Point, NS B0W 1M0, Canada. *Phone:* 902-769-2114 Ext. 116. *E-mail:* admission@usainteanne.ca.

University of Advancing Technology

Tempe, Arizona

http://www.uat.edu/

Contact: Admissions Office, University of Advancing Technology, 2625 West Baseline Road, Tempe, AZ 85283-1042. *Phone:* 602-383-8228. *Toll-free phone:* 800-658-5744. *Fax:* 602-383-8222. *E-mail:* admissions@uat.edu.

University of Alaska Anchorage

Anchorage, Alaska

http://www.uaa.alaska.edu/

Contact: Enrollment Services, University of Alaska Anchorage, PO Box 141629, 3901 Old Seward Highway, Anchorage, AK 99508-8046. *Phone:* 907-786-1480. *Fax:* 907-786-4888. *E-mail:* enroll@uaa.alaska.edu.

University of Alaska Anchorage, Kenai Peninsula College

Soldotna, Alaska

http://www.kpc.alaska.edu/

Contact: Ms. Shelly Love Blatchford, Admission and Registration Coordinator, University of Alaska Anchorage, Kenai Peninsula College, 156 College Road, Soldotna, AK 99669-9798. *Phone:* 907-262-0311. *Toll-free phone:* 877-262-0330.

University of Alaska Southeast

Juneau, Alaska

http://www.uas.alaska.edu/

Contact: Ms. Deema Ferguson, Admissions Clerk, University of Alaska Southeast, 11120 Glacier Highway, Juneau, AK 99801-8625. *Phone:* 907-796-6294 Ext. 6100. *Toll-free phone:* 877-465-4827. *Fax:* 907-796-6365. *E-mail:* admissions@uas.alaska.edu.

University of Arkansas at Monticello

Monticello, Arkansas

http://www.uamont.edu/

Contact: Ms. Mary Whiting, Director of Admissions, University of Arkansas at Monticello, Monticello, AR 71656. *Phone:* 870-460-1026. *Toll-free phone:* 800-844-1826. *E-mail:* admissions@uamont.edu.

University of Arkansas for Medical Sciences
Little Rock, Arkansas
http://www.uams.edu/
Contact: University of Arkansas for Medical Sciences, 4301 West Markham, Little Rock, AR 72205-7199. *Phone:* 501-686-5730.

University of Baltimore
Baltimore, Maryland
http://www.ubalt.edu/
Contact: David Waggoner, Associate Vice President of Admission, University of Baltimore, 1420 North Charles Street, Baltimore, MD 21201. *Phone:* 410-837-4777. *Fax:* 410-837-4793. *E-mail:* admission@ubalt.edu.

University of Calgary
Calgary, Alberta, Canada
http://www.ucalgary.ca/
Contact: Kim Vandam, Associate Director of Admissions, University of Calgary, 2500 University Drive NW, Calgary, AB T2N 1N4, Canada. *Phone:* 403-220-3825. *E-mail:* vandam@ucalgary.ca.

University of California, San Diego
La Jolla, California
http://www.ucsd.edu/
Contact: Ms. Mae Brown, Assistant Vice Chancellor, Admissions and Relations with Schools, University of California, San Diego, 9500 Gilman Drive, 0021, La Jolla, CA 92093-0021. *Phone:* 858-534-4831. *E-mail:* admissionsreply@ucsd.edu.

University of Detroit Mercy
Detroit, Michigan
http://www.udmercy.edu/
Contact: Office of Admissions, University of Detroit Mercy, 4001 West McNichols Road, Detroit, MI 48221-3038. *Phone:* 313-993-1245. *Toll-free phone:* 800-635-5020. *Fax:* 313-993-3326. *E-mail:* admissions@udmercy.edu.

University of Maine at Farmington
Farmington, Maine
http://www.umf.maine.edu/
Contact: Ms. Lisa Elrich, Associate Director of Admissions, University of Maine at Farmington, 246 Main Street, Farmington, ME 04938-1994. *Phone:* 207-778-7050. *Fax:* 207-778-8182. *E-mail:* umfadmit@maine.edu.

University of Management and Technology
Arlington, Virginia
http://www.umtweb.edu/
Contact: Vice President, University of Management and Technology, Suite 700, 1901 North Fort Meyers Drive, Arlington, VA 22209. *Phone:* 703-516-0035. *Toll-free phone:* 800-924-4883. *Fax:* 703-516-0985. *E-mail:* admissions@umtweb.edu.

University of Manitoba
Winnipeg, Manitoba, Canada
http://www.umanitoba.ca/
Contact: Mr. Peter Dueck, Director of Enrollment Services, University of Manitoba, Winnipeg, MB R3T 2N2, Canada. *Phone:* 204-474-6382.

University of Mary
Bismarck, North Dakota
http://www.umary.edu/
Contact: Mike Heitkamp, University of Mary, 7500 University Drive, Bismarck, ND 58504-9652. *Phone:* 701-355-8191. *Toll-free phone:* 800-288-6279. *Fax:* 701-255-7687. *E-mail:* mcheitkamp@umary.edu.

University of Maryland Eastern Shore
Princess Anne, Maryland
http://www.umes.edu/
Contact: University of Maryland Eastern Shore, Princess Anne, MD 21853-1299. *Phone:* 410-651-6410.

University of Mississippi Medical Center
Jackson, Mississippi
http://www.umc.edu/
Contact: Ms. Barbara Westerfield, Director of Student Records and Registrar, University of Mississippi Medical Center, 2500 North State Street, Jackson, MS 39216-4505. *Phone:* 601-984-1080. *Fax:* 601-984-1079.

University of Mount Olive
Mount Olive, North Carolina
http://www.umo.edu/
Contact: University of Mount Olive, 634 Henderson Street, Mount Olive, NC 28365. *Phone:* 919-658-2502 Ext. 3009. *Toll-free phone:* 800-653-0854.

University of Nebraska Medical Center
Omaha, Nebraska
http://www.unmc.edu/
Contact: University of Nebraska Medical Center, Nebraska Medical Center, Omaha, NE 68198. *Toll-free phone:* 800-626-8431 Ext. 6468.

University of New Mexico–Gallup
Gallup, New Mexico
http://www.gallup.unm.edu/
Contact: Ms. Pearl A. Morris, Admissions Representative, University of New Mexico–Gallup, 200 College Road, Gallup, NM 87301-5603. *Phone:* 505-863-7576.

University of Northern British Columbia
Prince George, British Columbia, Canada
http://www.unbc.ca/
Contact: Pamela Flagel, Associate Registrar Enrollment, University of Northern British Columbia, Office of the Registrar, 3333 University Way, Prince George, BC V2N 4Z9, Canada. *Phone:* 250-960-6300. *Fax:* 250-960-6330. *E-mail:* registrar-info@unbc.ca.

University of Northwestern Ohio

Lima, Ohio

http://www.unoh.edu/

Contact: Mr. Dan Klopp, Vice President for Enrollment Management, University of Northwestern Ohio, 1441 North Cable Road, Lima, OH 45805-1498. *Phone:* 419-227-3141. *Fax:* 419-229-6926. *E-mail:* klopp_d@unoh.edu.

University of Phoenix–Atlanta Campus

Sandy Springs, Georgia

http://www.phoenix.edu/

Contact: Marc Booker, Sr. Director, Office of Admissions and Evaluation, University of Phoenix–Atlanta Campus, 4035 South Riverpoint Parkway, Mail Stop CF-L101, Phoenix, AZ 85040. *Phone:* 602-557-4609. *Toll-free phone:* 866-766-0766. *Fax:* 480-643-1156.

University of Phoenix–Bay Area Campus

San Jose, California

http://www.phoenix.edu/

Contact: Marc Booker, Sr. Director, Office of Admissions and Evaluation, University of Phoenix–Bay Area Campus, 4035 South Riverpoint Parkway, Mail Stop CF-L101, Phoenix, AZ 85040-1958. *Phone:* 602-557-4609. *Toll-free phone:* 866-766-0766. *Fax:* 480-643-1156.

University of Phoenix–Boston Campus

Braintree, Massachusetts

http://www.phoenix.edu/

Contact: Marc Booker, Sr. Director, Office of Admissions and Evaluation, University of Phoenix–Boston Campus, 4035 South Riverpoint Parkway, Mail Stop CF-L101, Phoenix, AZ 85040. *Phone:* 602-557-4609. *Toll-free phone:* 866-766-0766. *Fax:* 480-643-1156.

University of Phoenix–Central Florida Campus

Orlando, Florida

http://www.phoenix.edu/

Contact: Marc Booker, Sr. Director, Office of Admissions and Evaluation, University of Phoenix–Central Florida Campus, 4035 South Riverpoint Parkway, Mail Stop CF-L101, Phoenix, AZ 85040. *Phone:* 602-557-4609. *Toll-free phone:* 866-766-0766. *Fax:* 480-643-1156.

University of Phoenix–Central Valley Campus

Fresno, California

http://www.phoenix.edu/

Contact: Marc Booker, Sr. Director, Office of Admissions and Evaluation, University of Phoenix–Central Valley Campus, 4035 South Riverpoint Parkway, Mail Stop CF-L101, Phoenix, AZ 85040. *Phone:* 602-557-4609. *Toll-free phone:* 866-766-0766. *Fax:* 480-643-1156.

University of Phoenix–Charlotte Campus

Charlotte, North Carolina

http://www.phoenix.edu/

Contact: Marc Booker, Sr. Director, Office of Admissions and Evaluation, University of Phoenix–Charlotte Campus, 4035 South Riverpoint Parkway, Mail Stop CF-L101, Phoenix, AZ 85040. *Phone:* 602-557-4609. *Toll-free phone:* 866-766-0766. *Fax:* 480-643-1156.

University of Phoenix–Chicago Campus

Schaumburg, Illinois

http://www.phoenix.edu/

Contact: Marc Booker, Sr. Director, Office of Admissions and Evaluation, University of Phoenix–Chicago Campus, 4035 South Riverpoint Parkway, Mail Stop CF-L101, Phoenix, AZ 85040-1958. *Phone:* 602-557-4609. *Toll-free phone:* 866-766-0766. *Fax:* 480-643-1156.

University of Phoenix–Cleveland Campus

Beachwood, Ohio

http://www.phoenix.edu/

Contact: Marc Booker, Sr. Director, Office of Admissions and Evaluation, University of Phoenix–Cleveland Campus, 4035 South Riverpoint Parkway, Mail Stop CF-L101, Phoenix, AZ 85040. *Phone:* 602-557-4609. *Toll-free phone:* 866-766-0766. *Fax:* 480-643-1156.

University of Phoenix–Colorado Campus

Lone Tree, Colorado

http://www.phoenix.edu/

Contact: Marc Booker, Sr. Director, Office of Admissions and Evaluation, University of Phoenix–Colorado Campus, 4035 South Riverpoint Parkway, Mail Stop CF-L101, Phoenix, AZ 85040. *Phone:* 602-557-4609. *Toll-free phone:* 866-766-0766. *Fax:* 480-643-1156.

University of Phoenix–Colorado Springs Downtown Campus

Colorado Springs, Colorado

http://www.phoenix.edu/

Contact: Marc Booker, Sr. Director, Office of Admissions and Evaluation, University of Phoenix–Colorado Springs Downtown Campus, 4035 South Riverpoint Parkway, Mail Stop CF-L101, Phoenix, AZ 85040. *Phone:* 602-557-4609. *Toll-free phone:* 866-766-0766. *Fax:* 480-643-1156.

University of Phoenix–Columbus Georgia Campus

Columbus, Georgia

http://www.phoenix.edu/

Contact: Marc Booker, Sr. Director, Office of Admissions and Evaluation, University of Phoenix–Columbus Georgia Campus, 4035 South Riverpoint Parkway, Mail Stop CF-L101, Phoenix, AZ 85040. *Phone:* 602-557-4609. *Toll-free phone:* 866-766-0766. *Fax:* 480-643-1156.

University of Phoenix–Dallas Campus

Dallas, Texas

http://www.phoenix.edu/

Contact: Marc Booker, Sr. Director, Office of Admissions and Evaluation, University of Phoenix–Dallas Campus, 4035 South Riverpoint Parkway, Mail Stop CF-L101, Phoenix, AZ 85040. *Phone:* 602-557-4609. *Toll-free phone:* 866-766-0766. *Fax:* 480-643-1156.

University of Phoenix–Hawaii Campus

Honolulu, Hawaii

http://www.phoenix.edu/

Contact: Marc Booker, Sr. Director, Office of Admissions and Evaluation, University of Phoenix–Hawaii Campus, 4035 South Riverpoint Parkway, Mail Stop CF-L101, Phoenix, AZ 85040. *Phone:* 602-557-4609. *Toll-free phone:* 866-766-0766. *Fax:* 480-643-1156.

University of Phoenix–Houston Campus

Houston, Texas

http://www.phoenix.edu/

Contact: Marc Booker, Sr. Director, Office of Admissions and Evaluation, University of Phoenix–Houston Campus, 4305 South Riverpoint Parkway, Mail Stop CF-L101, Phoenix, AZ 85040. *Phone:* 602-557-4609. *Toll-free phone:* 866-766-0766. *Fax:* 480-643-1156.

University of Phoenix–Idaho Campus

Meridian, Idaho

http://www.phoenix.edu/

Contact: Marc Booker, Sr. Director, Office of Admissions and Evaluation, University of Phoenix–Idaho Campus, 4305 South Riverpoint Parkway, Mail Stop CF-L101, Phoenix, AZ 85040. *Phone:* 602-557-4609. *Toll-free phone:* 866-766-0766. *Fax:* 480-643-1156.

University of Phoenix–Indianapolis Campus

Indianapolis, Indiana

http://www.phoenix.edu/

Contact: Marc Booker, Sr. Director, Office of Admissions and Evaluation, University of Phoenix–Indianapolis Campus, 4035 South Riverpoint Parkway, Mail Stop CF-L101, Phoenix, AZ 85040. *Phone:* 602-557-4609. *Toll-free phone:* 866-766-0766. *Fax:* 480-643-1156.

University of Phoenix–Kansas City Campus

Kansas City, Missouri

http://www.phoenix.edu/

Contact: Marc Booker, Sr. Director, Office of Admissions and Evaluation, University of Phoenix–Kansas City Campus, 4035 South Riverpoint Parkway, Mail Stop CF-L101, Phoenix, AZ 85040. *Phone:* 602-557-4609. *Toll-free phone:* 866-766-0766. *Fax:* 480-643-1156.

University of Phoenix–Las Vegas Campus

Las Vegas, Nevada

http://www.phoenix.edu/

Contact: Marc Booker, Sr. Director, Office of Admissions and Evaluation, University of Phoenix–Las Vegas Campus, 4305 South Riverpoint Parkway, Mail Stop CF-L101, Phoenix, AZ 85040. *Phone:* 602-557-4609. *Toll-free phone:* 866-766-0766. *Fax:* 480-643-1156.

University of Phoenix–Little Rock Campus

Little Rock, Arkansas

http://www.phoenix.edu/

Contact: Marc Booker, Sr. Director, Office of Admissions and Evaluation, University of Phoenix–Little Rock Campus, 4035 South Riverpoint Parkway, Mail Stop CF-L101, Phoenix, AZ 85040. *Phone:* 602-557-4609. *Toll-free phone:* 866-766-0766. *Fax:* 480-643-1156.

University of Phoenix–Maryland Campus

Columbia, Maryland

http://www.phoenix.edu/

Contact: Marc Booker, Sr. Director, Office of Admissions and Evaluation, University of Phoenix–Maryland Campus, 4035 South Riverpoint Parkway, Mail Stop CF-L101, Phoenix, AZ 85040. *Phone:* 602-557-4609. *Toll-free phone:* 866-766-0766. *Fax:* 480-643-1156.

University of Phoenix–Nashville Campus

Nashville, Tennessee

http://www.phoenix.edu/

Contact: Marc Booker, Sr. Director, Office of Admissions and Evaluation, University of Phoenix–Nashville Campus, 4035 South Riverpoint Parkway, Mail Stop CF-L101, Phoenix, AZ 85040. *Phone:* 602-557-4609. *Toll-free phone:* 866-766-0766. *Fax:* 480-643-1156.

University of Phoenix–New Mexico Campus

Albuquerque, New Mexico

http://www.phoenix.edu/

Contact: Marc Booker, Sr. Director, Office of Admissions and Evaluation, University of Phoenix–New Mexico Campus, 4035 South Riverpoint Parkway, Mail Stop CF-L101, Phoenix, AZ 85040. *Phone:* 602-557-4609. *Toll-free phone:* 866-766-0766. *Fax:* 480-643-1156.

University of Phoenix–North Florida Campus

Jacksonville, Florida

http://www.phoenix.edu/

Contact: Marc Booker, Sr. Director, Office of Admissions and Evaluation, University of Phoenix–North Florida Campus, 4035 South Riverpoint Parkway, Mail Stop CF-L101, Phoenix, AZ 85040. *Phone:* 602-557-4609. *Toll-free phone:* 866-766-0766. *Fax:* 480-643-1156.

University of Phoenix–Oklahoma City Campus

Oklahoma City, Oklahoma

http://www.phoenix.edu/

Contact: Marc Booker, Sr. Director, Office of Admissions and Evaluation, University of Phoenix–Oklahoma City Campus, 4035 South Riverpoint Parkway, Mail Stop CF-L101, Phoenix, AZ 85040-1958. *Phone:* 602-557-4609. *Toll-free phone:* 866-766-0766. *Fax:* 480-643-1156.

University of Phoenix–Online Campus

Phoenix, Arizona

http://www.uopxonline.com/

Contact: Marc Booker, Sr. Director, Office of Admissions and Evaluation, University of Phoenix–Online Campus, 4035 South Riverpoint Parkway, Mail Stop CF-L101, Phoenix, AZ 85040. *Phone:* 602-557-4609. *Toll-free phone:* 866-766-0766. *Fax:* 480-643-1156.

University of Phoenix–Oregon Campus

Tigard, Oregon

http://www.phoenix.edu/

Contact: Marc Booker, Sr. Director, Office of Admissions and Evaluation, University of Phoenix–Oregon Campus, 4035 South Riverpoint Parkway, Mail Stop CF-L101, Phoenix, AZ 85040. *Phone:* 602-557-4609. *Toll-free phone:* 866-766-0766. *Fax:* 480-643-1156.

University of Phoenix–Philadelphia Campus

Wayne, Pennsylvania

http://www.phoenix.edu/

Contact: Marc Booker, Sr. Director, Office of Admissions and Evaluation, University of Phoenix–Philadelphia Campus, 4035 South Riverpoint Parkway, Mail Stop CF-L101, Phoenix, AZ 85040. *Phone:* 602-557-4609. *Toll-free phone:* 866-766-0766. *Fax:* 480-643-1156.

University of Phoenix–Phoenix Campus

Tempe, Arizona

http://www.phoenix.edu/

Contact: Marc Booker, Sr. Director, Office of Admissions and Evaluation, University of Phoenix–Phoenix Campus, 4035 South Riverpoint Parkway, Mail Stop CF-L101, Phoenix, AZ 85040. *Phone:* 602-557-4609. *Toll-free phone:* 866-766-0766. *Fax:* 480-643-1156.

University of Phoenix–Puerto Rico Campus

Guaynabo, Puerto Rico

http://www.phoenix.edu/

Contact: Marc Booker, Sr. Director, Office of Admissions and Evaluation, University of Phoenix–Puerto Rico Campus, 4035 South Riverpoint Parkway, Mail Stop CF-L101, Phoenix, AZ 85040. *Phone:* 602-557-4609. *Toll-free phone:* 866-766-0766. *Fax:* 480-643-1156.

University of Phoenix–Richmond-Virginia Beach Campus

Glen Allen, Virginia

http://www.phoenix.edu/

Contact: Marc Booker, Sr. Director, Office of Admissions and Evaluation, University of Phoenix–Richmond-Virginia Beach Campus, 4035 South Riverpoint Parkway, Mail Stop CF-L101, Phoenix, AZ 85040. *Phone:* 602-557-4609. *Toll-free phone:* 866-766-0766. *Fax:* 480-643-1156.

University of Phoenix–Sacramento Valley Campus

Sacramento, California

http://www.phoenix.edu/

Contact: Marc Booker, Sr. Director, Office of Admissions and Evaluation, University of Phoenix–Sacramento Valley Campus, 4035 South Riverpoint Parkway, Mail Stop CF-L101, Phoenix, AZ 85040. *Phone:* 602-557-4609. *Toll-free phone:* 866-766-0766. *Fax:* 480-643-1156.

University of Phoenix–St. Louis Campus

St. Louis, Missouri

http://www.phoenix.edu/

Contact: Marc Booker, Sr. Director, Office of Admissions and Evaluation, University of Phoenix–St. Louis Campus, 4035 South Riverpoint Parkway, Mail Stop CF-L101, Phoenix, AZ 85040. *Phone:* 602-557-4609. *Toll-free phone:* 866-766-0766. *Fax:* 480-643-1156.

University of Phoenix–San Diego Campus

San Diego, California

http://www.phoenix.edu/

Contact: Marc Booker, Sr. Director, Office of Admissions and Evaluation, University of Phoenix–San Diego Campus, 4035 South Riverpoint Parkway, Mail Stop CF-L101, Phoenix, AZ 85040. *Phone:* 602-557-4609. *Toll-free phone:* 866-766-0766. *Fax:* 480-643-1156.

University of Phoenix–Southern Arizona Campus

Tucson, Arizona

http://www.phoenix.edu/

Contact: Marc Booker, Sr. Director, Office of Admissions and Evaluation, University of Phoenix–Southern Arizona Campus, 4035 South Riverpoint Parkway, Mail Stop CF-L101, Phoenix, AZ 85040-1958. *Phone:* 602-557-4609. *Toll-free phone:* 866-766-0766. *Fax:* 480-643-1156.

University of Phoenix–Southern California Campus

Costa Mesa, California

http://www.phoenix.edu/

Contact: Marc Booker, Sr. Director, Office of Admissions and Evaluation, University of Phoenix–Southern California Campus, 4035 South Riverpoint Parkway, Mail Stop CF-L101, Phoenix, AZ 85040. *Phone:* 602-557-4609. *Toll-free phone:* 866-766-0766. *Fax:* 480-643-1156.

University of Phoenix–South Florida Campus

Miramar, Florida

http://www.phoenix.edu/

Contact: Marc Booker, Sr. Director, Office of Admissions and Evaluation, University of Phoenix–South Florida Campus, 4035 South Riverpoint Parkway, Mail Stop CF-L101, Phoenix, AZ 85040. *Phone:* 602-557-4609. *Toll-free phone:* 866-766-0766. *Fax:* 480-643-1156.

University of Phoenix–Utah Campus

Salt Lake City, Utah

http://www.phoenix.edu/

Contact: Marc Booker, Sr. Director, Office of Admissions and Evaluation, University of Phoenix–Utah Campus, 4615 East Elwood Street, Mail Stop AA-K101, Phoenix, AZ 85040-1958. *Phone:* 602-557-4609. *Toll-free phone:* 866-766-0766. *Fax:* 480-643-1156.

University of Phoenix–Washington D.C. Campus

Washington, District of Columbia

http://www.phoenix.edu/

Contact: Marc Booker, Sr. Director, Office of Admissions and Evaluation, University of Phoenix–Washington D.C. Campus, 4035 South Riverpoint Parkway, Mail Stop CF-L101, Phoenix, AZ 85040. *Phone:* 602-557-4609. *Toll-free phone:* 866-766-0766. *Fax:* 480-643-1156.

University of Phoenix–Western Washington Campus

Tukwila, Washington

http://www.phoenix.edu/

Contact: Marc Booker, Sr. Director, Office of Admissions and Evaluation, University of Phoenix–Western Washington Campus, 4615 East Elwood Street, Mail Stop AA-K101, Phoenix, AZ 85040-1958. *Phone:* 602-557-4609. *Toll-free phone:* 866-766-0766. *Fax:* 480-643-1156.

University of Pittsburgh at Johnstown

Johnstown, Pennsylvania

http://www.upj.pitt.edu/

Contact: Office of Admissions, University of Pittsburgh at Johnstown, 157 Blackington Hall, Johnstown, PA 15904. *Phone:* 814-269-7050. *Toll-free phone:* 800-765-4875. *E-mail:* upjadmit@pitt.edu.

University of Prince Edward Island

Charlottetown, Prince Edward Island, Canada

http://home.upei.ca/

Contact: University of Prince Edward Island, 550 University Avenue, Charlottetown, PE C1A 4P3, Canada. *Phone:* 902-566-0634.

University of Puerto Rico in Aguadilla

Aguadilla, Puerto Rico

http://www.uprag.edu/

Contact: Ms. Melba Serrano Lugo, Admissions Officer, University of Puerto Rico in Aguadilla, PO Box 6150, Aguadilla, PR 00604. *Phone:* 787-890-2681 Ext. 280.

University of Puerto Rico in Arecibo

Arecibo, Puerto Rico

http://www.upra.edu/

Contact: University of Puerto Rico in Arecibo, PO Box 4010, Arecibo, PR 00613. *Phone:* 787-878-2830 Ext. 4101.

University of Puerto Rico in Carolina

Carolina, Puerto Rico

http://www.uprc.edu/

Contact: Ms. Celia Mendez, Admissions Officer, University of Puerto Rico in Carolina, PO Box 4800, Carolina, PR 00984-4800. *Phone:* 787-757-1485.

University of Puerto Rico in Cayey

Cayey, Puerto Rico

http://www.cayey.upr.edu/

Contact: University of Puerto Rico in Cayey, 205 Avenue Antonio R. Barcelo, Cayey, PR 00736. *Phone:* 787-738-2161 Ext. 2233.

University of Puerto Rico in Humacao

Humacao, Puerto Rico

http://www.uprh.edu/

Contact: Mrs. Elizabeth Gerena, Director of Admissions, University of Puerto Rico in Humacao, Call Box 860, Humacao, PR 00792. *Phone:* 787-850-9301. *Fax:* 787-850-9428. *E-mail:* elizabeth.gerena@upr.edu.

University of Puerto Rico in Utuado

Utuado, Puerto Rico

http://www.uprutuado.edu/

Contact: Mrs. Maria Robles Serrano, Admissions Officer, University of Puerto Rico in Utuado, PO Box 2500, Utuado, PR 00641-2500. *Phone:* 787-894-2828 Ext. 2240.

University of Puerto Rico, Mayagüez Campus

Mayagüez, Puerto Rico

http://www.uprm.edu/

Contact: Ms. Sheila Marty-Rodriquez, Director, Admissions Office, University of Puerto Rico, Mayagüez Campus, PO Box 9000, Mayagüez, PR 00681-9000. *Phone:* 787-265-5465. *Fax:* 787-265-5465. *E-mail:* smarty@uprm.edu.

University of Puerto Rico, Medical Sciences Campus

San Juan, Puerto Rico

http://www.rcm.upr.edu/

Contact: University of Puerto Rico, Medical Sciences Campus, PO Box 365067, San Juan, PR 00936-5067. *Phone:* 787-758-2525 Ext. 5214.

University of Puerto Rico, Río Piedras Campus

San Juan, Puerto Rico

http://www.uprrp.edu/

Contact: University of Puerto Rico, Río Piedras Campus, PO Box 23300, San Juan, PR 00931-3300. *Phone:* 787-764-0000 Ext. 85700.

University of Sioux Falls

Sioux Falls, South Dakota

http://www.usiouxfalls.edu/

Contact: Aimee Vander Feen, Director of Admissions, University of Sioux Falls, 1101 West 22nd Street, Sioux Falls, SD 57105. *Phone:* 605-331-6602. *Toll-free phone:* 800-888-1047. *Fax:* 605-331-6615. *E-mail:* admissions@usiouxfalls.edu.

The University of Texas Health Science Center at San Antonio

San Antonio, Texas

http://www.uthscsa.edu/

Contact: The University of Texas Health Science Center at San Antonio, 7703 Floyd Curl Drive, San Antonio, TX 78229-3900. *Phone:* 210-567-2659.

The University of Texas Medical Branch

Galveston, Texas

http://www.utmb.edu/

Contact: The University of Texas Medical Branch, 301 University Boulevard, Galveston, TX 77555. *Phone:* 409-772-1215.

University of the Sacred Heart

San Juan, Puerto Rico

http://www.sagrado.edu/

Contact: Mr. Luis Heviquez, Director of Admissions, University of the Sacred Heart, PO Box 12383, San Juan, PR 00914-0383. *Phone:* 787-728-1515 Ext. 3237.

University of the Southwest

Hobbs, New Mexico

http://www.usw.edu/

Contact: Ashley Taylor, Admissions Coordinator, University of the Southwest, 6610 North Lovington Highway, Hobbs, NM 88240. *Phone:* 575-492-2121. *Toll-free phone:* 800-530-4400. *Fax:* 575-392-6006. *E-mail:* ataylor@usw.edu.

University of Victoria

Victoria, British Columbia, Canada

http://www.uvic.ca/

Contact: Mr. Bruno Rocca, Student Recruitment Director, University of Victoria, PO Box 1700, STN CSC, Victoria, BC V8W 2Y2, Canada. *Phone:* 250-721-8121 Ext. 8109. *Fax:* 250-721-6225. *E-mail:* admit@uvic.ca.

The University of Winnipeg

Winnipeg, Manitoba, Canada

http://www.uwinnipeg.ca/

Contact: Mr. Colin Russell, Registrar, The University of Winnipeg, 515 Portage Avenue, Winnipeg, MB R3B 2E9, Canada. *Phone:* 204-786-9776. *Fax:* 204-786-8656. *E-mail:* admissions@uwinnipeg.ca.

U.T.A. Mesivta of Kiryas Joel

Monroe, New York

Contact: U.T.A. Mesivta of Kiryas Joel, 9 Nickelsburg Road, Unit 312, Monroe, NY 10950.

Vanguard College

Edmonton, Alberta, Canada

http://www.vanguardcollege.com/

Contact: Vanguard College, 11617 106 Avenue, NW, Edmonton, AB T5H 0S1, Canada. *Phone:* 780-452-0808 Ext. 231. *Toll-free phone:* 866-222-0808. *E-mail:* admissions@vanguardcollege.com.

Vatterott College

Des Moines, Iowa

http://www.vatterott.edu/

Contact: Mr. Henry Franken, Co-Director, Vatterott College, 7000 Fleur Drive, Suite 290, Des Moines, IA 50321. *Phone:* 515-309-9000. *Toll-free phone:* 888-553-6627. *Fax:* 515-309-0366.

Vatterott College

Berkeley, Missouri

http://www.vatterott.edu/

Contact: Ann Farajallah, Director of Admissions, Vatterott College, 8580 Evans Avenue, Berkeley, MO 63134. *Phone:* 314-264-1020. *Toll-free phone:* 888-553-6627.

Vatterott College

Sunset Hills, Missouri

http://www.vatterott.edu/

Contact: Director of Admission, Vatterott College, 12900 Maurer Industrial Drive, Sunset Hills, MO 63127. *Phone:* 314-843-4200. *Toll-free phone:* 888-553-6627. *Fax:* 314-843-1709.

Virginia College in Birmingham

Birmingham, Alabama

http://www.vc.edu/

Contact: Director of Admissions, Virginia College in Birmingham, 488 Palisades Boulevard, Birmingham, AL 35209. *Phone:* 205-802-1200.

Virginia College in Huntsville

Huntsville, Alabama

http://www.vc.edu/

Contact: Director of Admission, Virginia College in Huntsville, 2021 Drake Avenue SW, Huntsville, AL 35801. *Phone:* 256-533-7387. *Fax:* 256-533-7785.

Virginia University of Lynchburg

Lynchburg, Virginia

http://www.vul.edu/

Contact: Ms. Cheryl Glass, Director of Admissions, Virginia University of Lynchburg, 2058 Garfield Avenue, Lynchburg, VA 24501. *Phone:* 434-528-5276 Ext. 106. *Fax:* 434-528-4275. *E-mail:* cglass@vul.edu.

Wade College

Dallas, Texas

http://www.wadecollege.edu/

Contact: Wade College, INFOMart, 1950 Stemmons Freeway, Suite 4080, LB 562, Dallas, TX 75207. *Phone:* 214-637-3530. *Toll-free phone:* 800-624-4850.

Warner University

Lake Wales, Florida

http://www.warner.edu/

Contact: Mr. Jason Roe, Director of Admissions, Warner University, Warner Southern Center, 13895 Highway 27, Lake Wales, FL 33859. *Phone:* 863-638-7212 Ext. 7213. *Toll-free phone:* 800-309-9563. *Fax:* 863-638-1472. *E-mail:* admissions@warner.edu.

Washington Adventist University

Takoma Park, Maryland

http://www.wau.edu/

Contact: Elaine Oliver, Associate Vice President, Enrollment Services, Washington Adventist University, 7600 Flower Avenue, Takoma Park, MD 20912. *Phone:* 301-891-4502. *Toll-free phone:* 800-835-4212. *Fax:* 301-971-4230. *E-mail:* enroll@cuc.edu.

Western International University

Phoenix, Arizona

http://www.west.edu/

Contact: Ms. Melissa Machuca, Director of Enrollment, Western International University, 9215 North Black Canyon Highway, Phoenix, AZ 85021-2718. *Phone:* 602-943-2311. *E-mail:* Melissa.Machuca@west.edu.

Western New Mexico University

Silver City, New Mexico

http://www.wnmu.edu/

Contact: Matthew Lara, Director of Admissions, Western New Mexico University, PO Box 680, Silver City, NM 88062-0680. *Phone:* 505-538-6106. *Toll-free phone:* 800-872-WNMU. *Fax:* 505-538-6127. *E-mail:* tresslerd@wnmu.edu.

Westminster College

New Wilmington, Pennsylvania

http://www.westminster.edu/

Contact: Bradley Tokar, Director of Admissions, Westminster College, 319 South Market Street, New Wilmington, PA 16172-0001. *Phone:* 724-946-7100. *Toll-free phone:* 800-942-8033. *Fax:* 724-946-7171. *E-mail:* tokarbp@westminster.edu.

West Virginia University at Parkersburg

Parkersburg, West Virginia

http://www.wvup.edu/

Contact: Christine Post, Associate Dean of Enrollment Management, West Virginia University at Parkersburg, 300 Campus Drive, Parkersburg, WV 26104. *Phone:* 304-424-8223 Ext. 223. *Toll-free phone:* 800-WVA-WVUP. *Fax:* 304-424-8332. *E-mail:* christine.post@mail.wvu.edu.

Westwood College–Anaheim

Anaheim, California

http://www.westwood.edu/

Contact: Westwood College–Anaheim, 1551 South Douglass Road, Anaheim, CA 92806. *Phone:* 714-704-2721. *Toll-free phone:* 877-840-8999.

Westwood College–Annandale Campus

Annandale, Virginia

http://www.westwood.edu/

Contact: Westwood College–Annandale Campus, 7619 Little River Turnpike, 5th Floor, Annandale, VA 22003. *Phone:* 703-642-3633. *Toll-free phone:* 877-305-0049.

Westwood College–Arlington Ballston Campus

Arlington, Virginia

http://www.westwood.edu/

Contact: Westwood College–Arlington Ballston Campus, 4420 North Fairfax Drive, Arlington, VA 22203. *Phone:* 703-243-1662. *Toll-free phone:* 877-268-5278.

Westwood College–Atlanta Midtown

Atlanta, Georgia

http://www.westwood.edu/

Contact: Westwood College–Atlanta Midtown, 1100 Spring Street, Suite 102, Atlanta, GA 30309. *Phone:* 404-745-9862. *Toll-free phone:* 800-613-4595.

Westwood College–Atlanta Northlake

Atlanta, Georgia

http://www.westwood.edu/

Contact: Westwood College–Atlanta Northlake, 2309 Parklake Drive, NE, Building 10, Atlanta, GA 30345. *Phone:* 404-962-2998. *Toll-free phone:* 866-821-6145.

Westwood College–Chicago Du Page

Woodridge, Illinois

http://www.westwood.edu/

Contact: Westwood College–Chicago Du Page, 7155 Janes Avenue, Woodridge, IL 60517. *Phone:* 630-434-8250. *Toll-free phone:* 866-721-7647.

Westwood College–Chicago Loop Campus

Chicago, Illinois

http://www.westwood.edu/

Contact: Westwood College–Chicago Loop Campus, 1 North State Street, Suite 1000, Chicago, IL 60602. *Phone:* 312-739-0890. *Toll-free phone:* 800-693-5411.

Westwood College–Chicago O'Hare Airport

Chicago, Illinois

http://www.westwood.edu/

Contact: Westwood College–Chicago O'Hare Airport, 8501 West Higgins Road, Suite 100, Chicago, IL 60631. *Phone:* 773-380-6801. *Toll-free phone:* 866-235-2457.

Westwood College–Chicago River Oaks

Calumet City, Illinois

http://www.westwood.edu/

Contact: Westwood College–Chicago River Oaks, 80 River Oaks Drive, Suite 111, Calumet City, IL 60409. *Phone:* 708-832-9760. *Toll-free phone:* 888-549-4960.

Westwood College–Denver North

Denver, Colorado

http://www.westwood.edu/

Contact: Westwood College–Denver North, 7350 North Broadway, Denver, CO 80221-3653. *Phone:* 303-426-7000. *Toll-free phone:* 800-281-2978.

Westwood College–Denver South
Aurora, Colorado
http://www.westwood.edu/
Contact: Westwood College–Denver South, 350 Blackhawk Street, Aurora, CO 80011. *Phone:* 303-934-1122. *Toll-free phone:* 800-281-2978.

Westwood College–Inland Empire
Upland, California
http://www.westwood.edu/
Contact: Westwood College–Inland Empire, 20 West 7th Street, Upland, CA 91786. *Phone:* 909-931-7599. *Toll-free phone:* 866-221-5632.

Westwood College–Los Angeles
Los Angeles, California
http://www.westwood.edu/
Contact: Westwood College–Los Angeles, 3250 Wilshire Boulevard, 4th Floor, Los Angeles, CA 90010. *Phone:* 213-382-2328. *Toll-free phone:* 866-930-9256.

Westwood College–Online Campus
Westminster, Colorado
http://www.westwood.edu/
Contact: Westwood College–Online Campus, 10249 Church Ranch Way, Westminster, CO 80021. *Phone:* 720-887-8888.

Westwood College–South Bay Campus
Torrance, California
http://www.westwood.edu/
Contact: Westwood College–South Bay Campus, 19700 South Vermont Avenue, Suite 100, Torrance, CA 90502. *Phone:* 310-965-0877. *Toll-free phone:* 888-403-3308.

Wiley College
Marshall, Texas
http://www.wileyc.edu/
Contact: Ms. Alvena Jones, Interim Director of Admissions/Recruitment, Wiley College, 711 Wiley Avenue, Marshall, TX 75670-5199. *Phone:* 903-927-3222. *Toll-free phone:* 800-658-6889. *Fax:* 903-923-8878. *E-mail:* ajones@wileyc.edu.

Wilfrid Laurier University
Waterloo, Ontario, Canada
http://www.wlu.ca/
Contact: Wilfrid Laurier University, 75 University Avenue West, Waterloo, ON N2L 3C5, Canada. *Phone:* 519-884-0710 Ext. 6099.

William Carey University
Hattiesburg, Mississippi
http://www.wmcarey.edu/
Contact: Mr. William N. Curry, Dean of Enrollment Management, William Carey University, 498 Tuscan Avenue, Hattiesburg, MS 39401-5499. *Phone:* 601-318-6051. *Toll-free phone:* 800-962-5991. *Fax:* 601-318-6154. *E-mail:* admissions@wmcarey.edu.

Winston-Salem State University
Winston-Salem, North Carolina
http://www.wssu.edu/
Contact: Ms. Tomikia LeGrande, Assistant Vice Chancellor for Enrollment Services, Winston-Salem State University, 601 Martin Luther King, Jr. Drive, Thompson Center, Winston-Salem, NC 27110. *Phone:* 336-750-2070. *Toll-free phone:* 800-257-4052. *Fax:* 336-750-2079. *E-mail:* Legrandet@wssu.edu.

Yeshiva and Kolel Bais Medrash Elyon
Monsey, New York
Contact: Yeshiva and Kolel Bais Medrash Elyon, 73 Main Street, Monsey, NY 10952.

Yeshiva and Kollel Harbotzas Torah
Brooklyn, New York
Contact: Yeshiva and Kollel Harbotzas Torah, 1049 East 15th Street, Brooklyn, NY 11230.

Yeshiva Beth Moshe
Scranton, Pennsylvania
Contact: Dean, Yeshiva Beth Moshe, 930 Hickory Street, PO Box 1141, Scranton, PA 18505-2124. *Phone:* 717-346-1747.

Yeshiva Derech Chaim
Brooklyn, New York
Contact: Administrator, Yeshiva Derech Chaim, 1573 39th Street, Brooklyn, NY 11218. *Phone:* 718-438-5476.

Yeshiva D'Monsey Rabbinical College
Monsey, New York
Contact: Yeshiva D'Monsey Rabbinical College, 2 Roman Boulevard, Monsey, NY 10952.

Yeshiva Gedolah Imrei Yosef D'Spinka
Brooklyn, New York
Contact: Yeshiva Gedolah Imrei Yosef D'Spinka, 1466 56th Street, Brooklyn, NY 11219.

Yeshiva Gedolah of Greater Detroit
Oak Park, Michigan
Contact: Rabbi P. Rushnawitz, Director, Yeshiva Gedolah of Greater Detroit, 24600 Greenfield, Oak Park, MI 48237-1544.

Yeshiva Gedolah Rabbinical College
Miami Beach, Florida
Contact: Yeshiva Gedolah Rabbinical College, 1140 Alton Road, Miami Beach, FL 33139.

Yeshiva Karlin Stolin Rabbinical Institute
Brooklyn, New York
Contact: Director of Admissions, Yeshiva Karlin Stolin Rabbinical Institute, 1818 Fifty-fourth Street, Brooklyn, NY 11204. *Phone:* 718-232-7800 Ext. 26.

Yeshiva of Nitra Rabbinical College

Mount Kisco, New York

Contact: Administrator, Yeshiva of Nitra Rabbinical College, Pines Bridge Road, Mount Kisco, NY 10549. *Phone:* 718-384-5460. *Fax:* 718-387-9400.

Yeshiva of the Telshe Alumni

Riverdale, New York

Contact: Yeshiva of the Telshe Alumni, 4904 Independence Avenue, Riverdale, NY 10471.

Yeshiva Ohr Elchonon Chabad/West Coast Talmudical Seminary

Los Angeles, California

http://www.yoec.edu/

Contact: Rabbi Ezra Binyomin Schochet, Dean, Yeshiva Ohr Elchonon Chabad/West Coast Talmudical Seminary, 7215 Waring Avenue, Los Angeles, CA 90046-7660. *Phone:* 323-937-3763. *E-mail:* roshyeshiva@yoec.edu.

Yeshiva Shaarei Torah of Rockland

Suffern, New York

Contact: Yeshiva Shaarei Torah of Rockland, 91 West Carlton Road, Suffern, NY 10901.

Yeshiva Shaar Hatorah Talmudic Research Institute

Kew Gardens, New York

Contact: Assistant Dean, Yeshiva Shaar Hatorah Talmudic Research Institute, 117-06 84th Avenue, Kew Gardens, NY 11418-1469. *Phone:* 718-846-1940.

Yeshivas Novominsk

Brooklyn, New York

Contact: Yeshivas Novominsk, 1569 47th Street, Brooklyn, NY 11219.

Yeshivath Viznitz

Monsey, New York

Contact: Registrar, Yeshivath Viznitz, 25 Phyllis Terrace, Monsey, NY 10952. *Phone:* 914-356-1010.

Yeshivath Zichron Moshe

South Fallsburg, New York

Contact: Rabbi Abba Gorelick, Dean, Yeshivath Zichron Moshe, Laurel Park Road, South Fallsburg, NY 12779. *Phone:* 914-434-5240.

Yeshivat Mikdash Melech

Brooklyn, New York

Contact: Rabbi S. Beyda, Director of Admissions, Yeshivat Mikdash Melech, 1326 Ocean Parkway, Brooklyn, NY 11230-5601. *Phone:* 718-339-1090. *E-mail:* mikdashmelech@verizon.net.

Yeshiva Toras Chaim Talmudical Seminary

Denver, Colorado

Contact: Rabbi Israel Kagan, Dean, Yeshiva Toras Chaim Talmudical Seminary, 1555 Stuart Street, Denver, CO 80204-1415. *Phone:* 303-629-8200. *Fax:* 303-623-5949.

York College

York, Nebraska

http://www.york.edu/

Contact: Ms. Janae Parsons, York College, 1125 East 8th Street, York, NE 68467-2699. *Phone:* 402-363-5627. *Toll-free phone:* 800-950-9675. *Fax:* 402-363-5623. *E-mail:* enroll@york.edu.

Young Harris College

Young Harris, Georgia

http://www.yhc.edu/

Contact: Mr. Clinton G. Hobbs, Vice President for Enrollment Management, Young Harris College, PO Box 116, Young Harris, GA 30582-0098. *Phone:* 706-379-3111. *Toll-free phone:* 800-241-3754. *Fax:* 706-379-3108. *E-mail:* admissions@yhc.edu.

College Close-Ups

NOTICE: Certain portions of or information contained in this book have been submitted and paid for by the educational institution identified, and such institutions take full responsibility for the accuracy, timeliness, completeness and functionality of such content. Such portions or information include (i) each display ad in the "Profiles" section from pages 55 through 1334 that comprises a half or full page of information covering a single educational institution, and (ii) each two-page description in the "College Close-Up" section from pages 1336 through 1745.

A ★ indicates that the school has detailed information with a Premium Profile on Petersons.com.

ACADEMY OF ART UNIVERSITY

SAN FRANCISCO, CALIFORNIA

★ To read more about this school, visit http://petersons.to/academyofartuniversity

ACADEMY of ART UNIVERSITY®
FOUNDED IN SAN FRANCISCO 1929 BY ARTISTS FOR ARTISTS

The University

In 1929, Academy of Art University founder Richard S. Stephens, who was the advertising Creative Director of *Sunset* magazine, acted on his belief that "aspiring artists and designers, given proper instruction, hard work, and dedication, can learn the skills needed to become successful professionals." His new School of Advertising Art consisted of 46 students meeting in one room on San Francisco's Kearny Street.

The instructors, who were professional artists, brought real-world problems, situations, solutions, and practical experience to the students. Based on this idea, the school's philosophy was formulated: Hire established professionals to teach the art and design professionals of tomorrow. At that time, advertising consisted primarily of illustrations, photos, and copy. Consequently, it became necessary to teach beginning students the fundamentals of drawing, painting, color, light, and photography as well as layout and typography.

When Richard A. Stephens succeeded his father as President in 1951, the Foundations Department was added, ensuring all students mastered the basic principles of traditional art and design. Illustration soon expanded to include fine arts (drawing, painting, sculpture, and printmaking), and advertising design led to the School of Graphic Design. A Fashion School (design, knitwear, textiles, and merchandising) and an Interior Design School were also added. In 1966, the Academy officially became a college, and a decade later began offering the Master of Fine Arts degree. Later, five more buildings were purchased, and by 1992, the student body comprised more than 2,500 students.

The leadership of the Academy was then turned over to the third generation. Dr. Elisa Stephens, granddaughter of the school's founder, quickly determined that the school's small School of Web Design & New Media had enormous potential to prepare students for multimedia careers with such companies as Pixar, Adobe, and Walt Disney Productions. It is now one of the largest departments at the Academy. In 2004, the name of the school was changed from Academy of Art College to Academy of Art University, in recognition of its depth, scope, and quality.

Today, Academy of Art University is the largest accredited private art and design university in the nation. Nearly one third of the student body is made up of international students. The Academy has over 30 facilities that house classrooms, studios, galleries, and residence halls. The students, who are admitted through an open-enrollment policy, aspire to earn A.A., B.A., B.F.A., B.S., B.Arch. (currently in candidacy status), M.A., M.F.A., or M.Arch. degrees or an Art Teaching Credential. Students can study in San Francisco or through the Academy's flexible online programs.

The Academy maintains a system of courtesy shuttles to connect the different points of the campus, all of which are located within the city limits of San Francisco, one of the world's most vibrant and beautiful cities. The instructors, who are working art and design professionals from around the world, are drawn to the Academy and to the creative and intellectual center that is the Bay Area. Extensive senior-year internship programs allow students to gain valuable experience and develop strong portfolios in their chosen field prior to graduation.

Academy of Art University is an accredited member of the WASC Senior College and University Commission (WSCUC), National Association of Schools of Art and Design (NASAD), Council for Interior Design Accreditation (CIDA) for B.F.A.-IAD and M.F.A.-IAD, National Architectural Accrediting Board (NAAB) for M.Arch. and in candidacy for B.Arch., and California Commission on Teacher Credentialing (CTC).

Location

The city of San Francisco is one of the great cultural centers of the world; a melting pot of diversity, culture, and creativity that has spawned major museums and galleries, world-class opera and theaters, dance companies, film production and recording studios, technological innovation, performing artists ranging from classical to popular music, and numerous other cultural opportunities. The city's status as a tourist mecca located on the Pacific Rim ensures that one encounters people from all corners of the world.

The climate is moderate and offers kaleidoscopic blends of sunshine and fog most of the year. The Northpoint campus is located at the historic Cannery building near world-famous Pier 39, where students can view Alcatraz Island from their classroom windows. In addition, four campus buildings are located two blocks from historic Union Square, in the commercial heart of the city, and three others are located near the Financial District. Shop 657, a store in Union Square, opened in December 2014 to display AAU designs and provide merchandising students real-world experience.

The city offers myriad locations for field trips and studio visits. World-renowned artists display their creations in the Academy's five nonprofit art galleries, which are open to the public. The Academy is an urban institution that both draws upon and contributes to the cultural wealth of the community in which it resides.

Majors and Degrees

Academy of Art University offers A.A., B.A., B.F.A., B.S., B.Arch. (currently in candidacy status), M.A., M.F.A., and M.Arch. degrees and an Art Teaching Credential. Programs are available online and in San Francisco in the following: acting* (speech, improv, physical acting), advertising (creative strategy, art direction, copywriting, television commercials), animation & visual effects (background painting/layout design, character development, storyboard art, 3-D modeling, VFX/compositing), architecture (structures, materials and methods of construction, design process, structural and environmental systems), art education (learning to teach in museums, developmental psychology, teaching art in the community), art history (Renaissance art, American art history, ancient art history, looking at art, philosophy), art teaching credential (learning to teach both children and adults), costume design, fashion (design, knitwear, merchandising, textiles), fashion journalism (fashion writing, editorials for magazines, newspaper writing, fashion news), fashion styling, fine art (painting, printmaking, sculpture), game development (game engines, prototyping, level design, game art, 3-D modeling), game programming, graphic design (corporate and brand identity, package design, print and collateral), illustration (children's books, editorial, comic books), industrial design (furniture design, product design, toy design, transportation design), interior architecture & design (commercial and residential design, furniture design), jewelry & metal arts (fashion jewelry design, enameling, stone setting, casting, welded and fabricated sculpture), landscape architecture (plant design, elements in landscape, grading and drainage, urban open spaces), motion pictures & television (cinematography, directing, editing, producing, production design, screenwriting), multimedia communications (journalism, editing, short-form documentary), music production & sound design for visual media (harmony, arranging, orchestration, music production techniques, scoring for film), photography (architecture, advertising, digital documentary, editorial, fashion, fine art, landscape, photojournalism, portraiture), studio production for advertising & design, visual development (concept art for animation, film, and games; digital painting; character design; cinematic storytelling; Marquette sculpting; environment creation), web design & new media (user experience design, interactive design, new media, web design), and writing for film, television, & digital media.
* Acting degree program is currently not available online.

Academic Programs

The Bachelor of Fine Arts degree requires foundations courses, major courses, art electives, and liberal arts courses. Fundamental courses are related specifically to students' majors to prepare them to begin intense focus courses in their field by the sophomore year. All major courses of study are structured so the student builds upon skills learned the previous semester and advances to the next level of technical or creative proficiency. Some related major courses may be taken concurrently.

Liberal arts courses teach practical applications for forging a professional career in art and design. International students who come from countries where English is not the primary language may take additional ESL classes, as determined by English language proficiency testing. Students are advised to meet with departmental directors at least once during the academic year to have their progress assessed. Portfolios are reviewed before the junior year to determine whether or not a student has progressed sufficiently to continue study at the Academy.

Academic Facilities

Academy of Art University's state-of-the-art facilities offer students the tools they need to prepare for professional careers in art and design. The Academy invests in top-notch equipment to ensure it remains on the cutting edge of technology. Learning on industry-standard equipment, students gain hands-on experience.

Academy of Art University students have access to an array of digital tools. The School of Game Development and the School of Animation & Visual Effects provide the latest equipment, as well as a video and Cintiq lab, green screen studio, and sound booth. The School of Web Design & New Media houses a usability lab with the most current software, while the School of Music Production & Sound Design for Visual Media offers the latest sound design and video editing tools and is proud to have a new flagship mixing console, the Avid S6. The Academy is the first university in California to offer this new console and the second organization in California other than Skywalker Sound to own the console.

The School of Advertising is designed to look, feel, and function like an ad agency. Located in the heart of San Francisco's Financial District, the School of Graphic Design has the latest industry tools that enable students to have a seamless transition into the world of work following graduation. And the School of Illustration is housed in a unique historic building in San Francisco's Union Square District. The original libraries, meeting rooms, theater, and a ballroom have been transformed into drawing/painting studios and classrooms.

Undergraduate and graduate students in Architecture, Interior Architecture & Design, and Landscape Architecture share an 800-square-foot materials library and plotting room, as well as a model shop. The School of Industrial Design offers multiple shop facilities and a 3-D computer lab. The School of Landscape Architecture benefits from being located in San Francisco, the hub of urban landscape design.

Fashion students have access to studio facilities for women's, men's and children's wear, as well as textile design, knitwear design, and fashion merchandising and marketing. Surrounded by world-renowned museums and galleries, the School of Fine Art and the School of Art History facilities include thousands of square feet of studio space with everything their students need to bring their individual visions to life.

The School of Motion Pictures & Television and the School of Acting facilities include a postproduction area, green screen studio, screenwriting lab, and several soundstage studios. Students of the School of Multimedia Communications have access to a cutting-edge radio studio and television studio, complete with robotic cameras, anchor desks and interview sets, teleprompters, and green screens. School of Photography facilities are equipped with both traditional and digital photographic technology.

The library provides state-of-the-art digital tools, making it possible for students to access extensive art and design image resources and information on demand. The Academy Resource Center offers all students free learning support services including study hall tutoring, academic coaching, English as second language support programs, a writing lab, and a multimedia language lab.

Costs

As of December 2014, undergraduate tuition is $810 per credit unit. Full-time students must carry at least 12 units per Fall or Spring semester and 6 units per Summer semester. There is a nonrefundable $120 fee when applying—$100 is applicable toward tuition and $20 is for registration. Lab fees run from $25 to $400 per semester, depending on the class. Tuition and fees are subject to change at any time. Art supplies can run from $250 to $1,500 per semester, depending on the major. The Academy has most of the expensive technical equipment available for students to borrow or use in a lab.

Academy of Art University operates many residence halls within the city. Several housing options are offered, and costs vary from $7,640 to $14,670 per academic year (Fall and Spring semesters). For further information, students may contact the Department of Housing & Residence Life directly at 415-618-6335 or by e-mail at housing@academyart.edu.

Financial Aid

The Academy offers financial aid packages consisting of grants, loans, and work-study to eligible students with a demonstrated need. Low-interest loans are available to all eligible students, regardless of need. As financial aid programs, procedures, and eligibility requirements change frequently, applicants should contact the Financial Aid Office at financialaid@academyart.edu or 800-544-2787 (toll-free, U.S. only).

Faculty

The Academy averages 1,484 instructors in Fall/Spring semester, most of whom are full-time art and design professionals and part-time teachers. The student-teacher ratio for undergraduate classes averages 17:1.

Student Government

Although there is no formal student government, each department has between two and three student representatives who meet with the President as needed throughout the semester to discuss any student issues.

Admission Requirements

Applicants for the A.A., B.A., B.F.A., B.S., and B.Arch. (currently in candidacy status) programs must have a high school diploma or equivalent. There is no portfolio requirement. M.A., M.F.A., and M.Arch. applicants must have a bachelor's degree and submit a portfolio and statement of intent. International students take written and speech tests to determine which ESL classes may have to be completed. Most ESL classes can be taken in conjunction with art and design classes. All foundations classes offer specialized ESL sections with instructors trained for language assistance. The application fee is $100 for undergraduates. A $500 tuition deposit applies to international applicants.

What Sets Academy of Art University Apart

The Academy is one of the few art and design schools that believes in nurturing the whole artist; this includes developing athletic ability along with artistic talent. Students can participate in intercollegiate, intramural, and club sports. With Pacific West honors and national championships, the Academy offers basketball, baseball, softball, cross country, track & field, soccer, golf, volleyball, and tennis for its students to partake in. Furthermore, the Academy is proud to be the only art school in the NCAA Division II.

Application and Information

Students may apply to enter the Academy at the beginning of the Spring, Fall, or Summer semesters. Information in this profile is subject to change. Students should contact Academy of Art University for current information or visit www.academyart.edu to learn about total costs, median student loan debt, potential occupations, and other information.

Academy of Art University
79 New Montgomery Street
San Francisco, California 94105
Phone: 415-274-2200
800-544-2787 (U.S. only)
Fax: 415-618-6287
E-mail: info@academyart.edu
Website: www.academyart.edu
https://www.facebook.com/AcademyofArtUniversity
https://twitter.com/academy_of_art
https://plus.google.com/+academyofartuniversity/posts
http://www.pinterest.com/academyofartuni
http://academyofartu.tumblr.com
http://instagram.com/academy_of_art
http://www.youtube.com/user/academyofartu

Academy of Art University's downtown campus.

ADELPHI UNIVERSITY

GARDEN CITY, NEW YORK

ADELPHI UNIVERSITY

★ To read more about this school, visit http://petersons.to/adelphiuniversity

COLLEGE CLOSE-UPS

The University

Adelphi University, founded in 1896, is Long Island's first private coeducational institution of higher learning. A nonsectarian, independent university, Adelphi welcomes men and women of all backgrounds who display intellectual inquisitiveness, academic commitment, and a desire for achievement and purpose in life. The University enrolls 5,071 undergraduates and 2,539 graduate students. Thirty-five states and forty-two countries are represented in its diverse student body. The campus is located on 75 landscaped acres in Garden City, New York, 23 miles east of Manhattan and easily accessible by public transportation. The University also has four off-campus centers: the Manhattan Center in New York City; the Hudson Valley Center in Poughkeepsie, New York; the Hauppauge Education and Conference Center in Hauppauge, New York; and the Sayville Downtown Center in Sayville, New York.

Adelphi's schools and programs include the College of Arts and Sciences; the College of Nursing and Public Health; the Honors College; the Robert B. Willumstad School of Business; the Ruth S. Ammon School of Education; the School of Social Work; the Gordon F. Derner Institute of Advanced Psychological Studies; and adult academic programs in University College.

The University's seven residence halls provide all the comforts of home and include a Green Community and honors housing. The residential life staff at Adelphi is committed to bringing education to the residence halls. A lecture and discussion series brings faculty members together with students to examine events of the day and issues related to the classroom. In addition, about 200 seminars, workshops, and events are offered each year. Faculty and guest lecturers lead discussions on such topics as American and global politics, ethnic diversity, legal affairs, job interviewing, health and wellness, and more.

Opportunities for enhancing life beyond the classroom abound at Adelphi. Students take advantage of the many cultural and internship opportunities in Manhattan and on Long Island, and they can participate in intramural and 23 intercollegiate sports (including, but not limited to, men's and women's soccer, golf, softball, and baseball and men's basketball and lacrosse), drama productions, and more than eighty student clubs, community-service groups, and organizations. The Adelphi student newspaper (*The Delphian*) and the yearbook (*Oracle*) welcome writers and photographers. Students take advantage of thriving cultural arts programs, including plays, art exhibits, concerts, and lectures; the comprehensive sports and fitness services; and the breathtaking campus. Physical education facilities include a swimming pool; basketball courts; weight-training and exercise rooms; a large indoor running track; and fields for baseball, lacrosse, soccer, and softball. In addition, a vast array of activities such as movies, exhibits, cabarets, symposia, and field trips are scheduled every semester. These factors and more help account for Adelphi's ranking as a Best Buy in *The Fiske Guide to Colleges* for nine straight years, a Top College in the Northeast by The Princeton Review, and a Top College by *Forbes* magazine.

In the Ruth S. Harley University Center (UC)—a central meeting place on campus—Adelphi students can browse the full-service bookstore, refresh themselves and relax in one of the center's lounges (commuter students have a special lounge equipped with lockers), eat in the UC Café, and enjoy a vast array of activities, including movies, comedy shows, lectures, dance parties, and musical events. Cultural trips are also offered to such locations as Argentina, Australia, Costa Rica, Egypt, Italy, London, Spain, and more. The UC also houses Adelphi's numerous student organizations including academic clubs, community service and social action clubs, honor societies, and religious and special-interest organizations.

Location

Adelphi's main campus is located in Garden City, New York, a village of stately homes, historic buildings, and parks. The cultural and commercial resources of New York City—just 23 miles away—and the recreation and entertainment of Long Island are only a short distance away by public or private transit.

Majors and Degrees

Undergraduate studies leading to the degrees of Bachelor of Arts (B.A.), Bachelor of Business Administration (B.B.A.), Bachelor of Fine Arts (B.F.A.), Bachelor of Science (B.S.), and Bachelor of Social Work (B.S.W.) are offered at Adelphi. Programs of study at Adelphi include: accounting; African, Black, and Caribbean studies; anthropology/forensic anthropology; art history, fine arts and studio art* (ceramics, painting, photography, printmaking, sculpture) and graphic design*; art education; biochemistry; biology; business; chemistry; communications (journalism, media studies, moving image production); communication sciences and disorders; computer and management information systems; computer science (game development and information security); criminal justice; dance; economics; education studies, with programs of study in childhood education and adolescent education through the University's Scholar Teacher Education Program (S.T.E.P.); English (literature, creative writing); environmental studies; exercise science; finance; French; history; interdisciplinary studies; languages and international studies (political science, environmental studies, business); Latin American studies; management; marketing; mathematics; music**; music education**; nursing; philosophy; physical education; physical education/health education; physics; political science; psychology; social work; sociology; Spanish; sport management; and theatre arts** (acting and design technology).

* An art portfolio is required.

** An audition is required.

Five-year bachelor's/master's programs are offered in social work, psychology, and business, as well as S.T.E.P. in childhood education and adolescent education.

Adelphi students also take advantage of partnerships with prestigious institutions such as New York University and Columbia University for programs such as dentistry and engineering, respectively. Pre-professional studies and joint degree programs are available in pre-dental, pre-engineering, pre–environmental studies, pre-law, pre-medicine, pre-optometry, pre-pharmacy, pre–physical therapy/allied health, pre-podiatry, and pre–veterinary medicine.

Academic Programs

The goal of the academic programs at Adelphi is to provide higher education that fosters critical thinking and prepares students for the future. Consistent with the University's approach to liberal arts learning, students take part in the University's general education distribution requirements.

A minimum of 120 credits is required for a baccalaureate degree, with a specified number in the chosen major. Double majors and various minors may be elected. Seniors of superior academic ability may be admitted to graduate courses in their major field.

Off-Campus Programs

Adelphi University's Center for International Education offers study-abroad programs that can last several weeks or span an academic year. Students can participate in Adelphi-run programs in such locations as Australia, Costa Rica, Florence, India, and Peru, or join programs run by other educational institutions. Adelphi offers students the opportunity to participate in internship programs that provide access to a variety of industries and locations—in the local Long Island community, the surrounding Manhattan area, and beyond. Students can also take part in the Community Fellows Program, which pairs students with nonprofit organizations across Long Island and Manhattan, for 10-week, paid summer internships.

Academic Facilities

The University Libraries include the Swirbul Library, the Archives and Special Collections on the Garden City campus, and the libraries at the Manhattan Center, Hauppauge Education and Conference Center, and the Hudson Valley Center. The University's primary research holdings are at Swirbul Library and include 600,000 volumes (including bound periodicals and government publications), 806,000 items in microformats, 33,000 audiovisual items, and online access to more than 61,000 electronic journal titles and 221 research databases.

The Swirbul Library is also the center of information technology on campus. Its amenities include more than 100 computer workstations that are fully networked for student use and a faculty development lab. Adelphi's technology infrastructure reaches into every classroom and every part of the curriculum to provide web-based learning and other applications of communication and information media. Swirbul also houses a 3-D studio that features both large- and small-scale 3-D printers, a filament recycling machine, and work stations for scanning, editing, and modeling for 3-D projects.

The 18,000-square-foot Adele and Herbert J. Klapper Center for Fine Arts has greatly expanded Adelphi's art studio and classroom space and offers greater opportunity for nonmajors to take art courses. This is in addition to the current state-of-the-art digital graphics design studio and faculty offices and the expansion of drawing studios in Blodgett Hall.

The Adelphi University Performing Arts Center (AUPAC) showcases prestigious programs in acting, design/technical theater, and music and dance together under one roof. The center features a 500-seat concert hall, dance and recital rooms, music practice rooms, temperature-controlled instrument storage rooms, and a black box theater.

The Center for Recreation and Sports is the home of Adelphi's successful athletics programs. The center's three-story, three-court gym—that converts into a 2,200-seat arena for basketball games and other events—accommodates recreational and intercollegiate athletes and health and physical education students, and can host NCAA tournaments and championships.

In fall 2015, Adelphi is scheduled to open the Nexus Building and Welcome Center. The new home to the College of Nursing and Public Health, the building will contain administrative and academic space for the College, as well as classrooms and ultramodern simulation labs, a welcome center, the Office of University Admissions, and a below-grade parking garage for 200-plus cars with surface parking for 100 cars.

Costs

The 2014–15 tuition and fees for full-time undergraduates totalled $32,340. For students living on campus, additional costs included housing ($9,200 for a typical double room without air conditioning) and a meal plan ($3,770 for the gold meal plan).

Financial Aid

The Office of Student Financial Services administers federal and New York State programs that provide funds to assist students in pursuing their academic goals. In addition to grants based on need, Adelphi annually offers hundreds of its own scholarships based on merit, talent, and extracurricular excellence. Ninety-eight percent of Adelphi freshmen receive some form of financial aid each year. The average financial aid package award for a full-time undergraduate is approximately $20,900.

Faculty

At Adelphi, the quality of education is entrusted to its distinguished faculty members, who are noted for their serious commitment to students as well as for their research and professional contributions. Undergraduate courses are taught by professors, not graduate assistants, and students learn in small, intimate environments.

Student Government

The Student Government Association is the elected student group that represents the opinions of the full-time undergraduate body to the administration and other groups. The Student Government Association hosts speakers, sponsors awareness days, and serves as a voice for student concerns and interests.

Admission Requirements

Recommended admission qualifications include graduation from a four-year public or private high school or equivalent credentials, four years of English, three years of science, three years of mathematics, two to three years of a foreign language or languages, and 4 additional units chosen from the fields mentioned or from history and social studies. Official test results from the SAT or ACT with writing are required.

Personal interviews and campus tours are strongly recommended for all applicants. Arrangements can be made by calling 800-ADELPHI (233-5744).

Application and Information

The following admission credentials should be submitted by applicants: a completed online application for admission, the $40 nonrefundable application fee, an official secondary school transcript or GED certificate, official results of the SAT or ACT with writing, and a minimum of one letter of recommendation. Transfer students must submit official transcripts from all colleges previously attended.

Adelphi accepts applications on a rolling basis, with admission twice each year for the semesters beginning in September and January. Freshmen filing dates are December 1 for early action, February 1 for priority consideration for joint-degree programs, March 1 as the suggested deadline for regular admission to the fall semester (applications received later are reviewed on a rolling basis), and November 1 for regular admission for the spring semester (applications received later are reviewed on a rolling basis). The nonbinding early action plan is available only for the September term. An early action decision means that applicants who submit their completed applications by December 1 will receive a non-binding admissions decision by December 31. Early action applicants are fully considered for scholarships and financial aid.

For more information, students should contact:

Office of University Admissions
Adelphi University
One South Avenue
Garden City, New York 11530
Phone: 800-ADELPHI (233-5744, toll-free)
E-mail: admissions@adelphi.edu
Website: adelphi.edu

In fall 2015, Adelphi is set to open the Nexus Building and Welcome Center—the future home of the College of Nursing and Public Health. The new building will feature classrooms and at least ten examination rooms, including an intensive care room, a delivery room, and a home-care lab. The exam rooms will have closed-circuit TV to observe student performance.

AMRIDGE UNIVERSITY

MONTGOMERY, ALABAMA

★ To read more about this school, visit http://petersons.to/amridgeuniversity

AMRIDGE UNIVERSITY.edu

COLLEGE CLOSE-UPS

The University

Founded in 1967, Amridge University has been a long-time leader in online education. Distance learning is the primary instructional delivery system for all its programs. Amridge's focus is on supporting students from their first point of inquiry all the way through completion of their academic degree program. Its goal is to help students obtain their degree through a variety of student support services and rigorous academic support.

Amridge University is accredited by the Southern Association of Colleges and Schools Commission on Colleges (SACS-COC), sacscoc.org, to award bachelor's, master's, and doctoral degree programs in business, counseling, Biblical studies, and many more. Amridge is one of the most affordable private universities in the United States. It offers scholarships and incentive discounts for military students, first-time freshmen, sister institution staff, ministers, and corporate alliances.

With over forty-five years in higher education, Amridge University has taught in the online education arena since 1993. Through the vision of the leadership of the institution, Amridge was chosen as one of the first fifteen participants in the nation selected by the U.S. Department of Education to pilot distance education on a broad level, resulting in a change to the federal law to allow more students access to distance education.

Location

Amridge University is located in Montgomery, Alabama, the capital city of the state. The University is strategically located in the central part of the state between Huntsville, and Mobile. The city is clean and modern, with beautiful residential areas, parks, and playgrounds, and fine schools and universities. Students and families can also enjoy its museums, zoo, and facilities of the capitol building. Montgomery has two major U.S. Air Force installations: Maxwell Air Force Base and Gunter Annex. Maxwell is where the Air War College is located and is a strategic center for education. The metropolitan area has a population of more than 350,000 citizens. There are many churches and educational institutions. The city has an abundance of good housing in addition to other advantages. The Montgomery Regional Airport is located six miles southwest of the capital city of Montgomery.

Majors and Degrees

Undergraduate degrees are awarded in Biblical studies, business administration, human development, human resource management, liberal studies, management communication, and criminal justice. These degrees promote biblical and Christian ministry skills, human development skills, knowledge in the arts, and management communication skills.

Amridge University students are fully matriculated students of Amridge University with full student privileges, rights, and responsibilities. A student must fulfill the required semester hours in a program as well as the basic requirements of the core curriculum. All core and general education requirements can be received from the University. Amridge University is a participating member of GoArmyEd and is Military Friendly Higher Education Institution.

Academic Programs

Amridge University operates on a 15-week semester basis and uses an academic calendar to articulate important guidelines for students during the academic year. The fall semester runs from September to December, during which a 10-week and 8-week selection of courses is offered; the spring semester runs from January to April, including a 10-week and 8-week selection of courses; and the summer semester runs from April to August, including a 10-week and 8-week selection of courses. Distance learning is the primary instructional delivery system for all degree programs offered at Amridge and the University focuses on supporting students in the online learning format.

While Amridge University does have a campus, most students will not visit there unless they are doctoral students attending one-week residency seminars or attending graduation festivities. Amridge utilizes several state-of-the-art distance learning applications to provide services to its student learners.

Blackboard Learn™ and Blackboard Collaborate™: Amridge University uses Blackboard Learn for the delivery of all course materials and videos. Its course management system is hosted by Blackboard. The Blackboard portal is monitored locally by the Network Operations Center of Amridge University and is available 24/7 for student access. Amridge University uses Blackboard Collaborate as a course conferencing system and delivery technology for live-stream classes. This includes live-streamed seminars, live-streamed weekly classes, and live classes recorded as archives for later viewing. With Collaborate, a webcam, and a headset with microphone, students can see and hear their instructor, give class presentations, and engage in live discussions with classmates and instructors. Collaborate also allows instructors to display documents, slides, or write on a whiteboard. Students can chat with classmates, raise their hand (virtually) to ask a question, and receive files from their instructor or classmates. Collaborate is accessible within each Blackboard course. Setup and configuration support is provided by Amridge University technical support.

Blackboard Connect™: Blackboard Connect is a mass communication system that allows the University to send text, live voice messages, emergency alerts, and quick notifications. Students are added into the system on a semester basis. Because Amridge Connect is an alert system, students are not able to opt out.

Blackboard Mobile™ and Amridge Connect iPad Program: Amridge is committed to providing students with learning tools that give them access to course work and assignments from any location. As part of its commitment to embrace twenty-first century technology for education, the University has adopted the iPad as a technological tool for teaching and learning. During the course registration process, all students are given the opportunity to purchase a University-issued iPad to use as a resource for accessing courses when they are not seated in front of a desktop computer. Distance learners require a mobile and flexible style of learning and an iPad can be a valuable resource; students who have this technology will have ease of access to all student-related services available within the Amridge University mobile app, AU Mobile. The mobile app is available for free download with Apple IOS devices (e.g., iPhones, iPads) and Android devices (e.g., Samsung, Nexus, Kindle Fire, Kyocera, HP, and others). AU Mobile app is accessible on most devices.

The Amridge University App allows students to access the full version of Blackboard Learn through the Blackboard Mobile platform, where students can complete many of the assignments within their courses. Students can also view the University course schedule by term, view the academic calendar and events, look up faculty and staff contact information, and access the Library and e-books portal.

The policy of Amridge University is to provide reasonable accommodation for persons who are handicapped or disabled as designated in Section 504 of the Rehabilitation Act of 1973 and the Americans with Disabilities Act of 1990. Although the Morgan W. Brown building is not equipped with an elevator, the needs of the physically challenged can be met from the first floor. These include registration, counseling, library facilities, classroom facilities, restrooms, breakroom facilities, and others. Ample parking is provided.

Academic Facilities

Amridge University sits on a stately 9-acre campus adjoining Interstate 85. A beautiful building houses the administration offices, classrooms, and Library Resource Center.

Costs

Undergraduate tuition per semester hour is $365. First-time full-time students receive a reduced rate of $250 per semester hour. These rates are guaranteed through the student's degree program, as long as students maintain continuous full-time enrollment and are in good academic standing.

Financial Aid

More than 90 percent of all Amridge students receive financial aid in the form of grants, such as the Federal Pell Grant; scholarships from Amridge; and other sources. The amount of aid given is determined by the college's analysis of the Free Application for Federal Student Aid (FAFSA). All financial aid forms must be received by the Financial Aid department before a student can finalize enrollment.

Faculty

The instructional faculty members total approximately 100. Approximately 65 percent of the full-time faculty members hold doctoral degrees, 100 percent hold master's degrees, and 100 percent hold terminal degrees. Faculty members specialize in their areas and have exceptional training in distance learning delivery.

Student Government

Student volunteers serve as members of the Student Advisory Committee. Volunteers are appointed by the Student Services Team, with recommendations from the deans. The committee meets on a regular basis and is reorganized on an annual basis. Concerns, recommendations, and requests are presented directly from the committee to the appropriate University area.

Admission Requirements

Amridge University is open to all academically qualified persons. The University has developed a streamlined admissions process to help prospective students complete the process expeditiously so they can begin their studies. Students are strongly encouraged to work closely with University staff members to complete all steps to attain official (non-provisional) admission status for their respective degree program. Upon acceptance to the University, each student is assigned an academic adviser whose primary responsibility is to oversee the academic progress of each student and motivate them to succeed both inside and outside the classroom.

Application and Information

For further information, students may contact:
Admissions
Amridge University
1200 Taylor Road
Montgomery, Alabama 36117
Phone: 888-790-8080 (toll-free)
Fax: 334-387-3878
E-mail: cc@amridgeuniversity.edu
Website: http://www.amridgeuniversity.edu

Amridge University has been a leader in distance learning since 1993.

COLLEGE CLOSE-UPS

ANNA MARIA COLLEGE

PAXTON, MASSACHUSETTS

★ To read more about this school, visit http://petersons.to/annamariacollege

The College

Anna Maria College is a private, four-year, Catholic coeducational institution that was founded in 1946 by the Sisters of Saint Anne in Marlboro, Massachusetts. In 1952, AMC moved to its current 192-acre campus in Paxton, Massachusetts. Originally an elite women's college, AMC has been coeducational since 1973. The College has grown exponentially over the last sixty-seven years with a total enrollment of 1,500.

Anna Maria College is a close-knit community of teachers and learners. Small class sizes allow for mentor relationships to develop between faculty members and students. Freshman and sophomore classes generally have between 15 and 20 students; some upper-level classes have as few as 10 students. Faculty members teach and advise students based on their knowledge of each person as an individual. Students are supported when necessary and challenged at all times. Classes are never taught by graduate assistants.

In recent years the College has undergone significant change. Offerings have been enhanced, general education requirements have been revised, and extracurricular and athletic opportunities have grown, to ensure that students have access to the programs and services that will help develop their mind, body, and spirit. All majors are now organized under a school structure with six different schools: Business, Education, Fire and Health Sciences, Humanities, Justice and Social Sciences, and Visual and Performing Arts. An honors program with a unique international experience has become extremely popular. The recent addition of new programs in forensic criminology, health and community services, emergency management services, and marketing communications has added greatly to the wide range of professional offerings available to students.

As part of the master plan, AMC has already enhanced and revitalized the campus with an all-purpose athletic field and stadium; three new residence halls, one of which offers suite-style housing; a new fitness center facility; and a high-tech learning setting known as the Information Commons, which features computer stations and study areas for students. The College has also established the Student Success Center that brings tutoring, counseling, and support services together under one roof.

Anna Maria College is accredited by the New England Association of Schools and Colleges, the Council on Social Work Education, the American Music Therapy Association, and the Accreditation Commission for Education in Nursing, Inc. AMC is approved by the Board of Registration in Nursing in Massachusetts and the Massachusetts Department of Education.

Approximately 70 percent of Anna Maria College's undergraduates reside on campus in the residence halls. Students enjoy a full social life both on campus and within the college-city atmosphere of nearby Worcester, Massachusetts.

Anna Maria College's NCAA Division III athletic programs offer intercollegiate competition for men (baseball, basketball, cross-country, football, golf, lacrosse, and soccer,) and women (basketball, cross-country, field hockey, soccer, softball, tennis, and volleyball). Intramural athletics are also available to students who do not wish to participate on competitive sports teams.

Anna Maria College provides a wireless campus, with more than 500 computers linking classrooms, offices, the Student Success Center, labs, the Information Commons, and all residence hall rooms. In addition to College-owned computers, students have the opportunity to access the College network to gain access to the Internet from any location on campus via the College's wireless network and their own computers.

Location

Anna Maria College is located on a 192-acre campus in Paxton, Massachusetts, 8 miles from Worcester's vibrant downtown. The city offers numerous professional, cultural, and entertainment opportunities, and Boston, Providence, and Hartford are only an hour away.

Local attractions include big-name entertainment and minor league sports teams at the DCU Center; art, history, and science museums; classical and contemporary music performances and theatrical performances at the Hanover Theater and Mechanics Hall; and day and night skiing at Wachusett Mountain.

Majors and Degrees

Anna Maria College offers a four-year curriculum of undergraduate instruction leading to bachelor's degrees in the following areas: art; art education; art therapy; business administration; Catholic studies; criminal justice; early childhood education; elementary education; emergency management services, English; fire science; forensic criminology; graphic design; health and community services; health science; history; human development/human services; humanities (interdisciplinary program); law, politics, and society; liberal arts/general studies; music; music education; music therapy; nursing; paramedic science; psychology; secondary education; social work; sport management; and studio art.

Art and music therapy, business, criminal justice, fire science, education, nursing, social work, and sport management are the most popular majors. The Fifth Year Option allows undergraduate students in good academic standing a unique opportunity to earn both their undergraduate and graduate degrees in five years. Fifth-year master's options are available in business administration, counseling psychology, criminal justice, education, and fire science.

Academic Programs

When the Sisters of Saint Anne founded Anna Maria College in 1946, their mission was to increase access to high-quality education, educational innovation, and respect for service to others through the development of the total human being. That mission has not changed in over sixty-five years. As a Catholic college, the relationship between faith and reason is looked at closely. An AMC education is distinct because of its integration of rich tradition, diversity of knowledge, and the understanding of human history, institutions, and societies with Catholic teachings and traditions. The cornerstone of AMC's academic programs is the core curriculum, which integrates the Catholic character with a commitment to liberal arts education.

Students are encouraged to travel beyond their immediate interests to disciplines that may be connected by similar methods, history, theory, or application. The end result is a strong liberal arts foundation with a focused knowledge and professional preparation in a chosen area of concentration. AMC also encourages students to explore their own areas of interest and design their own majors.

While at AMC, students can gain practical experience and explore career options through internship programs, fieldwork, academic seminars, and summer programs. They also learn through required practicums, part-time work, and community service.

Off-Campus Programs

Anna Maria College is a member of the Higher Education Consortium of Central Massachusetts (HECCMA), a group of twelve area colleges (Anna Maria College, Assumption College, Becker College, Clark University, College of the Holy Cross, Massachusetts College of Pharmacy and Allied Health, Nichols College, Quinsigamond Community College, Tufts University School of Veterinary Medicine, University of Massachusetts Medical School, Worcester Polytechnic Institute, and Worcester State College). Students may enroll in non-major courses at any of the member institutions and have credits transferred at no additional cost.

AMC offers several off-campus opportunities for which academic credits are awarded. There are opportunities for study abroad, as well as an Urban Seminar course with travel to various locations worldwide. Students are also eligible to apply for Army and Air Force ROTC programs, available through HECCMA. A Washington, D.C. internship is offered for students in all majors, and a Disney internship is also available.

Academic Facilities

The Information Commons offers students a high-tech learning environment where they have access to the latest technologies in a setting that supports academic success. The traditional library is located in the lower level of the Information Commons. The Mondor-Eagan Library houses Anna Maria College's literary collection and archives. The library also links the combined material resources of central and western Massachusetts' libraries, making more than 4 million books and periodicals accessible to students.

Classrooms are located in Trinity Hall, Cardinal Cushing Hall, and Foundress Hall, which also houses the Zecco Performing Arts Center. Trinity Hall houses the Student Success Center. Other facilities include Madore Chapel, St. Joseph Hall for sciences, and Miriam Hall for music, performance, and art.

Costs

Costs for the 2015–16 academic year include tuition, $32,878; fees, $2,140; and room and board, $13,112.

Financial Aid

Ninety-seven percent of the most recent freshman class received financial aid in the form of scholarships, grants, loans, and work-study program awards. Some available sources of funds are the Federal Pell Grant, Federal Supplemental Educational Opportunity Grant, and Federal Perkins Loan programs. To apply for aid, students should submit the Free Application for Federal Student Aid (FAFSA), which can be found at http://www.fafsa.ed.gov. Aid is awarded on the basis of need. Non-need-based scholarships ranging in amount from $14,000 to $20,000 are also available. For further information, students should call 508-849-3366.

Faculty

Anna Maria College has 150 full- and part-time faculty members. Faculty members have a deep respect for scholarship and research and are dedicated to teaching and to the success of the student. The Center for Teaching Excellence provides opportunities for faculty to hone new skills and pursue their research.

Student Government

The Student Government Association (SGA) is the official representative of the student body, serving as the link between students and the administration. There are more than twenty clubs and organizations under the SGA, offering many activities and opportunities to participate in the extracurricular life of AMC.

Admission Requirements

At Anna Maria College, every application is considered individually and weighed on its own merits. Emphasis is placed on the applicant's transcript and recommendations. SAT and ACT scores are optional. Extracurricular activities and leadership positions are also important. Successful completion of a four-year college-preparatory program is required. Application for admission to AMC is encouraged for all academically qualified candidates regardless of race, religion, age, gender, or creed.

Application and Information

To apply, students should submit a completed application form (AMC is a member of the Common Application). An official high school transcript should be sent to the Office of Admission along with an essay and letter of recommendation. Prospective students can schedule a campus visit via the AMC website (www.annamaria.edu) or by calling 508-849-3360. AMC is on rolling admissions; however, the application priority deadline for financial aid is March 1. Students who apply after March 1 do not receive priority for financial aid. Transfer students must submit official transcripts of all postsecondary courses.

Anna Maria College invites students to learn more about AMC's community by visiting the campus. Students should call the Undergraduate Office of Admission to schedule an appointment. For detailed information about Anna Maria College's distinctive programs and campus community, prospective students should contact:

Peter Miller
Dean of Admission and Financial Aid
Anna Maria College
50 Sunset Lane
Paxton, Massachusetts 01612-1198
Phone: 508-849-3360
800-344-4586 Ext. 360 (toll-free)
Fax: 508-849-3362
E-mail: admission@annamaria.edu
Website: http://www.annamaria.edu

AMC students enjoy the beautiful New England Campus at Anna Maria College.

AQUINAS COLLEGE

GRAND RAPIDS, MICHIGAN

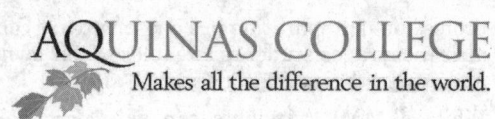

★ To read more about this school, visit http://petersons.to/aquinascollege

The College

Located on the eastern edge of the city of Grand Rapids, Aquinas enjoys all of the advantages of Michigan's second-largest city and is just a 3-hour drive from Detroit or Chicago. The Aquinas College campus is an interesting blend of early-nineteenth century architecture coupled with modern-day structures. The campus abounds with natural beauty; it has been called the most beautiful small campus in Michigan. Its 90 species of trees, winding woodland paths, and inviting creeks and ponds create a peaceful 117-acre environment that students of all ages find welcoming.

Founded by the Dominican Sisters of Grand Rapids in 1886, Aquinas has a Catholic heritage and a Christian tradition. For over 125 years, Aquinas College has inspired students to transform the world by providing a liberal arts education infused with the Catholic Dominican values of prayer, study, service, and community. It is lived out by Aquinas students who volunteer their time and talents in the Grand Rapids community and by those who travel to places such as the Dominican Republic; Appalachia, Kentucky; or any of a dozen other service-learning project sites. An ability to see the world from different perspectives is the hallmark of an Aquinas-educated student.

An Aquinas education makes graduates more employable. Each year, hundreds of Aquinas students find businesses, government agencies, and other organizations eager to offer field experience and internship opportunities. Students can find employment and internships with organizations such as the United States Senate, American Cancer Society, Detroit Red Wings, Disney World, Meijer, Grand Rapids Art Museum, Spartan Stores, Steelcase, and the Van Andel Institute, to name a few. Over 60 percent of applicants recommended by the Aquinas premedical advisory committee are admitted to medical school, and over 90 percent of Aquinas seniors find jobs or enroll in graduate school within six months after graduation.

Aquinas sees a liberal arts education as career preparation. The Aquinas general education plan exposes students to the necessary skills that enable them to become critical thinkers, articulate speakers, strong writers, and effective problem solvers. Aquinas faculty members insist that students carry values as well as skills into the workplace. The College's curriculum, with its more than 60 majors, is designed to provide students with both breadth and depth and to foster a thirst for knowledge and truth and a spirit of intellectual dialogue and inquiry. Coupled with nationally recognized internship programs, it prepares students to both live and work in the rapidly changing world of today and tomorrow.

Arriving from places as near as Grand Rapids, Chicago, and Detroit and as far as China and South America, the approximately 2,200 students include 1,600 full-time, 250 part-time, 150 graduate students, and almost 200 students in nursing, which is a collaborative program with University of Detroit Mercy. The Insignis program at Aquinas encourages students of exceptional academic ability to participate in social and intellectual activities such as lectures and receptions for visiting scholars and trips to places of cultural interest. Aquinas offers more than 60 student organizations, ranging from intramural teams and departmental clubs to a wide variety of musical groups, student publications, and service organizations.

In addition to its undergraduate degrees, Aquinas also offers Master in the Art of Teaching, Master in Education, Master of Management, and Master of Sustainable Business degrees.

Location

Aquinas' location in Grand Rapids allows students to reap the benefits of west Michigan's economic, educational, and cultural center. The city was named by acclaimed international travel website Lonely Planet as the top destination to visit in 2014. Grand Rapids combines big-city excitement and small-town charm. There are cosmopolitan amenities ranging from four-star hotels and restaurants to top-notch cultural facilities and entertainment venues. Established attractions include ArtPrize, Laughfest, the Gerald R. Ford Presidential Museum, the Van Andel Public Museum, the 10,000-seat Fifth Third Park for Whitecaps minor-league baseball, the 70-acre Fredrik Meijer Gardens, and the 12,000-seat Van Andel Arena, home to the Grand Rapids Griffins AHL hockey team and a venue for nationally known music concerts and performances. These major facilities add to the list of popular points of interest, festivals, and special events. With nearly half a million residents, there are abundant recreation, arts, and cultural opportunities available.

Majors and Degrees

Aquinas College offers the following undergraduate degree programs: Bachelor of Arts, Bachelor of Fine Arts, Bachelor of Arts in general education, Bachelor of Music Education, Bachelor of Science, Bachelor of Science in Business Administration, Bachelor of Science in sustainable business, and Bachelor of Science in International Business. A Bachelor of Science in Nursing degree program is offered in collaboration with the University of Detroit Mercy and Mercy Health St. Mary's.

Majors and programs of study are offered in accounting, accounting/business administration, art, art/business administration, art history, biology, business administration, business administration/chemistry, business administration/communication, business administration/music, business administration/sport management, chemical physics, chemistry, communication, community leadership, computer information systems, conductive education, drawing, economics, education, English, environmental studies, French, geography, German, health, history, international studies, Japanese, journalism/publications, learning disabilities, management information systems, mathematics, music, not-for-profit management, organizational communication, painting, philosophy, photography, physical education and recreation, physics, political science, pre-engineering, printmaking, psychology, sculpture, social science, sociology, Spanish, studio art, sustainable business, theater, theology, urban studies, visual arts administration, and women's studies. Pre-professional programs include dentistry, law, medicine, occupational therapy, physical therapy, and veterinary science.

Associate degrees are also available, including the Associate of Arts and the Associate of Science.

Academic Programs

In addition to their major and minor fields of study, students take a First Year Experience Course and an integrated skills course called Inquiry and Expression. This course spans the first semester of the freshman year and has an emphasis on writing integrated with reading critically, oral communication skills, critical thinking, library/electronic research methods, computer utilization, and basic quantitative reasoning. The thematic content is American Pluralism: The Individual in a Diverse America. Sophomores take a yearlong course in the humanities. As juniors, they are required to take 3 hours in Theological Foundation. Students are also required to be proficient in a second language through the 102 level. There also is a distribution plan in the general education plan covering social science, history/philosophy, natural world, artistic and creative studies, mathematics, technology, and health, physical education, and recreation. A career/professional development component is also a part of the curriculum and offers career planning courses and activities; topics include assessment of students' strengths, skills, and interests; development of goals, a learning plan, and setting a direction; focus on the individual—wellness, personal finances, and leadership/team skills; awareness of careers, professions, and graduate study; information on making and maintaining a professional portfolio and resume; participating in a professional/career mentor program; career fairs and networking; and experiential learning (choices include internship, service learning, service trips, and study abroad). The College follows a two-semester calendar with a summer session. Aquinas also accepts credit through CLEP, Advanced Placement, and International Baccalaureate.

Off-Campus Programs

Students have the option of participating in the Dominican College Campus Interchange Program. Cooperating colleges are Barry University in Miami, Florida; Dominican College in San Rafael, California; and St. Thomas Aquinas College in Sparkill, New York. Students can increase their foreign language skills through cultural-immersion programs in Costa Rica, France, Italy, Japan, Spain, or Germany. Two Aquinas faculty members accompany 30 students to Aquinas' study center in Tully Cross, Ireland. Students have the opportunity to earn a full semester of credit, travel abroad, and live in a rural Irish community. The curriculum is centered on several aspects of Irish studies.

Academic Facilities

The Grace Hauenstein Library is a $6-million facility with resources that include a public access catalog, audiovisual materials, circulation and course reserve materials, reference services, and interlibrary loan services (free access to more than 60 million books and documents from libraries across the country). Albertus Magnus Hall of Science features the handicapped-accessible Baldwin Observatory and a greenhouse. Other facilities include the Cook Carriage House student center and the Art and Music Center, featuring a 200-seat recital hall, an art gallery, and a sculpture studio. Five new apartment buildings have opened, providing more housing options. The Aquinas Performing Arts Center is a $7-million facility providing a state-of-the-art theater venue.

AQnet allows residents and commuters to wirelessly connect their personal computers or other devices to the Internet while on campus. Students will find centrally located kiosks and computer labs on campus in classrooms, residence halls, the Grace Hauenstein Library, and common areas. E-mail is powered by Google, and over 100 discipline-specific software applications are available as well as high-quality laser printing and access to multimedia technology.

Costs

For 2015–16, tuition is $28,426 and room and board are $8,558 for a total of $36,984. Other expenses, including books, travel, and personal supplies, average $2,000.

Financial Aid

Aquinas College awards both merit-based financial assistance and traditional need-based assistance to qualified students. The Spectrum Scholarship Program was developed to recognize students' achievements in academics, leadership, and service. More than 90 percent of entering freshmen receive some form of financial assistance. The College administers the traditional grant and loan programs, including Ford Federal Direct Loans and Federal PLUS loans. Athletic grants are also available. The College participates in an automatic payment program. This plan assists students in paying costs over a period of time. To apply for financial assistance, students must complete the Free Application for Federal Student Aid (FAFSA).

Faculty

Aquinas faculty members are teachers first: while research plays an important part in the Aquinas faculty's development, teaching remains the number-one priority. In addition to teaching, faculty members serve as academic advisers, mentors, and advisers to various clubs and organizations on campus. With a student-professor ratio of 13:1, faculty members give individual attention and assistance to students. All classes and labs are taught by faculty members, not graduate assistants. Approximately 90 percent of Aquinas faculty members have doctoral or terminal degrees.

Student Government

The Student Senate is the governing body of Aquinas students. Senators are chosen by securing twenty-five signatures of students in support of their involvement. These students have both voice and vote on issues facing the College's Academic Assembly. The senate is responsible for many of the academic, social, recreational, and cultural activities on the campus.

Admission Requirements

Freshman and transfer applications are received on a rolling basis. A candidate for admission to Aquinas is considered on the basis of academic preparation, scholarship, and character. Admission depends on a number of factors, including high school academic record and ACT or SAT test scores. Transfer students must present a minimum 2.0 grade point average on a 4.0 scale. The online application for admission does not require a fee. The admissions office reserves the right to review applications on a case-by-case basis. Curriculum, extracurricular activities, and any extenuating circumstances are considered in the decision. Letters of recommendation are encouraged but not required.

Application and Information

Prospective students may submit a free online application for admission at www.aquinas.edu/undergraduate.

For further information, interested students should contact:

Tom Mikowski
Associate Vice President of Admissions
Aquinas College
1607 Robinson Road, SE
Grand Rapids, Michigan 49506
Phone: 616-632-2900
800-678-9593 (toll-free)
E-mail: admissions@aquinas.edu
Website: http://www.aquinas.edu

Aquinas College Academic Building.

ARCADIA UNIVERSITY
GLENSIDE, PENNSYLVANIA

ARCADIA UNIVERSITY

★ To read more about this school, visit http://petersons.to/arcadiauniversity

The University

Arcadia is a top-ranked comprehensive private university offering bachelor's, master's, and doctoral degrees. Nearly 4,000 students choose from more than 65 fields of study. *U.S. News & World Report* ranks Arcadia University among the top 50 universities in the North, and the Institute of International Education's 2014 *Open Doors* report ranks Arcadia #1 for the percentage of undergraduate students studying abroad. Arcadia's diverse student population represents a cross section of cultural and socioeconomic backgrounds. Enrollment includes more than 2,500 undergraduate and 1,400 graduate students. At present, Arcadia students come from 46 states and 23 countries, and 82 percent of the full-time undergraduate population resides on campus.

Campus life, which includes more than 50 clubs and organizations, athletics, and cultural and social events, is rich and varied. Community service is an integral part of the Arcadia University experience. Students volunteer on neighborhood improvement projects, work at literacy or gerontology centers, and assist disadvantaged or disabled children. NCAA Division III intercollegiate competition is offered in basketball, field hockey, golf, lacrosse, soccer, softball, swimming, tennis, and volleyball for women and baseball, basketball, golf, lacrosse, soccer, swimming, and tennis for men. The equestrian team is coed and competes in the Intercollegiate Horse Show Association (IHSA). Cheerleading is offered as a club, while intramural sports provide other athletic opportunities.

Arcadia offers master's programs in business administration, counseling psychology, creative writing, education, English, forensic science, genetic counseling, health education, humanities, international peace and conflict resolution, international public relations, international relations and diplomacy, physician assistant studies, and public health. A Doctor of Physical Therapy (D.P.T.) and a Doctor of Education (Ed.D.) in Educational Leadership also are offered.

Location

Arcadia, located in suburban Philadelphia, features a beautiful rolling campus built around the National Historic Landmark Grey Towers Castle. The University is 12 miles from Center City Philadelphia and 90 minutes from the Jersey shore and Pennsylvania's Pocono Mountains. Students have access to dozens of museums, galleries, performing arts centers, and nightspots, as well as historic, government, and commercial sites in the metropolitan area. Convenient access to major rail lines and Philadelphia International Airport expand opportunities for educational experiences.

Majors and Degrees

Arcadia offers bachelor's degrees in accounting, acting (B.F.A.), actuarial science, art and design (B.A. or B.F.A.) (art education, ceramics, graphic design, interior design, metals and jewelry, painting, photography, pre–art therapy, printmaking, studio art), art history, biology (biomedical, conservation, molecular and biochemistry), business administration* (economics, finance, marketing), chemistry (biochemistry), communications* (corporate, print, video), computer science, computing technology (design, technical), criminal justice, cultural anthropology, education** (art education, elementary and early childhood, middle level, secondary, special education), engineering (3+2, 4+2 program with Columbia University or Washington University in St. Louis), English (including Creative Writing), forensic science (3+2, 4+2 with assured admission to Arcadia's Master of Science in Forensic Science (M.S.F.S.) program if prerequisites are met), French studies, global legal studies, global media (cultural studies, digital gaming systems, digital media, fashion studies, film production, media industries, media production, new media journalism, sound and music, visual cultures, visual journalism, world cinema), global security and emergency management, healthcare administration, history, interdisciplinary science, international business and culture*, international peace and conflict resolution (3+2, 4+2 with assured admission to Arcadia's Master of International Peace and Conflict Resolution program if prerequisites are met), international relations and diplomacy (3+2, 4+2 with assured admission to Arcadia's Master of International Relations and Diplomacy program if prerequisites are met), international studies* (Africa and the Middle East, the Americas, Europe and the Mediterranean, global health and human rights, social life of globalization, sustainable development), Italian studies, liberal studies (applied social science for the global citizen, individualized, leadership), mathematics, philosophy, political science (international politics, pre-law and political theory, U.S. politics and policy), pre-dentistry, pre-law (3+3, 4+3 with Drexel University), pre-medicine, pre-nursing (2+2 with Thomas Jefferson University), pre-optometry (3+4 with Salus University), pre–physician assistant (4+2, with assured admission into Arcadia's Master of Medical Science: Physician Assistant program if prerequisites are met), pre–physical therapy (4+D.P.T., with assured admission into Arcadia's Doctorate of Physical Therapy program if prerequisites are met), pre–veterinary medicine, psychology*, scientific illustration, sociology, Spanish, Spanish cultural studies, sport psychology, sports management, and theater studies.

*Arcadia also offers accelerated three-year bachelor's degrees in business administration, communications, international business and culture, international studies, and psychology. The format can include one summer of service learning and one summer internship at an international or U.S. location.

**Arcadia offers several five-year combined programs in education, including master's degrees in special education, literacy education/reading, literacy education/ESL, and technology education.

Academic Programs

Arcadia's undergraduate curriculum provides a distinctively global, integrative, and personal learning experience that prepares students to contribute and prosper in a diverse and dynamic world. The curriculum is designed to enable students to design their own path, explore the globe, make intellectual connections, and develop an area of expertise. There are opportunities to study around the world and make connections across disciplines and cultures. Every student pursues a major, participates in cultural experiences, explores areas of inquiry, and develops intellectual practices.

Highly qualified students may enhance their education through the Honors Program, which merges the best of Arcadia's academic traditions with innovative honors courses and features unique leadership and study-abroad opportunities.

Credit toward graduation is granted for scores of 3 or better on AP exams or earned through the College Level Examination Program (CLEP) and locally administered examinations at the discretion of the department.

Arcadia's academic year is divided into two semesters. Three summer sessions are offered, beginning in May and continuing through early August. Most full-time students carry four academic courses in each regular semester; 128 semester hours are required for graduation.

Off-Campus Programs

Arcadia is top-ranked in the nation for international study. With more than 150 programs around the world, The College of Global Studies supports and implements the University's commitment to international education. Students can spend a semester or full year abroad for approximately the same cost as remaining on campus. Many shorter-term options also are available.

Arcadia offers two distinct opportunities for students to study abroad during their first year. The University's Preview program enables first-year and new transfer students in good academic standing to earn two credits through a course that includes spending their spring break in countries such as Cuba, Ireland, France, England, Guatemala, China, South Korea, and Italy. Sites vary from year to year. The First-Year Study Abroad Experience (FYSAE) gives a select group of incoming freshmen the chance to spend their first or second semester in London, England, or Stirling, Scotland. Arcadia's FYSAE and Preview programs have been recognized as among the most innovative international programs in the country by the American Council on Education, *U.S. News & World Report,* and The Princeton Review.

Arcadia also offers seven Majors Abroad Programs (MAPs). Students in these majors spend a year (two semesters) abroad, taking general courses as well as major-related courses at an overseas institution.

Off-campus study in the Philadelphia area includes internships and fieldwork in most majors. The University requires students to partake in a global connections experience, which may occur overseas, through a domestic study away program, or locally.

Academic Facilities

The campus includes historical buildings as well as extensive modern facilities. A prime academic resource on Arcadia's campus is Landman Library, which offers students increased technology and access to resources both on campus and around the globe.

Arcadia's newly renovated Kuch Athletic and Recreation Center features the Alumni Gymnasium, which seats 1,500, and the Lenox Pool, with adjacent Jacuzzi. The Kuch Center also includes an indoor track that overlooks the gym, an aerobics/dance studio, a fitness center, locker rooms, saunas, and first aid/training rooms. The Commons student center features a game room, fireplace lounge, dining area, flexible meeting rooms, an art exhibit space, and more.

Wireless Internet access is available everywhere on campus and extends to every room in the residence halls. Computer labs—including a Mac lab—are available for student use.

Costs

For 2014–15, undergraduate tuition was $37,500. Room and board charges were $12,740 per year and annual student fees were $660.

Financial Aid

On average, 98 percent of full-time undergraduates receive need-based aid and merit-based grants and scholarships through the University. Every effort is made to see that students requiring financial assistance are able to attend Arcadia. Aid is awarded on the basis of need, as determined by the Free Application for Federal Student Aid (FAFSA) and the Arcadia University Financial Aid Application. Aid is available in the form of grants, loans, part-time campus employment, or some combination of the three. Scholarships are presented annually to entering first-year and transfer students who have achieved academic distinction or have been recognized for outstanding extracurricular accomplishments. Distinguished Scholarships, ranging from $70,000 to $92,000 over four years, and Achievement Awards, ranging from $4,000 to $66,000 over four years, recognize academic excellence, leadership, and extracurricular accomplishments. A limited number of full-tuition scholarships are available to the top entering first-year undergraduates. To receive full consideration, students should complete their applications by January 15. Subsequent to that date, scholarships are awarded on a rolling basis based on availability. Students should submit the FAFSA and Arcadia's Financial Aid Application by March 1.

Faculty

Arcadia University has a faculty with a primary commitment to teaching. The average class size is 16 students, and the student-faculty ratio is 12:1. This fosters an environment in which students and faculty members collaborate on research and writing and engage in informal discussions, field trips, and other activities outside the classroom. Eighty-nine percent of Arcadia faculty members hold terminal degrees, and all courses are taught by faculty members, not graduate assistants.

Student Government

Student participation in the management of undergraduate affairs takes place through the Student Government Organization (SGO) and through the Student Senate. Students serve on most major faculty committees and may even attend Board of Trustees meetings.

Admission Requirements

Students are selected on the basis of educational preparation, intellectual promise, and potential. Emphasis is placed on the candidate's academic record, including the type of program followed and the grades and class rank earned. Standardized test scores also carry significant weight. Counselor and teacher recommendations, participation in school and community activities, and other supporting credentials also are strongly considered.

Freshman applicants must submit an official high school transcript, standardized test scores (SAT or ACT), an admission essay, and school counselor and teacher recommendations. Students are encouraged to visit the campus for a student-guided tour and an information session or one-on-one meeting with an admissions counselor. Fall and Spring Open houses are offered each year.

Transfer applicants may apply for the fall term or at midyear and must submit official college transcripts. In some cases, transfer applicants are required to submit high school transcripts and SAT or ACT scores.

Application and Information

Prospective freshmen are encouraged to submit their applications as early as possible. Many apply in their junior year, but admission decisions begin August 1 of the summer prior to their senior year. Applicants for the B.F.A. in Acting must be approved for that major via audition. Applicants for the B.F.A. in Art and Design must submit an art portfolio. Admission decisions are made on a rolling basis, and applicants are usually notified within four to six weeks of the date of submission of the completed application. For freshman applicants, the priority admissions application deadline for Distinguished Scholarship consideration—as well as consideration for the Honors Program, First-Year Study Abroad Experience, and accelerated degree programs—is January 15. The priority admissions application deadline for Achievement Award consideration is March 1. The freshman admissions application deadline also is March 1. The transfer student deadline for portfolio review, Honors Program, Distinguished Scholarship consideration, and priority admissions is June 15 for fall-term admission.

Requests for further information should be directed to:

Office of Enrollment Management
Arcadia University
450 South Easton Road
Glenside, Pennsylvania 19038-3295
Phone: 215-572-2910
877-ARCADIA (877-272-2342, toll-free)
E-mail: admiss@arcadia.edu
Website: http://www.arcadia.edu/pet.asp

Grey Towers Castle.

COLLEGE CLOSE-UPS

ASSUMPTION COLLEGE

WORCESTER, MASSACHUSETTS

★ To read more about this school, visit http://petersons.to/assumptioncollege

ASSUMPTION COLLEGE

The College

Assumption College, established in 1904 by the Augustinians of the Assumption, is a coeducational institution known for its classic liberal arts curriculum and strong academic programs in business and professional studies. The College's 2,000 undergraduates choose among 42 majors and 48 minors, gaining a depth and breadth of knowledge that serves as a foundation for personal fulfillment and lifelong success. Students' educational experience is grounded in the rich Catholic intellectual tradition, which cultivates both the mind and the personal values students require to meet the demands of a constantly changing world. Undergraduates and graduate students are guided by faculty and staff members in a thriving community that develops individuals known for critical intelligence, thoughtful citizenship, and compassionate service.

The academic journey is characterized by individual attention and the quest for personal excellence. With a student-faculty ratio of just 12:1, Assumption's professors serve as mentors who challenge students to ask questions, find their own answers, and grow—intellectually, socially, and spiritually. Students are encouraged to pursue hands-on experience at internships and to participate in individual research projects. The result? Ninety-nine percent of the graduates who responded to a survey six months after graduation are either employed or enrolled in graduate school.

At Assumption, 90 percent of the undergraduates live on campus and housing is guaranteed for all four years. The campus is lively seven days a week with academic programming, activities sponsored by student clubs and organizations, community service opportunities, campus ministry programs, and intercollegiate, intramural, and club sports. The College's state-of-the-art recreation center offers a number of opportunities for students to exercise or participate in intramural sports.

Location

The College's 185-acre campus is situated in a beautiful, residential neighborhood just minutes from downtown Worcester, Massachusetts. Worcester, the second-largest city in New England, is a vibrant college town, home to 30,000 students. The city offers extensive opportunities for internships in virtually every field, as well as numerous entertainment and community service options. Great restaurants, cultural venues and programs, and retail shops provide students with an array of off-campus activities. Worcester is also centrally located to exciting urban areas such as Boston; Providence, Rhode Island; and Hartford, Connecticut only an hour's drive away. The mountains of Vermont and New Hampshire provide skiing, hiking, and sightseeing opportunities. There are numerous daily commuter trains to Boston as well as other transportation options.

Majors and Degrees

Assumption offers undergraduate and graduate degrees.

Undergraduates pursue Bachelor of Arts degrees. The most popular majors include English (concentrations in literature or writing and mass communications), history, political science, psychology, the natural sciences (biology, biotechnology and molecular biology, neuroscience, chemistry, and environmental science), education, human services and rehabilitation studies, and business disciplines such as accounting, international business, management, marketing, and organizational communication. Minors are offered in 48 areas. Pre-professional advising programs are available for medicine, law, and dentistry.

The College has also developed partnerships with a number of highly regarded institutions to provide students with additional options, including engineering with the University of Notre Dame, environmental science with Duke University, and law (3+3 programs with Duquesne, Vermont, and Western New England law schools). There are agreements for numerous medical professions as well, and joint seven-year programs are also available for those interested in podiatry or optometry.

Assumption College offers graduate degrees in business, special education, school counseling, counseling psychology, and rehabilitation counseling. A 6-in-5 combined bachelor's and master's program is offered in accounting, special education, school counseling, and rehabilitation counseling.

Academic Programs

The College's classic liberal arts curriculum promotes lively discussion of the books, ideas, people, and events that have shaped civilization. Faculty members and students explore the rich Catholic intellectual tradition together as they seek truth and the nature of the world.

Assumption also offers academic programs and courses that help students achieve their full potential. The College's first-year program, the Tagaste Project, links courses from two disciplines and offers activities that complement classroom experiences. Cohorts of 20 students take courses in the fall and spring semesters, enabling them to forge important intellectual connections, while getting to know other students. The Honors Program and the Fortin and Gonthier Foundations of Western Civilization Program encourage students to challenge themselves intellectually through intensive study and independent research. The SOPHIA (SOPHomore Initiative at Assumption) program is designed to help students discover a deeper connection between their spiritual, personal, and professional lives. Air Force and Army ROTC are also available at a neighboring institution.

Assumption College follows a traditional two-semester calendar, from late August to mid-May, as well as an optional January intersession. The Graduate Studies programs and the Center for Continuing and Career Education also offer two summer sessions for students.

Undergraduates complete a core curriculum that provides a strong foundation in the liberal arts, in addition to developing the skills and knowledge necessary for their professional career. Students must complete 120 credit hours in all academic programs to earn a degree.

Off-Campus Programs

The College and eleven other institutions of higher learning compose the Colleges of Worcester Consortium, which combines resources to offer the 30,000 college students in the area even greater academic and social opportunities. Assumption students may cross-register for academic credit at any of the participating colleges and enjoy their social and cultural events. Free transportation to and from other participating institutions is available.

Eligible students may choose to spend a semester or a year abroad. Assumption opened a campus in Rome in February 2013. The campus provides the opportunity for a close learning community where students live, study, and travel together in the city that forged the foundations of Western Civilization. The College's students have studied abroad in Australia, Austria, Chile, China, Costa Rica, the Czech Republic, England, France, Germany, Greece, Ireland, Italy, Japan, the Netherlands, Spain, and other locations. There are also numerous one- and two-week international experiences led by Assumption faculty.

Over 70 percent of Assumption students have undertaken at least one internship, where they explore their professional choices and broaden their workplace skills at local, regional, national, and international sites. In recent years, they have interned at PBS, the U.S. House of Representatives, Ralph Lauren, the Hungarian Embassy, Smith Barney, Fidelity, *The Rachel Ray Show*, *The Daily Show with Jon Stewart*, ABC News, PricewaterhouseCoopers, AT&T, Sony Japan, and countless other organizations.

Campus Facilities

The College has invested more than $80 million to enhance campus facilities, including implementing campuswide wireless Internet.

The Testa Science Center houses the Department of Natural Sciences and features multiuse classrooms with state-of-the-art technology, ten teaching laboratories, seven laboratories dedicated to faculty and student research, a greenhouse, and student lounge areas.

The Information Technology Center houses computer labs, technology-rich classrooms, and an experienced support staff. Students can learn Web authoring, graphics and animation, digital video, and multimedia production. The digital audio studio is available to all students and faculty members.

Assumption offers a variety of housing options to accommodate the 90 percent of students who choose to live on campus. There are traditional residence halls, suites, a living and learning residence, and apartments with full kitchens. All resident students have individual hard-wired and wireless Internet access in their rooms. The College's stadium and athletic facilities support Assumption's 23 NCAA Division II intercollegiate teams, recreational programs, and the physical well-being of the campus community.

Costs

For 2014–15, tuition was $35,510, room and board were $10,962, and student fees were $650. The board plan is required for all first-year students.

Financial Aid

The College offers financial aid based on demonstrated need and scholastic achievement. The College requires that students submit the Free Application for Federal Student Aid (FAFSA), which is available on January 1. This form should be filed by February 15, so that the College may consider the information as it makes financial aid awards.

All applicants for admission are considered for merit awards of up to $22,000 per year. Funds awarded through this program reflect the College's commitment to academic excellence and student leadership.

Faculty

More than 94 percent of the Assumption College faculty members hold the highest degree in their field. They are active scholars presenting their ideas and research at professional conferences, writing books and articles, and publishing in journals. With a student-to-faculty ratio of 12:1, professors work closely with students and challenge them to explore new paths of knowledge and make their own discoveries. All of Assumption's academic advisors are full-time faculty members.

Student Organizations and Government

There are more than 60 clubs and organizations on campus, offering students many opportunities in community service, sports, academics, leadership, and special interests. The Student Government Association (SGA), the elected representatives of the student body, coordinates official communication between the student community and the College administration and officially recognizes student clubs and activities.

Admission Requirements

All applicants must graduate from an accredited secondary school with a minimum of 18 academic units. These units should include 4 years of English, 3 years of mathematics, 2 years of a foreign language, 2 years of history, 2 years of science, and 5 additional academic units.

Admission to Assumption is test-score optional. When submitting an application, an essay and recommendations are required. Interviews are recommended, but not required.

The number of solid academic courses, including the number of honors-level or Advanced Placement–level courses, is considered during the application review process.

The Admissions Committee understands that grading standards vary from school to school and from one course to another. Class rank provides some context within which to place the grades of students applying from a given school, but is not the only factor weighed when considering a student for admission. Some schools also provide grade distribution charts. The Committee also considers whether the applicant's grade point average or rank in class is weighted or unweighted.

Application and Information

Campus visits are strongly recommended. Appointments can be scheduled Monday through Friday. Group Information Sessions are held most Saturdays in the fall.

Applicants must submit a completed application, a $50 application fee, official transcripts, a recommendation letter, and an essay. Applications for early action admission must be received by November 1. There is a second early action admission deadline of December 15. The deadline for regular admission is February 15. Students may complete the Common Application and Supplement at www.commonapp.org.

For more information, students should contact:

Office of Admissions
Assumption College
500 Salisbury Street
P.O. Box 15005
Worcester, Massachusetts 01609-1296
Phone: 508-767-7285
866-477-7776 (toll-free)
E-mail: admissions@assumption.edu
Website: www.assumption.edu
twitter.com/AssumptionNews
facebook.com/assumptioncollege

With a student-faculty ratio of just 12:1, Assumption's professors challenge students to ask questions, find their own answers, and grow.

COLLEGE CLOSE-UPS

BABSON COLLEGE

WELLESLEY, MASSACHUSETTS

★ To read more about this school, visit http://petersons.to/babsoncollege

BABSON

The College

Babson College is the educator, convener, and thought leader for Entrepreneurship of All Kinds™. As the only school to teach Entrepreneurial Thought and Action®, Babson shapes the leaders the world needs: those with strong functional knowledge and the skills and vision to navigate change, accommodate ambiguity, surmount complexity, and motivate teams in a common purpose. Every day, Babson students, faculty, alumni, and staff members address real-world business and societal problems, creating sustainable economic and social value in today's fast-paced global economy. Babson is accredited by the International Association for Management Education, AACSB International–The Association to Advance Collegiate Schools of Business, the New England Association of Schools and Colleges, and the European Quality Improvement System (EQUIS).

The 2014–15 undergraduate enrollment was 987 women and 1,120 men. Babson is a residential college and is a fast-paced community alive with intellectual, cultural, athletic, and social activities. Approximately 85 percent of the undergraduate student body lives on campus all four years in fourteen residence halls. Housing options include fraternity and sorority housing, and entrepreneurial, service-oriented, and other specialty-themed housing.

Babson College is an NCAA Division III school. Most of the College's intercollegiate teams compete in the New England Women's and Men's Athletic Conference (NEWMAC). There are twenty-two men's and women's varsity sports teams, with additional club and intramural sports available to all students. More information is available at www.babsonathletics.com.

The Webster Center features an indoor, 200-meter, six-lane track; a field house; a gymnasium with three basketball courts; a racquetball court; a 25-yard, six-lane pool with 1- and 3-meter diving boards; a fitness center; squash courts; and a dance/aerobics studio. The Babson Skating Center features a 600-seat skating arena. Outdoor facilities include eight tennis courts, an AstroTurf field, a game field, a renovated softball diamond, a baseball field, two sand-based varsity fields, and a club rugby field.

Location

Babson's beautiful 370-acre campus is in Wellesley, Massachusetts, 14 miles west of Boston, a city renowned for its cultural and recreational opportunities. More than sixty colleges and universities bring more than 250,000 college students to the Boston area, making it one of the world's best college towns for cultural exchange and research.

Majors and Degrees

Babson offers a Bachelor of Science degree, a Master of Business Administration degree, two Master of Science degree programs, and executive education programs for business professionals. Twenty-seven concentrations are available for undergraduate students to specialize their studies.

Academic Programs

Babson students earn a highly respected Bachelor of Science degree, recognized around the world by employers who appreciate the powerful combination of deep functional knowledge and the entrepreneurial mindset of Babson graduates.

First-year courses at Babson lay the groundwork for students' future courses—and careers—starting with the Foundations of Management and Entrepreneurship (FME) course, a yearlong immersion into the business world. A team of 10–15 students develops and manages an actual business or service organization, studying organizational behavior, marketing, entrepreneurship, and operations, while emphasizing the integrated role these functions have in a business. Students will have the chance to dabble in all areas of the organization, testing what disciplines and possible careers they would like to pursue further.

Students will also take integrated liberal arts foundation courses providing them with valuable analytic and communication skills and an appreciation for the arts and humanities. Throughout the year, students will develop a deeper understanding (and appreciation) of themselves and their goals, as they continue to prepare to excel in business and in life.

A weekly First-Year Seminar will ease each student's transition to college life by helping them develop an awareness of campus resources, providing a support group for challenges that arise, and teaching communication and study skills. Members of the Babson community—including alumni, faculty, staff members, and peer mentors—provide personal and professional support throughout all four years.

Second-year students take an integrated series of courses in finance, economics, marketing, information technology, management accounting, and operations management. These courses offer functional knowledge of each discipline, but because they are thematically linked, they also provide the broad perspective of a CEO.

Students look at actual business problems via case studies and get real-world experience by studying, touring, interacting with, and presenting to local companies. Pursuing topics more intensively allows students to focus on certain areas of concentration and begin to formulate ideas on what to pursue in life after college.

Throughout the third and fourth years at Babson, students begin to think about issues with increased confidence, independence, and creativity. There is flexibility to reflect on career options and to pursue courses that align with personal and professional goals. In addition to management and liberal arts electives, students gain field experience via internships or consulting programs. Students may also opt to take their education abroad for a semester or short elective during schools breaks and apply it to real-life situations in countries around the world.

Babson offers twenty-seven optional concentrations in both business and liberal arts disciplines; descriptions can be found at www.babson.edu/concentrations. Students may focus their course of study by choosing a concentration in their areas of interest. Special programs, such as the Weissman Scholarship program, the Honors Program, the Women's Leadership Program, the Management Consulting Field Experience, the Babson College Fund (student-managed endowment), Master of Science in Accounting (MSA), and independent research allow students to take advantage of customized learning opportunities at Babson.

Entering students may be granted credit or advanced course placement for successful scores on Advanced Placement (AP) examinations administered by the College Board as well as some courses in the International Baccalaureate (I.B.) curriculum.

Babson operates on a two-semester academic calendar. Semesters run from September to December and from late January through May. An optional credit-bearing three-week winter session is offered in January, and two summer sessions are offered—one from late May to early July and one from mid-July to mid-August.

Off-Campus Programs

Babson has a partnership with Wellesley College and the Franklin W. Olin College of Engineering, an independent institution located on a 70-acre site adjacent to Babson. Babson, Olin, and Wellesley are collaborating inside and outside the classroom in order to provide extraordinary opportunities in all aspects of the student experience, including joint academic and research programming, student life programming, and lecture series.

Babson's vibrant education abroad programs enable students to spend a summer, semester, or school break abroad. Currently, ninety-seven programs are offered in thirty-six countries, and full academic credit is given for approved management and liberal arts courses.

Academic Facilities

Horn Library houses an extensive business collection of print, media, and online information resources. Students have campus-wide access to library resources. Wireless access is available throughout the campus. Every incoming Babson undergraduate student receives a leased laptop computer, which is replaced after the sophomore year.

Other facilities are the Donald W. Reynolds Campus Center, the Richard W. Sorenson Family Visual Arts Center, the Stephen D. Cutler Center for Investments and Finance, the Glavin Family Chapel, and the Arthur M. Blank Center for Entrepreneurship.

Costs

For 2014–15, tuition was $45,120. The total estimated cost for books is $1,020 and other expenses (i.e. transportation and personal) is $1,750.

Financial Aid

Babson is committed to educating students from diverse backgrounds. Applying for financial aid does not affect a student's chances of being admitted to Babson College. Financial assistance is awarded on merit and demonstrated financial need. Assistance for students begins with consideration for student loans and work-study. Those with need beyond the loan and work-study amounts are also considered for Babson grants.

Half of Babson students receive some form of financial assistance. Need-based financial assistance is available to U.S. citizens and permanent residents of the United States. A small number of need-based scholarships are awarded each year to international students as part of the Global Scholars Program. Babson's merit scholarships include Weissman Scholarships, Presidential Scholarships, the Center for Women's Entrepreneurial Leadership Scholarship, and the Diversity Leadership Awards. Application for aid is made by submitting the Free Application for Federal Student Aid (FAFSA) and the Financial Aid PROFILE of the College Scholarship Service. The application deadline for first-year undergraduate students is February 15. For transfer students and September enrollment, the deadline is April 10, and November 15 for January enrollment.

Faculty

Because of Babson's close-knit community, students are able to form close relationships with the faculty. Of the 254 faculty members, 169 are full-time, and 88 percent of the full-time faculty members hold a doctoral degree or its equivalent. Faculty members are accomplished entrepreneurs, executives, scholars, authors, researchers, poets, and artists who bring an intellectual diversity that adds depth to Babson's educational programs and offers students a rich, challenging experience. Babson's student-faculty ratio is 14:1 and faculty members teach 100 percent of the courses. More information can be found at www.babson.edu/faculty.

Student Government

Students are encouraged to take an active role in campus activities and student government. The Student Government Association promotes students' interests; allocates funds to campus organizations for academic, social, and recreational activities; licenses student-run businesses; and helps formulate and maintain student regulations. There are over 115 student clubs and organizations currently on campus.

Admission Requirements

In selecting new students, the admission office considers each candidate based on academic factors such as high school record, recommendations, standardized test scores, and essays. Nonacademic factors are also considered, including extracurricular activities, demonstrated leadership abilities, character/personal qualities, volunteer work, work experience, creativity and enthusiasm, and a willingness to contribute to the Babson community in meaningful ways. Evaluation is based upon comparisons of the qualifications of those who apply. The degree of competition is set by the caliber of the applicants themselves. Consideration is given to the depth and rigor of each candidate's academic program, academic motivation and achievement, and progress from one year to the next. Prospective students are strongly encouraged to have completed or be currently enrolled in a pre-calculus math class.

Babson College offers three application plans: regular decision, early decision, and early action. For more information about these plans and their deadlines, prospective students should visit Babson's website at www.babson.edu/ugrad. Campus visits and group information sessions with an admission counselor are strongly recommended.

Application and Information

For further information or application forms, students should contact:

Lunder Undergraduate Admission Center
Babson College
Babson Park, Massachusetts 02457-0310
Phone: 781-239-5522
800-488-3696 (toll-free)
Fax: 781-239-4006
E-mail: ugradadmission@babson.edu
Website: www.babson.edu/ugrad
www.facebook.com/babsonadmission
www.twitter.com/BabsonAdmission

Tomasso Hall

BALDWIN WALLACE UNIVERSITY

BEREA, OHIO

★ To read more about this school, visit http://petersons.to/baldwinwallaceuniversity

BW BALDWIN WALLACE UNIVERSITY

The University

Founded in 1845, Baldwin Wallace University (BW) in Berea, Ohio, is an accredited institution affiliated with the United Methodist Church that blends the hallmarks of a traditional liberal arts education with an emphasis on professional preparation. Baldwin Wallace has a long history of diversity, as it was one of the first institutions of higher learning in Ohio to admit students without regard to race or gender. That spirit of inclusiveness has flourished and evolved into a personalized approach to education, one that stresses individual growth as students learn to learn, respond to new ideas, adapt to new situations, and prepare for the certainty of change.

With an enrollment of approximately 3,000 full-time undergraduate students, BW offers unique opportunities for engaged, transformative learning. The student profile shows that 20 percent of incoming first-year students come from the top 10 percent of their high school classes, with more than 50 percent in the top quarter. In addition to the traditional-aged college student, Baldwin Wallace has helped adult learners for more than fifty years to develop skills, redirect careers, and enhance lives. Today, 400 adult learners of all ages participate in evening and weekend classes in a variety of programs that are designed to accommodate the varying learning styles and schedules of busy adult learners. Another 600 students are enrolled in part-time graduate programs in education and business administration and 50 are enrolled full-time in an accelerated Bachelor of Nursing degree program and the physician assistant program.

Experiential learning is key to a Baldwin Wallace education and is a requirement for all undergraduates. A proven commitment to the liberal arts and sciences—characterized by excellence in teaching and learning—provides a strong foundation for internships, faculty-directed research, performance, and service-learning programs. Students work with faculty and staff to combine these opportunities in a way that prepares graduates for success after college.

In a postgraduation alumni survey, more than 93 percent of respondents found rewarding jobs or entered the graduate or professional school of their choice within nine months of graduation. Some programs—including athletic training, communication disorders, music therapy, and neuroscience—have close to 100 percent graduate school acceptance rates.

Several distinguished academic programs are offered. The international Society for Neuroscience (SfN) has named Baldwin Wallace University's neuroscience program its Undergraduate Program of the Year.

Baldwin Wallace is also home to a world-renowned Conservatory of Music. The undergraduate-only nature of the conservatory offers collaborative mentoring opportunities with a faculty of accomplished artists and extraordinary opportunities for performance in a variety of ensembles. The University hosts the country's oldest collegiate Bach Festival.

Baldwin Wallace University has entered into an early medical school acceptance agreement with Ohio University's Heritage College of Osteopathic Medicine and Lake Erie College of Osteopathic Medicine, aimed at developing a pipeline of premed students committed to primary care.

Location

BW students enjoy the best of both worlds. Berea, Ohio, with its tree-lined streets, picturesque homes, and population of 19,000, is an ideal college town. At the same time, students are only 20 minutes from the heart of Cleveland, which is home to Fortune 500 companies as well as outstanding museums and galleries, professional sporting events, a world-class orchestra, exciting nightlife, and an extensive park system.

Approximately 1,900 BW students live on campus in a variety of settings, ranging from residential learning communities to University-owned apartments for upperclassmen. A newly renovated residential complex featuring suite-style living opened in fall 2013. All full-time students are required to live on campus during their first and second years at Baldwin Wallace, with residency exemptions available for commuting students who live with their families.

Majors and Degrees

Baldwin Wallace offers the Bachelor of Arts (B.A.), Bachelor of Science (B.S.), Bachelor of Science in Education (B.S.E.), Bachelor of Music (B.M.), and Bachelor of Music in Education (B.M.E.) degrees. A Bachelor of Science in Nursing (B.S.N.) degree is offered in an accelerated format to students who have previously completed a bachelor's degree. Majors and programs include accounting, art studio, arts management, athletic training, biology, broadcasting and mass communication, business, chemistry, communication disorders, communication studies, computer information systems, computer science, criminal justice, digital media and design, economics, education, English, exercise science, film studies, finance, French, German, health-care management, health and physical education, history, human resource management, innovation and entrepreneurship, international business, international affairs, management, marketing, mathematical economics, mathematics, medical technology, national security, neuroscience, philosophy, physics, political science, pre-engineering, pre–physical therapy, psychology, public health, public history, public relations, religion, sociology, software engineering, Spanish, sport management, sustainability, and theater. The Conservatory of Music offers majors in music composition, music education, music history and literature, music performance, music theatre, music theory, and music therapy.

Academic Programs

More than sixty majors and several 3-2 cooperative and preprofessional programs are available to traditional BW undergraduates. The Honors Program offers unique learning opportunities to nearly 300 high-achieving students. Evening and weekend programs, designed for working adults, include sixteen majors and four certificate programs.

Off-Campus Programs

Baldwin Wallace University sends about 15 percent of its undergraduate student body abroad each year on over thirty different programs. BW has institutional (exchange) partnerships with institutions around the globe, where students can study for a semester or summer. International options include England, Australia, South Korea, Ecuador, Germany, Japan, China, Ireland, India, and Spain. Baldwin Wallace has many other opportunities including Semester at Sea for semester-long and summer programs. Semester at Sea sends students to ten different countries—such as Brazil, Egypt, India, Japan, and Vietnam—aboard a 23,000-ton ship with 600 other undergraduates.

In addition to traditional exchange programs, BW features a series of focused full-semester seminars that are led by BW faculty and staff members and examine specific topics or geographic regions. Quite literally, students learn while on the road. Full-semester seminars are offered in alternating academic years, and regular programs include Seminar in Europe and Seminar in Ecuador.

BW also sponsors faculty-led two- to three-week seminars for credit in May, which are perfect for students who seek an international experience but do not want to be away for extended periods of time. Past and current programs include travel to India, China, Costa Rica, Ireland and London.

Academic Facilities

Baldwin Wallace continues to invest in facilities for student learning. In August 2010, the University completed the $29-million renovation and expansion of the Thomas Family Center for Science and Innovation, a facility featuring a combined 100,000 square feet of comprehensive laboratory, research, and study space. This new complex includes the Center for Innovation and Growth, a facility that reflects the synergy of BW's cross-curricular academic offerings through entrepreneurial study and innovation.

In addition, BW opened renovated and expanded facilities for its Conservatory of Music in August 2011. This provides students with additional and improved rehearsal and performing spaces, while remaining home to the Jones Music Library and the Riemenschneider Bach Institute, where priceless Bach-related manuscripts and first editions are stored.

These new facilities complement the extensive offerings already available to students, including twenty campus computer labs; a 4,000-watt campus radio station; recently renovated recreation and athletic facilities; an on-campus gallery showcasing the work of student, faculty, and area artists; and the Burrell Memorial Observatory. A new campus master plan, already being implemented, will enhance facilities to support the University mission and create a pedestrian-friendly, environmentally responsible campus with inviting green spaces.

Costs

Baldwin Wallace's tuition ranks among the lowest and most affordable of private colleges in Ohio. In 2014–15, full-time (12–18 credit hours) liberal arts students paid $38,318 per academic year in tuition, room, board, and fees. Conservatory students paid $40,720 per academic year. These amounts also include a fully refundable board plan, as well as the cost of a student's books.

Baldwin-Wallace offers a four-year graduation guarantee—a promise that academically prepared students who follow predetermined benchmarks during their study at BW will earn their bachelor's degrees in four years or fewer. If a student who follows the agreement does not graduate in four years, BW will pay up to one year's additional tuition for the additional course work needed to graduate.

Financial Aid

To help students and their families meet the cost of a high-quality education, BW awards more than $50 million annually to students in the form of scholarships, grants, loans, and work-study opportunities. BW is committed to working with students and their families to offer financial support. Nearly all Baldwin Wallace students receive some sort of financial assistance.

Renewable merit scholarships ranging from $1,000 to $15,000 are awarded to academically exceptional incoming freshmen. The University also offers special and competitive awards, ranging from $1,000 to $4,000, as well as scholarships for transfer students.

Faculty

Close relationships are at the heart of the BW experience. Most classes average only 19 students, and the student-faculty ratio is 15:1. Professors share their wisdom and experience on a one-to-one basis, helping students choose classes or assisting students in their search for the perfect internship. From corporate executives and lifelong educators to environmentalists and practicing professionals, BW's more than 300 full-time and part-time faculty members bring impressive credentials from their fields. Nearly 80 percent have earned the highest degree in their field. They are dedicated and talented teachers who want to provide an educational experience that goes well beyond the textbook.

Student Clubs and Organizations

BW students participate in more than 100 clubs, professional organizations, and honor societies, ranging from community service and political action groups to student government and student-run media to marching band to fraternities and sororities. Almost a quarter of undergraduate student compete in one of 23 NCAA Division III varsity sports and many others participate in club sports, intramurals, and recreational activities.

Admission Requirements

Applicants must submit the completed application (electronic or paper), a high school transcript, a teacher recommendation, the Secondary School Record Request Form, and the $25 application fee (waived if applying online). SAT and ACT results are optional if a student has a cumulative GPA of 3.0 or better. (In lieu of standardized test results, students must submit a graded writing sample.) Transfer applicants also must submit college or university transcripts. Candidates applying to the Conservatory of Music also must complete the Conservatory Audition Portfolio.

Application and Information

The deadline for undergraduate admission is May 1. The priority admission and scholarship deadline is March 1. Applicants are notified, beginning November 1, on a rolling basis within four to six weeks of receipt of a completed application.

Office of Admission
Baldwin Wallace University
275 Eastland Road
Berea, Ohio 44017-2088
Phone: 440-826-2222
877-BW-APPLY (toll-free)
Fax: 440-826-3830
E-mail: admission@bw.edu
Website: http://www.bw.edu/admission

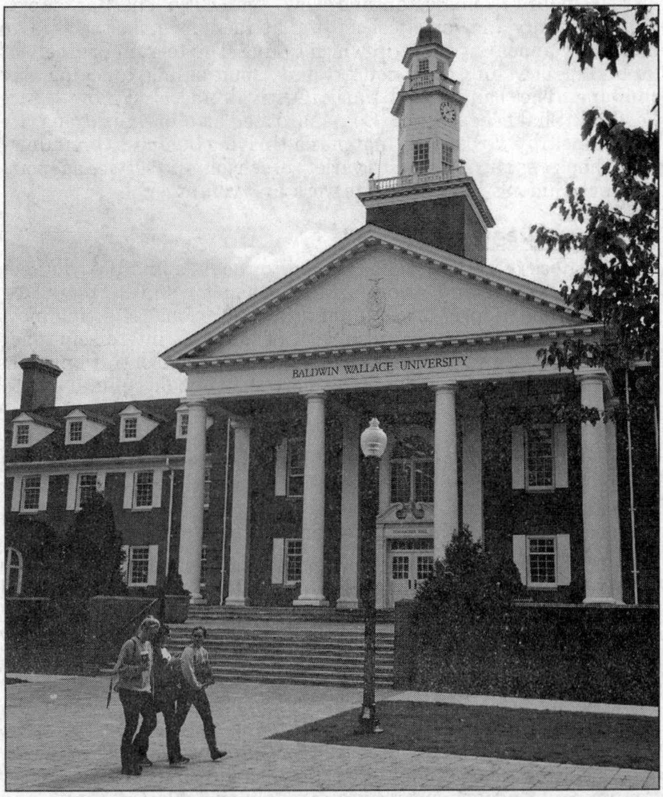

The student union building on the campus of Baldwin Wallace University.

BARD COLLEGE AT SIMON'S ROCK

GREAT BARRINGTON, MASSACHUSETTS

Bard College at SIMON'S ROCK the Early College

The College

Bard College at Simon's Rock | The Early College is the country's only four-year residential college of the liberal arts and sciences specifically designed to provide bright, highly motivated students with the opportunity to begin college after the tenth or eleventh grade. Students can earn an Associate of Arts (A.A.) degree after two years of study and a Bachelor of Arts (B.A.) degree after four. Merit scholarships and need-based aid are available. The average age of entering students is 16.

Founded in 1964 by Elizabeth Blodgett Hall, in 1979 Simon's Rock became a part of Bard College, located 50 miles away at Annandale-on-Hudson, New York.

Simon's Rock has served as a model for the growing U.S. early college movement. For forty-five years, Simon's Rock has demonstrated that highly motivated high school–age students are fully capable of college work; that they thrive intellectually and socially in a small-college environment; that serving these students well requires a faculty committed to distinction in teaching and scholarship, as well as active participation in the students' social and personal development; and that a coherent general education in the liberal arts and sciences should be the foundation for early college students.

Location

The College is located in Great Barrington, Massachusetts (population 8,500), named the Best Small Town in America in 2012 by *Smithsonian* magazine. Built on 275 rolling and wooded acres in the Berkshire Hills of western Massachusetts, Simon's Rock is just 2½ hours from Boston and New York City. The Berkshires' natural beauty and variety of cultural attractions make the area an unusually appealing place in which to live. The terrain is excellent for hiking, bicycling, cross-country and Alpine skiing, canoeing, and climbing. The Tanglewood Music Festival, Jacob's Pillow Dance Festival, Shakespeare and Co., and other arts organizations are located nearby. Great Barrington is a thriving business community with shops, restaurants, and a variety of schools and service agencies in which Simon's Rock students work and volunteer.

Majors and Degrees

Simon's Rock offers programs leading to the A.A. and B.A. degrees in the liberal arts and sciences. Students may complete their B.A. studies in one of forty-one different concentrations reflecting most traditional disciplines, choose one of several interdisciplinary concentrations, and/or design their own second concentration. Most Simon's Rock B.A. students study more than one discipline.

Academic Programs

The academic program at Simon's Rock combines a core curriculum in the liberal arts and sciences with extensive opportunities for students to pursue their own interests through electives, tutorials, independent studies, internships, and study abroad.

Because students begin college without completing high school, the College works to ensure that all students develop strong analytical abilities, skills in written and verbal expression, and knowledge across disciplines. The core curriculum comprises approximately half of students' total course load during their first two years. Requirements include a writing and thinking workshop, held the week before the regular semester begins; first-year, sophomore, and cultural perspectives seminars; and courses in the arts, mathematics, natural sciences, and foreign languages. The College also requires that students participate in the campus Active Community Engagement program, involving athletics, health and wellness programming, and community service opportunities on and off campus.

All new students are assigned a faculty adviser, who meets with them weekly during their first semester and regularly throughout the rest of their career at Simon's Rock. Classes are small, faculty members are accessible, and opportunities to pursue individual interests are extensive.

After earning the A.A., about 50 percent of students stay to complete their B.A. in one of forty-one concentrations. About 50 percent transfer, usually to highly competitive colleges and universities in the U.S. and abroad. Through the sophomore planning process, students receive individualized guidance from advisers and faculty as they explore options for their last two years of undergraduate study.

Students who stay for a B.A. apply for admission to a concentration through a process called Moderation. Students meet with a group of faculty in their area(s) of interest to review their accomplishments and plan their further education at Simon's Rock. Options include advanced course work at Simon's Rock, junior year study-away programs, independent study, involvement in faculty research projects, specialized tutorials, internships, and courses at Bard College's main campus, which offers more than 800 courses each year. Students may take classes, draw on the expertise of Bard faculty in the Moderation and Thesis processes, or arrange to spend a semester in residence at Bard.

The senior thesis is the focus of each B.A. student's final year. Drawing on the skills in analysis and synthesis acquired during the previous three years, students devote themselves wholeheartedly to the project, which is defined and developed under the guidance of 2 or more faculty members. Recent theses have taken many forms: critical studies in literature, psychological research, musical compositions, creative fiction, translations, scientific experiments, mathematical problem solving, artistic exhibitions and performances, and various combinations of these forms.

The regular academic program is supplemented by a number of signature programs. The Simon's Rock/Columbia University Engineering Program offers three years at Simon's Rock and two years at Columbia's School of Engineering and Applied Science, after which students receive both a B.A. from Simon's Rock and a B.S. from Columbia University. A similar arrangement exists with the engineering school at Dartmouth University.

Through Simon's Rock Scholars at Oxford, a select group of students is admitted to spend their junior year at Lincoln College or St. Catherine's College of the University of Oxford in England each year.

Simon's Rock has a half- or full-year program in creative writing at the Centre for New Writing at the University of Manchester in the UK. The College also has a relationship with Qingdao University in China, where students pursue Chinese language immersion study. Students interested in theater can spend a year at London Dramatic Academy; those interested in photography can study at the International Center of Photography in New York City.

Off-Campus Programs

Students work with the Office of Academic Affairs and the Win Resource Commons and Career Center to find study-abroad opportunities suited to their goals and interests. Established independent programs (the School for Field Studies, SEA Semester, Global Routes), programs through other schools (Oxford University, the Sorbonne), and special Simon's Rock programs (fieldwork in geography in China) provide immersive in-depth learning. Students have recently taken intensive math instruction at Central European University in Budapest, Hungary; helped build a school in a remote village in northern Thailand; and served as apprentices to dancers, drummers, mask carvers, and batik artists in Bali. Students can also take advantage of Bard's study-abroad and international programs, including special arrangements with universities in Germany, Russia, and South Africa, and intensive language immersion programs in China, France, Germany, Italy, Japan, Morocco, Mexico, and Russia. Programs can last for a semester, a full academic year, or shorter periods during breaks.

Academic Facilities

The Fisher Science and Academic Center houses the College's biology, chemistry, ecology, and physics laboratories; research labs for faculty members and students; classrooms and tutorial rooms; a sixty-seat lecture center; and faculty offices. The Daniel Arts Center incorporates a 350-seat theater and concert hall, a black box theater, and a dance studio and rehearsal facilities; painting, drawing, photography, ceramics, metalworking, printmaking, 3-D, video production, and digital arts studios; exhibition areas; and spaces for large-scale art and set construction. A music hall, a recording studio, and music practice rooms are also available to students in the arts. The Liebowitz International Center, which opened in 2011, houses faculty and programs focused on global issues, as well as two state-of-the-art classrooms. The campus library houses 104,020 volumes and collections of recordings and periodicals, a listening room, and a language laboratory. Simon's Rock students also have access to the Bard College library. An interlibrary loan system provides access to other college and university collections. The Kilpatrick Athletic Center includes squash courts, a basketball court, an elevated track, a swimming pool, a rock-climbing wall, and a full-service fitness center.

Costs

For 2014–15, tuition and fees were $47,442, and room and board were $13,198. There is also an $895 orientation fee for first-year students.

Financial Aid

Simon's Rock is committed to making an early college education available to a diverse group of highly motivated, academically qualified students. U.S. citizens and permanent residents are eligible to apply for federal and state financial assistance programs as well as institutional scholarships and grants. International students are eligible to receive Simon's Rock scholarships and grants. Approximately 85 percent of students receive some form of financial aid. Applications for admission and financial are considered on a rolling basis as long as space remains available; early application is encouraged. All applicants will be considered for any merit scholarships for which they are eligible; no additional application is required. Applicants typically hear a decision within six to eight weeks of completing their application. Students are also eligible for federal and state grants and loans that can cover up to the full cost of attendance.

Faculty

The College has approximately 40 full-time faculty members, all of whom hold either a doctorate or an equivalent degree in their field. Simon's Rock supplements this full-time faculty with visiting scholars, regular adjunct faculty members in music and studio arts, and part-time faculty members in other areas as needed. Faculty members are distinguished not only by their excellence in teaching and advising but also by their sensitivity to the particular developmental needs of the College's younger students.

Student Government

Students at Simon's Rock participate in the governance of the community through elected and appointed positions on College committees that oversee academic and social life. The campus is characterized by respect for individual rights and a strong sense of community.

Admission Requirements

Simon's Rock seeks students who are smart, independent-minded, self-directed, creative, and passionate about learning. The admission staff works closely with prospective students and their parents to ensure that the decision to enter Simon's Rock is the right one. The College understands that students are not defined solely by grades and scores. For this reason, essay responses and a personal interview are required of each applicant. The application also requires an official high school transcript, three letters of recommendation, and a parent's statement. Standardized test scores are optional for most applicants; international students for whom English is not a first language, or who have not studied for at least two years in a school in which English is the primary language of instruction, must submit TOEFL scores.

Application and Information

Candidates should submit their materials by May 31 for fall admission. Applications are reviewed on a rolling basis year-round. Early application is strongly encouraged. The Admission Committee generally notifies applicants of their decision within several weeks of receiving a completed application. The application fee is $50.

Bard College at Simon's Rock is on Facebook (http://www.facebook.com/simonsrock) and Twitter (http://twitter.com/SimonsRock).

To schedule an interview or request further information, students should contact:

Office of Admission
Bard College at Simon's Rock
84 Alford Road
Great Barrington, Massachusetts 01230-1978
Phone: 800-235-7186 (toll-free)
Fax: 413-541-0081
E-mail: startnow@simons-rock.edu
Website: simons-rock.edu

Did you know you can start college now, before earning a high school diploma or even taking the SATs?

COLLEGE CLOSE-UPS

BARNARD COLLEGE

NEW YORK, NEW YORK

★ To read more about this school, visit http://petersons.to/barnardcollege

The College

The founders of Barnard College were among the stalwart pioneers in the late nineteenth-century crusade who sought to make access to higher education available to women. Founded in 1889 and formally partnered with Columbia University since 1900, today Barnard serves more than 2,500 students from almost every state and more than fifty countries. It remains a partner of Columbia, with students at both schools regularly cross-registering for courses taught at either institution. Barnard students have access to the University's resources and graduates receive their degree from Columbia. Despite this close connection, Barnard College remains a small, independent liberal arts college, devoted solely to the undergraduate education of women. The College maintains its own Board of Trustees, faculty, administrative staff, endowment, admissions process, and sole ownership of its property and physical plant. It offers the intimacy of a small college with the added advantages of a large research university.

The self-contained Barnard campus occupies 4+ acres of urban property along Broadway between 116th and 120th streets and serves as an oasis from the hustle and bustle of New York City. An amalgam of styles comprise Barnard's architectural influences; the result is a blending of classic and modern. Barnard Hall, home of the Ethel S. LeFrak '41 and Samuel J. LeFrak Gymnasium, the Barnard Center for Research on Women, the Athena Center for Leadership Studies, and the Julius S. Held Lecture Hall, stands opposite the main gates of the College. The south end of the campus, referred to as the Quad, contains the Brooks, Reid, Hewitt, and Sulzberger residence halls; first-year students are housed in three of the four buildings in the Quad. Additional housing (twelve residence halls in total) provides those entering as first-years guaranteed housing for four years of continuous enrollment at Barnard. The latest campus addition, the Diana Center, a 70,000-square-foot student center, added a new element of design in 2010. Its seven-story glass structure stretches across campus, linking the historic gates of the entrance at the south end of campus, to one of the original campus buildings, Milbank Hall, on the north.

Location

Barnard is located north of Central Park on the upper west side of Manhattan, in the safe and student-friendly Morningside Heights neighborhood. It is directly across from Columbia University, and has six additional educational institutions as neighbors. Abounding with cultural, educational, internship, and professional opportunities and more than 500,000 college students, New York is Barnard's laboratory.

Majors and Degrees

Students can earn a Bachelor of Arts in the following subjects: Africana studies, American studies, ancient studies, anthropology, architecture, art history, Asian and Middle Eastern cultures, astronomy, biochemistry, biological sciences, chemistry, classics (Greek and Latin), comparative literature, computer science, dance, economics, education, English, environmental biology science or studies, European studies, film studies, French, German, history, human rights, Italian, Jewish studies, mathematics and applied mathematics, medieval and Renaissance studies, music, neuroscience, philosophy, physics, political science, psychology, religion, Russian and Slavic studies, sociology, Spanish and Latin American cultures, statistics, theater, urban studies, and women's, gender, and sexuality studies. The College provides an excellent education program, leading to teaching certification with a specific urban studies track, and prepares students for programs in health and medicine, law, and business, as well as further study in a variety of graduate programs.

Barnard College also offers double- and joint-degree programs in cooperation with other schools within the Columbia community. These include a five-year M.P.A./M.I.A. (3-2) program offered in conjunction with the School of International and Public Affairs. In cooperation with the School of Law, Barnard offers an accelerated program in interdisciplinary legal education, where select students can begin their legal studies after three years. Through the School of Engineering and Applied Science, Barnard students can pursue a five-year (3-2) program in all branches of engineering, leading to both an A.B. and a B.S. degree. In cooperation with the School of Dentistry, a limited number of students may enter the Columbia School of Dental and Oral Surgery after three years of undergraduate work. Outside the university, students may earn both an A.B. degree and a Master of Music (M.M.) in a five-year (3-2) program with the Juilliard School. Through an agreement with List College of the Jewish Theological Seminary, students can earn an A.B. degree from Barnard and a B.A. in Hebrew literature.

Academic Programs

Two required courses, First-Year Seminar and First-Year English, set the foundation for a Barnard education with small seminar classes, limited to 16 and 12 students, respectively. General education requirements are organized around the Nine Ways of Knowing, focusing on topics which reflect the breadth and depth of a true liberal arts education. The Ways of Knowing offer a flexible structure and a wide array of courses in ethics and values, social analysis, cultures in comparison, language, laboratory science, quantitative and deductive reasoning, historical studies, literature, and visual and performing arts. Barnard students shape their educational experience by choosing courses that enhance the way they view the world.

Advanced placement and I.B. credit are available. Barnard operates on a two-semester calendar, with classes beginning in early September. The fall semester ends in mid-December; classes resume for the spring semester in mid-January and end in mid-May.

Off-Campus Programs

As an independent partner of Columbia University, Barnard offers students open access to courses, libraries, and other facilities of the University. With special permission, students may also register for selected classes in Columbia's graduate and professional schools. In addition, two highly selective lesson exchange programs with the Juilliard School and the nearby Manhattan School of Music allow qualified Barnard students to take music lessons in a conservatory setting.

Barnard has a rich history and tradition of study abroad dating back to the 1930s. Today, qualified students are eligible to study in nearly 100 programs in more than fifty countries worldwide and nearly forty percent of Barnard students spend a semester or year abroad. Students are currently studying in Argentina, Australia, Austria, Bolivia, Brazil, Chile, China, Costa Rica, Czech Republic, Denmark, Ecuador, England, France, Germany, Greece, Hungary, Ireland, Israel, Italy, Japan, Jordan, Kenya, Madagascar, Netherlands, New Zealand, Panama, Peru, Russia, Scotland, Senegal, South Africa, Spain, Switzerland, and other locations. Students may also participate in a domestic exchange with Spelman College in Atlanta or Howard University in Washington, D.C.

Barnard's location offers its students a variety of work experiences through more than 2,500 internships. More than two thirds of Barnard students participate in internships throughout the academic year and/or summer.

Academic Facilities

Historic Milbank Hall anchors the north end of campus, topped by the 2,500-square-foot Arthur Ross Greenhouse, housing administrative and faculty offices in addition to the Minor Latham Playhouse. Sulzberger Tower and the residential quadrangle secure the south end of campus where most Barnard students reside. There are more than 400,000 volumes in the library in Lehman Hall (and nearly 12 million in the University library system) with a zine collection written by women (cisgender and transgender) with an emphasis on zines by women of color; dance studios and classrooms in Barnard Hall and its Annex; state-of-the-art science labs in the fourteen-story Altschul Hall; and architecture classrooms with a view in the multipurpose Diana Center, with its terra-cotta glass façade, black box theatre, and art gallery, among other remarkable features. At the heart of it all is the welcoming beauty of Barnard's beloved Lehman Lawn.

Costs

Tuition and fees for 2014–15 were $46,040. Room and board costs were an additional $14,660.

Financial Aid

Financial aid at Barnard is awarded based upon demonstrated need. Federal funds and institutional grants are administered as determined by federal and institutional methodology, assuming College aid is supplementary to family resources. Barnard gives no merit or athletic scholarships. Once need has been established, Barnard covers 100 percent of demonstrated need with a combination of grants, loans, and work-study or student employment. Approximately 50 percent of the students at Barnard receive some form of financial aid.

Barnard College has a need-blind admission policy in which all applications from first-years who are U.S. citizens or permanent residents are judged solely on merit without reference to financial circumstances. International and transfer students are considered for need-based aid from a limited pool of funding.

Faculty

Barnard College employs more than 300 teaching faculty members with a student-faculty ratio of 8:1 (10:1 FTE). Barnard's faculty includes editors of leading scholarly journals, prize-winning novelists and translators, and frequent winners of awards from respected foundations, corporations, and government agencies. They are actively engaged in research and publication in their respective fields, but they regard teaching as their primary commitment. From the start of their time at the College, all students have faculty advisers who assist them in selecting courses and designing individual academic programs, in addition to a vast network of decanal, staff, and peer advising.

Student Government

Barnard women have access to more than eighty clubs and organizations on the College campus alone. Add to this list the hundreds of additional dually recognized clubs with members from both Barnard and Columbia, provided for through Barnard's long-standing partnership with the University, and strong friendships develop among students from both sides of Broadway. Student groups include performance groups, academic and pre-professional, ethnic and cultural, language, community service, and publications. Social interaction and cooperation between Barnard and Columbia groups is virtually seamless, with Barnard women regularly joining and leading a variety of Columbia organizations. Students, faculty members, and administrators also serve on tripartite committees and share responsibility for policy on curriculum, housing, financial aid, orientation, and the library.

Admission Requirements

The Committee on Admissions selects women of proven academic strength who exhibit the potential for further intellectual growth. Careful consideration is given to candidates' high school records, recommendations, writing skills, standardized test scores, special abilities and interests, and personal and educational context.

Admission to Barnard is highly selective and candidates for admission to the first-year class are expected to have taken a highly rigorous college-preparatory program. Barnard also requires first-year candidates to submit scores from the SAT Reasoning Test, along with two SAT Subject Tests. Alternatively, they may submit scores from the ACT with writing in place of the SAT and Subject Tests. Transfers do not need to submit the results of Subject Tests. Students educated in a non-English-speaking setting or who have studied in English for less than five years must also take the TOEFL or IELTS exam. An interview is recommended for first-year students, but it is not required. Interviews are not part of the transfer admission process.

Application and Information

Applicants for first-year admission should apply in the fall of their senior year of high school. Applications must be received by January 1 and must include the nonrefundable application fee. Students are notified in late March. Well-qualified high school seniors who have selected Barnard as their first-choice college may instead apply under the binding early decision plan. Early decision applications must be submitted by November 1. Barnard accepts sophomore and junior transfer students. Transfer applications must be submitted by March 15 for consideration for September entrance and by November 1 for consideration for January.

For more information about Barnard College, students should contact:

Jennifer Fondiller
Dean of Enrollment Management
Barnard College, Office of Admissions
3009 Broadway
New York, New York 10027
Phone: 212-854-2014
Fax: 212-854-6220
E-mail: admissions@barnard.edu
Website: http://www.barnard.edu/admissions

A view of Milbank Hall from the Diana, Barnard's multipurpose student center.

BARRY UNIVERSITY

MIAMI SHORES, FLORIDA

Barry University

The University

Celebrating its 75th anniversary in 2015, Barry University is known for providing a higher education experience focusing on inspiring and training the next generation of change agents and leaders. Barry graduates apply what's learned in the classroom to a constantly changing and diverse world, while promoting civic engagement for the betterment of humanity.

Barry University, located in sunny Miami, Florida, is comprised of nine colleges and schools offering more than 100 bachelor's, master's, and doctoral degree programs. A university that values diversity, Barry's community includes approximately 9,000 students from nearly all fifty states and eighty countries; 52,000 alumni worldwide; and 1,700 faculty and staff members. Barry students gain vital hands-on experience, both locally and internationally, as they prepare to advance their careers in today's global market. Barry's use of service learning, which integrates coursework with community needs, engages students with real-world issues, and encourages them to help find solutions.

With degree programs in the arts and sciences, business, education, health sciences, human performance and leisure sciences, law, podiatric medicine, and social work, Barry students can quickly find their calling and acquire professional experience before graduation through internships and innovative service-learning programs.

Barry's palm-tree lined main campus is in Miami, but the university also includes the Dwayne O. Andreas School of Law in Orlando; College of Nursing and Health Sciences location in Hollywood, Florida; adult and continuing education programs at twenty additional locations throughout Florida; and graduate programs in the Caribbean.

Twenty-five percent of Barry students live on campus in ten residence halls and one apartment-style complex. Living-learning housing is available in five distinct areas: S.T.E.M., Honors Program, Transitions, Business Connections, and Pre-Nursing. The University's Office of Commuter Student Resources assists students who live off campus.

At the R. Kirk Landon Student Union, students have access to the bookstore, main dining hall, snack bar, game room, and more. A fully equipped fitness center features weight and cardio equipment and offers a variety of free fitness classes. Intramural sports include basketball, flag football, soccer, softball, and table tennis. Barry holds membership in 20 honor societies and hosts more than 60 student organizations, including the dance team, choir, Campus Activities Board, WBRY student radio station, as well as active fraternities and sororities.

Barry is accredited by the Southern Association of Colleges and Schools Commission on Colleges to award bachelor's, master's, specialist, and doctoral degrees. Barry also holds a number of accreditations from professional organizations for specific degree programs.

Location

Barry University is located the dynamic South Florida community, just minutes from downtown Miami and Miami Beach. At the crossroads of the Americas and the gateway to South America, Miami offers limitless experiences and opportunities that reflect its broad diversity. The international city of Miami is a center for business, tourism, and entertainment, providing a wide range of internship options and a vibrant cultural scene. Yearly events include the world-famous Art Basel Miami Beach contemporary art festival; Calle Ocho, the largest Hispanic street festival in the nation; the Miami International Book Fair; and the Miami International Film Festival. The New World Symphony and the Miami City Ballet provide a full season of performances, while the nearby Wynwood Arts District hosts a free art walk every second Saturday of the month.

South Florida is also home to the Miami Heat basketball team, the Miami Dolphins football team, the Miami Marlins baseball team, and the Florida Panthers hockey team. Miami's warm climate allows for swimming, sailing, scuba diving, golf, tennis, soccer, and other outdoor activities year-round, while the natural beauty of the Florida Keys, Everglades, and coral reefs are just a few hours away. Barry University's Center for Student Involvement regularly coordinates trips to help students experience the best that South Florida has to offer.

Majors and Degrees

Barry offers the Bachelor of Arts degree in advertising, art (art history, ceramics, graphic design, and painting and/or drawing), broadcast and emerging media, communication studies, English (literature and professional writing), general studies, history, international studies, music, philosophy, photography (biomedical/forensic), prelaw, public relations, Spanish (language and literature and translation and interpretation), theater (acting, dance theater, technical theater), and theology.

The Bachelor of Science degree is offered in accounting, athletic training (five-year seamless B.S. to M.S.), biology (marine, preprofessional), cardiovascular perfusion, clinical biology (histotechnology, medical technology), chemistry (biochemistry, preprofessional), computer information sciences, computer science, criminology, education (B.S. to M.S. option, infancy through early-childhood education, early- and middle-childhood education, special education, ESOL, and reading endorsements), exercise physiology (five-year seamless B.S. to M.S., pre-med, pre–physical therapy), finance, international business, management, marketing, mathematical sciences (computational, general, and statistics/actuarial science), political science, psychology (forensic, industrial/organizational), sociology, and sport management (diving industry, five-year seamless B.S. to M.S.).

Barry also offers the Bachelor of Science in Nursing, the Bachelor of Fine Arts (art and photography), the Bachelor of Music (instrumental performance, music education), and the Bachelor of Social Work.

Minor concentrations are available in specific subject areas as well as in the interdisciplinary areas of Africana studies, film studies, journalism, peace studies, social sciences, and women's studies. Certificates are also offered in Africana studies, photography, Spanish translation and interpretation, and women's studies.

Accelerated undergraduate degree programs are offered for working adults through Barry's evening and weekend programs.

Academic Programs

Barry operates on a semester plan. The first semester extends from the end of August to mid-December, and the second semester extends from mid-January to early May. Two 6-week sessions are offered during the summer. Students must maintain a minimum cumulative grade point average of 2.0 (or C) and earn a minimum of 120 credits for a degree. Of these 120 credits, 9 must be in philosophy and theology, 9 in communication—oral and written, 9 in humanities and arts, 9 in physical or natural sciences and mathematics, and 9 in social and behavioral sciences.

The traditional full-time academic load is 12 to 18 credits each semester and 6 credits each summer term. Candidates for degree programs may elect a major and area of specialization and must satisfy all requirements of the program that they choose to follow, including all professional preparation requirements. Internships are required for many majors.

An ELS Language Centers program is available to international students who need to increase language proficiency. The Center for Advanced Learning offers a program designed to assist students with learning disabilities who have the intellectual potential and motivation to complete a four-year degree.

The Honors Program offers an active, interdisciplinary honors curriculum designed to add breadth and depth to the educational experience.

Community Service

Faithful to its traditions, the Barry University experience fosters individual and communal transformation where learning leads to knowledge and truth, reflection leads to informed action, and a commitment to social justice leads to collaborative service. Rooted in its Catholic heritage, Barry promotes community service through organizations including Best Buddies International, Habitat for Humanity, Alternative Spring Break, and Pals-4-Paws animal rescue. Barry received the prestigious 2015 Community Engagement Classification from the Carnegie Foundation for the Advancement of Teaching. Colleges and universities that earn the distinction show evidence of improving and producing research that makes a difference in communities, revitalizing their civic and academic missions, and developing deeper community partnerships.

This is not the first time Barry has been recognized for its dedication to community service. Barry was recently named to the President's Honor Roll for Community Service for a third consecutive year after students logged more than 25,000 hours of community service. Barry's application process is managed by the Center for Community Service Initiatives, which serves as the university's community engagement clearinghouse, and functions as a catalyst to foster civic engagement among members of the Barry community.

Academic Facilities

Academic facilities include multimedia classrooms, the Monsignor William Barry Memorial Library, the Glenn Hubert Learning Center, a performing arts center, a full-service digital television production studio, art studios, photography and digital imaging labs, a human performance lab, an athletic training room, a biomechanics lab, a nursing lab and resource center, and several other labs dedicated to Barry's health, science, and education programs.

Costs

The following are average costs of attending Barry for the 2014–15 academic year. Tuition for full-time undergraduate students for the academic year was $28,160. Student services fees are included in tuition. Room and board costs averaged $10,400, based on a double-occupancy room. Expenses such as books, supplies, laboratory fees, and transportation are not included in these costs.

Financial Aid

All undergraduate students, U.S. citizens, permanent residents, and international students are automatically considered for financial aid once they have been accepted. Assistance options include scholarships and grants, federal financial aid, Stamps Leadership Scholars Program, and the Federal Work-Study program. Florida students have access to a wide assortment of state-funded assistance programs to attend college in-state. Students may be eligible for funds from the Florida Bright Futures Scholarship program, the Florida Resident Access Grant (FRAG), and the Florida Student Assistance Grant (FSAG).

Barry makes every effort to offer financial aid to students through a variety of federal, state, and institutional packages. Approximately 86 percent of Barry students receive some form of financial aid. The average package is $13,971.

For more information about receiving a financial aid at Barry, please visit: barry.edu/future-students/undergraduate/financial-aid.

Faculty

At Barry University, students experience a small community atmosphere where they can always rely on administrators and faculty for advice, encouragement, and personal attention. Barry has 358 full-time faculty members, 80 percent of whom hold terminal degrees; and 488 part-time faculty members. The student-faculty ratio is 13:1.

Athletics

Barry fields 12 intercollegiate athletic teams that participate in the NCAA Division II and the Sunshine State Conference. Over the years, the Buccaneers have won thirteen NCAA championships and have had 279 All-Americans, 321 Scholar All-Americans, and nine NCAA Women of the Year finalists, the most of any Division II school.

Barry's intercollegiate athletics program, as part of the School of Human Performance and Leisure Sciences, aims at achieving athletic triumphs and also helps student-athletes excel academically. As a member of the Sunshine State Conference, Barry currently has 12 varsity teams. Women's sports include basketball, golf, rowing, soccer, softball, tennis, and volleyball; men's sports include baseball, basketball, golf, soccer, and tennis. Barry's coaches have been awarded fifty "Coach of the Year" awards through the Sunshine State Conference, including nine national awards.

Campus Life

Barry students enjoy a vibrant, lively, campus community where engaged learners organize and participate in a wide variety of academic, athletic, and social experiences. College life is not just about the classroom. At Barry, students enjoy a full range of extracurricular activities including intramural sports, student government, and more than 60 clubs and organizations. The diversity of organizations and clubs on campus gives Barry students the chance to take the lessons they learn outside the classroom and make them part of their overall educational experience. From the GLO party and Founders' Week in the fall, to Homecoming and Festival of Nations in the spring, tradition abounds at Barry. Students, faculty, staff, and alumni gather throughout the year to connect Barry's past with its present to create a meaningful future.

Admission Requirements

In reviewing the credentials of students seeking admission, Barry University considers an applicant's composite efforts. Candidates must provide the following materials: the completed application form, official high school or college transcripts, and the results of the SAT or ACT.

Application and Information

Barry has a rolling admissions policy and reviews applications as they are completed. Students are notified of their acceptance once the admissions staff has reviewed all required documents. Prospective students are advised to apply early and may submit their application any time after completion of their junior year in high school. The student's completed application form and supporting credentials should be sent to the Office of Admissions. Students may also apply online at barry.edu/apply.

Barry University
Division of Enrollment Services
11300 Northeast Second Avenue
Miami, Florida 33161-6695
Phone: 305-899-3100
800-695-2279 (toll-free)
Fax: 305-899-2971
E-mail: admissions@barry.edu
Website: http://www.barry.edu
http://facebook.com/BarryUniversity (Facebook)
http://twitter.com/BarryUniversity (Twitter)

Barry students are full of school pride as they cheer on the Buccaneers at a home game.

COLLEGE CLOSE-UPS

BAY STATE COLLEGE

BOSTON, MASSACHUSETTS

★ To read more about this school, visit http://petersons.to/baystatecollege

Bay State College
Where Your Success Matters.

The College

Founded in 1946, Bay State College is a private, independent coeducational institution located in Boston's historic Back Bay. Since its founding, Bay State College has been preparing graduates for outstanding careers and continued education.

The College offers both associate degrees and bachelor's degrees. The educational experience offered through the variety of associate and bachelor's degree programs prepares students to excel in the career of their choice. The College gives students constant access to the people, places, and knowledge they need to succeed. Through the transformative power of its core values of quality, respect, and support, Bay State College has been able to assist students with setting and achieving goals that prepare them for careers and continued education. In fact, with its First-Year Experience, a 1-credit course all students must complete, Bay State College students are exposed to the concept of "action planning." The Bay State College action plan is designed to help students identify their goals and set about a course of action to achieve those goals. Students review their action plan each semester with their academic adviser and evaluate how they are progressing on their plan. This is just one method Bay State College graduates apply to their lives beyond college. The ability to identify, set, and achieve goals is a trait all people aspire to master.

Recognizing that one of the most important aspects of college is life outside the classroom, the Office of Student Affairs seeks to provide services to Bay State College students from orientation through graduation and beyond. There are many clubs and organizations on campus, such as the Criminal Justice Society, the Student Government Association, and the Entertainment Management Association. Bay State College students enjoy the opportunity to create clubs and organizations that meet their interests. Special events throughout the year include a fashion show and a host of events produced by the Entertainment Management Association. Students also enjoy professional sports teams such as the Boston Celtics and the Boston Red Sox.

One of the unique aspects of living at Bay State College is the residence halls. With their location in the historic Back Bay, the buildings are original Victorian town houses and brownstones. Each building has its own character and charm, making living on campus a distinctive experience. Each building has a computer lab with free Internet access, coin-operated laundry, vending machines, a house phone with free local calling, and a social lounge that includes cable television and a microwave oven. Each student room has basic cable service and wireless Internet access.

The Career Services office offers lifetime career assistance to both current students and alumni, continuing to provide assistance and support to them throughout their careers, with career-management counseling, workshops, career panels, guest speakers, resume and cover letter reviews, interview preparation, and job listings.

Bay State College is accredited by the New England Association of Schools and Colleges; is authorized to award the Associate in Science, Associate in Applied Science, and three Bachelor of Science degrees by the commonwealth of Massachusetts; and is a member of several professional educational associations. The College's medical assisting program is accredited by the Accrediting Bureau of Health Education Schools (ABHES). The College's nursing program is accredited by the Accreditation Commission for Education in Nursing. The physical therapist assistant studies program is accredited by the Commission on Accreditation in Physical Therapy Education (CAPTE) of the American Physical Therapy Association (APTA).

Location

Located in the historic city of Boston, Massachusetts, and surrounded by dozens of colleges and universities, Bay State College is an ideal setting in which to pursue a college degree. Tree-lined streets around the school are mirrored in the skyscrapers of the Back Bay. The College is located within walking distance of several major-league sports franchises, concert halls, museums, the Freedom Trail, Boston Symphony Hall, the Boston Public Library, and the Boston Public Garden. World-class shopping and major cultural and sporting events help make college life an experience that students will always remember. The College is accessible by the MBTA, commuter rail, and bus and is near Boston Logan International Airport.

Majors and Degrees

Bay State College is continually reviewing, enhancing, and adding new programs to help graduates remain industry-current in their respective fields.

Bachelor's degrees are offered in criminal justice, entertainment management, fashion merchandising, information technology, nursing (RN to B.S.N.), and management.

Associate degrees are offered in accounting, business administration, criminal justice, entertainment management (with a concentration in audio production), fashion design, fashion merchandising, health studies, medical assisting, nursing, physical therapist assistant studies, retail business management, and hospitality management.

Academic Programs

Bay State College operates on a semester calendar. The fall semester runs from early September to late December. The spring semester runs from late January to mid-May. A second campus is located in Taunton, Massachusetts.

Bay State College also offers courses on-ground and online to working adults in its Evening and Online Division. The courses, offered in eight-week sessions, allow more flexibility for students who must balance work and family commitments while pursuing their education.

Off-Campus Programs

The internship program, available in all major areas of study, provides students with practical field experience, enabling them to hone their skills and gain insight into the various technologies employed in their respective fields. Fieldwork is a requirement for many majors and is a great opportunity for students to build resumes, apply what they have learned in the classroom, and gain a competitive advantage in the job market.

Students from Bay State College are among the 250 students participating in the Walt Disney World College Program. During their stay at Walt Disney World, students receive on-the-job training and classroom experience. This is just one of the many internship possibilities for students each year at Bay State College.

Academic Facilities

The library has a combined book collection of approximately 5,300 books. In addition, Bay State College has 100 periodicals and 200 audiovisual titles. The College's sixty computers have access to the Internet and several databases for magazine and journal articles, including ProQuest Academic, LexisNexis Academic, JSTOR, Infotrac, Newsbank, EBSCO, the Internet Public Library, and the Library of Congress Research Tools. The library also participates in an interlibrary-loan program with the Boston Regional Library System.

Costs

Tuition for 2014–15 for full-time students was $26,280 per year (some costs vary by program). Room and board were $11,800 per year; student services fee, $400; and student activity fee, $50. The cost of books and additional fees varies by major. A residence hall security deposit of $300 and a technology fee of $300 are required of all resident students.

Financial Aid

Financial aid is available to those who qualify. The College's financial aid staff works one-on-one with every student to help them find what is best for their specific situation: scholarships, grants, loans, payment plans, or a combination of those. The College also offers numerous part-time employment and work-study opportunities during the academic year.

Faculty

There are 99 faculty members, with the majority holding advanced degrees. The student-faculty ratio is 18:1.

Student Government

The Student Association serves as the voice of the Bay State College student body. It consists of a group of elected student representatives from the various academic programs. Roles and responsibilities of Student Association members include providing input on College policies and procedures, assuming leadership roles on campus, acting as a voice of the student body, and planning activities and events.

Elections are held every fall, and all students are encouraged to vote. The group comprises representatives from each College department, club, and organization, and membership spans all four class years.

Admission Requirements

An applicant to Bay State College must be a high school graduate, a current high school student working toward graduation, or a recipient of a GED certificate. The Office of Admissions recommends that applicants to the associate degree programs have a minimum 2.0 GPA on a 4.0 scale; if available, applicants may submit SAT or ACT scores. Applicants must receive the recommendation of a Bay State College admissions officer. Applicants to the bachelor's degree programs must have a minimum 2.3 GPA on a 4.0 scale and must also submit SAT or ACT scores. A personal interview is highly recommended for all students, and parents are encouraged to attend. Students are responsible for arranging for their official high school transcripts, test scores, and letters of recommendation to be submitted to Bay State College. International applicants must also submit high school transcripts translated into English with an explanation of the grading system, a TOEFL score of at least 500 on the paper-based exam or 173 on the computer-based exam if English is not the native language, and financial documentation. The nursing, physical therapist assistant studies program, and Evening and Online Divisions have different or additional admission requirements. For more information about these programs, students should visit the website at http://www.baystate.edu.

The Bay State College Admissions Office notifies applicants of a decision within three weeks of receipt of the transcript and other required documents. When a student is accepted to Bay State College, there is a $100 nonrefundable tuition deposit required to ensure a place in the class, which is credited toward the tuition fee. Deposits are due within thirty days of acceptance. Once a student is accepted, a Bay State College representative creates a personalized financial plan that provides payment options for a Bay State College education.

Application and Information

Applications are accepted on a rolling basis. The fall tuition payment due date is July 1; the spring tuition payment due date is December 1.

Applications should be submitted to:

Admissions Office
Bay State College
122 Commonwealth Avenue
Boston, Massachusetts 02116
Phone: 800-81-LEARN (toll-free)
Fax: 617-249-0400
E-mail: admissions@baystate.edu
Website: http://www.baystate.edu
http://www.facebook.com/baystatecollege
http://twitter.com/baystatecollege

Giving students access is an essential part of a Bay State College education. Students have access to a community of support, experiential learning, faculty with real-world experience, and a dynamic location in the heart of the city.

BELOIT COLLEGE
BELOIT, WISCONSIN

Beloit College

The College

Beloit College students are challenged to know and to know-how. At this independent, residential college, students get a solid grounding in the liberal arts, while learning how to put their knowledge into practice. Beloit's focus is on teaching, then intentionally connecting and applying knowledge through internships, field work, study abroad, special summer programs, capstone courses, entrepreneurial projects, and lab-based courses in every field of study. Students also have ample opportunities to test and apply what they've learned by conducting research, publishing papers, presenting their work at symposiums, and taking advantage of entrepreneurial grants that send them around the world. Undergraduates at Beloit learn to approach problems ethically and critically in a collaborative academic community that values international and interdisciplinary perspectives.

Beloit is Wisconsin's first college, founded by New Englanders on the Midwestern frontier in 1846. Today, a geographically diverse population of 1,250 students is drawn to Beloit's residential campus from forty-six states and more than thirty countries. Ten percent come from countries outside the United States, 20 percent of U.S. students are non-Caucasian, and students represent many religious orientations and socioeconomic backgrounds.

Nearly all students reside on campus (95 percent) and may choose to live in traditional settings, on quiet or substance-free floors, in one of three fraternity houses or three sorority houses, or in special-interest houses. Two town-house complexes offer roomy, apartment-style living. Meals, served in two campus locations by premier food service provider Bon Appetit, include fresh, locally sourced, organic, vegetarian, and vegan meal options, often featuring student-grown produce. More than half of Beloit's students participate in some form of athletics—club, intramural, or varsity.

New students quickly become part of this active and diverse environment through the Beloit Initiatives program, which provides the framework for a Beloit education through two years of faculty advising designed to help students develop skills and perspectives that will help them create their educational trajectory while working one-on-one with a faculty mentor. Initiatives seminars begin the day students arrive and provide an academic grounding and a social network, starting with new student interdisciplinary seminars taught by experienced professors.

Location

Beloit's 65-acre campus is located on the border of Wisconsin and Illinois, 90 miles northwest of Chicago, 50 miles south of Madison, and 70 miles southwest of Milwaukee, in a small, diverse city of 36,000. Students take advantage of the resources of the three major metropolitan areas, and Beloit's businesses and civic and service organizations provide numerous internship, job shadowing, and community outreach opportunities. Beloit's academic buildings are clustered around lawns dotted with ancient North American Indian mounds, while residence halls on the other side of campus provide the base of the College's social scene. Karris Track & Field at Strong Stadium, a few blocks east of campus, features a new turf field and track where Beloit's varsity lacrosse teams played their first games in 2013.

Majors and Degrees

Beloit awards Bachelor of Arts and Bachelor of Science degrees in more than fifty fields of study. Students may major in anthropology, art/art history, biochemistry, biology, chemistry, classics, comparative literature, computer science, critical identity studies, economics, education and youth studies, English, environmental studies, geology, health and society, history, interdisciplinary studies (self-designed), international relations, mathematics, modern languages, music, philosophy, religious studies, physics, political science, psychology, science for elementary teaching, sociology, theatre, dance, and media studies. Students often create a unique interdisciplinary major or minor. The College offers an array of departmental minors; permanent interdisciplinary minors include African studies, American studies, ancient Mediterranean studies, Asian studies, critical identity studies, environmental studies, European studies, health and society, interdisciplinary studies, journalism, Latin American and Caribbean studies, legal studies, medieval studies, museum studies, performing arts, and Russian studies.

Beloit offers 3-2 programs in engineering and environmental management and forestry, and preprofessional programs in health professions and law. These programs complement a major in an appropriate discipline. Beloit students may also earn teaching certification.

Academic Programs

Beloit's academic calendar consists of two 14-week semesters with one-week midterm breaks. At the end of the sophomore year, students are required to declare a major and may add a second major, a minor, or teaching certification. Advising Practicum, a full-day series of workshops and discussions held every semester before advising week, is designed to help students develop an academic plan tailored to their individual interests and goals. Beloit requires students to complete five breadth requirements, a senior-year capstone experience, a liberal arts in practice experience outside the classroom, three writing-intensive courses, and an intercultural literacy course.

Off-Campus Programs

Beloit has a century-old tradition of domestic and international off-campus study opportunities, and more than half of new Beloit graduates will have studied and/or conducted research in such a program. Internships, field terms in the humanities and sciences, and summer employment opportunities are arranged through the Liberal Arts in Practice Center.

At Beloit College, approximately 40 percent of students study abroad. Whether through Beloit's own extensive programs or the Associated Colleges of the Midwest (ACM) and independent programs, Beloit students have studied in more than forty countries worldwide, from Australia to Zimbabwe.

Academic Facilities

Beloit's historic brick and stone buildings coexist with innovative contemporary structures such as the Center for the Sciences. Completed in 2008, the 117,000-square-foot center is LEED-certified Platinum and includes many sustainable features. The College's newest facility, the Hendricks Center for the Arts, opened in the fall of 2010 in downtown Beloit, in a historic building that formerly housed a public library. The 48,000-square-foot center provides a centralized home to the College's dance and music programs, and features studio classrooms, a state-of-the-art film classroom, faculty offices, rehearsal rooms, and design/staging labs. Beloit's Powerhouse activity and recreation center is set to be constructed in 2017. This one-of-a-kind adaptive reuse of an electric generating station will feature student life spaces, fitness and training facilities, a 200-meter training track and indoor turf field house, a competition pool, and a wellness center, all along the Rock River shoreline. The Logan Museum of Anthropology and the Wright Museum of Art are highly regarded teaching museums that offer students excellent resources for research and work experience. The Neese Performing Arts Theatre complex features a large thrust stage theater, a black-box theater, a scenic design studio, and a complete costume shop. The World Affairs Center is the hub of language and literature study. Beloit's library collection is in excess of half a million holdings and provides individual and group study areas and computer labs. A 6,000-square-foot center for entrepreneurship in downtown Beloit provides physical space, office resources, and a recording studio where students can put venture plans of their own design into action.

Costs

Tuition for the 2015–16 academic year is $44,590, fees are $460, a room is $4,490, and board (twenty-meal plan) is $3,400—for a total comprehensive fee of $52,940. While the cost of books and incidental expenses varies, it averages about $2,300.

Financial Aid

Beloit College is committed to making the Beloit experience affordable to all qualified students. The financial aid program recognizes two criteria—scholastic ability and financial need. During the 2014–15 academic year, more than 97 percent of enrolling first-year students received Beloit gift aid.

Beloit's attention to providing students high value has won the College recognition in the Princeton Review's guides, the *Fiske Guide to Colleges,* and *U.S. News & World Report* as among the nation's best buys in top colleges.

Faculty

The focus of Beloit's faculty is great teaching. Beloit professors are innovators who are committed to an educational environment that emphasizes collaborative, hands-on learning in small classes. Of the 110 full-time faculty members, 95 percent hold the highest academic degree in their field. All classes are taught by professors. In classrooms, it is easy for students and faculty members to become immersed in their work, since the student-faculty ratio is 10:1 and the average class size is 15 students.

Admission Requirements

Beloit seeks applicants with special qualities and talents, as well as those from diverse ethnic, geographic, and economic backgrounds. When reviewing applications, the transcript is the most important element. Beloit has no absolute secondary school requirements but recommends a rigorous college-preparatory program. This includes 4 years of English, 3 years of college-preparatory mathematics, 3 years of laboratory science, 3 years of history or social science, and at least 2 years of a foreign language. Applicants planning to major in the natural sciences should complete 4 years of high school mathematics and be prepared to begin calculus during their first year in college. Seventh-semester grades may be required. One teacher recommendation is required as part of the application. The essay component of Beloit's application is critical—there is no required topic, so students should write about a topic they believe will represent them well. SAT or ACT test scores are optional; however, TOEFL or IELTS scores are required for international students. Interviews are not required for admission but are encouraged. Off-campus alumni and staff interviews can be arranged if a student would like to interview but cannot travel to the campus. Transfer applications are considered for August or January entrance. Applicants must hold at least a B average at an accredited college or university.

Application and Information

Beloit offers a binding early decision plan with a deadline of November 1 and notification on or before November 30. In addition, there are two nonbinding early action plans with deadlines of either November 1 or December 1; notification is December 15 and January 15, respectively. The regular decision priority application deadline is January 15, with notification beginning in March. Applications received after January 15 will be given full consideration as space remains available. Beloit has no application fee. Test scores are optional for most students. Admitted students have until May 1 to reply to Beloit.

Review of transfer applications for the fall term begins March 15 and continues through the spring; the deadline for the spring term is October 15. Notification for transfer applications is rolling.

For more information, students should contact:

Admissions Office
Beloit College
700 College Street
Beloit, Wisconsin 53511
Phone: 608-363-2500
800-9-BELOIT (toll-free)
Fax: 608-363-2075
E-mail: admiss@beloit.edu
Website: http://www.beloit.edu
http://www.facebook.com/BeloitCollege
http://twitter.com/beloit_college

Beloit's residential campus is home to 1,250 students from 46 states and more than 30 countries.

COLLEGE CLOSE-UPS

BENTLEY UNIVERSITY

WALTHAM, MASSACHUSETTS

★ To read more about this school, visit http://petersons.to/bentleyuniversity

BENTLEY UNIVERSITY

The University

Bentley University believes that education should prepare students for whatever the world sends their way. That's why Bentley's one-of-a-kind curriculum starts with a core business foundation, infused with the kind of critical thinking and cultural understanding that comes from the study of the arts and sciences. As a result, Bentley students are highly sought after by today's leading organizations because of their professionalism, exposure to state-of-the-art research tools, and diverse, real-world experience. In its 2014 "Best Undergraduate Business Schools" issue, *Bloomberg Businessweek* ranked Bentley 20th among the country's top undergraduate business programs.

Located on a classic New England campus minutes from Boston, Bentley offers a wide variety of majors and minors, as well as optional liberal studies and business studies majors designed to create a modern intersection of the arts and sciences and business that's unique in higher education. This unique fusion of business fundamentals and liberal arts enables Bentley students to think outside of the box when faced with critical decisions in the workplace.

Bentley's career services office was recently ranked fourth in the country by the Princeton Review. The Miller Center for Career Services offers resources including an on-campus recruiting program involving 1,000 national and international companies; an online job and internship database; career fairs; workshops on topics such as interviewing and networking; and a newly developed Career Development Seminar (CDI 1901) for first-year students.

In addition, students can develop a customized four-year development plan, which contributes to the university's outstanding placement rates. In 2013, more than 95 percent of students found employment or enrolled in graduate school within six months of graduation. Their median annual salary was $52,000.

Approximately 98 percent of freshmen live on campus. Twenty-three residence halls provide a range of housing options: dorms, suites, and apartments. Housing is provided for all four years; all residence halls are air-conditioned and typically include study lounges, exercise facilities, TV lounges, and game rooms. Bentley has a variety of meal plans for students to choose from as they move into suites and apartments with kitchens. There are eleven places on campus to dine, offering an array of food options from buffet-style cafeterias to a Curitto to Dunkin' Donuts.

Students live and learn in a multicultural environment that prepares them to thrive in today's diverse world. International students representing nearly 100 countries make up a large percentage of the student body and bring valuable perspectives to the Bentley community.

Supporting Bentley's commitment to diversity are offices such as the Multicultural Center, Spiritual Life Center, Center for International Students and Scholars, Center for Women in Business, and the Women's Center.

The Student Center is the hub of campus activity and is home to the main dining room, the pub, eateries, student services, and more than 100 student organizations. These groups represent academics, the arts, media, fraternity and sorority life, and cultural interests.

Athletic programs are a Bentley hallmark and include intramurals, recreational sports, and more than 20 varsity teams in NCAA Divisions I and II. The Dana Athletic Center houses a weight and fitness complex, food court, locker rooms, a gym, a basketball court, volleyball and racquetball courts, a competition-size pool with a diving tank, and saunas. Outdoor facilities include soccer and baseball fields, a track, and tennis courts.

Location

Bentley's location in Waltham, Massachusetts—just minutes west of Boston—puts the city within easy reach. As the country's ultimate university town, Boston's options range from theater to art exhibits, dance clubs to concerts, and championship sports to world-class shopping. Bentley's free shuttle makes regular trips to Harvard Square in Cambridge, just a subway ride from Boston. Boston also offers many opportunities for internships and jobs after graduation.

Majors and Degrees

The Bentley curriculum is a groundbreaking integration of business and the arts and sciences that has been featured in the *Wall Street Journal*. "It's not about pitting lifelong learning skills against professional skills," President Gloria Larson told the paper. "A college degree should reflect both."

To that end, Bachelor of Science (B.S.) degree programs enable students to gain in-depth knowledge and skills in specific business disciplines: accountancy, actuarial science, computer information systems, corporate finance and accounting, economics–finance, finance, information design and corporate communication, information systems audit and control, management, managerial economics, marketing, and mathematical sciences.

Bentley also offers Bachelor of Arts (B.A.) degree programs with majors in global studies, health sciences, history, liberal arts, media and culture, philosophy, public policy, Spanish studies, and sustainable science. All Bachelor of Arts students gain business experience through either the Business Studies Major (BSM) or minor. All students can also choose from one of 36 minors, including entrepreneurial studies, law, and sports management.

The Liberal Studies Major (LSM), an optional double major, can be combined with any business program. It provides students with a competitive edge by building meaningful connections across and within disciplines. To complete the LSM, students do not need to take any extra courses beyond those normally required. It allows students to add another credential to their degree, helping them stand out to employers. LSM concentrations include American studies; earth, environment, and global sustainability; ethics and social responsibility; global perspectives; health and industry; media arts and society; and quantitative perspectives.

Academic Programs

The Bentley curriculum is a unique fusion of business and the liberal arts. The university's 4,200 undergraduates benefit from a breadth of programs and the ability to combine subjects to best fit their interests.

A Bentley education also focuses on gaining hands-on experience in the classroom. Students benefit from classes where they partner with outside companies to solve current business problems and present their solutions directly to company executives. Bentley also offers top applicants a chance to enroll in the Honors Program. Participants select honors-level courses each semester that offer extra intellectual challenge in a seminar atmosphere.

The Master's Candidate program enables students to earn a Bachelor of Business Administration degree and either an Emerging Leaders M.B.A. or Master of Science (M.S.) degree.

Off-Campus Programs

Hands-on experience is emphasized across the curriculum. Internships, study abroad, service-learning, and other opportunities allow students to apply classroom theory in the community.

Each year, more than 90 percent of students complete at least one internship, building valuable work experience and networking connections. Some of the top internship employers include Fidelity Investments, the TJX Companies, Liberty Mutual, Bain & Company, and all of the Big Four accounting firms.

Bentley students can gain insight into different cultures by studying abroad. Programs take place in more than 25 countries and vary in length from one week to a full academic year.

Through Bentley's Service-Learning Center, students build skills in business, communication, and teamwork while assisting nonprofit and community-based organizations both locally and internationally.

Academic Facilities

Concepts taught in the classroom are put to use in several high-tech learning laboratories.

Bentley's financial Trading Room combines state-of-the-art technology and real-time data to offer first-hand exposure to financial concepts in simulated trading sessions. Resources include Bloomberg, Capital IQ, Datastream, FactSet, Thomson One Analytics, Portfolio Analysis, MATLAB, S&P Compustat, and Worldscope.

The Center for Marketing Technology plays an integral role in marketing programs. Students gain a full grasp of software options, familiarity with research tools and techniques, and knowledge of new digital marketing frameworks.

The Accounting Center for Electronic Learning and Business Management (ACELAB) introduces cutting-edge technologies that are reshaping the accounting profession. Students have access to auditing and tax preparation software as well as other professional applications from industry leaders such as SAP and Oracle.

The Center for Languages and International Collaboration (CLIC) is a key resource for language courses, international studies majors, and students with an interest in global issues. The center promotes collaboration among Bentley students and their counterparts overseas.

The Media and Culture Labs and Studio feature resources for video production and editing as well as digital photography. The lab provides students with industry-standard software programs for screenwriting, sound mixing, graphic design, and DVD authoring.

The User Experience Center (UXC) features labs ideal for usability testing. Students use the applications employed by technical communicators, Web developers, user-interface designers, and usability specialists.

The CIS Learning and Technology Sandbox is a collaborative space for learning new technologies. Its resources include Google TVs, Xbox 360 with Kinect, study spaces, large-screen TVs, a smart board, specialized networking equipment, and tools such as Windows 8, Linux, and Android development software.

The Bentley Library is outfitted with computer workstations, group study rooms, and wireless network access. It also has an exceptional number of online database resources, research guides, and consultation appointments are available to assist students with their projects.

Costs

Tuition for resident and nonresident students during the 2014–15 academic year was $40,990. Room and board (double room, meal plan) costs were $13,949. Additional expenses include books, supplies, technology fee, and personal and travel expenses.

Financial Aid

Bentley's financial aid program includes both scholarships based on academic achievement, which are awarded through the admission process, as well as grants based on financial need. Bentley administered over $96 million in aid to undergraduate students last year. Well over half of that amount came in the form of grants and scholarships directly from Bentley. Significant institutional resources are committed each year so that all academically qualified students have access to a Bentley education regardless of their financial resources. Currently, more than 70 percent of undergraduates receive some type of financial assistance—either grants, scholarships, loans, and/or work study.

Faculty

Bentley faculty members are teacher-scholars known for their classroom skills and cutting-edge research. They bring practical, real-world experience to the classroom, based on years of professional involvement in their fields. Faculty research focuses on issues of prime importance to current business practice. Much of the research is conducted in partnership with leading organizations. A student-faculty ratio of 14:1 and average class size of 24 ensure a personal experience for students. All courses are taught by professors; there are no teaching assistants. Students often note that professors are accessible to them outside of the classroom.

Student Government

Bentley has a number of student governing groups, including the Student Government Association, Residence Hall Association, and the Graduate Student Association.

Admission Requirements

Applicants are encouraged to complete a competitive university preparatory program. Recommendations include four years of English, four years of mathematics (preferably algebra I and II, geometry, and pre-calculus or its equivalent), and three to four years each of history, laboratory science, and a foreign language.

Along with the application, students must submit a secondary school transcript, letters of recommendation from a teacher and a counselor, and official scores of either the SAT or ACT, including the ACT writing test. Bentley has special applications for international students and transfer students. Applicants who are nonnative speakers of English must also supply official scores of the Test of English as a Foreign Language (TOEFL).

Application and Information

Bentley University accepts the Common Application. Candidates for the fall semester are notified in late March; spring semester candidates and transfers are notified on a rolling basis.

Prospective students can visit bentley.edu/undergraduate/applying for application information and deadlines.

For more information, students should contact:

Office of Undergraduate Admission
Bentley University
175 Forest Street
Waltham, Massachusetts 02452-4705
Phone: 781-891-2244
800-523-2354 (toll-free)
Fax: 781-891-3414
E-mail: ugadmission@bentley.edu
Website: bentley.edu/undergraduate
facebook.com/bentleyadmission
twitter.com/bentleyu

Bentley students have access to professional research tools, cutting-edge software, and other valuable resources in seven high-tech learning labs and a state-of-the-art library.

BERKLEE COLLEGE OF MUSIC

BOSTON, MASSACHUSETTS

★ To read more about this school, visit http://petersons.to/berkleecollegeofmusic

The College

Berklee College of Music was founded on the revolutionary principle that the best way to prepare students for careers in music is through the study and practice of contemporary music. For nearly 70 years, the college has evolved to reflect the state of the art in music and the music business, leading the way with the world's first baccalaureate studies in jazz, rock, electric guitar, film scoring, songwriting, turntables, electronic production, and more than a dozen other genres and fields of study. Berklee serves distance learners worldwide through its award-winning online school, Berklee Online. The college's national after-school music program for underserved teens, the Berklee City Music Network, is in 41 cities and counting. Berklee's campus in Valencia, Spain, hosts the college's first graduate programs in contemporary performance; global entertainment and music business; scoring for film, television, and video games; and music technology innovation. With a diverse and talented student body representing nearly 100 countries, and alumni who have collectively won more than 310 Grammys and Latin Grammys, Berklee is the world's premier learning lab for the music of today—and tomorrow.

Berklee has proven its commitment to this approach by wholeheartedly embracing change. The musical landscape looks nothing like it did when Berklee was founded in 1945, but the college has remained current by supplementing its core curriculum with studies in emerging musical genres and indispensable new technology. Berklee also has responded to important developments in music education and music therapy, making good on its promise to improve society through music.

At Berklee, students acquire a strong foundation of contemporary music theory and technique, then build upon that foundation by learning the practical, professional skills needed to sustain a career in music. Students can earn either a fully accredited four-year baccalaureate degree or a professional diploma in music production and engineering, film scoring, music business/management, electronic production and design, songwriting, and music therapy, as well as the traditional mainstays of performance and composition. Perhaps more importantly, these disciplines prepare students for employment in the music industry.

Berklee attracts a diverse range of students who reflect the multiplicity of influences in today's music, including jazz, rock, hip-hop, country, gospel, electronica, Latin, and funk. The college is a magnet for aspiring musicians from every corner of the earth, which gives the school a uniquely international flavor. Of all U.S. colleges and universities, Berklee has one of the largest percentages of undergraduates from outside the United States—more than 30 percent. Reflecting the interplay between music and culture, Berklee creates an environment where aspiring music professionals learn how to integrate new ideas and showcase their distinctive skills in an evolving community.

The college's alumni form a wide network of industry professionals who use their openness, virtuosity, and versatility to take music in new directions. Notable alumni include Jeff Bhasker, Gary Burton, Terri Lyne Carrington, Bruce Cockburn, Juan Luis Guerra, Roy Hargrove, Amy Heidemann (Karmin), Quincy Jones, Diana Krall, Aimee Mann, Arif Mardin, Branford Marsalis, Danilo Pérez, John Scofield, Howard Shore, Alan Silvestri, Esperanza Spalding, Susan Tedeschi, and Gillian Welch.

Location

Berklee College of Music is located in Boston's Fenway Cultural District. An international hub of intellectual and creative exploration, the neighborhood includes many of the world's other great colleges and universities, treasure-filled museums and galleries, and world-class performing arts centers such as Symphony Hall and the Wang Center. Great performers appear at the Berklee Performance Center, and the college's all-ages venue, Cafe 939, highlights up-and-coming international performers in all genres. In addition to the music made at Berklee, there is a lively club and concert scene in the area with coffeehouses featuring folk and bluegrass music; neighborhood clubs offering jazz, reggae, and world music; and clubs specializing in rock, blues, dance, urban, and country music.

Berklee students participate in intramural sports and fitness programs at Berklee and at other ProArts Consortium member institutions; enjoy professional sporting events like baseball with the Boston Red Sox at Fenway Park, hockey with the Boston Bruins, basketball with the Boston Celtics, and football with the New England Patriots; attend theater, club, and concert hall events year-round throughout the city; and walk and bike through the city's many parks and public gardens. The college is on Boston's public transportation system, allowing students to take advantage of all that Boston has to offer.

In 2011, Berklee launched an international campus offering master's of music and art degrees in Valencia, Spain, in the heart of the City of Arts and Sciences complex in the Palau de les Arts. Valencia boasts the highest number of musicians per capita in Spain, and thousands of Valencians of all ages are involved in musical activities. With more than 500 symphonic bands throughout the region and representing countless music styles, including classical, rock, pop, and jazz, the Berklee campus in Valencia aims to be a main hub for the study, evolution, and global proliferation of many musical genres, including flamenco, in Europe, Latin America, the Middle East, and all over the world.

Majors and Degrees

Berklee offers a Bachelor of Music (B.M.) degree program and a four-year program leading to a professional diploma. Students may choose to major in composition, contemporary writing and production, electronic production and design, film scoring, jazz composition, music business/management, music education, music production and engineering, music therapy, performance, professional music, or songwriting. In addition, students may choose from 19 minors: acoustics and electronics, American roots music, audio design for video games, commercial record production, conducting, drama, English, history, instrument repair, music and society, music technology, performance studies in Latin music, philosophy, psychology, recording and production for musicians, theory of jazz and popular song, video game scoring, visual culture and new media studies, and writing for TV and new media. The college also offers a five-year, dual-major option in which students graduate with an even more marketable education that expands their career options in the music industry.

Academic Programs

The Bachelor of Music program offers a complete music curriculum combined with liberal arts courses in English, history, languages, mathematics, philosophy, and physical and social sciences. Intensive concentration in music subjects provides students with the necessary tools for developing their musical talents to the fullest and prepares them for the multifaceted and ever-changing demands of today's professional music. The degree program is especially appropriate for students who wish to earn a formal degree; are interested in pursuing a career in music education, music therapy, or music business/management; or want to continue their studies at the graduate level.

The diploma is designed for students who want to focus exclusively on contemporary music studies and still get the benefits of a Berklee experience, as well as students who have already earned a bachelor's degree at another institution.

All students must complete the core music curriculum, which consists of harmony, arranging, ear training, and introduction to music technology; instrumental studies; ensembles and instrumental labs; and the concentrate courses designated for each major. All degree candidates must complete the general education curriculum and traditional music studies courses.

Off-Campus Programs

Through the Professional Arts Consortium (ProArts), an association of six area institutions dedicated to the performing and visual arts, Berklee students can take courses at leading Boston arts institutions in communications, modern dance, visual arts, ballet, architectural and graphic design, theater arts, and liberal arts. The other members of the consortium are Boston Architectural Center, the Boston Conservatory, Emerson College, Massachusetts College of Art, and the School of the Museum of Fine Arts.

Students who major in music business/management may be eligible to receive credit for their Berklee course work toward an M.B.A. from Suffolk University.

The Berklee International Network is a shared endeavor designed to promote the effectiveness of contemporary music education among members and to advance the value of contemporary music education internationally. Berklee faculty and staff members visit network member schools annually to conduct workshops and clinics and to audition students for scholarships for full-time study at Berklee. There are currently 19 members of the network in Argentina, Australia, Brazil, Canada, Colombia, Ecuador, Finland, France, Germany, Greece, Hong Kong, Ireland, Israel, Japan, Korea, Malaysia, Puerto Rico, and Spain.

The college has a robust internship program, with students learning in music companies in Los Angeles, New York, Nashville, London, and beyond, as well as a semester-long global studies program at Berklee's campus in Valencia, Spain.

Academic Facilities

Berklee students have the opportunity to work in the college's state-of-the-art music technology facilities, using some of the most sophisticated recording and synthesis equipment currently available, in addition to facilities specifically designed for the areas of composition, arranging, and film scoring. The facilities at Berklee are furnished with the instruments and equipment that are being used in the world beyond the classroom. Berklee's performance facilities include the Berklee Performance Center, a 1,200-seat concert hall hosting more than 300 student, faculty, and other concerts each year; Cafe 939, a state-of-the-art, all-ages, student-run music venue and coffeehouse; four recital halls equipped with a variety of sound reinforcement systems; more than 40 ensemble rooms; over 80 private instruction studios; about 300 private practice rooms; and an outdoor concert pavilion.

Technological facilities include the Recording Studio Complex, consisting of 13 studio facilities that offer multitrack digital and analog recording capability, automated mix-down, digital audio editing, video postproduction, 5.1 multichannel surround mixing, and comprehensive signal processing equipment; electronic production and design labs, with nine facilities featuring hundreds of synthesizers, standard and alternate controllers, effects processors, recorders, mixers, computers, and software representing many of the industry's most progressive manufacturers; the Learning Center, a networked, computer-based training facility; the Professional Writing Division MIDI lab and advanced classroom, with 28 digital audio/MIDI work-stations; and film-scoring classroom, labs, and scoring studio complex, offering students the opportunity for hands-on study in the areas of film music composition, conducting, MIDI sequencing, and digital music editing. In January 2013, the college opened its state-of-the-art 160 Massachusetts Avenue Building, a 16-story tower that houses over 350 students and includes a ten-studio recording complex.

Costs

Information on costs is available online at berklee.edu/financial-aid/cost-of-attendance.

Financial Aid

A very large percentage of the student body receives some form of financial aid, so no student should allow financial barriers to stop him or her from applying to the college. Funds are available from many different sources, including Berklee and federal and state programs. Students are eligible for merit-based scholarships and, in cases of demonstrated need, federal assistance is provided. Subsidized loans, a tuition-installment plan, and campus employment are also available. Financial aid counselors are available to students and their families to discuss the various options available to them. Students should be aware that there are specific deadlines for federal and state fund applications and for scholarships. Berklee awards more than $35 million in scholarships each year to students from all over the world who demonstrate the potential to succeed in today's music industry.

Berklee's Office of Scholarships and Student Employment provides extensive opportunities for both domestic and international students to apply for merit-based scholarships via audition (entering students) or submission of an achievement portfolio (continuing and returning students who have successfully completed a minimum of two semesters).

Faculty

The personal attention students receive from teachers at Berklee guides them beyond the theoretical so that they can apply what they've learned in their next ensemble rehearsal, evening jam session, or gig. All instruction is administered by Berklee faculty members, the 600 teachers and talented artists who demonstrate their commitment to music education in the classroom and beyond. Most faculty members also write and arrange music, perform in concert halls and clubs, make recordings, or perform on television and radio, and some do it all. All faculty members bring to the classroom knowledge of music and the wisdom that comes from professional music experience.

Student Government

Berklee's broad-based system of governance relies on participation from all areas of the college community. The Council of Students represents the voice and perspectives of students regarding all of the issues reviewed by the college. Students are also asked to serve on a wide variety of college committees that advise administrators on such topics as the college's master plan, honorary degree recipients, the website, and academic and student policies. And many of Berklee's student leaders have the opportunity to meet with the president, vice presidents, and trustees during the academic year to discuss current issues, concerns, and institutional activities.

Admission Requirements

Berklee's board of admissions seeks students who show high potential—who are creative, collaborative, and who have something extra that sets them apart. The college considers every aspect of an applicant's strengths and looks for candidates who reflect the rich diversity of Berklee's curriculum, with high musical aptitude as players or writers; or in business, production, music therapy, or music education.

The college takes academics into consideration as well as musical aptitude. Berklee does not have specific GPA or test score requirements, nor does it have specific class rank requirements. The audition and interview process, along with a comprehensive and holistic evaluation of each applicant, provides a wealth of information to assess students' ability to succeed at Berklee.

Application and Information

Berklee uses fixed application deadlines for each semester of entry. Applying to the college is a three-step process. All applicants must submit an online application, participate in a live audition and interview, and mail in the appropriate transcripts to be considered for full-time enrollment at the college.

The online application asks that students provide their personal contact information, indicate whether they are a vocalist or instrumentalist; and name their preferred audition and interview location. A live audition and interview is required as part of the application. A complete listing of audition dates, deadlines, and locations throughout the world is available on Berklee's website.

The college also asks that students provide information about their musical and academic background. All supporting materials must be postmarked by the posted deadline date. To learn more about how to apply to the college, and information about the audition and interview experience, students should visit http://www.berklee.edu/admissions.

For further information, students should contact:

Office of Admissions
Berklee College of Music
1140 Boylston Street
Boston, Massachusetts 02215
Phone: 617-747-2221 (worldwide)
800-BERKLEE (toll-free in the U.S. and Canada)
Fax: 617-747-2047
E-mail: admissions@berklee.edu
Website: http://www.berklee.edu
http://www.facebook.com/berkleecollege
http://twitter.com/BerkleeCollege
http://www.youtube.com/berkleecollege

Berklee College of Music students using state-of-the-art music technology.

COLLEGE CLOSE-UPS

BOSTON COLLEGE

CHESTNUT HILL, MASSACHUSETTS

The University

Boston College (BC) was founded in 1863 by the Jesuits to serve the sons of Boston's Irish immigrants. Today a coeducational university on more than 239 acres in Chestnut Hill, BC may seem a world apart from the small school in the crowded heart of Boston that was its first home. Through more than fifteen decades of growth and change, however, BC has held fast to the Jesuit ideals that inspired its founders. A Jesuit education today, as a century ago, is grounded in the liberal arts and in a commitment to the service of others.

Undergraduates may enroll in the College of Arts and Sciences, the Wallace E. Carroll School of Management, the Connell School of Nursing, or the Lynch School of Education.

BC's approximately 9,000 undergraduates come from many backgrounds. The university draws from nearly all fifty states and more than fifty-five countries. Students' religious and cultural backgrounds are similarly diverse. Today, the university's AHANA (African American, Hispanic, Asian, and Native American) and international students make up approximately 30 percent of the undergraduate student body.

In today's complex and increasingly diverse world, the university believes that the best education is one that broadens a student's capacity to reason, think, and make critical judgments in a wide range of areas. Thus, each BC student fulfills a core of liberal arts courses from which he or she can pursue degrees in more than fifty areas of study and choose from more than 1,400 course offerings throughout the university.

According to several recent national publications, BC is in the top tier of the nation's colleges and universities. The foundation for that achievement is the university's scholars and researchers—758 full-time professionals who make up the faculty. The kinship between teachers and students is one of the hallmarks of a BC education; that relationship is nurtured by a student-teacher ratio of 13:1. The median class size at the university is 20 students.

At BC, learning continues beyond the classroom in more than 225 student-run organizations. These include student government, honor societies, language and cultural organizations, performance ensembles, political groups, preprofessional clubs, publications, and service organizations. BC also sponsors thirteen varsity teams for men and sixteen for women, all of which compete at the NCAA Division I level. The College also supports over sixty club and intramural sports.

Boston College's public affairs office maintains university profiles on three social networking sites. Prospective students can become a fan of BC on Facebook (http://www.facebook.com/BostonCollege) or follow BC on Twitter (http://twitter.com/BostonCollege) or explore BC's YouTube channel (http://www.youtube.com/bostoncollege). or Instagram (http://instagram.com/BostonCollege).

Location

Located in the Chestnut Hill section of Newton, BC sits on the doorstep of one of America's great cities, a center of culture and education for more than three centuries. It is an energetic, cosmopolitan city that draws life and enthusiasm from the more than 200,000 college students in residence during the academic year. Located just 6 miles from downtown Boston and with easy access to the city via the trolley system that stops at the foot of the campus, BC offers the best of both worlds: a scenic suburban setting neighboring an exciting metropolitan center.

Majors and Degrees

The College of Arts and Sciences (A&S) is the oldest and largest of the four undergraduate schools at BC. A&S students must complete thirty-eight 1-semester courses, thirty-two of which are in A&S departments. The normal course load is five courses per semester for the first three years and four courses per semester during the senior year. The undergraduate curriculum includes the university core curriculum and ten to twelve courses in the major field, with the remainder of courses chosen as electives. A&S offers degrees in the following areas: art history, biochemistry, biology, chemistry, classical studies, communication, computer science, economics, English, environmental geosciences, environmental studies, film studies, French, geology, geological studies, geophysics, German studies, Hispanic studies, history, independent major, international studies, Islamic civilizations and societies, Italian, linguistics, mathematics, music, philosophy, physics, political science, psychology, Russian, Slavic studies, sociology, studio art, theater, and theology. Preprofessional advisement is also available in medical, dental, veterinary, and legal programs. Students can also select from twenty-one departmental minors, or seventeen interdisciplinary minors.

The Carroll School of Management educates students to be leaders in business and industry and in public agencies, educational institutions, and service organizations. The Carroll School offers concentrations in accounting, accounting information systems, computer science, corporate reporting and analysis, economics, finance, general management, human resource management, information systems, management and leadership, marketing, and operations and strategic management.

The Lynch School of Education prepares students for education and human services professions. Programs provide a general education, professional preparation, and specialized education in the major field. Fieldwork in area schools is closely linked to course work in each specialization. The Lynch School awards degrees upon completion of thirty-eight courses, including the university core curriculum, a major field of study in education, and a second major in a subject field or an interdisciplinary area in A&S that complements the student's program. Areas of specialization include applied psychology and human development, elementary education, and secondary education. The Lynch School also offers interdisciplinary majors in American heritages, general science, mathematics/computer science, and perspectives on Spanish America.

The Connell School of Nursing offers a four-year program of study leading to a Bachelor of Science degree. The three major components to the curriculum are nursing major courses, electives, and the required university core curriculum. In all courses, principles of wellness, illness, rehabilitation, and health maintenance serve as a theoretical basis in preparing students for professional nursing practice. Nursing courses include traditional classes, simulated and audiovisual laboratory activities on campus, and clinical learning activities in health-care settings.

Academic Programs

Every BC education is centered on a core curriculum—a set of required courses. BC offers a core curriculum because it believes in the unity of knowledge. While the core, which is continually reviewed by a committee of faculty members, varies somewhat by school, its common elements include literature, natural science, writing, philosophy, theology, social science, modern European history, mathematics, fine arts, and the study of a non-European culture.

There are a wide variety of extraordinary academic programs available to BC students to enhance their educational experience. They include, among others, honors programs within each of the university's four undergraduate schools, Undergraduate Faculty Research Fellows, the Scholar of the College, PULSE, and Perspectives on Western Culture.

Off-Campus Programs

BC encourages all students to take part in internship programs. More than 80 percent of BC undergraduates participate in at least one internship or prepracticum placement during their college years. Internships can be paid or unpaid and may take place during the academic year or the summer; some carry academic credit.

BC students may take on the challenge of international study in more than sixty programs administered by BC at universities in more than forty countries. BC students who study abroad typically do so in their junior year, but there is also a range of full-year and summer-abroad opportunities. The Office of International Programs helps students with program selection and applications and maintains a library of reference books and professional evaluations of international study programs.

Academic Facilities

BC's eight libraries contain more than 3.1 million printed volumes, over 4.3 million items in microform, 454,666 e-books, 237,497 government documents, 39,347 serial subscriptions, and a wide collection of films and archival items. The resources of the library system range from some of Europe's earliest printed books to hundreds of computerized databases. Students with personal computers have dorm-room access to these databases as well as to Quest and other library information sources through Agora, the campus information network. BC also offers a 24/7 "Ask a Librarian" e-mail service and the capability to text questions to a librarian. In addition, all of BC's libraries and classrooms offer a wireless network that provides access to these resources and the Internet.

Research laboratories in the state-of-the-art science facilities have been specially designed to accommodate the advanced instrumentation required for modern science and to provide flexibility for accommodating new equipment. The $85-million expansion to the Higgins Biology and Physics Center was carefully designed to place classrooms, laboratories, computer facilities, and office space in proximity and to facilitate interaction among faculty members, researchers, and students. In addition to the Center's seventeen new teaching laboratories, special working labs are designed and outfitted for research and teaching in the fields of biology and physics.

Boston College opened Stokes Hall in January 2013. This $78-million facility was strategically designed to foster interdisciplinary collaboration among BC's humanities departments and enhanced student-faculty interaction, with thirty-six state-of-the-art classrooms and 200 faculty offices for the Classical Studies, English, History, Philosophy, and Theology departments. Stokes Hall also houses the Academic Advising Center, College of Arts and Sciences Honors Department, and Office of First Year Experience, as well as common areas, conference rooms, a coffee shop, and an outdoor garden and plaza that provide multiple meeting spaces to connect students and faculty.

Boston College is currently constructing new residence hall with 460 beds that is slated to open in 2016, as well as renovating a larger building to move the current museum of art to a bigger location featuring additional exhibit, function, and meeting space.

Costs

Tuition for the 2014–15 academic year was $46,670, which included a student activity fee and campus health fee of $766. The total for room and board was $13,186, which included the board plan. Freshman mandatory fees include a one-time required charge of $474 for first-year orientation and student identification.

Financial Aid

BC maintains a financial aid program to assist deserving and qualified students who might otherwise not be able to attend the university. Boston College is committed to providing funds to meet the full demonstrated need of every admitted student who applies for financial aid. Overall, 68 percent of students receive some form of financial aid with the University awarding over $110 million annually in need-based scholarships and grants. Assistance for freshmen alone included more than $19 million in need-based grants. The university offers financial aid to students based on need as demonstrated by completion of the College Scholarship Service's Financial Aid PROFILE and the Free Application for Federal Student Aid (FAFSA). All requirements and deadlines and complete instructions are available in BC admission literature. An application for financial aid in no way affects a decision on admission.

Each year, BC chooses 15 incoming freshmen as Presidential Scholars to receive merit-based, full-tuition scholarships. Students are selected from all candidates who apply through the early action program.

Faculty

BC has 758 full-time faculty members. Of these faculty members, 98 percent hold doctoral degrees. Over 60 Jesuits live on BC-owned property and make up one of the largest Apostolic Jesuit communities in the world. Approximately half of these members are active in the College's administration and teaching.

Student Government

The Undergraduate Government of Boston College (UGBC), formed in 1968, is led by the president and vice president, who are elected in the spring of each year by the entire student body. UGBC's goal is to serve the students by providing services and opportunities and by representing them in the best manner possible to the university community. To accomplish this goal, UGBC provides many educational, social, and cultural programs, such as concerts, lectures, roundtables, and more.

Admission Requirements

The undergraduate admission staff pays particular attention to students who have done well in a demanding college-preparatory curriculum, including Advanced Placement (AP) and honors courses when available. For the class of 2018, there were 23,223 applications for 2,288 places. The majority of incoming freshmen ranked comfortably in the top 10 percent of their high school class. The SAT scores of the middle half of admitted freshmen were 1910–2190. On the ACT, scores of the middle half were between 30 and 33.

Application and Information

Students applying to Boston College for a place in the freshman class must complete both the Common Application and the Boston College Supplemental Application. All applicants should submit the BC Supplemental Application as soon as they have decided to apply to Boston College. Students are encouraged to review the electronic application instructions on BC's website at http://www.bc.edu/content/bc/admission/undergrad/process.html and then apply at http://www.commonapp.org.

Students applying through the regular admission program must submit the Common Application and all other required forms, along with the $70 application fee, by January 1. Candidates are notified of action taken on their application in early April. Admitted students intending to matriculate are required to forward a confirmation fee to the Admission Office postmarked by May 1.

Students with superior academic credentials who view Boston College as a top choice may apply through the nonbinding early action program. These applicants must submit both application forms, along with the $70 application fee, by November 1. Candidates learn of their admission decision before December 25 but have the standard deadline (May 1) to reserve their places as freshmen. Boston College does permit students to apply under early action if they have applied to an early decision college.

BC accepts approximately 125 transfer students each year. Transfer candidates should request applications for transfer admission from the Office of Undergraduate Admission or via the website at http://www.bc.edu/transfer. In addition to high school records and standardized test results, transfer applicants must furnish transcripts from all postsecondary institutions they have attended.

For more information, students should contact:

Office of Undergraduate Admission
Devlin Hall 208
Boston College
Chestnut Hill, Massachusetts 02467
Phone: 617-552-3100
800-360-2522 (toll-free)
Fax: 617-552-0798
Website: http://www.bc.edu

BOSTON UNIVERSITY
BOSTON, MASSACHUSETTS

BOSTON UNIVERSITY

The University

Boston University (BU) is a private teaching and research university ranked #42 in the nation and #37 in the world by *U.S. News & World Report*. Students study with world-renowned faculty, including Fulbright Scholars, Pulitzer Prize winners, a MacArthur Fellow, Nobel Prize winners, and a former Poet Laureate. With an average class size of 27 and a 13:1 student-to-faculty ratio, these amazing professors become more than just a face students see in class. There are hundreds of research projects that allow undergraduates to work directly with faculty as early as freshman year through the Undergraduate Research Opportunities Program (UROP). With ten undergraduate schools and colleges; over 250 majors and minors, more than 600 in-depth, global courses; and one of the top 20 study-abroad programs in the country, the challenges at BU are vast and varied.

Among the academic opportunities at BU are several top-ranked programs such as biomedical engineering, occupational therapy, archaeology, business, and deaf studies. High-achieving students can also pursue dual degrees, combined B.A./M.A. programs, or be admitted to the prestigious Arvind and Chandan Nandlal Kilachand Honors College. BU students come from all fifty states and more than 100 countries; they are bright, driven, and inquisitive.

Located in the heart of Boston, students experience the city as an extension of the campus for study, internships, employment, and cultural and recreational activities. With four years of guaranteed campus housing, and 80 percent of undergraduates living on campus all four years, the campus feels like a true residential community in the heart of Boston.

Location

Boston provides an environment rich in intellectual and cultural stimuli; no other city in the world can compete with Boston's remarkable concentration of higher education institutions, world-renowned medical centers, and historic and cultural attractions. Students make up 20 percent of Boston's population during the academic year, enhancing the atmosphere of learning and excitement. The city provides many opportunities for impressive internship and research positions and is a world-class center for attractions including the Museum of Fine Arts, Fenway Park, the Boston Symphony Orchestra, and a thriving theater district.

Majors and Degrees

Boston University grants the B.A., B.S., B.S.B.A., B.L.S., Mus.B., and B.F.A. degrees. Of the University's seventeen schools and colleges, ten offer opportunities for undergraduate study.

As BU's largest academic division, the College of Arts and Sciences (CAS) offers a diverse learning community with world-class research faculty. Students may major in American studies; ancient Greek; ancient Greek and Latin; anthropology; anthropology and religion; archaeology; architectural studies; astronomy; astronomy and physics; biochemistry and molecular biology; biology; biology with a specialization in behavioral biology; biology with a specialization in cell biology, molecular biology, and genetics; biology with a specialization in ecology and conservation biology; biology with a specialization in neurobiology; biology with a specialization in quantitative biology; chemistry; chemistry with specialization in biochemistry; chemistry with specialization in teaching; Chinese language and literature; cinema and media studies (also offered in COM); classical civilization; classics and philosophy; classics and religion; comparative literature; computer science; earth sciences; economics; economics and mathematics; English; environmental analysis and policy; environmental science; French and linguistics; French studies; geography with a specialization in human geography; geography with a specialization in physical geography; geophysics and planetary sciences; German language and literature; Hispanic language and literature; history; history of art and architecture; Italian studies; Japanese and linguistics; Japanese language and literature; Latin; linguistics; linguistics and philosophy; marine science; mathematics (includes statistics); mathematics and computer science; mathematics and mathematics education; mathematics and philosophy; music (nonperformance); neuroscience; philosophy; philosophy and physics; philosophy and political science; philosophy and psychology; philosophy and religion; physics; political science; pre-dentistry; pre-law; pre-medicine; pre–veterinary medicine; psychology; religion; Russian language and literature; sociology; and Spanish and linguistics. Special curricula include seven-year accelerated programs in liberal arts medicine or liberal arts dentistry; the Modular Medical Integrated Curriculum (MMEDIC); the BU dual-degree program; the CFA/CAS double-degree program; the SED/CAS double-degree program; and various combined B.A./M.A. degree programs.

The College of Fine Arts (CFA) offers programs in the School of Music (composition and theory, music education, music-nonperformance, musicology, and performance), the School of Theatre (acting, design, stage management, production, and theater arts/performing), and the School of Visual Arts (art education, graphic design, painting, printmaking, and sculpture). There is also a double-degree program that allows students to earn two bachelor's degrees simultaneously in the CFA and the CAS.

The College of General Studies (CGS) offers a demanding, two-year program in the liberal arts and sciences that features an integrated core curriculum. It stresses an interdisciplinary approach to teaching. After two years, students continue into one of BU's degree-granting schools or colleges to complete their studies.

Located in one of the largest media markets in the nation, the College of Communication (COM) offers majors in cinema and media studies (also offered in CAS); communication (advertising, public relations, communication); film and television (production, writing, management); and journalism (with specialization available in broadcast, magazine, news-editorial, online, and photojournalism).

Majors in the College of Engineering (ENG) include biomedical engineering (a program ranked fourteenth in the country by *U.S. News & World Report*), computer engineering, electrical engineering, mechanical engineering, mechanical engineering with specialization in aerospace, and mechanical engineering with specialization in manufacturing.

The College of Health and Rehabilitation Sciences: Sargent College (SAR) is one of the oldest and top-ranked health sciences schools in the country. It offers programs in athletic training; behavior and health; health science; human physiology; nutrition; and speech, language, and hearing sciences. Also offered are a six-year B.S./D.P.T. program and a six-year program resulting in a B.S. in athletic training/D.P.T.

The Frederick S. Pardee School of Global Studies is housed within the College of Arts & Sciences and is dedicated to advancing human progress and improving the human condition. The School's education, research, and initiatives aim to produce globally competent citizens and leaders. Consisting of two divisions—international studies and regional studies—the School offers programs in Asian studies, European studies, international relations, Latin American studies, and Middle East and North Africa studies.

Areas of concentration in the School of Education (SED) include deaf studies, early childhood education, elementary education, English education, mathematics education, modern foreign languages education, science education, social studies education, and special education. The SED/CAS double-degree program is also offered.

Located in one of the hospitality and tourism capitals of the world, the School of Hospitality Administration (SHA) offers a rigorous program in the management of hotels, restaurants, food and beverage service, travel and tourism, and entertainment.

With a unique global curriculum, the School of Management (SMG) offers majors in accounting, entrepreneurship, finance, general management (business), international management, law, management information systems, marketing, operations and technology management, and organizational behavior.

Academic Programs

A Boston University education combines the elements of a traditional liberal arts education with training for the professions. There are 250 programs of study to choose from, including BU's top-ranked biomedical engineering, occupational therapy, deaf studies, economics, international relations, management information systems, journalism, theatre, and archeology programs. Highly qualified freshmen may also be invited to participate in the prestigious Arvind and Chandan Nandlal Kilachand Honors College.

Boston University has more than ninety study-abroad opportunities that take students around the world for courses, internships, and fieldwork. Opportunities are offered on six continents, in over thirty countries, and in cities such as Auckland, Beijing, Dresden, London, Los Angeles, Madrid, Paris, Sydney, and Washington, D.C. Programs offered include studies in art/architecture, business/economics, engineering, health and human services, journalism/communications, visual/performing arts, and many more. Fieldwork programs may be found in locations that include Ecuador and Spain, with study-abroad options that include programs in Grenoble, Padova, Quito, and Venice. Summer study programs are available in Argentina, Australia, China, England, France, Ireland, Italy, Peru, Spain, and the United States.

BU's Center for Career Development provides students the resources they need to select a major or get internships or part-time jobs in any number of fields.

Boston University operates on a calendar of two semesters and two summer terms. Students generally take four courses each semester; thirty-two courses are required for graduation. Most degree programs are built around a core of humanities and social and natural sciences. Concentrations require eight to thirteen courses. Electives generally total 30–40 percent of the courses taken, allowing for interdisciplinary study.

Academic Facilities

The new Yawkey Center for Student Services is home to BU's Center for Career Development, Educational Resource Center, Pre-professional Advising Center with pre-med and pre-law advising services, and the two-story Marciano Commons dining hall. The Engineering Product Innovation Center (EPIC) is a 15,000-square-foot facility where undergraduates can experiment with developing new products, from design to manufacturing. West campus now features the modern Student Village, including Agganis Arena; the Fitness and Recreation Center, complete with a 35-foot rock-climbing wall; and high-rise, apartment-style dorms. BU also has a life science and engineering facility with 187,000-square-feet of laboratory and research space for the biology, bioinformatics, chemistry, and bioengineering departments. The state-of-the-art Photonics Center features classroom and laboratory space for the College of Engineering as well as labs designed to support industry partners who seek to develop new photonics-based products. The School of Management building also offers technologically advanced educational facilities, with a dedicated career center and management library.

Through Boston University Information Services and Technology, students have access to public computing facilities equipped with workstations, terminals, and laser printers as well as a high-speed campus network. An 890-seat proscenium theater, studio space for visual arts students, practice rooms for music, and a 575-seat music performance center are indicative of BU's support for the arts. More than 2.8 million library volumes and over 4.7 million microform units are contained in Mugar Memorial Library, where the Twentieth-Century Archives are held, including the papers of Dr. Martin Luther King, Jr., Theodore Roosevelt, Robert Frost, and Bette Davis.

Costs

Tuition for 2014–15 was $45,686, estimated room and board costs were $14,030, and University and college fees are $978. These costs are exclusive of books, supplies, transportation, and personal expenses.

Financial Assistance

Boston University helps students realize their dreams with several different kinds of financial aid: BU scholarships, federal and state grants, federal loans, federal work-study awards, and financing and payment plan options. Financial aid is offered on the basis of calculated financial eligibility, and two or more types of aid are often combined in award packages. Approximately 78 percent of students who apply for aid and enroll at BU receive assistance. Students must submit the FAFSA and the CSS PROFILE by established deadlines to be considered. In addition, the Trustee Scholarship (full tuition) and the Presidential Scholarship ($20,000) are offered to the highest achieving students who apply for admission.

The University makes every effort to assist students with calculated financial eligibility, however funds are limited. All applicants who anticipate the need for financial aid are encouraged to apply.

Faculty

Seventy-eight percent of BU faculty members have a Ph.D. or equivalent and include Nobel Prize winners, Guggenheim scholars, Emmy Award winners, and Sloan Research Fellows. In addition to fulfilling their classroom responsibilities, faculty members are accessible as academic and career advisers who assist students in obtaining internships as well research opportunities.

Admission Requirements

The Board of Admissions considers each candidate individually. Primary emphasis is placed on the strength of the secondary school record, but required test scores, character, breadth of interest, school recommendations, and other personal qualifications are also carefully evaluated. Students are required to submit the SAT or the ACT (with writing). SAT Subject Tests are recommended, but not required, for students submitting the SAT. A full listing of the standardized testing requirements can be found in the requirements and standards chart at www.bu.edu/admissions/apply/freshman/program-requirements. Secondary school graduation or an equivalency diploma is required of all candidates; for the College of Fine Arts a prescreening, audition, or a portfolio may be required, depending on the program of interest. For certain programs, interviews and SAT Subject Test scores are required. Boston University offers programs of early decision (binding agreement), early admission, and deferred admission.

Transfer applicants are considered for September or January admission. Transfer students are not eligible for admission to the accelerated liberal arts medical or dental programs or the six-year, combined Bachelor of Science in Health Studies/Doctor of Physical Therapy and Bachelor of Science in Athletic Training/Doctor in Physical Therapy programs. January admission to the College of Fine Arts School of Theatre is also not available to transfer students.

Boston University admits qualified students to all its programs and activities regardless of their race, color, national origin, religion, sex, age, or disability.

Application and Information

Boston University requires the Common Application. Information on applying is available online at www.bu.edu/admissions/apply. The deadline for regular decision applications is January 1. Applicants for early decision must apply by November 1. Accelerated medical and dental program applications are due November 15. The deadline for the Trustee Scholarship (full tuition) and the Presidential Scholarship ($20,000) is December 1. Students must submit the College Scholarship Service (CSS) Financial Aid PROFILE and the Free Application for Federal Student Aid (FAFSA) between January 1 and February 15.

Transfer students applying for September admission should submit their applications, CSS PROFILE and FAFSA forms by March 1 or by November 1 for January admission.

Boston University Admissions
233 Bay State Road
Boston, Massachusetts 02215
Phone: 617-353-2300
E-mail: admissions@bu.edu
Website: http://www.bu.edu/admissions
http://www.facebook.com/BUadmissions
https://twitter.com/ApplyToBU

Students at Boston University find that nothing separates them from Boston's world-class museums, vibrant culture, legendary sports teams, rich history, or world-renowned scientific and medical communities.

COLLEGE CLOSE-UPS

BRADLEY UNIVERSITY

PEORIA, ILLINOIS

BRADLEY UNIVERSITY

★ To read more about this school, visit http://petersons.to/bradleyuniversity

COLLEGE CLOSE-UPS

The University

Bradley University is a four-year, private, independent university in Peoria, Illinois, offering more than 100 academic programs to 5,700 students. Students enjoy extensive resources not available at most small colleges and personal attention not commonly found at large universities. In addition to the traditional liberal arts and sciences, academic programs include business, communications, education, engineering, fine and performing arts, health sciences, and technology. Bradley offers innovative and popular programs in entrepreneurship, game design, hospitality leadership, interactive media, nursing, sports communication, and physical therapy.

Located on an 85-acre campus in the heart of Peoria's historic West Bluff neighborhoods, Bradley offers a traditional, residential environment just 1 mile from downtown and 8 miles from the Peoria International Airport.

Founded in 1897 by Lydia Moss Bradley, the University has a long and distinguished tradition of academic excellence and a focus on practical skill development through internships, practicums, experiential learning, and dynamic student life. For her part in establishing this reputation, along with her many other philanthropic and humanitarian achievements, Mrs. Bradley was inducted into the National Women's Hall of Fame.

Bradley's five academic colleges and graduate school are fully accredited by the North Central Association of Colleges and Universities. Students may pursue more than 100 undergraduate academic programs. In addition, the Graduate School offers master's degrees in more than thirty areas of study. Bradley students are encouraged to take advantage of a wealth of internships, co-ops, practicums, and other real-world experiences. Bradley's retention, graduation, career outcomes, and placement rates are among the highest in the nation.

In addition to modern academic facilities, there are ten residence halls, which house first-year students as well as upperclassmen; a residential apartment complex for students with junior standing through graduate school; a student center that includes a food court, and a movie theater; two student cafeterias; and two performing arts facilities.

The new Markin Family Student Recreation Center includes four basketball courts for intramural and recreational games, a championship basketball court, a 1/8-mile running/walking track, a climbing wall, an indoor pool, a weight room, and exercise rooms.

Bradley's active cocurricular environment includes more than 240 student organizations, Greek life, a comprehensive student government system, and NCAA Division I athletic programs including baseball, basketball, cross-country, golf, soccer, and track for men and basketball, cross-country, golf, softball, tennis, track, and volleyball for women.

Location

Bradley University is located in Peoria, Illinois, a diverse metropolitan community of approximately 365,000 residents located along the Illinois River. Peoria is home to several multinational corporations, businesses, and the Downstate Medical Center of Illinois, which offer numerous internships and opportunities for practicums and cooperative education. The greater Peoria area is the largest metropolitan area in downstate Illinois. In addition, Peoria offers an abundance of fine and performing arts, cultural attractions, shopping, entertainment, and professional sports teams. Chicago, Indianapolis, and St. Louis are just 3-hour drives.

Majors and Degrees

The College of Education and Health Sciences awards bachelor's degrees in community wellness, dietetics, early childhood education, elementary education, family and consumer sciences education, general family and consumer sciences, health science (leads to Bradley's doctoral degree in physical therapy and other health professions), hospitality leadership, learning behavior specialist studies, nursing, retail merchandising, secondary education, and special education.

The Caterpillar College of Engineering and Technology awards the Bachelor of Science degree in civil engineering, construction, electrical engineering, electrical engineering with computer option, industrial engineering, manufacturing engineering, manufacturing engineering technology, mechanical engineering, and mechanical engineering with an energy or biomedical concentration.

The Foster College of Business awards bachelor's degrees in accounting (includes a 3-2 B.S./M.S. option), actuarial science–business, economics, entrepreneurship, finance, international business, management and leadership (with concentrations in human resource management and legal studies in business), management information systems, and marketing (a concentration in global supply chain management, professional selling, or social media marketing is available).

Bradley University's College of Liberal Arts and Sciences offers programs in actuarial science–mathematics, biochemistry, biology, cell and molecular biology, chemistry, computer information systems, computer science, criminal justice studies, economics, English, environmental science, French, history, international studies, mathematics, medical laboratory science, philosophy, physics, political science, prelaw, premedicine, psychology, religious studies, social work, sociology, and Spanish.

The Slane College of Communications and Fine Arts awards bachelor's degrees in art (with concentrations in ceramics, drawing, graphic design, painting, photography, printmaking, and sculpture), art education, art history, communication (with concentrations in advertising, journalism, organizational communication, public relations, sports communication, and television arts), interactive media (with concentrations in animation, game design and web design), music, music business, music composition, music education, music performance, theater performance, and theater production.

Students may select minor areas of study from throughout the five colleges in African-American studies, anthropology, applied ergonomics, art history, Asian studies, biology, business studies, chemistry, computer science and information systems, computer game technology, creative writing, criminal justice studies, decision analysis, economics, entrepreneurship and innovation, family and consumer science, fine arts, French, game design, German, health, history, interactive media, internal auditing, international studies, journalism, Latin American studies, leadership studies, literature, management and leadership, management information systems, manufacturing engineering, marketing, mathematics, interactive media, music, organizational communication, philosophy, physics, political science, professional selling, professional writing, quality engineering, religious studies, Russian and East European studies, social media marketing, sociology, Spanish, studio art, theater arts, Western European studies, and women's studies.

Academic Programs

Although Bradley is in session year-round, the traditional academic year consists of two semesters. All students complete a set of general education requirements that blend course work from throughout the University in order to provide each student with a well-rounded education. General education courses include English composition, speech, mathematics, Western and non-Western civilization, literature, art, philosophy, the social sciences, and physical sciences. Considerable freedom is permitted in the selection of this course work. All undergraduate programs are designed so that students can complete their degree in four years.

Bradley also offers a dynamic honors program for selected recipients of Bradley's prestigious Presidential Scholarship.

The Academic Exploration Program (AEP) allows students who are undecided about a major to receive academic advisement to assist them in declaring a major during their first year of enrollment. There are also special programs for new students who are undecided about which area of study to choose in engineering, business, or communications.

Off-Campus Programs

More than 15 percent of Bradley students take advantage of a study-abroad experience. Bradley has established formal relationships with universities around the world, and students regularly study in Austria, China, Denmark, Germany, India, Ireland, Mexico, and Spain as well as a variety of other countries. Most academic programs encourage international travel and assist students in scheduling international study.

Bradley students also enjoy collaborative learning opportunities in the city of Peoria, including laboratory research at Caterpillar, Inc.; the Downstate Medical Center of Illinois; and the USDA National Center for Agricultural Utilization Research. In addition, the Bradley men's basketball and baseball teams play in professional facilities located in downtown Peoria.

Academic Facilities

The Cullom-Davis Library supports all of the University's programs and offers extensive opportunities for print and computerized research, including online and wireless resources and a Learning Assistance Center. Inside the Caterpillar Global Communications Center, students have access to multimedia classrooms and labs, television and radio studios, video and audio editing suites, and a world-class telecommunication facility. Olin Hall of Science is home to some of the finest undergraduate laboratory facilities in the nation, while Jobst Hall includes robotic and automotive labs and a wind tunnel for engineering students. Historic facilities include Westlake Hall, Constance Hall, the Hartmann Center for the Performing Arts, Dingeldine Recital Hall, and Bradley Hall.

Costs

Tuition for the 2014–15 academic year was $30,500. Room and board for the year was $9,420. Students also pay a $344 health and activity fee. Books and supplies vary by major and year in school, but they average approximately $1,300.

Financial Aid

The Office of Financial Assistance provides many resources to assist families in managing the cost of a Bradley education. Academic scholarships, which are competitive and renewable, are divided into three categories: the Presidential Scholarship, the Dean's Scholarship, and the University Scholarship. Each of these awards is based on a comprehensive review of the student's high school academic record, standardized test scores, cocurricular involvement, letters of recommendation, and personal statement. Bradley also offers scholarships to encourage talent in the fine and performing arts, and athletic achievement. The University participates in federally sponsored aid programs, such as the Pell Grant, Work-Study, and Stafford Student Loan. In order to be considered for these sources of financial assistance, students must submit the Free Application for Federal Student Aid (FAFSA).

Faculty

Bradley University is home to nearly 350 full-time teaching faculty members. The student-faculty ratio is 12:1, and the average class size is just 21 students. Bradley University is nationally recognized for the excellence of its faculty members, who not only teach undergraduates but also are active researchers and consultants in the academic and professional disciplines.

Student Life

Bradley students are involved in more than 240 student organizations including more than 50 dedicated to student leadership and community service. Some of the most active groups on campus include the national champion speech team, fraternities, sororities, intramural and club sports, and more than 60 academic and honorary societies.

Admission Requirements

Bradley University encourages applications from qualified students of all backgrounds who feel that they can contribute to the University's diverse intellectual and social environment. Students who have demonstrated past academic achievement and show promise and aptitude for successful performance at Bradley are encouraged to apply for admission. First-time college students are considered for admission based on a review of their high school transcript, standardized test scores (ACT or SAT), cocurricular involvement, letters of recommendation, and personal statement or essay.

Transfer students in good academic standing are encouraged to apply for admission to Bradley. Transfer students must submit a completed application and official transcripts from all colleges or universities attended. Several majors include additional requirements unique to transfer students.

Application and Information

To be considered for admission, students must submit the Application for Undergraduate Admission during one of three application periods. Bradley strongly encourages students to apply as early as possible during fall of their senior year. The application-review process begins each August. Applications received prior to February 1 are given priority consideration.

An application and additional information may be submitted online or by contacting:

Office of Admissions
Bradley University
1501 West Bradley Avenue
Peoria, Illinois 61625
United States
Phone: 309-677-1000
E-mail: admissions@bradley.edu
Website: bradley.edu/admissions

For more than 100 years Bradley students have worked and learned in the classrooms of Westlake Hall, the second-oldest building on campus and, after a two-year renovation project, a state-of-the-art learning facility.

BRIAR CLIFF UNIVERSITY

SIOUX CITY, IOWA

BRIAR CLIFF university
the catholic franciscan learning place

The University

Nurturing personal growth and professional promise—that's the goal of Briar Cliff University. Perched on a hilltop in Northwest Iowa, Briar Cliff University (BCU) is a private Catholic Franciscan learning place rooted firmly in the liberal arts and sciences, welcoming students of all faiths. In addition to offering top-quality academics, the University believes the best education shapes more than students' résumés; it also shapes their character.

At Briar Cliff, it's all about the students. Education is more than academics—a Briar Cliff education focuses on the whole student: mind, body, and spirit. Part of the University's mission is to provide a values-based experience that teaches students personal integrity, service, and social responsibility. BCU's core values are integrated in its culture and make a difference in students' lives at Briar Cliff University and beyond. While at BCU, students exceed their own expectations, becoming leaders and doers. Young men and women of diverse talents and interests share a common commitment to serve those in need.

Briar Cliff University is ranked among the 2015 America's Best Regional Colleges by *U.S. News & World Report.* Home to more than 1,100 students from 38 states and 13 countries, BCU provides a powerful sense of community, where the dignity of every individual is recognized. The focus of Briar Cliff's entire faculty and staff is on the students—even the University's president knows students by name. This exceptional student service sets Briar Cliff University and its graduates apart.

At Briar Cliff, freshmen are integrated into the University's social atmosphere with ease. Freshmen have access to Peer Advising Leaders, qualified student leaders who assist new students as they adjust to campus life. In addition, a first-year experience curriculum, which includes living and learning communities, helps students learn in relationship to others while engaging in service projects and hands-on learning assignments.

Throughout the college experience, Briar Cliff University prepares its students to embark on successful career paths as leaders and doers in the real world. That's why the majority of BCU students find jobs in their chosen fields or advance to graduate schools within six months of commencement.

Location

When students select a college, they're choosing a second home. With approximately 120,000 area residents, Sioux City, Iowa is a great place to call home. Sioux City is a larger community with a small-town atmosphere. Students also appreciate the city's low crime rate, moderate cost of living, and the region's Midwestern hospitality.

Find a Sense of Belonging: In this safe home away from home, Briar Cliff offers students the opportunity to shape their own world on the 70-acre hilltop university campus. Students of Briar Cliff literally have a view from the top, so from where students sit, the future looks bright. Surrounded by friends who become an extension of family, Briar Cliff creates a sense of community. Students also have access to newly renovated learning facilities, apartment-style living, high-tech science labs, and state-of-the-art classrooms.

Academic Programs

At Briar Cliff, students experience a liberal arts education that prepares them for real life. A mix of classes ranging from science and math to history and communication gives students a foundation of skills necessary for the real world, while also helping them discover the right degree path. Over 30 areas of study are offered so students can pursue their unique passion. Graduate programs are also available in nursing, business, health care, human resource management, and behavioral analysis.

Off-Campus Programs and Internships

Through a wide variety of internships locally, regionally, in the U.S., and abroad, Briar Cliff students apply classroom learning to real-work situations. The region offers a wealth of internships and employment opportunities with nature centers, insurance companies, hospitals, clinics, semi-pro sports teams, the court system, law enforcement agencies, forensics, social service agencies, news media, accounting firms, banking institutions, and athletic training facilities. Many students also have internships in their hometowns.

Academic Facilities

Briar Cliff has transformed the student experience with the completion of a more than $11-million renovation and construction project for the University's main academic center, Heelan Hall. As a result, students enjoy new inviting spaces on campus, conducive to learning and gathering. This includes new classrooms equipped with the latest digital technology; state-of-the-art nursing, biology, and chemistry laboratories; a state-of-the-art cadaver lab; lab prep rooms; and a multimedia lab in a sophisticated mass communications suite. With the Java City™ Coffee Shop and the installation of energy-efficient geothermal heating and cooling system for the entire facility, students experience an inspiring atmosphere to study and gather with other students.

With several new labs, Briar Cliff's biology and chemistry departments offer abundant opportunities for research and experimentation. The Heelan Hall addition expanded the nursing simulation labs and classrooms for enhanced learning. Briar Cliff's cadaver lab has doubled in size, allowing more students to take part in this valuable learning experience.

The Bishop Mueller Library offers access to over 350,000 print and electronic resources. Most of these materials are available for users on and off campus. The library is designed with collaboration in mind. A computer lab, study rooms, and comfortable casual seating are readily available. Wireless

Internet campuswide makes library resources accessible anywhere on campus. The library also has laptops, iPads, and other digital media for checkout by anyone with a Briar Cliff University ID.

Costs

Briar Cliff's full-time tuition for the 2015–16 academic year is $27,010.

Financial Aid

A degree at Briar Cliff can be made very affordable. At Briar Cliff, 100 percent of full-time, undergraduate students receive financial assistance, in the form of scholarships, grants, and state and federal aid. On average, a student receives $60,000 in scholarships over four years.

The University understands the financial needs of families and works with them to provide significant scholarships and financial assistance with college tuition, including the following: Presidential Scholarships (full tuition), Academic Achievement Scholarships, Fine Arts Scholarships, Athletic Scholarships, Transfer Scholarships, Connection Scholarships, Iowa Tuition Grants, Federal Pell Grants, Federal Perkins Loans, Federal SEOG Grants, Federal Direct Loans, Federal Work-Study awards, Federal PLUS Loans, and need-based grants. To receive scholarships and grants, students must fill out the FAFSA. The Briar Cliff FAFSA code is 001846. Additional information regarding scholarship awards and other financial aid is available online at www.briarcliff.edu.

Faculty

Briar Cliff offers an average student-to-faculty ratio of 12 to 1. This means professors can focus on the specific needs of each student. Experts in their fields, Briar Cliff professors conduct research, publish articles, maintain strong professional networks, and hold degrees from the nation's finest institutions.

Student Activities

Campus life is rich with a wide variety of competitive sports, social activities, cultural events, international travel, spiritual growth, service-learning, and mission experiences. At Briar Cliff, a majority of full-time students participate in at least one of over 30 co-curricular activities. In addition, BCU has 18 men's and women's intercollegiate athletic teams with a strong history of excellence in intercollegiate sports. Varsity student-athletes enjoy NAIA action in the highly competitive Great Plains Athletic Conference (GPAC).

The arts are also a big draw at Briar Cliff University. BCU's choirs are acclaimed regionally, nationally, and internationally and perform a wide variety of choral literature that embraces all genres. Many Briar Cliff students also participate in the creation of BCU's award-winning literary magazine, *The Briar Cliff Review*. Widely acclaimed for its literary and artistic content, *The Briar Cliff Review* has published the works of thousands of writers and artists from the United States and around the world.

Admission Requirements

Students applying to Briar Cliff University should have graduated from an accredited high school with 16 units of high school work, including English, natural sciences, foreign language, social studies, and mathematics. The requirements can be found in the course catalog under Academics at www.briarcliff.edu.

Applicants should also have satisfactory scores on the American College Test (ACT) or Scholastic Aptitude Test (SAT). This requirement is waived if the student has been out of high school for five years or more. Full-time students whose test scores or GPA are below standard requirements may request a review. These students may be asked to submit letters of recommendation.

Information for international students is available at www.briarcliff.edu under Admissions.

Application and Information

Briar Cliff University's application and additional information about degree programs, scholarships, and student life are available at www.briarcliff.edu.

For additional information, students should contact:

Office of Admissions
Briar Cliff University
3303 Rebecca Street
Sioux City, Iowa 51104
United States
Phone: 712-279-5200
800-662-3303 (toll-free)
Fax: 712-279-1632
E-mail: admissions@briarcliff.edu
Website: http://www.briarcliff.edu

Focused on the personal and professional goals of its students, a Briar Cliff University education prepares students for the global future. A majority of Briar Cliff graduates are accepted at first-rate graduate schools or start careers in their fields upon graduation.

COLLEGE CLOSE-UPS

BRYN MAWR COLLEGE

BRYN MAWR, PENNSYLVANIA

★ To read more about this school, visit http://petersons.to/brynmawrcollege

BRYN MAWR COLLEGE

The College

Every year 1,300 undergraduate women and 400 graduate students from around the world gather on Bryn Mawr College's historic campus to study with leading scholars, conduct advanced research, and expand the boundaries of what's possible.

The undergraduate college is known as one of the most academically rigorous liberal-arts colleges in the nation and consistently ranks among the top feeder schools to the world's premier graduate programs and professional schools.

Bryn Mawr's, Leadership, Innovation and Liberal Arts Center (LILAC), Office of Civic Engagement, and the Praxis Program, which integrates fieldwork with theoretical study, provide students with extensive opportunities for internships in nearby Philadelphia and beyond, where they may apply their knowledge outside the classroom. Many students pursue independent and interdepartmental majors with faculty permission. Joint academic programs also exist with Haverford, Swarthmore, and the University of Pennsylvania.

Through advanced research projects, summer internships, and collaborative research with faculty members, students are involved in the local, national, and global communities.

Bryn Mawr offers a unique interdisciplinary experience, 360°, in which a cohort of students takes several courses together to engage multiple aspects of a topic or theme, giving students an opportunity to investigate thoroughly and thoughtfully a multitude of perspectives. Typical 360°s focus on the history, economic concerns, cultural intersections, and political impact of an era, decision, event, policy, or important scientific innovation. 360° participants hone their arguments and insights through writing and research, develop strategies for teamwork that push the limits of their talents and creativity, and work with professors and scholars to promote big-picture thinking.

Bryn Mawr's prestigious alumnae include the first woman to be president of Harvard University, one of the first women to receive the Nobel Peace Prize, the first woman neurosurgeon, and the first and only woman to receive four Academy Awards.

Diversity is central to Bryn Mawr's mission as an extraordinary liberal-arts college, improving the academic experience and enriching the campus community. Students of color and international students make up nearly 56 percent of the undergraduate enrollment. Bryn Mawr's student body is composed of women from forty-two states and fifty-seven other countries.

Above all else, Bryn Mawr women share a tremendous respect for individual differences, not merely a passive tolerance of other lifestyles and points of view. The result is a community that resounds with the energy, healthy friction, and range of perspectives that can only come from true cultural and ideological diversity.

The diversity that Bryn Mawr students experience, in and out of the classroom, helps prepare them to be confident global citizens and leaders.

Bryn Mawr women share a commitment to a community that is based on inclusion and support, reinforced by the College's Honor Code, a set of principles stressing personal integrity and mutual respect. In the words of one graduating senior, "This is a place where being yourself makes you feel part of something larger than yourself. A strong sense of self is what we all have in common."

Bryn Mawr is a charter member of the Centennial Conference and is home to twelve NCAA varsity athletic teams. Students may compete in badminton, basketball, crew, cross-country, field hockey, lacrosse, soccer, swimming, tennis, indoor track and field, outdoor track and field, and volleyball. The Bern Schwartz Fitness and Athletic Center offers enhanced spaces for training, fitness, and aquatics.

The recently renovated Goodhart Hall serves as a hub for the College's performing arts scene and boasts a theater for 500+, a teaching theater, scene shop, music rooms, and several performance spaces. Other performance spaces include the Pembroke Dance Studio and the Denbigh Studio.

Bryn Mawr students participate in more than 100 active student organizations. The tricollege community of Haverford, Swarthmore, and Bryn Mawr also sponsors many student groups and activities.

Location

Students at Bryn Mawr have the best of it all in terms of location. The campus itself is such a picture-perfect example of Collegiate Gothic that it has been used as the backdrop for many motion pictures. A quick 5-minute walk into the suburban town of Bryn Mawr finds an eclectic mix of funky independent and favorite franchise coffee shops, eateries, and retailers; an historic movie theater; and a commuter train that can take students to the heart of Philadelphia in less than 20 minutes.

Philadelphia has a bustling arts scene and nightlife and is home to more than 250,000 college students. Bryn Mawr women enjoy a rich academic and social life on their own campus and at neighboring tricollege partners, Haverford and Swarthmore Colleges, as well as the University of Pennsylvania.

Bryn Mawr's relationship with Haverford College is particularly close and students participate in many bicollege extracurricular activities, including the orchestra, the chorus, the drama program, and a bicollege newspaper. A 20-minute walk or a 5-minute ride on the bicollege Blue Bus brings students from one campus to the other.

Almost all students live on campus in one of thirteen main residence halls. Two of the buildings are listed on the National Register of Historic Places, and one is also a National Historic Landmark.

Majors and Degrees

Bryn Mawr College grants the Bachelor of Arts (A.B.) degree with majors, minors, and concentrations in more than forty areas: Africana studies; anthropology; astronomy; biochemistry; biology; chemistry; child and family studies; Chinese; classical and Near Eastern archaeology; classical culture and society; classical languages; comparative literature; computational methods; computer science; creative writing; dance; East Asian languages and cultures; economics; education; English; environmental studies; film studies; fine arts; French and Francophone studies; gender and sexuality; geoarchaeology; geology; German and German studies; Greek; growth and structure of cities; Hebrew and Judaic studies; health studies; history; history of art; international studies; Italian studies; Japanese; Latin; Latin American; Latino and Iberian people and cultures; linguistics; mathematics; Middle East studies; music; neurosciences; peace, conflict, and social justice studies; philosophy; physics; political science; psychology; religion; Romance languages; Russian; sociology; Spanish; and theater studies. In consultation with faculty and academic advisers, students may apply to the following partnership degree programs: a 3-2 engineering degree through the California Institute of Technology; a 4+1 engineering degree via the University of Pennsylvania; or a 3-2 City and Regional Planning degree, also from the University of Pennsylvania.

There are nearly 3,000 course exchanges between Bryn Mawr and Haverford each year, selected from a jointly published course list. Bryn Mawr students may major in any of Haverford's coordinate departments or in astronomy, classics, fine arts, music, or religion while earning a Bachelor of Arts degree from Bryn Mawr. Students may also apply to obtain their master's through the combined A.B./M.A. program in chemistry, classical and Near Eastern archaeology, French, Greek studies, Latin language and Roman studies, classical studies, history of art, mathematics, and physics.

Academic Programs

The Bryn Mawr curriculum is designed to encourage breadth of learning and training in the fundamentals of scholarship. At some point during their first three years at Bryn Mawr, students are required to complete Approaches to Inquiry, a curriculum designed to introduce possibilities and problems in scientific investigation, critical interpretation, cross-cultural analysis, and inquiry into the past. Many options are available to fulfill these requirements and students are encouraged to explore. Innovative curricular options include the growth and structure of cities program; the Middle East Studies program; 360°; and Focus Courses, which are demanding, half-semester courses that may ignite a new intellectual passion. Mature, sophisticated, in-depth study in a major program during the last two years is designed to prepare students for the lifelong pleasure and responsibility of educating themselves and playing an active role in contemporary society. The curriculum encourages independence within a rigorous but flexible framework. Each student chooses and plans her major in consultation with her dean and faculty adviser. Some students take advantage of this freedom to design an independent major, while others fashion their own intellectual perspectives by enrolling in courses that span academic fields or assisting with a faculty member's research project.

With certain restrictions, full-time Bryn Mawr students may also take courses at Swarthmore College, the University of Pennsylvania, and Villanova University during the academic year without paying additional fees.

Off-Campus Programs

Bryn Mawr is only 20 minutes by car or seven short stops by train from the vast cultural and professional resources of Philadelphia, the nation's sixth-largest city. Philadelphia is an incredible resource for Bryn Mawr—a truly accessible city, rich with cultural and professional opportunities, including the Philadelphia Museum of Art, the Philadelphia Orchestra, the Pennsylvania Ballet, numerous theaters, professional sports teams, and some of the nation's most important historic sites. Students may also take advantage of internship opportunities in Center City law firms, art galleries, government agencies, hospitals, TV studios, banks, and schools. When Philadelphia seems too small, 1 in 3 Bryn Mawr students take advantage of one of Bryn Mawr's many study-abroad options.

Academic Facilities

Bryn Mawr ranks among the top 15 of all U.S. colleges and universities in the percentage of female graduates going on to earn a Ph.D. Bryn Mawr students have unlimited access to libraries and laboratories equal to those of many graduate programs, allowing students to pursue independent research at a level unavailable at most undergraduate institutions. These resources include an extensive array of laboratory equipment for the study of science, such as a robotics lab, laser with rangefinder, DNA analyzers, and a geological subsurface profiling system. More than 1 million volumes in a network of open-stack libraries are available to Bryn Mawr students, as well as access to the libraries of both Haverford and Swarthmore Colleges via the Tripod Library System.

In addition, the College has recently enhanced several of its buildings to support student inquiry in all of the liberal arts, including a $19-million renovation of the Marjorie Goodhart Theater which consists of a new state-of-the-art theater, practice rooms, a teaching theater, and scene shop; the upgrade of Dalton Hall, home to Bryn Mawr's social science labs and classrooms; and Bettws-y-Coed, a center for the study of psychology complete with new labs, faculty offices, and meeting rooms. Four former faculty residences have also been renovated to house the student activities village, Cambrian Row.

Costs

In 2015–16, Bryn Mawr tuition, room and board, and fees total $61,990.

Financial Aid

To apply for financial aid, students must submit the Free Application for Federal Student Aid (FAFSA), the College Scholarship Service (CSS) PROFILE form, and if applicable, the CSS Noncustodial Parent PROFILE. The College also requires a signed copy of the custodial and noncustodial parents' and student's most recent federal income tax returns, including W-2 forms, and all schedules and attachments. Tax returns must be submitted to The College Board's Institutional Documentation Service (IDOC). Applicants who are not citizens of the U.S. may file the (CSS) PROFILE or may instead submit the International Student Financial Aid Application directly to the Financial Aid Office. Non–U.S. citizens must also submit letters (in English) from their parents' employers stating gross income and the value of any perquisites, subsidies, and benefits directly to the Financial Aid Office. Prospective freshmen are notified of admission and financial aid decisions simultaneously.

Faculty

The Bryn Mawr faculty has 149 full-time members, of whom 53 percent are women and 18 percent are professors of color. The College's student-faculty ratio is 8:1. Few colleges or universities can genuinely claim the intellectual curiosity, intensity, and passion found at Bryn Mawr. Classes are small (many have fewer than 15 students), and faculty members come to know their students as individuals. That means more than just being on a first-name basis. In fact, Bryn Mawr faculty members, world-renowned leaders in their fields, regard their students as junior colleagues, fully capable of working at a high level, developing their own ideas, and making important contributions. It is in this way that, perhaps more than at any other school, Bryn Mawr feels like a graduate school on an undergraduate level.

Student Government

Bryn Mawr's culture of innovative leadership dates back to 1892 and the founding of the Student Self-Government Association (SGA), the oldest undergraduate governing body in the country. SGA gives Bryn Mawr students the responsibility of running many campus organizations and activities and participating in discussions and resolutions of important issues, such as curriculum and faculty appointments.

Admission Requirements

Every year, Bryn Mawr receives many more outstanding applications for admission than can be admitted into the first-year class of about 360 students. As members of the Common Application, Bryn Mawr practices holistic review, with admission decisions based on a number of factors. Strength of the applicant's high school curriculum within the context of the high school and academic performance are of significant importance. Other factors considered are a student's writing, recommendations from the high school counselor and academic teachers, test scores (optional), involvement in school and community, and diverse or unique perspectives and talents a student might bring to the Bryn Mawr community.

Basic high school academic requirements include 4 years of English, 3 years of mathematics, at least 1 year each of a laboratory science and history, and a solid foundation in at least one foreign language. However, most applicants are well prepared for the academic rigor of Bryn Mawr and have taken at least three lab science courses as well as mathematics courses that include trigonometry. Standardized test scores for U.S. applicants or U.S. permanent residents are not required. Non-U.S. citizens and non-U.S. permanent residents are required to submit standardized test scores (SAT I or ACT) as well as either the TOEFL or IELTS if their primary language is not English and/or their language of instruction over the past four years has not been English. Complete details may be found on the Bryn Mawr website.

An interview, either at the College or with a local alumnae representative, is also strongly recommended.

Bryn Mawr exclusively accepts the Common Application and waives the $50 application fee when students apply online. Application forms should be submitted by November 15 for fall early decision applicants, by January 1 for winter early decision applicants, and by January 15 for regular decision applicants.

Transfer students must complete a minimum of two years of work at Bryn Mawr to qualify for the A.B. degree.

Application and Information

The Office of Admissions is open from 9 a.m. to 5 p.m. on weekdays and some Saturdays throughout the year. Please visit the College website http://www.brynmawr.edu/admissions to plan a visit. Bryn Mawr accepts the Common Application, which can be found online (http://www.commonapplication.org). For additional information, prospective students should contact:

Bryn Mawr College Office of Admissions
101 North Merion Avenue
Bryn Mawr, Pennsylvania 19010-2899
Phone: 610-526-5152
Fax: 610-526-7471
E-mail: admissions@brynmawr.edu
Websites: http://www.brynmawr.edu
http://www.brynmawr.edu/admissions/
http://www.facebook.com/BrynMawrCollege
http://twitter.com/BrynMawrCollege

CALIFORNIA INSTITUTE OF THE ARTS

CalArts

VALENCIA, CALIFORNIA

The Institute

CalArts educates professional artists in a unique learning environment founded on the principles of art-making excellence, experimentation, critical reflection, and independent inquiry. Throughout its history, CalArts has sought to advance the practice of art and promote its understanding in a broad social, cultural, and historical context. CalArts offers students the knowledge and expertise of leading professional artists and scholars and a full complement of art-making tools. In return, it asks for the highest artistic and academic achievement. Reflecting its longstanding commitment to new forms and expressions in art, CalArts invites creative risk-taking and urges active collaboration and exchange among artists, artistic disciplines, and cultural traditions.

CalArts is the first higher educational institution in the United States to offer undergraduate and graduate degrees in both visual and performing arts. It was established in 1961 by Walt and Roy Disney through the merger of two professional schools, the Los Angeles Conservatory of Music and the Chouinard Art Institute.

Since its founding, CalArts has been recognized internationally as a leader in every discipline in which it provides instruction. Its artists and alumni have defined, and continue to extend, the very forefront of creative practice.

The total enrollment of the Institute is approximately 1,489 men and women, of whom 982 are undergraduates. The student body is gender balanced and geographically diverse, with students hailing from fifty states and thirty-one different countries.

Location

Thirty miles north of downtown Los Angeles, CalArts occupies 60 acres on hills overlooking the city of Santa Clarita. Rapid development in this peaceful suburban area has resulted in new residential communities and an ever-increasing population of more than 150,000. Los Angeles, the second-largest city in the United States and an important international hub for the arts, offers a vast array of professional and cultural resources.

Majors and Degrees

California Institute of the Arts grants the Bachelor of Fine Arts (B.F.A.) degree in art, dance, film/video, music, and theater. At the graduate level, the Institute grants the Master of Fine Arts (M.F.A.) degree in art, dance, film/video, theater, and creative writing and the Master of Arts (M.A.) degree in aesthetics and politics, and a Doctor of Musical Arts (D.M.A.) degree in performer-composer. Graduate programs take one, two, or three years to complete, depending on the individual program. Certificates and advanced certificates are also offered.

Academic Programs

Students must apply to and enroll in a specific program within a particular school. A modified, nontraditional grading system is utilized, with each school's curriculum being determined by the specific demands of the discipline. Instruction proceeds according to the student's preparation and need, with the student receiving guidance from a faculty mentor.

Undergraduate programs take four years or eight semesters and a minimum of 120 semester units to complete. All undergraduate students must fulfill the Critical Studies Requirements (40 percent of the total curriculum), which include courses in the humanities, social sciences, cultural studies, and natural sciences. These courses are intended to inform and influence each student's artistic practice.

Academic Facilities

Open 24 hours a day, the campus houses classrooms, art studios, animation studios, rehearsal rooms, and dance studios; galleries; theaters for drama, dance, and film; a music performance hall; costume, scenery, and machine shops; photo labs; computer and media labs; editing suites for film and video; and digital recording studios.

CalArts students also take advantage of a variety of special initiatives designed to respond to the realities of the social and cultural world today. These range from the Community Arts Partnership (CAP), which offers students a chance to teach in community and public school settings, to the Cotsen Center for Puppetry and the Arts, which allows students to explore the potential of puppetry in their art-making, and from the groundbreaking Center for New Performance, the professional wing of CalArts' Schools of Performance where students and faculty members collaborate on professionally presented performances, to the Institute's contemporary art journal *Afterall,* copublished with London's Central Saint Martins College of Art and Design, and the literary magazine *Black Clock,* published in association with CalArts' M.F.A. Writing Program.

The most momentous of these initiatives is the Roy and Edna Disney/CalArts Theater, or REDCAT, part of the Walt Disney Concert Hall complex in downtown Los Angeles. Designed by Frank Gehry, REDCAT includes a state-of-the-art, flexible performance space, a 3,000-square-foot gallery, and a café. REDCAT plays host to interesting new experimental theater, dance, music, art, film and video, and literature from Southern California, the nation, and the world. In the process, CalArts brings new resources to its students' education through performances, master classes, and residencies by visiting artists and helps its students make a seamless transition into the local, national, and international arts communities.

The library contains a collection designed especially for the visual and performing arts. In addition to holding more than 95,000 volumes, the library includes musical scores, sound recordings, films, videotapes, and slides that enable students to progress on their own in obtaining knowledge relevant to their specific studies.

Costs

Tuition for the 2015–16 academic year is $43,400 for full-time enrollment. Residence hall charges range from $6,100 to $8,900 per year, and meals are estimated at $4,500. The cost of books and supplies varies according to major.

Financial Aid

The Office of Financial Aid at CalArts is dedicated to helping students manage the cost of attendance at the Institute. Funds made available through the Office of Financial Aid are awarded on a combination of need and artistic merit. Need is determined by completing and submitting the FAFSA (Free Application for Federal Student Aid) and a CSS/Financial Aid PROFILE. To be considered for both merit- and need-based awards, applicants must complete both the FAFSA and a CSS PROFILE. Additional information on CalArts financial aid is available online at http://calarts.edu/financial-aid/prospective-students.

CalArts offers the following financial aid programs: Institute scholarships and grants, Federal Pell Grants, Federal Supplemental Educational Opportunity Grants, Federal Work-Study Program awards, Federal Perkins Loans, Federal Direct Loans, and Cal Grants. Details of these financial aid programs are available from the Financial Aid Office.

Faculty

The faculty numbers approximately 300, including both full- and part-time members. The student-faculty ratio is approximately 8:1. Faculty members maintain active, often prolific, careers in their respective disciplines. Their approach to teaching combines rigorous instruction with careful guidance and individualized attention, a process that empowers students to define their own artistic objectives. Every student works closely with an assigned faculty mentor.

Student Government

Student government is conducted through the Student Council, whose members are elected by the student body. In addition, students are active participants in a variety of Institute-wide standing committees, the composition of which also includes a Board of Trustees, faculty members, and staff members.

Admission Requirements

CalArts welcomes application for admission from any individual engaged in the visual and performing arts. The main criterion for admission is artistic merit, as assessed by the faculty of the individual programs. An artist statement, letters of recommendation, and school transcripts are also required.

Application and Information

For application forms and additional information, prospective students should visit http://calarts.edu/admissions or contact:

Office of Admissions
California Institute of the Arts
24700 McBean Parkway
Valencia, California 91355
Phone: 661-255-1050
E-mail: admissions@calarts.edu
Website: http://www.calarts.edu

The 60-acre campus of CalArts. 30 miles north of Los Angeles, overlooks the city of Santa Clarita.

CARLOW UNIVERSITY
PITTSBURGH, PENNSYLVANIA

CARLOW UNIVERSITY

The University

Founded in 1929, Carlow University is a coeducational, private, Catholic, master's comprehensive university looking for young women and men who are committed to making the world a better place for themselves and others.

Listed among the Top 20 Best Bang-for-the-Buck private colleges by *Washington Monthly,* and ranked in the Top 100 by Educate to Career for preparing students to find well-paying jobs in their fields after graduation, Carlow provides students with more than just an education. At Carlow, teachers become mentors, classmates become friends, and friends become family. And when it's time to leave, students are career-ready, prepared not just for a career when they graduate, but for opportunities that don't even exist yet. Carlow provides and helps students build connections—through alumni, faculty, internships, and programs—that will last a lifetime.

Carlow works hard to foster the intellectual and emotional growth of students both inside and outside the classroom. To make all of this possible, the University invests in small classes, passionate teachers, and a supportive learning environment that allows for flexibility and self-discovery—because knowledge is gained not only through formal instruction but also through experience, collaboration, conversation, and reflection.

Outside the classroom environment, students have the opportunity to explore a wide range of internship opportunities available in Pittsburgh's corporate community, its many health care institutions, nonprofit organizations, and an abundance of arts organizations.

Current enrollment exceeds 2,300 students. Carlow's students have various backgrounds and come mainly from the Middle Atlantic states; the majority are from Western Pennsylvania.

Career planning begins during New Student Orientation—each student is encouraged (with careful guidance from the Career Development Office) to develop a four-year plan that includes internships and other professional experiences that will lead to employment or placement in graduate school.

Other support services for students include: free professional and peer tutoring; workshops on handling stress, time management, research, writing, and more; disabilities services; a student health and wellness center with health-care services and personal counseling programs; and an active campus ministry.

Cocurricular organizations at Carlow include the Student Government Association, the Campus Activities Board, the Commuter Student Association, the *Carlow Chronicle* newspaper, Black Student Union, Gay Straight Alliance, and many others.

Carlow students can take volunteerism to a new level, exercise their civic responsibility, and increase their understanding of social issues and problems by working on various service-learning projects, a unique feature of a Carlow education. Each year, hundreds of Carlow students participate in Alternative Spring Break to take part in service projects. Past projects have taken students to Jamaica, the Virgin Islands, Arizona, Arkansas, Texas, Ireland, and many other locations.

Academic- or career-oriented organizations include Alpha Phi Omega (national service/honor society), American Chemical Society, Beta Beta Beta (biology club), Business Leaders of Carlow, Kappa Delta Epsilon (for education majors), Social Work Organization, Women in Communication (WIC), Student Nurses Association of Pennsylvania, Psi Chi (international psychology honor society), and the Psychology Club.

Special-interest groups at Carlow include the Carlow Mercy Leaders; Student Promotion and Recruitment Team (S.P.iR.iT.); Dance Division; Student Athlete Association; Strong Women, Strong Girls; Theater Group; Blessed, the Gospel choir; social sororities and fraternities; and many more.

Carlow sponsors eight intercollegiate teams: men's and women's basketball and cross-country and women's soccer, softball, tennis, and volleyball. Carlow is affiliated with the National Association of Intercollegiate Athletics (NAIA) and the United States Collegiate Athletics Association (USCAA), which provides opportunities for postseason competition and national recognition for athletic and academic achievements. The Carlow Celtic athletic teams consistently rank in the nation's top 25 for outstanding grade point averages, and have had continued success on the field, as well. Carlow also offers a number of club-level sports.

In addition to organized athletics, the University offers a selection of physical education courses, including aerobics, fitness and weight control, martial arts/self-defense, modern dance, water aerobics, weight training, and yoga. Wellness and fitness services at Carlow include two fitness centers, individual health assessment, fitness programming, and nutrition counseling.

Popular campus events include an annual fashion show benefiting Big Brothers Big Sisters of Greater Pittsburgh; live entertainment; film screenings; carnivals; poetry readings; art shows; tailgating before athletic events; trips to local attractions such as malls, ski resorts, amusement parks, etc.; Mercy Founders Fortnight; a St. Patrick's Day celebration and parade; Black History Month events; Women's History Month events; and theater productions.

Carlow University is situated is on a small hilltop just overlooking downtown Pittsburgh. The private, self-enclosed campus features seven tranquil gardens, a waterfall, and several art installations. The University's central location gives students opportunities for internships in various businesses and agencies. Students in health-related fields complete their clinical experiences in the many fine teaching hospitals and private health-care facilities in the city of Pittsburgh. City buses stop in front of the campus, and campus parking is available for commuting students.

Location

Carlow University is located on a 17-acre campus in the heart of Oakland, one of the nation's biggest college towns and the educational, cultural, and medical center of Pittsburgh. Nine other colleges and universities at which students can cross-register are within walking distance or just minutes away by bus. Schenley Park, Carnegie Library and Museums, Phipps Conservatory, Carnegie Music and Lecture Halls, and the Oakland shopping district are all a short walk from the campus. Downtown Pittsburgh is only a 10-minute bus ride away. Greater Pittsburgh International Airport is a 30-minute drive from the Carlow campus.

Majors and Degrees

With more than fifty undergraduate majors, Carlow offers a wide variety of programs, concentrations, and certificates that turn a spark of curiosity into real-world skills that make a difference.

Ranging from the classic (philosophy, history, English, liberal studies, art) to the practical (nursing, education, business) to the cutting-edge (biology with a concentration in autopsy specialist, forensic accounting, respiratory care), students are sure to find a specialty that suits their needs.

Carlow University grants the undergraduate degrees of Bachelor of Arts, Bachelor of Science, Bachelor of Science in Nursing, and Bachelor of Social Work. Programs include accounting, art, art/art education, art/art history, art/ceramics, art/graphic design, art/interactive media design, art/painting and drawing, art/photography, art therapy preparation, biology (with concentrations in forensic medical and legal investigations/ autopsy specialization, human biology, molecular cell and biotechnology, and organismal/ecological biology), business management, chemistry, communication and media, corporate communication, creative writing, criminal justice, early childhood education, early development and learning, English, forensic accounting, history, human resource management and technology, liberal studies, management in health services, mathematics, middle level education (with various certifications) nursing, philosophy, political science, psychology (with concentrations in counseling, human development, and crisis and trauma), social work (with concentrations in behavioral health services and crisis and trauma), sociology, special education, and theology. An independent major, designed by the student, may also be arranged.

Certification programs are offered in accounting, forensic accounting, perfusion technology (biology majors only), middle level education (English/language arts, English/language arts and mathematics, English/language arts and science, mathematics, science, science and mathematics, social studies, social studies and mathematics, and social studies and science), and autism spectrum disorders.

The University offers three dual-degree programs with Duquesne University: 3/3 J.D. law, biology/biotechnology, and biology/environmental science and management.

Students can also save time and money by working toward their graduate degree as an undergraduate student in Carlow's accelerated programs, which include: B.A./B.S. to M.B.A. business administration, B.A./B.S. to M.S. in fraud and forensics, B.A./B.S. to M.S. in professional counseling, B.A. to M.Ed. with certification in special education, and an RN-B.S.N. to M.S. in nursing.

Graduate programs include master's degrees in business, counseling, creative writing, education, fraud and forensics, and nursing, and two professional doctoral programs, the Psy.D. in counseling psychology and the D.N.P. in nursing.

Academic Programs

Carlow's primary concern is the development of the student as a lifelong learner. To this end, members of the Carlow community—students, faculty, and staff—recognize the integrity and value of each person in the daily life and work of the University. The academic programs are broad and flexible, including opportunities for double majors, minors, certificate programs, and changes of major. Transferring to Carlow is seamless, with up to 88 credits accepted from other institutions.

The University operates on the two-semester system, August to December and January to May. Summer sessions, a variable number of weeks in length, are offered every year. Most courses carry 3 credits (laboratory courses, among others, carry 4 credits). Students typically take five courses each semester. Each student must demonstrate basic competence in English composition, speech and interpersonal communication, reading comprehension, and mathematics. Required of all students is one course each in a lab science, history, literature, mathematics, social/behavioral science (such as psychology or sociology), theology, fine arts, philosophy, women's and gender studies, and political science or economics, as well as one global perspective course. Students are also required to take an interdisciplinary course, which is selected from a variety of subject areas. Students in nursing, education, social work, psychology, management, and perfusion technology are required to do fieldwork as part of their program. Field placements and internships are guaranteed and encouraged in all areas of study. An honors program is open to eligible students. After the first semester of the first year, one course per semester (outside of the major) may be taken on a pass-fail basis. Some courses may be challenged, for credit or exemption, by passing an examination. CLEP general exam credits may be used for this purpose as well.

The University gives women and men the opportunity to return to the classroom at various stages of their lives. Adult learners may enroll in full-time and part-time degree programs, noncredit enrichment courses, seminars, and workshops. Scheduling options include day, evening, accelerated, weekend, and online courses.

Academic Facilities

In fall 2015, Carlow celebrated the opening of a new University Commons building, a five-level, multipurpose learning and gathering center in the heart of the campus, complete with lounge and study areas, café, art gallery, computer labs, and an innovative multipurpose room for campus activities and events. The Commons also houses the offices of the President and Provost, the Center for Academic Achievement, the Center for Global Learning, the mailroom, the bookstore, Academic Affairs, student organization offices, the Office of Career Development, and Campus Ministry.

Grace Library, also housed inside the new University Commons, contains more than 100,000 books, subscribes to over 350 print journals, and offers access to more than 4,500 online journals.

Curran Hall houses the Nursing Department and includes a nursing simulation and skills lab, conference rooms, and seminar rooms. Frances Warde Hall is a residence hall that also houses the Education Department. Antonian Hall houses the 1,000-seat Rosemary Heyl Theatre, the College for Leadership and Social Change, the art department, and classrooms as well as administrative offices for admissions, financial aid, advising, the registrar, and student accounts.

The dining hall and The Campus School of Carlow University (preschool through grade eight) are located in Tiernan Hall. St. Joseph Hall houses the gymnasium, fitness center, and swimming pool. Aquinas Hall houses classrooms, the Humanities Department, and faculty and staff offices.

Carlow's A. J. Palumbo Hall of Science and Technology houses state-of-the-art teaching/research laboratories for physics, organic and advanced chemistry, genetics, cell biology, and gross anatomy; a cadaver laboratory; a STEM digital learning laboratory; a respiratory care laboratory and simulation center; a herbarium to store dry plant specimens; a greenhouse; and an amphitheater for scientific presentations.

Costs

Tuition for 2015–16 is $26,604 for full-time students. Room and board charges for the year are $10,572 for double occupancy.

Financial Aid

Financial aid in the form of grants, scholarships, loans, and student employment is available to eligible applicants. Many Carlow students and their families rely on financial aid to pay for their education—in fact, more than 90 percent of Carlow students receive financial assistance, including many who thought they couldn't afford to attend college. Carlow is dedicated to making education affordable and financial aid staff members are happy to help students estimate costs, determine eligibility, and navigate the financial aid process. The University expects that most aid recipients assume a portion of their expenses through loans and/or part-time employment. Job opportunities are available on campus in a wide variety of positions, and students are placed, whenever possible, in positions that coincide with their skills and interests. Basketball, soccer, softball, tennis, and volleyball scholarships are also available.

Faculty

At Carlow, classes are taught by faculty members who are not only experts in their fields, but who exhibit an ardent, deeply-rooted commitment to the practice of teaching. With a student-faculty ratio of 11:1, faculty members are readily available to help plan individualized programs of study, provide assistance relating to field placements and internships, and assist with career preparation. The student's major adviser is normally a faculty member in the department.

Student Government

All registered students are members of the Student Government Association (SGA). Through the SGA, students act as equal participants with the administration, faculty, and staff in general governance. The SGA promotes the general welfare of the students and is the advocate to ensure that the academic, social, and spiritual needs of students are met. SGA is empowered to charter all student organizations.

Admission Requirements

Applicants are evaluated on the basis of their secondary school record, class rank, and scores on the SAT or ACT. The Admissions Committee recognizes that school curricula vary greatly and always gives careful consideration to the application of an able student whose course work or grading scale is more challenging or whose preparation differs from the traditional program. Overnight visits; campus tours; and individual visit opportunities are available and interested students and families are strongly encouraged to attend. At each Admissions event, candidates can tour the campus; meet faculty, staff, and current Carlow students; and learn more about academic programs, financial aid, and the admissions process.

Application and Information

Although Carlow subscribes to the rolling admission plan, high school students are encouraged to submit an application early in the first semester of the senior year. Students interested in early notification should apply by September 30. The University's priority admission and scholarship deadline is February 15.

Students may apply online or request an application form by contacting:

Office of Admissions
Carlow University
3333 Fifth Avenue
Pittsburgh, Pennsylvania 15213
Phone: 412-578-6059
800-333-2275 (toll-free)
E-mail: admissions@carlow.edu
Website: http://www.carlow.edu

Carlow University is a small campus located in one of the largest, most vibrant college towns in the United States.

CARROLL UNIVERSITY
WAUKESHA, WISCONSIN

CARROLL UNIVERSITY

The University

Carroll University is Wisconsin's pioneer college. From 1846 forward, Carroll has been helping generations of students discover their unique place in the world.

With 2,700 undergraduate students and 80 areas of study, Carroll is large enough that students will be challenged academically, yet small enough that they don't become lost. Students know their teachers at Carroll and will have personal advisers from the day they are admitted.

The historic campus, just minutes from Milwaukee and 100 miles from Chicago, ensures a vibrant cultural scene and endless opportunities for internships, and work and clinical placements. And true to the University's heritage as pioneers, Carroll is tirelessly innovating and improving. A new $24-million Science Center is slated to open in 2016, on the heels of a multimillion-dollar renovation of the athletic field house. Three new apartment-style residence halls have also been added in the past several years.

In addition to the bachelor's degrees Carroll offers, the University also grants master's degrees in business, community health education, education, exercise physiology, graphic communication, physician assistant studies, and software engineering, as well as a clinical doctorate in physical therapy.

Location

The University is located in the city of Waukesha, a residential community of 68,000 people, just 18 miles west of Milwaukee and 100 miles north of Chicago.

Majors and Degrees

Carroll University grants the Bachelor of Arts, Bachelor of Science, Bachelor of Music Education, and Bachelor of Science in Nursing degrees. Areas of study include accounting, actuarial science, animal behavior, applied physics and engineering, art, athletic training, biochemistry, biology, book art, business administration, chemistry, communication, computational science, computer science, criminal justice, diagnostic medical sonography, education, English, environmental science, exercise science, forensic science, global studies, graphic communication, health care administration, history, information technology, journalism, marine biology, mathematics, modern languages and literatures, music, music education, nursing, organizational leadership, philosophy, politics and economics, photography, physical education, physical therapy, political science, pre-dental, pre-law, pre-medicine, pre–occupational therapy, pre–veterinary studies, professional writing, psychology, public health, public relations, radiologic technology, religious studies, self-designed major, sociology, sociology of sustainability, sport and recreation management, theatre arts, and writing.

Academic Programs

The University operates on a semester calendar. All students must complete 128 credits with a minimum 2.0 grade point average or better. A major, generally consisting of no more than 64 credits, must be completed. General education requirements include the Cultural Seminar, Writing Seminar, liberal studies distribution courses, a cross-cultural development course, a cross-cultural experience, a mathematics course, and a Global Perspectives Colloquium. B.A. students must take two years of a modern language or the equivalent. Students may also select a second major or they may select a minor, which generally requires 16 to 28 credits. The honors program offers intensive sections of courses in the arts and sciences for academically talented students.

Advanced placement credit might be granted to students who have completed the appropriate College Board Advanced Placement examinations. Credit may be granted for a score at or above the 75th percentile on the humanities, natural science, or social science general examination of the College-Level Examination Program (CLEP). Scores on CLEP subject examinations may also qualify to be approved for credit. A total of not more than 48 credit hours may be awarded through CLEP general and subject examinations.

Off-Campus Programs

Carroll believes that the world is the true classroom. Students have opportunities to enhance the awareness of their own cultural conditioning, assumptions, and perspectives by interacting with people who have backgrounds significantly different from their own.

The Cross-Cultural Experience (CCE) is at the heart of Carroll's Pioneer Core curriculum, which examines the place of culture in modern life and provides students the opportunity to experience firsthand another society, through domestic or international travel and study. In addition to semester- and year-long study abroad opportunities, Carroll students may select from a variety of courses that explore aspects of other cultures. All told, Carroll students have hundreds of cross-cultural program options available to them.

Domestic off-campus programs include the Washington Semester and the United Nations Semester. In addition, career internships are provided in the Milwaukee and Waukesha areas for students interested in gaining practical work experience in their proposed career field. All of these programs carry degree credit; the amount depends upon the nature and duration of the experience.

Academic Facilities

The University library offers a collection of books, compact disks and DVDs, and other materials, as well as electronic databases that allow Carroll students access to more than 140,000 journals. It also has the Learning Commons for free peer-led academic support services, including subject tutoring, supplemental instruction, workshops, Math Center, Writing Center, and Career Services.

Barstow Building has classes for communication and education. Rankin Hall houses the departments of biology and psychology. Chemistry and physics laboratories are in Lowry Hall. A new $24-million state-of-the-art science center is scheduled to open in 2016. Main Hall houses classrooms for all academic areas. MacAllister Hall has offices for faculty of English, history, political science, modern languages, religion, and philosophy.

Shattuck Music Center houses a recital hall that seats 150, an auditorium that seats 1,350, and a Schantz 72-stop pipe organ. The Department of Music has a large band practice room, teaching studios, a multisensing room, a computerized music laboratory, and classrooms. The Humphrey Building houses the art department and Humphrey Memorial Chapel. The University's health sciences classes are located adjacent to the University's athletic complex. A state-of-the-art nursing lab is in the lower level of Otteson Theatre. A Center for Graduate Studies is located about 3 miles east of the main campus.

Costs

For 2015–16, the annual tuition is approximately $28,825 and room and board are $9,032.

Financial Aid

Approximately 98 percent of Carroll's students receive some form of financial aid. Aid is based on need, as determined by the U.S. Department of Education's Free Application for Federal Student Aid (FAFSA), as well as on scholastic ability and achievement. Generally, students receive a package consisting of a scholarship, a grant, a loan, and/or campus employment. Carroll awarded students more than $40 million in institutional aid in the 2015–16 academic year.

Various merit scholarships are available to students. Merit scholarships range from $48,000 to $68,000 over four years and are determined by a student's ACT or SAT scores and class rank. Students who attend high schools that do not rank are not excluded from consideration for any academic scholarships. Additional scholarships are awarded to qualified students who are interested in music, theater, history, art, math, or the sciences. Students should contact the Financial Aid Office for details.

Faculty

The average class size at Carroll is 21 students. Nearly 70 percent of faculty members hold a terminal degree in their specialized area of study. There are more than 135 full-time faculty members at Carroll. The University's focus is on teaching and learning; no classes are taught by teaching assistants. Some faculty members teach at the undergraduate and graduate levels.

Student Government

Through election to the Student Senate and College Activities Board, students have responsibility for nonacademic matters affecting their lives at the University. In addition, there is voting student representation on all University committees, and there are student observers on the Board of Trustees.

Admission Requirements

Carroll's admission procedure is intended to ensure academic and personal success for accepted students. Each candidate is evaluated individually; evidence of the interest in and ability to do college-level work is important. The University exercises careful selection, but no candidate is disqualified because of race, color, religion, sex, national origin, age, disability, sexual orientation, or veteran status.

Application and Information

To be considered, each candidate for freshman admission must submit the following materials: a completed application for admission, a transcript from an accredited high school showing progress toward or completion of 15 units of work and graduation, a personal statement, a satisfactory personal evaluation from the high school, and scores on the SAT or ACT. Transfer students must submit a completed application, a transcript from every college attended previously, a personal statement, and a statement of good standing. Admission decisions are made on a rolling basis until the class is filled. There are no deadlines, but early application is recommended.

Admission to the University may be granted following the completion of three years of high school work, provided that the high school indicates that this is in the applicant's best interest. The candidate may or may not have completed the course work required for high school graduation at the time of admission, but he or she must show unusual promise and achievement.

For more information about Carroll University, prospective students should contact:

Admission Office
Carroll University
100 North East Avenue
Waukesha, Wisconsin 53186
Phone: 262-524-7220
800-CARROLL (toll-free)
E-mail: info@carrollu.edu
Web site: http://www.carrollu.edu
http://facebook.com/carroll.university (Facebook)
http://twitter.com/carrollu (Twitter)

Students seeking a friendly college and personalized education find the right fit at Carroll University. Main Hall, built in 1887, is a national historic landmark and signature building on a campus that is continually evolving and being updated.

CARSON-NEWMAN UNIVERSITY

JEFFERSON CITY, TENNESSEE

★ To read more about this school, visit http://petersons.to/carsonnewmanuniversity

The University

Carson-Newman University, a nationally ranked university founded in 1851, is where students can find their lifework and experience all that higher education can be.

This liberal arts institution integrates academic excellence with faith and learning in a life-changing and rigorous teaching environment where students come first. Carson-Newman's faculty members are scholar-mentors who imbue their students with critical thinking skills that help them reach their full potential as educated citizens and worldwide servant leaders. The University's 15:1 student-to-faculty ratio ensures a nurturing academic community in and out of the classroom, whether students are studying on campus or online.

Carson-Newman had a record total undergraduate and graduate enrollment of 2,362 in 2014–15. The University offers vast study-abroad and mission opportunities, a thriving honors program, and a nationally ranked honor society. In 2013, it created the Eagles Scholars program for all student-athletes.

The University was named the seventh-best "Baccalaureate College" in the nation in 2014 by *Washington Monthly* and is ranked by The Princeton Review as a "Best in the Southeast." Carson-Newman was also recently ranked number one in service in the nation by U.S. Department of Education. More than 95 percent of Carson-Newman's students receive financial aid, and in 2014 the University was been named a "Great School at a Great Price" and an "Up-and-Coming School" by *U.S. News & World Report*.

Carson-Newman is also a diverse campus community with students from more than 24 countries and most states. It offers students 70 campus organizations, 40 intramural sports, and 18 NCAA Division II sports.

Location

Carson-Newman offers a spectacular location in one of America's most scenic regions. It is situated nearby the Great Smoky Mountains National Park, the Oak Ridge National Laboratory and Tennessee's third-largest city, Knoxville.

Majors and Degrees

Carson-Newman offers fifty undergraduate majors and eleven graduate degree programs. The University awards Bachelor of Arts, Bachelor of Music, Bachelor of Science, and Bachelor of Science in Nursing degrees.

Majors are available in art (art, photography), business (accounting, business administration, finance economics, management, marketing), computer science, communication studies and theater (advertising/public relations, media studies, film, speech), education (athletic coaching, elementary education, physical education/health, secondary certification, special education), English (creative writing, literature), exercise science, family and consumer sciences (child and family studies, consumer services, [fashion design and merchandising], foods and nutrition, interior design, retail), early childhood education, exercise science, foreign language (biblical languages, Spanish), general studies, history, human services, mathematics, music (church music, music composition, music education, music theory, music with an outside field, piano and organ performance, vocal performance), natural and physical science (biochemistry, biology, chemistry, physics), nursing, philosophy (philosophy, philosophy/religion), political science, psychology (applied psychology, general psychology, social entrepreneurship), religion (biblical studies, leadership and ethics, ministry studies, missions, pastoral ministry, spirituality and the arts, youth and recreation ministry), R.N. to B.S.N. (online), and sociology.

Carson-Newman offers extremely strong curricula in preparation for professional and health professions. Preparatory programs are offered in dentistry, law, medicine, and physical therapy. Carson-Newman offers binary programs in pharmacy.

Carson-Newman supports a growing number of flexible undergraduate, graduate, and adult studies programs which are offered online and on campus, allowing nontraditional and adult students to create educational experiences compatible with their lives.

Academic Programs

Carson-Newman University operates on a traditional semester system. May term is a three-week intensive period of study giving students the opportunity to earn 3 credit hours. Summer terms are also offered.

All baccalaureate degrees require completion of 128 semester hours. Students must complete the Carson-Newman liberal arts core requirements and a total of 36 semester hours at the junior/senior level. Specific course requirements vary depending on major and degree program. Honors courses, independent study, and internships are available to students who qualify. Advanced credit is available for students who achieve required scores on AP exams, CLEP tests, and Carson-Newman departmental examinations.

New students are assigned a faculty adviser, who assists with course selection and student concerns. Career planning and tutoring services are also available through the Student Success Center at the Learning Commons. Carson-Newman's exceptionally high placement rate in professional programs in medicine, law, business, and theological study is a testimony to the excellence of its rigorous academic program.

Off-Campus and Study-Abroad Programs

Students can spend an entire semester abroad by participating in the London Semester and other study-abroad opportunities. Carson-Newman, along with International Enrichment, Inc., provides all academic and nonacademic support services.

The Washington Semester is available as an internship program primarily for political science and prelaw majors. Through the program, students earn credit for work in the nation's capital. Art and foreign language majors may earn credit while studying and traveling throughout Europe during the three-week May term.

Carson-Newman's film program offers students the opportunity to earn college credit while participating in internships with regional filmmakers. Through a partnership with the Los Angeles Film Studies Center, accepted students have an opportunity to live in L.A. and participate in a program that offers the chance to work and study with Hollywood filmmakers. Carson-Newman is also a sponsor of the highly-popular Knoxville Film Festival and its students have been honored in film competitions.

Academic Facilities

Carson-Newman offers the resources necessary for the enrichment of each student's education. Facilities include numerous computer labs, a campus-wide computer network, a media service center, a Digital Café, two theaters for drama production, Thomas Recital Hall, two art galleries and 23 individual art studios, the Stephens-Burnett Library, and the Maddox Student Activities Center. Recent construction projects have added two academic buildings to campus. These include Blye-Poteat Hall, home to the Department of Family and Consumer Sciences, and Ted Russell Hall, which houses the Department of Business.

Costs

The annual cost at Carson-Newman, including room, board, and tuition, is well below the national average for four-year private universities. Tuition and fees for 2014–15 were $24,460, room and board averaged $7,160, and the student activity fee was approximately $520.

Financial Aid

Carson-Newman allocates thousands of dollars each year to help supplement the resources of families. Financial aid awards are tailored to assist in meeting students' economic needs. Carson-Newman participates in all state and federal aid programs and awards aid based on demonstrated need as documented by a need analysis form, such as the Free Application for Federal Student Aid (FAFSA). Carson-Newman also awards merit academic scholarships based on achievement. The priority deadline for filing financial assistance forms is February 1. Additional information is available at cn.edu/administration/financial-assistance.

Faculty

Carson-Newman faculty members are known for their strong interaction with students both inside and outside of classes, walking alongside students during their college journey. Faculty members are also involved in scholarly pursuits such as authoring books, leading national scholastic organizations, and research.

Student Government

The Student Government Association (SGA) represents the entire student body by voicing student concerns in campus affairs. The SGA promotes the welfare of every student through justice, to protect individual rights and freedoms, to encourage high standards of conduct, and to train students in the general principles of self-government.

Admission Requirements

Carson-Newman seeks applicants who demonstrate academic preparation and who possess an appreciation of a Christian education and a liberal arts curriculum. Carson-Newman accepts applications for freshman and transfer admission for each term of enrollment (fall, spring, and summer). Prospective students can obtain additional admissions information online at cn.edu/admissions.

Application and Information

Applicants must submit all required application materials (application, official transcripts, and test scores) in order to be considered for admission. Admission decisions are made on a rolling basis, and students are notified within two weeks of receipt of all required documents.

For more information, prospective students should contact the Office of Undergraduate Admissions at 865-471-3223, admitme@cn.edu or visit cn.edu online.

Students may also follow Carson-Newman admissions on Facebook (www.facebook.com/cncollege) or Twitter (twitter.com/cneagles).

For additional information, contact:

Office of University Admissions
Carson-Newman University
Jefferson City, Tennessee 37760
Phone: 865-471-3223
800-678-9061 (toll-free)
E-mail: admitme@cn.edu
Website: http://www.cn.edu
facebook.com/CNcollege
twitter.com/cnadmissions

Operated through Carson-Newman's Communication Department, the Digital Café serves as a student development center for digital storytelling. Students are encouraged to explore innovative ways to tell multimedia stories.

CASE WESTERN RESERVE UNIVERSITY

CLEVELAND, OHIO

CASE WESTERN RESERVE EST. 1826 UNIVERSITY
think beyond the possible®

The University

Ranking consistently among the top private universities in the United States, Case Western Reserve University (CWRU) offers unlimited opportunities for motivated students. Its faculty members challenge and support students to help them flourish, and its partnerships with world-class cultural, educational, and scientific institutions ensure that undergraduate education extends beyond the classroom.

Challenging and innovative academic programs and experiential learning opportunities are at the core of the undergraduate experience. More than 4,600 undergraduates are enrolled in the University's programs in the arts, engineering, humanities, management, natural sciences, nursing, and social and behavioral sciences. Students access CWRU's graduate and professional schools in these areas as well as dental medicine, law, medicine, and social work.

Students are involved in more than 160 student organizations, including athletic, performance, religious, cultural, media, and community-service organizations. Greek life consists of eighteen fraternities and eight sororities, with approximately 35 percent of undergraduate students participating. Residence halls are coeducational, and more than 80 percent of students reside on campus.

A charter member of the University Athletic Association, an NCAA Division III conference, the Spartans have won championships in baseball, cross-country, football, softball, track and field, and wrestling. Twenty percent of undergraduates participate in varsity athletics, and 70 percent join an intramural team. Club sports include fencing, golf, ice hockey, skiing, and Ultimate (Frisbee).

Location

CWRU is located in Cleveland's University Circle, a unique cultural district comprising 550 acres of parks, gardens, museums, schools, hospitals, religious institutions, and human-service organizations. The Cleveland Museum of Art, the Cleveland Botanical Garden, the Cleveland Museum of Natural History, the Museum of Contemporary Art, and Severance Hall, home of the Cleveland Orchestra, are within walking distance; downtown Cleveland is 10 minutes away by car or public transportation. Partnerships in education and research among University Circle institutions enable students to make full use of resources beyond those of the University itself, and students receive free access to these and other local institutions.

Majors and Degrees

CWRU has a single-door admission policy—once students are admitted, they can pursue any major(s) they wish. Programs of study leading to the Bachelor of Arts degree include anthropology, art history, Asian studies, astronomy, biochemistry, biology, chemistry, chemical biology, classics, cognitive science, communication sciences, computer science, dance, economics, English, environmental geology, French, French and Francophone studies, geological sciences, German, German studies, history, history and philosophy of science, international studies, Japanese studies, mathematics, music, nutrition, nutritional biochemistry and metabolism, philosophy, physics, political science, psychology, religious studies, sociology, Spanish, statistics, theater, women's and gender studies, and world literature. The following B.A. programs are available as a second major: American studies, environmental studies, evolutionary biology, gerontological studies, natural sciences, pre-architecture, and teacher education.

Majors leading to the Bachelor of Science degrees are offered in the following fields: accountancy, aerospace engineering, applied mathematics, art education, astronomy, biochemistry, biology, biomedical engineering, chemical engineering, chemistry, civil engineering, computer engineering, computer science, electrical engineering, engineering physics, finance, geological sciences, marketing, materials science and engineering, mathematics, mathematics and physics, mechanical engineering, music education, nursing, nutrition, nutritional biochemistry and metabolism, physics, polymer science and engineering, statistics, systems and control engineering, systems biology, and an undesignated engineering major.

Minor areas of concentration are offered in most areas of major study, as well as art studio, artificial intelligence, banking and finance, business management, childhood studies, Chinese, computer gaming, creative writing, electronics, entrepreneurial studies, ethics, ethnic studies, film, health communication, Italian, Japanese, Judaic studies, leadership, mechanical design and manufacturing, public policy, Russian, social work, and sports medicine.

Students may work toward a combined B.A./B.S. degree or integrate undergraduate and graduate studies to complete both the bachelor's and master's degrees in five years or less. Students who are interested in both the liberal arts and engineering can benefit from the 3–2 Binary Program. Students spend three years at one of forty participating liberal arts colleges and then spend two years at CWRU studying engineering or a related field. Graduates of this program receive both a B.A. and a B.S. degree.

Academic Programs

Students in all majors participate in SAGES, the Seminar Approach to General Education and Scholarship program. SAGES consists of four engaging seminars that emphasize written and verbal communication skills and concludes with a senior capstone project. Through a combination of core curricula, major requirements, and minors or approved course sequences, all undergraduates receive a broad educational base as well as specialized knowledge in their chosen fields.

At Case Western Reserve University, hands-on learning comes in many forms. More than 95 percent of graduates say they took advantage of at least one of the many hands-on learning opportunities available, including:

Co-op: CWRU has one of only eleven co-op programs in the U.S. recognized by the Accreditation Council for Cooperative Education (ACCE). Students studying engineering, science, management, and accounting are eligible.

Clinicals: CWRU nursing students begin clinical placements during their first semester on campus. Upon graduation, students accrue more than 1,600 clinical hours—nearly double the national average.

Internships: Many students utilize the resources of the Career Center to help them find internships in their field of study. On-campus job fairs and employer visits also help students network and find opportunities.

Research: CWRU is among the country's leading independent research universities, ranking among the top 15 private universities receiving federal funding for research. The SOURCE (Support of Undergraduate Research and Creative Endeavors) office allows students to engage in research relevant to their academic study and provides guidance on acquiring research funding.

Service Learning: CWRU offers numerous volunteer opportunities connected to a student's academic interests. The Center for Civic Engagement and Learning connects students with community partners.

Study Abroad: CWRU offers many different types of study-abroad programs. Students have the opportunity to spend a full year or a semester in a traditional immersion arrangement or can choose from shorter-term programs.

Off-Campus Programs

More than one third of CWRU undergraduates take advantage of opportunities to have an educational experience abroad. The University offers short-term programs during winter, spring, and summer breaks, as well as more traditional semester-long study-abroad programs in several countries. Some students also choose to complete internships, research and co-ops abroad.

Academic Facilities

The Kelvin Smith Library is home to more than 1.7 million items and located in the heart of campus. Through reciprocal borrowing arrangements, CWRU students have access to the holdings of the Cleveland Public Library as well as the libraries of five University Circle institutions; the members of OhioLINK, a network that includes state colleges and universities; the State Library of Ohio; and several private institutions. CWRU is classified by the Carnegie Foundation as a university with very high research activity (RU/VH), and its lab facilities are state of the art. The University operates two astronomical observatories, a biological field station, a $6-million undergraduate engineering lab, and nearly 100 other designated research centers and laboratories, including think[box], the University invention center where budding entrepreneurs create prototypes and test new products. The University's high-speed communications network links every residence hall room with computing centers, libraries, and databases on and off campus. CWRU's wireless network is one of the largest in the country.

The University Farm, located in nearby Hunting Valley, Ohio, offers educational opportunities in natural settings. Its 389 acres encompass a variety of deciduous forests, ravines, waterfalls, meadows, ponds, and a self-contained natural watershed.

Costs

For 2014–15, tuition totalled $42,766. Room and board cost an average of $13,376. Other required fees totalled $887.

Financial Aid

Financial aid consisting of grants, loans, and work assistance is awarded on the basis of a student's need. Applicants are required to file the Free Application for Federal Student Aid (FAFSA) and the CSS/Financial Aid PROFILE. Students are automatically considered for merit-based scholarships when they apply to the University; these awards typically range from $10,000 to $30,000. Students also are encouraged to apply separately for a select number of scholarships that require applicants to audition, provide additional information, or respond to an essay prompt.

Faculty

The undergraduate student-faculty ratio at CWRU is 9:1. Ninety-five percent of credit hours are taught by faculty members, not graduate students. Each school and the College of Arts and Sciences provides advisers who are available for both academic and personal advice. Once a student has chosen a major, a member of the department in which the student is majoring acts as his or her academic adviser. Undergraduate students have several opportunities to partner with faculty members on research or special projects, allowing for valuable learning opportunities, mentoring, networking, and personal development.

Student Government

CWRU's Undergraduate Student Government represents all undergraduate students. The assembly acts as a liaison between undergraduate students and the faculty, administration, and other groups; grants recognition to undergraduate organizations; and has the responsibility and authority to allocate funds from student activity fees to student organizations. The Residence Hall Association is a governing body for on-campus living; the University Program Board plans special events; and the Interfraternity Congress and Panhellenic Council govern the Greek community.

Admission Requirements

Case Western Reserve University reviews each application for admission carefully, taking into consideration academic background, life experiences, and interests. There is no minimum test score or GPA range used to gauge a student's potential for admission. In terms of meeting academic requirements for admission, CWRU looks for students who have been successful in a variety of challenging classes. The admission staff understands that every school is different, so staff evaluates student transcripts specifically against their high school's curriculum.

Prior to high school graduation, it is recommended that students pursue 4 units of English, 3 units of math, 3 units of science (2 of which must be laboratory science), 3 units of social studies, and 2 units of foreign language. The University recommends that applicants interested in engineering and the sciences have an additional unit of math and laboratory science. For students interested in the liberal arts, it is recommended that students take an additional unit of social studies and foreign language.

The University requires an essay, submitted via the Common Application. An interview is not a required part of the admission process, but it is strongly recommended. To receive full consideration for admission and scholarships, students must take the SAT or ACT prior to their selected application deadline.

Application and Information

Application instructions and deadlines can be found at admission.case.edu/apply. First-year U.S. students must apply via the Common Application and supply an official high school transcript, school report with counselor recommendation, two teacher recommendations, and an SAT or ACT with writing score. Additional instructions for international students, transfer students, Pre-Professional Scholars program applicants, and home-schooled students can be found at admission.case.edu/apply.

Interviews with admission professionals and alumni, campus visits, group information sessions, and other resources are available to prospective students at admission.case.edu.

For more information, students should contact:

Office of Enrollment Management
Case Western Reserve University
10900 Euclid Avenue
Cleveland, Ohio 44106-7055
Phone: 216-368-4450
E-mail: admission@case.edu
Website: http://admission.case.edu
http://facebook.com/cwruadmission
http://twitter.com/cwruadmission

Aerial view of Case Western Reserve University's campus and its surroundings in Cleveland's University Circle.

COLLEGE CLOSE-UPS

CASTLETON STATE COLLEGE
CASTLETON, VERMONT

Castleton
VERMONT'S FIRST COLLEGE

The College

Since Castleton first opened its doors in 1787, it has been dedicated to providing a quality level of higher education to those eager to learn. Vermont's first college, and the eighteenth oldest in the United States, the 165-acre campus is located in Castleton, a historic Vermont village. Sixty-five percent of the 1,900 full-time undergraduate students at the College are Vermonters with the balance of the student population coming across the United States and nineteen countries, while New England and the Middle Atlantic states make up a majority of the out-of-state population.

Castleton is committed to providing an undergraduate education in which the liberal arts and career preparation complement each other. A commitment to community engagement, and experiential learning through civic-mindedness and internship has become central to the Castleton mission, providing students with a unique experience. Through an innovative program called Soundings, first-year students earn academic credit by attending a series of special events that include theater, music, dance, film, debate, and opinion from influential people. New students also participate in the First-Year Seminar, giving them the opportunity to develop the skills of a successful college student. First-year students may apply for the College's honors program.

There are eleven major residence halls which are not just dormitories, but communities where students are challenged to interact with others, learn respect and appreciation for differences, become involved in community governance, and receive support for their academic endeavors. Together, the residences accommodate nearly 1,100 students. Each residence hall room is equipped with at least two wired broadband Internet hookups and wireless access. There is no additional charge for this service. Off-campus housing is available in the Castleton, Fair Haven, and Rutland areas through private landlords. The College does not own any off-campus housing. All students have access to three dining options on campus: Huden Dining Hall, Fireside Café, and the Coffee Cottage. All students are allowed to have automobiles on campus.

More than fifty clubs and organizations provide a wide variety of student activities that include club sports, an FM radio station, the student newspaper, and an active outing club. Other clubs relate to college majors and future careers; still others serve the College or local community. Men compete in baseball, basketball, cross-country, football, golf, ice hockey, lacrosse, alpine skiing, Nordic skiing, soccer, tennis, and track and field. Women compete in basketball, cross-country, field hockey, golf, ice hockey, lacrosse, alpine skiing, Nordic skiing, soccer, softball, tennis, track and field, and volleyball. Nearly 500 students compete for Castleton on a varsity sports team, while countless others take advantage of the robust intramural and recreational sports programs offered.

Since 2002 Castleton has invested nearly $75 million in infrastructure improvements including a $25.7-million project that included the construction of Spartan Stadium, renovation and expansion of the Campus Center and the Spartan Athletic Complex, and improvements to the baseball and softball fields. In 2012, Castleton debuted new lighted tennis courts, a facilities barn, the renovation of Huden Dining Hall, the construction of Hoff Hall, a LEED Gold-certified residence hall with room for more than 160 students, and the impressive Castleton Pavilion, the largest indoor-outdoor venue of its kind in the state of Vermont.

This past year also saw the inauguration of "Castleton on the Move," a strategic plan and blueprint for the College's next ten years. Highlighted by new and enhanced graduate programs and a vision to become Vermont's public master's institution, the plan also includes incremental enrollment growth; a focus on international enrollment; and increased opportunities for students in Rutland through entrepreneurial ventures such as the Castleton Downtown Gallery, the Castleton Polling Institute, and Castleton Downtown, which is home to the Center for Community Engagement, Center for Entrepreneurial Programs, and Center for Schools.

Location

The campus is 12 miles west of Rutland, one of Vermont's largest cities. Montreal, Boston, Hartford, Albany, and New York City are all within easy driving distance. Amtrak passenger trains to and from New York City stop in the village of Castleton. Killington and Pico ski areas, Lake Bomoseen, and the Green Mountains provide excellent recreational opportunities and an exceptional living and learning environment.

Majors and Degrees

Castleton State College offers B.A. or B.S. degrees in more than thirty areas of study: accounting, American literature, art, athletic training, biology, chemistry, children's literature, computer information systems, communication, criminal justice, digital media, elementary education, environmental science, exercise science, forensic psychology, geology, health education, health science, history, journalism, management, marketing, mass media, mathematics, music, music education, nursing, physical education, psychology, public relations, secondary education, social work, sociology, Spanish, special education, sports administration, theater arts, and world literature. Associate degrees can be earned in business, communication, computer programming, criminal justice, or general studies.

Academic Programs

The Castleton curriculum is designed to provide the student with a strong liberal arts background plus the opportunity for career preparation in a specific area. Classes are small and students receive individual attention from faculty. Castleton's curriculum is based on the belief that a well-rounded education that expands students' horizons and teaches them how to write and to solve problems creatively is critical in preparation for all careers. All four-year students are required to complete a core of general education requirements during the four-year degree program. The first year of study can be used by the undecided student to explore various areas of interest. The student with a specific career interest may begin study in the major field as a first-year student, although four-year students are not required to formally declare their major until the end of the sophomore year.

Castleton students typically enroll in five courses each semester. The academic calendar consists of two 15-week semesters and three 4-week summer sessions. Grading is traditional, and a pass/no-pass option is available. Internships and field experiences complement the academic programs at Castleton and are a requirement for graduation in many.

Students may transfer internally from two-year to four-year programs in business, communication, computer information systems, criminal justice, and general studies. Students who transfer to Castleton after graduating from an accredited two-year college are granted full transfer credit for all academic work up to 64 credits or the number required for the associate degree.

First-year students achieving at least a 3.5 grade point average in their first year at Castleton are recognized by the Castleton Chapter of Phi Eta Sigma, a national honor society that recognizes first-year scholastic achievement in colleges throughout the country. Outstanding junior and senior scholars are recognized by the Castleton Chapter of Alpha Chi. Pinnacle, the honor society for nontraditional students, honors qualified candidates. There are honor societies in business administration, women's studies, history, science and mathematics, theater arts, education, psychology, and Spanish. Students who have achieved a 4.0 grade point average are named to the President's List and those with a 3.5 grade point average or better to the Dean's List.

Academic Facilities

The Calvin Coolidge Library houses a collection of more than 500,000 books, periodicals, microforms, and nonprint media. Access to Castleton's library resources and outside scholarly sources is made possible through numerous online and CD databases; a sophisticated, networked electronic library system; the Internet; and strong consortial relationships within the state of Vermont. An audiovisual media facility provides a wide range of audiovisual equipment, including digital video editing, digital cameras, and presentation equipment.

Castleton's Stafford Academic Center houses the Academic Computing Center, a high-tech multimedia lecture hall, and the departments of education, mathematics, and nursing.

The Spartan Athletic Complex houses Glenbrook Gymnasium, the athletic training rooms, a swimming pool, two racquetball courts, two fitness centers, and a large indoor activity area. Spartan Arena, the home of the men's and women's ice hockey teams, as well as a new fitness center, is a short drive away in Rutland Town.

The Fine Arts Center houses the 500-seat Casella Theater; facilities for art, drama, dance, and music. A new television studio opened in 2010 as part of an addition to Leavenworth Hall.

The Jeffords Center houses science classrooms and laboratories, a state-of-the-art auditorium, laboratories for faculty and student research projects, and a greenhouse. An astronomical observatory is a short walk away.

There are more than 225 personal computers designated for student use located in labs across the campus.

Costs

Costs for 2015–16 are as follows: tuition for Vermont residents, $10,248, and for nonresidents, $25,656. Room and board expenses total $9,696. Annual fees are $1,034.

Financial Aid

Eighty percent of Castleton's full-time undergraduate students receive financial assistance from federal, state, College, or other sources. Grants, loans, and work-study jobs are available for qualified students. Applicants for financial aid should file the Free Application for Federal Student Aid (FAFSA) form by April 1 of the senior year in high school. All financial aid awards are based on need.

Castleton offers an array of scholarships for first-year, transfer, international, and returning students.

For new students, Castleton Admissions reviews each applicant holistically; all application materials submitted are taken into consideration for initial acceptance. New Student Scholarships further recognize students' commitment to and success in academic and extra-curricular involvement.

Amounts range from $1,000 to $10,000 per year. Any individual who can provide proof of valedictorian status from a regionally accredited or state-approved public or independent high school will be eligible for the full tuition Valedictorian Scholarship and may be invited to participate in honors programming. There are also special scholarships for students wishing to study music or Spanish.

Faculty

The full-time faculty at Castleton consists of 103 men and women, 96 percent of whom hold terminal degrees in their field. Adjunct faculty members, many of them local businesspeople and members of the professions, complement the efforts of the full-time faculty. The student-faculty ratio is 14:1. Each student has a faculty member as an adviser.

Student Government

The Student Government Association (SGA) at Castleton operates with three branches of power, which are the Congress, the College Court, and the Campus Activities Board (CAB). All students participating in any facet of these groups are automatically members of the SGA.

As the student government of Castleton, the SGA represents the interests of Castleton students and administers the Student Activity Fee. This fee is assessed to all students and is used to fund activities on campus as well as numerous clubs and organizations.

Admission Requirements

Applicants are evaluated on the basis of their secondary school records, standardized test scores, and recommendations. Admission is granted to those applicants who have demonstrated their ability and potential to meet the challenges of a postsecondary learning experience.

Application and Information

Students may apply for admission through the Common Application. Under Castleton's rolling admission policy, applications are processed throughout the year, and candidates are notified of the admission decision as soon as their files are complete. Students are admitted in the fall and spring semesters.

For more information about Castleton State College or to arrange a campus visit, students should contact:

Office of Admissions
Castleton State College
Castleton, Vermont 05735
Phone: 802-468-1213
800-639-8521 (toll-free)
Fax: 802-468-1476
E-mail: info@castleton.edu
Website: http://www.castleton.edu

The Castleton campus is nestled at the base of the Green Mountains, and has a panoramic view of every season.

COLLEGE CLOSE-UPS

CEDAR CREST COLLEGE
ALLENTOWN, PENNSYLVANIA

★ To read more about this school, visit http://petersons.to/cedarcrestcollege

The College

Cedar Crest College was founded in 1867 and for more than 145 years has taken a bold approach to education by providing women with the competitive edge needed to succeed. A liberal arts college by design, Cedar Crest prepares women to lead in a global society. Approximately 1,600 students attend the College annually, representing twenty-seven states and twenty countries. Current students, alumnae, and future students maintain an active presence on the Cedar Crest Twitter and Facebook pages.

Cedar Crest College has more than thirty academic programs and faculty members who put a unique spin on traditional majors such as business and marketing, communication, English, and performing arts. In addition, Cedar Crest College has renowned programs in forensic science (one of fourteen accredited programs in the country and the only one affiliated with a women's college), social work (the only accredited program in the Lehigh Valley), and genetic engineering (one of the oldest programs in the country).

The College's health and wellness program has received a gold award for student health, wellness, and counseling from the National Association of Student Personnel Administrators. Their health and wellness initiative includes personal sports training; nutrition counseling; and a full schedule of dance, yoga, and aerobics classes. The Rodale Aquatic Center for Civic Health, a state-of-the-art, two-pool complex, offers health and fitness opportunities for the entire campus community. The campus also has tennis courts; regulation fields for field hockey, lacrosse, soccer, and softball; and a fitness center.

Cedar Crest students participate in nine NCAA Division III intercollegiate sports: basketball, cross-country, field hockey, lacrosse, soccer, softball, swimming, tennis, and volleyball. The College athletic department also supports club sports including equestrian, and cheerleading. The Falcons belong to the Colonial States Athletic Conference (CSAC) and compete against institutions in Pennsylvania, New Jersey, and Delaware. Cedar Crest student-athletes are held to high academic standards and have proven that it's possible to succeed both on the court and in the classroom. The CSAC recently awarded Cedar Crest student-athletes the first institutional achievement award for earning the highest grade point average in the Conference, and Cedar Crest teams have won several national academic awards. In 2011, basketball center Lizzy Sunderhause was recognized with the Jostens Trophy, awarded for excellence on the court and in the classroom and community.

Cedar Crest students hold leadership positions in more than forty clubs and organizations on campus. Student clubs range from the Student Government Association and Student Activities Board to the Literary Club and Biology Club. The College prepares women to lead in their future careers, community, and in life. Leadership retreats and community service opportunities are held throughout the year. The campus completes more than 20,000 hours in community service annually. Service opportunities are available throughout the Lehigh Valley at schools, hospitals, animal shelters, and Habitat for Humanity. At Cedar Crest, students serve early and often.

Cedar Crest upperclass students have the opportunity to live and learn together in the College's living-learning communities. These communities focus on a variety of relevant and timely topics such as global social justice, environmental ethics, entrepreneurship, and the arts. They bring together students who share a common interest, regardless of major or career focus. Sharing perspectives and lifestyles in this group setting enhances the students' educational journey as they gain intellectual appreciation and global awareness, apply and hone leadership skills, and make a difference locally and globally. These communities are the epitome of the seamless college experience as students live together, take a house class together, travel together, and develop close relationships with a faculty member affiliated with the community.

Through the Career Planning Office, students are placed in competitive internships near the campus and in major cities.

Cedar Crest's academic programs are fully accredited by the Middle States Association of Colleges and Schools and, where appropriate, by the American Academy of Forensic Science, American Medical Association, American Dietetic Association, American Bar Association, National League for Nursing Accrediting Commission, National Council on Social Work Education, and the Departments of Education of New York, New Jersey, and Pennsylvania. The College offers master's degrees in three fields: education, forensic science, and nursing.

Location

Students enjoy Cedar Crest's park-like campus, nestled in the heart of the Lehigh Valley in the West End of Allentown, Pennsylvania. The campus is a beautiful 84-acre nationally registered arboretum with more than 130 species of trees. The College is within easy distance of the extensive Allentown park system, high-end retail shopping, well-known restaurants, cultural activities, and the Pocono ski and outdoor resorts.

Cedar Crest is located in College Valley, home to more than 32,000 students at eight colleges within 20 minutes of campus. Students can participate in student- and faculty-led trips to nearby Philadelphia (less than 1 hour from campus) and New York City (less than 2 hours away). Students can explore the metropolitan areas of the East Coast, including Washington, D.C., Baltimore, and Boston, while enjoying the benefits of a small, suburban campus.

Majors and Degrees

Cedar Crest offers more than thirty fields of study in the arts, humanities, social sciences, business, and sciences. The combination of majors and course offerings provides students with a strong liberal arts background. The College also offers preprofessional programs in dentistry, law, medicine, and veterinary medicine. These well-respected academic programs provide individual support for students as they create an academic experience that is both personal and practical. Students are expected to be involved in planning their academic pathway from the very beginning.

Academic Programs

Self-designed majors, double majors, minors, and individual and group research projects are available and reflect the academic emphasis at the undergraduate level. Students may begin conducting research as early as their first year on campus. Students can also begin writing for the campus newspaper or hosting their own radio shows early in their college career.

The honors program at Cedar Crest is cross-disciplinary and designed for women who have demonstrated a record of high academic achievement. The honors program offers students a unique opportunity for growth and enrichment. Honors courses are marked by their engaging classroom environment, diverse and challenging coursework, and graduate-level research experiences.

Through a consortium with the Lehigh Valley Association of Independent Colleges, Cedar Crest upperclass students may cross-register and take courses at Lehigh and DeSales Universities and Lafayette, Moravian, and Muhlenberg Colleges at no additional cost.

Off-Campus Programs

Cedar Crest students are encouraged to pursue internships in their area of study. Internships enable students to gain practical experience at major corporations, small businesses, national nonprofit organizations, and top health-care facilities. Cedar Crest students have served internships with CNN, as a foreign correspondent with the United Nations, and with the FBI, working on a database for DNA fingerprinting.

The College stresses the importance of global awareness and encourages students to take advantage of study-abroad opportunities. Cedar Crest also offers courses with a short trip-abroad component lasting one to two weeks.

Academic Facilities

Learning spaces include hospital simulation labs, a ceramic studio, a state-of-the art nutrition laboratory, music practice rooms, *The Crestiad* newsroom, dance and art studios and workshops, theaters, genetic engineering laboratories, forensic science laboratories, a papermaking studio, media convergence lab, and a greenhouse.

Cedar Crest students socialize and dine in the Tompkins College Center, the hub of student activity. The center is home to Samuels Theatre, club meeting rooms, the dining hall, and the Falcon's Nest café.

Costs

For 2014–15, tuition was $33,904; room and board were $10,549.

Financial Aid

Student applications are reviewed for scholarship eligibility at the time of acceptance. The College's scholarships are awarded based on high school merit, leadership, and service. The College also holds an annual scholarship competition that awards one high-achieving student a full tuition scholarship for four years.

The financial aid program at Cedar Crest is based on financial need and includes grants, loans, and employment. Students applying for need-based financial aid should file the Free Application for Federal Student Aid (FAFSA).

Students are encouraged to use Cedar Crest's student aid calculator to receive a fast, accurate estimate of their financial aid package, including scholarships, grants, and loans. This calculator is available at http://www.cedarcrest.edu/calculator.

Faculty

Cedar Crest faculty members demand excellence, creating a challenging and supportive environment that allows students to grow and thrive. Faculty members are working artists, published writers, accomplished actors, international business professionals, and scientists making discoveries that will impact us all. They strive to ensure that student learning extends beyond the classroom.

Cedar Crest students meet one-on-one with a faculty mentor to build course schedules and discuss future plans. Students also work closely with faculty on groundbreaking research in all disciplines. This research can lead to national presentations and professional publications.

Admission Requirements

Cedar Crest welcomes applications from first-year students entering after high school and those seeking to transfer from another college or university. The admissions process looks at the entire student, from academic course work and standardized test scores to leadership potential, volunteer service, employment, and special talents.

Application and Information

Students are encouraged to visit the campus as they begin the application process, and can register for a visit at unleashed.cedarcrest.edu/visit. Applications are reviewed on a rolling basis, so they are processed and evaluated as soon as all materials have been received. Applicants are notified of their admissions decision beginning September 15 for the following fall semester. The priority deadline to apply for scholarship review is February 15.

Students can apply online at unleashed.cedarcrest.edu/apply-now or through the Common Application at https://www.commonapp.org.

Admissions Office
Cedar Crest College
100 College Drive
Allentown, Pennsylvania 18104-6196
Phone: 800-360-1222 (toll-free)
Fax: 610-606-4647
E-mail: admissions@cedarcrest.edu
Website: unleashed.cedarcrest.edu
www.facebook.com/CedarCrestCollege
twitter.com/cedarcrestcolle

Cedar Crest College is a great place to live and learn! The campus community comprises smart, creative women who will shape the world.

CHAMPLAIN COLLEGE
BURLINGTON, VERMONT

CHAMPLAIN COLLEGE

The College

Career-minded students have been the focus of Champlain College since its founding in 1878. Today, as a private, nonprofit college with 2,000 full-time residential undergraduate students, as well as online adult undergraduate and master's degree students, Champlain delivers a rigorous, interdisciplinary and career-focused education that endows students with the professional, intellectual and life-management skills to have gratifying careers and remarkable lives.

In addition to its main campus in Burlington, Vermont, Champlain College has two international campuses: one in Montreal, Canada, and the other in Dublin, Ireland. Champlain College is accredited by the New England Association of Schools and Colleges.

The undergraduate student body represents forty-one states and twenty-two countries. Class sizes are small (averaging 17 students), with an overall student to faculty ratio of 12:1. More than 50 student clubs and organizations, ranging from the Ski and Ride Club to the Quidditch team, from the Equestrian Team to the Dance Team, keep students involved and engaged in campus life (champlain.edu/activities-clubs).

Champlain's 22-acre campus is situated in the heart of Burlington's historic Hill Section neighborhood, overlooking Lake Champlain and the Adirondacks of New York. Many of the College's residence halls are restored Victorian-era mansions, which give students a unique atmosphere in which to learn and live. Other facilities are newly constructed or recently renovated and feature the latest in technology and resources.

Champlain's radically pragmatic education is underscored by over eighty career-focused majors, minors, and specializations in the Robert P. Stiller School of Business, as well as its three other academic divisions: Communication & Creative Media, Education & Human Studies, and Information Technology & Sciences. Champlain also offers eleven master's degree programs as well as online professional certificate programs.

In addition to professionally focused academics, Champlain students gain invaluable hands-on career experience through its Centers for Excellence, on-campus experiential learning centers, including the Build Your Own Business (BYOBiz) program, the Emergent Media Center and MakerLab, the Senator Patrick Leahy Center for Digital Investigation, and the Champlain College Publishing Initiative (champlain.edu/centers).

Champlain's Upside-Down curriculum allows students to begin taking internships as early as the summer after their first year at Champlain. Champlain students frequently complete multiple internships prior to graduation. Students from Champlain are highly prized by employers in the greater Burlington area because of their deep skill sets and professional training (champlain.edu/internships).

Providing students with a career-focused and relevant education is Champlain College's primary mission. Outcome data demonstrates that Champlain's approach is highly effective. Based on data collected from 87 percent of the class of 2013, 93 percent of traditional undergraduates were employed less than one year after graduating; of those, 90 percent were already working in jobs related to their career goals.

Champlain appears regularly in the nation's premier Best Colleges rankings. The College was included in the Princeton Review's *Guide to 332 Green Colleges*. Champlain College was described as the "ideal college" by *The Atlantic*. It is included in The Princeton Review's *Best 379 Best Colleges: 2015 Edition* and was named a top Up-and-Coming college in *U.S. News & World Report*'s 2014 Best Colleges. *SC Magazine* named Champlain as having the Best Cyber Security Higher Education Program in the nation.

Location

Champlain's residential campus is in the center of Burlington, Vermont's largest city, located on the eastern shore of Lake Champlain with New York's Adirondack Mountains to the west and Vermont's Green Mountains to the east. Burlington is home to 43,000 residents (in a metro area of 211,000), including nearly 15,000 college students. The Church Street Marketplace, the commercial heart of the city located just a few blocks from the campus, attracts both locals and tourists to its numerous shops, coffee bars, and restaurants. Montreal, Quebec, is 94 miles to the north, Boston is 220 miles to the southeast, and New York City is 285 miles to the south.

Burlington is frequently cited in national media as being one of the nation's best college towns and best places to live and work (champlain.edu/burlington). The area is home to five colleges, as well as UVM Medical Center, one of the leading medical centers in the East. There is an international airport; an Amtrak passenger train route with connections to Montreal, New York City, and Washington, D.C.; and long-distance bus service to Boston, Hartford, and New York City.

Champlain also has international campuses in Montreal, Canada, and Dublin, Ireland (champlain.edu/champlainabroad).

Majors and Degrees

Champlain College offers Bachelor of Fine Arts (B.F.A.), Bachelor of Science (B.S.), Bachelor of Science in Business Administration (B.S.B.A.), and Bachelor of Social Work (B.S.W.) degree programs with career-focused majors in arts and design, business, communication, computer forensics and cybersecurity, creative media, education, game development, information technology, legal studies, management, and social sciences. Students may also apply as an undeclared/undecided major. The undergraduate curriculum offering also includes specialization options within particular majors as well as career-focused minors open to all students. In addition, Champlain offers a degree program in radiography.

Academic Programs

Champlain's Upside-Down Curriculum allows students to take courses in their major starting in their first semester. Beyond the Upside-Down Curriculum, Champlain takes a multidimensional academic approach that encompasses the professional, academic, and practical knowledge students need to grow personally and professionally and to thrive in an ever-changing world. The Major Dimension gives students career-focused majors and prepares them for their career in all four years; it also includes extensive experiential learning, internships, and field study. The Core Dimension is the College's four-year innovative liberal arts education, offering courses in humanities, sciences, and economics that form the foundation of critical thinking and intellectual leadership. The Life Experience & Action Dimension (LEAD) teaches lifelong career management skills, as well as a financial and interpersonal understanding that prepares students for a well-managed and meaningful life.

As a career-focused institution, Champlain emphasizes the value of real-time experiences in a chosen field before graduation, and the curriculum and Career Services Office support all students in taking at least one professional internship, preferably more. Champlain gives students an immersive program in professional development, featuring specific professional career preparation such as portfolio development, hands-on learning, and on-campus recruitment events.

Champlain has graduate school admission agreements with New York Law School and New York University's School of Continuing and Professional Studies.

Off-Campus Programs

The Office of International Education ensures that students graduate prepared to be globally engaged citizens with international experience and global perspective. In addition to Champlain's international campuses in Montreal, Canada, and Dublin, Ireland, the College also has global partners in Buenos Aires, Argentina; Shanghai, China; Ifrane, Morocco; and Auckland, New Zealand. Students can also study abroad through approved third-party providers at other locations. More than 50 percent of Champlain students study abroad.

Academic Facilities

Champlain's main academic facilities continue to expand and evolve each year, incorporating the latest equipment and technology to match the nature and requirements of the College's career-focused majors. Students have access to campus computer labs, 3-D animation and game production labs, multimedia classrooms, the Metz Studio Barn, and the Emerging Media Center and MakerLab, among other lab spaces.

The new Center for Communication and Creative Media, scheduled to open in August 2015, is a 75,000 square-foot facility that will include new game and audio labs, studio spaces, gallery and exhibit areas, a traditional and digital photo lab, and a film soundstage. The S. D. Ireland Family Center for Global Business and Technology is home to the Robert P. Stiller School of Business as well as the David L. Cooperrider Center for Appreciative Inquiry.

The Holly D. and Robert E. Miller Information Commons received the 2012 Excellence in Academic Libraries Award from the Association of College and Research Libraries (ACRL). It combines the features of a traditional library with advanced technologies such as multimedia laboratories, specialized electronic classrooms, and online learning systems.

Costs

Tuition for 2015–16 is $37,436; room and board is $14,050. Total standard cost of attendance including tuition, fees, room, and board totals $51,664.

Financial Aid

Champlain invests in its students and recognizes academic achievement each year through need- and merit-based scholarships and financial aid. Each year, Champlain students receive more than $25 million in scholarships. More than 85 percent of students received scholarship funds to help pay their educational costs.

Special efforts are made to include support for new Americans, U.S. veterans, single parents, Vermont students who are the first in their family to attend college, women interested in studying in technology fields, and student entrepreneurs.

Students interested in receiving need-based financial aid must complete the Free Application for Federal Student Aid (FAFSA).

Faculty

Champlain's faculty members bring outstanding academic credentials to the classroom, but have also built their careers in the workplace, bringing practical professional experience to the educational experience. Champlain College employs 106 full-time professors as well as adjunct instructors, who in addition to their academic credentials have ongoing professional experience in the fields in which they teach. All classes are taught by faculty members; students will never have a class taught by a teaching assistant.

Admission Requirements

For first-year applicants, the College requires an official high school transcript, SAT or ACT scores, two letters of recommendation, and a completed application form in order to be considered for admission. Graduation from a recognized secondary school is required (or an equivalency certificate/GED) as a condition of acceptance. Personal interviews are not required but a campus visit is strongly recommended. Students applying to major in game design, game art & animation, graphic design & digital media, filmmaking, or creative media must submit a portfolio. Students may earn advanced standing by submitting appropriate scores on Advanced Placement and International Baccalaureate examinations.

Students can apply either through the early- or regular-decision program. Early Decision is a binding agreement, and students are encouraged to apply through this program only if Champlain College is their first choice. Deadlines are: November 15 for Early Decision I; January 15 for Early Decision II; and February 1 for Regular Decision.

Candidates for transfer admission are required to submit an official high school transcript with SAT or ACT scores, official college transcript(s), and a completed application form in order to be considered for admission.

Champlain College uses the Common Application as well as the Champlain College application for enrollment in fall or spring semesters. Transfer applicants can apply on a rolling basis. Links to applications can be found at www.champlain.edu/apply.

Champlain College admits students without regard to race, creed, color, national and ethnic origin, religion, age, gender, sexual orientation, or qualified disability, and does not discriminate in the administration of its educational and admission policies, scholarships and loan programs, or other College-administered programs. Champlain College makes reasonable accommodations to the disabilities of otherwise-qualified students, applicants or employees.

Application Information

Director of Admissions
Champlain College
163 South Willard Street
P.O. Box 670
Burlington, Vermont 05402-0670
Phone: 802-860-2727
800-570-5858 (toll-free)
Fax: 802-860-2767
E-mail: admission@champlain.edu
Website: champlain.edu

The Champlain College campus, home to 2,000 career-focused undergraduates, combines renovated historic buildings and modern facilities in a pedestrian-friendly campus overlooking Lake Champlain and the top college town of Burlington, Vermont.

CHAPMAN UNIVERSITY

ORANGE, CALIFORNIA

★ To read more about this school, visit http://petersons.to/chapmanuniversity

CHAPMAN UNIVERSITY

The University

During its more than 150-year history, Chapman University has evolved from a small, traditional liberal arts college into a comprehensive university distinguished for its extraordinary blend of liberal arts, science, and professional programs. Film and television production, business and economics, theatre, dance, music, education, and the natural and applied sciences—Chapman boasts a breadth of fields usually only found at larger institutions. Chapman University's mission is to develop global citizen-leaders who are distinctively prepared to improve their community and their world.

With beautiful grounds and stately buildings, Chapman is one of the oldest schools on the West Coast, yet its park-like campus is also one of the most modern. More than a dozen buildings have been built or renovated in just the last two decades, with four more on the drawing board. Architecturally impressive residence halls and apartment buildings offer students exciting lifestyle amenities within a vibrant Southern California setting.

Chapman University's academic structure includes the AACSB International–accredited Argyros School of Business and Economics; the CTC-approved College of Educational Studies; the Dodge College of Film and Media Arts; the Crean College of Health and Behavioral Sciences; the Wilkinson College of Humanities and Social Sciences; the College of Performing Arts, which includes the NASM-accredited Hall-Musco Conservatory of Music, the NAST-accredited Department of Theatre, and the NASD-accredited Department of Dance; the Schmid College of Science and Technology; the School of Pharmacy; and the ABA-accredited Fowler School of Law.

With its central Orange County, California, location and nearly 8,000 undergraduate, graduate, and professional school students, the University environment is alive with activity. In addition to the temperate climate, Chapman students enjoy a dynamic, eclectic, and outdoor-oriented lifestyle, both on campus and off. Students come from all walks of life; from across the country and from all over the world, each student brings his or her own unique view of what makes a true global citizen. In recent years, Chapman students have been named Truman, Fulbright, Soros, and Rotary scholars; *USA Today* All-USA College Academic Team members; NCAA All-Americans; and NCAA Academic All-Americans.

Chapman's long and distinguished heritage in intercollegiate athletics includes six NCAA national championships in baseball, tennis, and softball. In the last 12 years, the baseball program has been to the NCAA championship finals nine times, winning one national title. The Panthers compete in the NCAA Division III Southern California Intercollegiate Athletic Conference (SCIAC) and field teams in baseball, basketball, cross-country, football, golf, lacrosse, soccer, softball, swimming, tennis, track and field, volleyball, and water polo. Approximately 20 percent of Chapman's student body participates in intercollegiate athletics, intramurals, and club sports.

More than 120 clubs and organizations are recognized on campus, many with commitments to a wide range of community service efforts. Chapman's Greek system includes nine nationally chartered fraternities for men and eight nationally chartered sororities for women. Intramural sports, on-campus intercollegiate athletic events, as well as music, art, and theatre productions provide students with plenty to do outside of class. And that's just on campus—with San Diego to the south and Los Angeles to the north, the only hard thing is deciding what to do.

Prominent Chapman alumni include the Honorable Loretta Sanchez '88, member of Congress; the Honorable David Bonior '72, member of Congress; CNBC World anchorwoman Bettina Chua '88; television and film producers John Copeland '73, Jon Garcia '93, and John David Currey '98; cinematographer Gene Jackson '70; Miss California 2011, Noelle Freeman '11; St. John's University basketball coach Steve Lavin '88; Major League Baseball executive Gordon Blakely '76; Major League Baseball Cy Young Award winner Randy Jones '72; Tony Award nominee and star of Broadway's *Showboat,* Michel Bell '68; resident tenor at the Staatsoper-Vienna John Nuzzo '91; and former U.S. Ambassador to Spain and philanthropist George L. Argyros '59.

Location

Orange County, California, has been rated by *Places Rated Almanac* as "the number one place to live in North America," citing superior climate and cultural, recreational, educational, and career-entrée opportunities. Orange County's central location between two major cities means there is never a lack of entertainment choices. It is, in fact, home to the happiest place on Earth—Disneyland is literally minutes from campus.

The Segerstrom Center for the Arts, Major League Baseball's Los Angeles Angels of Anaheim, and the National Hockey League's Anaheim Ducks are all nearby Chapman's campus in Old Towne Orange. Pristine West Coast beaches are less than 10 miles from the campus, and seasonal snow skiing is 90 minutes away. The average year-round temperature on campus is 71°F, and the daily sea breeze from the nearby Pacific Ocean keeps the air cool, clean, and smog free.

Majors and Degrees

Chapman awards undergraduate degrees in the fields of accounting, art, art history, biochemistry and molecular biology, biological sciences, business administration, chemistry, communication studies, computer information systems, computer science, creative producing, creative writing, dance, digital arts, economics, English, environmental science and policy, film production, film studies, French, graphic design, health sciences, history, integrated educational studies, kinesiology, mathematics, mathematics and civil engineering, music, music composition, music education, music performance, news and documentary, peace studies, philosophy, physics and computational science, political science, psychology, public relations and advertising, religious studies, screen acting, screenwriting, sociology, Spanish, strategic and corporate communication, television writing and production, theatre, and theatre performance. In addition, Chapman offers preprofessional programs in health, law, and pharmacy. Chapman's graduate program offerings include degrees in accounting (M.S.); athletic training (M.S.); business (M.B.A.); communication sciences and disorders (M.S.); computational and data sciences (M.S., Ph.D.); creative writing (M.F.A.); documentary filmmaking (M.F.A.); economic systems design (M.S.); education (M.A., Ph.D.); English (M.A.); film and television producing (M.F.A., M.F.A./M.B.A., M.F.A./J.D.); film production (M.F.A.); film production design (M.F.A.); film screenwriting (M.F.A.); film studies (M.A.); food science (M.S., M.S./M.B.A.); health and strategic communication (M.S.); international studies (M.S.); law (J.D.); leadership development (M.A.); marriage and family therapy (M.A.); pharmaceutical sciences (M.S., Pharm.D.); and war and society (M.A.).

Academic Programs

For many, college is a time of uncertainty. The Academic Advising Center is a place students can come for information, resources, and referrals. Chapman's Academic Advising Center offers personalized services for all students, supporting and helping them to shape their educational goals. Students are encouraged to develop individualized plans for realizing the goals they set. The center is responsible for advising in all majors and serves all undeclared students. General academic counseling is offered, plus placement testing services. Individual appointments are available, though students can stop by any time, or access many of the center's resources online. Advising workshops are regularly available. The Tutoring, Learning, and Testing Center also offers students peer tutoring, study technique development, and advocacy services.

A wide variety of study and research opportunities are available through Chapman's academic and research centers. These include the Anderson Center for Economic Research; the Schweitzer Institute; the Rodgers Center for Holocaust Education; the Fowles Center for Creative Writing; the Leatherby Center for Entrepreneurship and Business Ethics; the Schmid Center for International Business; the Hoag Center for Real Estate and Finance; the Institute for the Study of Religion, Economics, and Society; the Economic Science Institute; and the Institute for Quantum Studies.

Requirements for graduation are commensurate with the philosophy of education fostered at Chapman. The program of studies is designed to ensure a breadth of selection in the liberal arts, as well as depth of preparation in the student's major field. The minimum graduation requirements include successful completion (C average) of 124 semester credits, of which 36 must be earned in the upper division. Competence in reading, written communication, oral communication, computation, and library usage is required of all students. Chapman's general education sequence provides a broad introduction to the humanities, social sciences, and natural sciences. Students select general education classes with the guidance of their faculty adviser. A maximum of 32 semester credits may be gained through Advanced Placement (AP), College-Level Examination Program (CLEP), and departmental examinations.

Chapman's academic year operates on a 4-1-4 modified semester system. January is reserved for an optional four-week interterm during which students can take a traditional course in an accelerated time frame or take more experiential courses, such as travel-study or travel abroad opportunities. Ample opportunities are available for alternative learning experiences. Internships and cooperative education programs are recommended. Students may also undertake in-depth individual study or research in their major field in conjunction with a faculty member.

Academic Facilities

Chapman's stunning campus continues to grow by leaps and bounds. The newest addition is the Digital Media Arts Center, housing state-of-the-art tools and equipment for digital arts majors including the Student Creative Commons, a 1,500-square-foot screening room with 3-D projection and a studio art space. Major additions to the campus over the past several years include the 100,000-square-foot Leatherby Libraries complex, housing eight discipline-specific individual libraries, a cyber courtyard, and a 24-hour study commons and coffee bar. The Oliphant Hall addition to the Conservatory of Music is a 24,000-square-foot space featuring fourteen teaching studios, a 60-seat lecture hall, music therapy laboratory, and orchestra hall. In addition to the Conservatory of Music's Bertea and Oliphant Halls, the College of Performing Arts facilities include the Moulton Fine Arts Complex featuring the 250-seat repertory-style Waltmar Theatre, a black box theatre, the Guggenheim Art Gallery, and the Partridge Dance Center. Also under construction and anticipated to open in 2016 is the Musco Center for the Arts, an 11,000-seat, state-of-the-art auditorium capable of housing Broadway-scale productions. The Fish Interfaith Center features the 12,500-square-foot Wallace All-Faiths Chapel, recognized by *Architectural Digest* for innovation in design. The 200,000-square-foot Sandhu Residence and Conference Center houses the primary on-campus dining facility for resident students, as well as a conference center and residence hall. The 90,000-square-foot Argyros Forum includes the newly expanded Student Union with additional campus dining options, as well as conference and classroom facilities. The 800-seat Chapman Memorial Auditorium, within Memorial Hall, is the primary performance and assembly venue on campus and is listed on the National Register of Historic Places. Athletic facilities include the 2,500-seat Hutton Sports Center; the 2,000-seat Ernie Chapman Stadium for football, lacrosse, and soccer; and the 500-seat Allred Aquatics Center swim stadium/Olympic pool complex. Beckman Hall is the center for business and information technology—the newly opened Janes Financial Center with its twelve Bloomberg terminals is housed here. The Hashinger Science Center features laboratories for nuclear science, radiation, crystallography, genetics, food science, physics, and computational sciences.

Costs

For the 2014–15 academic year, full-time tuition and fees (including accident and health services fee and associated student membership fee) were $44,710. Annual room and board costs averaged $12,954, while the estimated yearly cost for books and supplies was $1,560.

Financial Aid

More than 85 percent of Chapman students benefit from some form of financial aid or scholarship assistance. Need-based financial awards include a combination of grants, scholarships, loans, and work-study jobs on campus. Awards are renewable, assuming that students complete the annual application process on time. By using a combination of Chapman's internal resources and federal and state funding, an individual financial aid package can be tailored in an effort to meet the student's financial need. Merit and talent scholarship awards, regardless of financial need, round out the impressive financial assistance that Chapman offers.

Faculty

The University's faculty is composed of some 794 individuals, 86 percent of whom hold doctoral or other terminal degrees. Their primary commitment is to undergraduate teaching, although most are also actively involved in scholarly research and publication. Teaching assistants or graduate assistants are typically not used for the instruction of undergraduate classes, a fact upon which Chapman prides itself. Chapman's enviable student-faculty ratio of 14:1 allows extensive interaction between the faculty members and students.

Student Government

Chapman has an annually elected associated student government that actively participates in the administration of the University.

Admission Requirements

Admission to Chapman is selective. In 2014, admission was granted to 46 percent of the applicant pool. The University is interested in admitting students whose prior records indicate that they will be successful in a competitive collegiate environment. Freshman applicants are considered for admission based primarily on the nature and sequence of their high school course work, grade point average achieved, their results on either the SAT or ACT examination, co-curricular involvements, and personal characteristics. Transfer candidates are considered for admission on the basis of their course work and cumulative grade point average earned at other regionally accredited postsecondary institutions, their co-curricular involvements, and personal characteristics.

Application and Information

Chapman University exclusively uses the Common Application (http://www.commonapp.org), as well as a Chapman-specific section with questions and short answers, and an art supplement for those applying to the art, dance, film and media arts, music, or theatre programs. Candidates are strongly encouraged to visit and tour the campus and participate in an information session led by an admission officer. Arrangements for a group information session and campus tour can be made through the Office of Admission.

Freshman applicants can choose either a nonbinding November 1 early action application deadline or the January 15 regular application deadline. Transfer applicants must apply before the March 15 transfer deadline. Freshman candidates who apply after January 15 and transfer candidates who apply after March 15 are considered on a space-available basis.

For further information, students should contact:

Office of Admission
Chapman University
One University Drive
Orange, California 92866
Phone: 714-997-6711
888-CUAPPLY (toll-free)
Fax: 714-997-6713
E-mail: admit@chapman.edu
Website: http://www.chapman.edu
http://www.facebook.com/ChapmanUniversity

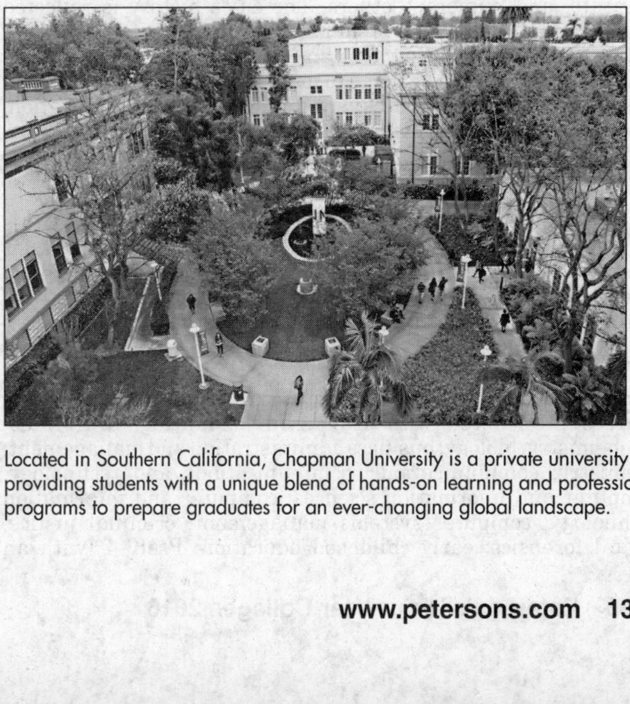

Located in Southern California, Chapman University is a private university providing students with a unique blend of hands-on learning and professional programs to prepare graduates for an ever-changing global landscape.

COLLEGE CLOSE-UPS

CHESTNUT HILL COLLEGE

PHILADELPHIA, PENNSYLVANIA

★ To read more about this school, visit http://petersons.to/chestnuthillcollege

CHESTNUT HILL COLLEGE

The College

Chestnut Hill College is a four-year, coeducational, Catholic liberal arts college. Founded in 1924 by the Sisters of St. Joseph, the mission of the college centers on the growth of the whole student, academically and personally.

Located in Philadelphia, the campus is situated on 75 acres overlooking the Wissahickon Creek. Students have the dual benefit of an idyllic campus and access to a cultural metropolis.

Enrolling more than 2,000 students, Chestnut Hill College is a diverse community of learners. Traditional students comprise the School of Undergraduate Studies. Working adults are enrolled in the School of Continuing and Professional Studies, which offers accelerated undergraduate programs. Chestnut Hill College awards the M.Ed., M.A., and M.S. in the School of Graduate Studies, and the college also awards a doctoral degree in clinical psychology (Psy.D.).

When it comes to activities, students enthusiastically engage in numerous clubs, organizations, and programming available. From community service to theater, special interest clubs, and most notably Quidditch, Chestnut Hill College offers a unique social outlet for everyone.

The college is a member of NCAA Division II and competes in baseball (men), basketball (men and women), cross-country (men and women), golf (men and women), indoor track (men and women), lacrosse (men and women), outdoor track (men and women), soccer (men and women), softball (women), tennis (men and women), and volleyball (women). A swimming pool, a gymnasium, a state-of-the-art fitness center, as well as outdoor basketball and tennis courts, provide excellent athletic facilities for Chestnut Hill's students.

Location

Chestnut Hill College is located in the northwest corner of Philadelphia—where city meets suburbs.

The college is bordered by the wooded hills of Fairmount Park, yet only a 20-minute ride by train or car to Center City Philadelphia where students can enjoy a wide variety of dining, cultural, and sporting events. Among the many attractions are the museums that grace Philadelphia, from its landmark Museum of Art to the Rodin Museum, the Living History Museum, the Franklin Institute, and numerous others. The city's history is reflected throughout, but is most prominent in the areas surrounding Independence Hall, Society Hill, and Penn's Landing. The greater Philadelphia area is also home to more than seventy colleges and universities, which offer further opportunities for socialization, student internships, and an extensive range of activities.

The heart of the Philadelphia neighborhood, Chestnut Hill, is just one mile beyond the college campus.

An official historic district reminiscent of a colonial village, this section of Philadelphia provides convenient opportunities for shopping, dining, and transportation to downtown Philadelphia. Chestnut Hill College is a school in a safe suburban setting with all the advantages of a cosmopolitan experience.

Majors and Degrees

Bachelor of Arts, Bachelor of Science, and Bachelor of Music degrees are offered with majors in accounting; art studio; biochemistry; biology; business administration and management; chemistry; communications; communications and technology; computer and information sciences; computer and information technology; computer systems management; criminal justice; digital forensics; early childhood education: PreK–4 (with an option of Montessori certification); middle level education: 4–8; secondary education: 7–12 (with a co-major in a specific content area); English literature; English literature and communications; environmental sciences; forensic biology; forensic chemistry; French; global affairs; history; human services; international business, language, and culture; marketing; mathematics; mathematical and computer science; molecular biology; music; music education; political science; psychology; sociology; and Spanish.

Combined bachelor's/master's programs are offered in education; administration of human services; psychology; instructional technology; and international business, language, and cultures.

Dual-degree programs in radiological sciences, bioscience technologies, and physician assistant studies are offered in partnership with Thomas Jefferson University and Arcadia University.

Academic Programs

As a liberal arts college, Chestnut Hill offers courses of study that provide the student with a broad background in the fine arts and humanities, a knowledge of science, and a keen awareness of the social problems of the day, as well as intensive, in-depth study in a major field. The academic year at the College consists of two 15-week semesters along with two optional 6-week summer sessions.

Chestnut Hill College confers a B.A., B.M., or B.S. degree to students who earn 120 semester hours of credit and satisfy specific requirements set by the faculty. A student with the ability and proper motivation may be permitted to major in two disciplines. It is understood that the student will satisfy the requirements of both departments. A student may also choose to create an individualized major to fit the needs of distinctive academic pursuits.

Each year, select students are invited into an interdisciplinary honors program that challenges intellectual initiative and provides the opportunity for independent study and seminar discussion. Students may apply for admission prior to first year enrollment or before the start of sophomore year. Sophomores of high scholastic standing are invited by the department chairs to engage in a program of independent study during their junior and senior years. This opportunity for independent study and original research culminates in an honors thesis, which is a prerequisite for the conferring of honors at graduation.

Off-Campus Programs

At Chestnut Hill College, students have many opportunities and options for when and where to study abroad. Whether for a year, a semester, a summer session, or spring break, there is a program to fit the needs of each student. With the assistance of advisors and professors, students can use their imagination and interests to develop an off-campus program.

Chestnut Hill College participates in a consortium arrangement with seven colleges throughout the nation, founded by the Sisters of Saint Joseph. As participants, students can study at any other member institution for a semester or a year, while maintaining status as full-time Chestnut Hill students.

In recent years, Chestnut Hill College students have enrolled in institutions in England, Belgium, France, Mexico, and other world economic centers. Chestnut Hill College maintains numerous agreements around the world with partner organizations including Catholic University of Oporto (Portugal), Universidad de Autònomadel Estado de Higalo (Mexico), Universidad Católica de la Santísima Concepción (Chile), Groupe IBS (France), Cesine Business School (Spain), Business Academy Aarhus (Denmark), Pyeongtaek University (South Korea), Howest University College West Flanders (Belgium), and Regents College (United Kingdom).

The growing interest of students in acquiring on-the-job experience while still in college has prompted the development of many departmental internship programs, which provide students with the opportunity to gain professional experience in their major while earning academic credit. Chestnut Hill College also has an office of career development, through which professionals assist students in finding jobs that correspond to their career interests, personal skill set, and academic pursuits.

Academic Facilities

The Logue Library houses approximately 140,000 volumes and offers students access to an innumerable number of e-books and periodicals. It is also home to a rare book room that contains first editions and special editions, the Gruber Theater, the Brimmer Curriculum Library for elementary education, and an Irish literature collection.

Well-equipped science laboratories, a math center, a multimedia technology center, a writing enrichment center, individual practice rooms for music students, a spacious art studio, a planetarium, and an observatory are among the many other outstanding facilities on campus.

Martino Hall, which opened in 2000 and was designed to maintain the architectural history of the college, provides room for a performance center, gymnasium, or convocation center. The second and third floors house "smart" classrooms. Fitzsimmons Hall, one of five on-site residence facilities, opened its doors in fall 2006 offering resident students suite-style living accommodations.

The College recently acquired the neighboring 35-acre Sugarloaf Mansion estate and has renovated the existing buildings. This new facility offers additional resident housing, classrooms, a second student dining facility, and office areas, along with conference and meeting facilities.

Costs

Tuition for the 2015–16 academic year is $30,210; room and board rates start at $9,620.

Financial Aid

Financial aid is available in the form of academic scholarships, service awards, loans, work-study grants, state grants, federal grants and loans, and Chestnut Hill College grants. Merit-based scholarships and awards are granted for academic achievement. All other types of aid are based on financial need and are awarded in financial aid packages that combine various forms of aid and are tailored to each student's need. More than 75 percent of Chestnut Hill College students receive financial aid to meet college costs. All applicants are encouraged to file the Free Application for Federal Student Aid (FAFSA). Merit-based scholarships and awards are granted for academic achievement.

Faculty

Evidence of Chestnut Hill's vitality can be seen in its faculty. While their primary interest is teaching, faculty members are also engaged in research, publication, travel, and other professional activities. More than 82 percent of the faculty members hold terminal degrees. The men and women who make up this group are deeply interested in both their subject and their students. Their qualifications include international degrees from Bangalore University (India), the University of London, and the University of Paris, and domestic degrees from Boston College, Bryn Mawr College, Catholic University of America, Columbia University, Creighton University, Duke University, Fordham University, Harvard University, Middlebury College, the New School for Social Research, New York University, Purdue University, Saint Louis University, Temple University, and the Universities of Arizona, Delaware, Massachusetts, Minnesota, Montana, New Mexico, North Carolina, Notre Dame, and Pennsylvania. Chestnut Hill College's faculty-student ratio is 1:11.

Student Government

A student at Chestnut Hill College has the opportunity to think independently and approach decisions creatively. Students, in conjunction with members of the faculty and administration, make judgments concerning all collegiate affairs. Several organizations provide structure for the decision-making process. Students join members of the faculty and administration on the Curriculum Committee and the College Council. The Academic, Social-Cultural, and Student Affairs Committees of the Student Organization identify, represent, and meet campus needs.

Admission Requirements

Chestnut Hill College welcomes students whose aptitudes and academic records show a desire to accept a challenge. Applications are judged by the Admissions Committee on the basis of intellectual ability, academic achievement (class rank and performance in high school, including completion of 16 academic units), and SAT or ACT results.

Students should submit a completed application, application fee, SAT or ACT scores, and a high school transcript. Letters of recommendation, a personal statement, and other supporting documentation are strongly encouraged. An interview is recommended and may be required. A student wishing to transfer to Chestnut Hill College is required to submit transcripts from all colleges previously attended.

Application and Information

Applications are processed on a rolling admission cycle. To arrange an interview, schedule a campus visit, or to obtain more detailed information about any academic program, students should contact:

Office of Admissions
School of Undergraduate Studies
Chestnut Hill College
9601 Germantown Avenue
Philadelphia, Pennsylvania 19118
Phone: 215-248-7001
800-248-0052 (toll-free)
E-mail: admissions@chc.edu
Website: http://www.chc.edu

Just minutes from downtown Philadelphia, Chestnut Hill College offers 75 acres of safe and scenic beauty to its success-focused student body.

CLEMSON UNIVERSITY

CLEMSON, SOUTH CAROLINA

★ To read more about this school, visit http://petersons.to/clemsonuniversity

The University

A top-20 public university with a reputation for excellence that's known worldwide, Clemson University leads the way in providing a hands-on education—in the lab, in the arts, and in the field. Clemson was founded in 1889 with a mission to be a "high seminary of learning" dedicated to teaching, research, and service. Today, Clemson is one of the country's most selective public research universities, and these three concepts remain prevalent, providing the framework for an exceptional educational experience.

At Clemson University, professors take the time to get to know students and explore innovative ways of teaching. Exceptional teaching is one reason Clemson's retention and graduation rates rank among the highest in the country for public universities.

Exceptional teaching is also why Clemson continues to attract an increasingly talented student body. In 2013, more than half of the entering freshmen were ranked in the top 10 percent of their high school classes, and the freshman class averaged 1253 on the SAT, placing Clemson in the top 18 public universities in the nation for critical reading and top 20 for math (*U.S. News & World Report*, 2015).

Clemson is committed to world-class research. Research expenditures in 2013 totaled nearly $101 million. The University is also invested in the success of its students. Student retention at Clemson is consistently more than 90 percent. Much of this is due to the Academic Success Center (ASC). Established in 2001, the ASC has been recognized nationally and internationally by organizations related to tutoring, supplemental instruction, and collegiate learning. The ASC moved into a new facility in 2012 where it offers free one-on-one tutoring services for more than 80 courses and provides tutoring for additional courses as the need arises. Supplemental instruction, academic skills workshops, and academic counseling are also available—free to all Clemson students. It is estimated that more than 50 percent of freshmen use ASC services during their first semester.

Clemson has also received national recognition for its innovative Communication Across the Curriculum (CAC) program; it is one of only 11 public colleges and universities identified as making writing across all disciplines a priority per *U.S. News & World Report*, 2015. At Clemson, CAC also has become a standard teaching method used in nearly every department. Professors use CAC to focus on providing real-life challenges that require students to think and communicate effectively.

From cheering the Tigers at a football game to socializing at the Hendrix Student Center, Clemson students can participate in a wide variety of activities outside the classroom. The more than 400 campus clubs and organizations include fraternities and sororities, as well as honorary, international, military, performing arts, political, professional, religious, service, social interest, special interest, sports and fitness, and student media programs and activities.

With 19 intercollegiate sports, Clemson offers exciting spectator sports year-round. Clemson is a charter member of the Atlantic Coast Conference (ACC) and is an NCAA Division I school. Admission to most regular-season home events is included in University fees for full-time students.

Clemson University is accredited by the Commission on Colleges of the Southern Association of Colleges and Schools to award bachelor's, master's, specialist, and doctoral degrees. Questions about the accreditation of Clemson University can be directed to the Commission on Colleges at 1866 Southern Lane, Decatur, Georgia 30033-4097; phone: 404-679-4500.

Location

Approximately midway between Charlotte, North Carolina, and Atlanta, Georgia, Clemson University is located on 1,400 acres in the foothills of the Blue Ridge Mountains and along the shores of Hartwell Lake. Great weather and proximity to natural wonders and large cities offer year-round recreational opportunities.

The University's enrollment of more than 20,000 undergraduate and graduate students makes it a defining presence in Clemson, South Carolina, a town of about 14,000. Students may live on campus in one of the 21 residence halls and four apartment complexes, most of which are within a 10-minute walk to class or downtown. More than 99 percent of students live on campus their freshman year.

Majors and Degrees

Clemson offers more than 80 undergraduate and 119 graduate degree programs through five academic colleges and the Eugene T. Moore School of Education: Agriculture, Forestry, and Life Sciences; Architecture, Arts, and Humanities; Business and Behavioral Science; Engineering and Science; and Health, Education, and Human Development. Undergraduate students can earn B.A., B.S., or preprofessional degrees in accounting; agribusiness; agricultural education; agricultural mechanization and business; animal and veterinary sciences; anthropology; architecture; art; biochemistry; bioengineering; biological sciences; biosystems engineering; chemical engineering; chemistry; civil engineering; communication studies; computer engineering; computer information systems; computer science; construction science and management; early childhood education; economics; electrical engineering; elementary education; English; environmental and natural resources; environmental engineering; financial management; food science; forest resource management; genetics; geology; graphic communications; health science; history; horticulture; industrial engineering; landscape architecture; language and international health; language and international trade; management; marketing; materials science and engineering; mathematical sciences; mathematics teaching; mechanical engineering; microbiology; modern languages (American Sign Language, Chinese, French, German, Italian, Japanese, and Spanish); nursing; packaging science; Pan African studies; parks, recreation, and tourism management; philosophy; physics; plant and environmental sciences; political science; prepharmacy; preprofessional health studies; prerehabilitation sciences; preveterinary medicine; production studies in performing arts; psychology; religious studies; science teaching; secondary education; sociology; soils and sustainable crop systems; special education; sports communication; turfgrass; wildlife and fisheries biology; and women's leadership.

Academic Programs

Clemson's academic year is divided into two semesters. The fall semester begins in mid-August and the spring semester starts in early January. Three summer sessions and four mini-semesters are also available. Students average 16 credit hours per semester, and Clemson requires all students to complete some general education classes specified by the University before graduation. The number of completed credit hours required for graduation varies, depending on the major.

Calhoun Honors College is a University-wide program that combines the strengths of a public, land-grant university with those of a highly selective small college. Calhoun Scholars may choose to pursue departmental honors within their specific academic discipline. In addition, EUREKA! (Experiences in Undergraduate Research, Exploration, and Knowledge Advancement) is a unique and exciting program that enables honors students to pursue research and scholarly activities with faculty members across all disciplines. The advantages of membership in the Honors College include priority registration, extended library loan privileges, honors research grants, and a special living-learning community.

The National Scholars Program is a highly selective program for exceptional students who strive to meet their highest intellectual potential. One of its goals is to develop the interests and talents students need to compete for Rhodes, Marshall, and Truman scholarships; Fulbright Grants; National Science Foundation Graduate Fellowships; and other prestigious international fellowships. In 2013, 11 Clemson students received National Science Foundation Graduate Fellowships. Three recent Clemson graduates received Fulbright grants to conduct research or teach abroad, and three students were named Goldwater Scholars.

Clemson's Creative Inquiry (CI) program allows undergraduate students to engage in research about problems that spring from their own curiosity, from a professor's challenge, or from the pressing needs of the world around them. Team-based investigations are led by a faculty mentor and typically span two to four semesters. Students take ownership of their projects and take the risks necessary to solve problems and get answers. This invaluable experience produces exceptional graduates, capable of thinking critically, solving problems as a team, and communicating and presenting their ideas to others. In 2013–14, 3,439 students participated in 519 CI teams.

Clemson's nationally recognized Programs for Educational Enrichment and Retention (PEER) is committed to improving the academic performance of underrepresented students in engineering and science.

Off-Campus Programs

Clemson's students are strongly encouraged to incorporate a study-abroad experience in their overall Clemson journey. Programs are available on six continents for all disciplines and interests. These include faculty-led programs, exchange programs, and programs available through Clemson's partnerships with study-abroad providers and institutions.

Students in a variety of majors also have opportunities at other Clemson campuses around the world, including the Archbold Center in Dominica; the Daniel Center in Genoa, Italy; and the Clemson University Brussels Center in Belgium. There are other campuses around South Carolina, including Greenville, Greenwood, and Charleston.

The Cooperative Education program provides an opportunity for students to alternate periods of academic study with semesters of paid, career-related, engaged-learning experiences to bridge the gap between academic study and its application in professional practice. Clemson's Center for Career and Professional Development helps to pair students with companies seeking interns or co-op students. The Princeton Review ranks Clemson's career services program as the number-five career office in the nation, and with help from the career center, about 2,200 students participate in academic internships and co-ops annually. Because co-op experiences have been proven to enhance academic performance and provide a competitive edge when seeking full-time employment, Clemson students can now add on-campus internship experiences to their resumes. Students can work part- or full-time, with many in full-time positions having the option of earning credit. The University has made an investment to fund a portion of these experiences, so these on-campus jobs are paid positions.

Academic Facilities

The Clemson campus is a blend of historic buildings and advanced research facilities surrounded by stately trees and lush greenery.

Clemson's main library, the Robert M. Cooper Library, is located at the center of campus and provides a variety of services and up-to-date collections. The University's wireless networking capability lets students communicate with professors and classmates, read online course materials, check e-mail, and conduct research—all from their own laptops.

The campus offers an array of facilities and programs designed to enhance a student's entire educational experience. These include the Pearce Center for Professional Communication, Class of 1941 Studio for Student Communication, Rutland Center for Ethics, and the Academic Success Center.

Clemson real estate holdings also include more than 32,000 acres of forestry and agricultural lands throughout the state, the majority of which are dedicated to the University's research and service missions.

Costs

For the 2014–15 academic year, undergraduate tuition and fees were $13,054 for South Carolina residents and $30,488 for out-of-state residents. Room and board costs were approximately $8,142, and books and supplies were around $1,112. Estimated personal and transportation expenses were $3,520, and the one-time laptop computer cost was about $1,900.

Financial Aid

Financial aid is usually awarded on the basis of need to supplement the amount students and their parents can contribute to college expenses. The University also awards some scholarships based entirely on academic merit. Clemson offers financial aid in the form of grants, scholarships, loans, and part-time employment, and 88 percent of first-time students receive financial aid at Clemson.

Entering freshmen are evaluated on a competitive basis for scholarships using the admission application. There is no separate scholarship application. For academic recruiting scholarships, selection of domestic students is based on test scores, high school class rank, and other academic factors. Stipends for in-state residents range from $500 per year to the full cost of attendance. Merit scholarships for out-of-state students range from $7,500 per year to the full cost of attendance. Academic recruiting scholarships are available only to entering freshmen and are renewable for three additional years provided that the minimum standards are maintained. The application for admission is the first step for prospective freshmen to be considered for merit awards.

General scholarships are awarded to both entering freshmen and upperclassmen. These may have special criteria set up by the donor, such as a certain residency, major, or career interest. Because of the restrictions on many of these scholarships, it is impossible to predict the recipients. The scholarship selection process is very competitive. Stipends range from $250 to $7,500.

Faculty

Clemson has more than 1,000 full-time faculty members, with around 88 percent holding a Ph.D. or terminal degree in their fields. In addition, the University has more than 100 part-time faculty members. Faculty honors include the Fulbright Scholarship, Guggenheim Fellowship, National Science Foundation CAREER Award, National Institutes of Health Senior Scientist Award, and membership in the American Academy of Arts and Sciences. The average class size is 30, and the student-to-faculty ratio is 17:1.

Admission Requirements

In 2014, the University received about 20,756 applications for a fall freshman class of more than 3,400. Transfer applications were received from 2,477 students, 1,147 of whom enrolled. Undergraduate applications are available online at clemson.edu/admissions.

For freshman applicants, the following factors are considered: class standing, standardized test scores (SAT or ACT), high school curriculum, grades, and choice of major. All entering freshmen must have completed 4 credits of English, 3 credits of mathematics, 3 credits of laboratory science, 3 credits of a foreign language (in the same language), 3 credits of social sciences, 1 credit of U.S. history, 1 credit of physical education or ROTC, and 1 credit of fine arts.

To be considered for transfer admission, candidates must have completed a full year of college study (a minimum of 30 semester hours or 45 quarter hours of transferable work completed after secondary school conclusion), earned a minimum cumulative GPA of at least 2.5 on a 4.0 scale (3.0 preferred), and completed freshman-level courses in English, science, and mathematics for their intended major at Clemson. Students may also transfer into Clemson after successful completion of their freshman year through the Bridge to Clemson program, a collaborative first-year academic and residential life partnership between Clemson University and Tri-County Technical College. Bridge is available by invitation only to qualified Clemson freshman applicants who have the potential to be successful at Clemson but, due to its competitive admissions landscape, could not be admitted directly into the University for their freshman year.

Application and Information

Application deadlines for freshman admissions are December 1 (priority date for fall semester), May 1 (fall semester), and December 15 (spring semester). For transfer admissions, the application deadlines are July 1 (fall semester) and December 15 (spring semester).

Office of Admissions
Clemson University
105 Sikes Hall, Box 345124
Clemson, South Carolina 29634-5124
Phone: 864-656-2287
Fax: 864-656-2464
E-mail: cuadmissions@clemson.edu
Website: http://www.clemson.edu/admissions

Hands-on research and real-world experiences make Clemson students exceptionally prepared for postgraduate education and future career opportunities. Here, landscape architecture students collaborate on a design project. In many cases, students travel to present their findings at conferences, in front of professors and peers alike.

COLLEGE OF MOUNT SAINT VINCENT

RIVERDALE, NEW YORK

★ To read more about this school, visit http://petersons.to/collegeofmountsaintvincent

The College

The College of Mount Saint Vincent is a rigorous and inclusive, ecumenical liberal arts college in the Catholic tradition, with nationally recognized undergraduate and graduate programs. Founded by the Sisters of Charity of New York in 1847, the College is located on the Hudson River in the Riverdale neighborhood of New York City. About 55 percent of full-time undergraduates live on campus. The current full-time undergraduate student enrollment is approximately 1,500 men and women.

Career, academic, and personal counseling; academic support; and health services are available to all students. At Mount Saint Vincent, students develop one-on-one relationships with professors who know what they need to thrive and make sure they get it, whether that means an added challenge, a push in a new direction, a little help getting acclimated to college life, or extra support with coursework. The Center for Undergraduate Research provides opportunities for students to take research projects to the next level.

The Mount has more than 40 different clubs and organizations on campus. There's something for everyone—from cultural awareness and community service to journalism, athletics, and theater. Students can also start their own clubs or organizations. There are many ways to hone leadership skills on campus: be an orientation leader or resident assistant, join student government, or play a bigger part in a club or as the captain of an athletic team. In addition, 15 academic honor societies have chapters on campus.

Mount Saint Vincent is an active member of the National Collegiate Athletic Association (NCAA), the Eastern College Athletic Conference (ECAC), the Hudson Valley Men's and Women's Athletic Conference, and the Skyline Conference. The Mount boasts 15 Division III varsity teams and a popular intramural sports program. Student athletes demonstrate strong character, both on and off the field.

In recent years, the College has invested in improving its athletic and recreation facilities, including the Peter Jay Sharp Athletic and Recreation Center and a new natural turf athletic field. All students have access to on-campus athletic facilities, including a state-of-the-art fitness center.

Members of the College community seek to share the best parts of themselves with others and constantly look for new ways to give back to the surrounding community. Students and faculty further the Sisters of Charity mission of active responsibility toward others, on campus and beyond. Students participate in Habitat for Humanity, Midnight Run, Alternative Spring Break, Relay for Life, Part of the Solution (POTS) soup kitchen, and on-campus clothing and food drives, among others.

The College offers master's degrees in urban and multicultural education, international development and service, and nursing, as well as a well-regarded M.B.A. program. All programs are designed to promote academic excellence and professional leadership and reflect a commitment to service.

The graduate nursing program offers three areas of study: family nurse practitioner, nursing education, and nursing administration. These programs prepare nurses for the complex decision-making process necessary in today's health-care environment. A registered nurse license and baccalaureate degree in nursing are required for application.

The graduate program in teacher education results in a Master of Science in urban and multicultural education. It is a values-centered program reflecting the belief that learning and culture are inseparable, as are relationships among learner, teacher, environment, and purpose for learning. A bachelor's degree and a provisional or initial teaching certificate are required for application.

Location

Overlooking the Hudson River, the 70-acre campus of Mount Saint Vincent encompasses rolling lawns, stone walls, wooded fields, and several buildings designated as historic landmarks of the city of New York. The campus is a mere 20 minutes from midtown Manhattan, so students have easy access to internships and other professional and cultural opportunities.

Majors and Degrees

The College of Mount Saint Vincent offers majors in accounting, art history, biochemistry, biology, business, business administration, chemistry, communication, visual arts and experimental media, economics, English, French, history, liberal arts, mathematics, modern foreign languages, nursing, philosophy, psychology, religious studies, sociology, teacher education, and Spanish. Students can pursue minors in biochemistry, biology, business, chemistry, communication, dance, economics, English, French studies, history, international studies, mathematics, philosophy, political science, psychology, religious studies, sociology, Spanish, studio art, theatre, women's studies, and writing.

The Department of Teacher Education offers programs for prospective teachers in elementary, middle, secondary, special education, and TESOL. In addition, there are dual certification programs, a five-year B.A./M.S., and a master's program in urban and multicultural education. Students may specialize in areas such as early childhood, childhood, or adolescence education. Students pursuing adolescence education may obtain certification in one of seven fields: biology, chemistry, English, French, history, mathematics, or Spanish. A five-year combined B.A./M.S. program in urban and multicultural education is also available.

Certificate programs are offered in a variety of programs.

Academic Programs

The regular academic year is divided into two semesters, with intersessions in January and three summer sessions.

A core curriculum builds every student's skills. Through a range of classes, students graduate with a repertoire of analytical skills, critical thinking, clear expression, and moral and religious thought. A liberal arts foundation develops a well-rounded individual that sets students apart professionally.

Candidates for the B.A. must earn 120 credits, and candidates for the B.S. must earn 126 credits, distributed according to the requirements of the curriculum pursued. The selection of elective courses is planned with guidance from the student's academic adviser, according to the student's goals and interests. Students who are preparing to teach after graduation follow a program outlined by the Department of Teacher Education.

Students may prepare for careers in dentistry, law, medicine, physical and occupational therapy, optometry, and podiatry through the Mount's preprofessional programs. The College also supports an honors program for academically talented and dedicated students, providing a supportive community that encourages critical thinking and independent scholarship so that participants can realize their scholarly potential.

The Mount prepares graduates for a career, not just a job. When it comes to starting a career, what matters most are connections, experience, and familiarity with the professional world. The Oxley Career Education Program is committed to assisting students with making connections between their academic experience and career paths by identifying their interests, skills, and professional goals. The Oxley Career Education Program provides personalized advice on resume and cover letter preparation, interview coaching, and support with graduate school applications.

Off-Campus Programs

The College of Mount Saint Vincent encourages students to live and learn in other countries and believes it is a transformative element of a liberal arts education. The Mount's study-abroad programs broaden cultural and intellectual horizons and deepen the student's perspective on the world. The College currently offers semester-long programs and short courses in South America, England, Turkey, Greece, and Spain, among others. The College also partners with a number of consortiums for international study and service opportunities.

Academic Facilities

The Elizabeth Seton Library provides traditional and innovative resources, and it holds more than 170,000 volumes, 616 current periodical subscriptions, 9,850 microfilms, 6,150 audiovisual units (recordings, films, and cassettes), and numerous electronic databases. From books and ebooks to journals, databases, and videos, the library makes it easy to connect the resources students need. With computer access, printing, study space, and expert research help available, the library is at students' service all year round.

The newly renovated and expanded Maryvale Hall houses the Communication and Fine Arts Departments and includes two art studios, a radio station, and a state-of-the-art TV production studio. The three-story Science Hall contains recently renovated laboratories, a lecture hall, classrooms, darkrooms, and environmental research facilities in addition to classrooms. The Administration Building is the main building on campus, housing most of the administrative and faculty offices, classrooms, general computer labs, Academic Advisement, and other support services.

Costs

Tuition and fees for the 2015–16 year are $22,490; room and board are $8,120.

Financial Aid

The College awards academic merit scholarships; distinguished scholarships; and federal, state, and institutional financial aid. Among the full-tuition scholarships are the Corazon C. Aquino Scholarship and the Fonthill Writing Award.

To be eligible for any merit or distinguished scholarship, freshman applicants must have a completed application for admission on file with the Admissions Office by March 1. In addition to providing College scholarships, Mount Saint Vincent participates in all available federal and state programs of financial assistance, including Federal Pell Grants, Federal Supplemental Educational Opportunity Grants, Federal Work-Study awards, federal and New York State student loans, and New York State Tuition Assistance Program (TAP) awards. Mount Saint Vincent also participates in the Higher Education Opportunity Program (HEOP).

To be eligible for all forms of financial aid, freshman applicants must submit the Free Application for Federal Student Aid (FAFSA) by April 1; transfer applicants should submit the FAFSA by June 15. Eligibility for these programs is based on need. More than 90 percent of the students at Mount Saint Vincent receive aid from government or private agencies.

Faculty

The College of Mount Saint Vincent has 225 faculty members who, in addition to their teaching responsibilities, act as academic advisers and moderate student activities. The student-faculty ratio is 13:1, with an average class size of 20 students.

Student Government

Students participate in College governance through a strong student government with elected representatives on most major governing bodies of the College, including the College Senate, the Undergraduate and Graduate Committees, the Policies and Procedures Council, the Orientation Committee, and the Commencement Committee. Student government leaders make most decisions regarding the disbursement of student activity fees and budgeted funds for clubs and organizations. Students also play a central role in discipline through an elected Student Judicial Council. This constitutionally ensured involvement guarantees that students have direct access to information and multiple opportunities to present student views and articulate student needs to both faculty and administrators.

Admission Requirements

Applicants to the College of Mount Saint Vincent must have graduated from an accredited secondary school; should rank in the upper half of their class; and must achieve satisfactory scores on the SAT, ACT, or TOEFL. International students who qualify for admission are welcome to apply. Students attending a community college or another four-year college may apply for transfer admission. It is recommended that prospective students phone or e-mail for an interview and tour.

Students may apply online by visiting the College's website (www.mountsaintvincent.edu/admission/undergraduate-college-admission/apply-high-school-students/) or by using the Common Application (www.commonapp.org). The College holds an annual open house in the fall and regularly hosts tours and information sessions. To schedule a tour or interview, prospective students are encouraged to visit www.mountsaintvincent.edu/admission/visit-the-mount/request-a-tour-and-interview/.

Application and Information

In order to be evaluated for admission, a candidate must present the following: an application fee of $35 (waived if the student applies online); a completed application; scores on the SAT, ACT, or TOEFL; an essay; a letter of recommendation; and a high school transcript. Transfer applicants should submit all college transcripts.

The Admission Committee operates on a rolling admission basis. Starting December 1, candidates are notified within four weeks of completing their application. The deadline is April 1, after which admission is considered on the basis of space availability. Early action—a nonbinding, flexible admission program—is also offered. The deadline for applying early action is November 1, and notifications arrive by December 1. Scholarship award letters are mailed simultaneously with acceptance letters. Recommended transfer application guidelines are June 1 for fall and December 1 for spring.

Information, brochures, and application forms for admission and financial aid may be obtained by contacting:

Daniel Gallagher
Vice President/Dean of Admission and Financial Aid
College of Mount Saint Vincent
6301 Riverdale Avenue
Riverdale, New York 10471-1093
United States
Phone: 718-405-3267
E-mail: admissions@mountsaintvincent.edu
Website: http://www.mountsaintvincent.edu

On a 70-acre campus overlooking the Hudson River, just 12 miles from midtown Manhattan, the College of Mount Saint Vincent offers exceptional academic and professional programs to more than 1,800 undergraduate and graduate students.

THE COLLEGE OF NEW JERSEY

EWING TOWNSHIP, NEW JERSEY

★ To read more about this school, visit http://petersons.to/tcnj

TCNJ
THE COLLEGE OF
NEW JERSEY

The College

The College of New Jersey (TCNJ) welcomes students who have the talent and motivation to succeed in a highly rigorous academic environment. A public institution founded in 1855, the College enrolls about 6,500 full-time undergraduates, two thirds of whom reside on campus. Today it is heralded by *U.S. News & World Report* as well as *Barron's* as one of the most competitive schools in the nation, public or private. TCNJ serves a diverse student body, preparing graduates to excel as leaders in their chosen fields.

TCNJ has set the standard for public higher education. Students report they find TCNJ large enough to provide a full range of academic and extracurricular choices, yet small enough to be a genuine residential community of friends and fellow learners. With professors committed to collaboration in and out of the classroom and facilities of enviable quality, TCNJ represents an exceptional value in higher education.

The College of New Jersey's academic approach combines aspects of both traditional liberal arts schools and professional schools. A liberal learning curriculum ensures that all students are grounded in the beliefs and values of civic engagement and intellectual and scholarly growth and that they benefit from a well-rounded academic experience. Interdisciplinary studies, internships, research, and faculty mentoring are all part of an educational approach designed to develop successful leaders. While a very high percentage of graduates find immediate employment related to their fields of study, more than 20 percent continue to pursue their academic passions in graduate schools across the country.

All first- and second-year students are guaranteed on-campus housing, and most juniors and seniors continue to live on campus. Rooming arrangements are quite flexible, from doubles in freshman residence halls to suites and single rooms and on-campus town houses or apartments for upper class students. A nationally recognized residence life program and more than 200 student organizations offer numerous opportunities for leadership development, community engagement, and the cultivation of lifelong friendships. An exceptional 96 percent of first-year students return for their sophomore year.

The arts flourish in two theaters, a recital hall, an art gallery, and numerous other campus venues. Student performances, professional groups on tour, and a large variety of films, lectures, local bands, and solo entertainers fill the academic year with opportunities for cultural enrichment.

Student wellness is given high priority at the College, with many facilities for recreation and physical conditioning. In Packer Hall, the campus has access to a comprehensive fitness center, a 25-meter swimming and diving pool, and a basketball court. The Student Recreation Center offers racquetball courts, four tennis courts that are convertible for basketball or volleyball use, a weight room, and an indoor track. Other facilities include a lighted field with an artificial surface, eight lighted outdoor tennis courts, an outdoor beach volleyball court, and numerous athletic fields. In addition to these recreational resources, TCNJ employs dieticians, nutritionists, and other specialists committed to promoting healthy lifestyles and overall wellness in the realms of mind, body, and spirit.

As a Division III member of the National Collegiate Athletic Association, TCNJ offers twenty sports: ten for men and ten for women. Since 1979, TCNJ student-athletes have amassed forty national championships and over thirty runner-up awards, giving the College an aggregate of more than seventy first- and second-place finishes. That figure tops the figures of the nation's 400-plus Division III colleges and universities over the past thirty years. TCNJ has produced 44 individual national champions and 58 CoSIDA Academic All-Americans. Over the past seventeen years, TCNJ has finished in the top ten of the Learfield Sports Director's Cup races sixteen times. The ranking is based on the cumulative performance of each sport of all competing NCAA Division III institutions.

In addition to its NCAA athletics, TCNJ offers a wide variety of recreation programs for intramural competition and self-governing sports clubs. More than 3,500 students play with these less demanding, but still spirited and competitive teams, each year, some of which have intercollegiate schedules.

The College's undergraduate programs are accredited by the Middle States Association of Colleges and Schools and by professional associations in business, chemistry, computer science, education, education of the deaf, engineering, music, and nursing.

Location

Students at The College of New Jersey live and learn on a picturesque, 289-acre campus located in suburban Ewing Township, approximately 15 minutes from downtown Princeton; 10 minutes from Bucks County, Pennsylvania; and 5 miles from the state capital of Trenton. Woodlands and lakes surround major academic and residential buildings, which have a strong Neoclassical Georgian Colonial aesthetic. The campus is 30 miles from the theaters and museums of Philadelphia and 60 miles from those in New York City. In 2013, TCNJ broke ground on Campus Town, a series of residential and commercial establishments along the edge of campus, scheduled to be completed in summer 2015.

Majors and Degrees

The College of New Jersey offers rigorous, personalized programs culminating in the Bachelor of Arts, Bachelor of Fine Arts, Bachelor of Music, Bachelor of Science, Bachelor of Science in Engineering, and Bachelor of Science in Nursing degrees.

TCNJ grants degrees in the following majors: Accountancy, Art Teacher Preparation (K–12), Art History, Biomedical Engineering, Biology*, Business Administration (specializations in finance, interdisciplinary business, management, and marketing), Chemistry*, Civil Engineering, Communication Studies, Computer Engineering, Computer Science, Criminology, Early Childhood Education, Education of the Deaf and Hard of Hearing, Economics*, Electrical Engineering, Elementary Education, Engineering Science (students may specialize in engineering management or policy and society), English*, Global Business, Health and Exercise Science, Health and Physical Education (teacher preparation K–12), History*, Interactive Multimedia, International Studies, i-STEM (integrative science, technology, engineering, and mathematics), Mathematics*, Mechanical Engineering, Music (options in performance and K–12 teacher preparation), Nursing, Philosophy, Physics*, Political Science, Psychology, Sociology and Anthropology, Special Education, Spanish*, Technology Education /Pre-Engineering (K–12), Urban Education, Visual Arts (options in fine arts, graphic design, and lens-based art), and Women and Gender Studies. **Programs in which students may prepare for teacher certification*

TCNJ offers a number of 5-year combined Master of Arts in Teaching degrees with dual certification in Elementary Education, and either Special Education, Urban Education, or Deaf and Hard-of-Hearing Education. Students may also enroll in a seven-year B.S./M.D. degree program with New Jersey Medical School (Newark) or a seven-year B.S./O.D. degree program with the State University of New York College of Optometry. The College also offers a Medical Careers Advisory Committee for premed students and a Pre-Law Advisement Committee for students planning a career in law.

Academic Programs

All academic courses contain significant out-of-class requirements, which foster deeper student-faculty collaboration. All baccalaureate degrees require at least thirty-two courses, including a core curriculum in the traditional arts and sciences. The average class size for freshman-level lectures is 24 students; it is 22 students for upper-division lectures.

The thirty-week year is divided into fall and spring semesters; a summer session offers courses in two 5-week sessions and one 6-week session. Winter Session guarantees all of the benefits of a full-time TCNJ course in a more compact time frame, in addition to study-abroad opportunities. For those students who find that they cannot fit study abroad into their standard semester, Winter Session offers courses everywhere from New Orleans to London.

All first-year students participate in a First Seminar Program that links residential learning with small classes taught by full-time faculty members. Seminars, independent studies, and capstone courses give many students the opportunity for challenging advanced study in close collaboration with faculty mentors. Many TCNJ students publish the results of these endeavors or present them at national and regional conferences.

The Honors Program offers students highly intensive academic experiences without adding extra obstructions on the path toward degree completion. Honors courses promote an interdisciplinary perspective and curriculum, concentrating on central themes within significant periods in the cultural development of civilization. Honors courses within specific majors consist of either specially designated discussion groups or independent study. All honors classes are small, personalized, and stimulating.

Off-Campus Programs

TCNJ offers students a variety of full-year and one-semester programs of study abroad as well as study at other state colleges and universities within the United States. Exchange programs are available in 80 cities in Australia, Austria, Canada, Denmark, France, Germany, Greece, Israel, Japan, Mexico, the United Kingdom, and numerous other countries. National exchanges are available at more than 130 participating institutions in the United States, the U.S. Virgin Islands, Puerto Rico, and Guam. The College of New Jersey is proud to host the New Jersey State Consortium for International Studies.

Academic Facilities

TCNJ has been nationally recognized as one of the most beautiful campuses in the nation. Within the past several years, TCNJ has built and opened a Science Complex, Biology Building, Social Science Building, College Spiritual Center, Art and Interactive Media Building, Education Building, student apartments, and a state-of-the-art library, which serves as the intellectual and social hub of campus. The College is also in the planning stages for construction of a new, comprehensive STEM (science, technology, engineering, and mathematics) building, with completion scheduled for 2017. Campuswide networking provides full Internet accessibility from all residence hall rooms and more than twenty student computing laboratories.

Costs

For up-to-date information on in-state and out-of state tuition and fees costs, as well as room and board figures, prospective students should go online to http://www.tcnj.edu/~sfs/tuition/index.html.

Financial Aid

Over 50 percent of full-time undergraduates receive some form of financial aid, such as federal, state, and institutional grants; merit scholarships; student employment; and loan assistance. The Free Application for Federal Student Aid (FAFSA) or Renewal FAFSA is used to apply for need-based aid at the federal and state levels. The CSS/Financial Aid Profile is used to apply for institutional need-based aid.

Scholarships and grants include The College of New Jersey Merit Scholars Program, Bonner Scholars, Chairman of the Board Merit Scholars, the New Jersey Tuition Aid Grant, Federal Pell Grants, Federal Supplemental Educational Opportunity Grants (FSEOG), Educational Opportunity Fund (EOF) Promise Award, and Army and Air Force ROTC Scholarships, as well as other institutional scholarships. Loans include the Federal Subsidized and Unsubsidized Stafford Loans, the Federal Perkins Loan, the Federal Parent Loan for Undergraduate Students (PLUS), the New Jersey CLASS Loan, private/alternative loans, nursing loans, and short-term emergency loan funds. Student employment options include the need-based Federal Work-Study Program (on- and off-campus positions) as well as institutionally supported campus jobs.

Faculty

The approximately 335 full-time members of the College of New Jersey faculty are teachers and scholars possessing terminal degrees in their respective fields. While teaching is their primary commitment, they are also active researchers, authors, artists, performers, and regular contributors in their academic disciplines. No classes are taught by graduate assistants. The student-faculty ratio is 12:1. From their first day, students study with faculty members who may be researching new ways to use solar energy, writing a new play or novel, or investigating the life cycle of desert ferns. Members of the faculty have attracted many significant grants, fellowships, and awards, including the Bancroft Prize in history, Fulbright Scholarships, and grants from the National Science Foundation, the National Institute for Advanced Study, the Guggenheim Foundation, and the National Endowment for the Humanities. Faculty members mentor their students, preparing them for careers, graduate and professional schools, and prestigious fellowships such as the Fulbright, Truman, and Marshall Fellowships.

Student Governance and Programming

The Student Government Association, comprising all undergraduate students at the College, is governed by elected representatives. The Residence Hall Association provides the mechanism for student input into campus housing policies, and members of the Student Finance Board oversee and administer approximately $500,000 in student funds. The College Union Board sponsors a wide range of special events, including recent visits by Seth Meyer, Cornel West, Nick Offerman, and John Oliver.

Admission Requirements

The College of New Jersey seeks students who can succeed in highly selective academic programs and who show intellectual curiosity, academic talent, and the potential to contribute to the life of the College. The College is committed to attracting students from diverse economic, racial, social, and geographic backgrounds. A high school record of college-preparatory credits, high school class rank, SAT scores, and special interests, skills, and qualities can be influential in application review. Certain departments, such as art, interactive multimedia, and music, waive the SAT/ACT submission requirement and use additional criteria such as portfolio submissions and auditions to evaluate candidates seeking admission into their programs. The College of New Jersey reviews candidates holistically and takes into consideration the variations in high schools and communities in which the applicants reside.

Application and Information

The College of New Jersey is a member of the Common Application. The deadline for applications for Spring enrollment is November. The Regular Decision application deadline for Fall enrollment is February 1. There is a $75 application fee. Candidates who apply only to The College of New Jersey under the Early Decision plan may apply before November 1 and will be notified on or before December 1. Early Decision applicants may also choose to apply before January 1 and receive notification on or before February 1. Students applying to the seven-year Accelerated Medical program must apply by December 1. For Fall enrollment, the College requires incoming students to pay an enrollment deposit of $600 no later than May 1.

For more information, students should contact:

The College of New Jersey
P.O. Box 7718
Ewing, New Jersey 08628-0718
United States
Phone: 609-771-2131
Website: http://www.tcnj.edu

The campus of The College of New Jersey, a marvel of Neoclassical Georgian Colonial architecture, is one of the most beautiful campuses in the United States.

COLLEGE OF SAINT BENEDICT AND SAINT JOHN'S UNIVERSITY

ST. JOSEPH AND COLLEGEVILLE, MINNESOTA

COLLEGE OF Saint Benedict

Saint John's UNIVERSITY

★ To read more about this school, visit http://petersons.to/csb-sju

The Colleges

The College of Saint Benedict (CSB) and Saint John's University (SJU) are nationally leading liberal arts colleges whose unique partnership provides students with a highly engaged learning experience, preparing them for leadership in a global society. The colleges' Catholic and Benedictine tradition and an extraordinary sense of community enliven the student experience.

With nearly 4,000 undergraduate students, CSB (for women) and SJU (for men) form the largest liberal arts college in the nation. Students at CSB/SJU have full access to the campuses, courses, faculty, facilities, and programs of two colleges. Together, CSB/SJU offer the opportunities, course selection, and extensive curriculum of a large university while retaining the close-knit community and personal attention expected from a top liberal arts college.

Students travel between the two campuses on the LINK, a free and frequent shuttle that runs throughout the day on an easy-to-remember schedule, making it simple to travel to either campus as needed. Students from both colleges eat at any of the four dining centers on the two campuses.

Through a focus on full-time, undergraduate students, CSB/SJU provide a highly engaging college experience. Eighty percent of CSB/SJU seniors report being involved on campus compared to just 50 percent at liberal arts colleges nationwide. The colleges' high level of student engagement combined with a residential campus community leads to a vibrant, 24/7 living experience.

The colleges' four-year residential program provides on-campus housing for approximately 90 percent of students including all first-year and sophomore students. Almost all first-year students reside in two-person rooms. Upperclass students live in a variety of residences including two-person rooms, suites, and apartments.

The colleges prepare students for leadership in a global society. CSB/SJU enroll 200 international students from thirty countries, and are ranked third in the nation among undergraduate colleges for the number of students who participate in semester-long study abroad programs. CSB/SJU received the Senator Paul Simon Award in 2012 for comprehensive internationalization—one of only a few liberal arts schools to claim this distinction. The award recognizes schools that demonstrate excellence in integrating an international and global perspective into all aspects of college life. A third of CSB/SJU professors have led a study-abroad program, and 200 courses offered throughout the year incorporate an international component.

The Benedictine communities that founded the colleges in the nineteenth century continue to shape the Catholic character of CSB/SJU. Today, Benedictine women and men remain actively involved on campus. Their presence in community life provides the stable sense of home for which the colleges are so well known. CSB/SJU are guided by the Benedictine values distilled from the *Rule of Saint Benedict*, written in the sixth century by Saint Benedict, the founder of the Benedictine monastic order.

Ninety-nine percent of last year's CSB/SJU graduates were employed, continuing their education, or engaged in a full-time volunteer program within one year of graduation—the searchable database at www.csbsjuresults.com gives an indication of what these graduates are doing. And 97 percent of CSB/SJU alums rate their college experience as good or excellent.

Location

CSB/SJU are located on 3,000 acres of woods and lakes in central Minnesota just west of St. Cloud (metro population 160,000) and an hour northwest of Minneapolis/St. Paul via Interstate 94. The campuses are ideally suited for active, outdoor-minded students, and include 15 miles of hiking trails, an on-campus beach, and an outdoor challenge course. Students can check out canoes and outdoor equipment from the Outdoor Leadership Center at SJU and Intramural Desk at CSB. The colleges were crowned champion of the 2014 Outdoor Nation Campus Challenge, a competition sponsored by The North Face in which colleges earned points through the outdoor activities of community members.

Majors and Degrees

CSB/SJU offer a Bachelor of Arts degree along with a Bachelor of Science degree in nursing. The colleges have more than 60 areas of study, with 37 majors and 33 minors. Major area of study include accounting, art, Asian studies, biochemistry, biology, business (global business leadership), chemistry, classics, communication, computer science, economics, education, engineering (dual-degree program), English, environmental studies, European studies, finance, French studies, gender studies, German studies, history, humanities, mathematics, music, natural science, numerical computation, nursing, peace studies, philosophy, physics, political science, psychology, social science, sociology, Spanish, theater, and theology.

Academic Programs

CSB/SJU share one combined academic curriculum—students from both colleges take classes together on both campuses. The colleges are on a semester schedule. As part of the colleges' core curriculum, all students enroll in a yearlong first-year seminar—composed of 16 students, the course focuses on critical thinking, reading, discussion, research, and other skills for successful college work. In addition to other core curriculum requirements, all CSB/SJU students enroll in a capstone course in ethics and complete at least one experiential learning activity such as undergraduate research, internships, study abroad, or community service.

Off-Campus Programs

The colleges rank third nationally among undergraduate colleges for the number of students participating in semester-long study abroad. CSB/SJU offer 19 semester-long, faculty-led international study programs in fifteen countries: Australia, Austria, Chile, China, England, France, Germany, Greece, Guatemala, India, Ireland, Italy, Japan, Spain, and South Africa. In addition, the colleges sponsor over 20 short-term international programs around the world each year. A growing number of study-abroad programs provide students with opportunities for on-site internships.

The CSB/SJU Washington Summer Study program provides students with an opportunity to live and work in the Washington D.C., area while earning academic credit. Participants serve in a Congressional office, on a committee staff, in a government agency, in a nonprofit organization, or with a public affairs group. In addition to the work experience, participants attend seminars and supplemental meetings with alumni and other professionals.

Academic Facilities

Students from both colleges use classrooms, libraries, labs, and art facilities on both campuses. CSB/SJU share one, joint library system and coordinate in the development of academic facilities across the two campuses.

All residence hall rooms are wired to the high-speed campus network backbone. Every residence hall has a computer cluster with access to the same applications as those in classrooms, labs, and access areas. Computer access areas are available for student use seven days a week, with PCs and laser printers. Wireless access is available in all academic buildings including libraries, most inner campus outdoor green spaces, and the majority of residence hall lounges.

A comprehensive virtual tour of the campuses is available at www.csbsjutour.com.

Costs

Tuition and fees for 2015–16 are $40,846 (CSB) and $40,226 (SJU). Average room and meal plan is $10,229 (CSB) and $9,604 (SJU).

Financial Aid

Financial aid is available to students who qualify based on the results of the Free Application for Federal Student Aid (FAFSA) and the CSB/SJU Financial Aid Application. Ninety-three percent of CSB/SJU students receive scholarship or grant assistance to help pay for college. Ninety percent of CSB/SJU graduates finish in four years.

Merit-based aid is awarded to students based on a combination of their test scores, GPA, curriculum, extracurricular involvement and volunteer work. CSB/SJU offer fine arts scholarships to students who plan to continue their involvement in art, music, or theater in college. Additional scholarships are available for students interested in biochemistry, chemistry, computer science, math, and physics. CSB/SJU are home to the Fighting Saints Army Battalion and offer an Army ROTC Scholarship.

Faculty

The heart of the CSB/SJU undergraduate experience is rooted in a lively and sustained engagement between students and faculty, both in the classroom and beyond. Professors actively encourage students to take responsibility for and own their education. Discussion-based classes and active learning teaching practices typify CSB/SJU classrooms and curricular challenges.

CSB/SJU offer students the opportunity to learn from experienced, well-prepared teacher/mentors who are recognized scholars in their own fields and committed to continued growth within their own disciplines. More than 85 percent of students stress the importance of faculty role models and mentors in their positive educational experiences at CSB/SJU. A 12:1 student-to-faculty ratio and an average class size of 19 allow for close interaction between faculty and students. A larger-than-average faculty in comparison to many liberal arts colleges translates into a more extensive range of courses available in many departments.

The CSB/SJU faculty includes 297 full-time and 51 part-time members. Eighty-five percent of full-time faculty members have the highest degree in their field. Faculty members teach all classes and labs.

Student Activities

CSB/SJU sponsor 100 student clubs and organizations. All campus-sponsored clubs are open to all students. An involvement fair at the beginning of each school year provides a perfect venue for new students to get connected with campus opportunities.

The colleges are members of the Minnesota Intercollegiate Athletic Association and participate in NCAA Division III. Women's intercollegiate sports include basketball, cross-country, golf, hockey, soccer, softball, swimming and diving, tennis, track and field, and volleyball. Men's intercollegiate sports include baseball, basketball, cross-country, football, golf, hockey, soccer, swimming and diving, tennis, track and field, and wrestling. The colleges also field competitive club sport teams including crew, dance, lacrosse, Nordic skiing, rugby, and Ultimate Frisbee.

With exceptional performing arts facilities and art galleries, CSB/SJU serve as a hub for the arts in central Minnesota. The colleges' Fine Arts Series annually attracts approximately 40 national and international touring acts and art exhibits to the campuses with dramatically reduced ticket prices for students.

The Joint Events Council, composed of students from both colleges, plans a full slate of campus events. Annual campus traditions include the Fruit at the Finish Triathlon, a polar bear plunge, Thanksgiving dinner at SJU, Christmas dinner at CSB, and the annual Pines music festival.

Students explore spirituality through a variety of options on campus, including Benedictine Friends, Companions on a Journey, Praise in the Pub, and Men's Spirituality groups. Campus Ministry offers both national and international service trips. In addition, urban plunges, prison ministry, and Alternative Break Experiences are a few of the many ways that students live out the Benedictine values.

Admission Requirements

CSB/SJU strive to attract a diverse student body, and enroll students from across the United States and around the world. Applicants are required to submit a high school transcript, standardized test scores (ACT/SAT/TOEFL), a writing sample, and a letter of recommendation. The admission office completes a holistic review of applicants, considering strength of curriculum, academic trends, and leadership potential in its admission decisions.

Application and Information

Students may apply to CSB/SJU using the colleges' online application or using the Common Application. Deadlines include: Early Action I, November 15; Early Action II, December 15; and regular decision, January 15. The colleges review applications after January 15 on a rolling basis.

For further information, prospective students should contact:

Office of Admission
College of Saint Benedict
Saint John's University
2850 Abbey Plaza
P.O. Box 7155
Collegeville, Minnesota 56321
United States
Phone: 320-363-5060
800-544-1489 (toll-free)
Fax: 320-363-5650
E-mail: admission@csbsju.edu
Website: www.twocolleges.com
www.facebook.com/twocolleges
twitter.com/csbsju

With nearly 4,000 full-time, residential, undergraduate students, CSB/SJU are a great fit for students looking to be highly engaged in their college experience.

COLLEGE OF STATEN ISLAND OF THE CITY UNIVERSITY OF NEW YORK

STATEN ISLAND, NEW YORK

★ To read more about this school, visit http://petersons.to/collegeofstatenisland

The College and the University

Founded in 1976 from the merger of two existing colleges, the College of Staten Island (CSI) is a four-year senior college within the City University of New York (CUNY) and is Staten Island's only public institution of higher learning. CSI is dedicated to access and excellence and currently serves over 14,300 students.

Offering over eighty programs and areas of study, the College ensures that students receive a thorough liberal arts education through core requirements that include classes in the arts and humanities, mathematics, sciences, and social sciences.

In addition to the exciting array of undergraduate degrees and majors available, CSI also awards master's degrees in the following disciplines: Accounting; Biology; Business Management; Cinema and Media Studies; Clinical Mental Health Counseling; Computer Science; Education; English; Environmental Science; History; Liberal Studies; Neuroscience, Mental Retardation, and Developmental Disabilities; Nursing; and Social Work. CSI also offers the following post-master's and advanced certificates: Adult-Gerontological Health Nursing, Autism Spectrum Disorders, Business Analytics of Large-Scale Data, Cultural Competence, and Leadership in Education. CSI proudly confers the Clinical Doctorate of Physical Therapy (D.P.T.) and the Doctorate of Nursing Practice in Adult Gerontological Health Nursing. Additional doctoral programs offered jointly with the CUNY Graduate School include Biochemistry, Biology, Polymer Chemistry, Computer Science, and Physics.

Housing: CSI offers students an opportunity to live on campus in luxury apartment-style housing. Located in two brand-new buildings, Dolphin Cove North and South contain 133 furnished apartments housing 454 residents. The buildings offer both private and semi-private bedroom accommodations with semi-private bathrooms and full kitchens. Other amenities include a study lounge, fitness center, and convenient parking. Housing is filled on a first-come, first-served basis.

Location

CSI is located on a sprawling 204-acre campus located in the heart of Staten Island. The campus is the largest single site for a college, public or private, within New York City. Classrooms and academic offices are located in fourteen neo-Georgian buildings that form two quadrangles connected by the campus walk, which extends between the Library and the Campus Center. The Library, Dolphin Cove North and South, the Campus Center, the Biological Sciences/Chemical Sciences building, the Center for the Arts, and the Sports and Recreation Center provide outstanding facilities for scholastic and community activities.

CSI's location offers students the better of two worlds, with Staten Island providing a suburban environment with some of the most interesting landscapes in the metropolitan area and Manhattan, the center of cultural and social life in the city, being only 25 minutes from the Island by ferry. In addition, the Verrazano-Narrows Bridge provides direct access between Staten Island and Brooklyn.

Majors and Degrees

CSI offers the following associate degrees: Business (A.A.S.): Accounting, Finance, Information Systems, International Business, Management, and Marketing specializations; Computer Technology (A.A.S.): Programming and Information Science sequences; Electrical Engineering Technology (A.A.S.); Engineering Science (A.S.); Liberal Arts and Sciences (A.A./A.S.); and Nursing (A.A.S.).

CSI offers the following bachelor's degree programs: Accounting (B.S.); African and African Diaspora Studies (B.A.); American Studies (B.A.); Art (B.A./B.F.A.): Studio Art and Photography concentrations; Biochemistry (B.S.); Biology* (B.S.): Bioinformatics option; Business (B.S.): Finance, International Business, Management, and Marketing concentrations; Chemistry* (B.S.); Cinema Studies (B.A.): Critical Studies and Production concentrations; Communications (B.S.): Journalism, Media Studies, Design and Digital Media, and Corporate Communications concentrations; Computer Science (B.S.); Computer Science/Mathematics (B.S.); Dramatic Arts (B.S.); Economics (B.A./B.S.): Business and Finance specializations; Education: Early Childhood, Childhood, and Adolescence programs; Electrical Engineering (B.S.); Engineering Science (B.S.): Computer, Electrical, and Mechanical specializations; English* (B.A.): Writing, Linguistics, Literature, and Dramatic Literature concentrations; Geography (B.A.); History* (B.A.); International Studies (B.A.); Italian Studies* (B.A.); Mathematics* (B.S.): Pure and Applied Mathematics emphases; Medical Technology (B.S.); Music (B.A./B.S.): Classical Performance, Literature and Theory, Music Technology, Jazz Studies, and Performance concentrations; Nursing (B.S.); Philosophy (B.A.); Philosophy and Political Science (B.A., dual major); Physics* (B.S.); Political Science (B.A.); Pre-Professional Preparation: Dentistry, Law, Medicine, Optometry, Physical Therapy, and Podiatry programs; Psychology (B.A./B.S.); Science Letters and Society (B.A.): Early Childhood sequence (Birth–2) and Childhood sequence (1–6); Social Work (B.S.S.W.); Sociology–Anthropology (B.A.); Spanish* (B.A.); and Women's, Gender, and Sexuality Studies (B.A.).

**Adolescent Education track (grades 7–12) available.*

Academic Programs

CSI offers two-year programs in career areas and in liberal arts and sciences and four-year programs with majors in the traditional fields of study. General education requirements have been established for all degrees. Credit may be awarded for internships, research, and experiential learning. Students may graduate with honors in most bachelor's degree majors.

The College offers classes scheduled during both the day and evening, seven days a week. The Office of Weekend and Evening Services offers a variety of course combinations leading to associate and bachelor's degrees, providing opportunities for nontraditional students to pursue a college education at more convenient times. CSI also offers intensive summer and winter sessions.

Honors Programs: The College offers several honors programs. Programs include Macaulay Honors College at CSI (MHC), the College's most selective full scholarship program*; The Verrazano School, a local honors program that creates learning communities and provides scholarships for study abroad; and Teacher Education Honors Academy at CSI (TEHA), a scholarship program designed to highly train select students to teach mathematics and science in New York City Department of Education middle and high schools.

**Scholarship receipt subject to eligibility requirements.*

Off-Campus Programs

CSI students may use the resources of and receive credit for courses taken at other CUNY colleges to support their education. The College also gives a number of courses for credit at off-campus locations throughout the city through internships at major corporations and other sites. Exceptional study-abroad opportunities are available through CSI's Center for International Service, which offers students the option of earning academic credit for study in Australia, Belgium, China, Costa Rica, Denmark, Ecuador, England, France, Greece, Ireland, Italy, Japan, Spain, or St. John, U.S. Virgin Islands. Students may also pursue study-abroad programs in additional countries through the College Consortium for International Studies (CCIS).

Academic Facilities

The academic buildings are designed to house approximately 300 state-of-the-art laboratories and classrooms; each has its own computer lab, study lounge for students, and faculty offices.

The Campus Center is where students can relax, dine, and be entertained. The two-story rotunda at the heart of the structure contains the main dining facilities, the College's health services, a bookstore, offices for student organizations, study lounges, a small performance/café space, game rooms with the latest game consoles, and the state-of-the-art student-operated studios of WSIA 88.9, the only FM radio station on Staten Island.

The Center for the Arts complex provides facilities for teaching in the instructional wing and performance spaces in the public wing. The complex of public facilities includes a 911-seat auditorium, a 442-seat fully equipped theater, a 156-seat recital hall, a 142-seat lecture hall, an experimental Black Box Theater, art galleries, and a conference center. Classrooms, lecture halls, studios, screening rooms, and offices for faculty members are located in the instructional wing.

The CSI Library is staffed with librarians trained in every discipline offered at the College, who also hold faculty status and rank. The Library's total collection consists of approximately 499,910 books and ebooks, 53,158 electronic journals, 210 electronic resources, 15,500 films and videos, and 5,000 sound recordings. The Library's online catalog provides complete access to the collections, including access to holdings of other CUNY libraries. Students also have electronic access to database and research tools 24 hours a day via the Internet. In addition, the Library maintains a collection of current textbooks donated by the CSI Student Government. These and other course materials are available at the Reserve Desk. Wireless laptops are loaned to students for use throughout the Library. The Library building also houses the Office of Academic Support and the Cybercafé, which offers Starbucks® coffee.

The laboratory science building provides facilities for teaching and for two research centers: the Center for Environmental Science and the Center for Developmental Neuroscience and Developmental Disabilities. It consists of a research wing and an instructional wing. State-of-the-art laboratories serve students and faculty members in their teaching and research.

The CSI Astrophysical Observatory is a world-class resource that has been recognized by the International Astronomical Union as an official asteroid-tracking station.

CSI is dedicated to keeping its campus up-to-date during these technology-centric times. Planned updates include the highly innovative Interdisciplinary High-Performance Computational Center and expansions to the Library and Campus Center.

Costs

For 2015–16, undergraduate tuition for New York State (NYS) residents is $275 per credit for resident part-time matriculated students, $3,165 per semester for resident full-time matriculated students, and $400 per credit for resident non-degree students. Nonresident full- and part-time students are charged $560 per credit, and nonresident non-degree students are charged $840 per credit. Graduate NYS resident tuition is $5,065 per semester for students attending the College full-time and $425 per credit for resident part-time students. Nonresidents are charged $780 per credit for full- and part-time attendance.

Financial Aid

Financial aid is available through state and federal programs and includes the New York State Tuition Assistance Program (TAP) awards, Federal Pell Grants, Supplemental Educational Opportunity Grants (SEOG), Search for Elevation and Education through Knowledge (SEEK) awards, Federal Work-Study Program awards, and student loan programs. Information about programs, application procedures, and deadlines is available from the Financial Aid Office.

The CSI Scholarship is awarded annually to incoming freshmen, transfer, and current students with a 90.00 or 3.25 (or higher) GPA. Further information about scholarships is available from the Career and Scholarship Center.

Faculty

The College has a full-time faculty of 352, of whom approximately 90 percent hold a doctoral degree or the highest attainable degree in their field. Numerous faculty members have made significant contributions in many areas of scholarship, creativity, and public service and have received prestigious grants and awards.

Student Government

A single body, the Senate, is composed of 25 elected students and represents the interests of the College's students, serving as liaison to faculty and administrators. The Senate derives funding from the Student Activity Fee and sponsors many academic and nonacademic programs benefiting students.

Admission Requirements

A freshman applicant seeking admission to a bachelor's degree program must pass the CUNY Assessment Tests (CATs) in reading, writing, and mathematics unless he or she qualifies for exemption based on their high SAT, ACT, or Regents Examination scores. Admission to a bachelor's degree program is determined by the applicant's high school courses, academic average, and the combined verbal and mathematics SAT scores. The College accepts applicants whose scores reach or exceed the College's minimum bachelor's degree program requirements. A faculty admissions committee may consider admitting applicants whose scores approach the College's minimum requirements. Entering first-year students may be admitted to associate-level programs if they have graduated from an accredited high school or have earned a high school equivalency diploma. A transfer applicant with 30 or more credits completed at the time of application must have a minimum cumulative GPA of 2.00. Applicants with fewer than 30 credits must have a GPA of at least 2.00 and must meet freshman entrance criteria.

Application and Information

Requests for further information and application materials should be directed to:

College of Staten Island/The City University of New York
Office of Recruitment and Admissions, Building 2A, Room 103
Staten Island, New York 10314
Phone: 718-982-2010
E-mail: admissions@csi.cuny.edu
Website: www.csi.cuny.edu

The CSI Library offers access to over 499,000 books and 53,000 electronic journals. All CSI students may also use the libraries and databases of other CUNY schools, allowing them access to millions of resources.

COLLEGE CLOSE-UPS

COLUMBIA UNIVERSITY
Columbia College/The Fu Foundation School of Engineering and Applied Science
NEW YORK, NEW YORK

The University

Columbia College and The Fu Foundation School of Engineering and Applied Science (Columbia Engineering) offer their students unique advantages; they are at the same time small, selective colleges and integral components of a major research university. Students benefit from over 250 years of rich history and distinction, easy access to the immense resources of New York City and a dynamic residential community where "Columbia Blue" is worn with pride at events ranging from Lions' basketball games to the World Leaders Forum, from the Varsity Show to late-night study sessions in the dorms.

The Columbia College student body is composed of approximately 4,500 students; the Columbia Engineering student body is roughly 1,500. Students come from all fifty states and over ninety countries. They represent a dazzling array of ethnic, social, economic, cultural, religious, and geographic backgrounds. The diversity of Columbia's student body reflects the diversity of New York City, the world's most international city.

Columbia guarantees four years of on-campus housing to all entering first-year students. Nearly all undergraduates remain in University residence halls for all four years.

Columbia students take part in extracurricular groups of all kinds: artistic (theater, music, dance, film, and visual arts), athletic (thirty-one Division I varsity sports and dozens of club and intramural sports), communications (the *Columbia Daily Spectator,* the *Columbia Journal of Literary Criticism*, WKCR-FM, a campus television station, and many others), community service (Amnesty International, Big Brother/Big Sister programs, after-hours tutoring programs, a volunteer ambulance squad, and partnerships with dozens of hospitals, soup kitchens, and homeless shelters), and preprofessional (the Charles Drew Pre-Medical Society, the National Society of Black Engineers, and more). Other groups represent students' ethnic, religious, political, and gender identities. There are twenty-eight fraternities and sororities. Alfred Lerner Hall houses office and meeting space for student organizations, a black box theater, a cinema, the Center for Student Advising, and many dining options.

Location

Columbia shares its Manhattan neighborhood, Morningside Heights, with a number of other notable institutions: Barnard College, the Cathedral of St. John the Divine, Union Theological Seminary, Jewish Theological Seminary, and the Manhattan School of Music, to name a few. Many faculty members from Columbia and the other surrounding schools make their homes in the neighborhood. Morningside Heights is an area known for bookstores, wonderfully varied restaurants, and merchants that cater to student tastes, student budgets, and student hours.

Students are encouraged to and assisted in making full use of New York's breathtaking variety of cultural, recreational, and professional resources. Through the Columbia Arts Initiative, students can receive discounted tickets to Broadway shows, film screenings, art galleries, and a multitude of cultural events in New York City. Passport to NYC offers students free access to over thirty museums throughout the city. Columbia students can be found any day of the week exploring the Metropolitan Museum of Art, the Museum of Modern Art, the Guggenheim Museum, the Museum of African Art, the Museo del Barrio, or the Asia Society. They might be discovering the theatrical offerings on, off, or "off-off" Broadway (or on campus); attending the opera, ballet, or symphony at Lincoln Center; enjoying jazz in Greenwich Village or blues at the Apollo; sampling *pai gwat* in Chinatown; or biking or jogging in Central Park. Columbia's Center for Career Education offers students opportunities to explore career pathways in depth; nowhere else in the world does the concentration of industries allow such a range of possibilities for internships and post-graduate employment. New York's public transportation system puts the entire city within easy reach of Columbia students; the campus is directly served by a subway line and five bus routes.

Majors and Degrees

Columbia College grants the B.A. degree in more than eighty programs of study in the humanities, social sciences, and pure sciences, including many interdisciplinary majors. Columbia Engineering grants the B.S. degree in sixteen engineering fields. A five-year program that begins in either school allows students to receive both a B.A. from Columbia College and a B.S. from Columbia Engineering.

Joint degree programs offer selected students the opportunity to combine their undergraduate work with study in Columbia University's schools of law and international affairs and with the Juilliard School.

Academic Programs

Columbia College is known for its Core Curriculum, a set of common courses required of all undergraduates and considered the necessary general education for students, irrespective of their choice in major. The communal learning—with all students encountering the same texts and issues at the same time—and the critical dialogue experienced in small seminars are the distinctive features of the Core. Begun in the 1919, the Core Curriculum is one of the founding experiments in liberal higher education in the United States, and it remains vibrant nearly a century later. One of the signature courses in the Core is Contemporary Civilization, a year-long historical survey of Western civilization's religious, political, and moral philosophies; another is Literature Humanities, a year-long introduction to Western culture's most seminal and meaningful literary works. A second year of humanities offers a semester each of music and art appreciation, encouraging students to experience the cultural treasures of New York City. The Global Core requirement enlarges the scope of inquiry beyond the Western focus in order to promote learning and thought about the variety of cultures and the diversity of traditions that interact in the United States and the world today. Frontiers of Science outlines the approaches that scientists take to answer compelling problems in the natural world and introduces students to scientific research methods. University Writing equips students with the ability and thoughtfulness to read and write essays in order to participate in the academic conversations that form Columbia's intellectual community. The Core Curriculum exposes Columbia's multicultural student body to a variety of disciplines, preparing them for the complex questions and issues of modern society.

The strength of Columbia Engineering's education is in its uniquely broad curriculum, preparing students not only to be world-class engineers but also to be global leaders across industries who are equipped and motivated to address the world's most pressing challenges. In addition to taking rigorous math and science courses typically offered at top undergraduate programs, Columbia Engineering students benefit from programming that fosters innovation and entrepreneurship, and are also required to take courses in the liberal arts alongside their College counterparts, providing them with interdisciplinary tools for real-world problem solving. This type of broad academic exposure is what alumni often cite as the foundation of their later academic and professional success. Another hallmark of the Columbia Engineering education is the Art of Engineering, where students are introduced to the field through interactive lectures, group projects, and guest speakers. A key component of the course is a semester-long, hands-on group project. Past examples of projects include mathematically modeling the U.S. elections, designing vital signs monitors, and modifying a laser pointer to transmit digital data over long distances. In addition to the technical issues discussed in the course, other key issues of importance in professional engineering such as ethics, project management, and societal impact are addressed.

Off-Campus Programs

Columbia maintains a network of global centers, developing opportunities for research, scholarship, teaching, and service across borders. With eight international locations ranging from Turkey to Chile and from Kenya to China, undergraduate options include summer Arabic language programs in Amman, Jordan or a semester-long French literature program in Paris at Columbia's Reid Hall. Columbia also has direct enrollment agreements with many partner institutions abroad, as well as a growing number of exchange programs with universities abroad.

Columbia was the first U.S. college to offer an integrated year-abroad program with the Universities of Oxford and Cambridge. Other programs allow students to work at the University of Kyoto in Japan or at the Free University of Berlin in Germany.

Altogether, Columbia students, with the help of advisers from the Office of Global Programs, may choose from over 150 study-abroad programs on nearly every continent.

Academic Facilities

Columbia has the fifth-largest research library system in the world, consisting of 12 million volumes and 26 million manuscripts within 3,000 collections. Included in the twenty-two libraries are the collections of the Avery Architectural and Fine Arts Library, the Starr East Asian Library, the Rare Book and Manuscript Library, and the Burke Library of Union Theological Seminary. All divisions are open to Columbia undergraduates. The majority of campus has wireless access including all residence halls. The LEED Gold–certified Northwest Corner Building houses cutting-edge labs that bring together researchers in biology, chemistry, physics, and engineering, as well as a science library, lecture hall, and café. Students may also make use of an electronic music lab, a cyclotron, an oral history collection, the facilities and programs of the Lamont-Doherty Earth Observatory, and oceanographic research ships.

Costs

Tuition for the 2014–15 academic year was $51,008. Room and board for all first-year students were $12,432. With typical fees, books, and supplies, the total cost of a year at Columbia was approximately $67,125.

Financial Aid

All first-year candidates who are U.S. citizens or have U.S. permanent resident or political refugee status are considered for admission without regard to their financial need. International students who do not fit into the above categories should be aware that their admissions process is not need-blind; their financial need is taken into account at the time of admission. Regardless of citizenship, Columbia meets the full demonstrated need of every student admitted as a first-year or transfer student. Columbia has eliminated loans for all students receiving financial aid and replaced them with University grant money. Parental contributions have also been significantly reduced for a large portion of students receiving financial aid. Prospective students should go to http://cc-seas.financialaid.columbia.edu/ for information on specific requirements and deadlines. All financial aid at Columbia is based on need; no aid is given in the form of academic, athletic, artistic, or other merit awards. The Office of Financial Aid and Educational Financing believes that cost should not be a barrier to students pursuing their educational dreams.

Faculty

The student-to-faculty ratio is 6:1. Core Curriculum classes are capped at 22 students, and 80 percent of classes have 20 students or fewer. The Columbia faculty is committed to both teaching and research, and all faculty members teach undergraduates, including the president of the University. All faculty members maintain office hours, and each student receives a faculty adviser from the department that he or she chooses as a major.

Admission Requirements

The Columbia first-year class of 1,400 students is selected from a much larger pool of applicants through a holistic, committee-based review process. There are no specific course requirements for admission, but applicants must present evidence that they are prepared for college work in a variety of disciplines as required for the Columbia degree. Accordingly, the following preparation is strongly recommended: 4 years of English, including meaningful work in literature and writing; 3 (preferably 4) years of mathematics, including precalculus and calculus where offered; 3 (preferably 4) years of history and social studies; 3 or more years of the same foreign language; and 3 (preferably 4) years of laboratory science (including chemistry and physics where available). Modifying the preparatory program just outlined—by taking more work in some subjects and less in others—is not only acceptable but may be desirable in individual cases.

Standardized tests are required for admission, according to the following guidelines. Students must take *either* the SAT and two SAT Subject Tests *or* the ACT with Writing. Students who take the SAT more than once are evaluated on the highest score they receive in any individual section. Applicants taking the ACT more than once are evaluated on the highest composite score they receive. The writing component of the ACT is mandatory for candidates for Columbia.

As noted above, students who take the SAT must also take two SAT Subject Tests. For Columbia College, they may take any two tests; for The Fu Foundation School of Engineering and Applied Science, they must take any mathematics test and either the biology, physics, or chemistry test.

Students who attend a school that does not give conventional grades or who are homeschooled must take two additional SAT Subject Tests in addition to all requirements outlined above for Columbia College or The Fu Foundation School of Engineering and Applied Science.

Applicants to either Columbia College or The Fu Foundation School of Engineering Applied Science should have the testing service report their standardized test scores directly to the Office of Undergraduate Admissions (SAT code 2116, ACT code 2717).

Transfer students may enter Columbia in the fall term only.

The College has a Visiting Students Program, which allows students to attend for one or both semesters of their sophomore, junior, or senior year.

Application and Information

Students may apply via the Common Application or the Columbia First-Year Application. Students for whom Columbia is their definite first choice are encouraged to apply early decision. The early decision deadline is November 1, and candidates are notified by mid-December. Candidates admitted to Columbia under early decision are required to withdraw their applications to other colleges. The regular decision deadline is January 1, and candidates are notified by April 1. Admitted candidates must respond to Columbia's offer of admission by May 1.

For further information, interested students should contact:

Office of Undergraduate Admissions
Columbia University
1130 Amsterdam Avenue, MC2807
New York, New York 10027
Phone: 212-854-2522
Fax: 212-854-1209
E-mail: ugrad-ask@columbia.edu
Website: http://undergrad.admissions.columbia.edu/
http://www.facebook.com/columbiaadmissions

COLUMBIA UNIVERSITY SCHOOL OF GENERAL STUDIES

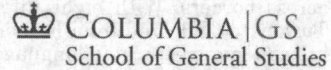

COLUMBIA | GS
School of General Studies

NEW YORK, NEW YORK

★ To read more about this school, visit http://petersons.to/columbiauniversitysgs

The University and The School

The School of General Studies (GS) of Columbia University is one of the finest liberal arts colleges in the United States created specifically for returning and nontraditional students seeking a rigorous, traditional, Ivy League undergraduate education full or part time. Most students at GS have, for personal or professional reasons, interrupted their educations, never attended college, or are only able to attend part time. GS is unique among colleges of its type, because its students are fully integrated into the Columbia undergraduate curriculum: they take the same courses, with the same faculty members, and earn the same degree as all other Columbia undergraduates.

GS students come from a variety of backgrounds. Many students work full time while pursuing a degree, and many have family responsibilities; others attend classes full time and experience Columbia's more traditional college life. In the classroom, the diversity and varied personal experience of the student body promote discussion and debate, fostering an environment of academic rigor and intellectual development. GS has approximately 1,800 undergraduate degree candidates and more than 450 Postbac Premed students. The average age of the GS student body is 28. More than 70 percent of GS students attend classes full time.

In addition to its bachelor's degree program, GS offers combined undergraduate/graduate degree programs with Columbia's Schools of Engineering and Applied Science, Social Work, International and Public Affairs, Law, Business, Dental Medicine, Teachers College, Public Health, and the College of Physicians and Surgeons. More than 70 percent of the students go on to earn advanced degrees after graduation.

Location

Columbia University is located in Morningside Heights, on the Upper West Side of Manhattan. The University's neighbors include the Union Theological Seminary, the Jewish Theological Seminary, the Manhattan School of Music, St. Luke's Hospital, Riverside Church, and the Cathedral of St. John the Divine. The diversity of intellectual and social activities offered by these institutions is one of Columbia's great assets as a university; another is New York City itself, which offers Columbia students a rich and almost boundless variety of social, cultural, and recreational opportunities that are themselves an education.

Majors and Degrees

The School of General Studies grants a B.A. degree and offers more than eighty majors and concentrations, which include: African studies; African American studies; American studies; ancient studies; anthropology; applied mathematics; archaeology; architecture; architecture, history and theory; art history; art history–visual arts; astronomy; astrophysics; biochemistry; biology; biophysics; business management; chemical physics; chemistry; classics; comparative literature and society; computer science; computer science–mathematics; computer science–statistics; creative writing; dance; drama and theater arts; earth and environmental science; East Asian studies; ecology, evolution, and environmental biology; economics; economics–mathematics; economics–philosophy; economics–political science; economics–statistics; education; English; environmental biology; environmental chemistry; environmental science; ethnicity and race studies; evolutionary biology of the human species; film and media studies; financial economics; French; French and Francophone studies; German literature and cultural history; Hispanic studies; history; human rights; information science, Italian cultural studies; Italian language and literature; jazz studies; Jewish studies; Latin American and Caribbean studies; Latin American and Iberian culture; linguistics; mathematics; mathematics–statistics; medieval and renaissance studies; Middle Eastern, South Asian, and African studies; modern Greek studies; music; neuroscience and behavior; philosophy; physics; political science; political science–statistics; Portuguese studies; premedical sciences; psychology; regional studies; religion; Russian language and culture; Russian literature and culture; Slavic language and culture; sociology; statistics; sustainable development; urban studies; visual arts; women's and gender studies; and Yiddish studies.

GS is home to the oldest and largest Postbaccalaureate Premedical Program in the United States, as well as dual-degree programs with the French University Sciences Po, Hong Kong's City University, and the Jewish Theological Seminary. Students enrolled in these interdisciplinary programs can earn two bachelor's degrees from two schools over four years.

The Dual BA Program Between Columbia University and Sciences Po is an intensive, transatlantic course of study in which undergraduate students earn bachelor's degrees from both Sciences Po and Columbia University in four years. Students who matriculate following their high school graduation, spend two years at one of three Sciences Po campuses, each of which is devoted to a particular region of the world and offers a heavy linguistic and cultural focus. After completing Sciences Po's interdisciplinary social sciences curriculum, Dual BA students matriculate at GS to complete the requirements for a major, as well as fulfill core distribution requirements in a variety of disciplines, including literature, art, music, science, and the humanities. Upon graduation, Dual BA Program students are eligible for guaranteed admission to a graduate program at Sciences Po. Admission to the program is highly competitive, and high school seniors are eligible to apply.

The Joint Bachelor's Degree Program between City University of Hong Kong and Columbia University offers students an international undergraduate educational experience—a program spanning two continents, in cosmopolitan cities that allow students to engage directly with the world around them. Joint Bachelor's Degree Program students will earn two bachelor's degrees, one from City University of Hong Kong and one from Columbia University. Students who wish to be considered for admission to the Joint Bachelor's Degree Program must first apply and be accepted to the City University of Hong Kong, at which time they will be eligible for consideration for the program.

Academic Programs

The School of General Studies offers a traditional liberal arts education designed to provide students with the broad knowledge and intellectual skills that foster continued education and growth in the years after college as well as providing a sound foundation for positions of responsibility in the professional world.

Requirements for the bachelor's degree comprise three elements: (1) core requirements, intended to develop in students the ability to write and communicate clearly; to understand the modes of thought that characterize the humanities, social sciences, and sciences; to gain familiarity with central cultural ideas through literature, fine arts, and music; and to acquire a working proficiency in a foreign language; (2) major requirements, designed to give students sustained and coherent exposure to a particular discipline in an area of strong intellectual interest; and (3) elective courses, in which students pursue particular interests and skills for their own personal growth or for their relationship to future professional or personal objectives. Students are required to complete a minimum of 124 points for the bachelor's degree; 60 of these may be in transfer credit, but at least 64 points (including the last 30 points) must be completed at Columbia. In addition to the usual graduation honors (cum laude, magna cum laude, and summa cum laude), honors programs for superior students are available in a majority of the University's departments.

Off-Campus Programs

Columbia students may enhance their academic experiences through various study abroad programs around the world. For example, students may spend a term at the Reid Hall Program in the Montparnasse district of Paris, the Berlin Consortium for

German Studies, the Kyoto Consortium for Japanese Studies, or the Language Program in Beijing, China. In addition, students may apply to participate in one of the dozens of Columbia-approved study abroad programs located in countries around the world.

Academic Facilities

The Columbia University Libraries constitute the nation's fifth-largest academic library system, with a collection of more than 12 million volumes; over 160,000 journals and serials; and an extensive array of electronic resources, manuscripts, rare books, microforms, maps, and graphic and audio-visual materials. Of the twenty-two libraries in the system, five are designated Distinctive Collections because of their unusual depth and nationally recognized excellence. All library divisions are available to GS students. The University's Computer Center is one of the largest and most powerful university installations in the world and has remote units and terminals in several parts of the campus to enhance its accessibility. The Fairchild Life Sciences Building houses research facilities, laboratories, electron microscopes, and a vast amount of biochemical equipment used for teaching and research. The University's physics building has been the scene of many important developments in the recent history of physics, including the invention of the laser and the first U.S. demonstration of nuclear fission.

Costs

For the 2014–15 academic year, tuition was $1,570 per point, and annual living (room and board) and personal expenses (books, local commuting costs, and miscellaneous expenses) were $22,685.

Financial Aid

The School of General Studies awards financial aid based upon need and academic ability. Approximately 70 percent of GS degree candidates receive some form of financial aid, including Federal Pell Grants, New York State TAP Grants, Federal Stafford and unsubsidized Stafford Loans, Federal Perkins Loans, General Studies Scholarships, and Federal Work-Study Program awards. Priority application deadlines for new students are March 1 (early action) and June 1 (regular decision) for the fall semester and October 1 (early action) and November 1 (regular decision) for the spring semester. The average scholarship award ranges from $8,000 to $10,000 for first-year students.

Faculty

Students in the School of General Studies take courses with professors who are members of the Columbia University Faculty of Arts and Sciences. These distinguished scholars in virtually every discipline also teach students in Columbia College, the Graduate School of Arts and Sciences, and the School of International and Public Affairs. Full-time and part-time students have many opportunities to work closely with faculty members, both in small classes and in research projects. Faculty members also serve as advisors to students majoring in their area of study and maintain regular office hours to see students.

Student Government

One student of the School represents GS students in the University Senate, a decision-making body comprising students, faculty members, and administrative staff members from each division of the University. In addition, two GS students sit as voting members on the Committee on Instruction, which oversees the curriculum of the School. The General Studies Student Council elects officers each year and sponsors activities for students. The Premedical Association (PMA) sponsors events related to the medical school admissions process.

Admission Requirements

The GS admission policy is geared to the maturity and varied backgrounds of its students. Aptitude and motivation are considered along with past academic performance, standardized test scores, and employment history. The School's admission decisions are based on a careful review of each application and reflect the Admissions Committee's considered judgment of the applicant's maturity, academic potential, and present ability to undertake course work at Columbia.

Admission requirements include a completed application form; a 1,500- to 2,000-word autobiographical statement describing the applicant's past educational history and work experience, present situation, and future plans; two letters of recommendation from academic or professional evaluators; an official high school transcript; official transcripts from all colleges and universities attended; official SAT or ACT scores (applicants may take the General Studies Admissions Examination); and a nonrefundable application fee of $80.

Students from outside the United States may apply to the School of General Studies to start or complete a baccalaureate degree. In addition to the materials previously described, international applicants must submit official TOEFL scores or take the Columbia University American Language Program Essay Exam.

Application and Information

Fall early action applications completed by January 15 will receive a March 1 decision; applications completed by March 1 will receive a decision by May 1. Spring early action applications completed by September 1 will receive an October 1 decision; applications completed by October 1 will receive a decision by November 15 Applications are reviewed as they are completed, and applicants are notified of decisions shortly thereafter.

For more information, students should contact:

Curtis M. Rodgers, Vice Dean
Office of Admissions and Educational Financing
School of General Studies
408 Lewisohn Hall
2970 Broadway
Columbia University, Mail Code 4101
New York, New York 10027
Phone: 212-854-2772
E-mail: gsdegree@columbia.edu
Website: http://gs.columbia.edu
http://facebook.com/ColumbiaGS
http://twitter.com/ColumbiaGS
http://youtube.com/GSColumbia

Columbia University, Low Memorial Library.

THE CULINARY INSTITUTE OF AMERICA

HYDE PARK, NEW YORK

★ To read more about this school, visit http://petersons.to/culinaryinstituteofamerica

THE WORLD'S PREMIER CULINARY COLLEGE

The College

The Culinary Institute of America (CIA) is a private, not-for-profit college dedicated to providing the world's best undergraduate education, with bachelor's degrees in management, culinary science, and applied food studies and associate degrees in culinary arts and baking and pastry arts. Guided by its core values of excellence, leadership, professionalism, ethics, and respect for diversity, the CIA strives to foster an atmosphere where students can develop both professionally and personally. At the CIA, aspiring food professionals gain the general knowledge and specific skills they need to grow into positions of leadership in the foodservice and hospitality industry, the second-largest private employer in the United States.

Founded in 1946, The Culinary Institute of America today enrolls more than 2,800 students from virtually every state and thirty countries around the world, all united by their shared passion for food.

As the world's premier culinary college, the CIA is renowned for its gold-standard degree programs, expert faculty, and world-class educational facilities. CIA classes span the culinary globe, exploring great cultures, cooking techniques, and cuisines to prepare students for the diversity and creativity of the foodservice industry. These studies culminate in operations courses that give students both kitchen and front-of-the-house experiences in the college's famous restaurants. Bachelor's degree management students also focus more deeply on the business side of food, with a broad range of business management and liberal arts courses; culinary science students apply a science-based understanding of the culinary arts to improve food production systems, food delivery systems, and customer satisfaction; and applied food studies students gain expertise in food policies, food systems, environmental issues, sustainability, and more so they can lead and influence policy in the food world.

CIA students enjoy an active campus life, with a variety of year-round fitness programs, intercollegiate and intramural sports, student clubs, and extracurricular activities such as ski and camping trips, on-campus live entertainment events, presentations by leading chefs and industry executives, and cook-offs. The college's Student Commons includes the Student Recreation Center, featuring a six-lane pool, a gymnasium, racquetball courts, an indoor track, a yoga and Pilates room, a cardio center, and free-weight and circuit training areas; The Egg, an extensive student dining area; and the Student Affairs Wing. The campus also features outdoor tennis courts and a soccer/softball field. Four coed residence halls, six lodges, and three townhouses provide on-campus housing for more than 1,700 students. The college's dining plan provides students with points equivalent to two meals per instructional day, with the option to purchase points for additional meals.

The Culinary Institute of America is accredited by the Middle States Commission on Higher Education, 3624 Market Street, Philadelphia, Pennsylvania 19104 (telephone: 215-662-5000), an institutional accrediting agency recognized by the U.S. Secretary of Education and the Council for Higher Education Accreditation.

Location

The CIA's scenic 170-acre campus is set along the east bank of the Hudson River in Hyde Park, New York, conveniently located 1½–2 hours from New York City and Albany.

The Mid-Hudson region's attractions and recreational opportunities offer something for everyone. Students can taste wines at local vineyards, visit farmer's markets, and pick apples at area orchards. The nearby Catskill and Shawangunk Mountains provide many opportunities for hiking, skiing, rock climbing, mountain biking, and sightseeing. Concerts, plays, films, and other cultural and special events are offered regularly throughout the Hudson Valley and Catskill regions. In addition, students can take advantage of the campus's proximity to New York City to experience the culture, arts, and nightlife of this exciting city and food mecca.

Majors and Degrees

At its New York campus, The Culinary Institute of America awards the Bachelor of Professional Studies (BPS) degree in management, culinary science, and applied food studies, as well as the Associate in Occupational Studies (AOS) degree in culinary arts and in baking and pastry arts.

Academic Programs

CIA students receive more than 1,300 hours of hands-on instruction in its kitchens and bakeshops and develop the managerial skills and creative thinking that today's food industry professional requires. They gain invaluable experience in a paid externship program and by cooking and serving in the college's bakery café or in some of the four public restaurants on campus. Bachelor's degree management students also take courses in marketing, communications, psychology, foreign languages and cultures, accounting, and human resources management. Students in the culinary science bachelor's program compare traditional techniques of food production and food delivery systems with new methods using modern equipment technologies, and broaden their knowledge and skills in science-related classes. Applied food studies bachelor's students research and analyze the ecology of food, food history, and anthropology of food as they participate in and conduct hands-on, practical projects related to food studies. Bachelor's management students can also focus their education with targeted concentrations in topics such as advanced wines and beverages, farm-to-table cooking, intrapreneurship, Latin cuisines, Asian cuisines, and advanced concepts in baking and pastry. Most of these include a semester at the CIA's California, Texas, or Singapore campuses.

Students must earn 132 total credits in management or culinary science or 120 total credits in applied food studies to graduate with a bachelor's degree. Students must earn 69 total credits in culinary arts or in baking and pastry arts to graduate with an associate degree. Students who earn their associate degrees at the CIA's California or Texas campuses can transfer to the New York campus to complete the bachelor's degree program.

Off-Campus Programs

All students work in externships for 15 consecutive weeks (600 hours). These externships provide students with valuable on-the-job experience at one of more than 1,200 top foodservice and hospitality properties such as hotels, restaurants, and resorts. Bachelor's degree students can also participate in a travel experience to one of a number of exciting destination choices, such as Spain, Italy, China, France, Peru, and the United States.

Academic Facilities

CIA students at the New York campus learn the fundamentals of the culinary and baking and pastry arts in the college's 41 professionally equipped production kitchens and bakeshops and four student-staffed public restaurants on campus—American Bounty Restaurant, The Bocuse Restaurant, Ristorante Caterina de' Medici, and Apple Pie Bakery Café. Most classes are centered in Roth Hall, the Shunsuke Takaki School of Baking and Pastry, the General Foods Nutrition Center, and the Colavita Center for Italian Food and Wine. The CIA regularly hosts world-renowned chefs for conferences, lectures, cooking demonstrations, and discussions with students in its Marriott Pavilion, Danny Kaye Theatre, Anheuser-Busch Theatre, and Ecolab Theatre.

Other valuable academic resources include the 86,000-volume Conrad N. Hilton Library, which contains the largest culinary collection of any culinary school; audiovisual programs; computer labs and workstations; and a campus-wide wireless network.

Costs

Freshman tuition for academic year 2015–16 is $27,930. Board is $1,400 per semester, which includes two meals per instructional day. Housing costs range from $3,200 to $4,025 per semester, depending on the room assigned.

Additional required fees for the freshman year include a confirmation fee of $100, equipment fees of $2,020 for culinary supplies or $1,875 for baking and pastry supplies, and a general fee of $660 per semester, which includes student activity and exam fees. The CIA offers students a tuition installment plan. Details are available from the college's Student Financial and Registration Services Office.

Financial Aid

Approximately 90 percent of the CIA's students receive financial aid in the form of scholarships, grants, loans, and work-study. Federal programs offered at the college include the Federal Pell Grant, Federal Supplemental Educational Opportunity Grant (SEOG), Federal Direct Loans (Subsidized and Unsubsidized), Federal Perkins Loan, Federal Work-Study Program, Federal PLUS, and veterans' benefits. Students should also investigate their own state's programs and apply if those grants or scholarships can be used in New York State.

Students who have applied for admission or who are currently enrolled at the CIA may apply for scholarships offered by various organizations in the foodservice industry. A list of these scholarships, which are administered by the college, is available from the Student Financial and Registration Services Office.

Faculty

The college's faculty is composed of more than 170 chefs and instructors from seventeen countries whose credentials and industry experience are unmatched in culinary education. The 17:1 student-faculty ratio in hands-on classes provides student support and mentoring, while giving students the opportunity to work in an environment closely representative of the foodservice industry.

Student Government

All students in good standing are members of the Student Government Association (SGA). The association's Executive Board acts as a liaison between students and the administration. The SGA helps support student activities and funds all student clubs and committees.

Admission Requirements

The Admissions Committee seeks candidates who have demonstrated a commitment to a culinary career and who have the personal initiative, confidence, and motivation to succeed. The basic requirements are successful completion of a secondary school education or its equivalent and some experience in the foodservice and hospitality industry. The applicant's educational record is evaluated on the basis of overall performance and the type of program taken. Academics and leadership ability are key requirements for the bachelor's degree program. SATs or ACTs are strongly recommended but not required.

Preference is given to candidates who have worked in foodservice, particularly in a kitchen that offers a varied menu. Before entering the program, students are required to have had six months of work in either the front-of-house or back-of-house at a non-fast-food establishment with a professional kitchen. Students can also gain the required experience through one year in a high school culinary program active in SkillsUSA, FCCLA, or ProStart, or through a semester of college-level work in hands-on cooking or baking classes. Candidates do not need this experience to apply for admission—the requirement must be met before they enter the CIA.

Applicants must submit a formal application for admission, a nonrefundable $50 application fee, an official secondary school transcript (not a student copy), responses to short essay questions from the college, and an official college transcript, if applicable. Students applying directly from high school may include an optional secondary school report. In addition, students must provide one recommendation.

Application and Information

Students may apply for admission to the CIA year-round, as the college offers multiple enrollment seasons. The CIA's Senior Edge Program, an early application program for high school seniors, offers a number of benefits including an early admission decision if students apply by November 1.

For information, to schedule a tour, or to participate in an Admissions Information Session, students should contact:

Admissions Office
The Culinary Institute of America
1946 Campus Drive
Hyde Park, New York 12538-1499
Phone: 1-800-CULINARY (toll-free)
E-mail: admissions@culinary.edu
Website: http://www.ciachef.edu/admissions

Set along the banks of the Hudson River, The Culinary Institute of America's New York campus lies on 170 scenic acres in historic Hyde Park.

CURRY COLLEGE

MILTON, MASSACHUSETTS

★ To read more about this school, visit http://petersons.to/currycollege

The College

Curry College is a private institution that offers academic majors in liberal arts disciplines and professional fields. The College's curriculum and programs focus on the two hallmarks of a Curry education: a high respect for the individuality of every student and an approach to learning that maximizes opportunities for achievement.

Students are attracted to Curry's friendly and caring academic community. One-on-one faculty-student relationships provide many opportunities for personalized instruction and close interaction. The average class size is 20 students, and the student-faculty ratio is 11:1. The student body consists of approximately 2,100 traditional undergraduate students. Approximately 1,450 students reside on the Curry campus.

Curry students have access to a wide range of cocurricular and extracurricular activities, including participation in the student newspaper and other campus media; performing arts programs, including theater and dance; and intramural sports or one of fourteen NCAA Division III athletic teams. Varsity sports for men are baseball, basketball, football, ice hockey, lacrosse, soccer, and tennis; women's varsity sports are basketball, cross-country, lacrosse, soccer, softball, tennis, and volleyball.

Curry College is accredited by the New England Association of Schools and Colleges; its nursing programs are accredited by the Commission on Collegiate Nursing Education (CCNE).

The College was founded in Boston in 1879 and moved to its present campus in Milton in 1952. The internationally acclaimed Program for Advancement of Learning (PAL) was established in 1970 as the nation's first college-level program for students with language-based learning differences. In 1974, the College absorbed the Perry Normal School, which prepared teachers for careers, and in 1977 it entered into a collaborative relationship with Children's Hospital Medical Center, which resulted in the establishment of Curry's Division of Nursing Studies.

Curry offers four master's degree programs, including a Master of Education (M.Ed.) established in 1981; a Master of Arts (M.A.) in criminal justice established in 1998; a Master of Business Administration (M.B.A.) established in 2005; and a Master of Science in Nursing (M.S.N) established in 2008.

As at its founding, Curry remains a dynamic and forward-looking institution committed to providing a highly individualized educational experience.

Location

Curry is located in Milton, Massachusetts, a residential suburb near the exceptional resources of Boston. Students enjoy the benefits of a traditional, 131-acre, wooded New England campus that also offers access to the amenities of a large city. The greater Boston area provides students with a diversity of cultural, educational, recreational, and sports activities. A wide variety of corporations, hospitals, agencies, broadcasting stations, and schools offer excellent internship and job opportunities for Curry students. The College operates a shuttle bus to the MBTA trains that run into Boston.

Majors and Degrees

Curry College awards the following Bachelor of Arts (B.A.) degrees: biology; business management (with concentrations in accounting, entrepreneurship, finance, human resources, marketing, residential property management, and sports management); child, youth, and community education; communication (with concentrations in corporate communication, film, multimedia journalism, multimedia sports journalism; public relations, radio broadcasting/audio production, relational communication, television/digital video, and theater); criminal justice; early childhood education; elementary education; English (with concentrations in American studies, creative writing, literary genre and movements, traditional literary heritage, journalism, professional writing, and women in literature); environmental science; graphic design; information technology; integrated liberal studies; mobile application development; philosophy; politics and history; psychology (with concentrations in counseling, developmental psychology, gerontology, health, and substance-abuse counseling); sociology (with concentrations in ethnic and gender studies and service in the community); special education; and visual arts (with a concentration in studio arts).

Curry College awards the following Bachelor of Science (B.S.) degrees: biochemistry, community health and wellness, and nursing.

Special minors are available in numerous areas, including dance, music, religion, Spanish, women's studies, and writing. For students with design majors, provision is made in the areas in which they have a special interest.

Curry College also offers academic programs of study in prehealth, prelaw, and premedicine.

Academic Programs

A central liberal arts curriculum, which is required for all students, incorporates a variety of academic disciplines into every student's plan of study. Curry's programs integrate theoretical classroom learning with a wide variety of field internships.

Curry College operates on a two-semester calendar with a summer session. To graduate, students must complete at least 120 credit hours for a B.A. or B.S. degree. In both cases, a minimum 2.0 cumulative average must be achieved.

Many academic programs enrich and facilitate a Curry education. The First-Year Seminar, the Honors Program, the Women's Studies Program, and the Internship Program are representative of that focus on special interests and diverse learning needs.

The Program for Advancement of Learning (PAL) is a credited program designed to help intelligent, motivated, language-based learning-disabled students to achieve at the college level. PAL provides individual or small-group instruction, textbooks on tape, and untimed examinations, as well as a variety of other applied technologies. Students must apply to the PAL program in order to take advantage of PAL's services. Students receive credit for enrollment in the program for the first year and are able to continue in the program as long as needed.

Off-Campus Programs

Curry students may earn up to 30 credit hours for field internships. In consultation with faculty members, students develop learning contracts that articulate their educational and personal goals and establish criteria for the evaluation of their field experience. Students may also arrange to study abroad or at another institution within the United States while enrolled at Curry.

Academic Facilities

The Levin Memorial Library houses tens of thousands of print volumes, electronic books, electronic journals, and other serial subscriptions. Levin Library is equipped with three computer labs containing PCs and Macintosh computers, laser printers, color printers, and state-of-the-art optical scanning equipment. The library houses the Academic Enrichment Center, where students may secure assistance in reading, writing, mathematics, and the development of study skills and is also home to the Educational Technology Center full of resources and materials for education students.

The Science Building includes five laboratories. The Kennedy Academic Center houses a simulated hospital room for use as a nursing laboratory; the Nursing Resource Center, which is equipped with an interactive video lab; and a laboratory for experimental psychology equipped with biofeedback, computer control, and animal and human learning facilities. The Webb Learning Center, with its own computer lab, maintains a complete tape library of all textbooks used at the College. The Hafer Academic Center features the Hirsh Communication Center and its state-of-the-art television studio. Curry students operate WMLN-FM 91.5, the College's award-winning, 172-watt radio station. WMLN-FM 91.5 also streams online at http://streaming.curry.edu/wmln-online.

The Academic and Performance Center features a 250-seat multipurpose auditorium, classrooms equipped with wireless laptop connectivity and SMART Board technology, breakout conference rooms, a stock-trading classroom, and a café-style food court.

The Student Center is an 84,000-square-foot facility that includes state-of-the-art areas for studying, co-curricular and extracurricular activities, dining, and athletics.

Costs

Tuition for the 2014–15 academic year was $33,750. Room and board were $13,510 (based on a standard double rate and a fourteen-meal-per week plan). The cost of the Program for Advancement of Learning (PAL) was $6,940. The cost of books, supplies, and personal expenses varies from $900 to $2,000.

Financial Aid

Curry provides financial assistance for students who need funding in order to attend college. The financial aid program consists of federal, state, and Curry College scholarships, grants, work-study awards, student assistant jobs, and loans. Approximately 90 percent of the student body receives some form of financial aid. All students applying for financial aid must submit the Free Application for Federal Student Aid (FAFSA) by March 1. Students applying for financial aid should contact the Financial Aid Office.

Faculty

There are 122 full-time faculty members at Curry, 73 percent of whom hold terminal degrees in their fields. In addition, each year the College hires highly qualified part-time faculty members and visiting lecturers to augment its teaching staff. Although primarily a teaching faculty, Curry's faculty members are also engaged in writing, research, and consulting.

Student Government

The purpose of the Student Government Association (SGA) is the advancement of the College community and the promotion of the general welfare of students. SGA seeks to increase student involvement in the formulation of College policies, communicate effectively with all constituencies of the College, and promote student participation within the institution. Members of SGA host an annual campus meeting with the College President and the senior management of the College.

Admission Requirements

Curry College accepts students who have the necessary preparation and educational background to meet the requirements of the College, regardless of race, religion, national or ethnic origin, age, sex, sexual orientation, or physical handicap. First-year students are selected on the basis of a combination of the following: secondary school record, scores on the SAT or ACT, recommendation of the secondary school, and the candidate's readiness for college. To be considered for admission, students must generally present at least 16 units of high school work, preferably at the college-preparatory level, from an approved secondary school. A recommended program of studies includes the following: 4 years of English, at least 3 years of mathematics, 2 years of a foreign language, 2 years of science (including at least 1 year of a laboratory science), and 2 years of social studies. Applicants should contact the Admission Office to discuss any possible exceptions to these requirements. A GED certificate is acceptable in lieu of a high school diploma. Curry College seeks well-rounded students who can contribute to the Curry community in athletic, artistic, and social endeavors, as well as in the academic sphere.

Application and Information

Curry's recommended application deadline is April 1; however, Curry operates on a rolling admission basis. The College also offers a nonbinding early action plan with a December 1 deadline. All early action candidates are notified of an admission decision by December 15. Students may apply for September or January entrance. Applicants for the nursing program may only apply for the fall semester. Applicants must submit an application and fee, an official high school transcript, scores from the SAT or ACT, and a counselor's recommendation. Transfer students must also submit official college transcripts, along with a College Official's Report form. If English is not the primary language of the applicant, then results of the Test of English as a Foreign Language (TOEFL) must be submitted. An interview is optional, but not required. The Admission Committee evaluates each application as soon as all required credentials are received, beginning in October. The College is a member of the Common Application.

Applicants to the Program for Advancement of Learning (PAL) must submit a completed application by March 1. PAL applicants must also submit the results of a recently administered Wechsler Adult Intelligence Scale (WAIS-R) test. Achievement testing in reading comprehension, written language, and math must also be submitted. The SAT or ACT requirement is waived for PAL applicants. Final decisions on admission to the program are made once all credentials are complete.

For more information about Curry College, students should contact:

Jane Patricia Fidler
Dean of Admission
Curry College
Milton, Massachusetts 02186
Phone: 617-333-2210
800-669-0686 (toll-free)
Fax: 617-333-2114
E-mail: curryadm@curry.edu
Website: http://www.curry.edu
http://on.fb.me/CurryColl_adm
http://twitter.com/CurryAdmission

The suburban campus of Curry College is just minutes away from the city of Boston.

COLLEGE CLOSE-UPS

DAEMEN COLLEGE

AMHERST, NEW YORK

DAEMEN COLLEGE
A World of Opportunity

★ To read more about this school, visit http://petersons.to/daemencollege

The College

Daemen College is a private, independent, coeducational college located in suburban Amherst, New York which was founded in 1947. Students choose Daemen because of its quality academic programs, generous scholarships, friendly faculty and staff, small campus with a 15:1 student-faculty ratio, and beautiful suburban location. Attributes at the heart of a Daemen education include: courage, curiosity, creativity, critical thinking, imagination, knowledge, innovation, professionalism, and success.

Daemen College prepares students for twenty-first century careers and service to the local and global community. The College offers rigorous academic programs that are aligned with current market demands that develop the liberal arts–based skills and competencies necessary for professional excellence. Daemen strengthens career readiness through professional development initiatives. It fosters the global competency of its students and faculty by increasing global content in the curriculum, increasing participation in experiential learning opportunities, and continuing to grow its population of students and faculty from international and other diverse backgrounds.

Daemen has approximately 2,000 undergraduate and 1,000 graduate students. Students come from all over New York and the United States, as well as from fifty other countries. Modern apartment-style residence halls provide separate housing for male and female students, in addition to a five-story traditional residence hall. More than fifty student organizations, themed dinners, movie nights, internationally famous speakers, and more contribute to a dynamic campus life.

The Center for Veterans and Veteran Family Services at Daemen provides a comprehensive support system. Daemen has been designated a Military Friendly School.

The Wildcats are a member of the United States Collegiate Athletic Association (USCAA) and have entered the provisional year of the NCAA Division II membership process. Daemen offers men's and women's basketball, cross-country, soccer, tennis, and track and field (indoor/outdoor), as well as men's golf and women's volleyball.

Location

Daemen's beautiful suburban 39-acre campus is located in Amherst, New York, just minutes from the city of Buffalo. Renowned for the arts, Buffalo offers exceptional theater, music, art, restaurants, and major league sports; it is also very close to scenic Niagara Falls and Canada. The campus is easily accessible by the major rail, plane, and motor routes that serve Buffalo.

Majors and Degrees

Daemen's Division of Arts and Sciences is just the place for students interested in becoming anything from a novelist to an occupational psychologist. In the visual and performing arts programs, students learn to see like a professional: websites, children's books, and intensive studio experience. Students interested in foreign languages can receive personalized instruction and become fluent in French, Spanish, or Chinese. History and political science majors examine everything from ancient history to the politics of globalization, leading to careers in public affairs, foreign correspondence, law, and more. English majors become acquainted with everything from syntax to Shakespeare, and move on to professions such as magazine journalist and high school teacher. A math degree can lead to careers in teaching, research, architecture, meteorology, and banking, among others. Those studying natural sciences can major in biochemistry, biology, and natural science; a chemistry minor is also available. Biology students can specialize in environmental studies, while other specialties include health sciences, forensic science, and individual studies. Career opportunities range from wildlife biologist to doctor and dentist. Paralegal studies students learn critical analysis, legal writing, research, and legal argument to prepare them for the legal field. Students can explore Christianity, Buddhism, Islam, Judaism, and more in the philosophy and religious studies program, perhaps leading to work ranging from library research to interfaith advisement. Psychology majors have the opportunity to study topics ranging from neuropsychology to human sexuality, in preparation for careers in family therapy, school counseling, law enforcement, and other challenging areas.

The Division of Health and Human Services offers career paths that lead to many destinations for students from special education teachers to athletic trainers, and tax accountants to parole officers. Accounting majors crunch numbers, but they also consider global issues to become financial analysts, company comptrollers, tax accountants, and more. Athletic training lets students assume responsibility for overseeing an athlete's total health care—through a five-year B.S./M.S. program. Business administration majors focus on economics, accounting, and marketing, but also on diversity and global management. Graduates work as market research analysts, HR managers, and more. Future teachers in the education program study childhood/early childhood and special education and visual arts education, with certification opportunities in several areas. Health-care studies covers all aspects of practical health-care delivery. Students can choose from one of three concentrations and leverage exceptional service-learning opportunities and professional internships. The nursing partner program allows future nurses to earn both their associate degree (from the partner school) and bachelor's degrees in four years. The physical therapy program is nationally recognized and offers a doctorate after six years. Studies span orthopedics/sports medicine, pediatrics, geriatrics, vestibular, cardiopulmonary, wound care, and more. Daemen's physical therapy students have a first-time pass rate on the National Exam that exceeds both New York State and national averages, with a current three-year weighted average ultimate pass rate of 100 percent. The physician assistant program prepares students to become licensed to practice medicine with physician supervision. Service-learning opportunities include an annual trip to the Dominican Republic. Daemen's program is one of only 191 in the country to be accredited. The rigor of Daemen's program is evident in the 98 percent first attempt pass rate on the NCCPA Certification Exam (the national average is 92–94 percent). Students interested in shaping communities can choose Daemen's social work program, with an abundance of practical service learning opportunities. Graduates enjoy careers as counselors, therapists, probation/parole officers, school social workers, and in other human service areas. Interdisciplinary programs include global and local sustainability.

Majors at Daemen include: accounting (B.S./M.S.); animation; art, with an emphasis in applied theatre, drawing, graphic design, illustration, painting/sculpture, or visual arts education K–12; arts administration (B.S./M.S.), with an emphasis in comprehensive arts, fine arts, or theater; athletic training (B.S./M.S.); biology, with an emphasis available in adolescence education 7–12 or environmental studies; biology/cytotechnology (B.S./M.S.), biochemistry, with several pre-professional programs available; business administration, with an emphasis available in human resource management, international business, marketing, or sport management; education, with an emphasis in childhood education 1–6, childhood education/special education 1–6, or early childhood education/special education B–2; English, with an emphasis available in adolescence education 7–12 or communication/public relations; French, with an emphasis available in adolescence education 7–12; health-care studies, with an emphasis available in community health, complementary and alternative health-care practices, or health and fitness training; history; history and political science, with an emphasis available in adolescence education 7–12 or environmental studies; mathematics, with an emphasis available in adolescence education 7–12; natural sciences, with an emphasis available in environmental studies, forensic science, health science; nursing (partner program),RN–B.S.; paralegal studies; physical therapy (B.S.N.S./D.P.T.); physician assistant studies (B.S./M.S.); political science; psychology; religious studies; social work (B.S./M.S.); and Spanish, with an emphasis available in adolescence education 7–12; and sustainability (global and local).

Academic Programs

Daemen has been named a College of Distinction for its exemplary commitment to engaged students, great teaching, vibrant communities, and successful outcomes.

Daemen College recognizes that education needs to prepare students for professional, intellectual, and civic leadership. The key to fostering the development of these skills is the core curriculum—a common educational experience for all students, regardless of major. The core is designed to strengthen students' abilities to become intellectually curious, acquire professional rewards, become responsible citizens, and deal with change. The seven core competencies are introduced at the freshman level, and are emphasized across the entire curriculum so that students develop a greater understanding of, appreciation for, and practice of these important life skills through their academic work. Research is carried out on a host of different fronts, from an innovative student/faculty think tank, to a high-profile wound therapy initiative. General research projects that include an enormous diversity of interests are showcased annually in the College's increasingly popular Academic Festival, held each spring. The honors program meets the intellectual needs of the best students, ensuring that the Daemen experience challenges their minds and fosters their potential to contribute both to the community and to society at large.

Off-Campus Programs

Career Services works with students to create a personalized Individual Career Action Plan (iCAP) and helps students to find an internship or co-op position to gain real-world experience in their area of interest. Daemen students say this chance to gain more insight into their fields prepares them better for employment after graduation. Internships are available in a wide range of fields, including business, sports, the arts, industry, government, health-related entities, nonprofit organizations, educational institutions, and cultural organizations. These can be local, national, or international and include excellent opportunities with the Washington Internship Institute.

Daemen's Office of Global Programs coordinates distinctive international programs. In today's global economy, it is vital that students learn about different cultures, political systems, and histories. International study is a staple of the Daemen experience. Students choose from semesters abroad, summer programs, and accelerated January term trips.

Daemen believes strongly in learning through service. All undergraduate students at Daemen engage in various service learning activities. Students participate as individuals or groups in short- and long-term projects or assignments that benefit the local, national, or global communities.

Academic Facilities

The Research and Information Commons, a green building, is a technological showcase—a hub of academic research, as well as the academic and social heart of the campus.

The Center for Visual & Performing Arts is a dramatic new space which features a spacious gallery, studios, a performance/lecture space, production area, computer labs, and an outdoor classroom.

The International Center for Excellence in Animation is located off campus. The 17,000-square-foot center is equipped with five studios, three editing rooms, a library/video library, and screening room.

Costs

For the 2014–15 academic year, tuition and fees were $24,990, and room and board were $11,430.

Financial Aid

Daemen creates individualized financial aid packages. Generous scholarships make attending the College very affordable. Over 93 percent of full-time undergraduates received some kind of financial assistance. Daemen awards merit scholarships based on academic and leadership achievement.

Faculty

Daemen has approximately 300 faculty members (full- and part-time). Small class sizes and a 15:1 student-faculty ratio ensure that students will have an engaging and interactive classroom experience.

Admission Requirements

Daemen offers a rolling admissions policy. The average student enrolled has a 91 GPA and 1060 SAT. Daemen has a test-optional policy which provides students with a choice regarding the submission of standardized test scores.

The admissions staff helps guide students through the process from start to finish. Students can create a personalized Daemen Connection web page at daemen.edu/admissions.

Application and Information

Prospective students can apply for free online at daemen.edu/apply or commonapp.org.

Daemen College
4380 Main Street
Amherst, New York 14226
Phone: 716-839-8225
800-462-7652 (toll-free)
716-218-8830 (text)
E-mail: admissions@daemen.edu
Website: daemen.edu

Visit Daemen—that's the best way to really get a feel for what the College has to offer.

No person shall, on the basis of sex, race, color, ethnic and national origin, handicap, religion, or age, be denied admission or be subjected to discrimination in admission to Daemen College

COLLEGE CLOSE-UPS

DEAN COLLEGE

FRANKLIN, MASSACHUSETTS

DEAN COLLEGE
DISCOVER THE DIFFERENCE

The College

Founded in 1865, Dean is a unique New England college awarding both four-year baccalaureate and two-year associate degrees. Students may choose from nearly two-dozen academic programs supported by state-of-the-art facilities, a dedicated teaching faculty, and professional advising known for exceptional personalized academic support.

Located 45-minutes outside Boston in the town of Franklin, Massachusetts, Dean's attractive 100-acre campus is home to WGAO-FM, the Joan Phelps Palladino School of Dance, and several buildings listed on the National Register of Historic Places. There are two fitness centers, a gymnasium, athletic fields, and indoor pool as well as a library learning commons, an advising center, a 214-seat theater, and dance studios.

Nearly all of Dean's 1,100 full-time students live on campus, and housing is available for all four years. The student body is impressively diverse with more than 30 states and 25 countries represented (and an additional 500 part-time students). The College sponsors 10 championship-caliber athletic teams, an Honors Program, internship and study abroad opportunities, an executive lecture series, and dozens of clubs, performance groups, and student organizations.

Dean College graduates are very successful. Of those receiving a bachelor's degree last year, 85 percent were employed or attending graduate school within 3 months—95 percent within six months. Among associate degree graduates, 98 percent were accepted as transfers to highly selective universities across the United States or had plans to continue their bachelor's degree at Dean.

Location

Dean's home town, Franklin, is a charming, historic Massachusetts community. The suburban setting is safe and convenient to downtown Boston with sufficient stores and restaurants to support an active college campus. The Commuter Rail—just three blocks from Dean—provides frequent train service to the city center, and students can reach popular destinations such as baseball's Fenway Park, the TD Garden, Museum of Fine Arts, and Harvard Square in less than an hour. Providence, Rhode Island, is even closer (40 minutes) where students can shop at Providence Place or see events at the Dunkin' Donuts Center and Rhode Island Center for the Performing Arts.

The area's biggest attractions are only minutes from Dean: Patriot Place and Gillette Stadium (home of the New England Patriots), the fashionable Wrentham Outlets, and Comcast Center outdoor amphitheater. For day trips, students can easily get to the beaches on Cape Cod, see Newport's mansions, or reach the mountains in nearby New Hampshire and Vermont.

Majors and Degrees

Dean College provides a wide range of programs across four academic schools: the School of Liberal Arts & Sciences, School of the Arts, School of Business, and the Joan Phelps Palladino School of Dance.

Bachelor's degrees are available in arts and entertainment management (with concentrations in dance, media studies, and theatre), business (with concentrations in management, sport management, human resource management, and public relations), dance (with concentrations in performance/choreography, dance education, and studio management), liberal arts and studies (including English, history, psychology, sociology, and individually designed), and theatre (with concentrations in acting, technical theatre, and musical theatre).

Dean also offers associate degree programs in business, criminal justice, dance, early childhood education, English, general studies, health sciences (including pre-nursing), history, mathematics, media studies and communications, psychology, science, sociology, sport fitness studies (with concentrations in athletic training, exercise science, physical education, and sports management), and theatre/musical theatre.

Academic Programs

Dean is accredited by the New England Association of Schools and Colleges. Graduation requirements include a 2.0 cumulative grade point average (GPA) and demonstrate competency in reading/writing, mathematics, and computers. Bachelor's degree candidates must complete a required internship or other experiential learning opportunity related to their major.

Unique to Dean is a special first semester course entitled Dean 100-Dean Foundations. Designed to assist new students with the academic and personal transition to college, this course covers a variety of learning and study strategies essential for collegiate success. Students apply these strategies to their daily experience as a college student and develop an individual plan that promotes a successful student transition.

The Honors Program at Dean offers academically talented students an opportunity to engage in stimulating and challenging courses, seminars, and colloquia. Students who meet the honors entrance criteria enroll in special course sections reserved for honors students or may enhance non-honors courses with additional intensive readings and analysis approved by the instructors. The Honors Program also offers exciting academic and cultural activities outside the traditional classroom environment.

Study-abroad and study-away opportunities are increasingly popular at Dean. Students may choose programs across the globe through cooperative arrangements facilitated by the College or take advantage of Dean's relationship with the Washington Center Program for study and internships in Washington, D.C.

The Dean Leadership Institute sponsors an Executive Lecture Series that brings leaders in business, media, and the arts to campus. Featured speakers share their insights into post-graduate opportunities and help build each student's career network. Recent guests include Bert Jacobs (Life is Good), Bob Kraft (Kraft Group/New England Patriots), Anne Finucane (Bank of America), and James Roosevelt (Tufts Health Plan).

The Arch Learning Community provides comprehensive support for students with diagnosed learning differences. Arch students receive dedicated academic advising and a cohort educational model specially designed to help LD students maximize their academic and personal potential and find success within the rigors of a traditional college curriculum.

Academic Facilities

Students have access to a wide range of facilities, including the newly renovated Green Family Library-Learning Commons and E. Ross Anderson Library, Berenson Writing Center, and Morton Family Learning Center—all housed under one roof. Together, these form the hub of Dean's academic support efforts. There are print and online resources for class projects, academic coaches to provide professional one-on-one mentoring, peer tutoring services, the Technology Service Center, and space for weekly faculty drop-in sessions where students can participate in group or individual advising.

Other academic facilities include the A.W. Pierce Technology and Science Center, which houses science and computer labs as well as the Alden Center high-tech master classroom; the Dean College Children's Center, an on-campus pre-school, which doubles as a learning laboratory for student teachers; and Campus Center, where students can find the Advising Center, Main Stage Theater, Guidrey Center multipurpose room, student activities office, and newly renovated classrooms featuring SmartBoard technology.

Costs

The basic costs related to attending Dean College for 2015–16 are $35,420 for tuition and fees and $15,200 for room and board.

Financial Aid

Last year, the College provided more than $19 million of merit-based financial aid; an astonishing 90 percent of Dean students receive some form of merit-based aid with an average award of $17,000 per year. These awards are based solely on the information students provide in their application for admission—not financial need—and help to reduce the average cost of attendance by more than 30 percent.

Approximately 90 percent of all full-time students receive academic grants not based on demonstrated financial need. Since the mission of Dean College is to nurture the potential within its students, these scholarships focus on current performance as well as future potential. They are based on academic or athletic performance, performing arts talent, place of residence, and academic promise. In addition, most students apply for—and receive—federal and state financial aid, which is separate from (and can be added to) Dean's scholarship awards.

Student financial aid packages are generally a combination of grants, loans, and work-study, contingent upon demonstrated financial need and the availability of funds. The College participates in all Federal Title IV and Federal Family Education Loan Programs. Students must submit the Free Application for Federal Student Aid (FAFSA) in order to be considered for need-based aid. Upon receipt of a valid FAFSA, full-time students are considered for all of the financial aid programs that Dean administers. Residents of Massachusetts and other reciprocal states may also be eligible for state scholarships, grants, or loans.

Faculty

Dean's dedicated faculty members, advisers, and educational specialists—some of the best in their respective fields—offer direct, personal involvement to help students obtain the full value of their college experience. The student-faculty ratio is 16:1.

Student Government

The Student Government Association serves as a liaison between the student body and Dean College administration. It disseminates information about College policies, seeks out student opinion, allocates funds collected from the activities fee to clubs and organizations through a budget request process, and coordinates the activities of various clubs, groups, and organizations campus wide.

Admission Requirements

Every application to Dean is carefully reviewed by the Admission Committee. In addition to the application form, students must submit an official high school transcript, a letter of recommendation from a guidance counselor or teacher, a personal statement or essay, and SAT or ACT scores. Interviews are not required but are strongly recommended. Students applying for the dance and theatre programs must audition.

Application and Information

Students who identify Dean as a top choice may choose to apply under the early action plan, with an application deadline of December 1. The College accepts applications on a rolling basis thereafter, though it is recommended that applications be submitted by March 15 to ensure access to the highest level of financial aid and priority in housing and class registration. Once an application is complete, an admissions decision is typically made within two weeks.

For more information, contact:

Office of Admissions
Dean College
99 Main Street
Franklin, Massachusetts 02038
Phone: 508-541-1508
877-TRY-DEAN (toll-free)
E-mail: admissions@dean.edu
Website: http://www.dean.edu

Dean Hall, built in 1865 when Dean College was established.

DOMINICAN UNIVERSITY OF CALIFORNIA

SAN RAFAEL, CALIFORNIA

★ To read more about this school, visit http://petersons.to/dominicanuniversityofcalifornia

DOMINICAN UNIVERSITY of CALIFORNIA 1890

The University

Dominican University of California's mission is to educate and prepare students to be ethical leaders and socially responsible global citizens who incorporate the Dominican values of study, reflection, community, and service into their lives. The University is committed to diversity, sustainability, and the integration of the liberal arts, the sciences, and professional programs.

Located in a community known for its extraordinary creative and entrepreneurial energy, Dominican's commitment to integrating the liberal arts and the professions prepares students for lives of purpose. The University balances academics with extensive practical, hands-on experiences, including service-learning, research, and internships with some of the Bay Area's largest and fastest-growing companies. Upon graduation, students are well-prepared to enter professional life or continue their studies in medical or graduate school.

Located in San Rafael, California, Dominican has approximately 2,000 students, including 1,480 undergraduates and 528 graduate students. With over 357 full- and part-time faculty members and a 10:1 student-faculty ratio, Dominican provides students with an exceptional level of support and mentorship. Founded in 1890, The University enjoys a century-long reputation for excellence in scholarship, research, and community outreach, and was named to the President's Higher Education Community Service Honor Roll and was cited as a Community Engagement institution by the Carnegie Foundation for the Advancement of Teaching. Dominican has also been recognized as a "College of Distinction."

Dominican supports eleven intercollegiate teams that compete in the NCAA's Pacific Western Conference: men's and women's basketball, golf, cross-country, and soccer; and women's softball, tennis, and volleyball. In addition to being fierce competitors, Dominican's Penguins are dedicated student athletes. The school's teams have earned the Pacific West Conference Academic Achievement Award in each of the last five years. In 2014, the men's lacrosse team joined the Western Collegiate Lacrosse League (WCLL) competing against Berkeley, Stanford, UC Santa Clara, and other top West Coast programs.

Activities: Students can get involved in Student Government (ASDU), Campus Ministry, or other clubs and organizations on campus. After a fun activity, students head to their residence halls for some rest, the dining hall for a quick snack, the Conlan Recreation Center for a workout, or attend one of the many lectures Dominican hosts featuring prominent speakers.

Dominican's residence halls vary in architectural style. There is a dining hall for resident students and others who wish to purchase meals on campus. The Conlan Recreation Center hosts basketball and volleyball games and seats over 1,000 fans. Conlan also features a weight-training and fitness room, a multipurpose room, lockers, athletic department offices, and conference rooms. Outside Conlan there is a lane pool surrounded by picturesque gardens. The John F. Allen Athletics Complex was built in 2012 and features Kennelly Field, a new multipurpose artificial turf field and the Castellucci Family Tennis Center, featuring six brand-new regulation tennis courts.

In addition to its undergraduate programs, Dominican also offers the following graduate programs: biological sciences (M.S.), business administration (M.B.A.) with three concentrations, counseling psychology (M.S., M.F.T.), education (M.S.), humanities (M.A.), and occupational therapy (M.S.O.T.).

Location

San Francisco, the mountains, the ocean—everything is within reach. Located in San Rafael, California, 12 miles north of the Golden Gate Bridge, Dominican's proximity to San Francisco offers students immediate access to a wide range of internship, service, employment, cultural, and recreational opportunities. In addition, Dominican's campus, located at the base of a mountain and a short drive to the beach, is a nature lover's dream.

Majors and Degrees

Dominican offers students twenty-four majors and thirty minors. There are four schools within the University: the School of Arts, Humanities, and Social Sciences; the Barowsky School of Business; the School of Education and Counseling Psychology; and the School of Health and Natural Sciences.

Undergraduate degrees (B.A., B.S., B.S.N., and B.F.A.) are awarded, and there are several specialty degree programs offered at Dominican, including multiple academic honors societies and honors programs. Some of these include the B.F.A. in dance, a nursing program, a five-year program leading to the Bachelor of Science in health science and the Master of Science in occupational therapy, the 4+1 M.B.A. program, and the Dual Degree/Dual Credential Program.

Academic Programs

The General Education Program offers exposure to the major areas of knowledge in the humanities, arts, and natural and social sciences. It is designed to provide a sequence of courses with a thematic focus that integrates the wisdom and perspectives of several disciplines. The focus assists students in discovering relationships between areas of knowledge, beliefs, cultures, and peoples that differ globally and historically, as well as in acquiring an awareness of tradition, a love of discovery, a respect for the diversity of the human condition, and a realization of human interdependence. Courses within the General Education Program also expose students to a variety of learning experiences, including discussion, lectures, seminars, simulations, and practicums.

Dominican University of California's incoming first-year students spend their first year exploring the origins and evolution of the universe in an interactive, multidisciplinary course based on Big History. Throughout the year, students gain a greater understanding of today's issues by studying the many links between nature and humankind. Big History is an emerging academic discipline that provides a unifying overview of the 14-billion-year history of the universe, from the big bang to the present day. Big History synthesizes history, astronomy, chemistry, biology, geology, sociology, and other fields to provide a cohesive picture, to scale, of the history of the human race and its relationship to the planet.

Opportunities to Engage the World

Japan, Australia, Spain, Sweden, Indonesia, South Africa—the world is at Dominican students' fingertips. Fostering an appreciation of cultural diversity and global interdependence is a fundamental part of a Dominican education. The University encourages students to develop a rich understanding of different cultural perspectives and experiences, and there is no better way to do that than by spending time living, learning, and working in another country.

Dominican encourages students to study abroad for two reasons: personal growth and professional development. There is a growing demand, across industries and geographic locations, for professionals who are multilingual and multicultural. Studying abroad and learning a new language can give students the competitive edge that they will need once they graduate.

A hallmark of a Dominican education is the belief that the most important aspect of a quality education is the personal interaction between professor and student. A program of engaged learning builds on this premise, incorporating active, collaborative learning in the classroom with enriching educational experiences beyond the physical classroom. These high-impact practices actively engage students in the learning process, enhancing their experience with the content, making the interaction personal and memorable.

Engaged learning at Dominican includes study abroad, internships, leadership, undergraduate research programs, and service learning initiatives. These experiences are interwoven with Dominican's distinctive programs, offering students a multitude of outlets to better understand themselves and the world around them.

Costs

Undergraduate full-time tuition (12–17 units per semester) was $41,280 per year for the 2014–15 year. Fees were $450; room and board (a fourteen-meal-per-week plan) costs were approximately $13,000 for the year.

Financial Aid

Financial aid is awarded on the basis of need and merit. Merit awards are available for both first-year and transfer students based on academic achievement. Dominican participates in various federal and state need-based financial aid programs and also has its own financial aid funds available, donated by generous alumni and friends, to help meet University costs.

Need-based financial aid comes in the form of scholarships, grants, part-time employment, and loans. The federal and state financial aid programs are the Federal Supplemental Educational Opportunity Grant, Teacher Education Assistance for College and Higher Education (TEACH) Grant, Federal Pell Grant, Federal Work-Study Program, Federal Direct Stafford Student Loans, Federal Direct PLUS loans, and Cal Grants A and B. Eligibility for need-based aid is determined after the student, who must be a citizen or permanent resident of the United States, files the Free Application for Federal Student Aid (FAFSA). The need-based financial aid deadline for first-priority consideration is March 2, although late applications are accepted. (Residents of California must file by March 2 to be eligible for Cal Grant consideration.)

Faculty

Students find themselves intellectually challenged by faculty members who hold degrees from colleges and universities throughout the world. The faculty is committed to individualized teaching and careful supervision of students' development. Seventy-three percent of Dominican's full-time faculty members hold doctorates or other terminal degrees. The student-faculty ratio is 10:1, ensuring students receive a highly personal education.

Student Government

The primary group that helps students plan and provide campus activities, distributes activity funds, initiates changes in policy, and represents themselves to the University's administration and the broader community is ASDU. This group of elected student representatives serves both as the student activities association and the student government board. The members of the ASDU Senate are representatives from all four class levels of regular day-program students.

Admission Requirements

Dominican University of California welcomes applications from prospective students of all ages, religions, races, and national origins. The University believes that academic potential is measured by more than grades alone. Each candidate for admission is given individual consideration and is evaluated by the Office of Admissions on the basis of the student's past scholastic record, present motivation, and potential intellectual development, as indicated by all of the admission materials submitted.

The application materials for first-year students include the following: a completed application; an official high school transcript to date; one letter of recommendation from a teacher, administrator, or counselor; scores from either the SAT or ACT; and a personal essay, as described in the application. Transfer students must submit a completed application and their high school transcript and official test scores if they have fewer than 24 transfer units. In addition, they must send official college transcripts to date; a personal essay as described in the application; proof of high school graduation; and one academic letter of recommendation or one professional letter of reference. Applications for admission are reviewed on a rolling basis; the sooner the student completes the application, the sooner the student will receive an admission decision. The priority deadline for the fall semester is February 1, and for the spring semester the deadline is November 1.

Application and Information

Students may apply online at the University's website (www.dominican.edu), or by using the Common Application. Students may also obtain admissions information by contacting:

Dominican University of California
Office of Admissions
50 Acacia Avenue
San Rafael, California 94901-2298
Phone: 415-485-3204
888-323-6763 (toll-free)
Fax: 415-485-3214
E-mail: enroll@dominican.edu
Website: dominican.edu

DOWLING COLLEGE

OAKDALE, NEW YORK

★ To read more about this school, visit http://petersons.to/dowlingcollege

DOWLING COLLEGE

The College

Dowling College, on the South Shore of Long Island, is an independent, comprehensive institution in the liberal arts tradition that specializes in truly personalized education: small classes, teachers who focus on one-on-one and collaborative work with their students, hands-on learning, and career-oriented programs in the arts and sciences, aviation, business, and education. With nearly fifty years of experience, Dowling offers both residential and commuter students the opportunity to join a welcoming family of learners and to forge a pathway to future success.

Dowling believes that education is personal and that personal attention from committed, full-time faculty is the key to academic success. There are no lecture halls, and no classroom holds more than 35 students; average class size is 15, even for introductory classes. Every student has a full-time faculty adviser, and students and professors get to know each other personally. While all faculty members engage in research, Dowling's primary focus is on teaching and learning.

Learning, however, doesn't only take place in the classroom. Dowling's programs emphasize hands-on experience through internships, collaborative learning, and service programs with internship opportunities in companies throughout the New York metropolitan area. In addition, academic programs stress hands-on learning. Students majoring in earth sciences have travelled to Iceland to study volcanoes and glaciers, and have researched horseshoe crabs through CEECOM (The Center for Estuarine, Environmental and Coastal Oceans Monitoring). Students in communication arts write copy for TV channels that include Nickelodeon and others, and sport management students become marketing interns with local sports teams such as the New York Mets and the New York Islanders.

Location

Located on the beautiful South Shore of Long Island (just 50 minutes from Manhattan and minutes from ocean beaches), Dowling's main campus sits on the banks of the Connetquot River, which is on the lush grounds of the former summer mansion of William K. Vanderbilt. A spacious 105-acre second campus—with classrooms, residential dorms, aviation facilities, and athletic fields—is located 15 miles east of the main campus in Shirley, adjacent to Brookhaven Airport. Dowling offers free shuttle bus service between the campuses.

Majors and Degrees

Dowling offers forty undergraduate career-oriented degree programs in arts and sciences, aviation, business, and education, as well as eleven graduate degree programs (six M.B.A. programs and five M.S. programs in education and sport management), and two Ed.D. degrees in educational administration. In addition, the College offers advanced certificates (both in-class and online), for educators and business executives who want to expand their training.

Dowling has recently developed new, career-oriented majors and programs. New programs include the B.S. in criminal justice management, the B.A. in gerontology, and the B.S. in TESOL (teaching English to speakers of other languages). Future programs being considered include a B.A. in game theory and a biology/psychology track oriented toward occupational therapy.

Dowling's School of Arts and Sciences offers majors in the arts and humanities, math and science, and social sciences. Dowling's vibrant creative writing program boasts its own student art/literary magazine, *Riverrun*, as well as writing and spoken word clubs, and a yearly writers' conference. Cutting-edge programs in graphic design and digital arts and communication arts offer internship components. Psychology, one of the College's most popular majors, offers fascinating courses that range from "Psychological Science Fiction in Film" to "Forensic Psychology and Law."

Dowling College's School of Education is one of the largest teacher and administration preparation programs in New York, with more than 5,000 teachers working on Long Island having received their education degrees from Dowling College. Students interested in becoming teachers can obtain teaching certification in areas such as special education, literacy education, or early childhood education. For those seeking a career in sports or sports management, Dowling offers a popular B.S. in physical education and sport management.

Students enrolled in the Townsend School of Business develop the skills necessary to prepare them for the challenges in today's competitive marketplace. Dowling tailors its program to accommodate the working population, offering a completely online B.B.A. in management and leadership and M.B.A. degrees, both online and on weekends. *U.S. News & World Report* lists Dowling's online graduate business degree as one of the top online programs in the nation. Dowling's graduates become motivated entrepreneurs and executives, taking full advantage of the business opportunities and trends in today's business world.

The School of Aviation trains students for careers in air traffic control, aviation management, and commercial piloting. Dowling graduates are recruited by employers who know that the students have received a balanced liberal arts background, as well as experience with the industry's most advanced equipment. Situated at Brookhaven Airport, the School of Aviation offers extensive flying opportunities with close proximity to some of the world's most varied and demanding airspace.

Academic Programs

Dowling has recently revised its core curriculum to allow for enhanced student flexibility, moving toward a system of distribution requirements that allows major and minor courses to count toward the core, giving students many ways to broaden their academic horizons. Students choose a First Year Experience Seminar and a capstone Senior Seminar in subjects ranging from earthquakes to sport in world culture to veterans affairs, as well as courses that stress fundamental skills in writing and math. These classes ensure that students graduate with a solid grounding in the liberal arts, along with the skills that are essential for success.

Academic Facilities

With over $50 million invested in the campus infrastructure since 2000, Dowling's facilities are designed to enhance every student's learning experience.

One thing students will not find on campus is a single lecture hall; this helps create a more personal learning environment. Smart classrooms bring the curriculum to life with Internet access, digital projectors, and the Blackboard Learning System, which enables students to access and share documents from anywhere in the world. A new science laboratory, flight and air traffic control simulators, new classrooms, a newly converted Music House, and a newly redesigned library are just some of the exciting improvements around the Dowling College campus.

On-campus amenities include the Lion's Den student lounge, a convenient fitness center, and two cafeterias—with the Oakdale cafeteria overlooking the scenic Connetquot River.

Costs

Full-time undergraduate tuition and fees are $29,100. Graduate tuition is $1,220 per credit hour. Housing costs range from $9,930 to $10,790 per year for dormitories in Oakdale or Brookhaven. Tuition for the distance-learning M.B.A. is $857 per credit hour. Doctoral program tuition is $52,000 for the full program. Tuition for the Saturday M.B.A. is $39,000 for the full program.

Financial Aid

There are numerous sources of financial aid available to help students achieve their goal of earning a degree from Dowling College. More than 75 percent of Dowling students receive some sort of financial aid to cover all or part of their educational costs. Numerous designated or endowed scholarships are available, including the Honors Scholarship, the Dowling College Faculty Scholarship, the Myrka Gonzalez and David Ochoa Latino Student Endowed Scholarship, and Presidential Endowed Scholarships. Dowling's goal is to bring its high-quality education within the financial reach of all its students.

Faculty

Dowling prides itself on the quality of its faculty and the personal one-on-one relationship between faculty and students. Over 95 percent of full-time faculty members hold a Ph.D. or the highest degree in their field. All classes at Dowling are taught by dedicated full-time faculty or exceptionally qualified adjunct faculty—not teaching assistants. Every faculty member serves as both instructor and mentor to his/her students, with all faculty serving as advisers, and many working one-on-one with their students.

Student Government and Organizations

Through the elected Student Government Association (SGA), students participate in self-government and promote student-run activities. With more than forty clubs and organizations, as well as frequent events and outings, Dowling offers a vibrant community for students. Fifteen highly competitive varsity teams compete in NCAA Division II at the beautiful state-of-the-art fields at the Brookhaven campus. Dowling's men's lacrosse team won the 2012 national championship and in 2012, the women's basketball team made it to the NCAA finals. In recent years, the Golden Lions have compiled an overall record of 178–98–6 in ECC-sponsored sports, earning regular season championships in volleyball, women's basketball, and women's lacrosse. Varsity teams include men's and women's basketball, cross-country, lacrosse, rowing, soccer, and tennis; men's baseball and golf; and women's volleyball and softball. Club sports include cheerleading, equestrian, and dance team.

There's always something happening at Dowling. Students can paddle one of the campus kayaks in front of historic Fortunoff Hall, take part in an intramural sport, or check out art exhibits at Dowling's Anthony Giordano Gallery.

Admission Requirements

Prospective students or applicants must provide evidence of a strong high school academic performance, a personal statement, and one or more letter(s) of recommendation from a high school or college guidance counselor, teacher, or school-based administrator. Dowling also accepts transfer students from both community and four-year colleges, allowing the transfer of up to 75 credits from a two-year college and up to 90 from a four-year college.

Application and Information

Dowling accepts students on a rolling basis but encourages early application (by March 1 for the fall semester and by December 15 for the spring semester). To ensure consideration for a wide range of scholarships, Dowling also encourages students to consider applying under its early action application program by submitting materials by December 31 (with a decision guaranteed by January 31).

The best way to discover Dowling is to experience it first-hand. Prospective students can meet with an enrollment counselor, sit in on a class, talk with a full-time faculty member in their proposed field of study, or schedule a tour of the College's historic Vanderbilt mansion at the Rudolph-Oakdale campus, or at the airport runways and athletic fields of the 105-acre Brookhaven Campus. Prospective students can call 631-244-3303 for application information or to schedule a visit. They are also invited to visit the College's website at www.dowling.edu, and to follow Dowling via Twitter or Facebook.

Office of Admission
Dowling College
150 Idle Hour Boulevard
Fortunoff Hall, Room 225
Oakdale, New York 11769
Phone: 631-244-3303
Fax: 631-244-1078
E-mail: admissions@dowling.edu
Website: http://www.dowling.edu

Dowling offers students the opportunity to join a welcoming family of learners and to forge a pathway to future success.

DREXEL UNIVERSITY

PHILADELPHIA, PENNSYLVANIA

★ To read more about this school, visit http://petersons.to/drexeluniversity

Drexel UNIVERSITY

The University

Drexel University is a private, nonsectarian, coeducational university that has maintained a reputation for academic excellence since its founding in 1891. The University's technologically focused approach to learning prepares undergraduates for a variety of careers and graduate school. Cooperative education is a vital part of a Drexel education. Students gain professional experience in jobs related to their career interests by alternating classroom study with periods of full-time employment. The 2014 undergraduate enrollment numbered 14,365 full-time students representing 47 states and 105 other countries. International students compose about 15 percent of the undergraduate population. Drexel University grants associate, bachelor's, master's, and doctoral degrees and certificates in a variety of programs.

Nine residential halls house more than 4,000 students on campus. Both the Campus Activities Board (CAB) and Drexel's nearly 30 active fraternities and sororities sponsor events such as dances, lectures, excursions, community service projects, and free movie screenings. Students can also take part in performing arts groups in dance, theater, and music; a variety of extracurricular activities; and over 300 student organizations. Drexel offers 18 Division I varsity athletic programs and competes in the Colonial Athletic Association Conference. The University also sponsors intramural and club sports.

Location

Drexel is located in the heart of Philadelphia, the nation's fifth-largest city, and shares its University City neighborhood with the University of Pennsylvania and the University of the Sciences. With thousands of student residents, University City is a great place for students to spend their college years in an urban campus setting, surrounded by the amenities of the city and the diversity of their peers. Philadelphia is home to some of the nation's best historical and cultural attractions and offers the vibrant nightlife, choice restaurants, dynamic arts, and major league athletics of a first-class city. Drexel's location offers easy access to public transportation and the Drexel shuttle provides convenient, free transportation between campuses for Drexel students. Adjacent to Drexel's University City Campus, Amtrak's 30th Street Station is a hub for trains and buses to the Philadelphia suburbs, New York City, Washington, D.C., and the Philadelphia International Airport.

Majors and Degrees

Whatever their interests, students at Drexel are at the forefront of their fields. Drexel offers more than 90 undergraduate majors and over 20 accelerated degree programs. Academic majors include accounting, animation and visual effects, anthropology, architectural engineering, architecture, behavioral health counseling, biological sciences, biomedical engineering, business analytics, business and engineering, business for Still-Deciding Students®, chemical engineering, chemistry, civil engineering, communication, computer engineering, computer science, construction management, criminology and justice studies, culinary arts, culinary science, custom-designed major, dance, design and merchandising, design for Still-Deciding Students®, economics, electrical engineering, elementary education, engineering, engineering for Still-Deciding Students®, engineering technology, English, entertainment and arts management, entrepreneurship, environmental engineering, environmental science, environmental studies, fashion design, film and video, finance, game art and production, general business, general humanities and social sciences for Still-Deciding Students®, geoscience, graphic design, health services administration, history, hospitality management, information systems, information technology, interactive digital media, interior design, international area studies, international business, invasive cardiovascular technology, legal studies, management information systems, marketing, materials science and engineering, mathematics, mechanical engineering, media for Still-Deciding Students®, music industry, nursing, nutrition and foods, operations and supply chain management, pathway to health professions, philosophy, photography, physics, political science, product design, property management, psychology, public health, radiologic technology, science for Still-Deciding Students®, screenwriting and playwriting, secondary education, sociology, software engineering, sport management, and TV production & media management.

Accelerated degree programs allow students to earn both a bachelor's and an advanced degree in a shortened period of time. Drexel's accelerated degree options include the B.A./B.S./J.D. in law; B.A./B.S./M.D. in medicine; B.S./D.P.T. in physical therapy; B.S./M.H.S. in physician assistant studies; B.S./M.P.H. in public health; B.S./M.B.A. programs in business, culinary arts, culinary science, design and merchandising, entertainment and arts management, hospitality management, information systems, information technology, and music industry; B.S./M.S. programs in accounting, biomedical engineering, communication, computing and informatics, education, engineering, and psychology; and B.A./B.S. in history/M.S. in library and information sciences.

Academic Programs

Qualified students can apply to the Honors program, which is open to students in every academic discipline. The Honors program offers special living communities designed for the exceptional student and opportunities for social activities, traveling, and independent projects. Specific classes for Honors students and Honors sections of general and required courses are available. Students who satisfy the program requirements qualify for Graduation with Honors or Graduation with Distinction.

Drexel students have opportunities to conduct research. The STAR (Students Tackling Advanced Research) Scholars program invites qualified students to participate in faculty-mentored research projects in their chosen fields as early as freshman year. Students who take part in research may be eligible for stipends or academic credit.

Off-Campus Programs

Classroom study is essential, but experience makes all the difference. Through Drexel Co-op, students have the opportunity to test-drive their degree in a professional setting by alternating periods of full-time work with periods of classroom study. Students can earn up to 18 months of workplace experience before graduation in paid full-time positions with employers such as Fortune 500 companies, major pharmaceutical companies, and top design firms, as well as nonprofit agencies and government organizations. More than 1,600 employers in 33 states and 48 international locations participate in the Drexel Co-op program. The average six-month paid co-op salary is nearly $17,000.

Drexel has an active Study Abroad program in more than two dozen countries around the world that allows students from all majors to spend a term or several terms studying abroad, earning credit toward their degrees and gaining valuable international experience. Freshman Frontiers: First Term in Dublin is a selective program that enables students in qualifying majors to study at the Dublin Business School and School of Arts for the first term of their freshman year. With any Drexel-sponsored program, students pay Drexel tuition rates and receive financial aid while abroad.

Academic Facilities

Drexel has four campus locations: University City Campus, Center City Campus, Queen Lane Campus, and Drexel University Sacramento. The University's library system comprises the W. W. Hagerty Library, the Library Learning Terrace, the Legal Research Center, and three health sciences libraries. The W. W. Hagerty Library, the University's central library located on the University City campus, maintains subscriptions to nearly 12,000 electronic journals, which are accessed via the library website, along with academic journals and 200 databases. Students may borrow laptops for use in the library. The Library Learning Terrace, a 3,000-square-foot flexible learning space located in a residence hall and staffed by librarians, enables students to learn and research collaboratively through a variety of technologies. The Legal Research Center on the third floor of the law school shares University databases while continuing to acquire new material. The additional libraries on the health sciences campuses provide study space, 75,000 books, and network access to the same set of online journals and databases.

The University recently expanded through the addition of several new, state-of-the-art buildings. The twelve-story 177,500-square-foot Gerri C. LeBow Hall, which houses the LeBow College of Business, opened in 2013, along with the Chestnut Square complex, which features mixed-use housing and retail, including a Shake Shack. Opened in fall 2012, the URBN Center houses the Westphal College of Media Arts & Design and provides space for exhibitions, labs, studios, and a black box theater. The five-story, 130,000-square-foot Papadakis Integrated Sciences Building features North America's largest biowall and opened in 2011. Currently under construction, The Summit at University City will provide more student housing and mixed-use commercial space.

Costs

Cost of attendance is made up of two different costs: direct and indirect. Direct costs are those that Drexel will bill students for and include tuition, fees, and University housing and dining plans (room and board). Indirect costs are those not charged to students by the University, but costs that they may incur as a result of additional living expenses at Drexel. For the 2015–16 academic year, Drexel's estimated cost of attendance for a full-time undergraduate student starting as a freshman would include $46,386 in tuition, $2,405 in fees, $14,367 in room and board, and $4,948 in indirect costs, personal expenses, and travel expenses. Note that book costs vary based on the program of study.

Financial Aid

Freshmen eligible for merit and/or need-based funds were awarded financial aid in the 2014–15 academic year. The average financial assistance package (including academic, athletic, or performing arts scholarships; grants; loans; part-time work-study employment; and federal programs) for these students was $33,000. All incoming students are encouraged to submit both the CSS Profile and the Free Application for Federal Student Aid (FAFSA) by specific deadlines. Financial aid notifications to students begin mid-December for students accepted during Early Action. The Drexel Liberty Scholarship also provides 50 full-tuition and fees scholarships to low-income students who are Philadelphia residents and who attend Philadelphia high schools.

Faculty

The University requires faculty members engaged in research and graduate-level teaching to also teach at the undergraduate level, allowing all students to benefit from the research activities of the faculty. Specially selected faculty members serve as advisors for freshmen. The student–faculty ratio is 10:1.

Admission Requirements

All colleges within the University require completion of a college-preparatory program in high school that includes at least 3 years of mathematics and 1 year of laboratory science. Students applying to major in the sciences or business and engineering are required to take 4 years of mathematics (through trigonometry) and 2 years of laboratory science. Engineering requires 4 years of mathematics (through trigonometry and precalculus), chemistry, and physics. The quality of academic performance is more important than merely meeting minimum requirements. The strength of preparation is judged primarily by rank in class or relative grade point average (GPA), by the degree of improvement in the quality of the academic record, and by the comments and recommendations from principals, school counselors, or teachers. Freshman applicants are required to take the SAT or the ACT. Students who were accepted and enrolled in the fall of 2014 had an average unweighted GPA of 3.4 on a 4.0 scale, an average SAT math score (25th–75th percentiles) of 570–670, and an average SAT critical reading score (25th–75th percentiles) of 530–630. An essay or personal statement is required, the subject of which is dependent on the major and program. Transfer applicants should complete a minimum of 24 college credits from a regionally accredited institution. Transfer applicants who have fewer than 24 college credits and graduated from high school less than two years prior to their application will also need to submit their high school transcript and SAT or ACT scores.

Application and Information

Applications are accepted through the Common Application only. The application fee is $50 and all Common Application waivers are honored. Students may choose to apply under the Early Action or Regular Decision options. Early Action means that students can apply by an earlier deadline to receive an admission decision earlier than students who apply Regular Decision. Early Action admission is not binding. The Early Action I deadline is November 4, with admission decisions rendered in mid-December. The Early Action II deadline is December 2, with admission decisions rendered in mid-January. Applications for Regular Decision full-time undergraduate status are due January 13, with admission decisions rendered no later than April 1. Applications for the B.A./B.S./M.D. accelerated degree program are due November 4. Drexel subscribes to the College Board candidates reply date of May 1. Transfer student deadlines vary by major and term of entry. For transfer application deadlines, please visit drexel.edu/undergrad/apply/deadlines.

Undergraduate Admissions
Drexel University
3141 Chestnut Street
Philadelphia, Pennsylvania 19104-2876
Phone: 215-895-2400
800-2-DREXEL (toll-free)
Fax: 215-895-1285
E-mail: enroll@drexel.edu
Website: drexel.edu/admissions (admissions)
drexel.edu/undergrad/apply (application)
facebook.com/drexeladmission (Facebook)
twitter.com/DrexelAdmission (Twitter)

Drexel's mascot, Mario the Dragon, faces Market Street and the Recreation Center.

COLLEGE CLOSE-UPS

D'YOUVILLE COLLEGE

BUFFALO, NEW YORK

★ To read more about this school, visit http://petersons.to/dyouvillecollege

D'Youville COLLEGE
Educating for life

COLLEGE CLOSE-UPS

The College

D'Youville College is a leading institution of higher learning for traditional and nontraditional undergraduate, master's, and doctoral level students from around the world. A significant number of the students come from Western New York and Canada. Students receive a well-rounded general education and specific training and experiences to improve the quality of life across the globe. D'Youville is a nurturing community that seeks to ensure the success of each student in diverse fields such as health care, education, and business. D'Youville offers the diversity and academic excellence of a large school, and the attention and sincerity of a small one.

D'Youville is a private, coeducational, liberal arts and professional college that has offered students an education of high quality since 1908. The College was the first in western New York to offer baccalaureate degrees to women. Its current enrollment is 3,000 men and women. Students may choose from thirty undergraduate and graduate degree programs that are enhanced by a 12:1 student-faculty ratio. The College is committed to helping its students to grow not only in academics but also in the social and personal areas of their college experience.

Students residing in Marguerite Hall or the new student apartment complex have a scenic view of the Niagara River and Lake Erie, which separate the U.S. and Canadian shorelines. The Koessler Administration Building, which once housed the entire college, now contains administrative offices, the chapel, Kavinoky Theatre, and the Learning Center. The Student Center, the focal point of leisure and extracurricular activities, has a new gymnasium, a swimming pool, fitness and wellness area, a training room, a dance studio, a general recreation center, and the main dining facilities. Student organizations and regularly scheduled activities, including intramural sports, NCAA Division III intercollegiate sports (baseball, basketball, crew, volleyball, golf, cross-country, soccer, and softball), a club hockey team, a ski club, the College newspaper, the yearbook, and social organizations, as well as academic programs, all help to make up an active campus life.

Location

D'Youville is situated on Buffalo's residential west side. The College is within minutes of many local attractions, including the downtown shopping center, the Kleinhans Music Hall, the Albright-Knox Art Gallery, two museums, and several theaters that offer stage productions. Seasonal changes in the area offer a variety of recreational opportunities. Buffalo is only 90 miles from Toronto and 25 minutes from Niagara Falls, making it a gateway to recreation areas in western New York and Ontario. Holiday Valley, a skier's paradise, is an hour's drive away. The city is served by the New York State Thruway, Amtrak, Greyhound and Trailways bus lines, and most major airlines.

D'Youville enjoys a diversified interchange with the community due to its affiliations with schools, hospitals, and social agencies in the area. College students in the Buffalo area number more than 60,000.

Majors and Degrees

D'Youville offers the degrees of Bachelor of Arts (B.A.), Bachelor of Science (B.S.), and Bachelor of Science in Nursing (B.S.N.). Majors include accounting, biology, business management, chemistry, chiropractic, dietetics, education (elementary, secondary, and special), English, exercise and sports studies, global studies, health analytics, health services management, history, international business, liberal studies for education, mathematics, nursing, occupational therapy, pharmacy, philosophy, physical therapy, physician assistant, preprofessional studies (dental, law, medicine, and veterinary studies), psychology, public health, RN to B.S.N. online program, and sociology. Five-year combined bachelor's/master's (B.S./M.S.) programs are offered in accounting (B.S)/international business (M.S.), dietetics (B.S./M.S.), education (B.S. + M.S.), international business (B.S./M.S.), occupational therapy (B.S./M.S.), and physician assistant (B.S./M.S.). A six-year B.S./D.P.T. program is offered in physical therapy. A seven-year B.S./D.C. program is offered in chiropractic studies. The Doctor of Pharmacy program began in 2010 with an early assurance program for prepharmacy students.

Academic Programs

The area of concentration recognizes individual differences and varying interests but still provides sufficient specialization in one discipline to form a foundation for graduate studies and professional careers. Students attending D'Youville are expected to complete the requirements of their chosen concentration while earning a minimum of 120 credit hours. Core requirements include humanities, 24 hours; social science, 12 hours; science, 7 hours; mathematics/computer science, 6 hours; and electives, 9 hours. A cumulative average of at least 2.0 must be maintained to meet graduation requirements. Sixteen credit hours, or five or six courses per semester, are considered a normal workload. Internships to meet specific career goals may be arranged in any major.

The College offers a Career Discovery Program that was purposely designed for the undecided student. This program, which can last for two years, offers credit courses and internships meeting two years of study in any major.

The academic year is composed of two semesters, each lasting approximately fifteen weeks. The first semester, including final examinations, ends before the Christmas holidays. During the eight-week summer sessions, programs of selected courses are given at all levels on a daily basis.

Off-Campus Programs

The baccalaureate program in nursing is affiliated with thirteen area hospitals and public health agencies. The education program is affiliated with local elementary, junior high, and secondary schools and with special education centers in the area for purposes of student teaching. The chiropractic, occupational therapy, physical therapy, and physician assistant programs are affiliated with appropriate clinical settings throughout the United States.

Academic Facilities

D'Youville's modern Montante Family Library offers state-of-the-art computer reference capabilities for both in-house and off-site users, including access to over seventy online databases. The multimillion-dollar Alt Health Science Building houses laboratories, including those for anatomy, organic chemistry, and gross anatomy; activity and daily living labs for the health professions; and additional laboratories for physics, chemistry, quantitative analysis, and computer science. It also houses classrooms, faculty member offices, and development centers, including one for career development. This is augmented by the modern Bauer Family Academic Center, which provides state-of-the-art classrooms, laboratories, and faculty offices.

Costs

For 2014–15, tuition was $11,550 per semester, and room and board cost $5,400 per semester. A general college fee of $370 is required and is based on credit hours taken; a Student Association fee of $40 per semester is applied toward concerts, yearbooks, activities, and guest lectures. A $100 deposit ($150 for dietetics, physician assistant studies, occupational therapy, and physical therapy programs), credited toward tuition, must be submitted by all candidates who accept an offer of admission.

Financial Aid

D'Youville attempts to provide financial aid for students who would not otherwise be able to attend. Determination of aid is based on the Free Application for Federal Student Aid. Aid is available in the form of grants, loans, and employment on campus. D'Youville automatically offers scholarships for academic achievement to all eligible incoming students.

All students may qualify for D'Youville's Academic Scholarship Program, which offers scholarships with total values up to $70,000. Students who apply, are accepted, and meet the criteria instantly qualify for one of these scholarships, all of which are renewable annually. These scholarships are not based on need. The three scholarship programs are the Honors Scholarship, the Academic Distinction Scholarship, and the Achievement Scholarship. The Honors Scholarship requires an 88 academic average, a minimum SAT score of 1100 (math and critical reading) or an ACT score of at least 24, and awards 50 percent off tuition and 25 percent of room and board costs. The Academic Distinction Scholarship requires SAT scores of at least 1000 (math and critical reading) or ACT scores of 21 to 23 and an academic average of at least 85. It awards 25 percent of tuition and 50 percent of room and board costs. The Achievement Scholarship criteria include SAT scores of 900 to 1090 (math and critical reading) or ACT scores of 19 to 23 and an academic average of 80 to 84. This scholarship awards $1,000–$5,000. The Transfer Honors Scholarship is based on a starting GPA of 2.75. This scholarship's award ranges from $1,000 to $5,000.

Faculty

The ratio of faculty members to students is 1:12. All members of the full-time instructional staff hold a doctorate or another advanced degree. Faculty members act as advisers and are available for consultation with students.

Student Government

The Student Association (SA), a representative form of student self-government, seeks to inspire in its members dedication to the intellectual, social, and moral ideals of the College and works closely with the administration and faculty. All students of D'Youville are considered members of the SA and may be elected to the executive council and the student senate. There are seventeen academic and social clubs affiliated with the SA.

Admission Requirements

An applicant must be a high school graduate or have a high school equivalency diploma before matriculating. The applicant should have a college-preparatory background, including required English and history courses and a sequence in either mathematics or science. Scores on the SAT or the ACT are also required for admission. High school advanced placement credit is acceptable and transferable. The admission decision is based on high school grade point average, rank in class, and scores on the SAT or ACT. Students who have difficulty meeting normal admission standards may be admitted with a reduced academic load.

The College Learning Center offers academic assistance to students whose education has been interrupted or has not prepared them adequately for college courses. The Tutor Bank, a system of peer tutoring, offers the assistance of qualified students to those who need help in specific academic disciplines.

Application and Information

D'Youville admits students on a rolling admission basis; therefore, applications are reviewed as they are received by the admissions office. Transfer students who have a quality point average of at least 2.0 are encouraged to apply by December 1 for the spring semester and by July 1 for the fall semester. A brochure listing course offerings and giving details about costs and room and board is available upon request.

Steve Smith
Director of Admissions
D'Youville College
One D'Youville Square
320 Porter Avenue
Buffalo, New York 14201-1084
Phone: 716-829-7600
800-777-3921 (toll-free)
Fax: 716-829-7900
E-mail: admissions@dyc.edu
Website: http://www.dyc.edu
http://www.dyc.edu/facebook
http://www.dyc.edu/twitter

ELIZABETHTOWN COLLEGE

ELIZABETHTOWN, PENNSYLVANIA

★ To read more about this school, visit http://petersons.to/elizabethtowncollege

Elizabethtown College

The College

Founded in 1899, and located in Lancaster County, Pennsylvania, Elizabethtown College offers its students more than fifty academic programs in liberal arts, sciences, and professional studies. A selective, private institution, the College is driven by its motto, "Educate for Service," and links classroom instruction with experiential learning through Signature Learning Experiences (SLEs). Each student is guaranteed to experience at least two of five SLEs, which supplement classroom learning and include choices in supervised research, cross-cultural experiences, community-based learning, internships, and capstone courses. When combined, SLEs prepare students for lives of purpose and are the hallmarks of the Elizabethtown experience.

Home to more than 1,900 traditional students from twenty-seven states and twenty-three countries, 88 percent of students live on the 200-acre campus in residence halls, senior townhouses and apartments, and college-owned houses called student-directed learning communities, where students commit to community-focused service work. Wireless access is available in all campus buildings.

In addition to an active intramural and club sports program, Blue Jay Athletics fields ten NCAA Division III teams for men (baseball, basketball, cross-country, golf, lacrosse, soccer, swimming, tennis, track and field, and wrestling) and ten for women (basketball, cross-country, field hockey, lacrosse, soccer, softball, swimming, tennis, track and field, and volleyball).

The Center for Student Success offers academic advising, personal counseling, and health and wellness programming. Career Services provides students of all class years with professional and career development services. The Center for Student Involvement houses the following offices: Student Activities (OSA), International Student Services, Diversity, and Chaplain/Religious Life.

The campus offers four dining venues: a traditional dining space, a deli/quick-serve/convenience store, a coffee shop, and a late-night food truck. Recreational spaces and offerings include The Body Shop, Thompson Gymnasium, fitness classes, an outdoor track, a pool, and lots of paths and green space. Koon's Activity Venue is a multipurpose entertainment and educational space. Leffler Chapel and Performance Center features an 840-seat auditorium. The campus events calendar boasts more than 125 arts and cultural happenings each academic year, not including student-run programming from OSA and the 80+ campus clubs.

Elizabethtown holds accreditations from the Middle States Commission for Higher Education, American Chemical Society for Clinical Lab Services, National Association of Schools of Music, National Council on Social Work Education, Accreditation Council for Occupational Therapy Education, and the Accreditation Board for Engineering and Technology Inc.

In addition to its traditional undergraduate programs, Elizabethtown also offers a Master of Science degree in occupational therapy and, through its School of Continuing and Professional Studies, a Master of Business Administration.

Location

Elizabethtown borough is a community of 20,000 people located in historic Lancaster County in south-central Pennsylvania, within 20 minutes of Harrisburg (the state capital), Hershey, and Lancaster; 90 minutes from Philadelphia and Baltimore; and a few hours from New York and Washington, D.C. Elizabethtown is easily accessible by Amtrak train service from New York, Philadelphia, and Pittsburgh, and the Harrisburg International Airport is 15 minutes away.

Majors and Degrees

Bachelor of Arts degrees are awarded in communications, economics, engineering, English, fine arts, French, German, history, international business, Japanese, music, philosophy, political philosophy and legal studies, political science, psychology, religious studies, secondary education, social work, sociology-anthropology, Spanish, and theatre.

Bachelor of Science degrees are offered in accounting, actuarial science, biochemistry, biology, biotechnology, business administration, chemistry, computer engineering, computer science, elementary education, engineering, environmental science, forestry and environmental management, general science education, health and occupation, industrial engineering management, information systems, mathematics, physics, secondary education, social sciences, and social studies.

Bachelor of Music degrees are offered in music education and music therapy.

Elizabethtown College offers more than ninety minors and concentrations, including Asian studies, as well as seven secondary education certification programs.

The College offers a variety of cooperative programs that allow qualified students to combine undergraduate studies with direct admission into graduate school. These include the Doctor of Physical Therapy programs at Thomas Jefferson University and Widener University, the Doctor of Osteopathic Medicine program at Philadelphia College of Osteopathic Medicine, Temple University's School of Dentistry, and the Master of Molecular Medicine program with Drexel University College of Medicine.

The Primary Care Pre-Admissions Program through the Pennsylvania State University College of Medicine at the Milton S. Hershey Medical Center provides options for Elizabethtown students who are Pennsylvania residents and are pursuing careers in internal medicine, family practice, and pediatrics.

The College also offers a Law Early Admissions program (LEAP) with Drexel University's Earle Mack School of Law and Widener University School of Law.

Academic Programs

An interdisciplinary first-year seminar and a strong core curriculum create a solid foundation for a student's chosen area of study. The core develops critical analysis and communication skills that ensure adaptability in the ever-changing global job market. Independent and directed studies, undergraduate research, and internships are available.

The Elizabethtown College Honors Program offers top students a highly selective program of study with the opportunity for a stipend to fund professional development, research, or travel-related study.

Called to Lead is a leadership-building program that helps students aspire to lead a purposeful life. Scholarship and Creative Arts Day, held each spring, gives students of all majors and class years the chance to showcase their research or creative works. The Center for Global Understanding and Peacemaking, Bowers Writers House, and The Young Center for Anabaptist and Pietist Studies offer various academic programming. The Momentum program, a pre-orientation program helps first-generation college students prepare for the academic expectations of Elizabethtown.

The College operates on a semester calendar. First-year students arrive in the last week of August, and examinations are given prior to the winter break. The spring semester begins in the middle of January and runs through early May. Students may earn credit toward graduation through Advanced Placement examinations,

College-Level Examination Program tests, or tests administered by the individual departments.

Off-Campus Programs

Elizabethtown offers its students high-impact, real-world learning experiences, and guarantees the opportunity to pursue at least two of the following: undergraduate research, study abroad, community-based learning, and internships/fieldwork.

Students may study abroad for a semester in twenty-six different locations on six continents through the College's affiliate programs. Short-term academic study tours or service-learning trips are also available. The Center for Community and Civic Engagement offers numerous community-based learning experiences locally and beyond.

Academic Facilities

The High Library's four stories contain more than 250,000 volumes and an extensive collection of journals and other research materials, plus Wi-Fi; computers and printers; conference rooms; and private, individual, and group study areas. Librarians help students with research projects and teach classes in using library resources effectively.

The campus features numerous academic buildings, including the James B. Hoover Center for Business and The Masters Center for Science, Mathematics, and Engineering. The student center, Brossman Commons, is home to the Tempest Theatre and a dance studio, and Zug Memorial Hall houses a recital hall and private and group practice rooms. Steinman Center for Communications and Arts features a television studio and radio station. The College houses three art galleries and the Masters Mineral Gallery.

Elizabethtown is home to The Young Center for Anabapstist and Pietist Studies, a world-renowned research center focusing on the Amish and other similar religions. The S. Dale High Center for Family Business, a local research and resource center for family-owned businesses, often partners with academic departments for events and programs.

Costs

For 2014–15, tuition was $39,920 and room and meals were $9,820, for a total comprehensive fee of $49,740. Students should also plan on an additional cost of about $2,000 for books, transportation, and personal expenses, for a total cost of $51,740. Financial aid is based on this figure.

Financial Aid

Elizabethtown College works with students and their families to make education affordable. Ninety-three percent of students receive some form of aid; packages are typically a combination of scholarships, grants, loans, and student employment. More than half of Elizabethtown's first-year students with the strongest academic credentials receive renewable merit-based scholarships, which are awarded on a competitive basis and without regard to need.

To apply for aid, students must file the Free Application for Federal Student Aid (FAFSA) and the Elizabethtown College need-based financial aid application. Students are assigned a personal financial aid counselor to help them throughout their years at the College. Elizabethtown's deadline for financial consideration is March 15.

Faculty

Elizabethtown has a teaching faculty of 131 full-time professors. The student-faculty ratio is 12:1. More than 90 percent of the full-time faculty members hold a Ph.D. or the highest earned degree in their field. In addition to being assigned a faculty adviser through the First-Year Seminar program, when students declare a major, they are also assigned a new faculty adviser within that department.

Student Government

Students play an active role in campus governance through the Student Senate, the Campus Residence Association, and other organizations. Members of the Student Senate are elected from each class to advocate for students, coordinate special events, and allocate funds for student activities and more than ninety student-run clubs and organizations. Students Working to Entertain E-town (S.W.E.E.T.) allocates funding for weekend programs, campus social activities, and entertainment for the College community.

Admission Requirements

Elizabethtown considers the right fit to be more than SAT scores and GPA; other factors considered at the College are academic fit, co-curricular fit, and social fit. Admissions decisions are made without regard to sex, sexual orientation, race, religion, physical handicap, or place of residence. On average, 60 percent of all applicants are accepted. The middle 50 percent of enrolled students scored between 1040 and 1240 on the critical reading and mathematics sections of the SAT, and 36 percent were in the top 10 percent of their high school class.

The College seeks diversity and students who display leadership abilities or special talents are considered highly desirable. Campus interviews are highly recommended but not required for most students, although the College reserves the right to require interviews in special cases. Applicants to the Honors Program and occupational therapy program are required to interview. Auditions are required for music students.

Early admission is available for highly qualified high school juniors.

Application and Information

The College operates on a rolling admission basis—applications are processed as they are received—and the application deadline is March 1. Students can apply using the Common Application or online at the College's website. Applicants must submit a high school transcript, first-quarter grades, SAT or ACT scores, two letters of recommendation, and a personal statement, essay, or graded paper. Early application is strongly recommended. Accepted students should notify the College of their decision to attend by May 1; matriculation after that date is on a space-available basis. Students who are interested in the Elizabethtown College Honors Program must submit a completed application by January 15.

For more information, students should contact:

Debra Murray
Director of Admissions
Elizabethtown College
One Alpha Drive
Elizabethtown, Pennsylvania 17022-2298
Phone: 717-361-1400
Fax: 717-361-1365
E-mail: admissions@etown.edu
Website: http://www.etown.edu

Elizabethtown College, home to about 1,900 students, offers more than fifty majors and more than ninety minors and concentrations.

COLLEGE CLOSE-UPS

ELMIRA COLLEGE
ELMIRA, NEW YORK

★ To read more about this school, visit http://petersons.to/elmiracollege

ELMIRA COLLEGE

The College

Students get to "Share in a tradition that transforms lives" at a small, private, coeducational college that is recognized for its emphasis on education of high quality in the liberal arts and preprofessional programs. One of the oldest colleges in the United States, Elmira was founded in 1855. The College has always produced graduates interested in both community service and successful careers. Friendliness, personal attention, strong college spirit, and support for learning beyond the classroom help to make Elmira a unique community. Elmira College is one of only 280 colleges in the nation to be granted a chapter of the prestigious Phi Beta Kappa honor society.

The full-time undergraduate enrollment is approximately 1,200 men and women. The students at Elmira represent more than thirty-five states, primarily those in the Northeast, with the highest representation coming from New York, New Jersey, Massachusetts, Connecticut, Maine, and Pennsylvania. International students from more than twenty countries are enrolled. Ninety percent of the full-time undergraduates live in College residence halls. Wireless access is available campuswide.

The intercollegiate sports program includes men's and women's basketball, golf, ice hockey, lacrosse, soccer, tennis, and volleyball; women's cheerleading, field hockey, and softball; and men's baseball. Men's cross-country will have its inaugural season in fall 2015. Intramural programs are also available. Emerson Hall houses the student fitness center, a pool, and a gym capable of seating 1,000, as well as the Gibson Theatre, which has a state-of-the-art sound and lighting system. Professional societies; clubs; music, dance, and drama groups; a student-operated FM radio station; and the student newspaper, yearbook, and literary magazine also provide numerous opportunities for extracurricular activity.

Location

Elmira College is located in the city of Elmira, which has a population of 30,000, in the Finger Lakes region of New York. The campus is a 10-minute walk from downtown Elmira. The relationship between the College and the local community is excellent, and numerous community activities and facilities are open to students, including the Elmira Symphony and Choral Society, the Elmira Little Theatre, clubs and civic groups, museums, movies, and a performing arts center. Excellent recreational areas are available in the Finger Lakes region, Western New York, and nearby Pennsylvania.

Majors and Degrees

Elmira College offers programs leading to the bachelor's degree in more than thirty-five majors, including accounting, American studies, art, art education, biology, biochemistry, business administration, chemistry, classical studies, clinical laboratory science, community health and wellness education, criminal justice, economics, special education, childhood and adolescent education, English literature, environmental studies, finance, French, general studies, history, human services, individualized studies, international studies, mathematics, music, nursing, philosophy and religion, political science, psychology, social studies, sociology and anthropology, Spanish, speech and hearing, speech and language disabilities, and theater. Secondary teaching certification is offered in several areas. 4+1 M.B.A. programs are available with Alfred University, Clarkson University, Rochester Institute of Technology, and Union College. Army and Air Force ROTC are available through respective units at Cornell University.

Preprofessional preparation is offered in education, clinical laboratory science, nursing, and speech pathology and audiology. Faculty advisers assist those who seek preparation for graduate study in dentistry, law, medicine, or pharmacy in choosing appropriate course work. Nearly 50 percent of Elmira graduates pursue graduate study.

Academic Programs

The College's calendar is composed of two 12-week terms followed by a six-week term in the spring. Students enroll for four subjects during the twelve-week terms, completing the first term by mid-December and the second during the first week of April. Term III, the six-week term, running from mid-April through May, may be devoted to a particular project involving travel, internship, research, or independent study. Students are required to participate in internships in order to gain practical and meaningful experience related to their program of study. Credit is awarded for these experiences. Forty percent of Elmira College students study abroad at least once during their four years of study.

Special opportunities for outstanding students include participation in thirteen national honorary societies on campus and a chance to assist faculty members in research. The College also offers an accelerated three-year graduation option for outstanding students, and an Advanced Placement Program is available.

Off-Campus Programs

Through the study-abroad programs, students may study in the United Kingdom, France, Spain, and Japan, as well as in other countries throughout Europe and Asia. Students from Elmira may spend Term III studying marine and island ecology or doing sociological research on the island of San Salvador in the Bahamas. The six-week Term III permits students in any major to study abroad, and students are able to participate in this program starting in their freshman year. Students have the opportunity to spend their junior year abroad studying for either one term or three years in any foreign country.

Academic Facilities

The Elmira campus offers exceptional academic facilities in a beautiful setting. The Gannett-Tripp Library's collections include more than 320,000 volumes of books, media, journals and microforms with access to over 146,000 eBooks, 86 subscription databases, and 30,000 eJournal titles. The library includes the Mark Twain Archive, the Student Learning Commons (Career Services, Writing Center, Tutoring Center, Information Technology, Finance Trading Center), two technology-enhanced conference rooms, nine collaborative study rooms, a quiet study room, computer labs, five classrooms, and photography and multimedia facilities.

A Center for Mark Twain Studies has been established at Quarry Farm, the author's summer home, which is located only a few miles from campus. The College also operates a Speech and Hearing Clinic on campus, which serves the public and provides valuable clinical experience for undergraduate students. Excellent facilities for drama and music are available.

Elmira College is in the midst of completing construction on the Elmira College Health Sciences Center, located in historic Cowles Hall. The Center, with its state-of-the-art technology and innovative educational programs, positions the College as a leader in the delivery of health sciences education.

The third floor of the Center is complete and features clinical simulation labs and the finest of today's medical learning equipment from top medical training products manufacturers. This equipment provides students with a technological edge in simulated training experiences. In addition to modern classrooms and wireless Internet access throughout the building, the new space is designed with teaching laboratories used for specific skill learning and student practice. These laboratories are unsurpassed in functionality and technology in comparison with other nursing programs in the region. The laboratories include a physical assessment skills lab, hospital unit labs, and a four-bed, high-tech simulation unit with control room.

The second and fourth floors are due to be complete in the fall of 2015, putting the Center in full use by that time.

Costs

Tuition for 2014–15 was $36,600, room was $6,300, board is $5,500, and fees were $1,550.

Financial Aid

Financial aid is available for both freshmen and transfer students. Awards are based upon the Free Application for Federal Student Aid (FAFSA) as well as the student's past academic performance. Types of aid include grants, scholarships, loans, and work opportunities. Sources of aid include college, federal, state, and private dollars. In addition, superior students may qualify for non-need-based Elmira College Honors Scholarships, which are available to both freshmen and transfer students and range from $13,000 to $26,000, with full-tuition scholarships available to Valedictorians and Salutatorians of graduating high school classes. Scholarships are renewable throughout 4 years of study at EC. About 97 percent of students receive merit or need-based financial aid from the College.

Faculty

Members of the faculty are chosen for their ability in and dedication to teaching. All full-time faculty members serve as advisers. Currently, the full-time faculty consists of 9 full professors, 37 associate professors, 15 assistant professors, and 5 instructors/lecturers. Approximately 90 percent of the full-time faculty hold the Ph.D. or terminal degree.

Student Government

Student government, an important part of the educational system at Elmira College, prepares students for active and responsible citizenship in society. Student government organizations include the Student Senate, the Judicial Board, and the Student Activities Board.

Admission Requirements

The Office of Admissions at Elmira College uses a rolling admission system. Each applicant is evaluated individually on the basis of his or her total application, including academic record, rank in class, SAT or ACT scores, essay, activities, letters of recommendation, and goals. The College strongly advises a personal interview. The recommendations of teachers and guidance counselors are also important. Special consideration is given to applicants from distant states and other countries, applicants with special skills, and applicants who are prepared to become actively involved in the campus community.

Elmira has two early decision programs available to students.

Application and Information

For further information, applicants should contact:

Dean of Admissions
Elmira College
Elmira, New York 14901
Phone: 800-935-6472 (toll-free)
E-mail: admissions@elmira.edu
Website: http://www.elmira.edu.

Elmira College, founded in 1855, celebrates 160 years of transforming lives!

EMBRY-RIDDLE AERONAUTICAL UNIVERSITY

DAYTONA BEACH, FLORIDA

★ To read more about this school, visit http://petersons.to/erau

The University

Embry-Riddle Aeronautical University's reputation as the leader in aviation and aerospace education is recognized worldwide. The University's history and legacy date back almost to the time of the Wright brothers, and in 2009 the University introduced the nation's first and only Ph.D. program in aviation. Embry-Riddle is an independent, nonsectarian, not-for-profit, coeducational university serving culturally diverse students seeking careers in aviation, aerospace, engineering, business, and related fields. Residential campuses in Daytona Beach, Florida, and Prescott, Arizona, provide education in a traditional setting, while the worldwide campus provides instruction through more than 150 centers in the United States, Europe, Canada, and the Middle East and through online learning.

Approximately 5,000 undergraduate students and 600 graduate students are currently enrolled at the 185-acre Daytona Beach residential campus. Students come from all fifty states, and nearly 100 countries are represented, making Embry-Riddle a truly international university.

Currently thirty undergraduate degree programs, fourteen graduate programs, and five doctoral programs are offered at the Daytona Beach campus. Embry-Riddle's premier aeronautical science (professional pilot) program and award-winning aerospace engineering program are the largest on campus and among the largest of their type in the nation.

Embry-Riddle conducts applied research and is leading the development of the Next Generation Air Transportation System along with the Federal Aviation Administration, Lockheed Martin, Boeing, and other high-tech organizations. Student research projects include development of green technologies like Embry-Riddle's EcoCAR and the world's first-of-its-kind hybrid aircraft. Alumni are leaders in every facet of the aviation and aerospace industries and serve as a strong network and resource for students.

Students at the Daytona Beach campus enjoy a wide array of activities and clubs, many focused on aviation and aerospace, as well as fraternities, sororities, and athletic opportunities. Forty-three percent of students live on campus.

Embry-Riddle's award-winning precision flight demonstration teams offer students the opportunity to compete nationally in air and ground events. Embry-Riddle also has the largest all-volunteer Air Force ROTC detachment in the country and among the fastest-growing Navy ROTC units and Army ROTC battalions. Embry-Riddle athletes compete in intercollegiate and intramural sports, including baseball, basketball, crew, cross-country, golf, lacrosse, soccer, tennis, track, volleyball, and ice hockey.

The 68,000-square-foot ICI Center contains two full-size NCAA basketball courts, a fitness center, and a weight room. The ICI Center provides a place to host sporting events and assemblies. The University sports complex also includes a two soccer fields, the Sliwa Stadium ballpark, the Ambassador William Crotty Tennis Center, and the Track and Field Complex. The Tine Davis Fitness Center is adjacent to the pool and features comprehensive fitness services and wellness programs. Recent expansions to athletic facilities include a softball complex for the newest athletic offering in women's fast-pitch softball, as well as two artificial turf fields for intramural competition.

The 5,300-square-foot Center for Faith and Spirituality accommodates the variety of faiths represented by the student body of Embry-Riddle. It consists of a 140-seat nondenominational worship area and four prayer rooms (Catholic, Jewish, Muslim, and Protestant).

Location

The year-round clear flying weather and the resort communities surrounding Embry-Riddle's residential campus in Daytona Beach, Florida, offer students an excellent environment in which to study, fly, and enjoy recreational activities. The campus, which is located adjacent to the Daytona Beach International Airport, is only 3 miles from what is called the world's most famous beach. The high-technology industries located in nearby Orlando and Kennedy Space Center provide the University with an outstanding support base. In addition, Walt Disney World and other theme parks are about an hour's drive from campus.

Majors and Degrees

The Daytona Beach campus of Embry-Riddle awards undergraduate degrees at the baccalaureate and associate level. Bachelor of Science degrees are offered in a variety of areas, each with a focus on the aviation, aerospace, and related industries. The newest major in unmanned aircraft systems science (open only to U.S. citizens) combines Embry-Riddle's expertise in flight, air traffic management, safety and engineering. The College of Engineering offers majors in aerospace engineering, civil engineering, computer engineering, electrical engineering, mechanical engineering, and software engineering.

All engineering programs, including Engineering Physics, are ABET accredited. Students who are interested in business administration may elect to major in management, accounting and finance, or marketing. An aviation business administration major is also available. The College of Aviation awards degrees in aeronautical science (professional piloting), air traffic management, applied meteorology, aviation maintenance science, and aerospace and occupational safety. Other majors include interdisciplinary studies (design your own major), communication, computational mathematics, global conflict studies, homeland security, human factors psychology, space physics, and commercial space operations. Students entering Embry-Riddle with an undecided major have the opportunity to explore a variety of academic pursuits before making a commitment to a specific track.

Academic Programs

Even a field as specialized as aviation requires a broad educational background. General education courses required of all students who are pursuing a baccalaureate program include communication skills, such as English composition, literature, and technical report writing; humanities; social sciences; mathematics; physical science; economics; and computer science. To ensure academic success, Embry-Riddle provides free tutorial services.

The academic year is divided into two semesters of fifteen weeks each, with the summer session divided into two terms. The average course load for each fall or spring semester is 15 credit hours.

Study abroad offers students the opportunity to better understand the global nature of the aviation and aerospace industries. Cooperative education adds value to the educational experience and allows students to gain real-world career skills.

Academic Facilities

The College of Aviation building at the Daytona Beach campus provides an unsurpassed environment for aviation education and research. The multimillion-dollar simulation laboratories duplicate the components and functions in the national airspace system, including capabilities to replicate actual weather reporting, airports, airways, air traffic control, flow control, and pilot and aircraft performance as found in the national air transportation system. Flight instruction is provided in the Embry-Riddle fleet of sixty-plus aircraft and a wide array of flight training devices. Aircraft are equipped with Automatic Dependent Surveillance-Broadcast (ADS-B) technology that decreases hazards associated with traffic, weather, and terrain. The High-Altitude Normobaric Lab allows students to experience the symptoms of high-altitude hypoxia to better enable them to recognize and recover from this threat. Embry-Riddle is the first university in the nation to acquire this technology.

The Advanced Flight Simulation Center gives Embry-Riddle students the opportunity to train in world-class simulators. The center, with more than 20,000 square feet of space and four high bays, currently houses two advanced aviation training devices

(AATDs), eight Cessna 172S NAVIIIs (Skyhawk), two Diamond DA42 TAE Twin Stars, two Diamond DA42 L360s, and one Canadair Regional Jet (CRJ-200). These devices duplicate the actual cockpit, adverse weather conditions, a full range of emergency situations, and virtually any flight pattern and complement flight training done in actual aircraft. Flight simulation enables students to learn aircraft performance, experience aerodynamic effects, and perform flight maneuvers immediately and without risk. Qualified to Level 6, the University's devices faithfully reproduce Embry-Riddle's fleet of single-engine and multiengine aircraft and are equipped with 220-degree panoramic visual theaters. In addition, the Aviation Building houses air traffic control and tower simulators, one motion-based disorientation trainer, and six basic aviation training devices (BATDs).

The James Hagedorn Aviation Complex, completed in the fall of 2011, includes 96,000 square feet in a three-building facility and is home to flight training operations, aircraft maintenance training, and a fleet maintenance hangar. The Emil Buehler Aviation Maintenance Science building's cutting-edge labs dedicated to aircraft systems, turbine engines, metallic and composite materials, and avionics electronics prepare students to become maintenance professionals. The facility includes classrooms, a licensed engine-repair station, a machine shop, offices, and a third-floor observation deck overlooking the flight line and Daytona Beach International Airport runways.

The Lehman Engineering and Technology Center is home to the College of Engineering. Labs include the advanced vehicles green garage, autonomous systems lab, wind tunnel lab, materials testing lab, structures lab, aerospace composites lab, real time lab, aerospace engineering and design lab, microcomputer and digital lab, circuits and power lab, electricity and magnetism thermo lab, and many more. Students use the labs to work in teams to develop hands-on projects. Research is conducted by faculty members and graduate and undergraduate students.

The newest academic facility is the 140,000-square-foot College of Arts and Sciences building, the largest structure on campus and home to the largest university-based telescope in the state of Florida. The building contains twenty-five labs dedicated to astronomy, astrophysics, atmospheric and space physics, control theory, and engineering physics.

The 18,500-square-foot Capt. Willie Miller Instructional Center, a lecture auditorium and classroom complex, provides space for large audience events, including presentations by distinguished lecturers and speakers.

The College of Business academic building features the aviation operations simulation lab, which is used to develop and evaluate aviation/airline operational strategies and processes. In addition, the College's Teaching Airport, a partnership between Embry-Riddle and Daytona Beach International Airport, is focused on teaching, research, and public outreach.

The Jack R. Hunt Memorial Library houses more than 230,000 volumes and book titles, and more than 340,000 items of microfiche, periodicals, documents, newspapers, and media programs. Among the library's resources is a historical aviation collection that includes a continuous run of *Aviation Week & Space Technology* dating from 1916 to the present and a complete set of *Jane's All the World's Aircraft* dating from 1909 to the present. The library provides rapid interlibrary loan service and wireless access points as well as computer terminals for research.

Costs

For the 2014–15 academic year, tuition and fees were $15,974 per semester. Flight fees are charged in addition to tuition. On-campus room and board costs were approximately $4,925 per semester. Personal expenses, books, and fees are in addition to the above. Costs are subject to change.

Financial Aid

Applicants for financial aid are required to complete the Department of Education's Free Application for Federal Student Aid (FAFSA) and any other documents requested by the University. Students are encouraged to apply early if they wish to be considered for all types of programs. Florida residents may also apply for several additional programs that are available through the state. All applicants are automatically reviewed for merit scholarship eligibility.

Faculty

The faculty members provide an excellent balance of professional experience and academic achievement. There is also a healthy balance between maturity and youth among the faculty. Faculty members who teach in the specialized and major programs have had professional experience in their areas of instruction. The student-faculty ratio is 16:1, and the average class size is 25. The primary concern of each faculty member is personalized teaching in classrooms and laboratories, on the flight line, and in student advising.

Student Government

The University places great emphasis on student self-government. The Student Government Association supports publication of the weekly newspaper and oversees the Touch 'n Go Office that organizes campus entertainment and broadcast of the student radio station, WIKD-FM. In addition, the president of the Student Government Association is a voting member of the University's Board of Trustees.

Admission Requirements

Admission is open to any qualified applicant, regardless of creed, sex, race, national origin, handicap, or geographical location. When evaluating an applicant for admission, Embry-Riddle takes into consideration a student's high school academic record (both courses taken and overall grade point average), rank in class, and activities. Embry-Riddle values individual academic achievement, initiative, talent, and character above standardized testing. Therefore, submission of standardized test scores (SAT or ACT) is optional for admission. If scores are submitted, they will be treated as supplemental information through the evaluation process. Students who do not feel that their scores accurately reflect their abilities do not need to submit them. Scores are not used for placement in freshman classes. Transfer students are required to submit transcripts from all colleges and universities attended. High school transcripts are not required if the student has earned 30 college credits or more.

Application and Information

Embry-Riddle requires each applicant to submit an application form and fee, two letters of recommendation, and an official high school/college transcript. Flight students must provide an FAA Class I or Class II medical certificate. When a student is accepted for admission, tuition and housing deposits are required by May 1. Embry-Riddle operates on a rolling admissions basis and admission decisions are rendered throughout the year.

University Admissions
Embry-Riddle Aeronautical University
P.O. Box 11767
Daytona Beach, Florida 32120-1767
Phone: 386-226-6100
800-862-2416 (toll-free nationwide)
E-mail: daytonabeach@erau.edu
Website: http://www.daytonabeach.erau.edu
http://twitter.com/ERAUniv
http://www.youtube.com/EmbryRiddleUniv

Embry-Riddle Aeronautical University's Daytona Beach, Florida, campus.

COLLEGE CLOSE-UPS

EMBRY-RIDDLE AERONAUTICAL UNIVERSITY

PRESCOTT, ARIZONA

EMBRY-RIDDLE
Aeronautical University
PRESCOTT, ARIZONA

★ To read more about this school, visit http://petersons.to/erauprescott

COLLEGE CLOSE-UPS

The University

Embry-Riddle Aeronautical University's Prescott, Arizona, campus is recognized and respected worldwide for cutting-edge instruction and training for tomorrow's aviation, aerospace, and security and intelligence leaders.

Embry-Riddle is a private, independent, four-year university accredited by SACS. All programs offer a special emphasis on aviation, aerospace, and related fields of global influence. The coed student population of just over 2,000 undergraduates comes from all fifty states and over thirty different nations.

There are more than 100 student clubs and organizations, including professional associations, fraternities, sororities, specialty clubs, and intramural sports. The National Association of Intercollegiate Athletics (NAIA) teams compete regionally and nationally as members of the CalPac Conference. Men's and women's teams include soccer, cross-country, and golf, along with men's wrestling, men's basketball, women's volleyball, and women's softball. The Golden Eagles flight team has consistently ranked among the top in the country in the Safety and Flight Evaluation Conference (SAFECON) competitions and has captured the national championship title nine times.

Within a year of graduation, 96 percent of graduates from all campuses are either employed or are continuing their education.

Location

Prescott is a mile-high city, and its climate reflects seasonable weather that is excellent for flying. Daytime averages are 80°F in the summer and 45°F in the winter. The local mountains reflect the spirit of the West, where students enjoy snow skiing, hiking, mountain biking, kayaking, rock climbing, and tours of the Grand Canyon.

Majors and Degrees

Twenty-three majors are offered through four different colleges: Arts and Sciences, Aviation, Engineering, and the nation's first College of Security and Intelligence.

Aeronautical Science, the professional pilot program, emphasizes hands-on training to prepare students for a career in the aviation industry with airlines, corporate and commercial aviation, or the military. Fixed-wing and rotary-wing flight options are offered.

Aeronautics is designed to build upon pre-existing experience or training in aviation or other technical fields. It also allows the flexibility to build a major with an aviation focus and a professional outcome.

Aerospace Engineering allows students to focus on the design of either aircraft or spacecraft. The program focuses primarily on the engineering of mission-oriented vehicles for atmospheric or space flight.

Air Traffic Management blends simulation training with rigorous academic study. Hands-on simulated air traffic training prepares students for a career as an air traffic controller with the Federal Aviation Administration (FAA).

Applied Meteorology provides a practical understanding of the physics and dynamics of the atmosphere to understand and forecast complex phenomena. This program offers areas of concentration in flight, meteorology for aviation operations, military meteorology, and research.

Astronomy emphasizes both a hands-on and theoretical education in astronomy and astrophysics. The Campus Observatory Complex, as well as Prescott's excellent viewing conditions, enhance education beyond the classroom.

Aviation Business Administration integrates in-depth studies of aviation, transportation, and government interface with a strong business foundation. The aviation business administration program is approved by the Aviation Accreditation Board International (AABI).

Business Administration students will have several opportunities to enjoy a unique hands-on learning approach as they take their education outside of the classroom by consulting with actual clients through a faculty-led student team to produce start-up business plans, strategic management plans, or conduct fraud risk analysis.

Computer Engineering provides a broad background in the design of digital hardware and software systems including communications systems, computers, and devices that contain computers. A senior design project will closely follow the development cycle of an engineering project in the industry.

Cyber Intelligence and Security equips students with the education necessary to lead, manage, administer, and create organizations in cyber security. Students will study computer forensics, information warfare, and technical intelligence while utilizing the University's state-of-the-art Hacker Lab.

Electrical Engineering is a systems-oriented program of study that includes analog and digital circuits, communication systems, computers, control systems, electromagnetic fields, energy sources and systems, and electronic materials and devices related to aerospace and avionics.

Forensic Biology combines the disciplines of biology, chemistry, and law to give students the background required in forensic science laboratories, law enforcement, and legal contexts. Hands-on activities include evidence collection, crime scene investigation, tissue sampling and analysis, and a heavy emphasis on DNA techniques. This major also fulfills pre-med requirements.

Global Business equips students for success in international management. Classroom topics include global events and issues related to transportation, trade, public policy, technology, resources, energy, and the environment. International cultures are studied with a focus on emerging markets.

Global Security and Intelligence Studies (GSIS) prepares graduates to become problem-solvers with expertise in such issues as terrorism and asymmetrical warfare, transportation security, threats to manufacturing facilities and corporate offices, and threats to computer systems and telecommunications infrastructure. Graduates are prepared for careers in the FBI, CIA, State Department, military intelligence, and private sectors. Students will follow a standard or Mandarin Chinese track, and languages include Arabic and Spanish as well.

Industrial Psychology and Safety explores the disciplines essential to the practice of safety: aviation safety, occupational safety, industrial hygiene, ergonomics, and quantitative methods.

Interdisciplinary Studies is a unique option allowing students to customize their undergraduate curriculum to match their specific career goals and interests by choosing three minor areas of study to create their own major.

Mechanical Engineering focuses on the design of robotic, propulsion, and energy systems. The program prepares students for careers in analysis, design, testing, and operation of mechanical systems.

Software Engineering teaches students to design and develop software. A unique cyber security track prepares graduates to support the nation's need for those skilled in cyber security to protect a company's proprietary information.

Space Physics is an applied physics program designed to prepare students for graduate studies in physics and astrophysics, as well as for work in space and aerospace-related industries.

Unmanned Aerial Systems prepares students for success in the design, operation, and business components of the emerging unmanned aerial vehicles industry. The focus of this program is on practical applications that humans could not, should not, or will not engage in, such as search and rescue, first responder, hazardous surveillance, evaluation of emergency situations, etc.

Wildlife Science is the only undergraduate environmental science program in the country with a focus on the aviation and aerospace industries. Graduates have the knowledge and technical skills needed to tackle the unique environmental and safety problems found in these industries.

Academic Programs

Along with their major, students may opt to select a minor from many fields, such as unmanned aircraft systems (UAS), air traffic control, Asian studies, aviation safety, or computer security; or they may work toward an Aircraft Dispatcher certificate. Army and Air Force Reserve Officer Training Corps (ROTC) courses are also available to all Embry-Riddle students. Embry-Riddle produces more Air Force officers and aviators than any institution except the Air Force Academy.

Education at Embry-Riddle goes far beyond the classroom. Through participation in internships and cooperative education arrangements, students in all fields of study gain valuable work experience with companies such as Delta Air Lines, the Federal Aviation Administration, Honeywell, Gulfstream, Lockheed Martin, NASA, the CIA, Raytheon, and more.

Faculty

Among Embry-Riddle's greatest strengths is its faculty. Faculty members, rather than graduate students, teach all classes. The average class size is 21, with an overall student-faculty ratio of 14:1. Faculty members bring both teaching and industry backgrounds to the classroom; most have extensive practical experience in their field, along with outstanding academic credentials.

Academic Facilities

Abundant hands-on experiences are what distinguish an Embry-Riddle education. Numerous laboratories and state-of-the art equipment provide students ample opportunity to explore and investigate, conduct experiments, build projects, and participate in undergraduate research.

The Robertson Aviation Safety Center houses the nation's only university-level accident investigation laboratory. This outdoor facility features an in-the-field investigation lab for studying wreckage sites of actual aircraft accidents.

The Glen Doherty Center for Security and Intelligence—named after an alumnus and fallen hero of the Benghazi tragedy—serves as a laboratory for students of the nation's first College of Security and Intelligence to simulate exercises in emergency management and homeland security. Related labs include the Computer Security and Forensics Laboratory and Forensic Science Laboratory, where students run forensic tests on crime scene evidence.

Classroom buildings for space physics and astronomy majors contain particle physics, exotic propulsion, optics, and remote sensing labs. There is also a campus observatory housing a CCD (charged coupled device) debris telescope.

The aerospace and mechanical engineering students spend a lot of time in the Aerospace Experimentation and Fabrication Building (AXFAB), a 20,000-square-foot facility comprised of numerous laboratories and equipment such as a two-axis electromagnetic shaker, vacuum chambers to simulate space environment, and 3-D printers. Additional buildings include the Aerial Robotics Laboratory for the research and development of unmanned systems; the Aerodynamics Laboratory, which houses five wind tunnels; and the Propulsion Laboratory housing a micro-turbojet.

The King Engineering and Technology Center is home for the computer, electrical, and software engineering programs. It includes a design suite for autonomous vehicles, a communications lab, control theory lab, power lab, digital circuits lab, and linear circuits lab.

The Flight Training Center is located at the Prescott Municipal Airport 2 miles from campus. The Prescott fleet includes Cessna 172s, Diamond DA42 NGs, an American Champion Super Decathlon for extreme attitude recovery, and two Cessna 150s for the flight team. All aircraft are ADS-b equipped, and the Cessnas are furnished with Garmin G1000 navigation systems. Also at the flight line are three Frasca 172 level 6 flight-training devices with 220° visual displays.

Additional College of Aviation facilities include an Air Traffic Control Lab, the Student Innovation Lab for unmanned aerial systems research and development, and a weather center which includes radar and a balloon launch facility.

Athletic facilities include an activities hub with indoor volleyball and basketball courts, a fitness center, a multipurpose gym, and a matted room for wrestling. Other facilities include a softball field, intercollegiate soccer field, tennis courts, sand volleyball courts, a 25-yard swimming pool, racquetball courts, a climbing wall, a running track, and a multisport recreation field. All facilities are available free of charge to all students.

Costs

The 2014–15 academic year tuition for all programs was $15,824 per semester for full-time students. Flight fees are charged in addition to tuition. The average on-campus housing accommodation rate for first-year students is $2,700 per semester; the required meal plan for freshmen is $2,158 per semester. Students also need to account for the cost of books, transportation, and personal expenses.

Financial Aid

Students and their families can find many sources of aid available to assist with meeting costs. Filing the FAFSA is an important part of this process. In addition, Embry-Riddle provides assistance in the form of academic scholarships, need-based grants, on-campus jobs, veterans' educational benefits (Embry-Riddle is a Yellow Ribbon school), and ROTC incentives.

Admission Requirements

Each student receives individual consideration for admission, based on a variety of factors and circumstances. Completion of the Embry-Riddle application for admission begins this process; students also need to submit official transcripts, score reports for either the SAT or ACT (not required but highly recommended), and two letters of recommendation.

Application and Information

For additional information students should contact:

Embry-Riddle Aeronautical University Admissions
3700 Willow Creek Road
Prescott, Arizona 86301
United States
Phone: 928-777-6600
800-888-3728 (toll-free)
E-mail: prescott@erau.edu
Website: http://prescott.erau.edu

The beautiful Prescott, Arizona campus glows in front of its dramatic, picturesque Granite Mountain backdrop.

EVANGEL UNIVERSITY
SPRINGFIELD, MISSOURI

EU EVANGEL UNIVERSITY

The University

Evangel University is one of the top Christian universities in the country. As a comprehensive institution, Evangel is the first Assemblies of God university to offer courses of study from the undergraduate to doctoral levels. Evangel is a residential university, drawing more than 2,100 students from all fifty states and many foreign countries.

The embedded Assemblies of God Theological Seminary (AGTS) at Evangel University trains men and women to be servant leaders through graduate programs. AGTS produces leaders with knowledge, skill, and passion to revitalize the church and evangelize the world in the power of the Spirit.

The Evangel campus is more than just buildings. It is a network of classmates who become lifelong friends as well as staff and faculty members who become mentors. The Activities Board, made up of members of the student body, presents activities throughout the year to create lifelong memories. Highlights include Harvest Fest, Spring Fling, homecoming events, and end-of-the-year banquets. Intramural athletic teams are a great outlet for stress relief after class and provide a chance to meet people from across campus. Residence halls encourage healthy relationships by providing hall-wide and individual floor activities. Roommates and hall mates become more than friends; they become family.

Evangel students may choose to be members of the marching band, a rare opportunity for a Christian college campus. Opportunities also abound for involvement in campus theatrical productions and musicals.

Evangel is part of the Heart of America Athletic Conference and has intercollegiate sports teams for men in football, basketball, baseball, track and field, cross-country, and golf. Women can participate in volleyball, basketball, softball, track and field, cross-country, and tennis. Evangel has also announced the launch of men's and women's soccer programs for the 2015–16 academic year.

Athletes are also actively involved in outreach through the athletic ministries program. T.E.A.M. (The Evangel Athletics Ministry) gives athletes the opportunity to serve local agencies and experience short-term international ministry trips. T.E.A.M. gives student athletes the chance to blend a passion for their sports with a passion for serving others.

Athletes plan and organize the T.E.A.M. trips with their teams and coaches. Trips often include competitions against local teams, educational experiences, service projects, team-building activities, and exciting cultural excursions. Students often return from their trips with renewed focus on their relationships with God and with others. They have a deeper appreciation for their experiences in the United States and are more aware of the depth and meaning of their calling and their Evangel academic and athletic career.

At Evangel, students' spiritual growth is encouraged through chapel services, biblical teaching, and a wide range of service opportunities on campus and in the community. Residence hall directors, the campus pastor, professors, and staff members are all available to lend a listening ear or provide direction as students progress through the formative years of young adulthood. Friends are there to encourage and inspire one another. Doctrine is not dictated, but one's beliefs are strengthened, supported, and clarified through the community of faith at Evangel.

Evangel graduates enjoy great acceptance in the marketplace and graduate schools throughout the United States and abroad. Recent graduates have secured positions in all areas of the workforce—from classrooms to Top 5 accounting firms. Some have made the choice to matriculate at prestigious universities, from Cambridge to Yale to the Washington University School of Medicine.

The value of a Christian college education is evidenced in the lives of more than 24,000 alumni who are serving around the world. These alumni include such prominent people as renowned cardiothoracic surgeon and artificial heart pioneer Dr. James Long; acclaimed singer/songwriter and author Sara Groves; *New York Times* best-selling author Beverly Lewis; the Honorable Sam Der-Yeghiayan, U.S. federal judge for the Northern District of Illinois; Bob Ferguson, Vice President, Global Cadillac at General Motors; Steve Poppen, Vice President of Finance of the NFL's Minnesota Vikings; Don Zimmerman, Senior Vice President/Chief Information Officer, Wendy's/Arby's Group, Inc.; Phil Stanton, founding member of "Blue Man Group;" Dr. Barry Corey, President of Biola University in La Mirada, California; and Darin Stahl, Special Agent, U.S. Secret Service.

Location

Evangel is located at the heart of one of the fastest-growing—yet safest and cleanest—cities in the nation. Rated one of the Top 10 Places to Live and Work by *Employment Review* magazine and "Missouri's #1 Sports town" by *Sports Illustrated,* Springfield is a medium-sized city with abundant job opportunities, as well as hotels, shopping, coffeehouses, restaurants, and many churches. It is also only an hour away from the lakes and entertainment of Branson, Missouri.

Majors and Degrees

There are more than 100 academic programs available at Evangel University through ten academic departments. They offer Bachelor of Arts (B.A.), Bachelor of Fine Arts (B.F.A.), Bachelor of Business Administration (B.B.A.), Bachelor of Music (B.M.), Bachelor of Science (B.S.), and Bachelor of Social Work (B.S.W.) degrees.

The **School of Theology and Church Ministries** delivers enhanced ministerial education in a variety of traditional, hybrid, and accelerated formats, all the way from bachelor's to doctoral degrees. The School offers majors in biblical languages, biblical studies, youth ministries, church leadership, preaching, and intercultural studies (missions).

The **Behavioral Sciences Department** offers majors in criminal justice, psychology, and social work.

The **Business Department** offers majors in accounting, business education, finance, management, marketing, and nonprofit business and social enterprise.

The **Communication Department** offers majors in advertising and public relations, broadcasting, communication studies, digital arts, film, journalism, and political communication.

The **Education Department** offers majors in art education (K–12), biology education, business education, chemistry education, early childhood education, elementary education, English education, mathematics education, middle school education, music education, physical education, Spanish education, and theatre/speech education.

The **Humanities Department** offers majors in art (graphic design), art (studio track), art education (K–12), English, English education, Spanish, Spanish education (K–12), theatre, theatre/music, and theatre/speech education.

The **Kinesiology Department** offers majors in athletic training, exercise science, physical education (K–12), and sport management.

The **Music Department** offers majors in music (B.A.), music industry (recording technology or music business), music (worship leadership), music education (K–12), and music performance.

The **Science and Technology Department** offers majors in biological chemistry, biology, biology education, chemistry, chemistry education, computer information systems, computer science, environmental science, health-care/nursing, mathematics, mathematics education, and medical technology. Pre-professional programs (taken as a biology, chemistry, biological chemistry, or mathematics major) are available in chiropractic studies, dentistry, engineering, medicine, occupational therapy, optometry, pharmacy, physical therapy, physician assistant, and veterinary science.

The **Social Sciences Department** offers majors in government (political science), history, international studies, public administration, social science, and social studies education. A pre-professional program in legal studies (pre-law and paralegal) is available for government majors.

For further details, visit www.evangel.edu/academics/undergraduate/programs-list/.

Accreditation

The University holds accreditation, not only with the Higher Learning Commission (North Central Association of Colleges and Schools), but also with the National Council for Accreditation of Teacher Education, National Association of Schools of Music, and the Council on Social Work Education. Evangel also is in candidacy status for accreditation with the Accreditation Council for Business Schools and Programs (ACBSP).

Off-Campus Programs

Learning at Evangel is not limited to the classroom. Each year, hundreds of students travel throughout the United States and abroad with music groups, service teams, or study-abroad programs. During the past 28 years, the concert choir and concert orchestra have both toured in the 48 contiguous states, Canada, the Bahamas, and 15 countries in Europe. In addition, the concert choir has performed for 2 U.S. presidents and has been honored with four solo performances at Carnegie Hall.

Academic Facilities

The University recently completed an extensive campus development program, with nine major construction projects since 1997, including two 3-story academic buildings, a student fitness center, the state-of-the-art Barnett Fine Arts Center, and Riggs Hall, the administration building.

When Evangel University was founded, its leaders demonstrated their commitment to academic achievement by building the Klaude Kendrick Library as the first permanent structure on campus. The building was completed in 1963. This commitment to research and scholarship has remained a priority as the University continually seeks to improve library services and adopt electronic and technological resources. Evangel students have access to a wide variety of innovative library and media services, as well as assistance from a committed staff of trained library professionals who are committed to students' academic success.

Faculty

Professors are committed to teaching from a biblical worldview. The integration of faith, learning, and life has been the focus of the institution since its formation in 1955. The student-teacher ratio is 15:1, which allows for individualized attention for students and provides for a rich, academic experience where faculty members often serve as mentors and form lifelong bonds with their students.

Costs

As one of the most affordable Christian universities in the nation, Evangel is committed to providing the best possible academic experience at a reasonable cost. For the 2015–16 academic year, the estimated cost per semester is $14,449. This includes tuition (12–18 credits), $10,133; room and board (double-room occupancy and 19-meal plan), $3,791; and additional fees.

Financial Aid

Evangel University not only strives for academic excellence, but it also strives to keep costs low. In addition, approximately 90 percent of Evangel students receive financial aid. The University offers a wide variety of scholarships and grants designed to help students finance their education at EU. For more information, students should visit www.evangel.edu/financial/scholarships/.

Admissions Requirements

As a committed Christian campus devoted to the highest standard of academic excellence, Evangel University is guided by a set of admissions requirements meant to provide the best spiritual and academic environment for its students. General requirements include the following:

- **Faith**—As a boldly Christian university, all students must make a profession of faith in Jesus Christ as their personal Lord and Savior.
- **Diploma**—Graduation from high school, or having the equivalent of a high school diploma such as the General Education Development (GED) examination
- **Core Subjects**—A minimum 2.0 GPA in core college-prep classes (English, math, social sciences, and science with a lab)
- **Grade Average**—A minimum "C" average (Students with a weak academic record may be considered; however to remain at Evangel, students must meet academic standards.)
- **Standardized Tests**—ACT or SAT test scores should be reported to the University.

For more information, prospective students should go online to www.evangel.edu/admissions/requirements/.

Application Information

Evangel does everything it can to make a prospective student's admissions process a fun and exciting experience. EU Preview Days are premier group visit opportunities that occur on Fridays throughout the year, offering tracks for both parents and prospective students. Customized visits are available most other weekdays. To schedule a visit to EU's campus, visit www.evangel.edu/admissions/campus-visits/.

Applications are available online at www.evangel.edu/admissions/apply-online/.

Evangel University has a rolling deadline. The application process opens September 1 for the following academic year, and the application fee is waived online from September 1 to November 15.

For more information, prospective students should contact:

Office of Enrollment Management
Riggs Hall, Suite 203
Evangel University
1111 N. Glenstone Avenue
Springfield, Missouri 65802
Phone: 417-865- 2811 Ext. 7346
E-mail: admissions@evangel.edu
Website: www.evangel.edu

Evangel is a comprehensive Christian university with a seminary, located in Springfield, Missouri, that draws more than 2,000 students from all fifty states. The focus of Evangel is to educate students for leadership positions in business, government, education, and church through a commitment to the integration of faith, learning, and life. Evangel offers 65 undergraduate majors. and, with the Assemblies of God Theological Seminary, a variety of master's and doctoral degrees.

COLLEGE CLOSE-UPS

FARMINGDALE STATE COLLEGE

FARMINGDALE, NEW YORK

★ To read more about this school, visit http://petersons.to/farmingdalestatecollege

Farmingdale State College

State University of New York

COLLEGE CLOSE-UPS

The University

Farmingdale State College is the State University of New York (SUNY)'s largest college of technology with more than 8,300 undergraduate students. It is dedicated to educating students in the areas of business, applied arts and sciences, health sciences, and engineering technology. A rich history of more than 92,000 graduates makes Farmingdale State a college with a legacy of excellence. Farmingdale State students enjoy small, personalized classes with dedicated faculty members who provide individual attention. Students are prepared for successful futures through real-life applications of knowledge, critical thinking, and a sound liberal arts education to help them pursue rewarding and successful careers.

Founded in 1912, Farmingdale State was Long Island's first public college and has a long and distinguished heritage. A four-year college offering more than thirty degrees, Farmingdale State offers students the opportunity to study in small classes taught by distinguished professors. The relationship formed between student and professor ensures that students receive the individual attention necessary for a successful college experience.

Students can commute to campus, or they can reside on campus in one of the residence halls. Orchard Hall, a suite-style building, opened in 2005. It features kitchen and laundry facilities on each floor. An active student life is important to the college experience, and making friends and building personal relationships are integral parts of life at Farmingdale State. Students can join one of the forty student clubs, hang out in the Campus Center, relax in the Books 'n Beans near the library, work out in the fitness center, or find a peaceful place to study in Greenley Library.

Farmingdale State offers unique courses of study that prepare students to assume responsible positions in a wide variety of careers. All programs operate within four schools: Health Sciences, Engineering Technology, Business, and Arts and Sciences. Because of its ideal location along the high-technology corridor on Long Island, many students benefit by combining their academic study with internships at local companies.

Farmingdale State College offers a comprehensive athletic program as an NCAA Division III school and is a member of the prestigious Skyline Conference. Farmingdale State's intercollegiate program is one of the finest in the country, with many teams receiving national and regional recognition.

Location

At Farmingdale State, students can enjoy the benefits of a traditional 380-acre northeast campus that is rich in historical buildings. Its central location in the heart of Long Island allows numerous opportunities for recreational and cultural pursuits or internship opportunities with leading local companies. Unique to the campus are the ornamental horticulture teaching gardens, the Solar Carport/Charging Station, the Solar Energy Center, the Aviation Center at Republic Airport, the Institute for Research and Technology Transfer, and New Media Design, an in-house advertising agency. Farmingdale State is only 50 minutes from New York City, where students can revel in the unique cultural and social environment, and it is only 20 minutes from the beautiful ocean beaches for which Long Island is famous.

Majors and Degrees

There are currently almost thirty bachelor's degrees including aeronautical science–professional pilot, applied economics, applied mathematics, applied psychology, architectural engineering technology, automotive management technology, aviation administration, bioscience, business management, computer engineering technology, computer programming and information systems, construction management engineering technology, criminal justice, dental hygiene, electrical engineering technology, facility management technology, global business management, manufacturing engineering technology, mechanical engineering technology, medical technician, nursing, professional communications, security systems technology, science, technology and society (liberal arts), software technology, sport management, telecommunications technology, urban horticulture and design, and visual communications (graphic design). In addition, eight associate degrees are offered in automotive technology, criminal justice–law enforcement, dental hygiene, landscape development, liberal arts and science, mechanical engineering technology, medical laboratory technician studies, and ornamental horticulture.

Athletic Programs

The Farmingdale State College athletics program is highly successful, with many teams receiving national and regional recognition. Eighteen teams include men's and women's basketball, cross-country, indoor track, lacrosse, outdoor track, soccer, and tennis; men's baseball and golf; and women's softball and volleyball.

The College's indoor athletic facilities include the newly renovated George E. Nold Hall which houses team and general locker rooms, officials' and staff locker rooms, three classrooms, three indoor racquetball courts, a new auxiliary gymnasium, a state-of-the-art weight training complex and sports medicine facility. The Walter A. Lynch Sports Center, a 94,000 square-foot gymnasium with a seating capacity of 4,000, houses three regulation basketball courts, five volleyball courts, four tennis courts, and an indoor track.

In addition, the outdoor facilities at the College include six tennis courts, a 20-station golf driving range, an outdoor track/lacrosse/soccer complex, a softball field, and baseball stadium. The baseball stadium is a state-of-the-art FieldTurf facility which includes seating for 1,000, dugouts, lights, batting cages, two bullpens, and a press box. The softball field features new dugouts and fencing, a revamped warning track, and bleachers behind the backstop. The outdoor track/lacrosse/soccer complex is a FieldTurf field surrounded by an eight-lane outdoor track. The tennis courts, renovated in 2009, feature six all-weather tennis courts with seating in the middle for easy viewing of either side of the courts.

Off-Campus Programs

Farmingdale State graduates are in high demand for their advanced technology skills, real-life experiences, and strong communications skills. Strategic partnerships with many companies result in active recruitment of students for internships and full-time careers. Farmingdale State also focuses on applied research, such as solar energy, fuel cells, medical research, robotics, and manufacturing. Students may have the opportunity to be involved in cutting-edge research with faculty members and industry partners.

In addition, there are opportunities to study abroad and to participate in short-term international travel/study programs, such as art tours of Italy and Greece.

Academic Facilities

The Farmingdale campus features several buildings of note. Technology-enhanced classrooms fill the campus. Hale Hall houses modern art studios and biology laboratories. Greenley Library houses an extensive collection of print and electronic resources. The Renewable Energy and Sustainability Center offers unique research opportunities in solar energy, wind turbine technology, solar thermal, plug-in hybrid electrical vehicle technology and fuel-cell development, or the opportunity to work with thermal spray and rapid prototyping technologies. For both students and faculty, the Sustainable Garden and 8-acre Ornamental Horticulture Teaching Gardens provide a living laboratory which has been featured in *House & Garden* magazine. The Security Systems Laboratories include specialized teaching and research labs in access control, closed-circuit television, computer forensics, and intrusion detection. In addition, there are twenty-three other academic buildings, including an on-campus children's center, and a new Campus Center, which contains food services, the bookstore, and plenty of spots to study and engage with other members of the community.

Costs

As part of the State University of New York system, Farmingdale State College offers a high-quality education at a very affordable cost and has extensive financial aid for qualified students. For the 2014–15 academic year, annual costs for full-time attendance at Farmingdale State were $6,170 for tuition (plus fees that brought the total to $7,483), $12,000 for room and board, and $1,000 for books and supplies. Tuition for out-of-state students was over $15,000.

Financial Aid

Almost 55 percent of Farmingdale State students receive some type of financial aid. Loans, grants, and scholarships are available through various federal, state, and private programs. To apply for financial aid, students must file the Free Application for Federal Student Aid (FAFSA) as early as possible, but no later than April 1.

Financial aid is based on a review of a student's financial circumstances. The FAFSA form should be completed soon after January 1. Farmingdale State is dedicated to providing high-quality, personal services to all applicants to assist them in funding their college education. An extensive network of services and resources is offered to help applicants with the financial aid process, and each student is assigned his or her own financial aid adviser. Financial aid advisers help students apply for financial aid and develop financial aid awards tailored to meet college expenses. Scholarships are available.

Faculty

Farmingdale State offers small, personalized classes with dedicated faculty members. The relationships formed between students and professors ensure individual attention. The faculty is composed of more than 211 full-time and 429 part-time members ready to help students grow academically and personally. One hundred and twenty-one members of the faculty and staff have won Chancellor's Awards for Excellence, including 16 who have been promoted to the rank of Distinguished Teaching/Service Professors. In addition, almost 100 students have similarly been honored. Farmingdale State's faculty represents an outstanding group of individuals dedicated to teaching, research, and scholarship. Farmingdale State offers students a relatively low faculty-student ratio (1:19) in order to maximize the student's individual experience. All classes are taught by faculty members; there are no teaching assistants at Farmingdale State.

Student Government

The Student Government Association (SGA) has authority over all student organizational and elected officers. Sixteen senators and seven executive board members compose the governing board, which acts in matters promoting the interests of the University and its students.

Admission Requirements

Farmingdale State seeks accomplished students with well-rounded backgrounds and competitive SAT scores. Applicants must have graduated from high school or hold a high school equivalency certificate. The SAT or ACT is required. Decisions are based primarily on grades earned in academic courses. The review process takes into account the applicant's individual overall background, including available data such as test scores, rank in class, and teacher or counselor recommendations. A personal interview is not required. While the school offers rolling admissions, it is highly recommended that applications be submitted by June 1. With more than 9,000 applications a year, Farmingdale State's admissions requirements are increasingly competitive.

Application and Information

Candidates must submit the State University of New York application form available online at www.farmingdale.edu and in New York State high school guidance offices.

Requests for further information should be addressed to:

Admissions Office
Laffin Hall
Farmingdale State College
2350 Broadhollow Road
Farmingdale, New York 11735-1021
United States
Phone: 631-420-2200
Website: http://www.farmingdale.edu

Bioscience students conduct research with their professors.

FASHION INSTITUTE OF TECHNOLOGY
State University of New York
NEW YORK, NEW YORK

★ To read more about this school, visit http://petersons.to/fit

FIT Fashion Institute of Technology
State University of New York

COLLEGE CLOSE-UPS

The College

The Fashion Institute of Technology (FIT) is New York City's celebrated urban college for creative and business talent. A State University of New York (SUNY) college of art and design, business, and technology, FIT is a dynamic mix of innovative achievers, original thinkers, and industry pioneers, with more than forty programs of study leading to the Associate of Applied Science (A.A.S.), Bachelor of Fine Arts (B.F.A.), and Bachelor of Science (B.S.) degrees. The School of Graduate Studies offers seven programs leading to a Master of Arts (M.A.), Master of Fine Arts (M.F.A.), or Master of Professional Studies (M.P.S.) degree. FIT is accredited by the Middle States Commission on Higher Education, the National Association of Schools of Art and Design, and the Council for Interior Design Accreditation. FIT serves approximately 10,000 students from the greater metropolitan area, New York State, across the country, and around the world, offering full- and part-time study options, evening/weekend degree programs, and online studies.

The college provides a singular approach to higher education—blending a real-world-based curriculum and hands-on instruction with a rigorous liberal arts foundation, marrying design and business, supporting individual creativity in a collaborative environment, and encouraging faculty members to match teaching expertise with professional experience. FIT's mission is to produce well-rounded graduates prepared for career success: doers and thinkers who become the next generation of business pacesetters and creative icons.

FIT offers a complete college experience with a vibrant student and residential life. The college's four residence halls house 2,300 students in fully furnished traditional and suite-style accommodations with a full meal plan option. Residential counselors and student staff members live in the residence halls, helping students adjust to college life and New York City.

The college is home to more than sixty student organizations, including academic societies, athletic teams, major-related organizations, and special-interest clubs. Student-run publications include a campus newspaper and a literary and art magazine.

FIT has intercollegiate teams in cross-country, half marathon, track and field, table tennis, tennis, women's soccer, swimming and diving, and women's volleyball. Athletics and Recreation offers students a full array of group fitness classes, including aerobics, dance, spin, and yoga at no extra cost. Students can also work out in a 5,000-square-foot fitness center. Open gym activities allow students to participate in both team and individual sports.

The David Dubinsky Student Center houses student lounges, a game room, a full-service dining hall and café, a student radio station, a student-run boutique, student government and club offices, health services, gyms, a dance studio, a fitness center, a counseling center, disability services, studios, and laboratories.

Location

Occupying an entire block in Manhattan's Chelsea neighborhood, FIT's campus places students at the heart of the fashion, advertising, visual arts, design, business, and communications industries. Students gain unparalleled exposure to their field through internships, field trips, and professional connections. A wide range of cultural and entertainment options—from dining to galleries to theater—are available within walking distance of the campus, which also offers convenient access to subway and bus lines and major rail and bus transportation hubs.

Majors and Degrees

FIT offers fifteen Associate in Applied Science (A.A.S.) and twenty-six baccalaureate programs. All first-time students complete a two-year A.A.S. program in their major area of study and then typically continue in a related, two-year Bachelor of Fine Arts (B.F.A.) or Bachelor of Science (B.S.) program. Some students choose to begin their careers after earning the A.A.S., which qualifies them for entry-level positions in their chosen field. All programs include a required liberal arts component. In addition, FIT has a variety of liberal arts minors that students may elect to complete.

The School of Art and Design offers ten A.A.S. and fourteen B.F.A. programs, the Jay and Patty Baker School of Business and Technology offers four A.A.S. and ten B.S. programs, and the School of Liberal Arts offers one A.A.S. and two B.S. programs and twenty-one minors.

The fifteen A.A.S. programs, all of which provide the foundation for one or more corresponding baccalaureate-level programs, are accessories design*, advertising and marketing communications*, communication design foundation*, fashion design*, fashion merchandising management* (with an online option), film and media, fine arts, illustration, interior design, jewelry design, menswear, photography, production management: fashion and related industries, textile development and marketing*, and textile/surface design*. Programs with an * are also available as a one-year option for students with acceptable transferable credits, and the one-year fashion merchandising management A.A.S. program is offered fully online.

The fourteen B.F.A. programs are accessories design, advertising design, computer animation and interactive media, fabric styling, fashion design (specializations in children's wear, intimate apparel, knitwear, special occasion, and sportswear), fine arts, graphic design, illustration, interior design, packaging design, photography and the digital image, textile/surface design, toy design, and visual presentation and exhibition design.

The twelve B.S. programs are advertising and marketing communications, art history and museum professions, cosmetics and fragrance marketing, direct and interactive marketing, entrepreneurship for the fashion and design industries, fashion merchandising management, film and media, home products development, international trade and marketing for the fashion industries, production management: fashion and related industries, technical design, and textile development and marketing.

Nine of the degree programs are also available through evening/weekend study: advertising and marketing communications (A.A.S. and B.S.), communication design foundation (A.A.S.), fashion design (A.A.S.), fashion merchandising management (A.A.S. and B.S.), graphic design (B.F.A.), illustration (B.F.A.), and international trade and marketing for the fashion industries (B.S.). The international trade and marketing degree (B.S.) is also available fully online.

Academic Programs

Each undergraduate program includes a core of traditional liberal arts courses. The School of Liberal Arts offers FIT students the opportunity to minor in a variety of liberal arts areas in two forms: traditional subject-based minors and interdisciplinary minors unique to the FIT liberal arts curriculum. Selected minors include film and media, economics, English literature, international politics, psychology, Latin American studies, and ethics and sustainability.

The Career and Internship Center offers lifetime placement services to graduates. Internships are a required element of most programs and are available to all students. Nearly one-third of FIT student interns are offered employment on completion of their internships.

The Presidential Scholars honors program, available to academically exceptional students in all disciplines, offers special liberal arts courses, projects, colloquiums, extracurricular activities, and off-campus visits designed to broaden horizons and stimulate discourse. Presidential Scholars are also awarded priority course registration and an annual merit stipend.

Precollege programs (Saturday Live, Sunday Live, and Summer Live) are available to middle and high school students during the fall, spring, and summer. More than 100 courses provide the chance to learn in an innovative environment, to develop art and design portfolios, to explore the business and technological sides of a wide range of creative careers, and to discover natural talents and abilities.

The Center for Continuing and Professional Studies provides courses for students and working professionals who want to pursue a certificate or further their knowledge in a particular area, as well as a wide range of classes for high school students on weekends and in the summer.

Off-Campus Programs

FIT has two campuses in Italy—one in Milan, one in Florence—where students study fashion design or fashion merchandising management and gain firsthand experience in the dynamics of European fashion. The study-abroad experience allows students to immerse themselves in diverse cultures and prepares them to live and work in a global community. Australia, China, England, France, and Mexico are some of the other countries where FIT offers study-abroad courses. Students can study abroad during the winter or summer sessions, or for a semester or a full academic year.

Academic Facilities

FIT provides its students with an urban campus of classrooms, laboratories, and studios that reflect the most advanced educational and professional practices. The Fred P. Pomerantz Art and Design Center houses studios, a printmaking room, display and exhibition design rooms, a model-making workshop, and a graphics printing service bureau. The Peter G. Scotese Computer-Aided Design and Communications Center allows students to explore the latest advancements in technology and their integration in design, photography, and computer graphics and animation. The fragrance studio, a professionally equipped fragrance development laboratory, is the only one of its kind on a U.S. college campus. Cutting and sewing laboratories offer the most advanced design and cutting machinery among educational facilities in the United States. The lighting laboratory, an educational and professional development facility, features more than 400 commercially available lighting fixtures. Other college facilities include a broadcasting studio, knitting and weaving labs, a multimedia foreign language laboratory, forty-six computer labs containing nearly 1,200 Mac and PC workstations, and several additional labs with computers reserved for students in specific programs.

The Museum at FIT is New York City's only museum dedicated to fashion. Students, designers, and historians use it for research and inspiration. The museum, which is accredited by the American Alliance of Museums, operates year-round, and its exhibitions are free and open to the public. The Gladys Marcus Library provides more than 300,000 volumes of print, nonprint, and electronic materials. The newspaper and periodicals collection includes 500 current subscriptions. Online resources include more than 90 searchable databases. The library also offers specialized resources, such as clipping files, fashion and trend forecasting services, and sketch collections.

Also on campus are three multimedia venues—the Katie Murphy Amphitheatre, the Morris W. and Fannie B. Haft Auditorium, and the John E. Reeves Great Hall—used for student presentations, industry panels, conferences, and special events.

Costs

For 2014–15, the associate-level tuition per semester was $2,250 for in-state residents and $6,750 for nonresidents. Baccalaureate-level tuition per semester was $3,085 for in-state residents and $8,905 for nonresidents. Housing costs ranged from $6,485 to $6,680 per semester for traditional residence hall accommodations with mandatory meal plan and from $6,060 to $10,095 for apartment-style accommodations. Meal plans varied from $1,745 to $2,233 per semester. Textbook costs and other nominal fees, such as locker rental or laboratory use, vary per program. Costs are subject to change.

Financial Aid

FIT attempts to remove financial barriers to college entrance by providing scholarships, grants, loans, and work-study employment for students in financial need. Over two-thirds of full-time, matriculated students who complete the federal financial aid application process receive some type of assistance through loans and/or grants. The college directly administers its own institutional grants and scholarships, which are provided by the FIT Foundation.

College-administered federal funding includes Federal Pell Grants, Federal Perkins Loans, Federal Supplemental Educational Opportunity Grants, Federal Work-Study, and Federal Family Educational Loans, which include student and parent loans. New York State residents who meet state guidelines for eligibility may also receive Tuition Assistance Program (TAP) and/or Educational Opportunity Program (EOP) grants.

Financial aid applicants must file the Free Application for Federal Student Aid (FAFSA). Students are also encouraged to apply for all available outside sources of aid. Additional documentation may be requested by the Financial Aid Services office. Applications for financial aid should be completed prior to February 15 for fall applicants or prior to November 1 for spring applicants.

Faculty

FIT's faculty is drawn from top professionals who bring their experience to the classroom and introduce students to the real-world opportunities and challenges of their disciplines through field trips, guest lectures, and sponsored competitions. Academic departments consult with industry advisory boards in their fields, ensuring that the curriculum and classroom technology reflect evolving industry practice. Student-instructor interaction is encouraged, with no class larger than 25 and more often smaller, and courses are structured to foster participation, independent thinking, and self-expression.

Student Government

The Student Council, the governing body of the FIT Student Association, gives all students the privileges and responsibilities of citizens in a self-governing college community. Many faculty committees include student representatives, and the president of the student government sits on FIT's Board of Trustees.

Admission Requirements

Applicants for admission must be either candidates for or recipients of a high school diploma or a General Educational Development (GED) certificate. Admission is based on strength and performance in college-preparatory course work and the student essay. A portfolio evaluation is required for art and design majors. Specific portfolio requirements are explained on FIT's website. SAT and ACT scores are required for placement in math and English classes and for students applying to the Presidential Scholars honors program. International applicants whose native language is not English must submit scores from TOEFL or IELTS examinations.

Transfer students must submit official transcripts for admission and credit evaluation. Students may qualify for the one-year A.A.S. option if they hold a baccalaureate degree from an accredited college or if they have a minimum of 30 transferable credits from an accredited college, including 24 credits that are equivalent to FIT's liberal arts requirements.

Students seeking admission to a B.F.A. or B.S. program must hold an A.A.S. degree from FIT or an equivalent degree from an accredited college. They must also meet the appropriate prerequisites for the specific major and must have completed FIT's liberal arts requirements. Further requirements may include an individual interview with a department committee, review of academic standing, and a portfolio review (for applicants to B.F.A. programs). Any student who applies for transfer to FIT from a four-year program must have completed a minimum of 60 credits, including the requisite art or technical courses and the liberal arts requirements.

Application and Information

Students wishing to visit FIT are encouraged to attend an information session and take a tour of FIT's campus. The visit schedule is available online at fitnyc.edu/visitfit. A virtual tour of the campus can be found online at fitnyc.edu/virtualtour. Interested candidates may apply online at fitnyc.edu/admissions.

For more information, students should contact:

Admissions
Fashion Institute of Technology
227 West 27th Street, Room C139
New York, NY 10001-5992
Phone: 212-217-3760
800-GO-TO-FIT (toll-free)
E-mail: fitinfo@fitnyc.edu
Website: http://www.fitnyc.edu
http://www.facebook.com/FashionInstituteofTechnology

FIDM/FASHION INSTITUTE OF DESIGN & MERCHANDISING

LOS ANGELES, CALIFORNIA

★ To read more about this school, visit http://petersons.to/fidm

The Institute

FIDM offers a highly focused education that prepares students for the professional world of fashion, interior design, digital arts, and entertainment. Students can choose from twenty-six specialized creative business and design majors. Among the degrees granted are Bachelor of Arts, Bachelor of Science, Associate of Arts (A.A.), A.A. Professional Designation, and A.A. Advanced Study. FIDM is accredited by the Senior College and University Commission of the Western Association of Schools and Colleges (WASC) and the National Association of Schools of Art and Design (NASAD).

Career planning and job placement are among the most important services offered by the college. Career assistance includes job search techniques, preparation for employment interviews, resume preparation, virtual portfolios, and job adjustment assistance. FIDM's full-time advisors in the Career Center department partner one-on-one with current students and graduates to help them move forward on their career paths, within their chosen major. Employers post over 23,000 jobs a year on FIDM's alumni job search site, which is available 24/7 exclusively to FIDM students and graduates. FIDM Career Advisors connect students to internships and directly to people in the industry. FIDM also offers Job Fairs, Open Portfolio Days, and networking days to allow students to meet alumni and industry leaders face-to-face. Because of the college's long-standing industry relationships, many firms come to FIDM first to recruit its students. Some of FIDM's successful graduates include celebrity designers Nick Verreos, Monique Lhuillier, and the cofounder of Juicy Couture, Pamela Skaist-Levy, as well as notable Hollywood costume designers Trish Summerville, Marlene Stewart, and Mona May.

Student Life: FIDM's ethnically and culturally diverse student body attracts students from around the world. The current population includes students from more than thirty different countries. The Student Activities Department plans and coordinates social activities, cultural events, and community projects. Student organizations include the ASID Student Chapter, Cross-Cultural Student Alliance, American Association of Textile Chemists and Colorists, Phi Theta Kappa Honor Society, and the Alumni Association. Students from all majors and campuses collaborate to produce *FIDM MODE™*, a glossy lifestyle magazine that promotes awareness about the design industry, current events, alumni news, and FIDM student life. The current issue is available for viewing online at FIDMMODE.com.

Location

FIDM's main campus is in the heart of the gentrified South Park neighborhood of downtown Los Angeles, between the STAPLES Center and the famed California Market Center and Fashion District. There are additional California campuses in San Francisco, Orange County, and San Diego. A virtual tour of the campuses and their locations is available at http://fidm.edu/visit-fidm/virtual-tour/.

FIDM Los Angeles is nestled at the center of an incredibly vibrant apparel and entertainment hub, surrounded by the fashion, entertainment, jewelry, and financial districts. It is situated next to beautiful Grand Hope Park, a tree-filled oasis amid the hustle and bustle of downtown Los Angeles. Newly renovated by acclaimed architect Clive Wilkinson, **FIDM San Francisco** stands in the heart of historic Union Square. The country's third-largest shopping area and stimulating atmosphere combined with the industry-based staff and faculty make this campus as incredible as the city in which it is located.

FIDM Orange County is a dynamic visual experience with ultra-modern lofts, an indoor/outdoor student lounge, eye-popping colors, and a one-of-a-kind audio-visual igloo. Also designed by world-renowned architect Clive Wilkinson, this campus has received several prestigious architectural awards and has been featured in numerous national magazines. **FIDM San Diego**'s gorgeous campus overlooks PETCO Park and is near the historic Gaslamp district and the San Diego harbor. FIDM's newest campus is sophisticated, stylish, and tech savvy, reflecting the importance of California's fastest-growing city and its appeal to the global industry.

Majors and Degrees

FIDM's twenty-six majors are all pathways to careers in the creative industries. Taught by working professionals, with an emphasis on hands-on learning and internships, FIDM degrees lead to careers in the fashion, interior, digital media, and entertainment industries.

FIDM's Admissions Advisors help students explore the career paths available and choose the right one.

Associate degree programs include:

- **Associate of Arts:** Two years of specialized education in Apparel Industry Management, Beauty Industry Merchandising & Marketing, Digital Media, Fashion Design, Fashion Knitwear Design, Graphic Design, Interior Design, Jewelry Design, Merchandise Marketing, Merchandise Product Development, Social Media, Textile Design, and Visual Communications.
- **Associate of Arts Professional Designation:** One-year programs designed for transfer students and college grads. Specialties include Apparel Industry Management, Beauty Industry Merchandising & Marketing, Digital Media, Fashion Design, Fashion Knitwear Design, Graphic Design, Interior Design, Jewelry Design, Merchandise Marketing, Merchandise Product Development, Social Media, Textile Design, and Visual Communications.
- **Associate of Arts Advanced Study:** For students holding an A.A. degree from FIDM in a related discipline, programs include: Advanced Fashion Design, Beauty Industry Management, Entertainment Set Design & Decoration, Film & TV Costume Design, Footwear Design, International Manufacturing & Product Development, Menswear, Textile Production & Development, and Theatre Costume Design.

Bachelor's degree programs are geared for students holding an A.A. degree from FIDM in a related discipline. Bachelor of Arts (B.A.) and Bachelor of Science (B.S.) degrees include:

- **B.A. degrees in:** Design, Digital Media, Graphic Design, Interior Design, Professional Studies (both A.A. and A.A. Advanced Study required), and Social Media.
- **B.S. degrees in:** Apparel Technical Design and Business Management.

For specific information and requirements concerning the above programs, prospective students should contact an Admissions Advisor at any FIDM campus.

Academic Programs

FIDM operates on a four-quarter academic calendar. Students can choose from twenty-six specialized creative business and design majors. New students may begin their studies at the start of any quarter throughout the year. Detailed information about FIDM majors is also available online at http://fidm.edu/en/Majors/.

Department chairs and trained advisers assist students in selecting the correct sequence of courses to complete degree requirements. The counseling department provides personal guidance and referral to outside counseling services and matches peer tutors to specific students' needs. Individual Development and Education Assistance (IDEA) Centers at each campus provide students with additional educational assistance in the areas of writing, mathematics, computer competency, study skills, research skills, and reading comprehension.

FIDM's eLearning program includes the B.S. in Business Management, the A.A. Professional Designation in Merchandise Marketing, and various classes in other majors. Students can check with the Admissions Office to determine the availability of FIDM's eLearning program in their area. The online courses are designed to replicate the experience of classes on campus. Students in the eLearning program are granted the same high-quality education as students on campus and have immediate access to valuable campus resources, including the FIDM Library, Career Advisors, and instructors.

Off-Campus Programs

Internships are available within each major. Paid and volunteer positions provide work experience for students to gain practical application of classroom skills. Among the companies that recruit FIDM interns are: Smashbox, Stila, Saks Fifth Avenue, BCBG, GUESS?, Rachel Zoe, Old Navy, Alexander McQueen, NBC Universal, Mattel, and Charlotte Russe.

FIDM provides the opportunity for students to participate in academic study tours in Europe, Asia, and New York. These tours are specifically designed to broaden and enhance the specialized education offered at FIDM. Participants may earn academic credit under faculty-supervised directed studies. Exchange programs are also available with L'Accademia Internazionale d'Alta Moda e d'Arte del Costume Koefia, Rome; Instituto Europeo di Design, Milan, Turin, Rome, Barcelona; Créapole, École de Création Management, Paris; Janette Klein Instituto de la Moda, Mexico City; Pearl Academy of Fashion, New Delhi; and RMIT University, Melbourne, Australia.

Academic Facilities

FIDM's award-winning campuses feature design studios with computer labs and innovative study spaces, spacious classrooms, imaginative common areas, and state-of-the-industry technology. Computer labs support and enhance the educational programs of the Institute. Specialized labs offer computerized cutting and marking; graphic, interior, and textile design; word processing; and database management.

The FIDM Library goes beyond traditional sources of information. It houses a print and electronic collection of over 2.5 million titles encompassing all subject areas, with an emphasis on fashion, interior design, retailing, and costume. The library subscribes to over 160 national and international periodicals, providing the latest information on art, design, graphics, fashion, beauty, business, and current trends. The FIDM Library also features an international video library, subscriptions to major predictive services, interior design workrooms, textile samples, a Textiles and Design Research Room, and access to the Internet.

The FIDM Museum & Galleries Permanent and Study Collections contain more than 12,000 garments from the eighteenth century to present day, including film and theatre costumes. One of the largest collections in the United States, it features top designer holdings including Chanel, Yves Saint Laurent, Dior, and Lacroix. The collection also includes items from the California Historical Society (First Families), the Hollywood Collection, and the Rudi Gernreich Collection.

Costs

For the 2014–15 academic year, tuition, fees, books, and most supplies started at $30,205, depending on the selected major. First-year application fees range from $225 for California residents to $525 for international students.

Financial Aid

There are several sources of financial funding available to eligible students, including federal financial aid and education loan programs, California state aid programs, institutional loan programs, and FIDM awards and scholarships. The FIDM Student Financial Services Office and FIDM Admissions Advisors work one-on-one with students and parents to help them find funding for their FIDM education. More information on FIDM scholarships and financial aid can be found at http://fidm.edu/go/fidmscholarships.

Faculty

FIDM faculty members are specialists in their fields, working professionals with impressive resumes and invaluable connections. They bring daily exposure from their industries into the classroom for the benefit of the students. In pursuit of the best faculty members, consideration is given to both academic excellence and practical experience.

Admission Requirements

Students are accepted into one of FIDM's specialized Associate of Arts degree programs packed with 16–25 challenging courses per major. Associate of Arts programs are designed for high school graduates or applicants with strong GED scores. They offer the highly specialized curriculum of a specific major, as well as a traditional liberal arts/ general studies foundation. Official transcripts from high school/secondary schools and all colleges/universities attended are needed to apply. International students must send transcripts accompanied by official English translations. Three recommendations from teachers, counselors, or employers are also required for admission. FIDM provides a reference request form on its website in the Admissions section under "How To Apply." All references must be sealed and mailed to the school when applying. An admissions essay portion and portfolio/entrance project requirement, which is specific to the student's selected major, are also available on the website's Admissions section under "How To Apply." For more information on the application process, prospective students can go online to www.fidm.edu. Admission to the Bachelor's degree programs is contingent on completion of an A.A. degree from FIDM.

Applications and Information

Applications are accepted on an ongoing basis. All prospective students should contact:

FIDM/Fashion Institute of Design & Merchandising
919 South Grand Avenue
Los Angeles, California 90015
Phone: 800-624-1200 (toll-free)
213-624-1201 (outside the United States)
Fax: 213-624-4799
Website: http://www.fidm.edu
http://www.facebook.com/home.php/#!/FIDMCollege
http://twitter.com/#!/FIDM

FIDM Los Angeles campus exterior.

COLLEGE CLOSE-UPS

FITCHBURG STATE UNIVERSITY

FITCHBURG, MASSACHUSETTS

★ To read more about this school, visit http://petersons.to/fitchburgstateuniversity

FITCHBURG STATE UNIVERSITY

The University

Fitchburg State University is a public, liberal arts center of learning, dedicated to teaching, with thriving career-oriented and professional education programs. The University prepares its graduates for jobs in their fields and continues to place more than 70 percent of its graduates in their chosen professions within six months of graduation.

Fitchburg State's excellent academic reputation and graduate placement can be attributed to a nationally recognized faculty and a strong commitment to teaching. The University enrolls approximately 3,800 undergraduate students in its day and evening divisions and another 3,500 students in its graduate and continuing education programs. The average undergraduate class size is 21, and the overall student-teacher ratio remains low at 15:1. Each student is assigned to an academic adviser to assist with planning an individualized program of study. In addition, each department has access to state-of-the-art equipment and there is an extensive internship network that spreads throughout New England and across the country.

Student life at Fitchburg State is active and fun. There are numerous and varied opportunities for student leadership and involvement. More than sixty student-run clubs and organizations are on campus, including academic, cultural, and ethnic; profession-oriented; performance; sports and fitness; social and volunteer; fraternities and sororities; student government; and academic honor societies. Hundreds of popular and well-attended activities take place during the year, including films, lectures, concerts, seminars, coffeehouses, pub entertainment, recreational tournaments, a performing arts series, and visual arts exhibits, to name just a few. The University's students participate in exciting Division III athletics, offering sixteen intercollegiate varsity sports teams for both men and women, and there is a variety of intramural sports for all students. The beautiful, well-equipped Recreation Center has all the equipment and activities students need to stay healthy and have fun.

In addition to Bachelor of Arts and Bachelor of Science degrees, Fitchburg State confers the Master of Arts; the Master of Arts in Teaching (M.A.T.); the Master of Business Administration (M.B.A.); the Master of Education (M.Ed.) in several disciplines; and the Master of Science (M.S.) in applied communication, computer science, mental health and school counseling, and forensic nursing. Several Certificate of Advanced Graduate Studies (C.A.G.S.) and other graduate-level certificate programs are available as well.

Location

The University is located in a residential area near the center of Fitchburg, a city with a population of 41,000, which serves as the hub of the commercial and industrial life of north-central Massachusetts. Fitchburg State owns the Wallace Civic Center which is home to the University's ice hockey team and provides many activities each year, such as exhibits, fairs, performances, free public ice skating, local hockey events, and lectures. The City of Fitchburg offers many opportunities for study and practical experience in the areas of sociology, psychology, health, computer technology, business, industry, political organization, and community service. Outdoor activities, including skiing, camping, hiking, canoeing, and fishing, are just minutes from the campus.

The historic and literary centers of Lexington and Concord and the city of Boston are only about an hour from the University. It's very easy to get to Boston—the commuter rail station is right on the edge of campus. The city of Worcester, the second largest in New England, is only one-half hour to the south. Fitchburg offers students the convenience of a residential campus with easy access to all the amenities that the surrounding area offers.

Majors and Degrees

Fitchburg State University offers the Bachelor of Arts, Bachelor of Science, and Bachelor of Science in Education degrees and offers the following undergraduate programs: accounting; architectural technology; biology; biotechnology; business administration; chemistry; clinical exercise physiology; cognitive science; communications media studies; computer information systems; computer science; construction technology; criminal justice (Police Certification option); developmental psychology; earth systems science; economics; education, with teacher education programs available in early childhood education, elementary education, middle school education, secondary education (with emphases in biology, English, history, chemistry, and mathematics), special education with emphases in severe disabilities (all levels) and moderate disabilities (pre-K–8), and technology education; electronics engineering technology; English studies; environmental biology; exercise and sports science; energy management; film/video production; fitness management; game design; geographic science and technology; graphic design; health sciences; history; human services; interactive media; humanities–interdisciplinary studies (pre-law option in 3+3 B.A./J.D. program linked with the University of Massachusetts School of Law); industrial technology; international business and economics; literature; management; manufacturing engineering technology; marketing; mathematics; nursing (RN, RN to B.S.N., LPN to B.S.N.); photography; political science; professional communication; professional writing; psychology; sociology; technical theatre arts; theater; undeclared/pre-major; and the following pre-professional programs: dentistry, law, medicine, and veterinary medicine.

Academic Programs

The University operates on a two-semester calendar. The first semester begins in early September and ends in mid-December, and the second semester begins in mid-January and ends in mid-May.

The curriculum has a strong liberal arts and sciences requirement, which provides a solid foundation for either further academic study or a career. Students obtain practical experience through numerous internships in social agencies, government offices, hospitals, and corporations related to their interests. Some major programs require an extensive supervised practicum to complete degree requirements. For education and nursing majors, a broad spectrum of student teaching and clinical experience is incorporated into their respective programs of study. The University's four-year honors program culminates in a senior thesis or project.

Off-Campus Programs

Fitchburg State is one of nine state universities under the jurisdiction of the Massachusetts Department of Higher Education. Through this affiliation, students may participate in the College Academic Program Sharing program, which allows study for a semester or a year at another university. For a rewarding cultural exchange experience, the Office of International Education provides undergraduate students the opportunity to study abroad at a variety of colleges and universities all over the world. Programs vary in length from a few weeks to as long as a semester or a year. Some of the locations in the exchange program include Australia, China, Costa Rica, England, France, Italy, Japan, New Zealand, and Russia.

Academic Facilities

The University has a number of special facilities. A well-equipped Academic Success Center includes offices for academic advising, career services, disability services, math and writing centers, multicultural student services, and peer tutoring. The McKay Arts Academy is a pre-K through eighth grade elementary school located on the campus, which gives education majors direct experience in a fully operational school. An outstanding $58-million Science Center opened in September 2013 and features state-of-the-art laboratories and equipment for science students. The Instructional Media Center has extensive, modern, well-equipped facilities, which support the industrial education and industrial technology programs. The nursing program utilizes an on-campus clinical lab that simulates a hospital setting with several computerized training models: SimMan, SimBaby, and SimNewB. The communications media program possesses a full range of the latest equipment, such as media/film composers, digital audio workstations, a full-color dye-sublimation printer, CD recording and slide-scanning equipment, multiple editing rooms, a production studio, darkrooms, and graphic design and game design computer labs and a motion-capture room for game design students. Communication students at Fitchburg State have access to many of the labs and facilities as early as their freshman year.

Costs

Fitchburg State University seeks to provide a very affordable education. Annual tuition for residents of Massachusetts was $970 per year in 2014–15; out-of-state tuition was $7,050. Required annual fees in 2014–15 totaled $8,290. The estimated annual total for a full-time, on-campus student from Massachusetts was $18,280 and for an out-of-state student, it was $24,360. Fees are subject to change.

Financial Aid

Many sources of financial aid are available to Fitchburg State students. The University participates in federal and state programs. Packages consisting of grants, loans, work-study awards, and scholarships are given to students demonstrating financial need and academic merit. All students who submit a completed application for admission by February 1 will automatically be considered for all available merit scholarships for the fall semester. Financial aid applications (including the FAFSA) for the fall semester must be completed by the preceding March 1 to be given priority consideration. Over $34 million in financial aid is granted annually to approximately 80 percent of Fitchburg State students making a quality education affordable for many deserving students.

Faculty

More than 92 percent of Fitchburg State's 192 full-time faculty members hold earned doctoral or other terminal degrees. Full professors teach freshman classes as well as advanced courses and serve as academic advisers to students majoring in their respective programs. Faculty members are accessible, engaging, and available to teach and advise students throughout their four years at the University.

Student Government

All full-time undergraduate students are members of the Student Government Association (SGA). The purpose of the SGA is to encourage responsibility and cooperation in democratic self-government; to form an official body for expressing the judgments of students and fostering activities and matters of general student interest; and to promote full understanding and cooperation among the students, the faculty members, and the administration in order to further the welfare of the University.

The governing body of the SGA consists of 6 SGA officers and a General Council, which includes these officers and 55 elected representatives of classes and residence halls, as well as the commuter student population. The SGA operates through a number of standing and ad hoc committees; membership is open to all students.

A 14-member All-University Committee, representing students, the faculty, and the administration, makes recommendations to the president of the University concerning matters of campus-wide policy.

Admission Requirements

As part of the Massachusetts State University system, Fitchburg State evaluates each applicant from any state, based on standards set by the Massachusetts Department of Higher Education and the University. The University considers high school curriculum, grade point average, SAT and/or ACT scores, school and community service, recommendations, application essay, life experience, special talents, and learning styles. The state admissions standards place significant attention on the student's high school record and SAT or ACT scores. The record of achievement in high school is the single most important item in the applicant's academic credentials. Freshman applicants should have completed a college-preparatory program that includes 16 college-preparatory units, with 4 units in English, 2 units in the same foreign language, 2 units in social studies, 3 units in mathematics (algebra I and II and geometry or trigonometry), 3 units in the natural sciences (2 of which must be laboratory courses), and 2 college-preparatory electives. Please note that for freshman students enrolling in the Fall 2016 semester and later, 4 units in mathematics will be required: algebra I and II and geometry or trigonometry or comparable course work, including mathematics in the final year of high school.

An essay is required; however, interviews are not required. Applicants who have questions about the programs and admission procedures at the University are encouraged to contact the Admissions Office to speak with a counselor.

The University encourages applications from transfer students and enrolls over 400 each year. An official transcript from each college previously attended must be submitted along with the application for admission.

International students are also encouraged to apply. Official evaluations of all international transcripts and translations of international transcripts must be submitted in addition to the application for admission. Additional information for international students is available on the University's website.

Application and Information

Fitchburg State University reviews applications on a rolling basis, sending its first set of admission decisions for the fall semester by mid-December. The priority deadline for applications is March 1. Applicants to the communications media, game design, and nursing programs are reviewed against a higher set of admissions standards and are strongly encouraged to submit their applications by the January 1 priority deadline. In addition, applicants who wish to be considered for merit scholarships and the Honors Program must complete their admission and financial aid application process (i.e., submit all required materials) by February 1.

Transfer applicants are encouraged to apply by April 15 for the fall and by November 1 for the spring semester. International applicants applying for the fall semester must complete the application process by March 15 if they require on-campus housing and by June 1 if they are not in need of campus housing. Applicants for the spring semester must complete their applications for admission by October 1.

For further information, students should contact:

Admissions Office
Fitchburg State University
160 Pearl Street
Fitchburg, Massachusetts 01420
Phone: 978-665-3144
800-705-9692 (toll-free)
Fax: 978-665-4540
E-mail: admissions@fitchburgstate.edu
Website: www.fitchburgstate.edu
www.facebook.com/FitchurgStateUniversity
twitter.com/FITCHBURG_STATE

FLORIDA ATLANTIC UNIVERSITY

BOCA RATON, FLORIDA

★ To read more about this school, visit http://petersons.to/floridaatlanticuniversity

The University

Florida Atlantic University (FAU) offers students a world-class education in a beautiful subtropical setting in Boca Raton, Florida. FAU is currently serving over 30,000 students at sites throughout its six-county service region in southeast Florida, with state-of-the-art student housing available on the Boca Raton and Jupiter campuses.

Student life as an FAU Owl has never been better. From a football team playing in the on-campus stadium to over 300 organizations that serve every academic and leisure-time interest, there's something for everyone at FAU. The University has an outstanding faculty of more than 1,000 accomplished scholars and researchers who are known for their excellence in teaching and mentoring. Enrichment opportunities abound, including honors education, internships, hands-on research, and study-abroad experiences. FAU offers 19 varsity sport teams plus cheer and dance. Students learn in beautiful campus environments, and the beach is just a few miles away.

The University offers more than 180 undergraduate and graduate degree programs in fields that span the arts and humanities, the sciences, medicine, nursing, accounting, business, education, public administration, social work, architecture, engineering, computer science, and more.

Florida Atlantic University is accredited by the Commission on Colleges of the Southern Association of Colleges and Schools to award associate, bachelor's, master's, and doctoral degrees. In addition, it is accredited by 14 professional agencies. FAU is also a member of the National Association of State Universities and Land-Grant Colleges and the Council of Graduate Schools in the United States.

FAU has exchange agreements with international schools in locations such as France, Germany, Japan, Sweden, Brazil, Finland, Ireland, Spain, Portugal, South Korea, Thailand, and many other locations.

The **Boca Raton campus** is FAU's first and largest campus. It occupies more than 850 acres just east of I-95, only 3 miles from the Atlantic Ocean. The campus features state-of-the-art labs and classrooms, suite-style student housing, and vibrant campus life. FAU's recreation and fitness center includes an aquatic center, three indoor basketball/volleyball courts, and a cardio/free-weight area. The recreation and wellness complex includes tennis courts, a track, and a variety of fields for club and intramural sports competition. It is home to the Florida Atlantic Research and Development Park and the nation's largest Lifelong Learning Society.

FAU's second-largest campus, the **Davie campus,** offers a wide variety of 2+2 programs in partnership with Broward College. The campus is also the base of operations for FAU's Everglades research and restoration efforts.

FAU Jupiter is home to the John D. MacArthur campus, which offers a wide range of upper division and graduate programs. The Harriet L. Wilkes Honors College, the Center for Environmental Studies, the Hibel Museum of Art, the research facility for Scripps Florida, and the Max Planck Florida Institute are all located on the Jupiter campus.

FAU Harbor Branch Oceanographic Institution's 600-acre campus is located in Fort Pierce. The institute features a 40,000-square-foot Marine Sciences Building, which houses specially equipped labs and classrooms. It provides an ideal setting for marine science research and teaching.

FAU Fort Lauderdale is part of an evolving, dynamic urban community that provides a laboratory for the professional degree program in architecture. The campus is located in downtown Fort Lauderdale.

Location

All of Florida Atlantic University's campuses are located in South Florida.

South Florida's climate is subtropical, with an average year-round temperature of 75 degrees. FAU's campuses are within easy driving distance of major airports, restaurants, shopping, cultural activities, and some of the most beautiful beaches and recreational facilities to be found anywhere.

Majors and Degrees

FAU offers programs leading to the Bachelor of Arts (B.A.), Bachelor of Science (B.S.), and specialized bachelor's degrees. A minimum of 120 credit hours is required for a bachelor's degree.

The College for Design and Social Inquiry offers majors in architecture, criminal justice, public management, public safety administration, social work, urban design, and urban and regional planning.

The Dorothy F. Schmidt College of Arts and Letters offers majors in anthropology; art: ceramics, painting, photography, printmaking, and sculpture; arts and humanities; commercial music; communication studies; English; French studies; graphic design; history, Italian studies; Jewish studies; linguistics; multimedia studies; music; music education; philosophy; political science; sociology; Spanish studies; theatre and dance; and visual arts and art history.

The College of Business offers majors in accounting, economics, finance, health administration, hospitality management, international business and trade, management leadership and entrepreneurship, management information systems, and marketing.

The Harriet L. Wilkes Honors College in Jupiter offers a liberal arts and sciences education in a highly selective environment. Concentrations include American studies, anthropology, biological sciences/pre-med, chemistry, economics, English literature, environmental studies, history, interdisciplinary critical theory, international studies, Latin American studies, law and society, marine biology, mathematics, mathematical sciences, medical humanities, philosophy, physics, political science, psychology, Spanish, and women's studies.

The College of Medicine and FAU's Wilkes Honors College offer select students early provisional admission to medical school, making it possible to receive both a bachelor's degree and an M.D. from FAU in only seven or eight years. Incoming freshmen who are accepted into the Wilkes Medical Scholars Program will begin their undergraduate programs already assured of a spot in FAU's medical school, provided they complete all program requirements.

The University Honors Program at the Boca Raton campus provides exceptional and rewarding learning opportunities through special honors seminars. The goal of the program is to give students a learning experience that will prepare them to continue their education throughout their lives.

The College of Education offers majors in art education, biology education, chemistry education, early care and education, elementary education, English education, exceptional student education, exercise science and health promotion, French education, math education, music education, physics education, social science education, and Spanish education.

The College of Engineering and Computer Science offers majors in computer science as well as civil, computer, electrical, environmental, geomatics, mechanical, and ocean engineering. FAU established the nation's first ocean engineering degree program in 1965 and now conducts millions of dollars in research annually.

The Christine E. Lynn College of Nursing offers a B.S. in Nursing degree and is nationally and internationally known for developing innovative approaches to nursing education within a caring philosophy.

The Charles E. Schmidt College of Science has majors in biological science, chemistry, geography, geology, mathematics, neuroscience and behavior, physics, and psychology. The Charles E. Schmidt College of Science also offers a pre-health professions certificate for any students interested in pursuing careers in dentistry, general medicine, optometry, pharmacy, physical therapy, and veterinary medicine.

Academic Facilities

FAU offers a multitude of academic resources. The Dorothy F. Schmidt College of Arts and Letters features a 75,000-square-foot, three-building complex comprising a performance arts center, an art gallery, a theater, a visual arts center, lecture halls, classrooms, and offices. The College of Business occupies a four-story building including wireless classrooms with a simulated trading room floor. The College of Education's four-story, 90,000-square-foot facility houses its academic departments and offers a teaching gymnasium, an early childhood center, and the A. D. Henderson University School operated by the College of Education. There is also a marine sciences center, Gumbo Limbo, located between the Intracoastal Waterway and the Atlantic Ocean; it provides teaching and research facilities. The Christine E. Lynn College of Nursing is housed in a state-of-the-art building, which is LEED-certified Gold. The five-story S. E. Wimberly Library houses a large collection of monographs, serials, and other academic resources. Computer labs, study lounges, a media center and tutoring services also provide valuable academic support for students.

Additional facilities include the Marleen and Harold Forkas Alumni Center; the College of Engineering and Computer Science facility, which has received LEED Platinum certification; the Culture and Society building, which includes the Living Room Theaters, a 200-seat digital movie complex; and Parliament Hall, a new 614-bed state-of-the-art freshman residence hall.

Costs

For the 2014–15 academic year, in-state tuition was $201.29 per credit hour and out-of-state tuition was $719.84 per credit hour. Average on-campus room and board costs are $11,556. Approximate expenses are $1,220 for books, $2,217 for personal items, and $3,167 for transportation for off-campus students. Fees are subject to change.

Financial Aid

Approximately $191 million in financial aid is awarded each year. A comprehensive program of student financial aid includes scholarships, grants, loans, and work-study that may provide assistance from initial enrollment through graduate study. As a member of the College Scholarship Service of the College Board, the University is guided by the principles and policies of that organization. Students who are interested in applying for need-based aid must complete the Free Application for Federal Student Aid (FAFSA), which is available online at http://www.fau.edu/finaid. Students are strongly encouraged to complete the FAFSA in January for fall admission. The process of applying for aid normally takes six to eight weeks. The priority deadline is March 1.

There are a variety of scholarships for academic, athletic, or artistic talent. Students should visit the Admissions website at http://www.fau.edu/admissions for more information on academic scholarships and should check with individual departments for information on athletic or artistic scholarships.

Faculty

Recognizing that the excellence of its faculty is the true measure of the worth of a university, FAU has brought together a distinguished group of scholars who hold a balanced dedication to both teaching and research. Faculty members come from more than thirty states and several countries. The majority hold a doctorate or professional degree. They all represent a high level of professional experience and academic attainment and are committed to the development of a vigorous educational program of the highest caliber.

Student Government

FAU gives students an active role on virtually all University and faculty committees, including the Curriculum Committee, the Board of Trustees, college advisory councils, the Student Government Association, and Residence Hall Councils, as well as the interclub, interfraternity, and Panhellenic groups. Students also serve on the University Senate along with faculty and staff members.

Admission Requirements

Admission to the University is selective and limited to applicants who have graduated from regionally accredited high schools or who have achieved a certain level on the GED certificate exam. Evaluation is based on the academic course grade point average and rigor of curriculum combined with acceptable results on the SAT or ACT. Candidates for admission should have the 18 required academic high school units. An application, a non-refundable $30 application fee, official transcripts, and the official results of the SAT or ACT are required to be considered for admission.

For detailed additional requirements and additional information, students should visit http://www.fau.edu/admissions.

Application and Information

Office of Undergraduate Admissions
Florida Atlantic University
777 Glades Road
Boca Raton, Florida 33431
Phone: 561-297-3040
E-mail: admissions@fau.edu
Website: http://www.fau.edu

Florida Atlantic University Boca Raton entrance, 3 miles from the beach.

FLORIDA SOUTHERN COLLEGE

LAKELAND, FLORIDA

FLORIDA SOUTHERN COLLEGE

The College

The oldest private college in the state, Florida Southern College (FSC) was chartered in 1883 and settled on the shores of the spectacular Lake Hollingsworth in Lakeland in 1922.

Today, Florida Southern is a nationally ranked, residential, coeducational, and comprehensive college recognized for its commitment to providing engaged learning experiences to its students. Florida Southern's 2,200 students represent nearly every state and fifty countries. Students choose Florida Southern because of its national reputation for dynamic, hands-on learning in an atmosphere that is friendly and personal.

Experiencing the world beyond the classroom is an essential part of a Florida Southern education. Along with providing ample opportunities to conduct lab and field research, become involved in community service, and perform, Florida Southern guarantees each student an internship and study-abroad experience. Florida Southern also guarantees its students will graduate in four years.

Members of the community take great pride in the beautiful campus, a historic landmark and home to the world's largest single-site collection of buildings designed by renowned architect Frank Lloyd Wright.

As a residential community, Florida Southern provides its students with a wide range of housing options, including all-female and all-male halls, coed halls, suite-style living arrangements, and off-campus apartments. The College also dedicates spaces to various majors, honors students, and fraternity and sorority life. Accommodations are well equipped and feature stunning views of the lake, contemporary student lounges, modern kitchens and bathrooms, and wireless Internet access.

Athletic facilities are first rate. The George Jenkins Field House includes a three-court gymnasium, a weight room, and an athletic training room. The popular Nina B. Hollis Wellness Center, the hub of student life, offers a fully equipped fitness center, an aerobics/dance studio, an intramural gymnasium, racquetball courts, and a competition-sized swimming pool. Directly across from the Wellness Center is Lake Hollingsworth, which offers kayaks, paddleboats, and waterskiing.

The student body is extremely involved. With more than eighty clubs, Florida Southern offers countless ways for students to pursue their interests while making lasting connections. Florida Southern is also home to thirteen national Greek fraternities and sororities. FSC's Moccasins are members of NCAA Division II. The nineteen varsity programs, including men's and women's lacrosse teams and a nationally-ranked water skiing team, have won twenty-eight national championship titles. Other popular student activities are intramural sports; water sports, such as kayaking, on Lake Hollingsworth; drama and music groups; publications; and organizations related to academic and political, religious, and social interests. A high percentage of students are involved in volunteer programs in the community, state, and internationally.

Location

Florida Southern's campus consists of approximately 113 acres on the shore of Lake Hollingsworth in Lakeland, Florida, a dynamic suburban community of about 120,000 residents in the heart of Florida's high-tech corridor. The campus is within walking distance of Lakeland's historic downtown, and Lakeland is just 45 minutes from Tampa and an hour from Orlando. Within an hour's drive of the state's major recreational attractions, including Walt Disney World and award-winning beaches, the College is ideally situated for internships and job opportunities with leading corporations that tap into one of the largest markets in the United States. Students enjoy Festival of Fine Arts series performances in music, dance, and drama; distinguished speakers; and business symposiums. The local Lakeland Center also offers many cultural and entertainment opportunities.

Majors and Degrees

Florida Southern College offers Bachelor of Arts, Bachelor of Fine Arts, Bachelor of Music, Bachelor of Music Education, Bachelor of Science, and Bachelor of Science in Nursing degrees in more than fifty majors including accounting, art (art education, art history, graphic design, and studio art), biochemistry and molecular biology, biology, biotechnology, business administration (career tracks in finance, international business, management, and marketing), chemistry, citrus, communication (advertising and public relations; broadcast, print, and online media; interpersonal communication; political communication; and sports communication), computer science, criminology, dance, education (elementary, music, and secondary), English, exercise science, finance and economics, free enterprise, history, healthcare administration, health science, marine biology, mathematics, music (music education, music management, and music performance), nursing, philosophy, political economy, political science, psychology, religion, Spanish, sport management, theater arts (musical theater and technical theater/design), and youth ministry. Divisional majors are available in humanities and social science.

Outstanding preprofessional programs are offered in dentistry, engineering, law, medicine, pharmacy, physical therapy, theology, and veterinary medicine. Florida Southern's pre-law program boasts a 100 percent acceptance rate into law school, with similar results for pre-med students. One hundred percent of accounting majors pass the CPA exam and go on to find jobs. The School of Education and School of Health Sciences also have 100 percent placement rates for their education and nursing majors, respectively.

An honors program provides special opportunities for a select group of entering first-year students to explore topics of common interest in an integrated and interdisciplinary fashion.

Academic Programs

Florida Southern's rigorous degree programs require the satisfactory completion of a minimum of 124 semester hours with a minimum grade point average of 2.0. Students and professors work together in discussion-based classes featuring debate, collaborative projects, and other forms of engaged learning. The College operates on the semester system, with two 15-week semesters, and summer sessions. The average course load is 16 hours per semester. Along with course work in their major, students are required to complete a general education curriculum designed to help develop knowledge, communication, and critical-thinking skills, as well as attitudes for lifelong success, in addition to their major course work.

As part of FSC's engaged-learning model, students work collaboratively with faculty on research, fieldwork, and service projects. For example, business students have established strategic plans and operational reports for corporate and nonprofit organizations, nursing students have delivered babies in Tanzania, and chemistry students have collaborated with faculty members to become published in national academic journals, such as *The Journal of Physical Chemistry*. Fine arts students have performed alongside talented faculty and visiting performers. Regardless of their course of study, Florida Southern student graduate with the real-world experience employers seek.

The FSC experience is career focused from day one. The College's career counselors help students explore their strengths and provide continual evaluation of career options with personalized guidance on resume building, interviewing, and landing the ideal first post-college job.

An honors program provides special opportunities for a select group of entering first-year students to explore topics of common interest in an integrated and interdisciplinary fashion.

Approximately 20 percent of Florida Southern graduates opt to continue their studies in graduate school.

Off-campus Programs

Entering first-year students are guaranteed a travel-study opportunity during their junior or senior year at Florida Southern. Students have traveled to Africa, the Caribbean, China, Costa Rica, England, France, Italy, Mexico, Washington, D.C., and other exciting destinations.

Florida Southern College is also affiliated with The Washington Center (TWC), a highly regarded, nonpartisan internship provider with international scope. As the only private institution of higher education in the state to affiliate with TWC, FSC students have access to prestigious and valuable field experiences. Programs range from tailored internships that are academic and work-experience based for governmental, international, corporate, and nonprofit organizations, to intensive-learning academic seminars focused on timely topics.

Academic Facilities

Situated within an orange grove overlooking scenic Lake Hollingsworth, the FSC campus combines beautiful landscape with modern buildings designed by world-famous architects.

The campus's newest addition is the 40,000-square-foot Becker Business Building, designed by renowned architect Robert A. M. Stern. This premiere business education center features high-tech classrooms equipped with the latest educational technology and houses a simulated trading floor that will function as a laboratory in which students can learn first-hand about investment analysis and trading strategies. The technologically advanced Joe K. and Alberta Blanton Nursing Building, home to the College's growing School of Nursing, features patient simulators in the state-of-the art treatment simulation laboratory. The Dr. Marcene H. and Robert E. Christoverson Humanities Building comprises contemporary classrooms along with language labs and the film studies center. Recently renovated, Frank Lloyd Wright's Polk Science Building is home to FSC's natural science and premedical programs and is outfitted with a wide range of cutting-edge instrumentation, such as a nuclear magnetic resonance spectrometer, the preeminent device in determining the structure of chemical compounds. The building also features the world's only Wright-designed planetarium.

The Marshall and Vera Lea Rinker Technology Center is the nucleus for learning on campus. It houses the College's main computer lab, classrooms, and small group study areas and provides students with the latest technologies.

An integral part of the intellectual life of the College, FSC's E. T. Roux Library provides access to a rich collection of materials, including print and digital books; periodicals; electronic databases; a media collection that includes CDs, DVDs, and CD-ROMs; a substantial microforms collection; and seating for almost 500 students. The Library is also home to TûTû's Cyber Café, a comfortable venue for club meetings as well as late-night study groups. Adjacent is the Sarah D. and L. Kirk McKay, Jr., Archives Center which houses the archival materials of the Florida Conference of the United Methodist Church, the Center for Florida History collection, the Florida Citrus Archives, along with the College's collection of Frank Lloyd Wright memorabilia.

The campus also boasts a fine arts complex, which includes Branscomb Memorial Auditorium (seating 1,800 and nationally known for its perfect acoustics), the Marjorie M. McKinley Music Building, the Melvin Art Gallery, and the Loca Lee Buckner Theater.

Florida Southern is also home to a preschool lab and the Roberts Academy, the first transitional school for children with dyslexia in the state of Florida, and a preschool lab, each providing an opportunity for students majoring in elementary education to observe and teach.

Costs

The comprehensive cost for 2015–16 is $41,670 per year ($31,460 for tuition and standard fees and $10,210 for room and board). FSC estimates that $1,150 is adequate for books and supplies, and $1,500 should cover personal expenses, exclusive of travel to and from home.

Financial Aid

Consistently rated as a best value, 98 percent of all FSC students receive financial assistance. Each year, Florida Southern offers more than $20 million in college aid on the basis of academic merit; talent in athletics (baseball, basketball, cross-country, golf, soccer, softball, swimming, tennis, volleyball, or lacrosse), fine arts, theater, leadership, or community service; student need; and other factors. The College's most talented applicants are invited to apply for several of the College's Prestige Scholarships, which cover up to the full cost of tuition and fees, as well as additional stipends for study abroad.

Florida Southern understands that everyone's financial situation is different and offers students assistance in meeting their educational expenses through scholarships, grants, loans, and campus employment. To demonstrate need, an applicant is required to file the Free Application for Federal Student Aid (FAFSA). Applicants for aid must reapply each year. Florida Southern participates in the Federal Perkins Loan, Federal Supplemental Educational Opportunity Grant, and Federal Work-Study college-based programs. All applicants are expected to apply for any entitlement grant for which they are eligible, such as a Federal Pell Grant and, for Florida residents, the Florida Student Assistance Grant. The Federal Stafford Direct Student Loan Program is also available. The completed FAFSA and the College's financial aid application must be filed with the Financial Aid Office by April 1. Early application is encouraged for students seeking academic scholarships.

Faculty

FSC faculty members are more than professors—they also function as advisers, mentors, and a true partner in a student's learning. The student-faculty ratio is 13:1 and 85 percent of Florida Southern's faculty members have doctoral or other terminal degrees. Not only are they top scholars in their fields, but they are also devoted to providing students with personalized attention and a truly outstanding education. Faculty members are selected for their teaching abilities and their ability to relate to the needs and concerns of their students.

Admission Requirements

Florida Southern looks for two things in applicants: performance and promise. The majority of students who have been accepted have a weighted GPA of 3.6 or better in college-preparatory courses (including four courses in English, three in mathematics, and the balance divided among science, foreign language, and social science); and have earned between 1040 and 1200 (combined reading and math scores) on the SAT or a composite score between 23 and 28 on the ACT. All applicants must graduate from an accredited high school.

The Admissions Office is committed to reviewing individual applicants on their own merits based on the level of challenge attempted, patterns of grades over time, recommendations from references, and an applicant's own assessment of the learning environment best suited to his or her needs. Evidence of leadership and community service also are typical attributes of a successful applicant. Applicants are encouraged to visit campus and meet with an Admissions Counselor. (Qualified high school juniors may apply for early admission if they have the recommendation of their secondary school and have had a personal interview with the Dean of Admissions.)

Florida Southern welcomes applications from students resuming their education and from older students who have delayed their entrance into college and typically enrolls 100 transfer students annually. Transfer applicants should have a minimum 2.5 grade point average and be graduates of or eligible to return to their former institutions. Transfer students with fewer than 25 semester hours must submit high school transcripts and standardized test scores. Applicants who hold Associate of Arts degrees from regionally accredited two-year institutions are typically granted junior standing. All applicants are encouraged to interview; an interview may be required for some candidates.

Credit by examination is awarded on the basis of successful scores on Advanced Placement tests, the International Baccalaureate (I.B.), Advanced International Certificate of Education (AICE), and College-Level Examination Program (CLEP) tests.

Application and Information

An application is considered by the Admissions Committee when it has been received with required test scores, references, and transcripts from each school attended. Because all students are required to live on campus unless they are seniors, married, or living with their parents, early application is desirable to ensure that housing is available. The freshman application priority date is March 1. The deadline for early decision applicants is December 1.

For more information about Florida Southern College, prospective students should contact:

Office of Admissions
Florida Southern College
111 Lake Hollingsworth Drive
Lakeland, Florida 33801-5698
Phone: 800-274-4131 (toll-free)
E-mail: fscadm@flsouthern.edu
Website: http://www.flsouthern.edu

Students enjoying the Florida sun in front of the classic Joseph-Reynolds Residence Hall, constructed in 1922.

FRANKLIN COLLEGE
FRANKLIN, INDIANA

The College

As an innovative scientist, diplomat, thinker, writer, and leader, Benjamin Franklin's remarkable life and accomplishments left a mark on not only a young nation, but also the world. Named in the spirit of this extraordinary American icon, Franklin College continues his legacy of exploration and knowledge.

Since its founding in 1834, Franklin College has a long history of preparing students for lives committed to excellence, leadership, and service. With a comprehensive liberal arts curriculum combined with a leading-edge professional development program, Franklin College prepares graduates to think independently, to lead responsibly, and to serve with integrity in their professions, their communities, and the world.

Small classes and dedicated faculty members ensure that students get the attention needed to succeed, and Franklin's career and graduate school admission rates prove this. Franklin combines liberal arts training with preprofessional development like no other college. Students can develop the competencies and resources necessary to be successful in their personal and professional lives through Franklin's innovative Professional Development Program (PDP). This exciting program gives them the opportunity to dine with corporate executives, network with national and community leaders, learn the finer points of corporate communication, and develop a level of polish and sophistication that sets them apart from other college graduates.

Location

Located in the heart of the Midwest, Franklin College offers students the best of both a small community and a big city's excitement.

Franklin, Indiana, is only 20 miles south of Indianapolis, which is the state's capital city and the twelfth largest city in the U.S. It offers a wide variety of internship opportunities, as well as athletic, cultural, and entertainment events that appeal to all students.

Majors and Degrees

Flagship programs at Franklin College include the sciences, athletic training, business, journalism, and education.

Franklin College confers more than fifty-five Bachelor of Arts degrees in the following areas: accounting, art (art history and studio art), athletic training, biology, business (finance, general, international business, management, and marketing), chemistry, computer science/computer information systems, creative writing, economics, education (elementary and secondary), engineering (computer, electrical, and mechanical), English, exercise science, French, history, mathematical science (applied, pure, and quantitative analysis), multimedia journalism (broadcasting and news-editorial), music (instrumental and vocal), philosophy, physical education, political science, psychology, religious studies, sociology (criminology and social work), Spanish, and theater. Franklin also offers forty-one different minors, including areas like leadership, neuroscience, coaching, and physics.

Preparation for graduate school is exceptional, with 85 percent of students gaining admission to medical school and 90 percent of applicants accepted to law school.

Students considering a career in dentistry, medical technology, medicine, occupational therapy, optometry, pharmacy, physical therapy, or veterinary medicine arrange their program with the advice of the preprofessional adviser of the science division.

One-hundred percent of athletic training majors are employed six months after graduation.

Business students repeatedly score in the top 5 percent on the National College Business Examination.

The Pulliam School of Journalism is one of a few comprehensive journalism schools housed at a small liberal arts institution. Student media opportunities include a student-run PR agency, a student newspaper, magazine, and radio show. Franklin's journalism students also have the opportunity to work at the Indiana Statehouse Bureau in downtown Indianapolis.

Students planning a career in secondary education may elect an academic area of concentration that will satisfy the state requirements for a teaching major. The Education Department is endorsed and approved by the Indiana Professional Standards Board and the National Council for Accreditation of Teacher Education (NCATE). After graduation, education majors are placed at 97 percent or higher in the classroom.

Engineering is offered as a 3+2 program. Students earn a Bachelor of Arts degree from Franklin College and a Bachelor of Science degree in one of the engineering disciplines from the Purdue School of Engineering and Technology (IUPUI).

Academic Programs

Academic programming is built around applied learning. Active engagement is at the core, giving students fundamental skills for the workplace and graduate school. Franklin College is committed to engaging every student in collaborative, hands-on learning. Approximately one third of each student's total course work is composed of the prescribed and exploratory courses that make up the general education core curriculum.

All of Franklin's academic departments offer individualized study, allowing a student to pursue his or her field of interest in depth. Students interested in pursuing a major not offered at Franklin may submit a proposal for their individualized major.

Franklin College operates on a 4-1-4 academic calendar, which allows tremendous opportunities for students throughout the academic year. The fall semester begins toward the end of August and ends before Christmas; the spring semester begins in February and ends in the middle of May. The two semesters are broken up by a special four-week Winter Term program during the month of January. Winter Term is designed to allow students to study in areas of particular interest to them, either within or outside their major field of study. Some January classes offer students the opportunity to travel to locations such as Belize, England, France, Italy, and Mexico.

Students can also take advantage of internship opportunities during Winter Term, offering practical experience under the supervision of a professional. Internships are available during Winter Term, summer, fall semester, and spring semester. The location of the college in proximity to downtown Indianapolis allows students to complete internships with nationally known Fortune 500 companies. One-hundred percent of Franklin College students complete an internship or significant undergraduate research prior to graduation.

Franklin gives credit in seventeen academic areas for successful scores on CLEP subject examinations; credit is also granted for successful scores on the Advanced Placement tests of the College Board. The Running Start Program enables talented high school students to get an early start on their college education.

Study-Away-From-Campus Programs

Franklin College students can participate in a variety of international and domestic study-away-from-campus opportunities. Students at the college have the opportunity to study away beginning as early as their freshman year. This experience is a key component of a liberal arts education. Not only does it allow students to learn about other cultures and countries of the world, it also helps them develop problem-solving and cross-cultural communication skills. In a global economy, this experience can be invaluable upon graduation.

Franklin College offers many ways for students to broaden their horizons, including a semester or year away, a Winter Term travel course, or a summer away. Options range from two weeks to a full year. Students can take courses for their major, earn credits for electives, complete an internship, or take part in a service-learning experience.

Academic Facilities

Franklin College has two campus buildings listed on the National Historic Register. Old Main, the original home of the college, and Shirk Hall, home of the Pulliam School of Journalism, are footholds of the rich past and recent renovation of the Franklin College campus. Classrooms and administrative, business, and professorial offices, along with computer laboratories, occupy Old Main; Shirk Hall also houses classrooms and the radio station.

Barnes Science Hall houses all physics, biology, and chemistry department classrooms and laboratories. The Spurlock Center gymnasium and fitness center provide workout and weight equipment to students in order to maintain a healthy lifestyle.

The Dietz Center for Professional Development is the home of the Professional Development Program. State-of-the-art conference rooms and computer facilities enhance Franklin's career programming commitment to its students.

The B. F. Hamilton Library, containing more than 117,000 volumes and collections of microfilm, slides, art reproductions, recordings, and periodicals, is a member of P.A.L.N.I. (Private Academic Library Network of Indiana). The library also houses the Academic Resource Center (ARC), where students can receive help with their individual studies. The Johnson Center for Fine Arts provides classrooms and practice and performance accommodations, and it houses the facilities and meeting rooms for the Leadership Program.

Costs

The direct cost for the 2015–16 academic year is $38,065. This amount is derived from tuition, which is $28,840; residence hall, which is $5,150; student fees of $185; and Winter Term meal fees of $390 plus the meal plan, which is $3,500.

Financial Aid

The Franklin College financial aid program assists students who might not otherwise be able to attend college and rewards applicants for excellent academic achievement in high school. Awards are based on scholarship, curricular and extracurricular activities, and financial need. Aid involving financial need includes Franklin College grants, loans, and employment. Franklin participates in the Federal Stafford Student Loan and Federal Work-Study programs. Merit-based scholarships ranging from $2,500 to full tuition are awarded to students based on academic performance, activities, and standardized test scores. Scholarships are renewable for each of the recipient's four academic years at Franklin, provided students maintain specific GPA requirements and advance in class status each year. Franklin College encourages all students and families to file the Free Application for Federal Student Aid (FAFSA) in order to receive additional financial aid.

Faculty

The 12:1 student-faculty ratio allows Franklin faculty members to provide excellent instruction in small classes that promote participatory learning. Nearly 90 percent of current faculty members have obtained the highest degree in their field. Faculty members serve as advisers and provide supplemental attention outside the classroom. While many faculty members carry on research and publish their work, their main emphasis is teaching. No classes are taught by graduate students or teaching assistants.

Student Organizations

Franklin College offers more than sixty clubs and organizations such as Student Congress, Black Student Union, Greek Life, and Student Entertainment Board. These organizations allow students to plan on-campus concerts/events, represent the student body to change campus policies, and volunteer their time with the college's Habitat for Humanity programs from the first year. In addition to the existing organizations, the college allows students to set up new groups of their interests.

Admission Requirements

Applications for admission to Franklin College are evaluated on an individual basis. A student's potential academic and personal contributions to the college, recommendations, school and community activities, academic record, and standardized test scores are taken into consideration by the Admissions Committee. A student should complete a strong college-preparatory program. Candidates for admission are urged to visit the campus in order to experience the college community. Franklin offers a variety of visit opportunities, from personal visits to open houses, all providing opportunities to meet current students, professors, and coaches, and to take a campus tour.

Application and Information

To be considered for admission, an applicant must submit a completed application (paper or online), a transcript of all secondary school and college work attempted, and either SAT or ACT scores. A decision regarding acceptance is made after the college receives all necessary credentials. Notification is sent immediately after the Enrollment Committee has acted.

Office of Admissions
Franklin College
101 Branigin Boulevard
Franklin, Indiana 46131
Phone: 317-738-8075
888-852-6471 (toll-free)
Fax: 317-738-8274
E-mail: admissions@FranklinCollege.edu
Website: http://www.franklincollege.edu/admissions/
http://www.facebook.com/fcadmissions

Old Main is the oldest academic building on the Franklin College campus.

COLLEGE CLOSE-UPS

FRANKLIN UNIVERSITY SWITZERLAND

LUGANO, SWITZERLAND

★ To read more about this school, visit http://petersons.to/franklinuswitzerland

The University

Franklin University Switzerland (FUS), named for the United States' first and most illustrious ambassador to Europe, was founded in 1969 as Franklin College, a nonprofit, independent, postsecondary institution. The University takes as its cornerstone Benjamin Franklin's vigorous support of intellectual interchange between nations. An American liberal arts institution in an international environment, Franklin is accredited in the United States by the Commission on Higher Education of the Middle States Association of Colleges and Schools and in Switzerland by the Swiss University Conference.

Franklin places a strong emphasis on cross-cultural perspectives, advocating that international studies should be an integral part of an education. Franklin defines higher education from its beginning as the experience of thinking internationally. Its emphasis on global perspectives, both academic and social, is designed to affect the direction and meaning of a student's educational experience, life, and career.

The essence of a Franklin education is the exposure of its students to cultures other than their own, providing them with a better understanding of others, the world, and their place in the world. The University's location in Lugano, a vibrant Swiss city that is part of the cultural milieu of northern Italy, ensures a constant commingling of cultures in a quadrilingual nation.

Close faculty-student contact is essential to Franklin's educational philosophy. Teaching is designed to promote engaging student-teacher interaction from the beginning. The exceptional student-faculty ratio of just over 10:1 makes learning at Franklin University Switzerland an intensive and personal endeavor.

Students and faculty members, many of whom have a cross-cultural background, come to FUS from every corner of the globe, further strengthening international study and experiences. Approximately 60 percent of the students come from the United States; the remaining 40 percent are from Europe, Asia, Africa, South America, and the Middle East. Bringing diverse experiences and perspectives to university life, students live in University residences both on and near the campus. All residences have kitchens available, and two campus dining facilities provide regular meal service and a diverse meal plan. Resident Assistants supervise all campus buildings.

Campus activities are varied. Franklin's Student Government Association (SGA) promotes a student newspaper; a literary magazine; a drama club; cultural, language, and sports clubs; and numerous social events that take advantage of southern Switzerland's extensive recreational resources. There are competitive sports teams and student-organized games, which include basketball, soccer, and volleyball. In addition, the Office of Student Life connects interested students with a considerable number of local Swiss clubs and teams that welcome newcomers: basketball, ice hockey, soccer, and volleyball teams, as well as crew, fencing, flying, golf, hang gliding, ice skating, judo, parachuting, riding, rock climbing, sailing, swimming, tennis, track, and windsurfing clubs. By joining these local groups, Franklin students become part of the region's local community; they are themselves essential to the cross-cultural learning the University promotes.

Location

Franklin University Switzerland's campus is in the community of Sorengo, a section of the city of Lugano, southern Switzerland's principal business, banking, medical, and cultural center. Easily accessible from the campus either by public transportation or on foot, downtown Lugano and its surrounding lakeside villages are renowned for their scenic beauty and Mediterranean climate.

Throughout the year, Lugano features outstanding cultural activities The Swiss-Italian radio station hosts its own permanent symphony orchestra, and the International Convention Center attracts guest performers from around the world. Several music festivals are held throughout the summer, covering classical, jazz, and pop music. Nine public museums, many art galleries, several movie theaters, and a multitude of restaurants and discotheques make for a range of recreational choices normally found only in a large city. A covered ice rink, swimming pools, and a wide range of other sports facilities are maintained by local sports clubs; Lugano and the southern part of Switzerland offer access to an extraordinary variety of sports activities. In the spring and fall, Ticino's most popular recreation is hiking. In winter, skiing is available in San Bernardino and Andermatt, about an hour from the campus, or in the fabled St. Moritz, Davos, Klosters, and Zermatt.

Academic Programs

Franklin offers a Bachelor of Arts program with majors in art history and visual culture, communication and media studies, comparative literary and cultural studies, environmental studies, French studies, history, international banking and finance, international economics, international management, international relations, Italian studies, literature, psychology, and visual and communication arts, with combined and double majors in a number of study areas. Since 2012, the University also offers a master's degree program in international management and additional graduate programs are under development.

Franklin's curriculum promotes international awareness and critical thinking, while being interdisciplinary in the highest tradition of a liberal arts education. The courses of study explore the diverse disciplines that enlighten an educated human being.

All B.A. degree candidates must demonstrate a foreign language proficiency in a language other than their mother tongue equivalent to three years of university-level instruction in one of the languages taught at Franklin. This requirement is met by successfully completing appropriate courses at Franklin or by passing an equivalency test administered by the language department.

In addition to their major field of study, students may minor in another course of study. The number of credit hours (12 to 15) and the program of courses are subject to departmental approval.

FUS operates on a two-semester calendar, with classes starting in late August and mid-January; two 4-week intensive summer sessions are also available. A required orientation program for all new students is held in August and mid-January.

Off-Campus Programs

Franklin's renowned Academic Travel program is a fully integrated part of the regular curriculum. Each semester, all Franklin undergraduate students participate in two weeks of faculty-led study visits to various destinations around the globe—an excellent opportunity to learn through experience. Recent Academic Travel destinations have included Austria, Botswana, Croatia, Cyprus, Czech Republic, England, France, Germany, Holland, Iceland, India, Republic of Ireland and Northern Ireland, Italy, Malawi, Morocco, Mozambique, Oman, Poland, Qatar, Romania, Scotland, Serbia, Slovenia, South Africa, Spain, Switzerland, Thailand, Turkey, and the United Arab Emirates.

Franklin students also often undertake internships during the course of their studies. Undergraduate students may apply for an internship after two semesters of residence at Franklin, either by asking to be considered for one of the internships provided by the University or by arranging for an appointment themselves. At the graduate level, internships are a core requirement to obtain the degree.

Students in good standing who major in modern languages are also eligible for study in a country where the target language is spoken; such study is limited to one semester at an approved institution.

Academic Facilities

Franklin's libraries contain over 38,000 volumes in English and six other languages, as well as over 100 print newspapers and journals. In addition to the print and multimedia collections, the libraries subscribe to many online indexes and full-text databases, including ProQuest, EBSCO, LexisNexis University, MarketLine, Columbia International Affairs Online (CIAO), and ARTstor. Public Internet-access computers are available in the libraries and computer lab for student research use.

Costs

The comprehensive fee for the 2014–15 academic year was $64,000. This figure includes the cost of tuition, room and board, Academic Travel, and student fees. The estimated cost of personal expenses and incidentals, including textbooks, is $6,500 per year. The estimated cost range to fly round-trip from the United States is from $1,100 to $1,400.

Financial Aid

Franklin University Switzerland offers academic merit awards and need-based financial aid to qualified students. U.S. applicants for financial aid must submit the FAFSA for evaluation. Veterans' and Social Security benefits are also available to eligible students. Federal Stafford Student Loans and PLUS loans may be obtained through the Department of Education's Direct Loan Program. International students must submit an International Student Financial Aid Form. Campus scholarships are also available. Students interested in applying for one can do so by requesting information about available Life Long Learning Scholarships through the Office of Student Life at the beginning of each semester.

Faculty

Franklin University Switzerland has 53 full-time and part-time professors, approximately half of whom are American or British; others are of various nationalities. The majority have advanced degrees from prestigious universities; most have lived, studied, worked, and taught in a variety of countries. Franklin's teaching staff characterizes the cross-cultural essence of the University. Franklin professors are committed to global arenas of study; are knowledgeable about particular countries enough to organize and lead rewarding Academic Travel courses; are usually competent in more than one language; and are dedicated to the personal, discursive style of teaching required by a small liberal arts institution with small classes. The faculty members also advise the various student activities, lead local excursions, and regularly contribute to the University's co-curricular program of lectures. In addition, each faculty member acts as academic counselor to a number of students. The faculty-conducted Academic Travel program promotes the intellectual friendship between teacher and student essential to a liberal arts education. Franklin's student-faculty ratio is approximately 10:1.

Student Government

The student body elects the members of the Student Government Association (SGA). The SGA sponsors several interest groups including the Franklin Business Society, the *Franklin Voice* (student newspaper), Sustainability Club, and AIESEC, as well as several social events. In addition, the SGA collaborates with the local community to host events, such as a biannual blood drive. The SGA is actively involved in campus governance by appointing members to participate in meetings of the Curriculum Committee, Faculty Assembly, and the Appeals Board.

Admission Requirements

Franklin University Switzerland seeks students who are eager to meet the challenge of studying and living in Europe, serious about undertaking university-level learning, and prepared to contribute positively to the intellectual life of the institution. To identify such students, and also to ensure a diverse student population, the FUS Admissions Committee considers both academic and personal factors, including the student's academic record, evaluations by teachers and counselors, standardized test scores, extracurricular interests and talents, and academic distinctions. Admission to FUS is limited and therefore competitive. To achieve the best match between the student and Franklin, a personal interview is strongly recommended; one can be arranged by contacting the Admissions Office in Lugano or New York. Applicants to the first-year class must submit a completed application form (using either the Franklin application or the Common Application) with a nonrefundable fee of $90; an essay and personal statement; an official transcript of their secondary school record; SAT or ACT scores, either included on transcripts or forwarded by the testing service to Franklin University (CEEB code number 0922; ACT code number 5223); and three letters of academic evaluation. Applicants whose first language is not English must submit their score on either the SAT or ACT, or Test of English as a Foreign Language (TOEFL)/International English Language Testing System (IELTS). TOEFL scores should be at least 79 (Internet-based test) or 550 (paper-based test). IELTS scores should be above 6.0. Transfer applicants and institute applicants are required to submit a completed application and a nonrefundable application fee of $90, an official transcript of their academic records, a dean's report from the dean of students, and one letter of academic recommendation. The application fee is waived for all applicants who apply by January 15.

Application Deadlines and Information

The priority application deadline for scholarships and for fall entry is December 1 for applicants to the freshman class and June 15 for transfer and study-abroad applicants. The final application deadline is June 15. The priority application deadline for the spring semester is November 1. Admission decisions are made on a rolling basis, allowing consideration for enrollment after the priority deadline. All inquiries and applications should be directed to the nearest Admissions Office.

Franklin University Switzerland
U.S. Office, Suite 2746
420 Lexington Avenue
New York, NY 10170
United States
Phone: 212-922-9650
Fax: 212-922-9870
E-mail: info@fus.edu

Peter Dorthe
Director of Admissions
Franklin University Switzerland
Via Ponte Tresa, 29
6924 Sorengo/Lugano
Switzerland
Phone: 41-91-986-3613
Fax: 41-91-993-3906
E-mail: info@fus.edu
Website: www.fus.edu
www.facebook.com/franklinuniversityswitzerland

Franklin students enjoying terrace dining at the Grotto, Franklin University Switzerland's casual dining area.

GANNON UNIVERSITY

ERIE, PENNSYLVANIA

★ To read more about this school, visit http://petersons.to/gannonuniversity

The University

Gannon University is a Catholic, Diocesan university founded in 1925 and dedicated to excellence in teaching, scholarship and service. The faculty and staff prepare students to be global citizens through programs grounded in the liberal arts and sciences and professional specializations. Inspired by the Catholic Intellectual Tradition, Gannon offers a comprehensive, values-centered learning experience that emphasizes faith, leadership, inclusiveness, and social responsibility.

Gannon consistently receives high marks from *U.S. News & World Report*; the 2015 edition of *America's Best Colleges* ranks Gannon as a "Best Value School" in the North Region, placing Gannon ninth on the list. This is the ninth consecutive year that Gannon has been named to the list.

Situated in downtown Erie, Pennsylvania, Gannon is close to businesses, organizations, and government agencies that are active partners in helping its students receive a hands-on education. The urban campus also places students within walking distance of shops, restaurants, theaters, and professional sports venues. The campus includes the Recreation and Wellness Center which recently underwent a 65,000-square-foot expansion project that included a complete interior renovation, new cardio equipment, and new locker rooms. Gannon's residence halls, apartments, academic buildings, administrative offices and chapel are centered around the Waldron Campus Center—the heart of Gannon's campus—where members of the University's close-knit community meet, dine, study, and socialize.

Student athletes excel at Gannon in NCAA Division II intercollegiate athletics. Men's teams include baseball, basketball, cross-country, football, golf, soccer, swimming and diving, water polo, and wrestling. Women's teams include acrobatics and tumbling, basketball, competitive cheer, cross-country, golf, lacrosse, soccer, softball, swimming and diving, volleyball, and water polo. Many of Gannon's athletes utilize the Gannon University Field, a multipurpose athletic facility that is conveniently located on campus. In addition, the Recreation and Wellness Center renovation included a 51,300-square-foot field house that features an 80-yard practice facility for all teams and students to use. Gannon also offers students a broad intramural sports program that runs throughout the entire year.

The student body consists of more than 4,400 students, 3,300 of whom are undergraduates, with a 14:1 student/faculty ratio. The Student Success Center provides students with internship placement, career development, employment assistance, and tutoring services.

Location

Gannon is located in Pennsylvania's fourth-largest city and one of the busiest ports on the Great Lakes. Gannon's urban campus, in the middle of downtown Erie, is within a 2-hour drive of Cleveland, Buffalo, and Pittsburgh. Its unique location and facilities create a special atmosphere conducive to learning, scholarship, research, service, and personal growth. The campus is within 5 miles of Interstates 79 and 90 and 5 miles from Erie International Airport. Erie is also serviced by rail and bus transportation.

Majors and Degrees

In the College of Humanities, Education, and Social Sciences, areas of study are: advertising communication, communication arts, criminal justice, English (with concentrations in applied communications, literature, and writing), foreign language and international studies, foreign language and literature, health communications, history, interdisciplinary studies, international studies, journalism communications, legal studies, mortuary science, philosophy, political science, prelaw, a 3+3 prelaw program that includes early admission to Duquesne University, psychology, social work, theater, theater and communication arts, and theology.

In the School of Education, the areas of study from which students may select a major are early childhood education Pre-K–4, early childhood education PreK–4/special education PreK–8, middle level education 4–8, middle level education 4–8/special education PreK–8, secondary education (in biology, English, mathematics, and social studies).

The Morosky College of Health Professions and Sciences offers degrees in the health professions and sciences. The degrees offered in the health professions include athletic training (master's), medical technology, nursing (master's programs and a doctorate program available as well), nutrition and human performance, occupational therapy (master's), physical therapy (doctorate), physician assistant (master's), radiologic sciences, respiratory care, sport and exercise science (master's), and undecided health science.

The School of Sciences offers degrees in biochemistry, biology, chemistry, environmental science, freshwater and marine biology, mathematics, and science. Also offered are preprofessional programs for students who wish to enter chiropractic, dental, medical, optometry, podiatry, or veterinary school, as well as accelerated and cooperative medical programs in allopathy, osteopathy, optometry, podiatry, and pharmacy.

The College of Engineering and Business offers degrees in a variety of areas. Students may choose from majors in bioinformatics, biomedical engineering, chemical engineering (cooperative program), computer science, electrical engineering, electrical engineering (five-year co-op program), environmental engineering, industrial engineering, information systems, mechanical engineering, mechanical engineering (five-year co-op program), and software engineering. Business options include accounting, entrepreneurship, finance, healthcare management, international management, management, marketing, risk management and insurance, sports management and marketing, and supply chain management. All business students are encouraged to participate in an internship before graduation.

The associate degree program offers Associate of Science and Associate of Arts degrees. Areas of study in which students may major are accounting, business administration, criminal justice, early childhood education, legal studies, radiologic sciences, and respiratory care.

Academic Programs

Each undergraduate program has its own sequence of requirements. Students in all programs must complete credits in liberal studies. A faculty adviser is assigned to each student to assist with academic planning. A department chairperson and faculty adviser also assist each student in selecting courses that fulfill requirements and best meet the student's desired career objectives. The basic graduation requirements for bachelor's degree candidates are 128 credit hours, including completion of requirements for their major and the liberal studies program. To earn an associate degree, students must usually complete 60 to 68 credit hours, depending on the program. Students may receive credit through the Advanced Placement program.

Gannon offers a program for students with learning disabilities (PSLD) and an Army ROTC program that is open to interested students.

Gannon's academic calendar consists of two full semesters, running from August to December and from January to May. There are also optional summer classes.

Academic Facilities

The A. J. Palumbo Academic Center houses the College of Humanities, Education and Social Sciences. From education to foreign language programs, the faculty members and facilities in Palumbo provide high-quality education. The University's honors program as well as all support services are also located in Palumbo.

There are three new academic buildings on campus: the Forensic Investigation Center, the School of Communication and the Arts, and the Center for Business Ingenuity. Students in Gannon's criminal justice program utilize the Forensic Investigation Center that features classroom space, a forensic laboratory, a firearms training simulator, and space to reenact crimes.

Programs such as advertising communication, communication arts, journalism, and theater are housed in the School of Communication Arts. This building provides state-of-the-art technology and houses Gannon's award-winning radio station, WERG-FM, 90.5, its television studio, and its student newspaper, *The Gannon Knight*.

All business courses are now held in the Center for Business Ingenuity, which is also home to the Small Business Development Center and the Erie Technology Incubator. The proximity of these operations and the hands-on opportunities they offer have a tremendous impact on the student experience. In addition, the business curriculum now incorporates the same SAP software that many European businesses use.

The recently remodeled Zurn Science Center has laboratories for research in biology, anatomy, physics, chemistry, and engineering. The building also houses an open engineering computer lab as well as additional computer labs for student use. There are numerous classrooms and two auditoriums in the building.

The Morosky College of Health Professions and Sciences is located in the Robert H. Morosky Academic Center. This 99,000-square-foot facility includes classrooms, labs, and faculty offices. It also includes a 5,800-square-foot state-of-the-art Patient Simulation Center.

Other academic buildings include Scottino Hall, home of the Schuster Theatre; and the Nash Library, the hub of academic life at Gannon.

Costs

For 2014–15, full-time tuition was $13,880 per semester ($14,715 for engineering and health sciences), or $27,760 per academic year ($29,430 for engineering and health sciences). Tuition for part-time students was $670 per credit hour. Room and board range from $4,950 to $6,730 per semester. The total cost for the academic year at Gannon was between $28,368 and $30,038 for commuting students and $38,598 and $43,498 for resident students, depending on the program of study.

Financial Aid

The University offers an integrated financial aid program of scholarships, grants, loans, and employment. Gannon's financial aid program is open to all full-time students attending classes during the period from August to May. It is highly recommended that all students seeking financial aid should file the admissions and financial aid applications by the preferred deadline of March 15. Numerous scholarship opportunities are available to qualified students. Each year the University offers its top incoming freshmen the ability to compete for full tuition scholarships. Application deadline for this competition is December 15 with on-campus competition taking place in late January.

Faculty

Gannon's faculty consists of 200 lay and religious men and women, and 72 percent of the full-time faculty members have either doctoral or terminal degrees. The student-faculty ratio is about 14:1, and average class size is approximately 25 students in each class. Most faculty members assist in the faculty adviser program, giving each student individual attention and counseling on academic and personal matters.

Student Government

The Student Government Association (SGA) is composed of students elected by members of their class. Through the SGA, students can play a responsible role in the planning and working of the University. SGA has voting representatives on all of the standing committees of the University. Members of the SGA not only research existing policies and problems, they also look for new ways to improve the academic life of students. The SGA also plans social events for the student body.

Admission Requirements

Gannon University actively recruits students of all races, creeds, and ages from all geographic regions. Transfer and international students are encouraged to seek admission. Applicants are required to submit scores (including senior-year scores) on either the SAT or ACT; an up-to-date transcript of the high school record, showing rank in class if available (plus a college transcript for transfer applicants); a completed application form; and a nonrefundable $25 fee. Admission decisions are based upon numerous factors, central of which is the strength of the high school record, as demonstrated through grades and relative class standing and SAT and/or ACT scores and other test scores that may be available. Recommendations and personal statements also affect admission decisions. Transfer and international students should check with the admissions office for special application procedures.

Application and Information

Students applying for admission in the fall semester should start the application process at the beginning of their senior year in high school. Gannon operates on a rolling admissions basis, which means that there is no deadline for filing applications, with the exceptions of the physician assistant program, LECOM (Lake Erie College of Osteopathic Medicine) and PCOM (Philadelphia College of Osteopathic Medicine) 4+4 Medical Programs and the accelerated pharmacy options, which have a deadline of November 1 for the fall semester. Due to the competitiveness of the program, students who are interested in the nursing or occupational therapy programs are highly encouraged to file their applications in September. Early applications are recommended, as are enrollment deposits.

For further information, students should contact:

Office of Admissions
Gannon University
109 University Square
Erie, Pennsylvania 16541
Phone: 814-871-7240
800-GANNON-U (426-6668, toll-free)
Fax: 814-871-5803
E-mail: admissions@gannon.edu
Website: http://www.gannon.edu

The new Recreation and Wellness Center opened in August 2014, featuring nearly 52,000 square feet of subdivided indoor space for year-round athletic, intramural, open recreation, and fitness activities.

COLLEGE CLOSE-UPS

THE GEORGE WASHINGTON UNIVERSITY

WASHINGTON, D.C.

THE GEORGE WASHINGTON UNIVERSITY

WASHINGTON, DC

The University

Located just four blocks from the White House, the George Washington University (GW) is the largest institution of higher education in the nation's capital. Founded in 1821 by an Act of Congress, GW is a private nonsectarian coeducational institution accredited by the Middle States Association of Colleges and Universities. GW prides itself in being at the forefront of major research endeavors, while providing a stimulating intellectual environment where students and faculty members put knowledge into action.

The student population at GW consists of approximately 10,400 undergraduates and 14,600 graduates. Students hail from all fifty states, the District of Columbia, Puerto Rico, the Virgin Islands, and 120 countries. The undergraduate student population is 10.8 percent Asian American, 5.0 percent African American, 8.0 percent Hispanic American, and 9.9 percent international.

GW comprises two fully integrated campuses, the Foggy Bottom campus and the Mount Vernon campus. Both campuses are located in historic D.C. neighborhoods that offer vibrant and distinctive residential options to freshmen and continuing students. The Foggy Bottom campus is situated in the center of downtown D.C., neighbored by the Kennedy Center, the Watergate complex, the State Department, and the White House. The 26-acre Mount Vernon campus is home to outdoor athletic facilities and is surrounded by embassy and diplomatic residences.

GW guarantees housing for entering freshmen, sophomores, and juniors and houses 75 percent of undergraduates in thirty-five residence halls. GW offers a number of living arrangements, including apartment-style living for upperclassmen and residential town houses. GW's academic residential communities' philosophy guarantees that residence hall life is a valuable extension of the undergraduate academic experience. With nearly 100 percent of the entering class living in university housing, the atmosphere proves to be academically as well as socially stimulating.

GW hosts a strong intercollegiate varsity athletic program with twenty-seven teams participating in the NCAA Division I and Atlantic 10 Conference. They include men's baseball, basketball, cross-country, golf, rowing, sailing, soccer, squash, swimming, tennis, and water polo, and women's basketball, cross-country, gymnastics, lacrosse, rowing, soccer, softball, swimming and diving, tennis, volleyball, and water polo. Students interested in playing sports, but not quite up to the varsity level, may join a number of university-supported club and intramural sports.

There are more than 450 student-created and student-run organizations at GW. These organizations run the spectrum from academic to cultural, spiritual to recreational, and political to artistic. In addition to these special-interest organizations, GW is home to twenty-six national sororities and fraternities, eight multicultural Greek chapters, the Student Association (details in the Student Government section), the Program Board, the *GW Hatchet* (GW's independent newspaper), and WRGW (the campus radio station). The Division of Student Affairs plans hallmark program events for students on campus, ranging from Welcome Week to the Excellence in Student Life Awards.

Location

Many students at GW also choose to immerse themselves in the excitement of Washington, D.C., which has been called the most livable city on the East Coast and one of the best college towns in the United States. Washington, D.C., offers an infinite array of internships and cooperative education experiences, allowing GW students to explore their career aspirations outside of the four walls of the classroom. GW students have interned at the White House, the World Bank, IBM, the U.S. House of Representatives and Senate, NASA, the National Zoo, the Smithsonian Institution, and CNN, among many other world famous organizations.

Almost 19 million tourists flock to Washington, D.C., every year, and they experience the vibrant college town and young professional social scene of the nation's capital. There are more than 50,000 college students in the D.C. metropolitan area.

Majors and Degrees

GW offers a wide range of undergraduate programs in seven undergraduate schools: the Columbian College of Arts and Sciences, the Elliott School of International Affairs, the School of Business, the School of Engineering and Applied Science, the School of Media and Public Affairs, the Corcoran School of the Arts and Design, and the Milken Institute School of Public Health.

GW offers more than 1,800 courses in over 70 majors, and yet, the average class size is only 28. Students may earn an undergraduate degree in a single field of study, or they may choose to double major, major in one field and minor in another, participate in an interdisciplinary program, or create their own individualized field of study.

The university awards an array of bachelor's degrees, including Bachelor of Arts (B.A.), Bachelor of Science (B.S.), Bachelor of Accountancy (B.Accy.), Bachelor of Fine Arts (B.F.A.), and Bachelor of Business Administration (B.B.A.).

A variety of joint-degree programs are available to undergraduates. In addition to a seven-year accelerated B.A/M.D. program, the university offers nearly fifty 5-year bachelor's/master's combined programs.

Academic Programs

Most undergraduate students must complete 120 credit hours to be eligible for graduation, which means that the average student carries 15 credit hours (five courses) per semester. All students at GW are required to participate in the university's writing program. In addition, each school has general curriculum requirements, ranging from 17 to 45 credit hours.

GW is home to twelve honor societies, including Phi Beta Kappa and Golden Key National Honor Society. GW offers a variety of specialized academic programs. The University Honors Program, which does not replace a regular program of study but rather enhances it with intellectually challenging analysis and discussion, consists of approximately 500 undergraduates.

The seven-year accelerated B.A./M.D. program is designed for students who wish to obtain a strong foundation in the liberal arts prior to becoming physicians, enabling them to accomplish that goal in a shorter amount of time than a traditional program of study.

Off-Campus Programs

GW students are encouraged to study abroad in order to expand their worldview and their educational opportunities. GW offers study abroad centers in Madrid, Paris, England, and Latin America (Chile and Argentina), as well as affiliated and exchange programs. More than 2,000 GW undergraduates study abroad in over sixty countries.

Many GW students also take advantage of cooperative education (co-op), which provides students with an opportunity to gain valuable paid work experiences directly related to their major. The Center for Career Services manages the program, in partnership with area employers, to ensure that co-op experiences are substantive and well-supervised. Similarly, most GW students engage in internships, which serve as a means for students to gain practical, professional experience and to augment their academic knowledge. Internships can be paid or unpaid, offered for academic credit, and can last for as long (or short) as the student and employer choose. The Center for Career Services also acts as a clearinghouse for internship positions.

Academic Facilities

The Gelman Library houses more than 2 million volumes and, as a member of the Washington Research Library Consortium (WRLC), offers GW students access to more than 12 million items at nine area universities. Gelman Library is open 24 hours a day, offering study lounges, group discussion rooms, computer labs, walk-up reference consultation, and an interlibrary loan service. GW provides on-site and remote access to ALADIN, the shared online catalogue of WRLC libraries, plus databases indexing periodical articles and some full-text journals. GW is also home to the Eckles Library, the Jacob Burns Law Library, the Himmelfarb Health Sciences Library, and the Virginia Science and Technology Campus Library.

GW's state-of-the-art facilities enhance academic and campus life experiences. Completed and planned projects include the Science and Engineering Hall; the Milken Institute School of Public Health building; The George Washington University Museum and The Textile Museum; and an 850-bed residence hall with faculty suites, affinity housing, and retail space.

Costs

In response to family concerns about paying for college, GW has instituted a fixed tuition plan. Under this plan, the tuition remains the same each year for students who remain enrolled in full-time status during their undergraduate programs. Therefore, except for marginal increases in housing costs, cost of attendance will not rise. Students who entered in fall 2014 have tuition costs of $48,700 per year for four years. Room and board costs are approximately $11,700.

Financial Aid

The ability to finance a GW education is a priority, so the Office of Student Financial Assistance seeks to assist students and their families in meeting the costs to attend the university. The university budgets $170 million for undergraduate financial assistance, which includes scholarships and need-based assistance. In addition, GW offers families the opportunity to participate in a ten-month payment plan.

By applying for admission, students with outstanding academic credentials are automatically considered for merit scholarships. More than 65 percent of freshmen receive need-based assistance with an average package of over $35,943.

The Presidential Scholars in the Arts Program awards scholarships to, and encourages the work of, entering freshmen who have shown promise in the fine arts (ceramics, design, drawing, painting, photography, and sculpture), music, theater, technical theater, directing, dance, and choreography.

More information about financial aid at GW can be obtained online at http://financialaid.gwu.edu.

Faculty

There is 1 faculty member for every 13 students at GW. Ninety-one percent of GW's full-time faculty members hold a doctoral degree. Part-time and adjunct faculty members are often leaders in their fields of expertise. GW professors are engaging, eminently qualified, and well connected, which allows for a robust intellectual community.

Student Government

The Student Association (SA) is an organization chartered by GW's Board of Trustees to represent students and their concerns. Any person registered for any academic credit at GW is a member of the SA. The SA undertakes initiatives related to academics, community service, neighborhood relations, and student activities.

Admission Requirements

GW receives more than 19,000 applications for freshman admission and aims to recruit a class of 2,350. Admitted students have strong academic records and the demonstrated ability to achieve success in their college endeavors. To be considered for admission, applicants must submit the following credentials: the Common Application and fee, high school transcripts, essays, letters of recommendation from a teacher and a guidance counselor, and either SAT or ACT scores. Students applying to the Corcoran School of the Arts and Design must submit a portfolio in lieu of SAT or ACT scores. Details can be obtained online at http://undergraduate.admissions.gwu.edu. Freshman interviews are not required, but may be helpful.

Application and Information

GW has a number of application options: regular decision, early decision I, and early decision II. Students apply to GW using the Common Application. Prospective students should consult the website (http://undergraduate.admissions.gwu.edu) for more information and deadlines.

Office of Admissions
The George Washington University
2121 I Street, NW, Suite 201
Washington, D.C. 20052
Phone: 202-994-6040
E-mail: gwadm@gwu.edu
Website: http://www.gwu.edu

Kogan Plaza on the GW campus.

COLLEGE CLOSE-UPS

GODDARD COLLEGE

PLAINFIELD, VERMONT

★ To read more about this school, visit http://petersons.to/goddardcollege

Goddard College

The College

With its main campus nestled in rural Vermont, Goddard College is recognized for innovation in education. Its mission is to advance the theory and practice of learning by undertaking new experiments based upon the ideals of democracy and the principles of progressive education asserted by John Dewey. At Goddard, students are regarded as unique individuals who will take charge of their learning and collaborate with other students, staff, and faculty to build a strong community. Goddard encourages students to become creative, passionate, lifelong learners, working and living with an earnest concern for others and the welfare of the Earth.

Goddard's semester format comprises an intensive eight-day residency on campus followed by 16 weeks of independent work and self-reflection in close collaboration with a faculty adviser. A student's semester studies are carried out where the student is, be that in their home community, engaged in a service project, traveling, and so on. Faculty evaluations form the basis of the narrative transcript, which—in place of letter grades—provides external readers with a precise, detailed synopsis of the student's learning.

Goddard offers Bachelor of Arts (B.A.) degree programs in education, health arts and sciences, individualized (self-designed) studies, psychology, and sustainability, as well as a Bachelor of Fine Arts (B.F.A.) degree in creative writing. The College also offers graduate study options in community education, clinical mental health counseling, consciousness studies, creative writing, dual language early childhood education, health arts and sciences, psychology, social innovation and sustainability, teacher licensure, transformative language arts, and individualized (self-designed) studies.

Goddard College is accredited by the New England Association of Schools and Colleges, through its Commission on Institutions of Higher Education, to offer bachelor's and master's degrees.

Location

Goddard College is located on the grounds of a late-nineteenth-century model farm in Plainfield, Vermont, just outside Montpelier. The Greatwood Farm and Estate consists of shingle-style buildings and gardens designed by noted American architect, Arthur Shurcliff. The campus buildings were added to the National Register of Historic Places in 1996.

Goddard also has satellite campuses in Seattle, Washington, and at the Fort Worden State Park in Port Townsend, Washington.

Majors and Degrees

Goddard offers the Bachelor of Arts in community education, dual language early childhood education, health arts and sciences, psychology, sustainability, teacher licensure, and individualized (self-designed) studies. The college offers the nation's only low-residency Bachelor of Fine Arts in Creative Writing degree program.

Academic Programs

Students must accumulate 120 semester-hour credits to earn the Bachelor of Arts or Bachelor of Fine Arts degree from Goddard College.

Students may apply to transfer up to 75 semester hour credits toward a Goddard undergraduate degree. This can be a combination of credit from regionally accredited colleges and universities, Advanced Placement (AP) examinations, and College Level Examination Program (CLEP) examinations.

Instead of taking traditional classes in a given set of academic areas, students demonstrate progression toward meeting degree requirements through the submission of Progress Review Portfolios following the first year and prior to the final year of study.

All students produce a senior study, or thesis, prior to earning the baccalaureate degree.

B.F.A. in Creative Writing: Students study fiction, poetry, memoir and nonfiction, and hybrid forms in the first low-residency B.F.A. degree program in the country. Students may seek sole vocations in writing, or integrate their creative writing into professions such as psychology, social work, library science, or education. With the B.F.A. in Creative Writing degree program, students may also go on to pursue graduate work in creative writing, literature, or professional writing.

Goddard's creative writing program is a 120-credit degree program open to transfer students who have already completed approximately 60 liberal arts credits. Students may be eligible to bring a combination of transfer credits and/or credits awarded for prior learning and experience into the degree program. Students wishing to enter the degree program without 60 credits may enter Goddard's individualized studies program to gain credits.

The senior project is completed at the end of the program. Students prepare their manuscripts, study papers on the topics of their choosing, annotated bibliographies, and readings of their works to the residents of the college. All students leave the program with complete drafts of finished manuscripts.

B.A. in Education: The Bachelor of Arts in Education degree program is of special interest to educators, parents, or community/cultural workers who seek knowledge in the field of educational pedagogy and progressive education. Students may pursue an individualized focus in education, teacher licensure, dual language early childhood education, or community education. Goddard College's B.A. in Education program licensure degree option is approved by the Vermont Agency of Education to offer initial Vermont teacher licensure in the following endorsement areas: early childhood (birth to age 6, K to grade 3 or both); elementary (K–6); art (pre-K to 6, 7 to 12, or pre-K to 12); middle grades (5–9); secondary English; and secondary social studies.

The low-residency B.A. in Education degree program is a 120-credit program open to transfer students who have already completed approximately 60 liberal arts credits and who wish to extend their knowledge in the field of education to meet personal or professional goals. Students may be eligible to bring a combination of transfer credits and/or credits awarded for prior learning and experience into the degree program.

The B.A. in Education degree program is available as a licensure program (on the Vermont campus only) or as a nonlicensure option (on both the Vermont and Seattle, Washington campuses).

B.A. in Health Arts and Sciences: Student work in health arts combines integrative health studies, holistic sciences, health philosophy, multicultural perspectives, social change, self-awareness, and self-care practices to bridge nature, culture, and healing. Potential course subjects include community and environmental health, women's health and midwifery, men's health, botanical medicine and ethnobotany, nutritional health, expressive arts, body and movement therapies, integrative health, integrative nursing, mind-body health, ecopsychology, and cross-cultural healing.

The low-residency B.A. in Health Arts and Sciences degree program is a 120-credit degree program open to transfer students who have already completed approximately 60 liberal arts credits.

Individualized B.A. degree program: The individualized studies degree program at Goddard emphasizes personal and social transformation, meditative action, positive self-development, and a wide breadth of knowledge. Students may bring up to 75 approved credits into the program through a combination of transfer or credits earned through an assessment of prior learning.

B.A. in Sustainability: Working closely with faculty advisers, students design courses of study that are individualized and interdisciplinary, practical as well as visionary. Students understand that the earth and its people face unprecedented environmental and social challenges, as well as unparalleled opportunities to build a sustainable future. Goddard welcomes students who are determined to create just lives and livelihoods as partners with the earth and its peoples. Topics of study include alternative energy, soil science, local food systems, waste management, and the ethical dimensions of international trade.

The low-residency B.A. in Sustainability degree program is a 120-credit degree program open to transfer students who have already completed approximately 60 liberal arts credits.

B.A. in Psychology: Goddard's B.A./M.A. fast-track degree program in psychology and counseling is a low-residency accelerated degree program that affords learners a seamless path to obtain their bachelor's and master's degrees over a shorter period of time. Students pursue standard undergraduate degrees in psychology with the final semester counting for both the B.A. degree program and as the first 15 hours of the M.A. degree program.

The low-residency B.A. in Psychology is a 120-credit degree program open to transfer students who have already completed approximately 60 liberal arts credits.

Academic Facilities

Goddard's campus includes a library, dormitories, and meeting spaces. Students and faculty are dispersed, but students enjoy intense relationships with their faculty advisors, which both students and faculty experience as rewarding and intimate, in the best sense of that word. The college relies on web-based communications to connect the dispersed Goddard community. Each student has a completely individualized curriculum, with as many curricula as we have students.

Costs

Tuition varies by degree. For the most up-to-date information, prospective students should visit www.goddard.edu/admissions/tuition-and-fees.

Financial Aid

Eighty-five percent of all Goddard students receive federal financial aid. Among undergraduate students, 63 percent receive the Pell Grant. The highest level of aid comes in the form of subsidized and unsubsidized federal loans, though Goddard awarded $454,000 in institutional aid in 2013–14 academic year.

Faculty

Goddard maintains a low 8:1 student-faculty ratio. Faculty serve as mentors and collaborators in student's individualized curriculum. The Goddard faculty members have longstanding presence in the College and bring to their work a host of professional skills, expertise, and interests.

Student Government

The Student Council acts as a conduit for the student voice by responding to, and advocating for, the needs of students, as individuals or groups, along with serving as liaisons to the greater Goddard community, including prospective students, staff, faculty, administration, and the Board of Trustees. Students elect Student Council members as representatives from their unique programs.

Admission Requirements

Applications receive a holistic review. Goddard does not require a minimum GPA or standardized test scores. Applications should demonstrate an understanding of Goddard's student-driven, low-residency model. The application essay should articulate why Goddard is the right fit. The College also seeks students who are willing to think critically about their personal and academic experiences, who express a willingness to take responsibility for their learning, and whose academic record demonstrates sufficient preparation for writing-intensive, independent, and critical work in the liberal arts and sciences.

Application and Information

Goddard's rolling admission process allows students to apply and receive notification at any time in the year before the semester in which they would like to enter. Application deadlines are thirty days before the semester begins.

For further information, prospective students should contact:

Admissions Office
Goddard College
123 Pitkin Road
Plainfield, Vermont 05667
United States
Phone: 800-906-8312 (admissions)
E-mail: admissions@godddard.edu
Website: http://www.goddard.edu

All of Goddard's degree programs are highly individualized, guided by students' particular learning needs and professional goals.

GRACELAND UNIVERSITY

LAMONI, IOWA

★ To read more about this school, visit http://petersons.to/gracelanduniversity

GRACELAND UNIVERSITY

The University

Graceland University (GU) provides challenging academic programs rooted in the liberal arts tradition, with a strong emphasis on career preparation. Since 1895, the University has maintained a tradition of academic excellence based on the Christian view of wholeness, worth, and dignity for every person. The 2014–15 class hailed from forty-five states and twenty-six countries, and there are approximately 1,000 students on Graceland's Lamoni, Iowa campus.

The Graceland experience combines a personalized education and an ongoing adventure, intended to last throughout the student's lifetime. Graduates go on to careers in the sciences, arts, nursing, education, business, athletics, and humanitarian service. Alumni say that Graceland helped focus their passions and shape their futures. The Graceland alumni network creates a strong web of resources for a lifetime of success.

Graceland's house residential system makes students feel at home instantly. Residence halls are divided into floors known as houses, where students live with friends from day one through graduation. Each house has its own traditions and every student becomes a part of the traditions of tomorrow. Members of each house elect a council to plan social, intramural, religious, and academic-support activities.

Leadership is defined in many ways at Graceland. Hands-on experiences allow students to cultivate skills and prepare for future leadership positions. Students hold more than 200 leadership posts on campus that provide skills for an added edge in the job market and graduate school. Graceland was named a 2015 Best College in the Midwestern region by the Princeton Review and a first-tier university by *U.S. News & World Report,* which serves as evidence of the University's leadership in higher education today.

Location

Lamoni is located in the rolling hills of south-central Iowa on Interstate 35. Shops, restaurants, a vintage theater, a cozy downtown district, and a scenic bike trail are all within walking or biking distance of the campus. It is a safe, friendly, small town where students always feel welcome. Graceland also has a stunning urban campus in Independence, Missouri, home to a wide array of online programs and its award-winning School of Nursing. The Graceland website (www.graceland.edu) offers more information about the students, alumni, the university, and the welcoming community. The University's Facebook page (www.facebook.com/GracelandUniversity) is another way to connect with GU, along with active Instagram and Twitter social media accounts.

Majors and Degrees

GU offers more than fifty academic majors and programs.

Graceland awards the Bachelor of Arts, Bachelor of Science, and Bachelor of Science in Nursing degrees. Concentrations in the arts include accounting, agricultural business, art, business administration, communications, corrective exercise and performance enhancement, criminal justice, economics, elementary education, English, health, health care management, history, human services, international studies, liberal studies, mathematics, music, organizational leadership, physical education, psychology, publication writing and design, recreation, religion and philosophy, social media marketing, Spanish, sport management, theatre, theatre and film, visual communication, and web design. The first two years of the Bachelor of Science in Nursing program are offered on the Lamoni campus, while the junior and senior years are on the Independence, Missouri campus. Bachelor of Science programs and majors include basic science, biology, chemistry, computer science and information technology, nursing, and preprofessional programs.

Graceland also offers degree programs at satellite campus locations. Through a partnership with North Central Missouri College in Trenton, Missouri, Graceland offers undergraduate degrees in liberal studies and elementary education. Through a partnership with Indian Hills Community College in Centerville, Iowa, Graceland offers an undergraduate degree in elementary education. The undergraduate elementary education program is also offered at the Independence campus.

Graduate programs include the Master of Arts in Religion, Master of Education, Master of Science in Nursing, and a Doctor of Nursing Practice. Graceland also offers a postgraduate Family Nurse Practitioner Certificate and a postgraduate Nurse Educator Certificate as well as a postbaccalaureate Differentiated Instruction Certificate, postbaccalaureate Management in a Quality Classroom Certificate, and postbaccalaureate Literacy Certificate.

Graceland's Edmund J. Gleazer School of Education offers a Master of Education degree with an emphasis in six areas: collaborative learning and teaching, curriculum and instruction in a quality classroom, differentiated instruction, literacy, management in a quality classroom, mild/moderate special education, and technology integration.

The Master of Education program is offered online. Graceland's graduate online education program was rated fifth by *U.S. News & World Report* for 2015.

Graceland offers many options for distance learners. Programs offered online by the School of Nursing include a bachelor's degree in health-care management, RN-B.S.N., RN-M.S.N., and M.S.N. programs. The M.S.N. program has three tracks: family nurse practitioner, nurse educator, and health-care administrator. Graceland was ranked by *U.S. News & World Report* as ninth in the nation for best graduate online nursing program in 2015.

The Community of Christ Seminary at Graceland offers the Master of Arts in Religion degree with a blended-delivery system from the Independence, Missouri campus.

Graceland University is accredited by the Higher Learning Commission (30 North LaSalle Street, Suite 2400, Chicago, Illinois 60602-2504; phone: 800-621-7440; website: http://www.ncahigherlearningcommission.org). All teacher-education programs at GU are approved by the Iowa Department of Education. The Bachelor of Arts (B.A.) in education and Master of Education (M.Ed.) programs in collaborative teaching and learning, quality education, and special education are accredited by the National Council for Accreditation of Teacher Education (NCATE; 2010 Massachusetts Avenue NW, Suite 500, Washington, D.C. 20036; phone: 202-466-7496; website: http://www.ncate.org). All GU nursing programs are accredited by the Iowa and Missouri Departments of Education and the Commission on Collegiate Nursing Education (CCNE; One DuPont Circle NW, Suite 530, Washington, D.C. 20036; http://www.aacn.nche.edu). The athletic training program is accredited by the Commission on Accreditation of Athletic Training Education Programs (CAATE; 2201 Double Creek Drive, Suite 5006, Round Rock, Texas 78664; phone: 512-733-9700; website: http://www.caate.net). These academic standards ensure that a degree from Graceland University is recognized by educational, business, and professional communities.

Academic Programs

Graceland is committed to helping develop the lives of its students—intellectually, socially, physically, and ethically—through a curriculum that is strongly rooted in the liberal arts. General education requirements are based on ten core competencies and can be satisfied by course selections, internships, portfolios, proficiency exams, work experience, independent studies, performance, and achievement. Graceland programs foster conceptual thinking, encourage team building, develop communication skills, and accommodate growth and enrichment.

Two programs at Graceland provide attention to special needs of students. The honors program is designed for highly motivated students who want to expand their learning beyond the traditional academic curriculum by developing and completing honors theses or projects. Trio is a program for students who clearly have the aptitude for university education but have experienced learning challenges and may benefit from individual attention.

Off-Campus Programs

Off-campus Summer Term experiences range from marine-life exploration in Grand Cayman to touring the great art museums of France to humanitarian work in Zambia. Summer Term is also an opportune time for students to explore career interests through internships and job shadowing.

Students who major in a foreign language may study abroad during their junior or senior year under the auspices of a recognized academic program. Graceland sponsors an International Health Center that provides opportunities for students to interact with health workers in villages in Africa and Asia. School of Nursing and School of Education students may participate in international humanitarian aid missions during Summer Term.

Academic Facilities

The Resch Science and Technology Hall was completed in 2009 and provides superb infrastructure and industry-standard lab equipment. The beautiful facility offers Graceland students some of the best science, math, and technology facilities in the Midwest.

The Helene Center for the Visual Arts includes 29,000 square feet of classrooms, galleries, and numerous studios. It includes large, north-facing windows to allow optimum light for artists.

The Shaw Center has a 650-seat performance auditorium, a 150-seat studio theater, a world-class Casavant pipe organ, a Steinway concert grand piano in the acoustically perfect Carol Hall, an art gallery, and a scene-and-wardrobe shop. The Shaw Center received a beautiful new recital hall, a black box experimental theater, a new gallery, a stunning glass-front atrium, and student gathering area in 2012.

The Eugene E. and Julia Travis Closson Physical Education Center includes an indoor pool; indoor track; weight and training room; new locker rooms; and basketball, tennis, volleyball, and racquetball courts. The Sports Complex includes an outdoor track, a $1-million artificial-turf football field, and three outstanding soccer fields. The campus borders a nine-hole golf course and has a highly regarded disc golf course where Midwest tournaments are held.

Costs

Full-time tuition for 2015–16 is $25,420, making Graceland one of the most affordable private universities in the Midwest.

Financial Aid

Graceland students receive academic and athletic scholarships, performance grants, work-study opportunities, federal and state grants, and government loans. Grants are available for achievement in athletics and performing arts, and for international students. The University offers significant scholarships to members of its sponsoring church, the Community of Christ.

Faculty

Students work closely with professors. The student-faculty ratio is 15:1. Graceland's faculty are both teachers and scholars; 85 percent hold Ph.D.'s or terminal degrees. They are experts, by experience and education. Their passion is to share their knowledge with students. Faculty members are active in their professional fields but consider teaching their primary responsibility.

Student Government

Students are actively involved in the decision-making process of the University. Student-elected executive members of the Graceland Student Government attend faculty meetings and participate with voice and vote. Each academic department has student representatives who participate in business sessions and serve on faculty search committees. Students provide leadership for Graceland's house residential and campus social programs. There are numerous ways for students to gain practical leadership experience.

Admission Requirements

High school graduates must meet two of the following criteria: rank in the upper 50 percent of their class, have a minimum 2.5 GPA, or have either a minimum composite ACT score of 21 or a minimum SAT combined score of 960.

Application and Information

Interested students can request admissions information online at www.graceland.edu/requestinformation or www.graceland.edu/apply.

For more information, prospective students should contact:

Admissions Office
Graceland University
1 University Place
Lamoni, Iowa 50140
United States
Phone: 641-784-5196
866-GRACELAND (toll-free in the United States and Canada)
Fax: 641-784-5480
E-mail: admissions@graceland.edu
Website: http://www.admissions.graceland.edu

Student success is the top priority at Graceland University.

COLLEGE CLOSE-UPS

GRAND VIEW UNIVERSITY

DES MOINES, IOWA

★ To read more about this school, visit http://petersons.to/grandviewuniversity

COLLEGE CLOSE-UPS

The University

Grand View University is a liberal arts institution affiliated with the Evangelical Lutheran Church in America. Founded more than 100 years ago, Grand View offers a high-quality education to a diverse student body in a career-oriented, liberal arts–grounded curriculum at two campus locations in greater Des Moines. Grand View welcomes traditional students, adult learners, and graduate students representing a wide range of religious and cultural backgrounds.

At Grand View, students find a winning combination of high-quality programs, experienced professors, and caring individuals. With 2,200 students and an average class size of 17, students get to know their professors and other students well. They learn independence and seek responsibility in Grand View's educational environment. Learning is an interactive process at Grand View—students engage in lively discussions, work on real-world projects, and participate in career-related work experiences.

Grand View stands out from other universities because of its partnerships with leading businesses and organizations in Des Moines, which has led to challenging internships. Grand View is known for its ability to connect students with exciting and challenging career opportunities. For more than two decades, nearly 100 percent of students found jobs right after graduation or continued their education.

Students are encouraged to develop leadership and team skills through involvement in campus organizations, which include intercollegiate and intramural athletics, speech and theater groups, major department clubs, student government, and musical ensembles. Active honorary societies include Alpha Chi, Alpha Mu Gamma, Alpha Psi Omega, Alpha Sigma Lambda, Beta Beta Beta, Phi Eta Sigma, Sigma Theta Tau, and Theta Alpha Kappa among others. Grand View's student leadership program provides opportunities for students without leadership experience to seek and develop critical thinking, interpersonal, and networking skills.

Student athletes compete in men's baseball, basketball, bowling, cross-country, football, golf, soccer, tennis, track and field, volleyball, and wrestling, and women's basketball, bowling, competitive cheer, competitive dance, cross-country, golf, soccer, softball, tennis, track and field, and volleyball. Grand View participates in the Midwest Collegiate Conference of the National Association of Intercollegiate Athletics. Athletic scholarships are available.

Two locations offer Grand View students convenient scheduling options for their program of study. Weekend and evening classes are offered at the main campus in Des Moines and at Grand View's campus in Johnston, Iowa. For motivated students seeking to complete their degree quickly, accelerated schedules are offered for several of sixteen evening majors.

Location

Grand View is located in Des Moines, a metropolitan area of more than half a million people in central Iowa. Des Moines is the state capital and serves as the communications hub for Iowa. Nationally recognized organizations that have their corporate offices in Des Moines include Pioneer Hi-Bred International, Inc.; the Principal Financial Group; Meredith Corporation; and the *Des Moines Register*.

In essence, Grand View's campus is the entire city of Des Moines—as part of the Grand View community, students are not limited by the confines of a small school or small town. In a given day, students can catch an Iowa Cubs professional baseball doubleheader, head down to the Court Avenue district for great food and nightlife, or take in a concert at Wells Fargo Arena.

A thriving arts program in Des Moines features the Des Moines Metro Opera, Ballet Iowa, the Des Moines Symphony, the Des Moines Art Center, and the Des Moines Playhouse. The summer Des Moines Arts Festival is ranked third in the nation.

Des Moines features four distinct and beautiful seasons. Except for a month or so of bundle-up, see-your-breath weather, the climate is ideal for outdoor activities. Grand View students can take advantage of terrific recreational opportunities, including several golf courses, Saylorville Lake, and many city parks and state forests.

Easily accessible from Interstates 35 and 80, Grand View is 4 hours from Minneapolis, 6 hours from Chicago, and 3 hours from Kansas City.

Majors and Degrees

Grand View University grants the Bachelor of Arts degree and offers forty majors in areas such as accounting, applied mathematics, art education, biology, biochemistry, biotechnology, business administration (with concentrations in areas such as finance, human resource management, management, marketing, and real estate), church music, computer science, criminal justice, digital media production, elementary education, English, graphic design, graphic journalism, health promotion and kinesiology, history, human services, individualized major, journalism and public relations, liberal arts, management information systems, multimedia communication, music, music education, organizational studies, paralegal studies, physical education, political studies (prelaw or public administration), psychology, secondary education, service management, Spanish for careers and professionals, studio arts, theater arts, and theology. Grand View also offers a Bachelor of Science degree in nursing, as well as an RN to B.S.N. program. In addition, the University offers certificate programs in art therapy, human resource management, and Spanish essentials, as well as a postbaccalaureate certificate in accounting.

The University offers four master's degree programs: the Master of Science in organizational leadership, the Master of Science in Nursing (clinical nurse leadership and nursing education), the Master of Education, and a Master of Science in sport management.

Academic Programs

Grand View operates on a 4-4-1 academic calendar. The first semester runs from late August to December. The second semester begins in early January and ends in late April. Three one-month summer sessions are offered in May, June, and July, as is a summer trimester evening program.

Grand View's general education core takes an innovative, integrated approach to developing essential abilities employers seek in graduates, such as writing, speaking, analysis, problem-solving, and critical thinking. Through their coursework, students can gain the personal and intellectual depth that will help them thrive in today's knowledge-based economy and in their communities.

The Logos Honors Program augments the general education core. By invitation, freshman and sophomore students enrolled in this program complete a series of courses designed to challenge exceptional students.

An active study-abroad program gives students opportunities to learn in an international setting, particularly through a partnership with the Danish Institute for Study Abroad.

The Grand View academic mission is to provide a diverse student body with an academically rigorous education. In order to meet this commitment, Grand View provides a variety of learning environments and teaching techniques. The university's academic support programs and services were lauded as a national model by the examining team from the North Central Association of Colleges and Schools during reaccreditation in 2005, when the University received complete ten-year accreditation with no follow-up required.

Costs

For 2014–15, the comprehensive cost for freshmen living on campus was approximately $31,070, which included tuition, an activity fee, a technology fee, a parking fee, and room and board. Students have several residential and meal plan options that affect cost. Health services and Internet access are also included in the comprehensive fee.

Financial Aid

Typically, most full-time Grand View students received financial assistance. The average freshman full-time award package is usually around $22,000 with about $15,000 in grants and scholarships, and the remainder in work-study and student loans. The amount of aid is determined through a combination of merit and analysis of need as determined through the Free Application for Federal Student Aid. The priority deadline for financial aid is March 1. Students receive notification of financial aid packages following acceptance of admission to the University and receipt of their financial aid analysis of need.

Faculty

There are approximately 90 full-time faculty members and 90 part-time faculty members. More than 70 percent hold terminal degrees. All classes are taught by professors; no graduate or teaching assistants instruct Grand View classes.

Student Government

Students participate in University governance. The Student Activities Council and Viking Council plan student activities that promote educational, social, cultural, and recreational aspects of student life. Students serve as representatives on faculty and staff search committees, programming committees, and student life committees.

Admission Requirements

Applicants' files are reviewed to determine their preparedness for a Grand View education. Official high school transcripts and submission of ACT or SAT scores are required for applicants with less than 24 semester hours of college credit. Applicants transferring from another college are required to submit official transcripts from all colleges previously attended.

Application and Information

For more information about Grand View, students should contact:

Admissions Office
Grand View University
1200 Grandview Avenue
Des Moines, Iowa 50316
Phone: 515-263-2810
800-444-6083 (toll-free)
Fax: 515-263-2974
E-mail: admissions@grandview.edu
Website: http://www.admissions.grandview.edu
http://www.facebook.com/pages/Grand-View-University/31506809l675 (Facebook)

Grand View students on their way to class.

GROVE CITY COLLEGE

GROVE CITY, PENNSYLVANIA

★ To read more about this school, visit http://petersons.to/grovecitycollege

GROVE CITY COLLEGE

The College

Because Faith and Freedom Matter

The beautifully landscaped campus of Grove City College stretches more than 180 acres and includes nearly thirty neo-Gothic buildings valued at more than $100 million. The campus is considered one of the loveliest in the nation. While the College has changed to meet the needs of the society it serves, its basic philosophy has remained unchanged since its founding in 1876. It is a Christian liberal arts and sciences institution of ideal size and dedicated to the principle of providing the highest-quality education at the lowest possible cost. Wishing to remain truly independent and to retain its distinctive qualities as a private school governed by private citizens (trustees), it is one of the very few colleges in the country that does not accept any federal funding. Although historically affiliated with the Presbyterian Church it is not narrowly denominational; the College believes that to be well educated a student should be exposed to the central ideas of the Christian faith. A 20-minute chapel program offered Tuesday and Thursday mornings, along with a Sunday evening worship service, challenges students in their faith. Sixteen chapel services per semester are required out of over fifty opportunities. Christian organizations and activities exist to provide fellowship and spiritual growth.

Grove City attracts students from all over the United States. While most come from Pennsylvania, Ohio, New Jersey, Virginia, and New York, forty-one states and eleven other countries were represented in the fall 2014 term. In the average freshman class (of those submitting a rank), 96 percent of the women and 95 percent of the men rank in the top fifth of their high school class. The average SAT combined score is 1225 (combining only the critical reading and math scores); the average ACT composite score was 27.

Ninety-five percent of the 2,509 students live in separate men's and women's residence halls. All others are commuters or participants in a study-abroad program. A full program of cultural, professional, athletic, and social activities is offered. An arena, Crawford Auditorium, and the J. Howard Pew Fine Arts Center are used for athletics, concerts, movies, plays, and lectures. The Physical Learning Center is one of the finest among the nation's small colleges and includes the Grove City College Arena, James E. Longnecker competition pool, a recreational pool, an eight-lane bowling alley, handball/racquetball courts, an intramural room, fitness rooms with free weights, aerobic equipment and Cybex machines, and an indoor three-lane running track. The Breen Student Union provides an eatery; mailroom; bookstore; commuters' lounge; and a commons area for dining, studying, and socializing. The Ketler and South Hall Recreation Lounges are also available for cooking, games, and socializing. There are more than 150 organizations and special interest groups, including local fraternities and sororities. The athletic activities include extensive intramural, club, and varsity sports programs that provide nineteen intercollegiate teams that compete at the NCAA Division III level for men and women. No alcohol or drugs are permitted on campus.

The College's well-established placement services, ranked recently by The Princeton Review as sixteenth in the nation, are used constantly by students. A complete file of personal data, scholastic records, and recommendations is prepared for each participant. These files are available to the scores of prospective employers who visit the campus annually to interview the graduating seniors. One of Grove City's strengths is placing students in business, industrial, and teaching positions, as well as in professional institutions such as medical schools.

Prospective students may check out Grove City College's web page at www.gcc.edu.

Location

Grove City, a town of 8,000 people, is 60 miles north of Pittsburgh and is located 4 miles from restaurants, hotels, and a 140-store outlet mall. Convenient to I-79 and I-80, Grove City is only a day's drive from Chicago, New York City, Toronto, and Washington, D.C. The municipal airport has a 4,500-foot runway, and there is bus service to the bus and train stations and airport located in Pittsburgh.

Majors and Degrees

Grove City College offers undergraduate degrees in liberal arts, sciences, engineering, and music. The Bachelor of Arts (B.A.) is offered with majors in Biblical and religious studies, communication studies, economics, English, history, modern language (French and Spanish), philosophy, political science, psychology, and sociology. Pre-professional students in law or theology usually earn the B.A. degree. Interdisciplinary major programs are also available for qualified students.

The Bachelor of Science (B.S.) is granted with majors in accounting, biochemistry, biology, business economics, business management, chemistry, chemistry secondary education, chemistry/general science education, computer information systems, computer science, PreK–4 elementary education, PreK–8 special education, entrepreneurship, exercise science, finance, industrial management, international business, marketing management, mathematics, middle level education, physics, physics/computer, physics/general science secondary education, and psychology. Pre-professional students often select one of these majors for dentistry, medicine, or other health fields.

The Bachelor of Science in Mechanical Engineering (B.S.M.E.) degree is also offered. The Bachelor of Science in Electrical Engineering (B.S.E.E.) degree provides for concentration areas in either electrical or computer engineering. Both engineering degree programs are accredited by the Engineering Accreditation Commission of the Accreditation Board for Engineering and Technology, Inc. (ABET).

The Bachelor of Music (B.M.) degree is awarded to those who major in music, music/business, music/performing arts, music/religion, and music education.

In addition to the majors listed above, secondary education (grades 7–12) certification is also available in biology/general science, English, English/communication, math, physics, and social science. Grades 7–12 certification is available in biology/general science/environmental science, French, and Spanish.

Academic Programs

Grove City College's goal is to assist young men and women in developing as complete individuals—academically, spiritually, and physically. The general education requirements provide all students with a high level of cultural literacy and communication skills. They include 46 semester hours of courses with emphases in the humanities, social sciences, and natural sciences; in quantitative and logical reasoning; physical education; and in science, faith, and technology, as well as a language requirement for all majors except engineering and science. Degree candidates must also complete the requirements in their field of concentration and electives. To graduate, a student must have completed a minimum 128 semester hours as well as the chapel attendance requirement. On average, 78 percent of those entering as freshmen stay and receive a diploma in four years and 82 percent in six years.

A distinctive liberal arts–engineering program includes engineering courses plus courses in the humanities to provide students with a well-grounded preparation for entering the engineering field, as well as the civic and cultural life of society. The Austrian economics program exposes students to all economic philosophies, yet it strongly advocates economic freedoms and free markets.

Grove City follows the semester calendar plan. Academic credit may be granted to incoming freshmen on the basis of scores on appropriate Advanced Placement tests, International Baccalaureate tests, or College-Level Examination Program tests. Honors courses, independent study, seminars, and the opportunity for students to study abroad for credit are also offered.

Academic Facilities

The Hall of Arts and Letters is a state-of-the-art teaching facility featuring a 200-seat lecture hall, forty classrooms (including multimedia-equipped rooms and tiered "case study" rooms), eighty faculty offices, the Early Education Center, the Curriculum Library, and language, computer, and video production labs.

The College library houses 162,000 books and serials; 3,600 audio/video tapes, CDs, and DVDs; and 112 current serial subscriptions. In addition, the College has access to 58,885 journal titles through its collection of full-text journal databases.

The College owns an observatory and the remote structure is utilized for astronomy classes as well as faculty and student research. Modern, well-equipped laboratories for biology, chemistry, engineering, and physics are available on campus, as are facilities for language, art, and music studies.

The Weir C. Ketler Technological Learning Center consists of computers for walk-up access, a lecture hall, video production lab, the College's FM radio station, and the campus print shop. It also houses the computer help desk and repair center that support the student technology initiative. All freshmen receive their own tablet PC and color printer/scanner/copier.

The J. Howard Pew Fine Arts Center has art, photography, and music studios; a rehearsal hall; a small theater; a museum; an art gallery; music practice rooms; and a 675-seat, acoustically tunable auditorium and stage large enough to accommodate the most elaborate drama productions and concerts. An addition contains additional classrooms, practice rooms, and a 180-seat recital hall.

Costs

As a relatively small, financially sound college, Grove City College is able to charge an unusually low tuition in comparison to other independent institutions of similar quality. The 2014–15 annual tuition charge was $15,550 for all degrees. The cost of a tablet PC for all freshmen is included in the tuition fees. There is no comprehensive fee. Part-time tuition was $486 per credit. Room and board were $8,472. Expenses for books, laundry, transportation, and personal needs vary considerably with the lifestyle of the individual.

Financial Aid

Because the College's tuition charges are low, every student, in effect, receives significant financial assistance. Seventy percent of the freshmen received some form of financial aid for the 2014–15 school year. Students applying for financial assistance must complete Grove City College's financial aid form. Job opportunities are available both on and off campus.

Faculty

The focus of the Grove City College faculty members is on teaching students, although many members are involved with research and writing. Eighty percent of the full-time faculty members hold doctoral or other terminal degrees. Many of the administrative staff members also teach part-time in various departments. The student-faculty ratio is approximately 14:1. Faculty members emphasize teaching and attention to the students' individual needs; they also participate extensively in the College's extracurricular programs.

Student Government

The Student Government Association provides an opportunity for direct student interaction with the faculty members and administration in matters relating to campus activities. Students serve on regular College committees (library, publications, religious activities, and student activities) and also on the Men's and Women's Governing Board and the Discipline Committee.

Admission Requirements

The College seeks academically qualified students without regard to age, race, color, creed, sex, marital status, disability, or national/ethnic origin. An applicant for admission should be a high school graduate with the following recommended units: English, 4; foreign language, 3; mathematics, 3; history, 2; and science, 3. Engineering, science, and mathematics majors should have 4 units each in both mathematics and science. An interview is highly recommended, especially for those who live within a day's drive (400 miles). Auditions are required for music majors.

Transfer students may receive advanced standing if they have maintained good academic standing at their previous institution(s).

Application and Information

An early decision applicant should take the SAT and/or ACT in the eleventh grade, visit the College for an interview, and submit the application by November 1; notification of the admission decision is mailed on December 15. The application should include scores on the SAT or the ACT; a high school transcript; two letters of recommendation (one academic and one character or spiritual reference); and a nonrefundable application fee of $50. Approved early decision applicants must accept by January 15 and submit a nonrefundable deposit of $250.

Students applying for the early action deadline must submit their application and supporting documents by December 1; notification of the admission decision will be mailed on January 15, and the student has until May 1 to make their decision and send a nonrefundable deposit of $250. Priority consideration for merit-based scholarships will be given to students who apply for either the early decision or early action deadlines

A regular admission applicant should take the SAT or ACT by October or November of the senior year in high school. Applicants seeking regular decision must submit the completed application and supporting documents by February 1 of their senior year. Notification of the admission decision is mailed on March 15. Students who are offered admission should reply as soon as possible, but no later than May 1, and include a nonrefundable deposit of $250. Applications received after February 1 are considered as space permits.

Additional information may be obtained from:

Sarah E. Gibbs
Director of Admissions
Grove City College
100 Campus Drive
Grove City, Pennsylvania 16127-2104
Phone: 724-458-2100
Fax: 724-458-3395
E-mail: admissions@gcc.edu
Website: http://www.gcc.edu
www.facebook.com/GCCAdmissions (Facebook)
http://twitter.com/GroveCtyCollege (Twitter)
instagram.com/GroveCityAdmissions (Instagram)
http://www.youvisit.com/tour/grovecitycollege?pl=v
(YouVisit virtual tour)

Chapel is just one aspect of an authentically Christian environment at Grove City College.

GWYNEDD MERCY UNIVERSITY

GWYNEDD VALLEY, PENNSYLVANIA

★ To read more about this school, visit http://petersons.to/gwyneddmercyuniversity

Gwynedd Mercy University

COLLEGE CLOSE-UPS

The University

Gwynedd Mercy University is a Catholic University with a strong foundation in the liberal arts. Its academic distinction lies in the intersection of excellent programs in health care, arts and sciences, education, and business administration, which prepare students to become leaders in the region's powerful and growing life-sciences industry. Located just 30 minutes from Philadelphia and with an enrollment of nearly 3,000 students, Gwynedd Mercy University is large enough to offer a vibrant campus life but small enough that professors can develop mentoring relationships with students. The University educates students in the Mercy tradition of service to society; preparing graduates who not only are recruited for jobs but also create lives and careers with deep meaning.

Gwynedd Mercy University offers prestigious undergraduate, graduate, and doctoral degrees in accelerated, traditional, and online formats. More than thirty associate, bachelor's, master's, and doctoral degree programs are offered on a full- and part-time basis.

In the 2015 edition of *U.S. News & World Report's* "Best Colleges," Gwynedd Mercy University ranked in the first tier of its category, in part because of its high graduation and retention rates. In addition, Gwynedd Mercy University was ranked eleventh in the nation on its listing of "college/university that adds the most value" by *Money* magazine. *The Washington Post* named Gwynedd Mercy University as one of its "top colleges for producing graduates who make the world a better place" for 2014. Finally, the *Philadelphia Business Journal* ranked the University as one of the top business schools in Philadelphia for the 2013–14 academic year.

At the graduate level, Gwynedd Mercy University offers master's degree programs in business (M.B.A.), education (educational administration, school counseling, special education, and a Master Teacher program), and nursing (nurse educator, nurse practitioner, and clinical nurse specialist). The University also offers the Doctor in Nursing Practice (D.N.P.) degree.

Gwynedd Mercy University has nineteen NCAA Division III athletic teams. The University also offers more than thirty clubs and organizations, including campus ministry, a nationally renowned choir, and social committees. Students can write for the University newspaper, the *Gwynmercian,* which has received a first-place rating with special merit from the American Scholastic Press Association. Through the on-campus chapter of the Mercy Works Program, students can help the poor with fundraising efforts and adopt-a-family programs at Thanksgiving and Christmas. Some students decide to give a year of service after graduation to Mercy Volunteer Corps' nationwide outreach program.

On campus, students can choose from four styles of residence halls and dine at several eateries that offer full meals, sandwiches, pizza, salads, breakfast and coffee. The Late Night Lounge has events every weekend, including movie nights, dances, comedians, rock band competitions, and game parties. The University also offers the Griffin Loop, a shuttle service to the best attractions, shopping, and restaurants the area has to offer.

Location

Gwynedd Mercy University's idyllic 160-acre campus is located in Gwynedd Valley, Pennsylvania, a suburb 30 miles from downtown Philadelphia. Old City, South Street, and sports arenas are a 25- to 30-minute car or train ride from the campus. The University is just minutes from several major highways, including the Pennsylvania Turnpike. In addition to the vibrant city life of Philadelphia, students can travel to the New Jersey beaches, Pocono Mountains, Washington D.C., and New York City; all are only 2 hours from campus.

Majors and Degrees

Gwynedd Mercy University offers baccalaureate degrees in accounting, behavioral/social gerontology, biology, communication, computer information science, criminal justice, elementary education, English, finance, history, human resource management, human services, management, marketing, mathematics, medical laboratory science, nursing, philosophy, psychology, radiologic technology, radiation therapy, respiratory care, special education, and sports management.

Associate degrees are awarded in liberal studies, natural science, and respiratory care.

Academic Programs

The academic year is divided into two semesters, and most baccalaureate degree programs require the completion of a minimum of 125 credit hours. Gwynedd Mercy University maintains a strong liberal arts component in all of its degree programs. Whether the student chooses to major in one of the liberal arts or to pursue a professionally oriented degree, courses are required in language, literature and the fine arts, humanities, and behavioral, social, and natural sciences. Students have access to the Academic Resource Center for free class tutoring and assistance with improving their writing skills.

Individualized internships and work experience programs are available and recommended in all majors to give students firsthand experience in their chosen major. Nearby Fortune 500 companies offer a variety of experiences to students in business and accounting. Through these internships, the students earn credit while gaining valuable experience in challenging positions. TAP, the Teacher Assistance Program, places every education major in the classroom one day a week beginning in their first year. All allied health and nursing programs require clinical experience. The 3+1 program—with an associate degree to bachelor's degree progression—offers respiratory care students the opportunity to gain employment in their field while continuing toward the baccalaureate degree.

Students are encouraged to develop a global perspective through various study abroad opportunities. In 2010, the University launched a study abroad program to Brescia, Italy.

Off-Campus Programs

The excellent on-campus laboratory facilities are extended by affiliations with more than 200 hospitals and health-care agencies in Pennsylvania, New Jersey, and Delaware, where students may complete their clinical experience. Merck provides a one-semester industrial laboratory experience for qualified biology majors. Gwynedd Mercy University maintains a close relationship with nearby companies, including Johnson & Johnson, McNeil, and Sun Company, for work experience programs.

Academic Facilities

Gwynedd Mercy University has expanded its physical facilities as its student enrollment has increased. The Sister Isabelle Keiss Center for Health and Science houses the Schools of Nursing and Allied Health Professions and the Division of Natural Sciences. The 50,000-square-foot state-of-the-art facility offers laboratories for areas such as nursing skills, respiratory care, radiation therapy, organic chemistry, and microbiology.

Gwynedd Mercy University continues to "discover the Next" with the addition of the new University Hall academic building which opened in the spring of 2014. The building is the new shared home for the Schools of Business and Education. University Hall is equipped with state-of-the-art technology to further enhance educational opportunities, including the Financial Trading Room, equipped with a real-time stock ticker.

The Griffin Complex houses the University's recreation facilities, including a full gymnasium and track, racquetball court, and weight room. Theaters include the Julia Ball Auditorium and an upgraded TV production studio. The Student Technology Center is equipped with personal computers and printers and the latest software for student use. The Valie Genuardi Hobbit House, a fully licensed nursery school and prekindergarten where students in the School of Education are trained, is situated on campus.

The Keiss Hall Library and Learning Commons is a best practice in higher education, partnering academic support services and library services to provide a one-stop academic center that facilitates student success.

Costs

The 2015–16 academic year tuition for full-time students (12 to 18 credits per semester) is $30,760. The tuition for allied health and nursing students is $32,260. Room and board costs average $10,500. Professional liability fees for students enrolled in clinical components and lab fees are extra.

Financial Aid

Gwynedd Mercy University's financial aid program is designed to provide financial assistance to academically qualified students whose resources are inadequate to meet the costs of attending the University. The student Financial Aid Committee endeavors to assist as many students as possible, using Gwynedd Mercy University funds as well as federal, state, and other available funds. Aid is awarded on the basis of demonstrated financial need, academic proficiency, and responsible campus citizenship. In 2013–14, 92 percent of the University's full-time students received some form of financial aid.

Faculty

The student-faculty ratio is 13:1, allowing for personal contact, advising, and after-class instruction. This is a widely acknowledged strength of the Gwynedd Mercy University experience. For nursing students in the clinical setting, there are never more than 8 students to 1 clinical adviser; in the allied health programs, there often is one-to-one instruction. The quality of teaching is enhanced by the diversified interests of the faculty. The 181 faculty members teach both day and evening classes, allowing students the greatest flexibility in scheduling. Free tutoring is available in all disciplines.

Student Government

All students are encouraged to take part in the responsibilities of student government. This student participation and shared responsibility for the welfare of the University are promoted through a framework of committees.

Admission Requirements

Admission to Gwynedd Mercy University is based on a student's high school record, rank in class, SAT or ACT scores, counselor's recommendation, and choice of major. Entrance requirements vary with the program. The rolling admission policy allows the student to be informed of the admission decision within two to three weeks of submitting their application.

Gwynedd Mercy University awards credit for satisfactory completion of Advanced Placement courses. The exam score must be 3 or above.

A minimum 2.0 grade point average (on a 4.0 scale) is generally required to transfer from another institution. Gwynedd Mercy University does, however, retain the right to require a higher GPA for admission to some programs.

Gwynedd Mercy University does not discriminate on the basis of race, age, national origin, religion, sex, or disability in the administration of its educational, admission, scholarship, or loan policies.

Application and Information

All prospective applicants are urged to visit the campus to meet and talk with an admission counselor, dean, or program director. To apply for admission, applicants should complete the online application available at www.gmercyu.edu. First-time freshmen must also submit an official high school transcript or equivalency certificate; a written recommendation from a principal, teacher, guidance counselor, or employer; and results of the SAT or ACT (for recent high school graduates). All applicants should verify that they meet the specific requirements and have the necessary high school prerequisites for admission.

Students who wish to transfer to Gwynedd Mercy University should submit the same online application, high school and college transcripts, and a letter of recommendation.

For additional information or to schedule campus tours and visits, students are encouraged to register with the Enrollment Support Services Office at admissions@gmercyu.edu or contact the office at 800-342-5462.

For more information, contact:

Office of Admissions
Gwynedd Mercy University
1325 Sumneytown Pike
P.O. Box 901
Gwynedd Valley, Pennsylvania 19437-0901
Phone: 800-342-5462 (toll-free)
E-mail: admissions@gmercycu.edu
Website: http://www.gmercyu.edu/admissions-aid/
https://twitter.com/GMercyU
https://www.facebook.com/GMercyU

Students walk to and from classes in University Hall, the newest academic building on campus.

HARDING UNIVERSITY

SEARCY, ARKANSAS

★ To read more about this school, visit http://petersons.to/hardinguniversity

COLLEGE CLOSE-UPS

The University

As an institution rooted in Christian principles and a liberal arts tradition since 1924, Harding University challenges its students to pursue scholarship, service, teamwork, excellence, and commitment. Harding is ranked by *U.S. News and World Report* and Princeton Review as one of the top liberal arts universities in the South and attracts exceptional high school students from almost every U.S. state and more than 44 countries.

The University is accredited by 15 organizations, including the Higher Learning Commission of the North Central Association of Colleges and Schools. Housed within nine colleges, including the Honors College, students can choose from a wide range of majors: from humanities and theology to business and education to natural and health sciences. The University allows students the opportunity to study in more than 100 academic majors, 14 preprofessional programs, 21 graduate programs, two specialist degrees, and four doctoral-level degrees. With a student-teacher ratio of 17 to 1, strong relationships are built in and out of the classroom.

Students can cultivate friendships and interests with 120 academic and professional organizations and 31 social clubs. Ranging from the arts, music, politics, business, diversity, children, missions, service, and the environment, the clubs on campus offer a variety of interests to explore.

Provided with a Christian perspective through which to appreciate various disciplines, students excel as scholars and develop leadership skills. As a result, Harding alumni display character, conviction, and a competitive edge and are prepared for success at prestigious graduate schools and companies throughout the nation.

Location

Harding is located in Searcy, Arkansas, and offers students a hometown feeling with easy access to major cities. The University is about an hour away from Little Rock, Arkansas, and the Bill and Hillary Clinton National Airport and is about 2 hours away from Memphis, Tennessee.

Majors and Degrees

The University offers more than 100 academic majors, including 14 preprofessional programs, taught by top instructors.

Within the College of Allied Health, students may earn a Bachelor of Arts degree in communication sciences and disorders, a Master of Science degree in speech-language pathology, a Master of Science degree in physician assistant studies, and a Doctor of Physical Therapy degree.

The College of Arts and Humanities offers a wide range of degrees in the humanities, arts, English language and literature, foreign language and international studies, history and social science, mass communication, music, oral communication, and theater.

In the College of Bible and Ministry, there are degrees in Bible and religion, biblical languages, Christian education, missions, preaching, and youth and family ministry.

Students in the Paul R. Carter College of Business Administration may receive degrees in accounting, economics, finance, global economic development, health care management, international business management, management information systems, marketing, and professional sales.

Those interested in teaching may earn degrees in early childhood P–4, middle childhood/early adolescence English/language arts/social science 4–8, middle childhood/early adolescence math/science 4–8, secondary education, and special education endorsement (P–3) in the Cannon-Clary College of Education.

The Carr College of Nursing offers a Bachelor of Science in Nursing, enabling students to take the NCLEX-RN exam after graduation. There is also a Master of Science in Nursing degree program, preparing students to be family nurse practitioners.

Students can earn a Doctor of Pharmacy degree through the University's four-year program in the College of Pharmacy.

Lastly, the College of Sciences allows students to study health sciences, behavioral sciences, biology, chemistry, computer science, engineering and physics, exercise and sport sciences, family and consumer sciences, kinesiology, and mathematics.

Academic Programs

For the basic requirements necessary for each degree, prospective students should visit the Harding University online catalog at www.harding.edu/catalog.

Students may apply and participate in the Honors College with acceptance based on acceptance to the University and an ACT score of 27 or higher or an SAT score of 1220 or higher. These students may take honors-level courses and graduate with honors.

In addition, various majors may allow students to receive their teaching licensure in the process.

Off-Campus Programs

Harding offers seven study abroad programs in Australia, Chile, England, France, Greece, Italy, and Zambia that will help expand cultural awareness and understanding. Nearly 50 percent of each graduating class takes advantage of one of these semester-long programs. At each location, students are accompanied and taught by University faculty. Costs are based on 16 tuition hours and include housing and meals.

Academic Facilities

Harding's campus consists of 13 academic buildings, cafeteria, 2 auditoriums, a library, a performing arts center, a student center, student health services, 14 residence halls, and 6 apartment complexes.

Costs

The basic undergraduate, on-campus cost for 2014–15 for 15 hours of enrollment per semester was $8,280 for a semester and $16,560 for the year. Tuition was $552 per course hour. Students paid $480 a year for a required technology fee, $3,290 for a standard dorm room, and $3,226 for a standard meal plan of 210 meals plus a $200 declining cash balance. The overall total came to $23,556.

Financial Aid

On average, 93 percent of Harding University freshman students receive financial assistance. In 2013–14, Harding awarded students more than $12 million in institutional need-based grants and more than $23 million in institutional scholarships. In addition, students received nearly $9 million in federal, state, and externally funded scholarships and grants.

Admission Requirements

Students wishing to apply to Harding must have a 19 ACT or 900 SAT and 3.0 high school GPA (on a 4.0 scale). In addition, high school graduates should have completed at least 15 units in academic subjects. Specifically, an applicant should have completed 4 units of English, 3 units of mathematics (taken from general math, geometry, algebra, trigonometry, precalculus, or calculus), 3 units of social studies (taken from civics, American history, world history, or geography), and 2 units of natural science (taken from physical science, biology, physics, or chemistry). Students planning to major in any area of health care are strongly encouraged to take one or more chemistry courses while in high school. Although not required for admission, two years of foreign language is recommended. The additional units may come from any academic area.

Application and Information

Prospective students may apply online at www.harding.edu/apply/.

Because Harding receives so many applications, it recommends that students apply before the fall of their senior year of high school—even if they haven't taken the ACT or SAT. Admissions advisers are glad to help students through this process.

For more information, prospective students should contact:

Harding University
Box 12255
Searcy, Arkansas 72143-5615
Phone: 501-279-4407
Website: http://www.harding.edu
http://www.facebook.com/HardingU
http://www.twitter.com/HardingU

Each year Harding University's student population comes from almost all 50 states and more than 44 other nations. With more than 6,000 students, Harding is the largest private college or university in Arkansas.

HAVERFORD COLLEGE

HAVERFORD, PENNSYLVANIA

★ To read more about this school, visit http://petersons.to/haverfordcollege

HAVERFORD COLLEGE

The College

Founded in 1833 as the first college established by members of the Society of Friends (Quakers), Haverford College has chosen to remain small, undergraduate, and residential in order to offer students remarkable classroom and research opportunities while maintaining a strong sense of community. Haverford's Honor Code, created and implemented by students, is an important part of the College's identity. The Code allows students to directly confront academic and social issues in a spirit of cooperation and mutual respect.

Haverford's 1,187 students represent forty-four states, Puerto Rico, the District of Columbia, and thirty-eight countries. Thirty-five percent of the students are students of color and 10 percent are international students.

Haverford is a residential campus with 99 percent of the students and 61 percent of the faculty living on campus. Housing on Haverford's campus is single-sex or coed, and residence halls vary in accommodations from 4-person apartments to suites and singles. Other choices of residence facilities include the Ira De A. Reid House (Black Cultural Center), La Casa Hispanica, Quaker House, and an environmental house.

Haverford's athletic teams participate in NCAA Division III. Intercollegiate sports include baseball, basketball, cricket, cross-country, fencing, field hockey, lacrosse, soccer, softball, squash, tennis, track and field, and volleyball. Haverford also sponsors several club and intramural sports teams. Athletic facilities include the Douglas B. Gardner Integrated Athletic Center, the Alumni Field House, the John A. Lester Cricket Pavilion, and Swan Field—Haverford's turf field.

Location

The College is located 8 miles (16 kilometers) west of Center City Philadelphia on a wooded campus of 216 acres. Haverford's proximity to the fifth-largest city in the United States allows its students to take advantage of the many social, cultural, and educational resources that this historic area offers. Extensive public transportation allows students easy access to the city and environs.

Majors and Degrees

Haverford offers forty majors, including anthropology, archaeology, astronomy, biology, chemistry, classics, comparative literature, computer science, East Asian studies (including Chinese and Japanese), economics, English, fine arts, French, geology, German, growth and structure of cities, history, history of art, Italian, linguistics, mathematics and statistics, music, philosophy, physics, political science, psychology, religion, Romance languages, Russian, sociology, and Spanish. Students may minor, arrange an interdepartmental or double major, or design an individual major. Approximately 30 percent of the students major in the sciences or mathematics, 40 percent in the social sciences, and 30 percent in the humanities. Ten percent have double, interdepartmental, or special majors. Master's degree partnerships, like the 4+1 engineering or bioethics programs with the University of Pennsylvania, a 4+1 finance program with Claremont McKenna College, and a 4+1 Latin American studies program with Georgetown University, are available to students who qualify.

Other programs and concentrations that students may incorporate into their curricula include Africana studies; biochemistry and biophysics; creative writing; dance; education; environmental studies; gender and sexuality studies; Hebrew and Judaic studies; health studies; Hispanic and Hispanic American studies; international economic relations; Latin American and Iberian studies; linguistics; mathematical economics; neuroscience; peace, justice, and human rights; pre-business; prelaw; pre-medicine; scientific computing; and theater.

Academic Programs

The academic experience at Haverford is centered around a deep commitment to the core values of a liberal arts education and its emphasis on the dual pursuit of a breadth of study and in-depth work. While the College mandates that all students take classes across the academic spectrum, there is no core curriculum of specific required courses. Instead, Haverford's system of distribution requirements ensures that students will take at least three classes in each of the divisions of the College (humanities, natural sciences, and social sciences) while allowing them the flexibility to choose courses they find truly interesting. In addition, students must fulfill requirements in foreign language, writing, and quantitative course work. Majors are selected at the end of the sophomore year.

Haverford's small size and exclusive focus on undergraduate education allow students to count on discussion-based classes and research opportunities that students at most colleges would not be able to experience until graduate school. It is common for Haverford students to pursue independent study and approximately half will study abroad, typically during the junior year.

Haverford's three academic centers—the John B. Hurford Humanities Center, the Marian E. Koshland Integrated Natural Sciences Center, and the Center for Peace and Global Citizenship—provide opportunities for integrated learning, bringing students and faculty in related fields together and promoting conversation and collaboration across disciplines. The centers also help to bring an outward view to students' education by sponsoring speaker series, artists in residence, and colloquia on campus.

One of Haverford's distinctive features is its extensive academic and social cooperation with Bryn Mawr College. Students may take courses or major at either school, live on either campus, and eat on either campus. There are more than 2,000 cross-registrations annually. Both colleges jointly operate a weekly newspaper, a drama club, a radio station, an orchestra, social action groups, and intramural sports. A free bus service between the two campuses, which are a mile apart, facilitates cooperative arrangements. Haverford and Bryn Mawr also share library resources with nearby Swarthmore College. All three college libraries are linked electronically, and students have instant access to library resources through the campus computer network. Combined holdings are in excess of 1.5 million volumes.

Off-Campus Programs

Haverford students may take advantage of course offerings at Swarthmore College and the University of Pennsylvania in addition to courses at Bryn Mawr. Students may also enhance their college experiences by arranging study abroad at one of seventy-six programs overseas or study away at Claremont McKenna, Fisk, Spelman, or Pitzer colleges.

Academic Facilities

Major facilities include the James P. Magill Library (580,000 volumes); computer centers; the Koshland Integrated Natural Sciences Center for the physical sciences, biology, and psychology; the Strawbridge Observatory for astronomy; the Music Center; Gest Center for Cross-Cultural Study of Religion; the Fine Arts Center; Marshall Auditorium; and the Language Learning Center. Academic buildings and dormitories are linked by a campuswide computer network.

Costs

The total approximate costs for 2014–15 were $61,784. This consisted of $46,790 for tuition, $14,350 for room and board, and a student activity fee of $424. New students have a one-time orientation fee of $220.

Financial Aid

Fifty-eight percent of Haverford's students receive financial aid, which is awarded solely based on need. Candidates for Haverford College–funded aid must file the online College Board PROFILE application and the online Free Application for Federal Student Aid (FAFSA), along with other forms. Complete information on forms and deadlines to apply for financial aid at Haverford, including links to the PROFILE and FAFSA, are available at www.haverford.edu/financialaid. Early decision applicants must file for financial aid by November 15 and regular decision applicants by January 31. Further details are available on the website. Haverford's PROFILE code is 2289, and the FAFSA code is 003274.

Faculty

The student-faculty ratio is 9:1. The faculty devotes its full teaching time to undergraduates. There are no graduate assistants. The regular faculty is supplemented by 90 to 100 scholars, artists, and public figures who visit the College annually under the auspices of seven specially endowed funds.

Student Government

The Students' Association has responsibility for nearly all aspects of student life. The Haverford Honor Code, established and administered by students, has been in existence since 1897. The Honor Code makes possible a climate of trust, concern, and respect, which produces a campus atmosphere conducive to learning and personal growth. The code provides for students' academic and social freedom within the confines of agreed-upon community standards. Exams are not proctored, and the students schedule their own final exams. The code is administered by an elected Honor Council of 16 students, 4 from each class at the College. Each year, the students meet to discuss resolutions and changes in the Honor Code and to approve its adoption. The students also elect several members of the student body to serve on faculty committees and as nonvoting representatives to the Board of Managers (trustees).

Admission Requirements

Admission to Haverford is highly competitive. Admitted students have strong academic records and represent a diversity of backgrounds and interests. The primary criteria for admission are academic and personal qualities as shown by the school record, standardized test scores, extracurricular achievement, and personal recommendations. A combination of qualities that indicate academic and personal promise and potential for growth at Haverford is more significant than any single factor. Of the most recent first-year class, 94 percent rank in the top 10 percent of their high school class, and their SAT scores range from 500 to 800. The mean SAT ranges are 680–780 critical reasoning, 670–770 math, and 680–770 writing. All candidates are required to take the ACT with writing or the SAT Reasoning Test and two SAT Subject Tests. A visit to campus to meet students, observe classes, and have an interview is recommended. Students who live within 150 miles of the campus are strongly recommended to arrange an on-campus interview. A first-choice early decision plan and a deferred matriculation plan are offered.

Admission of transfer students to Haverford is also highly competitive. A limited number of transfer students are accepted each year. Candidates must have completed one full year of college, with a minimum grade point average of 3.0 (B). Campus visits are strongly recommended for those wishing to transfer. A transfer student must spend a minimum of two years at Haverford in order to receive a degree.

Application and Information

The application deadlines for admission are November 15 for early decision candidates, January 15 for regular decision candidates, and March 31 for transfer candidates. Haverford uses the Common Application, which is available in school guidance offices and online. The admission office is open from 9 a.m. to 5 p.m. on weekdays (8:30 a.m. to 4:30 p.m. from May 15 through Labor Day) and, during the fall, from 10 a.m. to 1 p.m. on Saturday.

For more information or to arrange an interview or tour appointment, students should contact:

Office of Admission and Financial Aid
Haverford College
370 Lancaster Avenue
Haverford, Pennsylvania 19041-1392
Phone: 610-896-1350
610-896-1436 (TTY/TDD)
Fax: 610-896-1338
E-mail: admission@haverford.edu (Admission)
finaid@haverford.edu (Financial Aid)
Website: http://www.haverford.edu

Haverford is consistently ranked among the top academic institutions in the country. The rigorous academic program focuses on individual growth, intellectual exploration, and pushing the boundaries of each discipline. Most classes are taught seminar style with an emphasis on discussion and debate.

HILLSDALE COLLEGE

HILLSDALE, MICHIGAN

HILLSDALE COLLEGE
PURSUING TRUTH · DEFENDING LIBERTY SINCE 1844

The College

Hillsdale College is a private, independent, nonsectarian institution of higher learning founded in 1844 by men and women who described themselves as "grateful to God for the inestimable blessings" resulting from civil and religious liberty and as "believing that the diffusion of learning is essential to the perpetuity of those blessings." The College has maintained institutional independence since its founding by refusing to accept aid from or control by federal authorities. Far-reaching private support from a national constituency has enabled Hillsdale to continue its trusteeship of the intellectual and spiritual inheritance derived from the Judeo-Christian faith and Greco-Roman culture.

The undergraduate enrollment for fall 2014 was 1,437, of whom 48 percent were men. The College draws students from forty-nine states and nine other countries. Approximately 34 percent of students are from Michigan. The entering freshman class in 2014 had an average high school grade-point average of 3.81 and mean ACT (29) and SAT (1933) scores well above national averages. Hillsdale students are housed in dormitories, fraternity and sorority houses, and various off-campus dwellings. Single and double rooms are available on campus; there are no coed dormitories. Each College-owned residence hall is supervised by a resident director and resident advisers. All freshmen (except commuters) are required to live on campus; upperclass students seeking to live off campus must apply to the dean of men or dean of women for this privilege.

Hillsdale's Charger athletes compete in 14 intercollegiate NCAA Division II varsity sports as part of the Great Lakes Intercollegiate Athletic Conference (GLIAC). Since 1998, the College has produced 107 athletic All-Americans and 28 conference champions, and Hillsdale teams have qualified for national tournaments nineteen times. Thirty-four athletes have earned national academic honors in their respective sports as well. An active intramural program is also available. Four national fraternities, three national sororities, and more than 100 other social, academic, spiritual, and service organizations provide Hillsdale students with a diverse array of cocurricular opportunities. A resident drama troupe and dance company, a concert choir and chamber chorale, a jazz program with big band and combos, instrumental chamber ensembles from string quartets to percussion ensemble, and a symphony orchestra and band constitute the College's performing arts organizations.

Special student services provided by the College include career planning and placement counseling, academic advising and tutoring, and a health service staffed by a physician and a resident nurse.

Location

Hillsdale College is located amidst the hills, dales, and lakes of south-central Michigan. The Indiana and Ohio turnpikes are each 30 minutes away, and the College is within close reach of such metropolitan areas as Detroit, Chicago, Cleveland, Toledo, Ft. Wayne, and Indianapolis. The town of Hillsdale is a county seat with a population of 10,000. Stores, churches, restaurants, and movie theaters are all within walking distance of the campus.

Majors and Degrees

Hillsdale awards Bachelor of Arts and Bachelor of Science degrees in accounting, art, biochemistry, biology, chemistry, classical studies, computational mathematics, economics, education, English, exercise science, financial management, French, German, Greek, history, Latin, marketing/management, mathematics, music, music education, philosophy, physical education, physics, politics, psychology, religion, Spanish, speech, sport management, sport psychology, and theater. Interdisciplinary majors in American studies, Christian studies, comparative literature, European studies, international studies in business and foreign language, political economy, and sociology and social thought are also available. Preprofessional programs are offered in allied health services (including optometry, pharmacy, physical therapy, nursing, and medical technology), dentistry, engineering, environmental sciences, forestry, law, medicine, osteopathy, theology, and veterinary medicine.

Academic Programs

Hillsdale operates on a two-semester schedule, with the fall term beginning in late August and ending in mid-December and the spring term beginning in mid-January and ending in mid-May. Two 3-week summer sessions are also offered.

The College believes that a sound classical liberal arts education includes study in the humanities, natural sciences, and social sciences, and each student is required to complete a structured core of courses in these areas. All students declare a major by the end of the sophomore year. To graduate, students must complete a minimum 124 hours of course work and fulfill the requirements of at least one major field. The B.A. program includes a foreign language proficiency requirement. The B.S. program requires additional studies in mathematics and the natural sciences.

The honors program enables exceptionally talented students interested in an interdisciplinary community of learning to develop their intellectual potential through an accelerated college core and honors seminars in the junior and senior years. Discussions, guest lectures, and travel opportunities contribute to the social cohesiveness of the group. All honors students complete a senior thesis on an interdisciplinary topic of their choosing.

The Center for Constructive Alternatives conducts four weeklong symposia during the academic year and is one of the largest college lecture series in America. These programs, with themes ranging from historical to political, business, science, and the arts, bring to the campus distinguished scholars and public figures of national and international renown. All students are required to enroll in one seminar for credit.

Off-Campus Programs

For forty years, the Washington Hillsdale Internship Program (WHIP) has provided students the opportunity to participate in full-time, academically intensive internships in the nation's capital. The program has been significantly bolstered with the 2008 establishment of the Hillsdale College Allan P. Kirby, Jr. Center for Constitutional Studies and Citizenship in Washington, D.C. Past interns and fellows have been placed in locations as challenging and rewarding as the U.S. House of Representatives, the U.S. Senate, the White House, various think tanks including the Heritage Foundation, news and media outlets, national security agencies, lobbying firms, international trade and relations organizations, and private sector companies.

Through the College's affiliations with the Center for Medieval and Renaissance Studies and the Oxford Study Abroad Program, Hillsdale students are able to study abroad for a summer or a year at one of the more than thirty colleges of Oxford University. Hillsdale offers a summer business program in cooperation with Regent's College in London, England, and the opportunity to study at the University of St. Andrews in St. Andrews, Scotland. Science students benefit from Hillsdale's 685-acre field research laboratory in northern Michigan, as well as from a marine biology program in the Florida Keys, and internship opportunities with the Omaha Zoo. Foreign language students frequently study abroad in Argentina, France, Germany, and Spain. Qualified individual students who wish to study in another country for a semester or a year are assisted by their faculty adviser and the registrar in planning a program that enables them to gain academic credit as well as take full advantage of their experience.

Academic Facilities

The Hillsdale College Mossey Library is a three-floor facility with a collection of more than 1,000,000 volumes. In addition to the main study and research collections, the Library also contains a number of rare and special holdings, including the Ludwig von Mises, Russell Kirk, Richardson Heritage, and Richard Weaver collections. Connected to other Michigan libraries through MelCat, and with college libraries nationwide via interlibrary loan, students have access to most any material necessary for on-campus research. Numerous individual study areas and group study rooms are available for students, as well as computer research terminals.

Lane and Kendall Halls at the front of campus serve as the primary academic facilities in the humanities and contain classroom space and faculty offices, as well as a special laboratory for experimental psychology. The Strosacker Science Center houses the departments of biology, chemistry, and physics. The Joseph H. Moss Family Laboratory Wing, completed in 2008, is a 17,000-square-foot addition that includes a microbiology/cell biology lab, anatomy/physiology lab with human cadaver access, conservation genetics lab, water lab, greenhouse, and organic/general chemistry labs. The 32,000-square-foot Herbert Henry Dow Science Building provides additional classrooms, research laboratories, animal rooms, and a computer lab. The Mary Randall Preschool is a circular laboratory school in which nursery school children are taught by students specializing in early childhood education and psychology. Experts in the field have called this building "a model for the nation." The Hillsdale Academy, a K–12 private model school, provides additional opportunities for classroom observation.

The Roche Sports Complex is a facility available to varsity athletes and the general student body alike. The building houses the 60,000-square-foot Dawn Tibbetts Potter Arena, which features a student fitness center and basketball/volleyball courts. The building also houses the John "Jack" McAvoy Natatorium for swimming and diving, an exercise physiology and sports medicine facility, four racquetball courts, extensive locker room space, and a weight/fitness room. Adjacent is the 7,000-seat capacity Frank "Muddy" Waters Stadium, which features an artificial surface football field; all-weather, Olympic-quality eight-lane running track; outdoor tennis courts; and fields for soccer, baseball, and women's softball. The new Margot V. Biermann Athletic Center houses a six-lane track and four tennis courts.

The Sage Center for the Arts is home to the departments of art, theater, and speech. This 47,000-square-foot facility contains studios, classroom space, an exhibition gallery, a prop- and scene-construction shop, a sound studio, graphics lab, black box theatre, and the Markel Auditorium, a 353-seat performance hall (with orchestra pit). Completed in 2003, the 32,809-square-foot Howard Music Hall houses office, studio, classroom, rehearsal, and performance space for the John E. N. and Dede Howard Department of Music. Notable features include the McNamara Rehearsal Hall, Conrad Recital Hall, and studio space for percussion and jazz studies. Lower-level practice rooms are available to students during business hours without reservation.

Dedicated in January 2008, the 53,000-square-foot Grewcock Student Union is the center of student life. The two-story structure houses the cafeteria, bookstore, student mail center, offices for student activities and publications, a lounge with a 100-inch flat screen television, a formal lounge and conference room, AJ's Café, and a game area. The entire building is wireless, and any Hillsdale student can check out a laptop at the main desk.

Costs

Annual tuition for the 2014–15 academic year was $22,920, room was $4,570, board was $4,680, and mandatory fees were $696. Books, supplies, and personal expenses (including travel, recreation, and clothing) are estimated at $3,000 per year.

Financial Aid

Financial aid at Hillsdale is available in many forms. Academic scholarships are awarded on a competitive basis, regardless of financial need, to students who rank in the top 10 percent of their high school class and have standardized test scores in the top 10 percent according to national test norms. The priority deadline for academic scholarship consideration is January 1. The application for admission also serves as the Hillsdale application for merit-based aid. Athletic scholarships are available on a competitive basis in men's baseball and football; men's and women's basketball, track, and cross-country; and women's swimming and volleyball. The departments of art and music also award a select number of scholarships based on strength of portfolio/audition. To apply for aid on the basis of financial need, students are required to file Hillsdale's Confidential Family Financial Statement (CFFS) in January or February of the year of prospective enrollment at Hillsdale. Grants and loans are available from the College.

Faculty

The faculty consists of 133 full-time members. No classes are taught by graduate students. The size and closeness of the College community enable personal attention and faculty mentorship inside the classroom and during office visits after class. Each student has a faculty adviser for core and major coursework who directs the program of study and provides academic and career counseling. Hillsdale's faculty considers teaching their first priority. Many faculty members also engage in research and scholarly writing, supported by summer and sabbatical leaves funded by the College, and are often invited to comment on the national scene in lecture programs and media outlets.

Student Government

Hillsdale's student government and campus organizations offer students special opportunities to develop leadership skills that enrich both their collegiate experience and lives after graduation. The governing organization of the student body is the Student Federation, which is composed of 18 elected representatives. This group funds student organizations, sponsors all-College entertainment, and acts upon matters of concern to the student community.

Admission Requirements

Admission is a privilege extended to students who will benefit from, and contribute to, the academic, social, and spiritual environments of the College. Important determinants for admission are intellectual curiosity, ambition, leadership, and volunteerism. Accordingly, grade-point average, test scores, class rank, strength of curriculum, extracurricular activities, interviews, self-evaluations, writing samples in the form of two essays, and recommendations are all reviewed carefully and are important in the evaluation process. An admissions interview is strongly encouraged. Although some factors are necessarily more important than others, seldom is any single criterion, however important, decisive.

Transfer students must submit the standard application, including the high school record, SAT or ACT scores, transcripts from all colleges previously attended, and a transfer form from the dean of students of the most recent college attended. Applications by transfers are evaluated similarly to nontransfers.

Candidates for admission from other countries follow the regular entrance procedures. Students who come from a non-English-speaking country must demonstrate proficiency in English by satisfactory performance on the Test of English as a Foreign Language (TOEFL) or the Michigan Test of English Proficiency or at an ESL Center.

Application and Information

Students may apply to Hillsdale College any time after the completion of the junior year of high school. A formal application includes a completed application form accompanied by a nonrefundable fee of $35 (free if submitted online) and all required credentials. Application plans include early decision (November 15), early action (December 15), and regular decision (February 15). Hillsdale College has been distinguished since its founding in 1844 by voluntarily adhering to a nondiscriminatory policy regarding race, religion, sex, and national or ethnic origin—long before the government began regulating such matters.

All records and forms should be mailed to:

Admissions Office
Hillsdale College
33 East College Street
Hillsdale, Michigan 49242-1298
Phone: 517-607-2327
Fax: 517-607-2223
E-mail: admissions@hillsdale.edu
Website: http://www.hillsdale.edu

HOFSTRA UNIVERSITY

HEMPSTEAD, NEW YORK

★ To read more about this school, visit http://petersons.to/hofstrauniversity

HOFSTRA UNIVERSITY
prideandpurpose

COLLEGE CLOSE-UPS

The University

Hofstra University is one of the largest private colleges on Long Island, New York, and one of only three universities in the New York metropolitan area with schools of medicine, law, and engineering. Since its founding in 1935, Hofstra has evolved into a nationally and internationally renowned university that is consistently recognized by *U.S. News & World Report,* the Princeton Review, *Fiske, Washington Monthly,* and *Forbes.*

The Hofstra North Shore–LIJ School of Medicine at Hofstra University welcomed its third class of students in August 2013, shortly after breaking ground on a 65,000-square-foot addition that will be completed in 2015, more than doubling the size of the school. In addition, Hofstra has invested $11 million in equipment and labs, including Big Data and robotics labs, for its new School of Engineering and Applied Science. The school also offers an innovative co-op program to give students real-world work experience. The new School of Health Sciences and Human Services launched a Master of Public Health program in 2012.

Hofstra's diverse and driven student body of nearly 11,000 can choose from 143 undergraduate and 156 graduate program options in liberal arts and sciences, business, engineering, communication, teacher education, law, health and human services, and honors studies. Hofstra offers more than 100 dual-degree programs that allow students to earn both an undergraduate and graduate degree in less time than if each degree was pursued separately. More information is available at hofstra.edu/academics or hofstra.edu/dualdegree.

Hofstra hosts hundreds of social, academic, and cultural events each year. Notably, Hofstra is only the second school to ever host two consecutive U.S. Presidential debates, in 2008 and 2012. Hofstra also hosted the New York state gubernatorial debate in 2010. These events help foster a connection between classroom work and extracurricular interests, as well as encourage civic engagement among its students.

In addition, Hofstra offers 17 intercollegiate athletic programs that compete at the NCAA Division I level and more than 200 academic, fraternal/sororal, media, multicultural, performance, pre-professional, religious, social, social/political, and sports clubs and organizations. The David S. Mack Sports and Exhibition Complex, a 93,000-square-foot facility, is home to the Hofstra Pride men's and women's basketball teams and wrestling, and is also the site for events such as commencements, exhibitions, trade shows, televised political events, and concerts. Other on-campus recreational and athletic facilities include a renovated state-of-the-art fitness center, featuring an Olympic-sized swimming pool, an indoor track, an aerobics room, and weight and cardiovascular facilities, as well as access to various athletic playing fields.

Each year, the University is visited by more than 400 employers who recognize how much Hofstra students have to offer. In addition to the plentiful networking opportunities on campus, students may choose to do an internship at a top company on Long Island or in New York City, thus gaining critical work experience that will give them an edge in a competitive job market.

At Hofstra, students join a network of more than 126,000 graduates, including outstanding alumni such as Academy Award–winning film director and producer Francis Ford Coppola; best-selling author Nelson DeMille; vascular surgeon Dr. Donna Mendes; president of the New York Yankees Randy Levine; creator, executive producer, and writer Philip Rosenthal and actress Monica Horan from *Everybody Loves Raymond*; actresses Lainie Kazan and Susan Sullivan; and New York State Comptroller Thomas P. DiNapoli.

At Hofstra, it's all about choice. Students can live in one of the 37 residence halls, each with a unique flair and life of its own, including living/learning communities. Hofstra students also have 20 on-campus dining facilities.

Location

Hofstra is located only 25 miles east of New York City—a short train ride from all the cultural, recreational, internship, and career opportunities the city has to offer. The University, which blends longstanding traditions with twenty-first-century resources, is home to both ivy-covered classrooms buildings and modern, elegant facilities. Students will find exceptional and technologically advanced classrooms, six theaters, a state-of-the-art fitness center, an accredited museum, modern athletic facilities, and an impressive 11-floor library that holds more than 1 million print volumes and 24/7 electronic access to more than 125,000 journals and books—all on a campus that is a nationally recognized arboretum.

Majors and Degrees

The Bachelor of Arts (B.A.) is awarded in African studies, American studies, anthropology, art history, Asian studies, biology, chemistry, Chinese, Chinese studies, classics, comparative literature and languages, computer science, criminology, dance, drama, early childhood and childhood education (with dual major in another discipline), early childhood education (with dual major in another discipline), economics, elementary education (with dual major in another discipline), engineering science, English, English education, film studies and production, fine arts, foreign language education (French, German, Italian, Russian, Spanish), French, geography, geology, German, global studies, Hebrew, history, Ibero-American studies, Italian, Japanese and Japanese studies, Jewish studies, journalism, labor studies, Latin, Latin American and Caribbean studies, liberal arts, linguistics, mass media studies, math education (with a dual major in another discipline), mathematical economics, mathematics, music, philosophy, physics, political science, pre-health with a concentration in humanities and social sciences, psychology, public relations, radio production and studies, religion, Russian, science education (biology, chemistry, earth science, physics), social studies education (with a dual major in another discipline), sociology, Spanish, speech communication and rhetorical studies, speech-language-hearing sciences, sustainability studies, urban ecology, video/television, and women's studies.

The Bachelor of Business Administration (B.B.A.) is awarded in accounting, entrepreneurship, finance, information technology, international business, legal studies in business, management, marketing, and supply chain management.

The Bachelor of Science (B.S.) is offered in applied physics, athletic training, biochemistry, biology, business economics, chemistry, community health, computer engineering, computer science, computer science and mathematics (dual major), electrical engineering, environmental resources, exercise science, fine arts, forensic science, geology, health education, health science, industrial engineering, mathematical business economics, mathematics, mechanical engineering, music, philosophy, physics, pre-medical, sustainability studies, urban ecology, video/television, video/television and business, and video/television and film.

The Bachelor of Science in Education (B.S.Ed.) is offered with specializations in dance, fine arts, music, and physical education.

The Bachelor of Engineering (B.E.) is offered in engineering science with specializations in biomedical engineering and civil engineering.

The Bachelor of Fine Arts (B.F.A.) is awarded in theater arts with specializations in performance and production.

Combined (dual) degrees offered include Bachelor of Arts/Juris Doctor (B.A./J.D.) in collaboration with the Maurice A. Deane School of Law at Hofstra University, B.S./M.S. in physician assistant studies, B.S./M.D. and B.A./M.D., through the Hofstra North Shore–LIJ School of Medicine at Hofstra University, and various majors and concentrations leading to the B.A./M.B.A., B.S./M.B.A., B.A./M.S.Ed., B.A./M.A., B.A./M.S., B.S./M.S., B.B.A./M.S.Ed., B.B.A./M.S., and B.B.A./M.B.A.

Academic Programs

Requirements for graduation vary among schools and majors. A liberal arts core curriculum is an integral part of all areas of concentration. The University calendar is organized on a traditional semester system, and also includes one January session and three summer sessions.

Hofstra offers innovative programs designed to meet the needs of its diverse student body. These include Hofstra University Honors College, Legal Education Accelerated Program (LEAP), Hofstra 4+4 Program, First-Year Connections, and living/learning communities.

Hofstra's Honors College provides a rich academic and extracurricular experience for students who show exceptional potential. Honors students can elect to study in any of the University's undergraduate programs and are involved in all fields of advanced study.

The Legal Education Accelerated Program allows students to earn both a B.A. and a J.D. in just six years.

The Hofstra 4+4 Program allows students to earn both a bachelor's degree (B.A. or B.S.) and M.D. in eight years in collaboration with the Hofstra North Shore-LIJ School of Medicine.

First-Year Connections, an integrated academic and social program, helps first-year students connect with one another as well as with all the resources and opportunities offered at the University. The program offers seminars and course clusters and features small classes taught by distinguished faculty. These courses introduce students to the intellectual and social life of the University and satisfy the general education requirements for all majors.

Through Hofstra's living/learning communities, learning is not limited to a classroom's four walls, or even to the borders of the campus. Here, students are exposed to environments that are intellectually stimulating, supportive, and conducive to building lasting friendships and a memorable first-year experience. These living/learning communities are associated with several first-year clusters and seminars, giving students the opportunity to live with many students who are in their classes and who share their interests.

Off-Campus Programs

Hofstra extends learning beyond the classroom through varied internship programs and study-abroad opportunities. The internship programs take advantage of Hofstra's proximity to New York City, allowing students to gain on-the-job experience in areas such as finance, business, media, advertising, and entertainment. Through study-abroad programs in Europe, Asia, South America, and other locations, students can explore the world while earning college credits. More information is available at hofstra.edu/studyabroad.

Academic Facilities

Hofstra students live and learn on a campus that is home to state-of-the-art facilities and resources. C. V. Starr Hall, home to the Frank G. Zarb School of Business, features the Martin B. Greenberg Trading Room, which has 34 Bloomberg terminals and is among the largest academic training facilities in the world. The Lawrence Herbert School of Communication contains one of the largest broadcast facilities in the northeastern United States as well as a converged newsroom and multimedia classroom. Plus, Hofstra students benefit from real-world experience at the nationally recognized on-campus radio station, WRHU 88.7 FM (Radio Hofstra University), which is the only college radio station in the nation that is the flagship for a professional sports franchise, the NHL's New York Islanders. In 2014, WRHU was ranked by the Princeton Review as the number-one college radio station in the United States and also won the National Association of Broadcasters (NAB) Marconi Award for the top noncommercial radio station in the country. Hagedorn Hall, where the School of Education is located, features a technologically robust learning environment complete with interactive whiteboards, computer-driven instructor stations and wireless communication.

Costs

The 2014–15 annual tuition and fees at Hofstra University for a full-time undergraduate student were $37,850. The cost of housing and dining plan was approximately $13,960. Books and supplies cost approximately $1,000; personal expenses and transportation generally amount to $3,089. For the full tuition and fees schedule, students should visit hofstra.edu/tuition.

Financial Aid

Hofstra University works hard to make a private college education affordable for students and families, and offers several financial aid options for new undergraduates, including interest-free payment plans and a money-saving four-year locked-in rate for tuition and fees (hofstra.edu/lockedintuitionrate) that can help students manage costs from admission through graduation. For detailed information, students should visit hofstra.edu/FinancialAid.

Faculty

Hofstra's hardworking, ambitious students are taught by Guggenheim Fellows and Fulbright scholars; Emmy Award recipients; prize-winning scientists; leaders in business, education and the health sciences; and knowledgeable and insightful thinkers. Students at Hofstra learn from faculty members—not graduate students. With an average undergraduate class size of 21 and a student-to-faculty ratio of 14:1, Hofstra students are challenged and encouraged to think critically in an open and diverse learning environment.

Student Government

The Student Government Association is a student-run governing body that supervises and coordinates all student activities and serves as a liaison with the faculty and administration. The Student Government Association sends representatives to the committees of the University Senate. A judicial board has responsibility for promoting justice in the conduct of student affairs.

Admission Requirements

Hofstra is a competitive institution that seeks to enroll students who demonstrate academic ability, intellectual curiosity, and the motivation to be successful and contribute to the campus community. Careful consideration is given to a student's high school record, types of courses taken, SAT or ACT scores, letters of recommendation, extracurricular involvement, and the personal essay. The most competitive applicants will have followed a rigorous college preparatory curriculum, and will have taken advantage of honors and advanced placement level courses where appropriate. The Office of Admission prefers to see a high school curriculum that includes 4 years of English, 3 to 4 years of social studies, 2 to 3 years of foreign language, 3 years of mathematics, and 3 years of science. Prospective engineering majors need at least 4 years of mathematics, 1 year of chemistry, and 1 year of physics. Campus visits are strongly recommended. Hofstra accepts applications from first-year, transfer, and international students.

For students whose first choice is Hofstra, there are two early action periods: when an application is submitted by November 15, notification is made to the student by December 15; when an application is submitted by December 15, notification is made to the student by January 15. Students applying for regular decision are considered on a rolling basis.

First-year applicants must submit an application, $70 application fee ($60 online fee), high school transcript, SAT or ACT scores, essay, and letter of recommendation. Hofstra accepts applications via mail or online and participates in the Common Application.

For more information, students should contact:

Application and Information

Hofstra University
Office of Undergraduate Admission
100 Hofstra University
Hempstead, New York 11549-1000
Phone: 516-463-6700
Fax: 516-463-5100
E-mail: admission@hofstra.edu
Website: http://www.hofstra.edu/admission

Hofstra students live, work, and play on a beautiful, state-of-the-art campus that's only a short commute from New York City. The 240-acre campus is lush, green, and spacious, with ivy-covered buildings and great facilities, just minutes from all the adventure and opportunity the New York metropolitan region has to offer.

HUNTER COLLEGE OF THE CITY UNIVERSITY OF NEW YORK

NEW YORK, NEW YORK

HUNTER
The City University of New York

COLLEGE CLOSE-UPS

The College

In 1870, Thomas Hunter founded Hunter College to train young women to become school teachers. Their contributions helped make New York City's schools among the most highly regarded public school systems in the world. Today, Hunter College is a coeducational liberal arts college serving 21,000 undergraduate and graduate students of all racial, ethnic, and cultural backgrounds. Wide offerings in the liberal arts and sciences and three professional schools—education, health sciences, and social work—meet the highest academic standards. A distinguished faculty encourages intellectual and personal growth in each student.

Location

Hunter students study in the heart of Manhattan. Many of the world's finest museums, libraries, concert halls, cultural centers, and theaters are just a quick walk away.

Majors and Degrees

Hunter College offers bachelor's and master's degrees in the arts and sciences, education, health professions, nursing, and social work, along with several combined (B.A./M.A. or B.A./M.S.) degrees. The following programs of study are available: accounting, Africana and Puerto Rican/Latino studies, anthropology, archaeology, art history, biological sciences, chemistry, Chinese language and literature, classical studies, community health education, comparative literature, computer science, dance, economics, elementary education, environmental studies, English, English language arts, film, French, geography, German, Greek, Hebrew, history, honors curriculum, Italian, Jewish social studies, Latin, Latin American and Caribbean Studies, Latin and Greek, mathematics, media studies, medical laboratory sciences, music, nursing, nutrition and food science, philosophy, physics, political science, psychology, religion, Romance languages, Russian, secondary education, sociology, Spanish, statistics, studio art, theater, urban studies, and women's studies. Secondary education programs are for grades 7–12 unless otherwise noted and include biology, chemistry, Chinese, dance (pre-K–12), English, French, German, Hebrew, Italian, mathematics, music (pre-K–12, accelerated B.A./M.A. program only), physics, Russian, social studies, and Spanish.

Special programs in anthropology, biological sciences/environmental and occupational health sciences, biopharmacology, biotechnology, economics, English, history, mathematics, music, physics, sociology/social research, and statistics and applied mathematics lead to the combined bachelor's/master's degree, enabling highly qualified students to earn both degrees more quickly.

Hunter College also provides preprofessional advisement and preparation for advanced study in chiropractic, dentistry, engineering, law, medicine, optometry, osteopathy, pharmacy, podiatry, and veterinary medicine.

Academic Programs

Hunter instills a rich and informed sense of the possibilities of humanity in its students and expects them to carry their liberal arts education forward in their careers, their public responsibilities, and their personal lives.

The College trains its students in the sciences, the humanities, and a number of professional fields. As they strive to achieve their career goals, students are expected to perceive their chosen fields of study as only a part of a wider realm of knowledge. Undergraduate programs of study at Hunter consist of four parts, totaling 120 credits: a general education requirement, a pluralism and diversity requirement, a concentration of in-depth study (major), and elective courses.

Undergraduate students at Hunter who exhibit intellectual curiosity and exceptional ability may apply to the Thomas Hunter Scholars Program, an interdisciplinary program that individualizes study according to needs and interests and grants a Bachelor of Arts degree.

Students may earn sophomore standing (up to 30 credits) if they score well on the College-Level Examination Program (CLEP) subject tests, the Advanced Placement examinations of the College Board, and the Regents College Examination (RCE) Program of New York State.

Off-Campus Programs

Hunter College taps Manhattan to allow innumerable internships. Hosts have included Atlantic Records, CNN, the Council on Foreign Relations, DreamWorks SKG, Madison Square Garden, Metropolitan Museum of Art, New York City Council, Simon & Schuster, and many more. Interns perform curatorial and administrative work in museums, research and production work on TV news shows and newspapers, design work in commercial graphics, and booking, managing, and technical work in theaters.

Academic Facilities

The College is made up of five sites in Manhattan. The largest, a modern complex of buildings connected by skywalks at 68th Street and Lexington Avenue, sits above a convenient subway stop. This campus offers programs in the arts and sciences and in teacher education.

Downtown on East 25th Street, the Brookdale Campus houses the Division of the Schools of the Health Professions, which includes the Hunter-Bellevue School of Nursing, one of the nation's largest nursing programs, and the School of Health Sciences.

Uptown on East 119th Street is the Silberman School of Social Work at Hunter College. This campus also houses the CUNY School of Public Health at Hunter College.

Downtown on Manhattan's West Side, Hunter's brand new Studio Art Building houses a 7,000-square-foot gallery and provides M.F.A. students with individual studios that are among the best in the city.

At East 94th Street, the Campus Schools house an elementary school and a high school for the intellectually gifted that are renowned, as is the College itself, for a long tradition of academic excellence.

All locations are minutes from Grand Central Terminal, Penn Station, and the New York/New Jersey Port Authority Bus

Terminal, making Hunter easily accessible from Connecticut, Westchester, New Jersey, and Long Island.

The collections of the Hunter College libraries are housed in the newly renovated Jacqueline Grennan Wexler Library, as well as at the branch libraries at the Brookdale Campus and the Silberman School of Social Work. The libraries hold over 800,000 volumes, 5,000 periodicals, a nonprint collection of more than 1 million microforms, and over 250,000 art slides in addition to records, tapes, scores, music CDs, and videos. Recently, Hunter installed new computer, multimedia, and Internet labs and its first CD-ROM network. The CD-ROM network provides access to indexes, abstracts, and complete texts and multimedia resources, and Internet labs make the World Wide Web accessible.

Costs

Hunter College is affordable. In fall 2015, New York State residents enrolled as full-time, matriculated students are slated to pay $3,015 per semester ($260 per credit part-time). Nonresidents enrolled as full-time, matriculated students will pay $535 per credit. All students pay a student activity fee ($85.10 per semester for full-time students and $55.05 per semester for part-time students) and a $15-per-semester consolidated fee.

Financial Aid

Hunter College participates in all state and federal financial aid programs. Financial aid is available to matriculated students in the form of grants, loans, and work-study. Grants provide funds that do not have to be repaid. Loans must be repaid in regular installments over a prescribed period of time. Work-study consists of part-time employment, either on campus or in an outside agency. More information is available from the Office of Financial Aid at 212-772-4820.

Entering freshmen whose high school records indicate a high level of academic achievement may apply to the Macaulay Honors College at Hunter College. This prestigious program offers a generous financial aid package, including a full academic scholarship, as well as extensive benefits, including a free room at the Hunter College Residence Hall for two years. In addition, Hunter College offers a wide array of other scholarships.

Faculty

Thanks to its location in the heart of New York City, Hunter College attracts a special kind of faculty member. Some are well-known scholars and researchers in their fields, such as biologists involved in advanced research on genetic structure. Others are professionals with active careers in the city, including well-known painters, sculptors, architects, and urban design experts. Hunter's faculty also includes environmental health scientists who work on occupational health and safety issues, nursing administrators who work in the country's leading hospitals, and film directors, theater critics, and musicians who are engaged in New York City's cultural milieu. Many members of the faculty are nationally renowned; they maintain Hunter's reputation for academic excellence through outstanding teaching and cutting-edge publications and by securing millions of dollars in annual grants for research.

Student Government

Several governing assemblies involve students in Hunter's governance. The College Senate, the legislative body of the College, includes faculty members, students, and administrators. Two student governments (undergraduate and graduate) also play essential roles in the life of the College. Students with voting power sit on faculty and administrative committees.

Admission Requirements

Candidates for freshman admission are considered based on the overall strength of their academic preparation, cumulative high school averages, and SAT or ACT scores. Freshman students who entered in fall 2014 had a high school academic grade point average of 88.6 and an SAT score of 1203 (math and verbal only). The College recommends 4 years of English, 4 years of social studies, 3 years of mathematics, 2 years of a foreign language, 2 years of laboratory sciences, and 1 year of performing or visual arts as the minimum academic preparation for success in college.

Students are considered transfer applicants if they have previously attended any college, university, and/or proprietary school since graduating from high school or secondary school. This applies whether or not the student is seeking transfer credit. Transfer students in fall 2014 had a cumulative grade point average of 3.20 with an average of 79.0 credits attempted. For more information, applicants should visit Hunter College's website.

Application and Information

Applicants are considered for fall (September) and spring (February) admission. Applications for the fall must be filed no later than September 15 and for spring, no later than February 1. All applications must be filed on the CUNY website at http://www.cuny.edu.

Welcome Center
Hunter College
695 Park Avenue, Room 100N
New York, New York 10065
Phone: 212-772-4490
E-mail: admissions@hunter.cuny.edu
Website: http://www.hunter.cuny.edu/ugprospects
http://www.facebook.com/groups/263613092099
(Welcome Center)

Students at Hunter College enjoy the convenience of skywalks that connect all four buildings at the 68th Street campus. Hunter's Upper East Side location provides easy access to some of New York's finest offerings; Central Park and the Metropolitan Museum of Art are just blocks away.

COLLEGE CLOSE-UPS

IMMACULATA UNIVERSITY

IMMACULATA, PENNSYLVANIA

IMMACULATA UNIVERSITY

The University

Immaculata University (IU), a comprehensive Catholic liberal arts university for students of all faiths, offers a high-quality education that is firmly grounded in values and tradition. Immaculata graduates are known for their skills and knowledge and for their desire to serve. The University was founded in 1920 and has since grown to enroll almost 4,000 students in bachelor's, master's, and doctoral degree programs and accelerated degree-completion and online programs.

Approximately 1,000 traditional-age men and women attend the College of Undergraduate Studies. The College of Lifelong Learning includes undergraduate programs that are open to adult men and women. Students represent seventeen states and twenty-seven countries, giving the campus both ethnic and geographic diversity. Resident students live in four residence halls containing double rooms. A new apartment housing complex, opened in fall 2014, is also available. Both resident and nonresident students participate in more than sixty student clubs and organizations that represent interests in athletics, student government, academic disciplines, community action, music, dance, theater, and student publications.

Intercollegiate sports include women's basketball, cross-country, field hockey, lacrosse, soccer, softball, tennis, track and field, and volleyball and men's baseball, basketball, cross-country, golf, lacrosse, soccer, tennis, and track and field. Immaculata competes in Division III athletics as part of the Colonial States Athletic Conference. A turf field, stadium, indoor batting cages, gymnasium, fitness room, and pool are available for student use and provide numerous opportunities for physical activities and wellness programs. The Student Association of Immaculata University provides the unity, enthusiasm, and leadership that are integral parts of the traditional undergraduate experience.

Immaculata University celebrates unique traditions as a part of the overall collegiate experience, such as Sophomore pinning and Junior ring ceremonies. Carol Night, one of Immaculata's best-loved traditions, involves students, faculty members, alumni, and families singing around the Christmas tree in the Rotunda of Villa Maria Hall.

The main building, Villa Maria Hall, is of neo-Renaissance architecture in gray stone with a red tile roof. The other thirteen major campus buildings are also of gray stone with red tile roofs, unifying the aesthetic appearance of the campus.

Graduate degrees offered in the College of Graduate Studies include the Master of Arts in counseling psychology, cultural and linguistic diversity, educational leadership and administration, music therapy, nursing, nutrition education, and organization leadership. Doctoral degrees are offered in educational administration, higher education, clinical psychology, and school psychology. IU's online degree-completion programs include an Associate in Science degree in business administration, and Bachelor of Science degrees in business management, emergency planning and management, finance, health care management, health information management, human performance management, human resource management, marketing management, and an RN to B.S.N. in Nursing.

Location

Immaculata's 375-acre campus is located in historic Chester County, 20 miles west of Philadelphia and 10 miles south of Valley Forge. The area is primarily suburban, with numerous colleges and universities offering a wide range of cultural and social activities. Many places of interest in Philadelphia and Lancaster are easily reached by car, train, or bus. The campus is 15 minutes from the King of Prussia Mall, the second largest mall in the U.S. Southern New Jersey shore resorts and New York City are within 1½ hours by car, with Pocono Mountain ski resorts and Washington, D.C., only 2½ hours away by car or train. The University provides numerous opportunities for internships in the business, educational, and scientific communities throughout the area.

Majors and Degrees

The College of Undergraduate Studies at Immaculata offers the Bachelor of Arts, Bachelor of Music, Bachelor of Science, Associate of Arts, and Associate of Science degrees. Undergraduate major fields of study include accounting, allied health, athletic training, biology, biology/psychology, business administration, chemistry, communication, criminology/sociology, education, English, exercise science, family and consumer sciences, fashion merchandising, finance, general science, history, information systems, interactive digital media, international business/foreign language, marketing management, mathematics, mathematics–data sciences, music, music education, music performance, music therapy, nursing, nutrition/dietetics, political science/international relations, prelaw, premedicine, pre–physical therapy, pre–veterinary medicine, psychology, sociology, social work, Spanish, Spanish/psychology, Spanish/social work, theology, and undecided. Allied health concentrations include: clinical laboratory science, diagnostic medical sonography, invasive cardiovascular technology, nuclear medicine technology, and surgical technology. IU also offers partnership programs with Thomas Jefferson University (TJU) in physical therapy, occupational therapy, bioscience technologies, and radiologic sciences. These programs allow students to seamlessly matriculate into TJU after three years of study at IU.

Academic Programs

Two factors are emphasized in the educational program at Immaculata: a comprehensive liberal arts background and a major field of concentration that prepares students to begin a career or to attend graduate school. The honors program offers an array of courses designed to give those who participate a special involvement in the learning process.

The Mary Bruder Center houses the offices for personal, career, and graduate study counseling and for educational and career testing. Workshops and seminars in resume writing, interviewing, career options, internship opportunities, and graduate fellowships are offered at regular intervals.

Off-Campus Programs

Both summer-abroad and junior-year-abroad programs combine travel with academic study to heighten the experience of students who seek these opportunities. Students can study in England and Ireland through IU and in other countries through the University's collaboration with Arcadia University.

Every undergraduate major department offers numerous internship opportunities for students in agencies, businesses, institutions, or corporations related to their study. Some majors, such as nutrition, fashion merchandising, and music therapy, require a multi-week internship for the degree to be granted.

Academic Facilities

The Gabriele Library houses 145,000 volumes, 3,500 audiovisual items, 40 electronic databases, and 300 periodical subscriptions. In addition to the computer center, students have access to networked computers in the library, an interactive language lab with a video screen, and a multifaceted science lab with computer-simulated experiments; they also have Internet/Intranet access from their residence halls. Well-equipped laboratories, art studios, media centers, and a 1,150-seat theater give students a variety of settings in which to pursue their interests.

State-of-the-art computer labs include the Campus Learning and Language Laboratory, the Sister Maria Socorro Studio Laboratory for Mathematics and Science, a new biology laboratory, and the Loyola Executive Technology Center. Classrooms and the library utilize wireless technology in the smart classrooms.

Costs

For 2015–16, tuition and fees are $33,280 and room and board are $13,200. An additional $1,000 is estimated to cover books and personal spending.

Financial Aid

Financial aid is available in the form of scholarships, grants, loans, and part-time campus employment through the resources of Immaculata, federal and state governments, and private endowments. Scholarships are awarded for academic excellence. Approximately 90 percent of the students receive some form of aid, and all students who demonstrate need are offered financial aid packages. The University requires that students submit the Free Application for Federal Student Aid (FAFSA) to be considered for financial aid. The University sends financial aid packages to accepted students as their files are completed by the end of February. The FAFSA reporting code is 003276.

Faculty

The faculty has more than 100 full-time and 200 part-time members, more than half of whom hold doctorates. Several members of the Immaculata faculty conduct research and present papers in various disciplines, both nationally and internationally. High-quality teaching is of the greatest importance to Immaculata's academic program. Full-time faculty members serve as academic counselors and activity moderators. The student-faculty ratio is 9:1.

Student Government

The Student Government Association of Immaculata University (SGA) governs most aspects of student life for both resident and commuter students. The resident assistant program moderates residence life by holding open meetings to discuss safety issues and to set residence hall regulations. Students serve on the various University policymaking committees and handle all student activity funds.

Admission Requirements

In order to be considered for admission to the College of Undergraduate Studies, students must submit an official secondary school transcript indicating course selection for the senior year and SAT or ACT scores. The reporting code for the SAT is 2320, and the reporting code for the ACT is 3596. An essay and recommendations are required. The Admission Committee requires 14 or more course units, as follows: 4 units of English, 2 units of social science, 2 units of mathematics, 2 units of science (1 lab), and 2 consecutive years of the same foreign language. Most candidates exceed this curriculum. The mid-range GPA for the past two years was 3.2.

All admission credentials should be sent to the College of Undergraduate Studies. Students can apply online at the University's website, http://www.immaculata.edu/admissions. The application fee of $35 is waived for students who apply online or who visit the campus and complete an application during their visit. Students also have the option to apply through the Common Application, http://www.commonapp.org, which is free as well.

Application and Information

Applications are accepted from prospective freshman and transfer students on a rolling admissions basis, and decisions are made three to four weeks after an applicant's file is complete. The only exceptions are those students applying for nursing and the Thomas Jefferson University programs. The application deadline for Thomas Jefferson is December 15. All of the credentials required for admission must be received and the file completed by that date.

For further information, students should contact:

Nicola DiFronzo-Heitzer, Ed.D., Director of Admission
Immaculata University
P.O. Box 642
Immaculata, Pennsylvania 19345-0642
United States
Phone: 610-647-4400 Ext. 3060
877-42-TODAY (toll-free)
Fax: 610-640-0836
E-mail: admiss@immaculata.edu
Website: http://www.immaculata.edu

Immaculata's beautiful Rotunda in Volla Maria Hall is where students often gather to celebrate various IU traditions.

COLLEGE CLOSE-UPS

JOHN CABOT UNIVERSITY

ROME, ITALY

★ To read more about this school, visit http://petersons.to/johncabotuniversity

The University

John Cabot University (JCU) was founded in 1972 and is the first overseas American university in Italy with regional accreditation by the Middle States Commission of Higher Education. JCU is a four-year liberal arts college following the American system of education with a distinctive European and international character. Located in the historic center of Rome, the University has unparalleled access to history, culture, and the active diplomatic and international communities associated with both the United Nations organizations and embassies to Italy and the Holy See. JCU's international setting, commitment to a serious liberal arts education, and unique relationship with leading multinational corporations, media, cultural, and other international organizations, provides degree-seeking students the academic training and opportunities to participate in exclusive internships and enter directly into demanding careers, or continue their studies at prestigious graduate programs.

The University has a diverse and unique student body, composed of American, Italian, and international degree-seeking students from more than sixty countries. This group is complemented by visiting American students from major universities across the United States. The visiting American students bring to Rome their own regional diversity which complements the European diversity at JCU resulting in a dynamic and engaging student body. JCU's commitment to creating a student community of both four-year degree and visiting students provides degree students with the friendly, close community of a small campus, with the active and energetic networks that come from studying with a larger pool of students from across the United States.

The average class size is 15 students, and there are approximately 100 full- and part-time faculty members with advanced degrees from universities all over the world. Students work closely with professors and receive the individual attention needed to develop their academic talents and abilities. With a student-centered approach to both education and human relationships, the University offers an active learning environment while also teaching the essential ethical standards for responsibility and leadership in today's world. JCU graduates are accepted into a wide array of graduate programs in the United States, United Kingdom, and Italy, such as Columbia University, Johns Hopkins University, London School of Economics, and Università Bocconi.

The University is licensed by the Delaware Department of Education to award its degrees and is authorized by the Italian Ministry of Research and Instruction to operate as an institution of American higher education in Rome. John Cabot University was accredited in 2003 by the Middle States Commission on Higher Education (http://www.msche.org). The University also offers a dual American/Italian Communications degree through the University of Milan, in addition to honors classes in various disciplines.

Location

John Cabot University is located in Rome, Italy, in the picturesque Trastevere neighborhood, just down the river from St. Peter's Basilica and the Vatican and a short walk from the Colosseum and Roman Forum. John Cabot University has two campuses within a 5-minute walk of each other and a residence dorm with 24/7 security, also a 5-minute walk away. The Frank J. Guarini Campus, a former convent, consists of a central main building of three floors and an adjacent wing connected by terraces and courtyards. The original separate chapel now serves as a wing of the library. The property offers students a tranquil atmosphere in which to study and interact, while historic, bustling Rome is just a few steps away. Surrounded by the green gardens of the Accademia dei Lincei (the National Academy of Sciences, of which Galileo was an early member) and next door to the Villa Farnesina of Raphael's famous frescoes, the Guarini Campus is buttressed by the Aurelian Wall of the Roman Empire. The Guarini Campus is approached through the Porta Settimiana, which was built in the third century and later rebuilt by Pope Alexander VI Borgia in 1498, giving it the look it has today. John Cabot also has spacious classrooms and a cafeteria in the Tiber Campus, located along the banks of the famous Tiber River. Both campuses are equipped with Wi-Fi and classrooms furnished with multimedia equipment. The JCU Frohing Library is one of the most impressive English language libraries in Italy. JCU's fine arts and art history classes often meet at famous monuments such as the Colosseum and the Forum, which are within easy reach of JCU. In effect, all of Rome is John Cabot University's campus, and students take advantage of JCU's urban setting, meeting with friends and faculty at local cafés and trattorias as well as in many of the piazzas that are hidden within the small streets of Rome's historic center.

Majors and Degrees

John Cabot University offers the Bachelor of Arts degree in thirteen majors: art history, business administration, classical studies, communications, economics and finance, English literature, history, humanistic studies, international affairs, international business, Italian studies, marketing, and political science. JCU also offers a joint degree in Communications with the University of Milan, allowing students to simultaneously earn an American and European Bachelor of Arts degree. Students may select minors in all of the major areas, as well as in creative writing, entrepreneurship, philosophy, and psychology. John Cabot also offers the Associate of Arts degree in all major fields of study.

Each of these programs is designed to develop the characteristics of the individual student through a unique learning and living experience in a setting rich in history, culture, and geopolitical interaction. All majors are complemented by internship opportunities at the United Nations, museums, and international firms in Rome. JCU's Career Services Center offers support for students' preparation and transition into post-graduate activities, offering over 500 internship and job opportunities each year. JCU's 10,000 member alumni network located across the world provides additional opportunities for graduates to continue their career development through international connections, valued in today's global world.

Academic Programs

Unlike most European university systems, the American system of higher education encourages experimentation and breadth, particularly during the first two years of the university experience. The curricula of the University's programs are, therefore, divided into two basic categories: the general distribution requirements of the first two years of study, which give the student a broad exposure to the basic disciplines of the liberal arts educational experience, and the specific, additional requirements of each degree awarded by the University.

The general distribution and other introductory courses equip the student to select an area of specialization as a degree candidate. Within each degree program, there are specific requirements that must be met by the student who wishes to earn a degree at John Cabot. These requirements include ten to twelve core courses deemed by faculty members to be essential to the discipline of the degree and comparable to the requirements for the same degree at recognized and accredited colleges and universities in the American system of higher education. In addition to the core requirements, other requisites include electives that support the core program and offer opportunities to take courses in other discipline areas of particular interest or need.

The academic year is divided into two semesters of fifteen weeks each, beginning in September and January (see the academic calendar for more details). In one semester, a student normally takes five courses, earning 15 credits in the semester and 30 credits in the year. Two 5-week summer sessions allow students to take one or two additional courses. To earn the Bachelor of Arts degree, a student must complete 120 credits (forty courses); to earn the Associate of Arts degree, a student must complete 60 credits (twenty courses).

John Cabot University accepts up to 60 transfer credits, including the IB diploma, AP exams, UK A-Levels, and other college-level courses.

Special programs include English language preparation for university study (ENLUS), after which students who successfully complete the program may transfer directly into one of JCU's degree programs.

Off-Campus Programs

The Go Global program at JCU offers degree-seeking students the opportunity to study at universities in the United States as well as a variety of other international locations in Europe, Africa, Asia, and the Americas. This enriching opportunity contributes to educational growth and cultural awareness in general and helps prepare students for careers in international fields.

Academic Facilities

The Frohring Library, constructed in 1999, provides the latest in online access to academic journals and indexes and is the University center for research in support of the academic programs as well as a quiet place for study and pleasure reading. The University's four computer laboratories contain desktop computers and Macs equipped with the latest software as well as high-speed printers and a full-color scanner. The University is equipped with high speed WiFi across campus, a studio art facility, a fitness center, a cafeteria, and a digital media lab.

Costs

Tuition for 2015–16 is $23,900 and housing costs begin at $4,800 per semester.

Financial Aid

U.S. citizens attending a college or university outside the United States are eligible to apply for Title IV Federal Financial Aid, including the Parent Loan for Undergraduate Students (PLUS), the Stafford Loan programs, and the U.S. Department of Education's Direct Lending Program. Academic scholarships are awarded each year based on merit and need. Institutional scholarships include the Presidential Scholarships, the Financial Assistance Grant, the Dean's List Scholarship, and the Italian Merit Scholarship. A number of work-study assistantships are available for students who are interested in and capable of assisting the various administrative offices and academic departments of the University.

Faculty

The University has a distinguished faculty of approximately 100 part- and full-time professors from around the world who are actively engaged in research. In addition to teaching, faculty members take part in academic advising; planning and monitoring a student's progress through the academic program; and extracurricular activities, such as field trips, fund-raising events, and lectures and seminars.

Student Government

Student government at John Cabot University contributes significantly to the quality of student life. A Student Senate is elected each year to coordinate activities. During the year, the Student Government sponsors a number of programs, such as the International Student Government Conference, which brings together student leaders from Italy, Europe, and the Middle East. The Student Government works with a faculty adviser and staff adviser in planning social, cultural, intellectual, and sports activities to respond to students' interests and needs. Student Government also sponsors social events to raise funds for charitable activities.

Admission Requirements

Admission is selective. Successful applicants must have a scholastic record demonstrating a commitment to their studies and the ability to succeed at college-level work.

Each applicant is considered as an individual, and no single factor can guarantee acceptance to the University. The previous school's documentation of the applicant's academic ability, motivation, character, and contribution to school life is very important. This information should be reflected in the student's academic record and letters of recommendation. The University does not prescribe a fixed secondary school course of study but considers both the quality and breadth of the student's record. The University is open to all applicants without regard to race, national origin, religion, or gender.

For applicants coming from the U.S. secondary school system, a standard college-preparatory program is expected. For applicants from other national systems, an essential requirement is successful completion of a secondary school program permitting university admission in the respective system. Students holding the Italian Diploma di Maturità, the International Baccalaureate, or other equivalent academic credentials may be granted advanced standing. Results of the SAT or the ACT are required for high school students graduating from an American secondary school.

Applicants whose first language is not English or who did not attend a secondary school where classes were taught in English must demonstrate sufficient preparation in the English language. Standardized test scores, such as the Test of English as a Foreign Language (TOEFL) or the International English Language Testing System (IELTS), are useful in assessing a student's language capability. A minimum score of 550 on the TOEFL (213 on the computer-based exam or 85 on the Internet-based test), a minimum score of 6.5 on the IELTS, or an equivalent passing score on the John Cabot English Proficiency Test are accepted as evidence of sufficient preparation in the English language.

Application and Information

Admissions decisions are based on the review of official transcripts, results of standardized tests, the student's GPA, final examination results, a personal statement, an interview, and letters of recommendation from teachers or professors. Transfer students from another university must be in good academic standing. An application form completed in its entirety must be accompanied by a nonrefundable application fee of $50 or €50. Students may complete the application online or apply through the Common Application. The University has three application deadlines for fall: November 15 (Early Action), March 1 (Regular Decision), and June 1 (Late Decision). The spring application deadline is October 15. Candidates are urged to submit their application and supporting documents as early as possible, as greater scholarship funds may be available.

Students may apply online at https://netcommunity.johncabot.edu/application#.

For additional information, prospective students should contact:

Admissions Office
John Cabot University
Via della Lungara, 233
00165 Rome
Italy
Phone: 655-JCU ROMA
Fax: 39-06-683-2088
E-mail: admissions@johncabot.edu
Website: http://www.johncabot.edu
https://www.facebook.com/JohnCabotUniversity
http://twitter.com/#!/JohnCabotRome
http://instagram.com/johncabotuniversity
http://www.youtube.com/user/JohnCabotU

John Cabot University is located in the picturesque Trastevere neighborhood, just down the river from St. Peter's Basilica and the Vatican and a short walk from the Colosseum and Roman Forum.

COLLEGE CLOSE-UPS

JOHNS HOPKINS UNIVERSITY
Krieger School of Arts and Sciences and Whiting School of Engineering
BALTIMORE, MARYLAND

JOHNS HOPKINS UNIVERSITY

★ To read more about this school, visit http://petersons.to/johnshopkins

COLLEGE CLOSE-UPS

The University

Johns Hopkins University (JHU) was founded in 1876 as the first American research university, committed to the idea that knowledge should be discovered, rather than merely transmitted. Daniel Coit Gilman, the first president of Johns Hopkins, stated that the object of the University was "not so much to impart knowledge as to whet the appetite, exhibit methods, develop powers, strengthen judgment, and invigorate the intellectual and moral forces." Today, Johns Hopkins continues to stress creative scholarship by providing research-oriented education for undergraduates. Students in all disciplines are encouraged to explore intellectual questions and discover new ideas within a supportive environment.

Johns Hopkins students come from all across the United States and abroad. Of the total undergraduate enrollment of approximately 5,000 students, about 49 percent are women and 51 percent are men. All freshmen and sophomores live in campus residence halls. In addition, University-owned housing is available for juniors and seniors and is located directly across from the University on North Charles Street, making the campus community strong. Upperclassmen may also live in private housing or in Greek housing. Johns Hopkins has thirteen fraternities and nine sororities.

The Homewood campus is active and engaged, with many different events such as films, concerts, seminars, and athletic games being offered each week. More than 300 student-run clubs and organizations offer many opportunities to get involved. From the performing arts to hobby-centered clubs, there are many opportunities for students of all interests. The Student Council runs a number of activities, including a popular Spring Fair each year. Men's varsity teams compete in twelve sports. In the fall, men's teams compete in cross-country, football, soccer, and water polo. In the winter, basketball, fencing, swimming, and wrestling are offered. The big sports season at Johns Hopkins is spring, with baseball, lacrosse, tennis, and track and field. The men's and women's lacrosse teams compete at the Division I level, and the men have won forty-four national championships. Women's varsity sports also include basketball, cross-country, fencing, field hockey, soccer, swimming, tennis, track and field, and volleyball. An extensive and popular intramural program is also available. The O'Connor Recreation Center contains basketball and volleyball courts, a running track, racquetball courts, a rock-climbing wall, a weight room, and fitness and aerobic areas.

Location

Johns Hopkins University's Homewood campus is on 140 acres of lush greenery, bounded on all sides by residential areas. Johns Hopkins offers the best of both worlds—the tranquil seclusion of the campus plus the amenities of a big urban environment. Located just 3 miles from the heart of downtown Baltimore, students take advantage of nearby entertainment and academic opportunities, including two university-owned museums and The Baltimore Museum of Art, which is located right next to campus. The theater, symphony, and opera are 10 minutes away, as are Oriole Park at Camden Yards and M&T Bank Stadium. Weekend activities include visiting Baltimore's Inner Harbor, home to the National Aquarium and many other attractions, enjoying an ethnic festival by the water, sailing on the Chesapeake Bay, and hiking around the Maryland countryside. Washington, D.C. is a 50-minute drive by car or a 1-hour train ride.

Majors and Degrees

Majors are offered in Africana studies; anthropology; applied mathematics and statistics; archaeology; behavioral biology; biology; biomedical engineering; biophysics; chemical and biomolecular engineering; chemistry; civil engineering; classics; cognitive science; computer engineering; computer science; earth and planetary sciences; East Asian studies; economics; electrical engineering; engineering mechanics; English; environmental engineering; film and media studies; French; general engineering; geography; German; global environmental change and sustainability; history; history of art; history of science and technology; interdisciplinary studies; international studies; Italian; Latin American studies; materials science and engineering; mathematics; mechanical engineering; medicine, science, & the humanities; molecular and cellular biology; natural sciences; Near Eastern studies; neuroscience; philosophy; physics; political science; psychology; public health studies; Romance languages; sociology; Spanish; and the Writing Seminars. In addition, forty-three minors and various certificates are available.

Accelerated bachelor's/master's degree programs are offered in biophysics, classics, German, global environmental change & sustainability, history, international studies, mathematics, molecular & cellular biology, neuroscience, and public health studies. Accelerated B.S./M.S.E. programs are offered in all engineering departments. A dual-degree program leading to a Bachelor of Arts or Bachelor of Science degree and a Bachelor of Music degree is available in cooperation with the University's Peabody Institute and Conservatory of Music.

Academic Programs

Johns Hopkins has a flexible program, with no core curriculum. While students must fulfill distribution requirements as well as the requirements for their major, they will find the academic freedom to combine majors, programs, and minors to create an educational experience that is unique and meaningful to them. Students in all majors are encouraged to conduct research or engage in hands-on learning through internships, study abroad, and other experiential opportunities.

In most majors, 120 credits are required for graduation. Johns Hopkins has a 4-1-4 calendar.

The University offers the Army ROTC program on campus and the Air Force ROTC program in cooperation with the University of Maryland, College Park.

Off-Campus Programs

Many students study abroad, normally during the junior year. Programs are offered at Johns Hopkins' international center in Bologna, Italy, as well as in Paris, France; Madrid, Spain; Berlin, Germany; and Latin America and through independent study-abroad programs with Johns Hopkins credit. During any given year, there are more than 400 students studying abroad in nearly thirty countries. The University also participates in a cooperative program with other colleges in the Baltimore area. Undergraduates may take courses at the other divisions of Johns Hopkins University, including the Peabody Conservatory, the School of Nursing, the Bloomberg School of Public Health, the Nitze School of Advanced International Studies, the School of Education, the Carey Business School, and the School of Medicine.

Academic Facilities

Two recent additions to campus highlight opportunities for collaborative study and research. Opened in 2012, the Brody Learning Commons is a place for students to gather, study, and work together. The building connects to the Milton S. Eisenhower Library and contains the latest learning technology, including TeamSpot, interactive projectors that allow students to write on walls; Lifecam cameras; and video teleconferencing capabilities, all to support collaborative work. The building, constructed with current student input, features ample natural light and has achieved LEED Silver certification. Another recent addition to campus, the Undergraduate Teaching Labs, were unveiled in 2013. The 105,000-square-foot facility is equipped with the latest lab technology and enables synergistic, cross-disciplinary partnerships and research opportunities. The Milton S. Eisenhower Library on the Homewood campus is part of the University's Sheridan Libraries, which comprise the Milton S. Eisenhower Library, the John Work Garrett Library, the Albert D. Hutzler Undergraduate Reading Room, and the George Peabody Library. Together, these libraries provide one of the most comprehensive learning resources in the world.

The Mattin Student Arts Center contains the Swirnow Theater, a dance studio, music practice rooms, film and digital labs, darkrooms, a café, art studios, and spaces for students to gather. Hodson Hall includes classrooms, a meeting room for the Board of Trustees, the archives of the Hodson Trust, and a 500-seat auditorium, in which every seat is wired to the Internet. Clark Hall houses a state-of-the-art research and teaching facility for biomedical engineering. Charles Commons, a 618-person residential complex and dining facility, also houses the University's two-story Barnes and Noble bookstore.

The Brown Foundation Digital Media Center offers an environment where students can bring artistic inspiration to life using digital tools. It features twelve high-end computers that enable digital and audio composition and editing, animation, virtual painting, and 3-D modeling. All campus buildings are networked with each other and the other Johns Hopkins campuses.

Costs

Costs for 2014–15 were $47,060 for tuition and $14,246 for room and board, and $1,223 for books plus personal expenses. Travel expenses vary.

Financial Aid

Financial aid is based on demonstrated eligibility, as determined by the Free Application for Federal Student Aid (FAFSA) at the time of acceptance. Approximately 44 percent of students receive financial assistance, with the average need-based package for freshmen at $35,000. Annually, JHU offers over $74 million in aid for all undergraduates. Students must reapply for financial aid each year with the FAFSA and the College Scholarship Service (CSS) Financial Aid PROFILE. Johns Hopkins offers several merit-based scholarships. Johns Hopkins also offers Army ROTC scholarships worth up to full tuition. The Baltimore Scholars Program provides full-tuition scholarships to eligible Baltimore City public high school graduates. In addition, several scholarships and grants allow undergraduates to pursue research opportunities, even as freshmen.

Faculty

The University's intellectual reputation is based on the strength of its faculty, of whom 92 percent hold a doctorate. The student-faculty ratio is 12:1, which means that students receive a great deal of personal attention both in and out of the classroom. Professors at Johns Hopkins are enthusiastic about their students' success and teach both undergraduate and graduate students. Johns Hopkins has a large number of notable professors, including 51 American Academy of Arts and Sciences fellows, 4 National Medal of Science winners, 2 Presidential Medal of Freedom winners, 6 MacArthur Fellows, and 1 Pulitzer Prize winner. Faculty members are always accessible to advise and assist students and to work with them on research projects.

Student Government

Johns Hopkins students enjoy the benefits of a well-organized and far-reaching student government, which is led by a dedicated Student Council. The council is composed of elected class representatives and officers, but it relies on the active participation of many students in its numerous committees, boards, and commissions. Through the Student Activities Commission, the University encourages initiative and independence by giving students full responsibility and control of funds for various clubs and organizations.

Admission Requirements

The University looks for students who will take advantage of the resources and support a Johns Hopkins education offers, and who will contribute to the campus community. A student's intellectual interests and accomplishments are of primary importance, and the Admissions Committee carefully examines each applicant's scholastic record, standardized test results, essays, and recommendations from secondary school officials. However, the student's character, intellectual curiosity, seriousness of purpose, and range of extracurricular involvement play the most significant role in application review. The application essays are an important part of how the Admissions Committee learns more about students during the application review process. Two teacher recommendations are required. In addition, the SAT or the ACT with writing test is required. For students submitting SAT scores, Johns Hopkins recommends the submission of SAT Subject Tests, and if submitted, requests results from three tests. Students should consult www.apply.jhu.edu/apply for additional requirements. Every year, the University enrolls a first-year class of approximately 1,300 men and women from all parts of the United States and a number of other countries. In addition, transfer students from other colleges and universities are admitted to the sophomore and junior classes. Advanced-standing credit is granted from college-level work completed at an accredited college or through the Advanced Placement and International Baccalaureate programs.

Application and Information

Johns Hopkins accepts the Common Application and the Universal College Application, both with a Johns Hopkins supplement. The application deadline is usually January 1—additional information is available online at apply.jhu.edu. If applicants consider Johns Hopkins to be their first choice, they may apply under the Early Decision plan. This requires that the application be filed by November 1. Notification is given by April 1 for Regular Decision students and by December 15 for those applying under the Early Decision plan. Students wishing to enroll in the biomedical engineering (BME) program must indicate BME as their first choice of major on their application. First-year students who are BME majors are admitted into the program at the time of their admission to Johns Hopkins University.

Office of Undergraduate Admissions
Johns Hopkins University
Mason Hall
3400 North Charles Street
Baltimore, Maryland 21218-2683
Phone: 410-516-8171
Fax: 410-516-6025
E-mail: gotojhu@jhu.edu
Website: http://apply.jhu.edu

Johns Hopkins students enjoy class in front of Gilman Hall.

KETTERING UNIVERSITY

FLINT, MICHIGAN

Kettering UNIVERSITY

★ To read more about this school, visit http://petersons.to/ketteringuniversity

The University

Founded in 1919, Kettering University is a private university specializing in science, technology, engineering, math (STEM), and business degrees. The school enrolls about 1,900 undergraduate students and offers a 13:1 student-faculty ratio. Most classes have fewer than 20 students and are taught by Ph.D.-level professors, not teaching assistants. This combination of small class size and highly qualified teaching staff ensures students a much more personalized learning experience.

Kettering is a highly acclaimed university with the one of the country's most modern cooperative education and experiential learning programs. Whatever major is chosen, students alternate between study terms and full-time work terms. During study terms, students learn material in small, intense classes taught by University professors. During work terms, students work as paid professionals at corporations related to their studies and interests. Kettering students have done everything from testing ballistic systems for the U.S. government to reengineering crowd management at Disney World. Kettering has the only cooperative education and experiential learning program of its kind where students begin working as early as their freshman year. By graduation from Kettering, students have up to 2½ years of professional experience and impressive resumes. Traditionally, nearly all Kettering students graduate with job offers or grad school acceptances in hand.

Kettering University's cooperative education and experiential learning program pairs hands-on education with real-world experience—all undergraduate students alternate between on-campus study terms and full-time terms of employment with one of more than 500 corporate partners. This unique system of education prepares students to be technology innovators—professionals with cutting-edge skills who are ready to compete in tomorrow's business environment.

Kettering University is accredited by the North Central Association of Colleges and Schools, the Accreditation Board for Engineering and Technology (ABET), and the Association of Collegiate Business Schools and Programs (ACBSP). Kettering is also a member of the National Commission of Cooperative Education (NCCE) and the Association of Independent Technological Universities.

Besides being academically ahead of the game, Kettering students bring a wide range of skills and interests with them to campus. To make sure that students get a life along with an education, Kettering offers more than fifty student organizations, including thirteen fraternities and six sororities, an active student government, a state-of-the-art recreation and fitness facility, and very competitive intramural sports. Recreation facilities include athletic fields, tennis courts, and a recreation center with an Olympic-size, six-lane swimming pool; aerobic fitness rooms; a full line of Nautilus equipment; and basketball, tennis, and racquetball courts.

Kettering also offers Master of Science degree programs in engineering, engineering management, operation management, lean manufacturing and an M.B.A. program. Graduate certificates in global leadership, green business, and supply chain management are also available.

Professional counseling, support services, and health-care services are available. To learn more about Kettering, potential students may visit the University's site on Facebook at http://www.facebook.com/KetteringUniversity or on Twitter at http://www.twitter.com/KetteringU.

Location

Kettering University is located in Flint, Michigan, which is 60 miles west of Lake Huron and 60 miles north of Detroit. Flint has approximately 102,000 residents and a metropolitan area population of 420,000.

Flint is particularly proud of its Cultural Center, which is only 10 minutes from Kettering's campus. Built and endowed entirely by the gifts of private citizens, the Cultural Center includes the Alfred P. Sloan Museum, the Whiting Auditorium (home of the Flint Symphony and host to leading stage shows and entertainers), the Robert T. Longway Planetarium (Michigan's largest and best-equipped sky show facility), the Flint Institute of Arts, the F. A. Bower Theater, the Dort Institute of Music, Mott Community College, and the Flint Public Library. Nearby is the University of Michigan–Flint campus.

The area also offers numerous outdoor and indoor recreational opportunities. Within a few minutes' drive are downhill and cross-country skiing facilities, lakes for the entire range of water sports, a wide selection of good public golf courses, excellent indoor and outdoor skating rinks, and plentiful shopping facilities and restaurants

Majors and Degrees

Kettering University offers a 4½-year, professional cooperative education and experiential learning program with Bachelor of Science degrees in applied biology, applied mathematics, applied physics, biochemistry, bioinformatics, business administration, chemical engineering, chemistry, computer engineering, computer science, electrical engineering, engineering physics, industrial engineering, and mechanical engineering.

Kettering also offers a variety of dual-degree programs and more than fifty minors, specialties, and concentrations, to ensure that students' degrees are custom-fit to their interests and career goals. Examples include computer gaming, system and data security, premed, and prelaw.

Academic Programs

Although each program at Kettering University has its own requirements, 160 credit hours are generally required for graduation. The program involves nine academic terms and nine work terms, two of which are focused on the capstone thesis project, which is a major work project assigned by the employer. Students alternate between eleven-week periods of academic study on the campus in Flint and twelve-week periods of related work experience with their corporate employer. The academic year consists of two 3-month academic terms on campus and two 3-month terms of paid work experience.

Academic Facilities

Kettering University offers some of the best facilities, labs, and educational resources in the world, and students start using them as early as their freshman year. The Crash Safety Center, for example, is the only one of its kind in the nation used in an undergraduate program. The University also offers labs in areas such as fuel-cell research, polymer optimization, machining, acoustics, and more.

Kettering is fully networked and allows 24-hour access to computer resources and the Internet from dorms and labs. A 445-student residence hall and an apartment complex are located on the campus for student housing. The library offers more than 100,000 cataloged volumes and 540 periodicals. And through online resources like Kettering Connect and Blackboard, students can always be in touch with professors and University staff members.

Costs

For 2014–15, tuition costs were $36,980 and room and board cost $7,240.

Kettering now offers fixed-rate tuition, and is the first STEM university in Michigan to do so. For students making normal progress towards their degrees, tuition rates will not change during their course of study, removing some of the guesswork associated with budgeting for college costs.

Financial Aid

Kettering University wants to invest in its students, so it does what it takes to help finance their education through scholarships, loans, and work-study opportunities. More than 98 percent of the students receive some sort of financial aid. Factor in co-op earnings—between $40,000 and $65,000 over the course of the college career—and the new fixed-rate tuition guarantee, and students are looking at one of the best values in education today. In addition, Kettering's Merit Scholarship program awards students with extremely generous scholarship packages. Students should fill out the Free Application for Federal Student Aid (FAFSA) and request a copy of the analysis to be sent to Kettering University. The University works to create a financial aid package for based on those results.

Faculty

Kettering University's 118 full-time faculty members have teaching as their main responsibility. Most professors have industrial experience in addition to academic credentials and maintain contact with industry through consulting, sponsored research, and advising on student thesis projects. More than 85 percent of faculty members hold a doctorate. Because only half of the students are on campus at any one time, class sizes are small, and opportunities for enrichment and extra help are readily available.

Admission Requirements

Admission to Kettering University is competitive and based on scholastic achievement and extracurricular interests, activities, and achievements. Applicants are required to have earned the following: 3 years of English, 2 years algebra, 1 year of geometry, 1 semester of trigonometry, 2 years of lab science (1 must be physics or chemistry; both are recommended). Applicants must submit results of the SAT or ACT (Kettering's ACT code number is 1998 and the SAT code number is 1246).

Most Kettering University students are in the top 10 percent of their graduating class. Kettering University also welcomes students wishing to transfer from other colleges and universities. The transfer alternative is an excellent way to gain admission for students who do not enroll as freshmen.

Application and Information

Students can apply online at http://www.kettering.edu/apply. Students should call 800-955-4464 ext. 7865 for assistance.

Kettering officials review applications and let students know if they have been accepted. Although Kettering accepts and processes applications throughout the year, it is best to apply as early as possible. Once accepted, students receive information on programs and the professional co-op program, which are only available to admitted students. Students should complete the co-op registration (resume) online and pay a $300 tuition deposit (to be credited to the first-semester tuition). The deposit shows that a student is as serious about Kettering as Kettering is about the student and ensures a place in the entering class and eligibility to begin the co-op employment search process.

For more information, prospective students should contact:

Admissions Office
Kettering University
1700 University Avenue
Flint, Michigan 48504
United States
Phone: 810-762-7865
800-955-4464 Ext. 7865 (toll-free in the United States and Canada)
E-mail: admissions@kettering.edu
Website: http://www.kettering.edu/admissions
http://www.facebook.com/KetteringAdmissions
http://www.twitter.com/Ready4Kettering

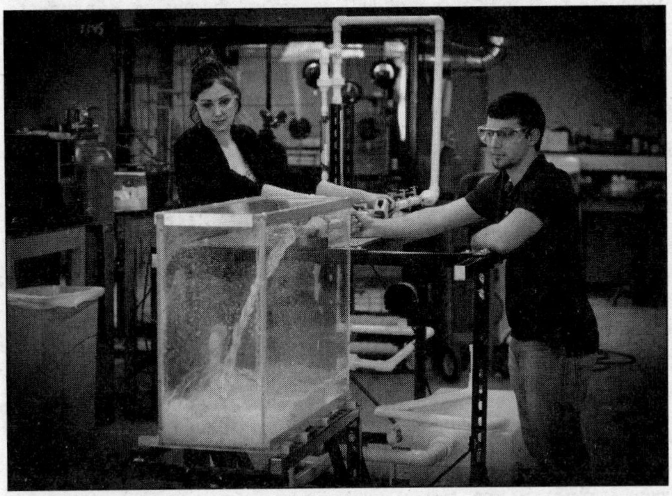

Kettering students major in experience.

COLLEGE CLOSE-UPS

THE KING'S COLLEGE

NEW YORK, NEW YORK

★ To read more about this school, visit http://petersons.to/thekingscollege

THE KING'S COLLEGE
NEW YORK CITY

The University

The King's College, founded in 1938, has been providing high-quality undergraduate education for more than sixty years. King's seeks ambitious students who want to make a difference in the world. The College aims to contribute to American society by producing graduates who have a command of the important intellectual traditions, who think critically about the social and political issues that confront them today, who write with force and flair, who speak with eloquence, and who are eager to exchange ideas in open debate with those who espouse different views.

The King's College educates students to lead with honor as they aspire to make America better. To The King's College, leadership requires facility in complex ideas and the sophistication to guide the strategic institutions of society—government, commerce, law, the media, civil society, education, the arts, and the church. The College teaches a compelling worldview rooted in the Bible and informed by close study of great works of philosophy, political theory, and economics.

King's places a high value on helping students develop their spiritual lives. Students entering the College are at various places in their spiritual journeys, but they grow in significant ways during their time at King's. To that end, King's provides a number of opportunities designed for Christian spiritual growth. Small group Bible studies and discipleship groups occur on campus weekly and are designed to help students meet, encourage, and challenge one another. In addition, King's students are invited to participate in retreats, conferences, and missions projects in New York City, throughout the United States, and around the world.

The King's College has more than 500 undergraduates, 62 percent of whom are women. Five percent are international students representing thirteen countries.

New Student Orientation (NSO) is held each year during the week before fall classes start. NSO delivers a first installment of the College's mission. Students connect with their classmates and King's faculty and staff members. Important College policies and systems are explained. Attendance at NSO is required.

Students at The King's College live in nearby luxury apartments. Approximately 90 percent of the student body lives on campus. King's offers studios and one-bedroom apartments on an as-available basis. Returning and full-time students are given first priority. Housing contracts are for one school year unless otherwise stipulated.

House System: Each new student at the King's College becomes a member of one of ten Houses, each named for a notable leader who embodies the ideals of The King's College.

House involvement shapes virtually every aspect of student experience at The King's College. The Houses are led by students and driven by a mission to support, encourage, and develop. Students build close friendships, join together to explore New York City, and grow spiritually and intellectually. Each House has an Executive Team to welcome, acclimate, and encourage others. Caring teamwork and genuine friendship support personal honor and academic success.

The Houses are the defining dimensions of student life. For upperclassmen and incoming students alike, they are the perpetual centerpieces of life at The King's College. More than any other initiative, the House System fundamentally shapes The King's College experience.

The King's College is accredited by the Middle States Commission on Higher Education. The Middle States Commission on Higher Education is an institutional accrediting agency recognized by the U.S. Secretary of Education and the Council for Higher Education Accreditation.

Location

Located in the heart of the Financial District in Manhattan, The King's College is strategically positioned to take advantage of all New York City has to offer. Home to more than 8 million people, the city has some of the nation's most influential institutions and significant landmarks, including Wall Street, the United Nations, Times Square, Broadway, Madison Square Garden, all four of the major American broadcast television networks (ABC, CBS, Fox, and NBC), the Statue of Liberty, and Ellis Island.

In fact, the City is often referred to as the "capital of the world." Some have described New York City as one of the global economy's major "command centers."

A diverse collection of world-class museums, art galleries, music groups, and performing arts venues converge to make New York City one of the world's most popular tourist destinations. The Metropolitan Museum of Art is one such attraction, with more than 2 million works of art from around the world, representing 5,000 years of history. Just down the street are the iconic Museum of Modern Art (MoMA) and the Guggenheim Museum.

Across town, the Lincoln Center of the Performing Arts offers a myriad of artistic expressions, ranging from ballet to jazz to opera. Employment opportunities in New York City are numerous. Because of its ideal location in the heart of Wall Street, The King's College offers proximity to many work environments, which makes combining both education and professional employment possible. It is no coincidence that The King's College chose New York City as its campus. The city influences and shapes culture: not just in the United States, but also in the entire world.

Majors and Degrees

The King's College offers four degree programs—the Bachelor of Arts in Politics, Philosophy, and Economics (PPE), the Bachelor of Science in Business Management, the Bachelor of Science in Finance, and the Bachelor of Arts in Media, Culture, and the Arts (MCA). Students are required to declare a major in one of these four degree programs before registering for their third semester.

Academic Programs

The King's College was created to prepare students for a particular kind of cultural, political, and economic leadership. Students who aspire to change the key institutions of society for the better need to know the best ideas, the most important arguments, and the most influential traditions. Students must also achieve excellence in the written and the spoken word.

The Common Core is a classical answer to these challenges—it recognizes that some subjects are more fundamental than others, that subjects are best learned in a specific sequence, and that truly advanced courses must be built on secure foundations. The core consists of twenty courses in a particular sequence. Students are required to take the first ten during the freshman year. Altogether, the Common Core accounts for half the courses a student needs to graduate from King's.

Every spring semester, The King's College takes time out from regular classes to spend time on a single intellectual theme of both philosophical depth and current public importance for a campuswide event called Interregnum.

Off-Campus Programs

King's wants all full-time students to be a part of at least one cross-cultural trip during their time in college. By taking advantage of such trips, students are better prepared for Christian leadership in today's world, wherever they live. New York City has incredible opportunities for ministry and service. King's has created strategic opportunities with key partners to provide avenues for students to have an impact. A listing of current opportunities can be found in the Student Handbook.

Academic Facilities

The Rosezella Battles Library, with its distinctive lighting and beautiful furniture, provides a quiet setting conducive to study. The library's collection is particularly strong in a biblical worldview and the integration of faith and learning. The library also houses hundreds of educational videos and dozens of academic journals. Through its catalog on the student web page, the library provides 24-hour access to virtual study halls, reference desks, and reading lounges.

The Battles Library also offers such helpful services as reference assistance, classroom instruction in academic research methods, group tours of nearby public libraries, access to the Internet, and borrowing privileges from other libraries. Students have access to millions of books housed in three New York Public Libraries, all within walking distance of the College as well as library shares with both NYU and Columbia.

The media lab contains a number of computers (each has the Adobe suite), DSLRs, and video cameras for student use. Students have used the media lab to create podcasts, record songs, make videos, and edit photos.

Costs

Tuition, fees, and room costs are $23,135 per semester in 2015–16.

Financial Aid

Nearly all students receive some form of financial aid. In 2015, award packages ranged between $5,000 and $26,500. Assistance is available in the form of scholarships, grants, and loans. Scholarships are awarded based on academic abilities, leadership potential, and character. Grants and loans are awarded based on both merit and financial need. Institutional financial aid awards are made on a yearly basis. The College does participate in federal financial aid programs; therefore, students who file the FAFSA may be eligible for additional federal funds.

Faculty

More than half of the College's faculty members are full-time, and King's student-faculty ratio is 17:1. Business management classes are taught by both full-time faculty members and individuals currently working in the fields they teach. Faculty members include venture capitalists, an award-winning *Wall Street Journal* reporter, a former bank executive, and a Wall Street investment specialist.

Student Government

The goal of the student government is to enable, advance, and serve the College's community, primarily through responsibly distributing available funds to student-led organizations and planning events consistent with the College's vision and goals.

Admission Requirements

Admission to The King's College is based primarily upon previous academic success. Students should have earned a high school diploma, with a minimum of 16 academic units, including 4 of standard English courses, 3 each of mathematics and science, and 2 each in foreign language, social studies, and history. Students who have successfully completed a college-preparatory curriculum that includes at least two years of a modern language are given preference. Those who have attained a GED certificate should contact the admissions office directly regarding admission. Applicants must submit the completed application, official high school transcripts, and official SAT or ACT scores. An interview is required for enrollment.

International Student Requirements: Each year, The King's College welcomes students from all around the world to its NYC campus. King's international students contribute diverse ideas to classroom discussions and enrich the student body. International students should submit an online application (King's does not accept the Common Application) and the following supporting documents to be considered for admission:

- High School Transcript with graduation date, signature of school official, and sealed by the school. The transcript should be translated into English if necessary.
- College Transcripts (if applicable and translated if necessary)
- SAT scores if the student plans to apply for merit-based financial aid
- TOEFL score (83 minimum on the IBT) or IELTS score equivalent
- Completed essay requirement
- Completed phone or Skype entrance interview

The TOEFL/IELTS requirement may be waived only after a phone interview and the student submits the writing requirement. Prospective international students should contact their admissions counselor for details regarding admissions requirements. Merit and need-based financial aid is available to King's international students.

Transfer Student Requirements: Transfer students make up an important part of The King's College student body. Admissions counselors work with transfer students to ensure a smooth transition to the college. Transfer credits are evaluated on a course-by-course level and are carefully reviewed to ensure the maximum amount of credits come through. Students must send the transcript for each issuing institution in order for the credits to be considered. Transfer students should submit the Regular Admissions application via King's website with the following requirements to be considered for admission:

- Below 30 completed credits:
  - SAT or ACT scores
  - High School Transcript
  - College Transcript(s)
  - Entrance Interview (via phone or Skype)
- 30 completed credits or above:
  - College Transcript(s)
  - Entrance Interview (via phone or Skype)
  - Possible writing sample and/or Letter of Recommendation upon request of the admissions counselor

Application and Information

The deadline for early admission is December 15. Regular admissions applications are accepted on a rolling basis. Students who complete their admission application by November 15 receive an admission decision by December 15. A Visit Scholarship is awarded to those students who visit the campus.

For more information, prospective students should contact:

Luke Smith, Director of Admissions
The King's College
56 Broadway
New York, New York 10004
United States
Phone: 212-659-3610
Fax: 877-349-0231
E-mail: admissionsoffice@tkc.edu
Web site: http://www.tkc.edu
Facebook: https://www.facebook.com/TheKingsCollege.NYC
Twitter: @TheKingsCollege

The King's College is strategically positioned to take advantage of all New York City has to offer.

KING'S COLLEGE

WILKES-BARRE, PENNSYLVANIA

★ To read more about this school, visit http://petersons.to/kingscollege

The College

King's College is an independent, coed, four-year Catholic college with 2,100 students. Founded in 1946 by the Holy Cross Priests and Brothers from the University of Notre Dame, King's prepares students for a purposeful life, with an education that integrates the human values inherent in a broadly based liberal arts curriculum. The College encourages the religious, moral, personal, and social development of its students.

In addition to the undergraduate degrees, King's College offers a Master of Science (M.S.) degree in health-care administration, a Master of Education (M.Ed.) degree in reading or curriculum and instruction, and a five-year physician assistant studies program leading to a master's degree.

Academic advising begins before students enroll and continues with an innovative program of career development across the curriculum. King's Academic Skills Center includes a nationally certified tutoring program and a faculty-staffed writing center. More than 70 percent of students who attend King's graduate from the College, which is well above the national average, and 99 percent are employed or attend graduate school within six months of graduation.

The quaint urban campus comprises eight city blocks and features many buildings and centers that house King's numerous academic programs, including the Charles E. and Mary Parente Life Sciences Center, the Mulligan Physical Sciences Center, and the William G. McGowan School of Business. The 15-acre campus also includes Monarch Court; the Sheehy-Farmer Campus Center, which offers an art gallery, an outdoor waterfall and patio, a student restaurant, and marketplace dining; the J. Carroll McCormick Campus Ministry Center; and the William S. Scandlon Physical Education Center, which features a 3,200-seat basketball arena, wrestling facilities, racquetball and handball courts, an Olympic-size swimming pool, a wellness center, and a state-of-the-art sports medicine facility. In addition, an expansion of the Scandlon Center was recently completed, which includes three multipurpose courts as well as new offices, meeting rooms, and additional sports medicine facilities.

The new King's on the Square facility is a vibrant and dynamic center for learning and living in the heart of downtown Wilkes-Barre. King's on the Square is home to a number of in-demand programs, including physician assistant studies, athletic training, and exercise science. The new center also includes attractive and safe student residences that bring students in direct contact with the downtown environment; a community-centered art and cultural display center; and a casual restaurant for students, faculty, staff, and the downtown community. King's on the Square has quickly established itself as a safe, productive, and bustling downtown anchor.

The six-story administration and science buildings form a unit that houses the College's newly renovated theater, the Susquehanna Room dining hall and coffee bar, administrative offices, science laboratories, and classrooms. Residence halls have cable television, wireless Internet access, and 24-hour computer labs. Many of King's athletic teams train and compete just 2 miles from campus at the Robert L. Betzler Athletic Complex, a 33.5-acre athletic facility that includes McCarthy Stadium; a field house; and fields for baseball, softball, men's and women's soccer, football, and field hockey.

There are fifty student organizations that provide King's students with the opportunity to explore interests outside of the classroom. King's has 19 NCAA Division III teams including men's baseball, basketball, football, golf, lacrosse, soccer, swimming, tennis, and wrestling; women's basketball, field hockey, lacrosse, soccer, softball, swimming, tennis, and volleyball; and coed cross-country. The College offers cheerleading, ice hockey, and track and field as club sports. Intramural sports include basketball, flag football, indoor soccer, racquetball, and dodgeball. Other cocurricular activities include: academic clubs in almost every department, the King's Players (theater), Cantores Christi Regis (choir), Campus Ministry, the Experiencing the Arts Series, *The Crown* (student newspaper), the *Regis* (yearbook), and the *SCOP* (literary magazine).

Location

The King's campus is located in a residential area near downtown Wilkes-Barre, Pennsylvania, a city of approximately 50,000 on the banks of the Susquehanna River. A growing city, Wilkes-Barre has developed both economically and culturally, yet it has avoided many typical urban problems. Shopping malls, multiplex theaters, a brand new riverfront park, art galleries, and restaurants are nearby. Two blocks from King's is the F. M. Kirby Center, which has hosted national performances, music groups, traveling theater, and more. National recording acts regularly perform in nearby venues.

King's is a short drive from several ski resorts, state parks, and major lakes where students can participate in many seasonal outdoor activities. Students can also enjoy professional sports action including the New York Yankees' AAA baseball team, the Pocono International Raceway which hosts two NASCAR races each season, and the Pittsburgh Penguins' minor-league ice hockey team. The Mohegan Sun Arena is the host to many concerts and events, and is the site of the King's commencement. The campus is close to major metropolitan areas including New York City and Philadelphia (each a 2½-hour drive); Washington, D.C., and the attractions of New England are within a 4-hour drive.

Majors and Degrees

King's awards the Master of Science, Master of Education, Bachelor of Arts, Bachelor of Science, Associate of Arts, and Associate of Science degrees. The College's thirty-six major programs are offered in the arts and sciences and the William G. McGowan School of Business, which is accredited by AACSB International—The Association to Advance Collegiate Schools of Business.

Arts and sciences include the humanities and social sciences division (computers and information systems, criminal justice, economics, English–literature, English–professional writing, French, history, mass communications, philosophy, political science, psychology, sociology, Spanish, theater, and theology); the education division, which is accredited by NCATE (preschool–grade 4, secondary certification, and special education); the science division (biology, chemistry, computer science, engineering, environmental science, environmental studies, general science, mathematics, neuroscience, and physics); and the allied health division (clinical lab science, physician assistant studies, exercise science, and athletics training education/sports medicine accredited by CAAHEP). Available majors in the William G. McGowan School of Business are accounting, finance, human resources management, international business, management, and marketing. King's offers pre-professional programs in chiropractic, dentistry, law, medicine, optometry, pharmacy, and veterinary science. The engineering program is a 3+2 dual-degree program with the University of Notre Dame, in which students spend three years at King's and then two years at Notre Dame.

Academic Programs

The general education program at King's is recognized nationwide by its peers. King's is included in *Barron's Best Buys in College Education* and has been honored in nineteen consecutive issues of *U.S. News & World Report's Best Colleges Guide.* The College was also recognized by the John Templeton Foundation Honor Roll for Character-Building Colleges, the Forbes/CCAP list of America's best colleges, and is one of sixteen institutions nationwide named to the Greater Expectations initiative.

The honors program offers highly motivated students the challenge of learning in discussion-centered courses that explore distinctive subject matter with exciting and innovative approaches. Twenty honor societies encourage students to excel in their chosen fields and recognize students for their academic distinction; members are honored each year at the All-College Honors Convocation. Science students receive hands-on lab training much earlier than students at other institutions and work together with faculty members on real-world research projects.

Off-Campus Programs

Experiential learning (via internships) is available in conjunction with almost every major. King's students have interned at CNN, the New York Stock Exchange, PricewaterhouseCoopers, the U.S. House of Representatives, U.S. Senators' offices, the U.S. Department of Energy, Walt Disney World, and Xerox Corporation, among other places. Every year, students are placed with local, regional, and national companies around the globe.

Through the study-abroad program many of King's students have studied on campuses throughout Europe, Thailand, China, Australia, and various other countries.

Academic Facilities

King's facilities include the 51,000-square-foot, three-story D. Leonard Corgan Library, which contains several study rooms, a 160,000-volume collection, and a computerized catalog, which students can access from their home or residence hall. The library provides full-text databases from every computer on campus, and access to college and research libraries throughout the United States. Students and faculty members also have direct access to more than 1 million volumes through the local library cooperative (NEPBC).

King's features computer labs with more than 440 PCs, 24-hour labs in residence halls, e-mail accounts for all students, computerized library databases, multimedia classrooms with a variety of instructional aids, course discussions on Moodle, distance-learning facilities for teleconferencing, and cross-registration with area colleges that enables students to take courses complementary to their majors.

The Charles E. and Mary Parente Life Sciences Center, which contains a molecular biology laboratory and a genomics center, includes computer facilities, instrumentation rooms, a rooftop greenhouse, and environmental chambers. The Mulligan Physical Sciences Center includes modern research laboratories, computer facilities, and state-of-the-art instrumentation used for molecular identification. In 2014, the five-year physician assistant studies program (master's degree) will expand in size and scope and will occupy a brand new facility. The new King's on the Square facility includes a state-of-the-art gross anatomy lab, four clinical practice labs, and ten examination rooms.

Costs

For the 2014–15 academic year, tuition for full-time students was $31,816. Room and board totaled $11,658.

Financial Aid

King's assists all qualified students through its financial aid programs. Currently, more than 97 percent of King's students receive financial aid in the form of scholarships, grants, work-study, or loans. In 2014, the average financial aid award was $23,472, taking a significant amount of the financial obligation away from the student and their family. The average net cost of tuition, room, and board for 2014–15 was $20,322. Aid is awarded on the basis of demonstrated financial need, the difference between the total cost of education and the expected family contribution.

In addition to financial aid programs, installment payment plans are available, offering students and/or their families the ability to make monthly payments throughout the academic year. Students who wish to be considered for financial aid must fill out the Free Application for Federal Student Aid (FAFSA) and the King's College Financial Aid Application. The preferred filing deadline for new freshmen is March 1.

Faculty

King's College has 154 full-time and 89 part-time faculty members. Eighty-five percent of the full-time faculty members have a Ph.D. or an equivalent terminal degree. Graduate assistants do not teach courses. The student-faculty ratio is 12:1.

Student Government

The student government coordinates and participates in numerous activities for both the student body and the surrounding community. It regularly holds open forums for students and senior administrators at the College, coordinates informal socials for the students with the College president, and makes presentations at each meeting of the Board of Directors. In addition, the student government sponsors events that foster awareness for social and justice issues and a celebration of cultural diversity.

Admission Requirements

King's encourages applications from qualified high school students and those who wish to transfer from another institution. To be considered for admission, students must be prepared to successfully pursue a program of study at the College, as evidenced by the quality of previous academic and extracurricular performance, the recommendation of school officials and character references, and the student's display of personal promise, maturity, and motivation. King's admits students of any race, sex, color, creed, or national or ethnic origin.

Admission decisions are made for both high school students and transfer students with the understanding that all current courses and examinations will be completed satisfactorily. Candidates should complete 4 years of mathematics (through trigonometry or precalculus). One year each of high school chemistry, biology, and physics is also strongly recommended.

The Office of Admission offers two methods for candidates to apply for admission: the SAT/ACT Traditional Choice and the Test Optional Choice. Applicants are required to state their preference prior to the application review, and the decision is nonreversible. Students who select the SAT/ACT Traditional Choice must submit a completed application, official high school transcripts, SAT or ACT scores, guidance counselor recommendation, an essay, and the $30 application fee, which is waived if students apply online. Students who choose the Test Optional Choice must submit a completed application, official high school transcripts, an official graded writing sample from either their junior or senior year—submitted and notarized by the high school guidance office, guidance counselor recommendation, an essay, and the $30 application fee, which is waived if students apply online.

Application and Information

Applicants should forward a completed application and the $30 fee to the Office of Admission or apply online at www.kings.edu in order to waive the application fee. Secondary and postsecondary (if applicable) transcripts must be sent. Admission decisions are not made until all credentials are received. King's subscribes to a rolling admission policy. Decisions are announced within two weeks from the date of application. Upon notification of acceptance, a $200 nonrefundable deposit is requested to reserve a place in the class. The deposit deadline is May 1 but may be extended upon request. To schedule an interview, obtain an application form, or for more information, students should contact:

Office of Admission
King's College
133 North River Street
Wilkes-Barre, Pennsylvania 18711
Phone: 570-208-5858
888-KINGS-PA (toll-free)
E-mail: admissions@kings.edu
Website: http://www.kings.edu
http://www.facebook.com/kingscollegepa
http://twitter.com/KingsCollege_PA

KUTZTOWN UNIVERSITY OF PENNSYLVANIA

KUTZTOWN, PENNSYLVANIA

★ To read more about this school, visit http://petersons.to/kutztownuniversity

KUTZTOWN UNIVERSITY

The University

The Kutztown University (KU) community is defined by its bright, ambitious students; brilliant, dedicated faculty; and a diverse, vibrant learning atmosphere.

Kutztown University is a four-year public institution located 30 minutes from Allentown and Reading, 1½ hours from Philadelphia, and 2 hours from New York City. Founded in 1866, KU has nearly 9,500 undergraduate and graduate students, more than 100 areas of study, 200 student organizations, and 21 NCAA Division II athletic programs—all housed on a beautiful 289-acre campus.

Location

The University is located in a beautiful, rural Pennsylvania Dutch community, midway between the cities of Allentown and Reading. Both cities are a short drive from the campus and have major shopping and recreational facilities available. Kutztown borough, an easy walk from the campus, has ample stores and shops to meet the needs of students.

Majors and Degrees

Students can choose from over 100 majors and minors, many in today's fastest-growing fields, such as biochemistry, education, marketing, communication design, criminal justice, software development, and more.

College of Business: Programs are available in accounting, finance, management, marketing, and sports management and leadership development. Students can learn the fundamentals of business while taking advantage of programming and internship opportunities through KU's Entrepreneurial Leadership Center.

College of Education: KU offers programs in elementary and secondary education, instructional technology, and special education. KU's Special Education/Visual Impairment program and clinically based Reading program are among only three programs of this nature in the country. New this year is an Autism Certificate program.

College of Liberal Arts and Sciences: Majors include anthropology, biological sciences, chemistry, computer science, criminal justice, English, environmental science, geography, geology, German, history, marine science, mathematics, philosophy, physics, political science, professional writing, public administration, social work, sociology, and Spanish. Recent highlights from the College of Liberal Arts and Sciences include a National Science Foundation grant for environmental and marine science scholarships and programs, significant undergraduate research, and new and exciting internships.

College of Visual and Performing Arts: Programs in this college include art education, communication design, communication studies, crafts, an Emmy Award–winning electronic media program, music, music education, and studio art. Visual arts and music programs are housed in the Sharadin Arts Building and the recently renovated Schaeffer Auditorium. Students benefit from KU's proximity to vibrant arts communities in Philadelphia, New York City, Baltimore, and Washington, D.C.

Off-Campus Programs

Internships are designed to provide students with one semester of practical experience in their specialty. Students majoring in education spend one semester of their senior year student teaching in area schools under the guidance of an experienced teacher. Additional teaching field experiences are available in the junior year during the professional semester.

As an enhancement to course work, KU students have the opportunity to study away from campus, both nationally and internationally, through more than 150 student exchange programs.

Through a consortium arrangement with other colleges and universities in three states, Kutztown participates in the operation of a marine science research center at Wallops Island, Virginia, which has laboratories, research equipment, and coastal research ships. Through this facility, students in marine science classes are able to gain first-hand knowledge of the ocean environment.

Costs

In 2014–15, tuition was $6,820 for Pennsylvania residents and $17,050 for out-of-state residents. The average cost of room and board for an incoming freshman was $8,430, and fees were $2,013. Books, travel expenses, and other supplies are additional.

Financial Aid

KU believes that no student who is eligible to enroll at the University should be denied the opportunity for an education solely due to lack of funds. Financial assistance is available through grants, private and institutional scholarships, military officer training programs, on-campus part-time employment, and loans. Information describing financial aid opportunities is available on the KU website. Any student wishing to investigate financial aid opportunities should do so when applying for admission, as most programs have application deadlines. The only form needed to apply for financial aid is the FAFSA. KU has a priority filing date of March 1. Pennsylvania residents should file the FAFSA no later than May 1 to qualify for Pennsylvania state grants.

Faculty

Although many professors at KU are involved in important research and are leaders in their fields, their primary interest is in the classroom. The University has more than 370 full-time instructors and a f20:1 student-faculty ratio. The average class size is 29. Approximately 90 percent of the faculty members hold terminal degrees in their field of study. Upon enrollment in the University, each student is assigned a faculty adviser to help plan his or her academic career. Many faculty members are active in campus groups as members or advisers, creating a close and friendly working relationship with students.

Student Government

All students are members of the Student Government Association and elect representatives who form the Student Government Board (SGB). Students at Kutztown are regarded as mature individuals who can be, in great measure, responsible for the control of their own environment. For that reason, the SGB exercises considerable discretion in coordinating and funding student organizations. Most University committees, including the Council of Trustees, have student members with full voting rights.

Admission Requirements

The main criteria for admission are achievement as indicated on scholastic records and standardized tests. Candidates must have graduated from an approved secondary school or demonstrate equivalent preparation. Scores on either the SAT or the ACT are required and are regarded as evidence of ability to do university-level work. It is the responsibility of the applicant to request that his or her scores be forwarded to the Office of Admissions. Either test should be taken no later than the fall of the senior year; sitting for these exams during the junior year is encouraged. For admission to special programs, the candidate may be required to supply additional evidence of ability to succeed in the given field. Specific requirements and instructions are included in the admission application materials.

Application and Information

The completed application and all other required materials must be submitted to the Office of Admissions. No action is taken by the Admission Committee until all materials have been submitted. For additional information and application forms, students should contact:

Nancy Wunderly
Director of Admissions
Kutztown University of Pennsylvania
Kutztown, Pennsylvania 19530
United States
Phone: 610-683-4060
E-mail: admissions@kutztown.edu
Website: http://www.kutztown.edu/admissions
https://www.facebook.com/KUAdmissions
https://twitter.com/Admissions_KU

Old Main Clock Tower at Kutztown University.

LAFAYETTE COLLEGE
EASTON, PENNSYLVANIA

LAFAYETTE COLLEGE

The College

Classified as one of the nation's most academically competitive colleges, Lafayette focuses exclusively on undergraduates, offering a wide variety of academic choices in the humanities, social sciences, natural sciences, and engineering. The College is committed to providing the best education for men and women who possess the ability to benefit from the Lafayette experience, and the capacity to contribute to a vibrant campus community with no graduate programs and no graduate students.

The breadth and depth of Lafayette's curriculum are unusual and unexpected in a college of its size. One of just a few undergraduate colleges with fully accredited programs in engineering, Lafayette enrolls 2,400 students from more than forty U.S. states and territories, and more than fifty other countries. The College draws strength from the diversity of its students, who represent a wide range of backgrounds, special talents, and aspirations.

Lafayette is a residential college where learning continues outside the classroom. Living in college housing is guaranteed and required for all four years. About 95 percent of students live in College-owned residence halls, apartments, special-interest houses, fraternities, or sororities. An array of student organizations, arts and cultural events, social opportunities, NCAA Division I varsity athletics, and intramural sports programs are available to all students.

Recent trends indicate that approximately two thirds of Lafayette graduates obtain a graduate or professional degree. A large and growing number obtain practical experience through employment, and then undertake full-time study for an advanced degree, often with an employer's financial support. Others continue academic pursuits on a part-time basis. Strong internship and externship programs with alumni and parent mentors help pave the way to fulfilling careers for Lafayette graduates.

Location

Lafayette is located in a picturesque setting atop a hill overlooking the Delaware and Lehigh rivers and the progressive city of Easton, population 30,000, located 70 miles from New York City, and 60 miles from Philadelphia.

Easton, Allentown, and Bethlehem are the principal cities of the Lehigh Valley, Pennsylvania's third-largest metropolitan area, which has a population of about 800,000.

Shops, restaurants, and other business establishments that serve the needs of Lafayette students are located adjacent to the campus, and in nearby downtown Easton. Beyond Easton to the west and north are great ski slopes, top fishing rivers, and challenging hiking trails.

Majors and Degrees

Lafayette awards the Bachelor of Science (B.S.) degree in biochemistry, biology, chemical engineering, chemistry, civil engineering, computer science, electrical and computer engineering, environmental science, geology, mathematics, mechanical engineering, neuroscience, physics, and psychology.

The Bachelor of Arts (A.B.) degree is awarded with the following majors: Africana studies, American studies, anthropology and sociology, art, Asian studies, biochemistry, biology, chemistry, computer science, economics, engineering studies, English, environmental studies, film and media studies, French, geology, German, government and law, government and law and foreign language, history, international affairs, mathematics, mathematics-economics, music, philosophy, physics, policy studies, psychology, religion and politics, religious studies, Russian and East European studies, Spanish, theater, and women's and gender studies. Minors are offered in many of these fields.

In addition, Lafayette offers a two-degree program leading to a B.S. in one of four engineering disciplines and an A.B. in international studies.

Academic Programs

High-level research, rigorous small-class discussion, field experiences, community-based learning projects, and global studies—these elements of a Lafayette education attract active and engaged learners. Students from different majors and faculty members work together to solve real-world problems. This results in the high-impact learning for which Lafayette is known, leading to a distinct career advantage where 94 percent or more of recent graduating classes are employed, continuing their education, taking part in internships, or engaged in volunteer work within six months of graduation.

Interdisciplinary minor programs are offered in aging studies; architectural studies; biotechnology/bioengineering; classical civilization; computational methods; environmental science; health and life sciences; health care and society; Italian studies; Jewish studies; Latin American and Caribbean studies; medieval, Renaissance, and early modern studies; Russian; and writing.

Staff in the Office of Advising and Co-Curricular Programs mentor students in their academic development, provide support for students interested in careers in law and the health professions, and work with students to pursue prestigious undergraduate and post-graduate fellowships and awards.

The academic year is divided into two semesters with a January interim session, where courses are offered on and off campus, including study overseas.

Off-Campus Programs

Lafayette recognizes that we live in an increasingly complex and interrelated global environment, and connecting the classroom to the world outside our walls is at the core of the College's mission. Off-campus study combines academic rigor with experiential learning through immersion in an international or culturally significant domestic setting.

Semester-long programs led by Lafayette professors are offered at Jacobs University Bremen; Saint Louis University in Madrid; Goldsmith's College at the University of London; and the Universidad Veritas in Costa Rica. Lafayette students also choose from semester-long and yearlong programs, coordinated by affiliated institutions, in many countries.

During interim session, Lafayette faculty lead distinctive three-week courses around the world. Courses have been offered in Australia, China, East Africa, England, Guatemala, India, Italy, Japan, New Zealand, Russia, Scandinavia, Spain, South Africa, Thailand, Turkey, and the West Indies, among many other locations.

Academic Facilities

With an endowment per student that ranks among the top private colleges and universities nationally, the College has invested more than $200 million in new academic, residential, and recreational facilities recently, including a center for global studies, a science center, a center for psychology and neuroscience, a center for the visual arts, and a center for intramural and recreational sports. Improvements also include an expansion and transformation of the main library, a thorough modernization of the engineering complex, and new and renovated residence halls and athletic facilities. An expansion of the downtown arts campus is under way to include new facilities for theater and for film and media studies.

Costs

The tuition for 2015–16 is $46,590. Additional costs include a standard room fee of $8,610, board fee of $5,310 (twenty meals/week), activity/technology fee of $420, matriculation fee of $750 (for new students only), and an estimated $2,000 for books, travel, and miscellaneous expenses.

Financial Aid

An education that is personal—featuring faculty time with students on-task in the classroom and in student-faculty research—and emphasizes teams of students learning together across different majors will always be more costly to deliver than the traditional large, lecture-based classes taught by graduate students at large public or private research universities.

Lafayette is committed to partnering with students of all financial backgrounds to make its active, globally connected education affordable. Lafayette awarded over $40 million in College-funded grants and scholarships in 2014–15 and has budgeted over $41 million for 2015–16. Over half of the College's students are eligible for financial assistance and receive the aid they need to make a Lafayette education possible through grants, scholarships, loans, and/or work-study. Accepted students with demonstrated need whose total family earnings are less than $100,000 will realize a financial aid award that meets that need with scholarship, grant, work-study, and either no loan or a reduced loan.

Lafayette recognizes its most outstanding applicants with merit-based awards named for the Marquis de Lafayette. The Marquis Awards are offered to approximately 13 percent of our accepted applicants each year. The Marquis Scholarship is valued at $24,000 per year and the Marquis Fellowship is valued at $40,000 per year. Additional benefits include a stipend of $4,000 for one faculty-led off-campus course during an interim session. Marquis Fellows and Marquis Scholars seeking financial aid and whose demonstrated need exceeds the amount of their fellowship or scholarship award will receive a financial aid award, inclusive of the fellowship or scholarship, up to demonstrated need.

Detailed information regarding financial assistance is available from the Office of Student Financial Aid, Lafayette College, Easton, Pennsylvania 18042-1777 (phone: 610-330-5055).

Faculty

Lafayette's student-to-faculty ratio is 10:1. Ninety-six percent of the College's 224 full-time faculty members hold the doctorate or other terminal degree in their field. All faculty members—full professors and heads of departments as well as junior faculty members—teach courses and serve as academic advisers to students. Many have earned wide recognition for their research and scholarship and won awards for superior teaching. Grants from public and private agencies and foundations are supporting innovative approaches to teaching and learning.

Admission Requirements

Lafayette seeks to enroll students who have a compelling blend of intellectual dynamism, extra- and co-curricular talent, and meaningful experiences that will enhance life and learning for all members of the connected college community. The College seeks to enroll students from diverse backgrounds—from different cultures and ethnicities, from different parts of the country and the world, and from across the socioeconomic spectrum. The Admissions Office selects students with a wide variety of academic and extracurricular interests and talents, using a holistic evaluation process that employs no formulas. The most important aspect of the College's evaluation of applicants' ability to succeed academically at Lafayette is a review of the quality of the courses taken in high school and performance in those courses.

Applicants are required to submit scores from either the SAT reasoning test or ACT (with writing). SAT subject test results are recommended but not required. Prospective math, science, or engineering majors are encouraged to take subject tests in mathematics and science.

A campus interview or regional interview with an alumni representative is strongly encouraged, especially for applicants seeking merit scholarships.

Application and Information

The application deadline is January 15. Applicants are notified about admission decisions on or about April 1. May 1 is the National Candidate Reply Date, by which admitted students must reply to the College's offer of admission.

Students who have decided that Lafayette is their first choice may request consideration of their applications under early decision. The deadline for early decision I applications is November 15, with notification by December 15.

Applicants who decide that Lafayette is their first choice after November 15 may submit an early decision II application until January 15 or convert a regular decision application to early decision II until February 1. In these cases, notification will be made by February 15.

To be considered for early decision admission, students must sign and submit the early decision plan agreement. Applicants admitted under early decision must withdraw their applications to other institutions.

Office of Admissions
Lafayette College
Easton, Pennsylvania 18042-1770
Phone: 610-330-5100
Website: http://www.lafayette.edu

A view of Lafayette College's campus.

LEBANON VALLEY COLLEGE

ANNVILLE, PENNSYLVANIA

Lebanon Valley College

★ To read more about this school, visit http://petersons.to/lebanonvalleycollege

The College

These are exciting times at Lebanon Valley College as faculty and students advance programs and research that improve lives around the world. Located near Hershey in central Pennsylvania, Lebanon Valley College (LVC) is distinguished by innovative, high-impact, customizable learning experiences, and generous academic scholarships.

The College provides broad and challenging curriculum offerings that include in-demand, specialized majors, supported by technology with global reach. LVC's culture is one of warm, respectful, and supportive relationships that promote personal growth through creative risk taking. There is a College-wide commitment to community outreach.

LVC graduates are accomplished, confident citizens and leaders well prepared to make meaningful contributions to their professions and communities; the most recent governor of Pennsylvania is a graduate.

Founded in 1866, LVC was the first college east of the Alleghenies to offer higher education to men and women. Now, 149 years later, the College remains an innovative leader—enjoying the number three ranking on *U.S. News & World Report*'s Great Schools, Great Prices list, and ranking among the top baccalaureate colleges in its category for the twenty-first consecutive year. Lebanon Valley College is well-known for awarding generous academic scholarships to those whose high school records demonstrate a commitment to achievement. The College seeks the best students and rewards their hard work with scholarships and numerous additional financial support opportunities.

Lebanon Valley aims to educate its nearly 1,600 students to become people of broad vision, capable of making informed decisions, and prepared for a life of service to others. To that end, the College provides an education that imparts the knowledge, skills, and values necessary to live and work in a changing, diverse, and fragile world. In the process, they develop the desire and ability to think deeply, ask critical questions, solve complex problems, and communicate effectively, preparing themselves to be competitive and flexible in whatever career they pursue or challenge they encounter.

Lebanon Valley College professors strive to continue the College's proud tradition of inspired teaching with the dedication and commitment to community service that has long been an LVC hallmark. A supportive, sophisticated community and an 11:1 student-faculty ratio ensure that students have direct access to the men and women who teach and guide them; relationships beyond the classroom are common.

One of the most significant aspects of teaching and learning at LVC is inclusive research in the sciences and humanities. Each summer, dozens of LVC students work alongside their professors as funded research assistants, contributing to important discoveries while gaining invaluable skills and experiences. Many LVC students co-author articles in scientific or other academic journals or present their work at professional conferences while they are still in college. This experiential learning supports independent student research, internships, and student-faculty research/scholarly work across all disciplines, and provides opportunities seldom found at the undergraduate level.

LVC's strong advising, straightforward requirements, and outstanding student support services mean that the majority of students are able to graduate in four years. If a student is not able to earn the LVC bachelor's degree in four years because of a course scheduling problem, the College will cover the costs of any additional course work the student needs.

LVC's forty-eight buildings support every aspect of college life. The College's twenty-seven student residences include four apartment-style halls. Academic buildings feature enhanced classrooms with the latest technology. Two student centers, one of which recently benefitted from a $13.3-million renovation, support learning and development outside the traditional classroom, group study, and extracurricular interests. Students enjoy a recreational sports center; a varsity gymnasium; a newly completed all-sports turf stadium; soccer, baseball, and softball parks; and a state-of-the-art physical therapy facility.

LVC's Center for Career Development staff helps students research careers and establish contacts with potential employers, and offers seminars on résumé writing and interviewing skills. The Career Connections alumni database provides students direct access to successful alumni in their fields—men and women who have volunteered to mentor, advise, or otherwise assist LVC students or recent graduates. Eighty-six percent of 2013 graduates who responded to an annual survey were either employed full-time or attending graduate school within six months of graduation

Location

Annville is a town of approximately 5,000 residents located just 10 minutes east of Hershey and within a 2- to 3-hour drive of Philadelphia, Baltimore, New York, and Washington, D.C. Nestled in a beautiful valley, the College is located on a 357-acre site. A wide variety of internship opportunities, potential employment options, cultural events, and other activities are available on campus and within the surrounding communities.

Majors and Degrees

The College confers five baccalaureate degrees. The Bachelor of Arts is available in art and art history, criminal justice, economics, English, French, German, global studies, historical communications, history, music, music business, philosophy, politics, religion, sociology, Spanish, and certain self-designed majors.

The Bachelor of Science is available in accounting, actuarial science, athletic training, biochemistry and molecular biology, biology, business administration, chemistry, computer science, cooperative engineering, digital communications, early childhood education, early childhood/special education, exercise science, healthcare management, mathematics, music education, physics, psychobiology, psychology, and certain self-designed majors.

The Bachelor of Science in Chemistry, Bachelor of Science in Medical Technology, and Bachelor of Music (with an emphasis in music recording technology) are also available.

Minors, concentrations, and pre-professional programs are offered in American studies, art history, business technology, communications (digital and English), creative writing, dentistry, design, family studies, law, law and society, medicine, ministry, pharmacy, programming, studio art, theater, user experience, veterinary medicine, videography, and world classics.

Lebanon Valley offers master's degree programs in athletic training, business, music education, and science education; and a doctoral program in physical therapy.

Academic Programs

Lebanon Valley has long been known for the strength of its academic programs and the achievement of its faculty members and alumni. The sciences are a particular strength, with well-equipped and up-to-date laboratories. The College has won research grants from the National Science Foundation, National Institutes of Health, Dow, Exxon, and Merck/AAAS.

Other particularly well-known and respected programs include actuarial science (LVC graduates are employed by more than fifty firms nationwide), physical therapy (which offers a six-year doctoral program), music (the music recording technology major is especially popular), business (which provides the fundamentals of accounting and business administration within a strong liberal arts context), and education (alumni of which are in high demand throughout the region).

Each student's academic program is complemented by a wide range of extracurricular activities. The College's more than ninety clubs, organizations, and other student-run initiatives provide ample opportunities for leadership. Many students choose to participate in community outreach, often by volunteering in the surrounding communities. More than 30 percent of students play on one or more of LVC's twenty-four intercollegiate athletics teams, and many more participate in club or intramural sports. All students benefit from extensive campus programming that includes guest lectures, concerts, conferences, symposia, and a variety of cultural activities.

Off-Campus Programs

Students are encouraged to take advantage of numerous off-campus study opportunities offered by the College. Options abroad include programs in Argentina, Australia, China, Dominican Republic, England, France, Germany, Greece, Italy, New Zealand, Northern Ireland, and Spain, or several short-term, faculty-led options. Internship-based programs in Washington, D.C., and Philadelphia are also popular options. A student's scholarship funding and financial aid can be transferred to most of the programs, making study abroad available to most students, regardless of their family's financial situation.

Internships are another important aspect of experience-based learning at LVC. With guidance from professors and help from professional counselors, students in every major find internship placements, gain professional experiences, and build confidence, all of which helps when it comes time to apply for jobs.

Academic Facilities

Lebanon Valley's tree-lined walkways and beautiful gardens provide the perfect backdrop for academic and social facilities. The College's new $2.5 million Lebegern Learning Commons is a facility equipped with the latest in technology that serves as a gathering place for all students to learn, study, and collaborate. It houses the Center for Writing and Tutoring Resources, Center for Disability Resources, and Centers for Global Education and Career Development. The Bishop Library contains more than 225,000 books, CDs, and DVDs, as well as more than 3,000 electronic journal subscriptions, 130 online databases, and 31,000 full-text journals and newspapers. Well-equipped, up-to-date laboratories provide students with the tools and technologies they need to conduct cutting-edge research, independently or in partnership with faculty.

Costs

Annual tuition for the 2014–15 school year was $36,470. Room and board charges were $10,100 and fees were $1,000.

Financial Aid

Committed to helping all families afford the first-rate education it offers, Lebanon Valley College has a reputation for seeking talented, hard-working high school students and recognizing their achievements with academic scholarships and other opportunities for financial support.

Merit- and need-based financial assistance is also available. In 2014–15, the College committed more than $28,533,870 to merit- and need-based aid. Overall, 97 percent of LVC students receive some form of financial assistance from the College. Students and their families should complete the Free Application for Federal Student Aid (FAFSA) to determine eligibility. The priority deadline for filing for financial aid is March 1.

Faculty

The LVC faculty includes scientists, scholars, artists, and professionals in a wide range of fields, many of whom are respected contributors to their disciplines. LVC professors are dedicated to teaching and are drawn to the College for its close-knit community and for the opportunity to be actively involved in students' educational growth. Most faculty members are involved in research, scholarship, and professional organizations and play an active role in helping students find internships and start with their own research. Of LVC's 106 professors, 90 percent have earned a Ph.D. or equivalent terminal degree. The College is committed to maintaining a low student-teacher ratio of 11:1 (FTE). The average class size is 20, and all courses are taught by professors, not graduate students.

Student Government

Lebanon Valley students participate in the College's governing system through Student Government and the Student Programming Board. Student Government fosters understanding, communication, and cooperation among students, faculty, and administration. Different student groups and students meet regularly with LVC President Lewis Thayne, Ph.D., ensuring that there is a clear line of communication between the student body and the administration. The Student Programming Board organizes off-campus trips and schedules comedians, musicians, and other on-campus entertainment.

Admission Requirements

The LVC admission process is selective, and the applicant's academic record is the most important factor in admission decisions. The College seeks students from a variety of backgrounds as well as those who display leadership abilities, a commitment to community involvement, and special talents or interests that might benefit or enrich the LVC community. Competitive applicants will have pursued a challenging high school course of study that includes at least 4 courses in English, 2 in foreign language, 3 in mathematics, 2 in science, and 1 in social studies. Additional course work in math and science is strongly recommended. More than 75 percent of recent incoming LVC students rank among the top 30 percent of their high school class. Submission of SAT or ACT scores is optional. Advanced standing is offered through CLEP and AP examinations.

Application and Information

To apply, students should submit a completed application and official copies of their high school transcript. Lebanon Valley has both an early decision enrollment option and a rolling admission option. Early decision applicants must apply by November 1 and rolling admission students are encouraged to apply during the fall of their senior year. Personal visits to campus are encouraged.

For more information, applicants should contact:

Susan Jones
Senior Associate Director of Admission
Lebanon Valley College
101 North College Avenue
Annville, Pennsylvania 17003-1400
Phone: 866-LVC-4ADM (866-582-4236, toll-free)
Fax: 717-867-6026
E-mail: admission@lvc.edu
Website: www.lvc.edu

The Lebanon Valley College community is close-knit and welcoming.

LE MOYNE COLLEGE

SYRACUSE, NEW YORK

LE MOYNE
SPIRIT. INQUIRY. LEADERSHIP. JESUIT.

★ To read more about this school, visit http://petersons.to/lemoynecollege

The College

Le Moyne College is a four-year, coeducational Jesuit college of approximately 2,500 undergraduate students that uniquely balances a comprehensive liberal arts education with preparation for specific career paths or graduate study. Founded by the Society of Jesus in 1946, Le Moyne is the second youngest of the twenty-eight Jesuit colleges and universities in the United States. Its emphasis is on the education of the whole person and on the search for meaning and value as integral parts of an intellectual life. Le Moyne's personal approach to education is reflected in the quality of contact between students and faculty members.

A wide range of student-directed activities, athletics, clubs, and service organizations complement the academic experience. Intramural sports are very popular with Le Moyne students; nearly 85 percent of the students participate. Le Moyne also has twenty-one NCAA intercollegiate teams (ten for men and eleven for women). Athletic facilities include a new soccer/lacrosse turf field, softball and baseball fields; basketball, and racquetball courts; a weight-training and fitness center; practice fields; and two gymnasiums. A recreation center houses an Olympic-size indoor swimming pool, jogging track, indoor tennis and volleyball courts, and additional basketball, racquetball, and fitness areas.

Between 80 and 85 percent of students live in residence halls, apartments, and town houses on campus. The Residence Hall Councils and the Le Moyne Student Programming Board organize a variety of campus activities, including concerts, dances, a weekly film series, student talent programs, and special lectures as well as off-campus trips and skiing excursions. The College also has a plaza, which houses its bookstore, a café, and a pizzeria. The new Dolphin Den, which features a food court and a convenience store, is a popular space for students to meet, have a bite to eat, or just spend a quiet moment relaxing by the fireplace.

Location

Le Moyne's 160-plus acre, tree-lined campus is located in a residential setting 10 minutes from downtown Syracuse, the heart of New York State, whose metropolitan population is about 700,000. Syracuse is convenient to most major cities throughout the Northeast, New England, and Canada and offers a wide array of shopping centers and restaurants, many near Le Moyne. Syracuse offers year-round entertainment in the form of rock concerts at the Landmark Theatre, professional baseball and hockey, Bristol Omnitheatre, Syracuse Stage, Everson Museum of Art, and the Armory Square district downtown, which offers one-of-a-kind eateries, pubs, and coffeehouses in addition to a wide variety of social and cultural events. All are easily accessible via the excellent public transportation service, which schedules regular stops on Le Moyne's campus. Just a few miles outside the city are the rolling hills, picturesque lakes, and miles of open country for which central New York is renowned. An extensive network of state and county parks, recreational areas, and other facilities offer an abundance of recreational opportunities, including swimming, boating, hiking, downhill and cross-country skiing, snowboarding, and golf.

Majors and Degrees

Le Moyne College awards the Bachelor of Arts degree in biological sciences, communication (advertising, filmmaking, journalism, media studies, music and culture, music industry, music journalism, public relations, television/radio), computer science, criminology (human services, international affairs, law enforcement, research), economics, English (creative writing, literature), French, history, mathematics (actuarial science, pure mathematics, statistics), peace and global studies, philosophy, physics, political science, psychology, religious studies, sociology (anthropology, criminology, human services, research and theory), software applications and system development, Spanish, and theatre arts. The Bachelor of Science degree is awarded in biochemistry, biological sciences (health professions, molecular biology, neurobiology), chemistry, economics, environmental science systems, environmental studies, general science, physics, and psychology. The Bachelor of Science in business is awarded in accounting, business analytics, finance, human resource management, information systems, management and leadership, and marketing. A Bachelor of Science in nursing is also offered.

Students may minor in arts administration, business administration, Catholic studies, classical humanities, film, gender and women's studies, Irish literature, Italian, Latin, legal studies, health information systems, medieval studies, music, urban and regional studies, or visual arts as well as most of the major fields of study offered. Preprofessional programs are offered in dentistry, law, medicine, optometry, physical therapy, direct-entry physician assistant studies, podiatry, and veterinary science. Students may prepare for teaching careers through certification programs in adolescent education, dual adolescent/special education, dual childhood/special education, and TESOL.

Le Moyne College and the L. C. Smith College of Engineering and Computer Science at Syracuse University offer a dual-degree program in which students may earn a bachelor's degree from Le Moyne and a master's degree in engineering from Syracuse University in as few as five years. Concentrations include aerospace; chemical, electrical, and mechanical engineering; computer science; and other fields of engineering.

Formal accelerated 3-4 programs are offered in dentistry, optometry, and podiatry in cooperation with the State University of New York at Buffalo School of Dental Medicine, Pennsylvania College of Optometry at Salus University, and the New York College of Podiatric Medicine. Predental students may also participate in an early assurance program with the State University of New York at Buffalo School of Dental Medicine. Cooperative 3-2 dual-degree programs in engineering are available with Clarkson University, Manhattan College, and University of Detroit Mercy.

SUNY Upstate Medical University in Syracuse offers students pursuing careers in the health-related professions an accelerated 3-3 doctoral-level transfer program in physical therapy as well as two-year cooperative transfer programs in medical technology, and respiratory care. Premedical students at Le Moyne are also offered the opportunity to participate in a medical school early assurance program. An early assurance program for premedical students is also available through the State University of New York at Buffalo School of Medicine and formal agreements also exist with Fordham's School of Law and Syracuse University School of Law.

Academic Programs

While each major department has its own sequence requirements for the minimum 120 credit hours needed for the Le Moyne degree, the College is convinced that there is a fundamental intellectual discipline that should characterize the graduate of a superior liberal arts college. Le Moyne's core curriculum provides this foundation by including studies of English language and literature, philosophy, history, religious studies, natural sciences, and social sciences.

For exceptional students, Le Moyne offers an integral honors program that includes an interdisciplinary humanities sequence as well as departmental honors courses. Le Moyne also offers a part-time course of study during evening hours through its Center for Continuing Education.

Le Moyne students may enroll in Army and Air Force ROTC programs in conjunction with Syracuse University.

Off-Campus Programs

The study-abroad program allows qualified students to spend a semester or year in almost any country throughout the world. Le Moyne College has study-abroad programs or affiliations in the Czech Republic, Dominican Republic, England, Germany, Ireland, Scotland, and Spain. Students can also use partner programs to study in locations such as Australia, Costa Rica, Egypt, France, Italy, Japan, and South Africa. Le Moyne is a participant in the sixty-member New York State Visiting Student Program. As part of the mission of preparing future leaders, Le Moyne College places a strong emphasis on career preparation through internships and other forms of experiential education. Academic departments and the Office of Career Advising and Development both provide programs and services for students interested in interning part time and full time, both locally and in major cities such as New York and Washington, D.C. The Offices of Service Learning and the Academic Deans are also involved in experiential education to promote learning outside the classroom. In the sciences, students take part in campus research with mentor faculty members. Others receive assistance in pursuing outstanding opportunities off campus in leading research laboratories and health-care settings. The College has maintained a long-standing relationship with the Washington Center internship programs, where students from all majors complete full-time semester-long internships in Washington, D.C., with government, business, or major nonprofit organizations. Faculty members in the Political Science Department assist students interested in opportunities in Albany, the state's seat of government, with either the New York State Senate or Assembly. Finally, the education programs at Le Moyne put students into school classrooms starting immediately as freshmen and continuing each year until graduation.

Academic Facilities

Le Moyne students benefit from an ongoing commitment to technological excellence. The College's forty-two buildings are equipped with accounting, biology, chemistry, computer science, physics, psychology, and statistics laboratories. The W. Carroll Coyne Center for the Performing Arts houses generous production, performance, and classroom space; the latest light and sound technology; scene and costume shops; an aerobics and dance studio; and rehearsal rooms for instrumental and choral music. Academic facilities also include an extensively renovated color television studio; a radio/recording studio; a receiver-antenna satellite dish; transmission and scanning electron microscopes; a nuclear magnetic resonance spectrometer; a gas chromatograph/mass spectrophotometer; a 240,000-volume, open-stack library; and extensive on-site computer facilities. A fiber-optic network enables students to access the library system, the campus network, and the Internet from several computer labs around the campus or from their personal computers in their rooms. All classrooms are smart classrooms, with multimedia capabilities that expand and enrich the learning process. Le Moyne students have access to other libraries through the Central New York Library Resources Council, and the campus Academic Support Center is available to students for instructional support. In addition, Le Moyne recently opened a 48,000-square-foot addition to its existing science complex, and the Madden School of Business, featuring a state-of-the-art trading floor and analytics lab.

Costs

For 2014–15, Le Moyne's tuition was $30,350. Room and board charges were $12,130. Additional fees amounted to approximately $990, and books and supplies cost approximately $700.

Financial Aid

Financial aid is offered to a large percentage of Le Moyne's students through scholarships, grants, loans, and work-study assignments. Le Moyne offers a generous program of merit-based academic and athletic scholarships as well as financial aid based on a student's need and academic promise. Federal funds are available through the Federal Pell Grant, Federal Work-Study, Federal Supplemental Educational Opportunity Grant, and Federal Perkins Loan programs. A student's eligibility for need-based financial aid is determined from both the Free Application for Federal Student Aid (FAFSA) and the Le Moyne Financial Aid Application Form. It is recommended that these forms be mailed by February 1.

Faculty

The Le Moyne full-time faculty numbers 150 men and women; 94 percent have earned the highest degree in their field. With an average class size of 22, a student-faculty ratio of 13:1, and private offices for all full-time faculty members, the College promotes a personal as well as an academic relationship between students and faculty members. All classroom instruction is done by faculty members, and they are happy to assist and encourage students who wish to pursue undergraduate research through tutorials or senior research projects. These projects are carried out in an atmosphere free of competition from graduate students for books, laboratories, or professors' time. Le Moyne emphasizes advising and academic counseling for students throughout their four years.

Student Government

The College encourages student leadership in all activities. Positions of leadership are open to students in all class years. Students are represented by a Student Senate and have formal representation through the senate on most College-wide committees involved in decision making and policy formation.

Admission Requirements

Le Moyne seeks qualified students who are well prepared for serious academic study. Secondary school preparation must have included at least 17 college-preparatory high school units, 4 of which must be in English, 4 in social studies, 3–4 in mathematics, 3–4 in foreign language, and 3–4 in science. It is also recommended that prospective science and mathematics majors complete 4 units of mathematics and science. The SAT or ACT is required and should be taken no later than December or January of the senior year in high school. Campus visits are strongly recommended, as the admission process is a personal one. As bases for selection, academic achievement and secondary school recommendations are of primary importance. SAT or ACT scores are important as they relate to the record of achievement and to recommendations. Out-of-state students are encouraged to apply.

Application and Information

Le Moyne offers students the opportunity to apply in two ways: early action or regular admission. The early action program is nonbinding and provides high school students the opportunity to receive an admission decision by December 15 of their senior year. The early action application deadline is November 15. Regular admission applications are reviewed and admission decisions are made on a rolling basis beginning January 1. The priority deadline for applications is February 1; all students who wish to be considered for academic merit scholarships should have a completed application on file in the Office of Admission before this date. All students are encouraged to include Le Moyne (002748) on their FAFSA submission. Transfer students are encouraged to apply before June 1 for the fall semester and December 1 for the spring semester. Orientation programs for incoming freshmen take place in June and early July. Transfer student orientation programs are offered throughout the summer.

Mary Chandler
Senior Director of Admission
Le Moyne College
Syracuse, New York 13214-1399
Phone: 315-445-4300
800-333-4733 (toll-free)
E-mail: admission@lemoyne.edu
Website: http://www.lemoyne.edu
twitter.com/lemoynecollege

Grewen Hall, the College's oldest building, overlooks Le Moyne's beautiful 160-plus acre campus.

COLLEGE CLOSE-UPS

LEWIS & CLARK COLLEGE

PORTLAND, OREGON

Lewis & Clark College

The College

A private college with a public conscience, Lewis & Clark College has a global reach that extends well beyond its location in Portland, Oregon. Located on a 137-acre campus in a wooded residential area 6 miles from downtown, the College is a starting point for students to explore the wider world and find their place in it.

The student body is known for its geographic diversity. In fall 2014, of the 2,179 undergraduates, 21 percent were from Oregon, and 79 percent came from forty-seven other states plus the District of Columbia and represented seventy-six countries. Approximately 65 percent live in housing on campus, most of which is coed (91 percent). There are no fraternities or sororities.

The College offers numerous co-curricular activities, including twelve music groups; nine media organizations; twelve religious/spiritual life groups; seventeen international, cultural, and diversity clubs; and nearly seventy student organizations. Cultural events such as lectures, student-run symposia, art exhibits, theater productions, concerts, recitals, and dance performances occur on a regular basis. Currently, there are nineteen NCAA Division III varsity athletic teams, fourteen club teams, and numerous intramural sports. The renowned College Outdoors Program offers adventures such as backpacking, rafting, skiing, snowshoeing, caving, winter camping, sea kayaking, and environmental service projects in Oregon's and Washington's nearby wilderness areas.

Location

Portland has long been known for its livability and its excellent transportation system. Public buses and a free College shuttle run from the Lewis & Clark campus to downtown Portland. The vibrant metropolitan area (population 2.2 million) offers resources and opportunities for entertainment, study, work, and internships. The city has 10,447 acres of parks; diverse galleries, museums, music groups, and theater and dance companies; and a nationally recognized food scene. Professional sports teams compete in soccer, hockey, and NBA basketball. For those looking for outdoor pursuits, Mount Hood, offering skiing ten months per year, is 50 miles away, and Oregon's rugged coastline lies 90 miles to the west.

Majors and Degrees

Lewis & Clark offers programs leading to the Bachelor of Arts degree. Academic majors include art (art history and studio art), biochemistry and molecular biology, biology, chemistry, classics, computer science, computer science and mathematics, East Asian studies, economics (international, public policy, theory), English, environmental studies, foreign languages, French studies, German studies, Hispanic studies, history, international affairs, mathematics, music, philosophy, physics, political science, psychology, religious studies, rhetoric and media studies, sociology/anthropology, and theater. Students may also design a major or pursue a double major and numerous minors. Pre-professional preparation is available in the fields of law, medicine, business, entrepreneurship, and education.

Dual-degree (3-2 and 4-2) programs in engineering are offered in cooperation with Columbia University, Washington University (St. Louis), and the University of Southern California. A 4-2 B.A./M.B.A. program is offered in cooperation with the University of Rochester's Simon Graduate School of Business. A 4-1 B.A./M.A.T. program is offered through Lewis & Clark's Graduate School of Education and Counseling. In addition, there is a guaranteed admission agreement with Lewis & Clark's Law School for students meeting certain criteria.

Academic Programs

The liberal arts curriculum offers sufficient structure to ensure depth and breadth of study, but it also incorporates a high degree of freedom. In the four-year plan of study, approximately one third of a student's time is devoted to general education, one third to a major program, and one third to elective courses. Students are also encouraged to participate in departmental honors programs, undergraduate research, independent study, and internships.

The academic calendar consists of two 15-week semesters. A normal load is four 4 semester-hour academic courses, plus one or more activity courses. The fall semester begins early in September and ends before Christmas, and the spring semester begins in mid-January and ends in early May. A limited number of courses are offered during two summer sessions.

The community of scholars at Lewis & Clark College is dedicated to personal and academic excellence. Joining the Lewis & Clark community obligates each member to observe the principles of mutual respect, academic integrity, civil discourse, and responsible decision-making.

Off-Campus Programs

Lewis & Clark offers nationally recognized international and off-campus study opportunities. Usually, 20 to 24 students plus a faculty leader participate in each program. More than half of the College's graduates have taken advantage of these outstanding programs, often satisfying General Education or major requirements at the same time.

Overseas study may have either a general-culture focus or a specialized academic focus. Sites for overseas study programs from 2015 through 2018 are Australia, Chile, China, Cuba, Dominican Republic, East Africa, Ecuador, England, France, Germany, Ghana, Greece, India, Ireland, Italy, Japan, Morocco, New Zealand, Russia, Scotland, Senegal, Spain, Swaziland, and Vietnam. Domestic programs are available in the Arizona borderlands, New York, and Washington, D.C.

Academic Facilities

The Aubrey R. Watzek Library is open 24 hours per day when school is in session and offers individualized reference assistance for students. The library houses more than 740,000 items and its website provides access to its catalog as well as to a full range of electronic resources. The library is a member of Summit, a consortium of thirty-seven academic libraries that have a unified catalog that enables students to request and receive materials from member libraries within two days.

Music department facilities include a 410-seat recital hall equipped with an orchestra pit and stage elevator; an extensive collection of more than 4,000 records, CDs, and tape recordings; twenty-two practice rooms; forty-three pianos; two harpsichords; a Baroque organ; an electronic music studio; Zimbabwe marimbas; and an Indonesian gamelan orchestra. The 600-seat chapel houses an 85-rank Casavant organ.

The visual arts center is equipped with studio space for painting, drawing, ceramics, sculpture, design, and printmaking as well as a photography lab. The department also has a Visual Resources Collection of 50,000 slides and several thousand digital images representing artwork from a wide range of media, time periods, world regions, and cultures. The humanities and social sciences also enjoy state-of-the-art classrooms and lab facilities.

The natural science buildings are equipped with modern instrumentation to support collaborative student-faculty research. Among the notable facilities are laboratories for the study of astrophysics, the biomechanics of animal locomotion, human-computer interactions, molecular modeling and parallel computing, a scanning electron microscope, a modern greenhouse, and an astronomical observatory with Newtonian and solar telescopes, Ecological investigations and studies of the environmental impacts of human activity are conducted both on the College's heavily wooded campus and at the nearby Tryon Creek State Park.

Computer labs house more than 130 Macintosh and Microsoft Windows computers, along with peripherals such as scanners, printers, and digital video editing equipment. Digital, still and video cameras, digital audio recorders, and more are available for checkout. All residence halls have wireless networks. The institution has an 800 Mbps connection to the Internet.

Costs

Tuition and fees for 2014–15 were $43,382. The room and board charge was $10,906 for fourteen (flex) meals per week; other meal plans are also available. The estimate for books and personal expenses is $2,112.

Financial Aid

In 2013–14, 86 percent of the College's students received some form of financial assistance. A financial aid package may include institutional, state, and/or federal resources. Lewis & Clark College participates in a variety of federal aid programs that may include Federal Pell and Supplemental Educational Opportunity Grants, Federal Direct and Perkins loans, as well as Federal Work-Study. To receive priority consideration for need-based financial aid, students must meet appropriate deadlines for admission and should submit the Free Application for Federal Student Aid (FAFSA) and the CSS/Financial Aid PROFILE application by February 15.

Lewis & Clark offers renewable merit-based scholarships and participation awards to students who demonstrate the qualities of mind, self-discipline, and commitment to learning that characterize the best in Lewis & Clark students. These awards range from $1,000 to full tuition. Many of these scholarships are awarded through the admissions process and don't require a separate application. Others require additional paper work. Full details on merit-based scholarship opportunities can be found at go.lclark.edu/fao.

Faculty

The 155 full-time members of the faculty are committed to undergraduate teaching and advising and are also active in research, writing, and publishing. Involving students in the research process is of high priority. Ninety-six percent of the full-time faculty members hold a Ph.D. or the highest advanced degree in their discipline. The student-faculty ratio is 12:1. The average class size is 17, with 88 percent of classes having 29 or fewer students.

Student Government

The Associated Students of Lewis & Clark (ASLC) consists of a Student Senate, governing boards, and appointed students who serve on faculty constitutional, standing, and special committees. The 30 members of the Student Academic Affairs Board (SAAB) are appointed on a departmental basis to represent the student body in discussions concerning academics at the College and to support student academic initiatives through a grant program. Students may apply for one of four different types of grants: student-initiated research, academic conference attendance, visiting scholars program, and Arts and Expression.

Admission Requirements

Lewis & Clark College seeks first-year and transfer applicants who are committed to academic excellence and personal growth. Admission is competitive. Applications are carefully reviewed and examined for degree of academic preparation, ability to express ideas in essay form, participation in activities, citizenship and community service, and support given by the school through recommendations. Campus visits are encouraged. Interviews are available but not required. Recommended high school preparation includes 4 years of English, 3 to 4 years of history or social science, 4 years of mathematics, 3 years of laboratory science, 2 to 3 years of foreign language, and 1 year of fine arts. The SAT or ACT is required, unless the student is applying via the Test-Optional Portfolio Path.

Application and Information

First-year applicants should submit the Common Application online; a personal essay; an official academic transcript, including senior grades from the first marking period; one recommendation from a counselor; and at least one reference from an academic teacher. Application deadlines for the fall semester are November 1 for binding early decision (notification by December 15), November 1 for nonbinding early action (notification by January 1) and January 15 for regular decision (notification by April 1).

Transfer applicants are evaluated on a rolling basis. To ensure full consideration, the College strongly recommends that transfer students submit all credentials before the end of March.

The application deadline for first-year and transfer students for the spring semester is November 1 (notification within three weeks of file completion). The Test-Optional Portfolio Path admissions program provides an opportunity for applicants who have shown exceptional academic initiative to demonstrate the full extent of their pursuits by presenting a portfolio of their academic work. Under this plan, SAT or ACT scores are optional. More details about the Portfolio Path can be found online at go.lclark.edu/portfolio_path.

For more information about Lewis & Clark College or to arrange a visit, students should contact:

Office of Admissions
Lewis & Clark College
0615 SW Palatine Hill Road
Portland, Oregon 97219-7899
Phone: 503-768-7040
800-444-4111 (toll-free)
Fax: 503-768-7055
E-mail: admissions@lclark.edu
Website: www.lclark.edu

Lewis & Clark students learn through a rigorous curriculum that builds intellectual depth and breadth, creativity, and critical thinking skills in its graduates.

COLLEGE CLOSE-UPS

LIM COLLEGE

NEW YORK, NEW YORK

★ To read more about this school, visit http://petersons.to/limcollege

LIM COLLEGE

The College

Situated in the center of the fashion capital of the world, LIM College has been a major force in fashion and business education for over 75 years. Graduates can be found throughout all areas of the fashion industry, and its high quality of education has earned LIM College accreditation from the Middle States Association of Colleges and Schools. The College's B.B.A., B.P.S., and associate degrees are also accredited by the Accreditation Council of Business Schools and Programs (ACBSP).

LIM College offers a highly personal environment where students learn about the business of fashion, with an emphasis on academic and professional study. Lifelong friends are made at LIM College, as well as long-lasting careers. Although most students come to the College directly from high school or transfer from other colleges, there are also those of nontraditional college age who enroll. Students come to LIM College from many parts of the country and the world. The current undergraduate enrollment is approximately 1,550.

The Department of Experiential Education & Career Management is one of LIM College's chief assets. Each student receives extensive career advising throughout their time at the College, beginning in the first semester. This helps direct students to career opportunities within their field of study. This relationship is one intended to strengthen during the college years into post-graduation, as the department offers lifetime services.

The unique nature of LIM College's curriculum provides students with a foundation of core courses in the liberal arts and business while offering diverse and intensive hands-on preparation in the fashion industry. This affords graduates the opportunity to accept executive training, merchandising, management, marketing, visual, and communications positions in a wide variety of areas within the fashion and business worlds.

Support services are important at LIM College. In addition to academic and career advising, personal counseling is available. Because of the College's small size and the close relationships between students and staff members, any faculty member or administrator is readily accessible to help and advise all students.

Student life at LIM College is very dynamic. Active clubs include the Fashion Show Production Club, Student Life Activities Board, Student Leadership Council, Dance Team, and many more. There are also student publications including the *LIMLIGHT* yearbook and *The Lexington Line,* an online student magazine.

Located at 1760 Third Avenue, LIM College's state-of-the-art residence hall boasts a plethora of modern amenities. All rooms have private bathrooms, complementary wireless Internet access, phone service, and over 100 cable channels. Rooms are also equipped with full refrigerators and 25-inch flat-screen televisions. The facility also contains a private gym, game room, computer lab, and a brand new, state-of-the-art kitchen.

LIM College's Open House program offers students and their families the opportunity to tour the College's campus and learn not only about LIM College's unique academic programs, but also of the vast array of careers found in the fashion industry. The day also includes special presentations on financial aid, study abroad, clubs, and much more. Current LIM College students assist in hosting the event and are available to answer questions. LIM College also offers many other opportunities to visit including weekly information sessions, Transfer Services Days, mock classes for accepted students, and other periodically scheduled special events.

Location

LIM College is situated in three academic buildings—on East 53rd Street, East 45th Street, and on Fifth Avenue, one of the most fashionable locales in the world. With a residence hall on the Upper East Side, a whole world of fashion is at the College's doorstep and includes Bergdorf Goodman, MTV Networks, Hearst Publications, Christian Louboutin, and Universal Music Group. New York City is the headquarters for the garment, cosmetics, advertising, publishing, and textile industries, all of which are essential to the fashion industry and are visited regularly by LIM College students. The College incorporates all of these resources into the curriculum. For example, the Fashion Magazines course may include trips to photography studios, modeling agencies, or tours of magazine offices and advertising firms. New York City offers LIM College students an unparalleled learning experience.

Majors and Degrees

LIM College offers four-year programs in Fashion Merchandising, Management, Marketing, and Visual Merchandising, leading to the Bachelor of Business Administration (B.B.A.) degree and International Business leading to the Bachelor of Science (B.S.) degree. Also offered is a four-year Bachelor of Professional Studies (B.P.S.) program in Fashion Merchandising as well as two-year programs in Fashion Merchandising leading to the Associate in Applied Sciences (A.A.S.) and the Associate in Occupational Studies (A.O.S.) degrees. The Fashion Merchandising program offers tracks in apparel and accessories, home fashions, and retail buying and planning.

LIM College also offers four graduate programs: the Master of Professional Studies (M.P.S.) in Fashion Merchandising and Retail Management; the Master of Professional Studies (M.P.S.) in Fashion Marketing; the Master of Professional Studies (M.P.S.) in Global Fashion Supply Chain Management; and the Master of Professional Studies (M.P.S) in Visual Merchandising.

The College also offers a broad variety of concentrations, such as digital business strategy, entrepreneurship, event planning, fashion merchandising, international marketing, and styling, which allow students to pursue a focused area of study that complements their major.

Academic Programs

LIM College offers a combination of classroom education and supervised internships that have been designed to prepare students for executive training programs and other entry-level executive positions in various areas of the fashion industry.

Experiential education, or learning by doing, is an integral part of the LIM College curriculum. The internship program helps students become truly prepared for successful careers within fashion and fashion-related industries. All students are required to take three internships in order to earn their bachelor's degree at LIM College. Each internship has a prerequisite seminar attached to it that includes activities such as field trips, guest speakers, and portfolio-building that help students network with industry professionals and develop into dynamic business leaders.

Courses are sequential, each built upon the knowledge and experience a student gains through the process of learning. The experiential education program at LIM College commences with a course designed to increase a student's knowledge of the industry, hence building a foundation upon which to build a career in fashion. The program culminates with a nearly full-time Senior Co-op internship intended to be a real working experience while the student works closely with instructors and advisers to ensure the best chance of this becoming a real job upon graduation.

To graduate, students must complete 127 credits for the Bachelor of Science degree and 124 credits for the Bachelor of Business Administration and the Bachelor of Professional Studies degrees. Associate degree candidates must earn 67 credits. All students must have at least a GPA of 2.0 and satisfactory completion of all coursework and other curriculum requirements.

LIM College accepts qualified students as transfers throughout the four years. The maximum number of credits that LIM will accept is 65. Transfer students must complete the last consecutive 46 credits at LIM College, including the Senior Co-op semester.

The College calendar runs on a traditional semester format, offering both fall and spring start dates. Also offered are summer and Saturday Fashion Lab programs for high school students. The specially selected courses, such as Fashion Buying and Fashion Magazines, blend academics with hands-on experience and are a great way to explore the fashion industry.

Off-Campus Programs

From two-week immersion programs to semester-long study abroad experiences, LIM College offers students the opportunity to see the world and experience fashion on an international stage. With programs in Australia, China, England, France, Spain, and Italy, students are given a global education for a global industry.

Academic Facilities

Facilities include the 5,000-square-foot Adrian G. Marcuse Library, with over 14,583 books, 1,081 librarian-selected e-books, 203 scholarly journals and magazines, 780 bound volumes of magazine back issues, 1,135 DVDs, an archive of historic materials, and a large collection of fashion, business, and marketing books to assist students in their research. The library also has 42 CAD-enabled computers, copiers, and printers, both black and white and color. The 54 subscription databases located on the library-run website are available 24/7, on- or off-campus, and can be accessed by computer, iPad, iPhone, or any other Internet-ready device. The Math Center and Writing Center offer one-on-one tutoring for all students.

LIM College's facility on Fifth Avenue is equipped with two fashion merchandising studios. There are also two 1,100-square-foot visual merchandising studios, as well as a state-of-the-art Color and Materials Lab.

Costs

Tuition for the 2014–15 school year was $23,650 with additional mandatory fees of $575. Housing charges for the 2014–15 year were $15,850. Books and supplies expenses average around $900 per academic year and students living on campus may spend up to $4,000 a year on meal expenses. Students who commute spend from $1,200 to $2,000 for transportation, depending on distance traveled. Personal expenses for the academic year are estimated to be $1,500.

Financial Aid

LIM College believes that lack of funds should not keep students from attaining a degree; thus, admissions decisions and financial aid are totally separate, and a request for aid has no effect on admissions. About 80 percent of LIM College's students received some form of financial aid during the 2013–14 school year. Institutional scholarships, Federal Pell Grants, Federal Supplemental Educational Opportunity Grants, and New York State TAP grants are all available for eligible students. In addition, the College participates in the Federal Stafford Loan program for students and Federal PLUS Loan program for parents. The College also works with several private lenders to offer alternative education loans for students to supplement their federal loans. International students are eligible to apply for alternative loans with a credit-worthy U.S.-based co-signer. The Free Application for Federal Student Aid (FAFSA) should be filed by all domestic applicants by March 1 for priority consideration. Aid is granted on the basis of financial need and scholarships are merit based, although some awards take need into consideration. Details of the financial aid programs are available on the LIM College website or are available directly from the Office of Student Financial Services.

LIM College features a Merit Scholarship Program for incoming freshmen and transfer students. These scholarship monies are awarded for academic achievement in high school or college. Students can remain eligible for their scholarship throughout their stay at the College by maintaining a GPA of 3.0 or above.

Faculty

LIM College prides itself on its outstanding faculty members. LIM College faculty members include fashion industry leaders, whose up-to-the-minute knowledge of current trends keeps the College's focus sharp. LIM's liberal arts professors—accomplished journalists, poets, playwrights, and artists—make sure graduates are also well-rounded global citizens. With a student-faculty member ratio of 8:1 and an average class size of 16, LIM College offers a friendly, close-knit environment.

Student Activities

The Office of Student Life is the center of student activities and clubs at LIM College. One of LIM College's most popular clubs is the Fashion Show Production Club, which plans an annual fashion show attended by more than 1,000 people. Another popular activity is the online student magazine, *The Lexington Line*. LIM College's Office of Student Life plans many other activities including diversity programming, philanthropic service, and new student orientation.

Admission Requirements

All undergraduate applicants are required to submit high school transcripts, SAT or ACT scores, two letters of recommendation, an essay, and the completed application with the application fee. Transfer students must also submit all college transcripts. Undergraduate Admissions will waive the standardized test requirement if the student has satisfactorily earned 15 credit hours (21 on a quarter or trimester system) at the time of application. International students should review the LIM College website and contact the Office of Admissions for specific requirements. It is also strongly suggested that all applicants create an activity sheet or resume highlighting their experience, with emphasis on business and fashion activities.

Application and Information

LIM College's Admissions Committee recognizes that many intangibles go into the making of a successful student and it evaluates each applicant individually and holistically. The College uses a rolling admission policy. Applicants are informed of the admission decision within approximately four to six weeks after all admission requirements have been fulfilled. An application may be obtained from the LIM College website or by contacting the Admissions Office.

Kristina Ortiz
Dean of Admissions
LIM College
12 East 53rd Street
New York, New York 10022-5268
Phone: 212-752-1530
800-677-1323 (toll-free outside New York City)
Fax: 212-750-3432
E-mail: admissions@limcollege.edu
Website: http://www.limcollege.edu
http://www.facebook.com/LIMCollege
http://twitter.com/LIMcollege
http://instagram.com/LIMcollege

LIM College's flagship location, The Townhouse, is located right off Fifth Avenue in Midtown Manhattan.

LINDENWOOD UNIVERSITY

ST. CHARLES, MISSOURI

LINDENWOOD UNIVERSITY

★ To read more about this school, visit http://petersons.to/lindenwooduniversity

COLLEGE CLOSE-UPS

The University

An independent teaching university founded in 1827, Lindenwood is the second oldest university west of the Mississippi River. Lindenwood is a dynamic four-year liberal arts institution dedicated to excellence, delivering a high-quality education that leads to the development of the whole person and preparation for life and work after graduation, through more than 200 undergraduate and graduate degree programs.

Lindenwood University is a member of and/or is accredited by the Higher Learning Commission of the North Central Association of Colleges and Schools, the Accreditation Council for Business Schools and Programs, the Council on Social Work Education, the Commission on Accreditation of Athletic Training Education, and the Missouri Department of Elementary and Secondary Education, and it is fully endorsed by the Society for Human Resource Management. Lindenwood is a member of the Teacher Education Accreditation Council and the Council for Higher Education Accreditation.

Lindenwood University offers bachelor's, master's, Education Specialist, and Doctor of Education degrees. Lindenwood is an independent, public-serving, liberal arts university that has a historical relationship with the Presbyterian Church and is committed to the values inherent in the Judeo-Christian tradition. Lindenwood welcomes students from all religious denominations.

The University's 27 NCAA Division II athletic teams compete in the Mid-America Intercollegiate Athletics Association (MIAA), one of the top conferences in the division. Another 20 Student Life sports and competitive programs compete in an array of college-level organizations specific to the individual programs. Over the last 10 years, Lindenwood athletic teams have won more than 40 national championships. On-campus athletic facilities consist of the Robert F. Hyland Performance Arena, the Harlen C. Hunter Stadium, the new Student–Athlete Center, the Lou Brock Sports Complex for baseball and softball, and an eight-lane all-weather running track, recently renovated with a new surface and a grandstand and press box. Students also participate in an assortment of intramural sports at the University's Fitness Center and the Evans Commons.

More than 70 student organizations and clubs, including the Lindenwood Student Government Association and the Student Senate, provide avenues for extended personal growth, leadership, and community service. The University radio station, 50,000-watt KCLC-FM, and LUTV, Lindenwood's HD television station, are staffed by students, as is the *Lindenwood Legacy* student newspaper and LindenLink, an online source of news and feature content.

Students wishing to live on campus may choose from residence halls, houses, and apartment-style living. Eight new residence halls have opened since 2000, and in 2010, Lindenwood acquired the former Days Inn in St. Charles for student housing. Sibley Hall, named in honor of founders Mary Easton and George C. Sibley, was built in 1856 to replace the original log cabin that served as the first University building. It is listed on the National Register of Historic Places and is now a women's residence hall. All residential buildings have easy access to University facilities.

Location

The 500-acre main campus is located in St. Charles, Missouri, a city of about 55,000 people, situated 20 miles from Downtown St. Louis. Resting on the banks of the Missouri River, just south of the Mississippi, St. Charles is the site of Missouri's first state capital. The area offers a wide range of opportunities for all types of interests and is particularly rich in state heritage and attractions associated with the history of America's westward expansion. Lindenwood's proximity to a major city allows students to enjoy theme parks, a delightful zoo, professional sporting events, Broadway plays and theater, performances of a world-renowned symphony orchestra, state parks, and lakes. St. Louis–Lambert International Airport is located just 5 miles from Lindenwood University on Interstate 70.

Majors and Degrees

With a foundation as solid as the campus' century-old linden trees, the academic programs of Lindenwood University have a tradition of excellence and innovation. Lindenwood awards Bachelor of Arts, Bachelor of Fine Arts, and Bachelor of Science degrees with majors in sixty-five subject areas—from accounting to unified sciences.

Preprofessional courses are offered in chiropractic science, dentistry, engineering, health, law, medicine, optometry, nursing, and veterinary science. In addition, programs in engineering are available in conjunction with Washington University in St. Louis, the University of Missouri–Columbia, the University of Missouri—St. Louis, and the Missouri University of Science and Technology in Rolla. In fall 2013, the University launched a two-year Bachelor of Science in Nursing degree-completion program for RNs who already have a two-year associate degree in nursing. A Master of Science in Nursing degree was also added recently.

Academic Programs

The emphasis at Lindenwood University is on an individualized liberal arts education with career-oriented preparation. Students fulfill general education requirements, participate in the University's Work and Learn Program when qualified, and acquire an in-depth knowledge of at least one area of study as a major. Lindenwood requires the completion of 128 credit hours to earn a bachelor's degree.

Academic Facilities

The Margaret Leggat Butler Library houses volumes, microfilm items, and a computer lab and subscribes to hundreds of periodicals. Roemer Hall serves as the main administration building and has classrooms and faculty offices on the upper floors. Young Science Hall houses an auditorium, laboratories, and classrooms for natural science, mathematics, and computer science, as well as a theater that is home to the University's film series. The recently renovated and expanded Harmon Hall houses the School of Business and Entrepreneurship with classrooms, offices, and the Dunseth Auditorium. The Lindenwood University Cultural Center provides a 750-seat auditorium, classrooms, meeting rooms, and offices. It is the site of theatrical productions, concerts, convocations, and lectures and is the headquarters of the University's accelerated evening programs. In addition, the Spellmann Campus Center houses a state-of-the-art cafeteria, Macintosh and PC computer labs, classrooms, conference rooms, networking and campus life offices, career planning and placement services, and the studios of KCLC. In August 2011, Lindenwood opened the 119,000-square-foot Evans Common, which houses a variety of amenities for students, including basketball and multipurpose courts, an array of the latest fitness equipment, movie and music rooms, and a dining hall with a food court configuration, among others. The 132,000-square-foot J. Scheidegger Center for the Arts, completed in 2008, is home to Lindenwood's Theatre, Dance, and Music departments, as well as the 1,200-seat Lindenwood Family Theater, the 250-seat Emerson Black Box Theater, the Boyle Family Gallery, and the Charter Communications LUTV HD Studio.

Costs

For the academic year 2014–15, tuition was $15,230. Students who choose to live on campus pay $7,520 for room and board, plus $360 for communications service and $350 for a health and activity fee. There is a refundable $300 room deposit. Books and other supplies are extra.

Financial Aid

Financial aid is available to all qualified students. A student must submit the Free Application for Federal Student Aid (FAFSA). To qualify for the full amount of financial aid, students must submit their federal financial aid forms before April 1. As determined by the evaluation, a student's financial need may be met with a combination of federal, state, and institutional sources of aid. In addition, institutional awards are available in the areas of academics, leadership, athletics, drama, yearbook/newspaper, and music. Resident students may earn $2,400 toward their expenses by working on campus.

Faculty

Lindenwood has approximately 260 full-time faculty members, who serve as teachers, mentors, and advisers to their students. Faculty members advise students regarding majors and other matters to help them succeed academically.

Student Government

The Lindenwood Student Government Association (LSGA) is made up of representatives elected by the student body. LSGA has the responsibility of providing a balanced program of cultural, social, and recreational events and activities throughout the year. In addition, an elected Student Senate meets periodically with the University president regarding matters of interest to the student body.

Admission Requirements

To apply for admission, a student should submit a completed application form with a nonrefundable $30 application fee, a transcript of high school and/or college work, and ACT or SAT scores.

Applicants are evaluated on an individual basis, and admission is based on an analysis of the student's grade point average, ACT or SAT scores, extracurricular activities, recommendations, and personal qualifications. Students are admitted without regard to race, sex, or national origin.

Application and Information

Admission to Lindenwood is on a rolling basis; students are encouraged to apply by April 15 for the fall semester and by December 1 for the spring semester. Notification of the admission decision is mailed soon after all required materials are received and evaluated by the Office of Undergraduate Day Admissions.

Applications for admission, financial aid, and scholarships and other information about Lindenwood University can be obtained by contacting:

Undergraduate Day Admissions
Lindenwood University
209 South Kingshighway
St. Charles, Missouri 63301-1695
Phone: 636-949-4949
Fax: 636-949-4989
Website: www.lindenwood.edu
www.facebook.com/LUDayAdmissions

Student life at Lindenwood University.

LINFIELD COLLEGE

McMINNVILLE, OREGON

Linfield College

★ To read more about this school, visit http://petersons.to/linfieldcollege

The College

Linfield College (1858) is an independent, coeducational, residential, comprehensive liberal arts and sciences college dedicated to providing an educational environment conducive to learning and participation. There are 1,700 full-time students on the McMinnville campus. These students come primarily from the thirteen Western states (twenty-three states overall) but also from twenty-two other countries. Students of color make up 33 percent of the student body, and 4 percent of students are international. Most students are between 18 and 22. Linfield is primarily residential, with seventeen residence halls, each accommodating between 10 and 100 residents. Each hall establishes its own calendar of social, educational, and recreational events throughout the year. Students who reside on campus eat their meals in the College dining hall. Houses and apartments are available for upper-division students. Social clubs, professional organizations, four sororities and four fraternities, service clubs, and almost forty other organizations play an important role in the daily life of a Linfield student. Linfield's winning athletics tradition fosters participation at all levels of competition. Women compete in intercollegiate basketball, cross-country, golf, lacrosse, soccer, softball, swimming, tennis, track and field, and volleyball. Men compete in intercollegiate baseball, basketball, cross-country, football, golf, soccer, swimming, tennis, and track and field. Linfield also has an extensive and active year-round intramural program.

Linfield hosts the Oregon Nobel Laureate Symposium, one of five such symposiums worldwide. At each symposium, several Nobel laureates come to share their backgrounds and expertise within the context of a basic theme.

The Linfield–Good Samaritan School of Nursing, an academic unit of the College at its Portland campus, prepares students for careers in nursing. This campus, at the Good Samaritan Hospital and Medical Center, has residence facilities, food service options, and a residence life program. In 2006, the Portland campus programs became open only to transfer admission.

Location

Located in McMinnville, 40 miles southwest of Portland, Linfield College is a leader in the cultural, educational, and recreational events of the fast-growing community of 35,000. Linfield is situated on 193 acres with most classrooms no more than a 10-minute walk from any of the twenty-four on-campus apartment buildings and residence halls. With most students living on campus, Linfield offers a welcoming and lively community.

Coffeehouses, cinemas, boutiques, a community theater, the Evergreen Air and Space Museum (including an IMAX theater and water park), bowling alleys, and a wide variety of restaurants are within walking distance for Linfield students. The central Oregon coast is an hour to the west, and the outdoor activity areas of the Oregon Cascade Range, including year-round skiing at Mount Hood, are two hours to the east. Salem, the state capital of Oregon, is 25 miles to the southeast, and Eugene is 80 miles south. Rainfall in western Oregon averages 42 inches annually and the winter temperature averages 41°F.

Majors and Degrees

Linfield offers the Bachelor of Arts degree in communication arts, creative writing, electronic arts, Francophone African Studies, French studies, German, German studies, history, intercultural communication, international relations, Japanese, Japanese studies, Latin American/Latino studies, literature, mass communication, music, philosophy, political science, religious studies, sociology, Spanish, studio art, and theater arts. The Bachelor of Arts or Bachelor of Science degree is offered in accounting, anthropology, applied physics, athletic training, biochemistry and molecular biology, biology, business, chemistry, computing science, economics, elementary education, environmental studies, exercise science, finance, international business, marketing, management, mathematics, physical activity and fitness studies, physical education, physics, and psychology. A Bachelor of Science in Nursing (B.S.N.) is also available. The College has programs to prepare students for advanced study in any health profession, including medicine, as well as law. The education department offers a strong program of teacher certification at the secondary and elementary levels.

Academic Programs

The academic year is divided into two 15-week semesters (fall and spring) and a four-week winter term in January. The January Term, required for first-year students, but optional for students in subsequent years, offers regular departmental courses and off-campus and international study. Academic courses are assigned 1–5 semester credit hours each; 125 credits are required for a B.A. or a B.S. degree. Students divide their time equally among required general education courses, a major area of study, and elective subjects. The Linfield Curriculum courses, selected to provide a solid foundation in the liberal arts, require students to take 3 semester hours in each of the six Modes of Inquiry as well as one upper-division course in one of these areas. These Modes of Inquiry are as follows: Vital Past; Ultimate Questions; Individuals, Systems, and Societies; Natural World; Creative Studies; and Quantitative Reasoning. In addition, students are required to take a writing-intensive course, a course addressing global pluralisms, and a course dealing with United States pluralism. Individually designed majors are available with faculty approval. Students majoring in a foreign language spend an academic year in a country in which the language being studied is the native tongue.

The College offers courses in English through the English Language and Culture Program. These courses are designed to help international students whose native language is not English to achieve competence in academic and social English skills, so that they may work effectively in their undergraduate classes at Linfield.

Off-Campus Programs

Off-campus educational experiences include the Semester Abroad program, involving four months of study in Australia, Austria, China, Costa Rica, Ecuador, England, France, Germany, Ireland, Japan, New Zealand, Norway, Senegal, South Korea, and Spain. Transportation for the first round-trip is included in the cost of tuition, and most of these study programs cost the same as a semester on campus. January Term study-abroad programs for four weeks are also offered. Recent offerings included Health Care in Kenya; China's Solutions to Energy Issues in the Twenty-first Century; Art and Visual Culture of Catalonia, Spain; and Australia: From Colony to Asian Power.

Academic Facilities

Over the last decade, the College has opened two residence halls, six apartment buildings, the James F. Miller Fine Arts Center, the Marshall Theatre and communication arts facility, the Vivian A. Bull Center for Music, and the Nicholson Library. The library covers 56,000 square feet and combines traditional collections of books and journals with the new and changing digital and electronic technology to provide access to the web and web-based

designs. The studio theater has an audience seating capacity of up to 140 and includes space for set construction and design.

In 2011, Linfield reopened the former library to provide new classroom and office space for the departments of business, economics, English, and philosophy. This state-of-the-art facility, T. J. Day Hall, includes the College's writing center and the Linfield Center for the Northwest (LCN). The LCN cultivates regionally relevant partnerships for training, research, service learning, and cultural or artistic exchanges. These opportunities promote student engagement in regional issues and produce real-world change. T. J. Day Hall is Linfield's first LEED-certified Gold building, underscoring the College's commitment to sustainability and conservation.

Murdock and Graf Halls house the biology, chemistry, and physics departments and up-to-date laboratories and equipment. Other facilities include art galleries and studios, a 250-watt FM radio station, an experimental psychology lab, dance and music studios, a preschool, and a 425-seat auditorium that houses a three-manual, 48-rank Casavant pipe organ.

Linfield students benefit from a communications and technology network that includes phone service, voice mail, e-mail, and wireless Internet connections in each residence hall room. In addition, there is wireless access in the library and other academic areas of the campus.

The Health and Physical Education/Recreation Complex houses three gymnasiums; weight rooms; fitness laboratories with a hydrostatic weighing tank, a metabolic and pulmonary measuring system, and an electrocardiovascular exercise ECG system; an eight-lane, 25-yard indoor pool; handball and racquetball courts; classrooms; offices; and a 28,000-square-foot field house.

Costs

For 2014–15, tuition and fees were $37,000 per two-semester year, board was $4,720, and a double room was $5,610. There was a $219 per-credit fee for on-campus January Term classes.

Financial Aid

Eligibility for most of Linfield's assistance programs is based on need as determined by a federally approved needs analysis processor. The only form required for need-based programs is the Free Application for Federal Student Aid (FAFSA). Linfield participates in the federal grant, loan, and work programs, and other forms of financial assistance on the basis of demonstrated need.

The College awards scholarships to full-time students based on scholastic achievement, independent of financial need. These academic scholarships vary from 30 to 60 percent of tuition. A number of criteria are used when determining scholarships, including grade point average, strength of curriculum, and standardized test scores. Linfield sponsors special scholarships for National Merit finalists. The College also sponsors an annual Competitive Scholarship Day in February. Participation is limited to high school seniors who meet particular academic requirements and apply by December 1. Each academic department offers prizes ranging from $12,000 to $20,000, divided over the student's four years at Linfield. Scholarships are also available to students from the departments of music, theater, and communication who demonstrate outstanding leadership and community service. Financial assistance for non–U.S. citizens is limited to partial-tuition scholarships and the opportunity to work part-time on campus.

Faculty

There are 129 faculty members, each of whom is committed to undergraduate teaching and scholarship. Ninety-one percent have doctoral or other terminal degrees within their field. The student-faculty ratio is 11:1, and faculty members serve as academic advisers. There are no teaching assistants.

Student Government

Students have a significant voice in establishing and changing College policies and regulations. The Student Senate, chosen through campus elections, is the focus of student opinion and debate. Students are represented on most College governing councils and committees with faculty members and trustees, and they are encouraged to express and implement their ideas on academic or extracurricular matters.

Admission Requirements

Admission to Linfield College is selective. Admission is granted to students who are likely to grow and succeed in a personal and challenging liberal arts environment. Each applicant is judged on individual merit, based on high school performance, a writing sample, recommendations from teachers and counselors, precollege standardized test results (ACT or SAT), and the depth and quality of an applicant's involvement in community and school activities. Linfield is a member of the Common Application Association.

International students whose education has been in a language other than English must submit certified English translations of their academic work. Proficiency in English is required, as demonstrated by an official TOEFL score report or other English proficiency exam.

Application and Information

The early action deadline is November 15 (with notification by January 15) and the regular decision priority deadline is February 15 (with notification by April 1).

Interviews are not required, but students are encouraged to visit. Appointments should be made in advance and can be requested online at http://www.linfield.edu/stopby. The Linfield website provides students with information on academic programs, student life, and athletics.

Interested students are encouraged to contact:

Office of Admission
Linfield College
900 SE Baker Street
McMinnville, Oregon 97128
Phone: 503-883-2213
800-640-2287 (toll-free)
Fax: 503-883-2472
E-mail: admission@linfield.edu
Website: http://www.linfield.edu/admission
http://www.facebook.com/linfieldadmit
http://twitter.com/linfieldadmit

Linfield College is located 1 hour southwest of Portland, Oregon's largest city, on nearly 200 acres. Nearly sixty buildings, many built in Georgian colonial style, house forty academic departments among a grove of oak trees.

LOYOLA UNIVERSITY MARYLAND

BALTIMORE, MARYLAND

★ To read more about this school, visit http://petersons.to/loyolauniversityinmaryland

LOYOLA
UNIVERSITY MARYLAND

The University

Loyola University Maryland is a Jesuit, Catholic comprehensive university committed to the educational and spiritual traditions of the Society of Jesus and the development of the whole person. Accordingly, the University inspires students to learn, lead, and serve in a diverse and changing world.

Loyola's current full-time undergraduate enrollment is 4,084; 81 percent of the student body lives on campus with most first-year students participating in Messina, Loyola's living-learning program. The University encourages co-curricular activities that contribute to the academic, social, and spiritual growth of the student. These include social and cultural organizations, student government activities, an ROTC program, national honor societies, and Patriot League Division I athletic programs such as basketball, cross-country, golf, lacrosse, soccer, swimming and diving, tennis, track, and volleyball. The majority of the student body participates in the wide variety of club and intramural sports offered.

In recent years, Loyola's campus has undergone significant expansion. Thirteen apartment complexes and four first-year residence halls provide Loyola students with on-campus housing. In 2011, the Donnelly Science Center was expanded, making it the largest academic building on the Evergreen campus. The Andrew White Student Center offers several dining choices, as well as spacious meeting and recreational space. The Student Center also provides facilities for athletics, the communication department, and the fine arts, including the McManus Theatre and Reitz Arena, which holds as many as 3,000 people for various events. The Center also has an art gallery, classrooms, black box theater, and music, photography, and studio art labs. Loyola's recreational sports facility is the Fitness and Aquatic Center. This 115,000-square-foot state-of-the-art athletic facility provides an indoor pool, basketball courts, squash courts, a climbing wall, fitness equipment, tracks, and outdoor playing fields. The Ridley Athletic Complex, completed in spring 2010, is a 6,000-seat grandstand stadium with locker rooms, a weight-training suite, concession areas, and memorabilia for sale on-site.

Location

The Loyola campus is located in a residential area of north Baltimore, 5 miles from the Inner Harbor area. This location offers students the advantage of quiet residential living with the attractions of city life. The metropolitan area has a wide variety of theaters, museums, professional and intercollegiate sports events, and historical points of interest. Other colleges and universities in the vicinity help to expand the social calendar and academic life.

Majors and Degrees

Loyola offers more than 32 majors and more than 48 minors. The Bachelor of Arts degree is awarded in art history, classical civilization, classics, communication, comparative cultures and literary studies, computer science, economics, elementary education, English, fine arts, French, German, global studies, history, philosophy, political science, psychology, sociology, Spanish, speech pathology/audiology, theology, and writing. The Bachelor of Business Administration degree is awarded in accounting, business economics, finance, general business, information systems, international business, management, and marketing. The Bachelor of Science degree is awarded in biology, chemistry, computer science, engineering science, mathematical science, statistics, and physics.

Academic Programs

The curriculum at Loyola is divided into three parts: the core, the major, and electives. The core contains those courses that Loyola considers essential to the liberal arts curriculum. These courses, which are required of all students regardless of major, are completed throughout the four years. The core consists of a classical or modern language, English literature, writing, mathematics and natural science, social science, fine arts, history, philosophy, ethics, and theology. The major enables students to pursue their specialized area of study in depth. Electives give students the opportunity to broaden their intellectual and cultural background in areas of special interest. To prepare for graduate study, students may enroll in one of four pre-professional programs: dental, law, medical, or veterinary.

Messina, Loyola's universal living-learning program, is a unique, first-year experience designed to help students adjust quickly to college-level work and forge a clear path to success at Loyola and in the life and career that will follow. Messina offers a similarly distinctive and powerful beginning, an opportunity to explore a wide range of disciplines, appreciate their interconnectedness, and take to heart the importance of learning in a student's personal and intellectual growth.

Off-Campus Programs

Loyola University Maryland participates in a cooperative program with Notre Dame of Maryland University, Johns Hopkins University, Goucher College, Morgan State University, Towson University, the Peabody Conservatory of Music, and the Maryland Institute College of Art. Loyola students may cross-register at any of these area colleges and universities.

Students in good academic standing may pursue studies abroad through Loyola's programs in Accra, Ghana; Copenhagen, Denmark; Glasgow, Scotland; Leuven, Belgium; Bangkok, Thailand; Alcalá, Spain; Melbourne, Australia; Newcastle, England; Auckland, New Zealand; Beijing, China; Cork, Ireland; Rome, Italy; Paris, France; and San Salvador, El Salvador. Loyola also participates in exchange programs with eight other countries, offers summer and winter study tours, and assists students in applying to a variety of non-Loyola affiliated international study programs each year.

Academic Facilities

Loyola celebrated the completion of the Donnelly Science Center expansion in September 2011. The 15,000-square-foot addition provides class laboratory spaces, research laboratories, offices, a conference room for the natural sciences, storage, a vivarium, a microscopy center, and a robotics laboratory. Spacious hallways connecting the building's wings on all levels include spaces for science displays and gathering areas for students and faculty in biology, chemistry, physics, computer science, and engineering.

The Sellinger School of Business and Management is Loyola's AACSB-accredited business school. Highlights of this school include experiential learning requirements, the Sellinger Scholars honors program, many student associations, and the Student Experiential Learning Lab, a state-of-the-art trading room that allows students access to the three most widely used databases in the finance industry—Reuters, Morningstar, and Bloomberg—and features a six-screen video display for breaking news and real-time market updates and a scrolling price ticker.

Costs

For 2015–16, tuition for all undergraduate students is $43,800 per year. Room for first-year students is $9,680. Student fees are estimated at $1,400.

Financial Aid

The University strives to make a Loyola education accessible for qualified students of all socioeconomic backgrounds. Financial aid is awarded based on academic ability and financial need. Seventy-two percent of the student body receives financial assistance in the forms of Loyola University Maryland grants and scholarships, state scholarships, Federal Supplemental Educational Opportunity Grants, Federal Pell Grants, Federal Perkins Loans, and Federal Work-Study Program opportunities. To apply for financial assistance, students must submit the Free Application for Federal Student Aid (FAFSA) and the CSS/Financial Aid PROFILE through the College Scholarship Service in Princeton, New Jersey. The financial aid application deadline is February 15.

Faculty

Loyola intends to maintain its faculty-student ratio of approximately 1:12 and an average class size of 20 students to ensure its continued focus on students as individuals. Of the 354 full-time faculty members, 84 percent have a Ph.D. or terminal degree in their field and 75 percent are tenured or on the tenure track. No classes are taught by graduate students or teaching assistants.

Student Government

The Student Government serves three chief functions, which make its existence not only valuable but also necessary. These functions are to represent the student body outside the University, to provide leadership within the student body, and to perform services, both social and academic, for the students. Responsibility for budgeting activities also rests with the Student Government. The president of the Student Government is a member of the College Academic Council.

Admission Requirements

The admission evaluation at Loyola combines an analysis of academic information submitted along with a review of recommendations, the record of extracurricular involvement and evidence of special talent, leadership, and service. The admission committee does not use a formula or have strict cutoffs. Instead, the admission office's goal is to conduct a balanced and holistic review, taking a number of factors into account. Submission of SAT and ACT scores is optional for all first-year applicants, excluding home-school students. Students who choose not to submit standardized test scores must submit an additional letter of recommendation or personal essay. Students may apply early decision (binding), early action (nonbinding), or regular decision. The University welcomes applications from students of character, intelligence, and motivation, without discrimination on the grounds of race or religious belief.

Application and Information

Interested students seeking to enroll at Loyola may apply online using the Loyola Application or the Common Application. Each applicant must submit a school counselor letter of recommendation, a teacher letter of recommendation, and a personal statement. Applicants for financial aid must file the Free Application for Federal Student Aid (FAFSA) to be considered for federal student aid and also file the CSS Profile application to be considered for all forms of institutionally funded need-based aid. A $60 application fee must accompany the application for admission.

For additional information, students are encouraged to contact:

Undergraduate Admission Office
Loyola University Maryland
4501 North Charles Street
Baltimore, Maryland 21210-2699
Phone: 410-617-5012
800-221-9107 (toll-free)
Website: http://www.loyola.edu/undergraduate
http://www.facebook.com/LoyolaMarylandAdmission
https://twitter.com/chooseloyola
https://instagram.com/chooseloyola

Loyola University Maryland is located in residential Baltimore, 5 miles from the Inner Harbor and less than an hour from Washington, D.C., giving students access to an array of cultural events, restaurants, shops, and internship opportunities.

COLLEGE CLOSE-UPS

LUTHER COLLEGE

DECORAH, IOWA

★ To read more about this school, visit http://petersons.to/luthercollege

The College

Luther College, founded in 1861 by Norwegian immigrants, is a four-year residential liberal arts college of the Lutheran church (ELCA). The College is an academic community of faith and learning where students of promise from all beliefs and backgrounds have the freedom to learn, to express themselves, to perform, to compete, and to grow. Located in Decorah, Iowa, the College is home to nearly 2,400 students from forty states and sixty-one countries. Thirty percent of the students are from Iowa; 84 percent come from the four-state area of Iowa, Minnesota, Wisconsin, and Illinois. In 2014–15, 146 international students choose to study at Luther.

In keeping with its liberal arts tradition, the College requires students to develop a depth of knowledge in their chosen major and a breadth of knowledge through exposure to a wide range of subjects and intellectual approaches (general requirements). Learning at Luther is about engagement: faculty members who are passionate in their teaching and scholarship; students who are bright, active, and involved; and a College community characterized by personal attention, hands-on experiences, academic challenge, and community support. At Luther, all students become immersed in the liberal arts through the College's Paideia program. This program, which is uncommon in its approach, helps train students' minds and develop their research and writing skills as they explore human cultures and history. In addition, Luther offers a Phi Beta Kappa chapter and departmental honor societies, evidence of the quality of teaching and learning on campus.

At Luther, students are encouraged to seek out connections between their lives in the classroom and their lives outside the classroom. The College provides a stimulating cultural and educational atmosphere by bringing distinguished public figures, theater groups, musicians, and educators to the campus. Cocurricular activities are an important part of college life. The College sponsors six choirs, three orchestras, three bands, two jazz bands, and a full theater and dance program. Numerous student organizations and societies provide ample opportunities for student involvement in meaningful activities. As a community of faith, students can participate in chapel, weekly Sunday worship, and outreach teams.

Nineteen intercollegiate sports are offered. Men may participate in ten sports: baseball, basketball, cross-country, football, golf, soccer, swimming, tennis, track and field, and wrestling. Women compete in nine intercollegiate sports: basketball, cross-country, golf, soccer, softball, swimming, tennis, track and field, and volleyball. Club sports include Ultimate (Frisbee), rugby, and women's lacrosse. Seventy percent of the student body is involved in an extensive intramural and recreational sports program. Available for recreational use are twelve outdoor tennis courts, an eight-lane polyurethane 400-meter track, numerous cross-country running and ski trails, and 15 acres of intramural fields. The well-equipped Regents Center houses four hardwood basketball courts, a wrestling complex, three racquetball courts, and a 3,000-seat gymnasium. A sports forum accommodates a six-lane, 200-meter indoor track; six indoor tennis courts; locker rooms; and athletic training facilities. The Legends Fitness for Life Center provides the latest fitness equipment and a 30-foot-high rock-climbing wall. A new aquatic center opened in the fall of 2013 that features an eight-lane stainless steel pool complete with diving well.

Location

The College is located in Decorah, a city of 8,100 people in the scenic bluff country of northeast Iowa. The Upper Iowa River, which runs through the campus, is designated as a National Scenic and Recreational River. Rich in Scandinavian heritage, Decorah is a popular recreation area, providing opportunities for canoeing, kayaking, fishing, hunting, cross-country skiing, camping, hiking, biking, and spelunking. Three airports are located within a 75-mile radius of Decorah: in Rochester, Minnesota; Waterloo, Iowa; and La Crosse, Wisconsin.

Majors and Degrees

Luther College grants the Bachelor of Arts (B.A.) degree and offers majors in accounting, Africana studies, anthropology, art, athletic training, Biblical languages, biology, business (management), chemistry, classics, communication studies, computer science, dance, economics, elementary education, English, environmental studies, French, German, health and fitness promotion, health education–teaching, history, intermedia arts, international studies, management, mathematics, mathematics/statistics, music, nursing, philosophy, physical education–exercise physiology, physical education–teaching, physics, political science, psychology, religion, Russian studies, Scandinavian studies, secondary education, social work, sociology, Spanish, theater, and women and gender studies. Preprofessional preparation is offered in dentistry, engineering, law, medicine, optometry, pharmacy, physical therapy, seminary, and veterinary medicine.

Academic Programs

Luther operates on a 4-1-4 academic calendar. The first semester runs from September to December, followed by a three-week January Term and the second semester, which runs from February to May. Two four-week summer sessions are offered in June and July. All students must complete at least thirty regular courses and two January-term courses in order to graduate from Luther. Other requirements for graduation include four common foundational courses: Paideia (111 and 112); foreign language (typically one or two courses); religion (two courses, one of which must be in biblical studies); and wellness (two 1-credit courses). In addition to a focused area of study (the major, which usually requires eight to ten courses), Luther requires all students to take courses in three general fields of inquiry: the natural world (two courses); human behavior (two courses); and human expression (two courses). Before graduating, students are required to bring together all they have learned in two culminating experiences: senior project (one course); and Paideia 450. Luther students also develop the perspectives and skills they will utilize in their lives as citizens and professionals equipped for distinguished service. Qualified students may develop interdisciplinary majors with faculty advisers.

Off-Campus Programs

Luther operates under the belief that the best education connects students with global issues and helps them engage with the larger world. Luther is consistently ranked among the top baccalaureate colleges in the nation for the number of students studying abroad prior to graduation.

Luther's off-campus programs not only span the globe, but also offer in-depth and immersive study in a wide variety of subjects. Students may participate in programs during fall and spring semesters, the January Term, and summer sessions.

The College's signature off-campus programs include an academic-year program in Nottingham, England; a semester program in Sliema, Malta; a semester program in Münster, Germany; and a semester program in Coldigioco, Italy. In addition, Luther is part of a thirteen-college consortium which runs a successful Washington Semester in Washington, D.C. Students also have options for urban study at several centers in Chicago.

Each January Term, 300–400 Luther students study on twenty to twenty-five faculty-led domestic and international programs.

Finally, Luther students have a wide variety of off-campus options through Luther-affiliated programs, such as those sponsored by the Associated Colleges of the Midwest, Institute for Study

Abroad–Butler University, the Institute for the International Education of Students (IES), and International Studies Abroad (ISA), among others.

Academic Facilities

The 1,000-acre campus includes the Preus Library, housing 340,812 volumes, 525 print periodicals, 150,000 electronic books, and the College art collection. The library's circulation desk, Research Help Desk, Technology Help Desk, and Digital Media Center connect students with the resources they need. Two science teaching facilities, Sampson Hoffland Laboratories and Valders Hall of Science, feature modern, well-equipped labs as well as a planetarium, a greenhouse, a herbarium, a live-animal center, a human anatomy laboratory, a natural history museum, and a psychology sleep laboratory. Within easy walking distance of the campus, the field study area offers an ideal setting for studies in aquatic biology, ecology, and field biology. Five ponds, two reestablished prairies, marshes, wooded areas, and agricultural lands are available for classwork and independent study. The College has wired and wireless networking support throughout the campus. Residence halls, classrooms, and labs are outfitted with computers, printers, and academic software. Multiple connections to the Internet provide high bandwidth and reliable connectivity.

Luther College maintains radio station KWLC-AM, and the College's affiliate station, KLSE-FM, is part of the Minnesota Public Radio network. Luther is also home to one of the largest archaeological research centers in Iowa. In addition to computer facilities and video screening rooms, the Language Learning Center houses a foreign language media library with over 800 foreign language films, audio books, and print books for language learners.

The economics and business, mathematics, and computer science departments are located in the impressive F. W. Olin Building.

The award-winning Jenson-Noble Hall of Music contains 32,000 square feet of classrooms, studios, practice rooms, and rehearsal rooms for keyboard, vocal, and instrumental music. The Center for Faith and Life (CFL) houses a 42-stop/62-rank organ in the 1,600-seat auditorium for the performing arts. A 200-seat recital hall, a 24-hour meditation chapel, and one of four campus art galleries are located in the CFL as well. The Center for the Arts serves as the home for theater, dance, and the visual arts.

Costs

For 2014–15, the comprehensive fee was $45,260, which included tuition, facilities fees, room, board, subscription to student publications, and admission to College-supported concerts, lectures, and other events. A room telephone, cable TV, computer access from residence hall rooms, and a health-service program were also included. Private music lessons are $425 per semester. It is estimated that an additional $3,000 is adequate for books, clothing, entertainment, and other personal expenses.

Financial Aid

More than 98 percent of all Luther students receive financial aid in the form of grants, scholarships, low-interest loans, and work-study jobs on campus. Luther awards Founders, President's, and Dean's Scholarships to students demonstrating superior academic achievement. The amount of aid given is determined by an analysis of the Free Application for Federal Student Aid (FAFSA).

Faculty

There are 179 full-time faculty members; 93 percent hold a Ph.D., first professional, or other terminal degree. The student-faculty ratio is 12:1.

Student Government

Students share in the governance of the College and participate in social and cultural programming. They have full membership on most College committees, majority representation in the Community Assembly, and nonvoting representation on the Board of Regents.

Admission Requirements

Admission is selective. An applicant must be a graduate of an accredited high school and have completed at least 4 units of English, 3 units of mathematics, 3 units of social science, and 2 units of natural science. It is strongly recommended that the applicant have at least two years of a foreign language. Sixty-three percent of entering students rank in the top quarter of their high school class. Transfer students may enroll at the beginning of the fall or spring semester or the January term.

Application and Information

An application, SAT or ACT scores, an educator's reference, and a transcript of previous academic work are required for admission. On-campus interviews are recommended but not required. For more information about Luther, students should contact:

Admissions Office
Luther College
700 College Drive
Decorah, Iowa 52101-1042
Phone: 563-387-1287
800-458-8437 (toll-free)
Fax: 563-387-2159
E-mail: admissions@luther.edu (admissions)
finaid@luther.edu (financial aid)
global@luther.edu (international)
Website: http://admissions.luther.edu
http://www.facebook.com/luthercollege1861
http://twitter.com/luthercollege

Luther College students learn in a community that emphasizes rigorous academics, a world-class music program, competitive athletics, and opportunities to put their classroom learning to the test through internships, independent research, and study abroad. Typically, 98 percent of Luther graduates are employed, attending graduate school, or engaged in an internship or volunteer work within eight months of graduation.

COLLEGE CLOSE-UPS

LYNCHBURG COLLEGE
LYNCHBURG, VIRGINIA

Lynchburg College

COLLEGE CLOSE-UPS

The College

Lynchburg College provides a dynamic learning experience for its 2,500 undergraduate and graduate students. A fully accredited, coeducational, residential college affiliated with the Christian Church (Disciples of Christ), Lynchburg College (LC) offers forty undergraduate majors, fifty-two minors, and fourteen pre-professional programs, all supported by a strong liberal arts foundation. The College's graduate studies program includes two doctoral degrees and fourteen master's programs. Lynchburg College is nationally recognized by such publications as The Princeton Review's *The Best 376 Colleges: 2014 edition* and is one of the forty colleges featured in Loren Pope's *Colleges That Change Lives*.

LC's student body is composed of students from thirty-six states and fourteen foreign countries. The College community is largely residential with 75 percent of the full-time undergraduate student body living on campus.

The 250-acre campus is considered one of the most beautiful in the South with thirty-seven buildings of mostly Georgian Colonial style against a backdrop of the majestic Blue Ridge Mountains. A $12-million expansion and renovation of the Drysdale Student Center has resulted in ample and attractive space for students to gather for dining, fitness, student activities, and club and organization meetings.

The LC community is a busy place, with a wide variety of activities including service and honor organizations, such as the national Bonner Leaders Program; more than 100 clubs and organizations; three fraternities; seven sororities; and opportunities to participate in dramatic productions, student publications, religious activities, and musical performances. The Outdoor Leadership Program provides adventure-based leadership and team-building opportunities for individuals and groups. Community service (www.lynchburg.edu/volunteering-and-service) is a distinguishing feature of Lynchburg College students, staff, and faculty, who last year contributed more than 70,000 volunteer hours to the community through such projects as Habitat for Humanity, Camp Jaycees, Special Olympics, and other programs, earning the College a place on the 2014 President's Higher Education Community Service Honor Roll.

The varsity athletic program (http://athletics.lynchburg.edu) includes twenty-one sports for men and women. In 2014, LC's women's soccer team won the NCAA Division III championship, bringing home the first team national championship in the history of the College. LC is a charter member of the Old Dominion Athletic Conference (ODAC) and supports several intramural and club sports for men and women. The Turner Athletic Facility includes exercise and fitness areas, a dance studio, and one of the top exercise physiology labs in Virginia.

At the heart of LC athletic facilities is the newly renovated Shellenberger Field complex for men's and women's soccer, lacrosse, track and field, and field hockey, as well as intramural and club sports. The facility features a large, new artificial turf field, a new state-of-the-art eight-lane track, night lighting, and a 3,000-spectator capacity stadium with chair and bleacher seating. Moon Field is home to LC's softball team and the track and field events of javelin, hammer, shot put, and discus. Fox Field is one of the nicest baseball fields in the ODAC, with batting cages, a press box, and seating for up to 1,000 fans.

Location

Lynchburg College (www.lynchburg.edu) is located in central Virginia, 100 miles from Richmond, Virginia, 180 miles southwest of Washington, D.C., and 50 miles east of Roanoke, Virginia. Air, bus, and railroad transportation place Lynchburg within easy reach of any urban center. Greater Lynchburg is a growing business and industrial center with a population of more than 240,000. The city is noted for its climate, culture, historic landmarks, and proximity to the Blue Ridge Mountains.

Majors and Degrees

Lynchburg College offers the Bachelor of Arts degree in: accounting, art (graphic design or studio art), business administration, communication studies (convergent journalism, social influence, electronic media or public relations), economics (financial or general), English (literature or writing), French, history, international relations, liberal arts studies, management, marketing, music (instrumental or vocal education, instrumental or vocal performance), philosophy, political science, religious studies, sociology (cultural studies, deviance and crime, human services), Spanish, sports management, and theater. The Bachelor of Science degree is offered in: athletic training, biology, biomedical science, chemistry, computer science, environmental science, exercise physiology, health promotion, human development and learning (elementary education or special education), mathematics, nursing, physics, and psychology. For more information, prospective students should visit www.lynchburg.edu/majors-and-minors.

Pre-professional and professional courses are available for students who want preparation for careers in art therapy, dentistry, engineering, forestry and wildlife management, law, library science, medicine, ministry and ministry-related occupations, occupational therapy, optometry, pharmacy, physical therapy, and veterinary medicine.

Graduate programs include: Doctor of Physical Therapy; Doctor of Education in Leadership Studies; Master of Business Administration; Master of Arts in history and music; Master of Education in clinical mental health and school counseling, curriculum and instruction, educational leadership, educational studies, reading, science education, and special education; and the Master of Science in Nursing. A Master of Physician Assistant Medicine program is scheduled to begin in June 2015. Lynchburg College has applied for provisional accreditation from the Accreditation Review Commission on Education for the Physician Assistant (ARC-PA).

Three new master's degree programs will launch in the fall of 2015 that will not only increase the skill level of successful graduates but will also be beneficial to the communities they will serve. The new programs are Master of Criminal Justice Leadership, Master of Nonprofit Leadership Studies, and Master of Public Health.

Seven graduate certificates provide professional development opportunities to graduate students in the areas of literacy studies, applied behavior analysis, earth science, counseling, and special education.

Academic Programs

To be eligible for a degree, a student must complete at least 124 semester hours of college-level academic work with a grade point average of at least 2.0 or higher on all work undertaken in the major field.

The curriculum at Lynchburg College is divided into two general areas: general education requirements (GERs) and the major. GERs are selected from the broad disciplines of world literature, fine arts, philosophy, religious studies, mathematics, history, social science, laboratory science, foreign languages, and health and movement science. Additional hours are available for students to explore coursework in free elective hours of their choice or students may devote their free elective hours to a minor.

Outstanding students may be selected to participate in the College's Westover Honors Program (www.lynchburg.edu/westoverhonors), designed to attract, stimulate, challenge, and fulfill academically gifted students. The program offers a challenging curriculum that promotes intellectual curiosity and independent thinking and places strong emphasis on creative problem solving.

Off-Campus Programs

Various agency and intercollegiate exchange programs are available and students are encouraged to engage in foreign-study programs, particularly LC's study-abroad program (www.lynchburg.edu/study-abroad).

Internships, organized through the Academic and Career Services Office, are available locally, nationally, and internationally (www.lynchburg.edu/career-services). More than 1,000 internships are already established, and new sites are developed each year. As members of the Tri-College Consortium of Virginia, Lynchburg College, Randolph College, and Sweet Briar College maintain cooperative relationships for sharing facilities and offerings.

Academic Facilities

Lynchburg College has twenty-three computer labs with both PCs and Macs. New students may bring a computer of their own or utilize one of the many available on campus. All students are assigned an e-mail account and have access to the Internet. All residence hall rooms are wired for network access and the Intranet, which serves the College community. Wireless Internet access is available in most areas of the campus.

The Hobbs Science Center provides an outstanding learning environment for students studying biology, chemistry, physics, biomedical sciences, environmental science, psychology, mathematics, and computer science. A cadaver lab, cutting-edge research labs, online weather station, GIS and remote sensing software, and digitizer are just some of the learning tools available. This facility is also used during the summer by the Virginia Governor's School for Math and Science to provide programming for selected high school students.

Schewel Hall, a $12-million classroom and laboratory facility, houses the School of Business and Economics, the Communication Studies program, foreign languages, and performing arts. This 67,000-square-foot facility includes technology-based classrooms, computer laboratories, and specialized teaching-learning settings, including a model stock exchange room, a digital darkroom, and a multimedia development center with television and recording studios. Sydnor Performance Hall provides an excellent venue for concerts, lectures, and other programs, with seating for 250 people.

The Daura Art Gallery (www.lynchburg.edu/daura-gallery) is the major repository of more than 1,000 works of Pierre Daura, the Catalan-American artist for whom the Gallery is named. Each year, The Daura Gallery features traveling exhibitions throughout the academic year and is the site for the Senior Art Show where selected student works are exhibited.

The Claytor Nature Study Center provides an outdoor classroom and laboratory for hands-on, field-based environmental study and research. Located at the foot of the Blue Ridge Mountains in Bedford County, the Claytor Center was run as a farm from the late 1700s until the mid-1990s, when it was given to Lynchburg College by the late A. Boyd Claytor III, a member of the LC Board of Trustees. The property has lakes, woodlands, wetlands, grasslands, rare plants, formal gardens, a primitive campground, and three miles of hiking trails. The land is now managed for environmental conservation and restoration through agreements with the Virginia Outdoors Foundation and the USDA's Natural Resources Conservation Service.

The A. Boyd Claytor III Education and Research Facility, a 7,700-square-foot multipurpose building, offers LC students and regional K–12 students and teachers an ideal location for learning with seminar, laboratory, classroom, conference, and retreat space.

The Belk Astronomical Observatory sits at one of the highest points on the Claytor Nature Study Center property (approximately 960 feet above sea level) and is one of the most publicly accessible dark sky observatories in Virginia. The observatory features an RC Optical Systems 20-inch (0.51 meter) Truss Ritchey-Chrétien telescope with a 177-square-foot dome housing, an observation deck equipped with twelve piers for mounting smaller telescopes, and a control room with instrumentation that allows LC to conduct extensive stellar and planetary research and pursue astronomical research with other regional colleges and universities.

The Chandler Eco-Lodge, a 2,100-square-foot lodge, provides accommodations for 14 to 16 people to stay at Claytor Nature Study Center and study outside the classroom. The lodge is built with energy-efficiency and low-impact design and includes a constructed wetland to handle wastewater.

Costs

Total charges for resident students for the 2014–15 session were $43,075: $33,600 tuition, $8,530 room and board, and $945 student fees (www.lynchburg.edu/undergraduate-admission/tuition-fees).

Financial Aid

Lynchburg College administers a financial aid program of more than $26 million. These resources are awarded to students for meritorious achievement and/or for demonstrated need. Lynchburg College offers academic scholarships (www.lynchburg.edu/financial-aid/scholarships) that range from $10,000 to $20,000 and are based on performance and accomplishments at the high school or community college level. These awards are renewable each year until the student graduates, as long as the recipient maintains a qualifying minimum academic average each year. Students are identified to receive these scholarships through the admission application; no separate application is necessary. Free early aid estimates are available for students. More than 98 percent of last year's entering class received academic and/or need-based financial aid. The average amount of aid received was $23,500.

To determine eligibility for need-based financial aid, the student should complete the Free Application for Federal Student Aid (FAFSA), which may be obtained at most high schools and at the College. The FAFSA results determine the student's eligibility for federally funded grants and loans and other support such as work-study opportunities. In addition, students from Virginia are eligible to apply for the Virginia Tuition Assistance grant.

Faculty

Lynchburg College faculty members are outstanding scholars who are leaders in their disciplines. Of the 181 full-time members, 82 percent hold the doctorate or terminal degree in their fields. The student-faculty ratio is 12:1, which allows for personal attention and student-faculty collaborative research, both of which are essential to the LC experience. While LC faculty are involved in various research and writing projects, College policy requires that teaching will be their top priority.

Admission Requirements

A candidate for admission to Lynchburg College (www.lynchburg.edu/undergraduate-admission) should be a graduate of an approved secondary school with a minimum of 16 academic units or the equivalent, as shown by examination. It is required that the academic work include major emphases in the areas of English, foreign language, social science, natural sciences, and mathematics. An applicant must demonstrate above-average academic ability in all areas of study, as admission is competitive. In support of the record, a student must present satisfactory scores on the ACT or SAT (critical reading and math scores are used to determine admission decisions and merit scholarship awards). It is recommended that all students have a personal interview and visit the campus beginning the spring semester of their junior year or during their senior year. Enrollment Office hours during the academic year are 9 a.m. to 5 p.m. Monday through Friday and 10 a.m. to noon on Saturday during the academic year.

Application and Information

The College operates on an early semester calendar. The first semester begins in late August and ends before Christmas, and the second semester runs from mid-January to early May. An optional winter term abroad is also offered.

Early decision admission applications must be received by November 15 (www.lynchburg.edu/undergraduate-admission/freshman-application-steps); notification of acceptance is made by December 15. All other applications are processed on a rolling admissions basis. Applicants are notified of the status of their application usually within two to four weeks of the date their application file is completed.

For information, students should contact:

Sharon Walters-Bower, Director of Admissions
Lynchburg College
1501 Lakeside Drive
Lynchburg, Virginia 24501
Phone: 434-544-8300
800-426-8101 (toll-free)
Fax: 434-544-8653
E-mail: admissions@lynchburg.edu
Website: http://www.lynchburg.edu
http://www.facebook.com/lynchburgcollege
http://twitter.com/lynchburg
http://www.youtube.com/lynchburgcollege
http://www.flickr.com/photos/lynchburgcollege

Schewel Hall is a popular campus meeting place housing classrooms, meeting and study rooms, and technology studios like the multi-camera television studio and digital control room.

COLLEGE CLOSE-UPS

MANHATTAN COLLEGE

RIVERDALE, NEW YORK

★ To read more about this school, visit http://petersons.to/manhattancollege

MANHATTAN COLLEGE

The College

Manhattan College has more than sixty programs that build upon a strong liberal arts foundation and offer professional preparation in arts, business, education and health, science, and engineering. Learning extends beyond the classroom through internships in New York City and beyond.

The College is one of only a few U.S. colleges to have chapters of all five of these distinguished national honor societies: Phi Beta Kappa, Beta Gamma Sigma, Kappa Delta Pi, Sigma Xi, and Beta Pi.

Manhattan placed fifteenth among 900 U.S. colleges and universities on the 2014 College Return on Investment (ROI) Report and ranked in the top 1 percent of private universities for ROI in the Million Dollar ROI ranking.

Following in the Lasallian Catholic tradition, many Manhattan College students actively define their commitment to social justice by balancing their traditional lifestyles with immersion and service experiences around the city, country, and world.

Each year, Campus Ministry and Social Action (CMSA) organizes several L.O.V.E. programs (Lasallian Outreach Volunteer Experience), which give students the opportunity to travel to some of the world's poorest areas in New Orleans, West Virginia, Kenya, Ecuador, and the Dominican Republic to volunteer with people of very different socioeconomic backgrounds.

Manhattan College Jaspers do not have to travel far to lend a helping hand throughout the semester. The Lasallian Collegians group volunteers on campus and in New York City by arranging school blood drives, toy drives, soup kitchen trips, and food runs. In addition, the Arches, a learning-living resident program, offers first-year students the opportunity to live in community, attend two classes together, and experience New York City through service projects in the city.

The tight-knit College community is comprised of 3,675 students. With a 12:1 student-to-faculty ratio, professors know students personally and care about their success. The majority of students live on the traditional collegiate campus, which is just a subway ride from midtown Manhattan.

Location

Manhattan College's 22-acre campus is located 10 miles north of midtown Manhattan in the suburban Riverdale section of the Bronx, about a mile from Westchester County. The College is located in the world's greatest cultural hub, where renowned museums and landmarks serve as off-campus classrooms. Students have access to internship and job opportunities at some of the country's most prestigious companies.

Majors and Degrees

Arts: The liberal arts curriculum of the School of Arts provides programs that lead to a Bachelor of Arts or Bachelor of Science degree with majors in the humanities and the social sciences, including art history, communication, economics, English, fine arts, government, history, labor studies, modern foreign languages, philosophy, psychology, religious studies, and sociology. Interdisciplinary majors include international studies, peace studies, and urban studies.

Science: In the School of Science, programs lead to a Bachelor of Science or Bachelor of Arts degree with majors in biochemistry, biology, chemistry, computer science, environmental science, mathematics, and physics. Pre-medical, pre-dental, and pre-veterinary studies programs are also available.

Engineering: The School of Engineering has a well-deserved reputation as one of the best college engineering schools in the nation and offers programs leading to a Bachelor of Science degree in chemical, civil, computer, electrical, and mechanical engineering. The program is fully accredited by the Educational Accreditation Commission of ABET. Graduate programs are also available in chemical, civil, computer, electrical, environmental, and mechanical engineering.

Business: The School of Business, accredited by AACSB International, has programs leading to a Bachelor of Science in Business Administration degree with majors in accounting, business analytics, computer information systems, economics, finance, global business studies, management, and marketing. In addition, Manhattan College also offers the following graduate programs: the Bachelor of Science in Professional Accounting/Master of Business Administration and the Bachelor of Science in Business/Master of Business Administration, which offer students the opportunity to complete a five-year multiple award program.

Education and Health: The School of Education and Health offers a curriculum leading to a Bachelor of Arts degree in childhood education, childhood/special education (dual program), and adolescent education. The kinesiology curriculum leads to a Bachelor of Science degree in physical education and exercise science. The health curriculum leads to a Bachelor of Science degree in allied health, with a concentration in health-care administration, health counseling, or scientific foundations. Curricula in radiological and health sciences lead to a Bachelor of Science in radiation therapy, radiologic technology, or nuclear medicine technology. In addition, the School of Education and Health offers the five-year childhood/special education program, which allows the student to receive a bachelor's and master's degree with eligibility to pursue certification for grades 1–6 in regular and special education. The School of Education and Health also offers master's degrees and professional diplomas in school counseling, mental health counseling, special education, and school building leadership. All programs are approved by the New York State Education Department and accredited by the Teacher Education Accreditation Council (TEAC).

Academic Programs

The core curriculum shared by the School of Arts and the School of Science studies some of the vital works of humankind, explores new ideas, examines the meaning of scientific experimentation, and encourages a student to develop his or her thinking and leadership abilities. The major programs offer advanced work in specific humanistic and scientific disciplines and opportunities to work on research projects in collaboration with faculty scholars.

In the School of Engineering, all engineering students follow a common core curriculum during the first two years and choose a major at the beginning of the junior year. Each curriculum includes a generous selection of courses in basic sciences, the engineering sciences, humanistic studies, and mathematics.

The School of Business prepares students for positions of executive responsibility in business, government, and nonprofit organizations. The business curriculum is based on a strong commitment to liberal education and is well balanced between professional business courses, humanities, sciences, and social sciences. This is a reflection of the school's belief that executives should be broadly educated and should involve themselves, as well as their organizations, in efforts to solve social problems.

The School of Education and Health prepares students for teaching, counseling, and health professions. Students complete the College's core curriculum in liberal arts and sciences and then complete a major in various programs in the school's three departments: education, kinesiology, and radiological and health professions. All programs include internships/practicums in schools, hospitals, or other institutions. Graduates of the school's teacher-preparation programs receive New York State provisional teaching certification. The school also offers a five-year B.A./M.S. program in childhood/special education and special education.

Off-Campus Programs

Manhattan College also offers study-abroad programs in many countries; arrangements can be made to study in a country of choice. Students in the School of Business may participate in the International Field Studies Seminar. As participants, they spend time in another country studying the effect of that environment on international firms. Career services and co-op education integrate classroom theory with the practical experience of a job in industry, business, the social services, the arts, or government. Portions of the education courses are conducted in New York City schools, so that student teachers may gain experience in urban education at an early stage.

Academic Facilities

There are more than forty scientific and engineering laboratories at Manhattan, including the Research and Learning Center, as well as a modern language laboratory and a computer information systems laboratory. Manhattan's O'Malley Library is a state-of-the-art facility featuring modern accommodations for study and research.

The Raymond W. Kelly ('63) Student Commons, which opened in the fall of 2014, is a 70,000-square-foot building, which has quickly become a focal point on campus. It enhances the College's ability to integrate academics and student life, and provides space for fitness and wellness programming, cultural and community events, dining, student activities, and student collaboration.

Costs

For 2015–16, the tuition for Manhattan College is $35,600 per year plus program fee. Room and board for the year is $14,430.

Financial Aid

Manhattan grants or administers financial assistance in the form of tuition awards to students on the basis of need and/or ability. Need is evaluated by submitting the FAFSA. In addition to a merit scholarship fund, Manhattan offers endowed scholarships, special category scholarships and student athletic grants, Federal Pell Grants, Federal Supplemental Educational Opportunity Grants, student loans, Federal Work-Study Program awards, and New York State financial assistance are also available to students who qualify. Forty-eight percent of all students receive merit aid with 94 percent of the students receiving aid.

Faculty

Manhattan's faculty has 219 full-time faculty members. Ninety-three percent of the faculty members hold doctorates. Faculty members serve on the college senate, the council for faculty affairs, and numerous faculty and campus committees. They are available to students for informal guidance and counseling and also serve as official moderators of many campus organizations.

Admission Requirements

Manhattan has a long-standing policy of nondiscrimination. No applicant is refused admission because of race, color, religion, age, national origin, sex, or disability. All applicants must present an academic diploma from an accredited high school and must offer a minimum of 16 credits in academic subjects. At the discretion of the Committee on Admissions, quantitative requirements may be modified for applicants with especially strong records who show promise of doing well in college. In the selection process, attention is given to scholastic ability, as indicated by grades and rank in class, as well as to standardized test scores and recommendations from teachers and counselors. All candidates must submit either SAT or ACT results. An interview with a member of the admission staff can be arranged but is not required. Applicants may submit scores on the General Educational Development test in lieu of a formal high school diploma; however, all such applicants must submit the results of the appropriate College Board tests. Manhattan College offers early acceptance for high school seniors, admission to advanced standing, advanced placement, and credit by examination. Junior college or other transfer students are welcome. Manhattan College requires applicants whose native language is not English to take the Test of English as a Foreign Language (TOEFL), IELTS, the SAT, or ACT exam. The average SAT scores of entering freshmen in 2013 were 554 in mathematics and 536 in the verbal portion.

Application and Information

Application forms are furnished by the Admission Office on request and available on the Manhattan College website. The Common Application, which is available in many high school guidance offices and online, may also be used. Students must send the application to the admission office at Manhattan College. The high school report, recommendation letters, and transcript must be submitted by the high school guidance counselor. This should be done after six terms of high school or right after the seventh term. There is a rolling admissions policy and a March 1 deadline for financial aid applications. A nonrefundable application fee of $60 is required.

For more information, contact:

William J. Bisset
Vice President for Enrollment Management
Manhattan College
Riverdale, New York 10471
United States
Phone: 718-862-7200
800-MC2-XCEL (toll-free)
E-mail: admit@manhattan.edu
Website: http://www.manhattan.edu

Manhattan College centers a great deal of its campus activity around the main quadrangle.

COLLEGE CLOSE-UPS

MANHATTANVILLE COLLEGE

PURCHASE, NEW YORK

Manhattanville COLLEGE®

The College

While the 100 beautiful acres that make up Manhattanville are located in a quiet suburban setting, the culture, entertainment, and excitement of New York City are only 30 miles away. The private coeducational college founded in 1841 draws its 1,700 students from more than fifty countries and thirty states. Manhattanville College is ranked in the *Princeton Review* and *Newsweek* as one of the best colleges for undergraduate study. Manhattanville College has created a small global village. This richly diverse community embodies the College's mission: to educate students to be ethical and socially responsible leaders in a global community.

Learning is at the heart of Manhattanville, and the College's proximity to New York City creates a constant flow of opportunity that brings learning to life. Manhattanville students know how to have fun, but they also have a sense of purpose. The College's social conscience is informed by a commitment to serving the community. The Corporation for National and Community Service has named Manhattanville College in the 2013 President's Higher Education Community Service Honor Roll for excellent services. The Duchesne Center serves as the coordinator and catalyst for service learning, community outreach, culture, and leadership across the College campus and around the world. Last year, students participated in 30,000 hours of community service. Manhattanville students actively seek opportunities to serve humanitarian causes in the developing world.

The College's global perspective is enriched by its role as a Non-Governmental Organization of the United Nations. Select students have an opportunity to intern at the UN and to study with an ambassador.

Location

Manhattanville's campus lies in the heart of Westchester County, bordered on the east by Long Island Sound and on the west by the Hudson River. From the roof of Reid Castle, which serves as the campus's main hall, the skyline of Manhattan is visible. This proximity to the city that calls itself the "Capital of the World" is one of Manhattanville's many assets. The College provides free transportation to the city on Saturdays and to Manhattan-bound commuter trains seven days a week so students can take advantage of all New York City has to offer.

Majors and Degrees

Manhattanville College offers undergraduate degrees in more than fifty academic concentrations in the arts and sciences, including Bachelor of Arts (B.A.), Bachelor of Science (B.S.), Bachelor of Fine Arts (B.F.A.), and Bachelor of Music (B.Mus.) degrees; a self-designed major; a double major with teacher certification; and preparation for professional and graduate study (pre-law, pre-medical, pre–physical therapy, and pre–speech language pathology).

Students may choose from the following areas of study: accounting, African studies, American studies, art history, art (studio), biochemistry, biology, business management, chemistry, classical civilizations, communications studies, computer science, creative writing, criminal law, dance and theatre, dance therapy, digital media production, economics, education, English, environmental studies, film studies, finance, French, German, history, Holocaust and genocide studies, human resource management, international management, international studies, Irish studies, Italian, Latin American studies, legal studies, marketing, mathematics, museum studies, music, music education, music business, musical theatre, music technology, neuroscience, philosophy, political science, pre-dental, pre-health, pre-law, pre-medical, pre–physical therapy, pre–speech language pathology, psychology, self-designed major, social justice, sociology and anthropology, Spanish, sport studies, women's studies, world literature, and world religions.

This listing can be found online at http://www.Manhattanville.edu/Academics.

Academic Programs

Manhattanville College offers full-time, part-time, and accelerated opportunities for study as well as dual-degree programs. The Manhattanville curriculum nurtures intellectual curiosity and independent thinking. Students and professors form close collaborative relationships beginning with the first year program, an interdisciplinary survey of the liberal arts that is required of all freshmen.

Under the guidance of a faculty adviser, the student maps an academic and co-curricular program, establishing a major from different branches of the liberal arts. The student may begin studies in the chosen field as early as the freshman year. Over the course of four years of study, the student assembles a portfolio consisting of study plans, evidence of academic proficiency in written critical analysis and qualitative research, annual evaluations, transcripts, and examples of the student's best work.

A special option for B.A. candidates is the self-designed major. If a student's interests direct them beyond existing departmental majors, they may propose a program of study to the Board of Academic Standards. Manhattanville students also have the opportunity to earn academic credit for internships in New York City.

Manhattanville College offers college credit for A-level exams, International Baccalaureate, and Advanced Placement examinations.

Off-Campus Programs

Manhattanville offers more than 100 study-abroad opportunities through either direct exchange programs or study-abroad providers at various levels of language proficiency, including Argentina, Belgium (internship at the European Union), Chile, England, France, Germany, Ireland, Italy, Japan, South Africa, Mexico, and Spain, among others. There is also a world of over 650 domestic and international internship possibilities with leading groups such as Apple, Condé Nast, IBM, and MasterCard.

Academic Facilities

Manhattanville is one of the first colleges in the U.S. to outsource a service that enables students to interact online with experienced reference librarians at any time of the day or night from anywhere in the world. The virtual research service, "Ask a Librarian 24/7," uses co-browsing to connect students with professional librarians who can answer questions about research and help students navigate the College's extensive array of subscription databases and other library resources. Manhattanville's teaching library, which supports the School of Education, ranks among the foremost undergraduate teaching libraries in the country. The Menendez Language Laboratory includes videos and record libraries that provide materials for class instruction and individual practice in French, Spanish, Russian, Italian, German, Chinese, Japanese, Hindi, Marathi, Modern Hebrew, and English as a second language. The College provides a writing clinic, a reading clinic, audiovisual facilities, and a bibliographic instruction program. The library building is open 24 hours a day, seven days a week through most of the fall and spring semesters, and it has computer labs, quiet study areas, group-study rooms, and a café where students and faculty members can meet informally.

Among the College's other academic facilities and resources are the art studio, science laboratories, the performing arts facilities, and student media facilities.

The College has state-of-the-art computers, computer labs, and campus networking for student use and instruction. In addition, advanced music technology systems offer performing arts students limitless opportunities for creativity.

Costs

For the 2014–15 academic year, tuition was $34,870 and the average room and board costs were $14,520.

Financial Aid

Manhattanville College offers both merit scholarships and need-based financial aid. Over 90 percent of students receive financial awards. The Free Application for Federal Student Aid (FAFSA) is required. The types of awards available are honors, merit, arts, and community service scholarships; Manhattanville grants and scholarships; Federal Perkins Loans; Federal Stafford Student Loans; Federal Pell Grants; Federal Supplemental Educational Opportunity Grants; Federal Work-Study Program awards; and Tuition Assistance Program awards.

For scholarship information and advice about financial aid eligibility, prospective students should visit www.manhattanville.edu/FinancialAid.

Faculty

Nearly 90 percent of faculty members have Ph.D. or terminal degrees in their fields. Many faculty members live on the campus. The Manhattanville curriculum nurtures intellectual curiosity and independent thinking. The student-faculty ratio of 16:1 promotes close and collaborative relationships between faculty members and students, aided by the structure of the curriculum and the Portfolio System, which fosters collaboration between student and faculty adviser. Faculty members, not teaching assistants, teach all Manhattanville classes, and 84 percent of the classes have 20 or fewer students.

Student Government

Students in large measure shape the quality of life on the Manhattanville campus. Elected representatives of the student body run the student government, which serves as a principal means of communication among the administration, faculty members, and students. Its board of directors is responsible for formulating policy on student life and for implementing this policy through various committees. Student government members also serve on the College's policymaking and ad hoc committees.

Admission Requirements

Manhattanville College admits candidates for undergraduate degrees if their academic records indicate a competence to engage in a challenging liberal arts curriculum. Admission to the College is selective, and the most important consideration is the student's secondary school performance. When weighing this aspect, the admissions committee evaluates the quality of the school, the strength of the student's program, and success in those studies. Next, the committee considers the various recommendations that are submitted on behalf of the student, along with standardized test scores if submitted (Manhattanville is a test-optional institution) and the student's personal statement. A campus interview is strongly recommended. Students who plan to specialize in music or dance and theater should come to Manhattanville for an audition or should secure permission to submit a DVD. Students who plan to apply for the B.F.A. degree program should present portfolios to the art department for evaluation. Students who plan to study in these areas may audition for scholarships.

Application and Information

Applying is straightforward—submit the completed application, official high school transcript, letters of recommendation, a personal statement, and optional SAT or ACT scores. Transfer applicants should submit an official transcript from each school attended. Admission is rolling with a priority deadline of March 1 for all enrollment. Early action deadline is December 1. For details, students should visit Manhattanville.edu or contact the College via e-mail at admissions@mville.edu or by phone at 800-328-4553 (toll-free) or 914-323-5464.

The College subscribes to the Candidates Reply Date. Applications should be submitted as early in the senior year as possible. Candidates may apply online at www.manhattanville.edu/Apply.

Manhattanville College is committed to equality of educational opportunity, and is an equal opportunity employer. The College does not discriminate against current or prospective students and employees on the basis of race, color, sex, national and ethnic origin, religion, age, disability, or any other legally protected characteristic. This College policy is implemented in educational and admissions policies, scholarship and loan programs, athletic and other school-administered programs, and in employee-related programs.

For further information, students should contact:

Office of Undergraduate Admissions
Manhattanville College
2900 Purchase Street
Purchase, New York 10577
United States
Phone: 914-323-5464
800-32-VILLE (toll-free)
E-mail: admissions@mville.edu
Website: http://www.manhattanville.edu
http://www.facebook.com/Manhattanville
http://www.twitter.com/Mville_College

Reid Hall (The Castle) is the centerpiece of the Manhattanville College campus.

MARLBORO COLLEGE

MARLBORO, VERMONT

Marlboro College

★ To read more about this school, visit http://petersons.to/marlborocollege

COLLEGE CLOSE-UPS

The College

Marlboro College, founded in 1946, is a small community of self-directed learners with a passion for intellectual engagement and a desire to create a course of study tailored to their own interests. Tucked away in the foothills of Vermont's Green Mountains, Marlboro offers a rigorous liberal arts curriculum through small classes and advanced individualized study. Marlboro's goal is to teach students to think clearly and learn independently, develop a command of concise and correct writing, and aspire to academic excellence, all while participating responsibly in a self-governing community. The college's 7:1 student-faculty ratio sparks dynamic exchanges between students and faculty members both in and out of the classroom, and fosters a close-knit community in which asking questions is more important than knowing the right answers.

The fields and woodlands that make up Marlboro's rural 300-plus-acre campus include the original cluster of barns and other farm buildings that were converted by the first students and faculty members into classrooms and dormitories. The Outdoor Program offers instruction and equipment for backpacking, canoeing, cross-country skiing, kayaking, rock climbing, skating, snow-shoeing, and other outdoor recreational opportunities that bring students in touch with the surrounding environment. The soccer team competes with other colleges, and more impromptu volleyball, basketball, softball, and Ultimate (Frisbee) teams play on an informal basis. In addition, Marlboro's broomball (a game akin to hockey) tournament takes place each winter, with prizes for the winning teams and those with the best costumes. Campus committees organize many events both on and off campus, including concerts, lectures, poetry and fiction readings, art shows, and trips to Boston, Montreal, and New York for museum visits, shopping, and baseball games. Other activities that enrich campus life include parties, dances, plays, and film screenings.

Marlboro is—and intends to remain—one of the nation's smallest liberal arts colleges, with some 300 students on average. Students come from nearly forty states and approximately six other countries. Transfer students—who make up one quarter of each incoming class—bring an important perspective to the campus community. More than 80 percent of all students live in campus housing, which consists of small dormitories, several four-bedroom cottages, and a renovated country inn.

Location

The village of Marlboro, just 2 miles from the college, consists of a post office, a town clerk's office, and an inn. The total population of the town is 1,200 residents, more in the summer during the famous Marlboro Music Festival. The town of Brattleboro, 12 miles away, is a lively cultural and commercial center with bookstores, restaurants, coffee shops, a community food cooperative, and a movie theater. The college is 2 hours by car from Boston and 4 hours from New York City and Montreal.

Areas of Study and Degrees

Marlboro confers the Bachelor of Arts and Bachelor of Science degrees in 34 fields. Marlboro also confers the Master of Arts, Master of Science, and related certificates through six graduate programs offered at its Brattleboro campus. Students have the freedom to design their own majors, which allows them to make interdisciplinary connections and pursue individualized research. The college also offers Bachelor of Arts and Bachelor of Science degrees in International Studies through its World Studies Program (WSP).

Areas of study offered at Marlboro include American studies, anthropology, art history, Asian studies, astronomy, biochemistry, biology, ceramics, chemistry, classics, computer science, cultural history, dance, drama, economics, environmental studies, film/video studies, gender studies, history, international studies, languages, literature, mathematics, music, painting, philosophy, photography, physics, political science, psychology, religion, sculpture, sociology, theater, visual arts, world studies, and writing.

Academic Programs

In the first two years, Marlboro students study broadly, discover new interests, and begin to see the connections that lead many to pursue interdisciplinary work. Each new student is paired with a faculty adviser and joins an advising group of students with similar interests. Students learn from each other, as well as from their engaging professors, in seminar-style classes.

Marlboro believes that clear writing both reflects and engenders clear thinking. The college requires each new student to pass a Clear Writing Requirement within three semesters of enrolling. Designated writing courses, faculty advisers, and student writing tutors all help new students meet the requirement.

More than any other academic component, Marlboro's Plan of Concentration sets the college apart from other undergraduate programs. Undertaken by all Marlboro students in their junior and senior years, the Plan is the collection of related projects and papers that form the final product of the student's academic work at Marlboro. It is an individualized program of classes, research, experiences, one-to-one study, and original thought, driven by the student's interests and academic goals and designed in close collaboration with faculty sponsors. Final evaluation of the student's Plan is conducted by her or his faculty advisers and an outside examiner who is a recognized expert in the student's field.

Off-Campus Programs

Marlboro College sponsors multiple academic adventures and humanitarian trips each year, ranging from community service work in South Carolina and Cambodia to interdisciplinary research in Cuba, China, Kenya, and Vietnam. Students working on their Plan of Concentration often travel abroad or attend other institutions for a period of time to augment their academic work. Marlboro faculty members may help plan these pursuits and frequently aid students in securing internships in their academic fields.

The World Studies Program is a four-year program leading to a Bachelor of Arts or Bachelor of Science degree in International Studies. The program involves intensive study on campus as well as a six- to eight-month internship abroad. In addition, WSP sponsors regular on-campus activities, which include a themed international dinner, music from around the world, and guest lectures and films related to current world issues.

Academic Facilities

Marlboro's academic facilities offer small classrooms and inviting faculty offices for students to meet in small groups and individually with their professors. Facilities are open 24 hours a day, supporting student research and creative explorations in a DNA lab, a black-and-white darkroom, a digital film-editing studio, two pottery studios, and an astronomical observatory. The Rudolf and Irene Serkin Performing Arts Center offers more than 10,000 square feet for music, dance, and drama rehearsals and performances. Marlboro's Total Health Center provides additional space for medical and psychological counseling services as well as a fitness room. The Snyder Center for the Visual Arts, slated to open in 2015, will include studios, classrooms, gallery space, and a new digital media lab.

Costs

Tuition and fees at Marlboro were $38,110 for the 2014–15 academic year. Room and board costs were $10,280.

Financial Aid

More than 80 percent of all Marlboro students receive financial help. The college is committed to helping any student who qualifies for admission assemble the financial resources necessary to attend, and need is not a factor in the admission decision. Merit scholarships and grants are also available.

Faculty

Marlboro's 40 full-time faculty members are committed first and foremost to teaching. The lively exchange of ideas between teachers and students is the cornerstone of the Marlboro curriculum.

Student Government

All students and faculty and staff members are equal members of the college Town Meeting. Since the founding of Marlboro College in 1946, the community has come together every month to debate and decide budget initiatives, college policies, and other issues that affect daily life. A board of selectpersons, elected by the college community, serves the college's interests and is responsible for drafting Town Meeting rules and regulations. Students serve with faculty and staff members on more than 30 college committees, including those that make faculty-hiring decisions. Other important committees include the social committee and the Community Court, which is responsible for enforcing campus regulations.

Admission Requirements

The Admissions Committee seeks students with intellectual promise; a high degree of motivation, self-discipline, personal stability, and social concern; and the ability and desire to contribute to the college community. All applicants are considered without regard to race, creed, sex, sexual orientation, gender identity or its expression, national or ethnic origin, age, or disability. Homeschoolers, transfers, veterans, and older or returning students are encouraged to apply.

Like most colleges, Marlboro requires students to submit a variety of documentation, from high school transcripts to teacher recommendations. The Admissions Committee evaluates each applicant as a unique individual who possesses qualities that are not necessarily quantifiable.

A campus visit is strongly recommended for all applicants, and interviews are required. Many campus interviews are conducted by faculty members in the applicant's area of interest. Marlboro does not use a formulaic approach in making admission decisions. Applicants are encouraged to demonstrate their particular strengths; the goal is a successful match between the student and the college.

Application and Information

New students and transfers are admitted for either the spring or the fall semester. Applicants for the fall semester have a choice of three admission plans. The early decision plan is for those students who have thoroughly researched Marlboro and for whom Marlboro is the first choice. Applicants should be aware that early decision is binding. The early decision deadline for first-year students to submit application materials is November 15, and applicants are notified by December 15. Early action, a nonbinding plan, has a deadline of January 15. These applicants are notified of a decision on February 1. The regular admission deadline is March 1. The deadline for transfer students to submit applications materials for the fall semester is April 1, and for the spring semester it is November 15.

Students can apply to Marlboro through the Common Application or directly through Marlboro College's website. All applications should include the Marlboro College supplement form with a "Why Marlboro" personal statement, a $50 application fee, complete transcripts from all secondary schools and colleges currently or previously attended, an analytical writing sample, and two letters of recommendation. SAT or ACT test scores are not required, but will be taken into consideration if submitted by the prospective student. The Admissions Committee welcomes applications from homeschooled students. In lieu of a high school transcript, homeschooled students must submit a detailed description of their curriculum (including reading lists and academic study areas).

Office of Admissions
Marlboro College, 2582 South Road
Marlboro, Vermont 05344-0300
United States
Phone: 802-257-4333
800-343-0049 (toll-free)
Fax: 802-451-7555
E-mail: admissions@marlboro.edu
Website: http://www.marlboro.edu

Marlboro College cultivates a close-knit, intentionally small learning community where independent thinkers can explore their deepest interests.

COLLEGE CLOSE-UPS

MARYWOOD UNIVERSITY

SCRANTON, PENNSYLVANIA

Marywood UNIVERSITY

★ To read more about this school, visit http://petersons.to/marywooduniversity

The University

Marywood University is coeducational, comprehensive, residential, and Catholic. Founded in 1915 by the Sisters, Servants of the Immaculate Heart of Mary, the University serves men and women from a variety of backgrounds and religions. The University enrolls more than 3,100 students in an array of undergraduate and graduate programs. Marywood provides a framework for educational excellence that enables students to develop fully as persons and to master professional and leadership skills that are necessary for meeting human needs.

Students at Marywood have the opportunity to build on their academic interests and proactively shape their educational experience. Students' energy and intellectual curiosity guides their work, growth, and success. Marywood believes in the power of the individual and in the premise that education is the most empowering tool.

Marywood is fully accredited by the Commission on Higher Education of the Middle States Association of Colleges and Schools. Accreditations/approvals have been granted by Accreditation Review Committee on Education for the Physician Assistant, American Psychological Association, American Art Therapy Association, American Music Therapy Association, Accreditation Council for Education in Nutrition and Dietetics, Council on Academic Accreditation, American Speech-Language-Hearing Association, Accreditation Council for Business Schools and Programs, Commission on Accreditation of Athletic Training Education, Council for Accreditation of Counseling and Related Educational Programs, Council on Social Work Education, National Association of Schools of Art and Design, National Association of Schools of Music, Council for the Accreditation of Educator Preparation, Accreditation Commission for Education in Nursing, and Commission on Collegiate Nursing Education.

The athletic program for women and men at Marywood provides students with opportunities to play on competitive intercollegiate, club, and intramural teams. Students compete on an intercollegiate basis in baseball, basketball, cross-country, field hockey, golf, lacrosse, soccer, softball, swimming/diving, tennis, track and field, and volleyball. Marywood is a member of NCAA Division III, the Colonial States Athletic Conference (CSAC), and the Eastern College Athletic Conference.

Prospective students can connect with Marywood through social networks including Facebook (http://facebook.com/marywoodu), Twitter (http://twitter.com/marywoodu), and YouTube (http://youtube.com/marywoodu).

Location

Marywood's scenic 115-acre main campus is part of an attractive residential area of the city of Scranton, in northeastern Pennsylvania. With a population of 78,000, Scranton is the fifth-largest city in Pennsylvania and is the county seat of Lackawanna County (the county population is approximately 213,000). Marywood is relatively close to many major cities of the Northeast; traveling by car, it is 1 hour to Binghamton; 2½ hours to New York and Philadelphia; 4 hours to Washington, D.C.; and 5½ hours to Boston. Several airlines serve the Wilkes-Barre/Scranton International Airport, which is 20 minutes from the campus. The Pocono Mountains, offering spectacular scenery and an abundance of outdoor recreational opportunities, including downhill skiing, are a short distance from the campus.

Majors and Degrees

Marywood University offers a variety of majors and minors at the undergraduate level. Individually designed majors, developed with faculty guidance, and double and interdisciplinary majors are also available. Several five-year bachelor's/master's degree programs are offered.

At the undergraduate level, Marywood University awards the Bachelor of Arts (B.A.), Bachelor of Architecture (B.Arch.), Bachelor of Business Administration (B.B.A.), Bachelor of Environmental Design in Architecture (B.E.D.A.), Bachelor of Fine Arts (B.F.A.), Bachelor of Music (B.M.), Bachelor of Science (B.S.), Bachelor of Science in Nursing (B.S.N.), and Bachelor of Social Work (B.S.W.).

Marywood offers majors and minors in the following areas of study: accounting, ad hoc (self-designed), advertising and public relations, architecture and interior architecture/design, art (studio: ceramics, painting, sculpture; design: graphic design, illustration, photography), art education, art therapy, arts administration (art, music, theater), aviation management, biology, biotechnology, clinical laboratory science, communication sciences and disorders (speech-language pathology), computer science, criminal justice, cybersecurity (information security), dance/movement (minor), digital media and broadcast production (broadcast, corporate), early childhood education, education (elementary, secondary), English, environmental science, family and consumer sciences education, financial planning, general science education, health and physical education (athletic training, education, exercise science), health services administration, history/political science, hospitality management, industrial/organizational psychology, international business, journalism, management, marketing, mathematics, multimedia (minor), music, music education, music therapy, nursing, nutrition and dietetics, performance, performing arts, philosophy, physician assistant studies, psychology, psychology/clinical practice, public administration, religious studies, retail business management, science, social sciences secondary education, sociology, social work, Spanish, special education/elementary education (dual certification), theater, and women's studies (minor).

Preprofessional programs are offered in chiropractic, communication sciences and disorders, dentistry, law, medicine, physician assistant studies, and veterinary medicine. A joint seven-year bachelor's/doctoral program in chiropractic involves three years of study on the Marywood campus and additional work at New York Chiropractic College, which is located in Seneca Falls, New York.

Marywood offers bachelor's to master's degree programs in accounting, architecture, biotechnology, communication arts, criminal justice, education, financial information services, health services administration, physician assistant studies, social work, and speech language pathology.

Academic Programs

Undergraduate degrees are offered in approximately sixty academic programs, including the arts, sciences, music, fine arts, social work, and nursing. All students are required to complete a core curriculum in the liberal arts in addition to the courses in their major. Opportunities for undergraduates abound through double majors, honors and independent-study programs, practicums, internships, and study abroad. Army and Air Force ROTC programs are available.

Off-Campus Programs

Study-abroad opportunities are available in countries such as Australia, Canada, England, France, Mexico, and Spain. Through Studio Art Centers International (SACI), art students may study in Florence, Italy.

Academic Facilities

In recent years, the University has made $100 million in improvements to the campus, including new athletic, residence hall, and dining facilities, and one of the finest studio arts facilities in the northeast. The Insalaco Center for Studio Arts features 60,000 square feet of fully equipped studios, labs, and classroom spaces for a broad variety of artistic disciplines. The Center for Architectural Studies offers students two levels of studio space in a spacious, adaptive re-use of Marywood's former gymnasium and pool space. A new library is scheduled to open in September 2015. Called the Learning Commons, it will include 72,000-square-feet of learning spaces, an emerging media center, an entrepreneur launch pad, and an automatic book retrieval system.

Costs

Tuition for full-time students (12–18 credits per semester) for the 2015–16 academic year is a flat fee of $30,942. There is also a general fee of $1,500 for full-time students. Costs for room and board for a full academic year are approximately $13,900, depending on which meal plan is selected and the desired room occupancy. Costs of books and supplies are estimated at $1,000.

Financial Aid

Marywood offers a comprehensive program of financial aid to assist students in meeting educational costs. Eligibility for federal and state programs is based on demonstrated financial need, as determined by a federal eligibility formula that analyzes family income and assets. In addition, approximately $32 million in institutional aid is awarded annually to Marywood students. Applicants to Marywood are considered for all financial assistance programs for which they qualify. Candidates are required to submit the Free Application for Federal Student Aid (FAFSA) and the Marywood application form, preferably by February 15.

Faculty

Among faculty members at Marywood, 167 are full-time, and 90 percent of these hold the Ph.D. or the highest degree in their field. The student-faculty ratio is 13:1. Faculty members are evaluated on their teaching and on their scholarly and artistic activities.

Student Government

All matriculated students in the undergraduate school are members of the Student Government Association (SGA). The SGA operates with a number of committees, including the Student Council, the Resident Committee, and the Commuter Committee. The association plays a key role in establishing a positive campus environment.

Admission Requirements

Candidates for admission should demonstrate reasonable progress toward graduation in an accredited secondary school, have graduated from a secondary school, or offer evidence of an equivalent secondary education. Each candidate should show satisfactory academic preparation in 16 units of subject matter, including 4 units of English, 3 units of social studies, 2 units of mathematics, 1 unit of science with laboratory, and 6 additional units. Either SAT or ACT scores are required for those who wish to enter as freshmen.

In addition to fulfilling general admission requirements, candidates for admission to a degree program in architecture, art, education, music, nursing, pre–physician assistant studies, and speech language pathology must meet special standards established by the department. Prior to enrollment, music, theater, and art candidates are required to audition or to present an art portfolio.

For certain programs, candidates without the recommended distribution of units may be eligible for admission if their course work as a whole and the results of their tests offer evidence of a strong foundation for college work. Candidates who are deficient in required course work may complete the appropriate work during the summer or the first year in college.

A student who demonstrates satisfactory academic performance at another college may apply for admission as a transfer student. Academic courses presented for transfer should be equivalents of courses required by the programs of study at Marywood. Students should have earned a grade of C or higher in their course work; C– will not transfer. A student should expect to earn a minimum of 60 credits at Marywood University; ordinarily, at least one half of the credits required for a major must also be earned at Marywood.

International candidates are required to meet the academic standards for admission, demonstrate proficiency in the use of the English language, and submit documentation of having sufficient funds to cover educational and living expenses for the duration of study. To certify proficiency in the use of English, international applicants whose primary language is not English must submit scores from the Test of English as a Foreign Language (TOEFL) or the IELTS.

Application and Information

Applications for admission are considered on a rolling basis; however, candidates are strongly encouraged to submit applications by March 1. Applications received after March 1 are considered on the basis of available space in particular programs. To be considered for admission, freshman applicants must submit to the Office of Admissions a completed application (paper or online), a nonrefundable $35 application fee (waived if applying online), an official high school transcript with an indication of class rank, an official report of scores from the SAT or ACT, and at least one letter of recommendation. Students can apply online at http://www.marywood.edu/admissions/applying/.

Transfer students must submit a completed application, a nonrefundable $35 application fee (waived if applying online), an official high school transcript, official academic transcript(s) reflecting all college course work for which the candidate has enrolled, and at least one letter of recommendation.

All submitted credentials become the property of Marywood and are not returnable to the applicant. Admission standards and policies are free of discrimination on grounds of race, color, national origin, sex, age, or disability.

For further information, interested students should contact:

Christian DiGregorio, Director
University Admissions
Marywood University
2300 Adams Avenue
Scranton, Pennsylvania 18509
Phone: 866-279-9663
Fax: 570-961-4763
E-mail: yourfuture@marywood.edu
Website: http://marywood.edu/admissions
http://www.facebook.com/marywoodu
http://www.twitter.com/marywoodu
http://www.youtube.com/marywoodu

The majestic Rotunda located in the Liberal Arts Center on Marywood's campus.

MIDAMERICA NAZARENE UNIVERSITY

OLATHE, KANSAS

★ To read more about this school, visit http://petersons.to/midamericanazarene

The University

MidAmerica Nazarene University (MNU) is a comprehensive liberal arts university of approximately 1,900 students. A faith-based university, MNU welcomes students of all religious backgrounds; approximately 35 percent of the student population is Nazarene.

MNU educates students for a life of purpose. With service-learning woven into course work and University-sponsored opportunities to minister in the local community, students prepare not only for a career, but to make the world a better place through servant-leadership. The University's most popular areas of study include nursing, business administration, kinesiology, ministry, psychology, sports management, elementary education, criminal justice, and athletic training. More information on MNU's academic programs is available online at www.mnu.edu/majors.

The average ACT score of incoming freshmen is 22; the average GPA is 3.32. Students hail from thirty-six states, five countries, and forty-plus denominations. The student to faculty ratio is 12:1.

MidAmerica Nazarene University offers NAIA Division I baseball, men's and women's basketball, men's and women's indoor/outdoor track and field, men's and women's cross-country, cheerleading, football, men's and women's soccer, softball, and volleyball. Detailed information about MNU's athletic programs can be found at www.mnusports.com.

Location

MidAmerica Nazarene University is located in Olathe, Kansas, a residential community of approximately 130,000 just 20 minutes from the heart of Kansas City, with all the cultural advantages of a major metropolitan area. Olathe offers a lifestyle of exceptional quality. The city's school district and healthcare system are routinely recognized among the best in the nation. Outdoor recreation offers a variety of activities, including running, jogging, bicycling, fishing, boating, team sports, and just relaxing. The proximity to downtown Kansas City provides internship opportunities in the areas of business, technology, the arts, creative services, and health care. Kansas City also boasts several professional sports teams, multiple shopping destinations, a brand new state-of-the-art performing arts center, and a great food and arts culture.

Majors and Degrees

Students can earn an Associate of Arts (A.A.) degree in general business or liberal arts.

The Bachelor of Arts (B.A.) degree is available in accounting, athletic training, Bible and theology, biology, biology education, business administration, business psychology, chemistry, corporate communication, criminal justice, elementary education, English, English language arts education, forensic biology, forensic chemistry, graphic design, history, history/government and social studies education, intercultural studies, kinesiology, marketing, mathematics, mathematics education, middle-level mathematics education, middle-level science education, ministry, multimedia, music, organizational leadership, physical education, psychology, recreation and leisure studies, sociology, speech/theatre education, sports management, and youth and family ministry.

MNU also offers the Bachelor of Music Education (B.M.Ed.) degree and the Bachelor of Science in Nursing (B.S.N.) degree. MNU offers accelerated bachelor's and graduate degree programs in business, counseling, education, and nursing.

Academic Programs

MNU students receive direction from advisors in choosing a major, discovering their interests, finding a mentor, and preparation for interviews.

At MNU, hands-on learning and real-world experience are core components of each student's education. For example, criminal justice majors learn in the University's own forensics lab, then intern for local police departments or laboratories. Communications students build public relations skills by helping nonprofit organizations, and nursing majors train on the latest medical technology including state-of-the-art patient simulators. Marketing and graphic design students propose creative and brand strategies for real-world businesses.

Off-Campus Programs

MNU Europe is the University's international program. Students travel to, live, and study in Busingen, Germany, a quaint European village with a small college campus. Courses may last a few weeks to an entire semester. Courses are taught by MNU professors and adjuncts in a variety of subjects fulfilling both general education and elective requirements.

As a member of the Council for Christian Colleges and Universities (CCCU), a national association of more than 100 Christian colleges and universities, MNU makes a number of off-campus learning opportunities available. Domestic programs are available in Washington, D.C.; Los Angeles; and Martha's Vineyard, Massachusetts. Students have also studied abroad in China, Costa Rica, Egypt, Germany, Russia, and the United Kingdom through this cooperative program.

Academic Facilities

The 40,000-square-foot Bell Cultural Events Center features state-of-the-art practice, recital, and performance facilities for the fine arts division, as well as a black-box theater and 500-seat performance hall for music and drama productions. Osborne Hall houses the Department of Science and Mathematics, while Lunn Hall houses administrative offices. Dobson Hall contains two art studios and a graphic-design computer lab. The largest facility on campus, the 70,000-square-foot Cook Center, houses Bell Family Arena, two practice gyms, and the Athletic Training and Athletics department offices. It is also home to MNU's School of Nursing and Health Science. Metz Hall houses the School of Behavioral Sciences and Counseling, School of Business, and School of Education. One of several on-campus computer labs is also located in this facility.

Costs

While fees vary according to course load, costs for a full-time student total around $31,800, which includes tuition ($24,250), and room and board ($7,550). Part-time tuition and fees vary according to course load.

Financial Aid

The perception that a private university isn't affordable is false—the truth is, any higher education requires a significant investment. In fact, 100 percent of first-year students at MNU receive some form of financial aid. MNU scholarships are available for academics, athletics and fine arts. Information and applications may be obtained from Student Financial Aid Services at 913-971-3298 or www.mnu.edu/financial-aid.

Faculty

MNU students receive personal attention from their instructors. It is not uncommon to find faculty members in residence hall rooms talking with students or even inviting students into their homes for dinner. MNU faculty members have decades of real-world experience in many industries and fields.

Student Government

Associated Student Government (ASG) exists to discover God's agenda as students serve God and the campus community. ASG offers plenty of opportunities for students to get involved through many different campus activities and service-learning opportunities.

Admission Requirements

Prospective students should complete the ACT or SAT exam. While the University does not require specific subjects for entrance, it does recommend that students complete 3 units of math, 4 units of English, 3 units of science, 3 units of social studies, and 1 unit of foreign language. Students over 18 who have not graduated from high school can submit GED scores.

Application and Information

Students must submit the completed application, official high school transcripts, ACT or SAT scores, and the housing questionnaire, provided by Admissions. International students must also submit TOEFL scores. The deadline for the fall semester is August 1; the spring semester deadline is December 15.

For more information on how to apply to MNU, prospective students should visit www.mnu.edu/apply or contact:

MNU Office of Admissions
MidAmerica Nazarene University
2030 East College Way
Olathe, Kansas 66062-1899
United States
Phone: 913-971-3380
800-800-8887 (toll-free)
E-mail: admissions@mnu.edu
Website: www.mnu.edu
www.facebook.com/MNUPioneers
www.vimeo.com/choosemnu

With over 40 majors, MNU students graduate ready to lead and serve, no matter what their field.

MILLERSVILLE UNIVERSITY OF PENNSYLVANIA

Millersville University

MILLERSVILLE, PENNSYLVANIA

★ To read more about this school, visit http://petersons.to/millersvilleuniversityofpennsylvania

The University

Millersville University is among the highest ranked public universities in its class in the North according to the *U.S. News & World Report*. Millersville University offers a wide range of programs and a commitment to high-quality undergraduate instruction. Millersville's student body of approximately 8,100, including 7,200 undergraduates, is large enough for the University to offer over 100 academic programs. Millersville's degree offerings also include master's and doctoral degrees. The University is small enough, however, to provide friendly service and individual attention. Students report that the relaxed, friendly campus atmosphere is one of the things they like best. The Millersville campus features a beautiful green and flowered landscape, a lake with resident swans, and clean, well-maintained facilities.

Millersville University was established more than 150 years ago, in 1855, as a normal school, the first one in Pennsylvania. It remained a teachers college until 1962, when it was authorized to offer liberal arts degrees. It has been Millersville University of Pennsylvania since 1983.

The two reasons students most frequently cite for choosing Millersville are its excellent academic reputation and affordable tuition. The most popular majors are education, business administration, psychology, biology, English, speech communications, and sociology. Millersville's undergraduates are diverse; 1 in 9 students attends part-time, 23 percent are members of a racial/ethnic minority group, and 10 percent are more than 25 years old. Thirty-three percent of Millersville undergraduates are from Lancaster County, 63 percent from elsewhere in Pennsylvania, 5 percent from out of state, and 2 percent from other countries.

The University offers 19 intercollegiate varsity sports in NCAA Division II, intramural, and club sports; special interest clubs; fraternities and sororities; musical organizations; publications; and broad cultural programs.

Thirty-one percent of undergraduates live in campus residence halls, with the rest commuting from home or living nearby. Coed dormitories and apartments are available for students. Freshmen and sophomores not commuting from home are required to live on campus. The possession, use, or sale of alcoholic beverages and illegal drugs is prohibited on the University campus. Smoking is prohibited in all academic and residential buildings on campus. Freshmen are permitted to have cars on campus.

Special services provided for students include free tutoring, academic advisement, career planning and placement, personal counseling, health services, wellness activities, and special facilities for commuters.

Location

Millersville is 3 miles from Lancaster city, a growing metro-politan area. Lancaster County is an exceptionally friendly and beautiful area with a large number of stores, restaurants, theaters, parks, and tourist attractions. The campus is served by the area bus system, and Lancaster has train and air service.

Lancaster County is one of the fastest-growing counties in Pennsylvania and has one of the lowest unemployment rates in the state. The local economy is unusually sound and diverse. Sixty percent of Millersville graduates settle within the county.

Millersville University is conveniently located to a number of major metropolitan areas in the Northeast. It's just 1½ hours from Philadelphia and Baltimore, 2½ hours from Washington D.C., and 3 hours from New York City.

Majors and Degrees

Millersville offers the Bachelor of Arts degree in anthropology, art, biology, chemistry, earth sciences, economics, English, environmental geology, French, geography, German, government and political affairs, history, international studies, mathematics, music, philosophy, physics, psychology, social work, sociology, and Spanish.

The Bachelor of Science degree is offered in allied health technology; applied engineering, safety and technology; biology; business administration; chemistry; communications and theatre; computer science; geology; mathematics; meteorology; occupational safety and environmental health; ocean sciences and coastal sciences; and physics.

The Bachelor of Science in Education degree with teaching certification is offered in art education, biology, chemistry, earth sciences, Pre-K–4 education, English, French, German, mathematics, middle level education, music education, physics, social studies, Spanish, special education, and technology education.

The University also offers the Bachelor of Fine Arts degree in art; the Bachelor of Science in nursing degree for RNs only (a fully online and on-campus modalities are available); and the Associate of Technology degree in applied engineering, safety and technology.

Two new academic programs add to the diversity of Millersville's offering—the Multidisciplinary studies major allows students to work with a faculty advisor to combine their unique areas of interest and create a custom degree focus, and the Paul H. Slaugh, Jr. entrepreneurship minor allows students to combine entrepreneurship with a major of their choosing. Students should refer to the website for a complete listing. More than sixty-five minors are offered along with 3-2 engineering programs for chemistry majors. Special advisement is available for students interested in pre-medicine and pre-law.

Academic Programs

Millersville University places a strong emphasis on the liberal arts. Nearly half of the courses required for all its undergraduate degrees, including those with technical or professional majors, are in the liberal arts. This prepares students for a lifetime of learning and gives them a background in writing, speaking, analysis, and critical thinking across a broad range of subjects.

Millersville's baccalaureate degree programs have four common curricular elements: proficiency requirements in English composition and speech; the general education program, which constitutes about half the curriculum; the major field of study; and elective courses, if needed, to meet the minimum of 120 credits required for graduation. Within this framework, students have many choices in developing programs of study.

The general education program has requirements in writing, speaking, humanities, natural sciences and mathematics, social sciences, and interdisciplinary and/or multicultural study. There is also a health and physical education requirement.

Millersville offers a University Honors College, departmental honors programs, independent study, a pass/fail option, and special advisement to students who are undecided about a major.

The University operates on a 4-1-4 academic calendar with summer sessions.

Off-Campus Programs

An exchange agreement with Franklin & Marshall College allows Millersville students to take select Franklin & Marshall courses not offered at Millersville. Cooperative education internships are available to students in most majors, and some majors offer or require specialized internships. Millersville has study-abroad programs in Australia, Chile, China, England, France, Germany, Ireland, Japan, Peru, Scotland, South Africa, Spain, and other countries. Qualified students who wish to study abroad elsewhere may do so through the University's cooperative arrangements with other colleges and universities. Students may also choose to student teach or participate in an internship abroad.

Academic Facilities

With numerous study areas, classrooms, and even a café, the new Dr. Francine G. McNairy Library and Learning Forum is a relaxing and visually pleasing place where students can study and work. Materials from other libraries are available through interlibrary loan.

The University's computing facilities support both PC and Apple platforms. There are more than 400 terminals and computer stations available in multiple computer labs across campus. On-campus access to the Internet is available for all faculty members and students. Wireless access is available in all buildings, residence halls, classrooms, and offices.

Other University facilities include an extensive scientific instrumentation inventory, industry and technology laboratories, a variety of art studios and galleries, two visual and performing arts centers, a state-of-the-art sound studio, three gymnasiums, two swimming pools, radio and television production facilities, soundproof music practice modules, and a language laboratory.

Costs

Annual tuition and fees in 2014–15 were $10,268 (based on 15 credits per semester) for Pennsylvania residents and $19,618 for out-of-state students. Annual room and board charges for 2014–15 were $9,884.

Financial Aid

Approximately 82 percent of Millersville undergraduates receive financial aid through grants, scholarships, employment, and loans. Scholarships are available on the basis of academic performance. Federal Pell, Federal Supplemental Educational Opportunity grants, and Pennsylvania Higher Education Assistance Agency (PHEAA) grants are awarded on the basis of need. Students may also qualify for Federal Perkins Loans and Federal Stafford Student Loans. On-campus and off-campus job opportunities are plentiful, with nearly one-third of students holding an on-campus job.

Students applying for a federal or state grant, Federal Work-Study, or a Federal Perkins Loan must complete the Free Application for Federal Student Aid. The forms are available from high school guidance offices, from the Financial Aid Office, or online at http://www.fafsa.ed.gov. Deadlines are given in the forms' instructions.

Faculty

Millersville University faculty members are dedicated to teaching and to offering individual attention. Ninety-eight percent of the 301 full-time faculty members hold a doctorate or the terminal degree in their field. The University keeps a relatively low student-faculty ratio of 22:1 and an average class size of approximately 25. No classes are taught by graduate or teaching assistants.

Student Government

Millersville University students participate in University governance through the Student Senate, faculty-student committees, and representation on the Faculty Senate, the Council of Trustees, and the Millersville Borough Council. The Student Senate works with faculty members and the administration on major University policies.

Admission Requirements

Millersville University admits approximately 60 percent of its applicants. More than 80 percent of its full-time freshmen rank in the top 40 percent of their high school class. Academic records are the most important factor in admission decisions. Applicants must have successfully completed at least 4 years of high school English, 3 years of social studies, 3 years of mathematics, and 3 years of science (1 unit must be a lab). In addition, 2 years of foreign language is strongly recommended.

Because an important part of the college experience is meeting people with backgrounds and interests different from one's own, Millersville University is committed to recruiting a diversified student body. SAT or ACT scores are required. Letters of recommendations are encouraged. Out-of-state, international, nontraditional, and transfer applicants are welcome. Exceptional high school students may apply for early admission at the end of their junior year. Admitted applicants may request to defer their admission for up to two semesters. Advanced standing is offered through CLEP and AP examinations.

Application and Information

To apply, students should submit an online application with a $40 processing fee and official copies of the high school record and SAT or ACT scores (freshman applicants only, transfer students must submit official transcripts from all previous institutions). The paper application fee is $50. The University has a rolling admission policy, and students are encouraged to apply early (by mid-November) in their senior year for fall admission. Applicants are usually notified of a decision within a month after a completed application and required materials are received.

For application forms and additional information, students should contact:

Office of Admissions
Millersville University of Pennsylvania
P.O. Box 1002
Millersville, Pennsylvania 17551-0302
Phone: 717-871-4625
800-MU-ADMIT (toll-free)
E-mail: admissions@millersville.edu
Website: www.millersville.edu
YouTube: www.youtube.com/millersvilleu
Facebook: www.facebook.com/villeadmissions
Twitter: https://twitter.com/VilleAdmissions
Virtual tour: www.youvisit.com/millersville

Millersville University offers a beautiful campus located in Lancaster County, Pennsylvania, with easy access to major metropolitan centers, such as New York, Philadelphia, and Washington, D.C.

MILLIGAN COLLEGE

MILLIGAN COLLEGE, TENNESSEE

MILLIGAN

The College

Milligan College is a four-year private Christian liberal arts college in northeast Tennessee. From its beginning in 1866, Milligan College has integrated academic excellence with a Christian worldview, and its mission is to educate men and women as Christian servant-leaders. A comprehensive humanities program and a core curriculum are complemented by specialized training in more than thirty majors and several master's degrees. Christian perspectives are integrated throughout the curriculum and student life activities as students are prepared intellectually and spiritually to change lives and shape culture.

Milligan's student body of 1,200 comes from more than thirty-five states and fifteen nations. Seventy percent of traditional students live on the campus. More than forty clubs and organizations provide opportunities to develop leadership skills. A wide variety of activities and campus events encourage social, cultural, and spiritual growth. Milligan College is affiliated with the independent Christian Churches/Churches of Christ, but the interdenominational student body is diverse.

All campus facilities are networked and have wireless access. Every residence hall room and apartment features a high-speed data connection to the campus network and the Internet as well as telephone service, voice mail, and cable TV.

Milligan is well recognized as an NAIA athletic powerhouse with a highly competitive athletic program in twenty-four varsity sports. In the past ten years, Milligan has won fifty conference titles and made sixty national tournament appearances. Men's varsity teams include baseball, basketball, cross-country, cycling, golf, soccer, swimming, tennis, volleyball, and indoor and outdoor track and field. Women's varsity teams include basketball, cheerleading, cross-country, cycling, dance, golf, soccer, softball, swimming, tennis, indoor and outdoor track and field, and volleyball.

Milligan is accredited by the Southern Association of Colleges and Schools' Commission on Colleges to award baccalaureate and master's degrees. Questions about the accreditation of Milligan College can be directed to the Commission on Colleges, 1866 Southern Lane, Decatur, Georgia 30033-4097; phone: 404-679-4500.

In addition to more than thirty undergraduate majors, Milligan offers a Master of Science in Counseling degree, a Master of Education degree, a Master of Science in Occupational Therapy degree, and a Master of Business Administration degree. In summer 2015 Emmanuel Christian Seminary will become part of Milligan, adding graduate-level options in divinity, religion, and Christian ministries as well as a Doctor of Ministry degree. Milligan frequently is recognized for affordability and value. The College continues to be named among the top 10 regional colleges in the South and Best Values in the South in *U.S. News & World Report*'s America's Best Colleges issue as well as among the top 20 baccalaureate colleges in the nation by *Washington Monthly* and the top 15 percent of Military-Friendly Schools by *G. I. Jobs* magazine.

Nearly 100 percent of Milligan graduates are employed or in graduate school within one year of graduation. Milligan's retention and graduation rates are 20 percent higher than other regional colleges and state universities, indicating students enjoy their experience and stay on track to finish on time, saving money and realizing their career goals more quickly.

Location

Milligan's picturesque 195-acre campus, which comprises more than twenty buildings of Colonial architecture, is located in the beautiful mountains of northeast Tennessee, just minutes from Johnson City and the dynamic Tri-Cities region. Students enjoy historical locations, theaters, parks, restaurants, and shops; explore the breathtaking Appalachian Mountains by hiking or camping in state parks near the campus; visit local lakes and rivers for outdoor recreation; or ski the nearby North Carolina slopes. Because Milligan believes leadership is about service, students are encouraged to be active in the local community. Many are employed in internships or part-time work in area businesses.

Majors and Degrees

The Bachelor of Science, Bachelor of Arts, Bachelor of Science in Nursing, and Bachelor of Social Work degrees are offered. Undergraduate majors include accounting, allied health science, applied finance and accounting, Bible (children's ministry, general studies, missions, pastoral ministry, youth ministry), biology, business administration (accounting, economics, general, health care administration, international business, legal studies, management, marketing, sports management), chemistry, child and youth development, communications (digital media, film studies, interpersonal and public communication, multimedia journalism, public relations and advertising), computer information systems, computer science, economics, education (professional teacher licensure), English, fine arts (art, film studies, music, photography, theater arts), history, humanities, human performance and exercise science (exercise science, fitness and wellness, physical education, sports management), interdisciplinary studies, language arts, mathematics, music (performance, jazz studies), music business, music education (licensure in vocal, instrumental), nursing, political science, psychology (general, preprofessional), public leadership and service, social work, sociology, and worship leadership. Both electrical and mechanical engineering majors are scheduled to be offered beginning in fall 2016.

Professional teacher licensure areas include early childhood, elementary education, K–12, middle grades, secondary, and special education. Preprofessional programs are available in dentistry, law, medicine, occupational therapy, optometry, pharmacy, and physical therapy. Accelerated programs for adults are available in business administration, early childhood education, and nursing, and the computer information systems major is offered online.

Academic Programs

Milligan College offers students a liberal arts education taught from a perspective of God's activity with humanity. The College's strong core curriculum educates students toward the world in an open and constructive way. The candidate for the bachelor's degree must have completed a major and electives to total a minimum of 128 semester hours of credit, with at least a 2.0 GPA. Core curriculum requirements include courses in humanities, the Bible, social sciences, ethnic studies, laboratory science, speech communication, mathematics, and health/fitness. The Milligan Honors Program complements and builds on Milligan's liberal arts curriculum by providing an advanced opportunity for high-achieving students from all major fields to deepen their intellectual scholarship, leadership, and service. Admission to the Honors Program is selective.

Realizing that not all college-level learning occurs in a college classroom, prior learning assessment programs provide a method by which other modes of learning can be evaluated for college credit. The Advanced Placement (AP) program, the College-Level Examination Program (CLEP), Defense Activity for Non-Traditional Educational Support (DANTES) programs, and the International Baccalaureate (I.B.) program are available to all students interested in receiving college credit for studies or work experience already completed.

Milligan College operates on a semester system (semesters begin in August and January) with two 4-week summer sessions in June and July or one 8-week term. Also available are short-term classes during January term (one week before the onset of the spring semester) and May term (the weeks between the spring semester and the summer sessions).

Off-Campus Programs

Students can go beyond geographical and cultural boundaries and earn up to 16 hours of credit with Milligan's Study Abroad Program or with the many off-campus learning opportunities sponsored by the Council for Christian Colleges & Universities. These include an

American Studies Program in Washington, D.C.; Australia Studies Centre; China Studies Program; Contemporary Music Center in Nashville; Disney College Program; India Studies Program; Latin American Studies Program in Costa Rica; Los Angeles Film Studies Center; Middle East Studies Program in Cairo; Oxford Summer Programme; Scholars' Semester in Oxford; Semester or Summer in London; Uganda Studies Program; and Washington Journalism Center.

Through an affiliation with the International Business Institute, business majors can earn college credit through an intensive ten-week summer program in Europe. Milligan also offers a three-week summer humanities tour in Europe, during which students explore the origins of Western civilization. In addition, internship opportunities offer students college credit and work experience in their field of interest.

Academic Facilities

Milligan College's library has extensive holdings and online access to other major libraries and databases. Special collections within the library contain materials on the history of the College, the Restoration Movement, and the local area. The library also participates in resource-sharing agreements with Emmanuel Christian Seminary and East Tennessee State University. The Writing and Study Skills Center offers access to resources, instruction, and tutoring for academic success. Television and radio production studios and an FM radio station provide on-site training for communication students. A darkroom and art gallery feature works by fine arts students. Standardized laboratory facilities, including a gross anatomy lab, are available for general and advanced work in the sciences.

A new housing village opened in fall 2013. Other recent on-campus projects include a new state-of-the-art theater and convocation facility; renovation of the College's main classroom building and several other lecture halls and labs; and the addition of a new education center, a new tennis complex, and a new wellness center.

Costs

Tuition for 2014–15 was $27,700. Room and board were $6,250. Additional fees were approximately $1,030. Typical annual miscellaneous costs (books, supplies, etc.) were approximately $1,300. As a private institution, Milligan supplements student fees with income from endowments and gifts from alumni, friends, and churches in order to keep tuition well below the national average of similar four-year private institutions.

Financial Aid

Approximately 98 percent of all students at Milligan College receive federal, state, institutional, and/or outside (such as from a church or private foundation) aid, including both academic scholarships and need-based grants. Milligan has increased its financial aid offerings each year, spending more than $10 million last year to assist in meeting students' financial needs. Financial assistance is allocated on the basis of need demonstrated by information supplied on the Free Application for Federal Student Aid (FAFSA), which should be completed by January 1 for priority consideration. Returning students must complete and submit a Milligan College Financial Aid Scholarship/Renewal Application. The Milligan College Office of Financial Aid begins mailing award letters between March 1 and March 15.

Faculty

Eighty percent of Milligan's faculty members have earned the highest degree in their field from well-respected colleges and universities in the United States and abroad. Professors integrate biblical truths into their classes and are active leaders both on and off the campus. The low student-faculty ratio and small classes put the student at the center of attention and allow faculty members to cultivate special mentoring relationships with students. Professors serve as advisers to students from registration to graduation and are often instrumental in helping students find employment or gain admission to graduate school following graduation. Milligan's faculty members are mature and caring scholars who are committed to world-class scholarship, excellence in teaching, and their students.

Student Government

The Student Government Association (SGA) serves as the official representative voice of Milligan students and promotes academic, social, and spiritual activities for the campus community. SGA operates under a constitution approved and supported by the administration of the College, promotes well-ordered conduct among students, and enforces the regulations of the College. SGA leadership is provided by an executive council and representatives from throughout the campus. As a Christian college, Milligan adopts basic moral and social principles and expects students to serve Christ in an atmosphere of trust, encouragement, and respect for one another.

Admission Requirements

Character, ability, preparation, and seriousness of purpose are the qualities emphasized in considering applicants for acceptance to Milligan College. Overall excellence of performance in high school subjects, as well as evidence of Christian commitment and academic potential, provide the basis for admission to Milligan College. These qualities are evaluated by consideration of each applicant's academic record (based on transcripts), a personal reference, ACT or SAT scores, and participation in extracurricular activities. Some majors, such as music and theater, may require auditions and interviews. All applicants should have a high school diploma or the equivalent and have completed a college-preparatory curriculum with course work in English, math, science, history and/or social sciences, foreign language, and some work in speech, music, or art in preparation for study in a liberal arts curriculum. Satisfactory scores on the ACT or SAT are required of all applicants to the freshman class. The average ACT score for the current first-year class is 24. Transfer students should have a grade point average of 2.5 or above and must follow the same application procedures as first-time students, with the addition of providing official transcripts of all previous college work. ACT or SAT scores and high school transcripts are not required for transfer students with at least 24 earned semester hours. International applicants are subject to additional submission requirements.

Application and Information

Applications are processed on a rolling basis, and early application is encouraged. Notification is also given on a rolling basis. An application packet, complete with detailed instructions and requirements, can be obtained from the Admissions Office.

For further information, students should contact:

Admissions Office
Milligan College
P.O. Box 210
Milligan College, Tennessee 37682
Phone: 423-461-8730
800-262-8337 (toll-free)
Fax: 423-461-8982
E-mail: admissions@milligan.edu (general)
visits@milligan.edu (visits)
Website: http://www.milligan.edu

Milligan College is a Christian liberal arts college that unites humanities, sciences, and fine arts with a Christian worldview.

MILLS COLLEGE

OAKLAND, CALIFORNIA

MILLS

★ To read more about this school, visit http://petersons.to/millscollege

COLLEGE CLOSE-UPS

The College

Located in the heart of the San Francisco Bay Area, Mills College offers a challenging liberal arts curriculum that encourages women to think creatively, prepares them to take well-calculated risks, and equips them to put their passions into practice. At Mills, students join a welcoming community that helps them work smarter by working together and supports their individual determination to improve themselves and the world around them.

With mentoring from accomplished professors and an 11:1 student-faculty ratio, Mills students learn how to examine every side of an argument so they can succeed in every type of situation. They gain the confidence to ask and the knowledge to answer, generating new ideas and sharing opinions in an inclusive learning environment with women from all ages and backgrounds. Mills students are encouraged to stand out by standing up for their ideas and empowered to find their voices and make a statement in their careers and their communities.

At Mills, students have access to a range of opportunities beyond the classroom that enable them to expand their leadership and communication skills. Students can work directly with nationally renowned faculty on undergraduate research projects, gain practical career experience through internships, or obtain a broader international perspective by studying abroad. Students also participate in the 50-plus clubs and organizations at Mills—many of which are dedicated to making a difference on campus or in the local community.

Students at Mills can keep active by competing in six intercollegiate sports—cross-country, rowing, soccer, swimming, tennis, and volleyball—as members of the National Collegiate Athletic Association (NCAA) Division III. They also can participate in recreational activity courses ranging from Zumba to karate to horseback riding.

Mills has been educating creative, independent women since 1852, two years after California became a state. Since then, Mills has been recognized as one of the top colleges in the West by *U.S. News & World Report* and as one of the best colleges in the nation by The Princeton Review. Historically a college for women only, Mills continues that proud tradition today at the undergraduate level while offering respected graduate programs for women and men. The College's 135-acre campus has been home to alumnae who have gone on to excel as authors, composers, lawyers, professors, ambassadors, news anchors, governors, congresswomen, and activists.

Location

Mills College students make their home on the beautiful, safe campus in Oakland, California, from which they enjoy easy access to the cultural, recreational, academic, and professional opportunities available in the vibrant San Francisco Bay Area. The College's deep connection to Oakland and the wider Bay Area—including Berkeley, San Francisco, Napa, and Silicon Valley—enables students to examine big-city social, economic, and political issues through the diverse perspectives represented at a liberal arts college. They also have the opportunity to put theory into practice with internships at organizations such as Google, the *San Francisco Chronicle*, and the Office of Congresswoman Barbara Lee, and by volunteering at places ranging from Highland Hospital to the Oakland Asian Cultural Center.

Majors and Degrees

With more than forty different majors to choose from, Mills students can dive deeply into their field of interest or discover the academic topics that most inspire them. Whatever their area of interest, Mills students will find themselves asking tough questions, challenging preconceived ideas, thinking critically, and shaping new solutions with support from their professors and classmates.

Mills offers the Bachelor of Arts (B.A.) degree in American studies; anthropology; art (history and studio); biochemistry and molecular biology; biology; biopsychology; business economics; chemistry; child development; computer science; dance; economics; English (creative writing and literature); environmental science; environmental studies; ethnic studies; French and Francophone studies; government; history; intermedia arts; international relations; Latin American studies; literary and cultural studies; mathematics; music; philosophy; political, legal, and economic analysis; psychology; public policy; sociology; Spanish and Spanish American studies; theater; and women's, gender and sexuality studies. The major in child development meets the requirements for a state child development permit for teaching in preschool and day-care centers and provides a strong basis for graduate school and for many other careers. Special pre-law and pre-medical advising is available.

Mills offers the Bachelor of Science (B.S.) degree in biochemistry and molecular biology, biology, biopsychology, chemistry, environmental science, and mathematics.

Students can also choose to create their own major, working with 3 faculty advisers to plan an individual program that draws courses from across the curriculum and creates an integrated educational experience.

Mills offers seven unique programs that enable students to earn both a bachelor's and a master's degree—increasing their career options after college. The bachelor's to master's accelerated degree programs are: B.A./M.B.A. business administration, B.A./M.A. early childhood education, B.A./M.A. infant mental health, B.A./M.A. interdisciplinary computer science, B.A./M.A. mathematics, B.A./M.P.P. public policy, and B.A./M.A./credential teacher education.

Academic Programs

To earn a Mills bachelor's degree, students complete 34 semester course credits (usually four courses each semester). Grading is traditional, and a pass-fail option is available outside the major.

The innovative General Education Program is guided by a thoughtfully constructed set of learning outcomes, instead of a list of required courses. Each student designs her own program with the guidance of her faculty adviser, tailoring it to the student's specific needs and interests. The program places the work a student does in her major in a larger context and ensures that she explores and appreciates realms of knowledge beyond her field. The general education requirements fall into three outcome categories: skills (written communication, quantitative and computational reasoning, and information literacy/information technology); perspectives (women and gender, and multicultural); and disciplinary experiences (creation and criticism in the arts, historical perspectives, natural sciences, and human institutions and behavior).

The Career Services Office offers a comprehensive career counseling and coaching program to assist students in clarifying their goals. Workshops, individual counseling sessions, an internship program, a strong alumnae network, and special opportunities to meet Bay Area business leaders and top professional women all help students to focus their interests and plan career goals.

Off-Campus Programs

To provide students with further academic experiences, the College has cross-registration agreements with many reputable institutions in the San Francisco Bay Area. Mills sophomores, juniors, and seniors may cross-register for one course per semester at schools including Berkeley City College; California College of the Arts; California State University, East Bay; Saint Mary's College of California; and University of California, Berkeley.

On the national level, Mills has exchange or visiting programs with eleven American colleges and universities, including Barnard, Manhattanville, Mount Holyoke, Simmons, Spelman, and Wellesley.

Mills also encourages adventurous students with a minimum 3.0 GPA to study internationally for a semester or a full academic year. The College has study-abroad programs in more than 70 countries across Europe, Africa, South America, Asia, and Australia, and has special exchange programs with universities in China, Japan, and South Korea.

Academic Facilities

The facilities at Mills reflect the breadth of the College's academic programs and cocurricular activities. The open-stack F. W. Olin Library provides students with access to more than 240,000 volumes in addition to more than 22,000 rare books and manuscripts. Students have access to more than 60 databases, including Academic Search, LexisNexis, PsycINFO, and Britannica Online—available 24 hours a day via the library's website.

The Betty Irene Moore Natural Sciences Building provides students in STEM fields with a state-of-the-art learning environment that is also a model of green construction. The LEED-certified Platinum facility features high-tech classrooms, multiple teaching laboratories, and a research lab.

The home of the Lorry I. Lokey Graduate School of Business hosts both undergraduate and graduate classes. Students enjoy smart classrooms and lecture halls with the latest educational technology and light-filled community areas that encourage student collaboration.

The Jeannik Méquet Littlefield Concert Hall features an expanded stage area for larger performances and enhanced acoustic features for improved performing and recording quality. Nearby Lisser Hall contains a flexible proscenium stage as well as a small experimental theater.

The Mills College Art Museum houses the largest permanent collection of any liberal arts college on the West Coast and presents a changing array of innovative exhibitions. The highly regarded Children's School at Mills College provides hands-on experience for students preparing for careers in early childhood education.

Costs

In 2015–16, tuition and fees are $44,258 and room and board are $13,200. Students should calculate the costs of travel, books, and personal expenses on an individual basis and learn about the financial aid support available from Mills, state and federal aid programs, and third-party organizations.

Financial Aid

The College is committed to ensuring that a Mills education is within reach for those who have the desire and the qualifications to attend. Financial aid options at Mills include grants and scholarships, loans, and student employment. Some are funded by Mills directly, and others are state and federal programs.

In fall 2014, more than 80 percent of undergraduates at the College received some type of financial assistance in the form of grants, scholarships, loans, or on-campus employment. Ninety-three percent of Mills students received some portion of their aid directly from Mills. Awards are based on need and academic merit. Mills makes a special effort to provide financial aid to all students who demonstrate need.

All first-year students and transfer candidates must file the Free Application for Federal Student Aid (FAFSA) and the Mills College Financial Aid Form to be considered for government aid and need-based Mills scholarship funds. The FAFSA is required for non-Mills aid, such as the Federal Pell Grant and the Federal Supplemental Educational Opportunity Grant. California residents must also file the Cal Grant GPA Verification Form to be considered for a Cal Grant. More than 50 percent of Mills students have some of their demonstrated need offset by such non-Mills awards.

Faculty

Nearly 70 percent of the Mills faculty members are women, enabling students to work with professional women mentors in every academic area. Faculty members are selected for their teaching ability and scholarly achievement; 93 percent of full-time faculty members hold the highest degrees in their fields. Nearly 30 percent of the full- and part-time faculty are members of minority groups.

Student Government

Mills values the development of communication and leadership skills, and participating in student government provides a unique opportunity to enhance those skills. The Associated Students of Mills College (ASMC) is run by an executive board of 9 elected or appointed positions. Following a student-drafted constitution, the board supports student organizations, student publications, campus-wide events, and various student initiatives. From academic issues to social events to honor code concerns, the ASMC is the voice of the student body to the College administration.

Admission Requirements

Most first-year students admitted to Mills have a B+ average and have followed a full college-preparatory course in their secondary school, including 4 years of English, 3 to 4 years of mathematics, 2 to 4 years of foreign languages, 2 to 4 years of social sciences, and 2 to 4 years of a laboratory science. Additional course work in fine arts is given positive consideration, as is evidence of special talents or interests. Mills is interested in individuals, not statistical averages, so each application is carefully reviewed. Credit may be awarded for the College Board Advanced Placement tests and the International Baccalaureate program's higher level examinations.

Applications from transfer students and women who have delayed their entrance to college or who wish to continue work on their bachelor's degrees are welcome at Mills. The SAT/ACT and high school transcript requirements are waived if 24 or more transferable semester hours are presented. For international students, SAT or ACT and TOEFL or IELTS are application requirements. Applications should be accompanied by transcripts, a letter of recommendation, and test scores. An interview, either on campus or online through Skype or FaceTime, is strongly recommended for all applicants.

Application and Information

For first-year students, fall admission application deadlines are November 15 for early action and January 15 for regular decision. All required materials are due by January 15.

For transfer students, fall admission application deadlines are March 1 for priority scholarship consideration and April 1 for regular decision.

The spring admission application deadline for both first-year and transfer students is November 1. Admission decisions are mailed on a rolling basis.

For more information, students should contact:

Office of Undergraduate Admissions
Mills College
5000 MacArthur Boulevard
Oakland, California 94613
Phone: 510-430-2135
800-87-MILLS (toll-free)
Fax: 510-430-3298
E-mail: admission@mills.edu
Website: http://www.mills.edu
http://www.facebook.com/millscollege (Facebook)
http://twitter.com/millscollege (Twitter)
http://instagram.com/millscollege (Instagram)
http://youtube.com/millscollege (YouTube)

Mills students become part of an inclusive community that welcomes women from all ages and backgrounds.

MISERICORDIA UNIVERSITY

DALLAS, PENNSYLVANIA

★ To read more about this school, visit http://petersons.to/misericordiauniversity

MISERICORDIA UNIVERSITY

The University

Misericordia University is a high-quality liberal arts and professional studies institution rooted in service to others and committed to challenging academics and the personal attention students deserve. Founded by the Religious Sisters of Mercy in 1924, Misericordia offers undergraduate and graduate programs to resident and commuter students, as well as adult students. Current enrollment is more than 3,000 men and women.

The University cultivates a spirit of community service and a lifelong love of learning in its students through extracurricular activities, experiential learning, and challenging academic programs. In the National Survey of Student Engagement, Misericordia students say they are more involved in learning and have better relationships with faculty members and peers than students at other similar institutions. Misericordia is also ranked in the top tier of *U.S. News & World Report's* America's Best Regional Universities–North Category 2015.

Misericordia operates twelve residential facilities, including five residence halls, a town house complex, and off-campus housing, with a total capacity of more than 1,100 students. This includes Michael and Tina MacDowell Hall, which opened in fall 2012. Three nearby homes are reserved for upper-level students. Residents have a number of options, including single rooms and wellness housing. Each residence hall offers study rooms, laundry facilities, and recreational lounges. The Metz Dining Hall is located in the Banks Student Life Center, which also houses the Cougar's Den coffeehouse and the renovated Student Union that features flat-screen televisions as well as pool and foosball tables.

There are numerous campus activities. Besides Student Government, there are 43 chartered student clubs and organizations. Cultural events, Campus Ministry, intramural and intercollegiate athletic programs, performing arts shows, art exhibits, and many other social activities complement the academic experience. The new Metz Field House provides enhanced facilities for student athletes. In keeping with the University's tradition of Mercy, Service, Justice, and Hospitality, students have opportunities to develop leadership potential through service projects. MU earned a spot on the President's National Community Service Honor Roll for the past several years.

On spring break, students have served the needy in rural Appalachia, the Gulf Coast, Texas, California, Philadelphia, and the South Bronx. Students have volunteered abroad in Jamaica, Guyana, and Romania.

Personalized attention is the key to the support available in the Student Success Center. A psychologist, counselors, therapists, and peer counselors conduct workshops each semester on a variety of topics, including test anxiety, stress management, time management, and goal setting. Many services are free of charge to students and contacts are confidential.

First-year students may join the Guaranteed Placement Program (GPP) through the Insalaco Center for Career Development. The GPP program includes academic standards, cocurricular activities (such as leadership and service projects), internships, resume development, etiquette development, and interviewing skills. If a student fulfills the program's requirements and is not employed in his or her field or enrolled in graduate or professional school within six months of graduation, a paid internship is assured. The center also co-presents the Choice Program, which offers special guidance for students who have not declared a major. Opportunities for career exploration, cooperative education, and internships help students develop the skills they need to be successful when they enter the working world.

Student Health Services staff members provide first aid, assessment and treatment of common illnesses, and referrals for more serious health conditions. Health center activities are directed by a nurse practitioner. A self-care room offers reference materials and up-to-date information on personal health concerns. All services are confidential.

A rapidly evolving world has increased the number of adults who seek higher education. Misericordia offers bachelor's, master's, and doctoral programs for adult learners in several formats. The Ruth Matthews Bourger Women with Children program provides housing and support services for single women with children who are working toward their undergraduate degree. Convenient evening, online, and weekend formats also are available for people with families and full-time jobs.

Master's degrees are available in education, nurse practitioner studies, occupational therapy, physician assistant studies, speech/language pathology, business administration, and organizational management. A doctoral program in physical therapy is available to students entering in a full-time format, and a doctoral program in occupational therapy is available for graduate students via part-time study, including online and in-class components. A Doctor of Nursing Practice (D.N.P.) degree program began in fall 2014.

The University is fully accredited by the Middle States Association of Colleges and Schools. The medical imaging, nursing, occupational therapy, physician assistant, physical therapy, social work, and speech-language pathology programs are accredited by the National League for Nursing Accrediting Commission, the Council on Social Work Education, the Joint Review Committee on Education in Radiologic Technology, the American Occupational Therapy Association, the American Physical Therapy Association, the American Speech-Language and Hearing Association, and the Accreditation Review Commission on Education for the Physician Assistant.

Location

Located in northeastern Pennsylvania, Misericordia University is the oldest four-year institution of higher education in Luzerne County. Expansive lawns and thick stands of trees dominate the 124-acre upper and expanding lower campuses. It is 9 miles from the city of Wilkes-Barre. The area offers shopping centers, malls, cinemas, skiing, professional sporting events, and a variety of cultural activities. Pennsylvania's largest natural lake and two state parks are nearby, as are Pocono ski resorts. Metropolitan New York and Philadelphia are each within a 3-hour drive. Public and university-sponsored transportation serves the campus.

Majors and Degrees

Misericordia University awards the Bachelor of Arts (B.A.) degree in English, history, communications, government, law and national security, and philosophy. The Bachelor of Science (B.S.) degree is awarded in accounting, applied behavioral science, biochemistry, biology, business administration, chemistry, clinical laboratory science, communications, computer science, diagnostic medical sonography, elementary education, health-care management, information technology, management, mathematics, medical imaging, medical science, professional studies, psychology, secondary education, special education, and sport management. After completing the medical science bachelor's degree, students can opt for seamless transition into the master's degree in physician assistant studies. A Bachelor of Science in Nursing (B.S.N.) is awarded to nursing majors, and a Bachelor of Science in Social Work (B.S.W.) is awarded to social work majors. Specializations in accounting, early childhood education, prelaw, special education, and preprofessional occupations are also available. Certification programs include addictions counseling, picture archiving and communications administrator, diagnostic medical sonography, geriatric care management, gerontology, health-care informatics, post-professional pediatrics certificate for occupational therapists and physical therapists, and secondary education. These may be taken in support of several degrees offered by Misericordia or as stand-alone programs.

The University also offers five-year entry-level graduate majors in occupational therapy and speech-language pathology. Students graduate with a master's degree in speech-language pathology or occupational therapy and a bachelor's degree in health sciences. The physical therapy program is a 6½-year doctoral program. Students graduate with a bachelor's degree in one of several areas and a Doctor of Physical Therapy (D.P.T.) degree.

Academic Programs

Candidates for the B.A., B.S., B.S.N., or B.S.W. must fulfill a 48-credit liberal arts core curriculum in addition to the requirements of their chosen major to graduate. They must earn at least 36 credit hours in a chosen field. For regularly enrolled students, the average requirement for a baccalaureate degree is a total of 126 credits. Other options include minors, specializations, certifications, and electives. Other degrees have specialized requirements. Interested students should consult the academic catalog for the most current information.

Courses are offered on a semester basis, beginning in August and January and ending in December and May. Summer, weekend, and accelerated courses are also available.

Academic Facilities

The chemistry, physics, and biology departments all have fully equipped research laboratories available to students in these fields. State-of-the-art equipment includes high-performance liquid chromatography (HPLC), a rotary evaporator, and a new gas chromatograph mass spectrometer. The science building contains a gross anatomy laboratory, a rare asset for a university of this size. The University also houses an energized radiation laboratory for the medical imaging program. The Passan Hall–College of Health Sciences provides classrooms and high-tech laboratories for the occupational therapy, physical therapy, speech-language pathology, and nursing programs in a facility devoted to these majors. Physician assistant labs are located in a renovated space in the Passan Hall annex.

In addition to the four main computer labs, most other campus buildings and common areas offer wireless Internet access. The University operates e-MU, a secure online portal where students can access e-mail, course schedules, class registration tools, and student account and registration information from a single sign-on.

Mercy Hall, the original administrative building, offers multi-purpose academic classrooms and facilities. Many key student service departments, including the registrar, student accounts, and financial aid are centralized in one area in Mercy Hall. Sandy and Marlene Insalaco Hall houses the Pauly Friedman Art Gallery, café, computer labs, an ensemble room, fine arts classroom, music teaching and practice areas, and the Assistive Technology Research Institute.

The new Michael and Tina MacDowell Residence Hall hosts three ultramodern classrooms on the first floor.

The three-story Mark Kintz Bevevino Library covers 37,500 square feet and houses stacks for 90,000 volumes. Materials include information and communication technology and a reference section that offers books, serials, and a variety of periodicals as well as reference search tools.

Costs

Full-time undergraduate tuition for 2014–15 was $27,470 per year. The general fee was $1,540. Housing options include traditional rooms, suites, town houses, and lower-campus housing. The median room cost was $7,280. All resident students must participate in a 10-, 14-, or 19-meal plan. In addition, town house residents are eligible to choose a five-meal plan. The median board cost is $4,570.

Financial Aid

All students applying for financial aid must complete the Free Application for Federal Student Aid (FAFSA) by May 1. This is used for Federal Pell Grants, Federal Supplemental Educational Opportunity Grants (FSEOG), subsidized and unsubsidized Federal Direct Student Loans, Federal Perkins Loans, nursing loans, and the Federal Work-Study Program. This application is also the basis upon which state and institutional aid is awarded. The University also offers a no-interest monthly payment plan. Many scholarships are available including $20 million in presidential scholarships based on academic ability and $4.6 million in McAuley Awards for students who have experience in leadership roles and volunteer service.

Faculty

There are 123 full-time faculty members. A student-faculty ratio of 13:1 results in students receiving a great deal of individual attention from a highly qualified faculty; 87 percent of the faculty members hold doctorates. Besides student academic advising, the faculty members also serve as advisers to clubs.

Student Government

An active student government organization serves as a liaison between the students and the faculty and staff members. The administration enables students to become involved by serving as student representatives on various University committees.

Admission Requirements

Misericordia University admits applicants based on their secondary school record, high school recommendation, extracurricular activities, and personal promise. The University requires SAT or ACT scores.

Transfer students with a cumulative average of at least 2.0 (4.0 scale) may be considered for admission and may receive advanced standing. Some majors require a 2.5 or higher cumulative average. Transfer students must submit official high school transcripts and a transcript of work completed at other colleges and universities.

Application and Information

Applicants must submit an official application form (available upon request), transcripts, and SAT or ACT scores. Applicants may also apply through the University's website. There is a nonrefundable application fee of $35, which is waived for students who visit the campus or apply online.

The University considers applications on a rolling basis. Usually, candidates are notified of the admission decision within three weeks of receipt of all required materials.

Office of Admissions
Misericordia University
301 Lake Street
Dallas, Pennsylvania 18612-1090
Phone: 570-674-6461
866-262-6363 (toll free)
Fax: 570-675-2441
E-mail: admiss@misericordia.edu
Website: http://admissions.misericordia.edu
www.twitter.com/misericordiau
www.facebook.com/misericordiauniversity

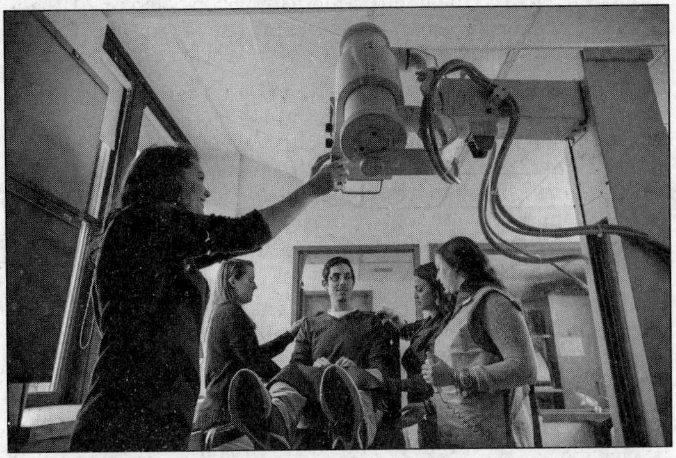

Misericordia University offers multiple medical and health science degree options on the undergraduate and graduate levels.

COLLEGE CLOSE-UPS

MOLLOY COLLEGE

ROCKVILLE CENTRE, NEW YORK

★ To read more about this school, visit http://petersons.to/molloycollege

The College

In 1955, 44 students became part of an exciting new tradition in higher education on Long Island. As the first freshman class of Molloy College, located in Rockville Centre, New York, these young students made a commitment to academic excellence. So did the College, which had a distinguished faculty of 15 and a library containing 5,000 books.

Today, Molloy offers students a rich and multidimensional education experience. The Long Island school encourages critical thinking and creative exploration in a personal community setting. Molloy combines the strengths of academic excellence and leadership with personal, compassionate mentoring to bring out the best in every student.

For over fifty years, Molloy College has evolved to become a dynamic learning institution with outstanding faculty, advanced technology, and a wide range of academic programs. In addition, Molloy has expanded its reach, offering graduate level courses at its Suffolk Center in East Farmingdale, New York, along with a number of on-site opportunities at area hospitals and school districts.

Molloy College students possess the confidence needed to live and work in this fast-paced, ever-changing world. The College has expanded its International Education program, where students travel from Rockville Centre and study abroad in Belgium, India, Italy, France, Spain, Thailand, and Australia. By traveling from Long Island and immersing themselves in cultures in other parts of the world, students gain knowledge while learning acceptance and understanding.

Closer to home, Molloy College students make a difference in Rockville Centre as well as other nearby local communities. For example, as part of Molloy's tradition of service, students become involved in a number of service projects that include BoxTown, a program to raise social consciousness about the issue of homelessness.

Athletics and academics go hand-in-hand at Molloy College, where students are known for both their athletic and scholastic success. The Long Island school has a winning tradition in a number of NCAA Division II athletic programs, and in 2013 and 2010 the women's softball team became one of only eight teams in the country to qualify for the College World Series.

Campus life in Rockville Centre, New York, is alive and vibrant, with more than fifty student clubs and honor societies. In 2011, Molloy opened its first residence hall, which houses more than 150 students. The College's second residence hall opened in fall 2014, giving Molloy more than 250 beds for on-campus living. In addition, a new student center (which also opened in 2011) provides new opportunities for Molloy students to study, interact with their fellow students, or simply relax.

Molloy College has become a focal point for civic discourse with key community forums. Top regional, national, and international leaders (including former Secretary of State Colin Powell and best-selling author Malcolm Gladwell) have come to Rockville Centre to visit the College and address critical and timely issues.

In recent years Molloy launched two new initiatives to enhance students' experience. The Sustainability Institute at Molloy College is Long Island's first-ever venture combining environmental advocacy and sustainability education within an academic institution, and the new sustainability minor provides students with a solid background in this critical subject. Molloy also started its new Irish Studies Institute recently with a presentation from Bertie Ahern, the former prime minister of Ireland.

Through Molloy College's diverse programs, personal attention from faculty, and commitment to improving both Long Island and the world, students develop an "I will" attitude that prepares them to enter the professional world, ready and able to make a difference.

Location

Located on a 30-acre campus in Rockville Centre, Long Island, Molloy College is close to metropolitan New York and all its diverse and rich resources. The College is easily accessible from all parts of Nassau, Suffolk, and Queens counties.

Majors and Degrees

Molloy College offers the A.A. degree in liberal arts; the A.A.S. degree in respiratory therapy and cardiovascular technology; and B.A., B.S., B.F.A., or B.S.W. degrees in accounting, art, biology, business management, communications, computer information systems, computer science, criminal justice, English, environmental studies, finance, history, interdisciplinary studies, international peace and justice studies, marketing, mathematics, modern languages, music, music therapy, new media, nuclear medicine technology, nursing, philosophy, political science, psychology, social work, sociology, speech-language pathology/audiology, theatre arts, and theology. Teacher certification programs are available in childhood (1–6), adolescence (7–12), and special education. Dual certification is available for birth–grade 2/childhood 1–6.

Special advisement is offered for students interested in pre-dental, pre-law, pre-medical, or pre–veterinary science programs.

On the graduate level, Molloy College offers a Master of Science degree as well as post-master's certification in nursing and education. M.B.A. programs are available in business, accounting, healthcare, and personal financial planning; a master's program in clinical mental health counseling was recently launched as well. A Master of Social Work is offered through Molloy's partnership with Fordham University. Molloy also offers graduate degrees in criminal justice, music therapy, and speech pathology. The College offers two doctoral programs, a Ph.D. in nursing and a Doctor of Nursing Practice (D.N.P.); other doctoral programs are in the planning stages.

The internship program at the College offers students the opportunity for on-the-job experience along with the classroom exposure so essential to the completely educated person. Internships are available in all areas of study.

Academic Programs

Advanced Placement credit is granted for a score of 3 or better on the AP exam. CLEP and CPE credit is also given. Molloy has a 4-1-4 academic calendar.

Academic Facilities

The Molloy campus has several new additions. The College has opened two new residence halls in recent years and there is also a new student center. In late 2011 Molloy also opened a new 550-seat performing arts theater, which serves the campus as well as the surrounding communities.

The James E. Tobin Library houses a collection of 110,000 volumes, along with hundreds of subscriptions to print journals and periodicals. Students and faculty members have access to the library's databases on campus and off campus as well as through the College's website. The library also houses a library instruction room, where librarians meet with professors and individual classes for instruction on the use of the databases and related research methods. The Tobin Library is a wireless facility. In the Media Center, over 3,000 DVDs and VHS tapes support the curriculum.

Students may use more than 300 computers located in nineteen labs and open space areas, including the Information Commons in the Public Square. The College has 100 percent wireless coverage for portable devices.

The Wilbur Arts Center features numerous art studios, music studios, a cable television studio, and the Lucille B. Hays Theatre. Molloy's new performing arts center opened in the Public Square student center in 2011, providing additional rehearsal and performance space for students, while bringing world-class performers to the College's campus.

Kellenberg Hall houses six science labs, a language lab, and the education resource center. The Casey Center houses two nursing labs, and the behavioral sciences research facility is located in Siena Hall.

Costs

For 2014–15, tuition was $25,800 and required fees were approximately $1,050. Students can expect to spend about $1,400 on books and supplies and approximately $2,400 in miscellaneous expenses.

Financial Aid

More than 85 percent of the student body of Molloy College is awarded financial aid in the form of scholarships, grants, loans, and Federal Work-Study Program employment. Financial aid awards are based on academic achievement and financial need. Completion of the Free Application for Federal Student Aid (FAFSA) is required. No-need scholarships and grants are also available.

Students who have attained a 95 percent or better high school average and a minimum combined score of 1280 on the SAT (composite math and verbal scores) are considered for the Molloy Scholars' Program, which awards full-tuition scholarships. Partial scholarships are available under Dominican, Community Service, and Fine Arts Scholarships. The Transfer Scholarship Program grants partial-tuition scholarships to students transferring into Molloy College with at least a 3.0 cumulative average. Athletic grants (Division II only) are awarded to full-time students based on athletic ability in a variety of sports. The Community Service Award is awarded to full-time freshmen demonstrating a commitment to their community and their school.

Faculty

The over 500 full-time and part-time faculty members at Molloy are dedicated as much to the students as to their respective fields. The 10:1 student-faculty ratio allows for small classes where students can receive the individual attention they deserve.

In addition to their teaching responsibilities, faculty members advise students in their fields to help them select courses that both satisfy major course requirements and lead to the attainment of career goals.

Student Government

Every member of the Molloy College student body belongs to the Molloy Student Association, whose elected leaders form the Molloy Student Government. This group of students provides the leadership necessary to keep extracurricular life at Molloy College alive, productive, and practical.

Admission Requirements

Recommended admission qualifications include graduation from a four-year public or private high school or equivalent (GED test) with a minimum of 18.5 units, including 4 in English, 4 in social studies, 3 in a foreign language, 3 in mathematics, and 3 in science. Nursing applicants must have taken courses in biology and chemistry. Mathematics applicants must have taken 4 units of math and 3 of science (including chemistry or physics). Biology applicants must have credits in biology, chemistry, and physics and 4 units of math. A portfolio is required of art applicants, and music students must audition. Social work applicants must file a special application with the director of the social work program.

The admissions committee bases its selection of candidates on the secondary school record, SAT or ACT scores, class rank, and the school's recommendation. A particular talent or ability can be important. Character and personality, extracurricular participation, and alumni relationships are all considered. On-campus interviews are recommended but not required.

The St. Thomas Aquinas Program may be an option for students not normally eligible for admission.

Molloy College also offers an honors program for a select group of academically gifted students. The program is open to entering freshmen in all majors (except for theatre arts).

Application and Information

To apply to Molloy College, students should submit the following credentials to the Admissions Office: a completed application for admission (the Common Application is accepted), a nonrefundable $40 application fee, an official high school transcript or GED score report, official results of the SAT or ACT, and official college transcripts (transfer students only).

The College uses a rolling admission system. Students are advised of an admission decision within a few weeks after the application filing process is complete.

For further information, prospective students should contact:

Dean of Admissions
Molloy College
1000 Hempstead Avenue
P.O. Box 5002
Rockville Centre, New York 11571-5002
Phone: 888-4-MOLLOY (toll-free)
Website: http://www.molloy.edu

Molloy College combines academic excellence and leadership with personal, compassionate mentoring to bring out the best in every student.

MONMOUTH UNIVERSITY

WEST LONG BRANCH, NEW JERSEY

★ To read more about this school, visit http://petersons.to/monmouth

MONMOUTH UNIVERSITY

The University

Monmouth University is a dynamic, top-tier, private university that empowers students to reach their full potential as leaders. Through small classes, individual attention, and innovative faculty members, students are afforded a challenging learning environment on one of the most beautiful campuses in New Jersey, which blends classic beauty with the latest technology.

The University has a diverse student body comprising approximately 6,400 undergraduate and graduate students. While many are from the Northeast, students come from all across the United States, as well as nations around the world. For those choosing University housing, Monmouth offers traditional residence halls and garden-style apartments. Some University-sponsored beachfront campus housing is also offered to students who meet certain requirements. Housing is guaranteed for first-year and sophomore students. First-year housing is guaranteed for students who submit the required enrollment deposit, housing deposit, and housing contract by May 1.

Students at Monmouth have an assortment of extracurricular activities to choose from, including more than 100 student-run clubs and organizations, such as the Student Government Association, the campus newspaper (*The Outlook*), the FM radio station (WMCX), the television station (Hawk TV), the online news portal (*The Verge*), the yearbook (*Shadows*), the literary magazine (*Monmouth Review*), and various sororities and fraternities. Special events are held throughout the year, including art exhibits, concerts, lectures, and sightseeing trips.

In addition, students can cheer on Monmouth's NCAA Division I athletics programs. Monmouth is proud to host a successful inter-collegiate athletics program that fields twenty-one men's and women's teams. The teams compete in the Metro Atlantic Athletic Conference (MAAC), with the exception of football, which competes in the full-scholarship Big South Conference. The University's basketball and track and field teams compete in the 153,200-square-foot Multipurpose Activity Center (MAC)—a modern, 4,100-seat mid-major sports arena. All Monmouth students have access to the MAC, which also houses a 200-meter, six-lane indoor track; fitness center; conference space; the University Store; and more.

Monmouth is a destination that offers something for everyone, and it strives to ensure that students have the resources and support to pursue their goals. For instance, the Center for Student Success (CSS) assists students through a variety of academic and career counseling services and programs. Furthermore, students who complete their degrees benefit from continued relationships with the Monmouth family. Many graduates return to campus to visit friends, discuss projects with faculty members, and even recruit the next generation of alumni.

Location

Monmouth University's location is a portal to the world. From its safe, suburban West Long Branch, New Jersey campus, students can easily connect to an abundance of experience, culture, knowledge, and more. Approximately 1 hour from both New York City and Philadelphia, and 1 mile from the coastal beaches of the Atlantic Ocean, the University is also close to Asbury Park, the city where music lives.

Economic and political centers of the country and the world are made real and accessible through fascinating internships, a robust study-abroad program, and multiple field experience opportunities. Corporate global headquarters, world-class museums, Madison Square Garden, and other sports hubs, shops, restaurants, and theaters are all within reach of the campus.

Students from every discipline are easily able to link academic interests with hands-on, real-world adventures that can be networked into lifelong career paths.

Majors and Degrees

Monmouth University offers thirty-two baccalaureate degree programs in six academic schools that share the University's commitment to providing the highest level of education through innovative techniques and personal attention. The **Leon Hess Business School** awards bachelor's degrees in business administration with concentrations in accounting; economics; finance; economics and finance; international business; management and decision sciences; marketing; marketing, management, and decision sciences; and real estate. The **School of Education** awards bachelor's degrees that allow students to earn certification as elementary and secondary school teachers; the school also offers various endorsements, such as English as a second language and teacher of students with disabilities. The **Wayne D. McMurray School of Humanities and Social Sciences** awards bachelor's degrees in anthropology, art, communication, criminal justice, English, fine arts, foreign language, history, homeland security, music, political science, psychology, and sociology. A Spanish and international business B.A. degree is awarded jointly through the Leon Hess Business School and the School of Humanities and Social Sciences. The **School of Science** awards bachelor's degrees in biology, chemistry, clinical laboratory sciences, computer science, marine and environmental biology and policy, mathematics, medical laboratory science, and software engineering. The **School of Social Work** awards the Bachelor of Social Work degree. The **Marjorie K. Unterberg School of Nursing and Health Studies** awards bachelor's degrees in health studies and health and physical education, as well as the Bachelor of Science in Nursing. A preprofessional advising program is available for students who intend to pursue careers in medicine, dentistry, or other healthcare fields. Monmouth also offers a number of Five-Year Baccalaureate/Master's programs, which enable qualified students to earn a bachelor's and a master's degree in five years in business, computer science, criminal justice, education (select programs), English, history, homeland security, political science/public policy, psychology/school counseling, social work, or software engineering.

Academic Programs

The curriculum at Monmouth is focused on creating the next generation of leaders who are attuned to today's globally oriented, technological society and yet are grounded in the liberal arts. The University also emphasizes writing, speaking, and other interpersonal skills that are critical to personal growth and professional success. Monmouth equips every student with technological literacy and experiential education—real-world experience that enhances classroom learning and academic progress.

Experiential education (Ex Ed) is an invaluable part of the curriculum for all Monmouth students, enabling them to gain experience in corporations, local businesses, nonprofits, government, and schools. The Ex Ed requirement at Monmouth can be completed in various ways; for instance, students have recently completed internships in New York City and Philadelphia, in places such as ESPN, JPMorgan Chase, NBCUniversal, and others. The University also partners with the Washington Center, allowing students to earn credit for experiential learning gained through internships and symposia in the nation's capital.

Genuine concern for the individual student characterizes the entire educational program at Monmouth. Professors, not teaching assistants, conduct all courses and supervise all laboratories. They also strive to help students develop values, such as citizenship and social responsibility, that enable graduates to make significant contributions to their communities and society.

In addition, the University's Honors School allows qualified students to participate in an educational environment that encourages and supports intellectual and personal excellence. First-year courses are clustered to enhance interactive learning, with professors who develop common themes and assignments. Honors classes are distinguished by in-depth coverage of material through discussion and writing, smaller class sizes, and a heightened student-faculty rapport. In their final year, each Honors School student researches, writes, and publicly presents an honors thesis, guided by a faculty member who serves as their academic mentor.

Academic Facilities

Monmouth's sixty-five buildings provide a synthesis of historical architecture and modern aesthetics. The campus' signature building is Woodrow Wilson Hall, a National Historic Landmark, which houses classrooms and administrative offices and served as Daddy Warbucks' mansion in the 1982 film *Annie*. Two other buildings on campus have rich histories: the Monmouth University Library and Lauren K. Woods Theatre. The library, the former mansion of Murry and Leonie Guggenheim, displays many charming architectural features and holds 290,000 print and online monographs, 166 databases (abstracts and full-text, e-books, motion picture, image, tools), over 61,000 electronic and print journal subscriptions, and over 1,000 media items. Woods Theatre, once the Guggenheim carriage house, features a variety of performances and lets students experience all phases of the theater arts.

One of Monmouth's most unique buildings is the Jules L. Plangere Jr. Center for Communication, which is home to the Department of Communication and provides state-of-the-art studios and editing facilities. The newest facility on campus is Joan and Robert Rechnitz Hall, which houses the Department of Art and Design, an art gallery, three Mac labs, a reception area, and an animation and editing studio.

All academic programs are amply supported by state-of-the-art computer hardware and software and classroom/laboratory facilities. The major components supporting Monmouth's academic programs include Windows, Mac OS, and Unix systems connected via an expansive wired and wireless network, which spans twenty-three buildings and encompasses more than 2,400 workstations including general and specialty labs and classrooms.

Costs

For 2014–15, tuition and fees were approximately $32,310 per year. Annual room and board costs are approximately $11,710; actual costs are determined by the type of room and meal plan selected. Costs are subject to change for 2015–16.

Financial Aid

A Monmouth University education is an investment that will pay off for the rest of a student's life. The value of a Monmouth education is found not only in its excellent academic programs, but in the personalized attention its students receive in and out of the classroom.

Monmouth is among the most affordable high-quality, comprehensive private educational institutions in New Jersey. It is found in the top tier of academic quality and the mid-tier in costs. At Monmouth, 99 percent of first-year students receive some form of financial aid; about 96 percent receive a scholarship or grant (federal, state, or University), and the average scholarship/grant package is $17,600; and the average financial aid package, including student loans and work study, is approximately $29,500. All this, combined with the fact that Monmouth awards more than $51 million in institutional aid to students each year, makes Monmouth an affordable option for many families.

A wide range of University scholarships and grants are offered to all prospective full-time, first-year, and transfer students on the basis of academic performance. Eligibility for University scholarship and grant funding varies according to the quality of the student's previous academic record. Award amounts range from $2,000 to $17,000.

The University also participates in all federal and state grant and loan programs. To establish eligibility for these programs and capitalize on available assistance, students should complete the Free Application for Federal Student Aid (FAFSA) as soon after January 1 as possible. Students and their families may call 732-571-3463, e-mail finaid@monmouth.edu, or visit the Financial Aid Office for assistance.

Students interested in attending Monmouth can get an estimate of their eligibility for federal, state, and institutional aid, even before submitting their application. To complete the University's Scholarship Inquiry Form and Net Price Calculator, students should visit www.monmouth.edu/scholarship and www.monmouth.edu/netpricecalculator.

Faculty

The University's professors are leaders in their fields and contribute through research, publishing, and consulting services to their respective academic areas. There are 288 full-time and 350 part-time faculty members. Approximately 80 percent of full-time faculty members have doctorates or terminal degrees in their fields. The average class size is 23, and the student-faculty ratio is 14:1.

Student Government

The Student Government Association (SGA) is an important and necessary voice in the University community; its views are recognized and respected. Monmouth students who wish to get involved with SGA can also do so as general members. This flexible form of involvement does not require a student to run for a position or participate in any one of the elections that are sponsored by SGA. More information is available at www.monmouth.edu/sga.

Admission Requirements

Many factors are considered in an admission application. For first-year applicants, a committee evaluates the required high school transcripts and SAT or ACT scores, one letter of recommendation, and a personal essay. A resume of activities including leadership positions held and other information supporting the application are also welcome. Campus tours and information sessions with admission counselors are available. Transfer students must submit official transcripts from all colleges attended. If transfer students have earned fewer than 24 transferable credits, they must fulfill first-year admission requirements as well. Nursing applicants must apply by December 1 and submit a nursing-specific essay.

Application and Information

Early action is a nonbinding option for students who wish to receive an early response from Monmouth. December 1 is the deadline for early action and nursing applicants, and admission decisions are mailed by January 15. The application deadline for regular decision is March 1, with an admission decision notification date prior to April 1. Applications received after March 1 are considered on a space-available basis. First-year housing is guaranteed for students who submit the required enrollment deposit, housing deposit, and housing contract by May 1. Students who submit their deposits and housing contract after May 1 may be placed on a wait list for admission and/or housing.

For further information, students should contact:

Office of Undergraduate Admission
Monmouth University
400 Cedar Avenue
West Long Branch, New Jersey 07764-1898
Phone: 732-571-3456
800-543-9671 (toll-free)
Fax: 732-263-5166
E-mail: admission@monmouth.edu
Website: http://www.monmouth.edu
http://www.facebook.com/monmouthuniversity
http://www.twitter.com/monmouthu
http://www.youtube.com/monmouthuniversity

Monmouth students enjoy a challenging learning environment on a campus that offers classical beauty and the latest technology.

MORNINGSIDE COLLEGE

SIOUX CITY, IOWA

MORNINGSIDE COLLEGE

The College

The Morningside College experience cultivates a passion for lifelong learning and a dedication to ethical leadership and civic responsibility. For 120 years, the goal of Morningside College has been to provide students with an education of the highest quality. Morningside is rooted in a strong church-related, liberal arts tradition, and its challenge is to prepare students to be flexible in thought, open in attitude, and confident in themselves.

Founded in 1894, Morningside College is a private, four-year, coeducational, liberal arts institution affiliated with the United Methodist Church. The College seeks both students and faculty members representing diverse social, cultural, ethnic, racial, and national backgrounds.

At the graduate level, Morningside confers a Master of Arts in Teaching, with professional educator or special education tracks.

Morningside College's nearly 1,300 full-time undergraduate students are encouraged to participate in a wide variety of activities, including departmental, professional, and religious organizations; honor societies; and sororities and fraternities. A newspaper, literary magazine, and campus radio station are all student directed. These activities provide students with many opportunities to develop leadership, interpersonal, and social skills. Since nearly all activities on campus are student initiated and student directed, ample opportunities for leadership development exist. Students interested in the performing arts can participate in a variety of vocal and instrumental ensembles, marching band, and theater productions. Intercollegiate athletics are available for men in baseball, basketball, bowling, cross-country, football, golf, soccer, swimming, tennis, track and field, volleyball, and wrestling and for women in basketball, bowling, cross-country, golf, soccer, softball, swimming, tennis, track, and volleyball. Cheer and dance squads are also part of the athletic department.

The Hindman-Hobbs Center includes a pool, saunas, racquetball courts, a weight room, basketball courts, a wrestling room, and a jogging track as well as classroom facilities and offices.

Location

Morningside College is located on a 68-acre campus in Sioux City, the fourth-largest city in Iowa. The campus is based in a residential section of the community, adjacent to a city park, and within 5 minutes of major regional shopping centers. The Sioux City metropolitan area offers a blend of urban shopping, commerce, and recreation in a scenic setting. Students find Morningside's Sioux City location to be advantageous in seeking internship opportunities and full- or part-time employment.

Majors and Degrees

The five undergraduate degrees conferred by Morningside College are the Bachelor of Arts, Bachelor of Science, Bachelor of Science in Nursing, Bachelor of Music, and Bachelor of Music Education. Career programs consist of accounting, advertising, applied agricultural and food studies, art, biology, business administration, chemistry, computer science, corporate communications, elementary education, engineering physics, English, graphic arts, history, interdisciplinary studies, marketing, mass communications, mathematics, music, nursing, philosophy, photography, political science, psychology, religious studies, Spanish, special education, and theater. Students choosing to teach in secondary school may be certified in most academic majors.

In cooperation with other institutions, Morningside offers preprofessional programs in dentistry, engineering, law, medical technology, medicine, the ministry, optometry, pharmacy, physical therapy, physician assistant studies, and veterinary medicine.

Academic Programs

Morningside operates on a two-semester system; sessions are held from late August to December and from January to early May. Evening classes are offered each semester. A three-week May Term and a six-week summer session are also available.

The Morningside College experience provides an education that develops the whole person through an emphasis on critical thinking, effective communication, cultural understanding, practical wisdom, spiritual discernment, and ethical action. By working with talented faculty members in a large number of majors, caring college staff members who provide numerous opportunities for valuable cocurricular experiences, and other exceptional and interesting students with whom they will form lifelong connections, Morningside students gain the knowledge, skills, and personal dispositions that will ensure their success.

Special opportunities include a voluntary Interdepartmental Honors Program, in which students meet weekly to discuss ideas that have shaped history from the ancient world into the future. Friday Is Writing Day, offered in a weekly discussion format, allows students and faculty members to read aloud and react to one another's writing.

Every entering full-time student is provided with a notebook computer that is used in classroom work. Student technology services include high-speed Internet connection, ports in all residence halls and classrooms, web-accessible personal e-mail accounts, a digital library accessible day and night, specialized computer labs to support academic programs, and wireless network access points across campus.

Off-Campus Programs

Morningside students who qualify have the opportunity to take advantage of special programs for off-campus study. Programs are available for a semester or the entire school year. The College has agreements with schools in Italy, England, Japan, and Northern Ireland.

Students participate in exchange programs with the Consortium Institute of Management and Business Analysis (CIMBA) in Italy; Kansai Gaidai University in Japan; Queen's University, the University of Ulster, Belfast Institute for Further and Higher Education, Stranmillis University College, and St. Mary's University College in Northern Ireland; and Edge Hill University, the Centre for Medieval and Renaissance Studies, Regent's American College London in England, the University of Teacher Education Central Switzerland in Lucerne, and the Beijing Center for Chinese Studies.

Morningside also offers a Spanish Studies Abroad program in various cities in Spain as well as Argentina and Puerto Rico. The Morningside in Italy program combines classroom study, research, and experiential learning opportunities.

A cooperative program with Central College in Pella, Iowa, allows Morningside students to study abroad in Austria, England, France, Mexico, the Netherlands, Spain, and Wales.

In addition, Morningside has opportunities for students to enroll for a semester at American University in Washington, D.C., to study the U.S. government in action. Students may also be nominated for a semester at Drew University in New Jersey to study the United Nations. Students who participate in these programs maintain their enrollment at Morningside College.

Academic Facilities

The Hickman-Johnson-Furrow Learning Center is the home of the library, the Writing Center, and the Academic Support Services Center. The library has more than 99,000 volumes, nearly 3,000 audio recordings and video materials, and nearly 440 current print periodical subscriptions. Online accessibility includes student/faculty access to more than 18,000 full-text journals. The library's web-based, integrated online system allows seamless access to numerous subscription databases as well as other online catalogs and websites. The library building also houses the Spoonholder Café, classrooms, the Mass Communication Department, and a computer lab.

Charles City College Hall is listed on the National Register of Historic Places and houses classrooms and offices for the History, Philosophy, Religious Studies, and Theatre Departments.

The Eugene C. Eppley Fine Arts Building, one of the finest music and art facilities in the Midwest, underwent an extensive remodel which was completed in the fall of 2013. The auditorium seats 1,300 and is noted for its acoustical qualities and the majestic Sanford Memorial Organ. The MacCollin Classroom Building, adjoining the auditorium, houses offices, art studios, practice rooms, and classrooms for music and art students.

The Helen Levitt Art Gallery adjoins the Eppley Auditorium and is home to the Levitt art collection, which includes work by internationally famous artists.

Lewis Hall, the second-oldest building on campus, is the site of the English and Modern Languages Department and the Economics, Political Science, and Sociology Department, as well as administrative offices.

The Robert M. Lincoln Center houses the College's Business Administration and contains a library, auditorium, a conference room, several classrooms, and the Center for Entrepreneurship Education.

The James and Sharon Walker Science Center features up-to-date laboratories and classrooms and houses offices for the Natural Sciences and Mathematics Division.

Buhler Rohlfs Hall was constructed in 2014 to house the Sharon Walker School of Education, the Nylen School of Nursing, and the Regina Roth Applied Agricultural and Food Studies Program.

Krone Advising Center, also constructed in 2014, houses offices for the full-time advisers who work with Morningside's first-year students.

Costs

Tuition and fees for 2014–15 were $27,180, and room and board were $8,250. These figures do not include books and personal expenses.

Financial Aid

In 2013–14, more than $37 million was awarded in financial aid to Morningside students, with an average financial aid package of $27,142 for a full-time student. The financial aid resources of federal, state, and College programs are available to Morningside students through a combination of scholarships, grants, loans, and work-study employment. Financial assistance is offered to 100 percent of full-time students.

Students are encouraged to submit the Free Application for Federal Student Aid (FAFSA) as early as possible. The College's code number is 001879. The annual priority deadline for need-based financial aid is March 1.

Faculty

Seventy-three percent of Morningside College's 83 full-time faculty members have earned the terminal degree in their chosen field. The College also employs 53 part-time instructors and has a 13:1 student-faculty ratio.

Student Government

Student government is directly responsible for regulation, supervision, and coordination of student campus activities. The president of the student body is a voting member of the Board of Directors, allowing for student input in decisions facing the Board.

Admission Requirements

Morningside College selects students for admission whose scholastic achievement and personal abilities provide a foundation for success at the college level. While the College seeks students who rank in the upper half of their graduating class, each application is considered on an individual basis. The student's academic record, class rank, and test scores are considered. Transfer students must have earned 24 transferable semester hours of a 2.25 or better cumulative GPA on previous college work to qualify for automatic admission. It is the policy and practice of Morningside College to not discriminate against persons on the basis of age, sex, religion, creed, race, color, gender identity, sexual orientation, marital status, disability, genetic information, or national origin.

Application and Information

Rolling admission allows for flexibility; however, prospective students are encouraged to apply as early as possible before the semester in which they wish to enroll. Transfer and international students are welcome. Catalogs, application forms, and financial aid forms are available from the Office of Admissions.

For further information, students should contact:

Office of Admissions
Morningside College
1501 Morningside Avenue
Sioux City, Iowa 51106
Phone: 712-274-5111
800-831-0806 (toll-free)
E-mail: mscadm@morningside.edu
Website: http://www.morningside.edu
http://www.facebook.com/morningside.edu

Morningside College students enjoy one of the most attractive campuses in the Midwest.

COLLEGE CLOSE-UPS

MOUNT ALOYSIUS COLLEGE

CRESSON, PENNSYLVANIA

★ To read more about this school, visit http://petersons.to/mountaloysiuscollege

The College

Mount Aloysius College is a private, accessible, and affordable Catholic liberal arts college sponsored by the Religious Sisters of Mercy. The College welcomes people of all faith traditions. Established in 1853, Mount Aloysius College offers both undergraduate and graduate education. Since the founding of the College, nearly 15,500 students have become proud Mount Aloysius alumni. The College is committed to providing small class sizes, and students benefit from accessible faculty and staff. Mount Aloysius students come mostly from throughout Pennsylvania and the mid-Atlantic Region. There are over 2,500 students enrolled (unduplicated headcount).

Mount Aloysius College is one of 18 Mercy Colleges nationwide. Students are encouraged to synthesize faith with learning, to develop competence with compassion, to apply their talents and gifts to the service of others, and to assume leadership in their community.

Student activities play a distinctive role in personal growth. At Mount Aloysius College, there are approximately 100 organized clubs, groups, honor societies, and an intramural sports program. Activities include a student newspaper, residence hall associations, student government, cheerleading, dance team, scholarship-funded theater and choir programs, and a student activities planning board. Mount Aloysius fun includes social events, intramural sports, athletic events, comedians, live music, theater, educational events, campus forums, and awesome guest lectures.

Mount Aloysius College is a member of NCAA Division III. Athletic programs involve both women and men and include basketball, cross-country, golf, soccer, and tennis. Men's baseball and women's bowling, softball, and volleyball are also offered. Athletes benefit from the Ray S. and Louise S. Walker Athletic Field Complex, which includes a softball field, one of the finest soccer fields in the area, and the Calandra-Smith baseball complex. Recently the Mountie Stables were opened to the College and to the community. The Stables add dugouts, lockers, showers, storage, and concession facilities to the school's athletic infrastructure.

Opened in autumn 2013, the new Athletic Convocation and Wellness Center is a spectacular 87,400-square-foot multipurpose facility on the western edge of the beautiful and expansive 193-acre campus. This facility takes Mount Aloysius athletics to a new level and adds a welcomed special events venue to the southern Allegheny Mountains. The Center houses a main gymnasium and events venue with seating for over 2,500, home and visitor locker rooms, and trainer facilities. There is also a full-size auxiliary gymnasium. Athletic offices, Institutional Advancement, Student Affairs, Business faculty offices, and fully integrated smart classrooms and conferencing facilities are also located in the building. On the ground floor, a new state-of-the-art wellness center offers both cardio and resistance training in a spacious, modern environment.

In spring 2014, an anonymous donor memorialized the late Sr. Virginia Bertschi, RSM by repurposing the former Health amd Fitness Center. The new Bertschi Center and Technology Commons—with open architecture, vivid colors, and glass walls offering great views of the campus and surrounding mountains—is an additional social, technology, and special events venue that serves both commuter and resident students.

The main campus building is a picturesque structure dating to 1897. It houses the admissions, financial aid, security, health, and academic offices, along with the Office of the President, classrooms, the region's premiere nursing simulation center, and the Wolf-Kuhn Art Gallery. Cosgrave Center is the hub of campus life. The building contains the dining hall, snack bar, bookstore, child-care center (part of the elementary education/early childhood program at the College), lounges, recreational rooms, student affairs offices, and meeting rooms. Ihmsen Halls are key housing facilities for residential students. Misciagna Residence is a state-of-the-art residence hall, providing 25 suites and private bathrooms. McAuley Hall features both double and single rooms and a large multipurpose room and study lounges on all three floors. Alumni Hall is a historic, multipurpose facility used for College drama, musicals, lectures, and performing arts events. The College operates 12 months per year and opens its facilities to the Southern Allegheny community.

The College is 100 percent wireless, and smart classrooms are located throughout the campus.

Mount Aloysius is fully accredited by the Middle States Association of Colleges and Schools and approved by the Pennsylvania Department of Education. All nursing and health studies programs are fully accredited by their professional accrediting bodies, including the National League for Nursing Accrediting Commission, the Commission on Accreditation for Programs of Diagnostic Medical Sonography, the Commission on Accreditation in Physical Therapy Education, the American Association of Medical Assistants, and the Joint Commission on Accreditation for Programs of Surgical Technology.

In addition to its undergraduate programs—both associate and bachelor's degrees—Mount Aloysius offers master's degree programs in business administration, behavioral specialist consulting, community counseling, and psychology.

Location

Mount Aloysius College is located in the scenic Southern Allegheny Mountains of west-central Pennsylvania, in the town of Cresson. Convenient and accessible from U.S. Route 22, the College's setting is rural but mere minutes from State College, Altoona, Johnstown, and Pittsburgh, Pennsylvania. The area has warm, beautiful summers; brisk, breathtaking autumns; invigorating winters; and cool, blooming springs. Facilities are available for biking, golfing, swimming, horseback riding, waterskiing, boating, hiking, spelunking, cross-country and downhill skiing, picnicking, and amusement parks. A well-kept system of State Parks is convenient to the College as are shopping malls, golf courses, and numerous historical sites.

Majors and Degrees

Mount Aloysius College awards bachelor's and associate degrees in the arts, sciences, and health studies fields in both career-oriented and traditional liberal arts programs. Baccalaureate degrees are available in accounting, American Sign Language/English interpreter education, behavioral and social science, biology and general science, business administration (includes a fifth-year MBA option), computer science, criminology, dentistry (4-4), elementary/early childhood education and secondary education (with certifications), English, general science, history/political science, humanities, information technology, math/science, medical imaging, nursing (RN-BSN program), nursing (2+2), occupational therapy (3-2), osteopathic medicine (3-4), pharmacy (3-3), physical therapy (4-3), physician assistant studies (3-2), prelaw, psychology, and undecided/exploratory. Associate degrees are offered in applied technology, business administration, criminology, early childhood studies, general studies, legal studies, liberal arts, medical assistant studies, nursing, physical therapist assistant studies, radiography/medical imaging, sign language/deaf studies, and surgical technology.

Academic Programs

Whether preparing students for careers upon graduation or for graduate school, Mount Aloysius recognizes the importance of a broad and liberal education. Thus, in addition to receiving solid preparation for a chosen career, every student at the College receives a foundation in the arts, sciences, and humanities through an outstanding core curriculum. Strong emphasis is placed on the specialized courses within each program of study, and many academic programs combine classroom experience with internships and related training at area clinical sites, agencies, and institutions. In addition to its regular academic programs, Mount Aloysius offers independent and directed study with a commitment to service, a central component of a Mercy education. The College has an excellent honors program and academic services area. The academic calendar has two traditional semesters and optional summer sessions.

Off-Campus Programs

An important feature of many academic programs is off-campus training. The majority of the College's programs of study require credit-yielding practicums at partnering hospitals, public and private schools, or health or human service agencies. Students in all health programs benefit from required clinical training during their time at the College.

Academic Facilities

In 1995, Mount Aloysius College opened both a new Library and a new era, signifying greater access to information for the College community. This state-of-the-art Library is the campus hub for technology and study. With a Buhl Electronic Classroom and more than 80,000 print and nonprint titles, the Library is an impressive, 31,000-square-foot facility with ample seating space, four group-study rooms, a reading lounge, a law library and classroom, an unparalleled 18,000-volume Ecumenical Collection donated by Pastor Gerald Myers, and ample room for expansion. This facility is completely automated, with an online catalog and access to remote libraries and the Internet through more than 30 workstations. The Library also houses the Information Technology Center, home to 15 multimedia workstations and the latest educational software.

Pierce Hall serves as the campus science center. A state-of-the-art, 31,000-square-foot facility, it was completed in 1997. Pierce Hall houses all science labs, health science centers, and the offices of science faculty. Academic Hall is home to the College Honors Program. It houses classrooms, labs, seminar rooms, faculty offices, and electronic classrooms. The College is proud of its bridge to the past and its progress in providing 21st Century learning facilities.

Costs

Annual tuition and fees for the 2014–15 academic year for full-time students were $19,790; room and board were $8,780. Up-to-date cost information is available online at www.mtaloy.edu/tuition_and_aid/tuition_and_fees.

Financial Aid

Mount Aloysius prides itself on affordability. Many MAC students hail from proud families of modest means and many are first-generation students. The College understands the expense involved in acquiring a quality education and encourages all students to apply for all available aid. Through the Office of Financial Aid, the College assists students in applying for state and federal grants, loans, work-study awards, merit scholarships and more. The College awards academic monies based on GPA and SAT or ACT scores. These awards are renewable over a four-year period and range from $1,000 to $12,000 per year. Mount Aloysius College participates in all federal and state programs; fully 94 percent of Mount Aloysius College students receive some form of financial aid. *U.S. News & World Report* has ranked Mount Aloysius College as one of the best-priced private liberal arts colleges in the United States.

Faculty

The Mount Aloysius faculty consists of approximately 175 members, whose primary responsibility is teaching and advising students. Many faculty members hold advanced or terminal degrees and are expected to maintain close instructional ties with students. Many professors hold national, professional certificates in such disciplines as criminology, education, law, and nursing. The Mount Aloysius student-faculty ratio of 13:1 allows close contact between students and faculty members, providing personal attention in a highly structured environment—a key ingredient in the College's academic philosophy.

Student Government

The Student Government Association (SGA) represents students on all issues that concern the College. The SGA appoints student representatives to all student-oriented College committees. The College encourages student participation in the general governance structure and other matters concerning the development and implementation of policies on residential student life.

Admission Requirements

The College enrolls a freshman class of approximately 350 students. The total class of 550 includes transfer students. Admission is selective, based on academic promise, as indicated by a student's secondary school performance and activities, standardized test scores, and special experience and talents. Applicants are required to have or expected to earn a diploma from an approved secondary school or a GED diploma. Submission of official transcripts and SAT or ACT scores is required. In addition to the general admission requirements, specific admission requirements exist for the health programs.

For further information, students should visit the College's website at http://www.mtaloy.edu. Prospective students are encouraged to visit the scenic 193-acre campus. The College is open Monday to Friday from 8:30 a.m. to 5 p.m. and on select Saturdays.

Application and Information

To apply for admission to Mount Aloysius College, candidates are encouraged to submit their application and $30 application fee to the Office of Undergraduate and Graduate Admissions. In addition, students may apply online.

For further information, students should contact:

Office of Undergraduate and Graduate Admissions
Mount Aloysius College
7373 Admiral Peary Highway
Cresson, Pennsylvania 16630
Phone: 814-886-6383
888-823-2220 (toll-free)
Fax: 814-886-6441
E-mail: admissions@mtaloy.edu
Website: http://www.mtaloy.edu

Mount Aloysius College, located on a beautiful 193-acre campus in Cresson, Pennsylvania provides a safe, vibrant learning community. Nestled in the southern Allegheny Mountains, Mount Aloysius is one of 18 US Mercy colleges and universities. Mount Aloysius offers year-round recreational and cultural opportunities. Students enjoy both the security of the campus and the proximity to State College to the east and Pittsburgh to the west. Mount Aloysius College is minutes away from all the amenities of Altoona and Johnstown, Pennsylvania. Interstate highways, the Pennsylvania Turnpike, AMTRAK train service, bus service, and several airports make Mount Aloysius College convenient from anywhere.

MOUNT MARY UNIVERSITY

MILWAUKEE, WISCONSIN

★ To read more about this school, visit http://petersons.to/mountmaryuniversity

Mount Mary UNIVERSITY

The University

Creativity is a part of Mount Mary University's identity—a big part. Students learn new and exciting ways to think, to collaborate, and to personalize their college experience in order to be at the leading edge of their future careers.

Students appreciate the surprises of discovery and focus less on finding a single perfect answer. Because at Mount Mary, creativity is about having an open mind—to different ways of learning, living, and looking at the world and interacting with it. At Mount Mary, students can create their own future.

Mount Mary University, one of fewer than fifty women's colleges in the nation, is home to nearly 1,500 undergraduate and graduate students. Located on a beautiful 80-acre wooded campus, only 15 minutes from downtown Milwaukee, students at Mount Mary are fully engaged both inside and outside of the classroom, learning not just the subject matter but also how to express opinions and develop leadership skills. Through exciting internships, club activities, community service, and campus ministry programs, students explore their interests and discover their skills. Special and professional interests are served by affiliates of national societies.

Caroline Hall, the student residence hall, provides accommodations for private occupancy and single and double suites. Over 90 percent of the rooms feature walk-in closets and over two thirds have private bathrooms. Every floor in Caroline Hall has newly renovated kitchens and lounge areas. All residence hall rooms have wireless computer access and are wired for cable television and telephone service. Mount Mary University sponsors many social activities including performances by comedians, holiday dances, and campus picnics.

Physical fitness and an interest in athletics are fostered through various activities, fitness programs, health and dance courses, and intramural and intercollegiate athletics. Mount Mary's Blue Angels are members of the NCAA Division III. The Blue Angels compete in basketball, cross-country, soccer, softball, tennis, and volleyball. Facilities on campus and in the Bloechl Recreation Center include a gymnasium, outdoor soccer fields and a fitness center. Bordering the campus is the Menomonee River Parkway, ideal for biking, jogging, cross-country skiing, and much more.

Academic and professional student services are available to all Mount Mary students, including free tutoring and assistance with tests through the Academic Resource Center; advising, resume writing, and career planning through the Advising and Career Development Center; and personal counseling through the Counseling Center.

Location

Mount Mary University is located in a residential area in northwestern Milwaukee, just 15 minutes from downtown and less than 5 minutes from one of Milwaukee's premier shopping malls. Students can access public transportation right in front of the campus. Several other private and public universities call Milwaukee home, making it a great environment to meet students from other universities.

Majors and Degrees

At Mount Mary, students can choose from more than thirty undergraduate programs and nine graduate programs. Mount Mary's focus on teaching students to think creatively enhances their leadership ability and creates greater success in the workplace. When students graduate, they have the confidence and open minds to imagine and experiment with innovative ideas that push organizations—and themselves—to the top of their fields.

Mount Mary offers programs in accounting, art, art therapy, behavioral science, biology, business administration, chemistry, communication arts, dietetics, education, English (literature, writing for new media, and education), fashion (design and merchandise management), graphic design, health sciences (preprofessional programs), history, interior design, interior merchandising, international studies, justice, mathematics, marketing, occupational therapy, philosophy, psychology/behavioral science, public relations, radiologic technology, social work, Spanish, student-designed, and theology. Special services are also available for undeclared students to help them find and focus on a major suited to their interests and talents.

In addition to undergraduate programs, Mount Mary also offers eight graduate programs in art therapy, business administration (M.B.A. in general management or health systems leadership), counseling (clinical mental health, clinical rehabilitation, and school), dietetics, education, English, and occupational therapy (master's and online post-professional doctorate). Mount Mary also offers the first Professional Doctorate of Art Therapy degree program in the nation.

Academic Programs

Mount Mary's curriculum integrates leadership skills into each student's educational experience, developing leaders who take individual responsibility for social justice. The curriculum and co-curricular activities promote self-knowledge and competence, an entrepreneurial sense of vision, effective oral and written communication skills, and the ability to strengthen leadership in others. In their professions, churches, and communities, Mount Mary students model collaborative leadership, enabling them to work effectively both in leadership positions and as supportive team members.

Many academic programs at Mount Mary University offer internships, which allow students to relate theory to practice and interact with professionals while learning life skills. The process encourages students to reflect on the skills and knowledge they hope to gain and allows them to tailor their practical experience to the career goals they have set for the future. Many of the programs incorporate a work experience into the curriculum. Work experience includes student teaching, clinicals, fieldwork, practicum, and internships. Several majors also offer study abroad components allowing students to gain hands on experience in their major along with learning about another culture.

Off-Campus Programs

Nearly 20 percent of Mount Mary students study abroad for a summer, a semester, a year, or over a break. Students can travel to places such as Nicaragua, Italy, France Spain, Nova Scotia, Japan, and more. Mount Mary works with students to make sure their international travels add to their program of study in as many ways as possible, without delaying graduation plans.

The Office of International Studies also aids students in finding an accredited program that meets their individual needs.

Costs

For the 2015–16 academic year, undergraduate tuition is $26,230 for full-time students and $795 per credit for part-time students. Accelerated programs are offered at $745 per credit. Additional information about tuition and fees can be found online at mtmary.edu/financialaid. All costs are subject to change.

Financial Aid

At Mount Mary University, 100 percent of full-time, first-year students receive an academic scholarship covering up to the full cost of tuition, room, and board. Mount Mary offers numerous scholarships and financial aid opportunities to help students afford their education including the Caroline Scholars Program, Grace Scholars Program, Legacy Award, student employment, and discipline-specific assistance. All full-time transfer students are also eligible to receive up to $15,000 in academic scholarships per year or reduced tuition.

Prospective students are required to file the FAFSA during the priority deadline between January 1 and March 1 in order to be eligible for all of Mount Mary's financial aid opportunities. Mount Mary's FAFSA code is 003869.

Faculty

Faculty members holding advanced degrees do all the teaching; no classes are taught by teaching assistants. In addition, every student is assigned a faculty advisor with whom they meet prior to registering each semester. With a total enrollment of nearly 1,500, Mount Mary offers a low student-to-faculty ratio of 13:1.

Student Government

Students are encouraged to participate in the governance of the University. Student Government makes recommendations about University policies and other matters of importance to students and serves as a liaison to the Mount Mary administration, faculty, and staff. Student Government also coordinates many on-campus events throughout the year.

Admission Requirements

Being challenged and encouraged at Mount Mary will prepare students for a successful life after college. Mount Mary reviews each applicant individually. At least 20 academic units of study in high school are recommended, including college preparatory math (2); electives (2); English (4); and history, world language, or social science (6). Satisfactory scores on the ACT or SAT are required and the Test of English as a Foreign Language (TOEFL) is required for international students for whom English is a second language. The average full-time undergraduate ACT score is 20.5 and high school GPA is 3.21. Consideration is given for AP and I.B. Courses.

Application and Information

Mount Mary offers rolling admission. It is recommended that students apply in the fall semester of their senior year in order to take advantage of as many scholarship opportunities as possible. Interested students should submit an online admission application, official high school transcripts, and ACT or SAT scores. Students can expect an application decision within two weeks of a completed submission.

Undergraduate, international, transfer, accelerated, postbaccalaureate, and graduate student applications and requirements can be found on the Mount Mary University website at mtmary.edu/apply.

Mount Mary does not discriminate against any individual for reasons of race, color, religion, age, national or ethnic origin, or disability. Mount Mary University is a women's university, which accepts men into postbaccalaureate certificate programs and graduate programs.

For further information, students should contact:

Admission Office
Mount Mary University
2900 North Menomonee River Parkway
Milwaukee, Wisconsin 53222-4597
United States
Phone: 414-256-1219
800-321-6265 (toll-free)
Fax: 414-256-0180
E-mail: mmu-admiss@mtmary.edu
Website: http://www.mtmary.edu
http://www.facebook.com/mountmary
http://twitter.com/MountMary

Mount Mary University is located on 80 acres in a residential Milwaukee neighborhood bordering Wauwatosa. Students have a safe, secure environment in which to live, learn, and create.

COLLEGE CLOSE-UPS

MUHLENBERG COLLEGE

ALLENTOWN, PENNSYLVANIA

★ To read more about this school, visit http://petersons.to/muhlenbergcollege

The College

Founded in 1848, Muhlenberg College aims to develop independent critical thinkers who are intellectually agile, characterized by a zeal for reasoned and civil debate, knowledgeable about the achievements and traditions of diverse civilizations and cultures, able to express ideas with clarity and grace, committed to lifelong learning, equipped with ethical values, and prepared for lives of leadership and service.

Muhlenberg students achieve the College's goals by assuming strong individual responsibility for intense involvement in vigorous academic work and for personal involvement within the College community. The more than 100 student organizations provide outlets for the diversified cultural, athletic, religious, social, leadership, and service interests of the students. The campus is primarily residential; more than 90 percent of the 2,200 students live on campus. A close sense of community develops naturally, one in which their diversified academic and personal interests enable students to contribute positively to the intellectual and personal growth of their peers.

Students are aided by an active Career Center in relating academic and personal knowledge and skills to appropriate career goals and in obtaining positions upon graduation. About one third of a typical graduating class proceeds immediately to graduate or professional school.

Location

Muhlenberg College is located on a campus of 82 acres in suburban west Allentown, an area made up primarily of attractive family homes and parks. The downtown area of Allentown, a city of approximately 105,000 people, is a 10-minute ride from the campus. The College is located 90 miles west of New York City and 60 miles north of Philadelphia.

Majors and Degrees

Muhlenberg offers the Bachelor of Arts (A.B.) degree in the following fields: accounting, American studies, anthropology, art, business, dance, economics, English, film studies, finance, French, history, history/government, international studies, Jewish studies, media and communication, music, philosophy, philosophy/political thought, political economy, political science, psychology, religious studies, Russian studies, social science, sociology, Spanish, and theater arts. The Bachelor of Science (B.S.) degree is offered in the following fields: biochemistry, biology, chemistry, computer science, environmental science, mathematics, natural sciences, neuroscience, physics, and public health. Students may also design their own major. Minors are offered in most of the major fields, as well as in Africana studies, creative writing, German studies, Latin American and Caribbean studies, women's studies, public health, sustainability studies, and Asian traditions.

In addition, students may receive certification to teach at the elementary and secondary levels. Other opportunities include a 4-4 dual-admission program with Drexel University College of Medicine; a 3-4 dental program with the University of Pennsylvania; a 3-3 B.S./Ph.D. program in physical therapy with Thomas Jefferson University; a 3-2 B.S./M.S. program in occupational therapy with Thomas Jefferson University; a 3-2/4-2 combined program in engineering, offered in cooperation with Columbia University; a 3-2 combined program in forestry, offered in cooperation with Duke University; and a 4-4 dual-admission program with SUNY College of Optometry.

Academic Programs

The A.B. and B.S. programs emphasize breadth of study in the liberal arts as well as in-depth study of a particular academic major. All students must fulfill requirements in the arts, foreign culture, the humanities, social sciences, and natural sciences. Strong achievement on Advanced Placement examinations may enable a student to receive advanced placement, possibly with credit. Scores of 4 or 5 earn automatic credit. Scores of 3 are evaluated by the appropriate department.

Students work closely with academic advisers to formulate programs well suited to their individual interests, abilities, needs, and goals. Generally, students are expected to declare their major at the end of the freshman year; however, many students later change their academic major with no difficulty. A double major is possible, and about a third of Muhlenberg students graduate with a double major. The College also enriches the freshman-year experience through more than thirty special-focus First-Year Seminars. Seniors have the opportunity to synthesize and integrate their academic experience through a Culminating Undergraduate Experience (CUE).

Off-Campus Programs

Study abroad is available through Muhlenberg's Semester-in-London Program, Netherlands semester, Dublin semester, or more than 160 affiliate agreements with international universities all over the world. In addition, the Lehigh Valley Association of Independent Colleges sponsors summer study-abroad options in England, France, Germany, Israel, and Spain. Credit for study-abroad programs sponsored by other institutions or by private agencies may also be transferred to Muhlenberg by special arrangement.

Students may participate in a variety of internships in local businesses, health-care facilities, schools, public agencies, theaters, broadcasting stations, and magazines. Government internships in Harrisburg, Pennsylvania, and Washington, D.C., and an Ethics and Public Affairs semester in Washington, D.C., as well as a New York City semester at Jewish Theological Seminary are also available.

Students may enroll in courses offered at any of the five other member institutions of the Lehigh Valley Association of Independent Colleges: Lafayette College, Lehigh University, Cedar Crest College, DeSales University, and Moravian College.

Academic Facilities

Muhlenberg's library collection contains more than 200,000 volumes as well as numerous government documents, periodicals, and electronic and online resources. The $12-million Harry C. Trexler Library, a state-of-the-art library facility, opened in 1988. Students may also use library materials owned by the other institutions participating in the Lehigh Valley Association of Independent Colleges.

The Baker Center for the Arts was designed for Muhlenberg by the well-known architect Philip Johnson. It houses a modern theater complex, a recital hall, classrooms, art studios, and a fine arts gallery. The Trexler Pavilion for Theater and Dance opened in 2000 and provides dance performance and studio space, a new theater, a Black Box, and additional arts spaces. The College augmented its arts facilities with the Rehearsal House in 2011.

Life science facilities include numerous laboratories, classrooms, two electron microscopes, a DNA sequencer, an isolation room used for growing and studying viruses, and a museum of natural history. Facilities supporting students in the physical sciences include equipment for optics, electronics, and atomic, nuclear, and solid-state physics. A new 40,000-square-foot addition to the science facilities opened in fall 2006. The College uses a UNIX/Windows computer system with Novell software, and supports both Microsoft and Apple applications throughout campus.

Costs

The comprehensive tuition and fees for the 2014–15 academic year was $44,145. The room and board fee averaged $10,335. The total cost for a resident student was approximately $54,480.

Financial Aid

Muhlenberg College endeavors to make its educational opportunities available to all qualified students regardless of their financial circumstances. While most financial aid at Muhlenberg is based on financial need as demonstrated by the College Scholarship Service Financial Aid PROFILE and FAFSA, there is also significant merit aid available. Typically, about 80 percent of Muhlenberg's students qualify for and receive financial aid.

Faculty

The Muhlenberg faculty consists of 171 full-time and 121 part-time members. Ninety percent of full-time faculty members hold doctoral or terminal degrees. While many faculty members are distinguished for their scholarly research, teaching is the main emphasis of their work. Professors at all levels work closely with students both inside and outside of the classroom. Many department heads teach introductory courses, and no courses are taught by graduate students or teaching assistants.

Student Government

Muhlenberg students are expected to demonstrate a high level of responsibility with regard to their own governance and to participate extensively in internal decision-making and communication processes throughout the campus. These responsibilities are coordinated by the United Student Government, which transacts all business pertaining to the student body. This organization is in charge of a student activities budget of more than $350,000. In addition, 2 students serve as representatives to the Board of Trustees, and students hold full voting privileges on many faculty committees.

Admission Requirements

The College selects students who give evidence of ability and scholastic achievement, seriousness of purpose, and the capacity to make constructive contributions to the College community. Approximately 70 percent of a typical freshman class ranked in the top fifth of their secondary school class. SAT scores for entering freshmen average approximately 610 verbal, 615 math, and 615 writing.

Submission of SAT or ACT scores is optional. An on-campus interview is strongly recommended for all applicants and required for students who choose not to submit standardized test scores.

Application and Information

Students who wish to be considered for admission should submit a completed application form as early as possible during their senior year of secondary school and no later than February 15. Regular decision candidates receive notice of admission decisions in late March. Early decision plans are available, and the College fills approximately half of its freshman class via early decision. Transfer admission is also possible.

For further information, interested students should contact:

Christopher Hooker-Haring
Dean of Admission and Financial Aid
Muhlenberg College
Allentown, Pennsylvania 18104-5586
Phone: 484-664-3200
E-mail: admissions@muhlenberg.edu
Website: http://www.muhlenberg.edu

The Bell Tower of the Haas College Center stands as the focal point of the Muhlenberg College campus.

NEUMANN UNIVERSITY

ASTON, PENNSYLVANIA

★ To read more about this school, visit http://petersons.to/neumannuniversity

The University

Neumann University (http://www.neumann.edu), a Catholic coeducational institution in the Franciscan tradition, recognizes the value of developing intellectual excellence, professional competence, and strong community life. As a university that balances the liberal arts with the professions, Neumann was founded to meet and expand the educational and professional horizons of men and women through instruction that is based on values, ethical behavior, and service to others. With its Living and Learning Center (multimedia-capable residences), Neumann University is able to serve a diverse geographic and demographic population.

Founded and sponsored by the Sisters of St. Francis of Philadelphia, the University is committed to a varied student body and welcomes students of all denominations. Current enrollment is 3,047.

The Life Center houses the Meagher Theatre, the Bruder Athletic Center, and the Crossroads Cafe dining facility. Intercollegiate sports include women's basketball, cross-country, field hockey, golf, ice hockey, indoor track, lacrosse, soccer, softball, tennis, track, and volleyball; and men's baseball, basketball, cross-country, golf, ice hockey, indoor track, lacrosse, soccer, tennis, and track. Neumann University competes as a member of the National Collegiate Athletic Association (NCAA) Division III, the Colonial States Athletic Conference, and the Eastern Collegiate Athletic Conference (ECAC). Intramural sports are available to all members of the campus community.

The Living and Learning Center is designed to provide a state-of-the-art residential experience, with a focus on education within a real-world living environment. Technologically smart, the center connects students to both faculty members and friends via wireless Internet, which is available in every suite and apartment. The system provides full access to campus resources and activities, as well as activities and resources worldwide. The center also houses a separate computer lab, a fitness center, a reflection room, various study rooms with warming kitchens for group study or meetings, and a laundry.

The University provides a full range of services to students, including career placement, career and personal counseling, a tutoring program, and health services.

Neumann students are involved in a wide variety of campus and community activities. Major and special interest clubs are available for student participation. Clubs bring together students who share common interests and help foster new friendships.

At Neumann, the spiritual dimension of one's life is recognized as integral to total human development. The Ministry Team provides a pastoral presence on campus and promotes a sense of community. The entire University community is invited to serve the needs of the poor and neglected in society through various outreach programs, with special attention to the need for peace and justice in the world today.

Neumann is well positioned to respond to the academic and extracurricular needs of students who are of traditional or nontraditional age, commuters or residents, and full-time or part-time.

In addition to undergraduate programs, Neumann confers master's degrees in accounting, education, nursing, organizational and strategic leadership, pastoral counseling, and sport and entertainment management as well as doctoral degrees in education (Ed.D.), pastoral counseling (Ph.D.), and physical therapy (D.P.T.).

Location

Neumann, with a beautiful 68-acre suburban campus in Aston, Delaware County, Pennsylvania, is a short distance from Philadelphia; Wilmington, Delaware; southern New Jersey; and Maryland. It is easily accessible from major arteries such as I-95, Route 476, Route 1, and the Pennsylvania Turnpike.

Majors and Degrees

Neumann offers strong academic majors leading to a Bachelor of Arts degree or a Bachelor of Science degree in accounting, arts production and performance, athletic training, biology, business administration, communication and digital media, computer and information management, criminal justice, education, English, international business, liberal arts, marketing, nursing, political science, psychology, social work, and sport and entertainment management. The education programs lead to teacher certification in early elementary (PK–4), special education (PK–8) or secondary education. Pre-professional programs in law and medicine are also available. An accelerated evening program for adults leads to an Associate of Arts, Bachelor of Arts, or Bachelor of Science degree in liberal studies or professional studies.

Academic Programs

The academic program at Neumann University is composed of a core curriculum (required of all students), a major area of study (chosen by each student), and a wide range of elective offerings. Students may also choose a minor area of study. The University's broad base of liberal arts offerings prepares students for the intellectual and social challenges they will face in the employment marketplace and throughout their lives. The core is intended to provide basic knowledge of the liberal arts and sciences; develop verbal, written, and symbolic communication skills; and stimulate interest in a broad range of topics for the purpose of enhancing the individual's contributions to society, thereby enabling the individual to realize full human potential.

Classroom instruction is supplemented by cooperative education and internships, through which students can earn credit and gain experience by working in a job related to their career interest. Fieldwork and student teaching are required of all education majors. Clinical practice for the nursing major occurs in a variety of health-care facilities in the tri-state area.

The honors program is an opportunity for academically talented students to explore imaginative and innovative perspectives on learning. It is also an opportunity to stimulate and motivate students to expand their knowledge and interest and to strive for greater excellence. Moreover, it is a reward for prior perseverance and dedication as well as an obligation to use skills and abilities in service to others. Admission to the honors program is by invitation.

Neumann University has transfer articulation agreements with numerous schools throughout the area.

Academic Facilities

The Child Development Center is a state-of-the-art, octagonal-shaped building, specifically designed to house an educational program for preschoolers. As a state-licensed day-care facility, it enrolls children of Neumann students, the faculty, and the community. The Child Development Center is part of the Division of Education and Human Services. Students enrolled in education courses use the center for observation, practical experience, and student teaching.

The Academic Computing Center is located on the ground floor of the University. The computers are viewed as tools to support all fields of study and all students and faculty members. Neumann University provides wireless access across campus. Computers are available to all students, as is software related to various academic disciplines.

The University library contains a balanced collection of more than 55,000 physical volumes and films, 20,000 e-books, and nearly

100,000 electronic journals. E-books and journals can be accessed from anywhere with an Internet connection. Collaboration with faculty and membership in local consortia (TCLC, SEPCHE) ensures access to the most relevant resources for academic success. Professional librarians provide in-person research support seven days a week and also create online Research Guides and video tutorials for around-the-clock assistance. Librarians also provide cutting-edge instruction to help develop essential 21st-century skills like critical thinking, technological literacy, and information management. Quiet study rooms, collaborative group spaces, and an open computer lab and Wi-Fi collectively support student study needs.

Costs

Tuition for full-time students (12 to 19 credits per semester) in 2014–15 was $24,800. Room and board were $11,800 (full meal plan).

Financial Aid

Typically, about 95 percent of Neumann undergraduate students receive some form of financial aid (scholarships, grants, and student loans).

Neumann offers a variety of renewable scholarships each year to entering full-time freshmen and transfer students. Interested applicants should contact the Office of Admissions and Financial Aid as soon as possible to determine eligibility.

In addition to Neumann scholarships, funds are available through the Federal Pell Grant, Federal Supplemental Educational Opportunity Grant, and Federal Work-Study Programs. Many states provide grant money to attend Neumann (non-Pennsylvania residents should check with their state's higher education agency for details). Veterans Administration benefits can be received by qualified veterans or their dependents. Federal Stafford Student Loans and Federal PLUS Program loans are available and can be applied for through Neumann's preferred lender or any participating bank. Neumann also offers institutional need-based grants. All students requesting financial aid must complete the Free Application for Federal Student Aid (FAFSA) each year to determine eligibility. In order to expedite processing, the FAFSA should be submitted by March 15 for the following school year. Financial aid funds are renewable annually based on need, as determined by the FAFSA results.

Faculty

Neumann students describe faculty members as sincere, hard-working, determined, and energetic. Faculty members view themselves, first, as teachers and are proud partners in their students' journeys toward professional careers. Each student has a faculty adviser, who assists in arranging a program designed to meet the student's educational goals. Many faculty members serve as moderators of student clubs. The student-faculty ratio is 14:1.

Student Government

The Student Government Association (SGA) is the representative body for all students. Its function is to implement the aims and purposes of the University, foster cooperation in student relationships, assist the University in being responsive to the needs of the student body, and encourage personal responsibility for an intelligent system of student self-government. Through the Student Activities Board, social functions are planned throughout the year. Students serve on various University committees, including the Student Affairs Committee of the Board, Academic Advising Committee, Honors Program Committee, Registration/Orientation Task Force, and Student Judicial Board. For full-time students, a Student Government Association fee of $85 per semester is required.

Admission Requirements

Neumann has a rolling admission policy and accepts applications throughout the year. Applicants are considered on the basis of high school record, SAT or ACT scores, recommendations, class rank, and other indicators of potential to succeed in university-level studies. Applications for admission are reviewed without regard to sex, race, creed, color, national origin, age, sexual orientation, pregnancy, military status, religion, or disability. Applicants should be graduates of an accredited high school (or present equivalent credentials) and have a recommended curriculum of 16 units of high school course work, distributed as follows: 4 in English, 2 to 3 in science, 2 in mathematics, 2 in social studies, 2 in foreign language, and 4 in electives. Students intending to pursue a major in biology or clinical laboratory science must have at least 1 year of high school biology and chemistry, and high school physics is highly recommended.

Neumann participates in the Advanced Placement (AP) Program and the College-Level Examination Program (CLEP).

An interview and tour of the campus are highly recommended for all prospective students and parents. Visits can be arranged by contacting the Office of Admissions.

Application and Information

Applicants for freshman admission are requested to have SAT or ACT scores and high school transcripts sent to the Office of Admissions. A nonrefundable $35 application fee should accompany the completed application. A free application is available online at http://www.neumann.edu.

Neumann University welcomes applications from students who have attended or are currently attending either two-year or four-year regionally accredited institutions of higher learning.

For further information, students should contact:

Office of Admissions
Neumann University
One Neumann Drive
Aston, Pennsylvania 19014-1298
United States
Phone: 610-558-5616
800-9NEUMANN (toll-free)
E-mail: neumann@neumann.edu
Website: http://www.neumann.edu

Students love the newest building on campus, the Mirenda Center for Sport, Spirituality, and Character Development.

NEW COLLEGE OF FLORIDA

SARASOTA, FLORIDA

The College

New College of Florida offers serious students the opportunity to pursue rigorous academic study in an environment designed to promote depth in thinking, free exchange of ideas, and highly individualized interaction with faculty members.

Study is focused in the arts and sciences and is highly accelerated and independent. A recent study of the College's graduates found that 80 percent pursue graduate or professional study, gaining admission to Harvard, Yale, MIT, Brown, Georgetown, Berkeley, and other leading graduate programs. New College is competitive with other top schools in the nation when it comes to the percentage of graduates who go on to earn the Ph.D., especially in the sciences.

New College is also known as one of the nation's top producers of Fulbright scholarship recipients, with 30 in the last five years alone, giving the College a better per-capita performance than almost all U.S. colleges and universities.

New College was founded as a private institution in 1960 with a devotion to the values implicit in a liberal arts and sciences education, and a dedication to creating an innovative academic program where talented students and outstanding faculty members could come together and pursue learning through small classes, seminars, and independent study to pursue advanced undergraduate research.

The College entered Florida's public university system in 1975 which served to strengthen and perpetuate the idealistic vision and academic mission of the College's founders. In 2001, New College was designated as the official Honors College in the liberal arts and sciences for the State University System of Florida. A public-private funding arrangement provides students at New College with a private honors college experience at a public college cost. As a result, the College is regularly featured in guidebooks as being among the nation's leading educational values and as one of the country's top small, public colleges.

New College's student population is 837, of whom approximately 57 percent are women. Approximately 20 percent of students are out-of-state or overseas residents. Through active recruitment of out-of-state students, the College is increasing its percentage of non-Florida residents.

The College's 110-acre bay front location on the Gulf of Mexico includes basketball, racquetball, tennis, and volleyball courts; a multipurpose soccer and athletic field; a running trail; a 25-meter swimming pool; and a comprehensive fitness center. The New College sailing team is part of the Inter-Collegiate Sailing Association of North America (ICSA), South Atlantic Interscholastic Sailing Association (SAISA) division. Students also compete in recreational and intramural sports including soccer, tennis, fencing, flag football, softball, and swimming. Sailboats, kayaks, and canoes are also available for use by students and faculty members free of charge.

Location

Situated along the coastline of the Gulf of Mexico in southwest Florida, New College serves as the northern gateway to Sarasota, a bustling city 50 miles south of Tampa. Sarasota is noted for its recreational, cultural, and artistic attractions, including beautiful white-sand beaches and an abundance of professional theater, art, and music venues. Notably, New College sits adjacent to the world-famous John and Mable Ringling Museum of Art, which offers students free entry to view its Baroque and Renaissance art collections.

The climate is semitropical, consisting of long, warm springs and autumns, with mild winters. Transportation from throughout the nation and within the city is readily accessible. Many major airlines serve Sarasota-Bradenton International Airport, which is adjacent to the College. Within the city, buses link the campus to downtown, shopping malls, parks, and beaches. While mass transit is available, bicycling is the favored means of transportation among students. The College's Office of Student Affairs offers group outings on a regular basis to the downtown Sarasota Farmers Market, grocery stores, and other venues around town.

Majors and Degrees

New College awards the Bachelor of Arts degree in liberal arts and sciences. Each of the College's nearly forty different areas of concentration (majors) is an individualized program of study that students design in consultation with, and with the approval of, faculty members. These include anthropology; applied mathematics; art; art history; biochemistry; biology; biopsychology; chemistry; Chinese language and culture; classics; computer science; economics; English; environmental studies; European studies; French; gender studies; German studies/German language and literature; history; humanities; international and area studies; literature; marine biology; mathematics; medieval and Renaissance studies; music; natural sciences; neurobiology; philosophy; physics; political science; psychology; public policy; religion; Russian language and literature; social sciences; sociology; Spanish language, literature, and culture; and urban studies. Partial areas of concentration include theater. Students may also pursue special program areas of concentration with faculty approval. Pre-medical, pre-law, pre-M.B.A., pre-veterinary, and other advanced-degree program advising and guidelines are provided by faculty members and by the Center for Engagement and Opportunity.

Academic Programs

New College of Florida's academic program aims to encourage academic excellence, creativity, and personal initiative and to provide essential tools for lifelong intellectual, personal, and professional growth. The College's distinctive curriculum enables students, in close consultation with faculty members, to develop programs of seminars, tutorials, independent research, internships, and off-campus experiences that meet each student's personal academic interests and goals.

At the end of each semester, rather than grades, students receive detailed narrative evaluations as well as satisfactory/unsatisfactory assessments of their work from individual faculty members. Graduation requirements include satisfactory completion of seven academic contracts (a set of academic courses and other goals for the semester, planned by the student and faculty adviser), three independent-study projects, a senior thesis or project, and an oral baccalaureate examination. In addition to the requirements for individual majors, students must complete eight courses within the liberal arts curriculum, with at least one course each in the humanities, social sciences, natural sciences, and diverse perspectives. Students must also meet basic proficiency in mathematics and English language and advanced proficiency in written and oral English language.

The College operates on a 4-1-4 calendar year. The College offers a January interterm when students undertake independent study projects in forms such as library, laboratory, or field research; internships; and performing arts projects, all of which they design and complete under faculty sponsorship.

Off-Campus Programs

Internships, fieldwork, and independent research away from the campus offer New College students the opportunity to gain new skills and evaluate career interests. New College believes that off-campus study can make a major contribution to an undergraduate education and facilitates such study through its flexible, individualized curriculum and special support services. New College is a member of the National Student Exchange, which provides access to nearly 200 universities with programs in the U.S. and abroad (many with comparable tuition costs) and the Consortium for Innovative Environments in Learning. Students may also participate in programs offered by independent providers, such as the School for International Training and AustraLearn, as well as international programs available through the State University System of Florida and Center for Cross Cultural Studies. With faculty approval, students may pursue off-campus independent study or participate in programs including Living Routes, which offers nontraditional venues for study abroad.

Academic Facilities

New College's wireless-equipped Jane Bancroft Cook Library is befitting of one of the country's leading colleges for the liberal arts and sciences and has an open stack arrangement that allows free access to most materials. Administration, trustees, faculty members, and the New College Library Association have implemented an ambitious acquisition program to expand the current holdings of approximately 274,000 volumes. An expansion of the library's visual image collection is also in the works. In total, the library subscribes to more than 900 serial titles, including 700 magazines and journals and many state, national, and international newspapers. In addition, through computer networks and other cooperative programs, New College students and faculty members have access to hundreds of online databases and electronic journals and newspapers, as well as numerous online document delivery services. Through a comprehensive online interlibrary loan system, New College students have convenient access to holdings throughout the State University System of Florida.

The Harry Sudakoff Conference Center on campus hosts visiting lecturers, meetings of campus and community organizations, and a wide range of special events. The Caples Fine Arts Complex includes the 264-seat Mildred Sainer Music and Arts Pavilion, which features student, local, and national performances; the Lota Mundy Music Building, which houses eight music practice rooms, plus the Benjamin and Barbara Slavin Electronic Music Studio; the Christianne Felsmann Fine Arts Building; the Betty Isermann Fine Arts Gallery and Studio; and a sculpture studio.

Science facilities include the R. V. Heiser Natural Sciences Complex, which houses laboratories, classrooms, offices, a state-of-the-art optical spectroscopy and nanomaterials laboratory, a research greenhouse, herbarium, a computer lab, two electron microscopes, and an auditorium, as well as the Rhoda and Jack Pritzker Marine Biology Research Center. The marine center, one of the leading marine research centers in southwest Florida, features culture rooms, laboratories, and aquariums with water drawn from Sarasota Bay. Saltwater effluent from the tanks is cleaned by means of a wetland constructed in 2001 as part of a New College senior thesis project.

The College's 35,000-square-foot Academic Center, which opened in 2011, was awarded LEED Gold certification by the U.S. Green Building Council. It includes a state-of-the-art computer lab, classrooms, faculty offices, and a student lounge. Outside the center is Koski Plaza with the Four Winds sculpture, Koski Bell Tower, built-in benches, and green space.

Costs

For the 2014–15 academic year, in-state tuition and fees at New College of Florida were $6,916 and out-of-state tuition and fees were $29,944. Room and board costs were $8,687.

Financial Aid

The actual cost of providing New College of Florida's highly individualized honors college experience is far greater than the state funding appropriated for support of the College. The New College Foundation secures independent funding to provide for the remaining costs. Part of the foundation's endowment produces income for scholarships.

Approximately 96 percent of New College students receive some form of financial assistance, including academic scholarships and need-based financial aid. To apply for financial aid, students should file the Free Application for Federal Student Aid (FAFSA). February 15 is the priority date for need-based financial aid. All freshmen who complete applications by April 15 and who are admitted to New College are guaranteed academic scholarship funding. April 15 is also the priority date for scholarship funding for transfer and international students. No additional scholarship application is necessary.

Faculty

Of New College's regular, full-time faculty members, 97 percent hold the highest degree awarded in their field of study, which in most cases is the doctorate. They have come to New College from the finest universities nationally and abroad, drawn to an environment that emphasizes excellence in teaching and fosters a close-knit community of scholars. Faculty members sponsor individual students in the formulation of their academic programs, gradually moving toward a form of mentorship through which joint research is sometimes pursued. A 10:1 student-faculty ratio is a key factor in the College's individualized approach to education. At New College, all classes are taught by faculty, not by teaching assistants.

Student Government

Student input is a decisive factor in campus governance. Elected student representatives serve on the Board of Trustees and most major policymaking committees, and are voting participants in divisional and campuswide faculty meetings. The New College Student Alliance, the College's student government, has authority over funding for recreational events, social events, student clubs and organizations on campus, and allocation of the Green Fee for environmentally friendly projects.

Admission Requirements

New College of Florida seeks highly capable students eager to take responsibility for their own education. The admissions staff reviews each candidate individually, assessing his or her potential for success within, and contribution to, the College's unique environment. Course selection, academic record, and writing ability are focal points of the committee's review. Over two-thirds of the first-year students entering in fall 2014 ranked in the top 20 percent of their high school class. The middle 50 percent of SAT takers had a combined score of 1200–1350 on the critical reading and math sections. The middle 50 percent of ACT takers had a composite score of 26–30.

All prospective students may apply for entrance to either the fall or the spring term. However, the College reserves the right to modify or cancel the spring admission cycle if its enrollment goals have been met. Candidates must submit an admission application, fee or fee waiver, official transcript(s), SAT or ACT scores, and a letter of recommendation. A campus visit and demonstrated interest are also recommended for all those with serious interest in applying.

Application and Information

Admissions application materials and descriptive literature are available through the New College Office of Admissions and Financial Aid. The deadline for priority admission is November 1. All students who meet this deadline will receive a decision by April 1, however some students will receive their decisions sooner. Applications will continue to be accepted on a rolling basis November 2 through April 15. Those students who apply during that time will receive their decisions on a rolling basis. A completed application and all supporting documents must be submitted to the Office of Admissions and Financial Aid before a candidate is considered for admission.

Inquiries and application requests should be directed to:

Kathleen M. Killion
Dean of Enrollment Services
New College of Florida
5800 Bay Shore Road
Sarasota, Florida 34243-2109
United States
Phone: 941-487-5000
Fax: 941-487-5001
E-mail: admissions@ncf.edu
Website: http://www.ncf.edu
http://www.facebook.com/newcollegeofflorida
http://twitter.com/NewCollegeofFL
http://www.youtube.com/user/NewCollegeofFL

New College of Florida's historic waterfront campus features spectacular sunsets, wetlands, an intertidal lagoon, and boat access.

THE NEW SCHOOL

NEW YORK, NEW YORK

★ To read more about this school, visit http://petersons.to/thenewschool

The University

An essential part of New York City's intellectual and creative life since 1919, The New School is a leading university that offers some of the country's most respected degree and nondegree programs in art and design, liberal arts and social sciences, management and policy, media studies, and the performing arts. Academics reflect The New School's growing prominence as a design-led university where students develop the critical-thinking and visual communication skills that make them competitive in the evolving workplace. Learning at The New School connects students with New York City's history, culture, energy, and—most importantly—opportunity.

Founded by progressive educators, The New School has long fostered free expression and embraced civic engagement and dissent in pursuit of a socially, economically, and environmentally just future. New School students continue to produce intellectually and creatively rich work, collaborating across disciplines to address many of the world's most pressing problems.

The New School is composed of five distinctive colleges offering arts and the humanities undergraduate programs: Parsons The New School for Design, Eugene Lang College The New School for Liberal Arts, Mannes College The New School for Music, The New School for Jazz and Contemporary Music, and The New School for Drama. In addition, The New School for Public Engagement offers undergraduate programs, on campus and online, that are tailored to the needs of adults and transfer students. New School programs expose students to an exciting and challenging course of study led by a faculty of artists, scholars, and professionals who practice what they teach. And new minors give students options to develop special skills and interests.

Location

New York City offers a range of cultural, artistic, intellectual, and commercial resources that make it one of the world's great urban centers. Most New School students attend classes downtown in Greenwich Village, where the surrounding community and streetscape become a kind of classroom.

At Parsons Paris, the university's European campus, students can take courses and pursue bachelor's and master's degrees taught in English. Located near the Louvre, the Palais Garnier, Gaîté Lyrique media arts center, and Notre Dame Cathedral, Parsons Paris offers students options to help them prepare for work in global contexts.

Majors and Degrees

Eugene Lang College The New School for Liberal Arts offers the B.A. in Anthropology, B.A. in the Arts (concentrations in arts in context, dance, and visual arts), B.A. in Contemporary Music, B.A. in Culture and Media, B.A. in Economics, B.A. in Education Studies, B.A./B.S. in Environmental Studies, B.A. in Global Studies, B.A. in History, B.A. in Global Studies, B.A. in Interdisciplinary Science (tracks in biology of health and science of the environment), B.A. in Journalism + Design, B.A./B.S. in Liberal Arts (self-designed program or optional guided areas of study in ethnicity and race, gender studies, Jewish studies, religious studies, and foreign languages), B.A. in Literary Studies (concentrations in literature and writing), B.A. in Philosophy, B.A. in Politics, B.A. in Psychology, B.A. in Sociology, B.A. in Theater, B.A. in Urban Studies, and a B.A.-B.F.A. Dual Degree with Parsons The New School for Design or The New School for Jazz and Contemporary Music.

Parsons The New School for Design in New York City offers the B.A. in Architectural Design, B.F.A. in Communication Design, B.F.A. in Design and Technology, B.F.A. in Fashion Design, B.F.A. in Fine Arts, B.F.A. in Illustration, B.F.A. in Integrated Design, B.F.A. in Interior Design, B.F.A. in Photography, B.F.A. in Product Design, B.B.A. in Strategic Design and Management, B.S. in Urban Design, and a B.A.-B.F.A. Dual Degree with Eugene Lang College. Parsons Paris offers the B.A. in Art and Design History and Theory; B.F.A. in Art, Media, and Technology; B.F.A. in Fashion Design; and B.B.A. in Strategic Design and Management.

Mannes College The New School for Music offers the B.M. (Bachelor of Music), B.S. (Bachelor of Science), and undergraduate diploma. Areas of study at Mannes are orchestral instruments, piano, harpsichord, orchestral conducting, choral conducting, voice, classical guitar, composition, and theory.

The New School for Jazz and Contemporary Music offers the B.F.A and a B.A.-B.F.A. Dual Degree with Eugene Lang College.

The New School for Drama offers the B.F.A. in Dramatic Arts.

Academic Programs

Parsons The New School for Design has been a forerunner in the field of art and design education since its founding in 1896; today, it is one of the nation's largest and most prestigious degree-granting colleges. Its intensive programs and distinguished faculty embrace innovation, pioneer new uses of technology, and instill in students a global perspective on design. Parsons' curricula combine a foundation in art and design with the critical reflection abilities one develops through liberal arts study, leading students to understand the social and economic implications of their work.

Eugene Lang College The New School for Liberal Arts brings together the advantages of a small, liberal arts college and the resources of a major university. Lang attracts smart, creative, and independent students who value the opportunity to tailor their own study path and be challenged in intimate seminar-style classes. Socially engaged leaders, scholars, and newsmakers teach these talented young people using interdisciplinary learning methods.

Lang enables students to accelerate their progress toward a master's degree by combining their undergraduate work with graduate study at one of The New School's graduate programs. Dual bachelor's-master's degrees offered at Lang include anthropology, economics, environmental policy and sustainability management, historical studies, international affairs, liberal studies, media studies, nonprofit management, organizational change management, philosophy, politics, psychology, sociology, teaching English to speakers of other languages, and urban policy analysis and management.

Mannes College The New School for Music is a preeminent conservatory of classical music for undergraduate and graduate students who want to master an area of focus while reimagining the field for the twenty-first century. The Mannes community is made up of collegial musicians who encourage collaboration and professional development under the guidance of world-class faculty. Mannes seeks to develop citizen-artists who engage with the world through music and in traditional and emerging forms of practice, developing opportunities and new audiences.

The New School for Jazz and Contemporary Music was founded on the principle that working artists should play a critical role in jazz education. For mentors, Jazz students have 75 of the city's leading musicians, and as peers, they have some of the world's most promising young performers. Scores of student ensembles and hundreds of public performances every year help jazz students develop their creative potential in a world center of jazz music.

The New School for Jazz and Contemporary Music also offers students the opportunity to combine their B.F.A. studies with a certificate program in creative arts therapies.

The New School for Drama offers students four-year B.F.A. program in dramatic arts, preparing them to be twenty-first–century artists and creative thinkers. Professionalism and community are at the core of the program, which provides a rich multidisciplinary, project-based investigation of theater arts that focuses on the development of critical thinking and collaborative skills.

The B.A.-B.F.A. program at The New School is a five-year, dual-degree program through which students can earn a Bachelor of Arts degree from Eugene Lang College The New School for Liberal Arts and a Bachelor of Fine Arts degree from either Parsons The New

School for Design or The New School for Jazz and Contemporary Music.

Off-Campus Programs

Situated in a world center of scholarship, commerce, and creativity, The New School gives students exciting opportunities to learn hands-on with partners throughout the city. With access to a wide array of internships, apprenticeships with industry leaders, and performance opportunities in venues from downtown clubs to Carnegie Hall, students can shape their education according to their interests and goals, taking advantage of all the university and the city have to offer.

New School students have landed internships at prestigious city agencies, organizations, and companies including the ACLU, Apple, Beth Israel Hospital, *The Colbert Report*, Condé Nast, DKNY, GLAAD, Guggenheim, HBO, Marvel, MTV, NFL, the NYC Department of Parks and Recreation, Open Society Institute, Random House, Sesame Workshop, Sony Entertainment, the *Village Voice*, and WNYC.

The New School also gives students exciting learning opportunities that prepare them for success in global contexts. Numerous undergraduate and study-abroad offerings provide students a competitive advantage.

Academic Facilities

New School students have access to the university's libraries—devoted to social sciences, art and design, and European and American classical music—and the Research Library Consortium of South Manhattan, one of the largest university library consortiums in the United States. State-of-the-art computing and media tools, including an advanced production facility with portable production equipment along with making facilities—CNC routers, 3-D printers, laser cutters, and traditional shop equipment—are available for student use. The university also provides studios and practice rooms for students of art and design, music, and dance. The New School's new sixteen-story University Center, which houses classrooms, a library–research center, an auditorium, a cafeteria and event café, and a 600-bed student residence, was described as "a celebration of the cosmopolitan city" by the *New York Times*.

Costs

Tuition varies by division and by program. Tuition for students entering full-time undergraduate programs in after fall 2014 ranged from $40,000 to $42,080, plus fees. More specific information regarding tuition and fees is available online at www.newschool.edu/registrar/tuition-and-fees.

Room and board total approximately $16,880, depending on the student's choice of meal plan and dormitory accommodations. Details about the cost of attendance can be found online at www.newschool.edu/student-financial-services/cost-of-attendance.

Financial Aid

Students are encouraged to apply for aid by filing the Free Application for Federal Student Aid (FAFSA) and requesting that a copy of the need analysis report be sent to The New School (FAFSA code number: 002780). Qualified college students are eligible for all federal and state financial aid programs in addition to university gift aid. University aid is awarded on the basis of need and merit and is part of a package consisting of both gift aid (grants and/or scholarships) and a self-help component (loans and Federal Work-Study Program awards). Aid is renewable each year if need continues and students maintain satisfactory academic standing at the college. Special attention is given to continuing students with exceptional academic achievement.

Faculty

At The New School, a small student-faculty ratio enables students to collaborate closely with faculty to develop bold, innovative ideas and creative approaches in all disciplines. Having the country's highest percentage of classes with fewer than 20 students has earned The New School a number one ranking in *U.S. News & World Report*'s Best Colleges editions for the past several years. Faculty members also connect students with prominent scholars and designers, prestigious arts presenters, and representatives from local commercial, nonprofit, and government organizations.

Student Government

The University Student Senate (USS) is the official student government of The New School. Elected from programs throughout the university, student senators present student concerns to administration, maintain a USS website, plan all-campus parties and events, and co-fund events thrown by other people.

Admission Requirements

The New School welcomes admission applications from students of diverse racial, ethnic, religious, and political backgrounds whose past performance and academic and personal promise make them likely to gain from and add to The New School community. The university seeks inquisitive, motivated students who are eager to engage in a distinctive, rigorous undergraduate program. Specific admission requirements vary by division. Admission requirements vary; information about requirements for specific programs is available at www.newschool.edu/admission.

Application and Information

Freshmen, transfers, and visiting students may apply for either the September (fall) or January (spring) semester for all New School programs except those offered by Mannes College and The New School for Drama. Application deadlines for freshman and transfer students vary by division. Details regarding fees, deadlines, and other application information can be found online at www.newschool.edu/admission.

For more information, students should contact:

The New School
Office of Admission
79 Fifth Avenue, 5th floor
New York, New York 10003
Phone: 212-229-5150
800-292-3040 (toll-free)
E-mail: admission@newschool.edu
Website: www.newschool.edu/admission

New York City is a laboratory that enriches academic study and artistic exploration.

COLLEGE CLOSE-UPS

NIAGARA UNIVERSITY

NIAGARA UNIVERSITY, NEW YORK

★ To read more about this school, visit http://petersons.to/niagarauniversity

NIAGARA UNIVERSITY
Education That Makes a Difference

The University

Niagara University (NU), founded in 1856, is a private, comprehensive university rooted in a Catholic and Vincentian tradition. The suburban campus combines the old and new; both ivy-covered buildings and modern architectural structures line its picturesque landscape. The University is easily accessible from every major city in the eastern and midwestern United States via the New York State Thruway, both the Buffalo and Niagara Falls international airports, and rail and bus service.

There are approximately 3,200 undergraduate and 825 graduate students enrolled at Niagara. A large percentage of these students take advantage of the more than 100 extracurricular and cocurricular activities offered. Volunteer work in the community is popular among the students and enhances learning and community relations. Students work with numerous organizations, including Habitat for Humanity, Special Olympics, Opportunities Unlimited, and the United Way.

University sports teams compete on the Division I level and are members of the NCAA, the Metro Atlantic Athletic Conference and the Atlantic Hockey Association. Intercollegiate sports for men include baseball, basketball, cross-country, golf, ice hockey, soccer, swimming and diving, and tennis. Intercollegiate sports for women include basketball, cross-country, golf, lacrosse, outdoor track and field, soccer, softball, swimming and diving, tennis, and volleyball. Club sports include cheerleading, danceline, hockey, martial arts, rugby, skiing, wrestling, and many others. The Kiernan Recreation Center offers a variety of sports and recreational facilities, including a multipurpose gymnasium, a swimming and diving pool, an indoor track, racquetball courts, free-weight and Nautilus rooms, and aerobics rooms. There are several outdoor athletic fields as well as basketball and tennis courts.

Additional student services include the Health Center, which provides inpatient and outpatient care during the day; the Office of Academic Support, which provides free tutoring services; and the Office of Career Services, which offers professional and career counseling. Other services include counseling, new student orientation, academic planning, career planning, veterans' affairs, and job placement.

Niagara University's housing accommodations include five residence halls, a grouping of five small cottages, and a student apartment complex.

The University offers graduate studies in business, counseling, criminal justice, education, finance, interdisciplinary studies, sport management and a Ph.D. in leadership and policy.

Location

Niagara University's picturesque 160-acre campus is located in the town of Lewiston, New York, two minutes off the I-190 on Route 104. The campus is situated on Monteagle Ridge overlooking the lower Niagara River, which connects the two Great Lakes of Erie and Ontario. The University's suburban campus setting is just a few miles from the world-famous Niagara Falls, 20 minutes from Buffalo, which offers a variety of cultural events, sports, and entertainment opportunities, and just 90 minutes from Rochester and Toronto, Canada's largest metropolitan area. In addition, the University is minutes away from the quaint village of Lewiston, New York, and the city of Niagara Falls, New York.

Majors and Degrees

The **College of Arts and Sciences** offers the Bachelor of Arts degree in art history with museum studies, chemistry (with a concentration in environmental studies), communication studies, English, French, gerontology, history, international studies, liberal arts, life sciences, mathematics, philosophy, political science (with a concentration in environmental studies), psychology, religious studies, social sciences, sociology, and Spanish. The Bachelor of Science degree is awarded in biochemistry (with a concentration in bioinformatics), biology (with concentrations in bioinformatics, biotechnology, and environmental studies), chemistry (with concentrations in computational chemistry and environmental studies), computer and information sciences, criminology and criminal justice, mathematics, nursing, and social work. This division also offers the Bachelor of Fine Arts degree in theatre studies (with concentrations in design technology, general theatre, and performance). Preprofessional programs are offered in dentistry, law, medicine, pharmacy, veterinary medicine, and Army ROTC. An Associate of Arts degree is available in general studies. Enrichment courses in fine arts and languages are also available. A combination five-year B.S./M.S. program is available to students in the criminal justice administration program; psychology majors can engage in a six-year B.A./M.S. program in clinical psychology; and an accelerated nursing program and an R.N. to B.S.N. program is offered for students who already have their R.N.

Preprofessional Partnerships: In addition to the programs listed above NU offers a number of preprofessional partnerships. These include a 3+4 partnership in pharmacy with the State University of New York at Buffalo (SUNY), a 2+3 partnership in pharmacy with Lake Erie College of Osteopathic Medicine (LECOM), a 3+4 partnership in medicine with LECOM, and a 3+4 partnership in dentistry with SUNY at Buffalo. Qualified premedical Niagara students are eligible to apply for the early assurance program sponsored by the SUNY at Buffalo.

Niagara University's **College of Business Administration** is accredited by AACSB International—The Association to Advance Collegiate Schools of Business and offers a B.B.A. and a combination B.B.A./M.B.A. degree (five-year program) in accounting. This division offers B.S. degrees in economics, finance, management (with concentrations in human resources, international business, and supply chain management), and marketing. In addition, an A.A.S. degree can be earned in business. Students gain real-world experiences through internships, study abroad, and via cooperative education programs as well as research being conducted in several business-focused campus centers. These centers include the Family Business Center, the Center for Supply Chain Management, the Center for International Accounting and Research, and the Technology Transfer Center.

Holding the highest accreditations possible in both the United States and Canada—the United States National Council for Teacher Education (NCATE) and Canada's Ontario College of Teachers—Niagara University's **College of Education** provides students with an option of earning dual certification to teach in both countries. The College of Education offers bachelor's degree programs leading to New York State initial certification in early childhood (birth–grade 6), childhood (grades 1–6), childhood and middle childhood (grades 1–9), middle childhood and adolescence (grades 5–12), adolescence (grades 7–12), certification for teaching students with disabilities (grades 1–6 childhood and grades 7–12 adolescence), and in Teaching English to Speakers of Other Languages (TESOL). All education majors pursue an academic concentration to establish expertise in one of the following subject areas: biology, business, chemistry, English, French, liberal arts, mathematics, social studies, and Spanish. Business education is offered only for grades 5–12. The academic concentration in liberal arts can only be pursued in the early childhood and childhood (birth–grade 6), and special education and childhood (grades 1–6). Most other states, and Puerto Rico, have reciprocity agreements with New York, so an NU education would qualify education majors to teach in those states as well. Committed to working with those with special needs, NU offers a bachelor's degree program in developmental disabilities. The College of Education also offers a bachelor's degree program in early childhood development and cognition, which prepares students for work in child care and preschool settings.

The **College of Hospitality and Tourism Management** provides a career-oriented curriculum leading to a B.S. degree in three specific areas: hotel and restaurant management (with concentrations in food and beverage management; luxury hospitality operations; and hotel planning, development, and operations), sport management (with concentrations in sport operations and revenue management), and tourism and recreation management (with concentrations in event and meeting management and tourism destination management). The College of Hospitality and Tourism Management offered the world's first bachelor's degree in tourism. NU's hotel and restaurant program, the second oldest in New York state, has the distinction of being the seventh program nationally to be accredited by the Accreditation Commission for Programs in Hospitality Administration by the Council of Hotel, Restaurant, and Institutional Education. The College introduces students to a comprehensive body of knowledge about the hotel, restaurant, tourism, and recreational areas and applies this knowledge to current industry challenges. The College requires that its students accumulate 800 hours of industry-related experience. These and other practical experiences offer NU students the knowledge necessary to advance in the field. Students work with industry leaders in classroom projects, join academic clubs and professional organizations, and participate in special trips to trade shows and conventions and specially designed study-abroad experiences, making NU a national leader in the area.

For students who are undecided about which major to choose, Niagara University offers its **Academic Exploration Program (AEP).** AEP provides a structured opportunity for students to participate in a thorough, organized process of selecting a major that meets their academic talents and career goals while fulfilling requirements to graduate with classmates on time.

Academic Programs

Niagara University's curricula enable students to pursue their academic preferences and to complete courses that lead to proficiency in other academic areas. Courses that have been considered upper-division courses are available to all students. This provides students with the opportunity to take more challenging courses early in their collegiate career. The honors program provides special academic opportunities that stimulate, encourage, and challenge participants. In addition, an accelerated three-year degree program is offered to qualified students.

Niagara grants credit for successful scores on the Advanced Placement, College-Level Examination Program, and the International Baccalaureate tests.

Internships, research, independent study, and cooperative education are available in many academic programs. An Army ROTC program is also offered.

The University operates on a two-semester plan (fall and spring). A comprehensive summer session offers a variety of courses.

NU is fully accredited by the Middle States Association of Colleges and Schools. The University's programs in the respective areas are accredited by the National Council for Accreditation of Teacher Education, AACSB International–The Association to Advance Collegiate Schools of Business, and the Council on Social Work Education. The chemistry department has the approval of the American Chemical Society. The travel, hotel, and restaurant administration program is accredited by the Commission for Programs in Hospitality Administration.

Off-Campus Programs

For those students who wish to study abroad, the University offers programs in Argentina, Australia, Chile, China, England, France, Ireland, Italy, Japan, Spain, Thailand, and many other countries. Students may choose from more than 200 programs in more than 30 countries available through the University's membership in the American Institute for Foreign Studies, Center for Cross-Cultural Study, College Consortium for International Studies, Global Learning Semesters, and Semester at Sea.

Academic Facilities

The University's library supports student learning and knowledge creation by providing assistance, access to technology, information resources, and individual and collaborative work and study space. The collection exceeds 145,000 print and audiovisual titles, 70 research databases, 35,000 journal titles, and 300,000 electronic books. In addition, the library's main floor is open 24 hours a day.

The B. Thomas Golisano Center for Integrated Sciences, the newest structural addition to Niagara's campus, offers 50,000-square-feet of learning space and cutting-edge equipment that encourages collaboration among scientific disciplines. The Academic Complex, the home to the College of Education and the College of Business Administration (Bisgrove Hall), is a state-of-the-art learning facility, with a simulated trading floor in the Glynn Atrium. Dunleavy Hall, outstanding both educationally and architecturally, includes a computerized lecture hall and TV production rooms. The University's facilities also include the Computer Center; St. Vincent's Hall; the Kiernan Center, NU's athletic and recreation center; the Elizabeth Ann Clune Center for Theatre; the Castellani Art Museum; and Dwyer Arena, a dual-rink ice hockey complex.

Costs

Tuition for 2014–15 was $27,700. Room and board (with a choice of meal plans) cost an additional $11,950 per year. Fees were estimated at $1,360 per year. Niagara estimates that an additional $2,500 to $3,050 per year is adequate for books, laundry, and other essentials, such as travel to and from home.

Financial Aid

Ninety-eight percent of the entering freshmen and transfer students received a financial aid package which may include merit-based scholarships, loans, grants, or campus employment. Students seeking financial aid should file the Free Application for Federal Student Aid (FAFSA). New York state residents should also file a Tuition Assistance Program (TAP) application.

Faculty

Niagara University has a dedicated, accessible faculty that genuinely cares about the academic and personal growth of their students. Their commitment to teaching is their primary concern. A student-to-faculty ratio of 12:1 and an average class size of approximately 20 allow personal attention and classroom interaction.

Admission Requirements

The University welcomes men and women who have demonstrated aptitude and academic achievement at the high school level. Either SAT or ACT test scores are required. International students are required to submit the results of their TOEFL examination and a translation of their academic documentation. Interviews are recommended. Transfer students are accepted in any semester. (Transfer credit is evaluated individually by the dean of each division.) Students who complete high school in less than four years are eligible for early admission. Students may also apply under an early action program. Economically and educationally disadvantaged students from New York State are eligible to apply for admission through the Higher Educational Opportunity Program (HEOP).

Application and Information

For all programs except the four-year nursing program, Niagara operates on a rolling admission basis and adheres to the College Board Candidates Reply Date. Nursing applicants must apply by mid-December of their senior year. A visit to the campus is encouraged, and overnight accommodations in a residence hall are available through the Niagara Nights program.

Information on all aspects of the University can be obtained by contacting the Office of Admissions or by visiting www.niagara.edu.

Mark Wojnowski
Director of Admissions
Niagara University
Niagara University, New York 14109-2011
Phone: 716-286-8700
800-462-2111 (toll-free)
Fax: 716-286-8710
E-mail: admissions@niagara.edu
Website: http://www.niagara.edu
http://www.facebook.com/niagarau
http://twitter.com/niagarauniv
http://instagram.com/NiagaraUniversity

Adjacent to the international border between the United States and Canada, Niagara University's 160-acre campus runs along the top of picturesque Monteagle Ridge, overlooking the Niagara River gorge just 4 miles north of the world-famous waterfalls.

NORTHEASTERN UNIVERSITY
BOSTON, MASSACHUSETTS

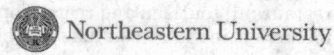

Northeastern University

The University

There's a certain energy about Northeastern University. It comes from the bright, ambitious students, exhibiting a strong sense of purpose in the classroom and while working or studying abroad. In the city of Boston—the ultimate college town—and across the globe, Northeastern students challenge themselves intellectually, investigate career options, participate in community service, and graduate both personally and professionally prepared for their future careers and graduate school.

Northeastern is a leader in interdisciplinary research, urban engagement, and the seamless integration of classroom learning with real-world experiences. The academic curriculum is enhanced by experiential learning opportunities including undergraduate research, professional work experience, global programs, and service learning options. Anchored by the world's largest, most innovative cooperative education program, Northeastern prepares students for a lifetime of achievement.

The current undergraduate enrollment of 17,506 is made up of students of all backgrounds and interests, giving Northeastern its distinctive culture. Students can join a cultural club, participate in cutting-edge research with faculty from various disciplines, or perform with an award winning a capella group. They can travel to nearby New Hampshire or Vermont for a ski club trip, play varsity or club basketball, tutor local children, volunteer at a local soup kitchen, and more. Students have countless opportunities to make lifelong friendships, to try something brand new—a class, a sport, or a career path—to hone their leadership skills, and have fun. Quiet corners of the campus feel far from city streets and give students a secluded haven to read, write, or relax in and around the 73-acre campus, a dynamic and welcoming stretch of leafy green in the heart of Boston.

Location

Northeastern's residential campus is located in the center of Boston, where the distinctive neighborhoods of the Back Bay, South End, Fenway, and Roxbury meet. Over half of the student body lives on campus and many of the residence halls have amazing views of the Boston skyline.

The Back Bay area, known for its many cultural and educational institutions, is just steps away from Symphony Hall, the New England Conservatory of Music, the Museum of Fine Arts, and the Isabella Stewart Gardner Museum. The South End is home to elegant Victorian row houses, a vibrant arts scene, hidden gardens, and some of the finest dining in Boston. The Fenway area, with its beautiful rose garden, bicycle and jogging paths, and Fenway Park (home of the Boston Red Sox) is also just a few blocks away.

Majors and Degrees

Northeastern's undergraduate programs are divided among eight colleges.

The College of Arts, Media and Design awards degrees in architecture, arts, media arts and design, communication studies, game design, journalism, media and screen studies, as well as music, studio art (in collaboration with the School of the Museum of Fine Arts), and theatre.

The D'Amore-McKim School of Business offers two degree options: the Bachelor of Science in Business Administration (B.S.B.A.) and the Bachelor of Science in International Business (B.S.I.B.), which includes language instruction as well as international study and work. D'Amore-McKim offers concentrations in accounting, entrepreneurship and innovation, finance and insurance, management, management information systems, marketing, and supply chain management.

The College of Computer and Information Science awards degrees in computer science and information science and also offers combined majors that pair computer science with biology, business, cognitive psychology, cyber operations, digital art, game design, interactive media, mathematics, music, and physics, and pair information science with business administration and cognitive psychology.

The College of Engineering offers degrees in chemical, civil, computer, electrical, industrial, and mechanical engineering.

The Bouvé College of Health Sciences awards degrees in communication sciences and disorders, health science, nursing, and pharmacy. The college also offers a six-year Doctor of Pharmacy degree and a six-year program leading to a Doctor of Physical Therapy.

The College of Science awards degrees in applied physics, behavioral neuroscience, biochemistry, biology, biomedical physics, chemistry, environmental science, environmental studies, linguistics, marine biology, mathematics, physics, and psychology.

The College of Social Sciences and Humanities awards undergraduate degrees in African American studies, American Sign Language, Asian studies, criminal justice, cultural anthropology, economics, English, history, human services, international affairs, Jewish studies (combined major only), philosophy, political science, religious studies, sociology, and Spanish.

The Program for Undeclared Students offers a wide array of academic opportunities designed to help students who want to explore their options before committing to any major(s). The program provides the support and guidance students need to discover and eventually choose one of Northeastern's undergraduate programs.

Academic Programs

Award-winning faculty mentors are at the heart of a Northeastern education, as well as a rigorous and innovative curriculum, undergraduate research opportunities, and global and professional experiences that challenge and transform. Northeastern's innovative programs encompass a wide range of majors, concentrations, and interdisciplinary studies along with honors, preprofessional, and study-abroad programs.

Northeastern's approach to educating its students is to integrate a challenging academic curriculum with experiential learning opportunities including research, global experiences, service learning, and the university's signature cooperative education program (co-op), enabling students to make deep connections between their field of study and the world around them. At Northeastern, Rigorous Academics + Immersive Experiences = Experiential Learning.

After completing their first year, Northeastern students integrate classroom learning with immersive six-month periods of full-time professional work, global study, service, or research experiences related to their major or interests. Northeastern's flexibility enables students to choose a four- or five-year path with up to eighteen months of experience, strengthening their professional network and giving them confidence—and a significant edge in the job market. Students learn what career is a good fit for them—and what careers are not—all before graduating. In addition, half the students are offered full-time jobs from co-op employers.

Northeastern partners with over 2,900 co-op employers around the globe, including some of the world's largest and most reputable companies: Pfizer, John Hancock, Google, Fidelity Investments, IBM, General Electric, Massachusetts General Hospital, Microsoft, and the Boston Globe, just to name a few.

Experiential learning opportunities are currently available in 128 countries around the world.

The University Honors Program allows a select group of students to participate in enriched opportunities and offers experiences that include honors sections of academic courses, seminars, independent research, and specialized study abroad programs.

The University Scholars Program is Northeastern's most prestigious scholarship program. Every scholar is provided with broad access to the university and the opportunity to design a tailored program that potentially spans colleges, departments, and global partner institutions to address each scholar's unique academic goals and career aspirations, as well as to advance their entrepreneurial ideas.

Academic Facilities

Northeastern is home to over 40 research centers and undergraduates have ample opportunities to work alongside their professors to aid and conduct research on a variety of topics.

The university library system is comprised of Snell Library, a 240,000-square-foot central library on the Boston campus, the School of Law Library, and a small supplemental collection at the Nahant Marine Science Center. Snell Library houses almost 875,000 print volumes, 399,488 e-books, 1,332,128 microfilms, and access to 60,270 licensed electronic journals, as well as 23,437 audio, video, and computer software items, and 5,712 linear feet of archival material as of June 2012.

Northeastern University provides a broad range of academic and administrative computer resources to students, faculty, and staff members. Many computing resources are available, including an extensive wireless network, technology-assisted classrooms, computer labs, and the myNEU portal, which allows students to access many administrative and academic functions online.

Costs

For 2014–15, tuition was $42,534, and room and board fees were $14,050. Regardless of time to degree, tuition is charged only while students are earning course credit.

Financial Aid

The university operates a substantial aid program designed to make attendance feasible for all qualified students. By coordinating the resources of the university and various public and private scholarship programs, the Office of Student Financial Services was able to provide more than $220 million in grant and scholarship assistance this past year. About 75 percent of students receive some form of financial aid. Northeastern participates in all federal aid programs. Financial aid is based on need and academic merit and may consist of grants, loans, work-study employment, or any combination of the three. To apply, students must file the Free Application for Federal Student Aid (FAFSA) and a CSS PROFILE form with the College Scholarship Service by the priority filing date of February 15.

Faculty

The university has more than 1,200 full-time faculty members with a wide variety of research and teaching interests and specialties. Academic advisers in each college work closely with students to assist them in developing programs suited to their interests and abilities. Co-op advisers assist students in resume-building, honing interview skills and tactics, and developing contacts with businesses and employers to support networking and professional opportunities.

Admission Requirements

Students may enter the university with advanced credit on the basis of test scores on Advanced Placement (AP) examinations, the International Baccalaureate (I.B.) examinations, or with successful completion of accredited college-level courses. In addition to the application for admission, prospective freshmen must submit official high school transcript(s) (or official GED score reports); official transcripts for any college-level coursework taken while a secondary-school student; written recommendations from their secondary school counselor and a teacher; and scores from the SAT (Northeastern's College Board code is 3667) or ACT, including the writing section. Please visit the university's website for additional admission details for specific student populations and transfer admissions requirements (northeastern.edu/admissions).

Application and Information

Admission to Northeastern is selective and competitive. For the freshman class entering in Fall 2015, the university received more than 50,535 applications for 2,800 seats in the freshman class. Students are reviewed in the context of their environment, with attention paid to their academic course selection and rigor, academic achievement, extracurricular involvement and impact, and their potential fit with Northeastern, including the demonstration of personal traits like leadership, adaptability, a global perspective, or an entrepreneurial spirit.

November 1 is the deadline for both the early action admission program and the binding early decision program. Students who have carefully explored their college options and have decided that Northeastern is where they want to enroll may choose to apply under the early decision program. The deadline for the regular admission program is January 1. Admitted students are required to pay a deposit by May 1 to secure a place in the class. For transfer students, the admission deadlines are April 1 for fall and October 1 for spring admission. Fall transfer and spring admission decisions are made on a space-available basis and are released online by June 15.

Northeastern offers a variety of visit options including information sessions and campus tours. For more information, or to register, visit northeastern.edu/admissions/visitcampus.

For more information, students should contact:

Office of Undergraduate Admissions
240 West Village F
Northeastern University
360 Huntington Avenue
Boston, Massachusetts 02115
Phone: 617-373-2200
E-mail: admissions@neu.edu
Website: http://www.northeastern.edu/admissions

Northeastern's campus skyline and Centennial Common, a typical quad where students relax, study, and hang out with friends.

NORTHERN KENTUCKY UNIVERSITY

HIGHLAND HEIGHTS, KENTUCKY

NKU NORTHERN KENTUCKY UNIVERSITY

The University

Northern Kentucky University (NKU) was founded in 1968 and is the newest of Kentucky's eight state universities. Nestled in a quiet suburb, NKU is just minutes from the entertainment and career opportunities of downtown Cincinnati. NKU has an enrollment of more than 15,000 students from forty-five states and fifty-nine countries and is accredited by the Southern Association of Colleges and Schools. The Salmon P. Chase College of Law is accredited by both the American Bar Association and the Association of American Law Schools.

There are more than 220 student organizations and NKU's athletic teams compete in the NCAA Division I Atlantic Sun Conference. Intercollegiate sports are offered for men and women in basketball, cross-country, track, golf, soccer, and tennis; for men in baseball; and for women in fast-pitch softball and volleyball. Intramural activities vary by semester, but include basketball, dodgeball, field hockey, flag football, ice hockey, racquetball, soccer, softball, taekwando, volleyball, and many others. A complete list can be found online at http://campusrec.nku.edu.

Majors and Degrees

NKU offers 72 bachelor's degrees; 6 associate degrees; 24 graduate programs; and the Juris Doctor, the Doctor of Education in Educational Leadership, and the Doctor of Nursing Practice degree, as well as 28 graduate certificates.

Academic Programs

NKU operates on a semester calendar. To receive a bachelor's degree, students must complete a minimum of 120 credit hours. At least 60 credit hours are required for the associate degree.

The University offers a variety of career planning and placement, internship, independent study, work-study, and cooperative-education programs. There is also an advising, counseling, and testing Center available. Other programs include an honors program, a program that allows for the dual enrollment of high school students, a program where students can combine their career interests in the liberal arts and engineering fields, and University 101, an orientation program for freshmen and transfer students.

NKU recognizes credit earned through the Advanced Placement (AP) Program and the general, subject, and institutional tests of specific College-Level Examination Program (CLEP). A maximum of 45 credit hours may be applied toward the bachelor's degree from the AP and CLEP examinations. The International Baccalaureate program allows students to earn credit in science, mathematics, psychology, and languages.

Off-Campus Programs

More than 330 students participated in study-abroad programs in twenty-six countries worldwide.

Academic Facilities

Among the academic facilities at NKU are an anthropology museum, a biology museum, and an art gallery with rotating exhibits. NKU also has a laser projection planetarium; laboratories for nursing, respiratory care, and radiologic technology; the 9,000-seat Bank of Kentucky Center; and the James C. and Rachel M. Votruba Student Union, a student-centered facility, and focal point for campus programs and student organizations.

NKU's Griffin Hall, the home of the College of Informatics, is designed to help students interested in communication and media, computer science, information technology, or management information systems become the new generation of professionals who will build the region's information economy. The W. Frank Steely Library contains 311,155 book titles and maintains 1,729 paper periodical subscriptions (additional periodicals are available in electronic format). Computer laboratories offer students opportunities to learn and utilize a variety of software programs. The Computer Science Department and Criminal Justice Department have collaborated to offer students a computer forensics minor to teach students how to handle digital evidence and how to present such evidence in court.

Costs

Tuition and fees for 2014–15 were $8,472 for Kentucky students, $12,936 for metro students, and $16,944 for nonresidents. Other costs included $7,000–$9,000 for room and meals, about $850 for books and supplies, and $3,000 for miscellaneous expenses.

Financial Aid

Northern Kentucky University awards more than $2 million in academic scholarships each year to the incoming freshman class. The University awards scholarships to highly motivated students who demonstrate strong academic performance. Students who achieve a 3.0 GPA and a 23 ACT or 1050

SAT are considered for academic awards. The University offers numerous scholarship levels. Each scholarship level has merit guidelines that students must meet to qualify. To be considered to academic scholarships, interested students need to apply for admission by January 15 (based on availability of funds). For fall 2015, there is no separate scholarship application for general Northern Kentucky University academic scholarships. Students who qualify for a scholarship received an award letter upon acceptance to NKU. Prospective students can visit scholarships.nku.edu for information on how to be considered for 2016 merit-based scholarships and which scholarships require an application, letters of recommendation, or an essay. There is no deadline for the University's financial aid application; however, students who wish to receive institutional aid must apply by February 1 for priority consideration. Applicants are notified of acceptance on a rolling basis.

Faculty

More than 82 percent of the faculty members at NKU hold a doctoral degree or the terminal degree in their field. Classes are small, with an average class size of 24 and a student-faculty ratio of 17:1. All classes are taught by faculty members; no classes are taught by graduate assistants.

Student Government

Student Government (SG) is the elected student assembly at Northern Kentucky University. It is the official student voice on campus and represents the student viewpoint on University committees. All SG meetings are open, and students are encouraged to attend.

Admission Requirements

Incoming freshmen must submit an application for admission; arrange for the official ACT, SAT, or COMPASS score report to be sent; and request that the high school send an official transcript. In order to be considered for regular admission, a student must meet precollege curriculum requirements for Kentucky and institutional admission standards. Out-of-state applicants must also meet the Kentucky precollege curriculum requirements.

Based on the review of official test results and the precollege curriculum, students are admitted into one of two categories: regular admission or admission with conditions. Students who have two or more deficiencies are encouraged to retake the ACT or SAT so an additional review can be completed. Students with two or more deficiencies may be asked to submit an essay, letters of recommendation, and an activities portfolio before an admission decision can be rendered. Students with two or more deficiencies who are offered admission will be required to participate in the Pathfinders Program, which is designed to enhance student engagement and provide tools needed for future academic achievement. The program includes: mandatory advising, completion of University 101 (Introduction to College) course, participation in study tables, tutoring, and college success workshops. Some degree programs require that students meet additional criteria; more information is available in the current catalog (http://www.nku.edu).

Application and Information

The $40 paper application fee may be waived for applicants with demonstrated need. The fall semester early action and scholarship deadline is January 15, assured consideration deadline is February 1, enrollment confirmation deadline is May 1, and the final deadline is July 1. The priority application deadline for the nursing program is January 31. The priority application deadline for the respiratory care program is February 15.

For more information, students should contact:

Office of Admissions
Northern Kentucky University
Highland Heights, Kentucky 41099
Phone: 859-572-5220
800-637-9948 (toll-free)
E-mail: admitnku@nku.edu
Website: http://admissions.nku.edu
http://www.facebook.com/nkuedu
http://twitter.com.nkuedu

Northern Kentucky University's modern campus is set in Highland Heights, just minutes from downtown Cincinnati.

NORWICH UNIVERSITY
NORTHFIELD, VERMONT

★ To read more about this school, visit http://petersons.to/norwichuniversity

NORWICH UNIVERSITY™ 1819
Expect Challenge. Achieve Distinction.

The University

Norwich University was established in 1819 as the first private military college in America. It was at Norwich that the idea of the citizen-soldier developed and eventually evolved into the Reserve Officer Training Corps (ROTC) program. Norwich was the first private college to offer civil engineering, and many University alumni were involved in the construction of the nation's continental railway system. In 1974, Norwich became one of the first military colleges to admit women into its Corps of Cadets, preceding the federal academies.

Norwich University offers a diverse blend of disciplines, teaching styles, and viewpoints. Students enrolled in the Corps of Cadets have a more disciplined, challenging, and structured path through college, while their civilian student classmates lead a more traditional collegiate lifestyle. However, both groups are coeducational and attend classes and participate in sports and other activities together.

In keeping with its mission, Norwich provides opportunities for all of its students to develop leadership skills with a strong commitment to community service. Both groups gain skills such as leadership, honor, and integrity, which are required to be successful in today's job market. These two diverse groups of students are very different and yet have much in common—they are Norwich.

Norwich University has an enrollment of 2,300 students from more than forty-five states and twenty countries. The University's minority enrollment is consistently higher (by percentage) than that of any other Vermont university or college.

The athletic facilities at Norwich are comparable to the best at any of New England's Division III universities. The main athletic complex, Andrews Hall, features a gymnasium, racquetball courts, a modernized athletic training room, an equipment room, and laundry facilities. Kreitzberg Arena is a multipurpose facility with a seating capacity of 1,500 and a fully equipped weight room. It was here that the University's men's hockey team won the Division III National Championship in 2003. The recently constructed 22,000-square-foot Doyle Hall facility connects the Kreitzberg Arena and Andrews Hall. Doyle Hall features a new Hall of Fame lobby at the main entrance into the athletic complex and includes a grand stairway, ticket booth, concessions area, and restroom facilities. The new facility also provides the athletic department with offices for coaches, team meeting rooms, and locker room facilities. In 2013, the renovation of Sabine Field transformed the once-natural football field to a state-of-the-art oversized turf field used for football, rugby, lacrosse, soccer, etc. The installation of lighting allows for evening competition as well.

Plumley Armory has a huge gym as well as an indoor track, weight and aerobics rooms, a wrestling room, and an indoor swimming pool. Shapiro Field House has 50,000 square feet of floor space and includes a 200-meter indoor track, tennis courts, and a climbing wall. The newly developed Shaw Outdoor Center at the base of Paine Mountain offers students a variety of outdoor recreational activities including trails for jogging, cross-country running races, hiking, snowshoeing, cross-country skiing, sledding, and mountain biking. Equipment to participate in these activities is available to students free of charge. The 1,200-acre campus includes numerous playing fields for baseball, football, rugby, soccer, and softball. Norwich also has a paintball course, a rappel tower, and an obstacle and confidence course.

Norwich has the only professional five-year Master of Architecture program in northern New England. The University also offers online graduate degrees in business administration, diplomacy, information assurance, nursing, public administration, business continuity, organizational leadership, civil engineering, history and military history.

Location

Norwich University is located in the heart of the Green Mountains of Vermont, right in the middle of ski country. Some of the nation's most popular resorts, such as Stowe, Sugarbush, and Killington, are located within an hour's drive. Vermont is world renowned as one of America's most beautiful states. Nature's playground is just outside the dorm room—skiing, snowboarding, telemark skiing, cross-country skiing, snowshoeing, rock climbing, hiking, mountain biking, canoeing, kayaking, and more are available.

The University campus is located in the small town of Northfield, Vermont. Northfield is 10 miles south of the state capital of Montpelier and is 50 miles from Burlington, the largest city in Vermont. Both Montpelier and Burlington are cultural centers for the arts. Burlington International Airport is within an hour's drive. In addition, the cities of Boston and Montreal are only a 3-hour drive from the campus.

Majors and Degrees

Norwich offers students more than thirty academic majors from which to choose. The Bachelor of Arts degree is awarded in Chinese, criminal justice, English, history, international studies, political science, studies in war and peace, psychology, and Spanish. The Bachelor of Science degree is awarded in accounting, architectural studies; biochemistry, biology, chemistry, civil engineering, communications, computer/electrical engineering, computer science, computer security and information assurance, education, engineering management, environmental science, geology, management, mathematics, mechanical engineering, nursing, physical education, physics, sports medicine, and strategic studies and defense analysis. Prelaw, premedical, and predental programs are also available.

Academic Programs

Norwich University is dedicated to the discovery, preservation, and dissemination of knowledge and the search for truth. Norwich is distinctive in that it maintains a strong emphasis on the development of leadership in both military and civilian pursuits and in providing for the educational needs of students. The University's mission is to foster in each student the growth of self-discipline, personal integrity, social responsibility, physical fitness, respect for law, and intellectual ability essential for full and effective participation in a free society.

For students enrolling in the Corps of Cadets, six semesters of Reserve Officer Training Corps are required. Norwich is considered the birthplace of ROTC; therefore, all four service branches can be found on campus. Prior to their junior year, cadets may elect to contract with their ROTC program and be considered upon graduation for a commission as officers in the Army, Navy, Air Force, or Marine Corps. Cadets not on an ROTC scholarship are not required to join the military.

Students typically take an average of five classes per semester. Each semester is sixteen weeks long, with holiday breaks at Thanksgiving, Christmas, and New Year's and in March during spring break. The academic year normally begins the last week in August and ends after the first week in May.

Academic Facilities

The academic facilities at Norwich are among the finest in New England. Completed in 1997, the math and science building was designed to keep classes small. Its labs hold no more than 16 students, and all of the classrooms are hardwired to allow for multimedia presentations. Students can find numerous computer labs across the campus, and the Kreitzberg library offers students plenty of resources, space, and technology. Students may research Norwich's facilities on the University's website.

Costs

For 2014–15, tuition and fees were $16,406 per semester. The cost of room and board was $5,992 per semester. Books and personal expenses average $1,250 per semester. Cadets pay a uniform fee of $1,050 per semester in each of their first two years.

Financial Aid

Most families assume they cannot afford a private college education and fall victim to sticker shock, but a Norwich education can often be an affordable option for a family. Last year, 98 percent of Norwich students shared in more than $70 million of financial aid from all sources, including ROTC scholarships. This included an aggressive need-based financial aid program that enabled deserving students to secure a private education at Norwich.

Norwich awards many institutional scholarships based on academic merit. A student's high school GPA and ACT or SAT scores determine the level of scholarship. These scholarships may pay from $7,000 to $20,000 of the student's tuition for all four years. Students are required to maintain a specified GPA in order to renew the scholarship each year. Norwich also offers scholarships to students who attend the University's Future Leader Camp, participate in National Drill Team competitions, and who are in leadership positions in the Civil Air Patrol. Prospective students should contact an admissions counselor for more details about these scholarships.

Norwich also offers a large number of institutional grants based on financial need. A student must file the Free Application for Federal Student Aid (FAFSA) to be considered for these grants.

Students who bring a three- or four-year ROTC scholarship to Norwich are eligible for the General I. D. White Scholarship, which covers the cost of room and board. Students who are interested in applying for an ROTC scholarship should visit the individual ROTC detachment's web page on the Norwich University website.

Faculty

The student-faculty ratio is 14:1. Faculty members are full-time instructors with advanced degrees; 72 percent hold a doctorate. Small classes help promote a close relationship between faculty members and students. Students are assigned faculty advisers within each academic division.

Student Government

The Norwich University Corps of Cadets is a military organization made up of and led by cadets under the supervision of the Commandant of Cadets. Members of the Corps and student body preside over the University Honor Council. The University's honor code binds all Norwich students. Members of the Corps and student body also participate on the Student Affairs Committee, whose members include the Dean of Students, members of the faculty, and the Senior Vice President and Commandant of Cadets. This committee serves as the voice of the Norwich community and provides a channel of communication for change.

Admission Requirements

Admission to Norwich is based on a review of the applicant's academic record, personal essay, letters of recommendation, and extracurricular activities. Students at Norwich are heavily involved in community service and leadership development activities. Applicants should be able to demonstrate participation in activities both inside and outside of their high school.

Norwich is looking for students who want to become leaders, serve others, and give back to their communities. While the admissions office uses a rolling admissions system (meaning applications may be submitted at any time), there is a priority deadline of February 1. Students applying for admission or financial aid after February 1 are admitted on a space-available basis.

Application and Information

Students can visit the University's website or contact the University for more information.

Admissions Office
Norwich University
158 Harmon Drive
Northfield, Vermont 05663
Phone: 800-468-6679 (toll-free)
Fax: 802-485-2032
E-mail: nuadm@norwich.edu
Website: http://www.norwich.edu
http://www.facebook.com/NorwichUniversity

Two lifestyles. One University.

NOTRE DAME COLLEGE

SOUTH EUCLID, OHIO

★ To read more about this school, visit http://petersons.to/notredamecollege

The College

Notre Dame College (NDC) offers stimulating academics, personalized attention, small class sizes, NCAA Division II intercollegiate athletics, and vibrant student life.

Founded in 1922 by the Sisters of Notre Dame, the College has grown strategically to keep pace with the rapidly changing needs of students and the dramatic changes in higher education. But it has never lost sight of its emphasis on teaching students not only how to make a good living but also how to live a good life.

Notre Dame College has rapidly become one of the finest small, Catholic, residential, liberal arts colleges in the Great Lakes region. Founded as an all-women's school, the College became coeducational in 2001. Since 2003, total enrollment has since grown from 875 to 2,029.

A snapshot of the fall 2014 traditional NDC student population shows 44 percent are female, 56 percent male; 55 percent are Catholic; 31 percent are from an ethnic minority group; 55 percent are student-athletes; and 53 percent live on campus. The mosaic of NDC students represents forty states and twenty-three foreign countries.

Notre Dame offers high quality academic programs in over thirty disciplines with majors based in five academic divisions: arts and humanities, business, education, nursing, and science and math.

A Catholic institution in the tradition of the Sisters of Notre Dame, the College educates a diverse population in the liberal arts for personal, professional, and global responsibility. The College believes that truly progressive education selectively blends traditional values with new ideas that represent real growth. Within the scope of a career-oriented liberal arts education, students can grow to meet the challenges of the present and the future.

A variety of clubs and activities enrich the overall experience of the 2,000+ students. Campus Ministry promotes the spiritual growth of the College community and facilitates community service, and the award-winning FalconCorps service program provides students opportunities to serve at local charities and national programs such as Habitat for Humanity.

Most on-campus events are free, and students often may purchase tickets at reduced rates for off-campus programs such as performances of the world-famous Cleveland Orchestra, the Cleveland Opera, and road shows of Broadway productions at the Cleveland Play House, the Palace Theatre, the State Theatre, and the Ohio Theatre at Playhouse Square.

Notre Dame is an NCAA Division II institution and an associate member of the Mountain East Conference, with 22 intercollegiate sports for men and women.

Location

Located in South Euclid, Ohio, the 48-acre campus is in a residential neighborhood just 25 minutes from downtown Cleveland and all the excitement and cultural wealth of the city, such as the Rock and Roll Hall of Fame and Museum, the Cleveland Metroparks, University Circle, several professional sports teams, and one of the richest cultural, theatrical, entertainment, healthcare, and employment regions in the nation. Only five minutes from Legacy Village and Beachwood Place, Cleveland's lifestyle retail centers, the area combines all the opportunities of a major urban and educational center with the relaxed atmosphere of a suburb.

The beautiful campus provides the perfect setting for the Clara Fritzsche Library; the historic Administration Building which houses classrooms, labs, and offices; Regina Hall and Regina Auditorium; Connelly Center, the dining hall and student center; Keller Center, the recreational and fitness facility; Falcon Café; and five residence halls that accommodate 650 students. Other students commute or reside in nearby off-campus housing.

Majors and Degrees

The College awards bachelor's degrees in arts and humanities (communication, criminal justice, English, graphic design, history, intelligence studies, political science, public relations, studio art, and theology), business (accounting, business administration, finance, human resources, information systems, international business, management, marketing, and sports management), education (adolescent, early childhood, middle childhood, mild/moderate intervention specialist, and visual arts), nursing (direct-entry program), and science and math (biology, chemistry, environmental science, and mathematics).

Notre Dame College also offers a Bachelor of Science in Nursing program and an online RN to B.S.N. completion program.

A Master of Education degree is offered with concentrations available in special education, reading, and critical and creative thinking. The College has an online Master of Arts in Security Policy Studies program and an online Master's of Science in Nursing.

Teacher licensure is available in early childhood education, middle childhood education, adolescent/young adult education, and multiage for mild/moderate intervention specialist studies. The College is accredited by both the North Central Association of Colleges and Schools and NCATE and is registered to award state teacher's licenses by the State of Ohio Department of Education.

Minors include biblical studies, coaching, computer programming, entrepreneurship, economics, fine arts, health education, performing arts, sociology, Spanish, theater, and more.

Concentrations are available in gaming design (graphic design), exercise science (biology), pre-law (English and history), engineering–binary program (math and chemistry), comprehensive biology (biology), and biochemistry (chemistry).

A student can also design his or her own major that leads to a bachelor's degree by combining two or three academic areas, such as graphic design, human resource management, and public relations.

The Finn Center for Adult, Graduate, Online, and Professional Programs unites all aspects of adult education at NDC, providing convenient, flexible programs for educational advancement on days, nights, weekends, and the Web. Housing the Office of Adult and Graduate Admissions and the Office of Professional Development, the Finn Center offers professional development classes, associate degrees, bachelor's degrees, postbaccalaureate programs, and master's degrees.

Academic Programs

For the bachelor's degree, students must earn 128 semester hours of credit, with a minimum cumulative grade point average of 2.0. From 36 to 68 semester hours of credit are required in the major field of study.

Through a cooperative education program, students can earn up to 6 credit hours for paid or volunteer work experience related to their academic field of study.

Advanced Placement credit is awarded to students who have demonstrated the ability to pursue coursework beyond the level of entering freshmen, as indicated by their scores on the Advanced Placement (AP) or College-Level Examination Program (CLEP) tests of the College Board. College credit is given on the basis of a decision made jointly by the academic dean and the department involved.

Academic Facilities

Students with documented learning differences, such as attention deficit disorder (ADD), attention deficit hyperactivity disorder (ADHD), dyslexia, Asperger syndrome, and specific learning disabilities (SLD) can enroll in NDC's Academic Support Center to receive comprehensive support services. These include tutoring, academic advising, and access to a large array of adaptive equipment. In order to be accepted into the Learning Differences Program, students must first meet the admission requirements of Notre Dame College. To participate in the Academic Support Center, students must submit documentation of a learning disability.

The Career Services Center coordinates cooperative education and internships for students and interacts with faculty to create meaningful programs that link academics to the workplace. It further offers graduate school advising, resume preparation assistance, interviewing and job search coaching, posting of positions available, and a resource library. On-campus recruiting opportunities attract employers to the College to meet with students firsthand.

The Clara Fritzsche Library has a capacity of 100,000 volumes. As a member of OhioLINK, the College also has online access to members throughout the state, with access to more than 31 million library items and more than 90 research databases.

The Dwyer Success Center consists of an electronic classroom, a student computer lab, a writing lab, a test proctoring room and a tutoring room. The writing lab is staffed by English faculty who provide professional writing assistance to students free of charge. The tutoring room is staffed with graduate assistants and upper-class peer tutors for one-on-one study skills and subject specific assistance.

Costs

For the 2015–16 academic year tuition and fee charges are $27,520. Room and board costs are $9,180 for double occupancy.

Financial Aid

Notre Dame believes that all qualified students should have the opportunity to attend college, and provides need-, merit-, and athletic-based aid to its students. A comprehensive financial assistance program of more than $25 million assists approximately 95 percent of all full-time students. Students applying for aid must submit the Free Application for Federal Student Aid (FAFSA).

Faculty

The College has 59 full-time faculty members, augmented by highly qualified instructors. Faculty members hold advanced degrees from more than thirty universities in the United States, Canada, and Europe.

Admission Requirements

Notre Dame College admits students who demonstrate potential for success in rigorous academic work. In fulfilling its mission, the College seeks to attract students of diverse religious, racial, and economic backgrounds. Candidates for admission as first-time, full-time freshmen are reviewed on an individual basis, and decisions are based on a broad range of criteria. The most important consideration is the candidate's high school performance, as demonstrated by her/his overall grade average, class rank, grade trends, and level of courses completed. Aptitude for verbal and mathematical reasoning, as measured by performance on standardized tests, is also considered. In addition, counselor and teacher recommendations are reviewed.

Notre Dame College recommends that students complete at least 16 units of high school credit in academic subjects as a prerequisite for matriculation in the College. The distribution of these subject areas and the units are as follows: English, 4; mathematics, 3 (to include algebra I, geometry, and algebra II); science, 3 (with laboratory experience); social studies, 3; foreign language, 2 (from the same language); and fine arts, 1. Applicants should generally rank in the upper half of their high school graduating class and have a minimum average of C+. Either ACT or SAT scores are accepted.

The College has a fair and generous policy on the transfer of academic credit earned within the preceding five years at a regionally accredited college or university. Students wishing to transfer from other regionally accredited colleges and universities are admitted to advanced standing upon presentation of satisfactory evidence of scholarship and character.

Special consideration may be granted to an applicant whose academic preparation is not consistent with the requirements stated above.

Notre Dame College strongly recommends that prospective students schedule an appointment to visit the campus and talk with an admissions counselor.

A free application is available online at NotreDameCollege.edu. The College maintains a rolling admission policy.

To apply, students should submit the completed application for undergraduate admission, an official transcript of their high school record and results of the ACT or SAT to:
Office of Admissions
Notre Dame College
4545 College Road
South Euclid, Ohio 44121
United States
Phone: 877-NDC-OHIO Ext. 5355 (toll-free)
Fax: 216-373-5278
E-mail: admissions@ndc.edu
Website: http://NotreDameCollege.edu

Fall semester is one of the most beautiful times of the year at Notre Dame College in South Euclid, Ohio.

OHIO NORTHERN UNIVERSITY

ADA, OHIO

NORTHERN
OHIO NORTHERN UNIVERSITY

COLLEGE CLOSE-UPS

The University

Ohio Northern University (ONU) has a 95 percent job and graduate school placement rate. Its long-standing success is partly because of excellent professors, partly because of ambitious students, and partly because the University always been rooted in the future. At ONU, students move toward a career long before they graduate—and ONU's alumni successes prove it. With top-ranked programs and opportunities outside the classroom, any path a student chooses at ONU will be grounded in concrete applications for the future. Established in 1871 and comprised of five colleges (Arts & Sciences, Business Administration, Engineering, Pharmacy, and Law), ONU's beautiful residential campus is made up of more than sixty modern residences and academic buildings and provides a vibrant campus experience.

Students can choose from a variety of campus activities including nearly 200 student organizations; four national sororities and five national fraternities; fine arts, music, and theatrical events; and intramural and club sports. Residence hall living is an integral part of the educational program, contributing to a student's personal development. There are nine residence halls on campus as well as eight campus apartment complexes and an Affinity Housing complex.

The ONU Polar Bears compete successfully at the NCAA Division III level in twenty-three varsity sports as part of the highly respected Ohio Athletic Conference. ONU has twelve men's teams (baseball, basketball, cross-country, football, golf, lacrosse (beginning in 2015–16), soccer, swimming and diving, tennis, indoor and outdoor track, and wrestling) and eleven women's teams (basketball, cross-country, fast-pitch softball, golf, lacrosse (beginning in 2015–16), soccer, swimming and diving, tennis, indoor and outdoor track, and volleyball).

Location

Ohio Northern University's campus is situated on 342 beautiful acres in the village of Ada (population 5,500). Located in northwestern Ohio, ONU is easily accessible by major highways and conveniently located near major cities such as Columbus, Dayton, Toledo, and Fort Wayne, Indiana.

Majors and Degrees

Ohio Northern University offers the undergraduate degrees: Bachelor of Arts, Bachelor of Fine Arts, Bachelor of Music, Bachelor of Science, Bachelor of Science in Business Administration, Bachelor of Science in Civil Engineering, Bachelor of Science in Medical Laboratory Science, Bachelor of Science in Computer Engineering, Bachelor of Science in Electrical Engineering, Bachelor of Science in Mechanical Engineering, and Bachelor of Science in Nursing. In addition to the undergraduate programs, ONU offers a Master of Professional Practice in Accounting; Juris Doctor; Doctor of Pharmacy (Pharm.D.), which is an 0-6, direct entry program; and the Master of Laws (LL.M.) in Democratic Governance and Rule of Law. The 3+3 Law Admissions Program will be offered for the first time to incoming freshmen and transfer students who enroll for the first time in the fall 2015–16 semester. This program leads to an approved bachelor's degree plus a juris doctorate degree. Majors considered for the 3+3 Admissions Program include business administration, chemistry, English, history, philosophy, political science, religion, and sociology.

Majors are offered in accounting; advertising design; applied mathematics; art education; athletic training; biochemistry; biology; chemistry; civil engineering; communication studies; computer engineering; computer science; construction management; creative writing; criminal justice; early childhood education; electrical engineering; engineering education; environmental and field biology; exercise physiology; forensic biology; French; German; graphic design; history; language arts education; literature; management; manufacturing technology; marketing; mathematical statistics; mathematics; mechanical engineering; medical laboratory science; middle childhood education; molecular biology; multimedia journalism; music; music education; musical theatre; music performance; nursing; pharmaceutical business; pharmacy; philosophy; philosophy, politics, and economics; physics; political science; professional writing; psychology; public relations; religion; risk management and insurance; social studies; sociology; Spanish; sport management; studio arts; technology education; theatre; theatre design and production; youth ministry; undecided business; undecided general studies; and undecided sciences.

Special preprofessional programs are available in dentistry, law, medicine, occupational therapy, physical therapy, physician assistant, seminary, and veterinary medicine. Teacher licensure programs are offered at the early childhood, middle childhood, adolescent/young adult, and multiage levels within 16 programs and two endorsement areas.

Changes in programs of study are updated at www.onu.edu.

Academic Programs

The Getty College of Arts & Sciences creatively combines a traditional liberal arts education with cutting-edge preprofessional studies. The college offers more than 50 majors in 17 academic departments, and students can earn a Bachelor of Arts, Bachelor of Fine Arts, Bachelor of Music, Bachelor of Science, Bachelor of Science in Medical Laboratory Science, or Bachelor of Science in Nursing.

Students in the sciences have been honored by the Barry M. Goldwater Scholarship and Excellence in Education Foundation for ten consecutive years. The college has also been recognized as one of the top 200 programs in the nation for creative students in *Creative Colleges: A Guide for Student Actors, Artists, Dancers, Musicians and Writers.*

Working closely with dedicated faculty members, students complete the general education requirements, delve deeply into advanced courses, and engage in high-impact learning through research, internships, practicum experiences, study abroad, and more.

The Dicke College of Business Administration focuses on creating ethical, entrepreneurial, and engaged business and civic leaders. The college offers a rigorous academic curriculum with signature programs in pharmaceutical business and risk management and insurance. Internships are required by the college and are available year-round. There are international programs, including study abroad, work abroad, and study tours. An office of experiential learning supports students looking for these opportunities. The course of study for the Bachelor of Science in Business Administration includes a four-year business core experience themed around strategic business planning. Personal attention and mentoring from faculty members, small intimate classes, and active student organizations combine with an emphasis on experiential learning, global awareness, and the entrepreneurial spirit. The college is accredited by the AACSB International—The Association to Advance Collegiate Schools of Business. The Dicke College of Business Administration is ranked by *Bloomberg Businessweek* among the top 100 undergraduate business programs in the United States and the top private school business program in Ohio.

The T. J. Smull College of Engineering is noted for its hands-on learning; small, intimate classes; dedicated, accessible professors; and world-class, top-ranked instruction. Ranked forty-first in the nation for undergraduate engineering programs by *U.S. News & World Report*, ONU's engineering and computer science programs prepare graduates who think critically, lead confidently, and have solid technical foundations upon which to build successful long-term careers. From strong lab components to a host of experiential learning opportunities, ONU's faculty is committed to helping its students achieve their educational goals and realize their dreams. The college features six accredited, disciplinary majors in civil, computer, electrical, and mechanical engineering; computer science; and engineering education, a degree option supporting the demand for high school math teachers with engineering degrees.

The courses for the first academic year are essentially the same for each degree program, offering students an easy track to move from one program to another if initially uncertain which disciplines they prefer to study.

An optional five-year co-op program is available for students in each program, provided they maintain a minimum 2.5 GPA. The college focuses on high-impact learning as an essential part of an engineering education; thus, in addition to a co-op program, students apply their classroom learning in freshman design projects, senior capstone projects, national design competitions, and numerous engineering projects in community services (EPICS). Further, many opportunities are available for valuable work experience through the co-op and internship programs, with a historically high job-placement rate for graduates.

For more than 130 years, the Raabe College of Pharmacy has offered distinctive, challenging, and comprehensive training for some of the nation's most talented pharmacists. This University signature program features a six-year Doctor of Pharmacy (Pharm.D.) degree accredited by the American Council on Pharmaceutical Education. This program is direct-entry, admitting students immediately from high school into the college's professional program. This approach enables students to take pharmacy courses from the very first day. A rigorous curriculum utilizes an innovative modular format to organize learning around the human body systems and patient care implementation.

Cutting-edge clinical facilities include the Pharmacy Skills Center, where students access state-of-the-art compounding/counseling pods with portable OTC simulation stations. Students gain considerable experience through a strong undergraduate research program and may pursue minors or dual majors in other areas. Faculty members are teaching-focused but remain current in their research disciplines. Upon graduation, students are well schooled in every aspect of pharmacy and have a high placement rate.

Off-Campus Programs

Many majors may take part in study-abroad programs developed in consultation with faculty members. Field experiences and internships are available to most majors. Externships are required of all pharmacy majors and place students in retail and clinical experiences. Teacher licensure requires one semester of primary or secondary classroom teaching experience under the supervision of practicing teachers. Additional opportunities include computer science and mathematics co-op programs (professional practice), engineering co-op programs (professional practice, domestic and international), and an honors program. All off-campus learning experiences carry credit.

Academic Facilities

Among the nineteen modern academic buildings on campus, the newest is the Mathile Center for the Natural Sciences, which expands the science-learning environment. This 95,145-square-foot student-centered academic research and learning facility blends hands-on teaching excellence with advanced technology in a functional modern environment.

The College of Business Administration's Dicke Hall offers students a modern setting for high-tech classrooms, meeting rooms and a 150-seat lecture forum.

ONU's Heterick Memorial Library and the Taggart Law Library provide information resources and services to support course offerings and foster independent study.

The Freed Center for the Performing Arts houses Communications and Theatre Arts classrooms and features a 550-seat theater/concert hall, a 120-seat studio theater, and television and radio production facilities. WONB-FM is the commercial-free voice of ONU.

Costs

A result of the Ohio Northern Promise—a 20–25 percent tuition reset—tuition charges for the 2015–16 year are $27,500 for the colleges of Arts & Sciences and Business Administration; $31,500 for the College of Engineering; and $32,500 for the College of Pharmacy. These totals do not include room, board, or fees.

Financial Aid

Even with one of the highest returns on investment in the nation, ONU invests more than $45 million toward merit-based scholarships and need-based resources. To be considered, the student should submit the FAFSA to the University along with the admission application.

Faculty

More than 210 full-time faculty members bring extensive academic, work, travel, and life experience to their classrooms. Ohio Northern values excellence, innovation, technology, diversity, and its people. With a 12:1 student-faculty ratio, students get lots of personal attention from professors who are passionate about teaching and mentoring.

Student Government

The Student Senate provides self-government in many areas of student life and seeks to further ideals of character and service to the University. The Student Senate serves as the official representative group of the student body to the University administration and agencies in matters pertaining to the student body.

Admission Requirements

High school students applying for admission to the University should present an official transcript indicating at least 16 total units of study, including work in specific academic areas as indicated by each college. Applicants are also required to submit scores on the ACT and/or SAT. For scholarship purposes, the traditional sections of the ACT and the SAT are considered. An on-campus interview is also recommended.

Application and Information

In the colleges of Arts & Sciences, Business Administration, and Engineering, a student's file is considered complete when it contains the application, official high school transcript, and ACT and/or SAT scores. The College of Pharmacy requires a personal statement and a recommendation in addition to the previous items.

The College of Pharmacy's application deadline is December 1 for entering freshmen. A campus visit is strongly encouraged for consideration for admittance into this college.

Requests for catalogs or additional information should be directed to:

Office of Admissions
Ohio Northern University
525 South Main Street
Ada, Ohio 45810
Phone: 888-408-4668 (toll-free)
Fax: 419-772-2821
E-mail: admissions-ug@onu.edu
Website: www.onu.edu
www.facebook.com/ohionorthern
www.twitter.com/ohionorthern

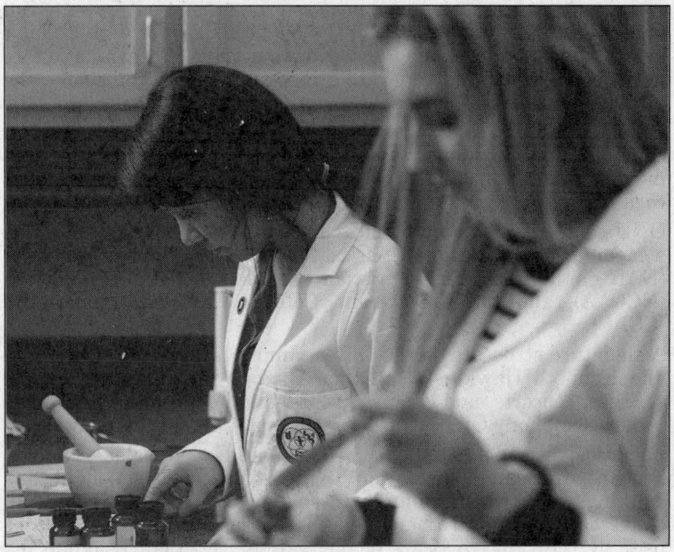

An Ohio Northern University education is based on experiential, hands-on learning, and students are guided by professors who know them personally and care about their lifelong success.

COLLEGE CLOSE-UPS

OLIVET NAZARENE UNIVERSITY

BOURBONNAIS, ILLINOIS

★ To read more about this school, visit http://petersons.to/olivetnazareneuniversity

The University

Olivet Nazarene University (ONU) is a private, Christian liberal arts university with a strong emphasis on academic excellence and Christ-centered living. Olivet's 250-acre Bourbonnais campus offers world-class facilities for learning, personal development, entertainment, and all aspects of student life. The atmosphere promotes academic rigor, fun, relationship building, career preparation, and spiritual growth.

The student body of 4,900—including 2,900 undergraduates—represents more than 40 denominations, most U.S. states, and more than 20 countries. Olivet operates on a two-semester schedule from August to May, and two summer sessions are available.

Faculty, staff, and administration are dedicated to teaching, encouraging, and mentoring each student as a whole person—academically, socially, and spiritually. Olivet's high retention, graduation, and employment/placement rates demonstrate the University's commitment to student success.

In addition to traditional undergraduate programs, Olivet offers more than 20 master's degree programs, a Doctor of Education in ethical leadership, and degree-completion continuing studies programs through the School of Graduate and Continuing Studies (SGCS). Programs are designed to facilitate a seamless transition from undergraduate to master's programs. As it strives to meet the needs of adults returning to school, the SGCS also helps working adults complete degree requirements without interrupting their employment. Courses and programs also provide resources to help enhance students' personal and professional lives.

The SGCS offers courses on the main campus in Bourbonnais and throughout the Chicago area, Indianapolis, Northeast Indiana, and Michigan. Students benefit from robust online programming, as well as courses offered in more than 150 churches, schools, hospitals, and other locations convenient to their homes or workplaces.

Another expression of ONU's commitment to preparing students for their future is the University's leadership in founding the Catalyst Innovation Center, a cooperative educational, business, and research venture to provide comprehensive services and programs to support academic programs, business growth, and entrepreneurial opportunities. The University is the lead collaborator with a major health care employer and a regional economic organization to develop programs and renovate a historic building to become the physical home of the center.

Outside the classroom, Olivet students participate in more than 80 clubs and organizations, including 30 intramural sports, the 200-member marching band, two orchestras, 28 musical ensembles, theater groups, clubs, and ministries.

ONU competes in 21 intercollegiate men's and women's sports as a member of the National Association of Intercollegiate Athletics (NAIA), the National Christian College Athletic Association (NCCAA), and the Chicagoland Collegiate Athletic Conference (CCAC).

A signature structure on the Olivet campus is the 3,046-seat Betty and Kenneth Hawkins Centennial Chapel, the venue for chapel services, concerts, and campus events, and home to the Kankakee Valley Symphony Orchestra.

Facilities also include the 168,000-square-foot Douglas E. Perry Student Life and Recreation Center, featuring an eight-lane running track, two swimming pools, a four-story rock climbing wall, basketball courts, and other amenities that include workout facilities used by the Chicago Bears of the National Football League. The ONU campus is home to the Chicago Bears' summer training camp, which annually draws national and local media coverage as well as thousands of fans to Olivet's campus.

The University is also home to Shine.FM, a top-rated contemporary 'hristian U.S. radio network. Olivet-owned Shine.FM broadcasts in Chicago area, Indianapolis, Northwest Indiana, and Lansing, igan. Olivet students studying broadcast journalism and radio broadcasting work alongside seasoned professionals in operating the station.

Location

Olivet's main campus is located just 50 miles south of Chicago's Loop, in the historic village of Bourbonnais, Illinois. The area offers shopping, restaurants, entertainment, and outdoor recreation through the Kankakee River State Park system.

Students benefit from ONU's proximity to Chicago's cultural, sports, and entertainment attractions. Plentiful professional internships and employment opportunities are additional advantages.

Other ONU locations include Rolling Meadows and Oak Brook, Illinois; Indianapolis, Indiana; Grand Rapids and Grand Ledge, Michigan; and Hong Kong.

Majors and Degrees

Olivet confers Bachelor of Arts (B.A.) and/or Bachelor of Science (B.S.) degrees in more than 120 areas of study (majors, minors, and concentrations), including accounting, actuarial science, art, art education, athletic coaching, athletic training, biblical languages, biblical studies, biochemistry, biology, broadcast journalism, business administration, business administration–not-for-profit management, business information systems, chemistry, child development, children's ministry, Christian education, coaching, commercial graphics/marketing, communication studies, computer science, corporate communication, criminal justice, dietetics, digital media: graphics, digital media: photography, drawing and illustration, early childhood education, earth and space science teaching, economics and finance, elementary education, engineering (electrical, mechanical, computer, geological), English, English as a second language, English education, environmental science, exercise science, family and consumer sciences, family and consumer sciences education, family studies, fashion merchandising, film studies, finance, forensic chemistry, French, general studies, geography, geological sciences, geology, Greek, health education, Hebrew, history, history teaching, hospitality, information systems, information technology, interior design, intercultural studies, international business, international marketing, journalism, leadership studies, legal studies, literature, management, marketing, marketing management, mass communication, mathematics, mathematics education, media production, military affairs, military science, ministerial missions, missions and intercultural studies, multimedia studies, music, music composition, music education, music ministry, music performance, musical theatre, nursing, painting, pastoral ministry, philosophy and religion, physical education and health teaching, physical science, political science, pre–art therapy, pre-dental, pre-law, pre-medicine, pre-optometry, pre-pharmacy, pre–physical therapy, pre–physician's assistant studies, pre-seminary, pre–veterinary science, print and online journalism, psychology, public policy, public relations, radio broadcasting, recreation, sports and fitness, religion, religious studies, science education, secondary education, social science, social science education, social work, sociology, Spanish, Spanish education, special education, sport management, television video production, theatre, writing, youth ministry, and zoology.

Academic Programs

Olivet is dedicated to "An Education with a Christian Purpose." This commitment to Christ-centered learning mandates nothing less than the highest-quality academic programs. Olivet's liberal arts curriculum requires that students complete 45 to 58 hours of general-education courses. With the addition of major and minor programs of study, students must complete a minimum of 128 credit hours to earn a bachelor's degree. Credit may be earned through advanced placement (AP) and College Level Examination Program (CLEP) tests. Students may also participate in the on-campus U.S. Military Reserve Officers' Training Corps (ROTC).

In 2013, Olivet engineering students who took the Fundamentals of Engineering exam administered by the National Council of Examiners for Engineering and Surveying registered a 90 percent first-time pass rate, compared to the national-average of 76 percent.

Students completing Olivet's nursing program have a 90 percent pass rate for the National Council Licensure Exam (NCLEX-RN) measuring preparedness to enter the field.

In fine arts, Olivet's School of Music earned the Apple Distinguished Program designation for 2014 through 2016 for its iLearn@Olivet initiative, which provides an iPad to every member of the Tiger marching band and all music majors, as well as faculty and staff members.

Off-Campus Programs

Each sester, ONU offers off-campus study programs, including the Council for Christian Colleges and Universities BestSemester programs, such as American Studies Program in Washington, D.C., Australia Studies Centre, China Studies Program, Contemporary Music Center, India Studies Program, Latin American Studies Program, Los Angeles Film Studies Center, Middle East Studies Program, Oxford Summer Programme, Scholar's Semester in Oxford, and Uganda Studies Program.

Other study programs include AuSable Institute, International Business Institute, ISA Spain (Barcelona), Nazarene International Language Institute, Oxford Summer Program, Quetzal Education Research Center (QERC), Environmental Studies (Costa Rica), and Tokyo Christian University. Costs are usually comparable to a semester at Olivet, and students earn academic credit for these programs. Some financial aid is available.

Numerous educational and mission-oriented, short-term trips are available to ONU students during the Christmas, spring, and summer breaks. More than 250 Olivet students participate in mission trips each year.

Academic Facilities

ONU continues to expand and refine its main campus facilities to anticipate the needs of the University's steadily increasing student population.

In 2014, to accommodate the growing engineering program, the University completed an expansion and renovation of Reed Hall of Science. The building has a new three-story wing dedicated to studying technology and innovation, and two former lecture halls are new, state-of-the-art engineering design labs. As of 2015, plans call for another Reed expansion—for the natural sciences program—as well as expansion and renovation of Larsen Fine Arts Center and Wisner Hall of Nursing and Health Sciences.

State-of-the-art academic facilities include Benner Library and Resource Center, information hub for digital and print research and communication; and Strickler Planetarium, renovated in 2008 with the same technology in Chicago's Adler Planetarium and one of the Midwest's few all-digital planetariums.

Costs

The cost of an Olivet education continues to be competitive for private colleges nationwide. A full year's tuition for 2015–16 is $31,950, based on 12 to 18 credit hours. Room and board are estimated at $7,900 for the year, based on double occupancy and a meal plan. Additional fees are $840 for the year. Olivet offers two interest-free payment plans: a 10-month plan for the year or four payments per semester.

Financial Aid

For the 2014–15 academic year, Olivet awarded $101.9 million in financial aid. Each year, approximately 99 percent of ONU's traditional undergraduates receive a collective total of $38.7 million in federal and state grants and institutional scholarships. The University participates in all federal and state financial aid programs. To apply for aid, students must fill out the Free Application for Federal Student Aid (FAFSA). Priority deadline for FAFSA filing is February 15. The University creates a financial aid package once a student is an accepted ONU applicant.

Faculty

For more than 120 full-time ONU faculty members, teaching is a ministry. These dedicated Christian leaders are the key to excellent education inside and outside the classroom. Olivet's 17:1 student-faculty ratio gives faculty the opportunity to teach, mentor, and encourage students with personal attention. Faculty members are deeply committed and involved in campus life, whether sponsoring social organizations and clubs, participating in talent shows, tutoring in their offices, or talking with students over lunch in the dining room. Faculty as well as ONU staff members also work side-by-side with students in local and regional ministry projects. Beyond spiritual modeling, course instruction, and service roles, faculty members maintain an agenda for professional growth through staying current in their respective fields of study, professional leadership, and published scholarship projects.

Student Government

The Associated Student Council (ASC) is the ONU student government organization on campus. The executive council consists of a president, vice president of finance, vice president of spiritual life, vice president of social affairs, vice president of publicity, vice president of women's residential life, vice president of men's residential life, and vice president of office management, as well as the editors of *The GlimmerGlass* newspaper and *Aurora* yearbook. These students work alongside the University's administrative team to ensure the welfare and promotion of campus activities and organizations.

Admission Requirements

Admission to Olivet is moderately difficult. Students are considered for admission on the basis of high school GPA and ACT or SAT scores. An ACT score is required for placement in courses. For international students, TOEFL results are also considered. Students with low test scores and GPA may be admitted on a provisional basis. A campus visit and interview are strongly recommended for all prospective students.

Application and Information

Applications are processed on a rolling basis. Application deadline is May 1. For some scholarships, an early decision is required. Students may apply through Olivet's website or by mail. The process includes the written or electronic application, high school transcripts, ACT or SAT scores, and a health form. An enrollment deposit is collected to prioritize student housing and class registration.

For more information or to arrange a campus visit, contact:

Office of Admissions
Olivet Nazarene University
One University Avenue
Bourbonnais, Illinois 60914
Phone: 800-648-1463 (toll-free)
E-mail: admissions@olivet.edu
Website: http://www.olivet.edu
http://www.facebook.com/olivetnazareneuniversity
http://twitter.com/OlivetNazareneU
http://www.youtube.com/olivetnazareneu
http://www.flickr.com/photos/olivet/collections
http://instagram.com/olivetnazarene
http://vimeo.com/olivetnazarene

Now in its 108th year, Olivet Nazarene University sits on a park-like campus just 50 miles south of Chicago's loop, boasting a combination of beautiful historic buildings and modern architecture.

COLLEGE CLOSE-UPS

PACE UNIVERSITY

NEW YORK CITY AND WESTCHESTER, NEW YORK

★ To read more about this school, visit http://petersons.to/paceuniversity

The University

Founded in 1906, Pace University is a leading private metropolitan university that offers an exceptional liberal arts education combined with superior professional preparation, two strategic undergraduate New York locations, and robust scholarships and financial aid. The diverse student population of 8,289 undergraduates (5,289 in New York City and 3,000 in Westchester) is enrolled in more than 3,000 courses across 100-plus majors and combined, accelerated bachelor's and graduate degree programs. These are offered through five undergraduate schools and colleges: the Lubin School of Business, the Dyson College of Arts and Sciences, the Seidenberg School of Computer Science and Information Systems, the School of Education, and the College of Health Professions. Pace facilitates more than 4,000 internships, co-op experiences, practicums, field experiences, and clinical assignments every year.

Many student-led clubs and organizations are active on the campus, including the Pace Advertising Club, African Students Association, the Pace Association for Collegiate Entrepreneurs, the Student Government Association, and the Collegiate Psychology Club. Pace also offers many campus activities, including student government associations, fraternities, sororities, two campus newspapers, two literary magazines, two yearbooks, and two campus broadcasting systems. Athletic facilities are available for students, and intercollegiate sports include baseball, basketball, cross-country, cheerleading, dance, women's field hockey, football, lacrosse, women's soccer, women's softball, swimming and diving, and women's volleyball.

The student body is diverse, representing forty-eight states, five U.S. territories, and more than 100 countries.

Location

Pace University is a multicampus institution with campuses in both New York City and Westchester, New York. Both locations are within reach of cultural, business, and social resources and opportunities. The New York City campus is located in the heart of the Financial District in lower Manhattan, and within a short walking distance of Wall Street and the South Street Seaport. Lincoln Center, Broadway theaters, museums, and many world-famous attractions are minutes away by public transportation. Located 35 miles north of New York City, the Westchester campus offers a traditional college experience: state-of-the-art science and video production labs, competitive athletics, fraternities and sororities, and access to internship opportunities at many Fortune 500 companies.

Students can take courses at either campus, and housing is available in both New York City and Westchester. Residence halls are equipped with complimentary cable TV, telephone, and high-speed Internet access.

Majors and Degrees

The following programs are offered at both the New York City and Westchester campuses. The Bachelor of Business Administration (B.B.A.) is offered with majors in accounting–general, accounting–public, finance, general business, information systems, international management, management (with concentrations in business, entrepreneurship, health care, and human resources), and marketing (with concentrations in advertising and integrated marketing communications, global marketing management, and sports marketing). In addition, a five-year combined B.B.A./M.B.A in public accounting is available for qualified students. The Bachelor of Arts (B.A.) degree is granted in adolescent education (with concentrations in biology, chemistry, earth science, English, history/social studies, mathematics, and Spanish), American studies, applied psychology and human relations, biology, computer science, economics, environmental studies, film and screen studies, health science, history, information systems, liberal studies, mathematics, philosophy and religious studies, political science, and psychology. The Bachelor of Science (B.S.) degree is offered in biochemistry, biology, business economics, chemistry, computer science, criminal justice, environmental science, information systems, information systems, information technology, mathematics, professional computer studies, and professional studies.

Certain programs are available only on one campus. The B.S. programs in biology–pre-professional (occupational therapy, optometry, and podiatry) and forensic science; the B.B.A. programs in arts and entertainment management, hospitality and tourism management, and quantitative business analysis; the B.F.A. programs in acting, art, commercial dance, musical theater, and production and design for stage and screen; and the B.A. programs in acting; art; art history; communication science and disorders; communication studies; directing; English language and literature; language, culture, and world trade; global Asia studies; global professional studies; Latin American studies; modern languages and culture; sociology-anthropology; Spanish; stage management; teaching students with speech and language disabilities; theater arts (acting and design/technical); and women's and gender studies are offered only at the New York City campus. The B.A. programs in biological psychology, childhood education, communication arts and journalism, communications, digital/journalism, digital cinema and filmmaking, English, English and communications, education, and personality and social psychology, and the B.S. programs in nursing and physics are available at the Westchester campus only.

Pace University offers a five-year engineering programs in cooperation with Manhattan College and Rensselaer Polytechnic Institute. Students attend Pace for three years and either Manhattan College or Rensselaer for two years. Upon successful completion, students receive a B.S. degree in chemistry from Pace and either a Bachelor of Chemical Engineering (B.C.E.) in chemical engineering from Manhattan or a B.S. degree in engineering from Rensselaer.

Academic Programs

At Pace University, an innovative core curriculum allows students to develop critical thinking and communication skills by studying subject areas that are integrated around a theme. Students can choose from civic engagement and public values, critical writing, world traditions and cultures, and public speaking. Students also participate in community-based learning where they are given opportunities to practice their skills in real-life settings. Selective academic programs in the University are preparatory for professional training in dentistry, law, medicine, and veterinary science.

The Pforzheimer Honors College is a highly esteemed opportunity at Pace—a community of talented undergraduate scholars studying under the distinguished faculty of the University's five undergraduate schools and colleges. It is a place to excel and realize potential.

Pace University's internship program is nationally recognized and offers qualified students the opportunity to gain experience in their field of study while earning a four-year degree. Students can choose full-time, part-time, or summer positions working in an area directly related to their major course of study. Over 4,000 Pace students participate each year in internships, faculty-sponsored research, consulting projects, fieldwork, and practicums—Pace's Career Services team is one of the largest in the New York Metropolitan area.

Academic Facilities

The Pace University Library is a comprehensive teaching library and student learning center, a virtual library that combines strong core collections with ubiquitous access to global Internet resources to support broad and diversified curricula. Reciprocal borrowing and access accords, traditional interlibrary loan services, and commercial document delivery options supplement the aggregate library. Pace offers Instructional Services librarians, a state-of-the-art electronic classroom, digital reference services, and multimedia applications. Pace's computer resource centers are linked to high-speed data networks and feature sophisticated hardware and software to facilitate active learning. Pace supports high-speed Internet and Internet2 access on every campus—residence facilities are wired, and most public areas are enabled for wireless connectivity. Full-motion videoconference facilities enable remote delivery of instruction between campus sites for synchronous learning applications.

Costs

For the 2015–16 academic year, undergraduate tuition is $39,728 per year for full-time study. The cost for an on-campus double-occupancy room and board is $15,010–$17,938, with different housing options available.

Financial Aid

Pace University strives to provide opportunities to students of diverse backgrounds and varied circumstances and is committed to offering financial aid to students to the fullest extent of its resources. University-sponsored scholarships are awarded to students on the basis of academic merit, service to the community, and financial need. The goal is to offer every student as much financial assistance as possible, based upon availability and need. Last year, Pace students received more than $310 million in aid. Pace's comprehensive student financial aid assistance program includes scholarships, grants, on-campus employment, student loans (federal and alternative plans), and tuition payment plans. Pace participates in all federal financial aid programs and the New York State Tuition Assistance Program (TAP) and honors awards from other states' incentive grant programs.

Students should submit the Free Application for Federal Student Aid (FAFSA) by February 15 for priority consideration for the fall semester. Pace University's new Net Price Calculator (www.pace.edu/calculator) is an online tool designed to help students and their families estimate their financial aid package. Many find that Pace is actually more affordable than similar public and private colleges due to the scholarship and financial aid awards offered to families.

Faculty

First and foremost, Pace University professors are dedicated teachers. All Pace classes are taught by professors. Students will never take a course taught by a teaching assistant. Faculty members also bring real-world experience and scholarship into the classroom through their work with outside companies and organizations and by leading cutting-edge research projects. Faculty members come from the best graduate and doctoral programs in the country. Professors—86 percent of whom hold Ph.D.'s—have earned degrees from the University of Pennsylvania, Harvard, Brown, Columbia, and Yale. Pace professors work closely with students to not only broaden their academic horizons, but to show how their work in the classroom is applicable to their future careers.

Admission Requirements

A minimum of 16 academic units from an accredited secondary school, or equivalent, are required. Academic subjects in high school should be distributed as follows: 4 years of English, 3–4 years of college-preparatory mathematics, 2 years of foreign language, 3–4 years of history/social science, 2 years of laboratory science, and 2–3 units of academic electives. All domestic applicants are required to take either the SAT or ACT examination and have results forwarded to the University. International students are required to take the TOEFL, IELTS, or PTE.

Application and Information

The freshman application deadline is February 15. Transfer applications are reviewed on a rolling basis. Requests for application forms and information for both the New York City and Westchester campuses should be addressed to:

Application Processing Center
Pace University
861 Bedford Road
Pleasantville, New York 10570-2799
Phone: 800-874-7223 (toll-free)
E-mail: infoctr@pace.edu
Website: http://www.pace.edu

PACIFIC UNIVERSITY

FOREST GROVE, OREGON

★ To read more about this school, visit http://petersons.to/pacificuniversity

The University

Pacific University is a private, fully accredited university with more than sixty undergraduate fields of study and sixteen graduate and professional programs. With colleges in the Arts and Sciences, Optometry, Education, Health Professions and Business, the University's four Oregon campuses draw more than 3,500 students.

Students come from around the United States and abroad for a wide variety of programs, but they share a common Pacific University experience: small classes, a nurturing environment, and personal attention. Students learn from the university's full-time faculty members, who are devoted to teaching and to forming close mentoring relationships with their students. Recent graduates at both the undergraduate and graduate level say that access to the high-quality faculty is a hallmark of the University.

As the first chartered university west of the Mississippi, Pacific University has a long history of excellence. At every level, its curriculum emphasizes real-world experience, service learning, and preparation to contribute to a global community.

The Forest Grove Campus is Pacific University's residential campus, where most undergraduate students study.

The campus is home to six residence halls and a student apartment complex; the newest residence hall opened in fall 2014. Many of the newer buildings feature double-occupancy rooms or suites, as well as shared study spaces, kitchens, and game rooms. The residential nature of the campus creates a vibrant living environment, where students develop close, lifelong friendships.

There are more than sixty student interest groups at Pacific University, including student media, academic societies, religious and political organizations, and service clubs. One of the largest student organizations, Nā Haumāna O Hawai'i, unites Pacific's significant population of students from Hawai'i and presents an authentic lu'au each year. Pacific University also is home to an active Greek system.

Pacific University also is a member of the NCAA Division III Northwest Conference. The campus athletic center houses a gymnasium, fitness center, state-of-the-art indoor field house featuring FieldTurf, handball/racquetball courts, wrestling room, and a sports medicine training facility. The Lincoln Park Athletic Complex, a partnership with the City of Forest Grove, features a 1,100-seat stadium with a nine-lane, 400-meter track, a FieldTurf soccer/football/lacrosse field, a Bond baseball field, and a varsity softball field.

Almost a third of undergraduate students participate in varsity athletics. Men's sports include baseball, basketball, cross-country, football, golf, soccer, swimming, tennis, track and field, and wrestling. Women compete in basketball, cross-country, golf, lacrosse, rowing, soccer, softball, swimming, tennis, track and field, volleyball, and wrestling.

Informal sports also are a highlight of the Pacific University student experience. Students compete in intramural sports, and they also enjoy outdoor recreation opportunities through the Pacific Outback, which offers training, equipment, and organized trips for snowboarding and skiing, rock climbing, camping, kayaking, and much more. Students also can rent bicycles for a semester or for the year from the Outback to get around the bike-friendly Forest Grove area.

Locations

Pacific University was founded in Forest Grove, Oregon, in 1849. The historic college town, population 22,000, is now home to the 55-acre oak-covered campus on the west side of the Portland Metro Area. About 25 miles from downtown Portland and an hour from the beach or Mount Hood, Forest Grove is the perfect home base for exploring the best of Oregon's urban and outdoor adventures.

Pacific University also offers health professions and graduate business courses on its growing campus in Hillsboro, Oregon, the fifth-largest city in the state. Located on the regional light-rail line in the Hillsboro Health and Education District, the Hillsboro Campus connects students with world-class learning opportunities and real-world experience as they connect with local businesses, hospitals, and nonprofit organizations.

Undergraduate and graduate teaching programs are offered at Pacific University's campus in Eugene, as well as a new Master of Social Work program.

Pacific University's newest campus is in Woodburn, one of the most diverse and fastest-growing communities in Oregon. The College of Education has a science, technology, engineering, and math teaching program embedded in the local school district and also offers a degree track in elementary education and English language learning at the Woodburn Campus.

Majors and Degrees

Pacific University is known for its excellent liberal arts foundation, as well as the superior preparation its students receive to go on to careers and advanced study. In particular, the University is heralded for its graduate programs in health professions, as well as its undergraduate preparation for healthcare fields and medical school.

Pacific emphasizes the education benefits of research projects, internships, study-abroad experiences, and service learning. Most freshmen participate in a semester-long first-year seminar program designed to introduce students to college-level writing and research expectations. The core curriculum emphasizes writing, reasoning, and communication skills, as well as global perspectives and service. Pacific University also requires most students to complete a senior capstone, a year-long research project designed and implemented by students and culminating in a presentation to the University community.

Most undergraduate programs operate on a two-semester calendar with an optional January term and limited summer courses. Most graduate and professional programs have year-round calendars.

The Pacific University College of Arts and Sciences offers most undergraduate majors, including programs in anthropology/sociology, applied science, art, bioinformatics, biology, chemistry, computer science, criminal justice, dance, economics, English, environmental science, exercise science, history, international studies, mathematics, media arts, modern languages, music, philosophy, physics, politics and government, psychology, public health, social work, and theatre. The College of Arts and Sciences also offers a nationally recognized, low-residency Master of Fine Arts in writing program, and a new Master of Social Work program.

The College of Business offers undergraduate tracks in accounting, finance, international business, marketing, and business administration. Master's programs in finance and in business administration opened in 2014.

The College of Health Professions provides an undergraduate program in dental health science, as well as graduate programs in athletic training, audiology, healthcare administration, occupational therapy, pharmacy, physical therapy, physician assistant studies, and professional psychology. Also available are graduate-level certificate programs in gerontology and healthcare compliance, as well as a new bachelor's degree program in health science.

The College of Education offers an undergraduate major in education and learning, as well as a Bachelor of Education in elementary education and English language learning. Graduate programs in the College of Education include a fifth-year Master of Arts in Teaching, a Master of Arts in teaching special education, a Master of Education, and several endorsement options. Also available is a master's degree in speech-language pathology, as well as an undergraduate minor in communication sciences and disorders that prepares students for the speech-language pathology program.

The College of Optometry offers a Doctor of Optometry program, as well as a master's degree in vision science.

Costs

Tuition and fees for the 2015–16 school year are $39,858 for undergraduates in the College of Arts and Sciences. Room and board are $11,448 for a double room and a University meal plan. Pacific University was named a Best Value School by *U.S. News & World Report*.

Financial Aid

Financial assistance at Pacific is awarded on the basis of demonstrated need, academic merit, and talent. The Free Application for Federal Student Aid (FAFSA) is used in evaluating need. Prospective students are encouraged to apply for financial assistance by submitting the FAFSA to the federal processor as soon after January 1 as possible. Pacific provides financial assistance through grants, scholarships, loans, and part-time employment. For more information prospective students can e-mail financialaid@pacificu.edu.

Faculty

Pacific's outstanding faculty members provide the foundation for the University's academic program. A student-faculty ratio of 10:1 and an average class size of 19 students in undergraduate courses allows for personal attention from the professors. Pacific University does not use graduate or teaching assistants; all faculty members teach their own courses.

Admission Requirements

Pacific University is selective in considering new students. Primary consideration is given to a candidate's academic preparation and potential for successful study at the college level, as assessed by evaluating the student's transcripts of college-preparatory work, counselor and teacher recommendations, personal essay, SAT and/or ACT scores, and other student-submitted information. Transfer students must submit high school records and test scores if they have completed less than 30 semester hours, plus official transcripts from any institution previously attended.

Application and Information

Students may apply early and may be notified early through the modified rolling admissions plan. Pacific University is an exclusive member of the Common Application. The regular priority deadline for admission is February 1. For additional information, interested students should contact:

Office of Admissions
Pacific University
2043 College Way
Forest Grove, Oregon 97116
Phone: 503-352-2218
800-677-6712 (toll-free)
E-mail: admissions@pacificu.edu
Website: http://www.pacificu.edu
http://www.facebook.com/pacificu

Pacific University is home to the unique and legendary Boxer mascot. Based on an ancient Chinese statue, Boxer is a mythical creature that resembles both a dog and a dragon. The original statue has been missing for decades, but the spirit of Boxer—representing pride, honor, and cultural diversity—is very much alive at Pacific University.

PEPPERDINE UNIVERSITY
Seaver College
MALIBU, CALIFORNIA

PEPPERDINE

COLLEGE CLOSE-UPS

The University and The College

Pepperdine University is a private, faith-based university committed to the highest standards of academic excellence and Christian values, where students are strengthened for lives of purpose, service, and leadership.

Seaver College, Pepperdine's undergraduate liberal arts college, is comprised of approximately 3,200 students, 57 percent of which come from California. Thirty-three percent hail from the other forty-nine states, and 10 percent are international. The 2014–15 freshmen class had an average high school GPA of 3.61. It's this diversity of backgrounds and worldviews that helps contribute to Pepperdine's unique educational experience.

Nestled between the Santa Monica Mountains and the Pacific Ocean, Pepperdine's Malibu campus provides fantastic on-campus housing options for all students. Students are required to live on campus during their first and second years, and also have premium residence halls available as upperclassmen.

Students have a wide range of extracurricular activities and organizations to choose from, including social, honor, service, spiritual, professional, divisional, and special interest clubs. Pepperdine provides students with interests in communications and media the chance to be involved with the campus radio station, weekly student newspaper and television broadcast.

Pepperdine has 17 Division One men's and women's athletic programs that have won an impressive 13 national team championships and 10 individual national championships. As a member of the West Coast Conference, the University houses a 3,500-seat gymnasium, an Olympic-size swimming pool, a tennis pavilion and sixteen additional tennis courts, an intramural field, and a 2,000-seat baseball stadium.

Pepperdine's graduate schools include The School of Law, School of Public Policy, School of Education and Psychology, and the George L. Graziado School of Business and Management. These distinguished programs offer master's degrees in law, dispute resolution, public policy, business, and more.

Location

Overlooking the Pacific Ocean in scenic Malibu, California, and less than an hour from downtown Los Angeles, Seaver's Malibu campus offers both the benefits of a small coastal community and the advantages of proximity to a major metropolitan area.

Malibu is a pristine beach community with excellent restaurants, a movie theater, and shopping centers complete with banking facilities and industry-leading brands. The winding seashore and rugged beauty of Malibu connects students to a litany of nightlife options in Santa Monica, Hollywood, and Los Angeles. Malibu's clean air provides an environment conducive to study, while the moderate climate permits year-round outdoor recreation. In addition to making use of the physical education facilities on campus, students can enjoy swimming, surfing, horseback riding, fishing, hiking, boating, kayaking, and other activities in the vicinity. As an international epicenter of culture, industry, and trade, Los Angeles provides students with a one-of-a-kind living experience.

Majors and Degrees

Students can choose from forty-four majors and thirty-seven minors. Seaver College awards the Bachelor of Arts in advertising, art, art history, biology, chemistry, communication, creative writing, economics, English, film studies, French, German, Hispanic studies, history, integrated marketing communication, international studies, Italian, journalism, liberal arts, math education, media production, music, natural science, philosophy, political science, psychology, public relations, religion, sociology, Spanish, sport administration, sports medicine, theater and music, theater and television, and theater arts.

The Bachelor of Science is awarded in accounting, biology, business administration, chemistry, computer science and mathematics, international business, mathematics, nutritional science, physics, and sports medicine. A teacher education program offers credentials in single or multiple subjects.

Academic Programs

The academic programs at Seaver College provide students with a liberal arts education in a Christian atmosphere that sharpens critical thinking, improves information literacy, and builds a learning community. Students must complete 128 units for the B.A. or B.S. degree, including 64 units in general education requirements and 40 or more in upper-division studies.

Major requirements may be fulfilled through three basic arrangements. Students who specialize in a discipline must complete at least 24 units of upper-division work in their chosen discipline. Students may choose an interdisciplinary major, entailing at least 40 units of upper-division work, with courses ranging broadly across disciplinary lines within a division and on occasion crossing divisional lines, in one of the following fields of study: communication, English, humanities, international studies, liberal arts, or religion. Alternatively, students may initiate a contract major by presenting an application for specific upper-division courses to the Dean of Seaver College.

Seaver College functions on a semester plan; the regular academic year consists of two semesters from late August to April. In addition to the regular academic year, summer sessions run from late April to early August.

At Seaver, instruction and study are adapted both to students' abilities and to the nature of the course content, instead of utilizing only the traditional lecture method. Programs involve several types of learning experiences: seminars, integrated lectures, individual study, fieldwork, and laboratories. Students are never taught by a teacher's assistant at Pepperdine; the average class size is 19 students and a student-to-faculty ratio of 13:1 fosters an environment where professors are invested in the growth and success of their students.

The Dean's List of undergraduate students is published each semester, comprised of the top 10 percent of the class with a grade point index no lower than 3.5. Other honors include cum laude for students graduating with a scholastic level of at least 3.5, magna cum laude for 3.7, and summa cum laude for 3.9.

Off-Campus Programs

At Seaver, students have the opportunity to study abroad in Buenos Aires, Argentina; Florence, Italy; Heidelberg, Germany; Lausanne, Switzerland; London, England; and Shanghai, China. The academic programs emphasize European, Latin American, or Asian history and culture. Seaver also offers summer special interest programs in Fiji, Scotland, and East Africa. Classes are taught by Seaver faculty members. Serious study and the daily experiences of living in another country give students a special depth of understanding of other cultures and a broader world perspective.

The Buenos Aires program accommodates approximately 60 students who live in the homes of carefully selected host families.

The Florence program houses approximately 55 students who live in a Florentine villa and residential complex with classrooms, a library, a computer facility, and recreational facilities. The Heidelberg program has space for approximately 50 students at the Moore Haus, located near the city's famous castle. Classes are held in modern facilities in downtown Heidelberg. The Lausanne program accommodates about 70 students. The Pepperdine facility is located in La Croisée near the center of Lausanne, which has a picturesque view of Lake Geneva and the French Alps. The London program has space for approximately 40 students in the Knightsbridge area. In addition to living quarters, the facility includes classrooms, a library, a computer room, offices, and a student center. The Shanghai program accommodates approximately 40 students who live in the Pepperdine-owned jia, meaning "house," which is located in the French Concession area near the American Consulate. The majority of the international program facilities are University-owned.

Academic Facilities

The Malibu campus is home to academic complexes containing seminar and lecture rooms, art studios, communication facilities, science and computer laboratories, mini-theaters, a recital hall, and administrative offices. The Payson Library is the global gateway to knowledge and provides students access to thousands of online journals, articles, and periodicals through various databases. Payson Library serves as a sanctuary for study, learning, and research by encouraging discovery, contemplation, social discourse, and creative expression.

The 300-seat George Elkins Auditorium is used for public presentations and lectures. The Center for the Arts facility includes the renowned Frederick R. Weisman Museum of Art and the Smothers Theatre, which seats 450 people and is used for dance, music, and theater performances. The Center for Communication and Business building houses a state-of-the-art radio and television production center where students have the opportunity to work on Pepperdine's cable television and radio stations.

Costs

Costs for the 2014–15 academic year were $46,440 for tuition, $13,390 for room and board, and $252 for additional fees.

Financial Aid

Approximately 80 percent of Seaver's students receive some form of financial assistance through scholarships, loans, grants, work-study programs, or jobs within the University. To be eligible for financial assistance from institutional resources, an undergraduate student must be enrolled in at least 12 units. An applicant must be admitted to the University before being awarded assistance, but the financial assistance application may be submitted with an admission application. To ensure full consideration, the Pepperdine financial assistance application should be submitted by February 15 for the fall semester and October 15 for the spring semester. Students are also responsible for applying for the California State Scholarship (California residents only) and Federal Pell Grant by submitting the Free Application for Federal Student Aid (FAFSA) in addition to Pepperdine's one-page financial assistance form.

Faculty

Seaver College's faculty includes men and women of high academic distinction whose primary focus is instruction with a secondary focus on research. Fifty-four percent of faculty members are full-time, and 90 percent of full-time faculty members hold a doctorate or terminal degree in their field. Upon enrollment, each student is assigned an academic adviser from among the faculty members. A qualified counseling staff is also available to assist with personal, professional, and academic needs.

Student Government

The Student Government Association (SGA) is composed of student leaders dedicated to providing Pepperdine's students with quality representation through innovative advocacy programs. SGA serves as the voice of the students to the Seaver administration and works in coordination with the Student Activities Office in establishing activities and maintaining school policies. SGA coordinates over 150 on-campus events each year including movies, sightseeing trips, guest performances, dances, speakers, and more. Pepperdine has eight nationally recognized sororities and five fraternities and there are over sixty different student organizations on campus that focus on a range of interests, including academic, language, art, music, dance, drama, sports, and politics.

Admission Requirements

Applicants are admitted on the basis of their academic record, SAT or ACT scores, and personal information and references. Transfer applicants are high school graduates who have taken any transferable college units after graduating high school. Students who took colleges courses prior to graduating high school are not considered transfer students and should apply as a first-year student. To ensure full consideration for the fall semester, students should apply by the January 5 deadline. October 15 is the regular deadline for the spring semester. Decision letter dates are announced in the current application form.

Seaver College seeks to enroll a diverse student body. As such, Pepperdine University does not unlawfully discriminate on the basis of any status or condition protected by applicable federal or state law in the administration of its educational policies, admission, financial assistance, employment, educational programs, or activities.

Application and Information

To request information, students should contact:

Laura Kalinkewicz, Associate Dean of Enrollment Management,
Director of Admission
Seaver College
Pepperdine University
Malibu, California 90263-4392
Phone: 310-506-4392
Fax: 310-506-4861
Website: http://seaver.pepperdine.edu/admission
http://on.fb.me/Seaver_Admission (Facebook)
http://twitter.com/#!/SeaverAdmission (Twitter)
http://instagram.com/seaveradmission# (Instagram)
http://bit.ly/YouTube_Pepperdine (YouTube)
http://pinterest.com/seaveradmission/ (Pinterest)
http://seaveradmission.tumblr.com (Tumblr)

The 830-acre Malibu campus of Pepperdine University, Seaver College, overlooks the Pacific Ocean, 30 miles west of Los Angeles, California.

COLLEGE CLOSE-UPS

PILLAR COLLEGE

NEWARK AND SOMERSET, NEW JERSEY

PILLAR COLLEGE

The College

Pillar College educates, inspires, and equips students for excellent scholarship, service, and leadership. Rooted in and committed to Christian faith and love, Pillar College fosters intellectual, spiritual, and social development among its diverse student population at various instructional sites. Founded in 1908, Pillar College is New Jersey's only evangelical Christian college, and holds the highest accreditation available to any college or university. The College provides classes in Newark, Somerset, and other instructional sites in New Jersey.

Pillar College offers a unique blend of spiritual enrichment, academic excellence, and social fulfillment. The student body includes a broad spectrum of ages, races, interests, and personalities, reflecting the wide diversity of the metropolitan corridor of the Northeast. Through Godly instructors, rich curricula in career-shaping majors, spiritually enthusiastic students, valuable enriching internships, and global learning experiences, Pillar College offers students what they need to be equipped for their future.

Location

Pillar College is a non-residential college with instructional sites in Newark and Somerset County, New Jersey. Its Newark Campus occupies over 25,000 square feet of classroom, administrative, and conference/community space on the first, seventh and twentieth floors of the Military Park Building in the heart of downtown Newark. Both locations enjoy easy access to public transportation and major state and Interstate highways. Pillar College sites are a short drive from New York City, state parks, historical sites, hiking trails, professional and minor league sports, and New Jersey beaches.

Majors and Degrees

Pillar College offers three degree programs.

- The Bachelor of Arts (B.A.) in Biblical studies, with optional concentrations in worship, music, and media or youth leadership.
- The Bachelor of Arts in psychology and counseling, with optional concentrations in Christian counseling or marriage and family counseling.
- The Bachelor of Arts in business administration and management with optional concentrations in entrepreneurship, or organizational leadership.

Academic Programs

Committed to providing accredited college degrees for all qualified, motivated students, Pillar College has developed unique and flexible programs of study designed to meet the needs of diverse students in all stages of life. Besides traditional Fall and Spring semester classes, the College also offers courses in condensed nine-week modules in evenings and on Saturdays. Many adult students choose the College's Life Enhancing Accelerated Degree (LEAD) program. Students form small groups, attend class one night per week, and earn college credits for life experiences and competencies.

Pillar College's newest innovation is Programa BLEND (BiLingual Entry Degree) designed for Spanish-speaking students. BLEND enables students to take general education and other core classes taught in Spanish for two years while completing English as a Second Language (ESL). Students can then complete their bachelor's degree in Psychology and Counseling, Business Administration and Management, or Biblical studies in English.

Academic Facilities

The Newark Campus occupies two floors of the Military Park Building, 60 Park Place. Located one block south of the Performing Arts Center (PAC) and four blocks north of the Prudential Center, the Military Park Building is a prestigious high-rise building that hosts an interesting array of professional corporations. Both Pillar locations boast beautiful student lounges and state-of-the-art classroom and media center facilities. The Newark Campus features student service offices, a library, and the College's administrative offices.

Costs

Pillar College is committed to providing an excellent, cost-effective education for its students. Tuition and fee rates, payable each semester, are set annually according to economic conditions within the College and industry standards. Tuition and fees for full-time traditional students in the 2014–15 academic year were $8,988 per semester.

Financial Aid

Pillar College operates a full student financial aid program, including grants, scholarships, loans, and employment, allowing any student a realistic opportunity to finance their college education. More than 95 percent of all Pillar College students who apply for financial assistance to further their education receive it. The College is aware that each family has a unique financial situation and the financial aid staff is available to work with students to find the resources to fund their education.

Student Government

The Student Government seeks to fairly represent the interests and concerns of each member of the student body. Its purpose is to address student needs efficiently and effectively, uphold the code of conduct of the community, and to initiate positive activities and programs for the benefit of Pillar College students. The Student Government, working in close cooperation with the College's Vice President of Student Life, brings the students as a community into a closer and more vital relationship with the rest of the College community.

Admission Requirements

Pillar College admits all qualified students of any race, color, disability, national or ethnic origin to all the rights, privileges, programs, and activities available through the College. Pillar College does not discriminate on the basis of gender, race, color, disability, national or ethnic origin in administration of its educational policies, admission policies, financial aid, or other school-administered programs. In addition to enrolling, students enter into a covenant of respect for the Faith Statement and agree to adhere to the Ethos Statement. Prospective students and other persons interested in learning more about the College are cordially invited to arrange for a campus visit. Admissions requirements include an application, two recommendations, a personal statement, and official transcripts from all previous institutions. Pillar College, in compliance with the New Jersey Administrative Code (N.J.A.C. 8:57-6.5-6.9) and Health Department regulations, requires persons born January 1, 1957, or later to show proof of vaccinations for measles, mumps, rubella, and Hepatitis-B prior to arrival at school.

Application and Information

For an application form, catalog, and all forms required for admissions, students can contact:

Pillar College
60 Park Place, Suite 701
Newark, New Jersey 07102
Phone: 800-234-9305 (toll-free)
E-mail: info@pillar.edu
Website: http://www.pillar.edu

Pillar College offers students a unique blend of spiritual enrichment, academic excellence, and social fulfillment, which prepares students to become transformational leaders in communities, churches, and businesses.

PRATT INSTITUTE

BROOKLYN, NEW YORK

★ To read more about this school, visit http://petersons.to/prattinstitute

Pratt

COLLEGE CLOSE-UPS

The Institute

Industrialist and philanthropist Charles Pratt founded Pratt Institute in 1887 to educate students for various professions on a non-degree level. As the educational preparation necessary for various professions expanded, Pratt Institute moved to offer baccalaureate degrees with its first granted in 1938 and its first graduate degree granted in 1950. Now, with twenty-seven undergraduate majors and concentrations, Pratt offers students a wide variety of programs in which to major or take elective courses.

With all of its undergraduate ranked programs in art, design, and architecture ranked among the top ten in the country, Pratt has been ranked among the top design schools in the United States by *Business Week*. Pratt was also ranked number one in the country for its fine arts and studio programs by *USA Today*.

In addition to the four-year programs on its Brooklyn campus, Pratt offers students several additional locations to pursue their education: a two-year program in Utica, New York, at PrattMWP; and an associate degree program in fine art, graphic design, illustration, and digital design as well as a two- and four-year degree in construction management in Manhattan.

Although the characteristics and educational requirements of the professions for which Pratt prepares students have changed over the course of a century, the Institute has succeeded in pursuing its abiding purpose—to blend theoretical learning with professional and humanistic development—and has kept its curricula current by hiring practicing professionals to teach. Standards are high, modeled after the professional world. Faculty members connect students with internships and eventually jobs after graduation. Industry projects and internships provide students with real-world experience.

Pratt Institute offers four-year bachelor's, two-year associate, and master's degrees. Pratt's national and international reputation that attracts undergraduate and graduate students from forty-eight U.S. states and over eighty countries. Students who choose Pratt are committed to the study of art, design, architecture, or creative writing and to their career objectives.

A short subway or bus ride from the museums, galleries, and design centers of both Manhattan and Brooklyn, Pratt Institute's main campus in Brooklyn, New York features twenty-five buildings of differing architectural styles spread throughout a beautifully landscaped 25-acre campus. The campus was ranked by *Architectural Digest* as one of the top ten campuses nationwide with the best architecture. It includes a contemporary sculpture garden (ranked among the top ten campus art collections by *Public Art Review*), an athletic center, residence halls, dining halls, outstanding studio facilities, and historic buildings. Nineteen of the buildings house studios, classrooms, laboratories, administrative offices, auditoria, sports facilities, food services, and student centers. A new green LEED gold-certified building houses student administrative services including admissions, undergraduate and graduate digital arts programs, and various administrative offices, including student financial services and the registrar's offices. Six buildings are student residences, including the Stabile Hall freshman residence, which provides studio space on each floor. There are adequate parking facilities for residents and commuters. Student services include career planning and placement, health and counseling, and student development. More than sixty student organizations are available including fraternities and sororities, honorary societies, professional societies, and clubs.

Location

Pratt Institute, the country's premier college of art, design, writing, and architecture, has its main campus in the Clinton Hill section of Brooklyn, just minutes from downtown Manhattan. Ninety percent of Pratt's freshmen and over half of its undergraduates live on the tree-lined Brooklyn campus. Minutes from the Brooklyn Museum and the Brooklyn Academy of Music, Pratt is ideally located, providing students with a green oasis just minutes from the art capital of the world, Manhattan. The Manhattan campus is located in Chelsea. The Utica campus, home to two-year programs in fine art, communications design, photography, and art and design education (teacher certification), is located in upstate New York.

Majors and Degrees

Pratt Institute offers the Bachelor of Architecture, Bachelor of Fine Arts, Bachelor of Art, Bachelor of Industrial Design, Bachelor of Professional Studies, Bachelor of Science, Associate of Occupational Studies, and Associate of Applied Science degrees.

The Bachelor of Architecture degree program is a five-year, accredited program. For the Bachelor of Fine Arts degree, a candidate may choose to major in art and design education (teacher certification), art history, communications design (advertising art direction, graphic design, illustration), digital arts (traditional and digital animation, interactive arts), fashion design, film, fine arts (ceramics, drawing, jewelry, painting, printmaking, sculpture), interior design, photography, or writing. The Bachelor of Arts is offered in critical and visual studies and art history. The Bachelor of Industrial Design is offered for students interested in car, product, and furniture design. In the Bachelor of Professional Studies degree program, the major is in construction management. Students seeking the Bachelor of Science degree can major in construction management or professional services management.

The two-year Associate of Occupational Studies degree is offered in digital design and interactive media, graphic design, and illustration. The Associate of Applied Science is offered in painting/drawing and graphic design/illustration. The two-year Associate of Applied Science degree is transferable to a four-year program.

Students may also earn combined bachelor's/master's degrees. Programs include the B.F.A./M.S. in art and design education as well as art history.

Academic Programs

Educating artists and creative professionals to be responsible contributors to society has been the mission of Pratt Institute since it assembled its first group of students in 1887. Within the structure of that professional education, Pratt students are encouraged to acquire the diverse knowledge that is necessary for them to succeed in their chosen fields including sustainability. In addition to the professional studies, the curriculum in each of Pratt's schools includes a broad range of liberal arts courses. Students from all schools take these courses together and have the opportunity to examine the interrelationships of art, science, technology, and human need.

At the time of graduation, students in the associate degree programs have completed 67 credit hours of course work. In the bachelor's programs, credit-hour requirements range from 132 to 135 credits, depending on the particular program. For the Bachelor of Architecture degree, 170 credits are required.

Pratt's academic calendar consists of two semesters plus optional summer terms that allow students to choose alternative courses or various options usually not offered during the fall or spring semester.

Off-Campus Programs

Pratt Institute offers credit for a wide variety of off-campus study programs. The internship program offers qualified students challenging on-the-job experience related to their major fields of interest; this extension of the classroom and laboratory into the professional world adds a practical dimension to periods of on-campus study.

International programs, available during all academic sessions, have included art and design offerings in the cities of Copenhagen and Rome and in the countries of England, France, Italy, and South Africa. Architecture programs have been held in Italy, Finland, and Japan. New programs are developed regularly in these and other countries. A semester-long program is offered in Rome each year.

Academic Facilities

Founded as the first free library in Brooklyn, the Pratt Institute Library has more than 176,674 bound volumes, 84,604 art books, 237 print and online art and art history journals, a rare book collection, and subscriptions to journals online through JSTOR, EBSCO, and others. The library also has serial backfiles and other material, including government documents; 251,603 audiovisual materials; and 3,996 microforms and subscribes to 925 periodicals—the largest collection of any independent art school. With their ID cards, Pratt students also have access to numerous college libraries in the metropolitan area.

Extensive studio and state-of-the-art computer lab facilities are provided for all Pratt students. In the School of Art and Design, these include studio, shop, and technical facilities for work in all media, from the traditional to the most experimental. Gallery space, both on campus and at Pratt Manhattan, is extensive, showing the work of students, alumni, faculty members, staff members, and other well-known artists, architects, and designers.

Costs

Tuition for the 2015–16 academic year is $44,580. Room charges are $7,430 per academic year. A meal plan is available, and costs about $4,066 for the year. The fees are approximately $2,006. The estimated cost of books and supplies is $1,750 per academic year. Students should allow an additional $3,000 for transportation and personal expenses. For an updated list of tuition and fees, prospective students should visit www.pratt.edu/admissions/financing-your-education/financing-undergraduate/cost-of-attendance.

Financial Aid

Pratt Institute offers a large number of merit-based scholarships, need-based grants, loans, and awards based on academic achievement, talent, financial need, or all three. More than 75 percent of Pratt students receive financial assistance through one or more of these kinds of aid.

Faculty

The faculty at Pratt Institute is exceptional in that a large number of practicing professionals augment the regular full-time faculty. There are 150 full-time and 918 part-time faculty members. In small classes and studios, students have easy access to professors whose natural environment is the design studio, the architectural office, or the industrial research department. Faculty members often connect students with internships and eventually jobs.

Student Government

The Student Government Association (SGA) maintains primary responsibility for all student interests and involvement at Pratt. All undergraduate students are encouraged to become involved in the SGA, whose main functions are allocating and administering funds collected through the student activities fee, scheduling student activities, and representing the student viewpoint to the rest of the Pratt community.

Admission Requirements

Pratt Institute attracts and enrolls highly motivated and talented students from diverse backgrounds. Applications are welcome from all qualified students, regardless of age, sex, race, color, religion, national origin, or handicap. Admission standards at Pratt are high. One of the major components for admission consideration in art, design, or architecture is the evaluation of a student's art or writing portfolio, which must be submitted along with the other required documents.

All applicants to four-year programs must submit official transcripts, test scores, and a visual or writing portfolio with the exception of construction management applicants who are not required to submit a portfolio. Instructions may be found at www.pratt.edu/apply.

The admission committee bases its decisions on careful reviews of all credentials submitted by applicants in relation to the requirements of the program to which students seek admission. International students must submit TOEFL or IELTS scores or SAT scores, but not both. In certain cases, extraordinary talent may offset a low grade or a test score.

Application and Information

Pratt has two admissions deadlines: November 1 for early action and January 5 for regular admissions. To receive full consideration, students must submit their applications by January 5 for anticipated entrance in the fall semester and by October 1 for anticipated entrance in the spring semester.

For more information about Pratt Institute, students should contact:

Office of Admissions
Pratt Institute
200 Willoughby Avenue
Brooklyn, New York 11205
Phone: 718-636-3514
800-331-0834 (toll-free)
E-mail: admissions@pratt.edu
Website: www.pratt.edu
www.pratt.edu/request (Catalog request)
http://on.fb.me/pratt_admissions (Facebook)

Pratt's campus in the spring. *© 2014 Bob Handelman*

QUINNIPIAC UNIVERSITY

HAMDEN, CONNECTICUT

★ To read more about this school, visit http://petersons.to/quinnipiac

QUINNIPIAC UNIVERSITY

The University

Quinnipiac University offers four-year and graduate-level degree programs leading to careers in health sciences, nursing, business, communications, engineering, natural sciences, education, liberal arts, law, and medicine. A curriculum that combines a career focus with a globally oriented liberal arts background prepares graduates for the future, whether they start their careers right after commencement or opt to pursue advanced study.

Quinnipiac is coeducational and nonsectarian and currently enrolls 6,335 full-time undergraduates, 1,331 full-time graduate law and medical students, and 1,369 part-time students in its undergraduate, graduate, and professional programs. Twenty-five percent of the students are residents of Connecticut; the rest represent primarily the northeast corridor, in all a total of thirty states including Alaska, California, and Texas and thirty countries. Quinnipiac is big enough to sustain a wide variety of people and programs but small enough to keep students from getting lost in the shuffle. Life on campus emphasizes students' personal, as well as academic, growth. The approximately 120 student organizations and extracurricular activities, including intramural and intercollegiate (NCAA Division I) athletics, give students a chance to exercise their talents, muscles, and leadership skills. The University has a student newspaper, TV station, and an FM radio station (WQAQ) and twenty-one intercollegiate teams in men's baseball, basketball, cross-country, ice hockey, lacrosse, soccer, and tennis, and in women's acrobatics and tumbling, basketball, cross-country, field hockey, golf, ice hockey, lacrosse, rugby, soccer, softball, tennis, track (indoor and outdoor), and volleyball. Teams compete in the MAAC conference; men's and women's ice hockey teams are members in the ECAC. The men's ice hockey team was ranked #1 in the country for much of 2013 and played in the "Frozen Four" finals, the women's basketball team won the NEC and the MAAC championships, and women's rugby was undefeated in 2013.

The University has three distinct campus settings. The 250-acre Mount Carmel campus has fifty buildings including the Arnold Bernhard Library, academic facilities, an athletic and recreation center, and twenty-five residence halls of different styles, mainly for freshmen and sophomores, with traditional double and quad (4-person) rooms, suites, and multilevel suites and apartments with kitchens. About 95 percent of all freshmen and 75 percent of the total undergraduate population live in Quinnipiac housing. The nearby 250-acre York Hill campus includes the TD Bank Sports Center with twin 3,500-seat arenas for ice hockey and basketball; a suite-style with single and double rooms 1,500-bed residence halls and townhouses for juniors and seniors; "Rocky Top," a lodge-like student center; spectacular views; and a multilevel parking garage for 2,000 vehicles. Seniors may also live in University-owned houses or apartments. A free shuttle takes students between the two campuses. The 104-acre North Haven campus is just 4 miles away and provides state-of-the-art facilities for graduate and upper division offerings in several programs in the Schools of Health Sciences, Nursing, Education, Law, and Medicine. The Center for Medicine, Nursing, and Health Sciences offers a cooperative learning environment geared to educate the health-care team.

The Athletic and Recreation Center on the Mount Carmel campus includes a 24,000-square-foot recreation/fitness facility with a large free-weight room; an exercise machine center; aerobics studios; basketball, volleyball, and tennis courts; and a suspended indoor track. There are also lighted tennis courts, playing fields, and miles of scenic routes for running and biking. A second fitness center is located on York Hill.

Career planning takes place in each of the schools with assistance from the deans' offices. It begins with faculty advisement, along with career exploration, a strong focus on internships and clinical placements, exploration of various major and job fields, and exposure to prospective employers and job preparation. Approximately 30 percent of the undergraduate student population remains at Quinnipiac for their graduate degree in combined or direct entry majors, particularly in education, business, physical and occupational therapy, physician assistant, and social work programs. A particularly innovative Business 4 year (3+1) program offers academically talented applicants to the School of Business the opportunity to complete both a B.S. and an M.B.A. in just four years.

Graduate programs lead to the Master of Science (M.S.) degree in accounting, information technology, interactive media, journalism, molecular and cell biology, organizational leadership, public relations, and teacher leadership; the Master of Health Science in anesthesiologist assistant, medical lab sciences, cardiovascular perfusion, pathologist assistant, and physician assistant; a Master of Science in Nursing plus the Doctor of Nursing Practice in adult and family nursing and nurse anesthesia; the Doctor of Physical Therapy, the Master of Business Administration; the Master of Business Administration in Health Care Management; the Master of Business Administration–Chartered Financial Analyst; and the Master of Arts in Teaching and the Master of Social Work. The Quinnipiac University School of Law offers full-time and part-time programs leading to a J.D. degree or J.D./M.B.A. degree in combination with the School of Business. Several of the graduate degree programs are offered online or in a hybrid format. The Frank H. Netter MD School of Medicine focuses on developing doctors as part of a health-care team with a focus on primary care, rehabilitative medicine, and global health.

Location

Situated at the foot of Sleeping Giant Mountain in Hamden, Connecticut, Quinnipiac provides the best of the suburbs and the city. The University is only 8 miles from New Haven, 30 minutes from Hartford (the state capital), and less than 2 hours from New York City and Boston. Bordering the campus is the 1,700-acre Sleeping Giant State Park, for walking and hiking. The free campus shuttle takes students to shopping and restaurants in nearby Hamden and North Haven, plus to New Haven, where they can visit various art and science museums, attend a performance at the Shubert or Long Wharf Theater (which hosts productions by Quinnipiac's Theater Department), find great restaurants, and have easy access to Metro North and Amtrak at the New Haven train station.

Majors and Degrees

The Schools of Health Sciences and Nursing grant bachelor's degrees in athletic training/sports medicine, biomedical science, health and science studies, microbiology/immunology, and nursing. Combined B.S./graduate degree programs include occupational therapy (5½-year entry-level master's), physical therapy (6- or 7-year entry-level doctorate), physician assistant studies (6-year freshman entry-level master's), and radiologic science and diagnostic medical sonography (both can be a 3-year accelerated B.S.). Students who wish to prepare for entry into medical, dental, chiropractic, veterinary, or other medical schools work with a premed adviser and the pre-health advisory committee.

The School of Business and Engineering (accredited by AACSB International and ranked 66 in the top 100 Best Undergraduate Business Schools in 2014 *Bloomberg BusinessWeek*) offers bachelor's degree programs in accounting, advertising, biomedical marketing, economics, entrepreneurship, finance, computer information systems, international business, management, and marketing. The school offers an innovative Business 4-year (3+1) B.S./M.B.A. program to highly qualified business students, also a fast-track, five-year combined-degree program in which students may gain preadmission to the M.B.A. program, allowing them to fast-track through their M.B.A. in 12–14 months after earning their bachelor's degree. They complete their undergraduate degree plus the M.B.A. in just five years by taking several undergraduate and graduate business courses while undergraduates, are awarded a B.A. in the College of Arts and Sciences or Communications or the B.S. degree in Health Sciences, Engineering or Business and then complete their graduate degree in accounting, business administration, or computer information systems (M.S. or M.B.A.). The Engineering program has majors in mechanical, industrial, civil, and software engineering.

The College of Arts and Sciences offers bachelor's degree programs in behavioral neuroscience, biochemistry, biology, chemistry, computer science, criminal justice, economics, English, gerontology, history, interactive digital design, legal studies (paralegal), liberal studies, mathematics, philosophy, political science, psychology, social services, sociology, Spanish, and theater. Qualified students can go on to the Master of Science in molecular and cell biology program or pursue graduate programs in education, business, law, health sciences, journalism, interactive media, medicine, and social work.

The School of Communications offers undergraduate majors in communications/media studies; film, video, and interactive media; interactive digital design; journalism; and public relations, plus a B.F.A. in film and graduate programs in journalism, public relations, sports journalism, and interactive media. One highlight is a Los Angeles location with a faculty member in residence for summer/fall/spring internships for communications and business students in particular, but open to all undergraduate and graduate Quinnipiac students.

The School of Education's five-year program for undergraduates provides certification for teaching elementary and secondary grades through a B.A./Master of Arts in Teaching (M.A.T.) program (accredited by NCATE). Students complete a B.A. or B.S. in a subject area in the College of Arts and Sciences and begin the M.A.T. course work in their junior year and complete the degree in a final graduate year.

Academic Programs

The Quinnipiac Learning Paradigm begins at orientation, involving students in identifying their strengths and goals, and follows through to graduation. Students begin their electronic portfolio to track their accomplishments and learning. The foundation of the University Curriculum encourages students to explore a variety of options when selecting a major, double major, major and minor, or combined undergraduate/graduate degrees. The Writing Across the Curriculum initiative (WAC) stresses the improvement in writing skills in all subject areas. The University honors program addresses the needs and interests of the most academically talented and committed students. Advanced placement, credit, or both are given for appropriate scores on Advanced Placement tests and CLEP general and subject examinations as well as for scores of 4 or higher in the International Baccalaureate higher-level subjects.

Off-Campus Programs

Students can study abroad in a variety of countries. Most students choose a study-abroad option in their sophomore year, many at our affiliated program in Ireland. Students in any of the five under-graduate schools can also get hands-on experience in their field through off-campus internships and clinical placements in the health sciences. Academic credit is available for internships and affiliations, which are often part of degree requirements.

Academic Facilities

Academic life focuses on the Bernhard Library. This attractive facility provides individual carrels and small rooms for group study and is open 24/7 during the fall and spring semesters. A wireless network provides access to automated library systems and extensive Web-based resources. The Learning Commons, located in the north wing, offers individual tutoring assistance along with helpful learning workshops.

The multimedia and video laboratories in the School of Communications Center each have the latest Mac workstations and software. The computer cluster in the Financial Technology Center at the School of Business is a high-tech, simulated trading floor providing students with the opportunity to access real-time financial data, conduct interactive trading simulations, and develop financial models in preparation for careers in finance.

Engineering uses the active classroom for engineering, an advanced automation and production lab, the computer-aided engineering lab, plus the environmental and hydraulics lab, geotechnical lab, machine shop, and thermodynamics and heat transfer lab.

The Lender School of Business Center has satellite capabilities and the Ed McMahon Mass Communications Center, and contains a state-of-the-art, fully digital, high-definition TV production studio; audio production, print journalism, and desktop publishing laboratories; and a media innovation classroom and lab.

The Center for Medicine, Nursing, and Health Sciences on the North Haven campus provides state-of-the-art facilities for the Schools of Medicine, Nursing, Health Sciences, Law, and Education. In addition to a breathtaking location and expansive exterior and interior spaces, there are specialized facilities and equipment for each program, such as movement study/motion analysis and biomechanics labs; the ergonomics and assistive technology lab; a model adaptive apartment; an orthopedics lab; several rehabilitative sciences labs; CT scan, MRI, radiography, ultrasound, and mammography facilities; and the latest clinical skills simulation labs for adults and pediatric/neonatal patients including an intensive care unit, physical diagnosis lab, physical exam suite, health assessment labs, gross anatomy lab, and two operating suites. Medical and health science and nursing students are educated in an inter-professional atmosphere.

Costs

The 2015–16 cost is $57,090, of which tuition and fees (12–16 credits per semester) are $42,270. Room and board average $14,820 (which includes $2,040 allocated to the meal plan). Other expenses, estimated at $2,000 per year, include books, laboratory, course fees associated with specific courses, and personal travel expenses.

Financial Aid

Quinnipiac designs financial aid packages to include need-based grants and merit-based scholarships that do not have to be repaid, plus self-help financial aid programs such as federal and University-based work study, and loans. Students and families seeking need-based aid will file the College Scholarship Service's Financial Aid CSS PROFILE plus the Free Application for Federal Student Aid (FAFSA) to determine need. Transfer students are eligible for the same need-based financial aid consideration as first-time freshmen.

Faculty

The faculty is characterized by its teaching competence and outstanding academic qualifications. Of the 369 full-time faculty members, 85 percent have earned a Ph.D. or the appropriate terminal degree in their field. The faculty also includes a number of part-time teachers who are practicing professionals and experts in their fields. Classes are taught by these scholars and professionals and not by student instructors, and a low student-faculty ratio promotes close associations among faculty members and students.

Student Government

The Student Government is the student legislative body of Quinnipiac. It represents student opinion, promotes student welfare, supervises student organizations, appropriates funds for student groups, and provides voting student representation on the Board of Trustees.

Admission Requirements

Quinnipiac seeks students from a broad range of backgrounds. On average, freshman students have a 3.4 GPA or better average in college-preparatory courses (transfer students generally have a 2.5 GPA or better), rank in the top 25 percent of their high school class, and have an average combined score of 1100 on the SAT (critical reading plus math) or an ACT composite of 25. Visits to the campus for an interview, open house, group information session, or a campus tour are strongly encouraged. Transfer students are welcome to make an appointment to discuss requirements and the transfer of credit from previous institutions. Quinnipiac sponsors four open house programs during the year and several Saturday morning information sessions followed by a campus tour.

Application and Information

Quinnipiac generally receives about 21,000 applications for admission and admits about 65 percent, to enroll an incoming class of 1,800 freshmen and 200 transfer students. Quinnipiac has a rolling admission policy for its undergraduate programs and therefore recommends that freshman applicants submit their application materials starting early in the fall of their senior year and well before the deadline of February 1. Students applying to the physical therapy, nursing, and physician assistant studies programs should submit their applications by November 15. An early decision (binding) option is available in all majors with an application deadline of November 1. Applications begin to be reviewed as soon as they are complete, and the University begins notifying students of decisions in December. Quinnipiac is a member of the Common Application and recommends that applications be submitted online. Students placed on a waiting list are notified of any openings by June 1. Quinnipiac subscribes to the May 1 Candidates Reply Date Agreement. For information about full-time undergraduate study, students should contact:

Office of Undergraduate Admissions
Quinnipiac University
Hamden, Connecticut 06518-1940
Phone: 203-582-8600
800-462-1944 (toll-free)
Fax: 203-582-8906
E-mail: admissions@quinnipiac.edu
Website: http://www.quinnipiac.edu
http://www.facebook.com/QuinnipiacUniversity
http://twitter.com/QU_Admissions
http://quadmissions.blogspot.com/
http://www.youtube.com/quinnipiacuniversity
http://www.quinnipiac.edu/rss.xml

For information regarding transfer and part-time study:

Office of Transfer and Part-time Admissions
Quinnipiac University
Hamden, Connecticut 06518-1940
Phone: 203-582-8612
Fax: 203-582-8906
E-mail: transferadmissions@quinnipiac.edu

REED COLLEGE

PORTLAND, OREGON

★ To read more about this school, visit http://petersons.to/reedcollege

The College

Reed College is foremost an intellectual community, committed to a free exchange of ideas and predicated on personal responsibility and mutual respect. Since classes began in 1911, Reed has attracted students and faculty who seek to contribute to this type of environment. For its 1,394 students and 151 faculty members, the College offers a setting where a high degree of self-discipline and a genuine enthusiasm for academic work and intellectual challenge are valued commodities. More than four fifths of Reed's students come from outside the Northwest, with one fifth from the Northeast and one tenth from outside the United States. Over 30 percent of Reed's students identify with historically underrepresented racial and ethnic backgrounds. Reed's twenty-three residence halls enable approximately 70 percent of students to live on campus.

Campus social opportunities are open to all, with no closed clubs or organizations; there are no sororities or fraternities at Reed. Community life is full of activity and variety with more than seventy student organizations. Although there are competitive club sports at Reed, such as rugby, soccer, and Ultimate (Frisbee), there are no NCAA or NAIA athletic teams. Fitness and the development of lifelong skills take precedence over competition.

Location

Reed's 116-acre wooded campus is located in a quiet, residential section of southeast Portland. The nearby ocean and mountains of the Pacific Northwest provide a balance to the social and cultural offerings of the Portland metropolitan area. Reed is an hour and a half away from both the coast and the ski slopes on Mount Hood, where Reed owns a ski cabin for use by the Reed community. Portland is a comfortable, welcoming metropolis of 1.5 million people, offering every urban opportunity, crisscrossed by bike paths and excellent public transportation. The city is home to a great local music and theater scene, diverse restaurants and food carts, tranquil Japanese and Chinese gardens, noisy downtown clubs, a plethora of bridges, the largest independent bookstore in the world, and 30-pound salmon swimming past the city lights.

Majors and Degrees

Reed College awards the Bachelor of Arts degree in a wide variety of fields, based on work in traditional departments or in interdisciplinary combinations. Students may select from the following majors: American studies, anthropology, art, biochemistry and molecular biology, biology, chemistry, chemistry-physics, Chinese literature, Chinese studies, classics, classics-religion, comparative literature, dance-theater, economics, English literature, environmental studies, French literature, German literature, history, history-literature, international and comparative policy studies, linguistics, literature-theater, mathematics, mathematics-computer science, mathematics-economics, mathematics-physics, mathematics-statistics, music, philosophy, physics, political science, psychology, religion, Russian literature, sociology, Spanish literature, and theatre.

Students may also design additional interdisciplinary majors. The approval of such special programs, which link two or more disciplines, is reviewed by the student's adviser and the departments concerned.

Reed offers several combined 3-2 programs, which allow the student to earn both a bachelor's degree from Reed and a professional degree from the cooperating institution. Science programs and institutions include engineering (California Institute of Technology, Columbia University, and Rensselaer Polytechnic Institute), computer science (University of Washington), and environmental sciences (Duke University). The College also has a combined program in fine arts (Pacific Northwest College of Art).

Academic Programs

Hallmarks of academic life at Reed include the small-group conference method of teaching and its reliance on active student participation, a de-emphasis of grades, a yearlong interdisciplinary humanities program, and an integrated academic program that balances the breadth of traditional course content and distribution requirements with flexibility in designing an in-depth senior thesis. The development of skills in preparation for a life of learning takes precedence over the memorization of facts. In addition to fulfilling the requirements for the major, taking the humanities course, and writing the senior thesis, students must satisfy a distributional requirement, consisting of two core classes from each of the following academic groups: literature, philosophy, and the arts; history, social sciences, and psychology; the natural sciences; and math, foreign language, logic, and linguistics. Students must also take two classes from one other department outside their major course of study.

Off-Campus Programs

Reed participates in domestic exchange programs with Howard University in Washington, D.C.; Sarah Lawrence College in New York; and Sea Education Association in Massachusetts. In addition, Reed provides study-abroad opportunities for students in Australia, Argentina, China, Costa Rica, Cuba, Ecuador, Egypt, France, Germany, Greece, Hungary, Ireland, Israel, Italy, Kenya, Lebanon, Morocco, Palestine, Russia, South Africa, Spain, Turkey, Turks and Caicos, and the United Kingdom. Students may also arrange independent study plans in consultation with appropriate faculty members, the director for off-campus studies, and the registrar.

Academic Facilities

Students have access to Reed's substantial library collection by searching the online catalog in the library or from any computer on the campus network. Through its participation in PORTALS (Portland Area Library System) and Summit, a union catalog of Oregon and Washington academic libraries, Reed provides online access to other library catalogs and databases. Students may borrow materials directly from academic libraries in the Portland area, as well as from collections worldwide through interlibrary loan. In addition, the Reed library accommodates a first-rate art gallery, a language lab, and a multimedia resource facility. The Reed library is open 18 hours most days and 24 hours a day during examinations.

Computer technology is highly developed at Reed and widely used for instruction, research, and communication by all members of the College community. A state-of-the-art campus network links all residence halls, classrooms, laboratories, offices, and the library to one another and to the global Internet. The Educational Technology Center houses more than 100 computers and a variety of other teaching and technology resources that are used by students and faculty and staff members. The science laboratories at Reed are among the best equipped of any undergraduate college in the United States. These include the A. A. Knowlton Laboratory of Physics, the Arthur F. Scott Laboratory of Chemistry, and the L. E. Griffin Memorial Biology Building. Reed's research nuclear reactor (the only such reactor in the country that is staffed primarily by undergraduates) and radiochemistry lab are actively used for student research, instruction, and training. For those interested in the arts, the campus houses studio art facilities that recently saw a $2-million expansion, performing arts facilities, twenty instrumental practice rooms, a computer music laboratory, a recording system, and an 800-seat auditorium. In fall 2013, Reed opened a new $28-million Performing Arts Building; a major step forward in the College's commitment to the important role the arts play at Reed. For the first time in Reed's history, the departments of music, dance, and theatre are housed in one building that includes rehearsal and performance space, offices, scene and costume studios, collaborative spaces, and a multimedia lab. Other popular facilities include a radio station and a modern sports center.

Costs

Tuition for 2014–15 was $47,500, and room and board was $12,200. The student body fee was $260, bringing the yearly total cost to approximately $59,960. The cost of books and incidental expenses averages approximately $2,000.

Financial Aid

About half of the Reed student body receives financial assistance from the College. A full need-based financial aid program makes Reed accessible to students from a wide range of economic backgrounds. The College guarantees to meet the full demonstrated need of all continuing students in good academic standing who complete their financial aid applications on time. Reed's own funds are the primary source of grants to students. The College budgeted more than $29 million for this purpose in 2014–15. Reed also administers federal and state grants as well as federally subsidized loan programs. Campus employment and work-study programs are available. The size of a financial aid award is based solely upon analysis of the student's need. The average amount awarded to students receiving financial aid in 2014–15 was $44,147, which includes grants, loans, and work opportunities. Reed students' average graduating loan debt for all four years is $19,151, well below the national average.

Faculty

All classes at Reed are taught by professors, about 90 percent of whom hold the highest degree in their field. The average class has 15 students. Reed students point to the opportunity to work closely with faculty members as one of the great benefits of a Reed education. Reed faculty members point to the opportunity to work with students who are serious scholars as one of the great benefits of teaching at Reed. Faculty members commit themselves primarily to teaching, with scholarly and scientific research furthering this primary goal; they view students as partners in learning, often serving as coauthors and co-investigators on professional papers and research projects. This close association is due, in large part, to a 9:1 student-faculty ratio and the one-on-one relationship between thesis adviser (a professor) and student during the senior year.

Student Government

The Student Senate is the central body in student governance. The Senate consists of the student body president, vice president, and 8 student representatives, all elected by the students. Its two primary functions are to allocate student body funds and to represent student interests and concerns to the faculty, administration, and Board of Trustees. The Senate distributes approximately $40,000 each semester to the many student organizations on campus. As agreed under the community constitution, students participate fully in discussions and decisions on a wide variety of issues. The Student Committee on Academic Policy and Planning participates in debate about the curriculum at Reed; many other committees, from the Library Board to the Reactor Committee, have substantial student input. The Senate and student body president make all student appointments to such committees.

Admission Requirements

Reed welcomes applications from freshman and transfer candidates who are genuinely committed to the pursuit of a liberal arts education and a rigorous academic program. Those applicants are admitted who, in the view of the Admission Committee, are most likely to become successful members of and contribute significantly and honorably to the Reed community. The College is committed to maintaining a student body distinguished by its intellectual passion, yet diversified in its range of backgrounds, interests, and talents.

Admission decisions are based on many integrated factors, but academic accomplishments and talents are given the greatest weight in the selection process. A strong secondary school preparation, including honors and advanced courses where available, improves a student's chances for admission. Such a program usually includes: 4 years of English and 3 to 4 years of mathematics (through pre-calculus), science, foreign language, and history or social studies. Given the wide variation in high school programs and quality, however, there are no fixed requirements for secondary school courses. Applicants are expected to have obtained a secondary school diploma prior to enrollment, although exceptions are occasionally made. There are no cutoff points for high school or college grades or for test scores.

Reed recognizes the qualities of character—in particular, motivation, intellectual curiosity, individual responsibility, and community and social consciousness—as important considerations in the selection process, beyond a demonstrated commitment to academic excellence. Thus, the Admission Committee looks for students whose accomplishments and interests in various fields of endeavor will contribute to the overall liveliness of the Reed community. Personal interviews, either on or off campus, are not a requirement in the admission process but are strongly recommended whenever possible. Applications for early decision should be submitted by November 15 (Option I) or December 20 (Option II), regular freshman admission by January 15, and transfer candidates by March 1.

Application and Information

The Office of Admission is open Monday through Friday from 8:30 a.m. until 5 p.m. (Pacific time) all year, except for major holidays. The Admission Office is also open on select Saturdays in the spring and fall. Reed College uses the Common Application, and students may find a complete list of application requirements online at http://www.reed.edu/apply/guide-to-applying.

For further information or to arrange a campus tour, overnight stay, information session, or interview, students should contact:

Office of Admission
Reed College
3203 Southeast Woodstock Boulevard
Portland, Oregon 97202-8199
Phone: 503-777-7511
800-547-4750 (toll-free)
Fax: 503-777-7553
E-mail: admission@reed.edu
Website: http://www.reed.edu

Students at Reed College have a great appreciation for intellectual inquiry and passionate discussion, wherever it can be found.

COLLEGE CLOSE-UPS

THE RESTAURANT SCHOOL AT WALNUT HILL COLLEGE

PHILADELPHIA, PENNSYLVANIA

★ To read more about this school, visit http://petersons.to/therestaurantschoolatwalnuthillcollege

The School

Established in 1974, The Restaurant School at Walnut Hill College is dedicated to inspiring the future of the restaurant and hotel industry through dynamic, timely, and insightful training with an emphasis on service to its students. The Restaurant School at Walnut Hill College combines both intensive classroom training and practical experience; students use their knowledge while they learn.

A student's education is cultivated by the College's philosophy that hands-on training is an essential part of the educational process. This approach has multiple benefits—it enhances learning abilities, creates marketable skills and experience for a resume, brings education to life, and most importantly, puts the student at the center of it all.

The Restaurant School at Walnut Hill College is accredited by the Accrediting Commission of Career Schools and Colleges of Technology, certified for veteran's training by the Veterans Administration, approved by the United States Department of Justice to grant student visas, and recognized as a Professional Management Development Partner of the Educational Foundation of the National Restaurant Association.

There is a diverse population at the Restaurant School at Walnut Hill College, with students coming from all over the United States and abroad, ranging in age from the high school graduate to the adult who is changing careers.

Whether it is at a celebrity chef's cooking demonstration, dinner and a tour at a notable restaurant or hotel, or a winery tour and tasting, students at Walnut Hill College are exposed to the very best Philadelphia has to offer. Students will find a vibrant campus culture with daily activities and special events sponsored by the school's numerous student clubs. The Student Culinary Team has been the winner of several major competitions in recent years, both nationally and internationally. Activities are both educational and fun, combining opportunities to learn and to establish camaraderie and professional development. Events are listed on the school's website, posted to social media channels, and sent to students in a daily e-mail blast.

Location

Philadelphia is a great place to live and learn. As the fifth-largest city in the United States, Philadelphia has much to offer and is a city of firsts—the first public library, the first college, and the first zoo—all in a first-class city.

The Restaurant School at Walnut Hill College is located in the University City section of Philadelphia, neighboring both the University of Pennsylvania and Drexel University. Located just across the Schuylkill River from Center City, University City has a wonderful college-town ambiance. Restaurants, museums, shops, and theaters abound, with many local merchants offering discounts to students. The Amtrak train station is within walking distance of the campus, and the airport is just 20 minutes away by car.

Center City is located just minutes from campus. Here students find a bustling shopping and business district, complete with award-winning restaurants, luxury hotels, and exclusive boutiques.

Diversity abounds in this city of neighborhoods, including Chinatown, complete with exotic restaurants and shops; South Philadelphia, with its famed Italian market and trendy East Passyunk Square restaurants; and the ever-eclectic South Street, with blocks of restaurants, galleries, shops, and entertainment—not to mention the Historic District, which was the birthplace of the nation, and a waterfront that features an exciting nightlife.

Philadelphia is rich in culture and heritage. Students will find world-class art and science museums, theaters that feature major Broadway shows and renowned regional productions, and musical performances that include everything from jazz to pop to the internationally acclaimed Philadelphia Orchestra.

Majors and Degrees

The College offers associate and bachelor's degrees in four program majors: hotel management (95.5 A.S. and 185 B.S. credits), restaurant management (99.5 A.S. and 189 B.S. credits), culinary arts (96.5 A.S. and 194 B.S. credits), and pastry arts (94 A.S. and 187.5 B.S. credits). Each major provides students with a broad-based knowledge of the overall workings of a fine restaurant or hotel. Beyond that, the programs prepare students with the day-to-day skills and specific knowledge required as they develop careers as restaurant managers, chefs, pastry chefs, hotel managers, or restaurateurs. In partnership with the Educational Foundation of the National Restaurant Association, the College's curriculum includes up to eight nationally recognized food service and hospitality management courses. Upon successful completion of the courses and the certification exam, students receive national certification.

Academic Programs

All students must successfully complete twelve 10-week terms to be awarded a Bachelor of Science degree or six 10-week terms to be awarded an Associate of Science degree in their field of study. Each academic year consists of three terms. A student must fulfill the required term hours in a major as well as the basic requirements of the core curriculum. All students are required to participate in special service programs prior to graduating.

Off-Campus Programs

The Restaurant School at Walnut Hill College was one of the first schools in the country to offer a travel experience as part of its curriculum. Culinary and pastry arts students participate in an eight-day tour of France, and hotel and restaurant management students participate in an eight-day Orlando resort and cruise tour. This travel experience enhances both the students' training and resumes.

A capstone program to England is in place for all baccalaureate students. Potential students may contact the College for detailed information.

Academic Facilities

The Restaurant School at Walnut Hill College is poised to offer one of the most dynamic hands-on learning opportunities in the country. The dining experience, situated in the breathtakingly restored 1855 Allison Mansion, turns into a dining event with the addition of four theme restaurants. The Italian Trattoria is a casual Italian restaurant that features classic pasta presentations in an Italian terrace setting. Diners can enjoy a selection of handmade pasta.

Guests looking for a more diverse dining experience can choose to dine in the main restaurant and enjoy an international menu under the twinkling lights in the European courtyard.

American cuisine is presented in an innovative new style of the American Heartland. Depicting a country farm with a painted blue sky and cornfields, this restaurant allows students to explore some of America's best cooking while guests enjoy the comfort of a country dining or veranda setting.

Most notable is the elegant Great Chefs of Philadelphia restaurant. The dining room features all-white decor with glittering mirrors and thousands of glass balls—and a menu inspired by the world's greatest chefs. Guests enjoy high-end cuisine and service designed by some of Philadelphia and America's top chefs.

The mansion also houses the Student Resource Center, featuring computer lab stations as well as the Alumni Library, which includes thousands of books, magazines, and DVDs on cooking, management, and wine. The building also houses a student conference room and a wine lab.

Early each morning, pastry arts students enter the kitchen classrooms to prepare buttery croissants, crisp French baguettes, and glistening pastries for the on-campus Pastry Shop and Café. Meanwhile, culinary arts students are busy preparing a selection of pastas, salads, soups, and entrees for lunch service in the European Courtyard.

Student learning is centered in two buildings on campus—Allison Mansion and the Center for Hospitality Studies. They house six modern classroom kitchens, four lecture halls, and the College's purchasing center and school store.

The educational experience is enhanced by on-campus student support services. The College's Offices of Admissions, Financial Aid, and Independent Student Housing are located in Hunter Hall, a turn-of-the-century masterpiece that features magnificent carved mahogany, marble, and fireplaces.

Costs

Tuition for students who start September 2015 is $6,550 per academic term for the full-time program. Technology and lab fees cost $1,070 per term. Equipment, culinary whites, and management dining room attire are covered with a one-time fee of approximately $845. Interested students may contact the College for information on on-campus housing.

Financial Aid

Financial aid programs are available for those who qualify. It is recommended that students apply early. The College participates in the Federal Pell Grant, the Pennsylvania PHEAA State Grant, the subsidized Federal Stafford Student Loan, and parents' Federal PLUS Loan, in addition to other alternative loans. Financial aid officers assist students and their families with the creation of a personal plan that outlines expenses and identifies financial resources available to incoming students. For more specific information, students may contact the College.

Faculty

Learning comes to life under the guiding hands and encouragement of the highly trained, technically skilled faculty. The faculty members are seasoned professionals, having logged numerous years of experience in restaurants and food service. Through their instruction, students gain professional insight which gives them a competitive edge upon entering the hospitality field. The chefs and instructors are committed to helping students achieve academic, personal, and career success. As professionals, they continuously keep pace with current trends in the hospitality industry and convey their professional dedication and work ethic to their students.

Admission Requirements

Typically, the admissions procedure begins with a visit to the College. At that time, prospective students and their families tour the campus, watch hands-on classes in action, and get a feel for campus life. Application for admission to the College is available to any individual with a high school diploma or its equivalent and who has an interest in developing a career in the fine restaurant, food service, or hospitality field. Applicants are evaluated on their educational background and demonstrated or stated interest in their chosen field. Two references are required, as are high school transcripts and an essay.

Students may contact the College for information on the early decision program for high school juniors and seniors.

Application and Information

The Restaurant School at Walnut Hill College practices rolling admission; qualified applicants are accepted at any time. Applications for admission are submitted with a $50 application fee and a $150 registration fee. Prospective students should contact:

Office of Admissions
The Restaurant School at Walnut Hill College
4207 Walnut Street
Philadelphia, Pennsylvania 19104
United States
Phone: 215-222-4200 Ext. 3011
877-925-6884 Ext. 3011 (toll-free)
Fax: 215-222-4219
E-mail: info@walnuthillcollege.edu
Website: http://www.walnuthillcollege.edu

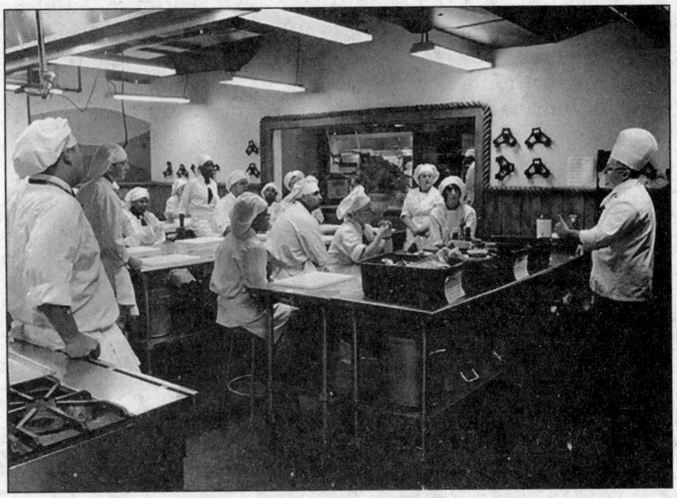

Students at The Restaurant School at Walnut Hill College receive instruction and hands-on training from expert chef instructors.

RICHMOND, THE AMERICAN INTERNATIONAL UNIVERSITY IN LONDON

LONDON, ENGLAND

RICHMOND
THE AMERICAN INTERNATIONAL
UNIVERSITY
IN LONDON

★ To read more about this school, visit http://petersons.to/richmond

The University

Richmond, The American International University in London, prepares men and women to serve with purpose and generosity in an interdependent and multicultural world. Richmond offers a strong academic program with many choices of fields of study, an exceptional faculty, superb campus life, and fellow students from all over the world. In the United States, Richmond is accredited by the Commission on Higher Education of the Middle States Association of Colleges and Schools, a regional accrediting body recognized by the U.S. Department of Education. Richmond is accredited in the United Kingdom by the Open University and holds related degree validation. The University's undergraduate and graduate degrees are designated by the United Kingdom's Department of Education and Employment. The University is a comprehensive American liberal arts and professional university. In addition to the undergraduate degree programs described below, Richmond offers M.A. and M.B.A. degrees in a range of different subjects.

Freshmen and sophomores study and live at the Richmond campus, 7 miles from central London. Junior and senior years are spent at the Kensington campus in one of London's most beautiful residential and historic districts. As part of their four-year B.A. degree program, students may spend a semester or a year studying at one of the University's two international study centers in Florence and Rome, Italy. Richmond currently enrolls over 1,000 students from more than 100 countries. Approximately 48 percent of the degree students are from Europe and the United Kingdom, 4 percent are from Asia, 6 percent are from the Middle East, 6 percent of the student body represents the continent of Africa, and 1 percent is from South America. The remaining 35 percent of the degree students are from North America. About 350 study-abroad students from various universities are enrolled for a semester or a year at Richmond.

Small classes, averaging 17–20 students, enable students to receive personal attention from professors in a supportive environment. The curriculum and academic advising system are structured to enable students to choose courses that provide broad knowledge, relevant skills, and an understanding of the world's many cultures and nations.

Richmond students supplement academic programs with activities that complement and balance the classroom experience. Many extracurricular and cocurricular programs are available to students, including student government, the Green Project, Model United Nations, Amnesty International, Richmond Free Press, Top of the Hill music club, and sports and business clubs.

Location

The Richmond Hill campus in the London suburb of Richmond offers a variety of entertainment, shopping, cultural, and recreational opportunities. Only yards from the University campus is Richmond Park, more than 2,200 acres of rolling hills and lush woodland, where one can ride horses, play tennis, jog, or simply relax. The journey from Richmond into Central London takes approximately 30 minutes using public transportation.

The Kensington campus is located in the heart of London's Borough of Kensington, which has fine museums, libraries, theatres, concert halls, historic buildings, and well-known cultural and educational resources. The University takes full advantage of London's cultural and social resources through selected academic courses, work experience placements with multinational corporations, and special visits to museums, art galleries, theatres, and concert halls.

Majors and Degrees

Richmond operates its academic program on the American system. The University offers the four-year Bachelor of Arts (B.A.) degree in more than twenty majors, with a further choice of twenty minors. Majors offered by the University include: art, design, and media; business administration (entrepreneurship, fashion management and marketing, finance, international business, marketing); communications; development economics, development studies; economics; film studies; financial economics; history; international journalism and media; international relations; performance and theatre arts; political science; and psychology.

Academic Programs

In order to graduate with the dual-validated U.S. and U.K. degree [B.A./B.A. (Honors)], students must earn a minimum of 120 credits. Usually, this means taking a full load for four years, or eight semesters. Within these 120 credits, students must complete all course requirements for their majors. Students must also meet the University's Language Proficiency and General Education requirements. In addition, valuable work experience for credit is offered through the International Internship program. Placements have been at the International Herald Tribune, General Electric, The House of Commons, CNN, the United Nations, Lloyds Bank, the Museum of London, and Sony Music Corporation.

Credit is also awarded for Advanced Placement tests (6 credits for each subject grade of 3, 4, or 5); a grade of A, B, or C on the A Level exams is awarded 9 credits (6 for D or E). Credit is also awarded for the International Baccalaureate, the Baccalauréat de l'Enseignement du Second Degré (France), the Abitur/Reifzuegnis (Germany), the Diploma di Maturità (Italy), and the School Leaving Diploma (Denmark, Finland, Norway, and Sweden).

The fall semester begins in early September and ends in mid-December. The spring semester begins in mid-January and runs through mid-May. A session of summer school runs from mid-May to late June.

Off-Campus Programs

Students may complement their studies in London with a semester, year, or summer at one of two international study centers. The centers are located in Florence and Rome, Italy, and each offer an intensive study of the language and culture of the country. The Florence Study Center emphasizes studio and fine arts. The Rome Study Center offers courses in Italian language and culture, art history, economics, and political science.

Academic Facilities

Information technology is integrated into the curriculum in ways that are natural to the discipline under study. Supporting this are eight student computer laboratories with more than 140 current-specification computers, which connect to the Internet and are networked for student, faculty, and administrative use. Wireless network access is also available on campus.

Richmond's libraries support the courses taught at each campus. Students may use either campus library. The libraries house over 95,000 items including books, DVDs, music CDs, company annual reports, and student theses. In addition, the libraries have subscriptions to a number of journal and magazine titles, along with a variety of national and international newspapers. Richmond students also have access to the many specialized libraries within the London area.

Costs

Tuition for the 2015–16 academic year is $36,000. Room and board costs start at $10,200. Personal expenses, books and supplies, clothing, recreation, and travel costs also need to be factored in as these are not included in tuition and room and board fees.

Financial Aid

Merit-based scholarships are awarded annually to students of high academic ability. Financial aid for U.S. citizens includes Federal Direct Stafford Student Loans and Federal PLUS loans. All U.S. citizens must file the Free Application for Federal Student Aid (FAFSA) to qualify for federal loans. The FAFSA school code for Richmond is G10594. Need-based Richmond grants are also available. Students should contact the admissions office for details regarding application procedures for scholarships and financial aid.

Faculty

The student-faculty ratio of 10:1 enables optimum interaction and individualized instructional assistance. The 118 faculty members (50 full-time, 68 part-time) have professional degrees from top European and American universities such as Harvard, the University of California (Berkeley), the University of Michigan, Cambridge, Oxford, the London School of Economics, the Royal College of Art, and the University of Bonn.

Student Government

The Richmond Student Union acts as a resource for all students, student organizations, and clubs to voice their opinions and ideas. The Student Union functions as a network between the student body and the administration. Using student ideas, it holds events and seeks to feature student talent while enhancing the overall University experience. The Student Union is ongoing in its development and thus offers possibilities for students to shape and change it. It is an organization directed by students for students and is structured to provide flexibility as well as the opportunity for all students to become involved.

Admission Requirements

Applicants are admitted on the basis of academic performance, references, intended major, and career interests. The required autobiographical essay is of paramount importance. Applicants to Richmond have usually completed a total of twelve years of primary and secondary school with a minimum grade of C+ (2.5 out of 4.0) in the American high school grading system, or its equivalent. British system students should have attained a minimum of three A levels (grades BBC) in acceptable academic subjects. Equivalent qualifications gained under other educational systems are also considered for the purpose of admission.

Students must submit a completed application form and application fee, an essay, transcripts of all secondary and postsecondary school work, and one confidential letter of academic recommendation. SAT or ACT scores are optional. The ATP code for Richmond is 0823L. The ACT code is 5244. Evidence of proficiency in the English language is required from students whose first language is not English or who did not attend English-speaking schools. Standardized test scores, such as the IELTS are considered in assessing students' language capability.

Richmond admits students on a rolling basis, and applicants are encouraged to submit their application at the earliest opportunity. All documents in languages other than English must be accompanied by official translations. Applicants are usually notified of a decision within three to four weeks.

Application and Information

An application for admission and further information may be submitted online at www.richmond.ac.uk using either the Richmond Direct Application or the Common Application, or UCAS.

Applicants residing in North America should contact:

Office of Admissions
Richmond, The American International University in London
343 Congress Street, Suite 3100
Boston, Massachusetts 02210-1214
Phone: 617-450-5617
Fax: 617-450-5601
E-mail: usadmissions@richmond.ac.uk
Website: http://www.richmond.ac.uk

Applicants residing in all other countries outside of North America should contact:

UK Office of Admissions
Richmond, The American International University in London
Queens Road, Richmond
Surrey TW10 6JP
England
Phone: 44-20-8332-9000
Fax: 44-20-8332-1596
E-mail: enrol@richmond.ac.uk
Website: http://www.richmond.ac.uk

Students outside Richmond University in London.

RIPON COLLEGE

RIPON, WISCONSIN

COLLEGE CLOSE-UPS

The College

Ripon College is a private undergraduate liberal arts and sciences college located in the historic town of Ripon, Wisconsin.

Founded in 1851 by former New York State Legislator David Mapes and townspeople, the College has a long tradition of excellence in facilitating transformational interdisciplinary learning within its beautiful century-old buildings and in communities near and far. The intentionally small residential campus enrolls some 1,000 bright, high-achieving young men and women from nearly every state and from countries around the world.

The rigorous liberal arts and sciences curriculum and active residential campus prepares students of diverse interests for lives of productive, socially responsible citizenship. Coursework challenges students to examine questions in-depth, identify patterns of logic and reasoning, think critically, consider multiple contexts, and pursue independent research and present findings publicly.

Ripon ensures students will graduate in four years if they remain in good academic standing and do not change majors late in their academic career.

All courses are taught by faculty members, 97 percent of whom have a Ph.D. or other terminal degree in their chosen field. Students benefit from intimate class sizes, 70 percent of which include fewer than 20 students. With an average student-to-faculty ratio of 11:1, professors get to know students and their strengths and capabilities extraordinarily well. They tailor course work to make sure students are always challenged to perform at the top of their game, yet they are always ready to provide extra support when needed. An overwhelming majority of students (95 percent) indicate they are satisfied or very satisfied with the amount of attention they receive from faculty, who also provide direct academic, internship, career, and club advising, and collaborate on serious research pursuits.

Ripon is host to 21 NCAA Division III varsity athletic teams as part of the Midwest Conference, with 37 percent of the student body participating. Men's varsity sports include baseball, basketball, cross-country, cycling, football, indoor and outdoor track and field, soccer, swimming and diving, and tennis. Women's varsity sports include basketball, cross-country, cycling, dance, indoor and outdoor track and field, soccer, softball, swimming and diving, tennis, and volleyball. Students also may participate in more than a dozen intramural sports teams and activities and join more than 50 student-led clubs and organizations.

In addition, Ripon provides more than 40 opportunities for off-campus study, whether as part of a semester-long program; an alternative fall, winter, or spring break; or one of the College's three-week Liberal Arts In Focus programs.

Graduates of Ripon College go on to serve in a variety of roles and have achieved recognition at the highest levels of national and international government, politics, medicine, finance, the arts, business and a host of other professional fields. A Ripon education can take graduates anywhere. A student could study psychology and play basketball and then become a seven-time Grammy winner like jazz singer Al Jarreau '62; guide a space shuttle into orbit like Jeff Bantle '80, a chief flight director with NASA; or become an international opera star like Gail Dobish '76. A student could set milestones in medical science like neonatologist Dr. Jonathan Muraskas '78, who is on record for saving the world's smallest premature baby; or a student might end up studying at Oxford University as a Rhodes Scholar like Zach Morris '02, who also found time to play touch football with former President Bill Clinton and spend an evening at Buckingham Palace with the Queen of England.

An impressive 96 percent of graduates are employed, student teaching, or attending graduate or professional school within six months of graduation, and the five-year average acceptance rate to medical school is 82 percent—twice the national average.

Location

Nestled in the heart of the Green Lake region of Wisconsin—a premier year-round destination for outdoor enthusiasts—Ripon's 250-acre, tree-lined campus is adjacent to historic downtown Ripon, and is centrally located within an hour to an hour-and-a-half drive of each of the state's three largest cities: Milwaukee, Madison, and Green Bay. The nearest airport is 45 minutes away in Appleton, Wisconsin.

Majors and Degrees

Majors include anthropology, art history, biology, business management, chemistry, chemistry–biology, communication, computer science, economics, educational studies, English, environmental studies, exercise science, French, German, global studies, history, Latin American and Caribbean studies, mathematics, music, philosophy, physical science, physics, politics and government, psychobiology, psychology, religion, sociology, Spanish, studio art, and theatre.

Minor programs are also available in classical studies, communication and civic advocacy, dramatic literature, early childhood education, entrepreneurship, environmental biology, health, Latin, law and society, military leadership, museum studies, national security studies, nonprofit management, socially responsible leadership, sports medicine/athletic training, theatre production, and women's and gender studies.

Preprofessional programs include chiropractic medicine, dentistry, engineering, forestry and environmental studies, journalism, law and society, library and information science, medicine, ministry, nursing, optometry, physical therapy, and veterinary medicine.

Dual-degree programs with other institutions include engineering and forestry.

Teacher licensure programs include early childhood/middle childhood; middle childhood/early adolescence; early adolescence/adolescence in language arts, mathematics, social studies, and science subjects; and early childhood/adolescence in art, music, theatre, foreign language, and physical education.

Academic Programs

Ripon's liberal arts and sciences curriculum is designed to introduce students to a wide variety of disciplines. About 40 percent of the students complete double or triple majors, whereas some create self-designed majors. Excellent communications skills—written and oral—as well as critical-thinking and problem-solving skills are the hallmark of a Ripon education, regardless of major. In addition, the innovative Center for Social Responsibility provides a strong foundation for leadership skills. An Army ROTC program is also available.

Off-Campus Programs

Ripon offers more than 40 off-campus programs of varying lengths, each officially sanctioned by and affiliated with Ripon.

Although most programs are connected with a major or minor program, all are open to every Ripon student, regardless of major.

U.S. programs include Chicago Arts, Entrepreneurship, and Urban Studies; Chicago Urban Education; Teach Chicago!; Chicago Newberry Seminar in the Humanities; Fisk University–Ripon Exchange Program; Tennessee Oak Ridge Science; Kentucky ROTC Leader's Training Course; American Indian Reservation Student Teaching Program; Washington, D.C.; Laboratory at Sea; and Laboratory at Woods Hole.

International programs include study in: Cordoba, Argentina; Botswana; Brazil; Costa Rica; London, England; Montpellier, France; Paris, France; Bonn, Germany; Budapest, Hungary; Pune, India; Coldigioco, Italy; Florence, Italy; Tokyo, Japan; Amman, Jordan; St. Petersburg, Russia; St. Andrews, Scotland; Alicante, Spain; Madrid, Spain; Seville, Spain; Toledo, Spain; Tanzania; Bangor, Wales; and Swansea, Wales.

Ripon also offers a variety of three-week Liberal Arts In Focus programs at the end of spring semester. Taught in short, intensive blocks, In Focus courses offer students an immersion experience bridging the theory and coursework of traditional classes to their real-world applications through problem-solving, creative work, and practical experience. Programs include: Intensive Field Studies on the Ecology of the Boreal Forest (Boundary Waters, Minnesota); Old Italy, New Italy (Rome, Italy); Exploring Sustainability and Development in Costa Rica (Costa Rica); Munich-Vienna: Music, Museums, Memorials (Germany); Peace Studies in Jamaica (Hagley Gap, Jamaica); and Ethology of Killer Whales: Field Experience (San Juan Island, Washington).

Academic Facilities

Constant additions and improvements, such as a recent multimillion-dollar apartment-style residence hall, the renovation and classroom expansion of Todd Wehr Hall, and upgrades to upperclass residence halls, the library, the bookstore, dining facilities, and a coffee shop, maintain Ripon's ability to meet the needs of today and tomorrow. Technology services include high-speed Internet, Wi-Fi, e-mail, and video communication. Intranet and Internet services are accessible through a campuswide network which provides access from every room and several wireless hot spots in key areas.

The library staff provides friendly, efficient circulation, reference, instruction, and interlibrary loan services that aid in research. The library provides access to multiple reading rooms for group and silent study, more than 180,000 volumes, and a variety of electronic databases supporting the research needs of the College. The library also houses the College archives and a computer lab.

C. J. Rodman Center for the Arts is home to a theater with a state-of-the-art computerized lighting system, a recital hall with one of only 50 existing Bedient organs, an art gallery, and a sculpture garden.

J. M. Storzer Athletic Center includes an Olympic-size pool, a first-class gymnasium, tennis and racquetball courts, a dance studio, training facilities, and a weight room. The outdoor playing fields and courts are among the best in their class. In addition, a large, modern exercise facility was recently added in the main student residence area.

Costs

Tuition for 2014–15 was $33,207, room and board was $9,085, and fees were $275, for a total cost of $42,567.

Financial Aid

Ripon has been consistently recognized as a best value by all of the national ranking organizations. More than 98 percent of Ripon students receive some form of merit-based scholarship and/or need-based grants and loans.

Ripon recognizes and rewards students' success in high school with its institutionally funded scholarships, based not only on academic merit but also on special achievements in other areas, such as the creative arts. The scholarships range from $1,000 to full tuition. Ripon participates in all federal and state need-based financial aid programs. The financial aid counselors work individually with students and their families to investigate every possible financial resource for which they are eligible.

Faculty

Ripon has 69 full-time and 45 part-time faculty members. Ninety-seven percent of the full-time faculty members have Ph.D.'s or other terminal degrees in their field.

Admission Requirements

Ripon College encourages applications from those students who are best prepared to benefit from and contribute to both the academic and extracurricular programs that it offers. In evaluating applications, attention is paid to evidence of academic achievement, as indicated both by the distribution of courses taken in secondary school and by performance in those courses. More information on admission requirements can be found at http://www.ripon.edu/admission/requirements.

Application and Information

The faculty committee on academic standards establishes the criteria for admission. The school considers a variety of factors, including secondary school record, standardized test scores (SAT or ACT), recommendations, a written essay, and extracurricular or community service activities. Ripon's admission process reflects the personal attention students can expect to receive during their college careers, and applicants are encouraged to provide any additional information they consider helpful.

For further information, students should contact:

Leigh D. Mlodzik
Dean of Admission
Ripon College
300 Seward Street
P.O. Box 248
Ripon, Wisconsin 54971-0248
Phone: 800-947-4766 (toll-free)
E-mail: adminfo@ripon.edu
Website: http://www.ripon.edu

The beauty of the Ripon College campus is accentuated with vibrant colors each fall.

RIVIER UNIVERSITY

NASHUA, NEW HAMPSHIRE

The University

Rivier University, a private Catholic university founded in 1933 by the Sisters of the Presentation of Mary, has earned a reputation for excellence with distinguished academic programs. Rivier offers many of the region's leading programs at the undergraduate, graduate, postgraduate, and doctoral levels.

"Nashua is our home and the world is our classroom," is the University's guiding force to providing students a Rivier experience that ensures students develop an awareness and appreciation of diverse cultures in New England and around the world. The Rivier community also offers a dynamic student leadership experience, with service opportunities integrated in the curriculum, in the campus culture, and in the hearts and minds of students as stated in the University's mission.

Rivier's School of Undergraduate Studies enrolls approximately 1,520 students, including more than 776 full-time day students. With a 23:1 student-faculty ratio, day students have plenty of opportunities to connect with faculty and become active members of the academic community.

The majority of undergraduate students enroll from the six New England states. Rivier also attracts students from all over the United States as well as international students representing countries in Africa, Asia, Europe, the Middle East, and South America. Students who live on campus reside in four modern residence halls, some with suite-style options. Rivier also provides substance-free housing and honors housing. The Dion Center houses the University's student center and the newly renovated Dining Center which offers a healthy upscale dining experience. The commuter lounge, a campus store, student development offices, and meeting rooms are also available in the Dion Center.

The Office of Student Development, the Student Government Association, and more than 17 student clubs and organizations provide a calendar of social, cultural, and recreational activities, including concerts, live entertainment, films, and sporting events. The University and student organizations frequently organize outings, including trips to locations such as Boston and New York. Students also enjoy a variety of performances by the Rivier Theater Company.

Rivier's orientation for new students introduces them to the University's wide array of services, such as academic advisers, the Writing and Resource Center, and peer tutors. The Health Services Center and Counseling Center ensure students' physical and emotional well-being. A full-time chaplain and Campus Ministry team coordinate spiritual activities and service opportunities, while a comprehensive career development service helps students prepare for employment after graduation.

Rivier is a Division III member of the NCAA and sponsors 13 intercollegiate sports. Rivier Raiders compete in men's and women's soccer, volleyball, cross-country, basketball, and lacrosse; men's baseball; and women's field hockey and softball. The men's volleyball team has been nationally ranked every year since 2001. The Muldoon Health and Fitness Center is home to Rivier's varsity athletics, fitness activities, and recreation programs including volleyball, floor hockey, basketball, weight training, indoor soccer, and more. The campus also has a turf rectangular field and a natural grass softball field, as well as a beach volleyball court and cross-country trail. Student athletes can take advantage of an on-campus athletic training clinic for injury assessment and rehab.

Location

Nashua (population 87,000) is located in southern New Hampshire. The city of Boston lies within easy access 40 miles to the south. Local access to public transportation provides for easy travel to and from the campus. Recreational activities abound year-round at nearby lakes and ski areas, in the White Mountains to the north, and at the seacoast, just an hour's drive to the east. The Manchester airport is a 15-minute drive from campus, convenient for students who must access air travel.

Majors and Degrees

Rivier University awards Bachelor of Arts and Bachelor of Science degrees in the following areas: biology (allied health and environmental science), biology education, business, criminal justice, early childhood education, education and community leadership, elementary education, English, English education, finance, global studies, history, homeland and international security, human development, liberal studies, marketing, marketing communications, mathematics, mathematics education, modern languages (modern language education and Spanish), nursing, political science, psychology, public health, secondary education, social studies education, sociology, and special education. The University offers preprofessional programs in law, dentistry, medicine, and veterinary medicine.

Academic Programs

Rivier University offers both professional studies and liberal arts programs to prepare students for a fast-changing, highly technological, and global society. The broad-based curriculum focuses on preparing students for challenging and rewarding careers and furthering their personal growth. The University launched a new core curriculum in 2013, offering opportunities for service learning, servant leadership, civic engagement, and community service to support the intellectual growth of students and enhance student leadership. Students choose from courses in three areas: humanities and social sciences, mathematics and natural sciences, and languages in the core complement. The new core is aligned with the Association of American Colleges and Universities' (AAC&U) essential learning outcomes, which provide Rivier graduates with the strong intellectual and practical skills that are in demand in the workplace. The bachelor's degree requires a minimum of 120 credits with a grade point average of at least 2.0. For the associate degree, the student must complete a minimum of 60 credits with a grade point average of at least 2.0.

All departments encourage qualified students to pursue internships in their field of study during their junior or senior year. Students in Rivier's new public health major will work alongside public health professionals and agencies, and a study-abroad component will offer first-hand global perspective and experience. Education specialists student teach in local schools. Nursing majors complete clinical rotations in healthcare facilities throughout southern New Hampshire and northern Massachusetts. History, law, and political science majors may work in a law office, business, legal-assistance agency, or government agency, and the University's global studies program offers students a global perspective and opportunities. Sociology and psychology majors work with local social service agencies. English and marketing communications majors work in public relations, broadcasting, or corporate communications positions. Business majors work in marketing, management, and technology. The homeland and international security program prepares students for today's changing world by closely examining global security issues, especially emerging transnational threats such as terrorism, weapons of mass destruction, regional and ethnic conflicts, and international crime.

Honors and awards for students include placement on the dean's list, membership in Kappa Gamma Pi, listing in *Who's Who Among Students in American Universities and Colleges*, listing in *The National Dean's List*, and degrees with honors. Academically talented students may also apply to the four-year honors program.

The academic year is divided into two 15-week semesters, with first-semester examinations held before Christmas break. Students usually take five courses each semester. Academic credit may be granted to incoming freshmen on the basis of scores on Advanced

Placement tests and CLEP examinations. Students may also "challenge" courses and receive credit by special examination.

Off-Campus Programs

Through Rivier University's membership in the New Hampshire College and University Council, a sixteen-member consortium of senior and two-year colleges, Rivier students may register for courses at any of the member colleges and receive transfer credits.

Academic Facilities

Academic facilities include Memorial Hall, which houses 14 classrooms, the Office of Global Engagement, faculty offices, a lecture hall, a behavioral science lab, and Rivier's art gallery. The Academic Computer Center features up to 68 workstations with a full range of cutting-edge software and Internet/e-mail access. Regina Library houses approximately 90,000 print volumes and more than 50,000 e-books, and provides access to more than 3 million volumes in 12 area libraries, as well as online access to licensed databases in virtually every academic subject. The Writing and Resource Center offers assistance from professional writing consultants as well as student tutors. Other academic facilities include nursing and science laboratories; a physical assessment lab and nursing skills simulation lab, which provide nursing students with practical experience using blood pressure cuffs, ophthalmoscopes, IV pumps, high-fidelity patient simulators, and more; the McLean Center for Finance and Economics; the BAE Student Research Lab; a clinical psychology lab; electronic classrooms offering multimedia learning tools; and the Benoit Education Center, which houses the eight-classroom Landry Early Childhood Center, observation rooms, and an educational resource center.

Costs

Tuition and fees for the academic year 2015–16 are $28,800; room and board, $11,310; and books and supplies, approximately $1,200. Students should expect to pay a $300 activities fee each semester.

Financial Aid

Financial aid is awarded on the basis of the financial need of the student and family. Approximately 98 percent of Rivier's full-time undergraduate students receive financial aid from the University or from government or private sources. Federal aid includes Federal Pell Grants, Federal Supplemental Educational Opportunity Grants, Federal Perkins Loans, Federal Direct Stafford Student Loans, the Federal Direct PLUS loan program, and the Federal Work-Study Program. To be considered for financial aid, a student must file the Free Application for Federal Student Aid (FAFSA) with the federal government as soon as possible after January 1 for the coming year. FAFSA results should be on file with the University Financial Aid Office prior to March 1 for the following academic year. Each applicant is assessed individually to determine the best combination of grant, work, scholarship, and loan amounts to meet the need of the student. The University awards more than $8 million in institutional merit-based scholarships and grants annually. For more information, students should contact the Office of Financial Aid.

Faculty

The University employs 71 full-time faculty members. The full-time student–faculty ratio is 23:1. Part-time instructors in specialized areas are working professionals who bring current knowledge and expertise in their field to their classes. All classes are taught by faculty members, and department chairs serve as academic advisers to students in their major programs.

Student Government

Every full-time day student automatically becomes a member of the Student Government Association (SGA) upon registration and payment of the student activity fee. The main goals of the SGA are to stimulate active participation in all University functions, to establish and maintain effective channels of communication among members of the University community and the community at large, and to foster a mutual trust, encourage a spirit of cooperation, and initiate new endeavors. The SGA also supervises student clubs and organizations and oversees their finances. The SGA Executive Board serves as the channel of communication through which the views of the students on institutional policies reach the University administration.

Admission Requirements

Applicants for admission should ordinarily have completed, in an accredited high school, a minimum of 16 academic units, including 4 in English, 2 in a modern foreign language, 3 in mathematics, 2 in social science, 2 in science, and 3 in electives. The most successful candidates are in the upper half of their class, with at least a B average. The University requires SAT or ACT scores as part of the student's overall admissions file. Average SAT scores trend around 1340. A personal interview is strongly recommended but not required.

Rivier welcomes applications from qualified transfer candidates from accredited institutions, as well as applications from international students. Transfer students must forward transcripts of all previous college work and a high school transcript. International students must fulfill the requirements for general admission; they may also be required to submit Test of English as a Foreign Language (TOEFL) scores. Deferred admission may be granted to students who wish to postpone entrance for up to one year, provided they have not been enrolled full-time at another postsecondary institution.

Application and Information

Applications must be accompanied by an essay, SAT scores, one letter of recommendation, and a high school transcript. The School of Undergraduate Studies employs a system of rolling admission that allows qualified students to be admitted approximately one month after their application is completed. Transfers should apply by June 1 for fall admission and by December 1 for spring admission. Those applying for financial aid should observe the March 1 deadline. Interviews are arranged through the Admissions Office. Students may apply online at the University's website.

For an application or additional information, please contact:

Office of Undergraduate Admissions
Rivier University
420 South Main Street
Nashua, New Hampshire 03060
Phone: 603-897-8507
800-44-RIVIER (toll-free)
Fax: 603-891-1799
E-mail: admissions@rivier.edu
Website: http://www.rivier.edu

Students enjoy Rivier's great location in the heart of New England—approximately an hour's drive from Boston, the mountains, and the seacoast.

ROBERT MORRIS UNIVERSITY

MOON TOWNSHIP, PENNSYLVANIA

★ To read more about this school, visit http://petersons.to/robertmorrisuniversity

The University

A private university in Pittsburgh's suburban hills, Robert Morris University (RMU) is set on a 230-acre former estate that is a short drive from the cultural and commercial opportunities of a major city. Founded in 1921, RMU offers more than sixty undergraduate programs and twenty graduate programs, including many online options, providing more than 5,400 students academic excellence with a professional focus.

The University built its reputation in the business fields of accounting, finance, marketing, and management. It has grown to include programs in communications, information systems, engineering, mathematics, science, education, social sciences, and nursing. RMU uses a student engagement transcript to document internships, service-learning activities, study abroad, leadership roles, and other learning outside the classroom. This focus on engaged learning contributes to the 92 percent placement rate of graduates within a year of graduation.

RMU is a teaching-centered institution featuring small classes taught by professors and a student-faculty ratio of 15:1. The campus is growing, with new buildings for both the School of Business and the School of Communications and Information Systems, and a new nursing simulation center due to open in 2015. New residence halls accommodate a growing student population. More than 85 percent of freshmen live in campus housing.

Visiting international scholars and a variety of opportunities to study abroad—for a semester or just a few weeks—enrich students' global perspectives. Students can participate in any of nearly 100 clubs and organizations. The Student Life Office organizes dances, parties, movie screenings, comedy acts, health and wellness fairs, educational programs, and day trips. Business organizations, professional clubs, and honor societies provide students with career preparation opportunities.

The University's competitive athletics program fields sixteen NCAA Division I teams, and the Colonials have won numerous titles and championships. The men's basketball team famously upset the reigning NCAA champion Kentucky Wildcats in the Charles Sewall Center in the first round of the 2013 NIT. Coach John Banaszak, former Pittsburgh Steeler and three-time Super Bowl winner, leads the football team at Joe Walton Stadium. Nationally ranked Division I men's and women's ice hockey teams play at the RMU Island Sports Center, a 32-acre sports and recreation complex with two ice rinks, two multipurpose rinks, an indoor golf driving range, a miniature golf course, a pro shop, and a restaurant and banquet facility. Students can also participate in a number of club and intramural sports on campus.

Location

The 230-acre main campus is located in Moon Township, Pennsylvania, just 15 minutes from Pittsburgh International Airport and 17 miles from downtown Pittsburgh. The RMU Island Sports Center is 15 minutes from campus on Neville Island.

Majors and Degrees

Robert Morris University offers more than sixty undergraduate programs of study: accounting, actuarial science, advertising, biology, biomedical engineering, business, communication, competitive intelligence systems, computer information systems, corporate communication, cyber forensics and information security, economics, education (specializing in grades preK–4, 4–8, or 7–12), engineering, English, environmental science, finance, graphic design, health services administration, history, hospitality and tourism management, industrial engineering, information sciences, intelligence systems, journalism, management, manufacturing engineering, marketing, mathematics, mechanical engineering, media arts, nuclear medicine technology, nursing, organizational leadership, photography, political science, pre-medicine, professional communications/information systems, psychology, public relations, social science, sociology, software development, software engineering, special education, sport management, sport psychology, theater, TV/video production, web design, and writing.

Fully online bachelor's degree programs are available in business, cyber forensics and information security, English, health services administration, hospitality and tourism management, organizational leadership, psychology, and RN–M.S.N.

The University offers five-year integrated bachelor's/master's degree programs, medical school affiliation, cooperative education programs, an integrated 3+3 J.D. program with Duquesne University School of Law, and an honors program.

Academic Programs

Robert Morris operates on a two-semester schedule with various summer sessions. A total of 120 credits are required for most bachelor's degrees. Internship or co-op credits of 3 to 12 hours may be used toward degree requirements. The University participates in a cross-registration program with nine local colleges through the Pittsburgh Council on Higher Education consortium.

Academic Facilities

Learning resources include a traditional library with more than 137,000 bound volumes, 80 reference databases, and 600 periodical subscriptions.

The Academic Media Center, with full production facilities, provides students with opportunities to collaborate on projects in all areas of media, including television/video production, audio production, and photography.

State-of-the-art laboratory facilities support the engineering, mathematics, science, and nursing programs. The new business school facility features a simulated stock trading floor and videoconferencing center. The nursing school utilizes patient simulators. Students in media arts have new, well-equipped studio and display space.

Costs

Annual tuition for the 2014–15 year was a $25,380 flat rate, based on a 24- to 36-credit, two-semester schedule. Annual room and board was $10,250 based on double occupancy and the Patriot meal plan.

Financial Aid

Eighty-nine percent of RMU undergraduates receive some sort of financial aid, including scholarships, grants, loans, and work-study programs. Both need-based and achievement-based awards are available. All applicants must complete the admissions application, the Free Application for Federal Student Aid, and the grant forms from their own state.

Faculty

The University has more than 450 full- and part-time faculty members; 81 percent of full-time faculty members hold terminal degrees. The student-faculty ratio is 15:1 and the average class size is 24. Students may take advantage of the expertise offered by the faculty in academic advisement and counseling, as well as counseling from the staff at the Center for Student Success.

Student Government

The Student Government Association represents all student organizations, including fraternities and sororities. Members participate in the planning of all social and cultural events on campus.

Admission Requirements

First-time freshmen must submit an application for admission with a $30 application fee (waived for online applicants), official high school transcripts or GED credential, and official SAT or ACT scores. Preference is given to applicants with a minimum 3.0 high school GPA and a combined SAT score of 1000 (Reading + Math) or a composite ACT score of 22.

Transfer students who have earned credits from another regionally accredited institution must submit transcripts from all postsecondary institutions attended and must have a minimum 2.0 GPA. Students with less than 30 college credits must also submit high school transcripts or GED credential.

Certain select academic programs have higher admissions criteria. Students are encouraged to arrange for a campus visit with an admissions counselor.

Application and Information

Students are encouraged to submit applications in the fall of their senior year of high school. Official transcripts and counselor recommendations should accompany the application; there is a $30 application processing fee that is waived for online applicants.

Robert Morris uses a rolling admission system; students are considered for acceptance as soon as all application materials have been received and evaluated.

For additional information and application materials, students should contact:

Kellie Laurenzi
Dean of Admissions
Robert Morris University
6001 University Boulevard
Moon Township, Pennsylvania 15108
Phone: 800-762-0097 (toll-free)
Website: http://www.rmu.edu
http://www.facebook.com/RMUpgh
http://twitter.com/rmu
http://www.youtube.com/RMUNewsTube

Robert Morris University's 230-acre campus in suburban Pittsburgh is a scenic place to live, learn, and play within easy reach of one of America's favorite cities.

ROCHESTER INSTITUTE OF TECHNOLOGY

ROCHESTER, NEW YORK

R·I·T

The Institute

Rochester Institute of Technology (RIT) is among the world's leading career-oriented, technological universities. RIT offers more than ninety undergraduate programs in areas such as engineering, computing and information sciences, engineering technology, business, hospitality, science, art, design, photography, biomedical sciences, game design and development, and the liberal arts including psychology, advertising and public relations, and public policy. Students may choose from more than eighty different minors to develop personal and professional interests that complement their academic program. RIT is a world leader in experiential education, which includes cooperative education, internships, study abroad, and undergraduate research. As home to the National Technical Institute for the Deaf (NTID), RIT is a leader in providing access services for deaf and hard-of-hearing students. RIT enrolls students from every state and more than 100 countries.

Close to 70 percent of RIT's approximately 12,050 full-time undergraduate students live on the campus in residence halls or campus apartments.

Each year, RIT's more than 300 student organizations sponsor over 1,300 on-campus activities. RIT offers 23 varsity sports, including Division I men's and women's hockey. Recreational facilities are exceptional and include two ice rinks, an aquatics center, a field house with an indoor track, and fitness facilities.

Location

The greater Rochester area has a population of about 800,000. Per-capita income is among the highest in the nation for metropolitan centers. The area's many internationally known industries employ a high proportion of scientists, technologists, and skilled workers. Rochester's industries have always been closely associated with RIT's programs and progress. Rochester is also a hub for higher education with twelve colleges and universities in the area.

Majors and Degrees

The College of Applied Science and Technology offers the Bachelor of Science (B.S.) degree in civil engineering technology, computer engineering technology, electrical engineering technology, electrical/mechanical engineering technology, manufacturing engineering technology, and mechanical engineering technology. It also grants the Bachelor of Science in environmental sustainability, health and safety, international hospitality and service management, and packaging science. An undeclared option allowing freshmen to delay selecting a major for up to a year is available in the School of Engineering Technology.

The E. Philip Saunders College of Business offers the B.S. in accounting, finance, new media marketing, international business, management, management information systems, and marketing. A 4+1 M.B.A. option is available, as are several minors, including entrepreneurship and digital business. An undeclared option allowing freshmen to delay the selection of their major for up to one year is available.

The B. Thomas Golisano College of Computing and Information Sciences offers the B.S. in computer science, game design and development, information technology, information security and forensics, networking and systems administration, new media interactive development, and software engineering. The college also offers a computing exploration option for undeclared freshman students.

The Kate Gleason College of Engineering grants the B.S. in biomedical engineering, chemical engineering, computer engineering, electrical engineering, industrial and systems engineering, mechanical engineering, and microelectronic engineering. Degree options in aerospace, automotive, bioengineering, biomedical, energy and environment, ergonomics, information systems, manufacturing, and software engineering are also offered within the college. Accelerated B.S./M.S. options are available. The Engineering Exploration Program, which allows freshmen to delay the selection of their major for up to one year, is available.

The College of Health Sciences and Technology offers B.S. programs in biomedical sciences, diagnostic medical sonography, nutrition management, and a five-year physician assistant B.S./M.S. program.

The College of Imaging Arts and Sciences offers the Bachelor of Fine Arts in advertising photography, ceramics and ceramic sculpture, film and animation, fine art photography, fine arts studio, glass, graphic design, illustration, industrial design, interior design, medical illustration, metals and jewelry design, new media design and imaging, photojournalism, 3-D digital graphics, visual media, and woodworking. The college also offers B.S. programs in biomedical photographic communications, digital media, graphic media, imaging and photographic technology, motion picture science, and new media/publishing. An undeclared option allowing freshmen to delay the selection of their major for up to one year is available in the School of Art, the School of Design, the School for American Crafts, and the School of Photographic Arts and Sciences.

The College of Liberal Arts offers B.S. programs in advertising and public relations, communication, criminal justice, economics, journalism, international and global studies, museum studies, philosophy, psychology, public policy, and sociology and anthropology. The Liberal Arts Exploration Program is designed to help undecided students formulate education and career plans.

The College of Science offers B.S. programs in applied mathematics, applied statistics, biology, biochemistry, bioinformatics, biotechnology and molecular bioscience, chemistry, computational mathematics, environmental science, imaging science, and physics. Special options are available in premedical studies (medicine, dentistry, veterinary medicine). Minors are available in astronomy, exercise science, imaging science, mathematics, physics, and statistics. Accelerated B.S./M.S. and B.S./M.B.A. programs are available. General Science Exploration allows freshmen to delay the selection of their major for up to one year.

Home of the National Technical Institute for the Deaf, RIT is a world leader in providing educational opportunities and access services for deaf and hard-of-hearing students. NTID awards associate degree programs and offers pre-baccalaureate studies for deaf and hard-of-hearing students. The associate degree programs prepare students for immediate employment after graduation or transfer into one of RIT's bachelor's degree programs. The pre-baccalaureate studies program prepares students for entry into RIT's bachelor's degree programs. Nearly 500 of the 1,200 deaf and hard-of-hearing students at RIT are enrolled in bachelor's degree programs in the other eight colleges.

Academic Programs

Most students entering as freshmen enroll directly in the academic program of their choice. Options for undeclared students are offered by most colleges as described above. A University Studies program is available for entering freshmen who wish to explore programs in two or more colleges. Undergraduates may choose from more than eighty different minors. Double-majors and accelerated dual-degree (combined bachelor's/masters) options are available. The RIT honors program admits approximately

150 freshmen annually. Air Force and Army ROTC programs are available on the campus. A Naval ROTC program is offered jointly with the University of Rochester.

Every academic program at RIT offers some form of experiential education opportunity, including cooperative education, internships, study abroad, undergraduate research, and industry-sponsored projects. Co-op students alternate periods of full-time study with periods of full-time paid work experience directly related to their field of study and career interests. Last year, more than 4,100 students completed co-op assignments with nearly 2,100 employers, earning collectively in excess of $33 million.

Off-Campus Programs

RIT has four international branch campuses. RIT Croatia is located in Dubrovnik and Zagreb, Croatia and offers undergraduate degree programs in hospitality and service management, information technology, and international business. The American University of Kosovo in Pristina provides career-oriented programs that foster links between the university, industry, and government in support of workforce development. RIT Dubai offers graduate and undergraduate programs in business, engineering, service leadership, and information sciences.

Academic Facilities

Excellent facilities add to the quality of academic life. Students have access to some of the most up-to-date microelectronic, telecommunications, and computer engineering facilities in the U.S. RIT's Wallace Library is a true multimedia learning center. Its collections are exceptionally extensive in the areas of art and design, education for the deaf, photography, and printing.

Students use state-of-the-art computer equipment regardless of their major. Central computer systems can be accessed via a high-speed data network connecting the library, academic facilities, residence hall rooms, and on-campus apartments. There are more than sixty locations campuswide, with wireless networking connectivity utilizing 802.11b technology. The RIT campus network is served by two OC3 connections, each operating at a data rate of 155 Mbps, and one T3 connection operating at 45 Mbps. RIT is among a select group of institutions with access to the Internet2 research network, a collaborative research and development effort led by more than 170 U.S. universities working in partnership with industry and government.

Costs

For 2014–15, undergraduate tuition for the academic year (three academic quarters) was $35,256. Fees, including the activities and health fees, are $512. Room and board (twenty meals per week) cost $11,568.

Financial Aid

Approximately 77 percent of RIT's full-time undergraduates receive some form of financial aid that includes RIT scholarships, alumni or industry-supported scholarships, and state and federal government grants. A variety of loans and part-time work positions are available. The FAFSA must be submitted by March 1. Giving full recognition to scholarship apart from financial need, RIT awards a number of academic scholarships based on grades, test scores, and activities. Freshmen applying by February 1 and transfers applying by March 1 are considered for these scholarships.

Faculty

There are 1,049 full-time faculty members, 508 part-time faculty members, and an administrative and supporting staff of more than 2,200. Approximately 70 percent of the faculty members have earned a Ph.D. or the terminal degree in their field.

Student Government

The Student Government is the representative body for students. It works with RIT administration, faculty, and staff members to communicate the needs and desires of the student body and to communicate decisions of the administration to students. Fraternity and sorority members, off-campus and hearing-impaired students, and students from minority groups elect special representative bodies. All full-time and part-time undergraduate and graduate students are represented in Student Government.

Admission Requirements

Admission to RIT is competitive and varies from selective to highly selective depending on the desired program of study. The major factors determining freshman admission are strength of academic program, high school performance, and ACT or SAT test results. College performance is the main factor for transfer candidates. Students applying for many programs in art, design, and crafts must submit a portfolio as part of the application process.

RIT promotes and values diversity and admits qualified men and women of any race, color, national or ethnic origin, religion, sexual orientation, gender identity, gender expression, or marital status. RIT does not discriminate on the basis of handicap in the recruitment or admission of students or in the operation of any of its programs or activities, as specified by federal laws and regulations.

Application and Information

An application, a nonrefundable processing fee of $60, official transcripts of all secondary school or college records, and SAT or ACT scores (for prospective freshmen) should be forwarded to RIT. Freshman applicants who provide all required materials for fall entry by February 1 receive admission notification by March 15. Prospective freshmen who apply after February 1 are considered on a space-available basis; all transfer students are notified of the admission decision on a rolling basis four to six weeks after their applications are complete. A binding early decision plan is offered to prospective freshmen who have completed applications and credentials filed by December 1 to receive notification by January 15.

For application forms, students should contact:

Director of Undergraduate Admissions
Rochester Institute of Technology
60 Lomb Memorial Drive
Rochester, New York 14623-5604
Phone: 585-475-6631
Fax: 585-475-7424
E-mail: admissions@rit.edu
Website: http://www.rit.edu
http://www.facebook.com/RITfb
http://twitter.com/RITAdmissions

A view of the campus.

SAINT ANSELM COLLEGE

MANCHESTER, NEW HAMPSHIRE

★ To read more about this school, visit http://petersons.to/saintanselmcollege

SAINT ANSELM COLLEGE 1889

The College

Saint Anselm College is a nationally-ranked private, Catholic, undergraduate institution with approximately 2,000 students. Founded in 1889 by the world's oldest religious order, the Benedictines—a Catholic order that has endured and thrived for more than 1,500 years—Saint Anselm is accredited by the New England Association of Schools and Colleges and holds membership in the Association of American Colleges, The American Council on Education, the National Catholic Educational Association, and the National Association of Independent Colleges and Universities. It is the third-oldest Catholic college in New England.

Saint Anselm College prepares students for life. With a liberal arts education, graduates are ready for real career experience, and for the challenges that lie ahead. They take their Saint Anselm experience with them to think critically, communicate effectively, and solve problems creatively.

Saint Anselm graduates are CEOs, doctors, lawyers, nurses, engineers, teachers, marketers, and researchers. They are humanitarians, healers, and philanthropists. They graduate Saint Anselm with the drive to achieve, empowered to make the world a better place. In fact, 98 percent of the class of 2013 was employed, in graduate school, or engaged in service within six months of graduation.

There's much to see and do on campus from open skate nights at Sullivan Arena to spring concerts on the quad. Academic buildings, such as the Goulet Science Center and Gadbois Hall, house innovative labs where remarkable research happens every day. There are cell culture labs, climate-controlled environmental chambers, a greenhouse, a sleep lab, SimMan labs, and more. In the library, students have access to the latest technological advances and a range of workspaces for individuals and groups.

Recreational facilities include the Carr Center with basketball courts and the recently renovated 9,000-square-foot, three-level fitness center. Saint Anselm College boasts some of the top athletic facilities in the Northeast-10 Conference. The College's twenty intercollegiate athletic teams play all of their home contests on campus (with the exception of the golf team) at Grappone Stadium, Sullivan Arena, or Melucci Field.

Ninety-two percent of Saint Anselm students live on campus in traditional residence halls, suites, townhouses, or apartments. A new 47,000-square-foot, 150-bed residence hall was completed in August 2014 offering students an innovative, living-learning community. Whether students live on campus or commute, everyone has access to Saint Anselm College's amazing food, ranked twelfth in the nation by the Princeton Review.

New Hampshire Institute of Politics: Saint Anselm is home to the New Hampshire Institute of Politics & Political Library (NHIOP), which offers unparalleled opportunities for students to be in the front row of the democratic process. Its auditorium, West Wing, TV studio, and classrooms are where students meet today's prominent political policy thinkers and researchers, journalists and authors, scientists, industry executives, global leaders, and presidential candidates. The Institute, nationally known to political scholars and strategists, is an essential campaign stop for presidential candidates. All of the U.S. presidents in the last fifty years have visited Saint Anselm.

Location

Saint Anselm College is located on 380 acres in Manchester, New Hampshire and is an hour drive from Boston, the Atlantic Ocean and New Hampshire seacoast, and the White Mountains. Just minutes from downtown Manchester, students can find all the venues a small city has to offer: great restaurants and coffee shops, a theater, museum, minor league baseball and hockey teams, and the Verizon Wireless Arena to name a few. The Manchester-Boston Regional Airport is also just minutes from the College.

Majors and Degrees

At Saint Anselm College, students may earn a Bachelor of Arts degree in the following academic programs and majors: accounting, American studies, biochemistry, biology, business, chemistry, classics, classical archaeology, communication, computer science, computer science with business, computer science with mathematics, criminal justice, economics, education (secondary and elementary), engineering physics (3-2 program), English, environmental politics and sustainability, environmental science, finance, fine arts (art history, music, and studio art), forensic science, French, German studies, history, international business, international relations, integrated studies in the Great Books, mathematics, mathematics with economics, natural science, peace and justice studies, philosophy, physics (applied), physics, politics, psychology, sociology, Spanish, and theology. The College also offers a Bachelor of Science in Nursing (B.S.N.) through a traditional, undergraduate nursing program and a hybrid RN-to-B.S.N. program.

Saint Anselm students may pursue preprofessional programs in dentistry, law, medicine, theology, and veterinary medicine.

The engineering physics (3-2) program partners with the University of Notre Dame, University of Massachusetts-Lowell, Catholic University of America, and Manhattan College. More information is available online at www.anselm.edu/engineering.

Students in the health sciences enjoy a partnership with Massachusetts College of Pharmacy and Health Sciences for graduate programs in physical therapy, pharmacy, physician assistant studies, or optometry.

Off-Campus Programs

At Saint Anselm College, a liberal arts education gives students a solid foundation for any career, but opportunities outside the classroom give students a competitive edge and real job experience.

Students find all kinds of experiential learning opportunities at Saint Anselm including internships, research, study abroad, and volunteering. Students of all majors and interests can find opportunities for internships through the Office of Career Services, which also brings employers to campus and advises students throughout their job search.

Internships are offered in Boston, New York City, Washington, D.C., Manchester, and beyond. Some recent internships opportunities have included: the Boston Bruins, United States Secret Service, Fidelity Investments, the United States Senate, Fox News, and the American Cancer Society.

Many students work closely on research projects with faculty members on campus to gain valuable lab skills, but there are also opportunities at local hospitals and businesses.

Students interested in study abroad can travel the world visiting such places as Thailand, Morocco, and South Africa. In recent years, students have studied marine biology on Australia's Great Barrier Reef, art history in the museums of Florence, finance in London, language in Spain and France, the culture of peace in Peru, and political history in Ireland. In spring 2016, Saint Anselm College will offer a semester abroad in Orvieto, Italy, with classes taught by Saint Anselm College faculty. If studying abroad for an entire semester seems too long, Saint Anselm students have traveled with faculty members on week-long trips to places such as China, Panama, and Vietnam.

Saint Anselm students have gained essential leadership and organizational skills through volunteering, doing everything from teaching English to new Americans to working the crisis hotline at the YWCA. In addition, every winter and spring break, Saint Anselm students travel to organizations around the country to volunteer at service sites through Service & Solidarity Mission trips. These service trips challenge students, giving them valuable perspectives and changing their views on the world.

Costs

For the 2014–15 academic year, tuition was $35,396, room and board was $13,040, and fees were $940.

Financial Aid

Saint Anselm provides students with financial aid opportunities through both private and federal aid programs. The College provides financial aid to offset the reasonable monetary investment that the student and family are expected to contribute. Ninety-seven percent of the College's undergraduates receive some degree of financial aid. Saint Anselm's financial aid opportunities include grants, loans, scholarships, and employment positions.

Merit awards are awarded to outstanding students. Two forms are required in applying for aid; the student must submit the CSS/Financial Aid PROFILE and the Free Application for Federal Student Aid (FAFSA) by March 15.

Faculty

With an average class size of 18 and a student-faculty ratio of 11 to 1, students receive individual attention in small classes. With 198 professors and no teaching assistants, Saint Anselm faculty members are committed to the success of their students.

Student Clubs

With more than sixty-five clubs and organizations, twenty varsity athletic teams, a performing arts center, and an art gallery, Saint Anselm students have plenty of activities to explore. From the soccer club to the mock trial team to the Muslim Student Association, there is a club for every interest, cultural to academic.

Students interested in service will be right at home volunteering through the Meelia Center for Community Engagement or through Campus Ministry. Saint Anselm students volunteered more than 50,926 hours last year. Service & Solidarity Mission trips, held during each winter and spring break, allow Saint Anselm students to volunteer at locations around the country.

Saint Anselm College is part of the Division II Northeast-10 and ECAC Conferences and offers men's intercollegiate baseball, basketball, cross-country, football, golf, ice hockey, lacrosse, skiing, soccer, and tennis; and women's basketball, cross-country, field hockey, ice hockey, lacrosse, skiing, soccer, softball, tennis, and volleyball. Saint Anselm also has a variety of club, recreational, and intramural sports teams.

Admission Requirements:

In reviewing applicants for the first-year class, admission considers each prospective student carefully. Counselors assess each applicant's secondary school performance, SAT or ACT scores (optional for non-nursing majors, nursing majors must submit scores), recommendation letters, and the written essay. Of highest priority is the applicant's secondary school transcript, with a specific focus on both the rigor of course study and the marks received. Saint Anselm invites transfer and international students to apply.

Saint Anselm College has the following admission deadlines:

- Early action—November 15
- Nursing majors—November 15
- Regular decision—February 1

Saint Anselm College invites students and families to visit campus for a tour, information session, and/or interview.

For more information, prospective students should contact:

Office of Admission
Saint Anselm College
100 Saint Anselm Drive
Manchester, New Hampshire 03102
Phone: 603-641-7500
888-426-7356 (toll-free)
E-mail: admission@anselm.edu
Website: http://www.anselm.edu

Saint Anselm's campus is home to students, instructors, researchers, and administrators, all striving to create a community where learning shapes living and where the search for knowledge takes place in an environment that values critical thinking, multicultural exchange, and service to humanity.

ST. BONAVENTURE UNIVERSITY

ST. BONAVENTURE, NEW YORK

ST. BONAVENTURE UNIVERSITY

The University

St. Bonaventure University provides a values-based education with individual attention from professors, a beautiful residential setting, and a friendly, close-knit atmosphere. Of the 2,200 students enrolled, 1,800 are undergraduates. More than 74 percent of the undergraduates are full-time residents. Complementing St. Bonaventure's traditions are innovative degree programs, computerized career placement aids, comprehensive student life activities, and modern academic facilities. Among major campus events during the academic year are concerts and coffeehouse acts, indoor and outdoor recreational programs, film offerings, and dramatic and musical plays. Aspiring writers and broadcasters from all academic majors—Bonaventure has produced 6 Pulitzer Prize winners—find challenging and plentiful opportunities working with one of the five University media: WSBU-88.3 FM-The Buzz, the nationally ranked campus radio station; *The Bona Venture,* the weekly newspaper; *The Bonadieu,* the yearbook; *The Intrepid,* the online-only news medium; and *The Laurel,* which marked its 115th anniversary in 2014. Other organizations on campus include academic fraternities and honor societies, a variety of club and intramural sports (including nationally ranked men's and women's rugby), and arts organizations that include choral, instrumental, dance, and drama ensembles. The Thomas Merton Center is open 24 hours a day and aims to foster a community of friendship and mutual service. Many students take the opportunity to serve as Bona Buddies to area children or senior citizens; help with the nation's oldest student-run soup kitchen The Warming House; or volunteer in one of many service organizations, including ENACTUS and BonaResponds, one of the most active collegiate disaster relief organizations in the nation. Volunteer opportunities include immersion experiences and service opportunities with the poor, both in the United States and abroad.

St. Bonaventure University students enjoy two athletic facilities: the state-of-the-art Richter Center, which is open 24 hours a day, features three basketball courts, a running/walking track, racquetball/squash/wallyball courts, an aerobics room, a recreational area for roller hockey, a weight room, a cardiovascular fitness room, locker rooms, an equipment check-out, a reception area, and a climbing wall; and the Reilly Center, housing a 5,500-seat sports arena, swimming pool, and weight room. Also available are outdoor tennis courts; a field-turf complex for baseball, soccer, lacrosse, and rugby; and a nine-hole golf course. NCAA Division I athletics for men are baseball, basketball, cross-country, golf, soccer, swimming, and tennis. Division I competition for women includes basketball, cross-country, lacrosse, soccer, softball, swimming, and tennis. St. Bonaventure is a member of the Atlantic 10 conference, and both basketball teams made their NCAA tournaments in 2012.

In addition to its undergraduate programs, St. Bonaventure offers the Master of Arts degree in English. A Master of Science in Education program includes adolescence education, counselor education, differentiated instruction, educational leadership, literacy, school building leader, and school district leader. Master's programs in business administration, integrated marketing communications (with online option), and strategic leadership (online only) are also offered.

Location

St. Bonaventure is located on Route 417 between Olean, a city of approximately 14,000 residents, and Allegany, a village with about 2,000 residents. Shops, restaurants, and movie theaters are all within walking distance. The campus is spread over 500 acres in a valley surrounded by the Allegheny Mountains. The free Bona Bus connects the campus with Olean and Allegany, carrying students to and from the area attractions. The region around St. Bonaventure provides a beautiful setting for many outdoor activities. Holiday Valley, a renowned ski resort, is just 20 miles away, and nearby Allegany State Park offers excellent facilities for hiking, water sports, and cross-country skiing. Buffalo/Niagara International is the nearest major airport.

Majors and Degrees

St. Bonaventure University grants the Bachelor of Arts degree with majors in art, art history, classical languages, English, history, interdisciplinary studies, international studies, journalism and mass communication, strategic communication and digital media, modern languages (French and Spanish), music, philosophy, political science, professional and creative writing, psychology, sociology, theater, theology, and women's studies. The Bachelor of Science is granted with majors in biochemistry, bioinformatics, biology, chemistry, childhood studies, computer science, early childhood education, elementary/special education (dual certification), engineering physics, environmental studies, interdisciplinary studies, mathematics, physical education, physics, psychology, and sport studies. The Bachelor of Business Administration is granted with majors in accounting, finance, industrial management, management, and marketing. St. Bonaventure's dual-admission/combined-degree programs offer unique opportunities for students pursuing careers in medicine, dentistry, pharmacy, and physical therapy.

Academic Programs

Students in all majors begin their intellectual journey in Clare College, St. Bonaventure's nationally acclaimed core curriculum, which offers a values-based education grounded in the vision of Saints Francis, Clare, and Bonaventure.

A candidate for a bachelor's degree must complete at least 120 credit hours, with a cumulative index of 2.0 or better in the major field and the overall program. A pass/fail grade option, available to all upperclass students, may be elected for one course per semester, but not for courses in a student's major field.

Advanced credit is granted for grades of C or better on either the College Proficiency Examination or the College-Level Examination Program (CLEP) tests. Advanced placement is granted on the basis of scores obtained on the College Board's Advanced Placement (AP) examinations.

Men and women may also elect to participate in the University's Army ROTC program.

Off-Campus Programs

Through St. Bonaventure's membership in the College Consortium for International Studies (CCIS), St. Bonaventure students have access to six continents. More than sixty semester-long international study programs, including study in Italy, Spain, Ireland, and Australia, are available to students in good academic standing in their junior year. Faculty-directed, short-term opportunities include a three-week intersession in China and the Francis E. Kelly Oxford summer program. For further information, students should contact the Office of International Studies. Fieldwork or internships are available in several major programs.

Academic Facilities

Friedsam Memorial Library houses more than 250,000 volumes and includes a tri-level resource center with a curriculum center, the University archives, and digital media and conferencing centers, as well as world-class special collections—most notably, the University's remarkable rare books collection in the new Holy Name Library addition to Friedsam.

The William F. Walsh Science Center opened in 2008 and doubled the space for science studies. It houses state-of-the-art computer science, laboratory and classroom space, biology labs, organic and general chemistry labs, a Natural World lab, a 150-seat indoor amphitheater, and faculty offices integrated with lab space for better student-teacher accessibility. It is attached to historic De La Roche Hall, which received a major face-lift in 2008.

The John J. Murphy Professional Building is home to the Russell J. Jandoli School of Journalism and Mass Communication. The Bob Koop Broadcast Journalism Laboratory features a television studio with an anchor desk, digital and videotape editing bays, while a remote TV production studio allows for live broadcasting of athletic events. A fiberoptic network connects microcomputers in academic and administrative areas. There are seven labs for student use with more than 100 Macintosh systems. St. Bonaventure students also have wireless Internet access across campus.

The state-of-the-art Swan Business Center opened in 2013. The two-story building, with its unique glass-walled atrium and signature Bonaventure tile roof, gives students in the School of Business access to state-of-the-art technology and amenities that cater to the school's personalized, collaborative approach to business education.

An annex to Plassmann Hall houses computer-adaptable education classrooms, seminar rooms, and offices for the education faculty. An observatory allows students access to three compact telescopes, two 8-inch Celestron telescopes, and one 11-inch Schmidt-Cassegrain telescope, and a heated classroom.

The Regina A. Quick Center for the Arts provides acoustically designed classroom space for music courses and painting and drawing studios. The center also includes a musical instrument digital interface lab, a 325-seat theater, and an atrium that is often used for receptions and impromptu musical performances. The F. Donald Kenney Museum and Art Study Wing includes four climate-controlled galleries offering nationally acclaimed traveling exhibits, works from the University's permanent collections, and student exhibits.

Historic Hickey Dining Hall received a spectacular makeover in 2006, and a 5,500-square-foot coffee café and gourmet deli opened in spring 2007.

Costs

For 2014–15, the annual costs were $29,510 for tuition and $965 for fees. Room and meal plans averaged $10,786 per year.

Financial Aid

Students who qualify for financial aid normally receive a package consisting of a combination of scholarships, grants, loans, and work-study awards. An average financial aid package for an incoming freshman is more than $21,000. Athletic grants-in-aid are available for men in baseball, basketball, cross-country, golf, soccer, swimming, and tennis; and for women in basketball, cross-country, lacrosse, soccer, softball, swimming, and tennis. Students must file the Free Application for Federal Student Aid (FAFSA) to be considered for financial assistance. For more complete details, a student should contact the director of financial aid at the University.

Faculty

Like the student body, the 154 full-time and 69 part-time faculty members at St. Bonaventure come from a wide range of geographic, ethnic, and religious backgrounds. The student-faculty ratio of 11:1 allows faculty members the time to help each student to understand different modes of thinking, develop as a person, and lay a foundation for lifelong learning. Seventy-five percent of the full-time faculty members hold the terminal degree in their field. Franciscan friars, many of whom teach and live on campus, add to the unique atmosphere of St. Bonaventure.

Student Government

Life at St. Bonaventure is centered on the residence halls, and the foundation of student government begins in the dormitories with the Residence Hall Councils. The elected council members determine the norms by which the residents are guided in their daily lives. The Student Government, whose members are elected from the student body, serves as the general student-governing unit, and its members serve on every major University board and committee.

Admission Requirements

St. Bonaventure University welcomes applications for admission from all serious candidates from a variety of backgrounds. St. Bonaventure University provides equal opportunity without regard to race, creed, color, gender, age, national or ethnic origin, marital status, veteran status, or disability in admission, employment, and in all of its educational programs and activities. Applicants, who are welcome to apply online, must show evidence of academic achievement to be selected for admission. The criteria used in making admission decisions, in order of importance, are quality of the high school curriculum, grade point average in college-preparatory courses, ACT (preferred) or SAT scores, class rank, recommendations from high school teachers and counselors, and extracurricular activities.

Application and Information

For more information about St. Bonaventure University, prospective students should contact:

Office of Admission
St. Bonaventure University
P.O. Box D
St. Bonaventure, New York 14778
Phone: 716-375-2400
800-462-5050 (toll-free)
E-mail: admissions@sbu.edu
Website: http://www.sbu.edu

Basketball games are a rite of passage for students at St. Bonaventure, which plays in the Atlantic 10, one of the nation's best conferences.

COLLEGE CLOSE-UPS

ST. FRANCIS COLLEGE

BROOKLYN HEIGHTS, NEW YORK

ST. FRANCIS COLLEGE
THE SMALL COLLEGE OF BIG DREAMS

The College

Founded more than 150 years ago by the Franciscan Brothers, the mission of St. Francis College has always been to help young people achieve their life dreams of personal and professional success by making a top quality college education more affordable.

U.S. News & World Report ranks St. Francis College as one of the best regional colleges in the north as well as the fifth most diverse college in the north (2015). The College has been included by Forbes.com on its America's Best Colleges list, and was most recently named to *Money* magazine's Best Value for Your Money list.

St. Francis College offers more than seventy-two academic programs, majors, minors, and concentrations and serves more than 2,800 students. It strives to graduate students who are prepared to make a meaningful contribution to their chosen careers and to society, by offering a wide range of interests, which includes courses in the humanities, social sciences, natural sciences, nursing and fine arts. An academically challenging honors program offers a series of small, intensive seminars, various field trips, and other activities that build toward a senior thesis. The B.S./M.S. degree in accounting has positioned graduates to get jobs at both Big Four accounting firms and private companies.

As part of the NCAA Northeast Conference, students participate on nineteen Division I athletic teams, including men's basketball, cross-country, golf, soccer (NEC Conference champions, 2013, 2014), swimming and diving, tennis, indoor/outdoor track, and the nationally ranked water polo team (NCAA Final Four, 2013, 2014) Women compete in basketball, volleyball, bowling, cross-country, golf, tennis, indoor/outdoor track, swimming and diving, and water polo.

Student activities offer opportunities to get involved with extracurricular activities, as well as intramural sports. With more than 35 clubs and organizations, numerous active fraternities and sororities, honor societies including the Duns Scotus Honor Society, and a vast selection of national societies, students who participate are given the opportunity to grow socially and intellectually and further enhance their leadership skills.

Transfer students will find that St. Francis is the best place to complete their education and with up to 98 credits accepted, the College's personal approach will help ease the student's transition. A generous scholarship program is dedicated to transfers.

Location

Travel & Leisure magazine named Brooklyn Heights as one of America's most beautiful neighborhoods and also ranks nearby Brooklyn Bridge Park as one of the best spots, not just in the city, but in America, for its iconic quality; it's also the home field to the St. Francis College men's soccer team. Students consider Brooklyn Heights and Manhattan as their extended campus with access to museums, historical societies, cultural activities, theater, shopping, restaurants, and sports arenas offering abundant experiences for personal enrichment.

Featuring newly renovated and amenity-rich rooms, the College's off-campus housing at the St. George Residence offers safe, secure, and fully furnished rooms with private bathrooms, high-speed Internet, phone service, TV with DVD player, and refrigerator. Communal spaces include state-of-the-art kitchens, lounges, Wi-Fi, and a fitness center.

Majors and Degrees

Bachelor's and master's degree programs are offered in accounting (B.S., B.S./M.S., M.S.), adolescence education 7–12 (B.A., B.S.), childhood education 1–6 (B.A., B.S.), communication arts (B.A.–advertising/public relations; English and communications; digital media: film, broadcasting, and journalism; performance studies), criminal justice (B.S.), economics (B.A.–finance, international economics, public policy), English (B.A.), health promotion and science (B.S.), healthcare management (B.S.), history (B.A.), information technology (B.S.), international cultural studies (B.A.–international business, Latin American/Caribbean studies, Western European studies), management (B.S.–e-commerce, finance, general business, international business, marketing), mathematics (B.S.), nursing (B.S.), philosophy (B.A.), physical education K–12 (B.S.), physician assistant studies (B.S.), political science (B.A.), professional studies (B.S.–organizational management and leadership, management of technology), psychology (B.A., B.A./M.A.), religious studies (B.A.), social studies (B.A.), sociology (B.A. social work), and Spanish (B.A.).

Bachelor's degree programs for pre-health professions include the Bachelor of Science in nursing program (B.S.N.) offered to qualified freshmen and transfer students interested in preparing for the NCLEX Exam. The RN to B.S.N. program is also offered to those who already have their RN certificates.

Associate degrees programs are available in business administration (A.A.S.), criminal justice (A.A.S.), and liberal arts (A.A.).

Certificate programs are offered in American studies, information systems, instructional technology, entrepreneurship, and insurance. A graduate certificate program in project management is also available. Numerous minors are also available with the newest being entrepreneurship.

Academic Programs

The core curriculum is the academic cornerstone of the College, offering big opportunity in a small community and providing support every step of the way. The Office of Freshman Studies coordinates advisement and scheduling for all first-year students making sure that each student reaches their academic goals. During their first year, freshmen are enrolled in Freshman Seminar, which teaches time and stress management, success strategies, and how to search for a major and a career. Many go on to take a sophomore year life-lessons course that provides practical advice on how to search for a job or graduate school, prepare for an interview, and make and keep connections with successful graduates of St. Francis. Students must choose a major by the end of their sophomore year. If a student decides to obtain a minor designation, a minimum requirement of nine credits shall apply unless otherwise specified. All graduation requirements must be met for the completion of a degree program.

The Academic Enhancement Center provides tutoring, intensive reading and writing courses, and workshops to achieve academic success and independence at all levels of the student's college career.

The College calendar is organized on a traditional semester system, including one January Intersession, May Intersession, and three summer sessions.

Off-Campus Programs

Participating in an internship related to the student's career path offers hands-on experience. The College's Career Center provides services, tools, and an up-to-date listing of New York metropolitan area companies that offer internships, all designed to help students reach their goals, enhance learning outside the classroom, and prepare for a rewarding career.

Opportunities to go global are readily available at St. Francis College. As a member of the College Consortium for International Studies, students who wish to study abroad have great flexibility as to where they would like to travel and study. Students can study in places such as Paris, Madrid, Rome, Prague, Costa Rica, Australia, and even a Semester at Sea. They can also explore the world of learning through the faculty-led program in various other countries. Each year, 2 students also have the opportunity to experience a Franciscan pilgrimage to Assisi, Italy, and other places associated with Saint Francis and Saint Clare. This ten-day annual pilgrimage will allow these qualified students to learn more about the Franciscan history, values, and traditions associated with the College.

Academic Facilities

The Frank and Mary Macchiarola Academic Center is the newest building on the St. Francis campus. This 35,000-square-foot building houses the College's library, an HDTV studio and edit suite, black box theater, state-of-the-art classrooms, computer labs, and seminar rooms. The $20-million building emphasizes the College's commitment to small class size by limiting all new classrooms to no more than 35 students. The library provides 24/7 access from virtually anywhere to more than 200,000 in print and online books, 26,000 e-journals, and 40 subject-specific and multi-disciplinary databases. The collection has been developed specifically to support student research needs and departmental curricula. Much of it is downloadable to mobile devices. The library also offers than 50 computers in two labs, 40 netbooks that can be loaned out, dedicated study spaces, and reference help. Librarians provide one-on-one and group instruction for research projects using library resources. The library also includes a smart classroom and group study rooms with plasma screens for students to view films or practice multimedia presentations. As part of the Academic Center, the Maroney Forum for Arts, Culture and Education is a 90-seat theater for plays, musical performances, workshops, and lectures. The theater is equipped with an HDTV projector to play high-definition movies and videos created by students in the HDTV production studio. The theater has excellent acoustics, a catwalk to help adjust lighting, a control room, green room, and a sympodium that allows professors to include multimedia in their lectures. The College's HDTV studio is equipped with everything needed to produce a complete live program and features three Ikegami HD studio cameras, a lighting grid, professional switching and character generator equipment, and a chroma key curtain. Communication arts majors who are in production classes also have the opportunity to write, shoot, and edit their own video projects with the department's HD cameras and Final Cut Pro editing software loaded onto all the Macs.

The Eileen C. Dugan Life Sciences Center is a newly designed state-of the-art addition to the College that features the biology, chemistry and physics labs, which offer safe and appropriate places to conduct experiments in a wide variety of sciences for pre-med and science majors.

The cutting-edge nursing lab is equipped with real-world medical simulators SimMan, SimMom, and SimBaby, which let nursing students diagnose and treat illnesses as they would encounter them on the job.

Division I athletic teams take great pride as they play in the Generoso Pope Athletic Complex. Other recreational facilities include the fitness center, aquatics center, and the Anthony J. Genovesi Center.

Costs

For 2014–15, the annual tuition and fees for a full-time commuter student was $22,300 and rates for off-campus housing ranged from $13,130–16,280 (nine-month term). Tuition, fees, and housing rates are all subject to change. The most up-to-date and complete tuition and fee schedule is available online at www.sfc.edu/tuitionandfees.

Financial Aid

St. Francis College prides itself on offering both academic excellence and value—it is one of the most affordable private colleges in the New York City area. Nearly 95 percent of SFC students receive some form of financial aid including federal and state grants, federal loans, and institutional scholarships. Merit-based scholarships that cover near-full tuition for graduating high school students with a 1200 on their SATs are the cornerstones of the College's financial aid program. During 2013–14, the College awarded more than $17 million in institutionally funded scholarships and grants with amounts that ranged from $5,000 to 10,000. Additional partial scholarships, academic achievement grants, and transfer student scholarships are also part of the generous aid packages.

Faculty

St. Francis College professors have a strong commitment to developing each student's potential and helping them reach their goals. With a student-faculty ratio of 18:1, the small class setting allows for personalized attention and support, which increases personal achievement. Professors bring current theories and knowledge to the classroom and create opportunities for students to participate in active and ongoing learning. St. Francis College faculty members are also well-versed in the Franciscan tradition, which ensures an educational environment that supports students and helps develop the whole person.

St. Francis College professors also believe learning is more than just a classroom activity. Several of them have expanded on their own research by creating institutes and centers dedicated to their interests and expertise including, Center of Excellence in Project Management, Institute for International and Cross-Cultural Psychology, Institute of E-government and Global Sustainability, Center for Crime and Popular Culture, Women's Studies Center, Center for Entrepreneurship, Institute for Peace and Justice, Institute of E-Governance and Sustainability, and Pinniped Ecology and Cognition.

Student Government

Student government serves as a sounding board for all student interests, while also providing efficient and productive leadership for the student body. Its goals are to facilitate student communication, coordinate and encourage student participation, provide means for responsible and effective student participation in appropriate decision-making processes of the College.

Admission Requirements

St. Francis College seeks to admit students who can successfully pursue courses leading to a degree. Students must submit evidence of successful high school completion, acceptable SAT or ACT scores, and an application for admission. While admission to St. Francis College is competitive, the admissions committee seeks a student body that is ethnically and socially diverse with the potential to succeed in college rather than meeting any prescribed pattern of entrance units. The office of admissions expects applicants to have pursued a challenging high school curriculum by taking advantage of honors and advanced placement classes where appropriate. Applicants seeking an associate or bachelor's degree must present a transcript from an approved secondary school. All applicants who are currently enrolled in secondary school are required to take the SAT or ACT and submit their test scores to the College.

Transfer students must submit official transcripts from the previously attended schools as well as a secondary school transcript or certificate of graduation. A catalogue from the colleges previously attended may be requested.

Application and Information

Students are encouraged to visit the campus and meet with an admissions counselor before applying. Students may apply online at no charge: www.sfc.edu/apply. A virtual tour is available at www.sfc.edu.

For more information, students should contact:

St. Francis College
Office of Admissions
180 Remsen Street
Brooklyn Heights, New York 11201-9864
Phone: 718-489-5200
Fax: 718-802-0453
E-mail: admissions@sfc.edu
Website: http://www.sfc.edu
https://www.facebook.com/SFCNY

With a vibrant campus community and more than 70 academic programs, St. Francis College puts students on the path to success.

SAINT FRANCIS UNIVERSITY

LORETTO, PENNSYLVANIA

★ To read more about this school, visit http://petersons.to/saintfrancisuniversity

SAINT FRANCIS UNIVERSITY
FOUNDED 1847

The University

Saint Francis University is a small, coeducational, liberal arts university. The University was founded in 1847 and is conducted under the tradition of the Franciscan Friars of the Third Order Regular. The University is concerned with the development of each student for the world of today. For more than 160 years, the University's philosophy of education and student life has continued to emphasize two values: high-quality instruction and respect for the student as an individual. The University believes that a liberal arts education, encompassing a major field of study, is the soundest kind of preparation a student can have for a productive life. In recent years, Saint Francis University has garnered recognition for advances in study abroad and outreach in health care. The University is accredited by the Middle States Association of Colleges and Schools. Departmental accreditations include the Accreditation Review Commission on Education for the Physician Assistant, Inc., ABET (engineering accreditation commission), International Assembly for Collegiate Business Education, and others. A complete list of accreditations may be found in the University catalog.

Students at Saint Francis University can find a number of outlets for their talents, interests, and abilities. Departmental clubs; volunteer organizations; social, business, and service fraternities; social sororities; and a service sorority are part of campus life. Athletics have played a major role in the University's history, and the athletics program offers twenty-two NCAA Division I sports for men and women as well as intramural sports. The university is a member of the Northeast Conference and competes in the Atlantic 10 Conference for field hockey, and the Eastern Intercollegiate Volleyball Association for men's volleyball. The Student Activities Organization sponsors an impressive program of lectures, films, and concerts. The Southern Alleghenies Museum of Art, separately chartered, is located on the campus as well.

The full-time undergraduate enrollment is 630 men and 940 women; the University as a whole enrolls approximately 2,400 students. Saint Francis University offers Associate of Science degrees in business administration, and religious education. On the graduate level, Saint Francis grants a Master of Arts degree in Human Resource Management. The University also offers the Master of Business Administration, Master of Education, Master of Educational Leadership, Master of Health Science, Master of Medical Science, Master of Physician Assistant Science, and Master of Science in Occupational Therapy degrees. A doctoral degree in physical therapy is also available. Postbaccalaureate certificates are offered in accounting, computer systems management, and paralegal studies.

Location

Saint Francis University is situated on 600 acres in the heart of the Allegheny Mountains. The campus is located in the borough of Loretto, which has a population of approximately 1,400. The campus is 6 miles from the county seat of Ebensburg, which has a population of 4,000. The cities of Johnstown and Altoona are within 25 miles of Loretto and have populations of 35,000 and 55,000, respectively. The University is a 90-minute drive east of Pittsburgh.

Majors and Degrees

Saint Francis University grants the Bachelor of Arts degree and offers majors in arts and letters, aquarium and zoo science, biology, chemistry, communications, environmental studies, engineering (3-2 program), English, fermentation arts, history, international studies, mathematics, philosophy, political science, psychology, public administration/government service, public health, religious studies, Spanish, and sociology. The Bachelor of Science degree is also granted, with majors in accounting, biology, chemistry, computer science, economics and finance, early childhood education, environmental engineering, exercise physiology, management, management information systems, marketing, mathematics, medical technology, middle childhood education, nursing, occupational therapy (five-year master's), petroleum and natural gas engineering, pharmacy (2+3 or 2+4), physical therapy (six-year doctoral degree), physician assistant science (five-year master's), podiatric science, psychology, public administration/government service, public health, social work, and sociology.

Areas of pre-professional study include chiropractic studies, dentistry, engineering (3-2 program), law, medicine, optometry, pharmacy, podiatry, and veterinary medicine. Areas of concentration within majors include bioinformatics, computer science, criminal justice, environmental science, forensics, gaming/new media design and production, healthcare management, information technology and security, international studies, marine education, molecular biology, political communications, public management, and public relations. The University also grants secondary education certification in the areas of biology, chemistry, English, general science, history, mathematics, and social studies. A 3-2 cooperative program with Duke University in forestry and environmental management, a 3+4 accelerated program in primary care, a 2+3 accelerated program and a 3+3 program in pharmacy with Lake Erie College of Osteopathic Medicine, and a 3+4 accelerated program leading to the baccalaureate and Doctor of Dental Medicine degrees with Temple University are also offered.

It is possible for students to major in one area and minor in another or to have a double major. A self-designed major program is available as well. The University offers an honors program to challenge intellectually ambitious students from all disciplines. While pursuing their major field of study, students enroll in the full four-year curriculum, which allows in-depth, creative study in a variety of subject areas.

A continuing education program provides credit and noncredit courses on campus, online, and in the communities surrounding Loretto. The Office of Adult Degree and Continuing Studies offers a variety of academic programs ranging from certificate programs to bachelor's degree programs. Areas of study include business, computer systems management, health sciences, and religious studies.

Academic Programs

The program of study leading to a bachelor's degree is usually completed in eight semesters. To qualify for graduation, a student must follow a program of study approved by the Office of the Provost that totals at least 128 credits distributed among liberal arts courses, major requirements, collateral requirements, and general electives. All students, regardless of major, are required to complete the University's general education program of 58 credits.

The academic calendar is divided into two semesters and three summer sessions.

Electronic capabilities at Saint Francis University enable students to access library holdings and communicate with professors, fellow students, and the world through the use of personal computers via e-mail and the Internet. Every classroom and residence hall room is wired for Internet access or can be accessed through the wireless network. The University has several classrooms equipped with state-of-the-art equipment that allows videoconferencing. All students receive a laptop computer as part of their tuition.

Off-Campus Programs

Students at Saint Francis University may, with permission of the University's administration, spend their junior year of study abroad or may earn credit for participation in summer programs conducted in Canada, France, Germany, Spain, and other countries by accredited American colleges and universities.

Students are encouraged to take advantage of the University's study abroad facility in Ambialet, France anytime throughout their academic career. The Semester in France program offers study for students within any major for the same tuition costs as studying on campus.

A number of departments offer students the opportunity for off-campus study. For some majors, such as nursing, occupational therapy, physical therapy, physician assistant science, education, medical technology, and social work, internships and/or clinical rotations are required. Saint Francis University strongly encourages students in all other academic majors to complement their field of study with an internship, study abroad, a community service experience, or academic research with a faculty member.

Academic Facilities

Recently the University's School of Science began operations in a new 70,000-square-foot-Science Center. This center, with its state-of-the-art laboratories and research facilities, is a tremendous complement to Saint Francis' already high-quality instruction and serves as the campus' flagship facility for science and technology programs. The DiSepio Institute for Rural Health & Wellness, a 30,000-square-foot education and research center, also opened recently. The facility includes a human performance laboratory, a state-of-the-art fitness facility, and rehabilitation services. The final phase of a campus-wide master plan involves the renovation of Sullivan Hall to house modern classroom and lab space, tailored to meet the needs of the University's highly regarded health science programs. An additional project centered on academic facilities includes the renovation of Schwab Hall in order to house the entire School of Business.

Costs

For 2015–16, tuition is $31,078, room and board are $11,190, and the technology fee is $1,050—for a total of $43,318. The technology fee provides each student with a Lenovo ThinkPad supported by the on-campus Information Technology staff.

Financial Aid

Approximately 98 percent of the Saint Francis University student body receives financial aid. In addition to participating in federal and state need-based student aid programs, Saint Francis University offers its own substantial grant program and a generous scholarship program that is based on SAT or ACT scores, high school average, and class rank. Academic awards range from $1,000 to $16,000 annually.

Faculty

Faculty members are chosen for their knowledge of subject matter, as well as for their ability to communicate. Of the teaching faculty at Saint Francis University, 90 percent hold a doctorate or the highest degree attainable in their specific field of expertise. No teaching assistants or graduate students teach classes at Saint Francis University.

Student Government

The Student Government Association's Steering Committee involves students who are interested in self-government. Students also serve on a number of committees in the Faculty Senate. The Student Government offices are located in the John F. Kennedy Student Center, which also houses a 600-seat auditorium, a campus bookstore and post office, a study lounge, and a café.

Admission Requirements

The admission committee considers applicants and renders decisions on the basis of the secondary school record, the recommendation of the secondary school principal or counselor, and the results of the SAT or ACT. Applicants to the School of Health Science should be aware of specified application requirements and deadlines. Applicants should have a minimum of 16 academic units and are strongly encouraged to visit the University campus for an admission interview and tour. Interviews and campus tours are available Monday through Friday throughout the year and select Saturday mornings while classes are in session.

Transfer students must submit a formal transfer application and a college clearance form in addition to official transcripts from each high school and college previously attended. Transfer students receive an advanced standing evaluation after an offer of admission has been made.

Saint Francis University, an equal opportunity/affirmative action employer, complies with applicable federal and state laws regarding nondiscrimination and affirmative action, including Title IX of the Educational Amendments of 1972, Titles VI and VII of the Civil Rights Act of 1964, and Section 504 of the Rehabilitation Act of 1973. Saint Francis University is committed to a policy of non-discrimination and equal opportunity in employment, education programs and activities, and admissions that includes all persons regardless of race, gender, color, religion, national origin or ancestry, age, marital status, disability, or Vietnam-era veteran status. Inquiries or complaints may be addressed to the University's Director of Human Resources/Affirmative Action/Title IX Coordinator, Saint Francis University, Loretto, Pennsylvania 15940; telephone: 814-472-3264. For other University information, students should call 814-472-3000 or visit the website at www.francis.edu.

Application and Information

The University operates under a rolling admission policy. The occupational therapy, physical therapy, and physician assistant science program have a December 1 priority application date. For more information about Saint Francis University, students should contact:

Vice President for Enrollment Management
Saint Francis University
P.O. Box 600
Loretto, Pennsylvania 15940
Phone: 814-472-3100
866-342-5738 (toll-free)
E-mail: admissions@francis.edu
Website: http://www.francis.edu
http://www.facebook.com/SaintFrancisUniversity(Facebook)
http://twitter.com/SaintFrancisPA (Twitter)

Saint Francis University's 70,000-square-foot flagship facility for science and technology programs houses state-of-the-art classrooms, laboratories, and research facilities; advanced chemical instrumentation and youth outreach areas; and additional space for students and faculty to gather, study, and learn. This is also the home to the newly added petroleum and natural gas engineering program.

COLLEGE CLOSE-UPS

ST. JOSEPH'S COLLEGE, LONG ISLAND CAMPUS

PATCHOGUE, NEW YORK

★ To read more about this school, visit http://petersons.to/stjosephscollegelongisland

The College

Founded in 1916, St. Joseph's is an independent, coeducational college with campuses in Long Island and Brooklyn, New York. St. Joseph's has earned national recognition for affordability and value, dedicated to putting a top-quality private education within reach of every student who applies. The College offers one of the lowest tuition rates of any private college in the Northeast, delivering a personal, practice oriented-education rooted in the liberal arts.

With exceptionally high graduation rates—the best among Long Island institutions—St. Joseph's College helps students gain great return on their investment and turn aspirations into accomplishments. The College's relevant and extensive degree offerings ensure that graduates are ready for multiple careers and place them on a fast track to success. In addition to offering a liberal arts education of the highest quality, St. Joseph's offers students an unrivaled degree of personal attention, encouraging them to lead lives characterized by integrity, a commitment to upholding intellectual and spiritual values, social responsibility, and service to others.

At St. Joseph's College, students are taught by a renowned faculty made up of scholars and experienced professionals. The faculty members keep their curriculum exciting and relevant, offering a depth of knowledge with valuable hands-on professional preparation and career-building experiences for students at every level. Through numerous internship opportunities, St. Joseph's students are placed into their future careers. Recently, students gained invaluable experience interning at the offices of local politicians, as well as top businesses such as Viacom (MTV), Major League Baseball, the Brooklyn Navy Yard, and several accounting firms, including Grant Thornton LLP. Some of the College's accounting internships have led to full-time positions upon completion. For high-achieving students, St. Joseph's offers an enriched and rigorous academic experience through the Honors Program, as well as the opportunity to be inducted into several honor societies. Greek life is also available for those interested in service.

In addition to its undergraduate programs, St. Joseph's College offers a wide range of graduate and adult professional programs. St. Joseph's understands an advanced degree can help build new skills, acquire essential knowledge, and accelerate career advancement to leadership positions. It also lets employers know their employees are not only qualified but are persistent, determined, and equipped to handle new challenges. St. Joseph's College helps turn professional dreams into reality with programs that are relevant, exciting, and designed to accommodate even the most hectic schedules.

The 30-acre lakeside Long Island Campus—home of the Golden Eagles—is an ideal setting for studying, socializing, and partaking in extracurricular activities. Students can participate in 18 different varsity sports at the campus in Suffolk County, including equestrian, track and field, softball, and baseball.

In addition to sports, St. Joseph's College is a diverse campus community alive with theater, music, social activism, and countless opportunities to build enduring friendships. Students can find a club for every interest—political affairs, Asian awareness, science, drama, dance, journalism, and more. Joining a club or organization emphasizes leadership, community service, and effective communication.

St. Joseph's College has been repeatedly recognized for its commitment to providing individualized, high-quality education to students. For the thirteenth consecutive year, St. Joseph's College has been ranked among America's Best Colleges by *U.S. News & World Report,* and it has been named to *Forbes'* America's Top College list for seven straight years.

Location

Miles of white, sandy beaches, championship golf courses, shopping malls, exciting nightlife, and a prime location for innovative careers and people—Long Island has a pulse of its own. The remarkable growth of St. Joseph's Long Island Campus has kept pace with the island's and the village it resides in. Patchogue, New York, has successfully been revitalized and become a center of activity throughout the year. Just off Sunrise Highway, the College is easily accessible from all parts of Long Island. The campus is just 50 miles from Manhattan and 60 miles from Montauk Point.

Majors and Degrees

Through individual attention, interactive teaching, and intensive advising, St. Joseph's meets students where they are academically and then guides them through the essential next steps to help them stretch intellectually, personally, and professionally. St. Joseph's offers four-year programs leading to B.A. and B.S. degrees, with majors in accounting, biology, business administration, chemistry, computer information technology, criminal justice, education, English, history, hospitality and tourism management, human relations, journalism and new media studies, marketing, mathematics, mathematics/computer science, medical technology, nursing, political science, psychology, recreation, social sciences, sociology, Spanish, and speech communications.

No matter what major students choose, they can also earn additional certificates designed to help them delve deeper into specific interests and give them a head start when entering the workforce. Certificate programs include business administration and marketing, human services, mathematics and computer science, psychology, and social sciences.

For students interested in a fast track to an advanced degree after completing their undergraduate studies, St. Joseph's offers special affiliated programs where students can earn a B.S./M.B.A. degree in accounting, a B.A./M.A. in Mathematics Education, or a B.A. or B.S. in Adolescence Education/M.A. in Special Education within five years, or they can choose to pursue pre-professional programs in accounting, business administration, recreation, law, teaching, and numerous health fields, including dentistry, medicine, and veterinarian studies. In addition, the College has several dual-degree programs, which give students the opportunity to earn a bachelor's and master's degree in just five years.

Adult learners with nontraditional academic backgrounds or with professional training and experience can pursue degrees in accounting, computer information technology, criminal justice, general studies, health administration, hospitality and tourism management, human services, medical technology, nursing, and organizational management.

Academic Programs

Each campus operates on the semester system, with additional courses offered in January and during the summer. St. Joseph's students take a core curriculum that offers a wide range of choices and allows them to tailor their academic programs to their personal and professional needs. The College recognizes the Advanced Placement (AP) Program and offers credit and placement for scores of 3 or above on AP tests. In each case, the score is reviewed by the registrar and/or department chairperson to determine credit and placement. Students who will be receiving AP, IB or college credit through a college or university are required to send in these grades and/or transcripts in order to receive credit at St. Joseph's College.

For working adults, the College offers flexible schedules, summer programs, and online courses to meet the needs of working students. Courses may meet for a semester or for six- or twelve-week sessions.

Academic Facilities

The Long Island Campus features state-of-the-art facilities, including the Business Technology Center and the John A. Danzi Athletic Center as well as the Clare Rose Playhouse, the Callahan Library, and the new 24.8-acre Outdoor Field Complex, located approximately one mile east of the main campus.

Costs

The 2015–16 annual full-time tuition rate for undergraduates is $23,500.

Financial Aid

St. Joseph's offers generous scholarship opportunities and grants-in-aid. Eighty-three percent of St. Joseph's undergraduate students receive some form of financial aid. Students who wish to apply for either form of assistance must file the Free Application for Federal Student Aid (FAFSA) and a state aid form. After a student has been accepted to the College and all financial aid forms are processed, the Office of Financial Aid prepares aid packages that usually consist of federal, state, and College funds. St. Joseph's is fully approved for veterans. Campus work-study programs are also available.

Faculty

With nearly 600 faculty members who are widely respected scholars in their fields and a student-faculty ratio of 12:1, St. Joseph's students benefit from close professional and personal working relationships with their professors. Faculty members serve as academic advisers, are active on student affairs committees, and act as moderators in student organizations.

Admission Requirements

St. Joseph's College seeks a diverse student body and welcomes applications from high school students, transfer students, and adult learners who may have a nontraditional academic background. The College offers programs to serve all of these groups.

Students who wish to enter as freshmen are expected to have completed at least 18 units of college-preparatory work by the end of their senior year. This should include the following distribution: 4 years of English, 2 years of foreign language, 3 years of mathematics, 3 years of science, and 4 years of social studies. Applicants interested in accounting, allied health fields, biology, business administration, chemistry, or mathematics should have more extensive backgrounds in mathematics and science. In addition, the College accepts the submission of official results from the critical reading and math sections of the SAT, as well as ACT scores.

St. Joseph's College accepts a block transfer of credits from students holding an A.A. or A.S. degree in certain majors from an accredited junior or community college. All other transfers are considered on an individual basis.

Application and Information

Admission is offered on a rolling basis. Applications and supporting documents should be submitted online or to the appropriate school. The College reviews each application carefully and usually sends a decision one month after receiving all necessary credentials. For more information and an online application, students can access the website at http://www.sjcny.edu.

For additional information, prospective students should contact:

Director of Admissions
St. Joseph's College
155 West Roe Boulevard
Patchogue, New York 11772
Phone: 631-687-4500
Website: http://www.sjcny.edu
http://www.facebook.com/SJCNY
http://twitter.com/#!/SJCNY

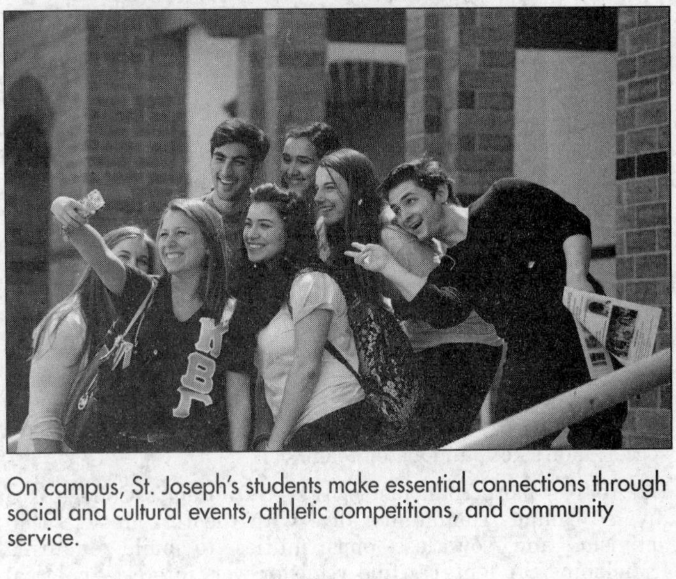

On campus, St. Joseph's students make essential connections through social and cultural events, athletic competitions, and community service.

ST. JOSEPH'S COLLEGE, NEW YORK

BROOKLYN, NEW YORK

★ To read more about this school, visit http://petersons.to/stjosephscollegenewyork

The College

Founded in 1916, St. Joseph's College is an independent, coeducational college with campuses in Brooklyn and Long Island, New York. St. Joseph's has earned national recognition for affordability and value and is dedicated to putting a top-quality private education within reach of every student who applies. It offers one of the lowest tuition rates of any private college in the Northeast, delivering a personal, practice oriented-education rooted in the liberal arts.

St. Joseph's College helps students turn aspirations into accomplishments by offering exceptional academic programs for undergraduate and graduate students, as well as adult learners. In addition to offering a liberal arts education of the highest quality, championship athletics, and an arts culture in the heart of Brooklyn, St. Joseph's offers students an unrivaled degree of personal attention, encouraging them to lead lives characterized by integrity, a commitment to upholding intellectual and spiritual values, social responsibility, and service to others.

At St. Joseph's College, students are taught by a renowned faculty made up of scholars and experienced professionals. They keep their curriculum exciting and relevant, offering a depth of knowledge with valuable hands-on professional preparation and career-building experiences for students at every level. Through numerous internship opportunities, St. Joseph's students are placed into their future careers. Recently, students gained invaluable experience interning at the offices of local politicians, as well as top businesses such as Viacom (MTV), Major League Baseball, the Brooklyn Navy Yard, and several accounting firms, including Grant Thornton LLP. Some of the College's accounting internships have led to full-time positions upon completion.

In addition to undergraduate programs, St. Joseph's College offers a wide range of graduate and adult professional programs. St. Joseph's understands an advanced degree can help students build new skills, acquire essential knowledge, and accelerate career advancement to leadership positions. It also signals to employers that their employees are not only qualified, but persistent, determined, and equipped to handle new challenges. St. Joseph's College helps turn professional dreams into reality with programs that are relevant, exciting, and designed to accommodate even the most hectic schedules.

St. Joseph's competes in NCAA Division III and is a member of the Skyline Conference. Students are able to choose from thirteen different varsity sports—six for men and seven for women. A variety of club sports are offered including women's soccer, men's golf, and a step team.

But there's more than just sports—St. Joseph's College is a diverse campus community alive with theater, music, social activism, and countless opportunities to build enduring friendships. Students can find a club for every interest—political affairs, Asian awareness, science, drama, dance, journalism and more. Joining a club or organization builds leadership skills, teaches effective communication, and provides valuable community service.

St. Joseph's College has repeatedly been recognized for its commitment to providing individualized, quality education to students. For the thirteenth consecutive year, St. Joseph's College has been ranked among America's Best Colleges by *U.S. News & World Report* and named to *Forbes'* America's Top College list for seven straight years.

Location

If there's one place that can match a student's energy and enthusiasm, it's Brooklyn—from Prospect Park and Coney Island to the Brooklyn Academy of Music and the Brooklyn Museum of Art. St. Joseph's is center stage in one of the borough's most successfully revitalized neighborhoods, historic Clinton Hill, where elegant brownstones and vest-pocket gardens lead to lively DeKalb Avenue, lined with cafés, bookstores, and boutiques. Just a few blocks away, the Barclays Center offers the best in entertainment and sporting events and is home to the Brooklyn Nets. This convenient location allows students to enjoy the freedom of a safe, well-landscaped campus and surroundings easily accessible to New York City by car or public transportation.

Majors and Degrees

Through individual attention, interactive teaching, and intensive advising, St. Joseph's meets all students (undergraduate, graduate, and adult learners) where they are academically, then guides them through the essential next steps to help them stretch intellectually, personally, and professionally. St. Joseph's offers four-year programs leading to B.A. and B.S. degrees, with majors in accounting, biology, business administration, chemistry, computer information technology, criminal justice, economics, education, English, history, hospitality and tourism management, human relations, journalism and new media studies, marketing, mathematics, medical technology, nursing, political science, psychology, recreation, social sciences, sociology, recreation, psychology, social sciences: economics, sociology, Spanish, and speech communications. Among these majors are a variety of minors from which students can choose.

No matter what major students choose, they can also earn additional certificates designed to help them delve deeper into specific interests and give them a head start when entering the workforce. Certificate programs include business administration and marketing, criminal justice, human services, mathematics and computer science, and religious studies.

For students interested in a fast track to an advanced degree after completing their undergraduate studies, St. Joseph's offers two special affiliated programs. One is an accelerated biomedical program in cooperation with the New York College of Podiatric Medicine, which allows students to receive a B.S. in biology and a doctorate in podiatric medicine within six years. The other allows students to earn B.S./M.B.A. degrees in accounting within five years, or they can choose to pursue pre-professional programs in accounting, business administration, recreation, law, teaching, and numerous health fields, including dentistry, medicine, and veterinary science. In addition, the College has several dual-degree programs, which give students the opportunity to earn a bachelor's and master's degree in just five years.

Adult learners with nontraditional academic backgrounds or with professional training and experience can pursue degrees in accounting, computer information technology, criminal justice, general studies, health administration, hospitality and tourism management, human services, marketing, medical technology, nursing, and organizational management.

Academic Programs

Each campus operates on the semester system, with additional courses offered in January and during the summer. St. Joseph's students take a core curriculum of 128 credits to graduate; a wide range of choices allows students to tailor their academic programs to their personal and professional needs. The College recognizes the Advanced Placement (AP) Program and offers credit and placement for scores of 3 or above on AP tests. In each case, the score is reviewed by the registrar and/or department chairperson to determine credit and placement.

For working adults, the College offers flexible schedules, summer programs, and online courses to meet the needs of working students. Courses may meet for a semester or for six- or twelve-week sessions.

Academic Facilities

The Brooklyn campus is composed of nine buildings, including historic landmark buildings. Students majoring in the widely recognized child-study program use the Dillon Child Study Center, which is a laboratory preschool enrolling approximately 100 students and a teaching and observation resource right on campus. McEntegart Hall, a modern five-level structure, houses the library, audiovisual resource center, curriculum library, archives, and computer labs. Other academic facilities include top-notch biology, chemistry, computer, physics, and psychology research laboratories. The Hill Center, a new state-of-the-art multipurpose complex, including an NCAA gymnasium and dance studio, opened in 2014.

A high-speed fiber-optic network connects all offices, institutional facilities, computer laboratories, and libraries on the campus. Direct Internet access is available to all students and faculty and staff members through the College's server. The integrated online library system enables students to locate and check out books at either campus and provides links to online databases and other electronic information sources.

Costs

The 2015–16 annual full-time tuition rate for undergraduates is $23,500.

Financial Aid

St. Joseph's offers scholarships and grants-in-aid. Eighty-three percent of St. Joseph's undergraduate students receive some form of financial aid. Students who wish to apply for either form of assistance must file the Free Application for Federal Student Aid (FAFSA) and a state aid form. After a student has been accepted to the College and all financial aid forms are processed, the Financial Aid Office prepares aid packages that usually consist of federal, state, and College funds. St. Joseph's is fully approved for veterans. Campus work-study programs are also available.

Faculty

With nearly 600 faculty members who are widely respected scholars in their fields and a student-faculty ratio of 12:1, St. Joseph's students benefit from close professional and personal working relationships with their professors. Faculty members serve as academic advisers, are active on student affairs committees, and act as moderators in student organizations.

Admission Requirements

St. Joseph's College seeks a diverse student body and welcomes applications from high school students, transfer students, and adult learners who may have a non-traditional academic background. The College offers programs to serve all of these groups.

Students who wish to enter as freshmen are expected to have completed at least 18 units of college-preparatory work by the end of their senior year. This should include the following distribution: 4 years of English, 2 years of foreign language, 3 years of mathematics, 2 years of science, and 4 years of social studies. Applicants interested in accounting, allied health fields, biology, business administration, chemistry, or mathematics should have more extensive backgrounds in mathematics and science. In addition, the College requires the submission of official results from the critical reading and math sections of the SAT.

St. Joseph's College accepts a block transfer of credits from students holding an A.A. or A.S. degree in certain majors from an accredited junior or community college. All other transfers are considered on an individual basis.

Application and Information

Admission is offered on a rolling basis. Applications and supporting documents should be submitted online or to the appropriate school. The College reviews each application carefully and usually sends a decision one month after receiving all necessary credentials.

For more information and an online application, students can access the website at http://www.sjcny.edu.

For additional information, prospective students should contact:

Office of Admissions
St. Joseph's College
245 Clinton Avenue
Brooklyn, New York 11205
Phone: 718-940-5800
Website: http://www.sjcny.edu
http://www.facebook.com/SJCNY
https://twitter.com/sjcnybkug

St. Joseph's offers programs in business, government, health care, and education, all available in nearby Manhattan, easily accessible by car or public transportation.

ST. LAWRENCE UNIVERSITY

CANTON, NEW YORK

★ To read more about this school, visit http://petersons.to/stlawrenceuniversity

The University

St. Lawrence University invites students to learn new ways of seeing the world, voicing ideas, and connecting with others. Graduates have the tools with which to think clearly, express themselves persuasively, and step into the world community with an understanding of their responsibility to all people and to the planet.

Founded in 1856, St. Lawrence is the oldest continuously coeducational degree-granting institution of higher learning in New York State. Initially established as a theology school for the Universalist Church, it quickly evolved into the liberal arts college that it is today. St. Lawrence is a private, nonsectarian university of approximately 2,400 undergraduate men and women, with a small graduate program in education. St. Lawrence is known for its residential/academic First-Year Program, its international study opportunities and area studies programs, its students' strong interest in the environment and the outdoors, and its strong sense of community.

St. Lawrence students are self-starters. The self-designed major is popular, intramural sports leagues are always full, and more than 100 student organizations serve broad interests, from communication to community service and creativity to social action. The University routinely hosts well-known speakers, while concerts, plays, and films are regulars on the weekly events calendar.

St. Lawrence students have historically placed high value on athletic activity, and a large number participate in varsity, intramural, or club sports. Most of the 32 varsity men's and women's teams compete at the NCAA Division III level, with the exception of men's and women's ice hockey, which compete in Division I, and riding, Alpine skiing, Nordic skiing, squash, and men's crew. Recreational facilities include cross-country ski and running trails; indoor and outdoor tennis courts; an athletic complex with a gymnasium, two field houses, a 133-station fitness center, a three-story climbing wall, and a pool; an ice rink; an equestrian center; a boathouse; a golf course; a nine-lane all-weather track; an artificial-turf field for lacrosse and field hockey; ten squash courts; and performance fields for soccer, football, baseball, and softball.

Residential life is an important aspect of the St. Lawrence experience. The University's innovative and highly regarded First-Year Program creates communities in which groups of approximately 30–35 first-year students live and learn together. In the upperclass years, students can choose from traditional residence halls, Greek chapter houses, suites, and theme cottages that focus on student interests such as low-impact living and community service. Seniors may also choose townhouses. St. Lawrence sponsors a full range of student services, from counseling to career planning.

Location

St. Lawrence is situated on a 1,000-acre campus in the village of Canton, New York (population 6,400), the seat of St. Lawrence County. Canton, with its Victorian homes, tree-lined streets, village green, farmer's market, restaurants, and small shops, is typical of college towns throughout the Northeast. Students and residents often mix in stores, at athletic events, and in community projects. Ottawa, Canada's capital, is 75 minutes to the north, while Lake Placid, one of America's hiking and skiing meccas, is 90 minutes to the southeast.

Majors and Degrees

St. Lawrence offers the Bachelor of Arts and Bachelor of Science degrees; students can choose from 35 majors and have the option of picking one of 38 minors. Combined five-year programs with other institutions are in place in engineering and management, and specialized advising is offered in preparation for postgraduate work in dentistry, law, medicine, nursing, physical therapy, and veterinary medicine.

Academic Programs

St. Lawrence's foremost mission is to provide its students with a liberal arts education. Students complete requirements in six areas and concentrated work in a major field as well as demonstrating competence in writing. Close faculty-student interaction is a hallmark of a St. Lawrence education. Every semester, many students engage in independent or honors projects, often working with professors on joint research projects that lead to publication in leading scholarly journals. A senior project is required in most majors.

Off-Campus Programs

St. Lawrence University supports a variety of off-campus programs on six continents that allow students to enrich their majors, expand their world, gain cross-cultural skills, and prepare to be responsible global citizens. More than 50 percent of St. Lawrence students study in one of the University's international programs during their collegiate careers. St. Lawrence operates programs in Australia, Austria, Canada, China, Costa Rica, the Czech Republic, Denmark, England, France, India, Italy, Japan, Jordan, Kenya, New Zealand, Spain, Thailand, and Trinidad and Tobago. The Kenya program is based at the University-owned and operated campus in the suburbs of Nairobi. The program strives to provide students with a unique study-abroad experience. In addition, the University's membership in the International Student Exchange Program permits students to directly enroll in universities in more than 32 additional countries. St. Lawrence operates programs at two other campuses in the United States: Fisk University in Nashville, Tennessee, and American University in Washington, D.C. St. Lawrence also administers its own Adirondack Semester Program, Sustainability Semester Program, and New York City Semester Program. The University also enrolls students in The Washington Center internship program, located in Washington, D.C.

Academic Facilities

Owen D. Young Library and Launders Science Library contain more than a million volumes as well as electronic resources and ample space for reading and research. Griffiths Arts Center is the home of the University's art and art history, performance, and communication studies academic programs as well as two theaters; an art gallery in which selections from St. Lawrence's 7,000-piece permanent collection are frequently shown; and the Peterson-Kermani Performance Hall, a 19,000-square-foot space for the performing arts. A unified science complex houses the departments of Biology, Chemistry, Physics, Psychology, Geology, and Mathematics, Computer Science and Statistics and is connected via a covered hallway to the science library and computing center. The 130,000-square-foot Johnson Hall of Science was the first LEED-certified gold science building in New York State. Richardson Hall, St. Lawrence's oldest building and on the National Register of Historic Places, is home to the English and religious studies departments. Other departments can be found in academic buildings clustered on one part of the campus, so classrooms are not far apart.

Costs

The comprehensive fee for 2014–15 was $59,982, including tuition, fees, room, and board.

Financial Aid

St. Lawrence awards both merit scholarships and need-based financial aid. More than 97 percent of the University's students receive some form of financial assistance, including scholarships, grants, student loans, and campus jobs. St. Lawrence is committed to assisting as many students as possible and recognizes academic and personal achievement in making financial aid decisions. To apply for need-based financial aid, students must file the Free Application for Federal Student Aid (FAFSA) between January 1 and March 1 and request that the results be sent directly to St. Lawrence.

Faculty

The 211 members of St. Lawrence's faculty are teachers and scholars who pride themselves on not just knowing student names, but knowing students. While teaching and advising are their primary responsibilities, they are also active researchers, artists, performers, and regular contributors in their academic disciplines. Faculty members teach all courses at St. Lawrence; no undergraduate courses are taught by graduate students. Active teaching assistants and tutoring programs, involving qualified upperclass students, are closely supervised by faculty members. The student-faculty ratio is about 11:1. Faculty members hold regular office hours, serve as academic advisers to students, and frequently take part in extracurricular activities on campus.

Student Government

The Thelomathesian Society, comprised of all students on campus, is governed by a senate of elected representatives. The senate distributes funds in support of student activities and provides two student delegates to the University's Board of Trustees.

Admission Requirements

St. Lawrence seeks students who can be successful in a demanding academic program and who can contribute to the quality of life of the community. The University is committed to enrolling students who represent the widest possible diversity of economic, social, ethnic, and geographic backgrounds. Academic preparation and ability are the most important criteria, but demonstrated ability in the creative arts, athletics, and/or social service is also a measure of a student's potential to benefit the St. Lawrence community. Candidates may choose whether or not to submit standardized test scores (SAT or ACT); University admissions are test-optional for domestic students. International students are required to submit SAT scores. A campus visit is strongly encouraged, and interviews may be scheduled on campus or off campus in certain areas.

Although there is no set distribution of required high school courses, successful applicants typically show strong preparation in the humanities, social sciences, mathematics, and natural sciences. Honors, Advanced Placement, and International Baccalaureate courses are opportunities for applicants to demonstrate intellectual maturity and curiosity, qualities highly valued in the admission process.

Application and Information

St. Lawrence uses the Common Application as its sole application form. The application processing fee is $60, which is waived if candidates have made an official visit to campus. Regular decision applications should be submitted by February 1, with notification in mid-March. Students who decide that St. Lawrence is their first choice may apply early decision. The priority deadline for early decision begins November 1; students may commit to early decision up until February 1. Early decision candidates will generally be notified within two weeks of receipt of a completed application.

Transfer candidates should submit applications no later than November 1 for the spring semester or March 1 for the fall semester.

For additional information, students should contact:

Office of Admissions and Financial Aid
St. Lawrence University
23 Romoda Drive
Canton, New York 13617
Phone: 315-229-5261 (admissions)
800-285-1856 (admissions, toll-free)
315-229-5265 (financial aid)
800-355-0863 (financial aid, toll-free)
E-mail: admissions@stlawu.edu or finaid@stlawu.edu
Website: http://www.stlawu.edu
http://twitter.com/StLawrenceU
http://instagram.com/StLawrenceU
http://www.youtube.com/StLawrenceU

The Johnson Hall of Science opened in 2007 and is LEED Gold certified. The 130,000-square-foot building includes teaching and research labs for biology, chemistry, psychology, biochemistry, and neuroscience.

SAINT LEO UNIVERSITY

SAINT LEO, FLORIDA

★ To read more about this school, visit http://petersons.to/saintleouniversity

SAINT LEO UNIVERSITY.

The University

Founded in 1889, Saint Leo University is recognized as one of the nation's leading Catholic teaching universities and a school of international consequence. The University Campus in Saint Leo, Florida, serves the educational needs of over 2,200 traditional-age undergraduate students. The University also offers a variety of dynamic graduate programs, a weekend and evening program for working adults, and both undergraduate and graduate degree programs at more than 40 education centers and offices in seven states and through the Center for Online Learning, which houses the University's cutting-edge online degree programs.

The University College student body represents 45 states and territories, as well as 61 countries. International students make up 13 percent of the student population. Minority students represent 38 percent of the University College enrollment. Approximately 63 percent of traditional full-time students live in one of thirteen residence halls.

Students can participate in the nationally recognized honors program and the more than seventy different clubs and organizations on campus, including national fraternities and sororities. The Student Government Union and various campus organizations also sponsor movies, concerts, art exhibits, lectures, dances, and other special events throughout the academic year.

Saint Leo is a member of the Sunshine State Conference and competes in NCAA Division II intercollegiate athletics for men and women. Men's sports include baseball, basketball, cross-country, golf, lacrosse, soccer, swimming, tennis, and track. Women compete in basketball, cross-country, golf, lacrosse, soccer, softball, swimming, tennis, track, and volleyball. Students can also participate in a wide variety of intramural athletics. Campus recreational facilities include lighted racquetball and tennis courts; soccer, baseball, lacrosse, and softball fields; a weight room/fitness center; and a heated outdoor competition-size swimming pool. The campus is bordered by a 154-acre lake and an eighteen-hole golf course.

Saint Leo is committed to giving its students an education that prepares them for the future. The goal of the University is to develop the whole person, both academically and personally, by providing a values-based education in the Benedictine tradition. In a recent satisfaction survey, 98 percent of respondents said they would recommend Saint Leo to a friend.

Saint Leo University is accredited by the Southern Association of Colleges and Schools Commission on Colleges to award the associate, bachelor's, master's, specialist's, and doctoral degrees. Saint Leo University's bachelor's and master's degree programs in social work are accredited by the Commission on Accreditation of the Council on Social Work Education (B.S.W. level). The Donald R. Tapia School of Business received initial accreditation by the International Assembly for Collegiate Business Education (IACBE) in September 1999. Saint Leo's undergraduate Sport Business program and M.B.A. Sport Business concentration are accredited by the Commission on Sport Management Accreditation (COSMA). Saint Leo University also has Teacher Education Programs approval by the State of Florida Department of Education.

In addition to associate and bachelor's degrees, Saint Leo University offers a Master of Accounting (M.Acc.); Master of Business Administration (M.B.A.) degree; a Master of Education (M.Ed.) degree; Master of Science (M.S.) degrees in criminal justice, cybersecurity, critical incident management, and instructional design; a Master of Arts (M.A.) degree in theology; a Master of Social Work (M.S.W.); and an education specialist degree. The University also began offering a Doctor of Business Administration (D.B.A.) degree in 2013.

Location

Saint Leo is located 35 minutes north of Tampa and 90 minutes west of Orlando. The scenic lakeside campus occupies 259 acres of rolling hills and wooded grounds. The resort-like setting is conducive to academic success and the University is located near metropolitan areas that give students the advantage of a wide variety of social and professional opportunities.

Majors and Degrees

Saint Leo University offers more than 50 traditional majors, pre-professional studies, specializations, endorsements, and programs. Undergraduate degrees offered are the Bachelor of Arts, Bachelor of Science, and Bachelor of Social Work.

The Donald R. Tapia School of Business offers degrees in accounting, communication management, computer information systems, computer science, economics, health care management, hospitality management, human resources management, management, marketing, multimedia management, and sport business. The School of Arts and Sciences offers majors in biology, English, global studies, history, mathematics, political science, psychology, religion, and sociology. The School of Education and Social Services offers majors in criminal justice, elementary education, middle grades education, secondary education, and social work.

Specialized advising is available for students interested in pursuing professional or graduate study in the fields of law, medicine, dentistry, osteopathy, nursing, and veterinary science.

Academic Programs

Saint Leo's new University Explorations general education program ensures that all graduates have a solid grounding in theories, issues, and knowledge to prepare them for successful careers and graduate work. The program develops the skills that are the foundation of a liberal arts education and that today's employers demand. Students learn essential skills in critical thinking and decision making, effective communication, problem solving, analysis, and creativity. Students complete foundation courses in English composition, mathematics, and computer skills. Students then select courses of interest from liberal arts learning clusters including The Human Adventure, The Human Mosaic, Science in a Changing World, The Creative Life, and The Reflective and Spiritual Life.

Saint Leo has an academic skills program to assist first-year students in their adjustment to university life. Included in this program are freshman studies, tutoring, and advising.

Students who demonstrate course mastery for any course listed in the catalog have the opportunity to receive up to 40 hours of credit through examination. Detailed information about credit by examination is available through the Registrar's Office.

Most students at Saint Leo earn the credits needed for their bachelor's degree through a four-year program of study. All major programs require a 2.0 minimum grade point average for graduation.

Off-Campus Programs

Saint Leo University is committed to helping students expand their horizons through study-abroad programs. Students have the opportunity to spend semesters studying at more than a dozen international universities, including schools in France, Italy, Ecuador, Spain, Australia, Ireland, England, Scotland, Greece, and more. Articulation agreements also afford study opportunities throughout Asia and the Pacific Rim. A partnership with the Semester at Sea program gives students the unique opportunity to spend a semester studying and traveling aboard the *MV Explorer*.

Students are also able to work with their professors and academic advisor to identify and pursue a wide variety of internship options, further enhancing the real-world experience component of their education.

Academic Facilities

The Cannon Memorial Library contains 105,508 volumes, and provides access to 355,685 e-books (non-unique e-book titles),

477 print periodical subscriptions, 126,364 unique e-journal titles, and 75 online databases. Also located in the library are the Hugh Culverhouse Computer Instruction Center classrooms, a student computer lab, and two VTT-equipped instruction/conference rooms.

Lab facilities include three teaching labs and one research lab for biology; two teaching labs, one research lab, and an instrumentation room for chemistry; and one physics lab. Labs have undergone comprehensive renovations, the most recent in 2012. The state-of-the-art building housing the Donald R. Tapia School of Business opened in fall 2011 and features SMART board technology, a Mac computer lab, and a broadcast studio. In 2014, the BB&T Center for Innovation & Technology was completed in the Donald R. Tapia School of Business. The Center houses the Cybersecurity Laboratory, which supports the teaching of the university's new master's degree in the field, and the Collaboration Zone, where business students work on real-world projects for area companies and nonprofits. The former Plant Operations building was renovated to serve as the new Fine Arts Building, completed and opened in spring 2015. Construction began spring 2014 on a new 48,000-square-foot academic building scheduled to be completed for fall semester 2015.

Students are encouraged to utilize the University's Learning Resource Center (LRC). The LRC is housed in the Student Activities Building and features study and meeting space for small groups as well as such technology as high-speed laser printers. Professional and peer tutoring services are available to students and may be scheduled through the LRC. Central to campus is the Student Community Center, which houses the dining hall, campus bookstore, student lounge, and Lion's Lair snack shop, as well as substantial meeting space for groups of various sizes.

The University's campus is a mostly wireless environment. All students who reside in campus housing receive a state-of-the-art laptop computer or iPad. For students living off campus, computers are available for use free of charge in the library and Learning Resource Center.

Costs

For the 2015–16 school year, tuition is $20,150; freshman room and board costs are $9,870, and mandatory fees are $680. Miscellaneous indirect costs for the year (such as books, personal living expenses, insurance, and travel) are estimated at $4,272.

Financial Aid

Saint Leo University offers generous financial aid packages which may include federal, state, and/or institutional aid in the form of grants, scholarships, and loans. Financial aid is allocated on the basis of academic performance and need, as determined by the federal government from the financial information provided on the Free Application for Federal Student Aid (FAFSA). On-campus jobs are available for students, with priority given to students with demonstrated financial need. Ninety-three percent of students receive some form of financial aid.

Faculty

At Saint Leo University, outstanding teaching and active learning go hand in hand. Caring and capable faculty members provide students with knowledge, guidance, academic support, and a broad range of learning opportunities both in and outside the classroom. Students enjoy small classes (average class size is 19) and develop close relationships with experienced, well-qualified professors. At Saint Leo, 84 percent of full-time instructional faculty members hold a terminal degree in their field.

Student Government

A significant contribution to the University comes from the activities initiated by the Student Government Union (SGU). The SGU is an annually elected body organized and conducted in accordance with democratic procedures. This organization strives to foster leadership and loyalty among the students, to formulate recommendations for student life, and to recognize all extracurricular activities.

Admission Requirements

All candidates for admission should be, or expect to be, graduates of secondary schools accredited by a regional or state accrediting agency. Applicants should show successful progress toward graduation with a minimum of 16 academic units of course work: 4 units of English, 3 units of mathematics (algebra I and II and geometry), 3 units of social studies, 2 units of science, 2 units of a foreign language, and 2 units of electives. All domestic applicants are recommended to take the SAT or the ACT examination, although the University does offer a test-optional policy for admission. A letter of recommendation from the student's guidance counselor is also required. Average SAT score (math and critical reading) for students entering in fall 2014 was 1000; average composite ACT score was 22; average GPA was 3.39. Students may request to be considered for admission under the test-optional policy that requires additional credentials in lieu of standardized test scores. Students who do not meet regular admission criteria are reviewed by the Admissions Committee for the Learning Enhancement for Academic Progress (LEAP) program, a preparatory program that has a summer attendance component.

Once the applicant has submitted the application with the $40 application fee (fee is waived if application is submitted online), high school transcripts, test scores (if not utilizing test-optional policy), and letter of recommendation, the file is reviewed and a decision is rendered. Notification is on a rolling basis. The priority application deadline is January 15; all applicants are encouraged to apply early.

Transfer and international students are also encouraged to apply. International students for whom English is not the primary language of instruction must have a score of at least 550 (paper-based test) or 78 (Internet-based test) on the TOEFL, a minimum of 6.0 on the IELTS, or a minimum of 450 on the verbal component of the SAT. The Bridge program is available to international students who fall just below the minimum language proficiency requirements.

Campus visits are strongly recommended. The Office of Admissions is open Monday through Friday from 8 a.m. to 5 p.m. and on select Saturdays during the academic year from 9 a.m. to noon. Appointments are preferred. Campus tours are available Monday, Tuesday, Thursday, and Friday at 9:30 a.m. and 1:30 p.m. as well as on Wednesdays at 9:30 a.m. and 4 p.m. Tours are also offered at 9:30 a.m. on select Saturdays during the academic year. Summer tours are available Monday through Friday at 9:30 a.m. and 1 p.m. as well. The Office of Admissions is closed on Sunday.

Application and Information

Additional information and application forms can be obtained by contacting the Office of Admissions. Candidates may apply online at www.saintleo.edu/apply.

Reggie Hill
Assistant Vice President of Enrollment
Office of Admissions—MC2008
Saint Leo University
P.O. Box 6665
Saint Leo, Florida 33574-6665
Phone: 352-588-8283
800-334-5532 (toll-free)
Fax: 352-588-8257
E-mail: admissions@saintleo.edu
Website: http://www.saintleo.edu

Students at the Saint Leo University campus in Saint Leo, Florida.

COLLEGE CLOSE-UPS

ST. LOUIS COLLEGE OF PHARMACY

ST. LOUIS, MISSOURI

★ To read more about this school, visit http://petersons.to/stlouiscollegeofpharmacy

ST. LOUIS COLLEGE of PHARMACY
EST. 1864

The College

Founded in 1864, St. Louis College of Pharmacy is the third oldest continuously operating college of pharmacy in the nation. Members of the first board of trustees included pharmacists, physicians, and business leaders, such as Henry Shaw, founder of the Missouri Botanical Garden, and John O'Fallon, nephew of explorer William Clark. *U.S. News & World Report* ranked the College as one of the top four private colleges of pharmacy in the country in 2012.

St. Louis College of Pharmacy is an independent college that primarily admits students directly from high school and the curriculum integrates the liberal arts and sciences with a professional program leading to a Doctor of Pharmacy (Pharm.D.) degree with an integrated Bachelor of Science degree.

More than 1,360 students from 32 states are currently enrolled at the College. Its 6,900 alumni practice in 48 states and 15 different countries. Three out of four practicing pharmacists in the St. Louis metropolitan area are graduates of the College and practice in a variety of areas: community or hospital pharmacies, managed care, consultant pharmacies, the pharmaceutical industry, military, academia, or pharmacy associations.

Location

Located in the heart of one of the world's most prestigious bio-medical, research, and patient-care centers, St. Louis College of Pharmacy provides innovative education, research, and career opportunities for students. The campus is one block from Forest Park, with its 1,300 acres of green space, tennis courts, ice-skating rink, golf course, and world-class museums, zoo, outdoor opera theater, and science center. Students at the College are near the cultural and entertainment scene of St. Louis on a safe, 8-acre campus within a block of public transportation.

Academic Programs

St. Louis College of Pharmacy's academic program includes three years of undergraduate work and a four-year professional program leading to a Doctor of Pharmacy (Pharm.D.) degree with an integrated Bachelor of Science degree. Students are admitted directly from high school into the College's preprofessional program and progress into the professional program without additional testing or reapplying, as long as progression requirements are met. Transfer students may enter into any of the College's preprofessional years or the first professional year.

The curriculum prepares students to take on the expanding role of pharmacists on patient-centered health care teams and includes significant preparation in the sciences, including basic and advanced courses in biology, chemistry, and pharmaceutical sciences as well as courses in the liberal arts and social and behavioral sciences.

The program provides an innovative teaching model, which integrates coursework across foundational subject areas to improve learning and advance patient care. Students are also able to identify and incorporate specialty areas into their studies to prepare them for the wide variety of career options available for pharmacists. Offerings include professional elective tracks and a graduate certificate in business administration or an MBA degree through a collaborative agreement with the University of Missouri–St. Louis. Introductory pharmacy practice experiences (IPPEs) throughout the curriculum give students the opportunity to apply their education and develop knowledge, communication skills, and professional values through interaction with other health care providers and patients. During the final year of the curriculum, students choose from more than 600 settings across the country to participate in a series of eight 5-week advanced pharmacy practice experiences (APPEs), or rotations.

After three preprofessional years and one professional year in the program, students earn a Bachelor of Science degree that recognizes their strong preparation in math and science as well as a well-rounded education in the liberal arts.

St. Louis College of Pharmacy's Doctor of Pharmacy degree is accredited by the Accreditation Council for Pharmacy Education and the North Central Association of Colleges and Schools.

Off-Campus Programs

St. Louis College of Pharmacy offers APPEs and international experiences in South Africa, China, Ethiopia, Mexico, and Saudi Arabia through its Office of International Programs. Students impact health care worldwide through several initiatives, such as working in hospital and outpatient HIV/AIDS clinics, developing pharmacy assistant programs, and participating in student exchange programs. Students are also able to enroll in courses, such as International Service Learning, that provide opportunities to help build houses with Habitat for Humanity in many locations, including Guatemala, Costa Rica, and Poland.

Students volunteer thousands of hours in the community each year, and the College was recognized for that effort by being named to the 2013 President's Higher Education Community Service Honor Roll by the Corporation for National and Community Service—the highest honor a college or university can receive for its commitment to volunteering, service learning, and civic engagement. The College has spearheaded numerous off-campus service events, such as the St. Louis Medication Disposal Initiative, the Asthma-Friendly Pharmacies program, and Boo Fest, a sugar-free Halloween event for children with Type 1 diabetes and their families.

Facilities

St. Louis College of Pharmacy is undergoing a physical transformation to better meet the needs of students, faculty, and staff. Construction is underway on a new, six-story, 213,000-square-foot academic and research building, scheduled for completion in June 2015. The new academic building will house faculty and staff offices, classrooms, teaching laboratories, research laboratories, the library, enrollment services, and auditorium spaces. Other plans for campus include new spaces for residential life, dining, a student center, recreation center, and gymnasium.

Residence Hall is at the center of the 8-acre campus and houses 265 students and 10 resident assistants. Students are part of a small, supportive environment that emphasizes community and personal development. Residence Life staff organize social and educational activities designed to help students be successful at St. Louis College of Pharmacy and in life outside of the College.

Assistance is offered in many ways, including individual counseling, tutoring, individual coaching, student-to-student mentoring, and disability accommodations.

Costs

For the 2014–15 academic year, tuition for students in year one was $26,192, in year two was $25,877, and in years three through six was $29,250. A notebook computer (issued to all new students) and lab fees are included in tuition costs. Room and board costs for the academic year were $9,317 for shared units and $8,915 for suites. Additional costs, including books, student activity fees, student health fees, professional program fees, and new student program fees vary each year but average $1,090 per semester.

Financial Aid

The College offers merit- and need-based scholarships to new students by performing a holistic evaluation of students' academic achievement, financial need, community service, and leadership experience. Most scholarships awarded to new students are renewable. The average institutional financial aid received by freshmen in 2014 was $8,900.

The College participates in all applicable federal and state financial aid programs. Scholarships, grants, loans, and student employment are offered to help qualified students pay for college expenses.

Students planning to attend the College in the fall semester should submit the Free Application for Federal Student Aid (FAFSA). The College begins awarding financial aid in March and continues until all funds are exhausted.

Student Government, Clubs, and Organizations

St. Louis College of Pharmacy provides a full student-life experience, including more than 50 professional and social fraternities, intramurals, club sports, pharmacy organizations, and special interest groups. The College participates in 12 NAIA sports: men's and women's cross-country, men's and women's basketball, women's softball, men's and women's track and field, men's and women's tennis, men's and women's soccer, and women's volleyball.

Some campus organizations include: Adventure Club, Campus Crusade for Christ (CRU), Catholic Students Organization, ConjuRings (literary magazine), EUTS Dance Team, Gay/Straight Alliance (GSA), GEARS (Gaming, Electronics, Anime, Rec, Sci-Fi), International Students Organization (ISO), Pharmakon (school newspaper), Prescripto (yearbook), Roller Hockey, Society of Apothecaries and Dreamers, STLCOP Book Club ("Booksies"), Student Alumni Association, Student Body Union (SBU), Student Organization for Drug and Alcohol Awareness (SODAA), and theater.

The Student Body Union (SBU) serves as the governing body of students at the College. SBU is responsible for student appointments to administrative and faculty committees. SBU oversees disbursement of student activity funds, which are used to support student publications, social activities, theater and musical productions, and provide support for student organizations.

Admission Requirements

All students applying for admission to St. Louis College of Pharmacy must present evidence of the satisfactory completion of a four-year course of study in, and graduation from, a high school approved by a recognized accrediting body. The high school course of study should include 4 units of English; 4 units of math, including algebra 1 and 2 and geometry; and at least 3 units of science, including biology/lab and chemistry/lab.

Required application materials include the following: completed application and $55 nonrefundable application fee; statement of commitment; high school transcripts including cumulative GPA and senior-year class rank; official ACT or SAT results; guidance counselor recommendation; science teacher recommendation; technical standards form; personal essay; declaration of finances form (international students only); English language test results, such as TOEFL (only U.S. and non-U.S. citizens whose native language is not English); a copy of U.S. Citizenship and Immigration Service status (international students only); and test results from the Pharmacy College Admission Test (transfer students only).

Early decision students who wish to accept an offer of admission must confirm their intention to enroll by submitting a $500 tuition deposit within 15 business days of acceptance notification. Regular decision students must submit a $300 deposit within 15 business days of acceptance of notification. The application deadline for transfer students is February 1. The PharmCAS deadline for submission of all admission materials is February 1. Transfer students are accepted into any of the undergraduate years and the first year of the professional program.

Application and Information

Application deadlines can be found online at www.stlcop.edu.

For additional information or to apply, students should contact:
Registrar/Director of Admissions
St. Louis College of Pharmacy
4588 Parkview Place
St. Louis, Missouri 63110
Phone: 314-367-8700 Ext. 8313
800-278-5267 (toll-free)
E-mail: admissions@stlcop.edu
Website: http://www.stlcop.edu
http://www.facebook.com/STLCOP
http://twitter.com/STLCOPedu

Located in the heart of one of the world's finest biomedical research and patient-care centers, St. Louis College of Pharmacy provides innovative education, research, and career opportunities for students.

SAINT MARY'S COLLEGE

NOTRE DAME, INDIANA

The College

Saint Mary's College is a community of bright, talented women who are on the path to self-discovery. Saint Mary's curriculum is challenging, not only in the student's chosen area of study, but also within the liberal arts foundation unique to Saint Mary's called the Sophia Program, the writing proficiency and senior comprehensive programs, and the development of exceptional critical thinking skills. Ninety-three percent of the school's graduates complete their degrees in four years, and whether they choose new careers, graduate school, or postgraduate service, Saint Mary's alumnae are prepared for life.

Founded by the Sisters of the Holy Cross in 1844, Saint Mary's is a pioneer in the education of women. Saint Mary's holds true to her Catholic values by providing leadership development and a focus on social responsibility.

With more than 1,500 students from forty states and seventeen countries, Saint Mary's brings together women from a wide range of backgrounds and experiences. International and diverse students compose 18.7 percent of the student body.

Saint Mary's unique relationship with the University of Notre Dame provides access to the exciting atmosphere of a large university—just across the street. Students at both schools can take courses at either institution. Saint Mary's students can audition for Notre Dame's legendary marching band or work for the *The Observer*, the daily newspaper published jointly by Notre Dame and Saint Mary's. In addition, students participate in dances, concerts, lectures, and social organizations on both campuses.

Saint Mary's residential campus becomes the students' second home. Saint Mary's five residence halls include Opus Hall, which offers apartment-style living for seniors on campus. Residence halls host events such as dances and coffee nights with the College president, and compete with each other in intramural athletics. All residence halls have chapels, and the Church of Loretto, the main worship space, offers daily Mass.

As an NCAA Division III school and a member of the Michigan Intercollegiate Athletic Association, Saint Mary's sponsors varsity teams in basketball, cross-country, golf, lacrosse, soccer, softball, tennis, and volleyball. Club sports, cosponsored with Notre Dame, include gymnastics and figure skating. In addition, Saint Mary's offers many intramural sports. Angela Athletic Facility has multipurpose courts and a training and fitness center with weight and cardio machines, a rock-climbing wall, and fitness classes for every level.

Location

Saint Mary's beautiful 100-acre campus, set alongside the Saint Joseph River, is across the street from the University of Notre Dame, minutes north of the city of South Bend (population 101,000), and 90 miles from Chicago. The South Bend community provides opportunities for internships, field practicums, and volunteer service. Eighty percent of Saint Mary's students engage in service by the time they graduate (the national average is approximately 55 percent).

Majors and Degrees

Saint Mary's College offers five degree programs: Bachelor of Arts, Bachelor of Science, Bachelor of Business Administration, Bachelor of Fine Arts, and Bachelor of Music.

The Bachelor of Arts degree program includes majors in art (concentrations in art history and studio art); biology; chemistry; communication studies; communicative sciences and disorders; economics; elementary education; English literature; English literature and writing; English writing; French; gender and women's studies; global studies; history (including a concentration in women's history); humanistic studies; Italian; mathematics; music; philosophy; political science; psychology; religious studies; social work; sociology; Spanish; statistics and actuarial mathematics; and theater. Also offered for approved, qualified students is a student-designed major.

Students may obtain a Bachelor of Science degree in biology (concentrations in cellular/molecular biology, ecology, evolution, environmental biology, and integrative biology), chemistry (including a concentration in biochemistry), computational mathematics, mathematics, nursing, statistics and actuarial mathematics, and a student-designed major for approved, qualified students.

The Bachelor of Business Administration degree program offers majors in accounting, business administration, and management information systems. Concentrations in the business administration program include accounting, finance, international business, management, management information systems, and marketing.

The Bachelor of Fine Arts degree offers specializations in ceramics, fiber, new media art, painting, photo media, printmaking, and sculpture.

The Bachelor of Music degree program offers majors in music and music education. The College is a member of the National Association of Schools of Music.

A five-year, dual-degree engineering program is offered in cooperation with the University of Notre Dame and leads to a bachelor's degree from Saint Mary's College and a Bachelor of Science in Engineering degree from Notre Dame in aerospace, chemical, civil, computer, electrical, environmental, or mechanical engineering.

Saint Mary's education department, accredited by the National Council for Accreditation of Teacher Education, offers an elementary education major (grades K–6) and a secondary education minor (grades 5–12). With an elementary education major, students can also receive mild intervention licensure (K–6) and an Indiana reading licensure (P–12). Minors in English as a second language and early childhood education are also offered. In addition, the department offers programs for those interested in teaching the visual arts or music. Secondary education requires a major in one of the following: English, modern languages (French, Spanish), mathematics, science (science majors must complete licensing requirements in chemistry or life science), history (history majors must complete additional course work in political science and one of the following: sociology, psychology, economics), and political science (political science majors must complete additional course work in history and one of the following: sociology, psychology, economics).

The College offers more than forty minors, including American history, anthropology, computer science, environmental studies, justice studies, Latin American studies, and women's studies.

Academic Programs

In addition to completing the required credit hours in her chosen field, every student completes a senior comprehensive in her major (a thesis, a research or creative project, or a written or oral examination). All students must also complete a writing-intensive "W" course, usually in the first year, and an advanced portfolio of writing in the major discipline, usually in the senior year.

Off-Campus Programs

Intercultural competence is a cornerstone of the liberal arts education. Saint Mary's combines that with travel and adventure through study-abroad experiences in sixteen locations: Argentina, Australia, Austria, China, Ecuador, England, France, Greece, Honduras, Ireland, Italy, Morocco, South Africa, South Korea, Spain, and Uganda. Saint Mary's students may also study in other countries through a cooperative program with the University of Notre Dame. Domestic programs include a semester at American University in

Washington, D.C. for political science majors, opportunities for student teachers in Native American communities, and the Catalyst Trip, a journey to sites significant to the history of social justice.

Academic Facilities

Several buildings have computer labs in addition to computer "collaboratories," where students and faculty members can conduct online research in classroom settings.

The Cushwa-Leighton Library houses a collection of more than 228,000 volumes. Also located in the library are the Trumper Computer Center, the Instructional Technology Resource Center, and a rare-book room.

Laboratory facilities are available for biology, chemistry, physics, psychology, and foreign language students. Art studios, music practice rooms, the O'Laughlin Auditorium, and Moreau's Little Theatre provide space for fine arts creation, practice, and performance. The Spes Unica academic building provides students with technology-equipped classrooms, group and individual study spaces, and presentation spaces.

The Early Childhood Development Center provides education and psychology majors with a unique opportunity to work with young children on campus. Other facilities include the Madeleva classroom building, Science Hall, Havican nursing facility, and Moreau Art Galleries.

Costs

Expenses for the 2014–15 academic year included tuition and fees, $35,970; room and board, $10,930 (average); and miscellaneous expenses (books, transportation, and living costs), $2,500.

Financial Aid

The College strives to make a Saint Mary's education available for every admitted student by offering financial aid packages that might include institutional need-based assistance, merit scholarships, and work-study opportunities in addition to state and federal grants and loans. Last year, more than 95 percent of Saint Mary's students received financial aid totaling more than $24 million in College grants and scholarships.

All applicants for financial aid must complete the College Board PROFILE and the Free Application for Federal Student Aid (FAFSA) by March 1 for each year that they desire assistance.

Faculty

Saint Mary's professors are experts in their fields of study and mentors to their students inside and outside the classroom. Of the full-time faculty members, 83 percent hold earned doctorates or other terminal degrees. Saint Mary's also has 73 part-time faculty members.

Student Government

The Student Government Association (SGA) is a dynamic student-led organization that sponsors extracurricular and co-curricular activities including service projects, social events, and learning experiences. It provides student participants with leadership opportunities that often include leadership training. SGA has voting representatives on the president's two highest advisory boards, the Student Affairs Council and the Academic Affairs Council. A student is also a voting member of the College's Board of Trustees.

Admission Requirements

Applicants for admission to Saint Mary's College should be graduates of an accredited high school. Home-schooled students are encouraged to apply. All applicants must complete a four-year, college-preparatory curriculum that consists of a minimum of 16 academic (Carnegie) units where one unit represents one full year of study. The minimum requirements are: 4 units of English literature and composition, 2 units of the same foreign language, 3 units of college-preparatory mathematics (beginning with algebra I), 2 units of laboratory science, and 2 units of history or social science. The remaining required units should consist of three additional units in the above listed subjects.

Applications must include an academic transcript showing current rank (if available) and senior-year courses, a secondary school report, SAT or ACT scores, and an essay. There is no application fee, and Saint Mary's is a member of the Common Application.

Saint Mary's encourages students to visit the campus for a tour and interview. An interview with an admission counselor is recommended. Arrangements to attend classes, stay overnight, or have an admission interview via phone (for students who do not visit campus) can be made through the Office of Admission.

Application and Information

Saint Mary's has two application and notification programs: early decision and modified rolling admission. Highly qualified students who have selected Saint Mary's as their first choice for admission may apply under the early decision program. The application deadline is November 15, and the notification date is December 15. Students who apply for modified rolling admission, and those whose application files are complete on or before December 1, are notified of the admission decision by mid-January. Applications received after December 1 are reviewed in the order in which they become complete. The priority application deadline for regular admission is February 15. Applications are accepted, however, as long as space is available.

Interested students are encouraged to contact:

Office of Admission
Saint Mary's College
Notre Dame, Indiana 46556-5001
Phone: 574-284-4587
800-551-7621 (toll-free)
Fax: 574-284-4841
E-mail: admission@saintmarys.edu
Website: www.saintmarys.edu
facebook.com/saintmaryscollegeadmission

We promise you discovery. Discovery of yourselves, discovery of the universe, and your place in it.
—Sister Madeleva Wolfe, CSC,
President of Saint Mary's College from 1934–1961

COLLEGE CLOSE-UPS

SAINT MICHAEL'S COLLEGE

COLCHESTER, VERMONT

★ To read more about this school, visit http://petersons.to/saintmichaelscollege

The College

What matters?

Saint Michael's College believes that a college education should prepare students not only for a meaningful career, but also for a meaningful life.

That's why Saint Michael's students start by building a strong liberal studies foundation, then dive deep into their majors. By the time they graduate, Saint Michael's students have developed essential skills and knowledge that will help ensure success in any field. And in the meantime, they've also been active in service (through the popular MOVE program), in the great outdoors (with Saint Michael's pioneering Wilderness Program and Smuggs' Ski Pass), and with the close campus community in ways that educate the body, mind, and spirit.

And happiness matters. Saint Michael's abounds with bright, engaged, friendly, happy students and faculty. The College's formula for happiness is its close campus environment, its perspective-changing exploration of the liberal arts with experiential learning, its legacy of faith and service, and its stunning Vermont location.

All this happiness and engagement underscores Saint Michael's successes: The College is among only 10 percent of colleges and universities nationwide that host a prestigious Phi Beta Kappa chapter on campus. Recent graduates are Rhodes Scholars, Pickering Fellows, medical students, law students, dental students, medical researchers, pharmacists, new media specialists, sports writers, nonprofit directors, and more. Alumni include a U.S. Senator; one of the founders of MTV; and noted authors, scientists, investment bankers, doctors, social workers, teachers, professors, and journalists. No matter what career paths they choose, Saint Michael's alumni take with them a solid liberal arts foundation, a strong sense of self, and a desire to give back to their communities.

Students at Saint Michael's are seriously involved with life on campus, taking on leadership roles, rallying support for worthy causes, and generally making things happen. Because everyone lives on campus (student housing is guaranteed for all four years), there's a profound sense of community, and students always find someone ready for whatever adventures they have in mind—from taking on a research project to rock climbing. Over one third of St. Mike's students study abroad for a semester, an academic year, or a summer. The Dion Family Student Center and residence hall opened in fall 2013, adding more than 50 additional rooms and four stories of living space, including a cafe, digital lounge, gym, game room and meditation space.

Location

Saint Michael's beautiful, safe 440-acre campus is just 3 miles from Burlington, Vermont's largest city, and highly ranked by *Travel + Leisure* as one of America's best college towns. Burlington is a vibrant college town that is home to 14,000 students who attend five local colleges and universities. Downtown Burlington is a thriving city center of businesses that offer great opportunities for hands-on learning through internships. There are tons of shops, restaurants, and cafés, the Church Street Marketplace, and a lively music scene as well as numerous places to ski, skate, kayak, and bike. The Smuggs' Pass gives students access to some of the best skiing in the East at an incredibly affordable price, and Saint Michael's renowned Wilderness Program delivers dozens of outdoor adventure opportunities. Saint Michael's Cultural Pass gives students deep discounts to fine arts performances at Burlington's famous Flynn Center.

The Burlington International Airport, Amtrak station, Megabus stop, and Greyhound bus station are all only a 10-minute drive from the campus.

Majors and Degrees

Saint Michael's College offers Bachelor of Arts and Bachelor of Science degrees in 36 majors in the following areas: accounting, American studies, art, art education, biochemistry, biology, business administration, chemistry, classics, computer science, economics, elementary and secondary education, engineering (3+2), English, environmental science, environmental studies, French, gender studies, history, information systems, international relations, mathematics, media studies/journalism/digital arts, music, neuroscience, philosophy, physics, political science, pre-pharmacy, psychology, religious studies, sociology/anthropology, Spanish, and theater. In addition, advising programs for pre-medicine, pre-law, pre-dentistry, pre–physical therapy, and pre–veterinary studies are available in addition to 37 minors, including interdisciplinary areas.

Dual-degree programs are available in engineering through the University of Vermont (Burlington, Vermont) and Clarkson University (Potsdam, New York), and pharmacy through Albany College of Pharmacy's Burlington campus. A 4+1 M.S.A. program is offered in conjunction with Boston College, Northeastern University, Syracuse University, and Clarkson University (M.S.A. and M.B.A.).

Academic Programs

Saint Michael's prepares its students for success after college with a dynamic curriculum designed to foster intellectual curiosity and exploration, including a highly competitive Honors Program and many opportunities for self-directed study. The College's curriculum includes an experiential learning requirement and emphasizes a solid understanding of building blocks of a meaningful life as a well-rounded, thoughtful person: humanities, social sciences, religious studies, philosophy, natural sciences, mathematics, and fine arts. Saint Michael's students develop excellent communication skills through writing intensive courses and foreign language requirements. And the curriculum pays serious attention to questions of ethics and responsible citizenship.

The Saint Michael's academic year consists of two semesters and an optional accelerated summer session. The College's focus is on undergraduate instruction, and its small classes support this primary emphasis. Saint Michael's has a strong faculty-student research tradition and provides competitive opportunities for research for academic credit and with faculty during the academic year, as well as paid research over the summer.

Saint Michael's mission is most evident in its service-learning and experiential-learning opportunities. These are credit-bearing, educational experiences where students in an academic course participate in a thoughtfully organized service activity that meets identified community needs. Students reflect on the service activities in ways that develop further understanding of course content, a broader appreciation of the discipline, and an enhanced sense of civic responsibility.

Off-Campus Programs

At Saint Michael's, students can gain hands-on experience with an internship related to their career goals and majors.

Internships are available both locally and in other selected areas around the United States and abroad. Sites include scientific research laboratories, brokerage houses, hospitals, schools, newspapers, and accounting firms. Saint Michael's students are given free access to the county's public transportation system which grants them easy access to the city of Burlington.

More than a third of Saint Michael's students study abroad for a semester or an academic year. Unique Saint Michael's programs include study-abroad experiences at University of the Americas, Mexico; College of Ripon and York St. John, England; Kansai Gaidai University, Japan; and a Washington, D.C., semester program. In recent years, many students have studied abroad in locations such as Botswana, China, France, Ghana, Ireland, Italy, Nepal, Samoa, and Spain.

Through the Association of Vermont Independent Colleges, Saint Michael's students can take a semester at other private colleges in Vermont, including Middlebury, Bennington, Marlboro, Sterling, and Green Mountain College.

Academic Facilities

Saint Michael's has a Main Campus and a North Campus. Main Campus is home to almost all academic and administrative buildings. Durick Library provides students with state-of-the-art technology for research and a perfect environment for study. Collections include over 430,000 books and e-books, 120,000 online journals, and 5,000 DVDs. Students can log in to library research databases from on or off campus, even when studying abroad.

Students have access to approximately 500 computers connected to the College's campus-wide information technology network. All campus areas have wireless Internet access.

Cheray Science Center has up-to-date facilities for the study of biochemistry, biology, chemistry, environmental science, and physics.

Saint Edmund's Hall, an impressive academic complex, includes a Mac lab, media labs, psychology labs, computer facilities, and language labs, in addition to traditional classroom and lecture hall space.

Costs

Tuition and residence fees for the 2015–16 academic year are $51,175. The residence fee includes housing and meals and is based on a standard double room and a standard meal plan. Nearly 100 percent of students live on campus, and on-campus housing is both guaranteed and required. Housing options include traditional residence halls, apartment-style housing, theme housing, and suites.

Financial Aid

Approximately 90 percent of admitted students receive financial aid in the form of loans, grants, scholarships, and work-study dollars. Students must file the FAFSA by February 1 for fall-semester enrollment. Saint Michael's students have a 2.9 percent default rate compared to the national average default rate of 13.7 percent.

Faculty

Saint Michael's faculty members are known not only for being experts in their fields but for sharing that expertise effectively with their students. Their doors are always open, too—it's not unusual to join professors for coffee or lunch, or to be invited to their homes for dinner. Students find faculty members at fundraisers and on the sidelines of athletic games. Chances are excellent that they'll know every student's name by the end of the first week of class. Saint Michael's remarkable faculty includes 152 full-time professors, 88 percent of whom have the doctoral or terminal degree in their field. Many have been recipients of grants, awards, and honors in recent years. While undergraduate instruction is the focus of the College, faculty members remain active in their field through research and publication.

Student Government

The Student Association (SA), an active and important part of campus life, is an elected body of students that authorizes and funds most other student activities and organizations. Representatives from the SA sit on many campus-wide committees, including the Curriculum Committee and various committees of the Board of Trustees.

Admission Requirements

Successful applicants to Saint Michael's typically rank in the top 25 percent of their high school class and have a strong college-preparatory background. Students should have completed 16 units in English, foreign language, mathematics, science, and social science. SAT or ACT scores are optional. Of those who opted to submit them, the average SAT score last year ranged between 1600 and 1900, and the average ACT score was 26. Applicants wishing to be considered for merit-based aid are strongly advised to submit test scores if they fall within those ranges. In addition, students should submit a counselor recommendation and any teacher recommendations they choose. Transfer applicants must submit transcripts of all college work in addition to their final high school transcript.

Application and Information

Saint Michael's offers an Early Action admission program deadline (nonbinding) of either November 1 or December 1, as well as a regular action deadline of February 1. The transfer application deadline is April 15. Students should consult the website for application deadlines and information. First-year candidates for the fall semester are notified of their admission decision on or before April 1. A limited number of students may be admitted to the spring semester and should have their applications in by November 1. The College adheres to the Candidates Reply Date of May 1 for the fall semester.

For further information, students should contact:
Office of Admission
Saint Michael's College
One Winooski Park, Box 7
Colchester, Vermont 05439
Phone: 800-762-8000 (toll-free)
Fax: 802-654-2906
E-mail: admission@smcvt.edu
Website: www.smcvt.edu

The Dion Family Student Center contains meeting rooms, student life offices, Einstein's Bagels, a meditation room, WWPV (the campus radio station), and a variety of great study spaces.

COLLEGE CLOSE-UPS

ST. NORBERT COLLEGE

DE PERE, WISCONSIN

COLLEGE CLOSE-UPS

The College

With over $100 million in new construction and renovations during the past seven years, St. Norbert College is the place where students connect their passions with the needs of the world. The riverfront campus is part of the thriving corporate, entertainment, educational, arts, and cultural environment of northeastern Wisconsin. Learning takes place in residence halls and classrooms, in the community, and, literally, around the world.

The St. Norbert learning community helps students become critical thinkers, strong writers, and able communicators, in a setting that encourages student-faculty collaborations. The graduate-level work done by St. Norbert undergraduates, even as first-year students, is notable and puts them ahead of their peers when heading to graduate school or the workforce.

St. Norbert seeks to challenge student viewpoints and encourage exploration of new or different ideas, in an environment where students from around the world come together in exploration of local and global perspectives.

Faculty members at St. Norbert are active researchers and creators who make ongoing contributions to their fields. They're also compassionate individuals who care not only about their students' grades, but also about their growth, making time for one-on-one conversations with students on a daily basis. Student success is their top priority, and they regularly give out their home or cell phone numbers for easy student access.

St. Norbert offers more than forty programs of study, including several pre-professional programs. Students can also design their own major. Opportunities to study abroad abound, with numerous service opportunities for students locally, nationally, and internationally.

Each St. Norbert student is paired with an adviser who helps ensure that the student is on track with classes and will graduate in four years. St. Norbert's innovative career services office provides service throughout college and beyond. When students are surveyed nine months after graduation, 92 percent are employed or attending graduate school.

Student life offers a blend of learning and fun. Students flourish within the academically challenging environment, but with more than seventy clubs and organizations on campus, there's no shortage of ways to become involved outside the classroom. The twenty Division III athletics teams produce conference champions, national champions, and more Academic All-Americans than any school in the Midwest Conference.

Students frequently comment on the sense of community and worldwide opportunities available at St. Norbert. They talk about the challenges of the classroom and the heartfelt rewards of service opportunities. Graduates value the friendships with peers and faculty members that started at St. Norbert and may last a lifetime. Some students love the campus so much they refer to St. Norbert as their home.

Location

The St. Norbert campus, approximately 108 acres, is located on the banks of the Fox River in De Pere, Wisconsin, just minutes south of Green Bay, a metropolitan area of about 300,000 people. Rich culture, arts, and entertainment are present in historic De Pere and the greater Green Bay area, recognized as one of the 100 best communities for young people by America's Promise Alliance. The campus is part of a vibrant eighteen-county region of 1.2 million people, with paid internship opportunities at Fortune 500 companies, hospitals, schools, and service organizations.

ST. NORBERT COLLEGE 1898 DE PERE, WISCONSIN

Majors and Degrees

St. Norbert offers programs leading to the Bachelor of Arts, Bachelor of Science, Bachelor of Music, and Bachelor of Business Administration degrees.

Programs of study at St. Norbert include: accounting, American studies, art–fine arts, art–graphic design, biology–biomedical, biology–organismal, business administration, chemistry, chemistry–biochemistry, classical studies, communication and media studies, computer science, computer science–business information systems, computer science–graphic design and implementation, economics, education, English, English–creative writing, environmental science, French, geography, geology, German, history, human services (social work), international business and language area studies, international studies, Japanese, leadership studies, mathematics, military science/ROTC, music, natural sciences, peace and justice, philosophy, physics, political science, pre-dental, pre-engineering, pre-law, pre-medical, pre-nursing, pre-pharmacy, pre-veterinary, psychology, religious studies, religious studies–youth ministry, sociology, Spanish, teacher education, theatre studies, and women's and gender studies.

Graduate Programs: Through the college's Donald J. Schneider School of Business and Economics, founded in 2014, St. Norbert now offers an M.B.A. program. The Schneider School seeks to become the region's center for the study of sound business practices, championing principles and methods that will contribute to a thriving northeast Wisconsin.

In addition, the college offers Master of Arts in Liberal Studies and Master of Theological Studies degrees.

Academic Programs

As a liberal arts institution, the college prepares students for a lifetime of challenges and opportunities by equipping them with exceptional communication abilities, as well as critical-thinking, problem-solving, and leadership skills. An honors program offers additional challenge in areas of general education to those of superior ability. St. Norbert holds the highest four-year graduation rate in Wisconsin over the past ten years, backed by a four-year graduation guarantee.

Several St. Norbert students are recipients of full Army ROTC scholarships each year. Among the college's alumni are an impressive 12 Army generals who completed ROTC at St. Norbert.

Off-Campus Programs

St. Norbert students, regardless of major, can spend a summer, a semester, or a year abroad. In fact, 30 percent of St. Norbert students spend at least one semester abroad during their four years compared to less than 4 percent nationally. The college has more than seventy-five study-abroad program sites in thirty countries on six continents. An international study component is a part of majors in French, Spanish, and German, and both the international business program and the international studies major. All approved international study carries regular academic credit. St. Norbert scholarship assistance and other financial aid carry over to overseas study.

St. Norbert considers international experience vital to today's graduates and it is a key component of the college's educational mission. St. Norbert's international curriculum, taught by a faculty committed to global learning, prepares students to live in a global society. A Washington semester is also available through American University in Washington, D.C.

Additional service-learning opportunities are available throughout the year. Students can participate in the TRIPS (Turning Responsibility into Powerful Service) program in local, national, and international locations, or participate in a variety of other off-campus service opportunities.

Academic Facilities

A state-of-the-art library houses more than 250,000 volumes. The 80,000-square-foot library features enhanced technology, flexible study and classroom spaces, and a 24-hour computer study area. A studio on the lower level of the library opened in 2013 and has become a favorite place for students to collaborate.

The F. K. Bemis International Center provides students with opportunities to prepare for careers with greater international emphasis. Students from nearly twenty countries attend St. Norbert College annually. The center also serves as a resource for K–12 schools and Wisconsin businesses for language instruction, translation, and interpretation.

The stunning new $40 million Gehl Mulva Science Center houses the science programs as well as the Medical College of Wisconsin's northeast Wisconsin campus.

The recently completed Cassandra Voss Center offers innovative, holistic programming about gender and diversity, attracting leading figures in the field as speakers.

Thirteen residence halls provide the link between living and learning at St. Norbert. Some residence halls focus on community service or feature campus programs, such as the honors program. A recently completed apartment-style residence hall offers upperclassmen a transitional experience to living on their own. Many halls have chapels for students.

An enviable outdoor athletics complex provides the practice and competition venue for football, soccer, and track and field. Michels Commons, completed in 2012, is where students eat their meals and gather in Dale's Sports Lounge on evenings and weekends. Chefs prepare meals in front of the students and are able to get immediate feedback on favorite recipes.

Costs

For 2014–15, tuition and required fees for full-time students totaled $33,023 for the year. Room and board costs averaged $8,455 per year.

Financial Aid

Students share in more than $50 million of financial aid each year, including scholarships and grants, campus jobs, and educational loans. More than 95 percent of St. Norbert students receive financial aid, with the average aid amount of more than $24,000 per year. There are both need-based and merit-based awards.

Need-based awards are made on the basis of the Free Application for Federal Student Aid (FAFSA; St. Norbert College's code is 003892) and the St. Norbert College institutional application for financial aid. First-year applicants should submit their FAFSA by March 1 of their senior year of high school.

A multitude of work-study positions exist on campus as well as paid campus and community internships. St. Norbert students graduate with an average indebtedness of about $31,438.

Faculty

The St. Norbert faculty is composed of 204 men and women, with 88 percent of the full-time faculty members holding the doctoral or other terminal degree in their field. The student-faculty ratio is 14:1, and student success is a top priority of the faculty. They work closely with students in their major area of study, help students prepare for graduate school, write letters of recommendation, and work with those who seek independent study and research opportunities. Research fellowships and collaborations with faculty members are available to all students—as early as their first year—who may ultimately have the opportunity to present their research findings collaboratively with faculty members at national conferences. Faculty members also work with Career Services in its professional practice program.

Student Government

The college's Student Government Association (SGA) is active on campus, with representation extending as far as the college's board of trustees. The president of the college and his cabinet respect the voice of the student body, and openly discuss issues that impact students and the college community. There are more than seventy organizations for students to get involved in.

Admission Requirements

St. Norbert College welcomes enrollment from a diverse group of students who are prepared academically and who will make a contribution to the college's living and learning community. The whole student is considered, not just their grades and test scores. Students who are likely to succeed in this environment are accepted. The average GPA of admitted students was 3.5, and the average ACT composite score was 25. Students with superior scores and grades are invited to enroll in the honors program. The college encourages and welcomes applications from international, transfer, and diversity students.

Application and Information

Because the college gives preference to students according to the date of admission and enrollment deposit, it benefits students to apply as early as possible in their senior year. Notification of the admission decision is made on a rolling basis beginning in late September. A $350 nonrefundable deposit is required to confirm enrollment.

For more information about St. Norbert College, students should contact:

Edward Lamm
Vice President of Enrollment Management and Communications
St. Norbert College
100 Grant Street
De Pere, Wisconsin 54115
Phone: 920-403-3005
800-236-4878 (toll-free)
E-mail: admit@snc.edu
Website: http://www.snc.edu
http://www.snc.edu/go/socialmedia
http://twitter.com/stnorbert

A welcoming, supportive community greets first-year students at Convocation.

COLLEGE CLOSE-UPS

ST. THOMAS AQUINAS COLLEGE

SPARKILL, NEW YORK

★ To read more about this school, visit http://petersons.to/stthomasaquinascollege

The College

St. Thomas Aquinas College (STAC) was founded in 1952 as a three-year teacher-training college with 30 students. Today, the College offers more than 100 different majors, minors, specializations, and dual degree programs and has a total student body of 2,800 in all programs, on and off campus. Much growth and development has taken place over the College's history. The College offers a Master of Science in Education, with concentrations in autism, literacy, special education, and educational leadership as well as postgraduate certificate programs in autism (online), literacy, special education, and teacher leadership (online). The College also offers a Master of Business Administration (M.B.A.) program with concentrations in finance, management, and marketing; and an online M.B.A. in general studies. St. Thomas offers a Master of Science in Teaching program for individuals without a background in teacher education who are seeking a career change. Certification is offered in childhood education, grades 1–6; childhood education and special education, grades 1–6; adolescence education, grades 7–12; and adolescence education and students with disabilities, grades 7–12. The College is home to New York University's Master in Social Work program.

The suburban campus includes two residential complexes: Aquinas Village, which consists of self-contained townhouse units that house 300 students, and the McNelis Commons, which consists of townhouse residential units that house 375 students and a common dining hall and laundry building. Approximately 40 percent of the College's full-time student population resides on campus.

Extracurricular activities are provided through forty different organizations, including the Spartan Volunteers, a community service program; a student-run radio station (WSTK); the Laetare Players dramatic and musical club; and the student-edited campus newspaper and yearbook. The College has excellent sports facilities, and several of its athletic teams have competed in national championships. The College has 18 NCAA Division II teams in men's and women's cross-country, indoor and outdoor track and field, basketball, soccer, lacrosse, and tennis; women's field hockey and softball; and men's baseball and golf. There are a number of club sports including ice hockey, cheerleading and dance, bowling, and ski and snowboarding, as well as intramural athletics.

The College has a campus ministry office, a health office, and residence life, career development, and counseling services.

Location

The College is located in Sparkill, a hamlet in southern Rockland County, New York, 16 miles north of New York City and adjacent to Bergen County, New Jersey.

Majors and Degrees

St. Thomas Aquinas College's School of Business offers accounting (and accounting as a dual degree with an M.B.A. degree), finance, management, marketing, and sports management. Minors are offered in business management, marketing, economics, human resource management, international business, and management information systems. Specializations are in management relations/industrial and organizational psychology.

The School of Arts & Sciences offers degrees in the humanities, mathematics, natural sciences, and social sciences. Programs are available in art therapy, art and graphic design, communication arts, creative writing, English, journalism, philosophy and religious studies, Romance languages, Spanish, mathematics, computer sciences, biochemistry, biology, forensic science, medical technology, natural sciences, criminal justice, psychology, therapeutic recreation, social science, and history. There are specializations in biology, chemistry, and physics. Minors include art therapy, biology, chemistry, communication arts, computer information science, criminal justice, English, fine arts, graphic design, history, journalism, mathematics, performing arts, physics, public relations, religious studies, social media, sociology, Spanish, therapeutic recreation, and writing. A full listing of all programs can be found online at www.stac.edu.

The School of Education offers programs in grades 1–6 childhood education, the same plus special education, and grades 7–12 adolescence education, the latter offering certification in biology, English, history, mathematics, natural science with either biology or chemistry, social sciences, and Spanish. An art education program with certifications in grades K–12 is offered as well as a middle school extension that adds to either the elementary or secondary degree, enabling the student to certify for all middle school grades. The School of Education also offers several dual-degree programs: B.S./B.A. and M.S.Ed. in childhood (B.S.) and special education (M.S.Ed.), grades 1–6; mathematics (B.S.) and special education (M.S.Ed.), grades 7–12; social sciences (B.S.) and special education (M.S.Ed.), grades 7–12; and Spanish (B.A.) and special education (M.S.Ed.), grades 7–12.

The College offers a five-year dual-degree program in mathematics/engineering with The George Washington University (GWU) or Manhattan College. Students study at St. Thomas for three years. After completion of their final two years at either GWU or Manhattan, they earn a B.S. in mathematics from STAC and a B.S. in engineering from one of the other two institutions. The College also offers several dual-degree options in biology: a dual degree in biology (B.S. from STAC) and biomedical engineering (M.S. from Polytechnic University), a dual degree in biology (B.S. from STAC) and physical therapy (D.P.T. from New York Medical College), a dual degree in biology (B.S. from STAC) and chiropractic (D.C. from New York Chiropractic College), and a dual degree in biology (B.S. from STAC) and podiatry (D.P.M. from New York College of Podiatric Medicine). There are several other strategic alliances, such as preferred admission to St. John's University School of Law in New York and a similar program with Barry University School of Law in Florida that includes scholarship funds. St. Thomas also has strategic agreements with St. John's University for an M.P.S. in sport management and a Master of Public Health. St. Thomas seeks out additional strategic opportunities for its undergraduate and graduate students on a regular basis; students should contact the College for information about new alliances.

Academic Programs

The College strives to develop students who are not only generally educated but also possess advanced knowledge in specialized areas, are prepared for further study, and have the background to undertake fulfilling careers. To earn a bachelor's degree, students must complete a total of 120 semester hours, including a minimum of 51 credits in a core curriculum; complete all requirements for the specific major; and complete the final 30 hours at St. Thomas. The College awards up to 30 credits for life experience and up to 30 credits for achievement on the College-Level Examination Program (CLEP). The College operates on a semester calendar (quarterly on the M.B.A. level). Students may enroll in classes in the fall, winter (a one-month session), spring, and summer (three separate sessions). Undergraduate students can apply for the fall and spring semesters. Graduate education students can apply for the fall, spring, and summer semesters. M.B.A. students can apply for any of the four quarters that classes are offered. Classes are scheduled during the day and evening, and students are permitted considerable academic flexibility in planning their programs.

Students can pursue independent study and internships, and many majors require a field practicum. The College maintains an active Center for Academic Excellence as a resource for enhancing academic performance, and students are encouraged to meet regularly with faculty advisers for academic guidance and career direction.

Several programs supplement the traditional academic areas. The College has a widely recognized program for college-age learning-disabled students, called the Pathways Program (at an additional cost). The College also participates in the New York State Higher

Education Opportunity Program and provides an honors program (freshman applicants only) for exceptionally qualified students with a limited number of 70 percent scholarships. The honors program includes summer study at Oxford University. The Aquinas Leaders Work Scholarship program is for qualified students (freshmen applicants only) with strong academic abilities and a desire to gain work experience each semester that can be related to academic pursuits. Aquinas Leaders receive financial awards that cover approximately 60 percent of tuition costs over four years.

Off-Campus Programs

The College offers a campus interchange program involving other fully accredited colleges (Barry University in Miami Shores, Florida; Dominican College of San Rafael in San Rafael, California; Aquinas College in Grand Rapids, Michigan; and Kyung Hee University, Korea) through which a student may enroll in courses at one of the participating colleges for a semester or set time frame. The College also offers a number of study-abroad opportunities for students throughout the entire year with as short a period as one week for a communication arts class in London.

The study-abroad program provides opportunities at colleges and universities in such places as Brazil, Canada, England, France, Hungary, Ireland, Italy, Morocco, and Spain. Several other locations are also available.

The College offers courses for an associate degree program at West Point for eligible students at the United States Military Academy.

Academic Facilities

Borelli Hall, a green-designed, LEED-certified Silver building, features new classrooms with interactive board technologies. Costello Hall houses the science laboratories, technology theaters, and Azarian-McCullough Art Gallery. Spellman Hall houses a multiroom technology corridor, with a state-of-the-art communication studio where students produce their own news show, and technology and language labs. Lougheed Library provides a variety of online research opportunities for students. Aquinas Hall houses athletic facilities and a fitness center. Maguire Hall is home to classrooms, art studios, and the Sullivan Theater. Additional meeting areas are provided in the Romano Student-Alumni Center and in the two residence complexes, McNelis Commons and Aquinas Village. There is an after-hours club in the McNelis Commons dining hall for student activities.

Costs

For 2014–15, the tuition for full-time study (12 to 16 credits per semester) was $27,130; annual fees are $500. Room and board at the College Commons were $11,680. Certain studio, laboratory, and computer courses carry fees.

Financial Aid

In 2013–14, 85 percent of the student body received financial aid. The College is committed to providing competent but needy students with the resources necessary to continue their education. Students must submit the Free Application for Federal Student Aid each year. The College awards academic and merit scholarships from $5,000 up to 70 percent scholarships and provides need-based aid from the College as well as athletic grants and all federal and New York State aid programs.

St. Thomas strives to partner with the student to make college education affordable. The College has one of the lowest private college tuition rates in New York State, and scholarships make it even more affordable. The College is also a member of the Yellow Ribbon program for veterans enabling a qualified veteran to study with a full tuition scholarship.

Faculty

The faculty has 70 full-time and 55 part-time members; 80 percent have terminal degrees. The student-faculty ratio is 18:1. All faculty members participate in the academic advising of students and serve on College committees. Many serve as advisers to extracurricular activities.

Student Government

The Student Government consists of elected members who officially represent the student body, are responsible for planning and implementing student-originated programs, and coordinate and oversee all extracurricular organizations. Through its various offices, students play a vital part in offering consultation on new policies, planning social and cultural events, managing student funds, and operating the judicial system. In addition, the College Forum, which is composed of elected students, faculty members, alumni, administrators, and trustees, meets regularly to discuss policies, procedures, long-range plans, and any problems affecting the College.

Admission Requirements

All applicants must have successfully completed an approved secondary school program or the equivalent, including 4 years in English, 3 years in mathematics, 3 years in science, 2 years of foreign language, and 4 years of social studies. Applicants whose high school background varies from the recommended pattern are considered. Freshman applicants must submit the application for admission, including an essay, high school transcripts, SAT and/or ACT scores, and a letter of recommendation. Transfer students must submit the application and official transcripts of all previous college work. An academic evaluation is prepared for every matriculant. The College is a member of the Common Application and students are strongly encouraged to apply online through that service.

Application and Information

Candidates should submit completed application forms to the Admissions and Financial Aid Office and must request that their official transcripts be sent to the Admissions Office from their school. Students are notified of the admission decision on a rolling basis upon receipt of all the necessary credentials. The College is a member of the Common Application and students can find the link to apply on its website, http://www.stac.edu/apply.

St. Thomas Aquinas College does not discriminate in its educational programs, activities or employment practices based on race, color, national origin, sex, sexual orientation or expression, disability, age, religion, ancestry, genetic information, marital status, veteran status or any other legally-protected category. Announcement of this policy is in accordance with State and with Federal law, including Title VI and Title VII of the Civil Rights Act of 1964, Title IX of the Education Amendments of 1972, Section 504 of the Rehabilitation Act of 1973, the Age Discrimination in Employment Act of 1967 and the Americans with Disabilities Act of 1990. For more information, please contact: EEO, Section 504/ADA and Title IX Compliance Officer, 125 Route 340, Sparkill, New York 10976; phone: 845-398-4044.

For more information or an application, students should contact:

Admissions and Financial Aid Office
St. Thomas Aquinas College
125 Route 340
Sparkill, New York 10976-1050
Phone: 845-398-4100
E-mail: admissions@stac.edu
Website: http://www.stac.edu

St. Thomas Aquinas College's Costello Hall in the fall.

SAINT VINCENT COLLEGE

LATROBE, PENNSYLVANIA

★ To read more about this school, visit http://petersons.to/saintvincentcollege

The College

Founded in 1846, Saint Vincent College is the first Benedictine college in the United States. It is an educational community rooted in the tradition of the Catholic faith, the heritage of Benedictine monasticism, and the love of values inherent in the liberal approach to life and learning. There are 1,560 full-time undergraduate students and 66 part-time students, of whom 73 percent reside on campus. The College welcomes students from twenty-eight states and ten other countries. In addition to more than fifty programs in the liberal arts and sciences, the College offers the Master of Science degrees in education: in counselor education, curriculum and instruction, instructional design and technology, science education, special education, and school administration and supervision. The College also offers postbaccalaureate and certification programs in special education, instructional technology specialist, principal, early childhood director, English as a second language, and online teaching. Other graduate and professional programs include a Master of Science in management: operational excellence and a Doctor of Nurse anesthesia practice.

Student services include advising, athletics, career placement and planning, computer assistance, and a wellness center. Students choose from more than sixty social, political, cultural, service, recreational, and religious student organizations. Saint Vincent College is accredited by the Department of Education of the Commonwealth of Pennsylvania, the Middle States Association of Colleges and Schools, and the Association of Collegiate Business Schools and Programs.

Location

Saint Vincent College is located on 200 acres in the Laurel Highlands of southwestern Pennsylvania. Noted for its beautiful countryside, the region offers abundant opportunities for outdoor recreation and adventure. Excellent sites for hiking, mountain biking, skiing, camping, and white-water rafting are less than half an hour from the campus in ten state forests. Pittsburgh, a regional center of culture and the arts, is only 35 miles to the west. The city offers music, museums, theater, shopping, nightlife, and sports.

Majors and Degrees

The College offers fifty degree programs; the most popular majors are biology, communication, education, management, and psychology. The College is organized into four schools: the Alex G. McKenna School of Business, Economics, and Government; the Herbert W. Boyer School of Natural Sciences, Mathematics, and Computing; the School of Humanities and Fine Arts; and the School of Social Sciences, Communication, and Education.

The McKenna School includes majors in the areas of accounting, business education information technology, economics, finance, international business, joint economics and mathematics, management, marketing, politics, and public policy. The School of Natural Sciences, Mathematics, and Computing offers degrees in biochemistry, bioinformatics, biology, chemistry, computing and information science, engineering science, environmental chemistry, environmental science, mathematics, mathematics/engineering, and physics/physics education. The School of Humanities and Fine Arts offers majors in art administration (performing arts or visual arts), art education, art history, English, graphic design, history, liberal arts, music, music performance, philosophy, Spanish, studio arts, and theology. The School of Social Sciences, Communication, and Education offers degrees in anthropology, communication, criminology, law and society, education (early childhood or middle grades), pre-law, psychology and sociology. Middle grade certification is offered in language arts, mathematics, science, and social studies, while minors in K–12 and secondary education include art, biology, business/computing and information technology, chemistry, Chinese, English, French, mathematics, physics, social studies, and Spanish.

The College offers a law school 3+3 program in cooperation with Duquesne University. Students complete their requirements in English, history, political science, public policy analysis, and sociology at Saint Vincent College. In addition, in conjunction with university schools of engineering, the College offers a five-year cooperative liberal arts and engineering program, as well as a four-year degree in engineering science.

Saint Vincent offers pre–health training in accelerated osteopathic medicine, accelerated podiatric medicine, allopathic medicine, chiropractic medicine, dental medicine, occupational therapy, optometry, pharmacy, physician assistant studies, physical therapy, and veterinary medicine in cooperation with various professional schools.

Students may select minor areas of study in accounting, anthropology, art history, arts administration, biochemistry, biology, biotechnology, chemistry, children's literature, children's studies, Chinese language and culture, communication, computing and information science, economics, education, English, environmental chemistry, environmental science, finance, fine arts, forensic science (computer security, financial investigations, or natural science), French, German, graphic arts, history, international business, international studies, Italian, Latin, liberal arts, management: operational excellence, marketing, mathematics, music, music history, philosophy, physics, political science, public administration, psychology, sociology, Spanish, studio arts, and theology.

Academic Programs

An academic year consists of two semesters, fall and spring, with the opportunity to earn credits in the summer. Saint Vincent College requires each student to complete a minimum of 124 credits, satisfy the requirements for the major(s) as specified by the department(s) or school(s), achieve an overall grade point average of at least 2.0 as well as a grade point average of at least 2.0 in the major, and satisfy the capstone requirement as specified by the major department(s) or school(s). Each student must complete a core curriculum. The core curriculum provides all students with a broadly based education that provides a general body of knowledge in the humanities, social sciences, natural sciences, and mathematics; an interdisciplinary view of that knowledge base; and the skills to increase that general body of knowledge throughout their lives. Special programs include national and international academic honor societies, a cooperative education and internship program, an interdisciplinary writing program, and an honors program. An annual Academic Conference allows students to showcase their work across a variety of disciplines.

Off-Campus Programs

Saint Vincent students may choose to learn in surrounding communities, those across the country, or around the world.

Service plays a prominent role in the life of the campus—almost two-thirds of seniors take part in a service project, and every student organization completes at least one service project each year. There are numerous local service opportunities, as well as service trips to Alaska, Appalachia, New Jersey, and abroad in Brazil, China, Guatemala, Haiti, Italy, and Taiwan.

Students can study abroad for a semester, an academic year, summer, or spring break in places as diverse as Argentina, Australia, China, Egypt, Great Britain, France, India, Italy, Japan, Poland, Russia, South Africa, Taiwan, and Turkey. In addition to options in dozens of other countries, the College has affiliations with nine Chinese colleges and universities.

From the breadth of the liberal arts curriculum to the excitement of hands-on learning, Saint Vincent's goal is to encourage a love for learning that endures.

Academic Facilities

Saint Vincent College has invested more than $75 million in campus facilities during the past five years, including the new $39-million Dupré Science Pavilion, where every student takes at least one class.

The result is a modern, student-friendly campus that features accessible computer laboratories and workstations; fiber-optic cabling between buildings; Wi-Fi across campus and specialized laboratories for the study of astronomy, ecology, genetics, geology, human anatomy, life sciences, microbiology, optics, organic chemistry, physiology, and other subjects. From the multimedia computer lab to the nature reserve (created by golfing legend and College supporter Arnold Palmer) to the $14-million Fred Rogers Center for Early Learning and Children's Media, Saint Vincent offers many resources to help students intensify their learning.

Traditionally, Benedictine institutions have granted a place of honor to the library. Open 89 hours a week, the Latimer Family Library offers access to more than 250,000 printed volumes; 99,000 microforms such as microfilm, microfiche, and cards; 3,000 musical scores; 400 periodical subscriptions; and online access to electronic journals through 19 different databases. The library also houses a collection of rare books and incunabula (pre-1500 imprints). It also provides plentiful space for quiet studying.

The Robert S. Carey Student Center, covering more than 2 acres, contains the Frank and Elizabeth Resnik Swimming Pool, a gymnasium, performing arts center, wellness center, bookstore, fitness center, locker rooms and training rooms, snack bar, student lounge, chapel, billiards room, art gallery, art studios, and music practice rooms.

Costs

Tuition and fees at Saint Vincent for 2015-16 are $16,480 per semester, and room and board costs average $5,239 per semester, depending on accommodations and meal plan. Books and supplies cost $1,000–$1,500 per year. Costs are subject to change.

Financial Aid

Saint Vincent College offers a comprehensive program of financial aid in the form of scholarships, grants, loans, part-time employment, and deferred-payment schedules and coordinates programs from the federal and state financial aid program. In 2014–15, 100 percent of first-year students who applied for financial aid were offered assistance. The College annually awards qualified freshmen academic scholarships of up to $20,000 per year, renewable for up to four years, for excellence in academic achievement. In addition, the College offers first-generation grants, out-of-state grants, and grants to graduates of Catholic high schools and Benedictine parishes, among others. Other financial aid opportunities include Federal Direct Student Loans and Federal PLUS loans. Residents of Pennsylvania may be eligible for the Pennsylvania Higher Education Assistance Agency Grant program. In order to be considered for financial aid, students must complete the Free Application for Federal Student Aid (FAFSA).

Faculty

The faculty numbers 102 members, of whom 89 percent hold terminal degrees. Members of the faculty have earned doctorates or terminal degrees at such schools as Catholic University of America, Cornell, Duke, École Biblique, Fordham, Northwestern, Notre Dame, NYU, Stanford, Yale, and the Universities of California, Chicago, and Pennsylvania. Faculty members are engaged as principal investigators in research and other projects funded through government agencies such as the National Science Foundation and the U.S. Department of Education and private foundations. The student-faculty ratio is 12:1, and no classes are taught by teaching assistants. Faculty members have chosen to teach at Saint Vincent in part because they value the quality of student-teacher interaction, specifically the emphasis on high standards, personalized learning, fieldwork, hands-on experience, and the high level of classroom participation.

Student Government and Student Activities

The Student Government Association (SGA) builds community at the College by providing opportunities for the students, faculty members, and administrators to share in their common interests. All class officers, senators, and representatives can vote in the unicameral senate that makes up the student government.

The sense of community that Saint Vincent is known for is fostered from the day students arrive on campus. Orientation lasts five weeks and involves more than 150 upperclassmen whose mission is to make freshmen feel at home. Every student is matched with an upperclassman who serves as a big brother or big sister throughout the first year. In the residence halls (where more than 70 percent of students live), trained prefects foster a safe living environment and provide guidance and advice, along with activities and educational programs.

The College community is proud of the Catholic, Benedictine tradition that has shaped life on the campus for nearly 170 years. In keeping with the tradition of hospitality, Saint Vincent welcomes students of all faiths or of no faith. The campus includes places for prayer, as it is an important part of life for many of our administrators, faculty members, and students—no matter their faith traditions.

Admission Requirements

Saint Vincent College has a rolling admission policy. Adequate preparation for college is an important determinant for a successful college education. Fifteen secondary school academic units are required for admission to Saint Vincent College. These 15 units must include 4 units of English, 3 or more units of college-preparatory mathematics, 1 unit of laboratory science, and 3 units of social science; 2 units of a foreign language are preferred among 5 elective units. Engineering students must have 1 unit in plane geometry, 1 unit in intermediate algebra, 1 unit in physics, and ½ unit in trigonometry in addition to those listed above. Art education, art studio, and graphic design majors must submit a portfolio for acceptance to the Fine Arts Department, and music and music performance students must audition for acceptance.

Transfer students are invited to apply to Saint Vincent College, which awards generous scholarships to academically capable transfer students. The applicant's academic achievement and personal history at the postsecondary schools previously attended are of primary importance in the decision for admission.

Application and Information

To be considered for admission, a freshman applicant must submit a completed application form with the nonrefundable $25 application fee, an official transcript sent directly to Saint Vincent College from the guidance office at the secondary school of graduation, and an official copy of the test results from the SAT or ACT.

An application and additional information may be obtained by contacting:

Office of Admission and Financial Aid
Saint Vincent College
300 Fraser Purchase Road
Latrobe, Pennsylvania 15650-2690
Phone: 800-782-5549 (toll-free)
E-mail: admission@stvincent.edu
Website: http://www.stvincent.edu
https://www.facebook.com/saintvincentcollege (Facebook)
https://twitter.com/MySaintVincent (Twitter)
https://www.youtube.com/user/saintvincentcollege (YouTube)
https://instagram.com/SaintVincentCollege (Instragram)

Saint Vincent College offers a warm and welcoming atmosphere combined with technologically advanced facilities including the $39-million Sis and Herman Dupré Science Pavilion, dedicated in 2013.

SEATTLE UNIVERSITY

SEATTLEU

SEATTLE, WASHINGTON

★ To read more about this school, visit http://petersons.to/seattleuniversity

The University

Located in the heart of a city with incomparable access to innovation and culture, Seattle University (SU) attracts students who are inspired, open-minded, socially and environmentally conscious, and have an interest in social justice. Students are transformed at this distinctive Jesuit, Catholic institution that encourages a lifelong capacity to create a more just and humane world.

Seattle produces some of the world's most influential and renowned nonprofits and companies such as Microsoft, the Gates Foundation, Starbucks, Amazon, and Costco. Seattle University is an independent school of action with an ever-growing impact on the city, the community, and the world.

Being near the center of a major metropolitan hub provides opportunities for on-the-job training through internships and job shadowing. This also means SU reflects the remarkable climate of its home base, with long-standing community and international partnerships that enrich the education here and help shape future leaders.

The greatest successes at Seattle University are the result of people coming together and standing united to bring about change. For example, the Seattle University Youth Initiative, the University's largest-ever community engagement project, which continues to grow as it transforms academic achievement at the city's most underserved public elementary school. The lure of the Youth Initiative is compelling—so much so that an increasing number of incoming students say it's the top reason they chose SU. Worldwide, other universities—20 and counting—see the Youth Initiative as a successful prototype. The White House also noticed, and honored the Youth Initiative with a pair of awards for community service in recent years.

In a state like Washington, where dozens of different languages are spoken and every race, religion, and perspective is represented, Seattle University's 4,500 undergraduate students from 53 states and territories and 89 nations fit right in. Fall quarter 2014 had a freshman class of 936, with 65 percent coming from outside Washington state. The ethnic breakdown for the undergraduate student body in 2014 was 57 percent white, 22 percent Asian American, and 15 percent African American, Latino, and Native American. International students make up about 11 percent of the student body. Ninety-one percent of freshmen live on campus in six residence halls and apartment complexes. Students are required to live on campus for both their freshman and sophomore years unless they commute from home.

The lively, urban 50-acre Seattle University campus is pesticide-free and continues to win awards for its commitment to environmental leadership, energy conservation, and recycling and composting programs. In addition, the University's Center for Environmental Justice and Sustainability is housed in the greenest commercial building in the world.

Seattle University has more than 130 extracurricular clubs and organizations. SU Athletics (www.goseattleu.com) are NCAA Division I, with 8 varsity teams for men (baseball, basketball, cross-country, golf, soccer, swimming, tennis, and track) and 10 for women (basketball, cross-country, golf, rowing, soccer, softball, swimming, tennis, track, and volleyball).

Connolly Athletic Center, the major facility for varsity and intramural athletics and recreation, features two swimming pools, two full-size gymnasiums, and locker-room saunas. A six-acre complex provides fields for outdoor sports. The William F. Eisiminger Fitness Center, which opened in fall 2011, provides 21,000 square feet of fitness and cardio equipment, weights, and studio and classroom spaces.

Location

Some cities claim to thrive, but Seattle feels more like it pulses. Music, art, and culture are everywhere. There's the breathtaking skyline from the top of the iconic Space Needle or the Seattle Great Wheel, a 175-foot Ferris wheel on the Seattle waterfront. It's easy to hop a sightseeing ferry across Puget Sound or wander through Pike Place Market, the Olympic Sculpture Park or the Experience Music Project Museum, all a short trek from campus.

Students can catch a professional sporting event such as Sounders FC soccer or Mariners baseball. And the Super Bowl–winning Seahawks football team has given the whole city reason to consider itself the 12th Man.

A short walk from campus, students frequently people-watch at a café, take in an author reading at a quirky bookstore, or browse through one of the area's many thrift shops. And there are plenty of ethnic eateries and restaurants nearby.

On clear days, Seattle residents take in mountain views of the Cascades to the east and the Olympics to the west. From the city, wooded hiking trails and ski slopes aren't far.

Numerous lakes, the largest of which are Lake Washington and Lake Union, also are part of the territory. With the blast of a cannon and a parade of boats, Seattle rings in Opening Day of boating season. There's also Seafair featuring a flight demonstration by the Blue Angels and the famous Seafair Pirates.

Majors and Degrees

Seattle University offers 64 undergraduate programs in five colleges and schools. Pre-professional programs at SU include dentistry, law, medicine, optometry, and veterinary medicine.

Academic Programs

Central to the academic excellence at SU is the Core Curriculum, which enriches academic rigor and engages new students quickly, deeply, and thoughtfully. The Core offers a glimpse at how SU inspires insightful and creative thinkers and serves as an important foundation for studies in the various majors and minors.

Designed to help students develop intellectual abilities, there's a strong liberal arts focus with broad exposure to the humanities, social sciences, natural sciences, and arts. Instead of broad survey courses, Core courses focus on specific questions. The study of those questions gives students a closer look at a discipline and how knowledge is pursued. Theology and philosophy play critical roles. There's also a focus on global engagement so students can examine their roles in local, regional, national, and transnational cultures and communities.

Seattle University offers two honors program options for students who seek rigorous academic challenges.

Seattle University operates on a quarter calendar. The fall quarter begins in mid-September; winter quarter in early January; spring quarter in late March; and summer quarter in mid-June.

Off-Campus Programs

Seattle University offers an array of short- and long-term educational and service programs abroad in more than 40 countries. Students also have an opportunity to intern with nongovernmental organizations in Asia, Africa, and Latin America through the distinctive International Development Internship Program (IDIP), which embodies the university's emphasis on social justice and global awareness. Additional education-abroad programs in other nations, in conjunction with overseas programs at other institutions, also are offered. Arrangements are made through the Education Abroad Office.

Academic Facilities

The Seattle University campus has undergone more than $200 million in recent improvements. Twelve academic buildings house classrooms, 34 instructional laboratories, 25 specialized laboratories, computer facilities, and other instructional equipment to support state-of-the-art instruction.

The newly renovated Lemieux Library and McGoldrick Learning Commons has nearly 300,000 volumes and 2,700 current serial subscriptions, 1,300 online databases, and microforms periodicals. The library's Media Production Center houses a recording studio, control room, audio/video editing facilities, and a theater-style screening room.

The College of Nursing's 20,000-square-foot clinical performance laboratory is among the most technically advanced clinical laboratories in the country. It joins two clinical practice rooms and a suite of laboratories.

The Lee Center for the Arts is a showcase for theater and musical performances. This modern building seats 135 and includes a prop room, dressing room, costume shop, and professional lighting and sound booths that give students career-building technical skills.

The Chapel of St. Ignatius is Seattle University's spiritual center. This award-winning structure is recognized as a place of beauty, contemplation, and Catholic worship.

Costs

For academic year 2015–16, tuition is $38,970; room and meals are $11,120. The estimate for books, fees, and personal expenses is $6,390. Costs are subject to change.

Financial Aid

Seattle University awarded $102 million in financial aid to fall 2013 freshmen, including merit scholarships ranging from $7,000 to $20,000. The average financial aid package was $24,699. Students are required to apply for financial aid by February 1, as awards are made early each spring for the following fall quarter. Applications received after this deadline are evaluated in the order received for any remaining aid. Students must submit the Free Application for Federal Student Aid (FAFSA) and be accepted for admission to be considered for financial assistance. Scholarships are awarded on the basis of academic achievement, extracurricular involvement, and community service.

Faculty

There are 500 full-time faculty members. All classes are taught by faculty with an average class size of 19 and a faculty-to-student ratio of 1:13. Faculty members are available to provide assistance outside of class, to help students with research, and to assist in arranging internships. Faculty advisers provide guidance, direction, and encouragement throughout a student's academic career. New students are assigned faculty advisers prior to registration according to their major.

Student Government

All undergraduates belong to the Student Government of Seattle University (SGSU), the central student organization on campus. SGSU has an elected president, executive vice president, vice president of finance, and activities vice president. A 14-member representative council is responsible for policy making and providing diverse activities to meet the needs of Seattle University's student body. In addition, SGSU communicates student needs to the administration and faculty.

Admission Requirements

Freshman applicants are required to have completed a college-preparatory program upon high school graduation, including 4 years of English, 3 years of social studies/history, 3 years of mathematics, 2 years of laboratory science, and 2 years of a foreign language. Some programs may have additional requirements for direct entry. Additional information is available online at www.seattleu.edu/undergraduate-admissions.

ACT or SAT scores, an official high school transcript, a counselor recommendation, a teacher recommendation, and an essay also are required for freshman admission consideration. The middle 50 percent of 2014 freshmen had GPAs between 3.3 and 3.9 on a 4.0 scale and ACT scores between 24 and 29 or SAT scores between 530 and 640 (critical reading), 520 and 630 (math), and 520 and 630 (writing). College credit is awarded to those who have successfully completed Advanced Placement or International Baccalaureate examinations. Qualifying scores can be obtained by contacting the Office of the Registrar.

Application and Information

Students can apply directly online at www.commonapp.org; the forms also can be downloaded from the Seattle University website at www.seattleu.edu.

High school students applying for early action consideration must apply by November 15 of their senior year. Those applying for regular admission consideration must apply by January 15. The priority application deadline for fall transfer applicants is March 1.

Campus visits can be scheduled Monday through Friday and many Saturdays. Prospective students should contact Admissions for availability. With two weeks' notice, visitors can attend a class, meet with a faculty adviser, participate in a campus tour, and speak individually with an Admissions representative.

For more information students should contact:

Admissions Office
Seattle University
901 12th Avenue
Seattle, Washington 98122-1090
Phone: 206-220-8040
800-426-7123 (toll-free)
E-mail: admissions@seattleu.edu
Website: http://www.seattleu.edu
http://www.facebook.com/seattleu
http://twitter.com/seattleu

From the heart of Seattle and its innovative and forward-thinking culture, Seattle University dares its students to know more, do more, and be more! Students are challenged to become greater than the sum of their parts, to impact locally, and shape the global environment.

COLLEGE CLOSE-UPS

SETON HALL UNIVERSITY

SOUTH ORANGE, NEW JERSEY

★ To read more about this school, visit http://petersons.to/setonhalluniversity

SETON HALL UNIVERSITY 1856

The University

As one of the nation's leading Catholic universities, Seton Hall provides over ninety rigorous academic programs that are highly ranked by the Princeton Review, *U.S. News & World Report,* and *Bloomberg Businessweek*. Seton Hall offers all the advantages of a large research university—national reputation; challenging academic programs; notable alumni; state-of-the-art facilities; renowned faculty; and extensive opportunities for internships, research, and scholarship—with all the benefits of a small, supportive, and nurturing environment. The 14:1 student-to-faculty ratio and average class size of 21 students means faculty members know more about each student than just their name.

The University's accomplished faculty members include Fulbright Scholars, prominent researchers, authors, artists, filmmakers, former school superintendents and principals, leaders in nursing, former ambassadors, analysts, and lawmakers—all of whom are dedicated to their fields and their students. They have graduated from some of the nation's leading institutions, including Seton Hall, Harvard, Columbia, Yale, Princeton, and Dartmouth. While faculty members shine in the lecture halls and on the national stage every day, they also meet regularly with students outside the classroom and help them learn to think critically.

Seton Hall offers more than 15,000 internship opportunities, and over 80 percent of students have an internship—or two—on their resume before graduation. This is just one of the reasons Seton Hall graduates have an employment rate of 86 percent, almost 20 percent higher than the national average. Seton Hall was recently ranked in the top 5 in the nation for providing internship opportunities. This national reputation coupled with the University's stellar academic programs draws over 550 employers to campus each year to recruit graduates.

Seton Hall is a Catholic university with an almost 160-year tradition of educational excellence. A welcoming community, Seton Hall embraces students of all faiths and inspires them to become servant-leaders who make a difference in the world. The University community performs over 40,000 hours of community service annually.

Location

Nestled in the suburban village of South Orange, New Jersey, Seton Hall provides small-town charm combined with big-city opportunities. The University's 58-acre, suburban, park-like campus sits proudly in this picturesque town with tree-lined streets; historic, gracious homes; and quaint shops just 14 miles from New York City—close to all the action, but not engulfed by it.

The bustling town center—with diners, pizzerias, banks, pharmacies, Starbucks, Cold Stone Creamery, a gourmet marketplace, South Orange Performing Arts Center, a movie theater, and more—is just a 5-minute walk from campus. The train station, right in the center of town, provides a direct link to NYC's Penn Station, just 30 minutes away.

The University takes full advantage of all the Big Apple has to offer; after all, it's where the worlds of entertainment, art, publishing, global finance, international diplomacy, and fashion collide. NYC is also one of the world's largest job markets, brimming with internship and job placement opportunities in a variety of companies. Seton Hall students have interned at leading companies like Goldman Sachs, American Express, CNN, the U.S. Secret Service, the United Nations, *The New York Times*, NBC, Sony Music, JPMorgan Chase, and more.

One of the wealthiest states in the nation, New Jersey is brimming with opportunity. Seton Hall's backyard boasts a powerhouse corporate corridor of more than fifty Fortune 500 companies, pharmaceutical giants, and major corporations. For students, this means networking, internships, and career opportunities.

Academic Programs

Seton Hall is a place where leaders learn. This is evident in the nearly two dozen student and alumni national scholars and fellows, including nearly 20 prestigious Fulbright Scholars since 2009, as well as Rhodes, Udall, Pickering, Marshall, Critical Language, and Truman Scholars and more than 100,000 alumni who are now successful as CEOs, judges, doctors, principals, CFOs, journalists, nurses, diplomats, and more. About 1,000 Seton Hall graduates have served in executive positions at firms like Oppenheimer, Visiting Nurse Service of New York, American Express, and Merrill Lynch. They have served as elected officials in Washington, D.C., and in hundreds of state capitals and town halls throughout the country. In New Jersey alone, almost 20 percent of the state legislators holds a Seton Hall degree.

Seton Hall's commitment to academic excellence is evident in the more than ninety academic programs offered through six undergraduate schools and colleges. In addition, the University has recently announced plans to form a medical school in partnership with Hackensack University Medical Center; the first class is scheduled to begin in the fall of 2017. A joint degree program for direct admission as a freshman applicant is also planned.

Majors and Degrees

- Accounting•
- Accounting (5-year B.S./M.S. dual-degree∞)
- Africana Studies•
- American Humanics√
- Ancient Greek†
- Anthropology•
- Applied Scientific Mathematics†
- Arabic†
- Archaeology†
- Art (Art History•, Fine Arts•, Graphic Interactive and Advertising Design•)
- Asian Studies•
- Athletic Training (5-year B.S./M.S. or B.A./M.S. dual-degree)∞
- Biochemistry
- Biology (B.A. or B.S.)
- Broadcasting, Visual and Interactive Media•
- Business Administration•‡
- Catholic Studies•‡
- Catholic Theology•
- Chemistry•
- Classical Culture†
- Classical Languages†
- Classical Studies•
- Communication Studies•
- Computer Graphics√
- Computer Science•
- Creative Writing
- Criminal Justice•
- Data Visualization and Analysis√
- Digital Media and Video√
- Digital Media Production for the Web√
- Diplomacy and International Relations•
- Early Childhood (integrated with elementary and special education)
- Elementary Education (integrated with early childhood and special education)
- Education with Speech Language Pathology (6-year B.S.E./M.S. dual- degree)∞
- Economics (B.A. or B.S.)
- Engineering (Biomedical, Chemical, Civil, Computer, Electrical, Industrial, Mechanical)§
- English•
- Entrepreneurial Studies√
- Environmental Sciences†
- Environmental Studies•
- Ethics and Applied Ethics†
- Finance
- French•
- Gerontology√
- History•
- Information Technologies√
- Information Technology Management‡
- International Business†
- Italian•
- Italian Studies†
- Journalism and Public Relations•
- Latin†
- Latin America and Latino/Latina Studies•
- Law (dual admission program with Seton Hall Law)∞
- Legal Studies in Business†
- Liberal Studies
- Management
- Marketing
- Mathematical Finance
- Mathematics•
- M.B.A. (5-year B.S./M.B.A. or B.A./ M.B.A. dual-degree)∞
- Modern Languages
- Music (Comprehensive Music/Music Education, Music Performance•)

Musical Theatre†
Nonprofit Studies†
Nursing
Occupational Therapy (6-year B.A./M.S. dual-degree)∞
Online Course Development and Management√
Philosophical Theology√
Philosophy•
Physical Therapy (7-year B.S./D.P.T. dual-degree)∞
Physician Assistant (6-year B.S./M.S. dual-degree)∞
Physics (B.A. or B.S.)•
Political Science•
Pre-Dental*
Pre-Law*
Pre-Medical*
Pre-Optometry*
Pre-Veterinary*
Psychology (B.A. or B.S.)•
Religion•
Russian†
Russian and East European Studies†√
Secondary Education (optional integration with special education)
Social and Behavioral Sciences
Social Work•
Sociology•
Spanish•
Special Education (integrated with early childhood, elementary, and secondary education)
Speech Language Pathology (6-year B.S.E./M.S. dual- degree)∞
Sport Management•
Supply Chain Management√
Theatre and Performance•
Web Design√
Women and Gender Studies†
Writing†
Undecided

• Minor also available
† Minor only
√ Certificate program only
‡ Certificate program also available
§ Dual-degree program with New Jersey Institute of Technology
∞ Seton Hall dual-degree program
* Pre-professional programs (students must also select a major)

Campus Facilities

Seton Hall places a strong emphasis on the use of state-of-the-art technology, facilities, and support services to aid in its students' development. Many investments have been made to the campus infrastructure, including the recent construction of a new academic classroom building, new residence hall space, a new parking deck, a Dunkin' Donuts, and a new recreation and fitness center. In addition, the campus boasts a state-of-the-art research library complete with a computerized catalog and 200 computer terminals. The Science and Technology Center is home to state-of-the-future biology and chemistry labs, an atrium, and auditorium, as well as an observatory and greenhouse.

The campus also offers many unique learning labs, such as a Mock Trading Room, Patient Simulation Laboratory, Market Research Center, a student-run radio station, and Sport Polling Center. All incoming students are provided a new, fully loaded laptop computer.

Costs

Seton Hall offers a flat-tuition rate for students taking between 12 and 18 credit hours. The 2014–15 tuition and fees were $37,226. Room and board costs vary depending on meal plans; however, the average rate is $12,254.

Financial Aid

Paying for college is a major investment. Seton Hall University has been rated as one of the best schools in the nation for return on investment and is committed to providing students with the resources needed to make their dreams a reality. The University gives over $75 million in aid each year; 98 percent of students receive some form of financial aid, and 97 percent receive scholarships or grants directly from the University. Most scholarships are automatically awarded upon admission and do not require separate applications. However, there are also several special scholarships for which students can apply; more information on those is available online at www.shu.edu/go/scholarships. Seton Hall also provides need-based aid to eligible students who complete the Free Application for Federal Student Aid (FAFSA) form by March 1.

Student Organizations and Activities

On campus, Seton Hall leaders learn to put their ideas into action; discover something new; become part of a community; and build trust, spirit, and lasting friendships. Extracurricular activities abound, with over 130 clubs and organizations, twenty-two Greek societies, fourteen Division 1 Big East athletic teams, and extensive club and intramural sports. Students can audition for one of the many theater productions each year; broadcast at the award-winning, student-run radio station, WSOU-FM, which attracts more than 120,000 listeners a week from the NYC area; be part of the Brownson Speech and Debate team, which has been ranked among the top 20 college and university forensic teams for years; or write for one of three student newspapers. More than two thirds of Seton Hall students participate in clubs and organizations and over 50 percent participate in club or intramural sports.

Admissions Process

Seton Hall takes a holistic approach to reviewing applications for admission, considering academic performance in high school, grades and the rigor of the curriculum, and SAT and/or ACT scores. These are essential indicators of a potential student's ability to succeed at Seton Hall. A personal essay, recommendations, and extracurricular activities are also considerations.

The typical student who entered Seton Hall last year had an average GPA of 3.4 (B+), an average SAT score of 1130 (Critical Reading and Math), and/or an average ACT score of 25.

Application and Information

Potential students are encouraged to visit Seton Hall in person. Tours are offered Mondays through Fridays at 10 a.m. and 2 p.m. and on Saturdays at 10 a.m., noon, and 2 p.m. Open houses are offered in mid-October, mid-November, mid-February, and late April. Visits can be scheduled online at www.shu.edu/visiting

For more information, prospective students should contact:

Office of Undergraduate Admissions
Seton Hall University
400 South Orange Avenue
South Orange, New Jersey 07079
Phone: 800-THE-HALL (843-4255; toll-free)
E-mail: thehall@shu.edu
Website: http://www.admissions.shu.edu

Students enjoy a spring day on the University Green, the scenic pathway located at the heart of Seton Hall's campus.

SIMPSON COLLEGE

INDIANOLA, IOWA

SIMPSON COLLEGE

★ To read more about this school, visit http://petersons.to/simpsoncollege

The College

Founded in 1860, Simpson College is a private liberal arts college affiliated with the United Methodist Church. Simpson produces successful students by combining the best of a liberal arts education with outstanding career preparation and extracurricular programs. With 1,400 full-time students and a student to faculty ratio of 13:1, students have the opportunity to work closely with their professors. Simpson's faculty members are as dedicated to their fields of study as they are to teaching—and it shows in the classroom. When this type of dedication and passion is combined with well-prepared and motivated students, the potential for success is virtually unlimited.

The campus is located just minutes from Iowa's capital city, Des Moines, which recently was ranked as the top city for business and careers. The proximity to Des Moines allows Simpson students to take advantage of an abundance of internship opportunities. Whether working with Fortune 500 companies, spending time in an elementary school, or gaining resume-building experiences in a medical field, students learn to push their own boundaries. Simpson's guaranteed internship program gives students an advantage in today's competitive job market.

Simpson's beautiful, tree-lined campus in Indianola provides small-town friendliness and safety, while the campus facilities are continually enhanced and updated for academic and recreational opportunities. Recent multimillion-dollar projects include the renovation and expansion of Blank Performing Arts Center (2011), renovation of outdoor athletic facilities (2011), and the addition of a stunning new student center (2012). A $6-million expansion and renovation of the Cowles Athletic and Carse Fitness Center was completed in January 2014.

Simpson's 4-4-1 academic calendar includes a May Term that provides students with unique learning opportunities in the classroom, internship settings, or while studying abroad. Throughout the year, students take advantage of Simpson's innovative Engaged Citizenship Curriculum. The curriculum allows students to gain skills and experiences valued most by employers while choosing classes that interest them. Simpson's "SC in 3" pathway allows high school students entering college with 24 or more college credits to finish a full, high-quality Simpson degree in three years, decreasing the cost of college and increasing their earning potential.

Extracurricular activities at Simpson are designed to supplement and reinforce the academic program and contribute toward a total learning experience. Activities range from an award-winning music program to nationally recognized NCAA Division III athletic teams. Students have the opportunity to participate in student government, campus publications, religious life, music, theater, departmental clubs, and various other organizations. Simpson competes in 19 intercollegiate sports and has an extensive intramural program. Simpson has seven Greek chapters on campus, including three national fraternities, one local fraternity, and three national sororities; each with their own house.

Location

Simpson is located in Indianola, a residential community with a population of 14,400. Indianola is 12 miles south of Des Moines, with easy access to Interstates 35 and 80. The Des Moines International Airport is 20 minutes from campus. Indianola is host to nationally known events including the Des Moines Metropolitan Opera and the National Balloon Classic. The vibrant, small-town community has many choices for entertainment and recreation including Lake Ahquabi State Park, Summerset Trail, and unique restaurants and shops within walking distance of campus on the town square. Indianola's proximity to Des Moines gives students plenty of distinct advantages. Within minutes, students are right in the heart of some of the best entertainment and employment options Iowa and the Midwest have to offer.

Majors and Degrees

Simpson College grants Bachelor of Arts and Bachelor of Music degrees. Majors include accounting, actuarial science, applied philosophy, art, athletic training, biochemistry, biology, chemistry, computer information systems, computer science, criminal justice, economics, education (elementary and secondary including art), English, environmental science, exercise science, forensic science/biochemistry, French, German, graphic design, history, interdisciplinary studies, international management, international relations, management, marketing, mathematics, multimedia journalism, music, music education, music performance, neuroscience, philosophy, physical education, physics, political science, psychology, public relations, religion, sociology, Spanish, sports administration, studio art, and theater arts.

Simpson also offers pre-professional programs in dentistry, engineering, law, medicine, optometry, pharmacy, physical therapy, theology/ministry, and veterinary medicine. Concentration areas such as early childhood education and ethics are available, as well as many additional minors, including women's studies, social work, human resources management, Latin American studies, and coaching endorsements.

Academic Programs

Simpson College operates on a 4-4-1 academic calendar. The first semester starts in late August and ends in mid-December; the second semester starts in mid-January and ends in late April. A three-week session takes place during the month of May. During this period, students participate in a field experience/internship, study abroad, or take a course on campus with a hands-on focus.

The First Year Program is an extensive program of orientation, team building, mentoring, community service, advising, and course work structured to help new students adapt to their first year of college. The program begins with summer orientation and continues throughout the academic year. The academic component of the First-Year Program is the Simpson Colloquium, a joint classroom and advising concept that is unique among first-year programs. These courses are small in size—no more than 18 first-year students each—and all are taught by each student's faculty adviser.

With Simpson's Engaged Citizenship Curriculum, students delve deeper in their courses and focus more on projects that provide hands-on understanding of the subject matter. These courses allow students to work closely and build strong relationships with faculty members, one of the hallmarks of a Simpson education. The curriculum encourages students to take advantage of Simpson's community partnerships, hold internships, study abroad, or conduct independent research. It was developed in response to research that indicates future employers are looking for effective communicators, innovators, and problem solvers. Simpson is on the forefront of providing the kind of experiential, liberal arts education that college graduates need to succeed in their careers and achieve fulfillment in their lives.

Off-Campus Programs

Simpson provides many opportunities for studying abroad, with the choice of a semester-long program or a three-week May Term. Simpson's semester-long, faculty-led study-abroad programs include London, England; Schorndorf, Germany; Chiang Mai, Thailand; Tahiti, French Polynesia; Adelaide, Australia; and Rosario, Argentina. Students also have the opportunity for semester study-abroad programs in France, Spain, Italy, Australia, and more locations.

In addition, 10 to 15 travel courses are offered each May Term. Recent destinations include Africa, Central America, Great Britain, France, Greece, Ireland, New Zealand, the Galapagos Islands, Brazil, Argentina, and Scandinavia. May Term study abroad courses are led by Simpson faculty members and give students the opportunity to experience a different culture while gaining a stronger global perspective. Simpson has been recognized as one of the top colleges in the nation for its percentage of students who study abroad.

The Capitol Hill Internship Program (CHIP) provides students with the opportunity to spend either the fall or spring semester in Washington, D.C. Past participants have had various experiences including interning for members of Congress, the Smithsonian Institution, the Republican National Committee, the Justice Department, CNN, the Australian Embassy, and FOX News.

Academic Facilities

Simpson has a wireless campus network with high-speed Internet access. There are numerous computer labs throughout campus where students can use standard office suite applications or specialized, discipline-specific applications.

The Carver Science Center, named after Simpson's most distinguished alumnus George Washington Carver, provides state-of-the-art research facilities, computer labs, a cadaver lab, and classrooms.

The Henry H. and Thomas H. McNeill Hall houses classrooms for management, accounting, and economics. In addition, the hall houses a seminar room and the Pioneer Hi-Bred International Conference Center.

The Amy Robertson Music Center is home to Simpson's acclaimed music department and contains the Sven and Mildred Lekberg Recital Hall, ten studios, twenty-two practice rooms, a music computer lab, and the band rehearsal room. The Salsbury Wing includes a choral rehearsal room, a classroom, and studios.

Dunn Library, a modern academic learning resource center, contains over 175,000 items including books, periodicals, videos/DVDs, and CDs. Many resources (print and online) can be located from the library website. Additional materials for research can be obtained through a national interlibrary loan network. The Hawley Academic Resource and Advising Center, which provides free academic support services to all students, is located in Dunn Library.

The A. H. and Theo Blank Performing Arts Center underwent a multimillion-dollar expansion and renovation in 2011. The center accommodates Simpson's well-known programs in theater arts and opera. It includes the magnificent 500-seat Pote Theatre, with both proscenium and hydraulically controlled thrust stages, a studio theater, the Barborka Gallery, technical facilities, and shops and classrooms.

Wallace Hall, named to the National Register of Historic Places in 1991, contains facilities for education, sociology, and applied social science.

Mary Berry Hall houses the psychology department as well as faculty offices, six labs, a control room for observation and data processing, and an animal care space. In addition, the building is home to humanities classrooms, a language lab, and the Farnham Art Galleries.

The Gaumer Center contains offices for Multimedia Communication and Art and provides space for *The Simpsonian*, the college newspaper, and radio station KSTM.

Faculty

Simpson offers one professor for every 13 students. Simpson's faculty members serve as academic advisers as well as teachers. Their commitment goes beyond the classroom as they often attend college plays, operas, and athletic events, reinforcing their sincere interest in the lives of the students and their ultimate success.

Costs

Tuition and fees for 2015–16 are $34,175; room charges are $3,860; and board is $4,103. These figures do not include books, music fees, or personal expenses.

Financial Aid

Simpson College is dedicated to making it financially feasible for qualified students to experience the advantages of a Simpson education. In fact, 99 percent of Simpson students receive some form of financial assistance. Generous gifts from alumni, trustees, and friends of the College—in addition to state and federal student aid programs—make this opportunity possible. Simpson offers financial assistance on both a need and non-need basis. Need is determined by filing the Free Application for Federal Student Aid.

Financial assistance granted on a non-need basis includes generous academic scholarships (awarded on the basis of prior academic records) and talent scholarships (available in theater, music, and art). The talent scholarships are determined by audition/portfolio.

Also, specific scholarships such as the John C. Culver Fellowship, the Iowa History Center Scholarship, and the Wesley Service Scholarship can be obtained through application.

Admission Requirements

A strong academic record is essential. Applications are acted upon by an admissions committee, which is elected by the faculty. These faculty members consider the college-preparatory courses taken and the grades received in those courses, rank in class, and standardized test scores (ACT and/or SAT), including test sub scores, as well as a high school report form and guidance counselor recommendation.

Transfer applicants are accepted on the basis of successful completion of academic work at an accredited college or university.

Application and Information

Applications are accepted on a rolling basis beginning in early fall and continuing on a space-available basis. Simpson's rolling admission policy allows flexibility; however, early application is recommended. Application information can be found at www.simpson.edu/apply.

For additional information or to obtain application materials, students should contact:

Office of Admissions
Simpson College
701 North C Street
Indianola, Iowa 50125
Phone: 515-961-1624
800-362-2454 Ext. 1624 (toll-free)
E-mail: admiss@simpson.edu
Website: http://www.simpson.edu
http://www.facebook.com/simpsoncollege
http://twitter.com/simpsoncollege
http://www.youtube.com/simpsonweb
http://instagram.com/simpsoncollege

Simpson's $14-million Kent Campus Center opened in fall 2012 and is the prime meeting place for students.

SKIDMORE COLLEGE

SARATOGA SPRINGS, NEW YORK

★ To read more about this school, visit http://petersons.to/skidmorecollege

The College

Skidmore College is an independent liberal arts college of 2,400 men and women from 50 states and 50 countries that prides itself on its creative approaches to just about everything. Hence, the College's belief that "Creative Thought Matters." Founded by Lucy Skidmore Scribner as the Skidmore School of Arts in 1911, it became Skidmore College in 1922. In addition to being accredited by the Middle States Association of Colleges and Schools, the College has a chapter of Phi Beta Kappa and program accreditation with the Council on Social Work Education and the National Association of Schools of Art and Design. Throughout its history, Skidmore has displayed a spirit of innovation and imagination in response to need and opportunity. In the 1960s the College built an entirely new campus; in 1971 it became coeducational; in 1983 it completely revised its curriculum, creating a comprehensive liberal studies program focused on interdisciplinarity (revised again in 2005 with the creation of the First-Year Experience program); and in 1993, it installed the Master of Arts in Liberal Studies program, primarily for adult learners. Skidmore has embraced change, seeing in it the opportunity to serve the needs and aspirations of its students. By expanding and refining its programs, the College has broadened its educational mission to respond to the opportunities and challenges of a global society.

Students enjoy a full schedule of intellectual, cultural, and social activities, such as lectures, visiting scholars in residence, art exhibits, concerts, and dance and theater performances. There are approximately 100 student organizations, including a weekly newspaper, radio and TV stations, numerous ethnic and cultural associations, an art and literary journal, and a student-volunteer network. There are no fraternities or sororities, which helps ensure an inclusive environment. A strong NCAA Division III intercollegiate sports program for men and women—nineteen teams in all—includes baseball, basketball, field hockey, golf, ice hockey, lacrosse, riding, rowing, soccer, softball, swimming and diving, tennis, and volleyball. Skidmore competes in the Liberty League, which also includes Bard, Clarkson, Hobart and William Smith, Rensselaer Polytechnic Institute, Rochester Institute of Technology, St. Lawrence, Union, and Vassar. The College has vigorous intramural; club sport; and health, fitness, and wellness programming.

Skidmore's campus includes more than fifty buildings. The Williamson Sports and Recreation Complex has a pool and diving well, racquet-sport courts, basketball and volleyball courts, several intramural gyms, three dance studios, a weight room, a fitness center, and a human performance laboratory. Adjacent to the complex are Wachenheim Field, a small stadium with an artificial turf field for soccer, lacrosse, and intramurals, and a 400-meter all-weather track; dedicated softball and field hockey turf fields; and the lighted Wenger Tennis Courts. The Frances Young Tang Teaching Museum and Art Gallery, unique in its interdisciplinary approach to exhibits and programming, opened in 2000.

Two major additions were made to the campus in 2006. The "green" Northwoods Apartments opened with 380 single-room units in ten new buildings. A completely renovated dining hall, Murray-Aikins, also opened, offering extensive vegetarian, vegan, and international options, freshly made pasta, locally grown organic items, and a broad array of daily choices. The Arthur Zankel Music Center, an award-winning, state-of-the-art music building with a 600-seat auditorium, opened in 2010. Construction of new 238-bed residence hall facilities, Sussman Village, was completed in late 2013 and is now open to students.

Location

Saratoga Springs, 30 miles north of Albany, New York's state capital, is perennially short-listed as one of the most interesting and vibrant small cities in the U.S. Famed for health, history, and horses—its mineral waters, Revolutionary War battlefield, and the nation's oldest thoroughbred racetrack—Saratoga is equally renowned as an arts and cultural destination. In 2014, *Travel + Leisure* named Saratoga Springs one of America's Best College Towns. The Saratoga Performing Arts Center is summer home to the New York City Ballet, Philadelphia Orchestra, and Lake George Opera, and is a performing venue for top rock and jazz musicians. The city's downtown is just a 10-minute walk from Skidmore and is brimming with galleries, clubs, shops, coffeehouses, and restaurants. The city's location near the foothills of the Adirondack Mountains puts an abundance of outdoor recreational opportunities—major ski areas, state parks, large lakes, and mountainous regions of eastern New York, Vermont, and western Massachusetts—within an hour's drive. Boston, New York City, and Montreal are each approximately 180 miles from the campus.

In terms of transportation, bus service is available from Saratoga Springs to New York City, Montreal, Boston, and other major cities. There are daily trains to and from New York City and Montreal. Rental cars are available at the Albany International Airport, which is served by major airlines. The College is located near Exit 15 of I-87 (the Northway).

Majors and Degrees

Skidmore College grants degrees in nearly 60 different academic disciplines, including a Bachelor of Arts degree in the following liberal arts subjects: American studies, anthropology, Asian studies, biology, chemistry, classics, computer science, economics, English, environmental studies, foreign languages and literatures (French, German, and Spanish), French area studies, gender studies, geosciences, government, history, history of art, international affairs, mathematics, music, neuroscience, philosophy, physics, psychology, religious studies, and sociology. The Bachelor of Science degree is granted in areas of a more professional nature, including business, dance, education studies, exercise science, social work, studio art, and theater. There are more than 10 interdepartmental majors, economics-sociology and government-Spanish being just two examples. Self-determined majors, double majors, and minors are also available. In keeping with the College's creative spirit and the realities of the marketplace, more than half of Skidmore students choose a second major or minor.

Through partnerships with other institutions, Skidmore offers enhanced program/degree offerings in business, education, engineering, nursing, and physical and occupational therapy. These include 4+1 M.B.A. programs with Clarkson University, Rochester Institute of Technology, and Union Graduate College; the Whitman MBA Advantage program with Syracuse University; 4+1 M.S.A. and M.S.F. programs with Syracuse; 3+2 programs in engineering with Dartmouth College and Clarkson; 4+1/4+2 programs in physical therapy and/or occupational therapy (Sage Graduate School), and a 4+1 nursing program (New York University School of Nursing). Skidmore also has certification programs in teaching and social work and pre-professional programs in law and medicine.

Academic Programs

The Skidmore journey begins with the First-Year Experience, which introduces students to the rigorous interdisciplinary academic program and overall approach to learning and connects them with a faculty adviser/mentor. Talented but economically disadvantaged students who have been accepted into the Opportunity Program (Higher Education Opportunity Program or Academic Opportunity Program) participate in a month-long summer program. A small percentage of students opt to apply for entry into Skidmore's Honors Forum on the basis of academic achievement and aspirations, leadership qualities, and civic commitment.

Generally, students choose a major by the end of sophomore year. In the interest of breadth, they are also expected to take one to two courses in both quantitative reasoning and expository writing, and at least one course in each of the following: lab science, social science, arts, humanities, and culture. There is plenty of academic support through Student Academic Services. In addition there are specific programs for prelaw and premed students. In their junior and senior years, students often add value to their courses of study through faculty-student collaborative research, internships, volunteerism, service learning, and off-campus study.

Off-Campus Programs

About 60 percent of Skidmore's students spend a semester or year off campus. In addition to Skidmore programs in China, England, France, and Spain, students can access approximately 140 international programs through the College's Approved Programs structure, including programs in Africa, Asia, Europe, Latin America, and Australia. Students can also study at some 200 other U.S. campuses, thanks to Skidmore's affiliation with National Student Exchange. All academic majors and minors can be accommodated and transfer credits are guaranteed for students studying on an Approved Program. Financial aid is transferable to most off-campus study programs. The College also offers a Washington Semester (internship in conjunction with American University) and a semester at the Marine Biological Laboratory in Woods Hole, Massachusetts.

Arrangements for student internships (for academic credit) are made through Skidmore's academic departments or the Office of Career Development. More than 50 percent of students are involved in volunteer work, much of it local. There are also up to 50 courses each semester with service-learning components.

Academic Facilities

Skidmore's 890-acre campus offers more than 50 buildings, designed and arranged to blend with the natural surroundings and to foster intellectual and social interaction. The newest academic building, the Arthur Zankel Music Center, features a spectacular 600-seat recital hall and a state-of-the-art recording studio. Skidmore's visual and performing arts space includes the Saisselin Art Building, with studios and the Schick Art Gallery; the Janet Kinghorn Bernhard Theater, with a seating capacity of 350, and an experimental black box theater; and the Dance Center. The Tang Museum provides a focal point for cross-disciplinary study through the visual arts. The Dana Science Center offers state-of-the-art teaching and research space, including a center for microscopy imaging. Dana links the College's science departments to the Department of Mathematics and Computer Science in neighboring Harder Hall, which features a Linux lab with more than 20 workstations for advanced computer science projects.

Costs

In 2014–15, tuition was $47,314, room fees ranged from $7,466 for a traditional residence hall to $8,066 for single occupancy and $9,598 for an on-campus apartment, and board fees were $5,162.

Financial Aid

About half of Skidmore's students receive some form of financial assistance. Aid is awarded on the basis of demonstrated financial need and is provided in the form of a student-aid package that usually includes a grant, campus job, and loan. Students interested in applying for admission are encouraged to do so regardless of their intention to seek financial aid. The FAFSA, a copy of the federal income tax form, and the CSS PROFILE must be filed each year. The College hosts an annual Filene Music Scholarship Competition to award four $48,000 ($12,000 per year) scholarships on the basis of musical ability without regard to financial need. Five to seven $15,000 scholarships ($60,000 over four years) in math and science are also awarded annually. Information concerning scholarships, grants, loans, and/or work awards can be obtained through the Office of Financial Aid.

Faculty

Skidmore College has some 250 faculty members and 70 part-time members, 84 percent of whom hold the doctoral degree or the highest degree in their field. The student-to-faculty ratio is about 9:1 and the average class size is 16. Although actively engaged in research and publication in their individual fields, the Skidmore faculty members regard teaching as their primary commitment. All students have faculty advisers who assist them in selecting courses and in designing individual academic programs.

Student Government

Students at Skidmore play an active role in College governance. Through the Student Government Association (SGA) and membership on a number of major College committees, they participate in academic and social life. The SGA operates under the authority granted by the Board of Trustees and is dedicated to democratic self-government and responsible citizenship. Within the association, elected faculty members and student representatives serve on the All-College Council, the Academic Integrity Board, and the Social Integrity Board. Broad concerns of the SGA include educational policy, elections, social and student events, first-year orientation, student publications, and student clubs and organizations.

Admission Requirements

Those seeking admission to Skidmore's first-year class should complete a secondary school curriculum that includes at least 16 credits in college-preparatory courses. The Admissions Committee is also pleased to consider applications from qualified high school juniors who plan to accelerate and enter college early. Applicants typically have completed 4 years of English, 4 years of a foreign language, 4 years of mathematics, 4 years of social studies, and 3–4 years of laboratory science. Applicants must provide a secondary school transcript, standardized test scores (SAT with writing or ACT with writing), letters of recommendation from two teachers of academic subjects, and a report from their guidance counselor. Skidmore recommends that applicants submit scores for three SAT Subject Tests. A campus visit and interview is also recommended.

Through its participation in the Higher Education Opportunity Program (HEOP) Skidmore enrolls capable, energetic, and ambitious New York state residents who, because of their academic and financial situations, would not otherwise gain admission to the College under traditional requirements.

Application and Information

Applicants for admission must complete the Common Application—online at www.commonapp.org—and submit it with a $65 fee or request a fee waiver from their adviser. All information should be postmarked by January 15. Applications from early decision candidates should be submitted by November 15 for the Round I early decision plan or by January 15 for the Round II early decision plan. Transfer candidates are urged to apply by April 1 for the next fall term and by November 15 for the next spring term. In addition to a high school transcript and standardized test scores, transfer candidates are required to submit, by the appropriate deadlines, an official transcript of all college-level work completed, recommendations from two professors, and a statement regarding personal and academic standing from the dean of students at the current college. International students are given special attention throughout the admissions process. Applicants whose first language is not English are encouraged to submit the results of the Test of English as a Foreign Language (TOEFL). There are a limited number of need-based financial aid awards available for outstanding international students.

Mary Lou W. Bates
Vice President and Dean of Admissions and Financial Aid
Skidmore College
815 North Broadway
Saratoga Springs, New York 12866
Phone: 518-580-5570
800-867-6007 (toll-free)
E-mail: admissions@skidmore.edu
Website: http://www.skidmore.edu
http://www.facebook.com/SkidmoreCollege
http://twitter.com/skidmorecollege
http://www.youtube.com/skidmorecollege

Autumn view of Skidmore's campus: Haupt Pond in the foreground, Case Center at left, and Scribner Library at right.

SOUTHERN ILLINOIS UNIVERSITY CARBONDALE

CARBONDALE, ILLINOIS

★ To read more about this school, visit http://petersons.to/southernillinoisuniversitycarbondale

The University

Southern Illinois University Carbondale (SIU), chartered in 1869, is a comprehensive, state-supported institution with nationally and internationally recognized instructional, research, and service programs. SIU is fully accredited by the North Central Association of Colleges and Schools.

SIU offers more than 200 undergraduate majors, minors, and specializations; three associate degree programs; 103 baccalaureate degree programs; 78 master's degree programs; 34 doctoral programs; and professional degrees in law and medicine. SIU is a multicampus university that includes the Carbondale campus as well as the SIU School of Medicine at Springfield.

During the 2014 academic year, SIU's enrollment was 17,989, which included 13,461 undergraduate students, 3,850 graduate students, and 635 professional students. The average age of undergraduates is 23. International students account for 10.1 percent of SIU's total enrollment. Of U.S. undergraduate students, 19.9 percent are African-American, 0.24 percent are American Indian/Alaskan, 1.7 percent are Asian or Pacific Islander, and 7.7 percent are Hispanic.

Students who are ready to start college but not ready to commit to a specific major can enroll in SIU's Exploratory Student-Undeclared (EXPU) program. Advisers and career counselors help these students plan their education and careers. SIU faculty members, staff members, and alumni help students arrange internships, cooperative education programs, and work-study programs.

All single students under the age of 21 not residing with their parents or legal guardians, and with fewer than 26 credit hours earned after high school, are required to live in University-owned and operated residence halls. SIU offers four on-campus residential areas for single students, each with a dining hall, post office, and laundry facilities. Learning Resource Centers are available on both sides of campus and offer writing centers, computer labs, and student lounges. University Housing Residence Hall Dining provides all-you-care-to-eat meals and late-night dining. Residence Hall Dining offers a variety of menus, vegetarian and light entrees, display cooking, and a full-time dietitian to help students with special dietary needs. Apartment housing is available for sophomore-, junior- and senior-level undergraduates, graduate students, and students with families.

SIU intercollegiate sports teams compete at the NCAA Division I level (football is Division I-FCS). Conference affiliations include the Missouri Valley Conference and the Missouri Valley Football Conference. Intercollegiate sports teams include men's and women's basketball, cross-country, diving, golf, swimming, tennis, and track and field; men's baseball and football; and women's softball and volleyball. The campus has various playing fields, several tennis courts, and a campus lake with a beach and boat dock. SIU's Student Recreation Center offers an Olympic-size pool; indoor tracks; handball/racquetball and squash courts; a climbing wall; weight rooms; basketball, volleyball, and tennis courts; outdoor equipment rental; an aerobic area; wallyball; martial arts; and dance and cardio studios.

The Student Center is one of the largest in the United States without a hotel. It holds a bookstore, several restaurants, a craft shop, facilities for bowling and billiards, headquarters for 400 student organizations and the student government office, four ballrooms, and an auditorium. On-campus events throughout the year include concerts, plays, festivals, guest speakers, and musicals.

Location

Carbondale is 6 hours south of Chicago, 2 hours southeast of St. Louis, and 3 hours north of Nashville. Four large recreational lakes, two great rivers (the Mississippi and the Ohio), and the spectacular 270,000-acre Shawnee National Forest are within reach of the campus. The mid-South climate is ideal for year-round outdoor activities.

Carbondale is a city of 26,000 that supports one large enclosed mall, several mini-malls, and theaters and restaurants. Students frequent the shops and restaurants that line Illinois and Grand Avenues.

Majors and Degrees

The University offers Associate in Applied Science degree programs at the College of Applied Sciences and Arts in aviation flight and physical therapist assistant studies.

The College of Applied Sciences and Arts offers bachelor's degree programs in architectural studies, automotive technology, aviation management, aviation technologies, dental hygiene, electronic systems technologies, fashion design and merchandising, fire service management (off-campus only), health care management, information systems technologies, interior design, mortuary science and funeral service, radiologic sciences, and technical resources management.

The College of Agricultural Sciences offers bachelor's degree programs in agribusiness economics, agricultural systems and education, animal science, forestry, hospitality and tourism administration, horticulture, human nutrition and dietetics, and plant and soil science.

The College of Business offers bachelor's degree programs in accounting, business and administration, business economics, finance, management, and marketing.

The College of Education and Human Services offers bachelor's degree programs in athletic training, communication disorders and sciences, early childhood education, elementary education, exercise science, health education, physical education teacher education, recreation, rehabilitation services, social work, special education, sport administration, and workforce education and development. Teacher preparation is available in art, biological sciences, English, French, German, health education, mathematics, physical education, secondary education, social sciences with designations in history and social studies, Spanish, and special education.

The College of Engineering offers bachelor's degree programs in civil engineering, computer engineering, electrical engineering, engineering technology, industrial technology, mechanical engineering, and mining engineering.

The College of Liberal Arts offers bachelor's degrees in anthropology, art, classics, criminology and criminal justice, design, economics, English, foreign language and international trade, French, geography and environmental resources, German, history, linguistics, mathematics, music, musical theater, paralegal studies, philosophy, political science, psychology, sociology, Spanish, speech communication, theater, and university studies.

The College of Mass Communication and Media Arts offers bachelor's degrees in cinema and photography, journalism, and radio-television.

The College of Science offers bachelor's degree programs in biological sciences, chemistry and biochemistry, computer science, geology, mathematics, microbiology, physics, physiology, plant biology, zoology, and preprofessional programs in dentistry, medicine, nursing, optometry, pharmacy, physical therapy, physician assistant studies, podiatry, and veterinary medicine.

In addition to the many majors offered at SIU, specializations are offered in all colleges in many areas.

Academic Programs

Each bachelor's degree candidate must earn a minimum of 120 semester hours of credit, including at least 60 at a senior-level institution and the last 30 at SIU. Each student must maintain at least a C average in all course work at SIU, fulfill the University core curriculum, and the specific requirements of their degree programs. SIU awards credit through qualifying extension and correspondence programs, military experience, the High School Advanced Placement program, the College-Level Examination Program (CLEP), SIU's proficiency examination program, and work experience.

SIU offers honors course work and special recognition for students who demonstrate exceptional academic achievement. The Air Force and Army offer ROTC programs at SIU. SIU offers fall and spring semesters, and a summer term.

Off-Campus Programs

At Southern Illinois University Carbondale, distance education courses are offered in interactive, print-based, and Web-based formats. Print-based (correspondence) and Web-based courses are offered by the Individualized

COLLEGE CLOSE-UPS

Learning Program (ILP). Web-based courses and two-way interactive video courses are offered through the Office of Distance Education. Many of the courses offered through the ILP and other distance education courses can be taken to complete the University Studies Degree (B.A.) in the College of Liberal Arts.

Off-campus credit programs are designed to meet the educational needs of adults wishing to pursue a degree but who are unable to travel to the Carbondale campus. Faculty members who teach off-campus courses travel to distant sites to teach SIU courses.

Contractual services are provided and include specialized educational services to groups, organizations, governmental agencies, and businesses on a cost-recovery basis. These services are provided regionally, nationally, and internationally.

All credit courses offered through these programs carry full SIU academic credit and are taught by faculty members appointed by the academic departments of the university. Additional information can be found on the online at http://www.dce.siu.edu.

Academic Facilities

In addition to the 2.6 million volumes, 3.6 million microfilms, and more than 43,000 current periodicals and serials available in Morris Library, students and faculty members have access to more than 53,000 full-text electronic journals. More details are available online at http://www.lib.siu.edu.

Students learn and practice in the Transportation Education Center based at the Southern Illinois Airport, outdoor laboratories, the student-run *Daily Egyptian* newspaper, WSIU-TV, WSIU-FM, art and natural history museums, a literary magazine, McLeod Theater, Memorial Hospital, a vivarium, plant biology greenhouses, University Farms, and Touch of Nature Environmental Center.

Costs

Tuition and fee charges for the 2014–15 academic year (fall and spring) for students enrolled in 15 or more semester hours were $12,251 for Illinois residents and $24,874 for out-of-state residents, including international students. Room and board totaled $9,694. (All costs are subject to change.) New freshman, transfer, and graduate students from Arkansas, Indiana, Kentucky, Missouri, and Tennessee qualify for a reduced tuition rate equal to the Illinois in-state rate. (As of the fall 2014 semester, new incoming students from Iowa and Wisconsin also qualify for the in-state tuition rate.) The cost of books and school supplies varies among programs. The average cost is $1,100 per academic year. Some courses require that students purchase special materials.

Financial Aid

More than $282 million in financial aid was distributed to 79 percent of SIU students in fiscal year 2014 through federal, state, and institutionally funded financial aid programs.

To apply for financial aid at SIU, students should complete the Free Application for Federal Student Aid (FAFSA). Applications that are filed before April 1 receive priority consideration for campus-based aid. The FAFSA can be completed electronically at the U.S. Department of Education's website (http://www.fafsa.ed.gov). When completing the FAFSA, students should list Southern Illinois University Carbondale (Federal School Code 001758) as a school of choice.

SIU has one of the largest student employment programs in the country, with about 4,000 students employed each year in a wide variety of job classifications. SIU offers competitive scholarships based on talent and academic achievement.

Faculty

Faculty members are dedicated to excellence in teaching and to their advancement of knowledge in a wide variety of disciplines and professions. Many faculty members are well-known nationally and internationally for their varied research contributions. The student-faculty ratio is 16:1. There are 1,252 full-time and 193 part-time instructional faculty members.

Teaching assistants at SIU are graduate students who assist faculty members in teaching. While some teach introductory undergraduate classes, others provide support to faculty members by assisting in laboratories, monitoring tests, and helping students.

Student Government

The Undergraduate Student Government consists of a president, vice president, chief of staff, and treasurer. Under the vice president, there are 44 senators (one senator per 340 students). Each student has at least 2 representatives: 1–9 for their residential area, 1–5 for the college in which they are enrolled, and 2 representing fraternity and sorority life. Senators serve on three committees: the Internal Affairs Committee, tasked with approving student organizations and senate accountability; the External Affairs Committee, tasked with informing the student body on the actions of the Undergraduate Student Government; and the Student Funding Board, which is tasked with allocating about $350,000 to student organizations on campus. Senators also may serve on external campus advisory committees, representing the interests of the student body. The Undergraduate Student Government writes and passes legislation on University policies, event funding, student organizations, and other matters that affect the students and the University.

Admission Requirements

Freshman applicants whose ACT composite score is at or above 23 (SAT score at or above 1070) and whose high school grade point average at or above 2.0 (on a 4.0 scale) are admitted to the University. Applicants also can be admitted with an ACT composite score at or above 18 (SAT score at or above 870) and a high school GPA at or above 3.0 (on a 4.0 scale). All other applicants who meet the course subject pattern requirements will undergo a holistic review to determine potential admissibility. Admission of students who do not meet automatic admission requirements may be subject to conditions. Freshman applicants must meet course pattern requirements: 4 years of English, 3 years of mathematics, 3 years of laboratory science, 3 years of social science, and 2 years of electives.

Transfer applicants must have an overall grade point average of at least 2.0 on a 4.0 scale, based on work attempted at all institutions and calculated by SIU grading policies. Transfer applicants must also be eligible to continue at the last institution attended.

Some programs have higher admission requirements or require additional screening for admission. Undergraduates can apply online at http://www.admissions.siu.edu.

Application and Information

Admission is granted on a rolling basis. Application priority deadlines for freshmen and transfer students are May 1 for the summer term and fall semester, and Dec. 1 for the spring semester. The application fee is $40.

For more information, prospective students should contact:

Undergraduate Admissions
Mail Code 4710
1263 Lincoln Drive
Southern Illinois University Carbondale
Carbondale, Illinois 62901
Phone: 618/536-4405
E-mail: admissions@siu.edu
Website: http://www.siu.edu
http://www.facebook.com/SouthernIllinoisUniversityCarbondale
http://twitter.com/siuc

SIU Carbondale, ranked among the top 5 percent of the nation's public research institutions, offers 227 degree and certificate programs encompassing every major academic discipline. Centrally located, diverse, and featuring remarkable amenities and hands-on learning opportunities, SIU provides 8,474 acres of possibilities.

SOUTHERN NEW HAMPSHIRE UNIVERSITY

MANCHESTER, NEW HAMPSHIRE

★ To read more about this school, visit http://petersons.to/snhu

The University

At Southern New Hampshire University (SNHU) there are no limits to what a student can do, be, or achieve. As an institution, there are seemingly no limits to what SNHU can achieve as well.

In 2012, SNHU was named the 12th most innovative company in the world by Fast Company, ranking ahead of industry giants like Google, Starbucks, and LinkedIn. SNHU was the only educational institution on the list—an impressive achievement for a university that is committed to consistently reinventing the way that education is delivered and received.

Academic programs are created with the real world in mind, so students are prepared to launch successful careers when they graduate. Classes are taught by highly credentialed faculty who have professional experience and remain current in their fields. Academic and personal support is readily available, both inside and outside the classroom. With small classes, students are able to get to know their professors and not be just a name or a student number inside the classroom. If students need help, faculty and staff will rally around them quickly to work toward mastering material and gaining success.

The University operates on the belief that college should change students' lives, not break the bank—a private university education should be affordable. That's why students with high school GPAs of 2.5 and higher can earn up to $17,000 in academic scholarships in addition to generous financial aid packages. More than 90 percent of the students at SNHU receive some type of financial aid.

The University has about 2,900 traditional, full-time undergraduate day students. Offering 48 undergraduate programs in business, culinary arts, education, and arts and sciences and more than 60 graduate programs, students can gain a variety of experiences inside and outside of the classroom that will better prepare them for the real world.

SNHU is the first carbon-neutral school in New Hampshire. Always looking to improve and provide innovative facilities that enhance the student experience, SNHU continues to update the campus to provide a top-notch environment for students to learn, engage, and have the best college experience possible. A new Library Learning Commons opened in the fall of 2014. In addition to housing library services, the Library Learning Commons also includes an IT help desk, The Learning Center, a café, and the Innovation Lab and Makerspace. This new 50,000-square-foot, $18-million building is located at the center of campus and provides a beautiful state-of-the-art facility for students to conduct their academic work. In the fall of 2013, a new 300-bed freshman residence hall opened. The building features a sustainable design, high-efficiency lighting systems, and individual temperature controls in the rooms. Additional campus features include a state-of-the-art academic center (built in 2009), a 47,700-square-foot dining center (built in 2010), a completely renovated student center (opened in 2013), updated dorms and apartment buildings, a simulated stock trading room, multimedia classrooms, an auditorium, the museum-quality McIninch Art Gallery, science labs, technology-ready buildings, a fitness center that rivals private commercial gyms, athletic fields, cooking labs, a bakery, and the award-winning student-run restaurant, The Quill.

Students can participate in one of the University's more than 65 student clubs and organizations or start new ones. Intercollegiate teams compete in Division II of the NCAA, and the Northeast-10 Conference. Sports include baseball, men's and women's basketball, cheerleading, men's and women's cross-country, men's golf, ice hockey, men's and women's lacrosse, men's and women's soccer, softball, men's and women's tennis, and women's volleyball. In 2013, the men's soccer team won the prestigious NCAA Division II national championship and won the NE-10 Division championship in 2014. SNHU recently announced plans to add women's bowling, field hockey, golf, and outdoor track and field. Intramural sports, including basketball, flag football, indoor soccer, and volleyball are also extremely popular. SNHU's powerful athletic teams dominate on the field—and in the classroom. The University's student-athletes earned honors from the NCAA and *USA Today* for high grades and 100 percent graduation rates.

Athletic facilities include an indoor, 25-meter competition-size swimming pool, a racquetball court, an aerobic studio, cardiovascular equipment, four outdoor lighted tennis courts, outdoor basketball and beach volleyball courts, a soccer/lacrosse turf field, baseball and softball fields, and two indoor gymnasiums with four basketball courts and areas for indoor soccer, indoor tennis, volleyball, and other activities. The fitness center has 4,000 square feet of strength equipment and a 1,500-square-foot cardio deck. A new athletics complex is expected to be built in 2016.

The Wellness Center provides short-term health care, health education, and counseling services for students. Buildings and facilities on campus are accessible to people with disabilities. In addition, the Wellness Center develops a robust schedule of events around issues ranging from bullying and domestic violence prevention to nutrition and physical fitness.

The Career Development Center provides assistance with resume development, letter writing, company research, networking, and informational interviewing, in addition to facilitating internships and job attainment. Lifetime career services and counseling are available to all current students as well as alumni.

Location

The University is ideally located, with easy access to downtown Manchester, New Hampshire's largest city. Manchester has also been named one of the top college towns in the country. Public transportation is available, and students may keep cars on campus beginning in their freshman year. The mountains, beaches, and Boston are only an hour away. CQ Press has repeatedly named New Hampshire one of the nation's most livable states.

Majors and Degrees

The University has three schools: the School of Arts and Sciences, the School of Business, and the School of Education. The University offers associate, bachelor's, master's, and doctoral degrees. Undergraduate programs provide students with a strong general education foundation and the knowledge and skills they need to succeed in their careers.

The School of Arts and Sciences offers degrees in communication, computer information technology (B.A. option), creative writing, English language and literature, environmental management, environmental science, game art and development, graphic design and media arts, history, justice studies, justice studies/crime & criminology, justice studies/law & legal process, justice studies/policing & law enforcement, justice studies/terrorism & homeland security, liberal arts, mathematics, law and politics, psychology, psychology/child and adolescent development, psychology/forensic psychology, psychology/mental health, and sociology.

The School of Business majors include accounting, accounting/finance, accounting/information systems, baking & pastry arts (A.S.), business administration, business studies, computer information technology (B.S. option), culinary arts (A.S.), culinary management (B.S.), fashion merchandising (A.S.), fashion merchandising and management (B.S.), finance/economics, game programming and development (B.S. option), hospitality business, hospitality management, international business, marketing, sport management, technical management, and the unique Degree in Three program—offered in accounting/finance, business administration, economics/finance, hospitality business, international business, marketing, operations/project management, and sport management. Students are able to earn a Bachelor of Science degree in three years through a blend of traditional and non-classroom experiences in the real world. The overall goal of the program is to foster and enhance effective communications, critical thinking, and teamwork. The program enables students to save more than $40,000 in tuition, room, and board; take a traditional course load of five classes per semester; graduate in six semesters with no night, weekend, or summer courses; secure internships and participate in community events; and pursue interests—graduate school, employment, study abroad, etc.—instead of their fourth year.

The School of Education majors include early childhood education, elementary education, English education, middle school mathematics education, middle school science education, music education, social studies education, and special education.

A University honors program, a prelaw program, and a pre-M.B.A. program are also available for students seeking additional challenges in their academic experience.

Academic Programs

At Southern New Hampshire University, undergraduate students receive a broad education in the liberal arts and intense practice in oral and written communication, coupled with the specific knowledge and skills they need to succeed in their chosen fields.

Recognizing that successful leaders must be able to view problems from a variety of perspectives, the University mandates that all students complete courses in writing, the fine arts, the social sciences, mathematics, science, and public speaking. Students also have the opportunity to take elective courses in whatever areas capture their curiosity and may elect to concentrate their electives to earn a minor. The University curriculum offers both structure and flexibility so that students can own their education.

One component of the core curriculum is the SNHU Experience sequence. A three-year, three-course curriculum, these classes introduce students to college and college-level work, help prepare them for life after college (including resume and cover-letter writing preparation), and help them demonstrate their academic, personal, and professional development throughout their SNHU experience.

Off-Campus Programs

Southern New Hampshire University is adept at mixing academic theory with practical experience inside and outside the classroom. Undergraduates participate in off-campus cooperative education experiences/internships, earning 3 to 12 academic credits. Such opportunities are based on a student's major and career goals and typically are taken during a student's junior or senior year. Students work with faculty members and the Career Development Office to find appropriate assignments.

The University has established relationships with a number of respected, high-profile employers who provide internship and job opportunities, including Fidelity Investments, Google, IBM, New York Life, Walt Disney World, LEGO Systems, the Boston Celtics, the Boston Red Sox, and Marriott International.

Students also work with real-world off-campus partners in their courses. For example, marketing students have created media campaigns for area businesses and education students assist local teachers in their classrooms. The University's graduates are in demand because businesses know they have been prepared to contribute both on the job and in their communities.

At SNHU, students are able to learn both inside and outside of the classroom. Going beyond the campus, students have many opportunities for studying abroad at a number of partnering institutions in countries around the world. In terms of tuition and room and board, studying abroad will not cost more than if a student lived on campus. SNHU will also pick up the tab for a student's flight (up to $1,000) and the full cost of travel health insurance. All of the credits and grades earned overseas at a partner university will apply directly towards an SNHU degree.

Costs

For the 2014–15 academic year, undergraduate costs totaled $41,066 ($29,604 for tuition and fees and $11,462 for room and board). Students should plan to budget funds for books, supplies, travel, and personal expenses. Culinary arts students also need to purchase uniforms and knife sets.

Financial Aid

More than 90 percent of the University's students receive some form of financial aid, which may include need-based grants, academic and merit scholarships, work-study funds, and loans. In 2013–14, the average financial aid totaled $22,782, including a combination of scholarships, grants, and federal aid.

The University participates in the Federal Work-Study Program and the Federal Supplemental Educational Opportunity Grant Program. The school is also eligible under the Federal Stafford Student Loan Program and the Federal Pell Grant Program. Aid applicants must complete the Free Application for Federal Student Aid (FAFSA) by the priority deadline of March 15. The One Stop/Financial Aid Office can provide the appropriate forms, or students can go online to http://www.fafsa.ed.gov. Academic, athletic, and leadership scholarships are available for students who qualify.

Faculty

The University has more than 128 full-time faculty members and more than 200 part-time instructors. The student-faculty ratio is 15:1. A majority of the full-time faculty members at SNHU hold Ph.D.'s or the equivalent in their areas of expertise.

Programs at SNHU blend theory with practice to stimulate students' professional development and personal growth. Faculty members bring extensive academic, work, travel, and life experiences to their classrooms. Although their primary goal is teaching, faculty members remain current in their disciplines. Outside the classroom, faculty members are management consultants, CPAs, analysts, small-business owners, economists, accountants, marketing professionals, entrepreneurs, innkeepers, chefs, world travelers, artists, poets, novelists, psychologists, and much more.

Student Government

The Student Government Association is led by 25 students, including 5 officers, who represent all the students at the University. Its primary function is to represent the student body in campus affairs and to dispense student activity funds. One student is appointed to represent the student body on the Board of Trustees. Students are also appointed to most other standing committees, including the Dining Services Committee, Residence Life Committee, Public Safety Committee, the Curriculum Advisory Committee, and the Library Committee.

Admission Requirements

Applicants for admission are evaluated individually on the basis of academic credentials and personal characteristics. When reviewing applicants, primary emphasis is placed on a student's academic record, as demonstrated by the quality and level of college-preparatory course work and achievement attained. Most successful candidates admitted to SNHU present a program of study consisting of 16 college-preparatory courses, including 4 years of English, 3 or more years of mathematics (up through successful completion of algebra II), 2 or more years of science, and 2 or more years of social science. Separate consideration is given to admission decisions for transfer, 3Year Honors Program, nontraditional, and international applicants. Students may apply online at www.snhu.edu or via the Common Application.

Application and Information

Applicants for undergraduate day programs must submit an application (Common Application or online at www.snhu.edu/apply), college essay, $40 application fee, official high school transcript, and one letter of recommendation from a school counselor or teacher. SNHU is a test-optional institution and SAT/ACT scores are not required.

Freshman applicants can apply before November 15 to be considered for the early action deadline. The University operates on a rolling admission basis; however, there is a priority application deadline of March 15. Admission and scholarship decisions are made within 30 days of receiving all required admission materials.

For more information about Southern New Hampshire University, students should contact:

Office of Admission
Southern New Hampshire University
2500 North River Road
Manchester, New Hampshire 03106-1045
Phone: 603-645-9611
Fax: 603-645-9693
Website: http://www.snhu.edu
http://www.facebook.com/snhuoncampus
http://www.twitter.com/snhuoncampus

SPRINGFIELD COLLEGE

SPRINGFIELD, MASSACHUSETTS

★ To read more about this school, visit http://petersons.to/springfieldcollege

The College

Real-world experience through fieldwork and internships, combined with outstanding academic preparation, gives Springfield College graduates a competitive advantage when they move on to careers or graduate education. Students perform fieldwork, internships, or service learning as early as their first semester, gaining valuable experience while following the College's mission of leadership in service to others.

Internationally renowned for educating leaders in health sciences, human and social services, sports and movement studies, education, business, and the arts and sciences, Springfield College offers bachelor's, master's, and doctorate degree programs, and it is accredited by the New England Association of Schools and Colleges (NEASC) and numerous other disciplinary accrediting bodies. Springfield College is annually recognized in the top tier of its category in *U.S. News & World Report*'s listing of "America's Best Colleges."

The Mission: Springfield College is a private, coeducational institution that was founded in 1885 with its Humanics philosophy: "to educate students, in spirit, mind, and body for leadership in service to others." Humanics has remained the College mission to this day, and students, faculty members, and administration are committed to that mission.

The College has been named to the President's Higher Education Community Service Honor Roll, has received Carnegie Foundation Community Engagement Classification, and has won the Jostens/NADIIIAA Award of Merit for community service by student athletes. The Institute for International Sport named it one of the fifteen most influential educators through sport in America. Springfield College is designated by the YMCA of the USA as a premier leadership development center.

Student Population: A diverse student body of 3,286 undergraduate and graduate students at the main campus comes from across the country and around the world.

Cocurricular Activities: Enriching the undergraduate experience is an array of cocurricular activities, health and wellness programs, arts and cultural events; an extensive campus recreation program; and one of the nation's largest athletics programs for a midsized college. There are more than 100 organizations and opportunities for involvement. More than 80 percent of undergraduates participate in some form of athletics, including varsity teams, intramurals, or club sports. Approximately 44 percent of males and 32 percent of females enrolled in the traditional undergraduate programs on the Springfield College campus participate in intercollegiate athletics. There are men's and women's teams in basketball, cross-country, gymnastics, lacrosse, soccer, swimming, diving, tennis, track and volleyball; women's teams in field hockey and softball; and men's teams in baseball, football, golf, and wrestling. Approximately 90 percent of the student body uses the Wellness Center and 35 to 40 percent of students participate in intramurals or clubs specifically.

Campus Facilities: Ten campus residence halls provide guaranteed on-campus housing. Options include traditional residence halls and suite-style accommodations with private rooms for 2 to 4 students along with a shared lounge, kitchen, and bathrooms. There are single-gender and coeducational residences. Seniors may choose to live off campus. The main student dining facility features a range of fresh food options. There are snack and other light-fare services around the campus, including a food court in a two-story atrium.

Recreational Facilities: The award-winning Wellness & Recreation Complex facilities represent the best in collegiate recreational centers. The complex includes the Wellness Center, Field House, and Athletic Training/Exercise Science Complex with 160,560 square feet of instructional, athletic, and recreational space adjoining the Physical Education Complex and Art Linkletter Natatorium. The buildings support the College's degree programs in athletic training, physical education, exercise science, sport management, and related areas. They also contain and support the center for campus recreation and wellness with its comprehensive programming serving the entire campus community.

Location

Springfield College's picturesque, 182-acre campus includes several new and newly renovated state-of-the-art facilities that blend with traditional campus architecture. On the shores of Lake Massasoit in the Pioneer Valley, Springfield College is located in Springfield, the third-largest city in Massachusetts and fourth-largest in New England (Boston, Worcester, and Providence are larger). A wide range of social, cultural, and athletic activities enhance the valley, as well as twelve other colleges and universities. For example, Springfield Symphony Hall is the site of concerts, plays, musicals, and dance performances; the MassMutual Center in Springfield is home to the American Hockey League's Springfield Falcons; and the Naismith Memorial Basketball Hall of Fame is an international attraction.

Nearby cities and towns offer many additional attractions. Northampton bustles with trendy shops, coffee houses, galleries, theater productions, health food stores, nightclubs, and restaurants. The Berkshire Hills offer hiking, skiing, biking, and other outdoor activities. Boston lies 90 miles to the east, New York City is less than a 3-hour drive away, Vermont is 1 hour away, and Bradley International Airport is 20 miles south.

Majors and Degrees

Springfield College offers Bachelor of Science or Bachelor of Arts degrees in the following: accounting, American studies, applied exercise science, art, art therapy, athletic training/Doctor of Physical Therapy (seven-year dual-degree program), biology, communications/sports journalism, communication sciences and disorders, computer and information sciences, computer graphics/digital arts, criminal justice, dance, early childhood education, elementary education, emergency medical services management, English, finance, general business (opportunity for a unique 4 + 1 program culminating in an M.B.A.), general studies, health care management, health science/general studies, health services administration, health education (health studies), history, management, marketing, mathematics, mathematics and computer technology, nutritional sciences, occupational therapy, physical education (movement and sport studies), physical therapy (entry-level 6½-year program culminating in a Doctor of Physical Therapy degree), physician assistant (entry-level six-year program culminating in a Master of Science degree), psychology, recreation management, rehabilitation and disability studies, secondary education, sociology, special education, sport management, sports biology, and youth development. Undeclared majors receive help in determining their path in First-Year Seminar.

Academic Program

Consistent with the unique Springfield College Humanics philosophy, undergraduate education takes a holistic approach and prepares the student—in spirit, mind, and body—for a life of leadership in fields that help others.

The College has a two-semester academic calendar. To graduate, students must complete 120 credits including required courses for the major field of study, electives, and required courses for all students (writing, computer applications, arts and humanities, analytical and natural sciences, social sciences, international/multicultural studies, social justice, and physical education). Students may also earn credit for successful completion of Advanced Placement (AP) high school courses, and through the DANTES subject standard test and the College-Level Examination Program (CLEP) administered by the College Board.

Springfield College has agreements with several medical schools, which guarantee acceptance of its qualified students. In addition, many Springfield College programs allow undergraduates to take graduate-level courses.

There are campus chapters of the following honor societies: Beta Beta Beta (biology), Kappa Delta Pi (education), Phi Alpha (social work), Phi Epsilon Kappa (health, physical education, recreation or safety), and Psi Chi (psychology).

Off-Campus Programs

From their very first semester, Springfield students benefit from fieldwork, internships, and service learning. The College maintains relationships with businesses, nonprofits, public and private agencies, and schools, and students benefit from real-world experience early and often. Sites have included the Naismith Memorial Basketball Hall of Fame, American Hockey League, *The Boston Globe*, YMCAs, American Heart Association, MassMutual, Hilton Head Crowne Plaza, Reebok Health and Fitness Center, Baystate Medical Center, children's hospitals, parks and recreation departments, and more. The Springfield College Career Center assists students and alumni with exploring career options, identifying career-related experiential learning, refining job search skills, identifying employment opportunities, preparing for admission to graduate and professional schools, and networking with alumni.

Extensive study-abroad programs are available. Students may also enroll in courses at some of the other colleges in the Springfield area.

Academic Facilities

Technologically up-to-date, the campus is wireless and has smart classrooms, computer labs, a videoconferencing facility, a conference center, a language laboratory, a television studio, a journalism lab, a radio station, and more.

Science facilities include the Schoo-Bemis Science Center with state-of-the-art equipment; the Athletic Training/Exercise Science Complex, cited as one of the most outstanding in the nation; and the Health Sciences Center, with a human anatomy laboratory and sophisticated equipment for physical testing, analysis, and treatment. Herbert P. Blake Hall contains labs, testing, and treatment facilities, including the medical simulation laboratory, or sim lab, that features high-fidelity 3G adult and baby patient-simulator mannequins that respond like humans, allowing students to experience realistic, hands-on training and complicated medical techniques. Locklin Hall contains a well-equipped rehabilitation assessment and counseling services center.

For arts studies and programs, the renovated Fuller Arts Center and Appleton Auditorium is the site of performances, and the Visual Arts Center contains studio workspace and a public exhibition center.

The East Campus comprises an 82-acre forest ecosystem with camping facilities and lake shoreline. It supports the programs of Springfield College through purposefully designed, outdoor experiential-learning opportunities. The Springfield College Child Development Center is an exceptional fieldwork facility for students of education and psychology.

Babson Library, well known for its resources in physical education, psychology, education, and health and human services, contains a rich collection of full-text print and digital materials. Library staff members assist, and students have access to a full range of information sources.

Costs

For the 2014–15 academic year, tuition and fees were $33,455. Room and board costs were $11,210.

Financial Aid

Students are encouraged to apply for grants, loans, and student employment. Springfield College financial aid is awarded based on need and academic achievement. The College gives full consideration to students who submit the Free Application for Federal Student Aid (FAFSA) and the Springfield College Financial Aid Application by March 15 for first-year students and May 1 for transfer students. Students not eligible for financial aid may be considered for campus employment.

Faculty

Most of the 208 faculty members hold doctorates or other terminal degrees. The student-teacher ratio is 13:1.

Student Government

The Student Government Association, managed by elected students, promotes students' interests and welfare. It guides and finances more than 30 student organizations, adopts policies affecting students, and is a liaison between students and the College administration.

Admission Requirements

Springfield College evaluates applicants on the basis of academic and personal factors. Applications for regular admission or early decision must be submitted to the Office of Undergraduate Admissions and include a completed application form, a high school transcript, one personal reference, and SAT or ACT scores. Transfer students must also submit a transcript and a dean's report from each college attended.

Application due dates are as follows: undergraduate applicants, April 1; transfer students, August 1; athletic training and physical therapy programs, December 1; and physician assistant and occupational therapy programs, January 15.

Members of the Springfield College faculty and staff are interested in meeting each applicant and encourage candidates to visit the College and experience campus life. The College offers personal interviews, campus tours, and open-house programs and also facilitates contact with alumni and current students.

Application and Information

Springfield College accepts the Common Application. The Springfield College Admissions Committee reviews applications upon receiving them.

Application forms and information may be obtained from:

Office of Admissions
Springfield College
263 Alden Street
Springfield, Massachusetts 01109
Phone: 413-748-3136
800-343-1257 (toll-free)
E-mail: admissions@springfieldcollege.edu
Website: springfieldcollege.edu

Faculty members make time so students make the grade. The student-to-faculty ratio is 13:1, so faculty members get to know their students, and can provide assistance and guidance throughout their studies at Springfield College.

COLLEGE CLOSE-UPS

STATE UNIVERSITY OF NEW YORK AT OSWEGO

OSWEGO, NEW YORK

★ To read more about this school, visit http://petersons.to/sunyoswego

The University

Founded in 1861, SUNY Oswego is a comprehensive college with an excellent academic reputation and commitment to teaching, learning, research, and service. Total enrollment, including part-time and graduate students, is approximately 8,000 students. Approximately 6,800 students are currently enrolled as full-time undergraduates. More than 110 liberal arts and career-oriented programs are offered through the College of Liberal Arts and Sciences; School of Business; School of Communication, Media, and the Arts; and School of Education. The School of Education is nationally accredited by the National Council for the Accreditation of Teacher Education (NCATE), and the School of Business is internationally accredited by AACSB–The Association to Advance Collegiate Schools of Business. Other individual programs within the College of Liberal Arts and Sciences and the School of Communication, Media, and the Arts are accredited by specific discipline-oriented accrediting organizations.

Located on 696 acres on the southern shore of Lake Ontario, the spacious tree-lined campus consists of over fifty academic and residential buildings. Twelve residence halls and The Village townhouse complex, offer a variety of on-campus housing opportunities to all degree-seeking students. More than 180 registered extracurricular organizations cover a wide range of social, academic, cultural, and intellectual interests. Theater, art, film, music, dance, and discussion events fill the campus cultural calendar throughout the school year as well. There is a full slate of twenty-four NCAA Division III intercollegiate sports for men and women, along with a full complement of competitive club sports and intramural athletics.

Oswego, a selective college, receives over 13,000 applications for some 2,000 freshman and transfer openings each fall. Accredited by the Middle States Association of Colleges and Schools, Oswego has been recognized by a number of authoritative guides for its outstanding academic opportunities and high academic standards. In recent years, SUNY Oswego has been cited for excellence and selectivity in *U.S. News & World Report's Best Colleges Guide, Colleges of Distinction,* and in both the Princeton Review's *Best Northeastern Colleges* and their *Best Value Colleges* for 2014. The Princeton Review ranks Oswego among the "Best in the Northeast." In 2014, for the third consecutive year, the Princeton Review and *USA Today* named SUNY Oswego to their "Best Value" listing of colleges and universities in the nation. Oswego is also included on *Kiplinger's Personal Finance* magazine's list of 100 best values in public colleges for 2015. The ranking cites four-year schools that combine outstanding academics with affordable cost.

The Oswego campus is undergoing a facilities renaissance with over $800 million invested in campus construction and renovations in recent years. Recently completed projects include the $118-million Richard S. Shineman Center for Science, Engineering, and Innovation; a new Biological Field Station lab facility; renovation and conversion of Romney Field House; and major renovations and additions to the School of Education's Park and Wilber Halls. Other projects completed in recent years include construction of The Village student townhouse complex along with development of the Marano Campus Center.

Location

With a population of nearly 20,000, the city of Oswego is a modest-sized, friendly upstate New York community. It is the country's oldest freshwater port and one of the leading ports on the Great Lakes and St. Lawrence Seaway. The city and its surrounding area are known for summer and winter recreation, including camping, boating, sailing, fishing, tennis, golf, ice skating, alpine and cross-country skiing, snowboarding, and sledding. It is at the heart of the booming sports fishing industry, with a thriving tourism scene. The campus is conveniently located 35 miles northwest of Syracuse and 65 miles east of Rochester. Students traveling by rail or air may utilize bus service to Oswego through the Regional Transportation Center located adjacent to one of the largest malls in the northeast, Destiny USA in Syracuse.

Majors and Degrees

SUNY Oswego awards the Bachelor of Arts (B.A.), Bachelor of Science (B.S.), and Bachelor of Fine Arts (B.F.A.) degrees.

Through the College of Liberal Arts and Sciences, students can earn a baccalaureate degree in American studies, anthropology, applied mathematics, applied mathematical economics, biochemistry, biology, chemistry, cinema and screen studies, cognitive science, computer science, creative writing, economics, electrical and computer engineering, English, French, gender and women's studies, geochemistry, geology, German, global and international studies, history, human development, information science, language and international trade, linguistics, mathematics, meteorology, philosophy, philosophy-psychology, physics, political science, psychology, public justice, sociology, software engineering, Spanish, and zoology.

The School of Business offers B.S. degree programs in accounting, business administration, finance, human resource management, marketing, operations management and information systems, and risk management and insurance.

The School of Communication, Media, and the Arts offers baccalaureate degree programs in art, broadcasting and mass communication, communication and social interaction, graphic design, journalism, music, public relations, and theater.

The School of Education offers B.S. degree programs in adolescence education, childhood education, teaching English to speakers of other languages (TESOL), technology education, technology management, vocational-teacher preparation, and wellness management.

In addition, three innovative five-year combined bachelor's and master's programs are available: a bachelor's degree in accounting with an M.B.A., a bachelor's in psychology with an M.B.A., and a bachelor's in psychology with a master's in human computer interaction.

Cooperative programs include a 2+2 program leading to a B.S. in medical imaging sciences, as well as a 3+3 program leading to a B.S./D.P.T. in physical therapy from SUNY Upstate Medical University; and a 3+4 pre-optometry program leading to a bachelor's in chemistry from Oswego and an O.D. in optometry from SUNY College of Optometry.

Academic Programs

Oswego offers students a broad range of courses in the liberal arts and in preprofessional and professional studies. In addition to core courses within a major, all students must satisfy general education requirements designed to strengthen basic writing and analytical proficiency, give students awareness of their cultural heritage, and provide a level of literacy in the social and behavioral sciences, natural sciences, and humanities. By completing these general education requirements during their first two years of study, students are able to select a major with a sense of confidence and purpose. Students who are certain of their academic interest may begin working on their major program in their first year.

Before arriving on campus, students are assigned an adviser from either their major area or the college's Student Advisement Center. Advisers assist students who have not declared a major; help with academic, personal, and career concerns; and collaborate in scheduling courses needed for graduation. In addition, most students are matched with a first-year peer adviser, an older student, to help them face the challenges of their first year. The college has more than 500 undeclared students; many drawn by Oswego's reputation for helping learners find their way in education and life.

Students may be selected for the college's honors program, which provides a challenging academic experience for high achievers regardless of major. Students also have the option of receiving credit through proficiency CLEP and Advanced Placement examinations while still in high school.

Off-Campus Programs

Opportunities exist for students to broaden their knowledge of other countries by participating in one of eighty different summer or semester overseas academic programs offered. Programs are available throughout the world, and costs are held as close as possible to the cost of an average semester on the Oswego campus. A newer option is short study-abroad quarter courses offering an intensive curriculum followed by a one-to-two-week experience in a foreign country. Through cooperative arrangements, Oswego also participates in semester programs in Albany and Washington D.C.

Internships and other field experiences are available for students from all disciplines through the Center for Experiential Learning. In addition, a formalized cooperative education program (co-op) is available to students from over twenty-five major areas. Each year, more than 1,000 Oswego students participate in internships, co-ops, and other career-awareness activities on campus, in the local area, and throughout the Northeast, the country, and the world.

Academic Facilities

Penfield Library is a high-tech information center supporting the curriculum, teaching, and research of SUNY Oswego. The library houses a collection of over 450,000 bound volumes, including partial U.S. and New York State government documents depositories, and provides access to nearly 26,000 print and/or electronic journals, magazines, and newspapers. Through Interlibrary Loan, Penfield can provide additional materials from libraries all over the world. The library's listening area has more than 12,000 recordings, cassettes, and CDs. Additional facilities include the Lake Effect Café, an online catalog, a 24-hour study room with computers, study carrels, wireless Internet access, and computer labs.

Campuswide computer technology services support students in their classroom, residence, and Internet activities. Students receive an account at the time of enrollment that can be activated online to access e-mail and other web services. High-speed Internet service is available from all residence hall rooms via Ethernet and wireless networks. Wireless access is also available throughout the campus. Other services include technology training workshops, Internet troubleshooting via an active help desk, web support for student clubs and organizations, free antivirus software and campuswide Gmail. The campus maintains hundreds of Macintosh and Windows-based computers in ten public-access labs. Students also have access to more than 500 computers and numerous Sun workstations in forty specialized departmental labs.

Adjacent to the campus, the college maintains the 330-acre Rice Creek Field Station, with its new $5.5-million, 7,200-square-foot lab facility which opened its doors in the fall of 2013. The facility has two lab/classrooms, a lecture room, and exhibit areas with an indoor viewing gallery, providing a unique vista of the creek and pond. College classes and community education programs are regularly held at the field station, which ranks among the five most extensively used facilities of its kind in the country.

Tyler Hall, Oswego's fine arts center, has two art galleries that feature annual traveling exhibitions, locally produced theme exhibitions, and the best work of students and faculty members. Tyler Hall's Waterman Theatre hosts student plays, musical performances, and productions by internationally renowned traveling artists. The building is undergoing a $22.2-million rejuvenation, scheduled for completion in spring 2016, to provide students with a more approachable, flexible and high-tech home for the performing fine arts.

The WRVO Stations, the college's 50,000-watt public radio outlet, provides outstanding on-campus internship opportunities. Communication Department facilities also include two new all-digital television studios, a modern radio lab, and two new journalism labs in Lanigan Hall. Student-run TV and radio stations and the college newspaper are located in the new Campus Center facilities.

Costs

Tuition for 2014–15 was $3,085 per semester for New York State residents and $7,910 per semester for nonresidents. Room and board charges were approximately $6,345 per semester for entering students, depending on the meal plan, and additional fees totaled approximately $840 per semester. SUNY Oswego guarantees that a student's initial first-year costs for room and board will be frozen for up to four consecutive years. Although many activities on campus are free of charge, students need to budget for personal expenses.

Financial Aid

Need-based financial assistance consists of grants, loans, and part-time employment. Oswego offers approximately $80 million in aid to its students annually. Students interested in financial aid must file a Free Application for Federal Student Aid (FAFSA). New York State residents also need to file an application for the state's Tuition Assistance Program (TAP). Priority is given to applications on file by March 1 for the fall term and November 15 for the spring term.

Oswego offers a very generous merit scholarship program. Students receive over $4 million annually in merit scholarships and approximately 35 percent of the entering freshman class receives one. The average four-year renewable scholarship is more than $2,800 per year. For scholarship qualifications and details, students should visit http://www.oswego.edu/admissions/scholarships.

Faculty

Consisting of more than 300 full-time members, Oswego's faculty is dedicated to undergraduate students. With approximately 88 percent of them holding doctoral or other terminal degrees from many of the finest institutions in the country, students can be assured of the opportunity for an outstanding undergraduate education. The student-faculty ratio is approximately 18:1. While dedicated to teaching first and foremost, Oswego's faculty members are also actively engaged in research—often in partnership with undergraduate students—as well as publications and public service.

Student Government

Students at SUNY Oswego are represented by the Student Association, which has as its aim the efficient and intelligent governance of a democratic student body. The functions of the Student Association are divided among various committees that allocate funds to student organizations, intercollegiate and intramural athletics, the student newspaper, literary magazine, TV studios, and radio station, as well as various social, cultural, and intellectual activities on campus.

Admission Requirements

Admission to Oswego is competitive, with high school average, academic program, and standardized test scores being the most important criteria for applicants. Special talents such as artistic, musical, athletic, and creative writing skills are also considered. The Committee on Admissions accepts results of either the ACT or the SAT. A campus admissions visit is encouraged.

Transfer students in good standing are encouraged to apply for admission. The average GPA for entering transfer students is 3.0.

Application and Information

Oswego accepts both The Common Application and the SUNY Application for admission. Both applications are available online at http://www.oswego.edu/apply. Oswego evaluates applications as they are completed and as space remains available. Applications completed by January 15 for the fall term or October 15 for the spring term are ensured equal consideration. Applications received after those dates are welcomed, although considered as space remains available.

Prospective students and their parents are encouraged to visit the campus to participate in a student-guided tour and speak with an admissions counselor. Visits can be scheduled online at www.oswego.edu/admissions. Interested candidates can also call the Office of Admissions in advance to schedule a visit.

For further information, students should contact:

Office of Admissions
229 Sheldon Hall
SUNY Oswego
Oswego, New York 13126
Phone: 315-312-2250
Fax: 315-312-3260
E-mail: admiss@oswego.edu
Website: http://www.oswego.edu

SUNY Oswego is located on 696 acres on the southern shore of Lake Ontario.

COLLEGE CLOSE-UPS

STATE UNIVERSITY OF NEW YORK COLLEGE OF ENVIRONMENTAL SCIENCE AND FORESTRY

SYRACUSE, NEW YORK

★ To read more about this school, visit http://petersons.to/collegeofenvironmentalscienceandforestry

COLLEGE CLOSE-UPS

The College

The SUNY College of Environmental Science and Forestry (ESF) is one of the nation's largest and most widely recognized environmental colleges. Founded in 1911, the College has grown beyond its original emphasis on forestry to include professional education in environmental science, landscape architecture, environmental studies, and engineering in addition to distinguished programs in the biological and physical sciences. Throughout its history, the College has focused on addressing the environmental issues of the time in its three mission areas—instruction, research, and public service. ESF graduates are well-prepared for environmental careers through specialized academic programs and a holistic approach to solving today's environmental and resource problems.

A leader in its field, ESF is one of the specialized doctoral degree–granting colleges within the State University of New York System. The College currently supports undergraduate and graduate degree programs in more than thirty environmentally-related disciplines. Graduate programs lead to the Master of Science (M.S.), Master of Landscape Architecture (M.L.A.), Master of Professional Studies (M.P.S.), and Doctor of Philosophy (Ph.D.) degrees. ESF's research program is conducted throughout the world and research funding totals more than $15 million per year.

ESF's main campus is located on 12 acres adjacent to Syracuse University and SUNY Upstate Medical University in an urban residential setting. There are 1,700 undergraduate and 600 graduate students enrolled at ESF. The College's unique partnership with Syracuse University offers ESF students the opportunity to take additional classes there for academic diversity and depth, and to participate in cultural events, student clubs, fraternities and sororities, and professional organizations.

ESF recently opened two new buildings on campus. Centennial Hall, is an environmentally friendly residence hall that houses more than 500 ESF students in a combination of double rooms and student apartments and the Gateway Center is a hub for campus events that serves as a showcase for the College's sustainability efforts. The center features a wood pellet–fueled heat-and-power plant designed to generate enough energy for five campus buildings.

Location

Syracuse, a metropolitan area of more than 730,000 people, is a leader in the health care and education industries and is recognized as one of the nation's emerging centers for the development of green technologies. It offers many cultural, recreational, and educational opportunities, including museums, live theater, college and professional sports, and historic points of interest. Syracuse is centrally located at the crossing point of two Northeast superhighways. The driving time to Syracuse from New York City, Philadelphia, Boston, Toronto, and Montreal is about 5 hours; from Buffalo and Albany, about 3 hours. The city is served by a modern international airport and major bus and rail lines.

Majors and Degrees

The SUNY College of Environmental Science and Forestry offers three undergraduate degrees: the Bachelor of Science (B.S.), the Bachelor of Landscape Architecture (B.L.A.), and the Associate in Applied Science (A.A.S.). The B.S. degree is awarded in aquatic and fisheries science, bioprocess engineering, biotechnology, chemistry, conservation biology, construction management, environmental biology, environmental education and interpretation, environmental health, environmental resources engineering, environmental science, environmental studies, forest ecosystem science, forest health, forest resources management, natural resources management, paper engineering, paper science, sustainable energy management, and wildlife science. A number of options and concentrations are offered within specific curricula. The B.L.A. degree, which requires a semester of off-campus study, is awarded in landscape architecture. Two-year A.A.S. degrees are awarded in forest technology, land surveying technology, and environmental and natural resources conservation at ESF's Ranger School campus in Wanakena, New York.

Academic Programs

All students at ESF have opportunities for specialized study as well as research and field experience. The Department of Environmental and Forest Biology is the largest department on campus and encompasses seven different majors, including biotechnology, conservation biology, wildlife science, aquatic and fisheries science, forest health, and environmental education and interpretation. Biology students are required to complete a four-week period of summer field study, usually at ESF's Cranberry Lake Biological Station, following their sophomore or junior year. Options for specialization within the chemistry program include biochemistry, environmental chemistry, and natural and synthetic polymer chemistry.

The construction management program teaches management, analysis, and design skills used in today's green construction process, with an emphasis on environmental and engineering issues.

Environmental resources engineering students learn skills in such areas as biological, environmental, and water resources engineering; mapping science; and geographic information systems.

The closely related environmental science program also deals with engineering science, along with areas of focus in watershed science, health and the environment, earth and atmospheric systems science, environmental analysis, and renewable energy. The new environmental health program focuses on the study of the intersection of human health and the physical environment. Analysis, prevention, and mitigation of potential environmental hazards are also studied.

Bioprocess engineering students focus on the engineering, biology, and chemistry of ecologically sound industrial technologies and processes, giving students career opportunities in areas such as chemical engineering and bioengineering, pharmaceuticals, and renewable energy.

The forest resources management curriculum offers areas of focus in forest management, measurement, and policy, along with forest ecology and biology. The program includes a minor in management offered in conjunction with Syracuse University. Natural resources management students can concentrate in specialized areas such as recreation or water resources management. Students in sustainable energy management focus on energy resources management, markets and policies, energy systems and sustainability, and renewable energy technologies. Forest and natural resources management students are required to complete a four-week period of summer field study at ESF's Wanakena campus prior to the junior year.

The environmental studies major offers specializations in environmental communication and society; biological science applications; and environmental policy, planning, and law.

The landscape architecture program is a five-year bachelor's degree that is accredited by the ASLA to provide preparation to enter this licensed profession. Students study site design, urban and regional planning, historic preservation, community and environmental design, and computer applications. During the first semester of the fifth year, the landscape architecture curriculum requires participation in off-campus independent study. Paper engineering students can study process and product design and environmental engineering applied to the pulp, paper, and related chemical industries, while paper science students focus on a variety of industry-specific research and management areas. In addition, ESF offers excellent preparation for graduate study in health professions, law, veterinary science, and medicine; the College has a joint admission agreement with the College of Medicine at nearby SUNY Upstate Medical University.

Academic Facilities

Specialized facilities and equipment include electron microscopes, plant-growth chambers, climate-controlled greenhouses, an animal environmental simulation chamber, a bioacoustical laboratory, a radioisotope laboratory, numerous computer labs, nuclear magnetic resonance spectrometers, gas chromatography apparatus, a mass spectrometer, ultracentrifuges, and X-ray and infrared spectrophotometers. The photogrammetric and geodetic facilities of the environmental resources engineering department are among the most extensive available in the United States. The paper science and engineering laboratory has a semi-commercial paper mill with accessory equipment. The sustainable construction management and engineering department has a strength-of-materials laboratory, a pilot-scale plywood laboratory, and a machining laboratory. The landscape architecture faculty has a one-of-a-kind environmental simulation laboratory. The greenhouses and forest insectary in Illick Hall are used to produce plant and insect materials for the classroom and laboratory. Extensive collections are available, including wood samples from all over the world, botanical materials, insects, birds, mammals, and fishes. The Roosevelt Wildlife Collection contains more than 10,000 species of well-preserved vertebrate and invertebrate animals and also recognizes the environmental interests and contributions of U.S. president Theodore Roosevelt.

The F. Franklin Moon Library includes the Academic Success Center for tutorial support in mathematics, writing, and other courses. Moon Library contains more than 100,000 specialized catalog items, including more than 1,800 research journals. The library also provides comprehensive abstract and indexing services relevant to the College's programs. Library facilities and services are supplemented by the collections at Syracuse University and the SUNY Upstate Medical University, both within walking distance.

ESF's regional campuses in Tully, Warrensburg, Cranberry Lake, Newcomb, and Wanakena, New York, offer a great diversity of forest sites that are used as outdoor teaching laboratories and for intensive research. ESF operates numerous field stations and provides students and faculty with access to over 25,000 acres of College-owned forest properties to support its instruction, research, and public service programs. These special properties make ESF one of the largest college campuses in the world.

Costs

Estimated costs for the 2014–15 academic year included resident tuition and fees of $7,398 and out-of-state tuition and fees of $17,048. Room and board expenses were $14,610. Books, personal expenses, and travel are estimated at $2,450.

Financial Aid

A wide variety of financial aid is available for ESF students, and more than 85 percent of the students receive some type of support. The forms of financial aid include merit- and need-based scholarships, grants, low-interest student loans, and student employment programs. All students are encouraged to apply for financial aid by completing the Free Application for Federal Student Aid (FAFSA).

Faculty

Faculty members at ESF are highly trained and dedicated to the College's teaching, research, and public-service missions. There are close to 140 full-time and 46 adjunct faculty members. Many are nationally and internationally recognized for their expertise in specialized fields. Nearly all regular faculty members hold twelve-month appointments. Just over 80 percent are tenured, and more than half are full professors, of whom 93 percent have earned doctorates. There is no distinction between the undergraduate and graduate faculty. Faculty members teach at both levels, and no courses are taught by teaching assistants. Faculty members serve as advisors to students and student groups and encourage excellence in scholarship and research. The student-faculty ratio is about 12:1.

Student Government

The College has a representative Undergraduate Student Association, and student representatives also participate in a counterpart association at Syracuse University. The ESF student government organizes and presents social activities, and its representatives attend College administrative meetings, communicate students' concerns and ideas to the administration, and serve as a conduit of information back to the student body. ESF students are obligated to abide by Syracuse University's rules and regulations when accessing classes or student services there.

Admission Requirements

Students who are interested in ESF have four enrollment options: early decision, regular freshman admission, guaranteed transfer admission, and regular transfer admission.

Outstanding high school seniors who have selected SUNY-ESF as their top choice may apply for early decision, a binding, first-choice application/early notification program for fall-entry freshmen. Students considering early decision admission must file an application and provide all supporting credentials to SUNY-ESF by the December 1 deadline. Students applying for early decision are notified by January 15.

Regular freshman admission is a second option for applicants who want to enroll immediately following high school. These candidates should demonstrate strong academic performance in a college-preparatory program, with emphasis on mathematics and science preparation. Students applying for regular freshmen entry are notified by March 1. All freshman candidates apply for admission to their intended programs of study.

Guaranteed transfer admission (GTA) candidates apply to ESF as high school seniors but are offered admission for either their sophomore or junior year. Students who plan to attend another college prior to transferring to ESF select this option to ensure a place at ESF for their chosen entry date. This option may also be offered to students who do not meet the freshman admission criteria. Those who are accepted for guaranteed transfer admission receive a letter of acceptance, contingent upon the successful completion of all the prerequisite courses required for the curriculum they have selected. The prerequisite courses are outlined and described in an enclosure with the student's acceptance letter and can also be found on the College's website at http://www.esf.edu.

Students are considered for admission to ESF on the basis of their previous college course work, overall academic aptitude, and interest in the College's programs. Consideration is given to both the quality and the appropriateness of each student's prior academic experience. The College has developed cooperative transfer programs with two-year colleges in New York, Connecticut, Massachusetts, New Jersey, and Pennsylvania.

Application and Information

Students may apply for fall or spring admission. Admission decisions are made on a rolling basis until the class is filled. ESF accepts either the State University of New York Application form or the Common Application. Links to both applications can be found online at http://www.esf.edu/admissions/freshman/apply.htm. Requests for more information should be directed to:

Office of Undergraduate Admissions
State University of New York College of Environmental Science and Forestry
1 Forestry Drive
Syracuse, New York 13210-2779
Phone: 315-470-6600
Fax: 315-470-6933
E-mail: esfinfo@esf.edu
Website: http://www.esf.edu
http://www.facebook.com/sunyesf
http://twitter.com/sunyesf/
http://www.youtube.com/user/SUNYESFVIDEO

The SUNY College of Environmental Science and Forestry is enhancing the student experience with the addition of a new residence hall, Centennial Hall, and the Gateway Center, which houses a student and event center.

COLLEGE CLOSE-UPS

SUNY POLYTECHNIC INSTITUTE

UTICA, NEW YORK

SUNY POLYTECHNIC INSTITUTE

★ To read more about this school, visit http://petersons.to/polytechnicinstitute

The Institute

SUNY Polytechnic Institute (SUNY Poly) is New York's globally recognized, high-tech educational ecosystem and a dynamic member of the largest comprehensive university system in the country, the State University of New York. Formed from the merger of the SUNY College of Nanoscale Science and Engineering and SUNY Institute of Technology, SUNY Poly is committed to academic excellence. As the world's most advanced, university-driven research enterprise, SUNY Poly is ranked number one in the nation in higher education research and development funding by businesses, ahead of such well-respected institutions as Duke University (#2), MIT (#3), and Stanford University (#7), according to the National Science Foundation. More than $20 billion in high-tech investments, over 300 corporate partners, and multiple technology and innovation hubs that span upstate New York, provide limitless opportunities for students.

SUNY Poly offers undergraduate and graduate degrees in the emerging disciplines of nanoscience and nanoengineering, as well as cutting-edge nanobioscience and nanoeconomics programs at its Albany campus, and degrees in technology, professional studies, and the arts and sciences at its Utica/Rome campus. The 1.3-million-square-foot Albany NanoTech megaplex is home to more than 3,500 scientists, researchers, engineers, students, faculty, and staff, in addition to Tech Valley High School. The Utica/Rome campus offers a unique high-tech learning environment, providing academic programs in technology, including engineering, cybersecurity, computer science, and the engineering technologies; professional studies, including business, communication, and nursing; and arts and sciences, with degrees and course offerings in natural sciences, mathematics, humanities, and social sciences. Thriving athletic, recreational, and cultural programs, events, and activities complement the campus experience.

Location

SUNY Poly's main campuses are located in Utica, at the foothills of the Adirondack Mountains, and in Albany, the capital of New York State. SUNY Poly founded and manages the Computer Chip Commercialization Center (Quad-C) on its Utica campus. In addition, SUNY Poly operates the Smart Cities Technology Innovation Center (SCiTI) at Kiernan Plaza in Albany, the Solar Energy Development Center in Halfmoon, CNSE's Central New York Hub for Emerging Nano Industries in Syracuse, the Photovoltaic Manufacturing and Technology Development Facility in Rochester, and the Smart System Technology and Commercialization Center (STC) in Canandaigua. SUNY Poly also manages the $500-million New York Power Electronics Manufacturing Consortium, with nodes in Albany and Rochester, as well as the Buffalo High-Tech Manufacturing Innovation Hub at RiverBend, Buffalo Information Technologies Innovation and Commercialization Hub, and Buffalo Medical Innovation and Commercialization Hub.

Majors and Degrees

SUNY Poly awards the following baccalaureate degrees: Bachelor of Professional Studies (B.P.S.), Bachelor of Science (B.S.), Bachelor of Arts (B.A.), and Bachelor of Business Administration (B.B.A.). At the graduate level, the Master of Science (M.S.) and Master of Business Administration (M.B.A.) degrees are awarded.

Academic majors available to undergraduate students include accounting, applied mathematics, applied computing, biology, business administration, civil engineering, civil engineering technology, community and behavioral health, communication and information design, computer and information science, computer engineering technology, computer information systems, electrical engineering, electrical engineering technology, health information management, interdisciplinary studies, mechanical engineering, mechanical engineering technology, nanoscale engineering, nanoscale science, network and computer security, nursing, psychology, and sociology.

A number of options and concentrations within specific curricula are also available, as are minors in accounting, anthropology, biology, computer and information science, communication and information design, computer information systems, criminal justice, entrepreneurship, finance, health information management, human resources management, marketing, mathematics, nanotechnology, network and computer security, physics, psychology, sociology, and technology and culture.

Academic Programs

SUNY Poly's academic year is divided into two semesters and runs from late August through May. Summer sessions are also available.

Baccalaureate degree requirements vary from program to program but usually consist of a combination of specific major courses and liberal arts studies. Specializations and other options exist within the Colleges of Arts and Sciences, Health Sciences and Management, Engineering, Nanoscale Sciences, and Nanoscale Engineering and Technology Innovation. Specializations are developed through the use of electives and individual advisement.

Off-Campus Programs

Internship and cooperative education experiences are integral to effective career planning and job search strategies. These experiences can influence career plans by providing an opportunity for occupational exploration, developing marketable career-related skills and characteristics, and establishing a network of contacts that can provide relevant and timely information critical to the career decision-making process. In addition, employers are increasingly using internships and cooperative education programs as training opportunities leading to full-time permanent employment. All students, regardless of major, are encouraged to consider gaining experience in their chosen field that complements classroom learning. For additional information, students should contact the academic department or the Office of Career Services.

Costs

Costs for the 2014–15 academic year included state resident tuition and fees of $7,440. Out-of-state tuition and fees were $17,090. Room and board costs were $11,236; personal expenses, books, supplies, and travel cost approximately $4,200. The total expenses were $22,876 for New York State residents and $32,526 for out-of-state students. Costs may be subject to change. Graduate student costs will vary; more information is available on the SUNY Poly website, www.sunypoly.edu.

Financial Aid

A wide variety of financial aid is available to students at SUNY Poly. Academic scholarships are awarded for the entering fall class, and are based on merit, personal achievement, and other factors. Additional financial aid is awarded on the basis of need, as determined by an assessment of the Free Application for Federal Student Aid. At present, approximately 85 percent of the students receive financial assistance. The forms of financial aid available include Tuition Assistance Program awards (for New York State residents only), Federal Supplemental Educational Opportunity Grant, Federal Pell Grant, Federal Work-Study Program employment, Federal Perkins Loan, Federal Nursing Student Loan, Federal Direct Student Loans, and a broad range of private scholarships and grants. Students with a cumulative transfer GPA of 3.25 or better or a high school average of 90 are automatically considered for merit scholarships at the time of their application.

Faculty

SUNY Poly's growing faculty has a synergistic blend of industrial experience and academic credentials, with an emphasis on research with real-world applications. Faculty members have experience at some of most esteemed industrial and national laboratories, including GE, IBM, Lockheed-Martin, and Berkeley National Labs. They hold Ph.D.s in a broad range of disciplines, including business, computer science, mathematics, physics, chemistry, material science, nursing, and engineering. SUNY Poly faculty members come from all over the world and are committed to teaching, research, and service to the community.

Student Government

All full-time undergraduates are members of the SUNY Poly Student Association. Its primary functions are to develop and monitor the student-activity-fee budget, to approve and oversee all student organizations, to debate issues of concern to students and take action as needed, and to develop programs of interest to all students. Student government consists of a 7-person executive committee and 11 senators. Students are encouraged to take an active role in the governance process, and many opportunities for involvement, in addition to those listed above, are available for interested students.

Admission Requirements

Generally, freshman applicants to programs at the Utica campus of SUNY Poly should carry a B/B+ average in a college-preparatory program and have achieved an SAT score in the 1000–1190 range (or approximately 22–26 composite ACT score). Admission is based on high school average, SAT or ACT scores, strength of course work, and other relevant information. For applicants to the Colleges of Nanoscale Science and Engineering in Albany, a B+ average and above in a college-prep program, with SAT scores in the 1300–1450 range, or ACT scores of 29–32 are expected. For the nanoscale science programs in Albany, a minimum GPA of 3.0 is required for admission consideration.

For transfer students to the Utica campus, most programs require a minimum GPA of 2.7 for guaranteed admission; some programs require a higher GPA or additional application materials. Transfer students below a 2.7 GPA but who have earned an A.A., A.S., or A.A.S. degree may be admitted under special circumstances. Transfer students are required to furnish an official transcript from all previous colleges they attended.

Students with a cumulative GPA of at least 3.25 are automatically considered for merit scholarships; no separate application is required.

Application and Information

The deadline for all applications is July 15 for fall entry and December 1 for spring entry. Prospective students are encouraged to apply early as programs may close prior to application deadlines. Those interested in scholarship opportunities should apply by February 1 for fall admission.

All applications are reviewed on an individual basis. All EOP applicants are also required to complete a supplemental application and are encouraged to apply for fall semester by December 1. The recommended application deadline for EOP and regular admission is February 15. However, applications received after that date will be considered on a rolling basis. Notification of admissions decisions begins on December 15.

SUNY Poly participates in the SUNY early action program. Early action students must submit their application by November 1 and complete their application by November 15; applications are reviewed and students are notified of admission by December 15. Students admitted under early action are required to submit a deposit by May 1.

Students who wish to apply should apply online through the SUNY Poly website, www.sunypoly.edu. SUNY Poly accepts the Common Application or the SUNY application. A copy of the State University of New York application booklet can be obtained from a two-year college, a local high school, or the Admissions Office. Application forms for international students may also be obtained through the SUNY Poly website or the Admissions Office.

SUNY Poly adheres to the principle that all persons should have equal opportunity and access to its educational facilities without regard to race, creed, sex, or national origin.

Official transcripts from all previously attended high schools and colleges should be sent to the Director of Admissions. All communications and requests for additional information should also be directed to:

Director of Admissions
SUNY Polytechnic Institute
100 Seymour Road
Utica, New York 13502
Phone: 315-792-7500
Fax: 315-792-7837
E-mail: admissions@sunyit.edu
Website: http://www.sunypoly.edu

A student relaxes on the second floor of the Student Center, a short walk from the main SUNY Poly academic building on the Utica campus, Donovan Hall.

STERLING COLLEGE

CRAFTSBURY COMMON, VERMONT

★ To read more about this school, visit http://petersons.to/sterlingcollege

Sterling College
Working Hands. Working Minds.

The College

Sterling College is the leader in environmental stewardship education. Sterling's environmental focus, and its commitment to grassroots sustainability make the college unique. Whether offered on campus in a laboratory or seminar room, on the side of a mountain, or in a barn or pasture, classes at Sterling are small and foster experiential learning and deep inquiry through close relationships between faculty members and students.

Sterling College removes the barriers between living one's life and learning. It is for the student who wants to commit to becoming an environmental steward and looks forward to the rigor and challenge of working with both hands and mind.

"I came to Sterling to . . . learn about the people and places of the rural Northeast. My future goal is to do nonprofit community work in rural America by organizing communities that are fighting battles of environmental and social justice, and helping them determine their own destinies. By actually participating in environmental justice with fellow students and faculty while studying environmental law and land use planning in class, I have learned a lot about the political process." —*Ira Powsner '13*

Academics: Sterling students are invested in solving the biggest issues of the 21st century: our food, our water, our air, and our energy. In classrooms and laboratories, in fields and community, working alongside faculty and staff, the College's students are tackling how to rethink humanity's relationship with the natural world.

Sterling College offers Bachelor of Arts degrees in ecology, environmental humanities, outdoor education, sustainable agriculture, and sustainable food systems. Students can also choose to design their own majors—some examples include agroecology, environmental justice, conservation education, and international agriculture and business.

A highlight of a Sterling education is a ten-week, 6-credit internship anywhere in the world. Internships in agriculture, cross-cultural education, ecotourism, environmental education, hydrology, land and resource management, outdoor education, and wildlife rehabilitation and research are popular options.

The typical class size at Sterling is 10, and the student-to-faculty member ratio is 7:1. Sterling's faculty is composed of 17 full-time members and 17 part-time members. Eighty-five percent of the faculty hold advanced degrees. All new students, accompanied by 5 to 6 faculty members, take part in Winter Expedition, a four-day, three-night trek along the ridge of the nearby Lowell Mountain Range. Expedition has been a tradition at Sterling College for 50 years.

Students and faculty collaborate on research projects, engage in real-world problem solving, and develop practical solutions to local and global environmental issues. Sterling is a destination for speakers, activists, and professionals who come to campus to share knowledge about sustainable systems and environmental stewardship. Academic inquiry at Sterling is strongly interdisciplinary and grounded in the liberal arts, with interrelated coursework drawn from all five majors. Core requirements include Ecology, A Sense of Place, Tools and their Applications, and a series of experiences focused on wilderness survival and group dynamics.

Authentic Sustainability: Sterling was among the very first colleges in the United States to link the liberal arts to ecology, outdoor education, environmental humanities, and sustainable agriculture. Sterling believes that the wellbeing of humanity depends on small, interconnected communities committed to conscientious practices in agriculture and energy use, and in stewardship of the air, soil, and water.

In 2013, Sterling College became the third college in the United States, and the first college in Vermont, to announce its intention to divest its endowment from fossil fuels. In 2015, the Real Food Challenge ranked Sterling as number one in the nation for eating food that is local, sustainable, humane, and fair trade.

Work: Students are part of the daily work of the college. All students work together to support each other and to build community. Regardless of financial need, all students work on campus, whether in the kitchen, on the farm, in the woodshop, or elsewhere. Sterling College is one of only seven colleges recognized by the federal government as a Work College—a college where student work is an integral and mandatory part of the educational process, as opposed to being an appended requirement. Sterling is also the only federally recognized Work College in the northeast.

Community: At Sterling, students, faculty members, and staff members not only live together, they work to create community together. Sterling College strives to be an educational community in which people of all backgrounds and experiences feel at home, where differences are embraced, and where individuals take responsibility for furthering the dignity of all.

Sterling is small, and will remain so by design. It is the only college in the nation where the entire community of students and faculty members sit together each week for community meeting. Everyone is on a first-name basis, including the president, deans, and faculty members.

Sterling College currently has three athletic teams on campus: Nordic skiing, shooting sports, and the nation's first collegiate mountain and trail running team.

Community life is informal. Sterling College students are likely to enjoy a long weekend of hiking, a lively evening of contra dancing, caring for beehives with friends, snowshoeing at the Craftsbury Outdoor Center, or sitting by a bonfire at the College's lean-tos above the Black River.

Location

Sterling's rural location is one of the College's most prized characteristics. The campus boasts 130 acres, with an additional 300 acres of boreal research forest.

This region of Vermont is known as the "Northeast Kingdom," and is an international destination for outdoor sports and adventure. There are four ski areas within 45 minutes of the college. When city life beckons, however, Burlington is about an hour or so away.

Majors and Degrees

Sterling College offers Bachelor of Arts degrees in ecology, environmental humanities, outdoor education, sustainable agriculture, and sustainable food systems. Students can also choose to design their own major.

Off-Campus Programs

A Sterling education is both local and global. Through Global Field Studies, students and faculty have the opportunity to travel together to look at issues related to environmental stewardship and to experience rich ecological and cultural diversity. Recent programs have included experiences in the Bahamas, Belize, Canada, Maine, Mexico, and the Sierra Nevada.

Academic Facilities

The campus has sixteen residential, administrative, and classroom buildings. Facilities include a woodshop, four computer labs, two greenhouses, and the Brown Library.

Outdoor teaching facilities include a challenge course with a climbing wall, a managed wood lot and sugarbush, recreation and nature trails, large organic gardens, a sugar house, and a diverse livestock farm for draft horses with solar- and wind-powered barns. Students spend about 40 percent of their class time outside the traditional classroom setting.

Costs

Tuition for the 2014–15 academic year was $29,992, room and board were $8,796, and fees were $3,500.

Financial Aid

College is a big investment, but Sterling College offers robust financial aid packages, and the Offices of Admission and Financial Aid works closely with students and families to plan an affordable path to graduation. Sterling College also awards over $1 million each year in need- and merit-based grants and scholarships. All students determined to have financial need receive assistance, and participation in the Work Program earns each student additional funds that help offset the cost of attendance.

Admission Requirements

Sterling College endeavors to enroll a diverse student population reflecting a broad range of interests and lived experiences. Good students who have demonstrated a commitment to the values that underlie Sterling's mission—a concern for environmental stewardship, social justice, and personal integrity—are strongly encouraged to apply.

Sterling College offers admission to both first-time college applicants and transfer applicants. Application review at Sterling is a highly individualized process, characterized by a personal approach. In arriving at an admission decision, the College looks for evidence of a combination of the following characteristics:

- Academic preparation, intellectual curiosity, and creativity
- Passion for environmental stewardship and social justice
- Enthusiasm for hard work and interest in seeking out challenges
- Interest in experiential education and intrepid outlook on learning
- Desire to be part of a small community in a rural location

Application and Information

High school seniors who wish to receive an early response to their application may apply for Early Action or Early Decision. For Early Decision, a completed application must be on file by November 15 to be notified of a decision on or before December 15. For Early Action, a completed application must be on file on or before December 15 to be notified of a decision on or before January 15. All other applicants are encouraged to submit applications before June 1 for fall enrollment, January 1 for spring enrollment, and April 1 for summer enrollment. Once completed, an application is reviewed for admission within two weeks.

Students should contact:

Tim Patterson, Director of Admission
Sterling College
P.O. Box 72
Craftsbury Common, Vermont 05827
United States
Phone: 802-586-7711
800-648-3591 (toll-free)
Fax: 802-586-2596
E-mail: admission@sterlingcollege.edu
Website: http://www.sterlingcollege.edu
www.facebook.com/SterlingCollegeVT
www.twitter.com/SterlingCollegeVT

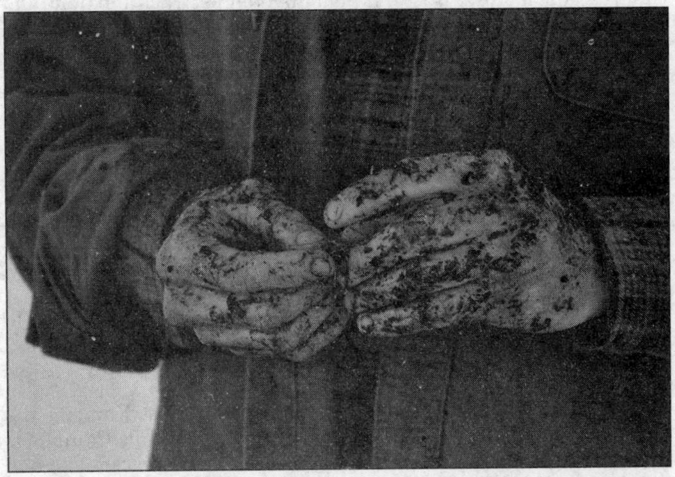

Sterling College is the leading voice in higher education for environmental stewardship. It was among the first colleges to focus on sustainability. Sterling College students are invested in solving the biggest issues of the 21st century: our food, our water, our air, and our energy.

STEVENSON UNIVERSITY

STEVENSON AND OWINGS MILLS, MARYLAND

★ To read more about this school, visit http://petersons.to/stevensonuniversity

STEVENSON UNIVERSITY
Imagine your future. Design your career.®

The University

Stevenson University (SU), formerly Villa Julie College, is a coeducational, independent institution dedicated to providing its 4,300 undergraduate and graduate students with a career-focused liberal arts education. Individual attention from faculty members, extensive career preparation gained through real-world training, and two ideal locations just north of Baltimore, Maryland, in Stevenson and Owings Mills, make the University truly unique.

At SU, academic quality is viewed as a personalized education that fosters intellectual growth and prepares students to thrive in the working world after graduation. With a student-faculty ratio of 15:1, it is easy to understand why students often cite the congenial rapport with faculty members as one of the University's strong points.

Through Stevenson University's concept of Learning Beyond, students step outside of the classroom to take their learning to the next level. Experiential learning opportunities include study abroad, service learning, field placements, internships, and independent research. In addition, through an approach known as Career Architecture℠, each student develops a professional career plan based on their values, skills, and strengths.

Stevenson's graduates maintain a placement rate that tops 92 percent each year, with students acquiring jobs or going on to further their education within six months of graduation.

At SU, students enjoy more than fifty clubs and organizations, multiple honor societies, and NCAA Division III athletics. The following sports are offered: men's and women's basketball, cross-country, golf, lacrosse, soccer, swimming, tennis, track and field, and volleyball; men's baseball, and football; and women's field hockey, ice hockey, and softball. Cheerleading, dance, and intramural sports are also extremely popular.

In addition to its undergraduate programs, the University offers a Master of Science degree in the following programs: business and technology management, communication studies, forensic science, cyber forensics, forensic studies, healthcare management, and nursing; and a Master of Arts degree in teaching.

Location

Stevenson University has two beautiful campuses in the heart of Maryland, in Stevenson and Owings Mills. SU students truly appreciate the beauty of a rural campus as well as the convenience and appeal of a more urban setting.

The original 60-acre Greenspring Campus is nestled among the rolling hills in Stevenson, Maryland. The Owings Mills Campus is a thriving center of student activity and offers both academic and residential facilities. Classes are held on both campuses, and the University provides a free shuttle service that runs between these locations.

In fall 2013, Stevenson expanded its campus with the addition of the 28-acre Owings Mills North campus, which is the current home of the School of Design and is slated to be the future home of the School of the Sciences.

Majors and Degrees

Stevenson University offers the following bachelor's degree programs: accounting; applied mathematics; biochemistry; biology; biotechnology; business administration; business communication; business information systems; chemistry; computer information systems; criminal justice; digital marketing; early childhood education: liberal arts and technology; elementary education: liberal arts and technology; English language and literature; environmental science; fashion design; fashion merchandising; film and moving image; human services; interdisciplinary studies; medical technology; middle school education; nursing; nursing: RN to B.S. (adult accelerated only); paralegal studies; psychology; public history; theatre and media performance; and visual communication design.

Stevenson's B.S. to M.S. option allows students to earn both a bachelor's and a master's degree in as few as five years. Graduate study begins in the spring semester of the junior year and runs concurrently with undergraduate work until the end of the spring semester of the senior year. All subsequent course work is at the graduate level.

Academic Programs

At SU, academic quality is regarded as a personalized curriculum that prepares students to enter the working world with the knowledge and skills that employers value. SU infuses the traditional liberal arts education with a distinct career focus. The University's goal is to prepare students for employment, graduate study, and productive involvement in today's world.

Academic Facilities

From recent enhancements to the Greenspring Campus to brand-new facilities at the Owings Mills Campus, the University provides modern facilities that serve the needs of all students.

The University's Greenspring Campus includes a 350-seat theater, multiple computer labs and classrooms, video and graphic studios, science laboratories, a student union, and athletic facilities. Each classroom and laboratory on the campus is capable of multimedia projection and computer-assisted learning.

The Owings Mills Campus hosts the University's newest facilities, including an expansive student center and dining hall, a 10,000-square-foot community center, an expansive athletic complex with a new gymnasium, multiple classrooms and study spaces, a fitness center, and additional athletic fields. The state-of-the art 3,500-seat Mustang Stadium opened in 2011.

The Howard S. Brown School of Business and Leadership offers twelve traditional classrooms and seven seminar halls. The facility also includes two distance-learning labs where students are able to interact with other learners worldwide, six computer labs utilizing the most up-to-date equipment, a student lounge, a law library, and a high-tech digital mock trial courtroom.

In 2013, campus facilities expanded with the opening of Owings Mills North, a 28-acre addition which houses the state-of-the-art School of Design, including a 3-D printer, studio space equipped with a green screen, twelve private edit bays, a soundstage, and a prop room. Owings Mills North is slated to become the new home of the School of the Sciences in 2015.

The University's library, located on the Greenspring Campus, has an extensive collection of more than 100,000 printed volumes, periodicals, videotapes and audiotapes, CDs, and microfilm and microfiche selections and an interlibrary loan consortium. In addition to the electronic databases it owns, the library has access to thousands of outside databases, such as LexisNexis Academic Universe, WESTLAW, Dialog, and Dow Jones News Retrieval.

Costs

Stevenson is among the most affordable universities in the state of Maryland. For the 2014–15 academic year, tuition and fees for full-time students were $28,980. Room and board for the 2014–15 year were $12,490.

Financial Aid

Stevenson University offers financial assistance to qualified students in the form of grants, scholarships, loans, student employment, and a special payment plan. On average, approximately 90 percent of the University's students receive some form of financial assistance. The University has a generous scholarship program and reviews all applicants for four levels of awards based on academic merit. SU participates in all major federal aid programs as well as all Maryland state programs. Applicants are required to file the Free Application for Federal Student Aid (FAFSA). The priority deadline for filing is February 15.

Stevenson offers the Presidential Fellowship, a full-tuition scholarship, to students who have the potential to make a lasting impact on the Stevenson community as shown by their commitment to academic excellence along with proven leadership in school-based achievements, community service, and/or athletics. A separate application is required. The deadline to apply for the Presidential Fellowship is November 1.

Faculty

The faculty at Stevenson University is primarily a teaching faculty. The University's 15:1 student-teacher ratio demonstrates the institution's dedication to personalized education. A majority of the full-time faculty members have the doctoral or terminal degree offered in their field, and a significant number are widely published. In addition, many are concurrently employed as professional specialists in their fields.

Student Government

The Student Government Association (SGA) facilitates an environment that encourages students to express their thoughts and opinions concerning Stevenson University, its policies, and sponsored activities. The SGA serves as the principal governing body of all campus clubs and activities. In conjunction with the Office of Student Affairs, the SGA organizes an array of campuswide events that promote the social aspects of college life. Each student at Stevenson is welcome and encouraged to participate in all SGA functions.

Admission Requirements

Applications for admission to Stevenson University are reviewed on a rolling basis. In evaluating each applicant, the University considers the applicant's high school academic record, SAT or ACT scores, recommendations, writing sample, and any other special talents or personal interests. Admission to the University is determined without regard for race, color, sex, religion, national or ethnic origin, or handicap. SU complies with all applicable laws and federal regulations regarding discrimination and accessibility on the condition of handicap, age, veteran status, or otherwise.

Application and Information

Applications for admission to undergraduate programs should be received by March 1 for fall-semester entry and October 1 for spring-semester entry. Scholarship consideration adheres to earlier deadlines. Applications received after these dates are reviewed on a space-available basis. Students applying to the University as freshmen must submit official high school transcripts, standardized test scores, the Counselor Recommendation Form, typed responses to the essay questions listed on the application, and a $40 nonrefundable application fee. The application fee is waived for all students who apply online at www.stevenson.edu/apply or via the Common Application. Transfer students must submit official transcripts from all colleges or universities they have attended and should contact the Transfer Admissions Counselor to discuss additional credential requirements.

For further information and application forms, students should contact:

Admissions Office
Garrison Hall, Suite 200
Stevenson University
100 Campus Circle
Owings Mills, Maryland 21117-7804
Phone: 410-486-7001
877-468-6852 (toll-free)
Fax: 443-352-4440
E-mail: admissions@stevenson.edu
Website: http://www.stevenson.edu

The residences at Stevenson University offer spacious apartments and suites with extensive amenities.

COLLEGE CLOSE-UPS

STOCKTON UNIVERSITY

GALLOWAY, NEW JERSEY

STOCKTON UNIVERSITY

★ To read more about this school, visit http://petersons.to/stocktonuniversity

The University

Thinking translates into doing at Stockton. Students can get hands-on experience in nursing, public health, occupational therapy, or physical therapy at the two hospitals on campus; conduct computational science research at nearby technology centers; "live" a hospitality and tourism internship 24/7 at the Seaview, Stockton's world-class resort; use cutting-edge marine technology to preserve historic underwater wreck sites or analyze the seafloor's ecosystems; study artistic techniques firsthand through a partnership with the nearby Noyes Museum of Art and at the Philadelphia Museum of Art; or bask in the beautiful, 2,000-acre campus in the Pinelands Natural Reserve just minutes from the ocean, natural labs perfect for Stockton's nationally recognized marine and environmental science programs.

Stockton students engage fully with faculty. Small classes allow for discussion, debate, and discovery—guided by Fulbright scholars, the most-published scientist in the world, and professors who care as much about teaching as research.

Rooted in a deep social and environmental consciousness, Stockton offers extensive service learning opportunities and has become an international leader in alternative energy research and conservation efforts.

Founded in 1969, The Richard Stockton College of New Jersey was named for one of the signers of the Declaration of Independence. In February 2015, Stockton celebrated a new designation and name change to Stockton University. Stockton already has a tradition of anticipating and leading changes that other universities and colleges follow; the name change highlights Stockton's tremendous overall growth. The University offers bachelor's, master's, and doctoral degree programs designed to challenge the brightest students, providing many of the academic, technological, and cultural advantages of a large university, but with the community spirit typical of smaller colleges.

Stockton enrolls over 8,500 students from New Jersey, the Mid-Atlantic states, and foreign countries, providing distinctive educational programs and experiences that extend learning beyond the classroom. The curriculum develops the students' analytic and creative capabilities and encourages individually planned courses of study.

Over 10,000 events, more than 130 clubs and organizations, Greek life, and academic and honor societies enhance the Stockton experience. Extensive intramural and club sports; NCAA Division III sports teams including men's baseball, basketball, lacrosse, and soccer, women's basketball, crew, field hockey, lacrosse, soccer, softball, tennis, and volleyball, and men's and women's cross-country and track and field; and a multipurpose Sports Center provide exercise for the body as well as the mind. Students who participate in cocurricular activities have their experiences documented through the ULTRA (Undergraduate Learning, Training, and Awareness) program, culminating in a co-curricular transcript.

The 154,000-square-foot Campus Center is the hub for student, staff, and visitor activity. It is a one-stop shop for conducting University business, bookstore purchases, student organization meetings, and larger all-University events, as well as performances and lectures in the 255-seat theater, a food court, coffee shop, game room, and plenty of space for students to meet and socialize.

The Residential Life Center offers more gathering space within two student housing areas. With meeting rooms, convenience store, and computer lab, the center encourages both organized and informal student groups.

Lakeside Lodge has a convenience store, snack bar, outdoor concert area, computer lab, multipurpose room for large programs, smaller meeting room, and a lakefront beach.

Stockton provides on-campus housing for more than 4,000 students in traditional residence halls, apartments, and at Stockton Seaview. All complexes are furnished and air conditioned, with cable TV and Internet access. Other students choose to live off campus in nearby townhouse and apartment complexes or winter rentals in one of the local seashore towns.

In addition to its undergraduate programs, Stockton offers the following graduate degrees: Doctor of Physical Therapy; Master of Arts in American studies, criminal justice, Holocaust and genocide studies, education, educational leadership, and instructional technology; Master of Business Administration; Master of Science in communication disorders, computational science, nursing, occupational therapy, and social work; and a Professional Science Master's in environmental science. Certificate and endorsement programs are offered in bilingual/bicultural education, ESL (English as a second language), family nurse practitioner, forensic psychology, health professions prep, homeland security, learning disabilities teacher consultant, middle school endorsement, New Jersey standard supervisor endorsement, preschool–grade 3 endorsement, reading specialist, special education, and student assistance coordinator.

Stockton University is accredited by the Commission on Higher Education of the Middle States Association of Colleges and Schools. In addition, the social work program is accredited by the Council on Social Work Education; teacher education is approved by the New Jersey Department of Education, the National Association of State Directors of Teacher Education and Certification, and the Teacher Education Accreditation Council; nursing is accredited by the New Jersey Board of Nursing and the Commission on Collegiate Nursing Education; chemistry is accredited by the American Chemical Society; physical therapy is accredited by the Commission on Accreditation in Physical Therapy Education of the American Physical Therapy Association; environmental health/public health is accredited by the National Environmental Health Sciences and Protection Accreditation Council; health administration is accredited by the Association of University Programs in Health Administration; occupational therapy is accredited by the Accreditation Council for Occupational Therapy Education of the American Occupational Therapy Association; communication disorders is accredited by the American Speech-Language-Hearing Association and Council on Academic Accreditation in Audiology and Speech-Language Pathology; and criminal justice programs are accredited by the Academy of Criminal Justice Sciences.

Location

Stockton is located on a stunning 2,000-acre campus in Galloway, New Jersey, nestled in the environmentally protected Pinelands National Reserve, just minutes west of Atlantic City and Jersey Shore beaches; an hour from Philadelphia and 2 hours from New York City. Courses are also offered online and at the Atlantic City, Hammonton, Manahawkin, and Woodbine Instructional Sites. The Stockton Seaview Resort and its two championship golf courses allow for expanding the hospitality and tourism management program while preserving an iconic landmark in the region. Collaboration with the Sam Azeez Museum of Woodbine Heritage and the Noyes Museum of Art provides enriching exhibitions and educational programs. Concerts, art exhibitions, lectures, recreation, and sports on campus are complemented by nearby Jersey Shore resort destinations. Within a 15-minute drive, students find shopping, dining, and cultural attractions, as well as the entertainment of Atlantic City.

Majors and Degrees

The Bachelor of Arts, Bachelor of Fine Arts, and Bachelor of Science degrees are offered in studies in the arts (visual and performing), biochemistry/molecular biology, biology, business (accounting, finance, financial planning, management, marketing), chemistry, communications, computer science and information systems, criminal justice (forensic psychology/investigation, homeland security), economics, education, environmental science, geology, health sciences, historical studies, hospitality and tourism management, languages and culture studies, liberal studies, literature, marine science, mathematics, nursing, philosophy and religion, physics, political science, psychology, public health, sociology and anthropology, social work, and sustainability.

Stockton also offers preprofessional preparation in dentistry, law, medicine, pharmacy, veterinary medicine, communication disorders (speech therapy), occupational therapy, physical therapy, and physician assistant studies, with the master's in occupational therapy, communication disorders, and doctorate in physical therapy completed at Stockton. The University also has accelerated seven-year dual-degree articulation agreements with Rowan School of Osteopathic Medicine, Rutgers School of Medicine, Rutgers School of Dental Medicine, and Temple School of Podiatry; an accelerated dual-degree program in pharmaceutical engineering with New Jersey Institute of Technology; articulation programs with Cornell University for hospitality and tourism management; and five-year, dual-degree programs with New Jersey Institute of Technology, Rowan University, and Rutgers University for engineering. In addition, students can graduate from Stockton with a Bachelor of Science degree in biochemistry/molecular biology or biology and finish their Doctor of Pharmacy degree through the Ernest Mario School of Pharmacy at Rutgers University.

Academic Programs

To earn a baccalaureate degree from Stockton, a student must satisfactorily complete a minimum of 128 semester credits. Degree programs include a combination of general studies and program (major) studies. Bachelor of Arts students must earn 64 credits in general studies; Bachelor of Science students must earn 48. General studies courses are cross-disciplinary courses designed to introduce students to all major areas of the curriculum and to the intellectual skills necessary for success in college. Students must select courses from each major curricular area. The only required courses within general studies are basic studies (up to three); students may be exempt from these courses based on testing. Bachelor of Arts students must earn 64 credits in major studies; Bachelor of Science students must earn 80. Requirements are carefully structured and emphasize sequences of specific courses.

Stockton students have the opportunity to influence what and how they learn. The preceptorial system enables students to work on a personalized basis with a faculty-staff preceptor in planning and evaluating courses and in exploring various career alternatives.

Off-Campus Programs

Off-campus experiences for credit are a requirement for most programs. Internships, research projects, and field studies extend learning beyond the classroom. Study abroad, Semester at Sea, and an honors program are also available.

Stockton sends more students to the Washington Internship Program than any other college or university outside the Washington, D.C., area.

Coordination of off-campus internship programs is provided by academic offices as well as the Career Center; coordination of foreign study is provided by the Office of Global Engagement.

Academic Facilities

Stockton's campus serves as a living-learning center, with academic, recreational, and living spaces mixed to promote interaction among students, faculty, and staff. Facilities include several large classroom/office buildings, an extensive library, lecture hall/auditorium, art gallery, performing arts center, and a new, state-of-the-art 66,000+-square-foot science center with a 54,000-square-foot expansion project underway.

The library contains 261,300 volumes, 41,354 paper and electronic periodical subscriptions, 351,000 government documents and 438,800 government microforms, 712,200 microforms, a 15,700-piece media collection, and subscriptions to 71 electronic databases. The library also houses a special New Jersey Pine Barrens collection; depository for federal, state, and Atlantic City documents; and the Sara and Sam Schoffer Holocaust Resource Center.

Costs

Costs for the 2014–15 academic year were $12,569 for in-state students and $19,089 for out-of-state students (flat-rate tuition up to 40 credits per year, fees); on-campus housing and board were $11,202 (double-occupancy residence room, Ultimate meal plan). Books, supplies, transportation, and personal items are extra. Costs are subject to change.

Financial Aid

Financial aid is available as scholarships, grants, loans, and work-study. Need-based financial aid is awarded according to student and family need. Students seeking financial aid should file the Free Application for Federal Student Aid (FAFSA) by March 1. Stockton offers aggressive and generous merit-based aid awards to academically talented freshmen and transfer students based on standardized test scores, grade point average, high school class rank, and college-level performance.

Faculty

Stockton's faculty represent highly diverse academic, training, and social backgrounds, with 96 percent holding terminal degrees in their field. Faculty members work closely with students through small class sizes and individual research opportunities and share social, recreational, and cultural programs and activities with students and staff members. This arrangement supports the exceptional rapport and learning relationships among students and faculty members.

Student Government

The Stockton University Student Senate consists of 25 student members. The advisory council is made up of 1 faculty member and 2 staff members. Student senators hold office for one year. The Student Senate reviews and makes recommendations on budgets of funded student organizations and acts as the official representative of the student body.

Admission Requirements

Stockton operates on rolling admission. Fall admission deadline is May 1 for most freshmen. Students should check the website for special program deadlines. Transfer deadline for fall admission is June 1. Spring (January) admission deadline for all students is December 1. Students may apply for admission to the fall or spring term and are notified of the admission decision as soon as their application file has been completed and reviewed. Freshman applicants must submit ACT and/or SAT scores. All students must submit official transcripts from all educational institutions attended. Admission is selective.

Early acceptance may be offered for highly qualified high school students in their junior year. Armed Services veterans and those who have been away from formal education for some time are also invited to apply for admission. Stockton makes no distinction between part- and full-time students in offering admission.

Stockton offers special admission to a limited number of New Jersey students from educationally and financially disadvantaged backgrounds. Students wishing to explore this opportunity should contact the Admissions Office.

Application and Information

For more information, prospective students should contact:

Dean of Enrollment Management
Stockton University
101 Vera King Farris Drive
Galloway, New Jersey 08205-9441
Phone: 609-652-4261
866-RSC-2885 (toll-free)
Fax: 609-626-5541
E-mail: admissions@stockton.edu
Website: Stockton.edu
Facebook.com/StocktonUniversity
Twitter.com/#!/Stockton_edu

Stockton University offers quality, value, distinction, and location. The personal attention and hands-on opportunities of a private, liberal arts education (at a public price) are available at Stockton, New Jersey's distinctive public university.

COLLEGE CLOSE-UPS

STONEHILL COLLEGE

EASTON, MASSACHUSETTS

LUX ET SPES STONEHILL COLLEGE

The College

Stonehill College provides the knowledge and experience students need to succeed in their chosen field along with a liberal arts foundation that fosters the kind of well-rounded and adaptable thinkers that today's leading organizations demand. Stonehill is a coed Catholic college with a welcoming, academically challenging community of more than 2,400 students on a beautiful, active campus 22 miles south of Boston. The College offers thirty-nine majors and forty-six minors in the humanities, natural and social sciences, business, education, and pre-professional advising programs to prepare students for a life of purposeful learning, leadership, and responsible citizenship. More than 90 percent of Stonehill students complete an internship, practicum, field experience, or study abroad by the time they graduate.

More than 80 percent of Stonehill students participate in at least one sport on campus. Stonehill competes in the Northeast-10 Conference, the largest NCAA Division II conference in the country, and offers twenty different varsity sports, including baseball, lacrosse, football, basketball, and soccer. There are twenty-one sports in the intramural program, including basketball, flag football, floor hockey, and softball, as well as indoor and outdoor soccer. Several are offered at two levels to accommodate various levels of ability. Club sports such as rugby and volleyball are yet another option, offering a spirited, fun experience without the demands of NCAA conference-sanctioned athletics.

Founded by the Congregation of Holy Cross in 1948, Stonehill's mission is "to educate the whole person so that each graduate thinks, acts, and leads with courage toward the creation of a more just and compassionate world." The idea of making the world a better place is part of the Catholic faith and an intrinsic element of the Stonehill experience. Each year, more than 2,000 Stonehill students (about 80 percent of the student body) participate in community service, providing more than 95,000 hours of service.

Stonehill consistently receives nationwide recognition as one of the country's top colleges. *U.S. News & World Report* recently ranked Stonehill 105th nationally among liberal arts colleges. The Princeton Review has also singled out Stonehill as one of the best in the nation for career services, most accessible professors, intramural sports, study abroad, and more.

Location

Stonehill is in Easton, Massachusetts, a friendly residential community nestled between New England's largest capital cities. Just 22 miles from Boston, America's number-one college town, and 37 miles from Providence, it is perfectly situated for internships, service opportunities, and job prospects, as well as enjoying museums, professional sports, cultural events, and more.

Whether the countless trees are in full bloom in the spring or the leaves are bursting into reds and golds in New England's colorful fall, Stonehill is beautiful every season of the year. Encompassing 384 acres, the campus features traditional landscaping, ponds, wooded trails, and Georgian-style architecture.

Majors and Degrees

Students may receive Bachelor of Arts degrees in American studies, art history, arts administration (museum studies and performing arts concentrations), biology, Catholic studies, chemistry, communication (communication studies and mediated communication concentrations), criminology, economics, education (early childhood/elementary and secondary education minor), English, environmental studies, foreign languages, French, gender and sexuality studies, graphic design, healthcare administration, history, interdisciplinary studies, mathematics, philosophy, physics (generalist and astronomy concentrations), political science and international studies (government and politics, international relations, and public administration and public policy concentrations), psychology, religious studies, sociology, Spanish, studio arts, as well as visual and performing arts (generalist and music concentrations).

Bachelor of Science degrees are offered in biochemistry, biology, chemistry, computer science, environmental science, mathematics, neuroscience, and physics. Bachelor of Science in Business Administration degrees are offered in accounting, finance, international business, management, and marketing. Stonehill's business department is accredited by the AACSB. In addition, Stonehill College partners with the University of Notre Dame to offer a combination 3+2 program in engineering with concentrations in aerospace, chemical, civil, computer, electrical, environmental engineering, environmental earth sciences, and mechanical engineering.

Pre-professional advising programs are offered in dentistry, education, law, medicine, veterinary science, and medical technology. Students interested in the field of education can pursue programs in early childhood education, elementary education, and secondary education, which lead to initial teacher licensure from the Commonwealth of Massachusetts. Students may pursue a double major as well as design their own major by combining various departmental courses into a comprehensive multidisciplinary program.

Academic Programs

The core of Stonehill's liberal arts curriculum is the Cornerstone Program, which leads students to examine themselves, society, culture, and the natural world through courses in ethics, sciences, language, and more.

Stonehill's students and alumni succeed because the entire college community collaborates to help them develop the knowledge, skills, and character to meet their professional goals and to live lives of purpose and integrity. Graduates can be found around the world enrolled in top graduate programs, enjoying meaningful careers, and working to improve their communities.

Within one year of graduation, 98 percent of Stonehill graduates over the last five years were employed, doing service work, or in graduate school. Nearly 50 percent of the class of 2013 had secured jobs by graduation (the national average for colleges is 30 percent) at organizations such as Goldman Sachs, the New England Patriots, and Brigham and Women's Hospital. Others joined or applied for yearlong volunteer service programs such as the Peace Corps, Teach for America, AmeriCorps, and World Teach.

On average, Stonehill students graduate at a higher rate and in less time than students at many other colleges and universities. About 80 percent of Stonehill students graduate within four years. Stonehill's four-year graduation rate is higher than at public institutions where the national average is five years.

Off-Campus Programs

At Stonehill, students are given experiential learning opportunities that allow them in-depth exploration of what they learn in the classroom and the opportunity to apply it in the real world. The National Survey of Student Engagement has ranked Stonehill in the top 10 percent of colleges nationwide for its enriching educational experiences such as competitive internships, nationally ranked study-abroad opportunities, and cocurricular programs.

Students take part in interdisciplinary Learning Communities (LCs), which combine two academic courses from different disciplines with a team-taught seminar that explores an interrelated topic. Some LCs even incorporate travel to places such as Ireland, Italy, the Florida Everglades, and the deserts of the Southwest.

In addition, Stonehill is consistently ranked among the top twenty baccalaureate institutions in the nation for student participation in semester-long study abroad programs, according to the Institute of

International Education's Open Doors Survey. Nearly 40 percent of Stonehill students study abroad before graduation in dozens of countries, including Argentina, Australia, China, Denmark, England, Ireland, Italy, Morocco, New Zealand, Spain, and South Africa.

Academic Facilities

Stonehill is dedicated to developing programs and projects that will continually improve quality of life for everyone on campus. Its $34 million science center, opened in 2009, provides state-of-the-art labs, observation rooms, and research areas, as well as a café and atrium, which is a popular meeting place for faculty, staff, and students.

More than 90 percent of Stonehill's students live on campus and very few leave on the weekends. In addition, all resident students are guaranteed housing for all four years. Students can choose from a variety of living options, including suites, townhouses, and double- and triple-occupancy rooms, and take advantage of amenities such as communal TV lounges, kitchen and laundry facilities, recreation rooms, pool tables, basketball courts, beach volleyball courts, and outdoor grills for barbeques.

Costs

For the 2015–16 academic year, Stonehill's costs are $38,550 for tuition and $14,720 for room and board.

Financial Aid

Stonehill is committed to helping each qualified student find the resources to make the dream of a Stonehill education become reality. Stonehill offers loans, grants, scholarships, employment programs, and tuition payment plans to help students become a part of the community here. In the 2013–14 academic year, Stonehill distributed $37 million in merit scholarships and need-based grants, and 94 percent of full-time students received some form of aid. On average, students received $26,192 each in scholarships, grants, loans, and work-study. A wide range of competitive merit-based scholarships is also available to outstanding students who do not demonstrate a financial need.

To file for Stonehill scholarship and/or financial aid consideration, students should complete the online CSS PROFILE form at https://profileonline.collegeboard.com. Stonehill's CSS PROFILE code is 3770. In addition, students must file the Free Application for Federal Student Aid (FAFSA) online at http://www.fafsa.ed.gov to be considered for government funds. Stonehill's FAFSA code is 002217.

Faculty

With a student-faculty ratio of 12:1 and an average class size of 19, Stonehill sees individual attention as a key component of our academic programs. Stonehill's accomplished faculty champions its students throughout all four years and is dedicated to teaching and conducting publishable research with students to help develop their professional portfolio. Students benefit from graduate-level access to high-tech equipment, attend professional academic conferences, and coauthor in-depth papers, while guided by faculty mentors. Stonehill students take advantage of collaborating one-on-one with their professors on a regular basis and they are always be taught by a faculty member, not a teaching assistant or graduate student.

Student Government

From enjoying on-campus activities to just hanging out with friends, students have plenty of opportunities for fun at Stonehill. The Student Government Association (SGA) is one of the country's most active—its programming won an award from the National Association of Campus Activities—so there's always something happening, from concerts and guest speakers to contests and game shows. Eighty clubs and organizations are available, including the College's arts and entertainment magazine *Rolling Stonehill*, the Ski/Snowboard Club, and the Neuroscience Society.

Stonehill also offers free transportation to Boston's public subway system, allowing easy access to the excitement of the city. And with Stonehill's unique Fun Fund, students can get up to $200 to pay for entertainment with friends, such as a show in New York City, a pottery class, or a Red Sox game.

Admission Requirements

Last year, Stonehill enrolled 610 students into the class of 2018. The College actively seeks an academically strong and geographically, culturally, and ethnically diverse student body. In the admission process, all information on each applicant is carefully considered, but academic performance and high school curriculum are given the greatest weight. The Admission Committee evaluates the depth and strength of each applicant's course selection and the consistency of their grades. Competitive students should have completed a strong academic program from among their high school's most challenging offerings. Stonehill admission is test optional, but students may choose to submit scores from either the SAT or ACT. The Admission Committee also evaluates extracurricular activities, work, volunteer and community activities, recommendations, and writing samples. Stonehill awards credit for strong scores on AP, CLEP, and higher-level International Baccalaureate exams.

Application and Information

Aspirants for Stonehill, as first-year, transfer, or international students may apply online at https://www.commonapp.org. The Common Application is also available in paper form at high school guidance offices.

Stonehill offers three admission plans for first-year candidates: early decision (binding), early action (nonbinding), and regular decision. November 1 is the deadline for early action and January 15 is the deadline for regular decision.

Office of Admission
Stonehill College
320 Washington Street
Easton, Massachusetts 02357-5610
United States
Phone: 888-694-4554
Fax: 508-565-1545
E-mail: admission@stonehill.edu
Website: http://www.stonehill.edu/admission/ (Admission)

Stonehill College is set on 384 acres of stately buildings and beautifully landscaped grounds, minutes from Boston and Providence.

SUSQUEHANNA UNIVERSITY

SELINSGROVE, PENNSYLVANIA

Susquehanna UNIVERSITY

The University

Susquehanna University educates enterprising, independent thinkers. No matter their major or career plans, students graduate with the broad-based academic foundation and 21st-century job skills—critical thinking, writing, teamwork, and communication skills—that employers and graduate schools seek. Ninety-four percent of Susquehanna's students find jobs or pursue graduate study within six months of graduation.

Susquehanna educates about 2,100 students from thirty-five states and twenty-two countries in liberal arts and science or preprofessional programs offered by the School of Arts and Sciences and the Sigmund Weis School of Business. With more than sixty majors and minors—and self-designed majors—available, students can easily combine their talents and interests with their career aspirations.

Susquehanna offers students a global perspective. Nine out of ten employers cite intercultural skills as a desirable trait for new employees, and Susquehanna's nationally recognized Global Opportunities (GO) program prepares graduates for the cultural competencies needed in today's global marketplace. Susquehanna is one of only a handful of universities to require a domestic or overseas study-away experience, which makes students more culturally aware and better prepared to be leaders in a diverse, dynamic, and interdependent world.

Susquehanna faculty members are dedicated scholars and passionate teachers. Because Susquehanna is an undergraduate-only institution, students learn from expert faculty members and not graduate assistants. Many disciplines offer hands-on collaborative research opportunities beginning in the first year of study. Ninety-two percent of full-time faculty have earned the highest degrees in their fields and pride themselves on being committed to student success. Susquehanna's student-teacher ratio is 12:1, allowing for close interactions with faculty and classmates. Inside or outside the classroom, professors become mentors and lifelong supporters.

Susquehanna offers a total collegiate experience. The University's deep-rooted commitment to the intellectual, personal, and professional growth of every student is evident on Susquehanna's residential campus. Outside the classroom students can choose from 145 student organizations and co-curricular activities, collaborative research, service learning, internships, student leadership opportunities, and 23 NCAA Division III sports. Susquehanna provides an inclusive and increasingly diverse community where students gain valuable leadership, social, and interpersonal skills—and memories to last a lifetime.

Location

In the central Pennsylvania town of Selinsgrove, nestled beside the Susquehanna River, students are able to walk downtown to businesses and restaurants. They also enjoy shopping malls, restaurants, and a 12-screen cinema within 15 minutes of campus. The area is rich with hiking, golfing, tubing, kayaking, and caving activities, with a zoo and amusement park nearby, also.

Selinsgrove is a 2½-hour drive from Philadelphia and Baltimore, a 3-hour drive from New York City and Washington, D.C., and 4 hours from Pittsburgh. Pennsylvania's capital city of Harrisburg and Harrisburg International Airport (MDT) are about 60 miles from the campus. Car rentals and limo and car services are available from the airport. The Penn Valley Airport in Selinsgrove accommodates private and charter aircraft and has a car rental agency.

Majors and Degrees

Susquehanna students pursue a Bachelor of Arts, Bachelor of Music, or Bachelor of Science degree in the following areas: accounting, anthropology, art history, biochemistry, biology, business administration, chemistry, communications (emphasis in digital multimedia with tracks in broadcasting, journalism, and sports media; emphasis in strategic communication with tracks in advertising and marketing communications, corporate communications, and public relations; and emphasis in communication arts with tracks in speech communications, communications studies, and teacher certification), computer science, creative writing, earth and environmental sciences, ecology, economics (emphasis in financial economics, general economics and global economy, and financial markets), education (certification in early childhood, pre-K through 4, or secondary 7–12 in many areas), English (with related majors in literature, publishing and editing, and professional and civic writing), environmental studies, finance, French, German, global management, graphic design, history, information systems, international studies (emphasis in Asian studies, comparative cultural studies, developing world studies, diplomacy, European studies, international trade and development, or sustainable development), Italian, luxury brand marketing and management, marketing, mathematics, music, music composition, music education, music performance, neuroscience, philosophy, physics, political science, psychology, public policy, religious studies, sociology, Spanish, studio art (painting and drawing or photography), and theatre (emphasis in performance or production and design).

Preprofessional programs are offered in dentistry, engineering, law, medicine, ministry, optometry, pharmacy, physical therapy, podiatry, teaching and veterinary medicine and include one-on-one advising, related internships, and test preparation for the MCAT and LSAT. Cooperative programs in allied health are offered with Thomas Jefferson University in Philadelphia, in dentistry with Temple University School of Dental Medicine in Philadelphia, and in engineering and applied science with Columbia University. Minors are available in almost every major area and in numerous additional areas.

Academic Programs

Susquehanna provides students the winning combination of a solid liberal arts education plus professional experiences such as internships and research opportunities. Critical-thinking skills and ethics, oral and written communications, teamwork, and other essential workplace skills are emphasized, and 78 percent of students get professional experience before graduation, which prepares them for postgraduate success. In 2014–15, the Council on Undergraduate Research recognized Susquehanna University as a leader among institutions nationwide for providing so many students the opportunity to present their research at the National Conference on Undergraduate Research (NCUR). Acceptance into the conference is competitive. Susquehanna students have presented at NCUR in various fields, including biology, chemistry, ecology, earth and environmental science, history, math, neuroscience, philosophy, political science, and psychology.

The nearby Susquehanna River provides unparalleled access to field research for students. A new research center opened in spring 2015 to support Susquehanna's Freshwater Research Initiative is an exciting development for faculty and student researchers. The Sigmund Weis School of Business is AACSB-accredited, a marker of excellence that places it among the top 5 percent of business programs worldwide. Eight Susquehanna graduates were named Fulbright scholars in 2013 and 2014; their international experiences will be extraordinary opportunities for personal growth and their future careers.

Off-Campus Programs

The University is recognized nationally for its Global Opportunities (GO) program. All students complete a cross-cultural experience lasting two weeks to a full semester in the United States or abroad and reflect on how their experience better prepares them for global citizenship. GO broadens students' perspectives and prepares them for professional success.

GO is flexible and affordable. Susquehanna currently offers more than 85 GO Long programs and 32 GO Short programs, with more in development. Most forms of financial aid, including scholarships, are available during GO experiences.

The majority of Susquehanna's students participate in nationally recognized community service projects, logging an average of 30,000 hours of community service each year.

Academic Facilities

Susquehanna's campus has been named one of the most beautiful in the nation, due in part to first-rate facilities that blend historic and new buildings. Two campus buildings are on the National Register of Historic Places. The academic buildings are designed for collaborative learning, such as the new Natural Sciences Center that houses the biology, chemistry, and earth and environmental sciences programs. It demonstrates the University community's strong commitment to sustainability and environmental responsibility, having earned the U.S. Green Building Council's LEED silver-level certification. Because science education is a part of the Central Curriculum, all students take classes there. Students also frequent the former science building, Fisher Hall, now renovated and housing several academic departments, in addition to the Center for Academic Achievement and the Career Development Center.

Other outstanding academic facilities include Apfelbaum Hall, home to the Sigmund Weis School of Business and the Department of Communications. Apfelbaum houses a television studio with green-screen technology, multimedia classrooms, a presentation room, and numerous small-group study rooms. Cunningham Center for Music and Art offers contemporary art and music teaching facilities and flexible practice and performance space, including Stretansky Concert Hall, a 320-seat venue designed to optimize choral and instrumental music. Weber Chapel Auditorium is home to a classic, 1,500-seat theater, with a revolving stage and recording studio for students studying music technology. Additional performance space for theater students is available in the Degenstein Center Theater, which features a modern 450-seat proscenium teaching theater with a counterweight fly system and an intimate, black-box studio theater.

Blough-Weis Library was renovated in 2014 and now offers ample study space, including seminar and study rooms and a reading and snack nook. The library houses the Media Center, 108 computers for student use, and library holdings totaling more than 193,000 print volumes, nearly 222,000 e-books, and approximately 67,000 electronic and print subscriptions.

Costs

Tuition and fees for 2015–16 are $42,040. Room and board costs are $11,170. A student's personal expenses, including books, travel, and other costs, are estimated at $2,290 per year.

Financial Aid

Susquehanna works with students and families to develop and customize personalized financial plans. The expert financial aid staff is knowledgeable and helpful regarding the federal, state, and Susquehanna financial aid programs, as well as other options such as payment plans and scholarship opportunities.

About 98 percent of Susquehanna students receive some form of financial aid. All students are encouraged to apply for need-based financial aid by filing the Free Application for Federal Student Aid (FAFSA). All students who are accepted are automatically considered for academic merit scholarships. Susquehanna is a participant in the Tuition Exchange program for children of employees at participating institutions and also participates in the Yellow Ribbon Program for veterans of the wars in Iraq and Afghanistan.

Faculty

Susquehanna's faculty members serve as advisers and creative mentors to their students both in the classroom and beyond. Whether meeting one-on-one with a student for more in-depth instruction after class or making their homes available for barbecues, faculty members make themselves accessible to students in a variety of formal and informal settings. Susquehanna professors value the opportunity to live and learn alongside their students. By graduation, many Susquehanna students have shared a stage with faculty members, whether through a recital or a national conference presentation.

Of the 140 full-time professors, 92 percent hold a doctorate or terminal degree in their field. The student-faculty ratio is 12:1.

Student Government

Susquehanna's Student Government Association is a self-governing organization providing representation of the student body in University affairs. The main function of the legislative body is the allocation of student activities fees to recognized clubs, student groups, campus projects, and University activities. Senators are elected each year and serve as student representatives to various offices and groups on campus.

Admission Requirements

Susquehanna students come from many different places and varied backgrounds. But what they share in common is a motivation to succeed and a record of academic and personal achievement. They are enterprising, independent thinkers who are ready to be academically challenged, socially engaged and mentally prepared to succeed in the 21st century. Accepted students earn an average GPA of 3.38 in a competitive college-prep curriculum. For those students who choose to submit test scores, the midrange SAT score is 1040–1190, and the midrange ACT score is 22–28. Because standardized test scores aren't always representative of a student's abilities, applicants who believe their test scores do not reflect their abilities may apply Test Score Optional in lieu of submitting SAT or ACT scores.

Susquehanna believes there is no better way than a campus visit to determine if Susquehanna will be a good fit. Prospective students are invited to schedule a personalized visit to campus or attend one of the special visit programs held throughout the year. Visitors have an opportunity to learn more about the University's programs during an information session, an interview with a member of the admissions staff, and by exploring the beautiful grounds and facilities. Prospective students can also request to visit a class or lab; meet with faculty, coaches, and students; or attend a campus event.

Application and Information

Susquehanna accepts the Common Application and the Susquehanna Success Application, both of which are free to file online. Early Decision and Early Action options are offered. Admission is competitive, but the University evaluates (and values) more than grades and test scores. Students applying to the Bachelor of Music degree program are required to audition. Students applying to major in graphic design or creative writing are required to submit a portfolio of their work.

For more information, prospective students should contact:

Office of Admissions
Susquehanna University
514 University Avenue
Selinsgrove, Pennsylvania 17870-1164
Phone: 570-372-4260
800-326-9672 (toll-free)
Fax: 570-372-2722
E-mail: suadmiss@susqu.edu
Website: http://www.susqu.edu

Apfelbaum Hall and Fisher Hall at Susquehanna University.

TEMPLE UNIVERSITY
PHILADELPHIA, PENNSYLVANIA

The University

Over its 130-year history, Temple University has developed a reputation for providing an affordable, high-quality education that prepares students for the real world. At this vibrant urban, public research university, passionate students turn opportunities into accomplishments: World-class labs are the proving grounds for world-changing ideas. A classroom doubles as the boardroom of a tech startup. Professors become mentors through graduate school and beyond. All because Temple students are driven to take action, and at Temple they find everything they need to achieve their goals.

Cutting-edge facilities, including the new 247,000-square-foot Science Education and Research Center, more than 3,500 engaged faculty members, and top-ranked programs combine to create a dynamic academic environment that attracts students from across the country and around the world. With seventeen schools and colleges, nine campuses, and 38,000 students, Temple is the forty-second-largest university in the United States.

More than 75 percent of freshmen live on campus, where they are a short walk from class, fitness facilities, food trucks, and the many cultural, sports, and academic events that take place every day at Temple. There are more than 300 clubs, activities, and student organizations to choose from, and the University's 10,200-seat entertainment complex hosts NCAA Division I basketball games as well as concerts—Kanye West, Sam Smith, and Bob Dylan have all performed there. The view isn't bad either: Temple's newest residential and dining complex, the twenty-seven-floor Morgan Hall, offers a breathtaking vista of the Philadelphia skyline.

But a Temple education goes beyond campus. The city is an extension of the classroom, and opportunities for hands-on learning are everywhere, from museums and technology meet-ups to internships in business, healthcare, and the arts. Learning in the real world means students are ready for the real world when they graduate, and the University's nearly 300,000 alumni form a powerful support network.

Location

Temple's Main Campus is located just 1.5 miles from the center of Philadelphia, the second-largest city on the East Coast. By train or on foot—Philadelphia is among the most walkable cities in the U.S.—students can explore all the city has to offer, including more than 100 museums, a thriving restaurant scene, numerous sports teams, and the largest landscaped park in the country. The professional world is also right outside Temple's door: There are thousands of opportunities for hands-on learning and internships in the Philadelphia area, and Temple's more than 100,000 alumni in the region love to hire Temple students.

Temple's other eight campuses include the largest and oldest American university in Japan and a location in Rome, Italy. Temple's campus in Ambler, Pennsylvania, is the hub of the University's environmental programs and home to a 187-acre arboretum that serves as a living laboratory. In addition to Main Campus, Temple's Philadelphia campuses are the Health Sciences Center, the Center City campus in downtown Philadelphia, and the Podiatric Medicine campus. Temple University Harrisburg is located in the heart of Pennsylvania's capital city.

Majors and Degrees

Temple offers 129 undergraduate majors, making it easy for students to follow, or discover, their passion. Students who need time to decide on a major can explore their interests through the University Studies program. Those who would like to accelerate their education can apply to one of Temple's many dual-degree programs.

The **Tyler School of Art** offers a B.A. with concentrations in ceramics/glass, fibers, graphic and interactive design, metals/jewelry/CAD-CAM, painting, photography, printmaking, and sculpture; a B.A. in art history and visual studies; and a B.S. in art education. Tyler's Architecture Program confers a B.S. in architecture (preprofessional), architectural preservation, and facilities management.

The **Fox School of Business** offers a B.B.A. in accounting, actuarial science, business management, economics, entrepreneurship, finance, human resource management, international business administration, legal studies, management information systems, marketing, real estate, and risk management and insurance.

The **College of Education** offers a B.S. in adult and organizational development, career and technical education, early childhood education, middle-grades education, and secondary education.

The **College of Engineering** offers a B.S. in engineering in civil engineering, electrical engineering, engineering (general program), and mechanical engineering. A B.S. is also offered in bioengineering, construction management technology, and general engineering technology.

The **College of Liberal Arts** offers a B.A. in African-American studies, American studies, anthropology, Asian studies, classics, criminal justice, economics, English, environmental studies, French, geography and urban studies, German, history, Italian, Jewish studies, Latin American studies, mathematical economics, neuroscience, philosophy, political science, psychology, religion, sociology, Spanish, and women's studies.

The **School of Media and Communication** offers a B.A. in advertising, communication studies, journalism, media studies and production, and strategic communication.

The **Boyer College of Music and Dance** offers a Bachelor of Music in composition, dance, jazz studies, music education, music history, music therapy, performance (specific instrument or voice), and theory; the B.F.A. is offered in dance.

The **College of Public Health** offers a B.S. in athletic training; health information management; kinesiology; linguistics; nursing; public health; speech, language, and hearing; and therapeutic recreation.

The **College of Science and Technology** offers a B.S. in applied mathematics, biochemistry, biology, biophysics, chemistry, computer science, environmental science, geology, information science and technology, mathematical economics, mathematics, physics, neuroscience (cell and molecular), and pre-pharmacy.

The **School of Social Work** offers the B.S.W. degree.

The **Division of Theater, Film, and Media Arts** offers a B.A. in theater and film and media arts.

The **School of Tourism and Hospitality Management** offers a B.S. in sport and recreation management and in tourism and hospitality management.

In addition, the **School of Environmental Design at Ambler** offers B.S. programs in horticulture and landscape architecture and in community and regional planning.

Academic Programs

Students passionate about learning are attracted to Temple because of its variety of academic programs: more than 400 are offered, including 143 bachelor's degree programs. The University provides all of the resources and opportunities of a large, world-class research institution and the individual attention of a small college—average class size is just 27 students, with a 14:1 student-to-faculty ratio.

All students complete the General Education curriculum, a cross-section of courses that form the intellectual foundation of a Temple education. But every student's experience at Temple is a unique and transformative one.

Some students pursue common interests in Living and Learning Communities, groups that live and learn together. Academically qualified students gain extra intellectual challenge through the Honors Program. Temple's study abroad programs offer the opportunity to take learning beyond campus and around the world. Students might find their niche earning course credit while running Temple's cooperative, locavore café. The Hatchery is the Tyler School of Art's design incubator, where entrepreneurial students transform projects into real products.

Students have opportunities to work directly with world-class faculty on research and creative projects and have presented at professional conferences, published in peer-reviewed journals, and premiered music and dance at venues across the world.

A degree from Temple doesn't just fill a transcript or create lines on a resume. Temple empowers students to spark change in themselves and prepares them to charge forward into the real world.

Academic Facilities

Whether in a high-tech classroom or the University's new Science Education and Research Center (SERC), Temple students learn in world-class facilities. At SERC, which is home to sixty-eight research and teaching labs and leading-edge technologies, students work with faculty on real-world projects, making the connection between understanding science and putting advanced research techniques into practice.

At the TECH Center—the largest student computing lab in the country—students can collaborate in a breakout room, edit video in a specialized lab, get assistance from the 24-hour help desk, or work on one of 700 computers. There are more than 100 other computer labs on campus, 3,600 student workstations, and 450 technology-enabled classrooms.

With the equivalent of more than 4 million bound volumes and an extensive special collection of rare books and archives, Temple's libraries rank among the top research libraries in North America. The intersection of collections, services, and library staff propel learning and research success.

Costs

Tuition and fees for the 2014–15 academic year were $14,696 for Pennsylvania residents and $24,722 for out-of-state residents (tuition rates can vary by major). Room and board for the academic year were about $10,700.

Financial Aid

Temple leads the charge with bold and innovative ways to make college affordable. A variety of scholarships, grants, loans, and work-study programs are available; 70 percent of first-year students receive need-based financial aid, and 42 percent receive an academic scholarship. Four-year academic merit scholarships for talented freshmen range from $3,000 to full tuition, and several include summer stipends for research, internships, and study abroad.

Temple's Fly in 4 program, which helps students limit their debt by graduating in four years, awards four-year grants to 500 eligible students in each incoming class in order to reduce their need to work for pay.

Faculty

From their first semester, students at Temple have contact with faculty at the forefront of their fields—winners of prestigious teaching and research awards, scientists doing groundbreaking research, and working artists who show all over the world.

Temple faculty members are also known for their practical experience—a marketing class may be led by a successful entrepreneur or music lessons given by a member of the Philadelphia Orchestra. Marine biologists, newspaper editors, published authors, practicing architects, and healthcare professionals all bring their expertise to the classroom.

And the roster of outstanding faculty members is growing. Temple has hired, on average, 57 new faculty members per year for the past decade, from leading universities and research centers including Princeton University, MIT, and the Cleveland Clinic.

Admission Requirements

The Temple Option is a new admissions path for tenacious students who have the ability to succeed in college but may not perform well on standardized tests. Students can opt to submit SAT or ACT scores, or they can choose the Temple Option and respond to short-answer questions.

For freshman admissions, high-school grades (quality of courses, grade trends), standardized test scores or the Temple Option responses, and other factors are considered. Temple uses a sliding scale rather than absolute cutoffs. SAT subject tests and personal interviews are not required. Official copies of high-school transcripts and standardized test scores must be sent directly to the admissions office.

The deadline for spring admission is November 1. Temple offers rolling admissions and early action decision plans for the fall semester. Those interested in early action must submit a completed application by November 1 and will receive notification by mid-January. The rolling admissions deadline is March 1; freshman decisions begin in early fall. Temple's admissions process is holistic; every aspect of the student's academic history is considered. Typically, students with a B+ average or better in a strong, college-prep curriculum in grades 9–12 and in the top 30 percent of their graduating classes are accepted. For students submitting SAT scores, all three sections are considered—admitted students average 500–600 on each section. Students who opt to take the ACT must also complete the writing section.

The application fee is $55; most students apply online through Temple or the Common Application.

Applicants are considered transfer students if they have attempted 15 or more college-level credits after high school. If this is not the case, they should apply as freshman students. In admissions decisions, careful consideration is given to the quality of a student's program, number of credits earned, and GPA. The average GPA for new transfer students is a 3.1 (on a 4.0 scale). The architecture, nursing, and pharmacy programs have higher minimum GPA requirements. For most programs, transfer students must complete the application process by June 1 for the fall semester or by November 1 for the spring semester. The fall priority deadline for the health information management and nursing programs is February 15. SAT or ACT scores are not required if an applicant has earned at least 15 college-level credits.

Application and Information

A completed file contains an application form accompanied by a nonrefundable application fee, a secondary-school transcript (sent by the student's school), and SAT or ACT scores or responses to the Temple Option questions.

For additional information, students may contact:

Office of Undergraduate Admissions
Temple University
Philadelphia, Pennsylvania 19122-6096
United States
Phone: 215-204-7200
888-340-2222 (toll-free)
E-mail: askanowl@temple.edu
Websites: admissions.temple.edu
nextstop.temple.edu
Facebook: facebook.com/TempleU
Twitter: @admissionsTU
Instagram: @admissionsTU
Snapchat: @TempleUniv

At Temple University, students share an uncommon drive.

TRINE UNIVERSITY

ANGOLA, INDIANA

★ To read more about this school, visit http://petersons.to/trineuniversity

TRINE UNIVERSITY

The University

Trine University has a reputation for producing work-ready graduates who are in demand, as proven by Trine's 97 percent job placement rate that surpasses the national average. The placement rate, along with the well-maintained campus, welcoming community and opportunities to excel in and out of the classroom are just some of the reasons why many students choose Trine.

Students can expect a well-rounded college experience with challenging courses taught by engaged and experienced faculty members who are eager to help students excel. Small class size is conducive to personalized attention.

Other facts about the University:

- Trine is private, independent, and coeducational.
- Trine offers associate, baccalaureate, and doctoral degrees to students in more than thirty-five programs, including engineering, mathematics, forensic science, pre–physical therapy, business, education, communication, exercise science, criminal justice, and golf management.
- In January 2015, Trine created the College of Engineering and Business to enhance the strengths of the Allen School of Engineering and Technology and the Ketner School of Business. The move also reflects the growing collaboration between professional engineers and business leaders.
- Trine offers a five-year combined Bachelor of Science and Master of Engineering program with majors in civil engineering.
- In 2014 Trine launched several new programs: Bachelor of Arts in professional writing and English studies, Bachelor of Science in cybersecurity, Master of Science in Engineering Management, Master of Business Administration, and Doctor of Physical Therapy. A physician assistant program is being developed.

Enhancing the campus is a priority. In recent years, Trine has invested more than $20 million in campus upgrades. The 170-bed Reiners Residence Hall is under construction, while Ford Hall, home of the Ketner School of Business, is being fully refurbished. Both are scheduled to open in fall 2015.

In fall 2014, the school set an enrollment record with more than 600 new students, which contributed to a record-setting 1,700-plus students on the main campus.

The student body at Trine breaks down as follows:

- Academic averages for the freshmen class include a 3.5 GPA, 1056 SAT, and 24 ACT. Thirty-one percent were in the top 10 percent of their high school graduating class and 57 percent were in the top 25 percent.
- Students represent thirty states and sixteen countries.
- Engineering is the most popular program with 46 percent of students enrolled in the major.
- Forty percent of students are involved in NCAA Division III athletics.

The 450-acre campus offers an inviting and safe atmosphere that complements the seriousness and determination with which Trine students pursue their academic goals. Students enjoy opportunities to develop friendships and to build leadership and teamwork skills in organizations and athletics. Trine has more that sixty-five academic, cultural, service, and Greek organizations and varsity athletic teams for men and women.

Trine is a member of National Collegiate Athletic Association (NCAA) Division III and the Michigan Intercollegiate Athletic Association (MIAA), the nation's oldest athletic conference. Men's sports include baseball, basketball, cross-country, football, golf, lacrosse, soccer, tennis, track, and wrestling. Women's sports include basketball, cross-country, golf, lacrosse, soccer, softball, tennis, track, and volleyball. Many students also participate on intramural sports teams.

In addition to succeeding on the field, Trine students also excel in and out of the classroom.

- Chemical engineering seniors have won the American Institute of Chemical Engineers national individual design competition several times and have won the national safety award seven times in the past eight years.
- Trine's Tau Alpha Omicron chapter of the American Criminal Justice Association annually wins regional and national awards for marksmanship, crime scene investigation, and physical agility. In 2014, it won sixteen awards.
- In 2014, Trine's softball team made school history by capturing the MIAA Tournament and NCAA Regional, earning a trip to the NCAA National Championship in Tyler, Texas.
- Trine student-athletes have been named to MIAA teams and individuals and teams have earned all-academic honors.

Location

Trine is in Angola, Indiana, the heart of northeast Indiana's scenic lake resort region, halfway between the metropolitan areas of Chicago and Cleveland. Just a 45-minute drive from Fort Wayne, Indiana, Trine offers the safety and ease of a small-town environment, near some of the nation's most vital cities.

Majors and Degrees

The Allen School of Engineering & Technology awards Bachelor of Science degrees in biomedical, chemical, civil, computer, electrical, computer, and mechanical engineering and design engineering technology. Minors are offered in aeronautical, biomedical, bioprocess, energy, environmental, metallurgical, plastics, software, and structural engineering.

The Ketner School of Business awards Bachelor of Science in business administration degrees with majors in accounting, finance, golf management, international business, management, marketing, and sport management.

The Franks School of Education awards Bachelor of Science degrees in elementary, health and physical, mathematics, science, and social studies education.

The Jannen School of Arts and Sciences awards Bachelor of Arts degrees with majors in general studies (pre-legal, self-designated, and social studies), professional writing and English studies, and psychology. The school also awards Bachelor of Science degrees with majors in biology, chemistry, communication, criminal justice, cybersecurity, forensic science, informatics, mathematics, and music.

The School of Health Sciences offers a Bachelor of Science degree in exercise science and pre–physical therapy and pre-medical professional tracks, and a doctoral degree in physical therapy.

The School of Professional Studies, with eight education centers in Indiana and Michigan, awards associate, bachelor's, and master's degrees in nine programs. Classes are geared toward busy, working adults and are seated, online, and blended.

Trine University, Peoria, Arizona, awards bachelor's degrees in more than thirty programs

Academic Programs

All programs combine classroom learning with a broad range of practical experience. Students learn from professionals with advanced degrees and industry expertise, and get hands-on experience in laboratories stocked with state-of-the-art equipment and in other professional environments.

Trine University is accredited by the Higher Learning Commission and a member of the North Central Association (www.hlcommission.org; phone: 312-263-0456). Trine's programs in chemical engineering, civil engineering, computer engineering, electrical engineering, and mechanical engineering are accredited by the Engineering Accreditation Commission of ABET (111 Market Place, Suite 1050, Baltimore, Maryland 21202-4012; phone: 410-347-7700).

All teacher preparation programs are accredited by the Council for the Accreditation of Educator Preparation (www.caepnet.org) and the Indiana Department Education/Office of Educator Licensing and Development (www.doe.ingov/licensing). The Ketner School of Business, Bachelor of Science in business administration program is accredited by the Accreditation Council for Business Schools and Programs (www.acbsp.org). Associate degree programs in accounting and business administration are also accredited.

Effective July 29, 2014, the Doctor of Physical Therapy Program at Trine University has been granted candidate for accreditation status by the Commission on Accreditation in Physical Therapy Education (1111 North Fairfax Street, Alexandria, Virginia, 22314; phone: 703-706-3245; e-mail: accreditation@apta.org). Candidate for accreditation is a pre-accreditation status of affiliation with the Commission on Accreditation in Physical Therapy Education that indicates that the program may matriculate students in technical/professional courses and that the program is progressing toward accreditation. Candidate for accreditation is not an accreditation status nor does it assure eventual accreditation.

Off-Campus Programs

Trine's Career Services office works with a long list of diverse companies to provide co-op and internship opportunities. Semesters of classroom study are alternated with professional work experience, which can give students a competitive edge in the job market and offset college expenses. Often, co-ops and internships launch careers as they lead to full-time employment.

Academic Facilities

The John G. Best Hall of Science, home of the Jannen School of Arts & Sciences, contains classrooms and science laboratories.

The Jim and Joan Bock Center for Innovation and Biomedical Engineering, a $6-million, nearly 25,000-square-foot facility, opened in August 2013. The Bock Center houses laboratories to support the Allen School of Engineering & Technology and Innovation One (i1), an incubator for technology and business. Experiential learning for students in all majors is also available through i1.

The Thomas L. Fawick Hall of Engineering, home to the Allen School of Engineering & Technology, features classrooms and laboratories, all providing students access to technology from day one.

The Perry T. Ford Memorial Building is being refurbished and is slated to open in fall 2015. The home of the Ketner School of Business will boast technology-rich classrooms and a design that mimics a business setting. A laboratory will have up-to-the-minute information about stocks being traded and other business news.

The T. Furth Center for Performing Arts, which opened in May 2014, is the result of a $7.8-million renovation of the former First Christian Church. The center is home to Trine's music program and the Ryan Concert Hall is the venue for a variety of concerts.

The Rick L. and Vicki L. James University Center is the hub for student activity, including a library stocked with plenty of computers, Fabiani Theatre, radio station WEAX, and the newly expanded Whitney Commons dining hall.

William D. Shambaugh Hall, home of the Franks School of Education, offers a juvenile literature and school curriculum collection, kits, and audio-visual resource materials, as well as workspace and materials to support education students.

The Charles and Nancy Taylor Hall of Humanities houses the Department of Humanities & Communication as well as classrooms, the Wells Gallery, the Humanities Institute, the Fine Arts Library, and Wells Theater, home of the University's drama club.

Costs

Tuition for the academic year (two semesters) in 2014–15 was $29,300 ($31,600 for engineering). Room and standard meal plan (nineteen meals per week) for the academic year cost $8,650 (double occupancy).

Financial Aid

Financial aid may be awarded in the form of scholarships, grants, loans, or campus employment. Any of these aids or any combination may supplement family and student resources to meet basic educational expenses. Trine requires the Free Application for Federal Student Aid (FAFSA) and recommends its submission by March 1.

Trine stands out in this area because:

- Ninety-eight percent of students receive some form of financial aid.
- Annually, $23 million is awarded in institutional aid.
- Average financial aid per student is $23,500.
- The school has been recognized for graduating students with the least amount of debt.

Faculty

Trine has a full-time faculty of 97 members; most have doctoral degrees and professional experience. The student-faculty ratio is 13:1.

Student Government

The student senate is organized for the purpose of providing funding and formulating policies for campus organizations. Representatives to the senate are elected by each class.

Admission Requirements

Graduation from an approved high school or equivalent preparation is required for admission. Selection is made without regard to race, religion, or gender. Applicants are required to take the ACT or SAT prior to approval for admission (writing sections are optional).

Admission requirements for engineering include 4 years of English, 1 year of chemistry, 1 year of physics, 1 year of social studies, 2 years of algebra, 1 year of geometry, and ½ year of trigonometry. All other applicants must have 4 years of English, 3 years of mathematics, 3 years of science, and 3 years of social studies.

Graduates of pre-professional or college-parallel programs at approved community or junior colleges are eligible for transfer. Credit may be allowed in subjects that parallel Trine programs, provided the student earned a grade of C or better in the course.

Application and Information

Trine University's online application is free and available at www.trine.edu. The University admits applicants on the basis of scholastic achievement and academic potential. Admission decisions are made on a rolling basis. Applicants are notified of their status within two weeks of receipt of their application, high school record, and test scores. Transfer students must also submit an official copy of their college transcript(s).

Interested students and their parents are encouraged to visit the campus. Arrangements can be made by contacting the Office of Admission.

For additional information, students should call or write:

Office of Admission
Trine University
One University Avenue
Angola, Indiana 46703-1764
United States
Phone: 260-665-4100
800-347-4878 (toll-free within continental United States)
E-mail: admit@trine.edu
Website: www.trine.edu
www.facebook.com/trineadmissions
www.youtube/trineuniversity

Trine University provides a safe and comfortable environment for learning and intellectual growth as well as for athletics and diverse activities.

TRINITY COLLEGE

HARTFORD, CONNECTICUT

★ To read more about this school, visit http://petersons.to/trinitycollege

The College

Since its founding in 1823, Trinity has provided an undergraduate education of uncommon quality. Widely acknowledged as one of the top liberal arts colleges in the country, Trinity has been recognized by a panel of national education editors for its bold and innovative ideas to advance the cause of higher education and ensure greater access.

In its commitment to the rigorous pursuit of the liberal arts and to instruction that is personal and conversational, Trinity is an ideal college. At the same time, Trinity is in close touch with the world beyond its campus. In that respect and in terms of the outstanding opportunities Trinity's capital city location offers students, a Trinity education is indeed a real education.

While remaining faithful to the classic liberal arts tradition, Trinity offers a distinctive educational experience that prepares students for the challenges and opportunities of the 21st century. Building on its traditional strengths in the arts and humanities and exceptional offerings in science and engineering, Trinity engages students in a conversation with the world through its Center for Urban and Global Studies, study-abroad programs, interdisciplinary programs, and innovative, rigorous programs that draw on the rich cultural, educational, and professional assets of Hartford. State-of-the-art electronic facilities support Trinity's advanced use of information technology in classrooms. The heart of a Trinity education, however, remains the personal encounter between professor and student, the intellectual partnership that discovers a world of ideas and ignites a passion for learning.

Trinity's students come from 44 states and 62 countries. The College believes that a diverse community makes learning flourish. Trinity's undergraduate enrollment of approximately 2,200 students is composed of 47 percent women and 53 percent men. Approximately 90 percent of undergraduates live on campus in College housing. Trinity is engaged in continuing campus revitalization programs that preserve its impressive Gothic buildings as it also develops a campus for the 21st century.

Trinity offers a rich array of extracurricular activities—films, plays, concerts, musical theater, sports, academic symposia, and visits by nationally and internationally known writers, speakers, and performers. Participation is an important word on campus, and Trinity students have abundant opportunities to lead and to be involved in numerous student clubs; special interest groups; theater, dance, and music groups; debate; academic programs; the campus cinema; Trinity's radio station; and many student publications. With 19 acres of playing fields, Trinity also offers an extensive athletic program. About 40 percent of the student body participates on 29 men's and women's varsity teams (Division III) and a roster of intramural sports. The Ferris Athletic Center features a swimming pool, a fully equipped fitness center, crew tanks, 10 international-size squash courts, basketball courts, and an indoor track.

Location

Situated on a beautiful 100-acre campus in the center of Hartford, the capital of Connecticut, Trinity offers the best of both worlds—a supportive and active campus community located in a city that provides students with myriad opportunities for internships, community service, and cultural exploration. Hartford's businesses, cultural organizations, governmental agencies, and nonprofit institutions offer Trinity students hundreds of opportunities to explore careers through the College's extensive internship program. Hartford has a number of cultural institutions, including the Wadsworth Atheneum (the oldest public art museum in the nation), Mark Twain House, Harriet Beecher Stowe Center, Hartford Symphony, Hartford Stage, and a number of smaller theaters and clubs that provide a cultural stew of dance, theater, and music. The shopping districts of Hartford and surrounding suburbs are nearby. The impressive Connecticut coast is easily accessible, and Boston and New York are each about 2 hours from campus. Off campus, Trinity students have access to a field station in Ashford, Connecticut, dedicated to research in the natural sciences and a wide range of environmental educational endeavors.

Majors and Degrees

On the undergraduate level, the College offers a Bachelor of Arts degree and a Bachelor of Science degree. Trinity offers 39 majors, including American studies; anthropology; art history; biochemistry; biology; chemistry; classical studies; computer science; economics; educational studies; engineering; English; environmental science; French studies; German studies; Hispanic studies; history; interdisciplinary computing; international studies; Italian studies; Jewish studies; language and culture studies (Arabic, Chinese, Hebrew, Japanese); mathematics; music; neuroscience; philosophy; physics; political science; psychology; public policy and law; religion; Russian; sociology; student-designed interdisciplinary major; studio arts; theater and dance; urban studies; women, gender, and sexuality; and world literature and culture studies.

Academic Programs

Featuring more than 900 courses, Trinity's curriculum provides a framework within which students may explore the many dimensions of an undergraduate education. At the same time, the curriculum offers each student flexibility to experiment, to deepen old interests and develop new ones, and to acquire specialized training in a major field. Students must demonstrate proficiency in writing, mathematics, and a second language and fulfill a five-part distribution requirement that consists of at least one course in each of the following categories: arts, humanities, natural sciences, numerical and symbolic reasoning, and social sciences. They must satisfy a writing intensive requirement, take a first-year seminar, and complete at least one course that focuses on global engagement.

Off-Campus Programs

Trinity College is a leading institution in the area of study away, offering nine of its own Trinity-administered semester/year programs in Barcelona, Buenos Aires, Cape Town, New York City, Paris, Rome, Trinidad, Shanghai, and Vienna. These programs provide rigorous academic offerings for students from all academic disciplines. Students also may select from more than 90 approved study-away programs throughout the world. More than 50 percent of students study away at some point prior to graduation.

Academic Facilities

The Raether Library and Information Technology Center is the central research facility of the College. The Raether Center houses the Trinity College Library, which contains more than 1.2 million books (in print and online) and includes the Watkinson Library (rare books and special collections). The Watkinson holds more than 150,000 books ranging in date from the eleventh century to the present, maintains the College archives, and is a regular contributor to the library's digital repository. Information Technology Services (ITS) is also located in the Raether Center and offers the latest in information and media-related technologies.

The campus is fully wired, with every student room connected to the College network and the Web. Public access computers are also available 24 hours a day in select facilities.

Costs

Costs for the 2015–16 academic year are $48,446 for tuition, $13,144 for room and board, and $2,380 for fees.

Financial Aid

Each student admitted to Trinity who qualifies for aid receives a package that fully meets his or her calculated need. Students must file the Free Application for Federal Student Aid (FAFSA) as well as the Financial Aid PROFILE of the College Scholarship Service. Admissions applications are due by January 1; FAFSA and PROFILE applications are due by February 1. Students are notified of admission and aid decisions by late March. Normally, need is met with a financial aid package that includes grant assistance, work-study, and federal student loans. Federal funds for which accepted students are eligible include Pell Grants, Perkins Loans, Stafford Loans, and PLUS Loans. State scholarships and private grants are also available. The College administers a large student employment program, and most students who demonstrate need are granted an on-campus job as part of their financial aid package. The ratio of grant assistance to loans and work-study aid is sometimes affected by the academic strength of the student's record. Trinity continues to expand its aid budget to keep pace with the College's goal to increase the socioeconomic and ethnic diversity on campus. More than 40 percent of the students receive financial aid.

Faculty

The distinctive strength of a Trinity education has always been the close interaction between students and a faculty of devoted teacher-scholars. A student-faculty ratio of 10:1 enables supportive yet challenging educational experiences that establish a foundation for lifetime learning and enables students to pursue academic interests with passion. Students have numerous opportunities to collaborate with faculty members in conducting research; many students have made joint presentations at local, national, or international symposia and/or have published jointly prepared papers. All courses are taught by Trinity faculty members, not graduate assistants.

Although the first calling of Trinity's professors is teaching, they are also active publishing scholars of national and international distinction. History professor Joan Hedrick, for example, won the Pulitzer Prize for her biography of Harriet Beecher Stowe. Other notable professors include Susan Masino, a psychologist and neuroscientist whose research has been funded by the National Science Foundation and the National Institutes of Health; Dan Lloyd, acclaimed philosopher and author of *Radiant Cool*; Pablo Delano, an accomplished photographer; and Samuel Kassow, a distinguished historian. Trinity professors pride themselves on their accessibility and keen interest in helping students.

Student Government

Trinity fosters the growth of future leaders by providing students with many opportunities to exercise and test their leadership skills. The Student Government Association (SGA), for example, provides students a strong voice in social, cultural, and—through membership on faculty committees—academic matters. Composed of elected class representatives, the SGA constantly seeks the expertise and insights of all interested students, and its committees offer enterprising students many chances to participate and to develop leadership skills.

Admission Requirements

Trinity seeks an ethnically and geographically diverse group of highly motivated students who have completed a rigorous course of study in secondary school and have demonstrated energy, talent, and leadership in a variety of extracurricular activities. Trinity has no specific GPA minimums or test-score cutoffs. The College is highly selective, and its candidates typically have a B+ high school average. At least 16 academic units of college-preparatory course work are recommended, including a minimum of 4 years of English, 3 years of foreign language, 2 years of laboratory science, 2 years of algebra, 1 year of geometry, and 2 years of history. Last year, more than 7,000 men and women from all over the nation and world applied for admission to the College, which enrolls an entering class of approximately 610 students. Transfer students with a 3.0 GPA in a strong course of study at another accredited college or university are considered for admission to the sophomore or junior classes.

Admissions officers review each application individually; decisions are based on each candidate's academic record (curriculum and GPA), evaluations from secondary school teachers and counselors, test scores, personal strengths, talents, activities, and application.

Application and Information

Students must submit completed applications to the Admissions Office. Application deadlines are November 15 for Early Decision I applicants (with notification by mid-December), January 1 for Early Decision II applicants (with notification by mid-February), and January 1 for Regular Decision applicants (with notification by late March). Transfer applicants must submit applications by April 1 for admission in the following fall semester (with notification by mid-June) and by November 15 for admission in the following spring semester (with notification by early January). Prospective students may submit an electronic Common Application at http://www.commonapp.org.

Inquiries should be made to:

Office of Admissions and Financial Aid
Trinity College
Hartford, Connecticut 06106-3100
Phone: 860-297-2180
Fax: 860-297-2287
E-mail: admissions.office@trincoll.edu
Website: http://www.trincoll.edu/admissions
http://www.facebook.com/trincoll
http://www.youtube.com/trincoll
http://www.twitter.com/trincolladmiss

Trinity's historic Long Walk buildings are the heart of the campus. Photo by Bob Handleman.

TRUMAN STATE UNIVERSITY

KIRKSVILLE, MISSOURI

★ To read more about this school, visit http://petersons.to/trumanstateuniversity

The University

Truman has forged a national reputation for offering an exceptionally high-quality undergraduate education at a competitive price. For the eighteenth consecutive year, *U.S. News & World Report* has ranked Truman as the number one public institution in the Midwest offering bachelor's and master's degrees. In addition, Truman is recognized by *Kiplinger's Personal Finance* as one of the nation's best values in public education.

A commitment to student achievement and learning is at the core of everything Truman does. This commitment is evidenced by faculty and staff members who recognize the importance of providing students with the opportunity to interact with their professors both in and out of the classroom. With class sizes averaging only 24 students and 80 percent having fewer than 30 students, scholars find ample opportunity to ask questions of professors as well as interact with their multitalented peers. Truman's academic environment is enhanced by a student body that achieves at remarkable levels. The 2014 freshman class had an ACT midrange of 25 to 30 and an average GPA of 3.76 on a 4.0 scale. In addition, numerous opportunities exist for students to engage in undergraduate research. Each year, approximately 1,200 students work alongside professors on University research projects, gaining confidence, knowledge, and skill in their chosen disciplines. The University offers these students the opportunity to present the results of their research at the annual Student Research Conference. In addition, selected students travel to the National Undergraduate Research Symposium to present their research findings. Undergraduate research stipends are also available.

Students wishing to attend Truman to become a teacher must first complete a bachelor's degree in an academic discipline and then apply for admission into professional study at the master's level to obtain a Master of Arts in Education (M.A.E). Through this program, certification can be achieved for elementary education, middle school education, secondary education, and special education.

With more than 240 University organizations available to students, encompassing service, Greek, honorary, professional, religious, social, political, and recreational influences, Truman students have tremendous opportunities to become involved while enrolled at the University. Truman's Student Activities Board provides special guests such as Olympic gold medalist Shawn Johnson, comic acts such as Vanessa Bayer and Judah Friedlander, and musical artists like B.o.B., Lee Brice, and Phillip Phillips. In addition, admission to all varsity athletic events, Truman theater productions, and Lyceum Series events is free to Truman students. Recent theater productions have included *Spring Awakening*, *Rebel Voices*, and *Bedroom Farce*.

Location

Truman is located in Kirksville, a town of approximately 17,000 nestled in the northeast corner of Missouri. The town square, located within walking distance of the Truman campus, provides a connection to Kirksville's past. A multiplex movie theater is located on the town square; local merchants operate specialized gift, book, and clothing stores; and several restaurants offer a wide selection of American and international cuisine.

The Kirksville Aquatic Center is a great place to have fun and get fit. This indoor/outdoor pool complex offers a variety of activities, classes, and programs designed to appeal to people of all ages. The complex includes a six-lane indoor swimming pool, perfect for swimming, relaxing, or playing a game of water-basketball. The outdoor pool is designed with a zero-depth entry, a 1-meter diving board, and four 25-yard outdoor lap lanes as well as a 20-foot water slide.

The northeast region of Missouri is also home to Thousand Hills State Park. A 3,252-acre state park and 573-acre lake for camping, hiking, biking, fishing, swimming, boating, and waterskiing is located within 10 minutes of the Truman campus.

Majors and Degrees

Undergraduate degrees offered by Truman include the Bachelor of Arts (B.A.), Bachelor of Science (B.S.), Bachelor of Music: Performance (B.M.), Bachelor of Fine Arts (B.F.A.), and Bachelor of Science in Nursing (B.S.N.). Truman offers more than forty areas of study in the following disciplines: accounting, agricultural science, athletic training, art, art history, biology, business administration, chemistry, classics, communication, communication disorders, computer science, creative writing, economics, English, exercise science, French, German, health science, history, interdisciplinary studies, justice systems, linguistics, mathematics, music, music: performance, nursing, philosophy and religion, physics, political science, psychology, Romance languages, Russian, sociology/anthropology, Spanish, and theatre.

Professional paths include but are not limited to dentistry, engineering, law, medicine, optometry, pharmacy, physical therapy, and veterinary medicine.

Academic Programs

Truman is Missouri's premier liberal arts and sciences university and the only highly selective public institution in the state. The Liberal Studies Program is the heart of Truman's curriculum and is intended to serve as a foundation for all major programs of study offered by the University. Truman's mission is to offer an exemplary undergraduate education, grounded in the liberal arts and sciences, in the context of a public institution of higher learning. Truman seeks to provide the kind of education in the liberal arts and sciences that has historically been offered only at private colleges. The program is a blend of two intellectual traditions in higher education, one that emphasizes the traditional thought and learning of the culture, as reflected in the classical works produced by it, and the other that emphasizes personal investigation and freedom of discovery. The philosophy behind the Liberal Studies Program is based on a commitment that Truman has made to provide students with essential skills needed for lifelong learning, breadth across the traditional liberal arts and sciences through exposure to various discipline-based modes of inquiry, and interconnecting perspectives that stress interdisciplinary thinking and integration as well as linkage to other cultures and experiences. All students graduating from Truman must complete 63 or more credit hours in liberal arts and sciences courses.

Truman also offers an especially challenging Honors Scholar Program. This program provides students with the opportunity to select the most rigorous honors courses to satisfy the liberal arts component of their respective programs. Students who successfully complete this program benefit from an even richer academic experience and also receive special recognition at graduation and distinction on their academic transcripts. Departmental honors are also available in several disciplines.

Off-Campus Programs

Each year, approximately 400 Truman students participate in enriching and life-changing study-abroad experiences. Truman's own study-abroad programs, combined with programs offered through Truman's membership in the College Consortium for International Studies, International Student Exchange Program, AustraLearn, and the Council on International Educational Exchange, provide students with study-abroad opportunities in more than sixty countries worldwide, including Australia, China, England, Finland, France, Italy, Russia, Spain, and Thailand.

In cooperation with the Washington Center for Internships and Academic Seminars, Truman offers a wide variety of experiential internships in Washington, D.C. Included are work-experience opportunities in such areas as public administration, the fine and performing arts, foreign affairs/diplomacy, government affairs, criminal justice, international relations, health and human services, environmental policy, business administration, and communications as well as other areas. Placement sites include nonprofit groups, media organizations, the State Department, Congress, museums, and much more.

Truman requires internships in education, health science, and exercise science and annually offers internship opportunities with the Missouri State Legislature. In recent years, students have completed internships with United States senators, the governor of Missouri, business and industry managers, zoos, broadcast and print media professionals, accountants, advertising agencies, physical therapists, musicians, artists, and the United States Supreme Court.

Academic Facilities

The Truman campus is beautifully situated on an expanse of 140 acres near downtown Kirksville. Featured among the forty facilities on campus is Pickler Memorial Library. This 460,116-volume facility provides a state-of-the-art library resource for students and faculty members alike. Materials not available in Pickler Memorial Library can be obtained through the Interlibrary Loan Office and MOBIUS.

Recent improvements to campus facilities include the expansion of the Pershing Building with the new health sciences wing, which was completed for the fall 2011 semester. Facility improvements included the new Fontaine C. Piper Movement Analysis Lab, a human performance lab, an expanded clinic for communication disorders, athletic training rooms, and a brand-new nursing simulation center. The renovations to the Student Union Building were completed in 2008 with an expanded Center for Student Involvement, new technology, mural restoration, and a completely renovated university bookstore.

The West Campus Suites opened to students in 2006. Each suite is equipped with a living room, two bedrooms housing 2 students each, closet space, a large bathroom, and central air conditioning. Recent renovations to Missouri Hall include a 2,500-square-foot addition, laundry facilities on every floor, and individually controlled heating and cooling in each room. Renovations are also complete on Blanton/Nason/Brewer Hall, Dobson Hall, and Ryle Hall; and Centennial Hall's renovation was completed in fall 2014.

Additional campus facilities include a student media center with a TV studio, a radio station, print media production facilities, a biofeedback laboratory, an organic chemistry lab, an analytical chemistry lab, an observatory, a greenhouse, a 5,000-seat football stadium, a soccer field, tennis courts, softball and baseball diamonds, a 3,000-seat arena with three basketball courts, an Olympic-size swimming pool, a multicultural affairs center, a writing center, a student success center, and a career center.

Costs

Tuition for Missouri residents for the 2014–15 academic year was $7,096; out-of-state tuition was $13,160. Room and board totals for both Missouri residents and nonresidents start at $7,420. Additional fees included a $315 freshman orientation fee, an annual $84 activities fee, a $54 Student Health Center fee, an annual $100 athletic fee, a $115 parking fee for those with a vehicle, and the costs of books and personal expenses.

Financial Aid

Truman offers automatic scholarships ranging from $500 to $5,000. Competitive scholarship awards vary from $500 up to full tuition, room and board, plus a $4,000 study-abroad stipend. The application for admission also serves as the application for the automatic and competitive scholarship programs.

Several scholarships are awarded to students for excellence in music, theatre, debate/forensics, or art. These scholarships are available for instrumental or vocal music; acting or dramatic production; speech or debate; and studio art or art history. Of special interest to piano students is the Truman Piano Fellowship Competition.

The National Collegiate Athletic Association and the University authorize a limited number of grants to outstanding athletes. The value of this aid may vary with each individual recipient.

Truman accepts the Free Application for Federal Student Aid (FAFSA) and participates in all Federal Title IV financial aid programs. Financial aid estimates are available upon request.

Faculty

Truman State University is committed to teaching the academically talented undergraduate student. The University has 312 full-time faculty members and 50 part-time faculty members. Of these, 98 percent teach undergraduates and graduate teaching assistants only teach 1 percent of classes. Most major graduate institutions are represented among the Truman faculty, including Harvard, Princeton, Yale, Brown, Cornell, Oxford, and the Sorbonne. The student-faculty ratio at Truman is 16:1.

Student Government

Student Senate is the official elected governing body of the Student Association, representing approximately 5,800 students. Its mission is to represent the views of the Student Association in the formulation of the University policy through legislation and membership on all University committees; to facilitate communication and mutual understanding among the Student Association, faculty and staff members, and administration; to maintain a cohesive vision for the future of the University; and to actively participate in the fulfillment of the University's mission as an exemplary public liberal arts and sciences university.

Admission Requirements

Admission to Truman is competitive. Each applicant is evaluated for admission based upon academic and cocurricular record, ACT or SAT results, and the admission essay. Truman requires the following high school core: 4 units of English, 3 units of mathematics (4 recommended), 3 units of social studies/history, 3 units of natural science, 1 unit of fine arts, and 2 units of the same foreign language.

Application and Information

The priority application date for admission is December 1. Students who have applied by this date are considered for all applicable competitive scholarships. Applications are processed on a rolling basis. There is no application fee. Students may apply online at the University's website.

For further information or to schedule a campus visit, students should contact:

Admission Office
Ruth W. Towne Museum and Visitors Center
Truman State University
100 East Normal
Kirksville, Missouri 63501
Phone: 660-785-4114
800-892-7792
Fax: 660-785-7456
E-mail: admissions@truman.edu
Website: http://admissions.truman.edu

Pickler Memorial Library is a state-of-the-art resource for the whole campus.

UNITED STATES MERCHANT MARINE ACADEMY

KINGS POINT, NEW YORK

The Academy

The United States Merchant Marine Academy is a four-year, tuition-free federal service academy that was founded in 1943 to educate and train maritime shipping industry (merchant marine) officers, officers on active duty in the armed forces, and leaders in the maritime and intermodal transportation industry. It is an accredited, degree-granting college whose students are commissioned as ensigns in the Navy Reserve upon graduation. The Academy is one of the world's foremost institutions in the field of maritime education and is operated under the Maritime Administration (MARAD) of the U.S. Department of Transportation.

There are approximately 975 men and women enrolled as midshipmen at the Academy. Their daily routine at Kings Point is very demanding. The academic day begins at 7:30 a.m. and concludes at 4 p.m. After classes, midshipmen are free to participate in recreational activities until dinnertime. After dinner, they are required to devote their time to study and academic preparation.

The extracurricular program is broad and varied. In addition to varsity athletics in twenty-five intercollegiate sports, the Academy has an extensive intramural program that permits all students to enjoy physical activity and competition.

The nonathletic activities are also wide ranging and abundant, falling into as many categories as there are individual interests. Publications and the Drill Team, Glee Club, Regimental Band, Scuba-Diving Club, Eagle Scout Association, International Relations Club, and Fencing Club are but a few of the pursuits available to the midshipmen. Regimental and class dances and informal mixers provide the midshipmen with an interesting social program.

Midshipmen are granted liberty on weekends, leave at Thanksgiving, winter holidays (December), spring trimester break, and annual leave in June–July after graduation and before the next academic term begins. Perhaps the most unusual and exciting part of the Academy curriculum is the Shipboard Training Program (Sea Year). Each midshipman, during three trimesters of the sophomore and junior years, serves 300–360 days at sea aboard commercially operated American-flag merchant ships. This exceptional work-study program takes the midshipmen to many parts of the world and provides them with practical experience on several different types of vessels. It can be said that the world is their campus during their three trimesters of sea service.

Location

The Academy is located on 80.5 acres of land at Kings Point, on the North Shore of Long Island. Kings Point is a suburban residential community only 20 miles east of midtown New York City, close to various cultural and recreational facilities.

Majors and Degrees

A graduate of the U.S. Merchant Marine Academy receives a Bachelor of Science degree, a merchant marine license as a third mate or third assistant engineer, and a commission as an ensign in the U.S. Navy Reserve. Graduates may apply to the Army, Navy, Air Force, Marine Corps, Coast Guard, or National Oceanic and Atmospheric Administration (NOAA) to serve on active duty. Five major programs are offered: marine transportation for the preparation of deck officers; marine engineering for students interested in becoming engineering officers; marine engineering systems, which, in addition to leading to a license as a third assistant engineer, is accredited by the Accreditation Board for Engineering and Technology (ABET) and includes a curriculum with greater depth in mathematics and a significant component of engineering design, as compared to the marine engineering curriculum; marine engineering and shipyard management, which is also accredited by ABET; and logistics and intermodal transportation, a marine transportation program focusing on logistics and intermodal systems management.

Academic Programs

During the first trimester of the plebe (or freshman) year, all students take a common program of mathematics, science, English, and professional courses. This background enables midshipmen to determine intelligently the area of their special interest. After the first trimester, midshipmen select their major and from then on concentrate on a program aligned with their career choice. The professional majors each consist of required core courses in technical and general education areas as well as selected electives. The option program consists of six courses for marine transportation and marine engineering majors, who have a choice of taking a series of related elective courses in a specific area of concentration or any individual elective course for which they qualify. These courses include such specialized fields as nuclear engineering, management science, computer science, chemistry, and naval architecture. By choosing to take the series of related courses, midshipmen can develop a proficiency in a subspecialty, supplementing their major field of study. Students in the marine engineering systems majors are not offered the choice of electives because of the required course load in their programs. General education courses make up about one third of each of the professional curriculums, and all midshipmen are required to take naval science courses prescribed by the Department of the Navy.

Thus, the Academy provides a balanced program of theoretical and practical study designed to provide the undergraduate with technical competence, leadership skills, and the well-rounded general education so essential for responsible citizenship in contemporary society.

Exemption credit may be awarded for college-level work completed at an accredited college if the course is equivalent to a course offered at the Academy.

Academic Facilities

With the exception of Wiley Hall, the former residence of Walter P. Chrysler and now an administration building, all the buildings of the Academy have been constructed since 1942. The interfaith chapel was dedicated in 1961, a three-story library was completed in 1968, and an indoor swimming pool and an engineering and science wing have been added since 1972. A modernization of all other academic buildings was completed in 1982. The Dean ('45) and Barbara White Admissions Center was dedicated in 2004. Upgrades to the dormitories and other facilities are currently under way, with five of the six company berthing buildings already renovated.

Costs

Tuition, room and board, and medical and dental care are provided by the U.S. government. In addition, the government pays for books and the initial issue of uniforms. Each midshipman also receives $1,017 per month during periods when they are assigned aboard ship for training. Entering plebes are required to pay a little more than $2,500 to cover the initial cost of a laptop computer as well as lab fees, equipment, and service, license, and activity fees. Upperclass members are also charged for service, license, and activity fees for the trimesters they are on campus (when they are not at sea).

Financial Aid

In effect, each midshipman receives a four-year scholarship from the U.S. government. Financial assistance is also available through the Federal Pell Grant Program, the Federal Stafford Student Loan Program, and the Federal PLUS (parent loan) Program. Students may also use outside scholarships to defray their costs.

Faculty

The Academy has 84 full-time faculty members and a student-faculty ratio of approximately 11:1. One third of the faculty members are licensed deck or engineering officers. Most hold advanced degrees in an academic discipline: 90 percent of the total faculty members hold master's degrees or higher; 50 percent have earned doctorates.

Student Government

The student body at the Academy is organized along military lines as a regiment, consisting of two battalions. Regimental life at the Academy is a form of student government and is an important part of the midshipman's total educational and leadership learning experience. The first classmen, or seniors, under the direction of the Commandant of Midshipmen, are responsible for exercising military command of the regiment and for administering the daily routine of the midshipmen. The military program is designed to develop leadership ability, self-discipline, and a sense of responsibility—attributes that are essential for effective citizenship as well as for a successful career as an officer.

Admission Requirements

Candidates for admission must be American citizens, be at least 17 years of age, must not have passed their twenty-fifth birthday by July 1 of the year of entry into the Academy, and be of good moral character. Candidates must be nominated by a U.S. representative or senator and must compete for vacancies allocated to their state in proportion to its representation in Congress. Candidates must achieve qualifying scores on the standard administration (timed) SAT or ACT. Candidates must have successfully completed chemistry or physics (including lab), as well as mathematics up to and including one semester of trigonometry or precalculus. Candidates' competitive standing is determined by their College Board score, their high school academic record and extracurricular participation, and their overall leadership potential. All candidates must meet the physical requirements for appointment as a midshipman in the Navy Reserve. Although not required, all applicants are strongly encouraged to perform a day or overnight visit to learn firsthand about midshipman life and academics. Visits are arranged through the Admissions Office when classes are in session, which is from mid-August to May.

Application and Information

Prospective candidates should write to the Admissions Office. They are sent detailed information on the nomination process, required tests, application procedures, and specific requirements. It is advisable to apply for a nomination during the late spring of the junior year in high school. The deadline for applications is March 1 of the year of desired entry.

Further information may be obtained by contacting:

Director of Admissions
U.S. Merchant Marine Academy
300 Steamboat Road
Kings Point, New York 11024-1699
Phone: 516-726-5640
866-546-4778 (toll-free)
Fax: 516-773-5390
E-mail: admissions@usmma.edu
Website: http://www.usmma.edu

An aerial view of the 80.5 acre "sea campus" of the U.S. Merchant Marine Academy at Kings Point, Long Island, on the shores of Long Island Sound.

UNIVERSITY OF ALASKA FAIRBANKS

FAIRBANKS, ALASKA

★ To read more about this school, visit http://petersons.to/universityofalaskafairbanks

UAF UNIVERSITY OF ALASKA FAIRBANKS

The University

The University of Alaska Fairbanks (UAF) draws students into a welcoming community, offering inspiring and transformational educational challenges—from the personal to the global—in the vast laboratory that is Alaska. Founded in 1917, UAF is Alaska's top teaching and research university. Total enrollment is more than 10,000 students; 84 percent are from Alaska and 16 percent are from the rest of the United States and 45 other countries.

The 2,250-acre Fairbanks campus, located near the center of Alaska, offers limitless opportunities for activity and recreation. Academic buildings and residences make up the core of campus, and just beyond are miles of trails, two lakes, and a boreal forest research and recreational area. Most of the UAF's research institutes, including the Geophysical Institute and the International Arctic Research Center, are clustered on the West Ridge, with incredible views of the Tanana Valley and Alaska Range. The university's Agricultural and Forestry Experiment Station is on campus, as are a Cooperative Fish and Wildlife Research Unit and various state and federal agencies and laboratories. The new Margaret Murie Building, with 100,000 square feet of life science classrooms and laboratories, opened its doors to students and researchers in 2013. A new six-story engineering building, currently under construction, will double the space available for College of Engineering and Mines labs, classrooms, and offices.

The Student Recreation Center and Patty Center house a variety of sports and physical activity facilities, including multipurpose areas for aerobics, badminton, calisthenics, dance, gymnastics, judo, karate, tennis, and volleyball; a rifle and pistol range; courts for handball, racquetball, and squash; an elevated 200-meter, three-lane jogging track; a swimming pool; weight-training and modern fitness equipment areas; an ice arena for recreational skating and hockey; and a three-story climbing wall. There is also an outdoor rock/ice climbing wall and a ski and snowboard terrain park.

The student union, the William Ransom Wood Center, is the focus of numerous activities for students and faculty members. The center houses meeting and exhibit rooms, lounges and television areas, student government offices, campus information, a pub, bowling alley, games room, cafeteria, snack bar, and an espresso bar. A major expansion of the Wood Center dining facilities was completed in fall 2014.

Intercollegiate athletics include men's and women's basketball, cross-country running and skiing, men's ice hockey, and women's volleyball and swim teams. The university also has an outstanding rifle team that has produced several Olympic athletes and earned 10 NCAA championships.

Location

The campus of the University of Alaska Fairbanks is situated on a ridge overlooking the Tanana River valley and the city of Fairbanks. With a population of more than 99,000 in the metro area, Fairbanks is a major trade center for outlying towns and villages in Interior Alaska. The city is connected to the rest of the state and the lower 48 states by air and highway. Municipal bus service is available between downtown Fairbanks, the surrounding area, and campus. A convenient shuttle bus service is available on campus. UAF students can also ride the city bus at no charge.

Fairbanks offers the sophistication of larger cities while maintaining the atmosphere of a smaller, more personal town. Denali National Park and Preserve and other vast wilderness areas are close at hand, and Anchorage is 350 miles south via the Parks Highway. Members of the Fairbanks and UAF communities unite to perform in the Fairbanks Symphony, Arctic Chamber Orchestra, and many other musical and theatrical programs.

Majors and Degrees

The University of Alaska Fairbanks awards occupational endorsements, certificates, A.A., A.S., A.A.S., B.A., B.A.S., B.B.A., B.E.M., B.F.A., B.M., B.S., and B.T. degrees in accounting; administrative assistant; airframe studies; Alaska Native studies; anthropology; applied accounting; applied business; applied physics; apprenticeship technology; art; arts and sciences; automotive technology; aviation maintenance technology; aviation technology; basic carpentry; behavioral health aide; biological sciences; bookkeeping technician; business administration; chemistry; child development and family services; civil engineering; communication; community health; computer science; culinary arts; diesel/heavy equipment; dental assisting; drafting technology; early childhood education; earth science; economics; electrical engineering; elementary education; English; entry-level welder; Eskimo (Inupiaq and Yup'ik); facility maintenance; film; financial services representative; fire science; fisheries; foreign languages; general science; geography; geological engineering; geology; health care reimbursement; high latitude range management; history; homeland security; homeland security and emergency management; human services; information technology specialist; instrumentation technology; interdisciplinary studies; Japanese studies; journalism; justice; law enforcement academy; linguistics; mathematics; mechanical engineering; medical assistant; medical billing; medical coding; medical office reception; mining applications and technologies; mining engineering; music; Native language education; natural resources management (including forestry); northern studies; nurse aide; paralegal studies; paramedic academy; paramedicine; petroleum engineering; philosophy; phlebotomy; physics; political science; power plant; power generation; process technology; professional piloting; psychology; renewable resources; rural development; rural human services; rural utilities business management; Russian studies; safety, health, and environmental awareness technology; secondary education; social work; sociology; sustainable energy; technology; theater; tribal justice; tribal management; welding and materials technology; wildland fire science; and wildlife biology and conservation.

Pre-professional opportunities and advising are available in dentistry, law, library science, medicine, pharmacy, physical therapy, physician assistant studies, and veterinary medicine.

Academic Programs

The academic year is divided into two semesters; registration begins in early April for the fall semester and in November for the spring semester. Preregistration is available for returning students. In addition, there are three-week, six-week, and 12-week summer sessions and between-semester two-week sessions in January and May.

The university is organized into the colleges of Engineering and Mines, Liberal Arts, Natural Science and Mathematics, Rural and Community Development, and the schools of Education, Fisheries and Ocean Sciences, Management, and Natural Resources and Extension. A minimum of 120 credits must be completed for the four-year baccalaureate degree programs.

Students who receive scores of 3 or higher on the College Board's Advanced Placement tests may be awarded credit by the university. Students graduating from any school offering the International Baccalaureate Programme should review a comprehensive list of transfer credits available at www.uaf.edu/catalog/current/

admissions/table9.html. Enrolled students may challenge courses for credit by successfully completing College-Level Examination Program examinations or by completing locally prepared examinations. Requests for advanced placement credit and credit by examination are coordinated through the Office of Admissions and the Registrar.

The Office of Undergraduate Research and Scholarly Activity supports and develops UAF's diverse and robust programs to engage undergraduate students in research and creative scholarship. URSA helps students pursue research from a single credit of first-year seminar to independent scholarly investigations or a senior thesis.

The honors program is designed for highly motivated undergraduate students who wish to acquire an advanced understanding of the natural and social sciences, the arts, and the humanities. Prospective honors students need a minimum ACT plus writing composite score of 27 or a minimum combined SAT score of 1820.

Off-Campus Programs

The university maintains active exchange programs with universities around the world. Membership in the University of the Arctic's north2north exchange program provides UAF students an extensive array of placement opportunities throughout the circumpolar North. UAF also offers a variety of study-abroad programs, including the Northwest Council on Study Abroad, which provides study opportunities with UAF and other U.S. faculty members worldwide. Additional study programs and internships are available through affiliates maintaining sites in numerous countries. UAF is also a member of the National Student Exchange, participating with more than 200 colleges and universities throughout the United States, in U.S. territories, and at ten locations in Canada.

Academic Facilities

The Fine Arts Complex features a 480-seat theater, a 1,072-seat concert hall, FM public radio (KUAC) and educational television (PBS) studios, an art gallery, and the Elmer E. Rasmuson Library. The library collection contains more than 1.75 million items, including many in the prestigious Alaska and Polar Regions Collection. Electronic catalogs provide access to collections in 11,000 libraries nationwide.

Students have free use of the university's academic computing facilities and wireless network, in labs, classrooms, dorm rooms, and other campus locations.

The University of Alaska Museum of the North attracts nearly 100,000 visitors each year to Interior Alaska and is located on the Fairbanks campus. The museum collects, preserves, and exhibits materials from Alaska and the North.

Costs

In 2015–16, tuition and fees are $6,609 annually for full-time (30 credits) students. Nonresident students will pay $20,329 annually for 30 credits of tuition each semester. Generally, to qualify as a resident, a student must show proof they have been living in Alaska for two years. Residents of Alaska, and of cities having sister-city agreements with any Alaska city, are eligible for resident tuition rates.

The approximate cost per semester for books and supplies is $1,400. A double-occupancy residence hall room on campus and a meal plan cost $8,100 per academic year during the 2015–16 academic year. All costs are subject to change.

If the student lives in a Western Undergraduate Exchange state (http://www.uaf.edu/admissions/other/wue), tuition is approximately 1.5 times that of an Alaska resident.

Financial Aid

A large portion of financial aid is derived from the Alaska Supplemental Education Loan Program, which is available to all students attending UAF, regardless of residency. Three kinds of aid are available: grants and scholarships (which need not be repaid), loans, and part-time employment. Inquiries should be sent by e-mail to the Financial Aid Office at financialaid@uaf.edu. Academic Merit and Human Achievement scholarships are one-year scholarships ranging from $2,500–$15,000 that are awarded by the Office of Admissions and the Registrar. To apply, students should submit for review a scholarship application, an application for admission, a high school transcript, and test scores. Questions about this scholarship should be directed to the Office of Admissions and the Registrar. The deadline for University of Alaska and UAF-funded scholarships is February 15. Prospective students should check the financial aid website (www.uaf.edu/finaid) for information about grants, loans, other aid, and applicable due dates.

Faculty

Seventy-seven percent of full-time faculty members and 50 percent of part-time faculty hold doctoral or terminal degrees, and many are engaged in research. In keeping with university policy, faculty members provide academic counseling for students. The combination of a student-faculty ratio of 11:1 and ready access to instructors for help outside of class leads to an excellent educational experience for students.

Admission Requirements

For admission to a baccalaureate program, applicants must be high school graduates with a GPA of at least 2.5 with 16 credits of high school core curriculum and a cumulative grade point average of at least 3.0. A GPA between 2.5 and 3.0 requires an ACT plus writing score of 18 or SAT score of 1290. Transfer students must also have a minimum grade point average of 2.0 in all previous college work.

Applicants for a major in a scientific or technical field may be required to present a higher grade point average and to have completed specific background courses before being accepted into the major department.

Application and Information

The application deadlines are May 1 for the summer semester, June 15 for the fall semester, and November 1 for the spring semester. A $50 application fee is required when the application is submitted. Applicants are notified of the admission decision once all application materials have been received.

For more information, applicants should contact:

Office of Admissions and the Registrar
University of Alaska Fairbanks
P.O. Box 757480
Fairbanks, Alaska 99775-7480
Phone: 907-474-7500
800-478-1823 (toll-free)
E-mail: admissions@uaf.edu
Website: http://www.uaf.edu/admissions
https://uaonline.alaska.edu (to apply)

Students make their way across campus on a November afternoon.

UNIVERSITY OF CENTRAL FLORIDA

ORLANDO, FLORIDA

UCF Stands For Opportunity

The University

The University of Central Florida (UCF) is a comprehensive research university with approximately 60,000 students. As one of the nation's fastest-growing universities in the South and the second largest in the nation, UCF enrolls an academically talented and diverse student body representing all fifty states and more than 120 countries. The University offers educational and research programs that complement the regional economy, with strong components in aerospace engineering, business, education, film, health, hospitality management, medicine, nursing, and social sciences. UCF's programs in communication and the fine arts help to meet the cultural and recreational needs of a growing metropolitan area. The University also offers many graduate programs leading to master's and doctoral degrees, including a doctorate of physical therapy. The UCF College of Medicine offers the M.D. degree.

UCF is accredited by the Commission on Colleges of the Southern Association of Colleges and Schools. In addition, a number of scientific, professional, and academic bodies confer accreditation in specific disciplines and groups of disciplines.

UCF has established extensive partnerships with businesses and industries in the central Florida area that provide students with research and learning experiences. These partnerships bring practical learning environments to UCF students through co-op, internship programs, and joint curriculum development strategies.

The on-campus and campus-affiliated housing facilities include traditional residence halls, apartment-style options, and Greek housing that accommodates approximately 11,500 students. In addition, several thousand students live in apartments located within walking distance of the campus.

Students participate in approximately 600 student organizations, including special-interest clubs, multicultural organizations, fraternities and sororities, honor societies, and academic and preprofessional organizations. The Office of Student Involvement schedules a wide array of extracurricular programs, including concerts, movies, and guest speakers.

The University of Central Florida is a member of the NCAA and competes in the American Athletic Conference (AAC). All teams compete on the NCAA Division I level. UCF's men's teams compete in intercollegiate baseball, basketball, football, golf, soccer, and tennis. Women's teams compete in basketball, cross-country, golf, rowing, soccer, softball, tennis, track and field, and volleyball. Intercollegiate coed club activities include championship cheerleading, crew, and waterskiing teams. The University offers an extensive intramural sports program.

Location

The University of Central Florida is located on 1,415 acres approximately 13 miles east of downtown Orlando. In addition to the academic programs offered on the Orlando campus, upper-division students can work toward a degree at ten locations around the central Florida area.

Majors and Degrees

The University offers the degrees of Bachelor of Applied Science, Bachelor of Arts, Bachelor of Arts in Business Administration, Bachelor of Design, Bachelor of Engineering Technology, Bachelor of Fine Arts, Bachelor of Music, Bachelor of Music Education, Bachelor of Science, Bachelor of Science in Business Administration, Bachelor of Science in Education, Bachelor of Science in Engineering, Bachelor of Science in Nursing, Bachelor of Social Work, and Bachelor of Science in Social Sciences. These degrees are available in the colleges listed below, with majors or areas of specialization as indicated.

The College of Arts and Humanities offers degrees in art, architecture, digital media, English, film, French, history, humanities and cultural studies, Latin American studies, music, philosophy, photography, religion and cultural studies, Spanish, theatre studies, and writing and rhetoric.

The College of Business Administration offers degrees in accounting, business economics, economics, finance, general business, management, marketing, and real estate.

The College of Education offers degrees in art education, early childhood development and education, elementary education, English language arts education, world languages education, mathematics education, science education, social science education, sport and exercise science, and technical education and industry training.

The College of Engineering and Computer Science offers degrees in aerospace engineering, civil engineering, computer engineering, computer science, construction engineering, electrical engineering, environmental engineering, industrial engineering, information technology, and mechanical engineering.

The College of Health and Public Affairs offers degrees in athletic training, communication sciences and disorders, criminal justice, health informatics and information management, health services administration, health sciences, legal studies, public administration, and social work.

The College of Medicine and the Burnett School of Biomedical Sciences offers degrees in biomedical sciences, biotechnology, and medical laboratory sciences.

The College of Nursing offers degrees in nursing.

The College of Optics and Photonics offers degrees in photonic science and engineering.

The College of Sciences offers degrees in advertising/public relations, anthropology, biology, chemistry, forensic science, human communication, international and global studies, journalism, mathematics, physics, political science, psychology, radio/television, sociology, social sciences, and statistics.

The Rosen College of Hospitality Management offers degrees in event management, hospitality management, and restaurant and foodservice management.

Preprofessional programs are offered in chiropractic, dentistry, medicine, optometry, pharmacy, physical assistant studies, physical therapy, podiatry, and veterinary medicine.

A degree in interdisciplinary studies is available through the Office of Undergraduate Studies.

Academic Programs

UCF provides a total education through a core curriculum of 36 hours of general education courses. In addition to fulfilling the general education requirement, each student must complete the necessary major and/or minor requirements to reach the minimum of 120 semester hours necessary for graduation.

Several special programs help students reach their academic and leadership potential. The Burnett Honors College at UCF encourages students to achieve academic excellence through small classes and interactive symposia. The innovative LEAD Scholars Academy fosters leadership and service commitment through a comprehensive student development program for freshmen. The Major Exploration Program (MEP) helps entering freshmen define their career goals and develop an academic strategy to reach those goals. The University also offers an increasing number of online courses and degree programs.

UCF offers Air Force and Army ROTC programs.

Off-Campus Programs

Career Services and Experiential Learning offers programs in which students alternate semesters of classroom study with equal periods of paid employment in government, industry, or business. The Department of Modern Languages offers summer study-abroad programs. Courses are available in the subject areas of language (all levels), art, and civilization. UCF is also a participant in the National Student Exchange Consortium.

Academic Facilities

In addition to the academic programs offered on the Orlando campus, upper division students can work toward a degree at ten campuses located throughout Central Florida. These regional campuses work cooperatively with local state colleges to provide all four years of course work in many academic areas. The library houses over 2.4 million volumes and subscribes to more than 43,000 periodicals and journals (40,500 in electronic format). Students have access to an online computer catalog that provides information on the collections of the State University System libraries. An extensive online network of more than 600 computers (both PC and Mac) cover the campus. The Institute for Simulation and Training gives students the opportunity to pursue undergraduate research. The College of Optics and Photonics allows faculty members and students to work directly with industry personnel in conducting basic and applied research at the regional and national levels. The Central Florida Research Park, adjacent to the UCF campus, houses more than ninety high-technology firms and agencies. This proximity fosters relationships between industry and the University, which strengthens the academic programs at UCF.

Costs

For Florida residents, the cost of tuition and fees in 2014–15, based on a full-time course load, was $6,368 for the year; for out-of-state residents, the cost was $22,466. Room and board were approximately $9,570 per year, books and supplies cost approximately $800.

Financial Aid

Financial aid is awarded according to each student's demonstrated financial need in relation to college costs and may include grants, loans, scholarships, and part-time employment. Programs based upon need include the Federal Perkins Loan, Federal Pell Grant, Florida Student Assistance Grant, Federal Work-Study, Florida College Career Work-Study Program, and Federal Stafford Student Loan. To qualify for these programs, students must complete the Free Application for Federal Student Aid (FAFSA). The priority application deadline is March 1. Seventy-six percent of UCF students receive some form of financial assistance.

Faculty

The University's teaching faculty consists of 1,961 full-time members and adjunct members. Seventy-seven percent of the full-time faculty members hold a doctoral degree. Undergraduate instruction is given primarily by the full-time and adjunct faculty members; graduate students play a minor role in undergraduate instruction. Students are assigned to a faculty adviser in their area of specialization for assistance in academic matters. The student-faculty ratio is 31:1.

Student Government

UCF's Student Government Association provides an opportunity for students to become involved at UCF. Every UCF student is encouraged to voice his or her opinion through senate representatives. Student Government is divided into three branches—the student-elected executive branch, the student-elected legislative branch, and the appointed judicial branch. Student Government is responsible for the allocation of all activity and service fees paid by students as a part of their tuition. This money goes toward student services, including the online Macintosh lab, homecoming activities, campus activities board, legal services, and funding for clubs and organizations. Admission is free to all events directly sponsored by the Student Government.

Admission Requirements

A freshman applicant is a student with fewer than 12 hours of college course work after high school graduation. The most important criteria in the admission decision for these applicants are the high school academic record, rigor of course work, grade point average, grade trends, and SAT or ACT Plus Writing test scores. UCF operates on a rolling admission basis. Students are generally notified of their initial admission decision within two to three weeks after receipt of the application and all official supporting documents. If the number of qualified applicants exceeds the number that the University is permitted to enroll, a waiting list is established.

All applicants must have earned a minimum of 18 high school academic units (yearlong courses that are not remedial in nature). These include 4 units of English (3 must include substantial writing), 4 units of mathematics at or above algebra I, 3 units of natural science (2 must include a laboratory), 3 units of social science, 2 units of one world language, and 2 units of academic electives. Grades in honors, International Baccalaureate, Advanced Placement, AICE, dual-enrollment, pre-AP, pre-IB, and pre-AICE courses are given additional weight in the GPA computation. Students must meet the Florida Department of Education minimum eligibility to be considered for admission. Applicants should understand that the satisfaction of minimum requirements does not guarantee admission to UCF.

Transfer applicants with fewer than 60 semester hours of college course work must submit official high school transcripts, SAT or ACT Plus Writing test scores, and all official college transcripts. Transfer students with more than 60 semester hours or who have earned an Associate in Arts degree or a statewide articulated Associate in Science degree from a Florida public community or state college need only submit all official college transcripts. A transfer credit summary evaluation is provided to students once they are offered admission to UCF.

Application and Information

Students are encouraged to apply several months in advance and can apply online at http://admissions.ucf.edu. It is recommended that freshman students apply early during the fall semester of their senior year. Applications are accepted up to one year prior to the start of the term for which enrollment is desired. Priority application deadlines are May 1 for the fall term (July 1 for transfers), November 1 for the spring term, and March 1 for the summer term.

The Campus Visit Experience, which includes an information session and a campus tour, is offered Monday through Friday at 10 and 2 (except holidays). Students can sign up for a campus visit online at http://admissions.ucf.edu.

For more information, contact:

Office of Undergraduate Admissions
University of Central Florida
P.O. Box 160111
Orlando, Florida 32816-0111
Phone: 407-823-3000
E-mail: admission@ucf.edu
Website: http://www.ucf.edu

The Charging Knight symbolizes UCF's excellence in academics, partnerships, and athletics.

UNIVERSITY OF DALLAS
IRVING, TEXAS, AND ROME, ITALY

UNIVERSITY OF DALLAS
The Catholic University for Independent Thinkers

The University

The University of Dallas (UD) is a private, Catholic liberal arts university dedicated to the pursuit of wisdom, truth, and virtue as the proper and primary ends of education. Approximately 1,380 undergraduate students from 49 states and 22 countries make up the undergraduate student body, with more than half coming from outside Texas. In addition, 82 percent of undergraduate students identify themselves as Catholic.

UD's academics are intensive and highly directed, making it an ideal program for serious students. While students engage in a full complement of extracurricular activities and independent study, it is the act of learning in association with professors that shapes their college years. Because the undergraduate college is small and largely residential, students easily form a close-knit community.

Spiritual life is an important aspect of the undergraduate experience. The university's core values include embracing the Catholic intellectual tradition and maintaining a dialogue between faith and reason; these values have a significant role both inside and outside of the classroom. The primary church on campus, the Church of the Incarnation, offers daily Mass as well as frequent reconciliation and adoration. Holy Trinity Seminary, St. Albert the Great Priory, and Cistercian Abbey, all within walking distance, also provide opportunities for students to participate in Mass and other spiritual growth activities. In addition, Campus Ministry offers a wide variety of spiritual and service opportunities for students of all faiths and backgrounds, such as lectures and Alternative Spring Break.

Location

The university's 244-acre campus core is located approximately 15 minutes from downtown Dallas in Irving, Texas, population 228,600. Dallas/Fort Worth, the nation's fourth-largest metropolitan area, offers a diverse mix of cultural and entertainment attractions that range from the Dallas Museum of Art to the Dallas Cowboys. The region is also home to major league teams in hockey, soccer, basketball, and baseball. A thriving economy provides students opportunities to connect with businesses and nonprofit organizations, including 18 Fortune 500 companies headquartered in the Dallas/Fort Worth area.

UD is conveniently located between two major airports, Dallas Love Field and Dallas/Fort Worth International. In addition, the campus has its own stop on the Orange Line of the Dallas Area Rapid Transit (DART) light rail system, providing easy access to downtown Dallas and many other destinations. The university encourages students to become involved in the community and take advantage of the area's arts and entertainment offerings. Through a program called Dallas Year, students have access to highly discounted tickets to area events such as the State Fair of Texas and Dallas Mavericks basketball games. Transportation is provided to and from the events.

The University of Dallas' 12-acre Eugene Constantin Campus is located just south of Rome, Italy, and includes amenities such as a working vineyard, a swimming pool, tennis courts, classrooms, a library, a suite-style residence hall, and a cappuccino bar. The majority of undergraduates spend a semester studying abroad on the Rome campus.

Academic Programs

UD students thrive in a rigorous academic program distinguished by the university's nationally recognized Core curriculum. Based on the belief that truth and virtue exist and are the proper objects of search in an education, the Core curriculum is a two-year course of study through which every UD student directly encounters Western civilization's greatest authors, leaders, and artists by reading original, classic works. Every student becomes familiar with the same works of literature and the same great books and concepts, fostering a natural understanding and exchange of ideas. The Core curriculum is comprehensive, encompassing English, philosophy, mathematics, fine arts, sciences, modern languages, American civilization, Western civilization, politics, economics, and theology.

Majors and Degrees

Choosing a specific major affords students an opportunity to further their curiosity in a particular area of study. UD offers 29 majors, which can be combined into double majors to match each student's interest. Thirty-three concentrations (minors) are available to broaden academic expertise. In addition, cooperative degree programs in nursing and engineering allow students to earn dual degrees from the University of Dallas and local partner universities.

Pre-professional programs in architecture, dentistry, engineering, law, medicine, ministry, and physical therapy also are available to prepare students academically for rigorous graduate programs and demanding professions. Undergraduate and post-baccalaureate certification is available to students interested in teaching at the elementary, middle, or secondary school level.

Regardless of major, all UD undergraduate students are required to complete major-specific capstone projects that culminate their undergraduate careers. Whether their specific projects entail conducting research and writing an extensive thesis, preparing for and taking comprehensive exams, or completing an intensive practicum, students find they are well-prepared to succeed upon graduation.

Rome Program

The academic experience is heightened and enriched by spending a semester abroad on the Eugene Constantin Campus in the Roman countryside. Because of the accessibility and affordability of the Rome program, all students are encouraged to participate, and most do, usually during their sophomore year. The Rome curriculum is a coherent and integral part of the undergraduate education. The courses, which include Art and Architecture of Rome and Western Theological Tradition, among others, are part of the Core curriculum and deepen the students' understanding and appreciation of Western civilization by allowing them to experience history and culture firsthand. Because the Rome semester courses are part of UD's Core curriculum, the academic integrity is maintained, students stay on schedule for graduation, and a seamless academic transition from Irving to Rome is possible.

Faculty members lead students on overnight trips around Italy, as well as a 10-day trip to Greece. Students are encouraged to travel independently on weekends and during their 10-day break.

Costs

Annual tuition and fees for the 2014–15 academic year are $34,430. Room and board costs are approximately $11,070. Costs are the same for both in-state and out-of-state students.

Financial Aid

Approximately 96 percent of UD undergraduates receive some type of merit- or need-based aid to help offset the cost of attendance. The application for admission serves as the application for institutional scholarships, which range from $7,000 up to full tuition and are based on GPA and test scores (ACT or SAT). Academic merit scholarships are renewable for four years, providing eligibility requirements set forth in the scholarship letter are met.

A limited number of other scholarships are available to students who excel in a particular area of study or have received academic distinctions such as being named National Merit Finalists, National Achievement Scholars, National Hispanic Scholars, or Phi Theta Kappa members.

All students who submit a Free Application for Federal Student Aid (FAFSA) are considered for financial assistance based on their family's finances. These forms of assistance include federal, state, or institutional grants; low-interest student loans; and work-study programs. Priority is given to applicants whose FAFSAs are received by UD on or before March 1.

Faculty

The University of Dallas has 139 full-time faculty members, 90 percent of whom hold a doctorate or equivalent highest academic degree in their discipline. As top scholars in their fields, professors value the academic freedom the university offers, allowing them to unreservedly explore intellectual inquiries both within and outside of their disciplines. UD students benefit from a 10:1 student-to-faculty ratio and an average class size of 16 students, providing all students with deserved individual attention and mentoring.

Student Government, Clubs, and Organizations

Through the elected Student Government (SG) Senate, students are responsible for all nonacademic matters that affect their life at UD. Guided by the mission of the university and in accordance with the teachings and principles of the Catholic Church, the SG representatives are dedicated to enhancing the quality of student life by promoting both the academic and social traditions of the university.

UD also offers more than 50 clubs and organizations that encourage students to become involved in areas of extracurricular or academic interest as well as develop vital leadership skills. From Best Buddies to the Pre-Health Society to Crusaders for Life, students can choose to get involved in many different ways. In addition, if several students have a shared interest that is not represented by current clubs and organizations, they are encouraged to start a new club.

UD competes in NCAA Division III athletics and is a member of the Southern Collegiate Athletic Conference. Sports include baseball (M), basketball (M, W), cross-country (M, W), golf (M), lacrosse (M, W), soccer (M, W), softball (W), track and field (M, W), and volleyball (W). Intramural sports are also offered to all students.

Admission Requirements

The University of Dallas performs a holistic review of applications, so no rigid cutoff for test scores or GPA is adhered to in the admission process. For the fall 2014 incoming freshman class, the average SAT score was approximately 1200 (on a 1600 scale), and the average ACT score was 27. The average high school GPA was 3.79 on a 4.0 scale.

The university seeks students who are not only academically well-prepared to succeed, but who will also contribute to the UD community. Letters of recommendation, the essay, and the answers to the UD member questions are all considered in determining a student's overall fit for the university. Interviews are not required, but students are highly encouraged to schedule a campus visit and meet with an admission counselor to discuss the admission process, as well as any opportunities for scholarships or financial aid.

Application and Information

Applicants are required to submit the following items: application (Common Application or Apply Texas), UD member questions, $50 application fee or fee waiver, essay, counselor recommendation, official high school transcript, and official test scores (ACT or SAT). The Early Action I deadline is November 1; the Early Action II deadline is December 1. The Freshman Priority Scholarship deadline is January 15, and the regular admission deadline is March 1. Rolling admission is March 2–August 1.

Students interested in transferring to the University of Dallas must submit transcripts from all colleges previously attended. Transfer students should apply by January 1 for spring entry or July 1 for fall entry.

For more information, students should contact:

Office of Undergraduate Admission & Financial Aid
University of Dallas
1845 East Northgate Drive
Irving, Texas 75062
Phone: 972-721-5266
800-628-6999 (toll-free)
Website: www.udallas.edu/admissions
www.facebook.com/udallas
https://twitter.com/UDallasUGA

The University of Dallas is located in the Irving/Las Colinas area of Dallas/Fort Worth, a metropolitan area of approximately 7 million that is home to scores of Fortune 500, Fortune 1000, and privately held companies.
(Photo: University of Dallas Marketing & Communications)

UNIVERSITY OF DENVER

DENVER, COLORADO

The University

Since its founding in 1864—2014 marked a sesquicentennial celebration of 150 years of tradition and legacy—the University of Denver (DU) has grown into one of the West's premier private universities, blending the friendliness and personal attention of a small college with the resources and intellectual diversity of an advanced research institution. As the oldest private university in the Rocky Mountain region, the University is home not only to a top-ranked undergraduate program but also to a number of world-renowned research centers and professional programs, including the Josef Korbel School of International Studies, the Sturm College of Law, and the Daniels College of Business.

The 125-acre campus brings together 5,212 traditional undergraduate students and 6,261 graduate students from fifty states and over eighty countries. In an environment that prizes innovation, cross-disciplinary exploration, and adventurous learning partnerships between students and faculty, students embark on a personalized educational journey inspired and framed by a spirit of exploration and openness.

Whatever their backgrounds and majors, DU students are engaged and active, taking advantage of the region's many recreation and cultural opportunities—everything from world-class skiing and white-water rafting to award-winning professional theater at the Denver Center for the Performing Arts and alternative music shows at Red Rocks Amphitheater. On campus, students attend performances at the three-venue Newman Center for the Performing Arts and cheer for the 17 varsity teams that compete in NCAA Division I Athletics at the Ritchie Center for Sports & Wellness.

The University of Denver is accredited by the North Central Association of Colleges and Schools. The Carnegie Foundation classifies the University of Denver as a Doctoral/Research University–Extensive.

Location

Located just 8 miles from bustling downtown Denver and mere minutes from the Rocky Mountain foothills, the University of Denver's tree-shaded campus is surrounded by pleasant urban neighborhoods offering coffee shops, retail stores, and diverse restaurants. The institution is located along a light-rail line and major bus lines, providing access to the city's arts districts, shopping centers, sports arenas, and an extensive network of parks. DU students can ride all public transportation for free, using their University-supplied Smart Cards.

Majors and Degrees

The University of Denver offers twelve bachelor's degrees in over 100 programs of study, including the arts, business, computer science, engineering, humanities, international studies, mathematics, natural sciences, and social sciences. Students who are interested in pre-professional programs can choose from law, medical, dental, and veterinary programs that prepare them for professional study beyond their undergraduate degree.

In addition, the University offers 4+1 and 3+2 dual-degree programs that allow students to complete both a bachelor's and master's degree in five years or less. These dual-degree programs are currently offered in business, education, social work, engineering, art history, international studies, public policy, and natural sciences. A six-year B.A. or B.S./J.D. program in conjunction with DU's Sturm College of Law has recently been established as well.

Academic Programs

Undergraduate programs at the University—which operates on the quarter system—emphasize experiential, dynamic, and cross-disciplinary learning, providing students with the culture and tools to create a positive impact and make meaningful, lasting contributions to their communities and professions.

First-year students enroll in a first-year seminar. Generally limited to 20 students, these seminars focus on a topic that reflects the professor's research interests. This professor, who serves as a mentor throughout the student's first year, introduces the class to university-level work and inquiry, while also advising students on everything from time management to University procedures. The seminar is complemented by a two-quarter writing sequence that trains students to conduct research, construct arguments, and write persuasively for the academic setting. The University's emphasis on writing continues throughout the next three years, with upper-division writing-intensive classes across the disciplines. By the time they graduate, DU students have developed the communication skills that are essential for career success.

Undergraduate students also complete foundations courses in mathematics and computer science, the arts and humanities, natural sciences, and social sciences. DU's common curriculum ensures that students have a wide base of knowledge upon graduation.

Because the University believes in the value of hands-on learning, students are encouraged to collaborate with faculty members and peers on research projects and creative endeavors. Through the Partners in Scholarship (PinS) program, the University sponsors student work through grants that fund field studies, research trips, and special materials. At year's end, students share their research and findings at a special symposium for their peers.

Thanks to opportunities like these, the University's academic programs earn high marks from students. In the 2012 National Survey of Student Engagement (NSSE), first-year students and seniors at 546 participating U.S. colleges and universities reported their satisfaction with their own campus. National results revealed that DU students reported significantly higher levels of satisfaction than the average of students at all other participating doctoral-extensive schools for level of academic challenge, involvement in active and collaborative learning, interaction with faculty members, and enriched educational experiences.

Off-Campus Programs

To groom students for the challenges of global citizenship, the University of Denver sponsors Cherrington Global Scholars, a for-credit program that aims to send every eligible junior and senior abroad for at least a quarter of study. The University believes so strongly in this opportunity to expand understanding and foster connections that it ensures qualifying students pay no more for the experience than for a quarter spent on campus. The University budgets about $10 million each year in support of this outstanding program. Just over 70 percent of all DU students participate in study-abroad programs, the highest percentage in the nation.

Academic Facilities

In the last decade, the University has invested over $500 million in new buildings and learning centers to ensure that students can prepare for the challenges awaiting them after graduation. These include the Robert and Judi Newman Center for the Performing Arts, home to the University's celebrated Lamont School of Music and host to a performing arts series known for its adventurous offerings; the Daniels College of Business, which houses eleven case-style meeting rooms, nine seminar classrooms, and an Advanced Technology Center; the Knoebel School of Hospitality Management, home to a full-production kitchen, a beverage-management center, a 120-person dining hall, a student-run coffee shop, and a student-faculty-staff commons; and the Anderson Academic Commons, which serves as the new library and hub of the University with a central campus location, multimedia software support services, and a full complement of individual and group study areas and rooms. Construction is well under way on the Daniel Felix Ritchie School of Engineering and Computer Science, which will allow dramatic expansion of both current programming and new STEM initiatives.

Other facilities support the University's commitment to community living and wellness, such as the Nelson Residence Hall which features suites, common kitchens on each floor, a central courtyard, a grand dining hall, and an outdoor dining patio. The Ritchie Center for Sports and Wellness brings students and members of the Denver community together to work out, try new sports, and watch the Pioneer athletic teams. With a state-of-the-art fitness center, a natatorium, a field house, two ice arenas, a gymnastics venue, a lacrosse stadium, a newly remodeled soccer stadium, and a tennis pavilion, the Ritchie Center complex supports the active lifestyle that DU students value.

Nagel Residence Hall serves as a campus gathering place, welcoming students and faculty at its food court, providing numerous locations for group study sessions, and offering studio space for students wanting to explore their artistic side. In keeping with the University's far-reaching sustainability initiative, the green building is LEED certified, meaning it uses key resources more efficiently than conventional buildings.

In recent years the University also completed construction on a spectacular new home for both the Morgridge College of Education and the Marsico Institute for Early Learning and Literacy. The influential institute serves as a regional and national nucleus for research and policy analysis on issues related to improving learning environments for young children.

Costs

For the 2014–15 academic year, tuition was $41,112, fees were estimated at $978, and on-campus room and board costs were $11,307—for a total cost of $53,397. Because the University of Denver is a private institution, costs are the same for in-state and out-of-state students.

Financial Aid

The University of Denver offers two types of financial assistance to students: need-based aid, which includes scholarships, grants, loans, and work-study based on financial need; and merit-based awards, which include scholarships based on merit or special talent. Each year, the Financial Aid office awards over $100 million in need- and merit-based assistance to undergraduate students. About 44 percent of full-time DU undergraduates demonstrate financial need and receive some form of need-based assistance.

To recognize achievement in the classroom, the sports arena, leadership, and in music, theater, and art, the University sponsors a number of merit-based scholarships. Although the requirements vary from scholarship to scholarship, most are renewable each year if the student maintains a specified minimum GPA. A complete listing of scholarships is posted at http://www.du.edu/financialaid.

Need-based financial aid is computed using a number of factors, including family income, assets, size, and the number of family members attending college at the same time. DU utilizes both the CSS PROFILE and the Free Application for Federal Student Aid (FAFSA) to determine need-based aid. Need-based awards generally combine scholarships, grants, loans, and work-study opportunities from a variety of federal, state, and institutional sources. The financial aid offer may also include any competitive scholarships the student has been awarded at the point of admission. To help determine how much need- and merit-based aid might be available to a prospective student and his or her family, DU offers access to a comprehensive net price calculator, found at www.du.edu/estimator.

The priority deadline for applying for financial aid is February 15. Because financial aid funds are limited, students who complete their financial aid applications in a timely manner are more likely to maximize financial aid resources. The student's financial aid package cannot be determined until he or she is officially admitted to DU. More information on applying for financial aid at DU is available at http://www.du.edu/financialaid.

Faculty

DU professors teach 99 percent of undergraduate courses, ensuring students work closely with faculty members and the intensity of the learning environment is maximized. The average class size is 21 students; 87 percent of undergraduate classes have fewer than 30 students and 96 percent of classes have fewer than 50 students.

Committed teachers, innovative researchers, and prolific publishers, University of Denver professors often include undergraduate students in their research projects and fieldwork. It is not uncommon for an undergraduate student to share publication credit with a professor or to participate in groundbreaking research with tangible, transformational benefits for humankind.

Student Government

At the University of Denver, the student population is represented by the Undergraduate Student Government (USG), whose elected representatives participate in the University's legislative process and communicate student issues to the administration. In addition, the USG oversees the allocation of the student activities fee and the licensing of DU's 100-plus student organizations. In the past few years this group has worked extensively on issues ranging from sustainability to diversity and academic affairs to spirit on campus.

The USG includes senators from each major, each geographic area (on-campus, off-campus), and each class (senior, junior, etc.). The USG Executive Board includes an advisor, graduate advisor, president, vice president, and a cabinet of members.

Admission Requirements

Admission to the University of Denver is selective. Students are evaluated individually on the basis of their academic record, test scores, essay, and recommendations. In making its admission decisions, the University seeks to foster an academic community of geographically, ethnically, and economically diverse learners. The admission committee seeks students who are committed to integrity, innovation, inclusiveness, leadership, academic excellence, and community engagement.

Applicants are required to submit either the Common Application or the DU Pioneer Application—both are posted on the DU website. In addition, applicants are required to submit their high school transcripts, scores from either the SAT or ACT (DU uses the superscore system), an essay, and a high school counselor recommendation. Students may also submit a teacher recommendation, although it is not required.

Application and Information

The University of Denver offers two application programs for first-year domestic students seeking fall quarter admission. Early Action (deadline of November 1) is a nonbinding program leading to an admission decision in late December. Regular Decision (deadline of January 15), also nonbinding, is the final admission deadline for fall quarter consideration. Regular Decision applicants receive their admission decision in mid-March.

To learn more about the University of Denver, students should contact:

Undergraduate Admission
University of Denver
2197 South University Boulevard
Denver, Colorado, 80208-9401
United States
Phone: 303-871-2036
E-mail: admission@du.edu
Website: http://www.du.edu/admission
http://www.youtube.com/uofdenver
http://www.facebook.com/uofdenveradmission
http://twitter.com/uofdenver

University of Denver

COLLEGE CLOSE-UPS

UNIVERSITY OF DUBUQUE

DUBUQUE, IOWA

UNIVERSITY *of* DUBUQUE

★ To read more about this school, visit http://petersons.to/universityofdubuque

The University

The University of Dubuque (UD) is a private, Presbyterian, professional university with a focus in the liberal arts, comprised of an undergraduate college, a graduate professional school, and a theological seminary, located in Iowa's first city—Dubuque. The Key City is on the Mississippi River at the point where the borders of Wisconsin, Illinois, and Iowa meet. Founded in 1852, the University's mission of encouraging intellectual, moral, and spiritual development dates back to its founding.

Throughout its history, the University has been known as a place of educational opportunity. Even today, a large portion of its students are from first-generation, underserved, or underrepresented populations. The University of Dubuque's welcoming interfaith community of approximately 2,200 students comes from across the country and around the globe.

Because students from many nations attend the University of Dubuque, UD offers students a cosmopolitan atmosphere. Students living in today's world are better prepared for life if they have a global perspective. American and international student interaction on campus, as well as the movement of faculty members and students across international boundaries, is essential for a meaningful education, human enrichment, and intercultural global awareness.

Location

The University of Dubuque's scenic 77-acre campus, located in northeast Iowa, is in the heart of the Midwest. Dubuque is a city for all seasons. From bluffs blazing with autumn oranges and reds, to the river sparkling with summer's blues and greens, the area scenery is spectacular year-round. Dubuque, the oldest city in Iowa, is a dynamic community built along the majestic Mississippi River and surrounded by dramatic bluffs. The setting is ideal for outdoor enthusiasts, with four seasons of ample outlets for recreation, including hiking, biking, boating, skiing, camping, golfing, climbing, and caving.

Dubuque offers the amenities of a larger city with the security and comfort of a smaller town. A lively cultural scene includes the Grand Opera House, the Dubuque Symphony Orchestra, and the Dubuque Museum of Art. The National Mississippi River Museum and Aquarium and the National Farm Toy Museum provide glimpses of the area's past. The city's theater productions, boutiques, restaurants, and Mississippi River Walk are wonderful ways to take a study break.

Nearby are some of the Midwest's most interesting cities, an easy drive for a weekend road trip. Historic Galena offers quaint shops and period architecture, while vibrant Chicago is famous for its museums and nightlife. Madison, Milwaukee, and Minneapolis–St. Paul are only hours away.

Majors and Degrees

With thirty-one undergraduate majors, the University prepares students for careers in a variety of fields. From future teachers and corporate leaders to aspiring pilots, biologists, and nurses, the University of Dubuque helps students achieve their career goals and live out their dreams.

The University's business and education departments have the most majors. The education department's future teachers graduate with twice as many field-experience hours as required by the state of Iowa.

Academic departments encourage internships as an experiential component to complement classroom learning. For example, environmental science majors take advantage of the natural classroom of the Mississippi River, where students study the interaction between people and the environment. Aviation majors complete internships at the Dubuque Regional Airport or with major airlines in addition to flying the most recent aircraft and learning on state-of-the-art equipment from UD's Garlick Flight Operations Center.

Academic Programs

The University of Dubuque education aims at helping students develop patterns of scholarship that make them effective learners throughout life. UD students are nurtured in the virtues of scholarship: the desire for understanding different peoples and cultures, an interest in learning, the skills to use multiple resources to explore ideas and find answers for life's questions, an understanding of conceptual connections, and the ability to reason and communicate effectively. Each graduate develops depth of knowledge in a particular field of study based on an integration of this field, the liberal arts, and his or her values.

University of Dubuque students begin to understand their chosen field of study by experiencing how it relates to other areas of knowledge. The process of exploring a variety of interests and possibilities in course work and in University activities results in the choice of a major. Current trends indicate that today's graduates change jobs and/or careers several times during their lifetimes. Therefore, professional preparation is more than a narrow, vocationally oriented process through which students prepare for one specific job. Rather, it is the development of transferable skills and attributes that allow students to succeed in a changing job market.

In the University of Dubuque community, the arts foster intellectual, emotional, and spiritual development. In literature, the visual arts, dance, drama, and music, students not only find aesthetic pleasure but also learn about other people's ideas, beliefs, and experiences, coming to deeper understandings of their own.

Because of the University's location near the Mississippi—one of the world's great river systems—students have an appreciation of environmental issues. Through academic endeavors involving formal and experiential learning, students develop an understanding of the basic processes that underpin various ecological communities and of the complex interaction of human activities on the environment. The University of Dubuque encourages individuals to integrate their knowledge of the environment into personal, ethical, and spiritual guidelines, which can be used to improve their lives, their communities, and society.

The Lester G. and Michael Lester Wendt Character Initiative, supported by a substantial endowment, integrates virtues and values such as truthfulness, honesty, fairness, and the Golden Rule across the curriculum and throughout the University.

The University's Learning Institute for Fulfillment and Engagement (LIFE) offers an accelerated degree program for adult learners age 22 and over. The UD LIFE program is designed to offer a flexible format, allowing students to earn a bachelor's degree in as few as three years and a master's degree in as few as eighteen months. Offering classes on weekday evenings as well as online, the program helps adults balance their studies, career, and family life.

Off-Campus Programs

The University of Dubuque offers its students the opportunity to attend and receive credit for courses at Clarke University and Loras College, also in the city, thus providing access to the many different faculty members, professional societies, educational opportunities, and social activities of combined campuses of more than 4,500 students.

The University of Dubuque affirms the value of an international/intercultural experience and considers it to be an important component of any student's education. Overseas travel, exchanges, and study programs are available to help increase the global perspective of the students and to promote cross-cultural education.

Academic Facilities

Veterans Memorial Training Center, a multipurpose facility that benefits a wide array of athletics programs was completed in January 2014. The facility is nearly 40,000 square feet with a 180-foot by 210-foot Mondo Synthetic Turf playing surface that simulates the feel and performance of real grass. The facility plays host to in-season and off-season workouts for numerous Spartans sports programs and for intramural recreational sports during times of inclement weather.

Chlapaty Hall is the newest residence hall at the University of Dubuque having opened in fall 2014. The facility incorporates a pod-style design intended to bolster close-knit communities within the building and on campus. The new 4-story structure is designed with 11 pods that include 7 double bedrooms, a bathroom, kitchenette, lounge, and study niche. The exterior of the building is intended to blend with the campus vernacular, through the use of brick and cast stone masonry.

Heritage Center, an 80,000-square-foot fine and performing arts, worship, and campus center, opened in May 2013. The facility is central to the University of Dubuque campus, and provides a multitude of venues to serve students, faculty, staff, and the public. "Art by osmosis" is the overarching theme of the new building, inviting people of all walks to happen upon art in its myriad forms, intentionally and accidentally, as they visit Heritage Center for their work, study, recreation, and entertainment. The primary functions of the building can be categorized as a casual student campus center and formal public areas, with overlapping meant to encourage interaction and interest. The student areas are designed to provide educational spaces, group and individual study settings, student services, offices, and hospitality; the public areas provide performance venues, associated gathering spaces, gallery space, heritage display, offices, and hospitality.

Costs

Tuition costs for the 2015–16 academic year are $26,630. Average room and board costs are $8,850. These costs do not include books, supplies, personal expenses, and travel.

Financial Aid

Ninety-six percent of the University of Dubuque's students receive financial assistance through scholarships, awards and grants, loans, or work-study programs. The average financial assistance package for 2014–15 was $22,959. All levels of household incomes receive financial assistance.

To apply for financial assistance, applicants must submit a completed application package for admission to the University of Dubuque, file a FAFSA after January 1 and before April 1 (the priority deadline), and send or fax a copy of the completed FAFSA to the University of Dubuque Office of Student Financial Planning. Institutional, federal, state, and alternative loan programs are all available as forms of financial assistance.

Faculty

Seventy percent of University of Dubuque faculty members have earned a Ph.D. or other terminal degree. The student-faculty ratio is 15:1.

Student Government

The Student Government Association (SGA) represents the student body through general election of individual student representatives. The SGA sponsors more than sixty campus organizations, including the University Program Council (UPC), the Spartan Spirit Club, and Under The Bell Tower (student newspaper). SGA provides student representatives for a number of key administrative committees.

Admission Requirements

An applicant for admission to the University of Dubuque undergraduate program is a graduate of a high school or equivalent (GED) and presents a minimum of 15 high school units, of which 10 are from academic fields (English, social studies, natural science, mathematics, foreign language). Either ACT or SAT scores are required. The Admission Committee looks at the application and transcript for indications of school achievement as well as aspiration, creativity, and adventurousness. Applicants to the University are usually active in cocurricular activities and these, as well as leadership qualities and character, are considered. An on-campus visit is encouraged. Two recommendations and an essay are requested and read with care.

Application and Information

First-year students are admitted to the University on a rolling basis. When the application and all supporting materials (e.g., transcripts and teacher and counselor recommendations) have been received, admission decisions are made by the Admission Committee and students are advised of the University's decision.

Transfer students who are enrolled or who were previously enrolled at another college or university may apply for transfer to the University of Dubuque. The University considers transfer applications for fall and spring semesters.

In addition to completing the application materials required for first-year applicants, transfer applicants must submit a complete official transcript for all college courses taken and grades received and a complete official transcript for all secondary school courses taken and grades received.

For further information, students should contact:

Office of Admission
University of Dubuque
2000 University Avenue
Dubuque, Iowa 52001
Phone: 563-589-3000
800-722-5583 (toll-free)
E-mail: admssns@dbq.edu
Website: http://www.dbq.edu

Heritage Center, the University's fine and performing arts, worship, and campus center, opened in May 2013.

THE UNIVERSITY OF FINDLAY

FINDLAY, OHIO

FINDLAY
THE UNIVERSITY OF FINDLAY

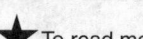

★ To read more about this school, visit http://petersons.to/universityoffindlay

The University

Since its founding as Findlay College in 1882, the University of Findlay's calling has been to help students find their calling. The exceptional quality of its academic programs, a focus on hands-on learning, and robust campus life and athletic programs have made Findlay one of the best private universities in the Midwest.

The University's mission is to prepare students for meaningful lives and productive careers. The curriculum, internships and placement initiatives, campus experiences, and undergraduate research and international opportunities prepare its 4,000 students to be leaders in their chosen career field.

The University of Findlay (UF) believes the learning that takes place outside of the classroom is as important as the foundational experiences that the outstanding faculty provides students inside the classroom. All the academic programs have an experiential learning component built in. Students participate in faculty-guided undergraduate research, learning labs that take place in real world settings, and mentorship opportunities. UF's college-specific career placement specialists work with students to prepare them for the professional world and establish the connections needed to land an internship and full-time job.

The University of Findlay has a great tradition of offering academic programs that fill niche needs in the professional world, and being flexible enough to develop academic offerings as industries evolve. Findlay has gained a national reputation for the quality of many of its academic programs including animal science, health professions, equestrian studies, environmental sciences, nuclear medicine and forensic science. UF's College of Business has incorporated the industry-leading enterprise resource planning software, SAP, in all levels of the curriculum. This gives students a competitive advantage at major corporations that use the powerful software.

Students at Findlay are engaged in the community and perform many types of service to learn about social issues, community building, and environmental challenges. UF works in the surrounding community to assist its neighbors and develop a sense of pride.

The University of Findlay offers nearly sixty bachelor's degree programs and nine master's degree programs, and doctoral degrees in education, pharmacy, and physical therapy. Findlay also has a robust online university that includes degree completion, M.B.A., and environmental, safety, and health programs.

The largest programs at Findlay are animal science/pre–veterinary medicine, equestrian studies, pharmacy, business administration, and education. Majors in the sciences and health professions include athletic training, chemistry, computer science, equestrian studies (English, western, and equine business management), nuclear medicine, occupational therapy, physical therapy, and animal science/pre–veterinary medicine. Business degrees are founded in a comprehensive core program with eleven different majors.

Students come to the University of Findlay from all over the world, with more than 30 states and 41 countries represented. With nearly 600 international students on campus, Findlay provides students, both domestic and international, with the educational and cultural experiences needed to thrive in our global society.

Resident students live in eight modern residence halls and several town-house-style apartments. With more than 100 clubs, organizations, academic honor societies, and mentorship opportunities, the University of Findlay helps student leaders develop the skills, resume material, and networks to become leaders in their industry.

Athletic programs are affiliated with NCAA Division II and the Great Lakes Intercollegiate Athletic Conference, with the exception of the equestrian teams, which have won national championships in the Intercollegiate Horse Show Association. Findlay offers ten intercollegiate sports for men: baseball, basketball, cross-country, football, golf, indoor and outdoor track and field, soccer, swimming and diving, tennis, and wrestling. It has eleven varsity sports for women: basketball, cheerleading, cross-country, golf, indoor and outdoor track and field, lacrosse, soccer, softball, swimming and diving, tennis, and volleyball. UF also has two mixed sports, western and English equestrian riding. Athletic scholarships are available.

The Croy Physical Education Center has a 25-meter swimming pool, a gymnasium, offices, and classrooms. The 130,000-square-foot Koehler Recreation and Fitness Complex contains a six-lane, NCAA-regulation track; sand pits for long jump; state-of-the-art timing system; wrestling room; four multipurpose courts; locker rooms; and offices for the athletic department. Also under the same roof is a general student recreation center, which includes a cardio center; basketball, volleyball, and tennis courts; a rock-climbing wall; a game room; and more.

Student services include career and placement counseling, the Cosiano Health Center, the Oiler Success Center, academic tutoring and personal counseling, and study skills assistance through the Academic Support Center.

Location

Findlay was voted the most livable micropolitan city in Ohio and scored among the top twelve 12 in the United States. It is within easy driving distance of Toledo, Columbus, Detroit, and Fort Wayne. Interstate 75 and the Ohio Turnpike (Interstates 80 and 90) are major highways serving the area. Airports in Toledo, Columbus, and Detroit are convenient. The town of Findlay has 40,000 residents and is home to Marathon Oil Corporation and Cooper Tire and Rubber Company. The Findlay campus consists of more than 388 acres on several sites. A 152-acre campus-owned farm houses the pre–veterinary medicine and western equestrian studies programs, including a 31,000-square-foot animal science center with two 50-seat classrooms, a laboratory, a pharmacy, a student lounge, locker rooms, offices, instructional demonstration areas, holding pens, and other animal servicing areas. A second 32-acre facility houses the English riding program. Approximately 350 horses are stabled and trained at the equestrian facilities, which offer barns and indoor and outdoor riding arenas.

Many opportunities exist for students who want business-related and social service agency experience. The University has established strong relationships with the community, which supports athletic and cultural events on the campus. Besides the full program of on-campus activities, off-campus trips to cultural and entertainment events are scheduled. The city of Findlay, which has an excellent business climate, offers part-time job opportunities, volunteer service organizations, and the chance to be involved with the larger civic community. Findlay's campus is attractive, safe, comfortable, and friendly.

Majors and Degrees

The Bachelor of Arts (B.A.) degree is awarded in the following majors: adolescent/young adult/integrated English/language arts, adolescent/young adult/integrated social studies, art, art management, children's book illustration, criminal justice, diagnostic medical sonography, English, English as an international language, graphic design, history, Japanese, journalism, law and the liberal arts, middle childhood/language arts/social studies, multiage/drama/theater, multiage/Japanese, multiage/Spanish, multiage/visual arts, philosophy/applied philosophy, political science, psychology, public relations, religious studies, social work, sociology, Spanish, studio art, teaching English to speakers of other languages, and theater. Minors are offered in numerous areas.

The Bachelor of Science (B.S.) degree is granted in accounting; adolescent/young adult/earth science; adolescent/young adult/integrated mathematics; adolescent/young adult/life science; animal science; biology (recommended for those interested in physician assistant or medical studies); business administration; business management; chemistry; computer science; early childhood; economics; environmental, safety, and occupational health management; equestrian studies (English and Western emphases); equine business management; finance; forensic science; health and physical education; health science (in preparation for occupational therapy or physical therapy); healthcare management; hospitality management; human resource management; international business; intervention specialist/mild to moderate disabilities; marketing; mathematics; medical laboratory science; middle childhood/language arts/math; middle childhood/language arts/science; middle childhood/math/science; middle childhood/math/social studies; middle childhood/science/social studies; multiage/health education; multiage/physical education; nuclear medicine technology; operations and logistics; physical education; positron emission tomography/computer technology; sport and event management and strength and conditioning.

The Associate of Arts degree is available in accounting, computer science, diagnostic medical sonography, English as an international language, equestrian studies (English and western riding), financial management, human resource management, management information systems, nuclear medicine technology, personal training, positron emission tomography/computed tomography (PET/CT), sales/retail management, and small business/entrepreneurship. Certificate programs are available in a variety of areas.

Academic Programs

Findlay operates on the semester system. Students must complete at least 124 semester hours with a minimum overall grade point average of 2.0 to earn a bachelor's degree. General education requirements and competency requirements in English, computer literacy, and speech must be fulfilled. The Gateway Program offers students the chance to develop those skills in writing, reading, and thinking needed for their success as college students. Study skills, time management, and academic advising are included. Students are selected for this program at the time of admission. The honors program provides additional challenge to those students who qualify on the basis of academic credentials. Study- and travel-abroad programs are offered by various departments. Credit and/or placement can be earned through Advanced Placement (AP) exams.

The equestrian program is a well-recognized program of its kind and serves approximately 280 students from throughout the United States and abroad. Majors in equine business management and in English and western riding are offered. The instruction, both in the classroom and on horseback, makes use of the expertise of recognized national equestrian champions.

The pre–veterinary medicine program, using the farm facilities, offers the advantages of hands-on experience with livestock and an internship program in a distinctive curriculum. Graduates of the pre-veterinary program have been accepted to all twenty-eight veterinary schools in the United States, and several internationally.

The Nuclear Medicine Institute provides the training necessary to qualify students for careers in nuclear medicine technology, a growing health-related career field.

Academic Facilities

The focal point of the Findlay campus is Old Main, which houses classrooms, faculty and administrative offices, the computer center, facilities for various student activities, the Oiler Success Center, and the Ritz Auditorium. Shafer Library is a member of a consortium that provides extensive resources to students. The Virginia B. Gardner Fine Arts Pavilion houses the Mazza Museum of International Art from Children's Books, the first and largest teaching museum in the world dedicated to literacy and children's book art. The Davis Building serves as home to the College of Education, the College of Pharmacy, and numerous science research labs. Other academic buildings include the Frost Science Center and the Egner Center for the Performing Arts, which houses a 200-seat theater.

Costs

Tuition for the 2014–15 academic year was $29,716. Room and board costs were $9,350. There are additional tuition charges for equestrian studies and pre–veterinary medicine.

Financial Aid

Assistance is based on need as well as scholastic achievement. In 2014–15, 99 percent of UF students received financial aid. The average need-based financial aid package for freshmen was more than $20,000 in fall 2014. Work-study jobs are available. Scholarships for high-achieving students and student athletes are offered.

Faculty

The 16:1 student-faculty ratio results in small classes, with an average class size of 20 students. Professors know their students, and every student has a faculty adviser.

Student Government

The Student Government Association (SGA) and the Campus Program Board are involved in planning and implementing student activities. SGA provides leadership experience for students and enhances cooperation among faculty members, the administration, and students. A representative from SGA sits on the Board of Trustees. The Campus Program Board plans activities for recreation and cultural enrichment.

Admission Requirements

The University of Findlay considers each applicant on an individualized basis. The University accepts applications on a rolling basis, but it encourages students to complete applications by January 15, as the class fills rapidly. Application deadlines are August 1 for the fall semester and December 15 for the spring semester. Major factors associated with rendering a decision include GPA, standardized test scores, and strength of curriculum. Although it is not required, a campus admission visit is encouraged. Applicants to Findlay should have a college-preparatory high school background, including 4 years of English, 3 to 4 years of mathematics, 2 to 3 years of social studies, and 2 years of science. A foreign language is recommended but not required. Results of the ACT or SAT should be submitted with the application for admission. Transfer students must be eligible to return to the institution last attended and must submit transcripts of all college work. For students not meeting regular minimum admission requirements, Findlay has a Gateway Program, which provides skill building and academic support during the first semester of the freshman year. Findlay is an equal opportunity institution in admission and employment.

Application and Information

For application forms and other information, students may contact:

Office of Admissions
The University of Findlay
1000 North Main Street
Findlay, Ohio 45840
Phone: 419-434-4732
800-548-0932 (toll-free)
E-mail: admissions@findlay.edu
Website: http://www.findlay.edu
http://www.facebook.com/universityfindlay (Facebook)
ufindlay (Twitter)

The University of Findlay's Old Main is an original building on campus and houses the College of Business and many student support services.

UNIVERSITY OF GUELPH

GUELPH, ONTARIO, CANADA

The University

The University of Guelph is ranked in the 2015 *U.S. News & World Report's* Best Global Universities and is consistently recognized as one of Canada's top Comprehensive Universities. It is a high-quality, student-focused, residential university that is committed to innovative programs and research, dynamic student-faculty interaction, and an integration of learning and research. It offers a wide range of undergraduate and graduate programs in the arts, humanities, social sciences, engineering, and natural sciences. Building on these core disciplines, Guelph also has a strong commitment to interdisciplinary programs, to a selected range of professional and applied programs, and to agriculture and veterinary medicine as areas of special responsibility.

Established in 1964 when three century-old founding colleges joined with a new college of arts and science, the University of Guelph is a vital community of more than 22,000 students on a campus of historical and modern buildings connected by red brick walkways. By Canadian standards, Guelph is of medium size, offering a wide range of academic programs while providing a safe, accommodating environment. On-campus living is available for more than 5,000 students, with new first-semester students guaranteed on-campus housing if they apply and submit a deposit before the deadline.

Guelph features state-of-the-art athletic facilities that include a double arena with an Olympic-size ice surface, two pools, a field house and indoor track, aerobic and weight-training gymnasiums, six squash courts, and a climbing wall. Guelph offers thirty varsity sports teams and in recent years has fielded national and provincial championship football, hockey, rowing, rugby, track and field, and wrestling teams.

Guelph ensures a personal approach to learning with a 1:23 faculty-student ratio. The success of the Center for New Students, which assists students with the transition from secondary school to university, is reflected in Guelph's 91.7 percent student retention rate and a 93.8 percent graduate employment rate, both well above the Canadian national average.

For graduate students, the University of Guelph offers a Doctor of Veterinary Medicine degree as well as several graduate diploma programs and more than eighty master's and doctoral degree programs. The graduate calendar is available on the Web at http://www.uoguelph.ca/GraduateStudies.

Location

The University of Guelph's main campus is located in the southwestern Ontario region the *New York Times* calls Canada's Technology Triangle, a locale known for its high-caliber educational institutions and innovative companies. This city of more than 121,000 features internationally recognized folk, jazz, and writers' festivals as well as a multipurpose performing arts center and a sports and entertainment center. Positioned within an hour's drive of Toronto, Canada's largest city, Guelph offers the comfort of small-community living with the excitement of an international metropolis at its doorstep. In addition to the main campus, the University of Guelph offers many dynamic degrees in Toronto at the University of Guelph–Humber and diploma programs in Ridgetown at the regional campus.

Majors and Degrees

The University of Guelph offers a number of undergraduate degree programs. Programs followed by an asterisk (*) indicate degrees that students can pursue in a traditional four-year or in a five-year co-op format. Co-ops offer students the opportunity to work in three to five different companies in paid work placements that result in one year of full-time work as a part of the degree experience.

The University of Guelph offers Bachelor of Arts degrees in anthropology; art history; classical studies; criminal justice and public policy; economics*; English; environmental governance; European studies; food, agriculture, and resource economics; French studies; geography; Hispanic studies; history; information systems and human behavior; international development; major to be determined; mathematical economics*; mathematics; music; philosophy; political science; psychology*; sociology; studio art; and theater studies. In addition, a Bachelor of Arts and Sciences degree is available to students who excel in both arts/social sciences and sciences.

Bachelor of Applied Science degrees are available in applied human nutrition; child, youth, and family*; and adult development*.

Bachelor of Commerce degrees are available in accounting*, food and agricultural business*, hotel and food administration*, leadership and organizational management, management economics and finance*, marketing management*, public management*, real estate and housing*, tourism management, and undeclared (first year only).

Bachelor of Bio-Resource Management degrees are available in environmental management and equine management.

The Bachelor of Computing degrees are available in computer science* and software engineering*.

Bachelor of Engineering degrees are available in biological engineering*, biomedical engineering*, computer engineering*, environmental engineering*, engineering systems and computing*, mechanical engineering*, water resources engineering*, and undeclared (first year only).

Bachelor of Science degrees are available in animal biology, biochemistry*, biodiversity, biological science, biological and pharmaceutical chemistry*, biological and pharmaceutical physics*, biomedical science, biomedical toxicology, chemical physics*, chemistry*, environmental biology, environmental geoscience and geomatics, food science*, human kinetics, marine and freshwater biology, microbiology*, molecular biology and genetics, nanoscience*, nutritional and nutraceutical sciences, physical science, physics*, plant science, psychology: brain and cognition, theoretical physics, wildlife biology and conservation, and zoology.

Bachelor of Science in Agriculture degrees are available in animal science; crop, horticulture, and turfgrass sciences; honors agriculture; and organic agriculture.

Bachelor of Science in Environmental Sciences degrees are among the top in the world and are available in ecology*, environment and resource management*, environmental economics and policy*, and environmental sciences*.

University of Guelph also offers a Bachelor of Landscape Architecture degree, a Doctor of Veterinary Medicine degree, and associate diplomas.

University of Guelph–Humber programs include honors degrees with integral work placements in business administration (accounting, finance, international business, marketing, and small business management and entrepreneurship); applied science (early childhood services, family and community social services, justice studies, kinesiology, or psychology); and applied arts in media studies (journalism, public relations, digital communications, and image arts).

Academic Programs

The academic year is divided into three semesters: fall (September through December), winter (January through April), and summer (May through August), with the majority of students in attendance during the fall and winter semesters. Fall is the normal entry point for all semester one students. However, transfer students who apply by deadlines are considered for many programs at all entry points.

Four-year honors degrees require the completion of eight semesters. Three-year general degrees require the completion of six semesters. A typical full-time semester totals 2.5 credits.

Off-Campus Programs

An important part of Guelph's mission is to attract students from around the world and develop a global perspective in its students. The campus attracts nearly 1,000 international students from over

100 countries, maintains fifty-six exchange programs with thirty countries, and offers six semester-abroad options. In addition, approximately 500 Guelph students study, research, or work each year in Africa, Australia, Europe, and South and Central America.

Over 2,000 students participate in co-op work semesters, making the co-op program at the University of Guelph one of the highest in co-op student enrollments among Ontario universities. Guelph also offers more than 100 distance degree credit courses to nearly 8,000 Open Learning course registrants.

Academic Facilities

Guelph's two libraries are linked with libraries at two other universities in the region, providing students with access to 7.5 million items through a state-of-the-art automated library system. Guelph's library holdings include Canada's largest collection of theater archives, extensive Scottish study materials, and one of the best collections of postcolonial African literature in Canada.

A 30-acre research park adjacent to the campus is home to a growing number of research-intensive industries. Industry and government trust Guelph's faculty members to meet their research needs, offering approximately Can$130 million annually for research that ranges from workplace efficiency to developing better approaches to food packaging and marketing to ensuring the availability of clean water.

All students receive free central computing accounts, which allow access to the University's integrated electronic services from on or off campus. Services include e-mail, access to the Internet, computer-assisted instruction, conferencing, course selection, and high-quality laser printing. Student residences are directly connected to the Internet via the campus high-speed network. Off-campus students have access to chargeable high-speed Internet providers.

The campus also features two art galleries; a sculpture park; two performance stages; a covered field house; a Can$144-million Science Complex; a Can$44.6-million engineering facility expansion; the Guelph Institute for the Environment; the Biodiversity Institute of Ontario, which is the world's first center for high-volume DNA barcoding; and the Can$70-million pathobiology/animal health laboratory. The 408-acre arboretum on the west side of the campus has nearly 5 miles of jogging trails and nature paths.

Costs

Full-time tuition for the 2014–15 academic year ranged from Can$3011 to Can$5466 per semester for Canadian residents and from Can$9214 to Can$11,932 per semester for international students. Doctor of Veterinary Medicine tuition ranged from Can$4292 per semester for Canadian residents to Can$27,042 per semester for international students. Mandatory fees totaled approximately Can$530 per semester, with slight variations according to each college. International students must purchase health-care coverage through the University. The cost for international students to attend Guelph for two semesters, including tuition and academic fees, health coverage, housing, clothing, food, and books, totaled between Can$32,546 and Can$37,961.

Financial Aid

The University of Guelph is committed to ensuring that a university education remains an attainable goal. In total, Can$17.3 million in annual student financial aid is given in the form of scholarships, awards, bursaries, and work-study opportunities. There are scholarships (ranging from Can$5500 to Can$8500) and bursaries specifically designed for international students who are allowed to work on and off campus.

Faculty

The percentage of Guelph's 830 full-time professors who hold the Ph.D. degree or its equivalent is 98.3 percent, and all strive to bring the excitement and process of research into the learning environment. More than 100 professors have been recognized for excellence in teaching by external agencies, their peers, and students. No comparably sized university in the country has more 3M awards, Canada's most prestigious university teaching honor. Guelph has 19 Fellows of the Royal Society of Canada among its researchers.

Student Government

Students are involved at all levels of University government, from the residence council to the Senate and the Board of Governors. The Central Student Association (CSA), which represents all undergraduate students, oversees more than fifty student clubs that range from political to recreational. In addition, there are more than fifty academic and other student-government organizations located on campus. Students also have access to a number of service groups on campus, which range from the Ontario Public Interest Research Group to a community radio station to Engineers without Borders and Habitat for Humanity.

Admission Requirements

Ontario applicants must present the Ontario Secondary School Diploma (OSSD), with a minimum of six 4U or 4M courses and specific subject requirements for the degree program desired. English 4U is required for all degree programs. For those outside Ontario, the secondary graduation certificate that would admit a student to a university in his or her home country is normally acceptable. Applicants must also satisfy the specific subject requirements for the program desired. Applicants who have completed the International Baccalaureate (I.B.) are granted credit for higher-level courses with grades of 5 or better to a maximum of 2.0 credits. Applicants who have completed Advanced Placement (AP) exams with a minimum grade of 4 are eligible to receive University credit to a maximum of 2.0 credits, which is subject to the discretion of the appropriate faculty. United States applicants are required to have a minimum unweighted cumulative grade point average of 3.0 and a combined SAT score of at least 1100 (critical reading and math components) or an ACT score of at least 24. Applicants should include specific subject requirements at the highest secondary school level offered.

Interested students should call Admission Services or refer to its website at http://admission.uoguelph.ca for application and deadline dates, detailed admission information, and downloadable application forms.

Students interested in University of Guelph–Humber programs should contact Admission Services at http://www.guelphhumber.ca.

Application and Information

For additional information about admissions, academic programs, or University visits and tours, students should contact:

Admission Services
Office of Registrarial Services
Third Floor, University Centre
University of Guelph
Guelph, Ontario N1G 2W1
Canada
Phone: 519-821-2130 or 519-824-4120 Ext. 58721
Fax: 519-766-9481
E-mail: internat@uoguelph.ca (International inquiries)
usa@uoguelph.ca (U.S. inquiries)
admission@registrar.uoguelph.ca (Canadian inquiries)
Website: http://admission.uoguelph.ca
http://www.guelphhumber.ca

The University of Guelph's facilities include a mix of traditional and modern lecture halls, labs, and study space.

COLLEGE CLOSE-UPS

UNIVERSITY OF HARTFORD

WEST HARTFORD, CONNECTICUT

UNIVERSITY OF HARTFORD

★ To read more about this school, visit http://petersons.to/universityofhartford

The University

The University of Hartford is a fully accredited, independent, nonsectarian institution. The University is composed of seven degree-granting schools and colleges: the College of Arts and Sciences; College of Engineering, Technology, and Architecture; College of Education, Nursing, and Health Professions; Hillyer College; the Barney School of Business; the Hartford Art School; and The Hartt School.

The current full-time undergraduate enrollment is approximately 4,600 men and women. With an average class size of about 20–25 students, each one benefits from additional personalized attention from faculty members. Students can expect to get to know not only their classroom professors, but also all faculty members in their department. Faculty members focus on helping students apply what they learn in the classroom to real-world scenarios and provide the mentoring necessary to push students past perceived limits. A wide range of interests, goals, and backgrounds is found among the students, who represent fifty states and forty countries. There are about 100 organized student groups, including clubs devoted to special interests or to political, professional, religious, or civic activities as well as service learning and community service activities and groups. Intercollegiate (NCAA Division I) and intramural athletics, student publications, and AM and FM radio stations provide further opportunities for extracurricular involvement. In addition, The Hartt School, the Hartford Art School, and the University Players present a variety of concerts, exhibitions, and theatrical productions each year. Recreational and fitness needs of the University community as well as intramural and intercollegiate sports are served by a well-equipped 130,000-square-foot sports center and outdoor athletic facilities.

More than 66 percent of all full-time undergraduates reside on campus. The University offers a wide array of residence halls, from traditional dormitory-style to fully equipped town house–style apartments.

Location

The University is located in the residential suburb of West Hartford. Whether it's to eat at the Cheesecake Factory and catch a movie at Criterion Cinemas, or shop at Ann Taylor or REI, West Hartford is a great place to visit. The Hartford area also boasts an impressive array of entertainment and cultural resources including the Comcast Theatre and the Bushnell Performing Arts Center. The campus is easily accessible by both train and bus and is located about 25 minutes from Bradley International Airport.

Majors and Degrees

About 25 percent of students apply undecided which, at the University of Hartford, is an opportunity to explore many academic interests among the more than 100 areas of study. Students receive support from offices such as Career Services, the Student Success Center, and a Dialogue course which allows them to meet with and learn from other undecided students. The College of Arts and Sciences offers majors in biology, chemistry, chemistry-biology, cinema, communication, computer science, criminal justice, economics, English, history, international studies, Judaic studies, mathematics, philosophy, physics, politics and government, psychology, and sociology.

Within the College of Education, Nursing, and Health Professions, there are majors in early childhood education, elementary education, integrated special education/elementary education, secondary education with a concentration in English or mathematics, health sciences, nursing (for registered nurses only), radiologic technology, respiratory therapy, a combined B.S. in health science, and doctorate in physical therapy (B.S./D.P.T.) program, as well as a combined B.S. in health science and a Master of Science in Prosthetics and Orthotics (B.S./M.S.P.O.) program.

The Hartford Art School offers Bachelor of Fine Arts degrees in ceramics, design, drawing, illustration, media arts, painting, photography, printmaking, sculpture, and visual communication as well as a Bachelor of Arts in art history.

At the Hartt School, students can major in actor training, applied music (guitar, orchestral instrument, organ, piano, pre–cantorial studies, and voice), composition, dance (ballet pedagogy or performance emphases), jazz studies, music, music education, music history, music management, music production and technology, music theater, music theory, and performing arts management (interdisciplinary program offered in conjunction with the Barney School of Business). There are also five-year double majors offered within the Hartt School.

Majors for the Bachelor of Science in Business Administration (B.S.B.A.) degree in the Barney School of Business are accounting, economics and finance, entrepreneurial studies, finance and insurance, management, and marketing.

Additional B.S. programs, offered by the College of Engineering, Technology, and Architecture include ABET-EAC accredited programs in electrical, mechanical, civil, computer, and biomedical engineering, and acoustical engineering and music. The newest offering in the mechanical engineering department is a concentration in energy engineering and sustainable design. The most popular B.S.E. options are acoustical engineering and music (interdisciplinary program in conjunction with the Hartt School) and biomedical engineering. In addition, the college offers interdisciplinary B.S.E. options. Technology programs include the Bachelor of Science in architectural engineering technology, audio engineering technology, computer engineering technology, electronic engineering technology, and mechanical engineering technology as well as the Associate in Applied Science in electronic engineering technology (A.S.) and the Associate in Applied Science in computer engineering technology (A.S.). New to the technology majors in 2014 is a B.S. in electromechanical engineering technology. The programs in architecture, electronics, and mechanical engineering are ABET-ETAC accredited.

Hillyer College provides the general education course work required to complete most of the University's baccalaureate programs. Particular emphasis is placed on the development of academic skills through small classes and close faculty-student interaction.

University Studies offers the Bachelor of University Studies, a B.A. degree program created for the part-time adult student who typically has previous college experience and seeks to complete a baccalaureate degree. Also offered is a B.A. degree program in multimedia website design and development for full-time undergraduates. Created for students who want to learn how to use and develop multimedia technologies that fit into today's wired world, this program combines courses across several disciplines where students create and use technology with user interaction in mind.

Academic Programs

The University of Hartford enjoys a national reputation for the breadth and depth of its academic programs. As highlighted above, about 100 programs of study are offered through seven schools and colleges. Students are encouraged to sample a variety of academic areas. Those who have special interests can develop interdisciplinary majors that combine courses from the different schools within the University. Academic advisers are assigned to all students to help guide them in curriculum choices, career exploration, and the transition to University life. The University also has a special program to assist students who may be undecided about a major. A reading and writing center provides individual support to help students increase their proficiency in writing, research, reading comprehension, and speed as well as study and test-taking skills. Further help in math is given through the Math Tutoring Lab, which is staffed by full-time faculty members and math majors. Career Services provides vocational counseling and information on occupations, employers, testing, and graduate schools; serves as a reference and credential source; and provides an on-campus recruiting program for graduating students. The Adult Academic Services Office addresses the needs of the part-time adult learner through courses, programs, and educational counseling. A trained counseling staff is available to assist part-time students in planning their education and resolving their special concerns and needs. Selected students are encouraged to participate in the honors program. Honors students have the opportunity to excel at college and add value to their education at no extra cost. Students in the honors program can enjoy smaller class sizes, special awards and scholarships, honor society membership, and can graduate with an honors degree.

Off-Campus Programs

Intercampus registration through the Hartford Consortium for Higher Education permits University of Hartford students to take certain courses at the School of the Hartford Ballet, Saint Joseph College, and Trinity College. Teaching majors in the College of Education, Nursing, and Health Professions have opportunities for field and/or clinical experiences where applicable. A central internship and cooperative education office is available to custom-tailor work experiences within many of the University's programs. The study-abroad office works with students to arrange international learning experiences that promote cultural exploration and lifelong memories. The University of Hartford has garnered affiliations with schools in more than sixty different countries, making study abroad a vast and popular option on campus.

Academic Facilities

Seven schools and colleges are housed on the main campus. The Harry Jack Gray Center houses the William H. Mortensen Library; the Mildred P. Allen Memorial Library; the Museum of American Political Life; the Harry J. Gray Conference Center; the Joseloff Gallery; the University Bookstore; studios for architecture, art, radio, and television; and the communication department. The library has approximately 600,000 reference items, including books, musical scores, recordings, periodicals, journals, and microfilm units as well as high-speed and wireless Internet access. Extensive resources are also available through the Hartford Consortium for Higher Education, the Hartford Library, and the Interlibrary Loan systems.

The new state-of-the-art Mort and Irma Handel Performing Arts Center, located 5 minutes from the main campus, is a 55,000-square-foot facility that houses five dance studios, four theater rehearsal studios, two black box theaters, a small dining facility, and faculty and staff offices. The Handel Performing Arts Center provides a rehearsal and performance environment for the Hartt School's dancers.

The University of Hartford Computer Center houses the central computer systems and operates a high-performance campus-wide network, which connects all student residential housing, all academic buildings on campus, and the University's remote locations. The University's network is connected via a high-speed telecommunication link to the Internet. The residential network gives each student resident his or her own high-speed Ethernet connection to the campus network and the Internet. All of the University network resources may be accessed on campus in any University facility and off campus by using computers with network connectivity.

Public access computing labs, used by all students of the University, are provided at various locations around the campus. In addition, college-specific labs are available to students. All labs are equipped with microcomputers (both PCs and Macs) and are connected to the campus network and the Internet. Typical microcomputer software includes word processing, spreadsheet, database management, and graphics programs; programming languages; and web browsers for accessing the Internet. Help is available from on-duty lab assistants. In addition to these computer labs, there are specialized computer facilities for instruction and learning. Wireless Internet access is available in all academic buildings, libraries, and dining facilities.

Costs

Tuition for incoming students was $32,758 for the 2014–15 academic year; fees, $2,686; on-campus room costs, $7,548; and board, $3,970. A variety of on-campus housing accommodates the University's residential student population.

Financial Aid

Financial aid for University of Hartford students totals approximately $98 million annually, including student loans. Scholarships, grants, loans, and work-study opportunities are provided through the federal government, private agencies, interested individuals, and University funds. University funds are disbursed based on the college or school in which the student is enrolled, availability of funds, applicant pool, and competition for funds. About 93 percent of new full-time undergraduate students receive some type of University assistance; the average out-of-pocket expense is $17,999 (estimate) per year. Partial-tuition scholarships are awarded to entering students who have demonstrated outstanding academic achievement or talent.

Faculty

There are 845 full-time and adjunct faculty members. The undergraduate and graduate faculties are essentially the same group, and 86 percent of the members hold the terminal degree in their field. Academic and personal advisory service is readily available. Each new student is assigned to a faculty adviser during summer orientation.

Student Government

The student governing body that represents all full-time students is the Student Government Association, through which students and faculty join in developing and coordinating the co-curricular activities of the University. Students are also represented on all major administrative committees, including the Board of Regents.

Admission Requirements

The Office of Admission considers the quality of the secondary school curriculum, academic performance in secondary school, ACT or SAT results, evidence of a desire to succeed, and leadership qualities shown by academic and extracurricular activities. Auditions, portfolios, and other tests are required of music and art applicants.

Application and Information

The University employs a rolling admission policy. For further information, students should visit the University on the Internet at http://admission.hartford.edu or contact:

Office of Admission
University of Hartford
West Hartford, Connecticut 06117
Phone: 860-768-4296
800-947-4303 (toll-free)
Fax: 860-768-4961
E-mail: admission@hartford.edu
Website: http://admission.hartford.edu

Find yourself here. Your talent will follow.

COLLEGE CLOSE-UPS

UNIVERSITY OF INDIANAPOLIS

INDIANAPOLIS, INDIANA

UIndy

UNIVERSITY OF INDIANAPOLIS

The University

The University of Indianapolis (UIndy) seeks to inspire excellence with a personal approach to education and a commitment to academic quality. Outstanding faculty members inspire students in small class sizes that allow individual attention. Students are encouraged to apply their knowledge to real-world situations through internships, active learning in the classroom, and community service. A private, residential, comprehensive university founded in 1902 and affiliated with the United Methodist Church, the University of Indianapolis welcomes students of many nations and faiths from around the world. Every year, more than 5,400 full-time and part-time students, both undergraduate and graduate, benefit from the University's commitment to offering outstanding academic programs in more than eighty major fields of study. The University of Indianapolis accepts qualified applicants for admission without regard to race, color, gender, sexual orientation, age, religion, creed, marital status, and ethnic or national origin.

Students indicate that they chose UIndy because of its challenging yet supportive atmosphere, relatively small class sizes, and the advantages of its location in the distinctive southside area of a thriving state capital city. As a result, there is a great sense of unity and pride on campus. The University helps students to determine and achieve their individual academic goals. UIndy has experienced much growth and has instituted many enhancements recently, including a four-story Health Pavilion (scheduled to open in fall 2015) to enhance classroom learning with real-life clinical experiences and simulations in health-related fields.

More than 3,000 full-time undergraduate students are enrolled. There are students from more than sixty countries and thirty-five states. Approximately 80 percent of freshmen live in on-campus housing. The warmth and sensitivity of the faculty, staff members, and students alike enable those who are a part of the campus to feel a strong sense of community. The most popular programs in the undergraduate division include pre–physical therapy, pre–occupational therapy, business, athletic training, communication, nursing, education, pre-medical studies, psychology, and music.

In addition to the undergraduate division, the University also offers a graduate division, including the nationally recognized Krannert School of Physical Therapy. The University of Indianapolis offers twenty-seven master's programs and five doctoral programs, including those in the College of Health Sciences, which rank among the finest in the nation.

Social life is organized through the numerous social, common-interest clubs available for students who wish to become involved in extracurricular activities. There are seven residence halls: six house both men and women, and one is only for women. Two-bedroom, one-bathroom apartments are also available to upperclassmen. Students must be admitted on a full-time basis in order to be assigned housing. NCAA Division II sports for men include baseball, basketball, cross-country, football, golf, soccer, swimming and diving, tennis, track and field (indoor and outdoor), and wrestling. NCAA Division II sports for women include basketball, cross-country, golf, soccer, softball, swimming and diving, tennis, track and field (indoor and outdoor), and volleyball. In spring 2016, Division II men's and women's lacrosse will be added. Intramural sports are also offered for men and women in flag football, basketball, softball, soccer, volleyball, indoor soccer, Ultimate (Frisbee), and wiffleball.

Location

The University is located in the University Heights neighborhood on the south side of Indianapolis, which is the nation's second-largest capital city. Indianapolis and the surrounding area constitute a metropolis of nearly 2 million people. The city offers numerous valuable internship and service-learning experiences as well as recreational and cultural opportunities for students. The campus is extremely accessible, just a few blocks from two major interstate highways (I-65 and I-465). IndyGo bus service is the city's public transportation system. Nonlocal options include Greyhound Bus Lines, Amtrak trains, and Megabus that arrive daily in downtown Indianapolis just 10 minutes from the campus. The Indianapolis International Airport is about 20 minutes away.

Majors and Degrees

The undergraduate programs are offered through the College of Arts and Sciences, College of Health Sciences, School of Business, School of Education, School of Nursing, and School of Psychological Sciences. The degrees awarded are the Associate in Arts, Associate in Science, Bachelor of Arts, Bachelor of Fine Arts, Bachelor of Music, Bachelor of Science, Bachelor of Science in Nursing, and Bachelor of Social Work.

Baccalaureate and pre-professional fields of study include accounting (CPA/non-CPA), actuarial science, anthropology, archeology, art, athletic training, biology, business administration, chemistry, communication, community health education, computer engineering (dual degree), computer science, criminal justice, digital media studies, earth-space sciences, economics, electrical engineering (dual degree), elementary education, English, entrepreneurship, environmental science, environmental sustainability, exercise science, experience design, finance, French, German, global leadership, history, human biology, human resource management, information systems, international business, international relations, management, marketing, mathematics, mechanical engineering (dual degree), medical laboratory science, music, music performance, nursing, operations and supply chain management, philosophy, physics, political science, pre-art therapy, pre-dental, pre-optometry, pre-pharmacy, pre-law, pre-medical studies, pre-occupational therapy, pre-pharmacy, pre-physical therapy, pre-theology, pre-veterinary science, psychology, religion, respiratory therapy, secondary education, social work, sociology, Spanish, sports information, sports management, sports marketing, studio art, theater, and visual communication design.

Teaching majors are offered in business education (all grades), chemistry, earth-space science, English, French, life science, mathematics, music (all grades), physical education (all grades), physics, social studies, Spanish, speech communication, theater, and visual arts (grades 5–12).

Associate degrees are awarded in business administration, chemistry, emergency and disaster management, information systems, life science, and physical therapist assistant studies.

The University also offers the Healthy Diploma that provides students with the skills, knowledge, and motivation to achieve and/or maintain a healthy lifestyle as students and employees.

Academic Programs

The University of Indianapolis provides a top-notch education that combines a liberal arts and career-oriented curriculum that graduates describe as life changing. Students find a powerful combination of features designed to inspire them to excellence. Faculty and staff members take a personal interest in students and encourage them to explore their interests and apply what they learn, so they can excel when it comes time to make their place in the world.

The goal of the liberal arts core classes is to provide learning above and beyond the student's major field; therefore students study topics and cultures that pique their interest in unexpected ways.

Students appreciate the curriculum because of the practical application of knowledge learned in the classroom. University of Indianapolis students have time—before they graduate—to practice what they learn. Most majors offer practical experiences, which give students an edge in the job market. The Indianapolis location is an excellent resource when it comes to finding internships, field experiences, service-learning opportunities, or part-time employment. Internships let students sample their future careers and gain some of the knowledge and experience they admire in their professors. The University offers a host of possibilities for virtually any major. The Professional Edge Center helps students identify career pathways, interact with professionals in their area of study, and develop professional and interpersonal skills.

Off-Campus Programs

UIndy has partnerships and extension sites for direct credit including Israel, Belize, and the People's Republic of China. Other off-campus study opportunities take place during Spring Term, a three-week course held in May, including assorted overseas travel options.

Academic Facilities

Krannert Memorial Library (renovated in 2015), which operates an online card catalog, houses more than 175,000 volumes, more than 1,000 periodicals, more than 19,000 microfilm/microform/ microfiche records, and the Indianapolis Mayoral Archives. The library is home to a full media center. The communication department, with new state-of-the-art equipment for its radio station and television studio, is located in Esch Hall. The UIndy Health Pavilion, set to open Fall 2015, will contain outstanding resources for the Schools of Nursing, Physical Therapy, Occupational Therapy, and Psychology, as well as the Departments of Social Work and Kinesiology, and the Athletic Training Program. Access to computers is available in all of the academic buildings. Students have access to the campus-wide information system from their rooms in the residence halls, and the entire campus is wireless. Ransburg Auditorium, with seating for nearly 800, is the setting for concerts, recitals, and theatrical productions. The Christel DeHaan Fine Arts Center features state-of-the-art music and art facilities; an art gallery; and a 502-seat, Viennese-style concert hall.

Costs

Direct costs for the 2014–15 academic year were $25,154 for tuition and $9,550 for room and board. Indirect costs are estimated at $1,250 for books and supplies, an average of $1,140 for transportation, and $2,000 to $4,200 for miscellaneous and personal expenses.

Financial Aid

All applicants for admission are eligible to apply for financial aid. Indiana residents should file the Free Application for Federal Student Aid (FAFSA) by March 10 to qualify for State of Indiana financial aid programs. All students should file the FAFSA along with the University of Indianapolis Application for Financial Aid by March 10 for priority consideration. For the 2014–15 academic year, about 88 percent of the enrolled full-time students received financial aid with an average financial aid package of $19,850 for entering students.

Faculty

UIndy's student-faculty ratio is 12:1 and the average class size is 18. Graduate students do not teach any undergraduate classes, instead the classes are taught by faculty members.

Student Government

The Indianapolis Student Government (ISG) consists of students elected to leadership positions plus student representatives from each class, chosen for a one-year term in an annual student body election. ISG's main focus is to pass resolutions regarding student concerns.

Admission Requirements

Applicants for admission must be high school graduates or have a GED certificate and are expected to have taken a college-preparatory curriculum in high school. Applicants for regular admission should have completed a minimum of 4 years of English, 3 years of mathematics, 3 years of laboratory science, 2 years of social science (U.S. history and government,), and 2 years of any foreign language. In addition, applicants for full-time admission without restrictions should rank in the upper half of their class and have average to above-average SAT or ACT scores. Essays are not required for admission. For immediate consideration, transfer applicants must have achieved a good overall record and have earned at least a C average in previous college or university work. An on-campus visit is recommended any time after the junior year of high school. To apply for admission, the Application for Admission, official high school transcript, official college transcript (if applicable), and official SAT or ACT scores should be forwarded to the Office of Admissions.

Application and Information

All applications are reviewed on a rolling basis—an admission decision is made as soon as all documents are received, and notifications are mailed immediately thereafter. There is no deadline for applications, but high school seniors are encouraged to apply during the fall semester of their senior year. Scholarships are also awarded on a rolling basis. Admitted students are notified of scholarships they have been awarded shortly after they have been accepted.

Requests for appointments and information about the University should be directed to:

University of Indianapolis
1400 East Hanna Avenue
Indianapolis, Indiana 46227-3697
United States
Phone: 866-421-7173 (toll-free)
317-788-3216
Fax: 317-788-3300
E-mail: admissions@uindy.edu
Website: uindy.edu
facebook.com/uindy
twitter.com/uindy
youtube.com/uindytv

Overlooking Smith Mall, located in the heart of campus, with Lilly Science Hall and the Schwitzer Student Center along the horizon.

UNIVERSITY OF MAINE

ORONO, MAINE

The University

The University of Maine (UMaine) offers the extensive academic opportunities expected from a major research university, with the close-knit feel of a small college. As Maine's flagship university, UMaine offers the state's most comprehensive academic experience, with more than 90 undergraduate majors and academic programs, 75 master's degree programs, and 30 doctoral programs. All majors benefit from a firm foundation in the liberal arts. Top students are invited to join UMaine's Honors College, one of the country's oldest and most prestigious.

The University of Maine is ranked 105 in the National Science Foundation's top research universities, and its facilities and faculty have an international reputation for excellence.

UMaine students have extraordinary opportunities to gain real-world experience through research and experiential learning. SPIFFY, the student investment club, manages a $2-million real-money portfolio. Wildlife ecology majors learn about bear behavior by going out and tagging cubs. Engineering majors secure co-ops and internships that often lead to employment after graduation. Education majors take advantage of urban, rural, and international student-teaching opportunities.

Location

There's no place like Maine, and UMaine students explore the great outdoors whenever they can. There are 15 miles of walking, biking, and cross-country skiing trails on campus. Some of the best skiing in the Northeast is located within easy driving distance of campus, as are Bar Harbor, Acadia National Park, and Baxter State Park, the northern terminus of the Appalachian Trail.

Orono is a classic college town, bounded by the Stillwater and Penobscot Rivers, located in the heart of Maine. The University of Maine is 10 minutes from the state's third-largest city, Bangor, and its international airport.

UMaine's campus was designed by legendary landscape architect Frederick Law Olmsted, who also designed Central Park in New York City and the U.S. Capitol grounds in Washington, D.C. It is a traditional New England campus, with ivy-covered brick buildings, towering pines, and incredible fall foliage.

Majors and Degrees

UMaine offers more than 90 majors and programs across five colleges—the College of Education and Human Development; the College of Engineering; the College of Liberal Arts and Sciences; the College of Natural Sciences, Forestry, and Agriculture; and the Honors College—as well as the Maine Business School. In addition, the Explorations program is designed to help undecided students identify a major from across UMaine's colleges while making progress toward their degree. The Division of Lifelong Learning offers online classes and distance-learning opportunities for students who need a flexible class schedule.

Academic Programs

UMaine provides a comprehensive academic and student experience, yielding graduates who are well educated, well adjusted, and well prepared to assume leadership roles in society. The university seeks to foster excellence and innovation through inspired, dedicated teaching and the discovery of new knowledge.

Students at the University of Maine benefit from a solid liberal arts foundation. They develop and refine the qualities they need to more fully engage with the world around them—critical thinking, curiosity, a sense of discovery, and a broader perspective—no matter what discipline they choose.

UMaine's Honors College provides an in-depth, academically challenging curriculum for qualified students in any major.

Undergraduate research is a priority and a point of pride. UMaine is the state's largest research university and graduate degree-granting institution, providing rich and varied opportunities for undergraduates to participate in research. Students publish, travel, and work alongside UMaine's world-class scholars and scientists. The Center for Undergraduate Research connects students with faculty projects that suit their interests. For many, research provides an opportunity for a mentor-mentee relationship different from—and often richer than—that of teacher-student. Skills developed through research and scholarship make students more competitive in the workplace and graduate school.

Off-Campus Programs

When UMaine students travel, they don't just go to Boston for the weekend. They go global, through study abroad, international volunteerism, and the worldwide research opportunities available to undergraduates. In recent semesters, UMaine students have traveled to China to learn more about the country's emerging financial markets, to Italy to explore Renaissance art history at the source, to Turkey to study film, and to Brazil to learn about a sensitive and diverse ecosystem from one of the world's leading conservation biologists (who also happens to be a UMaine professor and alumnus).

Academic Facilities

UMaine is home to state-of-the-art research facilities, classrooms, and teaching laboratories. Among the highlights are the Climate Change Institute, which has been featured on 60 Minutes; the Laboratory for Surface Science and Technology, which is a hub for cutting-edge sensor and nanotechnology research; and the Advanced Structures and Composites Center, which is leading the nation in deepwater offshore wind energy development.

Fogler Library, the state's largest library, houses more than 1.4 million volumes, 2.38 million microforms, and 2.3 million U.S. and Canadian government publications, and offers access to more than 200,000 e-books, 92,000 online serials, and 200 databases.

Completely renovated in 2013, Stewart Commons houses the Innovative Media Research and Commercialization Center (IMRC) and the Wyeth Family Studio Art Center. The IMRC contains facilities for training, research, development, and commercialization, such as a fabrication studio, electronics lab, and high-performance computer cluster that supports video and audio production, animation, 3-D design, and prototype production. The Wyeth Center features a suite of studios for painting, drawing, printmaking, photography, and design and allows the Department of Art's two-dimensional media to be housed under one roof.

The University of Maine is also a cultural hub. It is home to the region's premier performing arts center, the Collins Center for the Arts, as well as several museums and galleries.

Costs

The University of Maine System Board of Trustees adjusts costs annually. For the 2015–16 academic year, tuition is estimated at $279 per credit hour for undergraduate state residents and $888 per credit hour for nonresident students. The average credit load for full-time students is 15 credit hours per semester or 30 credit hours for the academic year. Canadian and nonresident students who qualify for the New England Regional Program will pay an estimated $419 per credit hour. Required university fees (about $2,240 per year for a full-time student) include the unified fee, which provides a variety of health-care services and admission to cultural, recreational, and athletic events. Books and supplies average about $1,000 for the academic year. Room and board charges for the academic year are about $9,575. These costs are subject to change.

Financial Aid

UMaine requires all financial aid applicants to file the Free Application for Federal Student Aid (FAFSA). The priority deadline to apply for aid is March 1. Awards usually consist of a combination of several types of aid, ranging from grants and scholarships to work-study jobs and student loans. In addition, students who apply through the early action admissions program (complete application submitted by December 15) will be considered for UMaine merit scholarships based on high school achievement, as demonstrated by high school rank, grade point average, and standardized test results (SAT and ACT).

Faculty

There's a common misconception that if students choose a university rather than a small college, they'll get lost in the shuffle. They'll never see a professor—only teaching assistants—until they're in grad school. But at the University of Maine, the majority of undergraduate classes are taught by professors, and many of those faculty members go on to become friends and mentors to their students. UMaine's professors are known for having an open-door policy. Students have opportunities to work alongside some of the most renowned scholars and scientists in the world, whether they're talking civil engineering over lunch at the Bear's Den or traversing an Antarctic ice sheet with researchers from UMaine's Climate Change Institute.

Student Government

Student Government, Inc. is the independent, representative body for UMaine's undergraduate students. An elected president, vice president, and vice president of financial affairs direct and coordinate Student Government programs at the University of Maine. Student Government works closely with the Office of the Vice President for Student Affairs and appoints 200 student representatives to various university committees involved with the planning and implementation of residence hall programs, student discipline, athletics, and cultural activities on campus.

Admission Requirements

Admission to the University of Maine is a selective process. Successful applicants are those whose scholastic achievement, intellectual curiosity, and established study habits promise success in a comprehensive university environment. Strength of the high school curriculum, grades received, class rank, counselor recommendation, and either SAT or ACT scores are the primary criteria for admission. Essays and information regarding school and community activities provide additional information that may help the admissions committee evaluate potential for success.

UMaine recognizes advanced work completed in secondary schools by means of Advanced Placement tests and honors classes. In addition, students who demonstrate advanced knowledge may be exempted from certain courses and requirements if they pass examinations specially developed by the university's academic departments.

Application and Information

Applicants may submit electronic or paper versions of the Common Application or the University of Maine System application. Additional required documents for all applicants include official high school transcripts and counselor recommendations. Traditional-age applicants are required to submit scores from either the SAT or ACT.

The University of Maine has an early action deadline of December 15. Students whose complete applications are postmarked by December 15 are reviewed by the end of January. Early action candidates are given first consideration for the Honors College and merit scholarships awarded by the Admissions Office.

All other applicants are encouraged to submit their applications and all supporting documents by February 1 and are notified by rolling admission.

Students applying for the spring semester are encouraged to submit applications by December 1. Applications after these dates are processed on a space-available basis. Applications and all supporting documents should be sent to UMS Processing, P.O. Box 412, Bangor, Maine 04402-0412.

For additional information, students should contact:

Office of Admissions
5713 Chadbourne Hall
University of Maine
Orono, Maine 04469-5713
Phone: 207-581-1561
877-486-2364 (toll-free)
Fax: 207-581-1213
E-mail: umaineadmissions@maine.edu
Website: go.umaine.edu
facebook.com/UMaineAdmissions
twitter.com/GoUMaine

The Mall is the heart of the University of Maine campus.

COLLEGE CLOSE-UPS

UNIVERSITY OF MAINE AT MACHIAS

MACHIAS, MAINE

★ To read more about this school, visit http://petersons.to/universityofmaineatmachias

The University

Located on the pristine Bold Coast of Maine, the University of Maine at Machias (UMM) is New England's only public environmental liberal arts college. The college was incorporated in 1909 and is a member of the University of Maine system. Small classes (the average is 16 students), hands-on learning opportunities, and a faculty-student ratio of 1:13 contribute to an academic atmosphere that is intimate and intense and where independent thinking is encouraged.

As Maine's Coastal University, UMM places an emphasis on the environment, distinctive programs, and a location that attracts students from the New England, mid-Atlantic, Midwest, and Southern regions of the country.

Location

Machias, Maine, is a classic New England town located on the tidal Machias River, with a town center that includes a number of retail stores, restaurants (including fast food), a supermarket, a natural foods store, and churches of various denominations. The greater Machias–area population is 5,000. The region is a popular outdoor recreation destination with ocean beaches, inland lakes and streams, and miles of mountains, forests, and trails.

Downeast Maine has been a source of inspiration for generations for artists, outdoor enthusiasts, mariners, and environmentalists. UMM's coastal location provides a unique learning environment, with excellent opportunities for fieldwork, hands-on learning, and cooperative education that prepares students for future careers.

Majors and Degrees

UMM awards Bachelor of Arts and Bachelor of Science degrees in biology (concentrations in fisheries biology; wildlife biology; and pre-professional preparation in dentistry, medicine, optometry, pharmacy, and veterinary medicine); business and entrepreneurial studies (concentrations in accounting, business sustainability, management, and sport and fitness management); college studies (self-designed program option); education (elementary education, environmental literacy education, secondary education, and special education); English, creative writing, and book arts (concentrations in book arts, creative writing, and literary studies); environmental recreation and tourism management (areas of specialization in conservation law, leisure programming, recreation and natural resources, and sport and fitness management); environmental studies; interdisciplinary fine arts (concentrations in book arts, creative writing, music, and visual arts); interdisciplinary studies; marine biology; and psychology and community studies (disabilities in youth concentration).

Academic Programs

Bachelor's degree candidates must complete at least 120 credit hours with a minimum cumulative grade point average of 2.0 and must also complete the core requirements in business studies, fine arts, humanities, physical education, science/mathematics, and social sciences.

Academic Facilities

All of the University's academic buildings are of modern construction and include a well-equipped science building with laboratories, a greenhouse, marine science aquariums, and a marine teaching and research laboratory. A Geographic Information Systems Laboratory and Service Center is located in Torrey Hall. Computer labs, some of which are open 24 hours a day, seven days a week for student use, house the latest in technology hardware and software. Located off-campus, UMM has an ongoing partnership with the Downeast Institute for Applied Marine Research and Education, where students conduct shellfish and finfish research.

Merrill Library provides a 24-hour study center with computer workstations for students, houses a collection of more than 100,000 volumes, and is linked to other libraries and educational resources throughout the state. A computer center with cross-campus networking and multiple computer labs enhances all of UMM's programs and provides access to the Internet and the web. Individual computer access is also available in every residence hall room. The University of Maine at Machias Student Support Center provides faculty, peer, and professional assistance as well as computer and audiovisual aids for all students. A residence facility with contemporary suites and single rooms was completed in 2003.

The Reynolds Athletic Center includes a large gymnasium, an aquatics center with a competition-size pool, a state-of-the-art fitness center, racquetball/handball courts, and a recreational equipment center, in which students may check out canoes, kayaks, snowshoes, cross-country skis, bicycles, and camping equipment. The Flaherty Early Care and Education Center provides child-care facilities for the community and the University; it also provides an on-campus site for UMM elementary teacher education students to participate in field studies.

A wide variety of student activities, from meetings to coffeehouses and other social events, are accommodated in the Student Center. Located in the same building, the campus radio station, WUMM, is run entirely by students. The Performing Arts Center, a 358-seat amphitheater auditorium, is host to numerous campus and community meetings, seminars, festivals, and performing arts and theatrical presentations.

Costs

The basic expenses for the 2014–15 academic year (based on a 15-credit-hour load per semester) were $6,660 per year for in-state tuition and $18,480 per year for out-of-state tuition. The University of Maine at Machias participates in the New England Board of Higher Education Regional Student (NEBHE) program, which allows reduced tuition ($9,990 per year) for students from the other New England states who are enrolled in specific academic programs.

Financial Aid

The University of Maine at Machias offers scholarships, loans, grants, and work-study funds. Merit scholarships are awarded at the time of acceptance based on academic merit. Eligibility for all other financial aid is determined by receipt of the Free Application for Federal Student Aid (FAFSA). Students meeting federal eligibility requirements are encouraged to apply for federal student aid regardless of income status. UMM uses the FAFSA to determine eligibility for University need-based grants. Funds from this program may be available to students whose EFC is too high to receive federal funds, but only if the FAFSA is filed. March 1 is UMM's priority funding deadline.

Faculty

Nearly all University of Maine at Machias faculty members hold the highest degree in their professional field. The faculty-student ratio is 1:13. All faculty members work as advisers and mentors to students within their areas of academic expertise. Faculty members know students on a first-name basis and develop a close relationship with them during their years of study at UMM and beyond.

Student Organizations

UMM students are engaged in many student organizations including Student Senate, Residence Hall Association, Science Club, and eight fraternities and sororities. Student Senate and Residence Hall Association members serve as advocates for students, propose changes to institutional policies, and provide programs and events.

Admission Requirements

Graduation from secondary school or a high school equivalency diploma is the basic requirement for admission. Applicants to the University should have followed a college-preparatory high school program with 4 years of English, 3 years of math, 3 lab sciences, 2 social sciences, a foreign language, and computer utilization. If a student is entering one of the business programs, consideration is given to business courses taken in high school. However, college-preparatory English, math, science, and social science courses are still necessary. Scores from the SAT or ACT are not required for admission. Applicants should rank in the top half of their high school class and have an overall grade average of B or better.

The University of Maine at Machias does not discriminate on the basis of race, creed, color, sex, sexual orientation, gender orientation, or national origin and is an Equal Opportunity/Affirmative Action Employer.

Application and Information

The University of Maine at Machias operates on a rolling admission system. Candidates should complete their applications as early as possible. Students may apply for early admission, through which they may be admitted directly into the University after completing three years of secondary school. Candidates for this program must have recommendations of support from their guidance counselor, principal, superintendent, and/or school board. Their high school grades should place them in the top 15 percent of their class. UMM accepts applications from transfer students. Transfer applicants should complete their applications by August 1 for the fall term or by January 1 for the spring term.

Application materials and additional information may be obtained by contacting:

UMM Admissions
University of Maine at Machias
116 O'Brien Avenue
Machias, Maine 04654
Phone: 207-255-1318
888-468-6866 (toll-free)
Fax: 207-255-1363
E-mail: ummadmissions@maine.edu
Website: machias.edu

Students at the University of Maine at Machias engaged in experiential learning on the coast of Maine.

COLLEGE CLOSE-UPS

UNIVERSITY OF MASSACHUSETTS BOSTON

BOSTON, MASSACHUSETTS

★ To read more about this school, visit http://petersons.to/umassboston

UMASS BOSTON

The University

The University of Massachusetts Boston (UMass Boston) has provided access to superior public education at a modest cost in the state's capital city of Boston since 1964. With more than 16,000 commuting students in its undergraduate, graduate, and Advancing and Professional Studies programs, UMass Boston is the second-largest campus in the University of Massachusetts system, and comprises a community of scholars who take pride in academic excellence, diversity, research, and service. The school's academic research and scholarship are tightly woven into the public and community service needs of Boston and modern metropolitan life.

UMass Boston's students represent an extraordinary range of economic, political, spiritual, and ethnic backgrounds, talents, and interests. Many come straight from high school. Others transfer from two- and four-year colleges. And while most come from within the Commonwealth of Massachusetts, many grew up in other states and countries.

UMass Boston has a vibrant student life. No matter what a student's social and intellectual interests, he or she can find engaging activities. From student government to student literary endeavors; from a champion chess team to working with inner-city youth; from academically affiliated clubs and athletic opportunities to a unique course-credit-based leadership development program, students are sure to find the right activities to complement their own classroom experiences.

The University's student body shares a strong motivation to succeed academically and to relate their classroom pursuits to career aspirations. The University Advising Center helps by providing comprehensive academic support, planning, and career advising services. A team of professional counselors provides personalized assistance for students to design their course of study, utilize tutorial and mentoring services, choose a major and career path, and develop interviewing, resume-writing, and job-search skills.

Location

From its peninsula on Boston Harbor, the University overlooks Dorchester Bay and the harbor islands. It shares the peninsula with the John F. Kennedy Presidential Library and Museum, the Massachusetts State Archives and Commonwealth Museum, and the new Edward M. Kennedy Institute for the Study of the United States Senate.

Just half a mile off Interstate Route 93, the campus and its stunning water vistas are easily accessed by both public transportation and automobile. The Office of Undergraduate Admissions provides a number of free parking spaces for day visitors. A free shuttle bus runs every few minutes between the Massachusetts Bay Transit Authority's (MBTA) JFK/UMass Red Line "T" stop and the front door of the school's Campus Center. Student MBTA discount passes are available for frequent users. Another free shuttle provides a regular transportation loop for those using the campus's auxiliary parking lot at the nearby Bayside Center.

Many students commute from home, while others utilize the Office of Student Housing for help finding a rental property and/or roommates. The University wants all its students to be at home at UMass Boston.

Boston itself, with its worldwide standing as a cultural center and well-earned reputation as a premier American college town, offers UMass Boston students a wealth of resources for academics, exploration, and entertainment. Everything, from Fenway Park and TD Garden to Symphony Hall and the Museum of Fine Arts, is easily accessible from UMass Boston.

Majors and Degrees

Five undergraduate colleges award bachelor's degrees: the College of Liberal Arts (with twenty-six majors and eighteen minors and programs of study), the College of Science and Mathematics (with ten majors, sixteen minors and programs of study, and three certificate programs), the College of Management (with two majors and eleven concentrations), the College of Nursing and Health Sciences (with a B.S.N., an online RN-to-B.S.N., and an accelerated B.S.N. program, as well as the B.S. program in exercise and health sciences), and the College of Public and Community Service (with one major and two certificate programs). In addition, the College of Advancing and Professional Studies offers a major in global affairs and community development, and the College of Education and Human Development offers both licensure and non-licensure bachelor's degree options in early education and care in inclusive settings (EECIS), as well as a program of study for those interested in earning teacher licensure during their undergraduate years. Also offered are premed and prelaw programs, programs for honors study, credit by examination, and advanced placement.

A joint arts or science bachelor's/master's degree program in business is available for high academic achievers, as is a bachelor's degree in liberal arts or science with a minor in management.

Academic Programs

The academic calendar runs from early September through the end of May. There is also an optional, month-long winter session in January, and summer school sessions are available beginning in May, June, and July. Matriculating students may choose to attend full- or part-time and may adjust their schedules from semester to semester. A minimum of 30 credits must be earned at UMass Boston as a residency requirement for graduation.

The College of Liberal Arts and the College of Science and Mathematics each require 120 credits to graduate. The general education curriculum comprises three elements: the distribution requirement, the core curriculum requirement, and the writing requirement. In addition, requirements of the major must be fulfilled. Both colleges offer an individual major option.

In the College of Management, the 120-credit undergraduate program leads to a B.S. degree in management or information technology. By fulfilling the general education, management, and elective course work requirements, students build a liberal arts foundation and receive the theoretical, technical, and functional training needed to succeed in the business world.

The College of Advancing and Professional Studies offers a 120-credit B.A. program in global affairs and community development, comprising a 33-credit major added to a world culture, world language, and diversity-based general education core plus electives.

The College of Nursing and Health Sciences' traditional B.S. program in nursing requires 123 credits for graduation, including general education courses and 63 credits of intensive study in the principles and practices of nursing. The exercise and health sciences B.S. program prepares students for the technical aspects of a professional discipline and gives them a solid foundation in the liberal arts.

The College of Public and Community Service (CPCS) offers a B.A. program in human services. Students may draw upon a variety of supplemental learning options in pursuit of their degree, including classroom study, self-directed study, and project-based learning.

The College of Education and Human Development (CEHD) offers both licensure and non-licensure B.A. programs in early childhood education and care in inclusive settings.

UMass Boston has also established the Honors College for curious, ambitious, reflective, and independent-minded students. The intensive academic offerings, outstanding honors faculty, individual advising, honors seminars, and all other honors benefits are open to first-year and transfer students of any major in any of the other colleges, based on an individual assessment of qualifications.

Off-Campus Programs

The National Student Exchange Program offers UMass Boston students the opportunity to study at one of more than seventy participating colleges and universities in forty states at a cost comparable to the cost of attending UMass Boston. The school's study-abroad program is available for students with a 3.0 GPA or better who seek international travel and academic experiences, and it offers summer and winter session programs in other countries as well. UMass Boston participates in the New England Regional Student Program and the Boston Five-College Exchange Program.

Cooperative education and internship programs place students in work assignments related directly to their fields of study so that they may apply what they learn in the classroom to practical work settings. Under the co-op program, students are placed in full-time, paid positions for six-month work periods. In the internship program, students are placed on a part-time basis, usually 15 to 20 hours per week, during a semester or over the summer months. Some are paid internships; others are volunteer opportunities. Both co-op and internship placements combine relevant practical learning, valuable work experience, career awareness, resume enhancement, personal and professional growth and, in many instances, opportunities for academic credit, good pay, and a permanent job after graduation.

Academic Facilities

The Joseph P. Healey Library (http://www.umb.edu/library) holds a collection of more than 600,000 print volumes, over 500,000 electronic journals and newspapers, more than 500,000 electronic books, 127 databases, and over 60,000 academic videos, DVDs, and films related to the campus's academic programs and degrees. The library's electronic resources are available on and off campus, 24/7 using a library bar code. UMass Boston is an active member of the Boston Library Consortium, the Fenway Libraries Online, Massachusetts Commonwealth Consortium of Libraries in Public Higher Education Institutions (MCCLPHEI), and is also a partner in nationwide resource-sharing networks with over 30 million volumes available locally, and many more nationwide, via point-and-click. Students may obtain a library consortium card to check out books from any of the consortia libraries.

The Information Technology Services Division (ITSD) provides seven-day-a-week access to general-use computer labs, including the Adaptive Computing Lab and Graduate Research Center, all located within the Healey Library Information Commons, which also houses the IT Service Desk. All classrooms are equipped with technology to enhance teaching and learning, and auditoria are equipped with state-of-the-art audiovisual equipment and lecture capture services. ITSD provides wireless access in most public spaces, ensuring that a wide variety of information technology and data communications resources is available to students. Students have access to Office365 (MS office suite including Outlook for e-mail) on laptops and tablets, as well as software applications such as SPSS, MatLab, Mathematica, STATA, etc. via the virtual computer lab.

The John F. Kennedy Presidential Library is linked to the University by a variety of educational programs, enabling students to conduct research utilizing the extensive resources of that library's archives. Next door, the Archives of the Commonwealth of Massachusetts are also a rich informational depository, covering more than 5½ centuries of Massachusetts history. The new Edward M. Kennedy Institute for the Study of the United States Senate provides further academic research opportunities.

The Campus Center provides easy access to student services, dining services, and spectacular meeting spaces, along with computer terminals and wireless Internet access. The new Integrated Sciences Complex has been designed to provide enhanced academic opportunities for scientific study, research, and development for UMass Boston students and faculty. And a new academic building—housing additional classroom, office, meeting, dining, conference and performance spaces, and providing room for further program and study growth—opens in 2015.

Costs

Tuition and fees for the spring 2015 semester were $5,983 for Massachusetts residents studying full-time (12 or more credits) or $14,195 for out-of-state students. Students enrolling part-time were charged tuition according to the number of credits taken, with Massachusetts residents paying tuition at $71.50 per credit and out-of-state residents paying $406.50 per credit. Annual mandatory fees for in-state residents ranged up to $10,252 and up to $18,632 for out-of-state students.

Financial Aid

Financial aid is based on need and/or merit. Applicants must complete the Free Application for Federal Student Aid (FAFSA), keeping in mind a priority deadline of March 1 for the fall semester and November 1 for the spring semester. Need-based aid is awarded to students who demonstrate financial need as determined by federal methodology. Aid may consist of grants, waivers, and merit scholarships, as well as self-help in the form of loans and work-study employment. An on-time applicant is automatically considered for all financial assistance options administered by UMass Boston.

Faculty

UMass Boston is proud of its 1,219 distinguished faculty members, some 93 percent of whom have terminal degrees in their field. UMass Boston has a student-faculty ratio of about 16:1 and a small class size averaging but 28 students. The faculty's top priority is teaching and advising students, although they also conduct research, publish materials, and participate in grant activities and professional organizations. Faculty members maintain office hours for students and make themselves accessible as mentors. Faculty and academic issues are governed by the Faculty Council.

Student Government

The undergraduate Student Senate consists of elected members from the undergraduate colleges and programs, and it participates fully in matters related to the quality of student life and the allocation of the student activities trust fund. Students are represented on numerous University- and college-based committees and councils that initiate major policy and procedural recommendations, forwarding those recommendations to governance bodies and the administration for enactment.

Admission Requirements

A freshman candidate for admission to the University should have earned a minimum of 16 academic units in high school that include 4 years of English, 4 years of mathematics, 3 years of science (including 2 with laboratory requirements), 2 years of social science (including 1 of U.S. history), 2 years of a single foreign language, and 2 years of electives in the arts or computer science (excluding vocational training). The student must also present satisfactory scores on either the SAT or ACT. The University looks for students with a strong academic background, as determined by a recalculated grade point average, and each candidate's academic program choices, motivation, achievement, and annual progress are closely scrutinized.

UMass Boston encourages qualified international students to apply for admission. Submission of a separate Declaration of Finances (DCF) form is required, along with supporting documents. Test of English as a Foreign Language (TOEFL) scores are required of all students educated in a non-English-language educational system.

Transfer students are considered based on a review of all college academic credentials. Several academic majors and programs have specific higher requirements for transfer students, but, in general, a minimum 2.5 GPA is required.

Participation in a campus tour and group information session with an admissions counselor (offered twice daily, Monday through Friday, by the Office of Undergraduate Admissions) is strongly encouraged.

Application and Information

For information about the application process, deadlines, and informational materials, students should explore www.umb.edu/admissions or contact

Office of Undergraduate Admissions
University of Massachusetts Boston
100 Morrissey Boulevard
Boston, Massachusetts 02125-3393
Phone: 617-287-6000
617-287-6010 (TTY/TDD)
Fax: 617-287-5999
E-mail: enrollment.info@umb.edu
Website: http://www.umb.edu
http://on.fb.me/UMassBoston (Facebook)
http://twitter.com/umassboston (Twitter)

UMass Boston is situated on a scenic peninsula just south of downtown Boston.

COLLEGE CLOSE-UPS

UNIVERSITY OF MASSACHUSETTS DARTMOUTH

DARTMOUTH, MASSACHUSETTS

UMass | Dartmouth

The University

The University of Massachusetts Dartmouth is a premier research institution that offers excellent, personalized undergraduate education in 83 fields of study, and more than two dozen graduate and doctoral degrees in an array of areas. The campus culture promotes student success by integrating theoretical knowledge with practical experiences to catalyze intellectual, social, and personal development, as well as economic progress within the region and around the globe.

UMass Dartmouth traces its roots to 1895 when the Massachusetts legislature chartered the New Bedford Textile School and the Bradford Durfee Textile School in Fall River. Today, there are five colleges and three graduate schools under the egis of UMass Dartmouth: College of Arts & Sciences with a School of Education, Charlton College of Business, College of Engineering, College of Nursing, College of Visual and Performing Arts, the School for Marine Science and Technology, and the UMass Law School. The faculty members pride themselves on their high level of research productivity that complements their personal commitment to teaching students.

There is a strong culture of community service, and the University is ranked in the top 3 percent on the President's Higher Education Community Service Honor Roll—one of 16 finalists for community service, with distinction in economic development and interfaith initiatives. It also was awarded the Community Engagement Classification from the Carnegie Foundation for the Advancement of Teaching for its commitment to service, donating more than 200,000 hours of service each year. UMass Dartmouth has consistently ranked on *U.S. News & World Report*'s list of the best colleges in the northern region of the United States; the entire University of Massachusetts system has a world ranking on the *Times* of London's prestigious "World University Rankings" list.

UMass Dartmouth enrolls approximately 7,500 undergraduates and 1,500 graduate students; and 60 percent of undergraduates reside on campus. While 88 percent are from Massachusetts, there is a growing number from other states and countries outside the United States. The residential campus offers a 110 different student organizations, 23 Division III athletic programs, and numerous cultural opportunities and activities. UMass Dartmouth fosters personal development, diversity, and responsible citizenship.

Location

Located in an historic and scenic southeastern Massachusetts coastal community, the campus is situated on 710 acres, with easy access to Boston, Providence, Fall River, New Bedford, and Cape Cod. Nearby shopping, entertainment, restaurants, museums, and theaters make this a vibrant hub. Recreational sites are minutes away, including beaches and hiking. Students who want other options can drive to New York City in 4 hours, and the mountains of New Hampshire and Vermont in 3–4 hours. Public transportation is available from campus to nearby communities and Boston.

Majors and Degrees

The five colleges within the University offer 83 fields of undergraduate study in the liberal arts and sciences, business, engineering, technology, nursing, art history, and various art forms including graphic design and music. One of the newest undergraduate offerings is an interdisciplinary data science degree.

In addition, honors programs, interdisciplinary studies, prelaw, premedical advising, and a number of different minors and options are available. The University offers Bachelor of Arts, Bachelor of Fine Arts, and Bachelor of Science degrees at the undergraduate level. A 3+3 program in conjunction with the UMass School of Law allows qualified students to complete 3 undergraduate years and then move on to law school. At the end of the first year of law school, they earn their undergraduate degree.

A complete list of undergraduate academic programs is available at www.umassd.edu/undergraduate/fieldsofstudy.

Academic Programs

The University Studies curriculum provides students in each of the colleges with a breadth of study that is the hallmark of a liberal education. Students study both the natural and social sciences, gain a broad worldview, enhance their analytical and communication skills, and learn how to integrate these varied fields.

Internships and undergraduate research opportunities are an important part of the educational experience at UMass Dartmouth as they prepare students to enter their careers or graduate school. Internships are available through the colleges and the office of Career Development. Undergraduate research opportunities are offered throughout the academic year and in the summer.

Other learning opportunities include independent study, contract learning, directed study, as well as credit by examination. UMass Dartmouth students can cross-register at six other local education institutions, including Stonehill and Wheaton College. They can take advantage of study-abroad agreements with partner institutions in a number of countries including Australia, Belgium, China, Egypt, England, France, Germany, Ireland, Italy, and Spain, to name a few. UMass has its own program in Lisbon, Portugal, making it extremely cost-efficient for students to study abroad. Students may also take the initiative to find other programs.

The University operates on a two-semester calendar, with the fall semester beginning the first week of September and concluding in mid-December and the spring semester beginning in late January and concluding in mid-May. A three-week intersession is offered between semesters. Summer-term courses are offered in May, June, July, and early August. Undergraduate students usually enroll in four or five courses each semester, and a typical course earns 3 credits. An undergraduate degree requires a minimum of 120 credits (there are a few majors that require more credits); a student can complete degree requirements for a specified major within a department or an approved interdepartmental major (30 credits).

Academic Facilities

Ground is being broken in 2015 for the new Charlton Learning Pavilion, a state-of-the-art addition to the Charlton College of Business. In addition, UMass Dartmouth is in the planning stage for a new $55-million academic building, with construction expected to start in 2016. Students are already benefitting from a campus-wide $175-million building and renovation program that has upgraded and improved academic facilities. A $45-million renovation to the library created a state-of-the-art, energy-efficient space that serves as both the intellectual and social heart of campus. The University library houses banks of computers, group-study spaces, and hundreds of thousands of publications and periodicals. A large interlibrary loan network and delivery system makes millions of volumes available to the students. A coffee shop in the lobby provides students the necessary fuel for classes and study sessions.

The Star Store arts campus in historic downtown New Bedford offers outstanding studio and gallery space for undergraduate and graduate art students. Important collaboration space on campus includes the Innovation, Design, Engineering, and Art Studio (IDEA Studio)—a digital, multimedia workspace for engineering and art students—and the Center for Scientific Computing and Visualization Research, where the data capabilities stretch the imagination.

Access to technology is an integral part of the curriculum. The campus is wireless, and computing clusters, located in the library and in most classroom buildings, support the classwork of students. Multiple computer labs (Apple and PC) are readily available throughout campus. Each of the five colleges within the University has facilities designed for its specific purposes with classrooms, laboratories, study spaces, galleries, faculty offices, and lounges.

Costs

In-state tuition and fees for 2014–15 were $11,681; non-Massachusetts resident tuition and fees were $24,619. Room and board expenses were $11,435 (based on a 19-meal plan and a double room for a year). Books and supplies cost approximately $1,200 a year depending on a student's courses. Specific fees may be assessed, depending on a student's course of study. UMass Dartmouth offers an Ocean State Proximity Program with discounted tuition and fees for all Rhode Island residents, and there are discounted tuition and fee rates for specific academic programs for students from other New England states as well.

Financial Aid

Nearly all students are eligible for some type of financial aid. UMass Dartmouth awards financial aid based on federal, state, and institutional guidelines; students must submit the Free Application for Federal Student Aid (FAFSA). In determining need, the Financial Aid Services Office considers the total costs of attending the University (tuition, fees, books, room and board, the cost of commuting, and an allowance for living and personal expenses). The difference between total University cost and the estimate of expected family contribution is the amount that the financial aid staff considers to be financial need. In 2014–15, UMass Dartmouth financial aid awarded 90 percent of a student's demonstrated need. Students are encouraged to submit their FAFSA by March 1 for priority consideration in the awarding process. More information about UMass Dartmouth financial aid and scholarships is available online at www.umassd.edu/financialaid.

Faculty

The faculty, numbering 376 full-time members, is distributed over 41 departments in five colleges and three graduate schools. Eighty-five percent of the faculty members hold the terminal degree in their chosen discipline (e.g., business, fine arts, education). The average class size at UMass Dartmouth is 27 students. Faculty members are actively engaged in advising students, providing guidance throughout a student's academic career.

Student Government

The Student Senate is the governing body offering a forum for debate on matters of importance to the student body. The Student Judiciary, a system of courts or judicial agencies, provides students and organizations with the protection of due process in all disciplinary matters. A student is also elected to the University of Massachusetts Board of Trustees. Students serve on the Board of Governors, policy makers for the Campus Center; the Resident Hall Congress; and the Student Activities Board. Students are active, voting participants on policymaking committees that regulate both academic and social aspects of the University.

Admission Requirements

Admission is selective. Applicants are evaluated both by the general standards of the University and by the special standards of the academic areas that they request. In addition, the Board of Higher Education sets guidelines governing admission standards for the University. Admission to some colleges or majors may be limited by spaces available. Students can apply either Early Action (November 15 deadline) or Regular Decision (March 1 priority deadline). Qualified Early Action candidates are notified by mid-December and qualified Regular Decision candidates are accepted on a rolling basis until the capacity has been reached in the program of choice. Each applicant's record is assessed on the basis of the depth and rigor of the secondary school program, rank in class and grade point average, SAT or ACT results, college-level records for transfer applicants, and other appropriate measures.

The University realizes its commitment to equal access through standard, as well as alternative admission programs. For College Now and START (for students interested in engineering, computer science, math, or physics), UMASS Dartmouth's alternative admission programs, Massachusetts applicants must meet at least one of two eligibility criteria: low-income status or first generation in the family to attend college.

All applicants for freshman admission to the University are required to submit an application form with the $60 application fee, a transcript of the secondary school record, SAT or ACT results, a letter of recommendation, an essay, and any other information that candidates consider important for the admissions committee to review. Transfer students, who compose approximately one quarter of the new student population every year, are required to submit records for all college-level work completed in addition to the application form. Additional information is required if the transfer student has completed fewer than 24 credits. The admission process is virtually the same for transfer candidates, with primary emphasis on the student's previous college/university record. UMass Dartmouth participates in the Mass Transfer program for students from Massachusetts who are transferring from a public two-year institution, as well as several joint admission partnerships with regional two-year colleges. More information can be found online at www.umassd.edu/transfer.

Application and Information

Students are invited to visit the University for a campus tour and an information session with an admissions officer. Some majors, such as nursing, may close early due to enrollment capacity. Nursing applicants are encouraged to apply by February 1 for priority consideration. UMass Dartmouth practices rolling admission with its Regular Decision candidates, and most decisions are made within four weeks of the completion of an application. Application forms and related information is available at www.umassd.edu/apply.

For more information, contact:

Office of Admissions
UMass Dartmouth
285 Old Westport Road
Dartmouth, Massachusetts 02747-2300
Phone: 508-999-8605
Fax: 508-999-8755
E-mail: admissions@umassd.edu
Website: www.umassd.edu/admissions

The dramatic UMass Dartmouth campus is the work of renowned architect Paul Rudolph, former dean of the Yale University School of Art and Architecture.

UNIVERSITY OF MASSACHUSETTS LOWELL

LOWELL, MASSACHUSETTS

★ To read more about this school, visit http://petersons.to/umasslowell

UMASS LOWELL

The University

The University of Massachusetts Lowell (UMass Lowell) is a doctoral-level public research university ranked in the top tier of *U.S. News & World Report's* national universities. Founded in 1894, the university is built on a tradition of innovation and entrepreneurship. Extensive partnerships with industry and community advance research, provide public service, and enrich the student experience. UMass Lowell graduates are ready to contribute meaningfully in the workplace, build lives around the principles and passions they develop in college, and make a difference in the world.

The university is part of the University of Massachusetts system and comprises the Francis College of Engineering; the College of Fine Arts, Humanities and Social Sciences (includes the School of Criminology and Justice Studies); the College of Health Sciences (includes the School of Nursing); the College of Sciences; the Graduate School of Education; the Manning School of Business; and the Honors College. Together, the colleges offer more than 100 bachelor's, 39 master's and 33 doctoral degrees, and dozens of certificate programs. All programs are accredited at the highest levels and incorporate vigorous hands-on learning and personalized attention. Students in all undergraduate disciplines who participate in the Honors College and complete its program requirements graduate with a Commonwealth Honors designation on their degrees.

UMass Lowell maintains a student-faculty ratio of 18:1 and focuses on putting the lessons of the classroom into practice in real-world settings through co-ops, internships, service learning, and research. A growing number of interdisciplinary programs, such as the biomedical engineering and technology minor offered jointly by the colleges of Engineering, Sciences, and Health Sciences, reflect emerging fields in the global economy. Dozens of accelerated bachelor's-to-master's programs allow students to earn two degrees in as few as five years. All academic programs are accredited and meet the most rigorous board standards in higher education.

Approximately 50 percent of undergraduate classes have fewer than 20 students. All first-year students belong to academic learning communities. Optional Living-Learning Communities in the residence halls include: honors, art, music, women in science and engineering, pre-med, business innovation, health professions, DifferenceMakers, criminal justice, creative arts, and veterans. The Centers for Learning offers tutoring and academic support programs. The Career Services and Cooperative Education Center helps students prepare for the transition to the working world. The DifferenceMaker program encourages student teams to address real-world problems through entrepreneurial action and sponsors the annual $25,000 Idea Challenge pitch contest.

The campus community is ethnically, culturally, and economically diverse with a female-to-male ratio of approximately 40:60. Students come from 30 states and 50 countries. Twenty-nine percent of undergraduates identify as students of color. Approximately 40 percent of each incoming class is transfer students. The majority of freshmen choose to live in university housing, which includes traditional residence halls, apartments, suites, and a former downtown hotel. Housing is guaranteed for freshmen and available to most returning and transfer students who want it. More than 200 active student organizations including a gaming group, dance and sport clubs, leadership societies, and a student-run FM radio station. The campus features over a dozen eateries, including Sal's Pizza, Starbucks, Subway, Red Mango, and traditional dining halls. The vibrant campus life includes supporting 18 Division I athletics teams, which compete in the America East and Hockey East conferences. The Campus Recreation Center runs intramural sports, fitness classes, and an outdoor adventure program. The 7,800-seat Tsongas Center at UMass Lowell is a popular venue for national acts and hosts the university's men's hockey team.

Location

The university is clustered along the Merrimack River in Lowell, a city of 110,000 that has gained national attention by successfully leveraging its history, ethnic diversity, and entrepreneurial spirit to create a vital urban center. The site of a unique, urban National Historical Park, Lowell is also home to an acclaimed professional theater company, literary, and folk festivals, and numerous restaurants and museums. Lowell is located 25 miles from Boston and Cambridge and within the region's major business corridors, which provide internship and co-op opportunities for students. It is also within easy reach of major outdoor recreational areas via major highways and regional train and bus service.

Majors and Degrees

Dual majors are permitted. Dual B.A./B.S. degrees and bachelor's-to-master's degree programs (indicated with an asterisk in the lists below) are available in all fields. Pre-medical, pre-law and other pre-professional advising is available to interested students in all majors. Many of the majors offered have additional program options available, as noted in parentheses below.

The College of Fine Arts, Humanities and Social Sciences offers baccalaureate programs in: American studies; criminal justice and criminology* (corrections, homeland security, information technology, police, violence), economics*, English (creative writing, journalism and professional writing, literature, theatre arts), fine arts (animation, painting, printmaking, sculpture, photography, graphic design, web design, interactive media), history, legal studies, liberal arts (art history, Asian studies, comparative arts, cultural studies, economics, education, English/literature, environment and society, environmental studies, gender studies, history, languages, legal studies, music, philosophy, political science, psychology, sociology, theatre arts, writing), modern languages (French, Spanish, French/Spanish, Italian/Spanish), music business, music performance (instrumental, vocal), music studies (instrumental, vocal), peace and conflict studies*, philosophy (communication and critical thinking), political science, psychology*, sociology, and sound recording technology*.

The College of Sciences offers baccalaureate programs in: biology* (bioinformatics, biotechnology, ecology), chemistry (cheminformatics, forensics), computer science* (bioinformatics/cheminformatics), environmental science (atmospheric science [meteorology], environmental studies, geoscience), mathematics* (applied computational mathematics, bioinformatics, business applications, computer science, probability and statistics, teaching), and physics* (general, optics, radiological health).

The James B. Francis College of Engineering offers baccalaureate programs in: chemical engineering* (biological engineering, computer-aided process design and controls, engineered materials, nanomaterials engineering, nuclear engineering, paper engineering), civil and environmental engineering*, electrical and computer engineering*, mechanical engineering*, and plastics engineering*. Engineering programs are accredited by the Accreditation Board for Engineering and Technology, Inc.

The College of Health Sciences and School of Nursing offer baccalaureate programs in: clinical laboratory and nutritional sciences (clinical laboratory sciences, clinical science, medical laboratory science, nutritional science), community health and sustainability (community health, environmental health), exercise physiology, nursing, and public health. A B.S. degree-completion program for RNs is offered through the Division of Online and Continuing Education. Accreditation is by the National Accrediting Agency for Clinical Laboratory Sciences and the National League for Nursing Accrediting Commission.

The Manning School of Business offers baccalaureate programs in: business administration* (accounting, corporate finance, entrepreneurship, financial markets, general finance, international business, management, management information systems, marketing, and supply chain/operations management). A one-year M.B.A. is available as a bachelor's-to-master's program. All programs are accredited by the Association to Advance Collegiate Schools of Business (AACSB) International.

The university's Graduate School of Education offers widely respected master's and doctoral programs as well as a range of initial certification courses. Undergraduates in STEM majors who are considering teaching can get classroom experience and a teaching minor through UTeach, a national teacher-training program whose only Northeast chapter is at UMass Lowell. Bachelor's-to-master's programs with initial Massachusetts teacher licensure are also available through the Fast Track to Teaching program.

The Division of Online and Continuing Education offers a wide range of programs that are delivered online and on campus in the evening.

Intercollegiate programs in aerospace studies, robotics, and joint military studies are available.

Academic Programs

The university calendar includes two semesters, a three-week intersession in January, and a summer term with two sessions. Full-time undergraduates generally take five courses each semester. A minimum of 120 credits is required for baccalaureate degrees; the minimum credits required for professional degree programs are generally higher. A general education requirement is imposed for all baccalaureate programs. Majors require 30 to 60 credits. Elective course options vary widely by major. Professional degree program options and requirements follow specific accreditation guidelines. Maximum curricular freedom is permitted in B.A. programs. Qualified students in all majors are invited to join the Honors College. The academic climate is serious and competitive and requires self-motivation.

Off-Campus Programs

Extensive opportunities for study abroad with credit include faculty-led courses, affiliate programs, exchanges, and more than 120 partnerships with prestigious institutions in 40 countries. Recent faculty-led courses include seminars on health care in Peru; business in China; crime, law, and asset protection in Hong Kong and Macau; and innovation and entrepreneurship in India. Professional co-ops, internships, and service-learning also take place off campus.

Academic Facilities

The campus is in the midst of a bold expansion. Ten new facilities have opened in the last five years, including the Mark and Elisia Saab Emerging Technologies and Innovation Center, the Health and Social Sciences Building (criminal justice and criminology, psychology and nursing), two suite-style residence halls, and two parking garages. A new writing center, a television studio, and a 14,500-square-foot anatomy and physiology lab opened in January 2014. University Crossing, the hub of student services and activities, opened in summer 2014 and connects the university's three campuses to the downtown business and cultural district. Construction is underway for a new building to house the Manning School of Business. Both libraries feature new learning commons with areas for quiet and group study as well as Starbucks cafés. Other academic facilities include six sound recording technology studios.

Costs

The annual costs for 2014–15 for full-time undergraduate residents of Massachusetts were $12,447 per year; for nonresidents of Massachusetts, they were $27,400 per year. Room and board charges were $11,278 per year. Accident insurance is covered by fees; health insurance that meets the comparable benefits established by the state of Massachusetts is required. Books and supplies are estimated at $400 to $600, depending on program. Quoted rates are subject to change.

Financial Aid

The university is committed to making higher education accessible to all qualified students. The university participates in federal and state programs, assisting students through grants-in-aid, loans, employment opportunities, and scholarships. The amount of a financial aid award is determined by need, as indicated by the Free Application for Federal Student Aid (FAFSA), which should be filed by March 1. The university awards a growing number of merit-based scholarships. More than $139 million in financial aid was awarded to students in the 2012–13 academic year, meeting approximately 92 percent of need.

Faculty

Faculty members are respected researchers who value their commitment to teaching and extend the learning experience beyond the classroom. The full-time faculty members number 541. The part-time day faculty members number approximately 462. Ninety-two percent of faculty members hold a Ph.D. or the terminal degree in their field. Most undergraduate courses are taught by faculty members. Graduate teaching assistants also hold part-time instructional positions, particularly as discussion section leaders and laboratory teaching assistants.

Student Government

The Student Government Association and the Residence Hall Association provide opportunities in student government at the all-campus level. Leadership opportunities are provided in residence halls and student organizations. Students also participate in the disciplinary system and in most university committees.

Admission Requirements

All undergraduate day applicants must have a high school or a general equivalency diploma and satisfactory SAT scores. Admissions standards vary by program. Last year's incoming freshmen had an average GPA of 3.44 and SAT scores of 1150 (reading and math).

Transfer students are considered for fall or spring semester admissions. Transcripts of completed work must be on file prior to acceptance. Depending on the number of transfer credits and college GPA, transfer students who seek admission as matriculating day students may be asked to provide a high school record and SAT scores.

Special-entrance programs that provide nontraditional admissions pathways for international students are available.

Application and Information

The university admits students through early action, regular admission, and transfer admission. Entering freshmen are admitted for the fall or spring semesters. The early action deadline for freshmen is November 15; the regular admission deadline is February 15. Applicants to the School of Nursing are encouraged to apply by the early action deadline. The preferred deadline for transfer applications is August 15 for the fall and January 7 for the spring. The Common Application or the UMass Lowell application is accepted; both require an essay and a letter of recommendation and are available online at www.uml.edu/apply.

For application forms and further information, students should contact:

Office of Undergraduate Admissions
University of Massachusetts Lowell
University Crossing, Suite 420
200 Pawtucket Street
Lowell, Massachusetts 01854-2874
Phone: 978-934-3931
Website: http://www.uml.edu
http://www.facebook.com/umlowell
http://www.twitter.com/umasslowell
http://www.youtube.com/user/umasslowell
http://instagram.com/umasslowell

University Crossing is the hub of student services and activities and connects the university's three campuses to the downtown business and cultural district.
UMass Lowell photo by Jim Higgins

The University of Massachusetts Lowell is an Equal Opportunity/Affirmative Action, Title IX employer.

UNIVERSITY OF MEMPHIS
MEMPHIS, TENNESSEE

The University

Located on a beautifully landscaped campus in the heart of one of the South's largest and most progressive cities, the University of Memphis (U of M) is the flagship institution of the Tennessee Board of Regents System. Since its beginning in 1912, the University has matured into a major public, metropolitan university recognized regionally and nationally for its academic, research, and athletic programs. The U of M offers more than 250 areas of study from which to choose.

The University campus comprises 1,654 acres at nine sites, including the Lambuth Campus in Jackson, Tennessee. In addition to the main campus, the Park Avenue campus contains spacious living accommodations for married students, a research park, and outstanding varsity athletic training facilities. U of M also owns the Meeman Biological Field Station, a 623-acre tract used for biological and ecological studies.

The University of Memphis is an Equal Opportunity/Affirmative Action institution committed to the education of a diverse student body. It has a total enrollment of 21,059 students, including 17,068 undergraduates from almost every state and many other countries. Approximately 44 percent of University of Memphis students are under the age of 22, and members of minority groups account for 49 percent of the enrollment.

Location

The greater Memphis area has a population of approximately 1.3 million, which makes the city the twentieth largest in the country. Centrally located on the Mississippi River, Memphis is an active hub for business, agriculture, and the transportation industry. The city has the Mid-South's largest medical center and offers many cultural and entertainment opportunities. Major museum exhibits, sporting events, concerts, art shows, lectures, and even barbecue contests take place throughout the year. The AAA baseball team, the Redbirds, and the NBA team, the Grizzlies, both make their homes in Memphis. With its many businesses, industries, and schools, Memphis provides students with employment opportunities in a variety of fields during and after their college careers.

Majors and Degrees

The College of Arts and Sciences offers undergraduate majors organized into three concentration groups: the humanities, the natural and mathematical sciences, and the social sciences. Three degree programs are offered: the Bachelor of Arts, the Bachelor of Science, and the Bachelor of Science in Chemistry. Majors include African and African-American studies, anthropology, biology, chemistry, computer science, criminology and criminal justice, earth sciences, economics, English, foreign languages and literatures, history, international studies, mathematical sciences, philosophy, physics, political science, psychology, social work, and sociology. Minors are available in each of those areas, as well as interdisciplinary minors in aerospace studies, Asian studies, emergency management, environmental studies, Judaic studies, legal thought and liberal arts, military science, naval science, pre–health studies, public and nonprofit administration, religious studies, and women's and gender studies.

The Fogelman College of Business and Economics (FCBE), an AACSB accredited institution, comprises six departments (School of Accountancy; Economics; Finance, Insurance, and Real Estate; Management Information Systems; Management; and Marketing and Supply Chain Management) and academic programs at all levels—undergraduate, master's, and Ph.D. The Fogelman College differentiates itself by providing a unique Complete Professional Program that holistically prepares students with the tools to achieve both personal and professional excellence. Through the Avron B. Fogelman Professional Development Center, FCBE provides training on ethics, healthy living habits, business etiquette, resume building, professionalism, philanthropic activities, and more.

The College of Communication and Fine Arts is made up of the Departments of Architecture, Art, Communication, Journalism, Theatre and Dance, and the Rudi E. Scheidt School of Music. Majors include architecture, art, art history, communication, interior design, journalism, music, music industry, and theater. The college offers three undergraduate degrees: the Bachelor of Arts, the Bachelor of Fine Arts, and the Bachelor of Music.

The founding program of the University of Memphis, the College of Education, Health, and Human Sciences (CEHHS) dates back to 1912 when West Tennessee State Normal School opened its doors. Today fifty-seven degree programs prepare students for varied career paths offered through the four departments within CEHHS. The college is home to fourteen research centers and institutes that are as diverse in their focus as the partnerships faculty and departments have built with the dynamic communities it serves. The College also is home to the Barbara K. Lipman Early Childhood School and Research Institute and the Campus School.

The Herff College of Engineering offers undergraduate degrees in biomedical, civil, computer, electrical, and mechanical engineering and engineering technology. High-ability students have the opportunity to work alongside faculty members on world-class research and participate in a paid Cooperative Education/Internship Program for global companies such as FedEx; for governmental organizations such as the U.S. Army Corps of Engineers; or for premier biomedical firms such as Medtronic, Smith & Nephew, and Wright Medical Technology. In addition, Herff offers a Living Learning Community dedicated to giving students a unique, inclusive residential learning experience that connects classroom learning to residential life.

The University College offers two nontraditional degrees, the Bachelor of Liberal Studies and the Bachelor of Professional Studies, for students with experience, talents, and interests served through personally designed or multidisciplinary programs. Through its experiential learning credit program, the college allows previously earned college credit or credit-worthy experiences to count toward a diploma, providing an affordable way to accelerate one's education and earning potential.

The University of Memphis also offers specialized degree programs. The Loewenberg School of Nursing offers a Bachelor of Science in Nursing degree. The program is accredited by the Commission on Collegiate Nursing Education (CCNE) and is a member of the American Association of Colleges of Nursing, National League for Nursing, and Southern Council for Collegiate Education in Nursing. Students benefit from exceptional learning opportunities at healthcare agencies in the Memphis area, including ten major hospitals.

Preprofessional training is offered for students who intend to enter law school or a college of dentistry, medicine, nursing, optometry, pharmacy, physical therapy, or veterinary medicine. The University also offers Air Force, Army, and Navy ROTC programs.

The University of Memphis has joined forty-six Tennessee Board of Regents institutions in offering Regents Online Degree Programs. The U of M offers four degree programs: the Bachelor of Liberal Studies in interdisciplinary studies, the Bachelor of Professional Studies in information technology, the Bachelor of Professional Studies in organizational leadership, and the Bachelor of Professional Studies in international organizational leadership. These degree programs are entirely online and are transferable among the participating institutions.

Academic Programs

Freshmen who have not declared a major are advised through the Academic Counseling Center in preparation for formal enrollment in one of the degree-granting colleges. Those freshmen who have chosen a major are assigned to their degree-granting college immediately for academic advising. Each student initially selects courses from the General Education Program, which offers classes ensuring the acquisition of breadth as well as depth of knowledge in various fields. In addition to meeting the requirements of the General Education Program, all students must meet the requirements for their specific degree. The Helen Hardin Honors Program, designed for academically ambitious and talented students, is the largest in the state. There is also an active Emerging Leaders program.

The academic year begins in late August and is divided into two semesters and a summer session. The fall semester ends in mid-December, and the spring semester begins in mid-January. Courses are also offered during shorter sessions within the semesters.

Off-Campus Programs

Students at the University of Memphis have the opportunity to participate in study-abroad programs and the National Student Exchange program. These programs allow students to study in more than fifty other countries as well as in other locations within the continental United States. The University also offers credit and noncredit courses at various locations throughout west Tennessee.

Academic Facilities

The University Libraries of the University of Memphis comprise the Ned R. McWherter Library and four branch libraries: Communications Sciences, Mathematics, Music, and the Lambuth Campus in Jackson, Tennessee. The University Libraries' collections include 1.3 million bound volumes, 10.2 million manuscripts, 109,017 electronic books, 3.78 million microfilms and microfiches, 635,640 government documents, 16,079 CDs, 1,984 DVDs, and additional holdings in other formats. Patrons also have access to more than 150 electronic indexes/full-text resources. The libraries also serve the general public and maintain a strong user-instruction program. The Learning Commons extends throughout the McWherter Library, with a Commons Room on the first floor where the Research and Information Services desk is located. The McWherter Library has wireless capabilities supporting the 168 public-use computers that give users access to all University-provided software applications. Laptop computers are available for loan to students. The University Libraries house the Regional Federal Depository Library for the State of Tennessee and receive all publications, maps, and electronic data distributed by the U.S. Government Printing Office. The Libraries' Preservation and Special Collections Department has holdings on the history and culture of the South, the lower Mississippi River Valley, the Mid-South, Tennessee, the Civil War, and African-American history, including the Civil Rights Movement.

The Department of Theatre and Dance and the Rudi E. Scheidt School of Music, in their adjoining facilities, make an appreciable contribution to campus activities with live drama and concert series, films, and programming over WUMR, the student-staffed campus radio station. Included among the many research facilities at the University of Memphis are the Benjamin L. Hooks Institute for Social Change, the Integrated Microscopy Center, the FedEx Center for Supply Chain Management, the Institute for Artificial Intelligence, the Ground Water Institute, and the Barbara K. Lipman Early Childhood School and Research Institute.

The state of Tennessee has designated five Centers of Excellence at the University: the Center for Applied Psychological Research, the Center for Research Initiatives and Strategies for the Communicatively Impaired, the Center for Research in Educational Policy, the Institute of Egyptian Art and Archaeology, and the Center for Earthquake Research and Information.

Costs

In 2014–15, for both fall and spring terms, in-state students paid a maintenance fee of $294 per hour for part-time study until they reached 12 hours ($3,528), when the maintenance fee was lowered to $59 per hour for additional hours over 12. Out-of-state students paid a maintenance fee of $907 per hour for part-time study until they reached 12 hours ($10,884), when the maintenance fee rate was reduced to $182 per hour for additional hours over 12. All part-time students paid an additional program service fee of $82.50 per hour for part-time study until they reached 6 hours, when the program service fee was highest at $628. On-campus residence hall rates ranged from $3,690 to $6,640 for an academic year.

Financial Aid/Scholarships

Financial assistance is provided through four basic sources: scholarships, grants, loans, and employment. Scholarships are offered through the Scholarship Office as well as through various academic, performance, and athletic departments. These include scholarships for Emerging Leaders and First Scholars. Residents of Tennessee may be eligible for the state's HOPE Scholarship. An application for admission is required to be considered for general and distinguished academic scholarship programs. Applicants for financial aid must submit the completed Free Application for Federal Student Aid (FAFSA) to the Financial Aid Office, which places the student under consideration for all financial aid programs. The priority deadline for filing the FAFSA is March 1. More than $200 million is awarded annually. The University operates two programs of student employment: the Federal Work-Study Program and a regular work program.

Faculty

The University of Memphis has 896 full-time faculty members. In addition, many adjunct professors are hired from the community to teach in their fields of expertise.

Student Government

The Student Government Association consists of officers, a senate, a cabinet, and a judiciary elected annually by the student body. Its goals are to present the opinions of the student body to the administration, to enact legislation beneficial to the students, and to promote a broad range of student activities.

Admission Requirements

The admission of entering freshmen is based on the transcript of a four-year course of study at an approved or accredited high school that includes prescribed units of English, mathematics, natural/physical sciences, U.S. history, social studies, foreign language, and visual/performing arts. The General Educational Development test and high school equivalency diploma are accepted when applicable. The admissions process is a competitive one and is based on a student's cumulative high school grade point average and ACT or SAT scores. The average ACT for the fall 2013 freshman class was 22.69, and the average GPA was 3.37. The admission of transfer students is based on the applicant's grade point average, academic standing at a former institution, and scores on any required admission tests. Transfer students may be required to provide a high school transcript, depending upon the total of their transfer credit hours.

Application and Information

Inquiries about admission and requests for information about any undergraduate college of the University should be addressed to the Office of Admissions/Recruitment and New Student Services. While the established application deadlines are July 1 for the fall semester, December 1 for the spring semester, and May 1 for the summer session, early application is strongly encouraged so applicants can be considered for scholarship opportunities and take advantage of early registration. A student must apply and be accepted by December 1 to receive priority consideration for academic merit scholarships. Additional scholarships may have earlier deadlines. Prospective students are encouraged to visit the University for a campus tour, which can be scheduled at http://www.memphis.edu/admissions/visitcampus.php or by contacting the Office of Admissions/Recruitment and New Student Services.

For more information, contact:

Office of Admissions/Recruitment and New Student Services
University of Memphis
101 John Wilder Tower
Memphis, Tennessee 38152-3520
Phone: 901-678-2169
800-669-2678 (toll-free)
Website: http://www.memphis.edu
http://on.fb.me/UofMemphis (Facebook)
http://www.twitter.com/uofmemphis

COLLEGE CLOSE-UPS

UNIVERSITY OF NEW ENGLAND

BIDDEFORD AND PORTLAND, MAINE AND TAGNIER, MOROCCO

UNE UNIVERSITY OF NEW ENGLAND

★ To read more about this school, visit http://petersons.to/une

COLLEGE CLOSE-UPS

The University

The University of New England (UNE) is an innovative health sciences university grounded in the liberal arts, with two distinctive coastal Maine campuses and a third campus in Tangier, Morocco. UNE has internationally recognized scholars in the sciences, health, medicine, and humanities; offers more than forty undergraduate, graduate, and professional degree programs; and is home to Maine's only medical school and the only college of dental medicine in Northern New England. The University fosters critical inquiry through a student-centered academic environment rich in research, scholarship, creative activity, and service while providing opportunities for acquiring and applying knowledge in select clinical, professional, and community settings.

UNE's student body of 6,429 includes 2,749 undergraduates, 1,477 doctor's degree–professional practice students, and 2,203 graduate students. UNE's total twelve-month student enrollment for the 2013–14 academic year was 9,679, which included all degree- and non–degree-seeking, full-and part-time, and online students. There were 5,468 undergraduate students; 3,002 graduate students; and 1,209 professional students. Students enroll in a wide variety of academic programs in UNE's six colleges: the College of Arts and Sciences, the College of Dental Medicine, the College of Osteopathic Medicine, the College of Pharmacy, the Westbrook College of Health Professions, and the online College of Graduate and Professional Studies. At the undergraduate level students represent thirty-five different states and several other countries in over forty undergraduate degree programs.

The University of New England's philosophy of education and student life places emphasis on the quality of instruction and the practical application of academic material. Each program includes the opportunity for learning in a community-based setting. Internships, co-ops, clinicals, and student teaching provide the practical experiences that allow students at UNE to apply the skills learned in the classroom to real job situations.

UNE traces its history to 1831 with the founding of Westbrook College, one of Maine's oldest institutions of learning. Today's University represents a union of three unique higher education institutions through the combining of St. Francis College and the New England College of Osteopathic Medicine in 1978 and Westbrook College in 1996.

UNE's Student Academic Success Center provides a wide range of services to assist with student health, academic support, educational and career planning, and equal opportunities during their academic experience. The Office of Career Services provides academic and career exploration assistance, assistance in applying to graduate schools, self-assessment and personal interest exploration.

The University offers a variety of cultural and social events and encourages students to become involved in activities, clubs, and sports. Popular interests include scuba diving, skiing, hiking, biking, varsity and intramural sports, swimming, surfing, music, theater, and community service programs. Opportunities for such activities are available at on-campus facilities such as the Harold Alfond Forum, a 106,000-square-foot facility featuring an ice hockey rink, basketball court, classroom and lab space, fitness center, and multipurpose courts.

The UNE Department of Athletics operates an NCAA Division III varsity athletics program. Varsity sports for men are basketball, cross-country, golf, ice hockey, lacrosse, and soccer. Varsity sports for women are basketball, cross-country, field hockey, ice hockey, lacrosse, soccer, softball, swimming, and volleyball.

Location

The University of New England currently has three campuses. The oceanside Biddeford Campus is located on a beautiful site in Biddeford, Maine, where the Saco River flows into the Atlantic Ocean. With more than 4,000 feet of water frontage, enjoying the ocean comes naturally to students. The 540-acre Biddeford Campus is home to the College of Arts and Sciences, the College of Osteopathic Medicine, the Harold Alfond Center for Health Sciences, and the Marine Science Center.

Twenty miles to the north is UNE's Portland Campus, a 41-acre quintessential historic New England campus in Portland, Maine. The campus is home to the Westbrook College of Health Professions, the College of Pharmacy, the College of Dental Medicine, and the College of Graduate and Professional Studies. The UNE Art Gallery, the Maine Women Writers Collection, the Oral Health Center, and the Dental Hygiene Clinic are also on the Portland Campus.

Students at both Maine campuses enjoy the vibrant social life offered in Portland, a city regularly recognized as one of the nation's most livable small cities, and the dynamic outdoor recreational activities that have made Maine a prime tourist destination. Southern Maine is conveniently serviced by a number of airlines at the Portland International Jetport as well as by bus and train.

UNE opened its third campus in Tangier, Morocco in 2014. At no additional cost, UNE students may choose to spend a semester or a year at UNE's Tangier Campus learning about the culture and languages while taking their college courses in English.

Majors and Degrees

UNE offers highly competitive undergraduate and graduate programs in a variety of areas. On the undergraduate level, the University confers Bachelor of Arts and Bachelor of Science degrees. Qualified undergraduate students also have the opportunity to move directly into a master's level or doctoral program through the Graduate Pathways to Success (GPS) program.

Bachelor's degrees are offered in animal behavior, applied exercise science, applied mathematics, applied social and cultural studies, aquaculture and aquarium science, art and design media, art education, athletic training, biochemistry, biological sciences, business, chemistry, communications, dental hygiene, elementary education, English, environmental science, environmental studies, health, wellness and occupational studies, history, laboratory science, liberal studies (including pre-law), marine sciences, medical biology (pre-dental, pre-medicine, pre-optometry, pre–physician assistant studies, and pre–veterinary science), neuroscience, nursing, ocean studies and marine affairs, political science, pre-pharmacy, pre–physical therapy, psychology, public health, secondary education, sociology, and sport and recreation management.

Master's degrees are offered in biological sciences, education, marine sciences, medical education leadership, nurse anesthesia, occupational therapy, physician assistant studies, public health, and social work.

Doctoral degrees offered include dental medicine (D.M.D.), education leadership (Ed.D.), osteopathic medicine (D.O.), pharmacy (Pharm.D.), and physical therapy (D.P.T.).

Academic Programs

UNE's academic programs ensure that students have plenty of opportunities for extensive fieldwork, clinical experiences, research, internships, and global experiences at both the undergraduate and graduate levels. All undergraduate programs at UNE have a core curriculum that provides a foundation in the liberal arts. The core reflects the values of each college and is designed to prepare students for living informed, thoughtful, and active lives in a complex and changing society.

Off-Campus Programs

UNE is committed to supplementing the traditional learning process with practical applications. All students are encouraged to participate in cooperative education programs, field placements, and practicums. These experiences provide valuable learning situations and increase a student's exposure to job-related opportunities, and they are required for graduation by most majors. Students also have the opportunity to arrange a study-abroad experience.

Academic Facilities

On UNE's Biddeford Campus, classroom and office spaces are housed in several facilities across campus. The Department of Creative and Fine Arts offers a dedicated building that provides faculty offices and studio space for drawing, painting, printmaking, sculpting, and photography. Several research facilities are on campus, including the Marine Science Center; the Harold Alfond Center for Health Sciences, with biology and chemistry labs as well as lecture halls, classrooms, a gross anatomy lab, and UNE's medical school facilities; the Pickus Center for Biomedical Research; and the Peter and Cécile Morgane Hall, a science center providing additional classrooms and an undergraduate teaching laboratory.

On the University's Portland Campus, Ludcke Auditorium is used for a variety of academic programs. Coleman Dental Hygiene Building houses classroom, clinic, and faculty space. The Blewett Science Center, home to UNE's nursing program, consists of science labs, classrooms, and the Clinical Simulation Program (CSP), which provides customized training and education for students and health professionals. Proctor Hall is also a classroom building and is home to the Proctor Learning and Career Center. The Josephine S. Abplanalp Library houses study space and a computer lab, as well as the Maine Women Writers Collection. The College of Pharmacy is a LEED-certified academic and research facility with teaching and research laboratories and a lecture hall. The College of Dental Medicine has its administration offices in historic Goddard Hall and its clinical home, the Oral Health Center, is a teaching clinic and simulation facility.

Costs

The costs for undergraduate students per academic year for 2014–15 were: tuition, $32,880; room and board, $12,670; and fees, $1,200.

Financial Aid

In 2013–14, approximately 98 percent of all full-time students received some form of financial assistance. The average package was $26,000 including scholarships, grants, loans, and employment. The University of New England has an extensive academic scholarship program. Merit awards range from $3,000 to $18,000 per year.

Faculty

The personal attention students receive from faculty both in and out of class, and the quality of faculty as experts in their fields are key strengths of the UNE experience. Students appreciate their faculty members as mentors, and trust them as accomplished scholars who impact their fields. From designing coastal trails and restoring wetlands on campus to caring for patients in need at the Biddeford Free Clinic, UNE faculty members not only work side-by-side with their students, but are recognized by their peers and other leaders for their expertise. UNE faculty members are national award recipients, Fulbright scholars, authors, and world-class researchers, and they share their knowledge unselfishly with their students.

Admission Requirements

Students applying for admission should submit a completed application, a $40 nonrefundable application fee, transcripts of all academic work (high school and college), and scores on either the ACT or SAT. Students who do not use English as their primary language must submit TOEFL scores. Students applying for admission should have completed a curriculum that includes English, mathematics, science, and social sciences. International students must also complete the International Student Supplemental Application. All prospective students are strongly encouraged to visit the campuses of the University of New England for an information session and tour. Information sessions and tours are held daily Monday through Friday; Saturday tours are also available. Prospective students can register for a tour at www.une.edu/admissions/undergrad/visit-une.

Application and Information

The undergraduate freshman admission application deadline is February 15; applications received after that date are reviewed on a space-available basis. There is a nonbinding December 1 early action application deadline with a December 31 notification date. Applications for the spring term are accepted through December 1.

For application information, students should contact:

University of New England
Office of Undergraduate Admissions
11 Hills Beach Road
Biddeford, Maine 04005
Phone: 207-602-2847
800-477-4863 (toll-free)
Fax: 207-602-5900
E-mail: admissions@une.edu
Website: www.une.edu

With 4,000 feet of water frontage on UNE's Biddeford Campus, students' education and college experiences are enriched both inside and outside the classroom.

COLLEGE CLOSE-UPS

UNIVERSITY OF NEW HAMPSHIRE

DURHAM, NEW HAMPSHIRE

University of New Hampshire

The University

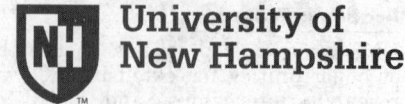

The University of New Hampshire (UNH) is a top-100 national public research university that draws students from nearly every state and 85 countries. The University has a sizeable undergraduate population of approximately 12,800 but still feels cozy and intimate. This is due in part to a campus layout that is manageable and beautiful—with college greens, water, and a pleasing mix of classic and modern buildings that gradually give way to 2,600 acres of woods, fields, and farms. It is also due to the school's traditions of strong student-faculty interaction and active student culture. As one student put it, "It's easy to meet people and get involved in campus activities here. You need to have some initiative, but student leaders, residence hall staff, and others also seek you out."

UNH is largely residential and offers students a variety of housing options, including halls of 100 to 600 students and two on-campus apartment complexes. Themed housing, such as honors, first-year experience, or international, is offered by dorm or floor. Ninety-one percent of freshmen and approximately half of undergraduate students live on campus. Others commute from home or from off-campus housing nearby. UNH's award-wining dining is available at three main dining halls, including Holloway Commons (HOCO), a spectacular dining and conference facility with seating for 850 and an after-hours café. HOCO will undergo an expansion during the summer of 2015.

The Memorial Union Building (MUB) is the University's community center. Housed in the MUB are two movie theaters, the UNH Bookstore, the Ticket Office, lounge/study space for both nontraditional and graduate students, and Granite Square Station, the undergraduate mail center. Computing and Information Services provides a computer cluster and a help desk with walk-in service. The MUB Food Court offers expanded dining options, and food service is also available in the Coffee Office. The Student Senate Office, Office of Multicultural Student Affairs, WUNH-radio, *The New Hampshire* student newspaper, and more than 200 other student organizations are based in the MUB.

Students at the University participate in a rich cultural life. Numerous lectures, films, concerts, exhibitions, meet-the-artist receptions, master classes, dance performances, and theatrical productions are offered throughout the year. The UNH Celebrity Series, the Art Gallery, and the Departments of Music, Theater and Dance, and Art and Art History bring artists of international stature to campus. Most events are free for students.

Many opportunities for athletics and recreation, regardless of skill or ability, are offered through Campus Recreation. The Hamel Student Recreation Center, available to all full-time matriculating students, offers two multipurpose courts, a group exercise studio, a club/martial art studio, an 8,000-square-foot fitness center with more than 100 exercise stations, three basketball/volleyball courts, an indoor track, a climbing wall, a lounge, several classrooms, locker rooms, towel and lock service at the equipment room, and saunas. An expansion to the Rec Center, including a complete renovation of UNH's distinctive outdoor pool, is slated for completion in 2016. Campus Recreation offers a variety of activities designed to help students reach personal fitness goals and have fun, including Zumba, cycling, cardio kickboxing, Pilates, yoga, tai chi, a climbing wall, racquetball, personal training, and massage therapy. Noncredit courses are also offered, including CPR and first aid. The intramural sports program consists of more than twenty different sports and activities offered to men's, women's, and co-ed teams that reflect the diverse interests of campus community members. Some clubs are intensely competitive, requiring a daily commitment to workouts and conditioning and compete either on an intercollegiate basis with New England teams or sponsor University tournaments. Other clubs meet on a casual come-when-you-can basis. In addition, Campus Recreation offers ice skating, manages a large outdoor recreation facility with its own sailing and canoe center, runs a children's camp (Camp Wildcat) in the summer, and supports men's and women's sport club rowing. UNH also has twenty different men's and women's Division I sports teams, including football, which is Division I-FCS.

Location

Nestled in New Hampshire's seacoast region, Durham is close to the Atlantic coast and several charming working-port cities. With a nonstudent population of 8,000, Durham is a classic college town that caters to the student clientele. Durham's Main Street includes restaurants, coffeehouses, a bookstore, pizza shops, and other student hangouts. Popular road trips for students include Boston (about an hour), Portsmouth (about 20 minutes), and the White Mountains (about an hour). There is an Amtrak stop on campus (Downeaster Line) with service between Portland, Maine, and Boston. UNH Wildcat Transit eco-buses run frequently on campus and to nearby towns and shopping areas.

Majors and Degrees

The University of New Hampshire comprises seven colleges and schools: College of Liberal Arts, College of Engineering and Physical Sciences, College of Health and Human Services, College of Life Sciences and Agriculture, Paul College of Business and Economics, Thompson School of Applied Science (which offers two-year associate degree programs), and the University of New Hampshire at Manchester, the University's urban campus. The University offers more than 100 majors through these fully accredited academic divisions. UNH enjoys a strong reputation in a wide range of academic fields, with biology, business administration, English, communication, engineering, environmental studies, history, hospitality management, kinesiology, marine and animal sciences, performing arts, political science, and psychology among those topping the list. The business school offers several options under the business administration major that include accounting, entrepreneurial venture creation, information systems, international business and economics, management, and a student-designed track. UNH Manchester recently launched the region's first on-campus, bachelor's degree program in data analytics, one of just a handful of such programs in the country.

Academic Programs

The Discovery Program, which encompasses the University's general education requirements, provides students with a broad foundation in the liberal arts and an introduction to the methods of inquiry needed for academic success. All students must complete ten courses which include writing skills; quantitative reasoning; biological and physical sciences; historical perspectives; world cultures; fine and performing arts; social science; humanities; and environment, technology, and society. A senior year capstone experience as well as inquiry courses allow students to reflect on their education and synthesize knowledge and skills gained from the Discovery Program. Depending on their academic program, students may begin course work in their major as early as their first year.

A major research university, UNH produces graduates who have had meaningful research experiences with a world-class faculty. Programs such as the Undergraduate Research Opportunities Program and International Research Opportunities Program provide research grants each year for undergraduates to work closely with faculty members, on campus or abroad, on original projects. Over 1,300 students typically participate in the UNH Undergraduate Research Conference on campus each year. The Office of Fellowships helps students identify and apply for national research fellowships, and the Center for International Education helps students participate in more than 500 programs for study or research abroad. As New Hampshire's major public institution, the University is involved in a wide range of outreach programs with state and industry groups. These partnerships provide abundant opportunities for students interested in internships.

Academic Facilities

The new Peter T. Paul College of Business and Economics building, completed in 2013, features a soaring lobby with study areas and a café, flexible classrooms with the latest instructional technologies, small breakout rooms, and an innovative lab for rapid prototyping. Parsons Hall, a chemistry teaching and research facility, underwent a $50-million renovation in 2009.

The Dimond Library, the state's only public university research library, offers three grand reading rooms, seating for 1,200 students, and state-of-the-art technology, including wireless and Internet. The Parker Adaptive Technology Room provides an array of technological options for patrons who have learning, mobility, or vision disabilities. Through ResNet, students who live on-campus have high-speed Internet access to UNH library resources, class software and information, e-mail, and other services. The Environmental Technology Building is a multidisciplinary science and engineering research facility with a focus on environmental technology development. Most of the University's cultural events take place in the Paul Creative Arts Center, which houses two theaters, dressing rooms, a well-equipped scene shop, a costume shop, a green room, storage facilities, classrooms, and the faculty and staff offices. New Hampshire Hall contains the Newman Dance Studio and a smaller stage studio. Hamilton Smith Hall, the iconic home of UNH's English Department and other complementary programs, will undergo a complete renovation beginning in 2015.

Costs

The 2014–15 tuition and fees for undergraduate in-state students were $16,553. For out-of-state students, tuition and fees were $29,532. Room (double) and board (unlimited meal plan) cost $10,360.

Financial Aid

Approximately 65 percent of students receive some form of need-based financial assistance from UNH. University merit scholarships ranging from $1,000 to $10,000 are awarded automatically (no additional application required) to qualified first-year applicants. Amounts are subject to change. Other scholarships are awarded by individual academic departments. The average financial aid package, including gift, loan, and employment assistance, was $13,252 for New Hampshire residents and $18,630 for nonresidents. The University participates in the Federal Pell Grant program, the Federal Supplemental Educational Opportunity Grant program, the Federal Perkins Loan program, the Federal Work-Study Program, and the Federal Stafford Student Loan program. Students seeking financial aid are required to submit the Free Application for Federal Student Aid (FAFSA) by March 1.

Faculty

The University of New Hampshire has 610 full-time and 422 part-time faculty members. The student-faculty ratio is 19:1 and 70 percent of classes have fewer students. Undergraduate teaching is a primary focus at UNH, and the vast majority of lecture courses are taught by faculty members. The UNH faculty includes recipients of the Pulitzer Prize, Guggenheim awards, MacArthur Fellowships (genius grants), and many other prestigious awards and honors. The University ranks among the top campuses in the nation in the percentage of faculty members who have won Fulbright scholarships. This research productivity has a powerful effect on students, who can share the experience of discovery.

Student Government

The Student Senate comprises a governing body of student officers and senators. They are the voice of the student body, representing student opinion to members of the faculty, staff, and administration as well as the University community and the state legislature. The Senate believes that all students have the right to participate in University decisions and policy making. Committees of the Senate include areas in academics, residential life, commuters, health and human services, judicial affairs, and community change. They also approve and monitor the rates and uses of all mandatory student fees.

Admission Requirements

Admission to a bachelor's degree program is based upon successful completion of a strong secondary school program of college-preparatory course work. Primary consideration is given to the academic record, as demonstrated by the quality of the candidate's secondary school course selection and achievement. Consideration is also given to the student's recommendation, personal essay, additional information, character, initiative, leadership, special talents, and SAT or ACT with writing component results. Most successful candidates present at least 4 years of English and mathematics and 3 or more years of laboratory science, social science, and foreign language. Recommended mathematics preparation includes the equivalent of algebra I, geometry, algebra II, and trigonometry or advanced math. Students who plan to specialize in health, physical sciences, life sciences, engineering, or mathematics should present at least 4 years of mathematics, including trigonometry as well as laboratory course work in chemistry and/or physics. Students pursuing business-related studies should also have completed 4 years of mathematics.

All candidates for admission to bachelor's degree programs are required to submit SAT or ACT scores with writing component results. SAT Subject Tests are not required. A foreign language SAT Subject Test may satisfy the foreign language requirement of the Bachelor of Arts degree programs. Required scores vary by test. International students whose primary language is not English must submit TOEFL or IELTS results. The recommended minimum TOEFL score is 213 (computer-based) or 550 (paper-based) or 80 (Internet-based). The minimum IELTS score is 6.5.

Candidates applying for programs in the Department of Music must make arrangements with the department chairperson for an audition (603-862-2404).

Application and Information

High school students who seek fall-semester admission may apply anytime after the start of the senior year and before the February 1 regular decision deadline. Admission notifications are provided on a continuous basis through April. Admitted first-year students have until May 1 to confirm their intent to enroll at the University. The review of a candidate's application begins with the receipt of all required materials. The Early Action (EA) Program allows candidates to receive a response by mid-January of their senior year; EA candidates must submit admission applications by November 15. In some cases, the Admission Committee requests senior mid-year grade reports in order to make a final admission decision. All positive admission decisions made prior to the completion of a candidate's course work in progress are considered provisional and are subject to the verification of satisfactory senior-year achievement when final high school transcripts are reviewed.

Office of Admissions
University of New Hampshire
3 Garrison Avenue
Durham, New Hampshire 03824-3501
Phone: 603-862-1360
Fax: 603-862-0077
Website: http://www.unh.edu/admissions
http://www.facebook.com/universityofnewhampshire (Facebook)
http://www.twitter.com/uofnh (Twitter)
http://www.youtube.com/unhvideo (YouTube)
http://www.instagram.com/uofnh (Instagram)

UNH combines the look and feel of a New England liberal arts college with the academic breadth and depth of a major research university.

UNIVERSITY OF NEW HAVEN

WEST HAVEN, CONNECTICUT

★ To read more about this school, visit http://petersons.to/universityofnewhaven

University of New Haven

The University

The University of New Haven's (UNH) mission is to prepare career-ready graduates for meaningful roles in today's global economy and to nurture the pursuit of lifelong learning. Founded in 1920, the University of New Haven is a private, independent institution focused on combining experience-based learning with liberal arts and sciences. UNH is committed to educational innovation, continuous improvement in career and professional education, and support of scholarship and personal development. UNH became a four-year college in 1958. UNH moved to its present location in West Haven in 1960 and has since rapidly expanded its programs, facilities, and faculty, attracting a student body that now stands at over 6,300—including the current enrollment of 4,600 full-time undergraduates.

The University is fully accredited by the New England Association of Schools and Colleges (NEASC). Individual programs, departments, and schools hold various forms of national professional accreditation. Seven of the University of New Haven's bachelor's degree programs—chemical, civil, electrical, system, computer, and mechanical engineering and computer science—are fully accredited by the Engineering Accreditation Commission of the Accreditation Board for Engineering and Technology, Inc. (EAC/ABET).

Despite a broad academic program, UNH is small enough to accommodate individualized educational needs. Programs evolve and adapt to meet changing career interests as well as the requirements of business, industry, and professional fields. Small classes foster close student-faculty relationships. Accelerated weekend and evening programs in business and convenient evening hours provide access for part-time students in engineering, computers, public safety, and the arts and sciences.

The main campus is in West Haven, Connecticut, on a hillside close to Long Island Sound. UNH also operates four satellite branches: the Lyme Academy College of Fine Arts in Old Lyme, Connecticut; the Southeastern Center in New London, Connecticut; a graduate business campus in Orange, Connecticut; and an international campus in Prato, Italy. Main campus administrative and classroom buildings support the University's four academic colleges: the College of Arts and Sciences, the College of Business, the Tagliatela College of Engineering, and the Henry C. Lee College of Criminal Justice and Forensic Sciences. Following the addition of the Graduate School in 1969, New Haven College was designated a university. Thirty master's degree programs attract full- and part-time graduate students, while just over 100 associate and bachelor's degree programs are available to entering freshmen and transfer students in a great variety of academic disciplines.

Other main campus buildings include the Marvin K. Peterson Library, the Henry C. Lee Institute of Forensic Science, Echlin Hall, the Bayer Hall admissions building, the Campus Bookstore, new residence halls and apartments, and Bartels Hall, the campus center, which houses dining facilities and student activities. The Charger Gymnasium and athletic fields are located on the North Campus, just two short blocks from Maxcy Hall, the main administration building. The David A. Beckerman Recreational Center, a state-of-the-art athletic facility for the benefit of all students, opened in fall 2007.

The University of New Haven has one of the most respected and successful NCAA Division II athletics programs in the country, with Charger teams combining to make over 120 post-season tournament appearances. UNH is a member of the Northeast-10 Conference, one of the most prestigious and celebrated conferences in the nation. UNH and its student athletes have won numerous conference, regional, and national awards, both athletically and academically. The University offers sixteen varsity sports: men's baseball, basketball, cross-country, football, soccer, indoor and outdoor track and field; and women's basketball, cross-country, lacrosse, soccer, softball, tennis, indoor and outdoor track and field, and volleyball.

Over 75 percent of the full-time undergraduate day students live on campus in the twelve residence halls. More than 170 clubs and organizations are open to students. Included are student chapters of professional societies, religious organizations, social groups, special-interest clubs, student councils, cultural groups, and fraternities and sororities.

Location

West Haven is contiguous to New Haven. There are theaters that attract star performers from the entertainment world, a deepwater harbor and beaches, fine restaurants, museums, and galleries in the area. Numerous social and cultural programs are presented by the many colleges and universities in the area. New Haven is served by a local airport and major railroads, and its location at the junction of two interstate highways places the University of New Haven within easy driving distance of New York, Boston, Cape Cod, and the ski areas of New England.

Majors and Degrees

The College of Arts and Sciences offers a Bachelor of Arts degree in art, chemistry, communication, English, global studies, graphic design, history, interior design, liberal studies, mathematics, music, music and sound recording, music industry, political science, and psychology; and a Bachelor of Science degree in biology, biotechnology, dental hygiene, environmental science, marine biology, mathematics, music and sound recording, and nutrition and dietetics.

The College of Business offers the Bachelor of Science degree in accounting, business management, economics, finance, hospitality and tourism management, management of sports industries, and marketing. In addition, the College of Business offers a fast-track study program allowing academically strong students the opportunity to earn a Bachelor of Science degree in business and a Master of Business Administration (M.B.A.) in just four years.

The Tagliatela College of Engineering offers a Bachelor of Science degree in chemical engineering, chemistry, civil engineering, computer engineering, computer science, electrical engineering, general engineering, information technology, mechanical engineering, and system engineering.

The Henry C. Lee College of Criminal Justice and Forensic Sciences offers a Bachelor of Science degree in criminal justice, fire protection engineering, fire science, forensic science, legal studies, national security studies, and paramedicine.

The Lyme Academy College of Fine Arts offers a Bachelor of Fine Arts degree in drawing, illustration, painting, and sculpture.

Academic Programs

The University of New Haven offers a broad range of programs in both liberal arts and professional areas. Experiential learning is emphasized, and there are diverse and numerous opportunities for internships, cooperative education, independent study, and industrial projects. Certain types of professional experience

COLLEGE CLOSE-UPS

are required in a number of degree programs. The Center for Learning Resources offers a tutoring service open to all students.

The undergraduate division operates on a 4-1-4 calendar. Credit is given for successful scores on the CLEP, International Baccalaureate, and Advanced Placement examinations. A University honors program provides outstanding study opportunities in most undergraduate disciplines. The residence requirement for all degrees is 30 credit hours.

UNH believes that all students pursuing a bachelor's degree should develop a common set of skills; the University's goal is to prepare all graduates for the complex lives they will lead in a changing world. This can best be done through the University Core Curriculum, which consists of a minimum of 40 credit hours in six basic competencies.

Academic Facilities

The Marvin K. Peterson Library contains more than 400,000 volumes in hard copy and provides access to about 20,000 electronic books and 20,000 e-journals from the library website and Voyager online catalog. Databases are available on a wide variety of subjects, with a focus on business, criminal justice/ forensic science, engineering, and psychology, as well as general arts and sciences. Through interlibrary loan services, the University community has access to the holdings of more than 8,650 libraries.

Communication majors participate in workshops along with studying sound, film, and television production and radio broadcasting techniques in well-equipped radio/television studios and laboratories. The Tagliatela College of Engineering has modern laboratories and equipment to support its programs. The College of Arts and Sciences maintains art studios, state-of-the-art recording studios, music practice rooms, and science, psychology, and language labs. Hands-on instruction and demonstrations are available in kitchen facilities for students in the hospitality and tourism and the nutrition and dietetics programs. Dental hygiene students gain experience in the Dental Hygiene Clinic.

There are more than a dozen computer labs for student use and teaching on campus. One of these is devoted to forensic computing instruction for the Henry C. Lee College of Criminal Justice and Forensic Sciences.

Costs

Estimated full-time undergraduate tuition for the 2015–16 academic year, including all fees, is $35,655; room and board cost $14,730.

Financial Aid

UNH offers a comprehensive financial aid program that includes University resources as well as state, federal, and private-aid programs. Approximately 90 percent of full-time undergraduate students receive some form of assistance. Students receive federal aid through the Federal Pell Grant, Federal Supplemental Educational Opportunity Grant, Federal Work-Study, Federal Perkins Loan, Federal Direct Student Loan, and Federal Direct PLUS loan programs. The University also administers programs sponsored by the state of Connecticut for Connecticut residents attending the University. Some students also qualify for financial aid from other states and from private companies, organizations, and foundations.

Faculty

It is a long-standing University policy that the faculty members teach a mix of undergraduate and graduate courses in order to preserve academic quality at all levels. Faculty members are selected and promoted primarily on the basis of teaching effectiveness, professional qualifications and performance, and contributions to the academic community. No classes are taught by teaching assistants. Some faculty members hold administrative positions and continue to teach. There are over 230 full-time and 400 part-time faculty members, making the student-faculty ratio 16:1. The majority of full-time faculty members (more than 90 percent) hold terminal degrees in their disciplines.

Student Government

The Undergraduate Student Government Association supervises annual expenditures by undergraduate clubs and organizations, directs liaison committees, supports student publications and the student-operated FM radio station, and schedules cultural and social events. Student representatives are elected annually to the University's Board of Governors.

Admission Requirements

To be eligible for admission, one must be a high school graduate or present evidence of equivalent preparation and have submitted all necessary application documents for consideration. The admissions decision is based on an applicant's high school transcript, SAT or ACT results, letter(s) of recommendation, and personal essay. Out-of-state residents are considered for admission on the same basis as in-state residents. The University of New Haven does not discriminate on the basis of age, color, sex, religion, race, sexual orientation, national origin, or disability in admission or treatment of students, administration or distribution of financial aid, or recruitment of employees.

Application and Information

To apply to the University of New Haven, one must submit a completed application via the Common Application (with $50 fee), official records of all academic enrollment, SAT or ACT results, a letter of recommendation (from an academic source), and a personal statement (250–500 words). International students are required to demonstrate proficiency in English and provide documentation of financial support. The University of New Haven is authorized under federal law to enroll nonimmigrant alien students who meet the university's academic and English proficiency standards. Application documents are considered on a rolling admissions basis with the opportunity to apply for early action and early decision.

For more information, contact:

Undergraduate Admissions
University of New Haven
300 Boston Post Road
West Haven, Connecticut 06516
Phone: 203-932-7319
E-mail: admssions@newhaven.edu
Website: http://www.newhaven.edu

Maxcy Hall on the main campus of the University of New Haven.

COLLEGE CLOSE-UPS

THE UNIVERSITY OF NORTH CAROLINA WILMINGTON

WILMINGTON, NORTH CAROLINA

★ To read more about this school, visit http://petersons.to/northcarolinawilmington

The University

The University of North Carolina Wilmington (UNCW), a public, comprehensive university, combines a small-college commitment to excellence in teaching with a research university's opportunities for student involvement in significant faculty scholarship. The University provides a personal learning environment that integrates teaching and mentoring with research and service, and promotes cultural diversity, community engagement, and individual growth and development. The school is named among 2014's Best in the Southeast by The Princeton Review for the eighth consecutive year, and it was one of the top three Best Values in North Carolina according to *Kiplinger's* in 2013. *Forbes'* 2010 list of America's Best College Buys ranks UNCW seventeenth in the nation. UNCW offers sixty majors, thirty-four graduate degree programs, and two doctoral degrees. The University is accredited by the Commission on Colleges of the Southern Association of Colleges and Schools and is one of the seventeen constituent institutions that comprise the public university system in the state of North Carolina.

UNCW enrolls nearly 15,000 students in seventy-three baccalaureate degree concentrations and thirty-six graduate degree programs. Of the 2,100 freshman students, approximately three fourths surveyed said the school was their first choice. Moreover, the University has the fourth-highest freshman SAT (critical reading and math only) average (1190), the fourth-highest freshman retention rate (84.4 percent), and the third-highest six-year graduation rate (70.5 percent) in the UNC system. With an average GPA of 3.9, incoming students have already demonstrated their motivation and ability to succeed in an academic setting.

At UNCW, students as well as faculty and staff members take full advantage of the University's proximity to the coast and its connections to the community. The internationally respected biology and marine biology programs have created promising research and development opportunities in the biotechnology, pharmacology, and mariculture fields. The Watson College of Education works closely with more than 100 area schools and agencies to improve the quality of public schools in the region. The School of Nursing has settled into a new, high-tech building equipped with patient simulation labs that replicate clinic, hospital, and home health care settings. The labs prepare students with extensive training prior to their placement in a wide range of clinical-practice experiences.

Campus life is a vibrant part of the UNCW experience. Students can live in one of twelve residential campus communities, with numerous options among residence halls, suites, and apartment buildings. Students enjoy a variety of cutting-edge cuisines at the University's fifteen dining locations. Students may participate in more than 250 student organizations, including political, academic, professional, sports, service, ethnic, religious, and student media groups. As a member of NCAA Division I, UNCW fields fifteen varsity teams, including men's and women's basketball, cross-country, golf, soccer, swimming and diving, and tennis; women's softball and volleyball; and men's baseball.

Several facilities serve as hubs for the entire campus community. The Fisher Student Center and the Fisher University Union include a two-story bookstore, a 360-seat movie theater, offices for student organizations, student lounges, a large game room, an art exhibition gallery and display spaces, a convenience store, and dining areas. Nearby, Randall Library's technology resource and assistance centers connect students, faculty, and staff to extensive collections of information, both on campus and in the world at large. The Campus Commons features a lake with lighted fountains, a network of sidewalks, a clock tower, and an open-air amphitheater. Monthly exhibitions of paintings, sculptures, and graphic arts are held in a variety of spaces on campus, including Claude Howell Gallery, Randall Library, Cultural Arts Building, Warwick Center, and the Ann Flack Boseman Gallery.

The Department of Campus Recreation offers numerous activities to support students' health and well-being. The University has recently added a new wing to the Student Recreation Center, which has doubled its original size. The facility currently includes multipurpose courts; a group exercise room; climbing wall; an elevated, multilane walking and jogging track; and a large selection of elliptical trainers, stair climbers, treadmills, weight machines, and more. Other facilities include the Gazebo Complex, which features four tennis courts, three basketball courts, two volleyball courts, and a softball field; and a natatorium with an eight-lane swimming pool and an adjacent diving tank.

Location

The campus occupies 660 acres in the southeastern part of North Carolina, midway between the Cape Fear River and the Atlantic Ocean. The city of Wilmington is situated on the east bank of the Cape Fear River, about 15 miles from Carolina Beach and 5 miles from Wrightsville Beach. Several main highways lead into the city, and a nearby airport (ILM) provides easy access from the city to other destinations.

Wilmington combines historical beauty and modern convenience. Visitors can visit many art galleries, museums, and historical landmarks; enjoy an evening of theater, music, and nightlife; or visit the city's many shops and restaurants. Ocean breezes and the nearness of the Gulf Stream give Wilmington a delightful year-round climate. Nature lovers can go biking, hiking, or bird watching in one of Wilmington's parks or play golf on one of the city's six courses. Wilmington's proximity to the river and the ocean makes it an ideal haven for water lovers, whether they prefer taking a riverboat cruise or spending the day surfing and swimming at the beach.

Majors and Degrees / Academic Programs

The College of Arts and Sciences offers degree programs in Anthropology, Art History, Biology, Chemistry, Communication Studies, Computer Science, Creative Writing, Criminology, English, Environmental Science, Environmental Studies, Film Studies, French, Geography, Geology, Geosciences, German Studies, History, International Studies, Information Technology, Marine Biology, Mathematics, Music, Music Education, Music Performance, Oceanography, Philosophy and Religion, Physics, Political Science, Psychology, Sociology, Spanish, Statistics, Studio Art, and Theatre.

Degree programs in the College of Health and Human Services include Athletic Training; Exercise Science; Physical Education and Health; Public Health Studies; Recreation, Sport Leadership, and Tourism Management; Recreation Therapy; Clinical Research; Professional Nursing; and Social Work.

Degree programs available in the Cameron School of Business include Business Administration, Accountancy and Business Law, Economics, Entrepreneurship and Business Development, Finance, Human Resource Management, International Business, Management and Leadership, Management Information Systems, Marketing, and Operations Management.

Degree programs available in the Watson College of Education include Education of Young Children, Elementary Education, Middle Grades Education, Special Education, and Secondary Education.

Off-Campus Programs

Academic areas across campus sponsor study-abroad programs that are designed to strengthen relationships between the University and the international community, including international students and institutions in other countries. For example, the Cameron School of Business offers an International Master of Business Administration (I.M.B.A.), the Watson College of Education conducts programs in Belize, and the School of Nursing partners with a rural health clinic in Peru. Many of the University's study-abroad programs are coordinated by the Office of International Programs. These may last a few weeks, a semester, or an entire academic year; several occur during the summer. The University has developed more than 500 programs in over fifty countries, including Argentina, Ghana, Israel, Thailand, Italy, and China.

The University also coordinates travel experiences that include more than study, such as internships that may consist of a combination of course work and/or supervised work experience in a government agency, profit or nonprofit agency, or company. Students and recent graduates may work abroad as family caretakers or English-language teachers, either in exchange for room and board or for a salary. Volunteer opportunities in other countries may involve health care, agriculture, community development, language training, youth camps, or house-building projects.

Academic Facilities

The William Madison Randall Library holds more than 2.1 million items, including more than 1 million books, journals, and government documents; more than 65,000 multimedia items; and a vast microform collection. In addition, the library provides extensive indexes and full texts for thousands of journals and books, including NC LIVE, LexisNexis, Science Direct, and JSTOR. The library's specialized collections include the Rare Book Collection and the Southeastern North Carolina Collection, devoted to publications about or written by residents of the Lower Cape Fear region. In addition, the library is a selective depository for United States government publications and a full depository for North Carolina documents.

Costs

In 2015–16, full-time undergraduate tuition and fees total $6,647 per year for in-state residents and $20,513 for nonresidents. Students living on campus can also expect to spend $9,862 per academic year on room and board, $1,082 on books and supplies, $1,690 on transportation, $1,604 on health insurance if not covered under another policy, and $1,554 on miscellaneous costs. Room, board, and transportation costs for commuters vary. Students enrolled part-time pay according to the number of credit hours earned each semester; costs range from $677.36 to $2,329.39 for in-state students and $2,064.74 to $6,491.51 for nonresidents.

Financial Aid

In order to be considered for the maximum amount of financial assistance, prospective students should submit the Free Application for Federal Student Aid (FAFSA) as early as possible; the priority deadline is March 1st. The University awards millions of dollars each year to assist students. Most of this aid is need-based, but a number of merit-based scholarships are available for the most outstanding students.

The University offers several scholarships—including scholarships specifically for incoming freshmen and students enrolled in specific programs—that have been generously donated in honor of individuals or organizations. Award amounts and eligibility criteria vary, but most of these scholarships are renewable as long as the student is enrolled in a degree program and continues to meet the eligibility requirements. For students with exceptional financial need, the University developed the S.O.A.R program designed to help eligible participants reduce student loan debt. The Federal Pell Grant Program and the Federal Supplemental Educational Opportunity Grant (FSEOG) Program along with several North Carolina state programs also help offset the cost of attendance for low-income families. Some programs are limited to in-state students only.

Several federal loan programs are available for students who require additional assistance. Loan amount limits are established by the federal government. Some students also participate in federal work-study, which awards money to students who work up to 20 hours per week on campus.

Faculty

The University seeks to attract and maintain a faculty of outstanding individuals who are capable of contributing to the enrichment of its diverse and comprehensive instructional and research programs. Of the nearly 1,000-strong faculty members, almost 86 percent hold terminal degrees and over 60 percent are tenured. Faculty members come from all geographic regions of the United States and several foreign countries, bringing a rich variety of educational experiences, training, and scholarship.

Student Government

The Student Government Association is devoted to the best interest of the University and committed to upholding a high standard of morals and conduct. Student activity fees support the Student Government Association in its objectives and activities. The student body president and class representatives are elected by the student body, and the president appoints an executive board, which includes a chief of staff, treasurer, and secretary.

Admission Requirements

All prospective students must meet the following minimum course requirements for enrollment: 6 course units in language (including 4 units in English and 2 units of the same foreign language); 4 units of mathematics (one for which algebra II is a prerequisite); 3 units in science (including at least 1 unit in biology, 1 unit in the physical sciences, and 1 laboratory course); and 2 units in social science (including 1 unit in United States history).

Prospective students are required to submit the following materials: a completed application for admission, official transcripts from all high schools attended, answer to the essay and short answer question on the application, official SAT or ACT scores, letter of recommendation, and a $75 application fee. When reviewing a freshman application, the admissions committee looks carefully at the applicant's academic achievements including rigorous course work, writing, grade point average, standardized test scores, and extracurricular activities. Students admitted to the University had a mean SAT combined math and critical reading score of 1190 and/or an ACT composite average of 25.

Application and Information

Students applying for early action should have their applications submitted online by November 1 or earlier and are notified on or around January 20. Regular decision applications must be submitted by February 1; students are notified of the University's decision on or around April 1.

Transfer applicants applying for summer or fall entry must have their applications submitted by March 1. Transfer applicants applying for spring must apply by October 15. Decision letters are mailed on a rolling basis.

For additional information, students can create a SeaLevel account found on the UNCW website.

Office of Admissions
University of North Carolina Wilmington
601 South College Road
Wilmington, North Carolina 28403-5904
United States
Phone: 910-962-3243
Fax: 910-962-3038
E-mail: admissions@uncw.edu
Website: http://www.uncw.edu/
https://www.facebook.com/UNCWOfficeofAdmissions
https://twitter.com/UNCW_Admissions

The Class of 2018 celebrates their Convocation Ceremony by stopping briefly at UNCW's Clock Tower Lawn for a class photo and to raise the 2018 Class Flag.

UNIVERSITY OF PITTSBURGH AT BRADFORD

BRADFORD, PENNSYLVANIA

University of Pittsburgh Bradford
you can go beyond

★ To read more about this school, visit http://petersons.to/universityofpittsburghatbradford

The University

The University of Pittsburgh at Bradford (Pitt-Bradford) can take students beyond—beyond the classroom by offering internships and research opportunities; beyond the degree by providing a robust Career Services Office and an informal alumni network; beyond 9-to-5 by offering an active student life, a friendly residence-life environment, excellent athletic and cultural facilities, and a wide range of recreational opportunities; beyond place by exposing students to the world and offering many study-abroad opportunities; and beyond students' expectations by giving them a college experience that can transform them.

At Pitt-Bradford, students live and learn on a safe, intimate campus, where they receive individual and personalized attention from committed professors who work at their side. In addition, students earn a degree from the University of Pittsburgh, which commands respect around the world.

Students can work out in a state-of-the-art fitness center or swim in the six-lane swimming pool in the Richard E. and Ruth McDowell Sport and Fitness Center. The building also houses facilities for intercollegiate and intramural athletic events.

The Frame-Westerberg Commons offers a place to eat, gather, and participate in campus life. The building houses the dining hall, where students can help themselves to a wide assortment of meals; a bookstore, which features an after-hours convenience store; offices for many student clubs and organizations; and areas to read or relax.

There are more than fifty clubs and organizations, from the campus radio station and newspaper to academic clubs, honor societies, and fraternities and sororities. Pitt-Bradford competes in Division III of the NCAA and fields seven men's teams in baseball, basketball, cross-country, golf, soccer, swimming, and tennis and eight women's teams in basketball, bowling, cross-country, soccer, softball, swimming, tennis, and volleyball.

Location

Pitt-Bradford encompasses 317 acres in the foothills of the Allegheny Mountains, only steps from the Allegheny National Forest. Pitt-Bradford also is a short drive from larger cities such as Buffalo, New York (80 miles north); Pittsburgh (160 miles southeast); and Erie, Pennsylvania (90 miles west). Pitt-Bradford can also be reached easily by car and plane.

At Pitt-Bradford, students have many opportunities to participate in co-curricular opportunities in the region, including cross-country and downhill skiing, snowboarding, snowshoeing, ice skating, biking, fishing, hiking, and hunting.

Majors and Degrees

Students may pursue four-year degrees in accounting, applied mathematics, athletic training, biology, biology education 7–12, broadcast communications, business, computer and information technology K–12, business management, chemistry, chemistry education 7–12, computer information systems and technology, criminal justice, early level education preK–4, economics, energy science and technology, English, English education 7–12, environmental studies, exercise science, general studies, health and physical education K–12, history/political science, hospitality management, human relations, interdisciplinary arts, mathematics education 7–12, nursing, physical sciences, psychology, public relations, radiological science, social sciences, social studies education 7–12, sociology, sport and recreation management, and writing.

Pitt-Bradford also offers associate degrees in engineering science, information systems, liberal studies, nursing (RN), and petroleum technology.

Students may also study engineering for up to two years at Pitt-Bradford and then complete a program at the Oakland campus in bioengineering, chemical and petroleum engineering, civil and environmental engineering, electrical and computer engineering, industrial engineering, materials science and engineering, or mechanical engineering.

Pitt-Bradford also provides programs offered in conjunction with the University of Pittsburgh School of Dental Medicine and the Pennsylvania College of Optometry. Students begin their studies at Pitt-Bradford and, after three years, transfer to the appropriate graduate school to complete four more years of study.

Pitt-Bradford also offers the first two years of study leading to the doctorate in pharmacy. Students must complete the program at the Oakland campus, where admission is competitive. The Pittsburgh School of Pharmacy pre-admits some qualified high school seniors, pending completion of the first two years of the pre-professional program at Pitt-Bradford.

The University also has an agreement with Lake Erie College of Osteopathic Medicine (LECOM), which allows qualifying students to continue their education in medicine at LECOM after their third year at Pitt-Bradford. Students who have successfully completed their first year of medical school classes at LECOM will receive their bachelor's degree from Pitt-Bradford. They will then continue at LECOM to finish their medical studies.

Academic Programs

The academic programs stress critical-thinking and communication skills and encourage hands-on learning through field experience, internships, and faculty-student collaboration on research. A Pitt-Bradford bachelor's degree requires 120–128 credit hours (requirements differ slightly among programs). Students need to complete between 60 and 70 credit hours to earn an associate degree.

The accounting major prepares students for the workplace, which has a growing need for accountants. The major also prepares students to earn a master's degree in either professional accountancy or business administration.

The biology program prepares students for careers in health-related professions, education, and research; technical positions in governmental agencies; and careers with food, pharmaceutical, chemical, and biotechnology companies. Most students interested in medicine, dentistry, optometry, pharmacy, osteopathy, physical therapy, occupational therapy, podiatry, chiropractic medicine, veterinary medicine, preclinical dietetics and nutrition, and a variety of careers in health and rehabilitation sciences are biology majors.

Students who choose to major in broadcast communications, English, public relations, or writing are able to work on the award-winning student newspaper, *The Source;* broadcast over the college radio station, WDRQ; and publish original works in the award-winning student literary magazine, *Baily's Beads.* Students also have access to an all-digital television studio and two digital radio facilities.

Students who choose a major in computer information systems and technology will get a broad IT background and gain hands-on lab experiences. Students will learn programming applications, network development, systems design and analysis, web technologies, multimedia applications, database development, and systems administration.

In the criminal justice program, students are able to intern with local and regional police departments, county court and probation offices, and a federal prison. State-of-the-art crime-scene investigatory tools enable students to work a crime scene using many of the same tools as professional law enforcement agents. In the Crime Scene Investigation (CSI) House students can process simulated crime scenes and collect evidence just like the pros.

An education major prepares a student for a career as a teacher in a world of rapid political, economic, scientific, and cultural change. The Education Department seeks to graduate students who have general knowledge and specific content knowledge, as well as sound theory and practice.

The nursing program at Pitt-Bradford offers an Associate of Science degree that can be completed in two years and a Bachelor of Science in Nursing degree that requires two additional years. Students may commence this program upon completion of the associate degree.

In psychology, students gain knowledge in the scientific and theoretical aspects of psychology as well as the application of this knowledge. The major prepares students for graduate work in psychology and related disciplines and for employment in social service agencies, mental health centers, industries, and not-for-profit and governmental agencies.

Students may relocate to another University of Pittsburgh campus to complete academic programs not offered at Pitt-Bradford, but they may earn no more than 70 credits before transferring. All students in the arts and sciences may relocate, provided they are in good standing. Engineering students may relocate if they maintain a grade point average of at least 3.0.

Academic Facilities

In addition to the T. Edward and Tullah Hanley Library on campus, Pitt-Bradford students have online access to the entire University of Pittsburgh library system.

Blaisdell Hall, the fine arts and communication arts building, houses the art, communication arts, theater, and music programs and features state-of-the-art equipment. Students can find a computer graphics lab, two art studios, a music/theater rehearsal hall, and a radio and television studio. The building also houses a multipurpose theater and serves as the cultural center for the region by housing plays, concerts, lectures, and other arts-related events.

Fisher Hall houses the science programs, such as biology, chemistry, engineering, engineering science and technology, petroleum technology, and physics. The science labs are filled with up-to-date scientific equipment, enabling students to perform a variety of experiments. The building also has two computer-aided learning centers and, on the roof, a campus greenhouse.

In Swarts Hall, students take courses in business, education, sociology, anthropology, psychology, history/political science, languages, English, writing, and criminal justice. The building also houses a nursing suite and multimedia classrooms that can turn a typical class into an audio and visual experience.

There is more to the Richard E. and Ruth McDowell Sport and Fitness Center than sports. The building also houses the athletic training, exercise science, and sport and recreation management programs, along with a human performance lab and an athletic training room.

In the Ceramic Studio, students get their hands dirty—literally. Students have sixteen motorized pottery wheels, a manual kick wheel, a work table, and a kiln to help turn slabs of clay into art.

Costs

For 2014–15, tuition for full-time students was $6,226 per fifteen-week term for Pennsylvania residents and $11,634 for nonresidents. Nursing tuition was $7,976 per term for Pennsylvania residents and $14,836 for nonresidents. Room and board expenses were $4,390 per term. Other costs include an activity fee of $100 per term, a health fee of $50 per term, a parking and transportation fee of $40 per term, and a computer fee of $175 per term. Books and supplies cost approximately $500 per term.

Financial Aid

Pitt-Bradford believes that the cost of a college education should not be a deterrent to any student regardless of family financial circumstances. About 94 percent of students receive some form of financial aid, including grants, scholarships, loans, and work-study opportunities are administered through the Financial Aid Office. During 2014–15, the average financial aid award was roughly $17,489 for Pennsylvania students and $19,500 for out-of-state students. All aid applicants must submit the Free Application for Federal Student Aid (FAFSA) by March 1 to receive priority consideration. Pennsylvania residents who complete the FAFSA by March 1 are also eligible for Pennsylvania Higher Education Assistance Agency (PHEAA) grants. Students who live outside of Pennsylvania should contact their state agency to learn more about the prerequisites for grants.

The University awards merit-based scholarships to those who demonstrate exceptional academic achievement. The University ROTC program is another possible source of aid. The University encourages veterans to contact the VA about educational benefits.

To learn more about financial assistance, students should contact the Financial Aid Office or visit the financial aid website at http://www.upb.pitt.edu/financialaid.

Faculty

Pitt-Bradford's 63 full-time faculty members hold doctorates and master's degrees from some of the most prestigious universities in the nation, including Cornell, Harvard, Stanford, and the University of Pittsburgh. Teaching is the primary activity of the faculty, and personal attention is emphasized in the classroom. Faculty members welcome the chance to meet with their students and know them by name. The student-faculty ratio is 18:1.

Student Government

Because Pitt-Bradford is a personalized campus, opportunities for leadership abound. Many students become campus leaders as early as their sophomore year. Regardless of students' background or interests, most find many places to become involved at Pitt-Bradford.

The Student Activities Council schedules comedy performances, lectures, art exhibits, movies, and trips to such cities as Toronto, Niagara Falls, Cooperstown, and New York City.

Admission Requirements

The Admissions Committee considers three primary factors in evaluating an applicant's ability to succeed in college work: the high school record, the results of standardized tests (SAT or ACT), and the high school's recommendations. In addition, personal qualifications, extracurricular activities, and potential to contribute to the college community may be taken into consideration.

Application and Information

Pitt-Bradford has a rolling admissions program, and students may apply at any time. All candidates are notified as soon as action is taken on their application.

Candidates for admission should complete and return the application with a nonrefundable $45 fee. Students must also submit an official copy of their high school record and scores from either the SAT or ACT. In addition to fulfilling the above requirements, transfer applicants must submit all official college transcripts and must have a minimum cumulative grade point average of 2.0.

The Office of Admissions welcomes campus visits by students and their families; such visits help students arrive at a final decision about Pitt-Bradford. Interviews and tours are scheduled Monday through Friday, 9 a.m. to 3 p.m., and on selected Saturdays. Arrangements can be made by contacting the Office of Admissions or by going online to http://www.upb.pitt.edu/visit.

For application forms, catalogs, and further information, students should contact:

Office of Admissions
University of Pittsburgh at Bradford
300 Campus Drive
Bradford, Pennsylvania 16701-2898
Phone: 814-362-7555
800-872-1787 (toll-free)
Website: http://www.upb.pitt.edu
http://www.facebook.com/PittBradford
https://twitter.com/PittBradford

Criminal justice students check for fingerprints at a mock crime scene at the Crime Scene Investigation House.

COLLEGE CLOSE-UPS

UNIVERSITY OF PUGET SOUND

TACOMA, WASHINGTON

The College

Since 1888, University of Puget Sound has been committed to the liberal arts and sciences, superb teaching, and the recognition of each student as an individual. A nationally acclaimed faculty, top-notch facilities, and a limited enrollment ensure excellence in education.

Puget Sound, the only national liberal arts college in Western Washington, ranks in the top 10 percent of colleges for alumni who go on to earn doctorate degrees, and many graduates have received undergraduate and postgraduate honors, including Rhodes, National Science Foundation, Fulbright, Rotary, Watson, Phi Kappa Phi, Truman, Goldwater, and National Endowment for the Humanities fellowships and scholarships. Equally impressive, among national colleges and universities with fewer than 5,000 undergraduate students, Puget Sound is consistently named among the top small colleges for number of alumni serving as Peace Corps volunteers worldwide.

Puget Sound enrolls 2,600 students, with more than 75 percent coming from outside Washington State. In addition, 44 states and 16 countries are represented in the student body. The student-to-faculty ratio is 12:1, and the average class size is 19. Professors (not teaching assistants) teach all courses and commonly go to great lengths to make themselves available outside the classroom.

Puget Sound is a vibrant residential community with nearly all of the student body living on or near campus. Special theme houses and halls are available for students with common interests. Commencement Hall, the campus' newest residence hall, is a five-story, 55,000-square-foot facility featuring themed residence options with areas of emphasis such as humanities, entrepreneurship, environmental outdoor leadership, international and global education, and honors. Athletic facilities include Memorial Fieldhouse and Pamplin Fitness Center (which includes an indoor tennis pavilion), Wallace Pool, Peyton Field at Baker Stadium, an indoor climbing wall, and numerous varsity and intramural athletic fields.

Athletics include 23 varsity teams, various club teams, and numerous intramural teams. In addition, students are involved in more than 100 clubs and associations, including forensics, theater, music, KUPS (the university's radio station, which received an award from mtvU for best college radio station in the nation), art and literary magazines, weekly newspaper, yearbook, Student Senate, religious groups, Black Student Union, Hui-O-Hawai`i, Earth Activists, Queer Alliance, Asian Pacific American Student Union, Community for Hispanic Awareness, and Habitat for Humanity. Seventy-five percent of students participate in community service activities.

Location

Home for Puget Sound is a residential neighborhood in the historic North End of Tacoma, 35 miles south of Seattle and easily accessible from Interstate 5 and SEA-TAC International Airport. Tacoma is a dynamic city of 200,000 people located on the shores of the Puget Sound, a short distance from ski slopes and the Pacific Ocean. It was ranked by *Money* magazine as one of the most livable medium-sized cities in the country. Tacoma also features many parks and museums, an entrepreneurial downtown, and a theater district. The college itself occupies 39 buildings on a 97-acre campus. The architecture is Tudor Gothic, with its distinctive red-brick pattern arches and porticoes.

Majors and Degrees

Puget Sound offers academic programs in more than 50 areas of study leading to the Bachelor of Arts, Bachelor of Science, and Bachelor of Music degrees. Academic programs include art and art history; anthropology; Asian languages and cultures (majors are offered in Chinese, Japanese, and East Asian languages); Asian studies; biochemistry; bioethics; biology; business; chemistry; classics; communication studies; computer science; computer science in business; economics; education; English; exercise science; French studies; geology; German studies; global development studies; health professions (pre-med, pre-dental, pre-veterinary); Hispanic studies; history; international political economy; mathematics; molecular and cellular biology; music; natural science; philosophy; physics; politics and government; pre-law; psychology; religion; science, technology, and society; sociology; and theatre arts. Minors are offered in Latina/o studies, Latin American studies, African American studies, environmental policy and decision making, gender and queer studies, humanities, neuroscience, and many other areas. The special interdisciplinary major allows exceptional students the opportunity to pursue a degree in a recognized interdisciplinary or emergent field. Puget Sound also offers a dual-degree program in engineering, leading to a joint Bachelor of Arts/Bachelor of Science degree in engineering. Graduate degrees offered include the Master of Occupational Therapy, Doctor of Physical Therapy, Master of Arts in Teaching, and Master of Education.

Academic Programs

Academic rigor, freedom to take courses from across the curriculum, and opportunities for interdisciplinary study characterize the academic experience. The emphasis throughout a student's undergraduate education is on the acquisition of intellectual skills: the ability to express oneself clearly, orally and in writing; the ability to reason quantitatively; and to think logically, critically, and independently.

A particularly well-designed curriculum for the first year and a model program of academic advising and career counseling enable each student to develop his or her own skills and interests in preparation for a lifetime of creative work. Puget Sound's highly successful and award-winning student orientation—Prelude, Passages and Perspectives—is a nine-day program that allows new students to become involved in writing and experiential seminars, academic workshops, community service, and a three-day adventure to the nearby Olympic Peninsula.

The academic year is divided into two semesters, beginning in late August and mid-January. A normal academic load is 4 units (typically four courses) per semester. Each unit of credit is equivalent to 6 quarter hours or 4 semester hours. Thirty-two units are required for graduation.

Off-Campus Programs

Puget Sound offers an outstanding selection of international opportunities for its students, with over 130 study-abroad programs in 45 countries, including Australia, England, Scotland, Spain, France, Germany, Italy, Ghana, Austria, China, Japan, Madagascar, Taiwan, Argentina, Tanzania, and Chile, among others. The Pacific Rim/Asia Study-Travel Program offers students an intense year of study and travel in six to eight Asian countries.

Puget Sound's location in one of the fastest-growing regions of the country places its internship program at the forefront of national liberal arts colleges. Opportunities for undergraduate research abound, as students may apply for summer research grants in the sciences, social sciences, humanities, and the arts.

Academic Facilities

Collins Memorial Library contains more than 530,000 volumes of books and periodicals plus a sizable collection of federal and Washington state government publications, maps, microforms, videotapes, cassettes, compact discs, and other media materials. These resources are strengthened through participation in the Orbis-Cascade Alliance, a consortium of more than 35 public and private institutions of higher education in the Pacific Northwest, with combined holdings of more than 22 million volumes. Other major academic facilities include Harned and Thompson halls, together forming the Science Center at Puget Sound, Kittredge Gallery, Schneebeck Concert Hall, Norton Clapp Theatre, Wyatt Hall, and Slater Museum of Natural History. The William T. and Gail T. Weyerhaeuser Center for Health Sciences opened in 2011, housing undergraduate programs in psychology, neuroscience, and exercise science, along with graduate programs in occupational and physical therapy.

Students of environmental science and marine biology work and learn in a superb outdoor laboratory. Equipment and facilities in the science center include a modern greenhouse; an observatory; an aquarium with a tidal cycle; a state-of-the-art genetics laboratory; a scanning electron microscope and transmission electron microscope; ultraviolet, visible, fluorescence, infrared, and nuclear magnetic resonance spectrophotometric equipment; and a seismograph. Students also have access to human cadavers. Special facilities are available for students of occupational and physical therapy, education, counseling, foreign languages, and psychology. The music building houses Schneebeck Concert Hall and provides a keyboard and music lab and 28 practice rooms, including a "V-Room," a unique facility in which the musician can change the acoustic properties of the room.

Wireless Internet access is available throughout campus. In addition, students have access to computer labs and state-of-the-art video editing facilities.

Costs

Tuition and student government fees were $43,200 and $228, respectively, for the 2014–15 academic year. Room and board cost $11,180.

Financial Aid

More than 90 percent of Puget Sound students receive financial aid in one or a combination of the following forms: scholarships, grants, low-interest loans, and part-time employment. Applicants are automatically considered for renewable merit scholarships that range in amount from $5,000 to $20,000 per year. All incoming first-year students are invited to apply for the prestigious Matelich and Lillis scholarships, which cover full tuition, room, and board at Puget Sound for all four years. In addition, Puget Sound offers many other scholarships by application or audition in music, theater, art, selected academic areas, and forensics/debate.

Faculty

Members of the faculty work closely with individual students both in the classroom and in student-originated research projects within and across the disciplines. Eighty-nine percent of the faculty members teach full time; 99 percent of tenured faculty members hold a Ph.D. or an equivalent terminal degree. In recent years professors at Puget Sound have been recognized for their academic and teaching achievements through awards and distinctions, including the Graves Award in the Humanities and fellowships from various organizations, such as the National Endowment for the Humanities, American Council of Learned Societies, and Danforth Foundation. Seven Puget Sound professors have been named Washington State Professor of the Year by the Carnegie Foundation for the Advancement of Teaching. Puget Sound has received more of these awards than any other college or university in the state.

Admission Requirements

Each applicant to University of Puget Sound is considered individually and is admitted on the basis of his or her qualifications and achievements. In considering applicants for first-year admission, the Admission Committee evaluates the following: high school course selection, high school grade point average, rank in graduating class (if available), SAT or ACT scores, a counselor's and an academic teacher's recommendations, an essay, an interview (recommended), and extracurricular activities. College credit is awarded to students who have earned scores of 4 or higher on Advanced Placement examinations. Credit for a score of 3 is available for selected examinations only. Credit is also available for a score of 5, 6, or 7 on the International Baccalaureate higher-level examinations.

Application and Information

Prospective first-year students may apply for admission anytime after the beginning of the senior year in high school using the Common Application for freshmen. The application deadline is January 15. Admission decisions are mailed on or before April 1. Students who have decided that Puget Sound is their first-choice college may choose one of two early decision plans. Early Decision I has a November 15 application deadline, with admission and tentative financial aid notification by December 15. Early Decision II has a January 1 application deadline, with admission and tentative financial aid notification by February 15. Transfer students are admitted in both semesters. Students applying for transfer admission should submit the Common Application for Transfer Students.

For more information about Puget Sound, students should contact:

Office of Admission
University of Puget Sound
1500 North Warner Street, #1062
Tacoma, Washington 98416-1062
Phone: 253-879-3211
E-mail: admission@pugetsound.edu
Website: pugetsound.edu

Commencement Hall, University of Puget Sound.

COLLEGE CLOSE-UPS

UNIVERSITY OF REDLANDS

REDLANDS, CALIFORNIA

★ To read more about this school, visit http://petersons.to/universityofredlands

The University

The University of Redlands has, for more than 100 years, offered its students a tradition of superior liberal arts education. While students may select from a variety of programs that prepare them for professional or graduate school, the heart and foundation of Redlands is in liberal studies. Its outstanding faculty, educated in the world's finest colleges and universities, provides students with extraordinary opportunities for learning and growth through excellent teaching and close, informal interaction. Intense intellectual activity is balanced by opportunities for quiet reflection, fun, and recreation.

The University College of Arts and Sciences enrolls more than 2,700 students. Sixty percent of the freshman class comes from California and the remainder from forty-three other states and eleven countries. In addition to a strong academic program in the liberal arts, the sciences, pre-professional programs, and the arts, many extracurricular programs are available to the student, including music, drama, dance, and athletics. Internships are available for students in many academic programs. The School of Music and the Department of Theatre Arts provide a rich selection of cultural events throughout the year. Prominent speakers are invited to the campus each year to give major addresses and participate in classes and public discussion groups, and many social functions are organized by the Office of Student Life and individual residence halls. Additional social opportunities are provided for interested students by local nonresidential fraternities and sororities. The student services center provides assistance in the areas of career and personal counseling and academic support.

Seventy percent of the students live on campus in residence halls that offer a variety of accommodations, including single gender, coed by separate wings, and coed by alternate suites.

The University of Redlands is one of a select number of schools that have a chapter of Phi Beta Kappa, the nation's oldest and most prestigious academic honor society. In addition, 15 Redlands students have been awarded Fulbright awards within the past seven years.

The University of Redlands offers master's programs in the fields of business, communicative disorders, education, geographic information systems, and music. The School of Education offers a Doctorate in Leadership for Educational Justice Ed.D. program.

Location

The University is located in the city of Redlands within the San Bernardino Valley. Overlooking the 160-acre campus are the two highest mountains in southern California, Mt. San Gorgonio and Mt. San Bernardino, each more than 10,000 feet high. Redlands has a population of 70,000 and is situated at an elevation of 1,500 feet. Metropolitan Los Angeles to the west and Palm Springs to the east are both about an hour's drive away by freeway.

Majors and Degrees

The B.A. degree is offered in the academic areas of Asian studies, biology, business administration, communicative disorders, creative writing, economics, English literature, environmental business, environmental studies, French, German, government, history, international relations, liberal studies, managerial studies, music, philosophy, psychology, race and ethnic studies, religion, sociology/anthropology, Spanish, studio art, theater arts, women's and gender studies, and visual and media studies. The B.S. degree is offered in accounting, biochemistry and molecular biology, biology, business administration, chemistry, economics, environmental policy and management, environmental science, mathematics, and physics. The professional degree of Bachelor of Music (B.M.) is offered by the School of Music. Primary and secondary credentials are granted by the School of Education. Strong interdisciplinary programs in Latin American studies, pre-law, and pre-medicine are also available.

Academic Programs

Academic majors are offered in the spirit of a liberal arts program, with emphasis on developing the whole student. In addition to the standard academic program, international-study programs, independent study, and an honors program are offered to provide greater diversity.

A liberal arts education, by definition, is an exposure to a wide variety of academic disciplines. Typically, such exposure carries no underlying theme but is distributed among broad categories such as the humanities, arts, social sciences, and natural sciences. The University of Redlands has never considered itself typical and, as a result, has developed an unusual approach to the implementation of its liberal arts philosophy by restructuring the general education requirements to provide a contemporary curriculum. This common experience emphasizes competence in writing, computing, problem solving, and creative skills, all of which are fundamental to a lifetime of learning and career development. In addition, the requirements include a first-year seminar that integrates the academic program and close personal relationships between students and faculty members. The overriding emphasis of this innovative curriculum is on a thorough investigation of human values as they affect the individual and society. An examination of the worth of the individual, respect for nature and life, free inquiry, and the understanding of other cultures are a few of the topics covered through various courses. The University hopes that this experience will broaden each student's understanding and better equip them to deal with today's dynamic society.

The Johnston Center for Integrative Studies provides a nontraditional approach for a select group of highly motivated students. Johnston Center students are exempted from most of the academic structure of Redlands and instead negotiate their entire course of study with a faculty/peer committee. Drawing from the Redlands curriculum as well as from courses created each semester by the Johnston community, each student proposes an individually designed general studies program and an area of concentration. Course performance is evaluated in a narrative format rather than with letter grades. These students live in the Johnston Center Complex, a living/learning community that includes student rooms, faculty offices, classrooms, and space for weekly community meetings. Students who are enrolled in the Johnston Center are expected to contribute to the life of the center's community.

The academic calendar divides the school year into a 4-4-1 plan, providing a fall semester, a spring semester, and a May term. The four classes taken in the fall semester are completed prior to the third Friday in December. The spring semester begins in January and runs through April. The four-week May term offers students the chance to pursue one subject in depth. Extensive off-campus opportunities, including internships, international study, and on-campus independent study, are available.

Academic Facilities

The institution has facilities with a mix of Greek, Spanish, and modern California architecture. The newly renovated ground floor of the Armacost Library includes rooms for collaboration and learning, the Fletcher Jones Computing Center, a student study area, the Bulldog café, and an Internet lounge. Other facilities include the Stauffer Complex for Science, Mathematics, and Environmental Studies; and the Center for the Arts, featuring the Glen Wallichs Theatre, Frederick Loewe Performance Hall, and an art gallery. The library houses 400,000 publications and online databases such as Dialog, ABI/INFORM, PsychLIT, ERIC, Wilson Indexes, and the Music Index. These facilities and surrounding common spaces also have access to a wireless network.

Costs

Tuition for 2014–15 was $42,836, and room and board costs were $12,500.

Financial Aid

Recognizing that many worthy and capable students find it impossible to obtain a college education without financial assistance, the University has established a program of aid. Most aid is need-based, but no-need scholarships based on academic achievement in high school and/or college are available. Presidential Scholarships are also available, based on grades and test scores, as are Achievement Awards. Talent Awards, ranging from $500 to $10,000 each, are available in art, creative writing, music, and theater.

Students seeking financial assistance should inquire through the Office of Admissions when applying for admission. The Free Application for Federal Student Aid (FAFSA) should be submitted by March 2. FAFSA forms received after this date are evaluated subject to the availability of funding. Forms may be obtained online at http://www.fafsa.gov.

Faculty

The highly qualified full-time faculty numbers 198 men and women, 83 percent of whom hold doctorates or other terminal degrees in their field. The wide variety of academic backgrounds represented in the faculty provides students with an excellent opportunity to live and work in an atmosphere of intellectual inquiry. Academic advising is handled by faculty members, and all students are assigned an adviser in the area of their major interest.

Student Government

Authority and responsibility for student government is delegated to the Associated Students of the University of Redlands by the president and the faculty to make possible genuine participation by students in the governance of the University. The organization is composed of all students in the college, and its officers are chosen by the student body. More than sixty positions of representation are open to students on faculty, administrative, trustee, and alumni committees. Among other activities and responsibilities, the student government finances and operates a student-union complex, on-campus shuttle, information center, vending program, convocation series, Internet radio station, and weekly newspaper.

Admission Requirements

Graduation from an accredited high school or the equivalent is necessary for admission. No set pattern of courses in high school is required, but applicants should have had 4 years of work in English and should have completed an academic program strongly emphasizing such studies as foreign language, science, mathematics (including algebra II), and social science. An average grade of at least B should have been maintained in the high school program. Applicants are requested to submit the results of the SAT or the ACT. The writing portion is used for placement in English classes but not admission. SAT Subject Tests are not required. Standardized test scores are not required of transfers who bring at least 24 transferable units to the University. International students, for whom English is not their first language, must submit the results from any of the following exams: TOEFL, IELTS, APIEL, PTE-A, iTEP, University of Cambridge ESOL examinations, or the International Baccalaureate Higher Level English exam.

Transfer students should have maintained a minimum 2.8 grade point average and may transfer up to 66 units of credit from a community college and 96 units from a four-year institution.

Application and Information

Applications are processed in two phases and on a space-available basis. Those wishing to be considered for an academic or merit scholarship should apply by the early action deadline of November 15. Those applying for need-based financial aid should apply by the regular decision deadline of January 15. Transfer applicants should apply by March 1. Applications made after this date are considered on a space-available basis.

Further inquiries should be addressed to:

Office of Admissions
University of Redlands
P.O. Box 3080
Redlands, California 92373-0999
Phone: 800-455-5064 (toll-free)
Fax: 909-335-4089
E-mail: admissions@redlands.edu
Website: http://www.redlands.edu

The University of Redlands stands out brilliantly against the majestic San Bernardino Mountains.

COLLEGE CLOSE-UPS

UNIVERSITY OF SAN FRANCISCO

SAN FRANCISCO, CALIFORNIA

★ To read more about this school, visit http://petersons.to/universityofsanfrancisco

UNIVERSITY OF SAN FRANCISCO
CHANGE THE WORLD FROM HERE

The University

From its beginnings as a one-room schoolhouse, founded in 1855 by the Jesuits, the University of San Francisco (USF) has developed into one of the premier Jesuit Catholic universities on the West Coast. Throughout its history, USF has been committed to preparing students to improve the world in which they live. With more than 10,000 undergraduate and graduate students, the University has remained faithful to the Jesuit tradition and has maintained its small class size and low student-faculty ratio. Its programs in the arts, the sciences, business, education, nursing, and law foster a love of learning grounded by the challenge to serve society. The University's foundation encompasses academic excellence; the Jesuit, Catholic learning tradition; a diverse community; and a global perspective that is rooted in San Francisco, which offers unparalleled opportunities for internships, service, and professional connections.

USF is one of the most diverse university campuses in the United States. Living and learning with a student body that consists of students from forty-nine states and eighty-seven other countries is a unique opportunity. All new incoming freshmen under the age of 21 are required to live on the campus, unless they live within 40 miles of the University. More than 90 percent of the incoming freshmen and 35 percent of all undergraduates live on-campus.

The University offers five on-campus residence halls, two on-campus apartment-style residences, and one off-campus traditional residence hall. Gillson, Hayes-Healy, and Phelan house freshmen, while Lone Mountain houses sophomores and upper-division students. Fromm Hall is the only all-female residence hall for first- and second-year students. Located just twelve blocks from the USF campus, Pedro Arrupe Hall is the off-campus traditional residence hall offered to upper-division students. Loyola Village is a residential community that features apartment-style living for third-year, fourth-year, and graduate students. Each residence hall has laundry facilities, study rooms, community kitchens, television lounges, and 24-hour front desk staff.

On the campus, students have access to various University facilities. The Koret Health and Recreation Center is an exciting complex that provides facilities for exercise, racquetball, court games, weight training, massage, personal training, and various aquatic activities in an Olympic-size pool. Tai Chi, yoga, Zumba, and spinning are just some of the classes offered at Koret. Outdoor adventures include horseback riding, camping, sailing, and sea kayaking. Intramural and club sports are offered in the fall and spring semesters and include basketball, boxing, flag football, fencing, karate, soccer, lacrosse, rugby, and co-ed volleyball. Special aquatic sports include a Masters swim team and a water polo club. NCAA Division I sports include baseball, basketball, cross-country, golf, soccer, tennis, track and field, and women's volleyball and sand volleyball.

Dining facilities are located all over campus and are within walking distance of the residence halls and classrooms. Located on the main campus, The Market Café offers a food court experience with a variety of choices, including global, vegan, homestyle classics, and vegetarian options. Other dining options include Outtakes Café, Outtahere Café, Crossroads Café, Club Ed in the School of Education, and Kendrick Café at the Law School.

Undergraduates keep busy by participating in over 100 on-campus, student-run associations, including fraternities, sororities, honor societies, and clubs. Among these are the oldest continuously performing theater group west of the Mississippi River, an entire consortium of culturally focused organizations, and a literary magazine.

For students interested in giving back to the community, the Leo T. McCarthy Center for Public Service and the Common Good forms a partnership between the local community and USF. Students may participate in service-learning projects that include socially-just urban design, outreach to underprivileged children in local schools, and habitat restoration.

Location

The University of San Francisco is located on a stunning 58-acre campus in a residential neighborhood just minutes from downtown San Francisco, the Financial District, Fisherman's Wharf, and the Pacific Ocean. The hilltop campus, renowned for its beautiful landscaping, borders the 1,000-acre Golden Gate Park and offers spectacular panoramic views of the city. The dynamic city of San Francisco keeps students entertained with concerts, the ballet, opera, museum exhibits, theater, and sporting events. Because of the diversity and geographical compactness of San Francisco, students find research facilities, opportunities for community involvement, and employment experiences that cannot be matched by most cities.

Majors and Degrees

The College of Arts and Sciences offers both B.A. and B.S. degrees. Popular majors include advertising, architecture and community design, art history/arts management, biology, chemistry, communication studies, comparative literature and culture, computer science, design, economics, economics 4+1, English, environmental science, environmental studies, exercise and sports science, fine arts, French studies, history, international and development economics 4+1, Japanese studies, Latin American studies, mathematics, media studies, performing arts and social justice, philosophy, physics, physics/engineering (dual-degree, 3+2 program), politics, psychology, sociology, Spanish, theology and religious studies, undeclared arts, and undeclared science. The School of Management offers Bachelor of Science degrees in accounting, business administration, entrepreneurship, finance, hospitality industry management, international business, marketing, and organizational behavior and leadership. The School of Nursing and Health Professions offers a direct-entry, four-year Bachelor of Science in Nursing for qualified high school and transfer applicants.

USF has seventy-seven minors and offers unique programs that enhance the learning experience at USF. Special programs include astronomy; African and African-American studies; Asia Pacific studies; Catholic studies and social thought; ethnic studies; film studies; honors program in the humanities; journalism; Judaic studies; Latino/a and Chicano/a Studies; Middle Eastern studies; neuroscience; 4+3 dual degrees in law, military science, premedical, and other pre-professional health studies; public relations; a five-year dual-degree teacher preparation program that results in teacher certification at the elementary or secondary level; and the School of Management honors cohort program.

Academic Programs

The University of San Francisco is committed to providing students with the essentials of a well-rounded education. A baccalaureate degree is issued upon the successful completion of a 128-unit curriculum. The curriculum consists of 44 units of core courses chosen from six specified categories in addition to 80–85 units that are divided among departmental major requirements and electives. An honors program is available for select students seeking a strong academic challenge. The academic year is based on the two-semester system, with summer sessions and a winter intersession also available.

In an effort to encourage high school students to move rapidly into the study of subjects now customarily reserved for colleges, the University of San Francisco honors advanced placement credits, as certified by the College Board's Advanced Placement Program exams and the International Baccalaureate program. The University also cooperates with the College-Level Examination Program (CLEP). Students in the College of Arts and Sciences can also accelerate the traditional undergraduate process and earn a bachelor's degree in three years with a combination of advanced placement credits and an academically rigorous schedule.

The USF Pre-Professional Health Committee serves to guide and recommend students to medical and dental professional health schools as well as to schools for pharmacy, optometry, veterinary medicine, and podiatry. A student may complete the premedical or other pre–health science requirements as part of, or in addition to, the requirements of an academic major. The Pre-Professional Health Committee assists students with the application process, develops a professional file for each student, collects and mails recommendations to professional schools, conducts interviews in preparation for application, and endorses approved candidates via a committee letter of recommendation sent to all professional schools selected by the student.

The St. Ignatius Institute has an integrated core curriculum based on the great books of Western civilization and an emphasis on critical analysis to promote the common good. Any undergraduate student at the University, regardless of major, may take courses through the Institute to meet general education requirements. The University also offers Army ROTC. ROTC scholarships are available for qualified applicants and continuing students.

Off-Campus Programs

The University of San Francisco's Center for Global Education has numerous study-abroad programs available to academically eligible undergraduate students. Exchanges with Jesuit universities include locations in Japan, Mexico, China, Spain, Philippines, El Salvador, and Chile. USF's St. Ignatius Institute program includes an exchange with Oxford University in England. Affiliations with other Jesuit universities make travel to other countries possible, e.g., Gonzaga University's study-abroad program in Florence, Italy, and Loyola University of Chicago's program in Rome. USF is also an associate member of the Institute of European and Asian Studies, which offers programs in Durham and London, England; Paris, Dijon, and Nantes, France; Berlin and Freiburg, Germany; Vienna, Austria; Madrid and Salamanca, Spain; Milan, Italy; Tokyo and Nagoya, Japan; Moscow, Russia; Adelaide and Canberra, Australia; Beijing, China; and Singapore. Numerous other study-abroad opportunities are also available. USF assists students in selecting a location, applying to programs, making financial arrangements, registering for academic credit, securing a passport and visa, and making travel plans.

Academic Facilities

University of San Francisco students have access to Gleeson Library's nearly 1.8 million holdings and Lo Schiavo Center for Science and Innovation, which houses a digital lecture hall, ample space for collaborative learning, and labs for chemistry, toxicology, advanced biotechnology, and mathematics. Cowell Hall, the base for nursing classes and the Nursing Skills Laboratory, also includes the Instructional Media Center. Malloy Hall, headquarters for the School of Management, houses an additional computer laboratory and special seminar rooms. Kalmanovitz Hall houses all programs in the humanities and social sciences and features state-of-the-art classrooms, a rooftop sculpture garden, and seventeen laboratories for language, writing, media, and psychology.

Costs

Tuition for the 2014–15 school year was $40,996. Room and board were $13,320 for the academic year. Books, travel, and other expenses are about $5,100 per year.

Financial Aid

A variety of financial aid programs are available at the University, including scholarships, merit awards, grants, loans, and campus employment opportunities. Domestic students who wish to be considered for financial aid must file the Free Application for Federal Student Aid (FAFSA) and College Scholarship Service Profile (CSS) by February 1. More than two thirds of all USF students receive some type of financial aid.

The University Scholars Program is available to new domestic freshmen applicants who have an exceptional cumulative GPA, SAT combined score, or ACT composite score. Scholars are awarded a non-need-based scholarship that pays a significant percentage of the cost of tuition for four years of undergraduate study. To remain eligible, University Scholars are expected to maintain a competitive GPA while enrolled. Eligible students are identified during the admission process and can apply as early action, early decision, or regular action applicants.

Faculty

The University has 1,043 full- and part-time faculty members; 92 percent of full-time faculty hold doctoral or terminal degrees in the field they teach. The University of San Francisco fosters a close relationship between students and faculty members. This is reflected in the small size of classes, the low student-faculty ratio, and the faculty members' availability for advising. Classes are not taught by student teachers or teachers' assistants.

Student Government

All undergraduates are members of the Associated Students of the University of San Francisco (ASUSF). ASUSF is the official representative body of undergraduate students at USF. The ASUSF government has three functions: to represent the official student viewpoint, to recommend policies, and to fund activities and services. ASUSF consists of three branches: the executive branch, the Student Senate, and the Student Court. The Senate comprises an executive board and student senators.

Admission Requirements

The University seeks students who are sincerely interested in pursuing a well-rounded education. The admission process is selective, and each application is reviewed individually. To enhance the quality and diversity of its student body, the University of San Francisco encourages men and women of all races, nationalities, and religious beliefs to apply. Eligibility is based on high school course work and GPA, the application essay, an academic recommendation, extracurricular involvement, and satisfactory test scores. Domestic applicants are required to submit SAT or ACT test scores. International applicants are required to submit TOEFL or IELTS test scores; however, if an international applicant submits sufficient SAT or ACT test scores, the TOEFL or IELTS may be waived.

Application and Information

A completed application includes the application form, the application fee, a personal essay, all academic transcripts, standardized test scores, and one letter of recommendation. For the fall semester, the application deadlines are November 15 for early action and early decision (freshmen only) and January 15 for regular action (freshmen and transfers).

Inquiries should be addressed to:

Office of Admission
University of San Francisco
2130 Fulton Street
San Francisco, California 94117-1080
Phone: 415-422-6563
800-CALL-USF (toll-free outside California)
Fax: 415-422-2217
E-mail: admission@usfca.edu
Website: http://www.usfca.edu
http://www.facebook.com/University.of.San.Francisco
http://twitter.com/USFCA
http://www.youtube.com/usfcalifornia

The University of San Francisco—change the world from here.

UNIVERSITY OF SOUTHERN INDIANA

EVANSVILLE, INDIANA

★ To read more about this school, visit http://petersons.to/universityofsouthernindiana

The University

Established in 1965, the University of Southern Indiana (USI) is a comprehensive public university supported by the state of Indiana. In the United States, institutions supported by the state government offer the most affordable programs in higher education. USI offers a quality education at an excellent price. Surrounded by lakes and woods, the 1,400-acre campus is known for its natural beauty, modern facilities, and friendly atmosphere.

Nearly 9,500 students attend USI. In fall of 2014, the University welcomed students from all across Indiana, 36 other states, and 51 other nations.

Campus community: USI offers a safe and friendly campus. The University has fourteen major buildings and provides modern apartments and suite-style housing for students living on campus. More than 2,800 students live in USI housing—near classes, the library, friends, and campus activities. USI's modern campus accommodations are extremely popular with students. A staff of housing professionals and student resident assistants helps students adjust to independent living and make the most of their college experience outside the classroom. Students living on campus enjoy easy access to academic and recreational facilities, and a campus convenience store serves their needs.

USI provides an ideal environment for students to get involved beyond the classroom. Students use the University Center, the expansive campus, and the recreational facilities to get together informally or to participate in intramurals, campus organizations, or other activities. Cultural activities include theater, musical events, and presentations by recognized speakers and performers.

The heart of recreation activity on campus is the newly expanded Recreation, Fitness, and Wellness Center. More than 3,000 students take part each semester in intramural programs, which include a wide range of activities such as soccer, table tennis, and rock climbing.

Accreditation: USI is accredited by the Higher Learning Commission of the North Central Association of Colleges and Secondary Schools (NCA). The College of Business is accredited by the Association to Advance Collegiate Schools of Business (AACSB), the highest standard of achievement for business schools which is achieved by only 15 percent of the world's business schools. The University's program in engineering is accredited by ABET. In addition, programs in chemistry, education, health professions, communications, and social work are accredited by the appropriate professional organizations and state agencies.

Location

The University of Southern Indiana is located in southwestern Indiana, often called "The Crossroads of America" because of its central location. About 6 million people live in Indiana. The capital of the state is Indianapolis, home of the famous Indianapolis 500 automobile race. Indiana is an important farming and manufacturing state and is rich in natural resources, including coal and limestone.

City of Evansville: USI's wooded campus is situated in beautiful rolling hills on the edge of Evansville, Indiana's third-largest city. A cultural and economic hub for the region, Evansville is located on the banks of the Ohio River. The climate of the region is moderate, offering four distinct seasons throughout the year.

While the city offers many urban attractions, it retains the friendliness and charm of a smaller town. Numerous recreational activities are available in the city, including live concerts, theatrical productions, and sports.

Evansville offers a lower cost of living and a much lower crime rate than other major U.S. cities. Evansville has been listed among the *100 Best Communities for Young People* by America's Promise Alliance, and has also been designated an All-America City by the National Civic League. In addition, Evansville was selected as one of 50 Smartest Cities in Which to Live by Kiplinger's Personal Finance.

Evansville's Regional Airport (airport code EVV) is serviced by several major airlines, with connecting flights from Chicago, Detroit, Atlanta, Charlotte, and Dallas.

Majors and Degrees

More than eighty undergraduate and graduate academic programs are offered through four colleges: the Romain College of Business Administration; the Pott College of Science, Engineering, and Education; the College of Liberal Arts; and the College of Nursing and Health Professions.

Bachelor's degree programs are offered in Accounting; Advanced Manufacturing; Anthropology; Art (art history, graphic design, illustration, interactive media design, photography, studio art); Art History; Art Teaching (elementary/secondary); Biochemistry; Biology; Biophysics; Business Administration; Chemistry; Communication Studies; Computer Information Systems; Computer Science; Criminal Justice Studies; Dental Hygiene; Early Childhood (nonteaching);Early Childhood Education; Economics; Elementary Education; Engineering; English; English (teaching); Environmental Science; Exercise Science; Finance; Food and Nutrition; French Studies; French Studies (teaching); Geology; German Studies; German Studies (teaching); Health Services; History; Industrial Supervision; International Studies; Journalism; Kinesiology; Management; Marketing; Mathematics; Nursing; Philosophy; Physical Education P–12 (teaching); Political Science; Psychology; Public Relations and Advertising; Radio and Television; Radiologic and Imaging Sciences; Science (teaching); Science (teaching), Secondary; Social Work; Sociology; Spanish Studies; Spanish Studies (teaching); Special Education; Sport Management; Theatre Arts; and Visual Art P–12 (teaching).

Academic Programs

Students at USI have access to a world-class education with state-of-the-art laboratory, research, and classroom facilities. In addition, students have many opportunities to work with professors on undergraduate research and creative projects to gain inspired perspectives and solve real-world challenges. USI's professors are accessible, engaging, and most importantly, committed to teaching.

The academic year (August through May) is organized into two semesters. The fall semester begins in late August and runs through mid-December; the spring semester begins in January and ends in May.

From May through August, the University has three 5-week summer sessions. Students can complete one or two courses during each summer session. Some students enroll during the summer in order to complete their degree in less than four years.

Off-Campus Programs

USI offers study-abroad opportunities in more than sixty countries around the globe. With advance planning, it is possible for students in virtually any major to participate in an overseas program. Programs offer a variety of experiences, from specialized courses taught entirely in English to direct enrollment in the foreign university. Students receive USI credit for the course work completed during the summer, semester, or academic year at an approved USI study-abroad location.

Costs

Undergraduate tuition (30 hours/year) for the 2015–16 academic year (two semesters) is estimated at $7,585 for Indiana residents and $17,330 for nonresidents, including international students. The cost for campus housing and a full meal plan is $8,276 for two semesters. The estimated cost of the Intensive English program (four 8-week sessions) is $12,740.

Financial Aid

Indiana residents should file the Free Application for Federal Student Aid (FAFSA) by March 10 to determine eligibility for State of Indiana financial assistance. Further information about the financial aid process for U.S. students is available from the Office of Student Financial Assistance (http://www.usi.edu/financial-aid).

Well-qualified international students may be considered for international scholarships, ranging from $1,000 to $4,000 per year. These awards are based on the student's academic record as well as financial need. In addition, a limited number of Global Leader Scholarships are granted to qualified international students who exhibit leadership potential and a desire to serve as a cultural ambassador during their academic program. Global Leader Scholarships are equivalent to in-state tuition waivers (approximately $9,500 per academic year).

Faculty

USI's top priority is teaching undergraduate students. USI invests tuition dollars in knowledgeable and qualified faculty who want to be in the classroom. The average class size is 25 students and the student-faculty ratio is 18:1. Small classes encourage dialogue and interaction and allow faculty to develop a working relationship with students.

Student Organizations

The University of Southern Indiana offers a wide range of student clubs and organizations; experiential learning, service, and volunteer opportunities; recreation and fitness events; education and fine art events; and entertainment. There are plenty of ways for students to engage in the campus community and connect with other students with similar interests.

There are over 120 students clubs and organizations at USI that represent a wide range of interests such as academic and professional organizations; special-interest clubs; club sports; and social, political and religious organizations.

Admission Requirements

Each freshman applicant is reviewed on an individual basis and is evaluated on the following areas from his/her high school transcript:

- 4 years of English
- 3 to 4 years of laboratory science
- 3 years of social studies
- 3 to 4 years of mathematics

The Admission Committee also considers the following:

- SAT and/or ACT composite scores
- Academic achievement (grade point average, class rank, course work)
- Extracurricular involvement
- Recommendations from counselors

USI prefers that students graduating from an Indiana accredited high school complete Core 40 requirements. The University prefers students have a 2.5 cumulative grade point average (on a 4.0 scale) and a minimum composite SAT score of 820 (critical reading/math combined) or a minimum composite ACT score of a 17 for admission.

Transcripts recording any course work completed while in high school that could be consider for college credit including university-level/dual-credit courses, Advanced Placement (AP), College Level Examination Program (CLEP), or International Baccalaureate (IB), should be submitted with the Application for Undergraduate Admission.

For international applicants: An international student should apply well in advance of the semester in which the student plans to enter. In order to receive consideration for admission the student must submit original official transcripts from all secondary schools and universities (and an English translation of those documents if necessary). International students whose native language is not English must provide proof of English language proficiency (TOEFL, IELTS). USI requires either the ACT or SAT score in lieu of TOEFL or IELTS for students whose native language is English.

To receive a student visa, international students must also provide information showing the ability to cover their educational costs for one year. In order for transfer credit to be accepted at USI, the foreign education institution must be recognized by the Ministry of Education (or other accrediting body) of the respective country. Upon acceptance of admission, the University of Southern Indiana will notify students regarding transfer credit as soon as possible.

Application and Information

Although undergraduate applications are reviewed on a rolling basis throughout the year, students are encouraged to apply during the first semester of their senior year in high school.

The online application form and requirements can be found at www.usi.edu/admission.

For more information, prospective students should contact:

Office of Admissions
University of Southern Indiana
8600 University Boulevard
Evansville, Indiana 47712
United States
Phone: 812-464-8600
E-mail: enroll@usi.edu (U.S. students)
i.apply@usi.edu (international students)
Website: www.usi.edu

View of the University Center and the library from the quad.

COLLEGE CLOSE-UPS

UNIVERSITY OF THE CUMBERLANDS

WILLIAMSBURG, KENTUCKY

The University

Chartered in 1888, Cumberland College became University of the Cumberlands on July 1, 2005, reflecting the diversity and excellence of options offered in high-quality education. The University is committed to providing a superior education within an exceptional Christian atmosphere at an affordable cost. Recognition by *U.S. News & World Report* in its list of America's Best Colleges and by the John Templeton Foundation as a member of its Honor Roll of Character Building Colleges signals that a University of the Cumberlands (UC) education is an exceptional value. Emphasizing the growth of the individual student, the University strives to instill in students the desire to be agents of change in the world and to use knowledge for the benefit of others as well as themselves.

UC is one of the few institutions where all students complete a leadership program. All students participate in community service as a component of this program.

University of the Cumberlands is a four-year, coed, liberal arts institution for higher education that offers a broad curriculum with more than thirty-five programs of undergraduate study, including eight preprofessional programs for professional and health science careers. Graduates enjoy a high acceptance rate to graduate and professional schools, particularly in science, business, and education. In fact, within five years of graduation, 66 percent of UC's alumni have completed or are pursuing a graduate or professional degree.

Graduate studies at University of the Cumberlands offer individual graduate courses as well as a Master of Arts in Teaching and a Master of Arts in Education degree programs with certification or concentration in various areas. Other master's programs include business administration (M.B.A.), professional counseling (M.A.P.C.), physician assistant studies (M.P.A.S.), Christian studies (M.A.C.S.), justice administration, and information systems security. Doctoral programs include educational leadership and clinical psychology.

One of the largest private institutions in the state of Kentucky, UC serves a diverse body of more than 1,800 undergraduate students from forty states and thirty countries. Primarily a residential campus, UC provides on-campus housing for about 75 percent of its students in the University's ten residence halls. A director, assisted by student staff members, supervises each hall.

Extracurricular activities abound. More than forty clubs and organizations provide students with a wide variety of activities, including a debate team, theater, musical performance groups, academic societies, an FM radio station, a student newspaper, student government, Baptist Campus Ministries, Appalachian Ministries, Mountain Outreach, Patriot Adventure Club, departmental clubs, and intramural sports.

University of the Cumberlands participates in intercollegiate competition. UC is a member of the NAIA Division I Mid-South Conference and offers opportunities in women's basketball, bowling, cross-country, golf, lacrosse, soccer, softball, swimming, tennis, track and field, volleyball, and wrestling; men's baseball, basketball, bowling, cross-country, football, golf, lacrosse, soccer, swimming, tennis, track and field, and wrestling; and coed archery and cheerleading. The O. Wayne Rollins Convocation/Physical Education Center houses a 2,700-seat athletic arena, the Dinah Taylor Aquatic Center, an indoor batting cage, a weight room, an indoor walking/jogging track, locker rooms, an intramural gymnasium, athletic training facilities, athletic offices, and classrooms.

The James H. Taylor II Stadium complex, which seats 2,400, includes a football field; an eight-lane, 400-meter all-weather track and field; the Patriot Pavilion; and a football practice field.

The Doyle Buhl Stadium and James Keelty Field are the home of Patriot baseball, with dugouts and locker rooms.

UC also has separate golf, soccer, softball, tennis, and wrestling facilities.

Location

One of the state's oldest cities, Williamsburg is located in southern Kentucky, 185 miles south of Cincinnati, Ohio, and 70 miles north of Knoxville, Tennessee. Williamsburg is known for its beautiful homes and the hospitality of its people. The University of the Cumberlands campus is situated on three hills above the town and, about 1 mile from exit 11, is easily accessed from I-75. UC has a well-kept campus that blends stately old buildings with new ones and has a panoramic view of the surrounding mountains and the Cumberland River Valley, an area known throughout the country for its lovely waterfalls, forests, and lakes. Famed Cumberland Falls State Resort Park is just 20 minutes from campus.

Majors and Degrees

University of the Cumberlands is accredited by the Commission on Colleges of the Southern Association of Colleges and Schools to award baccalaureate, master's, and doctoral degrees. It is approved by the Kentucky State Department of Education for teacher education and certification. Inquiries concerning the accreditation status of the University may be directed to the Commission on Colleges at 1866 Southern Lane, Decatur, Georgia 30033-4097 or by calling 404-676-4500.

Major fields of study are accounting, art, biology, business administration, chemistry, church music, Christian ministries, Christian studies, communication arts, criminal justice, education, English, exercise and sport science, fitness and sport management, health, history, human services, journalism and public relations, management information systems, mathematics, missions, music, philosophy, physics, political science, psychology, public health, religion, Spanish, special education, and theater arts.

Minor fields can be chosen from the major fields or in biblical languages or French.

Preprofessional and special curricula are offered in military science, pre-dentistry, pre-engineering, pre-law, pre-medicine, pre-optometry, pre-pharmacy, pre–physical therapy, pre–physician assistant studies, pre–veterinary medicine, and religious vocations.

Academic Programs

University of the Cumberlands seeks to provide academic specialization within a broad framework of a liberal arts education. To supplement the in-depth knowledge acquired within each major, 37 semester hours of general studies from the areas of Christian faith and values, cultural and aesthetic values, the English language, humanities, leadership and community service, natural and mathematical sciences, physical education, and social sciences are required. Students must earn at least 128 semester hours to graduate with a bachelor's degree.

The academic year begins in late August, with the first semester ending in mid-December. The second semester runs from early January to early May. Two 4-week undergraduate summer sessions and two 4-week graduate summer sessions are also offered. Orientation, preregistration, and academic advising by faculty members begin in the summer preceding entrance.

Students may receive credit for successful scores on the Advanced Placement examinations of the College Board, the College-Level Examination Program (CLEP), and special departmental tests. Through the honors program, highly qualified students have the opportunity to undertake advanced independent study.

Students benefit from such special services as free tutorial assistance and those offered by the Career Services Center, the Center for Leadership Studies, and the Academic Resource Center.

Academic Facilities

The University of the Cumberlands campus contains thirty-five buildings reflecting antebellum architectural style. The Correll Science Complex features state-of-the-art biology, chemistry, and physics labs providing graduate-level research opportunities.

The McGaw Music Building contains individual rehearsal and studio areas as well as a recital hall. The Norma Perkins Hagan Memorial Library houses thousands of book titles, periodical subscriptions, and microform titles. Sophisticated computer equipment provides access to millions of items from many of the nation's outstanding libraries. The instructional media center includes a children's library, a computerized language lab, and a listening library.

Other special academic features include a computer center, an art gallery, a word processing center for English composition, a theater, a 600-seat chapel, four large lecture halls, and the Distance Learning Laboratory.

Recent additions to the campus include the state-of-the-art Hutton School of Business, a 27,000-square-foot addition to the Science Building, and Harth Hall, a women's residence hall.

Costs

For 2015–16, the basic academic year expenses are $22,000 for tuition and fees and $8,500 for room and board, for a total of $30,500. There are no additional fees for out-of-state students. The average cost for books and supplies is approximately $500 per semester.

Financial Aid

University of the Cumberlands sponsors a large financial aid program that coordinates monies from federal, state, private, and University sources. Ninety-five percent of UC students share more than $30 million in aid.

To apply for financial aid, it is necessary to complete the Free Application for Federal Student Aid (FAFSA). For further information about financial aid opportunities, students should contact the Director of Financial Planning at 800-343-1609 (toll free). Applications made by March 1 are given priority for the fall semester.

Numerous scholarships and grants are available.

Faculty

There are 112 full-time and 33 part-time faculty members who are respected scholars and whose primary responsibility is to teach. Graduate assistants do not teach courses. The student-faculty ratio is 15:1, enabling students to receive ample attention and assistance from professors. Faculty members also serve as advisers to help students in planning their academic programs.

Admission Requirements

In compliance with federal law, including provisions of Title IX of the Educational Amendments of 1972 and Section 504 of the Rehabilitation Act of 1973, University of the Cumberlands does not illegally discriminate on the basis of race, sex, color, national or ethnic origin, age, disability, or military service in its administration of education policies, programs, or activities; admissions policies; or employment. Under federal law, the University reserves the right to discriminate on the basis of sex in its undergraduate admissions programs. Further, the University reserves the right to deny admission to any applicant whose academic preparation, character, or personal conduct is determined to be inconsistent with the purpose and objectives of the University. Where possible, the University will seek to reasonably accommodate a student's disability. However, the University's obligation to reasonably accommodate a student's disability ends where the accommodation would pose an undue hardship on the University or where the accommodation in question would fundamentally alter the academic program. Inquiries or complaints should be directed to the Vice President for Academic Affairs.

The purpose of the admission process is to identify applicants who are likely to succeed academically at University of the Cumberlands and at the same time contribute positively to the campus community. The process considers such factors as high school records (including courses taken, grade trends, and rank in class), college records (if transferring from another institution), scores on the ACT or SAT, extracurricular activities and honors, and personal conduct.

Campus tours are available on weekdays by appointment and on selected Saturdays. Prospective students can take a tour of the beautiful campus; talk with students, professors, and coaches; spend the night in the residence halls; attend an athletic or extracurricular event; and get answers to questions during a session with an admissions counselor.

Application and Information

Applicants may apply online at http://www.ucumberlands.edu or may contact the Office of Admissions for an application form. Return the completed form to the University, along with the appropriate application fee, official transcripts of all high school and college work, and a copy of ACT or SAT scores. Each student is notified regarding official admission within ten working days after the application procedure has been completed.

Students accepted for admission must submit the required enrollment deposit.

Additional information can be obtained at:

Office of Admissions
University of the Cumberlands
816 Walnut Street
Williamsburg, Kentucky 40769
Phone: 606-539-4241
800-343-1609 (toll-free)
E-mail: admiss@ucumberlands.edu
Website: http://www.ucumberlands.edu
http://twitter.com/#!/UCumberlandsKy
http://www.youtube.com/UCumberlandsMedia

University of the Cumberlands offers individualized learning and research opportunities.

UNIVERSITY OF THE INCARNATE WORD

SAN ANTONIO, TEXAS

★ To read more about this school, visit http://petersons.to/uiw

The University

Consistently rated among the top liberal arts universities in the Southwest, the University of the Incarnate Word (UIW) welcomes prospective students seeking a challenging and diverse Catholic university atmosphere. The university seeks students who value small classes, interaction with faculty members, and dynamic learning experiences. Founded in 1881 as Incarnate Word College by the Sisters of Charity of the Incarnate Word, the school achieved university status in 1996. The university has a population of close to 10,000 students, with more than 4,000 students seeking baccalaureate degrees on the main campus and over 2,000 students seeking graduate, doctoral, or professional degrees. UIW currently offers nearly eighty undergraduate and graduate programs of study in a variety of fields. The student body at the University of the Incarnate Word reflects the rich cultural diversity of south Texas—54 percent of students are Hispanic American, 22 percent are Caucasian, 8 percent are African American, 4 percent are Asian, 5 percent are other, 6 percent are Non-Resident Alien, and 1 percent two or more races. Students at the university come from forty-eight states and Puerto Rico as well as seventy-eight other countries. Many students reside on campus with housing options that include traditional dormitories, suites, and apartments. There are multiple dining facilities on campus, including a full-service cafeteria, a second limited offerings cafeteria, a Chick-fil-A, and two coffee shops featuring Starbucks coffees. There are more than 70 different student groups and organizations on campus, including fraternities and sororities, honors organizations, *The Logos* campus newspaper, Internet radio station KUIW, UIWtv, as well as theater and musical ensembles.

The School of Graduate Studies offers the following degrees: Master of Arts (M.A.) in biology, communication arts, education, mathematics teaching, multidisciplinary sciences, multidisciplinary studies, fashion design and religious studies; Master of Arts in Administration (M.A.A.); Master of Arts in Teaching (M.A.T.); Master of Business Administration (M.B.A.); Master of Education (M.Ed.); Master of Science in Nursing (M.S.N.); Master of Health Administration (M.H.A.); Master of Physician Assistant Studies (M.P.A.S.); and Master of Science (M.S.) in accounting, biology, kinesiology, nutrition, research statistics, and sport management. Doctoral programs include Doctor of Business Administration (D.B.A.); Doctor of Nursing Practice (D.N.P.); and Doctor of Philosophy in Vision Science and a Doctor of Philosophy in Education (Ph.D.). In addition, the Feik School of Pharmacy launched a Doctor of Pharmacy (Pharm.D.) program in 2006, quickly followed by the Rosenberg School of Optometry and the School of Physical Therapy. A physician assistant program is set to begin in the fall of 2015, and UIW recently announced plans to build a new osteopathic medical school in 2016. It is poised to be the second OD school in the state.

The University of the Incarnate Word is fully accredited by the Southern Association of Colleges and Schools, Texas Education Agency, Council of Baccalaureate and Higher Degree Programs of the National League for Nursing, Committee on Accreditation of Allied Health Education (CAAHE), American Dietetic Association, Joint Review Committee on Educational Programs in Nuclear Medicine, Joint Review Committee on Education Programs in Athletic Training, American Association for Music Therapy, National Association of Schools of Theatre, Board of Nurse Examiners for the State of Texas, and Commission for Collegiate Nursing Education. The university is affiliated with the American Association of Colleges for Teacher Education, Association of Collegiate Business Schools and Programs, Association of Texas Colleges and Universities, Association of Texas Graduate Schools, and National Catholic Education Association.

The University of the Incarnate Word is an equal opportunity institution and an Affirmative Action employer.

Location

The University of the Incarnate Word is located in the Alamo Heights area of San Antonio—an area replete with artisans, studios, specialty shops, cafés, and coffeehouses. The 154-acre campus of rolling hills is filled with live oak and pecan trees and many varieties of blooming trees and flowers. In addition, the waters of the San Antonio River flow through the campus, originating from natural springs located nearby. Within walking distance are the Witte Museum, San Antonio Zoo, Brackenridge Park, Sunken Garden Theatre, and the San Antonio Botanical Gardens. San Antonio, the "City of Fiesta" and America's seventh-largest city, boasts an international reputation for beauty and excitement—the Alamo, Paseo del Rio (Riverwalk), historic missions, Market Square, Institute of Texan Cultures, Sea World of Texas, and Six Flags Fiesta Texas are among its largest attractions. San Antonio is also home to four military bases, numerous cultural and civic groups, a symphony orchestra, the five-time NBA champion San Antonio Spurs, the WNBA's Silver Stars, major concerts, and many festivals and celebrations. The San Antonio International Airport and downtown San Antonio are just 10 minutes from the university and easily accessed via public transportation.

Majors and Degrees

The Bachelor of Arts (B.A.) degree is offered in art, biology, chemistry, communication arts, criminal justice, cultural studies, English, fashion management, government, history, interdisciplinary studies, interior design, international affairs, mathematics, music, music industry studies, pastoral ministry, philosophy, psychology, religious studies, sociology, Spanish, and theater arts.

The Bachelor of Business Administration (B.B.A.) degree is offered in accounting, business economics, finance, financial economics, general business, international business, management, management information systems, marketing, political economics, professional golf management, as well as sport management.

The Bachelor of Fine Arts (B.F.A.) degree is offered in art, fashion design, and graphic design.

The Bachelor of Music (B.M.) is offered in music education and music therapy.

The Bachelor of Science (B.S.) is offered in biochemistry, biology, broadcast meteorology, chemistry, computer information systems, engineering, environmental science, kinesiology, mathematics, meteorology, nuclear medicine science, nutrition, rehabilitative sciences, and vision science. The Bachelor of Science in Nursing (B.S.N.) and a Bachelor of Science in Athletic Training are also offered.

The university offers teacher certification and pre-professional programs, such as pre-dentistry, pre-engineering, pre-law, pre-medicine, pre-optometry, pre-pharmacy, and pre–veterinary science.

Academic Programs

To receive any degree from the UIW, a student must fulfill the requirements of the university's core curriculum in addition to course work specific to the major. The University of the Incarnate Word recognizes the core curriculum as the heart of the institution. Its mission of producing critical thinkers, effective communicators, ethical leaders, responsible citizens, and caring individuals is well demonstrated in the many successful graduates of UIW. The core is composed of approximately 43 hours of course work in rhetoric, literature and arts, foreign language, wellness development, mathematics and natural science, and computer literacy. Students must complete 45 hours of community service to receive their diploma.

The Bachelor of Arts degree entails a minimum of 120 hours of specified course work; the Bachelor of Business Administration requires a minimum of 120 hours; the Bachelor of Music specifies 137 hours; the Bachelor of Science in Nursing requires 129 hours; and the Bachelor of Science specifies a minimum of 120 hours. Graduation requirements for individual programs may vary depending on the minor sought, teacher certification requirements, clinical requirements, and credits transferred.

Academic credit is granted to students who achieve a score of 3 or higher on the College Board Advanced Placement examination. The university routinely administers examinations in the College-Level Examination Program (CLEP) for credit purposes. UIW operates on a semester calendar with two summer sessions.

Off-Campus Programs

The School of Extended Studies operates education sites at several locations in the city of San Antonio. UIW's burgeoning Adult Degree Completion Program (ADCaP) assists working adults who seek to complete their bachelor's degree. The UIW's Online program offers Internet-based courses, allowing students with busy or varied schedules to pursue an associate, bachelor's, or master's degree at UIW from anywhere in the world. Consortium agreements allow UIW students access to libraries at eight local colleges and universities. In addition, students may cross-register with three of these institutions for course work if necessary.

The University of the Incarnate Word recognizes the importance of providing opportunities for students to gain employment experience in their major field before graduation. As a result UIW students are involved in numerous challenging and rewarding internship and cooperative education ventures. With a diverse student body, UIW is a leader in international education with more than 140 sister schools around the world. The university also operates a campus in Mexico City, Miguel Angel–Incarnate Word, which is one of the first schools to offer degrees that are accredited both in the U.S. and in Mexico.

Academic Facilities

The library at the university houses 235,000 volumes and 3,048 periodical titles. Information systems currently available to students include CINAHL and HaPI for nursing majors; ERIC for education students; ABI/INFORM for business majors; and OCLC online system, Info Trac, National Newspaper and Dissertation Abstract, Books in Print, Dynix, and the Internet for general student use. All housing units are computer accessible. The Learning Assistance Center (LAC) underscores the university's commitment to student achievement.

Study groups, tutors, and special services are coordinated through the LAC as well. The university's fine arts complex is among the most impressive in south Texas. A state-of-the-art music building, complete with a full recording studio and private practice booths, was recently completed and full renovations on three theaters (including a downstage) is nearing completion as well. Construction on the new Student Engagement Center began in the summer of 2015. This new facility will house multiple offices, a new student center, dining facilities, and a recreation area. The commitment to technology extends beyond classrooms and dormitories. UIW has PC and Macbook laptops and tablets available for purchase by all students.

Costs

For the 2015–16 academic year, full-time resident students pay $40,362 for tuition, room and board, books, and fees. Full-time students who commute to campus pay $28,998 for tuition, books, and fees.

Financial Aid

More than 96 percent of all students at the university receive some type of financial assistance, and more than $91 million is spent annually in scholarships, work-study, loans, and grants. The university awards Presidential/Academic, performance/visual arts, and athletic scholarships, none of which are need-based. Presidential/Academic scholarships are awarded based on high school grade point average and SAT/ACT test scores. All other forms of financial assistance are awarded based on financial need as determined by the Free Application for Federal Student Aid (FAFSA). Other federal/state/institutional financial assistance awarded includes the Federal Pell Grant, Federal Supplemental Educational Opportunity Grant, Texas Equalization Grant, UIW Grant, Federal Perkins Loan, Federal Subsidized and Unsubsidized Stafford Loans, Federal Parent Loan, Texas College Access Loan, Federal Work-Study, Texas Work-Study, and Institutional Employment.

Faculty

The University of the Incarnate Word prides itself on a 125-year tradition of teaching excellence. The university's 400-plus faculty members include scholars with a variety of backgrounds and experiences. Eighty-five percent of the full-time faculty members possess either a doctorate or terminal degree. Faculty members at the university insist on playing an active role in the students' learning process. Small class sizes facilitate the dialogue and interaction that faculty members and students enjoy most.

Student Government

The Student Government Association (SGA) has a long and productive history at UIW. Student representatives are included on every policy-making body, including the Board of Trustees. SGA initiatives include a number of forums each year on issues of student concern and workshops/seminars on events of significance (Black History Month, Women's History Month, Earth Day, and the annual Golden Harvest). SGA also approves funding allocations for student clubs and organizations. Elections are held in April of each year for president and executive officers and in September for individual representatives.

Admission Requirements

The University of the Incarnate Word actively recruits students who can enrich and be enriched by a small, private, selective, Catholic liberal arts atmosphere. Applicants are evaluated using a number of criteria: GPA, course difficulty, class rank, SAT and/or ACT scores, letters of recommendation, and extracurricular activities (including part-time work). Prospective students are strongly encouraged to visit the campus and meet with an admissions counselor. Applicants with nontraditional or disadvantaged backgrounds are encouraged to apply. Prospective freshmen are advised to complete a minimum of 16 Carnegie units of work in high school, including 4 units of English, 2 units of mathematics, 2 units of natural science, 2 units of language, and 1 unit of the fine arts. Favorable consideration is given to students who enroll in courses at the honors or advanced placement (AP) level. High school graduates within less than two years of the entrance date must submit either SAT or ACT test scores. Applicants must submit an official transcript of high school work completed or General Educational Development (GED) test scores. Transfer students must submit official transcripts of all college-level work attempted. Those with fewer than 24 college credits completed must submit official high school transcripts and ACT or SAT scores as well. The university requires a minimum 2.5 cumulative GPA for consideration as a transfer student. It is recommended that international students apply no later than three months prior to the beginning of the intended semester of attendance. The Test of English as a Foreign Language (TOEFL) is required of international students. An intensive English program, which is administered by the Berlitz Company, is available on campus.

Application and Information

Applications for admission are accepted on a rolling basis. February 1, 2016, is the early application deadline. If any student applies for the fall 2016 semester on or before February 1, 2016, the application fee is waived. April 1 is the priority deadline for financial assistance. A complete application file is processed within three to four weeks.

For more information, prospective students should contact:

Office of Admissions
University of the Incarnate Word
4301 Broadway
San Antonio, Texas 78209
United States
Phone: 210-829-6005
800-749-WORD (toll-free)
Fax: 210-829-3921
E-mail: admis@uiwtx.edu
Website: http://www.uiw.edu/admissions

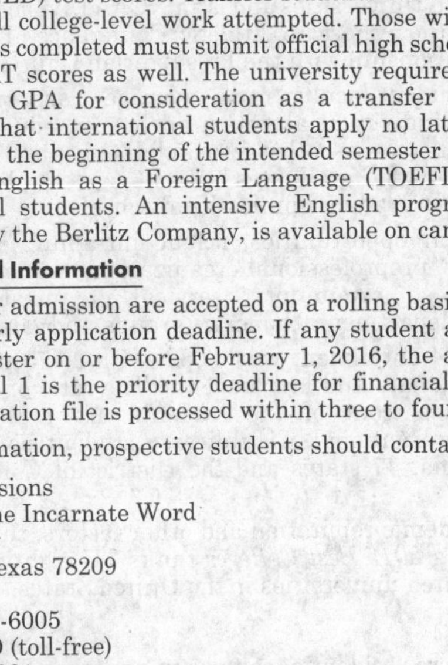

As a student ambassador, I love being able to tell prospective students about my school and all the ways you can get involved here. I've discovered my true potential, and now I work to help others find theirs.
Tenna Montana, UIW Undergraduate

THE UNIVERSITY OF TULSA

TULSA, OKLAHOMA

The University

The University of Tulsa (TU) is a private, comprehensive degree-granting university that provides high-quality education in the arts, humanities, sciences, engineering, business, education, applied health sciences, and law. TU comprises four undergraduate colleges—the Henry Kendall College of Arts and Sciences, the Collins College of Business, the College of Engineering and Natural Sciences, and the College of Health Sciences—along with a College of Law and a Graduate School.

The University is fully accredited by the North Central Association of Colleges and Universities and is an NCAA Division IA participant currently in the American Athletic Conference. TU maintains a covenant relationship with the Presbyterian Church (U.S.A.).

TU's 11:1 student-faculty ratio, average class size of 20, and emphasis on individual attention anchor an educational culture where students receive both rigorous challenges and comprehensive support. In 2014, TU graduates had a 96 percent placement rate in full-time jobs or graduate/professional schools.

Extracurricular opportunities include intramural sports, special interest clubs, preprofessional organizations, national fraternities and sororities, community service organizations, student government, departmental honorary groups, and campus ministries.

Total fall 2014 enrollment was 4,682, with 3,473 undergraduates and 1,209 graduate and law students. The ratio of men to women is 57:43, 16 percent of the students are multicultural, and 20 percent international. TU's diverse student population comes from Oklahoma, 47 states and the District of Columbia, and 81 countries.

Based on academic reputation and other factors, the *U.S. News & World Report*'s *2015 Best Colleges* ranks TU eighty-eighth among doctoral/research universities in the United States.

Location

TU is a 216-acre residential campus in midtown Tulsa, Oklahoma. Tulsa's prominent industries include energy, telecommunications, technology, data processing, manufacturing, health care, aerospace, transportation, and education, all of which provide TU students with opportunities for internships and employment after graduation. The Tulsa metropolitan area has about 550,000 residents. Cultural assets include the Performing Arts Center, BOK Center (venue for popular entertainers), acclaimed ballet and opera companies, a symphony, Philbrook Museum, Gilcrease Museum, Brady Arts District, and cultural festivals. Professional sports in Tulsa include baseball, basketball, and hockey. The River Parks system provides facilities for outdoor activities with jogging and biking trails, while Guthrie Green is a popular arts, music, and food truck destination.

Majors and Degrees

The Henry Kendall College of Arts and Sciences grants the Bachelor of Arts, Bachelor of Fine Arts, Bachelor of Music, Bachelor of Music Education, and Bachelor of Science degrees with majors in anthropology, art, art history, arts management, Chinese studies, communication, deaf education, economics, elementary education, English, environmental policy, film studies, French, German, history, music, musical theatre, organizational studies, philosophy, political science, psychology, religion, Russian studies, sociology, Spanish, theater, women's and gender studies, and self-designed majors. Minors include most disciplines as well as advertising, Chinese, classics, creative writing, dance, early childhood intervention, film scoring, Latin, Portuguese, and Russian. Secondary teacher certification is available in designated disciplines. Interdisciplinary certificate programs offer a way for students to focus their interests in advertising, African American studies, classics, creative writing, international studies, journalism studies, Judaic studies, museum studies, political philosophy, and visual studies.

The Collins College of Business awards the Bachelor of Science in Business Administration degree in accounting, economics, energy management, finance, management, management information systems, and marketing; and a Bachelor of Science in international business and language. Minors are available in most disciplines plus business administration (for non-majors), coaching, health care informatics, and international business (for business majors only). Certificate programs are available in accounting, finance, management information systems, not-for-profit administration, and sports administration. Management majors may choose specializations in business law, entrepreneurship and family business management, or human resource management. The college is home to several specialized centers, including the Energy Management Program, Family Owned Business Institute, the Genave King Rogers Center for Business Law, and the Williams Risk Management Center.

The College of Health Sciences offers the Bachelor of Science degree in nursing, athletic training, and exercise and sport science, as well as a Bachelor of Arts degree in speech pathology.

The College of Engineering and Natural Sciences offers the Bachelor of Science degree in applied mathematics, biochemistry, biogeosciences, biological science (options in pre-medicine, pre-dentistry, and pre–veterinary science), chemical engineering, chemistry, computer science, computer simulation and gaming, earth and environmental science, electrical and computer engineering, electrical engineering, engineering physics, geology, geophysics, information technology, mathematics, mechanical engineering, petroleum engineering, and physics. Minors are available in the science and computational science disciplines. The college features state-of-the-art research facilities for all majors. Since 1995, more than 50 TU engineering students have received the prestigious Barry M. Goldwater Scholarship, the nation's premier award for undergraduate students in engineering, math, or science.

Academic Programs

The Tulsa Curriculum links a broad, humanities-based core and writing-across-the-curriculum approach for all students with a highly flexible group of majors, minors, concentrations, and certificate programs. TU students can receive an education that is well-rounded, in-depth, and uniquely personalized. Candidates for graduation must complete at least 124 semester hours of course work, with more hours required of engineering and business administration majors.

The Honors Program engages students in a critical examination of the major epochs and ideas of Western thought and culture through careful study of primary texts. The acclaimed Tulsa Undergraduate Research Challenge (TURC) program combines advanced research in most disciplines, scholarship, and community service.

The TU Institute for Information Security is developing defenses against cyber-attacks and comprised infrastructure. The center supports the University's National Security Agency (NSA)–accredited certificate program in information assurance, a curriculum that integrates information security with computer law and policy issues. TU has been designated a Center of Excellence in information assurance by the NSA and is one of six pioneer institutions selected by the National Science Foundation for the Federal Cyber Service Initiative (Cyber Corps).

Air Force ROTC is available through a satellite program.

Qualified students may receive credit through Advanced Placement testing. Students who complete the International Baccalaureate diploma can receive up to 30 college credit hours.

The University of Tulsa operates on a semester calendar. The fall term begins in late August and the spring term in mid-January.

Off-Campus Programs

The University is supportive of study-abroad and internship experiences. The Center for Global Education helps students locate the perfect program, whether for TU credit or as an intern or volunteer. Students choose from hundreds of opportunities offered around the world through a direct exchange with an international university, an affiliate-sponsored program, or as part of a faculty-led course. Internship opportunities are also available in Tulsa and throughout the nation.

Academic Facilities

TU's libraries, historic McFarlin Library and Mabee Legal Information Center, house more than 4 million items. McFarlin holdings include over 920,000 volumes, 620,000 titles, 120,000 e-books, 40,000 electronic periodicals, 7,500 videos, and 10,000 recordings. McFarlin's special collections rare book holdings number over 125,000 volumes and are internationally recognized, particularly for holdings of Native American history and law, along with nineteenth- and twentieth-century Irish, English, and American literature. McFarlin is home to the papers of 2001 Nobel Laureate V. S. Naipaul. The 12,000-square-foot Academic Technology Center annex was dedicated in 2009, adding computer labs, a coffee shop, and restored reading rooms.

Recently the College of Engineering and Natural Sciences added J. Newton Rayzor Hall, a $14-million home for the Tandy School of Computer Science and Department of Electrical Engineering with twenty-four integrated classrooms and state-of-the-art teaching/research laboratories; and Stephenson Hall, the new 38,600-square-foot home for the Department of Mechanical Engineering and McDougall School of Petroleum Engineering. The University's flagship Keplinger Hall will soon undergo renovation. Additional research facilities are housed at Tulsa's North Campus where government- and industry-funded research consortia explore innovations and solve problems faced by the petroleum industry while fostering student learning.

The Mary K. Chapman Center for Communicative Disorders serves the community with its clinical facility and is the learning center for the Department of Communication Disorders. The department has the latest equipment and instrumentation available for use in research, diagnostic, and therapy activities.

Helmerich Hall, which houses the Collins College of Business, was renovated to add innovative learning spaces such as the Williams Students Services Center and Studio Blue. The Williams Risk Management Center, an advanced learning environment in the Collins College of Business, combines the latest in trading-floor technology and advanced study in risk management theories and techniques.

The Roxana Rózsa and Robert Eugene Lorton Performance Center is home to the School of Music and the Department of Film Studies, the 77,000-square-foot facility includes a 600-seat concert hall, specialized rehearsal and practice rooms, and a film production suite with postproduction editing and scoring capabilities.

Kendall Hall is home to the Department of Theatre and Musical Theatre and features two fully equipped theaters, a scene shop, costume shop, and computer-design lab.

The Donald W. Reynolds Center is the campus arena and convocation center. This $28-million facility is the home for the intercollegiate basketball and volleyball programs and has cutting-edge facilities for video editing and training.

The Chapman Student Union was recently renovated and offers many dining options. Meals and snacks are also available in the Pat Case Dining Center, the Collins Fitness Center, and the McFarlin Library Café.

Dedicated in 2007, the 29,000-square-foot Case Athletic Complex is home to the Golden Hurricane football program and adjoins the renovated H. A. Chapman Stadium where players enjoy one of the nation's elite college football training and playing environments.

The University's 34-acre sports and recreation complex features a 64,000-square-foot fitness center, the Michael Case Tennis Center, track, NCAA soccer and softball fields, and intramural fields.

TU manages the acclaimed Gilcrease Museum, home to the world's largest collection of art and artifacts of the American West. The two entities have expanded into the Brady Arts District to open the Henry Zarrow Center for Art and Education, providing classes and studio space.

Costs

For 2014–15, the typical cost for students living on campus was $46,331, including $35,050 for tuition, $10,426 for room and board, and fees of $855. Additional miscellaneous expenses (including books) average about $3,600 per year.

Financial Aid

In 2014, 91 percent of entering students received some form of financial aid (including grants, scholarships, work-study, and loans). TU offers a limited number of highly competitive Presidential Scholarships that cover full tuition, room, and board. All applicants may be considered for a range of University scholarships based on academic merit. Performance scholarships are available in music and theater by audition. The University of Tulsa participates in National Merit and National Achievement Scholarship Corporation's Finalist program and the National Hispanic Scholar Program. Applicants for aid should submit the Free Application for Federal Student Aid (FAFSA) by February 1 for priority consideration.

Faculty

The University has 334 full-time faculty members, with 96 percent having earned the highest degree in their field of study. The faculty is primarily a teaching faculty, although most of its members are also involved in funded research or publishing activities.

Admission Requirements

The University of Tulsa seeks students whose academic background indicates potential for success in the university's rigorous academic environment. Performance in high school college-preparatory subjects and scores on the SAT or ACT are key factors in the admission evaluation, but each applicant is reviewed holistically. Each applicant's counselor recommendation; extracurricular activities; and indicators of leadership, creativity, and focus are all taken into consideration. Campus visits and interviews are highly recommended but not required.

Application and Information

TU has a nonbinding, early action freshman admission plan with an application deadline of November 1. Decisions are mailed within five weeks. Applications received after November 1 are reviewed under a rolling admission process with notifications made on an ongoing basis after mid-December.

An application, high school transcript, ACT or SAT score results, and a guidance counselor recommendation are required. TU accepts the Common Application or its own online or paper application form. TU adheres to the national Candidate's Reply Date of May 1.

For more information, students should contact:

Office of Undergraduate Admission
The University of Tulsa
800 South Tucker Drive
Tulsa, Oklahoma 74104-3189
Phone: 918-631-2307 (in Tulsa)
800-331-3050 (toll-free)
Fax: 918-631-5008
E-mail: admission@utulsa.edu
Website: http://www.utulsa.edu/admission
http://www.utulsa.edu/admissionblog

Bayless Plaza is home to the iconic Kendall Bell. Graduating seniors honor tradition by ringing it following the completion of their last final exam.

UNIVERSITY OF WASHINGTON BOTHELL

BOTHELL, WASHINGTON

W UNIVERSITY *of* WASHINGTON BOTHELL

The University

The University of Washington Bothell (UW Bothell) opens the door to a nationally and internationally ranked university experience that inspires innovation and creativity. UW Bothell is one of three University of Washington campuses. Through providing distinctive offerings, its graduates earn a fully accredited UW degree. Faculty members are passionate about the knowledge they bring to the classroom and seek to provide a student-centered education in a collaborative learning environment. With 4,900 full-time students and approximately 360 faculty members, UW Bothell offers modest-sized classes, (average class size is 31 students), perfectly suited for meaningful interaction and critical thinking. Students take an active role in their educational experience, discover their own strengths and abilities, and ultimately learn how to fulfill their academic and personal goals. About three quarters of UW Bothell faculty involve undergraduates in hands-on research experiences.

The campus is located in the thriving, dynamic, and globally engaged greater Seattle area, home to some of the world's most iconic and entrepreneurial corporations, foundations, and arts organizations.

The curriculum emphasizes close student-faculty interactions, collaboration among students, and hands-on learning. Outstanding regional connections present students with unique opportunities for projects, internships, and research with leading businesses and organizations. At UW Bothell, students earn a University of Washington degree while building a solid foundation of relevant knowledge, practical skills, and professional preparation.

In additional to its undergraduate degree programs, UW Bothell offers several graduate programs in disciplines including accounting, business, computing and software systems, cultural studies, cyber security engineering, education, nursing, policy studies, and fine arts.

Location

UW Bothell is located in Bothell, Washington, approximately 20 minutes northeast of Seattle. Bothell is a suburban community conveniently located in an area full of both urban adventures and natural escapes. The UW Bothell campus sits atop a 128-acre plot of picturesque land overlooking protected wetlands and the Cascades beyond. Fifty-eight acres of campus house one of the largest and most complex floodplain restorations in Washington State that is now a sustainable functioning floodplain ecosystem.

Majors and Degrees

UW Bothell offers more than thirty-six degrees through a variety of programs as well as the School of Business; School of Science, Technology, Engineering, and Mathematics; and the School of Interdisciplinary Arts and Sciences. UW Bothell is proud of its reputation for innovative, specialized degree options.

Students can choose from an array of undergraduate degrees in disciplines including:

- American and Ethnic Studies
- Applied Computing
- Biology
- Business Administration (with many options and concentrations)
- Chemistry
- Climate Science and Policy
- Community Psychology
- Computer Engineering
- Computing Science and Software Engineering
- Culture, Literature, and the Arts
- Electrical Engineering
- Environmental Science
- Environmental Studies
- Global Studies
- Health Studies
- Interactive Media Design
- Interdisciplinary Arts
- Law, Economics and Public Policy
- Mathematics
- Mechanical Engineering
- Media and Communication Studies
- Nursing
- Science, Technology and Society
- Society, Ethics and Human Behavior

Postbaccalaureate programs include K–8 teacher certification as well as professional certification.

Off-Campus Programs

Students attending UW Bothell are able to take part in a variety of exceptional educational and technical programs made possible through collaborative efforts with a broad range of community partners. These opportunities are helpful in addressing workforce needs, as well as local and global challenges. Closer community ties will foster a better understanding of the skills and programs students and employers need, while enriching the education of the University's students by providing real-world experiences to learn from and the opportunity to give back to local communities.

UW Bothell takes advantage of the region's extraordinary capacity for creativity and innovation by connecting students to career-building experiences. Committed to the greater good, UW Bothell builds regional partnerships, inspires change, creates knowledge, shares discoveries, and prepares students for leadership in the state of Washington and beyond. Additional information is available at www.uwb.edu/cblr.

Academic Facilities

Although thoroughly modern, UW Bothell buildings were designed to complement the land's natural beauty; they are environmentally friendly and are equipped with advanced technology for faculty and student use. The UW Bothell campus is well known for its eco-friendly award-winning architecture, state-of-the-art technology, and breathtaking views. Its stunning architecture and landscaping garnered the American Institute of Architects 2002 Honor Award for Washington architecture.

UW Bothell takes its reputation as a green campus very seriously. Sustainability efforts are more than a concept to be studied. Instead, practicing consistent environmental caretaking is the norm. Examples abound, and include everything from LEED-certified buildings and solar panels to worm-assisted composting and pesticide-free landscape maintenance.

UW Bothell offers outstanding student support services: an award-winning on-campus library with access to the full UW library system, a career center, writing center, personal counseling, computer support, and mentoring available for first-generation students and English language learners (ELL).

As a result of generous support from private donors, the student body, and the State of Washington, the UW Bothell campus is experiencing unprecedented growth. The recently completed Sports Field and Recreation Complex was a student-led and funded project that includes a multipurpose synthetic turf sports field, tennis courts, basketball court, and a sand volleyball court. Also new in 2013 was the Sarah Simonds Green Conservatory. The conservatory includes education and exhibit space for historical displays and interpretive materials, as well as a greenhouse to support plant propagation. Discovery Hall, the new $68-million, 74,000 square-foot science and academic building, opened for classes in the fall of 2014. This new state-of-the art building provides space for eleven new science labs, several classrooms, gathering space, and a 200-person lecture hall. Construction has begun on the new student Activities and Recreation Center (ARC), expected to open in fall 2015. The Activities and Recreation Center is another student-led and funded project that will become the center of campus life and include open, flexible space for student government and club offices, an expanded fitness center with shower and locker facilities, and multipurpose and gathering spaces. More information about campus construction, including building renderings, is available online at www.uwb.edu/about/construction.

Costs

Tuition rates for 2014–15 for full-time (10 to 18 credits) undergraduate studies were $3,971 per quarter for Washington residents and $11,010 per quarter for nonresidents. Tuition rates for graduate and nondegree programs vary depending upon the individual program. Updated tuition information is available online at www.uwb.edu/tuition.

Financial Aid

As part of the University of Washington, UW Bothell participates in the Husky Promise Program, which is a vital part of the comprehensive financial aid program. The UW offers more than $160 million in financial aid each year, with about 60 percent of all undergraduates receiving aid. Each year, over 5,000 University of Washington students—both undergraduate and graduate—receive more than $20 million in scholarships alone through grants, gifts, or endowed funds.

Approximately 45 percent of UW Bothell first-year students will be the first in their families to earn a bachelor's degree, and 30 percent of students come from families below the median income for the state of Washington. Since fall quarter 2007, more than 5,000 UW students—nearly 20 percent of all undergraduates—have been covered under the Husky Promise. Both the total number of students and the overall percentage covered by the Husky Promise are among the highest in the country when compared to similar programs at comparable institutions.

In addition to the Husky Promise Program, UW Bothell offers a variety of scholarship, fellowship, and financial aid opportunities. The UW Bothell Purple and Gold Scholar Awards (up to $15,000 per year, renewable) are available to U.S. residents from outside the state of Washington who have demonstrated extraordinary scholarship and aptitude. Detailed information about financial aid and scholarship opportunities are available in the web version of the UW Bothell Financial Aid and Scholarships Guide at www.uwb.edu/financialaid.

Faculty

At UW Bothell the educational relationship between faculty members and their students is paramount. Modest class sizes and a student-faculty ratio of 19:1 provide ample opportunity for students to engage with their professors in an environment that is inspiring yet challenging. Faculty members are encouraged to be innovative and creative in the classroom, and are supported in their desire to pursue research and other endeavors as well.

Above all, UW Bothell faculty members pay attention to the changing needs and interests of their students. Students are not only allowed a voice in the classroom, but are strongly encouraged to share their ideas and help shape classroom dynamics.

In today's technologically advanced world, adaptability is the key to ultimate success. With this in mind, UW Bothell faculty members utilize innovative teaching methods and interdisciplinary approaches, thus providing hands-on preparation for real life and career.

Campus Student Housing

More than 270 students live in UW Bothell student housing and enjoy all the conveniences of apartment-style living along with residence life programming, a vibrant community of learners, and a safe environment to student success. This provides an opportunity for students to interact with diverse individuals, form study groups, and learn more about themselves. UW Bothell student residents socialize, thrive, and create lasting memories and friendships. On-campus student housing is located within a short distance from classrooms and services, as well as downtown Bothell shops, restaurants, and parks. Additional information is available online at www.uwb.edu/housing.

Student Government

Located within the Office of Student Life, the Associated Students of UW Bothell (ASUWB) serve as a voice for all students. The goal is to empower the student body through promoting clear communication between faculty members, administration, and students. ASUWB is the sole governing body for students, and its officers are elected.

ASUWB members strive to create an open, friendly campus atmosphere where students can get involved, make a difference, and have fun. There is a diverse selection of more than 90 clubs and groups focusing on academic and recreational interests.

More information can be found online at www.uwb.edu/studentlife.

Admission Requirements

Admission requirements vary depending on specific program of interest. All first-year applicants must complete studies in the following minimum College Academic Distribution Requirements (advanced studies in each subject are encouraged): English, 4 years; mathematics, 3 years; social science, 3 years; lab science, 2 years (including one algebra-based lab); foreign language (includes American sign language), 2 years; fine, visual, or performing arts, ½ year; and academic electives, ½ year.

The UW Bothell admissions website (www.uwb.edu/admissions) provides additional details about these and other requirements.

Application and Information

Application deadlines vary depending on specific program of interest. A detailed list of these dates can be found at www.uwb.edu/admissions/application-dates.

For additional information, contact:

UW Bothell Enrollment Management
Box 358500
18115 Campus Way NE
Bothell, Washington 98011-8246
Phone: 425-352-5000
425-352-5303 (TDD)
E-mail: info@uwb.edu
Website: http://www.uwb.edu

University of Washington Bothell—inspiring innovation and creativity.

UNIVERSITY OF WYOMING

LARAMIE, WYOMING

★ To read more about this school, visit http://petersons.to/universityofwyoming

The University

Established in 1886 as a land grant university, the University of Wyoming has grown into a nationally recognized research institution with accomplished faculty and world-class facilities, all on a picturesque campus. UW provides a unique learning environment with more than 200 areas of study, 250 student organizations, one of the nation's most extensive study-abroad programs, and tremendous opportunities for outdoor sports. UW's 13,600 students hail from all 50 states and 94 countries.

Research done by UW professors and students pushes the boundaries of modern science and technology resulting in the University's classification as a Carnegie Doctoral/High Research institution. UW offers 89 undergraduate degree programs and more than 90 graduate degree programs through seven colleges and two schools. UW's academic programs of distinction are focused in broad areas: science and technology, the arts and humanities, the environment and natural resources, life sciences, and professions critical to the state and region. With a low student-faculty ratio of 14:1 and an average class size of 29 students, UW is a community of scholars and learners committed to excellence.

Students can experience the camaraderie of 250-plus recognized student clubs and organizations, including national fraternities and sororities, honor and professional societies, political and faith-based organizations, and special interest groups. Students also have the opportunity to participate in more than sixty different intramural and club sports. UW is a NCAA Division I-A school with seventeen men's and women's sports competing in the Mountain West Conference.

UW has experienced tremendous growth in new academic, campus recreation, and student life facilities. UW's recently expanded $54-million College of Business building features behavioral and multimedia labs, and a state-of-the-art trading room where students manage a seven-figure portfolio. Students can engage their creative talents at UW's new visual arts center featuring 79,000 square feet of studio space for ceramics, drawing, painting, sculpting, and print making. Campus recreational facilities include the Wyoming Union, offering the UW bookstore, eating establishments, student computers, and study areas. Additional facilities on campus include the recently expanded Half Acre Gym with a 35-foot pinnacle climbing wall, an eighteen-hole golf course, tennis and racquetball courts, weight rooms, and two swimming pools.

UW houses 2,400 students in six residence halls. First-year students are required to live on campus. The residence halls offer unique living environments, including quiet/study floors, special-interest floors, honors floors, and single-gender floors. A variety of different Freshman Interest Groups (FIGS), which are living communities comprised of students who share common classes and academic interests, are also available. Interested students can explore UW's residential experience online at www.uwyo.edu/reslife-dining/.

Location

UW's 785-acre campus is located at the foot of the Rocky Mountains in Laramie, a scenic town of 30,000 at an elevation of 7,220 feet in southeastern Wyoming. No matter the time of year, UW students are outdoors. Many enjoy skiing, boarding, snowmobiling, hiking, camping, hunting, fishing, rock climbing, and mountain biking. UW was recently recognized by *Outside* magazine as the fifteenth-best college campus in the country for outdoor adventure. Laramie—with its blue skies, clean air, and 320 days of sunshine a year—is a friendly university town, 45 miles west of Cheyenne, and 130 miles northwest of Denver, Colorado.

Majors and Degrees

UW offers more than 200 areas of study within six colleges, leading to B.A. and B.S. degrees.

The College of Agriculture and Natural Resources offers undergraduate degree programs in Agricultural Business, Agricultural Communications, Animal and Veterinary Sciences, Family and Consumer Science, Microbiology, Molecular Biology, Organizational Leadership/Applied Science, Rangeland Ecology, and Watershed Management.

The College of Arts and Sciences offers undergraduate degree programs in African American and Diaspora Studies, American Indian Studies, American Studies, Anthropology, Art, Astronomy and Astrophysics, Biology, Botany, Chemistry, Communication, Criminal Justice, English, Environmental Geology and Geohydrology, French, Gender and Women's Studies, Geography, Geology, Geology and Earth Science, Geology and Water Resources, German, History, Humanities/Fine Arts, International Studies, Journalism, Mathematics, Mathematics/Science, Music (with options in education and performance), Philosophy, Physics, Physiology, Political Science, Psychology, Religious Studies, Russian, Social Science, Sociology, Spanish, Statistics, Theatre and Dance, Wildlife and Fisheries Biology and Management, and Zoology.

The College of Business offers undergraduate degree programs in Accounting, Business Administration, Economics, Finance, Management, and Marketing.

The College of Education offers undergraduate degree programs in Elementary Education (options in creative arts, early childhood, environmental studies, and international educational studies/American cultural diversity), and secondary education (options in agriculture, art, English, mathematics, modern languages, sciences, social studies, and industrial technology education).

The College of Engineering and Applied Science offers undergraduate degree programs in Architectural Engineering, Chemical Engineering, Civil Engineering, Computer Engineering, Computer Science, Electrical Engineering, Energy Systems Engineering, Mechanical Engineering, and Petroleum Engineering.

The College of Health Sciences offers degree programs in Dental Hygiene; Kinesiology and Health; Nursing; Pharmacy; Physical Education Teaching; Social Work; and Speech, Language and hearing sciences.

UW offers undergraduate preprofessional programs in Dentistry, Law, Medicine, Nursing, Occupational Therapy, Optometry, Pharmacy, Physical Therapy, and Veterinary Medicine.

The School of Environment and Natural Resources offers interdisciplinary studies that can be combined with course work in seven other fields of study, including the humanities, physical sciences, and social sciences.

The School of Energy Resources offers degree program in Energy Resource Management and Development (with options in fossil fuels; renewable energy; energy air, land, and water management; and professional land management).

Academic Programs

The UW academic calendar consists of two semesters and a complete summer session. Depending on the degree program, students are required to complete approximately 120 credit hours for graduation. Undergraduate programs for most majors can be completed in four years. Students may choose to double major. Minors are also available in many areas. All students are required to complete the University Studies Program, a core curriculum that assists students in developing their knowledge of oral and written communication, mathematics, science, diversity, global awareness, government, and culture.

The University Honors Program provides academically ambitious undergraduates innovative and intellectual learning opportunities. Award-winning faculty members, unique and challenging course work, and senior research projects are the hallmarks of this program.

Off-Campus Programs

UW has over 800 international students and close to 100 international researchers/scholars representing over 94 countries. The International Students and Scholars Office provides support through an extensive orientation program, the Friendship Families program, and the International Student Association, which arranges International Education Week and a weekly International Coffee Hour.

UW partners with over 400 exchange sites or study-abroad programs, allowing students to go almost anywhere in the world and study in English or a foreign language. International Programs also coordinates the National Student Exchange (NSE), a domestic student exchange consortium of U.S. colleges and universities.

The UW Outreach School extends the university learning experience to Wyoming and the nation through credit and noncredit programs. Courses are delivered online, via compressed video, audio teleconferencing, correspondence study, and on-site instruction. Select programs are offered, and degree availability may be limited.

Academic Facilities

The University Libraries' collections number nearly 1.5 million volumes, 2.3 million e-books, and offer links to a variety of library service collections. William Robertson Coe Library is the flagship library. Other library facilities include a geology library (Learning Resource Center), a plant research center (Rocky Mountain Herbarium Library), and a compact shelving facility (Library Annex) which houses the majority of UW Libraries' bound periodicals and government documents. Additional on-campus collections are housed in the American Heritage Center and the George W. Hopper Law Library.

Costs

UW annual tuition and fees for full-time undergraduates during the 2015–16 academic year are $4,891 for Wyoming residents and $15,631 for nonresidents (based on an average class load of 15 credit hours). Room and board (double occupancy, unlimited meal plan) costs are $10,037. Estimated expenses include $1,200 for books and supplies, $840 for travel costs, and $2,200 for personal expenses.

Financial Aid

More than 90 percent of all UW students receive financial assistance. More than $105 million is available in the form of scholarships, loans, grants, and work-study opportunities. The Free Application for Federal Student Aid (FAFSA) is required for need-based assistance (loans, grants, work-study) and for many scholarships. The priority deadline for FAFSA is March 1. Most scholarships at UW are based on academic merit. UW participates in the Western Undergraduate Exchange (WUE) program. The Rocky Mountain Scholars Award is available to nonresident students. Prospective students should visit uwyo.edu/scholarships for complete scholarship deadlines and application information.

Faculty

More than 700 faculty members from the world's most respected colleges and universities have come to teach at UW. Recognized nationally and internationally as experts, 82 percent of faculty members hold the highest degree in their field. UW professors are deeply committed to the success of their students. Ninety-one percent of undergraduate courses are taught by professors or professional lecturers, and many of the most distinguished and accomplished professors at UW teach first-year courses.

Admission Requirements

The University of Wyoming is an exceptional place. All students are welcome to apply at uwyo.edu/admissions. Each student is considered on their individual academic achievement. For assured admission, high school graduates and new first-year students with fewer than 30 transferable college credit hours should have a cumulative high school GPA of 3.0 or above. Students should also have a composite ACT score of 21 or greater or an SAT critical reading/math score of 980 or greater. In addition, all students need to complete 4 years of English, 4 years of mathematics, 4 years of science (including a physical science), 3 years of a social science, 2 years of the same foreign language, and 2 years of additional coursework (behavioral or social sciences, visual arts, performing arts, or humanities). Students who are unable to qualify for assured admission may be admissible with support. Freshman students admitted with support will be required to take part in Synergy, a national award-winning mentoring and support program that assists in the transition to college and increases the academic success rate for participants. Additional details can be found online at uwyo.edu/admissions. Transfer students with 30 or more transferable semester credit hours must have a minimum cumulative college GPA of 2.0.

Application and Information

Students must submit a completed UW Application for Admission, official high school or college transcripts, ACT or SAT scores, and a $40 nonrefundable application fee. Students may apply and pay the application fee online at www.uwyo.edu/apply. UW strongly encourages all prospective students and their parents to visit the campus. Explore www.uwyo.edu/visit to check out UW's various visit options and programs.

Admissions Office
Department 3435
University of Wyoming
1000 East University Avenue
Laramie, Wyoming 82071
United States
Phone: 307-766-5160
E-mail: admissions@uwyo.edu
Website: uwyo.edu/admissions

UW students stroll across campus on a warm fall day.

VANDERBILT UNIVERSITY

NASHVILLE, TENNESSEE

★ To read more about this school, visit http://petersons.to/vanderbilt

VANDERBILT UNIVERSITY

The University

In 1873, on the heels of the Civil War, Commodore Cornelius Vanderbilt gave $1 million to the university that now bears his name, with the hope that it would "contribute to strengthening the ties which should exist between all sections of our common country." Since then, Vanderbilt has enrolled America's most talented students and challenged them to expand their intellectual horizons in an inclusive environment based on open inquiry and respect. Vanderbilt's comprehensive interdisciplinary approach to education allows students to pursue a wide array of academic and curricular interests outside of their main focus of study and the University's progressive financial aid policies assure that it is often cited among the country's best values in national universities.

Consistently ranked among the top 20 universities in the country by *U.S. News & World Report,* Vanderbilt is a private research university that features four undergraduate schools and six graduate and professional schools. Each year, 1,600 first-year students join the University, bringing the total undergraduate population to approximately 6,800 students. Vanderbilt students come from across the country and around the world, and represent a rich diversity of backgrounds. Among undergraduates, 6.2 percent are international students, 31.3 percent are minority students, and 65 percent receive some type of financial aid.

Vanderbilt's 8:1 student-faculty ratio gives students access to faculty members of prominence in every area of academic study. Nearly 50 percent of undergraduates at Vanderbilt collaborate with professors on research projects that span almost every academic field, including natural and social sciences, humanities, engineering, and education. Full-time faculty members share their perspectives as instructors and advisers united by one goal: providing a challenging, comprehensive education that encourages broad perspectives and critical thinking.

Known for the rolling splendor of its 330-acre campus, which is classified as a national arboretum, Vanderbilt offers a top-ranked residential experience for its undergraduates, nearly all of whom live on campus all four years. First-year students live and learn in The Martha Rivers Ingram Commons, a collection of ten residence halls, or Houses, clustered along one side of campus (seven of the Houses are LEED-certified). The Ingram Commons incorporates more than just bricks and mortar. Faculty members—including the dean of The Ingram Commons and faculty heads of house—and their families live there, facilitating easy and meaningful interactions between students and professors. Frequent educational and social programming at The Ingram Commons invites students and faculty to explore current events and social issues. After their first year, students have many housing options, including apartment-style living and two new residential colleges, Warren and Moore.

Vanderbilt students take full advantage of student life in over 530 student organizations, a full range of study-abroad programs, Division I Athletics, and a variety of internship opportunities.

Location

Vanderbilt University is located in Nashville, the capital of Tennessee. Ranked number one for Friendliest People and Music Scene (*Travel + Leisure*, 2014), Nashville boasts a rich mosaic of cultures, vibrant arts, business, health and education sectors, and an array of recreational opportunities. Nashville hosts thousands of live concerts each year in every conceivable genre and is recognized as a top college city in America and an excellent location for businesses. Nashville's booming cultural scene, striking natural beauty, and thriving economy attract people from around the world.

Majors and Degrees

College of Arts and Science: African American and Diaspora Studies; American Studies; Anthropology; Art; Asian Studies; Biological Sciences; Chemistry; Cinema and Media Arts; Classical Civilizations; Classical Languages; Classics; Communication of Science and Technology; Communication Studies; Earth and Environmental Sciences; Ecology, Evolution, and Organismal Biology; Economics; Economics and History; English; European Studies; French; French and European Studies; German; German and European Studies; History; History of Art; Italian and European Studies; Jewish Studies; Latin American Studies; Latino and Latina Studies; Mathematics; Medicine, Health, and Society; Molecular and Cellular Biology; Neuroscience; Philosophy; Physics; Political Science; Psychology; Public Policy Studies; Religious Studies; Russian; Russian and European Studies; Sociology; Spanish; Spanish and European Studies; Spanish and Portuguese; Spanish, Portuguese, and European Studies; Theater; Women's and Gender Studies; and unique interdisciplinary majors, designed by students with faculty support.

Blair School of Music: Composition, Musical Arts, Musical Arts/Teacher Education, and Performance.

School of Engineering: Biomedical Engineering, Chemical Engineering, Civil Engineering, Computer Engineering, Computer Science, Electrical Engineering, Engineering Science, and Mechanical Engineering.

Peabody College of Education and Human Development: Child Development, Child Studies, Cognitive Studies, Early Childhood Education, Elementary Education, Human and Organizational Development, Secondary Education, and Special Education.

Graduate/Professional Schools: Divinity School, Graduate School, Vanderbilt University Law School, Vanderbilt Owen Graduate School of Management, School of Medicine, and School of Nursing.

Pre-professional advising is available for undergraduate students interested in pursuing graduate degrees in architecture, business, law, or health professions.

Academic Programs

Students apply for admission to one of the four schools that offer undergraduate programs: the College of Arts and Science, the School of Engineering, Peabody College of Education and Human Development, or the Blair School of Music. In all four schools, honors programs and opportunities for independent study and internships are available. Nearly one third of undergraduate students pursue double majors within or across the four undergraduate schools. This leads to some diverse combinations, such as pre-med students who study Spanish, engineers who study violin, math majors who study songwriting, or chemistry majors who study art history.

The College of Arts and Science provides many opportunities to experience a wide range of academic disciplines and subjects. Within the requirements of the AXLE (Achieving eXcellence in Liberal Education) curriculum, students refine their skills in writing, mathematics, foreign language, the humanities, natural sciences, social sciences, history, and culture.

The Blair School of Music offers the Bachelor of Music degree in composition, musical arts, musical arts/teacher education, and performance. Instruction is available in every instrument of the orchestra as well as piano, organ, euphonium, multiple woodwinds, saxophone, classical guitar, and voice. Unlike many schools of music, Blair has no graduate students. The curriculum combines intensive musical training with liberal arts studies. Students take approximately one third of their courses outside of the music school. The Blair School also offers a music minor and a wide variety of courses, private instruction, and performing organizations for nonmajors.

For more than 125 years, the School of Engineering has educated engineers for practice in industry, government, consulting, teaching, and research careers. In addition to technical courses, each student's program includes a rich complement of course work in the humanities and social sciences, resulting in a balanced foundation for future achievement and the assumption of leadership roles in their chosen fields. All programs leading to a Bachelor of Engineering degree are ABET-accredited, and students can earn a Bachelor of Science degree while majoring in Computer Science or Engineering Science.

Ranked the number one or number two graduate school of education (according to *U.S. News & World Report*) for seven years running, Peabody College offers degree programs in education, child development, child studies, cognitive studies, and human and organizational development. The degree reflects a strong liberal arts foundation combined with a solid program of preprofessional courses and a multitude of internship and practicum opportunities. All undergraduates must complete requirements in communications, the humanities, mathematics, the natural sciences, and the social sciences. Moreover, students have an abundance of field experiences throughout their four years.

Off-Campus Programs

Study-abroad programs allow students to immerse themselves in languages and cultures around the world. Vanderbilt offers more than 120 programs in countries such as Argentina, Australia, Austria, Chile, China, Costa Rica, the Czech Republic, Denmark, the Dominican Republic, Egypt, England, France, Germany, Israel, Italy, Japan, Russia, Singapore, South Africa, and Spain. In these Vanderbilt-approved programs, students receive direct credit for their courses, and the cost of tuition is usually the same as for study on campus in Nashville. In addition, any scholarships, grants, or loans a student has been awarded apply to Vanderbilt study-abroad programs. Students may also participate in programs sponsored by other universities by working with an adviser.

Academic Facilities

Students and faculty members take advantage of Vanderbilt's extensive library resources, obtaining easy access to books, periodicals, documents, microforms, and reference materials. The Jean and Alexander Heard Library is supported by ten major resource centers, including special collections, University Archives, and more than 8 million items.

Costs

The estimated costs for 2015–16 include: tuition, $43,620; housing, $9,580; meals, $5,090; books and supplies, $1,370; student activities and recreation fee, $1,092; personal expenses allowance, $2,780; first-year experience fee, $718; new student transcript fee, $30; engineering lab fee*, $650; and engineering laptop allowance*, $1,500. Travel allowances are variable. *The engineering laptop allowance and laboratory fee apply to engineering students only. First-year engineering students are required to either purchase a laptop from Vanderbilt or provide their own computer that meets published requirements.

Financial Aid

Through Opportunity Vanderbilt, the University makes three important commitments reflecting a strong dedication to making a Vanderbilt education possible: Vanderbilt is need-blind for all U.S. citizens and eligible non-citizens; Vanderbilt meets 100 percent of demonstrated need for all admitted students; and Vanderbilt's financial aid packages do not include loans. These three commitments combined place Vanderbilt among a small number of universities to adopt such progressive policies.

In the 2014–15 school year, 65 percent of Vanderbilt's undergraduate students received some type of financial aid. Need-based aid is awarded according to the evaluation of the FAFSA and the CSS/Financial Aid PROFILE.

Vanderbilt also awards merit-based scholarships to selected first-year applicants who demonstrate exceptional accomplishment and intellectual promise. Three signature scholarship programs comprise the majority of these honor scholarships: the Ingram Scholarship Program (for students who plan to combine a professional or business career with an exceptional commitment to community service), the Cornelius Vanderbilt Scholarship Program (for students who combine outstanding academic achievements with strong leadership and contributions outside the classroom), and the Chancellor's Scholarship Program (for students who have worked to build strong high school communities by bridging gaps among economically, socially, and racially diverse groups).

Faculty

Excluding the Schools of Medicine and Nursing, Vanderbilt has 1,033 full-time faculty members. All undergraduate faculty members, many of whom hold awards for distinguished scholarship, are required to teach undergraduates. A low student-faculty ratio of 8:1 provides for an intimate academic experience between students and professors who are recognized nationally and worldwide for their research. Ninety-one percent of classes have fewer than 50 students.

Student Government

The Vanderbilt Student Government provides students with an opportunity to participate actively in maintaining a high quality of life on campus. It works with many of the more than 530 student organizations to bring nationally prominent speakers to campus and provides an interesting and diverse array of programming throughout the year. A vital part of life at Vanderbilt is the honor system, which is governed entirely by students through representatives on the Honor Council. Each year, a senior is selected as a Young Alumni Trustee of the University's Board of Trust.

Admission Requirements

Vanderbilt uses a holistic admissions process—there are no cutoffs based on standardized testing or grade point averages. The Admissions Committee evaluates students' academic records, test scores (either the SAT or ACT is required, including the writing subscore), extracurricular involvement, counselor and teacher recommendations, and personal essay. Applicants to the Blair School of Music are required to submit a separate application and a prescreening video, and may be invited to audition.

Vanderbilt seeks students with high standards of scholarship and character. Most competitive applicants have a strong academic profile—including excellent grades in the context of a rigorous course load, strong test scores, and positive academic letters of recommendation. In addition, most successful applicants demonstrate significant levels of engagement and leadership outside the classroom.

Campus visits are highly recommended, though student interest is not used as a measure of admissibility. In addition to daily information sessions and campus tours, the Admissions Office offers various half-day and full-day visit programs for prospective students. For more information and to register, visit vu.edu/visit.

Application and Information

Students whose first choice is Vanderbilt may apply under one of Vanderbilt's early decision plans. Applications are due by November 1 for Early Decision I and by January 1 for Early Decision II; notification is made by December 15 for Early Decision I and by February 15 for Early Decision II. Regular Decision applications are due January 1. Students are informed of the admission decision by April 1. Students seeking transfer admission should submit application materials by March 15 for fall semester entry.

Office of Undergraduate Admissions
Vanderbilt University
2305 West End Avenue
Nashville, Tennessee 37203-1727
Phone: 615-322-2561
800-288-0432 (toll-free)
E-mail: admissions@vanderbilt.edu
Website: admissions.vanderbilt.edu
facebook.com/vanderbiltadmissions
twitter.com/vanderbiltu
instagram.com/vanderbiltadmissions
vanderbiltadmissions.tumblr.com

Kirkland Hall, Vanderbilt's oldest and most historic building.

COLLEGE CLOSE-UPS

VILLANOVA UNIVERSITY

VILLANOVA, PENNSYLVANIA

★ To read more about this school, visit http://petersons.to/villanova

VILLANOVA UNIVERSITY

The University

Since 1842, Villanova University's Augustinian Catholic intellectual tradition has been the cornerstone of an academic community in which students learn to think critically, act compassionately, and succeed while serving others. There are more than 10,000 undergraduate, graduate, and law students in the College of Liberal Arts and Sciences, the Villanova School of Business, the College of Engineering, the College of Nursing, the College of Professional Studies, and the Villanova University School of Law. As students grow intellectually, Villanova prepares them to become ethical leaders who create positive change everywhere life takes them.

Villanova offers more than 50 rigorous academic programs and features more than 265 student organizations and 36 national honor societies on campus. Undergraduate full-time enrollment is 6,553; total University enrollment is 10,735.

Located just 12 miles (20 kilometers) west of Philadelphia, Villanova's picturesque campus has 65 buildings, including 26 residence halls. Award-winning dining services are available in 3 residence dining halls and 16 à la carte eateries, all with many culinary options. Students have access to several athletic and fitness facilities on campus; the newest is the Davis Center for Athletics, with state-of-the-art cardio machines, weight equipment, and free weights. Group exercise classes, including yoga and Pilates, are also offered regularly. Villanova has 44 club and intramural sports on campus, and nearly 20 percent of the student body participates in varsity or club athletics.

To help facilitate the transition to college life, first-year students are encouraged to join a themed Learning Community. Community members live in the same residence halls, take their year-long Augustine and Culture Seminar together, and participate in co-curricular activities. These activities typically include lectures, plays, themed dinners, rich cultural events, and engaging trips. Through Learning Communities, students often form deeper, often lifelong, relationships with their classmates and professors, and become more fully engaged in their studies.

Location

Villanova students reap all the benefits of living within the beautiful and tranquil Philadelphia Main Line suburb, while the University's convenient proximity to Philadelphia also provides endless opportunities to complement campus life with cultural, recreational, and social activities found only in a vibrant major metropolitan area. Whether it's visiting world-class art and science museums, touring historic sites, sampling the impressive restaurant scene, browsing through countless stores and shops, or cheering on local professional sports teams, there is something for everyone to enjoy.

Majors and Degrees

Villanova's College of Liberal Arts and Sciences grants a Bachelor of Arts in Arab and Islamic Studies, Art History, Classical Studies, Communication, Criminology, Cultural Studies, Economics, Education and Counseling, English, Environmental Studies, French and Francophone Studies, Gender and Women's Studies, Geography, Global Interdisciplinary Studies, History, Humanities, Italian, Latin American Studies, Liberal Arts, Philosophy, Political Science, Psychology, Secondary Education, Sociology, Spanish Studies, and Theology and Religious Studies. The college grants a Bachelor of Science in Astrophysics and Planetary Science, Biochemistry, Biology, Chemistry, Cognitive and Behavioral Neuroscience, Comprehensive Science, Computing Science, Environmental Science, Mathematics and Statistics, and Physics.

Villanova School of Business (VSB) offers a Bachelor of Business Administration in Accountancy, Economics, Finance, Management, Management Information Systems, and Marketing. VSB also offers co-majors in International Business and Real Estate.

Through the College of Engineering, Villanova grants a Bachelor of Science in Chemical Engineering, Civil Engineering, Computer Engineering, Electrical Engineering, and Mechanical Engineering.

Villanova offers a Bachelor of Science in Nursing through the College of Nursing and also offers the following Health Science Affiliation programs: Drexel University College of Medicine, Doctor of Medicine; Jefferson College of Health Professions of Thomas Jefferson University, Doctor of Physical Therapy and Master of Science in Occupational Therapy; Pennsylvania College of Optometry at Salus University, Doctor of Optometry; and University of Pennsylvania School of Dental Medicine, Doctor of Dental Medicine.

Villanova offers a comprehensive four-year Honors Program of challenging seminars, research opportunities, service projects, and cultural and social events designed to bring together exceptional students and dedicated faculty. In addition, accelerated bachelor's/master's degree programs are available in the following areas: Applied Statistics, Biology, Chemical Engineering, Chemistry, Civil Engineering, Classical Studies, Communication, Computer Engineering, Computing Science, Electrical Engineering, Human Resource Development, Liberal Studies, Mathematics, Mechanical Engineering, Nursing, Political Science, Psychology, Public Administration, Software Engineering, and Theology.

Academic Programs

Villanova, through the College of Liberal Arts and Sciences, is one of the few institutions in the country that offers an undergraduate program in Astrophysics and Planetary Science, and one of only 18 Catholic colleges or universities in the nation to have a chapter of Phi Beta Kappa, the prestigious liberal arts and sciences honor society. It also is home to the Waterhouse Institute for the Study of Communication and Society—the only institute of its kind in the United States—which provides students with opportunities to explore the ethical dimensions of communication.

Highly ranked nationally, the Villanova School of Business is home to the Applied Finance Lab, where students have access to many of the real-time technologies available to Wall Street traders. The Clay Center at VSB assists students with important decisions regarding course selections, major and minors, and international experiences, and it helps coordinate internships and co-ops, which often lead to full-time job offers.

The College of Engineering, ranked among the best engineering programs in the nation, is home to three research units: the Center for Advanced Communications, the Center for Nonlinear Dynamics and Control, and the Center for the Advancement of Sustainability in Engineering. The Villanova Center for Engineering Education and Research houses state-of-the-art instructional and research labs, including the new Multidisciplinary Design Lab, and the 10,000-square-foot Structural Engineering Teaching and Research Laboratory offers additional engineering-related facilities.

The College of Nursing, designated a Center for Excellence in Nursing Education by the National League for Nursing, is housed in an advanced facility that features a 200-seat auditorium and a 200-seat lecture hall; future-oriented clinical simulation labs for health assessment, adult health, maternal/child health, anesthesia, and critical care; simulation labs for standardized patient observation and testing; a center for nursing research and scholarship; places for prayer and reflection; space for global health studies and international student activities; and areas for student, faculty, and alumni events and social interaction.

Naval and Marine Reserve Officers Training Corps (ROTC) programs are available on campus. Villanova has had an NROTC program for more than 50 years, and it is structured to complement a normal college lifestyle. Midshipmen are encouraged to participate fully in their academic programs as well as in extracurricular activities.

Off-Campus Programs

Villanova has a rich study abroad program. Each year, approximately 750 students take advantage of international study opportunities in nearly 40 nations, including Ireland, Switzerland, Peru, England, France, Germany, Italy, China, Chile, Russia, Poland, Thailand, Spain, Australia, Rwanda, the West Indies, Madagascar, and Samoa.

Academic Facilities

Villanova's state-of-the-art classrooms and labs are complemented with a vast array of learning and career resources. Falvey Memorial Library contains more than 1,000,000 items and offers access to numerous databases. The Office of Learning Support Services assists students with learning disabilities, neurologically based disorders, and chronic illnesses. The Villanova Career Center helps students set and reach their professional development goals. Ninety-nine percent of the Villanova Class of 2014 was employed or enrolled in graduate school within six months of degree completion. Approximately 6,500 jobs are posted on Villanova's job boards each year, and the average starting salary for recent graduates is $54,345.

Technology is widely available at Villanova. All residence halls are connected to the campus network. Students can participate in learning experiences across campus; receive curricular advising services; and access tests, webcasts, and library reserves online. Through Villanova's student portal, they can keep track of deadlines, class schedules, and financial aid information. Villanova's technology also provides easy access to meal plans, parking registration, laundry reservations, voting processes, ride sharing/carpooling, and basketball ticket lotteries. Students and parents can also sign up for NOVA Alert, the University's emergency notification system.

Costs

For the 2014–15 academic year, the average tuition was $45,376, and room and board were $12,278.

Financial Aid

For the 2014–15 freshman class, 83 percent of those eligible for need-based assistance received Villanova Grants. More than $19.4 million in Villanova Grants was awarded, with an average award amount of $27,148. The average assistance package for students with demonstrated need (combining grants, scholarships, loans, and student employment) was $37,602.

Villanova offers a Presidential Scholarship program to attract academic, civic, and cultural leaders who represent diverse intellectual, social, racial, and economic backgrounds, including students from families in which few or no members have attended college. Successful candidates are awarded this renewable scholarship—which covers tuition, general fee, room and board, and books—for eight consecutive semesters.

Faculty

Villanova has nearly 620 full-time faculty members; nearly 90 percent of them hold doctoral degrees. The student-to-faculty ratio is 12:1 and the average class size is 22.

Student Government

Empowering the Villanova student body since 1925, the Student Government Association (SGA) has three branches (administrative, community, and student relations) and twelve committees. The SGA provides opportunities for student leaders to serve the Villanova community as liaisons, representatives, and student senators.

Admission Requirements

Admission to Villanova is competitive. In addition to attracting academically talented, well-rounded students, Villanova seeks applicants who are compassionate and want to transform the world and make it a better place.

Villanova is a Common Application member institution. Prospective students are also required to complete the Villanova Supplement for Undergraduate Admission and submit an official high school transcript and Common Application School Report. Applicants must have their standardized test scores (SAT or ACT) reported directly by the College Board or ACT.

In the Villanova admissions process, high school performance is an extremely important selectivity factor. Each student's high school record, GPA, and class rank, along with each student's demonstration of character and personal abilities, are carefully considered. Extracurricular and volunteer activities are helpful to applicants in this regard. Another important factor is the personal essay. Since interviews are not part of the admission process, a well-crafted essay is essential for prospective students to explain who they are and why they should be selected to become Villanovans. (A recommendation from the secondary school counselor is also carefully considered.)

Prospective students who are not from the United States are encouraged to apply for admission to Villanova. Non-native English speakers must take the TOEFL or IELTS evaluations and have scores reported directly from the College Board. Villanova's International Student Services Office supports enrolled international students in areas including immigration rights and responsibilities; educational, social, and personal counseling; cultural adjustment issues; and campus and community activities.

Transferring to Villanova is possible, but selective. A completed transfer application, official transcripts from each postsecondary school attended, and a completed Dean of Students Transfer Evaluation form are required.

Application and Information

The deadline for early action and health affiliation program applications is November 1; regular decision deadline is January 15.

Villanova Office of University Admission
800 Lancaster Avenue
Villanova, Pennsylvania 19085-1672
Phone: 610-519-4000
Fax: 610-519-6450
E-mail: gotovu@villanova.edu
Website: http://www.villanova.edu
http://virtualvisit.villanova.edu (virtual visit)

St. Thomas of Villanova Church, Villanova University.

WALSH UNIVERSITY

NORTH CANTON, OHIO

WALSH UNIVERSITY
A Catholic University of Distinction

The University

Walsh University is a fully accredited, liberal arts and sciences Catholic university in North Canton, Ohio, offering sixty majors, seven graduate programs, and an accelerated-degree program for working adults. With 2,982 students and a 13:1 student-faculty ratio, the University offers a very friendly, supportive, and safe campus and a unique broad-based curriculum with close student-faculty interaction. Most residence halls and academic buildings on Walsh's 136-acre campus are new or have been renovated within the last several years, providing state-of-the-art facilities for students. Walsh also offers generous financial aid packages to 98 percent of full-time students.

Active and involved in campus and community life, more than 60 percent of Walsh students participate in extracurricular programs. Students also have the opportunity to participate in a variety of intramural sports. Walsh is an NCAA Division II member and offers twenty intercollegiate sports.

Walsh University welcomes students from around the world of all faiths and backgrounds. The University currently has students from thirty-four countries and looks forward to continued growth.

Walsh University was founded in 1960 by the Brothers of Christian Instruction and is accredited by the North Central Association/Higher Learning Commission, Accreditation Commission for Education in Nursing, Commission for Collegiate Nursing Education, the Commission on Accreditation in Physical Therapy Education, Council for Accreditation of Counseling and Related Educational Programs, and the National Council for Accreditation of Teacher Education. Walsh is a member of the Ohio College Association, the National Association of Independent Colleges and Universities, and the Association of Catholic Colleges and Universities, among other organizations.

In addition to its undergraduate degree programs, Walsh offers seven graduate degree programs that include a twelve-month M.B.A., a Master of Science in Nursing, Master of Arts in Counseling and Human Development, Master of Arts in Education (M.A.Ed.), Master of Arts in Theology, Doctor of Nursing Practice (D.N.P.), and a Doctor of Physical Therapy.

Location

Walsh University has a beautiful, tree-lined campus located just 3 miles east of I-77 in North Canton, a safe, pleasant residential suburban community. Canton, which is about 5 miles south of the Walsh campus, is a city of 84,000 that offers a wide array of cultural, recreational, and athletic activities. Home of the Professional Football Hall of Fame, the President McKinley National Memorial, and the National First Ladies Library, the city also hosts a symphony orchestra, an art museum, and a civic opera, theater guild, and ballet. A number of major companies are headquartered in Stark County, including the Timken Company and Diebold, Inc. Walsh also has campuses in Medina, Canfield, and Akron, Ohio as well as a campus in Castel Gandolfo, Italy just outside of Rome and a Master of Arts in Education program in Uganda.

Majors and Degrees

Bachelor of Arts and Bachelor of Science degrees are offered in the following majors: accounting (general and specialized CPA tracks), biochemistry, bioinformatics, biology, business management, chemistry, clinical laboratory science, communication, comprehensive science, computer science, corporate communication, counseling, criminal justice–sociology, education (early childhood, middle childhood, adolescence to young adulthood, integrated language arts, integrated mathematics teacher licensure, integrated science teacher licensure, integrated social studies teacher, intervention specialist, life science/biology teacher licensure, life science/biology and chemistry teacher licensure, multiage physical education, and physical education), English, environmental science, exercise science, family studies–sociology, French, general studies, global business, graphic design, history, international relations, marketing, mathematics, museum studies, nursing, philosophy/theology, physical education, political science, psychology, psychology–community/clinical, research methods and data analysis–sociology, Spanish, Spanish for healthcare, and theology.

Walsh offers preprofessional programs in dentistry, medicine, occupational therapy, optometry, pharmacy, physical therapy, and veterinary science. Each is developed within the context of a regular academic major. Walsh's physical therapy graduates have the option to continue their studies by entering Walsh's accredited Doctor of Physical Therapy degree program. Students enrolled in the University's B.A./M.A. program can earn a bachelor's degree in behavioral science and a master's degree in counseling and human development.

In addition, Walsh offers the Associate of Arts degree in accounting, finance, human services, liberal arts, management, and marketing.

Academic Programs

The student's academic program comprises courses within the liberal arts, a major field of study, and elective courses. Major course work, constituting one fourth or more of a student's program of studies, is designed to help students prepare for their careers. Forty percent of a student's program of studies is within the liberal arts. Elective courses, which constitute the remaining portion of a student's program of studies, enable students to develop personal interests, take more courses within their major field, or enroll in additional core courses. The University encourages students to give careful thought to selecting a program of study and a major. While many students select double majors as a way to improve their career opportunities, the design of individual programs requires consultation with a faculty adviser and a division chair. To earn a bachelor's degree, students must successfully complete 125 semester hours.

Designed for the academically gifted, the honors program offers challenges that lead students to achieve academic excellence. Honors students take advantage of such offerings as special seminars, independent studies, internships, and research projects.

Students in Walsh's global learning program may choose to study for a semester or a summer at the University's Rome campus, Tanzania, Uganda, or many other international locations through Walsh's partnership with CCSA. The University's School for Professional Studies Program is for working adults who have earned college credits and who wish to earn their bachelor's degree in an accelerated format. Classes are scheduled on nights and weekends to accommodate busy schedules.

Academic Facilities

A member of OhioLINK, the Walsh Library contains 132,890 volumes and 226 paper subscriptions, as well as thousands of audiovisual items and streaming videos. Students have access to 105,520 electronic journals, 142,705 electronic books, and more than 200 specialized databases. Library staff members give introductory lectures on research techniques. The library has a quiet study room and a snack lounge. All library resources are available via the Internet.

Faculty

Walsh University fosters close working relationships between faculty members and students. Beyond classroom teaching, faculty members serve as student counselors and tutors and take on roles as advisers for student organizations. The Walsh faculty is composed of full-time, part-time, and adjunct members. The student-faculty ratio is 13:1. The majority of full-time faculty members hold Ph.D.'s or terminal degrees in their respective fields.

Student Government

Walsh University Student Government provides capable, responsible student governance. Through its executive, legislative, and judicial branches, it fosters student involvement in the governance of the University, serves as a forum for student opinion, and functions as a liaison between students, faculty and staff members, and the administration. Along with the Student Affairs staff, it plans student activities and community projects.

Costs

Tuition for the 2014–15 academic year was $25,350. Tuition, fees, and room and board charges total approximately $35,850 per year and vary by residence hall. Books and personal expenses cost an estimated $700–$900 for the year. The University reserves the right to change the cost structure without notice.

Financial Aid

Walsh is dedicated to providing outstanding liberal arts education at an affordable price. The primary purpose of Walsh University's financial aid program is to assist deserving students who cannot otherwise meet the costs of a college education. Financial aid takes the form of scholarships, work-study awards, grants, or loans, depending upon the resources available. The University offers a number of scholarships in amounts from $1,500 to full tuition, in addition to institutional need-based grants. The Alumni Association offers scholarships as well. State and federal grants and loans are available to students along with the University's work-study program that provides work compatible with a student's academic schedule. Financial aid is awarded for one year and is renewable in subsequent years if the student shows a continuing need and maintains an appropriate academic record.

Applicants for admission may apply for financial aid by submitting the Walsh University Application for Financial Aid, which is available via the Walsh website and in the financial aid and admissions offices on the Walsh campus. In addition, students must complete the Free Application for Federal Student Aid (FAFSA), which is available online.

Admission Requirements

Every student seeking admission to Walsh University is reviewed individually to assess the student's ability to meet the rigors of the University's curriculum. The composition of high school classes, grades achieved, class rank, and standardized test scores are all taken into consideration before an admission decision is rendered. Essays and interviews are highly recommended but not required.

Walsh grants credit for college-level work completed in high school and for credits earned through the College Level Examination Program. Qualified high school juniors and seniors may enroll for college credit under the University's postsecondary enrollment program. The University seeks a diverse student body.

Application and Information

Early application is recommended. Walsh University operates under a rolling admissions policy. The completed admission application, $25 application fee, ACT or SAT scores, and a high school transcript are required for a student's application to be considered for admission. Transfer students must also submit transcripts from all colleges and universities attended.

Interested students are encouraged to contact:

Brett Freshour
Vice President for Enrollment Management
Walsh University
2020 East Maple Street NW
North Canton, Ohio 44720-3336
Phone: 330-492-7172
800-362-9846 (toll-free)
Fax: 330-490-7165
E-mail: admissions@walsh.edu
Website: http://www.walsh.edu
http://www.facebook.com/walshu
http://www.twitter.com/walshuniversity
http://www.youtube.com/ohiowalshuniversity

On the campus of Walsh University.

COLLEGE CLOSE-UPS

WEBBER INTERNATIONAL UNIVERSITY

BABSON PARK, FLORIDA

★ To read more about this school, visit http://petersons.to/webberinternationaluniversity

The University

Webber International University was founded in 1927 by Roger Babson, who was an internationally known economist in the early 1900s. The four-year independent coeducational university is located on a beautiful 110-acre campus along the shoreline of Crooked Lake, 45 minutes from Disney World, Legoland, and many other attractions. Webber is accredited by the Southern Association of Colleges and Schools and internationally by the International Assembly for Collegiate Business Education. The University offers associate, bachelor's, and graduate degrees. The Master of Business Administration (M.B.A.) program offers options in accounting, criminal justice management, international business (online), management, and sport business management. Built on a strong tradition that sets it apart, the University exemplifies integrity, high standards, and achievement. Webber International University provides an environment that encourages success through academic excellence and hard work. About 650 students are enrolled as undergraduates at Webber; 64 percent of the students are from Florida; 28 percent are international and represent forty-seven different countries; and 8 percent are from out-of-state, representing twenty-six states. Webber's student population is 66 percent male and 34 percent female.

Webber International University offers day, evening, weekend, and online classes with the flexibility to fit any busy schedule. Webber's off-campus internship programs provide a real-world business environment for Webber students. Field trips also supplement students' business education. Webber has on-campus housing options available to all students. Housing is reserved on a first-come, first-served basis. All freshmen are required to live on-campus for their first year. After the first year, on-campus housing is optional.

The University offers intercollegiate sports in baseball, basketball, beach volleyball, bowling, cross-country, football, golf, soccer, tennis, track and field and triathlon for men and basketball, beach volleyball, bowling, cheerleading, cross-country, golf, soccer, softball, tennis, track and field, triathlon, and volleyball for women. For the musically talented student, the University has a marching band. Intramural athletics are also available for all students. The University's physical education complex includes a gymnasium, two fitness rooms, a soccer field, a junior Olympic-size swimming pool, beach volleyball courts, and tennis courts. Webber students also enjoy lakeside activities such as beach volleyball, canoeing, fishing, and kayaking. Among the wide variety of social organizations and clubs are Phi Beta Lambda, a student leadership organization, an international club, Webber ambassadors, the Society of Hosteurs, a marketing club, FCA, a sport management club, and athletic boosters. These groups and others help to sponsor the various social functions at Webber.

Location

The town of Babson Park, a very small rural residential community, is located in the heart of Florida's citrus country near a chain of freshwater lakes. The area has a relaxed and friendly atmosphere. Babson Park is conveniently near many major recreational facilities and national tourist attractions in central Florida. Grocery stores, restaurants, and banks are a short 10-minute drive from campus. Webber is located about 45 minutes south of Orlando and an hour east of Tampa. The nearest airport is Orlando International Airport.

Majors and Degrees

Webber International University offers bachelor's and associate degrees in business administration, with ten different majors: accounting, computer information systems management, corporate communications, criminal justice management, finance, hospitality and tourism management, management, marketing, pre-law, and sport business management. The University also offers a Bachelor of Science degree in general business studies and a Bachelor of Arts degree in elementary education.

Academic Programs

The school operates on the semester system with two 15-week semesters, a six-week Summer Term A, and a six-week Summer Term B. A majority of Webber's courses are available online through its e-learning program. The University requires the completion of 60 credit hours for the Associate of Science degree and 120 credit hours for the Bachelor of Science degree. The average course load is 15 hours per semester. Students in the Bachelor of Science degree program are required to complete approximately 30 hours in their major, 36 hours in the business core, 36 hours in the general education core, and 18 hours of tailored electives. Students in the Associate of Science degree program are required to complete 27 hours in the business core, 18 hours in the general education core, and 15 hours in the major and tailored elective.

The Bachelor of Science degree in general business studies requires the completion of 45 hours in the general business studies core, 39 hours in the general education core, and 36 hours of tailored electives.

All students must complete 30 of the last 33 hours at Webber International University to receive a degree. Credit is awarded for successful scores on Advanced Placement (AP) and College-Level Examination Program (CLEP) general tests.

Off-Campus Programs

The hospitality and marketing departments have arrangements for internship programs with major hotels and restaurants in the Orlando area and major retail stores, both in-state and out-of-state.

The finance department places student interns in various financial institutions and financial departments of local corporations.

Other off-campus experiences include elective courses in which students observe and analyze business operations and functions of local companies and present their findings in a project format comparable to a professional business consultant's.

The departmental field trip is an opportunity for students in all twelve majors to travel abroad during a summer semester and to discover business techniques in an international environment.

Academic Facilities

The Grace and Roger Babson Learning Center, located in the central part of the campus, is a modern and comprehensive business library facility. An all-electronic collection provides a variety of databases with a wide selection of research materials for both the academic and business curriculum. The library houses several computers for student use but its resources are available wherever the student may be. The three computer resources centers are data processing centers and teaching facilities whose microcomputers offer the latest modern technology for developing student excellence in business, communication, and creativity.

Costs

In 2015–16, the total annual fee, which includes tuition, room and board, and insurance, is approximately $33,504. For commuting students, the total annual fee is $24,792. Tuition is $22,326 per year. Housing ranges from $5,404 to $9,508 per year depending on the housing option. There are two meal plan options: meal plan A, covering all meals, is $3,120 per year, and meal plan B, 200 meals of choice, is $2,606 per year. All freshmen are required to be on meal plan A. These figures are subject to change. The University estimates that $1,206 is adequate for books and supplies. Laboratory fees are additional.

Financial Aid

The Student Financial Aid Department offers students its counsel and assistance in meeting their educational expenses. Aid is awarded on the basis of an applicant's need, academic performance, and promise. Approximately 90 percent of the students at Webber International University receive financial assistance. To demonstrate need, applicants are required to file the Free Application for Federal Student Aid (FAFSA). Various types of aid, such as scholarships, grants, loans, and Federal Work-Study awards, are used to meet student needs. A limited number of no-need scholarships are available; these awards are based on academic performance, on community and college service, or on athletic ability as determined by the sport's coach. Applicants for aid must reapply each year. Webber participates in the Federal Perkins Loan, Federal Supplemental Educational Opportunity Grant, and Federal Work-Study programs. All applicants are expected to apply for any entitlement grant for which they are eligible, such as the Federal Pell Grant; Florida residents must apply for a Florida Student Assistance Grant and the Florida Resident Access Grant. Federal Student Loans are also available. Webber is nationally recognized as a military-friendly school and accepts the Post-9/11 GI Bill as well as a variety of other veteran's education benefits. Financial aid applicants should submit their requests and forms before April 1 in order to be eligible for certain financial aid programs.

Faculty

More than 70 percent of Webber's full-time faculty members hold doctoral degrees. The faculty-student ratio is 1:24, and all students are assigned a faculty adviser. All faculty members have posted office hours and are available for consultation and advising. Many of Webber's faculty members have a minimum of five years' actual professional work experience in their area of specialization in addition to their years of classroom teaching. This combination of applied and classroom work experience gives them a unique ability to relate to the needs and concerns of their students.

Admission Requirements

Applicants must have graduated from high school with a standard high school diploma. Most accepted candidates rank in the top 50 percent of their high school class. Scores on the SAT or ACT are required for admission. International applicants must submit proof of English proficiency, such as the Test of English as a Foreign Language (TOEFL).

Applications from transfer students are welcome, as are those from students resuming their education or adult students who have delayed their entrance to college. Transfer students must be in good standing at their former institution. They must also submit transcripts from all previous institutions.

Applicants who fail to meet regular admission requirements may be considered on an individual basis for the Fresh Start program by the Fresh Start admissions committee. An interview is required for all Fresh Start applicants.

Application and Information

An application is ready for consideration by the Admissions Committee when it has been received with a $35 application fee for domestic students and $75 for international students, the required test scores and references, and transcripts from each school attended. The University uses a system of rolling admissions. It is recommended that applications be submitted as early as possible, since on-campus housing is limited. Freshmen are required to live in the dormitory unless they reside with a parent, guardian, or spouse.

For application forms, catalogs, and additional information, students should contact:

Webber International University
1201 North Scenic Highway
P.O. Box 96
Babson Park, Florida 33827
Phone: 863-638-2910
E-mail: admissions@webber.edu
Website: http://www.webber.edu

Students enjoying the beautiful lakefront beach.

WEBB INSTITUTE

GLEN COVE, NEW YORK

The Institute

Webb Institute was founded in 1889 to provide an opportunity for worthy young students to obtain an education in the "art and science of designing ships and their propulsion systems." The Institute has followed this basic objective to the present, and its graduates are active throughout the United States in the ship design, ship construction, yacht design, marine operations and offshore industries, and in appropriate government offices.

The 26-acre campus is the former estate of Herbert L. Pratt and is located on Long Island Sound. Because of the Institute's small size and intensive academic program, varsity sports are limited. However, Webb participates in intercollegiate basketball, sailing, soccer, tennis, and volleyball, for which ample facilities are provided. The campus has a gymnasium, tennis courts, playing fields, and a beach. Golf and swimming facilities are available near campus. The school also has a running club and both a choral group and community service group.

Webb Institute maintains an enrollment that ranges from 80 to 95 students who come from all over the world and all of whom live on campus.

Location

Glen Cove is a city of more than 25,000 residents and is located on Long Island's North Shore, which is nearly an hour from New York City. Convenient train service from Glen Cove to New York brings the variety of cultural, educational, and recreational activities available in the city within easy reach of Webb students.

Majors and Degrees

Webb Institute offers an engineering program in ship design, which involves both naval architecture and marine engineering. The undergraduate degree awarded is the Bachelor of Science in naval architecture and marine engineering.

Academic Programs

The engineering program in ship design consists of fundamental foundation courses in mathematics, science, and engineering sciences, capped by extensive professional design courses. A coherent program in humanities supplements the technical program to round out undergraduate education.

In addition, students have a two-month, cooperative job experience each year in the U.S. marine and maritime industry. During this period, freshmen work as helper mechanics in shipyards, sophomores obtain seagoing experience aboard ship, and juniors and seniors work as engineering assistants in design and technical offices of various marine firms around the country and abroad. This important part of the program provides excellent articulation of the educational and career experiences. Innovative engineering ideas are encouraged in the thesis required during the last year. The program is fully accredited. Graduates are well equipped to pursue postgraduate studies.

Semesters run from late August to mid-December and from late February to late June. January and February are winter work periods, and the period from late June to late August is designated for vacation.

Academic Facilities

Full laboratory support is provided for chemistry, physics, metallurgy, and various engineering courses. A ship-model testing tank is available for ship and boat hull studies. The Livingston Library contains extensive holdings in naval architecture, marine engineering, and general engineering, as well as collections in literature, arts, social sciences, and music.

Costs

All U.S. citizens and green card holders admitted to Webb will receive scholarship money covering the full cost of tuition. For non-citizens, the tuition fee for the 2015–16 year is $44,000. Room and board costs are $14,050. Books and supplies costs vary from year to year, ranging from $150 to $800 per year. A $150 room deposit fee is payable on entry and refunded, less any breakage costs, on departure. The Student Organization requires a $100 deposit on entry, also refundable on departure.

Financial Aid

As stated, a full scholarship that covers tuition and fees is awarded to all accepted candidates who are U.S. citizens or green card holders. The winter work co-op in industry provides income for students that significantly assists in covering other expenses. Supplementary aid opportunities are available through the Federal Pell Grant, Federal Stafford Student Loans, and in-house grant programs. Students requiring financial assistance must submit the Free Application for Federal Student Aid (FAFSA) after March 31 but not later than July 1 of the year of entry.

Faculty

Webb Institute has a highly qualified faculty. Many members possess engineering licenses and engage in sponsored research programs, consult for commercial firms, and research and write technical papers. Classes are limited to no more than 28 students, and the student-faculty ratio is 8:1. Each student is assigned a faculty adviser, and consultation with individual faculty members is encouraged.

Student Government

The Student Organization is highly active in student administrative, social, and educational affairs. It is supplemented by an Honor Council and honor system. Together, these entities provide students with a high degree of responsibility for ordering and conducting student life.

Admission Requirements

Admission to Webb is highly competitive. The qualifying requirements for admission are graduation from high school with a B+ (87) or better average in 16 credits of basic high school subjects. Admission selections are based on high school standing (generally in the upper 10 percent) and scores on the College Board's SAT and Subject Tests in Mathematics (Level 1 or 2), and Physics or Chemistry. The ACT with writing is accepted in lieu of the SAT, but the SAT is still preferred. The final selection follows a personal interview conducted at Webb during the candidate's overnight visit and class observation.

All application papers must be submitted by October 15 for early decision consideration or by February 15 for the regular decision consideration, and all required College Board tests must be taken before that date. Advanced placement is not given in any of the course offerings. Campus visits by interested students are strongly recommended; prior appointments must be made.

Webb Institute does not discriminate in admission in the areas of gender, race, or religion. Academic qualities and career motivation are the only criteria.

Application and Information

For a catalog and application forms, students may contact:

Office of Admissions
Webb Institute
Glen Cove, New York 11542
Phone: 516-671-8355, Ext. 1107
E-mail: admissions@webb.edu
Website: http://www.webb.edu

The academic facilities of Webb Institute are located on Long Island Sound in the former residence of Herbert L. Pratt.

WELLS COLLEGE

AURORA, NEW YORK

★ To read more about this school, visit http://petersons.to/wellscollege

Wells College

The College

Wells College is ranked among the nation's top liberal arts colleges that offer high-quality education at an affordable price and has one of the most beautiful campuses in the United States. The College was established in 1868 by Henry Wells, who also founded the Wells Fargo and American Express companies.

At Wells, professors are dedicated to teaching, and because of the intimate nature of the campus community (the student body is 600), they get to know their students as individuals in and outside the classroom. Students frequently collaborate with their professors on original research and creative projects. At most other schools, these opportunities are only available to graduate students. Because faculty members at Wells know their students so well, they are especially effective advisers and mentors. Therefore, Wells students have a competitive edge entering careers and top graduate and professional schools.

Another aspect of the Wells tradition is hands-on learning. In addition to dynamic classroom teaching, Wells students have a variety of other experiential opportunities: internships, service, study abroad, and off-campus study. Professors encourage students to apply theory in practical settings and to discover what they want to do in life through involvement.

Wells currently fields intercollegiate teams at the NCAA Division III level in men's and women's cross-country, field hockey, men's and women's lacrosse, men's and women's soccer, men's and women's swimming, men's and women's basketball, men's and women's volleyball, and women's tennis. There are also a number of intramural opportunities, including basketball, soccer, swimming, skiing, tennis, and volleyball. Athletic facilities include indoor and outdoor tennis courts, a gymnasium, a newly renovated fitness center, a nine-hole golf course, and a campus boathouse and dock used in teaching sailing, canoeing, and lifeguarding.

Wells has a full range of active student organizations, including a literary magazine and newspaper, music and drama groups, environmental and political organizations, and abundant opportunities for community service, among others. A busy calendar of cultural events, symposia, and lectures enhances the academic and social life of the College.

Location

Wells is located in the village of Aurora on the eastern shore of Cayuga Lake—part of New York's scenic Finger Lakes region. The area is well known for its high concentration of prestigious colleges and universities, including Cornell University, Ithaca College, Hobart and William Smith Colleges, Colgate University, Hamilton College, and Syracuse University. Aurora is 25 miles from Ithaca and 60 miles from both Rochester and Syracuse. Students have abundant opportunities for outdoor recreation and sports, including sailing, swimming, horseback riding, skiing, and hiking.

Majors and Degrees

Wells offers majors and concentrations in anthropology, art history, biochemistry and molecular biology, biology, book arts, chemistry, computer science, creative writing, dance, economics and management, English, environmental policies and values, environmental science, film and media studies, history, international studies, literature, management, mathematics, philosophy, physics, political science, psychology, sociology, Spanish, studio art, theater and dance, visual arts, and women's and gender studies. Students also have the option of a self-designed major. In addition, they can choose minors from a list of more than forty programs.

Wells has also added an innovative Center for Business and Entrepreneurship, founded upon the tradition of liberal arts: learning that emphasizes critical thinking and problem solving. The role of the center is to help students build the skills and develop the discernment to know how and where they most want to serve society. As such, the center will offer students the opportunity to explore growing fields like arts administration, green businesses, not-for-profit organizations, and hospitality.

The College has pre-professional programs in education, engineering, law, medicine, teaching, and veterinary medicine. Wells has a cross-registration agreement with nearby Ithaca College, Cayuga Community College, and Cornell University and affiliations with Cornell's engineering school.

Wells awards the Bachelor of Arts degree and has a number of programs through which students can earn their bachelor's degree at Wells and a graduate or professional degree from an affiliated university. Participating schools are Clarkson University, Columbia University, Cornell University (engineering), and the University of Rochester (business, community health, and education).

Academic Programs

All Wells students benefit from an academic environment similar to honors programs available to only a small number of students at other schools. The College has a tradition of preparing students for leadership in their chosen fields, and the breadth of knowledge they gain and the range of life experiences they encounter enable them to achieve their career goals and establish a foundation for a rich and fulfilling life.

To learn more about the academic program and requirements for graduation, prospective students should visit the Wells College website.

Off-Campus Programs

Students can spend January term, a semester, or even a year in another college or university abroad or in the United States. Typically, Wells students choose to study off campus for a semester during the junior year, but many different possibilities are available depending on a student's academic program and interests.

The College offers affiliated study-abroad experiences in a wide variety of disciplines and specializations at prestigious institutions around the world. These off-campus study experiences are flexible as well as financially and academically accessible. After at least one semester at Wells, a student's financial aid applies to one semester of off-campus study.

Wells provides off-campus study options in the United States through its affiliations with American University, serving a wide range of academic and internship interests in Washington, D.C.; the Salt Institute for Documentary Studies, offering documentary field studies in Portland, Maine; and the Public Leadership Education Network (PLEN), providing leadership development through seminars and internships in Washington, D.C. As part of the PLEN affiliation, students can spend a semester studying at the London School of Economics and Political Science and hold an internship in the British government. Through the School for Field Studies, Wells offers semester-long study-abroad experiences in Africa, Australia, the Caribbean, and other locations. The College also offers credit-bearing courses during the January term that take students to a single destination in the U.S. or abroad for intensive study that requires travel in a region or country with a faculty member.

Academic Facilities

From the contemporary elegance of Weld House to the nineteenth-century Glen Park mansion, the former home of College founder Henry Wells, the residence halls encompass enough variety to satisfy every taste. Students eat their meals together in the majestic Tudor-style dining hall in Main Building.

The Louis Jefferson Long Library has received numerous awards for its architectural design. Facilities include an online computer center, individual study carrels, seminar and group-study rooms, and an art gallery. There are department libraries in art, economics, English, mathematics, music, philosophy, and the sciences located across the campus.

Home to the new Center for Sustainability and the Environment and the Sullivan Center for Business and Entrepreneurship, Zabriskie Hall provides newly renovated space for faculty offices, classrooms, and seminar rooms; Mac and PC labs; a media arts lab; a social science lab; student collaboration lounges; the Wall Street–style trading room; and more. Facilities for printmaking, painting, ceramics, sculpture, and photography are located in the Campbell Arts Building. The Cleveland Hall of Languages contains state-of-the-art equipment for learning foreign languages. Stratton Science Hall, completed in 2007, houses state-of-the-art laboratories for chemistry, biology, environmental science, and physics as well as a computer laboratory. Morgan Hall houses the Book Arts Center and the Wells College Press. Macmillan Hall has classrooms, faculty and administrative offices, several computer laboratories, and department libraries. The east wing of Macmillan contains the Margaret Phipps Auditorium, a theater facility used for teaching, concerts, lectures, and dramatic productions.

Costs

Wells is ranked among the best liberal arts colleges in the nation and has a long-term commitment to providing talented students with access to the best education. The College offers excellence at an affordable price.

The cost of a Wells education for the 2014–15 academic year was $35,200 for tuition, $12,700 for room and board, and $1,500 for fees.

Financial Aid

Approximately 99 percent of Wells students receive financial aid packaged in the form of grants, scholarships, loans, and work-study opportunities. The College works closely with students and their families to design a financial aid package that meets their needs and their budgets.

Award determinations are made on a rolling basis following acceptance. College financial aid is complex; however, Wells College's well-informed financial aid and admissions professionals are always pleased to answer questions and discuss methods of financing higher education with prospective students.

Applicants are considered for merit aid that is based largely on academic achievements and leadership abilities.

Faculty

At Wells, learning takes place in small, seminar-style classes where students are partners with faculty members in the learning process. Starting immediately in their first semester, students take classes with scholars who are recognized experts in their fields, not teaching assistants.

Nearly all Wells professors hold terminal degrees in their areas of expertise. They have been educated at the world's leading research universities, including Harvard, Yale, the University of California at Berkeley, Cornell, Brown, Rutgers, and Stanford. What students discover in Wells' classes is the importance of exploring ideas with others.

Wells is student centered, and academic programs focus on collaborative learning and teaching that meets the needs of students' different learning styles. As one would expect at a nationally recognized liberal arts college, professors are also engaged in research and a full range of scholarly activities. Their books are published by leading academic presses, their articles appear in top journals, and they are a presence at national and international conferences. Due to close faculty-student interaction, students have numerous opportunities to collaborate with faculty members on research, publications, and presentations.

Student Government

The student body is self-governing through the Collegiate Association. The three main governing bodies of the association are the Student-Faculty Administration Board, the Collegiate Council, and the Community Court. Students serve on faculty committees that make decisions concerning administrative and curricular matters.

Leadership development is an inherent part of the Wells experience, and students are encouraged to take an active role in student government and in the life of the campus community.

Admission Requirements

Wells admits students on the basis of the strength of their academic preparation. A student is expected to possess intellectual curiosity, motivation, and maturity to profit from the experience. In all cases, the College seeks students who have followed a solid college-preparatory program throughout high school.

Wells seeks students from varied backgrounds with diverse interests and talents in order to promote a stimulating learning community. Every admissions decision is made on an individual basis.

Wells students share an enthusiasm for academic pursuits and a serious intent to use their education in the future to enhance both their lives and the communities in which they choose to live.

Application and Information

Applications should be received early in the senior year of high school and not later than March 1 of the year in which entrance is desired. Applications from early decision and early action candidates must be received by December 15.

Transfer applications are reviewed on a rolling basis. Transfer students are eligible for merit scholarships and financial aid.

A campus visit is highly recommended for prospective students. For more information about Wells College or to schedule a campus visit, students should contact:

Admissions Office
Wells College
Aurora, New York 13026
Phone: 800-952-9355 (toll-free)
E-mail: admissions@wells.edu
Website: http://www.wells.edu
http://www.facebook.com/wellscollege

Aerial view of Wells College.

WENTWORTH INSTITUTE OF TECHNOLOGY

BOSTON, MASSACHUSETTS

★ To read more about this school, visit http://petersons.to/wentworthinstituteoftechnology

The Institute

Wentworth Institute of Technology was founded in 1904 to provide education in technology. Today, Wentworth has a current undergraduate full-time enrollment of approximately 3,600 men and women. The education acquired at Wentworth enables graduates to assume creative and responsible careers in business and industry. Wentworth is located on a 31-acre campus on Huntington Avenue in Boston.

Wentworth provides dormitory and suite-style residence halls on campus for men and women. Students in the residence halls are on a full meal plan with a full cafeteria, snack bar, and convenience store options on campus. Students living in a suite-style residence hall may prepare their own meals in their kitchen space.

Career counseling and placement assistance are available to all alumni and to students who have completed at least one semester of study at the Institute. While many graduates of Wentworth are employed in the Boston area, alumni have secured positions throughout the United States and abroad.

In addition to Wentworth's undergraduate programs, master's degree programs are awarded in architecture, construction management, and facility management.

Location

Boston is the educational center of New England. It is a city of charm, tradition, and elegance—a major center of art, science, music, history, medicine, and education. Wentworth is situated near the heart of Boston and is surrounded by institutions that provide the cultural advantages for which the city is famous. The Museum of Fine Arts, with its store of art treasures, is diagonally across the street, and admission is free to any student with a Wentworth ID card. Symphony Hall is just a few blocks away. The Harvard Medical School, the New England Conservatory of Music, Emmanuel College, Simmons College, Massachusetts College of Pharmacy and Health Sciences University, Massachusetts College of Art and Design, Roxbury Community College, and Northeastern University are among the many educational institutions within a few blocks of the campus.

Majors and Degrees

Degree programs are offered in the fields of applied mathematics, architecture, business management, computer science, construction management, design, engineering, and engineering technology. Bachelor of Science (B.S.) degrees are awarded in the following majors: applied mathematics, architecture, biomedical engineering, business management (optional concentrations in entrepreneurship or technology project management), civil engineering, computer engineering, computer engineering technology, computer information systems, computer networking, computer science, construction management, electromechanical engineering (optional concentration in biomedical systems engineering), electrical engineering, electronic engineering technology, engineering (interdisciplinary), facility planning and management, industrial design, interior design, and mechanical engineering. Baccalaureate degrees in architecture and interior design are designated as first professional degrees. Completion of a Wentworth baccalaureate degree usually requires four years (five years for the electromechanical engineering degree; applied mathematics is a three-year program with a four-year option).

Academic Programs

At Wentworth, college-level study in technological fundamentals and principles is combined with appropriate laboratory, field, and studio experience. Students apply theory to practical problems, and they acquire skills and techniques by using, operating, and controlling equipment and instruments that are particular to their area of specialization. In addition, study in the social sciences and humanities provides a balanced understanding of the world in which graduates work. Wentworth's programs of study are more practical than theoretical in approach, and the Institute's academic requirements demand extensive time and effort.

During the first two years of study in a degree program at Wentworth, students lay the foundation for more advanced study in the third and fourth (and fifth, where applicable) years. While nearly all majors allow continuous study from the freshman through the senior year, the architecture major requires a petition for acceptance to the baccalaureate program during the sophomore year.

All bachelor's degree programs are conducted as cooperative (co-op) education programs: upon entering their third year, students alternate semesters of academic study at Wentworth with semester-long periods of employment in industry. Two semesters of co-op employment are required; one additional (summer) semester of co-op is optional. Both students and the companies that hire them are enthusiastic about the co-op program and agree that it is a mutually valuable experience.

Off-Campus Programs

Students have the option to study abroad in Wentworth's established programs in Germany and Ireland. As part of various programs and classes, Wentworth students have also traveled to many destinations, such as Nicaragua, the United Kingdom, Italy, Austria, the Czech Republic, Russia, and throughout Scandinavia.

Wentworth's membership in the Colleges of the Fenway (COF) gives students the intimacy of a small college community and the resources of a major university. The COF consortium members are Emmanuel College, Massachusetts College of Art and Design, Massachusetts College of Pharmacy and Health Sciences University, Simmons College, Wentworth Institute of Technology, and Wheelock College. The consortium offers the benefits of cross-registration and access to social events, intramural teams, dance and theater troupes, a chorus and orchestra, professional activities, libraries, and campus facilities at five other colleges within walking distance of one another. The COF's Global Education Opportunities Center provides access to exchange programs and overseas institutions as well as cross-registration for faculty-led travel courses.

Academic Facilities

Wentworth's twenty-nine buildings house classrooms, studios, laboratories, administrative offices, and other facilities. Beatty Hall houses the Flanagan Campus Center, Schumann Fitness Center, Alumni Library, cafeteria, computer center, classrooms, recreation room, and office space. State-of-the-art laboratories, such as the Center for Sciences and Biomedical Engineering and the Manufacturing Center, are situated throughout the campus.

Costs

For 2015–16, tuition is $30,760, books and supplies are approximately $1,500, and the average room and board cost is about $14,160 (this figure varies according to accommodation). Tuition includes a brand new laptop that is outfitted with the complete suite of software used in the student's academic program.

Financial Aid

Scholarships are available to students who demonstrate need and academic promise. Merit-based scholarships are also available. Wentworth also provides federal and state financial assistance, such as Federal Pell and Federal Supplemental Educational Opportunity Grants, Federal Perkins Loans, Federal Work-Study Program awards, Gilbert Matching Grants, and Massachusetts No-Interest Loans, to students with financial need in accordance with federal and state guidelines.

Wentworth participates in the Federal Direct Lending program. As a result, students are eligible to borrow under the Federal Direct Stafford Student Loan program and parents may borrow under the Federal Direct PLUS program. Individuals participating in these programs borrow money directly from the federal government rather than through lending institutions.

In addition to these need-based programs, Wentworth also participates in the MEFA loan program sponsored by the Massachusetts Educational Financing Authority. Wentworth offers several payment options through payment plans and alternative loan financing.

To apply for financial aid, new students should complete the Free Application for Federal Student Aid (FAFSA) by March 1. Applications received after that date are considered as funds allow.

Faculty

Wentworth's faculty includes 145 full-time and 165 part-time members. The primary responsibility of every faculty member is teaching. Although professors may engage in some research and related work, student development remains the central mission of Wentworth's faculty. Upon entering Wentworth, every student is assigned a faculty adviser.

Student Government

Wentworth's Student Government performs an essential function as the official representative of the student body. Its purposes are to receive and express student opinion, to advance the best interests of the student body with the administration and faculty and with other institutions and associations, to support all extracurricular activities of the student body, and to serve as a bond between the student body and the faculty to foster cooperation and understanding. The Student Government is made up of elected representatives from each class section and the officers elected by the student body at large. The Student Government sponsors social functions and student organizations and serves as an advocate for student concerns.

Admission Requirements

Applicants must be graduates of secondary schools (or have passed the GED test) and must meet specific entrance requirements. All programs require four years of English, a laboratory science, and mathematics through algebra II in a college-preparatory program. Both the electromechanical engineering and the computer science programs require a background in precalculus or trigonometry. All programs require the submission of SAT or ACT scores. International students and transfers are welcome.

Application and Information

Students are admitted to Wentworth for September and January enrollment. Notification of admission is made on a rolling basis. The preferred method for applying is online at http://www.wit.edu/apply. The online application fee is $50. An application form, the application fee, transcripts from the secondary school and any colleges previously attended, SAT or ACT scores, a personal statement, and a letter of recommendation should be sent to:

Admissions Office
Wentworth Institute of Technology
550 Huntington Avenue
Boston, Massachusetts 02115
Phone: 617-989-4000
800-556-0610 (toll-free)
Fax: 617-989-4010
E-mail: admissions@wit.edu
Website: http://www.wit.edu
http://twitter.com/WITadmissions
http://facebook.com/wentworthadmissions

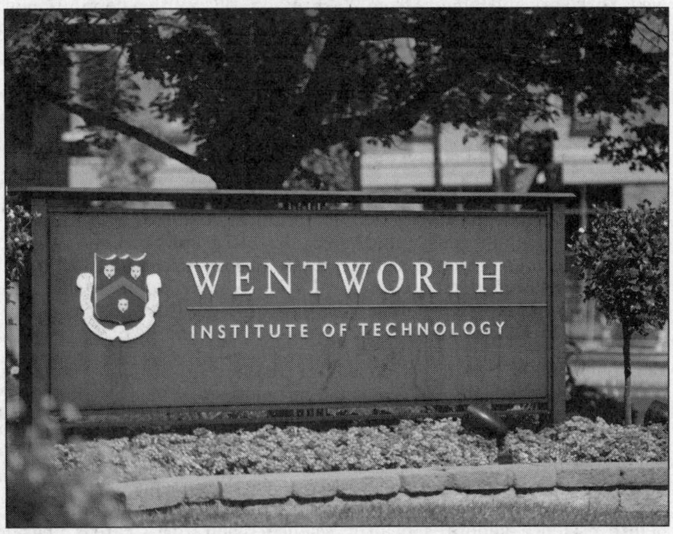

COLLEGE CLOSE-UPS

WEST CHESTER UNIVERSITY OF PENNSYLVANIA

WEST CHESTER, PENNSYLVANIA

WCU
WEST CHESTER UNIVERSITY

The University

West Chester University of Pennsylvania (WCU) is a leading public comprehensive university that excels in teacher education, business, health, natural and social sciences, music, and the arts. Founded in 1871, WCU has a total population of more than 16,000 (approximately 13,500 undergraduate and 2,500 graduate students) and is committed to high quality education at every level through more than 180 undergraduate and graduate programs, including a doctorate in nursing practice. The University's 406-acre campus has well-maintained facilities, including eleven residence halls, which range from singles and suites to apartment-style living, a new performing arts center, and a student recreation center. In keeping with West Chester's rich heritage, the University's Quadrangle buildings, part of the original campus, are on the National Register of Historic Places.

The University attracts its students from Pennsylvania, New Jersey, New York, and Delaware, as well as from states across the nation and from more than seventy countries around the world.

Each year, the University community hosts an impressive series of events, including programs with well-known musicians, authors, political figures, and more. The University also boasts more than 250 clubs and organizations on campus for those interested in everything from music, theater, and athletics to fraternities and sororities, service organizations, and honor societies. The University offers twenty-four intercollegiate NCAA Division II athletic teams (among the largest DII programs in the country), thirty club sports for men and women, and a variety of intramural sports including beach volleyball and street hockey. There are many athletic facilities across campus to support the University's various athletic programs, including a three-story climbing wall, a 13,000-square-foot fitness center, several gyms and pools, and athletic training facilities.

Location

The University is located in West Chester, a quaint but bustling community in southeastern Pennsylvania. West Chester retains much of its historical charm in its buildings and unspoiled countryside, yet it offers the twenty-first-century advantages of a town in the heart of a thriving suburban area. West Chester is just 25 miles west of Philadelphia and 17 miles north of Wilmington, Delaware, putting the museums, cultural stops, entertainment, restaurants, coffee shops, and historical sites of both cities within easy reach. It is also only 2 hours from New York City and 3 hours from Washington, D.C. With a population of about 20,000, the University nearly doubles West Chester's population, creating the feeling of a true college town.

Majors and Degrees

West Chester University offers more than 180 undergraduate and graduate programs of study, including degrees and certifications.

The Bachelor of Arts is offered in American studies, anthropology, art, biology, communication studies, communicative disorders, English, French, geography–geographic analysis, geography–urban/regional planning, German, history, Latin, liberal studies, literature, mathematics, philosophy, political science, political science–international relations, political science–applied public policy, psychology, Russian, sociology, Spanish, theater arts, and women's studies.

The Bachelor of Science is offered in accounting, athletic training, biochemistry, biology, biology–cell and molecular biology, biology–ecology, biology–medical technology, biology–microbiology, business management, chemistry, chemistry–biology (premed), computer science, criminal justice, economics, exercise science, finance, forensic and toxicological chemistry, geoscience–earth systems, geoscience–environmental, geosciences–geology, health and physical education, health science–general, health science–respiratory care, liberal studies–science and mathematics, liberal studies–professional studies, marketing, mathematics, nutrition and dietetics, pharmaceutical product development, physics, physics–engineering, public health–environmental, and public health–health promotion.

The Bachelor of Science in Nursing, the Bachelor of Fine Arts (studio arts), the Bachelor of Music (music education, performance, theory and composition, studies in an outside field), and the Bachelor of Social Work degrees are also offered.

The Bachelor of Science in Education degree is offered in biology, chemistry, communication–media, communication–speech, communication–theatre emphasis, early childhood education, earth-space science–astronomy, earth-space science–geology, elementary education, English, mathematics, physics, and special education.

Paraprofessional studies are available in medicine. WCU also offers early admission assurance programs with Drexel School of Medicine, Pennsylvania State University College of Medicine, Temple University School of Medicine, Temple University School of Dentistry, and Arcadia University Physician Assistant Program. In cooperation with Pennsylvania State University, West Chester University offers a 3+2 dual-degree program combining liberal arts, physics, and engineering. A similar, dual-degree cooperative physics/engineering program is available through affiliation with the School of Engineering and Textiles of Philadelphia University. As a member of the State System of Higher Education (PASSHE), special admission opportunities for scholarships to the Widener School of Law–Harrisburg Campus are also available.

Teacher certification programs are available in biology, chemistry, communications, early childhood education, elementary education, English, French, general science, German, health and physical education, Latin, mathematics, music education, physics, Russian, secondary education, social studies, Spanish, and special education. Certificates are also available in adapted physical education, athletic training, biology–medical technology, education for sustainability, and Russian studies.

Interdisciplinary areas of study include computer security certificate, ethnic studies, Honors College, Latin American studies, and Russian studies. Minors are available in most majors and in several interdisciplinary areas. The University also offers ROTC programs with cross-enrollment agreement with Widener University for Army ROTC and with St. Joseph's University for Air Force ROTC.

Academic Programs

Through the Study Abroad Program, students may spend one or more semesters in countries such as England, Italy, France, Australia, Spain, and Ireland. West Chester also sponsors a number of annual courses that include study abroad during spring, summer, and winter breaks.

West Chester University participates in the National Student Exchange Program, in which students spend up to a year at any one of more than 170 member schools across the United States, broadening their cultural and academic horizons. Automatic transfer of credit is arranged.

Off-Campus Programs

Through WCU's Study Abroad Program, students may spend a week, a semester, or even a year in countries around the world including England, Italy, France, Australia, Spain, and Ireland. The University also sponsors a number of faculty-led courses that include study abroad during spring, summer, and winter breaks and focus on a variety of topics including language immersion and program-specific courses.

West Chester University also participates in the National Student Exchange Program, in which students spend up to a year at any one of more than 170 member schools across the United States, broadening their cultural and academic horizons. Automatic transfer of credit is arranged.

Academic Facilities

There are two libraries on campus: the Francis Harvey Green Library and the Presser Music Library. Library collections include more than 1,416,480 print and electronic volumes; 2,000 print journal subscriptions; 926,000 microforms; 52,500 sound recordings; 10,300 films, videos, and DVDs; 3,500 maps; Internet access to more than 130 databases (including 27,000 titles of streaming video and 67,700 albums of streaming audio); and the full-text from more than 67,700 journals. Unique digital collections include University graduate and undergraduate catalogs from 1874 to date; title pages and autographs from the Philips Autograph Library; the letters of General Anthony Wayne; historic postcards, and other materials relating to the University and to local history. Services include free interlibrary loan, electronic and print reserves, more than one hundred public computer workstations, forty-six laptops for use in the library, and a Starbucks coffee shop.

The University's extensive computer facilities include more than 1000 PC and Mac workstations that are available to students in more than 72 portable/fixed computer labs. The majority of the buildings and the entire campus outdoors are wireless zones and Internet access is available in residence halls and computer labs. Students can use the computing facilities 16 hours a day during weekdays and open hours are available during the weekends.

The Merion Science Center, with modern multimedia lecture halls, extensive laboratories, and study areas where students can work together, connects to the Schmucker Science Center, which houses a fully equipped observatory and planetarium. The Center's extensive laboratories have a variety of advanced instruments such as a single-side band microscope—the world's second—as well as field inversion electrophoresis equipment for DNA analysis, and equipment for RFLP, PCR and DNA sequencing. The GIS computer lab has a first-order community base station and mobile GPS units to support coursework in geography, marketing and other subjects. Undergraduates have hands-on access to this equipment, as well as automated spectrophotometers, electron analytical equipment, atomic absorption spectrometers, and a variety of chromatographs, including gas chromatograph–mass spectrometers.

The campus includes a 100-acre natural area for environmental studies; speech and hearing and reading clinics; two theaters; music facilities with practice, rehearsal, and listening rooms; a large health and physical education complex; dance studios; research laboratories; physical therapy rooms; saunas; and a planetarium. The University also recently transitioned to geothermal energy and made room for green roofs on several buildings as well as plenty of flowering trees and gardens campuswide.

West Chester University is committed to providing barrier-free facilities for persons with impaired mobility.

Costs

West Chester University provides a high-quality education at an affordable cost. Full-time undergraduate students who are legal residents of Pennsylvania paid $6,820 for annual tuition for 12 to 18 semester hours in 2014–15. For more than 18 semester hours or fewer than 12, the cost was $284 per semester hour. Out-of-state students paid $17,050 per year for 12 to 18 semester hours and $710 per semester hour for more than 18 or fewer than 12. Room and board, on average, are $11,826 per year for on-campus residents in University-owned residence halls. Student fees for full-time students were $1,902 per year, plus a technology fee of $422 for in-state students and $642 for out-of-state students. Tuition is determined by the Board of Governors.

Financial Aid

Financial aid is available to students through work-study programs, grants, loans, special awards, and scholarships. A limited number of merit scholarships are awarded based on the student's academic standing and accomplishments in high school. Students who qualify are invited to apply. About 70 percent of all full-time undergraduate students receive some form of aid.

Faculty

West Chester University has a faculty of over 750 members. The majority hold doctoral degrees, and many are engaged in research and serve as consultants in their field of expertise. The student-faculty ratio is 20:1.

Student Government

The Student Government Association represents all students on the West Chester campus. In addition, the Residence Hall Association represents resident students, and the Off Campus and Commuter Association represents commuting students.

Admission Requirements

Applicants to West Chester University are evaluated on the basis of scholarship, character, and potential for achievement in the programs to which they apply. Freshman admission consideration includes graduation, with satisfactory scholarship, from an approved secondary school, approval from the Pennsylvania Homeschoolers Accreditation Agency, or by the applicant's Board of Education; satisfactory scores on either the SAT, ACT, or TOEFL (for international applicants); and completion of a personal statement. The University offers special admissions programs, including the Academic Development Program for Pennsylvania residents and a fall reduced course load program. Based on the scores received on Advanced Placement (AP) tests and subject examinations administered through the College-Level Examination Program (CLEP), students may receive advanced placement or credit.

Transfer applicants must have a minimum cumulative grade point average of 2.0 for admissions consideration. Certain academic programs require specific grade point averages above a 2.0 and may require an interview or specific course prerequisites. Transfer admission consideration includes the review of official college transcripts from all institutions attended and the completion of a personal statement. Applicants with fewer than 30 earned credits will also be reviewed on the basis of their high school achievements and standardized test scores. Those transfer applicants who graduated from high school more than three years ago are not required to submit SAT or ACT scores.

Application and Information

Students are admitted for the fall or spring semester. Freshman applicants for the fall semester are encouraged to apply electronically and urged to begin the application process early in their senior year of high school. Transfers should begin the process beginning in January for the fall semester. Applicants for the spring semester should apply by no later than November 15, however certain academic programs can close early. International students must apply by March 1 for the fall semester and September 1 for the spring semester. The Office of Admissions at West Chester University completes a preliminary evaluation of applicants once all information has been received and processed. The admissions committee reviews every application individually and each aspect of a student's file is considered. The admissions committee prioritizes applicants with the strongest academic credentials during the review process and notifies them of its decision as quickly as possible upon the completion of their file. Students are encouraged to visit WCU's campus. To arrange a visit or to attend an information session, or request additional information, students should visit www.wcupa.edu/admissions.

For additional information and required forms, students may contact:

Office of Admissions
Emil J. Messikomer Hall
West Chester University of Pennsylvania
100 West Rosedale Avenue
West Chester, Pennsylvania 19383
Phone: 610-436-3411
877-315-2165 (toll-free)
E-mail: ugadmiss@wcupa.edu
Transfer: ugtransfer@wcupa.edu
International: uginternational@wcupa.edu
Website: http://www.wcupa.edu/admissions

Philips Memorial Building is one of the many beautiful, historic buildings on West Chester University's main campus.

WESTERN CONNECTICUT STATE UNIVERSITY

DANBURY, CONNECTICUT

★ To read more about this school, visit http://petersons.to/westernconnecticutstateuniversity

The University

Founded in 1903, Western Connecticut State University (Western) is dedicated to providing both a high-quality university education and a memorable campus experience at an affordable cost. With programs in the fine arts, arts and sciences, business, and professional studies, Western takes pride in providing an outstanding education to more than 4,500 full-time undergraduates and nearly 2,000 graduate or part-time students.

Western offers excellent educational programs through five academic divisions: the Ancell School of Business, the Macricostas School of Arts and Sciences, the School of Professional Studies, the School of Visual and Performing Arts, and the Division of Graduate Studies and External Programs. The most popular majors include communication, theatre arts, education, business, justice and law administration, music, and nursing.

The university is also rich in a number of learning and social activities beyond the classroom. Students run academic and fraternal organizations, publish a newspaper and yearbook, and run a radio station. Western students also stage theater and musical productions, participate in cooperative education and internship programs, and administer their own campus government association.

The university provides accommodations for learning-disabled students, as well as study abroad, a University Scholars program, pre-collegiate and access initiatives, international student services, and community service learning opportunities. NCAA Division III men's and women's sports are represented on campus, and students enjoy intramural sports and premier recreation facilities, including a swimming pool, weight and cardiovascular machines, and basketball and tennis courts. The campus also features a child-care center, a counseling center, a health services office, a career development center, and campus ministries.

Western is accredited by the New England Association of Schools and Colleges; the American Chemical Society; the Commission on Collegiate Nursing Education; the Council on Social Work Education (baccalaureate level); the Council for Accreditation of Counseling and Related Educational Programs; and the National Association of Schools of Music.

Location

Western offers two campuses in Danbury, which is in the heart of western Connecticut, as well as a satellite campus in Waterbury. Danbury is a major city in Fairfield County in the foothills of the Berkshire Mountains, just 65 miles north of Manhattan and 50 miles west of Hartford.

In Danbury, the Midtown campus is a 34-acre, 15-building campus with an interesting mix of old and new architecture, and it offers easy access to downtown entertainment, restaurants, and shopping. The 364-acre Westside campus is ideal for hikers and nature buffs who want to discover its woodland wonders while enjoying state-of-the-art facilities. The Western-at-Waterbury campus offers a convenient location closer to the center of the state, with the same level of excellent service.

Majors and Degrees

The Ancell School of Business offers the Bachelor of Business Administration in Accounting, Finance, Management, Management Information Systems, and Marketing, as well as the Bachelor of Science in Justice and Law Administration programs.

The Macricostas School of Arts and Sciences offers the Associate in Science, Bachelor of Arts, and Bachelor of Science degree programs. The Associate in Science is offered in liberal arts. The Bachelor of Arts is offered in American Studies, Anthropology/Sociology, Biology, Chemistry, Communication, Computer Science, Earth and Planetary Sciences–Astronomy, Economics, English, English/Professional Writing, History, Mathematics, Political Science, Psychology, Social Sciences, and Spanish. The Bachelor of Science is offered in Medical Technology and Meteorology.

The School of Professional Studies offers the Bachelor of Arts and Bachelor of Science degree programs. The Bachelor of Arts is offered in Social Work. The Bachelor of Science is offered in Elementary Education, Health Education, Health Promotion Studies, Nursing, and Secondary Education.

The School of Visual and Performing Arts offers the Bachelor of Arts, Bachelor of Science, and Bachelor of Music degree programs. The Bachelor of Arts is offered in Art, Music, and Theatre Arts. The Bachelor of Science is offered in Music Education, and the Bachelor of Music is offered with options in Classical: Voice or Instrument or in Jazz Studies. Auditions are required for entrance into any of the music degree options.

In addition to the university's full menu of undergraduate programs, the Ancell School of Business offers the Master of Business Administration, Master of Health Administration, and Master of Science in Justice Administration. Programs in the School of Arts and Sciences include the Master of Arts in Biological and Environmental Sciences, Earth and Planetary Sciences, English, History, and Mathematics; and the Master of Fine Arts is offered in Professional Writing. The School of Professional Studies offers the Master of Science in Counselor Education, Elementary Education, Nursing, and Secondary Education programs; also offered is the Doctor of Education (Ed.D.) in Instructional Leadership and an Ed.D. in Nursing Education. Western's newest school, the School of Visual and Performing Arts, offers the Master of Fine Arts in Visual Arts and the Master of Science in Music Education programs.

Academic Programs

The university has developed a diverse mix of programs designed to inspire students. From enlightening arts to specialized fields of education, the emphasis is on the individual student's learning experience. Special offerings at Western include a program in Computer Information Security Management and the only licensed Meteorology program in Connecticut.

Academic Facilities

A number of facilities contribute to academic life on campus. The newly renovated and expanded library holds more than 200,000 volumes and 400,000-plus bound periodicals, microforms, government documents, music scores, electronic resources, and audiovisual items. Western's Science Building opened in 2005 to great acclaim for its ecology-friendly green design and cutting-edge lab and classroom equipment. The newest building on campus, the Visual and Performing Arts Center, opened in 2014 with two theaters, a concert hall and art studios, and exhibition space. The building was listed as ninth on a list of the 25 Most Amazing Campus Arts Centers and the university's Bachelor of Arts in Theatre Arts program was ranked as one of the ten best in the country in 2015.

Costs

As part of the Connecticut State Colleges & Universities system, Western provides a high-quality private university education at an exceptionally reasonable public school cost. A full-time, in-state undergraduate student who lived on campus paid approximately $19,800 for 2014–15. A full-time, out-of-state undergraduate student who lived on campus paid approximately $31,305 for 2014–15. These annual costs included tuition, fees, and room and board. Books, laboratory fees, health insurance, and personal expenses were not included in the estimate.

Western participates in the New England Regional Student Program of the New England Board of Higher Education. This program offers residents of other New England states the opportunity to enroll at Western at Connecticut resident-tuition rates, plus an additional fee, in programs that are not available in their home states.

Financial Aid

Any student who is matriculated at Western and registered for at least 6 credits per semester may apply for student aid, which includes federal, state, and institutional funding. Students must complete the Free Application for Federal Student Aid (FAFSA) and be sure to list Western's school code of 001380 in the college release section. If the student's file is selected for verification, appropriate signed copies of federal income tax returns must be submitted. Academic scholarships are available to students with superior academic credentials. Students with demonstrated financial need also have the opportunity to participate in work-study programs. For more information, students should contact the Financial Aid Office at 203-837-8580 or wcsufinancialaid@wcsu.edu.

Faculty

Western's faculty members and administrators are nationally respected and continually cited for scholarly achievement. The faculty-student ratio is 1:13.7, and nearly 90 percent of the university's full-time faculty members have doctoral or terminal degrees.

Admission Requirements

Western welcomes applications from all qualified individuals. Admission to the four undergraduate schools is competitive. University admissions criteria include GPA, types of courses taken, extracurricular activities, and standardized test results. Applications are reviewed by admissions professionals. If an applicant feels that individual circumstances warrant special consideration, a personal letter explaining those circumstances may be submitted with the application.

Academic preparation is the most important factor in determining admission. Freshman candidates for admission must have a high school diploma from an accredited secondary school or an equivalency diploma. General Educational Development (GED) test scores must be converted into a State of Connecticut Equivalency Diploma.

Western applicants should present evidence of successful completion of the following academic units in high school with a cumulative grade average of B-minus (80) or higher: 4 years of English, including writing skills and literature; 3 years of mathematics, including algebra I, geometry, and algebra II; 2 years of social sciences, including U.S. history; 2 years of laboratory sciences; and 2 to 3 years of a single foreign language (3 years are recommended). Academic course work in computer science, visual arts, theater, music, or dance may be substituted for one of the areas above. Those applicants who do not meet these guidelines may be considered under the Educational Achievement and Access Program. For more information about the program, students should contact the Office of University Admissions.

For specific information about transfer student admission, early admission, freshman entrance with advanced standing, special transfer arrangements for associate degree recipients, guest student admission, re-admit admission, fresh-start admission, and international student admission, students should contact the Office of University Admissions.

Interviews are not required, but candidates are encouraged to attend an information session before they enroll. These sessions provide information about the university and the admissions process and allow students to assess how the university can help them meet their educational goals. They also afford students the opportunity to meet with professors, other potential students, and current students. Student-guided tours are available. Students are able to visit the library, the residence halls, science and computer laboratories, the student center, and the recreation center. For information about appointments and campus visits, students should call the Office of University Admissions.

Application and Information

Western seeks to enroll students who will benefit from and contribute to the university. Rolling admission for the fall semester begins December 1, with class spaces filled on a first-come, first-served basis. Rolling admission for the spring semester begins October 1, with class spaces filled on a first-come, first-served basis. To apply, students should obtain an application from the Office of University Admissions or from a secondary school or community college guidance office. Western welcomes transfer and international student applications.

For application forms and more information, students should contact:

Office of University Admissions
Western Connecticut State University
181 White Street
Danbury, Connecticut 06810
Phone: 203-837-9000
877-837-WCSU (toll-free)
E-mail: admissions@wcsu.edu
Website: http://www.wcsu.edu
http://www.facebook.com/WestConn
http://twitter.com/West

WESTMONT COLLEGE

SANTA BARBARA, CALIFORNIA

WESTMONT

The College

Westmont College, a nationally ranked liberal arts college committed to historic Christianity, remains focused on undergraduate education. One of the country's most dynamic interdenominational Christian colleges, Westmont combines a world-class education with an unbeatable Southern California coastal location to prepare students for fulfilling lives of leadership and service.

Residence life, athletics, off-campus programs, and opportunities for local and international outreach contribute to balanced personal and spiritual development. Alumni enter a wide variety of professions and vocations and pursue professional-, master's-, and doctoral-level programs at the world's finest research universities, including UCLA, Stanford, Harvard, Yale, Princeton, Cambridge, the University of Chicago, and many others. Westmont's 1,200 students come to Westmont from the majority of states and many countries throughout the world, with the highest percentage from California. About 60 percent are women, 32 percent are students of color, and 2 percent are international students. Eighty-five percent of the students live in the five residence halls on campus or the apartment complex off campus.

As a member of the National Association of Intercollegiate Athletics and the Golden State Athletic Conference, Westmont provides intercollegiate sports for men and women in basketball, cross-country, soccer, tennis, and track and field. Men also compete in intercollegiate baseball, club polo, club rugby, club soccer, club volleyball, club Ultimate (Frisbee), and club golf. In addition, women participate in intercollegiate volleyball, polo, club cheer, and club golf. The intramural program offers a wide variety of activities as well.

The numerous clubs and organizations include a student newspaper, literary magazine, yearbook, choral and music ensembles, intercultural clubs, political organizations, theater productions, community service groups, and Christian service, mission, and outreach programs. The Ruth Kerr Memorial Student Center houses the campus dining facilities. Chapel, an integral part of a Westmont education, offers speakers and programs that inspire and challenge students to continue growing in their relationship with Christ. Students are required to attend chapel three days a week.

Location

Westmont is located on a 111-acre campus, rich with pine, oak, and eucalyptus trees in Montecito, a Santa Barbara neighborhood between the Pacific Ocean and the Santa Ynez Mountains. Students enjoy the beach and mountain trails year-round. A wealth of history and culture, theaters, libraries, community concerts, and other civic offerings await students just minutes from the campus.

Majors and Degrees

Westmont awards Bachelor of Arts (B.A.) and Bachelor of Science (B.S.) degrees in 28 liberal arts majors. These include alternative major, art, art history, biology, chemistry, communication studies, computer science, economics and business, education, engineering physics, English, English and modern languages, European studies, French, history, kinesiology, liberal studies mathematics, music, philosophy, physics, political science, psychology, religious studies, social science, sociology and anthropology, Spanish, and theater arts. The college offers a teacher-preparation program, which is approved by the California Commission for Teacher Preparation and Licensing, enabling students to qualify for either the single-subject or the multiple-subject credential. Pre-professional programs include athletic training, dentistry, engineering, law, medicine, ministry and missionary studies, pharmacy, physical therapy, and veterinary studies.

Academic Programs

All majors and programs of study feature thought-provoking and inspiring ways to integrate belief, thought, and action to reach a deeper, more accurate understanding of the world. Westmont demonstrates its commitment to academic freedom in courses that demand students' best critical thinking and through a wide range of opportunities and organizations that explore the world of ideas. Students consider issues of science and religion through the Pascal Society and attend lectures in the humanities sponsored by the Erasmus Society. As an exclusively undergraduate college, Westmont seeks to actively engage students in significant ideas and issues. Professors, staff members, and alumni want to help students grow through their questions toward an ever-deeper faith.

Off-Campus Programs

Off-campus programs include **Europe Semester,** which provides the broadest geographical scope. **England Semester,** offered every other year, combines travel and residential study in the British Isles for students of literature. **Westmont in Istanbul** allows students to live in a city that blends the past and the future, grace and grit, culture and politics, faith and skepticism. Students attending **Westmont in Mexico** gain skills for effective cross-cultural living, experience incarnational ministry, and improve their Spanish language abilities. **Semesters in France and Spain** offer French and Spanish majors the opportunity to study these languages in their home countries, as does the **Latin American Studies Program,** which combines the study of Spanish culture and language in Belize, Chile, Costa Rica, and Honduras. Similar programs are offered at Jerusalem University College in Israel; the **Middle East Studies Program** at the American University in Cairo, Egypt; and in the **Russian Studies Program** in Moscow, Nizhni Novgorod, and St. Petersburg (through Westmont's membership in the Council for Christian Colleges and Universities). Participants in the **International Business Institute program** visit the major economic and political capitals of Europe and Asia. The **Westmont Economics and Business Program in Asia** introduces students to the diverse economic growth in the Pacific Rim. The **East Asia Program** addresses contemporary world issues in China, Japan, and Taiwan. An additional summer program in Asia offers students an opportunity to study life and culture in Sri Lanka. Domestic off-campus programs include **Westmont in San Francisco,** which explores American urban society and offers internships; the **Washington Semester,** highlighting national political processes and incorporating internships in national, international, and economic policy, justice, and journalism; the **Consortium Visitor Program,** enabling students to study at any of the Christian College Consortium's 12 other member colleges; and other programs sponsored by the Council for Christian Colleges and Universities.

Academic Facilities

New buildings consist of the Adams Center for the Visual Arts, which includes a museum, studios, offices and classrooms; Winter Hall for Science and Mathematics; and the Westmont Observatory with the powerful Keck Telescope. The tri-level Roger John Voskuyl Library, named for Westmont's third president, provides access to information resources and services to support the research and information needs of faculty, staff, students and the surrounding community. The library collections include 237,000 books, media items, music scores, and microforms; 300 print periodical titles; and 105 online databases with access to 12,000 online periodicals. The Westmont community has access to additional resources through the Gold Coast Library Network, Camino and Interlibrary Loan Services. Westmont's network consists of both wired and wireless components. Wireless coverage extends through all campus buildings and most outdoor areas, with a total Internet bandwidth of 135 Mb/s. Students obtain Google Apps accounts through Westmont, providing e-mail, a calendar, document sharing, and 4 GB storage per student.

The college provides a general access computer lab with 27 dual-platform iMacs located on the main floor of the library. Westmont's Learning Commons is also housed in the library. This 21st-century space brings together library, technology, and other campus services in an environment designed to foster collaborative and creative work and social interaction. Voskuyl Library also houses departments that provide student support services: the Office of Life Planning, Academic Advising and Disability Services, Internship Programs, Writer's Corner, and Information Technology. Porter Theatre contains state-of-the-art equipment for dramatic productions and concerts. The Mericos H. Whittier Science Building and Winter Hall for Science and Mathematics house the college's science program and equipment, including an ultracentrifuge, a liquid scintillation counter for measuring radioactivity, physiographic units and other equipment for advanced physiological studies.

Costs

Tuition and fees for 2015–16 are $40,320, and room and board for the academic year are $13,040. The cost of books and personal expenses is estimated at $3,000.

Financial Aid

Westmont provides a strong financial aid program, so no student should hesitate to apply for lack of financial resources. Eighty-five percent of Westmont's students receive some form of financial assistance. Westmont offers full-tuition Monroe Scholarships, available only to first-year applicants who apply via the early action (nonbinding) process. A select group of these applicants are invited to the campus to participate in a formal competition. Students should contact the Office of Admission for more information. Other merit awards in the financial aid program—Dean's, Provost's, and President's Scholarships—range from $10,000 to $15,000. Transfer students may be eligible to receive scholarships ranging from $7,000 to $10,500. These merit scholarships are awarded to students who have demonstrated impressive academic achievement. Westmont also gives awards to students who demonstrate strength in art, music, theater arts, dance, cultural diversity, and athletics. After submitting the Free Application for Federal Student Aid (FAFSA), students may be eligible for generous state grants, aid from federal programs, institutional grants, loans, and work-study programs.

Faculty

One of the highest priorities at Westmont is attracting and retaining outstanding Christian teachers and scholars. The college's professors are dedicated to integrating faith and learning, and being actively involved in the lives of students. There are 96 full-time and 58 part-time faculty members. The student-faculty ratio is 11:1; the average class size is 18. Ninety-six percent of tenure-track faculty members hold a terminal degree. Westmont's professors are committed to teaching at the undergraduate level, and advise either incoming first-year students or majors in their department. A director of first-year programs oversees the advising and orientation of new students. Although teaching is their primary scholarly activity, many faculty members engage in research, write books, and publish articles in leading journals and periodicals.

Student Government

The Westmont College Student Association (WCSA) is an entirely self-governing body. Students elect their own WCSA representatives, who are responsible for organizing social, cultural, and educational activities. They actively participate in and are voting members on almost all faculty committees, and they allocate the student budget to various clubs and organizations. Westmont Student Ministries, another student-managed organization, organizes on- and off-campus ministries and mission opportunities.

Admission Requirements

Westmont selects candidates for admission from those prospective students who produce evidence they are prepared for the academic stimulation and spiritual vitality central to the character of Westmont. All applicants must submit one academic letter of recommendation, official high school or college transcripts, and official SAT or ACT scores. A pastoral/character reference is optional. An interview is strongly encouraged. For transfer students from an accredited two- or four-year college or university or a Bible college or university that is accredited by the American Association of Bible Colleges, the evaluation is based on achievement in solid, transferable course work; an assessment of the personal areas covered by the application (as stated above); and the quality of the written responses. High school records must be submitted if the applicant has completed fewer than 24 college-level credits at the time of application.

Application and Information

Students may enroll at Westmont at the beginning of either the fall or spring semester. The college offers an early action plan. High school seniors interested in applying for early action must submit an application by November 15; notifications are mailed on January 1. The priority deadline for regular decision is February 15 for first-year applicants and March 15 for transfers; notifications are mailed on a rolling basis. Applications should be submitted online via the Common Application or with the Westmont application, with an application fee of $50. The Office of Admission encourages prospective students to complete the application process as early as possible.

Visitors are welcome any time. Campus visitors can stay overnight in the residence halls, attend classes and chapel, speak with professors or coaches, audition for a music program, share a portfolio with the art department, and eat meals with Westmont students. Several Preview Day events occur each semester. Westmont seeks to enroll a well-rounded and balanced first-year class. One of the college's goals is creating a dynamic and culturally and traditionally diverse community of learners with a variety of attributes, accomplishments, backgrounds, and interests.

For more information regarding admissions students should contact:

Office of Admission
Westmont College
955 La Paz Road
Santa Barbara, California 93108
Phone: 800-777-9011 (toll-free)
Fax: 805-565-6234
E-mail: admissions@westmont.edu
Website: http://www.westmont.edu/
http://www.facebook.com/westmont
http://twitter.com/westmontnews

Nestled in the beautiful hills of Santa Barbara, California, Westmont is home to 1,200 undergraduate scholars, all seeking to engage the academy, church, and world.

COLLEGE CLOSE-UPS

WEST VIRGINIA WESLEYAN COLLEGE

BUCKHANNON, WEST VIRGINIA

WEST VIRGINIA WESLEYAN

The College

Founded in 1890, West Virginia Wesleyan College is a coeducational, residential, liberal arts college in Buckhannon, West Virginia. The College has an enrollment of 1,400 undergraduate students from thirty-five states and twenty-one countries. The average class size is 19 and the student-faculty ratio is 14:1. More than 75 percent of the faculty members hold the highest degree in their respective teaching field. Each fall, West Virginia Wesleyan enrolls approximately 415 freshmen and 50 transfers. Fifty-five percent of students originate from West Virginia, and the ratio of men to women is 1:1. Approximately 17 percent of the students are minority or international students. More than 85 percent of students live on campus, and housing is required for all four years of study. Housing options include residence halls, suites, on-campus apartments, and campus-adjacent residence units.

Among the many services available to students is the Academic and Career Center, which helps students with job placement, class scheduling, selection of a major program of study, internship opportunities, and international travel. The center also provides preparatory help for professional or graduate entrance exams such as the LSAT, GRE, or GMAT. The Health and Counseling Center allows students to receive personal and educational guidance, as well as health services. The Learning Center provides comprehensive learning resources for all students, as well as robust services for students with diagnosed learning differences and is one of the foremost programs of its type in the country.

In addition to challenging academic curriculum and innovative technology, Wesleyan offers a balanced and comprehensive student-life program. Co-curricular activities include twenty-two NCAA Division II varsity sports, intramurals, and outdoor recreation adventures. More than seventy campus organizations include vocal and instrumental musical ensembles, theatre arts, dance, community service, clubs, special interest groups, Greek life, and spiritual and religious life programming. On-campus media opportunities include a campus radio station, student newspaper, and yearbook. The student-run Bobcat Entertainment Board schedules cultural and social entertainment every week during the academic year.

Location

Situated in the foothills of the Allegheny Mountains, Wesleyan's picturesque 100-acre campus is located in the historic town of Buckhannon, West Virginia. Buckhannon is located two hours south of Pittsburgh, Pennsylvania, and 90 minutes north of Charleston, West Virginia. It is easily accessible by interstate highways. Buckhannon has been included in Norman Crampton's book, *The Top 100 Best Small Towns in America* and *The 120 Best College Towns in America*. Students are drawn to the attractive and friendly setting and the many restaurants, social events, and outdoor adventures available within a short distance from campus.

Majors and Degrees

The College awards Bachelor of Arts, Bachelor of Science, Bachelor of Science in Nursing, and Bachelor of Music Education degrees, in addition to a number of master's-level degrees. Majors include: accounting, art, arts administration, athletic training, biology, business administration, five-year bachelor's + master's in business administration, chemistry, Christian formation, communication studies, computer information science, computer science, criminal justice, economics, education (combined elementary/secondary, elementary, or secondary), engineering 3-2, English (literature, education, or writing), environmental science, environmental studies, exercise science, gender studies, graphic design, history, international business, international studies, management, marketing, mathematics, music (applied or theory), music education, musical theatre, nursing, painting and drawing, petroleum and natural gas geophysics, philosophy, physics, political science, psychology, public relations, religion, sociology, sport business, and theatre arts.

Preprofessional study programs are offered in dentistry, law, medicine, optometry, pharmacy, physical therapy, and veterinary medicine. The degrees are determined by the content of the student's program.

West Virginia Wesleyan also offers the following master's degrees: Master of Science in Athletic Training, Master of Business Administration, Master of Fine Arts in Creative Writing, Master of Education, and Master of Science in Nursing.

Academic Programs

Students are required to complete 120 credit hours of course work to become eligible for graduation. Approximately one third of those hours are taken in a student's major, one third in the general studies curriculum requirement, and one third in electives. The general studies and elective courses are taken to develop and enhance a student's worldview.

Wesleyan operates on a traditional semester system. The optional May Term is a three-week intensive period of study giving students the opportunity to earn three credit hours. International travel opportunities are popular options during May Term.

The honors program is offered for superior students who meet the specific requirements and are willing to commit themselves to a rigorous and enriching curriculum that affirms the highest ideals of a liberal arts institution. Challenging classes and cultural outings are an integral part of the honors program and are offered throughout the academic year.

Advanced credit is available for students who achieve required scores on Advanced Placement exams, International Baccalaureate exams, and CLEP tests.

New students are assigned a faculty adviser who assists with course selection and student concerns. All first-year students are required to successfully complete a four-hour First Year Seminar course. In addition to helping students adapt to college life, the First Year Seminar courses are topical and apply credit toward a general studies requirement.

Off-Campus Programs

Study abroad is highly encouraged and is an important part of the Wesleyan student's experience. In the recent past, students have studied in such countries as Australia, Austria, Bolivia, Bulgaria, England, Ireland, Italy, Kenya, Korea, Spain, and Wales, but there are a number of other countries in which students may study. Internships are required for many majors and highly encouraged for others. They are available locally, as well as in cities such as Pittsburgh, New York, Washington, D.C., and others around the globe. These off-campus opportunities can be taken for a complete semester, during the May Term, or during the summer.

Academic Facilities

Wesleyan's twenty-four buildings, including eleven modern residence hall units, house some of the most impressive facilities in the region. Residence hall facilities include Fleming Hall, which was completely remodeled in 2008, and Dunn Hall, a new residence hall that opened to students in 2011. Other recent campus construction includes the Virginia Thomas Law Center for the Performing Arts and the Reemsnyder Research Center for the sciences. A brand-new wellness center with Nautilus equipment, full cardio theater, separate workout rooms, and locker room facilities opened in 2012. In 2014 the College opened a new Welcome Center and over the next five years will remodel every major academic classroom through funding received from a Title III grant program. This $10-million grant also provides for a Student Success Center and Center for Teaching and Learning, providing Wesleyan unparalleled support services.

The Annie Merner Pfeiffer Library houses more than 105,000 volumes, 700 periodicals, and 10,000 media materials. More than 220 million additional resources worldwide can be accessed through a number of online databases from students' own residence halls 24 hours a day. Located in the center of the campus is Wesley Chapel, the largest sanctuary in West Virginia, and the Martin Religious Center. The Benedum Campus and Community Center houses a convenience store, bookstore, swimming pool, the Cat's Claw restaurant, the campus radio station, and student services offices.

The Rockefeller Health and Physical Education Center includes a main gymnasium that seats 3,700, an intramural gymnasium, weight-training rooms, and an indoor Astroturf training and recreational area. Other key campus buildings include Christopher Hall of Science and the adjacent Reemsnyder Research Center, which houses state-of-the-art laboratories and classrooms to complement the Christopher's planetarium, herbarium, and greenhouse; Loar Hall, which includes a 165-seat recital hall and state-of-the-art computer music lab; Middleton Hall, which houses the admission offices and department of nursing; Haymond Hall of Science; and the Lynch-Raine Administration Building.

Costs

The 2015–16 costs at Wesleyan are $27,614 for tuition, $8,066 for room and board, and $1,174 for fees. Students should allow $800 for books per year. Wesleyan offers a 10-month interest-free monthly payment plan during the academic year.

Financial Aid

Wesleyan allocates nearly $15 million each year to help supplement the financial needs of students and their families. Merit scholarships are available for students who demonstrate excellence in the classroom, as well as those who demonstrate talent in the arts and athletics. Scholarship opportunities are available for students who have a strong commitment to community service and for those who have a comprehensive co-curricular resume. A variety of need-based programs are also available, including government grants and loans, institutional grants, and student employment. All students and their families should file the Free Application for Federal Student Aid by February 15. The institutional code for West Virginia Wesleyan is 003830.

Faculty

The faculty members at Wesleyan have a primary goal of teaching and advising. More than 75 percent of the full-time faculty members hold the highest degree in their respective fields. With a 13:1 student-faculty ratio, classes are small, and personal attention is evident in all departments. Not only are faculty members teachers and advisers, but they are also mentors and friends.

Student Government

The Student Senate is structured to encourage and promote student participation. The four peer-elected officers are elected by their respective classes or representative student organizations. Student Senate meets biweekly, along with faculty members, administration, and staff members, and is recognized as the driving force behind many initiatives and decisions on campus.

Admission Requirements

Wesleyan seeks students who have proven academic credentials, combined with achievements and talents that enhance the quality of life on campus. Students are selected by the Office of Admission on the basis of their high school transcripts, college entrance exam results, letters of recommendation, campus interviews, and other supportive information. All applicants must take the SAT or ACT and submit secondary school transcripts from all schools attended, along with the application for admission. Candidates are considered on an individual basis without regard to race, color, national origin, sex, sexual orientation, age, disability, or religious affiliation. Essays and campus interviews are strongly encouraged and may be required in some instances.

Transfer students from accredited institutions are considered for admission. All official college transcripts must be submitted, along with high school transcripts and college entrance exam results.

Applicants who complete their secondary education through an alternative program (e.g., home schooling) must present evidence that they have been adequately prepared for college work to be considered for admission. SAT or ACT results are also required.

Application and Information

Applicants must submit an application for admission, official transcripts, and ACT or SAT scores. The application review period opens each year on October 1. Applying online is free of charge at http://apply.wvwc.edu. A paper application is also available and can be submitted along with a $35 nonrefundable fee. Admission decisions are made on a rolling basis, and students are notified within three weeks of receipt of all required documents. The preferred application deadline is March 1 for the fall semester, and December 1 for the spring semester. Applicants who wish to be considered for merit scholarships must apply before March 1. Interviews, campus tours, faculty and staff appointments, and class visits are encouraged and may be arranged through the Office of Admission.

For additional information, students should contact:

Office of Admission
West Virginia Wesleyan College
59 College Avenue
Buckhannon, West Virginia 26201
Phone: 304-473-8510
800-722-9933 (toll-free)
E-mail: admission@wvwc.edu
Website: http://www.wvwc.edu

The Central Campus Green is one of many outdoor gathering spaces where students meet, study, and pass through on their way to classes and co-curricular activities.

WHEATON COLLEGE

WHEATON, ILLINOIS

Wheaton College
For Christ and His Kingdom

The College

Ranked by *U.S. News & World Report* as one of the nation's top liberal arts colleges, Wheaton College attracts exceptional students from all fifty states and more than fifty countries. An interdenominational Christian liberal arts college, Wheaton takes the pursuit of faith and learning seriously. In addition to upholding an academically rigorous curriculum, Wheaton is committed to being a community that fearlessly pursues God's truth; invests in developing whole, well-rounded students; and prepares its graduates to lead lives that make a difference in the world.

Interdenominational and international in constituency, the student body at Wheaton College consists of approximately 2,400 undergraduates (including 200 students in the Conservatory of Music). Approximately 80 percent of the undergraduate students come from outside Illinois.

Wheaton College's 150-year history demonstrates the benefits of stable leadership in private Christian higher education—it has had only 8 presidents since it was founded in 1860. Wheaton has been faithful to its original precepts, and its legacy is shown in the lives of its graduates. Many distinguished graduate schools currently enroll Wheaton graduates in the dramatic arts, education, law, medicine, music, philosophy, science, and sociology. These include Notre Dame, Princeton, SMU, Yale, and the Universities of Chicago and Missouri–Kansas City; several of the Big Ten music schools; and the A.R.T./MXAT Institute for Advanced Theater Training at Harvard. Wheaton alumni also excel in a wealth of endeavors around the world, with many holding positions in business and finance, government and foreign service, teaching, ministry, law, medicine, and the arts. Wheaton graduates actively contribute to their communities and churches, and no matter what position they hold, they strive to make a difference in the world around them.

Wheaton offers a rich, life-changing education, with graduates trained for life, not just jobs. Students are taught to think, reason, and express themselves effectively. They should be able to attain knowledge and measure it against the truth of God's word, understand the importance of service, and value faith that embraces both right belief and right action. Developing strong, life-long relationships—with classmates, professors, and Jesus Christ—is a priority. Graduates are well-positioned for whatever they want to pursue and prepared to face the challenges of life. The Wheaton experience is distinctive and living and learning at Wheaton is extraordinary.

Location

Wheaton's 80-acre campus is located in a residential suburb (population 55,000) 25 miles west of Chicago. The educational and cultural features of the Chicago metropolitan area are easily accessible by train and regularly visited by students.

Majors and Degrees

Wheaton grants the Bachelor of Arts and Bachelor of Science degrees and, through the Wheaton Conservatory of Music, the Bachelor of Music and Bachelor of Music Education degrees.

The following majors are available in the arts and sciences: ancient languages, anthropology, applied health science, archaeology, art, biblical and theological studies, biology, business/economics, chemistry, Christian education and ministry, communication, computer science, economics, education, English, environmental studies, geology, history, interdisciplinary studies, international relations, mathematics, modern languages (French, German, and Spanish), music, philosophy, physics, political science, psychology, sociology, and urban studies. Also, 3-2 programs are offered in engineering and nursing, alongside a five-year cooperative engineering program with Illinois Institute of Technology and other engineering schools.

The Wheaton Conservatory of Music offers a full range of professional music majors, including composition, education, history/literature, performance, music with elective studies in an outside field, and music with an emphasis in a music-related field (such as media/film music, pedagogy, conducting, and collaborative piano). Students seeking these professional music degrees are accepted directly into the program by audition.

An on-campus program in military science leads to a commission in the U.S. Army at graduation. In addition to the majors offered, Wheaton has programs leading to teacher certification and to athletic training certification as well as programs preparing students for careers in business, health professions, law, and ministry.

Academic Programs

Wheaton is a distinctively Christian college where faculty members and students work together, both inside and outside the classroom, to apply Christian principles and values to the needs and problems of the individual and society. The vigorous search for knowledge and wisdom in any area of human activity is based on the belief that all truth is God's truth.

The academic curriculum combines with artistic, athletic, religious, service, and social activities to achieve a lively interaction of faith, learning, and living. Because of the College's strong commitment to developing effective servant/leaders for society worldwide and the church, there is a particularly strong integration of faith and learning in all degree programs.

A student's major is selected during the third semester of general education courses taken to meet competency and area requirements. Students must demonstrate competence (either by examination or by taking prescribed courses) in foreign language, mathematics, speech, and writing. All students must complete area requirements in applied health science, art, biblical studies, history, literature, music, natural science, philosophy, and social science. A student may be granted advanced placement or college credit on the basis of examination (SAT Subject Tests or AP). The number of credits granted and the level of placement are determined by the registrar and the chair of the department in which the course is taught.

Wheaton offers ten natural science majors—applied health science, biology, chemistry, computer science, environmental studies, geology, liberal arts engineering, liberal arts nursing, mathematics, and physics—in six academic departments. The Wheaton faculty members engage the study of science authoritatively, enthusiastically, and creatively in the classrooms and laboratories and beyond the campus. They are creative and offer more than two dozen general education courses in the natural sciences as well as the majors listed above. The programming includes the use of state-of-the-art technologies and techniques on the main Wheaton campus, cutting edge geological and biological studies in a large science station in the scientifically rich area of the Black Hills of South Dakota, and marine biology studies in Belize.

Off-Campus Programs

Wheaton offers a variety of off-campus opportunities to enhance students' programs of study. The Wheaton Passage program is a popular camp experience available to new students at the College's Honey Rock Camp in northern Wisconsin. Another program, Human Needs and Global Resources (HNGR), combines classroom study with a six-month, field-based, service-learning internship in the Global South. A similar program in urban studies, Wheaton in Chicago, focuses on urban issues in U.S. cities and includes a semester living in College-owned housing in urban Chicago.

Other special summer programs for credit include field study at the Wheaton College Science Station in the Black Hills of South Dakota; working with youth at Honey Rock Camp; interdisciplinary study in East Asia; the study of English literature in England; language study in France, Germany, and Spain; the Wheaton in the Holy Lands program, involving biblical and archaeological studies; the Arts in London program, which includes course work in music, theater, and art; and an international study program based in England and the Netherlands, offering courses in economics, political science, and psychology. Wheaton is a member of the Council of Christian Colleges and Universities, based in Washington, D.C. The council's activities increase students' learning opportunities by bringing special programs to campus and by providing off-campus study.

Off-campus programs include American Studies in Washington, D.C.; the Washington Journalism Center in Washington, D.C.; the Los Angeles Film Studies Center; the Contemporary Music Center in Martha's Vineyard; Latin American Studies in Costa Rica; Middle East Studies in Cairo; the Australia Studies Center; China Studies Program; the Scholar's Semester in Oxford; Russia Studies Program; and Uganda Studies Program. Wheaton has also recently affiliated with the International Sustainable Development Studies Institute in Thailand. In addition, Wheaton's membership in the Christian College Consortium allows students a semester of study at one of the other twelve consortium colleges.

Cooperative programs in social science are available at American and Drew Universities, and students may participate in a European seminar conducted by Gordon College.

Academic Facilities

An $80-million science and mathematics facility opened in fall 2010. The 128,000-square-feet of space includes eight teaching labs and research space designed to promote collaborative teacher-student research.

In 2009, an $11 million renovation of Adams Hall added art gallery and studio space. Edman Chapel, often the venue for concerts by world-class musicians, has undergone a $9 million renovation that added rehearsal space, including a large rehearsal room named for alum John Nelson, former conductor of Ensemble Orchestral de Paris.

In 2008, Wheaton's Memorial Student Center reopened after an extensive renovation to house the J. Dennis Hastert Center for Economics, Government, and Public Policy. The facility provides classroom, research, and public discussion space geared toward the study of economics, politics, and values in business, government, and ministry. Other recent additions to campus facilities include the Todd Beamer Student Center (2004); the Wade Center (2001), which houses the books and papers of seven British authors, including C. S. Lewis and J. R. R. Tolkien; and the Sports and Recreation Complex (2000).

Costs

Tuition for the 2015–16 year is $32,950; room and board for the year is $9,290.

Financial Aid

Realizing that a private college education is a sizable investment, Wheaton is committed to providing the necessary need-based financial aid so students can attend. Last year Wheaton awarded over $25 million in grants and scholarships.

The average need-based aid package for freshmen is about $20,000 and some merit aid is also available. The Career Development Center helps students to secure part-time jobs, as well as future employment.

Faculty

Over 94 percent of Wheaton's 198 full-time faculty members hold earned doctorates, and more than one third graduated from the top twenty-five graduate schools as designated in *U.S. News & World Report*. The professors' primary commitment as educators and advisers is enriched by their considerable research, publishing, and artistic activities. In addition, the professors are active Christians who strive to show how a profound commitment to God's word structures a vision of all of life, including intellectual life. They are dedicated to honoring a Christian perspective and to modeling Christ's love to their students.

All undergraduate courses are taught by faculty members.

To ensure a rich range of perspectives and expertise, every department at Wheaton has at least 3 full-time professors, and most have 5 to 10. The student-faculty ratio is 12:1.

Student Government

Student Government ensures a student voice in institutional affairs and provides a wide range of opportunities to develop leadership abilities. Student Government's vision is "To further the educational, spiritual, and relational development of the Wheaton College community as elected servant leaders representing student initiative, concern, creativity, and enthusiasm."

Besides Student Government, there are over forty academic, cultural, social justice, and entertainment student groups on campus. In addition, the Office of Christian Outreach provides opportunities for student ministry through student-run mission trips and ministries in urban and suburban Chicago.

Admission Requirements

Wheaton is a selective college that seeks to enroll students who evidence a vital Christian experience, high moral character, personal integrity, social concern, strong academic ability and motivation, and the desire to pursue Christian higher education as defined in the aims and objectives of the College. These qualities are evaluated by consideration of each applicant's academic record, autobiographical essays, test scores, recommendations, optional interview, and participation in extracurricular activities. For students applying to the Conservatory of Music, strong consideration is given to the evaluation of the required audition.

Applicants must have a high school diploma or the equivalent, and at the time of graduation should have completed a college-preparatory curriculum with a minimum of 18 acceptable units.

Satisfactory scores on the SAT or on the ACT examination are required of all applicants to the freshman class. The middle 50 percent range of scores for those admitted is 27–32 (ACT) and 1230–1400 (SAT composite math and verbal scores).

Application and Information

An application packet, complete with detailed instructions and requirements, can be obtained from the Admissions Office or online. For early action (nonbinding), students seeking admission in the fall term should apply to either the College of Arts and Sciences or the Conservatory of Music by November 1. The regular action deadline is January 10; the transfer application deadline is March 1. An admissions counselor can provide more information about Wheaton in general or the application process in particular.

Further information is available from:

Admissions Office
Wheaton College
501 College Avenue
Wheaton, Illinois 60187
Phone: 630-752-5005
800-222-2419 (toll-free)
E-mail: admissions@wheaton.edu
Website: http://www.wheaton.edu
http://www.wheaton.edu/Admissions-and-Aid/Undergrad

Historic Blanchard Hall overlooks Wheaton's front of campus.

WHITMAN COLLEGE

WALLA WALLA, WASHINGTON

WHITMAN COLLEGE

The College

Challenging students to excel in the sciences, humanities, art, and social sciences, Whitman College is a nationally recognized liberal arts college. It combines the educational prestige of the best Eastern liberal arts colleges with the unpretentious values of the Pacific Northwest. Since 1882, students have chosen Whitman because of its commitment to undergraduate education. With 1,500 students and an average class size of 16, Whitman encourages students to be active participants in their education. In 1913, the College led the nation by requiring students to successfully complete comprehensive oral and written evaluations in their major field of study. The installation of a chapter of Phi Beta Kappa in 1919 marked the recognition of the high quality of Whitman's curriculum and the standards of teaching and learning that distinguish the College. Seventy percent of Whitman graduates enroll in graduate school within five years of earning their undergraduate degree.

Enrollment includes students from forty-eight states and thirty countries. As a residential college, approximately 70 percent of Whitman students live on campus. A variety of residence hall living options are available, including coeducational housing, apartment-style living, eleven special-interest houses, four fraternity houses, and an all-women's residence hall that houses, among others, the members of four national sororities. First-year students and sophomores are required to live on campus.

Whitman has an extremely engaged student body. "Whitties" participate in more than 130 interest groups, clubs, and organizations. The debate team often ranks first in the country in parliamentary. The highly acclaimed theater department produces eight to ten shows each academic year, while the music department supports more than two dozen musical groups on campus. The College fields fifteen varsity teams and offers thirteen club sports and sixteen intramural activities. The Whitman club cycling team and men's and women's Ultimate (Frisbee) teams have won national championships in recent years. Several varsity teams have been nationally ranked in recent years, including men's and women's tennis, swimming, golf, and women's basketball, which held the number-one ranking throughout much of the 2014 season and finished as national runner-up.

Location

Whitman is located in Walla Walla, a historic community of 35,000 nestled in the foothills of the Blue Mountains of southeastern Washington. The Walla Walla Valley has four distinct seasons and enjoys more than 200 days of sunshine a year. With rich natural terrain at its doorstep, outdoor activities abound. These include cross-country and downhill skiing, backpacking, hiking, kayaking, rafting, and rock climbing. Whitman hosts a wide array of cultural activities on campus, including concerts, art exhibits, environmental forums, internationally renowned speakers and performers, and cinema arts films. Students also perform with the community symphony, browse in the area's seventeen art galleries, and act in the community theater. Parents appreciate the vibrant arts culture of the town as well as the wine and restaurant scene. Walla Walla is home to more than 100 wineries and is a popular tourist destination.

Majors and Degrees

Whitman College confers the Bachelor of Arts (B.A.) degree, with departmental majors in anthropology; art (history, studio, and visual culture studies); Asian studies; biochemistry, biophysics, and molecular biology (BBMB); biology; chemistry; classics; economics; English; foreign languages and literatures (French, German studies, or Spanish); film and media studies; gender studies; geology; history; Latin American studies; mathematics; music; philosophy; physics; politics; psychology; religion; rhetoric studies; sociology; and theater. Combined or interdepartmental major study programs are offered in Asian studies, astronomy-geology, biology-geology, chemistry-geology, economics-mathematics, environmental studies (emphasis in biology, chemistry, economics, geology, physics, politics, or sociology), geology-physics, mathematics-physics, and physics-astronomy. Minors are available in each of the departmental programs as well as Chinese, Japanese, Latin American and Caribbean literature, Latin American Studies, and world literature. Students with special interests may develop combined or interdepartmental major programs, subject to faculty approval. Whitman offers cooperative programs in engineering with Caltech, Columbia, Duke, the University of Washington, and Washington University in St. Louis; in environmental management or forestry with Duke; and oceanography with the University of Washington.

Academic Programs

Whitman's goal is to provide an atmosphere in which students can learn how to learn. At the heart of Whitman's academic curriculum is the general studies program. Through this program, students develop skills in intellectual reasoning, critical analysis of major works, effective writing, solid understanding of humanity's cultural and historic roots, valid bases for judgment of values, and confident abilities to ask tough questions. The general studies program consists of a first-year Encounters course and certain distribution requirements. Encounters is a two-semester course examining contact between peoples and cultures and the formation and transformation of dominant and competing worldviews. To satisfy distribution requirements, students complete at least 6 semester credits in fine arts, humanities, science, and social sciences; take 2 courses dealing with alternative voices; and take at least 1 course in quantitative analysis. Every candidate for graduation must complete at least 124 credits in appropriate course work with acceptable grades and a senior assessment. Whitman helps fund student research and internships, and approximately 200 students present professional-level research at the Annual Whitman Undergraduate Conference. Scores of 4 and 5 on the College Board's Advanced Placement tests are accepted for credit (the economics, English, and history departments accept only a score of 5). Whitman observes a two-semester calendar with a weeklong break for Thanksgiving, a month off over the winter holiday, and two weeks for spring break.

Off-Campus Programs

Whitman has strong study-abroad and domestic off-campus study programs. Each year, nearly 40 percent of the junior class studies off campus. There are 88 different programs available, spanning six of the seven continents (excluding Antarctica). In addition to academic course work, many students pursue internships and research opportunities. The College is formally affiliated with the Institute for the International Education of Students, with programs in Australia, Austria, China, England, France, Germany, and Italy. The school for field studies has opportunities in Australia, the Caribbean, Costa Rica, Kenya, and Mexico. Students may study at the Universities of East Anglia and York in England; St. Andrews University in Scotland; Doshisha University in Kyoto, Japan; and the University of Otago in Dunedin, New Zealand, and at programs in Argentina, Botswana, China, Costa Rica, Egypt, Greece, India, Ireland, Italy, Japan, Mexico, Spain, Sri Lanka, and Taiwan. Each year, 4 Whitman graduates are selected to teach English to university students in Kunming or Xi'an in the People's Republic of China. The College offers urban-semester programs in Philadelphia and Washington, D.C. Students may participate in one of more than 300 science research internships available through the College. Semester in the West, a signature program, is a semester-long, interdisciplinary traveling field-study program that investigates a myriad of issues throughout the intermountain West.

Academic Facilities

To enhance Whitman's learning environment, students have access to exceptional facilities and cultural resources. Penrose Memorial Library, open 24/7, houses more than 350,000 volumes and 2,000 subscriptions. In addition, the ORBIS Cascade Alliance provides access to approximately 3.5 million volumes that can be delivered to Whitman in less than 72 hours. Reid Campus Center, a 51,000-square-foot campus building, features a ballroom, cyberlounge, coffeehouse performance space, and flexible dining and meeting facilities. Olin Hall of Humanities features an audiovisual center, a foreign-language learning lab, and the Donald Sheehan Art Gallery. A newer addition to Olin houses the computing equipment and is the center for the campus-wide fiber-optic network. Maxey Hall, expanded in 2011, houses the social sciences, includes a natural history and anthropology museum, a 350-seat auditorium, and animal demonstration labs. The Hall of Science houses a sophisticated physics lecture/demonstration hall and laboratory, expanded chemistry work stations, the Clise Planetarium, and support facilities for electron microscopes. It also contains laboratories for botany, ecology, vertebrate biology, physiology and developmental biology, and biochemistry and genetics; preparation and display cases for the herbarium and the preserved animal collections; a seismograph; and well-equipped student research laboratories. Some of the newest features include organic chemistry and geology labs, computer stations, and new greenhouse spaces. The 105,000-square-foot Hall of Science has more student-faculty research labs, and enhanced classroom space. Off campus, Whitman operates an observatory and the Johnston Wilderness Center—a 27-acre mountain property serving as an environmental studies field station. The Hall of Music houses an acoustically perfect performance hall and twenty-seven practice rooms that are open 24 hours a day. After a comprehensive renovation in 2011, Harper Joy Theater consists of two main stages, black box theaters, and new classrooms. Cordiner Hall is a 1,500-seat auditorium featuring a 3,000-pipe Holtkamp organ. The Fouts Center for the Arts, a 38,000-square-foot visual arts facility, opened in fall 2008.

Costs

Tuition for 2014–15 was $44,440. Room and board cost was $11,228. The estimated cost of books, supplies, and incidentals was $1,400. The associated student body fee was $360.

Financial Aid

Financial aid usually combines scholarships, student employment opportunities, and low-interest loans. In 2014–15, Whitman provided more than $23 million in scholarships. Forty-four percent of Whitman students qualified for need-based aid. Roughly 50 percent of the students are employed on campus. Whitman also has an extensive merit scholarship program that rewards students who have demonstrated excellence in academics. These scholarships range from $5,000 to $14,000 and are renewable for four years. Scholarships are also available for students with exceptional talent in art, music, debate, theater, and leadership. To apply for financial aid, students must submit the Free Application for Federal Student Aid (FAFSA) and the CSS PROFILE. Early decision candidates should apply for financial aid by January 1; regular decision and transfer candidates must apply by February 1.

Faculty

Whitman College's faculty is comprised of individuals selected, retained, and promoted for demonstrated effectiveness as teachers as well as for leadership within their chosen fields. Ninety-one percent of faculty members hold a doctoral degree or terminal degree in their field, and all serve as academic advisers. The student-faculty ratio is 8.6:1. Recognized nationally for faculty accessibility, Whitman offers personal attention outside the classroom, setting it apart from peer institutions. Students collaborate with professors on research projects, compete with them on athletic fields, serve with them on College committees, and dine in their homes. In the past five years, Whitman faculty members have distinguished themselves by receiving awards, honors, and fellowships from the National Institute of Mental Health, National Endowment for the Humanities, Battelle Research Institute, Washington State Arts Commission, Burlington Northern Foundation, Department of Health and Human Services, and Department of Energy.

Student Government

The College encourages students to participate and take leadership roles in self-governing campus organizations. The largest of these is the Associated Students of Whitman College (ASWC), in which every student is a member. ASWC acts through an elected student congress and executive council and is responsible for the *Whitman Pioneer* (a weekly student newspaper), choral contest, Renaissance Faire, campus radio station KWCW (90.5 FM), and a multitude of all-campus concerts, speakers, films, and social events.

Admission Requirements

Whitman is a highly selective college that seeks academic excellence and diversity within its student body. Competition for admission is keen; in a typical year, approximately 60 percent of entering first-year students rank in the top 10 percent of their high school class and about 90 percent are in the top quarter. The Admission Committee looks for evidence of intellectual achievement, motivation, creativity, responsibility, and maturity. The median SAT scores for the class of 2018 were: 660 critical reading, 670 math, and 660 writing. The median ACT score was 31. The minimum TOEFL scores for international students are 85 on the Internet-based test and 560 on the paper test. The following pattern of high school subjects is highly recommended: 4 years of English, mathematics, science, and history or social sciences; at least 2 years of a foreign language; and 1 year of an art elective. Students who have decided early in their senior year that Whitman is their first-choice school are encouraged to apply for admission through early decision.

Application and Information

The application deadlines and notification dates for admission to Whitman are: early decision candidates apply by November 15 or January 1 and receive notification of admission by December 20 or February 1; regular decision applicants for the fall semester apply by January 15, and letters are postmarked by April 1; transfer students apply by March 1 and receive notification by April 20; and spring-semester candidates (if space is available) apply by November 15 and receive notification by December 15. First-year candidates are required to submit the following credentials: the Common Application, including the School Report Form; secondary school transcript; one teacher recommendation; and an application fee of $50. Application fees are waived for regular decision applications received before December 1. Whitman also requires test scores (SAT or ACT) and a personal supplement (a selection of writing prompts).

For more information, students should contact:

Office of Admission
Whitman College
345 Boyer Avenue
Walla Walla, Washington 99362-2046
Phone: 509-527-5176
877-462-9448 (toll-free)
Fax: 509-527-4967
E-mail: admission@whitman.edu
Website: http://www.whitman.edu

Students pursue their passions at Whitman, where they're provided with state-of-the-art facilities and discover their home away from home with a supportive community of inspiring teachers and peers.

WILKES UNIVERSITY

WILKES-BARRE, PENNSYLVANIA

WILKES UNIVERSITY

The University

Wilkes University offers the opportunities of a large university and the personal attention of a small institution. Its unique program mix and variety of extracurricular activities let students build their educational experience to suit their goals and interests.

Students may notice something unexpected: professors genuinely interested in their thoughts and aspirations. All Wilkes students have opportunities to gain real-world experience, whether starting a business, conducting research, or using high-tech instruments that even graduate students at other institutions rarely touch.

Located at the foothills of the Pocono Mountains, along the shore of the Susquehanna River and within walking distance of downtown Wilkes-Barre, Pennsylvania, Wilkes University is a private, comprehensive institution with about 2,200 undergraduate students.

The University includes the College of Arts, Humanities, and Social Sciences; the College of Science and Engineering; the Nesbitt School of Pharmacy; the School of Nursing; the Sidhu School of Business and Leadership; the School of Education; and University College (for undecided students). Wilkes offers bachelor's and master's degrees in the humanities, social and natural sciences, engineering, business administration, nursing, and education as well as the Master of Fine Arts, Doctor of Pharmacy, Doctor of Education, and Doctor of Nursing Practice degrees.

The Wilkes campus features a parklike quadrangle surrounded by modern classroom buildings and historic nineteenth-century mansions that have been restored as student residences and academic buildings. Facilities include the new Cohen Science Center, a sports and conference center, and a newly renovated home for the business school.

Programs provide students with a liberal arts foundation that cultivates independent thinking and prepares them for professional life or for graduate or professional school. Academic advising integrated with career planning is stressed, and hands-on experiences are provided in laboratory, internship, and cooperative education settings. Free tutorial services are available to all students.

The University is accredited by the Middle States Association of Colleges and Schools and has specialized accreditation in the sciences, engineering, nursing, education, and business. Ninety-seven percent of students are employed or attending graduate/professional school within one year of receiving their degrees.

First-year students enrolling prior to May 1 are guaranteed housing, and all students may have cars on campus. Campus housing is available for all four years. Residence halls include modern, multifloor buildings and historic mansions.

Student activities complement academic life. Intercollegiate athletics encompass 20 Division III sports, including swimming and lacrosse. Nearly 70 clubs and organizations recognize student achievement and provide opportunities for leadership development, professional growth, and community service. The award-winning e-mentor program links current students with incoming freshmen to ease the transition to college life.

Location

Wilkes-Barre is a medium-sized city of about 43,000. Nearby recreational facilities include PNC Field, home of a Triple A baseball team; the Mohegan Sun Arena, home to a professional hockey team; Pocono Mountain ski resorts; golf courses; state parks; tennis courts; and harness racing.

The University is located in the historic district, which features a performing arts center, the Wilkes University/King's College Barnes and Noble bookstore, a fourteen-screen movie complex, a nightclub, and numerous shops and restaurants. Other offerings include art galleries, ethnic and community festivals, and libraries and museums. The city is approximately 2 hours from New York City and Philadelphia.

Wilkes-Barre lies near the intersection of Interstates 80, 81, and 476 and within 6 hours of Washington, D.C. and Boston. The Wilkes-Barre/Scranton International Airport is about 20 minutes from campus.

Majors and Degrees

Wilkes University offers Bachelor of Arts, Bachelor of Business Administration, and Bachelor of Science degrees. Majors offered are: accounting; applied and engineering sciences; biochemistry; biology; chemistry; communication studies; computer information systems; computer science; criminology; earth and environmental sciences; electrical engineering; education (elementary and early childhood, middle-level, secondary minor with a subject-area major, and special education certification); engineering management; English (new concentration in digital humanities); entrepreneurship; environmental engineering; finance; history; integrative media; international studies; management; marketing; mathematics; mechanical engineering; medical laboratory sciences; musical theatre; nursing; philosophy; physics; political science; psychology; public administration; sociology; Spanish; sports and event management; and theatre arts. Wilkes also offers a guaranteed-seat pharmacy program.

Premedical and prelaw preparation programs are strong. Other preprofessional programs include dentistry, occupational therapy, optometry, physical therapy, physician assistant, podiatry, and veterinary science. A full-time health sciences coordinator advises students who wish to continue study in a professional health-care field. The University offers affiliated programs in medicine with the Philadelphia College of Osteopathic Medicine and The Commonwealth Medical College; in optometry with the Pennsylvania College of Optometry and the State University of New York (SUNY) College of Optometry; in podiatry with Temple University School of Podiatric Medicine; in occupational therapy with Temple University; in physical therapy with Drexel University, Temple University, and Widener University; in medical technology/medical laboratory sciences with Robert Packer Hospital; and in psychology with Widener University.

Academic Programs

Through a rigorous curriculum that emphasizes hands-on experience and training, Wilkes helps prepare students in all majors to adapt to a technologically and socially evolving world. To graduate, students must complete a core curriculum from 120 to 136 credits, depending on their major. Graduates demonstrate mastery of the fundamental intellectual skills and essential concepts and techniques of their field.

The University operates on a dual-semester calendar, with optional summer sessions and a January intersession. Advanced Placement test credits, College Level Examination Program (CLEP) credits, and International Baccalaureate (I.B.) credits are accepted.

Off-Campus Programs

A cooperative education (internship) program is available to all students, with credit applicable in most majors. Many government offices and private businesses in northeastern Pennsylvania, as well as in New York City, Philadelphia, Harrisburg, and Washington, D.C., employ Wilkes students. The study-abroad adviser works with interested students, placing them in the situation best suited to their academic pursuits. Students have recently attended programs in Costa Rica, England, Malaysia, Spain, Tanzania, Turkey, and Uganda.

Academic Facilities

The 72,500-square-foot Cohen Science Center opened in fall 2013, as did the University's new clinical nursing simulation center. The Eugene S. Farley Library has more than 200,000 volumes of books and bound journals, 430 journal and newspaper subscriptions, and 10,000 full-text online journals. Students also have access to 68 desktop computers and 14 wireless laptops that can be used anywhere within the library's wireless environment. Complete laboratory facilities are available for biology, chemistry, earth and environmental sciences, engineering, nursing, pharmacy, and psychology. Student-produced programming is broadcast from WCLH-FM and a television studio. The Dorothy Dickson Darte Center for the Performing Arts contains a 500-seat main theater and a 45-seat black box theater for presentation of plays, concerts, ballet, and other performances and lectures. Breiseth Hall accommodates computer facilities, psychology research laboratories, an integrative media lab, and modern classrooms with the latest audiovisual equipment.

Costs

For the 2014–15 academic year, tuition and fees were $31,262 per year, and room and board were $12,695. Books cost approximately $900 per year.

Financial Aid

Financial aid is available to those students who demonstrate quality academic ability and/or financial need, as verified by the Free Application for Federal Student Aid (FAFSA). Merit-based and need-based aid is available from Wilkes University for qualified students. Scholarships ranging from $8,000 to $15,000 per year are available to students solely on the basis of academic ability. Approximately 90 percent of the student body receive some type of financial assistance, including scholarships, grants, loans, and work-study awards.

Faculty

Wilkes University has a nationally recruited full-time faculty of 166 members, approximately 90 percent of whom have earned Ph.D.'s or terminal degrees in their chosen field. Faculty evaluation criteria emphasize teaching excellence and effective advising, while recognizing continued scholarly activities. The student-faculty ratio is 14:1.

Student Government

An active student government provides a structure for student participation in University governance and student discipline. The Inter-Residence Hall Council and Commuter Council coordinate extracurricular activities for on-campus and commuter students.

Admission Requirements

SAT or ACT scores are required. In cases where a student has taken the examination more than once, scores from the highest testing in each category are used. Freshman applicants should either have completed or be in the process of completing a college-preparatory course of study, including 3 to 4 years of mathematics, social studies, science, and English. Additional courses should be elected in academic subjects according to individual interests. Acceptable electives include foreign language and computing, among others. Students who have not followed this pattern may still qualify for admission if there is other strong evidence of preparation for college work. Letters of recommendation are not required but may be submitted. Students intending to pursue a major in pharmacy should have completed algebra I and II, geometry, and trigonometry prior to enrollment. Students intending to major in nursing should have completed courses in biology and chemistry. An audition is required for all prospective musical theatre and theatre arts students. Transfer students must submit a transcript from every college previously attended. Students individually receive academic advisement at the time of registration and throughout their enrollment.

Wilkes University is an Equal Opportunity/Affirmative Action institution. No applicant shall be denied admission to the University because of race, color, gender, religion, national or ethnic origin, sexual orientation, or handicap.

Application and Information

Applications for admission should be completed early in the senior year of secondary school. Applications are reviewed after all of the student's credentials have been received. Review begins on September 15, and notification of the University's decision reaches the student two to four weeks after the application file is complete. Priority deadline for all applications is March 1; applications for the Guaranteed Seat Pharmacy Program must be received by February 1. Other health science programs may have additional deadlines.

Prospective students should contact the Admissions Office for more information.

Admissions Office
Wilkes University
84 West South Street
Wilkes-Barre, Pennsylvania 18766
Phone: 570-408-4400
800-945-5378 Ext. 4400 (toll-free)
Website: http://www.wilkes.edu

The Sidhu School of Business and Leadership's home includes a financial trading room, complete with stock ticker.

WILLIAM PEACE UNIVERSITY

RALEIGH, NORTH CAROLINA

★ To read more about this school, visit http://petersons.to/williampeaceuniversity

The University

William Peace University (WPU), located in downtown Raleigh, North Carolina, is regarded as one of the best private academic institutions in the southeast. The University is ranked number one in the nation for student internships (according to a 2013 study by *U.S. News & World Report*), and is ranked in the top 10 percent nationally for student engagement (according to the 2013 National Survey for Student Engagement).

The school's mission is to prepare its students for careers in the organizations of tomorrow, emphasizing a skill-based curriculum rooted in the liberal arts. Because of that mission, the University consistently boasts a high job/graduate school placement rate. In fact, 97 percent of William Peace University's 2013 graduates found jobs or were enrolled in graduate school within a year of graduation (according to 2014 University data). The school believes in quality over quantity, employing industry professionals and professors and placing them in small classes (student to faculty ratio of 15:1) in order to provide students with hands-on experience.

The institution has been ranked among the nation's best in value-added gains in three of the four categories from the Collegiate Learning Assessment. This national assessment measures the improvement in critical thinking and analytical writing test scores of individual students between their freshman and senior years to determine how much they have learned while enrolled.

In addition, WPU offers countless clubs, activities, and intramural sports, along with 100 percent financial aid for its students. The school was founded in 1857 and named in honor of founding benefactor William Peace, an elder of the First Presbyterian Church of Raleigh.

Location

William Peace University offers the comfort of a small school with the backdrop of a big city. Surrounded by beautiful oak trees and a large front lawn, the historic campus has carved out its own niche in downtown Raleigh, the capital of North Carolina. The University is just a short distance from the state capitol, museums, music halls, restaurants, theaters, and nightlife—all accessible by foot and the R-Line, a free bus service that circulates throughout the capital city.

Raleigh is consistently regarded as one of the nation's best places to live because of its economic, cultural and professional opportunities. In addition to being ranked number one on *Businessweek*'s list of America's 50 Best Cities in 2011, Raleigh is also ranked one of the five Hottest Job Markets for Young Adults, a Top 10 Technology Town, a Top 10 City for Singles, and a Top 10 Best City to Live.

Majors and Degrees

William Peace University offers dozens of majors and concentrations, including biology, business administration, communication, criminal justice, education, English, environmental studies, global studies, liberal studies, political science, pre-law, pre-med, psychology, simulation and game design, sport management, theatre, and writing.

A Bachelor of Fine Arts degree in musical theatre is also offered.

A new core curriculum focuses on ethical decision making and emphasizes basic knowledge needed beyond graduation. In addition, there are mandatory courses in personal financial management, media literacy, and four years of writing courses within the English department. Students are also required to take a series of three classes focusing on career and professional development.

William Peace University also offers evening, online, and/or Saturday classes through its School of Professional Studies. Students can earn a Bachelor of Arts degree in education, liberal studies, or psychology or a Bachelor of Science degree in business administration, all without spending virtually any time on campus. Courses are taught by experienced faculty members in seven-week accelerated formats and include many opportunities for individualized academic advising. Classes are geared toward the unique needs of nontraditional students and working professionals.

Academic Programs

An academic internship related to the student's major is required in order to combine educational theory with job experience. Students are required to complete internships within their field of study during their junior or senior years (100 percent of graduating students have had an internship). Internships are offered in conjunction with classes that include biweekly meetings with the faculty. Recent student internship sites include Duke University Medical Center, Mothers Against Drunk Driving, the governor's office, and the North Carolina General Assembly. On average, more than 60 percent of WPU graduates report that their internship experience resulted in a job offer.

Eligible WPU students have the opportunity to join several national honor societies such as Omicron Delta Kappa, Sigma Tau Delta, Alpha Chi, Psi Chi, and TriBeta.

Students can also join the University's honors program that includes academic challenges, enriching experiences outside of the classroom, and opportunities to work on undergraduate research. The program allows academically talented and motivated students to study, conduct research, and exchange ideas in a challenging and supportive academic environment. It brings outstanding students and dynamic faculty together in courses that arouse curiosity and promote intellectual discovery and development. Program members can choose from a variety of courses that fulfill liberal education requirements, such as psychology, biology, cultural and physical anthropology, literature, and public speaking.

Students also have lifetime access to the Career Services Office, which provides career counseling, listings of internship options, workshops, mock interviews, and a resource library.

International study programs are offered in several parts of the world, including Costa Rica, Italy, Mexico, Qatar, and Spain. Other opportunities are available annually in a variety of other locations for short-term work or internships, or for a semester abroad.

Academic Facilities

William Peace University is a wireless campus. Students have access to courses and library facilities and online databases of other Raleigh colleges and universities through the Cooperating Raleigh Colleges (CRC) consortium.

Computer laboratories, the library, and the student publications area are equipped with state-of-the-art computer hardware and software. There are specialized computer laboratories in the biology, business, media, physics, simulation and game design, theatre, and visual communication departments. Student laboratories in the chemistry, general biology, and molecular and cellular biology departments are also available.

A recital hall, the Leggett Theatre and a studio are available for students in the fine arts department.

Costs

Tuition and fees at William Peace University for the 2014–15 academic year were as follows: tuition, $24,450; room, $6,400; board, $3,050; and an annual student activity fee of $200. Costs are the same for both in-state and out-of-state students.

Financial Aid

William Peace University strongly believes that everyone should have access to a college education; therefore, the University is committed to making it as affordable as possible. At a time where colleges across the country have raised prices, WPU has actually lowered its costs.

Every accepted student is automatically considered for merit- and need-based aid (with a submitted FAFSA), and 100 percent of students receive financial aid. Academic awards are available for the performing arts, community service, leadership, extracurricular activities, and more.

Through a combination of financial aid packaging, pursuit of scholarship and grant opportunities, and on-campus work-study groups, WPU works to make its educational program available to all qualified students, regardless of financial need. Information about payment options and the necessary forms are available online. Prospective students may call 919-508-2214 or e-mail finaid@peace.edu for more information on how to pay for college.

Faculty

William Peace University maintains a student-faculty ratio of 15:1. The average class size is 17 students (according to 2014 University data).

Student Organizations and Activities

William Peace University offers more than 30 student clubs and organizations, including publications, performance groups and academic honor societies. Some of them include: Anthropology Club, cheer/drill collaboration, Campus Activities Board (CAB), Commuter Student Association, Helping Hands, intramural sports, MOSAIC (multicultural association), *Peace Times* (student newspaper), Student Government Association (SGA), Student Recreation Association, Society for Human Resource Management, Spectrum (LGBTQ), Student Athlete Advisory Committee, and William Peace University Singers.

Admission Requirements

William Peace University seeks to enroll individuals who will benefit from the academic programs and who will contribute to university life—a community upheld by the honor system, which requires students to maintain academic and personal integrity. The University encourages individuals with varied talents and interests representative of all social, economic, ethnic, and racial backgrounds to apply. Admission decisions are made on a rolling basis. The University does not discriminate in its recruitment and admission of students, regardless of gender, race, creed, color, religion, age, national and ethnic origin, sexual orientation, disability, or veteran status.

Admission requirements/procedures for students are defined by five categories: traditional first-year student (high school senior or graduate), high school student applying as a junior for early entrance, transfer student, international student, or former student (readmission).

Applications are reviewed individually and decisions are based on the following credentials: GPA in academic courses, SAT (verbal and math only) or ACT scores, course selection, rank in class, and an interview with an admissions representative, if requested. Further consideration will be given to an applicant's personal qualifications, co-curricular activities, community involvement, and overall potential for success. Consideration of a students' acceptance will also be granted upon the discretion of the Vice President for Enrollment and Marketing.

Application and Information

Admissions decisions are made on a rolling basis. The Admissions Committee begins reviewing applications in July for the following fall. Applications received after April 1 for the fall semester and after November 1 for the spring semester are reviewed on a space-available basis.

The University requires each first-year applicant to submit an application, a nonrefundable $35 fee, SAT or ACT scores (senior-year scores are preferred), and an official transcript of all courses taken in high school. Transfer applicants must also submit official transcripts from all colleges and/or universities attended.

Inquiry cards and application forms may be completed online at www.peace.edu. Application forms and additional information may be obtained by contacting:

Office of Admissions
William Peace University
15 East Peace Street
Raleigh, North Carolina 27604
Phone: 919-508-2214
Fax: 919-508-2306
Website: http://www.peace.edu

William Peace University takes a different approach to higher education, going beyond lecture-based instruction and involving students more directly in their learning. William Peace students don't graduate college looking for any job; they graduate ready to enter the fields they went to college for in the first place.

WORCESTER POLYTECHNIC INSTITUTE

WORCESTER, MASSACHUSETTS

★ To read more about this school, visit http://petersons.to/wpi

WPI

COLLEGE CLOSE-UPS

The University

Following its founding motto of "Theory and practice," Worcester Polytechnic Institute (WPI) offers a unique project-based curriculum that prepares students to take on the world's great challenges. Students not only take rigorous classes, but also complete distinctive hands-on projects that address real issues in communities across the globe. In addition, small classes, one-on-one interaction with professors, and a spirit of innovation and teamwork encourage students to think creatively, collaborate across disciplines, and put their ideas into practice.

While many students attend WPI for its top-notch engineering and science programs, about 20 percent of students enter undeclared, and it is not uncommon for students to change their major at least once. WPI provides a comprehensive academic advising program and a wide array of academic support services, including a first-year Insight Program and a robust career services center that was recently ranked seventeenth in the nation by the Princeton Review.

WPI has been widely recognized for its distinct academic programs and the success of its graduates. It is consistently ranked among the top national universities by *U.S. News & World Report* and the Princeton Review. According to the National Association of Colleges and Employers, the starting salaries of WPI graduates are 27 percent higher than those of many other college graduates; Payscale.com ranked WPI as having the fifth-highest average starting salaries among national research universities. WPI was also ranked eighteenth in the nation for return on investment by Payscale.com and was recently ranked twenty-ninth on the Princeton Review's 2015 list of "Top 50 Colleges that Pay You Back."

Top-tier employers seek out WPI graduates for their real-world experience and ability to work collaboratively. More than 90 percent of students are in full-time jobs or attending graduate school within several months of graduation. Students are recruited by leading organizations such as Pfizer, General Electric, Fidelity Investments, and IBM. Each year, WPI graduates are accepted at many prestigious graduate schools, including MIT, Yale, Princeton, Johns Hopkins, and Tufts University Medical School.

Location

With its beautiful architecture, grassy quad, and ivy-covered walls, WPI provides a traditional New England campus situated on 95 acres in a hilltop residential neighborhood. Students stop and chat with faculty members on tree-lined paths, study by the fountain in Reunion Plaza, grab a coffee at the Rubin Campus Center, and watch live entertainment at the Goat's Head restaurant.

Home to nine other colleges and universities and more than 35,000 college students, Worcester is a true college town. It is ranked ninth on *Forbes*' list of "America's Most Livable Cities" and ninth on *Businessweek*'s list of "Best Cities for Gen Ys." Late-night diners, clubs, museums, concert venues, and theaters are just minutes from WPI, while Boston is less than an hour away by commuter rail. There is also skiing and snowboarding at nearby Wachusett Mountain and easy access to New York City, the Berkshires, Providence, and Cape Cod.

Majors and Degrees

WPI offers Bachelor of Science (B.S.) and Bachelor of Art (B.A.) degrees, as well as a combined B.S./M.S. program that enables students to begin studying toward a master's degree in their senior year. Students can major in a wide variety of engineering and science disciplines, as well as subject areas in the humanities and arts, social sciences, and business. They can also design their own majors or choose from interdisciplinary programs such as interactive media and game development, bioinformatics and computational biology, and robotics engineering (WPI's was the first undergraduate program in robotics in the nation). Additional information is available online at admissions.wpi.edu/+academics.

WPI also offers preprofessional programs in dentistry, law, medicine, veterinary medicine, and teacher licensure. More details on these programs can be found at wpi.edu/+prehealth.

Academic Programs

At WPI most students take three courses during each of the four 7-week terms (two in the fall and two in the spring). In keeping with WPI's motto of theory and practice, classes aim to provide a balance between academic content and hands-on projects and group work. WPI's academic program also encourages collaboration, not competition—students can get grades of A, B, C, or no credit, but do not receive failing grades.

Regardless of their majors, all students must meet a humanities and arts requirement that encourages them to broaden their thinking and explore new areas of performance, creativity, and culture by taking courses in disciplines such as music, art, theatre, foreign language, history, and literature.

WPI Projects Program

Projects are at the heart of the WPI curriculum. First-year students gain an introduction to project work through Great Problems Seminars, which focuses on themes of current global importance. All students complete a junior-year project in which they work with a team to address a problem at the intersection of science, technology, and society—from designing bicycle paths in WPI's hometown of Worcester to creating a mentoring program for children in Morocco. As seniors, students undertake an intensive capstone project related to their major field of study.

Through WPI's Global Perspective Program, over 60 percent of undergraduates complete at least one project off campus and overseas at more than 40 project centers around the world, including centers in Thailand, Australia, South Africa, Nova Scotia, Switzerland, and Costa Rica. Students immerse themselves in other cultures while working to solve real-world problems in partnership with government, corporate, and nonprofit sponsors.

Students, alumni, and employers praise WPI's project model for helping students develop professional and personal skills including problem solving, teamwork, communication, and leadership abilities, as well as increased global awareness and enriched personal lives. WPI's off-campus programs were recently recognized by the Princeton Review, which ranked WPI second for most popular study abroad program in the 2015 edition of *The Best 379 Colleges*. Additional information is available at admissions.wpi.edu/+global.

Academic Facilities

There are many teaching, research, and project facilities available to undergraduates at WPI. The Life Sciences and Bioengineering Center at Gateway Park is a state-of-the-art 130,000-square-foot facility for research and teaching in biology and biotechnology, biomedical engineering, chemistry and biochemistry, and chemical engineering.

In addition, undergraduates have access to over 40 state-of-the-art research centers and laboratories, including two atomic-force microscopes, medical imaging laboratories, a fire science laboratory, a laser holography lab, a computer music lab, a satellite navigation lab, and a research library with over half a million print and digital resources.

WPI also has an exceptional computer and networking infrastructure, including hundreds of computers in open-access 24/7 labs, powerful UNIX workstations, access to specialized scientific and engineering software, and a campuswide high-speed data network.

Costs

For 2015–16, full-time tuition is $44,970. Room and board charges are $13,410.

Financial Aid

Over 90 percent of students at WPI receive financial assistance in the form of need- and merit-based aid. Need-based aid includes financial aid packages, on-campus jobs, and loan programs. More information is available from WPI's Office of Financial Aid at wpi.edu/+finaid.

All admitted applicants to WPI are also considered for academic scholarships based upon academic performance, standardized test scores, leadership, extracurricular involvement, and community service. More information is available at wpi.edu/+scholarships.

Faculty

WPI's 478 full- and part-time faculty members are passionate teachers as well as committed researchers and scholars with world-class credentials. They are leading contributors to the fields of bioengineering, cybersecurity, robotics, energy and sustainability, materials science, and more. Fourteen members of the current faculty are Fulbright Scholars and 23 have won the CAREER Award, the National Science Foundation's most prestigious honor for young faculty members.

With a 14:1 student-faculty ratio, WPI prides itself on offering small classes where students have ample opportunity to join discussions, work in teams, and interact with professors. The National Survey of Student Engagement ranks WPI number one for student-faculty interaction, and *U.S. News & World Report* ranks WPI forty-second among national universities for faculty resources, including salary, class size, and student-faculty ratio.

Student Activities

At WPI, students work hard but play hard too—undergraduates at all levels take part in more than 200 clubs and organizations, ranging from music and theater ensembles to cultural and religious organizations, community service clubs, and professional groups. More than 85 percent of students are involved in sports programs, including twenty varsity (NCAA Division III) athletics teams and nearly forty club and intramural sports. Students also work out at the university's state-of-the art sports and recreation center, which was built in 2012 and contains a four-court gymnasium, indoor jogging track, racquetball and squash courts, and competition pool.

WPI "gets Greek life right," according to BestCollegesOnline.com—which may account for the fact that more than 30 percent of students participate in one of the 19 fraternities and sororities on campus. The Student Government Association also gives a voice to undergraduates within WPI's close-knit community.

Admission Requirements

WPI has high standards for applicants but also looks for more than just outstanding academic performance. They take care to admit students who will likely thrive at the university. These students tend to be creative and curious; like to work in teams; are comfortable making their own decisions; love math and science but feel just as passionate about literature, music, movies, and the arts; and are ready to make a positive impact on the world around them.

Applicants to WPI can choose to either submit SAT or ACT scores, or submit representative academic work or extracurricular projects through WPI's Flex Path (wpi.edu/+flexpath). Full admissions requirements can be found at admissions.wpi.edu.

Application and Information

The Common Application is the only way to apply to WPI. The deadline for early action round 1 is November 1, with notification by December 20. The deadline for early action round 2 is January 1, with notification by February 10. The regular decision deadline is February 1, with notification by April 1. More information is available at admissions.wpi.edu/apply.

Students are encouraged to visit the WPI campus to learn more about the university, see its facilities, and hear firsthand about the WPI experience. They can also view an interactive online tour at wpi.edu/+tour.

To schedule a visit or request more information, students should contact:

Bartlett Center
Worcester Polytechnic Institute
100 Institute Road
Worcester, Massachusetts 01609-2280
Phone: 508-831-5286
Fax: 508-831-5875
E-mail: admissions@wpi.edu
Website: http://admissions.wpi.edu
http://www.facebook.com/WPI
http://twitter.com/WPI

WPI is situated on an 80-acre campus, 40 miles west of Boston in a residential section of Worcester, Massachusetts, the second largest city in New England and home to ten colleges.

Indexes

Majors

ACCOUNTING

Abilene Christian U (TX)
Adams State U (CO)
Adelphi U (NY)
Alabama State U (AL)
Albany State U (GA)
Albertus Magnus Coll (CT)
Albion Coll (MI)
Albright Coll (PA)
Alcorn State U (MS)
Alma Coll (MI)
Alvernia U (PA)
American Intl Coll (MA)
American Public U System (WV)
American U (DC)
The American U in Cairo (Egypt)
The American U in Dubai (United Arab Emirates)
Anderson U (IN)
Andrews U (MI)
Angelo State U (TX)
Appalachian State U (NC)
Aquinas Coll (MI)
Arcadia U (PA)
Arizona State U at the Tempe campus (AZ)
Arizona State U at the West campus (AZ)
Arkansas State U (AR)
Arkansas Tech U (AR)
Asbury U (KY)
Ashland U (OH)
Assumption Coll (MA)
Athens State U (AL)
Auburn U (AL)
Auburn U at Montgomery (AL)
Augsburg Coll (MN)
Augustana Coll (IL)
Augustana Coll (SD)
Ave Maria U (FL)
Averett U (VA)
Avila U (MO)
Azusa Pacific U (CA)
Babson Coll (MA)
Baker Coll (MI)
Baker U (KS)
Baldwin Wallace U (OH)
Ball State U (IN)
Barry U (FL)
Baruch Coll of the City U of New York (NY)
Baylor U (TX)
Bay Path U (MA)
Belhaven U (MS)
Belmont Abbey Coll (NC)
Belmont U (TN)
Bemidji State U (MN)
Benedictine Coll (KS)
Benedictine U (IL)
Bentley U (MA)
Berkeley Coll, Woodland Park (NJ)
Berkeley Coll–New York City Campus (NY)
Berry Coll (GA)
Bethany Coll (WV)
Bethel Coll (IN)
Bethune-Cookman U (FL)
Binghamton U, State U of New York (NY)
Biola U (CA)
Blackburn Coll (IL)
Black Hills State U (SD)
Bloomfield Coll (NJ)
Bloomsburg U of Pennsylvania (PA)
Bluefield Coll (VA)
Bluefield State Coll (WV)
Bluffton U (OH)
Bob Jones U (SC)
Boston Coll (MA)
Boston U (MA)
Bowie State U (MD)
Bowling Green State U (OH)
Bradley U (IL)
Brenau U (GA)
Bridgewater State U (MA)
Bryant U (RI)
Buena Vista U (IA)
Butler U (IN)
Cabrini Coll (PA)
Caldwell U (NJ)
California Baptist U (CA)
California Lutheran U (CA)
California State U, Dominguez Hills (CA)
California State U, Fresno (CA)
California State U, Fullerton (CA)
California State U, Long Beach (CA)
California State U, San Bernardino (CA)
California State U, San Marcos (CA)
California State U, Stanislaus (CA)
California U of Pennsylvania (PA)
Calumet Coll of Saint Joseph (IN)
Calvin Coll (MI)
Cameron U (OK)
Campbellsville U (KY)
Canisius Coll (NY)
Cape Breton U (NS, Canada)
Capital U (OH)
Cardinal Stritch U (WI)
Caribbean U (PR)
Carlow U (PA)
Carroll Coll (MT)
Carson-Newman U (TN)
Case Western Reserve U (OH)
Castleton State Coll (VT)
Catawba Coll (NC)
The Catholic U of America (DC)
Cazenovia Coll (NY)
Cedar Crest Coll (PA)
Cedarville U (OH)
Central Coll (IA)
Central Connecticut State U (CT)
Central Methodist U (MO)
Central Michigan U (MI)
Central Penn Coll (PA)
Central State U (OH)
Central Washington U (WA)
Champlain Coll (VT)
Chapman U (CA)
Charleston Southern U (SC)
Chatham U (PA)
Chestnut Hill Coll (PA)
Cheyney U of Pennsylvania (PA)
Chowan U (NC)
Christian Brothers U (TN)
Christopher Newport U (VA)
Claremont McKenna Coll (CA)
Clark Atlanta U (GA)
Clarke U (IA)
Clayton State U (GA)
Clearwater Christian Coll (FL)
Cleveland State U (OH)
Coastal Carolina U (SC)
Coe Coll (IA)
The Coll at Brockport, State U of New York (NY)
Coll of Charleston (SC)
The Coll of Idaho (ID)
The Coll of New Jersey (NJ)
Coll of Saint Benedict (MN)
The Coll of Saint Rose (NY)
The Coll of St. Scholastica (MN)
Coll of Staten Island of the City U of New York (NY)
Coll of the Holy Cross (MA)
Coll of the Ozarks (MO)
The Coll of Westchester (NY)
The Coll of William and Mary (VA)
Colorado Mesa U (CO)
Colorado State U (CO)
Colorado State U–Pueblo (CO)
Columbia Coll (MO)
Columbia Coll (SC)
Columbus State U (GA)
Concordia Coll (MN)
Concordia Coll–New York (NY)
Concordia U (QC, Canada)
Concordia U Chicago (IL)
Concordia U, Nebraska (NE)
Concordia U, St. Paul (MN)
Concordia U Wisconsin (WI)
Concord U (WV)
Corban U (OR)
Cornerstone U (MI)
Creighton U (NE)
Culver-Stockton Coll (MO)
Cumberland U (TN)
Daemen Coll (NY)
Dakota State U (SD)
Dalhousie U (NS, Canada)
Dallas Baptist U (TX)
Daniel Webster Coll (NH)
Davenport U, Grand Rapids (MI)
Defiance Coll (OH)
Delaware State U (DE)
Delta State U (MS)
DePaul U (IL)
DeSales U (PA)
DeVry U, Phoenix (AZ)
DeVry U, Pomona (CA)
DeVry U, Westminster (CO)
DeVry U, Miramar (FL)
DeVry U, Orlando (FL)
DeVry U, Decatur (GA)
DeVry U, Kansas City (MO)
DeVry U, Houston (TX)
DeVry U, Arlington (VA)
DeVry U, Federal Way (WA)
Dickinson State U (ND)
Dixie State U (UT)
Doane Coll (NE)
Dominican Coll (NY)
Dominican U (IL)
Dowling Coll (NY)
Drake U (IA)
Drexel U (PA)
Drury U (MO)
Duquesne U (PA)
East Central U (OK)
Eastern Connecticut State U (CT)
Eastern Illinois U (IL)
Eastern Kentucky U (KY)
Eastern Michigan U (MI)
Eastern New Mexico U (NM)
East Tennessee State U (TN)
Edgewood Coll (WI)
Elizabethtown Coll (PA)
Elizabethtown Coll School of Continuing and Professional Studies (PA)
Ellis U (IL)
Elmhurst Coll (IL)
Elmira Coll (NY)
Elms Coll (MA)
Elon U (NC)
Emmanuel Coll (MA)
Emory & Henry Coll (VA)
Emporia State U (KS)
Endicott Coll (MA)
Eureka Coll (IL)
Excelsior Coll (NY)
Fairfield U (CT)
Fairleigh Dickinson U, Coll at Florham (NJ)
Fairleigh Dickinson U, Metropolitan Campus (NJ)
Fairmont State U (WV)
Faulkner U (AL)
Fayetteville State U (NC)
Ferris State U (MI)
Ferrum Coll (VA)
Fisher Coll (MA)
Fitchburg State U (MA)
Flagler Coll (FL)
Florida Ag and Mech U (FL)
Florida Atlantic U (FL)
Florida Gulf Coast U (FL)
Florida Intl U (FL)
Florida National U (FL)
Florida Southern Coll (FL)
Florida State U (FL)
Fordham U (NY)
Fort Hays State U (KS)
Fort Lewis Coll (CO)
Framingham State U (MA)
Franciscan U of Steubenville (OH)
Francis Marion U (SC)
Franklin Coll (IN)
Franklin Pierce U (NH)
Franklin U (OH)
Friends U (KS)
Frostburg State U (MD)
Furman U (SC)
Gallaudet U (DC)
Gannon U (PA)
Geneva Coll (PA)
George Mason U (VA)
Georgetown Coll (KY)
Georgetown U (DC)
The George Washington U (DC)
Georgia Coll & State U (GA)
Georgian Court U (NJ)
Georgia Regents U (GA)
Georgia Southern U (GA)
Georgia Southwestern State U (GA)
Georgia State U (GA)
Gonzaga U (WA)
Gordon Coll (MA)
Goshen Coll (IN)
Governors State U (IL)
Grace Coll (IN)
Graceland U (IA)
Grambling State U (LA)
Grand Valley State U (MI)
Grand View U (IA)
Greensboro Coll (NC)
Greenville Coll (IL)
Grove City Coll (PA)
Guilford Coll (NC)
Gustavus Adolphus Coll (MN)
Gwynedd Mercy U (PA)
Hamline U (MN)
Hampton U (VA)
Hannibal-LaGrange U (MO)
Harding U (AR)
Hardin-Simmons U (TX)
Harris-Stowe State U (MO)
Hartwick Coll (NY)
Hastings Coll (NE)
Hawai`i Pacific U (HI)
HEC Montreal (QC, Canada)
Heidelberg U (OH)
Hendrix Coll (AR)
Heritage U (WA)
High Point U (NC)
Hilbert Coll (NY)
Hillsdale Coll (MI)
Hofstra U (NY)
Holy Family U (PA)
Hope Coll (MI)
Houghton Coll (NY)
Houston Baptist U (TX)
Howard Payne U (TX)
Howard U (DC)
Hult Intl Business School (United Kingdom)
Hunter Coll of the City U of New York (NY)
Huntingdon Coll (AL)
Husson U (ME)
Huston-Tillotson U (TX)
Illinois Coll (IL)
Illinois State U (IL)
Illinois Wesleyan U (IL)
Immaculata U (PA)
Indiana State U (IN)
Indiana U of Pennsylvania (PA)
Indiana U–Purdue U Fort Wayne (IN)
Inter American U of Puerto Rico, Aguadilla Campus (PR)
Inter American U of Puerto Rico, Bayamón Campus (PR)
Inter American U of Puerto Rico, Fajardo Campus (PR)
Inter American U of Puerto Rico, Guayama Campus (PR)
Inter American U of Puerto Rico, Ponce Campus (PR)
Inter American U of Puerto Rico, San Germán Campus (PR)
Iona Coll (NY)
Iowa State U of Science and Technology (IA)
Ithaca Coll (NY)
Jackson State U (MS)
Jacksonville State U (AL)
Jacksonville U (FL)
James Madison U (VA)
John Brown U (AR)
John Carroll U (OH)
Johnson & Wales U (RI)
Johnson & Wales U - Charlotte Campus (NC)
Johnson State Coll (VT)
Judson U (IL)
Juniata Coll (PA)
Kansas State U (KS)
Kansas Wesleyan U (KS)
Kean U (NJ)
Keiser U, Fort Lauderdale (FL)
Kennesaw State U (GA)
Kent State U (OH)
Kentucky Wesleyan Coll (KY)
Keuka Coll (NY)
Keystone Coll (PA)
King's Coll (PA)
King U (TN)
Kuyper Coll (MI)
LaGrange Coll (GA)
Lake Erie Coll (OH)
Lamar U (TX)
Langston U (OK)
La Roche Coll (PA)
La Salle U (PA)
Lasell Coll (MA)
La Sierra U (CA)
Lebanon Valley Coll (PA)
Lee U (TN)
Lehigh U (PA)
Lehman Coll of the City U of New York (NY)
Le Moyne Coll (NY)
Lenoir-Rhyne U (NC)
LeTourneau U (TX)
Lewis U (IL)
Liberty U (VA)
Limestone Coll (SC)
Lincoln Memorial U (TN)
Lincoln U (MO)
Lincoln U (PA)
Lindenwood U (MO)
Linfield Coll (OR)
Lipscomb U (TN)
Lock Haven U of Pennsylvania (PA)
Long Island U–LIU Brooklyn (NY)
Long Island U–LIU Post (NY)
Loras Coll (IA)
Louisiana Coll (LA)
Louisiana State U and A&M Coll (LA)
Louisiana State U in Shreveport (LA)
Lourdes U (OH)
Loyola Marymount U (CA)
Loyola U Chicago (IL)
Loyola U New Orleans (LA)
Lubbock Christian U (TX)
Luther Coll (IA)
Lycoming Coll (PA)
Lynchburg Coll (VA)
Madonna U (MI)
Malone U (OH)
Manchester U (IN)
Manhattan Coll (NY)
Manhattanville Coll (NY)
Mansfield U of Pennsylvania (PA)
Maranatha Baptist U (WI)
Marian U (IN)
Marian U (WI)
Marietta Coll (OH)
Marist Coll (NY)
Marquette U (WI)
Marshall U (WV)
Mars Hill U (NC)
Marymount Manhattan Coll (NY)
Maryville U of Saint Louis (MO)
Marywood U (PA)
Massachusetts Coll of Liberal Arts (MA)
The Master's Coll and Sem (CA)
McKendree U (IL)
McMurry U (TX)
McNeese State U (LA)
Medaille Coll (NY)
Medgar Evers Coll of the City U of New York (NY)
Menlo Coll (CA)
Mercer U, Macon (GA)
Meredith Coll (NC)
Merrimack Coll (MA)
Messiah Coll (PA)
Metropolitan State U (MN)
Miami U (OH)
Michigan State U (MI)
Michigan Technological U (MI)

MidAmerica Nazarene U (KS)
Middle Tennessee State U (TN)
Midwestern State U (TX)
Milligan Coll (TN)
Millikin U (IL)
Millsaps Coll (MS)
Minnesota State U Mankato (MN)
Minnesota State U Moorhead (MN)
Minot State U (ND)
Misericordia U (PA)
Mississippi State U (MS)
Mississippi U for Women (MS)
Mississippi Valley State U (MS)
Missouri Baptist U (MO)
Missouri State U (MO)
Missouri Valley Coll (MO)
Missouri Western State U (MO)
Molloy Coll (NY)
Monmouth Coll (IL)
Montana State U Billings (MT)
Montclair State U (NJ)
Moravian Coll (PA)
Morehead State U (KY)
Mount Allison U (NB, Canada)
Mount Aloysius Coll (PA)
Mount Marty Coll (SD)
Mount Mary U (WI)
Mount Mercy U (IA)
Mount St. Joseph U (OH)
Mount Saint Mary Coll (NY)
Mount Saint Mary's U (CA)
Mount St. Mary's U (MD)
Mount Vernon Nazarene U (OH)
Muhlenberg Coll (PA)
Murray State U (KY)
National U (CA)
National U Coll, Bayamón (PR)
Nazareth Coll of Rochester (NY)
Nebraska Wesleyan U (NE)
Neumann U (PA)
Newberry Coll (SC)
Newbury Coll (MA)
New England Coll (NH)
Newman U (KS)
New Mexico Highlands U (NM)
New Mexico State U (NM)
New York Inst of Technology (NY)
New York U (NY)
Niagara U (NY)
Nichols Coll (MA)
Norfolk State U (VA)
North Carolina Ag and Tech State U (NC)
North Carolina Central U (NC)
North Carolina State U (NC)
North Carolina Wesleyan Coll (NC)
North Central Coll (IL)
North Dakota State U (ND)
Northeastern Illinois U (IL)
Northeastern State U (OK)
Northeastern U (MA)
Northern Arizona U (AZ)
Northern Illinois U (IL)
Northern Kentucky U (KY)
Northern Michigan U (MI)
Northern State U (SD)
North Greenville U (SC)
Northwest Christian U (OR)
Northwestern Coll (IA)
Northwestern Oklahoma State U (OK)
Northwest Missouri State U (MO)
Northwest Nazarene U (ID)
Northwest U (WA)
Northwood U, Michigan Campus (MI)
Northwood U, Texas Campus (TX)
Norwich U (VT)
Nova Southeastern U (FL)
Nyack Coll (NY)
Oakland U (MI)
Oglethorpe U (GA)
Ohio Dominican U (OH)
Ohio Northern U (OH)
The Ohio State U (OH)
Ohio U (OH)
Ohio Valley U (WV)
Ohio Wesleyan U (OH)
Oklahoma Baptist U (OK)
Oklahoma Christian U (OK)
Oklahoma City U (OK)
Oklahoma State U (OK)
Old Dominion U (VA)
Olivet Nazarene U (IL)
Oregon State U (OR)
Our Lady of the Lake U of San Antonio (TX)
Pace U (NY)
Pacific U (OR)
Palm Beach Atlantic U (FL)
Park U (MO)
Peirce Coll (PA)
Penn State Abington (PA)
Penn State Altoona (PA)
Penn State Beaver (PA)
Penn State Berks (PA)
Penn State Brandywine (PA)
Penn State DuBois (PA)
Penn State Erie, The Behrend Coll (PA)
Penn State Fayette, The Eberly Campus (PA)
Penn State Greater Allegheny (PA)
Penn State Hazleton (PA)
Penn State Lehigh Valley (PA)
Penn State Mont Alto (PA)
Penn State New Kensington (PA)
Penn State Schuylkill (PA)
Penn State Shenango (PA)
Penn State U Park (PA)
Penn State Wilkes-Barre (PA)
Penn State Worthington Scranton (PA)
Penn State York (PA)
Pennsylvania Coll of Technology (PA)
Pepperdine U, Malibu (CA)
Peru State Coll (NE)
Philadelphia U (PA)
Pittsburg State U (KS)
Plymouth State U (NH)
Point Loma Nazarene U (CA)
Point U (GA)
Portland State U (OR)
Post U (CT)
Prairie View A&M U (TX)
Providence Coll (RI)
Purdue U (IN)
Purdue U Calumet (IN)
Queens Coll of the City U of New York (NY)
Quincy U (IL)
Quinnipiac U (CT)
Radford U (VA)
Ramapo Coll of New Jersey (NJ)
Randolph-Macon Coll (VA)
Rasmussen Coll Bloomington (MN)
Rasmussen Coll Brooklyn Park (MN)
Rasmussen Coll Eagan (MN)
Rasmussen Coll Fargo (ND)
Rasmussen Coll Fort Myers (FL)
Rasmussen Coll Kansas City/ Overland Park (KS)
Rasmussen Coll Lake Elmo/ Woodbury (MN)
Rasmussen Coll Land O' Lakes (FL)
Rasmussen Coll Mankato (MN)
Rasmussen Coll Moorhead (MN)
Rasmussen Coll New Port Richey (FL)
Rasmussen Coll Ocala (FL)
Rasmussen Coll Rockford (IL)
Rasmussen Coll St. Cloud (MN)
Rasmussen Coll Tampa/Brandon (FL)
Rasmussen Coll Topeka (KS)
Regent U (VA)
Regis U (CO)
Reinhardt U (GA)
Rhode Island Coll (RI)
Rider U (NJ)
Robert Morris U (PA)
Robert Morris U Illinois (IL)
Roberts Wesleyan Coll (NY)
Rochester Inst of Technology (NY)
Rockford U (IL)
Roger Williams U (RI)
Roosevelt U (IL)
Rosemont Coll (PA)
Rutgers, The State U of New Jersey, Camden (NJ)
Rutgers, The State U of New Jersey, Newark (NJ)
Rutgers, The State U of New Jersey, New Brunswick (NJ)
Sacred Heart U (CT)
The Sage Colls (NY)
Saginaw Valley State U (MI)
Saint Anselm Coll (NH)
Saint Augustine's U (NC)
St. Bonaventure U (NY)
St. Catherine U (MN)
St. Edward's U (TX)
St. Francis Coll (NY)
Saint Francis U (PA)
St. Gregory's U, Shawnee (OK)
St. John Fisher Coll (NY)
Saint John's U (MN)
St. John's U (NY)
Saint Joseph's Coll (IN)
St. Joseph's Coll, Long Island Campus (NY)
St. Joseph's Coll, New York (NY)
Saint Joseph's U (PA)
Saint Leo U (FL)
Saint Martin's U (WA)
Saint Mary-of-the-Woods Coll (IN)
Saint Mary's Coll (IN)
St. Mary's U (TX)
Saint Mary's U of Minnesota (MN)
Saint Michael's Coll (VT)
St. Norbert Coll (WI)
Saint Peter's U (NJ)
St. Thomas Aquinas Coll (NY)
St. Thomas U (FL)
Saint Vincent Coll (PA)
Salem Coll (NC)
Salisbury U (MD)
Salve Regina U (RI)
Samford U (AL)
Sam Houston State U (TX)
San Diego State U (CA)
San Francisco State U (CA)
San Jose State U (CA)
Santa Clara U (CA)
Savannah State U (GA)
Scripps Coll (CA)
Seattle Pacific U (WA)
Seattle U (WA)
Seton Hill U (PA)
Shaw U (NC)
Shepherd U (WV)
Shippensburg U of Pennsylvania (PA)
Siena Coll (NY)
Siena Heights U (MI)
Silver Lake Coll of the Holy Family (WI)
Simpson Coll (IA)
Simpson U (CA)
Slippery Rock U of Pennsylvania (PA)
South Carolina State U (SC)
Southeastern Louisiana U (LA)
Southeastern Oklahoma State U (OK)
Southeastern U (FL)
Southeast Missouri State U (MO)
Southern Adventist U (TN)
Southern Arkansas U–Magnolia (AR)
Southern California Inst of Technology (CA)
Southern Connecticut State U (CT)
Southern Illinois U Carbondale (IL)
Southern Illinois U Edwardsville (IL)
Southern Methodist U (TX)
Southern New Hampshire U (NH)
Southern Oregon U (OR)
Southern Utah U (UT)
Southwest Baptist U (MO)
Southwestern Adventist U (TX)
Southwestern Assemblies of God U (TX)
Southwestern Coll (KS)
Southwestern U (TX)
Southwest Minnesota State U (MN)
Spalding U (KY)
Spring Hill Coll (AL)
State U of New York at Fredonia (NY)
State U of New York at New Paltz (NY)
State U of New York at Oswego (NY)
State U of New York at Plattsburgh (NY)
State U of New York Coll at Geneseo (NY)
State U of New York Coll at Old Westbury (NY)
State U of New York Polytechnic Inst (NY)
Stephen F. Austin State U (TX)
Stetson U (FL)
Stevenson U (MD)
Stonehill Coll (MA)
Stratford U, Glen Allen (VA)
Stratford U, Newport News (VA)
Stratford U, Woodbridge (VA)
Suffolk U (MA)
Sullivan U (KY)
Susquehanna U (PA)
Syracuse U (NY)
Tarleton State U (TX)
Taylor U (IN)
Temple U (PA)
Tennessee State U (TN)
Tennessee Wesleyan Coll (TN)
Texas A&M Intl U (TX)
Texas A&M U (TX)
Texas A&M U–Commerce (TX)
Texas A&M U–Corpus Christi (TX)
Texas A&M U–Kingsville (TX)
Texas Christian U (TX)
Texas Lutheran U (TX)
Texas Southern U (TX)
Texas State U (TX)
Texas Tech U (TX)
Texas Wesleyan U (TX)
Texas Woman's U (TX)
Thiel Coll (PA)
Thomas More Coll (KY)
Tiffin U (OH)
Tougaloo Coll (MS)
Towson U (MD)
Transylvania U (KY)
Trevecca Nazarene U (TN)
Trine U (IN)
Trinity Christian Coll (IL)
Trinity U (TX)
Troy U (AL)
Truman State U (MO)
Tulane U (LA)
Union Coll (KY)
Union Coll (NE)
Union U (TN)
Universidad del Turabo (PR)
Universidad Metropolitana (PR)
Université de Sherbrooke (QC, Canada)
Université du Québec en Outaouais (QC, Canada)
U at Albany, State U of New York (NY)
U at Buffalo, the State U of New York (NY)
The U of Akron (OH)
The U of Alabama (AL)
The U of Alabama at Birmingham (AL)
The U of Alabama in Huntsville (AL)
U of Alaska Fairbanks (AK)
U of Alberta (AB, Canada)
The U of Arizona (AZ)
U of Arkansas (AR)
U of Arkansas at Little Rock (AR)
U of Arkansas at Pine Bluff (AR)
U of Bridgeport (CT)
The U of British Columbia (BC, Canada)
The U of British Columbia–Okanagan Campus (BC, Canada)
U of Central Arkansas (AR)
U of Central Florida (FL)
U of Central Oklahoma (OK)
U of Charleston (WV)
U of Cincinnati (OH)
U of Colorado Boulder (CO)
U of Dayton (OH)
U of Delaware (DE)
U of Denver (CO)
U of Dubuque (IA)
U of Evansville (IN)
The U of Findlay (OH)
U of Florida (FL)
U of Georgia (GA)
U of Great Falls (MT)
U of Guam (GU)
U of Guelph (ON, Canada)
U of Hartford (CT)
U of Hawaii at Hilo (HI)
U of Hawaii at Manoa (HI)
U of Hawaii–West Oahu (HI)
U of Houston (TX)
U of Houston–Clear Lake (TX)
U of Houston–Downtown (TX)
U of Houston–Victoria (TX)
U of Idaho (ID)
U of Illinois at Chicago (IL)
U of Illinois at Springfield (IL)
U of Indianapolis (IN)
The U of Iowa (IA)
U of Jamestown (ND)
The U of Kansas (KS)
U of Kentucky (KY)
U of La Verne (CA)
U of Lethbridge (AB, Canada)
U of Louisiana at Lafayette (LA)
U of Louisville (KY)
U of Maine (ME)
U of Maine at Augusta (ME)
U of Maine at Machias (ME)
U of Maine at Presque Isle (ME)
U of Mary Hardin-Baylor (TX)
U of Maryland, Coll Park (MD)
U of Maryland U Coll (MD)
U of Massachusetts Amherst (MA)
U of Massachusetts Dartmouth (MA)
U of Memphis (TN)
U of Miami (FL)
U of Michigan–Dearborn (MI)
U of Michigan–Flint (MI)
U of Minnesota, Crookston (MN)
U of Minnesota, Duluth (MN)
U of Minnesota, Twin Cities Campus (MN)
U of Mississippi (MS)
U of Missouri (MO)
U of Missouri–Kansas City (MO)
U of Missouri–St. Louis (MO)
U of Mobile (AL)
The U of Montana (MT)
U of Montevallo (AL)
U of Mount Union (OH)
U of Nebraska–Lincoln (NE)
U of Nevada, Las Vegas (NV)
U of Nevada, Reno (NV)
U of New Brunswick Saint John (NB, Canada)
U of New Haven (CT)
U of New Orleans (LA)
U of North Alabama (AL)
U of North Carolina at Asheville (NC)
The U of North Carolina at Charlotte (NC)
The U of North Carolina at Greensboro (NC)
The U of North Carolina at Pembroke (NC)
U of North Dakota (ND)
U of Northern Iowa (IA)
U of North Florida (FL)
U of North Georgia (GA)
U of North Texas (TX)
U of Northwestern–St. Paul (MN)
U of Notre Dame (IN)
U of Oklahoma (OK)
U of Oregon (OR)
U of Ottawa (ON, Canada)
U of Pennsylvania (PA)
U of Pittsburgh (PA)
U of Pittsburgh at Bradford (PA)
U of Pittsburgh at Greensburg (PA)
U of Portland (OR)
U of Puerto Rico in Ponce (PR)
U of Regina (SK, Canada)
U of Rhode Island (RI)
U of Richmond (VA)
U of Rio Grande (OH)
U of St. Francis (IL)
U of Saint Francis (IN)
U of Saint Joseph (CT)
U of Saint Mary (KS)
U of St. Thomas (MN)
U of St. Thomas (TX)
U of San Diego (CA)
U of San Francisco (CA)
U of Saskatchewan (SK, Canada)
The U of Scranton (PA)
U of South Alabama (AL)
The U of South Dakota (SD)
U of Southern California (CA)
U of Southern Indiana (IN)
U of Southern Maine (ME)
U of Southern Mississippi (MS)
U of South Florida (FL)
U of South Florida, St. Petersburg (FL)
U of South Florida Sarasota-Manatee (FL)
The U of Tampa (FL)
The U of Tennessee (TN)
The U of Tennessee at Martin (TN)
The U of Texas at Arlington (TX)
The U of Texas at Austin (TX)
The U of Texas at Dallas (TX)
The U of Texas at El Paso (TX)

The U of Texas at San Antonio (TX)
The U of Texas at Tyler (TX)
The U of Texas of the Permian Basin (TX)
The U of Texas–Pan American (TX)
U of the Cumberlands (KY)
U of the District of Columbia (DC)
U of the Incarnate Word (TX)
U of the Virgin Islands (VI)
The U of Toledo (OH)
U of Toronto (ON, Canada)
The U of Tulsa (OK)
U of Utah (UT)
The U of Virginia's Coll at Wise (VA)
U of Washington (WA)
U of Washington, Bothell (WA)
U of Washington, Tacoma (WA)
U of Waterloo (ON, Canada)
The U of West Alabama (AL)
The U of Western Ontario (ON, Canada)
U of West Florida (FL)
U of West Georgia (GA)
U of Windsor (ON, Canada)
U of Wisconsin–Eau Claire (WI)
U of Wisconsin–Green Bay (WI)
U of Wisconsin–La Crosse (WI)
U of Wisconsin–Madison (WI)
U of Wisconsin–Milwaukee (WI)
U of Wisconsin–Oshkosh (WI)
U of Wisconsin–Parkside (WI)
U of Wisconsin–Platteville (WI)
U of Wisconsin–River Falls (WI)
U of Wisconsin–Stevens Point (WI)
U of Wisconsin–Superior (WI)
U of Wisconsin–Whitewater (WI)
U of Wyoming (WY)
Upper Iowa U (IA)
Urbana U (OH)
Ursuline Coll (OH)
Utah State U (UT)
Utah Valley U (UT)
Utica Coll (NY)
Valdosta State U (GA)
Valparaiso U (IN)
Vanguard U of Southern California (CA)
Villanova U (PA)
Virginia Commonwealth U (VA)
Virginia Polytechnic Inst and State U (VA)
Virginia State U (VA)
Virginia Union U (VA)
Viterbo U (WI)
Voorhees Coll (SC)
Wagner Coll (NY)
Wake Forest U (NC)
Walden U (MN)
Walla Walla U (WA)
Walsh Coll of Accountancy and Business Administration (MI)
Walsh U (OH)
Wartburg Coll (IA)
Washburn U (KS)
Washington & Jefferson Coll (PA)
Washington and Lee U (VA)
Washington State U (WA)
Washington State U Vancouver (WA)
Washington U in St. Louis (MO)
Waynesburg U (PA)
Wayne State U (MI)
Webber Intl U (FL)
Weber State U (UT)
Webster U (MO)
Wesleyan Coll (GA)
West Chester U of Pennsylvania (PA)
Western Carolina U (NC)
Western Illinois U (IL)
Western Kentucky U (KY)
Western Michigan U (MI)
Western New England U (MA)
Western State Colorado U (CO)
West Liberty U (WV)
Westminster Coll (MO)
Westminster Coll (UT)
West Texas A&M U (TX)
West Virginia U (WV)
West Virginia U Inst of Technology (WV)
West Virginia Wesleyan Coll (WV)
Wheeling Jesuit U (WV)
Whitworth U (WA)
Wichita State U (KS)
Widener U (PA)
Wilberforce U (OH)
Wilkes U (PA)
William Jewell Coll (MO)
William Paterson U of New Jersey (NJ)
William Penn U (IA)
William Woods U (MO)
Wilmington U (DE)
Wingate U (NC)
Winona State U (MN)
Wittenberg U (OH)
Wofford Coll (SC)
Wright State U (OH)
Xavier U (OH)
Xavier U of Louisiana (LA)
Yeshiva U (NY)
York Coll of Pennsylvania (PA)
York Coll of the City U of New York (NY)
Youngstown State U (OH)

ACCOUNTING AND BUSINESS/MANAGEMENT
Babson Coll (MA)
Canisius Coll (NY)
Chaminade U of Honolulu (HI)
Chestnut Hill Coll (PA)
East Carolina U (NC)
EDP U of Puerto Rico (PR)
EDP U of Puerto Rico–San Sebastian (PR)
Ellis U (IL)
Hope Coll (MI)
Husson U (ME)
Maranatha Baptist U (WI)
Mercy Coll (NY)
National U (CA)
Rasmussen Coll Appleton (WI)
Rasmussen Coll Fort Myers (FL)
Rasmussen Coll Green Bay (WI)
Rasmussen Coll Land O' Lakes (FL)
Rasmussen Coll New Port Richey (FL)
Rasmussen Coll Ocala (FL)
Rasmussen Coll Tampa/Brandon (FL)
Rasmussen Coll Wausau (WI)
Rocky Mountain Coll (MT)
St. Francis Coll (NY)
Santa Clara U (CA)
Spalding U (KY)
U of Great Falls (MT)
The U of Western Ontario (ON, Canada)
Walla Walla U (WA)
Washington and Lee U (VA)
Western State Colorado U (CO)

ACCOUNTING AND COMPUTER SCIENCE
Bethany Coll (WV)
Fordham U (NY)
Grove City Coll (PA)
Saint Mary-of-the-Woods Coll (IN)
Southern New Hampshire U (NH)

ACCOUNTING AND FINANCE
Babson Coll (MA)
Bentley U (MA)
Bethel U (MN)
Bridgewater State U (MA)
Bucknell U (PA)
Clarkson U (NY)
DEREE - The American Coll of Greece (Greece)
Drake U (IA)
Eastern U (PA)
Elmira Coll (NY)
Ferris State U (MI)
Granite State Coll (NH)
Hiram Coll (OH)
Holy Family U (PA)
Lourdes U (OH)
Maryville Coll (TN)
Mercy Coll (NY)
Northern Michigan U (MI)
Saint Francis U (PA)
Southern New Hampshire U (NH)
Tabor Coll (KS)
U of North Dakota (ND)
U of Southern Maine (ME)
U of Waterloo (ON, Canada)
The U of Western Ontario (ON, Canada)
U of Windsor (ON, Canada)
Western New England U (MA)
Western State Colorado U (CO)

ACCOUNTING RELATED
Brigham Young U (UT)
Central Michigan U (MI)
Eastern Michigan U (MI)
Franklin U (OH)
Maryville U of Saint Louis (MO)
McDaniel Coll (MD)
North Dakota State U (ND)
Northern Michigan U (MI)
Rocky Mountain Coll (MT)
State U of New York at New Paltz (NY)
State U of New York at Oswego (NY)

ACCOUNTING TECHNOLOGY AND BOOKKEEPING
Bowling Green State U (OH)
Ferris State U (MI)
Intl Business Coll, Fort Wayne (IN)
Post U (CT)
Rowan U (NJ)
St. Edward's U (TX)

ACTING
Acad of Art U (CA)
Arcadia U (PA)
Ashland U (OH)
Augsburg Coll (MN)
Baldwin Wallace U (OH)
Barry U (FL)
Baylor U (TX)
Belmont U (TN)
Bennington Coll (VT)
Bethany Coll (WV)
Boston U (MA)
Bradley U (IL)
Brigham Young U (UT)
California State U, Long Beach (CA)
Central Michigan U (MI)
Central Washington U (WA)
Chapman U (CA)
Coker Coll (SC)
Coll of the Ozarks (MO)
Columbia Coll Chicago (IL)
Cornish Coll of the Arts (WA)
Dalhousie U (NS, Canada)
DePaul U (IL)
Drake U (IA)
Elon U (NC)
Emerson Coll (MA)
Emory & Henry Coll (VA)
Five Towns Coll (NY)
Florida Southern Coll (FL)
Florida State U (FL)
Greensboro Coll (NC)
Hofstra U (NY)
Illinois Wesleyan U (IL)
Ithaca Coll (NY)
Johnson State Coll (VT)
Kean U (NJ)
Keene State Coll (NH)
Lindenwood U (MO)
Lipscomb U (TN)
Marymount Manhattan Coll (NY)
Nazareth Coll of Rochester (NY)
Nebraska Wesleyan U (NE)
Oakland U (MI)
Ohio U (OH)
Oklahoma City U (OK)
Old Dominion U (VA)
Penn State Abington (PA)
Penn State Altoona (PA)
Penn State Beaver (PA)
Penn State Berks (PA)
Penn State Brandywine (PA)
Penn State DuBois (PA)
Penn State Erie, The Behrend Coll (PA)
Penn State Fayette, The Eberly Campus (PA)
Penn State Greater Allegheny (PA)
Penn State Hazleton (PA)
Penn State Lehigh Valley (PA)
Penn State Mont Alto (PA)
Penn State New Kensington (PA)
Penn State Schuylkill (PA)
Penn State Shenango (PA)
Penn State U Park (PA)
Penn State Wilkes-Barre (PA)
Penn State Worthington Scranton (PA)
Penn State York (PA)
Pepperdine U, Malibu (CA)
Purdue U (IN)
Rhode Island Coll (RI)
Roosevelt U (IL)
St. Edward's U (TX)
Seton Hill U (PA)
Shenandoah U (VA)
Slippery Rock U of Pennsylvania (PA)
Stevenson U (MD)
Syracuse U (NY)
Temple U (PA)
Texas Christian U (TX)
Towson U (MD)
Trinity U (TX)
U of Alberta (AB, Canada)
U of Hartford (CT)
U of Lethbridge (AB, Canada)
U of Maryland, Baltimore County (MD)
U of Miami (FL)
U of Nevada, Las Vegas (NV)
U of Northern Iowa (IA)
U of Regina (SK, Canada)
U of Southern California (CA)
The U of the Arts (PA)
U of Washington (WA)
U of Windsor (ON, Canada)
Webster U (MO)
Western Michigan U (MI)
Wright State U (OH)

ACTUARIAL SCIENCE
Appalachian State U (NC)
Arcadia U (PA)
Arizona State U at the Tempe campus (AZ)
Ashland U (OH)
Ball State U (IN)
Baruch Coll of the City U of New York (NY)
Bentley U (MA)
Bethany Coll (WV)
Binghamton U, State U of New York (NY)
Bob Jones U (SC)
Bowling Green State U (OH)
Bradley U (IL)
Brigham Young U (UT)
Bryant U (RI)
Butler U (IN)
Central Coll (IA)
Central Michigan U (MI)
Central Washington U (WA)
Concordia U (QC, Canada)
Concordia U Wisconsin (WI)
Drake U (IA)
Eastern Michigan U (MI)
Elmhurst Coll (IL)
Georgia State U (GA)
High Point U (NC)
Indiana U Northwest (IN)
Indiana U South Bend (IN)
Lebanon Valley Coll (PA)
Maryville U of Saint Louis (MO)
The Master's Coll and Sem (CA)
Michigan State U (MI)
Milwaukee School of Eng (WI)
Mount Mercy U (IA)
New York U (NY)
North Central Coll (IL)
Northwestern Coll (IA)
Oakland U (MI)
Ohio Northern U (OH)
The Ohio State U (OH)
Ohio U (OH)
Olivet Coll (MI)
Penn State Abington (PA)
Penn State Altoona (PA)
Penn State Beaver (PA)
Penn State Berks (PA)
Penn State Brandywine (PA)
Penn State DuBois (PA)
Penn State Erie, The Behrend Coll (PA)
Penn State Fayette, The Eberly Campus (PA)
Penn State Greater Allegheny (PA)
Penn State Hazleton (PA)
Penn State Lehigh Valley (PA)
Penn State Mont Alto (PA)
Penn State New Kensington (PA)
Penn State Schuylkill (PA)
Penn State Shenango (PA)
Penn State Wilkes-Barre (PA)
Penn State Worthington Scranton (PA)
Penn State York (PA)
Purdue U (IN)
Queens Coll of the City U of New York (NY)
Robert Morris U (PA)
Roosevelt U (IL)
St. John's U (NY)
Saint Joseph's U (PA)
Saint Mary's U of Minnesota (MN)
Siena Coll (NY)
Simon Fraser U (BC, Canada)
Simpson Coll (IA)
Slippery Rock U of Pennsylvania (PA)
Temple U (PA)
Texas Christian U (TX)
Thiel Coll (PA)
Université de Montréal (QC, Canada)
U at Albany, State U of New York (NY)
U of Alberta (AB, Canada)
U of California, Santa Barbara (CA)
U of Central Oklahoma (OK)
The U of Iowa (IA)
U of Michigan–Flint (MI)
U of Minnesota, Twin Cities Campus (MN)
U of Nebraska–Lincoln (NE)
U of Pennsylvania (PA)
U of Regina (SK, Canada)
U of St. Thomas (MN)
The U of Texas at Dallas (TX)
The U of Texas at San Antonio (TX)
The U of Toledo (OH)
U of Toronto (ON, Canada)
U of Waterloo (ON, Canada)
The U of Western Ontario (ON, Canada)
U of Wisconsin–Madison (WI)
U of Wisconsin–Milwaukee (WI)
Valparaiso U (IN)
Worcester Polytechnic Inst (MA)
Xavier U (OH)

ADMINISTRATIVE ASSISTANT AND SECRETARIAL SCIENCE
Campbellsville U (KY)
EDP U of Puerto Rico (PR)
EDP U of Puerto Rico–San Sebastian (PR)
Faith Baptist Bible Coll and Theological Sem (IA)
Intl Business Coll, Fort Wayne (IN)
Mount Vernon Nazarene U (OH)
North Carolina Ag and Tech State U (NC)
Tennessee State U (TN)
The U of Montana (MT)
Valdosta State U (GA)
Weber State U (UT)

ADULT AND CONTINUING EDUCATION
Auburn U (AL)
Eastern Illinois U (IL)
Fisher Coll (MA)
Louisiana Coll (LA)
Louisiana State U and A&M Coll (LA)
Mars Hill U (NC)
Tennessee State U (TN)
U of Alberta (AB, Canada)
U of Central Oklahoma (OK)
U of Minnesota, Twin Cities Campus (MN)
U of Regina (SK, Canada)
U of San Francisco (CA)
U of the Fraser Valley (BC, Canada)
Urbana U (OH)
Welch Coll (TN)

ADULT AND CONTINUING EDUCATION ADMINISTRATION
Concordia Coll–New York (NY)
Marshall U (WV)
Penn State Abington (PA)
Penn State Altoona (PA)
Penn State Beaver (PA)
Penn State Berks (PA)
Penn State Brandywine (PA)
Penn State DuBois (PA)
Penn State Erie, The Behrend Coll (PA)
Penn State Fayette, The Eberly Campus (PA)
Penn State Greater Allegheny (PA)
Penn State Hazleton (PA)
Penn State Lehigh Valley (PA)
Penn State Mont Alto (PA)

Penn State New Kensington (PA)
Penn State Schuylkill (PA)
Penn State Shenango (PA)
Penn State U Park (PA)
Penn State Wilkes-Barre (PA)
Penn State Worthington Scranton (PA)
Penn State York (PA)
U of the District of Columbia (DC)

ADULT DEVELOPMENT AND AGING
Bowling Green State U (OH)
Goddard Coll (VT)
Madonna U (MI)
Rhode Island Coll (RI)
St. Thomas U (NB, Canada)
U of Central Oklahoma (OK)
U of Guelph (ON, Canada)
York Coll of the City U of New York (NY)

ADULT HEALTH NURSING
Concordia Coll–New York (NY)
King U (TN)
Long Island U–LIU Brooklyn (NY)
Pennsylvania Coll of Technology (PA)
U of Rochester (NY)
Worcester State U (MA)

ADVERTISING
Acad of Art U (CA)
Adams State U (CO)
American Acad of Art (IL)
The American U in Dubai (United Arab Emirates)
Appalachian State U (NC)
Art Center Coll of Design (CA)
Barry U (FL)
Bowling Green State U (OH)
Bradley U (IL)
Brigham Young U (UT)
California State U, Fullerton (CA)
Central Michigan U (MI)
Champlain Coll (VT)
Columbia Coll Chicago (IL)
Drake U (IA)
Drury U (MO)
Emerson Coll (MA)
Fashion Inst of Technology (NY)
Ferris State U (MI)
Fontbonne U (MO)
Franklin Pierce U (NH)
Gannon U (PA)
Grand Valley State U (MI)
Hampton U (VA)
Harding U (AR)
Hastings Coll (NE)
Hawai`i Pacific U (HI)
Iona Coll (NY)
Iowa State U of Science and Technology (IA)
Johnson & Wales U (RI)
Kent State U (OH)
Lamar U (TX)
Lee U (TN)
Lindenwood U (MO)
Louisiana Coll (LA)
Loyola U Chicago (IL)
Marquette U (WI)
Metropolitan State U (MN)
Michigan State U (MI)
Minnesota State U Moorhead (MN)
Murray State U (KY)
New York Inst of Technology (NY)
Northwest Missouri State U (MO)
Oklahoma Christian U (OK)
Pace U (NY)
Penn State Abington (PA)
Penn State Altoona (PA)
Penn State Beaver (PA)
Penn State Berks (PA)
Penn State Brandywine (PA)
Penn State DuBois (PA)
Penn State Erie, The Behrend Coll (PA)
Penn State Fayette, The Eberly Campus (PA)
Penn State Greater Allegheny (PA)
Penn State Hazleton (PA)
Penn State Lehigh Valley (PA)
Penn State Mont Alto (PA)
Penn State New Kensington (PA)
Penn State Schuylkill (PA)
Penn State Shenango (PA)
Penn State U Park (PA)
Penn State Wilkes-Barre (PA)
Penn State Worthington Scranton (PA)
Penn State York (PA)
Pepperdine U, Malibu (CA)
Portland State U (OR)
Quinnipiac U (CT)
Rider U (NJ)
Rochester Inst of Technology (NY)
Rowan U (NJ)
St. John's U (NY)
San Diego State U (CA)
San Jose State U (CA)
South Dakota State U (SD)
Southern Adventist U (TN)
Southern Methodist U (TX)
Suffolk U (MA)
Syracuse U (NY)
Temple U (PA)
Texas State U (TX)
Texas Tech U (TX)
Texas Wesleyan U (TX)
Union U (TN)
The U of Alabama (AL)
U of Central Florida (FL)
U of Central Oklahoma (OK)
U of Florida (FL)
U of Georgia (GA)
U of Houston (TX)
U of Idaho (ID)
U of Miami (FL)
U of Missouri (MO)
U of Oklahoma (OK)
U of Oregon (OR)
U of San Francisco (CA)
U of Southern Indiana (IN)
U of Southern Mississippi (MS)
The U of Tennessee (TN)
The U of Texas at Arlington (TX)
The U of Texas at Austin (TX)
Washington State U (WA)
Washington U in St. Louis (MO)
Waynesburg U (PA)
Webster U (MO)
Wesleyan Coll (GA)
Western Kentucky U (KY)
Western Michigan U (MI)
Western New England U (MA)
West Texas A&M U (TX)
Widener U (PA)
Winona State U (MN)
Xavier U (OH)
Youngstown State U (OH)

AERONAUTICAL/AEROSPACE ENGINEERING TECHNOLOGY
Bowling Green State U (OH)
Utah State U (UT)

AERONAUTICS/AVIATION/AEROSPACE SCIENCE AND TECHNOLOGY
American Public U System (WV)
Arizona State U at the Polytechnic campus (AZ)
Averett U (VA)
Bridgewater State U (MA)
Delaware State U (DE)
Delta State U (MS)
Dowling Coll (NY)
Embry-Riddle Aeronautical U–Daytona (FL)
Embry-Riddle Aeronautical U–Prescott (AZ)
Embry-Riddle Aeronautical U–Worldwide (FL)
Everglades U, Sarasota (FL)
Florida Inst of Technology (FL)
Kansas State U (KS)
Kent State U (OH)
LeTourneau U (TX)
Liberty U (VA)
Middle Tennessee State U (TN)
The Ohio State U (OH)
Ohio U (OH)
Oklahoma State U (OK)
Polk State Coll (FL)
Purdue U (IN)
Saint Louis U (MO)
San Diego Christian Coll (CA)
San Jose State U (CA)
South Dakota State U (SD)
Texas Lutheran U (TX)
Texas Southern U (TX)
U of Minnesota, Crookston (MN)
U of North Texas (TX)
U of Oklahoma (OK)
Vaughn Coll of Aeronautics and Technology (NY)
Walla Walla U (WA)

AEROSPACE, AERONAUTICAL AND ASTRONAUTICAL/SPACE ENGINEERING
Arizona State U at the Tempe campus (AZ)
Auburn U (AL)
California Polytechnic State U, San Luis Obispo (CA)
California State Polytechnic U, Pomona (CA)
California State U, Long Beach (CA)
Capitol Technology U (MD)
Case Western Reserve U (OH)
Clarkson U (NY)
Cornell U (NY)
Daniel Webster Coll (NH)
Embry-Riddle Aeronautical U–Daytona (FL)
Embry-Riddle Aeronautical U–Prescott (AZ)
Florida Inst of Technology (FL)
Georgia Inst of Technology (GA)
Illinois Inst of Technology (IL)
Iowa State U of Science and Technology (IA)
Massachusetts Inst of Technology (MA)
Mississippi State U (MS)
Missouri U of Science and Technology (MO)
New Mexico State U (NM)
North Carolina State U (NC)
The Ohio State U (OH)
Oklahoma State U (OK)
Penn State Abington (PA)
Penn State Altoona (PA)
Penn State Beaver (PA)
Penn State Berks (PA)
Penn State Brandywine (PA)
Penn State DuBois (PA)
Penn State Erie, The Behrend Coll (PA)
Penn State Fayette, The Eberly Campus (PA)
Penn State Greater Allegheny (PA)
Penn State Hazleton (PA)
Penn State Lehigh Valley (PA)
Penn State Mont Alto (PA)
Penn State New Kensington (PA)
Penn State Schuylkill (PA)
Penn State Shenango (PA)
Penn State U Park (PA)
Penn State Wilkes-Barre (PA)
Penn State Worthington Scranton (PA)
Penn State York (PA)
Purdue U (IN)
Rensselaer Polytechnic Inst (NY)
Rochester Inst of Technology (NY)
Saint Louis U (MO)
San Diego State U (CA)
San Jose State U (CA)
Stanford U (CA)
Syracuse U (NY)
Texas A&M U (TX)
United States Air Force Acad (CO)
United States Naval Acad (MD)
U at Buffalo, the State U of New York (NY)
The U of Alabama (AL)
The U of Alabama in Huntsville (AL)
The U of Arizona (AZ)
U of California, Davis (CA)
U of California, Irvine (CA)
U of California, Los Angeles (CA)
U of Central Florida (FL)
U of Cincinnati (OH)
U of Colorado Boulder (CO)
U of Florida (FL)
The U of Kansas (KS)
U of Maryland, Coll Park (MD)
U of Miami (FL)
U of Michigan (MI)
U of Minnesota, Twin Cities Campus (MN)
U of Notre Dame (IN)
U of Oklahoma (OK)
U of Southern California (CA)
U of Tennessee (TN)
The U of Texas at Arlington (TX)
The U of Texas at Austin (TX)
U of Toronto (ON, Canada)
U of Virginia (VA)
U of Washington (WA)
Utah State U (UT)
Virginia Polytechnic Inst and State U (VA)
Western Michigan U (MI)
West Virginia U (WV)
West Virginia U Inst of Technology (WV)
Wichita State U (KS)
Worcester Polytechnic Inst (MA)

AFRICAN AMERICAN/BLACK STUDIES
Amherst Coll (MA)
Arizona State U at the Tempe campus (AZ)
Bard Coll at Simon's Rock (MA)
Bates Coll (ME)
Berea Coll (KY)
Binghamton U, State U of New York (NY)
Bowling Green State U (OH)
Brandeis U (MA)
Brown U (RI)
California State U, Dominguez Hills (CA)
California State U, Fresno (CA)
California State U, Fullerton (CA)
California State U, Long Beach (CA)
California State U, Los Angeles (CA)
Chicago State U (IL)
City Coll of the City U of New York (NY)
Claflin U (SC)
Claremont McKenna Coll (CA)
Cleveland State U (OH)
Coe Coll (IA)
Colby Coll (ME)
The Coll at Brockport, State U of New York (NY)
Coll of Charleston (SC)
Coll of Staten Island of the City U of New York (NY)
The Coll of William and Mary (VA)
The Coll of Wooster (OH)
Columbia U (NY)
Columbia U, School of General Studies (NY)
Cornell U (NY)
Dartmouth Coll (NH)
Denison U (OH)
DePaul U (IL)
DePauw U (IN)
Dominican U (IL)
Drew U (NJ)
Earlham Coll (IN)
East Carolina U (NC)
Eastern Illinois U (IL)
Eastern Michigan U (MI)
Florida Ag and Mech U (FL)
Fordham U (NY)
Georgia State U (GA)
Gettysburg Coll (PA)
Guilford Coll (NC)
Hamilton Coll (NY)
Hampshire Coll (MA)
Harvard U (MA)
Hobart and William Smith Colls (NY)
Howard U (DC)
Hunter Coll of the City U of New York (NY)
Indiana State U (IN)
Indiana U Bloomington (IN)
Indiana U Northwest (IN)
Indiana U–Purdue U Indianapolis (IN)
Johns Hopkins U (MD)
Kent State U (OH)
Knox Coll (IL)
Lehman Coll of the City U of New York (NY)
Loyola Marymount U (CA)
Loyola U Chicago (IL)
Luther Coll (IA)
Mercer U, Macon (GA)
Miami U (OH)
Mount Holyoke Coll (MA)
New York U (NY)
North Carolina State U (NC)
Northeastern U (MA)
Northwestern U (IL)
Oberlin Coll (OH)
The Ohio State U (OH)
Ohio U (OH)
Ohio Wesleyan U (OH)
Old Dominion U (VA)
Penn State Abington (PA)
Penn State Altoona (PA)
Penn State Beaver (PA)
Penn State Berks (PA)
Penn State Brandywine (PA)
Penn State DuBois (PA)
Penn State Erie, The Behrend Coll (PA)
Penn State Fayette, The Eberly Campus (PA)
Penn State Greater Allegheny (PA)
Penn State Hazleton (PA)
Penn State Lehigh Valley (PA)
Penn State Mont Alto (PA)
Penn State New Kensington (PA)
Penn State Schuylkill (PA)
Penn State Shenango (PA)
Penn State U Park (PA)
Penn State Wilkes-Barre (PA)
Penn State Worthington Scranton (PA)
Penn State York (PA)
Pomona Coll (CA)
Portland State U (OR)
Purdue U (IN)
Ramapo Coll of New Jersey (NJ)
Rhode Island Coll (RI)
Rhodes Coll (TN)
Roosevelt U (IL)
Rutgers, The State U of New Jersey, Camden (NJ)
Rutgers, The State U of New Jersey, Newark (NJ)
Saint Louis U (MO)
San Diego State U (CA)
San Francisco State U (CA)
San Jose State U (CA)
Scripps Coll (CA)
Smith Coll (MA)
Southern Illinois U Carbondale (IL)
Southern Methodist U (TX)
Stanford U (CA)
State U of New York at New Paltz (NY)
State U of New York Coll at Cortland (NY)
State U of New York Coll at Geneseo (NY)
Stony Brook U, State U of New York (NY)
Syracuse U (NY)
Temple U (PA)
Tougaloo Coll (MS)
Tufts U (MA)
U at Albany, State U of New York (NY)
U at Buffalo, the State U of New York (NY)
The U of Alabama (AL)
The U of Alabama at Birmingham (AL)
The U of Arizona (AZ)
U of California, Berkeley (CA)
U of California, Davis (CA)
U of California, Irvine (CA)
U of California, Los Angeles (CA)
U of California, Riverside (CA)
U of California, Santa Barbara (CA)
U of Central Arkansas (AR)
U of Cincinnati (OH)
U of Delaware (DE)
U of Florida (FL)
U of Georgia (GA)
U of Illinois at Chicago (IL)
The U of Iowa (IA)
The U of Kansas (KS)
U of Louisville (KY)
U of Maryland, Baltimore County (MD)
U of Maryland, Coll Park (MD)
U of Massachusetts Amherst (MA)
U of Massachusetts Boston (MA)
U of Memphis (TN)
U of Miami (FL)
U of Michigan (MI)
U of Michigan–Flint (MI)
U of Minnesota, Twin Cities Campus (MN)
U of Mississippi (MS)
The U of Montana (MT)
U of Nevada, Las Vegas (NV)
U of New Mexico (NM)

The U of North Carolina at Chapel Hill (NC)
The U of North Carolina at Charlotte (NC)
The U of North Carolina at Greensboro (NC)
U of Northern Colorado (CO)
U of Notre Dame (IN)
U of Oklahoma (OK)
U of Pennsylvania (PA)
U of Pittsburgh (PA)
U of Rhode Island (RI)
U of Rochester (NY)
U of Southern California (CA)
U of South Florida (FL)
The U of Texas at Austin (TX)
The U of Toledo (OH)
U of Virginia (VA)
U of Wisconsin–Madison (WI)
U of Wisconsin–Milwaukee (WI)
Vanderbilt U (TN)
Virginia Commonwealth U (VA)
Washington U in St. Louis (MO)
Wayne State U (MI)
Wesleyan U (CT)
Western Illinois U (IL)
Western Michigan U (MI)
Wheaton Coll (MA)
William Paterson U of New Jersey (NJ)
Wofford Coll (SC)
Wright State U (OH)
Yale U (CT)
York Coll of the City U of New York (NY)
Youngstown State U (OH)

AFRICAN LANGUAGES
U of California, Los Angeles (CA)
U of Wisconsin–Madison (WI)

AFRICAN STUDIES
Agnes Scott Coll (GA)
Augustana Coll (IL)
Bard Coll (NY)
Barnard Coll (NY)
Bowdoin Coll (ME)
Bowling Green State U (OH)
Carleton Coll (MN)
Columbia U, School of General Studies (NY)
Connecticut Coll (CT)
Dartmouth Coll (NH)
Davidson Coll (NC)
Dickinson Coll (PA)
Fordham U (NY)
Franklin & Marshall Coll (PA)
Hampshire Coll (MA)
Haverford Coll (PA)
Hobart and William Smith Colls (NY)
Hofstra U (NY)
Illinois Wesleyan U (IL)
Kennesaw State U (GA)
Kentucky State U (KY)
Lehigh U (PA)
Middlebury Coll (VT)
Northwestern U (IL)
The Ohio State U (OH)
Ohio U (OH)
Portland State U (OR)
Queens Coll of the City U of New York (NY)
Rowan U (NJ)
Rutgers, The State U of New Jersey, New Brunswick (NJ)
Simmons Coll (MA)
Tennessee State U (TN)
Tufts U (MA)
Tulane U (LA)
Union Coll (NY)
United States Military Acad (NY)
U of Chicago (IL)
The U of Iowa (IA)
The U of Kansas (KS)
U of Minnesota, Twin Cities Campus (MN)
U of Pennsylvania (PA)
U of Richmond (VA)
U of Toronto (ON, Canada)
Vassar Coll (NY)
Washington U in St. Louis (MO)
William Paterson U of New Jersey (NJ)
Yale U (CT)

AGRIBUSINESS
Abilene Christian U (TX)
Adams State U (CO)
American U of Beirut (Lebanon)
Andrews U (MI)
Angelo State U (TX)
Arkansas State U (AR)
Arkansas Tech U (AR)
Brigham Young U (UT)
Colorado State U (CO)
Cornell U (NY)
Eastern New Mexico U (NM)
Florida Ag and Mech U (FL)
Kent State U at Tuscarawas (OH)
Middle Tennessee State U (TN)
Mississippi State U (MS)
Missouri State U (MO)
Morrisville State Coll (NY)
New Mexico State U (NM)
North Carolina Ag and Tech State U (NC)
North Carolina State U (NC)
North Dakota State U (ND)
Northwest Missouri State U (MO)
Penn State Abington (PA)
Penn State Altoona (PA)
Penn State Beaver (PA)
Penn State Berks (PA)
Penn State Brandywine (PA)
Penn State DuBois (PA)
Penn State Erie, The Behrend Coll (PA)
Penn State Fayette, The Eberly Campus (PA)
Penn State Greater Allegheny (PA)
Penn State Hazleton (PA)
Penn State Lehigh Valley (PA)
Penn State Mont Alto (PA)
Penn State New Kensington (PA)
Penn State Schuylkill (PA)
Penn State Shenango (PA)
Penn State U Park (PA)
Penn State Wilkes-Barre (PA)
Penn State Worthington Scranton (PA)
Penn State York (PA)
Sam Houston State U (TX)
South Carolina State U (SC)
South Dakota State U (SD)
Southeast Missouri State U (MO)
Southwest Minnesota State U (MN)
Stephen F. Austin State U (TX)
Tarleton State U (TX)
Texas A&M U (TX)
Texas A&M U–Commerce (TX)
Texas A&M U–Kingsville (TX)
Texas State U (TX)
U of Arkansas (AR)
U of Central Missouri (MO)
U of Delaware (DE)
U of Georgia (GA)
U of Minnesota, Crookston (MN)
U of Minnesota, Twin Cities Campus (MN)
U of Saskatchewan (SK, Canada)
U of Wisconsin–River Falls (WI)
U of Wyoming (WY)
Vermont Tech Coll (VT)
West Texas A&M U (TX)

AGRICULTURAL AND DOMESTIC ANIMAL SERVICES RELATED
Saint Mary-of-the-Woods Coll (IN)
Tarleton State U (TX)

AGRICULTURAL AND EXTENSION EDUCATION
New Mexico State U (NM)
North Carolina State U (NC)
Northwestern Oklahoma State U (OK)
Penn State Abington (PA)
Penn State Altoona (PA)
Penn State Beaver (PA)
Penn State Berks (PA)
Penn State Brandywine (PA)
Penn State DuBois (PA)
Penn State Erie, The Behrend Coll (PA)
Penn State Fayette, The Eberly Campus (PA)
Penn State Greater Allegheny (PA)
Penn State Hazleton (PA)
Penn State Lehigh Valley (PA)
Penn State Mont Alto (PA)
Penn State New Kensington (PA)
Penn State Schuylkill (PA)
Penn State Shenango (PA)
Penn State Wilkes-Barre (PA)
Penn State Worthington Scranton (PA)
Penn State York (PA)
Tarleton State U (TX)
U of Arkansas (AR)
The U of Tennessee (TN)

AGRICULTURAL AND FOOD PRODUCTS PROCESSING
Angelo State U (TX)
Cornell U (NY)
Dalhousie U (NS, Canada)
Kansas State U (KS)
Morningside Coll (IA)
The Ohio State U (OH)
Texas A&M U (TX)
The U of British Columbia (BC, Canada)
U of Florida (FL)
U of Nebraska–Lincoln (NE)
Washington State U (WA)

AGRICULTURAL AND HORTICULTURAL PLANT BREEDING
Cornell U (NY)
Delaware State U (DE)

AGRICULTURAL BUSINESS AND MANAGEMENT
Alcorn State U (MS)
Arizona State U at the Polytechnic campus (AZ)
Brigham Young U (UT)
California Polytechnic State U, San Luis Obispo (CA)
California State Polytechnic U, Pomona (CA)
California State U, Chico (CA)
California State U, Fresno (CA)
Coll of the Ozarks (MO)
Colorado Mesa U (CO)
Cornell U (NY)
Delaware State U (DE)
Dickinson State U (ND)
Florida Southern Coll (FL)
Fort Hays State U (KS)
Hastings Coll (NE)
Iowa State U of Science and Technology (IA)
Kansas State U (KS)
Lincoln U (MO)
Louisiana State U and A&M Coll (LA)
Michigan State U (MI)
Montana State U (MT)
North Carolina Ag and Tech State U (NC)
The Ohio State U (OH)
Oklahoma State U (OK)
Oregon State U (OR)
Purdue U (IN)
Rocky Mountain Coll (MT)
Southern Arkansas U–Magnolia (AR)
Southwest Minnesota State U (MN)
State U of New York Coll of Agriculture and Technology at Cobleskill (NY)
Sul Ross State U (TX)
Tabor Coll (KS)
Texas A&M U (TX)
Texas Tech U (TX)
U of Alberta (AB, Canada)
The U of Arizona (AZ)
U of Delaware (DE)
U of Guelph (ON, Canada)
U of Hawaii at Hilo (HI)
U of Idaho (ID)
U of Minnesota, Twin Cities Campus (MN)
U of Missouri (MO)
U of Nebraska at Kearney (NE)
U of Nebraska–Lincoln (NE)
The U of Tennessee (TN)
The U of Tennessee at Martin (TN)
U of the Fraser Valley (BC, Canada)
U of Wisconsin–Madison (WI)
U of Wisconsin–Platteville (WI)
U of Wisconsin–River Falls (WI)
Upper Iowa U (IA)
Utah State U (UT)
Washington State U (WA)
West Texas A&M U (TX)

AGRICULTURAL BUSINESS AND MANAGEMENT RELATED
Delaware State U (DE)
Penn State New Kensington (PA)
U of California, Davis (CA)
U of Minnesota, Twin Cities Campus (MN)
Utah State U (UT)

AGRICULTURAL BUSINESS TECHNOLOGY
The U of Arizona (AZ)
U of Minnesota, Crookston (MN)
Washington State U (WA)
Wright State U (OH)

AGRICULTURAL COMMUNICATION/ JOURNALISM
Auburn U (AL)
California Polytechnic State U, San Luis Obispo (CA)
Kansas State U (KS)
North Dakota State U (ND)
The Ohio State U (OH)
Oklahoma State U (OK)
Purdue U (IN)
Sam Houston State U (TX)
South Dakota State U (SD)
Texas A&M U (TX)
Texas Tech U (TX)
U of Georgia (GA)
U of Idaho (ID)
U of Nebraska–Lincoln (NE)
U of Wisconsin–Madison (WI)
U of Wyoming (WY)
Washington State U (WA)
West Texas A&M U (TX)

AGRICULTURAL ECONOMICS
Alcorn State U (MS)
Auburn U (AL)
Brigham Young U (UT)
Colorado State U (CO)
Cornell U (NY)
Kansas State U (KS)
Langston U (OK)
Mississippi State U (MS)
North Carolina Ag and Tech State U (NC)
North Dakota State U (ND)
The Ohio State U (OH)
Oklahoma State U (OK)
Oregon State U (OR)
Purdue U (IN)
South Dakota State U (SD)
Southern Illinois U Carbondale (IL)
Tarleton State U (TX)
Texas A&M U (TX)
Texas Tech U (TX)
U of Alberta (AB, Canada)
U of Arkansas at Pine Bluff (AR)
U of Florida (FL)
U of Georgia (GA)
U of Guelph (ON, Canada)
U of Idaho (ID)
U of Kentucky (KY)
U of Maryland, Coll Park (MD)
U of Massachusetts Amherst (MA)
U of Minnesota, Twin Cities Campus (MN)
U of Missouri (MO)
U of Nebraska–Lincoln (NE)
U of Saskatchewan (SK, Canada)
U of Wisconsin–Madison (WI)
U of Wisconsin–River Falls (WI)
Utah State U (UT)
Virginia Polytechnic Inst and State U (VA)
Washington State U (WA)
West Virginia U (WV)

AGRICULTURAL ENGINEERING
Auburn U (AL)
California Polytechnic State U, San Luis Obispo (CA)
Cornell U (NY)
Dalhousie U (NS, Canada)
Florida Ag and Mech U (FL)
Iowa State U of Science and Technology (IA)
Kansas State U (KS)
Michigan State U (MI)
Missouri U of Science and Technology (MO)
North Carolina Ag and Tech State U (NC)
North Carolina State U (NC)
North Dakota State U (ND)
The Ohio State U (OH)
Oklahoma State U (OK)
Oregon State U (OR)
Penn State Abington (PA)
Penn State Beaver (PA)
Penn State Brandywine (PA)
Penn State DuBois (PA)
Penn State Erie, The Behrend Coll (PA)
Penn State Fayette, The Eberly Campus (PA)
Penn State Greater Allegheny (PA)
Penn State Hazleton (PA)
Penn State Lehigh Valley (PA)
Penn State Mont Alto (PA)
Penn State New Kensington (PA)
Penn State Schuylkill (PA)
Penn State Shenango (PA)
Penn State U Park (PA)
Penn State Wilkes-Barre (PA)
Penn State Worthington Scranton (PA)
Penn State York (PA)
Purdue U (IN)
Rutgers, The State U of New Jersey, New Brunswick (NJ)
South Dakota State U (SD)
State U of New York Coll of Environmental Science and Forestry (NY)
Texas A&M U (TX)
U of Arkansas (AR)
U of Georgia (GA)
U of Hawaii at Manoa (HI)
U of Kentucky (KY)
U of Maine (ME)
U of Maryland, Coll Park (MD)
U of Minnesota, Twin Cities Campus (MN)
U of Nebraska–Lincoln (NE)
U of Saskatchewan (SK, Canada)
The U of Tennessee (TN)
U of Wisconsin–Madison (WI)
U of Wisconsin–River Falls (WI)
Utah State U (UT)
Walla Walla U (WA)

AGRICULTURAL/FARM SUPPLIES RETAILING AND WHOLESALING
Tarleton State U (TX)
Texas A&M U (TX)

AGRICULTURAL MECHANIZATION
California Polytechnic State U, San Luis Obispo (CA)
Iowa State U of Science and Technology (IA)
Kansas State U (KS)
Montana State U (MT)
North Carolina Ag and Tech State U (NC)
North Carolina State U (NC)
North Dakota State U (ND)
Penn State Abington (PA)
Penn State Altoona (PA)
Penn State Beaver (PA)
Penn State Berks (PA)
Penn State Brandywine (PA)
Penn State DuBois (PA)
Penn State Erie, The Behrend Coll (PA)
Penn State Fayette, The Eberly Campus (PA)
Penn State Greater Allegheny (PA)
Penn State Hazleton (PA)
Penn State Lehigh Valley (PA)
Penn State Mont Alto (PA)
Penn State New Kensington (PA)
Penn State Schuylkill (PA)
Penn State Shenango (PA)
Penn State Wilkes-Barre (PA)
Penn State Worthington Scranton (PA)
Penn State York (PA)
Purdue U (IN)
Sam Houston State U (TX)
South Dakota State U (SD)
Stephen F. Austin State U (TX)
Tarleton State U (TX)
U of Idaho (ID)
U of Minnesota, Crookston (MN)
U of Missouri (MO)
U of Nebraska–Lincoln (NE)
U of Wisconsin–River Falls (WI)
Washington State U (WA)

AGRICULTURAL MECHANIZATION RELATED
U of Minnesota, Twin Cities Campus (MN)

AGRICULTURAL POWER MACHINERY OPERATION
U of Minnesota, Crookston (MN)

AGRICULTURAL PRODUCTION
Eastern Kentucky U (KY)
Stephen F. Austin State U (TX)

AGRICULTURAL PRODUCTION RELATED
Tarleton State U (TX)

AGRICULTURAL PUBLIC SERVICES RELATED
Oklahoma State U (OK)
South Dakota State U (SD)
U of Kentucky (KY)

AGRICULTURAL TEACHER EDUCATION
Arkansas Tech U (AR)
Auburn U (AL)
California Polytechnic State U, San Luis Obispo (CA)
California State Polytechnic U, Pomona (CA)
California State U, Fresno (CA)
Coll of the Ozarks (MO)
Colorado State U (CO)
Cornell U (NY)
Delaware State U (DE)
Eastern New Mexico U (NM)
Iowa State U of Science and Technology (IA)
Kansas State U (KS)
Louisiana State U and A&M Coll (LA)
Mississippi State U (MS)
Missouri State U (MO)
Montana State U (MT)
New Mexico State U (NM)
North Carolina Ag and Tech State U (NC)
North Carolina State U (NC)
North Dakota State U (ND)
Northwest Missouri State U (MO)
The Ohio State U (OH)
Oklahoma State U (OK)
Penn State U Park (PA)
Purdue U (IN)
South Dakota State U (SD)
Southeast Missouri State U (MO)
Southern Arkansas U–Magnolia (AR)
State U of New York at Oswego (NY)
Tarleton State U (TX)
U of Alberta (AB, Canada)
U of Arkansas (AR)
U of Arkansas at Pine Bluff (AR)
U of Delaware (DE)
U of Florida (FL)
U of Georgia (GA)
U of Idaho (ID)
U of Minnesota, Twin Cities Campus (MN)
U of Missouri (MO)
U of Nebraska–Lincoln (NE)
The U of Tennessee at Martin (TN)
U of Wisconsin–Platteville (WI)
U of Wisconsin–River Falls (WI)
U of Wyoming (WY)
Utah State U (UT)
Washington State U (WA)
West Virginia U (WV)

AGRICULTURE
Alcorn State U (MS)
American U of Beirut (Lebanon)
Angelo State U (TX)
Auburn U (AL)
Austin Peay State U (TN)
Berea Coll (KY)
California State U, Stanislaus (CA)
Cameron U (OK)
Cornell U (NY)
Dalhousie U (NS, Canada)
Delaware State U (DE)
Eastern New Mexico U (NM)
Ferrum Coll (VA)
Florida Ag and Mech U (FL)
Fort Hays State U (KS)
Hampshire Coll (MA)
Illinois State U (IL)
Iowa State U of Science and Technology (IA)
Kentucky State U (KY)
Lincoln U (MO)
McNeese State U (LA)
Mississippi State U (MS)
Missouri State U (MO)
Montana State U (MT)
Morehead State U (KY)
New Mexico State U (NM)
North Carolina Ag and Tech State U (NC)
North Carolina State U (NC)
North Dakota State U (ND)
Northwestern Oklahoma State U (OK)
Northwest Missouri State U (MO)
Oregon State U (OR)
Penn State Abington (PA)
Penn State Altoona (PA)
Penn State Beaver (PA)
Penn State Berks (PA)
Penn State Brandywine (PA)
Penn State DuBois (PA)
Penn State Erie, The Behrend Coll (PA)
Penn State Fayette, The Eberly Campus (PA)
Penn State Greater Allegheny (PA)
Penn State Hazleton (PA)
Penn State Lehigh Valley (PA)
Penn State Mont Alto (PA)
Penn State New Kensington (PA)
Penn State Schuylkill (PA)
Penn State Shenango (PA)
Penn State U Park (PA)
Penn State Wilkes-Barre (PA)
Penn State Worthington Scranton (PA)
Penn State York (PA)
Prairie View A&M U (TX)
Purdue U (IN)
Rutgers, The State U of New Jersey, New Brunswick (NJ)
Sam Houston State U (TX)
South Dakota State U (SD)
Southern Arkansas U–Magnolia (AR)
Southern Illinois U Carbondale (IL)
Southern Utah U (UT)
Stephen F. Austin State U (TX)
Sterling Coll (VT)
Tarleton State U (TX)
Tennessee State U (TN)
Texas A&M U (TX)
Texas A&M U–Commerce (TX)
Texas A&M U–Kingsville (TX)
Texas State U (TX)
Texas Tech U (TX)
Truman State U (MO)
U of Alberta (AB, Canada)
U of Arkansas at Pine Bluff (AR)
The U of British Columbia (BC, Canada)
U of Delaware (DE)
U of Georgia (GA)
U of Guam (GU)
U of Hawaii at Hilo (HI)
U of Lethbridge (AB, Canada)
U of Maryland, Coll Park (MD)
U of Minnesota, Twin Cities Campus (MN)
U of Missouri (MO)
U of Nebraska–Lincoln (NE)
The U of Tennessee at Martin (TN)
U of Vermont (VT)
U of Wisconsin–River Falls (WI)
Utah State U (UT)
Virginia State U (VA)
Washington State U (WA)
Western Illinois U (IL)
Western Kentucky U (KY)
West Texas A&M U (TX)

AGRICULTURE AND AGRICULTURE OPERATIONS RELATED
California State U, Stanislaus (CA)
Coll of the Atlantic (ME)
Murray State U (KY)
The Ohio State U (OH)
Penn State U Park (PA)
Tarleton State U (TX)
U of Alberta (AB, Canada)
The U of Arizona (AZ)
U of California, Davis (CA)
U of Kentucky (KY)
U of Minnesota, Twin Cities Campus (MN)
U of Nebraska–Lincoln (NE)

AGROECOLOGY AND SUSTAINABLE AGRICULTURE
Dalhousie U (NS, Canada)
The Evergreen State Coll (WA)
Green Mountain Coll (VT)
Prescott Coll (AZ)
Purdue U (IN)
St. Catharine Coll (KY)
Unity Coll (ME)
U of Maine (ME)
U of Minnesota, Crookston (MN)
U of New Hampshire (NH)
U of Wyoming (WY)
Xavier U (OH)

AGRONOMY AND CROP SCIENCE
Auburn U (AL)
California Polytechnic State U, San Luis Obispo (CA)
California State U, Fresno (CA)
Coll of the Ozarks (MO)
Colorado State U (CO)
Cornell U (NY)
Dalhousie U (NS, Canada)
Delaware State U (DE)
Fort Hays State U (KS)
Iowa State U of Science and Technology (IA)
Kansas State U (KS)
Mississippi State U (MS)
Missouri State U (MO)
New Mexico State U (NM)
North Carolina State U (NC)
Northwest Missouri State U (MO)
The Ohio State U (OH)
Oregon State U (OR)
Penn State Abington (PA)
Penn State Altoona (PA)
Penn State Beaver (PA)
Penn State Berks (PA)
Penn State Brandywine (PA)
Penn State DuBois (PA)
Penn State Erie, The Behrend Coll (PA)
Penn State Fayette, The Eberly Campus (PA)
Penn State Greater Allegheny (PA)
Penn State Hazleton (PA)
Penn State Mont Alto (PA)
Penn State New Kensington (PA)
Penn State Shenango (PA)
Penn State Wilkes-Barre (PA)
Penn State Worthington Scranton (PA)
Penn State York (PA)
Purdue U (IN)
South Dakota State U (SD)
State U of New York Coll of Agriculture and Technology at Cobleskill (NY)
Tarleton State U (TX)
Texas A&M U (TX)
Texas A&M U–Kingsville (TX)
Texas Tech U (TX)
U of Arkansas (AR)
U of Guelph (ON, Canada)
U of Kentucky (KY)
U of Minnesota, Crookston (MN)
U of Minnesota, Twin Cities Campus (MN)
U of Nebraska–Lincoln (NE)
U of Saskatchewan (SK, Canada)
The U of Tennessee at Martin (TN)
U of Vermont (VT)
U of Wisconsin–Madison (WI)
U of Wisconsin–Platteville (WI)
U of Wisconsin–River Falls (WI)
Utah State U (UT)
Virginia Polytechnic Inst and State U (VA)
Washington State U (WA)
West Texas A&M U (TX)

AIR AND SPACE OPERATIONS TECHNOLOGY
Embry-Riddle Aeronautical U–Daytona (FL)

AIRCRAFT POWERPLANT TECHNOLOGY
Embry-Riddle Aeronautical U–Daytona (FL)
Embry-Riddle Aeronautical U–Worldwide (FL)

AIR FORCE ROTC/AIR SCIENCE
Elms Coll (MA)
La Salle U (PA)
The U of Iowa (IA)

AIRFRAME MECHANICS AND AIRCRAFT MAINTENANCE TECHNOLOGY
Kansas State U (KS)
Lewis U (IL)
Southeastern Oklahoma State U (OK)
Vaughn Coll of Aeronautics and Technology (NY)

AIRLINE PILOT AND FLIGHT CREW
Auburn U (AL)
Baylor U (TX)
Bridgewater State U (MA)
California Baptist U (CA)
Central Washington U (WA)
Delaware State U (DE)
Delta State U (MS)
Eastern Kentucky U (KY)
Eastern Michigan U (MI)
Embry-Riddle Aeronautical U–Daytona (FL)
Farmingdale State Coll (NY)
Indiana State U (IN)
Jacksonville U (FL)
Kansas State U (KS)
LeTourneau U (TX)
Quincy U (IL)
Rocky Mountain Coll (MT)
Saint Louis U (MO)
Southeastern Oklahoma State U (OK)
Tarleton State U (TX)
U of Dubuque (IA)
U of Minnesota, Crookston (MN)
U of North Dakota (ND)
Utah Valley U (UT)
Western Michigan U (MI)
Westminster Coll (UT)

AIR TRAFFIC CONTROL
Arizona State U at the Polytechnic campus (AZ)
Daniel Webster Coll (NH)
Embry-Riddle Aeronautical U–Daytona (FL)
Embry-Riddle Aeronautical U–Prescott (AZ)
Hampton U (VA)
LeTourneau U (TX)
Lewis U (IL)
U of North Dakota (ND)

AIR TRANSPORTATION RELATED
California Baptist U (CA)
Florida Inst of Technology (FL)
Inter American U of Puerto Rico, Bayamón Campus (PR)
U of North Dakota (ND)

ALGEBRA AND NUMBER THEORY
U of New Brunswick Saint John (NB, Canada)

ALLIED HEALTH AND MEDICAL ASSISTING SERVICES RELATED
Bowling Green State U-Firelands Coll (OH)
Cedarville U (OH)
Coll of Saint Elizabeth (NJ)
The Ohio State U (OH)
The Ohio State U at Lima (OH)
Ramapo Coll of New Jersey (NJ)
Widener U (PA)

ALLIED HEALTH DIAGNOSTIC, INTERVENTION, AND TREATMENT PROFESSIONS RELATED
Fairleigh Dickinson U, Coll at Florham (NJ)
Fairleigh Dickinson U, Metropolitan Campus (NJ)
Georgian Court U (NJ)
Gwynedd Mercy U (PA)
Hofstra U (NY)
Immaculata U (PA)
Millersville U of Pennsylvania (PA)
Northern Michigan U (MI)
Point Loma Nazarene U (CA)
Rutgers, The State U of New Jersey, Newark (NJ)
Rutgers, The State U of New Jersey, New Brunswick (NJ)
Sacred Heart U (CT)
Tennessee Wesleyan Coll (TN)
U of Nebraska at Kearney (NE)

ALTERNATIVE AND COMPLEMENTARY MEDICINE RELATED
Everglades U, Sarasota (FL)
Johnson State Coll (VT)

AMERICAN GOVERNMENT AND POLITICS
Arizona Christian U (AZ)
Ave Maria U (FL)
Belmont Abbey Coll (NC)
Bridgewater State U (MA)
Drury U (MO)
Emmanuel Coll (MA)
Emory & Henry Coll (VA)
Fitchburg State U (MA)
Gallaudet U (DC)
Houston Baptist U (TX)
Lenoir-Rhyne U (NC)
The Master's Coll and Sem (CA)
Misericordia U (PA)
Oklahoma Christian U (OK)
Southeastern U (FL)
United States Military Acad (NY)
The U of Akron (OH)
The U of Montana (MT)
Western Michigan U (MI)

AMERICAN HISTORY
Charleston Southern U (SC)
The Coll of Saint Rose (NY)
Florida Coll (FL)
Gettysburg Coll (PA)
Howard Payne U (TX)
Keene State Coll (NH)
Morningside Coll (IA)
United States Military Acad (NY)
Université de Montréal (QC, Canada)
U of Washington, Tacoma (WA)
The U of Western Ontario (ON, Canada)

AMERICAN INDIAN/NATIVE AMERICAN STUDIES
Arizona State U at the Tempe campus (AZ)
Augsburg Coll (MN)
Bemidji State U (MN)
Black Hills State U (SD)
Concordia U (QC, Canada)
Creighton U (NE)
Dartmouth Coll (NH)
East Central U (OK)
The Evergreen State Coll (WA)
Fort Lewis Coll (CO)
Hampshire Coll (MA)
Humboldt State U (CA)
Inst of American Indian Arts (NM)
Northeastern State U (OK)
Northern Arizona U (AZ)
Northland Coll (WI)
Portland State U (OR)
St. Thomas U (NB, Canada)
San Diego State U (CA)
San Francisco State U (CA)
South Dakota State U (SD)
Stanford U (CA)
Trent U (ON, Canada)
U of Alaska Fairbanks (AK)
U of Alberta (AB, Canada)
U of California, Berkeley (CA)
U of California, Davis (CA)
U of California, Los Angeles (CA)
U of California, Riverside (CA)
U of Hawaii at Hilo (HI)
U of Hawaii at Manoa (HI)
U of Lethbridge (AB, Canada)
U of Minnesota, Duluth (MN)
U of Minnesota, Twin Cities Campus (MN)
The U of Montana (MT)
U of New Mexico (NM)
The U of North Carolina at Pembroke (NC)
U of North Dakota (ND)
U of Oklahoma (OK)
U of Ottawa (ON, Canada)
U of Regina (SK, Canada)
U of Saskatchewan (SK, Canada)

U of Science and Arts of Oklahoma (OK)
The U of South Dakota (SD)
U of Toronto (ON, Canada)
U of Washington (WA)
The U of Western Ontario (ON, Canada)
U of Wisconsin–Eau Claire (WI)
U of Wisconsin–Green Bay (WI)
U of Wyoming (WY)

AMERICAN LITERATURE
Castleton State Coll (VT)
U of California, Los Angeles (CA)
Washington U in St. Louis (MO)
Whittier Coll (CA)

AMERICAN NATIVE/NATIVE AMERICAN EDUCATION
The Coll of St. Scholastica (MN)
Northeastern State U (OK)
U of Alberta (AB, Canada)
U of Lethbridge (AB, Canada)
U of Regina (SK, Canada)

AMERICAN NATIVE/NATIVE AMERICAN LANGUAGES
Bemidji State U (MN)
U of Alaska Fairbanks (AK)
U of Regina (SK, Canada)

AMERICAN SIGN LANGUAGE (ASL)
Augustana Coll (SD)
California State U, Sacramento (CA)
Lamar U (TX)
Liberty U (VA)
Madonna U (MI)
Maryville Coll (TN)
Northeastern U (MA)
Rochester Inst of Technology (NY)
St. Catherine U (MN)
U of Houston (TX)
U of Rochester (NY)
Utah Valley U (UT)
William Woods U (MO)

AMERICAN SIGN LANGUAGE RELATED
Eastern Kentucky U (KY)

AMERICAN STUDIES
Albright Coll (PA)
American U (DC)
Amherst Coll (MA)
Arizona State U at the West campus (AZ)
Ashland U (OH)
Augustana Coll (SD)
Austin Coll (TX)
Ave Maria U (FL)
Bard Coll (NY)
Bard Coll at Simon's Rock (MA)
Barnard Coll (NY)
Bates Coll (ME)
Baylor U (TX)
Bennington Coll (VT)
Boston U (MA)
Bowling Green State U (OH)
Brandeis U (MA)
Brown U (RI)
Bryant U (RI)
Cabrini Coll (PA)
California State U, Fullerton (CA)
California State U, Long Beach (CA)
California State U, San Bernardino (CA)
Carleton Coll (MN)
Case Western Reserve U (OH)
Chowan U (NC)
Christopher Newport U (VA)
Claflin U (SC)
Claremont McKenna Coll (CA)
Clarkson U (NY)
Coe Coll (IA)
Colby Coll (ME)
Coll of Saint Elizabeth (NJ)
The Coll of Saint Rose (NY)
Coll of Staten Island of the City U of New York (NY)
The Coll of William and Mary (VA)
Columbia Coll (MO)
Columbia U (NY)
Columbia U, School of General Studies (NY)
Connecticut Coll (CT)
Cornell U (NY)
Creighton U (NE)
Cumberland U (TN)
DePaul U (IL)
Dickinson Coll (PA)
Dominican U (IL)
Eckerd Coll (FL)
Elmhurst Coll (IL)
Elmira Coll (NY)
Emmanuel Coll (MA)
Erskine Coll (SC)
Fairfield U (CT)
Fordham U (NY)
Franklin & Marshall Coll (PA)
Franklin Pierce U (NH)
Georgetown Coll (KY)
Georgetown U (DC)
The George Washington U (DC)
Gettysburg Coll (PA)
Goucher Coll (MD)
Hamilton Coll (NY)
Hampshire Coll (MA)
Hendrix Coll (AR)
Hillsdale Coll (MI)
Hobart and William Smith Colls (NY)
Hofstra U (NY)
Illinois Wesleyan U (IL)
Indiana U Bloomington (IN)
Kansas State U (KS)
Keene State Coll (NH)
Kent State U (OH)
Kentucky Wesleyan Coll (KY)
Kenyon Coll (OH)
Knox Coll (IL)
Lafayette Coll (PA)
Lake Forest Coll (IL)
Lehman Coll of the City U of New York (NY)
Lenoir-Rhyne U (NC)
Lesley U (MA)
Lindsey Wilson Coll (KY)
Lipscomb U (TN)
Long Island U–LIU Post (NY)
Lycoming Coll (PA)
Manhattanville Coll (NY)
Marist Coll (NY)
Mary Baldwin Coll (VA)
Miami U (OH)
Middlebury Coll (VT)
Mills Coll (CA)
Montreat Coll, Montreat (NC)
Mount Allison U (NB, Canada)
Mount Saint Mary's U (CA)
Muhlenberg Coll (PA)
Nazareth Coll of Rochester (NY)
Northwestern U (IL)
Occidental Coll (CA)
Oglethorpe U (GA)
Oklahoma State U (OK)
Oregon State U (OR)
Pace U (NY)
Penn State Abington (PA)
Penn State Berks (PA)
Penn State Brandywine (PA)
Penn State Erie, The Behrend Coll (PA)
Penn State Harrisburg (PA)
Penn State Lehigh Valley (PA)
Penn State Schuylkill (PA)
Penn State Worthington Scranton (PA)
Penn State York (PA)
Pomona Coll (CA)
Providence Coll (RI)
Purdue U (IN)
Queens Coll of the City U of New York (NY)
Ramapo Coll of New Jersey (NJ)
Reed Coll (OR)
Rider U (NJ)
Roger Williams U (RI)
Rowan U (NJ)
Rutgers, The State U of New Jersey, Newark (NJ)
Rutgers, The State U of New Jersey, New Brunswick (NJ)
The Sage Colls (NY)
Saint Francis U (PA)
St. John Fisher Coll (NY)
Saint Louis U (MO)
Saint Michael's Coll (VT)
St. Olaf Coll (MN)
Saint Peter's U (NJ)
Salve Regina U (RI)
San Francisco State U (CA)
Scripps Coll (CA)
Sewanee: The U of the South (TN)
Siena Coll (NY)
Skidmore Coll (NY)
Smith Coll (MA)
Stanford U (CA)
State U of New York at Fredonia (NY)
State U of New York at Oswego (NY)
State U of New York Coll at Geneseo (NY)
State U of New York Coll at Old Westbury (NY)
Stetson U (FL)
Stonehill Coll (MA)
Stony Brook U, State U of New York (NY)
Syracuse U (NY)
Temple U (PA)
Tennessee Wesleyan Coll (TN)
Texas State U (TX)
Towson U (MD)
Trinity Coll (CT)
Tufts U (MA)
Tulane U (LA)
Union Coll (NY)
U at Buffalo, the State U of New York (NY)
The U of Alabama (AL)
U of Arkansas (AR)
U of California, Berkeley (CA)
U of California, Davis (CA)
U of California, Santa Cruz (CA)
U of Dayton (OH)
U of Hawaii at Manoa (HI)
U of Idaho (ID)
The U of Iowa (IA)
The U of Kansas (KS)
U of Maryland, Baltimore County (MD)
U of Maryland, Coll Park (MD)
U of Mary Washington (VA)
U of Massachusetts Boston (MA)
U of Massachusetts Lowell (MA)
U of Miami (FL)
U of Michigan (MI)
U of Michigan–Dearborn (MI)
U of Minnesota, Twin Cities Campus (MN)
U of Missouri–Kansas City (MO)
U of Mount Union (OH)
U of New England (ME)
U of New Mexico (NM)
The U of North Carolina at Chapel Hill (NC)
U of Notre Dame (IN)
U of Pennsylvania (PA)
U of Pittsburgh at Greensburg (PA)
U of Richmond (VA)
U of Rio Grande (OH)
U of Rochester (NY)
U of San Francisco (CA)
U of Southern California (CA)
U of Southern Mississippi (MS)
U of South Florida (FL)
The U of Texas at Austin (TX)
The U of Texas at Dallas (TX)
The U of Texas at San Antonio (TX)
The U of Toledo (OH)
U of Toronto (ON, Canada)
U of Washington, Bothell (WA)
U of Washington, Tacoma (WA)
The U of Western Ontario (ON, Canada)
U of Wyoming (WY)
Ursinus Coll (PA)
Utah State U (UT)
Valparaiso U (IN)
Vanderbilt U (TN)
Vassar Coll (NY)
Virginia Wesleyan Coll (VA)
Warner Pacific Coll (OR)
Washington Coll (MD)
Washington U in St. Louis (MO)
Wesleyan Coll (GA)
Wesleyan U (CT)
Western Washington U (WA)
Wheaton Coll (MA)
Wheelock Coll (MA)
Whitworth U (WA)
Willamette U (OR)
Williams Coll (MA)
Wittenberg U (OH)
Yale U (CT)
Youngstown State U (OH)

ANALYTICAL CHEMISTRY
North Central Coll (IL)
The U of Western Ontario (ON, Canada)
West Chester U of Pennsylvania (PA)

ANATOMY
Andrews U (MI)
Howard U (DC)
Minnesota State U Mankato (MN)
Tulane U (LA)
U of Saskatchewan (SK, Canada)
The U of Western Ontario (ON, Canada)

ANCIENT/CLASSICAL GREEK
Amherst Coll (MA)
Augustana Coll (IL)
Bard Coll (NY)
Barnard Coll (NY)
Baylor U (TX)
Boston U (MA)
Brigham Young U (UT)
Bryn Mawr Coll (PA)
California State U, Long Beach (CA)
Canisius Coll (NY)
Carleton Coll (MN)
Columbia U (NY)
Dartmouth Coll (NH)
DePauw U (IN)
Duquesne U (PA)
Franklin & Marshall Coll (PA)
Gettysburg Coll (PA)
Hampden-Sydney Coll (VA)
Hillsdale Coll (MI)
Hobart and William Smith Colls (NY)
Hunter Coll of the City U of New York (NY)
Indiana U Bloomington (IN)
Kalamazoo Coll (MI)
Kenyon Coll (OH)
Knox Coll (IL)
Lawrence U (WI)
Loyola U Chicago (IL)
Loyola U New Orleans (LA)
Monmouth Coll (IL)
Mount Allison U (NB, Canada)
Mount Holyoke Coll (MA)
Multnomah U (OR)
Randolph Coll (VA)
Randolph-Macon Coll (VA)
Rice U (TX)
Rutgers, The State U of New Jersey, New Brunswick (NJ)
St. Olaf Coll (MN)
Samford U (AL)
Santa Clara U (CA)
Sewanee: The U of the South (TN)
Smith Coll (MA)
Southwestern U (TX)
Stanford U (CA)
Tufts U (MA)
U of California, Berkeley (CA)
U of California, Los Angeles (CA)
U of Georgia (GA)
The U of Iowa (IA)
U of Miami (FL)
U of Michigan (MI)
U of Minnesota, Twin Cities Campus (MN)
U of New Hampshire (NH)
U of Notre Dame (IN)
U of Richmond (VA)
U of Vermont (VT)
U of Washington (WA)
The U of Western Ontario (ON, Canada)
Wake Forest U (NC)
Washington U in St. Louis (MO)
Yale U (CT)

ANCIENT NEAR EASTERN AND BIBLICAL LANGUAGES
Baylor U (TX)
Belmont U (TN)
Carson-Newman U (TN)
Columbia Intl U (SC)
Concordia U (CA)
Concordia U Chicago (IL)
Concordia U Wisconsin (WI)
Cornerstone U (MI)
Howard Payne U (TX)
Luther Coll (IA)
The Master's Coll and Sem (CA)
Northwest Nazarene U (ID)
Northwest U (WA)
Oklahoma Baptist U (OK)
Toccoa Falls Coll (GA)
Union U (TN)
U of Chicago (IL)
U of Toronto (ON, Canada)
U of Valley Forge (PA)
U of Washington (WA)
Walla Walla U (WA)

ANCIENT STUDIES
Bates Coll (ME)
Boston U (MA)
Bowdoin Coll (ME)
Colby Coll (ME)
Columbia U (NY)
Columbia U, School of General Studies (NY)
Concordia U (QC, Canada)
Eckerd Coll (FL)
Lehigh U (PA)
Loyola Marymount U (CA)
Mount Holyoke Coll (MA)
Ohio Wesleyan U (OH)
Purdue U (IN)
Saint Joseph's U (PA)
St. Olaf Coll (MN)
Santa Clara U (CA)
U of Alberta (AB, Canada)
The U of Iowa (IA)
The U of Kansas (KS)
U of Maryland, Baltimore County (MD)
U of Miami (FL)
U of Michigan (MI)
U of Minnesota, Twin Cities Campus (MN)
U of Nebraska–Lincoln (NE)
U of Richmond (VA)
The U of Texas at Austin (TX)
Vanderbilt U (TN)
Washington U in St. Louis (MO)
Wesleyan U (CT)
Wheaton Coll (MA)

ANIMAL-ASSISTED THERAPY
Averett U (VA)
Carroll Coll (MT)

ANIMAL BEHAVIOR AND ETHOLOGY
Bucknell U (PA)
Canisius Coll (NY)
Franklin & Marshall Coll (PA)
Hampshire Coll (MA)
Indiana U Bloomington (IN)
Southwestern U (TX)
U of New England (ME)
U of Toronto (ON, Canada)
The U of Western Ontario (ON, Canada)

ANIMAL GENETICS
Cornell U (NY)
Dartmouth Coll (NH)
Jacksonville State U (AL)
Ohio Wesleyan U (OH)
Rutgers, The State U of New Jersey, New Brunswick (NJ)
U of Alberta (AB, Canada)
The U of British Columbia (BC, Canada)
U of Toronto (ON, Canada)
Worcester Polytechnic Inst (MA)

ANIMAL HEALTH
Dalhousie U (NS, Canada)
Sul Ross State U (TX)
U of Georgia (GA)

ANIMAL/LIVESTOCK HUSBANDRY AND PRODUCTION
Dalhousie U (NS, Canada)
Rutgers, The State U of New Jersey, New Brunswick (NJ)
Tarleton State U (TX)
Texas A&M U (TX)
The U of British Columbia (BC, Canada)
U of Minnesota, Twin Cities Campus (MN)

ANIMAL NUTRITION
Dalhousie U (NS, Canada)

ANIMAL PHYSIOLOGY
California State U, Fresno (CA)
Cornell U (NY)
Minnesota State U Mankato (MN)
Rutgers, The State U of New Jersey, New Brunswick (NJ)

The U of Akron (OH)
U of Minnesota, Twin Cities Campus (MN)
U of Toronto (ON, Canada)
Utah State U (UT)

ANIMAL SCIENCES
Abilene Christian U (TX)
Angelo State U (TX)
Arkansas State U (AR)
Auburn U (AL)
Berry Coll (GA)
California Polytechnic State U, San Luis Obispo (CA)
California State Polytechnic U, Pomona (CA)
California State U, Chico (CA)
California State U, Fresno (CA)
Coll of the Ozarks (MO)
Colorado State U (CO)
Cornell U (NY)
Delaware State U (DE)
Fort Hays State U (KS)
Iowa State U of Science and Technology (IA)
Kansas State U (KS)
Langston U (OK)
Louisiana State U and A&M Coll (LA)
Lubbock Christian U (TX)
Michigan State U (MI)
Middle Tennessee State U (TN)
Mississippi State U (MS)
Missouri State U (MO)
Montana State U (MT)
Morrisville State Coll (NY)
New Mexico State U (NM)
North Carolina Ag and Tech State U (NC)
North Carolina State U (NC)
North Dakota State U (ND)
Northwest Missouri State U (MO)
The Ohio State U (OH)
Oklahoma State U (OK)
Oregon State U (OR)
Penn State Abington (PA)
Penn State Altoona (PA)
Penn State Beaver (PA)
Penn State Berks (PA)
Penn State Brandywine (PA)
Penn State DuBois (PA)
Penn State Erie, The Behrend Coll (PA)
Penn State Fayette, The Eberly Campus (PA)
Penn State Greater Allegheny (PA)
Penn State Hazleton (PA)
Penn State Lehigh Valley (PA)
Penn State Mont Alto (PA)
Penn State New Kensington (PA)
Penn State Schuylkill (PA)
Penn State Shenango (PA)
Penn State U Park (PA)
Penn State Wilkes-Barre (PA)
Penn State Worthington Scranton (PA)
Penn State York (PA)
Purdue U (IN)
Rutgers, The State U of New Jersey, New Brunswick (NJ)
Sam Houston State U (TX)
South Dakota State U (SD)
Southeast Missouri State U (MO)
Southern Illinois U Carbondale (IL)
State U of New York Coll of Environmental Science and Forestry (NY)
Stephen F. Austin State U (TX)
Tarleton State U (TX)
Tennessee State U (TN)
Texas A&M U (TX)
Texas A&M U–Commerce (TX)
Texas A&M U–Kingsville (TX)
Texas State U (TX)
Texas Tech U (TX)
U of Alberta (AB, Canada)
The U of Arizona (AZ)
U of Arkansas (AR)
The U of British Columbia (BC, Canada)
U of California, Davis (CA)
U of Delaware (DE)
U of Denver (CO)
The U of Findlay (OH)
U of Florida (FL)
U of Georgia (GA)
U of Guelph (ON, Canada)
U of Hawaii at Hilo (HI)
U of Hawaii at Manoa (HI)
U of Idaho (ID)
U of Kentucky (KY)
U of Maine (ME)
U of Maryland, Coll Park (MD)
U of Massachusetts Amherst (MA)
U of Minnesota, Crookston (MN)
U of Minnesota, Twin Cities Campus (MN)
U of Missouri (MO)
U of Nebraska–Lincoln (NE)
U of New Hampshire (NH)
U of Rhode Island (RI)
U of Saskatchewan (SK, Canada)
The U of Tennessee (TN)
The U of Tennessee at Martin (TN)
U of Vermont (VT)
U of Wisconsin–Madison (WI)
U of Wisconsin–Platteville (WI)
U of Wisconsin–River Falls (WI)
U of Wyoming (WY)
Utah State U (UT)
Virginia Polytechnic Inst and State U (VA)
Washington State U (WA)
West Texas A&M U (TX)
West Virginia U (WV)

ANIMAL SCIENCES RELATED
Dalhousie U (NS, Canada)
North Carolina Ag and Tech State U (NC)
Penn State Abington (PA)
Penn State Beaver (PA)
Penn State Brandywine (PA)
Penn State DuBois (PA)
Penn State Erie, The Behrend Coll (PA)
Penn State Fayette, The Eberly Campus (PA)
Penn State Greater Allegheny (PA)
Penn State Hazleton (PA)
Penn State Lehigh Valley (PA)
Penn State Mont Alto (PA)
Penn State New Kensington (PA)
Penn State Schuylkill (PA)
Penn State Shenango (PA)
Penn State Wilkes-Barre (PA)
Penn State Worthington Scranton (PA)
Penn State York (PA)
U of California, Davis (CA)

ANIMATION, INTERACTIVE TECHNOLOGY, VIDEO GRAPHICS AND SPECIAL EFFECTS
Acad of Art U (CA)
American Acad of Art (IL)
Art Center Coll of Design (CA)
Becker Coll (MA)
Bennington Coll (VT)
Bradley U (IL)
Brigham Young U (UT)
California Coll of the Arts (CA)
Cleveland Inst of Art (OH)
Cogswell Polytechnical Coll (CA)
Coll for Creative Studies (MI)
Coll of the Atlantic (ME)
Concordia U (QC, Canada)
Davenport U, Grand Rapids (MI)
DePaul U (IL)
DigiPen Inst of Technology (WA)
Eastern Michigan U (MI)
East Tennessee State U (TN)
Emily Carr U of Art + Design (BC, Canada)
Fashion Inst of Technology (NY)
Florida State Coll at Jacksonville (FL)
George Mason U (VA)
Kansas City Art Inst (MO)
Laguna Coll of Art & Design (CA)
Loyola Marymount U (CA)
Massachusetts Coll of Art and Design (MA)
Missouri Western State U (MO)
New England Inst of Technology (RI)
New Mexico State U (NM)
North Central Coll (IL)
Northeastern U (MA)
Pacific Northwest Coll of Art (OR)
Pennsylvania Coll of Art & Design (PA)
Regent U (VA)
Ringling Coll of Art and Design (FL)
Rochester Inst of Technology (NY)
Rocky Mountain Coll of Art + Design (CO)
Sam Houston State U (TX)
Savannah Coll of Art and Design (GA)
School of the Art Inst of Chicago (IL)
State U of New York Coll of Technology at Alfred (NY)
Sullivan Coll of Technology and Design (KY)
U of Arkansas–Fort Smith (AR)
U of Dubuque (IA)
U of Lethbridge (AB, Canada)
U of Northwestern–St. Paul (MN)
The U of the Arts (PA)
U of the Incarnate Word (TX)
Villa Maria Coll (NY)
Webster U (MO)

ANTHROPOLOGY
Adelphi U (NY)
Agnes Scott Coll (GA)
Albion Coll (MI)
Alma Coll (MI)
American U (DC)
The American U in Cairo (Egypt)
Amherst Coll (MA)
Antioch Coll, Yellow Springs (OH)
Appalachian State U (NC)
Arizona State U at the Tempe campus (AZ)
Auburn U (AL)
Augustana Coll (IL)
Augustana Coll (SD)
Ball State U (IN)
Bard Coll (NY)
Barnard Coll (NY)
Bates Coll (ME)
Baylor U (TX)
Beloit Coll (WI)
Bennington Coll (VT)
Binghamton U, State U of New York (NY)
Biola U (CA)
Bloomsburg U of Pennsylvania (PA)
Boston U (MA)
Bowdoin Coll (ME)
Brandeis U (MA)
Bridgewater State U (MA)
Brown U (RI)
Bryn Mawr Coll (PA)
Bucknell U (PA)
Buffalo State Coll, State U of New York (NY)
Butler U (IN)
California State Polytechnic U, Pomona (CA)
California State U, Chico (CA)
California State U, Dominguez Hills (CA)
California State U, Fresno (CA)
California State U, Fullerton (CA)
California State U, Long Beach (CA)
California State U, Los Angeles (CA)
California State U, Sacramento (CA)
California State U, San Bernardino (CA)
California State U, San Marcos (CA)
California State U, Stanislaus (CA)
California U of Pennsylvania (PA)
Canisius Coll (NY)
Cape Breton U (NS, Canada)
Carleton Coll (MN)
Case Western Reserve U (OH)
The Catholic U of America (DC)
Central Coll (IA)
Central Connecticut State U (CT)
Central Michigan U (MI)
Central Washington U (WA)
City Coll of the City U of New York (NY)
Clarion U of Pennsylvania (PA)
Cleveland State U (OH)
Colby Coll (ME)
The Coll at Brockport, State U of New York (NY)
Coll of Charleston (SC)
The Coll of Idaho (ID)
Coll of the Holy Cross (MA)
The Coll of William and Mary (VA)
The Coll of Wooster (OH)
The Colorado Coll (CO)
Colorado State U (CO)
Columbia U (NY)
Columbia U, School of General Studies (NY)
Concordia U (QC, Canada)
Connecticut Coll (CT)
Cornell Coll (IA)
Cornell U (NY)
Creighton U (NE)
Dalhousie U (NS, Canada)
Dartmouth Coll (NH)
Davidson Coll (NC)
Denison U (OH)
DePaul U (IL)
DePauw U (IN)
Dickinson Coll (PA)
Drake U (IA)
Drew U (NJ)
Drexel U (PA)
Earlham Coll (IN)
East Carolina U (NC)
Eastern Kentucky U (KY)
Eastern Michigan U (MI)
Eastern New Mexico U (NM)
East Tennessee State U (TN)
Eckerd Coll (FL)
Edinboro U of Pennsylvania (PA)
Elon U (NC)
Florida Atlantic U (FL)
Florida Gulf Coast U (FL)
Fordham U (NY)
Fort Lewis Coll (CO)
Franciscan U of Steubenville (OH)
Franklin & Marshall Coll (PA)
Franklin Pierce U (NH)
Furman U (SC)
George Mason U (VA)
Georgetown U (DC)
The George Washington U (DC)
Georgia Regents U (GA)
Georgia Southern U (GA)
Georgia State U (GA)
Gettysburg Coll (PA)
Grand Valley State U (MI)
Grinnell Coll (IA)
Gustavus Adolphus Coll (MN)
Hamilton Coll (NY)
Hamline U (MN)
Hampshire Coll (MA)
Hanover Coll (IN)
Hartwick Coll (NY)
Harvard U (MA)
Haverford Coll (PA)
Hawai`i Pacific U (HI)
Hendrix Coll (AR)
Hobart and William Smith Colls (NY)
Hofstra U (NY)
Howard U (DC)
Humboldt State U (CA)
Hunter Coll of the City U of New York (NY)
Illinois State U (IL)
Illinois Wesleyan U (IL)
Indiana U Bloomington (IN)
Indiana U Northwest (IN)
Indiana U of Pennsylvania (PA)
Indiana U–Purdue U Fort Wayne (IN)
Indiana U–Purdue U Indianapolis (IN)
Indiana U South Bend (IN)
Inter American U of Puerto Rico, San Germán Campus (PR)
Iowa State U of Science and Technology (IA)
Ithaca Coll (NY)
Jacksonville State U (AL)
James Madison U (VA)
Johns Hopkins U (MD)
Johnson State Coll (VT)
Juniata Coll (PA)
Kansas State U (KS)
Kennesaw State U (GA)
Kent State U (OH)
Kenyon Coll (OH)
Knox Coll (IL)
Kutztown U of Pennsylvania (PA)
Lafayette Coll (PA)
Lake Forest Coll (IL)
Lawrence U (WI)
Lee U (TN)
Lehigh U (PA)
Lehman Coll of the City U of New York (NY)
Lincoln U (PA)
Lindenwood U (MO)
Linfield Coll (OR)
Longwood U (VA)
Louisiana State U and A&M Coll (LA)
Loyola U Chicago (IL)
Luther Coll (IA)
Macalester Coll (MN)
Mansfield U of Pennsylvania (PA)
Marquette U (WI)
Massachusetts Inst of Technology (MA)
Miami U (OH)
Michigan State U (MI)
Michigan Technological U (MI)
Middle Tennessee State U (TN)
Millersville U of Pennsylvania (PA)
Mills Coll (CA)
Minnesota State U Mankato (MN)
Minnesota State U Moorhead (MN)
Mississippi State U (MS)
Missouri State U (MO)
Monmouth Coll (IL)
Monmouth U (NJ)
Montana State U (MT)
Montclair State U (NJ)
Mount Allison U (NB, Canada)
Mount Holyoke Coll (MA)
Muhlenberg Coll (PA)
Nazareth Coll of Rochester (NY)
New Coll of Florida (FL)
New Mexico State U (NM)
New York U (NY)
North Carolina State U (NC)
North Central Coll (IL)
North Dakota State U (ND)
Northeastern Illinois U (IL)
Northern Arizona U (AZ)
Northern Illinois U (IL)
Northern Kentucky U (KY)
Northwestern U (IL)
Oakland U (MI)
Oberlin Coll (OH)
The Ohio State U (OH)
Ohio U (OH)
Oklahoma Baptist U (OK)
Oregon State U (OR)
Pacific Lutheran U (WA)
Penn State Abington (PA)
Penn State Altoona (PA)
Penn State Beaver (PA)
Penn State Berks (PA)
Penn State Brandywine (PA)
Penn State DuBois (PA)
Penn State Erie, The Behrend Coll (PA)
Penn State Fayette, The Eberly Campus (PA)
Penn State Greater Allegheny (PA)
Penn State Hazleton (PA)
Penn State Lehigh Valley (PA)
Penn State Mont Alto (PA)
Penn State New Kensington (PA)
Penn State Schuylkill (PA)
Penn State Shenango (PA)
Penn State U Park (PA)
Penn State Wilkes-Barre (PA)
Penn State Worthington Scranton (PA)
Penn State York (PA)
Pomona Coll (CA)
Portland State U (OR)
Princeton U (NJ)
Principia Coll (IL)
Purchase Coll, State U of New York (NY)
Purdue U (IN)
Queens Coll of the City U of New York (NY)
Radford U (VA)
Reed Coll (OR)
Rhode Island Coll (RI)
Rhodes Coll (TN)
Rice U (TX)
Ripon Coll (WI)
Rockford U (IL)
Rollins Coll (FL)
Rutgers, The State U of New Jersey, Newark (NJ)
Rutgers, The State U of New Jersey, New Brunswick (NJ)
Saint Francis U (PA)
St. John Fisher Coll (NY)
St. John's U (NY)
Saint Louis U (MO)
Saint Martin's U (WA)
St. Mary's Coll of Maryland (MD)

St. Thomas U (NB, Canada)
Saint Vincent Coll (PA)
San Diego State U (CA)
San Francisco State U (CA)
San Jose State U (CA)
Santa Clara U (CA)
Sarah Lawrence Coll (NY)
Scripps Coll (CA)
Seattle U (WA)
Sewanee: The U of the South (TN)
Skidmore Coll (NY)
Smith Coll (MA)
Southern Connecticut State U (CT)
Southern Illinois U Carbondale (IL)
Southern Illinois U Edwardsville (IL)
Southern Methodist U (TX)
Southern Oregon U (OR)
Southwestern U (TX)
Stanford U (CA)
State U of New York at New Paltz (NY)
State U of New York at Oswego (NY)
State U of New York at Plattsburgh (NY)
State U of New York Coll at Cortland (NY)
State U of New York Coll at Geneseo (NY)
State U of New York Coll at Potsdam (NY)
Stony Brook U, State U of New York (NY)
Susquehanna U (PA)
Syracuse U (NY)
Temple U (PA)
Texas A&M U (TX)
Texas Christian U (TX)
Texas State U (TX)
Texas Tech U (TX)
Transylvania U (KY)
Trent U (ON, Canada)
Trinity Coll (CT)
Trinity U (TX)
Troy U (AL)
Tufts U (MA)
Tulane U (LA)
Union Coll (NY)
Université de Montréal (QC, Canada)
U at Albany, State U of New York (NY)
U at Buffalo, the State U of New York (NY)
The U of Akron (OH)
The U of Alabama (AL)
The U of Alabama at Birmingham (AL)
U of Alaska Fairbanks (AK)
U of Alberta (AB, Canada)
The U of Arizona (AZ)
U of Arkansas (AR)
U of Arkansas at Little Rock (AR)
The U of British Columbia (BC, Canada)
The U of British Columbia–Okanagan Campus (BC, Canada)
U of California, Berkeley (CA)
U of California, Davis (CA)
U of California, Irvine (CA)
U of California, Los Angeles (CA)
U of California, Merced (CA)
U of California, Riverside (CA)
U of California, Santa Barbara (CA)
U of California, Santa Cruz (CA)
U of Central Florida (FL)
U of Chicago (IL)
U of Colorado Boulder (CO)
U of Colorado Colorado Springs (CO)
U of Colorado Denver (CO)
U of Delaware (DE)
U of Denver (CO)
U of Florida (FL)
U of Georgia (GA)
U of Guam (GU)
U of Guelph (ON, Canada)
U of Hawaii at Hilo (HI)
U of Hawaii at Manoa (HI)
U of Hawaii–West Oahu (HI)
U of Houston (TX)
U of Houston–Clear Lake (TX)
U of Idaho (ID)
U of Illinois at Chicago (IL)
U of Indianapolis (IN)
The U of Iowa (IA)
The U of Kansas (KS)
U of Kentucky (KY)
U of King's Coll (NS, Canada)
U of La Verne (CA)
U of Lethbridge (AB, Canada)
U of Louisiana at Lafayette (LA)
U of Louisville (KY)
U of Maine (ME)
U of Maryland, Baltimore County (MD)
U of Maryland, Coll Park (MD)
U of Mary Washington (VA)
U of Massachusetts Amherst (MA)
U of Massachusetts Boston (MA)
U of Memphis (TN)
U of Miami (FL)
U of Michigan (MI)
U of Michigan–Dearborn (MI)
U of Michigan–Flint (MI)
U of Minnesota, Duluth (MN)
U of Minnesota, Morris (MN)
U of Minnesota, Twin Cities Campus (MN)
U of Mississippi (MS)
U of Missouri (MO)
U of Missouri–St. Louis (MO)
The U of Montana (MT)
U of Nebraska–Lincoln (NE)
U of Nevada, Las Vegas (NV)
U of Nevada, Reno (NV)
U of New Hampshire (NH)
U of New Mexico (NM)
U of New Orleans (LA)
The U of North Carolina at Chapel Hill (NC)
The U of North Carolina at Charlotte (NC)
The U of North Carolina at Greensboro (NC)
The U of North Carolina Wilmington (NC)
U of North Dakota (ND)
U of Northern Colorado (CO)
U of Northern Iowa (IA)
U of North Florida (FL)
U of North Texas (TX)
U of Notre Dame (IN)
U of Oklahoma (OK)
U of Oregon (OR)
U of Ottawa (ON, Canada)
U of Pennsylvania (PA)
U of Pittsburgh (PA)
U of Pittsburgh at Greensburg (PA)
U of Regina (SK, Canada)
U of Rhode Island (RI)
U of Richmond (VA)
U of Rochester (NY)
U of San Diego (CA)
U of Saskatchewan (SK, Canada)
U of South Alabama (AL)
The U of South Dakota (SD)
U of Southern California (CA)
U of Southern Indiana (IN)
U of Southern Mississippi (MS)
U of South Florida (FL)
U of South Florida, St. Petersburg (FL)
The U of Tennessee (TN)
The U of Texas at Arlington (TX)
The U of Texas at Austin (TX)
The U of Texas at El Paso (TX)
The U of Texas at San Antonio (TX)
The U of Texas–Pan American (TX)
U of the District of Columbia (DC)
U of the Fraser Valley (BC, Canada)
The U of Toledo (OH)
U of Toronto (ON, Canada)
The U of Tulsa (OK)
U of Utah (UT)
U of Vermont (VT)
U of Virginia (VA)
U of Washington (WA)
U of Waterloo (ON, Canada)
The U of Western Ontario (ON, Canada)
U of West Florida (FL)
U of West Georgia (GA)
U of Wisconsin–Madison (WI)
U of Wisconsin–Milwaukee (WI)
U of Wisconsin–Oshkosh (WI)
U of Wyoming (WY)
Ursinus Coll (PA)
Utah State U (UT)
Vanderbilt U (TN)
Vanguard U of Southern California (CA)
Vassar Coll (NY)
Virginia Commonwealth U (VA)
Wagner Coll (NY)
Wake Forest U (NC)
Washburn U (KS)
Washington Coll (MD)
Washington State U (WA)
Washington State U Vancouver (WA)
Washington U in St. Louis (MO)
Wayne State U (MI)
Weber State U (UT)
Wells Coll (NY)
Wesleyan U (CT)
West Chester U of Pennsylvania (PA)
Western Carolina U (NC)
Western Illinois U (IL)
Western Kentucky U (KY)
Western Michigan U (MI)
Western Oregon U (OR)
Western State Colorado U (CO)
Western Washington U (WA)
Westminster Coll (MO)
Wheaton Coll (IL)
Wheaton Coll (MA)
Whitman Coll (WA)
Whittier Coll (CA)
Wichita State U (KS)
Widener U (PA)
Willamette U (OR)
William Paterson U of New Jersey (NJ)
William Peace U (NC)
Williams Coll (MA)
Wright State U (OH)
Yale U (CT)
York Coll of the City U of New York (NY)
Youngstown State U (OH)

ANTHROPOLOGY RELATED
Bridgewater State U (MA)
California Baptist U (CA)
Mary Baldwin Coll (VA)
U of Michigan (MI)
The U of Western Ontario (ON, Canada)
Ursinus Coll (PA)
Western Washington U (WA)

APPAREL AND ACCESSORIES MARKETING
Philadelphia U (PA)
Stephens Coll (MO)
U of Central Oklahoma (OK)
U of Rhode Island (RI)

APPAREL AND TEXTILE MANUFACTURING
Fashion Inst of Technology (NY)
FIDM/Fashion Inst of Design & Merchandising, Los Angeles Campus (CA)
Michigan State U (MI)

APPAREL AND TEXTILE MARKETING MANAGEMENT
Auburn U (AL)
Central Washington U (WA)
Colorado State U (CO)
Northwest Missouri State U (MO)
Savannah Coll of Art and Design (GA)
South Dakota State U (SD)
U of Nebraska–Lincoln (NE)
U of the Incarnate Word (TX)
Wayne State U (MI)

APPAREL AND TEXTILES
Appalachian State U (NC)
Auburn U (AL)
Bowling Green State U (OH)
California State Polytechnic U, Pomona (CA)
California State U, Long Beach (CA)
Cornell U (NY)
Delaware State U (DE)
East Carolina U (NC)
Framingham State U (MA)
Georgia Southern U (GA)
Indiana State U (IN)
Indiana U Bloomington (IN)
Iowa State U of Science and Technology (IA)
Jacksonville State U (AL)
Kansas State U (KS)
Lamar U (TX)
Liberty U (VA)
Lipscomb U (TN)
Michigan State U (MI)
Middle Tennessee State U (TN)
Missouri State U (MO)
New Mexico State U (NM)
North Carolina Ag and Tech State U (NC)
North Dakota State U (ND)
Northern Illinois U (IL)
The Ohio State U (OH)
Ohio U (OH)
Oregon State U (OR)
Philadelphia U (PA)
Rhode Island School of Design (RI)
Seattle Pacific U (WA)
South Dakota State U (SD)
Southern Illinois U Carbondale (IL)
The U of Akron (OH)
The U of Alabama (AL)
U of Alberta (AB, Canada)
U of Arkansas (AR)
U of California, Davis (CA)
U of Central Missouri (MO)
U of Central Oklahoma (OK)
U of Delaware (DE)
U of Hawaii at Manoa (HI)
U of Idaho (ID)
U of Kentucky (KY)
U of Minnesota, Twin Cities Campus (MN)
U of Missouri (MO)
U of Nebraska–Lincoln (NE)
The U of North Carolina at Greensboro (NC)
U of Northern Iowa (IA)
U of Rhode Island (RI)
U of Southern Mississippi (MS)
The U of Texas at Austin (TX)
U of Wisconsin–Madison (WI)
U of Wisconsin–Stout (WI)
Virginia Polytechnic Inst and State U (VA)
Washington State U (WA)
Western Kentucky U (KY)
Western Michigan U (MI)

APPAREL AND TEXTILES RELATED
Savannah Coll of Art and Design (GA)
Stephens Coll (MO)
U of Alberta (AB, Canada)

APPLIED AND PROFESSIONAL ETHICS
Mount Saint Mary's U (CA)
Nazarene Bible Coll (CO)
Simpson Coll (IA)
U of Michigan–Flint (MI)
Ursinus Coll (PA)
Western Michigan U (MI)

APPLIED BEHAVIOR ANALYSIS
Averett U (VA)
Florida Inst of Technology (FL)
Saint Joseph's U (PA)
U of North Texas (TX)
Western Michigan U (MI)

APPLIED ECONOMICS
Allegheny Coll (PA)
Augsburg Coll (MN)
Binghamton U, State U of New York (NY)
Brigham Young U (UT)
Bryant U (RI)
The Coll of St. Scholastica (MN)
Concordia U (QC, Canada)
Cornell U (NY)
Farmingdale State Coll (NY)
Flagler Coll (FL)
HEC Montreal (QC, Canada)
Illinois Inst of Technology (IL)
Ithaca Coll (NY)
Penn State Abington (PA)
Penn State Beaver (PA)
Penn State Brandywine (PA)
Penn State DuBois (PA)
Penn State Erie, The Behrend Coll (PA)
Penn State Fayette, The Eberly Campus (PA)
Penn State Greater Allegheny (PA)
Penn State Hazleton (PA)
Penn State Lehigh Valley (PA)
Penn State Mont Alto (PA)
Penn State New Kensington (PA)
Penn State Schuylkill (PA)
Penn State Shenango (PA)
Penn State Wilkes-Barre (PA)
Penn State Worthington Scranton (PA)
Penn State York (PA)
The U of Akron (OH)
The U of Arizona (AZ)
U of Central Oklahoma (OK)
U of Minnesota, Twin Cities Campus (MN)
U of Northern Iowa (IA)
U of Rhode Island (RI)
U of San Francisco (CA)
U of Waterloo (ON, Canada)
Ursinus Coll (PA)

APPLIED HORTICULTURE/ HORTICULTURAL BUSINESS SERVICES RELATED
Morrisville State Coll (NY)
North Dakota State U (ND)
U of Rhode Island (RI)

APPLIED HORTICULTURE/ HORTICULTURE OPERATIONS
Colorado State U (CO)
Farmingdale State Coll (NY)
Ferrum Coll (VA)
Iowa State U of Science and Technology (IA)
Kent State U at Salem (OH)
South Dakota State U (SD)
Texas A&M U (TX)
Texas Tech U (TX)
U of Georgia (GA)
U of Maine (ME)
U of Massachusetts Amherst (MA)

APPLIED LINGUISTICS
Mid-Atlantic Christian U (NC)
Portland State U (OR)

APPLIED MATHEMATICS
American U (DC)
American U of Beirut (Lebanon)
Arizona State U at the West campus (AZ)
Auburn U (AL)
Augustana Coll (IL)
Bard Coll at Simon's Rock (MA)
Baylor U (TX)
Belmont U (TN)
Biola U (CA)
Bloomfield Coll (NJ)
Bowie State U (MD)
Brown U (RI)
Bryant U (RI)
California State U, Fullerton (CA)
California State U, Long Beach (CA)
Carroll Coll (MT)
Case Western Reserve U (OH)
Central Michigan U (MI)
Charleston Southern U (SC)
Christopher Newport U (VA)
Clarkson U (NY)
Coastal Carolina U (SC)
The Coll of Idaho (ID)
Columbia U (NY)
Columbia U, School of General Studies (NY)
Concordia U, St. Paul (MN)
Creighton U (NE)
Dowling Coll (NY)
East Central U (OK)
Elon U (NC)
Endicott Coll (MA)
Farmingdale State Coll (NY)
Ferris State U (MI)
Fitchburg State U (MA)
Florida Inst of Technology (FL)
Geneva Coll (PA)
The George Washington U (DC)
Georgia Inst of Technology (GA)
Grand View U (IA)
Hampden-Sydney Coll (VA)
Harvard U (MA)
Hawai`i Pacific U (HI)
Humboldt State U (CA)
Illinois Inst of Technology (IL)
Indiana U South Bend (IN)
Inter American U of Puerto Rico, San Germán Campus (PR)
Iona Coll (NY)
Johns Hopkins U (MD)

Kent State U (OH)
Kettering U (MI)
La Salle U (PA)
Lasell Coll (MA)
Lehigh U (PA)
Lipscomb U (TN)
Long Island U–LIU Post (NY)
Loyola Marymount U (CA)
Marist Coll (NY)
Mary Baldwin Coll (VA)
Maryville U of Saint Louis (MO)
The Master's Coll and Sem (CA)
Metropolitan State U (MN)
Millsaps Coll (MS)
Missouri U of Science and Technology (MO)
Mount Allison U (NB, Canada)
New Coll of Florida (FL)
New Jersey Inst of Technology (NJ)
New York City Coll of Technology of the City U of New York (NY)
North Carolina Ag and Tech State U (NC)
North Carolina State U (NC)
North Central Coll (IL)
Northern Illinois U (IL)
Northwestern U (IL)
Oakland City U (IN)
Ohio U (OH)
Penn State Harrisburg (PA)
Purdue U (IN)
Quinnipiac U (CT)
Rice U (TX)
Robert Morris U (PA)
Rutgers, The State U of New Jersey, Newark (NJ)
Saginaw Valley State U (MI)
St. Thomas Aquinas Coll (NY)
San Diego State U (CA)
San Francisco State U (CA)
San Jose State U (CA)
Siena Heights U (MI)
Simon Fraser U (BC, Canada)
State U of New York at Oswego (NY)
State U of New York Polytechnic Inst (NY)
Stevenson U (MD)
Stony Brook U, State U of New York (NY)
Syracuse U (NY)
Temple U (PA)
Texas A&M U (TX)
Texas State U (TX)
Trent U (ON, Canada)
Trevecca Nazarene U (TN)
Tufts U (MA)
Universidad Metropolitana (PR)
Université de Montréal (QC, Canada)
U at Albany, State U of New York (NY)
U at Buffalo, the State U of New York (NY)
The U of Akron (OH)
U of Alberta (AB, Canada)
The U of British Columbia (BC, Canada)
U of California, Berkeley (CA)
U of California, Davis (CA)
U of California, Los Angeles (CA)
U of California, Merced (CA)
U of Central Oklahoma (OK)
U of Colorado Boulder (CO)
U of Colorado Colorado Springs (CO)
U of Houston–Downtown (TX)
U of Idaho (ID)
The U of Iowa (IA)
U of Jamestown (ND)
U of Massachusetts Lowell (MA)
U of Miami (FL)
The U of Montana (MT)
U of New Haven (CT)
The U of North Carolina at Chapel Hill (NC)
U of Northern Iowa (IA)
U of North Florida (FL)
U of Pittsburgh (PA)
U of Pittsburgh at Bradford (PA)
U of Pittsburgh at Greensburg (PA)
U of Rochester (NY)
U of South Carolina Aiken (SC)
The U of Tennessee at Chattanooga (TN)
The U of Texas at El Paso (TX)
U of the Virgin Islands (VI)
U of Toronto (ON, Canada)
The U of Tulsa (OK)
U of Utah (UT)
U of Waterloo (ON, Canada)
The U of Western Ontario (ON, Canada)
U of Windsor (ON, Canada)
U of Wisconsin–Madison (WI)
U of Wisconsin–Milwaukee (WI)
U of Wisconsin–Stout (WI)
Valdosta State U (GA)
Washington State U (WA)
Washington U in St. Louis (MO)
Weber State U (UT)
Wentworth Inst of Technology (MA)
Western Michigan U (MI)
Western Washington U (WA)
Wheaton Coll (IL)
William Paterson U of New Jersey (NJ)
William Penn U (IA)
Worcester Polytechnic Inst (MA)
Yale U (CT)

APPLIED MATHEMATICS RELATED
Arizona State U at the Tempe campus (AZ)
Averett U (VA)
Belmont U (TN)
Berea Coll (KY)
Bucknell U (PA)
DePaul U (IL)
Elizabethtown Coll (PA)
Georgia Inst of Technology (GA)
Inter American U of Puerto Rico, Bayamón Campus (PR)
Keene State Coll (NH)
Lycoming Coll (PA)
Temple U (PA)
U of Alberta (AB, Canada)
U of California, Santa Barbara (CA)
U of the District of Columbia (DC)
U of Washington (WA)
U of Waterloo (ON, Canada)
U of Wisconsin–Milwaukee (WI)
Willamette U (OR)

APPLIED PSYCHOLOGY
Arizona State U at the Polytechnic campus (AZ)
Belhaven U (MS)
Bryant U (RI)
Christian Brothers U (TN)
Columbia Coll (SC)
Farmingdale State Coll (NY)
Franklin U (OH)
Judson U (IL)
Kansas Wesleyan U (KS)
Loyola U Chicago (IL)
Morrisville State Coll (NY)
Mount Saint Mary's U (CA)
New York U (NY)
Pace U (NY)
Palo Alto U (CA)
State U of New York Coll of Technology at Canton (NY)
U of Michigan–Flint (MI)

AQUACULTURE
Auburn U (AL)
Cheyney U of Pennsylvania (PA)
Dalhousie U (NS, Canada)
U of New England (ME)

AQUATIC BIOLOGY/ LIMNOLOGY
Florida Inst of Technology (FL)
Gannon U (PA)
State U of New York Coll of Environmental Science and Forestry (NY)
Stetson U (FL)
Texas State U (TX)

ARABIC
American U (DC)
American U of Beirut (Lebanon)
Bard Coll (NY)
Baylor U (TX)
Binghamton U, State U of New York (NY)
California U of Pennsylvania (PA)
Dartmouth Coll (NH)
DePaul U (IL)
Georgetown U (DC)
Lebanese American U (Lebanon)
Michigan State U (MI)
Middlebury Coll (VT)
National U (CA)
The Ohio State U (OH)
Portland State U (OR)
Tufts U (MA)
United States Military Acad (NY)
United States Naval Acad (MD)
U of California, Los Angeles (CA)
U of Cincinnati (OH)
U of Georgia (GA)
U of Maryland, Coll Park (MD)
U of Minnesota, Twin Cities Campus (MN)
U of Notre Dame (IN)
U of Oklahoma (OK)
U of Ottawa (ON, Canada)
The U of Texas at Austin (TX)
U of Toronto (ON, Canada)
U of Utah (UT)
Washington U in St. Louis (MO)
Western Kentucky U (KY)

ARCHEOLOGY
The American U in Cairo (Egypt)
American U of Beirut (Lebanon)
The American U of Rome (Italy)
Biola U (CA)
Boston U (MA)
Bowdoin Coll (ME)
Bridgewater State U (MA)
Brown U (RI)
Bryn Mawr Coll (PA)
Coll of Charleston (SC)
The Coll of Wooster (OH)
Columbia U (NY)
Columbia U, School of General Studies (NY)
Cornell Coll (IA)
Cornell U (NY)
Dartmouth Coll (NH)
Dickinson Coll (PA)
Franklin Pierce U (NH)
The George Washington U (DC)
Hamilton Coll (NY)
Haverford Coll (PA)
Hunter Coll of the City U of New York (NY)
Johns Hopkins U (MD)
Lawrence U (WI)
New York U (NY)
Oberlin Coll (OH)
Penn State Abington (PA)
Penn State Altoona (PA)
Penn State Beaver (PA)
Penn State Berks (PA)
Penn State Brandywine (PA)
Penn State DuBois (PA)
Penn State Erie, The Behrend Coll (PA)
Penn State Fayette, The Eberly Campus (PA)
Penn State Greater Allegheny (PA)
Penn State Hazleton (PA)
Penn State Lehigh Valley (PA)
Penn State Mont Alto (PA)
Penn State New Kensington (PA)
Penn State Schuylkill (PA)
Penn State Shenango (PA)
Penn State U Park (PA)
Penn State Wilkes-Barre (PA)
Penn State Worthington Scranton (PA)
Penn State York (PA)
Simon Fraser U (BC, Canada)
Southern Adventist U (TN)
Stanford U (CA)
State U of New York Coll at Potsdam (NY)
Tufts U (MA)
Université de Montréal (QC, Canada)
The U of British Columbia (BC, Canada)
U of Cincinnati (OH)
U of Evansville (IN)
U of Indianapolis (IN)
U of Lethbridge (AB, Canada)
U of Missouri (MO)
The U of North Carolina at Chapel Hill (NC)
U of Saskatchewan (SK, Canada)
U of Southern California (CA)
The U of Texas at Austin (TX)
U of Toronto (ON, Canada)
U of Wisconsin–La Crosse (WI)
Washington State U (WA)
Washington U in St. Louis (MO)
Wesleyan U (CT)
Western Washington U (WA)
Wheaton Coll (IL)
Yale U (CT)

ARCHITECTURAL AND BUILDING SCIENCES
Georgia Inst of Technology (GA)
Pennsylvania Coll of Technology (PA)

ARCHITECTURAL ENGINEERING
Andrews U (MI)
Auburn U (AL)
California Polytechnic State U, San Luis Obispo (CA)
Drexel U (PA)
Illinois Inst of Technology (IL)
Kansas State U (KS)
Lawrence Technological U (MI)
Milwaukee School of Eng (WI)
Missouri U of Science and Technology (MO)
North Carolina Ag and Tech State U (NC)
Oklahoma State U (OK)
Penn State Abington (PA)
Penn State Altoona (PA)
Penn State Beaver (PA)
Penn State Berks (PA)
Penn State Brandywine (PA)
Penn State DuBois (PA)
Penn State Erie, The Behrend Coll (PA)
Penn State Fayette, The Eberly Campus (PA)
Penn State Greater Allegheny (PA)
Penn State Hazleton (PA)
Penn State Lehigh Valley (PA)
Penn State Mont Alto (PA)
Penn State New Kensington (PA)
Penn State Schuylkill (PA)
Penn State Shenango (PA)
Penn State U Park (PA)
Penn State Wilkes-Barre (PA)
Penn State Worthington Scranton (PA)
Penn State York (PA)
Rutgers, The State U of New Jersey, New Brunswick (NJ)
Tennessee State U (TN)
Texas A&M U–Kingsville (TX)
Tufts U (MA)
The U of Alabama (AL)
U of Cincinnati (OH)
U of Colorado Boulder (CO)
The U of Kansas (KS)
U of Miami (FL)
U of Nebraska–Lincoln (NE)
U of Oklahoma (OK)
The U of Texas at Austin (TX)
U of Wyoming (WY)
Worcester Polytechnic Inst (MA)

ARCHITECTURAL ENGINEERING TECHNOLOGY
Bluefield State Coll (WV)
Delaware State U (DE)
Farmingdale State Coll (NY)
Ferris State U (MI)
Fitchburg State U (MA)
Indiana U–Purdue U Indianapolis (IN)
New England Inst of Technology (RI)
Purdue U (IN)
Seminole State Coll of Florida (FL)
State U of New York Coll of Technology at Alfred (NY)
Texas Tech U (TX)
U of Hartford (CT)
U of Southern Mississippi (MS)
Vermont Tech Coll (VT)
Washington U in St. Louis (MO)

ARCHITECTURAL HISTORY AND CRITICISM
Brown U (RI)
Coll of the Holy Cross (MA)
Columbia U, School of General Studies (NY)
Cornell U (NY)
DePaul U (IL)
Lawrence Technological U (MI)
Savannah Coll of Art and Design (GA)
Syracuse U (NY)
The U of Kansas (KS)
U of Miami (FL)
U of San Diego (CA)
U of Virginia (VA)

ARCHITECTURAL TECHNOLOGY
Lawrence Technological U (MI)
New York City Coll of Technology of the City U of New York (NY)
New York Inst of Technology (NY)
U of Maine at Augusta (ME)
Washington U in St. Louis (MO)
Western Kentucky U (KY)

ARCHITECTURE
Acad of Art U (CA)
The American U in Dubai (United Arab Emirates)
American U of Beirut (Lebanon)
Andrews U (MI)
Arizona State U at the Tempe campus (AZ)
Auburn U (AL)
Ball State U (IN)
Barnard Coll (NY)
Bennington Coll (VT)
Boston Architectural Coll (MA)
California Coll of the Arts (CA)
California Polytechnic State U, San Luis Obispo (CA)
California State Polytechnic U, Pomona (CA)
The Catholic U of America (DC)
City Coll of the City U of New York (NY)
Columbia U (NY)
Columbia U, School of General Studies (NY)
Connecticut Coll (CT)
Cooper Union for the Advancement of Science and Art (NY)
Cornell Coll (IA)
Cornell U (NY)
Dalhousie U (NS, Canada)
Drexel U (PA)
Drury U (MO)
Florida Ag and Mech U (FL)
Florida Atlantic U (FL)
Georgia Inst of Technology (GA)
Hampshire Coll (MA)
Hampton U (VA)
Hobart and William Smith Colls (NY)
Howard U (DC)
Illinois Inst of Technology (IL)
Inter American U of Puerto Rico, San Germán Campus (PR)
Iowa State U of Science and Technology (IA)
Ithaca Coll (NY)
Judson U (IL)
Keene State Coll (NH)
Kent State U (OH)
Lawrence Technological U (MI)
Lebanese American U (Lebanon)
Lehigh U (PA)
Louisiana State U and A&M Coll (LA)
Marywood U (PA)
Massachusetts Coll of Art and Design (MA)
Massachusetts Inst of Technology (MA)
Miami U (OH)
Middlebury Coll (VT)
Mississippi State U (MS)
New Jersey Inst of Technology (NJ)
New York Inst of Technology (NY)
North Carolina State U (NC)
Northeastern U (MA)
Norwich U (VT)
The Ohio State U (OH)
Oklahoma State U (OK)
Penn State U Park (PA)
Philadelphia U (PA)
Polytechnic U of Puerto Rico (PR)
Portland State U (OR)
Prairie View A&M U (TX)
Pratt Inst (NY)
Princeton U (NJ)
Rensselaer Polytechnic Inst (NY)
Rhode Island School of Design (RI)
Rice U (TX)
Roger Williams U (RI)
Savannah Coll of Art and Design (GA)
Smith Coll (MA)
South Dakota State U (SD)

Southern California Inst of Architecture (CA)
Southern Illinois U Carbondale (IL)
State U of New York Coll of Technology at Alfred (NY)
Syracuse U (NY)
Temple U (PA)
Texas A&M U (TX)
Texas Tech U (TX)
Tulane U (LA)
Université de Montréal (QC, Canada)
U at Buffalo, the State U of New York (NY)
The U of Arizona (AZ)
U of Arkansas (AR)
U of California, Berkeley (CA)
U of California, Los Angeles (CA)
U of Central Florida (FL)
U of Cincinnati (OH)
U of Colorado Denver (CO)
U of Florida (FL)
U of Hawaii at Manoa (HI)
U of Houston (TX)
U of Idaho (ID)
U of Illinois at Chicago (IL)
The U of Kansas (KS)
U of Kentucky (KY)
U of Louisiana at Lafayette (LA)
U of Maryland, Coll Park (MD)
U of Massachusetts Amherst (MA)
U of Memphis (TN)
U of Miami (FL)
U of Michigan (MI)
U of Minnesota, Twin Cities Campus (MN)
U of Missouri–Kansas City (MO)
U of Nebraska–Lincoln (NE)
U of Nevada, Las Vegas (NV)
U of New Mexico (NM)
The U of North Carolina at Charlotte (NC)
U of Notre Dame (IN)
U of Oklahoma (OK)
U of Oregon (OR)
U of Pennsylvania (PA)
U of San Francisco (CA)
U of Southern California (CA)
The U of Tennessee (TN)
The U of Texas at Arlington (TX)
The U of Texas at Austin (TX)
The U of Texas at San Antonio (TX)
U of the District of Columbia (DC)
U of Toronto (ON, Canada)
U of Utah (UT)
U of Virginia (VA)
U of Washington (WA)
U of Waterloo (ON, Canada)
U of Wisconsin–Milwaukee (WI)
Virginia Polytechnic Inst and State U (VA)
Washington State U (WA)
Washington U in St. Louis (MO)
Wentworth Inst of Technology (MA)
Yale U (CT)

ARCHITECTURE RELATED

Case Western Reserve U (OH)
Columbia U (NY)
Lipscomb U (TN)
Mount Holyoke Coll (MA)
New Jersey Inst of Technology (NJ)
Northern Michigan U (MI)
School of the Art Inst of Chicago (IL)
State U of New York Coll of Technology at Delhi (NY)
The U of Arizona (AZ)
U of Illinois at Chicago (IL)
U of Louisiana at Lafayette (LA)
U of Minnesota, Twin Cities Campus (MN)
Washington U in St. Louis (MO)

AREA STUDIES RELATED

Appalachian State U (NC)
Augsburg Coll (MN)
Bridgewater State U (MA)
Castleton State Coll (VT)
Cornell U (NY)
Eastern Michigan U (MI)
Gannon U (PA)
Gettysburg Coll (PA)
Hofstra U (NY)
Illinois Wesleyan U (IL)
Lake Forest Coll (IL)
Lycoming Coll (PA)
Millersville U of Pennsylvania (PA)
New York U (NY)
Northeastern State U (OK)
Northwestern U (IL)
Ramapo Coll of New Jersey (NJ)
St. Francis Coll (NY)
Stanford U (CA)
State U of New York at Plattsburgh (NY)
U of Alaska Fairbanks (AK)
U of Alberta (AB, Canada)
U of California, Santa Barbara (CA)
U of Michigan–Dearborn (MI)
U of Minnesota, Twin Cities Campus (MN)
U of Oklahoma (OK)
U of Pittsburgh (PA)
U of Virginia (VA)
U of Washington (WA)
Utah State U (UT)
Virginia Commonwealth U (VA)
Washington U in St. Louis (MO)
Williams Coll (MA)

ARMY ROTC/MILITARY SCIENCE

Hampton U (VA)
Jacksonville State U (AL)
Jacksonville U (FL)
La Salle U (PA)
Minnesota State U Mankato (MN)
The U of Iowa (IA)
U of Minnesota, Twin Cities Campus (MN)

ARMY ROTC, MILITARY SCIENCE AND OPERATIONS RELATED

Calvary Bible Coll and Theological Sem (MO)
Western Kentucky U (KY)

ART

Alabama State U (AL)
Albany State U (GA)
Albertus Magnus Coll (CT)
Albion Coll (MI)
Albright Coll (PA)
Allegheny Coll (PA)
Alma Coll (MI)
Alverno Coll (WI)
American Acad of Art (IL)
The American U in Cairo (Egypt)
Anderson U (SC)
Andrews U (MI)
Appalachian State U (NC)
Aquinas Coll (MI)
Arcadia U (PA)
Arizona State U at the Tempe campus (AZ)
Arkansas State U (AR)
Arkansas Tech U (AR)
Armstrong State U (GA)
Athens State U (AL)
Auburn U at Montgomery (AL)
Augustana Coll (IL)
Augustana Coll (SD)
Austin Coll (TX)
Austin Peay State U (TN)
Averett U (VA)
Avila U (MO)
Baldwin Wallace U (OH)
Ball State U (IN)
Bard Coll (NY)
Bard Coll at Simon's Rock (MA)
Bates Coll (ME)
Baylor U (TX)
Belhaven U (MS)
Belmont U (TN)
Bemidji State U (MN)
Benedictine Coll (KS)
Berea Coll (KY)
Berry Coll (GA)
Bethany Lutheran Coll (MN)
Bethel Coll (IN)
Bethel U (MN)
Binghamton U, State U of New York (NY)
Biola U (CA)
Birmingham-Southern Coll (AL)
Blackburn Coll (IL)
Black Hills State U (SD)
Bluefield Coll (VA)
Bluffton U (OH)
Bowie State U (MD)
Bowling Green State U (OH)
Bradley U (IL)
Brown U (RI)
Bryn Mawr Coll (PA)
Bucknell U (PA)
Buena Vista U (IA)
Buffalo State Coll, State U of New York (NY)
Caldwell U (NJ)
California Coll of the Arts (CA)
California Lutheran U (CA)
California State Polytechnic U, Pomona (CA)
California State U, Chico (CA)
California State U, Dominguez Hills (CA)
California State U, Fresno (CA)
California State U, Fullerton (CA)
California State U, Long Beach (CA)
California State U, Los Angeles (CA)
California State U, Monterey Bay (CA)
California State U, Sacramento (CA)
California State U, San Bernardino (CA)
California State U, Stanislaus (CA)
California U of Pennsylvania (PA)
Calvin Coll (MI)
Cameron U (OK)
Campbellsville U (KY)
Capital U (OH)
Cardinal Stritch U (WI)
Carson-Newman U (TN)
Castleton State Coll (VT)
The Catholic U of America (DC)
Cedar Crest Coll (PA)
Centenary Coll of Louisiana (LA)
Central Coll (IA)
Central Connecticut State U (CT)
Central Michigan U (MI)
Central State U (OH)
Central Washington U (WA)
Chapman U (CA)
Cheyney U of Pennsylvania (PA)
Chicago State U (IL)
City Coll of the City U of New York (NY)
Claflin U (SC)
Clarion U of Pennsylvania (PA)
Clark Atlanta U (GA)
Clarke U (IA)
Cleveland State U (OH)
Coe Coll (IA)
Colby Coll (ME)
Colby-Sawyer Coll (NH)
The Coll at Brockport, State U of New York (NY)
The Coll of Idaho (ID)
The Coll of New Jersey (NJ)
Coll of Saint Benedict (MN)
Coll of Saint Elizabeth (NJ)
Coll of Saint Mary (NE)
The Coll of St. Scholastica (MN)
Coll of the Atlantic (ME)
The Coll of William and Mary (VA)
Colorado Mesa U (CO)
Columbia Coll (MO)
Columbia Coll (SC)
Columbia Coll Chicago (IL)
Concordia Coll (MN)
Concordia Coll–New York (NY)
Concordia U (CA)
Concordia U Chicago (IL)
Concordia U, Nebraska (NE)
Concordia U, St. Paul (MN)
Concordia U Wisconsin (WI)
Connecticut Coll (CT)
Cornell Coll (IA)
Cornish Coll of the Arts (WA)
Creighton U (NE)
Culver-Stockton Coll (MO)
Daemen Coll (NY)
Dallas Baptist U (TX)
Davidson Coll (NC)
Delaware State U (DE)
Denison U (OH)
DePaul U (IL)
Dickinson State U (ND)
Doane Coll (NE)
Dominican U of California (CA)
Drake U (IA)
Earlham Coll (IN)
East Central U (OK)
Eastern Connecticut State U (CT)
Eastern Illinois U (IL)
Eastern Kentucky U (KY)
Eastern Michigan U (MI)
Eastern New Mexico U (NM)
Eastern Oregon U (OR)
East Tennessee State U (TN)
Edgewood Coll (WI)
Edinboro U of Pennsylvania (PA)
Elmhurst Coll (IL)
Elmira Coll (NY)
Elon U (NC)
Emmanuel Coll (MA)
Emporia State U (KS)
Erskine Coll (SC)
Eureka Coll (IL)
Evangel U (MO)
The Evergreen State Coll (WA)
Fayetteville State U (NC)
Ferrum Coll (VA)
Florida Atlantic U (FL)
Florida Gulf Coast U (FL)
Florida Intl U (FL)
Fontbonne U (MO)
Fort Hays State U (KS)
Fort Lewis Coll (CO)
Framingham State U (MA)
Francis Marion U (SC)
Franklin Pierce U (NH)
Friends U (KS)
Furman U (SC)
The George Washington U (DC)
Georgia Coll & State U (GA)
Georgian Court U (NJ)
Georgia Southern U (GA)
Georgia Southwestern State U (GA)
Gettysburg Coll (PA)
Goddard Coll (VT)
Gonzaga U (WA)
Gordon Coll (MA)
Goshen Coll (IN)
Governors State U (IL)
Graceland U (IA)
Green Mountain Coll (VT)
Greensboro Coll (NC)
Greenville Coll (IL)
Grinnell Coll (IA)
Guilford Coll (NC)
Gustavus Adolphus Coll (MN)
Hampton U (VA)
Hannibal-LaGrange U (MO)
Hanover Coll (IN)
Hartwick Coll (NY)
Hastings Coll (NE)
Haverford Coll (PA)
Hendrix Coll (AR)
Hillsdale Coll (MI)
Hiram Coll (OH)
Hobart and William Smith Colls (NY)
Hollins U (VA)
Holy Cross Coll (IN)
Houghton Coll (NY)
Howard Payne U (TX)
Howard U (DC)
Humboldt State U (CA)
Hunter Coll of the City U of New York (NY)
Illinois Coll (IL)
Illinois State U (IL)
Illinois Wesleyan U (IL)
Indiana State U (IN)
Indiana U Bloomington (IN)
Indiana U East (IN)
Indiana U Kokomo (IN)
Indiana U of Pennsylvania (PA)
Indiana U–Purdue U Fort Wayne (IN)
Indiana U South Bend (IN)
Indiana U Southeast (IN)
Inter American U of Puerto Rico, San Germán Campus (PR)
Iowa State U of Science and Technology (IA)
Iowa Wesleyan Coll (IA)
Ithaca Coll (NY)
Jacksonville State U (AL)
Jacksonville U (FL)
James Madison U (VA)
Johnson State Coll (VT)
Judson Coll (AL)
Judson U (IL)
Juniata Coll (PA)
Kalamazoo Coll (MI)
Kansas State U (KS)
Kean U (NJ)
Kennesaw State U (GA)
Kentucky Wesleyan Coll (KY)
Knox Coll (IL)
Kutztown U of Pennsylvania (PA)
Lafayette Coll (PA)
Laguna Coll of Art & Design (CA)
Lake Forest Coll (IL)
La Sierra U (CA)
Lebanon Valley Coll (PA)
Lehigh U (PA)
Lehman Coll of the City U of New York (NY)
LeMoyne-Owen Coll (TN)
Lesley U (MA)
Lewis & Clark Coll (OR)
Lewis U (IL)
Lincoln Memorial U (TN)
Lindenwood U (MO)
Linfield Coll (OR)
Lock Haven U of Pennsylvania (PA)
Louisiana Coll (LA)
Louisiana State U in Shreveport (LA)
Lourdes U (OH)
Loyola U New Orleans (LA)
Lubbock Christian U (TX)
Luther Coll (IA)
Lycoming Coll (PA)
Lynchburg Coll (VA)
Lyon Coll (AR)
Macalester Coll (MN)
Manchester U (IN)
Mansfield U of Pennsylvania (PA)
Marietta Coll (OH)
Marist Coll (NY)
Marshall U (WV)
Mars Hill U (NC)
Mary Baldwin Coll (VA)
Marylhurst U (OR)
Marymount Manhattan Coll (NY)
Massachusetts Coll of Liberal Arts (MA)
McDaniel Coll (MD)
McKendree U (IL)
McNeese State U (LA)
Mercer U, Macon (GA)
Miami U (OH)
Michigan State U (MI)
Middle Tennessee State U (TN)
Midwestern State U (TX)
Millersville U of Pennsylvania (PA)
Mills Coll (CA)
Minnesota State U Mankato (MN)
Minnesota State U Moorhead (MN)
Minot State U (ND)
Mississippi Valley State U (MS)
Missouri Southern State U (MO)
Missouri State U (MO)
Missouri Valley Coll (MO)
Missouri Western State U (MO)
Monmouth Coll (IL)
Monmouth U (NJ)
Montana State U (MT)
Montana State U Billings (MT)
Montclair State U (NJ)
Moravian Coll (PA)
Mount Mary U (WI)
Mount Mercy U (IA)
Mount St. Joseph U (OH)
Mount Saint Mary's U (CA)
Mount St. Mary's U (MD)
Mount Vernon Nazarene U (OH)
Muhlenberg Coll (PA)
National U (CA)
Nazareth Coll of Rochester (NY)
Nebraska Wesleyan U (NE)
Newberry Coll (SC)
New England Coll (NH)
New Jersey City U (NJ)
New Jersey Inst of Technology (NJ)
Newman U (KS)
New Mexico Highlands U (NM)
Nicholls State U (LA)
Norfolk State U (VA)
North Carolina Ag and Tech State U (NC)
North Carolina Central U (NC)
North Central Coll (IL)
North Dakota State U (ND)
Northeastern Illinois U (IL)
Northeastern State U (OK)
Northeastern U (MA)
Northern Illinois U (IL)
Northern Michigan U (MI)
Northern State U (SD)
Northland Coll (WI)
Northwestern Coll (IA)
Northwestern U (IL)
Northwest Nazarene U (ID)
Notre Dame of Maryland U (MD)
Oakland City U (IN)

Oberlin Coll (OH)
Occidental Coll (CA)
Oglethorpe U (GA)
Ohio Dominican U (OH)
The Ohio State U (OH)
Ohio U (OH)
Oklahoma Baptist U (OK)
Oklahoma Christian U (OK)
Oklahoma City U (OK)
Oklahoma State U (OK)
Old Dominion U (VA)
Olivet Coll (MI)
Olivet Nazarene U (IL)
Oregon State U (OR)
Otis Coll of Art and Design (CA)
Our Lady of the Lake U of San Antonio (TX)
Pace U (NY)
Pacific U (OR)
Penn State Abington (PA)
Penn State Altoona (PA)
Penn State Beaver (PA)
Penn State Berks (PA)
Penn State Brandywine (PA)
Penn State DuBois (PA)
Penn State Erie, The Behrend Coll (PA)
Penn State Fayette, The Eberly Campus (PA)
Penn State Greater Allegheny (PA)
Penn State Hazleton (PA)
Penn State Lehigh Valley (PA)
Penn State Mont Alto (PA)
Penn State New Kensington (PA)
Penn State Schuylkill (PA)
Penn State Shenango (PA)
Penn State U Park (PA)
Penn State Wilkes-Barre (PA)
Penn State Worthington Scranton (PA)
Penn State York (PA)
Pepperdine U, Malibu (CA)
Peru State Coll (NE)
Piedmont Coll (GA)
Pittsburg State U (KS)
Plymouth State U (NH)
Pomona Coll (CA)
Portland State U (OR)
Pratt Inst (NY)
Presbyterian Coll (SC)
Purchase Coll, State U of New York (NY)
Radford U (VA)
Randolph Coll (VA)
Reed Coll (OR)
Regis U (CO)
Reinhardt U (GA)
Rhodes Coll (TN)
Rice U (TX)
Rider U (NJ)
Ripon Coll (WI)
Roanoke Coll (VA)
Roberts Wesleyan Coll (NY)
Rockford U (IL)
Rocky Mountain Coll (MT)
Roger Williams U (RI)
Rollins Coll (FL)
Rowan U (NJ)
Rutgers, The State U of New Jersey, Camden (NJ)
Rutgers, The State U of New Jersey, Newark (NJ)
Rutgers, The State U of New Jersey, New Brunswick (NJ)
Sacred Heart U (CT)
Saginaw Valley State U (MI)
St. Andrews U (NC)
Saint Anselm Coll (NH)
St. Catherine U (MN)
St. Edward's U (TX)
Saint John's U (MN)
Saint Joseph's U (PA)
St. Lawrence U (NY)
Saint Mary's Coll (IN)
St. Mary's Coll of Maryland (MD)
Saint Michael's Coll (VT)
St. Norbert Coll (WI)
St. Olaf Coll (MN)
Saint Peter's U (NJ)
St. Thomas Aquinas Coll (NY)
Salisbury U (MD)
Samford U (AL)
San Diego State U (CA)
San Francisco State U (CA)
San Jose State U (CA)
School of the Art Inst of Chicago (IL)
School of the Museum of Fine Arts, Boston (MA)
Scripps Coll (CA)
Seattle Pacific U (WA)
Shepherd U (WV)
Shippensburg U of Pennsylvania (PA)
Siena Heights U (MI)
Silver Lake Coll of the Holy Family (WI)
Simmons Coll (MA)
Simon Fraser U (BC, Canada)
Simpson Coll (IA)
Skidmore Coll (NY)
Slippery Rock U of Pennsylvania (PA)
Smith Coll (MA)
Southeastern Louisiana U (LA)
Southeastern Oklahoma State U (OK)
Southeast Missouri State U (MO)
Southern Adventist U (TN)
Southern Arkansas U–Magnolia (AR)
Southern Illinois U Carbondale (IL)
Southern Illinois U Edwardsville (IL)
Southern Oregon U (OR)
Southern Utah U (UT)
Southwest Baptist U (MO)
Southwestern U (TX)
Southwest Minnesota State U (MN)
Spelman Coll (GA)
Stanford U (CA)
State U of New York at Fredonia (NY)
State U of New York at Oswego (NY)
State U of New York at Plattsburgh (NY)
State U of New York Coll at Old Westbury (NY)
State U of New York Empire State Coll (NY)
Stephen F. Austin State U (TX)
Sterling Coll (KS)
Stetson U (FL)
Stony Brook U, State U of New York (NY)
Sul Ross State U (TX)
Tarleton State U (TX)
Taylor U (IN)
Temple U (PA)
Tennessee State U (TN)
Texas A&M U–Corpus Christi (TX)
Texas Lutheran U (TX)
Texas State U (TX)
Texas Tech U (TX)
Texas Woman's U (TX)
Thiel Coll (PA)
Tiffin U (OH)
Tougaloo Coll (MS)
Towson U (MD)
Transylvania U (KY)
Trinity Coll (CT)
Trinity U (TX)
Troy U (AL)
Truman State U (MO)
Tulane U (LA)
Union Coll (NE)
Union U (TN)
Université de Montréal (QC, Canada)
Université du Québec en Outaouais (QC, Canada)
U at Albany, State U of New York (NY)
U at Buffalo, the State U of New York (NY)
The U of Alabama at Birmingham (AL)
The U of Alabama in Huntsville (AL)
U of Alaska Fairbanks (AK)
U of Alberta (AB, Canada)
U of Arkansas (AR)
U of Arkansas at Little Rock (AR)
U of Arkansas at Pine Bluff (AR)
U of Arkansas–Fort Smith (AR)
U of California, Berkeley (CA)
U of California, Los Angeles (CA)
U of California, Riverside (CA)
U of California, Santa Cruz (CA)
U of Central Arkansas (AR)
U of Central Florida (FL)
U of Central Oklahoma (OK)
U of Charleston (WV)
U of Dallas (TX)
U of Delaware (DE)
U of Denver (CO)
U of Evansville (IN)
The U of Findlay (OH)
U of Georgia (GA)
U of Great Falls (MT)
U of Hawaii at Hilo (HI)
U of Hawaii at Manoa (HI)
U of Houston (TX)
U of Idaho (ID)
U of Indianapolis (IN)
The U of Iowa (IA)
U of Jamestown (ND)
U of La Verne (CA)
U of Louisiana at Lafayette (LA)
U of Maine at Machias (ME)
U of Maine at Presque Isle (ME)
U of Massachusetts Boston (MA)
U of Memphis (TN)
U of Miami (FL)
U of Michigan (MI)
U of Minnesota, Duluth (MN)
U of Minnesota, Twin Cities Campus (MN)
U of Missouri (MO)
U of Missouri–Kansas City (MO)
U of Mobile (AL)
The U of Montana (MT)
The U of Montana Western (MT)
U of Montevallo (AL)
U of Nebraska at Kearney (NE)
U of Nevada, Las Vegas (NV)
U of Nevada, Reno (NV)
U of New Hampshire (NH)
U of New Mexico (NM)
U of North Alabama (AL)
U of North Carolina at Asheville (NC)
The U of North Carolina at Charlotte (NC)
The U of North Carolina at Greensboro (NC)
U of North Dakota (ND)
U of Northern Iowa (IA)
U of North Florida (FL)
U of North Georgia (GA)
U of Oregon (OR)
U of Pikeville (KY)
U of Puget Sound (WA)
U of Rhode Island (RI)
U of Rio Grande (OH)
U of Saint Francis (IN)
U of Saint Mary (KS)
U of San Diego (CA)
U of San Francisco (CA)
U of Science and Arts of Oklahoma (OK)
U of South Alabama (AL)
U of Southern California (CA)
U of Southern Indiana (IN)
U of South Florida (FL)
U of South Florida, St. Petersburg (FL)
The U of Tampa (FL)
The U of Tennessee at Chattanooga (TN)
The U of Texas at Arlington (TX)
The U of Texas at Austin (TX)
The U of Texas at San Antonio (TX)
The U of Texas at Tyler (TX)
The U of Texas of the Permian Basin (TX)
U of the District of Columbia (DC)
U of the Incarnate Word (TX)
U of the Pacific (CA)
The U of Toledo (OH)
U of Utah (UT)
U of Virginia (VA)
The U of Virginia's Coll at Wise (VA)
U of Washington (WA)
The U of Western Ontario (ON, Canada)
U of West Florida (FL)
U of West Georgia (GA)
U of Windsor (ON, Canada)
U of Wisconsin–Eau Claire (WI)
U of Wisconsin–Green Bay (WI)
U of Wisconsin–La Crosse (WI)
U of Wisconsin–Madison (WI)
U of Wisconsin–Milwaukee (WI)
U of Wisconsin–Oshkosh (WI)
U of Wisconsin–Parkside (WI)
U of Wisconsin–Platteville (WI)
U of Wisconsin–River Falls (WI)
U of Wisconsin–Whitewater (WI)
U of Wyoming (WY)
Upper Iowa U (IA)
Ursinus Coll (PA)
Utah State U (UT)
Valdosta State U (GA)
Valley City State U (ND)
Valparaiso U (IN)
Villa Maria Coll (NY)
Virginia Polytechnic Inst and State U (VA)
Virginia Wesleyan Coll (VA)
Viterbo U (WI)
Wabash Coll (IN)
Wagner Coll (NY)
Walla Walla U (WA)
Walsh U (OH)
Warren Wilson Coll (NC)
Wartburg Coll (IA)
Washburn U (KS)
Washington & Jefferson Coll (PA)
Washington Coll (MD)
Washington U in St. Louis (MO)
Watkins Coll of Art, Design, & Film (TN)
Waynesburg U (PA)
Wayne State Coll (NE)
Wayne State U (MI)
Weber State U (UT)
Wells Coll (NY)
West Chester U of Pennsylvania (PA)
Western Carolina U (NC)
Western Illinois U (IL)
Western Michigan U (MI)
Western Oregon U (OR)
Western State Colorado U (CO)
Western Washington U (WA)
Westfield State U (MA)
Westminster Coll (UT)
West Texas A&M U (TX)
West Virginia State U (WV)
West Virginia U (WV)
West Virginia Wesleyan Coll (WV)
Wheaton Coll (IL)
Whitman Coll (WA)
Whittier Coll (CA)
Whitworth U (WA)
Willamette U (OR)
William Jessup U (CA)
William Jewell Coll (MO)
William Paterson U of New Jersey (NJ)
Williams Baptist Coll (AR)
Williams Coll (MA)
William Woods U (MO)
Winona State U (MN)
Winthrop U (SC)
Wright State U (OH)
Xavier U (OH)
Xavier U of Louisiana (LA)
Yale U (CT)
York Coll of the City U of New York (NY)
Youngstown State U (OH)

ART HISTORY, CRITICISM AND CONSERVATION

Acad of Art U (CA)
Adams State U (CO)
Adelphi U (NY)
Agnes Scott Coll (GA)
Albertus Magnus Coll (CT)
Albion Coll (MI)
Allegheny Coll (PA)
American U (DC)
American U of Beirut (Lebanon)
The American U of Paris (France)
The American U of Rome (Italy)
Aquinas Coll (MI)
Arcadia U (PA)
Assumption Coll (MA)
Augsburg Coll (MN)
Augustana Coll (IL)
Baker U (KS)
Baldwin Wallace U (OH)
Bard Coll (NY)
Bard Coll at Simon's Rock (MA)
Barnard Coll (NY)
Baylor U (TX)
Belmont U (TN)
Beloit Coll (WI)
Bennington Coll (VT)
Binghamton U, State U of New York (NY)
Birmingham-Southern Coll (AL)
Bloomsburg U of Pennsylvania (PA)
Boston Coll (MA)
Bowdoin Coll (ME)
Bowling Green State U (OH)
Bradley U (IL)
Brandeis U (MA)
Bridgewater State U (MA)
Brown U (RI)
Bryn Mawr Coll (PA)
Bucknell U (PA)
Buffalo State Coll, State U of New York (NY)
California State Polytechnic U, Pomona (CA)
California State U, Dominguez Hills (CA)
California State U, Fullerton (CA)
California State U, Long Beach (CA)
California State U, Stanislaus (CA)
Calvary Bible Coll and Theological Sem (MO)
Calvin Coll (MI)
Canisius Coll (NY)
Carleton Coll (MN)
Case Western Reserve U (OH)
Castleton State Coll (VT)
The Catholic U of America (DC)
Centre Coll (KY)
Chapman U (CA)
Chatham U (PA)
City Coll of the City U of New York (NY)
Clarke U (IA)
Clark U (MA)
Coe Coll (IA)
Colby Coll (ME)
Colby-Sawyer Coll (NH)
Coll of Charleston (SC)
The Coll of New Rochelle (NY)
Coll of the Holy Cross (MA)
The Coll of William and Mary (VA)
The Coll of Wooster (OH)
The Colorado Coll (CO)
Columbia U (NY)
Columbia U, School of General Studies (NY)
Concordia U (QC, Canada)
Connecticut Coll (CT)
Cornell Coll (IA)
Cornell U (NY)
Dartmouth Coll (NH)
Denison U (OH)
DePaul U (IL)
DePauw U (IN)
DEREE - The American Coll of Greece (Greece)
Dominican U (IL)
Dominican U of California (CA)
Drake U (IA)
Drew U (NJ)
Drury U (MO)
Duquesne U (PA)
East Carolina U (NC)
Eastern Michigan U (MI)
Elizabethtown Coll (PA)
Elon U (NC)
Emmanuel Coll (MA)
Fairfield U (CT)
Ferris State U (MI)
Flagler Coll (FL)
Florida Intl U (FL)
Florida Southern Coll (FL)
Florida State U (FL)
Fordham U (NY)
Fort Hays State U (KS)
Franklin & Marshall Coll (PA)
Furman U (SC)
Gallaudet U (DC)
George Mason U (VA)
Georgetown U (DC)
The George Washington U (DC)
Gettysburg Coll (PA)
Goucher Coll (MD)
Grand Valley State U (MI)
Gustavus Adolphus Coll (MN)
Hamilton Coll (NY)
Hamline U (MN)
Hampshire Coll (MA)
Hanover Coll (IN)
Hartwick Coll (NY)
Harvard U (MA)
Hastings Coll (NE)
Haverford Coll (PA)
Hiram Coll (OH)
Hobart and William Smith Colls (NY)
Hofstra U (NY)
Hollins U (VA)

Hope Coll (MI)
Humboldt State U (CA)
Hunter Coll of the City U of New York (NY)
Indiana U Bloomington (IN)
Indiana U–Purdue U Indianapolis (IN)
Ithaca Coll (NY)
Jacksonville U (FL)
James Madison U (VA)
John Cabot U (Italy)
John Carroll U (OH)
Johns Hopkins U (MD)
Juniata Coll (PA)
Kalamazoo Coll (MI)
Kansas City Art Inst (MO)
Kean U (NJ)
Kennesaw State U (GA)
Kent State U (OH)
Kenyon Coll (OH)
Knox Coll (IL)
Lafayette Coll (PA)
Lake Forest Coll (IL)
La Salle U (PA)
Lawrence U (WI)
Lebanon Valley Coll (PA)
Lehigh U (PA)
Lehman Coll of the City U of New York (NY)
Lewis & Clark Coll (OR)
Lindenwood U (MO)
Long Island U–LIU Post (NY)
Lourdes U (OH)
Loyola Marymount U (CA)
Loyola U Chicago (IL)
Lycoming Coll (PA)
Manhattanville Coll (NY)
Marian U (IN)
Marist Coll (NY)
Mars Hill U (NC)
Marymount Manhattan Coll (NY)
Massachusetts Coll of Art and Design (MA)
McDaniel Coll (MD)
Merrimack Coll (MA)
Messiah Coll (PA)
Miami U (OH)
Michigan State U (MI)
Middlebury Coll (VT)
Millsaps Coll (MS)
Mills Coll (CA)
Minnesota State U Mankato (MN)
Missouri State U (MO)
Moore Coll of Art & Design (PA)
Moravian Coll (PA)
Mount Allison U (NB, Canada)
Mount Holyoke Coll (MA)
Nazareth Coll of Rochester (NY)
New Coll of Florida (FL)
New York U (NY)
North Carolina State U (NC)
North Central Coll (IL)
Northern Illinois U (IL)
Northern Michigan U (MI)
Northwestern U (IL)
Oakland U (MI)
Oberlin Coll (OH)
Oglethorpe U (GA)
The Ohio State U (OH)
Ohio U (OH)
Ohio Wesleyan U (OH)
Old Dominion U (VA)
Pace U (NY)
Pacific Lutheran U (WA)
Paris Coll of Art (France)
Penn State Abington (PA)
Penn State Altoona (PA)
Penn State Beaver (PA)
Penn State Berks (PA)
Penn State Brandywine (PA)
Penn State DuBois (PA)
Penn State Erie, The Behrend Coll (PA)
Penn State Fayette, The Eberly Campus (PA)
Penn State Greater Allegheny (PA)
Penn State Hazleton (PA)
Penn State Lehigh Valley (PA)
Penn State Mont Alto (PA)
Penn State New Kensington (PA)
Penn State Schuylkill (PA)
Penn State Shenango (PA)
Penn State U Park (PA)
Penn State Wilkes-Barre (PA)
Penn State Worthington Scranton (PA)
Penn State York (PA)
Pepperdine U, Malibu (CA)
Plymouth State U (NH)
Pomona Coll (CA)
Portland State U (OR)
Pratt Inst (NY)
Presbyterian Coll (SC)
Princeton U (NJ)
Principia Coll (IL)
Providence Coll (RI)
Purchase Coll, State U of New York (NY)
Purdue U (IN)
Queens Coll of the City U of New York (NY)
Randolph Coll (VA)
Randolph-Macon Coll (VA)
Regis U (CO)
Rhode Island Coll (RI)
Rice U (TX)
Roanoke Coll (VA)
Rockford U (IL)
Roger Williams U (RI)
Rollins Coll (FL)
Rosemont Coll (PA)
Rutgers, The State U of New Jersey, New Brunswick (NJ)
St. Bonaventure U (NY)
St. Catherine U (MN)
Saint Louis U (MO)
St. Olaf Coll (MN)
Saint Peter's U (NJ)
Saint Vincent Coll (PA)
Salem Coll (NC)
Salve Regina U (RI)
San Diego State U (CA)
San Francisco Art Inst (CA)
San Jose State U (CA)
Santa Clara U (CA)
Sarah Lawrence Coll (NY)
Savannah Coll of Art and Design (GA)
School of the Art Inst of Chicago (IL)
Scripps Coll (CA)
Seattle U (WA)
Seton Hill U (PA)
Sewanee: The U of the South (TN)
Siena Heights U (MI)
Skidmore Coll (NY)
Smith Coll (MA)
Southern Connecticut State U (CT)
Southern Methodist U (TX)
Southern Utah U (UT)
Southwestern U (TX)
Stanford U (CA)
State U of New York at Fredonia (NY)
State U of New York at New Paltz (NY)
State U of New York Coll at Cortland (NY)
State U of New York Coll at Geneseo (NY)
State U of New York Coll at Potsdam (NY)
Stephen F. Austin State U (TX)
Stetson U (FL)
Stonehill Coll (MA)
Stony Brook U, State U of New York (NY)
Susquehanna U (PA)
Syracuse U (NY)
Temple U (PA)
Texas Christian U (TX)
Texas State U (TX)
Thomas More Coll (KY)
Towson U (MD)
Transylvania U (KY)
Trinity Coll (CT)
Trinity U (TX)
Truman State U (MO)
Tufts U (MA)
Tulane U (LA)
Université de Montréal (QC, Canada)
U at Albany, State U of New York (NY)
U at Buffalo, the State U of New York (NY)
The U of Akron (OH)
The U of Alabama (AL)
U of Alberta (AB, Canada)
The U of Arizona (AZ)
The U of British Columbia (BC, Canada)
The U of British Columbia–Okanagan Campus (BC, Canada)
U of California, Berkeley (CA)
U of California, Davis (CA)
U of California, Irvine (CA)
U of California, Los Angeles (CA)
U of California, Riverside (CA)
U of California, Santa Barbara (CA)
U of California, Santa Cruz (CA)
U of Central Oklahoma (OK)
U of Chicago (IL)
U of Cincinnati (OH)
U of Colorado Boulder (CO)
U of Dallas (TX)
U of Dayton (OH)
U of Delaware (DE)
U of Denver (CO)
U of Evansville (IN)
U of Florida (FL)
U of Georgia (GA)
U of Guelph (ON, Canada)
U of Hartford (CT)
U of Houston (TX)
U of Illinois at Chicago (IL)
The U of Iowa (IA)
The U of Kansas (KS)
U of Kentucky (KY)
U of La Verne (CA)
U of Lethbridge (AB, Canada)
U of Louisville (KY)
U of Maine (ME)
U of Maryland, Coll Park (MD)
U of Mary Washington (VA)
U of Massachusetts Amherst (MA)
U of Massachusetts Dartmouth (MA)
U of Memphis (TN)
U of Miami (FL)
U of Michigan (MI)
U of Michigan–Dearborn (MI)
U of Michigan–Flint (MI)
U of Minnesota, Duluth (MN)
U of Minnesota, Morris (MN)
U of Minnesota, Twin Cities Campus (MN)
U of Mississippi (MS)
U of Missouri (MO)
U of Missouri–Kansas City (MO)
U of Missouri–St. Louis (MO)
The U of Montana (MT)
U of Nebraska–Lincoln (NE)
U of Nevada, Las Vegas (NV)
U of Nevada, Reno (NV)
U of New Mexico (NM)
U of New Orleans (LA)
The U of North Carolina at Chapel Hill (NC)
The U of North Carolina at Charlotte (NC)
The U of North Carolina Wilmington (NC)
U of Northern Iowa (IA)
U of North Texas (TX)
U of Notre Dame (IN)
U of Oklahoma (OK)
U of Oregon (OR)
U of Ottawa (ON, Canada)
U of Pennsylvania (PA)
U of Pittsburgh (PA)
U of Regina (SK, Canada)
U of Rhode Island (RI)
U of Richmond (VA)
U of Rochester (NY)
U of Saint Joseph (CT)
U of St. Thomas (MN)
U of San Diego (CA)
U of San Francisco (CA)
U of Saskatchewan (SK, Canada)
U of Southern California (CA)
U of South Florida (FL)
The U of Tennessee (TN)
The U of Texas at Arlington (TX)
The U of Texas at Austin (TX)
The U of Texas at San Antonio (TX)
U of the Incarnate Word (TX)
U of the Pacific (CA)
The U of Toledo (OH)
The U of Tulsa (OK)
U of Utah (UT)
U of Vermont (VT)
U of Washington (WA)
U of Waterloo (ON, Canada)
The U of Western Ontario (ON, Canada)
U of West Florida (FL)
U of Windsor (ON, Canada)
U of Wisconsin–Madison (WI)
U of Wisconsin–Milwaukee (WI)
U of Wisconsin–Superior (WI)
Ursinus Coll (PA)
Ursuline Coll (OH)
Vanderbilt U (TN)
Vassar Coll (NY)
Villanova U (PA)
Virginia Commonwealth U (VA)
Wake Forest U (NC)
Washburn U (KS)
Washington and Lee U (VA)
Washington U in St. Louis (MO)
Wayne State U (MI)
Webster U (MO)
Wells Coll (NY)
Wesleyan Coll (GA)
Wesleyan U (CT)
Western Kentucky U (KY)
Western Michigan U (MI)
Western Washington U (WA)
West Virginia U (WV)
Wheaton Coll (MA)
Whitman Coll (WA)
Willamette U (OR)
William Paterson U of New Jersey (NJ)
Williams Coll (MA)
Winthrop U (SC)
Wittenberg U (OH)
Wofford Coll (SC)
Wright State U (OH)
Yale U (CT)
York Coll of the City U of New York (NY)
Youngstown State U (OH)

ARTIFICIAL INTELLIGENCE

Sullivan Coll of Technology and Design (KY)
U of Windsor (ON, Canada)
Worcester Polytechnic Inst (MA)

ARTS, ENTERTAINMENT, AND MEDIA MANAGEMENT

Anderson U (IN)
Belmont U (TN)
Butler U (IN)
Champlain Coll (VT)
Concordia U, Nebraska (NE)
Dixie State U (UT)
Drexel U (PA)
Drury U (MO)
Lindenwood U (MO)
Long Island U–LIU Post (NY)
National U (CA)
St. Edward's U (TX)
State U of New York at Fredonia (NY)
U of Kentucky (KY)
U of North Alabama (AL)
U of Pikeville (KY)
The U of Tulsa (OK)
U of Wisconsin–Green Bay (WI)
Western New England U (MA)

ARTS, ENTERTAINMENT, AND MEDIA MANAGEMENT RELATED

Belmont U (TN)
Delta State U (MS)
U of Southern California (CA)

ART TEACHER EDUCATION

Abilene Christian U (TX)
Acad of Art U (CA)
Adams State U (CO)
Adelphi U (NY)
Albright Coll (PA)
Alma Coll (MI)
Alverno Coll (WI)
Anderson U (SC)
Andrews U (MI)
Anna Maria Coll (MA)
Appalachian State U (NC)
Arcadia U (PA)
Arkansas Tech U (AR)
Armstrong State U (GA)
Asbury U (KY)
Ashland U (OH)
Augustana Coll (IL)
Augustana Coll (SD)
Averett U (VA)
Baker U (KS)
Baylor U (TX)
Belmont U (TN)
Beloit Coll (WI)
Bemidji State U (MN)
Benedictine Coll (KS)
Berea Coll (KY)
Berry Coll (GA)
Bethany Coll (WV)
Bethel U (MN)
Birmingham-Southern Coll (AL)
Blackburn Coll (IL)
Boston U (MA)
Bowling Green State U (OH)
Bradley U (IL)
Brenau U (GA)
Bridgewater State U (MA)
Buena Vista U (IA)
Buffalo State Coll, State U of New York (NY)
California Lutheran U (CA)
California State U, Long Beach (CA)
Calvin Coll (MI)
Campbellsville U (KY)
Capital U (OH)
Carlow U (PA)
Carson-Newman U (TN)
Case Western Reserve U (OH)
Castleton State Coll (VT)
Central Connecticut State U (CT)
Central Michigan U (MI)
Central State U (OH)
City Coll of the City U of New York (NY)
Claflin U (SC)
Clarke U (IA)
Coe Coll (IA)
Coker Coll (SC)
Colby-Sawyer Coll (NH)
Coll for Creative Studies (MI)
The Coll of New Jersey (NJ)
The Coll of New Rochelle (NY)
Coll of Saint Mary (NE)
The Coll of Saint Rose (NY)
Coll of the Ozarks (MO)
Colorado State U (CO)
Columbus State U (GA)
Concordia Coll (MN)
Concordia U (QC, Canada)
Concordia U Chicago (IL)
Concordia U, Nebraska (NE)
Concordia U, St. Paul (MN)
Concordia U Wisconsin (WI)
Concord U (WV)
Creighton U (NE)
Culver-Stockton Coll (MO)
Daemen Coll (NY)
Delaware State U (DE)
DePaul U (IL)
Dickinson State U (ND)
Dowling Coll (NY)
East Carolina U (NC)
East Central U (OK)
Eastern Michigan U (MI)
Edgewood Coll (WI)
Elmhurst Coll (IL)
Elmira Coll (NY)
Emory & Henry Coll (VA)
Escuela de Artes Plasticas de Puerto Rico (PR)
Evangel U (MO)
Fairmont State U (WV)
Fayetteville State U (NC)
Ferris State U (MI)
Flagler Coll (FL)
Florida Intl U (FL)
Florida Southern Coll (FL)
Fontbonne U (MO)
Fort Hays State U (KS)
Francis Marion U (SC)
Franklin Pierce U (NH)
Friends U (KS)
Gallaudet U (DC)
Georgia State U (GA)
Goddard Coll (VT)
Grace Coll (IN)
Graceland U (IA)
Grand Valley State U (MI)
Green Mountain Coll (VT)
Greensboro Coll (NC)
Gustavus Adolphus Coll (MN)
Hampton U (VA)
Hannibal-LaGrange U (MO)
Harding U (AR)
Hardin-Simmons U (TX)
Hastings Coll (NE)
Heritage U (WA)
Hofstra U (NY)
Holy Family U (PA)
Hope Coll (MI)
Houghton Coll (NY)

Houston Baptist U (TX)
Howard Payne U (TX)
Humboldt State U (CA)
Indiana State U (IN)
Indiana U Bloomington (IN)
Indiana U–Purdue U Fort Wayne (IN)
Indiana U–Purdue U Indianapolis (IN)
Indiana U South Bend (IN)
Inter American U of Puerto Rico, San Germán Campus (PR)
Ithaca Coll (NY)
Johnson State Coll (VT)
Kansas State U (KS)
Kansas Wesleyan U (KS)
Kennesaw State U (GA)
Kent State U (OH)
Kentucky Wesleyan Coll (KY)
Keystone Coll (PA)
Langston U (OK)
Lawrence U (WI)
Lee U (TN)
Lehman Coll of the City U of New York (NY)
Lincoln Memorial U (TN)
Lincoln U (MO)
Lindenwood U (MO)
Lindsey Wilson Coll (KY)
Lipscomb U (TN)
Long Island U–LIU Brooklyn (NY)
Long Island U–LIU Post (NY)
Louisiana Coll (LA)
Louisiana State U in Shreveport (LA)
Lubbock Christian U (TX)
Manchester U (IN)
Manhattanville Coll (NY)
Mansfield U of Pennsylvania (PA)
Marian U (WI)
Mars Hill U (NC)
Maryville U of Saint Louis (MO)
Marywood U (PA)
Massachusetts Coll of Art and Design (MA)
McKendree U (IL)
McMurry U (TX)
Meredith Coll (NC)
Messiah Coll (PA)
Miami U (OH)
Michigan State U (MI)
Middle Tennessee State U (TN)
Millikin U (IL)
Minnesota State U Mankato (MN)
Minnesota State U Moorhead (MN)
Minot State U (ND)
Mississippi U for Women (MS)
Missouri State U (MO)
Missouri Western State U (MO)
Molloy Coll (NY)
Montana State U Billings (MT)
Moore Coll of Art & Design (PA)
Morningside Coll (IA)
Mount Mary U (WI)
Mount Mercy U (IA)
Mount St. Joseph U (OH)
Mount Vernon Nazarene U (OH)
Nazareth Coll of Rochester (NY)
New Jersey City U (NJ)
Nicholls State U (LA)
North Carolina Ag and Tech State U (NC)
North Central Coll (IL)
Northeastern State U (OK)
Northern Illinois U (IL)
Northern Michigan U (MI)
Northern State U (SD)
Northwestern Coll (IA)
Northwest Missouri State U (MO)
Northwest Nazarene U (ID)
Nova Southeastern U (FL)
Oakland City U (IN)
Ohio Dominican U (OH)
Ohio Northern U (OH)
The Ohio State U (OH)
Ohio Wesleyan U (OH)
Oklahoma Baptist U (OK)
Olivet Coll (MI)
Pacific U (OR)
Palm Beach Atlantic U (FL)
Penn State Abington (PA)
Penn State Altoona (PA)
Penn State Beaver (PA)
Penn State Berks (PA)
Penn State Brandywine (PA)
Penn State DuBois (PA)
Penn State Erie, The Behrend Coll (PA)
Penn State Fayette, The Eberly Campus (PA)
Penn State Greater Allegheny (PA)
Penn State Hazleton (PA)
Penn State Lehigh Valley (PA)
Penn State Mont Alto (PA)
Penn State New Kensington (PA)
Penn State Schuylkill (PA)
Penn State Shenango (PA)
Penn State U Park (PA)
Penn State Wilkes-Barre (PA)
Penn State Worthington Scranton (PA)
Penn State York (PA)
Peru State Coll (NE)
Piedmont Coll (GA)
Plymouth State U (NH)
Point Loma Nazarene U (CA)
Pratt Inst (NY)
Purdue U (IN)
Queens Coll of the City U of New York (NY)
Rhode Island Coll (RI)
Rocky Mountain Coll (MT)
Rocky Mountain Coll of Art + Design (CO)
Saginaw Valley State U (MI)
St. Catherine U (MN)
St. Edward's U (TX)
Saint Joseph's Coll (IN)
Saint Joseph's U (PA)
Saint Mary-of-the-Woods Coll (IN)
Saint Mary's Coll (IN)
Saint Michael's Coll (VT)
Saint Vincent Coll (PA)
School of the Art Inst of Chicago (IL)
Seton Hill U (PA)
Shawnee State U (OH)
Siena Heights U (MI)
Silver Lake Coll of the Holy Family (WI)
Simpson Coll (IA)
Slippery Rock U of Pennsylvania (PA)
South Carolina State U (SC)
South Dakota State U (SD)
Southeastern Oklahoma State U (OK)
Southeast Missouri State U (MO)
Southern Adventist U (TN)
Southern Arkansas U–Magnolia (AR)
Southern Connecticut State U (CT)
Southern Utah U (UT)
Southwest Baptist U (MO)
Southwest Minnesota State U (MN)
State U of New York at New Paltz (NY)
Syracuse U (NY)
Taylor U (IN)
Temple U (PA)
Texas Christian U (TX)
Texas Lutheran U (TX)
Thomas More Coll (KY)
Towson U (MD)
Transylvania U (KY)
Trinity Christian Coll (IL)
Tusculum Coll (TN)
Union Coll (NE)
Union U (TN)
The U of Akron (OH)
U of Alberta (AB, Canada)
The U of Arizona (AZ)
The U of British Columbia (BC, Canada)
U of Central Florida (FL)
U of Central Missouri (MO)
U of Central Oklahoma (OK)
U of Denver (CO)
U of Evansville (IN)
The U of Findlay (OH)
U of Florida (FL)
U of Great Falls (MT)
U of Idaho (ID)
U of Illinois at Chicago (IL)
U of Indianapolis (IN)
The U of Iowa (IA)
The U of Kansas (KS)
U of Kentucky (KY)
U of Lethbridge (AB, Canada)
U of Maine (ME)
U of Maine at Presque Isle (ME)
U of Mary Hardin-Baylor (TX)
U of Maryland, Coll Park (MD)
U of Massachusetts Dartmouth (MA)
U of Michigan–Flint (MI)
U of Minnesota, Duluth (MN)
U of Minnesota, Twin Cities Campus (MN)
U of Missouri (MO)
The U of Montana (MT)
The U of Montana Western (MT)
U of New Mexico (NM)
The U of North Carolina at Charlotte (NC)
The U of North Carolina at Greensboro (NC)
The U of North Carolina at Pembroke (NC)
U of Northern Iowa (IA)
U of North Florida (FL)
U of North Georgia (GA)
U of Northwestern–St. Paul (MN)
U of Regina (SK, Canada)
U of Rio Grande (OH)
U of St. Francis (IL)
U of Saint Francis (IN)
U of St. Thomas (TX)
U of South Carolina Upstate (SC)
The U of South Dakota (SD)
U of Southern Maine (ME)
The U of Tennessee at Chattanooga (TN)
The U of Texas at El Paso (TX)
U of the Cumberlands (KY)
U of the District of Columbia (DC)
The U of Toledo (OH)
U of Vermont (VT)
U of Windsor (ON, Canada)
U of Wisconsin–La Crosse (WI)
U of Wisconsin–Madison (WI)
U of Wisconsin–Milwaukee (WI)
U of Wisconsin–Oshkosh (WI)
U of Wisconsin–River Falls (WI)
U of Wisconsin–Stout (WI)
U of Wisconsin–Superior (WI)
U of Wisconsin–Whitewater (WI)
Upper Iowa U (IA)
Ursuline Coll (OH)
Utah Valley U (UT)
Valdosta State U (GA)
Valley City State U (ND)
Valparaiso U (IN)
Virginia Commonwealth U (VA)
Virginia Wesleyan Coll (VA)
Viterbo U (WI)
Walla Walla U (WA)
Wartburg Coll (IA)
Washburn U (KS)
Washington & Jefferson Coll (PA)
Washington U in St. Louis (MO)
Wayne State Coll (NE)
Wayne State U (MI)
Weber State U (UT)
Western Carolina U (NC)
Western Michigan U (MI)
Western State Colorado U (CO)
Western Washington U (WA)
West Liberty U (WV)
West Virginia Wesleyan Coll (WV)
Whitworth U (WA)
William Paterson U of New Jersey (NJ)
Williams Baptist Coll (AR)
William Woods U (MO)
Winona State U (MN)
Xavier U of Louisiana (LA)
Youngstown State U (OH)

ART THERAPY
Albertus Magnus Coll (CT)
Alverno Coll (WI)
Anna Maria Coll (MA)
Arcadia U (PA)
Capital U (OH)
Carlow U (PA)
Cedar Crest Coll (PA)
Chowan U (NC)
The Coll of New Rochelle (NY)
DePaul U (IL)
Edgewood Coll (WI)
Emmanuel Coll (MA)
Harding U (AR)
Howard U (DC)
Lesley U (MA)
Lipscomb U (TN)
Long Island U–LIU Post (NY)
Marywood U (PA)
Millikin U (IL)
Mount Mary U (WI)
Nazareth Coll of Rochester (NY)
Prescott Coll (AZ)
St. Thomas Aquinas Coll (NY)
Seton Hill U (PA)
Southern Adventist U (TN)
U of Indianapolis (IN)
U of Saint Francis (IN)
U of Wisconsin–Superior (WI)
West Virginia Wesleyan Coll (WV)

ASIAN AMERICAN STUDIES
Arizona State U at the Tempe campus (AZ)
Binghamton U, State U of New York (NY)
California State U, Fullerton (CA)
California State U, Long Beach (CA)
California State U, Los Angeles (CA)
Columbia U (NY)
Cornell U (NY)
Pomona Coll (CA)
San Francisco State U (CA)
Scripps Coll (CA)
Stanford U (CA)
U of California, Berkeley (CA)
U of California, Davis (CA)
U of California, Irvine (CA)
U of California, Los Angeles (CA)
U of California, Riverside (CA)
U of California, Santa Barbara (CA)
U of Denver (CO)
U of Southern California (CA)

ASIAN HISTORY
Gettysburg Coll (PA)
U of the West (CA)
U of Washington, Tacoma (WA)

ASIAN STUDIES
Amherst Coll (MA)
Arizona State U at the Tempe campus (AZ)
Augustana Coll (IL)
Austin Coll (TX)
Bard Coll (NY)
Bard Coll at Simon's Rock (MA)
Barnard Coll (NY)
Baylor U (TX)
Belmont U (TN)
Bennington Coll (VT)
Berea Coll (KY)
Binghamton U, State U of New York (NY)
Birmingham-Southern Coll (AL)
Bowdoin Coll (ME)
Bowling Green State U (OH)
California State U, Chico (CA)
California State U, Long Beach (CA)
California State U, Los Angeles (CA)
California State U, Sacramento (CA)
Calvin Coll (MI)
Carleton Coll (MN)
Case Western Reserve U (OH)
City Coll of the City U of New York (NY)
Claremont McKenna Coll (CA)
Clark U (MA)
Coe Coll (IA)
Coll of the Holy Cross (MA)
The Colorado Coll (CO)
Cornell U (NY)
Dartmouth Coll (NH)
Elms Coll (MA)
Florida Intl U (FL)
Furman U (SC)
The George Washington U (DC)
Gonzaga U (WA)
Hamilton Coll (NY)
Hawai`i Pacific U (HI)
Hobart and William Smith Colls (NY)
Illinois Wesleyan U (IL)
Indiana U of Pennsylvania (PA)
John Carroll U (OH)
Kean U (NJ)
Kenyon Coll (OH)
Knox Coll (IL)
Lake Forest Coll (IL)
Lehigh U (PA)
Loyola Marymount U (CA)
Macalester Coll (MN)
Manhattanville Coll (NY)
Marietta Coll (OH)
McDaniel Coll (MD)
Mount Holyoke Coll (MA)
Nazareth Coll of Rochester (NY)
Northeastern U (MA)
Northwestern U (IL)
Ohio U (OH)
Old Dominion U (VA)
Pace U (NY)
Penn State U Park (PA)
Pepperdine U, Malibu (CA)
Pomona Coll (CA)
Purdue U (IN)
Randolph-Macon Coll (VA)
Rice U (TX)
St. John's U (NY)
Saint Joseph's U (PA)
St. Mary's Coll of Maryland (MD)
St. Olaf Coll (MN)
San Diego State U (CA)
Sarah Lawrence Coll (NY)
Scripps Coll (CA)
Seattle U (WA)
Sewanee: The U of the South (TN)
Skidmore Coll (NY)
Stanford U (CA)
State U of New York at New Paltz (NY)
Stony Brook U, State U of New York (NY)
Temple U (PA)
Texas State U (TX)
Trinity U (TX)
Tufts U (MA)
Tulane U (LA)
Union Coll (NY)
U at Albany, State U of New York (NY)
U at Buffalo, the State U of New York (NY)
The U of British Columbia (BC, Canada)
U of California, Berkeley (CA)
U of California, Riverside (CA)
U of California, Santa Barbara (CA)
U of Cincinnati (OH)
U of Colorado Boulder (CO)
U of Delaware (DE)
U of Hawaii at Manoa (HI)
The U of Iowa (IA)
U of Louisville (KY)
U of Maryland, Baltimore County (MD)
U of Maryland U Coll (MD)
U of Massachusetts Boston (MA)
U of Michigan (MI)
The U of Montana (MT)
U of Mount Union (OH)
U of Nevada, Las Vegas (NV)
U of New Mexico (NM)
The U of North Carolina at Chapel Hill (NC)
U of Northern Colorado (CO)
U of Oregon (OR)
U of Puget Sound (WA)
U of Richmond (VA)
U of San Francisco (CA)
The U of Texas at Austin (TX)
The U of Toledo (OH)
U of Toronto (ON, Canada)
U of Utah (UT)
U of Vermont (VT)
U of Washington (WA)
The U of Western Ontario (ON, Canada)
U of Wisconsin–Madison (WI)
Utah State U (UT)
Vanderbilt U (TN)
Vassar Coll (NY)
Washington State U (WA)
Washington U in St. Louis (MO)
Western Kentucky U (KY)
Wheaton Coll (MA)
Whitman Coll (WA)
Willamette U (OR)
William Paterson U of New Jersey (NJ)
Williams Coll (MA)

ASIAN STUDIES (EAST)
Austin Coll (TX)
Bates Coll (ME)
Binghamton U, State U of New York (NY)
Boston U (MA)
Brandeis U (MA)
Brown U (RI)
Bryn Mawr Coll (PA)

Bucknell U (PA)
Colby Coll (ME)
Columbia U (NY)
Columbia U, School of General Studies (NY)
Connecticut Coll (CT)
Davidson Coll (NC)
Denison U (OH)
DePaul U (IL)
DePauw U (IN)
Dickinson Coll (PA)
The George Washington U (DC)
Gettysburg Coll (PA)
Grand Valley State U (MI)
Hamline U (MN)
Hampshire Coll (MA)
Harvard U (MA)
Haverford Coll (PA)
Hofstra U (NY)
Indiana U Bloomington (IN)
John Carroll U (OH)
Johns Hopkins U (MD)
Kalamazoo Coll (MI)
Lawrence U (WI)
Lewis & Clark Coll (OR)
Miami U (OH)
Middlebury Coll (VT)
Minnesota State U Moorhead (MN)
Mount Holyoke Coll (MA)
New York U (NY)
North Central Coll (IL)
Oakland U (MI)
Oberlin Coll (OH)
Occidental Coll (CA)
Ohio Wesleyan U (OH)
Penn State Abington (PA)
Penn State Altoona (PA)
Penn State Beaver (PA)
Penn State Berks (PA)
Penn State Brandywine (PA)
Penn State DuBois (PA)
Penn State Erie, The Behrend Coll (PA)
Penn State Fayette, The Eberly Campus (PA)
Penn State Greater Allegheny (PA)
Penn State Hazleton (PA)
Penn State Lehigh Valley (PA)
Penn State Mont Alto (PA)
Penn State New Kensington (PA)
Penn State Schuylkill (PA)
Penn State Shenango (PA)
Penn State Worthington Scranton (PA)
Penn State York (PA)
Portland State U (OR)
Princeton U (NJ)
Queens Coll of the City U of New York (NY)
Rutgers, The State U of New Jersey, New Brunswick (NJ)
Simmons Coll (MA)
Smith Coll (MA)
Stanford U (CA)
Trinity U (TX)
Tufts U (MA)
United States Military Acad (NY)
Université de Montréal (QC, Canada)
U at Albany, State U of New York (NY)
U of Alberta (AB, Canada)
The U of Arizona (AZ)
U of Bridgeport (CT)
U of California, Davis (CA)
U of California, Irvine (CA)
U of Minnesota, Twin Cities Campus (MN)
U of Missouri (MO)
The U of Montana (MT)
U of Pennsylvania (PA)
U of Rochester (NY)
U of Southern California (CA)
U of Toronto (ON, Canada)
The U of Western Ontario (ON, Canada)
Ursinus Coll (PA)
Valparaiso U (IN)
Washington U in St. Louis (MO)
Wayne State U (MI)
Wesleyan U (CT)
Western Washington U (WA)
Wittenberg U (OH)
Yale U (CT)

ASIAN STUDIES (SOUTH)
Binghamton U, State U of New York (NY)
Brown U (RI)
Columbia U, School of General Studies (NY)
Concordia U (QC, Canada)
Gettysburg Coll (PA)
Hampshire Coll (MA)
Indiana U Bloomington (IN)
Middlebury Coll (VT)
Mount Holyoke Coll (MA)
The U of British Columbia (BC, Canada)
U of Chicago (IL)
U of Minnesota, Twin Cities Campus (MN)
U of Missouri (MO)
U of Pennsylvania (PA)
U of Toronto (ON, Canada)
U of Washington (WA)
U of Wisconsin–Madison (WI)

ASIAN STUDIES (SOUTHEAST)
Tufts U (MA)
U of California, Berkeley (CA)
U of California, Los Angeles (CA)
U of Washington (WA)

ASIAN STUDIES (URAL-ALTAIC AND CENTRAL)
Indiana U Bloomington (IN)

ASTRONOMY
Amherst Coll (MA)
Barnard Coll (NY)
Baylor U (TX)
Benedictine Coll (KS)
Bennington Coll (VT)
Boston U (MA)
Brigham Young U (UT)
Bryn Mawr Coll (PA)
Case Western Reserve U (OH)
Central Michigan U (MI)
Columbia U (NY)
Columbia U, School of General Studies (NY)
Cornell U (NY)
Dartmouth Coll (NH)
Drake U (IA)
Embry-Riddle Aeronautical U–Prescott (AZ)
Franklin & Marshall Coll (PA)
George Mason U (VA)
Hampshire Coll (MA)
Haverford Coll (PA)
Indiana U Bloomington (IN)
Lehigh U (PA)
Lycoming Coll (PA)
Minnesota State U Mankato (MN)
Mount Holyoke Coll (MA)
Northern Arizona U (AZ)
Northwestern U (IL)
The Ohio State U (OH)
Ohio Wesleyan U (OH)
Penn State Abington (PA)
Penn State Altoona (PA)
Penn State Beaver (PA)
Penn State Berks (PA)
Penn State Brandywine (PA)
Penn State DuBois (PA)
Penn State Erie, The Behrend Coll (PA)
Penn State Fayette, The Eberly Campus (PA)
Penn State Greater Allegheny (PA)
Penn State Hazleton (PA)
Penn State Lehigh Valley (PA)
Penn State Mont Alto (PA)
Penn State New Kensington (PA)
Penn State Schuylkill (PA)
Penn State Shenango (PA)
Penn State U Park (PA)
Penn State Wilkes-Barre (PA)
Penn State Worthington Scranton (PA)
Penn State York (PA)
Pomona Coll (CA)
Rice U (TX)
San Diego State U (CA)
San Francisco State U (CA)
Smith Coll (MA)
State U of New York at New Paltz (NY)
Stony Brook U, State U of New York (NY)
Tufts U (MA)
Union Coll (NY)
The U of Arizona (AZ)
The U of British Columbia (BC, Canada)
U of California, Santa Cruz (CA)
U of Colorado Boulder (CO)
U of Florida (FL)
U of Georgia (GA)
U of Hawaii at Hilo (HI)
U of Hawaii at Manoa (HI)
The U of Iowa (IA)
The U of Kansas (KS)
U of Maryland, Coll Park (MD)
U of Massachusetts Amherst (MA)
U of Michigan (MI)
U of Minnesota, Twin Cities Campus (MN)
The U of Montana (MT)
U of Oklahoma (OK)
U of Pittsburgh (PA)
U of Southern California (CA)
The U of Texas at Austin (TX)
The U of Toledo (OH)
U of Virginia (VA)
U of Washington (WA)
The U of Western Ontario (ON, Canada)
Valdosta State U (GA)
Valparaiso U (IN)
Vassar Coll (NY)
Villanova U (PA)
Washington State U (WA)
Wayne State U (MI)
Wesleyan U (CT)
Whitman Coll (WA)
Williams Coll (MA)
Yale U (CT)
Youngstown State U (OH)

ASTRONOMY AND ASTROPHYSICS RELATED
Butler U (IN)
Coll of Charleston (SC)
Florida Inst of Technology (FL)
Harvard U (MA)
Texas Christian U (TX)
U of Wyoming (WY)

ASTROPHYSICS
Agnes Scott Coll (GA)
Barnard Coll (NY)
Baylor U (TX)
Boston U (MA)
California Inst of Technology (CA)
Columbia U (NY)
Columbia U, School of General Studies (NY)
Franklin & Marshall Coll (PA)
Haverford Coll (PA)
Illinois Inst of Technology (IL)
Lehigh U (PA)
Lycoming Coll (PA)
Michigan State U (MI)
Ohio U (OH)
Ohio Wesleyan U (OH)
Princeton U (NJ)
Rice U (TX)
Rutgers, The State U of New Jersey, New Brunswick (NJ)
San Francisco State U (CA)
Tufts U (MA)
U of Alberta (AB, Canada)
U of California, Berkeley (CA)
U of California, Los Angeles (CA)
U of California, Santa Cruz (CA)
U of Cincinnati (OH)
U of Hawaii at Manoa (HI)
U of Minnesota, Twin Cities Campus (MN)
U of New Mexico (NM)
U of Oklahoma (OK)
The U of Western Ontario (ON, Canada)
U of Wisconsin–Madison (WI)
Villanova U (PA)
Whitman Coll (WA)
Williams Coll (MA)
Yale U (CT)

ATHLETIC TRAINING
Albion Coll (MI)
Alvernia U (PA)
Anderson U (IN)
Appalachian State U (NC)
Aquinas Coll (MI)
Arkansas State U (AR)
Ashland U (OH)
Augustana Coll (SD)
Averett U (VA)
Azusa Pacific U (CA)
Baldwin Wallace U (OH)
Baylor U (TX)
Benedictine Coll (KS)
Bethel Coll (KS)
Bethel U (MN)
Boston U (MA)
Bowling Green State U (OH)
Bridgewater Coll (VA)
Bridgewater State U (MA)
Brigham Young U (UT)
Buena Vista U (IA)
California State U, Fullerton (CA)
California State U, Long Beach (CA)
California U of Pennsylvania (PA)
Campbellsville U (KY)
Canisius Coll (NY)
Capital U (OH)
Castleton State Coll (VT)
Catawba Coll (NC)
Cedarville U (OH)
Central Coll (IA)
Central Connecticut State U (CT)
Central Methodist U (MO)
Central Michigan U (MI)
Chapman U (CA)
Clarke U (IA)
Coe Coll (IA)
Colby-Sawyer Coll (NH)
The Coll at Brockport, State U of New York (NY)
Coll of Charleston (SC)
Colorado Mesa U (CO)
Colorado State U (CO)
Concordia U (CA)
Concordia U Wisconsin (WI)
Concord U (WV)
Creighton U (NE)
Culver-Stockton Coll (MO)
Cumberland U (TN)
Defiance Coll (OH)
Delta State U (MS)
DePauw U (IN)
Dominican Coll (NY)
Duquesne U (PA)
East Carolina U (NC)
East Central U (OK)
Eastern Illinois U (IL)
Eastern Kentucky U (KY)
Eastern Michigan U (MI)
Eastern U (PA)
East Stroudsburg U of Pennsylvania (PA)
East Texas Baptist U (TX)
Emory & Henry Coll (VA)
Emporia State U (KS)
Endicott Coll (MA)
Erskine Coll (SC)
Eureka Coll (IL)
Florida Gulf Coast U (FL)
Florida Southern Coll (FL)
Florida State U (FL)
Fort Lewis Coll (CO)
Franklin Coll (IN)
Frostburg State U (MD)
George Mason U (VA)
Georgetown Coll (KY)
Georgia Coll & State U (GA)
Georgia Southern U (GA)
Graceland U (IA)
Grand Valley State U (MI)
Greensboro Coll (NC)
Gustavus Adolphus Coll (MN)
Harding U (AR)
Hardin-Simmons U (TX)
Heidelberg U (OH)
High Point U (NC)
Hofstra U (NY)
Hope Coll (MI)
Howard Payne U (TX)
Illinois State U (IL)
Indiana State U (IN)
Indiana U Bloomington (IN)
Indiana U of Pennsylvania (PA)
Ithaca Coll (NY)
James Madison U (VA)
Johnson State Coll (VT)
Kansas State U (KS)
Kean U (NJ)
Keene State Coll (NH)
Kent State U (OH)
King's Coll (PA)
King U (TN)
Lasell Coll (MA)
Lees-McRae Coll (NC)
Lee U (TN)
Lewis U (IL)
Liberty U (VA)
Limestone Coll (SC)
Lincoln Memorial U (TN)
Lindenwood U (MO)
Linfield Coll (OR)
Lock Haven U of Pennsylvania (PA)
Long Island U–LIU Brooklyn (NY)
Longwood U (VA)
Loras Coll (IA)
Louisiana Coll (LA)
Louisiana State U and A&M Coll (LA)
Lubbock Christian U (TX)
Luther Coll (IA)
Lynchburg Coll (VA)
Manchester U (IN)
Marietta Coll (OH)
Marist Coll (NY)
Marquette U (WI)
Marshall U (WV)
Mars Hill U (NC)
Marywood U (PA)
Massachusetts Coll of Liberal Arts (MA)
McKendree U (IL)
McMurry U (TX)
McNeese State U (LA)
Merrimack Coll (MA)
Messiah Coll (PA)
Miami U (OH)
Michigan State U (MI)
MidAmerica Nazarene U (KS)
Middle Tennessee State U (TN)
Midwestern State U (TX)
Millikin U (IL)
Minnesota State U Moorhead (MN)
Minot State U (ND)
Missouri State U (MO)
Missouri Valley Coll (MO)
Montclair State U (NJ)
Mount St. Joseph U (OH)
Murray State U (KY)
Nebraska Wesleyan U (NE)
Neumann U (PA)
New Mexico State U (NM)
North Carolina Central U (NC)
North Central Coll (IL)
Northern Illinois U (IL)
Northern Michigan U (MI)
Northwestern Coll (IA)
Northwest Nazarene U (ID)
Norwich U (VT)
Ohio Northern U (OH)
The Ohio State U (OH)
Ohio U (OH)
Oklahoma Baptist U (OK)
Oklahoma State U (OK)
Olivet Coll (MI)
Olivet Nazarene U (IL)
Oregon State U (OR)
Pacific U (OR)
Palm Beach Atlantic U (FL)
Park U (MO)
Penn State U Park (PA)
Piedmont Coll (GA)
Plymouth State U (NH)
Point Loma Nazarene U (CA)
Quinnipiac U (CT)
Radford U (VA)
Roanoke Coll (VA)
Rocky Mountain Coll (MT)
Rowan U (NJ)
Sacred Heart U (CT)
Saginaw Valley State U (MI)
Saint Augustine's U (NC)
St. Catharine Coll (KY)
Saint Joseph's Coll (IN)
Salisbury U (MD)
Samford U (AL)
Sam Houston State U (TX)
San Diego State U (CA)
Shawnee State U (OH)
Shaw U (NC)
Simpson Coll (IA)
Slippery Rock U of Pennsylvania (PA)
South Dakota State U (SD)
Southeastern Louisiana U (LA)
Southeast Missouri State U (MO)
Southern Arkansas U–Magnolia (AR)
Southern Connecticut State U (CT)
Southern Utah U (UT)
Southwest Baptist U (MO)
Southwestern Coll (KS)

State U of New York Coll at Cortland (NY)
Sterling Coll (KS)
Stony Brook U, State U of New York (NY)
Tabor Coll (KS)
Temple U (PA)
Texas A&M U–Corpus Christi (TX)
Texas Christian U (TX)
Texas Lutheran U (TX)
Texas State U (TX)
Texas Wesleyan U (TX)
Thomas More Coll (KY)
Towson U (MD)
Troy U (AL)
Truman State U (MO)
Tusculum Coll (TN)
Union Coll (KY)
Union U (TN)
Université de Sherbrooke (QC, Canada)
The U of Akron (OH)
The U of Alabama (AL)
U of Central Arkansas (AR)
U of Central Florida (FL)
U of Charleston (WV)
U of Cincinnati (OH)
U of Delaware (DE)
U of Evansville (IN)
U of Florida (FL)
U of Georgia (GA)
U of Idaho (ID)
U of Indianapolis (IN)
The U of Iowa (IA)
The U of Kansas (KS)
U of La Verne (CA)
U of Louisiana at Lafayette (LA)
U of Maine (ME)
U of Maine at Presque Isle (ME)
U of Miami (FL)
U of Michigan (MI)
U of Minnesota, Duluth (MN)
U of Mobile (AL)
U of Mount Union (OH)
U of Nebraska–Lincoln (NE)
U of Nevada, Las Vegas (NV)
U of New England (ME)
The U of North Carolina at Charlotte (NC)
The U of North Carolina at Pembroke (NC)
The U of North Carolina Wilmington (NC)
U of North Dakota (ND)
U of Northern Colorado (CO)
U of Northern Iowa (IA)
U of North Florida (FL)
U of North Georgia (GA)
U of Pittsburgh at Bradford (PA)
U of Puerto Rico in Ponce (PR)
U of Southern Maine (ME)
U of Southern Mississippi (MS)
U of South Florida (FL)
The U of Tampa (FL)
The U of Tennessee at Martin (TN)
The U of Texas at Arlington (TX)
The U of Texas at Austin (TX)
The U of Texas of the Permian Basin (TX)
U of the Incarnate Word (TX)
The U of Toledo (OH)
The U of Tulsa (OK)
U of Utah (UT)
U of Vermont (VT)
The U of West Alabama (AL)
U of Wisconsin–Eau Claire (WI)
U of Wisconsin–La Crosse (WI)
U of Wisconsin–Madison (WI)
U of Wisconsin–Milwaukee (WI)
U of Wisconsin–Stevens Point (WI)
Upper Iowa U (IA)
Urbana U (OH)
Valdosta State U (GA)
Valley City State U (ND)
Vanguard U of Southern California (CA)
Washburn U (KS)
Washington State U (WA)
Waynesburg U (PA)
Wayne State Coll (NE)
Weber State U (UT)
Welch Coll (TN)
West Chester U of Pennsylvania (PA)
Western Carolina U (NC)
Western Illinois U (IL)
Western Michigan U (MI)
Westfield State U (MA)
West Texas A&M U (TX)
West Virginia Wesleyan Coll (WV)
Wheeling Jesuit U (WV)
Whitworth U (WA)
Wichita State U (KS)
William Paterson U of New Jersey (NJ)
William Woods U (MO)
Wingate U (NC)
Winona State U (MN)
Wright State U (OH)
Xavier U (OH)
Youngstown State U (OH)

ATMOSPHERIC CHEMISTRY AND CLIMATOLOGY
Rutgers, The State U of New Jersey, New Brunswick (NJ)
U of Washington (WA)

ATMOSPHERIC SCIENCES AND METEOROLOGY
The Coll at Brockport, State U of New York (NY)
Cornell U (NY)
Creighton U (NE)
Dalhousie U (NS, Canada)
Embry-Riddle Aeronautical U–Daytona (FL)
Embry-Riddle Aeronautical U–Prescott (AZ)
Florida State U (FL)
George Mason U (VA)
Iowa State U of Science and Technology (IA)
Jackson State U (MS)
Millersville U of Pennsylvania (PA)
North Carolina Ag and Tech State U (NC)
North Carolina State U (NC)
Northern Illinois U (IL)
Ohio U (OH)
Penn State Abington (PA)
Penn State Altoona (PA)
Penn State Beaver (PA)
Penn State Berks (PA)
Penn State Brandywine (PA)
Penn State DuBois (PA)
Penn State Erie, The Behrend Coll (PA)
Penn State Fayette, The Eberly Campus (PA)
Penn State Greater Allegheny (PA)
Penn State Hazleton (PA)
Penn State Lehigh Valley (PA)
Penn State Mont Alto (PA)
Penn State New Kensington (PA)
Penn State Schuylkill (PA)
Penn State Shenango (PA)
Penn State U Park (PA)
Penn State Wilkes-Barre (PA)
Penn State Worthington Scranton (PA)
Penn State York (PA)
Plymouth State U (NH)
Purdue U (IN)
Rutgers, The State U of New Jersey, New Brunswick (NJ)
Saint Louis U (MO)
San Francisco State U (CA)
San Jose State U (CA)
State U of New York at Oswego (NY)
Stony Brook U, State U of New York (NY)
Texas A&M U (TX)
United States Air Force Acad (CO)
U at Albany, State U of New York (NY)
U of Alberta (AB, Canada)
The U of British Columbia (BC, Canada)
U of California, Berkeley (CA)
U of California, Davis (CA)
The U of Kansas (KS)
U of Louisville (KY)
U of Maryland, Coll Park (MD)
U of Miami (FL)
U of Michigan (MI)
U of Missouri (MO)
U of Nebraska–Lincoln (NE)
U of Nevada, Reno (NV)
U of North Carolina at Asheville (NC)
U of North Dakota (ND)
U of Utah (UT)
U of Washington (WA)
U of Waterloo (ON, Canada)
U of Wisconsin–Madison (WI)
Valparaiso U (IN)

ATMOSPHERIC SCIENCES AND METEOROLOGY RELATED
East Carolina U (NC)
U of California, Los Angeles (CA)
U of the Incarnate Word (TX)

ATOMIC/MOLECULAR PHYSICS
Columbia U (NY)
San Diego State U (CA)
U of Waterloo (ON, Canada)

AUDIOLOGY
American U of Beirut (Lebanon)
Biola U (CA)
California State U, Long Beach (CA)
Cleveland State U (OH)
Northwestern U (IL)
The Ohio State U (OH)
Stephen F. Austin State U (TX)
U of Montevallo (AL)

AUDIOLOGY AND SPEECH-LANGUAGE PATHOLOGY
Adelphi U (NY)
Andrews U (MI)
Arkansas State U (AR)
Auburn U (AL)
Augustana Coll (SD)
Ball State U (IN)
Biola U (CA)
Bloomsburg U of Pennsylvania (PA)
Boston U (MA)
Bowling Green State U (OH)
Buffalo State Coll, State U of New York (NY)
California State U, Fresno (CA)
California State U, Long Beach (CA)
California State U, Sacramento (CA)
Calvin Coll (MI)
The Coll of Idaho (ID)
The Coll of Saint Rose (NY)
Delta State U (MS)
East Carolina U (NC)
Eastern Kentucky U (KY)
Eastern New Mexico U (NM)
East Stroudsburg U of Pennsylvania (PA)
Elmhurst Coll (IL)
Elmira Coll (NY)
Emerson Coll (MA)
Fontbonne U (MO)
Fort Hays State U (KS)
The George Washington U (DC)
Hardin-Simmons U (TX)
Hofstra U (NY)
Hunter Coll of the City U of New York (NY)
Illinois State U (IL)
Indiana State U (IN)
Indiana U Bloomington (IN)
Indiana U of Pennsylvania (PA)
Indiana U–Purdue U Fort Wayne (IN)
Iona Coll (NY)
Ithaca Coll (NY)
Kent State U (OH)
La Salle U (PA)
Lehman Coll of the City U of New York (NY)
Long Island U–LIU Brooklyn (NY)
Long Island U–LIU Post (NY)
Longwood U (VA)
Louisiana State U and A&M Coll (LA)
Marquette U (WI)
Marymount Manhattan Coll (NY)
Marywood U (PA)
Mercy Coll (NY)
Miami U (OH)
Minnesota State U Mankato (MN)
Minnesota State U Moorhead (MN)
Missouri State U (MO)
Murray State U (KY)
Nazareth Coll of Rochester (NY)
New York U (NY)
Nicholls State U (LA)
Northeastern State U (OK)
Northeastern U (MA)
Northwestern U (IL)
The Ohio State U (OH)
Ohio U (OH)
Old Dominion U (VA)
Purdue U (IN)
St. John's U (NY)
South Carolina State U (SC)
Southeastern Louisiana U (LA)
Southern Connecticut State U (CT)
Southern Illinois U Edwardsville (IL)
State U of New York at Fredonia (NY)
State U of New York at Plattsburgh (NY)
State U of New York Coll at Cortland (NY)
Stockton U (NJ)
Temple U (PA)
Tennessee State U (TN)
Texas Woman's U (TX)
Thiel Coll (PA)
Université de Montréal (QC, Canada)
U at Buffalo, the State U of New York (NY)
The U of Alabama (AL)
U of Arkansas (AR)
U of Arkansas at Little Rock (AR)
U of Central Arkansas (AR)
U of Central Florida (FL)
U of Central Oklahoma (OK)
U of Florida (FL)
The U of Iowa (IA)
U of Kentucky (KY)
U of Louisiana at Lafayette (LA)
U of Minnesota, Twin Cities Campus (MN)
U of Mississippi (MS)
The U of Montana (MT)
U of New Mexico (NM)
The U of North Carolina at Greensboro (NC)
U of Northern Colorado (CO)
U of North Texas (TX)
U of Pittsburgh (PA)
U of Southern Mississippi (MS)
U of South Florida (FL)
The U of Tennessee (TN)
The U of Texas at Dallas (TX)
The U of Texas at El Paso (TX)
U of the District of Columbia (DC)
U of the Pacific (CA)
The U of Toledo (OH)
The U of Tulsa (OK)
U of Utah (UT)
U of Virginia (VA)
U of Washington (WA)
U of Wisconsin–Madison (WI)
U of Wisconsin–Milwaukee (WI)
U of Wisconsin–Oshkosh (WI)
U of Wisconsin–Stevens Point (WI)
U of Wyoming (WY)
Utah State U (UT)
Washington State U (WA)
West Chester U of Pennsylvania (PA)
Western Michigan U (MI)
Western Washington U (WA)
West Virginia U (WV)
Yeshiva U (NY)

AUDIOVISUAL COMMUNICATIONS TECHNOLOGIES RELATED
Coll of the Ozarks (MO)
Webster U (MO)

AUDITING
Babson Coll (MA)
Carlow U (PA)
Inter American U of Puerto Rico, Bayamón Campus (PR)
State U of New York Coll of Technology at Delhi (NY)

AUSTRALIAN/OCEANIC/PACIFIC LANGUAGES
U of Hawaii–West Oahu (HI)

AUTOBODY/COLLISION AND REPAIR TECHNOLOGY
Pennsylvania Coll of Technology (PA)

AUTOMATION ENGINEER TECHNOLOGY
Purdue U Calumet (IN)

AUTOMOBILE/AUTOMOTIVE MECHANICS TECHNOLOGY
Benjamin Franklin Inst of Technology (MA)
Morrisville State Coll (NY)
New England Inst of Technology (RI)
Walla Walla U (WA)

AUTOMOTIVE ENGINEERING TECHNOLOGY
Benjamin Franklin Inst of Technology (MA)
Colorado State U–Pueblo (CO)
Ferris State U (MI)
Indiana State U (IN)
Minnesota State U Mankato (MN)
Pennsylvania Coll of Technology (PA)
Pittsburg State U (KS)
Southern Illinois U Carbondale (IL)
Western Washington U (WA)

AVIATION/AIRWAY MANAGEMENT
Auburn U (AL)
Averett U (VA)
Bridgewater State U (MA)
California Baptist U (CA)
California State U, Los Angeles (CA)
Central Washington U (WA)
Daniel Webster Coll (NH)
Delaware State U (DE)
Dixie State U (UT)
Dowling Coll (NY)
Eastern Michigan U (MI)
Eastern New Mexico U (NM)
Embry-Riddle Aeronautical U–Prescott (AZ)
Embry-Riddle Aeronautical U–Worldwide (FL)
Everglades U, Sarasota (FL)
Fairmont State U (WV)
Farmingdale State Coll (NY)
Florida Inst of Technology (FL)
Hallmark U (TX)
Hampton U (VA)
Indiana State U (IN)
Inter American U of Puerto Rico, Bayamón Campus (PR)
Jacksonville U (FL)
LeTourneau U (TX)
Lewis U (IL)
Lynn U (FL)
Marywood U (PA)
Minnesota State U Mankato (MN)
Northern Kentucky U (KY)
The Ohio State U (OH)
Ohio U (OH)
Quincy U (IL)
Rocky Mountain Coll (MT)
Saint Louis U (MO)
South Dakota State U (SD)
Southern Illinois U Carbondale (IL)
Tarleton State U (TX)
Texas Southern U (TX)
U of Dubuque (IA)
U of North Dakota (ND)
U of the Fraser Valley (BC, Canada)
The U of Western Ontario (ON, Canada)
Vaughn Coll of Aeronautics and Technology (NY)
Western Michigan U (MI)
Westminster Coll (UT)
Wilmington U (DE)

AVIONICS MAINTENANCE TECHNOLOGY
Fairmont State U (WV)
Lewis U (IL)
Pennsylvania Coll of Technology (PA)
Southern Illinois U Carbondale (IL)
Vaughn Coll of Aeronautics and Technology (NY)
Western Michigan U (MI)

AYURVEDIC MEDICINE
Maharishi U of Management (IA)

BAKING AND PASTRY ARTS
Johnson & Wales U (CO)
Johnson & Wales U (FL)
Johnson & Wales U (RI)

Johnson & Wales U - Charlotte Campus (NC)
Stratford U (MD)

BALLET
Brigham Young U (UT)
Friends U (KS)
Indiana U Bloomington (IN)
Marymount Manhattan Coll (NY)
Texas Christian U (TX)
U of Utah (UT)

BANKING AND FINANCIAL SUPPORT SERVICES
Buena Vista U (IA)
Delaware State U (DE)
Husson U (ME)
National U Coll, Bayamón (PR)
Northwood U, Michigan Campus (MI)
Saint Peter's U (NJ)
Sam Houston State U (TX)
State U of New York Coll of Agriculture and Technology at Cobleskill (NY)
Texas Southern U (TX)
U of Nebraska–Lincoln (NE)
U of North Florida (FL)
The U of Texas at Arlington (TX)
U of the Incarnate Word (TX)
West Liberty U (WV)
Youngstown State U (OH)

BEHAVIORAL ASPECTS OF HEALTH
Goddard Coll (VT)
Taylor U (IN)
U of Southern California (CA)

BEHAVIORAL SCIENCES
Ambrose U Coll (AB, Canada)
American Baptist Coll of American Baptist Theological Sem (TN)
Andrews U (MI)
Athens State U (AL)
Bemidji State U (MN)
Brown U (RI)
California Baptist U (CA)
California State U, Dominguez Hills (CA)
Central Washington U (WA)
Chaminade U of Honolulu (HI)
Columbia Coll (SC)
Concordia Coll–New York (NY)
Concordia U (CA)
Concordia U, Nebraska (NE)
Duquesne U (PA)
Evangel U (MO)
Goddard Coll (VT)
Inter American U of Puerto Rico, San Germán Campus (PR)
Johns Hopkins U (MD)
Mars Hill U (NC)
Mercy Coll (NY)
Minnesota State U Mankato (MN)
Missouri Baptist U (MO)
Mount Mary U (WI)
Northern Michigan U (MI)
Nova Southeastern U (FL)
Purdue U Calumet (IN)
Rocky Mountain Coll (AB, Canada)
Saint Augustine's U (NC)
San Jose State U (CA)
Sterling Coll (KS)
Tabor Coll (KS)
Tennessee Wesleyan Coll (TN)
Trevecca Nazarene U (TN)
Tufts U (MA)
United States Air Force Acad (CO)
U of Houston–Clear Lake (TX)
The U of Kansas (KS)
U of La Verne (CA)
U of Maine at Fort Kent (ME)
U of Maine at Machias (ME)
U of Missouri (MO)
U of North Texas (TX)
U of Wisconsin–Green Bay (WI)
Walsh U (OH)
Widener U (PA)
Wilmington U (DE)
York Coll of Pennsylvania (PA)

BIBLICAL STUDIES
Abilene Christian U (TX)
Amridge U (AL)
Anderson U (IN)
Andrews U (MI)
Arizona Christian U (AZ)
Asbury U (KY)
Azusa Pacific U (CA)
The Baptist Coll of Florida (FL)
Baptist U of the Americas (TX)
Barclay Coll (KS)
Belhaven U (MS)
Belmont U (TN)
Bethel Coll (IN)
Bethel U (MN)
Beulah Heights U (GA)
Biola U (CA)
Bluefield Coll (VA)
Blue Mountain Coll (MS)
Bluffton U (OH)
Bob Jones U (SC)
Bryan Coll (TN)
Cairn U (PA)
California Baptist U (CA)
Calvary Bible Coll and Theological Sem (MO)
Calvin Coll (MI)
Campbellsville U (KY)
Canisius Coll (NY)
Carson-Newman U (TN)
Cedarville U (OH)
Cincinnati Christian U (OH)
Clearwater Christian Coll (FL)
Coll of Biblical Studies–Houston (TX)
Coll of the Ozarks (MO)
Columbia Bible Coll (BC, Canada)
Corban U (OR)
Cornerstone U (MI)
Covenant Coll (GA)
Crandall U (NB, Canada)
Crossroads Coll (MN)
Dallas Baptist U (TX)
Davis Coll (NY)
Eastern U (PA)
East Texas Baptist U (TX)
Evangel U (MO)
Faith Baptist Bible Coll and Theological Sem (IA)
Faulkner U (AL)
Florida Coll (FL)
Geneva Coll (PA)
Gordon Coll (MA)
Goshen Coll (IN)
Grace Coll (IN)
Great Lakes Christian Coll (MI)
Hannibal-LaGrange U (MO)
Harding U (AR)
Hardin-Simmons U (TX)
Hobe Sound Bible Coll (FL)
Hope Intl U (CA)
Houghton Coll (NY)
Houston Baptist U (TX)
Howard Payne U (TX)
John Brown U (AR)
Judson U (IL)
Kentucky Christian U (KY)
Kentucky Mountain Bible Coll (KY)
Kingswood U (NB, Canada)
King U (TN)
Kuyper Coll (MI)
Lee U (TN)
LeTourneau U (TX)
Liberty U (VA)
Lincoln Christian U (IL)
Lipscomb U (TN)
Lubbock Christian U (TX)
Malone U (OH)
Manhattan Christian Coll (KS)
Maranatha Baptist U (WI)
The Master's Coll and Sem (CA)
Master's Coll and Sem (ON, Canada)
Messiah Coll (PA)
MidAmerica Nazarene U (KS)
Mid-Atlantic Christian U (NC)
Milligan Coll (TN)
Montreat Coll, Montreat (NC)
Mount Vernon Nazarene U (OH)
Multnomah U (OR)
Nazarene Bible Coll (CO)
North Greenville U (SC)
Northwest Christian U (OR)
Northwest Nazarene U (ID)
Northwest U (WA)
Nyack Coll (NY)
Oakland City U (IN)
Ohio Valley U (WV)
Oklahoma Baptist U (OK)
Oklahoma Christian U (OK)
Oklahoma Wesleyan U (OK)
Palm Beach Atlantic U (FL)
Point Loma Nazarene U (CA)
Point U (GA)
Roberts Wesleyan Coll (NY)
Rocky Mountain Coll (AB, Canada)
Saint Louis Christian Coll (MO)
San Diego Christian Coll (CA)
Selma U (AL)
Shasta Bible Coll (CA)
Shiloh U (IA)
Simpson U (CA)
Southeastern Bible Coll (AL)
Southern Adventist U (TN)
Southern California Sem (CA)
Southwest Baptist U (MO)
Southwestern Assemblies of God U (TX)
Summit U (PA)
Toccoa Falls Coll (GA)
Truett-McConnell Coll (GA)
Union Coll (NE)
Union U (TN)
Universidad Teolgica del Caribe (PR)
Université de Montréal (QC, Canada)
U of Evansville (IN)
U of Mary Hardin-Baylor (TX)
U of Northwestern–St. Paul (MN)
U of Valley Forge (PA)
The U of Western Ontario (ON, Canada)
Vanguard U of Southern California (CA)
Waynesburg U (PA)
Welch Coll (TN)
Wheaton Coll (IL)
Williamson Christian Coll (TN)

BILINGUAL AND MULTILINGUAL EDUCATION
Boston U (MA)
California State U, Stanislaus (CA)
Calvin Coll (MI)
Canisius Coll (NY)
Chicago State U (IL)
Goddard Coll (VT)
Houston Baptist U (TX)
Loyola U Chicago (IL)
Midwestern State U (TX)
Mount Mary U (WI)
Northeastern Illinois U (IL)
Southwestern Assemblies of God U (TX)
State U of New York Coll at Old Westbury (NY)
Texas A&M Intl U (TX)
Texas Christian U (TX)
Texas Wesleyan U (TX)
U of Delaware (DE)
The U of Findlay (OH)
U of Regina (SK, Canada)
U of San Francisco (CA)
The U of Texas at San Antonio (TX)
Washington State U (WA)
Western Illinois U (IL)
York Coll of the City U of New York (NY)

BIOCHEMICAL ENGINEERING
Christian Brothers U (TN)
U of Colorado Boulder (CO)
U of Georgia (GA)

BIOCHEMISTRY
Abilene Christian U (TX)
Adams State U (CO)
Adelphi U (NY)
Agnes Scott Coll (GA)
Albion Coll (MI)
Albright Coll (PA)
Allegheny Coll (PA)
Alma Coll (MI)
Alvernia U (PA)
American Intl Coll (MA)
American U (DC)
Anderson U (IN)
Andrews U (MI)
Arizona State U at the Tempe campus (AZ)
Asbury U (KY)
Auburn U (AL)
Augustana Coll (IL)
Augustana Coll (SD)
Austin Coll (TX)
Ave Maria U (FL)
Azusa Pacific U (CA)
Barnard Coll (NY)
Bates Coll (ME)
Baylor U (TX)
Bay Path U (MA)
Belmont U (TN)
Beloit Coll (WI)
Benedictine Coll (KS)
Berry Coll (GA)
Bethany Coll (WV)
Binghamton U, State U of New York (NY)
Biola U (CA)
Boston Coll (MA)
Bowdoin Coll (ME)
Bowling Green State U (OH)
Bradley U (IL)
Brandeis U (MA)
Bridgewater State U (MA)
Brown U (RI)
Bucknell U (PA)
California Lutheran U (CA)
California Polytechnic State U, San Luis Obispo (CA)
California State U, Chico (CA)
California State U, Dominguez Hills (CA)
California State U, Fullerton (CA)
California State U, Long Beach (CA)
California State U, Los Angeles (CA)
California State U, San Marcos (CA)
Calvin Coll (MI)
Canisius Coll (NY)
Capital U (OH)
Case Western Reserve U (OH)
The Catholic U of America (DC)
Cedar Crest Coll (PA)
Central Coll (IA)
Central Connecticut State U (CT)
Central Michigan U (MI)
Central Washington U (WA)
Chaminade U of Honolulu (HI)
Chapman U (CA)
Charleston Southern U (SC)
Chatham U (PA)
Chestnut Hill Coll (PA)
Christian Brothers U (TN)
Christopher Newport U (VA)
City Coll of the City U of New York (NY)
Claflin U (SC)
Claremont McKenna Coll (CA)
Clarke U (IA)
Clark U (MA)
Coastal Carolina U (SC)
Coe Coll (IA)
Colby Coll (ME)
The Coll at Brockport, State U of New York (NY)
Coll of Saint Benedict (MN)
Coll of Saint Elizabeth (NJ)
The Coll of Saint Rose (NY)
The Coll of St. Scholastica (MN)
Coll of Staten Island of the City U of New York (NY)
The Coll of Wooster (OH)
The Colorado Coll (CO)
Colorado State U (CO)
Columbia Coll (SC)
Columbia U (NY)
Columbia U, School of General Studies (NY)
Connecticut Coll (CT)
Cornell Coll (IA)
Cornell U (NY)
Curry Coll (MA)
Daemen Coll (NY)
Dartmouth Coll (NH)
Denison U (OH)
DePauw U (IN)
DeSales U (PA)
Dickinson Coll (PA)
Doane Coll (NE)
Dominican U (IL)
Drake U (IA)
Drew U (NJ)
Duquesne U (PA)
Earlham Coll (IN)
East Carolina U (NC)
Eastern Connecticut State U (CT)
Eastern Michigan U (MI)
Eastern New Mexico U (NM)
Eastern Oregon U (OR)
Eastern U (PA)
East Stroudsburg U of Pennsylvania (PA)
Eckerd Coll (FL)
Elizabethtown Coll (PA)
Elon U (NC)
Emmanuel Coll (MA)
Fairfield U (CT)
Fairleigh Dickinson U, Coll at Florham (NJ)
Fairleigh Dickinson U, Metropolitan Campus (NJ)
Ferris State U (MI)
Florida Inst of Technology (FL)
Florida State U (FL)
Fort Lewis Coll (CO)
Franklin & Marshall Coll (PA)
Furman U (SC)
Gannon U (PA)
Geneva Coll (PA)
Georgetown Coll (KY)
Georgetown U (DC)
Georgia Inst of Technology (GA)
Georgian Court U (NJ)
Gettysburg Coll (PA)
Gonzaga U (WA)
Grand View U (IA)
Grinnell Coll (IA)
Grove City Coll (PA)
Gustavus Adolphus Coll (MN)
Hamilton Coll (NY)
Hamline U (MN)
Hanover Coll (IN)
Harding U (AR)
Hartwick Coll (NY)
Harvard U (MA)
Haverford Coll (PA)
Hawai`i Pacific U (HI)
High Point U (NC)
Hillsdale Coll (MI)
Hiram Coll (OH)
Hobart and William Smith Colls (NY)
Hofstra U (NY)
Holy Family U (PA)
Houghton Coll (NY)
Humboldt State U (CA)
Huntingdon Coll (AL)
Illinois Inst of Technology (IL)
Illinois State U (IL)
Indiana U Bloomington (IN)
Indiana U East (IN)
Indiana U Kokomo (IN)
Indiana U of Pennsylvania (PA)
Indiana U South Bend (IN)
Iona Coll (NY)
Iowa State U of Science and Technology (IA)
Ithaca Coll (NY)
John Brown U (AR)
Judson U (IL)
Juniata Coll (PA)
Kansas State U (KS)
Kennesaw State U (GA)
Kenyon Coll (OH)
Kettering U (MI)
Keuka Coll (NY)
King U (TN)
Knox Coll (IL)
Kutztown U of Pennsylvania (PA)
Lafayette Coll (PA)
LaGrange Coll (GA)
Lamar U (TX)
La Roche Coll (PA)
La Salle U (PA)
La Sierra U (CA)
Lawrence Technological U (MI)
Lawrence U (WI)
Lee U (TN)
Lehigh U (PA)
Lehman Coll of the City U of New York (NY)
Le Moyne Coll (NY)
Lewis & Clark Coll (OR)
Lewis U (IL)
Liberty U (VA)
Lipscomb U (TN)
Long Island U–LIU Brooklyn (NY)
Loras Coll (IA)
Louisiana State U and A&M Coll (LA)
Loyola Marymount U (CA)
Loyola U Chicago (IL)
Lubbock Christian U (TX)
Madonna U (MI)
Manchester U (IN)
Manhattan Coll (NY)
Manhattanville Coll (NY)
Mansfield U of Pennsylvania (PA)
Marietta Coll (OH)
Marist Coll (NY)
Marymount U (VA)
Maryville Coll (TN)

Maryville U of Saint Louis (MO)
McMurry U (TX)
Mercer U, Macon (GA)
Merrimack Coll (MA)
Messiah Coll (PA)
Miami U (OH)
Michigan State U (MI)
Middlebury Coll (VT)
Millsaps Coll (MS)
Mills Coll (CA)
Minnesota State U Mankato (MN)
Misericordia U (PA)
Mississippi State U (MS)
Missouri Baptist U (MO)
Missouri Southern State U (MO)
Missouri Western State U (MO)
Monmouth Coll (IL)
Montclair State U (NJ)
Moravian Coll (PA)
Mount Allison U (NB, Canada)
Mount Holyoke Coll (MA)
Mount St. Joseph U (OH)
Mount Saint Mary's U (CA)
Mount St. Mary's U (MD)
Muhlenberg Coll (PA)
Nazareth Coll of Rochester (NY)
New Coll of Florida (FL)
New Jersey Inst of Technology (NJ)
Newman U (KS)
New Mexico State U (NM)
New York U (NY)
Niagara U (NY)
North Carolina State U (NC)
North Central Coll (IL)
Northeastern U (MA)
Northern Michigan U (MI)
Northwestern U (IL)
Northwest Nazarene U (ID)
Oakland U (MI)
Oberlin Coll (OH)
Occidental Coll (CA)
Ohio Northern U (OH)
The Ohio State U (OH)
Oklahoma Baptist U (OK)
Oklahoma Christian U (OK)
Oklahoma City U (OK)
Oklahoma State U (OK)
Old Dominion U (VA)
Olivet Coll (MI)
Pace U (NY)
Penn State Abington (PA)
Penn State Altoona (PA)
Penn State Beaver (PA)
Penn State Berks (PA)
Penn State Brandywine (PA)
Penn State DuBois (PA)
Penn State Erie, The Behrend Coll (PA)
Penn State Fayette, The Eberly Campus (PA)
Penn State Greater Allegheny (PA)
Penn State Hazleton (PA)
Penn State Lehigh Valley (PA)
Penn State Mont Alto (PA)
Penn State New Kensington (PA)
Penn State Schuylkill (PA)
Penn State Shenango (PA)
Penn State U Park (PA)
Penn State Wilkes-Barre (PA)
Penn State Worthington Scranton (PA)
Penn State York (PA)
Philadelphia U (PA)
Point Loma Nazarene U (CA)
Portland State U (OR)
Presbyterian Coll (SC)
Providence Coll (RI)
Purchase Coll, State U of New York (NY)
Purdue U (IN)
Quinnipiac U (CT)
Ramapo Coll of New Jersey (NJ)
Reed Coll (OR)
Regis Coll (MA)
Regis U (CO)
Rice U (TX)
Rider U (NJ)
Ripon Coll (WI)
Roanoke Coll (VA)
Roberts Wesleyan Coll (NY)
Rochester Inst of Technology (NY)
Rockford U (IL)
Rockhurst U (MO)
Roger Williams U (RI)
Rollins Coll (FL)
Roosevelt U (IL)
Rose-Hulman Inst of Technology (IN)
Rosemont Coll (PA)
Rowan U (NJ)
Rutgers, The State U of New Jersey, New Brunswick (NJ)
The Sage Colls (NY)
Saginaw Valley State U (MI)
Saint Anselm Coll (NH)
St. Bonaventure U (NY)
St. Catherine U (MN)
St. Edward's U (TX)
Saint John's U (MN)
Saint Joseph's Coll (IN)
Saint Joseph's U (PA)
St. Lawrence U (NY)
Saint Louis U (MO)
St. Mary's Coll of Maryland (MD)
St. Mary's U (TX)
Saint Mary's U of Minnesota (MN)
Saint Michael's Coll (VT)
Saint Peter's U (NJ)
Saint Vincent Coll (PA)
Samford U (AL)
San Francisco State U (CA)
San Jose State U (CA)
Santa Clara U (CA)
Scripps Coll (CA)
Seattle Pacific U (WA)
Seattle U (WA)
Seton Hill U (PA)
Sewanee: The U of the South (TN)
Siena Coll (NY)
Simon Fraser U (BC, Canada)
Simpson Coll (IA)
Slippery Rock U of Pennsylvania (PA)
Smith Coll (MA)
South Dakota State U (SD)
Southern Adventist U (TN)
Southern Methodist U (TX)
Southern Oregon U (OR)
Southwestern Adventist U (TX)
Southwestern Coll (KS)
Southwestern U (TX)
Spelman Coll (GA)
Spring Hill Coll (AL)
State U of New York at Fredonia (NY)
State U of New York at New Paltz (NY)
State U of New York at Plattsburgh (NY)
State U of New York Coll at Geneseo (NY)
State U of New York Coll at Old Westbury (NY)
State U of New York Coll at Potsdam (NY)
State U of New York Coll of Environmental Science and Forestry (NY)
Stephen F. Austin State U (TX)
Stetson U (FL)
Stevenson U (MD)
Stockton U (NJ)
Stonehill Coll (MA)
Stony Brook U, State U of New York (NY)
Susquehanna U (PA)
Syracuse U (NY)
Tabor Coll (KS)
Temple U (PA)
Texas A&M U (TX)
Texas Christian U (TX)
Texas State U (TX)
Texas Tech U (TX)
Texas Wesleyan U (TX)
Texas Woman's U (TX)
Trent U (ON, Canada)
Trinity Christian Coll (IL)
Trinity Coll (CT)
Trinity U (TX)
Tufts U (MA)
Tulane U (LA)
Union Coll (NY)
United States Air Force Acad (CO)
Université de Montréal (QC, Canada)
Université de Sherbrooke (QC, Canada)
U at Albany, State U of New York (NY)
U at Buffalo, the State U of New York (NY)
The U of Akron (OH)
U of Alberta (AB, Canada)
The U of Arizona (AZ)
The U of British Columbia (BC, Canada)
The U of British Columbia–Okanagan Campus (BC, Canada)
U of California, Los Angeles (CA)
U of California, Riverside (CA)
U of California, Santa Cruz (CA)
U of Charleston (WV)
U of Cincinnati (OH)
U of Colorado Boulder (CO)
U of Colorado Colorado Springs (CO)
U of Dallas (TX)
U of Dayton (OH)
U of Delaware (DE)
U of Denver (CO)
U of Evansville (IN)
U of Guelph (ON, Canada)
U of Hawaii at Manoa (HI)
U of Houston (TX)
U of Idaho (ID)
U of Illinois at Chicago (IL)
The U of Iowa (IA)
U of Jamestown (ND)
The U of Kansas (KS)
U of King's Coll (NS, Canada)
U of Lethbridge (AB, Canada)
U of Maine (ME)
U of Mary Hardin-Baylor (TX)
U of Maryland, Coll Park (MD)
U of Massachusetts Boston (MA)
U of Miami (FL)
U of Michigan (MI)
U of Michigan–Dearborn (MI)
U of Michigan–Flint (MI)
U of Minnesota, Duluth (MN)
U of Minnesota, Twin Cities Campus (MN)
U of Mississippi (MS)
U of Missouri (MO)
U of Missouri–St. Louis (MO)
The U of Montana (MT)
U of Mount Union (OH)
U of Nebraska–Lincoln (NE)
U of Nevada, Las Vegas (NV)
U of Nevada, Reno (NV)
U of New England (ME)
U of New Hampshire (NH)
U of New Haven (CT)
U of New Mexico (NM)
The U of North Carolina at Greensboro (NC)
U of Northern Iowa (IA)
U of North Texas (TX)
U of Northwestern–St. Paul (MN)
U of Notre Dame (IN)
U of Oklahoma (OK)
U of Oregon (OR)
U of Ottawa (ON, Canada)
U of Pennsylvania (PA)
U of Puget Sound (WA)
U of Regina (SK, Canada)
U of Saint Joseph (CT)
U of St. Thomas (MN)
U of St. Thomas (TX)
U of San Diego (CA)
U of Saskatchewan (SK, Canada)
The U of Scranton (PA)
U of Southern California (CA)
U of Southern Indiana (IN)
The U of Tampa (FL)
The U of Texas at Arlington (TX)
The U of Texas at Austin (TX)
The U of Texas at Dallas (TX)
The U of Texas at San Antonio (TX)
U of the Incarnate Word (TX)
U of the Pacific (CA)
U of the Sciences (PA)
The U of Toledo (OH)
U of Toronto (ON, Canada)
The U of Tulsa (OK)
U of Vermont (VT)
U of Washington (WA)
U of Washington, Bothell (WA)
U of Waterloo (ON, Canada)
The U of Western Ontario (ON, Canada)
U of Windsor (ON, Canada)
U of Wisconsin–La Crosse (WI)
U of Wisconsin–Madison (WI)
U of Wisconsin–Milwaukee (WI)
U of Wisconsin–River Falls (WI)
U of Wisconsin–Stevens Point (WI)
Ursinus Coll (PA)
Valparaiso U (IN)
Vanguard U of Southern California (CA)
Vassar Coll (NY)
Villanova U (PA)
Virginia Polytechnic Inst and State U (VA)
Viterbo U (WI)
Wabash Coll (IN)
Walla Walla U (WA)
Wartburg Coll (IA)
Washburn U (KS)
Washington & Jefferson Coll (PA)
Washington and Lee U (VA)
Washington State U (WA)
Washington U in St. Louis (MO)
Wells Coll (NY)
West Chester U of Pennsylvania (PA)
Western Kentucky U (KY)
Western Michigan U (MI)
Western State Colorado U (CO)
Western Washington U (WA)
Westminster Coll (MO)
West Virginia U (WV)
Wheaton Coll (MA)
Whitman Coll (WA)
Whittier Coll (CA)
Widener U (PA)
Wilkes U (PA)
William Jewell Coll (MO)
Winona State U (MN)
Worcester Polytechnic Inst (MA)
Xavier U of Louisiana (LA)
Yeshiva U (NY)

BIOCHEMISTRY AND MOLECULAR BIOLOGY

Belmont U (TN)
Benedictine U (IL)
Bethany Coll (WV)
Boston U (MA)
California State U, Long Beach (CA)
Carroll Coll (MT)
Castleton State Coll (VT)
Centre Coll (KY)
Culver-Stockton Coll (MO)
Dalhousie U (NS, Canada)
The Evergreen State Coll (WA)
Florida Southern Coll (FL)
Goucher Coll (MD)
Harding U (AR)
Hardin-Simmons U (TX)
Hendrix Coll (AR)
Hope Coll (MI)
Lebanon Valley Coll (PA)
Lincoln U (PA)
Linfield Coll (OR)
Marquette U (WI)
Michigan State U (MI)
Michigan Technological U (MI)
Middlebury Coll (VT)
Minnesota State U Moorhead (MN)
Nebraska Wesleyan U (NE)
North Dakota State U (ND)
Oregon State U (OR)
Purdue U (IN)
Rhodes Coll (TN)
Simmons Coll (MA)
The U of British Columbia (BC, Canada)
U of California, Irvine (CA)
U of Georgia (GA)
U of Maryland, Baltimore County (MD)
U of Massachusetts Amherst (MA)
U of Minnesota, Duluth (MN)
U of New Hampshire (NH)
U of Regina (SK, Canada)
U of Waterloo (ON, Canada)
The U of Western Ontario (ON, Canada)
Whitman Coll (WA)
Wittenberg U (OH)

BIOCHEMISTRY, BIOPHYSICS AND MOLECULAR BIOLOGY RELATED

Amherst Coll (MA)
Blackburn Coll (IL)
California Baptist U (CA)
Indiana U Kokomo (IN)
Rensselaer Polytechnic Inst (NY)
Towson U (MD)
U of Miami (FL)
U of Waterloo (ON, Canada)
The U of Western Ontario (ON, Canada)
Xavier U (OH)

BIOENGINEERING AND BIOMEDICAL ENGINEERING

Alabama State U (AL)
Arizona State U at the Tempe campus (AZ)
Binghamton U, State U of New York (NY)
Boston U (MA)
Brown U (RI)
Bucknell U (PA)
California Baptist U (CA)
California Inst of Technology (CA)
California Polytechnic State U, San Luis Obispo (CA)
California State U, Long Beach (CA)
Case Western Reserve U (OH)
The Catholic U of America (DC)
Central Michigan U (MI)
City Coll of the City U of New York (NY)
The Coll of New Jersey (NJ)
Colorado School of Mines (CO)
Colorado State U (CO)
Columbia U (NY)
Dalhousie U (NS, Canada)
Delaware State U (DE)
Drexel U (PA)
Duquesne U (PA)
Elon U (NC)
Endicott Coll (MA)
Florida Gulf Coast U (FL)
Florida Inst of Technology (FL)
Florida Intl U (FL)
Gannon U (PA)
George Mason U (VA)
Georgia Inst of Technology (GA)
Harding U (AR)
Harvard U (MA)
Hofstra U (NY)
Illinois Inst of Technology (IL)
Indiana U–Purdue U Indianapolis (IN)
Johns Hopkins U (MD)
Lawrence Technological U (MI)
Lehigh U (PA)
LeTourneau U (TX)
Louisiana State U and A&M Coll (LA)
Marquette U (WI)
Massachusetts Inst of Technology (MA)
Miami U (OH)
Michigan Technological U (MI)
Milwaukee School of Eng (WI)
Mississippi State U (MS)
National U (CA)
New Jersey Inst of Technology (NJ)
New York U (NY)
North Carolina Ag and Tech State U (NC)
North Carolina State U (NC)
Northwestern U (IL)
The Ohio State U (OH)
Oregon State U (OR)
Penn State Abington (PA)
Penn State Altoona (PA)
Penn State Beaver (PA)
Penn State Berks (PA)
Penn State Brandywine (PA)
Penn State DuBois (PA)
Penn State Erie, The Behrend Coll (PA)
Penn State Fayette, The Eberly Campus (PA)
Penn State Greater Allegheny (PA)
Penn State Hazleton (PA)
Penn State Lehigh Valley (PA)
Penn State Mont Alto (PA)
Penn State New Kensington (PA)
Penn State Schuylkill (PA)
Penn State Shenango (PA)
Penn State U Park (PA)
Penn State Wilkes-Barre (PA)
Penn State Worthington Scranton (PA)
Penn State York (PA)
Purdue U (IN)
Rensselaer Polytechnic Inst (NY)
Rice U (TX)
Rochester Inst of Technology (NY)
Rose-Hulman Inst of Technology (IN)

Rowan U (NJ)
Rutgers, The State U of New Jersey, New Brunswick (NJ)
Saint Louis U (MO)
Santa Clara U (CA)
Southern California Inst of Technology (CA)
Stanford U (CA)
State U of New York Coll of Environmental Science and Forestry (NY)
Stony Brook U, State U of New York (NY)
Syracuse U (NY)
Temple U (PA)
Texas A&M U (TX)
Trinity Coll (CT)
Tufts U (MA)
Tulane U (LA)
Union Coll (NY)
U at Buffalo, the State U of New York (NY)
The U of Akron (OH)
The U of Alabama at Birmingham (AL)
The U of Arizona (AZ)
U of Arkansas (AR)
The U of British Columbia (BC, Canada)
U of California, Berkeley (CA)
U of California, Davis (CA)
U of California, Irvine (CA)
U of California, Merced (CA)
U of California, Riverside (CA)
U of California, Santa Cruz (CA)
U of Central Oklahoma (OK)
U of Cincinnati (OH)
U of Colorado Denver (CO)
U of Delaware (DE)
U of Florida (FL)
U of Guelph (ON, Canada)
U of Houston (TX)
U of Illinois at Chicago (IL)
The U of Iowa (IA)
U of Louisville (KY)
U of Maine (ME)
U of Massachusetts Dartmouth (MA)
U of Memphis (TN)
U of Miami (FL)
U of Michigan (MI)
U of New Hampshire (NH)
U of North Texas (TX)
U of Ottawa (ON, Canada)
U of Pennsylvania (PA)
U of Pittsburgh (PA)
U of Rhode Island (RI)
U of Rochester (NY)
U of Southern California (CA)
The U of Tennessee (TN)
The U of Texas at Arlington (TX)
The U of Texas at Austin (TX)
The U of Texas at Dallas (TX)
The U of Texas at San Antonio (TX)
U of the Pacific (CA)
The U of Toledo (OH)
U of Toronto (ON, Canada)
U of Utah (UT)
U of Virginia (VA)
U of Washington (WA)
U of Waterloo (ON, Canada)
U of Wisconsin–Madison (WI)
Vanderbilt U (TN)
Virginia Commonwealth U (VA)
Walla Walla U (WA)
Washington State U (WA)
Washington U in St. Louis (MO)
Wayne State U (MI)
Wentworth Inst of Technology (MA)
Western New England U (MA)
West Virginia U (WV)
Widener U (PA)
Worcester Polytechnic Inst (MA)
Wright State U (OH)
Yale U (CT)

BIOETHICS/MEDICAL ETHICS
Creighton U (NE)
U of Miami (FL)
U of Richmond (VA)
U of Rochester (NY)

BIOINFORMATICS
Arizona State U at the Tempe campus (AZ)
Baylor U (TX)
California State U, San Bernardino (CA)
Canisius Coll (NY)
Claflin U (SC)
The Coll of Saint Rose (NY)
Dalhousie U (NS, Canada)
Davenport U, Grand Rapids (MI)
Gannon U (PA)
Inter American U of Puerto Rico, Bayamón Campus (PR)
Iowa State U of Science and Technology (IA)
Kettering U (MI)
Lebanese American U (Lebanon)
Loyola U Chicago (IL)
Michigan Technological U (MI)
New Jersey Inst of Technology (NJ)
New York City Coll of Technology of the City U of New York (NY)
Portland State U (OR)
Ramapo Coll of New Jersey (NJ)
Rensselaer Polytechnic Inst (NY)
Rochester Inst of Technology (NY)
Rowan U (NJ)
St. Bonaventure U (NY)
St. Edward's U (TX)
Saint Vincent Coll (PA)
U at Buffalo, the State U of New York (NY)
U of Alberta (AB, Canada)
U of California, Irvine (CA)
U of California, Santa Cruz (CA)
U of Denver (CO)
U of Maryland, Baltimore County (MD)
U of Memphis (TN)
U of Northern Iowa (IA)
U of Pennsylvania (PA)
U of Pittsburgh (PA)
U of St. Thomas (TX)
U of Saskatchewan (SK, Canada)
U of Waterloo (ON, Canada)
The U of Western Ontario (ON, Canada)
U of Windsor (ON, Canada)
Virginia Commonwealth U (VA)
Wheaton Coll (MA)
Whitworth U (WA)

BIOLOGICAL AND BIOMEDICAL SCIENCES RELATED
Alvernia U (PA)
Bethel U (MN)
Biola U (CA)
Boston U (MA)
Central Michigan U (MI)
Central Washington U (WA)
Charleston Southern U (SC)
Christopher Newport U (VA)
Cornell U (NY)
Dakota State U (SD)
Delaware State U (DE)
Eastern U (PA)
Grand Valley State U (MI)
Guilford Coll (NC)
Hiram Coll (OH)
Indiana U Bloomington (IN)
Indiana U East (IN)
Kent State U (OH)
Kent State U at Salem (OH)
King U (TN)
Logan U (MO)
Loras Coll (IA)
Louisiana State U in Shreveport (LA)
Messiah Coll (PA)
Mount Aloysius Coll (PA)
New York Inst of Technology (NY)
Oklahoma City U (OK)
Park U (MO)
Penn State Abington (PA)
Penn State Altoona (PA)
Penn State Beaver (PA)
Penn State Berks (PA)
Penn State Brandywine (PA)
Penn State DuBois (PA)
Penn State Erie, The Behrend Coll (PA)
Penn State Fayette, The Eberly Campus (PA)
Penn State Greater Allegheny (PA)
Penn State Hazleton (PA)
Penn State Lehigh Valley (PA)
Penn State Mont Alto (PA)
Penn State New Kensington (PA)
Penn State Schuylkill (PA)
Penn State Shenango (PA)
Penn State U Park (PA)
Penn State Wilkes-Barre (PA)
Penn State Worthington Scranton (PA)
Penn State York (PA)
Rochester Inst of Technology (NY)
Rutgers, The State U of New Jersey, Newark (NJ)
The Sage Colls (NY)
San Jose State U (CA)
Trevecca Nazarene U (TN)
Union Coll (NY)
U of Maryland U Coll (MD)
U of Michigan (MI)
U of Minnesota, Twin Cities Campus (MN)
U of North Dakota (ND)
U of Ottawa (ON, Canada)
U of Puerto Rico in Ponce (PR)
U of Wisconsin–Parkside (WI)
Ursuline Coll (OH)
Utah State U (UT)
Washington U in St. Louis (MO)
Western State Colorado U (CO)

BIOLOGICAL AND PHYSICAL SCIENCES
Adelphi U (NY)
Alice Lloyd Coll (KY)
Allegheny Coll (PA)
Alvernia U (PA)
Averett U (VA)
Baldwin Wallace U (OH)
Bemidji State U (MN)
Bennington Coll (VT)
Bluefield State Coll (WV)
Brevard Coll (NC)
Buena Vista U (IA)
California State U, Fresno (CA)
Calvin Coll (MI)
Castleton State Coll (VT)
Charleston Southern U (SC)
Cheyney U of Pennsylvania (PA)
Clarion U of Pennsylvania (PA)
Coll of Saint Benedict (MN)
Coll of the Atlantic (ME)
Covenant Coll (GA)
Delta State U (MS)
DePaul U (IL)
Dominican U (IL)
Drexel U (PA)
Eastern Michigan U (MI)
East Stroudsburg U of Pennsylvania (PA)
Edinboro U of Pennsylvania (PA)
Elmira Coll (NY)
Eureka Coll (IL)
The Evergreen State Coll (WA)
Fairleigh Dickinson U, Metropolitan Campus (NJ)
Fordham U (NY)
Fort Hays State U (KS)
Gettysburg Coll (PA)
Grand Valley State U (MI)
Houghton Coll (NY)
Indiana U Kokomo (IN)
Indiana U of Pennsylvania (PA)
Indiana U–Purdue U Indianapolis (IN)
Iowa Wesleyan Coll (IA)
John Brown U (AR)
John Carroll U (OH)
Johns Hopkins U (MD)
Johnson C. Smith U (NC)
Keene State Coll (NH)
King's Coll (PA)
King U (TN)
Kutztown U of Pennsylvania (PA)
Le Moyne Coll (NY)
Lock Haven U of Pennsylvania (PA)
Long Island U–LIU Brooklyn (NY)
Louisiana State U in Shreveport (LA)
Mansfield U of Pennsylvania (PA)
Mars Hill U (NC)
Maryville U of Saint Louis (MO)
The Master's Coll and Sem (CA)
Michigan State U (MI)
Middle Tennessee State U (TN)
Minnesota State U Mankato (MN)
Mississippi State U (MS)
Moravian Coll (PA)
Mount Allison U (NB, Canada)
National U (CA)
North Carolina Wesleyan Coll (NC)
North Central Coll (IL)
Northwestern U (IL)
Northwest Missouri State U (MO)
Oakland City U (IN)
Olivet Coll (MI)
Penn State Abington (PA)
Penn State Altoona (PA)
Penn State Beaver (PA)
Penn State Berks (PA)
Penn State Brandywine (PA)
Penn State DuBois (PA)
Penn State Erie, The Behrend Coll (PA)
Penn State Fayette, The Eberly Campus (PA)
Penn State Greater Allegheny (PA)
Penn State Hazleton (PA)
Penn State Lehigh Valley (PA)
Penn State Mont Alto (PA)
Penn State New Kensington (PA)
Penn State Schuylkill (PA)
Penn State Shenango (PA)
Penn State U Park (PA)
Penn State Wilkes-Barre (PA)
Penn State Worthington Scranton (PA)
Penn State York (PA)
Peru State Coll (NE)
Philander Smith Coll (AR)
Portland State U (OR)
Purdue U (IN)
Quinnipiac U (CT)
Ramapo Coll of New Jersey (NJ)
Roberts Wesleyan Coll (NY)
Rockford U (IL)
Saint Anselm Coll (NH)
St. Gregory's U, Shawnee (OK)
Saint John's U (MN)
St. Mary's Coll of Maryland (MD)
St. Norbert Coll (WI)
Saint Peter's U (NJ)
Sam Houston State U (TX)
San Francisco State U (CA)
Scripps Coll (CA)
Simon Fraser U (BC, Canada)
Southern Arkansas U–Magnolia (AR)
Spalding U (KY)
State U of New York at Fredonia (NY)
State U of New York Coll of Environmental Science and Forestry (NY)
Stony Brook U, State U of New York (NY)
Texas State U (TX)
Texas Tech U (TX)
Trent U (ON, Canada)
Troy U (AL)
Union Coll (NY)
Union U (TN)
United States Air Force Acad (CO)
The U of Alabama at Birmingham (AL)
U of Alaska Fairbanks (AK)
U of Central Arkansas (AR)
U of Denver (CO)
U of Dubuque (IA)
The U of Findlay (OH)
U of Georgia (GA)
U of Houston–Downtown (TX)
U of Massachusetts Amherst (MA)
U of Northern Iowa (IA)
U of Oregon (OR)
U of Pittsburgh (PA)
U of Puget Sound (WA)
U of Regina (SK, Canada)
U of Saint Francis (IN)
U of Southern Indiana (IN)
U of Southern Mississippi (MS)
U of South Florida (FL)
The U of Texas at San Antonio (TX)
U of Waterloo (ON, Canada)
The U of West Alabama (AL)
U of West Florida (FL)
U of Windsor (ON, Canada)
U of Wisconsin–Platteville (WI)
U of Wisconsin–River Falls (WI)
U of Wisconsin–Stevens Point (WI)
U of Wisconsin–Superior (WI)
Upper Iowa U (IA)
Ursinus Coll (PA)
Vanguard U of Southern California (CA)
Virginia Commonwealth U (VA)
Walsh U (OH)
Warner Pacific Coll (OR)
Washington State U (WA)
Washington U in St. Louis (MO)
Wesleyan U (CT)
Western Washington U (WA)
Xavier U (OH)

BIOLOGICAL/BIOSYSTEMS ENGINEERING
Auburn U (AL)
Oakland U (MI)
The U of Arizona (AZ)
U of Arkansas (AR)
U of Florida (FL)
U of Georgia (GA)
U of Guelph (ON, Canada)
U of Idaho (ID)
U of Nebraska–Lincoln (NE)

BIOLOGY/BIOLOGICAL SCIENCES
Abilene Christian U (TX)
Adams State U (CO)
Adelphi U (NY)
Agnes Scott Coll (GA)
Alabama State U (AL)
Albany State U (GA)
Albertus Magnus Coll (CT)
Albion Coll (MI)
Albright Coll (PA)
Alcorn State U (MS)
Alice Lloyd Coll (KY)
Allegheny Coll (PA)
Alma Coll (MI)
Alvernia U (PA)
Alverno Coll (WI)
Ambrose U Coll (AB, Canada)
American Intl Coll (MA)
American U (DC)
The American U in Cairo (Egypt)
American U of Beirut (Lebanon)
Amherst Coll (MA)
Anderson U (IN)
Anderson U (SC)
Andrews U (MI)
Angelo State U (TX)
Anna Maria Coll (MA)
Appalachian State U (NC)
Aquinas Coll (MI)
Arcadia U (PA)
Arizona Christian U (AZ)
Arizona State U at the Polytechnic campus (AZ)
Arizona State U at the Tempe campus (AZ)
Arizona State U at the West campus (AZ)
Arkansas State U (AR)
Arkansas Tech U (AR)
Armstrong State U (GA)
Asbury U (KY)
Ashland U (OH)
Assumption Coll (MA)
Athens State U (AL)
Auburn U (AL)
Auburn U at Montgomery (AL)
Augsburg Coll (MN)
Augustana Coll (IL)
Augustana Coll (SD)
Austin Coll (TX)
Austin Peay State U (TN)
Ave Maria U (FL)
Avila U (MO)
Azusa Pacific U (CA)
Baker U (KS)
Baldwin Wallace U (OH)
Ball State U (IN)
Bard Coll (NY)
Bard Coll at Simon's Rock (MA)
Barnard Coll (NY)
Barry U (FL)
Bastyr U (WA)
Bates Coll (ME)
Baylor U (TX)
Bay Path U (MA)
Belhaven U (MS)
Belmont Abbey Coll (NC)
Belmont U (TN)
Beloit Coll (WI)
Bemidji State U (MN)
Benedictine Coll (KS)
Benedictine U (IL)
Bennett Coll (NC)
Bennington Coll (VT)
Berea Coll (KY)
Berry Coll (GA)
Bethany Coll (WV)
Bethany Lutheran Coll (MN)
Bethel Coll (IN)
Bethel Coll (KS)

Bethel U (MN)
Bethune-Cookman U (FL)
Binghamton U, State U of New York (NY)
Biola U (CA)
Birmingham-Southern Coll (AL)
Blackburn Coll (IL)
Black Hills State U (SD)
Bloomfield Coll (NJ)
Bloomsburg U of Pennsylvania (PA)
Bluefield Coll (VA)
Blue Mountain Coll (MS)
Bluffton U (OH)
Bob Jones U (SC)
Boston Coll (MA)
Boston U (MA)
Bowdoin Coll (ME)
Bowie State U (MD)
Bowling Green State U (OH)
Bradley U (IL)
Brandeis U (MA)
Brenau U (GA)
Brevard Coll (NC)
Bridgewater Coll (VA)
Bridgewater State U (MA)
Brown U (RI)
Bryan Coll (TN)
Bryant U (RI)
Bryn Mawr Coll (PA)
Bucknell U (PA)
Buena Vista U (IA)
Buffalo State Coll, State U of New York (NY)
Butler U (IN)
Cabrini Coll (PA)
Caldwell U (NJ)
California Baptist U (CA)
California Inst of Technology (CA)
California Lutheran U (CA)
California Polytechnic State U, San Luis Obispo (CA)
California State Polytechnic U, Pomona (CA)
California State U, Chico (CA)
California State U, Dominguez Hills (CA)
California State U, Fresno (CA)
California State U, Fullerton (CA)
California State U, Long Beach (CA)
California State U, Los Angeles (CA)
California State U, Monterey Bay (CA)
California State U, Sacramento (CA)
California State U, San Bernardino (CA)
California State U, San Marcos (CA)
California State U, Stanislaus (CA)
California U of Pennsylvania (PA)
Calumet Coll of Saint Joseph (IN)
Calvin Coll (MI)
Cameron U (OK)
Campbellsville U (KY)
Canisius Coll (NY)
Cape Breton U (NS, Canada)
Capital U (OH)
Cardinal Stritch U (WI)
Carleton Coll (MN)
Carlow U (PA)
Carroll Coll (MT)
Carson-Newman U (TN)
Case Western Reserve U (OH)
Castleton State Coll (VT)
Catawba Coll (NC)
The Catholic U of America (DC)
Cazenovia Coll (NY)
Cedar Crest Coll (PA)
Cedarville U (OH)
Centenary Coll of Louisiana (LA)
Central Coll (IA)
Central Connecticut State U (CT)
Central Methodist U (MO)
Central Michigan U (MI)
Central State U (OH)
Central Washington U (WA)
Centre Coll (KY)
Chaminade U of Honolulu (HI)
Chapman U (CA)
Charleston Southern U (SC)
Chatham U (PA)
Chestnut Hill Coll (PA)
Cheyney U of Pennsylvania (PA)
Chicago State U (IL)
Chowan U (NC)
Christian Brothers U (TN)
Christopher Newport U (VA)
The Citadel, The Military Coll of South Carolina (SC)
City Coll of the City U of New York (NY)
Claflin U (SC)
Claremont McKenna Coll (CA)
Clarion U of Pennsylvania (PA)
Clark Atlanta U (GA)
Clarke U (IA)
Clarkson U (NY)
Clark U (MA)
Clayton State U (GA)
Clearwater Christian Coll (FL)
Cleveland State U (OH)
Coastal Carolina U (SC)
Coe Coll (IA)
Coker Coll (SC)
Colby Coll (ME)
Colby-Sawyer Coll (NH)
The Coll at Brockport, State U of New York (NY)
Coll of Charleston (SC)
Coll of Coastal Georgia (GA)
The Coll of Idaho (ID)
The Coll of New Jersey (NJ)
The Coll of New Rochelle (NY)
Coll of Saint Benedict (MN)
Coll of Saint Elizabeth (NJ)
Coll of Saint Mary (NE)
The Coll of Saint Rose (NY)
The Coll of St. Scholastica (MN)
Coll of Staten Island of the City U of New York (NY)
Coll of the Atlantic (ME)
Coll of the Holy Cross (MA)
The Coll of William and Mary (VA)
The Coll of Wooster (OH)
The Colorado Coll (CO)
Colorado Mesa U (CO)
Colorado State U (CO)
Colorado State U–Pueblo (CO)
Columbia Coll (MO)
Columbia Coll (SC)
Columbia U (NY)
Columbia U, School of General Studies (NY)
Columbus State U (GA)
Concordia Coll (MN)
Concordia Coll–New York (NY)
Concordia U (CA)
Concordia U (QC, Canada)
Concordia U Chicago (IL)
Concordia U, Nebraska (NE)
Concordia U, St. Paul (MN)
Concordia U Texas (TX)
Concordia U Wisconsin (WI)
Concord U (WV)
Connecticut Coll (CT)
Cornell Coll (IA)
Cornell U (NY)
Cornerstone U (MI)
Covenant Coll (GA)
Crandall U (NB, Canada)
Creighton U (NE)
Culver-Stockton Coll (MO)
Cumberland U (TN)
Curry Coll (MA)
Daemen Coll (NY)
Dalhousie U (NS, Canada)
Dallas Baptist U (TX)
Dartmouth Coll (NH)
Davidson Coll (NC)
Defiance Coll (OH)
Delaware State U (DE)
Delta State U (MS)
Denison U (OH)
DePaul U (IL)
DePauw U (IN)
DeSales U (PA)
Dickinson Coll (PA)
Dickinson State U (ND)
Dixie State U (UT)
Doane Coll (NE)
Dominican Coll (NY)
Dominican U (IL)
Dominican U of California (CA)
Dowling Coll (NY)
Drake U (IA)
Drew U (NJ)
Drexel U (PA)
Drury U (MO)
Duquesne U (PA)
Earlham Coll (IN)
East Carolina U (NC)
East Central U (OK)
Eastern Connecticut State U (CT)
Eastern Illinois U (IL)
Eastern Kentucky U (KY)
Eastern Michigan U (MI)
Eastern New Mexico U (NM)
Eastern Oregon U (OR)
Eastern U (PA)
East Stroudsburg U of Pennsylvania (PA)
East Tennessee State U (TN)
East Texas Baptist U (TX)
Eckerd Coll (FL)
Edgewood Coll (WI)
Edinboro U of Pennsylvania (PA)
Elizabethtown Coll (PA)
Elmhurst Coll (IL)
Elmira Coll (NY)
Elms Coll (MA)
Elon U (NC)
Emmanuel Coll (GA)
Emmanuel Coll (MA)
Emory & Henry Coll (VA)
Emporia State U (KS)
Erskine Coll (SC)
Eureka Coll (IL)
Evangel U (MO)
The Evergreen State Coll (WA)
Excelsior Coll (NY)
Fairfield U (CT)
Fairleigh Dickinson U, Coll at Florham (NJ)
Fairleigh Dickinson U, Metropolitan Campus (NJ)
Fairmont State U (WV)
Farmingdale State Coll (NY)
Faulkner U (AL)
Fayetteville State U (NC)
Ferris State U (MI)
Ferrum Coll (VA)
Fitchburg State U (MA)
Florida Ag and Mech U (FL)
Florida Atlantic U (FL)
Florida Gulf Coast U (FL)
Florida Inst of Technology (FL)
Florida Intl U (FL)
Florida Southern Coll (FL)
Fontbonne U (MO)
Fordham U (NY)
Fort Hays State U (KS)
Framingham State U (MA)
Franciscan U of Steubenville (OH)
Francis Marion U (SC)
Franklin & Marshall Coll (PA)
Franklin Coll (IN)
Franklin Pierce U (NH)
Friends U (KS)
Frostburg State U (MD)
Furman U (SC)
Gallaudet U (DC)
Gannon U (PA)
Geneva Coll (PA)
George Mason U (VA)
Georgetown Coll (KY)
Georgetown U (DC)
The George Washington U (DC)
Georgia Coll & State U (GA)
Georgia Gwinnett Coll (GA)
Georgia Inst of Technology (GA)
Georgian Court U (NJ)
Georgia Regents U (GA)
Georgia Southern U (GA)
Georgia Southwestern State U (GA)
Georgia State U (GA)
Gettysburg Coll (PA)
Gonzaga U (WA)
Gordon Coll (MA)
Goshen Coll (IN)
Goucher Coll (MD)
Governors State U (IL)
Grace Coll (IN)
Graceland U (IA)
Grambling State U (LA)
Grand Valley State U (MI)
Grand View U (IA)
Green Mountain Coll (VT)
Greensboro Coll (NC)
Greenville Coll (IL)
Grinnell Coll (IA)
Grove City Coll (PA)
Guilford Coll (NC)
Gustavus Adolphus Coll (MN)
Gwynedd Mercy U (PA)
Hamilton Coll (NY)
Hamline U (MN)
Hampden-Sydney Coll (VA)
Hampshire Coll (MA)
Hampton U (VA)
Hannibal-LaGrange U (MO)
Hanover Coll (IN)
Harding U (AR)
Hardin-Simmons U (TX)
Harris-Stowe State U (MO)
Hartwick Coll (NY)
Harvard U (MA)
Harvey Mudd Coll (CA)
Hastings Coll (NE)
Haverford Coll (PA)
Hawai`i Pacific U (HI)
Heidelberg U (OH)
Hendrix Coll (AR)
Heritage U (WA)
High Point U (NC)
Hillsdale Coll (MI)
Hiram Coll (OH)
Hobart and William Smith Colls (NY)
Hofstra U (NY)
Hollins U (VA)
Holy Family U (PA)
Hope Coll (MI)
Houghton Coll (NY)
Houston Baptist U (TX)
Howard Payne U (TX)
Howard U (DC)
Humboldt State U (CA)
Hunter Coll of the City U of New York (NY)
Huntingdon Coll (AL)
Husson U (ME)
Huston-Tillotson U (TX)
Illinois Coll (IL)
Illinois Inst of Technology (IL)
Illinois State U (IL)
Illinois Wesleyan U (IL)
Immaculata U (PA)
Indiana State U (IN)
Indiana U Bloomington (IN)
Indiana U East (IN)
Indiana U Kokomo (IN)
Indiana U Northwest (IN)
Indiana U of Pennsylvania (PA)
Indiana U–Purdue U Fort Wayne (IN)
Indiana U–Purdue U Indianapolis (IN)
Indiana U South Bend (IN)
Indiana U Southeast (IN)
Inter American U of Puerto Rico, Aguadilla Campus (PR)
Inter American U of Puerto Rico, Bayamón Campus (PR)
Inter American U of Puerto Rico, Fajardo Campus (PR)
Inter American U of Puerto Rico, Guayama Campus (PR)
Inter American U of Puerto Rico, Ponce Campus (PR)
Inter American U of Puerto Rico, San Germán Campus (PR)
Iona Coll (NY)
Iowa State U of Science and Technology (IA)
Iowa Wesleyan Coll (IA)
Ithaca Coll (NY)
Jackson State U (MS)
Jacksonville State U (AL)
Jacksonville U (FL)
James Madison U (VA)
Jarvis Christian Coll (TX)
John Brown U (AR)
John Carroll U (OH)
Johns Hopkins U (MD)
Johnson C. Smith U (NC)
Johnson State Coll (VT)
Judson Coll (AL)
Judson U (IL)
Juniata Coll (PA)
Kalamazoo Coll (MI)
Kansas State U (KS)
Kansas Wesleyan U (KS)
Kean U (NJ)
Keene State Coll (NH)
Kennesaw State U (GA)
Kent State U (OH)
Kent State U at Stark (OH)
Kentucky Christian U (KY)
Kentucky State U (KY)
Kentucky Wesleyan Coll (KY)
Kenyon Coll (OH)
Kettering U (MI)
Keuka Coll (NY)
Keystone Coll (PA)
King's Coll (PA)
The King's U Coll (AB, Canada)
King U (TN)
Knox Coll (IL)
Kutztown U of Pennsylvania (PA)
Lafayette Coll (PA)
LaGrange Coll (GA)
Lake Erie Coll (OH)
Lake Forest Coll (IL)
Lamar U (TX)
Lane Coll (TN)
Langston U (OK)
La Roche Coll (PA)
La Salle U (PA)
La Sierra U (CA)
Lawrence U (WI)
Lebanese American U (Lebanon)
Lebanon Valley Coll (PA)
Lees-McRae Coll (NC)
Lee U (TN)
Lehigh U (PA)
Lehman Coll of the City U of New York (NY)
Le Moyne Coll (NY)
LeMoyne-Owen Coll (TN)
Lenoir-Rhyne U (NC)
LeTourneau U (TX)
Lewis & Clark Coll (OR)
Lewis U (IL)
Liberty U (VA)
Life U (GA)
Limestone Coll (SC)
Lincoln Memorial U (TN)
Lincoln U (MO)
Lincoln U (PA)
Lindenwood U (MO)
Lindsey Wilson Coll (KY)
Linfield Coll (OR)
Lipscomb U (TN)
Lock Haven U of Pennsylvania (PA)
Logan U (MO)
Long Island U–LIU Brooklyn (NY)
Long Island U–LIU Post (NY)
Longwood U (VA)
Loras Coll (IA)
Louisiana Coll (LA)
Louisiana State U and A&M Coll (LA)
Louisiana State U in Shreveport (LA)
Lourdes U (OH)
Loyola Marymount U (CA)
Loyola U Chicago (IL)
Loyola U New Orleans (LA)
Lubbock Christian U (TX)
Luther Coll (IA)
Lycoming Coll (PA)
Lynchburg Coll (VA)
Lynn U (FL)
Lyon Coll (AR)
Macalester Coll (MN)
Madonna U (MI)
Malone U (OH)
Manchester U (IN)
Manhattan Coll (NY)
Manhattanville Coll (NY)
Mansfield U of Pennsylvania (PA)
Maranatha Baptist U (WI)
Marian U (IN)
Marian U (WI)
Marietta Coll (OH)
Marist Coll (NY)
Marquette U (WI)
Marshall U (WV)
Mars Hill U (NC)
Mary Baldwin Coll (VA)
Marymount Manhattan Coll (NY)
Marymount U (VA)
Maryville Coll (TN)
Maryville U of Saint Louis (MO)
Marywood U (PA)
Massachusetts Coll of Liberal Arts (MA)
Massachusetts Inst of Technology (MA)
The Master's Coll and Sem (CA)
Mayville State U (ND)
McDaniel Coll (MD)
McKendree U (IL)
McMurry U (TX)
McNeese State U (LA)
Medaille Coll (NY)
Medgar Evers Coll of the City U of New York (NY)
Mercer U, Macon (GA)
Mercy Coll (NY)
Meredith Coll (NC)
Merrimack Coll (MA)

Messiah Coll (PA)
Metropolitan State U (MN)
Miami Dade Coll (FL)
Miami U (OH)
Michigan State U (MI)
Michigan Technological U (MI)
MidAmerica Nazarene U (KS)
Middlebury Coll (VT)
Middle Tennessee State U (TN)
Midwestern State U (TX)
Millersville U of Pennsylvania (PA)
Milligan Coll (TN)
Millikin U (IL)
Millsaps Coll (MS)
Mills Coll (CA)
Minnesota State U Mankato (MN)
Minnesota State U Moorhead (MN)
Minot State U (ND)
Misericordia U (PA)
Mississippi State U (MS)
Mississippi U for Women (MS)
Mississippi Valley State U (MS)
Missouri Baptist U (MO)
Missouri Southern State U (MO)
Missouri State U (MO)
Missouri U of Science and Technology (MO)
Missouri Valley Coll (MO)
Missouri Western State U (MO)
Molloy Coll (NY)
Monmouth Coll (IL)
Monmouth U (NJ)
Montana State U (MT)
Montana State U Billings (MT)
Montana Tech of The U of Montana (MT)
Montclair State U (NJ)
Montreat Coll, Montreat (NC)
Moravian Coll (PA)
Morehead State U (KY)
Morningside Coll (IA)
Morris Coll (SC)
Mount Allison U (NB, Canada)
Mount Aloysius Coll (PA)
Mount Holyoke Coll (MA)
Mount Marty Coll (SD)
Mount Mary U (WI)
Mount Mercy U (IA)
Mount St. Joseph U (OH)
Mount Saint Mary Coll (NY)
Mount Saint Mary's U (CA)
Mount St. Mary's U (MD)
Mount Vernon Nazarene U (OH)
Muhlenberg Coll (PA)
Murray State U (KY)
National U (CA)
Nazareth Coll of Rochester (NY)
Nebraska Wesleyan U (NE)
Neumann U (PA)
Newberry Coll (SC)
New Coll of Florida (FL)
New England Coll (NH)
New Jersey City U (NJ)
New Jersey Inst of Technology (NJ)
Newman U (KS)
New Mexico Highlands U (NM)
New Mexico Inst of Mining and Technology (NM)
New Mexico State U (NM)
New York Inst of Technology (NY)
New York U (NY)
Niagara U (NY)
Nicholls State U (LA)
Norfolk State U (VA)
North Carolina Ag and Tech State U (NC)
North Carolina Central U (NC)
North Carolina State U (NC)
North Carolina Wesleyan Coll (NC)
North Central Coll (IL)
North Dakota State U (ND)
Northeastern Illinois U (IL)
Northeastern State U (OK)
Northeastern U (MA)
Northern Arizona U (AZ)
Northern Illinois U (IL)
Northern Kentucky U (KY)
Northern Michigan U (MI)
Northern State U (SD)
North Greenville U (SC)
Northland Coll (WI)
Northwest Christian U (OR)
Northwestern Coll (IA)
Northwestern Oklahoma State U (OK)
Northwestern U (IL)
Northwest Missouri State U (MO)
Northwest Nazarene U (ID)
Norwich U (VT)
Notre Dame of Maryland U (MD)
Nova Southeastern U (FL)
Nyack Coll (NY)
Oakland City U (IN)
Oakland U (MI)
Oberlin Coll (OH)
Occidental Coll (CA)
Oglethorpe U (GA)
Ohio Dominican U (OH)
Ohio Northern U (OH)
The Ohio State U (OH)
The Ohio State U at Lima (OH)
Ohio U (OH)
Ohio Wesleyan U (OH)
Oklahoma Baptist U (OK)
Oklahoma Christian U (OK)
Oklahoma City U (OK)
Oklahoma State U (OK)
Oklahoma Wesleyan U (OK)
Old Dominion U (VA)
Olivet Coll (MI)
Olivet Nazarene U (IL)
Oregon State U (OR)
Our Lady of the Lake U of San Antonio (TX)
Pace U (NY)
Pacific Lutheran U (WA)
Pacific U (OR)
Palm Beach Atlantic U (FL)
Park U (MO)
Penn State Abington (PA)
Penn State Altoona (PA)
Penn State Beaver (PA)
Penn State Berks (PA)
Penn State Brandywine (PA)
Penn State DuBois (PA)
Penn State Erie, The Behrend Coll (PA)
Penn State Fayette, The Eberly Campus (PA)
Penn State Greater Allegheny (PA)
Penn State Hazleton (PA)
Penn State Lehigh Valley (PA)
Penn State Mont Alto (PA)
Penn State New Kensington (PA)
Penn State Schuylkill (PA)
Penn State Shenango (PA)
Penn State U Park (PA)
Penn State Wilkes-Barre (PA)
Penn State Worthington Scranton (PA)
Penn State York (PA)
Pepperdine U, Malibu (CA)
Peru State Coll (NE)
Philadelphia U (PA)
Philander Smith Coll (AR)
Piedmont Coll (GA)
Pine Manor Coll (MA)
Pittsburg State U (KS)
Plymouth State U (NH)
Point Loma Nazarene U (CA)
Point U (GA)
Pomona Coll (CA)
Portland State U (OR)
Post U (CT)
Prairie View A&M U (TX)
Presbyterian Coll (SC)
Principia Coll (IL)
Providence Coll (RI)
Purchase Coll, State U of New York (NY)
Purdue U (IN)
Purdue U Calumet (IN)
Queens Coll of the City U of New York (NY)
Quincy U (IL)
Quinnipiac U (CT)
Radford U (VA)
Ramapo Coll of New Jersey (NJ)
Randolph Coll (VA)
Randolph-Macon Coll (VA)
Reed Coll (OR)
Regis Coll (MA)
Regis U (CO)
Reinhardt U (GA)
Rensselaer Polytechnic Inst (NY)
Rhode Island Coll (RI)
Rhodes Coll (TN)
Rice U (TX)
Rider U (NJ)
Ripon Coll (WI)
Rivier U (NH)
Roanoke Coll (VA)
Robert Morris U (PA)
Roberts Wesleyan Coll (NY)
Rochester Inst of Technology (NY)
Rockford U (IL)
Rockhurst U (MO)
Rocky Mountain Coll (MT)
Roger Williams U (RI)
Rollins Coll (FL)
Roosevelt U (IL)
Rose-Hulman Inst of Technology (IN)
Rosemont Coll (PA)
Rowan U (NJ)
Rust Coll (MS)
Rutgers, The State U of New Jersey, Camden (NJ)
Rutgers, The State U of New Jersey, Newark (NJ)
Rutgers, The State U of New Jersey, New Brunswick (NJ)
Sacred Heart U (CT)
The Sage Colls (NY)
Saginaw Valley State U (MI)
St. Andrews U (NC)
Saint Anselm Coll (NH)
Saint Augustine's U (NC)
St. Bonaventure U (NY)
St. Catharine Coll (KY)
St. Catherine U (MN)
St. Edward's U (TX)
St. Francis Coll (NY)
Saint Francis U (PA)
St. Gregory's U, Shawnee (OK)
St. John Fisher Coll (NY)
Saint John's U (MN)
St. John's U (NY)
Saint Joseph's Coll (IN)
St. Joseph's Coll, Long Island Campus (NY)
St. Joseph's Coll, New York (NY)
Saint Joseph's U (PA)
St. Lawrence U (NY)
Saint Leo U (FL)
Saint Louis U (MO)
Saint Martin's U (WA)
Saint Mary-of-the-Woods Coll (IN)
Saint Mary's Coll (IN)
St. Mary's Coll of Maryland (MD)
St. Mary's U (TX)
Saint Mary's U of Minnesota (MN)
Saint Michael's Coll (VT)
St. Norbert Coll (WI)
St. Olaf Coll (MN)
Saint Peter's U (NJ)
St. Thomas Aquinas Coll (NY)
St. Thomas U (FL)
Saint Vincent Coll (PA)
Salem Coll (NC)
Salisbury U (MD)
Salve Regina U (RI)
Samford U (AL)
Sam Houston State U (TX)
San Diego Christian Coll (CA)
San Diego State U (CA)
San Francisco State U (CA)
San Jose State U (CA)
Santa Clara U (CA)
Sarah Lawrence Coll (NY)
Savannah State U (GA)
Scripps Coll (CA)
Seattle Pacific U (WA)
Seattle U (WA)
Selma U (AL)
Seton Hill U (PA)
Sewanee: The U of the South (TN)
Shawnee State U (OH)
Shaw U (NC)
Shenandoah U (VA)
Shepherd U (WV)
Shippensburg U of Pennsylvania (PA)
Siena Coll (NY)
Siena Heights U (MI)
Silver Lake Coll of the Holy Family (WI)
Simmons Coll (MA)
Simon Fraser U (BC, Canada)
Simpson Coll (IA)
Simpson U (CA)
Skidmore Coll (NY)
Slippery Rock U of Pennsylvania (PA)
Smith Coll (MA)
South Carolina State U (SC)
South Dakota State U (SD)
Southeastern Louisiana U (LA)
Southeastern Oklahoma State U (OK)
Southeastern U (FL)
Southeast Missouri State U (MO)
Southern Adventist U (TN)
Southern Arkansas U–Magnolia (AR)
Southern Connecticut State U (CT)
Southern Illinois U Carbondale (IL)
Southern Illinois U Edwardsville (IL)
Southern Methodist U (TX)
Southern Oregon U (OR)
Southern Utah U (UT)
Southwest Baptist U (MO)
Southwestern Adventist U (TX)
Southwestern Coll (KS)
Southwestern U (TX)
Southwest Minnesota State U (MN)
Spelman Coll (GA)
Spring Hill Coll (AL)
Stanford U (CA)
State U of New York at Fredonia (NY)
State U of New York at New Paltz (NY)
State U of New York at Oswego (NY)
State U of New York at Plattsburgh (NY)
State U of New York Coll at Cortland (NY)
State U of New York Coll at Geneseo (NY)
State U of New York Coll at Old Westbury (NY)
State U of New York Coll at Potsdam (NY)
State U of New York Coll of Environmental Science and Forestry (NY)
State U of New York Polytechnic Inst (NY)
Stephen F. Austin State U (TX)
Stephens Coll (MO)
Sterling Coll (KS)
Stetson U (FL)
Stevenson U (MD)
Stockton U (NJ)
Stonehill Coll (MA)
Stony Brook U, State U of New York (NY)
Suffolk U (MA)
Sul Ross State U (TX)
Susquehanna U (PA)
Syracuse U (NY)
Tabor Coll (KS)
Tarleton State U (TX)
Taylor U (IN)
Temple U (PA)
Tennessee State U (TN)
Tennessee Wesleyan Coll (TN)
Texas A&M Intl U (TX)
Texas A&M U (TX)
Texas A&M U–Commerce (TX)
Texas A&M U–Corpus Christi (TX)
Texas A&M U–Kingsville (TX)
Texas Christian U (TX)
Texas Lutheran U (TX)
Texas Southern U (TX)
Texas State U (TX)
Texas Tech U (TX)
Texas Wesleyan U (TX)
Texas Woman's U (TX)
Thiel Coll (PA)
Thomas More Coll (KY)
Toccoa Falls Coll (GA)
Tougaloo Coll (MS)
Towson U (MD)
Transylvania U (KY)
Trent U (ON, Canada)
Trevecca Nazarene U (TN)
Trine U (IN)
Trinity Christian Coll (IL)
Trinity Coll (CT)
Trinity U (TX)
Troy U (AL)
Truett-McConnell Coll (GA)
Truman State U (MO)
Tufts U (MA)
Tulane U (LA)
Tusculum Coll (TN)
Union Coll (KY)
Union Coll (NE)
Union Coll (NY)
Union U (TN)
United States Air Force Acad (CO)
United States Military Acad (NY)
Universidad del Turabo (PR)
Universidad Metropolitana (PR)
Université de Montréal (QC, Canada)
Université de Sherbrooke (QC, Canada)
U at Albany, State U of New York (NY)
U at Buffalo, the State U of New York (NY)
The U of Akron (OH)
The U of Alabama (AL)
The U of Alabama at Birmingham (AL)
The U of Alabama in Huntsville (AL)
U of Alaska Fairbanks (AK)
U of Alberta (AB, Canada)
The U of Arizona (AZ)
U of Arkansas (AR)
U of Arkansas at Little Rock (AR)
U of Arkansas at Pine Bluff (AR)
U of Arkansas–Fort Smith (AR)
U of Bridgeport (CT)
The U of British Columbia (BC, Canada)
The U of British Columbia–Okanagan Campus (BC, Canada)
U of California, Berkeley (CA)
U of California, Davis (CA)
U of California, Irvine (CA)
U of California, Los Angeles (CA)
U of California, Merced (CA)
U of California, Riverside (CA)
U of California, Santa Barbara (CA)
U of California, Santa Cruz (CA)
U of Central Arkansas (AR)
U of Central Florida (FL)
U of Central Missouri (MO)
U of Central Oklahoma (OK)
U of Charleston (WV)
U of Chicago (IL)
U of Cincinnati (OH)
U of Colorado Colorado Springs (CO)
U of Colorado Denver (CO)
U of Dallas (TX)
U of Dayton (OH)
U of Delaware (DE)
U of Denver (CO)
U of Dubuque (IA)
U of Evansville (IN)
The U of Findlay (OH)
U of Florida (FL)
U of Georgia (GA)
U of Great Falls (MT)
U of Guam (GU)
U of Guelph (ON, Canada)
U of Hartford (CT)
U of Hawaii at Hilo (HI)
U of Hawaii at Manoa (HI)
U of Houston (TX)
U of Houston–Clear Lake (TX)
U of Houston–Downtown (TX)
U of Houston–Victoria (TX)
U of Idaho (ID)
U of Illinois at Chicago (IL)
U of Illinois at Springfield (IL)
U of Indianapolis (IN)
The U of Iowa (IA)
U of Jamestown (ND)
The U of Kansas (KS)
U of Kentucky (KY)
U of King's Coll (NS, Canada)
U of La Verne (CA)
U of Lethbridge (AB, Canada)
U of Louisiana at Lafayette (LA)
U of Louisville (KY)
U of Maine (ME)
U of Maine at Augusta (ME)
U of Maine at Fort Kent (ME)
U of Maine at Machias (ME)
U of Maine at Presque Isle (ME)
U of Mary Hardin-Baylor (TX)
U of Maryland, Baltimore County (MD)
U of Maryland, Coll Park (MD)
U of Mary Washington (VA)
U of Massachusetts Amherst (MA)
U of Massachusetts Boston (MA)
U of Massachusetts Dartmouth (MA)
U of Massachusetts Lowell (MA)
U of Memphis (TN)
U of Miami (FL)
U of Michigan (MI)
U of Michigan–Dearborn (MI)
U of Michigan–Flint (MI)

U of Minnesota, Crookston (MN)
U of Minnesota, Duluth (MN)
U of Minnesota, Morris (MN)
U of Minnesota, Twin Cities Campus (MN)
U of Mississippi (MS)
U of Missouri (MO)
U of Missouri–Kansas City (MO)
U of Missouri–St. Louis (MO)
U of Mobile (AL)
The U of Montana (MT)
The U of Montana Western (MT)
U of Montevallo (AL)
U of Mount Union (OH)
U of Nebraska at Kearney (NE)
U of Nebraska–Lincoln (NE)
U of Nevada, Las Vegas (NV)
U of Nevada, Reno (NV)
U of New Brunswick Saint John (NB, Canada)
U of New England (ME)
U of New Hampshire (NH)
U of New Hampshire at Manchester (NH)
U of New Haven (CT)
U of New Mexico (NM)
U of New Orleans (LA)
U of North Alabama (AL)
U of North Carolina at Asheville (NC)
The U of North Carolina at Chapel Hill (NC)
The U of North Carolina at Charlotte (NC)
The U of North Carolina at Greensboro (NC)
The U of North Carolina at Pembroke (NC)
The U of North Carolina Wilmington (NC)
U of North Dakota (ND)
U of Northern Colorado (CO)
U of Northern Iowa (IA)
U of North Florida (FL)
U of North Georgia (GA)
U of North Texas (TX)
U of Northwestern–St. Paul (MN)
U of Notre Dame (IN)
U of Oregon (OR)
U of Ottawa (ON, Canada)
U of Pennsylvania (PA)
U of Pikeville (KY)
U of Pittsburgh (PA)
U of Pittsburgh at Bradford (PA)
U of Pittsburgh at Greensburg (PA)
U of Portland (OR)
U of Puget Sound (WA)
U of Regina (SK, Canada)
U of Rhode Island (RI)
U of Richmond (VA)
U of Rio Grande (OH)
U of Rochester (NY)
U of St. Francis (IL)
U of Saint Joseph (CT)
U of Saint Mary (KS)
U of St. Thomas (MN)
U of St. Thomas (TX)
U of San Diego (CA)
U of San Francisco (CA)
U of Saskatchewan (SK, Canada)
U of Science and Arts of Oklahoma (OK)
The U of Scranton (PA)
U of South Alabama (AL)
U of South Carolina Aiken (SC)
U of South Carolina Beaufort (SC)
U of South Carolina Upstate (SC)
U of Southern California (CA)
U of Southern Indiana (IN)
U of Southern Maine (ME)
U of Southern Mississippi (MS)
U of South Florida (FL)
U of South Florida, St. Petersburg (FL)
U of South Florida Sarasota-Manatee (FL)
The U of Tampa (FL)
The U of Tennessee (TN)
The U of Tennessee at Chattanooga (TN)
The U of Tennessee at Martin (TN)
The U of Texas at Arlington (TX)
The U of Texas at Austin (TX)
The U of Texas at Dallas (TX)
The U of Texas at El Paso (TX)
The U of Texas at San Antonio (TX)
The U of Texas at Tyler (TX)
The U of Texas of the Permian Basin (TX)
The U of Texas–Pan American (TX)
U of the Cumberlands (KY)
U of the District of Columbia (DC)
U of the Fraser Valley (BC, Canada)
U of the Incarnate Word (TX)
U of the Pacific (CA)
U of the Sciences (PA)
U of the Virgin Islands (VI)
The U of Toledo (OH)
U of Toronto (ON, Canada)
The U of Tulsa (OK)
U of Utah (UT)
U of Vermont (VT)
U of Virginia (VA)
The U of Virginia's Coll at Wise (VA)
U of Washington (WA)
U of Washington, Bothell (WA)
U of Waterloo (ON, Canada)
The U of West Alabama (AL)
The U of Western Ontario (ON, Canada)
U of West Florida (FL)
U of West Georgia (GA)
U of Windsor (ON, Canada)
U of Wisconsin–Eau Claire (WI)
U of Wisconsin–Green Bay (WI)
U of Wisconsin–La Crosse (WI)
U of Wisconsin–Madison (WI)
U of Wisconsin–Milwaukee (WI)
U of Wisconsin–Oshkosh (WI)
U of Wisconsin–Platteville (WI)
U of Wisconsin–River Falls (WI)
U of Wisconsin–Stevens Point (WI)
U of Wisconsin–Superior (WI)
U of Wisconsin–Whitewater (WI)
U of Wyoming (WY)
Upper Iowa U (IA)
Urbana U (OH)
Ursinus Coll (PA)
Ursuline Coll (OH)
Utah State U (UT)
Utah Valley U (UT)
Utica Coll (NY)
Valdosta State U (GA)
Valley City State U (ND)
Valparaiso U (IN)
Vanderbilt U (TN)
Vanguard U of Southern California (CA)
Vassar Coll (NY)
Villanova U (PA)
Virginia Commonwealth U (VA)
Virginia Military Inst (VA)
Virginia Polytechnic Inst and State U (VA)
Virginia State U (VA)
Virginia Union U (VA)
Virginia Wesleyan Coll (VA)
Viterbo U (WI)
Voorhees Coll (SC)
Wabash Coll (IN)
Wagner Coll (NY)
Wake Forest U (NC)
Waldorf Coll (IA)
Walla Walla U (WA)
Walsh U (OH)
Warner Pacific Coll (OR)
Warren Wilson Coll (NC)
Wartburg Coll (IA)
Washburn U (KS)
Washington & Jefferson Coll (PA)
Washington and Lee U (VA)
Washington Coll (MD)
Washington State U (WA)
Washington State U Vancouver (WA)
Washington U in St. Louis (MO)
Waynesburg U (PA)
Wayne State Coll (NE)
Wayne State U (MI)
Webster U (MO)
Wells Coll (NY)
Wesleyan Coll (GA)
Wesleyan U (CT)
West Chester U of Pennsylvania (PA)
Western Carolina U (NC)
Western Illinois U (IL)
Western Kentucky U (KY)
Western Michigan U (MI)
Western New England U (MA)
Western Oregon U (OR)
Western State Colorado U (CO)
Western Washington U (WA)
Westfield State U (MA)
West Liberty U (WV)
Westminster Coll (MO)
Westminster Coll (UT)
West Texas A&M U (TX)
West Virginia State U (WV)
West Virginia U (WV)
West Virginia U Inst of Technology (WV)
West Virginia Wesleyan Coll (WV)
Wheaton Coll (IL)
Wheaton Coll (MA)
Wheeling Jesuit U (WV)
Whitman Coll (WA)
Whittier Coll (CA)
Whitworth U (WA)
Wichita State U (KS)
Widener U (PA)
Wilberforce U (OH)
Wilkes U (PA)
Willamette U (OR)
William Jessup U (CA)
William Jewell Coll (MO)
William Paterson U of New Jersey (NJ)
William Peace U (NC)
William Penn U (IA)
Williams Baptist Coll (AR)
Williams Coll (MA)
William Woods U (MO)
Wingate U (NC)
Winona State U (MN)
Winthrop U (SC)
Wittenberg U (OH)
Wofford Coll (SC)
Worcester Polytechnic Inst (MA)
Worcester State U (MA)
Wright State U (OH)
Xavier U (OH)
Xavier U of Louisiana (LA)
Yale U (CT)
Yeshiva U (NY)
York Coll of Pennsylvania (PA)
York Coll of the City U of New York (NY)
Youngstown State U (OH)

BIOLOGY/BIOTECHNOLOGY LABORATORY TECHNICIAN

Cleveland State U (OH)
Delaware State U (DE)
Niagara U (NY)
Penn State Abington (PA)
Penn State Altoona (PA)
Penn State Beaver (PA)
Penn State Berks (PA)
Penn State Brandywine (PA)
Penn State DuBois (PA)
Penn State Erie, The Behrend Coll (PA)
Penn State Fayette, The Eberly Campus (PA)
Penn State Greater Allegheny (PA)
Penn State Hazleton (PA)
Penn State Lehigh Valley (PA)
Penn State Mont Alto (PA)
Penn State New Kensington (PA)
Penn State Schuylkill (PA)
Penn State Shenango (PA)
Penn State U Park (PA)
Penn State Wilkes-Barre (PA)
Penn State Worthington Scranton (PA)
Penn State York (PA)
State U of New York at Fredonia (NY)
Tusculum Coll (TN)
U of New Haven (CT)
Washburn U (KS)
Worcester Polytechnic Inst (MA)
York Coll of the City U of New York (NY)

BIOLOGY TEACHER EDUCATION

Abilene Christian U (TX)
Adams State U (CO)
Albion Coll (MI)
Alma Coll (MI)
Alvernia U (PA)
Arizona Christian U (AZ)
Arkansas State U (AR)
Arkansas Tech U (AR)
Ashland U (OH)
Augustana Coll (IL)
Averett U (VA)
Bay Path U (MA)
Bethany Coll (WV)
Bethune-Cookman U (FL)
Biola U (CA)
Blackburn Coll (IL)
Bluefield Coll (VA)
Blue Mountain Coll (MS)
Bowling Green State U (OH)
Bradley U (IL)
Bridgewater State U (MA)
Bryan Coll (TN)
Buena Vista U (IA)
Cabrini Coll (PA)
California State U, Long Beach (CA)
Calvin Coll (MI)
Campbellsville U (KY)
Canisius Coll (NY)
Carroll Coll (MT)
Cedarville U (OH)
Central Methodist U (MO)
Central Michigan U (MI)
Central Washington U (WA)
City Coll of the City U of New York (NY)
Clearwater Christian Coll (FL)
Coker Coll (SC)
The Coll of New Jersey (NJ)
Coll of Saint Mary (NE)
The Coll of Saint Rose (NY)
Coll of Staten Island of the City U of New York (NY)
Coll of the Ozarks (MO)
Colorado State U (CO)
Concordia Coll (MN)
Concordia U Chicago (IL)
Concordia U, Nebraska (NE)
Concordia U, St. Paul (MN)
Corban U (OR)
Cornerstone U (MI)
Culver-Stockton Coll (MO)
Cumberland U (TN)
Daemen Coll (NY)
Dakota State U (SD)
Dallas Baptist U (TX)
Daytona State Coll (FL)
Delaware State U (DE)
Dixie State U (UT)
Dominican Coll (NY)
Dowling Coll (NY)
East Central U (OK)
Eastern Kentucky U (KY)
Eastern Michigan U (MI)
East Texas Baptist U (TX)
Edgewood Coll (WI)
Elmhurst Coll (IL)
Elmira Coll (NY)
Emory & Henry Coll (VA)
Evangel U (MO)
Fayetteville State U (NC)
Ferris State U (MI)
Fitchburg State U (MA)
Florida Inst of Technology (FL)
Florida SouthWestern State Coll (FL)
Fordham U (NY)
Fort Lewis Coll (CO)
Franklin Coll (IN)
Friends U (KS)
Grace Coll (IN)
Grand Valley State U (MI)
Green Mountain Coll (VT)
Greensboro Coll (NC)
Greenville Coll (IL)
Gustavus Adolphus Coll (MN)
Harding U (AR)
Hastings Coll (NE)
Hofstra U (NY)
Holy Family U (PA)
Hope Coll (MI)
Houston Baptist U (TX)
Howard Payne U (TX)
Hunter Coll of the City U of New York (NY)
Huntingdon Coll (AL)
Husson U (ME)
Indiana U Bloomington (IN)
Indiana U Northwest (IN)
Indiana U–Purdue U Fort Wayne (IN)
Indiana U South Bend (IN)
Indiana U Southeast (IN)
Indian River State Coll (FL)
Inter American U of Puerto Rico, Aguadilla Campus (PR)
Inter American U of Puerto Rico, Fajardo Campus (PR)
Inter American U of Puerto Rico, Ponce Campus (PR)
Inter American U of Puerto Rico, San Germán Campus (PR)
Iona Coll (NY)
Ithaca Coll (NY)
Johnson State Coll (VT)
Kansas Wesleyan U (KS)
Keene State Coll (NH)
Kennesaw State U (GA)
Keuka Coll (NY)
King U (TN)
Lee U (TN)
Le Moyne Coll (NY)
Lincoln Memorial U (TN)
Lincoln U (MO)
Lincoln U (PA)
Lindenwood U (MO)
Lindsey Wilson Coll (KY)
Lipscomb U (TN)
Long Island U–LIU Post (NY)
Louisiana State U in Shreveport (LA)
Madonna U (MI)
Manchester U (IN)
Manhattanville Coll (NY)
Mansfield U of Pennsylvania (PA)
Maranatha Baptist U (WI)
Marist Coll (NY)
Maryville Coll (TN)
Marywood U (PA)
Mayville State U (ND)
McKendree U (IL)
McMurry U (TX)
Merrimack Coll (MA)
Messiah Coll (PA)
Metropolitan State U (MN)
Miami Dade Coll (FL)
Miami U (OH)
Michigan State U (MI)
MidAmerica Nazarene U (KS)
Millikin U (IL)
Minnesota State U Moorhead (MN)
Minot State U (ND)
Misericordia U (PA)
Missouri State U (MO)
Montana State U Billings (MT)
Morningside Coll (IA)
Morris Coll (SC)
Mount Mary U (WI)
Mount Vernon Nazarene U (OH)
Nazareth Coll of Rochester (NY)
Niagara U (NY)
North Carolina Ag and Tech State U (NC)
North Dakota State U (ND)
Northern Michigan U (MI)
Northwestern Coll (IA)
Northwest Missouri State U (MO)
Northwest Nazarene U (ID)
Northwest U (WA)
Oakland City U (IN)
Ohio Dominican U (OH)
Ohio Northern U (OH)
Ohio Wesleyan U (OH)
Pace U (NY)
Palm Beach Atlantic U (FL)
Peru State Coll (NE)
Pittsburg State U (KS)
Providence Coll (RI)
Rhode Island Coll (RI)
Rivier U (NH)
Roberts Wesleyan Coll (NY)
Rocky Mountain Coll (MT)
Rust Coll (MS)
Saginaw Valley State U (MI)
St. Catherine U (MN)
St. Edward's U (TX)
St. Francis Coll (NY)
Saint Francis U (PA)
St. Gregory's U, Shawnee (OK)
St. John Fisher Coll (NY)
St. John's U (NY)
St. Joseph's Coll, Long Island Campus (NY)
St. Joseph's Coll, New York (NY)
Saint Joseph's U (PA)
Saint Mary's U of Minnesota (MN)
Salve Regina U (RI)
Seattle U (WA)
Seton Hill U (PA)
Southeastern U (FL)
Southern Adventist U (TN)
Southern Utah U (UT)
Southwest Baptist U (MO)
Southwest Minnesota State U (MN)
Spring Hill Coll (AL)

State U of New York at New Paltz (NY)
State U of New York at Plattsburgh (NY)
State U of New York Coll at Cortland (NY)
State U of New York Coll at Old Westbury (NY)
State U of New York Coll at Potsdam (NY)
State U of New York Coll of Environmental Science and Forestry (NY)
Syracuse U (NY)
Tabor Coll (KS)
Texas A&M Intl U (TX)
Texas Wesleyan U (TX)
Trevecca Nazarene U (TN)
Trinity Christian Coll (IL)
Tusculum Coll (TN)
Union Coll (NE)
Universidad del Turabo (PR)
U of Alberta (AB, Canada)
U of Arkansas–Fort Smith (AR)
U of California, Irvine (CA)
U of Central Oklahoma (OK)
U of Charleston (WV)
U of Delaware (DE)
U of Dubuque (IA)
U of Evansville (IN)
U of Great Falls (MT)
U of Illinois at Chicago (IL)
The U of Iowa (IA)
U of Jamestown (ND)
U of Maine at Machias (ME)
U of Mary Hardin-Baylor (TX)
U of Maryland, Baltimore County (MD)
U of Minnesota, Twin Cities Campus (MN)
U of Missouri (MO)
U of Mobile (AL)
The U of Montana Western (MT)
U of Nebraska–Lincoln (NE)
The U of North Carolina at Greensboro (NC)
The U of North Carolina Wilmington (NC)
U of Regina (SK, Canada)
U of Rio Grande (OH)
U of Saint Francis (IN)
The U of South Dakota (SD)
The U of Tennessee at Martin (TN)
U of Waterloo (ON, Canada)
U of Windsor (ON, Canada)
U of Wisconsin–River Falls (WI)
U of Wisconsin–Superior (WI)
Utah State U (UT)
Utah Valley U (UT)
Utica Coll (NY)
Valley City State U (ND)
Valparaiso U (IN)
Viterbo U (WI)
Washburn U (KS)
Washington State U (WA)
Washington U in St. Louis (MO)
Waynesburg U (PA)
Wayne State Coll (NE)
Weber State U (UT)
Welch Coll (TN)
Western Michigan U (MI)
Western State Colorado U (CO)
Western Washington U (WA)
Widener U (PA)
William Woods U (MO)
Wingate U (NC)
Winona State U (MN)
Xavier U (OH)
Xavier U of Louisiana (LA)
York Coll of Pennsylvania (PA)
Youngstown State U (OH)

BIOMATHEMATICS, BIOINFORMATICS, AND COMPUTATIONAL BIOLOGY RELATED
Cedar Crest Coll (PA)
Florida Inst of Technology (FL)
Florida State U (FL)
Harvey Mudd Coll (CA)
Universidad Metropolitana (PR)
U of California, Los Angeles (CA)
Walsh U (OH)
Washington U in St. Louis (MO)
Worcester Polytechnic Inst (MA)

BIOMEDICAL SCIENCES
Adventist U of Health Sciences (FL)
Antioch Coll, Yellow Springs (OH)
Auburn U (AL)
Bridgewater State U (MA)
Brigham Young U (UT)
Brown U (RI)
Central Michigan U (MI)
Central Washington U (WA)
Christian Brothers U (TN)
City Coll of the City U of New York (NY)
Coll of the Ozarks (MO)
Colorado State U (CO)
Concordia Coll–New York (NY)
Concordia U Wisconsin (WI)
Edgewood Coll (WI)
Fitchburg State U (MA)
Florida Inst of Technology (FL)
Florida State Coll at Jacksonville (FL)
Heritage U (WA)
Inter American U of Puerto Rico, Ponce Campus (PR)
Jefferson Coll of Health Sciences (VA)
Keiser U, Fort Lauderdale (FL)
Keuka Coll (NY)
Lewis U (IL)
Liberty U (VA)
Lynchburg Coll (VA)
Madonna U (MI)
Marist Coll (NY)
Marquette U (WI)
Marymount Manhattan Coll (NY)
Maryville U of Saint Louis (MO)
McMurry U (TX)
Morehead State U (KY)
North Carolina Central U (NC)
North Carolina Wesleyan Coll (NC)
Northern Arizona U (AZ)
Oakland U (MI)
The Ohio State U (OH)
Oklahoma City U (OK)
Peru State Coll (NE)
Rochester Inst of Technology (NY)
Rowan U (NJ)
Rutgers, The State U of New Jersey, New Brunswick (NJ)
St. Francis Coll (NY)
St. Gregory's U, Shawnee (OK)
Saint Leo U (FL)
Sam Houston State U (TX)
Slippery Rock U of Pennsylvania (PA)
State U of New York at Fredonia (NY)
Tarleton State U (TX)
Texas A&M U (TX)
Texas A&M U–Corpus Christi (TX)
Texas A&M U–Kingsville (TX)
Troy U (AL)
Union Coll (NE)
Université de Montréal (QC, Canada)
U at Buffalo, the State U of New York (NY)
U of California, Riverside (CA)
U of Central Florida (FL)
U of Guelph (ON, Canada)
U of Michigan–Flint (MI)
U of Minnesota, Duluth (MN)
U of New England (ME)
U of New Hampshire (NH)
U of Ottawa (ON, Canada)
U of Pennsylvania (PA)
U of Saskatchewan (SK, Canada)
U of South Alabama (AL)
U of South Florida (FL)
Washington State U (WA)
Western Michigan U (MI)
Worcester Polytechnic Inst (MA)

BIOMEDICAL TECHNOLOGY
Andrews U (MI)
Cleveland State U (OH)
DeVry Coll of New York (NY)
DeVry U, Phoenix (AZ)
DeVry U, Miramar (FL)
DeVry U, Orlando (FL)
DeVry U, Decatur (GA)
DeVry U, Chicago (IL)
DeVry U, North Brunswick (NJ)
DeVry U, Columbus (OH)
DeVry U, Fort Washington (PA)
DeVry U, Irving (TX)
Indiana U–Purdue U Indianapolis (IN)
Lawrence Technological U (MI)
Long Island U–LIU Post (NY)
Rutgers, The State U of New Jersey, Camden (NJ)
Wright State U (OH)

BIOMETRY/BIOMETRICS
Cornell U (NY)
Rutgers, The State U of New Jersey, New Brunswick (NJ)
Stanford U (CA)
U of Delaware (DE)
U of Minnesota, Twin Cities Campus (MN)

BIOPHYSICS
Andrews U (MI)
Arizona State U at the Tempe campus (AZ)
Augsburg Coll (MN)
Brandeis U (MA)
Brigham Young U (UT)
Brown U (RI)
Centenary Coll of Louisiana (LA)
Claremont McKenna Coll (CA)
Columbia U (NY)
Columbia U, School of General Studies (NY)
Elon U (NC)
Haverford Coll (PA)
Illinois Inst of Technology (IL)
Iowa State U of Science and Technology (IA)
Johns Hopkins U (MD)
La Sierra U (CA)
Lipscomb U (TN)
Miami U (OH)
New Jersey Inst of Technology (NJ)
Northeastern U (MA)
Oakland U (MI)
Regent U (VA)
St. Bonaventure U (NY)
St. Lawrence U (NY)
Southern Adventist U (TN)
State U of New York Coll at Geneseo (NY)
Syracuse U (NY)
Temple U (PA)
U at Buffalo, the State U of New York (NY)
The U of British Columbia (BC, Canada)
U of California, Los Angeles (CA)
U of Michigan (MI)
U of Pennsylvania (PA)
U of San Diego (CA)
The U of Scranton (PA)
U of Southern California (CA)
U of Southern Indiana (IN)
U of Toronto (ON, Canada)
The U of Western Ontario (ON, Canada)
Walla Walla U (WA)
Washington & Jefferson Coll (PA)
Washington U in St. Louis (MO)
Whitman Coll (WA)

BIOPSYCHOLOGY
Augsburg Coll (MN)
Bucknell U (PA)
Columbia U (NY)
Geneva Coll (PA)
Grand Valley State U (MI)
Hastings Coll (NE)
Immaculata U (PA)
Life U (GA)
Messiah Coll (PA)
Monmouth Coll (IL)
Morningside Coll (IA)
Mount Allison U (NB, Canada)
Nebraska Wesleyan U (NE)
Oglethorpe U (GA)
Ohio Dominican U (OH)
Philadelphia U (PA)
Rider U (NJ)
Spring Hill Coll (AL)
Tufts U (MA)
U of California, Santa Barbara (CA)
U of Guelph (ON, Canada)
Viterbo U (WI)
Wagner Coll (NY)
Washington U in St. Louis (MO)

BIOSTATISTICS
Cornell U (NY)
Emmanuel Coll (MA)
National U (CA)
Simmons Coll (MA)
Tulane U (LA)
U of Minnesota, Twin Cities Campus (MN)
The U of North Carolina at Chapel Hill (NC)
The U of Western Ontario (ON, Canada)

BIOTECHNOLOGY
Ashland U (OH)
Assumption Coll (MA)
Bay Path U (MA)
California State Polytechnic U, Pomona (CA)
California State U, San Marcos (CA)
Calvin Coll (MI)
City Coll of the City U of New York (NY)
Claflin U (SC)
Colorado State U (CO)
Delaware State U (DE)
East Stroudsburg U of Pennsylvania (PA)
Elizabethtown Coll (PA)
Endicott Coll (MA)
Fayetteville State U (NC)
Ferris State U (MI)
Fitchburg State U (MA)
Florida Gulf Coast U (FL)
Florida Southern Coll (FL)
Grand View U (IA)
Hunter Coll of the City U of New York (NY)
Indiana U Bloomington (IN)
Indiana U East (IN)
Indiana U–Purdue U Indianapolis (IN)
Inter American U of Puerto Rico, Aguadilla Campus (PR)
Inter American U of Puerto Rico, Bayamón Campus (PR)
Inter American U of Puerto Rico, Ponce Campus (PR)
James Madison U (VA)
Keiser U, Fort Lauderdale (FL)
Kennesaw State U (GA)
Kent State U (OH)
Manhattan Coll (NY)
Marywood U (PA)
Massachusetts Coll of Liberal Arts (MA)
Missouri Baptist U (MO)
Missouri Western State U (MO)
Montana State U (MT)
New York Inst of Technology (NY)
North Dakota State U (ND)
Oregon State U (OR)
Plymouth State U (NH)
Rochester Inst of Technology (NY)
Roosevelt U (IL)
Rutgers, The State U of New Jersey, New Brunswick (NJ)
Santa Fe Coll (FL)
South Dakota State U (SD)
Southeastern Oklahoma State U (OK)
State U of New York Coll of Agriculture and Technology at Cobleskill (NY)
State U of New York Coll of Environmental Science and Forestry (NY)
Stevenson U (MD)
Syracuse U (NY)
Tufts U (MA)
U at Buffalo, the State U of New York (NY)
U of Alberta (AB, Canada)
The U of British Columbia (BC, Canada)
U of California, Davis (CA)
U of Central Florida (FL)
U of Georgia (GA)
U of Hawaii at Manoa (HI)
U of Houston (TX)
U of Houston–Downtown (TX)
U of Kentucky (KY)
U of Nevada, Reno (NV)
The U of North Carolina at Pembroke (NC)
U of Northern Iowa (IA)
U of Puerto Rico in Ponce (PR)
U of Saskatchewan (SK, Canada)
U of Waterloo (ON, Canada)
U of Windsor (ON, Canada)
U of Wisconsin–River Falls (WI)
Ursuline Coll (OH)
Utah Valley U (UT)
West Texas A&M U (TX)
Worcester State U (MA)
York Coll of the City U of New York (NY)

BLOOD BANK TECHNOLOGY
Rasmussen Coll St. Cloud (MN)

BOTANY/PLANT BIOLOGY
Andrews U (MI)
Auburn U (AL)
Bennington Coll (VT)
California State U, Long Beach (CA)
Coll of the Atlantic (ME)
Colorado State U (CO)
Connecticut Coll (CT)
Cornell U (NY)
Dalhousie U (NS, Canada)
Goddard Coll (VT)
Humboldt State U (CA)
Iowa State U of Science and Technology (IA)
Kent State U (OH)
Miami U (OH)
Michigan State U (MI)
North Carolina State U (NC)
North Dakota State U (ND)
The Ohio State U (OH)
Ohio U (OH)
Ohio Wesleyan U (OH)
Oklahoma State U (OK)
Oregon State U (OR)
Purdue U (IN)
Rutgers, The State U of New Jersey, Newark (NJ)
San Francisco State U (CA)
Southern Illinois U Carbondale (IL)
State U of New York Coll of Environmental Science and Forestry (NY)
The U of Akron (OH)
U of Alberta (AB, Canada)
U of California, Berkeley (CA)
U of California, Davis (CA)
U of California, Irvine (CA)
U of California, Riverside (CA)
U of Florida (FL)
U of Georgia (GA)
U of Great Falls (MT)
U of Hawaii at Manoa (HI)
U of Maine (ME)
U of Minnesota, Twin Cities Campus (MN)
The U of Montana (MT)
U of Nebraska–Lincoln (NE)
U of Oklahoma (OK)
The U of Texas at El Paso (TX)
U of Toronto (ON, Canada)
U of Vermont (VT)
U of Washington (WA)
U of Wisconsin–Madison (WI)
U of Wisconsin–Superior (WI)
U of Wyoming (WY)
Utah State U (UT)
Utah Valley U (UT)
Weber State U (UT)

BOTANY/PLANT BIOLOGY RELATED
Dalhousie U (NS, Canada)
Frostburg State U (MD)
U of Hawaii at Manoa (HI)
U of Minnesota, Twin Cities Campus (MN)

BRASS INSTRUMENTS
Houghton Coll (NY)
Liberty U (VA)
San Francisco Conservatory of Music (CA)
Syracuse U (NY)
The U of Kansas (KS)
U of Southern California (CA)
Vanderbilt U (TN)
Youngstown State U (OH)

BROADCAST JOURNALISM
Auburn U (AL)
Barry U (FL)
Belmont U (TN)
Bemidji State U (MN)
Biola U (CA)
Bluffton U (OH)

Bowie State U (MD)
Bowling Green State U (OH)
Brigham Young U (UT)
Buffalo State Coll, State U of New York (NY)
California State U, Long Beach (CA)
Cameron U (OK)
Central State U (OH)
Central Washington U (WA)
Champlain Coll (VT)
Chapman U (CA)
Chatham U (PA)
The Coll at Brockport, State U of New York (NY)
The Coll of New Rochelle (NY)
Columbia Coll Chicago (IL)
Delaware State U (DE)
Drake U (IA)
Drury U (MO)
Elon U (NC)
Emerson Coll (MA)
Evangel U (MO)
Five Towns Coll (NY)
Fordham U (NY)
Gettysburg Coll (PA)
Gonzaga U (WA)
Grand View U (IA)
Hampton U (VA)
Hannibal-LaGrange U (MO)
Harding U (AR)
Hastings Coll (NE)
Hawai`i Pacific U (HI)
Howard U (DC)
Humboldt State U (CA)
Ithaca Coll (NY)
John Brown U (AR)
Kuyper Coll (MI)
Langston U (OK)
La Salle U (PA)
Lincoln U (PA)
Lindenwood U (MO)
Louisiana Coll (LA)
Manchester U (IN)
Marywood U (PA)
Massachusetts Coll of Liberal Arts (MA)
Minnesota State U Moorhead (MN)
Morrisville State Coll (NY)
Mount Vernon Nazarene U (OH)
North Carolina Ag and Tech State U (NC)
Northern Kentucky U (KY)
North Greenville U (SC)
Ohio U (OH)
Ohio Wesleyan U (OH)
Oklahoma Christian U (OK)
Oklahoma City U (OK)
Pacific U (OR)
Point Loma Nazarene U (CA)
Quinnipiac U (CT)
Rust Coll (MS)
Southern Adventist U (TN)
Southwestern Assemblies of God U (TX)
State U of New York at Oswego (NY)
Suffolk U (MA)
Syracuse U (NY)
Troy U (AL)
Union U (TN)
U of Central Oklahoma (OK)
The U of Findlay (OH)
U of Georgia (GA)
U of La Verne (CA)
U of Miami (FL)
U of Missouri (MO)
U of Nebraska–Lincoln (NE)
U of North Texas (TX)
U of Oklahoma (OK)
The U of Scranton (PA)
U of Southern California (CA)
The U of Texas at El Paso (TX)
U of Wisconsin–Oshkosh (WI)
U of Wisconsin–River Falls (WI)
U of Wisconsin–Superior (WI)
Wartburg Coll (IA)
Washington State U (WA)
Western Kentucky U (KY)
West Texas A&M U (TX)
William Penn U (IA)

BUDDHIST STUDIES
U of the West (CA)

BUILDING/CONSTRUCTION FINISHING, MANAGEMENT, AND INSPECTION RELATED
California State U, Long Beach (CA)
John Brown U (AR)
Minnesota State U Mankato (MN)
Pratt Inst (NY)
U of the District of Columbia (DC)
Weber State U (UT)

BUILDING/CONSTRUCTION SITE MANAGEMENT
Pennsylvania Coll of Technology (PA)
Southern Utah U (UT)
The U of Texas at San Antonio (TX)

BUILDING CONSTRUCTION TECHNOLOGY
U of Massachusetts Amherst (MA)

BUSINESS ADMINISTRATION AND MANAGEMENT
Abilene Christian U (TX)
Adams State U (CO)
Adelphi U (NY)
Agnes Scott Coll (GA)
Alabama State U (AL)
Alaska Pacific U (AK)
Albany State U (GA)
Albertus Magnus Coll (CT)
Albion Coll (MI)
Albright Coll (PA)
Alcorn State U (MS)
Alice Lloyd Coll (KY)
Alma Coll (MI)
Alvernia U (PA)
Alverno Coll (WI)
Ambrose U Coll (AB, Canada)
American Intl Coll (MA)
American Public U System (WV)
American U (DC)
American U in Bulgaria (Bulgaria)
The American U in Cairo (Egypt)
The American U in Dubai (United Arab Emirates)
American U of Beirut (Lebanon)
The American U of Paris (France)
The American U of Rome (Italy)
Amridge U (AL)
Anderson U (IN)
Anderson U (SC)
Angelo State U (TX)
Anna Maria Coll (MA)
Antioch U Midwest (OH)
Appalachian State U (NC)
Aquinas Coll (MI)
Aquinas Coll (TN)
Arcadia U (PA)
Arizona Christian U (AZ)
Arizona State U at the Polytechnic campus (AZ)
Arizona State U at the Tempe campus (AZ)
Arizona State U at the West campus (AZ)
Arkansas State U (AR)
Arkansas Tech U (AR)
Ashland U (OH)
Assumption Coll (MA)
Athens State U (AL)
Auburn U (AL)
Auburn U at Montgomery (AL)
Augsburg Coll (MN)
Augustana Coll (IL)
Augustana Coll (SD)
Austin Coll (TX)
Averett U (VA)
Avila U (MO)
Azusa Pacific U (CA)
Babson Coll (MA)
Baker Coll (MI)
Baldwin Wallace U (OH)
Ball State U (IN)
The Baptist Coll of Florida (FL)
Baptist U of the Americas (TX)
Barclay Coll (KS)
Barry U (FL)
Baruch Coll of the City U of New York (NY)
Baylor U (TX)
Bay Path U (MA)
Beacon Coll (FL)
Becker Coll (MA)
Belhaven U (MS)
Belmont Abbey Coll (NC)
Belmont U (TN)
Bemidji State U (MN)
Benedictine Coll (KS)
Bennett Coll (NC)
Bentley U (MA)
Berea Coll (KY)
Berkeley Coll, Woodland Park (NJ)
Berkeley Coll–New York City Campus (NY)
Berkeley Coll–Westchester Campus (NY)
Berry Coll (GA)
Bethany Coll (WV)
Bethany Lutheran Coll (MN)
Bethel Coll (IN)
Bethel U (MN)
Bethune-Cookman U (FL)
Beulah Heights U (GA)
Binghamton U, State U of New York (NY)
Biola U (CA)
Birmingham-Southern Coll (AL)
Blackburn Coll (IL)
Black Hills State U (SD)
Bloomfield Coll (NJ)
Bloomsburg U of Pennsylvania (PA)
Bluefield Coll (VA)
Bluefield State Coll (WV)
Blue Mountain Coll (MS)
Bluffton U (OH)
Bob Jones U (SC)
Boston Coll (MA)
Boston U (MA)
Bowie State U (MD)
Bowling Green State U (OH)
Bowling Green State U-Firelands Coll (OH)
Bradley U (IL)
Brevard Coll (NC)
Bridgewater Coll (VA)
Bridgewater State U (MA)
Bryan Coll (TN)
Bryant U (RI)
Bucknell U (PA)
Buena Vista U (IA)
Buffalo State Coll, State U of New York (NY)
Cabrini Coll (PA)
Cairn U (PA)
Caldwell U (NJ)
California Lutheran U (CA)
California Polytechnic State U, San Luis Obispo (CA)
California State Polytechnic U, Pomona (CA)
California State U, Chico (CA)
California State U, Dominguez Hills (CA)
California State U, Fresno (CA)
California State U, Fullerton (CA)
California State U, Long Beach (CA)
California State U, Los Angeles (CA)
California State U, Monterey Bay (CA)
California State U, Sacramento (CA)
California State U, San Bernardino (CA)
California State U, San Marcos (CA)
California State U, Stanislaus (CA)
California U of Pennsylvania (PA)
Calumet Coll of Saint Joseph (IN)
Calvary Bible Coll and Theological Sem (MO)
Calvin Coll (MI)
Cameron U (OK)
Campbellsville U (KY)
Canisius Coll (NY)
Capital U (OH)
Capitol Technology U (MD)
Cardinal Stritch U (WI)
Caribbean U (PR)
Carlos Albizu U, Miami Campus (FL)
Carlow U (PA)
Carroll Coll (MT)
Carson-Newman U (TN)
Case Western Reserve U (OH)
Castleton State Coll (VT)
Catawba Coll (NC)
Cazenovia Coll (NY)
Cedar Crest Coll (PA)
Cedarville U (OH)
Centenary Coll of Louisiana (LA)
Central Coll (IA)
Central Connecticut State U (CT)
Central Methodist U (MO)
Central Michigan U (MI)
Central Washington U (WA)
Chaminade U of Honolulu (HI)
Champlain Coll (VT)
Chapman U (CA)
Charleston Southern U (SC)
Chatham U (PA)
Chestnut Hill Coll (PA)
Cheyney U of Pennsylvania (PA)
Chicago State U (IL)
Chipola Coll (FL)
Chowan U (NC)
Christian Brothers U (TN)
Christopher Newport U (VA)
The Citadel, The Military Coll of South Carolina (SC)
City Coll of the City U of New York (NY)
Claflin U (SC)
Clarion U of Pennsylvania (PA)
Clark Atlanta U (GA)
Clarke U (IA)
Clarkson U (NY)
Clark U (MA)
Clayton State U (GA)
Clearwater Christian Coll (FL)
Cleveland State U (OH)
Coastal Carolina U (SC)
Coe Coll (IA)
Coker Coll (SC)
Colby-Sawyer Coll (NH)
The Coll at Brockport, State U of New York (NY)
Coll of Charleston (SC)
Coll of Coastal Georgia (GA)
The Coll of Idaho (ID)
The Coll of New Jersey (NJ)
The Coll of New Rochelle (NY)
Coll of Saint Benedict (MN)
Coll of Saint Elizabeth (NJ)
Coll of Saint Mary (NE)
The Coll of Saint Rose (NY)
The Coll of St. Scholastica (MN)
Coll of the Ozarks (MO)
The Coll of Westchester (NY)
The Coll of William and Mary (VA)
Colorado State U (CO)
Columbia Centro Universitario, Yauco (PR)
Columbia Coll (MO)
Columbia Coll (SC)
Columbia Coll Chicago (IL)
Columbia Southern U (AL)
Columbus State U (GA)
Concordia Coll (MN)
Concordia Coll–New York (NY)
Concordia U (CA)
Concordia U (QC, Canada)
Concordia U Chicago (IL)
Concordia U, Nebraska (NE)
Concordia U, St. Paul (MN)
Concordia U Texas (TX)
Concordia U Wisconsin (WI)
Concord U (WV)
Corban U (OR)
Cornerstone U (MI)
Crandall U (NB, Canada)
Creighton U (NE)
Crossroads Coll (MN)
Culver-Stockton Coll (MO)
Curry Coll (MA)
Daemen Coll (NY)
Dakota State U (SD)
Dalhousie U (NS, Canada)
Dallas Baptist U (TX)
Daniel Webster Coll (NH)
Davenport U, Grand Rapids (MI)
Daytona State Coll (FL)
Defiance Coll (OH)
Delaware State U (DE)
Delta State U (MS)
DePaul U (IL)
DEREE - The American Coll of Greece (Greece)
DeSales U (PA)
DeVry Coll of New York (NY)
DeVry U, Phoenix (AZ)
DeVry U, Pomona (CA)
DeVry U, Westminster (CO)
DeVry U, Miramar (FL)
DeVry U, Orlando (FL)
DeVry U, Decatur (GA)
DeVry U, Chicago (IL)
DeVry U, Kansas City (MO)
DeVry U, North Brunswick (NJ)
DeVry U, Columbus (OH)
DeVry U, Fort Washington (PA)
DeVry U, Houston (TX)
DeVry U, Irving (TX)
DeVry U, Arlington (VA)
DeVry U, Federal Way (WA)
DeVry U Online (IL)
Dickinson State U (ND)
Dixie State U (UT)
Doane Coll (NE)
Dominican Coll (NY)
Dominican U (IL)
Dominican U of California (CA)
Dowling Coll (NY)
Drake U (IA)
Drew U (NJ)
Drury U (MO)
Dunwoody Coll of Technology (MN)
East Carolina U (NC)
East Central U (OK)
Eastern Connecticut State U (CT)
Eastern Illinois U (IL)
Eastern Kentucky U (KY)
Eastern Michigan U (MI)
Eastern New Mexico U (NM)
East Stroudsburg U of Pennsylvania (PA)
East Tennessee State U (TN)
Eckerd Coll (FL)
Edgewood Coll (WI)
Edinboro U of Pennsylvania (PA)
EDP U of Puerto Rico (PR)
EDP U of Puerto Rico–San Sebastian (PR)
Elizabethtown Coll (PA)
Elizabethtown Coll School of Continuing and Professional Studies (PA)
Ellis U (IL)
Elmhurst Coll (IL)
Elmira Coll (NY)
Elms Coll (MA)
Elon U (NC)
Embry-Riddle Aeronautical U–Worldwide (FL)
Emmanuel Coll (MA)
Emory & Henry Coll (VA)
Emporia State U (KS)
Endicott Coll (MA)
Erskine Coll (SC)
Eureka Coll (IL)
Evangel U (MO)
Everglades U, Sarasota (FL)
Excelsior Coll (NY)
Fairfield U (CT)
Fairleigh Dickinson U, Coll at Florham (NJ)
Fairleigh Dickinson U, Metropolitan Campus (NJ)
Fairmont State U (WV)
Farmingdale State Coll (NY)
Faulkner U (AL)
Fayetteville State U (NC)
Ferris State U (MI)
Ferrum Coll (VA)
FIDM/Fashion Inst of Design & Merchandising, Los Angeles Campus (CA)
Fisher Coll (MA)
Fitchburg State U (MA)
Five Towns Coll (NY)
Flagler Coll (FL)
Florida Ag and Mech U (FL)
Florida Atlantic U (FL)
Florida Coll (FL)
Florida Inst of Technology (FL)
Florida Intl U (FL)
Florida National U (FL)
Florida Southern Coll (FL)
Florida State U (FL)
Fontbonne U (MO)
Fordham U (NY)
Fort Hays State U (KS)
Fort Lewis Coll (CO)
Franciscan U of Steubenville (OH)
Francis Marion U (SC)
Franklin & Marshall Coll (PA)
Franklin Pierce U (NH)
Franklin U (OH)
Friends U (KS)
Frostburg State U (MD)
Furman U (SC)
Gallaudet U (DC)
Gannon U (PA)
Geneva Coll (PA)
George Mason U (VA)
Georgetown Coll (KY)
Georgetown U (DC)

The George Washington U (DC)
Georgia Coll & State U (GA)
Georgia Inst of Technology (GA)
Georgian Court U (NJ)
Georgia Regents U (GA)
Georgia Southern U (GA)
Georgia Southwestern State U (GA)
Georgia State U (GA)
Gettysburg Coll (PA)
Gonzaga U (WA)
Goodwin Coll (CT)
Gordon Coll (MA)
Goshen Coll (IN)
Goucher Coll (MD)
Governors State U (IL)
Grace Coll (IN)
Graceland U (IA)
Grambling State U (LA)
Grand View U (IA)
Granite State Coll (NH)
Green Mountain Coll (VT)
Greensboro Coll (NC)
Greenville Coll (IL)
Grove City Coll (PA)
Guilford Coll (NC)
Gustavus Adolphus Coll (MN)
Gwynedd Mercy U (PA)
Hallmark U (TX)
Hamline U (MN)
Hampton U (VA)
Hannibal-LaGrange U (MO)
Harding U (AR)
Hardin-Simmons U (TX)
Harris-Stowe State U (MO)
Hartwick Coll (NY)
Hastings Coll (NE)
Hawai`i Pacific U (HI)
HEC Montreal (QC, Canada)
Heidelberg U (OH)
Heritage U (WA)
Hickey Coll (MO)
High Point U (NC)
Hilbert Coll (NY)
Hiram Coll (OH)
Hofstra U (NY)
Holy Cross Coll (IN)
Holy Family U (PA)
Hope Coll (MI)
Hope Intl U (CA)
Houghton Coll (NY)
Houston Baptist U (TX)
Howard Payne U (TX)
Howard U (DC)
Hult Intl Business School (United Kingdom)
Humboldt State U (CA)
Huntingdon Coll (AL)
Husson U (ME)
Huston-Tillotson U (TX)
Illinois Coll (IL)
Illinois Inst of Technology (IL)
Illinois State U (IL)
Illinois Wesleyan U (IL)
Immaculata U (PA)
Indiana State U (IN)
Indiana U of Pennsylvania (PA)
Indiana U–Purdue U Fort Wayne (IN)
Inter American U of Puerto Rico, Fajardo Campus (PR)
Inter American U of Puerto Rico, Guayama Campus (PR)
Inter American U of Puerto Rico, Ponce Campus (PR)
Inter American U of Puerto Rico, San Germán Campus (PR)
Intl Business Coll, Fort Wayne (IN)
Iona Coll (NY)
Iowa State U of Science and Technology (IA)
Iowa Wesleyan Coll (IA)
Ithaca Coll (NY)
Jackson State U (MS)
Jacksonville State U (AL)
Jacksonville U (FL)
James Madison U (VA)
Jamestown Business Coll (NY)
Jarvis Christian Coll (TX)
John Brown U (AR)
John Cabot U (Italy)
John Carroll U (OH)
Johnson & Wales U (CO)
Johnson & Wales U (FL)
Johnson & Wales U (RI)
Johnson & Wales U - Charlotte Campus (NC)
Johnson C. Smith U (NC)
Johnson State Coll (VT)
Judson U (IL)
Kansas State U (KS)
Kansas Wesleyan U (KS)
Kean U (NJ)
Keene State Coll (NH)
Keiser U, Fort Lauderdale (FL)
Kennesaw State U (GA)
Kent State U (OH)
Kent State U at Ashtabula (OH)
Kent State U at Geauga (OH)
Kent State U at Salem (OH)
Kent State U at Stark (OH)
Kent State U at Trumbull (OH)
Kent State U at Tuscarawas (OH)
Kentucky Christian U (KY)
Kentucky Wesleyan Coll (KY)
Kettering U (MI)
Keuka Coll (NY)
Keystone Coll (PA)
The King's Coll (NY)
King's Coll (PA)
The King's U Coll (AB, Canada)
King U (TN)
Kutztown U of Pennsylvania (PA)
Kuyper Coll (MI)
LaGrange Coll (GA)
Lake Erie Coll (OH)
Lamar U (TX)
Lane Coll (TN)
Langston U (OK)
La Salle U (PA)
Lasell Coll (MA)
La Sierra U (CA)
Laurel U (NC)
Lawrence Technological U (MI)
Lebanese American U (Lebanon)
Lebanon Valley Coll (PA)
Lees-McRae Coll (NC)
Lee U (TN)
Lehman Coll of the City U of New York (NY)
Le Moyne Coll (NY)
LeMoyne-Owen Coll (TN)
Lenoir-Rhyne U (NC)
Lesley U (MA)
LeTourneau U (TX)
Lewis U (IL)
Liberty U (VA)
Life U (GA)
Limestone Coll (SC)
Lincoln Memorial U (TN)
Lincoln U (CA)
Lincoln U (MO)
Lincoln U (PA)
Lindenwood U (MO)
Lindsey Wilson Coll (KY)
Lipscomb U (TN)
Lock Haven U of Pennsylvania (PA)
Long Island U–LIU Brooklyn (NY)
Long Island U–LIU Post (NY)
Longwood U (VA)
Loras Coll (IA)
Louisiana Coll (LA)
Louisiana State U and A&M Coll (LA)
Louisiana State U in Shreveport (LA)
Lourdes U (OH)
Loyola Marymount U (CA)
Loyola U New Orleans (LA)
Lubbock Christian U (TX)
Luther Coll (IA)
Lycoming Coll (PA)
Lynchburg Coll (VA)
Lynn U (FL)
Lyon Coll (AR)
Madonna U (MI)
Maharishi U of Management (IA)
Maine Maritime Acad (ME)
Malone U (OH)
Manchester U (IN)
Manhattanville Coll (NY)
Mansfield U of Pennsylvania (PA)
Maranatha Baptist U (WI)
Marian U (IN)
Marian U (WI)
Marietta Coll (OH)
Marist Coll (NY)
Marquette U (WI)
Marshall U (WV)
Mars Hill U (NC)
Mary Baldwin Coll (VA)
Marylhurst U (OR)
Marymount California U (CA)
Marymount Manhattan Coll (NY)
Marymount U (VA)
Maryville Coll (TN)
Maryville U of Saint Louis (MO)
Marywood U (PA)
Massachusetts Coll of Liberal Arts (MA)
The Master's Coll and Sem (CA)
Mayville State U (ND)
McDaniel Coll (MD)
McKendree U (IL)
McMurry U (TX)
McNeese State U (LA)
Medaille Coll (NY)
Mercy Coll (NY)
Meredith Coll (NC)
Merrimack Coll (MA)
Messiah Coll (PA)
Metropolitan State U (MN)
Miami U (OH)
Michigan State U (MI)
Michigan Technological U (MI)
MidAmerica Nazarene U (KS)
Middle Tennessee State U (TN)
Midland Coll (TX)
Millersville U of Pennsylvania (PA)
Milligan Coll (TN)
Millikin U (IL)
Millsaps Coll (MS)
Milwaukee School of Eng (WI)
Minnesota State U Mankato (MN)
Minnesota State U Moorhead (MN)
Minot State U (ND)
Misericordia U (PA)
Mississippi State U (MS)
Mississippi U for Women (MS)
Mississippi Valley State U (MS)
Missouri Baptist U (MO)
Missouri State U (MO)
Missouri U of Science and Technology (MO)
Missouri Western State U (MO)
Mitchell Coll (CT)
Molloy Coll (NY)
Monmouth Coll (IL)
Monmouth U (NJ)
Montana State U Billings (MT)
Montclair State U (NJ)
Montreat Coll, Montreat (NC)
Moravian Coll (PA)
Morehead State U (KY)
Morningside Coll (IA)
Morris Coll (SC)
Morrisville State Coll (NY)
Mount Allison U (NB, Canada)
Mount Aloysius Coll (PA)
Mount Marty Coll (SD)
Mount Mary U (WI)
Mount Mercy U (IA)
Mount St. Joseph U (OH)
Mount Saint Mary Coll (NY)
Mount Saint Mary's U (CA)
Mount Vernon Nazarene U (OH)
Muhlenberg Coll (PA)
Murray State U (KY)
National U (CA)
Nazareth Coll of Rochester (NY)
Nebraska Wesleyan U (NE)
Neumann U (PA)
Newberry Coll (SC)
Newbury Coll (MA)
New England Coll (NH)
New England Inst of Technology (RI)
New Jersey City U (NJ)
New Jersey Inst of Technology (NJ)
Newman U (KS)
New Mexico Highlands U (NM)
New Mexico Inst of Mining and Technology (NM)
New Mexico State U (NM)
New York Inst of Technology (NY)
Niagara U (NY)
Nicholls State U (LA)
Nichols Coll (MA)
North Carolina Ag and Tech State U (NC)
North Carolina Central U (NC)
North Carolina State U (NC)
North Carolina Wesleyan Coll (NC)
North Central Coll (IL)
North Dakota State U (ND)
Northeastern Illinois U (IL)
Northeastern State U (OK)
Northeastern U (MA)
Northern Arizona U (AZ)
Northern Illinois U (IL)
Northern Kentucky U (KY)
Northern Michigan U (MI)
North Greenville U (SC)
Northland Coll (WI)
Northwest Christian U (OR)
Northwestern Coll (IA)
Northwestern Oklahoma State U (OK)
Northwest Missouri State U (MO)
Northwest Nazarene U (ID)
Northwest U (WA)
Northwood U, Michigan Campus (MI)
Northwood U, Texas Campus (TX)
Norwich U (VT)
Notre Dame of Maryland U (MD)
Nova Southeastern U (FL)
Nyack Coll (NY)
Oakland City U (IN)
Oglethorpe U (GA)
Ohio Dominican U (OH)
Ohio Northern U (OH)
The Ohio State U (OH)
The Ohio State U at Lima (OH)
The Ohio State U at Marion (OH)
The Ohio State U–Mansfield Campus (OH)
The Ohio State U–Newark Campus (OH)
Ohio U (OH)
Ohio Valley U (WV)
Ohio Wesleyan U (OH)
Oklahoma Christian U (OK)
Oklahoma City U (OK)
Oklahoma State U (OK)
Oklahoma Wesleyan U (OK)
Old Dominion U (VA)
Olivet Coll (MI)
Olivet Nazarene U (IL)
Oregon State U (OR)
Our Lady of the Lake U of San Antonio (TX)
Pace U (NY)
Pacific Lutheran U (WA)
Pacific U (OR)
Palm Beach Atlantic U (FL)
Palm Beach State Coll (FL)
Paris Coll of Art (France)
Park U (MO)
Peirce Coll (PA)
Penn Foster Coll (AZ)
Penn State Beaver (PA)
Penn State Brandywine (PA)
Penn State DuBois (PA)
Penn State Erie, The Behrend Coll (PA)
Penn State Fayette, The Eberly Campus (PA)
Penn State Greater Allegheny (PA)
Penn State Harrisburg (PA)
Penn State Hazleton (PA)
Penn State Mont Alto (PA)
Penn State New Kensington (PA)
Penn State Shenango (PA)
Penn State Wilkes-Barre (PA)
Penn State Worthington Scranton (PA)
Penn State York (PA)
Pennsylvania Coll of Technology (PA)
Pepperdine U, Malibu (CA)
Peru State Coll (NE)
Philadelphia U (PA)
Philander Smith Coll (AR)
Piedmont Coll (GA)
Pine Manor Coll (MA)
Plymouth State U (NH)
Point Loma Nazarene U (CA)
Point U (GA)
Polk State Coll (FL)
Polytechnic U of Puerto Rico (PR)
Portland State U (OR)
Post U (CT)
Prairie View A&M U (TX)
Presbyterian Coll (SC)
Principia Coll (IL)
Providence Coll (RI)
Purdue U (IN)
Purdue U Calumet (IN)
Quincy U (IL)
Quinnipiac U (CT)
Radford U (VA)
Ramapo Coll of New Jersey (NJ)
Rasmussen Coll Bismarck (ND)
Rasmussen Coll Bloomington (MN)
Rasmussen Coll Brooklyn Park (MN)
Rasmussen Coll Eagan (MN)
Rasmussen Coll Fargo (ND)
Rasmussen Coll Fort Myers (FL)
Rasmussen Coll Kansas City/Overland Park (KS)
Rasmussen Coll Lake Elmo/Woodbury (MN)
Rasmussen Coll Land O' Lakes (FL)
Rasmussen Coll Mankato (MN)
Rasmussen Coll Moorhead (MN)
Rasmussen Coll New Port Richey (FL)
Rasmussen Coll Ocala (FL)
Rasmussen Coll Rockford (IL)
Rasmussen Coll St. Cloud (MN)
Rasmussen Coll Tampa/Brandon (FL)
Rasmussen Coll Topeka (KS)
Regent U (VA)
Regis U (CO)
Reinhardt U (GA)
Rensselaer Polytechnic Inst (NY)
Rhode Island Coll (RI)
Rhodes Coll (TN)
Rice U (TX)
Ripon Coll (WI)
Rivier U (NH)
Roanoke Coll (VA)
Robert Morris U (PA)
Robert Morris U Illinois (IL)
Roberts Wesleyan Coll (NY)
Rochester Inst of Technology (NY)
Rockford U (IL)
Rockhurst U (MO)
Rocky Mountain Coll (MT)
Roger Williams U (RI)
Rosemont Coll (PA)
Rowan U (NJ)
Rust Coll (MS)
Rutgers, The State U of New Jersey, Camden (NJ)
Rutgers, The State U of New Jersey, Newark (NJ)
Rutgers, The State U of New Jersey, New Brunswick (NJ)
Sacred Heart U (CT)
The Sage Colls (NY)
Saginaw Valley State U (MI)
St. Andrews U (NC)
Saint Augustine's U (NC)
St. Bonaventure U (NY)
St. Catharine Coll (KY)
St. Catherine U (MN)
St. Edward's U (TX)
St. Francis Coll (NY)
Saint Francis U (PA)
St. Gregory's U, Shawnee (OK)
St. John Fisher Coll (NY)
Saint John's U (MN)
St. John's U (NY)
St. Joseph's Coll, Long Island Campus (NY)
St. Joseph's Coll, New York (NY)
Saint Joseph's U (PA)
Saint Leo U (FL)
Saint Louis U (MO)
Saint Martin's U (WA)
Saint Mary-of-the-Woods Coll (IN)
Saint Mary's Coll (IN)
St. Mary's U (TX)
Saint Michael's Coll (VT)
St. Norbert Coll (WI)
Saint Peter's U (NJ)
St. Thomas Aquinas Coll (NY)
St. Thomas U (FL)
Saint Vincent Coll (PA)
Salem Coll (NC)
Salisbury U (MD)
Salve Regina U (RI)
Samford U (AL)
Sam Houston State U (TX)
San Diego Christian Coll (CA)
San Diego State U (CA)
San Francisco State U (CA)
San Jose State U (CA)
Santa Fe U of Art and Design (NM)
Savannah State U (GA)
Seattle Pacific U (WA)
Seattle U (WA)
Selma U (AL)
Seminole State Coll of Florida (FL)
Seton Hill U (PA)
Shawnee State U (OH)
Shaw U (NC)
Shenandoah U (VA)
Shepherd U (WV)

Shippensburg U of Pennsylvania (PA)
Siena Heights U (MI)
Silver Lake Coll of the Holy Family (WI)
Simmons Coll (MA)
Simon Fraser U (BC, Canada)
Simpson Coll (IA)
Simpson U (CA)
Slippery Rock U of Pennsylvania (PA)
South Carolina State U (SC)
Southeastern Louisiana U (LA)
Southeastern Oklahoma State U (OK)
Southeastern U (FL)
Southeast Missouri State U (MO)
Southern Adventist U (TN)
Southern Arkansas U–Magnolia (AR)
Southern Connecticut State U (CT)
Southern Illinois U Carbondale (IL)
Southern Illinois U Edwardsville (IL)
Southern Methodist U (TX)
Southern New Hampshire U (NH)
Southern Oregon U (OR)
Southern Utah U (UT)
Southern Vermont Coll (VT)
Southwest Baptist U (MO)
Southwestern Adventist U (TX)
Southwestern Assemblies of God U (TX)
Southwestern Coll (KS)
Southwest Minnesota State U (MN)
Spring Hill Coll (AL)
State U of New York at Fredonia (NY)
State U of New York at New Paltz (NY)
State U of New York at Oswego (NY)
State U of New York at Plattsburgh (NY)
State U of New York Coll at Geneseo (NY)
State U of New York Coll at Old Westbury (NY)
State U of New York Coll at Potsdam (NY)
State U of New York Coll of Technology at Alfred (NY)
State U of New York Coll of Technology at Canton (NY)
State U of New York Polytechnic Inst (NY)
Stephen F. Austin State U (TX)
Stephens Coll (MO)
Sterling Coll (KS)
Stetson U (FL)
Stevenson U (MD)
Stevens–The Inst of Business & Arts (MO)
Stockton U (NJ)
Stonehill Coll (MA)
Stony Brook U, State U of New York (NY)
Stratford U, Falls Church (VA)
Stratford U, Glen Allen (VA)
Stratford U, Newport News (VA)
Stratford U, Woodbridge (VA)
Suffolk U (MA)
Sullivan U (KY)
Sul Ross State U (TX)
Summit U (PA)
Susquehanna U (PA)
Syracuse U (NY)
Tabor Coll (KS)
Tarleton State U (TX)
Taylor U (IN)
Tennessee State U (TN)
Tennessee Wesleyan Coll (TN)
Texas A&M Intl U (TX)
Texas A&M U (TX)
Texas A&M U–Commerce (TX)
Texas A&M U–Corpus Christi (TX)
Texas A&M U–Kingsville (TX)
Texas Lutheran U (TX)
Texas Southern U (TX)
Texas State U (TX)
Texas Tech U (TX)
Texas Wesleyan U (TX)
Texas Woman's U (TX)
Thiel Coll (PA)
Thomas More Coll (KY)
Tiffin U (OH)
Toccoa Falls Coll (GA)
Tougaloo Coll (MS)
Towson U (MD)
Trent U (ON, Canada)
Trevecca Nazarene U (TN)
Trine U (IN)
Trinity Christian Coll (IL)
Trinity U (TX)
Troy U (AL)
Truett-McConnell Coll (GA)
Truman State U (MO)
Tulane U (LA)
Union Coll (KY)
Union Coll (NE)
Union Inst & U (OH)
Union U (TN)
United States Air Force Acad (CO)
United States Military Acad (NY)
Universidad del Turabo (PR)
Universidad Metropolitana (PR)
Université de Sherbrooke (QC, Canada)
Université du Québec en Outaouais (QC, Canada)
U at Albany, State U of New York (NY)
U at Buffalo, the State U of New York (NY)
The U of Akron (OH)
The U of Alabama (AL)
The U of Alabama at Birmingham (AL)
The U of Alabama in Huntsville (AL)
U of Alaska Fairbanks (AK)
U of Alaska Southeast, Sitka Campus (AK)
U of Arkansas (AR)
U of Arkansas at Little Rock (AR)
U of Arkansas at Pine Bluff (AR)
U of Arkansas–Fort Smith (AR)
The U of British Columbia (BC, Canada)
The U of British Columbia–Okanagan Campus (BC, Canada)
U of California, Berkeley (CA)
U of California, Irvine (CA)
U of California, Merced (CA)
U of California, Riverside (CA)
U of Central Arkansas (AR)
U of Central Florida (FL)
U of Central Missouri (MO)
U of Central Oklahoma (OK)
U of Charleston (WV)
U of Colorado Boulder (CO)
U of Colorado Colorado Springs (CO)
U of Colorado Denver (CO)
U of Dallas (TX)
U of Denver (CO)
U of Dubuque (IA)
U of Evansville (IN)
The U of Findlay (OH)
U of Florida (FL)
U of Georgia (GA)
U of Great Falls (MT)
U of Guam (GU)
U of Hartford (CT)
U of Hawaii at Hilo (HI)
U of Hawaii at Manoa (HI)
U of Hawaii–West Oahu (HI)
U of Houston (TX)
U of Houston–Clear Lake (TX)
U of Houston–Downtown (TX)
U of Houston–Victoria (TX)
U of Idaho (ID)
U of Illinois at Chicago (IL)
U of Illinois at Springfield (IL)
The U of Iowa (IA)
U of Jamestown (ND)
The U of Kansas (KS)
U of La Verne (CA)
U of Lethbridge (AB, Canada)
U of Louisiana at Lafayette (LA)
U of Maine (ME)
U of Maine at Augusta (ME)
U of Maine at Fort Kent (ME)
U of Maine at Machias (ME)
U of Maine at Presque Isle (ME)
U of Mary Hardin-Baylor (TX)
U of Maryland U Coll (MD)
U of Mary Washington (VA)
U of Massachusetts Amherst (MA)
U of Massachusetts Boston (MA)
U of Massachusetts Dartmouth (MA)
U of Massachusetts Lowell (MA)
U of Memphis (TN)
U of Miami (FL)
U of Michigan (MI)
U of Michigan–Dearborn (MI)
U of Michigan–Flint (MI)
U of Minnesota, Crookston (MN)
U of Minnesota, Duluth (MN)
U of Minnesota, Morris (MN)
U of Minnesota, Twin Cities Campus (MN)
U of Mississippi (MS)
U of Missouri (MO)
U of Missouri–Kansas City (MO)
U of Missouri–St. Louis (MO)
U of Mobile (AL)
The U of Montana Western (MT)
U of Montevallo (AL)
U of Mount Union (OH)
U of Nebraska at Kearney (NE)
U of Nebraska–Lincoln (NE)
U of Nevada, Las Vegas (NV)
U of Nevada, Reno (NV)
U of New Brunswick Saint John (NB, Canada)
U of New England (ME)
U of New Hampshire (NH)
U of New Hampshire at Manchester (NH)
U of New Haven (CT)
U of New Mexico (NM)
U of New Orleans (LA)
U of North Alabama (AL)
U of North Carolina at Asheville (NC)
The U of North Carolina at Chapel Hill (NC)
The U of North Carolina at Charlotte (NC)
The U of North Carolina at Greensboro (NC)
The U of North Carolina at Pembroke (NC)
The U of North Carolina Wilmington (NC)
U of North Dakota (ND)
U of Northern Colorado (CO)
U of Northern Iowa (IA)
U of North Florida (FL)
U of North Georgia (GA)
U of Northwestern–St. Paul (MN)
U of Oklahoma (OK)
U of Pennsylvania (PA)
U of Pikeville (KY)
U of Pittsburgh at Bradford (PA)
U of Pittsburgh at Greensburg (PA)
U of Portland (OR)
U of Puget Sound (WA)
U of Regina (SK, Canada)
U of Rhode Island (RI)
U of Richmond (VA)
U of Rio Grande (OH)
U of St. Francis (IL)
U of Saint Francis (IN)
U of Saint Joseph (CT)
U of Saint Mary (KS)
U of St. Thomas (MN)
U of St. Thomas (TX)
U of San Diego (CA)
U of San Francisco (CA)
U of Saskatchewan (SK, Canada)
The U of Scranton (PA)
U of South Alabama (AL)
U of South Carolina Aiken (SC)
U of South Carolina Beaufort (SC)
U of South Carolina Upstate (SC)
U of Southern California (CA)
U of Southern Indiana (IN)
U of Southern Maine (ME)
U of Southern Mississippi (MS)
U of South Florida (FL)
U of South Florida Sarasota-Manatee (FL)
The U of Tampa (FL)
The U of Tennessee (TN)
The U of Tennessee at Chattanooga (TN)
The U of Tennessee at Martin (TN)
The U of Texas at Arlington (TX)
The U of Texas at Austin (TX)
The U of Texas at El Paso (TX)
The U of Texas at San Antonio (TX)
The U of Texas at Tyler (TX)
The U of Texas of the Permian Basin (TX)
The U of Texas–Pan American (TX)
U of the Cumberlands (KY)
U of the District of Columbia (DC)
U of the Fraser Valley (BC, Canada)
U of the Incarnate Word (TX)
U of the Pacific (CA)
U of the Virgin Islands (VI)
U of the West (CA)
The U of Toledo (OH)
U of Toronto (ON, Canada)
The U of Tulsa (OK)
U of Utah (UT)
U of Valley Forge (PA)
U of Vermont (VT)
The U of Virginia's Coll at Wise (VA)
U of Washington (WA)
U of Washington, Bothell (WA)
U of Washington, Tacoma (WA)
U of Waterloo (ON, Canada)
The U of West Alabama (AL)
The U of Western Ontario (ON, Canada)
U of West Florida (FL)
U of West Georgia (GA)
U of Windsor (ON, Canada)
U of Wisconsin–Eau Claire (WI)
U of Wisconsin–Green Bay (WI)
U of Wisconsin–La Crosse (WI)
U of Wisconsin–Madison (WI)
U of Wisconsin–Oshkosh (WI)
U of Wisconsin–Parkside (WI)
U of Wisconsin–Platteville (WI)
U of Wisconsin–River Falls (WI)
U of Wisconsin–Stevens Point (WI)
U of Wisconsin–Stout (WI)
U of Wisconsin–Superior (WI)
U of Wisconsin–Whitewater (WI)
U of Wyoming (WY)
Upper Iowa U (IA)
Urbana U (OH)
Ursinus Coll (PA)
Ursuline Coll (OH)
Utah State U (UT)
Utah Valley U (UT)
Utica Coll (NY)
Valdosta State U (GA)
Valley City State U (ND)
Vanguard U of Southern California (CA)
Vermont Tech Coll (VT)
Villanova U (PA)
Virginia Commonwealth U (VA)
Virginia Polytechnic Inst and State U (VA)
Virginia State U (VA)
Virginia Wesleyan Coll (VA)
Viterbo U (WI)
Voorhees Coll (SC)
Wagner Coll (NY)
Walden U (MN)
Waldorf Coll (IA)
Walla Walla U (WA)
Walsh Coll of Accountancy and Business Administration (MI)
Walsh U (OH)
Warner Pacific Coll (OR)
Wartburg Coll (IA)
Washburn U (KS)
Washington and Lee U (VA)
Washington Coll (MD)
Washington State U (WA)
Washington State U Vancouver (WA)
Washington U in St. Louis (MO)
Waynesburg U (PA)
Wayne State Coll (NE)
Webber Intl U (FL)
Weber State U (UT)
Webster U (MO)
Welch Coll (TN)
Wesleyan Coll (GA)
West Chester U of Pennsylvania (PA)
Western Carolina U (NC)
Western Illinois U (IL)
Western Kentucky U (KY)
Western Michigan U (MI)
Western New England U (MA)
Western State Colorado U (CO)
Western Washington U (WA)
Westfield State U (MA)
West Liberty U (WV)
Westminster Coll (MO)
West Texas A&M U (TX)
West Virginia State U (WV)
West Virginia U (WV)
West Virginia U Inst of Technology (WV)
West Virginia Wesleyan Coll (WV)
Wheeling Jesuit U (WV)
Whittier Coll (CA)
Whitworth U (WA)
Wichita State U (KS)
Widener U (PA)
Wilberforce U (OH)
Wilkes U (PA)
William Jessup U (CA)
William Jewell Coll (MO)
William Peace U (NC)
Williams Baptist Coll (AR)
William Woods U (MO)
Wilmington U (DE)
Wingate U (NC)
Winona State U (MN)
Winthrop U (SC)
Wittenberg U (OH)
Worcester Polytechnic Inst (MA)
Worcester State U (MA)
Wright State U (OH)
Xavier U (OH)
Xavier U of Louisiana (LA)
Yeshiva U (NY)
York Coll of Pennsylvania (PA)
York Coll of the City U of New York (NY)
Youngstown State U (OH)

BUSINESS ADMINISTRATION, MANAGEMENT AND OPERATIONS RELATED

Adams State U (CO)
Albany State U (GA)
Alverno Coll (WI)
The American U of Paris (France)
Anna Maria Coll (MA)
Augsburg Coll (MN)
Babson Coll (MA)
Bay Path U (MA)
Becker Coll (MA)
Benedictine U (IL)
Berkeley Coll, Woodland Park (NJ)
Blackburn Coll (IL)
Bowling Green State U (OH)
Bradley U (IL)
California State U, San Bernardino (CA)
Calumet Coll of Saint Joseph (IN)
Capital U (OH)
Cardinal Stritch U (WI)
Carlos Albizu U, Miami Campus (FL)
Central Michigan U (MI)
Central Washington U (WA)
Charleston Southern U (SC)
Clayton State U (GA)
Coll of Central Florida (FL)
Colorado Mesa U (CO)
Cornerstone U (MI)
Crossroads Coll (MN)
Delaware State U (DE)
DePaul U (IL)
DeVry Coll of New York (NY)
DeVry U, Phoenix (AZ)
DeVry U, Pomona (CA)
DeVry U, Westminster (CO)
DeVry U, Miramar (FL)
DeVry U, Orlando (FL)
DeVry U, Decatur (GA)
DeVry U, Chicago (IL)
DeVry U, Kansas City (MO)
DeVry U, North Brunswick (NJ)
DeVry U, Columbus (OH)
DeVry U, Fort Washington (PA)
DeVry U, Houston (TX)
DeVry U, Irving (TX)
DeVry U, Arlington (VA)
DeVry U, Federal Way (WA)
DeVry U Online (IL)
Dixie State U (UT)
Dominican U of California (CA)
Eastern Oregon U (OR)
Embry-Riddle Aeronautical U–Daytona (FL)
Embry-Riddle Aeronautical U–Prescott (AZ)
Embry-Riddle Aeronautical U–Worldwide (FL)
Florida Inst of Technology (FL)
Florida SouthWestern State Coll (FL)
Florida State Coll at Jacksonville (FL)
Franklin U (OH)
Gettysburg Coll (PA)
Grace Coll (IN)

Hallmark U (TX)
High Point U (NC)
Hodges U (FL)
Hofstra U (NY)
Holy Cross Coll (IN)
Howard Payne U (TX)
Huntingdon Coll (AL)
John Brown U (AR)
Judson U (IL)
Kansas Wesleyan U (KS)
Kettering U (MI)
La Roche Coll (PA)
Le Moyne Coll (NY)
Limestone Coll (SC)
Lincoln Christian U (IL)
Lincoln Coll of New England, Southington (CT)
Lincoln Memorial U (TN)
Malone U (OH)
Marquette U (WI)
Mayville State U (ND)
Mercer U, Macon (GA)
Mercy Coll (NY)
Miami Dade Coll (FL)
Millikin U (IL)
Missouri Baptist U (MO)
Missouri State U (MO)
Morris Coll (SC)
Morrisville State Coll (NY)
North Dakota State U (ND)
Oakland City U (IN)
Ohio Northern U (OH)
Olivet Nazarene U (IL)
Pennsylvania Coll of Technology (PA)
Pensacola State Coll (FL)
Plaza Coll (NY)
Polk State Coll (FL)
Prescott Coll (AZ)
Rider U (NJ)
Roosevelt U (IL)
Saint Leo U (FL)
San Jose State U (CA)
Santa Fe Coll (FL)
Shenandoah U (VA)
South Florida State Coll (FL)
State U of New York at New Paltz (NY)
Texas Tech U (TX)
Towson U (MD)
The U of Alabama at Birmingham (AL)
U of Alberta (AB, Canada)
U of Charleston (WV)
U of Houston–Clear Lake (TX)
U of Illinois at Springfield (IL)
U of Louisville (KY)
U of Maryland, Baltimore County (MD)
U of Maryland U Coll (MD)
U of Miami (FL)
U of Michigan–Dearborn (MI)
U of North Georgia (GA)
U of Ottawa (ON, Canada)
U of Pennsylvania (PA)
U of Puerto Rico in Ponce (PR)
U of St. Thomas (MN)
U of Southern Maine (ME)
U of the District of Columbia (DC)
U of the Incarnate Word (TX)
U of Waterloo (ON, Canada)
The U of Western Ontario (ON, Canada)
U of Wisconsin–River Falls (WI)
U of Wyoming (WY)
Ursuline Coll (OH)
Viterbo U (WI)
Washington U in St. Louis (MO)
Western Governors U (UT)
Widener U (PA)
Williamson Christian Coll (TN)

BUSINESS AND PERSONAL/ FINANCIAL SERVICES MARKETING
Anna Maria Coll (MA)
DeSales U (PA)
Dixie State U (UT)
Lindenwood U (MO)
Walla Walla U (WA)

BUSINESS AUTOMATION/ TECHNOLOGY/DATA ENTRY
East Carolina U (NC)
Mount Vernon Nazarene U (OH)

BUSINESS/COMMERCE
Adams State U (CO)
Alice Lloyd Coll (KY)
Alvernia U (PA)
American Coll of Thessaloniki (Greece)
Anderson U (SC)
Asbury U (KY)
Auburn U at Montgomery (AL)
Austin Coll (TX)
Austin Peay State U (TN)
Ave Maria U (FL)
Avila U (MO)
Baker U (KS)
Ball State U (IN)
Baylor U (TX)
Belmont U (TN)
Bentley U (MA)
Bethel Coll (KS)
Bloomsburg U of Pennsylvania (PA)
Bowling Green State U (OH)
Brandeis U (MA)
Brenau U (GA)
Bucknell U (PA)
California Baptist U (CA)
California State U, Dominguez Hills (CA)
Canisius Coll (NY)
Cardinal Stritch U (WI)
Caribbean U (PR)
The Catholic U of America (DC)
Central State U (OH)
Champlain Coll (VT)
Christian Brothers U (TN)
Clayton State U (GA)
Coll of Central Florida (FL)
The Coll of New Rochelle (NY)
Colorado Mesa U (CO)
Colorado State U–Pueblo (CO)
Columbia Centro Universitario, Caguas (PR)
Columbia Coll (MO)
Columbus State U (GA)
Concordia U, Nebraska (NE)
Concordia U Texas (TX)
Covenant Coll (GA)
Creighton U (NE)
Cumberland U (TN)
Dalhousie U (NS, Canada)
Davenport U, Grand Rapids (MI)
Delta State U (MS)
DeSales U (PA)
DeVry U, Phoenix (AZ)
DeVry U, Pomona (CA)
DeVry U, Westminster (CO)
DeVry U, Miramar (FL)
DeVry U, Orlando (FL)
DeVry U, Decatur (GA)
DeVry U, Chicago (IL)
DeVry U, Kansas City (MO)
DeVry U, Columbus (OH)
DeVry U, Fort Washington (PA)
DeVry U, Houston (TX)
DeVry U, Irving (TX)
DeVry U, Arlington (VA)
DeVry U, Federal Way (WA)
DeVry U Online (IL)
Drake U (IA)
Drexel U (PA)
Earlham Coll (IN)
East Central U (OK)
Eastern Connecticut State U (CT)
Eastern Michigan U (MI)
Eastern Oregon U (OR)
East Texas Baptist U (TX)
Edgewood Coll (WI)
Ellis U (IL)
The Evergreen State Coll (WA)
Florida State U (FL)
Framingham State U (MA)
Franklin Coll (IN)
Georgia Gwinnett Coll (GA)
Goshen Coll (IN)
Grace Coll (IN)
Grand Valley State U (MI)
Hawai`i Pacific U (HI)
HEC Montreal (QC, Canada)
Hillsdale Free Will Baptist Coll (OK)
Hofstra U (NY)
Hollins U (VA)
Houston Baptist U (TX)
Howard Payne U (TX)
Hult Intl Business School (United Kingdom)
Huntingdon Coll (AL)
Husson U (ME)
Indiana U Bloomington (IN)
Indiana U East (IN)
Indiana U Kokomo (IN)
Indiana U Northwest (IN)
Indiana U of Pennsylvania (PA)
Indiana U–Purdue U Fort Wayne (IN)
Indiana U–Purdue U Indianapolis (IN)
Indiana U South Bend (IN)
Indiana U Southeast (IN)
Iowa Wesleyan Coll (IA)
Ithaca Coll (NY)
Johns Hopkins U (MD)
Johnson State Coll (VT)
Judson Coll (AL)
Juniata Coll (PA)
Kalamazoo Coll (MI)
Kansas State U (KS)
Kentucky State U (KY)
Lamar U (TX)
La Sierra U (CA)
Lewis U (IL)
LIM Coll (NY)
Limestone Coll (SC)
Linfield Coll (OR)
Loras Coll (IA)
Lourdes U (OH)
Loyola Marymount U (CA)
Manchester U (IN)
Marymount Manhattan Coll (NY)
Maryville Coll (TN)
Maryville U of Saint Louis (MO)
Massachusetts Inst of Technology (MA)
McMurry U (TX)
Medgar Evers Coll of the City U of New York (NY)
Mercer U, Macon (GA)
Mercy Coll (NY)
Metropolitan Coll of New York (NY)
Midwestern State U (TX)
Milwaukee School of Eng (WI)
Mississippi U for Women (MS)
Missouri Southern State U (MO)
Missouri State U (MO)
Montana State U (MT)
Montana State U Billings (MT)
Montana Tech of The U of Montana (MT)
Morehead State U (KY)
Mount Allison U (NB, Canada)
Mount Mercy U (IA)
Mount St. Mary's U (MD)
Mount Vernon Nazarene U (OH)
Multnomah U (OR)
Murray State U (KY)
New Mexico State U (NM)
New York U (NY)
Niagara U (NY)
Nichols Coll (MA)
Norfolk State U (VA)
Northeastern Illinois U (IL)
Northeastern U (MA)
Northern Illinois U (IL)
Northern Kentucky U (KY)
Oakland U (MI)
Ohio Northern U (OH)
The Ohio State U at Lima (OH)
The Ohio State U at Marion (OH)
The Ohio State U–Newark Campus (OH)
Ohio Valley U (WV)
Oklahoma Christian U (OK)
Oklahoma Wesleyan U (OK)
Pace U (NY)
Penn State Abington (PA)
Penn State Altoona (PA)
Penn State Berks (PA)
Penn State Lehigh Valley (PA)
Penn State Schuylkill (PA)
Pittsburg State U (KS)
Plymouth State U (NH)
Purdue U Calumet (IN)
Randolph Coll (VA)
Regis Coll (MA)
Reinhardt U (GA)
Rochester Inst of Technology (NY)
Roosevelt U (IL)
Saginaw Valley State U (MI)
Saint Anselm Coll (NH)
Saint Joseph's Coll (IN)
St. Lawrence U (NY)
Saint Leo U (FL)
St. Mary's U (TX)
St. Thomas U (FL)
Saint Vincent Coll (PA)
Sam Houston State U (TX)
Savannah State U (GA)
Seattle Pacific U (WA)
Seattle U (WA)
Skidmore Coll (NY)
Southern Arkansas U–Magnolia (AR)
Southwestern U (TX)
Spalding U (KY)
State U of New York at New Paltz (NY)
State U of New York at Plattsburgh (NY)
State U of New York Empire State Coll (NY)
Stephen F. Austin State U (TX)
Tarleton State U (TX)
Temple U (PA)
Texas A&M U–Commerce (TX)
Texas A&M U–Kingsville (TX)
Texas Tech U (TX)
Transylvania U (KY)
Trinity Coll of Florida (FL)
Troy U (AL)
The U of Akron (OH)
U of Alberta (AB, Canada)
The U of Arizona (AZ)
U of Arkansas (AR)
U of Arkansas at Little Rock (AR)
U of Bridgeport (CT)
The U of British Columbia (BC, Canada)
U of Central Arkansas (AR)
U of Central Florida (FL)
U of Central Oklahoma (OK)
U of Delaware (DE)
U of Denver (CO)
U of Georgia (GA)
U of Hawaii at Manoa (HI)
U of Houston–Clear Lake (TX)
U of Houston–Downtown (TX)
The U of Kansas (KS)
U of Kentucky (KY)
U of Maine at Fort Kent (ME)
U of Maryland, Coll Park (MD)
U of Massachusetts Dartmouth (MA)
U of Minnesota, Twin Cities Campus (MN)
The U of Montana (MT)
U of Nevada, Reno (NV)
U of North Texas (TX)
U of Notre Dame (IN)
U of Oregon (OR)
U of Pittsburgh (PA)
U of Regina (SK, Canada)
U of Rhode Island (RI)
U of Rochester (NY)
U of San Francisco (CA)
U of Science and Arts of Oklahoma (OK)
U of South Alabama (AL)
The U of South Dakota (SD)
U of Southern Indiana (IN)
U of South Florida (FL)
U of South Florida Sarasota-Manatee (FL)
The U of Texas at Austin (TX)
The U of Texas at Dallas (TX)
The U of Texas at San Antonio (TX)
The U of Toledo (OH)
The U of Tulsa (OK)
U of Utah (UT)
U of Valley Forge (PA)
U of Virginia (VA)
The U of Western Ontario (ON, Canada)
U of West Florida (FL)
U of Windsor (ON, Canada)
U of Wisconsin–Milwaukee (WI)
U of Wisconsin–Whitewater (WI)
Utah State U (UT)
Villa Maria Coll (NY)
Virginia Commonwealth U (VA)
Wake Forest U (NC)
Waldorf Coll (IA)
Washburn U (KS)
Washington & Jefferson Coll (PA)
Washington State U (WA)
Washington U in St. Louis (MO)
Webber Intl U (FL)
Welch Coll (TN)
Western Michigan U (MI)
Western New England U (MA)
Western Oregon U (OR)
Western Washington U (WA)
West Texas A&M U (TX)
West Virginia U (WV)
Wheaton Coll (MA)
William Penn U (IA)
Wright State U (OH)
Youngstown State U (OH)

BUSINESS/CORPORATE COMMUNICATIONS
Aquinas Coll (MI)
Augustana Coll (SD)
Babson Coll (MA)
Bentley U (MA)
Chestnut Hill Coll (PA)
Christian Brothers U (TN)
Concordia U Chicago (IL)
Duquesne U (PA)
Elon U (NC)
Fort Hays State U (KS)
Hawai`i Pacific U (HI)
Lycoming Coll (PA)
Marietta Coll (OH)
Mercy Coll (NY)
MidAmerica Nazarene U (KS)
Morningside Coll (IA)
Mount Mary U (WI)
National U (CA)
Nichols Coll (MA)
North Dakota State U (ND)
Penn State Abington (PA)
Point Loma Nazarene U (CA)
Rockhurst U (MO)
Roosevelt U (IL)
Saint Leo U (FL)
Stephen F. Austin State U (TX)
Stevenson U (MD)
Trinity Christian Coll (IL)
The U of Findlay (OH)
U of Houston (TX)
U of New England (ME)
U of Rio Grande (OH)
The U of Western Ontario (ON, Canada)
Walden U (MN)
Walsh U (OH)

BUSINESS FAMILY AND CONSUMER SCIENCES/ HUMAN SCIENCES
Brigham Young U (UT)
The Ohio State U (OH)
U of Houston (TX)
Virginia Polytechnic Inst and State U (VA)

BUSINESS, MANAGEMENT, AND MARKETING RELATED
Adelphi U (NY)
American U (DC)
Arizona State U at the Polytechnic campus (AZ)
Arizona State U at the Tempe campus (AZ)
Arizona State U at the West campus (AZ)
Athens State U (AL)
Baylor U (TX)
Benedictine U (IL)
Bentley U (MA)
Bowling Green State U (OH)
Bridgewater State U (MA)
California State U, Dominguez Hills (CA)
Claflin U (SC)
Concordia Coll–New York (NY)
Corban U (OR)
Dowling Coll (NY)
Duquesne U (PA)
Eastern U (PA)
FIDM/Fashion Inst of Design & Merchandising, Los Angeles Campus (CA)
FIDM/Fashion Inst of Design & Merchandising, San Francisco Campus (CA)
Five Towns Coll (NY)
Greenville Coll (IL)
Hamline U (MN)
Hofstra U (NY)
Howard Payne U (TX)
Lehigh U (PA)
Loyola U Chicago (IL)
Mercy Coll (NY)
Messiah Coll (PA)
Missouri U of Science and Technology (MO)
Morrisville State Coll (NY)
Multnomah U (OR)
Nebraska Wesleyan U (NE)
New Jersey Inst of Technology (NJ)
New York U (NY)
Oklahoma Wesleyan U (OK)

Old Dominion U (VA)
Park U (MO)
Penn State U Park (PA)
Peru State Coll (NE)
Polytechnic U of Puerto Rico (PR)
Sacred Heart U (CT)
Saint Mary's U of Minnesota (MN)
Seton Hill U (PA)
Skidmore Coll (NY)
Southeastern U (FL)
Southern California Inst of Technology (CA)
Southern New Hampshire U (NH)
State U of New York at Plattsburgh (NY)
State U of New York Coll of Agriculture and Technology at Cobleskill (NY)
State U of New York Coll of Technology at Alfred (NY)
State U of New York Coll of Technology at Canton (NY)
State U of New York Coll of Technology at Delhi (NY)
State U of New York Maritime Coll (NY)
Trevecca Nazarene U (TN)
Troy U (AL)
U of Alberta (AB, Canada)
U of Louisiana at Lafayette (LA)
U of Minnesota, Crookston (MN)
U of Southern Mississippi (MS)
The U of Western Ontario (ON, Canada)
U of Wisconsin–Stout (WI)
U of Wisconsin–Whitewater (WI)
Utica Coll (NY)
Walla Walla U (WA)
Western State Colorado U (CO)
Xavier U (OH)

BUSINESS/MANAGERIAL ECONOMICS
Allegheny Coll (PA)
American Intl Coll (MA)
Anderson U (IN)
Andrews U (MI)
Arcadia U (PA)
Arkansas State U (AR)
Arkansas Tech U (AR)
Armstrong State U (GA)
Auburn U (AL)
Auburn U at Montgomery (AL)
Ball State U (IN)
Bard Coll (NY)
Baruch Coll of the City U of New York (NY)
Baylor U (TX)
Belmont U (TN)
Beloit Coll (WI)
Benedictine U (IL)
Bentley U (MA)
Berry Coll (GA)
Boston Coll (MA)
Bradley U (IL)
Buena Vista U (IA)
California Inst of Technology (CA)
California State U, Fullerton (CA)
California State U, Long Beach (CA)
Campbellsville U (KY)
Canisius Coll (NY)
Capital U (OH)
Carson-Newman U (TN)
Central Washington U (WA)
Chapman U (CA)
Charleston Southern U (SC)
Chatham U (PA)
Clarion U of Pennsylvania (PA)
Clark Atlanta U (GA)
Cleveland State U (OH)
Coastal Carolina U (SC)
The Coll of Wooster (OH)
Colorado State U–Pueblo (CO)
Delaware State U (DE)
DePaul U (IL)
Duquesne U (PA)
Eastern Michigan U (MI)
East Tennessee State U (TN)
Fordham U (NY)
Fort Hays State U (KS)
Fort Lewis Coll (CO)
Francis Marion U (SC)
Georgetown Coll (KY)
The George Washington U (DC)
Georgia Coll & State U (GA)
Georgia Inst of Technology (GA)
Georgia Southern U (GA)
Georgia State U (GA)
Gonzaga U (WA)
Grambling State U (LA)
Grand Valley State U (MI)
Green Mountain Coll (VT)
Greensboro Coll (NC)
Grove City Coll (PA)
Gustavus Adolphus Coll (MN)
Hampden-Sydney Coll (VA)
HEC Montreal (QC, Canada)
High Point U (NC)
Hofstra U (NY)
Hope Coll (MI)
Houston Baptist U (TX)
Husson U (ME)
Illinois Coll (IL)
Indiana U–Purdue U Fort Wayne (IN)
Inter American U of Puerto Rico, Bayamón Campus (PR)
Inter American U of Puerto Rico, San Germán Campus (PR)
Ithaca Coll (NY)
Jackson State U (MS)
James Madison U (VA)
Kennesaw State U (GA)
Kent State U (OH)
Kentucky Wesleyan Coll (KY)
Lake Forest Coll (IL)
Lamar U (TX)
La Salle U (PA)
Lehigh U (PA)
Lewis U (IL)
Limestone Coll (SC)
Lincoln Memorial U (TN)
Lipscomb U (TN)
Louisiana State U and A&M Coll (LA)
Louisiana State U in Shreveport (LA)
Loyola U Chicago (IL)
Loyola U New Orleans (LA)
Marquette U (WI)
Marshall U (WV)
Mars Hill U (NC)
Marymount Manhattan Coll (NY)
Miami U (OH)
Middle Tennessee State U (TN)
Midwestern State U (TX)
Mills Coll (CA)
Mississippi State U (MS)
Missouri Southern State U (MO)
Montana State U Billings (MT)
Morehead State U (KY)
Mount Allison U (NB, Canada)
New York U (NY)
Niagara U (NY)
Nichols Coll (MA)
North Carolina State U (NC)
Northern Arizona U (AZ)
Northern Kentucky U (KY)
Northern State U (SD)
Northwest Missouri State U (MO)
Oakland U (MI)
Oglethorpe U (GA)
The Ohio State U (OH)
The Ohio State U at Lima (OH)
The Ohio State U at Marion (OH)
The Ohio State U–Mansfield Campus (OH)
The Ohio State U–Newark Campus (OH)
Ohio U (OH)
Ohio Wesleyan U (OH)
Oklahoma State U (OK)
Oklahoma Wesleyan U (OK)
Old Dominion U (VA)
Olivet Coll (MI)
Park U (MO)
Patrick Henry Coll (VA)
Penn State Abington (PA)
Penn State Altoona (PA)
Penn State Beaver (PA)
Penn State Berks (PA)
Penn State Brandywine (PA)
Penn State DuBois (PA)
Penn State Erie, The Behrend Coll (PA)
Penn State Fayette, The Eberly Campus (PA)
Penn State Greater Allegheny (PA)
Penn State Hazleton (PA)
Penn State Lehigh Valley (PA)
Penn State Mont Alto (PA)
Penn State New Kensington (PA)
Penn State Schuylkill (PA)
Penn State Shenango (PA)
Penn State Wilkes-Barre (PA)
Penn State Worthington Scranton (PA)
Penn State York (PA)
Point Loma Nazarene U (CA)
Presbyterian Coll (SC)
Quinnipiac U (CT)
Randolph-Macon Coll (VA)
Rider U (NJ)
Sacred Heart U (CT)
Saginaw Valley State U (MI)
Saint Anselm Coll (NH)
Saint Louis U (MO)
Saint Peter's U (NJ)
Salisbury U (MD)
Samford U (AL)
Sam Houston State U (TX)
Seattle U (WA)
South Carolina State U (SC)
Southern Connecticut State U (CT)
Southern Illinois U Carbondale (IL)
Southern Illinois U Edwardsville (IL)
Spring Hill Coll (AL)
State U of New York at Plattsburgh (NY)
State U of New York Coll at Potsdam (NY)
Stephen F. Austin State U (TX)
Stetson U (FL)
Tarleton State U (TX)
Tennessee State U (TN)
Texas A&M Intl U (TX)
Texas State U (TX)
Troy U (AL)
Union Coll (NY)
Union U (TN)
Universidad Metropolitana (PR)
The U of Alabama (AL)
The U of Alabama at Birmingham (AL)
The U of Alabama in Huntsville (AL)
U of Alberta (AB, Canada)
The U of Arizona (AZ)
U of Arkansas (AR)
U of California, Irvine (CA)
U of California, Los Angeles (CA)
U of California, Riverside (CA)
U of California, Santa Cruz (CA)
U of Central Florida (FL)
U of Central Oklahoma (OK)
U of Dayton (OH)
U of Denver (CO)
U of Georgia (GA)
U of Guelph (ON, Canada)
U of Idaho (ID)
U of Indianapolis (IN)
The U of Iowa (IA)
U of Kentucky (KY)
U of Lethbridge (AB, Canada)
U of Louisiana at Lafayette (LA)
U of Louisville (KY)
U of Mary Hardin-Baylor (TX)
U of Memphis (TN)
U of Miami (FL)
U of Mississippi (MS)
U of Missouri (MO)
U of Nebraska–Lincoln (NE)
U of Nevada, Reno (NV)
U of North Alabama (AL)
The U of North Carolina at Charlotte (NC)
The U of North Carolina at Greensboro (NC)
U of North Dakota (ND)
U of North Florida (FL)
U of North Texas (TX)
U of Oklahoma (OK)
U of Rochester (NY)
U of San Diego (CA)
U of San Francisco (CA)
U of Saskatchewan (SK, Canada)
U of Southern Mississippi (MS)
U of South Florida (FL)
U of South Florida, St. Petersburg (FL)
The U of Tennessee (TN)
The U of Tennessee at Martin (TN)
The U of Texas at Arlington (TX)
The U of Texas at San Antonio (TX)
The U of Texas of the Permian Basin (TX)
U of the Incarnate Word (TX)
The U of Western Ontario (ON, Canada)
U of West Florida (FL)
U of West Georgia (GA)
U of Windsor (ON, Canada)
U of Wisconsin–Superior (WI)
U of Wyoming (WY)
Urbana U (OH)
Utica Coll (NY)
Valdosta State U (GA)
Villanova U (PA)
Virginia Commonwealth U (VA)
Virginia Polytechnic Inst and State U (VA)
Virginia State U (VA)
Washburn U (KS)
Washington U in St. Louis (MO)
Weber State U (UT)
West Chester U of Pennsylvania (PA)
Western Illinois U (IL)
Western Kentucky U (KY)
Western Michigan U (MI)
Western State Colorado U (CO)
West Liberty U (WV)
Westminster Coll (UT)
West Texas A&M U (TX)
West Virginia U (WV)
West Virginia Wesleyan Coll (WV)
Wheaton Coll (IL)
Widener U (PA)
William Jewell Coll (MO)
William Paterson U of New Jersey (NJ)
Wofford Coll (SC)
Wright State U (OH)
Xavier U (OH)
Youngstown State U (OH)

BUSINESS OPERATIONS SUPPORT AND SECRETARIAL SERVICES RELATED
Delaware State U (DE)

BUSINESS STATISTICS
Baylor U (TX)
Bryant U (RI)
HEC Montreal (QC, Canada)
Southern Oregon U (OR)
U of Central Missouri (MO)
U of Denver (CO)
The U of Tennessee (TN)

BUSINESS TEACHER EDUCATION
Adams State U (CO)
Appalachian State U (NC)
Arizona Christian U (AZ)
Arkansas State U (AR)
Arkansas Tech U (AR)
Auburn U (AL)
Avila U (MO)
Ball State U (IN)
Baylor U (TX)
Bethune-Cookman U (FL)
Black Hills State U (SD)
Bluefield Coll (VA)
Bowling Green State U (OH)
Buena Vista U (IA)
Buffalo State Coll, State U of New York (NY)
California State U, Dominguez Hills (CA)
Campbellsville U (KY)
Canisius Coll (NY)
Carson-Newman U (TN)
Central Michigan U (MI)
Coll of Saint Mary (NE)
Colorado State U (CO)
Concordia Coll (MN)
Concordia U, Nebraska (NE)
Concordia U Wisconsin (WI)
Concord U (WV)
Corban U (OR)
Dakota State U (SD)
Delaware State U (DE)
Dickinson State U (ND)
Doane Coll (NE)
Dowling Coll (NY)
East Carolina U (NC)
Eastern Kentucky U (KY)
Eastern Michigan U (MI)
Edgewood Coll (WI)
Emmanuel Coll (GA)
Emory & Henry Coll (VA)
Evangel U (MO)
Fairmont State U (WV)
Fayetteville State U (NC)
Fort Hays State U (KS)
Friends U (KS)
Grace Coll (IN)
Gwynedd Mercy U (PA)
Hampton U (VA)
Hannibal-LaGrange U (MO)
Hardin-Simmons U (TX)
Hastings Coll (NE)
Hofstra U (NY)
Howard Payne U (TX)
Illinois State U (IL)
Immaculata U (PA)
Indiana State U (IN)
John Brown U (AR)
La Salle U (PA)
Lee U (TN)
Lehman Coll of the City U of New York (NY)
LeTourneau U (TX)
Lincoln U (MO)
Lindenwood U (MO)
Louisiana Coll (LA)
Maranatha Baptist U (WI)
McKendree U (IL)
Middle Tennessee State U (TN)
Minot State U (ND)
Mississippi State U (MS)
Missouri Baptist U (MO)
Missouri State U (MO)
Morehead State U (KY)
Mount Vernon Nazarene U (OH)
National U Coll, Bayamón (PR)
Nazareth Coll of Rochester (NY)
Niagara U (NY)
Nicholls State U (LA)
Norfolk State U (VA)
North Carolina Ag and Tech State U (NC)
Northern Kentucky U (KY)
Northwestern Coll (IA)
Northwest Missouri State U (MO)
Oakland City U (IN)
Ohio Wesleyan U (OH)
Peru State Coll (NE)
Rider U (NJ)
Robert Morris U (PA)
Rust Coll (MS)
Saint Mary's Coll (IN)
Saint Vincent Coll (PA)
South Carolina State U (SC)
Southeast Missouri State U (MO)
Southern Arkansas U–Magnolia (AR)
Southern Utah U (UT)
Southwestern Adventist U (TX)
Tabor Coll (KS)
Tennessee State U (TN)
Thomas More Coll (KY)
Trevecca Nazarene U (TN)
Trinity Christian Coll (IL)
Tusculum Coll (TN)
Union Coll (NE)
Union U (TN)
U of Alberta (AB, Canada)
U of Arkansas at Pine Bluff (AR)
The U of British Columbia (BC, Canada)
U of Central Arkansas (AR)
U of Central Missouri (MO)
U of Central Oklahoma (OK)
The U of Findlay (OH)
U of Indianapolis (IN)
U of Lethbridge (AB, Canada)
U of Maine at Machias (ME)
U of Minnesota, Twin Cities Campus (MN)
U of Missouri (MO)
The U of Montana (MT)
The U of Montana Western (MT)
U of Nebraska at Kearney (NE)
U of Nebraska–Lincoln (NE)
U of Northern Iowa (IA)
U of Regina (SK, Canada)
U of Rio Grande (OH)
U of Saint Francis (IN)
U of Southern Indiana (IN)
U of Southern Mississippi (MS)
The U of Tennessee at Martin (TN)
The U of Toledo (OH)
U of Wisconsin–Superior (WI)
U of Wisconsin–Whitewater (WI)
Upper Iowa U (IA)
Utah State U (UT)
Utah Valley U (UT)
Utica Coll (NY)
Valley City State U (ND)
Virginia State U (VA)
Virginia Union U (VA)
Viterbo U (WI)

Walla Walla U (WA)
Wayne State Coll (NE)
Weber State U (UT)
Western Kentucky U (KY)
Western Michigan U (MI)
Winona State U (MN)
Wright State U (OH)

CAD/CADD DRAFTING/ DESIGN TECHNOLOGY
Eastern Michigan U (MI)
Ferris State U (MI)
Murray State U (KY)

CANADIAN GOVERNMENT AND POLITICS
The U of British Columbia (BC, Canada)

CANADIAN STUDIES
Dalhousie U (NS, Canada)
Mount Allison U (NB, Canada)
Trent U (ON, Canada)
U of Alberta (AB, Canada)
The U of British Columbia (BC, Canada)
U of Lethbridge (AB, Canada)
U of Ottawa (ON, Canada)
U of Toronto (ON, Canada)
U of Washington (WA)
U of Waterloo (ON, Canada)
The U of Western Ontario (ON, Canada)
Western Washington U (WA)

CARDIOVASCULAR TECHNOLOGY
Gwynedd Mercy U (PA)
Louisiana State U Health Sciences Center (LA)
Nebraska Methodist Coll (NE)
Pennsylvania Coll of Technology (PA)

CARIBBEAN STUDIES
Columbia U, School of General Studies (NY)
Hofstra U (NY)
Northwestern U (IL)

CASINO MANAGEMENT
Central Michigan U (MI)
National U (CA)

CELL AND MOLECULAR BIOLOGY
Adams State U (CO)
Bennington Coll (VT)
Binghamton U, State U of New York (NY)
Bradley U (IL)
Bridgewater State U (MA)
Bucknell U (PA)
Canisius Coll (NY)
Cedarville U (OH)
Central Washington U (WA)
Christopher Newport U (VA)
The Colorado Coll (CO)
Concordia U (QC, Canada)
Connecticut Coll (CT)
Florida State U (FL)
Fort Lewis Coll (CO)
Georgia Regents U (GA)
Grand Valley State U (MI)
Harvard U (MA)
Illinois State U (IL)
Johns Hopkins U (MD)
Liberty U (VA)
Limestone Coll (SC)
Marymount U (VA)
Missouri State U (MO)
Northwest Nazarene U (ID)
Ohio U (OH)
Oklahoma City U (OK)
Purdue U (IN)
Seattle Pacific U (WA)
Seattle U (WA)
Texas A&M U (TX)
Texas Tech U (TX)
Universidad Metropolitana (PR)
U of Alberta (AB, Canada)
The U of Arizona (AZ)
U of California, Berkeley (CA)
U of California, Irvine (CA)
U of California, Los Angeles (CA)
U of Colorado Boulder (CO)
U of Hawaii at Manoa (HI)
U of Michigan (MI)
U of Regina (SK, Canada)
U of Rhode Island (RI)
U of Saskatchewan (SK, Canada)
The U of Tennessee at Martin (TN)
U of Washington (WA)
U of Wisconsin–Superior (WI)
Western Washington U (WA)

CELL BIOLOGY AND ANATOMICAL SCIENCES RELATED
Rutgers, The State U of New Jersey, New Brunswick (NJ)
Tulane U (LA)
U of Mary Hardin-Baylor (TX)
Washington & Jefferson Coll (PA)
Yale U (CT)

CELL BIOLOGY AND ANATOMY
Dallas Baptist U (TX)
Huntingdon Coll (AL)
The U of Western Ontario (ON, Canada)
Western State Colorado U (CO)

CELL BIOLOGY AND HISTOLOGY
Beloit Coll (WI)
California State U, Dominguez Hills (CA)
California State U, Fresno (CA)
California State U, Long Beach (CA)
California State U, San Marcos (CA)
The Coll of Saint Rose (NY)
Humboldt State U (CA)
Johns Hopkins U (MD)
Long Island U–LIU Post (NY)
Mansfield U of Pennsylvania (PA)
Montana State U (MT)
Northwestern U (IL)
Rutgers, The State U of New Jersey, New Brunswick (NJ)
San Francisco State U (CA)
Tulane U (LA)
The U of British Columbia (BC, Canada)
U of California, Davis (CA)
U of California, Santa Cruz (CA)
U of Georgia (GA)
U of Minnesota, Duluth (MN)
U of Minnesota, Twin Cities Campus (MN)
U of Utah (UT)
Western Washington U (WA)
Worcester Polytechnic Inst (MA)

CELTIC LANGUAGES
U of California, Berkeley (CA)

CERAMIC ARTS AND CERAMICS
Adams State U (CO)
Aquinas Coll (MI)
Arcadia U (PA)
Bard Coll at Simon's Rock (MA)
Bennington Coll (VT)
Bowling Green State U (OH)
Bradley U (IL)
Brigham Young U (UT)
California Coll of the Arts (CA)
California State U, Long Beach (CA)
Central Washington U (WA)
Cleveland Inst of Art (OH)
Coll of the Atlantic (ME)
Coll of the Ozarks (MO)
Columbia Coll (MO)
Concordia U (QC, Canada)
Concord U (WV)
Emily Carr U of Art + Design (BC, Canada)
Franklin Pierce U (NH)
Hofstra U (NY)
Howard U (DC)
Inter American U of Puerto Rico, San Germán Campus (PR)
Kansas City Art Inst (MO)
Marywood U (PA)
Massachusetts Coll of Art and Design (MA)
Minnesota State U Mankato (MN)
Northern Michigan U (MI)
Northwest Nazarene U (ID)
Ohio Northern U (OH)
Ohio U (OH)
Pratt Inst (NY)
Providence Coll (RI)
Rhode Island Coll (RI)
Rhode Island School of Design (RI)
Rochester Inst of Technology (NY)
Rutgers, The State U of New Jersey, New Brunswick (NJ)
Salve Regina U (RI)
School of the Art Inst of Chicago (IL)
School of the Museum of Fine Arts, Boston (MA)
Seton Hill U (PA)
State U of New York at New Paltz (NY)
Syracuse U (NY)
Temple U (PA)
Texas Christian U (TX)
The U of Akron (OH)
U of Dallas (TX)
U of Hartford (CT)
The U of Iowa (IA)
The U of Kansas (KS)
U of Massachusetts Dartmouth (MA)
U of Miami (FL)
U of Michigan (MI)
U of Oregon (OR)
U of Regina (SK, Canada)
The U of Texas at El Paso (TX)
U of Washington (WA)
Washington U in St. Louis (MO)
Western State Colorado U (CO)
Western Washington U (WA)
West Virginia Wesleyan Coll (WV)

CERAMIC SCIENCES AND ENGINEERING
Missouri U of Science and Technology (MO)
Rutgers, The State U of New Jersey, New Brunswick (NJ)

CHEMICAL AND BIOMOLECULAR ENGINEERING
Johns Hopkins U (MD)
Massachusetts Inst of Technology (MA)
Milwaukee School of Eng (WI)
New York U (NY)
U of Washington (WA)

CHEMICAL ENGINEERING
American U of Beirut (Lebanon)
Arizona State U at the Tempe campus (AZ)
Auburn U (AL)
Brown U (RI)
Bucknell U (PA)
California Baptist U (CA)
California Inst of Technology (CA)
California State Polytechnic U, Pomona (CA)
California State U, Long Beach (CA)
Calvin Coll (MI)
Case Western Reserve U (OH)
Christian Brothers U (TN)
City Coll of the City U of New York (NY)
Clarkson U (NY)
Cleveland State U (OH)
Colorado School of Mines (CO)
Colorado State U (CO)
Columbia U (NY)
Cooper Union for the Advancement of Science and Art (NY)
Cornell U (NY)
Dalhousie U (NS, Canada)
Drexel U (PA)
Elon U (NC)
Florida Ag and Mech U (FL)
Florida Inst of Technology (FL)
Georgia Inst of Technology (GA)
Hampton U (VA)
Howard U (DC)
Illinois Inst of Technology (IL)
Iowa State U of Science and Technology (IA)
Johns Hopkins U (MD)
Kansas State U (KS)
Kettering U (MI)
Lafayette Coll (PA)
Lamar U (TX)
Lehigh U (PA)
Louisiana State U and A&M Coll (LA)
Manhattan Coll (NY)
Massachusetts Inst of Technology (MA)
Miami U (OH)
Michigan State U (MI)
Michigan Technological U (MI)
Mississippi State U (MS)
Missouri U of Science and Technology (MO)
Montana State U (MT)
New Jersey Inst of Technology (NJ)
New Mexico Inst of Mining and Technology (NM)
New Mexico State U (NM)
New York U (NY)
North Carolina Ag and Tech State U (NC)
North Carolina State U (NC)
Northeastern U (MA)
Northwestern U (IL)
The Ohio State U (OH)
Ohio U (OH)
Oklahoma State U (OK)
Oregon State U (OR)
Penn State Abington (PA)
Penn State Altoona (PA)
Penn State Beaver (PA)
Penn State Berks (PA)
Penn State Brandywine (PA)
Penn State DuBois (PA)
Penn State Erie, The Behrend Coll (PA)
Penn State Fayette, The Eberly Campus (PA)
Penn State Greater Allegheny (PA)
Penn State Hazleton (PA)
Penn State Lehigh Valley (PA)
Penn State Mont Alto (PA)
Penn State New Kensington (PA)
Penn State Schuylkill (PA)
Penn State Shenango (PA)
Penn State U Park (PA)
Penn State Wilkes-Barre (PA)
Penn State Worthington Scranton (PA)
Penn State York (PA)
Polytechnic U of Puerto Rico (PR)
Prairie View A&M U (TX)
Princeton U (NJ)
Purdue U (IN)
Rensselaer Polytechnic Inst (NY)
Rice U (TX)
Rochester Inst of Technology (NY)
Rose-Hulman Inst of Technology (IN)
Rowan U (NJ)
Rutgers, The State U of New Jersey, New Brunswick (NJ)
San Jose State U (CA)
South Dakota School of Mines and Technology (SD)
Stanford U (CA)
State U of New York Coll of Environmental Science and Forestry (NY)
Stony Brook U, State U of New York (NY)
Syracuse U (NY)
Texas A&M U (TX)
Texas Tech U (TX)
Thiel Coll (PA)
Trine U (IN)
Tufts U (MA)
Tulane U (LA)
United States Military Acad (NY)
Université de Montréal (QC, Canada)
Université de Sherbrooke (QC, Canada)
U at Buffalo, the State U of New York (NY)
The U of Akron (OH)
The U of Alabama (AL)
The U of Alabama in Huntsville (AL)
The U of Arizona (AZ)
U of Arkansas (AR)
The U of British Columbia (BC, Canada)
U of California, Berkeley (CA)
U of California, Davis (CA)
U of California, Irvine (CA)
U of California, Los Angeles (CA)
U of California, Riverside (CA)
U of California, Santa Barbara (CA)
U of Cincinnati (OH)
U of Colorado Boulder (CO)
U of Dayton (OH)
U of Delaware (DE)
U of Florida (FL)
U of Houston (TX)
U of Idaho (ID)
U of Illinois at Chicago (IL)
The U of Iowa (IA)
The U of Kansas (KS)
U of Kentucky (KY)
U of Louisiana at Lafayette (LA)
U of Louisville (KY)
U of Maine (ME)
U of Maryland, Baltimore County (MD)
U of Maryland, Coll Park (MD)
U of Massachusetts Amherst (MA)
U of Massachusetts Lowell (MA)
U of Michigan (MI)
U of Minnesota, Duluth (MN)
U of Minnesota, Twin Cities Campus (MN)
U of Mississippi (MS)
U of Missouri (MO)
U of Nebraska–Lincoln (NE)
U of Nevada, Reno (NV)
U of New Hampshire (NH)
U of New Haven (CT)
U of New Mexico (NM)
U of North Dakota (ND)
U of Notre Dame (IN)
U of Oklahoma (OK)
U of Ottawa (ON, Canada)
U of Pennsylvania (PA)
U of Pittsburgh (PA)
U of Rhode Island (RI)
U of Rochester (NY)
U of Saskatchewan (SK, Canada)
U of South Alabama (AL)
U of Southern California (CA)
U of South Florida (FL)
The U of Tennessee (TN)
The U of Tennessee at Chattanooga (TN)
The U of Texas at Austin (TX)
The U of Toledo (OH)
U of Toronto (ON, Canada)
The U of Tulsa (OK)
U of Utah (UT)
U of Virginia (VA)
U of Washington (WA)
U of Waterloo (ON, Canada)
The U of Western Ontario (ON, Canada)
U of Wisconsin–Madison (WI)
U of Wyoming (WY)
Vanderbilt U (TN)
Villanova U (PA)
Virginia Commonwealth U (VA)
Virginia Polytechnic Inst and State U (VA)
Washington State U (WA)
Washington U in St. Louis (MO)
Wayne State U (MI)
Western Michigan U (MI)
West Virginia U (WV)
West Virginia U Inst of Technology (WV)
Widener U (PA)
Worcester Polytechnic Inst (MA)
Xavier U (OH)
Yale U (CT)
Youngstown State U (OH)

CHEMICAL PHYSICS
Adams State U (CO)
Augustana Coll (SD)
Bowdoin Coll (ME)
Centre Coll (KY)
Columbia U, School of General Studies (NY)
Hamilton Coll (NY)
Harvard U (MA)
Hendrix Coll (AR)
LeTourneau U (TX)
Lewis U (IL)
Michigan State U (MI)
Saginaw Valley State U (MI)
Simon Fraser U (BC, Canada)
U of Guelph (ON, Canada)
U of Waterloo (ON, Canada)

CHEMICAL TECHNOLOGY
Inter American U of Puerto Rico, Guayama Campus (PR)
Norwich U (VT)
U of Regina (SK, Canada)

CHEMISTRY
Abilene Christian U (TX)

Adams State U (CO)
Adelphi U (NY)
Agnes Scott Coll (GA)
Alabama State U (AL)
Albany Coll of Pharmacy and Health Sciences (NY)
Albany State U (GA)
Albertus Magnus Coll (CT)
Albion Coll (MI)
Albright Coll (PA)
Alcorn State U (MS)
Allegheny Coll (PA)
Alma Coll (MI)
Alvernia U (PA)
Alverno Coll (WI)
American Intl Coll (MA)
American U (DC)
The American U in Cairo (Egypt)
American U of Beirut (Lebanon)
Amherst Coll (MA)
Anderson U (IN)
Andrews U (MI)
Angelo State U (TX)
Appalachian State U (NC)
Aquinas Coll (MI)
Arcadia U (PA)
Arizona State U at the Tempe campus (AZ)
Arkansas State U (AR)
Arkansas Tech U (AR)
Armstrong State U (GA)
Asbury U (KY)
Ashland U (OH)
Assumption Coll (MA)
Athens State U (AL)
Auburn U (AL)
Augsburg Coll (MN)
Augustana Coll (IL)
Augustana Coll (SD)
Austin Coll (TX)
Austin Peay State U (TN)
Azusa Pacific U (CA)
Baker U (KS)
Baldwin Wallace U (OH)
Ball State U (IN)
Bard Coll (NY)
Bard Coll at Simon's Rock (MA)
Barnard Coll (NY)
Barry U (FL)
Bates Coll (ME)
Baylor U (TX)
Belhaven U (MS)
Belmont U (TN)
Beloit Coll (WI)
Bemidji State U (MN)
Benedictine Coll (KS)
Benedictine U (IL)
Bennett Coll (NC)
Bennington Coll (VT)
Berea Coll (KY)
Berry Coll (GA)
Bethany Coll (WV)
Bethany Lutheran Coll (MN)
Bethel Coll (IN)
Bethel Coll (KS)
Bethel U (MN)
Bethune-Cookman U (FL)
Binghamton U, State U of New York (NY)
Biola U (CA)
Birmingham-Southern Coll (AL)
Blackburn Coll (IL)
Black Hills State U (SD)
Bloomfield Coll (NJ)
Bloomsburg U of Pennsylvania (PA)
Bluefield Coll (VA)
Bluffton U (OH)
Bob Jones U (SC)
Boston Coll (MA)
Boston U (MA)
Bowdoin Coll (ME)
Bowling Green State U (OH)
Bradley U (IL)
Brandeis U (MA)
Bridgewater Coll (VA)
Bridgewater State U (MA)
Brown U (RI)
Bryn Mawr Coll (PA)
Bucknell U (PA)
Buena Vista U (IA)
Buffalo State Coll, State U of New York (NY)
Butler U (IN)
Cabrini Coll (PA)
California Baptist U (CA)
California Inst of Technology (CA)
California Lutheran U (CA)
California Polytechnic State U, San Luis Obispo (CA)
California State Polytechnic U, Pomona (CA)
California State U, Chico (CA)
California State U, Dominguez Hills (CA)
California State U, Fresno (CA)
California State U, Fullerton (CA)
California State U, Long Beach (CA)
California State U, Los Angeles (CA)
California State U, Sacramento (CA)
California State U, San Bernardino (CA)
California State U, San Marcos (CA)
California State U, Stanislaus (CA)
California U of Pennsylvania (PA)
Calvin Coll (MI)
Cameron U (OK)
Campbellsville U (KY)
Canisius Coll (NY)
Cape Breton U (NS, Canada)
Capital U (OH)
Cardinal Stritch U (WI)
Carleton Coll (MN)
Carlow U (PA)
Carroll Coll (MT)
Carson-Newman U (TN)
Case Western Reserve U (OH)
Castleton State Coll (VT)
Catawba Coll (NC)
The Catholic U of America (DC)
Cedar Crest Coll (PA)
Cedarville U (OH)
Centenary Coll of Louisiana (LA)
Central Coll (IA)
Central Connecticut State U (CT)
Central Methodist U (MO)
Central Michigan U (MI)
Central State U (OH)
Central Washington U (WA)
Centre Coll (KY)
Chapman U (CA)
Charleston Southern U (SC)
Chatham U (PA)
Chestnut Hill Coll (PA)
Cheyney U of Pennsylvania (PA)
Chicago State U (IL)
Chowan U (NC)
Christian Brothers U (TN)
Christopher Newport U (VA)
The Citadel, The Military Coll of South Carolina (SC)
City Coll of the City U of New York (NY)
Claflin U (SC)
Claremont McKenna Coll (CA)
Clarion U of Pennsylvania (PA)
Clark Atlanta U (GA)
Clarke U (IA)
Clarkson U (NY)
Clark U (MA)
Clayton State U (GA)
Cleveland State U (OH)
Coastal Carolina U (SC)
Coe Coll (IA)
Coker Coll (SC)
Colby Coll (ME)
The Coll at Brockport, State U of New York (NY)
Coll of Charleston (SC)
The Coll of Idaho (ID)
The Coll of New Jersey (NJ)
The Coll of New Rochelle (NY)
Coll of Saint Benedict (MN)
Coll of Saint Elizabeth (NJ)
Coll of Saint Mary (NE)
The Coll of Saint Rose (NY)
The Coll of St. Scholastica (MN)
Coll of Staten Island of the City U of New York (NY)
Coll of the Holy Cross (MA)
Coll of the Ozarks (MO)
The Coll of William and Mary (VA)
The Coll of Wooster (OH)
The Colorado Coll (CO)
Colorado Mesa U (CO)
Colorado School of Mines (CO)
Colorado State U (CO)
Colorado State U–Pueblo (CO)
Columbia Coll (MO)
Columbia Coll (SC)
Columbia U (NY)
Columbia U, School of General Studies (NY)
Columbus State U (GA)
Concordia Coll (MN)
Concordia U (CA)
Concordia U (QC, Canada)
Concordia U Chicago (IL)
Concordia U, Nebraska (NE)
Concord U (WV)
Connecticut Coll (CT)
Cornell Coll (IA)
Cornell U (NY)
Covenant Coll (GA)
Creighton U (NE)
Dalhousie U (NS, Canada)
Dartmouth Coll (NH)
Davidson Coll (NC)
Delaware State U (DE)
Delta State U (MS)
Denison U (OH)
DePaul U (IL)
DePauw U (IN)
DeSales U (PA)
Dickinson Coll (PA)
Dickinson State U (ND)
Doane Coll (NE)
Dominican U (IL)
Dominican U of California (CA)
Dowling Coll (NY)
Drake U (IA)
Drew U (NJ)
Drexel U (PA)
Drury U (MO)
Duquesne U (PA)
Earlham Coll (IN)
East Carolina U (NC)
East Central U (OK)
Eastern Illinois U (IL)
Eastern Kentucky U (KY)
Eastern Michigan U (MI)
Eastern New Mexico U (NM)
Eastern Oregon U (OR)
Eastern U (PA)
East Stroudsburg U of Pennsylvania (PA)
East Tennessee State U (TN)
East Texas Baptist U (TX)
Eckerd Coll (FL)
Edgewood Coll (WI)
Edinboro U of Pennsylvania (PA)
Elizabethtown Coll (PA)
Elmhurst Coll (IL)
Elmira Coll (NY)
Elms Coll (MA)
Elon U (NC)
Emmanuel Coll (MA)
Emory & Henry Coll (VA)
Emporia State U (KS)
Erskine Coll (SC)
Eureka Coll (IL)
Evangel U (MO)
Fairfield U (CT)
Fairleigh Dickinson U, Coll at Florham (NJ)
Fairleigh Dickinson U, Metropolitan Campus (NJ)
Fairmont State U (WV)
Fayetteville State U (NC)
Ferris State U (MI)
Ferrum Coll (VA)
Fitchburg State U (MA)
Florida Ag and Mech U (FL)
Florida Atlantic U (FL)
Florida Gulf Coast U (FL)
Florida Inst of Technology (FL)
Florida Intl U (FL)
Florida Southern Coll (FL)
Florida State U (FL)
Fordham U (NY)
Fort Hays State U (KS)
Fort Lewis Coll (CO)
Framingham State U (MA)
Franciscan U of Steubenville (OH)
Francis Marion U (SC)
Franklin & Marshall Coll (PA)
Franklin Coll (IN)
Friends U (KS)
Frostburg State U (MD)
Furman U (SC)
Gallaudet U (DC)
Gannon U (PA)
Geneva Coll (PA)
George Mason U (VA)
Georgetown Coll (KY)
Georgetown U (DC)
The George Washington U (DC)
Georgia Coll & State U (GA)
Georgia Gwinnett Coll (GA)
Georgia Inst of Technology (GA)
Georgian Court U (NJ)
Georgia Regents U (GA)
Georgia Southern U (GA)
Georgia Southwestern State U (GA)
Georgia State U (GA)
Gettysburg Coll (PA)
Gonzaga U (WA)
Gordon Coll (MA)
Goshen Coll (IN)
Goucher Coll (MD)
Governors State U (IL)
Graceland U (IA)
Grambling State U (LA)
Grand Valley State U (MI)
Greensboro Coll (NC)
Greenville Coll (IL)
Grinnell Coll (IA)
Grove City Coll (PA)
Guilford Coll (NC)
Gustavus Adolphus Coll (MN)
Hamilton Coll (NY)
Hamline U (MN)
Hampden-Sydney Coll (VA)
Hampshire Coll (MA)
Hampton U (VA)
Hanover Coll (IN)
Harding U (AR)
Hardin-Simmons U (TX)
Hartwick Coll (NY)
Harvard U (MA)
Harvey Mudd Coll (CA)
Hastings Coll (NE)
Haverford Coll (PA)
Hawai`i Pacific U (HI)
Heidelberg U (OH)
Hendrix Coll (AR)
High Point U (NC)
Hillsdale Coll (MI)
Hiram Coll (OH)
Hobart and William Smith Colls (NY)
Hofstra U (NY)
Hollins U (VA)
Hope Coll (MI)
Houghton Coll (NY)
Houston Baptist U (TX)
Howard Payne U (TX)
Howard U (DC)
Humboldt State U (CA)
Hunter Coll of the City U of New York (NY)
Huntingdon Coll (AL)
Husson U (ME)
Huston-Tillotson U (TX)
Illinois Coll (IL)
Illinois Inst of Technology (IL)
Illinois State U (IL)
Illinois Wesleyan U (IL)
Immaculata U (PA)
Indiana State U (IN)
Indiana U Bloomington (IN)
Indiana U Kokomo (IN)
Indiana U Northwest (IN)
Indiana U of Pennsylvania (PA)
Indiana U–Purdue U Fort Wayne (IN)
Indiana U–Purdue U Indianapolis (IN)
Indiana U South Bend (IN)
Indiana U Southeast (IN)
Inter American U of Puerto Rico, San Germán Campus (PR)
Iona Coll (NY)
Iowa State U of Science and Technology (IA)
Ithaca Coll (NY)
Jackson State U (MS)
Jacksonville State U (AL)
Jacksonville U (FL)
James Madison U (VA)
Jarvis Christian Coll (TX)
John Brown U (AR)
John Carroll U (OH)
Johns Hopkins U (MD)
Johnson C. Smith U (NC)
Judson Coll (AL)
Judson U (IL)
Juniata Coll (PA)
Kalamazoo Coll (MI)
Kansas State U (KS)
Kansas Wesleyan U (KS)
Kean U (NJ)
Keene State Coll (NH)
Kennesaw State U (GA)
Kent State U (OH)
Kentucky State U (KY)
Kentucky Wesleyan Coll (KY)
Kenyon Coll (OH)
Kettering U (MI)
King's Coll (PA)
The King's U Coll (AB, Canada)
King U (TN)
Knox Coll (IL)
Kutztown U of Pennsylvania (PA)
Lafayette Coll (PA)
LaGrange Coll (GA)
Lake Erie Coll (OH)
Lake Forest Coll (IL)
Lamar U (TX)
Lane Coll (TN)
Langston U (OK)
La Roche Coll (PA)
La Salle U (PA)
La Sierra U (CA)
Lawrence Technological U (MI)
Lawrence U (WI)
Lebanese American U (Lebanon)
Lebanon Valley Coll (PA)
Lee U (TN)
Lehigh U (PA)
Lehman Coll of the City U of New York (NY)
Le Moyne Coll (NY)
LeMoyne-Owen Coll (TN)
Lenoir-Rhyne U (NC)
LeTourneau U (TX)
Lewis & Clark Coll (OR)
Lewis U (IL)
Liberty U (VA)
Limestone Coll (SC)
Lincoln Memorial U (TN)
Lincoln U (MO)
Lincoln U (PA)
Lindenwood U (MO)
Linfield Coll (OR)
Lipscomb U (TN)
Lock Haven U of Pennsylvania (PA)
Long Island U–LIU Brooklyn (NY)
Long Island U–LIU Post (NY)
Longwood U (VA)
Loras Coll (IA)
Louisiana Coll (LA)
Louisiana State U and A&M Coll (LA)
Louisiana State U in Shreveport (LA)
Loyola Marymount U (CA)
Loyola U Chicago (IL)
Loyola U New Orleans (LA)
Lubbock Christian U (TX)
Luther Coll (IA)
Lycoming Coll (PA)
Lynchburg Coll (VA)
Lyon Coll (AR)
Macalester Coll (MN)
Madonna U (MI)
Malone U (OH)
Manchester U (IN)
Manhattan Coll (NY)
Manhattanville Coll (NY)
Mansfield U of Pennsylvania (PA)
Marian U (IN)
Marian U (WI)
Marietta Coll (OH)
Marist Coll (NY)
Marquette U (WI)
Marshall U (WV)
Mars Hill U (NC)
Mary Baldwin Coll (VA)
Maryville Coll (TN)
Maryville U of Saint Louis (MO)
Massachusetts Coll of Liberal Arts (MA)
Massachusetts Inst of Technology (MA)
Mayville State U (ND)
McDaniel Coll (MD)
McKendree U (IL)
McMurry U (TX)
McNeese State U (LA)
MCPHS U (MA)
Mercer U, Macon (GA)
Meredith Coll (NC)
Merrimack Coll (MA)
Messiah Coll (PA)
Miami U (OH)
Michigan State U (MI)
Michigan Technological U (MI)
MidAmerica Nazarene U (KS)
Middlebury Coll (VT)
Middle Tennessee State U (TN)

Midwestern State U (TX)
Millersville U of Pennsylvania (PA)
Milligan Coll (TN)
Millikin U (IL)
Millsaps Coll (MS)
Mills Coll (CA)
Minnesota State U Mankato (MN)
Minnesota State U Moorhead (MN)
Minot State U (ND)
Misericordia U (PA)
Mississippi State U (MS)
Mississippi U for Women (MS)
Mississippi Valley State U (MS)
Missouri Baptist U (MO)
Missouri Southern State U (MO)
Missouri State U (MO)
Missouri U of Science and Technology (MO)
Missouri Western State U (MO)
Monmouth Coll (IL)
Monmouth U (NJ)
Montana State U (MT)
Montana State U Billings (MT)
Montana Tech of The U of Montana (MT)
Montclair State U (NJ)
Moravian Coll (PA)
Morehead State U (KY)
Morningside Coll (IA)
Mount Allison U (NB, Canada)
Mount Holyoke Coll (MA)
Mount Marty Coll (SD)
Mount Mary U (WI)
Mount St. Joseph U (OH)
Mount Saint Mary Coll (NY)
Mount Saint Mary's U (CA)
Mount St. Mary's U (MD)
Mount Vernon Nazarene U (OH)
Muhlenberg Coll (PA)
Murray State U (KY)
Nazareth Coll of Rochester (NY)
Nebraska Wesleyan U (NE)
Newberry Coll (SC)
New Coll of Florida (FL)
New Jersey City U (NJ)
New Jersey Inst of Technology (NJ)
Newman U (KS)
New Mexico Highlands U (NM)
New Mexico Inst of Mining and Technology (NM)
New Mexico State U (NM)
New York Inst of Technology (NY)
New York U (NY)
Niagara U (NY)
Nicholls State U (LA)
Norfolk State U (VA)
North Carolina Ag and Tech State U (NC)
North Carolina Central U (NC)
North Carolina State U (NC)
North Carolina Wesleyan Coll (NC)
North Central Coll (IL)
North Dakota State U (ND)
Northeastern Illinois U (IL)
Northeastern State U (OK)
Northeastern U (MA)
Northern Arizona U (AZ)
Northern Illinois U (IL)
Northern Kentucky U (KY)
Northern Michigan U (MI)
Northern State U (SD)
Northland Coll (WI)
Northwestern Coll (IA)
Northwestern Oklahoma State U (OK)
Northwestern U (IL)
Northwest Missouri State U (MO)
Northwest Nazarene U (ID)
Norwich U (VT)
Notre Dame of Maryland U (MD)
Nova Southeastern U (FL)
Oakland City U (IN)
Oakland U (MI)
Oberlin Coll (OH)
Occidental Coll (CA)
Oglethorpe U (GA)
Ohio Dominican U (OH)
Ohio Northern U (OH)
The Ohio State U (OH)
Ohio U (OH)
Ohio Wesleyan U (OH)
Oklahoma Baptist U (OK)
Oklahoma Christian U (OK)
Oklahoma State U (OK)
Oklahoma Wesleyan U (OK)
Old Dominion U (VA)
Olivet Coll (MI)
Olivet Nazarene U (IL)
Oregon State U (OR)
Our Lady of the Lake U of San Antonio (TX)
Pace U (NY)
Pacific Lutheran U (WA)
Pacific U (OR)
Park U (MO)
Penn State Abington (PA)
Penn State Altoona (PA)
Penn State Beaver (PA)
Penn State Berks (PA)
Penn State Brandywine (PA)
Penn State DuBois (PA)
Penn State Erie, The Behrend Coll (PA)
Penn State Fayette, The Eberly Campus (PA)
Penn State Greater Allegheny (PA)
Penn State Hazleton (PA)
Penn State Lehigh Valley (PA)
Penn State Mont Alto (PA)
Penn State New Kensington (PA)
Penn State Schuylkill (PA)
Penn State Shenango (PA)
Penn State U Park (PA)
Penn State Wilkes-Barre (PA)
Penn State Worthington Scranton (PA)
Penn State York (PA)
Pepperdine U, Malibu (CA)
Peru State Coll (NE)
Philadelphia U (PA)
Philander Smith Coll (AR)
Piedmont Coll (GA)
Pittsburg State U (KS)
Plymouth State U (NH)
Point Loma Nazarene U (CA)
Pomona Coll (CA)
Portland State U (OR)
Prairie View A&M U (TX)
Presbyterian Coll (SC)
Princeton U (NJ)
Principia Coll (IL)
Providence Coll (RI)
Purchase Coll, State U of New York (NY)
Purdue U (IN)
Purdue U Calumet (IN)
Queens Coll of the City U of New York (NY)
Quincy U (IL)
Quinnipiac U (CT)
Radford U (VA)
Ramapo Coll of New Jersey (NJ)
Randolph Coll (VA)
Randolph-Macon Coll (VA)
Reed Coll (OR)
Regis U (CO)
Rensselaer Polytechnic Inst (NY)
Rhode Island Coll (RI)
Rhodes Coll (TN)
Rice U (TX)
Rider U (NJ)
Ripon Coll (WI)
Roanoke Coll (VA)
Roberts Wesleyan Coll (NY)
Rochester Inst of Technology (NY)
Rockford U (IL)
Rockhurst U (MO)
Rocky Mountain Coll (MT)
Roger Williams U (RI)
Rollins Coll (FL)
Roosevelt U (IL)
Rose-Hulman Inst of Technology (IN)
Rosemont Coll (PA)
Rowan U (NJ)
Rust Coll (MS)
Rutgers, The State U of New Jersey, Camden (NJ)
Rutgers, The State U of New Jersey, Newark (NJ)
Rutgers, The State U of New Jersey, New Brunswick (NJ)
Sacred Heart U (CT)
The Sage Colls (NY)
Saginaw Valley State U (MI)
Saint Anselm Coll (NH)
Saint Augustine's U (NC)
St. Bonaventure U (NY)
St. Catherine U (MN)
St. Edward's U (TX)
St. Francis Coll (NY)
Saint Francis U (PA)
St. John Fisher Coll (NY)
Saint John's U (MN)
St. John's U (NY)
Saint Joseph's Coll (IN)
St. Joseph's Coll, Long Island Campus (NY)
St. Joseph's Coll, New York (NY)
Saint Joseph's U (PA)
St. Lawrence U (NY)
Saint Louis U (MO)
Saint Martin's U (WA)
Saint Mary's Coll (IN)
St. Mary's Coll of Maryland (MD)
St. Mary's U (TX)
Saint Mary's U of Minnesota (MN)
Saint Michael's Coll (VT)
St. Norbert Coll (WI)
St. Olaf Coll (MN)
Saint Peter's U (NJ)
St. Thomas U (FL)
Saint Vincent Coll (PA)
Salem Coll (NC)
Salisbury U (MD)
Salve Regina U (RI)
Samford U (AL)
Sam Houston State U (TX)
San Diego State U (CA)
San Francisco State U (CA)
San Jose State U (CA)
Santa Clara U (CA)
Sarah Lawrence Coll (NY)
Savannah State U (GA)
Scripps Coll (CA)
Seattle Pacific U (WA)
Seattle U (WA)
Seton Hill U (PA)
Sewanee: The U of the South (TN)
Shawnee State U (OH)
Shaw U (NC)
Shenandoah U (VA)
Shepherd U (WV)
Shippensburg U of Pennsylvania (PA)
Siena Coll (NY)
Siena Heights U (MI)
Simmons Coll (MA)
Simon Fraser U (BC, Canada)
Simpson Coll (IA)
Skidmore Coll (NY)
Slippery Rock U of Pennsylvania (PA)
Smith Coll (MA)
South Carolina State U (SC)
South Dakota School of Mines and Technology (SD)
South Dakota State U (SD)
Southeastern Louisiana U (LA)
Southeastern Oklahoma State U (OK)
Southeast Missouri State U (MO)
Southern Adventist U (TN)
Southern Arkansas U–Magnolia (AR)
Southern Connecticut State U (CT)
Southern Illinois U Carbondale (IL)
Southern Illinois U Edwardsville (IL)
Southern Methodist U (TX)
Southern Oregon U (OR)
Southern Utah U (UT)
Southwest Baptist U (MO)
Southwestern Adventist U (TX)
Southwestern Coll (KS)
Southwestern U (TX)
Southwest Minnesota State U (MN)
Spelman Coll (GA)
Spring Hill Coll (AL)
Stanford U (CA)
State U of New York at Fredonia (NY)
State U of New York at New Paltz (NY)
State U of New York at Oswego (NY)
State U of New York at Plattsburgh (NY)
State U of New York Coll at Cortland (NY)
State U of New York Coll at Geneseo (NY)
State U of New York Coll at Old Westbury (NY)
State U of New York Coll at Potsdam (NY)
State U of New York Coll of Environmental Science and Forestry (NY)
Stephen F. Austin State U (TX)
Stetson U (FL)
Stevenson U (MD)
Stockton U (NJ)
Stonehill Coll (MA)
Stony Brook U, State U of New York (NY)
Sul Ross State U (TX)
Susquehanna U (PA)
Syracuse U (NY)
Tabor Coll (KS)
Tarleton State U (TX)
Taylor U (IN)
Temple U (PA)
Tennessee State U (TN)
Tennessee Wesleyan Coll (TN)
Texas A&M Intl U (TX)
Texas A&M U (TX)
Texas A&M U–Commerce (TX)
Texas A&M U–Corpus Christi (TX)
Texas A&M U–Kingsville (TX)
Texas Christian U (TX)
Texas Lutheran U (TX)
Texas Southern U (TX)
Texas State U (TX)
Texas Tech U (TX)
Texas Wesleyan U (TX)
Texas Woman's U (TX)
Thiel Coll (PA)
Thomas More Coll (KY)
Tougaloo Coll (MS)
Towson U (MD)
Transylvania U (KY)
Trent U (ON, Canada)
Trevecca Nazarene U (TN)
Trine U (IN)
Trinity Christian Coll (IL)
Trinity Coll (CT)
Trinity U (TX)
Troy U (AL)
Truman State U (MO)
Tufts U (MA)
Tulane U (LA)
Tusculum Coll (TN)
Union Coll (KY)
Union Coll (NE)
Union Coll (NY)
Union U (TN)
United States Air Force Acad (CO)
United States Military Acad (NY)
United States Naval Acad (MD)
Universidad del Turabo (PR)
Universidad Metropolitana (PR)
Université de Montréal (QC, Canada)
Université de Sherbrooke (QC, Canada)
U at Albany, State U of New York (NY)
U at Buffalo, the State U of New York (NY)
The U of Akron (OH)
The U of Alabama (AL)
The U of Alabama at Birmingham (AL)
The U of Alabama in Huntsville (AL)
U of Alaska Fairbanks (AK)
U of Alberta (AB, Canada)
The U of Arizona (AZ)
U of Arkansas (AR)
U of Arkansas at Little Rock (AR)
U of Arkansas at Pine Bluff (AR)
U of Arkansas–Fort Smith (AR)
The U of British Columbia (BC, Canada)
The U of British Columbia–Okanagan Campus (BC, Canada)
U of California, Berkeley (CA)
U of California, Davis (CA)
U of California, Irvine (CA)
U of California, Los Angeles (CA)
U of California, Merced (CA)
U of California, Riverside (CA)
U of California, Santa Barbara (CA)
U of California, Santa Cruz (CA)
U of Central Arkansas (AR)
U of Central Florida (FL)
U of Central Missouri (MO)
U of Central Oklahoma (OK)
U of Charleston (WV)
U of Chicago (IL)
U of Cincinnati (OH)
U of Colorado Boulder (CO)
U of Colorado Colorado Springs (CO)
U of Colorado Denver (CO)
U of Dallas (TX)
U of Dayton (OH)
U of Delaware (DE)
U of Denver (CO)
U of Evansville (IN)
The U of Findlay (OH)
U of Florida (FL)
U of Georgia (GA)
U of Great Falls (MT)
U of Guam (GU)
U of Guelph (ON, Canada)
U of Hartford (CT)
U of Hawaii at Hilo (HI)
U of Hawaii at Manoa (HI)
U of Houston (TX)
U of Houston–Clear Lake (TX)
U of Houston–Downtown (TX)
U of Idaho (ID)
U of Illinois at Chicago (IL)
U of Illinois at Springfield (IL)
The U of Iowa (IA)
U of Jamestown (ND)
The U of Kansas (KS)
U of Kentucky (KY)
U of King's Coll (NS, Canada)
U of La Verne (CA)
U of Lethbridge (AB, Canada)
U of Louisiana at Lafayette (LA)
U of Louisville (KY)
U of Maine (ME)
U of Mary Hardin-Baylor (TX)
U of Maryland, Baltimore County (MD)
U of Maryland, Coll Park (MD)
U of Mary Washington (VA)
U of Massachusetts Amherst (MA)
U of Massachusetts Boston (MA)
U of Massachusetts Dartmouth (MA)
U of Massachusetts Lowell (MA)
U of Memphis (TN)
U of Miami (FL)
U of Michigan (MI)
U of Michigan–Dearborn (MI)
U of Michigan–Flint (MI)
U of Minnesota, Duluth (MN)
U of Minnesota, Morris (MN)
U of Minnesota, Twin Cities Campus (MN)
U of Mississippi (MS)
U of Missouri (MO)
U of Missouri–Kansas City (MO)
U of Missouri–St. Louis (MO)
The U of Montana (MT)
U of Montevallo (AL)
U of Mount Union (OH)
U of Nebraska at Kearney (NE)
U of Nebraska–Lincoln (NE)
U of Nevada, Las Vegas (NV)
U of Nevada, Reno (NV)
U of New Brunswick Saint John (NB, Canada)
U of New England (ME)
U of New Hampshire (NH)
U of New Haven (CT)
U of New Mexico (NM)
U of New Orleans (LA)
U of North Alabama (AL)
U of North Carolina at Asheville (NC)
The U of North Carolina at Chapel Hill (NC)
The U of North Carolina at Charlotte (NC)
The U of North Carolina at Greensboro (NC)
The U of North Carolina at Pembroke (NC)
The U of North Carolina Wilmington (NC)
U of North Dakota (ND)
U of Northern Colorado (CO)
U of Northern Iowa (IA)
U of North Florida (FL)
U of North Georgia (GA)
U of North Texas (TX)
U of Notre Dame (IN)
U of Oklahoma (OK)
U of Oregon (OR)
U of Ottawa (ON, Canada)
U of Pennsylvania (PA)
U of Pikeville (KY)
U of Pittsburgh (PA)
U of Pittsburgh at Bradford (PA)
U of Pittsburgh at Greensburg (PA)
U of Portland (OR)
U of Puget Sound (WA)
U of Regina (SK, Canada)

U of Rhode Island (RI)
U of Richmond (VA)
U of Rio Grande (OH)
U of Rochester (NY)
U of Saint Francis (IN)
U of Saint Joseph (CT)
U of Saint Mary (KS)
U of St. Thomas (MN)
U of St. Thomas (TX)
U of San Diego (CA)
U of San Francisco (CA)
U of Saskatchewan (SK, Canada)
U of Science and Arts of Oklahoma (OK)
The U of Scranton (PA)
U of South Alabama (AL)
U of South Carolina Aiken (SC)
U of South Carolina Upstate (SC)
The U of South Dakota (SD)
U of Southern California (CA)
U of Southern Indiana (IN)
U of Southern Maine (ME)
U of Southern Mississippi (MS)
U of South Florida (FL)
The U of Tampa (FL)
The U of Tennessee (TN)
The U of Tennessee at Chattanooga (TN)
The U of Tennessee at Martin (TN)
The U of Texas at Arlington (TX)
The U of Texas at Austin (TX)
The U of Texas at Dallas (TX)
The U of Texas at El Paso (TX)
The U of Texas at San Antonio (TX)
The U of Texas at Tyler (TX)
The U of Texas of the Permian Basin (TX)
The U of Texas–Pan American (TX)
U of the Cumberlands (KY)
U of the District of Columbia (DC)
U of the Fraser Valley (BC, Canada)
U of the Incarnate Word (TX)
U of the Pacific (CA)
U of the Sciences (PA)
U of the Virgin Islands (VI)
The U of Toledo (OH)
The U of Tulsa (OK)
U of Utah (UT)
U of Vermont (VT)
U of Virginia (VA)
The U of Virginia's Coll at Wise (VA)
U of Washington (WA)
U of Washington, Bothell (WA)
U of Waterloo (ON, Canada)
The U of West Alabama (AL)
The U of Western Ontario (ON, Canada)
U of West Florida (FL)
U of West Georgia (GA)
U of Windsor (ON, Canada)
U of Wisconsin–Eau Claire (WI)
U of Wisconsin–Green Bay (WI)
U of Wisconsin–La Crosse (WI)
U of Wisconsin–Madison (WI)
U of Wisconsin–Milwaukee (WI)
U of Wisconsin–Oshkosh (WI)
U of Wisconsin–Parkside (WI)
U of Wisconsin–Platteville (WI)
U of Wisconsin–River Falls (WI)
U of Wisconsin–Stevens Point (WI)
U of Wisconsin–Superior (WI)
U of Wisconsin–Whitewater (WI)
U of Wyoming (WY)
Upper Iowa U (IA)
Urbana U (OH)
Ursinus Coll (PA)
Utah State U (UT)
Utah Valley U (UT)
Utica Coll (NY)
Valdosta State U (GA)
Valley City State U (ND)
Valparaiso U (IN)
Vanderbilt U (TN)
Vanguard U of Southern California (CA)
Vassar Coll (NY)
Villanova U (PA)
Virginia Commonwealth U (VA)
Virginia Military Inst (VA)
Virginia Polytechnic Inst and State U (VA)
Virginia State U (VA)
Virginia Union U (VA)
Virginia Wesleyan Coll (VA)
Viterbo U (WI)
Wabash Coll (IN)
Wagner Coll (NY)
Wake Forest U (NC)
Walla Walla U (WA)
Walsh U (OH)
Warren Wilson Coll (NC)
Wartburg Coll (IA)
Washburn U (KS)
Washington & Jefferson Coll (PA)
Washington and Lee U (VA)
Washington Coll (MD)
Washington State U (WA)
Washington U in St. Louis (MO)
Waynesburg U (PA)
Wayne State Coll (NE)
Wayne State U (MI)
Weber State U (UT)
Wells Coll (NY)
Wesleyan Coll (GA)
Wesleyan U (CT)
West Chester U of Pennsylvania (PA)
Western Carolina U (NC)
Western Illinois U (IL)
Western Kentucky U (KY)
Western Michigan U (MI)
Western New England U (MA)
Western Oregon U (OR)
Western State Colorado U (CO)
Western Washington U (WA)
Westfield State U (MA)
West Liberty U (WV)
Westminster Coll (MO)
Westminster Coll (UT)
West Texas A&M U (TX)
West Virginia State U (WV)
West Virginia U (WV)
West Virginia U Inst of Technology (WV)
West Virginia Wesleyan Coll (WV)
Wheaton Coll (IL)
Wheaton Coll (MA)
Wheeling Jesuit U (WV)
Whitman Coll (WA)
Whittier Coll (CA)
Whitworth U (WA)
Wichita State U (KS)
Widener U (PA)
Wilkes U (PA)
Willamette U (OR)
William Jewell Coll (MO)
William Paterson U of New Jersey (NJ)
Williams Coll (MA)
Wingate U (NC)
Winona State U (MN)
Winthrop U (SC)
Wittenberg U (OH)
Wofford Coll (SC)
Worcester Polytechnic Inst (MA)
Worcester State U (MA)
Wright State U (OH)
Xavier U (OH)
Xavier U of Louisiana (LA)
Yale U (CT)
Yeshiva U (NY)
York Coll of Pennsylvania (PA)
York Coll of the City U of New York (NY)
Youngstown State U (OH)

CHEMISTRY RELATED
Alvernia U (PA)
Belmont U (TN)
Boston U (MA)
Bridgewater Coll (VA)
Bridgewater State U (MA)
Case Western Reserve U (OH)
Coll of Charleston (SC)
Connecticut Coll (CT)
Dartmouth Coll (NH)
Delaware State U (DE)
Duquesne U (PA)
Eastern U (PA)
Florida Inst of Technology (FL)
Florida State U (FL)
Harvard U (MA)
Inter American U of Puerto Rico, Bayamón Campus (PR)
Kansas Wesleyan U (KS)
Keene State Coll (NH)
LeTourneau U (TX)
Loras Coll (IA)
Loyola U New Orleans (LA)
Michigan Technological U (MI)
Northern Michigan U (MI)
Ohio Northern U (OH)
Palm Beach Atlantic U (FL)
Rhode Island Coll (RI)
Roger Williams U (RI)
Saginaw Valley State U (MI)
Saint Anselm Coll (NH)
Saint Vincent Coll (PA)
Stony Brook U, State U of New York (NY)
Taylor U (IN)
Union Coll (KY)
U at Buffalo, the State U of New York (NY)
U of California, Berkeley (CA)
U of California, Santa Barbara (CA)
U of Chicago (IL)
U of Denver (CO)
U of Houston–Downtown (TX)
U of Northern Iowa (IA)
U of Notre Dame (IN)
The U of Scranton (PA)
U of Southern Mississippi (MS)
U of the Pacific (CA)
U of Wisconsin–Eau Claire (WI)
U of Wisconsin–Milwaukee (WI)
Washington U in St. Louis (MO)
Wayne State U (MI)
Western Illinois U (IL)
Western Michigan U (MI)
Western State Colorado U (CO)
West Virginia Wesleyan Coll (WV)
Whitman Coll (WA)

CHEMISTRY TEACHER EDUCATION
Adams State U (CO)
Albion Coll (MI)
Alma Coll (MI)
Alvernia U (PA)
Arkansas State U (AR)
Ashland U (OH)
Augustana Coll (IL)
Bethany Coll (WV)
Bethune-Cookman U (FL)
Bluefield Coll (VA)
Boston U (MA)
Bowling Green State U (OH)
Bradley U (IL)
Buena Vista U (IA)
Cabrini Coll (PA)
Calvin Coll (MI)
Campbellsville U (KY)
Canisius Coll (NY)
Carroll Coll (MT)
Cedarville U (OH)
Central Methodist U (MO)
Central Michigan U (MI)
Central Washington U (WA)
City Coll of the City U of New York (NY)
Coker Coll (SC)
The Coll of New Jersey (NJ)
Coll of Saint Mary (NE)
The Coll of Saint Rose (NY)
Coll of Staten Island of the City U of New York (NY)
Coll of the Ozarks (MO)
Colorado State U (CO)
Concordia Coll (MN)
Concordia U Chicago (IL)
Concordia U, Nebraska (NE)
Concordia U, St. Paul (MN)
Creighton U (NE)
Delaware State U (DE)
Dowling Coll (NY)
East Central U (OK)
Eastern Michigan U (MI)
Edgewood Coll (WI)
Elmhurst Coll (IL)
Elmira Coll (NY)
Emory & Henry Coll (VA)
Evangel U (MO)
Ferris State U (MI)
Florida Inst of Technology (FL)
Fordham U (NY)
Fort Lewis Coll (CO)
Franklin Coll (IN)
Grand Valley State U (MI)
Greenville Coll (IL)
Gustavus Adolphus Coll (MN)
Hastings Coll (NE)
Hofstra U (NY)
Holy Family U (PA)
Hope Coll (MI)
Huntingdon Coll (AL)
Indiana U Bloomington (IN)
Indiana U Northwest (IN)
Indiana U–Purdue U Fort Wayne (IN)
Indiana U South Bend (IN)
Inter American U of Puerto Rico, San Germán Campus (PR)
Ithaca Coll (NY)
Juniata Coll (PA)
Kansas Wesleyan U (KS)
Keene State Coll (NH)
Kent State U (OH)
King U (TN)
Lee U (TN)
Le Moyne Coll (NY)
Lincoln Memorial U (TN)
Lincoln U (MO)
Lindenwood U (MO)
Lipscomb U (TN)
Long Island U–LIU Post (NY)
Louisiana State U in Shreveport (LA)
Madonna U (MI)
Manchester U (IN)
Manhattanville Coll (NY)
Mansfield U of Pennsylvania (PA)
Marist Coll (NY)
Maryville Coll (TN)
Mayville State U (ND)
McMurry U (TX)
Merrimack Coll (MA)
Messiah Coll (PA)
Miami Dade Coll (FL)
Miami U (OH)
Michigan State U (MI)
Millikin U (IL)
Minnesota State U Moorhead (MN)
Minot State U (ND)
Misericordia U (PA)
Missouri State U (MO)
Montana State U Billings (MT)
Morningside Coll (IA)
Mount Marty Coll (SD)
Mount Mary U (WI)
Mount Vernon Nazarene U (OH)
Nazareth Coll of Rochester (NY)
Nebraska Wesleyan U (NE)
New York U (NY)
Niagara U (NY)
North Carolina Ag and Tech State U (NC)
North Dakota State U (ND)
Northern Michigan U (MI)
Northwest Missouri State U (MO)
Northwest Nazarene U (ID)
Ohio Dominican U (OH)
Ohio Northern U (OH)
Ohio Wesleyan U (OH)
Olivet Coll (MI)
Pace U (NY)
Pepperdine U, Malibu (CA)
Peru State Coll (NE)
Pittsburg State U (KS)
Providence Coll (RI)
Rhode Island Coll (RI)
Roberts Wesleyan Coll (NY)
Saginaw Valley State U (MI)
St. Catherine U (MN)
St. Edward's U (TX)
St. Francis Coll (NY)
Saint Francis U (PA)
St. John Fisher Coll (NY)
St. Joseph's Coll, Long Island Campus (NY)
St. Joseph's Coll, New York (NY)
Saint Joseph's U (PA)
Saint Mary's U of Minnesota (MN)
Seattle U (WA)
Seton Hill U (PA)
Southern Adventist U (TN)
Southern Utah U (UT)
Southwest Baptist U (MO)
Southwest Minnesota State U (MN)
State U of New York at New Paltz (NY)
State U of New York at Plattsburgh (NY)
State U of New York Coll at Cortland (NY)
State U of New York Coll at Old Westbury (NY)
State U of New York Coll of Environmental Science and Forestry (NY)
Syracuse U (NY)
Tabor Coll (KS)
Transylvania U (KY)
Trevecca Nazarene U (TN)
Trinity Christian Coll (IL)
Union Coll (NE)
Universidad del Turabo (PR)
U of Alberta (AB, Canada)
U of Arkansas–Fort Smith (AR)
U of Central Oklahoma (OK)
U of Delaware (DE)
U of Evansville (IN)
U of Great Falls (MT)
U of Illinois at Chicago (IL)
The U of Iowa (IA)
U of Jamestown (ND)
U of Mary Hardin-Baylor (TX)
U of Maryland, Baltimore County (MD)
U of Michigan–Dearborn (MI)
U of Missouri (MO)
U of Nebraska–Lincoln (NE)
The U of North Carolina Wilmington (NC)
U of Regina (SK, Canada)
U of Saint Francis (IN)
U of St. Thomas (MN)
The U of Tennessee at Martin (TN)
U of Waterloo (ON, Canada)
U of Windsor (ON, Canada)
U of Wisconsin–River Falls (WI)
U of Wisconsin–Superior (WI)
Utah State U (UT)
Utah Valley U (UT)
Utica Coll (NY)
Valley City State U (ND)
Valparaiso U (IN)
Viterbo U (WI)
Washburn U (KS)
Washington State U (WA)
Washington U in St. Louis (MO)
Waynesburg U (PA)
Wayne State Coll (NE)
Weber State U (UT)
Western Michigan U (MI)
Western State Colorado U (CO)
Western Washington U (WA)
Widener U (PA)
Winona State U (MN)
Xavier U (OH)
Xavier U of Louisiana (LA)

CHILD-CARE AND SUPPORT SERVICES MANAGEMENT
Brigham Young U (UT)
Chestnut Hill Coll (PA)
Ferris State U (MI)
Messiah Coll (PA)
Purdue U Calumet (IN)
Rust Coll (MS)
Seton Hill U (PA)
Siena Heights U (MI)
State U of New York Coll of Agriculture and Technology at Cobleskill (NY)
U of Minnesota, Twin Cities Campus (MN)
The U of Texas–Pan American (TX)
U of the Fraser Valley (BC, Canada)

CHILD-CARE PROVISION
Brigham Young U (UT)
Southeastern Oklahoma State U (OK)
Wayne State Coll (NE)

CHILD DEVELOPMENT
Albertus Magnus Coll (CT)
Alcorn State U (MS)
Appalachian State U (NC)
Auburn U (AL)
Bennington Coll (VT)
Bowling Green State U (OH)
Brigham Young U (UT)
California State U, Fresno (CA)
California State U, Long Beach (CA)
California State U, Los Angeles (CA)
California State U, Sacramento (CA)
Cameron U (OK)
Carson-Newman U (TN)
Central Michigan U (MI)
Coll of the Ozarks (MO)
Concordia U, St. Paul (MN)
Delaware State U (DE)
East Carolina U (NC)
East Tennessee State U (TN)
Ellis U (IL)
Goddard Coll (VT)
Goodwin Coll (CT)

Hampton U (VA)
Hannibal-LaGrange U (MO)
Harding U (AR)
Houston Baptist U (TX)
Humboldt State U (CA)
Kansas State U (KS)
Kuyper Coll (MI)
Lesley U (MA)
Madonna U (MI)
Meredith Coll (NC)
Michigan State U (MI)
Milligan Coll (TN)
Minnesota State U Mankato (MN)
Missouri Baptist U (MO)
Mount Saint Mary's U (CA)
National U (CA)
North Carolina Ag and Tech State U (NC)
Oklahoma Christian U (OK)
Olivet Nazarene U (IL)
Point Loma Nazarene U (CA)
Point U (GA)
Portland State U (OR)
Post U (CT)
Quinnipiac U (CT)
St. Bonaventure U (NY)
Seton Hill U (PA)
Texas Tech U (TX)
Texas Woman's U (TX)
Tougaloo Coll (MS)
Tufts U (MA)
Union Inst & U (OH)
The U of Akron (OH)
U of Alaska Fairbanks (AK)
U of Central Oklahoma (OK)
U of Guelph (ON, Canada)
U of La Verne (CA)
U of Nevada, Reno (NV)
U of North Texas (TX)
U of Saint Joseph (CT)
U of Saint Mary (KS)
The U of Tennessee at Martin (TN)
The U of Texas at Arlington (TX)
U of the Incarnate Word (TX)
U of Virginia (VA)
The U of Western Ontario (ON, Canada)
Vanderbilt U (TN)
Weber State U (UT)
Western Michigan U (MI)
West Virginia U (WV)
Wheelock Coll (MA)
Whittier Coll (CA)
Youngstown State U (OH)

CHILDREN'S AND ADOLESCENT LITERATURE
Castleton State Coll (VT)
Central Michigan U (MI)

CHINESE
Bard Coll (NY)
Bates Coll (ME)
Beloit Coll (WI)
Bennington Coll (VT)
Boston U (MA)
Bryant U (RI)
California State U, Long Beach (CA)
California State U, Los Angeles (CA)
Calvin Coll (MI)
Coll of the Holy Cross (MA)
Concordia Coll (MN)
Connecticut Coll (CT)
Dartmouth Coll (NH)
Davidson Coll (NC)
Georgetown U (DC)
The George Washington U (DC)
Grinnell Coll (IA)
Hamilton Coll (NY)
Hobart and William Smith Colls (NY)
Hofstra U (NY)
Hunter Coll of the City U of New York (NY)
Lawrence U (WI)
Lehigh U (PA)
Macalester Coll (MN)
Messiah Coll (PA)
Michigan State U (MI)
Middlebury Coll (VT)
National U (CA)
Nazareth Coll of Rochester (NY)
New Coll of Florida (FL)
North Central Coll (IL)
Occidental Coll (CA)
The Ohio State U (OH)
Pacific U (OR)
Penn State U Park (PA)
Pomona Coll (CA)
Portland State U (OR)
Queens Coll of the City U of New York (NY)
Reed Coll (OR)
Rutgers, The State U of New Jersey, New Brunswick (NJ)
San Francisco State U (CA)
San Jose State U (CA)
Scripps Coll (CA)
Stanford U (CA)
Trinity Coll (CT)
Trinity U (TX)
Tufts U (MA)
Union Coll (NY)
United States Military Acad (NY)
United States Naval Acad (MD)
U of Alberta (AB, Canada)
The U of British Columbia (BC, Canada)
U of California, Berkeley (CA)
U of California, Davis (CA)
U of California, Irvine (CA)
U of California, Los Angeles (CA)
U of California, Santa Barbara (CA)
U of Colorado Boulder (CO)
U of Georgia (GA)
U of Hawaii at Manoa (HI)
U of Houston (TX)
The U of Iowa (IA)
U of Kentucky (KY)
U of Maryland, Coll Park (MD)
U of Massachusetts Amherst (MA)
U of Minnesota, Twin Cities Campus (MN)
U of Mississippi (MS)
The U of Montana (MT)
U of North Georgia (GA)
U of Notre Dame (IN)
U of Oklahoma (OK)
U of Oregon (OR)
U of Pittsburgh (PA)
U of Puget Sound (WA)
U of Regina (SK, Canada)
U of Rhode Island (RI)
U of Utah (UT)
U of Vermont (VT)
U of Washington (WA)
The U of Western Ontario (ON, Canada)
U of Wisconsin–Madison (WI)
Vassar Coll (NY)
Wake Forest U (NC)
Washington U in St. Louis (MO)
Western Kentucky U (KY)
Whittier Coll (CA)
Williams Coll (MA)
Wofford Coll (SC)
Yale U (CT)

CHINESE STUDIES
The Coll of William and Mary (VA)
DePaul U (IL)
Drew U (NJ)
Gettysburg Coll (PA)
Lindenwood U (MO)
Pacific Lutheran U (WA)
U at Albany, State U of New York (NY)
U of Alberta (AB, Canada)
U of California, Irvine (CA)
U of Minnesota, Duluth (MN)
U of North Dakota (ND)
U of Richmond (VA)
The U of Tulsa (OK)
U of Washington (WA)
The U of Western Ontario (ON, Canada)
Washington State U (WA)

CHIROPRACTIC ASSISTANT
Hawai`i Pacific U (HI)

CHRISTIAN STUDIES
Ambrose U Coll (AB, Canada)
Anderson U (SC)
Bethany Lutheran Coll (MN)
Bethel Coll (IN)
Bluefield Coll (VA)
Bryan Coll (TN)
California Baptist U (CA)
Canisius Coll (NY)
Coll of Biblical Studies–Houston (TX)
The Coll of St. Scholastica (MN)
Concordia U Wisconsin (WI)
Gordon Coll (MA)
Hardin-Simmons U (TX)
Hillsdale Coll (MI)
Inter American U of Puerto Rico, Guayama Campus (PR)
Iowa Wesleyan Coll (IA)
Lee U (TN)
Liberty U (VA)
Lindenwood U (MO)
Loyola U New Orleans (LA)
Marian U (IN)
McMurry U (TX)
Mercer U, Macon (GA)
Missouri Baptist U (MO)
Oklahoma Wesleyan U (OK)
Roanoke Coll (VA)
St. Edward's U (TX)
Saint Mary's U of Minnesota (MN)
St. Thomas U (NB, Canada)
Simpson U (CA)
Stonehill Coll (MA)
Tabor Coll (KS)
Tennessee Wesleyan Coll (TN)
Texas Wesleyan U (TX)
Toccoa Falls Coll (GA)
Truett-McConnell Coll (GA)
U of Mary Hardin-Baylor (TX)
U of the Cumberlands (KY)
Ursuline Coll (OH)

CINEMATOGRAPHY AND FILM/VIDEO PRODUCTION
Acad of Art U (CA)
American U (DC)
Anderson U (IN)
Art Center Coll of Design (CA)
Belmont U (TN)
Bennington Coll (VT)
Binghamton U, State U of New York (NY)
Biola U (CA)
Bob Jones U (SC)
Brigham Young U (UT)
California Inst of the Arts (CA)
California State U, Long Beach (CA)
Calvin Coll (MI)
Central Washington U (WA)
Chapman U (CA)
City Coll of the City U of New York (NY)
Cleveland State U (OH)
Columbia Coll Chicago (IL)
Concordia U (QC, Canada)
Cornell U (NY)
Cornerstone U (MI)
DePaul U (IL)
Drexel U (PA)
Eastern New Mexico U (NM)
Emerson Coll (MA)
Emily Carr U of Art + Design (BC, Canada)
The Evergreen State Coll (WA)
Fairleigh Dickinson U, Coll at Florham (NJ)
Fashion Inst of Technology (NY)
FIDM/Fashion Inst of Design & Merchandising, Los Angeles Campus (CA)
Fitchburg State U (MA)
Five Towns Coll (NY)
George Mason U (VA)
Hawai`i Pacific U (HI)
Houston Baptist U (TX)
Hunter Coll of the City U of New York (NY)
Inst of American Indian Arts (NM)
Ithaca Coll (NY)
John Brown U (AR)
John Paul the Great Catholic U (CA)
Keene State Coll (NH)
La Sierra U (CA)
Liberty U (VA)
Long Island U–LIU Post (NY)
Loyola Marymount U (CA)
Lynn U (FL)
Maharishi U of Management (IA)
Massachusetts Coll of Art and Design (MA)
Mercy Coll (NY)
Messiah Coll (PA)
Miami Dade Coll (FL)
Missouri Western State U (MO)
Montana State U (MT)
Montclair State U (NJ)
Mount Saint Mary's U (CA)
New England Inst of Technology (RI)
New Mexico Highlands U (NM)
New Mexico State U (NM)
New York U (NY)
Northern Michigan U (MI)
Ohio U (OH)
Oklahoma City U (OK)
Palm Beach Atlantic U (FL)
Pratt Inst (NY)
Purchase Coll, State U of New York (NY)
Quinnipiac U (CT)
Regent U (VA)
Ringling Coll of Art and Design (FL)
Rochester Inst of Technology (NY)
Rutgers, The State U of New Jersey, Newark (NJ)
San Francisco Art Inst (CA)
Santa Fe Coll (FL)
Santa Fe U of Art and Design (NM)
Savannah Coll of Art and Design (GA)
School of the Art Inst of Chicago (IL)
School of the Museum of Fine Arts, Boston (MA)
Southern Adventist U (TN)
Southern Illinois U Carbondale (IL)
Southern Methodist U (TX)
Stanford U (CA)
Stevenson U (MD)
Syracuse U (NY)
Taylor U (IN)
U of Central Arkansas (AR)
U of Central Florida (FL)
U of Illinois at Chicago (IL)
The U of Iowa (IA)
U of Miami (FL)
U of North Carolina School of the Arts (NC)
The U of North Carolina Wilmington (NC)
U of Regina (SK, Canada)
U of Rhode Island (RI)
U of Southern California (CA)
Vanguard U of Southern California (CA)
Virginia Commonwealth U (VA)
Walla Walla U (WA)
Wayne State U (MI)
Webster U (MO)
Wilmington U (DE)

CITY/URBAN, COMMUNITY AND REGIONAL PLANNING
Appalachian State U (NC)
Arizona State U at the Tempe campus (AZ)
Ball State U (IN)
Bridgewater State U (MA)
Buffalo State Coll, State U of New York (NY)
California Polytechnic State U, San Luis Obispo (CA)
California State Polytechnic U, Pomona (CA)
Concordia U (QC, Canada)
Cornell U (NY)
Dalhousie U (NS, Canada)
East Carolina U (NC)
Eastern Michigan U (MI)
Florida Atlantic U (FL)
Frostburg State U (MD)
Indiana U of Pennsylvania (PA)
Iowa State U of Science and Technology (IA)
Mansfield U of Pennsylvania (PA)
Massachusetts Inst of Technology (MA)
Miami U (OH)
Michigan State U (MI)
Minnesota State U Mankato (MN)
Missouri State U (MO)
The Ohio State U (OH)
Plymouth State U (NH)
Portland State U (OR)
Rowan U (NJ)
State U of New York Coll of Environmental Science and Forestry (NY)
Temple U (PA)
Texas A&M U (TX)
Texas State U (TX)
Tufts U (MA)
The U of Akron (OH)
U of Alberta (AB, Canada)
The U of Arizona (AZ)
U of California, Davis (CA)
U of Cincinnati (OH)
U of Missouri–Kansas City (MO)
The U of Montana (MT)
U of New Hampshire (NH)
U of San Francisco (CA)
U of Saskatchewan (SK, Canada)
U of Virginia (VA)
U of Washington (WA)
U of Waterloo (ON, Canada)
Western Michigan U (MI)
Westfield State U (MA)

CIVIL ENGINEERING
The American U in Dubai (United Arab Emirates)
American U of Beirut (Lebanon)
Arizona State U at the Tempe campus (AZ)
Arkansas State U (AR)
Auburn U (AL)
Bradley U (IL)
Bucknell U (PA)
California Baptist U (CA)
California Polytechnic State U, San Luis Obispo (CA)
California State Polytechnic U, Pomona (CA)
California State U, Chico (CA)
California State U, Fresno (CA)
California State U, Long Beach (CA)
California State U, Los Angeles (CA)
California State U, Sacramento (CA)
Calvin Coll (MI)
Caribbean U (PR)
Carroll Coll (MT)
Case Western Reserve U (OH)
The Catholic U of America (DC)
Central Connecticut State U (CT)
Christian Brothers U (TN)
The Citadel, The Military Coll of South Carolina (SC)
City Coll of the City U of New York (NY)
Clarkson U (NY)
Cleveland State U (OH)
The Coll of New Jersey (NJ)
Colorado School of Mines (CO)
Colorado State U (CO)
Columbia U (NY)
Concordia U (QC, Canada)
Cooper Union for the Advancement of Science and Art (NY)
Cornell U (NY)
Delaware State U (DE)
Drexel U (PA)
Florida Ag and Mech U (FL)
Florida Atlantic U (FL)
Florida Gulf Coast U (FL)
Florida Inst of Technology (FL)
Florida Intl U (FL)
George Mason U (VA)
The George Washington U (DC)
Georgia Inst of Technology (GA)
Georgia Southern U (GA)
Gonzaga U (WA)
Hofstra U (NY)
Howard U (DC)
Illinois Inst of Technology (IL)
Indiana U–Purdue U Fort Wayne (IN)
Iowa State U of Science and Technology (IA)
Jackson State U (MS)
Johns Hopkins U (MD)
Kansas State U (KS)
Lafayette Coll (PA)
Lamar U (TX)
Lawrence Technological U (MI)
Lebanese American U (Lebanon)
Lehigh U (PA)
LeTourneau U (TX)
Lipscomb U (TN)
Louisiana State U and A&M Coll (LA)
Loyola Marymount U (CA)
Manhattan Coll (NY)
Marquette U (WI)
Massachusetts Inst of Technology (MA)
Merrimack Coll (MA)
Michigan State U (MI)
Michigan Technological U (MI)

Milwaukee School of Eng (WI)
Minnesota State U Mankato (MN)
Mississippi State U (MS)
Missouri U of Science and Technology (MO)
Montana State U (MT)
New Jersey Inst of Technology (NJ)
New Mexico Inst of Mining and Technology (NM)
New Mexico State U (NM)
New York U (NY)
North Carolina Ag and Tech State U (NC)
North Carolina State U (NC)
North Dakota State U (ND)
Northeastern U (MA)
Northern Arizona U (AZ)
Northwestern U (IL)
Norwich U (VT)
Ohio Northern U (OH)
The Ohio State U (OH)
Ohio U (OH)
Oklahoma State U (OK)
Old Dominion U (VA)
Oregon State U (OR)
Penn State Abington (PA)
Penn State Altoona (PA)
Penn State Beaver (PA)
Penn State Berks (PA)
Penn State Brandywine (PA)
Penn State DuBois (PA)
Penn State Erie, The Behrend Coll (PA)
Penn State Fayette, The Eberly Campus (PA)
Penn State Greater Allegheny (PA)
Penn State Harrisburg (PA)
Penn State Hazleton (PA)
Penn State Lehigh Valley (PA)
Penn State Mont Alto (PA)
Penn State New Kensington (PA)
Penn State Schuylkill (PA)
Penn State Shenango (PA)
Penn State U Park (PA)
Penn State Wilkes-Barre (PA)
Penn State Worthington Scranton (PA)
Penn State York (PA)
Polytechnic U of Puerto Rico (PR)
Portland State U (OR)
Prairie View A&M U (TX)
Princeton U (NJ)
Purdue U (IN)
Purdue U Calumet (IN)
Quinnipiac U (CT)
Rensselaer Polytechnic Inst (NY)
Rice U (TX)
Rockhurst U (MO)
Rose-Hulman Inst of Technology (IN)
Rowan U (NJ)
Rutgers, The State U of New Jersey, New Brunswick (NJ)
Saint Louis U (MO)
Saint Martin's U (WA)
San Diego State U (CA)
San Francisco State U (CA)
San Jose State U (CA)
Santa Clara U (CA)
Seattle U (WA)
South Dakota School of Mines and Technology (SD)
South Dakota State U (SD)
Southern Illinois U Carbondale (IL)
Southern Illinois U Edwardsville (IL)
Southern Methodist U (TX)
Stanford U (CA)
State U of New York Polytechnic Inst (NY)
Stony Brook U, State U of New York (NY)
Syracuse U (NY)
Temple U (PA)
Tennessee State U (TN)
Texas A&M U (TX)
Texas A&M U–Kingsville (TX)
Texas Tech U (TX)
Trine U (IN)
Tufts U (MA)
United States Air Force Acad (CO)
United States Coast Guard Acad (CT)
United States Military Acad (NY)
Universidad del Turabo (PR)
Université de Sherbrooke (QC, Canada)
U at Buffalo, the State U of New York (NY)
The U of Akron (OH)
The U of Alabama (AL)
The U of Alabama at Birmingham (AL)
The U of Alabama in Huntsville (AL)
U of Alaska Fairbanks (AK)
The U of Arizona (AZ)
U of Arkansas (AR)
The U of British Columbia (BC, Canada)
The U of British Columbia–Okanagan Campus (BC, Canada)
U of California, Berkeley (CA)
U of California, Davis (CA)
U of California, Irvine (CA)
U of California, Los Angeles (CA)
U of Central Florida (FL)
U of Cincinnati (OH)
U of Colorado Boulder (CO)
U of Colorado Denver (CO)
U of Dayton (OH)
U of Delaware (DE)
U of Evansville (IN)
U of Florida (FL)
U of Georgia (GA)
U of Hartford (CT)
U of Hawaii at Manoa (HI)
U of Houston (TX)
U of Idaho (ID)
U of Illinois at Chicago (IL)
The U of Iowa (IA)
The U of Kansas (KS)
U of Kentucky (KY)
U of Louisiana at Lafayette (LA)
U of Louisville (KY)
U of Maine (ME)
U of Maryland, Coll Park (MD)
U of Massachusetts Amherst (MA)
U of Massachusetts Dartmouth (MA)
U of Massachusetts Lowell (MA)
U of Memphis (TN)
U of Miami (FL)
U of Michigan (MI)
U of Minnesota, Duluth (MN)
U of Minnesota, Twin Cities Campus (MN)
U of Mississippi (MS)
U of Missouri (MO)
U of Missouri–Kansas City (MO)
U of Missouri–St. Louis (MO)
U of Mount Union (OH)
U of Nebraska–Lincoln (NE)
U of Nevada, Las Vegas (NV)
U of Nevada, Reno (NV)
U of New Hampshire (NH)
U of New Haven (CT)
U of New Mexico (NM)
U of New Orleans (LA)
The U of North Carolina at Charlotte (NC)
U of North Dakota (ND)
U of North Florida (FL)
U of Notre Dame (IN)
U of Oklahoma (OK)
U of Ottawa (ON, Canada)
U of Pittsburgh (PA)
U of Portland (OR)
U of Rhode Island (RI)
U of Saskatchewan (SK, Canada)
U of South Alabama (AL)
U of Southern California (CA)
U of South Florida (FL)
The U of Tennessee (TN)
The U of Tennessee at Chattanooga (TN)
The U of Texas at Arlington (TX)
The U of Texas at Austin (TX)
The U of Texas at El Paso (TX)
The U of Texas at San Antonio (TX)
The U of Texas at Tyler (TX)
The U of Texas–Pan American (TX)
U of the District of Columbia (DC)
U of the Pacific (CA)
The U of Toledo (OH)
U of Toronto (ON, Canada)
U of Utah (UT)
U of Vermont (VT)
U of Virginia (VA)
U of Washington (WA)
U of Waterloo (ON, Canada)
The U of Western Ontario (ON, Canada)
U of Windsor (ON, Canada)
U of Wisconsin–Madison (WI)
U of Wisconsin–Milwaukee (WI)
U of Wisconsin–Platteville (WI)
U of Wyoming (WY)
Ursinus Coll (PA)
Utah State U (UT)
Valparaiso U (IN)
Vanderbilt U (TN)
Villanova U (PA)
Virginia Military Inst (VA)
Virginia Polytechnic Inst and State U (VA)
Walla Walla U (WA)
Washington State U (WA)
Wayne State U (MI)
Wentworth Inst of Technology (MA)
Western Kentucky U (KY)
Western Michigan U (MI)
Western New England U (MA)
West Texas A&M U (TX)
West Virginia U (WV)
West Virginia U Inst of Technology (WV)
Widener U (PA)
Worcester Polytechnic Inst (MA)
Youngstown State U (OH)

CIVIL ENGINEERING RELATED

Bradley U (IL)
California Polytechnic State U, San Luis Obispo (CA)
Embry-Riddle Aeronautical U–Daytona (FL)
Ohio Northern U (OH)
Oregon State U (OR)
U of Southern California (CA)

CIVIL ENGINEERING TECHNOLOGY

Bluefield State Coll (WV)
Central Connecticut State U (CT)
Colorado State U–Pueblo (CO)
Delaware State U (DE)
Fairleigh Dickinson U, Metropolitan Campus (NJ)
Fairmont State U (WV)
Georgia Southern U (GA)
Indiana State U (IN)
Lincoln U (MO)
Murray State U (KY)
Oklahoma State U Inst of Technology (OK)
Pennsylvania Coll of Technology (PA)
Rochester Inst of Technology (NY)
Savannah State U (GA)
South Carolina State U (SC)
State U of New York Coll of Technology at Canton (NY)
State U of New York Polytechnic Inst (NY)
Temple U (PA)
Texas Southern U (TX)
United States Military Acad (NY)
U of Houston–Downtown (TX)
U of Maine (ME)
U of Massachusetts Lowell (MA)
The U of North Carolina at Charlotte (NC)
Youngstown State U (OH)

CLASSICAL, ANCIENT MEDITERRANEAN AND NEAR EASTERN STUDIES AND ARCHAEOLOGY

Bard Coll (NY)
Bowdoin Coll (ME)
Butler U (IN)
Columbia U (NY)
Creighton U (NE)
Hampshire Coll (MA)
Hanover Coll (IN)
Kalamazoo Coll (MI)
Lycoming Coll (PA)
Randolph-Macon Coll (VA)
Saint Anselm Coll (NH)
Syracuse U (NY)
U of Alberta (AB, Canada)
U of California, Berkeley (CA)
U of California, Davis (CA)
U of California, Irvine (CA)
U of California, Los Angeles (CA)
U of Illinois at Chicago (IL)
U of Michigan (MI)
U of Ottawa (ON, Canada)
U of Toronto (ON, Canada)

CLASSICS AND CLASSICAL LANGUAGES

Agnes Scott Coll (GA)
Amherst Coll (MA)
Asbury U (KY)
Assumption Coll (MA)
Augustana Coll (IL)
Augustana Coll (SD)
Austin Coll (TX)
Ave Maria U (FL)
Ball State U (IN)
Barnard Coll (NY)
Baylor U (TX)
Belmont U (TN)
Beloit Coll (WI)
Binghamton U, State U of New York (NY)
Boston Coll (MA)
Boston U (MA)
Bowdoin Coll (ME)
Bowling Green State U (OH)
Brandeis U (MA)
Brown U (RI)
Bryn Mawr Coll (PA)
Bucknell U (PA)
Calvin Coll (MI)
Carleton Coll (MN)
Carroll Coll (MT)
Case Western Reserve U (OH)
The Catholic U of America (DC)
Centre Coll (KY)
Christendom Coll (VA)
Christopher Newport U (VA)
Claremont McKenna Coll (CA)
Clark U (MA)
Coe Coll (IA)
Colby Coll (ME)
Coll of Charleston (SC)
The Coll of New Rochelle (NY)
Coll of Saint Benedict (MN)
Coll of the Holy Cross (MA)
The Coll of William and Mary (VA)
The Coll of Wooster (OH)
The Colorado Coll (CO)
Columbia U (NY)
Columbia U, School of General Studies (NY)
Concordia Coll (MN)
Concordia U (QC, Canada)
Connecticut Coll (CT)
Cornell Coll (IA)
Cornell U (NY)
Creighton U (NE)
Dalhousie U (NS, Canada)
Dartmouth Coll (NH)
Davidson Coll (NC)
Denison U (OH)
DePauw U (IN)
Dickinson Coll (PA)
Drew U (NJ)
Duquesne U (PA)
Earlham Coll (IN)
The Evergreen State Coll (WA)
Fordham U (NY)
Franciscan U of Steubenville (OH)
Franklin & Marshall Coll (PA)
Furman U (SC)
Georgetown U (DC)
The George Washington U (DC)
Gettysburg Coll (PA)
Gonzaga U (WA)
Grand Valley State U (MI)
Grinnell Coll (IA)
Gustavus Adolphus Coll (MN)
Hamilton Coll (NY)
Hampden-Sydney Coll (VA)
Hanover Coll (IN)
Harvard U (MA)
Haverford Coll (PA)
Hendrix Coll (AR)
Hillsdale Coll (MI)
Hobart and William Smith Colls (NY)
Hofstra U (NY)
Hollins U (VA)
Hope Coll (MI)
Howard U (DC)
Hunter Coll of the City U of New York (NY)
Illinois Wesleyan U (IL)
Indiana U Bloomington (IN)
John Carroll U (OH)
Johns Hopkins U (MD)
Kenyon Coll (OH)
Knox Coll (IL)
La Salle U (PA)
Lawrence U (WI)
Lehigh U (PA)
Lehman Coll of the City U of New York (NY)
Lewis & Clark Coll (OR)
Loyola Marymount U (CA)
Loyola U Chicago (IL)
Loyola U New Orleans (LA)
Luther Coll (IA)
Macalester Coll (MN)
Manhattan Coll (NY)
Marquette U (WI)
Mercer U, Macon (GA)
Miami U (OH)
Middlebury Coll (VT)
Millsaps Coll (MS)
Monmouth Coll (IL)
Montclair State U (NJ)
Moravian Coll (PA)
Mount Allison U (NB, Canada)
Mount Holyoke Coll (MA)
New York U (NY)
North Central Coll (IL)
Northwestern U (IL)
Notre Dame of Maryland U (MD)
Oberlin Coll (OH)
The Ohio State U (OH)
Ohio U (OH)
Ohio Wesleyan U (OH)
Pacific Lutheran U (WA)
Penn State Abington (PA)
Penn State Altoona (PA)
Penn State Beaver (PA)
Penn State Berks (PA)
Penn State Brandywine (PA)
Penn State DuBois (PA)
Penn State Erie, The Behrend Coll (PA)
Penn State Fayette, The Eberly Campus (PA)
Penn State Greater Allegheny (PA)
Penn State Hazleton (PA)
Penn State Lehigh Valley (PA)
Penn State Mont Alto (PA)
Penn State New Kensington (PA)
Penn State Schuylkill (PA)
Penn State Shenango (PA)
Penn State U Park (PA)
Penn State Wilkes-Barre (PA)
Penn State Worthington Scranton (PA)
Penn State York (PA)
Pomona Coll (CA)
Princeton U (NJ)
Randolph Coll (VA)
Randolph-Macon Coll (VA)
Reed Coll (OR)
Rhodes Coll (TN)
Rice U (TX)
Rockford U (IL)
Rollins Coll (FL)
Rutgers, The State U of New Jersey, Newark (NJ)
Rutgers, The State U of New Jersey, New Brunswick (NJ)
Saint Anselm Coll (NH)
St. Bonaventure U (NY)
Saint John's U (MN)
Saint Louis U (MO)
Saint Michael's Coll (VT)
St. Olaf Coll (MN)
Saint Peter's U (NJ)
Samford U (AL)
San Diego State U (CA)
San Francisco State U (CA)
Santa Clara U (CA)
Scripps Coll (CA)
Sewanee: The U of the South (TN)
Siena Coll (NY)
Skidmore Coll (NY)
Smith Coll (MA)
Southwestern U (TX)
Stanford U (CA)
Syracuse U (NY)
Temple U (PA)
Texas A&M U (TX)
Texas Tech U (TX)
Transylvania U (KY)
Trent U (ON, Canada)
Trinity Coll (CT)
Trinity U (TX)
Truman State U (MO)
Tufts U (MA)
Tulane U (LA)
Union Coll (NY)
Université de Montréal (QC, Canada)

U at Buffalo, the State U of New York (NY)
The U of Akron (OH)
The U of Arizona (AZ)
U of Arkansas (AR)
The U of British Columbia (BC, Canada)
U of California, Berkeley (CA)
U of California, Irvine (CA)
U of California, Santa Barbara (CA)
U of California, Santa Cruz (CA)
U of Chicago (IL)
U of Cincinnati (OH)
U of Colorado Boulder (CO)
U of Dallas (TX)
U of Evansville (IN)
U of Florida (FL)
U of Georgia (GA)
U of Guelph (ON, Canada)
U of Hawaii at Manoa (HI)
U of Illinois at Chicago (IL)
The U of Iowa (IA)
The U of Kansas (KS)
U of Kentucky (KY)
U of King's Coll (NS, Canada)
U of Maryland, Coll Park (MD)
U of Mary Washington (VA)
U of Massachusetts Amherst (MA)
U of Massachusetts Boston (MA)
U of Miami (FL)
U of Michigan (MI)
U of Minnesota, Twin Cities Campus (MN)
U of Mississippi (MS)
U of Missouri (MO)
The U of Montana (MT)
U of Nebraska–Lincoln (NE)
U of New Brunswick Saint John (NB, Canada)
U of New Hampshire (NH)
U of New Mexico (NM)
U of North Carolina at Asheville (NC)
The U of North Carolina at Chapel Hill (NC)
The U of North Carolina at Greensboro (NC)
U of North Dakota (ND)
U of Notre Dame (IN)
U of Oklahoma (OK)
U of Oregon (OR)
U of Ottawa (ON, Canada)
U of Pennsylvania (PA)
U of Pittsburgh (PA)
U of Puget Sound (WA)
U of Regina (SK, Canada)
U of Rhode Island (RI)
U of Rochester (NY)
U of St. Thomas (MN)
The U of Scranton (PA)
U of Southern California (CA)
U of South Florida (FL)
The U of Tennessee (TN)
The U of Texas at Austin (TX)
The U of Texas at San Antonio (TX)
U of the Pacific (CA)
U of Toronto (ON, Canada)
U of Utah (UT)
U of Vermont (VT)
U of Virginia (VA)
U of Washington (WA)
U of Waterloo (ON, Canada)
The U of Western Ontario (ON, Canada)
U of Windsor (ON, Canada)
U of Wisconsin–Madison (WI)
U of Wisconsin–Milwaukee (WI)
Ursinus Coll (PA)
Valparaiso U (IN)
Vanderbilt U (TN)
Vassar Coll (NY)
Villanova U (PA)
Virginia Wesleyan Coll (VA)
Wabash Coll (IN)
Wake Forest U (NC)
Washington and Lee U (VA)
Washington U in St. Louis (MO)
Wayne State U (MI)
Wesleyan U (CT)
Wheaton Coll (MA)
Whitman Coll (WA)
Willamette U (OR)
Williams Coll (MA)
Wright State U (OH)
Xavier U (OH)
Yale U (CT)
Yeshiva U (NY)

CLASSICS AND CLASSICAL LANGUAGES RELATED
Austin Coll (TX)
Bryn Mawr Coll (PA)
California State U, Long Beach (CA)
Columbia U, School of General Studies (NY)
Eckerd Coll (FL)
Elmira Coll (NY)
Gonzaga U (WA)
Lawrence U (WI)
Marquette U (WI)
New Coll of Florida (FL)
Ohio U (OH)
Rutgers, The State U of New Jersey, Newark (NJ)
Tulane U (LA)
U of Alberta (AB, Canada)
U of California, Los Angeles (CA)
U of Chicago (IL)
Wheaton Coll (IL)
Wheaton Coll (MA)
Xavier U (OH)

CLINICAL, COUNSELING AND APPLIED PSYCHOLOGY RELATED
Lincoln U (PA)
St. Francis Coll (NY)

CLINICAL LABORATORY SCIENCE/MEDICAL TECHNOLOGY
Abilene Christian U (TX)
Albany Coll of Pharmacy and Health Sciences (NY)
American U of Beirut (Lebanon)
Anderson U (IN)
Andrews U (MI)
Arkansas State U (AR)
Arkansas Tech U (AR)
Armstrong State U (GA)
Auburn U (AL)
Auburn U at Montgomery (AL)
Augustana Coll (SD)
Austin Peay State U (TN)
Ball State U (IN)
Barry U (FL)
Baylor U (TX)
Belmont U (TN)
Bemidji State U (MN)
Benedictine U (IL)
Bethune-Cookman U (FL)
Blackburn Coll (IL)
Blue Mountain Coll (MS)
Bowling Green State U (OH)
Bradley U (IL)
Brigham Young U (UT)
Caldwell U (NJ)
California State U, Dominguez Hills (CA)
Cameron U (OK)
Campbellsville U (KY)
Canisius Coll (NY)
Carson-Newman U (TN)
Catawba Coll (NC)
The Catholic U of America (DC)
Coker Coll (SC)
The Coll at Brockport, State U of New York (NY)
Coll of Saint Elizabeth (NJ)
Coll of Saint Mary (NE)
The Coll of Saint Rose (NY)
Coll of Staten Island of the City U of New York (NY)
Coll of the Ozarks (MO)
Concord U (WV)
DePaul U (IL)
DeVry U, Phoenix (AZ)
DeVry U, Houston (TX)
Dixie State U (UT)
East Carolina U (NC)
East Central U (OK)
Eastern Illinois U (IL)
Eastern Kentucky U (KY)
Eastern Michigan U (MI)
Eastern New Mexico U (NM)
East Stroudsburg U of Pennsylvania (PA)
Edinboro U of Pennsylvania (PA)
Elmhurst Coll (IL)
Elmira Coll (NY)
Eureka Coll (IL)
Evangel U (MO)
Fairleigh Dickinson U, Coll at Florham (NJ)
Fairleigh Dickinson U, Metropolitan Campus (NJ)
Ferris State U (MI)
Florida Gulf Coast U (FL)
Fort Hays State U (KS)
Gannon U (PA)
George Mason U (VA)
The George Washington U (DC)
Georgian Court U (NJ)
Georgia Regents U (GA)
Graceland U (IA)
Grand Valley State U (MI)
Greensboro Coll (NC)
Gwynedd Mercy U (PA)
Hartwick Coll (NY)
Heritage U (WA)
Holy Family U (PA)
Houghton Coll (NY)
Howard U (DC)
Illinois Coll (IL)
Illinois State U (IL)
Indiana State U (IN)
Indiana U of Pennsylvania (PA)
Indiana U–Purdue U Fort Wayne (IN)
Indiana U–Purdue U Indianapolis (IN)
Indiana U Southeast (IN)
Inter American U of Puerto Rico, San Germán Campus (PR)
Kansas State U (KS)
Kean U (NJ)
Kent State U (OH)
Keuka Coll (NY)
King's Coll (PA)
King U (TN)
Lebanon Valley Coll (PA)
Lincoln Memorial U (TN)
Lincoln U (MO)
Lindenwood U (MO)
Long Island U–LIU Brooklyn (NY)
Long Island U–LIU Post (NY)
Louisiana Coll (LA)
Louisiana State U Health Sciences Center (LA)
Malone U (OH)
Manchester U (IN)
Mansfield U of Pennsylvania (PA)
Marian U (IN)
Marist Coll (NY)
Marquette U (WI)
Marshall U (WV)
Mary Baldwin Coll (VA)
Maryville U of Saint Louis (MO)
Marywood U (PA)
Mayville State U (ND)
McNeese State U (LA)
Mercy Coll (NY)
Miami U (OH)
Michigan State U (MI)
Michigan Technological U (MI)
Midwestern State U (TX)
Minnesota State U Mankato (MN)
Minnesota State U Moorhead (MN)
Minot State U (ND)
Misericordia U (PA)
Mississippi State U (MS)
Missouri Southern State U (MO)
Missouri State U (MO)
Missouri Western State U (MO)
Monmouth U (NJ)
Morningside Coll (IA)
Mount Marty Coll (SD)
Mount Mercy U (IA)
Mount Vernon Nazarene U (OH)
National U (CA)
Nazareth Coll of Rochester (NY)
Norfolk State U (VA)
North Dakota State U (ND)
Northeastern State U (OK)
Northern Illinois U (IL)
Northern Michigan U (MI)
Northern State U (SD)
Northwestern Coll (IA)
Northwest Missouri State U (MO)
Oakland U (MI)
Ohio Northern U (OH)
The Ohio State U (OH)
Oklahoma Christian U (OK)
Old Dominion U (VA)
Peru State Coll (NE)
Pittsburg State U (KS)
Purdue U (IN)
Purdue U Calumet (IN)
Quincy U (IL)
Ramapo Coll of New Jersey (NJ)
Rochester Inst of Technology (NY)
Rockhurst U (MO)
Roosevelt U (IL)
Rutgers, The State U of New Jersey, Camden (NJ)
Rutgers, The State U of New Jersey, Newark (NJ)
Rutgers, The State U of New Jersey, New Brunswick (NJ)
Saginaw Valley State U (MI)
St. Catherine U (MN)
St. Edward's U (TX)
St. Francis Coll (NY)
Saint Francis U (PA)
St. John's U (NY)
Saint Joseph's Coll (IN)
St. Joseph's Coll, Long Island Campus (NY)
St. Joseph's Coll, New York (NY)
Saint Leo U (FL)
Saint Louis U (MO)
Saint Mary-of-the-Woods Coll (IN)
Saint Mary's U of Minnesota (MN)
St. Thomas Aquinas Coll (NY)
Salem Coll (NC)
Salisbury U (MD)
Salve Regina U (RI)
Santa Fe Coll (FL)
Seton Hill U (PA)
South Dakota State U (SD)
Southeast Missouri State U (MO)
Southern Adventist U (TN)
Southern Arkansas U–Magnolia (AR)
Southwest Baptist U (MO)
Southwestern Adventist U (TX)
Spencerian Coll (KY)
State U of New York at Fredonia (NY)
State U of New York at Plattsburgh (NY)
Stevenson U (MD)
Stony Brook U, State U of New York (NY)
Tarleton State U (TX)
Tennessee State U (TN)
Texas Southern U (TX)
Texas State U (TX)
Texas Woman's U (TX)
Thiel Coll (PA)
Thomas More Coll (KY)
Union Coll (NE)
Union U (TN)
U at Buffalo, the State U of New York (NY)
The U of Akron (OH)
The U of Alabama at Birmingham (AL)
U of Alberta (AB, Canada)
U of Bridgeport (CT)
U of Central Arkansas (AR)
U of Central Florida (FL)
U of Central Missouri (MO)
U of Central Oklahoma (OK)
U of Cincinnati (OH)
U of Delaware (DE)
U of Evansville (IN)
The U of Findlay (OH)
U of Hartford (CT)
U of Hawaii at Manoa (HI)
U of Idaho (ID)
U of Illinois at Springfield (IL)
U of Indianapolis (IN)
The U of Iowa (IA)
U of Jamestown (ND)
The U of Kansas (KS)
U of Kentucky (KY)
U of Maine (ME)
U of Mary Hardin-Baylor (TX)
U of Massachusetts Dartmouth (MA)
U of Michigan–Flint (MI)
U of Minnesota, Twin Cities Campus (MN)
U of Mississippi (MS)
The U of Montana (MT)
U of Mount Union (OH)
U of New England (ME)
U of New Hampshire (NH)
The U of North Carolina at Chapel Hill (NC)
The U of North Carolina at Charlotte (NC)
U of North Dakota (ND)
U of North Texas (TX)
U of Regina (SK, Canada)
U of Rhode Island (RI)
U of Rio Grande (OH)
U of St. Francis (IL)
U of Saint Francis (IN)
The U of Scranton (PA)
U of Southern Mississippi (MS)
U of South Florida (FL)
The U of Tennessee (TN)
The U of Texas at Arlington (TX)
The U of Texas at El Paso (TX)
The U of Texas at San Antonio (TX)
The U of Texas at Tyler (TX)
The U of Texas–Pan American (TX)
U of the Sciences (PA)
The U of Toledo (OH)
U of Utah (UT)
U of Vermont (VT)
The U of Virginia's Coll at Wise (VA)
U of Washington (WA)
U of West Florida (FL)
U of Wisconsin–La Crosse (WI)
U of Wisconsin–Milwaukee (WI)
U of Wisconsin–Oshkosh (WI)
U of Wisconsin–Stevens Point (WI)
U of Wyoming (WY)
Utah State U (UT)
Virginia Commonwealth U (VA)
Wake Forest U (NC)
Walla Walla U (WA)
Walsh U (OH)
Wartburg Coll (IA)
Washburn U (KS)
Wayne State U (MI)
Weber State U (UT)
Western Illinois U (IL)
Western Kentucky U (KY)
West Liberty U (WV)
West Texas A&M U (TX)
West Virginia U (WV)
Wichita State U (KS)
Wilkes U (PA)
Winona State U (MN)
Wright State U (OH)
Xavier U (OH)
York Coll of Pennsylvania (PA)
York Coll of the City U of New York (NY)
Youngstown State U (OH)

CLINICAL/MEDICAL LABORATORY ASSISTANT
National U (CA)

CLINICAL/MEDICAL LABORATORY SCIENCE AND ALLIED PROFESSIONS RELATED
Allen Coll (IA)
Auburn U (AL)
Bloomfield Coll (NJ)
The Coll of Idaho (ID)
Hunter Coll of the City U of New York (NY)
New Jersey Inst of Technology (NJ)
Roosevelt U (IL)
Rutgers, The State U of New Jersey, Newark (NJ)
Rutgers, The State U of New Jersey, New Brunswick (NJ)
Saint Louis U (MO)
U of Alberta (AB, Canada)
U of Massachusetts Lowell (MA)

CLINICAL/MEDICAL LABORATORY TECHNOLOGY
Auburn U (AL)
Barry U (FL)
Clarion U of Pennsylvania (PA)
Delaware State U (DE)
Indiana U–Purdue U Fort Wayne (IN)
Northern State U (SD)
Penn State DuBois (PA)
Rhode Island Coll (RI)
St. Thomas Aquinas Coll (NY)
The U of British Columbia (BC, Canada)
U of Missouri–Kansas City (MO)
The U of Montana (MT)
U of New Mexico (NM)
U of Science and Arts of Oklahoma (OK)
Viterbo U (WI)
Washburn U (KS)
Weber State U (UT)
York Coll of the City U of New York (NY)

CLINICAL/MEDICAL SOCIAL WORK
Eastern New Mexico U (NM)
New Mexico Highlands U (NM)

CLINICAL NUTRITION
Kent State U (OH)
Life U (GA)
Long Island U–LIU Post (NY)
U of North Dakota (ND)

CLINICAL PSYCHOLOGY
Augsburg Coll (MN)
Biola U (CA)
Illinois Inst of Technology (IL)
LeTourneau U (TX)
Mansfield U of Pennsylvania (PA)
Roger Williams U (RI)
Simon Fraser U (BC, Canada)
Southern Adventist U (TN)
Tennessee State U (TN)
Tufts U (MA)
The U of British Columbia (BC, Canada)
U of Mary Hardin-Baylor (TX)
U of Michigan–Flint (MI)
U of Windsor (ON, Canada)
Western State Colorado U (CO)

COGNITIVE PSYCHOLOGY AND PSYCHOLINGUISTICS
Averett U (VA)
Brown U (RI)
Dartmouth Coll (NH)
Fitchburg State U (MA)
Lawrence U (WI)
Northwestern U (IL)
Scripps Coll (CA)
State U of New York at Oswego (NY)
Tulane U (LA)
U of California, Santa Cruz (CA)
Vassar Coll (NY)
Washington U in St. Louis (MO)
Welch Coll (TN)
Yale U (CT)

COGNITIVE SCIENCE
California State U, Fresno (CA)
California State U, Stanislaus (CA)
Canisius Coll (NY)
Case Western Reserve U (OH)
Hampshire Coll (MA)
Indiana U Bloomington (IN)
Johns Hopkins U (MD)
Lawrence U (WI)
Lehigh U (PA)
Massachusetts Inst of Technology (MA)
Millsaps Coll (MS)
Occidental Coll (CA)
Pomona Coll (CA)
Rensselaer Polytechnic Inst (NY)
Simon Fraser U (BC, Canada)
State U of New York at Oswego (NY)
Susquehanna U (PA)
United States Military Acad (NY)
The U of British Columbia (BC, Canada)
U of California, Berkeley (CA)
U of California, Irvine (CA)
U of California, Los Angeles (CA)
U of California, Merced (CA)
U of Delaware (DE)
U of Evansville (IN)
U of Georgia (GA)
U of Michigan (MI)
U of Pennsylvania (PA)
U of Richmond (VA)
U of Southern California (CA)
The U of Texas at Dallas (TX)
Vanderbilt U (TN)

COLLEGE STUDENT COUNSELING AND PERSONNEL SERVICES
Bowling Green State U (OH)
The U of North Carolina at Pembroke (NC)

COMMERCIAL AND ADVERTISING ART
Acad of Art U (CA)
American Acad of Art (IL)
Arcadia U (PA)
Arkansas State U (AR)
Art Center Coll of Design (CA)
Ashland U (OH)
Bemidji State U (MN)
Biola U (CA)
Black Hills State U (SD)
Bowling Green State U (OH)
Buena Vista U (IA)
Buffalo State Coll, State U of New York (NY)
California Coll of the Arts (CA)
California State U, Fresno (CA)
California State U, Long Beach (CA)
California U of Pennsylvania (PA)
Carson-Newman U (TN)
Clark U (MA)
Coll for Creative Studies (MI)
The Coll of New Jersey (NJ)
The Coll of Saint Rose (NY)
Columbia Coll Chicago (IL)
Columbus Coll of Art & Design (OH)
Concordia U Chicago (IL)
Concordia U Wisconsin (WI)
Dominican U (IL)
Drake U (IA)
Fairmont State U (WV)
Fashion Inst of Technology (NY)
Fontbonne U (MO)
Franklin Pierce U (NH)
Graceland U (IA)
Hampton U (VA)
Indiana U–Purdue U Fort Wayne (IN)
Iowa State U of Science and Technology (IA)
Keene State Coll (NH)
Kent State U (OH)
Kutztown U of Pennsylvania (PA)
Laguna Coll of Art & Design (CA)
Lewis U (IL)
Lipscomb U (TN)
Long Island U–LIU Brooklyn (NY)
Long Island U–LIU Post (NY)
Louisiana Coll (LA)
Loyola U New Orleans (LA)
Lycoming Coll (PA)
Marietta Coll (OH)
Marymount Manhattan Coll (NY)
Massachusetts Coll of Art and Design (MA)
Mercy Coll (NY)
Miami U (OH)
Millikin U (IL)
Minnesota State U Mankato (MN)
Minnesota State U Moorhead (MN)
New York City Coll of Technology of the City U of New York (NY)
New York Inst of Technology (NY)
Northern Kentucky U (KY)
Northwest Nazarene U (ID)
Ohio Northern U (OH)
Oklahoma Christian U (OK)
Otis Coll of Art and Design (CA)
Pennsylvania Coll of Art & Design (PA)
Pennsylvania Coll of Technology (PA)
Peru State Coll (NE)
Philadelphia U (PA)
Portland State U (OR)
Pratt Inst (NY)
Purchase Coll, State U of New York (NY)
Ringling Coll of Art and Design (FL)
Rochester Inst of Technology (NY)
Rutgers, The State U of New Jersey, New Brunswick (NJ)
St. Norbert Coll (WI)
St. Thomas Aquinas Coll (NY)
Sam Houston State U (TX)
Savannah Coll of Art and Design (GA)
Seattle U (WA)
Seton Hill U (PA)
Southwest Baptist U (MO)
State U of New York at Fredonia (NY)
State U of New York at Oswego (NY)
U of Central Missouri (MO)
U of Central Oklahoma (OK)
U of Cincinnati (OH)
U of Denver (CO)
U of Indianapolis (IN)
U of Massachusetts Dartmouth (MA)
U of Minnesota, Duluth (MN)
U of New Haven (CT)
U of North Georgia (GA)
U of North Texas (TX)
U of San Francisco (CA)
The U of Tennessee (TN)
The U of Texas at El Paso (TX)
The U of the Arts (PA)
U of the Pacific (CA)
U of Wisconsin–Stevens Point (WI)
Upper Iowa U (IA)
Villa Maria Coll (NY)
Walla Walla U (WA)
Wartburg Coll (IA)
Washington U in St. Louis (MO)
Waynesburg U (PA)
Weber State U (UT)
West Liberty U (WV)
William Paterson U of New Jersey (NJ)
York Coll of Pennsylvania (PA)

COMMERCIAL PHOTOGRAPHY
Appalachian State U (NC)
Fashion Inst of Technology (NY)
Rochester Inst of Technology (NY)
Rocky Mountain Coll of Art + Design (CO)

COMMUNICATION
Albion Coll (MI)
Alvernia U (PA)
Arizona Christian U (AZ)
Arkansas State U (AR)
Asbury U (KY)
Ashland U (OH)
Averett U (VA)
Bethany Lutheran Coll (MN)
Bethel U (MN)
Biola U (CA)
Bob Jones U (SC)
Boston Coll (MA)
Boston U (MA)
Carlow U (PA)
Cedarville U (OH)
Central Washington U (WA)
Cheyney U of Pennsylvania (PA)
Cleveland State U (OH)
The Coll of New Jersey (NJ)
Coll of the Ozarks (MO)
Concordia Coll (MN)
Concordia U (CA)
Cornell U (NY)
Dallas Baptist U (TX)
DEREE - The American Coll of Greece (Greece)
DeSales U (PA)
DeVry U, Pomona (CA)
DeVry U, Westminster (CO)
DeVry U, Miramar (FL)
DeVry U, Orlando (FL)
DeVry U, Decatur (GA)
DeVry U, Chicago (IL)
DeVry U, Kansas City (MO)
DeVry U, Fort Washington (PA)
DeVry U, Irving (TX)
DeVry U, Federal Way (WA)
DeVry U Online (IL)
Eastern Illinois U (IL)
Eastern New Mexico U (NM)
Edgewood Coll (WI)
Elizabethtown Coll School of Continuing and Professional Studies (PA)
Five Towns Coll (NY)
Florida Coll (FL)
Florida Inst of Technology (FL)
Fordham U (NY)
Frostburg State U (MD)
Geneva Coll (PA)
Granite State Coll (NH)
Hannibal-LaGrange U (MO)
Hardin-Simmons U (TX)
High Point U (NC)
Hiram Coll (OH)
Holy Cross Coll (IN)
Huntingdon Coll (AL)
Jacksonville State U (AL)
Kansas Wesleyan U (KS)
Lake Forest Coll (IL)
Lamar U (TX)
Lasell Coll (MA)
Lebanese American U (Lebanon)
Le Moyne Coll (NY)
Lenoir-Rhyne U (NC)
Liberty U (VA)
Limestone Coll (SC)
Lynn U (FL)
Marist Coll (NY)
Marymount Manhattan Coll (NY)
Marymount U (VA)
Massachusetts Coll of Liberal Arts (MA)
Misericordia U (PA)
National U (CA)
New Mexico State U (NM)
Northwest Christian U (OR)
Northwest Missouri State U (MO)
Nyack Coll (NY)
Oakland U (MI)
Oklahoma City U (OK)
Pepperdine U, Malibu (CA)
Portland State U (OR)
Post U (CT)
Purdue U (IN)
Randolph-Macon Coll (VA)
Regent U (VA)
Roanoke Coll (VA)
Rowan U (NJ)
Sacred Heart U (CT)
Saint Anselm Coll (NH)
St. John Fisher Coll (NY)
Saint Joseph's U (PA)
Saint Louis U (MO)
Saint Martin's U (WA)
Simpson Coll (IA)
Southwestern Coll (KS)
Spalding U (KY)
Spring Hill Coll (AL)
Stetson U (FL)
Tarleton State U (TX)
Texas A&M U (TX)
Texas A&M U–Kingsville (TX)
Thomas More Coll (KY)
Toccoa Falls Coll (GA)
Trinity U (TX)
U of Arkansas–Fort Smith (AR)
U of California, Santa Barbara (CA)
U of Central Oklahoma (OK)
U of Delaware (DE)
U of Evansville (IN)
U of Houston–Clear Lake (TX)
U of Houston–Downtown (TX)
U of Houston–Victoria (TX)
U of Illinois at Chicago (IL)
U of Illinois at Springfield (IL)
U of Maine (ME)
U of Mary Hardin-Baylor (TX)
U of Massachusetts Amherst (MA)
U of Massachusetts Boston (MA)
U of Michigan–Flint (MI)
U of Minnesota, Crookston (MN)
U of Mobile (AL)
U of Mount Union (OH)
U of North Dakota (ND)
U of Saint Francis (IN)
U of San Diego (CA)
The U of Tampa (FL)
The U of Texas at San Antonio (TX)
The U of Texas at Tyler (TX)
The U of Texas of the Permian Basin (TX)
The U of Texas–Pan American (TX)
U of Wisconsin–Eau Claire (WI)
U of Wisconsin–Green Bay (WI)
U of Wisconsin–Stevens Point (WI)
Walden U (MN)
Washington State U Vancouver (WA)
Wheeling Jesuit U (WV)
William Peace U (NC)
William Penn U (IA)
Wingate U (NC)
Xavier U (OH)
Youngstown State U (OH)

COMMUNICATION AND JOURNALISM RELATED
The American U in Dubai (United Arab Emirates)
The American U of Paris (France)
Auburn U (AL)
Augustana Coll (IL)
Benedictine U (IL)
Berry Coll (GA)
Bob Jones U (SC)
Bowling Green State U (OH)
Brigham Young U (UT)
California Lutheran U (CA)
Carlow U (PA)
Centenary Coll of Louisiana (LA)
Chestnut Hill Coll (PA)
Clarke U (IA)
Concordia U (QC, Canada)
Dalhousie U (NS, Canada)
Dominican U of California (CA)
Drexel U (PA)
Endicott Coll (MA)
Farmingdale State Coll (NY)
Flagler Coll (FL)
Florida Inst of Technology (FL)
Friends U (KS)
Hannibal-LaGrange U (MO)
Hawai`i Pacific U (HI)
Immaculata U (PA)
Lake Erie Coll (OH)
Lehman Coll of the City U of New York (NY)
Madonna U (MI)
Malone U (OH)
Marquette U (WI)
Mary Baldwin Coll (VA)
Mercer U, Macon (GA)
Mercy Coll (NY)
Merrimack Coll (MA)
Milwaukee School of Eng (WI)
Minot State U (ND)
Morehead State U (KY)
National U (CA)
Newberry Coll (SC)
Newbury Coll (MA)
Norfolk State U (VA)
Ohio Northern U (OH)
The Ohio State U (OH)
Oklahoma Christian U (OK)
Our Lady of the Lake U of San Antonio (TX)
Pace U (NY)
Penn State Abington (PA)
Penn State Altoona (PA)
Penn State Beaver (PA)
Penn State Berks (PA)
Penn State Brandywine (PA)
Penn State DuBois (PA)
Penn State Erie, The Behrend Coll (PA)
Penn State Fayette, The Eberly Campus (PA)
Penn State Greater Allegheny (PA)
Penn State Hazleton (PA)
Penn State Lehigh Valley (PA)
Penn State Mont Alto (PA)
Penn State New Kensington (PA)
Penn State Schuylkill (PA)
Penn State Shenango (PA)
Penn State U Park (PA)
Penn State Wilkes-Barre (PA)
Penn State Worthington Scranton (PA)
Penn State York (PA)
Quincy U (IL)
Quinnipiac U (CT)
Reinhardt U (GA)
Sacred Heart U (CT)
Siena Heights U (MI)
Southeastern Oklahoma State U (OK)
State U of New York Polytechnic Inst (NY)
Sterling Coll (KS)
Tiffin U (OH)
Trevecca Nazarene U (TN)
Universidad Metropolitana (PR)
U of Guam (GU)
U of Miami (FL)
U of Minnesota, Duluth (MN)
U of Minnesota, Twin Cities Campus (MN)
U of Wisconsin–Green Bay (WI)
Washington U in St. Louis (MO)
Webster U (MO)
West Virginia U (WV)
William Penn U (IA)

COMMUNICATION AND MEDIA RELATED
Acad of Art U (CA)
Adelphi U (NY)
Albion Coll (MI)
Alma Coll (MI)
American U of Beirut (Lebanon)
Ashland U (OH)
Auburn U (AL)
Austin Coll (TX)
Belmont U (TN)
Bennington Coll (VT)
Biola U (CA)
Butler U (IN)
Cameron U (OK)
Canisius Coll (NY)
Columbia Intl U (SC)
Concordia U (QC, Canada)
Curry Coll (MA)

DePaul U (IL)
DeSales U (PA)
Elizabethtown Coll School of Continuing and Professional Studies (PA)
Elon U (NC)
Fairleigh Dickinson U, Metropolitan Campus (NJ)
Flagler Coll (FL)
Florida State U (FL)
Georgetown Coll (KY)
Georgian Court U (NJ)
Greenville Coll (IL)
Hamilton Coll (NY)
Houghton Coll (NY)
Houston Baptist U (TX)
Judson U (IL)
King's Coll (PA)
Lane Coll (TN)
La Roche Coll (PA)
Lasell Coll (MA)
Lees-McRae Coll (NC)
Loyola U Chicago (IL)
Lycoming Coll (PA)
Marquette U (WI)
Marymount Manhattan Coll (NY)
Milligan Coll (TN)
Missouri Baptist U (MO)
Mitchell Coll (CT)
Molloy Coll (NY)
Montclair State U (NJ)
Montreat Coll, Montreat (NC)
Morehead State U (KY)
Neumann U (PA)
Newberry Coll (SC)
New Jersey Inst of Technology (NJ)
New York U (NY)
Northeastern Illinois U (IL)
Northwestern U (IL)
Oklahoma City U (OK)
Penn State Erie, The Behrend Coll (PA)
Reinhardt U (GA)
Rochester Inst of Technology (NY)
Roger Williams U (RI)
Rollins Coll (FL)
St. Edward's U (TX)
St. Thomas U (FL)
Salve Regina U (RI)
Southwestern Coll (KS)
Stanford U (CA)
Taylor U (IN)
Unity Coll (ME)
Universidad Metropolitana (PR)
Université de Sherbrooke (QC, Canada)
U of Central Missouri (MO)
U of Colorado Boulder (CO)
U of Miami (FL)
U of Mobile (AL)
U of the Incarnate Word (TX)
The U of West Alabama (AL)
The U of Western Ontario (ON, Canada)
U of Wisconsin–Superior (WI)
Virginia Wesleyan Coll (VA)
Waldorf Coll (IA)
Walsh U (OH)
Washington & Jefferson Coll (PA)
Wheelock Coll (MA)

COMMUNICATION DISORDERS SCIENCES AND SERVICES RELATED
Marquette U (WI)
U of Missouri (MO)
U of New Hampshire (NH)

COMMUNICATION SCIENCES AND DISORDERS
Appalachian State U (NC)
Arizona State U at the Tempe campus (AZ)
Auburn U (AL)
Augustana Coll (IL)
Baldwin Wallace U (OH)
Baylor U (TX)
Biola U (CA)
Bob Jones U (SC)
Bowling Green State U (OH)
Bridgewater State U (MA)
Butler U (IN)
California Baptist U (CA)
California State U, Chico (CA)
California State U, Fresno (CA)
California State U, Fullerton (CA)
California State U, Long Beach (CA)
California State U, Los Angeles (CA)
California U of Pennsylvania (PA)
Case Western Reserve U (OH)
Central Michigan U (MI)
Eastern Illinois U (IL)
Elms Coll (MA)
Emerson Coll (MA)
Fontbonne U (MO)
Governors State U (IL)
Hampton U (VA)
Harding U (AR)
Jacksonville U (FL)
Kansas State U (KS)
Lamar U (TX)
Maryville U of Saint Louis (MO)
Minnesota State U Mankato (MN)
Minot State U (ND)
Northern Illinois U (IL)
Northwestern U (IL)
Our Lady of the Lake U of San Antonio (TX)
Pace U (NY)
Penn State Abington (PA)
Penn State Altoona (PA)
Penn State Beaver (PA)
Penn State Berks (PA)
Penn State Brandywine (PA)
Penn State DuBois (PA)
Penn State Erie, The Behrend Coll (PA)
Penn State Fayette, The Eberly Campus (PA)
Penn State Greater Allegheny (PA)
Penn State Hazleton (PA)
Penn State Lehigh Valley (PA)
Penn State Mont Alto (PA)
Penn State New Kensington (PA)
Penn State Schuylkill (PA)
Penn State Shenango (PA)
Penn State U Park (PA)
Penn State Wilkes-Barre (PA)
Penn State Worthington Scranton (PA)
Penn State York (PA)
Portland State U (OR)
Queens Coll of the City U of New York (NY)
Radford U (VA)
Rhode Island Coll (RI)
Saint Louis U (MO)
Saint Mary's Coll (IN)
Samford U (AL)
San Diego State U (CA)
San Francisco State U (CA)
San Jose State U (CA)
Shaw U (NC)
Southeast Missouri State U (MO)
Southern Illinois U Carbondale (IL)
State U of New York at Fredonia (NY)
State U of New York at New Paltz (NY)
Stephen F. Austin State U (TX)
Syracuse U (NY)
Texas A&M Intl U (TX)
Texas A&M U–Kingsville (TX)
Texas State U (TX)
Truman State U (MO)
The U of Akron (OH)
The U of Arizona (AZ)
The U of British Columbia (BC, Canada)
U of Cincinnati (OH)
U of Colorado Boulder (CO)
U of Georgia (GA)
U of Houston (TX)
The U of Kansas (KS)
U of Maine (ME)
U of Maryland, Coll Park (MD)
U of Massachusetts Amherst (MA)
U of Minnesota, Duluth (MN)
U of Minnesota, Twin Cities Campus (MN)
U of Mississippi (MS)
U of Nebraska at Kearney (NE)
U of North Dakota (ND)
U of Oklahoma Health Sciences Center (OK)
U of Oregon (OR)
U of Rhode Island (RI)
U of South Alabama (AL)
The U of South Dakota (SD)
U of South Florida Sarasota-Manatee (FL)
The U of Texas at Austin (TX)
The U of Texas–Pan American (TX)
The U of Toledo (OH)
U of Vermont (VT)
U of Wisconsin–Eau Claire (WI)
U of Wisconsin–River Falls (WI)
U of Wisconsin–Stevens Point (WI)
U of Wisconsin–Whitewater (WI)
Wayne State U (MI)
Western Carolina U (NC)
Western Illinois U (IL)
Western Kentucky U (KY)
West Texas A&M U (TX)
Wichita State U (KS)
William Paterson U of New Jersey (NJ)
Winthrop U (SC)
Worcester State U (MA)
Xavier U of Louisiana (LA)

COMMUNICATIONS TECHNOLOGIES AND SUPPORT SERVICES RELATED
Alverno Coll (WI)
Bowling Green State U (OH)
Chestnut Hill Coll (PA)
Framingham State U (MA)
Lesley U (MA)
Lewis U (IL)
Minot State U (ND)
Salve Regina U (RI)
U of Central Oklahoma (OK)
U of Windsor (ON, Canada)
U of Wisconsin–Platteville (WI)

COMMUNICATIONS TECHNOLOGY
Eastern Michigan U (MI)
East Stroudsburg U of Pennsylvania (PA)
Hastings Coll (NE)
Inter American U of Puerto Rico, Bayamón Campus (PR)
Lawrence Technological U (MI)
Messiah Coll (PA)
Southern Adventist U (TN)
York Coll of the City U of New York (NY)

COMMUNITY HEALTH AND PREVENTIVE MEDICINE
Canisius Coll (NY)
Carroll Coll (MT)
Florida Gulf Coast U (FL)
George Mason U (VA)
Georgia Coll & State U (GA)
Governors State U (IL)
Hofstra U (NY)
Indiana U Bloomington (IN)
Mansfield U of Pennsylvania (PA)
Minnesota State U Moorhead (MN)
Moravian Coll (PA)
Murray State U (KY)
National U (CA)
Pine Manor Coll (MA)
Portland State U (OR)
Tufts U (MA)
U of Florida (FL)
U of Wisconsin–Eau Claire (WI)
U of Wisconsin–La Crosse (WI)
Western Kentucky U (KY)

COMMUNITY HEALTH SERVICES COUNSELING
Canisius Coll (NY)
Carroll Coll (MT)
Central Michigan U (MI)
Delaware State U (DE)
Indiana State U (IN)
Indiana U–Purdue U Fort Wayne (IN)
James Madison U (VA)
Johnson C. Smith U (NC)
Morris Coll (SC)
New Mexico State U (NM)
Northeastern Illinois U (IL)
Northern Illinois U (IL)
Northern Michigan U (MI)
Ohio U (OH)
Prairie View A&M U (TX)
Rhode Island Coll (RI)
Texas A&M U (TX)
The U of Arizona (AZ)
U of Central Arkansas (AR)
The U of Kansas (KS)
U of Massachusetts Lowell (MA)
U of Northern Iowa (IA)
U of Pennsylvania (PA)
The U of Western Ontario (ON, Canada)
U of West Florida (FL)
Western Washington U (WA)
Worcester State U (MA)
Youngstown State U (OH)

COMMUNITY ORGANIZATION AND ADVOCACY
Allegheny Coll (PA)
Alverno Coll (WI)
Bemidji State U (MN)
Bryant U (RI)
Cape Breton U (NS, Canada)
Central Michigan U (MI)
Cornell U (NY)
DePaul U (IL)
Elmira Coll (NY)
Emory & Henry Coll (VA)
Goddard Coll (VT)
Lewis U (IL)
Metropolitan Coll of New York (NY)
Miami U (OH)
Nazareth Coll of Rochester (NY)
New Mexico State U (NM)
New York U (NY)
Northern State U (SD)
Northland Coll (WI)
Northwestern U (IL)
Providence Coll (RI)
Rockhurst U (MO)
Saint Martin's U (WA)
Siena Heights U (MI)
Southern Arkansas U–Magnolia (AR)
State U of New York Empire State Coll (NY)
U of Alaska Fairbanks (AK)
U of Hartford (CT)
U of Massachusetts Boston (MA)
U of New Mexico (NM)
U of Saint Mary (KS)
The U of Texas at El Paso (TX)
West Virginia U Inst of Technology (WV)

COMMUNITY PSYCHOLOGY
Clayton State U (GA)
Goddard Coll (VT)
Kansas Wesleyan U (KS)
Montana State U Billings (MT)
Northwestern U (IL)
U of Miami (FL)
U of New Haven (CT)
U of Saint Mary (KS)
U of Washington, Bothell (WA)

COMPARATIVE LITERATURE
The American U in Cairo (Egypt)
The American U of Paris (France)
Arcadia U (PA)
Ave Maria U (FL)
Barnard Coll (NY)
Barry U (FL)
Beloit Coll (WI)
Binghamton U, State U of New York (NY)
Blackburn Coll (IL)
Boston U (MA)
Brandeis U (MA)
Brown U (RI)
Bryn Mawr Coll (PA)
California State U, Fullerton (CA)
California State U, Long Beach (CA)
Case Western Reserve U (OH)
Castleton State Coll (VT)
Cazenovia Coll (NY)
Chowan U (NC)
Christendom Coll (VA)
City Coll of the City U of New York (NY)
Clark U (MA)
Coll of the Atlantic (ME)
Coll of the Holy Cross (MA)
The Coll of Wooster (OH)
The Colorado Coll (CO)
Columbia U (NY)
Columbia U, School of General Studies (NY)
Cornell U (NY)
Dalhousie U (NS, Canada)
Dartmouth Coll (NH)
Earlham Coll (IN)
Eckerd Coll (FL)
Eureka Coll (IL)
Fordham U (NY)
Franklin Pierce U (NH)
Georgetown U (DC)
Gettysburg Coll (PA)
Goddard Coll (VT)
Graceland U (IA)
Hamilton Coll (NY)
Harrison Middleton U (AZ)
Harvard U (MA)
Hastings Coll (NE)
Haverford Coll (PA)
Hillsdale Coll (MI)
Hobart and William Smith Colls (NY)
Hofstra U (NY)
Houghton Coll (NY)
Hunter Coll of the City U of New York (NY)
Indiana U Bloomington (IN)
Inter American U of Puerto Rico, San Germán Campus (PR)
John Cabot U (Italy)
John Carroll U (OH)
Johnson State Coll (VT)
Lycoming Coll (PA)
Manchester U (IN)
Middlebury Coll (VT)
Mills Coll (CA)
Minnesota State U Mankato (MN)
Mount Allison U (NB, Canada)
National U (CA)
New Coll of Florida (FL)
New York U (NY)
Northwestern U (IL)
Northwest U (WA)
Oberlin Coll (OH)
The Ohio State U (OH)
Ohio Wesleyan U (OH)
Pacific U (OR)
Penn State Abington (PA)
Penn State Altoona (PA)
Penn State Beaver (PA)
Penn State Berks (PA)
Penn State Brandywine (PA)
Penn State DuBois (PA)
Penn State Erie, The Behrend Coll (PA)
Penn State Fayette, The Eberly Campus (PA)
Penn State Greater Allegheny (PA)
Penn State Hazleton (PA)
Penn State Lehigh Valley (PA)
Penn State Mont Alto (PA)
Penn State New Kensington (PA)
Penn State Schuylkill (PA)
Penn State Shenango (PA)
Penn State U Park (PA)
Penn State Wilkes-Barre (PA)
Penn State Worthington Scranton (PA)
Penn State York (PA)
Princeton U (NJ)
Purchase Coll, State U of New York (NY)
Purdue U (IN)
Queens Coll of the City U of New York (NY)
Quinnipiac U (CT)
Ramapo Coll of New Jersey (NJ)
Reed Coll (OR)
Rockford U (IL)
Rutgers, The State U of New Jersey, New Brunswick (NJ)
St. Catherine U (MN)
Saint Francis U (PA)
San Diego State U (CA)
San Francisco State U (CA)
Shimer Coll (IL)
Smith Coll (MA)
Stanford U (CA)
State U of New York Coll at Geneseo (NY)
State U of New York Coll at Old Westbury (NY)
Stony Brook U, State U of New York (NY)
Syracuse U (NY)
Trinity Coll (CT)
Tufts U (MA)
United States Military Acad (NY)
Université de Montréal (QC, Canada)
U of Alberta (AB, Canada)
U of California, Berkeley (CA)
U of California, Davis (CA)
U of California, Irvine (CA)
U of California, Los Angeles (CA)
U of California, Merced (CA)
U of California, Santa Barbara (CA)
U of California, Santa Cruz (CA)
U of Chicago (IL)
U of Delaware (DE)

U of Georgia (GA)
The U of Iowa (IA)
U of La Verne (CA)
U of Massachusetts Amherst (MA)
U of Michigan (MI)
U of Minnesota, Twin Cities Campus (MN)
U of New Mexico (NM)
The U of North Carolina at Chapel Hill (NC)
U of Oregon (OR)
U of Pennsylvania (PA)
U of Pittsburgh at Greensburg (PA)
U of Rochester (NY)
U of San Francisco (CA)
U of Saskatchewan (SK, Canada)
U of Southern California (CA)
The U of Texas at Dallas (TX)
U of Toronto (ON, Canada)
U of Utah (UT)
U of Virginia (VA)
U of Washington (WA)
The U of Western Ontario (ON, Canada)
U of Wisconsin–Madison (WI)
U of Wisconsin–Milwaukee (WI)
Washington U in St. Louis (MO)
Willamette U (OR)
William Paterson U of New Jersey (NJ)
Williams Coll (MA)
Yale U (CT)

COMPUTATIONAL AND APPLIED MATHEMATICS
American Public U System (WV)
Bryant U (RI)
Mary Baldwin Coll (VA)
Purdue U (IN)
U of Notre Dame (IN)
U of Southern California (CA)

COMPUTATIONAL BIOLOGY
Case Western Reserve U (OH)
Colby Coll (ME)
Massachusetts Inst of Technology (MA)

COMPUTATIONAL MATHEMATICS
Arizona State U at the Tempe campus (AZ)
Asbury U (KY)
California Inst of Technology (CA)
Christopher Newport U (VA)
Coll of Saint Benedict (MN)
Embry-Riddle Aeronautical U–Daytona (FL)
Hillsdale Coll (MI)
Indiana U–Purdue U Fort Wayne (IN)
Marquette U (WI)
McKendree U (IL)
Michigan State U (MI)
Rochester Inst of Technology (NY)
Saint John's U (MN)
Siena Coll (NY)
Southwestern U (TX)
U of California, Davis (CA)
U of California, Los Angeles (CA)
U of Washington (WA)
U of Waterloo (ON, Canada)

COMPUTATIONAL SCIENCE
American U (DC)
Anderson U (IN)
Canisius Coll (NY)
Stockton U (NJ)
U of South Carolina Beaufort (SC)

COMPUTER AND INFORMATION SCIENCES
Adelphi U (NY)
Albany State U (GA)
Alcorn State U (MS)
Alverno Coll (WI)
American U (DC)
American U in Bulgaria (Bulgaria)
Andrews U (MI)
Angelo State U (TX)
Anna Maria Coll (MA)
Aquinas Coll (MI)
Arcadia U (PA)
Arizona State U at the Tempe campus (AZ)
Arkansas State U (AR)
Arkansas Tech U (AR)
Armstrong State U (GA)
Assumption Coll (MA)
Athens State U (AL)
Auburn U (AL)
Austin Coll (TX)
Austin Peay State U (TN)
Avila U (MO)
Ball State U (IN)
Barnard Coll (NY)
Beacon Coll (FL)
Belmont U (TN)
Bennett Coll (NC)
Bennington Coll (VT)
Bentley U (MA)
Berea Coll (KY)
Bethel U (MN)
Binghamton U, State U of New York (NY)
Bloomfield Coll (NJ)
Bluefield State Coll (WV)
Boston Coll (MA)
Bowie State U (MD)
Bowling Green State U (OH)
Bryant U (RI)
Bucknell U (PA)
Butler U (IN)
Caldwell U (NJ)
California Lutheran U (CA)
California State U, Fresno (CA)
California State U, Los Angeles (CA)
California U of Pennsylvania (PA)
Calumet Coll of Saint Joseph (IN)
Cape Breton U (NS, Canada)
Capitol Technology U (MD)
Carroll Coll (MT)
Castleton State Coll (VT)
Catawba Coll (NC)
The Catholic U of America (DC)
Cedar Crest Coll (PA)
Central Connecticut State U (CT)
Central State U (OH)
Chaminade U of Honolulu (HI)
Champlain Coll (VT)
Chapman U (CA)
Chestnut Hill Coll (PA)
Cheyney U of Pennsylvania (PA)
Chowan U (NC)
The Citadel, The Military Coll of South Carolina (SC)
Clarion U of Pennsylvania (PA)
Clark Atlanta U (GA)
Clarke U (IA)
Cleveland State U (OH)
Coastal Carolina U (SC)
The Coll at Brockport, State U of New York (NY)
Coll of Charleston (SC)
The Coll of New Jersey (NJ)
Coll of Saint Elizabeth (NJ)
The Coll of Saint Rose (NY)
The Coll of St. Scholastica (MN)
The Coll of William and Mary (VA)
Colorado Mesa U (CO)
Colorado State U (CO)
Columbia Coll (MO)
Columbia Coll (SC)
Columbus State U (GA)
Concordia U Chicago (IL)
Concordia U, Nebraska (NE)
Cornell U (NY)
Covenant Coll (GA)
Curry Coll (MA)
Dakota State U (SD)
Dallas Baptist U (TX)
Delaware State U (DE)
DEREE - The American Coll of Greece (Greece)
Dickinson Coll (PA)
Dixie State U (UT)
Doane Coll (NE)
Dominican Coll (NY)
Dowling Coll (NY)
Earlham Coll (IN)
East Central U (OK)
Eastern Connecticut State U (CT)
Eastern Kentucky U (KY)
Eastern Michigan U (MI)
Eastern New Mexico U (NM)
Eastern Oregon U (OR)
East Stroudsburg U of Pennsylvania (PA)
East Tennessee State U (TN)
Edgewood Coll (WI)
Edinboro U of Pennsylvania (PA)
Elizabethtown Coll (PA)
Elms Coll (MA)
Elon U (NC)
Emmanuel Coll (GA)
Emporia State U (KS)
Eureka Coll (IL)
The Evergreen State Coll (WA)
Excelsior Coll (NY)
Fairfield U (CT)
Fairleigh Dickinson U, Coll at Florham (NJ)
Fisher Coll (MA)
Fitchburg State U (MA)
Florida Ag and Mech U (FL)
Florida Atlantic U (FL)
Florida Gulf Coast U (FL)
Florida Intl U (FL)
Fordham U (NY)
Framingham State U (MA)
Franciscan U of Steubenville (OH)
Francis Marion U (SC)
Franklin & Marshall Coll (PA)
Franklin Coll (IN)
Friends U (KS)
Gallaudet U (DC)
Gannon U (PA)
Geneva Coll (PA)
George Mason U (VA)
Georgetown Coll (KY)
The George Washington U (DC)
Georgia Inst of Technology (GA)
Georgia Regents U (GA)
Georgia Southern U (GA)
Georgia State U (GA)
Goshen Coll (IN)
Grand Valley State U (MI)
Greenville Coll (IL)
Guilford Coll (NC)
Gwynedd Mercy U (PA)
Hamilton Coll (NY)
Hannibal-LaGrange U (MO)
Hartwick Coll (NY)
Hastings Coll (NE)
Hawai`i Pacific U (HI)
Hiram Coll (OH)
Hope Coll (MI)
Howard Payne U (TX)
Husson U (ME)
Huston-Tillotson U (TX)
Illinois Inst of Technology (IL)
Indiana State U (IN)
Indiana U of Pennsylvania (PA)
Indiana U–Purdue U Fort Wayne (IN)
Inter American U of Puerto Rico, Fajardo Campus (PR)
Ithaca Coll (NY)
Jackson State U (MS)
Jacksonville State U (AL)
Jacksonville U (FL)
James Madison U (VA)
Johns Hopkins U (MD)
Johnson C. Smith U (NC)
Juniata Coll (PA)
Kalamazoo Coll (MI)
Kansas State U (KS)
Kansas Wesleyan U (KS)
Kean U (NJ)
Keene State Coll (NH)
Kennesaw State U (GA)
Kent State U (OH)
Kentucky State U (KY)
Kentucky Wesleyan Coll (KY)
King's Coll (PA)
Kutztown U of Pennsylvania (PA)
Kuyper Coll (MI)
LaGrange Coll (GA)
Lamar U (TX)
Lane Coll (TN)
La Roche Coll (PA)
La Salle U (PA)
Lehman Coll of the City U of New York (NY)
Le Moyne Coll (NY)
Lenoir-Rhyne U (NC)
Liberty U (VA)
Lincoln Memorial U (TN)
Lincoln U (PA)
Lindenwood U (MO)
Lock Haven U of Pennsylvania (PA)
Long Island U–LIU Brooklyn (NY)
Loyola Marymount U (CA)
Loyola U Chicago (IL)
Lubbock Christian U (TX)
Macalester Coll (MN)
Mansfield U of Pennsylvania (PA)
Marist Coll (NY)
Marquette U (WI)
Marshall U (WV)
Mars Hill U (NC)
Maryville Coll (TN)
Massachusetts Coll of Liberal Arts (MA)
The Master's Coll and Sem (CA)
Mayville State U (ND)
McDaniel Coll (MD)
McKendree U (IL)
McMurry U (TX)
Mercy Coll (NY)
Miami U (OH)
Michigan State U (MI)
Midwestern State U (TX)
Millersville U of Pennsylvania (PA)
Milligan Coll (TN)
Minot State U (ND)
Misericordia U (PA)
Mississippi State U (MS)
Missouri Southern State U (MO)
Missouri Western State U (MO)
Molloy Coll (NY)
Monmouth U (NJ)
Montclair State U (NJ)
Montreat Coll, Montreat (NC)
Morehead State U (KY)
Morrisville State Coll (NY)
Mount St. Mary's U (MD)
National U (CA)
Neumann U (PA)
Neumont U (UT)
New England Coll (NH)
New England Inst of Technology (RI)
New Jersey City U (NJ)
New Jersey Inst of Technology (NJ)
New Mexico Highlands U (NM)
New Mexico State U (NM)
New York Inst of Technology (NY)
New York U (NY)
Norfolk State U (VA)
North Carolina Wesleyan Coll (NC)
Northeastern Illinois U (IL)
Northeastern U (MA)
Northern Kentucky U (KY)
Northern Michigan U (MI)
Northwestern U (IL)
Northwest Missouri State U (MO)
Northwood U, Michigan Campus (MI)
Nova Southeastern U (FL)
Oakland U (MI)
The Ohio State U (OH)
Ohio U (OH)
Oklahoma Baptist U (OK)
Oklahoma City U (OK)
Oklahoma State U (OK)
Old Dominion U (VA)
Olivet Coll (MI)
Our Lady of the Lake U of San Antonio (TX)
Pace U (NY)
Park U (MO)
Penn State Abington (PA)
Penn State Altoona (PA)
Penn State Beaver (PA)
Penn State Berks (PA)
Penn State Brandywine (PA)
Penn State DuBois (PA)
Penn State Erie, The Behrend Coll (PA)
Penn State Fayette, The Eberly Campus (PA)
Penn State Greater Allegheny (PA)
Penn State Harrisburg (PA)
Penn State Hazleton (PA)
Penn State Lehigh Valley (PA)
Penn State Mont Alto (PA)
Penn State New Kensington (PA)
Penn State Schuylkill (PA)
Penn State Shenango (PA)
Penn State U Park (PA)
Penn State Wilkes-Barre (PA)
Penn State Worthington Scranton (PA)
Penn State York (PA)
Philadelphia U (PA)
Pittsburg State U (KS)
Polytechnic U of Puerto Rico (PR)
Portland State U (OR)
Prairie View A&M U (TX)
Principia Coll (IL)
Ramapo Coll of New Jersey (NJ)
Regis U (CO)
Rhode Island Coll (RI)
Rice U (TX)
Rider U (NJ)
Roanoke Coll (VA)
Rochester Inst of Technology (NY)
Rollins Coll (FL)
Rutgers, The State U of New Jersey, Camden (NJ)
Rutgers, The State U of New Jersey, Newark (NJ)
Sacred Heart U (CT)
Saginaw Valley State U (MI)
Saint Augustine's U (NC)
St. Bonaventure U (NY)
St. Catherine U (MN)
St. Edward's U (TX)
St. John Fisher Coll (NY)
St. John's U (NY)
Saint Joseph's Coll (IN)
Saint Joseph's U (PA)
St. Lawrence U (NY)
Saint Leo U (FL)
Saint Louis U (MO)
Saint Mary-of-the-Woods Coll (IN)
St. Mary's Coll of Maryland (MD)
St. Norbert Coll (WI)
Saint Peter's U (NJ)
St. Thomas Aquinas Coll (NY)
Saint Vincent Coll (PA)
Salisbury U (MD)
Sam Houston State U (TX)
Shaw U (NC)
Shepherd U (WV)
Shippensburg U of Pennsylvania (PA)
Siena Coll (NY)
Siena Heights U (MI)
Simmons Coll (MA)
Simpson Coll (IA)
Skidmore Coll (NY)
South Carolina State U (SC)
South Dakota State U (SD)
Southeastern Oklahoma State U (OK)
Southeast Missouri State U (MO)
Southern Arkansas U–Magnolia (AR)
Southern New Hampshire U (NH)
Southern Utah U (UT)
Southwest Baptist U (MO)
Southwestern U (TX)
Spring Hill Coll (AL)
State U of New York at New Paltz (NY)
State U of New York at Plattsburgh (NY)
State U of New York Coll at Old Westbury (NY)
State U of New York Polytechnic Inst (NY)
Stephen F. Austin State U (TX)
Sterling Coll (KS)
Stetson U (FL)
Stevenson U (MD)
Stony Brook U, State U of New York (NY)
Suffolk U (MA)
Syracuse U (NY)
Tarleton State U (TX)
Taylor U (IN)
Temple U (PA)
Tennessee Wesleyan Coll (TN)
Texas A&M U–Commerce (TX)
Texas A&M U–Kingsville (TX)
Texas Christian U (TX)
Texas Southern U (TX)
Texas State U (TX)
Texas Tech U (TX)
Texas Woman's U (TX)
Tiffin U (OH)
Towson U (MD)
Transylvania U (KY)
Trinity Christian Coll (IL)
Trinity U (TX)
Troy U (AL)
Truman State U (MO)
Tufts U (MA)
Tulane U (LA)
Union Coll (NE)
Union Coll (NY)
United States Military Acad (NY)
United States Naval Acad (MD)
Universidad del Turabo (PR)
U at Albany, State U of New York (NY)
The U of Alabama (AL)
The U of Alabama at Birmingham (AL)
The U of Alabama in Huntsville (AL)
U of Alaska Fairbanks (AK)
The U of Arizona (AZ)
U of Arkansas (AR)

U of Arkansas–Fort Smith (AR)
U of California, Irvine (CA)
U of California, Los Angeles (CA)
U of Central Arkansas (AR)
U of Central Florida (FL)
U of Central Missouri (MO)
U of Central Oklahoma (OK)
U of Cincinnati (OH)
U of Colorado Colorado Springs (CO)
U of Colorado Denver (CO)
U of Dayton (OH)
U of Delaware (DE)
U of Dubuque (IA)
U of Florida (FL)
U of Great Falls (MT)
U of Hartford (CT)
U of Hawaii at Manoa (HI)
U of Houston (TX)
U of Houston–Clear Lake (TX)
U of Houston–Downtown (TX)
The U of Kansas (KS)
U of Kentucky (KY)
U of Louisiana at Lafayette (LA)
U of Maine at Augusta (ME)
U of Mary Hardin-Baylor (TX)
U of Maryland, Coll Park (MD)
U of Maryland U Coll (MD)
U of Mary Washington (VA)
U of Massachusetts Boston (MA)
U of Massachusetts Dartmouth (MA)
U of Michigan (MI)
U of Michigan–Dearborn (MI)
U of Mississippi (MS)
U of Missouri (MO)
U of Mobile (AL)
The U of Montana (MT)
U of Nebraska at Kearney (NE)
U of Nebraska–Lincoln (NE)
U of Nevada, Reno (NV)
U of New Hampshire (NH)
U of New Haven (CT)
U of New Mexico (NM)
U of North Alabama (AL)
U of North Dakota (ND)
U of North Florida (FL)
U of North Georgia (GA)
U of North Texas (TX)
U of Notre Dame (IN)
U of Oregon (OR)
U of Ottawa (ON, Canada)
U of Pikeville (KY)
U of Pittsburgh at Greensburg (PA)
U of Puerto Rico in Ponce (PR)
U of Rhode Island (RI)
U of Richmond (VA)
U of Saint Mary (KS)
U of San Francisco (CA)
U of South Carolina Upstate (SC)
The U of South Dakota (SD)
U of Southern Indiana (IN)
U of Southern Mississippi (MS)
U of South Florida (FL)
The U of Tampa (FL)
The U of Texas at Austin (TX)
The U of Texas at Dallas (TX)
The U of Texas at San Antonio (TX)
The U of Texas at Tyler (TX)
The U of Texas of the Permian Basin (TX)
U of the Fraser Valley (BC, Canada)
U of the Incarnate Word (TX)
U of Vermont (VT)
U of Virginia (VA)
The U of Virginia's Coll at Wise (VA)
U of Washington, Bothell (WA)
U of Washington, Tacoma (WA)
The U of Western Ontario (ON, Canada)
U of West Florida (FL)
U of West Georgia (GA)
U of Windsor (ON, Canada)
U of Wisconsin–Eau Claire (WI)
U of Wisconsin–La Crosse (WI)
U of Wisconsin–Madison (WI)
U of Wisconsin–Milwaukee (WI)
U of Wisconsin–River Falls (WI)
U of Wisconsin–Stevens Point (WI)
U of Wisconsin–Superior (WI)
U of Wisconsin–Whitewater (WI)
Utah State U (UT)
Utica Coll (NY)
Valdosta State U (GA)
Valley City State U (ND)
Vassar Coll (NY)
Virginia Commonwealth U (VA)
Virginia Polytechnic Inst and State U (VA)
Wake Forest U (NC)
Walden U (MN)
Walsh Coll of Accountancy and Business Administration (MI)
Wartburg Coll (IA)
Washburn U (KS)
Washington State U (WA)
Washington U in St. Louis (MO)
Waynesburg U (PA)
Wayne State Coll (NE)
Wayne State U (MI)
Webber Intl U (FL)
Weber State U (UT)
Webster U (MO)
West Chester U of Pennsylvania (PA)
Western Illinois U (IL)
Western Kentucky U (KY)
Western Michigan U (MI)
Western Washington U (WA)
Westminster Coll (UT)
West Texas A&M U (TX)
West Virginia U Inst of Technology (WV)
West Virginia Wesleyan Coll (WV)
Wheeling Jesuit U (WV)
Widener U (PA)
Wilkes U (PA)
William Jessup U (CA)
William Penn U (IA)
Williams Baptist Coll (AR)
Worcester Polytechnic Inst (MA)
Worcester State U (MA)
Wright State U (OH)
Xavier U of Louisiana (LA)
Yale U (CT)
Yeshiva U (NY)
Youngstown State U (OH)

COMPUTER AND INFORMATION SCIENCES AND SUPPORT SERVICES RELATED

Amridge U (AL)
Arizona State U at the West campus (AZ)
Cabrini Coll (PA)
California State U, Los Angeles (CA)
Capitol Technology U (MD)
Champlain Coll (VT)
Coll of Staten Island of the City U of New York (NY)
Columbia Coll Chicago (IL)
DePaul U (IL)
Ferris State U (MI)
Hofstra U (NY)
Indiana U–Purdue U Indianapolis (IN)
Inter American U of Puerto Rico, Guayama Campus (PR)
Keene State Coll (NH)
Lehigh U (PA)
Limestone Coll (SC)
Long Island U–LIU Post (NY)
Mayville State U (ND)
Missouri U of Science and Technology (MO)
Morrisville State Coll (NY)
National U (CA)
Northern Kentucky U (KY)
Park U (MO)
Purdue U Calumet (IN)
Roberts Wesleyan Coll (NY)
Southern Adventist U (TN)
State U of New York Coll of Agriculture and Technology at Cobleskill (NY)
Tiffin U (OH)
U of Great Falls (MT)
U of Mount Union (OH)
U of New Hampshire (NH)
U of Northern Iowa (IA)
U of Notre Dame (IN)
U of Pittsburgh (PA)
U of Washington, Bothell (WA)
Utah State U (UT)
Valley City State U (ND)
Washington U in St. Louis (MO)
Western Governors U (UT)

COMPUTER AND INFORMATION SCIENCES RELATED

California State U, Dominguez Hills (CA)
California State U, Monterey Bay (CA)
Coll of Charleston (SC)
The Colorado Coll (CO)
Columbia U, School of General Studies (NY)
Eastern Illinois U (IL)
Granite State Coll (NH)
Kansas Wesleyan U (KS)
Limestone Coll (SC)
Maryville Coll (TN)
Missouri State U (MO)
Neumont U (UT)
Northern Kentucky U (KY)
Taylor U (IN)
Temple U (PA)
Université de Sherbrooke (QC, Canada)
U of Great Falls (MT)
U of Windsor (ON, Canada)
U of Wisconsin–Stout (WI)
Wagner Coll (NY)
West Virginia U (WV)

COMPUTER AND INFORMATION SYSTEMS SECURITY

Bay Path U (MA)
Central Washington U (WA)
Charter Oak State Coll (CT)
Columbia Southern U (AL)
Dakota State U (SD)
Davenport U, Grand Rapids (MI)
DePaul U (IL)
Donnelly Coll (KS)
Drexel U (PA)
East Stroudsburg U of Pennsylvania (PA)
Ferris State U (MI)
Franklin U (OH)
Frostburg State U (MD)
Hilbert Coll (NY)
Kennesaw State U (GA)
LeTourneau U (TX)
Lewis U (IL)
Limestone Coll (SC)
Lindenwood U (MO)
Lipscomb U (TN)
Loyola U Chicago (IL)
Marshall U (WV)
Marywood U (PA)
Mercy Coll (NY)
Metropolitan State U (MN)
Neumont U (UT)
Oklahoma State U Inst of Technology (OK)
Pennsylvania Coll of Technology (PA)
Rasmussen Coll Appleton (WI)
Rasmussen Coll Bismarck (ND)
Rasmussen Coll Blaine (MN)
Rasmussen Coll Bloomington (MN)
Rasmussen Coll Brooklyn Park (MN)
Rasmussen Coll Eagan (MN)
Rasmussen Coll Fargo (ND)
Rasmussen Coll Fort Myers (FL)
Rasmussen Coll Green Bay (WI)
Rasmussen Coll Kansas City/Overland Park (KS)
Rasmussen Coll Lake Elmo/Woodbury (MN)
Rasmussen Coll Land O' Lakes (FL)
Rasmussen Coll Mankato (MN)
Rasmussen Coll Moorhead (MN)
Rasmussen Coll New Port Richey (FL)
Rasmussen Coll Ocala (FL)
Rasmussen Coll St. Cloud (MN)
Rasmussen Coll Tampa/Brandon (FL)
Rasmussen Coll Topeka (KS)
Rasmussen Coll Wausau (WI)
Rochester Inst of Technology (NY)
St. John's U (NY)
Southeast Missouri State U (MO)
State U of New York Coll of Technology at Alfred (NY)
State U of New York Polytechnic Inst (NY)
Stratford U, Woodbridge (VA)
Sullivan Coll of Technology and Design (KY)
U of Cincinnati (OH)
U of Colorado Colorado Springs (CO)
U of Great Falls (MT)
U of Illinois at Springfield (IL)
U of Maryland U Coll (MD)
U of Miami (FL)
U of South Alabama (AL)
The U of Texas at San Antonio (TX)
Walla Walla U (WA)
Weber State U (UT)
Wilmington U (DE)

COMPUTER ENGINEERING

The American U in Dubai (United Arab Emirates)
American U of Beirut (Lebanon)
Arizona State U at the Tempe campus (AZ)
Auburn U (AL)
Bethune-Cookman U (FL)
Binghamton U, State U of New York (NY)
Boston U (MA)
Bradley U (IL)
Brown U (RI)
Bucknell U (PA)
California Baptist U (CA)
California Inst of Technology (CA)
California Polytechnic State U, San Luis Obispo (CA)
California State Polytechnic U, Pomona (CA)
California State U, Chico (CA)
California State U, Fresno (CA)
California State U, Fullerton (CA)
California State U, Long Beach (CA)
California State U, Sacramento (CA)
California State U, San Bernardino (CA)
Capital U (OH)
Capitol Technology U (MD)
Case Western Reserve U (OH)
Cedarville U (OH)
Central Michigan U (MI)
Christian Brothers U (TN)
Christopher Newport U (VA)
Claflin U (SC)
Clarkson U (NY)
Cleveland State U (OH)
The Coll of New Jersey (NJ)
Colorado State U (CO)
Columbia U (NY)
Concordia U (QC, Canada)
DigiPen Inst of Technology (WA)
Drexel U (PA)
Elizabethtown Coll (PA)
Elon U (NC)
Embry-Riddle Aeronautical U–Daytona (FL)
Embry-Riddle Aeronautical U–Prescott (AZ)
Fairfield U (CT)
Florida Ag and Mech U (FL)
Florida Atlantic U (FL)
Florida Inst of Technology (FL)
Florida Intl U (FL)
George Mason U (VA)
The George Washington U (DC)
Georgia Inst of Technology (GA)
Gonzaga U (WA)
Harding U (AR)
Hofstra U (NY)
Howard U (DC)
Illinois Inst of Technology (IL)
Indiana U–Purdue U Fort Wayne (IN)
Indiana U–Purdue U Indianapolis (IN)
Inter American U of Puerto Rico, Bayamón Campus (PR)
Iowa State U of Science and Technology (IA)
Jackson State U (MS)
Johns Hopkins U (MD)
Johnson & Wales U (RI)
Johnson C. Smith U (NC)
Kansas State U (KS)
Kettering U (MI)
Lawrence Technological U (MI)
Lebanese American U (Lebanon)
Lehigh U (PA)
LeTourneau U (TX)
Lewis U (IL)
Liberty U (VA)
Lipscomb U (TN)
Louisiana State U and A&M Coll (LA)
Manhattan Coll (NY)
Marquette U (WI)
Miami U (OH)
Michigan State U (MI)
Michigan Technological U (MI)
Midwestern State U (TX)
Milwaukee School of Eng (WI)
Minnesota State U Mankato (MN)
Mississippi State U (MS)
Missouri U of Science and Technology (MO)
Montana State U (MT)
New England Inst of Technology (RI)
New Jersey Inst of Technology (NJ)
New York Inst of Technology (NY)
New York U (NY)
North Carolina Ag and Tech State U (NC)
North Carolina State U (NC)
North Dakota State U (ND)
Northeastern U (MA)
Northwestern U (IL)
Norwich U (VT)
Oakland U (MI)
Ohio Northern U (OH)
The Ohio State U (OH)
Oklahoma Christian U (OK)
Oklahoma State U (OK)
Old Dominion U (VA)
Pacific Lutheran U (WA)
Penn State Abington (PA)
Penn State Altoona (PA)
Penn State Beaver (PA)
Penn State Berks (PA)
Penn State Brandywine (PA)
Penn State DuBois (PA)
Penn State Erie, The Behrend Coll (PA)
Penn State Fayette, The Eberly Campus (PA)
Penn State Greater Allegheny (PA)
Penn State Hazleton (PA)
Penn State Lehigh Valley (PA)
Penn State Mont Alto (PA)
Penn State New Kensington (PA)
Penn State Schuylkill (PA)
Penn State Shenango (PA)
Penn State U Park (PA)
Penn State Wilkes-Barre (PA)
Penn State Worthington Scranton (PA)
Penn State York (PA)
Polytechnic U of Puerto Rico (PR)
Portland State U (OR)
Princeton U (NJ)
Purdue U (IN)
Purdue U Calumet (IN)
Rice U (TX)
Rochester Inst of Technology (NY)
Rose-Hulman Inst of Technology (IN)
Rutgers, The State U of New Jersey, New Brunswick (NJ)
Saint Louis U (MO)
St. Mary's U (TX)
San Diego State U (CA)
San Francisco State U (CA)
San Jose State U (CA)
Santa Clara U (CA)
Shepherd U (WV)
South Dakota School of Mines and Technology (SD)
Southern Illinois U Carbondale (IL)
Southern Illinois U Edwardsville (IL)
Southern Methodist U (TX)
State U of New York at New Paltz (NY)
Stony Brook U, State U of New York (NY)
Suffolk U (MA)
Syracuse U (NY)
Taylor U (IN)
Texas A&M U (TX)
Texas Tech U (TX)
Trine U (IN)
Trinity Coll (CT)
Tufts U (MA)
Universidad del Turabo (PR)
Université de Sherbrooke (QC, Canada)

Université du Québec en Outaouais (QC, Canada)
U at Buffalo, the State U of New York (NY)
The U of Akron (OH)
The U of Alabama in Huntsville (AL)
U of Alaska Fairbanks (AK)
U of Arkansas (AR)
U of Bridgeport (CT)
The U of British Columbia (BC, Canada)
U of California, Irvine (CA)
U of California, Los Angeles (CA)
U of California, Merced (CA)
U of California, Riverside (CA)
U of California, Santa Barbara (CA)
U of California, Santa Cruz (CA)
U of Central Florida (FL)
U of Cincinnati (OH)
U of Colorado Boulder (CO)
U of Colorado Colorado Springs (CO)
U of Dayton (OH)
U of Delaware (DE)
U of Denver (CO)
U of Evansville (IN)
U of Florida (FL)
U of Georgia (GA)
U of Guelph (ON, Canada)
U of Hartford (CT)
U of Houston (TX)
U of Houston–Clear Lake (TX)
U of Idaho (ID)
U of Illinois at Chicago (IL)
U of Indianapolis (IN)
The U of Kansas (KS)
U of Kentucky (KY)
U of La Verne (CA)
U of Louisiana at Lafayette (LA)
U of Louisville (KY)
U of Maine (ME)
U of Maryland, Baltimore County (MD)
U of Maryland, Coll Park (MD)
U of Massachusetts Amherst (MA)
U of Massachusetts Boston (MA)
U of Massachusetts Dartmouth (MA)
U of Massachusetts Lowell (MA)
U of Memphis (TN)
U of Miami (FL)
U of Michigan (MI)
U of Minnesota, Twin Cities Campus (MN)
U of Missouri (MO)
U of Nebraska–Lincoln (NE)
U of Nevada, Las Vegas (NV)
U of Nevada, Reno (NV)
U of New Hampshire (NH)
U of New Haven (CT)
U of New Mexico (NM)
The U of North Carolina at Charlotte (NC)
U of Notre Dame (IN)
U of Oklahoma (OK)
U of Ottawa (ON, Canada)
U of Pennsylvania (PA)
U of Pittsburgh (PA)
U of Portland (OR)
U of Rhode Island (RI)
U of Saskatchewan (SK, Canada)
The U of Scranton (PA)
U of South Alabama (AL)
U of Southern California (CA)
U of South Florida (FL)
The U of Tennessee (TN)
The U of Texas at Arlington (TX)
The U of Texas at Dallas (TX)
The U of Texas at San Antonio (TX)
The U of Texas–Pan American (TX)
U of the Pacific (CA)
U of Toledo (OH)
U of Toronto (ON, Canada)
The U of Tulsa (OK)
U of Utah (UT)
U of Virginia (VA)
U of Washington (WA)
U of Washington, Bothell (WA)
U of Waterloo (ON, Canada)
The U of Western Ontario (ON, Canada)
U of West Florida (FL)
U of Wisconsin–Madison (WI)
U of Wisconsin–Milwaukee (WI)
U of Wisconsin–Stout (WI)
U of Wyoming (WY)
Utah State U (UT)
Valparaiso U (IN)
Vanderbilt U (TN)
Villanova U (PA)
Virginia Commonwealth U (VA)
Virginia Polytechnic Inst and State U (VA)
Virginia State U (VA)
Walla Walla U (WA)
Washington State U (WA)
Washington U in St. Louis (MO)
Wentworth Inst of Technology (MA)
Western Michigan U (MI)
Western New England U (MA)
West Virginia U (WV)
West Virginia U Inst of Technology (WV)
Wichita State U (KS)
Wilberforce U (OH)
Worcester Polytechnic Inst (MA)
Wright State U (OH)
Xavier U of Louisiana (LA)
York Coll of Pennsylvania (PA)

COMPUTER ENGINEERING RELATED
Auburn U (AL)
Ohio Northern U (OH)

COMPUTER ENGINEERING TECHNOLOGIES RELATED
Eastern Kentucky U (KY)
Inter American U of Puerto Rico, Bayamón Campus (PR)
U of Guelph (ON, Canada)

COMPUTER ENGINEERING TECHNOLOGY
Arizona State U at the Polytechnic campus (AZ)
Bowling Green State U (OH)
California State U, Long Beach (CA)
California U of Pennsylvania (PA)
Capitol Technology U (MD)
Central Connecticut State U (CT)
Central Washington U (WA)
DeVry Coll of New York (NY)
DeVry U, Phoenix (AZ)
DeVry U, Pomona (CA)
DeVry U, Westminster (CO)
DeVry U, Miramar (FL)
DeVry U, Orlando (FL)
DeVry U, Decatur (GA)
DeVry U, Chicago (IL)
DeVry U, Kansas City (MO)
DeVry U, Columbus (OH)
DeVry U, Fort Washington (PA)
DeVry U, Houston (TX)
DeVry U, Irving (TX)
DeVry U, Arlington (VA)
DeVry U, Federal Way (WA)
DeVry U Online (IL)
Eastern Michigan U (MI)
Farmingdale State Coll (NY)
Indiana State U (IN)
Indiana U–Purdue U Fort Wayne (IN)
Indiana U–Purdue U Indianapolis (IN)
LeTourneau U (TX)
Minnesota State U Mankato (MN)
Missouri Western State U (MO)
New York City Coll of Technology of the City U of New York (NY)
Norfolk State U (VA)
Rochester Inst of Technology (NY)
Sam Houston State U (TX)
Savannah State U (GA)
Shawnee State U (OH)
State U of New York Coll of Technology at Alfred (NY)
State U of New York Polytechnic Inst (NY)
Texas Southern U (TX)
U of Arkansas at Little Rock (AR)
U of Cincinnati (OH)
U of Hartford (CT)
U of Houston (TX)
U of Houston–Downtown (TX)
U of Memphis (TN)
U of Southern Mississippi (MS)
Utah State U (UT)
Vermont Tech Coll (VT)
Weber State U (UT)
Wentworth Inst of Technology (MA)

COMPUTER GRAPHICS
American Acad of Art (IL)
The Art Inst of Cincinnati (OH)
Baker Coll (MI)
Becker Coll (MA)
Bowie State U (MD)
California State U, Chico (CA)
Champlain Coll (VT)
Coll of the Atlantic (ME)
Concordia U (QC, Canada)
Dakota State U (SD)
DePaul U (IL)
Dixie State U (UT)
John Brown U (AR)
Lindenwood U (MO)
Los Angeles Film School (CA)
New York Inst of Technology (NY)
Oakland City U (IN)
Pratt Inst (NY)
Purdue U (IN)
Purdue U Calumet (IN)
Rochester Inst of Technology (NY)
Rocky Mountain Coll of Art + Design (CO)
School of the Art Inst of Chicago (IL)
School of the Museum of Fine Arts, Boston (MA)
Southern New Hampshire U (NH)
State U of New York at Fredonia (NY)
Sullivan Coll of Technology and Design (KY)
Texas A&M U (TX)
U of California, Santa Cruz (CA)
U of Dubuque (IA)
U of Great Falls (MT)
U of Houston (TX)
U of Mary Hardin-Baylor (TX)
U of Miami (FL)
U of Pennsylvania (PA)
Wilmington U (DE)

COMPUTER HARDWARE ENGINEERING
Auburn U (AL)
United States Naval Acad (MD)
Utah Valley U (UT)

COMPUTER/INFORMATION TECHNOLOGY SERVICES ADMINISTRATION RELATED
Anna Maria Coll (MA)
Berkeley Coll, Woodland Park (NJ)
Berkeley Coll–New York City Campus (NY)
Bloomsburg U of Pennsylvania (PA)
Champlain Coll (VT)
Chestnut Hill Coll (PA)
Concordia U, St. Paul (MN)
Dalhousie U (NS, Canada)
Florida State Coll at Jacksonville (FL)
Friends U (KS)
Frostburg State U (MD)
Granite State Coll (NH)
Hodges U (FL)
Limestone Coll (SC)
Marywood U (PA)
Missouri State U (MO)
National U (CA)
Robert Morris U (PA)
St. Francis Coll (NY)
St. Joseph's Coll, Long Island Campus (NY)
St. Joseph's Coll, New York (NY)
U of Great Falls (MT)
U of Guam (GU)
U of Maryland, Baltimore County (MD)
Washington U in St. Louis (MO)

COMPUTER INSTALLATION AND REPAIR TECHNOLOGY
Inter American U of Puerto Rico, Bayamón Campus (PR)

COMPUTER PROGRAMMING
Andrews U (MI)
Arcadia U (PA)
Baker Coll (MI)
Belmont U (TN)
Bowling Green State U (OH)
Capitol Technology U (MD)
Caribbean U (PR)
Champlain Coll (VT)
The Coll of Saint Rose (NY)
Creighton U (NE)
DePaul U (IL)
EDP U of Puerto Rico (PR)
EDP U of Puerto Rico–San Sebastian (PR)
Farmingdale State Coll (NY)
Franklin Pierce U (NH)
Gannon U (PA)
Hardin-Simmons U (TX)
Inter American U of Puerto Rico, San Germán Campus (PR)
Intl Business Coll, Fort Wayne (IN)
La Salle U (PA)
Le Moyne Coll (NY)
Limestone Coll (SC)
Morrisville State Coll (NY)
Neumont U (UT)
New England Inst of Technology (RI)
Saint Francis U (PA)
Southeast Missouri State U (MO)
Tufts U (MA)
Université de Sherbrooke (QC, Canada)
The U of Akron (OH)
U of Great Falls (MT)
U of Michigan–Dearborn (MI)
U of Mount Union (OH)
The U of Western Ontario (ON, Canada)
Walla Walla U (WA)
Youngstown State U (OH)

COMPUTER PROGRAMMING RELATED
Curry Coll (MA)
Neumont U (UT)
The U of Akron (OH)

COMPUTER PROGRAMMING (SPECIFIC APPLICATIONS)
Acad of Art U (CA)
DePaul U (IL)
DigiPen Inst of Technology (WA)
Neumont U (UT)
U of Alberta (AB, Canada)
U of Washington, Bothell (WA)
U of Windsor (ON, Canada)
Yale U (CT)

COMPUTER PROGRAMMING (VENDOR/PRODUCT CERTIFICATION)
Neumont U (UT)

COMPUTER SCIENCE
Abilene Christian U (TX)
Adams State U (CO)
Alabama State U (AL)
Albright Coll (PA)
Allegheny Coll (PA)
Alma Coll (MI)
American Coll of Thessaloniki (Greece)
The American U in Cairo (Egypt)
American U of Beirut (Lebanon)
The American U of Paris (France)
Amherst Coll (MA)
Anderson U (IN)
Andrews U (MI)
Appalachian State U (NC)
Arcadia U (PA)
Arizona State U at the Tempe campus (AZ)
Ashland U (OH)
Athens State U (AL)
Auburn U at Montgomery (AL)
Augsburg Coll (MN)
Augustana Coll (IL)
Augustana Coll (SD)
Austin Coll (TX)
Azusa Pacific U (CA)
Baker Coll (MI)
Baker U (KS)
Baldwin Wallace U (OH)
Bard Coll (NY)
Bard Coll at Simon's Rock (MA)
Barry U (FL)
Baylor U (TX)
Belmont U (TN)
Beloit Coll (WI)
Bemidji State U (MN)
Benedictine Coll (KS)
Benedictine U (IL)
Bennett Coll (NC)
Bennington Coll (VT)
Bethany Coll (WV)
Bethune-Cookman U (FL)
Binghamton U, State U of New York (NY)
Biola U (CA)
Blackburn Coll (IL)
Bloomsburg U of Pennsylvania (PA)
Bob Jones U (SC)
Boston Coll (MA)
Boston U (MA)
Bowdoin Coll (ME)
Bradley U (IL)
Brandeis U (MA)
Bridgewater Coll (VA)
Bridgewater State U (MA)
Brown U (RI)
Buena Vista U (IA)
California Baptist U (CA)
California Lutheran U (CA)
California Polytechnic State U, San Luis Obispo (CA)
California State Polytechnic U, Pomona (CA)
California State U, Chico (CA)
California State U, Dominguez Hills (CA)
California State U, Fresno (CA)
California State U, Fullerton (CA)
California State U, Long Beach (CA)
California State U, Los Angeles (CA)
California State U, Sacramento (CA)
California State U, San Bernardino (CA)
California State U, San Marcos (CA)
California State U, Stanislaus (CA)
Calvary Bible Coll and Theological Sem (MO)
Calvin Coll (MI)
Cameron U (OK)
Canisius Coll (NY)
Capital U (OH)
Cardinal Stritch U (WI)
Carleton Coll (MN)
Carroll Coll (MT)
Case Western Reserve U (OH)
The Catholic U of America (DC)
Cedarville U (OH)
Central Coll (IA)
Central Methodist U (MO)
Central Michigan U (MI)
Central Penn Coll (PA)
Central State U (OH)
Central Washington U (WA)
Centre Coll (KY)
Chaminade U of Honolulu (HI)
Champlain Coll (VT)
Chapman U (CA)
Charleston Southern U (SC)
Chicago State U (IL)
Christian Brothers U (TN)
Christopher Newport U (VA)
City Coll of the City U of New York (NY)
Claflin U (SC)
Clark Atlanta U (GA)
Clarkson U (NY)
Clark U (MA)
Clayton State U (GA)
Coe Coll (IA)
Coker Coll (SC)
Colby Coll (ME)
CollAmerica–Flagstaff (AZ)
Coll of Saint Benedict (MN)
Coll of Saint Elizabeth (NJ)
Coll of Staten Island of the City U of New York (NY)
Coll of the Holy Cross (MA)
Coll of the Ozarks (MO)
The Coll of Wooster (OH)
Colorado School of Mines (CO)
Columbia Coll (MO)
Columbia U (NY)
Columbia U, School of General Studies (NY)
Concordia U (QC, Canada)
Concordia U, Nebraska (NE)
Concordia U Texas (TX)
Concordia U Wisconsin (WI)
Concord U (WV)
Connecticut Coll (CT)
Cornell Coll (IA)
Cornell U (NY)
Creighton U (NE)
Dalhousie U (NS, Canada)
Dallas Baptist U (TX)
Daniel Webster Coll (NH)
Dartmouth Coll (NH)
Delaware State U (DE)

Denison U (OH)
DePaul U (IL)
DePauw U (IN)
DeSales U (PA)
Dickinson State U (ND)
Dixie State U (UT)
Doane Coll (NE)
Dominican U (IL)
Dowling Coll (NY)
Drake U (IA)
Drew U (NJ)
Drexel U (PA)
Drury U (MO)
Dunwoody Coll of Technology (MN)
Duquesne U (PA)
East Carolina U (NC)
Eastern Kentucky U (KY)
Eastern Michigan U (MI)
Eckerd Coll (FL)
Elmhurst Coll (IL)
Elon U (NC)
Embry-Riddle Aeronautical U–Daytona (FL)
Endicott Coll (MA)
Eureka Coll (IL)
Evangel U (MO)
Fairleigh Dickinson U, Metropolitan Campus (NJ)
Fairmont State U (WV)
Fayetteville State U (NC)
Fitchburg State U (MA)
Florida Inst of Technology (FL)
Florida Southern Coll (FL)
Fontbonne U (MO)
Fordham U (NY)
Fort Hays State U (KS)
Franciscan U of Steubenville (OH)
Franklin Coll (IN)
Franklin Pierce U (NH)
Franklin U (OH)
Frostburg State U (MD)
Furman U (SC)
George Mason U (VA)
Georgetown Coll (KY)
Georgetown U (DC)
The George Washington U (DC)
Georgia Coll & State U (GA)
Georgia Southwestern State U (GA)
Georgia State U (GA)
Gettysburg Coll (PA)
Gonzaga U (WA)
Gordon Coll (MA)
Goucher Coll (MD)
Governors State U (IL)
Graceland U (IA)
Grambling State U (LA)
Grand View U (IA)
Grinnell Coll (IA)
Grove City Coll (PA)
Gustavus Adolphus Coll (MN)
Hampden-Sydney Coll (VA)
Hampshire Coll (MA)
Hampton U (VA)
Hanover Coll (IN)
Harding U (AR)
Hartwick Coll (NY)
Harvard U (MA)
Harvey Mudd Coll (CA)
Hastings Coll (NE)
Haverford Coll (PA)
Hawai`i Pacific U (HI)
Heidelberg U (OH)
Hendrix Coll (AR)
Heritage U (WA)
High Point U (NC)
Hiram Coll (OH)
Hobart and William Smith Colls (NY)
Hofstra U (NY)
Houghton Coll (NY)
Howard U (DC)
Humboldt State U (CA)
Hunter Coll of the City U of New York (NY)
Huston-Tillotson U (TX)
Illinois Coll (IL)
Illinois Inst of Technology (IL)
Illinois State U (IL)
Illinois Wesleyan U (IL)
Indiana U Bloomington (IN)
Indiana U Northwest (IN)
Indiana U–Purdue U Indianapolis (IN)
Indiana U South Bend (IN)
Indiana U Southeast (IN)
Inter American U of Puerto Rico, Aguadilla Campus (PR)
Inter American U of Puerto Rico, Bayamón Campus (PR)
Inter American U of Puerto Rico, Ponce Campus (PR)
Inter American U of Puerto Rico, San Germán Campus (PR)
Iona Coll (NY)
Ithaca Coll (NY)
John Carroll U (OH)
Kennesaw State U (GA)
Kettering U (MI)
King's Coll (PA)
The King's U Coll (AB, Canada)
King U (TN)
Knox Coll (IL)
Lafayette Coll (PA)
Lake Forest Coll (IL)
Landmark Coll (VT)
Langston U (OK)
La Roche Coll (PA)
La Salle U (PA)
La Sierra U (CA)
Lawrence Technological U (MI)
Lawrence U (WI)
Lebanese American U (Lebanon)
Lebanon Valley Coll (PA)
Lehigh U (PA)
Lehman Coll of the City U of New York (NY)
LeMoyne-Owen Coll (TN)
LeTourneau U (TX)
Lewis & Clark Coll (OR)
Lewis U (IL)
Limestone Coll (SC)
Lindenwood U (MO)
Linfield Coll (OR)
Lipscomb U (TN)
Lock Haven U of Pennsylvania (PA)
Long Island U–LIU Post (NY)
Longwood U (VA)
Loras Coll (IA)
Louisiana State U and A&M Coll (LA)
Louisiana State U in Shreveport (LA)
Luther Coll (IA)
Lynchburg Coll (VA)
Madonna U (MI)
Maharishi U of Management (IA)
Malone U (OH)
Manchester U (IN)
Manhattan Coll (NY)
Manhattanville Coll (NY)
Mansfield U of Pennsylvania (PA)
Marietta Coll (OH)
Marist Coll (NY)
Mars Hill U (NC)
Marywood U (PA)
Massachusetts Coll of Liberal Arts (MA)
Massachusetts Inst of Technology (MA)
McKendree U (IL)
McNeese State U (LA)
Mercer U, Macon (GA)
Mercy Coll (NY)
Meredith Coll (NC)
Merrimack Coll (MA)
Messiah Coll (PA)
Metropolitan State U (MN)
Michigan Technological U (MI)
Middlebury Coll (VT)
Middle Tennessee State U (TN)
Milligan Coll (TN)
Millsaps Coll (MS)
Mills Coll (CA)
Minnesota State U Moorhead (MN)
Minot State U (ND)
Mississippi Valley State U (MS)
Missouri State U (MO)
Missouri U of Science and Technology (MO)
Missouri Valley Coll (MO)
Monmouth Coll (IL)
Montana State U (MT)
Montana Tech of The U of Montana (MT)
Moravian Coll (PA)
Mount Allison U (NB, Canada)
Mount Holyoke Coll (MA)
Mount Marty Coll (SD)
Mount Vernon Nazarene U (OH)
Murray State U (KY)
National U (CA)
Neumont U (UT)
Newbury Coll (MA)
New England Inst of Technology (RI)
New Jersey Inst of Technology (NJ)
New Mexico Inst of Mining and Technology (NM)
Niagara U (NY)
North Carolina Ag and Tech State U (NC)
North Carolina State U (NC)
North Central Coll (IL)
North Dakota State U (ND)
Northeastern Illinois U (IL)
Northeastern State U (OK)
Northeastern U (MA)
Northern Arizona U (AZ)
Northern Illinois U (IL)
Northwestern Coll (IA)
Northwestern Oklahoma State U (OK)
Northwestern U (IL)
Northwest Nazarene U (ID)
Norwich U (VT)
Nova Southeastern U (FL)
Nyack Coll (NY)
Oberlin Coll (OH)
Ohio Dominican U (OH)
Ohio Northern U (OH)
The Ohio State U (OH)
Ohio U (OH)
Ohio Wesleyan U (OH)
Oklahoma Baptist U (OK)
Oklahoma Christian U (OK)
Olivet Nazarene U (IL)
Oregon State U (OR)
Pace U (NY)
Pacific Lutheran U (WA)
Pacific U (OR)
Palm Beach Atlantic U (FL)
Park U (MO)
Penn State Erie, The Behrend Coll (PA)
Philadelphia U (PA)
Philander Smith Coll (AR)
Plymouth State U (NH)
Point Loma Nazarene U (CA)
Polytechnic U of Puerto Rico (PR)
Pomona Coll (CA)
Portland State U (OR)
Prairie View A&M U (TX)
Providence Coll (RI)
Purdue U (IN)
Purdue U Calumet (IN)
Queens Coll of the City U of New York (NY)
Quincy U (IL)
Quinnipiac U (CT)
Radford U (VA)
Randolph-Macon Coll (VA)
Rasmussen Coll Appleton (WI)
Rasmussen Coll Bismarck (ND)
Rasmussen Coll Blaine (MN)
Rasmussen Coll Bloomington (MN)
Rasmussen Coll Brooklyn Park (MN)
Rasmussen Coll Eagan (MN)
Rasmussen Coll Fargo (ND)
Rasmussen Coll Fort Myers (FL)
Rasmussen Coll Green Bay (WI)
Rasmussen Coll Lake Elmo/Woodbury (MN)
Rasmussen Coll Land O' Lakes (FL)
Rasmussen Coll Mankato (MN)
Rasmussen Coll Moorhead (MN)
Rasmussen Coll New Port Richey (FL)
Rasmussen Coll Ocala (FL)
Rasmussen Coll St. Cloud (MN)
Rasmussen Coll Tampa/Brandon (FL)
Rasmussen Coll Topeka (KS)
Rasmussen Coll Wausau (WI)
Reed Coll (OR)
Regis U (CO)
Rensselaer Polytechnic Inst (NY)
Rhodes Coll (TN)
Ripon Coll (WI)
Roanoke Coll (VA)
Rochester Inst of Technology (NY)
Rockford U (IL)
Rocky Mountain Coll (MT)
Roger Williams U (RI)
Roosevelt U (IL)
Rose-Hulman Inst of Technology (IN)
Rowan U (NJ)
Rust Coll (MS)
Sacred Heart U (CT)
Saginaw Valley State U (MI)
Saint Anselm Coll (NH)
Saint Augustine's U (NC)
St. Bonaventure U (NY)
St. Edward's U (TX)
Saint Francis U (PA)
Saint John's U (MN)
Saint Martin's U (WA)
St. Mary's U (TX)
Saint Mary's U of Minnesota (MN)
Saint Michael's Coll (VT)
St. Norbert Coll (WI)
St. Olaf Coll (MN)
St. Thomas U (FL)
Samford U (AL)
San Diego State U (CA)
San Francisco State U (CA)
San Jose State U (CA)
Scripps Coll (CA)
Seattle U (WA)
Seton Hill U (PA)
Sewanee: The U of the South (TN)
Shaw U (NC)
Silver Lake Coll of the Holy Family (WI)
Simon Fraser U (BC, Canada)
Simpson Coll (IA)
Slippery Rock U of Pennsylvania (PA)
Smith Coll (MA)
South Dakota School of Mines and Technology (SD)
Southeastern Louisiana U (LA)
Southern Adventist U (TN)
Southern California Inst of Technology (CA)
Southern Connecticut State U (CT)
Southern Illinois U Carbondale (IL)
Southern Illinois U Edwardsville (IL)
Southern Methodist U (TX)
Southern Oregon U (OR)
Southern Utah U (UT)
Southwest Baptist U (MO)
Southwestern Adventist U (TX)
Southwestern Coll (KS)
Southwest Minnesota State U (MN)
Spelman Coll (GA)
Stanford U (CA)
State U of New York at Fredonia (NY)
State U of New York at Oswego (NY)
State U of New York Coll at Old Westbury (NY)
State U of New York Coll at Potsdam (NY)
Stetson U (FL)
Stonehill Coll (MA)
Suffolk U (MA)
Susquehanna U (PA)
Taylor U (IN)
Tennessee State U (TN)
Texas A&M U (TX)
Texas Lutheran U (TX)
Texas State U (TX)
Texas Wesleyan U (TX)
Thiel Coll (PA)
Tougaloo Coll (MS)
Trent U (ON, Canada)
Trine U (IN)
Trinity Christian Coll (IL)
Trinity Coll (CT)
Tufts U (MA)
Tulane U (LA)
Union Coll (NE)
Union U (TN)
United States Air Force Acad (CO)
United States Naval Acad (MD)
Universidad Metropolitana (PR)
Université de Montréal (QC, Canada)
Université de Sherbrooke (QC, Canada)
Université du Québec en Outaouais (QC, Canada)
U at Albany, State U of New York (NY)
U at Buffalo, the State U of New York (NY)
The U of Akron (OH)
U of Alaska Fairbanks (AK)
U of Alberta (AB, Canada)
The U of Arizona (AZ)
U of Arkansas at Little Rock (AR)
U of Arkansas at Pine Bluff (AR)
U of Bridgeport (CT)
The U of British Columbia (BC, Canada)
The U of British Columbia–Okanagan Campus (BC, Canada)
U of California, Berkeley (CA)
U of California, Irvine (CA)
U of California, Riverside (CA)
U of California, Santa Barbara (CA)
U of California, Santa Cruz (CA)
U of Central Oklahoma (OK)
U of Chicago (IL)
U of Colorado Boulder (CO)
U of Dayton (OH)
U of Delaware (DE)
U of Denver (CO)
U of Dubuque (IA)
U of Evansville (IN)
The U of Findlay (OH)
U of Georgia (GA)
U of Great Falls (MT)
U of Guam (GU)
U of Guelph (ON, Canada)
U of Hawaii at Hilo (HI)
U of Hawaii at Manoa (HI)
U of Houston–Clear Lake (TX)
U of Houston–Victoria (TX)
U of Idaho (ID)
U of Illinois at Chicago (IL)
U of Illinois at Springfield (IL)
U of Indianapolis (IN)
The U of Iowa (IA)
U of Jamestown (ND)
U of King's Coll (NS, Canada)
U of La Verne (CA)
U of Lethbridge (AB, Canada)
U of Maine (ME)
U of Maine at Fort Kent (ME)
U of Mary Hardin-Baylor (TX)
U of Maryland, Baltimore County (MD)
U of Massachusetts Amherst (MA)
U of Massachusetts Lowell (MA)
U of Memphis (TN)
U of Miami (FL)
U of Michigan–Flint (MI)
U of Minnesota, Duluth (MN)
U of Minnesota, Morris (MN)
U of Minnesota, Twin Cities Campus (MN)
U of Missouri (MO)
U of Missouri–Kansas City (MO)
U of Missouri–St. Louis (MO)
The U of Montana (MT)
U of Nevada, Las Vegas (NV)
U of Nevada, Reno (NV)
U of New Brunswick Saint John (NB, Canada)
U of New Haven (CT)
U of New Orleans (LA)
U of North Carolina at Asheville (NC)
The U of North Carolina at Chapel Hill (NC)
The U of North Carolina at Charlotte (NC)
The U of North Carolina at Greensboro (NC)
The U of North Carolina at Pembroke (NC)
The U of North Carolina Wilmington (NC)
U of Northern Iowa (IA)
U of Oklahoma (OK)
U of Pittsburgh (PA)
U of Pittsburgh at Bradford (PA)
U of Portland (OR)
U of Puget Sound (WA)
U of Regina (SK, Canada)
U of Rio Grande (OH)
U of Rochester (NY)
U of St. Francis (IL)
U of St. Thomas (TX)
U of San Diego (CA)
U of San Francisco (CA)
U of Saskatchewan (SK, Canada)
The U of Scranton (PA)
U of South Alabama (AL)
U of Southern California (CA)
U of Southern Indiana (IN)
U of Southern Maine (ME)
The U of Tennessee (TN)
The U of Tennessee at Chattanooga (TN)
The U of Tennessee at Martin (TN)

The U of Texas at Arlington (TX)
The U of Texas at El Paso (TX)
The U of Texas at Tyler (TX)
The U of Texas–Pan American (TX)
U of the District of Columbia (DC)
U of the Pacific (CA)
U of the Virgin Islands (VI)
The U of Toledo (OH)
U of Toronto (ON, Canada)
The U of Tulsa (OK)
U of Utah (UT)
U of Vermont (VT)
U of Washington (WA)
U of Washington, Bothell (WA)
U of Waterloo (ON, Canada)
The U of Western Ontario (ON, Canada)
U of Windsor (ON, Canada)
U of Wisconsin–Green Bay (WI)
U of Wisconsin–Milwaukee (WI)
U of Wisconsin–Oshkosh (WI)
U of Wisconsin–Parkside (WI)
U of Wisconsin–Platteville (WI)
U of Wisconsin–River Falls (WI)
U of Wisconsin–Superior (WI)
U of Wyoming (WY)
Ursinus Coll (PA)
Utah Valley U (UT)
Valparaiso U (IN)
Vanderbilt U (TN)
Villanova U (PA)
Virginia Military Inst (VA)
Virginia Polytechnic Inst and State U (VA)
Virginia State U (VA)
Virginia Wesleyan Coll (VA)
Voorhees Coll (SC)
Wagner Coll (NY)
Walla Walla U (WA)
Walsh U (OH)
Wartburg Coll (IA)
Washington and Lee U (VA)
Washington Coll (MD)
Washington State U (WA)
Washington State U Vancouver (WA)
Washington U in St. Louis (MO)
Waynesburg U (PA)
Weber State U (UT)
Webster U (MO)
Wells Coll (NY)
Wentworth Inst of Technology (MA)
Wesleyan U (CT)
Western Carolina U (NC)
Western Michigan U (MI)
Western New England U (MA)
Western Oregon U (OR)
Western State Colorado U (CO)
Westfield State U (MA)
Westminster Coll (MO)
Westminster Coll (UT)
West Texas A&M U (TX)
West Virginia State U (WV)
West Virginia U (WV)
West Virginia U Inst of Technology (WV)
West Virginia Wesleyan Coll (WV)
Wheaton Coll (IL)
Wheaton Coll (MA)
Whitworth U (WA)
Widener U (PA)
Wilberforce U (OH)
Willamette U (OR)
William Paterson U of New Jersey (NJ)
William Penn U (IA)
Williams Coll (MA)
Winona State U (MN)
Wittenberg U (OH)
Wofford Coll (SC)
Worcester Polytechnic Inst (MA)
Xavier U (OH)
Xavier U of Louisiana (LA)
Yeshiva U (NY)
York Coll of Pennsylvania (PA)
York Coll of the City U of New York (NY)
Youngstown State U (OH)

COMPUTER SOFTWARE AND MEDIA APPLICATIONS RELATED
Champlain Coll (VT)
Coll of Charleston (SC)
DePaul U (IL)
Duquesne U (PA)
Florida State U (FL)
LeTourneau U (TX)
Limestone Coll (SC)
Loyola U Chicago (IL)
McKendree U (IL)
Morrisville State Coll (NY)
Neumont U (UT)
State U of New York Coll of Agriculture and Technology at Cobleskill (NY)
U of Denver (CO)
U of Great Falls (MT)
The U of Western Ontario (ON, Canada)
U of Wisconsin–Stout (WI)

COMPUTER SOFTWARE ENGINEERING
Allegheny Coll (PA)
Arizona State U at the Polytechnic campus (AZ)
Auburn U (AL)
Baldwin Wallace U (OH)
California Baptist U (CA)
Centennial Coll (ON, Canada)
Champlain Coll (VT)
Clarkson U (NY)
Concordia U (QC, Canada)
Dalhousie U (NS, Canada)
DeVry U, Phoenix (AZ)
DeVry U, Pomona (CA)
DeVry U, Westminster (CO)
DeVry U, Orlando (FL)
DeVry U, Decatur (GA)
DeVry U, Fort Washington (PA)
DeVry U, Irving (TX)
DeVry U, Arlington (VA)
DeVry U, Federal Way (WA)
DeVry U Online (IL)
DigiPen Inst of Technology (WA)
Drexel U (PA)
Embry-Riddle Aeronautical U–Daytona (FL)
Embry-Riddle Aeronautical U–Prescott (AZ)
Fairfield U (CT)
Florida Inst of Technology (FL)
Keiser U, Fort Lauderdale (FL)
Liberty U (VA)
Miami U (OH)
Michigan Technological U (MI)
Milwaukee School of Eng (WI)
Monmouth U (NJ)
Montana Tech of The U of Montana (MT)
National U (CA)
Nova Southeastern U (FL)
Ohio Dominican U (OH)
Oklahoma City U (OK)
Penn State Erie, The Behrend Coll (PA)
Point Loma Nazarene U (CA)
Quinnipiac U (CT)
Robert Morris U (PA)
Rochester Inst of Technology (NY)
Rose-Hulman Inst of Technology (IN)
Shippensburg U of Pennsylvania (PA)
State U of New York at Oswego (NY)
Stratford U, Woodbridge (VA)
U of Alberta (AB, Canada)
U of California, Irvine (CA)
U of Guelph (ON, Canada)
U of Miami (FL)
U of Minnesota, Crookston (MN)
U of Northern Colorado (CO)
U of Ottawa (ON, Canada)
U of Regina (SK, Canada)
The U of Texas at Arlington (TX)
The U of Texas at Dallas (TX)
U of Toronto (ON, Canada)
U of Waterloo (ON, Canada)
The U of Western Ontario (ON, Canada)
U of Wisconsin–Platteville (WI)
Utah Valley U (UT)
Vermont Tech Coll (VT)
Wichita State U (KS)
William Penn U (IA)

COMPUTER SOFTWARE TECHNOLOGY
Sam Houston State U (TX)

COMPUTER SYSTEMS ANALYSIS
Arizona State U at the Polytechnic campus (AZ)
Arkansas Tech U (AR)
Baldwin Wallace U (OH)
California Polytechnic State U, San Luis Obispo (CA)
Clayton State U (GA)
Concordia U (QC, Canada)
Daniel Webster Coll (NH)
Davenport U, Grand Rapids (MI)
DeVry Coll of New York (NY)
DeVry U, Phoenix (AZ)
DeVry U, Pomona (CA)
DeVry U, Westminster (CO)
DeVry U, Miramar (FL)
DeVry U, Orlando (FL)
DeVry U, Decatur (GA)
DeVry U, Chicago (IL)
DeVry U, Kansas City (MO)
DeVry U, North Brunswick (NJ)
DeVry U, Columbus (OH)
DeVry U, Fort Washington (PA)
DeVry U, Houston (TX)
DeVry U, Irving (TX)
DeVry U, Arlington (VA)
DeVry U, Federal Way (WA)
DeVry U Online (IL)
HEC Montreal (QC, Canada)
Johnson & Wales U (RI)
Kent State U (OH)
Northern Arizona U (AZ)
Pittsburg State U (KS)
Rochester Inst of Technology (NY)
Saginaw Valley State U (MI)
Seattle Pacific U (WA)
Shippensburg U of Pennsylvania (PA)
Taylor U (IN)
Texas Christian U (TX)
U of Denver (CO)
U of Great Falls (MT)
U of Houston (TX)
U of Illinois at Springfield (IL)
U of Louisiana at Lafayette (LA)
U of North Dakota (ND)
U of Vermont (VT)
U of Washington, Bothell (WA)
West Virginia U Inst of Technology (WV)

COMPUTER SYSTEMS NETWORKING AND TELECOMMUNICATIONS
Baldwin Wallace U (OH)
Bloomfield Coll (NJ)
Bowling Green State U (OH)
Cape Breton U (NS, Canada)
Centennial Coll (ON, Canada)
Champlain Coll (VT)
Chowan U (NC)
Concordia U (QC, Canada)
Davenport U, Grand Rapids (MI)
DePaul U (IL)
DeVry Coll of New York (NY)
DeVry U, Phoenix (AZ)
DeVry U, Pomona (CA)
DeVry U, Westminster (CO)
DeVry U, Miramar (FL)
DeVry U, Orlando (FL)
DeVry U, Decatur (GA)
DeVry U, Chicago (IL)
DeVry U, Kansas City (MO)
DeVry U, North Brunswick (NJ)
DeVry U, Columbus (OH)
DeVry U, Fort Washington (PA)
DeVry U, Houston (TX)
DeVry U, Irving (TX)
DeVry U, Arlington (VA)
DeVry U, Federal Way (WA)
DeVry U Online (IL)
EDP U of Puerto Rico (PR)
Ferris State U (MI)
Florida State Coll at Jacksonville (FL)
Illinois State U (IL)
Inter American U of Puerto Rico, Aguadilla Campus (PR)
Inter American U of Puerto Rico, Bayamón Campus (PR)
Inter American U of Puerto Rico, Ponce Campus (PR)
Iona Coll (NY)
Johns Hopkins U (MD)
Kansas State U (KS)
Kean U (NJ)
Keiser U, Fort Lauderdale (FL)
Lindenwood U (MO)
Michigan Technological U (MI)
Montana Tech of The U of Montana (MT)
Morrisville State Coll (NY)
Mount Vernon Nazarene U (OH)
Northern Michigan U (MI)
Northwestern Oklahoma State U (OK)
Ohio U (OH)
Pennsylvania Coll of Technology (PA)
Rochester Inst of Technology (NY)
Roosevelt U (IL)
Stevenson U (MD)
The U of Akron (OH)
The U of Findlay (OH)
U of Great Falls (MT)
U of Minnesota, Duluth (MN)
U of Minnesota, Twin Cities Campus (MN)
The U of North Carolina at Greensboro (NC)
U of Pennsylvania (PA)
U of the Incarnate Word (TX)
U of Toronto (ON, Canada)
U of Wisconsin–Stout (WI)
Utah Valley U (UT)
Virginia Union U (VA)
Weber State U (UT)
Wentworth Inst of Technology (MA)
Western Illinois U (IL)
Western State Colorado U (CO)

COMPUTER TEACHER EDUCATION
Abilene Christian U (TX)
Alma Coll (MI)
Baylor U (TX)
Bowling Green State U (OH)
Buena Vista U (IA)
Colorado State U (CO)
Concordia U Chicago (IL)
Concordia U, Nebraska (NE)
Dakota State U (SD)
Dallas Baptist U (TX)
Eastern Michigan U (MI)
Edgewood Coll (WI)
Hardin-Simmons U (TX)
Howard Payne U (TX)
McMurry U (TX)
Michigan State U (MI)
National U Coll, Bayamón (PR)
Olivet Coll (MI)
U of Alberta (AB, Canada)
U of Nebraska–Lincoln (NE)
U of Wisconsin–River Falls (WI)
Utica Coll (NY)
Western Washington U (WA)
Wright State U (OH)

COMPUTER TECHNOLOGY/ COMPUTER SYSTEMS TECHNOLOGY
Bowling Green State U (OH)
Colorado State U (CO)
Daytona State Coll (FL)
Florida Atlantic U (FL)
New England Inst of Technology (RI)
Prairie View A&M U (TX)
Rensselaer Polytechnic Inst (NY)
Wayne State U (MI)

CONDENSED MATTER AND MATERIALS PHYSICS
Rowan U (NJ)

CONDUCTING
Chapman U (CA)
McMurry U (TX)
Union Coll (NE)

CONSERVATION BIOLOGY
Boston U (MA)
Florida Inst of Technology (FL)
Philadelphia U (PA)
Prescott Coll (AZ)
St. Lawrence U (NY)
Seattle U (WA)
State U of New York Coll of Environmental Science and Forestry (NY)
Sterling Coll (VT)
U of Alberta (AB, Canada)
U of Idaho (ID)
U of Maine at Machias (ME)
The U of Western Ontario (ON, Canada)
U of Wisconsin–Madison (WI)

CONSTRUCTION ENGINEERING
The American U in Cairo (Egypt)
American U of Beirut (Lebanon)
Arizona State U at the Tempe campus (AZ)
Bradley U (IL)
California State U, Long Beach (CA)
Concordia U (QC, Canada)
Daniel Webster Coll (NH)
John Brown U (AR)
Lamar U (TX)
Marquette U (WI)
National U (CA)
New York U (NY)
North Carolina State U (NC)
North Dakota State U (ND)
Oregon State U (OR)
Purdue U (IN)
Texas A&M U–Commerce (TX)
Texas Tech U (TX)
The U of Alabama (AL)
U of Arkansas at Little Rock (AR)
U of Nebraska–Lincoln (NE)
U of New Mexico (NM)

CONSTRUCTION ENGINEERING TECHNOLOGY
Bemidji State U (MN)
Bowling Green State U (OH)
California Baptist U (CA)
California State Polytechnic U, Pomona (CA)
California State U, Chico (CA)
California State U, Fresno (CA)
California State U, Long Beach (CA)
California State U, Sacramento (CA)
Central Michigan U (MI)
Colorado Mesa U (CO)
Colorado State U (CO)
Fairleigh Dickinson U, Metropolitan Campus (NJ)
Farmingdale State Coll (NY)
Fitchburg State U (MA)
Florida Ag and Mech U (FL)
Florida Inst of Technology (FL)
Florida Intl U (FL)
Georgia Southern U (GA)
Indiana U–Purdue U Fort Wayne (IN)
John Brown U (AR)
Kansas State U (KS)
Michigan State U (MI)
Missouri Western State U (MO)
Montana State U (MT)
Norfolk State U (VA)
Northern Michigan U (MI)
The Ohio State U (OH)
Oklahoma State U (OK)
Pittsburg State U (KS)
Prairie View A&M U (TX)
Roger Williams U (RI)
Sam Houston State U (TX)
San Diego State U (CA)
Seminole State Coll of Florida (FL)
South Dakota State U (SD)
Texas A&M U (TX)
Texas State U (TX)
The U of Akron (OH)
U of Arkansas at Little Rock (AR)
U of Florida (FL)
U of Houston (TX)
U of Nebraska–Lincoln (NE)
U of Nevada, Las Vegas (NV)
U of North Florida (FL)
U of North Texas (TX)
The U of Toledo (OH)
Wayne State U (MI)
Western Carolina U (NC)
Western Kentucky U (KY)

CONSTRUCTION MANAGEMENT
Appalachian State U (NC)
Arizona State U at the Tempe campus (AZ)
California State U, Fresno (CA)
Central Connecticut State U (CT)
Central Washington U (WA)
Colorado State U (CO)
Drexel U (PA)

Dunwoody Coll of Technology (MN)
Eastern Kentucky U (KY)
Eastern Michigan U (MI)
Everglades U, Sarasota (FL)
Ferris State U (MI)
Hastings Coll (NE)
Illinois State U (IL)
Indiana State U (IN)
John Brown U (AR)
Kent State U (OH)
Lawrence Technological U (MI)
Louisiana State U and A&M Coll (LA)
Michigan State U (MI)
Michigan Technological U (MI)
Milwaukee School of Eng (WI)
Minnesota State U Moorhead (MN)
Mississippi State U (MS)
Missouri State U (MO)
National U (CA)
North Dakota State U (ND)
Northern Arizona U (AZ)
Northern Kentucky U (KY)
Ohio Northern U (OH)
The Ohio State U (OH)
Pittsburg State U (KS)
State U of New York Coll of Environmental Science and Forestry (NY)
State U of New York Coll of Technology at Alfred (NY)
State U of New York Coll of Technology at Delhi (NY)
U of Nevada, Las Vegas (NV)
U of Northern Iowa (IA)
U of Oklahoma (OK)
The U of Texas at Tyler (TX)
U of Washington (WA)
U of Wisconsin–Stout (WI)
Utah Valley U (UT)
Vermont Tech Coll (VT)
Virginia Polytechnic Inst and State U (VA)
Washington State U (WA)
Wentworth Inst of Technology (MA)
Western Carolina U (NC)
Western Illinois U (IL)
Western Nevada Coll (NV)

CONSTRUCTION TRADES
National U (CA)
Utica Coll (NY)

CONSTRUCTION TRADES RELATED
John Brown U (AR)

CONSUMER ECONOMICS
Delaware State U (DE)
South Dakota State U (SD)
U of Georgia (GA)
U of Kentucky (KY)
The U of Tennessee (TN)
U of Utah (UT)

CONSUMER MERCHANDISING/ RETAILING MANAGEMENT
Bradley U (IL)
Fontbonne U (MO)
HEC Montreal (QC, Canada)
Newbury Coll (MA)
Oregon State U (OR)
Purdue U (IN)
San Francisco State U (CA)
Savannah Coll of Art and Design (GA)
Simmons Coll (MA)
U of Central Oklahoma (OK)
U of Memphis (TN)

CONSUMER SERVICES AND ADVOCACY
Carson-Newman U (TN)
Tennessee State U (TN)
Texas State U (TX)

CORRECTIONS
Adams State U (CO)
Bowling Green State U (OH)
California State U, Stanislaus (CA)
California U of Pennsylvania (PA)
Coll of the Ozarks (MO)
Eastern Kentucky U (KY)
Ellis U (IL)
Jacksonville State U (AL)
Langston U (OK)
Minnesota State U Mankato (MN)
Oakland U (MI)
Southeast Missouri State U (MO)
Stephen F. Austin State U (TX)
Texas State U (TX)
Tiffin U (OH)
Tulane U (LA)
U of Arkansas at Pine Bluff (AR)
U of Central Oklahoma (OK)
U of Great Falls (MT)
U of Minnesota, Crookston (MN)
U of New Mexico (NM)
U of Pittsburgh (PA)
Washburn U (KS)
Weber State U (UT)
Western Oregon U (OR)
Winona State U (MN)
Youngstown State U (OH)

CORRECTIONS ADMINISTRATION
Inter American U of Puerto Rico, Fajardo Campus (PR)
U of Great Falls (MT)

CORRECTIONS AND CRIMINAL JUSTICE RELATED
Albany State U (GA)
Averett U (VA)
Bethune-Cookman U (FL)
Cameron U (OK)
Cedarville U (OH)
Concordia U, Nebraska (NE)
Corban U (OR)
Delaware State U (DE)
DeVry U, Arlington (VA)
Emporia State U (KS)
Eureka Coll (IL)
Hastings Coll (NE)
Keene State Coll (NH)
La Roche Coll (PA)
Limestone Coll (SC)
Morrisville State Coll (NY)
Northwestern Coll (IA)
Rasmussen Coll Bloomington (MN)
Rasmussen Coll Brooklyn Park (MN)
Rasmussen Coll Eagan (MN)
Rasmussen Coll Fargo (ND)
Rasmussen Coll Fort Myers (FL)
Rasmussen Coll Kansas City/ Overland Park (KS)
Rasmussen Coll Lake Elmo/ Woodbury (MN)
Rasmussen Coll Land O' Lakes (FL)
Rasmussen Coll Mankato (MN)
Rasmussen Coll Moorhead (MN)
Rasmussen Coll New Port Richey (FL)
Rasmussen Coll Ocala (FL)
Rasmussen Coll St. Cloud (MN)
Rasmussen Coll Tampa/Brandon (FL)
Rasmussen Coll Topeka (KS)
Roger Williams U (RI)
Saint Mary's U of Minnesota (MN)
Sam Houston State U (TX)
Savannah State U (GA)
Southern New Hampshire U (NH)
State U of New York Coll of Technology at Canton (NY)
The U of Alabama at Birmingham (AL)
U of Alaska Fairbanks (AK)
U of Great Falls (MT)
U of Michigan–Flint (MI)
U of Saint Francis (IN)
Vincennes U (IN)
Weber State U (UT)

COSTUME DESIGN
Acad of Art U (CA)
Greensboro Coll (NC)
Marymount Manhattan Coll (NY)
Stephens Coll (MO)

COUNSELING PSYCHOLOGY
Arizona Christian U (AZ)
Averett U (VA)
Avila U (MO)
Coker Coll (SC)
Crossroads Coll (MN)
Emmanuel Coll (MA)
Fort Lewis Coll (CO)
Grace Coll (IN)
Great Lakes Christian Coll (MI)
Hobe Sound Bible Coll (FL)
Hope Intl U (CA)
Johnson & Wales U (RI)
Kentucky Christian U (KY)
Lesley U (MA)
LeTourneau U (TX)
Maryville Coll (TN)
Mid-Atlantic Christian U (NC)
Midwestern State U (TX)
Morningside Coll (IA)
Mount Saint Mary's U (CA)
Newman U (KS)
Northwestern U (IL)
Point U (GA)
Prescott Coll (AZ)
San Diego Christian Coll (CA)
Southwestern Assemblies of God U (TX)
Tarleton State U (TX)
Toccoa Falls Coll (GA)
Universidad del Turabo (PR)
U of Jamestown (ND)
Wayne State Coll (NE)

COUNSELOR EDUCATION/ SCHOOL COUNSELING AND GUIDANCE
Bowling Green State U (OH)
Buena Vista U (IA)
Creighton U (NE)
East Central U (OK)
Florida Gulf Coast U (FL)
Houston Baptist U (TX)
Howard U (DC)
John Brown U (AR)
Marshall U (WV)
Midwestern State U (TX)
Tarleton State U (TX)
Université de Sherbrooke (QC, Canada)
U of Central Oklahoma (OK)
The U of North Carolina at Pembroke (NC)
The U of South Dakota (SD)
U of Windsor (ON, Canada)
U of Wisconsin–River Falls (WI)
Wright State U (OH)

CRAFTS, FOLK ART AND ARTISANRY
Bowling Green State U (OH)
Bridgewater State U (MA)
Brigham Young U (UT)
Coll for Creative Studies (MI)
Indiana U–Purdue U Fort Wayne (IN)
Kent State U (OH)
Kutztown U of Pennsylvania (PA)
Oregon Coll of Art & Craft (OR)
Rochester Inst of Technology (NY)
The U of the Arts (PA)
Virginia Commonwealth U (VA)

CREATIVE WRITING
Adams State U (CO)
Agnes Scott Coll (GA)
Albion Coll (MI)
Allegheny Coll (PA)
Arcadia U (PA)
Arkansas Tech U (AR)
Asbury U (KY)
Ashland U (OH)
Augsburg Coll (MN)
Augustana Coll (IL)
Austin Coll (TX)
Baldwin Wallace U (OH)
Bard Coll (NY)
Bard Coll at Simon's Rock (MA)
Belhaven U (MS)
Beloit Coll (WI)
Bennington Coll (VT)
Berry Coll (GA)
Bethany Coll (WV)
Binghamton U, State U of New York (NY)
Biola U (CA)
Bob Jones U (SC)
Bowie State U (MD)
Bowling Green State U (OH)
Brandeis U (MA)
Bridgewater State U (MA)
Brown U (RI)
Bucknell U (PA)
Butler U (IN)
California Coll of the Arts (CA)
California State U, Long Beach (CA)
Calvary Bible Coll and Theological Sem (MO)
Canisius Coll (NY)
Capital U (OH)
Carlow U (PA)
Carson-Newman U (TN)
Catawba Coll (NC)
Central Michigan U (MI)
Central Washington U (WA)
Chapman U (CA)
Chatham U (PA)
Christian Brothers U (TN)
City Coll of the City U of New York (NY)
Coe Coll (IA)
Colby Coll (ME)
Colby-Sawyer Coll (NH)
The Coll of Idaho (ID)
Coll of the Atlantic (ME)
The Colorado Coll (CO)
Colorado State U (CO)
Columbia Coll Chicago (IL)
Columbia U (NY)
Columbia U, School of General Studies (NY)
Concordia U (QC, Canada)
Corban U (OR)
Cornell Coll (IA)
Creighton U (NE)
Dartmouth Coll (NH)
Denison U (OH)
Dixie State U (UT)
Dominican U of California (CA)
Eastern Michigan U (MI)
Eckerd Coll (FL)
Emerson Coll (MA)
Emily Carr U of Art + Design (BC, Canada)
Emory & Henry Coll (VA)
Fairleigh Dickinson U, Coll at Florham (NJ)
Florida Southern Coll (FL)
Florida State U (FL)
Franklin & Marshall Coll (PA)
Franklin Coll (IN)
Franklin Pierce U (NH)
George Mason U (VA)
Gettysburg Coll (PA)
Goddard Coll (VT)
Green Mountain Coll (VT)
Hamilton Coll (NY)
Hamline U (MN)
Hampshire Coll (MA)
Hastings Coll (NE)
Hiram Coll (OH)
Hofstra U (NY)
Houghton Coll (NY)
Houston Baptist U (TX)
Huntingdon Coll (AL)
Inst of American Indian Arts (NM)
Ithaca Coll (NY)
Johns Hopkins U (MD)
Johnson State Coll (VT)
Kansas City Art Inst (MO)
Knox Coll (IL)
Lee U (TN)
Lehman Coll of the City U of New York (NY)
Linfield Coll (OR)
Loras Coll (IA)
Lubbock Christian U (TX)
Lycoming Coll (PA)
Malone U (OH)
Massachusetts Coll of Liberal Arts (MA)
Massachusetts Inst of Technology (MA)
McMurry U (TX)
Mercer U, Macon (GA)
Metropolitan State U (MN)
Miami U (OH)
Mills Coll (CA)
Minnesota State U Mankato (MN)
Moravian Coll (PA)
Morehead State U (KY)
Murray State U (KY)
New England Coll (NH)
North Central Coll (IL)
Northern Michigan U (MI)
Northland Coll (WI)
Oakland U (MI)
Oberlin Coll (OH)
Ohio Northern U (OH)
Ohio U (OH)
Ohio Wesleyan U (OH)
Oklahoma Christian U (OK)
Pacific U (OR)
Pepperdine U, Malibu (CA)
Pratt Inst (NY)
Providence Coll (RI)
Purchase Coll, State U of New York (NY)
Purdue U (IN)
Randolph Coll (VA)
Rhode Island Coll (RI)
Roanoke Coll (VA)
Rocky Mountain Coll (MT)
Saginaw Valley State U (MI)
St. Catherine U (MN)
Saint Joseph's Coll (IN)
Saint Mary-of-the-Woods Coll (IN)
Saint Mary's Coll (IN)
St. Thomas Aquinas Coll (NY)
Salem Coll (NC)
San Francisco State U (CA)
Santa Fe U of Art and Design (NM)
Sarah Lawrence Coll (NY)
School of the Art Inst of Chicago (IL)
Seattle U (WA)
Seton Hill U (PA)
Siena Heights U (MI)
Slippery Rock U of Pennsylvania (PA)
Southern Methodist U (TX)
Southern New Hampshire U (NH)
Southern Vermont Coll (VT)
Southwestern Coll (KS)
Southwest Minnesota State U (MN)
Spalding U (KY)
State U of New York at Oswego (NY)
State U of New York Coll at Potsdam (NY)
Stephen F. Austin State U (TX)
Stephens Coll (MO)
Susquehanna U (PA)
Texas Christian U (TX)
Trinity Coll (CT)
Truman State U (MO)
The U of Arizona (AZ)
The U of British Columbia (BC, Canada)
The U of British Columbia–Okanagan Campus (BC, Canada)
U of California, Riverside (CA)
U of Central Oklahoma (OK)
U of Cincinnati (OH)
U of Denver (CO)
U of Evansville (IN)
The U of Findlay (OH)
U of Great Falls (MT)
U of Houston (TX)
U of Idaho (ID)
U of Maine at Machias (ME)
U of Maine at Presque Isle (ME)
U of Miami (FL)
U of Michigan (MI)
The U of Montana (MT)
U of Mount Union (OH)
The U of North Carolina Wilmington (NC)
U of Pittsburgh (PA)
U of Pittsburgh at Bradford (PA)
U of Pittsburgh at Greensburg (PA)
U of Regina (SK, Canada)
U of St. Thomas (MN)
U of Southern California (CA)
The U of Texas at El Paso (TX)
The U of the Arts (PA)
U of Washington (WA)
The U of Western Ontario (ON, Canada)
U of Windsor (ON, Canada)
Valparaiso U (IN)
Waldorf Coll (IA)
Warren Wilson Coll (NC)
Washington U in St. Louis (MO)
Waynesburg U (PA)
Weber State U (UT)
Wells Coll (NY)
Western Michigan U (MI)
Western New England U (MA)
Western State Colorado U (CO)
Western Washington U (WA)
West Virginia Wesleyan Coll (WV)
Wheaton Coll (MA)
Wichita State U (KS)
Wofford Coll (SC)
Yeshiva U (NY)

CRIMINALISTICS AND CRIMINAL SCIENCE
Alabama State U (AL)
Bay Path U (MA)
Florida Gulf Coast U (FL)
Inter American U of Puerto Rico, Ponce Campus (PR)

Ohio Dominican U (OH)
Saint Leo U (FL)
Seattle U (WA)

CRIMINAL JUSTICE/LAW ENFORCEMENT ADMINISTRATION

Abilene Christian U (TX)
Adams State U (CO)
Albertus Magnus Coll (CT)
Alvernia U (PA)
American Public U System (WV)
Anderson U (IN)
Anderson U (SC)
Anna Maria Coll (MA)
Arcadia U (PA)
Arizona State U at the Downtown Phoenix campus (AZ)
Athens State U (AL)
Austin Peay State U (TN)
Averett U (VA)
Bay Path U (MA)
Becker Coll (MA)
Belhaven U (MS)
Bemidji State U (MN)
Berkeley Coll, Woodland Park (NJ)
Berkeley Coll–New York City Campus (NY)
Berkeley Coll–Westchester Campus (NY)
Blackburn Coll (IL)
Bluefield Coll (VA)
Bowie State U (MD)
Bowling Green State U (OH)
Bradley U (IL)
Brevard Coll (NC)
Buffalo State Coll, State U of New York (NY)
California Baptist U (CA)
California Lutheran U (CA)
California State U, Long Beach (CA)
California State U, Sacramento (CA)
Calumet Coll of Saint Joseph (IN)
Calvary Bible Coll and Theological Sem (MO)
Campbellsville U (KY)
Canisius Coll (NY)
Castleton State Coll (VT)
Catawba Coll (NC)
Chestnut Hill Coll (PA)
Cheyney U of Pennsylvania (PA)
The Citadel, The Military Coll of South Carolina (SC)
Claflin U (SC)
Clarion U of Pennsylvania (PA)
The Coll of New Jersey (NJ)
The Coll of Saint Rose (NY)
Columbia Coll (MO)
Concordia U Texas (TX)
Concordia U Wisconsin (WI)
Culver-Stockton Coll (MO)
Cumberland U (TN)
Delaware State U (DE)
DeVry U, Phoenix (AZ)
DeVry U, Pomona (CA)
DeVry U, Westminster (CO)
DeVry U, Miramar (FL)
DeVry U, Orlando (FL)
DeVry U, Decatur (GA)
DeVry U, Chicago (IL)
DeVry U, Kansas City (MO)
DeVry U, Houston (TX)
DeVry U, Federal Way (WA)
DeVry U Online (IL)
Drexel U (PA)
East Central U (OK)
Eastern Kentucky U (KY)
East Tennessee State U (TN)
East Texas Baptist U (TX)
Ellis U (IL)
Elmira Coll (NY)
Elms Coll (MA)
Emmanuel Coll (GA)
Evangel U (MO)
Excelsior Coll (NY)
Fairleigh Dickinson U, Metropolitan Campus (NJ)
Fayetteville State U (NC)
Ferris State U (MI)
Fisher Coll (MA)
Florida National U (FL)
Franklin Pierce U (NH)
Franklin U (OH)
Frostburg State U (MD)
The George Washington U (DC)
Georgia Coll & State U (GA)
Graceland U (IA)
Grand Valley State U (MI)
Grand View U (IA)
Greenville Coll (IL)
Gustavus Adolphus Coll (MN)
Hampton U (VA)
Hannibal-LaGrange U (MO)
Harris-Stowe State U (MO)
Hawai`i Pacific U (HI)
Huntingdon Coll (AL)
Husson U (ME)
Indiana U East (IN)
Inter American U of Puerto Rico, Guayama Campus (PR)
Iona Coll (NY)
Jacksonville State U (AL)
Johnson & Wales U (CO)
Johnson & Wales U (FL)
Johnson & Wales U (RI)
Judson Coll (AL)
Kansas Wesleyan U (KS)
Kean U (NJ)
Keiser U, Fort Lauderdale (FL)
Keuka Coll (NY)
Keystone Coll (PA)
Lake Erie Coll (OH)
Langston U (OK)
Lees-McRae Coll (NC)
LeMoyne-Owen Coll (TN)
Limestone Coll (SC)
Lincoln Coll of New England, Southington (CT)
Lincoln Memorial U (TN)
Lincoln U (MO)
Lindsey Wilson Coll (KY)
Lock Haven U of Pennsylvania (PA)
Long Island U–LIU Post (NY)
Lubbock Christian U (TX)
Lynn U (FL)
Mansfield U of Pennsylvania (PA)
Marist Coll (NY)
Mars Hill U (NC)
Marymount U (VA)
Marywood U (PA)
Medaille Coll (NY)
Mercy Coll (NY)
Merrimack Coll (MA)
Miami U (OH)
Michigan State U (MI)
MidAmerica Nazarene U (KS)
Middle Tennessee State U (TN)
Midwestern State U (TX)
Mississippi Valley State U (MS)
Missouri Southern State U (MO)
Missouri Valley Coll (MO)
Morris Coll (SC)
Mount Aloysius Coll (PA)
Mount Mary U (WI)
Mount Mercy U (IA)
Mount Vernon Nazarene U (OH)
National U (CA)
New England Coll (NH)
New England Inst of Technology (RI)
Newman U (KS)
New York Inst of Technology (NY)
Niagara U (NY)
North Carolina Wesleyan Coll (NC)
Northeastern State U (OK)
Northwest Christian U (OR)
Northwest Nazarene U (ID)
Norwich U (VT)
Oakland City U (IN)
Oakland U (MI)
Ohio Northern U (OH)
Oklahoma City U (OK)
Olivet Nazarene U (IL)
Pace U (NY)
Penn Foster Coll (AZ)
Penn State Abington (PA)
Penn State Altoona (PA)
Penn State Beaver (PA)
Penn State Berks (PA)
Penn State Brandywine (PA)
Penn State DuBois (PA)
Penn State Erie, The Behrend Coll (PA)
Penn State Fayette, The Eberly Campus (PA)
Penn State Greater Allegheny (PA)
Penn State Hazleton (PA)
Penn State Lehigh Valley (PA)
Penn State Mont Alto (PA)
Penn State New Kensington (PA)
Penn State Schuylkill (PA)
Penn State Shenango (PA)
Penn State U Park (PA)
Penn State Wilkes-Barre (PA)
Penn State Worthington Scranton (PA)
Penn State York (PA)
Peru State Coll (NE)
Piedmont Coll (GA)
Polk State Coll (FL)
Portland State U (OR)
Post U (CT)
Regent U (VA)
Rivier U (NH)
Roberts Wesleyan Coll (NY)
Rochester Inst of Technology (NY)
Rockhurst U (MO)
Roger Williams U (RI)
Rutgers, The State U of New Jersey, New Brunswick (NJ)
Sacred Heart U (CT)
The Sage Colls (NY)
Saint Augustine's U (NC)
St. Catharine Coll (KY)
Saint Francis U (PA)
St. John's U (NY)
St. Joseph's Coll, Long Island Campus (NY)
St. Joseph's Coll, New York (NY)
St. Mary's U (TX)
St. Thomas Aquinas Coll (NY)
St. Thomas U (FL)
Salve Regina U (RI)
San Francisco State U (CA)
Shenandoah U (VA)
Simpson Coll (IA)
South Carolina State U (SC)
Southeastern U (FL)
Southern Illinois U Carbondale (IL)
Southern Vermont Coll (VT)
Southwest Baptist U (MO)
Southwest Minnesota State U (MN)
State U of New York at Fredonia (NY)
State U of New York at Oswego (NY)
State U of New York Coll of Technology at Canton (NY)
Sterling Coll (KS)
Stevenson U (MD)
Sul Ross State U (TX)
Tarleton State U (TX)
Tennessee State U (TN)
Texas Southern U (TX)
Tiffin U (OH)
Trevecca Nazarene U (TN)
Trine U (IN)
Trinity Christian Coll (IL)
Tusculum Coll (TN)
Union Coll (KY)
Union Inst & U (OH)
Universidad Metropolitana (PR)
U at Albany, State U of New York (NY)
U of Arkansas–Fort Smith (AR)
U of Central Missouri (MO)
U of Central Oklahoma (OK)
U of Colorado Colorado Springs (CO)
U of Colorado Denver (CO)
U of Dayton (OH)
U of Dubuque (IA)
The U of Findlay (OH)
U of Georgia (GA)
U of Great Falls (MT)
U of Guam (GU)
U of Guelph (ON, Canada)
U of Hawaii–West Oahu (HI)
U of Louisville (KY)
U of Maine at Augusta (ME)
U of Maine at Presque Isle (ME)
U of Mary Hardin-Baylor (TX)
U of Massachusetts Lowell (MA)
U of Memphis (TN)
U of Minnesota, Crookston (MN)
U of Mississippi (MS)
U of Missouri–Kansas City (MO)
U of New Brunswick Saint John (NB, Canada)
U of New Haven (CT)
U of North Alabama (AL)
U of Oklahoma (OK)
U of Pittsburgh at Bradford (PA)
U of Pittsburgh at Greensburg (PA)
U of Regina (SK, Canada)
U of St. Francis (IL)
U of South Alabama (AL)
U of South Carolina Upstate (SC)
The U of South Dakota (SD)
The U of Tennessee at Chattanooga (TN)
The U of Tennessee at Martin (TN)
The U of Texas at El Paso (TX)
The U of Texas–Pan American (TX)
U of the Incarnate Word (TX)
U of Wisconsin–Oshkosh (WI)
U of Wisconsin–Parkside (WI)
U of Wisconsin–Platteville (WI)
Urbana U (OH)
Utah Valley U (UT)
Utica Coll (NY)
Villanova U (PA)
Virginia Commonwealth U (VA)
Voorhees Coll (SC)
Walden U (MN)
Waldorf Coll (IA)
Washburn U (KS)
Washington State U (WA)
Waynesburg U (PA)
Webber Intl U (FL)
Western Illinois U (IL)
Western Oregon U (OR)
West Liberty U (WV)
West Texas A&M U (TX)
West Virginia U Inst of Technology (WV)
West Virginia Wesleyan Coll (WV)
Widener U (PA)
William Peace U (NC)
Wilmington U (DE)
Wingate U (NC)
York Coll of Pennsylvania (PA)
Youngstown State U (OH)

CRIMINAL JUSTICE/POLICE SCIENCE

Armstrong State U (GA)
Bemidji State U (MN)
Bowling Green State U (OH)
Caribbean U (PR)
Coll of the Ozarks (MO)
Colorado Mesa U (CO)
Columbia Southern U (AL)
East Central U (OK)
Eastern Kentucky U (KY)
Elizabethtown Coll School of Continuing and Professional Studies (PA)
Fairmont State U (WV)
Ferris State U (MI)
George Mason U (VA)
Heidelberg U (OH)
Hilbert Coll (NY)
Howard U (DC)
Inter American U of Puerto Rico, San Germán Campus (PR)
Jacksonville State U (AL)
Louisiana Coll (LA)
Marian U (WI)
Metropolitan State U (MN)
Middle Tennessee State U (TN)
Minnesota State U Mankato (MN)
Newbury Coll (MA)
Northern State U (SD)
Northwestern Oklahoma State U (OK)
Ohio Northern U (OH)
Oklahoma City U (OK)
Rowan U (NJ)
St. Gregory's U, Shawnee (OK)
Southern Utah U (UT)
Stephen F. Austin State U (TX)
Texas A&M Intl U (TX)
Texas State U (TX)
U of Great Falls (MT)
U of Hartford (CT)
U of Pittsburgh at Greensburg (PA)
U of Regina (SK, Canada)
U of the Virgin Islands (VI)
U of Toronto (ON, Canada)
U of Washington, Tacoma (WA)
U of Wisconsin–Superior (WI)
Washington State U Vancouver (WA)
Weber State U (UT)
Western Oregon U (OR)

CRIMINAL JUSTICE/SAFETY

Adelphi U (NY)
Alabama State U (AL)
Albany State U (GA)
Alcorn State U (MS)
American Intl Coll (MA)
American Public U System (WV)
American U (DC)
Angelo State U (TX)
Appalachian State U (NC)
Athens State U (AL)
Auburn U at Montgomery (AL)
Baldwin Wallace U (OH)
Ball State U (IN)
Becker Coll (MA)
Belmont Abbey Coll (NC)
Benedictine U (IL)
Bethel Coll (IN)
Bloomsburg U of Pennsylvania (PA)
Bluefield State Coll (WV)
Blue Mountain Coll (MS)
Bluffton U (OH)
Bob Jones U (SC)
Bowling Green State U (OH)
Bowling Green State U-Firelands Coll (OH)
Bridgewater State U (MA)
Bryan Coll (TN)
Buena Vista U (IA)
Caldwell U (NJ)
California State U, Chico (CA)
California State U, Dominguez Hills (CA)
California State U, Fresno (CA)
California State U, Fullerton (CA)
California State U, Los Angeles (CA)
California State U, San Bernardino (CA)
California State U, Stanislaus (CA)
Calumet Coll of Saint Joseph (IN)
Carlos Albizu U, Miami Campus (FL)
Cazenovia Coll (NY)
Central Methodist U (MO)
Central Penn Coll (PA)
Central State U (OH)
Central Washington U (WA)
Chaminade U of Honolulu (HI)
Champlain Coll (VT)
Charleston Southern U (SC)
Chicago State U (IL)
Chowan U (NC)
Clark Atlanta U (GA)
Clayton State U (GA)
Clearwater Christian Coll (FL)
The Coll at Brockport, State U of New York (NY)
Colorado Mesa U (CO)
Columbus State U (GA)
Concordia U, St. Paul (MN)
Curry Coll (MA)
Dallas Baptist U (TX)
Defiance Coll (OH)
Delta State U (MS)
DeSales U (PA)
Dixie State U (UT)
Dominican Coll (NY)
East Carolina U (NC)
Eastern New Mexico U (NM)
Edgewood Coll (WI)
Edinboro U of Pennsylvania (PA)
Endicott Coll (MA)
Excelsior Coll (NY)
Ferrum Coll (VA)
Fisher Coll (MA)
Fitchburg State U (MA)
Florida Ag and Mech U (FL)
Florida Atlantic U (FL)
Florida Gulf Coast U (FL)
Florida Intl U (FL)
Florida National U (FL)
Fort Hays State U (KS)
Friends U (KS)
Frostburg State U (MD)
Gannon U (PA)
Georgia Gwinnett Coll (GA)
Georgian Court U (NJ)
Georgia Regents U (GA)
Georgia Southern U (GA)
Georgia State U (GA)
Gonzaga U (WA)
Goodwin Coll (CT)
Governors State U (IL)
Grace Coll (IN)
Grambling State U (LA)
Granite State Coll (NH)
Greensboro Coll (NC)
Guilford Coll (NC)
Hamline U (MN)
Harding U (AR)
Hardin-Simmons U (TX)
Harris-Stowe State U (MO)
Heritage U (WA)
High Point U (NC)
Holy Family U (PA)
Husson U (ME)

Huston-Tillotson U (TX)
Illinois State U (IL)
Immaculata U (PA)
Indiana U Bloomington (IN)
Indiana U Kokomo (IN)
Indiana U Northwest (IN)
Indiana U–Purdue U Indianapolis (IN)
Indiana U South Bend (IN)
Indiana U Southeast (IN)
Indian River State Coll (FL)
Inter American U of Puerto Rico, Aguadilla Campus (PR)
Inter American U of Puerto Rico, Fajardo Campus (PR)
Inter American U of Puerto Rico, Ponce Campus (PR)
Iowa Wesleyan Coll (IA)
Jackson State U (MS)
Judson U (IL)
Keiser U, Fort Lauderdale (FL)
Kennesaw State U (GA)
Kent State U (OH)
Kent State U at Ashtabula (OH)
Kent State U at East Liverpool (OH)
Kent State U at Salem (OH)
Kent State U at Stark (OH)
Kent State U at Trumbull (OH)
Kent State U at Tuscarawas (OH)
Kentucky State U (KY)
Kentucky Wesleyan Coll (KY)
King's Coll (PA)
King U (TN)
Kutztown U of Pennsylvania (PA)
Lamar U (TX)
Lane Coll (TN)
La Roche Coll (PA)
La Salle U (PA)
Lasell Coll (MA)
La Sierra U (CA)
Lewis U (IL)
Liberty U (VA)
Limestone Coll (SC)
Lincoln U (PA)
Lindenwood U (MO)
Longwood U (VA)
Loras Coll (IA)
Louisiana State U in Shreveport (LA)
Lourdes U (OH)
Loyola U Chicago (IL)
Madonna U (MI)
Marshall U (WV)
McNeese State U (LA)
Medaille Coll (NY)
Mercer U, Macon (GA)
Messiah Coll (PA)
Metropolitan State U (MN)
Michigan State U (MI)
Minnesota State U Moorhead (MN)
Minot State U (ND)
Missouri Baptist U (MO)
Missouri Western State U (MO)
Mitchell Coll (CT)
Molloy Coll (NY)
Monmouth U (NJ)
Montana State U Billings (MT)
Moravian Coll (PA)
Mount Marty Coll (SD)
Mount Vernon Nazarene U (OH)
Murray State U (KY)
National U (CA)
Neumann U (PA)
New Jersey City U (NJ)
New Mexico Highlands U (NM)
New Mexico State U (NM)
Nichols Coll (MA)
North Carolina Ag and Tech State U (NC)
North Carolina Central U (NC)
North Dakota State U (ND)
Northeastern Illinois U (IL)
Northeastern U (MA)
Northern Kentucky U (KY)
Northern Michigan U (MI)
Nova Southeastern U (FL)
Nyack Coll (NY)
Ohio Northern U (OH)
Olivet Coll (MI)
Our Lady of the Lake U of San Antonio (TX)
Penn State Abington (PA)
Penn State Altoona (PA)
Penn State Erie, The Behrend Coll (PA)
Penn State Fayette, The Eberly Campus (PA)
Penn State Harrisburg (PA)
Penn State Schuylkill (PA)
Penn State Wilkes-Barre (PA)
Pittsburg State U (KS)
Plymouth State U (NH)
Point U (GA)
Post U (CT)
Prairie View A&M U (TX)
Quincy U (IL)
Quinnipiac U (CT)
Radford U (VA)
Regis Coll (MA)
Rhode Island Coll (RI)
Rider U (NJ)
Roanoke Coll (VA)
Rochester Inst of Technology (NY)
Roosevelt U (IL)
Rosemont Coll (PA)
Rowan U (NJ)
Rutgers, The State U of New Jersey, Camden (NJ)
Rutgers, The State U of New Jersey, Newark (NJ)
Sacred Heart U (CT)
Saginaw Valley State U (MI)
Saint Anselm Coll (NH)
St. Edward's U (TX)
St. Francis Coll (NY)
Saint Joseph's Coll (IN)
Saint Leo U (FL)
Saint Martin's U (WA)
Saint Peter's U (NJ)
Samford U (AL)
Sam Houston State U (TX)
San Diego State U (CA)
San Jose State U (CA)
Seattle U (WA)
Seton Hill U (PA)
Shaw U (NC)
Shippensburg U of Pennsylvania (PA)
Siena Heights U (MI)
Southeastern Louisiana U (LA)
Southeastern Oklahoma State U (OK)
Southern Arkansas U–Magnolia (AR)
Southern Illinois U Edwardsville (IL)
Southwestern Assemblies of God U (TX)
Southwest Minnesota State U (MN)
State U of New York at Plattsburgh (NY)
State U of New York Coll at Potsdam (NY)
State U of New York Coll of Technology at Delhi (NY)
Sullivan U (KY)
Tarleton State U (TX)
Temple U (PA)
Tennessee Wesleyan Coll (TN)
Texas A&M U–Commerce (TX)
Texas A&M U–Kingsville (TX)
Texas Christian U (TX)
Texas State U (TX)
Texas Wesleyan U (TX)
Texas Woman's U (TX)
Thiel Coll (PA)
Thomas More Coll (KY)
Troy U (AL)
Truman State U (MO)
Universidad Metropolitana (PR)
The U of Akron (OH)
The U of Alabama (AL)
U of Arkansas (AR)
U of Arkansas at Little Rock (AR)
U of Bridgeport (CT)
U of Central Florida (FL)
U of Central Oklahoma (OK)
U of Cincinnati (OH)
U of Evansville (IN)
U of Great Falls (MT)
U of Hawaii at Hilo (HI)
U of Houston–Downtown (TX)
U of Houston–Victoria (TX)
U of Illinois at Chicago (IL)
U of Illinois at Springfield (IL)
U of Jamestown (ND)
U of Louisiana at Lafayette (LA)
U of Maryland U Coll (MD)
U of Massachusetts Boston (MA)
U of Michigan–Dearborn (MI)
U of Mount Union (OH)
U of Nebraska at Kearney (NE)
U of Nevada, Las Vegas (NV)
The U of North Carolina at Charlotte (NC)
The U of North Carolina at Pembroke (NC)
U of North Dakota (ND)
U of Northern Colorado (CO)
U of North Florida (FL)
U of North Georgia (GA)
U of North Texas (TX)
U of Northwestern–St. Paul (MN)
U of Pikeville (KY)
U of Regina (SK, Canada)
U of Richmond (VA)
The U of Scranton (PA)
U of Southern Indiana (IN)
U of Southern Mississippi (MS)
The U of Texas at Arlington (TX)
The U of Texas at San Antonio (TX)
The U of Texas at Tyler (TX)
The U of Texas of the Permian Basin (TX)
U of the Cumberlands (KY)
U of the Fraser Valley (BC, Canada)
U of the Incarnate Word (TX)
The U of Toledo (OH)
U of Valley Forge (PA)
The U of Virginia's Coll at Wise (VA)
U of West Florida (FL)
U of Wisconsin–Eau Claire (WI)
U of Wisconsin–Milwaukee (WI)
U of Wisconsin–Superior (WI)
U of Wyoming (WY)
Valdosta State U (GA)
Virginia State U (VA)
Virginia Wesleyan Coll (VA)
Viterbo U (WI)
Wayne State Coll (NE)
Wayne State U (MI)
Weber State U (UT)
West Chester U of Pennsylvania (PA)
Western Carolina U (NC)
Western Michigan U (MI)
Western New England U (MA)
Westfield State U (MA)
Westminster Coll (UT)
West Texas A&M U (TX)
West Virginia State U (WV)
Wheeling Jesuit U (WV)
Wichita State U (KS)
Wilkes U (PA)
William Paterson U of New Jersey (NJ)
William Penn U (IA)
William Woods U (MO)
Worcester State U (MA)
Xavier U (OH)
Youngstown State U (OH)

CRIMINOLOGY
Adams State U (CO)
Albright Coll (PA)
Arcadia U (PA)
Arkansas State U (AR)
Assumption Coll (MA)
Auburn U (AL)
Avila U (MO)
Barry U (FL)
Benedictine Coll (KS)
Biola U (CA)
Butler U (IN)
Cabrini Coll (PA)
California State U, Fresno (CA)
California State U, San Marcos (CA)
California State U, Stanislaus (CA)
Capital U (OH)
Carlow U (PA)
Castleton State Coll (VT)
Cedar Crest Coll (PA)
Central Connecticut State U (CT)
Chatham U (PA)
Cleveland State U (OH)
Coker Coll (SC)
Delaware State U (DE)
Dominican U (IL)
Drexel U (PA)
Drury U (MO)
Eastern Michigan U (MI)
Eastern U (PA)
Elizabethtown Coll School of Continuing and Professional Studies (PA)
Elmhurst Coll (IL)
Emmanuel Coll (MA)
Fairleigh Dickinson U, Coll at Florham (NJ)
Flagler Coll (FL)
Florida Southern Coll (FL)
Florida State U (FL)
Framingham State U (MA)
Geneva Coll (PA)
Gonzaga U (WA)
Hofstra U (NY)
Howard Payne U (TX)
Husson U (ME)
Indiana State U (IN)
Indiana U of Pennsylvania (PA)
Johnson C. Smith U (NC)
Lasell Coll (MA)
Lebanon Valley Coll (PA)
Lees-McRae Coll (NC)
Le Moyne Coll (NY)
LeTourneau U (TX)
Lindenwood U (MO)
Loyola U New Orleans (LA)
Lycoming Coll (PA)
Lynchburg Coll (VA)
Marquette U (WI)
Mary Baldwin Coll (VA)
Maryville U of Saint Louis (MO)
Mississippi State U (MS)
Missouri State U (MO)
Mount St. Joseph U (OH)
Mount Saint Mary's U (CA)
Mount St. Mary's U (MD)
Niagara U (NY)
North Carolina State U (NC)
Northern Arizona U (AZ)
Northwest Christian U (OR)
Notre Dame of Maryland U (MD)
The Ohio State U (OH)
The Ohio State U–Mansfield Campus (OH)
Ohio U (OH)
Oklahoma Wesleyan U (OK)
Old Dominion U (VA)
Regis U (CO)
Rivier U (NH)
St. Edward's U (TX)
Saint Francis U (PA)
St. John Fisher Coll (NY)
Saint Joseph's U (PA)
Saint Mary-of-the-Woods Coll (IN)
St. Mary's U (TX)
St. Thomas U (NB, Canada)
Saint Vincent Coll (PA)
Simon Fraser U (BC, Canada)
Slippery Rock U of Pennsylvania (PA)
Southern Oregon U (OR)
Spring Hill Coll (AL)
State U of New York Coll at Cortland (NY)
State U of New York Coll at Old Westbury (NY)
Stockton U (NJ)
Stonehill Coll (MA)
Texas A&M U–Kingsville (TX)
Universidad del Turabo (PR)
Université de Montréal (QC, Canada)
The U of Akron (OH)
U of California, Irvine (CA)
U of Delaware (DE)
U of Denver (CO)
U of Florida (FL)
U of Houston–Clear Lake (TX)
U of La Verne (CA)
U of Maryland, Coll Park (MD)
U of Massachusetts Dartmouth (MA)
U of Memphis (TN)
U of Miami (FL)
U of Minnesota, Duluth (MN)
U of Minnesota, Twin Cities Campus (MN)
U of Missouri–Kansas City (MO)
U of Missouri–St. Louis (MO)
U of Mount Union (OH)
U of Nevada, Reno (NV)
U of New Hampshire (NH)
U of Northern Iowa (IA)
U of Ottawa (ON, Canada)
U of Saint Mary (KS)
U of St. Thomas (MN)
U of Southern Maine (ME)
U of South Florida (FL)
U of South Florida, St. Petersburg (FL)
U of South Florida Sarasota-Manatee (FL)
The U of Tampa (FL)
The U of Texas at Dallas (TX)
The U of Texas of the Permian Basin (TX)
U of Toronto (ON, Canada)
The U of Western Ontario (ON, Canada)
U of West Georgia (GA)
U of Windsor (ON, Canada)
U of Wisconsin–Whitewater (WI)
Upper Iowa U (IA)
Valparaiso U (IN)
Virginia Union U (VA)
Virginia Wesleyan Coll (VA)
Walsh U (OH)
Western Kentucky U (KY)
Western State Colorado U (CO)
Wheeling Jesuit U (WV)
William Penn U (IA)
Wright State U (OH)

CRISIS/EMERGENCY/DISASTER MANAGEMENT
Adelphi U (NY)
American Public U System (WV)
Arkansas State U (AR)
Arkansas Tech U (AR)
Kansas Wesleyan U (KS)
North Dakota State U (ND)
Pennsylvania Coll of Technology (PA)
Post U (CT)
Saint Louis U (MO)
Southeast Missouri State U (MO)
State U of New York Coll of Technology at Canton (NY)
Texas Southern U (TX)
Union Inst & U (OH)
U of Alaska Fairbanks (AK)
U of North Texas (TX)

CRITICAL INFRASTRUCTURE PROTECTION
George Mason U (VA)

CROP PRODUCTION
Cornell U (NY)
North Dakota State U (ND)
U of Alberta (AB, Canada)
U of Massachusetts Amherst (MA)
U of Minnesota, Crookston (MN)
U of Minnesota, Twin Cities Campus (MN)
Washington State U (WA)

CULINARY ARTS
Coll of the Ozarks (MO)
Drexel U (PA)
Johnson & Wales U (CO)
Johnson & Wales U (FL)
Johnson & Wales U (RI)
Johnson & Wales U - Charlotte Campus (NC)
Newbury Coll (MA)
Nicholls State U (LA)
Southern New Hampshire U (NH)
Stratford U (MD)

CULINARY ARTS RELATED
Johnson & Wales U (CO)
Johnson & Wales U (FL)
Johnson & Wales U (RI)
Mississippi U for Women (MS)
Newbury Coll (MA)
U of Cincinnati (OH)
U of Nevada, Las Vegas (NV)
U of North Alabama (AL)

CULINARY SCIENCE
The Culinary Inst of America (NY)
Drexel U (PA)
Mississippi State U (MS)

CULTURAL ANTHROPOLOGY
Webster U (MO)

CULTURAL RESOURCE MANAGEMENT AND POLICY ANALYSIS
California State U, Dominguez Hills (CA)
U of Waterloo (ON, Canada)

CULTURAL STUDIES/ CRITICAL THEORY AND ANALYSIS
American Public U System (WV)
The American U in Dubai (United Arab Emirates)
Bard Coll at Simon's Rock (MA)

Bryant U (RI)
Goddard Coll (VT)
Howard Payne U (TX)
Northern Arizona U (AZ)
The U of British Columbia–Okanagan Campus (BC, Canada)
The U of Tampa (FL)
Western Kentucky U (KY)

CURRICULUM AND INSTRUCTION
Albertus Magnus Coll (CT)
Franklin Pierce U (NH)
Lasell Coll (MA)
LeTourneau U (TX)
Midwestern State U (TX)
Randolph Coll (VA)
Tarleton State U (TX)
U of Minnesota, Twin Cities Campus (MN)
The U of Montana (MT)
The U of South Dakota (SD)
The U of Western Ontario (ON, Canada)
Utah State U (UT)
Walden U (MN)
Welch Coll (TN)
Wright State U (OH)

CUSTOMER SERVICE MANAGEMENT
Drexel U (PA)
Ohio U (OH)
Southwest Baptist U (MO)

CYBER/COMPUTER FORENSICS AND COUNTERTERRORISM
Anna Maria Coll (MA)
Bloomsburg U of Pennsylvania (PA)
Champlain Coll (VT)
Chestnut Hill Coll (PA)
Christian Brothers U (TN)
Embry-Riddle Aeronautical U–Prescott (AZ)
Keiser U, Fort Lauderdale (FL)
Mercy Coll (NY)
Oakland U (MI)

CYBER/ELECTRONIC OPERATIONS AND WARFARE
Maryville U of Saint Louis (MO)
Northern Michigan U (MI)
United States Naval Acad (MD)
Webster U (MO)

CYTOGENETICS/GENETICS/CLINICAL GENETICS TECHNOLOGY
Northern Michigan U (MI)

CYTOTECHNOLOGY
Barry U (FL)
Edgewood Coll (WI)
Elmhurst Coll (IL)
Illinois Coll (IL)
Indiana U–Purdue U Indianapolis (IN)
Marian U (WI)
Marshall U (WV)
Oakland U (MI)
Saint Louis U (MO)
Saint Mary's U of Minnesota (MN)
Slippery Rock U of Pennsylvania (PA)
State U of New York at Plattsburgh (NY)
Thiel Coll (PA)
The U of Kansas (KS)
U of Massachusetts Dartmouth (MA)
U of North Dakota (ND)
Winona State U (MN)

DAIRY HUSBANDRY AND PRODUCTION
Coll of the Ozarks (MO)
Morrisville State Coll (NY)
U of Vermont (VT)

DAIRY SCIENCE
California Polytechnic State U, San Luis Obispo (CA)
Eastern New Mexico U (NM)
Iowa State U of Science and Technology (IA)
Morrisville State Coll (NY)
South Dakota State U (SD)
U of Georgia (GA)
U of Minnesota, Twin Cities Campus (MN)
U of Wisconsin–Madison (WI)
U of Wisconsin–River Falls (WI)
Utah State U (UT)
Virginia Polytechnic Inst and State U (VA)

DANCE
Adelphi U (NY)
Agnes Scott Coll (GA)
Alabama State U (AL)
Alma Coll (MI)
Amherst Coll (MA)
Anderson U (IN)
Appalachian State U (NC)
Arizona State U at the Tempe campus (AZ)
Ball State U (IN)
Bard Coll (NY)
Bard Coll at Simon's Rock (MA)
Barnard Coll (NY)
Bates Coll (ME)
Belhaven U (MS)
Beloit Coll (WI)
Bennington Coll (VT)
Brenau U (GA)
Butler U (IN)
California Inst of the Arts (CA)
California State U, Fresno (CA)
California State U, Fullerton (CA)
California State U, Long Beach (CA)
California State U, Los Angeles (CA)
California State U, Sacramento (CA)
Case Western Reserve U (OH)
Cedar Crest Coll (PA)
Chapman U (CA)
The Coll at Brockport, State U of New York (NY)
Coll of Charleston (SC)
The Colorado Coll (CO)
Colorado State U (CO)
Columbia Coll (SC)
Columbia Coll Chicago (IL)
Columbia U (NY)
Columbia U, School of General Studies (NY)
Concordia U (QC, Canada)
Connecticut Coll (CT)
Cornell U (NY)
Cornish Coll of the Arts (WA)
Creighton U (NE)
Denison U (OH)
DeSales U (PA)
Dickinson Coll (PA)
Dominican U of California (CA)
Drexel U (PA)
East Carolina U (NC)
Eastern Michigan U (MI)
Eastern U (PA)
Elon U (NC)
Florida Southern Coll (FL)
Florida State U (FL)
Fordham U (NY)
Franklin & Marshall Coll (PA)
George Mason U (VA)
The George Washington U (DC)
Georgian Court U (NJ)
Goucher Coll (MD)
Grand Valley State U (MI)
Gustavus Adolphus Coll (MN)
Hamilton Coll (NY)
Hampshire Coll (MA)
Hobart and William Smith Colls (NY)
Hofstra U (NY)
Hollins U (VA)
Hope Coll (MI)
Hunter Coll of the City U of New York (NY)
Indiana U Bloomington (IN)
Johnson State Coll (VT)
The Juilliard School (NY)
Keene State Coll (NH)
Kennesaw State U (GA)
Kent State U (OH)
Kenyon Coll (OH)
La Roche Coll (PA)
Lehman Coll of the City U of New York (NY)
Lindenwood U (MO)
Long Island U–LIU Brooklyn (NY)
Long Island U–LIU Post (NY)
Loyola Marymount U (CA)
Loyola U Chicago (IL)
Manhattanville Coll (NY)
Marymount Manhattan Coll (NY)
Meredith Coll (NC)
Messiah Coll (PA)
Middlebury Coll (VT)
Mills Coll (CA)
Montclair State U (NJ)
Mount Holyoke Coll (MA)
Muhlenberg Coll (PA)
Nazareth Coll of Rochester (NY)
New Mexico State U (NM)
New York U (NY)
Northwestern U (IL)
Nova Southeastern U (FL)
Oakland U (MI)
Oberlin Coll (OH)
The Ohio State U (OH)
Ohio U (OH)
Oklahoma City U (OK)
Pace U (NY)
Palm Beach Atlantic U (FL)
Pomona Coll (CA)
Purchase Coll, State U of New York (NY)
Radford U (VA)
Randolph Coll (VA)
Reed Coll (OR)
Rhode Island Coll (RI)
Rider U (NJ)
Rockford U (IL)
Roger Williams U (RI)
Rutgers, The State U of New Jersey, New Brunswick (NJ)
St. Gregory's U, Shawnee (OK)
St. Olaf Coll (MN)
Sam Houston State U (TX)
San Diego State U (CA)
San Francisco State U (CA)
San Jose State U (CA)
Sarah Lawrence Coll (NY)
Scripps Coll (CA)
Seton Hill U (PA)
Shenandoah U (VA)
Simon Fraser U (BC, Canada)
Skidmore Coll (NY)
Slippery Rock U of Pennsylvania (PA)
Smith Coll (MA)
Southern Methodist U (TX)
State U of New York at Fredonia (NY)
State U of New York Coll at Potsdam (NY)
Stephen F. Austin State U (TX)
Stephens Coll (MO)
Temple U (PA)
Texas Christian U (TX)
Texas State U (TX)
Texas Tech U (TX)
Texas Woman's U (TX)
Towson U (MD)
Trinity Coll (CT)
Troy U (AL)
Tulane U (LA)
U at Buffalo, the State U of New York (NY)
The U of Akron (OH)
The U of Alabama (AL)
The U of Arizona (AZ)
U of Arkansas at Little Rock (AR)
U of California, Berkeley (CA)
U of California, Irvine (CA)
U of California, Los Angeles (CA)
U of California, Santa Barbara (CA)
U of Central Oklahoma (OK)
U of Cincinnati (OH)
U of Colorado Boulder (CO)
U of Florida (FL)
U of Georgia (GA)
U of Hartford (CT)
U of Hawaii at Manoa (HI)
U of Houston (TX)
U of Idaho (ID)
The U of Iowa (IA)
The U of Kansas (KS)
U of Maryland, Baltimore County (MD)
U of Maryland, Coll Park (MD)
U of Massachusetts Amherst (MA)
U of Michigan (MI)
U of Michigan–Flint (MI)
U of Minnesota, Twin Cities Campus (MN)
U of Missouri–Kansas City (MO)
The U of Montana (MT)
U of Nebraska–Lincoln (NE)
U of Nevada, Las Vegas (NV)
U of New Mexico (NM)
The U of North Carolina at Charlotte (NC)
The U of North Carolina at Greensboro (NC)
U of North Carolina School of the Arts (NC)
U of North Texas (TX)
U of Oklahoma (OK)
U of Oregon (OR)
U of Richmond (VA)
U of Saint Francis (IN)
U of Southern California (CA)
U of Southern Mississippi (MS)
U of South Florida (FL)
The U of Texas at Austin (TX)
The U of Texas–Pan American (TX)
The U of the Arts (PA)
U of Utah (UT)
U of Washington (WA)
U of Wisconsin–Madison (WI)
U of Wisconsin–Milwaukee (WI)
U of Wisconsin–Stevens Point (WI)
Ursinus Coll (PA)
Utah State U (UT)
Utah Valley U (UT)
Valdosta State U (GA)
Virginia Commonwealth U (VA)
Washington U in St. Louis (MO)
Wayne State U (MI)
Weber State U (UT)
Webster U (MO)
Wells Coll (NY)
Wesleyan U (CT)
Western Kentucky U (KY)
Western Michigan U (MI)
Western Oregon U (OR)
Western Washington U (WA)
West Texas A&M U (TX)
Winthrop U (SC)
Wittenberg U (OH)
Wright State U (OH)

DANCE RELATED
Anderson U (IN)
Brigham Young U (UT)
California State U, Long Beach (CA)
Coker Coll (SC)
Drexel U (PA)
Marymount Manhattan Coll (NY)
Western Michigan U (MI)
Youngstown State U (OH)

DANCE THERAPY
Columbia Coll Chicago (IL)

DANISH
U of Washington (WA)

DATA MODELING/WAREHOUSING AND DATABASE ADMINISTRATION
Bryant U (RI)
Central Washington U (WA)
Lewis U (IL)
Limestone Coll (SC)
Neumont U (UT)
Pennsylvania Coll of Technology (PA)
Rochester Inst of Technology (NY)
U of Michigan (MI)

DATA PROCESSING AND DATA PROCESSING TECHNOLOGY
Arkansas State U (AR)
Bemidji State U (MN)
California State U, San Marcos (CA)
The Coll of Saint Rose (NY)
Delaware State U (DE)
U of Arkansas (AR)
U of Southern Mississippi (MS)

DEAF STUDIES
U of Valley Forge (PA)

DENTAL ASSISTING
Delaware State U (DE)

DENTAL HYGIENE
Clayton State U (GA)
Creighton U (NE)
Dalhousie U (NS, Canada)
Dixie State U (UT)
East Tennessee State U (TN)
Farmingdale State Coll (NY)
Ferris State U (MI)
Georgia Regents U (GA)
Howard U (DC)
Indiana U Northwest (IN)
Indiana U South Bend (IN)
Lewis U (IL)
Louisiana State U Health Sciences Center (LA)
MCPHS U (MA)
Metropolitan State U (MN)
Midwestern State U (TX)
Minnesota State U Mankato (MN)
New York U (NY)
Northern Arizona U (AZ)
The Ohio State U (OH)
The Ohio State U at Lima (OH)
Old Dominion U (VA)
Pennsylvania Coll of Technology (PA)
Rhode Island Coll (RI)
Southern Illinois U Carbondale (IL)
State U of New York Coll of Technology at Canton (NY)
Tennessee State U (TN)
Texas Woman's U (TX)
U of Arkansas–Fort Smith (AR)
U of Bridgeport (CT)
The U of British Columbia (BC, Canada)
U of Hawaii at Manoa (HI)
U of Louisville (KY)
U of Maine at Augusta (ME)
U of Michigan (MI)
U of Minnesota, Twin Cities Campus (MN)
U of Missouri–Kansas City (MO)
U of New England (ME)
U of New Haven (CT)
U of New Mexico (NM)
The U of North Carolina at Chapel Hill (NC)
U of Oklahoma Health Sciences Center (OK)
U of Pittsburgh (PA)
The U of South Dakota (SD)
U of Southern California (CA)
U of Southern Indiana (IN)
The U of Tennessee (TN)
The U of Texas Health Science Center at Houston (TX)
U of Washington (WA)
U of Wyoming (WY)
Utah Valley U (UT)
Vermont Tech Coll (VT)
Virginia Commonwealth U (VA)
Weber State U (UT)
Western Kentucky U (KY)
West Liberty U (WV)
West Virginia U (WV)
Wichita State U (KS)
Youngstown State U (OH)

DENTAL SERVICES AND ALLIED PROFESSIONS RELATED
Delaware State U (DE)
Indiana U–Purdue U Indianapolis (IN)
U of Minnesota, Twin Cities Campus (MN)

DESIGN AND APPLIED ARTS RELATED
Alverno Coll (WI)
Arizona State U at the Tempe campus (AZ)
Asbury U (KY)
Augsburg Coll (MN)
Azusa Pacific U (CA)
Bemidji State U (MN)
Berkeley Coll, Woodland Park (NJ)
Buffalo State Coll, State U of New York (NY)
Butler U (IN)
California Coll of the Arts (CA)
Columbia U, School of General Studies (NY)
Concordia U (QC, Canada)
Drexel U (PA)
Fashion Inst of Technology (NY)
Ferris State U (MI)
Franklin Pierce U (NH)
Hampshire Coll (MA)
Harding U (AR)
Hofstra U (NY)
Howard U (DC)
Inter American U of Puerto Rico, San Germán Campus (PR)
Laguna Coll of Art & Design (CA)

Mansfield U of Pennsylvania (PA)
McMurry U (TX)
Midwestern State U (TX)
Minnesota State U Mankato (MN)
Montclair State U (NJ)
New York Inst of Technology (NY)
Otis Coll of Art and Design (CA)
Penn State Altoona (PA)
Penn State Berks (PA)
Penn State U Park (PA)
Peru State Coll (NE)
Portland State U (OR)
Pratt Inst (NY)
Reinhardt U (GA)
Roberts Wesleyan Coll (NY)
Savannah Coll of Art and Design (GA)
School of the Art Inst of Chicago (IL)
School of the Museum of Fine Arts, Boston (MA)
Shawnee State U (OH)
Southern Methodist U (TX)
State U of New York at Fredonia (NY)
Taylor U (IN)
U of Alberta (AB, Canada)
U of California, Los Angeles (CA)
U of Illinois at Chicago (IL)
U of Massachusetts Dartmouth (MA)
U of Oregon (OR)
U of Saint Francis (IN)
U of Wisconsin–Stout (WI)
Washington U in St. Louis (MO)
Western Washington U (WA)
William Paterson U of New Jersey (NJ)

DESIGN AND VISUAL COMMUNICATIONS

Albright Coll (PA)
Alma Coll (MI)
American Acad of Art (IL)
American U (DC)
The American U in Dubai (United Arab Emirates)
Anderson U (IN)
Auburn U (AL)
Belmont U (TN)
Bennington Coll (VT)
Bethel Coll (IN)
Biola U (CA)
Bowling Green State U (OH)
Bowling Green State U-Firelands Coll (OH)
Bryant U (RI)
Buffalo State Coll, State U of New York (NY)
California Coll of the Arts (CA)
California Inst of the Arts (CA)
California State U, Chico (CA)
California State U, Monterey Bay (CA)
Cazenovia Coll (NY)
Central Connecticut State U (CT)
Coll of the Ozarks (MO)
Columbia Coll Chicago (IL)
Concordia U, St. Paul (MN)
Drury U (MO)
EDP U of Puerto Rico (PR)
Emily Carr U of Art + Design (BC, Canada)
Endicott Coll (MA)
Escuela de Artes Plasticas de Puerto Rico (PR)
Farmingdale State Coll (NY)
Holy Cross Coll (IN)
Houghton Coll (NY)
Iowa State U of Science and Technology (IA)
Iowa Wesleyan Coll (IA)
Jacksonville U (FL)
Kean U (NJ)
Laguna Coll of Art & Design (CA)
La Roche Coll (PA)
Lawrence Technological U (MI)
Lees-McRae Coll (NC)
Lehigh U (PA)
Lewis U (IL)
LIM Coll (NY)
Linfield Coll (OR)
Loyola U Chicago (IL)
Lubbock Christian U (TX)
Madonna U (MI)
Maryville Coll (TN)
Missouri State U (MO)
Mount St. Joseph U (OH)
Nazareth Coll of Rochester (NY)
New Mexico Highlands U (NM)
New York City Coll of Technology of the City U of New York (NY)
North Carolina State U (NC)
Northeastern State U (OK)
Northern Arizona U (AZ)
Northwest Coll of Art & Design (WA)
Ohio Dominican U (OH)
Ohio Northern U (OH)
The Ohio State U (OH)
Pacific Northwest Coll of Art (OR)
Paris Coll of Art (France)
Purdue U (IN)
Radford U (VA)
Rensselaer Polytechnic Inst (NY)
Robert Morris U (PA)
Rochester Inst of Technology (NY)
Saginaw Valley State U (MI)
Saint Mary-of-the-Woods Coll (IN)
San Francisco State U (CA)
Savannah Coll of Art and Design (GA)
School of the Art Inst of Chicago (IL)
Seattle Pacific U (WA)
Southern Illinois U Carbondale (IL)
Stevenson U (MD)
Syracuse U (NY)
Texas State U (TX)
Université du Québec en Outaouais (QC, Canada)
U of Alberta (AB, Canada)
U of Dayton (OH)
U of Evansville (IN)
U of Hartford (CT)
The U of Kansas (KS)
U of Mary Hardin-Baylor (TX)
U of Maryland, Baltimore County (MD)
U of Massachusetts Dartmouth (MA)
U of Michigan–Flint (MI)
U of Minnesota, Twin Cities Campus (MN)
U of North Texas (TX)
U of Notre Dame (IN)
U of Oklahoma (OK)
U of San Francisco (CA)
The U of Tennessee at Martin (TN)
The U of Texas at Austin (TX)
U of Washington (WA)
U of Wisconsin–Green Bay (WI)
U of Wisconsin–Stevens Point (WI)
Utah Valley U (UT)
Viterbo U (WI)
Washington U in St. Louis (MO)
Watkins Coll of Art, Design, & Film (TN)
Weber State U (UT)
Western Washington U (WA)
West Virginia U (WV)
Wilmington U (DE)

DESKTOP PUBLISHING AND DIGITAL IMAGING DESIGN

California Baptist U (CA)
Chowan U (NC)
EDP U of Puerto Rico (PR)
New England Inst of Technology (RI)
Rochester Inst of Technology (NY)
Saint Mary's U of Minnesota (MN)
Sullivan Coll of Technology and Design (KY)
Wilmington U (DE)

DEVELOPMENTAL AND CHILD PSYCHOLOGY

Antioch U Midwest (OH)
Bay Path U (MA)
Boston Coll (MA)
Bridgewater State U (MA)
California State U, Stanislaus (CA)
Carson-Newman U (TN)
Castleton State Coll (VT)
Colby-Sawyer Coll (NH)
Eastern Connecticut State U (CT)
East Texas Baptist U (TX)
Emmanuel Coll (MA)
Fitchburg State U (MA)
Hampton U (VA)
Houston Baptist U (TX)
Humboldt State U (CA)
LeTourneau U (TX)
Maryville Coll (TN)
Metropolitan State U (MN)
Mills Coll (CA)
Minnesota State U Mankato (MN)
Mount Saint Mary's U (CA)
Northern Michigan U (MI)
Quinnipiac U (CT)
Savannah State U (GA)
Texas Christian U (TX)
Tufts U (MA)
Université de Montréal (QC, Canada)
The U of British Columbia (BC, Canada)
U of California, Santa Cruz (CA)
The U of Kansas (KS)
U of Minnesota, Twin Cities Campus (MN)
U of Saint Francis (IN)
The U of Texas at Dallas (TX)
U of the District of Columbia (DC)
The U of Toledo (OH)
U of Windsor (ON, Canada)
U of Wisconsin–Green Bay (WI)
Utica Coll (NY)
Vanderbilt U (TN)
Western Washington U (WA)

DEVELOPMENTAL BIOLOGY AND EMBRYOLOGY

U of Alberta (AB, Canada)
U of California, Santa Barbara (CA)

DEVELOPMENT ECONOMICS AND INTERNATIONAL DEVELOPMENT

Brown U (RI)
Calvin Coll (MI)
Clark U (MA)
Dalhousie U (NS, Canada)
Georgia Southern U (GA)
Houghton Coll (NY)
Illinois Inst of Technology (IL)
John Brown U (AR)
Messiah Coll (PA)
Penn State Altoona (PA)
Penn State Berks (PA)
Point Loma Nazarene U (CA)
Seattle Pacific U (WA)
Taylor U (IN)
U of California, Los Angeles (CA)
U of Dayton (OH)
U of Guelph (ON, Canada)
U of King's Coll (NS, Canada)
U of New Brunswick Saint John (NB, Canada)
U of Ottawa (ON, Canada)
U of St. Thomas (TX)
U of San Francisco (CA)
U of the Fraser Valley (BC, Canada)
U of Vermont (VT)

DIAGNOSTIC MEDICAL SONOGRAPHY AND ULTRASOUND TECHNOLOGY

Adventist U of Health Sciences (FL)
Benedictine U (IL)
Bowling Green State U (OH)
Dalhousie U (NS, Canada)
The George Washington U (DC)
Lewis U (IL)
Long Island U–LIU Brooklyn (NY)
Marian U (WI)
Misericordia U (PA)
Nebraska Methodist Coll (NE)
Newman U (KS)
Nova Southeastern U (FL)
Rhode Island Coll (RI)
Rochester Inst of Technology (NY)
Seattle U (WA)
Trocaire Coll (NY)
U of Charleston (WV)
U of Missouri (MO)
U of Oklahoma Health Sciences Center (OK)
Washburn U (KS)
Weber State U (UT)

DIETETICS

Abilene Christian U (TX)
American U of Beirut (Lebanon)
Andrews U (MI)
Appalachian State U (NC)
Arkansas State U (AR)
Ashland U (OH)
Ball State U (IN)
Bastyr U (WA)
Bowling Green State U (OH)
Bradley U (IL)
Buffalo State Coll, State U of New York (NY)
California Polytechnic State U, San Luis Obispo (CA)
California State Polytechnic U, Pomona (CA)
California State U, Chico (CA)
California State U, Fresno (CA)
California State U, Long Beach (CA)
California State U, Los Angeles (CA)
California State U, San Bernardino (CA)
Carson-Newman U (TN)
Case Western Reserve U (OH)
Central Michigan U (MI)
Central Washington U (WA)
Coll of Saint Elizabeth (NJ)
Coll of the Ozarks (MO)
Delaware State U (DE)
Dominican U (IL)
East Carolina U (NC)
Eastern Michigan U (MI)
Florida Intl U (FL)
Fontbonne U (MO)
Georgia State U (GA)
Harding U (AR)
Immaculata U (PA)
Iowa State U of Science and Technology (IA)
Jacksonville State U (AL)
Kansas State U (KS)
Keene State Coll (NH)
Keiser U, Fort Lauderdale (FL)
Lehman Coll of the City U of New York (NY)
Life U (GA)
Lipscomb U (TN)
Mansfield U of Pennsylvania (PA)
Marshall U (WV)
Marywood U (PA)
Meredith Coll (NC)
Miami U (OH)
Michigan State U (MI)
Minnesota State U Mankato (MN)
Missouri State U (MO)
Mount Mary U (WI)
New Mexico State U (NM)
Nicholls State U (LA)
North Dakota State U (ND)
Northern Illinois U (IL)
Northwest Missouri State U (MO)
The Ohio State U (OH)
Ohio U (OH)
Olivet Nazarene U (IL)
Point Loma Nazarene U (CA)
Purdue U (IN)
Rutgers, The State U of New Jersey, New Brunswick (NJ)
St. Catherine U (MN)
Saint Louis U (MO)
San Diego State U (CA)
San Francisco State U (CA)
San Jose State U (CA)
Seton Hill U (PA)
Simmons Coll (MA)
South Dakota State U (SD)
Texas A&M U–Kingsville (TX)
Texas Christian U (TX)
Texas Southern U (TX)
Texas Tech U (TX)
The U of Akron (OH)
The U of Alabama (AL)
The U of British Columbia (BC, Canada)
U of Central Missouri (MO)
U of Central Oklahoma (OK)
U of Cincinnati (OH)
U of Dayton (OH)
U of Delaware (DE)
U of Florida (FL)
U of Georgia (GA)
U of Illinois at Chicago (IL)
U of Louisiana at Lafayette (LA)
U of Minnesota, Twin Cities Campus (MN)
U of Missouri (MO)
U of New Haven (CT)
U of North Dakota (ND)
U of Northern Colorado (CO)
U of Oklahoma Health Sciences Center (OK)
U of Pittsburgh (PA)
U of Rhode Island (RI)
U of Saskatchewan (SK, Canada)
U of Southern Mississippi (MS)
The U of Tennessee at Martin (TN)
The U of Texas at San Antonio (TX)
The U of Texas–Pan American (TX)
U of Vermont (VT)
The U of Western Ontario (ON, Canada)
U of Wisconsin–Stevens Point (WI)
U of Wisconsin–Stout (WI)
Viterbo U (WI)
Wayne State U (MI)
West Chester U of Pennsylvania (PA)
Western Carolina U (NC)
Youngstown State U (OH)

DIETETICS AND CLINICAL NUTRITION SERVICES RELATED

Coll of Saint Benedict (MN)
Coll of Saint Elizabeth (NJ)
Madonna U (MI)
Saint John's U (MN)
Texas Christian U (TX)
Universidad del Turabo (PR)
Western Michigan U (MI)

DIGITAL ARTS

Acad of Art U (CA)
Antioch Coll, Yellow Springs (OH)
Arizona State U at the Tempe campus (AZ)
Ashland U (OH)
Austin Coll (TX)
Bethany Lutheran Coll (MN)
Champlain Coll (VT)
Concordia U (QC, Canada)
Daemen Coll (NY)
DeSales U (PA)
Georgian Court U (NJ)
Greenville Coll (IL)
Hamline U (MN)
Huntingdon Coll (AL)
Kansas City Art Inst (MO)
King U (TN)
Lake Erie Coll (OH)
Lawrence Technological U (MI)
Long Island U–LIU Post (NY)
Marymount California U (CA)
Merrimack Coll (MA)
Moore Coll of Art & Design (PA)
Pennsylvania Coll of Art & Design (PA)
Rhode Island Coll (RI)
Santa Fe U of Art and Design (NM)
Southwestern Coll (KS)
Stetson U (FL)
Syracuse U (NY)
U of Central Florida (FL)
U of Florida (FL)
U of Massachusetts Dartmouth (MA)
U of New Mexico (NM)
U of Oregon (OR)
U of Saint Francis (IN)
U of Southern California (CA)
The U of Tampa (FL)
The U of Toledo (OH)
U of Wisconsin–Stout (WI)
U of Wisconsin–Whitewater (WI)

DIGITAL COMMUNICATION AND MEDIA/MULTIMEDIA

Abilene Christian U (TX)
The American U in Dubai (United Arab Emirates)
Ashland U (OH)
Baldwin Wallace U (OH)
Baylor U (TX)
Bennington Coll (VT)
Bethany Coll (WV)
Bradley U (IL)
Butler U (IN)
California Coll of the Arts (CA)
California Lutheran U (CA)
California State U, Dominguez Hills (CA)
Calvin Coll (MI)
Canisius Coll (NY)
Cedar Crest Coll (PA)
Cedarville U (OH)
Central Washington U (WA)
Clarkson U (NY)
Cleveland State U (OH)
Columbia Intl U (SC)
Concordia Coll–New York (NY)
Concordia U Wisconsin (WI)
Cornerstone U (MI)

Dallas Baptist U (TX)
Dixie State U (UT)
Endicott Coll (MA)
The Evergreen State Coll (WA)
Fitchburg State U (MA)
Florida Atlantic U (FL)
Franklin U (OH)
Georgia Inst of Technology (GA)
Georgian Court U (NJ)
Georgia Southern U (GA)
Granite State Coll (NH)
Harding U (AR)
Hilbert Coll (NY)
Howard Payne U (TX)
Indiana U Bloomington (IN)
Indiana U Kokomo (IN)
Indiana U–Purdue U Indianapolis (IN)
Inter American U of Puerto Rico, Bayamón Campus (PR)
John Brown U (AR)
Juniata Coll (PA)
Keene State Coll (NH)
Kutztown U of Pennsylvania (PA)
Lebanon Valley Coll (PA)
Lee U (TN)
Lewis U (IL)
Liberty U (VA)
Limestone Coll (SC)
Lindenwood U (MO)
Loyola U Chicago (IL)
Lubbock Christian U (TX)
Lycoming Coll (PA)
Manhattanville Coll (NY)
Marquette U (WI)
Marywood U (PA)
Mercy Coll (NY)
Messiah Coll (PA)
Miami U (OH)
Minnesota State U Moorhead (MN)
Mount Marty Coll (SD)
Mount Mercy U (IA)
National U (CA)
New York U (NY)
Northern Michigan U (MI)
Notre Dame of Maryland U (MD)
Ohio U (OH)
Rensselaer Polytechnic Inst (NY)
Rochester Inst of Technology (NY)
Saginaw Valley State U (MI)
St. Bonaventure U (NY)
St. Edward's U (TX)
St. John Fisher Coll (NY)
Saint Joseph's Coll (IN)
San Diego State U (CA)
Savannah Coll of Art and Design (GA)
School of the Art Inst of Chicago (IL)
Simpson Coll (IA)
Slippery Rock U of Pennsylvania (PA)
Southwestern Coll (KS)
State U of New York at New Paltz (NY)
Stevenson U (MD)
Sullivan Coll of Technology and Design (KY)
Taylor U (IN)
Texas A&M U (TX)
Tiffin U (OH)
Trevecca Nazarene U (TN)
Tusculum Coll (TN)
Universidad Metropolitana (PR)
U of Denver (CO)
U of Georgia (GA)
U of Idaho (ID)
U of Maine (ME)
U of Miami (FL)
U of Mississippi (MS)
U of Northern Iowa (IA)
U of Rochester (NY)
The U of Scranton (PA)
The U of Tampa (FL)
The U of Texas at Arlington (TX)
The U of Texas at Dallas (TX)
U of the Incarnate Word (TX)
U of Toronto (ON, Canada)
U of Valley Forge (PA)
U of Waterloo (ON, Canada)
The U of Western Ontario (ON, Canada)
Valparaiso U (IN)
Washington State U (WA)
Webster U (MO)
Wilkes U (PA)

DIRECTING AND THEATRICAL PRODUCTION
Augsburg Coll (MN)
Baldwin Wallace U (OH)
Belmont U (TN)
Bennington Coll (VT)
Binghamton U, State U of New York (NY)
Boston U (MA)
Bradley U (IL)
Brigham Young U (UT)
California Inst of the Arts (CA)
California State U, Long Beach (CA)
Cornish Coll of the Arts (WA)
Drake U (IA)
Emory & Henry Coll (VA)
Hofstra U (NY)
Keene State Coll (NH)
Lindenwood U (MO)
Lipscomb U (TN)
Marymount Manhattan Coll (NY)
Nebraska Wesleyan U (NE)
Pace U (NY)
Pepperdine U, Malibu (CA)
Rider U (NJ)
Saint Joseph's Coll (IN)
Texas Christian U (TX)
U of Chicago (IL)
U of Miami (FL)
The U of the Arts (PA)
U of Washington (WA)
Webster U (MO)

DISABILITY STUDIES
The U of Western Ontario (ON, Canada)

DIVINITY/MINISTRY
Azusa Pacific U (CA)
Barclay Coll (KS)
Belmont U (TN)
Bethel Coll (IN)
Biola U (CA)
Bluefield Coll (VA)
Calvary Bible Coll and Theological Sem (MO)
Campbellsville U (KY)
Christian Life Coll (IL)
Cincinnati Christian U (OH)
Corban U (OR)
Davis Coll (NY)
Faith Baptist Bible Coll and Theological Sem (IA)
Great Lakes Christian Coll (MI)
John Brown U (AR)
Judson U (IL)
Kansas Wesleyan U (KS)
Kingswood U (NB, Canada)
Kuyper Coll (MI)
Laurel U (NC)
The Master's Coll and Sem (CA)
Master's Coll and Sem (ON, Canada)
Nazarene Bible Coll (CO)
Nebraska Christian Coll (NE)
Northwest Nazarene U (ID)
Northwest U (WA)
Oakland City U (IN)
Oklahoma Baptist U (OK)
Providence Coll (RI)
Regent U (VA)
Roberts Wesleyan Coll (NY)
Rocky Mountain Coll (AB, Canada)
San Diego Christian Coll (CA)
Southwestern Assemblies of God U (TX)
Summit U (PA)
Toccoa Falls Coll (GA)
Trevecca Nazarene U (TN)
U of Valley Forge (PA)
Williams Baptist Coll (AR)

DOCUMENTARY PRODUCTION
Ithaca Coll (NY)
Mount Saint Mary's U (CA)
Syracuse U (NY)
U at Albany, State U of New York (NY)

DRAFTING AND DESIGN TECHNOLOGY
East Carolina U (NC)
East Central U (OK)
Johnson & Wales U (RI)
Northern Michigan U (MI)
Sam Houston State U (TX)
Texas Southern U (TX)
Trine U (IN)
U of Rio Grande (OH)
Weber State U (UT)
Western Michigan U (MI)

DRAFTING/DESIGN ENGINEERING TECHNOLOGIES RELATED
Central Michigan U (MI)
Murray State U (KY)
National U (CA)

DRAMA AND DANCE TEACHER EDUCATION
Adams State U (CO)
Austin Coll (TX)
Belmont U (TN)
Boston U (MA)
Bowling Green State U (OH)
Bradley U (IL)
Brenau U (GA)
Bridgewater State U (MA)
Catawba Coll (NC)
Central Washington U (WA)
Coll of the Ozarks (MO)
Columbia Coll (SC)
Columbus State U (GA)
Concordia U, Nebraska (NE)
East Carolina U (NC)
East Central U (OK)
East Texas Baptist U (TX)
Edgewood Coll (WI)
Emerson Coll (MA)
Greensboro Coll (NC)
Hardin-Simmons U (TX)
Hastings Coll (NE)
Hofstra U (NY)
Hope Coll (MI)
Howard Payne U (TX)
Jacksonville U (FL)
Johnson State Coll (VT)
Keene State Coll (NH)
Lees-McRae Coll (NC)
Lee U (TN)
Lipscomb U (TN)
Lubbock Christian U (TX)
Maryville Coll (TN)
Meredith Coll (NC)
Missouri Baptist U (MO)
Montclair State U (NJ)
Ohio Wesleyan U (OH)
Piedmont Coll (GA)
St. Catherine U (MN)
St. Edward's U (TX)
Southern Utah U (UT)
State U of New York Coll at Potsdam (NY)
Trevecca Nazarene U (TN)
The U of Akron (OH)
U of Alberta (AB, Canada)
U of Central Oklahoma (OK)
U of Evansville (IN)
The U of Iowa (IA)
U of Lethbridge (AB, Canada)
The U of North Carolina at Charlotte (NC)
The U of North Carolina at Greensboro (NC)
U of Regina (SK, Canada)
The U of South Dakota (SD)
The U of the Arts (PA)
U of Windsor (ON, Canada)
Utah Valley U (UT)
Valparaiso U (IN)
Viterbo U (WI)
Washington U in St. Louis (MO)
Wayne State Coll (NE)
Weber State U (UT)
Western Washington U (WA)
Xavier U (OH)

DRAMA THERAPY
Howard U (DC)
Virginia Union U (VA)

DRAMATIC/THEATER ARTS
Abilene Christian U (TX)
Adelphi U (NY)
Agnes Scott Coll (GA)
Alabama State U (AL)
Albertus Magnus Coll (CT)
Albion Coll (MI)
Albright Coll (PA)
Allegheny Coll (PA)
Alma Coll (MI)
Alvernia U (PA)
American Intl Coll (MA)
American U (DC)
The American U in Cairo (Egypt)
Amherst Coll (MA)
Angelo State U (TX)
Anna Maria Coll (MA)
Appalachian State U (NC)
Aquinas Coll (MI)
Arcadia U (PA)
Arizona State U at the Tempe campus (AZ)
Arkansas State U (AR)
Armstrong State U (GA)
Asbury U (KY)
Ashland U (OH)
Auburn U (AL)
Augsburg Coll (MN)
Augustana Coll (IL)
Augustana Coll (SD)
Averett U (VA)
Avila U (MO)
Baker U (KS)
Ball State U (IN)
Bard Coll (NY)
Bard Coll at Simon's Rock (MA)
Barnard Coll (NY)
Barry U (FL)
Bates Coll (ME)
Baylor U (TX)
Belhaven U (MS)
Belmont U (TN)
Beloit Coll (WI)
Bemidji State U (MN)
Benedictine Coll (KS)
Bennington Coll (VT)
Berea Coll (KY)
Bethany Lutheran Coll (MN)
Bethel Coll (IN)
Bethel U (MN)
Binghamton U, State U of New York (NY)
Biola U (CA)
Birmingham-Southern Coll (AL)
Bloomsburg U of Pennsylvania (PA)
Bluefield Coll (VA)
Bob Jones U (SC)
Boston Coll (MA)
Boston U (MA)
Bowling Green State U (OH)
Bradley U (IL)
Brandeis U (MA)
Brenau U (GA)
Brevard Coll (NC)
Bridgewater State U (MA)
Brown U (RI)
Bryan Coll (TN)
Bucknell U (PA)
Buffalo State Coll, State U of New York (NY)
Butler U (IN)
California Baptist U (CA)
California Lutheran U (CA)
California Polytechnic State U, San Luis Obispo (CA)
California State Polytechnic U, Pomona (CA)
California State U, Dominguez Hills (CA)
California State U, Fresno (CA)
California State U, Fullerton (CA)
California State U, Long Beach (CA)
California State U, Los Angeles (CA)
California State U, Sacramento (CA)
California State U, San Bernardino (CA)
California State U, Stanislaus (CA)
California U of Pennsylvania (PA)
Calvary Bible Coll and Theological Sem (MO)
Calvin Coll (MI)
Capital U (OH)
Cardinal Stritch U (WI)
Carleton Coll (MN)
Carroll Coll (MT)
Carson-Newman U (TN)
Case Western Reserve U (OH)
Castleton State Coll (VT)
Catawba Coll (NC)
The Catholic U of America (DC)
Cedar Crest Coll (PA)
Cedarville U (OH)
Centenary Coll of Louisiana (LA)
Central Coll (IA)
Central Methodist U (MO)
Central Michigan U (MI)
Centre Coll (KY)
Chapman U (CA)
Cheyney U of Pennsylvania (PA)
Chowan U (NC)
Christopher Newport U (VA)
City Coll of the City U of New York (NY)
Claremont McKenna Coll (CA)
Clarion U of Pennsylvania (PA)
Clarke U (IA)
Clark U (MA)
Clayton State U (GA)
Cleveland State U (OH)
Coastal Carolina U (SC)
Coe Coll (IA)
Coker Coll (SC)
Colby Coll (ME)
The Coll at Brockport, State U of New York (NY)
Coll of Charleston (SC)
The Coll of Idaho (ID)
Coll of Saint Benedict (MN)
Coll of Staten Island of the City U of New York (NY)
Coll of the Holy Cross (MA)
Coll of the Ozarks (MO)
The Coll of William and Mary (VA)
The Coll of Wooster (OH)
The Colorado Coll (CO)
Colorado Mesa U (CO)
Colorado State U (CO)
Columbia Coll Chicago (IL)
Columbia U (NY)
Columbia U, School of General Studies (NY)
Columbus State U (GA)
Concordia Coll (MN)
Concordia U (CA)
Concordia U (QC, Canada)
Concordia U Chicago (IL)
Concordia U, Nebraska (NE)
Concordia U, St. Paul (MN)
Connecticut Coll (CT)
Cornell Coll (IA)
Cornell U (NY)
Cornish Coll of the Arts (WA)
Covenant Coll (GA)
Creighton U (NE)
Culver-Stockton Coll (MO)
Cumberland U (TN)
Daemen Coll (NY)
Dalhousie U (NS, Canada)
Dartmouth Coll (NH)
Davidson Coll (NC)
Denison U (OH)
DePaul U (IL)
DePauw U (IN)
DeSales U (PA)
Dickinson Coll (PA)
Dickinson State U (ND)
Dixie State U (UT)
Dominican U (IL)
Drake U (IA)
Drew U (NJ)
Drury U (MO)
Duquesne U (PA)
Earlham Coll (IN)
East Carolina U (NC)
East Central U (OK)
Eastern Illinois U (IL)
Eastern Michigan U (MI)
Eastern New Mexico U (NM)
Eastern Oregon U (OR)
East Stroudsburg U of Pennsylvania (PA)
East Tennessee State U (TN)
East Texas Baptist U (TX)
Eckerd Coll (FL)
Edgewood Coll (WI)
Elizabethtown Coll (PA)
Elmhurst Coll (IL)
Elmira Coll (NY)
Elms Coll (MA)
Elon U (NC)
Emerson Coll (MA)
Emory & Henry Coll (VA)
Emporia State U (KS)
Eureka Coll (IL)
The Evergreen State Coll (WA)
Fairfield U (CT)
Fairleigh Dickinson U, Coll at Florham (NJ)
Fairmont State U (WV)
Faulkner U (AL)
Ferrum Coll (VA)
Fitchburg State U (MA)
Five Towns Coll (NY)
Flagler Coll (FL)

Florida Ag and Mech U (FL)
Florida Atlantic U (FL)
Florida Gulf Coast U (FL)
Florida Intl U (FL)
Florida Southern Coll (FL)
Florida State U (FL)
Fontbonne U (MO)
Fordham U (NY)
Fort Hays State U (KS)
Fort Lewis Coll (CO)
Franciscan U of Steubenville (OH)
Francis Marion U (SC)
Franklin & Marshall Coll (PA)
Franklin Coll (IN)
Franklin Pierce U (NH)
Friends U (KS)
Frostburg State U (MD)
Furman U (SC)
Gannon U (PA)
George Mason U (VA)
Georgetown Coll (KY)
The George Washington U (DC)
Georgia Coll & State U (GA)
Georgia Southern U (GA)
Georgia Southwestern State U (GA)
Gettysburg Coll (PA)
Gonzaga U (WA)
Gordon Coll (MA)
Goshen Coll (IN)
Goucher Coll (MD)
Governors State U (IL)
Grace Coll (IN)
Graceland U (IA)
Grand Valley State U (MI)
Grand View U (IA)
Greensboro Coll (NC)
Greenville Coll (IL)
Grinnell Coll (IA)
Guilford Coll (NC)
Gustavus Adolphus Coll (MN)
Hamilton Coll (NY)
Hamline U (MN)
Hampshire Coll (MA)
Hampton U (VA)
Hannibal-LaGrange U (MO)
Hanover Coll (IN)
Harding U (AR)
Hardin-Simmons U (TX)
Hartwick Coll (NY)
Hastings Coll (NE)
Heidelberg U (OH)
Hendrix Coll (AR)
High Point U (NC)
Hillsdale Coll (MI)
Hiram Coll (OH)
Hofstra U (NY)
Hollins U (VA)
Hope Coll (MI)
Howard Payne U (TX)
Howard U (DC)
Humboldt State U (CA)
Hunter Coll of the City U of New York (NY)
Illinois Coll (IL)
Illinois State U (IL)
Illinois Wesleyan U (IL)
Indiana State U (IN)
Indiana U Bloomington (IN)
Indiana U Northwest (IN)
Indiana U of Pennsylvania (PA)
Indiana U–Purdue U Fort Wayne (IN)
Indiana U South Bend (IN)
Iowa State U of Science and Technology (IA)
Ithaca Coll (NY)
Jacksonville State U (AL)
Jacksonville U (FL)
James Madison U (VA)
Johnson State Coll (VT)
The Juilliard School (NY)
Kalamazoo Coll (MI)
Kansas State U (KS)
Kansas Wesleyan U (KS)
Kean U (NJ)
Kennesaw State U (GA)
Kent State U (OH)
Kentucky Wesleyan Coll (KY)
Kenyon Coll (OH)
King's Coll (PA)
Knox Coll (IL)
Kuyper Coll (MI)
Lafayette Coll (PA)
LaGrange Coll (GA)
Lake Forest Coll (IL)
Lamar U (TX)
Lawrence U (WI)
Lees-McRae Coll (NC)
Lehigh U (PA)
Lehman Coll of the City U of New York (NY)
Le Moyne Coll (NY)
Lenoir-Rhyne U (NC)
Lewis & Clark Coll (OR)
Lewis U (IL)
Liberty U (VA)
Limestone Coll (SC)
Lindenwood U (MO)
Linfield Coll (OR)
Lipscomb U (TN)
Lock Haven U of Pennsylvania (PA)
Long Island U–LIU Post (NY)
Louisiana Coll (LA)
Louisiana State U and A&M Coll (LA)
Loyola Marymount U (CA)
Loyola U Chicago (IL)
Loyola U New Orleans (LA)
Lubbock Christian U (TX)
Luther Coll (IA)
Lycoming Coll (PA)
Lynchburg Coll (VA)
Lynn U (FL)
Lyon Coll (AR)
Macalester Coll (MN)
Manchester U (IN)
Marietta Coll (OH)
Marquette U (WI)
Mars Hill U (NC)
Mary Baldwin Coll (VA)
Marymount Manhattan Coll (NY)
Maryville Coll (TN)
Marywood U (PA)
McDaniel Coll (MD)
McMurry U (TX)
Mercer U, Macon (GA)
Meredith Coll (NC)
Merrimack Coll (MA)
Messiah Coll (PA)
Metropolitan State U (MN)
Miami U (OH)
Michigan State U (MI)
MidAmerica Nazarene U (KS)
Middlebury Coll (VT)
Middle Tennessee State U (TN)
Millikin U (IL)
Mills Coll (CA)
Minnesota State U Mankato (MN)
Minnesota State U Moorhead (MN)
Missouri Baptist U (MO)
Missouri Southern State U (MO)
Missouri State U (MO)
Missouri Valley Coll (MO)
Missouri Western State U (MO)
Molloy Coll (NY)
Monmouth Coll (IL)
Montana State U Billings (MT)
Montclair State U (NJ)
Morehead State U (KY)
Morningside Coll (IA)
Mount Allison U (NB, Canada)
Mount Holyoke Coll (MA)
Mount Marty Coll (SD)
Mount Vernon Nazarene U (OH)
Muhlenberg Coll (PA)
Murray State U (KY)
Naropa U (CO)
Nazareth Coll of Rochester (NY)
Nebraska Wesleyan U (NE)
Newberry Coll (SC)
New England Coll (NH)
New Mexico State U (NM)
New York U (NY)
Niagara U (NY)
North Carolina Ag and Tech State U (NC)
North Carolina Central U (NC)
North Carolina Wesleyan Coll (NC)
North Central Coll (IL)
North Dakota State U (ND)
Northeastern State U (OK)
Northeastern U (MA)
Northern Arizona U (AZ)
Northern Illinois U (IL)
Northern Kentucky U (KY)
Northern Michigan U (MI)
Northern State U (SD)
North Greenville U (SC)
Northwestern Coll (IA)
Northwestern U (IL)
Northwest Missouri State U (MO)
Northwest U (WA)
Nova Southeastern U (FL)
Oakland U (MI)
Oberlin Coll (OH)
Occidental Coll (CA)
Ohio Northern U (OH)
The Ohio State U (OH)
The Ohio State U at Lima (OH)
Ohio U (OH)
Ohio Wesleyan U (OH)
Oklahoma Baptist U (OK)
Oklahoma Christian U (OK)
Oklahoma City U (OK)
Oklahoma State U (OK)
Old Dominion U (VA)
Olivet Coll (MI)
Our Lady of the Lake U of San Antonio (TX)
Pacific Lutheran U (WA)
Pacific U (OR)
Palm Beach Atlantic U (FL)
Park U (MO)
Pepperdine U, Malibu (CA)
Piedmont Coll (GA)
Plymouth State U (NH)
Point Loma Nazarene U (CA)
Pomona Coll (CA)
Portland State U (OR)
Prairie View A&M U (TX)
Presbyterian Coll (SC)
Principia Coll (IL)
Providence Coll (RI)
Purchase Coll, State U of New York (NY)
Purdue U (IN)
Queens Coll of the City U of New York (NY)
Quinnipiac U (CT)
Radford U (VA)
Ramapo Coll of New Jersey (NJ)
Randolph Coll (VA)
Randolph-Macon Coll (VA)
Reed Coll (OR)
Rhode Island Coll (RI)
Rhodes Coll (TN)
Ripon Coll (WI)
Roanoke Coll (VA)
Rockford U (IL)
Rocky Mountain Coll (MT)
Rocky Mountain Coll (AB, Canada)
Roger Williams U (RI)
Rollins Coll (FL)
Roosevelt U (IL)
Rowan U (NJ)
Rutgers, The State U of New Jersey, Camden (NJ)
Rutgers, The State U of New Jersey, Newark (NJ)
Rutgers, The State U of New Jersey, New Brunswick (NJ)
The Sage Colls (NY)
Saginaw Valley State U (MI)
St. Bonaventure U (NY)
St. Catherine U (MN)
St. Edward's U (TX)
St. Gregory's U, Shawnee (OK)
Saint John's U (MN)
St. John's U (NY)
Saint Louis U (MO)
Saint Martin's U (WA)
Saint Mary's Coll (IN)
St. Mary's Coll of Maryland (MD)
Saint Mary's U of Minnesota (MN)
Saint Michael's Coll (VT)
St. Norbert Coll (WI)
St. Olaf Coll (MN)
Salisbury U (MD)
Salve Regina U (RI)
Samford U (AL)
Sam Houston State U (TX)
San Diego State U (CA)
San Francisco State U (CA)
San Jose State U (CA)
Santa Clara U (CA)
Santa Fe U of Art and Design (NM)
Sarah Lawrence Coll (NY)
Savannah Coll of Art and Design (GA)
Scripps Coll (CA)
Seattle Pacific U (WA)
Seattle U (WA)
Seton Hill U (PA)
Sewanee: The U of the South (TN)
Siena Heights U (MI)
Simon Fraser U (BC, Canada)
Simpson Coll (IA)
Skidmore Coll (NY)
Slippery Rock U of Pennsylvania (PA)
Smith Coll (MA)
South Carolina State U (SC)
South Dakota State U (SD)
Southeastern Oklahoma State U (OK)
Southeastern U (FL)
Southeast Missouri State U (MO)
Southern Arkansas U–Magnolia (AR)
Southern Connecticut State U (CT)
Southern Illinois U Carbondale (IL)
Southern Illinois U Edwardsville (IL)
Southern Methodist U (TX)
Southern Oregon U (OR)
Southern Utah U (UT)
Southwest Baptist U (MO)
Southwestern Assemblies of God U (TX)
Southwestern Coll (KS)
Southwestern U (TX)
Southwest Minnesota State U (MN)
Spelman Coll (GA)
Spring Hill Coll (AL)
Stanford U (CA)
State U of New York at Fredonia (NY)
State U of New York at New Paltz (NY)
State U of New York at Oswego (NY)
State U of New York at Plattsburgh (NY)
State U of New York Coll at Geneseo (NY)
State U of New York Coll at Potsdam (NY)
Stephen F. Austin State U (TX)
Stephens Coll (MO)
Sterling Coll (KS)
Stetson U (FL)
Stevenson U (MD)
Stony Brook U, State U of New York (NY)
Suffolk U (MA)
Sul Ross State U (TX)
Susquehanna U (PA)
Syracuse U (NY)
Tarleton State U (TX)
Taylor U (IN)
Tennessee Wesleyan Coll (TN)
Texas A&M U (TX)
Texas A&M U–Commerce (TX)
Texas A&M U–Corpus Christi (TX)
Texas Christian U (TX)
Texas Lutheran U (TX)
Texas Southern U (TX)
Texas State U (TX)
Texas Tech U (TX)
Texas Woman's U (TX)
Thomas More Coll (KY)
Towson U (MD)
Transylvania U (KY)
Trevecca Nazarene U (TN)
Trinity Coll (CT)
Trinity U (TX)
Truman State U (MO)
Tufts U (MA)
Tulane U (LA)
Union Coll (KY)
Union U (TN)
U at Buffalo, the State U of New York (NY)
The U of Akron (OH)
The U of Alabama (AL)
The U of Alabama at Birmingham (AL)
U of Alberta (AB, Canada)
The U of Arizona (AZ)
U of Arkansas (AR)
U of Arkansas at Little Rock (AR)
U of Arkansas–Fort Smith (AR)
The U of British Columbia (BC, Canada)
The U of British Columbia–Okanagan Campus (BC, Canada)
U of California, Berkeley (CA)
U of California, Irvine (CA)
U of California, Los Angeles (CA)
U of California, Riverside (CA)
U of California, Santa Barbara (CA)
U of California, Santa Cruz (CA)
U of Central Arkansas (AR)
U of Central Florida (FL)
U of Central Missouri (MO)
U of Central Oklahoma (OK)
U of Cincinnati (OH)
U of Colorado Boulder (CO)
U of Colorado Denver (CO)
U of Dallas (TX)
U of Dayton (OH)
U of Denver (CO)
U of Evansville (IN)
The U of Findlay (OH)
U of Florida (FL)
U of Georgia (GA)
U of Guelph (ON, Canada)
U of Hawaii at Manoa (HI)
U of Houston (TX)
U of Idaho (ID)
U of Illinois at Chicago (IL)
U of Indianapolis (IN)
The U of Iowa (IA)
U of Jamestown (ND)
The U of Kansas (KS)
U of Kentucky (KY)
U of King's Coll (NS, Canada)
U of La Verne (CA)
U of Lethbridge (AB, Canada)
U of Louisville (KY)
U of Maine (ME)
U of Maine at Machias (ME)
U of Maryland, Baltimore County (MD)
U of Maryland, Coll Park (MD)
U of Massachusetts Amherst (MA)
U of Massachusetts Boston (MA)
U of Memphis (TN)
U of Miami (FL)
U of Michigan (MI)
U of Michigan–Flint (MI)
U of Minnesota, Duluth (MN)
U of Minnesota, Morris (MN)
U of Minnesota, Twin Cities Campus (MN)
U of Mississippi (MS)
U of Missouri (MO)
U of Missouri–Kansas City (MO)
U of Missouri–St. Louis (MO)
U of Mobile (AL)
The U of Montana (MT)
U of Montevallo (AL)
U of Mount Union (OH)
U of Nebraska at Kearney (NE)
U of Nebraska–Lincoln (NE)
U of Nevada, Las Vegas (NV)
U of Nevada, Reno (NV)
U of New Hampshire (NH)
U of New Haven (CT)
U of New Mexico (NM)
U of New Orleans (LA)
U of North Carolina at Asheville (NC)
The U of North Carolina at Chapel Hill (NC)
The U of North Carolina at Charlotte (NC)
The U of North Carolina at Greensboro (NC)
The U of North Carolina at Pembroke (NC)
U of North Carolina School of the Arts (NC)
The U of North Carolina Wilmington (NC)
U of North Dakota (ND)
U of Northern Colorado (CO)
U of Northern Iowa (IA)
U of North Texas (TX)
U of Northwestern–St. Paul (MN)
U of Notre Dame (IN)
U of Oklahoma (OK)
U of Oregon (OR)
U of Ottawa (ON, Canada)
U of Pennsylvania (PA)
U of Pittsburgh (PA)
U of Portland (OR)
U of Puget Sound (WA)
U of Regina (SK, Canada)
U of Rhode Island (RI)
U of Richmond (VA)
U of Saint Mary (KS)
U of St. Thomas (TX)
U of San Diego (CA)
U of Saskatchewan (SK, Canada)
U of Science and Arts of Oklahoma (OK)
The U of Scranton (PA)
U of South Alabama (AL)
U of South Carolina Upstate (SC)
The U of South Dakota (SD)
U of Southern California (CA)
U of Southern Indiana (IN)

U of Southern Maine (ME)
U of Southern Mississippi (MS)
U of South Florida (FL)
The U of Tampa (FL)
The U of Tennessee (TN)
The U of Tennessee at Chattanooga (TN)
The U of Tennessee at Martin (TN)
The U of Texas at Arlington (TX)
The U of Texas at Austin (TX)
The U of Texas at El Paso (TX)
The U of Texas–Pan American (TX)
U of the Cumberlands (KY)
U of the District of Columbia (DC)
U of the Fraser Valley (BC, Canada)
U of the Incarnate Word (TX)
U of the Pacific (CA)
The U of Toledo (OH)
The U of Tulsa (OK)
U of Utah (UT)
U of Vermont (VT)
U of Virginia (VA)
The U of Virginia's Coll at Wise (VA)
U of Washington (WA)
U of Waterloo (ON, Canada)
U of West Florida (FL)
U of West Georgia (GA)
U of Windsor (ON, Canada)
U of Wisconsin–Eau Claire (WI)
U of Wisconsin–Green Bay (WI)
U of Wisconsin–La Crosse (WI)
U of Wisconsin–Madison (WI)
U of Wisconsin–Milwaukee (WI)
U of Wisconsin–Oshkosh (WI)
U of Wisconsin–Parkside (WI)
U of Wisconsin–River Falls (WI)
U of Wisconsin–Stevens Point (WI)
U of Wisconsin–Superior (WI)
U of Wisconsin–Whitewater (WI)
U of Wyoming (WY)
Ursinus Coll (PA)
Utah State U (UT)
Utah Valley U (UT)
Valdosta State U (GA)
Valparaiso U (IN)
Vanderbilt U (TN)
Vanguard U of Southern California (CA)
Vassar Coll (NY)
Virginia Commonwealth U (VA)
Virginia Polytechnic Inst and State U (VA)
Virginia Wesleyan Coll (VA)
Viterbo U (WI)
Wabash Coll (IN)
Wagner Coll (NY)
Wake Forest U (NC)
Waldorf Coll (IA)
Wartburg Coll (IA)
Washburn U (KS)
Washington and Lee U (VA)
Washington Coll (MD)
Washington U in St. Louis (MO)
Wayne State Coll (NE)
Wayne State U (MI)
Weber State U (UT)
Webster U (MO)
Wells Coll (NY)
Wesleyan U (CT)
West Chester U of Pennsylvania (PA)
Western Carolina U (NC)
Western Illinois U (IL)
Western Kentucky U (KY)
Western Oregon U (OR)
Western State Colorado U (CO)
Western Washington U (WA)
Westfield State U (MA)
Westminster Coll (UT)
West Texas A&M U (TX)
West Virginia U (WV)
West Virginia Wesleyan Coll (WV)
Whitman Coll (WA)
Whittier Coll (CA)
Whitworth U (WA)
Wichita State U (KS)
Wilkes U (PA)
Willamette U (OR)
William Jessup U (CA)
William Jewell Coll (MO)
William Paterson U of New Jersey (NJ)
William Peace U (NC)
Williams Coll (MA)
William Woods U (MO)
Winona State U (MN)
Winthrop U (SC)
Wittenberg U (OH)
Wofford Coll (SC)
Wright State U (OH)
Xavier U (OH)
York Coll of Pennsylvania (PA)
York Coll of the City U of New York (NY)
Youngstown State U (OH)

DRAMATIC/THEATER ARTS AND STAGECRAFT RELATED

Adams State U (CO)
Benedictine Coll (KS)
Brigham Young U (UT)
Catawba Coll (NC)
Charleston Southern U (SC)
Coastal Carolina U (SC)
Dalhousie U (NS, Canada)
DePaul U (IL)
Drake U (IA)
Fayetteville State U (NC)
Indiana U South Bend (IN)
Lee U (TN)
Lindenwood U (MO)
Meredith Coll (NC)
Nebraska Wesleyan U (NE)
North Central Coll (IL)
Pepperdine U, Malibu (CA)
Saint Augustine's U (NC)
Seton Hill U (PA)
Southern Illinois U Carbondale (IL)
Southwestern Coll (KS)
Southwest Minnesota State U (MN)
U of Miami (FL)
U of Michigan–Flint (MI)
U of Northern Colorado (CO)
U of Southern California (CA)
Western Kentucky U (KY)
Western Michigan U (MI)
Wheaton Coll (MA)

DRAWING

Adams State U (CO)
Albany State U (GA)
American Acad of Art (IL)
Aquinas Coll (MI)
Arcadia U (PA)
Bard Coll at Simon's Rock (MA)
Bennington Coll (VT)
Biola U (CA)
Birmingham-Southern Coll (AL)
Bowling Green State U (OH)
Bradley U (IL)
Brigham Young U (UT)
Buffalo State Coll, State U of New York (NY)
California Coll of the Arts (CA)
California State U, Long Beach (CA)
Carson-Newman U (TN)
Central Washington U (WA)
Cleveland Inst of Art (OH)
Coll of the Atlantic (ME)
Colorado State U (CO)
Columbus State U (GA)
Dixie State U (UT)
Drake U (IA)
Emily Carr U of Art + Design (BC, Canada)
Ferris State U (MI)
Georgia State U (GA)
Grace Coll (IN)
Indiana U–Purdue U Fort Wayne (IN)
Inter American U of Puerto Rico, San Germán Campus (PR)
Kansas Wesleyan U (KS)
Laguna Coll of Art & Design (CA)
Lewis U (IL)
Lindenwood U (MO)
Minnesota State U Mankato (MN)
Mount Allison U (NB, Canada)
New England Coll (NH)
Northern Michigan U (MI)
Oakland U (MI)
Otis Coll of Art and Design (CA)
Portland State U (OR)
Pratt Inst (NY)
Providence Coll (RI)
Rutgers, The State U of New Jersey, New Brunswick (NJ)
School of the Art Inst of Chicago (IL)
School of the Museum of Fine Arts, Boston (MA)
Seton Hill U (PA)
State U of New York at Fredonia (NY)
U of Hartford (CT)
The U of Iowa (IA)
U of Michigan (MI)
The U of Montana (MT)
U of New Haven (CT)
U of Regina (SK, Canada)
U of San Francisco (CA)
The U of Texas at El Paso (TX)
U of Windsor (ON, Canada)
Washington U in St. Louis (MO)
Western Washington U (WA)
West Virginia Wesleyan Coll (WV)

DRIVER AND SAFETY TEACHER EDUCATION

U of Wisconsin–Whitewater (WI)

DUTCH/FLEMISH

U of California, Berkeley (CA)

EARLY CHILDHOOD EDUCATION

Adams State U (CO)
Alabama State U (AL)
Albany State U (GA)
Alma Coll (MI)
Alvernia U (PA)
Anderson U (SC)
Anna Maria Coll (MA)
Antioch U Midwest (OH)
Arcadia U (PA)
Arizona State U at the Polytechnic campus (AZ)
Arizona State U at the Tempe campus (AZ)
Arizona State U at the West campus (AZ)
Arkansas State U (AR)
Arkansas Tech U (AR)
Armstrong State U (GA)
Auburn U (AL)
Baldwin Wallace U (OH)
Baylor U (TX)
Bay Path U (MA)
Becker Coll (MA)
Belmont U (TN)
Berry Coll (GA)
Bethel Coll (IN)
Bloomsburg U of Pennsylvania (PA)
Bob Jones U (SC)
Boston U (MA)
Bradley U (IL)
Bridgewater State U (MA)
Brigham Young U (UT)
Bucknell U (PA)
Butler U (IN)
California Baptist U (CA)
California State U, Chico (CA)
California State U, Dominguez Hills (CA)
California State U, Los Angeles (CA)
California State U, San Bernardino (CA)
California State U, Stanislaus (CA)
California U of Pennsylvania (PA)
Calvin Coll (MI)
Cameron U (OK)
Canisius Coll (NY)
Capital U (OH)
Cardinal Stritch U (WI)
Carlow U (PA)
The Catholic U of America (DC)
Cazenovia Coll (NY)
Cedar Crest Coll (PA)
Cedarville U (OH)
Central Methodist U (MO)
Central Michigan U (MI)
Central State U (OH)
Central Washington U (WA)
Chaminade U of Honolulu (HI)
Charleston Southern U (SC)
Chatham U (PA)
Chestnut Hill Coll (PA)
Cheyney U of Pennsylvania (PA)
Chicago State U (IL)
Christian Brothers U (TN)
City Coll of the City U of New York (NY)
Claflin U (SC)
Clarion U of Pennsylvania (PA)
Clark Atlanta U (GA)
Cleveland State U (OH)
Coastal Carolina U (SC)
Coker Coll (SC)
Colby-Sawyer Coll (NH)
Coll of Central Florida (FL)
Coll of Charleston (SC)
The Coll of New Jersey (NJ)
Coll of Saint Mary (NE)
Coll of the Ozarks (MO)
Colorado State U (CO)
Columbia Coll (SC)
Columbia Coll Chicago (IL)
Columbus State U (GA)
Concordia Coll–New York (NY)
Concordia U Chicago (IL)
Concordia U, Nebraska (NE)
Concordia U, St. Paul (MN)
Curry Coll (MA)
Daemen Coll (NY)
Delaware State U (DE)
DePaul U (IL)
DeSales U (PA)
Dominican U (IL)
Dowling Coll (NY)
Duquesne U (PA)
East Central U (OK)
Eastern Connecticut State U (CT)
Eastern Michigan U (MI)
Eastern New Mexico U (NM)
Eastern Oregon U (OR)
Eastern U (PA)
East Stroudsburg U of Pennsylvania (PA)
Edgewood Coll (WI)
Edinboro U of Pennsylvania (PA)
Elizabethtown Coll (PA)
Elon U (NC)
Endicott Coll (MA)
Evangel U (MO)
Fayetteville State U (NC)
Fitchburg State U (MA)
Florida Ag and Mech U (FL)
Florida Atlantic U (FL)
Florida Gulf Coast U (FL)
Florida Intl U (FL)
Florida State Coll at Jacksonville (FL)
Florida State U (FL)
Fort Lewis Coll (CO)
Francis Marion U (SC)
Frostburg State U (MD)
Gannon U (PA)
Georgia Coll & State U (GA)
Georgia Gwinnett Coll (GA)
Georgia Regents U (GA)
Gordon Coll (MA)
Governors State U (IL)
Granite State Coll (NH)
Greensboro Coll (NC)
Greenville Coll (IL)
Grove City Coll (PA)
Hannibal-LaGrange U (MO)
Harding U (AR)
Hardin-Simmons U (TX)
Harris-Stowe State U (MO)
Hastings Coll (NE)
Heritage U (WA)
Hofstra U (NY)
Holy Family U (PA)
Houston Baptist U (TX)
Illinois Coll (IL)
Illinois State U (IL)
Indiana U Bloomington (IN)
Indiana U Kokomo (IN)
Indiana U of Pennsylvania (PA)
Inter American U of Puerto Rico, San Germán Campus (PR)
Iona Coll (NY)
Iowa Wesleyan Coll (IA)
John Brown U (AR)
Judson U (IL)
Keene State Coll (NH)
Kennesaw State U (GA)
Kent State U (OH)
Kent State U at Salem (OH)
Kent State U at Tuscarawas (OH)
Keystone Coll (PA)
King's Coll (PA)
Kutztown U of Pennsylvania (PA)
LaGrange Coll (GA)
Lake Erie Coll (OH)
Lasell Coll (MA)
Lebanon Valley Coll (PA)
Lees-McRae Coll (NC)
Lee U (TN)
LeMoyne-Owen Coll (TN)
Limestone Coll (SC)
Lindenwood U (MO)
Long Island U–LIU Post (NY)
Louisiana State U and A&M Coll (LA)
Lourdes U (OH)
Loyola U Chicago (IL)
Lubbock Christian U (TX)
Madonna U (MI)
Malone U (OH)
Maranatha Baptist U (WI)
Marian U (WI)
Marywood U (PA)
Mayville State U (ND)
McMurry U (TX)
McNeese State U (LA)
Merrimack Coll (MA)
Messiah Coll (PA)
Metropolitan State U (MN)
Miami Dade Coll (FL)
Miami U (OH)
Michigan State U (MI)
Midwestern State U (TX)
Millersville U of Pennsylvania (PA)
Milligan Coll (TN)
Millikin U (IL)
Minnesota State U Moorhead (MN)
Misericordia U (PA)
Missouri Baptist U (MO)
Missouri State U (MO)
Missouri Western State U (MO)
Mitchell Coll (CT)
Morehead State U (KY)
Morris Coll (SC)
Mount Aloysius Coll (PA)
Mount St. Joseph U (OH)
Mount Saint Mary Coll (NY)
Mount Vernon Nazarene U (OH)
Murray State U (KY)
Naropa U (CO)
National U (CA)
Newberry Coll (SC)
New Jersey City U (NJ)
Newman U (KS)
New Mexico State U (NM)
New York U (NY)
Nicholls State U (LA)
Northeastern Illinois U (IL)
Northeastern State U (OK)
Northern Arizona U (AZ)
Northern Illinois U (IL)
North Greenville U (SC)
Northwest Christian U (OR)
Northwestern Oklahoma State U (OK)
Nyack Coll (NY)
Ohio Dominican U (OH)
Ohio Northern U (OH)
Ohio U (OH)
Ohio Wesleyan U (OH)
Oklahoma Baptist U (OK)
Oklahoma Christian U (OK)
Oklahoma City U (OK)
Oklahoma Wesleyan U (OK)
Park U (MO)
Penn State U Park (PA)
Peru State Coll (NE)
Piedmont Coll (GA)
Pine Manor Coll (MA)
Plymouth State U (NH)
Point U (GA)
Presbyterian Coll (SC)
Prescott Coll (AZ)
Purdue U (IN)
Reinhardt U (GA)
Rhode Island Coll (RI)
Ripon Coll (WI)
Rivier U (NH)
Roberts Wesleyan Coll (NY)
Rockford U (IL)
Roosevelt U (IL)
Rowan U (NJ)
Saint Vincent Coll (PA)
Salisbury U (MD)
Salve Regina U (RI)
San Diego State U (CA)
San Francisco State U (CA)
San Jose State U (CA)
Santa Fe Coll (FL)
Shawnee State U (OH)
Shippensburg U of Pennsylvania (PA)
Silver Lake Coll of the Holy Family (WI)
South Carolina State U (SC)
South Dakota State U (SD)
Southeastern Louisiana U (LA)
Southeast Missouri State U (MO)
Southern Arkansas U–Magnolia (AR)
Southern Connecticut State U (CT)
Southern Illinois U Carbondale (IL)

Southern Illinois U Edwardsville (IL)
Southern New Hampshire U (NH)
Southwest Baptist U (MO)
Southwestern Coll (KS)
Spalding U (KY)
Spring Hill Coll (AL)
State Coll of Florida Manatee-Sarasota (FL)
State U of New York Coll at Geneseo (NY)
State U of New York Coll at Old Westbury (NY)
Stephens Coll (MO)
Stevenson U (MD)
Tennessee Wesleyan Coll (TN)
Texas Christian U (TX)
Towson U (MD)
Trevecca Nazarene U (TN)
Troy U (AL)
Tufts U (MA)
Tusculum Coll (TN)
Union Coll (NE)
Universidad del Turabo (PR)
Universidad Metropolitana (PR)
The U of Akron (OH)
The U of Alabama (AL)
The U of Alabama at Birmingham (AL)
U of Arkansas (AR)
U of Arkansas at Little Rock (AR)
U of Arkansas–Fort Smith (AR)
U of Central Florida (FL)
U of Central Oklahoma (OK)
U of Colorado Colorado Springs (CO)
U of Dayton (OH)
U of Delaware (DE)
U of Georgia (GA)
U of Guam (GU)
U of Hartford (CT)
U of Hawaii at Manoa (HI)
U of Hawaii–West Oahu (HI)
The U of Kansas (KS)
U of Kentucky (KY)
U of Louisiana at Lafayette (LA)
U of Michigan–Dearborn (MI)
U of Minnesota, Crookston (MN)
U of Missouri (MO)
U of Missouri–Kansas City (MO)
U of Missouri–St. Louis (MO)
U of Mobile (AL)
The U of Montana Western (MT)
U of Mount Union (OH)
U of Nevada, Las Vegas (NV)
U of New Mexico (NM)
U of New Orleans (LA)
The U of North Carolina at Chapel Hill (NC)
The U of North Carolina at Greensboro (NC)
U of North Dakota (ND)
U of Northern Colorado (CO)
U of North Florida (FL)
U of North Georgia (GA)
U of Northwestern–St. Paul (MN)
U of Oklahoma (OK)
U of Regina (SK, Canada)
U of Science and Arts of Oklahoma (OK)
The U of Scranton (PA)
U of South Alabama (AL)
U of South Carolina Aiken (SC)
U of South Carolina Beaufort (SC)
U of South Carolina Upstate (SC)
U of Southern Indiana (IN)
U of South Florida (FL)
The U of Tennessee at Chattanooga (TN)
U of the District of Columbia (DC)
U of the Virgin Islands (VI)
The U of Toledo (OH)
The U of Tulsa (OK)
U of Valley Forge (PA)
U of Vermont (VT)
U of West Florida (FL)
U of Wisconsin–Stevens Point (WI)
U of Wisconsin–Stout (WI)
U of Wisconsin–Whitewater (WI)
Ursuline Coll (OH)
Valdosta State U (GA)
Vanderbilt U (TN)
Walsh U (OH)
Warner Pacific Coll (OR)
Washington State U (WA)
Wayne State Coll (NE)
Weber State U (UT)
Webster U (MO)
Welch Coll (TN)
Wesleyan Coll (GA)
West Chester U of Pennsylvania (PA)
Western Kentucky U (KY)
Western Michigan U (MI)
Western Washington U (WA)
Wheelock Coll (MA)
Widener U (PA)
Wilmington U (DE)
Worcester State U (MA)
Wright State U (OH)
Xavier U (OH)
Xavier U of Louisiana (LA)
Yeshiva U (NY)
York Coll of Pennsylvania (PA)
Youngstown State U (OH)

EARTH SCIENCE EDUCATION
Albion Coll (MI)
Calvin Coll (MI)
Central Michigan U (MI)
Eastern Kentucky U (KY)
Florida Inst of Technology (FL)
Long Island U–LIU Post (NY)
Minnesota State U Moorhead (MN)
Pace U (NY)
State U of New York Coll at Potsdam (NY)
Syracuse U (NY)
Western Michigan U (MI)

EAST ASIAN LANGUAGES
Arizona State U at the Tempe campus (AZ)
Austin Coll (TX)
Columbia U (NY)
Eckerd Coll (FL)
Indiana U Bloomington (IN)
Michigan State U (MI)
Smith Coll (MA)
U of Alberta (AB, Canada)
The U of Kansas (KS)
U of Pennsylvania (PA)
U of Puget Sound (WA)
U of Southern California (CA)
The U of Texas at Austin (TX)
The U of Western Ontario (ON, Canada)
Washington and Lee U (VA)

EAST ASIAN LANGUAGES RELATED
Columbia U, School of General Studies (NY)
Dartmouth Coll (NH)
Michigan State U (MI)
Northwestern U (IL)
U of Chicago (IL)
U of Florida (FL)
U of Minnesota, Twin Cities Campus (MN)
Washington U in St. Louis (MO)

ECOLOGY
Bard Coll at Simon's Rock (MA)
Barry U (FL)
Beloit Coll (WI)
Bemidji State U (MN)
Bennington Coll (VT)
California State U, Dominguez Hills (CA)
California State U, Fresno (CA)
California State U, Long Beach (CA)
California State U, San Marcos (CA)
Castleton State Coll (VT)
Central Washington U (WA)
Cheyney U of Pennsylvania (PA)
Christian Brothers U (TN)
Clark U (MA)
Coll of the Ozarks (MO)
Colorado State U (CO)
Concordia Coll–New York (NY)
Concordia U (QC, Canada)
Cornell U (NY)
Dartmouth Coll (NH)
Defiance Coll (OH)
The Evergreen State Coll (WA)
Fort Lewis Coll (CO)
Georgetown Coll (KY)
Georgia Regents U (GA)
Greensboro Coll (NC)
Iowa State U of Science and Technology (IA)
Jacksonville State U (AL)
Lawrence U (WI)
Le Moyne Coll (NY)
Manchester U (IN)
Medgar Evers Coll of the City U of New York (NY)
Minnesota State U Mankato (MN)
Molloy Coll (NY)
New Mexico State U (NM)
New York U (NY)
Northern Michigan U (MI)
Northwestern U (IL)
Oberlin Coll (OH)
Ohio U (OH)
Oklahoma State U (OK)
Prescott Coll (AZ)
Princeton U (NJ)
Rice U (TX)
Rocky Mountain Coll (MT)
Rutgers, The State U of New Jersey, New Brunswick (NJ)
Saint Leo U (FL)
Salisbury U (MD)
San Diego State U (CA)
San Francisco State U (CA)
Seattle Pacific U (WA)
State U of New York at Plattsburgh (NY)
State U of New York Coll of Environmental Science and Forestry (NY)
Sterling Coll (VT)
Stony Brook U, State U of New York (NY)
Susquehanna U (PA)
Towson U (MD)
Tufts U (MA)
Tulane U (LA)
Université de Montréal (QC, Canada)
Université de Sherbrooke (QC, Canada)
The U of Akron (OH)
U of California, Los Angeles (CA)
U of California, Santa Barbara (CA)
U of California, Santa Cruz (CA)
U of Delaware (DE)
U of Denver (CO)
U of Georgia (GA)
U of Guelph (ON, Canada)
U of Maine at Machias (ME)
U of Maryland, Coll Park (MD)
U of Michigan–Flint (MI)
U of Minnesota, Twin Cities Campus (MN)
U of Northern Iowa (IA)
U of North Texas (TX)
U of Pittsburgh (PA)
U of Rio Grande (OH)
U of Waterloo (ON, Canada)
The U of Western Ontario (ON, Canada)
Utah State U (UT)
Washington Coll (MD)
Washington U in St. Louis (MO)
William Paterson U of New Jersey (NJ)
Yale U (CT)

ECOLOGY AND EVOLUTIONARY BIOLOGY
Angelo State U (TX)
Bradley U (IL)
Colby Coll (ME)
The Colorado Coll (CO)
Columbia U, School of General Studies (NY)
Purdue U (IN)
The U of Arizona (AZ)
The U of British Columbia–Okanagan Campus (BC, Canada)
U of California, Irvine (CA)
U of Michigan (MI)
U of Pittsburgh (PA)
Vanderbilt U (TN)

ECOLOGY, EVOLUTION, SYSTEMATICS AND POPULATION BIOLOGY RELATED
Hofstra U (NY)
The Ohio State U (OH)
The U of British Columbia–Okanagan Campus (BC, Canada)
U of California, Davis (CA)
U of Colorado Boulder (CO)
U of Guelph (ON, Canada)
U of Regina (SK, Canada)
U of Washington (WA)

E-COMMERCE
Bloomfield Coll (NJ)
Creighton U (NE)
Delaware State U (DE)
DePaul U (IL)
Lewis U (IL)
Limestone Coll (SC)
Maryville U of Saint Louis (MO)
Philadelphia U (PA)
Seattle U (WA)
Thiel Coll (PA)
Tiffin U (OH)
Trevecca Nazarene U (TN)
The U of Akron (OH)
U of La Verne (CA)
U of Ottawa (ON, Canada)
U of Pennsylvania (PA)
The U of Scranton (PA)
The U of Toledo (OH)
U of Toronto (ON, Canada)
Western Michigan U (MI)
Winthrop U (SC)

ECONOMETRICS AND QUANTITATIVE ECONOMICS
Baldwin Wallace U (OH)
Bethany Coll (WV)
Bowdoin Coll (ME)
Bucknell U (PA)
The Colorado Coll (CO)
Hampden-Sydney Coll (VA)
High Point U (NC)
Hofstra U (NY)
Scripps Coll (CA)
Southern Methodist U (TX)
State U of New York at Oswego (NY)
United States Naval Acad (MD)
U of California, Irvine (CA)
U of California, Santa Barbara (CA)
U of Dayton (OH)
U of Guelph (ON, Canada)
U of Minnesota, Twin Cities Campus (MN)
U of Rhode Island (RI)
Wake Forest U (NC)
Weber State U (UT)
Western Kentucky U (KY)
Youngstown State U (OH)

ECONOMICS
Adams State U (CO)
Adelphi U (NY)
Agnes Scott Coll (GA)
Albion Coll (MI)
Albright Coll (PA)
Allegheny Coll (PA)
Alma Coll (MI)
American U (DC)
American U in Bulgaria (Bulgaria)
The American U in Cairo (Egypt)
The American U in Dubai (United Arab Emirates)
American U of Beirut (Lebanon)
Amherst Coll (MA)
Andrews U (MI)
Appalachian State U (NC)
Aquinas Coll (MI)
Arizona State U at the Tempe campus (AZ)
Arkansas State U (AR)
Armstrong State U (GA)
Ashland U (OH)
Assumption Coll (MA)
Auburn U (AL)
Augsburg Coll (MN)
Augustana Coll (IL)
Augustana Coll (SD)
Austin Coll (TX)
Ave Maria U (FL)
Babson Coll (MA)
Baker U (KS)
Baldwin Wallace U (OH)
Ball State U (IN)
Bard Coll (NY)
Barnard Coll (NY)
Barry U (FL)
Baruch Coll of the City U of New York (NY)
Bates Coll (ME)
Baylor U (TX)
Beloit Coll (WI)
Bemidji State U (MN)
Benedictine Coll (KS)
Benedictine U (IL)
Berea Coll (KY)
Bethany Coll (WV)
Bethel U (MN)
Binghamton U, State U of New York (NY)
Birmingham-Southern Coll (AL)
Bloomsburg U of Pennsylvania (PA)
Bluffton U (OH)
Boston Coll (MA)
Boston U (MA)
Bowdoin Coll (ME)
Bowie State U (MD)
Bowling Green State U (OH)
Bradley U (IL)
Brandeis U (MA)
Bridgewater Coll (VA)
Bridgewater State U (MA)
Brown U (RI)
Bryant U (RI)
Bryn Mawr Coll (PA)
Bucknell U (PA)
Buffalo State Coll, State U of New York (NY)
Butler U (IN)
Caldwell U (NJ)
California Inst of Technology (CA)
California Lutheran U (CA)
California Polytechnic State U, San Luis Obispo (CA)
California State Polytechnic U, Pomona (CA)
California State U, Chico (CA)
California State U, Fresno (CA)
California State U, Fullerton (CA)
California State U, Long Beach (CA)
California State U, Los Angeles (CA)
California State U, Sacramento (CA)
California State U, San Bernardino (CA)
California State U, San Marcos (CA)
California State U, Stanislaus (CA)
Calvin Coll (MI)
Campbellsville U (KY)
Canisius Coll (NY)
Cape Breton U (NS, Canada)
Capital U (OH)
Carleton Coll (MN)
Case Western Reserve U (OH)
Castleton State Coll (VT)
Catawba Coll (NC)
The Catholic U of America (DC)
Centenary Coll of Louisiana (LA)
Central Coll (IA)
Central Connecticut State U (CT)
Central Methodist U (MO)
Central Michigan U (MI)
Central State U (OH)
Central Washington U (WA)
Centre Coll (KY)
Charleston Southern U (SC)
Chicago State U (IL)
Chowan U (NC)
Christopher Newport U (VA)
City Coll of the City U of New York (NY)
Claremont McKenna Coll (CA)
Clarion U of Pennsylvania (PA)
Clark U (MA)
Cleveland State U (OH)
Coastal Carolina U (SC)
Coe Coll (IA)
Colby Coll (ME)
Coll of Charleston (SC)
The Coll of New Jersey (NJ)
The Coll of New Rochelle (NY)
Coll of Saint Benedict (MN)
Coll of Saint Elizabeth (NJ)
Coll of Staten Island of the City U of New York (NY)
Coll of the Atlantic (ME)
Coll of the Holy Cross (MA)
The Coll of William and Mary (VA)
The Coll of Wooster (OH)
The Colorado Coll (CO)
Colorado School of Mines (CO)
Colorado State U (CO)
Columbia U (NY)
Columbia U, School of General Studies (NY)
Concordia U (CA)
Concordia U (QC, Canada)
Concordia U Wisconsin (WI)
Connecticut Coll (CT)

Cornell Coll (IA)
Cornell U (NY)
Creighton U (NE)
Dalhousie U (NS, Canada)
Dartmouth Coll (NH)
Davidson Coll (NC)
Denison U (OH)
DePaul U (IL)
DePauw U (IN)
DEREE - The American Coll of Greece (Greece)
Dickinson Coll (PA)
Doane Coll (NE)
Dominican Coll (NY)
Dominican U (IL)
Dowling Coll (NY)
Drew U (NJ)
Drexel U (PA)
Drury U (MO)
Duquesne U (PA)
Earlham Coll (IN)
East Carolina U (NC)
Eastern Connecticut State U (CT)
Eastern Illinois U (IL)
Eastern Kentucky U (KY)
Eastern Michigan U (MI)
Eastern Oregon U (OR)
East Stroudsburg U of Pennsylvania (PA)
East Tennessee State U (TN)
Eckerd Coll (FL)
Edgewood Coll (WI)
Edinboro U of Pennsylvania (PA)
Elizabethtown Coll (PA)
Elmhurst Coll (IL)
Elmira Coll (NY)
Elon U (NC)
Emmanuel Coll (MA)
Emory & Henry Coll (VA)
Emporia State U (KS)
Fairfield U (CT)
Fairleigh Dickinson U, Coll at Florham (NJ)
Fairleigh Dickinson U, Metropolitan Campus (NJ)
Fairmont State U (WV)
Fitchburg State U (MA)
Flagler Coll (FL)
Florida Ag and Mech U (FL)
Florida Atlantic U (FL)
Florida Gulf Coast U (FL)
Florida Intl U (FL)
Florida Southern Coll (FL)
Florida State U (FL)
Fordham U (NY)
Fort Hays State U (KS)
Fort Lewis Coll (CO)
Framingham State U (MA)
Franciscan U of Steubenville (OH)
Francis Marion U (SC)
Franklin & Marshall Coll (PA)
Franklin Coll (IN)
Franklin U (OH)
Frostburg State U (MD)
Furman U (SC)
George Mason U (VA)
Georgetown Coll (KY)
Georgetown U (DC)
The George Washington U (DC)
Georgia Southern U (GA)
Georgia State U (GA)
Gettysburg Coll (PA)
Gonzaga U (WA)
Gordon Coll (MA)
Goucher Coll (MD)
Governors State U (IL)
Graceland U (IA)
Grand Valley State U (MI)
Grinnell Coll (IA)
Grove City Coll (PA)
Guilford Coll (NC)
Gustavus Adolphus Coll (MN)
Hamilton Coll (NY)
Hamline U (MN)
Hampden-Sydney Coll (VA)
Hampshire Coll (MA)
Hampton U (VA)
Hanover Coll (IN)
Harding U (AR)
Hardin-Simmons U (TX)
Hartwick Coll (NY)
Harvard U (MA)
Hastings Coll (NE)
Haverford Coll (PA)
Hawai`i Pacific U (HI)
Heidelberg U (OH)
Hendrix Coll (AR)
Hillsdale Coll (MI)
Hiram Coll (OH)
Hobart and William Smith Colls (NY)
Hofstra U (NY)
Hollins U (VA)
Hope Coll (MI)
Houston Baptist U (TX)
Howard U (DC)
Humboldt State U (CA)
Hunter Coll of the City U of New York (NY)
Illinois Coll (IL)
Illinois State U (IL)
Illinois Wesleyan U (IL)
Immaculata U (PA)
Indiana State U (IN)
Indiana U Bloomington (IN)
Indiana U Northwest (IN)
Indiana U of Pennsylvania (PA)
Indiana U–Purdue U Fort Wayne (IN)
Indiana U–Purdue U Indianapolis (IN)
Indiana U South Bend (IN)
Indiana U Southeast (IN)
Inter American U of Puerto Rico, San Germán Campus (PR)
Iona Coll (NY)
Iowa State U of Science and Technology (IA)
Ithaca Coll (NY)
Jacksonville State U (AL)
Jacksonville U (FL)
James Madison U (VA)
John Brown U (AR)
John Cabot U (Italy)
John Carroll U (OH)
Johns Hopkins U (MD)
Johnson C. Smith U (NC)
Juniata Coll (PA)
Kalamazoo Coll (MI)
Kansas State U (KS)
Kean U (NJ)
Keene State Coll (NH)
Kenyon Coll (OH)
King's Coll (PA)
King U (TN)
Knox Coll (IL)
Lafayette Coll (PA)
Lake Forest Coll (IL)
Langston U (OK)
La Salle U (PA)
La Sierra U (CA)
Lawrence U (WI)
Lebanese American U (Lebanon)
Lebanon Valley Coll (PA)
Lehman Coll of the City U of New York (NY)
Le Moyne Coll (NY)
Lenoir-Rhyne U (NC)
Lewis & Clark Coll (OR)
Limestone Coll (SC)
Lincoln Memorial U (TN)
Lincoln U (CA)
Lindenwood U (MO)
Linfield Coll (OR)
Long Island U–LIU Brooklyn (NY)
Long Island U–LIU Post (NY)
Longwood U (VA)
Loras Coll (IA)
Louisiana Coll (LA)
Louisiana State U and A&M Coll (LA)
Loyola Marymount U (CA)
Loyola U New Orleans (LA)
Lubbock Christian U (TX)
Luther Coll (IA)
Lycoming Coll (PA)
Lynchburg Coll (VA)
Lyon Coll (AR)
Macalester Coll (MN)
Manchester U (IN)
Manhattan Coll (NY)
Manhattanville Coll (NY)
Marian U (IN)
Marietta Coll (OH)
Marist Coll (NY)
Marquette U (WI)
Marshall U (WV)
Mars Hill U (NC)
Mary Baldwin Coll (VA)
Marymount U (VA)
Maryville Coll (TN)
Massachusetts Inst of Technology (MA)
McDaniel Coll (MD)
McKendree U (IL)
Mercer U, Macon (GA)
Meredith Coll (NC)
Merrimack Coll (MA)
Messiah Coll (PA)
Metropolitan State U (MN)
Miami U (OH)
Michigan State U (MI)
Michigan Technological U (MI)
Middlebury Coll (VT)
Middle Tennessee State U (TN)
Midwestern State U (TX)
Millersville U of Pennsylvania (PA)
Milligan Coll (TN)
Millsaps Coll (MS)
Mills Coll (CA)
Minnesota State U Mankato (MN)
Minnesota State U Moorhead (MN)
Mississippi State U (MS)
Missouri State U (MO)
Missouri U of Science and Technology (MO)
Missouri Valley Coll (MO)
Missouri Western State U (MO)
Monmouth Coll (IL)
Montana State U (MT)
Montclair State U (NJ)
Moravian Coll (PA)
Mount Allison U (NB, Canada)
Mount Holyoke Coll (MA)
Mount St. Mary's U (MD)
Muhlenberg Coll (PA)
Murray State U (KY)
Nazareth Coll of Rochester (NY)
Nebraska Wesleyan U (NE)
New Coll of Florida (FL)
New Jersey City U (NJ)
New Mexico State U (NM)
New York U (NY)
Niagara U (NY)
Nichols Coll (MA)
North Carolina Ag and Tech State U (NC)
North Central Coll (IL)
North Dakota State U (ND)
Northeastern Illinois U (IL)
Northeastern U (MA)
Northern Illinois U (IL)
Northern Michigan U (MI)
Northern State U (SD)
Northwestern Coll (IA)
Northwestern U (IL)
Northwest Missouri State U (MO)
Norwich U (VT)
Oakland U (MI)
Oberlin Coll (OH)
Occidental Coll (CA)
Oglethorpe U (GA)
Ohio Dominican U (OH)
The Ohio State U (OH)
Ohio U (OH)
Ohio Wesleyan U (OH)
Oklahoma City U (OK)
Oklahoma State U (OK)
Old Dominion U (VA)
Olivet Nazarene U (IL)
Oregon State U (OR)
Pace U (NY)
Pacific Lutheran U (WA)
Pacific U (OR)
Park U (MO)
Penn State Abington (PA)
Penn State Altoona (PA)
Penn State Beaver (PA)
Penn State Berks (PA)
Penn State Brandywine (PA)
Penn State DuBois (PA)
Penn State Erie, The Behrend Coll (PA)
Penn State Fayette, The Eberly Campus (PA)
Penn State Greater Allegheny (PA)
Penn State Hazleton (PA)
Penn State Lehigh Valley (PA)
Penn State Mont Alto (PA)
Penn State New Kensington (PA)
Penn State Schuylkill (PA)
Penn State Shenango (PA)
Penn State U Park (PA)
Penn State Wilkes-Barre (PA)
Penn State Worthington Scranton (PA)
Penn State York (PA)
Pepperdine U, Malibu (CA)
Pittsburg State U (KS)
Pomona Coll (CA)
Portland State U (OR)
Princeton U (NJ)
Principia Coll (IL)
Providence Coll (RI)
Purchase Coll, State U of New York (NY)
Purdue U (IN)
Purdue U Calumet (IN)
Queens Coll of the City U of New York (NY)
Quinnipiac U (CT)
Radford U (VA)
Ramapo Coll of New Jersey (NJ)
Randolph Coll (VA)
Randolph-Macon Coll (VA)
Reed Coll (OR)
Regis U (CO)
Rensselaer Polytechnic Inst (NY)
Rhode Island Coll (RI)
Rhodes Coll (TN)
Rice U (TX)
Rider U (NJ)
Ripon Coll (WI)
Roanoke Coll (VA)
Robert Morris U (PA)
Rochester Inst of Technology (NY)
Rockford U (IL)
Rockhurst U (MO)
Roger Williams U (RI)
Rollins Coll (FL)
Roosevelt U (IL)
Rose-Hulman Inst of Technology (IN)
Rosemont Coll (PA)
Rowan U (NJ)
Rutgers, The State U of New Jersey, Camden (NJ)
Rutgers, The State U of New Jersey, Newark (NJ)
Rutgers, The State U of New Jersey, New Brunswick (NJ)
Sacred Heart U (CT)
Saginaw Valley State U (MI)
Saint Anselm Coll (NH)
St. Catherine U (MN)
St. Edward's U (TX)
St. Francis Coll (NY)
Saint Francis U (PA)
St. John Fisher Coll (NY)
Saint John's U (MN)
St. John's U (NY)
Saint Joseph's Coll (IN)
Saint Joseph's U (PA)
St. Lawrence U (NY)
Saint Leo U (FL)
Saint Mary's Coll (IN)
St. Mary's Coll of Maryland (MD)
St. Mary's U (TX)
Saint Michael's Coll (VT)
St. Norbert Coll (WI)
St. Olaf Coll (MN)
Saint Peter's U (NJ)
St. Thomas U (FL)
St. Thomas U (NB, Canada)
Saint Vincent Coll (PA)
Salem Coll (NC)
Salisbury U (MD)
Salve Regina U (RI)
San Diego State U (CA)
San Francisco State U (CA)
San Jose State U (CA)
Santa Clara U (CA)
Sarah Lawrence Coll (NY)
Scripps Coll (CA)
Seattle Pacific U (WA)
Seattle U (WA)
Seton Hill U (PA)
Sewanee: The U of the South (TN)
Shepherd U (WV)
Shippensburg U of Pennsylvania (PA)
Siena Coll (NY)
Simmons Coll (MA)
Simon Fraser U (BC, Canada)
Simpson Coll (IA)
Skidmore Coll (NY)
Slippery Rock U of Pennsylvania (PA)
Smith Coll (MA)
South Dakota State U (SD)
Southeast Missouri State U (MO)
Southern Connecticut State U (CT)
Southern Illinois U Carbondale (IL)
Southern Illinois U Edwardsville (IL)
Southern Methodist U (TX)
Southern New Hampshire U (NH)
Southern Oregon U (OR)
Southern Utah U (UT)
Southwestern U (TX)
Spelman Coll (GA)
Stanford U (CA)
State U of New York at Fredonia (NY)
State U of New York at New Paltz (NY)
State U of New York at Oswego (NY)
State U of New York at Plattsburgh (NY)
State U of New York Coll at Cortland (NY)
State U of New York Coll at Geneseo (NY)
State U of New York Coll at Potsdam (NY)
Stephen F. Austin State U (TX)
Stetson U (FL)
Stockton U (NJ)
Stonehill Coll (MA)
Stony Brook U, State U of New York (NY)
Suffolk U (MA)
Susquehanna U (PA)
Syracuse U (NY)
Tarleton State U (TX)
Taylor U (IN)
Temple U (PA)
Texas A&M U (TX)
Texas A&M U–Corpus Christi (TX)
Texas Christian U (TX)
Texas Lutheran U (TX)
Texas Southern U (TX)
Texas State U (TX)
Texas Tech U (TX)
Thomas More Coll (KY)
Tougaloo Coll (MS)
Towson U (MD)
Transylvania U (KY)
Trent U (ON, Canada)
Trinity Coll (CT)
Trinity U (TX)
Troy U (AL)
Truman State U (MO)
Tufts U (MA)
Tulane U (LA)
Union Coll (NY)
Union U (TN)
United States Air Force Acad (CO)
United States Military Acad (NY)
United States Naval Acad (MD)
Université de Montréal (QC, Canada)
U at Albany, State U of New York (NY)
U at Buffalo, the State U of New York (NY)
The U of Akron (OH)
U of Alaska Fairbanks (AK)
U of Alberta (AB, Canada)
The U of Arizona (AZ)
U of Arkansas (AR)
The U of British Columbia (BC, Canada)
The U of British Columbia–Okanagan Campus (BC, Canada)
U of California, Berkeley (CA)
U of California, Davis (CA)
U of California, Irvine (CA)
U of California, Los Angeles (CA)
U of California, Merced (CA)
U of California, Riverside (CA)
U of California, Santa Barbara (CA)
U of California, Santa Cruz (CA)
U of Central Arkansas (AR)
U of Central Florida (FL)
U of Central Missouri (MO)
U of Central Oklahoma (OK)
U of Chicago (IL)
U of Cincinnati (OH)
U of Colorado Boulder (CO)
U of Colorado Colorado Springs (CO)
U of Colorado Denver (CO)
U of Dallas (TX)
U of Dayton (OH)
U of Delaware (DE)
U of Denver (CO)
U of Evansville (IN)
The U of Findlay (OH)
U of Florida (FL)
U of Guelph (ON, Canada)
U of Hartford (CT)
U of Hawaii at Hilo (HI)

U of Hawaii at Manoa (HI)
U of Hawaii–West Oahu (HI)
U of Houston (TX)
U of Idaho (ID)
U of Illinois at Chicago (IL)
U of Illinois at Springfield (IL)
The U of Iowa (IA)
The U of Kansas (KS)
U of Kentucky (KY)
U of King's Coll (NS, Canada)
U of La Verne (CA)
U of Lethbridge (AB, Canada)
U of Louisville (KY)
U of Maine (ME)
U of Maryland, Baltimore County (MD)
U of Maryland, Coll Park (MD)
U of Mary Washington (VA)
U of Massachusetts Amherst (MA)
U of Massachusetts Boston (MA)
U of Massachusetts Dartmouth (MA)
U of Massachusetts Lowell (MA)
U of Memphis (TN)
U of Miami (FL)
U of Michigan (MI)
U of Michigan–Dearborn (MI)
U of Michigan–Flint (MI)
U of Minnesota, Duluth (MN)
U of Minnesota, Morris (MN)
U of Minnesota, Twin Cities Campus (MN)
U of Mississippi (MS)
U of Missouri (MO)
U of Missouri–Kansas City (MO)
U of Missouri–St. Louis (MO)
The U of Montana (MT)
U of Mount Union (OH)
U of Nebraska at Kearney (NE)
U of Nebraska–Lincoln (NE)
U of Nevada, Las Vegas (NV)
U of New Brunswick Saint John (NB, Canada)
U of New Hampshire (NH)
U of New Haven (CT)
U of New Mexico (NM)
U of North Carolina at Asheville (NC)
The U of North Carolina at Chapel Hill (NC)
The U of North Carolina at Charlotte (NC)
The U of North Carolina at Greensboro (NC)
The U of North Carolina Wilmington (NC)
U of North Dakota (ND)
U of Northern Colorado (CO)
U of Northern Iowa (IA)
U of North Florida (FL)
U of North Texas (TX)
U of Notre Dame (IN)
U of Oklahoma (OK)
U of Oregon (OR)
U of Ottawa (ON, Canada)
U of Pennsylvania (PA)
U of Pittsburgh (PA)
U of Pittsburgh at Bradford (PA)
U of Portland (OR)
U of Puget Sound (WA)
U of Regina (SK, Canada)
U of Rhode Island (RI)
U of Richmond (VA)
U of Rio Grande (OH)
U of Rochester (NY)
U of St. Thomas (MN)
U of St. Thomas (TX)
U of San Diego (CA)
U of San Francisco (CA)
U of Saskatchewan (SK, Canada)
U of Science and Arts of Oklahoma (OK)
The U of Scranton (PA)
The U of South Dakota (SD)
U of Southern California (CA)
U of Southern Indiana (IN)
U of Southern Maine (ME)
U of South Florida (FL)
The U of Tampa (FL)
The U of Tennessee (TN)
The U of Tennessee at Chattanooga (TN)
The U of Tennessee at Martin (TN)
The U of Texas at Arlington (TX)
The U of Texas at Austin (TX)
The U of Texas at Dallas (TX)
The U of Texas at El Paso (TX)
The U of Texas at Tyler (TX)
The U of Texas–Pan American (TX)
U of the District of Columbia (DC)
U of the Fraser Valley (BC, Canada)
U of the Pacific (CA)
The U of Toledo (OH)
U of Toronto (ON, Canada)
The U of Tulsa (OK)
U of Utah (UT)
U of Vermont (VT)
U of Virginia (VA)
The U of Virginia's Coll at Wise (VA)
U of Washington (WA)
U of Waterloo (ON, Canada)
The U of Western Ontario (ON, Canada)
U of West Florida (FL)
U of West Georgia (GA)
U of Windsor (ON, Canada)
U of Wisconsin–Eau Claire (WI)
U of Wisconsin–Green Bay (WI)
U of Wisconsin–La Crosse (WI)
U of Wisconsin–Madison (WI)
U of Wisconsin–Milwaukee (WI)
U of Wisconsin–Oshkosh (WI)
U of Wisconsin–Parkside (WI)
U of Wisconsin–Platteville (WI)
U of Wisconsin–River Falls (WI)
U of Wisconsin–Stevens Point (WI)
U of Wisconsin–Superior (WI)
U of Wisconsin–Whitewater (WI)
Ursinus Coll (PA)
Utah State U (UT)
Utah Valley U (UT)
Utica Coll (NY)
Valparaiso U (IN)
Vanderbilt U (TN)
Vassar Coll (NY)
Villanova U (PA)
Virginia Military Inst (VA)
Virginia Polytechnic Inst and State U (VA)
Wabash Coll (IN)
Wagner Coll (NY)
Wake Forest U (NC)
Walla Walla U (WA)
Wartburg Coll (IA)
Washburn U (KS)
Washington & Jefferson Coll (PA)
Washington and Lee U (VA)
Washington Coll (MD)
Washington State U (WA)
Washington U in St. Louis (MO)
Wayne State U (MI)
Weber State U (UT)
Webster U (MO)
Wells Coll (NY)
Wesleyan Coll (GA)
Wesleyan U (CT)
Western Illinois U (IL)
Western Kentucky U (KY)
Western Michigan U (MI)
Western New England U (MA)
Western Oregon U (OR)
Western State Colorado U (CO)
Western Washington U (WA)
Westfield State U (MA)
Westminster Coll (MO)
West Virginia State U (WV)
West Virginia U (WV)
West Virginia Wesleyan Coll (WV)
Wheaton Coll (IL)
Wheaton Coll (MA)
Whitman Coll (WA)
Whittier Coll (CA)
Whitworth U (WA)
Wichita State U (KS)
Widener U (PA)
Willamette U (OR)
Williams Coll (MA)
Winona State U (MN)
Wittenberg U (OH)
Wofford Coll (SC)
Worcester Polytechnic Inst (MA)
Worcester State U (MA)
Wright State U (OH)
Xavier U (OH)
Yale U (CT)
Yeshiva U (NY)
York Coll of Pennsylvania (PA)
York Coll of the City U of New York (NY)
Youngstown State U (OH)

ECONOMICS RELATED

American Intl Coll (MA)
Augsburg Coll (MN)
Central Washington U (WA)
Centre Coll (KY)
The Colorado Coll (CO)
Columbia U, School of General Studies (NY)
Emory & Henry Coll (VA)
Florida Southern Coll (FL)
Lindenwood U (MO)
Muhlenberg Coll (PA)
Regis U (CO)
San Diego State U (CA)
U of Delaware (DE)
U of Maine (ME)
U of Minnesota, Duluth (MN)
U of Regina (SK, Canada)
U of Richmond (VA)
U of West Georgia (GA)
Valparaiso U (IN)
Washington & Jefferson Coll (PA)
Western Washington U (WA)
Wittenberg U (OH)
Xavier U (OH)

EDUCATION

Albertus Magnus Coll (CT)
Alma Coll (MI)
Alverno Coll (WI)
Anderson U (IN)
Andrews U (MI)
Anna Maria Coll (MA)
Arcadia U (PA)
Ashland U (OH)
Auburn U (AL)
Augsburg Coll (MN)
Avila U (MO)
Baker Coll (MI)
Ball State U (IN)
The Baptist Coll of Florida (FL)
Barnard Coll (NY)
Barry U (FL)
Baylor U (TX)
Becker Coll (MA)
Belmont Abbey Coll (NC)
Belmont U (TN)
Beloit Coll (WI)
Bemidji State U (MN)
Bennington Coll (VT)
Berea Coll (KY)
Bethel Coll (IN)
Bethune-Cookman U (FL)
Biola U (CA)
Birmingham-Southern Coll (AL)
Bloomfield Coll (NJ)
Bluefield Coll (VA)
Bowie State U (MD)
Bowling Green State U (OH)
Bowling Green State U-Firelands Coll (OH)
Brandeis U (MA)
Brown U (RI)
Bucknell U (PA)
Cabrini Coll (PA)
California Baptist U (CA)
Canisius Coll (NY)
Cape Breton U (NS, Canada)
Carson-Newman U (TN)
The Catholic U of America (DC)
Cedar Crest Coll (PA)
Central Methodist U (MO)
Central Washington U (WA)
Chapman U (CA)
Chipola Coll (FL)
Chowan U (NC)
Christian Brothers U (TN)
Cincinnati Christian U (OH)
City Coll of the City U of New York (NY)
Clark Atlanta U (GA)
Clarke U (IA)
Clark U (MA)
Coe Coll (IA)
Coker Coll (SC)
Colby Coll (ME)
The Coll of New Rochelle (NY)
Coll of Saint Mary (NE)
Coll of the Atlantic (ME)
The Colorado Coll (CO)
Colorado State U (CO)
Concordia Coll (MN)
Concordia Coll–New York (NY)
Concordia U (QC, Canada)
Concordia U Chicago (IL)
Concordia U, Nebraska (NE)
Concordia U, St. Paul (MN)
Concordia U Wisconsin (WI)
Concord U (WV)
Corban U (OR)
Cornell U (NY)
Crandall U (NB, Canada)
Cumberland U (TN)
Curry Coll (MA)
Defiance Coll (OH)
Dickinson State U (ND)
Dominican Coll (NY)
Duquesne U (PA)
East Texas Baptist U (TX)
Elmhurst Coll (IL)
Elms Coll (MA)
Elon U (NC)
Emmanuel Coll (MA)
Eureka Coll (IL)
The Evergreen State Coll (WA)
Fairmont State U (WV)
Ferrum Coll (VA)
Fitchburg State U (MA)
Five Towns Coll (NY)
Florida Gulf Coast U (FL)
Fontbonne U (MO)
Fordham U (NY)
Framingham State U (MA)
Franklin Pierce U (NH)
Furman U (SC)
Gallaudet U (DC)
Georgia Southern U (GA)
Gettysburg Coll (PA)
Goddard Coll (VT)
Goshen Coll (IN)
Graceland U (IA)
Greensboro Coll (NC)
Guilford Coll (NC)
Gustavus Adolphus Coll (MN)
Hampshire Coll (MA)
Hampton U (VA)
Hannibal-LaGrange U (MO)
Hardin-Simmons U (TX)
Harrison Middleton U (AZ)
Harris-Stowe State U (MO)
Hastings Coll (NE)
Haverford Coll (PA)
Heidelberg U (OH)
Heritage U (WA)
Hiram Coll (OH)
Houston Baptist U (TX)
Howard U (DC)
Humboldt State U (CA)
Huston-Tillotson U (TX)
Illinois Coll (IL)
Illinois Wesleyan U (IL)
Indiana U–Purdue U Fort Wayne (IN)
Inter American U of Puerto Rico, San Germán Campus (PR)
Iowa State U of Science and Technology (IA)
Iowa Wesleyan Coll (IA)
Jacksonville State U (AL)
John Brown U (AR)
John Carroll U (OH)
Johnson State Coll (VT)
Juniata Coll (PA)
Kent State U (OH)
Knox Coll (IL)
Lake Forest Coll (IL)
Langston U (OK)
La Salle U (PA)
Lasell Coll (MA)
Lebanese American U (Lebanon)
Lesley U (MA)
Limestone Coll (SC)
Lincoln Memorial U (TN)
Lindenwood U (MO)
Lindsey Wilson Coll (KY)
Lipscomb U (TN)
Loras Coll (IA)
Macalester Coll (MN)
Manchester U (IN)
Manhattan Coll (NY)
Manhattanville Coll (NY)
Mansfield U of Pennsylvania (PA)
Marian U (IN)
Marietta Coll (OH)
Mars Hill U (NC)
Maryville Coll (TN)
Massachusetts Coll of Liberal Arts (MA)
The Master's Coll and Sem (CA)
Mayville State U (ND)
Merrimack Coll (MA)
Miami Dade Coll (FL)
Michigan State U (MI)
Milligan Coll (TN)
Millsaps Coll (MS)
Minnesota State U Mankato (MN)
Mississippi Valley State U (MS)
Missouri Baptist U (MO)
Missouri Valley Coll (MO)
Monmouth U (NJ)
Montana State U Billings (MT)
Mount Marty Coll (SD)
Mount Mary U (WI)
Mount St. Joseph U (OH)
Mount Saint Mary's U (CA)
Mount Vernon Nazarene U (OH)
Nazareth Coll of Rochester (NY)
New England Coll (NH)
Newman U (KS)
New Mexico State U (NM)
Niagara U (NY)
North Carolina Ag and Tech State U (NC)
North Carolina State U (NC)
North Carolina Wesleyan Coll (NC)
North Central Coll (IL)
Northern Illinois U (IL)
Northern State U (SD)
Northwestern U (IL)
Northwest U (WA)
Notre Dame of Maryland U (MD)
Nova Southeastern U (FL)
Oakland City U (IN)
Ohio Dominican U (OH)
Ohio Northern U (OH)
Ohio Wesleyan U (OH)
Oklahoma Baptist U (OK)
Oklahoma City U (OK)
Oregon State U (OR)
Pacific Lutheran U (WA)
Pacific U (OR)
Peru State Coll (NE)
Piedmont Coll (GA)
Purdue U (IN)
Quinnipiac U (CT)
Regent U (VA)
Regis U (CO)
Reinhardt U (GA)
Ripon Coll (WI)
Rivier U (NH)
Rockford U (IL)
Roger Williams U (RI)
Rowan U (NJ)
Sacred Heart U (CT)
Saginaw Valley State U (MI)
St. Catherine U (MN)
Saint Francis U (PA)
Saint Louis U (MO)
Saint Martin's U (WA)
St. Mary's U (TX)
Saint Michael's Coll (VT)
St. Thomas Aquinas Coll (NY)
St. Thomas U (NB, Canada)
Salem Coll (NC)
San Diego Christian Coll (CA)
Seattle Pacific U (WA)
Shasta Bible Coll (CA)
Shawnee State U (OH)
Simmons Coll (MA)
Simon Fraser U (BC, Canada)
Simpson Coll (IA)
Skidmore Coll (NY)
Smith Coll (MA)
Southern New Hampshire U (NH)
Southwestern Assemblies of God U (TX)
Southwestern U (TX)
Southwest Minnesota State U (MN)
Spalding U (KY)
State U of New York at Fredonia (NY)
State U of New York at Oswego (NY)
State U of New York at Plattsburgh (NY)
State U of New York Coll at Geneseo (NY)
State U of New York Empire State Coll (NY)
Stetson U (FL)
Summit U (PA)
Tabor Coll (KS)
Tarleton State U (TX)
Tennessee State U (TN)
Tennessee Wesleyan Coll (TN)
Texas Lutheran U (TX)
Texas Wesleyan U (TX)
Tougaloo Coll (MS)
Trent U (ON, Canada)
Trine U (IN)
Trinity Coll (CT)

Union Coll (KY)
Union U (TN)
Université de Montréal (QC, Canada)
Université de Sherbrooke (QC, Canada)
Université du Québec en Outaouais (QC, Canada)
U of Arkansas (AR)
U of Arkansas at Little Rock (AR)
The U of British Columbia (BC, Canada)
The U of British Columbia–Okanagan Campus (BC, Canada)
U of California, Irvine (CA)
U of California, Santa Cruz (CA)
U of Central Missouri (MO)
U of Charleston (WV)
U of Colorado Denver (CO)
U of Dallas (TX)
The U of Findlay (OH)
U of Hawaii at Manoa (HI)
U of Indianapolis (IN)
U of Lethbridge (AB, Canada)
U of Maine at Machias (ME)
U of Maine at Presque Isle (ME)
U of Massachusetts Amherst (MA)
U of Massachusetts Boston (MA)
U of Miami (FL)
U of Michigan–Dearborn (MI)
U of Minnesota, Duluth (MN)
U of Minnesota, Morris (MN)
U of Minnesota, Twin Cities Campus (MN)
U of Missouri (MO)
U of Missouri–St. Louis (MO)
The U of Montana (MT)
U of Nevada, Las Vegas (NV)
U of New Brunswick Saint John (NB, Canada)
U of New England (ME)
U of North Texas (TX)
U of Oregon (OR)
U of Pittsburgh at Greensburg (PA)
U of Portland (OR)
U of Regina (SK, Canada)
U of Rio Grande (OH)
U of Saint Francis (IN)
U of Saint Mary (KS)
U of St. Thomas (TX)
U of San Francisco (CA)
U of Saskatchewan (SK, Canada)
The U of South Dakota (SD)
The U of Texas at San Antonio (TX)
U of the Pacific (CA)
The U of Toledo (OH)
U of Toronto (ON, Canada)
The U of Tulsa (OK)
U of Utah (UT)
U of Vermont (VT)
The U of Western Ontario (ON, Canada)
U of Windsor (ON, Canada)
U of Wisconsin–Green Bay (WI)
U of Wisconsin–Milwaukee (WI)
U of Wisconsin–Oshkosh (WI)
U of Wisconsin–Platteville (WI)
U of Wisconsin–River Falls (WI)
U of Wisconsin–Stevens Point (WI)
U of Wisconsin–Superior (WI)
Upper Iowa U (IA)
Urbana U (OH)
Valley City State U (ND)
Vanderbilt U (TN)
Vanguard U of Southern California (CA)
Vassar Coll (NY)
Viterbo U (WI)
Wagner Coll (NY)
Walden U (MN)
Walsh U (OH)
Washburn U (KS)
Washington & Jefferson Coll (PA)
Washington State U (WA)
Washington State U Vancouver (WA)
Washington U in St. Louis (MO)
Webster U (MO)
Welch Coll (TN)
Wells Coll (NY)
West Liberty U (WV)
West Virginia Wesleyan Coll (WV)
Wheeling Jesuit U (WV)
Wilkes U (PA)
William Jessup U (CA)
William Paterson U of New Jersey (NJ)
William Peace U (NC)
William Penn U (IA)
Williams Baptist Coll (AR)
William Woods U (MO)
Winona State U (MN)
Wittenberg U (OH)
Wofford Coll (SC)
Xavier U (OH)
Xavier U of Louisiana (LA)
Youngstown State U (OH)

EDUCATIONAL ADMINISTRATION AND SUPERVISION RELATED
Canisius Coll (NY)
Cornell U (NY)
Philander Smith Coll (AR)
The U of Western Ontario (ON, Canada)

EDUCATIONAL ASSESSMENT, EVALUATION, AND RESEARCH RELATED
Penn State Altoona (PA)
Penn State Berks (PA)
Penn State U Park (PA)

EDUCATIONAL, INSTRUCTIONAL, AND CURRICULUM SUPERVISION
Canisius Coll (NY)
U of Wisconsin–River Falls (WI)
Wright State U (OH)

EDUCATIONAL/ INSTRUCTIONAL TECHNOLOGY
Bowling Green State U (OH)
Bridgewater State U (MA)
Cameron U (OK)
Canisius Coll (NY)
Jackson State U (MS)
Jacksonville State U (AL)
LeTourneau U (TX)
Midwestern State U (TX)
National U (CA)
Post U (CT)
U of Central Oklahoma (OK)
The U of Toledo (OH)
The U of Western Ontario (ON, Canada)
Wayne State U (MI)
Western Illinois U (IL)
Western Oregon U (OR)
Widener U (PA)
Wilmington U (DE)

EDUCATIONAL LEADERSHIP AND ADMINISTRATION
Avila U (MO)
Canisius Coll (NY)
Creighton U (NE)
DePaul U (IL)
Hiram Coll (OH)
LeTourneau U (TX)
Midwestern State U (TX)
Tarleton State U (TX)
Tennessee State U (TN)
U of Central Oklahoma (OK)
U of Minnesota, Crookston (MN)
U of San Francisco (CA)
U of the Incarnate Word (TX)
Welch Coll (TN)
Wright State U (OH)

EDUCATIONAL PSYCHOLOGY
Bethany Coll (WV)
DePaul U (IL)
Jacksonville State U (AL)
Mississippi State U (MS)
Saint Vincent Coll (PA)
Tarleton State U (TX)
U of Pittsburgh (PA)

EDUCATIONAL STATISTICS AND RESEARCH METHODS
Bucknell U (PA)

EDUCATION (MULTIPLE LEVELS)
Adams State U (CO)
Assumption Coll (MA)
Augustana Coll (SD)
Austin Peay State U (TN)
Averett U (VA)
Biola U (CA)
Birmingham-Southern Coll (AL)
Bowling Green State U (OH)
Canisius Coll (NY)
Central State U (OH)
Coll of Charleston (SC)
Coll of Coastal Georgia (GA)
Coll of Saint Elizabeth (NJ)
Coll of Saint Mary (NE)
The Coll of St. Scholastica (MN)
Columbia Intl U (SC)
Columbia U (NY)
Concordia U Chicago (IL)
Concordia U, Nebraska (NE)
Concordia U Wisconsin (WI)
Crandall U (NB, Canada)
DePaul U (IL)
Dickinson State U (ND)
Dominican U (IL)
Dowling Coll (NY)
Eastern Oregon U (OR)
Emory & Henry Coll (VA)
Florida Southern Coll (FL)
Frostburg State U (MD)
Gannon U (PA)
Geneva Coll (PA)
Goddard Coll (VT)
Hamline U (MN)
Harding U (AR)
Heritage U (WA)
Hofstra U (NY)
Illinois Coll (IL)
Ithaca Coll (NY)
John Carroll U (OH)
Lindenwood U (MO)
Manchester U (IN)
Manhattan Coll (NY)
Martin Luther Coll (MN)
McKendree U (IL)
Merrimack Coll (MA)
Molloy Coll (NY)
Mount Mary U (WI)
Mount Saint Mary Coll (NY)
New England Coll (NH)
Northland Coll (WI)
Northwestern Coll (IA)
Nyack Coll (NY)
Ohio Dominican U (OH)
Ohio Northern U (OH)
Ohio Wesleyan U (OH)
Piedmont Coll (GA)
Quincy U (IL)
Saint Augustine's U (NC)
Saint Mary-of-the-Woods Coll (IN)
Samford U (AL)
San Diego Christian Coll (CA)
Shawnee State U (OH)
Spalding U (KY)
Spelman Coll (GA)
Stockton U (NJ)
Summit U (PA)
Tarleton State U (TX)
Tennessee Wesleyan Coll (TN)
Texas Lutheran U (TX)
Troy U (AL)
Universidad Metropolitana (PR)
U of Great Falls (MT)
U of Louisiana at Lafayette (LA)
U of Louisville (KY)
U of Maine at Fort Kent (ME)
U of Memphis (TN)
U of Minnesota, Duluth (MN)
U of Minnesota, Morris (MN)
The U of Montana Western (MT)
U of Nebraska–Lincoln (NE)
U of North Alabama (AL)
U of Rio Grande (OH)
U of South Florida (FL)
U of South Florida, St. Petersburg (FL)
The U of Tennessee at Martin (TN)
The U of Toledo (OH)
The U of West Alabama (AL)
U of Windsor (ON, Canada)
Utah State U (UT)
Virginia Wesleyan Coll (VA)
Wake Forest U (NC)
Walla Walla U (WA)
Washington State U (WA)
Washington U in St. Louis (MO)
Western Governors U (UT)
Western Kentucky U (KY)
West Virginia Wesleyan Coll (WV)
William Jewell Coll (MO)
Wright State U (OH)

EDUCATION RELATED
Albany State U (GA)
Arizona State U at the Downtown Phoenix campus (AZ)
Arizona State U at the Polytechnic campus (AZ)
Arizona State U at the Tempe campus (AZ)
Arizona State U at the West campus (AZ)
Bowling Green State U (OH)
Brigham Young U (UT)
Central State U (OH)
Concordia U, St. Paul (MN)
Delaware State U (DE)
DePaul U (IL)
Eastern Oregon U (OR)
Edgewood Coll (WI)
Elmira Coll (NY)
Grace Coll (IN)
Jackson State U (MS)
Lee U (TN)
Lindsey Wilson Coll (KY)
Madonna U (MI)
Mercer U, Macon (GA)
Midwestern State U (TX)
Mount Holyoke Coll (MA)
Nazarene Bible Coll (CO)
Northwest Missouri State U (MO)
Northwest Nazarene U (ID)
Ohio Northern U (OH)
Park U (MO)
Piedmont Coll (GA)
Prescott Coll (AZ)
Quincy U (IL)
Saginaw Valley State U (MI)
Saint Mary-of-the-Woods Coll (IN)
Saint Mary's U of Minnesota (MN)
Shaw U (NC)
Southern Adventist U (TN)
Southern New Hampshire U (NH)
State U of New York at New Paltz (NY)
Sterling Coll (VT)
Thomas More Coll (KY)
Towson U (MD)
Union Coll (NE)
U of Alberta (AB, Canada)
U of Miami (FL)
U of Minnesota, Duluth (MN)
U of Minnesota, Twin Cities Campus (MN)
U of Nevada, Reno (NV)
U of South Alabama (AL)
U of Washington (WA)
U of Waterloo (ON, Canada)
Vanderbilt U (TN)
Waldorf Coll (IA)
Wayne State U (MI)
Wright State U (OH)

EDUCATION (SPECIFIC LEVELS AND METHODS) RELATED
Anderson U (SC)
Anna Maria Coll (MA)
Ave Maria U (FL)
Boston U (MA)
Brigham Young U (UT)
Cairn U (PA)
Colorado State U (CO)
Columbia Coll Chicago (IL)
Concordia Coll–New York (NY)
Delaware State U (DE)
Emory & Henry Coll (VA)
Immaculata U (PA)
Inter American U of Puerto Rico, San Germán Campus (PR)
John Brown U (AR)
Lynchburg Coll (VA)
Roger Williams U (RI)
Rowan U (NJ)
Universidad Metropolitana (PR)
Washington U in St. Louis (MO)
Weber State U (UT)
Western Washington U (WA)
Wright State U (OH)
Xavier U (OH)

EDUCATION (SPECIFIC SUBJECT AREAS) RELATED
Appalachian State U (NC)
Augsburg Coll (MN)
Averett U (VA)
Avila U (MO)
Baylor U (TX)
Bowling Green State U (OH)
Brigham Young U (UT)
Cairn U (PA)
The Coll of Saint Rose (NY)
Columbia Coll Chicago (IL)
Eastern Kentucky U (KY)
Eastern Michigan U (MI)
Florida Inst of Technology (FL)
Graceland U (IA)
Indiana U Bloomington (IN)
Madonna U (MI)
Marywood U (PA)
Minot State U (ND)
Mississippi State U (MS)
Missouri State U (MO)
Missouri Western State U (MO)
Murray State U (KY)
Northern Kentucky U (KY)
Northern Michigan U (MI)
Northwest Missouri State U (MO)
Old Dominion U (VA)
Piedmont Coll (GA)
Pittsburg State U (KS)
Plymouth State U (NH)
Taylor U (IN)
Tusculum Coll (TN)
Union Coll (NE)
U of Central Oklahoma (OK)
U of Kentucky (KY)
U of Lethbridge (AB, Canada)
U of Minnesota, Duluth (MN)
U of Nebraska–Lincoln (NE)
The U of North Carolina Wilmington (NC)
U of Ottawa (ON, Canada)
U of Regina (SK, Canada)
U of Wisconsin–Eau Claire (WI)
U of Wisconsin–Stout (WI)
Utah State U (UT)
Wayne State Coll (NE)
Weber State U (UT)
Western Washington U (WA)
William Woods U (MO)
Wright State U (OH)

ELECTRICAL AND ELECTRONIC ENGINEERING TECHNOLOGIES RELATED
Capitol Technology U (MD)
Excelsior Coll (NY)
LeTourneau U (TX)
North Carolina Ag and Tech State U (NC)
Penn State Berks (PA)
Pennsylvania Coll of Technology (PA)
Rochester Inst of Technology (NY)
Southern Illinois U Carbondale (IL)
U of the District of Columbia (DC)
Vaughn Coll of Aeronautics and Technology (NY)
Virginia State U (VA)
Wayne State U (MI)
West Virginia U Inst of Technology (WV)

ELECTRICAL AND ELECTRONICS ENGINEERING
American Public U System (WV)
The American U in Cairo (Egypt)
The American U in Dubai (United Arab Emirates)
American U of Beirut (Lebanon)
Anderson U (IN)
Arizona State U at the Tempe campus (AZ)
Arkansas State U (AR)
Arkansas Tech U (AR)
Auburn U (AL)
Baylor U (TX)
Binghamton U, State U of New York (NY)
Bloomsburg U of Pennsylvania (PA)
Boston U (MA)
Bradley U (IL)
Brown U (RI)
Bucknell U (PA)
California Inst of Technology (CA)
California Polytechnic State U, San Luis Obispo (CA)
California State Polytechnic U, Pomona (CA)
California State U, Chico (CA)
California State U, Fresno (CA)
California State U, Fullerton (CA)
California State U, Long Beach (CA)
California State U, Los Angeles (CA)
California State U, Sacramento (CA)
Calvin Coll (MI)
Capitol Technology U (MD)
Caribbean U (PR)

Case Western Reserve U (OH)
The Catholic U of America (DC)
Cedarville U (OH)
Central Connecticut State U (CT)
Central Michigan U (MI)
Christian Brothers U (TN)
Christopher Newport U (VA)
The Citadel, The Military Coll of South Carolina (SC)
City Coll of the City U of New York (NY)
Clarkson U (NY)
Cleveland State U (OH)
The Coll of New Jersey (NJ)
Colorado School of Mines (CO)
Colorado State U (CO)
Columbia U (NY)
Concordia U (QC, Canada)
Cooper Union for the Advancement of Science and Art (NY)
Cornell U (NY)
Dalhousie U (NS, Canada)
Delaware State U (DE)
Dominican U (IL)
Drexel U (PA)
Embry-Riddle Aeronautical U–Daytona (FL)
Embry-Riddle Aeronautical U–Prescott (AZ)
Fairfield U (CT)
Fairleigh Dickinson U, Metropolitan Campus (NJ)
Florida Ag and Mech U (FL)
Florida Atlantic U (FL)
Florida Inst of Technology (FL)
Florida Intl U (FL)
Franklin W. Olin Coll of Eng (MA)
Gannon U (PA)
George Mason U (VA)
The George Washington U (DC)
Georgia Inst of Technology (GA)
Georgia Southern U (GA)
Gonzaga U (WA)
Grove City Coll (PA)
Hampton U (VA)
Harding U (AR)
Hofstra U (NY)
Howard U (DC)
Illinois Inst of Technology (IL)
Indiana U–Purdue U Fort Wayne (IN)
Indiana U–Purdue U Indianapolis (IN)
Inter American U of Puerto Rico, Bayamón Campus (PR)
Iowa State U of Science and Technology (IA)
Jackson State U (MS)
Jacksonville U (FL)
John Brown U (AR)
Johns Hopkins U (MD)
Johnson & Wales U (RI)
Kansas State U (KS)
Kettering U (MI)
Lafayette Coll (PA)
Lamar U (TX)
Lawrence Technological U (MI)
Lebanese American U (Lebanon)
Lehigh U (PA)
LeTourneau U (TX)
Liberty U (VA)
Louisiana State U and A&M Coll (LA)
Loyola Marymount U (CA)
Manhattan Coll (NY)
Marquette U (WI)
Massachusetts Inst of Technology (MA)
Merrimack Coll (MA)
Miami U (OH)
Michigan State U (MI)
Michigan Technological U (MI)
Milwaukee School of Eng (WI)
Minnesota State U Mankato (MN)
Mississippi State U (MS)
Missouri U of Science and Technology (MO)
Montana State U (MT)
Montana Tech of The U of Montana (MT)
National U (CA)
New England Inst of Technology (RI)
New Jersey Inst of Technology (NJ)
New Mexico Highlands U (NM)
New Mexico Inst of Mining and Technology (NM)
New Mexico State U (NM)
New York Inst of Technology (NY)
New York U (NY)
Norfolk State U (VA)
North Carolina Ag and Tech State U (NC)
North Carolina State U (NC)
North Dakota State U (ND)
Northeastern U (MA)
Northern Arizona U (AZ)
Northern Illinois U (IL)
Northwestern U (IL)
Norwich U (VT)
Oakland U (MI)
Ohio Northern U (OH)
The Ohio State U (OH)
Ohio U (OH)
Oklahoma Christian U (OK)
Oklahoma State U (OK)
Old Dominion U (VA)
Oregon State U (OR)
Penn State Abington (PA)
Penn State Altoona (PA)
Penn State Beaver (PA)
Penn State Berks (PA)
Penn State Brandywine (PA)
Penn State DuBois (PA)
Penn State Erie, The Behrend Coll (PA)
Penn State Fayette, The Eberly Campus (PA)
Penn State Greater Allegheny (PA)
Penn State Harrisburg (PA)
Penn State Hazleton (PA)
Penn State Lehigh Valley (PA)
Penn State Mont Alto (PA)
Penn State New Kensington (PA)
Penn State Schuylkill (PA)
Penn State Shenango (PA)
Penn State U Park (PA)
Penn State Wilkes-Barre (PA)
Penn State Worthington Scranton (PA)
Penn State York (PA)
Polytechnic U of Puerto Rico (PR)
Portland State U (OR)
Prairie View A&M U (TX)
Princeton U (NJ)
Purdue U (IN)
Purdue U Calumet (IN)
Rensselaer Polytechnic Inst (NY)
Rice U (TX)
Rochester Inst of Technology (NY)
Rockhurst U (MO)
Rose-Hulman Inst of Technology (IN)
Rowan U (NJ)
Rutgers, The State U of New Jersey, New Brunswick (NJ)
Saginaw Valley State U (MI)
Saint Louis U (MO)
St. Mary's U (TX)
San Diego State U (CA)
San Francisco State U (CA)
San Jose State U (CA)
Santa Clara U (CA)
Seattle Pacific U (WA)
Seattle U (WA)
Shippensburg U of Pennsylvania (PA)
South Dakota School of Mines and Technology (SD)
South Dakota State U (SD)
Southern California Inst of Technology (CA)
Southern Illinois U Carbondale (IL)
Southern Illinois U Edwardsville (IL)
Southern Methodist U (TX)
Stanford U (CA)
State U of New York at New Paltz (NY)
State U of New York at Oswego (NY)
State U of New York Maritime Coll (NY)
State U of New York Polytechnic Inst (NY)
Stony Brook U, State U of New York (NY)
Suffolk U (MA)
Syracuse U (NY)
Temple U (PA)
Tennessee State U (TN)
Texas A&M U (TX)
Texas A&M U–Kingsville (TX)
Texas State U (TX)
Texas Tech U (TX)
Trine U (IN)
Trinity Coll (CT)
Tufts U (MA)
Tulane U (LA)
Union Coll (NY)
United States Air Force Acad (CO)
United States Coast Guard Acad (CT)
United States Military Acad (NY)
United States Naval Acad (MD)
Universidad del Turabo (PR)
Université de Sherbrooke (QC, Canada)
U at Buffalo, the State U of New York (NY)
The U of Akron (OH)
The U of Alabama (AL)
The U of Alabama at Birmingham (AL)
The U of Alabama in Huntsville (AL)
U of Alaska Fairbanks (AK)
U of Arkansas (AR)
The U of British Columbia (BC, Canada)
The U of British Columbia–Okanagan Campus (BC, Canada)
U of California, Berkeley (CA)
U of California, Davis (CA)
U of California, Irvine (CA)
U of California, Los Angeles (CA)
U of California, Riverside (CA)
U of California, Santa Barbara (CA)
U of California, Santa Cruz (CA)
U of Central Florida (FL)
U of Central Oklahoma (OK)
U of Cincinnati (OH)
U of Colorado Boulder (CO)
U of Colorado Colorado Springs (CO)
U of Colorado Denver (CO)
U of Dayton (OH)
U of Delaware (DE)
U of Denver (CO)
U of Evansville (IN)
U of Florida (FL)
U of Hartford (CT)
U of Hawaii at Manoa (HI)
U of Houston (TX)
U of Idaho (ID)
U of Illinois at Chicago (IL)
The U of Iowa (IA)
The U of Kansas (KS)
U of Kentucky (KY)
U of Louisiana at Lafayette (LA)
U of Louisville (KY)
U of Maine (ME)
U of Maryland, Coll Park (MD)
U of Massachusetts Amherst (MA)
U of Massachusetts Boston (MA)
U of Massachusetts Dartmouth (MA)
U of Massachusetts Lowell (MA)
U of Memphis (TN)
U of Miami (FL)
U of Michigan (MI)
U of Michigan–Dearborn (MI)
U of Minnesota, Duluth (MN)
U of Minnesota, Twin Cities Campus (MN)
U of Mississippi (MS)
U of Missouri (MO)
U of Missouri–Kansas City (MO)
U of Missouri–St. Louis (MO)
U of Nebraska–Lincoln (NE)
U of Nevada, Las Vegas (NV)
U of Nevada, Reno (NV)
U of New Hampshire (NH)
U of New Haven (CT)
U of New Mexico (NM)
U of New Orleans (LA)
The U of North Carolina at Charlotte (NC)
U of North Dakota (ND)
U of North Florida (FL)
U of North Texas (TX)
U of Notre Dame (IN)
U of Oklahoma (OK)
U of Ottawa (ON, Canada)
U of Pennsylvania (PA)
U of Pittsburgh (PA)
U of Portland (OR)
U of Regina (SK, Canada)
U of Rhode Island (RI)
U of Rochester (NY)
U of St. Thomas (MN)
U of San Diego (CA)
U of Saskatchewan (SK, Canada)
The U of Scranton (PA)
U of South Alabama (AL)
U of Southern California (CA)
U of Southern Maine (ME)
U of South Florida (FL)
The U of Tennessee (TN)
The U of Tennessee at Chattanooga (TN)
The U of Texas at Arlington (TX)
The U of Texas at Austin (TX)
The U of Texas at Dallas (TX)
The U of Texas at El Paso (TX)
The U of Texas at San Antonio (TX)
The U of Texas at Tyler (TX)
The U of Texas–Pan American (TX)
U of the District of Columbia (DC)
U of the Pacific (CA)
The U of Toledo (OH)
U of Toronto (ON, Canada)
The U of Tulsa (OK)
U of Utah (UT)
U of Vermont (VT)
U of Virginia (VA)
U of Washington (WA)
U of Washington, Bothell (WA)
U of Waterloo (ON, Canada)
The U of Western Ontario (ON, Canada)
U of West Florida (FL)
U of Windsor (ON, Canada)
U of Wisconsin–Madison (WI)
U of Wisconsin–Milwaukee (WI)
U of Wisconsin–Platteville (WI)
U of Wyoming (WY)
Ursinus Coll (PA)
Utah State U (UT)
Valparaiso U (IN)
Vanderbilt U (TN)
Villanova U (PA)
Virginia Commonwealth U (VA)
Virginia Military Inst (VA)
Virginia Polytechnic Inst and State U (VA)
Walla Walla U (WA)
Washington State U (WA)
Washington U in St. Louis (MO)
Wayne State U (MI)
Wentworth Inst of Technology (MA)
Western Carolina U (NC)
Western Kentucky U (KY)
Western Michigan U (MI)
Western New England U (MA)
Western Washington U (WA)
West Virginia U (WV)
West Virginia U Inst of Technology (WV)
Wichita State U (KS)
Widener U (PA)
Wilberforce U (OH)
Wilkes U (PA)
Worcester Polytechnic Inst (MA)
Wright State U (OH)
Yale U (CT)
York Coll of Pennsylvania (PA)
Youngstown State U (OH)

ELECTRICAL, ELECTRONIC AND COMMUNICATIONS ENGINEERING TECHNOLOGY

Arizona State U at the Polytechnic campus (AZ)
Baker Coll (MI)
Bluefield State Coll (WV)
Bowling Green State U (OH)
Buffalo State Coll, State U of New York (NY)
California State Polytechnic U, Pomona (CA)
California State U, Long Beach (CA)
California U of Pennsylvania (PA)
Central Connecticut State U (CT)
Central Washington U (WA)
Cleveland State U (OH)
Daytona State Coll (FL)
Delaware State U (DE)
DeVry Coll of New York (NY)
DeVry U, Phoenix (AZ)
DeVry U, Pomona (CA)
DeVry U, Westminster (CO)
DeVry U, Miramar (FL)
DeVry U, Orlando (FL)
DeVry U, Decatur (GA)
DeVry U, Chicago (IL)
DeVry U, Kansas City (MO)
DeVry U, North Brunswick (NJ)
DeVry U, Columbus (OH)
DeVry U, Fort Washington (PA)
DeVry U, Houston (TX)
DeVry U, Irving (TX)
DeVry U, Arlington (VA)
DeVry U, Federal Way (WA)
DeVry U Online (IL)
Eastern Michigan U (MI)
Fairleigh Dickinson U, Metropolitan Campus (NJ)
Fairmont State U (WV)
Farmingdale State Coll (NY)
Ferris State U (MI)
Fitchburg State U (MA)
Florida Ag and Mech U (FL)
Georgia Southern U (GA)
Hampton U (VA)
Indiana State U (IN)
Indiana U–Purdue U Fort Wayne (IN)
Inter American U of Puerto Rico, Aguadilla Campus (PR)
Inter American U of Puerto Rico, San Germán Campus (PR)
Jacksonville State U (AL)
LeTourneau U (TX)
Miami Dade Coll (FL)
Michigan Technological U (MI)
Minnesota State U Mankato (MN)
Missouri Western State U (MO)
New York City Coll of Technology of the City U of New York (NY)
Norfolk State U (VA)
North Carolina Ag and Tech State U (NC)
Northern Kentucky U (KY)
Oklahoma State U (OK)
Penn State Erie, The Behrend Coll (PA)
Pittsburg State U (KS)
Prairie View A&M U (TX)
Purdue U (IN)
Purdue U Calumet (IN)
Savannah State U (GA)
South Carolina State U (SC)
South Dakota State U (SD)
State U of New York Coll of Technology at Alfred (NY)
State U of New York Coll of Technology at Canton (NY)
State U of New York Polytechnic Inst (NY)
Texas A&M U (TX)
Texas A&M U–Corpus Christi (TX)
Texas Southern U (TX)
Troy U (AL)
The U of Akron (OH)
U of Arkansas at Little Rock (AR)
U of Central Missouri (MO)
U of Cincinnati (OH)
U of Dayton (OH)
U of Hartford (CT)
U of Houston (TX)
U of Maine (ME)
U of Massachusetts Lowell (MA)
U of Memphis (TN)
U of New Hampshire (NH)
U of New Hampshire at Manchester (NH)
The U of North Carolina at Charlotte (NC)
U of North Texas (TX)
U of Southern Mississippi (MS)
The U of Toledo (OH)
Valencia Coll (FL)
Vaughn Coll of Aeronautics and Technology (NY)
Vermont Tech Coll (VT)
Wayne State U (MI)
Weber State U (UT)
Wentworth Inst of Technology (MA)
Western Carolina U (NC)
Youngstown State U (OH)

ELECTRICAL, ELECTRONICS AND COMMUNICATIONS ENGINEERING RELATED

Marquette U (WI)
The U of Arizona (AZ)
U of Miami (FL)

ELECTRICAL/ELECTRONICS EQUIPMENT INSTALLATION AND REPAIR

Cape Breton U (NS, Canada)

ELECTRICAL/ELECTRONICS MAINTENANCE AND REPAIR TECHNOLOGY RELATED
Sullivan Coll of Technology and Design (KY)

ELECTROMECHANICAL AND INSTRUMENTATION AND MAINTENANCE TECHNOLOGIES RELATED
Excelsior Coll (NY)
Sullivan Coll of Technology and Design (KY)

ELECTROMECHANICAL ENGINEERING
Wentworth Inst of Technology (MA)

ELECTROMECHANICAL TECHNOLOGY
Bowling Green State U (OH)
Buffalo State Coll, State U of New York (NY)
Excelsior Coll (NY)
John Brown U (AR)
Murray State U (KY)
Rochester Inst of Technology (NY)
State U of New York Coll of Technology at Alfred (NY)
U of Northern Iowa (IA)
The U of Toledo (OH)
Vermont Tech Coll (VT)
Wayne State U (MI)

ELEMENTARY AND MIDDLE SCHOOL ADMINISTRATION/ PRINCIPALSHIP
Berea Coll (KY)
Charleston Southern U (SC)
Creighton U (NE)
Philander Smith Coll (AR)

ELEMENTARY EDUCATION
Abilene Christian U (TX)
Alabama State U (AL)
Albright Coll (PA)
Alcorn State U (MS)
Alice Lloyd Coll (KY)
Alma Coll (MI)
Alverno Coll (WI)
American U (DC)
American U of Beirut (Lebanon)
Anderson U (IN)
Anderson U (SC)
Andrews U (MI)
Anna Maria Coll (MA)
Appalachian State U (NC)
Aquinas Coll (TN)
Arcadia U (PA)
Arizona Christian U (AZ)
Arizona State U at the Downtown Phoenix campus (AZ)
Arizona State U at the Polytechnic campus (AZ)
Arizona State U at the Tempe campus (AZ)
Arizona State U at the West campus (AZ)
Arkansas Tech U (AR)
Asbury U (KY)
Ashland U (OH)
Athens State U (AL)
Auburn U (AL)
Auburn U at Montgomery (AL)
Augsburg Coll (MN)
Augustana Coll (IL)
Augustana Coll (SD)
Austin Coll (TX)
Avila U (MO)
Baker U (KS)
Ball State U (IN)
The Baptist Coll of Florida (FL)
Barclay Coll (KS)
Barry U (FL)
Baylor U (TX)
Bay Path U (MA)
Becker Coll (MA)
Belhaven U (MS)
Belmont Abbey Coll (NC)
Belmont U (TN)
Beloit Coll (WI)
Bemidji State U (MN)
Benedictine Coll (KS)
Benedictine U (IL)
Bennett Coll (NC)
Bethany Coll (WV)
Bethany Lutheran Coll (MN)
Bethel Coll (IN)
Bethel Coll (KS)
Bethel U (MN)
Bethune-Cookman U (FL)
Biola U (CA)
Birmingham-Southern Coll (AL)
Blackburn Coll (IL)
Black Hills State U (SD)
Bluefield Coll (VA)
Bluefield State Coll (WV)
Blue Mountain Coll (MS)
Bluffton U (OH)
Bob Jones U (SC)
Boston Coll (MA)
Boston U (MA)
Bowie State U (MD)
Bowling Green State U (OH)
Bradley U (IL)
Brenau U (GA)
Bridgewater State U (MA)
Bryan Coll (TN)
Bucknell U (PA)
Buena Vista U (IA)
Buffalo State Coll, State U of New York (NY)
Butler U (IN)
Cabrini Coll (PA)
Cairn U (PA)
Caldwell U (NJ)
California U of Pennsylvania (PA)
Calumet Coll of Saint Joseph (IN)
Calvary Bible Coll and Theological Sem (MO)
Calvin Coll (MI)
Cameron U (OK)
Campbellsville U (KY)
Canisius Coll (NY)
Cardinal Stritch U (WI)
Caribbean U (PR)
Carlos Albizu U, Miami Campus (FL)
Carroll Coll (MT)
Carson-Newman U (TN)
Castleton State Coll (VT)
Catawba Coll (NC)
The Catholic U of America (DC)
Cedar Crest Coll (PA)
Central Coll (IA)
Central Connecticut State U (CT)
Central Methodist U (MO)
Central Michigan U (MI)
Central Washington U (WA)
Chaminade U of Honolulu (HI)
Champlain Coll (VT)
Charleston Southern U (SC)
Chatham U (PA)
Chestnut Hill Coll (PA)
Chicago State U (IL)
Chowan U (NC)
City Coll of the City U of New York (NY)
Claflin U (SC)
Clarion U of Pennsylvania (PA)
Clark U (MA)
Clearwater Christian Coll (FL)
Coastal Carolina U (SC)
Coe Coll (IA)
Coker Coll (SC)
Coll of Charleston (SC)
The Coll of New Jersey (NJ)
The Coll of New Rochelle (NY)
Coll of Saint Benedict (MN)
Coll of Saint Mary (NE)
The Coll of Saint Rose (NY)
The Coll of St. Scholastica (MN)
Coll of Staten Island of the City U of New York (NY)
Coll of the Atlantic (ME)
Coll of the Ozarks (MO)
Columbia Coll (SC)
Concordia Coll (MN)
Concordia Coll–New York (NY)
Concordia U (QC, Canada)
Concordia U Chicago (IL)
Concordia U, Nebraska (NE)
Concordia U, St. Paul (MN)
Concordia U Texas (TX)
Concordia U Wisconsin (WI)
Concord U (WV)
Corban U (OR)
Cornell Coll (IA)
Cornerstone U (MI)
Covenant Coll (GA)
Creighton U (NE)
Culver-Stockton Coll (MO)
Cumberland U (TN)
Curry Coll (MA)
Daemen Coll (NY)
Dakota State U (SD)
Dallas Baptist U (TX)
Daytona State Coll (FL)
Defiance Coll (OH)
Delaware State U (DE)
Delta State U (MS)
DePaul U (IL)
DePauw U (IN)
DeSales U (PA)
Dickinson State U (ND)
Dixie State U (UT)
Doane Coll (NE)
Dominican Coll (NY)
Dominican U (IL)
Donnelly Coll (KS)
Dowling Coll (NY)
Drake U (IA)
Drexel U (PA)
Drury U (MO)
East Carolina U (NC)
East Central U (OK)
Eastern Connecticut State U (CT)
Eastern Illinois U (IL)
Eastern Kentucky U (KY)
Eastern Michigan U (MI)
Eastern New Mexico U (NM)
East Stroudsburg U of Pennsylvania (PA)
East Texas Baptist U (TX)
Edgewood Coll (WI)
Elmhurst Coll (IL)
Elmira Coll (NY)
Elon U (NC)
Emmanuel Coll (GA)
Emmanuel Coll (MA)
Emporia State U (KS)
Endicott Coll (MA)
Erskine Coll (SC)
Eureka Coll (IL)
Evangel U (MO)
Fairmont State U (WV)
Faith Baptist Bible Coll and Theological Sem (IA)
Faulkner U (AL)
Fayetteville State U (NC)
Ferris State U (MI)
Fitchburg State U (MA)
Five Towns Coll (NY)
Flagler Coll (FL)
Florida Ag and Mech U (FL)
Florida Atlantic U (FL)
Florida Coll (FL)
Florida Gulf Coast U (FL)
Florida Intl U (FL)
Florida Southern Coll (FL)
Florida SouthWestern State Coll (FL)
Fontbonne U (MO)
Fordham U (NY)
Fort Hays State U (KS)
Fort Lewis Coll (CO)
Franciscan U of Steubenville (OH)
Francis Marion U (SC)
Franklin Coll (IN)
Franklin Pierce U (NH)
Friends U (KS)
Frostburg State U (MD)
Furman U (SC)
Geneva Coll (PA)
Georgetown Coll (KY)
Georgian Court U (NJ)
Georgia Southern U (GA)
Georgia Southwestern State U (GA)
Gettysburg Coll (PA)
Goddard Coll (VT)
Gonzaga U (WA)
Gordon Coll (MA)
Goshen Coll (IN)
Goucher Coll (MD)
Governors State U (IL)
Grace Coll (IN)
Graceland U (IA)
Grambling State U (LA)
Grand Valley State U (MI)
Grand View U (IA)
Granite State Coll (NH)
Great Basin Coll (NV)
Green Mountain Coll (VT)
Greensboro Coll (NC)
Greenville Coll (IL)
Guilford Coll (NC)
Gustavus Adolphus Coll (MN)
Gwynedd Mercy U (PA)
Hamline U (MN)
Hampton U (VA)
Hannibal-LaGrange U (MO)
Hanover Coll (IN)
Harding U (AR)
Harris-Stowe State U (MO)
Hastings Coll (NE)
Hawai`i Pacific U (HI)
Heidelberg U (OH)
Heritage U (WA)
High Point U (NC)
Hillsdale Free Will Baptist Coll (OK)
Hobe Sound Bible Coll (FL)
Hofstra U (NY)
Holy Cross Coll (IN)
Holy Family U (PA)
Hope Coll (MI)
Hope Intl U (CA)
Houghton Coll (NY)
Houston Baptist U (TX)
Howard Payne U (TX)
Humboldt State U (CA)
Hunter Coll of the City U of New York (NY)
Huntingdon Coll (AL)
Husson U (ME)
Huston-Tillotson U (TX)
Illinois Coll (IL)
Illinois State U (IL)
Illinois Wesleyan U (IL)
Immaculata U (PA)
Indiana State U (IN)
Indiana U Bloomington (IN)
Indiana U East (IN)
Indiana U Kokomo (IN)
Indiana U Northwest (IN)
Indiana U–Purdue U Fort Wayne (IN)
Indiana U–Purdue U Indianapolis (IN)
Indiana U South Bend (IN)
Indiana U Southeast (IN)
Inter American U of Puerto Rico, Aguadilla Campus (PR)
Inter American U of Puerto Rico, Fajardo Campus (PR)
Inter American U of Puerto Rico, Guayama Campus (PR)
Inter American U of Puerto Rico, Ponce Campus (PR)
Inter American U of Puerto Rico, San Germán Campus (PR)
Iona Coll (NY)
Iowa State U of Science and Technology (IA)
Iowa Wesleyan Coll (IA)
Jackson State U (MS)
Jacksonville State U (AL)
Jacksonville U (FL)
Jarvis Christian Coll (TX)
John Brown U (AR)
John Carroll U (OH)
Johnson State Coll (VT)
Judson Coll (AL)
Judson U (IL)
Kansas State U (KS)
Kansas Wesleyan U (KS)
Kean U (NJ)
Keene State Coll (NH)
Keiser U, Fort Lauderdale (FL)
Kennesaw State U (GA)
Kentucky Christian U (KY)
Kentucky Mountain Bible Coll (KY)
Kentucky State U (KY)
Kentucky Wesleyan Coll (KY)
Keuka Coll (NY)
King's Coll (PA)
The King's U Coll (AB, Canada)
Kingswood U (NB, Canada)
Knox Coll (IL)
Kuyper Coll (MI)
Langston U (OK)
La Roche Coll (PA)
La Salle U (PA)
Lasell Coll (MA)
Laurel U (NC)
Lees-McRae Coll (NC)
Lee U (TN)
Le Moyne Coll (NY)
Lenoir-Rhyne U (NC)
Lesley U (MA)
LeTourneau U (TX)
Lewis U (IL)
Limestone Coll (SC)
Lincoln Memorial U (TN)
Lincoln U (MO)
Lindenwood U (MO)
Lindsey Wilson Coll (KY)
Linfield Coll (OR)
Lipscomb U (TN)
Lock Haven U of Pennsylvania (PA)
Long Island U–LIU Brooklyn (NY)
Long Island U–LIU Post (NY)
Loras Coll (IA)
Louisiana Coll (LA)
Louisiana State U and A&M Coll (LA)
Louisiana State U in Shreveport (LA)
Loyola U Chicago (IL)
Luther Coll (IA)
Lynchburg Coll (VA)
Lynn U (FL)
Madonna U (MI)
Maharishi U of Management (IA)
Manchester U (IN)
Manhattan Coll (NY)
Manhattanville Coll (NY)
Mansfield U of Pennsylvania (PA)
Maranatha Baptist U (WI)
Marian U (IN)
Marian U (WI)
Marietta Coll (OH)
Marquette U (WI)
Marshall U (WV)
Mars Hill U (NC)
Martin Luther Coll (MN)
Marymount U (VA)
Maryville U of Saint Louis (MO)
Marywood U (PA)
The Master's Coll and Sem (CA)
Mayville State U (ND)
McKendree U (IL)
McMurry U (TX)
McNeese State U (LA)
Medaille Coll (NY)
Medgar Evers Coll of the City U of New York (NY)
Mercer U, Macon (GA)
Merrimack Coll (MA)
Messiah Coll (PA)
Metropolitan State U (MN)
Michigan State U (MI)
MidAmerica Nazarene U (KS)
Mid-Atlantic Christian U (NC)
Millikin U (IL)
Minnesota State U Mankato (MN)
Minnesota State U Moorhead (MN)
Minot State U (ND)
Misericordia U (PA)
Mississippi State U (MS)
Mississippi U for Women (MS)
Mississippi Valley State U (MS)
Missouri Baptist U (MO)
Missouri Southern State U (MO)
Missouri State U (MO)
Missouri Valley Coll (MO)
Missouri Western State U (MO)
Mitchell Coll (CT)
Molloy Coll (NY)
Monmouth Coll (IL)
Montana State U (MT)
Montana State U Billings (MT)
Montreat Coll, Montreat (NC)
Morehead State U (KY)
Morningside Coll (IA)
Morris Coll (SC)
Mount Marty Coll (SD)
Mount Mercy U (IA)
Mount Saint Mary's U (CA)
Mount St. Mary's U (MD)
Multnomah U (OR)
Murray State U (KY)
National U (CA)
Nazareth Coll of Rochester (NY)
Neumann U (PA)
Newberry Coll (SC)
New England Coll (NH)
New Jersey City U (NJ)
Newman U (KS)
New Mexico Highlands U (NM)
New Mexico State U (NM)
New York U (NY)
Niagara U (NY)
Nicholls State U (LA)
North Carolina Ag and Tech State U (NC)
North Carolina Central U (NC)
North Carolina State U (NC)
North Carolina Wesleyan Coll (NC)
North Central Coll (IL)
Northeastern Illinois U (IL)
Northeastern State U (OK)
Northern Arizona U (AZ)
Northern Illinois U (IL)
Northern Kentucky U (KY)
Northern Michigan U (MI)
Northern State U (SD)
North Greenville U (SC)

Northwest Christian U (OR)
Northwestern Coll (IA)
Northwestern Oklahoma State U (OK)
Northwest Missouri State U (MO)
Northwest Nazarene U (ID)
Northwest U (WA)
Notre Dame of Maryland U (MD)
Nova Southeastern U (FL)
Nyack Coll (NY)
Oakland City U (IN)
Oakland U (MI)
The Ohio State U at Lima (OH)
The Ohio State U at Marion (OH)
The Ohio State U–Mansfield Campus (OH)
The Ohio State U–Newark Campus (OH)
Ohio Valley U (WV)
Ohio Wesleyan U (OH)
Oklahoma Baptist U (OK)
Oklahoma Christian U (OK)
Oklahoma City U (OK)
Oklahoma State U (OK)
Oklahoma Wesleyan U (OK)
Olivet Nazarene U (IL)
Pace U (NY)
Pacific U (OR)
Palm Beach Atlantic U (FL)
Park U (MO)
Penn State Abington (PA)
Penn State Altoona (PA)
Penn State Beaver (PA)
Penn State Berks (PA)
Penn State Brandywine (PA)
Penn State DuBois (PA)
Penn State Erie, The Behrend Coll (PA)
Penn State Fayette, The Eberly Campus (PA)
Penn State Greater Allegheny (PA)
Penn State Harrisburg (PA)
Penn State Hazleton (PA)
Penn State Lehigh Valley (PA)
Penn State Mont Alto (PA)
Penn State New Kensington (PA)
Penn State Schuylkill (PA)
Penn State Shenango (PA)
Penn State U Park (PA)
Penn State Wilkes-Barre (PA)
Penn State Worthington Scranton (PA)
Penn State York (PA)
Peru State Coll (NE)
Pittsburg State U (KS)
Plymouth State U (NH)
Point Loma Nazarene U (CA)
Presbyterian Coll (SC)
Prescott Coll (AZ)
Purdue U (IN)
Purdue U Calumet (IN)
Queens Coll of the City U of New York (NY)
Quincy U (IL)
Regis U (CO)
Rhode Island Coll (RI)
Rider U (NJ)
Ripon Coll (WI)
Rivier U (NH)
Robert Morris U (PA)
Rockford U (IL)
Rockhurst U (MO)
Rocky Mountain Coll (MT)
Roger Williams U (RI)
Rollins Coll (FL)
Roosevelt U (IL)
Rosemont Coll (PA)
Rowan U (NJ)
Rust Coll (MS)
Sacred Heart U (CT)
The Sage Colls (NY)
Saginaw Valley State U (MI)
St. Andrews U (NC)
Saint Anselm Coll (NH)
St. Bonaventure U (NY)
St. Catharine Coll (KY)
St. Catherine U (MN)
Saint Francis U (PA)
St. Gregory's U, Shawnee (OK)
St. John Fisher Coll (NY)
Saint John's U (MN)
St. John's U (NY)
Saint Joseph's Coll (IN)
St. Joseph's Coll, Long Island Campus (NY)
St. Joseph's Coll, New York (NY)
Saint Joseph's U (PA)
Saint Leo U (FL)
Saint Martin's U (WA)
Saint Mary-of-the-Woods Coll (IN)
Saint Mary's Coll (IN)
Saint Mary's U of Minnesota (MN)
Saint Michael's Coll (VT)
St. Norbert Coll (WI)
Saint Peter's U (NJ)
St. Thomas Aquinas Coll (NY)
St. Thomas U (FL)
Salisbury U (MD)
Salve Regina U (RI)
San Diego Christian Coll (CA)
Seton Hill U (PA)
Shaw U (NC)
Shepherd U (WV)
Siena Heights U (MI)
Silver Lake Coll of the Holy Family (WI)
Simmons Coll (MA)
Simpson Coll (IA)
Skidmore Coll (NY)
Slippery Rock U of Pennsylvania (PA)
South Carolina State U (SC)
Southeastern Louisiana U (LA)
Southeastern Oklahoma State U (OK)
Southeastern U (FL)
Southeast Missouri State U (MO)
Southern Adventist U (TN)
Southern Connecticut State U (CT)
Southern Illinois U Carbondale (IL)
Southern Illinois U Edwardsville (IL)
Southern New Hampshire U (NH)
Southern Utah U (UT)
South Florida State Coll (FL)
Southwest Baptist U (MO)
Southwestern Adventist U (TX)
Southwestern Assemblies of God U (TX)
Southwestern Coll (KS)
Southwest Minnesota State U (MN)
Spalding U (KY)
Spring Hill Coll (AL)
State U of New York at Fredonia (NY)
State U of New York at New Paltz (NY)
State U of New York at Oswego (NY)
State U of New York at Plattsburgh (NY)
State U of New York Coll at Cortland (NY)
State U of New York Coll at Geneseo (NY)
State U of New York Coll at Old Westbury (NY)
State U of New York Coll at Potsdam (NY)
Sterling Coll (KS)
Stetson U (FL)
Stevenson U (MD)
Summit U (PA)
Susquehanna U (PA)
Tabor Coll (KS)
Tarleton State U (TX)
Taylor U (IN)
Temple U (PA)
Tennessee State U (TN)
Tennessee Wesleyan Coll (TN)
Texas Christian U (TX)
Texas Lutheran U (TX)
Thiel Coll (PA)
Thomas More Coll (KY)
Toccoa Falls Coll (GA)
Tougaloo Coll (MS)
Towson U (MD)
Transylvania U (KY)
Trent U (ON, Canada)
Trevecca Nazarene U (TN)
Trine U (IN)
Trinity Christian Coll (IL)
Trinity Coll of Florida (FL)
Troy U (AL)
Truett-McConnell Coll (GA)
Tufts U (MA)
Tusculum Coll (TN)
Union Coll (KY)
Union Coll (NE)
Union Inst & U (OH)
Union U (TN)
Universidad del Turabo (PR)
Universidad Metropolitana (PR)
Université de Montréal (QC, Canada)
Université de Sherbrooke (QC, Canada)
Université du Québec en Outaouais (QC, Canada)
The U of Alabama (AL)
The U of Alabama at Birmingham (AL)
The U of Alabama in Huntsville (AL)
U of Alaska Fairbanks (AK)
U of Alaska Southeast, Sitka Campus (AK)
U of Alberta (AB, Canada)
The U of Arizona (AZ)
U of Arkansas (AR)
U of Arkansas at Little Rock (AR)
The U of British Columbia (BC, Canada)
U of Central Florida (FL)
U of Central Missouri (MO)
U of Central Oklahoma (OK)
U of Charleston (WV)
U of Dallas (TX)
U of Delaware (DE)
U of Dubuque (IA)
U of Evansville (IN)
The U of Findlay (OH)
U of Florida (FL)
U of Great Falls (MT)
U of Guam (GU)
U of Hartford (CT)
U of Hawaii at Hilo (HI)
U of Hawaii at Manoa (HI)
U of Hawaii–West Oahu (HI)
U of Idaho (ID)
U of Illinois at Chicago (IL)
U of Indianapolis (IN)
The U of Iowa (IA)
U of Jamestown (ND)
The U of Kansas (KS)
U of Kentucky (KY)
U of Louisiana at Lafayette (LA)
U of Louisville (KY)
U of Maine (ME)
U of Maine at Machias (ME)
U of Maine at Presque Isle (ME)
U of Mary Hardin-Baylor (TX)
U of Maryland, Coll Park (MD)
U of Miami (FL)
U of Michigan (MI)
U of Michigan–Dearborn (MI)
U of Michigan–Flint (MI)
U of Minnesota, Crookston (MN)
U of Minnesota, Morris (MN)
U of Minnesota, Twin Cities Campus (MN)
U of Mississippi (MS)
U of Missouri (MO)
U of Missouri–Kansas City (MO)
U of Missouri–St. Louis (MO)
U of Mobile (AL)
The U of Montana (MT)
The U of Montana Western (MT)
U of Montevallo (AL)
U of Nebraska at Kearney (NE)
U of Nebraska–Lincoln (NE)
U of Nevada, Las Vegas (NV)
U of Nevada, Reno (NV)
U of New England (ME)
U of New Mexico (NM)
U of New Orleans (LA)
U of North Alabama (AL)
The U of North Carolina at Chapel Hill (NC)
The U of North Carolina at Charlotte (NC)
The U of North Carolina at Greensboro (NC)
The U of North Carolina at Pembroke (NC)
The U of North Carolina Wilmington (NC)
U of North Dakota (ND)
U of Northern Colorado (CO)
U of Northern Iowa (IA)
U of North Florida (FL)
U of Northwestern–St. Paul (MN)
U of Oklahoma (OK)
U of Pennsylvania (PA)
U of Pikeville (KY)
U of Pittsburgh at Bradford (PA)
U of Portland (OR)
U of Puerto Rico in Ponce (PR)
U of Regina (SK, Canada)
U of Rhode Island (RI)
U of Rio Grande (OH)
U of St. Francis (IL)
U of Saint Francis (IN)
U of Saint Mary (KS)
U of St. Thomas (TX)
U of San Francisco (CA)
U of Saskatchewan (SK, Canada)
U of Science and Arts of Oklahoma (OK)
The U of Scranton (PA)
U of South Alabama (AL)
U of South Carolina Aiken (SC)
U of South Carolina Beaufort (SC)
U of South Carolina Upstate (SC)
The U of South Dakota (SD)
U of Southern Indiana (IN)
U of Southern Mississippi (MS)
U of South Florida (FL)
U of South Florida Sarasota-Manatee (FL)
The U of Tampa (FL)
The U of Tennessee at Martin (TN)
The U of Texas at San Antonio (TX)
U of the Cumberlands (KY)
U of the District of Columbia (DC)
U of the Incarnate Word (TX)
U of the Virgin Islands (VI)
The U of Toledo (OH)
The U of Tulsa (OK)
U of Utah (UT)
U of Valley Forge (PA)
U of Vermont (VT)
The U of Western Ontario (ON, Canada)
U of West Florida (FL)
U of West Georgia (GA)
U of Windsor (ON, Canada)
U of Wisconsin–Eau Claire (WI)
U of Wisconsin–La Crosse (WI)
U of Wisconsin–Madison (WI)
U of Wisconsin–Oshkosh (WI)
U of Wisconsin–Platteville (WI)
U of Wisconsin–River Falls (WI)
U of Wisconsin–Stevens Point (WI)
U of Wisconsin–Superior (WI)
U of Wisconsin–Whitewater (WI)
U of Wyoming (WY)
Upper Iowa U (IA)
Urbana U (OH)
Utah State U (UT)
Utah Valley U (UT)
Utica Coll (NY)
Valley City State U (ND)
Valparaiso U (IN)
Vanderbilt U (TN)
Vanguard U of Southern California (CA)
Virginia Union U (VA)
Virginia Wesleyan Coll (VA)
Viterbo U (WI)
Wagner Coll (NY)
Waldorf Coll (IA)
Walla Walla U (WA)
Warner Pacific Coll (OR)
Wartburg Coll (IA)
Washburn U (KS)
Washington State U (WA)
Washington U in St. Louis (MO)
Waynesburg U (PA)
Wayne State Coll (NE)
Wayne State U (MI)
Weber State U (UT)
Webster U (MO)
Welch Coll (TN)
Wells Coll (NY)
West Chester U of Pennsylvania (PA)
Western Carolina U (NC)
Western Illinois U (IL)
Western Kentucky U (KY)
Western Michigan U (MI)
Western New England U (MA)
Western Washington U (WA)
Westfield State U (MA)
West Liberty U (WV)
Westminster Coll (MO)
Westminster Coll (UT)
West Texas A&M U (TX)
West Virginia State U (WV)
West Virginia U (WV)
West Virginia Wesleyan Coll (WV)
Wheaton Coll (IL)
Wheelock Coll (MA)
Whitworth U (WA)
Wichita State U (KS)
Widener U (PA)
Wilkes U (PA)
William Jewell Coll (MO)
William Paterson U of New Jersey (NJ)
William Penn U (IA)
Williams Baptist Coll (AR)
William Woods U (MO)
Wilmington U (DE)
Wingate U (NC)
Winona State U (MN)
Winthrop U (SC)
Worcester State U (MA)
Wright State U (OH)
Xavier U (OH)
Xavier U of Louisiana (LA)
Yeshiva U (NY)
York Coll of the City U of New York (NY)
Youngstown State U (OH)

EMERGENCY MEDICAL TECHNOLOGY (EMT PARAMEDIC)

Anna Maria Coll (MA)
Bowling Green State U (OH)
Central Washington U (WA)
Columbia Southern U (AL)
Concordia U Chicago (IL)
Creighton U (NE)
Eastern Kentucky U (KY)
The George Washington U (DC)
Jefferson Coll of Health Sciences (VA)
U of Maryland, Baltimore County (MD)
U of New Haven (CT)
U of New Mexico (NM)
U of South Alabama (AL)
U of Washington (WA)
Western Carolina U (NC)

ENERGY MANAGEMENT AND SYSTEMS TECHNOLOGY

Creighton U (NE)
Ferris State U (MI)
Fitchburg State U (MA)
Illinois State U (IL)
State Coll of Florida Manatee-Sarasota (FL)
Unity Coll (ME)
Vermont Tech Coll (VT)

ENGINEERING

Abilene Christian U (TX)
Albion Coll (MI)
Arizona State U at the Polytechnic campus (AZ)
Arkansas State U (AR)
Auburn U (AL)
Augsburg Coll (MN)
Ball State U (IN)
Barry U (FL)
Bates Coll (ME)
Baylor U (TX)
Beloit Coll (WI)
Benedictine Coll (KS)
Bethany Lutheran Coll (MN)
Bethel Coll (IN)
Binghamton U, State U of New York (NY)
Biola U (CA)
Bob Jones U (SC)
Boston U (MA)
Brown U (RI)
Buffalo State Coll, State U of New York (NY)
California Baptist U (CA)
California Inst of Technology (CA)
California State Polytechnic U, Pomona (CA)
California State U, Long Beach (CA)
California State U, Los Angeles (CA)
Calvin Coll (MI)
Cape Breton U (NS, Canada)
Case Western Reserve U (OH)
The Catholic U of America (DC)
Clarkson U (NY)
Clark U (MA)
Coll of Staten Island of the City U of New York (NY)
Colorado School of Mines (CO)
Colorado State U–Pueblo (CO)
Cooper Union for the Advancement of Science and Art (NY)
Cornell U (NY)
Dalhousie U (NS, Canada)
Dartmouth Coll (NH)

Daytona State Coll (FL)
Dominican U (IL)
Drexel U (PA)
East Carolina U (NC)
Elizabethtown Coll (PA)
Elon U (NC)
Embry-Riddle Aeronautical U–Daytona (FL)
Florida Inst of Technology (FL)
Franklin W. Olin Coll of Eng (MA)
Frostburg State U (MD)
Geneva Coll (PA)
The George Washington U (DC)
Gonzaga U (WA)
Grand Valley State U (MI)
Harvard U (MA)
Harvey Mudd Coll (CA)
Hiram Coll (OH)
Hope Coll (MI)
Illinois Inst of Technology (IL)
Indiana U–Purdue U Indianapolis (IN)
Inter American U of Puerto Rico, San Germán Campus (PR)
Iowa State U of Science and Technology (IA)
Jacksonville U (FL)
James Madison U (VA)
John Brown U (AR)
Johns Hopkins U (MD)
Lafayette Coll (PA)
LaGrange Coll (GA)
LeTourneau U (TX)
Lubbock Christian U (TX)
Maine Maritime Acad (ME)
Manchester U (IN)
Manhattan Coll (NY)
Marshall U (WV)
Maryville Coll (TN)
Massachusetts Maritime Acad (MA)
McKendree U (IL)
McNeese State U (LA)
Mercer U, Macon (GA)
Messiah Coll (PA)
Miami U (OH)
Michigan State U (MI)
Michigan Technological U (MI)
Mills Coll (CA)
Milwaukee School of Eng (WI)
Missouri U of Science and Technology (MO)
Montana State U (MT)
Montana Tech of The U of Montana (MT)
Moravian Coll (PA)
New Mexico Highlands U (NM)
North Carolina Ag and Tech State U (NC)
North Carolina State U (NC)
Northeastern U (MA)
Northland Coll (WI)
Northwestern U (IL)
Oglethorpe U (GA)
Ohio Northern U (OH)
The Ohio State U (OH)
Oklahoma Christian U (OK)
Old Dominion U (VA)
Olivet Nazarene U (IL)
Pacific Lutheran U (WA)
Princeton U (NJ)
Purdue U Calumet (IN)
Quinnipiac U (CT)
Rensselaer Polytechnic Inst (NY)
Robert Morris U (PA)
Rochester Inst of Technology (NY)
Roger Williams U (RI)
Rutgers, The State U of New Jersey, Camden (NJ)
Rutgers, The State U of New Jersey, Newark (NJ)
Saginaw Valley State U (MI)
Saint Anselm Coll (NH)
Saint Augustine's U (NC)
Saint Francis U (PA)
Saint Louis U (MO)
St. Thomas U (FL)
Saint Vincent Coll (PA)
San Jose State U (CA)
Seattle Pacific U (WA)
Seattle U (WA)
Spelman Coll (GA)
Stanford U (CA)
State U of New York Coll of Environmental Science and Forestry (NY)
State U of New York Polytechnic Inst (NY)
Stony Brook U, State U of New York (NY)
Temple U (PA)
Tennessee State U (TN)
Texas Christian U (TX)
Trinity Coll (CT)
Tufts U (MA)
United States Air Force Acad (CO)
United States Naval Acad (MD)
U at Buffalo, the State U of New York (NY)
The U of Akron (OH)
U of California, Irvine (CA)
U of Cincinnati (OH)
U of Colorado Boulder (CO)
U of Delaware (DE)
U of Denver (CO)
U of Hartford (CT)
U of Hawaii at Hilo (HI)
U of Hawaii at Manoa (HI)
The U of Iowa (IA)
U of Maryland, Baltimore County (MD)
U of Miami (FL)
U of Michigan (MI)
U of Minnesota, Twin Cities Campus (MN)
U of Mississippi (MS)
U of Missouri–Kansas City (MO)
U of Nebraska–Lincoln (NE)
U of Nevada, Las Vegas (NV)
U of New Brunswick Saint John (NB, Canada)
U of New Haven (CT)
U of North Carolina at Asheville (NC)
U of North Texas (TX)
U of Northwestern–St. Paul (MN)
U of Oklahoma (OK)
U of Portland (OR)
U of Regina (SK, Canada)
U of Rochester (NY)
U of Southern Indiana (IN)
The U of Tennessee at Chattanooga (TN)
The U of Tennessee at Martin (TN)
The U of Toledo (OH)
U of Toronto (ON, Canada)
U of Utah (UT)
U of Virginia (VA)
The U of Western Ontario (ON, Canada)
U of Windsor (ON, Canada)
Vaughn Coll of Aeronautics and Technology (NY)
Wake Forest U (NC)
Walla Walla U (WA)
Wartburg Coll (IA)
Washington U in St. Louis (MO)
Weber State U (UT)
Wells Coll (NY)
Wentworth Inst of Technology (MA)
Western Illinois U (IL)
Widener U (PA)
Wilkes U (PA)
Youngstown State U (OH)

ENGINEERING CHEMISTRY
Oakland U (MI)

ENGINEERING FIELDS RELATED
California State U, Chico (CA)

ENGINEERING/INDUSTRIAL MANAGEMENT
Arizona State U at the Tempe campus (AZ)
California State U, Long Beach (CA)
Christian Brothers U (TN)
Claremont McKenna Coll (CA)
Clarkson U (NY)
Columbia U (NY)
Eastern Kentucky U (KY)
Eastern Michigan U (MI)
Fort Lewis Coll (CO)
Grove City Coll (PA)
Illinois Inst of Technology (IL)
John Brown U (AR)
Kansas State U (KS)
Lawrence Technological U (MI)
LeTourneau U (TX)
Massachusetts Maritime Acad (MA)
Miami U (OH)
Middle Tennessee State U (TN)
Missouri Southern State U (MO)
Missouri State U (MO)
Missouri U of Science and Technology (MO)
Morehead State U (KY)
National U (CA)
Pittsburg State U (KS)
Purdue U Calumet (IN)
Saginaw Valley State U (MI)
Stanford U (CA)
State U of New York Coll of Technology at Canton (NY)
Texas State U (TX)
United States Merchant Marine Acad (NY)
United States Military Acad (NY)
Universidad del Turabo (PR)
The U of Arizona (AZ)
U of Illinois at Chicago (IL)
The U of Scranton (PA)
The U of Tennessee at Chattanooga (TN)
U of the Incarnate Word (TX)
U of the Pacific (CA)
U of Vermont (VT)
Washburn U (KS)
Western Michigan U (MI)
Widener U (PA)
Wilkes U (PA)
Worcester Polytechnic Inst (MA)

ENGINEERING MECHANICS
Carroll Coll (MT)
Columbia U (NY)
Johns Hopkins U (MD)
Lehigh U (PA)
United States Air Force Acad (CO)
U of Windsor (ON, Canada)
U of Wisconsin–Madison (WI)
Virginia Polytechnic Inst and State U (VA)
Worcester Polytechnic Inst (MA)

ENGINEERING PHYSICS/ APPLIED PHYSICS
Adams State U (CO)
Arkansas Tech U (AR)
Augustana Coll (IL)
Augustana Coll (SD)
Belmont U (TN)
Bemidji State U (MN)
Biola U (CA)
Bradley U (IL)
Brown U (RI)
California Inst of Technology (CA)
Case Western Reserve U (OH)
Central Washington U (WA)
Christian Brothers U (TN)
Colorado School of Mines (CO)
Colorado State U (CO)
Columbia U (NY)
Cornell U (NY)
Dartmouth Coll (NH)
Delaware State U (DE)
Eastern Michigan U (MI)
Elon U (NC)
Embry-Riddle Aeronautical U–Daytona (FL)
Fordham U (NY)
Fort Lewis Coll (CO)
Illinois Inst of Technology (IL)
Jacksonville U (FL)
John Carroll U (OH)
Juniata Coll (PA)
Kansas Wesleyan U (KS)
Kettering U (MI)
Lehigh U (PA)
LeTourneau U (TX)
Linfield Coll (OR)
Loras Coll (IA)
Loyola Marymount U (CA)
Miami U (OH)
Morningside Coll (IA)
Murray State U (KY)
New Mexico State U (NM)
New York U (NY)
North Carolina Ag and Tech State U (NC)
Northwest Nazarene U (ID)
Oakland U (MI)
The Ohio State U (OH)
Oregon State U (OR)
Point Loma Nazarene U (CA)
Providence Coll (RI)
Randolph Coll (VA)
Randolph-Macon Coll (VA)
Rensselaer Polytechnic Inst (NY)
Rose-Hulman Inst of Technology (IN)
Saint Louis U (MO)
Saint Mary's U of Minnesota (MN)
Samford U (AL)
Santa Clara U (CA)
Southeast Missouri State U (MO)
Stephen F. Austin State U (TX)
Tarleton State U (TX)
Taylor U (IN)
Thiel Coll (PA)
Trevecca Nazarene U (TN)
Tufts U (MA)
U at Buffalo, the State U of New York (NY)
The U of British Columbia (BC, Canada)
U of California, Berkeley (CA)
U of Central Oklahoma (OK)
U of Colorado Boulder (CO)
U of Illinois at Chicago (IL)
The U of Kansas (KS)
U of Maine (ME)
U of Massachusetts Boston (MA)
U of Michigan (MI)
U of Nevada, Reno (NV)
U of Northern Iowa (IA)
U of North Texas (TX)
U of Oklahoma (OK)
U of Pittsburgh (PA)
U of Saskatchewan (SK, Canada)
The U of Tennessee (TN)
U of the Pacific (CA)
The U of Toledo (OH)
The U of Tulsa (OK)
The U of Western Ontario (ON, Canada)
U of Wisconsin–Madison (WI)
U of Wisconsin–Platteville (WI)
Washington and Lee U (VA)
Whittier Coll (CA)
Worcester Polytechnic Inst (MA)
Wright State U (OH)
Xavier U (OH)
Yale U (CT)

ENGINEERING RELATED
Agnes Scott Coll (GA)
Anderson U (SC)
Auburn U (AL)
Benedictine Coll (KS)
Boston U (MA)
California State U, Chico (CA)
California State U, Long Beach (CA)
Claremont McKenna Coll (CA)
Cogswell Polytechnical Coll (CA)
The Coll of Idaho (ID)
Colorado State U–Pueblo (CO)
Eastern Illinois U (IL)
Gettysburg Coll (PA)
Hawai`i Pacific U (HI)
Indiana U–Purdue U Indianapolis (IN)
Iowa State U of Science and Technology (IA)
Lehigh U (PA)
LeTourneau U (TX)
Madonna U (MI)
Maryville U of Saint Louis (MO)
Mississippi State U (MS)
Morehead State U (KY)
New York U (NY)
Norfolk State U (VA)
Northern Michigan U (MI)
Northwestern U (IL)
Ohio Northern U (OH)
The Ohio State U (OH)
Ohio Wesleyan U (OH)
Park U (MO)
Penn State Altoona (PA)
Penn State Berks (PA)
Penn State U Park (PA)
Polytechnic U of Puerto Rico (PR)
Principia Coll (IL)
Purdue U (IN)
Rochester Inst of Technology (NY)
Rose-Hulman Inst of Technology (IN)
State U of New York at New Paltz (NY)
State U of New York at Oswego (NY)
Transylvania U (KY)
Tufts U (MA)
The U of Alabama in Huntsville (AL)
U of Alberta (AB, Canada)
U of California, Davis (CA)
U of Delaware (DE)
U of Maryland, Coll Park (MD)
U of Massachusetts Lowell (MA)
U of Miami (FL)
U of Michigan–Dearborn (MI)
U of New Hampshire (NH)
U of Pennsylvania (PA)
The U of Virginia's Coll at Wise (VA)
U of Washington (WA)
U of Waterloo (ON, Canada)
The U of Western Ontario (ON, Canada)
U of Wisconsin–Platteville (WI)
Washington U in St. Louis (MO)
Waynesburg U (PA)
Western Michigan U (MI)
Wheaton Coll (IL)
Worcester Polytechnic Inst (MA)
Wright State U (OH)
York Coll of Pennsylvania (PA)

ENGINEERING-RELATED TECHNOLOGIES
Rochester Inst of Technology (NY)
United States Merchant Marine Acad (NY)

ENGINEERING SCIENCE
Belmont U (TN)
Benedictine U (IL)
Bethel U (MN)
California Polytechnic State U, San Luis Obispo (CA)
Carroll Coll (MT)
The Coll of New Jersey (NJ)
Colorado State U (CO)
Concordia U, St. Paul (MN)
Hofstra U (NY)
Iowa State U of Science and Technology (IA)
Lamar U (TX)
New Jersey Inst of Technology (NJ)
Northwestern U (IL)
Ohio Wesleyan U (OH)
Penn State Abington (PA)
Penn State Altoona (PA)
Penn State Beaver (PA)
Penn State Berks (PA)
Penn State Brandywine (PA)
Penn State DuBois (PA)
Penn State Erie, The Behrend Coll (PA)
Penn State Fayette, The Eberly Campus (PA)
Penn State Greater Allegheny (PA)
Penn State Hazleton (PA)
Penn State Lehigh Valley (PA)
Penn State Mont Alto (PA)
Penn State New Kensington (PA)
Penn State Schuylkill (PA)
Penn State Shenango (PA)
Penn State U Park (PA)
Penn State Wilkes-Barre (PA)
Penn State Worthington Scranton (PA)
Penn State York (PA)
Rensselaer Polytechnic Inst (NY)
Rutgers, The State U of New Jersey, New Brunswick (NJ)
St. Mary's U (TX)
St. Thomas Aquinas Coll (NY)
Simon Fraser U (BC, Canada)
Smith Coll (MA)
Southern Utah U (UT)
Trinity U (TX)
Tufts U (MA)
Tulane U (LA)
United States Air Force Acad (CO)
U of California, Berkeley (CA)
U of Miami (FL)
U of Michigan (MI)
U of Michigan–Flint (MI)
U of New Mexico (NM)
U of Pittsburgh (PA)
U of Portland (OR)
U of Rochester (NY)
U of Toronto (ON, Canada)
The U of Western Ontario (ON, Canada)
Vanderbilt U (TN)
Wartburg Coll (IA)
Wheeling Jesuit U (WV)
Wright State U (OH)
Yale U (CT)

ENGINEERING TECHNOLOGIES AND ENGINEERING RELATED
Arkansas State U (AR)
Ball State U (IN)
Bowling Green State U (OH)
Cameron U (OK)
Capitol Technology U (MD)
East Carolina U (NC)
Excelsior Coll (NY)
Keene State Coll (NH)
LeTourneau U (TX)
New York Inst of Technology (NY)
North Carolina Ag and Tech State U (NC)
Northeastern State U (OK)
Old Dominion U (VA)
Pennsylvania Coll of Technology (PA)
Pittsburg State U (KS)
Shawnee State U (OH)
Silver Lake Coll of the Holy Family (WI)
State U of New York Coll of Technology at Alfred (NY)
United States Military Acad (NY)
The U of British Columbia (BC, Canada)
U of Hartford (CT)
U of Minnesota, Twin Cities Campus (MN)
The U of North Carolina at Charlotte (NC)
The U of West Alabama (AL)

ENGINEERING TECHNOLOGY
Austin Peay State U (TN)
Berry Coll (GA)
Buffalo State Coll, State U of New York (NY)
California State Polytechnic U, Pomona (CA)
California State U, Long Beach (CA)
California U of Pennsylvania (PA)
Drexel U (PA)
Eastern New Mexico U (NM)
East Tennessee State U (TN)
Fairmont State U (WV)
Grambling State U (LA)
Illinois State U (IL)
Indiana State U (IN)
Kansas State U (KS)
Kent State U (OH)
Kent State U at Tuscarawas (OH)
Lawrence Technological U (MI)
Lenoir-Rhyne U (NC)
LeTourneau U (TX)
Maine Maritime Acad (ME)
Miami U (OH)
Middle Tennessee State U (TN)
Midwestern State U (TX)
Morehead State U (KY)
New Jersey Inst of Technology (NJ)
New Mexico State U (NM)
New York Inst of Technology (NY)
Northern Illinois U (IL)
Southeastern Louisiana U (LA)
Southeast Missouri State U (MO)
Southern Illinois U Carbondale (IL)
Southern Utah U (UT)
Tarleton State U (TX)
Temple U (PA)
Texas A&M U (TX)
Texas State U (TX)
Texas Tech U (TX)
U of Delaware (DE)
U of Hartford (CT)
U of Memphis (TN)
U of Rochester (NY)
U of South Carolina Upstate (SC)
The U of Texas at Tyler (TX)
The U of West Alabama (AL)
U of West Florida (FL)
U of Wisconsin–Green Bay (WI)
U of Wisconsin–River Falls (WI)
U of Wisconsin–Stout (WI)
Walla Walla U (WA)
Wentworth Inst of Technology (MA)
Western Carolina U (NC)
Western Illinois U (IL)
West Texas A&M U (TX)
West Virginia U Inst of Technology (WV)
William Penn U (IA)
Youngstown State U (OH)

ENGLISH
Abilene Christian U (TX)
Adams State U (CO)
Adelphi U (NY)
Agnes Scott Coll (GA)
Alabama State U (AL)
Albany State U (GA)
Albertus Magnus Coll (CT)
Albion Coll (MI)
Albright Coll (PA)
Alcorn State U (MS)
Alice Lloyd Coll (KY)
Allegheny Coll (PA)
Alma Coll (MI)
Alvernia U (PA)
Alverno Coll (WI)
American Coll of Thessaloniki (Greece)
American Intl Coll (MA)
American Public U System (WV)
The American U in Cairo (Egypt)
American U of Beirut (Lebanon)
Amherst Coll (MA)
Anderson U (IN)
Anderson U (SC)
Andrews U (MI)
Angelo State U (TX)
Anna Maria Coll (MA)
Appalachian State U (NC)
Aquinas Coll (MI)
Aquinas Coll (TN)
Arcadia U (PA)
Arizona State U at the Polytechnic campus (AZ)
Arizona State U at the Tempe campus (AZ)
Arizona State U at the West campus (AZ)
Arkansas State U (AR)
Arkansas Tech U (AR)
Armstrong State U (GA)
Asbury U (KY)
Ashland U (OH)
Assumption Coll (MA)
Athens State U (AL)
Auburn U (AL)
Auburn U at Montgomery (AL)
Augsburg Coll (MN)
Augustana Coll (IL)
Augustana Coll (SD)
Austin Coll (TX)
Austin Peay State U (TN)
Ave Maria U (FL)
Averett U (VA)
Avila U (MO)
Azusa Pacific U (CA)
Baker U (KS)
Baldwin Wallace U (OH)
Ball State U (IN)
Bard Coll (NY)
Barnard Coll (NY)
Barry U (FL)
Baruch Coll of the City U of New York (NY)
Bates Coll (ME)
Baylor U (TX)
Belhaven U (MS)
Belmont Abbey Coll (NC)
Belmont U (TN)
Beloit Coll (WI)
Bemidji State U (MN)
Benedictine Coll (KS)
Benedictine U (IL)
Bennett Coll (NC)
Bennington Coll (VT)
Berea Coll (KY)
Berry Coll (GA)
Bethany Coll (WV)
Bethany Lutheran Coll (MN)
Bethel Coll (IN)
Bethel Coll (KS)
Bethel U (MN)
Bethune-Cookman U (FL)
Binghamton U, State U of New York (NY)
Biola U (CA)
Birmingham-Southern Coll (AL)
Blackburn Coll (IL)
Black Hills State U (SD)
Bloomfield Coll (NJ)
Bloomsburg U of Pennsylvania (PA)
Bluefield Coll (VA)
Blue Mountain Coll (MS)
Bluffton U (OH)
Bob Jones U (SC)
Boston Coll (MA)
Boston U (MA)
Bowdoin Coll (ME)
Bowie State U (MD)
Bowling Green State U (OH)
Bradley U (IL)
Brandeis U (MA)
Brenau U (GA)
Brevard Coll (NC)
Bridgewater Coll (VA)
Bridgewater State U (MA)
Brown U (RI)
Bryan Coll (TN)
Bryant U (RI)
Bryn Mawr Coll (PA)
Bucknell U (PA)
Buena Vista U (IA)
Buffalo State Coll, State U of New York (NY)
Butler U (IN)
Cabrini Coll (PA)
Cairn U (PA)
Caldwell U (NJ)
California Baptist U (CA)
California Inst of Technology (CA)
California Lutheran U (CA)
California Polytechnic State U, San Luis Obispo (CA)
California State Polytechnic U, Pomona (CA)
California State U, Chico (CA)
California State U, Dominguez Hills (CA)
California State U, Fresno (CA)
California State U, Fullerton (CA)
California State U, Long Beach (CA)
California State U, Los Angeles (CA)
California State U, Sacramento (CA)
California State U, San Bernardino (CA)
California State U, San Marcos (CA)
California State U, Stanislaus (CA)
California U of Pennsylvania (PA)
Calumet Coll of Saint Joseph (IN)
Calvary Bible Coll and Theological Sem (MO)
Calvin Coll (MI)
Cameron U (OK)
Campbellsville U (KY)
Canisius Coll (NY)
Cape Breton U (NS, Canada)
Capital U (OH)
Cardinal Stritch U (WI)
Carleton Coll (MN)
Carlow U (PA)
Carroll Coll (MT)
Carson-Newman U (TN)
Case Western Reserve U (OH)
Catawba Coll (NC)
The Catholic U of America (DC)
Cazenovia Coll (NY)
Cedar Crest Coll (PA)
Cedarville U (OH)
Centenary Coll of Louisiana (LA)
Central Coll (IA)
Central Connecticut State U (CT)
Central Methodist U (MO)
Central Michigan U (MI)
Central State U (OH)
Central Washington U (WA)
Centre Coll (KY)
Chaminade U of Honolulu (HI)
Chapman U (CA)
Charleston Southern U (SC)
Chatham U (PA)
Chestnut Hill Coll (PA)
Cheyney U of Pennsylvania (PA)
Chicago State U (IL)
Chowan U (NC)
Christian Brothers U (TN)
Christopher Newport U (VA)
The Citadel, The Military Coll of South Carolina (SC)
City Coll of the City U of New York (NY)
Claflin U (SC)
Claremont McKenna Coll (CA)
Clarion U of Pennsylvania (PA)
Clark Atlanta U (GA)
Clarke U (IA)
Clark U (MA)
Clayton State U (GA)
Clearwater Christian Coll (FL)
Cleveland State U (OH)
Coastal Carolina U (SC)
Coe Coll (IA)
Coker Coll (SC)
Colby Coll (ME)
Colby-Sawyer Coll (NH)
The Coll at Brockport, State U of New York (NY)
Coll of Charleston (SC)
The Coll of Idaho (ID)
The Coll of New Jersey (NJ)
The Coll of New Rochelle (NY)
The Coll of Saint Benedict (MN)
Coll of Saint Elizabeth (NJ)
Coll of Saint Mary (NE)
The Coll of Saint Rose (NY)
The Coll of St. Scholastica (MN)
Coll of Staten Island of the City U of New York (NY)
Coll of the Atlantic (ME)
Coll of the Holy Cross (MA)
Coll of the Ozarks (MO)
The Coll of William and Mary (VA)
The Coll of Wooster (OH)
The Colorado Coll (CO)
Colorado Mesa U (CO)
Colorado State U (CO)
Colorado State U–Pueblo (CO)
Columbia Coll (MO)
Columbia Coll (SC)
Columbia Intl U (SC)
Columbia U (NY)
Columbia U, School of General Studies (NY)
Columbus State U (GA)
Concordia Coll (MN)
Concordia Coll–New York (NY)
Concordia U (CA)
Concordia U (QC, Canada)
Concordia U Chicago (IL)
Concordia U, Nebraska (NE)
Concordia U, St. Paul (MN)
Concordia U Texas (TX)
Concordia U Wisconsin (WI)
Concord U (WV)
Connecticut Coll (CT)
Corban U (OR)
Cornell Coll (IA)
Cornell U (NY)
Covenant Coll (GA)
Crandall U (NB, Canada)
Creighton U (NE)
Culver-Stockton Coll (MO)
Cumberland U (TN)
Curry Coll (MA)
Daemen Coll (NY)
Dalhousie U (NS, Canada)
Dallas Baptist U (TX)
Dartmouth Coll (NH)
Davidson Coll (NC)
Defiance Coll (OH)
Delaware State U (DE)
Delta State U (MS)
Denison U (OH)
DePaul U (IL)
DePauw U (IN)
DEREE - The American Coll of Greece (Greece)
DeSales U (PA)
Dickinson Coll (PA)
Dickinson State U (ND)
Dixie State U (UT)
Doane Coll (NE)
Dominican Coll (NY)
Dominican U (IL)
Dominican U of California (CA)
Dowling Coll (NY)
Drake U (IA)
Drew U (NJ)
Drury U (MO)
Duquesne U (PA)
Earlham Coll (IN)
East Carolina U (NC)
East Central U (OK)
Eastern Connecticut State U (CT)
Eastern Illinois U (IL)
Eastern Kentucky U (KY)
Eastern Michigan U (MI)
Eastern New Mexico U (NM)
Eastern Oregon U (OR)
East Stroudsburg U of Pennsylvania (PA)
East Tennessee State U (TN)
East Texas Baptist U (TX)
Eckerd Coll (FL)
Edgewood Coll (WI)
Edinboro U of Pennsylvania (PA)
Elizabethtown Coll (PA)
Elmhurst Coll (IL)
Elmira Coll (NY)
Elms Coll (MA)
Elon U (NC)
Emmanuel Coll (GA)
Emmanuel Coll (MA)
Emory & Henry Coll (VA)
Emporia State U (KS)
Endicott Coll (MA)
Erskine Coll (SC)
Eureka Coll (IL)
Evangel U (MO)
The Evergreen State Coll (WA)
Fairfield U (CT)
Fairleigh Dickinson U, Coll at Florham (NJ)
Fairleigh Dickinson U, Metropolitan Campus (NJ)
Fairmont State U (WV)
Faulkner U (AL)
Fayetteville State U (NC)
Ferrum Coll (VA)
Fitchburg State U (MA)
Flagler Coll (FL)
Florida Ag and Mech U (FL)
Florida Atlantic U (FL)
Florida Gulf Coast U (FL)
Florida Intl U (FL)
Florida State U (FL)
Fontbonne U (MO)
Fordham U (NY)
Fort Hays State U (KS)
Fort Lewis Coll (CO)
Framingham State U (MA)
Franciscan U of Steubenville (OH)
Francis Marion U (SC)
Franklin & Marshall Coll (PA)
Franklin Coll (IN)
Franklin Pierce U (NH)
Friends U (KS)
Frostburg State U (MD)
Furman U (SC)
Gallaudet U (DC)
Geneva Coll (PA)
George Mason U (VA)
Georgetown Coll (KY)
Georgetown U (DC)
The George Washington U (DC)
Georgia Coll & State U (GA)
Georgia Gwinnett Coll (GA)
Georgian Court U (NJ)
Georgia Regents U (GA)
Georgia Southern U (GA)
Georgia Southwestern State U (GA)
Georgia State U (GA)
Gettysburg Coll (PA)
Gonzaga U (WA)
Gordon Coll (MA)
Goshen Coll (IN)
Goucher Coll (MD)
Governors State U (IL)
Grace Coll (IN)
Graceland U (IA)
Grambling State U (LA)
Grand Valley State U (MI)
Grand View U (IA)
Granite State Coll (NH)
Green Mountain Coll (VT)
Greensboro Coll (NC)
Greenville Coll (IL)
Grinnell Coll (IA)
Guilford Coll (NC)
Gustavus Adolphus Coll (MN)
Gwynedd Mercy U (PA)
Hamilton Coll (NY)
Hamline U (MN)
Hampden-Sydney Coll (VA)
Hampshire Coll (MA)
Hampton U (VA)
Hannibal-LaGrange U (MO)
Hanover Coll (IN)
Harding U (AR)
Hardin-Simmons U (TX)
Hartwick Coll (NY)
Harvard U (MA)
Hastings Coll (NE)
Haverford Coll (PA)
Hawai`i Pacific U (HI)
Heidelberg U (OH)
Hendrix Coll (AR)
Heritage U (WA)
High Point U (NC)
Hilbert Coll (NY)
Hillsdale Coll (MI)
Hiram Coll (OH)
Hobart and William Smith Colls (NY)

Hofstra U (NY)
Hollins U (VA)
Holy Cross Coll (IN)
Holy Family U (PA)
Hope Coll (MI)
Hope Intl U (CA)
Houghton Coll (NY)
Houston Baptist U (TX)
Howard Payne U (TX)
Howard U (DC)
Humboldt State U (CA)
Hunter Coll of the City U of New York (NY)
Huntingdon Coll (AL)
Husson U (ME)
Huston-Tillotson U (TX)
Illinois Coll (IL)
Illinois State U (IL)
Immaculata U (PA)
Indiana State U (IN)
Indiana U Bloomington (IN)
Indiana U East (IN)
Indiana U Kokomo (IN)
Indiana U Northwest (IN)
Indiana U of Pennsylvania (PA)
Indiana U–Purdue U Fort Wayne (IN)
Indiana U–Purdue U Indianapolis (IN)
Indiana U South Bend (IN)
Indiana U Southeast (IN)
Inter American U of Puerto Rico, San Germán Campus (PR)
Iona Coll (NY)
Iowa State U of Science and Technology (IA)
Iowa Wesleyan Coll (IA)
Ithaca Coll (NY)
Jackson State U (MS)
Jacksonville State U (AL)
Jacksonville U (FL)
James Madison U (VA)
Jarvis Christian Coll (TX)
John Brown U (AR)
John Cabot U (Italy)
John Carroll U (OH)
Johns Hopkins U (MD)
Johnson C. Smith U (NC)
Johnson State Coll (VT)
Judson Coll (AL)
Judson U (IL)
Juniata Coll (PA)
Kalamazoo Coll (MI)
Kansas State U (KS)
Kansas Wesleyan U (KS)
Kean U (NJ)
Keene State Coll (NH)
Kennesaw State U (GA)
Kent State U (OH)
Kent State U at Ashtabula (OH)
Kent State U at East Liverpool (OH)
Kent State U at Geauga (OH)
Kent State U at Salem (OH)
Kent State U at Stark (OH)
Kent State U at Trumbull (OH)
Kent State U at Tuscarawas (OH)
Kentucky State U (KY)
Kentucky Wesleyan Coll (KY)
Kenyon Coll (OH)
Keuka Coll (NY)
King's Coll (PA)
The King's U Coll (AB, Canada)
King U (TN)
Knox Coll (IL)
Kutztown U of Pennsylvania (PA)
Lafayette Coll (PA)
LaGrange Coll (GA)
Lake Erie Coll (OH)
Lake Forest Coll (IL)
Lamar U (TX)
Lane Coll (TN)
Langston U (OK)
La Roche Coll (PA)
La Salle U (PA)
Lasell Coll (MA)
La Sierra U (CA)
Lawrence Technological U (MI)
Lawrence U (WI)
Lebanese American U (Lebanon)
Lebanon Valley Coll (PA)
Lees-McRae Coll (NC)
Lee U (TN)
Lehigh U (PA)
Lehman Coll of the City U of New York (NY)
Le Moyne Coll (NY)
LeMoyne-Owen Coll (TN)
Lenoir-Rhyne U (NC)
Lesley U (MA)
LeTourneau U (TX)
Lewis & Clark Coll (OR)
Lewis U (IL)
Liberty U (VA)
Limestone Coll (SC)
Lincoln Memorial U (TN)
Lincoln U (MO)
Lincoln U (PA)
Lindenwood U (MO)
Lindsey Wilson Coll (KY)
Lipscomb U (TN)
Lock Haven U of Pennsylvania (PA)
Long Island U–LIU Brooklyn (NY)
Long Island U–LIU Post (NY)
Longwood U (VA)
Loras Coll (IA)
Louisiana Coll (LA)
Louisiana State U and A&M Coll (LA)
Louisiana State U in Shreveport (LA)
Lourdes U (OH)
Loyola Marymount U (CA)
Loyola U Chicago (IL)
Loyola U New Orleans (LA)
Luther Coll (IA)
Lycoming Coll (PA)
Lynchburg Coll (VA)
Lyon Coll (AR)
Macalester Coll (MN)
Madonna U (MI)
Maharishi U of Management (IA)
Malone U (OH)
Manchester U (IN)
Manhattan Coll (NY)
Manhattanville Coll (NY)
Mansfield U of Pennsylvania (PA)
Maranatha Baptist U (WI)
Marian U (IN)
Marian U (WI)
Marietta Coll (OH)
Marist Coll (NY)
Marquette U (WI)
Marshall U (WV)
Mars Hill U (NC)
Mary Baldwin Coll (VA)
Marylhurst U (OR)
Marymount Manhattan Coll (NY)
Marymount U (VA)
Maryville Coll (TN)
Maryville U of Saint Louis (MO)
Marywood U (PA)
Massachusetts Coll of Liberal Arts (MA)
Massachusetts Inst of Technology (MA)
The Master's Coll and Sem (CA)
Mayville State U (ND)
McDaniel Coll (MD)
McKendree U (IL)
McMurry U (TX)
McNeese State U (LA)
Medaille Coll (NY)
Mercer U, Macon (GA)
Mercy Coll (NY)
Meredith Coll (NC)
Merrimack Coll (MA)
Messiah Coll (PA)
Metropolitan State U (MN)
Miami U (OH)
Michigan State U (MI)
Michigan Technological U (MI)
MidAmerica Nazarene U (KS)
Middle Tennessee State U (TN)
Midwestern State U (TX)
Millersville U of Pennsylvania (PA)
Milligan Coll (TN)
Millikin U (IL)
Millsaps Coll (MS)
Mills Coll (CA)
Minnesota State U Mankato (MN)
Minnesota State U Moorhead (MN)
Minot State U (ND)
Misericordia U (PA)
Mississippi State U (MS)
Mississippi U for Women (MS)
Mississippi Valley State U (MS)
Missouri Baptist U (MO)
Missouri Southern State U (MO)
Missouri State U (MO)
Missouri U of Science and Technology (MO)
Missouri Valley Coll (MO)
Missouri Western State U (MO)
Molloy Coll (NY)
Monmouth Coll (IL)
Monmouth U (NJ)
Montana State U (MT)
Montana State U Billings (MT)
Montclair State U (NJ)
Montreat Coll, Montreat (NC)
Moravian Coll (PA)
Morehead State U (KY)
Morningside Coll (IA)
Morris Coll (SC)
Mount Allison U (NB, Canada)
Mount Aloysius Coll (PA)
Mount Holyoke Coll (MA)
Mount Marty Coll (SD)
Mount Mary U (WI)
Mount Mercy U (IA)
Mount St. Joseph U (OH)
Mount Saint Mary Coll (NY)
Mount Saint Mary's U (CA)
Mount St. Mary's U (MD)
Mount Vernon Nazarene U (OH)
Muhlenberg Coll (PA)
Multnomah U (OR)
Murray State U (KY)
Naropa U (CO)
National U (CA)
Nazareth Coll of Rochester (NY)
Nebraska Wesleyan U (NE)
Neumann U (PA)
Newberry Coll (SC)
New Coll of Florida (FL)
New Jersey City U (NJ)
Newman U (KS)
New Mexico Highlands U (NM)
New Mexico State U (NM)
New York Inst of Technology (NY)
New York U (NY)
Niagara U (NY)
Nicholls State U (LA)
Nichols Coll (MA)
Norfolk State U (VA)
North Carolina Ag and Tech State U (NC)
North Carolina Central U (NC)
North Carolina State U (NC)
North Carolina Wesleyan Coll (NC)
North Central Coll (IL)
North Dakota State U (ND)
Northeastern Illinois U (IL)
Northeastern State U (OK)
Northeastern U (MA)
Northern Arizona U (AZ)
Northern Illinois U (IL)
Northern Kentucky U (KY)
Northern Michigan U (MI)
Northern State U (SD)
North Greenville U (SC)
Northland Coll (WI)
Northwest Christian U (OR)
Northwestern Coll (IA)
Northwestern Oklahoma State U (OK)
Northwestern U (IL)
Northwest Missouri State U (MO)
Northwest Nazarene U (ID)
Northwest U (WA)
Norwich U (VT)
Notre Dame of Maryland U (MD)
Nova Southeastern U (FL)
Nyack Coll (NY)
Oakland U (MI)
Oberlin Coll (OH)
Occidental Coll (CA)
Oglethorpe U (GA)
Ohio Dominican U (OH)
The Ohio State U (OH)
The Ohio State U at Lima (OH)
The Ohio State U at Marion (OH)
The Ohio State U–Mansfield Campus (OH)
The Ohio State U–Newark Campus (OH)
Ohio U (OH)
Ohio Wesleyan U (OH)
Oklahoma Christian U (OK)
Oklahoma City U (OK)
Oklahoma State U (OK)
Oklahoma Wesleyan U (OK)
Old Dominion U (VA)
Olivet Coll (MI)
Olivet Nazarene U (IL)
Oregon State U (OR)
Our Lady of the Lake U of San Antonio (TX)
Pace U (NY)
Pacific Lutheran U (WA)
Pacific U (OR)
Palm Beach Atlantic U (FL)
Park U (MO)
Penn State Abington (PA)
Penn State Altoona (PA)
Penn State Beaver (PA)
Penn State Berks (PA)
Penn State Brandywine (PA)
Penn State DuBois (PA)
Penn State Erie, The Behrend Coll (PA)
Penn State Fayette, The Eberly Campus (PA)
Penn State Greater Allegheny (PA)
Penn State Harrisburg (PA)
Penn State Hazleton (PA)
Penn State Lehigh Valley (PA)
Penn State Mont Alto (PA)
Penn State New Kensington (PA)
Penn State Schuylkill (PA)
Penn State Shenango (PA)
Penn State U Park (PA)
Penn State Wilkes-Barre (PA)
Penn State Worthington Scranton (PA)
Penn State York (PA)
Pepperdine U, Malibu (CA)
Peru State Coll (NE)
Philander Smith Coll (AR)
Piedmont Coll (GA)
Pine Manor Coll (MA)
Pittsburg State U (KS)
Plymouth State U (NH)
Point Loma Nazarene U (CA)
Point U (GA)
Pomona Coll (CA)
Portland State U (OR)
Prairie View A&M U (TX)
Presbyterian Coll (SC)
Princeton U (NJ)
Principia Coll (IL)
Providence Coll (RI)
Purdue U Calumet (IN)
Queens Coll of the City U of New York (NY)
Quincy U (IL)
Quinnipiac U (CT)
Radford U (VA)
Randolph Coll (VA)
Randolph-Macon Coll (VA)
Reed Coll (OR)
Regent U (VA)
Regis Coll (MA)
Regis U (CO)
Reinhardt U (GA)
Rhode Island Coll (RI)
Rhodes Coll (TN)
Rice U (TX)
Rider U (NJ)
Ripon Coll (WI)
Rivier U (NH)
Roanoke Coll (VA)
Robert Morris U (PA)
Roberts Wesleyan Coll (NY)
Rockford U (IL)
Rockhurst U (MO)
Rocky Mountain Coll (MT)
Roger Williams U (RI)
Rollins Coll (FL)
Roosevelt U (IL)
Rosemont Coll (PA)
Rowan U (NJ)
Rust Coll (MS)
Rutgers, The State U of New Jersey, Camden (NJ)
Rutgers, The State U of New Jersey, Newark (NJ)
Rutgers, The State U of New Jersey, New Brunswick (NJ)
Sacred Heart U (CT)
The Sage Colls (NY)
Saginaw Valley State U (MI)
St. Andrews U (NC)
Saint Anselm Coll (NH)
Saint Augustine's U (NC)
St. Bonaventure U (NY)
St. Catharine Coll (KY)
St. Catherine U (MN)
St. Edward's U (TX)
St. Francis Coll (NY)
Saint Francis U (PA)
St. Gregory's U, Shawnee (OK)
St. John Fisher Coll (NY)
Saint John's U (MN)
St. John's U (NY)
Saint Joseph's Coll (IN)
St. Joseph's Coll, Long Island Campus (NY)
St. Joseph's Coll, New York (NY)
Saint Joseph's U (PA)
St. Lawrence U (NY)
Saint Leo U (FL)
Saint Louis U (MO)
Saint Martin's U (WA)
Saint Mary-of-the-Woods Coll (IN)
Saint Mary's Coll (IN)
St. Mary's Coll of Maryland (MD)
St. Mary's U (TX)
Saint Michael's Coll (VT)
St. Norbert Coll (WI)
St. Olaf Coll (MN)
Saint Peter's U (NJ)
St. Thomas Aquinas Coll (NY)
St. Thomas U (FL)
St. Thomas U (NB, Canada)
Saint Vincent Coll (PA)
Salem Coll (NC)
Salisbury U (MD)
Salve Regina U (RI)
Samford U (AL)
Sam Houston State U (TX)
San Diego Christian Coll (CA)
San Diego State U (CA)
San Francisco State U (CA)
San Jose State U (CA)
Santa Clara U (CA)
Savannah State U (GA)
Scripps Coll (CA)
Seattle Pacific U (WA)
Seattle U (WA)
Seton Hill U (PA)
Sewanee: The U of the South (TN)
Shawnee State U (OH)
Shaw U (NC)
Shenandoah U (VA)
Shepherd U (WV)
Shippensburg U of Pennsylvania (PA)
Siena Coll (NY)
Siena Heights U (MI)
Silver Lake Coll of the Holy Family (WI)
Simmons Coll (MA)
Simon Fraser U (BC, Canada)
Simpson Coll (IA)
Simpson U (CA)
Skidmore Coll (NY)
Slippery Rock U of Pennsylvania (PA)
Smith Coll (MA)
South Carolina State U (SC)
South Dakota State U (SD)
Southeastern Louisiana U (LA)
Southeastern Oklahoma State U (OK)
Southeastern U (FL)
Southeast Missouri State U (MO)
Southern Adventist U (TN)
Southern Arkansas U–Magnolia (AR)
Southern Connecticut State U (CT)
Southern Illinois U Carbondale (IL)
Southern Illinois U Edwardsville (IL)
Southern Methodist U (TX)
Southern New Hampshire U (NH)
Southern Oregon U (OR)
Southern Utah U (UT)
Southern Vermont Coll (VT)
Southwest Baptist U (MO)
Southwestern Adventist U (TX)
Southwestern Assemblies of God U (TX)
Southwestern Coll (KS)
Southwestern U (TX)
Southwest Minnesota State U (MN)
Spelman Coll (GA)
Spring Hill Coll (AL)
Stanford U (CA)
State U of New York at Fredonia (NY)
State U of New York at New Paltz (NY)
State U of New York at Oswego (NY)
State U of New York at Plattsburgh (NY)
State U of New York Coll at Cortland (NY)
State U of New York Coll at Geneseo (NY)
State U of New York Coll at Potsdam (NY)
Stephen F. Austin State U (TX)
Stephens Coll (MO)

Sterling Coll (KS)
Stetson U (FL)
Stevenson U (MD)
Stockton U (NJ)
Stonehill Coll (MA)
Stony Brook U, State U of New York (NY)
Suffolk U (MA)
Sul Ross State U (TX)
Susquehanna U (PA)
Syracuse U (NY)
Tabor Coll (KS)
Tarleton State U (TX)
Taylor U (IN)
Temple U (PA)
Tennessee State U (TN)
Tennessee Wesleyan Coll (TN)
Texas A&M Intl U (TX)
Texas A&M U (TX)
Texas A&M U–Commerce (TX)
Texas A&M U–Corpus Christi (TX)
Texas A&M U–Kingsville (TX)
Texas Christian U (TX)
Texas Lutheran U (TX)
Texas Southern U (TX)
Texas State U (TX)
Texas Tech U (TX)
Texas Wesleyan U (TX)
Texas Woman's U (TX)
Thiel Coll (PA)
Thomas More Coll (KY)
Tiffin U (OH)
Toccoa Falls Coll (GA)
Tougaloo Coll (MS)
Towson U (MD)
Transylvania U (KY)
Trent U (ON, Canada)
Trevecca Nazarene U (TN)
Trinity Christian Coll (IL)
Trinity Coll (CT)
Trinity U (TX)
Troy U (AL)
Truett-McConnell Coll (GA)
Truman State U (MO)
Tufts U (MA)
Tulane U (LA)
Tusculum Coll (TN)
Union Coll (KY)
Union Coll (NE)
Union Coll (NY)
Union U (TN)
United States Air Force Acad (CO)
United States Naval Acad (MD)
Université de Montréal (QC, Canada)
Université de Sherbrooke (QC, Canada)
U at Albany, State U of New York (NY)
U at Buffalo, the State U of New York (NY)
The U of Akron (OH)
The U of Alabama (AL)
The U of Alabama at Birmingham (AL)
The U of Alabama in Huntsville (AL)
U of Alaska Fairbanks (AK)
U of Alberta (AB, Canada)
The U of Arizona (AZ)
U of Arkansas (AR)
U of Arkansas at Little Rock (AR)
U of Arkansas at Pine Bluff (AR)
U of Arkansas–Fort Smith (AR)
U of Bridgeport (CT)
The U of British Columbia (BC, Canada)
The U of British Columbia–Okanagan Campus (BC, Canada)
U of California, Berkeley (CA)
U of California, Davis (CA)
U of California, Irvine (CA)
U of California, Los Angeles (CA)
U of California, Merced (CA)
U of California, Riverside (CA)
U of California, Santa Barbara (CA)
U of Central Arkansas (AR)
U of Central Florida (FL)
U of Central Missouri (MO)
U of Central Oklahoma (OK)
U of Charleston (WV)
U of Chicago (IL)
U of Colorado Boulder (CO)
U of Colorado Colorado Springs (CO)
U of Colorado Denver (CO)
U of Dallas (TX)
U of Dayton (OH)
U of Delaware (DE)
U of Denver (CO)
U of Dubuque (IA)
U of Evansville (IN)
The U of Findlay (OH)
U of Florida (FL)
U of Georgia (GA)
U of Great Falls (MT)
U of Guam (GU)
U of Guelph (ON, Canada)
U of Hartford (CT)
U of Hawaii at Hilo (HI)
U of Hawaii at Manoa (HI)
U of Hawaii–West Oahu (HI)
U of Houston (TX)
U of Houston–Clear Lake (TX)
U of Houston–Downtown (TX)
U of Houston–Victoria (TX)
U of Idaho (ID)
U of Illinois at Chicago (IL)
U of Illinois at Springfield (IL)
U of Indianapolis (IN)
The U of Iowa (IA)
U of Jamestown (ND)
The U of Kansas (KS)
U of Kentucky (KY)
U of King's Coll (NS, Canada)
U of La Verne (CA)
U of Lethbridge (AB, Canada)
U of Louisiana at Lafayette (LA)
U of Louisville (KY)
U of Maine (ME)
U of Maine at Fort Kent (ME)
U of Maine at Machias (ME)
U of Maine at Presque Isle (ME)
U of Mary Hardin-Baylor (TX)
U of Maryland, Baltimore County (MD)
U of Maryland, Coll Park (MD)
U of Maryland U Coll (MD)
U of Mary Washington (VA)
U of Massachusetts Amherst (MA)
U of Massachusetts Boston (MA)
U of Massachusetts Dartmouth (MA)
U of Massachusetts Lowell (MA)
U of Memphis (TN)
U of Miami (FL)
U of Michigan (MI)
U of Michigan–Dearborn (MI)
U of Michigan–Flint (MI)
U of Minnesota, Duluth (MN)
U of Minnesota, Morris (MN)
U of Minnesota, Twin Cities Campus (MN)
U of Mississippi (MS)
U of Missouri (MO)
U of Missouri–Kansas City (MO)
U of Missouri–St. Louis (MO)
U of Mobile (AL)
The U of Montana (MT)
The U of Montana Western (MT)
U of Montevallo (AL)
U of Mount Union (OH)
U of Nebraska at Kearney (NE)
U of Nebraska–Lincoln (NE)
U of Nevada, Las Vegas (NV)
U of Nevada, Reno (NV)
U of New Brunswick Saint John (NB, Canada)
U of New England (ME)
U of New Hampshire (NH)
U of New Hampshire at Manchester (NH)
U of New Haven (CT)
U of New Mexico (NM)
U of New Orleans (LA)
U of North Alabama (AL)
U of North Carolina at Asheville (NC)
The U of North Carolina at Chapel Hill (NC)
The U of North Carolina at Charlotte (NC)
The U of North Carolina at Greensboro (NC)
The U of North Carolina at Pembroke (NC)
The U of North Carolina Wilmington (NC)
U of North Dakota (ND)
U of Northern Colorado (CO)
U of Northern Iowa (IA)
U of North Florida (FL)
U of North Georgia (GA)
U of North Texas (TX)
U of Northwestern–St. Paul (MN)
U of Notre Dame (IN)
U of Oklahoma (OK)
U of Oregon (OR)
U of Ottawa (ON, Canada)
U of Pennsylvania (PA)
U of Pikeville (KY)
U of Pittsburgh at Bradford (PA)
U of Pittsburgh at Greensburg (PA)
U of Portland (OR)
U of Puget Sound (WA)
U of Regina (SK, Canada)
U of Rhode Island (RI)
U of Richmond (VA)
U of Rio Grande (OH)
U of Rochester (NY)
U of St. Francis (IL)
U of Saint Francis (IN)
U of Saint Joseph (CT)
U of Saint Mary (KS)
U of St. Thomas (MN)
U of St. Thomas (TX)
U of San Diego (CA)
U of San Francisco (CA)
U of Saskatchewan (SK, Canada)
U of Science and Arts of Oklahoma (OK)
The U of Scranton (PA)
U of South Alabama (AL)
U of South Carolina Aiken (SC)
U of South Carolina Beaufort (SC)
U of South Carolina Upstate (SC)
The U of South Dakota (SD)
U of Southern California (CA)
U of Southern Indiana (IN)
U of Southern Maine (ME)
U of Southern Mississippi (MS)
U of South Florida (FL)
U of South Florida, St. Petersburg (FL)
U of South Florida Sarasota-Manatee (FL)
The U of Tampa (FL)
The U of Tennessee (TN)
The U of Tennessee at Chattanooga (TN)
The U of Tennessee at Martin (TN)
The U of Texas at Arlington (TX)
The U of Texas at Austin (TX)
The U of Texas at El Paso (TX)
The U of Texas at San Antonio (TX)
The U of Texas at Tyler (TX)
The U of Texas of the Permian Basin (TX)
The U of Texas–Pan American (TX)
U of the Cumberlands (KY)
U of the District of Columbia (DC)
U of the Fraser Valley (BC, Canada)
U of the Incarnate Word (TX)
U of the Pacific (CA)
U of the Virgin Islands (VI)
U of the West (CA)
The U of Toledo (OH)
U of Toronto (ON, Canada)
The U of Tulsa (OK)
U of Utah (UT)
U of Valley Forge (PA)
U of Vermont (VT)
U of Virginia (VA)
The U of Virginia's Coll at Wise (VA)
U of Washington (WA)
U of Waterloo (ON, Canada)
The U of West Alabama (AL)
The U of Western Ontario (ON, Canada)
U of West Florida (FL)
U of West Georgia (GA)
U of Windsor (ON, Canada)
U of Wisconsin–Eau Claire (WI)
U of Wisconsin–Green Bay (WI)
U of Wisconsin–La Crosse (WI)
U of Wisconsin–Madison (WI)
U of Wisconsin–Milwaukee (WI)
U of Wisconsin–Oshkosh (WI)
U of Wisconsin–Parkside (WI)
U of Wisconsin–Platteville (WI)
U of Wisconsin–River Falls (WI)
U of Wisconsin–Stevens Point (WI)
U of Wisconsin–Superior (WI)
U of Wisconsin–Whitewater (WI)
U of Wyoming (WY)
Upper Iowa U (IA)
Urbana U (OH)
Ursinus Coll (PA)
Ursuline Coll (OH)
Utah State U (UT)
Utah Valley U (UT)
Utica Coll (NY)
Valdosta State U (GA)
Valley City State U (ND)
Valparaiso U (IN)
Vanderbilt U (TN)
Vanguard U of Southern California (CA)
Vassar Coll (NY)
Villanova U (PA)
Virginia Commonwealth U (VA)
Virginia Military Inst (VA)
Virginia Polytechnic Inst and State U (VA)
Virginia State U (VA)
Virginia Union U (VA)
Virginia Wesleyan Coll (VA)
Viterbo U (WI)
Wabash Coll (IN)
Wagner Coll (NY)
Wake Forest U (NC)
Waldorf Coll (IA)
Walla Walla U (WA)
Walsh U (OH)
Warner Pacific Coll (OR)
Warren Wilson Coll (NC)
Wartburg Coll (IA)
Washburn U (KS)
Washington & Jefferson Coll (PA)
Washington and Lee U (VA)
Washington Coll (MD)
Washington State U (WA)
Washington State U Vancouver (WA)
Washington U in St. Louis (MO)
Waynesburg U (PA)
Wayne State Coll (NE)
Wayne State U (MI)
Weber State U (UT)
Webster U (MO)
Welch Coll (TN)
Wells Coll (NY)
Wesleyan Coll (GA)
Wesleyan U (CT)
West Chester U of Pennsylvania (PA)
Western Carolina U (NC)
Western Illinois U (IL)
Western Kentucky U (KY)
Western Michigan U (MI)
Western New England U (MA)
Western Oregon U (OR)
Western State Colorado U (CO)
Western Washington U (WA)
Westfield State U (MA)
West Liberty U (WV)
Westminster Coll (MO)
Westminster Coll (UT)
West Texas A&M U (TX)
West Virginia State U (WV)
West Virginia U (WV)
West Virginia Wesleyan Coll (WV)
Wheaton Coll (IL)
Wheaton Coll (MA)
Wheeling Jesuit U (WV)
Whitman Coll (WA)
Whittier Coll (CA)
Whitworth U (WA)
Wichita State U (KS)
Widener U (PA)
Wilkes U (PA)
Willamette U (OR)
William Jessup U (CA)
William Jewell Coll (MO)
William Paterson U of New Jersey (NJ)
William Peace U (NC)
William Penn U (IA)
Williams Baptist Coll (AR)
Williams Coll (MA)
William Woods U (MO)
Wingate U (NC)
Winona State U (MN)
Winthrop U (SC)
Wittenberg U (OH)
Wofford Coll (SC)
Worcester State U (MA)
Wright State U (OH)
Xavier U (OH)
Xavier U of Louisiana (LA)
Yale U (CT)
Yeshiva U (NY)
York Coll of Pennsylvania (PA)
York Coll of the City U of New York (NY)
Youngstown State U (OH)

ENGLISH AS A SECOND/ FOREIGN LANGUAGE (TEACHING)

American U (DC)
Augsburg Coll (MN)
Bethel U (MN)
Brigham Young U (UT)
California State U, Stanislaus (CA)
Calvin Coll (MI)
Carroll Coll (MT)
The Catholic U of America (DC)
Concordia U (QC, Canada)
Concordia U, Nebraska (NE)
Concordia U, St. Paul (MN)
Concordia U Wisconsin (WI)
Davis Coll (NY)
Doane Coll (NE)
Dowling Coll (NY)
Goshen Coll (IN)
Granite State Coll (NH)
Hawai`i Pacific U (HI)
Houghton Coll (NY)
Inter American U of Puerto Rico, Aguadilla Campus (PR)
Inter American U of Puerto Rico, Fajardo Campus (PR)
Inter American U of Puerto Rico, Guayama Campus (PR)
Inter American U of Puerto Rico, Ponce Campus (PR)
Inter American U of Puerto Rico, San Germán Campus (PR)
Kent State U (OH)
Langston U (OK)
Lebanese American U (Lebanon)
Lee U (TN)
Le Moyne Coll (NY)
Lenoir-Rhyne U (NC)
Liberty U (VA)
Maryville Coll (TN)
Minnesota State U Moorhead (MN)
Multnomah U (OR)
Niagara U (NY)
Northwest U (WA)
Nyack Coll (NY)
Oklahoma Christian U (OK)
Oklahoma City U (OK)
Queens Coll of the City U of New York (NY)
Saint Joseph's U (PA)
Salisbury U (MD)
Simmons Coll (MA)
Southern Adventist U (TN)
Stony Brook U, State U of New York (NY)
Tarleton State U (TX)
Union U (TN)
The U of British Columbia (BC, Canada)
The U of Findlay (OH)
U of Guam (GU)
U of Hawaii at Manoa (HI)
U of Minnesota, Twin Cities Campus (MN)
The U of Montana (MT)
U of Nebraska–Lincoln (NE)
U of New Brunswick Saint John (NB, Canada)
U of Northern Iowa (IA)
U of Northwestern–St. Paul (MN)
The U of Texas at San Antonio (TX)
U of Wisconsin–Oshkosh (WI)
U of Wisconsin–River Falls (WI)
Washington State U (WA)
Wichita State U (KS)
Winona State U (MN)
Wright State U (OH)

ENGLISH/FRENCH AS A SECOND/FOREIGN LANGUAGE (TEACHING) RELATED

U of Ottawa (ON, Canada)

ENGLISH LANGUAGE AND LITERATURE RELATED

Binghamton U, State U of New York (NY)
Columbia U, School of General Studies (NY)
Concordia Coll–New York (NY)
Dakota State U (SD)
Doane Coll (NE)
Drexel U (PA)
Eastern U (PA)

Emmanuel Coll (MA)
Fort Lewis Coll (CO)
Harvard U (MA)
Hastings Coll (NE)
Heritage U (WA)
Hofstra U (NY)
Middlebury Coll (VT)
Milligan Coll (TN)
Ohio U (OH)
Olivet Coll (MI)
Patrick Henry Coll (VA)
Purdue U (IN)
Rowan U (NJ)
Saint Leo U (FL)
Saint Mary's U of Minnesota (MN)
State U of New York Empire State Coll (NY)
Thiel Coll (PA)
U of Great Falls (MT)
U of Maine at Augusta (ME)
U of Michigan (MI)
U of Pennsylvania (PA)
Viterbo U (WI)
Washington U in St. Louis (MO)
Webster U (MO)
Wesleyan U (CT)
Western Kentucky U (KY)

ENGLISH/LANGUAGE ARTS TEACHER EDUCATION
Abilene Christian U (TX)
Adams State U (CO)
Albion Coll (MI)
Alice Lloyd Coll (KY)
Alma Coll (MI)
Alvernia U (PA)
Alverno Coll (WI)
Anderson U (IN)
Anderson U (SC)
Anna Maria Coll (MA)
Appalachian State U (NC)
Aquinas Coll (MI)
Aquinas Coll (TN)
Arizona Christian U (AZ)
Arkansas State U (AR)
Arkansas Tech U (AR)
Auburn U (AL)
Augustana Coll (IL)
Averett U (VA)
The Baptist Coll of Florida (FL)
Barry U (FL)
Baylor U (TX)
Bennett Coll (NC)
Bethany Coll (WV)
Bethel Coll (IN)
Bethel U (MN)
Bethune-Cookman U (FL)
Blackburn Coll (IL)
Bluefield Coll (VA)
Blue Mountain Coll (MS)
Bob Jones U (SC)
Boston U (MA)
Bowling Green State U (OH)
Bradley U (IL)
Bridgewater State U (MA)
Bryan Coll (TN)
Buena Vista U (IA)
Buffalo State Coll, State U of New York (NY)
Cabrini Coll (PA)
Cairn U (PA)
California State U, Long Beach (CA)
Calumet Coll of Saint Joseph (IN)
Cameron U (OK)
Campbellsville U (KY)
Canisius Coll (NY)
Capital U (OH)
Carroll Coll (MT)
The Catholic U of America (DC)
Cedarville U (OH)
Central Michigan U (MI)
Central Washington U (WA)
Charleston Southern U (SC)
Claflin U (SC)
Clearwater Christian Coll (FL)
Coker Coll (SC)
Colby-Sawyer Coll (NH)
The Coll of New Jersey (NJ)
Coll of Saint Mary (NE)
The Coll of Saint Rose (NY)
Coll of Staten Island of the City U of New York (NY)
Coll of the Ozarks (MO)
Colorado State U (CO)
Columbus State U (GA)
Concordia U Chicago (IL)
Concordia U, Nebraska (NE)
Corban U (OR)
Cornerstone U (MI)
Covenant Coll (GA)
Culver-Stockton Coll (MO)
Daemen Coll (NY)
Dakota State U (SD)
Dallas Baptist U (TX)
Delaware State U (DE)
Delta State U (MS)
Dixie State U (UT)
Dominican Coll (NY)
Dowling Coll (NY)
Duquesne U (PA)
East Carolina U (NC)
East Central U (OK)
Eastern Kentucky U (KY)
Eastern Michigan U (MI)
East Texas Baptist U (TX)
Edgewood Coll (WI)
Elmhurst Coll (IL)
Elmira Coll (NY)
Emmanuel Coll (GA)
Emory & Henry Coll (VA)
Faith Baptist Bible Coll and Theological Sem (IA)
Fayetteville State U (NC)
Ferris State U (MI)
Fitchburg State U (MA)
Flagler Coll (FL)
Florida Ag and Mech U (FL)
Florida Atlantic U (FL)
Florida SouthWestern State Coll (FL)
Fordham U (NY)
Fort Lewis Coll (CO)
Franklin Coll (IN)
Friends U (KS)
Goddard Coll (VT)
Grace Coll (IN)
Grambling State U (LA)
Grand Valley State U (MI)
Grand View U (IA)
Granite State Coll (NH)
Green Mountain Coll (VT)
Greensboro Coll (NC)
Greenville Coll (IL)
Hannibal-LaGrange U (MO)
Harding U (AR)
Hardin-Simmons U (TX)
Hastings Coll (NE)
Heritage U (WA)
Hobe Sound Bible Coll (FL)
Hofstra U (NY)
Holy Family U (PA)
Hope Coll (MI)
Houston Baptist U (TX)
Howard Payne U (TX)
Huntingdon Coll (AL)
Husson U (ME)
Indiana U Bloomington (IN)
Indiana U Northwest (IN)
Indiana U–Purdue U Fort Wayne (IN)
Indiana U–Purdue U Indianapolis (IN)
Indiana U South Bend (IN)
Indiana U Southeast (IN)
Inter American U of Puerto Rico, San Germán Campus (PR)
Iona Coll (NY)
Ithaca Coll (NY)
Johnson State Coll (VT)
Judson Coll (AL)
Juniata Coll (PA)
Kansas Wesleyan U (KS)
Keene State Coll (NH)
Kennesaw State U (GA)
Kentucky Christian U (KY)
Keuka Coll (NY)
Keystone Coll (PA)
King U (TN)
La Roche Coll (PA)
Lee U (TN)
Le Moyne Coll (NY)
LeMoyne-Owen Coll (TN)
LeTourneau U (TX)
Limestone Coll (SC)
Lincoln U (MO)
Lincoln U (PA)
Lipscomb U (TN)
Long Island U–LIU Brooklyn (NY)
Long Island U–LIU Post (NY)
Louisiana State U in Shreveport (LA)
Madonna U (MI)
Malone U (OH)
Manchester U (IN)
Manhattanville Coll (NY)
Mansfield U of Pennsylvania (PA)
Maranatha Baptist U (WI)
Marian U (WI)
Marist Coll (NY)
Maryville Coll (TN)
Marywood U (PA)
Mayville State U (ND)
McKendree U (IL)
McMurry U (TX)
Medaille Coll (NY)
Merrimack Coll (MA)
Messiah Coll (PA)
Metropolitan State U (MN)
Miami U (OH)
MidAmerica Nazarene U (KS)
Midwestern State U (TX)
Millikin U (IL)
Minnesota State U Moorhead (MN)
Minot State U (ND)
Misericordia U (PA)
Missouri State U (MO)
Missouri Western State U (MO)
Montana State U Billings (MT)
Morningside Coll (IA)
Morris Coll (SC)
Mount Marty Coll (SD)
Mount Mary U (WI)
Mount Vernon Nazarene U (OH)
National U (CA)
Nazareth Coll of Rochester (NY)
Nebraska Wesleyan U (NE)
Nicholls State U (LA)
North Carolina Ag and Tech State U (NC)
North Carolina State U (NC)
North Dakota State U (ND)
Northeastern State U (OK)
Northern Michigan U (MI)
North Greenville U (SC)
Northwestern Coll (IA)
Northwestern Oklahoma State U (OK)
Northwest Missouri State U (MO)
Northwest Nazarene U (ID)
Northwest U (WA)
Nova Southeastern U (FL)
Nyack Coll (NY)
Ohio Dominican U (OH)
Ohio Northern U (OH)
The Ohio State U at Lima (OH)
The Ohio State U at Marion (OH)
The Ohio State U–Mansfield Campus (OH)
The Ohio State U–Newark Campus (OH)
Oklahoma Baptist U (OK)
Oklahoma Christian U (OK)
Oklahoma City U (OK)
Oklahoma Wesleyan U (OK)
Pace U (NY)
Palm Beach Atlantic U (FL)
Pepperdine U, Malibu (CA)
Peru State Coll (NE)
Piedmont Coll (GA)
Pittsburg State U (KS)
Providence Coll (RI)
Purdue U (IN)
Reinhardt U (GA)
Rhode Island Coll (RI)
Rivier U (NH)
Roberts Wesleyan Coll (NY)
Rocky Mountain Coll (MT)
Rust Coll (MS)
Saginaw Valley State U (MI)
St. Catherine U (MN)
St. Edward's U (TX)
St. Francis Coll (NY)
Saint Francis U (PA)
St. Gregory's U, Shawnee (OK)
St. John Fisher Coll (NY)
St. John's U (NY)
St. Joseph's Coll, Long Island Campus (NY)
St. Joseph's Coll, New York (NY)
Saint Mary's U of Minnesota (MN)
Samford U (AL)
Seattle Pacific U (WA)
Seton Hill U (PA)
Shaw U (NC)
Simpson U (CA)
Southeastern Louisiana U (LA)
Southeastern Oklahoma State U (OK)
Southeastern U (FL)
Southeast Missouri State U (MO)
Southern Adventist U (TN)
Southern New Hampshire U (NH)
Southern Utah U (UT)
Southwest Baptist U (MO)
Southwestern Assemblies of God U (TX)
Southwestern Coll (KS)
Southwest Minnesota State U (MN)
Spring Hill Coll (AL)
State U of New York at New Paltz (NY)
State U of New York at Plattsburgh (NY)
State U of New York Coll at Potsdam (NY)
Syracuse U (NY)
Tabor Coll (KS)
Taylor U (IN)
Temple U (PA)
Texas A&M Intl U (TX)
Texas Christian U (TX)
Texas Wesleyan U (TX)
Tiffin U (OH)
Toccoa Falls Coll (GA)
Trevecca Nazarene U (TN)
Trinity Christian Coll (IL)
Tusculum Coll (TN)
Union Coll (NE)
Universidad del Turabo (PR)
Universidad Metropolitana (PR)
The U of Akron (OH)
U of Alberta (AB, Canada)
U of Arkansas–Fort Smith (AR)
U of Central Florida (FL)
U of Central Oklahoma (OK)
U of Delaware (DE)
U of Dubuque (IA)
U of Evansville (IN)
U of Georgia (GA)
U of Great Falls (MT)
U of Idaho (ID)
U of Illinois at Chicago (IL)
U of Indianapolis (IN)
U of Jamestown (ND)
U of Lethbridge (AB, Canada)
U of Maine at Machias (ME)
U of Mary Hardin-Baylor (TX)
U of Michigan–Flint (MI)
U of Minnesota, Twin Cities Campus (MN)
U of Mississippi (MS)
U of Mobile (AL)
The U of Montana Western (MT)
U of Nebraska–Lincoln (NE)
The U of North Carolina at Greensboro (NC)
The U of North Carolina at Pembroke (NC)
The U of North Carolina Wilmington (NC)
U of Northwestern–St. Paul (MN)
U of Oklahoma (OK)
U of Regina (SK, Canada)
U of Rio Grande (OH)
U of St. Francis (IL)
U of Saint Francis (IN)
U of St. Thomas (MN)
The U of South Dakota (SD)
U of South Florida (FL)
The U of Tennessee at Chattanooga (TN)
The U of Tennessee at Martin (TN)
The U of Toledo (OH)
U of Vermont (VT)
U of Windsor (ON, Canada)
U of Wisconsin–River Falls (WI)
U of Wisconsin–Superior (WI)
Ursuline Coll (OH)
Utah Valley U (UT)
Utica Coll (NY)
Valley City State U (ND)
Valparaiso U (IN)
Viterbo U (WI)
Washburn U (KS)
Washington State U (WA)
Washington U in St. Louis (MO)
Waynesburg U (PA)
Wayne State Coll (NE)
Wayne State U (MI)
Weber State U (UT)
Webster U (MO)
Welch Coll (TN)
Western Carolina U (NC)
Western Michigan U (MI)
Western State Colorado U (CO)
Western Washington U (WA)
West Virginia Wesleyan Coll (WV)
Widener U (PA)
William Woods U (MO)
Wilmington U (DE)
Wingate U (NC)
Winona State U (MN)
York Coll of Pennsylvania (PA)
Youngstown State U (OH)

ENGLISH LITERATURE (BRITISH AND COMMONWEALTH)
Ambrose U Coll (AB, Canada)
American U of Beirut (Lebanon)
Bennington Coll (VT)
Concordia U (QC, Canada)
Excelsior Coll (NY)
Gannon U (PA)
Hunter Coll of the City U of New York (NY)
Indiana U–Purdue U Fort Wayne (IN)
Marian U (WI)
New York U (NY)
Pace U (NY)
Saint Mary's Coll (IN)
U of Pittsburgh (PA)
Washington U in St. Louis (MO)
Whittier Coll (CA)

ENTOMOLOGY
Cornell U (NY)
Iowa State U of Science and Technology (IA)
Michigan State U (MI)
The Ohio State U (OH)
Oklahoma State U (OK)
State U of New York Coll of Environmental Science and Forestry (NY)
Texas A&M U (TX)
U of California, Davis (CA)
U of California, Riverside (CA)
U of Delaware (DE)
U of Florida (FL)
U of Georgia (GA)
U of Minnesota, Twin Cities Campus (MN)
U of Nebraska–Lincoln (NE)
U of Wisconsin–Madison (WI)
Utah State U (UT)

ENTREPRENEURIAL AND SMALL BUSINESS RELATED
Babson Coll (MA)
Fairleigh Dickinson U, Coll at Florham (NJ)
Fairleigh Dickinson U, Metropolitan Campus (NJ)
Fashion Inst of Technology (NY)
Florida State U (FL)
Lipscomb U (TN)
Loyola U Chicago (IL)
New York Inst of Technology (NY)
State U of New York at Plattsburgh (NY)

ENTREPRENEURSHIP
American Public U System (WV)
The American U of Paris (France)
Anderson U (IN)
Arizona State U at the Tempe campus (AZ)
Ashland U (OH)
Avila U (MO)
Babson Coll (MA)
Baldwin Wallace U (OH)
Ball State U (IN)
Baylor U (TX)
Belmont U (TN)
Binghamton U, State U of New York (NY)
Bradley U (IL)
Brigham Young U (UT)
Bryant U (RI)
Buena Vista U (IA)
Butler U (IN)
California State U, Dominguez Hills (CA)
California State U, Fullerton (CA)
Canisius Coll (NY)
Cape Breton U (NS, Canada)
Central Michigan U (MI)
Clarkson U (NY)
Cogswell Polytechnical Coll (CA)
Coll of the Atlantic (ME)
Creighton U (NE)
Dalhousie U (NS, Canada)
Drexel U (PA)

Duquesne U (PA)
Eastern Michigan U (MI)
Eastern U (PA)
Ellis U (IL)
Elon U (NC)
Endicott Coll (MA)
Fairleigh Dickinson U, Coll at Florham (NJ)
Franklin U (OH)
Gannon U (PA)
Governors State U (IL)
Grove City Coll (PA)
Hampshire Coll (MA)
Hawai`i Pacific U (HI)
HEC Montreal (QC, Canada)
High Point U (NC)
Hofstra U (NY)
Hult Intl Business School (United Kingdom)
Husson U (ME)
Inter American U of Puerto Rico, Aguadilla Campus (PR)
Inter American U of Puerto Rico, Bayamón Campus (PR)
Inter American U of Puerto Rico, Ponce Campus (PR)
Inter American U of Puerto Rico, San Germán Campus (PR)
Iowa State U of Science and Technology (IA)
Jackson State U (MS)
John Paul the Great Catholic U (CA)
Johnson & Wales U (CO)
Johnson & Wales U (RI)
Juniata Coll (PA)
Kansas State U (KS)
Kent State U (OH)
Lake Erie Coll (OH)
Lamar U (TX)
Lasell Coll (MA)
Lenoir-Rhyne U (NC)
Lindenwood U (MO)
Lipscomb U (TN)
Loyola Marymount U (CA)
Lynn U (FL)
Marquette U (WI)
Mars Hill U (NC)
Marymount Manhattan Coll (NY)
Menlo Coll (CA)
Mercy Coll (NY)
Millikin U (IL)
Missouri State U (MO)
Morrisville State Coll (NY)
Northeastern State U (OK)
Northeastern U (MA)
Northern Kentucky U (KY)
Northern Michigan U (MI)
Northland Coll (WI)
Northwood U, Michigan Campus (MI)
Ohio Northern U (OH)
Oklahoma State U (OK)
Pace U (NY)
Point Loma Nazarene U (CA)
Quinnipiac U (CT)
Reinhardt U (GA)
Rider U (NJ)
Rowan U (NJ)
St. Edward's U (TX)
St. Mary's U (TX)
Saint Mary's U of Minnesota (MN)
Samford U (AL)
Sam Houston State U (TX)
Seton Hill U (PA)
Shenandoah U (VA)
South Dakota State U (SD)
Southern Vermont Coll (VT)
Stetson U (FL)
Suffolk U (MA)
Syracuse U (NY)
Temple U (PA)
Trine U (IN)
Trinity Christian Coll (IL)
Universidad Metropolitana (PR)
U of Alberta (AB, Canada)
The U of Arizona (AZ)
The U of British Columbia–Okanagan Campus (BC, Canada)
U of Central Arkansas (AR)
U of Dayton (OH)
U of Hartford (CT)
U of Hawaii at Manoa (HI)
U of Houston (TX)
U of Illinois at Chicago (IL)
U of Indianapolis (IN)
U of Maine at Machias (ME)
U of Massachusetts Lowell (MA)
U of Miami (FL)
U of Minnesota, Crookston (MN)
U of Minnesota, Duluth (MN)
U of Nevada, Las Vegas (NV)
The U of North Carolina at Greensboro (NC)
The U of North Carolina at Pembroke (NC)
U of North Dakota (ND)
U of North Texas (TX)
U of Notre Dame (IN)
U of Ottawa (ON, Canada)
U of Pittsburgh at Bradford (PA)
U of Regina (SK, Canada)
U of St. Francis (IL)
U of St. Thomas (MN)
U of San Francisco (CA)
U of Southern Indiana (IN)
U of South Florida, St. Petersburg (FL)
The U of Tampa (FL)
The U of Texas at San Antonio (TX)
The U of Toledo (OH)
U of Utah (UT)
U of Valley Forge (PA)
U of Vermont (VT)
U of Washington (WA)
The U of Western Ontario (ON, Canada)
U of Wisconsin–Whitewater (WI)
Virginia Union U (VA)
Washington State U (WA)
Washington U in St. Louis (MO)
Waynesburg U (PA)
Western Carolina U (NC)
Western Kentucky U (KY)
Western New England U (MA)
Western State Colorado U (CO)
Wichita State U (KS)
Wilkes U (PA)
Wittenberg U (OH)
Xavier U (OH)
York Coll of Pennsylvania (PA)

ENVIRONMENTAL BIOLOGY
Arcadia U (PA)
Barnard Coll (NY)
Beloit Coll (WI)
Bennington Coll (VT)
Blackburn Coll (IL)
Boston U (MA)
Bridgewater State U (MA)
California State Polytechnic U, Pomona (CA)
Cedar Crest Coll (PA)
Central Methodist U (MO)
Central Washington U (WA)
Chowan U (NC)
Christopher Newport U (VA)
Colby Coll (ME)
Coll of the Atlantic (ME)
Columbia U (NY)
Columbia U, School of General Studies (NY)
Cornerstone U (MI)
East Stroudsburg U of Pennsylvania (PA)
Elizabethtown Coll (PA)
Ferris State U (MI)
Fitchburg State U (MA)
Fort Lewis Coll (CO)
Franklin Pierce U (NH)
Friends U (KS)
Grace Coll (IN)
Greenville Coll (IL)
Heidelberg U (OH)
Houghton Coll (NY)
Humboldt State U (CA)
Inter American U of Puerto Rico, Bayamón Campus (PR)
Iona Coll (NY)
Jacksonville State U (AL)
Keystone Coll (PA)
Liberty U (VA)
Lindenwood U (MO)
Manchester U (IN)
The Master's Coll and Sem (CA)
McDaniel Coll (MD)
Michigan State U (MI)
Minnesota State U Mankato (MN)
Monmouth U (NJ)
Philadelphia U (PA)
Plymouth State U (NH)
Roberts Wesleyan Coll (NY)
Saint Mary's U of Minnesota (MN)
Sewanee: The U of the South (TN)
State U of New York Coll at Cortland (NY)
State U of New York Coll of Environmental Science and Forestry (NY)
Texas A&M U (TX)
Tulane U (LA)
Unity Coll (ME)
U of Alberta (AB, Canada)
The U of British Columbia (BC, Canada)
U of Dayton (OH)
U of Dubuque (IA)
U of Guelph (ON, Canada)
U of La Verne (CA)
U of Mount Union (OH)
U of New Brunswick Saint John (NB, Canada)
U of Regina (SK, Canada)
U of Saskatchewan (SK, Canada)
The U of Tennessee at Martin (TN)
U of Windsor (ON, Canada)
Viterbo U (WI)
Washington U in St. Louis (MO)
Western State Colorado U (CO)
William Penn U (IA)
Wingate U (NC)

ENVIRONMENTAL CHEMISTRY
Beloit Coll (WI)
Cardinal Stritch U (WI)
Castleton State Coll (VT)
Central Washington U (WA)
Colby Coll (ME)
Columbia U, School of General Studies (NY)
Lawrence Technological U (MI)
Rhode Island Coll (RI)
Roberts Wesleyan Coll (NY)
St. Edward's U (TX)
The U of British Columbia–Okanagan Campus (BC, Canada)
U of Georgia (GA)

ENVIRONMENTAL CONTROL TECHNOLOGIES RELATED
Delaware State U (DE)

ENVIRONMENTAL DESIGN/ ARCHITECTURE
Arizona State U at the Tempe campus (AZ)
Art Center Coll of Design (CA)
Auburn U (AL)
Ball State U (IN)
Bennington Coll (VT)
Boston Architectural Coll (MA)
Bowling Green State U (OH)
Coll of the Atlantic (ME)
Cornell U (NY)
Dalhousie U (NS, Canada)
Florida Atlantic U (FL)
Green Mountain Coll (VT)
Lawrence Technological U (MI)
Marywood U (PA)
Montana State U (MT)
North Carolina State U (NC)
North Dakota State U (ND)
Olivet Nazarene U (IL)
Otis Coll of Art and Design (CA)
Rutgers, The State U of New Jersey, New Brunswick (NJ)
State U of New York Coll of Environmental Science and Forestry (NY)
Stony Brook U, State U of New York (NY)
Syracuse U (NY)
U at Buffalo, the State U of New York (NY)
U of Colorado Boulder (CO)
U of Hawaii at Manoa (HI)
U of Houston (TX)
U of Massachusetts Amherst (MA)
U of Memphis (TN)
U of Minnesota, Twin Cities Campus (MN)
U of Missouri–Kansas City (MO)
U of New Mexico (NM)
U of Oklahoma (OK)
U of Pennsylvania (PA)

ENVIRONMENTAL EDUCATION
Coll of the Atlantic (ME)
Johnson State Coll (VT)
Prescott Coll (AZ)
State U of New York Coll of Environmental Science and Forestry (NY)
U of Maine at Machias (ME)
The U of Montana (MT)
Wright State U (OH)

ENVIRONMENTAL ENGINEERING TECHNOLOGY
Bowling Green State U (OH)
Brown U (RI)
California State U, Long Beach (CA)
City Coll of the City U of New York (NY)
Middle Tennessee State U (TN)
North Carolina State U (NC)
Shawnee State U (OH)
Tufts U (MA)
United States Military Acad (NY)
The U of British Columbia (BC, Canada)
U of Guelph (ON, Canada)
U of Wisconsin–Whitewater (WI)

ENVIRONMENTAL/ ENVIRONMENTAL HEALTH ENGINEERING
Arizona State U at the Polytechnic campus (AZ)
Bucknell U (PA)
California Polytechnic State U, San Luis Obispo (CA)
Central State U (OH)
Clarkson U (NY)
Colorado School of Mines (CO)
Colorado State U (CO)
Columbia U (NY)
Cornell U (NY)
Dalhousie U (NS, Canada)
Drexel U (PA)
Elon U (NC)
Florida Gulf Coast U (FL)
Florida Intl U (FL)
Gannon U (PA)
The George Washington U (DC)
Georgia Inst of Technology (GA)
Humboldt State U (CA)
Johns Hopkins U (MD)
Lafayette Coll (PA)
Lehigh U (PA)
Louisiana State U and A&M Coll (LA)
Manhattan Coll (NY)
Marquette U (WI)
Massachusetts Inst of Technology (MA)
Massachusetts Maritime Acad (MA)
Michigan Technological U (MI)
Missouri U of Science and Technology (MO)
Montana Tech of The U of Montana (MT)
New Jersey Inst of Technology (NJ)
New Mexico Inst of Mining and Technology (NM)
North Carolina State U (NC)
Northern Arizona U (AZ)
Northwestern U (IL)
The Ohio State U (OH)
Old Dominion U (VA)
Oregon State U (OR)
Penn State Abington (PA)
Penn State Altoona (PA)
Penn State Beaver (PA)
Penn State Berks (PA)
Penn State Brandywine (PA)
Penn State DuBois (PA)
Penn State Erie, The Behrend Coll (PA)
Penn State Fayette, The Eberly Campus (PA)
Penn State Greater Allegheny (PA)
Penn State Harrisburg (PA)
Penn State Hazleton (PA)
Penn State Lehigh Valley (PA)
Penn State Mont Alto (PA)
Penn State New Kensington (PA)
Penn State Schuylkill (PA)
Penn State Shenango (PA)
Penn State U Park (PA)
Penn State Wilkes-Barre (PA)
Penn State Worthington Scranton (PA)
Penn State York (PA)
Polytechnic U of Puerto Rico (PR)
Purdue U (IN)
Rensselaer Polytechnic Inst (NY)
Rice U (TX)
San Diego State U (CA)
Seattle U (WA)
South Dakota School of Mines and Technology (SD)
Southern Methodist U (TX)
Stanford U (CA)
State U of New York Coll of Environmental Science and Forestry (NY)
Suffolk U (MA)
Syracuse U (NY)
Tarleton State U (TX)
Taylor U (IN)
Texas A&M U–Kingsville (TX)
Texas Tech U (TX)
Tufts U (MA)
Tulane U (LA)
United States Air Force Acad (CO)
United States Military Acad (NY)
U at Buffalo, the State U of New York (NY)
The U of Alabama (AL)
U of California, Berkeley (CA)
U of California, Irvine (CA)
U of California, Merced (CA)
U of California, Riverside (CA)
U of Central Florida (FL)
U of Cincinnati (OH)
U of Colorado Boulder (CO)
U of Delaware (DE)
U of Florida (FL)
U of Georgia (GA)
U of Miami (FL)
U of Michigan (MI)
U of Nevada, Reno (NV)
U of North Dakota (ND)
U of Notre Dame (IN)
U of Oklahoma (OK)
U of Pennsylvania (PA)
U of Regina (SK, Canada)
U of Saskatchewan (SK, Canada)
U of Southern California (CA)
U of Vermont (VT)
U of Waterloo (ON, Canada)
The U of Western Ontario (ON, Canada)
U of Windsor (ON, Canada)
U of Wisconsin–Platteville (WI)
Utah State U (UT)
Wilkes U (PA)
Worcester Polytechnic Inst (MA)
Yale U (CT)

ENVIRONMENTAL HEALTH
American U of Beirut (Lebanon)
Baylor U (TX)
Bowling Green State U (OH)
Central Michigan U (MI)
Colorado State U (CO)
Drury U (MO)
East Carolina U (NC)
East Central U (OK)
Eastern Kentucky U (KY)
East Tennessee State U (TN)
Illinois State U (IL)
Mississippi Valley State U (MS)
Missouri Southern State U (MO)
Oakland U (MI)
Ohio U (OH)
State U of New York Coll of Environmental Science and Forestry (NY)
Texas Southern U (TX)
U of Arkansas at Little Rock (AR)
U of Georgia (GA)
U of Massachusetts Lowell (MA)
The U of North Carolina at Chapel Hill (NC)
U of Regina (SK, Canada)
U of Washington (WA)
Western Carolina U (NC)
Western Kentucky U (KY)
Wright State U (OH)
York Coll of the City U of New York (NY)

ENVIRONMENTAL PSYCHOLOGY
Embry-Riddle Aeronautical U–Daytona (FL)

ENVIRONMENTAL SCIENCE
Abilene Christian U (TX)
Alaska Pacific U (AK)
Albion Coll (MI)

Albright Coll (PA)
Allegheny Coll (PA)
Alverno Coll (WI)
American Public U System (WV)
American U (DC)
The American U of Paris (France)
Anna Maria Coll (MA)
Antioch Coll, Yellow Springs (OH)
Appalachian State U (NC)
Ashland U (OH)
Assumption Coll (MA)
Auburn U (AL)
Ave Maria U (FL)
Averett U (VA)
Barnard Coll (NY)
Baylor U (TX)
Belmont U (TN)
Benedictine U (IL)
Bennington Coll (VT)
Berry Coll (GA)
Bethany Coll (WV)
Bethel U (MN)
Bethune-Cookman U (FL)
Biola U (CA)
Blackburn Coll (IL)
Bradley U (IL)
Brevard Coll (NC)
Bridgewater Coll (VA)
Brigham Young U (UT)
Brown U (RI)
Bryant U (RI)
Bucknell U (PA)
Buena Vista U (IA)
California Baptist U (CA)
California Lutheran U (CA)
California State U, Fresno (CA)
California State U, Long Beach (CA)
California State U, Monterey Bay (CA)
California U of Pennsylvania (PA)
Calvin Coll (MI)
Canisius Coll (NY)
Capital U (OH)
Castleton State Coll (VT)
Catawba Coll (NC)
Cedarville U (OH)
Central Methodist U (MO)
Central Michigan U (MI)
Central Washington U (WA)
Chatham U (PA)
Chestnut Hill Coll (PA)
Cheyney U of Pennsylvania (PA)
Claflin U (SC)
Clarion U of Pennsylvania (PA)
Clarkson U (NY)
Cleveland State U (OH)
Coe Coll (IA)
Colby Coll (ME)
The Coll at Brockport, State U of New York (NY)
The Colorado Coll (CO)
Colorado Mesa U (CO)
Columbia Coll (MO)
Columbia U, School of General Studies (NY)
Concordia U (QC, Canada)
Concordia U Chicago (IL)
Concordia U, Nebraska (NE)
Concordia U Texas (TX)
Concord U (WV)
Creighton U (NE)
Curry Coll (MA)
Dalhousie U (NS, Canada)
Dallas Baptist U (TX)
Delaware State U (DE)
DePaul U (IL)
DEREE - The American Coll of Greece (Greece)
Dickinson Coll (PA)
Dominican U (IL)
Drake U (IA)
Drexel U (PA)
Drury U (MO)
Duquesne U (PA)
Earlham Coll (IN)
Eastern Connecticut State U (CT)
Eastern New Mexico U (NM)
Eastern U (PA)
Edgewood Coll (WI)
Edinboro U of Pennsylvania (PA)
Elon U (NC)
Emory & Henry Coll (VA)
Endicott Coll (MA)
Eureka Coll (IL)
The Evergreen State Coll (WA)
Fairleigh Dickinson U, Metropolitan Campus (NJ)
Flagler Coll (FL)
Florida Ag and Mech U (FL)
Florida Inst of Technology (FL)
Fordham U (NY)
Franklin & Marshall Coll (PA)
Frostburg State U (MD)
Gannon U (PA)
Geneva Coll (PA)
George Mason U (VA)
Georgia Coll & State U (GA)
Gettysburg Coll (PA)
Gonzaga U (WA)
Goshen Coll (IN)
Hardin-Simmons U (TX)
Hartwick Coll (NY)
Hawai`i Pacific U (HI)
Heidelberg U (OH)
Heritage U (WA)
Humboldt State U (CA)
Hunter Coll of the City U of New York (NY)
Husson U (ME)
Indiana U Bloomington (IN)
Indiana U–Purdue U Indianapolis (IN)
Inter American U of Puerto Rico, Bayamón Campus (PR)
Inter American U of Puerto Rico, Ponce Campus (PR)
Inter American U of Puerto Rico, San Germán Campus (PR)
John Brown U (AR)
Johns Hopkins U (MD)
Juniata Coll (PA)
Keuka Coll (NY)
King's Coll (PA)
Kutztown U of Pennsylvania (PA)
Lamar U (TX)
La Sierra U (CA)
Lewis U (IL)
Lincoln U (MO)
Lincoln U (PA)
Lindenwood U (MO)
Lipscomb U (TN)
Longwood U (VA)
Louisiana State U and A&M Coll (LA)
Lourdes U (OH)
Loyola Marymount U (CA)
Loyola U Chicago (IL)
Lynchburg Coll (VA)
Madonna U (MI)
Marietta Coll (OH)
Marshall U (WV)
Marylhurst U (OR)
Maryville U of Saint Louis (MO)
Marywood U (PA)
Massachusetts Coll of Liberal Arts (MA)
Massachusetts Maritime Acad (MA)
McDaniel Coll (MD)
Mercer U, Macon (GA)
Merrimack Coll (MA)
Messiah Coll (PA)
Miami U (OH)
Michigan State U (MI)
Michigan Technological U (MI)
Midwestern State U (TX)
Mills Coll (CA)
Monmouth Coll (IL)
Montana State U (MT)
Moravian Coll (PA)
Muhlenberg Coll (PA)
National U (CA)
Nazareth Coll of Rochester (NY)
New England Coll (NH)
New Jersey Inst of Technology (NJ)
New Mexico State U (NM)
North Carolina State U (NC)
Northeastern U (MA)
Northern Arizona U (AZ)
Northern Kentucky U (KY)
Northern Michigan U (MI)
Northwestern U (IL)
Northwest U (WA)
Nova Southeastern U (FL)
Oakland U (MI)
The Ohio State U (OH)
Oklahoma State U (OK)
Oregon State U (OR)
Pace U (NY)
Piedmont Coll (GA)
Point Loma Nazarene U (CA)
Post U (CT)
Purdue U (IN)
Queens Coll of the City U of New York (NY)
Ramapo Coll of New Jersey (NJ)
Randolph Coll (VA)
Regis U (CO)
Rensselaer Polytechnic Inst (NY)
Rhodes Coll (TN)
Rochester Inst of Technology (NY)
Rocky Mountain Coll (MT)
Roger Williams U (RI)
Rutgers, The State U of New Jersey, New Brunswick (NJ)
St. Bonaventure U (NY)
Saint Francis U (PA)
St. Mary's U (TX)
St. Norbert Coll (WI)
Saint Vincent Coll (PA)
Salisbury U (MD)
Samford U (AL)
San Diego State U (CA)
Santa Clara U (CA)
Scripps Coll (CA)
Seattle U (WA)
Siena Heights U (MI)
Simmons Coll (MA)
Simon Fraser U (BC, Canada)
Simpson Coll (IA)
Skidmore Coll (NY)
South Dakota State U (SD)
Southeast Missouri State U (MO)
Southern Methodist U (TX)
Southern New Hampshire U (NH)
Southwest Minnesota State U (MN)
State U of New York Coll at Cortland (NY)
State U of New York Coll of Environmental Science and Forestry (NY)
Stephen F. Austin State U (TX)
Stetson U (FL)
Stevenson U (MD)
Stonehill Coll (MA)
Suffolk U (MA)
Tarleton State U (TX)
Taylor U (IN)
Temple U (PA)
Texas A&M U (TX)
Texas A&M U–Commerce (TX)
Texas A&M U–Corpus Christi (TX)
Texas Christian U (TX)
Texas State U (TX)
Thomas More Coll (KY)
Trinity Coll (CT)
Troy U (AL)
United States Military Acad (NY)
Unity Coll (ME)
Universidad Metropolitana (PR)
U at Albany, State U of New York (NY)
The U of Alabama (AL)
U of Alberta (AB, Canada)
The U of Arizona (AZ)
U of Arkansas (AR)
U of California, Irvine (CA)
U of California, Los Angeles (CA)
U of California, Riverside (CA)
U of Delaware (DE)
U of Denver (CO)
U of Dubuque (IA)
U of Evansville (IN)
U of Florida (FL)
U of Georgia (GA)
U of Guelph (ON, Canada)
U of Hawaii at Hilo (HI)
U of Hawaii at Manoa (HI)
U of Houston (TX)
U of Houston–Clear Lake (TX)
U of Idaho (ID)
U of Illinois at Chicago (IL)
The U of Iowa (IA)
U of Lethbridge (AB, Canada)
U of Louisiana at Lafayette (LA)
U of Maine (ME)
U of Maryland, Baltimore County (MD)
U of Maryland, Coll Park (MD)
U of Massachusetts Amherst (MA)
U of Michigan–Dearborn (MI)
U of Michigan–Flint (MI)
U of Minnesota, Duluth (MN)
U of Mobile (AL)
The U of Montana Western (MT)
U of Mount Union (OH)
U of New England (ME)
U of New Hampshire (NH)
U of New Haven (CT)
U of New Mexico (NM)
The U of North Carolina at Chapel Hill (NC)
The U of North Carolina at Pembroke (NC)
The U of North Carolina Wilmington (NC)
U of Northern Iowa (IA)
U of Notre Dame (IN)
U of Oklahoma (OK)
U of Oregon (OR)
U of Ottawa (ON, Canada)
U of Rochester (NY)
U of St. Francis (IL)
U of Saint Francis (IN)
U of St. Thomas (TX)
U of San Francisco (CA)
U of Saskatchewan (SK, Canada)
The U of Scranton (PA)
U of Southern California (CA)
U of Southern Maine (ME)
U of South Florida (FL)
U of South Florida, St. Petersburg (FL)
The U of Tennessee at Chattanooga (TN)
The U of Texas at Arlington (TX)
The U of Texas at San Antonio (TX)
The U of Texas–Pan American (TX)
U of the District of Columbia (DC)
U of the Incarnate Word (TX)
U of the Sciences (PA)
The U of Toledo (OH)
U of Utah (UT)
U of Vermont (VT)
U of Virginia (VA)
U of Washington (WA)
U of Washington, Bothell (WA)
U of Washington, Tacoma (WA)
U of Waterloo (ON, Canada)
The U of Western Ontario (ON, Canada)
U of West Florida (FL)
U of Windsor (ON, Canada)
U of Wisconsin–Green Bay (WI)
U of Wisconsin–Madison (WI)
U of Wisconsin–Milwaukee (WI)
U of Wisconsin–River Falls (WI)
U of Wisconsin–Stout (WI)
U of Wisconsin–Whitewater (WI)
Upper Iowa U (IA)
Utah Valley U (UT)
Valparaiso U (IN)
Vassar Coll (NY)
Villanova U (PA)
Walla Walla U (WA)
Walsh U (OH)
Wartburg Coll (IA)
Washington Coll (MD)
Washington State U (WA)
Washington State U Vancouver (WA)
Washington U in St. Louis (MO)
Wayne State U (MI)
Wesleyan Coll (GA)
Western Carolina U (NC)
Western Washington U (WA)
Westfield State U (MA)
Westminster Coll (MO)
West Texas A&M U (TX)
West Virginia Wesleyan Coll (WV)
Wheaton Coll (IL)
Wheaton Coll (MA)
Wheeling Jesuit U (WV)
Whittier Coll (CA)
Willamette U (OR)
William Jessup U (CA)
Williams Coll (MA)
Winthrop U (SC)
Wittenberg U (OH)
Youngstown State U (OH)

ENVIRONMENTAL STUDIES

Adelphi U (NY)
Albion Coll (MI)
Allegheny Coll (PA)
American U (DC)
Amherst Coll (MA)
Anna Maria Coll (MA)
Appalachian State U (NC)
Arizona State U at the Tempe campus (AZ)
Augsburg Coll (MN)
Augustana Coll (IL)
Austin Coll (TX)
Bard Coll (NY)
Bard Coll at Simon's Rock (MA)
Bates Coll (ME)
Baylor U (TX)
Beloit Coll (WI)
Bemidji State U (MN)
Bennington Coll (VT)
Bethel U (MN)
Binghamton U, State U of New York (NY)
Birmingham-Southern Coll (AL)
Black Hills State U (SD)
Boston Coll (MA)
Bowdoin Coll (ME)
Bowling Green State U (OH)
Brandeis U (MA)
Brevard Coll (NC)
Brown U (RI)
Bucknell U (PA)
California State U, Monterey Bay (CA)
California State U, Sacramento (CA)
Calvin Coll (MI)
Canisius Coll (NY)
Cape Breton U (NS, Canada)
Carleton Coll (MN)
Carroll Coll (MT)
Case Western Reserve U (OH)
Castleton State Coll (VT)
Catawba Coll (NC)
Cazenovia Coll (NY)
Central Coll (IA)
Central Michigan U (MI)
Central Washington U (WA)
Centre Coll (KY)
Chaminade U of Honolulu (HI)
Champlain Coll (VT)
Chatham U (PA)
Christopher Newport U (VA)
City Coll of the City U of New York (NY)
Claremont McKenna Coll (CA)
Cleveland State U (OH)
Coe Coll (IA)
Colby Coll (ME)
Colby-Sawyer Coll (NH)
The Coll of Idaho (ID)
The Coll of New Rochelle (NY)
Coll of Saint Benedict (MN)
Coll of the Atlantic (ME)
Coll of the Holy Cross (MA)
The Coll of William and Mary (VA)
The Colorado Coll (CO)
Columbia Southern U (AL)
Columbia U (NY)
Concordia Coll (MN)
Concordia U, Nebraska (NE)
Concordia U Texas (TX)
Concordia U Wisconsin (WI)
Connecticut Coll (CT)
Cornell Coll (IA)
Dalhousie U (NS, Canada)
Dartmouth Coll (NH)
Davidson Coll (NC)
Denison U (OH)
DePauw U (IN)
Dickinson Coll (PA)
Dickinson State U (ND)
Doane Coll (NE)
Drake U (IA)
Drew U (NJ)
Drexel U (PA)
Drury U (MO)
Earlham Coll (IN)
Eastern Kentucky U (KY)
Eastern U (PA)
Eckerd Coll (FL)
Elmhurst Coll (IL)
Elmira Coll (NY)
Elon U (NC)
Emory & Henry Coll (VA)
Eureka Coll (IL)
The Evergreen State Coll (WA)
Ferrum Coll (VA)
Florida Ag and Mech U (FL)
Florida Intl U (FL)
Florida Southern Coll (FL)
Fort Lewis Coll (CO)
Framingham State U (MA)
Franklin & Marshall Coll (PA)
Franklin Pierce U (NH)
Furman U (SC)
Georgetown U (DC)
The George Washington U (DC)
Gettysburg Coll (PA)
Goddard Coll (VT)
Gonzaga U (WA)
Goodwin Coll (CT)

Goucher Coll (MD)
Green Mountain Coll (VT)
Guilford Coll (NC)
Gustavus Adolphus Coll (MN)
Hamilton Coll (NY)
Hamline U (MN)
Hampshire Coll (MA)
Hampton U (VA)
Harvard U (MA)
Hawai`i Pacific U (HI)
Heidelberg U (OH)
Hendrix Coll (AR)
Hiram Coll (OH)
Hobart and William Smith Colls (NY)
Hofstra U (NY)
Hollins U (VA)
Humboldt State U (CA)
Illinois Coll (IL)
Illinois Wesleyan U (IL)
Immaculata U (PA)
Indiana U Bloomington (IN)
Indiana U South Bend (IN)
Inter American U of Puerto Rico, San Germán Campus (PR)
Iowa State U of Science and Technology (IA)
Ithaca Coll (NY)
John Brown U (AR)
John Carroll U (OH)
Johns Hopkins U (MD)
Johnson State Coll (VT)
Judson U (IL)
Juniata Coll (PA)
Kansas Wesleyan U (KS)
Keene State Coll (NH)
King's Coll (PA)
The King's U Coll (AB, Canada)
Knox Coll (IL)
Lake Forest Coll (IL)
La Salle U (PA)
Lasell Coll (MA)
Lawrence U (WI)
Lehigh U (PA)
Le Moyne Coll (NY)
Lenoir-Rhyne U (NC)
Lesley U (MA)
Lewis & Clark Coll (OR)
Lincoln Memorial U (TN)
Lincoln U (PA)
Linfield Coll (OR)
Loyola U Chicago (IL)
Luther Coll (IA)
Lynchburg Coll (VA)
Lynn U (FL)
Macalester Coll (MN)
Maharishi U of Management (IA)
Manchester U (IN)
Manhattanville Coll (NY)
Mansfield U of Pennsylvania (PA)
Marietta Coll (OH)
Marymount Manhattan Coll (NY)
Maryville Coll (TN)
Maryville U of Saint Louis (MO)
Massachusetts Coll of Liberal Arts (MA)
Massachusetts Maritime Acad (MA)
McDaniel Coll (MD)
McKendree U (IL)
Mercer U, Macon (GA)
Meredith Coll (NC)
Michigan State U (MI)
Middlebury Coll (VT)
Mills Coll (CA)
Minnesota State U Mankato (MN)
Minnesota State U Moorhead (MN)
Mitchell Coll (CT)
Montana State U Billings (MT)
Montreat Coll, Montreat (NC)
Moravian Coll (PA)
Mount Allison U (NB, Canada)
Mount Holyoke Coll (MA)
Mount St. Mary's U (MD)
Naropa U (CO)
National U (CA)
New Coll of Florida (FL)
New Mexico Highlands U (NM)
New Mexico Inst of Mining and Technology (NM)
New York U (NY)
North Carolina Wesleyan Coll (NC)
Northeastern Illinois U (IL)
Northeastern U (MA)
Northern Arizona U (AZ)
Northern Illinois U (IL)
Northern State U (SD)
Northland Coll (WI)
Northwestern U (IL)
Norwich U (VT)
Oberlin Coll (OH)
Occidental Coll (CA)
Ohio Northern U (OH)
The Ohio State U (OH)
Ohio U (OH)
Ohio Wesleyan U (OH)
Oklahoma City U (OK)
Olivet Coll (MI)
Pace U (NY)
Pacific Lutheran U (WA)
Pacific U (OR)
Penn State Altoona (PA)
Penn State U Park (PA)
Plymouth State U (NH)
Pomona Coll (CA)
Portland State U (OR)
Post U (CT)
Prescott Coll (AZ)
Principia Coll (IL)
Purchase Coll, State U of New York (NY)
Queens Coll of the City U of New York (NY)
Ramapo Coll of New Jersey (NJ)
Randolph Coll (VA)
Randolph-Macon Coll (VA)
Reed Coll (OR)
Regis U (CO)
Rider U (NJ)
Ripon Coll (WI)
Roanoke Coll (VA)
Robert Morris U (PA)
Rocky Mountain Coll (MT)
Rollins Coll (FL)
Rowan U (NJ)
Rutgers, The State U of New Jersey, New Brunswick (NJ)
The Sage Colls (NY)
Saint Anselm Coll (NH)
St. Edward's U (TX)
Saint Francis U (PA)
Saint John's U (MN)
St. John's U (NY)
Saint Joseph's U (PA)
St. Lawrence U (NY)
Saint Louis U (MO)
Saint Michael's Coll (VT)
St. Olaf Coll (MN)
St. Thomas U (FL)
St. Thomas U (NB, Canada)
Saint Vincent Coll (PA)
Salve Regina U (RI)
San Diego State U (CA)
San Francisco State U (CA)
San Jose State U (CA)
Santa Clara U (CA)
Seattle U (WA)
Sewanee: The U of the South (TN)
Shenandoah U (VA)
Shepherd U (WV)
Shippensburg U of Pennsylvania (PA)
Siena Coll (NY)
Skidmore Coll (NY)
Smith Coll (MA)
Southern Methodist U (TX)
Southern New Hampshire U (NH)
Southern Oregon U (OR)
Southwestern U (TX)
Spelman Coll (GA)
Stanford U (CA)
State U of New York at Fredonia (NY)
State U of New York at Plattsburgh (NY)
State U of New York Coll at Cortland (NY)
State U of New York Coll at Potsdam (NY)
State U of New York Coll of Agriculture and Technology at Cobleskill (NY)
State U of New York Coll of Environmental Science and Forestry (NY)
Sterling Coll (VT)
Stockton U (NJ)
Stonehill Coll (MA)
Stony Brook U, State U of New York (NY)
Tarleton State U (TX)
Taylor U (IN)
Temple U (PA)
Tennessee Wesleyan Coll (TN)
Texas A&M U (TX)
Thiel Coll (PA)
Trent U (ON, Canada)
Trine U (IN)
Trinity U (TX)
Tufts U (MA)
Tulane U (LA)
Tusculum Coll (TN)
United States Military Acad (NY)
Université de Sherbrooke (QC, Canada)
U of Alberta (AB, Canada)
The U of Arizona (AZ)
The U of British Columbia (BC, Canada)
The U of British Columbia–Okanagan Campus (BC, Canada)
U of California, Davis (CA)
U of California, Irvine (CA)
U of California, Santa Barbara (CA)
U of California, Santa Cruz (CA)
U of Central Arkansas (AR)
U of Chicago (IL)
U of Cincinnati (OH)
U of Colorado Boulder (CO)
U of Delaware (DE)
U of Dubuque (IA)
U of Evansville (IN)
The U of Findlay (OH)
U of Guelph (ON, Canada)
U of Hawaii at Hilo (HI)
U of Illinois at Springfield (IL)
U of Indianapolis (IN)
The U of Iowa (IA)
The U of Kansas (KS)
U of Kentucky (KY)
U of Maine at Fort Kent (ME)
U of Maine at Machias (ME)
U of Maine at Presque Isle (ME)
U of Maryland, Baltimore County (MD)
U of Michigan (MI)
U of Michigan–Dearborn (MI)
U of Minnesota, Duluth (MN)
U of Minnesota, Twin Cities Campus (MN)
U of Missouri (MO)
U of Missouri–Kansas City (MO)
The U of Montana (MT)
U of Nebraska–Lincoln (NE)
U of Nevada, Las Vegas (NV)
U of New England (ME)
U of New Haven (CT)
U of North Carolina at Asheville (NC)
The U of North Carolina at Chapel Hill (NC)
The U of North Carolina Wilmington (NC)
U of North Dakota (ND)
U of Oklahoma (OK)
U of Oregon (OR)
U of Ottawa (ON, Canada)
U of Pennsylvania (PA)
U of Pittsburgh at Bradford (PA)
U of Portland (OR)
U of Regina (SK, Canada)
U of Rhode Island (RI)
U of Richmond (VA)
U of Rochester (NY)
U of Saint Francis (IN)
U of St. Thomas (TX)
U of San Diego (CA)
U of San Francisco (CA)
U of Southern California (CA)
U of Southern Indiana (IN)
U of Southern Maine (ME)
The U of Tampa (FL)
The U of Tennessee at Martin (TN)
U of the District of Columbia (DC)
U of the Pacific (CA)
The U of Toledo (OH)
U of Toronto (ON, Canada)
The U of Tulsa (OK)
U of Utah (UT)
U of Vermont (VT)
The U of Virginia's Coll at Wise (VA)
U of Washington (WA)
U of Washington, Bothell (WA)
U of Washington, Tacoma (WA)
U of Waterloo (ON, Canada)
The U of Western Ontario (ON, Canada)
U of Windsor (ON, Canada)
U of Wisconsin–Green Bay (WI)
U of Wisconsin–Madison (WI)
U of Wisconsin–River Falls (WI)
U of Wyoming (WY)
Ursinus Coll (PA)
Vassar Coll (NY)
Villanova U (PA)
Virginia Commonwealth U (VA)
Virginia Polytechnic Inst and State U (VA)
Virginia Wesleyan Coll (VA)
Walla Walla U (WA)
Warren Wilson Coll (NC)
Washington & Jefferson Coll (PA)
Washington and Lee U (VA)
Washington Coll (MD)
Washington U in St. Louis (MO)
Waynesburg U (PA)
Wells Coll (NY)
Wesleyan U (CT)
Western Michigan U (MI)
Western State Colorado U (CO)
Western Washington U (WA)
Westminster Coll (MO)
Westminster Coll (UT)
Wheelock Coll (MA)
Whittier Coll (CA)
Widener U (PA)
William Paterson U of New Jersey (NJ)
William Peace U (NC)
Williams Coll (MA)
Wofford Coll (SC)
Worcester Polytechnic Inst (MA)
Yale U (CT)

ENVIRONMENTAL TOXICOLOGY

Clarkson U (NY)
U of California, Davis (CA)

EPIDEMIOLOGY

U of Rochester (NY)
The U of Western Ontario (ON, Canada)

EQUESTRIAN STUDIES

Asbury U (KY)
Averett U (VA)
Becker Coll (MA)
Bethany Coll (WV)
Cazenovia Coll (NY)
Colorado State U (CO)
Emory & Henry Coll (VA)
Houghton Coll (NY)
Johnson & Wales U (RI)
Judson Coll (AL)
Lake Erie Coll (OH)
North Dakota State U (ND)
Post U (CT)
Rocky Mountain Coll (MT)
Rutgers, The State U of New Jersey, New Brunswick (NJ)
Saint Mary-of-the-Woods Coll (IN)
Stephens Coll (MO)
The U of Findlay (OH)
The U of Montana Western (MT)
U of Wisconsin–River Falls (WI)
West Texas A&M U (TX)

ETHICS

Bridgewater State U (MA)
Carroll Coll (MT)
Drake U (IA)
Syracuse U (NY)
U of Michigan–Flint (MI)
U of Ottawa (ON, Canada)
U of Washington, Bothell (WA)
The U of Western Ontario (ON, Canada)

ETHNIC, CULTURAL MINORITY, GENDER, AND GROUP STUDIES RELATED

Albion Coll (MI)
American U (DC)
Bard Coll at Simon's Rock (MA)
Beloit Coll (WI)
Bethel U (MN)
Bowling Green State U (OH)
California Polytechnic State U, San Luis Obispo (CA)
California State Polytechnic U, Pomona (CA)
California State U, Chico (CA)
California State U, Stanislaus (CA)
Central Michigan U (MI)
Chatham U (PA)
Christian Brothers U (TN)
The Colorado Coll (CO)
Columbia U, School of General Studies (NY)
Connecticut Coll (CT)
Cornell Coll (IA)
Davidson Coll (NC)
Emmanuel Coll (MA)
The Evergreen State Coll (WA)
Grinnell Coll (IA)
Hampshire Coll (MA)
Hawai`i Pacific U (HI)
Indiana U Bloomington (IN)
Indiana U South Bend (IN)
Lawrence U (WI)
Mills Coll (CA)
Mount Holyoke Coll (MA)
New York U (NY)
Northeastern Illinois U (IL)
Oregon State U (OR)
St. Francis Coll (NY)
Saint Michael's Coll (VT)
San Diego State U (CA)
Santa Clara U (CA)
Savannah State U (GA)
Skidmore Coll (NY)
Southern Adventist U (TN)
Stanford U (CA)
Stonehill Coll (MA)
U at Buffalo, the State U of New York (NY)
U of California, Berkeley (CA)
U of California, Irvine (CA)
U of California, Los Angeles (CA)
U of Chicago (IL)
U of Colorado Colorado Springs (CO)
U of Denver (CO)
U of Hawaii at Manoa (HI)
U of Houston (TX)
U of Illinois at Chicago (IL)
U of Kentucky (KY)
U of Nebraska–Lincoln (NE)
U of New Brunswick Saint John (NB, Canada)
U of Pittsburgh (PA)
U of Southern California (CA)
U of Utah (UT)
U of Washington (WA)
U of Washington, Tacoma (WA)
The U of Western Ontario (ON, Canada)
Washington State U (WA)
Washington U in St. Louis (MO)
Wayne State U (MI)
Wesleyan U (CT)
Western Kentucky U (KY)
Westfield State U (MA)
Whitman Coll (WA)
Williams Coll (MA)
Xavier U (OH)
Yale U (CT)

ETHNIC STUDIES

Arizona State U at the West campus (AZ)
Colorado State U (CO)
Edgewood Coll (WI)
Goddard Coll (VT)
Kansas State U (KS)
Lewis & Clark Coll (OR)
Messiah Coll (PA)
Metropolitan State U (MN)
Minnesota State U Moorhead (MN)
St. Olaf Coll (MN)
U of Colorado Boulder (CO)
U of Colorado Denver (CO)
U of Oregon (OR)
U of San Diego (CA)
The U of Texas at Austin (TX)

EUROPEAN HISTORY

Charleston Southern U (SC)
Gettysburg Coll (PA)
Howard Payne U (TX)
Keene State Coll (NH)
U of Washington, Tacoma (WA)

EUROPEAN STUDIES

American U in Bulgaria (Bulgaria)
The American U of Paris (France)
Amherst Coll (MA)
Bard Coll at Simon's Rock (MA)
Barnard Coll (NY)
Belmont U (TN)
Bennington Coll (VT)
Bowling Green State U (OH)
Brandeis U (MA)
Canisius Coll (NY)
Dalhousie U (NS, Canada)

Emory & Henry Coll (VA)
Fort Lewis Coll (CO)
Georgetown Coll (KY)
The George Washington U (DC)
Gettysburg Coll (PA)
Hampshire Coll (MA)
Hobart and William Smith Colls (NY)
Loyola Marymount U (CA)
Middlebury Coll (VT)
Millsaps Coll (MS)
New Coll of Florida (FL)
New York U (NY)
Ohio U (OH)
Pepperdine U, Malibu (CA)
Portland State U (OR)
Rutgers, The State U of New Jersey, New Brunswick (NJ)
Sacred Heart U (CT)
Saint Joseph's U (PA)
San Diego State U (CA)
Scripps Coll (CA)
Seattle Pacific U (WA)
Stony Brook U, State U of New York (NY)
Texas State U (TX)
Trinity U (TX)
Tufts U (MA)
United States Military Acad (NY)
U of Alberta (AB, Canada)
The U of British Columbia (BC, Canada)
U of California, Irvine (CA)
U of California, Los Angeles (CA)
U of Delaware (DE)
U of Guelph (ON, Canada)
The U of Kansas (KS)
U of King's Coll (NS, Canada)
U of Minnesota, Morris (MN)
U of Minnesota, Twin Cities Campus (MN)
U of Missouri (MO)
U of New Hampshire (NH)
U of New Mexico (NM)
The U of North Carolina at Chapel Hill (NC)
U of Richmond (VA)
The U of Texas at Austin (TX)
The U of Toledo (OH)
U of Toronto (ON, Canada)
U of Vermont (VT)
U of Washington (WA)
Vanderbilt U (TN)
Washington U in St. Louis (MO)
Webster U (MO)

EUROPEAN STUDIES (WESTERN)
Bates Coll (ME)
Illinois Wesleyan U (IL)
Seattle U (WA)
Tufts U (MA)
U of Nebraska–Lincoln (NE)

EVOLUTIONARY BIOLOGY
Bennington Coll (VT)
Case Western Reserve U (OH)
Coll of the Atlantic (ME)
Columbia U, School of General Studies (NY)
Dartmouth Coll (NH)
Harvard U (MA)
Rice U (TX)
Rutgers, The State U of New Jersey, New Brunswick (NJ)
Stony Brook U, State U of New York (NY)
Tulane U (LA)
U of Alberta (AB, Canada)
Yale U (CT)

EXECUTIVE ASSISTANT/ EXECUTIVE SECRETARY
Bowling Green State U (OH)
Caribbean U (PR)
U of Puerto Rico in Ponce (PR)

EXERCISE PHYSIOLOGY
Ave Maria U (FL)
Baldwin Wallace U (OH)
Baylor U (TX)
Bethany Lutheran Coll (MN)
Biola U (CA)
California Baptist U (CA)
Central Washington U (WA)
Coll of Charleston (SC)
The Coll of St. Scholastica (MN)
Concordia U Wisconsin (WI)
East Carolina U (NC)
Fitchburg State U (MA)
Gonzaga U (WA)
Lynchburg Coll (VA)
Marquette U (WI)
Mercy Coll (NY)
Merrimack Coll (MA)
Northwest Christian U (OR)
Ohio Northern U (OH)
Saint Francis U (PA)
Shenandoah U (VA)
U at Buffalo, the State U of New York (NY)
U of California, Davis (CA)
U of California, Irvine (CA)
U of Dayton (OH)
U of Delaware (DE)
U of Florida (FL)
U of Massachusetts Amherst (MA)
U of Miami (FL)
U of Southern Maine (ME)
Ursinus Coll (PA)
West Virginia U (WV)

EXPERIMENTAL PSYCHOLOGY
Northern Michigan U (MI)
Purdue U (IN)
Tiffin U (OH)
Tufts U (MA)
The U of British Columbia (BC, Canada)
U of California, Santa Barbara (CA)
U of Mary Hardin-Baylor (TX)
U of Michigan (MI)
U of Rochester (NY)
The U of Toledo (OH)

FACILITIES PLANNING AND MANAGEMENT
Eastern Michigan U (MI)
Missouri State U (MO)
New York City Coll of Technology of the City U of New York (NY)

FAMILY AND COMMUNITY SERVICES
Andrews U (MI)
Bowling Green State U (OH)
Coll of the Ozarks (MO)
East Carolina U (NC)
Harding U (AR)
Iowa State U of Science and Technology (IA)
John Brown U (AR)
La Roche Coll (PA)
Messiah Coll (PA)
Michigan State U (MI)
Mount St. Mary's U (MD)
Oklahoma Baptist U (OK)
Oklahoma Christian U (OK)
Prairie View A&M U (TX)
Stevenson U (MD)
Texas Tech U (TX)
Toccoa Falls Coll (GA)
Union U (TN)
U of California, Santa Cruz (CA)
U of Florida (FL)
U of Maine at Machias (ME)
U of Maryland, Coll Park (MD)
U of Miami (FL)
U of Minnesota, Twin Cities Campus (MN)
U of Northern Iowa (IA)
U of Wisconsin–Madison (WI)
William Penn U (IA)
Youngstown State U (OH)

FAMILY AND CONSUMER ECONOMICS RELATED
Andrews U (MI)
Bowling Green State U (OH)
Brigham Young U (UT)
California State U, Fresno (CA)
California State U, Sacramento (CA)
Carson-Newman U (TN)
Fairmont State U (WV)
Howard U (DC)
Iowa State U of Science and Technology (IA)
Louisiana Coll (LA)
Minnesota State U Mankato (MN)
Tennessee State U (TN)
U of Hawaii at Manoa (HI)
U of Minnesota, Twin Cities Campus (MN)
U of Missouri (MO)
U of Nebraska at Kearney (NE)
U of Nebraska–Lincoln (NE)
U of Northern Iowa (IA)
U of Wisconsin–Stevens Point (WI)
Utah State U (UT)
Virginia State U (VA)

FAMILY AND CONSUMER SCIENCES/HOME ECONOMICS TEACHER EDUCATION
Appalachian State U (NC)
Baylor U (TX)
Bowling Green State U (OH)
Bradley U (IL)
Carson-Newman U (TN)
Central Washington U (WA)
Colorado State U (CO)
East Carolina U (NC)
Eastern Kentucky U (KY)
Fairmont State U (WV)
Fontbonne U (MO)
Georgia Southern U (GA)
Hampton U (VA)
Harding U (AR)
Immaculata U (PA)
Iowa State U of Science and Technology (IA)
Jacksonville State U (AL)
Langston U (OK)
Marywood U (PA)
Messiah Coll (PA)
Michigan State U (MI)
Minnesota State U Mankato (MN)
Missouri State U (MO)
Mount Vernon Nazarene U (OH)
New Mexico State U (NM)
North Carolina Ag and Tech State U (NC)
North Dakota State U (ND)
Northern Illinois U (IL)
The Ohio State U (OH)
The Ohio State U at Lima (OH)
Ohio U (OH)
Pittsburg State U (KS)
Queens Coll of the City U of New York (NY)
St. Catherine U (MN)
Seton Hill U (PA)
South Dakota State U (SD)
Southeast Missouri State U (MO)
The U of Akron (OH)
U of Alberta (AB, Canada)
U of Arkansas at Pine Bluff (AR)
U of Central Arkansas (AR)
U of Central Oklahoma (OK)
U of Georgia (GA)
U of Guam (GU)
U of Minnesota, Twin Cities Campus (MN)
U of Saskatchewan (SK, Canada)
The U of Tennessee at Martin (TN)
U of Wisconsin–Stevens Point (WI)
U of Wisconsin–Stout (WI)
Utah State U (UT)
Virginia Polytechnic Inst and State U (VA)
Washington State U (WA)
Wayne State Coll (NE)
Western Kentucky U (KY)
Western Michigan U (MI)
Winthrop U (SC)
Youngstown State U (OH)

FAMILY AND CONSUMER SCIENCES/HUMAN SCIENCES
Auburn U (AL)
Ball State U (IN)
Baylor U (TX)
Berea Coll (KY)
Bowling Green State U (OH)
Bradley U (IL)
Bridgewater Coll (VA)
Brigham Young U (UT)
California State U, Long Beach (CA)
Carson-Newman U (TN)
Central Washington U (WA)
Coll of the Atlantic (ME)
Coll of the Ozarks (MO)
Colorado State U (CO)
Delaware State U (DE)
Delta State U (MS)
East Central U (OK)
Eastern Illinois U (IL)
East Tennessee State U (TN)
Fairmont State U (WV)
Fontbonne U (MO)
Framingham State U (MA)
Great Lakes Christian Coll (MI)
Harding U (AR)
Illinois State U (IL)
Indiana State U (IN)
Indiana U of Pennsylvania (PA)
Iowa State U of Science and Technology (IA)
Jacksonville State U (AL)
Kansas State U (KS)
Liberty U (VA)
Lipscomb U (TN)
Louisiana State U and A&M Coll (LA)
Madonna U (MI)
Marshall U (WV)
The Master's Coll and Sem (CA)
Meredith Coll (NC)
Michigan State U (MI)
Minnesota State U Mankato (MN)
Mississippi State U (MS)
Montana State U (MT)
Montclair State U (NJ)
Mount Vernon Nazarene U (OH)
New Mexico Highlands U (NM)
Nicholls State U (LA)
North Carolina Ag and Tech State U (NC)
North Carolina Central U (NC)
Northeastern State U (OK)
Olivet Nazarene U (IL)
Pittsburg State U (KS)
Point Loma Nazarene U (CA)
Prairie View A&M U (TX)
Purdue U (IN)
Queens Coll of the City U of New York (NY)
Rutgers, The State U of New Jersey, New Brunswick (NJ)
St. Catherine U (MN)
Sam Houston State U (TX)
San Francisco State U (CA)
Seattle Pacific U (WA)
Seton Hill U (PA)
Shepherd U (WV)
South Carolina State U (SC)
Southeastern Louisiana U (LA)
Southeast Missouri State U (MO)
Southern Utah U (UT)
Tarleton State U (TX)
Texas A&M U–Kingsville (TX)
Texas Southern U (TX)
Texas Tech U (TX)
Texas Woman's U (TX)
The U of Alabama (AL)
U of Alberta (AB, Canada)
U of Arkansas (AR)
U of Arkansas at Pine Bluff (AR)
The U of British Columbia (BC, Canada)
U of Central Arkansas (AR)
U of Central Missouri (MO)
U of Central Oklahoma (OK)
U of Kentucky (KY)
U of Minnesota, Twin Cities Campus (MN)
U of Montevallo (AL)
U of New Mexico (NM)
U of North Alabama (AL)
U of Saint Joseph (CT)
The U of Tennessee at Martin (TN)
The U of Texas at Austin (TX)
The U of Western Ontario (ON, Canada)
U of Wyoming (WY)
Washington State U (WA)
Wayne State Coll (NE)
Western Illinois U (IL)
Youngstown State U (OH)

FAMILY AND CONSUMER SCIENCES/HUMAN SCIENCES BUSINESS SERVICES RELATED
Brigham Young U (UT)

FAMILY AND CONSUMER SCIENCES/HUMAN SCIENCES COMMUNICATION
U of Georgia (GA)

FAMILY AND CONSUMER SCIENCES/HUMAN SCIENCES RELATED
Auburn U (AL)
California State U, Long Beach (CA)
Norfolk State U (VA)
U of Minnesota, Twin Cities Campus (MN)

FAMILY PRACTICE NURSING
Grand Valley State U (MI)
Michigan State U (MI)
The U of Virginia's Coll at Wise (VA)
The U of Western Ontario (ON, Canada)
U of Windsor (ON, Canada)

FAMILY PSYCHOLOGY
Arizona Christian U (AZ)
Corban U (OR)
Goddard Coll (VT)
Kansas Wesleyan U (KS)

FAMILY RESOURCE MANAGEMENT
Arizona State U at the Tempe campus (AZ)
Brigham Young U (UT)
Cornell U (NY)
Iowa State U of Science and Technology (IA)
Middle Tennessee State U (TN)
New Mexico State U (NM)
The Ohio State U (OH)
The Ohio State U at Lima (OH)
Ohio U (OH)
South Dakota State U (SD)
Texas Tech U (TX)
The U of Alabama (AL)
U of Georgia (GA)

FAMILY SYSTEMS
Anderson U (IN)
Bowling Green State U (OH)
Central Michigan U (MI)
Central Washington U (WA)
DeSales U (PA)
Goodwin Coll (CT)
John Brown U (AR)
Lipscomb U (TN)
Lubbock Christian U (TX)
Mid-Atlantic Christian U (NC)
Mississippi U for Women (MS)
Southern Adventist U (TN)
Towson U (MD)
The U of Akron (OH)
U of Central Oklahoma (OK)
U of Minnesota, Twin Cities Campus (MN)
U of Southern Mississippi (MS)
Weber State U (UT)
Western Michigan U (MI)

FARM AND RANCH MANAGEMENT
Cornell U (NY)
Iowa State U of Science and Technology (IA)
Johnson & Wales U (RI)
Lake Erie Coll (OH)
Purdue U (IN)
Tarleton State U (TX)
Texas A&M U (TX)
Texas Christian U (TX)
The U of Findlay (OH)
U of Minnesota, Crookston (MN)

FASHION AND FABRIC CONSULTING
Acad of Art U (CA)

FASHION/APPAREL DESIGN
Acad of Art U (CA)
Baylor U (TX)
Bennington Coll (VT)
Bob Jones U (SC)
Bowling Green State U (OH)
Brenau U (GA)
Buffalo State Coll, State U of New York (NY)
California Coll of the Arts (CA)
Cazenovia Coll (NY)
Clark Atlanta U (GA)
Columbia Coll Chicago (IL)
Columbus Coll of Art & Design (OH)
Dalhousie U (NS, Canada)
Dominican U (IL)
Drexel U (PA)
EDP U of Puerto Rico (PR)
Escuela de Artes Plasticas de Puerto Rico (PR)
Fashion Inst of Technology (NY)
Ferris State U (MI)
Fisher Coll (MA)
Hampton U (VA)
Howard U (DC)

Indiana U Bloomington (IN)
Iowa State U of Science and Technology (IA)
Kent State U (OH)
Lasell Coll (MA)
Lebanese American U (Lebanon)
Lindenwood U (MO)
Marist Coll (NY)
Marymount U (VA)
Massachusetts Coll of Art and Design (MA)
Meredith Coll (NC)
Michigan State U (MI)
Montclair State U (NJ)
Moore Coll of Art & Design (PA)
Mount Mary U (WI)
Otis Coll of Art and Design (CA)
Paris Coll of Art (France)
Philadelphia U (PA)
Pratt Inst (NY)
Purdue U (IN)
Rocky Mountain Coll of Art + Design (CO)
Sacred Heart U (CT)
St. Catherine U (MN)
Savannah Coll of Art and Design (GA)
School of the Art Inst of Chicago (IL)
Stephens Coll (MO)
Stevenson U (MD)
Syracuse U (NY)
Texas Tech U (TX)
Texas Woman's U (TX)
U of Cincinnati (OH)
U of Delaware (DE)
U of Minnesota, Twin Cities Campus (MN)
U of North Texas (TX)
U of the Incarnate Word (TX)
Ursuline Coll (OH)
Villa Maria Coll (NY)
Virginia Commonwealth U (VA)
Washington U in St. Louis (MO)

FASHION MERCHANDISING
Ashland U (OH)
Baylor U (TX)
Berkeley Coll, Woodland Park (NJ)
Berkeley Coll–New York City Campus (NY)
Bowling Green State U (OH)
Bradley U (IL)
Brenau U (GA)
Buffalo State Coll, State U of New York (NY)
California State U, Long Beach (CA)
Carson-Newman U (TN)
Central Michigan U (MI)
Cheyney U of Pennsylvania (PA)
Delaware State U (DE)
Dominican U (IL)
East Central U (OK)
Eastern Kentucky U (KY)
Eastern Michigan U (MI)
Fashion Inst of Technology (NY)
Fisher Coll (MA)
Fontbonne U (MO)
Hampton U (VA)
Harding U (AR)
Immaculata U (PA)
Indiana U of Pennsylvania (PA)
Johnson & Wales U (CO)
Johnson & Wales U (FL)
Johnson & Wales U (RI)
Johnson & Wales U - Charlotte Campus (NC)
Kent State U (OH)
Lasell Coll (MA)
LIM Coll (NY)
Lipscomb U (TN)
Louisiana State U and A&M Coll (LA)
Lynn U (FL)
Mars Hill U (NC)
Marymount Manhattan Coll (NY)
Marymount U (VA)
Meredith Coll (NC)
Mount Mary U (WI)
Newbury Coll (MA)
Northwood U, Michigan Campus (MI)
Olivet Nazarene U (IL)
Philadelphia U (PA)
Point Loma Nazarene U (CA)
Sacred Heart U (CT)
St. Catherine U (MN)
Sam Houston State U (TX)
Southern New Hampshire U (NH)
Stephen F. Austin State U (TX)
Stevenson U (MD)
Stevens–The Inst of Business & Arts (MO)
Texas Christian U (TX)
Texas State U (TX)
Texas Tech U (TX)
Texas Woman's U (TX)
U of Bridgeport (CT)
U of Central Oklahoma (OK)
U of Georgia (GA)
U of Minnesota, Twin Cities Campus (MN)
The U of Montana (MT)
U of North Texas (TX)
The U of Tennessee at Martin (TN)
Ursuline Coll (OH)
Utah State U (UT)
Youngstown State U (OH)

FIBER, TEXTILE AND WEAVING ARTS
Adams State U (CO)
Bowling Green State U (OH)
California Coll of the Arts (CA)
California State U, Long Beach (CA)
Coll of the Ozarks (MO)
Colorado State U (CO)
Cornell U (NY)
Kansas City Art Inst (MO)
Massachusetts Coll of Art and Design (MA)
Philadelphia U (PA)
Rhode Island School of Design (RI)
Savannah Coll of Art and Design (GA)
School of the Art Inst of Chicago (IL)
Temple U (PA)
The U of Kansas (KS)
U of Massachusetts Dartmouth (MA)
U of Michigan (MI)
U of Oregon (OR)
Western Washington U (WA)

FILIPINO/TAGALOG
U of Hawaii at Manoa (HI)

FILM/CINEMA/VIDEO STUDIES
The American U in Cairo (Egypt)
The American U of Paris (France)
The American U of Rome (Italy)
Augsburg Coll (MN)
Baldwin Wallace U (OH)
Bard Coll (NY)
Barnard Coll (NY)
Bennington Coll (VT)
Biola U (CA)
Boston Coll (MA)
Bowling Green State U (OH)
Brandeis U (MA)
Brigham Young U (UT)
Brown U (RI)
California Baptist U (CA)
California Coll of the Arts (CA)
California State U, Long Beach (CA)
California State U, Sacramento (CA)
Carleton Coll (MN)
Carson-Newman U (TN)
Central Washington U (WA)
Champlain Coll (VT)
Chapman U (CA)
Claremont McKenna Coll (CA)
Clark U (MA)
Coe Coll (IA)
Coll of Staten Island of the City U of New York (NY)
The Colorado Coll (CO)
Columbia Coll Chicago (IL)
Columbia U (NY)
Columbia U, School of General Studies (NY)
Concordia U (QC, Canada)
Connecticut Coll (CT)
Cornell U (NY)
Dartmouth Coll (NH)
Denison U (OH)
DeSales U (PA)
Dominican U (IL)
Eastern Michigan U (MI)
Eckerd Coll (FL)
Emerson Coll (MA)
The Evergreen State Coll (WA)
Florida State U (FL)
Georgia State U (GA)
Grace Coll (IN)
Grand Valley State U (MI)
Howard U (DC)
Hunter Coll of the City U of New York (NY)
Ithaca Coll (NY)
Jacksonville U (FL)
John Brown U (AR)
Johns Hopkins U (MD)
Judson U (IL)
Keene State Coll (NH)
Kenyon Coll (OH)
Lafayette Coll (PA)
La Salle U (PA)
La Sierra U (CA)
McDaniel Coll (MD)
Middlebury Coll (VT)
Minnesota State U Moorhead (MN)
Mount Holyoke Coll (MA)
Muhlenberg Coll (PA)
New York U (NY)
Northeastern U (MA)
Northwestern U (IL)
Northwest U (WA)
Oakland U (MI)
The Ohio State U (OH)
Pace U (NY)
Penn State Abington (PA)
Penn State Altoona (PA)
Penn State Beaver (PA)
Penn State Berks (PA)
Penn State Brandywine (PA)
Penn State DuBois (PA)
Penn State Erie, The Behrend Coll (PA)
Penn State Fayette, The Eberly Campus (PA)
Penn State Greater Allegheny (PA)
Penn State Hazleton (PA)
Penn State Lehigh Valley (PA)
Penn State Mont Alto (PA)
Penn State New Kensington (PA)
Penn State Schuylkill (PA)
Penn State Shenango (PA)
Penn State U Park (PA)
Penn State Wilkes-Barre (PA)
Penn State Worthington Scranton (PA)
Penn State York (PA)
Pepperdine U, Malibu (CA)
Purchase Coll, State U of New York (NY)
Purdue U (IN)
Queens Coll of the City U of New York (NY)
Quinnipiac U (CT)
Rhode Island Coll (RI)
Roger Williams U (RI)
Rutgers, The State U of New Jersey, New Brunswick (NJ)
Saint Augustine's U (NC)
San Francisco State U (CA)
Sarah Lawrence Coll (NY)
School of the Art Inst of Chicago (IL)
School of the Museum of Fine Arts, Boston (MA)
Seattle U (WA)
Simon Fraser U (BC, Canada)
Smith Coll (MA)
Southeastern U (FL)
Southwestern Coll (KS)
Stanford U (CA)
State U of New York at Fredonia (NY)
Stephens Coll (MO)
Stevenson U (MD)
Temple U (PA)
Université de Montréal (QC, Canada)
U at Buffalo, the State U of New York (NY)
U of Alaska Fairbanks (AK)
U of Alberta (AB, Canada)
The U of Arizona (AZ)
U of Arkansas at Little Rock (AR)
The U of British Columbia (BC, Canada)
U of California, Berkeley (CA)
U of California, Davis (CA)
U of California, Irvine (CA)
U of California, Los Angeles (CA)
U of California, Santa Barbara (CA)
U of California, Santa Cruz (CA)
U of Chicago (IL)
U of Colorado Boulder (CO)
U of Georgia (GA)
U of Hartford (CT)
The U of Iowa (IA)
The U of Kansas (KS)
U of Louisiana at Lafayette (LA)
U of Mary Hardin-Baylor (TX)
U of Maryland, Coll Park (MD)
U of Michigan (MI)
U of Minnesota, Twin Cities Campus (MN)
U of Nebraska–Lincoln (NE)
U of Nevada, Las Vegas (NV)
U of New Mexico (NM)
U of North Carolina School of the Arts (NC)
U of Oklahoma (OK)
U of Oregon (OR)
U of Pennsylvania (PA)
U of Pikeville (KY)
U of Pittsburgh (PA)
U of Regina (SK, Canada)
U of Richmond (VA)
U of Rochester (NY)
U of Southern California (CA)
The U of Tampa (FL)
The U of the Arts (PA)
The U of Toledo (OH)
The U of Tulsa (OK)
U of Utah (UT)
U of Vermont (VT)
U of Waterloo (ON, Canada)
The U of Western Ontario (ON, Canada)
U of Windsor (ON, Canada)
U of Wisconsin–Milwaukee (WI)
Vanderbilt U (TN)
Vassar Coll (NY)
Washington U in St. Louis (MO)
Watkins Coll of Art, Design, & Film (TN)
Wayne State U (MI)
Webster U (MO)
Wells Coll (NY)
Wesleyan U (CT)
Wheaton Coll (MA)
Whitman Coll (WA)
Wright State U (OH)
Yale U (CT)

FILM/VIDEO AND PHOTOGRAPHIC ARTS RELATED
Arizona State U at the Tempe campus (AZ)
Birmingham-Southern Coll (AL)
Brigham Young U (UT)
Calvary Bible Coll and Theological Sem (MO)
Chatham U (PA)
Cleveland State U (OH)
Coe Coll (IA)
Coll of the Atlantic (ME)
Columbus Coll of Art & Design (OH)
Fairfield U (CT)
Hampshire Coll (MA)
Hollins U (VA)
Kansas City Art Inst (MO)
La Roche Coll (PA)
Mount Saint Mary's U (CA)
Northern Michigan U (MI)
Nossi Coll of Art (TN)
Oklahoma City U (OK)
Paris Coll of Art (France)
Portland State U (OR)
Pratt Inst (NY)
Rhode Island School of Design (RI)
Saint Joseph's U (PA)
School of the Art Inst of Chicago (IL)
School of the Museum of Fine Arts, Boston (MA)
Scripps Coll (CA)
U of Illinois at Chicago (IL)
U of Minnesota, Twin Cities Campus (MN)
Western Michigan U (MI)

FINANCE
Abilene Christian U (TX)
Adams State U (CO)
Adelphi U (NY)
Alabama State U (AL)
Albertus Magnus Coll (CT)
Albion Coll (MI)
Albright Coll (PA)
Alma Coll (MI)
American U (DC)
The American U in Dubai (United Arab Emirates)
Anderson U (IN)
Angelo State U (TX)
Appalachian State U (NC)
Aquinas Coll (TN)
Arcadia U (PA)
Arizona State U at the Tempe campus (AZ)
Arkansas State U (AR)
Ashland U (OH)
Auburn U (AL)
Auburn U at Montgomery (AL)
Augsburg Coll (MN)
Ave Maria U (FL)
Avila U (MO)
Babson Coll (MA)
Baldwin Wallace U (OH)
Ball State U (IN)
Barry U (FL)
Baruch Coll of the City U of New York (NY)
Baylor U (TX)
Belmont U (TN)
Benedictine Coll (KS)
Benedictine U (IL)
Bentley U (MA)
Berry Coll (GA)
Bethany Coll (WV)
Binghamton U, State U of New York (NY)
Boston Coll (MA)
Boston U (MA)
Bowling Green State U (OH)
Bradley U (IL)
Bridgewater State U (MA)
Bryant U (RI)
Butler U (IN)
Cabrini Coll (PA)
California State U, Dominguez Hills (CA)
California State U, Fresno (CA)
California State U, Long Beach (CA)
California State U, San Marcos (CA)
California State U, Stanislaus (CA)
Canisius Coll (NY)
Cape Breton U (NS, Canada)
Carroll Coll (MT)
Case Western Reserve U (OH)
The Catholic U of America (DC)
Cedarville U (OH)
Central Connecticut State U (CT)
Central Michigan U (MI)
Central Washington U (WA)
Charleston Southern U (SC)
Cheyney U of Pennsylvania (PA)
Christopher Newport U (VA)
Clarion U of Pennsylvania (PA)
Cleveland State U (OH)
Coastal Carolina U (SC)
The Coll at Brockport, State U of New York (NY)
Coll of Charleston (SC)
The Coll of St. Scholastica (MN)
The Coll of William and Mary (VA)
Colorado State U (CO)
Columbia Coll (MO)
Columbus State U (GA)
Concordia U (QC, Canada)
Concordia U, St. Paul (MN)
Corban U (OR)
Cornerstone U (MI)
Creighton U (NE)
Culver-Stockton Coll (MO)
Dakota State U (SD)
Dalhousie U (NS, Canada)
Dallas Baptist U (TX)
Davenport U, Grand Rapids (MI)
Delaware State U (DE)
Delta State U (MS)
DePaul U (IL)
DeSales U (PA)
Dickinson State U (ND)
Dixie State U (UT)
Dominican Coll (NY)
Dominican U (IL)
Dowling Coll (NY)
Drake U (IA)
Drexel U (PA)
Drury U (MO)
Duquesne U (PA)
East Carolina U (NC)

East Central U (OK)
Eastern Illinois U (IL)
Eastern Kentucky U (KY)
Eastern Michigan U (MI)
East Tennessee State U (TN)
Ellis U (IL)
Elmhurst Coll (IL)
Elon U (NC)
Endicott Coll (MA)
Excelsior Coll (NY)
Fairfield U (CT)
Fairleigh Dickinson U, Coll at Florham (NJ)
Fairleigh Dickinson U, Metropolitan Campus (NJ)
Fairmont State U (WV)
Fayetteville State U (NC)
Ferris State U (MI)
Fitchburg State U (MA)
Florida Atlantic U (FL)
Florida Gulf Coast U (FL)
Florida Intl U (FL)
Florida State Coll at Jacksonville (FL)
Florida State U (FL)
Fordham U (NY)
Fort Hays State U (KS)
Fort Lewis Coll (CO)
Framingham State U (MA)
Francis Marion U (SC)
Franklin Pierce U (NH)
Franklin U (OH)
Friends U (KS)
Gannon U (PA)
George Mason U (VA)
Georgetown U (DC)
The George Washington U (DC)
Georgia Regents U (GA)
Georgia Southern U (GA)
Georgia State U (GA)
Gonzaga U (WA)
Gordon Coll (MA)
Grace Coll (IN)
Grand Valley State U (MI)
Grove City Coll (PA)
Hamline U (MN)
Hampton U (VA)
Harding U (AR)
Hardin-Simmons U (TX)
Hawai`i Pacific U (HI)
HEC Montreal (QC, Canada)
High Point U (NC)
Hillsdale Coll (MI)
Hofstra U (NY)
Holy Family U (PA)
Houston Baptist U (TX)
Howard Payne U (TX)
Howard U (DC)
Hult Intl Business School (United Kingdom)
Husson U (ME)
Illinois Coll (IL)
Illinois State U (IL)
Immaculata U (PA)
Indiana State U (IN)
Indiana U of Pennsylvania (PA)
Indiana U–Purdue U Fort Wayne (IN)
Inter American U of Puerto Rico, Bayamón Campus (PR)
Inter American U of Puerto Rico, Ponce Campus (PR)
Inter American U of Puerto Rico, San Germán Campus (PR)
Iona Coll (NY)
Iowa State U of Science and Technology (IA)
Ithaca Coll (NY)
Jackson State U (MS)
Jacksonville State U (AL)
Jacksonville U (FL)
James Madison U (VA)
John Cabot U (Italy)
John Carroll U (OH)
Johnson & Wales U (RI)
Juniata Coll (PA)
Kansas State U (KS)
Kean U (NJ)
Keiser U, Fort Lauderdale (FL)
Kennesaw State U (GA)
Kent State U (OH)
King's Coll (PA)
King U (TN)
Lake Erie Coll (OH)
Lake Forest Coll (IL)
Lamar U (TX)
La Roche Coll (PA)
La Salle U (PA)
Lasell Coll (MA)
La Sierra U (CA)
Lehigh U (PA)
Le Moyne Coll (NY)
Lenoir-Rhyne U (NC)
LeTourneau U (TX)
Lewis U (IL)
Lincoln Memorial U (TN)
Lincoln U (PA)
Lindenwood U (MO)
Linfield Coll (OR)
Long Island U–LIU Brooklyn (NY)
Loras Coll (IA)
Louisiana Coll (LA)
Louisiana State U and A&M Coll (LA)
Louisiana State U in Shreveport (LA)
Loyola Marymount U (CA)
Loyola U Chicago (IL)
Loyola U New Orleans (LA)
Lubbock Christian U (TX)
Lycoming Coll (PA)
Manchester U (IN)
Manhattan Coll (NY)
Manhattanville Coll (NY)
Marian U (IN)
Marian U (WI)
Marietta Coll (OH)
Marquette U (WI)
Marshall U (WV)
Mars Hill U (NC)
Marymount Manhattan Coll (NY)
The Master's Coll and Sem (CA)
McKendree U (IL)
McMurry U (TX)
McNeese State U (LA)
Menlo Coll (CA)
Mercer U, Macon (GA)
Mercy Coll (NY)
Merrimack Coll (MA)
Metropolitan State U (MN)
Miami U (OH)
Michigan State U (MI)
Michigan Technological U (MI)
Middle Tennessee State U (TN)
Midwestern State U (TX)
Minnesota State U Mankato (MN)
Minnesota State U Moorhead (MN)
Minot State U (ND)
Mississippi State U (MS)
Missouri State U (MO)
Missouri Western State U (MO)
Molloy Coll (NY)
Montana State U Billings (MT)
Morehead State U (KY)
Mount Mercy U (IA)
Mount Vernon Nazarene U (OH)
Murray State U (KY)
National U (CA)
Nazareth Coll of Rochester (NY)
New England Coll (NH)
New Mexico Highlands U (NM)
New Mexico State U (NM)
New York Inst of Technology (NY)
New York U (NY)
Nicholls State U (LA)
Nichols Coll (MA)
North Carolina Ag and Tech State U (NC)
North Central Coll (IL)
North Dakota State U (ND)
Northeastern Illinois U (IL)
Northeastern State U (OK)
Northeastern U (MA)
Northern Arizona U (AZ)
Northern Illinois U (IL)
Northern Kentucky U (KY)
Northern Michigan U (MI)
Northern State U (SD)
Northwest Missouri State U (MO)
Northwest Nazarene U (ID)
Northwood U, Michigan Campus (MI)
Nova Southeastern U (FL)
Oakland U (MI)
Ohio Dominican U (OH)
The Ohio State U (OH)
Ohio U (OH)
Oklahoma Baptist U (OK)
Oklahoma Christian U (OK)
Oklahoma City U (OK)
Oklahoma State U (OK)
Old Dominion U (VA)
Olivet Coll (MI)
Oregon State U (OR)
Our Lady of the Lake U of San Antonio (TX)
Pace U (NY)
Pacific U (OR)
Palm Beach Atlantic U (FL)
Penn State Abington (PA)
Penn State Altoona (PA)
Penn State Beaver (PA)
Penn State Berks (PA)
Penn State Brandywine (PA)
Penn State DuBois (PA)
Penn State Erie, The Behrend Coll (PA)
Penn State Fayette, The Eberly Campus (PA)
Penn State Greater Allegheny (PA)
Penn State Harrisburg (PA)
Penn State Hazleton (PA)
Penn State Lehigh Valley (PA)
Penn State Mont Alto (PA)
Penn State New Kensington (PA)
Penn State Schuylkill (PA)
Penn State Shenango (PA)
Penn State U Park (PA)
Penn State Wilkes-Barre (PA)
Penn State Worthington Scranton (PA)
Penn State York (PA)
Pepperdine U, Malibu (CA)
Philadelphia U (PA)
Pittsburg State U (KS)
Plymouth State U (NH)
Point Loma Nazarene U (CA)
Polytechnic U of Puerto Rico (PR)
Portland State U (OR)
Post U (CT)
Prairie View A&M U (TX)
Providence Coll (RI)
Queens Coll of the City U of New York (NY)
Quincy U (IL)
Quinnipiac U (CT)
Radford U (VA)
Regis U (CO)
Rhode Island Coll (RI)
Rider U (NJ)
Rivier U (NH)
Robert Morris U (PA)
Rochester Inst of Technology (NY)
Rockford U (IL)
Roger Williams U (RI)
Roosevelt U (IL)
Rowan U (NJ)
Rutgers, The State U of New Jersey, Camden (NJ)
Rutgers, The State U of New Jersey, Newark (NJ)
Rutgers, The State U of New Jersey, New Brunswick (NJ)
Sacred Heart U (CT)
Saginaw Valley State U (MI)
Saint Anselm Coll (NH)
St. Bonaventure U (NY)
St. Edward's U (TX)
Saint Francis U (PA)
St. Gregory's U, Shawnee (OK)
St. John Fisher Coll (NY)
St. John's U (NY)
Saint Joseph's U (PA)
St. Mary's U (TX)
Saint Mary's U of Minnesota (MN)
St. Thomas Aquinas Coll (NY)
St. Thomas U (FL)
Saint Vincent Coll (PA)
Salisbury U (MD)
Salve Regina U (RI)
Samford U (AL)
Sam Houston State U (TX)
San Diego State U (CA)
San Francisco State U (CA)
San Jose State U (CA)
Santa Clara U (CA)
Seattle U (WA)
Shippensburg U of Pennsylvania (PA)
Siena Coll (NY)
Simmons Coll (MA)
Slippery Rock U of Pennsylvania (PA)
Southeastern Louisiana U (LA)
Southeastern Oklahoma State U (OK)
Southeastern U (FL)
Southeast Missouri State U (MO)
Southern Adventist U (TN)
Southern Connecticut State U (CT)
Southern Illinois U Carbondale (IL)
Southern Methodist U (TX)
Southern Utah U (UT)
Southwest Baptist U (MO)
Southwestern Adventist U (TX)
Southwestern Coll (KS)
Southwest Minnesota State U (MN)
State U of New York at Fredonia (NY)
State U of New York at New Paltz (NY)
State U of New York at Oswego (NY)
State U of New York at Plattsburgh (NY)
State U of New York Coll at Old Westbury (NY)
State U of New York Coll of Technology at Canton (NY)
Stephen F. Austin State U (TX)
Stetson U (FL)
Stonehill Coll (MA)
Suffolk U (MA)
Syracuse U (NY)
Tarleton State U (TX)
Taylor U (IN)
Temple U (PA)
Tennessee Wesleyan Coll (TN)
Texas A&M Intl U (TX)
Texas A&M U (TX)
Texas A&M U–Commerce (TX)
Texas A&M U–Corpus Christi (TX)
Texas A&M U–Kingsville (TX)
Texas Christian U (TX)
Texas Lutheran U (TX)
Texas State U (TX)
Texas Tech U (TX)
Texas Wesleyan U (TX)
Texas Woman's U (TX)
Tiffin U (OH)
Trinity Christian Coll (IL)
Trinity U (TX)
Troy U (AL)
Tulane U (LA)
Union U (TN)
Université de Sherbrooke (QC, Canada)
The U of Alabama (AL)
The U of Alabama at Birmingham (AL)
The U of Alabama in Huntsville (AL)
U of Alberta (AB, Canada)
The U of Arizona (AZ)
U of Arkansas (AR)
U of Arkansas at Little Rock (AR)
U of Bridgeport (CT)
The U of British Columbia (BC, Canada)
The U of British Columbia–Okanagan Campus (BC, Canada)
U of Central Arkansas (AR)
U of Central Florida (FL)
U of Central Missouri (MO)
U of Central Oklahoma (OK)
U of Charleston (WV)
U of Cincinnati (OH)
U of Colorado Boulder (CO)
U of Dayton (OH)
U of Delaware (DE)
U of Denver (CO)
U of Evansville (IN)
The U of Findlay (OH)
U of Florida (FL)
U of Georgia (GA)
U of Guelph (ON, Canada)
U of Hartford (CT)
U of Hawaii at Manoa (HI)
U of Houston (TX)
U of Houston–Clear Lake (TX)
U of Houston–Downtown (TX)
U of Houston–Victoria (TX)
U of Idaho (ID)
U of Illinois at Chicago (IL)
The U of Iowa (IA)
The U of Kansas (KS)
U of Kentucky (KY)
U of Lethbridge (AB, Canada)
U of Louisiana at Lafayette (LA)
U of Louisville (KY)
U of Maine (ME)
U of Mary Hardin-Baylor (TX)
U of Maryland, Coll Park (MD)
U of Maryland U Coll (MD)
U of Massachusetts Amherst (MA)
U of Massachusetts Dartmouth (MA)
U of Memphis (TN)
U of Miami (FL)
U of Michigan–Dearborn (MI)
U of Michigan–Flint (MI)
U of Minnesota, Duluth (MN)
U of Minnesota, Twin Cities Campus (MN)
U of Mississippi (MS)
U of Missouri (MO)
U of Missouri–St. Louis (MO)
The U of Montana (MT)
U of Montevallo (AL)
U of Mount Union (OH)
U of Nebraska–Lincoln (NE)
U of Nevada, Las Vegas (NV)
U of Nevada, Reno (NV)
U of New Haven (CT)
U of New Orleans (LA)
U of North Alabama (AL)
The U of North Carolina at Charlotte (NC)
The U of North Carolina at Greensboro (NC)
U of Northern Iowa (IA)
U of North Florida (FL)
U of North Georgia (GA)
U of North Texas (TX)
U of Northwestern–St. Paul (MN)
U of Notre Dame (IN)
U of Oklahoma (OK)
U of Ottawa (ON, Canada)
U of Pennsylvania (PA)
U of Pittsburgh (PA)
U of Portland (OR)
U of Puerto Rico in Ponce (PR)
U of Regina (SK, Canada)
U of Rhode Island (RI)
U of St. Francis (IL)
U of St. Thomas (MN)
U of St. Thomas (TX)
U of San Diego (CA)
U of San Francisco (CA)
U of Saskatchewan (SK, Canada)
The U of Scranton (PA)
U of South Alabama (AL)
The U of South Dakota (SD)
U of Southern Indiana (IN)
U of Southern Maine (ME)
U of Southern Mississippi (MS)
U of South Florida (FL)
U of South Florida, St. Petersburg (FL)
U of South Florida Sarasota-Manatee (FL)
The U of Tampa (FL)
The U of Tennessee (TN)
The U of Tennessee at Martin (TN)
The U of Texas at Austin (TX)
The U of Texas at Dallas (TX)
The U of Texas at El Paso (TX)
The U of Texas at San Antonio (TX)
The U of Texas at Tyler (TX)
The U of Texas of the Permian Basin (TX)
The U of Texas–Pan American (TX)
U of the District of Columbia (DC)
The U of Toledo (OH)
U of Toronto (ON, Canada)
The U of Tulsa (OK)
U of Utah (UT)
U of Washington (WA)
U of Washington, Tacoma (WA)
The U of West Alabama (AL)
The U of Western Ontario (ON, Canada)
U of West Florida (FL)
U of West Georgia (GA)
U of Windsor (ON, Canada)
U of Wisconsin–Eau Claire (WI)
U of Wisconsin–La Crosse (WI)
U of Wisconsin–Madison (WI)
U of Wisconsin–Milwaukee (WI)
U of Wisconsin–Oshkosh (WI)
U of Wisconsin–Parkside (WI)
U of Wisconsin–River Falls (WI)
U of Wisconsin–Superior (WI)
U of Wisconsin–Whitewater (WI)
U of Wyoming (WY)
Utah State U (UT)
Utah Valley U (UT)
Valdosta State U (GA)
Valparaiso U (IN)
Vanguard U of Southern California (CA)
Villanova U (PA)
Virginia Polytechnic Inst and State U (VA)

Virginia Union U (VA)
Wagner Coll (NY)
Wake Forest U (NC)
Walla Walla U (WA)
Walsh Coll of Accountancy and Business Administration (MI)
Wartburg Coll (IA)
Washburn U (KS)
Washington State U (WA)
Washington State U Vancouver (WA)
Washington U in St. Louis (MO)
Waynesburg U (PA)
Wayne State U (MI)
Webber Intl U (FL)
Weber State U (UT)
Webster U (MO)
West Chester U of Pennsylvania (PA)
Western Carolina U (NC)
Western Illinois U (IL)
Western Kentucky U (KY)
Western Michigan U (MI)
Western New England U (MA)
Western Washington U (WA)
Westminster Coll (UT)
West Texas A&M U (TX)
West Virginia U (WV)
Wichita State U (KS)
Wilkes U (PA)
William Paterson U of New Jersey (NJ)
Wilmington U (DE)
Wingate U (NC)
Winona State U (MN)
Wittenberg U (OH)
Wofford Coll (SC)
Wright State U (OH)
Xavier U (OH)
Yeshiva U (NY)
York Coll of Pennsylvania (PA)
Youngstown State U (OH)

FINANCE AND FINANCIAL MANAGEMENT SERVICES RELATED
Babson Coll (MA)
Columbia U, School of General Studies (NY)
Hofstra U (NY)
Immaculata U (PA)
James Madison U (VA)
Minot State U (ND)
National U (CA)
Olivet Coll (MI)
San Jose State U (CA)
Simmons Coll (MA)
State U of New York at New Paltz (NY)
The U of Tampa (FL)
Virginia Commonwealth U (VA)
Westminster Coll (UT)

FINANCIAL FORENSICS AND FRAUD INVESTIGATION
Canisius Coll (NY)
Champlain Coll (VT)
Keiser U, Fort Lauderdale (FL)

FINANCIAL MATHEMATICS
American U (DC)
Asbury U (KY)
Bethany Coll (WV)
Concordia Coll (MN)
Knox Coll (IL)
Lindenwood U (MO)
Purdue U (IN)
Trevecca Nazarene U (TN)
Trinity U (TX)
U of California, Los Angeles (CA)
U of Cincinnati (OH)
U of Kentucky (KY)
U of Mount Union (OH)

FINANCIAL PLANNING AND SERVICES
Baylor U (TX)
Berkeley Coll, Woodland Park (NJ)
Berkeley Coll–New York City Campus (NY)
Brigham Young U (UT)
Bryant U (RI)
Central Michigan U (MI)
Creighton U (NE)
Franklin U (OH)
Kansas State U (KS)
Lubbock Christian U (TX)
Maryville U of Saint Louis (MO)
Marywood U (PA)
Northern Michigan U (MI)
Olivet Coll (MI)
Purdue U (IN)
Saint Joseph's U (PA)
San Diego State U (CA)
Southern Methodist U (TX)
State U of New York Coll of Technology at Alfred (NY)
The U of Akron (OH)
U of Jamestown (ND)
U of Maine at Augusta (ME)
U of Mount Union (OH)
U of Wisconsin–Madison (WI)
Utah Valley U (UT)
Western Michigan U (MI)
Widener U (PA)
William Paterson U of New Jersey (NJ)
Wright State U (OH)
Youngstown State U (OH)

FINE AND STUDIO ARTS MANAGEMENT
Anna Maria Coll (MA)
Aquinas Coll (MI)
Belhaven U (MS)
Bennett Coll (NC)
Brenau U (GA)
Buena Vista U (IA)
Butler U (IN)
Catawba Coll (NC)
Chatham U (PA)
Coll of Charleston (SC)
The Coll of Idaho (ID)
Columbia Coll Chicago (IL)
Culver-Stockton Coll (MO)
Daemen Coll (NY)
Delaware State U (DE)
DePaul U (IL)
Eastern Michigan U (MI)
Fashion Inst of Technology (NY)
Fontbonne U (MO)
Fort Lewis Coll (CO)
Indiana U Bloomington (IN)
Ithaca Coll (NY)
Lake Erie Coll (OH)
Lasell Coll (MA)
Lenoir-Rhyne U (NC)
Lipscomb U (TN)
Marian U (IN)
Mary Baldwin Coll (VA)
Marywood U (PA)
Massachusetts Coll of Liberal Arts (MA)
Messiah Coll (PA)
Minot State U (ND)
North Carolina State U (NC)
Purchase Coll, State U of New York (NY)
Randolph-Macon Coll (VA)
Rider U (NJ)
Ringling Coll of Art and Design (FL)
Saint Vincent Coll (PA)
Salem Coll (NC)
Seton Hill U (PA)
Spring Hill Coll (AL)
State U of New York at Fredonia (NY)
Tiffin U (OH)
The U of Iowa (IA)
U of San Francisco (CA)
The U of Tulsa (OK)
U of Waterloo (ON, Canada)
U of Wisconsin–Stevens Point (WI)
Upper Iowa U (IA)
Viterbo U (WI)
Wagner Coll (NY)
Wartburg Coll (IA)
Waynesburg U (PA)
Westminster Coll (UT)
Whitworth U (WA)

FINE ARTS RELATED
Adelphi U (NY)
Allegheny Coll (PA)
Anna Maria Coll (MA)
Art Center Coll of Design (CA)
Ball State U (IN)
Benedictine U (IL)
Birmingham-Southern Coll (AL)
Bowdoin Coll (ME)
Bowling Green State U (OH)
California State U, Long Beach (CA)
Cleveland Inst of Art (OH)
The Coll of Saint Rose (NY)
Columbus Coll of Art & Design (OH)
Cornish Coll of the Arts (WA)
Covenant Coll (GA)
Elmira Coll (NY)
Grand Valley State U (MI)
Grand View U (IA)
Hampden-Sydney Coll (VA)
Hampshire Coll (MA)
Heritage U (WA)
Huntingdon Coll (AL)
Jacksonville U (FL)
Kentucky Wesleyan Coll (KY)
Kenyon Coll (OH)
Lake Erie Coll (OH)
Lindenwood U (MO)
Long Island U–LIU Post (NY)
Loyola U New Orleans (LA)
Madonna U (MI)
Monmouth U (NJ)
New York U (NY)
Northern Kentucky U (KY)
Northern Michigan U (MI)
Oakland U (MI)
Oklahoma City U (OK)
Oregon Coll of Art & Craft (OR)
Pratt Inst (NY)
Providence Coll (RI)
Purchase Coll, State U of New York (NY)
Rhode Island School of Design (RI)
Rutgers, The State U of New Jersey, Newark (NJ)
St. John's U (NY)
School of the Art Inst of Chicago (IL)
School of the Museum of Fine Arts, Boston (MA)
Seattle U (WA)
Seton Hill U (PA)
Skidmore Coll (NY)
The U of Akron (OH)
U of California, Los Angeles (CA)
U of Denver (CO)
U of Guam (GU)
U of Hartford (CT)
U of Maryland, Baltimore County (MD)
U of Mary Washington (VA)
U of Massachusetts Dartmouth (MA)
U of Massachusetts Lowell (MA)
U of Michigan (MI)
U of Regina (SK, Canada)
The U of the Arts (PA)
U of Washington (WA)
U of Wisconsin–Milwaukee (WI)
Ursinus Coll (PA)
Washington State U Vancouver (WA)
Widener U (PA)

FINE/STUDIO ARTS
Abilene Christian U (TX)
Acad of Art U (CA)
Agnes Scott Coll (GA)
Albertus Magnus Coll (CT)
Albion Coll (MI)
Allegheny Coll (PA)
American Acad of Art (IL)
American U (DC)
The American U in Dubai (United Arab Emirates)
American U of Beirut (Lebanon)
The American U of Rome (Italy)
Amherst Coll (MA)
Angelo State U (TX)
Antioch Coll, Yellow Springs (OH)
Appalachian State U (NC)
Aquinas Coll (MI)
Arcadia U (PA)
Art Center Coll of Design (CA)
Asbury U (KY)
Ashland U (OH)
Assumption Coll (MA)
Auburn U (AL)
Augsburg Coll (MN)
Baker U (KS)
Baldwin Wallace U (OH)
Bard Coll (NY)
Bard Coll at Simon's Rock (MA)
Baylor U (TX)
Beacon Coll (FL)
Belmont U (TN)
Beloit Coll (WI)
Bemidji State U (MN)
Benedictine U (IL)
Bennington Coll (VT)
Bethany Coll (WV)
Bethany Lutheran Coll (MN)
Bethel Coll (KS)
Bethel U (MN)
Biola U (CA)
Birmingham-Southern Coll (AL)
Bloomsburg U of Pennsylvania (PA)
Bob Jones U (SC)
Boston Coll (MA)
Bowdoin Coll (ME)
Bowling Green State U (OH)
Bradley U (IL)
Brandeis U (MA)
Brevard Coll (NC)
Bridgewater Coll (VA)
Bridgewater State U (MA)
Brigham Young U (UT)
Brown U (RI)
Bucknell U (PA)
Buffalo State Coll, State U of New York (NY)
Caldwell U (NJ)
California Coll of the Arts (CA)
California Inst of the Arts (CA)
California Polytechnic State U, San Luis Obispo (CA)
California State U, Chico (CA)
California State U, Fullerton (CA)
California State U, Long Beach (CA)
California State U, Stanislaus (CA)
Calvin Coll (MI)
Canisius Coll (NY)
Carleton Coll (MN)
Carlow U (PA)
Cazenovia Coll (NY)
Cedarville U (OH)
Centenary Coll of Louisiana (LA)
Central Michigan U (MI)
Central Washington U (WA)
Centre Coll (KY)
Chapman U (CA)
Chatham U (PA)
Chestnut Hill Coll (PA)
Cheyney U of Pennsylvania (PA)
Chowan U (NC)
Christian Brothers U (TN)
Christopher Newport U (VA)
Claflin U (SC)
Clark U (MA)
Coastal Carolina U (SC)
Coe Coll (IA)
Coker Coll (SC)
Colby Coll (ME)
Colby-Sawyer Coll (NH)
Coll for Creative Studies (MI)
Coll of Charleston (SC)
The Coll of Idaho (ID)
The Coll of New Jersey (NJ)
The Coll of New Rochelle (NY)
Coll of Saint Benedict (MN)
Coll of Staten Island of the City U of New York (NY)
Coll of the Holy Cross (MA)
The Coll of Wooster (OH)
The Colorado Coll (CO)
Colorado State U (CO)
Colorado State U–Pueblo (CO)
Columbia Coll (SC)
Columbia Coll Chicago (IL)
Columbia U, School of General Studies (NY)
Concordia U (QC, Canada)
Concordia U, Nebraska (NE)
Concordia U, St. Paul (MN)
Concord U (WV)
Cooper Union for the Advancement of Science and Art (NY)
Cornish Coll of the Arts (WA)
Creighton U (NE)
Culver-Stockton Coll (MO)
Cumberland U (TN)
Curry Coll (MA)
Daemen Coll (NY)
Dartmouth Coll (NH)
Denison U (OH)
DePauw U (IN)
Dickinson Coll (PA)
Dominican U (IL)
Drake U (IA)
Drury U (MO)
East Carolina U (NC)
Eastern Kentucky U (KY)
Edinboro U of Pennsylvania (PA)
Elizabethtown Coll (PA)
Elms Coll (MA)
Emily Carr U of Art + Design (BC, Canada)
Emmanuel Coll (MA)
Emory & Henry Coll (VA)
Endicott Coll (MA)
The Evergreen State Coll (WA)
Fairfield U (CT)
Fashion Inst of Technology (NY)
Ferris State U (MI)
Flagler Coll (FL)
Florida Ag and Mech U (FL)
Florida Intl U (FL)
Florida Southern Coll (FL)
Florida State U (FL)
Fontbonne U (MO)
Fordham U (NY)
Fort Hays State U (KS)
Franklin & Marshall Coll (PA)
Franklin Pierce U (NH)
Frostburg State U (MD)
Furman U (SC)
Gallaudet U (DC)
Georgetown Coll (KY)
Georgetown U (DC)
The George Washington U (DC)
Gettysburg Coll (PA)
Goucher Coll (MD)
Graceland U (IA)
Grand View U (IA)
Green Mountain Coll (VT)
Grinnell Coll (IA)
Hamilton Coll (NY)
Hamline U (MN)
Hampden-Sydney Coll (VA)
Harding U (AR)
Hardin-Simmons U (TX)
High Point U (NC)
Hobart and William Smith Colls (NY)
Hofstra U (NY)
Holy Family U (PA)
Hope Coll (MI)
Houston Baptist U (TX)
Howard Payne U (TX)
Humboldt State U (CA)
Hunter Coll of the City U of New York (NY)
Huntingdon Coll (AL)
Illinois State U (IL)
Indiana State U (IN)
Indiana U Bloomington (IN)
Indiana U Kokomo (IN)
Indiana U Northwest (IN)
Indiana U of Pennsylvania (PA)
Indiana U–Purdue U Fort Wayne (IN)
Indiana U–Purdue U Indianapolis (IN)
Indiana U South Bend (IN)
Indiana U Southeast (IN)
Inst of American Indian Arts (NM)
Ithaca Coll (NY)
Jacksonville U (FL)
Johnson State Coll (VT)
Judson U (IL)
Juniata Coll (PA)
Kansas State U (KS)
Kean U (NJ)
Keene State Coll (NH)
Kentucky State U (KY)
Kenyon Coll (OH)
Keystone Coll (PA)
Knox Coll (IL)
Kutztown U of Pennsylvania (PA)
Lafayette Coll (PA)
Laguna Coll of Art & Design (CA)
Lamar U (TX)
Landmark Coll (VT)
La Sierra U (CA)
Lawrence U (WI)
Lebanese American U (Lebanon)
Lee U (TN)
Lewis & Clark Coll (OR)
Liberty U (VA)
Limestone Coll (SC)
Lincoln U (MO)
Lincoln U (PA)
Lindenwood U (MO)
Lindsey Wilson Coll (KY)
Linfield Coll (OR)
Lipscomb U (TN)
Lock Haven U of Pennsylvania (PA)
Long Island U–LIU Brooklyn (NY)
Louisiana Coll (LA)
Louisiana State U and A&M Coll (LA)
Loyola Marymount U (CA)
Loyola U Chicago (IL)
Lycoming Coll (PA)

Maharishi U of Management (IA)
Malone U (OH)
Manchester U (IN)
Manhattanville Coll (NY)
Marian U (IN)
Marian U (WI)
Marietta Coll (OH)
Marist Coll (NY)
Mars Hill U (NC)
Marylhurst U (OR)
Marymount Manhattan Coll (NY)
Marymount U (VA)
Maryville Coll (TN)
Maryville U of Saint Louis (MO)
Massachusetts Coll of Art and Design (MA)
McMurry U (TX)
Meredith Coll (NC)
Merrimack Coll (MA)
Messiah Coll (PA)
Middlebury Coll (VT)
Milligan Coll (TN)
Millikin U (IL)
Millsaps Coll (MS)
Mills Coll (CA)
Minnesota State U Mankato (MN)
Missouri Southern State U (MO)
Missouri Western State U (MO)
Molloy Coll (NY)
Montana State U (MT)
Montclair State U (NJ)
Moore Coll of Art & Design (PA)
Moravian Coll (PA)
Morehead State U (KY)
Morningside Coll (IA)
Mount Allison U (NB, Canada)
Mount Holyoke Coll (MA)
Murray State U (KY)
Naropa U (CO)
Nazareth Coll of Rochester (NY)
New Coll of Florida (FL)
New England Coll (NH)
New Mexico State U (NM)
New York Inst of Technology (NY)
New York U (NY)
Northeastern U (MA)
Northern Arizona U (AZ)
Northern Illinois U (IL)
Northern Kentucky U (KY)
North Greenville U (SC)
Nova Southeastern U (FL)
Oberlin Coll (OH)
Ohio Northern U (OH)
The Ohio State U (OH)
Ohio U (OH)
Ohio Wesleyan U (OH)
Oklahoma Baptist U (OK)
Oklahoma City U (OK)
Otis Coll of Art and Design (CA)
Pace U (NY)
Pacific Lutheran U (WA)
Pacific Northwest Coll of Art (OR)
Paier Coll of Art, Inc. (CT)
Palm Beach Atlantic U (FL)
Paris Coll of Art (France)
Park U (MO)
Pennsylvania Coll of Art & Design (PA)
Piedmont Coll (GA)
Plymouth State U (NH)
Pratt Inst (NY)
Presbyterian Coll (SC)
Prescott Coll (AZ)
Principia Coll (IL)
Providence Coll (RI)
Purdue U (IN)
Queens Coll of the City U of New York (NY)
Randolph Coll (VA)
Randolph-Macon Coll (VA)
Reed Coll (OR)
Rice U (TX)
Ringling Coll of Art and Design (FL)
Rochester Inst of Technology (NY)
Rocky Mountain Coll of Art + Design (CO)
Rosemont Coll (PA)
The Sage Colls (NY)
Saginaw Valley State U (MI)
St. Catherine U (MN)
Saint John's U (MN)
Saint Joseph's Coll (IN)
Saint Louis U (MO)
Saint Mary's U of Minnesota (MN)
Saint Peter's U (NJ)
St. Thomas Aquinas Coll (NY)
Saint Vincent Coll (PA)
Salem Coll (NC)
Salisbury U (MD)
Salve Regina U (RI)
Sam Houston State U (TX)
San Diego State U (CA)
San Jose State U (CA)
Santa Clara U (CA)
Santa Fe U of Art and Design (NM)
Sarah Lawrence Coll (NY)
School of the Art Inst of Chicago (IL)
School of the Museum of Fine Arts, Boston (MA)
Scripps Coll (CA)
Seattle U (WA)
Seton Hill U (PA)
Sewanee: The U of the South (TN)
Shawnee State U (OH)
Siena Coll (NY)
Simpson Coll (IA)
Slippery Rock U of Pennsylvania (PA)
Smith Coll (MA)
South Carolina State U (SC)
South Dakota State U (SD)
Southern Arkansas U–Magnolia (AR)
Southern Connecticut State U (CT)
Southern Illinois U Carbondale (IL)
Southern Illinois U Edwardsville (IL)
Southern Methodist U (TX)
Southern Utah U (UT)
Spalding U (KY)
Spring Hill Coll (AL)
Stanford U (CA)
State U of New York at Fredonia (NY)
State U of New York Coll at Cortland (NY)
State U of New York Coll at Potsdam (NY)
Stockton U (NJ)
Stonehill Coll (MA)
Suffolk U (MA)
Susquehanna U (PA)
Syracuse U (NY)
Tabor Coll (KS)
Tarleton State U (TX)
Texas A&M Intl U (TX)
Texas A&M U–Commerce (TX)
Texas A&M U–Kingsville (TX)
Texas Christian U (TX)
Texas Southern U (TX)
Texas State U (TX)
Thomas More Coll (KY)
Towson U (MD)
Trinity Christian Coll (IL)
Trinity Coll (CT)
Truman State U (MO)
Tufts U (MA)
Tulane U (LA)
Union Coll (NE)
Union Coll (NY)
Unity Coll (ME)
Université du Québec en Outaouais (QC, Canada)
U at Buffalo, the State U of New York (NY)
The U of Akron (OH)
The U of Alabama (AL)
The U of Arizona (AZ)
U of Arkansas at Little Rock (AR)
The U of British Columbia (BC, Canada)
U of California, Davis (CA)
U of California, Irvine (CA)
U of California, Riverside (CA)
U of California, Santa Barbara (CA)
U of Central Florida (FL)
U of Central Missouri (MO)
U of Central Oklahoma (OK)
U of Cincinnati (OH)
U of Colorado Boulder (CO)
U of Colorado Denver (CO)
U of Dallas (TX)
U of Dayton (OH)
U of Delaware (DE)
U of Florida (FL)
U of Georgia (GA)
U of Great Falls (MT)
U of Guelph (ON, Canada)
U of Houston–Clear Lake (TX)
U of Idaho (ID)
U of Illinois at Chicago (IL)
U of Illinois at Springfield (IL)
U of Indianapolis (IN)
U of Jamestown (ND)
The U of Kansas (KS)
U of Kentucky (KY)
U of Lethbridge (AB, Canada)
U of Louisville (KY)
U of Maine (ME)
U of Maine at Augusta (ME)
U of Maine at Presque Isle (ME)
U of Mary Hardin-Baylor (TX)
U of Maryland, Baltimore County (MD)
U of Maryland, Coll Park (MD)
U of Massachusetts Amherst (MA)
U of Massachusetts Dartmouth (MA)
U of Miami (FL)
U of Michigan–Flint (MI)
U of Minnesota, Duluth (MN)
U of Minnesota, Morris (MN)
U of Minnesota, Twin Cities Campus (MN)
U of Mississippi (MS)
U of Missouri–Kansas City (MO)
U of Missouri–St. Louis (MO)
U of Mount Union (OH)
U of Nebraska–Lincoln (NE)
U of New Hampshire (NH)
U of New Haven (CT)
U of New Orleans (LA)
U of North Carolina at Asheville (NC)
The U of North Carolina at Chapel Hill (NC)
The U of North Carolina at Charlotte (NC)
The U of North Carolina at Greensboro (NC)
The U of North Carolina at Pembroke (NC)
The U of North Carolina Wilmington (NC)
U of Northern Colorado (CO)
U of Northern Iowa (IA)
U of North Florida (FL)
U of North Georgia (GA)
U of North Texas (TX)
U of Northwestern–St. Paul (MN)
U of Notre Dame (IN)
U of Oklahoma (OK)
U of Oregon (OR)
U of Ottawa (ON, Canada)
U of Pennsylvania (PA)
U of Pittsburgh (PA)
U of Regina (SK, Canada)
U of Rhode Island (RI)
U of Richmond (VA)
U of Rochester (NY)
U of Saint Francis (IN)
U of St. Thomas (TX)
U of San Francisco (CA)
U of Saskatchewan (SK, Canada)
U of Science and Arts of Oklahoma (OK)
U of South Carolina Aiken (SC)
U of South Carolina Beaufort (SC)
U of South Carolina Upstate (SC)
U of Southern California (CA)
U of Southern Maine (ME)
U of Southern Mississippi (MS)
U of South Florida (FL)
The U of Tennessee (TN)
The U of Texas at Arlington (TX)
The U of Texas at Austin (TX)
The U of Texas at El Paso (TX)
The U of Texas at San Antonio (TX)
The U of Texas–Pan American (TX)
The U of the Arts (PA)
U of the Cumberlands (KY)
U of the District of Columbia (DC)
U of the Fraser Valley (BC, Canada)
U of the Incarnate Word (TX)
U of the Pacific (CA)
The U of Toledo (OH)
The U of Tulsa (OK)
U of Vermont (VT)
U of Waterloo (ON, Canada)
The U of Western Ontario (ON, Canada)
U of West Florida (FL)
U of Windsor (ON, Canada)
U of Wisconsin–Oshkosh (WI)
U of Wisconsin–Stevens Point (WI)
U of Wisconsin–Superior (WI)
Ursuline Coll (OH)
Vanderbilt U (TN)
Vassar Coll (NY)
Virginia Union U (VA)
Viterbo U (WI)
Wake Forest U (NC)
Walla Walla U (WA)
Washington and Lee U (VA)
Washington State U (WA)
Washington U in St. Louis (MO)
Watkins Coll of Art, Design, & Film (TN)
Webster U (MO)
Wells Coll (NY)
Wesleyan Coll (GA)
Wesleyan U (CT)
West Chester U of Pennsylvania (PA)
Western Carolina U (NC)
Western Illinois U (IL)
Western Kentucky U (KY)
Western Michigan U (MI)
Western State Colorado U (CO)
Westminster Coll (UT)
West Texas A&M U (TX)
West Virginia Wesleyan Coll (WV)
Whitworth U (WA)
Willamette U (OR)
William Paterson U of New Jersey (NJ)
Williams Baptist Coll (AR)
Wittenberg U (OH)
Wofford Coll (SC)
Xavier U (OH)
York Coll of Pennsylvania (PA)
Youngstown State U (OH)

FIRE/ARSON INVESTIGATION AND PREVENTION
Eastern Kentucky U (KY)

FIRE PREVENTION AND SAFETY TECHNOLOGY
Athens State U (AL)
Delaware State U (DE)
Eastern Kentucky U (KY)
Jefferson Coll of Health Sciences (VA)
Oklahoma State U (OK)
U of New Haven (CT)
West Texas A&M U (TX)

FIRE PROTECTION RELATED
The U of Akron (OH)

FIRE SCIENCE/FIREFIGHTING
Anna Maria Coll (MA)
Columbia Southern U (AL)
Embry-Riddle Aeronautical U–Worldwide (FL)
Hampton U (VA)
Madonna U (MI)
New Jersey City U (NJ)
Providence Coll (RI)
U of Florida (FL)
U of New Haven (CT)
Utah Valley U (UT)

FIRE SERVICES ADMINISTRATION
Albany State U (GA)
American Public U System (WV)
Bowling Green State U (OH)
California State U, Los Angeles (CA)
Colorado State U (CO)
Columbia Southern U (AL)
Eastern Kentucky U (KY)
Eastern Oregon U (OR)
Fayetteville State U (NC)
Holy Family U (PA)
Lewis U (IL)
Lindenwood U (MO)
St. Thomas U (FL)
Southern Illinois U Carbondale (IL)
U of Cincinnati (OH)
The U of North Carolina at Charlotte (NC)
U of the District of Columbia (DC)
Waldorf Coll (IA)
Western Illinois U (IL)
Western Oregon U (OR)

FISHING AND FISHERIES SCIENCES AND MANAGEMENT
Colorado State U (CO)
Delaware State U (DE)
Humboldt State U (CA)
Iowa State U of Science and Technology (IA)
Mansfield U of Pennsylvania (PA)
Michigan State U (MI)
The Ohio State U (OH)
Oregon State U (OR)
Purdue U (IN)
State U of New York Coll of Environmental Science and Forestry (NY)
Texas A&M U (TX)
U of Alaska Fairbanks (AK)
U of Arkansas at Pine Bluff (AR)
The U of British Columbia (BC, Canada)
U of Idaho (ID)
U of Minnesota, Twin Cities Campus (MN)
U of Missouri (MO)
U of Rhode Island (RI)
The U of Tennessee at Martin (TN)

FLIGHT INSTRUCTION
South Dakota State U (SD)
U of North Dakota (ND)

FOLKLORE
Goddard Coll (VT)
Indiana U Bloomington (IN)
U of Oregon (OR)

FOODS AND NUTRITION RELATED
California State U, Long Beach (CA)
Samford U (AL)
U of Alberta (AB, Canada)
The U of British Columbia (BC, Canada)
U of Guelph (ON, Canada)
Utah State U (UT)

FOOD SCIENCE
American U of Beirut (Lebanon)
Auburn U (AL)
California Polytechnic State U, San Luis Obispo (CA)
California State Polytechnic U, Pomona (CA)
Clarke U (IA)
Cornell U (NY)
Dalhousie U (NS, Canada)
Dominican U (IL)
Framingham State U (MA)
Kansas State U (KS)
Michigan State U (MI)
Mississippi State U (MS)
North Carolina Ag and Tech State U (NC)
North Carolina State U (NC)
North Dakota State U (ND)
The Ohio State U (OH)
Oklahoma State U (OK)
Oregon State U (OR)
Penn State Abington (PA)
Penn State Altoona (PA)
Penn State Beaver (PA)
Penn State Berks (PA)
Penn State Brandywine (PA)
Penn State DuBois (PA)
Penn State Erie, The Behrend Coll (PA)
Penn State Fayette, The Eberly Campus (PA)
Penn State Greater Allegheny (PA)
Penn State Hazleton (PA)
Penn State Lehigh Valley (PA)
Penn State Mont Alto (PA)
Penn State New Kensington (PA)
Penn State Schuylkill (PA)
Penn State Shenango (PA)
Penn State U Park (PA)
Penn State Wilkes-Barre (PA)
Penn State Worthington Scranton (PA)
Penn State York (PA)
Purdue U (IN)
Rutgers, The State U of New Jersey, New Brunswick (NJ)
San Jose State U (CA)
Simmons Coll (MA)
Texas Tech U (TX)
U of Arkansas (AR)
The U of British Columbia (BC, Canada)
U of California, Davis (CA)
U of Delaware (DE)
U of Florida (FL)
U of Georgia (GA)
U of Guelph (ON, Canada)
U of Idaho (ID)

U of Kentucky (KY)
U of Maine (ME)
U of Maryland, Coll Park (MD)
U of Massachusetts Amherst (MA)
U of Minnesota, Twin Cities Campus (MN)
U of Missouri (MO)
U of Nebraska–Lincoln (NE)
U of Saskatchewan (SK, Canada)
The U of Tennessee (TN)
U of Wisconsin–Madison (WI)
U of Wisconsin–River Falls (WI)
Virginia Polytechnic Inst and State U (VA)
Washington State U (WA)

FOOD SCIENCE AND TECHNOLOGY RELATED
Appalachian State U (NC)
North Dakota State U (ND)
U of Alberta (AB, Canada)
The U of British Columbia (BC, Canada)

FOOD SERVICE AND DINING ROOM MANAGEMENT
Johnson & Wales U (CO)
Johnson & Wales U (FL)
Johnson & Wales U - Charlotte Campus (NC)

FOOD SERVICE SYSTEMS ADMINISTRATION
Central Michigan U (MI)
Dominican U (IL)
Iowa State U of Science and Technology (IA)
Johnson & Wales U (RI)
Lamar U (TX)
Lipscomb U (TN)
Ohio U (OH)
Point Loma Nazarene U (CA)
Rochester Inst of Technology (NY)
Sam Houston State U (TX)
Simmons Coll (MA)
The U of North Carolina at Greensboro (NC)
U of Wisconsin–Stout (WI)
Western Michigan U (MI)

FOODS, NUTRITION, AND WELLNESS
Alcorn State U (MS)
Andrews U (MI)
Arizona State U at the Downtown Phoenix campus (AZ)
Auburn U (AL)
Bastyr U (WA)
Benedictine U (IL)
Bluffton U (OH)
Bowling Green State U (OH)
Bradley U (IL)
Bridgewater Coll (VA)
California State U, Fresno (CA)
California State U, Los Angeles (CA)
Carson-Newman U (TN)
Cedar Crest Coll (PA)
Coll of the Ozarks (MO)
Delaware State U (DE)
Dominican U (IL)
Eastern Kentucky U (KY)
Georgia Southern U (GA)
Goddard Coll (VT)
Howard U (DC)
Hunter Coll of the City U of New York (NY)
Indiana State U (IN)
Indiana U of Pennsylvania (PA)
Iowa State U of Science and Technology (IA)
Ithaca Coll (NY)
Jacksonville State U (AL)
James Madison U (VA)
Langston U (OK)
Lehman Coll of the City U of New York (NY)
Life U (GA)
Lincoln U (MO)
Madonna U (MI)
The Master's Coll and Sem (CA)
Middle Tennessee State U (TN)
Minnesota State U Mankato (MN)
Montclair State U (NJ)
Morrisville State Coll (NY)
Murray State U (KY)
New Mexico State U (NM)
New York U (NY)
North Carolina Ag and Tech State U (NC)
Northern Illinois U (IL)
The Ohio State U (OH)
Ohio U (OH)
Oklahoma State U (OK)
Point Loma Nazarene U (CA)
Prairie View A&M U (TX)
Purdue U (IN)
Radford U (VA)
St. Catherine U (MN)
Samford U (AL)
Sam Houston State U (TX)
Seattle Pacific U (WA)
South Carolina State U (SC)
South Dakota State U (SD)
State U of New York at Plattsburgh (NY)
Stephen F. Austin State U (TX)
Syracuse U (NY)
Texas A&M U (TX)
Texas State U (TX)
Texas Tech U (TX)
Texas Woman's U (TX)
Université de Montréal (QC, Canada)
The U of Akron (OH)
U of Arkansas (AR)
The U of British Columbia (BC, Canada)
U of Central Arkansas (AR)
U of Central Oklahoma (OK)
U of Delaware (DE)
U of Georgia (GA)
U of Idaho (ID)
U of Kentucky (KY)
U of Minnesota, Twin Cities Campus (MN)
U of Missouri (MO)
U of Nebraska–Lincoln (NE)
U of Nevada, Reno (NV)
U of New Mexico (NM)
The U of North Carolina at Chapel Hill (NC)
U of Northern Iowa (IA)
U of Ottawa (ON, Canada)
U of Saint Joseph (CT)
The U of Tennessee (TN)
The U of Texas at Austin (TX)
U of Toronto (ON, Canada)
The U of Western Ontario (ON, Canada)
Virginia Polytechnic Inst and State U (VA)
Waldorf Coll (IA)
Washington State U (WA)
Wayne State U (MI)
Youngstown State U (OH)

FOOD TECHNOLOGY AND PROCESSING
Brigham Young U (UT)
Iowa State U of Science and Technology (IA)
New Mexico State U (NM)
Purdue U (IN)
Tennessee State U (TN)

FOREIGN LANGUAGES AND LITERATURES
Arkansas State U (AR)
Arkansas Tech U (AR)
Assumption Coll (MA)
Auburn U (AL)
Auburn U at Montgomery (AL)
Augustana Coll (SD)
Austin Peay State U (TN)
Benedictine Coll (KS)
Bennington Coll (VT)
Bloomsburg U of Pennsylvania (PA)
Boston U (MA)
California Polytechnic State U, San Luis Obispo (CA)
Cameron U (OK)
Central Methodist U (MO)
The Citadel, The Military Coll of South Carolina (SC)
Clarion U of Pennsylvania (PA)
Colorado State U (CO)
Colorado State U–Pueblo (CO)
Covenant Coll (GA)
Delta State U (MS)
Duquesne U (PA)
Eastern Illinois U (IL)
East Tennessee State U (TN)
Elmira Coll (NY)
Elon U (NC)
Emporia State U (KS)
The Evergreen State Coll (WA)
Excelsior Coll (NY)
Framingham State U (MA)
Francis Marion U (SC)
Frostburg State U (MD)
Gannon U (PA)
George Mason U (VA)
Georgia Inst of Technology (GA)
Gordon Coll (MA)
Grace Coll (IN)
Hamilton Coll (NY)
Hastings Coll (NE)
Jackson State U (MS)
James Madison U (VA)
Juniata Coll (PA)
Kansas State U (KS)
Kenyon Coll (OH)
Knox Coll (IL)
Lake Erie Coll (OH)
Lamar U (TX)
Lewis & Clark Coll (OR)
Long Island U–LIU Brooklyn (NY)
Long Island U–LIU Post (NY)
Longwood U (VA)
Loyola U New Orleans (LA)
Lycoming Coll (PA)
Manchester U (IN)
Marshall U (WV)
Massachusetts Inst of Technology (MA)
McNeese State U (LA)
Middle Tennessee State U (TN)
Mississippi State U (MS)
Missouri Western State U (MO)
Monmouth U (NJ)
Montana State U (MT)
New Mexico State U (NM)
New York U (NY)
North Carolina State U (NC)
Northern Arizona U (AZ)
Notre Dame of Maryland U (MD)
Oakland U (MI)
Old Dominion U (VA)
Pace U (NY)
Penn State Berks (PA)
Penn State Lehigh Valley (PA)
Piedmont Coll (GA)
Plymouth State U (NH)
Presbyterian Coll (SC)
Principia Coll (IL)
Purdue U Calumet (IN)
Radford U (VA)
Roger Williams U (RI)
Rutgers, The State U of New Jersey, New Brunswick (NJ)
St. Mary's Coll of Maryland (MD)
Saint Peter's U (NJ)
Samford U (AL)
Scripps Coll (CA)
South Carolina State U (SC)
Southern Adventist U (TN)
Southern Illinois U Carbondale (IL)
Southern Illinois U Edwardsville (IL)
Stanford U (CA)
State U of New York Coll at Old Westbury (NY)
Stephen F. Austin State U (TX)
Stockton U (NJ)
Stonehill Coll (MA)
Suffolk U (MA)
Syracuse U (NY)
Texas A&M U (TX)
Texas Tech U (TX)
Towson U (MD)
Tufts U (MA)
Tulane U (LA)
Union Coll (NE)
Union Coll (NY)
Union U (TN)
The U of Alabama (AL)
The U of Alabama at Birmingham (AL)
The U of Alabama in Huntsville (AL)
U of Alaska Fairbanks (AK)
U of Arkansas at Little Rock (AR)
U of California, Riverside (CA)
U of California, Santa Cruz (CA)
U of Dayton (OH)
U of Delaware (DE)
U of Hartford (CT)
U of Houston (TX)
U of Idaho (ID)
U of Louisiana at Lafayette (LA)
U of Maine (ME)
U of Maryland, Baltimore County (MD)
U of Mary Washington (VA)
U of Massachusetts Lowell (MA)
U of Memphis (TN)
U of Minnesota, Twin Cities Campus (MN)
U of Missouri–Kansas City (MO)
U of Missouri–St. Louis (MO)
The U of Montana (MT)
U of Montevallo (AL)
U of New Mexico (NM)
U of New Orleans (LA)
U of North Alabama (AL)
The U of North Carolina at Chapel Hill (NC)
U of Northern Colorado (CO)
U of Ottawa (ON, Canada)
U of Puget Sound (WA)
The U of Scranton (PA)
U of South Alabama (AL)
U of Southern Mississippi (MS)
U of South Florida, St. Petersburg (FL)
The U of Tennessee (TN)
The U of Tennessee at Chattanooga (TN)
The U of Texas at Arlington (TX)
The U of Texas at San Antonio (TX)
The U of Texas at Tyler (TX)
The U of Virginia's Coll at Wise (VA)
U of Wisconsin–River Falls (WI)
Utica Coll (NY)
Virginia Commonwealth U (VA)
Washington Coll (MD)
Washington State U (WA)
Wayne State Coll (NE)
Wayne State U (MI)
West Chester U of Pennsylvania (PA)
Western Washington U (WA)
West Virginia U (WV)
Wichita State U (KS)
Widener U (PA)
Winthrop U (SC)
Wright State U (OH)
Youngstown State U (OH)

FOREIGN LANGUAGES RELATED
Arizona State U at the Tempe campus (AZ)
Augustana Coll (SD)
Averett U (VA)
Binghamton U, State U of New York (NY)
Excelsior Coll (NY)
Georgia Regents U (GA)
Georgia Southern U (GA)
Houston Baptist U (TX)
Indiana State U (IN)
Indiana U of Pennsylvania (PA)
Kennesaw State U (GA)
New York U (NY)
Occidental Coll (CA)
Purchase Coll, State U of New York (NY)
St. Lawrence U (NY)
U of Alaska Fairbanks (AK)
U of Alberta (AB, Canada)
U of California, Berkeley (CA)
U of California, Los Angeles (CA)
U of Delaware (DE)
U of Hawaii at Manoa (HI)
U of Lethbridge (AB, Canada)
U of West Georgia (GA)
Western Washington U (WA)
Yale U (CT)

FOREIGN LANGUAGE TEACHER EDUCATION
Arkansas State U (AR)
Arkansas Tech U (AR)
Ashland U (OH)
Auburn U (AL)
Baylor U (TX)
Boston U (MA)
Bowling Green State U (OH)
Buffalo State Coll, State U of New York (NY)
Calvin Coll (MI)
Cameron U (OK)
Central Methodist U (MO)
Coll of Staten Island of the City U of New York (NY)
Concordia Coll (MN)
Cornell U (NY)
Dowling Coll (NY)
Eastern Michigan U (MI)
Elmira Coll (NY)
Grand Valley State U (MI)
Greensboro Coll (NC)
Hastings Coll (NE)
Hofstra U (NY)
Indiana U Bloomington (IN)
Iona Coll (NY)
Lincoln U (PA)
Long Island U–LIU Post (NY)
Manchester U (IN)
Miami U (OH)
Nazareth Coll of Rochester (NY)
New York U (NY)
Northern Kentucky U (KY)
Ohio Northern U (OH)
Ohio Wesleyan U (OH)
Penn State Abington (PA)
Penn State Altoona (PA)
Penn State Beaver (PA)
Penn State Berks (PA)
Penn State Brandywine (PA)
Penn State DuBois (PA)
Penn State Erie, The Behrend Coll (PA)
Penn State Fayette, The Eberly Campus (PA)
Penn State Greater Allegheny (PA)
Penn State Mont Alto (PA)
Penn State Shenango (PA)
Penn State U Park (PA)
Penn State Worthington Scranton (PA)
Penn State York (PA)
Piedmont Coll (GA)
Providence Coll (RI)
Rhode Island Coll (RI)
Saint Francis U (PA)
Seton Hill U (PA)
Southeast Missouri State U (MO)
State U of New York Coll at Old Westbury (NY)
Temple U (PA)
U of Alberta (AB, Canada)
U of Central Florida (FL)
U of Dayton (OH)
U of Georgia (GA)
U of Mary Hardin-Baylor (TX)
U of Minnesota, Duluth (MN)
U of Nebraska–Lincoln (NE)
U of Nevada, Reno (NV)
U of Northern Iowa (IA)
U of Oklahoma (OK)
The U of South Dakota (SD)
U of South Florida (FL)
The U of Tennessee at Chattanooga (TN)
U of Vermont (VT)
U of Windsor (ON, Canada)
Valparaiso U (IN)
Vanderbilt U (TN)
Virginia Wesleyan Coll (VA)
Washington State U (WA)
Wayne State Coll (NE)
Youngstown State U (OH)

FORENSIC CHEMISTRY
Alabama State U (AL)
Arizona State U at the West campus (AZ)
Ashland U (OH)
Bethany Coll (WV)
Chestnut Hill Coll (PA)
Delaware State U (DE)
Emmanuel Coll (MA)
Lamar U (TX)
Maryville U of Saint Louis (MO)
Missouri Baptist U (MO)
Palm Beach Atlantic U (FL)
St. Edward's U (TX)
Sam Houston State U (TX)
Slippery Rock U of Pennsylvania (PA)
U of Central Oklahoma (OK)
U of Rhode Island (RI)
U of Saint Francis (IN)
Western Carolina U (NC)
Western New England U (MA)

FORENSIC PSYCHOLOGY
Bay Path U (MA)
Canisius Coll (NY)
Castleton State Coll (VT)
The Coll of Saint Rose (NY)
Florida Inst of Technology (FL)
Gwynedd Mercy U (PA)

Roger Williams U (RI)
Tiffin U (OH)
U of New Haven (CT)
Walden U (MN)
Walla Walla U (WA)
Western State Colorado U (CO)

FORENSIC SCIENCE AND TECHNOLOGY
Alvernia U (PA)
American Public U System (WV)
Bay Path U (MA)
Becker Coll (MA)
Bluefield Coll (VA)
Bryant U (RI)
Buffalo State Coll, State U of New York (NY)
Cedar Crest Coll (PA)
Cedarville U (OH)
Chaminade U of Honolulu (HI)
Chestnut Hill Coll (PA)
The Coll of Saint Rose (NY)
Columbia Coll (MO)
Defiance Coll (OH)
Delaware State U (DE)
Dixie State U (UT)
Eastern Kentucky U (KY)
Eastern New Mexico U (NM)
Ellis U (IL)
Embry-Riddle Aeronautical U–Prescott (AZ)
Farmingdale State Coll (NY)
Fayetteville State U (NC)
Friends U (KS)
George Mason U (VA)
Hilbert Coll (NY)
Hofstra U (NY)
Husson U (ME)
Indiana U–Purdue U Indianapolis (IN)
Inter American U of Puerto Rico, Aguadilla Campus (PR)
Inter American U of Puerto Rico, Bayamón Campus (PR)
Inter American U of Puerto Rico, Ponce Campus (PR)
Jacksonville State U (AL)
Keiser U, Fort Lauderdale (FL)
Keystone Coll (PA)
King U (TN)
Lewis U (IL)
Liberty U (VA)
Long Island U–LIU Post (NY)
Loyola U Chicago (IL)
Lynn U (FL)
Madonna U (MI)
Marian U (WI)
Marymount U (VA)
Mercy Coll (NY)
Miami U (OH)
Mount Marty Coll (SD)
Newman U (KS)
New Mexico Highlands U (NM)
Northwest Nazarene U (ID)
Olivet Coll (MI)
Pace U (NY)
Penn State Altoona (PA)
Penn State Berks (PA)
Penn State U Park (PA)
Piedmont Coll (GA)
Quincy U (IL)
Roberts Wesleyan Coll (NY)
The Sage Colls (NY)
St. Andrews U (NC)
Saint Augustine's U (NC)
St. Edward's U (TX)
Saint Francis U (PA)
St. Thomas Aquinas Coll (NY)
Savannah State U (GA)
Seton Hill U (PA)
Simpson Coll (IA)
State U of New York Coll of Technology at Alfred (NY)
Syracuse U (NY)
Texas A&M U (TX)
Thomas More Coll (KY)
Tiffin U (OH)
Towson U (MD)
Trine U (IN)
U of Central Florida (FL)
U of Central Oklahoma (OK)
The U of Findlay (OH)
U of Great Falls (MT)
U of Maryland U Coll (MD)
U of Nebraska–Lincoln (NE)
U of New Haven (CT)
U of North Dakota (ND)
The U of Scranton (PA)
U of Southern Mississippi (MS)
The U of Tampa (FL)
U of Toronto (ON, Canada)
U of Windsor (ON, Canada)
U of Wisconsin–Platteville (WI)
Utah Valley U (UT)
Virginia Commonwealth U (VA)
Washburn U (KS)
Waynesburg U (PA)
Weber State U (UT)
West Virginia U (WV)
West Virginia U Inst of Technology (WV)
Wichita State U (KS)
York Coll of Pennsylvania (PA)
Youngstown State U (OH)

FOREST ENGINEERING
Oregon State U (OR)

FOREST/FOREST RESOURCES MANAGEMENT
Elizabethtown Coll (PA)
Keystone Coll (PA)
North Carolina State U (NC)
Oregon State U (OR)
State U of New York Coll of Environmental Science and Forestry (NY)
Stephen F. Austin State U (TX)
U of Alberta (AB, Canada)
The U of British Columbia (BC, Canada)
U of California, Berkeley (CA)
U of Idaho (ID)
The U of Montana (MT)
U of Toronto (ON, Canada)
West Virginia U (WV)

FORESTRY
Albright Coll (PA)
Beloit Coll (WI)
California Polytechnic State U, San Luis Obispo (CA)
Coll of Saint Benedict (MN)
Delaware State U (DE)
Georgia Southern U (GA)
Humboldt State U (CA)
Iowa State U of Science and Technology (IA)
Lenoir-Rhyne U (NC)
Michigan State U (MI)
Michigan Technological U (MI)
Mississippi State U (MS)
New Mexico Highlands U (NM)
The Ohio State U (OH)
Oklahoma State U (OK)
Purdue U (IN)
Saint John's U (MN)
Southern Illinois U Carbondale (IL)
State U of New York Coll of Environmental Science and Forestry (NY)
Stephen F. Austin State U (TX)
Texas A&M U (TX)
The U of British Columbia (BC, Canada)
U of California, Berkeley (CA)
U of Florida (FL)
U of Georgia (GA)
U of Maine (ME)
U of Minnesota, Twin Cities Campus (MN)
U of Missouri (MO)
The U of Montana (MT)
U of Nevada, Reno (NV)
U of New Hampshire (NH)
The U of Tennessee (TN)
U of Toronto (ON, Canada)
U of Vermont (VT)
U of Wisconsin–Stevens Point (WI)
Utah State U (UT)
Virginia Polytechnic Inst and State U (VA)

FORESTRY RELATED
Northland Coll (WI)
Sterling Coll (VT)
U of Minnesota, Twin Cities Campus (MN)
Utah State U (UT)

FOREST SCIENCES AND BIOLOGY
Auburn U (AL)
Colorado State U (CO)
Northern Arizona U (AZ)
Ohio Northern U (OH)
Penn State Abington (PA)
Penn State Altoona (PA)
Penn State Beaver (PA)
Penn State Berks (PA)
Penn State Brandywine (PA)
Penn State DuBois (PA)
Penn State Erie, The Behrend Coll (PA)
Penn State Fayette, The Eberly Campus (PA)
Penn State Greater Allegheny (PA)
Penn State Hazleton (PA)
Penn State Lehigh Valley (PA)
Penn State Mont Alto (PA)
Penn State New Kensington (PA)
Penn State Schuylkill (PA)
Penn State Shenango (PA)
Penn State U Park (PA)
Penn State Wilkes-Barre (PA)
Penn State Worthington Scranton (PA)
Penn State York (PA)
Sewanee: The U of the South (TN)
State U of New York Coll of Environmental Science and Forestry (NY)
U of Alberta (AB, Canada)
U of Idaho (ID)
U of Kentucky (KY)
U of Maine (ME)
U of Wisconsin–Madison (WI)

FOREST TECHNOLOGY
Penn State Abington (PA)
Penn State Altoona (PA)
Penn State Beaver (PA)
Penn State Berks (PA)
Penn State Brandywine (PA)
Penn State DuBois (PA)
Penn State Erie, The Behrend Coll (PA)
Penn State Fayette, The Eberly Campus (PA)
Penn State Greater Allegheny (PA)
Penn State Hazleton (PA)
Penn State Lehigh Valley (PA)
Penn State Mont Alto (PA)
Penn State New Kensington (PA)
Penn State Schuylkill (PA)
Penn State Shenango (PA)
Penn State Wilkes-Barre (PA)
Penn State Worthington Scranton (PA)
Penn State York (PA)

FRANCHISING
St. Catherine U (MN)

FRENCH
Adelphi U (NY)
Agnes Scott Coll (GA)
Albion Coll (MI)
Albright Coll (PA)
Allegheny Coll (PA)
Alma Coll (MI)
American U (DC)
Amherst Coll (MA)
Andrews U (MI)
Aquinas Coll (MI)
Arcadia U (PA)
Arizona State U at the Tempe campus (AZ)
Asbury U (KY)
Ashland U (OH)
Assumption Coll (MA)
Auburn U (AL)
Augsburg Coll (MN)
Augustana Coll (IL)
Augustana Coll (SD)
Austin Coll (TX)
Baker U (KS)
Baldwin Wallace U (OH)
Ball State U (IN)
Bard Coll (NY)
Bard Coll at Simon's Rock (MA)
Barnard Coll (NY)
Barry U (FL)
Bates Coll (ME)
Baylor U (TX)
Belmont U (TN)
Beloit Coll (WI)
Benedictine Coll (KS)
Bennington Coll (VT)
Berea Coll (KY)
Berry Coll (GA)
Binghamton U, State U of New York (NY)
Boston Coll (MA)
Boston U (MA)
Bowdoin Coll (ME)
Bowling Green State U (OH)
Bradley U (IL)
Brandeis U (MA)
Bridgewater Coll (VA)
Brown U (RI)
Bryant U (RI)
Bryn Mawr Coll (PA)
Bucknell U (PA)
Buffalo State Coll, State U of New York (NY)
Butler U (IN)
Cabrini Coll (PA)
California Lutheran U (CA)
California State U, Chico (CA)
California State U, Fresno (CA)
California State U, Fullerton (CA)
California State U, Long Beach (CA)
California State U, Los Angeles (CA)
California State U, Sacramento (CA)
California State U, San Bernardino (CA)
California U of Pennsylvania (PA)
Calvin Coll (MI)
Canisius Coll (NY)
Cape Breton U (NS, Canada)
Capital U (OH)
Carleton Coll (MN)
Carroll Coll (MT)
Case Western Reserve U (OH)
The Catholic U of America (DC)
Centenary Coll of Louisiana (LA)
Central Coll (IA)
Central Connecticut State U (CT)
Central Michigan U (MI)
Central Washington U (WA)
Centre Coll (KY)
Chapman U (CA)
Chestnut Hill Coll (PA)
Chowan U (NC)
Christopher Newport U (VA)
City Coll of the City U of New York (NY)
Claremont McKenna Coll (CA)
Clarion U of Pennsylvania (PA)
Clark Atlanta U (GA)
Clark U (MA)
Cleveland State U (OH)
Coe Coll (IA)
Colby Coll (ME)
The Coll at Brockport, State U of New York (NY)
Coll of Charleston (SC)
The Coll of New Rochelle (NY)
Coll of Saint Benedict (MN)
Coll of the Holy Cross (MA)
The Coll of William and Mary (VA)
The Coll of Wooster (OH)
The Colorado Coll (CO)
Colorado State U (CO)
Columbia U (NY)
Columbia U, School of General Studies (NY)
Columbus State U (GA)
Concordia Coll (MN)
Concordia U (QC, Canada)
Connecticut Coll (CT)
Cornell Coll (IA)
Cornell U (NY)
Creighton U (NE)
Daemen Coll (NY)
Dalhousie U (NS, Canada)
Dartmouth Coll (NH)
Davidson Coll (NC)
Delaware State U (DE)
Denison U (OH)
DePaul U (IL)
DePauw U (IN)
Dickinson Coll (PA)
Doane Coll (NE)
Dominican U (IL)
Drew U (NJ)
Drury U (MO)
Earlham Coll (IN)
East Carolina U (NC)
Eastern Kentucky U (KY)
Eastern Michigan U (MI)
East Stroudsburg U of Pennsylvania (PA)
Eckerd Coll (FL)
Edgewood Coll (WI)
Elizabethtown Coll (PA)
Elmhurst Coll (IL)
Elon U (NC)
Emory & Henry Coll (VA)
Erskine Coll (SC)
Fairfield U (CT)
Fairleigh Dickinson U, Coll at Florham (NJ)
Fairleigh Dickinson U, Metropolitan Campus (NJ)
Fairmont State U (WV)
Florida Atlantic U (FL)
Florida Intl U (FL)
Fordham U (NY)
Fort Hays State U (KS)
Franciscan U of Steubenville (OH)
Franklin & Marshall Coll (PA)
Franklin Coll (IN)
Furman U (SC)
Georgetown Coll (KY)
Georgetown U (DC)
The George Washington U (DC)
Georgia Coll & State U (GA)
Georgia Southern U (GA)
Georgia State U (GA)
Gettysburg Coll (PA)
Gonzaga U (WA)
Gordon Coll (MA)
Goucher Coll (MD)
Grace Coll (IN)
Grand Valley State U (MI)
Greensboro Coll (NC)
Grinnell Coll (IA)
Grove City Coll (PA)
Guilford Coll (NC)
Gustavus Adolphus Coll (MN)
Hamilton Coll (NY)
Hampden-Sydney Coll (VA)
Hanover Coll (IN)
Harding U (AR)
Hartwick Coll (NY)
Haverford Coll (PA)
Hendrix Coll (AR)
High Point U (NC)
Hillsdale Coll (MI)
Hiram Coll (OH)
Hobart and William Smith Colls (NY)
Hofstra U (NY)
Hollins U (VA)
Hope Coll (MI)
Howard U (DC)
Humboldt State U (CA)
Hunter Coll of the City U of New York (NY)
Illinois Coll (IL)
Illinois State U (IL)
Illinois Wesleyan U (IL)
Immaculata U (PA)
Indiana U Bloomington (IN)
Indiana U Northwest (IN)
Indiana U–Purdue U Fort Wayne (IN)
Indiana U–Purdue U Indianapolis (IN)
Indiana U South Bend (IN)
Indiana U Southeast (IN)
Iona Coll (NY)
Iowa State U of Science and Technology (IA)
Ithaca Coll (NY)
Jacksonville State U (AL)
Jacksonville U (FL)
John Carroll U (OH)
Johns Hopkins U (MD)
Johnson C. Smith U (NC)
Juniata Coll (PA)
Kalamazoo Coll (MI)
Keene State Coll (NH)
Kent State U (OH)
Kenyon Coll (OH)
King's Coll (PA)
King U (TN)
Knox Coll (IL)
Lafayette Coll (PA)
Lake Erie Coll (OH)
Lake Forest Coll (IL)
Lane Coll (TN)
La Salle U (PA)
Lawrence U (WI)
Lebanon Valley Coll (PA)
Lee U (TN)
Lehigh U (PA)
Lehman Coll of the City U of New York (NY)
Le Moyne Coll (NY)
Lincoln U (PA)
Lindenwood U (MO)
Linfield Coll (OR)

Lipscomb U (TN)
Lock Haven U of Pennsylvania (PA)
Long Island U–LIU Post (NY)
Louisiana Coll (LA)
Louisiana State U and A&M Coll (LA)
Loyola Marymount U (CA)
Loyola U Chicago (IL)
Loyola U New Orleans (LA)
Luther Coll (IA)
Lycoming Coll (PA)
Lynchburg Coll (VA)
Macalester Coll (MN)
Manchester U (IN)
Manhattan Coll (NY)
Manhattanville Coll (NY)
Marian U (IN)
Marist Coll (NY)
Marquette U (WI)
Mary Baldwin Coll (VA)
Marywood U (PA)
McDaniel Coll (MD)
Mercer U, Macon (GA)
Merrimack Coll (MA)
Messiah Coll (PA)
Miami U (OH)
Michigan State U (MI)
Middlebury Coll (VT)
Millersville U of Pennsylvania (PA)
Mills Coll (CA)
Minnesota State U Mankato (MN)
Missouri Southern State U (MO)
Missouri State U (MO)
Missouri Western State U (MO)
Monmouth Coll (IL)
Montclair State U (NJ)
Moravian Coll (PA)
Morehead State U (KY)
Mount Allison U (NB, Canada)
Mount Holyoke Coll (MA)
Mount Saint Mary's U (CA)
Mount St. Mary's U (MD)
Muhlenberg Coll (PA)
Murray State U (KY)
Nazareth Coll of Rochester (NY)
Nebraska Wesleyan U (NE)
New Coll of Florida (FL)
New York U (NY)
Niagara U (NY)
North Carolina Ag and Tech State U (NC)
North Carolina State U (NC)
North Central Coll (IL)
North Dakota State U (ND)
Northeastern Illinois U (IL)
Northern Illinois U (IL)
Northern Kentucky U (KY)
Northern Michigan U (MI)
Northern State U (SD)
Northwestern U (IL)
Notre Dame of Maryland U (MD)
Oakland U (MI)
Oberlin Coll (OH)
Occidental Coll (CA)
Oglethorpe U (GA)
Ohio Northern U (OH)
The Ohio State U (OH)
Ohio U (OH)
Ohio Wesleyan U (OH)
Oklahoma City U (OK)
Oklahoma State U (OK)
Oregon State U (OR)
Pacific Lutheran U (WA)
Pacific U (OR)
Penn State Abington (PA)
Penn State Altoona (PA)
Penn State Beaver (PA)
Penn State Berks (PA)
Penn State Brandywine (PA)
Penn State DuBois (PA)
Penn State Erie, The Behrend Coll (PA)
Penn State Fayette, The Eberly Campus (PA)
Penn State Greater Allegheny (PA)
Penn State Hazleton (PA)
Penn State Lehigh Valley (PA)
Penn State Mont Alto (PA)
Penn State New Kensington (PA)
Penn State Schuylkill (PA)
Penn State Shenango (PA)
Penn State U Park (PA)
Penn State Wilkes-Barre (PA)
Penn State Worthington Scranton (PA)
Penn State York (PA)
Pepperdine U, Malibu (CA)
Pittsburg State U (KS)
Plymouth State U (NH)
Point Loma Nazarene U (CA)
Pomona Coll (CA)
Portland State U (OR)
Presbyterian Coll (SC)
Princeton U (NJ)
Principia Coll (IL)
Providence Coll (RI)
Purchase Coll, State U of New York (NY)
Purdue U (IN)
Queens Coll of the City U of New York (NY)
Randolph Coll (VA)
Randolph-Macon Coll (VA)
Reed Coll (OR)
Regis U (CO)
Rhode Island Coll (RI)
Rhodes Coll (TN)
Rice U (TX)
Rider U (NJ)
Ripon Coll (WI)
Roanoke Coll (VA)
Rockford U (IL)
Rockhurst U (MO)
Rollins Coll (FL)
Rutgers, The State U of New Jersey, Camden (NJ)
Rutgers, The State U of New Jersey, Newark (NJ)
Rutgers, The State U of New Jersey, New Brunswick (NJ)
Sacred Heart U (CT)
Saginaw Valley State U (MI)
Saint Anselm Coll (NH)
St. Bonaventure U (NY)
St. Catherine U (MN)
St. Edward's U (TX)
St. John Fisher Coll (NY)
Saint John's U (MN)
St. John's U (NY)
Saint Joseph's U (PA)
St. Lawrence U (NY)
Saint Louis U (MO)
Saint Mary's Coll (IN)
St. Mary's U (TX)
Saint Michael's Coll (VT)
St. Norbert Coll (WI)
St. Olaf Coll (MN)
St. Thomas U (NB, Canada)
Saint Vincent Coll (PA)
Salem Coll (NC)
Salisbury U (MD)
Salve Regina U (RI)
Samford U (AL)
San Diego State U (CA)
San Francisco State U (CA)
San Jose State U (CA)
Santa Clara U (CA)
Sarah Lawrence Coll (NY)
Scripps Coll (CA)
Seattle U (WA)
Sewanee: The U of the South (TN)
Shippensburg U of Pennsylvania (PA)
Siena Coll (NY)
Simmons Coll (MA)
Simon Fraser U (BC, Canada)
Simpson Coll (IA)
Skidmore Coll (NY)
Slippery Rock U of Pennsylvania (PA)
Smith Coll (MA)
South Dakota State U (SD)
Southern Adventist U (TN)
Southern Connecticut State U (CT)
Southern Methodist U (TX)
Southern Oregon U (OR)
Southern Utah U (UT)
Southwestern U (TX)
Spelman Coll (GA)
Stanford U (CA)
State U of New York at Fredonia (NY)
State U of New York at New Paltz (NY)
State U of New York at Oswego (NY)
State U of New York at Plattsburgh (NY)
State U of New York Coll at Cortland (NY)
State U of New York Coll at Geneseo (NY)
State U of New York Coll at Potsdam (NY)
Stetson U (FL)
Stonehill Coll (MA)
Stony Brook U, State U of New York (NY)
Suffolk U (MA)
Susquehanna U (PA)
Syracuse U (NY)
Temple U (PA)
Tennessee State U (TN)
Tennessee Wesleyan Coll (TN)
Texas A&M U (TX)
Texas Christian U (TX)
Texas State U (TX)
Texas Tech U (TX)
Transylvania U (KY)
Trent U (ON, Canada)
Trinity Coll (CT)
Trinity U (TX)
Truman State U (MO)
Tufts U (MA)
Tulane U (LA)
Union Coll (NE)
Union Coll (NY)
Union U (TN)
United States Military Acad (NY)
Université de Montréal (QC, Canada)
Université de Sherbrooke (QC, Canada)
U at Buffalo, the State U of New York (NY)
The U of Akron (OH)
U of Alberta (AB, Canada)
The U of Arizona (AZ)
U of Arkansas (AR)
U of Arkansas at Little Rock (AR)
The U of British Columbia (BC, Canada)
The U of British Columbia–Okanagan Campus (BC, Canada)
U of California, Berkeley (CA)
U of California, Davis (CA)
U of California, Irvine (CA)
U of California, Los Angeles (CA)
U of California, Riverside (CA)
U of California, Santa Barbara (CA)
U of Central Arkansas (AR)
U of Central Florida (FL)
U of Central Missouri (MO)
U of Central Oklahoma (OK)
U of Cincinnati (OH)
U of Colorado Boulder (CO)
U of Colorado Denver (CO)
U of Dallas (TX)
U of Dayton (OH)
U of Denver (CO)
U of Evansville (IN)
U of Florida (FL)
U of Georgia (GA)
U of Hawaii at Manoa (HI)
U of Houston (TX)
U of Idaho (ID)
U of Illinois at Chicago (IL)
U of Indianapolis (IN)
The U of Iowa (IA)
U of Jamestown (ND)
The U of Kansas (KS)
U of Kentucky (KY)
U of King's Coll (NS, Canada)
U of La Verne (CA)
U of Louisville (KY)
U of Maine (ME)
U of Maine at Fort Kent (ME)
U of Maryland, Coll Park (MD)
U of Massachusetts Amherst (MA)
U of Massachusetts Boston (MA)
U of Massachusetts Dartmouth (MA)
U of Miami (FL)
U of Michigan (MI)
U of Michigan–Dearborn (MI)
U of Michigan–Flint (MI)
U of Minnesota, Duluth (MN)
U of Minnesota, Morris (MN)
U of Minnesota, Twin Cities Campus (MN)
U of Mississippi (MS)
U of Missouri (MO)
The U of Montana (MT)
U of Mount Union (OH)
U of Nebraska at Kearney (NE)
U of Nebraska–Lincoln (NE)
U of Nevada, Las Vegas (NV)
U of Nevada, Reno (NV)
U of New Brunswick Saint John (NB, Canada)
U of New Hampshire (NH)
U of New Mexico (NM)
U of North Carolina at Asheville (NC)
The U of North Carolina at Charlotte (NC)
The U of North Carolina at Greensboro (NC)
The U of North Carolina Wilmington (NC)
U of North Dakota (ND)
U of North Georgia (GA)
U of North Texas (TX)
U of Notre Dame (IN)
U of Oklahoma (OK)
U of Oregon (OR)
U of Ottawa (ON, Canada)
U of Pennsylvania (PA)
U of Pittsburgh (PA)
U of Puget Sound (WA)
U of Regina (SK, Canada)
U of Rhode Island (RI)
U of Richmond (VA)
U of Rochester (NY)
U of St. Thomas (MN)
U of St. Thomas (TX)
U of San Diego (CA)
U of San Francisco (CA)
U of Saskatchewan (SK, Canada)
The U of Scranton (PA)
The U of South Dakota (SD)
U of Southern California (CA)
U of Southern Indiana (IN)
U of Southern Maine (ME)
U of South Florida (FL)
The U of Tennessee (TN)
The U of Tennessee at Martin (TN)
The U of Texas at Arlington (TX)
The U of Texas at Austin (TX)
The U of Texas at El Paso (TX)
The U of Texas at San Antonio (TX)
The U of Texas–Pan American (TX)
U of the Cumberlands (KY)
U of the Pacific (CA)
The U of Toledo (OH)
U of Toronto (ON, Canada)
The U of Tulsa (OK)
U of Utah (UT)
U of Vermont (VT)
U of Virginia (VA)
The U of Virginia's Coll at Wise (VA)
U of Washington (WA)
U of Waterloo (ON, Canada)
The U of Western Ontario (ON, Canada)
U of West Florida (FL)
U of Windsor (ON, Canada)
U of Wisconsin–Eau Claire (WI)
U of Wisconsin–Green Bay (WI)
U of Wisconsin–La Crosse (WI)
U of Wisconsin–Madison (WI)
U of Wisconsin–Milwaukee (WI)
U of Wisconsin–Oshkosh (WI)
U of Wisconsin–River Falls (WI)
U of Wisconsin–Stevens Point (WI)
U of Wisconsin–Whitewater (WI)
U of Wyoming (WY)
Ursinus Coll (PA)
Utah State U (UT)
Valdosta State U (GA)
Valparaiso U (IN)
Vanderbilt U (TN)
Vassar Coll (NY)
Villanova U (PA)
Virginia Polytechnic Inst and State U (VA)
Virginia Wesleyan Coll (VA)
Wabash Coll (IN)
Wake Forest U (NC)
Walla Walla U (WA)
Walsh U (OH)
Wartburg Coll (IA)
Washburn U (KS)
Washington & Jefferson Coll (PA)
Washington and Lee U (VA)
Washington Coll (MD)
Washington State U (WA)
Washington U in St. Louis (MO)
Weber State U (UT)
Webster U (MO)
Wesleyan Coll (GA)
West Chester U of Pennsylvania (PA)
Western Carolina U (NC)
Western Illinois U (IL)
Western Kentucky U (KY)
Western Michigan U (MI)
Western Washington U (WA)
Westminster Coll (MO)
Wheaton Coll (IL)
Wheeling Jesuit U (WV)
Whitman Coll (WA)
Whittier Coll (CA)
Whitworth U (WA)
Wichita State U (KS)
Widener U (PA)
Willamette U (OR)
William Jewell Coll (MO)
Williams Coll (MA)
Wittenberg U (OH)
Wofford Coll (SC)
Wright State U (OH)
Xavier U (OH)
Xavier U of Louisiana (LA)
Yale U (CT)
York Coll of the City U of New York (NY)
Youngstown State U (OH)

FRENCH AS A SECOND/ FOREIGN LANGUAGE (TEACHING)

Saginaw Valley State U (MI)
U of Alberta (AB, Canada)
U of Toronto (ON, Canada)
U of Windsor (ON, Canada)

FRENCH LANGUAGE TEACHER EDUCATION

Albion Coll (MI)
Alma Coll (MI)
Ashland U (OH)
Auburn U (AL)
Augustana Coll (IL)
Austin Coll (TX)
Bethel U (MN)
California Lutheran U (CA)
Calvin Coll (MI)
Canisius Coll (NY)
The Catholic U of America (DC)
Central Michigan U (MI)
Central Washington U (WA)
Colorado State U (CO)
Concordia Coll (MN)
Cornell U (NY)
Daemen Coll (NY)
Delaware State U (DE)
East Carolina U (NC)
Eastern Kentucky U (KY)
Eastern Michigan U (MI)
Edgewood Coll (WI)
Elmhurst Coll (IL)
Elmira Coll (NY)
Emory & Henry Coll (VA)
Franklin Coll (IN)
Grace Coll (IN)
Grand Valley State U (MI)
Harding U (AR)
Hofstra U (NY)
Holy Family U (PA)
Hope Coll (MI)
Indiana U Bloomington (IN)
Indiana U Northwest (IN)
Indiana U–Purdue U Fort Wayne (IN)
Indiana U–Purdue U Indianapolis (IN)
Indiana U South Bend (IN)
Iona Coll (NY)
Ithaca Coll (NY)
Juniata Coll (PA)
Keene State Coll (NH)
King U (TN)
Lee U (TN)
Le Moyne Coll (NY)
Lincoln U (PA)
Lindenwood U (MO)
Lipscomb U (TN)
Long Island U–LIU Post (NY)
Louisiana State U in Shreveport (LA)
Manchester U (IN)
Manhattanville Coll (NY)
Marist Coll (NY)
Marywood U (PA)
Messiah Coll (PA)
Miami U (OH)
Michigan State U (MI)
Missouri State U (MO)
Missouri Western State U (MO)
New York U (NY)
Niagara U (NY)
North Carolina Ag and Tech State U (NC)

North Carolina State U (NC)
North Dakota State U (ND)
Northern Michigan U (MI)
Ohio Northern U (OH)
Ohio U (OH)
Ohio Wesleyan U (OH)
Pittsburg State U (KS)
Providence Coll (RI)
Rhode Island Coll (RI)
St. Catherine U (MN)
St. John Fisher Coll (NY)
Saint Joseph's U (PA)
Salve Regina U (RI)
Southern Adventist U (TN)
Southern Utah U (UT)
State U of New York at New Paltz (NY)
State U of New York at Plattsburgh (NY)
State U of New York Coll at Cortland (NY)
Stony Brook U, State U of New York (NY)
The U of Akron (OH)
U of Alberta (AB, Canada)
U of Central Oklahoma (OK)
U of Delaware (DE)
U of Evansville (IN)
U of Illinois at Chicago (IL)
U of Indianapolis (IN)
The U of Iowa (IA)
U of Lethbridge (AB, Canada)
U of Michigan–Flint (MI)
U of Nebraska–Lincoln (NE)
The U of North Carolina at Greensboro (NC)
The U of North Carolina Wilmington (NC)
U of Regina (SK, Canada)
The U of South Dakota (SD)
The U of Tennessee at Martin (TN)
U of the Cumberlands (KY)
The U of Toledo (OH)
U of Toronto (ON, Canada)
U of Waterloo (ON, Canada)
U of Windsor (ON, Canada)
U of Wisconsin–River Falls (WI)
Valparaiso U (IN)
Washburn U (KS)
Washington State U (WA)
Washington U in St. Louis (MO)
Weber State U (UT)
Western Michigan U (MI)
Western Washington U (WA)
Widener U (PA)
Xavier U of Louisiana (LA)
Youngstown State U (OH)

FRENCH STUDIES
American U (DC)
Bard Coll (NY)
Bard Coll at Simon's Rock (MA)
Barnard Coll (NY)
Brown U (RI)
Carleton Coll (MN)
Case Western Reserve U (OH)
Coe Coll (IA)
The Colorado Coll (CO)
Columbia U (NY)
Columbia U, School of General Studies (NY)
Emory & Henry Coll (VA)
Fordham U (NY)
Lewis & Clark Coll (OR)
Linfield Coll (OR)
Mills Coll (CA)
Moravian Coll (PA)
New Coll of Florida (FL)
Rhode Island Coll (RI)
Saint Joseph's U (PA)
Skidmore Coll (NY)
Smith Coll (MA)
Suffolk U (MA)
U of Alberta (AB, Canada)
U of Guelph (ON, Canada)
U of New Hampshire (NH)
U of North Florida (FL)
The U of Scranton (PA)
U of Waterloo (ON, Canada)
The U of Western Ontario (ON, Canada)
U of Windsor (ON, Canada)
Wagner Coll (NY)
Wesleyan U (CT)
Wheaton Coll (MA)

FUNERAL DIRECTION/ SERVICE
Wayne State U (MI)

FUNERAL SERVICE AND MORTUARY SCIENCE
Cincinnati Coll of Mortuary Science (OH)
Gannon U (PA)
Lincoln Coll of New England, Southington (CT)
St. John's U (NY)
Southern Illinois U Carbondale (IL)
Thiel Coll (PA)
U of Central Oklahoma (OK)
U of Minnesota, Twin Cities Campus (MN)

FURNITURE DESIGN AND MANUFACTURING
Rhode Island School of Design (RI)

GAME AND INTERACTIVE MEDIA DESIGN
Abilene Christian U (TX)
Acad of Art U (CA)
Art Center Coll of Design (CA)
Cardinal Stritch U (WI)
Champlain Coll (VT)
Cleveland Inst of Art (OH)
Dakota State U (SD)
Daniel Webster Coll (NH)
DeSales U (PA)
Franklin U (OH)
Inter American U of Puerto Rico, Bayamón Campus (PR)
Laguna Coll of Art & Design (CA)
Los Angeles Film School (CA)
Neumont U (UT)
Oklahoma Christian U (OK)
Paris Coll of Art (France)
Quinnipiac U (CT)
Ringling Coll of Art and Design (FL)
Rochester Inst of Technology (NY)
Rocky Mountain Coll of Art + Design (CO)
St. Edward's U (TX)
Savannah Coll of Art and Design (GA)
Shawnee State U (OH)
Southern Arkansas U–Magnolia (AR)
Southwestern Coll (KS)
U of California, Irvine (CA)
U of Southern California (CA)
The U of Texas at Dallas (TX)
Webster U (MO)
William Peace U (NC)

GAY/LESBIAN STUDIES
Bennington Coll (VT)
Bryant U (RI)
Cornell U (NY)
Hampshire Coll (MA)
Mills Coll (CA)
Trinity Coll (CT)
The U of Western Ontario (ON, Canada)

GENERAL STUDIES
Albertus Magnus Coll (CT)
Ambrose U Coll (AB, Canada)
American Public U System (WV)
Anna Maria Coll (MA)
Antioch U Midwest (OH)
Aquinas Coll (MI)
Arkansas State U (AR)
Austin Coll (TX)
Austin Peay State U (TN)
Ball State U (IN)
Bay Path U (MA)
Bethel Coll (IN)
Bluefield State Coll (WV)
Brenau U (GA)
Buffalo State Coll, State U of New York (NY)
California State U, San Bernardino (CA)
California State U, San Marcos (CA)
Calumet Coll of Saint Joseph (IN)
Cameron U (OK)
The Catholic U of America (DC)
Champlain Coll (VT)
Chicago State U (IL)
Clearwater Christian Coll (FL)
Columbia Coll (MO)
Columbia Intl U (SC)
Concordia U, St. Paul (MN)
Concordia U Wisconsin (WI)
Cornell U (NY)
Delta State U (MS)
DePaul U (IL)
Drexel U (PA)
East Central U (OK)
Eastern Connecticut State U (CT)
Eastern Kentucky U (KY)
Eastern New Mexico U (NM)
East Tennessee State U (TN)
Emory & Henry Coll (VA)
Emporia State U (KS)
Fairfield U (CT)
Fairleigh Dickinson U, Coll at Florham (NJ)
Fairleigh Dickinson U, Metropolitan Campus (NJ)
Fisher Coll (MA)
Florida Inst of Technology (FL)
Fort Hays State U (KS)
Fort Lewis Coll (CO)
George Mason U (VA)
Georgia Southern U (GA)
Granite State Coll (NH)
Hampton U (VA)
Harding U (AR)
Holy Family U (PA)
Howard Payne U (TX)
Illinois State U (IL)
Indiana U Bloomington (IN)
Indiana U East (IN)
Indiana U Kokomo (IN)
Indiana U Northwest (IN)
Indiana U–Purdue U Fort Wayne (IN)
Indiana U–Purdue U Indianapolis (IN)
Indiana U South Bend (IN)
Indiana U Southeast (IN)
Jacksonville U (FL)
John Brown U (AR)
Kansas Wesleyan U (KS)
Kent State U (OH)
Kent State U at Ashtabula (OH)
Kent State U at East Liverpool (OH)
Kent State U at Geauga (OH)
Kent State U at Salem (OH)
Kent State U at Stark (OH)
Kent State U at Trumbull (OH)
Kent State U at Tuscarawas (OH)
Kentucky Wesleyan Coll (KY)
Kingswood U (NB, Canada)
Kutztown U of Pennsylvania (PA)
LaGrange Coll (GA)
Lamar U (TX)
La Roche Coll (PA)
La Salle U (PA)
Lasell Coll (MA)
Lee U (TN)
Lewis U (IL)
Liberty U (VA)
Lincoln Christian U (IL)
Lindenwood U (MO)
Lipscomb U (TN)
Louisiana State U in Shreveport (LA)
Loyola U Chicago (IL)
Loyola U New Orleans (LA)
Madonna U (MI)
Marshall U (WV)
Marywood U (PA)
Mayville State U (ND)
McNeese State U (LA)
Medaille Coll (NY)
Minot State U (ND)
Misericordia U (PA)
Montana Tech of The U of Montana (MT)
Morehead State U (KY)
Mount Marty Coll (SD)
Mount Mary U (WI)
Mount St. Joseph U (OH)
Murray State U (KY)
National U (CA)
New Coll of Florida (FL)
New Jersey Inst of Technology (NJ)
New Mexico Inst of Mining and Technology (NM)
New Mexico State U (NM)
Nicholls State U (LA)
Northeastern State U (OK)
Northern Kentucky U (KY)
Northwestern Oklahoma State U (OK)
Northwestern U (IL)
Northwest U (WA)
Nova Southeastern U (FL)
Ohio Dominican U (OH)
Ohio Northern U (OH)
Ohio Wesleyan U (OH)
Oklahoma State U (OK)
Oklahoma Wesleyan U (OK)
Palm Beach Atlantic U (FL)
Providence Coll (RI)
Quincy U (IL)
Roberts Wesleyan Coll (NY)
Sacred Heart U (CT)
Saginaw Valley State U (MI)
St. John's Coll (NM)
St. Lawrence U (NY)
Saint Louis U (MO)
Samford U (AL)
Sam Houston State U (TX)
San Diego State U (CA)
Savannah State U (GA)
Seattle Pacific U (WA)
Selma U (AL)
Seton Hill U (PA)
Shawnee State U (OH)
Shepherd U (WV)
Shimer Coll (IL)
Siena Heights U (MI)
Simon Fraser U (BC, Canada)
South Dakota State U (SD)
Southeastern Louisiana U (LA)
Southeastern Oklahoma State U (OK)
Southeast Missouri State U (MO)
Southern Arkansas U–Magnolia (AR)
Southern New Hampshire U (NH)
Southern Utah U (UT)
Southwestern Adventist U (TX)
Southwestern Coll (KS)
Southwest Minnesota State U (MN)
Spring Hill Coll (AL)
Sullivan U (KY)
Tabor Coll (KS)
Temple U (PA)
Texas A&M U–Commerce (TX)
Texas Christian U (TX)
Texas Southern U (TX)
Texas State U (TX)
Texas Tech U (TX)
Texas Woman's U (TX)
Tiffin U (OH)
Toccoa Falls Coll (GA)
Trinity Coll of Florida (FL)
Union Coll (NE)
U of Alberta (AB, Canada)
U of Arkansas–Fort Smith (AR)
U of Bridgeport (CT)
The U of British Columbia–Okanagan Campus (BC, Canada)
U of Central Florida (FL)
U of Central Oklahoma (OK)
U of Charleston (WV)
U of Delaware (DE)
U of Hartford (CT)
U of Idaho (ID)
U of Kentucky (KY)
U of Lethbridge (AB, Canada)
U of Louisiana at Lafayette (LA)
U of Maine at Machias (ME)
U of Mary Hardin-Baylor (TX)
U of Massachusetts Amherst (MA)
U of Memphis (TN)
U of Miami (FL)
U of Michigan (MI)
U of Michigan–Dearborn (MI)
U of Mississippi (MS)
U of Missouri (MO)
U of Missouri–Kansas City (MO)
U of Mobile (AL)
U of Nebraska at Kearney (NE)
U of Nevada, Reno (NV)
U of New Mexico (NM)
U of New Orleans (LA)
U of North Dakota (ND)
U of North Georgia (GA)
U of North Texas (TX)
U of St. Thomas (TX)
U of South Florida (FL)
U of South Florida Sarasota-Manatee (FL)
The U of Tennessee at Martin (TN)
The U of Texas at Arlington (TX)
The U of Texas at San Antonio (TX)
The U of Texas at Tyler (TX)
The U of Texas–Pan American (TX)
U of the Cumberlands (KY)
U of the Fraser Valley (BC, Canada)
U of the West (CA)
The U of Toledo (OH)
U of Utah (UT)
U of Washington (WA)
U of Washington, Bothell (WA)
U of Washington, Tacoma (WA)
U of Wisconsin–Stevens Point (WI)
Ursinus Coll (PA)
Valdosta State U (GA)
Warren Wilson Coll (NC)
Western Illinois U (IL)
Western Kentucky U (KY)
Western Washington U (WA)
West Texas A&M U (TX)
West Virginia State U (WV)
West Virginia U (WV)
West Virginia U Inst of Technology (WV)
Wheeling Jesuit U (WV)
Wichita State U (KS)
Widener U (PA)
Wilmington U (DE)
York Coll of Pennsylvania (PA)
Youngstown State U (OH)

GENETICS
Cedar Crest Coll (PA)
Iowa State U of Science and Technology (IA)
New Mexico State U (NM)
North Carolina State U (NC)
Ohio Wesleyan U (OH)
Purdue U (IN)
U of California, Davis (CA)
U of California, Irvine (CA)
U of Georgia (GA)
U of New Hampshire (NH)
The U of Western Ontario (ON, Canada)
U of Wisconsin–Madison (WI)
Washington State U (WA)

GENETICS RELATED
The George Washington U (DC)

GEOCHEMISTRY
Bowling Green State U (OH)
Bridgewater State U (MA)
Brown U (RI)
California Inst of Technology (CA)
The Coll of Saint Rose (NY)
Columbia U (NY)
Grand Valley State U (MI)
State U of New York at Fredonia (NY)
State U of New York at New Paltz (NY)
State U of New York at Oswego (NY)
State U of New York Coll at Cortland (NY)
State U of New York Coll at Geneseo (NY)
U of Waterloo (ON, Canada)
Washington U in St. Louis (MO)
Western Michigan U (MI)

GEOGRAPHIC INFORMATION SCIENCE AND CARTOGRAPHY
Arizona State U at the Tempe campus (AZ)
Auburn U at Montgomery (AL)
Binghamton U, State U of New York (NY)
Brigham Young U (UT)
Central Michigan U (MI)
Central Washington U (WA)
East Central U (OK)
Kennesaw State U (GA)
Michigan State U (MI)
Northern Michigan U (MI)
Northwest Missouri State U (MO)
Radford U (VA)
Rowan U (NJ)
South Dakota State U (SD)
Stephen F. Austin State U (TX)
Texas A&M U (TX)
Texas State U (TX)
The U of Akron (OH)
U of Cincinnati (OH)
U of Lethbridge (AB, Canada)
U of Minnesota, Duluth (MN)
U of Oklahoma (OK)
U of Ottawa (ON, Canada)
The U of Texas at Dallas (TX)
The U of Western Ontario (ON, Canada)
U of Wisconsin–Madison (WI)

U of Wisconsin–Platteville (WI)
Western Kentucky U (KY)

GEOGRAPHY
Adams State U (CO)
Appalachian State U (NC)
Aquinas Coll (MI)
Arizona State U at the Tempe campus (AZ)
Auburn U (AL)
Augustana Coll (IL)
Ball State U (IN)
Bard Coll at Simon's Rock (MA)
Bemidji State U (MN)
Binghamton U, State U of New York (NY)
Boston U (MA)
Bowling Green State U (OH)
Bridgewater State U (MA)
Bucknell U (PA)
Buffalo State Coll, State U of New York (NY)
California State Polytechnic U, Pomona (CA)
California State U, Chico (CA)
California State U, Dominguez Hills (CA)
California State U, Fresno (CA)
California State U, Fullerton (CA)
California State U, Long Beach (CA)
California State U, Los Angeles (CA)
California State U, Sacramento (CA)
California State U, San Bernardino (CA)
California State U, Stanislaus (CA)
California U of Pennsylvania (PA)
Calvin Coll (MI)
Castleton State Coll (VT)
Central Connecticut State U (CT)
Central Michigan U (MI)
Central State U (OH)
Central Washington U (WA)
Chicago State U (IL)
Chowan U (NC)
City Coll of the City U of New York (NY)
Clark U (MA)
Concordia U (QC, Canada)
Concordia U Chicago (IL)
Concordia U, Nebraska (NE)
Concord U (WV)
Dartmouth Coll (NH)
DePaul U (IL)
Dickinson State U (ND)
East Carolina U (NC)
Eastern Illinois U (IL)
Eastern Kentucky U (KY)
Eastern Michigan U (MI)
East Stroudsburg U of Pennsylvania (PA)
East Tennessee State U (TN)
Edinboro U of Pennsylvania (PA)
Elmhurst Coll (IL)
Emory & Henry Coll (VA)
Fayetteville State U (NC)
Fitchburg State U (MA)
Florida Atlantic U (FL)
Florida Intl U (FL)
Florida State U (FL)
Fort Hays State U (KS)
Framingham State U (MA)
Frostburg State U (MD)
George Mason U (VA)
The George Washington U (DC)
Georgia Coll & State U (GA)
Georgia Southern U (GA)
Grand Valley State U (MI)
Gustavus Adolphus Coll (MN)
Hofstra U (NY)
Humboldt State U (CA)
Hunter Coll of the City U of New York (NY)
Illinois State U (IL)
Indiana State U (IN)
Indiana U Bloomington (IN)
Indiana U of Pennsylvania (PA)
Indiana U–Purdue U Indianapolis (IN)
Indiana U Southeast (IN)
Jacksonville State U (AL)
Jacksonville U (FL)
James Madison U (VA)
Johns Hopkins U (MD)
Kansas State U (KS)
Keene State Coll (NH)
Kennesaw State U (GA)
Kent State U (OH)
Kutztown U of Pennsylvania (PA)
Lehman Coll of the City U of New York (NY)
Long Island U–LIU Post (NY)
Louisiana State U and A&M Coll (LA)
Macalester Coll (MN)
Mansfield U of Pennsylvania (PA)
Marshall U (WV)
Miami U (OH)
Michigan State U (MI)
Middlebury Coll (VT)
Millersville U of Pennsylvania (PA)
Minnesota State U Mankato (MN)
Missouri State U (MO)
Montclair State U (NJ)
Mount Allison U (NB, Canada)
Mount Holyoke Coll (MA)
New Mexico State U (NM)
Northeastern Illinois U (IL)
Northeastern State U (OK)
Northern Arizona U (AZ)
Northern Illinois U (IL)
Northern Kentucky U (KY)
Northern Michigan U (MI)
Northwestern U (IL)
Northwest Missouri State U (MO)
The Ohio State U (OH)
Ohio U (OH)
Ohio Wesleyan U (OH)
Oklahoma State U (OK)
Old Dominion U (VA)
Olivet Nazarene U (IL)
Park U (MO)
Penn State Abington (PA)
Penn State Altoona (PA)
Penn State Beaver (PA)
Penn State Berks (PA)
Penn State Brandywine (PA)
Penn State DuBois (PA)
Penn State Erie, The Behrend Coll (PA)
Penn State Fayette, The Eberly Campus (PA)
Penn State Greater Allegheny (PA)
Penn State Hazleton (PA)
Penn State Lehigh Valley (PA)
Penn State Mont Alto (PA)
Penn State New Kensington (PA)
Penn State Schuylkill (PA)
Penn State Shenango (PA)
Penn State U Park (PA)
Penn State Wilkes-Barre (PA)
Penn State Worthington Scranton (PA)
Penn State York (PA)
Pittsburg State U (KS)
Plymouth State U (NH)
Portland State U (OR)
Rhode Island Coll (RI)
Rowan U (NJ)
Rutgers, The State U of New Jersey, New Brunswick (NJ)
Salisbury U (MD)
Samford U (AL)
Sam Houston State U (TX)
San Diego State U (CA)
San Francisco State U (CA)
San Jose State U (CA)
Shippensburg U of Pennsylvania (PA)
Simon Fraser U (BC, Canada)
Slippery Rock U of Pennsylvania (PA)
South Dakota State U (SD)
Southern Connecticut State U (CT)
Southern Illinois U Carbondale (IL)
Southern Illinois U Edwardsville (IL)
State U of New York at New Paltz (NY)
State U of New York at Plattsburgh (NY)
State U of New York Coll at Cortland (NY)
State U of New York Coll at Geneseo (NY)
Stephen F. Austin State U (TX)
Stetson U (FL)
Syracuse U (NY)
Taylor U (IN)
Texas A&M U (TX)
Texas Christian U (TX)
Texas State U (TX)
Texas Tech U (TX)
Towson U (MD)
Trent U (ON, Canada)
United States Air Force Acad (CO)
United States Military Acad (NY)
Université de Montréal (QC, Canada)
U at Albany, State U of New York (NY)
U at Buffalo, the State U of New York (NY)
The U of Akron (OH)
The U of Alabama (AL)
U of Alaska Fairbanks (AK)
U of Alberta (AB, Canada)
The U of Arizona (AZ)
U of Arkansas (AR)
The U of British Columbia (BC, Canada)
The U of British Columbia–Okanagan Campus (BC, Canada)
U of California, Berkeley (CA)
U of California, Los Angeles (CA)
U of California, Santa Barbara (CA)
U of Central Arkansas (AR)
U of Central Missouri (MO)
U of Central Oklahoma (OK)
U of Chicago (IL)
U of Cincinnati (OH)
U of Colorado Boulder (CO)
U of Colorado Colorado Springs (CO)
U of Colorado Denver (CO)
U of Delaware (DE)
U of Denver (CO)
U of Florida (FL)
U of Georgia (GA)
U of Guelph (ON, Canada)
U of Hawaii at Hilo (HI)
U of Hawaii at Manoa (HI)
U of Houston–Clear Lake (TX)
U of Idaho (ID)
The U of Iowa (IA)
The U of Kansas (KS)
U of Kentucky (KY)
U of Lethbridge (AB, Canada)
U of Louisville (KY)
U of Maryland, Baltimore County (MD)
U of Maryland, Coll Park (MD)
U of Mary Washington (VA)
U of Massachusetts Amherst (MA)
U of Memphis (TN)
U of Miami (FL)
U of Minnesota, Duluth (MN)
U of Minnesota, Twin Cities Campus (MN)
U of Missouri (MO)
U of Missouri–Kansas City (MO)
The U of Montana (MT)
U of Nebraska at Kearney (NE)
U of Nebraska–Lincoln (NE)
U of Nevada, Reno (NV)
U of New Hampshire (NH)
U of New Mexico (NM)
U of North Alabama (AL)
The U of North Carolina at Chapel Hill (NC)
The U of North Carolina at Charlotte (NC)
The U of North Carolina at Greensboro (NC)
The U of North Carolina Wilmington (NC)
U of North Dakota (ND)
U of Northern Colorado (CO)
U of Northern Iowa (IA)
U of North Texas (TX)
U of Oklahoma (OK)
U of Oregon (OR)
U of Ottawa (ON, Canada)
U of Regina (SK, Canada)
U of Richmond (VA)
U of St. Thomas (MN)
U of Saskatchewan (SK, Canada)
U of South Alabama (AL)
U of Southern California (CA)
U of Southern Mississippi (MS)
U of South Florida (FL)
The U of Tennessee (TN)
The U of Tennessee at Martin (TN)
The U of Texas at Austin (TX)
The U of Texas at El Paso (TX)
The U of Texas at San Antonio (TX)
U of the Fraser Valley (BC, Canada)
The U of Toledo (OH)
U of Toronto (ON, Canada)
U of Utah (UT)
U of Vermont (VT)
U of Washington (WA)
U of Waterloo (ON, Canada)
The U of Western Ontario (ON, Canada)
U of West Georgia (GA)
U of Wisconsin–Eau Claire (WI)
U of Wisconsin–La Crosse (WI)
U of Wisconsin–Madison (WI)
U of Wisconsin–Milwaukee (WI)
U of Wisconsin–Oshkosh (WI)
U of Wisconsin–Parkside (WI)
U of Wisconsin–Platteville (WI)
U of Wisconsin–River Falls (WI)
U of Wisconsin–Stevens Point (WI)
U of Wisconsin–Whitewater (WI)
U of Wyoming (WY)
Utah State U (UT)
Valparaiso U (IN)
Vassar Coll (NY)
Villanova U (PA)
Virginia Polytechnic Inst and State U (VA)
Wayne State Coll (NE)
Weber State U (UT)
West Chester U of Pennsylvania (PA)
Western Carolina U (NC)
Western Illinois U (IL)
Western Kentucky U (KY)
Western Michigan U (MI)
Western Oregon U (OR)
Western Washington U (WA)
West Texas A&M U (TX)
West Virginia U (WV)
William Paterson U of New Jersey (NJ)
Worcester State U (MA)
Wright State U (OH)
Youngstown State U (OH)

GEOGRAPHY RELATED
Bridgewater State U (MA)
Brigham Young U (UT)
Central Washington U (WA)
Emory & Henry Coll (VA)
Northern Michigan U (MI)
Ohio U (OH)
Temple U (PA)
U of Alberta (AB, Canada)
U of California, Los Angeles (CA)

GEOGRAPHY TEACHER EDUCATION
Central Michigan U (MI)
Concordia U, Nebraska (NE)
Cumberland U (TN)
Grand Valley State U (MI)
Mayville State U (ND)
Michigan State U (MI)
Northern Michigan U (MI)
Rhode Island Coll (RI)
U of Delaware (DE)
The U of Tennessee at Martin (TN)
U of Windsor (ON, Canada)
Valparaiso U (IN)
Wayne State Coll (NE)
Western Michigan U (MI)

GEOLOGICAL AND EARTH SCIENCES/GEOSCIENCES RELATED
Allegheny Coll (PA)
Boston U (MA)
Bridgewater State U (MA)
Brigham Young U (UT)
California State U, Chico (CA)
California State U, Dominguez Hills (CA)
California State U, Fullerton (CA)
Cedarville U (OH)
Central Washington U (WA)
Cornell U (NY)
Earlham Coll (IN)
Eckerd Coll (FL)
Georgia Inst of Technology (GA)
Hamilton Coll (NY)
Lehigh U (PA)
Minnesota State U Moorhead (MN)
Old Dominion U (VA)
Oregon State U (OR)
Penn State Abington (PA)
Penn State Altoona (PA)
Penn State Beaver (PA)
Penn State Berks (PA)
Penn State Brandywine (PA)
Penn State DuBois (PA)
Penn State Erie, The Behrend Coll (PA)
Penn State Fayette, The Eberly Campus (PA)
Penn State Greater Allegheny (PA)
Penn State Hazleton (PA)
Penn State Lehigh Valley (PA)
Penn State Mont Alto (PA)
Penn State New Kensington (PA)
Penn State Schuylkill (PA)
Penn State Shenango (PA)
Penn State U Park (PA)
Penn State Wilkes-Barre (PA)
Penn State Worthington Scranton (PA)
Penn State York (PA)
Princeton U (NJ)
Salisbury U (MD)
San Jose State U (CA)
Stanford U (CA)
Texas A&M U (TX)
Texas Christian U (TX)
Towson U (MD)
Union Coll (NY)
U at Buffalo, the State U of New York (NY)
U of Alberta (AB, Canada)
U of California, Los Angeles (CA)
U of Guelph (ON, Canada)
U of Miami (FL)
U of Northern Iowa (IA)
U of Pittsburgh (PA)
U of Rhode Island (RI)
The U of Texas at Arlington (TX)
U of Utah (UT)
U of Washington (WA)
U of Wyoming (WY)
Utica Coll (NY)
Western State Colorado U (CO)
Western Washington U (WA)
Whitman Coll (WA)
Yale U (CT)

GEOLOGICAL/GEOPHYSICAL ENGINEERING
Colorado School of Mines (CO)
Michigan Technological U (MI)
Missouri U of Science and Technology (MO)
Montana Tech of The U of Montana (MT)
New Jersey Inst of Technology (NJ)
Rutgers, The State U of New Jersey, Newark (NJ)
South Dakota School of Mines and Technology (SD)
Tufts U (MA)
U of Alaska Fairbanks (AK)
The U of British Columbia (BC, Canada)
U of California, Berkeley (CA)
U of California, Los Angeles (CA)
U of Michigan (MI)
U of Minnesota, Twin Cities Campus (MN)
U of Mississippi (MS)
U of Nevada, Reno (NV)
U of North Dakota (ND)
U of Rochester (NY)
U of Saskatchewan (SK, Canada)
U of Toronto (ON, Canada)
U of Utah (UT)
U of Waterloo (ON, Canada)
U of Wisconsin–Madison (WI)

GEOLOGY/EARTH SCIENCE
Adams State U (CO)
Alaska Pacific U (AK)
Albion Coll (MI)
Allegheny Coll (PA)
American U of Beirut (Lebanon)
Amherst Coll (MA)
Angelo State U (TX)
Appalachian State U (NC)
Arizona State U at the Tempe campus (AZ)
Arkansas Tech U (AR)
Ashland U (OH)
Auburn U (AL)
Augustana Coll (IL)
Austin Peay State U (TN)
Ball State U (IN)
Bates Coll (ME)
Baylor U (TX)
Beloit Coll (WI)
Bemidji State U (MN)

Binghamton U, State U of New York (NY)
Bloomsburg U of Pennsylvania (PA)
Boston Coll (MA)
Boston U (MA)
Bowdoin Coll (ME)
Bowling Green State U (OH)
Bridgewater State U (MA)
Brown U (RI)
Bryn Mawr Coll (PA)
Bucknell U (PA)
Buffalo State Coll, State U of New York (NY)
California Inst of Technology (CA)
California Lutheran U (CA)
California Polytechnic State U, San Luis Obispo (CA)
California State Polytechnic U, Pomona (CA)
California State U, Chico (CA)
California State U, Fresno (CA)
California State U, Fullerton (CA)
California State U, Long Beach (CA)
California State U, Los Angeles (CA)
California State U, Sacramento (CA)
California State U, San Bernardino (CA)
California State U, Stanislaus (CA)
California U of Pennsylvania (PA)
Calvin Coll (MI)
Carleton Coll (MN)
Case Western Reserve U (OH)
Castleton State Coll (VT)
Cedarville U (OH)
Centenary Coll of Louisiana (LA)
Central Connecticut State U (CT)
Central Michigan U (MI)
Central State U (OH)
Central Washington U (WA)
City Coll of the City U of New York (NY)
Clarion U of Pennsylvania (PA)
Clark U (MA)
Colby Coll (ME)
The Coll at Brockport, State U of New York (NY)
Coll of Charleston (SC)
The Coll of William and Mary (VA)
The Coll of Wooster (OH)
The Colorado Coll (CO)
Colorado Mesa U (CO)
Colorado State U (CO)
Columbia U (NY)
Columbia U, School of General Studies (NY)
Columbus State U (GA)
Concordia U Chicago (IL)
Cornell Coll (IA)
Cornell U (NY)
Dalhousie U (NS, Canada)
Dartmouth Coll (NH)
Denison U (OH)
DePauw U (IN)
Dickinson Coll (PA)
Dickinson State U (ND)
Drexel U (PA)
East Carolina U (NC)
Eastern Illinois U (IL)
Eastern Kentucky U (KY)
Eastern Michigan U (MI)
Eastern New Mexico U (NM)
East Stroudsburg U of Pennsylvania (PA)
East Tennessee State U (TN)
Edinboro U of Pennsylvania (PA)
Emporia State U (KS)
Florida Atlantic U (FL)
Florida Intl U (FL)
Florida State U (FL)
Fort Hays State U (KS)
Fort Lewis Coll (CO)
Franklin & Marshall Coll (PA)
Frostburg State U (MD)
Furman U (SC)
George Mason U (VA)
The George Washington U (DC)
Georgia Southern U (GA)
Georgia Southwestern State U (GA)
Georgia State U (GA)
Grand Valley State U (MI)
Guilford Coll (NC)
Gustavus Adolphus Coll (MN)
Hamilton Coll (NY)
Hanover Coll (IN)
Hardin-Simmons U (TX)
Hartwick Coll (NY)
Harvard U (MA)
Haverford Coll (PA)
Hobart and William Smith Colls (NY)
Hofstra U (NY)
Hope Coll (MI)
Humboldt State U (CA)
Illinois State U (IL)
Indiana State U (IN)
Indiana U Bloomington (IN)
Indiana U Northwest (IN)
Indiana U of Pennsylvania (PA)
Indiana U–Purdue U Fort Wayne (IN)
Indiana U–Purdue U Indianapolis (IN)
Iowa State U of Science and Technology (IA)
Jackson State U (MS)
Jacksonville State U (AL)
James Madison U (VA)
Johns Hopkins U (MD)
Kansas State U (KS)
Kean U (NJ)
Keene State Coll (NH)
Kent State U (OH)
Keystone Coll (PA)
Kutztown U of Pennsylvania (PA)
Lafayette Coll (PA)
Lamar U (TX)
La Salle U (PA)
Lawrence U (WI)
Lehman Coll of the City U of New York (NY)
Lock Haven U of Pennsylvania (PA)
Long Island U–LIU Post (NY)
Louisiana State U and A&M Coll (LA)
Macalester Coll (MN)
Marietta Coll (OH)
Marshall U (WV)
Massachusetts Inst of Technology (MA)
Miami U (OH)
Michigan State U (MI)
Michigan Technological U (MI)
Middlebury Coll (VT)
Middle Tennessee State U (TN)
Midwestern State U (TX)
Millersville U of Pennsylvania (PA)
Millsaps Coll (MS)
Minnesota State U Mankato (MN)
Minot State U (ND)
Mississippi State U (MS)
Missouri State U (MO)
Missouri U of Science and Technology (MO)
Montana State U (MT)
Montclair State U (NJ)
Moravian Coll (PA)
Morehead State U (KY)
Mount Allison U (NB, Canada)
Mount Holyoke Coll (MA)
Murray State U (KY)
National U (CA)
New Jersey City U (NJ)
New Mexico Highlands U (NM)
New Mexico Inst of Mining and Technology (NM)
New Mexico State U (NM)
North Carolina State U (NC)
North Dakota State U (ND)
Northeastern Illinois U (IL)
Northeastern U (MA)
Northern Arizona U (AZ)
Northern Illinois U (IL)
Northern Kentucky U (KY)
Northern Michigan U (MI)
Northland Coll (WI)
Northwestern U (IL)
Northwest Missouri State U (MO)
Norwich U (VT)
Oberlin Coll (OH)
Occidental Coll (CA)
The Ohio State U (OH)
Ohio U (OH)
Ohio Wesleyan U (OH)
Oklahoma State U (OK)
Olivet Nazarene U (IL)
Pace U (NY)
Pacific Lutheran U (WA)
Penn State Abington (PA)
Penn State Altoona (PA)
Penn State Beaver (PA)
Penn State Berks (PA)
Penn State Brandywine (PA)
Penn State DuBois (PA)
Penn State Erie, The Behrend Coll (PA)
Penn State Fayette, The Eberly Campus (PA)
Penn State Greater Allegheny (PA)
Penn State Hazleton (PA)
Penn State Lehigh Valley (PA)
Penn State Mont Alto (PA)
Penn State New Kensington (PA)
Penn State Schuylkill (PA)
Penn State Shenango (PA)
Penn State U Park (PA)
Penn State Wilkes-Barre (PA)
Penn State Worthington Scranton (PA)
Penn State York (PA)
Piedmont Coll (GA)
Pomona Coll (CA)
Portland State U (OR)
Purdue U (IN)
Queens Coll of the City U of New York (NY)
Radford U (VA)
Rensselaer Polytechnic Inst (NY)
Rice U (TX)
Rider U (NJ)
Rocky Mountain Coll (MT)
Rutgers, The State U of New Jersey, Newark (NJ)
Rutgers, The State U of New Jersey, New Brunswick (NJ)
St. Lawrence U (NY)
Saint Louis U (MO)
St. Mary's U (TX)
St. Norbert Coll (WI)
Sam Houston State U (TX)
San Diego State U (CA)
San Francisco State U (CA)
San Jose State U (CA)
Savannah State U (GA)
Scripps Coll (CA)
Sewanee: The U of the South (TN)
Shawnee State U (OH)
Shippensburg U of Pennsylvania (PA)
Skidmore Coll (NY)
Slippery Rock U of Pennsylvania (PA)
Smith Coll (MA)
South Dakota School of Mines and Technology (SD)
Southern Connecticut State U (CT)
Southern Illinois U Carbondale (IL)
Southern Methodist U (TX)
Southern Oregon U (OR)
Southern Utah U (UT)
Stanford U (CA)
State U of New York at Fredonia (NY)
State U of New York at New Paltz (NY)
State U of New York at Oswego (NY)
State U of New York at Plattsburgh (NY)
State U of New York Coll at Cortland (NY)
State U of New York Coll at Geneseo (NY)
State U of New York Coll at Potsdam (NY)
Stephen F. Austin State U (TX)
Stockton U (NJ)
Stony Brook U, State U of New York (NY)
Sul Ross State U (TX)
Susquehanna U (PA)
Syracuse U (NY)
Tarleton State U (TX)
Taylor U (IN)
Temple U (PA)
Texas A&M U (TX)
Texas A&M U–Corpus Christi (TX)
Texas A&M U–Kingsville (TX)
Texas Christian U (TX)
Texas Tech U (TX)
Towson U (MD)
Trinity U (TX)
Tufts U (MA)
Tulane U (LA)
Union Coll (NY)
Université de Montréal (QC, Canada)
U at Buffalo, the State U of New York (NY)
The U of Akron (OH)
The U of Alabama (AL)
U of Alaska Fairbanks (AK)
U of Alberta (AB, Canada)
The U of Arizona (AZ)
U of Arkansas (AR)
U of Arkansas at Little Rock (AR)
The U of British Columbia (BC, Canada)
U of California, Berkeley (CA)
U of California, Davis (CA)
U of California, Irvine (CA)
U of California, Los Angeles (CA)
U of California, Merced (CA)
U of California, Riverside (CA)
U of California, Santa Barbara (CA)
U of California, Santa Cruz (CA)
U of Central Missouri (MO)
U of Cincinnati (OH)
U of Colorado Boulder (CO)
U of Dayton (OH)
U of Delaware (DE)
U of Florida (FL)
U of Georgia (GA)
U of Hawaii at Hilo (HI)
U of Hawaii at Manoa (HI)
U of Houston (TX)
U of Houston–Downtown (TX)
U of Idaho (ID)
U of Illinois at Chicago (IL)
U of Indianapolis (IN)
The U of Iowa (IA)
The U of Kansas (KS)
U of Kentucky (KY)
U of King's Coll (NS, Canada)
U of Louisiana at Lafayette (LA)
U of Maine (ME)
U of Maine at Presque Isle (ME)
U of Maryland, Coll Park (MD)
U of Massachusetts Amherst (MA)
U of Massachusetts Boston (MA)
U of Memphis (TN)
U of Miami (FL)
U of Michigan (MI)
U of Michigan–Dearborn (MI)
U of Minnesota, Duluth (MN)
U of Minnesota, Morris (MN)
U of Minnesota, Twin Cities Campus (MN)
U of Mississippi (MS)
U of Missouri (MO)
U of Missouri–Kansas City (MO)
The U of Montana (MT)
U of Mount Union (OH)
U of Nebraska–Lincoln (NE)
U of Nevada, Las Vegas (NV)
U of Nevada, Reno (NV)
U of New Brunswick Saint John (NB, Canada)
U of New Hampshire (NH)
U of New Mexico (NM)
U of New Orleans (LA)
The U of North Carolina at Chapel Hill (NC)
The U of North Carolina Wilmington (NC)
U of North Dakota (ND)
U of Northern Colorado (CO)
U of Northern Iowa (IA)
U of Oklahoma (OK)
U of Oregon (OR)
U of Ottawa (ON, Canada)
U of Pennsylvania (PA)
U of Pittsburgh (PA)
U of Puget Sound (WA)
U of Regina (SK, Canada)
U of Rhode Island (RI)
U of Rochester (NY)
U of St. Thomas (MN)
U of Saskatchewan (SK, Canada)
U of South Alabama (AL)
The U of South Dakota (SD)
U of Southern California (CA)
U of Southern Indiana (IN)
U of Southern Maine (ME)
U of Southern Mississippi (MS)
U of South Florida (FL)
The U of Tennessee (TN)
The U of Tennessee at Chattanooga (TN)
The U of Tennessee at Martin (TN)
The U of Texas at Arlington (TX)
The U of Texas at Austin (TX)
The U of Texas at Dallas (TX)
The U of Texas at El Paso (TX)
The U of Texas at San Antonio (TX)
The U of Texas of the Permian Basin (TX)
U of the Pacific (CA)
The U of Toledo (OH)
The U of Tulsa (OK)
U of Utah (UT)
U of Vermont (VT)
U of Washington (WA)
U of Waterloo (ON, Canada)
The U of Western Ontario (ON, Canada)
U of West Georgia (GA)
U of Windsor (ON, Canada)
U of Wisconsin–Eau Claire (WI)
U of Wisconsin–Green Bay (WI)
U of Wisconsin–Madison (WI)
U of Wisconsin–Milwaukee (WI)
U of Wisconsin–Oshkosh (WI)
U of Wisconsin–Parkside (WI)
U of Wisconsin–River Falls (WI)
U of Wisconsin–Stevens Point (WI)
U of Wyoming (WY)
Utah State U (UT)
Utah Valley U (UT)
Valdosta State U (GA)
Valparaiso U (IN)
Vanderbilt U (TN)
Vassar Coll (NY)
Virginia Polytechnic Inst and State U (VA)
Virginia Wesleyan Coll (VA)
Washington and Lee U (VA)
Washington State U (WA)
Washington U in St. Louis (MO)
Wayne State U (MI)
Weber State U (UT)
West Chester U of Pennsylvania (PA)
Western Carolina U (NC)
Western Illinois U (IL)
Western Kentucky U (KY)
Western Michigan U (MI)
Western State Colorado U (CO)
Western Washington U (WA)
West Texas A&M U (TX)
West Virginia U (WV)
Wheaton Coll (IL)
Whitman Coll (WA)
Wichita State U (KS)
Wilkes U (PA)
William Paterson U of New Jersey (NJ)
Williams Coll (MA)
Wittenberg U (OH)
Wright State U (OH)
York Coll of the City U of New York (NY)
Youngstown State U (OH)

GEOPHYSICS AND SEISMOLOGY

Baylor U (TX)
Boston Coll (MA)
Boston U (MA)
Bowling Green State U (OH)
Brown U (RI)
California Inst of Technology (CA)
Eastern Michigan U (MI)
Michigan State U (MI)
Michigan Technological U (MI)
Missouri U of Science and Technology (MO)
New Mexico Inst of Mining and Technology (NM)
Rice U (TX)
St. Lawrence U (NY)
Southern Methodist U (TX)
Stanford U (CA)
State U of New York at Fredonia (NY)
State U of New York Coll at Geneseo (NY)
Texas A&M U (TX)
The U of Akron (OH)
U of Alberta (AB, Canada)
The U of British Columbia (BC, Canada)
U of California, Los Angeles (CA)
U of California, Riverside (CA)
U of California, Santa Barbara (CA)
U of Chicago (IL)
U of Houston (TX)
U of Minnesota, Twin Cities Campus (MN)
U of Nevada, Reno (NV)
U of Oklahoma (OK)

U of Ottawa (ON, Canada)
U of Saskatchewan (SK, Canada)
The U of Texas at Austin (TX)
The U of Texas at El Paso (TX)
The U of Tulsa (OK)
U of Utah (UT)
U of Washington (WA)
U of Waterloo (ON, Canada)
Washington U in St. Louis (MO)
Western Michigan U (MI)
Western Washington U (WA)
West Virginia Wesleyan Coll (WV)

GERMAN
Agnes Scott Coll (GA)
Albion Coll (MI)
Allegheny Coll (PA)
Alma Coll (MI)
American U (DC)
Amherst Coll (MA)
Aquinas Coll (MI)
Arizona State U at the Tempe campus (AZ)
Auburn U (AL)
Augsburg Coll (MN)
Augustana Coll (IL)
Augustana Coll (SD)
Austin Coll (TX)
Baker U (KS)
Baldwin Wallace U (OH)
Ball State U (IN)
Bard Coll (NY)
Bard Coll at Simon's Rock (MA)
Barnard Coll (NY)
Bates Coll (ME)
Baylor U (TX)
Belmont U (TN)
Beloit Coll (WI)
Bemidji State U (MN)
Berea Coll (KY)
Berry Coll (GA)
Binghamton U, State U of New York (NY)
Boston Coll (MA)
Boston U (MA)
Bowdoin Coll (ME)
Bowling Green State U (OH)
Brandeis U (MA)
Brown U (RI)
Bryn Mawr Coll (PA)
Bucknell U (PA)
Butler U (IN)
California Lutheran U (CA)
California State U, Chico (CA)
California State U, Long Beach (CA)
Calvin Coll (MI)
Canisius Coll (NY)
Carleton Coll (MN)
Case Western Reserve U (OH)
The Catholic U of America (DC)
Central Connecticut State U (CT)
Central Michigan U (MI)
Central Washington U (WA)
Centre Coll (KY)
Christopher Newport U (VA)
Coe Coll (IA)
Colby Coll (ME)
Coll of Charleston (SC)
Coll of Saint Benedict (MN)
Coll of the Holy Cross (MA)
The Coll of William and Mary (VA)
The Coll of Wooster (OH)
The Colorado Coll (CO)
Colorado State U (CO)
Columbia U (NY)
Columbia U, School of General Studies (NY)
Concordia Coll (MN)
Concordia U Wisconsin (WI)
Cornell Coll (IA)
Cornell U (NY)
Creighton U (NE)
Dalhousie U (NS, Canada)
Dartmouth Coll (NH)
Davidson Coll (NC)
Delaware State U (DE)
Denison U (OH)
DePaul U (IL)
DePauw U (IN)
Dickinson Coll (PA)
Doane Coll (NE)
Drew U (NJ)
Drury U (MO)
Earlham Coll (IN)
East Carolina U (NC)
Eastern Michigan U (MI)
Elizabethtown Coll (PA)
Elmhurst Coll (IL)
Fairfield U (CT)
Fordham U (NY)
Fort Hays State U (KS)
Franciscan U of Steubenville (OH)
Franklin & Marshall Coll (PA)
Furman U (SC)
Georgetown U (DC)
The George Washington U (DC)
Georgia Southern U (GA)
Georgia State U (GA)
Gettysburg Coll (PA)
Gordon Coll (MA)
Grinnell Coll (IA)
Guilford Coll (NC)
Gustavus Adolphus Coll (MN)
Hamline U (MN)
Hampden-Sydney Coll (VA)
Hanover Coll (IN)
Hartwick Coll (NY)
Harvard U (MA)
Hastings Coll (NE)
Haverford Coll (PA)
Heidelberg U (OH)
Hendrix Coll (AR)
Hillsdale Coll (MI)
Hofstra U (NY)
Hope Coll (MI)
Howard U (DC)
Hunter Coll of the City U of New York (NY)
Illinois Coll (IL)
Illinois State U (IL)
Illinois Wesleyan U (IL)
Immaculata U (PA)
Indiana U–Purdue U Fort Wayne (IN)
Indiana U–Purdue U Indianapolis (IN)
Indiana U South Bend (IN)
Indiana U Southeast (IN)
Iowa State U of Science and Technology (IA)
Ithaca Coll (NY)
Jacksonville State U (AL)
John Carroll U (OH)
Johns Hopkins U (MD)
Juniata Coll (PA)
Kalamazoo Coll (MI)
Kent State U (OH)
Kenyon Coll (OH)
Knox Coll (IL)
Lafayette Coll (PA)
Lake Erie Coll (OH)
La Salle U (PA)
Lawrence U (WI)
Lebanon Valley Coll (PA)
Lehigh U (PA)
Lenoir-Rhyne U (NC)
Linfield Coll (OR)
Lipscomb U (TN)
Lock Haven U of Pennsylvania (PA)
Luther Coll (IA)
Lycoming Coll (PA)
Macalester Coll (MN)
Marquette U (WI)
McDaniel Coll (MD)
Mercer U, Macon (GA)
Messiah Coll (PA)
Miami U (OH)
Michigan State U (MI)
Middlebury Coll (VT)
Millersville U of Pennsylvania (PA)
Minnesota State U Mankato (MN)
Minot State U (ND)
Missouri Southern State U (MO)
Missouri State U (MO)
Montclair State U (NJ)
Moravian Coll (PA)
Mount Allison U (NB, Canada)
Mount St. Mary's U (MD)
Muhlenberg Coll (PA)
Murray State U (KY)
Nazareth Coll of Rochester (NY)
Nebraska Wesleyan U (NE)
New Coll of Florida (FL)
New York U (NY)
North Central Coll (IL)
Northern Illinois U (IL)
Northern Kentucky U (KY)
Northern State U (SD)
Northwestern U (IL)
Oakland U (MI)
Oberlin Coll (OH)
The Ohio State U (OH)
Ohio U (OH)
Ohio Wesleyan U (OH)
Oklahoma State U (OK)
Oregon State U (OR)
Pacific Lutheran U (WA)
Pacific U (OR)
Penn State Abington (PA)
Penn State Altoona (PA)
Penn State Beaver (PA)
Penn State Berks (PA)
Penn State Brandywine (PA)
Penn State DuBois (PA)
Penn State Erie, The Behrend Coll (PA)
Penn State Fayette, The Eberly Campus (PA)
Penn State Greater Allegheny (PA)
Penn State Hazleton (PA)
Penn State Lehigh Valley (PA)
Penn State Mont Alto (PA)
Penn State New Kensington (PA)
Penn State Schuylkill (PA)
Penn State Shenango (PA)
Penn State U Park (PA)
Penn State Wilkes-Barre (PA)
Penn State Worthington Scranton (PA)
Penn State York (PA)
Pomona Coll (CA)
Portland State U (OR)
Princeton U (NJ)
Purdue U (IN)
Queens Coll of the City U of New York (NY)
Randolph-Macon Coll (VA)
Reed Coll (OR)
Rhodes Coll (TN)
Rice U (TX)
Rider U (NJ)
Ripon Coll (WI)
Rutgers, The State U of New Jersey, Camden (NJ)
Rutgers, The State U of New Jersey, Newark (NJ)
Rutgers, The State U of New Jersey, New Brunswick (NJ)
Saint John's U (MN)
Saint Joseph's U (PA)
Saint Louis U (MO)
St. Norbert Coll (WI)
St. Olaf Coll (MN)
Samford U (AL)
San Diego State U (CA)
San Francisco State U (CA)
San Jose State U (CA)
Santa Clara U (CA)
Scripps Coll (CA)
Sewanee: The U of the South (TN)
Simpson Coll (IA)
Skidmore Coll (NY)
Smith Coll (MA)
South Dakota State U (SD)
Southern Connecticut State U (CT)
Southern Methodist U (TX)
Southwestern U (TX)
Stanford U (CA)
State U of New York at Oswego (NY)
State U of New York Coll at Cortland (NY)
Stetson U (FL)
Stony Brook U, State U of New York (NY)
Susquehanna U (PA)
Syracuse U (NY)
Temple U (PA)
Texas A&M U (TX)
Texas Christian U (TX)
Texas State U (TX)
Texas Tech U (TX)
Transylvania U (KY)
Trent U (ON, Canada)
Trinity Coll (CT)
Trinity U (TX)
Truman State U (MO)
Tufts U (MA)
Tulane U (LA)
Union Coll (NE)
Union Coll (NY)
United States Military Acad (NY)
Université de Montréal (QC, Canada)
U at Buffalo, the State U of New York (NY)
U of Alberta (AB, Canada)
The U of Arizona (AZ)
U of Arkansas (AR)
The U of British Columbia (BC, Canada)
U of California, Berkeley (CA)
U of California, Davis (CA)
U of California, Los Angeles (CA)
U of California, Santa Barbara (CA)
U of California, Santa Cruz (CA)
U of Central Missouri (MO)
U of Central Oklahoma (OK)
U of Chicago (IL)
U of Cincinnati (OH)
U of Dallas (TX)
U of Dayton (OH)
U of Denver (CO)
U of Evansville (IN)
U of Florida (FL)
U of Georgia (GA)
U of Hawaii at Manoa (HI)
U of Indianapolis (IN)
The U of Iowa (IA)
U of Jamestown (ND)
U of Kentucky (KY)
U of King's Coll (NS, Canada)
U of Lethbridge (AB, Canada)
U of Maine (ME)
U of Maryland, Coll Park (MD)
U of Miami (FL)
U of Michigan (MI)
U of Minnesota, Duluth (MN)
U of Minnesota, Morris (MN)
U of Minnesota, Twin Cities Campus (MN)
U of Mississippi (MS)
U of Missouri (MO)
The U of Montana (MT)
U of Mount Union (OH)
U of Nebraska at Kearney (NE)
U of Nebraska–Lincoln (NE)
U of Nevada, Las Vegas (NV)
U of New Brunswick Saint John (NB, Canada)
U of New Hampshire (NH)
U of New Mexico (NM)
U of North Carolina at Asheville (NC)
The U of North Carolina at Charlotte (NC)
The U of North Carolina at Greensboro (NC)
The U of North Carolina Wilmington (NC)
U of North Dakota (ND)
U of North Texas (TX)
U of Notre Dame (IN)
U of Oregon (OR)
U of Ottawa (ON, Canada)
U of Pennsylvania (PA)
U of Pittsburgh (PA)
U of Puget Sound (WA)
U of Regina (SK, Canada)
U of Rhode Island (RI)
U of Rochester (NY)
U of St. Thomas (MN)
U of Saskatchewan (SK, Canada)
The U of Scranton (PA)
The U of South Dakota (SD)
U of Southern Indiana (IN)
U of South Florida (FL)
The U of Tennessee (TN)
The U of Texas at Arlington (TX)
The U of Texas at Austin (TX)
The U of Texas at El Paso (TX)
U of the Pacific (CA)
The U of Toledo (OH)
U of Toronto (ON, Canada)
The U of Tulsa (OK)
U of Utah (UT)
U of Virginia (VA)
U of Waterloo (ON, Canada)
The U of Western Ontario (ON, Canada)
U of Windsor (ON, Canada)
U of Wisconsin–La Crosse (WI)
U of Wisconsin–Oshkosh (WI)
U of Wisconsin–Platteville (WI)
U of Wisconsin–River Falls (WI)
U of Wisconsin–Stevens Point (WI)
U of Wisconsin–Whitewater (WI)
U of Wyoming (WY)
Ursinus Coll (PA)
Utah State U (UT)
Valparaiso U (IN)
Vanderbilt U (TN)
Vassar Coll (NY)
Virginia Polytechnic Inst and State U (VA)
Virginia Wesleyan Coll (VA)
Wabash Coll (IN)
Wake Forest U (NC)
Wartburg Coll (IA)
Washburn U (KS)
Washington & Jefferson Coll (PA)
Washington and Lee U (VA)
Washington Coll (MD)
Washington U in St. Louis (MO)
Wayne State U (MI)
Weber State U (UT)
Webster U (MO)
West Chester U of Pennsylvania (PA)
Western Carolina U (NC)
Western Kentucky U (KY)
Western Michigan U (MI)
Western Oregon U (OR)
Western Washington U (WA)
Wheaton Coll (IL)
Wheaton Coll (MA)
Whitman Coll (WA)
Willamette U (OR)
Williams Coll (MA)
Wittenberg U (OH)
Wofford Coll (SC)
Wright State U (OH)
Xavier U (OH)
Yale U (CT)

GERMANIC LANGUAGES
Eastern Michigan U (MI)
Grand Valley State U (MI)
Indiana U Bloomington (IN)
New Coll of Florida (FL)
U of Alberta (AB, Canada)
U of Colorado Boulder (CO)
The U of Kansas (KS)
U of Oklahoma (OK)
The U of Texas at San Antonio (TX)
U of Washington (WA)
U of Wisconsin–Eau Claire (WI)
U of Wisconsin–Green Bay (WI)
U of Wisconsin–Madison (WI)
U of Wisconsin–Milwaukee (WI)
Washington U in St. Louis (MO)

GERMANIC LANGUAGES RELATED
Calvin Coll (MI)
Columbia U, School of General Studies (NY)
Ohio Northern U (OH)
U of Alberta (AB, Canada)

GERMAN LANGUAGE TEACHER EDUCATION
Albion Coll (MI)
Alma Coll (MI)
Auburn U (AL)
Augustana Coll (IL)
California Lutheran U (CA)
Calvin Coll (MI)
Canisius Coll (NY)
The Catholic U of America (DC)
Central Michigan U (MI)
Colorado State U (CO)
Concordia Coll (MN)
Concordia U Wisconsin (WI)
Delaware State U (DE)
East Carolina U (NC)
Eastern Michigan U (MI)
Elmhurst Coll (IL)
Grand Valley State U (MI)
Hastings Coll (NE)
Hofstra U (NY)
Hope Coll (MI)
Hunter Coll of the City U of New York (NY)
Indiana U Bloomington (IN)
Indiana U–Purdue U Fort Wayne (IN)
Indiana U–Purdue U Indianapolis (IN)
Indiana U South Bend (IN)
Ithaca Coll (NY)
Messiah Coll (PA)
Miami U (OH)
Michigan State U (MI)
Minot State U (ND)
Missouri State U (MO)
Ohio Northern U (OH)
Ohio U (OH)
Ohio Wesleyan U (OH)
Saint Joseph's U (PA)
U of Alberta (AB, Canada)
U of Central Oklahoma (OK)
U of Delaware (DE)
U of Evansville (IN)

U of Illinois at Chicago (IL)
The U of Iowa (IA)
U of Lethbridge (AB, Canada)
U of Nebraska–Lincoln (NE)
The U of South Dakota (SD)
The U of Tennessee at Martin (TN)
The U of Toledo (OH)
U of Windsor (ON, Canada)
U of Wisconsin–River Falls (WI)
Valparaiso U (IN)
Washburn U (KS)
Washington U in St. Louis (MO)
Weber State U (UT)
Western Michigan U (MI)
Western Washington U (WA)

GERMAN STUDIES
American U (DC)
Bard Coll (NY)
Bard Coll at Simon's Rock (MA)
Barnard Coll (NY)
Brown U (RI)
Case Western Reserve U (OH)
Central Coll (IA)
Coe Coll (IA)
Coll of the Holy Cross (MA)
The Coll of Wooster (OH)
Columbia U (NY)
Connecticut Coll (CT)
Cornell U (NY)
Fordham U (NY)
Franklin & Marshall Coll (PA)
Hamilton Coll (NY)
Ithaca Coll (NY)
Kutztown U of Pennsylvania (PA)
Lewis & Clark Coll (OR)
Linfield Coll (OR)
Moravian Coll (PA)
Mount Holyoke Coll (MA)
North Carolina State U (NC)
Northern Michigan U (MI)
Pomona Coll (CA)
Smith Coll (MA)
Stanford U (CA)
U of Alberta (AB, Canada)
U of California, Irvine (CA)
U of California, Riverside (CA)
U of Illinois at Chicago (IL)
U of Massachusetts Amherst (MA)
U of Pittsburgh (PA)
U of Richmond (VA)
The U of Scranton (PA)
The U of Western Ontario (ON, Canada)
U of Windsor (ON, Canada)
Wesleyan U (CT)
Wheaton Coll (MA)

GERONTOLOGY
Bethune-Cookman U (FL)
Bowling Green State U (OH)
California State U, Sacramento (CA)
California U of Pennsylvania (PA)
Canisius Coll (NY)
Case Western Reserve U (OH)
Concordia U, Nebraska (NE)
Dowling Coll (NY)
Gwynedd Mercy U (PA)
Ithaca Coll (NY)
John Carroll U (OH)
Langston U (OK)
Lindenwood U (MO)
Madonna U (MI)
Miami U (OH)
Minnesota State U Moorhead (MN)
Missouri State U (MO)
Mount Saint Mary's U (CA)
Quinnipiac U (CT)
St. Bonaventure U (NY)
St. Thomas U (NB, Canada)
San Diego State U (CA)
State Coll of Florida Manatee-Sarasota (FL)
Towson U (MD)
U of Maryland U Coll (MD)
U of Northern Iowa (IA)
U of North Texas (TX)
U of Regina (SK, Canada)
U of Southern California (CA)
U of South Florida (FL)
Weber State U (UT)
Wichita State U (KS)
York Coll of the City U of New York (NY)
Youngstown State U (OH)

GRAPHIC AND PRINTING EQUIPMENT OPERATION/ PRODUCTION
Chowan U (NC)
Fairmont State U (WV)
Georgia Southern U (GA)
Western Illinois U (IL)

GRAPHIC COMMUNICATIONS
Arizona State U at the Polytechnic campus (AZ)
California Polytechnic State U, San Luis Obispo (CA)
Chowan U (NC)
Grand View U (IA)
Illinois State U (IL)
Murray State U (KY)
New England Inst of Technology (RI)
Rochester Inst of Technology (NY)
Roger Williams U (RI)
School of the Art Inst of Chicago (IL)
U of Maryland U Coll (MD)
U of New Brunswick Saint John (NB, Canada)
U of North Dakota (ND)
U of Northern Iowa (IA)
Walla Walla U (WA)

GRAPHIC COMMUNICATIONS RELATED
Castleton State Coll (VT)
Rasmussen Coll Appleton (WI)
Rasmussen Coll Aurora (IL)
Rasmussen Coll Bismarck (ND)
Rasmussen Coll Blaine (MN)
Rasmussen Coll Bloomington (MN)
Rasmussen Coll Brooklyn Park (MN)
Rasmussen Coll Eagan (MN)
Rasmussen Coll Fargo (ND)
Rasmussen Coll Fort Myers (FL)
Rasmussen Coll Green Bay (WI)
Rasmussen Coll Lake Elmo/ Woodbury (MN)
Rasmussen Coll Land O' Lakes (FL)
Rasmussen Coll Mankato (MN)
Rasmussen Coll Mokena/Tinley Park (IL)
Rasmussen Coll New Port Richey (FL)
Rasmussen Coll Ocala (FL)
Rasmussen Coll Rockford (IL)
Rasmussen Coll Romeoville/Joliet (IL)
Rasmussen Coll St. Cloud (MN)
Rasmussen Coll Tampa/Brandon (FL)
Rasmussen Coll Wausau (WI)
Sullivan Coll of Technology and Design (KY)
U of Wisconsin–Stout (WI)

GRAPHIC DESIGN
Abilene Christian U (TX)
Acad of Art U (CA)
Adams State U (CO)
Albertus Magnus Coll (CT)
Alma Coll (MI)
American U (DC)
The American U in Dubai (United Arab Emirates)
American U of Beirut (Lebanon)
Anna Maria Coll (MA)
Appalachian State U (NC)
Arizona State U at the Tempe campus (AZ)
Arkansas Tech U (AR)
Art Center Coll of Design (CA)
Assumption Coll (MA)
Auburn U (AL)
Augsburg Coll (MN)
Augustana Coll (IL)
Baldwin Wallace U (OH)
Becker Coll (MA)
Belhaven U (MS)
Benedictine U (IL)
Berkeley Coll, Woodland Park (NJ)
Bethel U (MN)
Bluffton U (OH)
Bob Jones U (SC)
Boston U (MA)
Bradley U (IL)
Bridgewater State U (MA)
Brigham Young U (UT)
Cabrini Coll (PA)
Caldwell U (NJ)
California State Polytechnic U, Pomona (CA)
California State U, Dominguez Hills (CA)
California State U, Fresno (CA)
California State U, Long Beach (CA)
California State U, Sacramento (CA)
California U of Pennsylvania (PA)
Calvin Coll (MI)
Cardinal Stritch U (WI)
Castleton State Coll (VT)
Cedarville U (OH)
Central Michigan U (MI)
Central Washington U (WA)
Champlain Coll (VT)
Chapman U (CA)
Chatham U (PA)
Chowan U (NC)
City Coll of the City U of New York (NY)
Cleveland Inst of Art (OH)
Coastal Carolina U (SC)
Coker Coll (SC)
Colby-Sawyer Coll (NH)
Coll for Creative Studies (MI)
Coll of the Ozarks (MO)
Colorado Mesa U (CO)
Colorado State U (CO)
Columbia Coll (MO)
Concordia U (CA)
Concordia U, Nebraska (NE)
Concordia U Wisconsin (WI)
Concord U (WV)
Cornish Coll of the Arts (WA)
Creative Center (NE)
Creighton U (NE)
Culver-Stockton Coll (MO)
Daemen Coll (NY)
Defiance Coll (OH)
DePaul U (IL)
Dixie State U (UT)
Dominican U of California (CA)
Dowling Coll (NY)
Drake U (IA)
Drexel U (PA)
East Central U (OK)
East Stroudsburg U of Pennsylvania (PA)
Edgewood Coll (WI)
Elmhurst Coll (IL)
Emmanuel Coll (MA)
Emory & Henry Coll (VA)
Endicott Coll (MA)
Fashion Inst of Technology (NY)
Ferris State U (MI)
FIDM/Fashion Inst of Design & Merchandising, Los Angeles Campus (CA)
Fitchburg State U (MA)
Flagler Coll (FL)
Florida Ag and Mech U (FL)
Florida Southern Coll (FL)
Florida State U (FL)
Fort Hays State U (KS)
Georgia Southern U (GA)
Grace Coll (IN)
Grand View U (IA)
Harding U (AR)
Hardin-Simmons U (TX)
High Point U (NC)
Holy Family U (PA)
Indiana U–Purdue U Fort Wayne (IN)
Intl Business Coll, Fort Wayne (IN)
Iowa State U of Science and Technology (IA)
John Brown U (AR)
Judson U (IL)
Kansas City Art Inst (MO)
Kansas Wesleyan U (KS)
Kentucky Wesleyan Coll (KY)
Laguna Coll of Art & Design (CA)
Lamar U (TX)
Lasell Coll (MA)
Lawrence Technological U (MI)
Lebanese American U (Lebanon)
Lenoir-Rhyne U (NC)
Liberty U (VA)
Limestone Coll (SC)
Madonna U (MI)
Mansfield U of Pennsylvania (PA)
Marian U (IN)
Marian U (WI)
Marietta Coll (OH)
Mars Hill U (NC)
Marymount Manhattan Coll (NY)
Marymount U (VA)
Maryville U of Saint Louis (MO)
Marywood U (PA)
Mercer U, Macon (GA)
Meredith Coll (NC)
MidAmerica Nazarene U (KS)
Minnesota State U Moorhead (MN)
Missouri Western State U (MO)
Montclair State U (NJ)
Moore Coll of Art & Design (PA)
Moravian Coll (PA)
Morningside Coll (IA)
Mount Mary U (WI)
Mount Mercy U (IA)
Mount St. Joseph U (OH)
Mount Vernon Nazarene U (OH)
Newberry Coll (SC)
Newbury Coll (MA)
North Carolina Ag and Tech State U (NC)
North Carolina State U (NC)
North Central Coll (IL)
Northeastern U (MA)
Northern Michigan U (MI)
Northwestern Coll (IA)
Northwest Nazarene U (ID)
Nossi Coll of Art (TN)
Oakland U (MI)
Ohio Northern U (OH)
Ohio U (OH)
Oklahoma Baptist U (OK)
Pacific Northwest Coll of Art (OR)
Paier Coll of Art, Inc. (CT)
Palm Beach Atlantic U (FL)
Paris Coll of Art (France)
Park U (MO)
Penn State Abington (PA)
Penn State Altoona (PA)
Penn State Beaver (PA)
Penn State Berks (PA)
Penn State Brandywine (PA)
Penn State DuBois (PA)
Penn State Erie, The Behrend Coll (PA)
Penn State Fayette, The Eberly Campus (PA)
Penn State Greater Allegheny (PA)
Penn State Hazleton (PA)
Penn State Lehigh Valley (PA)
Penn State Mont Alto (PA)
Penn State New Kensington (PA)
Penn State Schuylkill (PA)
Penn State Shenango (PA)
Penn State U Park (PA)
Penn State Wilkes-Barre (PA)
Penn State Worthington Scranton (PA)
Penn State York (PA)
Pennsylvania Coll of Art & Design (PA)
Peru State Coll (NE)
Philadelphia U (PA)
Plymouth State U (NH)
Point Loma Nazarene U (CA)
Portland State U (OR)
Pratt Inst (NY)
Queens Coll of the City U of New York (NY)
Quincy U (IL)
Rhode Island Coll (RI)
Rhode Island School of Design (RI)
Rider U (NJ)
Ringling Coll of Art and Design (FL)
Robert Morris U Illinois (IL)
Rochester Inst of Technology (NY)
Rocky Mountain Coll of Art + Design (CO)
Sacred Heart U (CT)
The Sage Colls (NY)
Saginaw Valley State U (MI)
St. Edward's U (TX)
St. John's U (NY)
Saint Mary's U of Minnesota (MN)
St. Norbert Coll (WI)
St. Thomas Aquinas Coll (NY)
Saint Vincent Coll (PA)
Salve Regina U (RI)
Samford U (AL)
San Diego State U (CA)
San Jose State U (CA)
Santa Fe U of Art and Design (NM)
Savannah Coll of Art and Design (GA)
School of the Art Inst of Chicago (IL)
School of the Museum of Fine Arts, Boston (MA)
Siena Heights U (MI)
Simpson Coll (IA)
South Dakota State U (SD)
Southern Adventist U (TN)
Southern New Hampshire U (NH)
Southern Utah U (UT)
Spring Hill Coll (AL)
State U of New York at New Paltz (NY)
State U of New York Coll of Technology at Canton (NY)
Stephens Coll (MO)
Stonehill Coll (MA)
Sullivan Coll of Technology and Design (KY)
Susquehanna U (PA)
Syracuse U (NY)
Tabor Coll (KS)
Temple U (PA)
Texas Christian U (TX)
Trinity Christian Coll (IL)
Union Coll (NE)
Universidad del Turabo (PR)
The U of Akron (OH)
U of Arkansas–Fort Smith (AR)
U of Bridgeport (CT)
U of Central Oklahoma (OK)
U of Denver (CO)
U of Florida (FL)
U of Hartford (CT)
U of Houston (TX)
U of Illinois at Chicago (IL)
The U of Kansas (KS)
U of Mary Hardin-Baylor (TX)
U of Miami (FL)
U of Michigan (MI)
U of Nevada, Las Vegas (NV)
U of New Haven (CT)
U of North Dakota (ND)
U of Northwestern–St. Paul (MN)
U of Rio Grande (OH)
U of San Francisco (CA)
The U of Tampa (FL)
The U of Tennessee at Martin (TN)
The U of the Arts (PA)
U of the District of Columbia (DC)
U of the Incarnate Word (TX)
U of Wisconsin–Stout (WI)
Ursuline Coll (OH)
Villa Maria Coll (NY)
Virginia Commonwealth U (VA)
Walla Walla U (WA)
Walsh U (OH)
Washington U in St. Louis (MO)
Waynesburg U (PA)
Wayne State Coll (NE)
Western Michigan U (MI)
Western State Colorado U (CO)
West Texas A&M U (TX)
Wichita State U (KS)
William Woods U (MO)
Wright State U (OH)
Xavier U (OH)
Youngstown State U (OH)

GREENHOUSE MANAGEMENT
U of Minnesota, Crookston (MN)

HEALTH AND MEDICAL ADMINISTRATIVE SERVICES RELATED
Ave Maria U (FL)
Clayton State U (GA)
Concordia Coll–New York (NY)
Concordia U, St. Paul (MN)
Missouri Southern State U (MO)
Mount Mercy U (IA)
Northeastern U (MA)
Pennsylvania Coll of Technology (PA)
State U of New York Coll of Technology at Canton (NY)
Ursuline Coll (OH)
Washburn U (KS)
Weber State U (UT)
Western Michigan U (MI)
Wheeling Jesuit U (WV)

HEALTH AND PHYSICAL EDUCATION/FITNESS
Arkansas State U (AR)
Asbury U (KY)
Austin Peay State U (TN)
Averett U (VA)
Baker U (KS)
Baldwin Wallace U (OH)

Baylor U (TX)
Belmont U (TN)
Berea Coll (KY)
Bethel Coll (IN)
Bethel Coll (KS)
Biola U (CA)
Blackburn Coll (IL)
Black Hills State U (SD)
Bluffton U (OH)
Bob Jones U (SC)
Brevard Coll (NC)
Bridgewater Coll (VA)
Bryan Coll (TN)
California Polytechnic State U, San Luis Obispo (CA)
California State Polytechnic U, Pomona (CA)
California State U, Chico (CA)
California State U, Dominguez Hills (CA)
California State U, Fullerton (CA)
California State U, Monterey Bay (CA)
California State U, San Bernardino (CA)
California State U, San Marcos (CA)
California State U, Stanislaus (CA)
Cameron U (OK)
Capital U (OH)
Carroll Coll (MT)
Castleton State Coll (VT)
Catawba Coll (NC)
Cedarville U (OH)
Central Michigan U (MI)
Charleston Southern U (SC)
Claflin U (SC)
Cleveland State U (OH)
Coll of the Ozarks (MO)
The Coll of William and Mary (VA)
Concordia Coll (MN)
Concordia U (CA)
Concordia U, Nebraska (NE)
Concordia U, St. Paul (MN)
Concordia U Texas (TX)
Concordia U Wisconsin (WI)
Dallas Baptist U (TX)
Delaware State U (DE)
DePaul U (IL)
Doane Coll (NE)
East Central U (OK)
Eastern Michigan U (MI)
Eastern Oregon U (OR)
East Tennessee State U (TN)
East Texas Baptist U (TX)
Elmhurst Coll (IL)
Emory & Henry Coll (VA)
Evangel U (MO)
Ferrum Coll (VA)
Florida Ag and Mech U (FL)
Friends U (KS)
Georgia Southern U (GA)
Grand View U (IA)
Greensboro Coll (NC)
Hanover Coll (IN)
Hardin-Simmons U (TX)
Hastings Coll (NE)
Houghton Coll (NY)
Houston Baptist U (TX)
Howard Payne U (TX)
Husson U (ME)
Indiana U of Pennsylvania (PA)
Iowa State U of Science and Technology (IA)
Iowa Wesleyan Coll (IA)
Ithaca Coll (NY)
Jacksonville State U (AL)
Jacksonville U (FL)
James Madison U (VA)
Jarvis Christian Coll (TX)
John Brown U (AR)
Johnson State Coll (VT)
Keene State Coll (NH)
La Sierra U (CA)
Lee U (TN)
Liberty U (VA)
Lincoln Memorial U (TN)
Lincoln U (PA)
Linfield Coll (OR)
Lubbock Christian U (TX)
Luther Coll (IA)
Lynchburg Coll (VA)
Marian U (IN)
Maryville Coll (TN)
Marywood U (PA)
The Master's Coll and Sem (CA)
Mayville State U (ND)
McDaniel Coll (MD)
Miami U (OH)
Middle Tennessee State U (TN)
Milligan Coll (TN)
Minnesota State U Moorhead (MN)
Mississippi U for Women (MS)
Missouri Western State U (MO)
Monmouth Coll (IL)
Monmouth U (NJ)
Montana State U Billings (MT)
Morehead State U (KY)
New England Coll (NH)
North Carolina Central U (NC)
Northern Illinois U (IL)
Northern Michigan U (MI)
Northwest Nazarene U (ID)
The Ohio State U (OH)
Ohio U (OH)
Oklahoma Baptist U (OK)
Olivet Coll (MI)
Oregon State U (OR)
Pepperdine U, Malibu (CA)
Philander Smith Coll (AR)
Plymouth State U (NH)
Point Loma Nazarene U (CA)
Prairie View A&M U (TX)
Quincy U (IL)
Randolph Coll (VA)
Rhode Island Coll (RI)
Rocky Mountain Coll (MT)
Rowan U (NJ)
St. Catherine U (MN)
St. Gregory's U, Shawnee (OK)
Saint Joseph's Coll (IN)
San Diego State U (CA)
San Jose State U (CA)
Selma U (AL)
Shawnee State U (OH)
Slippery Rock U of Pennsylvania (PA)
South Carolina State U (SC)
South Dakota State U (SD)
Southeast Missouri State U (MO)
Southwest Baptist U (MO)
Southwestern Adventist U (TX)
Southwest Minnesota State U (MN)
Sterling Coll (KS)
Syracuse U (NY)
Tabor Coll (KS)
Tarleton State U (TX)
Tennessee Wesleyan Coll (TN)
Texas A&M Intl U (TX)
Texas A&M U–Kingsville (TX)
Texas Christian U (TX)
Truman State U (MO)
Union Coll (NE)
Universidad Metropolitana (PR)
U of Alberta (AB, Canada)
U of Arkansas (AR)
U of Delaware (DE)
The U of Findlay (OH)
U of Georgia (GA)
U of Great Falls (MT)
U of Guam (GU)
U of Hawaii at Manoa (HI)
The U of Iowa (IA)
The U of Kansas (KS)
U of Louisville (KY)
U of Massachusetts Boston (MA)
U of Michigan (MI)
U of Mobile (AL)
The U of Montana Western (MT)
U of Montevallo (AL)
U of New Orleans (LA)
The U of North Carolina at Chapel Hill (NC)
The U of North Carolina at Charlotte (NC)
The U of North Carolina at Pembroke (NC)
The U of North Carolina Wilmington (NC)
U of Northern Iowa (IA)
U of Northwestern–St. Paul (MN)
U of Ottawa (ON, Canada)
U of Regina (SK, Canada)
U of Rio Grande (OH)
U of San Francisco (CA)
U of Science and Arts of Oklahoma (OK)
U of Southern Maine (ME)
U of Southern Mississippi (MS)
The U of Tampa (FL)
The U of Tennessee at Martin (TN)
The U of Texas at Austin (TX)
The U of Texas at Tyler (TX)
U of the Cumberlands (KY)
U of Toronto (ON, Canada)
U of Utah (UT)
U of West Florida (FL)
U of Windsor (ON, Canada)
U of Wisconsin–La Crosse (WI)
U of Wisconsin–Stevens Point (WI)
U of Wisconsin–Superior (WI)
Ursinus Coll (PA)
Utah Valley U (UT)
Valley City State U (ND)
Valparaiso U (IN)
Vanguard U of Southern California (CA)
Walla Walla U (WA)
Walsh U (OH)
Weber State U (UT)
Welch Coll (TN)
West Chester U of Pennsylvania (PA)
Western Washington U (WA)
Westfield State U (MA)
West Virginia State U (WV)
West Virginia U (WV)
West Virginia Wesleyan Coll (WV)
Whittier Coll (CA)
William Penn U (IA)
Wingate U (NC)
Wright State U (OH)
Youngstown State U (OH)

HEALTH AND PHYSICAL EDUCATION RELATED

Adelphi U (NY)
Arizona State U at the Downtown Phoenix campus (AZ)
Averett U (VA)
Avila U (MO)
Bloomsburg U of Pennsylvania (PA)
Bowling Green State U (OH)
Bridgewater State U (MA)
California State U, Long Beach (CA)
Coe Coll (IA)
Coker Coll (SC)
Concordia Coll (MN)
Concordia U Wisconsin (WI)
Cornell Coll (IA)
East Carolina U (NC)
East Stroudsburg U of Pennsylvania (PA)
Edinboro U of Pennsylvania (PA)
Greensboro Coll (NC)
Gustavus Adolphus Coll (MN)
Ithaca Coll (NY)
John Brown U (AR)
Limestone Coll (SC)
Lincoln U (PA)
Lock Haven U of Pennsylvania (PA)
Mayville State U (ND)
Midwestern State U (TX)
Missouri Southern State U (MO)
Mount Vernon Nazarene U (OH)
Naropa U (CO)
North Greenville U (SC)
Regis Coll (MA)
Reinhardt U (GA)
Rocky Mountain Coll (MT)
South Dakota State U (SD)
Texas Lutheran U (TX)
Union Coll (NE)
U of Alberta (AB, Canada)
U of Central Oklahoma (OK)
The U of Iowa (IA)
U of New England (ME)
U of Utah (UT)
U of Wisconsin–Superior (WI)
Valdosta State U (GA)
Wayne State Coll (NE)

HEALTH AND WELLNESS

Antioch U Midwest (OH)
Arkansas State U (AR)
Canisius Coll (NY)
Chatham U (PA)
Creighton U (NE)
Daemen Coll (NY)
Georgetown Coll (KY)
Goddard Coll (VT)
Granite State Coll (NH)
Indiana U Kokomo (IN)
Jacksonville State U (AL)
Johnson C. Smith U (NC)
Keene State Coll (NH)
Lamar U (TX)
Maryville U of Saint Louis (MO)
Missouri Baptist U (MO)
National U (CA)
New York Inst of Technology (NY)
North Dakota State U (ND)
Point Loma Nazarene U (CA)
Rhode Island Coll (RI)
Sam Houston State U (TX)
State U of New York Coll at Potsdam (NY)
Texas A&M U (TX)
Texas Woman's U (TX)
U of Houston (TX)
U of Saint Francis (IN)
The U of Texas at San Antonio (TX)
The U of Texas–Pan American (TX)
U of Wisconsin–La Crosse (WI)
U of Wisconsin–Stout (WI)
U of Wisconsin–Superior (WI)
Viterbo U (WI)

HEALTH COMMUNICATION

Ashland U (OH)
Grand Valley State U (MI)
Juniata Coll (PA)
North Dakota State U (ND)
San Diego State U (CA)
Southeast Missouri State U (MO)
U of Houston (TX)

HEALTH/HEALTH-CARE ADMINISTRATION

Adams State U (CO)
Appalachian State U (NC)
Arcadia U (PA)
Arizona State U at the Polytechnic campus (AZ)
Auburn U (AL)
Augustana Coll (SD)
Averett U (VA)
Baldwin Wallace U (OH)
Belhaven U (MS)
Benedictine U (IL)
Berkeley Coll, Woodland Park (NJ)
Berkeley Coll–New York City Campus (NY)
Berkeley Coll–Westchester Campus (NY)
Black Hills State U (SD)
Bluefield State Coll (WV)
Bluffton U (OH)
Bowling Green State U (OH)
Brandeis U (MA)
Cabarrus Coll of Health Sciences (NC)
California Baptist U (CA)
California State U, Dominguez Hills (CA)
California State U, Long Beach (CA)
Carlow U (PA)
Central Michigan U (MI)
Charter Oak State Coll (CT)
Chestnut Hill Coll (PA)
Coastal Carolina U (SC)
Colby-Sawyer Coll (NH)
CollAmerica–Flagstaff (AZ)
The Coll of Westchester (NY)
Columbia Coll (MO)
Columbia Southern U (AL)
Concordia U (CA)
Concordia U, St. Paul (MN)
Concordia U Wisconsin (WI)
Corban U (OR)
Creighton U (NE)
Dallas Baptist U (TX)
Daniel Webster Coll (NH)
Davenport U, Grand Rapids (MI)
DeVry U, Pomona (CA)
DeVry U, Westminster (CO)
DeVry U, Miramar (FL)
DeVry U, Orlando (FL)
DeVry U, Decatur (GA)
DeVry U, Houston (TX)
DeVry U Online (IL)
Dominican Coll (NY)
Drexel U (PA)
East Carolina U (NC)
Eastern Kentucky U (KY)
Eastern Michigan U (MI)
Elizabethtown Coll School of Continuing and Professional Studies (PA)
Elms Coll (MA)
Ferris State U (MI)
Florida Ag and Mech U (FL)
Florida Atlantic U (FL)
Florida Intl U (FL)
Florida Southern Coll (FL)
Franklin U (OH)
Frostburg State U (MD)
Gannon U (PA)
Granite State Coll (NH)
Harding U (AR)
Harris-Stowe State U (MO)
Hastings Coll (NE)
Heidelberg U (OH)
Hodges U (FL)
Immaculata U (PA)
Indiana U–Purdue U Fort Wayne (IN)
Indiana U–Purdue U Indianapolis (IN)
Indian River State Coll (FL)
Iona Coll (NY)
Ithaca Coll (NY)
Jackson State U (MS)
James Madison U (VA)
Jefferson Coll of Health Sciences (VA)
King U (TN)
Langston U (OK)
Lebanon Valley Coll (PA)
Lee U (TN)
Lehman Coll of the City U of New York (NY)
LeTourneau U (TX)
Lewis U (IL)
Limestone Coll (SC)
Lindenwood U (MO)
Long Island U–LIU Post (NY)
Lourdes U (OH)
Loyola U Chicago (IL)
Madonna U (MI)
Malone U (OH)
Marian U (WI)
Mary Baldwin Coll (VA)
Marywood U (PA)
Mercy Coll of Health Sciences (IA)
Minnesota State U Moorhead (MN)
Misericordia U (PA)
Mississippi State U (MS)
Missouri Baptist U (MO)
Montana State U Billings (MT)
Mount Mercy U (IA)
National U (CA)
Newbury Coll (MA)
New England Coll (NH)
Norfolk State U (VA)
Northeastern State U (OK)
Ohio U (OH)
Oregon State U (OR)
Our Lady of the Lake U of San Antonio (TX)
Peirce Coll (PA)
Penn State Abington (PA)
Penn State Altoona (PA)
Penn State Beaver (PA)
Penn State Berks (PA)
Penn State Brandywine (PA)
Penn State DuBois (PA)
Penn State Erie, The Behrend Coll (PA)
Penn State Fayette, The Eberly Campus (PA)
Penn State Greater Allegheny (PA)
Penn State Hazleton (PA)
Penn State Lehigh Valley (PA)
Penn State Mont Alto (PA)
Penn State New Kensington (PA)
Penn State Schuylkill (PA)
Penn State Shenango (PA)
Penn State U Park (PA)
Penn State Wilkes-Barre (PA)
Penn State Worthington Scranton (PA)
Penn State York (PA)
Pennsylvania Coll of Health Sciences (PA)
Plaza Coll (NY)
Providence Coll (RI)
Rasmussen Coll Appleton (WI)
Rasmussen Coll Aurora (IL)
Rasmussen Coll Bismarck (ND)
Rasmussen Coll Blaine (MN)
Rasmussen Coll Bloomington (MN)
Rasmussen Coll Brooklyn Park (MN)
Rasmussen Coll Eagan (MN)
Rasmussen Coll Fargo (ND)
Rasmussen Coll Fort Myers (FL)
Rasmussen Coll Green Bay (WI)
Rasmussen Coll Kansas City/ Overland Park (KS)
Rasmussen Coll Lake Elmo/ Woodbury (MN)
Rasmussen Coll Land O' Lakes (FL)
Rasmussen Coll Mankato (MN)

Rasmussen Coll Mokena/Tinley Park (IL)
Rasmussen Coll Moorhead (MN)
Rasmussen Coll New Port Richey (FL)
Rasmussen Coll Ocala (FL)
Rasmussen Coll Rockford (IL)
Rasmussen Coll Romeoville/Joliet (IL)
Rasmussen Coll St. Cloud (MN)
Rasmussen Coll Tampa/Brandon (FL)
Rasmussen Coll Topeka (KS)
Rasmussen Coll Wausau (WI)
Regis U (CO)
Rhode Island Coll (RI)
Roberts Wesleyan Coll (NY)
Roger Williams U (RI)
Saint Leo U (FL)
Saint Louis U (MO)
Saint Mary-of-the-Woods Coll (IN)
Saint Peter's U (NJ)
St. Thomas U (FL)
Salve Regina U (RI)
Sam Houston State U (TX)
San Jose State U (CA)
Santa Fe Coll (FL)
Shippensburg U of Pennsylvania (PA)
Simpson U (CA)
Southeast Missouri State U (MO)
Southern Adventist U (TN)
Southern Illinois U Carbondale (IL)
Southern Vermont Coll (VT)
State U of New York Coll of Technology at Canton (NY)
Stonehill Coll (MA)
Stratford U, Glen Allen (VA)
Stratford U, Newport News (VA)
Tennessee State U (TN)
Texas Southern U (TX)
Texas State U (TX)
Thomas More Coll (KY)
Towson U (MD)
The U of Alabama at Birmingham (AL)
U of Central Florida (FL)
U of Evansville (IN)
U of Great Falls (MT)
U of Hawaii–West Oahu (HI)
U of Houston–Clear Lake (TX)
U of Kentucky (KY)
U of La Verne (CA)
U of Louisiana at Lafayette (LA)
U of Maryland U Coll (MD)
U of Massachusetts Dartmouth (MA)
U of Miami (FL)
U of Michigan–Dearborn (MI)
U of Michigan–Flint (MI)
U of Minnesota, Crookston (MN)
U of Minnesota, Duluth (MN)
U of Mount Union (OH)
U of Nevada, Las Vegas (NV)
U of New England (ME)
U of New Hampshire (NH)
The U of North Carolina at Chapel Hill (NC)
U of North Florida (FL)
U of Pennsylvania (PA)
U of Rhode Island (RI)
U of St. Francis (IL)
U of Saint Francis (IN)
The U of Scranton (PA)
U of Southern Indiana (IN)
U of South Florida (FL)
The U of Texas at El Paso (TX)
U of Virginia (VA)
U of Wisconsin–Eau Claire (WI)
Upper Iowa U (IA)
Ursuline Coll (OH)
Valdosta State U (GA)
Valparaiso U (IN)
Viterbo U (WI)
Walden U (MN)
Washington U in St. Louis (MO)
Waynesburg U (PA)
Weber State U (UT)
Webster U (MO)
Western Carolina U (NC)
Western Illinois U (IL)
Western Kentucky U (KY)
West Virginia U Inst of Technology (WV)
Wichita State U (KS)
Wilberforce U (OH)

HEALTH INFORMATION/ MEDICAL RECORDS ADMINISTRATION

Alabama State U (AL)
Arkansas Tech U (AR)
Bowling Green State U (OH)
Charter Oak State Coll (CT)
Chicago State U (IL)
Coll of Coastal Georgia (GA)
The Coll of St. Scholastica (MN)
Dakota State U (SD)
Dalhousie U (NS, Canada)
Davenport U, Grand Rapids (MI)
Duquesne U (PA)
East Carolina U (NC)
Eastern Kentucky U (KY)
Fairleigh Dickinson U, Metropolitan Campus (NJ)
Ferris State U (MI)
Florida Ag and Mech U (FL)
Georgian Court U (NJ)
Georgia Regents U (GA)
Granite State Coll (NH)
Gwynedd Mercy U (PA)
Illinois State U (IL)
Indiana U–Purdue U Indianapolis (IN)
Indiana U Southeast (IN)
Kean U (NJ)
Keiser U, Fort Lauderdale (FL)
Lincoln Coll of New England, Southington (CT)
Long Island U–LIU Post (NY)
Marymount U (VA)
Medaille Coll (NY)
Metropolitan Coll of New York (NY)
Missouri Western State U (MO)
Murray State U (KY)
The Ohio State U (OH)
The Ohio State U at Lima (OH)
Peirce Coll (PA)
Pennsylvania Coll of Technology (PA)
Rasmussen Coll Appleton (WI)
Rasmussen Coll Aurora (IL)
Rasmussen Coll Bismarck (ND)
Rasmussen Coll Blaine (MN)
Rasmussen Coll Bloomington (MN)
Rasmussen Coll Brooklyn Park (MN)
Rasmussen Coll Eagan (MN)
Rasmussen Coll Fargo (ND)
Rasmussen Coll Fort Myers (FL)
Rasmussen Coll Green Bay (WI)
Rasmussen Coll Kansas City/ Overland Park (KS)
Rasmussen Coll Lake Elmo/ Woodbury (MN)
Rasmussen Coll Land O' Lakes (FL)
Rasmussen Coll Mankato (MN)
Rasmussen Coll Mokena/Tinley Park (IL)
Rasmussen Coll Moorhead (MN)
Rasmussen Coll New Port Richey (FL)
Rasmussen Coll Ocala (FL)
Rasmussen Coll Rockford (IL)
Rasmussen Coll Romeoville/Joliet (IL)
Rasmussen Coll St. Cloud (MN)
Rasmussen Coll Tampa/Brandon (FL)
Rasmussen Coll Topeka (KS)
Rasmussen Coll Wausau (WI)
Regis U (CO)
Rutgers, The State U of New Jersey, New Brunswick (NJ)
Saint Louis U (MO)
State U of New York Polytechnic Inst (NY)
Stephens Coll (MO)
Stratford U, Glen Allen (VA)
Stratford U, Newport News (VA)
Sullivan U (KY)
Tennessee State U (TN)
Texas Southern U (TX)
Texas State U (TX)
Trevecca Nazarene U (TN)
The U of Alabama at Birmingham (AL)
U of Central Florida (FL)
U of Cincinnati (OH)
U of Illinois at Chicago (IL)
The U of Kansas (KS)
U of Louisiana at Lafayette (LA)
U of Pittsburgh (PA)
The U of Tennessee (TN)
The U of Toledo (OH)
U of Washington (WA)
U of Wisconsin–Green Bay (WI)
Weber State U (UT)
Western Carolina U (NC)
Western Kentucky U (KY)

HEALTH INFORMATION/ MEDICAL RECORDS TECHNOLOGY

Bowling Green State U (OH)
Davenport U, Grand Rapids (MI)
Fisher Coll (MA)
Franklin U (OH)
Gwynedd Mercy U (PA)
Keiser U, Fort Lauderdale (FL)
St. John's U (NY)
U of Saint Mary (KS)

HEALTH/MEDICAL PHYSICS

Belmont U (TN)
Bloomsburg U of Pennsylvania (PA)
Cabarrus Coll of Health Sciences (NC)
California State U, Dominguez Hills (CA)
Oregon State U (OR)
U of Guelph (ON, Canada)
U of Nevada, Las Vegas (NV)

HEALTH/MEDICAL PREPARATORY PROGRAMS RELATED

Abilene Christian U (TX)
Allegheny Coll (PA)
Arizona State U at the Downtown Phoenix campus (AZ)
Asbury U (KY)
Avila U (MO)
Baylor U (TX)
Benedictine U (IL)
Binghamton U, State U of New York (NY)
Bloomsburg U of Pennsylvania (PA)
Cleveland State U (OH)
Concordia U, Nebraska (NE)
Cornerstone U (MI)
Cumberland U (TN)
Drexel U (PA)
Duquesne U (PA)
Eastern Kentucky U (KY)
Emory & Henry Coll (VA)
Gannon U (PA)
Guilford Coll (NC)
Hodges U (FL)
Hofstra U (NY)
Ithaca Coll (NY)
Kent State U (OH)
Kent State U at Ashtabula (OH)
Lee U (TN)
Le Moyne Coll (NY)
Lipscomb U (TN)
Lock Haven U of Pennsylvania (PA)
Lubbock Christian U (TX)
Madonna U (MI)
Maryville U of Saint Louis (MO)
Mercer U, Macon (GA)
Meredith Coll (NC)
Northern Illinois U (IL)
Northern Michigan U (MI)
Saginaw Valley State U (MI)
Seattle Pacific U (WA)
Seattle U (WA)
Tusculum Coll (TN)
The U of Findlay (OH)
U of Michigan–Flint (MI)
U of Minnesota, Twin Cities Campus (MN)
U of Missouri (MO)
U of Regina (SK, Canada)
U of South Alabama (AL)
U of Waterloo (ON, Canada)
Utica Coll (NY)
Valley City State U (ND)
Western Washington U (WA)

HEALTH/MEDICAL PSYCHOLOGY

Bridgewater State U (MA)
Castleton State Coll (VT)
Greenville Coll (IL)
Jefferson Coll of Health Sciences (VA)
Kansas Wesleyan U (KS)
LeTourneau U (TX)
MCPHS U (MA)
U of Mary Hardin-Baylor (TX)

HEALTH OCCUPATIONS TEACHER EDUCATION

Baylor U (TX)
Midwestern State U (TX)
North Carolina State U (NC)
Northwest U (WA)
U of Central Oklahoma (OK)

HEALTH POLICY ANALYSIS

Mount Saint Mary's U (CA)

HEALTH PROFESSIONS RELATED

Alma Coll (MI)
Alvernia U (PA)
Armstrong State U (GA)
Athens State U (AL)
Azusa Pacific U (CA)
Baldwin Wallace U (OH)
Bastyr U (WA)
Boston U (MA)
Bowling Green State U (OH)
Bradley U (IL)
California State U, Fresno (CA)
California State U, Long Beach (CA)
California State U, Los Angeles (CA)
California State U, Sacramento (CA)
Caribbean U (PR)
Castleton State Coll (VT)
Cleveland State U (OH)
Concordia Coll–New York (NY)
Corban U (OR)
Creighton U (NE)
Curry Coll (MA)
Dalhousie U (NS, Canada)
DePaul U (IL)
DeSales U (PA)
East Tennessee State U (TN)
Elizabethtown Coll (PA)
Elmira Coll (NY)
Excelsior Coll (NY)
Fairmont State U (WV)
Ferris State U (MI)
Fisher Coll (MA)
Furman U (SC)
Gannon U (PA)
George Mason U (VA)
Georgetown U (DC)
Gettysburg Coll (PA)
Gwynedd Mercy U (PA)
Inter American U of Puerto Rico, Ponce Campus (PR)
Johnson State Coll (VT)
King's Coll (PA)
King U (TN)
Lock Haven U of Pennsylvania (PA)
Long Island U–LIU Brooklyn (NY)
Long Island U–LIU Post (NY)
Manchester U (IN)
Marquette U (WI)
Maryville U of Saint Louis (MO)
Marywood U (PA)
MCPHS U (MA)
Mercy Coll (NY)
Milligan Coll (TN)
Minnesota State U Mankato (MN)
Missouri Southern State U (MO)
Molloy Coll (NY)
Morrisville State Coll (NY)
Mount St. Mary's U (MD)
New Jersey City U (NJ)
Newman U (KS)
New York Inst of Technology (NY)
Northeastern State U (OK)
Northern Illinois U (IL)
Norwich U (VT)
Nova Southeastern U (FL)
Oakland U (MI)
The Ohio State U (OH)
Old Dominion U (VA)
Pacific U (OR)
Purdue U (IN)
Randolph Coll (VA)
Sacred Heart U (CT)
The Sage Colls (NY)
Saint Augustine's U (NC)
St. Catharine Coll (KY)
St. Francis Coll (NY)
St. John's U (NY)
Saint Joseph's U (PA)
Saint Mary-of-the-Woods Coll (IN)
Samford U (AL)
San Francisco State U (CA)
Southern Methodist U (TX)
State U of New York Coll at Cortland (NY)
Tennessee Wesleyan Coll (TN)
Towson U (MD)
The U of Alabama (AL)
U of Arkansas at Little Rock (AR)
U of Bridgeport (CT)
The U of British Columbia–Okanagan Campus (BC, Canada)
U of California, Santa Cruz (CA)
U of Central Arkansas (AR)
U of Charleston (WV)
U of Cincinnati (OH)
U of Colorado Colorado Springs (CO)
U of Delaware (DE)
U of Hartford (CT)
U of Maryland, Baltimore County (MD)
U of Nevada, Reno (NV)
U of New Brunswick Saint John (NB, Canada)
U of New England (ME)
The U of North Carolina Wilmington (NC)
U of Northern Iowa (IA)
U of Pennsylvania (PA)
U of Pittsburgh (PA)
U of Saint Francis (IN)
The U of Tennessee at Martin (TN)
The U of Texas at El Paso (TX)
The U of Texas at Tyler (TX)
U of Waterloo (ON, Canada)
The U of Western Ontario (ON, Canada)
U of Wisconsin–Parkside (WI)
U of Wisconsin–Stevens Point (WI)
Walla Walla U (WA)
Washington U in St. Louis (MO)
Wayne State U (MI)
West Liberty U (WV)
West Virginia State U (WV)
William Paterson U of New Jersey (NJ)
Worcester State U (MA)
Youngstown State U (OH)

HEALTH SERVICES ADMINISTRATION

Arizona State U at the Downtown Phoenix campus (AZ)
Bentley U (MA)
Chapman U (CA)
East Stroudsburg U of Pennsylvania (PA)
Florida National U (FL)
Indiana U Northwest (IN)
Indiana U–Purdue U Fort Wayne (IN)
Indiana U–Purdue U Indianapolis (IN)
Inter American U of Puerto Rico, Ponce Campus (PR)
Keiser U, Fort Lauderdale (FL)
McNeese State U (LA)
Northeastern State U (OK)
Rider U (NJ)
Robert Morris U (PA)
Slippery Rock U of Pennsylvania (PA)
State Coll of Florida Manatee-Sarasota (FL)
U of New Orleans (LA)
U of San Francisco (CA)
U of the District of Columbia (DC)
U of Washington, Tacoma (WA)
Ursuline Coll (OH)

HEALTH SERVICES/ALLIED HEALTH/HEALTH SCIENCES

Adventist U of Health Sciences (FL)
Albany Coll of Pharmacy and Health Sciences (NY)
Albion Coll (MI)
Alvernia U (PA)
American Intl Coll (MA)
Anna Maria Coll (MA)
Bay Path U (MA)
Biola U (CA)
Boston U (MA)
Brenau U (GA)
Brevard Coll (NC)
Butler U (IN)
California Baptist U (CA)
California State U, Chico (CA)

California State U, Dominguez Hills (CA)
California State U, Fullerton (CA)
California State U, San Bernardino (CA)
Canisius Coll (NY)
Carroll Coll (MT)
Cheyney U of Pennsylvania (PA)
Chicago State U (IL)
Chowan U (NC)
Colby-Sawyer Coll (NH)
The Coll at Brockport, State U of New York (NY)
The Coll of Idaho (ID)
The Coll of St. Scholastica (MN)
Coll of the Ozarks (MO)
Columbus State U (GA)
Corban U (OR)
Dalhousie U (NS, Canada)
DePaul U (IL)
Emmanuel Coll (MA)
The Evergreen State Coll (WA)
Fairleigh Dickinson U, Coll at Florham (NJ)
Ferrum Coll (VA)
Fisher Coll (MA)
Florida Ag and Mech U (FL)
Florida Gulf Coast U (FL)
Friends U (KS)
Goodwin Coll (CT)
Graceland U (IA)
Granite State Coll (NH)
Greensboro Coll (NC)
Gwynedd Mercy U (PA)
Heidelberg U (OH)
Hendrix Coll (AR)
Hofstra U (NY)
Keiser U, Fort Lauderdale (FL)
Kentucky Wesleyan Coll (KY)
Lasell Coll (MA)
Lebanon Valley Coll (PA)
Lee U (TN)
LeTourneau U (TX)
Lincoln U (CA)
Lincoln U (PA)
Madonna U (MI)
Marywood U (PA)
McKendree U (IL)
Mercy Coll (NY)
Mercy Coll of Health Sciences (IA)
Merrimack Coll (MA)
Messiah Coll (PA)
Miami Dade Coll (FL)
Misericordia U (PA)
Monmouth U (NJ)
National U (CA)
Nicholls State U (LA)
Northern Kentucky U (KY)
Olivet Coll (MI)
Pace U (NY)
Pennsylvania Coll of Health Sciences (PA)
Quinnipiac U (CT)
Rhode Island Coll (RI)
Rutgers, The State U of New Jersey, Newark (NJ)
The Sage Colls (NY)
Saginaw Valley State U (MI)
St. Catharine Coll (KY)
Saint Joseph's U (PA)
Saint Louis U (MO)
St. Luke's Coll (IA)
Sam Houston State U (TX)
San Diego State U (CA)
San Jose State U (CA)
Spalding U (KY)
Stephen F. Austin State U (TX)
Stetson U (FL)
Stockton U (NJ)
Stony Brook U, State U of New York (NY)
Texas Southern U (TX)
Texas Woman's U (TX)
Towson U (MD)
Union Coll (NE)
U of Central Florida (FL)
U of Florida (FL)
U of Hartford (CT)
U of Kentucky (KY)
U of Miami (FL)
U of Michigan–Flint (MI)
U of Minnesota, Crookston (MN)
U of Missouri–Kansas City (MO)
U of New England (ME)
U of Northern Colorado (CO)
U of North Florida (FL)
U of Oklahoma Health Sciences Center (OK)
U of Ottawa (ON, Canada)
U of San Francisco (CA)
U of Southern California (CA)
U of Southern Mississippi (MS)
U of South Florida (FL)
U of South Florida, St. Petersburg (FL)
The U of Texas at Dallas (TX)
U of the Incarnate Word (TX)
U of the Sciences (PA)
U of Utah (UT)
U of Washington, Bothell (WA)
The U of Western Ontario (ON, Canada)
U of West Florida (FL)
Ursuline Coll (OH)
Valparaiso U (IN)
Walden U (MN)
Washington U in St. Louis (MO)
West Chester U of Pennsylvania (PA)
Western Kentucky U (KY)
Western New England U (MA)
Westminster Coll (UT)
West Texas A&M U (TX)
Wheaton Coll (IL)
Wheeling Jesuit U (WV)
Whitworth U (WA)
Widener U (PA)
Wilmington U (DE)
Youngstown State U (OH)

HEALTH TEACHER EDUCATION
Alma Coll (MI)
Appalachian State U (NC)
Auburn U (AL)
Augsburg Coll (MN)
Averett U (VA)
Ball State U (IN)
Baylor U (TX)
Bemidji State U (MN)
Bethel U (MN)
Bluefield Coll (VA)
Bowling Green State U (OH)
Bridgewater State U (MA)
California State U, Stanislaus (CA)
Campbellsville U (KY)
Capital U (OH)
Central Michigan U (MI)
Concordia Coll (MN)
Concordia U, Nebraska (NE)
Concordia U, St. Paul (MN)
Concord U (WV)
Defiance Coll (OH)
Delaware State U (DE)
DePaul U (IL)
East Carolina U (NC)
Eastern Illinois U (IL)
Eastern Oregon U (OR)
East Stroudsburg U of Pennsylvania (PA)
Elon U (NC)
Fayetteville State U (NC)
George Mason U (VA)
Graceland U (IA)
Grand Valley State U (MI)
Gustavus Adolphus Coll (MN)
Hampton U (VA)
Harding U (AR)
Heidelberg U (OH)
Hofstra U (NY)
Houghton Coll (NY)
Hunter Coll of the City U of New York (NY)
Illinois State U (IL)
Indiana U Bloomington (IN)
Inter American U of Puerto Rico, San Germán Campus (PR)
Iowa State U of Science and Technology (IA)
Iowa Wesleyan Coll (IA)
Ithaca Coll (NY)
Jacksonville State U (AL)
John Brown U (AR)
Kansas Wesleyan U (KS)
Kent State U (OH)
Lee U (TN)
Lehman Coll of the City U of New York (NY)
Lincoln Memorial U (TN)
Linfield Coll (OR)
Long Island U–LIU Post (NY)
Louisiana Coll (LA)
Maryville Coll (TN)
Mayville State U (ND)
McKendree U (IL)
Michigan State U (MI)
Middle Tennessee State U (TN)
Minnesota State U Mankato (MN)
Minnesota State U Moorhead (MN)
Missouri Baptist U (MO)
Missouri Valley Coll (MO)
Montana State U Billings (MT)
Montclair State U (NJ)
Morehead State U (KY)
Murray State U (KY)
National U (CA)
National U Coll, Bayamón (PR)
New Mexico Highlands U (NM)
North Carolina Central U (NC)
North Dakota State U (ND)
Northern Illinois U (IL)
Northern Michigan U (MI)
Northern State U (SD)
Northwestern Oklahoma State U (OK)
Ohio Wesleyan U (OH)
Olivet Coll (MI)
Peru State Coll (NE)
Portland State U (OR)
Purdue U (IN)
Rhode Island Coll (RI)
Rocky Mountain Coll (MT)
Roger Williams U (RI)
Salisbury U (MD)
South Dakota State U (SD)
Southern Illinois U Carbondale (IL)
Southern Illinois U Edwardsville (IL)
Southern Oregon U (OR)
Southwest Baptist U (MO)
Southwest Minnesota State U (MN)
State U of New York at Oswego (NY)
State U of New York Coll at Cortland (NY)
Tabor Coll (KS)
Tennessee State U (TN)
Troy U (AL)
Union Coll (KY)
The U of Akron (OH)
The U of Alabama at Birmingham (AL)
U of Alberta (AB, Canada)
U of Charleston (WV)
U of Cincinnati (OH)
U of Great Falls (MT)
U of Kentucky (KY)
U of Maryland, Coll Park (MD)
U of Minnesota, Twin Cities Campus (MN)
The U of Montana (MT)
The U of Montana Western (MT)
U of Mount Union (OH)
U of Nevada, Las Vegas (NV)
U of New Mexico (NM)
U of Northern Iowa (IA)
U of Regina (SK, Canada)
U of Rio Grande (OH)
U of Saint Francis (IN)
U of St. Thomas (MN)
The U of South Dakota (SD)
U of the Cumberlands (KY)
U of the District of Columbia (DC)
The U of Toledo (OH)
U of Toronto (ON, Canada)
U of Windsor (ON, Canada)
U of Wisconsin–La Crosse (WI)
Urbana U (OH)
Utah State U (UT)
Utah Valley U (UT)
Valley City State U (ND)
Virginia Commonwealth U (VA)
Washington State U (WA)
Wayne State U (MI)
Western Illinois U (IL)
Western Michigan U (MI)
West Liberty U (WV)
West Virginia Wesleyan Coll (WV)
William Paterson U of New Jersey (NJ)
William Penn U (IA)
Winona State U (MN)
York Coll of the City U of New York (NY)
Youngstown State U (OH)

HEAVY EQUIPMENT MAINTENANCE TECHNOLOGY
Ferris State U (MI)

HEBREW
Bard Coll (NY)
Baruch Coll of the City U of New York (NY)
Binghamton U, State U of New York (NY)
Brandeis U (MA)
Brigham Young U (UT)
Concordia U Wisconsin (WI)
Dartmouth Coll (NH)
Hofstra U (NY)
Hunter Coll of the City U of New York (NY)
Lehman Coll of the City U of New York (NY)
Multnomah U (OR)
New York U (NY)
The Ohio State U (OH)
Queens Coll of the City U of New York (NY)
U of Cincinnati (OH)
U of Michigan (MI)
U of Minnesota, Twin Cities Campus (MN)
The U of Texas at Austin (TX)
U of Utah (UT)
Washington U in St. Louis (MO)
Yeshiva U (NY)

HERBALISM
Bastyr U (WA)

HISPANIC-AMERICAN, PUERTO RICAN, AND MEXICAN-AMERICAN/ CHICANO STUDIES
Arizona State U at the Tempe campus (AZ)
Boston Coll (MA)
Bowling Green State U (OH)
Brown U (RI)
California State U, Dominguez Hills (CA)
California State U, Fresno (CA)
California State U, Fullerton (CA)
California State U, Long Beach (CA)
California State U, Los Angeles (CA)
Cedar Crest Coll (PA)
Claremont McKenna Coll (CA)
The Colorado Coll (CO)
Columbia U (NY)
Columbia U, School of General Studies (NY)
Connecticut Coll (CT)
Dartmouth Coll (NH)
Gettysburg Coll (PA)
Hunter Coll of the City U of New York (NY)
Lewis & Clark Coll (OR)
Loyola Marymount U (CA)
Mills Coll (CA)
Pepperdine U, Malibu (CA)
Pomona Coll (CA)
Rutgers, The State U of New Jersey, Newark (NJ)
Rutgers, The State U of New Jersey, New Brunswick (NJ)
San Diego State U (CA)
San Francisco State U (CA)
Scripps Coll (CA)
Southern Methodist U (TX)
Stanford U (CA)
Trent U (ON, Canada)
Tulane U (LA)
Université de Montréal (QC, Canada)
U at Albany, State U of New York (NY)
U of Alberta (AB, Canada)
The U of Arizona (AZ)
U of California, Berkeley (CA)
U of California, Davis (CA)
U of California, Irvine (CA)
U of California, Los Angeles (CA)
U of California, Riverside (CA)
U of California, Santa Barbara (CA)
U of California, Santa Cruz (CA)
U of Michigan (MI)
U of Minnesota, Twin Cities Campus (MN)
U of New Mexico (NM)
U of Northern Colorado (CO)
The U of Scranton (PA)
U of Southern California (CA)
The U of Texas at El Paso (TX)
The U of Texas at San Antonio (TX)
The U of Texas–Pan American (TX)

HISPANIC AND LATIN AMERICAN LANGUAGES
Hamilton Coll (NY)
Molloy Coll (NY)
Pacific Lutheran U (WA)
Purdue U (IN)
U of California, Merced (CA)
U of Washington, Tacoma (WA)

HISTOLOGIC TECHNOLOGY/ HISTOTECHNOLOGIST
Oakland U (MI)

HISTORIC PRESERVATION AND CONSERVATION
Coll of Charleston (SC)
Delaware State U (DE)
Roger Williams U (RI)
Salve Regina U (RI)
Savannah Coll of Art and Design (GA)
Southeast Missouri State U (MO)
U of Delaware (DE)
U of Mary Washington (VA)
Ursuline Coll (OH)

HISTORY
Abilene Christian U (TX)
Adams State U (CO)
Adelphi U (NY)
Agnes Scott Coll (GA)
Alabama State U (AL)
Albany State U (GA)
Albertus Magnus Coll (CT)
Albion Coll (MI)
Albright Coll (PA)
Alcorn State U (MS)
Alice Lloyd Coll (KY)
Allegheny Coll (PA)
Alma Coll (MI)
Alvernia U (PA)
Alverno Coll (WI)
Ambrose U Coll (AB, Canada)
American Intl Coll (MA)
American Public U System (WV)
American U (DC)
American U in Bulgaria (Bulgaria)
The American U in Cairo (Egypt)
American U of Beirut (Lebanon)
The American U of Paris (France)
Amherst Coll (MA)
Anderson U (IN)
Anderson U (SC)
Andrews U (MI)
Angelo State U (TX)
Anna Maria Coll (MA)
Antioch Coll, Yellow Springs (OH)
Appalachian State U (NC)
Aquinas Coll (MI)
Aquinas Coll (TN)
Arcadia U (PA)
Arizona State U at the Polytechnic campus (AZ)
Arizona State U at the Tempe campus (AZ)
Arizona State U at the West campus (AZ)
Arkansas State U (AR)
Arkansas Tech U (AR)
Armstrong State U (GA)
Asbury U (KY)
Ashland U (OH)
Assumption Coll (MA)
Athens State U (AL)
Auburn U (AL)
Auburn U at Montgomery (AL)
Augsburg Coll (MN)
Augustana Coll (IL)
Augustana Coll (SD)
Austin Coll (TX)
Austin Peay State U (TN)
Ave Maria U (FL)
Averett U (VA)
Avila U (MO)
Azusa Pacific U (CA)
Baker U (KS)
Baldwin Wallace U (OH)
Ball State U (IN)
Bard Coll (NY)
Bard Coll at Simon's Rock (MA)
Barnard Coll (NY)
Barry U (FL)
Baruch Coll of the City U of New York (NY)
Bates Coll (ME)

Baylor U (TX)
Belhaven U (MS)
Belmont Abbey Coll (NC)
Belmont U (TN)
Beloit Coll (WI)
Bemidji State U (MN)
Benedictine Coll (KS)
Benedictine U (IL)
Bennington Coll (VT)
Bentley U (MA)
Berea Coll (KY)
Berry Coll (GA)
Bethany Coll (WV)
Bethany Lutheran Coll (MN)
Bethel Coll (IN)
Bethel Coll (KS)
Bethel U (MN)
Binghamton U, State U of New York (NY)
Biola U (CA)
Birmingham-Southern Coll (AL)
Blackburn Coll (IL)
Black Hills State U (SD)
Bloomfield Coll (NJ)
Bloomsburg U of Pennsylvania (PA)
Bluefield Coll (VA)
Blue Mountain Coll (MS)
Bluffton U (OH)
Bob Jones U (SC)
Boston Coll (MA)
Boston U (MA)
Bowdoin Coll (ME)
Bowie State U (MD)
Bowling Green State U (OH)
Bradley U (IL)
Brandeis U (MA)
Brenau U (GA)
Brevard Coll (NC)
Bridgewater Coll (VA)
Bridgewater State U (MA)
Brown U (RI)
Bryan Coll (TN)
Bryant U (RI)
Bryn Mawr Coll (PA)
Bucknell U (PA)
Buena Vista U (IA)
Buffalo State Coll, State U of New York (NY)
Butler U (IN)
Cabrini Coll (PA)
Caldwell U (NJ)
California Baptist U (CA)
California Inst of Technology (CA)
California Lutheran U (CA)
California Polytechnic State U, San Luis Obispo (CA)
California State Polytechnic U, Pomona (CA)
California State U, Chico (CA)
California State U, Dominguez Hills (CA)
California State U, Fresno (CA)
California State U, Fullerton (CA)
California State U, Long Beach (CA)
California State U, Los Angeles (CA)
California State U, Sacramento (CA)
California State U, San Bernardino (CA)
California State U, San Marcos (CA)
California State U, Stanislaus (CA)
California U of Pennsylvania (PA)
Calvary Bible Coll and Theological Sem (MO)
Calvin Coll (MI)
Cameron U (OK)
Campbellsville U (KY)
Canisius Coll (NY)
Cape Breton U (NS, Canada)
Capital U (OH)
Cardinal Stritch U (WI)
Carleton Coll (MN)
Carlow U (PA)
Carroll Coll (MT)
Carson-Newman U (TN)
Case Western Reserve U (OH)
Castleton State Coll (VT)
Catawba Coll (NC)
The Catholic U of America (DC)
Cedar Crest Coll (PA)
Cedarville U (OH)
Centenary Coll of Louisiana (LA)
Central Coll (IA)
Central Connecticut State U (CT)
Central Methodist U (MO)
Central Michigan U (MI)
Central State U (OH)
Central Washington U (WA)
Centre Coll (KY)
Chapman U (CA)
Charleston Southern U (SC)
Chatham U (PA)
Chestnut Hill Coll (PA)
Chicago State U (IL)
Chowan U (NC)
Christendom Coll (VA)
Christian Brothers U (TN)
Christopher Newport U (VA)
The Citadel, The Military Coll of South Carolina (SC)
City Coll of the City U of New York (NY)
Claflin U (SC)
Claremont McKenna Coll (CA)
Clarion U of Pennsylvania (PA)
Clark Atlanta U (GA)
Clarke U (IA)
Clarkson U (NY)
Clark U (MA)
Clayton State U (GA)
Clearwater Christian Coll (FL)
Cleveland State U (OH)
Coastal Carolina U (SC)
Coe Coll (IA)
Coker Coll (SC)
Colby Coll (ME)
The Coll at Brockport, State U of New York (NY)
Coll of Charleston (SC)
The Coll of Idaho (ID)
The Coll of New Jersey (NJ)
The Coll of New Rochelle (NY)
Coll of Saint Benedict (MN)
Coll of Saint Elizabeth (NJ)
The Coll of St. Scholastica (MN)
Coll of Staten Island of the City U of New York (NY)
Coll of the Holy Cross (MA)
Coll of the Ozarks (MO)
The Coll of William and Mary (VA)
The Coll of Wooster (OH)
The Colorado Coll (CO)
Colorado Mesa U (CO)
Colorado State U (CO)
Colorado State U–Pueblo (CO)
Columbia Coll (MO)
Columbia Coll (SC)
Columbia U (NY)
Columbia U, School of General Studies (NY)
Columbus State U (GA)
Concordia Coll (MN)
Concordia Coll–New York (NY)
Concordia U (CA)
Concordia U (QC, Canada)
Concordia U Chicago (IL)
Concordia U, Nebraska (NE)
Concordia U, St. Paul (MN)
Concordia U Texas (TX)
Concordia U Wisconsin (WI)
Concord U (WV)
Connecticut Coll (CT)
Corban U (OR)
Cornell Coll (IA)
Cornell U (NY)
Cornerstone U (MI)
Covenant Coll (GA)
Crandall U (NB, Canada)
Creighton U (NE)
Culver-Stockton Coll (MO)
Cumberland U (TN)
Daemen Coll (NY)
Dalhousie U (NS, Canada)
Dallas Baptist U (TX)
Dartmouth Coll (NH)
Davidson Coll (NC)
Defiance Coll (OH)
Delaware State U (DE)
Delta State U (MS)
Denison U (OH)
DePaul U (IL)
DePauw U (IN)
DEREE - The American Coll of Greece (Greece)
DeSales U (PA)
Dickinson Coll (PA)
Dickinson State U (ND)
Dixie State U (UT)
Doane Coll (NE)
Dominican Coll (NY)
Dominican U (IL)
Dominican U of California (CA)
Dowling Coll (NY)
Drake U (IA)
Drew U (NJ)
Drexel U (PA)
Drury U (MO)
Duquesne U (PA)
Earlham Coll (IN)
East Carolina U (NC)
East Central U (OK)
Eastern Connecticut State U (CT)
Eastern Illinois U (IL)
Eastern Kentucky U (KY)
Eastern Michigan U (MI)
Eastern New Mexico U (NM)
Eastern Oregon U (OR)
Eastern U (PA)
East Stroudsburg U of Pennsylvania (PA)
East Tennessee State U (TN)
East Texas Baptist U (TX)
Eckerd Coll (FL)
Edgewood Coll (WI)
Edinboro U of Pennsylvania (PA)
Elizabethtown Coll (PA)
Elmhurst Coll (IL)
Elmira Coll (NY)
Elms Coll (MA)
Elon U (NC)
Emmanuel Coll (MA)
Emory & Henry Coll (VA)
Emporia State U (KS)
Endicott Coll (MA)
Erskine Coll (SC)
Eureka Coll (IL)
Evangel U (MO)
Fairfield U (CT)
Fairleigh Dickinson U, Coll at Florham (NJ)
Fairleigh Dickinson U, Metropolitan Campus (NJ)
Fairmont State U (WV)
Faulkner U (AL)
Fayetteville State U (NC)
Ferris State U (MI)
Ferrum Coll (VA)
Fitchburg State U (MA)
Flagler Coll (FL)
Florida Ag and Mech U (FL)
Florida Atlantic U (FL)
Florida Coll (FL)
Florida Gulf Coast U (FL)
Florida Intl U (FL)
Florida Southern Coll (FL)
Florida State U (FL)
Fontbonne U (MO)
Fordham U (NY)
Fort Hays State U (KS)
Fort Lewis Coll (CO)
Framingham State U (MA)
Franciscan U of Steubenville (OH)
Francis Marion U (SC)
Franklin & Marshall Coll (PA)
Franklin Coll (IN)
Franklin Pierce U (NH)
Friends U (KS)
Frostburg State U (MD)
Furman U (SC)
Gannon U (PA)
Geneva Coll (PA)
George Mason U (VA)
Georgetown Coll (KY)
Georgetown U (DC)
The George Washington U (DC)
Georgia Coll & State U (GA)
Georgia Gwinnett Coll (GA)
Georgian Court U (NJ)
Georgia Regents U (GA)
Georgia Southern U (GA)
Georgia Southwestern State U (GA)
Georgia State U (GA)
Gettysburg Coll (PA)
Goddard Coll (VT)
Gonzaga U (WA)
Gordon Coll (MA)
Goshen Coll (IN)
Goucher Coll (MD)
Governors State U (IL)
Grace Coll (IN)
Graceland U (IA)
Grambling State U (LA)
Grand Valley State U (MI)
Grand View U (IA)
Granite State Coll (NH)
Great Lakes Christian Coll (MI)
Green Mountain Coll (VT)
Greensboro Coll (NC)
Greenville Coll (IL)
Grinnell Coll (IA)
Grove City Coll (PA)
Guilford Coll (NC)
Gustavus Adolphus Coll (MN)
Gwynedd Mercy U (PA)
Hamilton Coll (NY)
Hamline U (MN)
Hampden-Sydney Coll (VA)
Hampshire Coll (MA)
Hampton U (VA)
Hannibal-LaGrange U (MO)
Hanover Coll (IN)
Harding U (AR)
Hardin-Simmons U (TX)
Hartwick Coll (NY)
Harvard U (MA)
Hastings Coll (NE)
Haverford Coll (PA)
Hawai`i Pacific U (HI)
Heidelberg U (OH)
Hendrix Coll (AR)
High Point U (NC)
Hillsdale Coll (MI)
Hiram Coll (OH)
Hobart and William Smith Colls (NY)
Hofstra U (NY)
Hollins U (VA)
Holy Cross Coll (IN)
Holy Family U (PA)
Hope Coll (MI)
Houghton Coll (NY)
Houston Baptist U (TX)
Howard Payne U (TX)
Howard U (DC)
Humboldt State U (CA)
Hunter Coll of the City U of New York (NY)
Huntingdon Coll (AL)
Huston-Tillotson U (TX)
Illinois Coll (IL)
Illinois State U (IL)
Illinois Wesleyan U (IL)
Immaculata U (PA)
Indiana State U (IN)
Indiana U Bloomington (IN)
Indiana U East (IN)
Indiana U Northwest (IN)
Indiana U of Pennsylvania (PA)
Indiana U–Purdue U Fort Wayne (IN)
Indiana U–Purdue U Indianapolis (IN)
Indiana U South Bend (IN)
Indiana U Southeast (IN)
Inter American U of Puerto Rico, San Germán Campus (PR)
Iona Coll (NY)
Iowa State U of Science and Technology (IA)
Ithaca Coll (NY)
Jackson State U (MS)
Jacksonville State U (AL)
Jacksonville U (FL)
James Madison U (VA)
Jarvis Christian Coll (TX)
John Brown U (AR)
John Cabot U (Italy)
John Carroll U (OH)
Johns Hopkins U (MD)
Johnson C. Smith U (NC)
Johnson State Coll (VT)
Judson Coll (AL)
Judson U (IL)
Juniata Coll (PA)
Kalamazoo Coll (MI)
Kansas State U (KS)
Kansas Wesleyan U (KS)
Kean U (NJ)
Keene State Coll (NH)
Kennesaw State U (GA)
Kent State U (OH)
Kent State U at Stark (OH)
Kentucky Christian U (KY)
Kentucky Wesleyan Coll (KY)
Kenyon Coll (OH)
Keuka Coll (NY)
King's Coll (PA)
The King's U Coll (AB, Canada)
King U (TN)
Knox Coll (IL)
Kutztown U of Pennsylvania (PA)
Lafayette Coll (PA)
LaGrange Coll (GA)
Lake Erie Coll (OH)
Lake Forest Coll (IL)
Lamar U (TX)
Lane Coll (TN)
La Roche Coll (PA)
La Salle U (PA)
Lasell Coll (MA)
La Sierra U (CA)
Lawrence U (WI)
Lebanese American U (Lebanon)
Lebanon Valley Coll (PA)
Lees-McRae Coll (NC)
Lee U (TN)
Lehigh U (PA)
Lehman Coll of the City U of New York (NY)
Le Moyne Coll (NY)
LeMoyne-Owen Coll (TN)
Lenoir-Rhyne U (NC)
Lewis & Clark Coll (OR)
Lewis U (IL)
Liberty U (VA)
Limestone Coll (SC)
Lincoln Memorial U (TN)
Lincoln U (MO)
Lincoln U (PA)
Lindenwood U (MO)
Lindsey Wilson Coll (KY)
Linfield Coll (OR)
Lipscomb U (TN)
Lock Haven U of Pennsylvania (PA)
Long Island U–LIU Brooklyn (NY)
Long Island U–LIU Post (NY)
Longwood U (VA)
Loras Coll (IA)
Louisiana Coll (LA)
Louisiana State U and A&M Coll (LA)
Louisiana State U in Shreveport (LA)
Lourdes U (OH)
Loyola Marymount U (CA)
Loyola U Chicago (IL)
Loyola U New Orleans (LA)
Lubbock Christian U (TX)
Luther Coll (IA)
Lycoming Coll (PA)
Lynchburg Coll (VA)
Lyon Coll (AR)
Macalester Coll (MN)
Madonna U (MI)
Malone U (OH)
Manchester U (IN)
Manhattan Coll (NY)
Manhattanville Coll (NY)
Mansfield U of Pennsylvania (PA)
Marian U (IN)
Marian U (WI)
Marietta Coll (OH)
Marist Coll (NY)
Marquette U (WI)
Marshall U (WV)
Mars Hill U (NC)
Mary Baldwin Coll (VA)
Marymount Manhattan Coll (NY)
Marymount U (VA)
Maryville Coll (TN)
Maryville U of Saint Louis (MO)
Marywood U (PA)
Massachusetts Coll of Liberal Arts (MA)
Massachusetts Inst of Technology (MA)
The Master's Coll and Sem (CA)
McDaniel Coll (MD)
McKendree U (IL)
McMurry U (TX)
McNeese State U (LA)
Mercer U, Macon (GA)
Mercy Coll (NY)
Meredith Coll (NC)
Merrimack Coll (MA)
Messiah Coll (PA)
Metropolitan State U (MN)
Miami U (OH)
Michigan State U (MI)
Michigan Technological U (MI)
MidAmerica Nazarene U (KS)
Middlebury Coll (VT)
Middle Tennessee State U (TN)
Midwestern State U (TX)
Millersville U of Pennsylvania (PA)
Milligan Coll (TN)
Millikin U (IL)
Millsaps Coll (MS)
Mills Coll (CA)
Minnesota State U Mankato (MN)
Minnesota State U Moorhead (MN)

Minot State U (ND)
Misericordia U (PA)
Mississippi State U (MS)
Mississippi U for Women (MS)
Mississippi Valley State U (MS)
Missouri Baptist U (MO)
Missouri Southern State U (MO)
Missouri State U (MO)
Missouri U of Science and Technology (MO)
Missouri Valley Coll (MO)
Missouri Western State U (MO)
Molloy Coll (NY)
Monmouth Coll (IL)
Monmouth U (NJ)
Montana State U (MT)
Montana State U Billings (MT)
Montclair State U (NJ)
Montreat Coll, Montreat (NC)
Moravian Coll (PA)
Morehead State U (KY)
Morningside Coll (IA)
Morris Coll (SC)
Mount Allison U (NB, Canada)
Mount Holyoke Coll (MA)
Mount Marty Coll (SD)
Mount Mary U (WI)
Mount Mercy U (IA)
Mount St. Joseph U (OH)
Mount Saint Mary Coll (NY)
Mount Saint Mary's U (CA)
Mount St. Mary's U (MD)
Mount Vernon Nazarene U (OH)
Muhlenberg Coll (PA)
Multnomah U (OR)
Murray State U (KY)
National U (CA)
Nazareth Coll of Rochester (NY)
Nebraska Wesleyan U (NE)
Newberry Coll (SC)
New Coll of Florida (FL)
New England Coll (NH)
New Jersey City U (NJ)
New Jersey Inst of Technology (NJ)
Newman U (KS)
New Mexico Highlands U (NM)
New Mexico State U (NM)
New York U (NY)
Niagara U (NY)
Nicholls State U (LA)
Norfolk State U (VA)
North Carolina Ag and Tech State U (NC)
North Carolina Central U (NC)
North Carolina State U (NC)
North Carolina Wesleyan Coll (NC)
North Central Coll (IL)
North Dakota State U (ND)
Northeastern Illinois U (IL)
Northeastern State U (OK)
Northeastern U (MA)
Northern Arizona U (AZ)
Northern Illinois U (IL)
Northern Kentucky U (KY)
Northern Michigan U (MI)
Northern State U (SD)
North Greenville U (SC)
Northland Coll (WI)
Northwest Christian U (OR)
Northwestern Coll (IA)
Northwestern Oklahoma State U (OK)
Northwestern U (IL)
Northwest Missouri State U (MO)
Northwest Nazarene U (ID)
Northwest U (WA)
Norwich U (VT)
Notre Dame of Maryland U (MD)
Nova Southeastern U (FL)
Nyack Coll (NY)
Oakland U (MI)
Oberlin Coll (OH)
Occidental Coll (CA)
Oglethorpe U (GA)
Ohio Dominican U (OH)
Ohio Northern U (OH)
The Ohio State U (OH)
The Ohio State U at Lima (OH)
The Ohio State U at Marion (OH)
The Ohio State U–Newark Campus (OH)
Ohio U (OH)
Ohio Valley U (WV)
Ohio Wesleyan U (OH)
Oklahoma Baptist U (OK)
Oklahoma Christian U (OK)
Oklahoma City U (OK)
Oklahoma State U (OK)
Oklahoma Wesleyan U (OK)
Old Dominion U (VA)
Olivet Coll (MI)
Olivet Nazarene U (IL)
Oregon State U (OR)
Our Lady of the Lake U of San Antonio (TX)
Pace U (NY)
Pacific Lutheran U (WA)
Pacific U (OR)
Palm Beach Atlantic U (FL)
Park U (MO)
Patrick Henry Coll (VA)
Penn State Abington (PA)
Penn State Altoona (PA)
Penn State Beaver (PA)
Penn State Berks (PA)
Penn State Brandywine (PA)
Penn State DuBois (PA)
Penn State Erie, The Behrend Coll (PA)
Penn State Fayette, The Eberly Campus (PA)
Penn State Greater Allegheny (PA)
Penn State Hazleton (PA)
Penn State Lehigh Valley (PA)
Penn State Mont Alto (PA)
Penn State New Kensington (PA)
Penn State Schuylkill (PA)
Penn State Shenango (PA)
Penn State U Park (PA)
Penn State Wilkes-Barre (PA)
Penn State Worthington Scranton (PA)
Penn State York (PA)
Pepperdine U, Malibu (CA)
Peru State Coll (NE)
Piedmont Coll (GA)
Pittsburg State U (KS)
Plymouth State U (NH)
Point Loma Nazarene U (CA)
Point U (GA)
Pomona Coll (CA)
Portland State U (OR)
Prairie View A&M U (TX)
Presbyterian Coll (SC)
Princeton U (NJ)
Principia Coll (IL)
Providence Coll (RI)
Purchase Coll, State U of New York (NY)
Purdue U (IN)
Purdue U Calumet (IN)
Queens Coll of the City U of New York (NY)
Quincy U (IL)
Quinnipiac U (CT)
Radford U (VA)
Ramapo Coll of New Jersey (NJ)
Randolph Coll (VA)
Randolph-Macon Coll (VA)
Reed Coll (OR)
Regent U (VA)
Regis Coll (MA)
Regis U (CO)
Reinhardt U (GA)
Rhode Island Coll (RI)
Rhodes Coll (TN)
Rice U (TX)
Rider U (NJ)
Ripon Coll (WI)
Rivier U (NH)
Roanoke Coll (VA)
Roberts Wesleyan Coll (NY)
Rockford U (IL)
Rockhurst U (MO)
Rocky Mountain Coll (MT)
Roger Williams U (RI)
Rollins Coll (FL)
Roosevelt U (IL)
Rosemont Coll (PA)
Rowan U (NJ)
Rutgers, The State U of New Jersey, Camden (NJ)
Rutgers, The State U of New Jersey, Newark (NJ)
Rutgers, The State U of New Jersey, New Brunswick (NJ)
Sacred Heart U (CT)
The Sage Colls (NY)
Saginaw Valley State U (MI)
Saint Anselm Coll (NH)
Saint Augustine's U (NC)
St. Bonaventure U (NY)
St. Catherine U (MN)
St. Edward's U (TX)
St. Francis Coll (NY)
Saint Francis U (PA)
St. Gregory's U, Shawnee (OK)
St. John Fisher Coll (NY)
Saint John's U (MN)
St. John's U (NY)
Saint Joseph's Coll (IN)
St. Joseph's Coll, Long Island Campus (NY)
St. Joseph's Coll, New York (NY)
Saint Joseph's U (PA)
St. Lawrence U (NY)
Saint Leo U (FL)
Saint Louis U (MO)
Saint Martin's U (WA)
Saint Mary's Coll (IN)
St. Mary's Coll of Maryland (MD)
St. Mary's U (TX)
Saint Mary's U of Minnesota (MN)
Saint Michael's Coll (VT)
St. Norbert Coll (WI)
St. Olaf Coll (MN)
Saint Peter's U (NJ)
St. Thomas Aquinas Coll (NY)
St. Thomas U (FL)
St. Thomas U (NB, Canada)
Saint Vincent Coll (PA)
Salem Coll (NC)
Salisbury U (MD)
Salve Regina U (RI)
Samford U (AL)
Sam Houston State U (TX)
San Diego Christian Coll (CA)
San Diego State U (CA)
San Francisco State U (CA)
San Jose State U (CA)
Santa Clara U (CA)
Sarah Lawrence Coll (NY)
Savannah State U (GA)
Scripps Coll (CA)
Seattle Pacific U (WA)
Seattle U (WA)
Seton Hill U (PA)
Sewanee: The U of the South (TN)
Shawnee State U (OH)
Shenandoah U (VA)
Shepherd U (WV)
Shippensburg U of Pennsylvania (PA)
Siena Coll (NY)
Siena Heights U (MI)
Silver Lake Coll of the Holy Family (WI)
Simmons Coll (MA)
Simon Fraser U (BC, Canada)
Simpson Coll (IA)
Simpson U (CA)
Skidmore Coll (NY)
Slippery Rock U of Pennsylvania (PA)
Smith Coll (MA)
South Carolina State U (SC)
South Dakota State U (SD)
Southeastern Louisiana U (LA)
Southeastern Oklahoma State U (OK)
Southeastern U (FL)
Southeast Missouri State U (MO)
Southern Adventist U (TN)
Southern Arkansas U–Magnolia (AR)
Southern Connecticut State U (CT)
Southern Illinois U Carbondale (IL)
Southern Illinois U Edwardsville (IL)
Southern Methodist U (TX)
Southern New Hampshire U (NH)
Southern Oregon U (OR)
Southern Utah U (UT)
Southern Vermont Coll (VT)
Southwest Baptist U (MO)
Southwestern Adventist U (TX)
Southwestern Assemblies of God U (TX)
Southwestern Coll (KS)
Southwestern U (TX)
Southwest Minnesota State U (MN)
Spelman Coll (GA)
Spring Hill Coll (AL)
Stanford U (CA)
State U of New York at Fredonia (NY)
State U of New York at New Paltz (NY)
State U of New York at Oswego (NY)
State U of New York at Plattsburgh (NY)
State U of New York Coll at Cortland (NY)
State U of New York Coll at Geneseo (NY)
State U of New York Coll at Old Westbury (NY)
State U of New York Coll at Potsdam (NY)
State U of New York Empire State Coll (NY)
Stephen F. Austin State U (TX)
Sterling Coll (KS)
Stetson U (FL)
Stevenson U (MD)
Stockton U (NJ)
Stonehill Coll (MA)
Stony Brook U, State U of New York (NY)
Suffolk U (MA)
Sul Ross State U (TX)
Susquehanna U (PA)
Syracuse U (NY)
Tarleton State U (TX)
Taylor U (IN)
Temple U (PA)
Tennessee State U (TN)
Tennessee Wesleyan Coll (TN)
Texas A&M Intl U (TX)
Texas A&M U (TX)
Texas A&M U–Commerce (TX)
Texas A&M U–Corpus Christi (TX)
Texas A&M U–Kingsville (TX)
Texas Christian U (TX)
Texas Lutheran U (TX)
Texas Southern U (TX)
Texas State U (TX)
Texas Tech U (TX)
Texas Wesleyan U (TX)
Texas Woman's U (TX)
Thiel Coll (PA)
Thomas More Coll (KY)
Tiffin U (OH)
Toccoa Falls Coll (GA)
Tougaloo Coll (MS)
Towson U (MD)
Transylvania U (KY)
Trent U (ON, Canada)
Trevecca Nazarene U (TN)
Trinity Christian Coll (IL)
Trinity Coll (CT)
Trinity U (TX)
Troy U (AL)
Truett-McConnell Coll (GA)
Truman State U (MO)
Tufts U (MA)
Tulane U (LA)
Tusculum Coll (TN)
Union Coll (KY)
Union Coll (NE)
Union Coll (NY)
Union U (TN)
United States Air Force Acad (CO)
United States Naval Acad (MD)
Université de Montréal (QC, Canada)
Université de Sherbrooke (QC, Canada)
U at Albany, State U of New York (NY)
U at Buffalo, the State U of New York (NY)
The U of Akron (OH)
The U of Alabama (AL)
The U of Alabama at Birmingham (AL)
The U of Alabama in Huntsville (AL)
U of Alaska Fairbanks (AK)
U of Alberta (AB, Canada)
The U of Arizona (AZ)
U of Arkansas (AR)
U of Arkansas at Little Rock (AR)
U of Arkansas at Pine Bluff (AR)
U of Arkansas–Fort Smith (AR)
The U of British Columbia (BC, Canada)
The U of British Columbia–Okanagan Campus (BC, Canada)
U of California, Berkeley (CA)
U of California, Davis (CA)
U of California, Irvine (CA)
U of California, Los Angeles (CA)
U of California, Merced (CA)
U of California, Riverside (CA)
U of California, Santa Barbara (CA)
U of California, Santa Cruz (CA)
U of Central Arkansas (AR)
U of Central Florida (FL)
U of Central Missouri (MO)
U of Central Oklahoma (OK)
U of Charleston (WV)
U of Chicago (IL)
U of Cincinnati (OH)
U of Colorado Boulder (CO)
U of Colorado Colorado Springs (CO)
U of Colorado Denver (CO)
U of Dallas (TX)
U of Dayton (OH)
U of Delaware (DE)
U of Denver (CO)
U of Evansville (IN)
The U of Findlay (OH)
U of Florida (FL)
U of Georgia (GA)
U of Great Falls (MT)
U of Guam (GU)
U of Guelph (ON, Canada)
U of Hartford (CT)
U of Hawaii at Hilo (HI)
U of Hawaii at Manoa (HI)
U of Hawaii–West Oahu (HI)
U of Houston (TX)
U of Houston–Clear Lake (TX)
U of Houston–Downtown (TX)
U of Houston–Victoria (TX)
U of Idaho (ID)
U of Illinois at Chicago (IL)
U of Illinois at Springfield (IL)
U of Indianapolis (IN)
The U of Iowa (IA)
U of Jamestown (ND)
The U of Kansas (KS)
U of Kentucky (KY)
U of King's Coll (NS, Canada)
U of La Verne (CA)
U of Lethbridge (AB, Canada)
U of Louisiana at Lafayette (LA)
U of Louisville (KY)
U of Maine (ME)
U of Maine at Machias (ME)
U of Maine at Presque Isle (ME)
U of Mary Hardin-Baylor (TX)
U of Maryland, Baltimore County (MD)
U of Maryland, Coll Park (MD)
U of Maryland U Coll (MD)
U of Mary Washington (VA)
U of Massachusetts Amherst (MA)
U of Massachusetts Boston (MA)
U of Massachusetts Dartmouth (MA)
U of Massachusetts Lowell (MA)
U of Memphis (TN)
U of Miami (FL)
U of Michigan (MI)
U of Michigan–Dearborn (MI)
U of Michigan–Flint (MI)
U of Minnesota, Duluth (MN)
U of Minnesota, Morris (MN)
U of Minnesota, Twin Cities Campus (MN)
U of Mississippi (MS)
U of Missouri (MO)
U of Missouri–Kansas City (MO)
U of Missouri–St. Louis (MO)
U of Mobile (AL)
The U of Montana (MT)
The U of Montana Western (MT)
U of Montevallo (AL)
U of Mount Union (OH)
U of Nebraska at Kearney (NE)
U of Nebraska–Lincoln (NE)
U of Nevada, Las Vegas (NV)
U of Nevada, Reno (NV)
U of New Brunswick Saint John (NB, Canada)
U of New England (ME)
U of New Hampshire (NH)
U of New Hampshire at Manchester (NH)
U of New Haven (CT)
U of New Mexico (NM)
U of New Orleans (LA)
U of North Alabama (AL)
U of North Carolina at Asheville (NC)
The U of North Carolina at Chapel Hill (NC)
The U of North Carolina at Charlotte (NC)

MAJORS LISTING

The U of North Carolina at Greensboro (NC)
The U of North Carolina at Pembroke (NC)
The U of North Carolina Wilmington (NC)
U of North Dakota (ND)
U of Northern Colorado (CO)
U of Northern Iowa (IA)
U of North Florida (FL)
U of North Georgia (GA)
U of North Texas (TX)
U of Northwestern–St. Paul (MN)
U of Notre Dame (IN)
U of Oklahoma (OK)
U of Oregon (OR)
U of Ottawa (ON, Canada)
U of Pennsylvania (PA)
U of Pikeville (KY)
U of Pittsburgh (PA)
U of Pittsburgh at Bradford (PA)
U of Portland (OR)
U of Puget Sound (WA)
U of Regina (SK, Canada)
U of Rhode Island (RI)
U of Richmond (VA)
U of Rio Grande (OH)
U of Rochester (NY)
U of St. Francis (IL)
U of Saint Francis (IN)
U of Saint Joseph (CT)
U of Saint Mary (KS)
U of St. Thomas (MN)
U of St. Thomas (TX)
U of San Diego (CA)
U of San Francisco (CA)
U of Saskatchewan (SK, Canada)
U of Science and Arts of Oklahoma (OK)
The U of Scranton (PA)
U of South Alabama (AL)
U of South Carolina Aiken (SC)
U of South Carolina Beaufort (SC)
U of South Carolina Upstate (SC)
The U of South Dakota (SD)
U of Southern California (CA)
U of Southern Indiana (IN)
U of Southern Maine (ME)
U of Southern Mississippi (MS)
U of South Florida (FL)
U of South Florida, St. Petersburg (FL)
U of South Florida Sarasota-Manatee (FL)
The U of Tampa (FL)
The U of Tennessee (TN)
The U of Tennessee at Chattanooga (TN)
The U of Tennessee at Martin (TN)
The U of Texas at Arlington (TX)
The U of Texas at Austin (TX)
The U of Texas at Dallas (TX)
The U of Texas at El Paso (TX)
The U of Texas at San Antonio (TX)
The U of Texas at Tyler (TX)
The U of Texas of the Permian Basin (TX)
The U of Texas–Pan American (TX)
U of the Cumberlands (KY)
U of the District of Columbia (DC)
U of the Fraser Valley (BC, Canada)
U of the Incarnate Word (TX)
U of the Pacific (CA)
The U of Toledo (OH)
U of Toronto (ON, Canada)
The U of Tulsa (OK)
U of Utah (UT)
U of Vermont (VT)
U of Virginia (VA)
The U of Virginia's Coll at Wise (VA)
U of Washington (WA)
U of Washington, Tacoma (WA)
U of Waterloo (ON, Canada)
The U of West Alabama (AL)
The U of Western Ontario (ON, Canada)
U of West Florida (FL)
U of West Georgia (GA)
U of Windsor (ON, Canada)
U of Wisconsin–Eau Claire (WI)
U of Wisconsin–Green Bay (WI)
U of Wisconsin–La Crosse (WI)
U of Wisconsin–Madison (WI)
U of Wisconsin–Milwaukee (WI)
U of Wisconsin–Oshkosh (WI)
U of Wisconsin–Parkside (WI)
U of Wisconsin–Platteville (WI)
U of Wisconsin–River Falls (WI)
U of Wisconsin–Stevens Point (WI)
U of Wisconsin–Superior (WI)
U of Wisconsin–Whitewater (WI)
U of Wyoming (WY)
Urbana U (OH)
Ursinus Coll (PA)
Ursuline Coll (OH)
Utah State U (UT)
Utah Valley U (UT)
Utica Coll (NY)
Valdosta State U (GA)
Valley City State U (ND)
Valparaiso U (IN)
Vanderbilt U (TN)
Vanguard U of Southern California (CA)
Vassar Coll (NY)
Villanova U (PA)
Virginia Commonwealth U (VA)
Virginia Military Inst (VA)
Virginia Polytechnic Inst and State U (VA)
Virginia State U (VA)
Virginia Union U (VA)
Virginia Wesleyan Coll (VA)
Wabash Coll (IN)
Wagner Coll (NY)
Wake Forest U (NC)
Waldorf Coll (IA)
Walla Walla U (WA)
Walsh U (OH)
Warner Pacific Coll (OR)
Warren Wilson Coll (NC)
Wartburg Coll (IA)
Washburn U (KS)
Washington & Jefferson Coll (PA)
Washington and Lee U (VA)
Washington Coll (MD)
Washington State U (WA)
Washington State U Vancouver (WA)
Washington U in St. Louis (MO)
Waynesburg U (PA)
Wayne State Coll (NE)
Wayne State U (MI)
Weber State U (UT)
Webster U (MO)
Welch Coll (TN)
Wells Coll (NY)
Wesleyan Coll (GA)
Wesleyan U (CT)
West Chester U of Pennsylvania (PA)
Western Carolina U (NC)
Western Illinois U (IL)
Western Kentucky U (KY)
Western Michigan U (MI)
Western New England U (MA)
Western Oregon U (OR)
Western State Colorado U (CO)
Western Washington U (WA)
Westfield State U (MA)
West Liberty U (WV)
Westminster Coll (MO)
Westminster Coll (UT)
West Texas A&M U (TX)
West Virginia State U (WV)
West Virginia U (WV)
West Virginia U Inst of Technology (WV)
West Virginia Wesleyan Coll (WV)
Wheaton Coll (IL)
Wheaton Coll (MA)
Wheeling Jesuit U (WV)
Whitman Coll (WA)
Whittier Coll (CA)
Whitworth U (WA)
Wichita State U (KS)
Widener U (PA)
Wilkes U (PA)
Willamette U (OR)
William Jessup U (CA)
William Jewell Coll (MO)
William Paterson U of New Jersey (NJ)
William Penn U (IA)
Williams Baptist Coll (AR)
Williams Coll (MA)
William Woods U (MO)
Wingate U (NC)
Winona State U (MN)
Winthrop U (SC)
Wittenberg U (OH)
Wofford Coll (SC)
Worcester Polytechnic Inst (MA)
Worcester State U (MA)
Wright State U (OH)
Xavier U (OH)
Xavier U of Louisiana (LA)
Yale U (CT)
Yeshiva U (NY)
York Coll of Pennsylvania (PA)
York Coll of the City U of New York (NY)
Youngstown State U (OH)

HISTORY AND PHILOSOPHY OF SCIENCE AND TECHNOLOGY

Bard Coll (NY)
California Inst of Technology (CA)
Case Western Reserve U (OH)
Dalhousie U (NS, Canada)
Georgia Inst of Technology (GA)
Harvard U (MA)
Johns Hopkins U (MD)
U of Chicago (IL)
U of Oklahoma (OK)
U of Pennsylvania (PA)
U of Pittsburgh (PA)
U of Toronto (ON, Canada)
U of Washington (WA)
U of Wisconsin–Madison (WI)
Worcester Polytechnic Inst (MA)

HISTORY RELATED

The American U of Paris (France)
Arizona State U at the Polytechnic campus (AZ)
Bridgewater Coll (VA)
Bridgewater State U (MA)
Chaminade U of Honolulu (HI)
Delaware State U (DE)
Eureka Coll (IL)
Harvard U (MA)
Indiana U Kokomo (IN)
LeTourneau U (TX)
National U (CA)
The Ohio State U (OH)
The Ohio State U at Lima (OH)
The Ohio State U at Marion (OH)
The Ohio State U–Mansfield Campus (OH)
The Ohio State U–Newark Campus (OH)
Saint Mary's U of Minnesota (MN)
United States Military Acad (NY)
U at Albany, State U of New York (NY)
U of Alberta (AB, Canada)
U of California, Santa Barbara (CA)
U of Southern California (CA)
U of Washington (WA)
U of Washington, Tacoma (WA)
Vanderbilt U (TN)
Virginia Wesleyan Coll (VA)
Viterbo U (WI)
William Penn U (IA)

HISTORY TEACHER EDUCATION

Abilene Christian U (TX)
Albion Coll (MI)
Alma Coll (MI)
Anderson U (SC)
Appalachian State U (NC)
Aquinas Coll (TN)
Auburn U (AL)
Augustana Coll (IL)
Averett U (VA)
Biola U (CA)
Bluefield Coll (VA)
Bowling Green State U (OH)
Bradley U (IL)
Bryan Coll (TN)
Buena Vista U (IA)
Calvin Coll (MI)
Campbellsville U (KY)
Carroll Coll (MT)
The Catholic U of America (DC)
Central Michigan U (MI)
Central Washington U (WA)
Charleston Southern U (SC)
Coker Coll (SC)
The Coll of New Jersey (NJ)
Coll of Staten Island of the City U of New York (NY)
Coll of the Ozarks (MO)
Concordia U Chicago (IL)
Concordia U, Nebraska (NE)
Concordia U Wisconsin (WI)
Cornerstone U (MI)
Covenant Coll (GA)
Culver-Stockton Coll (MO)
Cumberland U (TN)
Dallas Baptist U (TX)
Dominican Coll (NY)
Dominican U (IL)
East Central U (OK)
Eastern Kentucky U (KY)
Eastern Michigan U (MI)
East Texas Baptist U (TX)
Elmhurst Coll (IL)
Emory & Henry Coll (VA)
Evangel U (MO)
Ferris State U (MI)
Fitchburg State U (MA)
Friends U (KS)
Grand Valley State U (MI)
Greenville Coll (IL)
Gwynedd Mercy U (PA)
Hannibal-LaGrange U (MO)
Hardin-Simmons U (TX)
Hastings Coll (NE)
Hobe Sound Bible Coll (FL)
Holy Family U (PA)
Hope Coll (MI)
Howard Payne U (TX)
Huntingdon Coll (AL)
Indiana U–Purdue U Fort Wayne (IN)
Inter American U of Puerto Rico, San Germán Campus (PR)
Ithaca Coll (NY)
Johnson State Coll (VT)
Kansas Wesleyan U (KS)
Keene State Coll (NH)
King U (TN)
Lee U (TN)
LeTourneau U (TX)
Lincoln Memorial U (TN)
Lindenwood U (MO)
Lipscomb U (TN)
Manchester U (IN)
Maranatha Baptist U (WI)
Maryville Coll (TN)
Mayville State U (ND)
McKendree U (IL)
McMurry U (TX)
Merrimack Coll (MA)
Michigan State U (MI)
MidAmerica Nazarene U (KS)
Minot State U (ND)
Missouri State U (MO)
Montana State U Billings (MT)
Morningside Coll (IA)
Mount Marty Coll (SD)
Mount Mary U (WI)
Mount Vernon Nazarene U (OH)
Nazareth Coll of Rochester (NY)
North Carolina Ag and Tech State U (NC)
North Dakota State U (ND)
Northern Michigan U (MI)
Northwest Nazarene U (ID)
Ohio Northern U (OH)
Ohio Wesleyan U (OH)
Peru State Coll (NE)
Piedmont Coll (GA)
Pittsburg State U (KS)
Providence Coll (RI)
Rhode Island Coll (RI)
Rocky Mountain Coll (MT)
Saginaw Valley State U (MI)
St. Edward's U (TX)
Saint Francis U (PA)
St. John Fisher Coll (NY)
Saint Joseph's U (PA)
Salve Regina U (RI)
Samford U (AL)
Southern Adventist U (TN)
Southern Utah U (UT)
Spring Hill Coll (AL)
Tabor Coll (KS)
Texas A&M Intl U (TX)
Texas Lutheran U (TX)
Texas Wesleyan U (TX)
Tiffin U (OH)
Toccoa Falls Coll (GA)
Trevecca Nazarene U (TN)
Trinity Christian Coll (IL)
Tusculum Coll (TN)
Union Coll (NE)
Universidad del Turabo (PR)
Universidad Metropolitana (PR)
The U of Akron (OH)
U of Arkansas–Fort Smith (AR)
U of Central Oklahoma (OK)
U of Delaware (DE)
U of Great Falls (MT)
U of Illinois at Chicago (IL)
The U of Iowa (IA)
U of Jamestown (ND)
U of Maine at Machias (ME)
U of Mary Hardin-Baylor (TX)
U of Michigan–Flint (MI)
U of Mobile (AL)
The U of Montana Western (MT)
U of Rio Grande (OH)
The U of South Dakota (SD)
The U of Tennessee at Martin (TN)
U of Windsor (ON, Canada)
U of Wisconsin–River Falls (WI)
U of Wisconsin–Superior (WI)
Utah Valley U (UT)
Utica Coll (NY)
Valley City State U (ND)
Valparaiso U (IN)
Wartburg Coll (IA)
Washburn U (KS)
Washington State U (WA)
Washington U in St. Louis (MO)
Wayne State Coll (NE)
Weber State U (UT)
Welch Coll (TN)
Western Michigan U (MI)
Western State Colorado U (CO)
Western Washington U (WA)
Widener U (PA)
William Woods U (MO)
Wingate U (NC)
Xavier U of Louisiana (LA)

HOLOCAUST AND RELATED STUDIES

Keene State Coll (NH)

HOME FURNISHINGS AND EQUIPMENT INSTALLATION

Brigham Young U (UT)

HOMELAND SECURITY

American Public U System (WV)
Angelo State U (TX)
Columbia Southern U (AL)
Daniel Webster Coll (NH)
Eastern Kentucky U (KY)
Embry-Riddle Aeronautical U–Daytona (FL)
Keiser U, Fort Lauderdale (FL)
Mercy Coll (NY)
Monmouth U (NJ)
National U (CA)
Oakland U (MI)
Saint Leo U (FL)
State Coll of Florida Manatee-Sarasota (FL)
State U of New York Coll of Technology at Canton (NY)
Tulane U (LA)
The U of Arizona (AZ)

HOMELAND SECURITY, LAW ENFORCEMENT, FIREFIGHTING AND PROTECTIVE SERVICES RELATED

Eastern Michigan U (MI)
Florida Atlantic U (FL)
Florida SouthWestern State Coll (FL)
Florida State Coll at Jacksonville (FL)
Franklin U (OH)
Lewis U (IL)
Madonna U (MI)
Marian U (WI)
Massachusetts Maritime Acad (MA)
Mercy Coll (NY)
Miami Dade Coll (FL)
Mitchell Coll (CT)
Neumann U (PA)
North Dakota State U (ND)
Northwestern Oklahoma State U (OK)
Penn State Altoona (PA)
Penn State Berks (PA)
Penn State U Park (PA)
Roberts Wesleyan Coll (NY)
Savannah State U (GA)
Tiffin U (OH)
Virginia Commonwealth U (VA)
Washburn U (KS)
Western Illinois U (IL)

HOMELAND SECURITY RELATED
Rivier U (NH)

HORSE HUSBANDRY/EQUINE SCIENCE AND MANAGEMENT
Averett U (VA)
Becker Coll (MA)
Johnson & Wales U (RI)
Morrisville State Coll (NY)
Saint Mary-of-the-Woods Coll (IN)
Tiffin U (OH)
U of Guelph (ON, Canada)
U of Kentucky (KY)
U of Minnesota, Crookston (MN)
Vermont Tech Coll (VT)
William Woods U (MO)

HORTICULTURAL SCIENCE
Auburn U (AL)
California State U, Fresno (CA)
Coll of the Ozarks (MO)
Colorado State U (CO)
Cornell U (NY)
Ferrum Coll (VA)
Iowa State U of Science and Technology (IA)
Kansas State U (KS)
Michigan State U (MI)
Mississippi State U (MS)
Missouri State U (MO)
Montana State U (MT)
Morrisville State Coll (NY)
New Mexico State U (NM)
North Carolina State U (NC)
Northwest Missouri State U (MO)
Oklahoma State U (OK)
Oregon State U (OR)
Penn State Abington (PA)
Penn State Altoona (PA)
Penn State Beaver (PA)
Penn State Berks (PA)
Penn State Brandywine (PA)
Penn State DuBois (PA)
Penn State Erie, The Behrend Coll (PA)
Penn State Fayette, The Eberly Campus (PA)
Penn State Greater Allegheny (PA)
Penn State Hazleton (PA)
Penn State Lehigh Valley (PA)
Penn State Mont Alto (PA)
Penn State New Kensington (PA)
Penn State Schuylkill (PA)
Penn State Shenango (PA)
Penn State Wilkes-Barre (PA)
Penn State Worthington Scranton (PA)
Penn State York (PA)
Purdue U (IN)
Sam Houston State U (TX)
Southeast Missouri State U (MO)
Stephen F. Austin State U (TX)
Tarleton State U (TX)
Temple U (PA)
The U of British Columbia (BC, Canada)
U of Cincinnati (OH)
U of Florida (FL)
U of Hawaii at Hilo (HI)
U of Idaho (ID)
U of Minnesota, Crookston (MN)
U of Minnesota, Twin Cities Campus (MN)
U of Nebraska–Lincoln (NE)
U of Saskatchewan (SK, Canada)
U of Vermont (VT)
U of Wisconsin–Madison (WI)
U of Wisconsin–River Falls (WI)
Utah State U (UT)
Virginia Polytechnic Inst and State U (VA)
Washington State U (WA)

HOSPITAL AND HEALTH-CARE FACILITIES ADMINISTRATION
American Intl Coll (MA)
Avila U (MO)
Black Hills State U (SD)
Champlain Coll (VT)
Clayton State U (GA)
Governors State U (IL)
Gwynedd Mercy U (PA)
Ithaca Coll (NY)
Langston U (OK)
Newman U (KS)
New York City Coll of Technology of the City U of New York (NY)
St. Joseph's Coll, Long Island Campus (NY)
St. Joseph's Coll, New York (NY)
Saint Joseph's U (PA)
The U of Alabama (AL)
U of Oklahoma (OK)
U of St. Francis (IL)
The U of South Dakota (SD)
The U of Toledo (OH)
U of Wisconsin–Milwaukee (WI)
Ursuline Coll (OH)
Youngstown State U (OH)

HOSPITALITY ADMINISTRATION
American Public U System (WV)
Appalachian State U (NC)
Arkansas Tech U (AR)
Ashland U (OH)
Auburn U (AL)
Beacon Coll (FL)
Belmont U (TN)
Boston U (MA)
Bowling Green State U (OH)
Bradley U (IL)
Buffalo State Coll, State U of New York (NY)
California State Polytechnic U, Pomona (CA)
Cape Breton U (NS, Canada)
Central Michigan U (MI)
Champlain Coll (VT)
Cheyney U of Pennsylvania (PA)
Coll of Charleston (SC)
Coll of the Ozarks (MO)
Colorado Mesa U (CO)
Columbia Southern U (AL)
Concordia U, St. Paul (MN)
Concord U (WV)
Dallas Baptist U (TX)
Delaware State U (DE)
Delta State U (MS)
DePaul U (IL)
East Carolina U (NC)
Eastern Michigan U (MI)
East Stroudsburg U of Pennsylvania (PA)
Endicott Coll (MA)
Fairleigh Dickinson U, Coll at Florham (NJ)
Fairleigh Dickinson U, Metropolitan Campus (NJ)
Ferris State U (MI)
Fisher Coll (MA)
Florida Atlantic U (FL)
Florida Intl U (FL)
Florida State U (FL)
Georgia State U (GA)
Grand Valley State U (MI)
Granite State Coll (NH)
Husson U (ME)
Indiana U Kokomo (IN)
Indiana U of Pennsylvania (PA)
Indiana U–Purdue U Fort Wayne (IN)
James Madison U (VA)
Johnson & Wales U (CO)
Johnson & Wales U (FL)
Johnson & Wales U (RI)
Johnson State Coll (VT)
Kansas State U (KS)
Kent State U (OH)
Kent State U at Ashtabula (OH)
Lasell Coll (MA)
Lebanese American U (Lebanon)
Lynn U (FL)
Madonna U (MI)
Marywood U (PA)
Metropolitan State U (MN)
Michigan State U (MI)
Missouri State U (MO)
Mitchell Coll (CT)
Montclair State U (NJ)
Morrisville State Coll (NY)
New Mexico State U (NM)
New York City Coll of Technology of the City U of New York (NY)
Nichols Coll (MA)
North Carolina Central U (NC)
North Dakota State U (ND)
Northern Arizona U (AZ)
Northern Michigan U (MI)
The Ohio State U (OH)
Oklahoma State U (OK)
Philander Smith Coll (AR)
Purdue U Calumet (IN)
Robert Morris U (PA)
Rochester Inst of Technology (NY)
Roosevelt U (IL)
Rutgers, The State U of New Jersey, Camden (NJ)
St. John's U (NY)
St. Joseph's Coll, Long Island Campus (NY)
St. Joseph's Coll, New York (NY)
Saint Leo U (FL)
San Diego State U (CA)
San Francisco State U (CA)
San Jose State U (CA)
Seton Hill U (PA)
South Dakota State U (SD)
Southern New Hampshire U (NH)
Southern Utah U (UT)
State U of New York Coll of Technology at Delhi (NY)
Stephen F. Austin State U (TX)
Stockton U (NJ)
Stratford U (MD)
Stratford U, Falls Church (VA)
Stratford U, Glen Allen (VA)
Stratford U, Newport News (VA)
Stratford U, Woodbridge (VA)
Sullivan U (KY)
Temple U (PA)
Tiffin U (OH)
U of Central Florida (FL)
U of Cincinnati (OH)
U of Delaware (DE)
U of Denver (CO)
U of Kentucky (KY)
U of Louisiana at Lafayette (LA)
U of Massachusetts Amherst (MA)
U of Memphis (TN)
U of Mississippi (MS)
U of Nebraska–Lincoln (NE)
U of Nevada, Las Vegas (NV)
U of New Brunswick Saint John (NB, Canada)
U of New Hampshire (NH)
U of New Haven (CT)
U of New Orleans (LA)
The U of North Carolina at Greensboro (NC)
U of North Texas (TX)
U of Pittsburgh at Bradford (PA)
U of San Francisco (CA)
U of South Alabama (AL)
U of South Carolina Beaufort (SC)
U of South Florida (FL)
U of South Florida Sarasota-Manatee (FL)
U of the Virgin Islands (VI)
U of West Florida (FL)
U of Wisconsin–Stout (WI)
Utah Valley U (UT)
Virginia State U (VA)
Washington State U (WA)
Washington State U Vancouver (WA)
Webber Intl U (FL)
Western Carolina U (NC)
Western Kentucky U (KY)
West Virginia U (WV)
York Coll of Pennsylvania (PA)
Youngstown State U (OH)

HOSPITALITY ADMINISTRATION RELATED
Auburn U (AL)
California State U, Dominguez Hills (CA)
California State U, Fullerton (CA)
Delaware State U (DE)
DEREE - The American Coll of Greece (Greece)
Harris-Stowe State U (MO)
Morrisville State Coll (NY)
Niagara U (NY)
Penn State Abington (PA)
Penn State Altoona (PA)
Penn State Beaver (PA)
Penn State Berks (PA)
Penn State Brandywine (PA)
Penn State DuBois (PA)
Penn State Erie, The Behrend Coll (PA)
Penn State Fayette, The Eberly Campus (PA)
Penn State Greater Allegheny (PA)
Penn State Hazleton (PA)
Penn State Lehigh Valley (PA)
Penn State Mont Alto (PA)
Penn State New Kensington (PA)
Penn State Schuylkill (PA)
Penn State Shenango (PA)
Penn State U Park (PA)
Penn State Wilkes-Barre (PA)
Penn State Worthington Scranton (PA)
Penn State York (PA)
Southern Illinois U Carbondale (IL)
U of Nevada, Las Vegas (NV)
U of Southern Mississippi (MS)
Widener U (PA)

HOSPITALITY AND RECREATION MARKETING
Cape Breton U (NS, Canada)
Ferris State U (MI)
Husson U (ME)
Rochester Inst of Technology (NY)
Saint Joseph's U (PA)
U of Minnesota, Twin Cities Campus (MN)

HOTEL/MOTEL ADMINISTRATION
Ashland U (OH)
Auburn U (AL)
Bethune-Cookman U (FL)
Buffalo State Coll, State U of New York (NY)
California State U, Long Beach (CA)
Concord U (WV)
Cornell U (NY)
Drexel U (PA)
Ferris State U (MI)
Georgia Southern U (GA)
Grand Valley State U (MI)
Hampton U (VA)
Howard U (DC)
Husson U (ME)
Indiana U–Purdue U Fort Wayne (IN)
Inter American U of Puerto Rico, Aguadilla Campus (PR)
Inter American U of Puerto Rico, Fajardo Campus (PR)
Inter American U of Puerto Rico, Ponce Campus (PR)
Intl Business Coll, Fort Wayne (IN)
Iowa State U of Science and Technology (IA)
Johnson & Wales U (CO)
Johnson & Wales U (FL)
Johnson & Wales U (RI)
Johnson & Wales U - Charlotte Campus (NC)
Kansas State U (KS)
Keuka Coll (NY)
Newbury Coll (MA)
New York U (NY)
Niagara U (NY)
Northwood U, Michigan Campus (MI)
The Ohio State U (OH)
Pace U (NY)
Purdue U (IN)
Rochester Inst of Technology (NY)
St. Thomas U (FL)
South Dakota State U (SD)
Southern Oregon U (OR)
Southwest Minnesota State U (MN)
State U of New York at Plattsburgh (NY)
Texas Tech U (TX)
U of Central Missouri (MO)
U of Central Oklahoma (OK)
U of Delaware (DE)
U of Denver (CO)
The U of Findlay (OH)
U of Guelph (ON, Canada)
U of Houston (TX)
U of Maine at Machias (ME)
U of Memphis (TN)
U of Missouri (MO)
U of New Haven (CT)
U of San Francisco (CA)
U of Southern Mississippi (MS)
The U of Tennessee (TN)
Virginia Polytechnic Inst and State U (VA)
Widener U (PA)

HOTEL, MOTEL, AND RESTAURANT MANAGEMENT
Endicott Coll (MA)
New York Inst of Technology (NY)

HOUSING AND HUMAN ENVIRONMENTS
Harding U (AR)
Missouri State U (MO)
Ohio U (OH)
Oklahoma State U (OK)
Oregon State U (OR)
The U of Akron (OH)
U of Georgia (GA)
U of Minnesota, Twin Cities Campus (MN)
U of Missouri (MO)
U of Northern Iowa (IA)
Utah State U (UT)

HOUSING AND HUMAN ENVIRONMENTS RELATED
Bob Jones U (SC)
U of Nevada, Reno (NV)

HUMAN BIOLOGY
Biola U (CA)
Hamline U (MN)
Indiana U–Purdue U Indianapolis (IN)
Scripps Coll (CA)
U of California, Irvine (CA)
U of California, Los Angeles (CA)
The U of Kansas (KS)
U of Southern California (CA)
U of Wisconsin–Green Bay (WI)

HUMAN COMPUTER INTERACTION
DigiPen Inst of Technology (WA)
U of Guelph (ON, Canada)

HUMAN DEVELOPMENT AND FAMILY STUDIES
Abilene Christian U (TX)
Antioch U Midwest (OH)
Auburn U (AL)
Baylor U (TX)
Bowling Green State U (OH)
Brigham Young U (UT)
California State U, Long Beach (CA)
California State U, San Bernardino (CA)
California State U, San Marcos (CA)
Colorado State U (CO)
Columbia Coll (SC)
Concordia U, St. Paul (MN)
Connecticut Coll (CT)
Cornell U (NY)
Cornerstone U (MI)
Eastern Kentucky U (KY)
Eckerd Coll (FL)
Florida State U (FL)
George Mason U (VA)
Georgia Southern U (GA)
Hope Intl U (CA)
Howard Payne U (TX)
Indiana State U (IN)
Indiana U of Pennsylvania (PA)
Kansas State U (KS)
Kent State U (OH)
Kent State U at Salem (OH)
Kent State U at Stark (OH)
Kentucky State U (KY)
Keystone Coll (PA)
Lamar U (TX)
Lesley U (MA)
Liberty U (VA)
Miami U (OH)
Missouri State U (MO)
Mitchell Coll (CT)
New Mexico State U (NM)
North Dakota State U (ND)
Northern Illinois U (IL)
Nova Southeastern U (FL)
The Ohio State U (OH)
Ohio U (OH)
Oklahoma State U (OK)
Oregon State U (OR)
Penn State Abington (PA)
Penn State Altoona (PA)
Penn State Beaver (PA)
Penn State Berks (PA)
Penn State Brandywine (PA)
Penn State DuBois (PA)
Penn State Erie, The Behrend Coll (PA)
Penn State Fayette, The Eberly Campus (PA)
Penn State Greater Allegheny (PA)
Penn State Harrisburg (PA)
Penn State Hazleton (PA)

Penn State Lehigh Valley (PA)
Penn State Mont Alto (PA)
Penn State New Kensington (PA)
Penn State Schuylkill (PA)
Penn State Shenango (PA)
Penn State U Park (PA)
Penn State Wilkes-Barre (PA)
Penn State Worthington Scranton (PA)
Penn State York (PA)
Purdue U (IN)
Purdue U Calumet (IN)
Rockford U (IL)
St. Joseph's Coll, Long Island Campus (NY)
St. Joseph's Coll, New York (NY)
Samford U (AL)
San Diego Christian Coll (CA)
Seattle Pacific U (WA)
South Dakota State U (SD)
State U of New York at Oswego (NY)
State U of New York at Plattsburgh (NY)
Stephens Coll (MO)
Syracuse U (NY)
Temple U (PA)
Texas State U (TX)
Texas Tech U (TX)
Texas Woman's U (TX)
The U of Alabama (AL)
The U of Arizona (AZ)
U of Arkansas (AR)
U of California, Davis (CA)
U of Georgia (GA)
U of Guelph (ON, Canada)
U of Houston (TX)
U of Idaho (ID)
U of Kentucky (KY)
U of Louisiana at Lafayette (LA)
U of Maine (ME)
U of Memphis (TN)
U of Missouri (MO)
U of Nevada, Reno (NV)
U of New Hampshire (NH)
U of New Mexico (NM)
The U of North Carolina at Greensboro (NC)
U of North Texas (TX)
U of Rhode Island (RI)
The U of Tennessee (TN)
The U of Texas at Austin (TX)
The U of Texas of the Permian Basin (TX)
U of the District of Columbia (DC)
U of Utah (UT)
U of Vermont (VT)
U of Waterloo (ON, Canada)
U of Wisconsin–Madison (WI)
Utah State U (UT)
Vanguard U of Southern California (CA)
Virginia Polytechnic Inst and State U (VA)
Walden U (MN)
Warner Pacific Coll (OR)
Washington State U (WA)
Wheelock Coll (MA)
Youngstown State U (OH)

HUMAN DEVELOPMENT AND FAMILY STUDIES RELATED
American Public U System (WV)
Auburn U (AL)
Ball State U (IN)
Binghamton U, State U of New York (NY)
Bowling Green State U (OH)
Harding U (AR)
Hope Intl U (CA)
LaGrange Coll (GA)
Merrimack Coll (MA)
The U of Alabama (AL)
U of South Carolina Upstate (SC)
U of Valley Forge (PA)
Washington State U Vancouver (WA)

HUMANITIES
Adelphi U (NY)
Albertus Magnus Coll (CT)
Anna Maria Coll (MA)
Antioch U Midwest (OH)
Aquinas Coll (TN)
Athens State U (AL)
Ave Maria U (FL)
Baptist U of the Americas (TX)
Baylor U (TX)
Belhaven U (MS)
Bemidji State U (MN)
Benedictine U (IL)
Bennington Coll (VT)
Biola U (CA)
Bluefield State Coll (WV)
Bob Jones U (SC)
Bowling Green State U (OH)
Bradley U (IL)
Bucknell U (PA)
Buffalo State Coll, State U of New York (NY)
California State U, Chico (CA)
California State U, Monterey Bay (CA)
California State U, Sacramento (CA)
California State U, San Bernardino (CA)
Calumet Coll of Saint Joseph (IN)
Chaminade U of Honolulu (HI)
Charleston Southern U (SC)
Chowan U (NC)
Clarkson U (NY)
Clearwater Christian Coll (FL)
Coll of Saint Benedict (MN)
Coll of Saint Mary (NE)
The Coll of Saint Rose (NY)
The Coll of St. Scholastica (MN)
Columbia Intl U (SC)
Concordia Coll (MN)
Concordia U (CA)
Concordia U (QC, Canada)
Concordia U Wisconsin (WI)
Corban U (OR)
Cornell U (NY)
Cornerstone U (MI)
DePaul U (IL)
Dominican Coll (NY)
Dominican U of California (CA)
Dowling Coll (NY)
Drexel U (PA)
Eastern Kentucky U (KY)
Eastern Oregon U (OR)
East Stroudsburg U of Pennsylvania (PA)
Eckerd Coll (FL)
The Evergreen State Coll (WA)
Fairleigh Dickinson U, Coll at Florham (NJ)
Fairleigh Dickinson U, Metropolitan Campus (NJ)
Faulkner U (AL)
Florida Inst of Technology (FL)
Florida Southern Coll (FL)
Florida State U (FL)
Fort Lewis Coll (CO)
Franciscan U of Steubenville (OH)
The George Washington U (DC)
Georgian Court U (NJ)
Goddard Coll (VT)
Harding U (AR)
Harrison Middleton U (AZ)
Hawai`i Pacific U (HI)
Hillsdale Free Will Baptist Coll (OK)
Holy Family U (PA)
Houghton Coll (NY)
Hunter Coll of the City U of New York (NY)
Indiana U East (IN)
Indiana U Kokomo (IN)
Jacksonville U (FL)
John Cabot U (Italy)
John Carroll U (OH)
Johnson State Coll (VT)
Juniata Coll (PA)
Kansas State U (KS)
Kent State U (OH)
Kentucky Christian U (KY)
The King's Coll (NY)
Lasell Coll (MA)
Lawrence Technological U (MI)
Lee U (TN)
LeMoyne-Owen Coll (TN)
Lesley U (MA)
Lincoln Memorial U (TN)
Long Island U–LIU Brooklyn (NY)
Long Island U–LIU Post (NY)
Loyola Marymount U (CA)
Lubbock Christian U (TX)
Maranatha Baptist U (WI)
Marshall U (WV)
Marylhurst U (OR)
Marymount Manhattan Coll (NY)
Messiah Coll (PA)
Michigan State U (MI)
Midwestern State U (TX)
Milligan Coll (TN)
Minnesota State U Mankato (MN)
Montclair State U (NJ)
Mount Allison U (NB, Canada)
New Coll of Florida (FL)
New York U (NY)
North Central Coll (IL)
Northland Coll (WI)
Northwestern Coll (IA)
Northwestern U (IL)
Northwest Missouri State U (MO)
Northwest Nazarene U (ID)
Nova Southeastern U (FL)
Oakland City U (IN)
The Ohio State U (OH)
Ohio Wesleyan U (OH)
Oklahoma Baptist U (OK)
Pacific U (OR)
Penn State Harrisburg (PA)
Plymouth State U (NH)
Point U (GA)
Portland State U (OR)
Providence Coll (RI)
Purchase Coll, State U of New York (NY)
Purdue U (IN)
Quincy U (IL)
Roberts Wesleyan Coll (NY)
Rockford U (IL)
Rollins Coll (FL)
The Sage Colls (NY)
St. Andrews U (NC)
Saint John's U (MN)
St. Lawrence U (NY)
Saint Louis U (MO)
Saint Mary-of-the-Woods Coll (IN)
Saint Mary's Coll (IN)
St. Norbert Coll (WI)
Saint Peter's U (NJ)
St. Thomas Aquinas Coll (NY)
San Diego State U (CA)
San Francisco State U (CA)
San Jose State U (CA)
Scripps Coll (CA)
Seattle U (WA)
Shimer Coll (IL)
Siena Heights U (MI)
Simon Fraser U (BC, Canada)
Spalding U (KY)
State U of New York Coll at Old Westbury (NY)
Stony Brook U, State U of New York (NY)
Suffolk U (MA)
Tennessee State U (TN)
Thomas More Coll (KY)
Trent U (ON, Canada)
Trinity U (TX)
Union Coll (NY)
United States Air Force Acad (CO)
United States Military Acad (NY)
Universidad del Turabo (PR)
U at Buffalo, the State U of New York (NY)
The U of Akron (OH)
U of Arkansas at Little Rock (AR)
U of Bridgeport (CT)
U of California, Irvine (CA)
U of California, Riverside (CA)
U of Central Florida (FL)
U of Central Oklahoma (OK)
U of Chicago (IL)
U of Colorado Boulder (CO)
U of Hawaii–West Oahu (HI)
U of Houston–Clear Lake (TX)
U of Houston–Downtown (TX)
U of Houston–Victoria (TX)
The U of Kansas (KS)
U of Lethbridge (AB, Canada)
U of Louisville (KY)
U of Massachusetts Amherst (MA)
U of Michigan (MI)
U of Michigan–Dearborn (MI)
U of Minnesota, Twin Cities Campus (MN)
U of Mobile (AL)
U of New Hampshire (NH)
U of New Hampshire at Manchester (NH)
U of New Mexico (NM)
U of Northern Iowa (IA)
U of Oklahoma (OK)
U of Oregon (OR)
U of Ottawa (ON, Canada)
U of Pennsylvania (PA)
U of Pittsburgh (PA)
U of Pittsburgh at Bradford (PA)
U of Pittsburgh at Greensburg (PA)
U of Regina (SK, Canada)
U of Richmond (VA)
U of Rio Grande (OH)
U of San Diego (CA)
U of Southern Maine (ME)
U of South Florida (FL)
The U of Tennessee at Chattanooga (TN)
The U of Texas at Austin (TX)
The U of Texas at San Antonio (TX)
The U of Texas of the Permian Basin (TX)
U of the Sciences (PA)
U of the Virgin Islands (VI)
The U of Toledo (OH)
U of Toronto (ON, Canada)
U of Utah (UT)
U of Washington (WA)
U of Washington, Bothell (WA)
U of Washington, Tacoma (WA)
U of West Florida (FL)
U of Wisconsin–Green Bay (WI)
U of Wisconsin–Parkside (WI)
U of Wyoming (WY)
Ursuline Coll (OH)
Valparaiso U (IN)
Villanova U (PA)
Virginia Wesleyan Coll (VA)
Walla Walla U (WA)
Washington Coll (MD)
Washington State U (WA)
Washington State U Vancouver (WA)
Washington U in St. Louis (MO)
Webster U (MO)
Welch Coll (TN)
Wesleyan Coll (GA)
Wesleyan U (CT)
Western Oregon U (OR)
Western Washington U (WA)
Wheelock Coll (MA)
Widener U (PA)
Willamette U (OR)
Wofford Coll (SC)
Worcester Polytechnic Inst (MA)
Yale U (CT)

HUMAN NUTRITION
Baylor U (TX)
Cape Breton U (NS, Canada)
Case Western Reserve U (OH)
Central Washington U (WA)
Colorado State U (CO)
Kansas State U (KS)
Life U (GA)
The Ohio State U (OH)
Penn State Abington (PA)
Penn State Altoona (PA)
Penn State Beaver (PA)
Penn State Berks (PA)
Penn State Brandywine (PA)
Penn State DuBois (PA)
Penn State Erie, The Behrend Coll (PA)
Penn State Fayette, The Eberly Campus (PA)
Penn State Greater Allegheny (PA)
Penn State Hazleton (PA)
Penn State Lehigh Valley (PA)
Penn State Mont Alto (PA)
Penn State New Kensington (PA)
Penn State Schuylkill (PA)
Penn State Shenango (PA)
Penn State U Park (PA)
Penn State Wilkes-Barre (PA)
Penn State Worthington Scranton (PA)
Penn State York (PA)
Purdue U (IN)
Rochester Inst of Technology (NY)
Southern Utah U (UT)
State Coll of Florida Manatee-Sarasota (FL)
Syracuse U (NY)
Tarleton State U (TX)
The U of British Columbia (BC, Canada)
U of Central Oklahoma (OK)
U of Dayton (OH)
U of Guelph (ON, Canada)
U of Houston (TX)
U of Kentucky (KY)
Washington State U (WA)

HUMAN RESOURCES DEVELOPMENT
Concordia U Texas (TX)
Hawai`i Pacific U (HI)
Houghton Coll (NY)
Limestone Coll (SC)
Midwestern State U (TX)
Nichols Coll (MA)
Northern Kentucky U (KY)
Oakland U (MI)
The Ohio State U (OH)
Park U (MO)
Texas A&M U (TX)
U of Arkansas (AR)
U of Houston (TX)
The U of Texas at Tyler (TX)
U of Wisconsin–Milwaukee (WI)
Washington State U Vancouver (WA)

HUMAN RESOURCES MANAGEMENT
Alvernia U (PA)
Anderson U (SC)
Antioch U Midwest (OH)
Arcadia U (PA)
Athens State U (AL)
Auburn U (AL)
Auburn U at Montgomery (AL)
Avila U (MO)
Baker Coll (MI)
Baldwin Wallace U (OH)
Ball State U (IN)
Baylor U (TX)
Belhaven U (MS)
Black Hills State U (SD)
Boston Coll (MA)
Bowling Green State U (OH)
Bradley U (IL)
Brigham Young U (UT)
Bryant U (RI)
Buena Vista U (IA)
Cabrini Coll (PA)
California State U, Fresno (CA)
California State U, Long Beach (CA)
Canisius Coll (NY)
Cape Breton U (NS, Canada)
Cardinal Stritch U (WI)
The Catholic U of America (DC)
Central Michigan U (MI)
Central Washington U (WA)
Chestnut Hill Coll (PA)
Coll of Saint Elizabeth (NJ)
Columbia Coll (MO)
Columbia Southern U (AL)
Concordia U (QC, Canada)
Concordia U, St. Paul (MN)
Concordia U Texas (TX)
Davenport U, Grand Rapids (MI)
Delaware State U (DE)
DePaul U (IL)
Dominican Coll (NY)
East Central U (OK)
Ellis U (IL)
Faulkner U (AL)
Ferris State U (MI)
Florida Intl U (FL)
Fort Hays State U (KS)
Franklin U (OH)
Friends U (KS)
The George Washington U (DC)
Georgia Southwestern State U (GA)
Granite State Coll (NH)
Hastings Coll (NE)
Hawai`i Pacific U (HI)
HEC Montreal (QC, Canada)
Holy Family U (PA)
Houghton Coll (NY)
Indiana State U (IN)
Indiana U of Pennsylvania (PA)
Inter American U of Puerto Rico, Aguadilla Campus (PR)
Inter American U of Puerto Rico, Bayamón Campus (PR)
Inter American U of Puerto Rico, Fajardo Campus (PR)
Inter American U of Puerto Rico, Guayama Campus (PR)
Inter American U of Puerto Rico, Ponce Campus (PR)
Inter American U of Puerto Rico, San Germán Campus (PR)
John Carroll U (OH)
Judson U (IL)
Juniata Coll (PA)
Kansas Wesleyan U (KS)
Keiser U, Fort Lauderdale (FL)
King's Coll (PA)

Lake Erie Coll (OH)
Lamar U (TX)
La Salle U (PA)
La Sierra U (CA)
Le Moyne Coll (NY)
LeTourneau U (TX)
Lewis U (IL)
Limestone Coll (SC)
Lindenwood U (MO)
Lipscomb U (TN)
Lourdes U (OH)
Loyola U Chicago (IL)
Lynchburg Coll (VA)
Madonna U (MI)
Mansfield U of Pennsylvania (PA)
Marian U (WI)
Marietta Coll (OH)
Marquette U (WI)
Marymount Manhattan Coll (NY)
Maryville Coll (TN)
McKendree U (IL)
Metropolitan State U (MN)
Michigan State U (MI)
Mount Mercy U (IA)
Nazareth Coll of Rochester (NY)
New York Inst of Technology (NY)
Niagara U (NY)
Nichols Coll (MA)
North Central Coll (IL)
Northeastern Illinois U (IL)
Oakland City U (IN)
Oakland U (MI)
The Ohio State U (OH)
Ohio U (OH)
Ohio Valley U (WV)
Oklahoma Wesleyan U (OK)
Our Lady of the Lake U of San Antonio (TX)
Pace U (NY)
Peirce Coll (PA)
Portland State U (OR)
Quinnipiac U (CT)
Rasmussen Coll Bismarck (ND)
Rasmussen Coll Bloomington (MN)
Rasmussen Coll Brooklyn Park (MN)
Rasmussen Coll Eagan (MN)
Rasmussen Coll Fort Myers (FL)
Rasmussen Coll Kansas City/Overland Park (KS)
Rasmussen Coll Lake Elmo/Woodbury (MN)
Rasmussen Coll Land O' Lakes (FL)
Rasmussen Coll Mankato (MN)
Rasmussen Coll Moorhead (MN)
Rasmussen Coll New Port Richey (FL)
Rasmussen Coll Ocala (FL)
Rasmussen Coll Tampa/Brandon (FL)
Rasmussen Coll Topeka (KS)
Regis U (CO)
Rhode Island Coll (RI)
Roberts Wesleyan Coll (NY)
Roosevelt U (IL)
Rowan U (NJ)
Rutgers, The State U of New Jersey, New Brunswick (NJ)
Saint Francis U (PA)
Saint Joseph's U (PA)
Saint Leo U (FL)
Saint Mary-of-the-Woods Coll (IN)
Saint Mary's U of Minnesota (MN)
Sam Houston State U (TX)
San Diego State U (CA)
San Jose State U (CA)
Seton Hill U (PA)
Silver Lake Coll of the Holy Family (WI)
Simpson U (CA)
Southern Adventist U (TN)
State U of New York at Oswego (NY)
State U of New York Coll of Technology at Alfred (NY)
Sullivan U (KY)
Tarleton State U (TX)
Temple U (PA)
Tennessee Wesleyan Coll (TN)
Texas Woman's U (TX)
Tiffin U (OH)
Université de Montréal (QC, Canada)
The U of Akron (OH)
U of Alberta (AB, Canada)
The U of Arizona (AZ)
The U of British Columbia–Okanagan Campus (BC, Canada)
U of Central Oklahoma (OK)
The U of Findlay (OH)
U of Guelph (ON, Canada)
U of Hawaii at Manoa (HI)
U of Idaho (ID)
The U of Iowa (IA)
U of Lethbridge (AB, Canada)
U of Maryland U Coll (MD)
U of Miami (FL)
U of Michigan–Dearborn (MI)
U of Michigan–Flint (MI)
U of Minnesota, Duluth (MN)
U of Minnesota, Twin Cities Campus (MN)
The U of North Carolina at Chapel Hill (NC)
U of North Dakota (ND)
U of Ottawa (ON, Canada)
U of Pennsylvania (PA)
U of Regina (SK, Canada)
U of St. Francis (IL)
U of St. Thomas (MN)
U of Saskatchewan (SK, Canada)
The U of Scranton (PA)
U of Southern Mississippi (MS)
The U of Tennessee (TN)
The U of Tennessee at Martin (TN)
The U of Texas at San Antonio (TX)
U of the Incarnate Word (TX)
The U of Toledo (OH)
U of Valley Forge (PA)
U of Washington (WA)
U of Waterloo (ON, Canada)
The U of Western Ontario (ON, Canada)
U of Windsor (ON, Canada)
U of Wisconsin–Parkside (WI)
U of Wisconsin–Whitewater (WI)
Urbana U (OH)
Ursuline Coll (OH)
Utah State U (UT)
Valley City State U (ND)
Washington U in St. Louis (MO)
Weber State U (UT)
Western Illinois U (IL)
Western Washington U (WA)
Wichita State U (KS)
William Penn U (IA)
Wilmington U (DE)
Winona State U (MN)
Wright State U (OH)
Xavier U (OH)
Youngstown State U (OH)

HUMAN RESOURCES MANAGEMENT AND SERVICES RELATED

Albertus Magnus Coll (CT)
Becker Coll (MA)
Bradley U (IL)
Carlow U (PA)
Elizabethtown Coll School of Continuing and Professional Studies (PA)
Grand Valley State U (MI)
Immaculata U (PA)
Menlo Coll (CA)
Moravian Coll (PA)
Niagara U (NY)
Park U (MO)
Simpson U (CA)
Université du Québec en Outaouais (QC, Canada)
The U of British Columbia (BC, Canada)
U of Mount Union (OH)
U of Oklahoma (OK)
U of Pittsburgh (PA)
Western Michigan U (MI)
Widener U (PA)
William Penn U (IA)

HUMAN SERVICES

Albertus Magnus Coll (CT)
American Baptist Coll of American Baptist Theological Sem (TN)
Anna Maria Coll (MA)
Antioch U Midwest (OH)
Arcadia U (PA)
Beacon Coll (FL)
Bethel Coll (IN)
Black Hills State U (SD)
California State U, Dominguez Hills (CA)
California State U, Fullerton (CA)
California State U, Monterey Bay (CA)
California State U, San Bernardino (CA)
Calumet Coll of Saint Joseph (IN)
Carson-Newman U (TN)
Cazenovia Coll (NY)
Central Washington U (WA)
Chestnut Hill Coll (PA)
Columbia Coll (MO)
Doane Coll (NE)
Dominican U (IL)
East Central U (OK)
East Tennessee State U (TN)
Elizabethtown Coll School of Continuing and Professional Studies (PA)
Elon U (NC)
Fairmont State U (WV)
Fisher Coll (MA)
Fitchburg State U (MA)
Fontbonne U (MO)
Geneva Coll (PA)
The George Washington U (DC)
Graceland U (IA)
Grand View U (IA)
Granite State Coll (NH)
Gwynedd Mercy U (PA)
Hardin-Simmons U (TX)
Hastings Coll (NE)
Hilbert Coll (NY)
Iowa Wesleyan Coll (IA)
Judson U (IL)
Kennesaw State U (GA)
Kentucky Wesleyan Coll (KY)
Lasell Coll (MA)
Lees-McRae Coll (NC)
Lenoir-Rhyne U (NC)
Lesley U (MA)
Liberty U (VA)
Lincoln Christian U (IL)
Lincoln U (PA)
Lindenwood U (MO)
Lindsey Wilson Coll (KY)
Loyola U Chicago (IL)
Marian U (WI)
Mercer U, Macon (GA)
Merrimack Coll (MA)
Metropolitan State U (MN)
Missouri Baptist U (MO)
Missouri Valley Coll (MO)
Montreat Coll, Montreat (NC)
Mount Marty Coll (SD)
Mount Saint Mary Coll (NY)
New York City Coll of Technology of the City U of New York (NY)
Northeastern U (MA)
Nova Southeastern U (FL)
Park U (MO)
Post U (CT)
Quincy U (IL)
Quinnipiac U (CT)
Rocky Mountain Coll (AB, Canada)
St. Joseph's Coll, Long Island Campus (NY)
St. Joseph's Coll, New York (NY)
Saint Mary-of-the-Woods Coll (IN)
Saint Mary's U of Minnesota (MN)
St. Thomas U (FL)
Seton Hill U (PA)
Siena Heights U (MI)
Southeastern U (FL)
Southwest Baptist U (MO)
Southwestern Assemblies of God U (TX)
Spelman Coll (GA)
State U of New York Coll at Cortland (NY)
Tennessee Wesleyan Coll (TN)
Texas A&M U–Kingsville (TX)
Tiffin U (OH)
Towson U (MD)
Troy U (AL)
U of Bridgeport (CT)
U of Delaware (DE)
U of Great Falls (MT)
U of Hartford (CT)
U of Maine at Machias (ME)
U of Massachusetts Boston (MA)
U of Minnesota, Morris (MN)
U of Nevada, Las Vegas (NV)
U of North Georgia (GA)
U of North Texas (TX)
U of Oregon (OR)
U of Saint Francis (IN)
The U of Scranton (PA)
U of South Florida (FL)
U of the Cumberlands (KY)
U of Wisconsin–Oshkosh (WI)
Upper Iowa U (IA)
Virginia Wesleyan Coll (VA)
Walden U (MN)
Waynesburg U (PA)
Wesleyan Coll (GA)
Western Washington U (WA)
William Penn U (IA)
Wingate U (NC)
Wright State U (OH)

HYDROLOGY AND WATER RESOURCES SCIENCE

The Coll at Brockport, State U of New York (NY)
Heidelberg U (OH)
Humboldt State U (CA)
Northland Coll (WI)
Rensselaer Polytechnic Inst (NY)
State U of New York Coll of Environmental Science and Forestry (NY)
Tarleton State U (TX)
The U of Arizona (AZ)
U of California, Davis (CA)
U of California, Santa Barbara (CA)
U of New Hampshire (NH)
The U of Texas at Austin (TX)
U of Toronto (ON, Canada)
U of Wisconsin–Stevens Point (WI)
Western Michigan U (MI)

ILLUSTRATION

Acad of Art U (CA)
American Acad of Art (IL)
Arcadia U (PA)
Art Center Coll of Design (CA)
Brigham Young U (UT)
California Coll of the Arts (CA)
California State U, Long Beach (CA)
Cleveland Inst of Art (OH)
Coll for Creative Studies (MI)
Columbus Coll of Art & Design (OH)
Cornish Coll of the Arts (WA)
Emily Carr U of Art + Design (BC, Canada)
Fashion Inst of Technology (NY)
Ferris State U (MI)
Grace Coll (IN)
John Brown U (AR)
Kansas City Art Inst (MO)
Laguna Coll of Art & Design (CA)
Lawrence Technological U (MI)
Marywood U (PA)
Moore Coll of Art & Design (PA)
Northeastern U (MA)
Northern Michigan U (MI)
Nossi Coll of Art (TN)
Pacific Northwest Coll of Art (OR)
Paier Coll of Art, Inc. (CT)
Paris Coll of Art (France)
Pennsylvania Coll of Art & Design (PA)
Pratt Inst (NY)
Rhode Island School of Design (RI)
Ringling Coll of Art and Design (FL)
Rochester Inst of Technology (NY)
Rocky Mountain Coll of Art + Design (CO)
St. John's U (NY)
Savannah Coll of Art and Design (GA)
School of the Art Inst of Chicago (IL)
School of the Museum of Fine Arts, Boston (MA)
Syracuse U (NY)
U of Hartford (CT)
The U of Kansas (KS)
U of Massachusetts Dartmouth (MA)
U of Michigan (MI)
U of New Haven (CT)
U of San Francisco (CA)
The U of the Arts (PA)
Virginia Commonwealth U (VA)
Washington U in St. Louis (MO)

IMMUNOLOGY

U of Saskatchewan (SK, Canada)

INDUSTRIAL AND ORGANIZATIONAL PSYCHOLOGY

Albright Coll (PA)
Avila U (MO)
Baldwin Wallace U (OH)
Baruch Coll of the City U of New York (NY)
Bridgewater State U (MA)
Canisius Coll (NY)
Concordia U (CA)
Corban U (OR)
Eastern Connecticut State U (CT)
Fitchburg State U (MA)
Fort Lewis Coll (CO)
Georgia Inst of Technology (GA)
Holy Family U (PA)
Ithaca Coll (NY)
Lincoln U (PA)
Maryville U of Saint Louis (MO)
Marywood U (PA)
Middle Tennessee State U (TN)
Morningside Coll (IA)
Northwest Missouri State U (MO)
Palo Alto U (CA)
Pepperdine U, Malibu (CA)
Southern Adventist U (TN)
The U of Tennessee at Martin (TN)
Washington U in St. Louis (MO)

INDUSTRIAL AND PHYSICAL PHARMACY AND COSMETIC SCIENCES

The U of Toledo (OH)

INDUSTRIAL AND PRODUCT DESIGN

Acad of Art U (CA)
Appalachian State U (NC)
Arizona State U at the Tempe campus (AZ)
Art Center Coll of Design (CA)
Auburn U (AL)
California Coll of the Arts (CA)
California State U, Long Beach (CA)
Cedarville U (OH)
Cleveland Inst of Art (OH)
Coll for Creative Studies (MI)
Columbia Coll Chicago (IL)
Columbus Coll of Art & Design (OH)
Drexel U (PA)
Emily Carr U of Art + Design (BC, Canada)
Escuela de Artes Plasticas de Puerto Rico (PR)
Fashion Inst of Technology (NY)
Ferris State U (MI)
FIDM/Fashion Inst of Design & Merchandising, Los Angeles Campus (CA)
Georgia Inst of Technology (GA)
Iowa State U of Science and Technology (IA)
Kean U (NJ)
Lawrence Technological U (MI)
Massachusetts Coll of Art and Design (MA)
Montclair State U (NJ)
New Jersey Inst of Technology (NJ)
North Carolina State U (NC)
The Ohio State U (OH)
Pennsylvania Coll of Technology (PA)
Philadelphia U (PA)
Pratt Inst (NY)
Purdue U (IN)
Rhode Island School of Design (RI)
Rochester Inst of Technology (NY)
San Francisco State U (CA)
San Jose State U (CA)
Savannah Coll of Art and Design (GA)
Stanford U (CA)
Syracuse U (NY)
Universidad del Turabo (PR)
Université de Montréal (QC, Canada)
U of Bridgeport (CT)
U of Cincinnati (OH)
U of Houston (TX)
U of Illinois at Chicago (IL)
The U of Kansas (KS)
U of Louisiana at Lafayette (LA)
U of Michigan (MI)
The U of the Arts (PA)
U of Washington (WA)
U of Wisconsin–Platteville (WI)
U of Wisconsin–Stout (WI)
Virginia Polytechnic Inst and State U (VA)

Walla Walla U (WA)
Wentworth Inst of Technology (MA)
Western Washington U (WA)

INDUSTRIAL ELECTRONICS TECHNOLOGY
Sullivan Coll of Technology and Design (KY)

INDUSTRIAL ENGINEERING
Arizona State U at the Tempe campus (AZ)
Auburn U (AL)
Binghamton U, State U of New York (NY)
Bradley U (IL)
California Polytechnic State U, San Luis Obispo (CA)
California State Polytechnic U, Pomona (CA)
California State U, Long Beach (CA)
Caribbean U (PR)
Columbia U (NY)
Concordia U (QC, Canada)
Cornell U (NY)
Dalhousie U (NS, Canada)
Elizabethtown Coll (PA)
Florida Ag and Mech U (FL)
Francis Marion U (SC)
Gannon U (PA)
Georgia Inst of Technology (GA)
Hofstra U (NY)
Inter American U of Puerto Rico, Bayamón Campus (PR)
Iowa State U of Science and Technology (IA)
Kansas State U (KS)
Kent State U (OH)
Kettering U (MI)
Lamar U (TX)
Lawrence Technological U (MI)
Lebanese American U (Lebanon)
Lehigh U (PA)
Liberty U (VA)
Louisiana State U and A&M Coll (LA)
Milwaukee School of Eng (WI)
Mississippi State U (MS)
Missouri Southern State U (MO)
Missouri U of Science and Technology (MO)
Montana State U (MT)
New Jersey Inst of Technology (NJ)
New Mexico State U (NM)
North Carolina Ag and Tech State U (NC)
North Carolina State U (NC)
North Dakota State U (ND)
Northeastern U (MA)
Northern Illinois U (IL)
Northwestern U (IL)
Oakland U (MI)
The Ohio State U (OH)
Ohio U (OH)
Oklahoma State U (OK)
Oregon State U (OR)
Penn State Abington (PA)
Penn State Altoona (PA)
Penn State Beaver (PA)
Penn State Berks (PA)
Penn State Brandywine (PA)
Penn State DuBois (PA)
Penn State Erie, The Behrend Coll (PA)
Penn State Fayette, The Eberly Campus (PA)
Penn State Greater Allegheny (PA)
Penn State Hazleton (PA)
Penn State Lehigh Valley (PA)
Penn State Mont Alto (PA)
Penn State New Kensington (PA)
Penn State Schuylkill (PA)
Penn State Shenango (PA)
Penn State U Park (PA)
Penn State Wilkes-Barre (PA)
Penn State Worthington Scranton (PA)
Penn State York (PA)
Polytechnic U of Puerto Rico (PR)
Purdue U (IN)
Quinnipiac U (CT)
Rensselaer Polytechnic Inst (NY)
Rochester Inst of Technology (NY)
Rutgers, The State U of New Jersey, New Brunswick (NJ)
St. Mary's U (TX)
San Jose State U (CA)
South Dakota School of Mines and Technology (SD)
Southern Illinois U Edwardsville (IL)
Stanford U (CA)
State U of New York Maritime Coll (NY)
Tennessee State U (TN)
Texas A&M U (TX)
Texas A&M U–Commerce (TX)
Texas A&M U–Kingsville (TX)
Texas State U (TX)
Texas Tech U (TX)
U at Buffalo, the State U of New York (NY)
The U of Alabama in Huntsville (AL)
The U of Arizona (AZ)
U of Arkansas (AR)
U of Central Florida (FL)
U of Houston (TX)
U of Illinois at Chicago (IL)
The U of Iowa (IA)
U of Louisville (KY)
U of Massachusetts Amherst (MA)
U of Miami (FL)
U of Michigan (MI)
U of Michigan–Dearborn (MI)
U of Minnesota, Duluth (MN)
U of Minnesota, Twin Cities Campus (MN)
U of Missouri (MO)
U of New Haven (CT)
U of Oklahoma (OK)
U of Pittsburgh (PA)
U of Regina (SK, Canada)
U of Rhode Island (RI)
U of San Diego (CA)
U of Southern California (CA)
U of South Florida (FL)
The U of Tennessee (TN)
The U of Texas at Arlington (TX)
The U of Texas at El Paso (TX)
The U of Texas–Pan American (TX)
The U of Toledo (OH)
U of Toronto (ON, Canada)
U of Vermont (VT)
U of Washington (WA)
U of Windsor (ON, Canada)
U of Wisconsin–Madison (WI)
U of Wisconsin–Milwaukee (WI)
U of Wisconsin–Platteville (WI)
Virginia Polytechnic Inst and State U (VA)
Wayne State U (MI)
Western Michigan U (MI)
Western New England U (MA)
West Virginia U (WV)
Wichita State U (KS)
Worcester Polytechnic Inst (MA)
Youngstown State U (OH)

INDUSTRIAL MECHANICS AND MAINTENANCE TECHNOLOGY
Sullivan Coll of Technology and Design (KY)

INDUSTRIAL PRODUCTION TECHNOLOGIES RELATED
Bowling Green State U (OH)
California U of Pennsylvania (PA)
Central Washington U (WA)
Delaware State U (DE)
Ferris State U (MI)
Georgia Southern U (GA)
Millersville U of Pennsylvania (PA)
Mississippi State U (MS)
Missouri State U (MO)
Pennsylvania Coll of Technology (PA)
Saginaw Valley State U (MI)
Tarleton State U (TX)
Valdosta State U (GA)
Wayne State Coll (NE)

INDUSTRIAL RADIOLOGIC TECHNOLOGY
Concordia U Wisconsin (WI)
Howard U (DC)

INDUSTRIAL SAFETY TECHNOLOGY
Central Washington U (WA)
Eastern Kentucky U (KY)
Mansfield U of Pennsylvania (PA)
Northeastern State U (OK)
U of Houston–Downtown (TX)
The U of Texas at Tyler (TX)

INDUSTRIAL TECHNOLOGY
Baker Coll (MI)
Ball State U (IN)
Bemidji State U (MN)
Black Hills State U (SD)
Bowling Green State U (OH)
Buffalo State Coll, State U of New York (NY)
California Polytechnic State U, San Luis Obispo (CA)
California State U, Fresno (CA)
California State U, Long Beach (CA)
California State U, Los Angeles (CA)
Central Connecticut State U (CT)
Central State U (OH)
Central Washington U (WA)
Clarion U of Pennsylvania (PA)
Dunwoody Coll of Technology (MN)
East Carolina U (NC)
Eastern Illinois U (IL)
Eastern Michigan U (MI)
Fairmont State U (WV)
Ferris State U (MI)
Fitchburg State U (MA)
Fort Hays State U (KS)
Illinois State U (IL)
Indiana State U (IN)
Indiana U–Purdue U Fort Wayne (IN)
Jackson State U (MS)
Jacksonville State U (AL)
Lamar U (TX)
Lawrence Technological U (MI)
Middle Tennessee State U (TN)
Millersville U of Pennsylvania (PA)
Mississippi State U (MS)
Mississippi Valley State U (MS)
Missouri Southern State U (MO)
North Carolina Ag and Tech State U (NC)
Northern Illinois U (IL)
Northern Michigan U (MI)
Ohio U (OH)
Pittsburg State U (KS)
Purdue U Calumet (IN)
Roger Williams U (RI)
Sam Houston State U (TX)
South Carolina State U (SC)
Southeastern Louisiana U (LA)
Southeast Missouri State U (MO)
Southern Arkansas U–Magnolia (AR)
Southern Illinois U Carbondale (IL)
Tarleton State U (TX)
Tennessee State U (TN)
Texas A&M U–Commerce (TX)
Texas A&M U–Kingsville (TX)
Texas Southern U (TX)
Texas State U (TX)
U of Arkansas at Pine Bluff (AR)
U of Dayton (OH)
U of Idaho (ID)
U of Louisiana at Lafayette (LA)
U of Massachusetts Lowell (MA)
U of North Dakota (ND)
U of Northern Iowa (IA)
U of Rio Grande (OH)
U of Southern Maine (ME)
U of Southern Mississippi (MS)
The U of Texas at Tyler (TX)
The U of Texas of the Permian Basin (TX)
U of Wisconsin–Platteville (WI)
Vincennes U (IN)
Western Kentucky U (KY)
Western Washington U (WA)
West Virginia U Inst of Technology (WV)
William Penn U (IA)

INFORMATICS
Arizona State U at the Tempe campus (AZ)
Drexel U (PA)
Indiana U Bloomington (IN)
Indiana U East (IN)
Indiana U Kokomo (IN)
Indiana U Northwest (IN)
Indiana U–Purdue U Indianapolis (IN)
Indiana U South Bend (IN)
Indiana U Southeast (IN)
Mount St. Joseph U (OH)
U of California, Irvine (CA)
U of Louisiana at Lafayette (LA)
U of Michigan (MI)
U of Washington (WA)

INFORMATION RESOURCES MANAGEMENT
Abilene Christian U (TX)
Athens State U (AL)
Chestnut Hill Coll (PA)
Lewis U (IL)
Lipscomb U (TN)
Lubbock Christian U (TX)
Metropolitan State U (MN)
Michigan State U (MI)
Mount St. Mary's U (MD)
Rasmussen Coll Land O' Lakes (FL)
Rasmussen Coll New Port Richey (FL)
Rasmussen Coll Ocala (FL)
Rasmussen Coll Tampa/Brandon (FL)
Salve Regina U (RI)
U of California, Irvine (CA)
U of Wisconsin–Eau Claire (WI)
Western Michigan U (MI)
Wilmington U (DE)

INFORMATION SCIENCE/ STUDIES
Adelphi U (NY)
Alabama State U (AL)
Albany State U (GA)
Albertus Magnus Coll (CT)
Albright Coll (PA)
Anderson U (IN)
Andrews U (MI)
Armstrong State U (GA)
Ashland U (OH)
Averett U (VA)
Barry U (FL)
Baruch Coll of the City U of New York (NY)
Belmont U (TN)
Bemidji State U (MN)
Benedictine U (IL)
Bethune-Cookman U (FL)
Bradley U (IL)
Buffalo State Coll, State U of New York (NY)
California Lutheran U (CA)
California State U, Stanislaus (CA)
Campbellsville U (KY)
Cape Breton U (NS, Canada)
Carson-Newman U (TN)
Central Coll (IA)
Chowan U (NC)
Christopher Newport U (VA)
Clarion U of Pennsylvania (PA)
Clayton State U (GA)
Coastal Carolina U (SC)
The Coll at Brockport, State U of New York (NY)
Coll of Charleston (SC)
Colorado State U (CO)
Colorado State U–Pueblo (CO)
Columbia U, School of General Studies (NY)
Concord U (WV)
Cornell U (NY)
Dakota State U (SD)
Delaware State U (DE)
DePaul U (IL)
Doane Coll (NE)
Drexel U (PA)
East Carolina U (NC)
Elizabethtown Coll (PA)
Elizabethtown Coll School of Continuing and Professional Studies (PA)
Elon U (NC)
Emporia State U (KS)
Excelsior Coll (NY)
Ferrum Coll (VA)
Fordham U (NY)
Fort Hays State U (KS)
Friends U (KS)
Frostburg State U (MD)
Gallaudet U (DC)
Georgia Southern U (GA)
Goshen Coll (IN)
Grambling State U (LA)
Grand Valley State U (MI)
Grand View U (IA)
Hampton U (VA)
Harris-Stowe State U (MO)
HEC Montreal (QC, Canada)
Heidelberg U (OH)
Howard U (DC)
Illinois Coll (IL)
Immaculata U (PA)
Indiana U–Purdue U Fort Wayne (IN)
Inter American U of Puerto Rico, Ponce Campus (PR)
Inter American U of Puerto Rico, San Germán Campus (PR)
James Madison U (VA)
Johnson & Wales U (RI)
Johnson State Coll (VT)
Kansas State U (KS)
Kennesaw State U (GA)
King U (TN)
La Salle U (PA)
La Sierra U (CA)
Lenoir-Rhyne U (NC)
LeTourneau U (TX)
Lewis U (IL)
Limestone Coll (SC)
Lincoln U (MO)
Lipscomb U (TN)
Long Island U–LIU Post (NY)
Louisiana State U in Shreveport (LA)
Mansfield U of Pennsylvania (PA)
Marietta Coll (OH)
McKendree U (IL)
Medaille Coll (NY)
Medgar Evers Coll of the City U of New York (NY)
Mercer U, Macon (GA)
Mercy Coll (NY)
Metropolitan State U (MN)
Michigan State U (MI)
Midwestern State U (TX)
Minnesota State U Mankato (MN)
Minnesota State U Moorhead (MN)
Missouri U of Science and Technology (MO)
Molloy Coll (NY)
Murray State U (KY)
National U (CA)
New Jersey Inst of Technology (NJ)
Newman U (KS)
New Mexico Highlands U (NM)
New York City Coll of Technology of the City U of New York (NY)
Niagara U (NY)
Northeastern U (MA)
Northern Kentucky U (KY)
Northwestern Coll (IA)
Northwestern Oklahoma State U (OK)
Northwestern U (IL)
Notre Dame of Maryland U (MD)
Oakland City U (IN)
Ohio Dominican U (OH)
The Ohio State U (OH)
Oklahoma Baptist U (OK)
Oklahoma Christian U (OK)
Olivet Nazarene U (IL)
Pace U (NY)
Penn State Abington (PA)
Penn State Altoona (PA)
Penn State Beaver (PA)
Penn State Berks (PA)
Penn State Brandywine (PA)
Penn State DuBois (PA)
Penn State Erie, The Behrend Coll (PA)
Penn State Fayette, The Eberly Campus (PA)
Penn State Greater Allegheny (PA)
Penn State Harrisburg (PA)
Penn State Lehigh Valley (PA)
Penn State Mont Alto (PA)
Penn State New Kensington (PA)
Penn State Schuylkill (PA)
Penn State Shenango (PA)
Penn State U Park (PA)
Penn State Wilkes-Barre (PA)
Penn State Worthington Scranton (PA)
Penn State York (PA)
Philadelphia U (PA)
Portland State U (OR)
Quincy U (IL)
Quinnipiac U (CT)
Radford U (VA)
Ramapo Coll of New Jersey (NJ)
Reinhardt U (GA)
Robert Morris U (PA)
Rutgers, The State U of New Jersey, Newark (NJ)
Rutgers, The State U of New Jersey, New Brunswick (NJ)

The Sage Colls (NY)
Saint Joseph's U (PA)
St. Mary's U (TX)
Saint Michael's Coll (VT)
Saint Peter's U (NJ)
St. Thomas Aquinas Coll (NY)
St. Thomas U (FL)
Salisbury U (MD)
San Francisco State U (CA)
Savannah State U (GA)
Silver Lake Coll of the Holy Family (WI)
Slippery Rock U of Pennsylvania (PA)
Southeastern Oklahoma State U (OK)
Southern Illinois U Carbondale (IL)
State U of New York at Fredonia (NY)
State U of New York at Oswego (NY)
State U of New York Coll at Old Westbury (NY)
State U of New York Polytechnic Inst (NY)
Stevenson U (MD)
Stockton U (NJ)
Stony Brook U, State U of New York (NY)
Stratford U, Woodbridge (VA)
Suffolk U (MA)
Susquehanna U (PA)
Syracuse U (NY)
Tarleton State U (TX)
Texas A&M Intl U (TX)
Texas A&M U–Commerce (TX)
Texas Lutheran U (TX)
Texas Tech U (TX)
Thiel Coll (PA)
Towson U (MD)
Tufts U (MA)
Tulane U (LA)
Union U (TN)
United States Military Acad (NY)
Universidad Metropolitana (PR)
Université de Sherbrooke (QC, Canada)
U at Albany, State U of New York (NY)
U at Buffalo, the State U of New York (NY)
U of Alberta (AB, Canada)
U of Arkansas at Little Rock (AR)
U of Bridgeport (CT)
U of California, Santa Cruz (CA)
U of Cincinnati (OH)
U of Colorado Boulder (CO)
U of Great Falls (MT)
U of Hartford (CT)
U of Houston (TX)
U of Illinois at Chicago (IL)
The U of Iowa (IA)
U of Kentucky (KY)
U of Mary Hardin-Baylor (TX)
U of Maryland, Baltimore County (MD)
U of Maryland, Coll Park (MD)
U of Maryland U Coll (MD)
U of Massachusetts Lowell (MA)
U of Miami (FL)
U of Michigan (MI)
U of Michigan–Flint (MI)
The U of Montana (MT)
U of Nevada, Las Vegas (NV)
U of New Haven (CT)
The U of North Carolina at Chapel Hill (NC)
U of North Georgia (GA)
U of North Texas (TX)
U of Oklahoma (OK)
U of Pittsburgh (PA)
U of San Francisco (CA)
The U of Scranton (PA)
U of South Alabama (AL)
U of South Carolina Upstate (SC)
U of South Florida (FL)
The U of Texas at Arlington (TX)
The U of Texas at El Paso (TX)
The U of Texas of the Permian Basin (TX)
U of the District of Columbia (DC)
U of the Pacific (CA)
The U of Toledo (OH)
The U of Tulsa (OK)
U of Vermont (VT)
U of Washington, Bothell (WA)
The U of Western Ontario (ON, Canada)
U of Wisconsin–Green Bay (WI)
U of Wisconsin–Milwaukee (WI)
U of Wisconsin–River Falls (WI)
U of Wisconsin–Superior (WI)
Utah State U (UT)
Utah Valley U (UT)
Valdosta State U (GA)
Virginia Commonwealth U (VA)
Virginia Polytechnic Inst and State U (VA)
Washington U in St. Louis (MO)
Wayne State Coll (NE)
Wayne State U (MI)
Weber State U (UT)
Wentworth Inst of Technology (MA)
Westfield State U (MA)
West Liberty U (WV)
West Virginia Wesleyan Coll (WV)
Widener U (PA)
Wilberforce U (OH)
Wilkes U (PA)
Worcester Polytechnic Inst (MA)
York Coll of the City U of New York (NY)

INFORMATION TECHNOLOGY
Abilene Christian U (TX)
American Public U System (WV)
Arkansas Tech U (AR)
Baylor U (TX)
Bluefield Coll (VA)
Bluffton U (OH)
Bob Jones U (SC)
Brigham Young U (UT)
Bryant U (RI)
Cabrini Coll (PA)
Caldwell U (NJ)
California Baptist U (CA)
California State U, Chico (CA)
California State U, Dominguez Hills (CA)
California State U, Fullerton (CA)
California State U, Los Angeles (CA)
California State U, San Bernardino (CA)
California State U, Stanislaus (CA)
Cameron U (OK)
Central Michigan U (MI)
Central Washington U (WA)
Christopher Newport U (VA)
Clayton State U (GA)
Coastal Carolina U (SC)
Coll of the Ozarks (MO)
Columbia Southern U (AL)
Columbus State U (GA)
Cornell U (NY)
Creighton U (NE)
Daytona State Coll (FL)
DePaul U (IL)
DEREE - The American Coll of Greece (Greece)
DeSales U (PA)
Dixie State U (UT)
East Carolina U (NC)
Fairleigh Dickinson U, Metropolitan Campus (NJ)
Ferris State U (MI)
Florida Ag and Mech U (FL)
Florida Intl U (FL)
Franklin U (OH)
Frostburg State U (MD)
Furman U (SC)
George Mason U (VA)
Georgia Gwinnett Coll (GA)
Georgia Regents U (GA)
Georgia Southwestern State U (GA)
Governors State U (IL)
Granite State Coll (NH)
Harding U (AR)
Humboldt State U (CA)
Illinois Inst of Technology (IL)
Illinois State U (IL)
Indiana State U (IN)
Indiana U–Purdue U Fort Wayne (IN)
Inter American U of Puerto Rico, Bayamón Campus (PR)
Johnson C. Smith U (NC)
Juniata Coll (PA)
Keiser U, Fort Lauderdale (FL)
Kentucky State U (KY)
Keystone Coll (PA)
La Roche Coll (PA)
Lawrence Technological U (MI)
Lehigh U (PA)
LeMoyne-Owen Coll (TN)
Liberty U (VA)
Life U (GA)
Limestone Coll (SC)
Lincoln U (PA)
Lindenwood U (MO)
Lipscomb U (TN)
Loyola U Chicago (IL)
Marian U (WI)
Marquette U (WI)
Marymount U (VA)
McKendree U (IL)
McMurry U (TX)
Merrimack Coll (MA)
Miami Dade Coll (FL)
Miami U (OH)
Missouri Baptist U (MO)
Missouri Western State U (MO)
Montclair State U (NJ)
Morrisville State Coll (NY)
Mount Aloysius Coll (PA)
Mount Marty Coll (SD)
Mount Saint Mary Coll (NY)
Murray State U (KY)
National U Coll, Bayamón (PR)
Neumont U (UT)
Newbury Coll (MA)
New England Inst of Technology (RI)
New Jersey Inst of Technology (NJ)
New Mexico Inst of Mining and Technology (NM)
New Mexico State U (NM)
New York Inst of Technology (NY)
Northern Kentucky U (KY)
Oakland U (MI)
Oklahoma State U (OK)
Olivet Coll (MI)
Peirce Coll (PA)
Plymouth State U (NH)
Purdue U (IN)
Regent U (VA)
Rensselaer Polytechnic Inst (NY)
Rivier U (NH)
Robert Morris U Illinois (IL)
Rochester Inst of Technology (NY)
Sacred Heart U (CT)
Saint Joseph's U (PA)
San Diego State U (CA)
San Jose State U (CA)
Seminole State Coll of Florida (FL)
Simmons Coll (MA)
Slippery Rock U of Pennsylvania (PA)
Southwest Minnesota State U (MN)
State U of New York Coll of Agriculture and Technology at Cobleskill (NY)
State U of New York Coll of Technology at Canton (NY)
Stephen F. Austin State U (TX)
Stratford U, Falls Church (VA)
Stratford U, Glen Allen (VA)
Stratford U, Newport News (VA)
Sullivan Coll of Technology and Design (KY)
Sullivan U (KY)
Syracuse U (NY)
Temple U (PA)
Texas Christian U (TX)
Thomas More Coll (KY)
Tiffin U (OH)
Towson U (MD)
Trevecca Nazarene U (TN)
Union Coll (KY)
United States Military Acad (NY)
Université de Sherbrooke (QC, Canada)
The U of British Columbia–Okanagan Campus (BC, Canada)
U of Central Florida (FL)
U of Central Oklahoma (OK)
U of Cincinnati (OH)
U of Denver (CO)
U of Great Falls (MT)
U of Houston–Clear Lake (TX)
U of Jamestown (ND)
The U of Kansas (KS)
U of Massachusetts Boston (MA)
U of Missouri–Kansas City (MO)
The U of Montana (MT)
U of New Hampshire (NH)
The U of North Carolina at Pembroke (NC)
The U of North Carolina Wilmington (NC)
U of North Texas (TX)
U of Rio Grande (OH)
U of St. Francis (IL)
U of Saint Mary (KS)
U of San Francisco (CA)
U of South Alabama (AL)
U of South Florida (FL)
U of South Florida Sarasota-Manatee (FL)
U of the District of Columbia (DC)
The U of Toledo (OH)
The U of Tulsa (OK)
U of Washington (WA)
U of Washington, Tacoma (WA)
The U of Western Ontario (ON, Canada)
U of West Florida (FL)
U of Wisconsin–Stevens Point (WI)
U of Wisconsin–Whitewater (WI)
Vanguard U of Southern California (CA)
Vermont Tech Coll (VT)
Washington & Jefferson Coll (PA)
Western Illinois U (IL)
Western Kentucky U (KY)
Western New England U (MA)
William Penn U (IA)
Youngstown State U (OH)

INFORMATION TECHNOLOGY PROJECT MANAGEMENT
Arizona State U at the Polytechnic campus (AZ)
National U (CA)
Pace U (NY)

INORGANIC CHEMISTRY
The U of Western Ontario (ON, Canada)

INSTITUTIONAL FOOD WORKERS
Cornell U (NY)
Immaculata U (PA)

INSTRUMENTATION TECHNOLOGY
Bowling Green State U (OH)
Northern Michigan U (MI)
Oklahoma State U Inst of Technology (OK)

INSURANCE
Appalachian State U (NC)
Baylor U (TX)
Bowling Green State U (OH)
Bradley U (IL)
Butler U (IN)
Delta State U (MS)
Excelsior Coll (NY)
Franklin U (OH)
Gannon U (PA)
Georgia State U (GA)
Howard U (DC)
Illinois State U (IL)
Illinois Wesleyan U (IL)
Indiana State U (IN)
Kent State U at Salem (OH)
Mississippi State U (MS)
Missouri State U (MO)
Northern Michigan U (MI)
Ohio Dominican U (OH)
The Ohio State U (OH)
Olivet Coll (MI)
St. John's U (NY)
Saint Joseph's U (PA)
Southern Methodist U (TX)
Temple U (PA)
U of Central Arkansas (AR)
U of Central Oklahoma (OK)
U of Cincinnati (OH)
U of Georgia (GA)
U of Hartford (CT)
U of Houston–Downtown (TX)
U of Louisiana at Lafayette (LA)
U of Minnesota, Twin Cities Campus (MN)
U of Mississippi (MS)
U of Nebraska–Lincoln (NE)
U of North Texas (TX)
U of Pennsylvania (PA)
U of Saint Francis (IN)
U of Wisconsin–La Crosse (WI)
U of Wisconsin–Madison (WI)
William Penn U (IA)

INTELLIGENCE
Coastal Carolina U (SC)
Henley-Putnam U (CA)

INTERCULTURAL/ MULTICULTURAL AND DIVERSITY STUDIES
Bard Coll at Simon's Rock (MA)
Biola U (CA)
Calvary Bible Coll and Theological Sem (MO)
Columbia Bible Coll (BC, Canada)
Columbia Intl U (SC)
Concordia U (QC, Canada)
Evangel U (MO)
The Evergreen State Coll (WA)
Goddard Coll (VT)
Judson U (IL)
Macalester Coll (MN)
Northwest U (WA)
Nyack Coll (NY)
Rocky Mountain Coll (AB, Canada)
St. Catherine U (MN)
Trevecca Nazarene U (TN)
U of Mobile (AL)
U of Regina (SK, Canada)
U of the Incarnate Word (TX)
U of Valley Forge (PA)
Vanguard U of Southern California (CA)
Villanova U (PA)
Western Oregon U (OR)
Wofford Coll (SC)

INTERDISCIPLINARY STUDIES
Agnes Scott Coll (GA)
Albright Coll (PA)
The American U of Rome (Italy)
Amherst Coll (MA)
Auburn U (AL)
Averett U (VA)
Bard Coll (NY)
Bard Coll at Simon's Rock (MA)
Barnard Coll (NY)
Bay Path U (MA)
Beloit Coll (WI)
Berry Coll (GA)
Bethany Coll (WV)
Biola U (CA)
Birmingham-Southern Coll (AL)
Blackburn Coll (IL)
Bloomfield Coll (NJ)
Bloomsburg U of Pennsylvania (PA)
Bluefield Coll (VA)
Boston Coll (MA)
Boston U (MA)
Bucknell U (PA)
California Lutheran U (CA)
California State U, Long Beach (CA)
California State U, Los Angeles (CA)
Calvin Coll (MI)
Carleton Coll (MN)
Carson-Newman U (TN)
Castleton State Coll (VT)
Centenary Coll of Louisiana (LA)
Central Methodist U (MO)
Chowan U (NC)
Christian Brothers U (TN)
Clark U (MA)
Coe Coll (IA)
Coll of the Atlantic (ME)
The Coll of William and Mary (VA)
The Coll of Wooster (OH)
Columbia Coll Chicago (IL)
Connecticut Coll (CT)
Corban U (OR)
Cornell Coll (IA)
Crandall U (NB, Canada)
DePauw U (IN)
Doane Coll (NE)
Drexel U (PA)
Earlham Coll (IN)
Eckerd Coll (FL)
Ellis U (IL)
Elmhurst Coll (IL)
Elms Coll (MA)
Emerson Coll (MA)
Fairleigh Dickinson U, Metropolitan Campus (NJ)
FIDM/Fashion Inst of Design & Merchandising, Los Angeles Campus (CA)
FIDM/Fashion Inst of Design & Merchandising, San Francisco Campus (CA)
Florida Ag and Mech U (FL)

Florida Inst of Technology (FL)
Geneva Coll (PA)
Georgetown U (DC)
The George Washington U (DC)
Gettysburg Coll (PA)
Goddard Coll (VT)
Green Mountain Coll (VT)
Greensboro Coll (NC)
Grinnell Coll (IA)
Guilford Coll (NC)
Gustavus Adolphus Coll (MN)
Hamilton Coll (NY)
Harris-Stowe State U (MO)
Hendrix Coll (AR)
Hillsdale Free Will Baptist Coll (OK)
Hollins U (VA)
Houghton Coll (NY)
Houston Baptist U (TX)
Huston-Tillotson U (TX)
Illinois Coll (IL)
Indiana U Bloomington (IN)
Indiana U East (IN)
Indiana U Kokomo (IN)
Indiana U Northwest (IN)
Indiana U–Purdue U Indianapolis (IN)
Indiana U South Bend (IN)
Indiana U Southeast (IN)
Iowa State U of Science and Technology (IA)
Ithaca Coll (NY)
Jacksonville U (FL)
John Brown U (AR)
John Carroll U (OH)
Johns Hopkins U (MD)
Judson Coll (AL)
Kalamazoo Coll (MI)
Keiser U, Fort Lauderdale (FL)
Keuka Coll (NY)
King U (TN)
Kuyper Coll (MI)
Lasell Coll (MA)
Lees-McRae Coll (NC)
Lehman Coll of the City U of New York (NY)
Lipscomb U (TN)
Louisiana Coll (LA)
Maranatha Baptist U (WI)
Mars Hill U (NC)
Martin Luther Coll (MN)
Marymount Manhattan Coll (NY)
Massachusetts Coll of Liberal Arts (MA)
Merrimack Coll (MA)
Middle Tennessee State U (TN)
Midwestern State U (TX)
Millersville U of Pennsylvania (PA)
Mills Coll (CA)
Minnesota State U Moorhead (MN)
Mount Allison U (NB, Canada)
Mount Saint Mary Coll (NY)
Mount Saint Mary's U (CA)
National U (CA)
Nebraska Wesleyan U (NE)
Newbury Coll (MA)
North Dakota State U (ND)
Northern Arizona U (AZ)
North Greenville U (SC)
Northland Coll (WI)
Northwestern U (IL)
Northwest U (WA)
Notre Dame of Maryland U (MD)
Nyack Coll (NY)
Oakland City U (IN)
Oberlin Coll (OH)
Oglethorpe U (GA)
Oklahoma Baptist U (OK)
Olivet Coll (MI)
Pennsylvania Coll of Technology (PA)
Piedmont Coll (GA)
Prairie View A&M U (TX)
Rhode Island Coll (RI)
Rhodes Coll (TN)
Ripon Coll (WI)
Rochester Inst of Technology (NY)
Rocky Mountain Coll (MT)
Rutgers, The State U of New Jersey, New Brunswick (NJ)
St. Andrews U (NC)
Saint Mary's Coll (IN)
St. Thomas U (NB, Canada)
Salem Coll (NC)
San Diego Christian Coll (CA)
Savannah State U (GA)
Simpson Coll (IA)
Slippery Rock U of Pennsylvania (PA)
Smith Coll (MA)
South Dakota School of Mines and Technology (SD)
Southern Oregon U (OR)
Southwestern Coll (KS)
Stanford U (CA)
State U of New York at Fredonia (NY)
Sterling Coll (KS)
Stevenson U (MD)
Tarleton State U (TX)
Tennessee Wesleyan Coll (TN)
Texas Christian U (TX)
Texas Southern U (TX)
Tougaloo Coll (MS)
Towson U (MD)
Trent U (ON, Canada)
Trinity Coll (CT)
Union Coll (KY)
United States Air Force Acad (CO)
Université de Montréal (QC, Canada)
Université de Sherbrooke (QC, Canada)
U at Albany, State U of New York (NY)
The U of Alabama (AL)
The U of Arizona (AZ)
U of Arkansas (AR)
U of Bridgeport (CT)
The U of British Columbia (BC, Canada)
U of California, Santa Barbara (CA)
U of Central Florida (FL)
U of Evansville (IN)
U of Guam (GU)
U of Hartford (CT)
U of Hawaii at Hilo (HI)
The U of Iowa (IA)
U of Kentucky (KY)
U of Memphis (TN)
U of Michigan–Flint (MI)
U of Minnesota, Duluth (MN)
U of Missouri (MO)
The U of Montana (MT)
U of Mount Union (OH)
U of New Mexico (NM)
U of North Alabama (AL)
U of North Dakota (ND)
U of North Florida (FL)
U of Oklahoma (OK)
U of Portland (OR)
U of Puget Sound (WA)
U of Richmond (VA)
U of Saint Mary (KS)
U of St. Thomas (MN)
U of San Francisco (CA)
U of South Alabama (AL)
U of South Carolina Upstate (SC)
The U of Tennessee at Chattanooga (TN)
The U of Tennessee at Martin (TN)
The U of Texas at Dallas (TX)
The U of Texas at El Paso (TX)
The U of Texas at Tyler (TX)
U of the Fraser Valley (BC, Canada)
U of the Pacific (CA)
The U of Toledo (OH)
The U of Tulsa (OK)
U of Vermont (VT)
The U of Virginia's Coll at Wise (VA)
U of Washington, Tacoma (WA)
U of Waterloo (ON, Canada)
The U of West Alabama (AL)
The U of Western Ontario (ON, Canada)
U of Wisconsin–Parkside (WI)
Vanguard U of Southern California (CA)
Vassar Coll (NY)
Virginia Polytechnic Inst and State U (VA)
Virginia State U (VA)
Virginia Wesleyan Coll (VA)
Walden U (MN)
Warren Wilson Coll (NC)
Wayne State Coll (NE)
Wesleyan Coll (GA)
Western Oregon U (OR)
Western State Colorado U (CO)
West Liberty U (WV)
William Woods U (MO)
Wittenberg U (OH)
Worcester Polytechnic Inst (MA)
Yeshiva U (NY)

INTERIOR ARCHITECTURE
Auburn U (AL)
Boston Architectural Coll (MA)
Bowling Green State U (OH)
California Coll of the Arts (CA)
Chatham U (PA)
Indiana State U (IN)
Lamar U (TX)
La Roche Coll (PA)
Lawrence Technological U (MI)
Lebanese American U (Lebanon)
Louisiana State U and A&M Coll (LA)
Miami U (OH)
Mississippi State U (MS)
Mount St. Joseph U (OH)
Philadelphia U (PA)
Rhode Island School of Design (RI)
Sam Houston State U (TX)
School of the Art Inst of Chicago (IL)
Stephen F. Austin State U (TX)
Texas Tech U (TX)
U of Houston (TX)
U of Louisiana at Lafayette (LA)
U of Missouri (MO)
U of Nebraska–Lincoln (NE)
U of Nevada, Las Vegas (NV)
U of New Haven (CT)
U of North Texas (TX)
U of Oregon (OR)
U of Southern Mississippi (MS)
The U of Texas at Arlington (TX)
The U of Texas at San Antonio (TX)
Villa Maria Coll (NY)

INTERIOR DESIGN
Abilene Christian U (TX)
Acad of Art U (CA)
The American U in Dubai (United Arab Emirates)
Anderson U (SC)
Appalachian State U (NC)
Arcadia U (PA)
Arizona State U at the Tempe campus (AZ)
Art Center Coll of Design (CA)
Auburn U (AL)
Baker Coll (MI)
Baylor U (TX)
Bay Path U (MA)
Berkeley Coll, Woodland Park (NJ)
Brenau U (GA)
California State U, Fresno (CA)
California State U, Long Beach (CA)
California State U, Sacramento (CA)
Carson-Newman U (TN)
Cazenovia Coll (NY)
Chaminade U of Honolulu (HI)
Cleveland Inst of Art (OH)
Coll for Creative Studies (MI)
Colorado State U (CO)
Columbia Coll Chicago (IL)
Columbus Coll of Art & Design (OH)
Concordia U Wisconsin (WI)
Cornish Coll of the Arts (WA)
Design Inst of San Diego (CA)
Drexel U (PA)
Dunwoody Coll of Technology (MN)
East Carolina U (NC)
Eastern Michigan U (MI)
East Tennessee State U (TN)
EDP U of Puerto Rico (PR)
Endicott Coll (MA)
Fashion Inst of Technology (NY)
Ferris State U (MI)
Florida Intl U (FL)
Florida State U (FL)
Fort Hays State U (KS)
Georgia Southern U (GA)
Hampton U (VA)
Harding U (AR)
High Point U (NC)
Howard U (DC)
Indiana U Bloomington (IN)
Indiana U of Pennsylvania (PA)
Indiana U–Purdue U Fort Wayne (IN)
Indiana U–Purdue U Indianapolis (IN)
Iowa State U of Science and Technology (IA)
Judson U (IL)
Kansas State U (KS)
Kean U (NJ)
Kent State U (OH)
Lebanese American U (Lebanon)
Marist Coll (NY)
Marylhurst U (OR)
Marymount U (VA)
Maryville U of Saint Louis (MO)
Marywood U (PA)
Meredith Coll (NC)
Michigan State U (MI)
Middle Tennessee State U (TN)
Moore Coll of Art & Design (PA)
Mount Mary U (WI)
Newbury Coll (MA)
New England Inst of Technology (RI)
New Jersey Inst of Technology (NJ)
New York Inst of Technology (NY)
New York School of Interior Design (NY)
North Dakota State U (ND)
Northern Arizona U (AZ)
The Ohio State U (OH)
Oklahoma Christian U (OK)
Oregon State U (OR)
Otis Coll of Art and Design (CA)
Paier Coll of Art, Inc. (CT)
Paris Coll of Art (France)
Park U (MO)
Philadelphia U (PA)
Point Loma Nazarene U (CA)
Polytechnic U of Puerto Rico (PR)
Pratt Inst (NY)
Ringling Coll of Art and Design (FL)
Rochester Inst of Technology (NY)
Rocky Mountain Coll of Art + Design (CO)
The Sage Colls (NY)
Salem Coll (NC)
Samford U (AL)
San Diego State U (CA)
San Francisco State U (CA)
San Jose State U (CA)
Savannah Coll of Art and Design (GA)
Seattle Pacific U (WA)
Seminole State Coll of Florida (FL)
South Dakota State U (SD)
Southern Illinois U Carbondale (IL)
Stephens Coll (MO)
Stevens–The Inst of Business & Arts (MO)
Suffolk U (MA)
Sullivan Coll of Technology and Design (KY)
Texas Christian U (TX)
Texas State U (TX)
Universidad del Turabo (PR)
The U of Alabama (AL)
U of Arkansas (AR)
U of Bridgeport (CT)
U of Central Arkansas (AR)
U of Central Missouri (MO)
U of Central Oklahoma (OK)
U of Charleston (WV)
U of Cincinnati (OH)
U of Florida (FL)
U of Idaho (ID)
The U of Kansas (KS)
U of Kentucky (KY)
U of Minnesota, Twin Cities Campus (MN)
The U of North Carolina at Greensboro (NC)
U of Northern Iowa (IA)
U of Oklahoma (OK)
The U of Tennessee (TN)
The U of Tennessee at Chattanooga (TN)
The U of Tennessee at Martin (TN)
The U of Texas at Austin (TX)
U of the Incarnate Word (TX)
U of Wisconsin–Madison (WI)
U of Wisconsin–Stevens Point (WI)
U of Wisconsin–Stout (WI)
Utah State U (UT)
Valdosta State U (GA)
Villa Maria Coll (NY)
Virginia Commonwealth U (VA)
Virginia Polytechnic Inst and State U (VA)
Washington State U (WA)
Watkins Coll of Art, Design, & Film (TN)
Wentworth Inst of Technology (MA)
Western Carolina U (NC)
Western Michigan U (MI)

INTERMEDIA/MULTIMEDIA
Art Center Coll of Design (CA)
Bard Coll at Simon's Rock (MA)
Bennington Coll (VT)
Biola U (CA)
Calumet Coll of Saint Joseph (IN)
Champlain Coll (VT)
City Coll of the City U of New York (NY)
The Coll of New Jersey (NJ)
Columbia Coll Chicago (IL)
Concordia U (QC, Canada)
Emerson Coll (MA)
The Evergreen State Coll (WA)
Georgia Regents U (GA)
Hawai`i Pacific U (HI)
Indiana U of Pennsylvania (PA)
Jacksonville U (FL)
Laguna Coll of Art & Design (CA)
Luther Coll (IA)
Marist Coll (NY)
Massachusetts Coll of Art and Design (MA)
Mills Coll (CA)
Missouri State U (MO)
Northeastern U (MA)
Pacific Northwest Coll of Art (OR)
Purchase Coll, State U of New York (NY)
Ramapo Coll of New Jersey (NJ)
Rochester Inst of Technology (NY)
San Francisco Art Inst (CA)
School of the Art Inst of Chicago (IL)
School of the Museum of Fine Arts, Boston (MA)
State U of New York at Fredonia (NY)
U of Hartford (CT)
U of Regina (SK, Canada)
The U of the Arts (PA)
The U of Toledo (OH)
Weber State U (UT)
Western Washington U (WA)
Worcester Polytechnic Inst (MA)

INTERNATIONAL AGRICULTURE
Cornell U (NY)
Dalhousie U (NS, Canada)
Iowa State U of Science and Technology (IA)
Tarleton State U (TX)
U of California, Davis (CA)
U of Missouri (MO)
Utah State U (UT)

INTERNATIONAL AND COMPARATIVE EDUCATION
Avila U (MO)

INTERNATIONAL AND INTERCULTURAL COMMUNICATION
Cedarville U (OH)
Linfield Coll (OR)
Michigan Technological U (MI)
Pepperdine U, Malibu (CA)
U of Valley Forge (PA)

INTERNATIONAL BUSINESS/ TRADE/COMMERCE
Adams State U (CO)
Albertus Magnus Coll (CT)
Albright Coll (PA)
Alverno Coll (WI)
American Intl Coll (MA)
The American U of Rome (Italy)
Anderson U (IN)
Angelo State U (TX)
Appalachian State U (NC)
Aquinas Coll (MI)
Arcadia U (PA)
Arkansas State U (AR)
Assumption Coll (MA)
Auburn U (AL)
Augsburg Coll (MN)
Augustana Coll (IL)
Austin Coll (TX)
Ave Maria U (FL)
Avila U (MO)
Babson Coll (MA)
Baker U (KS)

Baldwin Wallace U (OH)
Barry U (FL)
Baruch Coll of the City U of New York (NY)
Baylor U (TX)
Belmont U (TN)
Benedictine Coll (KS)
Benedictine U (IL)
Berkeley Coll, Woodland Park (NJ)
Berkeley Coll–New York City Campus (NY)
Berry Coll (GA)
Bethel Coll (IN)
Bethune-Cookman U (FL)
Binghamton U, State U of New York (NY)
Biola U (CA)
Birmingham-Southern Coll (AL)
Bowling Green State U (OH)
Bradley U (IL)
Bridgewater State U (MA)
Bryant U (RI)
Bucknell U (PA)
Buena Vista U (IA)
Butler U (IN)
Caldwell U (NJ)
California State U, Dominguez Hills (CA)
California State U, Fresno (CA)
California State U, Fullerton (CA)
California State U, Long Beach (CA)
California State U, San Marcos (CA)
Canisius Coll (NY)
Cardinal Stritch U (WI)
The Catholic U of America (DC)
Cedarville U (OH)
Central Coll (IA)
Central Michigan U (MI)
Chaminade U of Honolulu (HI)
Champlain Coll (VT)
Chatham U (PA)
Chestnut Hill Coll (PA)
Clarion U of Pennsylvania (PA)
Cleveland State U (OH)
The Coll at Brockport, State U of New York (NY)
Coll of Charleston (SC)
The Coll of Idaho (ID)
Coll of the Ozarks (MO)
Columbia Coll (MO)
Concordia Coll (MN)
Concordia Coll–New York (NY)
Concordia U (QC, Canada)
Concordia U Wisconsin (WI)
Cornell Coll (IA)
Cornerstone U (MI)
Creighton U (NE)
Dalhousie U (NS, Canada)
Davenport U, Grand Rapids (MI)
DEREE - The American Coll of Greece (Greece)
DeSales U (PA)
Dickinson Coll (PA)
Dickinson State U (ND)
Dominican Coll (NY)
Dominican U (IL)
Drake U (IA)
Drexel U (PA)
Dunlap-Stone U, Phoenix (AZ)
Duquesne U (PA)
Eastern Michigan U (MI)
Eastern U (PA)
Eckerd Coll (FL)
Elizabethtown Coll (PA)
Elmhurst Coll (IL)
Elms Coll (MA)
Elon U (NC)
Embry-Riddle Aeronautical U–Prescott (AZ)
Emory & Henry Coll (VA)
Endicott Coll (MA)
Excelsior Coll (NY)
Florida Atlantic U (FL)
Florida Inst of Technology (FL)
Florida Intl U (FL)
Fordham U (NY)
Fort Lewis Coll (CO)
Friends U (KS)
Gannon U (PA)
Georgetown U (DC)
The George Washington U (DC)
Georgia Southern U (GA)
Gettysburg Coll (PA)
Gonzaga U (WA)
Grace Coll (IN)
Graceland U (IA)
Grand Valley State U (MI)
Grove City Coll (PA)
Gustavus Adolphus Coll (MN)
Hamline U (MN)
Harding U (AR)
Hawai`i Pacific U (HI)
HEC Montreal (QC, Canada)
High Point U (NC)
Hilbert Coll (NY)
Hillsdale Coll (MI)
Hofstra U (NY)
Holy Family U (PA)
Houston Baptist U (TX)
Howard U (DC)
Husson U (ME)
Illinois State U (IL)
Illinois Wesleyan U (IL)
Indiana U of Pennsylvania (PA)
Iona Coll (NY)
Iowa State U of Science and Technology (IA)
Ithaca Coll (NY)
Jacksonville U (FL)
James Madison U (VA)
John Brown U (AR)
John Cabot U (Italy)
John Carroll U (OH)
Johnson & Wales U (CO)
Johnson & Wales U (RI)
Juniata Coll (PA)
Kean U (NJ)
Keiser U, Fort Lauderdale (FL)
Kennesaw State U (GA)
King's Coll (PA)
King U (TN)
Kuyper Coll (MI)
Lake Erie Coll (OH)
La Roche Coll (PA)
La Salle U (PA)
Lasell Coll (MA)
Lawrence Technological U (MI)
Lenoir-Rhyne U (NC)
LeTourneau U (TX)
Lewis U (IL)
LIM Coll (NY)
Lincoln U (CA)
Lindenwood U (MO)
Linfield Coll (OR)
Lipscomb U (TN)
Louisiana State U and A&M Coll (LA)
Loyola U Chicago (IL)
Loyola U New Orleans (LA)
Lynn U (FL)
Madonna U (MI)
Maine Maritime Acad (ME)
Mansfield U of Pennsylvania (PA)
Marietta Coll (OH)
Marshall U (WV)
Marymount Manhattan Coll (NY)
Maryville Coll (TN)
Maryville U of Saint Louis (MO)
Marywood U (PA)
Massachusetts Coll of Liberal Arts (MA)
Massachusetts Maritime Acad (MA)
Menlo Coll (CA)
Mercer U, Macon (GA)
Mercy Coll (NY)
Merrimack Coll (MA)
Messiah Coll (PA)
Metropolitan State U (MN)
Midwestern State U (TX)
Millikin U (IL)
Milwaukee School of Eng (WI)
Minnesota State U Mankato (MN)
Minot State U (ND)
Monmouth Coll (IL)
Monmouth U (NJ)
Moravian Coll (PA)
Mount Allison U (NB, Canada)
Mount Saint Mary's U (CA)
Mount Vernon Nazarene U (OH)
Murray State U (KY)
Nazareth Coll of Rochester (NY)
Nebraska Wesleyan U (NE)
Neumann U (PA)
Newbury Coll (MA)
New Jersey Inst of Technology (NJ)
New Mexico State U (NM)
New York Inst of Technology (NY)
New York U (NY)
Niagara U (NY)
Nichols Coll (MA)
North Central Coll (IL)
Northeastern State U (OK)
Northeastern U (MA)
Northern State U (SD)
North Greenville U (SC)
Northwest Missouri State U (MO)
Northwest Nazarene U (ID)
Northwood U, Michigan Campus (MI)
Notre Dame of Maryland U (MD)
Ohio Northern U (OH)
The Ohio State U (OH)
Ohio U (OH)
Ohio Wesleyan U (OH)
Oklahoma Baptist U (OK)
Oklahoma State U (OK)
Olivet Nazarene U (IL)
Our Lady of the Lake U of San Antonio (TX)
Pace U (NY)
Palm Beach Atlantic U (FL)
Penn State DuBois (PA)
Penn State Erie, The Behrend Coll (PA)
Penn State Harrisburg (PA)
Penn State Lehigh Valley (PA)
Penn State Schuylkill (PA)
Pepperdine U, Malibu (CA)
Philadelphia U (PA)
Pittsburg State U (KS)
Queens Coll of the City U of New York (NY)
Quinnipiac U (CT)
Ramapo Coll of New Jersey (NJ)
Rhode Island Coll (RI)
Rhodes Coll (TN)
Rider U (NJ)
Rochester Inst of Technology (NY)
Roger Williams U (RI)
Rollins Coll (FL)
Saginaw Valley State U (MI)
Saint Anselm Coll (NH)
St. Catherine U (MN)
St. Edward's U (TX)
Saint Francis U (PA)
Saint Joseph's U (PA)
St. Mary's U (TX)
Saint Mary's U of Minnesota (MN)
St. Norbert Coll (WI)
Saint Peter's U (NJ)
St. Thomas U (FL)
Saint Vincent Coll (PA)
Salem Coll (NC)
Salisbury U (MD)
Samford U (AL)
Sam Houston State U (TX)
San Diego State U (CA)
San Francisco State U (CA)
San Jose State U (CA)
Savannah State U (GA)
Seattle U (WA)
Seton Hill U (PA)
Simpson Coll (IA)
Southeastern U (FL)
Southeast Missouri State U (MO)
Southern Adventist U (TN)
Southern New Hampshire U (NH)
Southwestern Adventist U (TX)
Spring Hill Coll (AL)
State Coll of Florida Manatee-Sarasota (FL)
State U of New York at New Paltz (NY)
State U of New York at Plattsburgh (NY)
Stephen F. Austin State U (TX)
Stetson U (FL)
Stonehill Coll (MA)
Suffolk U (MA)
Tarleton State U (TX)
Taylor U (IN)
Temple U (PA)
Texas Christian U (TX)
Texas Tech U (TX)
Thiel Coll (PA)
Tiffin U (OH)
Trevecca Nazarene U (TN)
Trinity U (TX)
Union Coll (NE)
Université du Québec en Outaouais (QC, Canada)
U at Buffalo, the State U of New York (NY)
The U of Akron (OH)
U of Alberta (AB, Canada)
U of Arkansas (AR)
U of Arkansas at Little Rock (AR)
U of Bridgeport (CT)
The U of British Columbia (BC, Canada)
U of Central Oklahoma (OK)
U of Cincinnati (OH)
U of Dayton (OH)
U of Delaware (DE)
U of Denver (CO)
U of Evansville (IN)
The U of Findlay (OH)
U of Georgia (GA)
U of Hawaii at Manoa (HI)
U of Houston–Downtown (TX)
U of Indianapolis (IN)
U of Jamestown (ND)
U of La Verne (CA)
U of Lethbridge (AB, Canada)
U of Mary Hardin-Baylor (TX)
U of Maryland, Coll Park (MD)
U of Memphis (TN)
U of Miami (FL)
U of Michigan–Flint (MI)
U of Minnesota, Twin Cities Campus (MN)
U of Missouri (MO)
The U of Montana (MT)
U of Mount Union (OH)
U of Nebraska–Lincoln (NE)
U of Nevada, Las Vegas (NV)
U of Nevada, Reno (NV)
The U of North Carolina at Charlotte (NC)
The U of North Carolina at Greensboro (NC)
U of North Florida (FL)
U of Northwestern–St. Paul (MN)
U of Ottawa (ON, Canada)
U of Pennsylvania (PA)
U of Pittsburgh (PA)
U of Portland (OR)
U of Regina (SK, Canada)
U of Rhode Island (RI)
U of Rio Grande (OH)
U of St. Francis (IL)
U of St. Thomas (MN)
U of San Diego (CA)
U of San Francisco (CA)
The U of Scranton (PA)
U of Southern California (CA)
U of Southern Mississippi (MS)
U of South Florida (FL)
The U of Tampa (FL)
The U of Tennessee at Martin (TN)
The U of Texas at Arlington (TX)
The U of Texas at Dallas (TX)
The U of Texas at San Antonio (TX)
The U of Texas–Pan American (TX)
U of the Incarnate Word (TX)
The U of Toledo (OH)
The U of Tulsa (OK)
U of Valley Forge (PA)
U of Waterloo (ON, Canada)
The U of Western Ontario (ON, Canada)
U of Wisconsin–Eau Claire (WI)
U of Wisconsin–La Crosse (WI)
U of Wisconsin–Madison (WI)
U of Wisconsin–Whitewater (WI)
Utica Coll (NY)
Valdosta State U (GA)
Valparaiso U (IN)
Vanguard U of Southern California (CA)
Villanova U (PA)
Waldorf Coll (IA)
Walla Walla U (WA)
Wartburg Coll (IA)
Washington & Jefferson Coll (PA)
Washington State U (WA)
Washington U in St. Louis (MO)
Waynesburg U (PA)
Wayne State U (MI)
Wesleyan Coll (GA)
Western Kentucky U (KY)
Western New England U (MA)
Western Washington U (WA)
Westminster Coll (MO)
Westminster Coll (UT)
Whitworth U (WA)
Wichita State U (KS)
Widener U (PA)
William Paterson U of New Jersey (NJ)
Wright State U (OH)
Xavier U (OH)
Yeshiva U (NY)

INTERNATIONAL ECONOMICS

Albion Coll (MI)
The American U of Paris (France)
Austin Coll (TX)
Belmont U (TN)
Bethany Coll (WV)
The Coll of Idaho (ID)
The Colorado Coll (CO)
Elon U (NC)
Fitchburg State U (MA)
Georgetown U (DC)
Georgia State U (GA)
Gettysburg Coll (PA)
HEC Montreal (QC, Canada)
Howard U (DC)
John Carroll U (OH)
Lawrence U (WI)
Mary Baldwin Coll (VA)
Rhodes Coll (TN)
Rockford U (IL)
St. Catherine U (MN)
Salve Regina U (RI)
State U of New York at Oswego (NY)
Texas Christian U (TX)
Texas Tech U (TX)
Trinity U (TX)
U of California, Los Angeles (CA)
U of California, Santa Cruz (CA)
U of Puget Sound (WA)
U of Richmond (VA)
U of St. Thomas (MN)
U of West Georgia (GA)
Valparaiso U (IN)
Washington U in St. Louis (MO)
Weber State U (UT)
Youngstown State U (OH)

INTERNATIONAL FINANCE

The American U of Paris (France)
Babson Coll (MA)
Brigham Young U (UT)
The Catholic U of America (DC)
HEC Montreal (QC, Canada)
Lycoming Coll (PA)
Texas Christian U (TX)
Washington U in St. Louis (MO)

INTERNATIONAL/GLOBAL STUDIES

Abilene Christian U (TX)
Adelphi U (NY)
Albertus Magnus Coll (CT)
Albion Coll (MI)
The American U of Rome (Italy)
Appalachian State U (NC)
Arcadia U (PA)
Arizona State U at the Tempe campus (AZ)
Arkansas Tech U (AR)
Assumption Coll (MA)
Auburn U at Montgomery (AL)
Baker U (KS)
Baldwin Wallace U (OH)
Bard Coll (NY)
Belhaven U (MS)
Benedictine Coll (KS)
Benedictine U (IL)
Bennington Coll (VT)
Bentley U (MA)
Brandeis U (MA)
Bryant U (RI)
California Baptist U (CA)
Case Western Reserve U (OH)
Cedar Crest Coll (PA)
Cedarville U (OH)
Central Coll (IA)
Central Connecticut State U (CT)
Centre Coll (KY)
Chatham U (PA)
Chestnut Hill Coll (PA)
Chicago State U (IL)
City Coll of the City U of New York (NY)
Colby Coll (ME)
Coll of Charleston (SC)
The Coll of New Rochelle (NY)
Coll of Saint Elizabeth (NJ)
The Coll of St. Scholastica (MN)
Coll of Staten Island of the City U of New York (NY)
Coll of the Holy Cross (MA)
Colorado State U (CO)
Columbia Intl U (SC)
Concordia Coll (MN)
Concordia Coll–New York (NY)
Concordia U (CA)

Concordia U, Nebraska (NE)
Davis Coll (NY)
Doane Coll (NE)
Dominican U of California (CA)
Drexel U (PA)
Eastern Kentucky U (KY)
East Texas Baptist U (TX)
Emmanuel Coll (MA)
Endicott Coll (MA)
The Evergreen State Coll (WA)
Flagler Coll (FL)
Framingham State U (MA)
Frostburg State U (MD)
Gannon U (PA)
Georgia Inst of Technology (GA)
Goddard Coll (VT)
Greenville Coll (IL)
Hamline U (MN)
Hampshire Coll (MA)
Hanover Coll (IN)
Harding U (AR)
Hawai`i Pacific U (HI)
Hofstra U (NY)
Hope Coll (MI)
Illinois Wesleyan U (IL)
John Brown U (AR)
Juniata Coll (PA)
Kenyon Coll (OH)
Knox Coll (IL)
La Sierra U (CA)
Lebanon Valley Coll (PA)
Lehigh U (PA)
Le Moyne Coll (NY)
Long Island U–LIU Post (NY)
Louisiana State U and A&M Coll (LA)
Lubbock Christian U (TX)
Luther Coll (IA)
Macalester Coll (MN)
Malone U (OH)
Manchester U (IN)
Manhattanville Coll (NY)
Marymount Manhattan Coll (NY)
Maryville U of Saint Louis (MO)
McKendree U (IL)
Meredith Coll (NC)
Michigan State U (MI)
Midwestern State U (TX)
Minnesota State U Moorhead (MN)
Missouri State U (MO)
Missouri Western State U (MO)
Monmouth Coll (IL)
Morehead State U (KY)
Morningside Coll (IA)
Mount Mary U (WI)
National U (CA)
Nebraska Wesleyan U (NE)
New Coll of Florida (FL)
New York U (NY)
North Carolina State U (NC)
North Central Coll (IL)
North Dakota State U (ND)
The Ohio State U (OH)
Oregon State U (OR)
Pacific Lutheran U (WA)
Pepperdine U, Malibu (CA)
Point Loma Nazarene U (CA)
Presbyterian Coll (SC)
Providence Coll (RI)
Randolph Coll (VA)
Randolph-Macon Coll (VA)
Regent U (VA)
Reinhardt U (GA)
Rockford U (IL)
Roger Williams U (RI)
Sacred Heart U (CT)
Saginaw Valley State U (MI)
St. Bonaventure U (NY)
St. Edward's U (TX)
St. Lawrence U (NY)
Saint Leo U (FL)
Saint Mary's Coll (IN)
Saint Mary's U of Minnesota (MN)
St. Norbert Coll (WI)
Salisbury U (MD)
Salve Regina U (RI)
Samford U (AL)
Scripps Coll (CA)
Seattle U (WA)
Sewanee: The U of the South (TN)
Shippensburg U of Pennsylvania (PA)
South Dakota State U (SD)
Southeast Missouri State U (MO)
Southern Methodist U (TX)
State U of New York Coll at Cortland (NY)
Susquehanna U (PA)
Tabor Coll (KS)
Tarleton State U (TX)
Temple U (PA)
Tennessee Wesleyan Coll (TN)
Texas A&M U (TX)
Texas State U (TX)
Texas Tech U (TX)
Thomas More Coll (KY)
United States Air Force Acad (CO)
U at Albany, State U of New York (NY)
The U of Arizona (AZ)
U of California, Irvine (CA)
U of California, Los Angeles (CA)
U of California, Riverside (CA)
U of California, Santa Barbara (CA)
U of Central Arkansas (AR)
U of Central Florida (FL)
U of Colorado Boulder (CO)
U of Colorado Denver (CO)
U of Dayton (OH)
U of Florida (FL)
U of Illinois at Springfield (IL)
The U of Iowa (IA)
The U of Kansas (KS)
U of Kentucky (KY)
U of La Verne (CA)
U of Maryland, Baltimore County (MD)
U of Michigan (MI)
U of Nebraska–Lincoln (NE)
U of New Haven (CT)
U of New Mexico (NM)
U of New Orleans (LA)
The U of North Carolina at Chapel Hill (NC)
The U of North Carolina at Charlotte (NC)
The U of North Carolina Wilmington (NC)
U of North Dakota (ND)
U of Northern Colorado (CO)
U of North Florida (FL)
U of North Texas (TX)
U of Oklahoma (OK)
U of Oregon (OR)
U of Ottawa (ON, Canada)
U of Pennsylvania (PA)
U of Regina (SK, Canada)
U of Saint Joseph (CT)
U of Saskatchewan (SK, Canada)
U of South Alabama (AL)
The U of South Dakota (SD)
U of Southern California (CA)
The U of Texas at Arlington (TX)
The U of Texas at Austin (TX)
U of Utah (UT)
U of Washington, Bothell (WA)
U of Washington, Tacoma (WA)
U of Waterloo (ON, Canada)
U of Wisconsin–Madison (WI)
U of Wisconsin–Milwaukee (WI)
U of Wisconsin–River Falls (WI)
U of Wisconsin–Stevens Point (WI)
U of Wisconsin–Whitewater (WI)
U of Wyoming (WY)
Valparaiso U (IN)
Villanova U (PA)
Warren Wilson Coll (NC)
Washington & Jefferson Coll (PA)
Webster U (MO)
Western Carolina U (NC)
Western Michigan U (MI)
Western New England U (MA)
Westminster Coll (MO)
West Virginia State U (WV)
Wheeling Jesuit U (WV)
Whittier Coll (CA)
Willamette U (OR)
William Peace U (NC)
Winona State U (MN)

INTERNATIONAL MARKETING

Fashion Inst of Technology (NY)
Husson U (ME)
Oklahoma Baptist U (OK)
Pace U (NY)
Texas Christian U (TX)

INTERNATIONAL POLICY ANALYSIS

Southern Methodist U (TX)

INTERNATIONAL PUBLIC HEALTH

Allegheny Coll (PA)
American U (DC)
Bethel Coll (IN)
California Baptist U (CA)
Cornell U (NY)
Mercer U, Macon (GA)
Union Coll (NE)
The U of Iowa (IA)
U of Southern California (CA)

INTERNATIONAL RELATIONS AND AFFAIRS

Agnes Scott Coll (GA)
Allegheny Coll (PA)
Alverno Coll (WI)
American Coll of Thessaloniki (Greece)
American Intl Coll (MA)
American Public U System (WV)
American U (DC)
American U in Bulgaria (Bulgaria)
The American U in Dubai (United Arab Emirates)
The American U of Rome (Italy)
Aquinas Coll (MI)
Augsburg Coll (MN)
Augustana Coll (SD)
Austin Coll (TX)
Azusa Pacific U (CA)
Barry U (FL)
Baylor U (TX)
Belmont U (TN)
Beloit Coll (WI)
Benedictine U (IL)
Bennington Coll (VT)
Berry Coll (GA)
Bethany Coll (WV)
Bethel U (MN)
Bethune-Cookman U (FL)
Binghamton U, State U of New York (NY)
Bob Jones U (SC)
Boston U (MA)
Bowling Green State U (OH)
Bradley U (IL)
Bridgewater Coll (VA)
Bridgewater State U (MA)
Brown U (RI)
Bucknell U (PA)
Butler U (IN)
California Lutheran U (CA)
California State U, Chico (CA)
California State U, Long Beach (CA)
California State U, Monterey Bay (CA)
California State U, San Marcos (CA)
Calvin Coll (MI)
Canisius Coll (NY)
Capital U (OH)
Carleton Coll (MN)
Carroll Coll (MT)
Case Western Reserve U (OH)
Central Michigan U (MI)
Chaminade U of Honolulu (HI)
Chatham U (PA)
City Coll of the City U of New York (NY)
Claremont McKenna Coll (CA)
Clark U (MA)
Cleveland State U (OH)
The Coll at Brockport, State U of New York (NY)
The Coll of Idaho (ID)
The Coll of New Jersey (NJ)
Coll of Staten Island of the City U of New York (NY)
The Coll of William and Mary (VA)
The Coll of Wooster (OH)
Concordia Coll–New York (NY)
Connecticut Coll (CT)
Cornell Coll (IA)
Creighton U (NE)
Dalhousie U (NS, Canada)
Denison U (OH)
DePaul U (IL)
Dickinson Coll (PA)
Dominican U (IL)
Drake U (IA)
Drew U (NJ)
Drury U (MO)
Duquesne U (PA)
Eastern Michigan U (MI)
East Tennessee State U (TN)
Eckerd Coll (FL)
Edgewood Coll (WI)
Elmira Coll (NY)
Elon U (NC)
Embry-Riddle Aeronautical U–Prescott (AZ)
Emmanuel Coll (MA)
Fairfield U (CT)
Fairleigh Dickinson U, Metropolitan Campus (NJ)
Ferrum Coll (VA)
Fitchburg State U (MA)
Florida Intl U (FL)
Florida State U (FL)
Fordham U (NY)
Francis Marion U (SC)
George Mason U (VA)
Georgetown U (DC)
The George Washington U (DC)
Georgia Inst of Technology (GA)
Georgia Southern U (GA)
Gettysburg Coll (PA)
Gonzaga U (WA)
Gordon Coll (MA)
Goucher Coll (MD)
Graceland U (IA)
Grand Valley State U (MI)
Hamilton Coll (NY)
Hampden-Sydney Coll (VA)
Hampshire Coll (MA)
Hastings Coll (NE)
Hawai`i Pacific U (HI)
Heidelberg U (OH)
Hendrix Coll (AR)
High Point U (NC)
Hobart and William Smith Colls (NY)
Hollins U (VA)
Howard Payne U (TX)
Illinois Coll (IL)
Illinois Wesleyan U (IL)
Immaculata U (PA)
Indiana U Bloomington (IN)
Indiana U of Pennsylvania (PA)
Indiana U–Purdue U Indianapolis (IN)
Indiana U Southeast (IN)
Iona Coll (NY)
Iowa State U of Science and Technology (IA)
Jacksonville U (FL)
James Madison U (VA)
John Brown U (AR)
John Cabot U (Italy)
John Carroll U (OH)
Johns Hopkins U (MD)
Juniata Coll (PA)
Kennesaw State U (GA)
Kent State U (OH)
Knox Coll (IL)
Lafayette Coll (PA)
Lake Forest Coll (IL)
La Roche Coll (PA)
Lawrence U (WI)
Lebanese American U (Lebanon)
Lehigh U (PA)
Lenoir-Rhyne U (NC)
Lewis & Clark Coll (OR)
Lewis U (IL)
Liberty U (VA)
Lindenwood U (MO)
Linfield Coll (OR)
Lock Haven U of Pennsylvania (PA)
Loras Coll (IA)
Loyola U Chicago (IL)
Lynchburg Coll (VA)
Manhattan Coll (NY)
Mansfield U of Pennsylvania (PA)
Marshall U (WV)
Mary Baldwin Coll (VA)
Marymount Manhattan Coll (NY)
Maryville Coll (TN)
McKendree U (IL)
Mercer U, Macon (GA)
Mercy Coll (NY)
Meredith Coll (NC)
Miami U (OH)
Michigan State U (MI)
Middlebury Coll (VT)
Middle Tennessee State U (TN)
Mills Coll (CA)
Minnesota State U Mankato (MN)
Missouri Southern State U (MO)
Morningside Coll (IA)
Mount Allison U (NB, Canada)
Mount Holyoke Coll (MA)
Mount Mercy U (IA)
Mount St. Mary's U (MD)
Muhlenberg Coll (PA)
Murray State U (KY)
Nazareth Coll of Rochester (NY)
Newberry Coll (SC)
New York U (NY)
Niagara U (NY)
Northeastern U (MA)
Northern Arizona U (AZ)
Northern Kentucky U (KY)
Northern Michigan U (MI)
Northwestern U (IL)
Northwest Nazarene U (ID)
Norwich U (VT)
Notre Dame of Maryland U (MD)
Nova Southeastern U (FL)
Oakland U (MI)
Occidental Coll (CA)
Oglethorpe U (GA)
Ohio Northern U (OH)
The Ohio State U (OH)
Ohio U (OH)
Ohio Wesleyan U (OH)
Oklahoma Baptist U (OK)
Old Dominion U (VA)
Pacific U (OR)
Penn State Abington (PA)
Penn State Altoona (PA)
Penn State Beaver (PA)
Penn State Berks (PA)
Penn State Brandywine (PA)
Penn State DuBois (PA)
Penn State Erie, The Behrend Coll (PA)
Penn State Fayette, The Eberly Campus (PA)
Penn State Greater Allegheny (PA)
Penn State Hazleton (PA)
Penn State Lehigh Valley (PA)
Penn State Mont Alto (PA)
Penn State New Kensington (PA)
Penn State Schuylkill (PA)
Penn State Shenango (PA)
Penn State U Park (PA)
Penn State Wilkes-Barre (PA)
Penn State Worthington Scranton (PA)
Penn State York (PA)
Pomona Coll (CA)
Portland State U (OR)
Quinnipiac U (CT)
Reed Coll (OR)
Regis Coll (MA)
Rhodes Coll (TN)
Rider U (NJ)
Roanoke Coll (VA)
Rochester Inst of Technology (NY)
Rockhurst U (MO)
Rollins Coll (FL)
Roosevelt U (IL)
The Sage Colls (NY)
Saginaw Valley State U (MI)
Saint Anselm Coll (NH)
St. Catherine U (MN)
Saint Francis U (PA)
St. John Fisher Coll (NY)
Saint Joseph's Coll (IN)
Saint Joseph's U (PA)
Saint Louis U (MO)
St. Mary's U (TX)
Saint Michael's Coll (VT)
St. Norbert Coll (WI)
St. Thomas U (NB, Canada)
Salem Coll (NC)
Samford U (AL)
San Diego State U (CA)
San Francisco State U (CA)
Seton Hill U (PA)
Shawnee State U (OH)
Shaw U (NC)
Simmons Coll (MA)
Simpson Coll (IA)
Skidmore Coll (NY)
Southern Oregon U (OR)
Southwestern U (TX)
Spelman Coll (GA)
Spring Hill Coll (AL)
Stanford U (CA)
State U of New York at New Paltz (NY)
State U of New York at Oswego (NY)
State U of New York Coll at Cortland (NY)
State U of New York Coll at Geneseo (NY)
Stetson U (FL)
Syracuse U (NY)
Taylor U (IN)
Temple U (PA)
Texas Christian U (TX)

Texas State U (TX)
Tiffin U (OH)
Towson U (MD)
Trent U (ON, Canada)
Trinity Coll (CT)
Trinity U (TX)
Tufts U (MA)
Tulane U (LA)
United States Military Acad (NY)
The U of Alabama (AL)
U of Arkansas (AR)
U of Bridgeport (CT)
The U of British Columbia (BC, Canada)
The U of British Columbia–Okanagan Campus (BC, Canada)
U of California, Davis (CA)
U of Chicago (IL)
U of Cincinnati (OH)
U of Delaware (DE)
U of Denver (CO)
U of Evansville (IN)
U of Georgia (GA)
U of Hartford (CT)
U of Idaho (ID)
U of Indianapolis (IN)
U of La Verne (CA)
U of Maine (ME)
U of Mary Washington (VA)
U of Memphis (TN)
U of Miami (FL)
U of Minnesota, Duluth (MN)
U of Minnesota, Twin Cities Campus (MN)
U of Mississippi (MS)
U of Mount Union (OH)
U of Nebraska at Kearney (NE)
U of Nevada, Reno (NV)
U of New Brunswick Saint John (NB, Canada)
U of North Georgia (GA)
U of Ottawa (ON, Canada)
U of Pennsylvania (PA)
U of Richmond (VA)
U of Rochester (NY)
U of St. Thomas (TX)
U of San Diego (CA)
U of San Francisco (CA)
The U of Scranton (PA)
U of Southern California (CA)
U of Southern Indiana (IN)
U of Southern Mississippi (MS)
U of South Florida (FL)
The U of Tennessee at Martin (TN)
The U of Texas at San Antonio (TX)
U of the Incarnate Word (TX)
U of the Pacific (CA)
The U of Toledo (OH)
U of Toronto (ON, Canada)
U of Virginia (VA)
U of Waterloo (ON, Canada)
The U of Western Ontario (ON, Canada)
U of West Florida (FL)
U of West Georgia (GA)
U of Windsor (ON, Canada)
U of Wisconsin–Oshkosh (WI)
U of Wisconsin–Parkside (WI)
U of Wisconsin–Stevens Point (WI)
U of Wisconsin–Superior (WI)
Ursinus Coll (PA)
Utica Coll (NY)
Valparaiso U (IN)
Vassar Coll (NY)
Virginia Military Inst (VA)
Virginia Polytechnic Inst and State U (VA)
Virginia Wesleyan Coll (VA)
Wagner Coll (NY)
Walsh U (OH)
Wartburg Coll (IA)
Washington Coll (MD)
Washington U in St. Louis (MO)
Webster U (MO)
Wells Coll (NY)
Wesleyan Coll (GA)
Western Kentucky U (KY)
Western Oregon U (OR)
Westminster Coll (MO)
West Virginia Wesleyan Coll (WV)
Wheaton Coll (IL)
Wheaton Coll (MA)
Wheeling Jesuit U (WV)
Whitworth U (WA)
Widener U (PA)
Wilkes U (PA)
William Jewell Coll (MO)
Wittenberg U (OH)
Wright State U (OH)
Xavier U (OH)
Yale U (CT)
York Coll of Pennsylvania (PA)

INTERNATIONAL RELATIONS AND NATIONAL SECURITY RELATED
San Diego State U (CA)
U of Mount Union (OH)

INVESTMENTS AND SECURITIES
Babson Coll (MA)
Johnson & Wales U (RI)
Lynn U (FL)
Marymount Manhattan Coll (NY)
U of Nebraska–Lincoln (NE)
U of North Dakota (ND)

IRANIAN LANGUAGES
National U (CA)
U of Maryland, Coll Park (MD)
The U of Texas at Austin (TX)
U of Utah (UT)
Washington U in St. Louis (MO)

IRISH STUDIES
Bard Coll (NY)
Canisius Coll (NY)
Sacred Heart U (CT)

ISLAMIC STUDIES
Boston Coll (MA)
DePaul U (IL)
The Ohio State U (OH)
U of Minnesota, Twin Cities Campus (MN)
The U of Texas at Austin (TX)
U of Washington (WA)
The U of Western Ontario (ON, Canada)
Villanova U (PA)
Washington U in St. Louis (MO)

ITALIAN
The American U of Rome (Italy)
Arizona State U at the Tempe campus (AZ)
Bard Coll (NY)
Barnard Coll (NY)
Bennington Coll (VT)
Binghamton U, State U of New York (NY)
Boston Coll (MA)
Boston U (MA)
Brown U (RI)
Bryn Mawr Coll (PA)
California State U, Long Beach (CA)
Central Connecticut State U (CT)
Coll of Staten Island of the City U of New York (NY)
Coll of the Holy Cross (MA)
The Colorado Coll (CO)
Columbia U (NY)
Columbia U, School of General Studies (NY)
Concordia U (QC, Canada)
Connecticut Coll (CT)
Cornell U (NY)
Dartmouth Coll (NH)
DePaul U (IL)
Dominican U (IL)
Fairfield U (CT)
Florida Intl U (FL)
Fordham U (NY)
Georgetown U (DC)
Gettysburg Coll (PA)
Gonzaga U (WA)
Haverford Coll (PA)
Hofstra U (NY)
Hunter Coll of the City U of New York (NY)
Indiana U Bloomington (IN)
Iona Coll (NY)
Ithaca Coll (NY)
Johns Hopkins U (MD)
Lake Erie Coll (OH)
La Salle U (PA)
Lehman Coll of the City U of New York (NY)
Long Island U–LIU Post (NY)
Loyola U Chicago (IL)
Marist Coll (NY)
Middlebury Coll (VT)
Montclair State U (NJ)
Mount Holyoke Coll (MA)
Nazareth Coll of Rochester (NY)
New York U (NY)
Northwestern U (IL)
The Ohio State U (OH)
Penn State Abington (PA)
Penn State Altoona (PA)
Penn State Beaver (PA)
Penn State Berks (PA)
Penn State Brandywine (PA)
Penn State DuBois (PA)
Penn State Erie, The Behrend Coll (PA)
Penn State Fayette, The Eberly Campus (PA)
Penn State Greater Allegheny (PA)
Penn State Hazleton (PA)
Penn State Lehigh Valley (PA)
Penn State Mont Alto (PA)
Penn State New Kensington (PA)
Penn State Schuylkill (PA)
Penn State Shenango (PA)
Penn State U Park (PA)
Penn State Wilkes-Barre (PA)
Penn State Worthington Scranton (PA)
Penn State York (PA)
Pepperdine U, Malibu (CA)
Providence Coll (RI)
Queens Coll of the City U of New York (NY)
Rutgers, The State U of New Jersey, Newark (NJ)
Rutgers, The State U of New Jersey, New Brunswick (NJ)
St. John's U (NY)
Saint Joseph's U (PA)
Saint Louis U (MO)
Saint Mary's Coll (IN)
San Francisco State U (CA)
Santa Clara U (CA)
Scripps Coll (CA)
Smith Coll (MA)
Southern Connecticut State U (CT)
Stanford U (CA)
Stony Brook U, State U of New York (NY)
Susquehanna U (PA)
Syracuse U (NY)
Temple U (PA)
Trinity Coll (CT)
Tufts U (MA)
Tulane U (LA)
U at Buffalo, the State U of New York (NY)
U of Alberta (AB, Canada)
The U of Arizona (AZ)
The U of British Columbia (BC, Canada)
U of California, Berkeley (CA)
U of California, Davis (CA)
U of California, Los Angeles (CA)
U of Colorado Boulder (CO)
U of Delaware (DE)
U of Denver (CO)
U of Georgia (GA)
U of Houston (TX)
U of Illinois at Chicago (IL)
The U of Iowa (IA)
U of Maryland, Coll Park (MD)
U of Massachusetts Amherst (MA)
U of Massachusetts Boston (MA)
U of Michigan (MI)
U of Minnesota, Twin Cities Campus (MN)
U of Notre Dame (IN)
U of Oklahoma (OK)
U of Oregon (OR)
U of Ottawa (ON, Canada)
U of Pennsylvania (PA)
U of Pittsburgh (PA)
U of Rhode Island (RI)
The U of Scranton (PA)
U of Southern California (CA)
U of South Florida (FL)
The U of Tennessee (TN)
The U of Texas at Austin (TX)
U of Toronto (ON, Canada)
U of Virginia (VA)
U of Washington (WA)
The U of Western Ontario (ON, Canada)
U of Windsor (ON, Canada)
U of Wisconsin–Madison (WI)
U of Wisconsin–Milwaukee (WI)
Vassar Coll (NY)
Villanova U (PA)
Washington U in St. Louis (MO)
Yale U (CT)
York Coll of the City U of New York (NY)
Youngstown State U (OH)

ITALIAN STUDIES
Arcadia U (PA)
Assumption Coll (MA)
Bard Coll (NY)
Boston U (MA)
Brown U (RI)
Coll of the Holy Cross (MA)
The Colorado Coll (CO)
Columbia U (NY)
Columbia U, School of General Studies (NY)
Dalhousie U (NS, Canada)
Dickinson Coll (PA)
Fordham U (NY)
John Cabot U (Italy)
Merrimack Coll (MA)
Miami U (OH)
Purdue U (IN)
Saint Joseph's U (PA)
Scripps Coll (CA)
Southern Methodist U (TX)
Tufts U (MA)
Tulane U (LA)
U of Alberta (AB, Canada)
U of California, Santa Barbara (CA)
U of California, Santa Cruz (CA)
U of Richmond (VA)
U of San Diego (CA)
The U of Scranton (PA)
U of Vermont (VT)
The U of Western Ontario (ON, Canada)
U of Windsor (ON, Canada)
Wesleyan U (CT)
Wheaton Coll (MA)

JAPANESE
Ball State U (IN)
Bard Coll (NY)
Bates Coll (ME)
Beloit Coll (WI)
Bennington Coll (VT)
Boston U (MA)
California State U, Fullerton (CA)
California State U, Long Beach (CA)
California State U, Los Angeles (CA)
California State U, Monterey Bay (CA)
Calvin Coll (MI)
Central Washington U (WA)
Connecticut Coll (CT)
Dartmouth Coll (NH)
Eastern Michigan U (MI)
Elizabethtown Coll (PA)
Georgetown U (DC)
Gettysburg Coll (PA)
Gustavus Adolphus Coll (MN)
Hobart and William Smith Colls (NY)
Hofstra U (NY)
Lawrence U (WI)
Linfield Coll (OR)
Macalester Coll (MN)
Michigan State U (MI)
Middlebury Coll (VT)
Murray State U (KY)
North Central Coll (IL)
Oakland U (MI)
Occidental Coll (CA)
The Ohio State U (OH)
Pacific U (OR)
Penn State Abington (PA)
Penn State Altoona (PA)
Penn State Beaver (PA)
Penn State Berks (PA)
Penn State Brandywine (PA)
Penn State DuBois (PA)
Penn State Erie, The Behrend Coll (PA)
Penn State Fayette, The Eberly Campus (PA)
Penn State Greater Allegheny (PA)
Penn State Hazleton (PA)
Penn State Lehigh Valley (PA)
Penn State Mont Alto (PA)
Penn State New Kensington (PA)
Penn State Schuylkill (PA)
Penn State Shenango (PA)
Penn State U Park (PA)
Penn State Wilkes-Barre (PA)
Penn State Worthington Scranton (PA)
Penn State York (PA)
Pomona Coll (CA)
Portland State U (OR)
Purdue U (IN)
San Diego State U (CA)
San Francisco State U (CA)
San Jose State U (CA)
Scripps Coll (CA)
Stanford U (CA)
Temple U (PA)
Trinity Coll (CT)
Tufts U (MA)
U of Alaska Fairbanks (AK)
U of Alberta (AB, Canada)
U of California, Berkeley (CA)
U of California, Davis (CA)
U of California, Irvine (CA)
U of California, Los Angeles (CA)
U of California, Santa Barbara (CA)
U of Colorado Boulder (CO)
The U of Findlay (OH)
U of Georgia (GA)
U of Hawaii at Hilo (HI)
U of Hawaii at Manoa (HI)
The U of Iowa (IA)
U of Kentucky (KY)
U of Maryland, Coll Park (MD)
U of Massachusetts Amherst (MA)
U of Minnesota, Twin Cities Campus (MN)
The U of Montana (MT)
U of Mount Union (OH)
The U of North Carolina at Charlotte (NC)
U of Notre Dame (IN)
U of Oregon (OR)
U of Pittsburgh (PA)
U of Puget Sound (WA)
U of Regina (SK, Canada)
U of Rochester (NY)
U of San Francisco (CA)
U of the Pacific (CA)
U of Utah (UT)
U of Vermont (VT)
U of Washington (WA)
The U of Western Ontario (ON, Canada)
U of Wisconsin–Madison (WI)
Vassar Coll (NY)
Wake Forest U (NC)
Washington U in St. Louis (MO)
Western Michigan U (MI)
Western Washington U (WA)
Williams Coll (MA)
Yale U (CT)

JAPANESE STUDIES
Case Western Reserve U (OH)
Earlham Coll (IN)
Gettysburg Coll (PA)
Gustavus Adolphus Coll (MN)
Hofstra U (NY)
Hope Coll (MI)
Linfield Coll (OR)
U at Albany, State U of New York (NY)
U of Alberta (AB, Canada)
U of Hawaii at Hilo (HI)
U of San Francisco (CA)
U of Washington (WA)
U of Wisconsin–Whitewater (WI)
Willamette U (OR)

JAZZ/JAZZ STUDIES
Ashland U (OH)
Bard Coll (NY)
Bennington Coll (VT)
Bowling Green State U (OH)
Brigham Young U (UT)
Butler U (IN)
Capital U (OH)
Central State U (OH)
Central Washington U (WA)
City Coll of the City U of New York (NY)
Concordia U (QC, Canada)
Cornish Coll of the Arts (WA)
DePaul U (IL)
Drake U (IA)
Five Towns Coll (NY)
Florida State U (FL)
Hampton U (VA)
Hofstra U (NY)
Hope Coll (MI)

Ithaca Coll (NY)
Johnson State Coll (VT)
Liberty U (VA)
Limestone Coll (SC)
Loyola U New Orleans (LA)
Manhattan School of Music (NY)
Michigan State U (MI)
Minnesota State U Moorhead (MN)
New England Conservatory of Music (MA)
North Carolina Central U (NC)
North Central Coll (IL)
Northwestern U (IL)
Oberlin Coll (OH)
The Ohio State U (OH)
Peabody Conservatory of The Johns Hopkins U (MD)
Roosevelt U (IL)
Rutgers, The State U of New Jersey, New Brunswick (NJ)
Shenandoah U (VA)
Temple U (PA)
Texas State U (TX)
Université de Montréal (QC, Canada)
The U of Akron (OH)
U of Hartford (CT)
The U of Iowa (IA)
U of Miami (FL)
U of Michigan (MI)
U of Missouri–Kansas City (MO)
The U of North Carolina at Greensboro (NC)
U of North Florida (FL)
U of North Texas (TX)
U of Oregon (OR)
U of Rochester (NY)
U of Southern California (CA)
The U of Texas at Austin (TX)
U of Washington (WA)
Villa Maria Coll (NY)
Webster U (MO)
Western Michigan U (MI)
William Paterson U of New Jersey (NJ)
Youngstown State U (OH)

JEWISH/JUDAIC STUDIES
American U (DC)
Arizona State U at the Tempe campus (AZ)
Bard Coll (NY)
Barnard Coll (NY)
Bennington Coll (VT)
Binghamton U, State U of New York (NY)
Brown U (RI)
City Coll of the City U of New York (NY)
Clark U (MA)
Coll of Charleston (SC)
Concordia U (QC, Canada)
DePaul U (IL)
Dickinson Coll (PA)
Florida Atlantic U (FL)
The George Washington U (DC)
Gettysburg Coll (PA)
Hofstra U (NY)
Hunter Coll of the City U of New York (NY)
Indiana U Bloomington (IN)
Lehman Coll of the City U of New York (NY)
Northeastern U (MA)
Oberlin Coll (OH)
The Ohio State U (OH)
Penn State Abington (PA)
Penn State Altoona (PA)
Penn State Beaver (PA)
Penn State Berks (PA)
Penn State Brandywine (PA)
Penn State DuBois (PA)
Penn State Erie, The Behrend Coll (PA)
Penn State Fayette, The Eberly Campus (PA)
Penn State Greater Allegheny (PA)
Penn State Hazleton (PA)
Penn State Lehigh Valley (PA)
Penn State Mont Alto (PA)
Penn State New Kensington (PA)
Penn State Schuylkill (PA)
Penn State Shenango (PA)
Penn State U Park (PA)
Penn State Wilkes-Barre (PA)
Penn State Worthington Scranton (PA)
Penn State York (PA)
Purdue U (IN)
Queens Coll of the City U of New York (NY)
Rutgers, The State U of New Jersey, New Brunswick (NJ)
San Diego State U (CA)
San Francisco State U (CA)
Scripps Coll (CA)
Syracuse U (NY)
Temple U (PA)
Trinity Coll (CT)
Tufts U (MA)
Tulane U (LA)
U at Buffalo, the State U of New York (NY)
The U of Arizona (AZ)
U of California, Los Angeles (CA)
U of Chicago (IL)
U of Colorado Boulder (CO)
U of Florida (FL)
U of Hartford (CT)
U of Maryland, Coll Park (MD)
U of Massachusetts Amherst (MA)
U of Miami (FL)
U of Michigan (MI)
U of Minnesota, Twin Cities Campus (MN)
U of Oklahoma (OK)
U of Oregon (OR)
U of Pennsylvania (PA)
U of Southern California (CA)
The U of Texas at Austin (TX)
U of Washington (WA)
The U of Western Ontario (ON, Canada)
U of Wisconsin–Madison (WI)
U of Wisconsin–Milwaukee (WI)
Vanderbilt U (TN)
Vassar Coll (NY)
Washington U in St. Louis (MO)
Yale U (CT)
Yeshiva U (NY)

JOURNALISM
Abilene Christian U (TX)
Acad of Art U (CA)
American U (DC)
American U in Bulgaria (Bulgaria)
The American U in Cairo (Egypt)
The American U in Dubai (United Arab Emirates)
Andrews U (MI)
Angelo State U (TX)
Appalachian State U (NC)
Arkansas Tech U (AR)
Asbury U (KY)
Ashland U (OH)
Auburn U (AL)
Augustana Coll (SD)
Averett U (VA)
Ball State U (IN)
Barry U (FL)
Baruch Coll of the City U of New York (NY)
Baylor U (TX)
Belmont U (TN)
Bemidji State U (MN)
Benedictine Coll (KS)
Bethel U (MN)
Biola U (CA)
Boston U (MA)
Bowling Green State U (OH)
Bradley U (IL)
Brigham Young U (UT)
Buffalo State Coll, State U of New York (NY)
Butler U (IN)
California Baptist U (CA)
California Lutheran U (CA)
California Polytechnic State U, San Luis Obispo (CA)
California State U, Chico (CA)
California State U, Dominguez Hills (CA)
California State U, Fresno (CA)
California State U, Fullerton (CA)
California State U, Long Beach (CA)
California State U, Sacramento (CA)
Campbellsville U (KY)
Canisius Coll (NY)
Carson-Newman U (TN)
Castleton State Coll (VT)
Cedarville U (OH)
Central Connecticut State U (CT)
Central Michigan U (MI)
Central State U (OH)
Central Washington U (WA)
Chatham U (PA)
Cincinnati Christian U (OH)
Cleveland State U (OH)
The Coll of St. Scholastica (MN)
Coll of the Ozarks (MO)
Colorado State U (CO)
Columbia Coll (SC)
Columbia Coll Chicago (IL)
Concordia U (QC, Canada)
Concordia U Chicago (IL)
Concordia U, St. Paul (MN)
Corban U (OR)
Cornerstone U (MI)
Creighton U (NE)
Delaware State U (DE)
Delta State U (MS)
DePaul U (IL)
Doane Coll (NE)
Dominican U (IL)
Drake U (IA)
Drury U (MO)
Duquesne U (PA)
East Central U (OK)
Eastern Illinois U (IL)
Eastern Kentucky U (KY)
Eastern Michigan U (MI)
Edinboro U of Pennsylvania (PA)
Elon U (NC)
Emerson Coll (MA)
Five Towns Coll (NY)
Florida Ag and Mech U (FL)
Fort Hays State U (KS)
Franklin Coll (IN)
Franklin Pierce U (NH)
Gannon U (PA)
The George Washington U (DC)
Georgia Coll & State U (GA)
Georgia Southern U (GA)
Georgia State U (GA)
Gettysburg Coll (PA)
Gonzaga U (WA)
Goshen Coll (IN)
Grace Coll (IN)
Grand Valley State U (MI)
Grand View U (IA)
Hampton U (VA)
Harding U (AR)
Hastings Coll (NE)
Hawai`i Pacific U (HI)
Hofstra U (NY)
Howard U (DC)
Humboldt State U (CA)
Illinois State U (IL)
Indiana U Bloomington (IN)
Indiana U of Pennsylvania (PA)
Indiana U–Purdue U Indianapolis (IN)
Indiana U Southeast (IN)
Iona Coll (NY)
Iowa State U of Science and Technology (IA)
Ithaca Coll (NY)
John Brown U (AR)
Johnson State Coll (VT)
Kansas State U (KS)
Keene State Coll (NH)
Kent State U (OH)
Langston U (OK)
La Salle U (PA)
Lasell Coll (MA)
Lebanese American U (Lebanon)
Lee U (TN)
Lehigh U (PA)
Lewis U (IL)
Liberty U (VA)
Lincoln U (MO)
Lincoln U (PA)
Lindenwood U (MO)
Lock Haven U of Pennsylvania (PA)
Long Island U–LIU Brooklyn (NY)
Long Island U–LIU Post (NY)
Louisiana Coll (LA)
Loyola U Chicago (IL)
Lubbock Christian U (TX)
Lynn U (FL)
Madonna U (MI)
Mansfield U of Pennsylvania (PA)
Marietta Coll (OH)
Marquette U (WI)
Marshall U (WV)
Marymount Manhattan Coll (NY)
Massachusetts Coll of Liberal Arts (MA)
Mercer U, Macon (GA)
Mercy Coll (NY)
Messiah Coll (PA)
Miami U (OH)
Michigan State U (MI)
Minnesota State U Mankato (MN)
Minnesota State U Moorhead (MN)
Missouri State U (MO)
Mount Mercy U (IA)
Mount Saint Mary's U (CA)
Mount Vernon Nazarene U (OH)
Murray State U (KY)
New England Coll (NH)
New Mexico State U (NM)
New York U (NY)
Norfolk State U (VA)
North Carolina Ag and Tech State U (NC)
North Central Coll (IL)
Northeastern U (MA)
Northern Arizona U (AZ)
Northern Illinois U (IL)
Northern Kentucky U (KY)
North Greenville U (SC)
Northwestern Coll (IA)
Northwestern U (IL)
Oakland U (MI)
Ohio Northern U (OH)
The Ohio State U (OH)
Ohio U (OH)
Ohio Wesleyan U (OH)
Oklahoma Baptist U (OK)
Oklahoma Christian U (OK)
Oklahoma State U (OK)
Olivet Coll (MI)
Pace U (NY)
Pacific U (OR)
Palm Beach Atlantic U (FL)
Patrick Henry Coll (VA)
Penn State Abington (PA)
Penn State Altoona (PA)
Penn State Beaver (PA)
Penn State Berks (PA)
Penn State Brandywine (PA)
Penn State DuBois (PA)
Penn State Erie, The Behrend Coll (PA)
Penn State Fayette, The Eberly Campus (PA)
Penn State Greater Allegheny (PA)
Penn State Hazleton (PA)
Penn State Lehigh Valley (PA)
Penn State Mont Alto (PA)
Penn State New Kensington (PA)
Penn State Schuylkill (PA)
Penn State Shenango (PA)
Penn State U Park (PA)
Penn State Wilkes-Barre (PA)
Penn State Worthington Scranton (PA)
Penn State York (PA)
Pepperdine U, Malibu (CA)
Point Loma Nazarene U (CA)
Purchase Coll, State U of New York (NY)
Quinnipiac U (CT)
Radford U (VA)
Rider U (NJ)
Rochester Inst of Technology (NY)
Roosevelt U (IL)
Rowan U (NJ)
Rust Coll (MS)
Rutgers, The State U of New Jersey, Newark (NJ)
Rutgers, The State U of New Jersey, New Brunswick (NJ)
Saint Augustine's U (NC)
St. Bonaventure U (NY)
St. Catherine U (MN)
Saint Francis U (PA)
St. John's U (NY)
St. Joseph's Coll, Long Island Campus (NY)
St. Joseph's Coll, New York (NY)
Saint Mary's U of Minnesota (MN)
St. Thomas Aquinas Coll (NY)
St. Thomas U (NB, Canada)
Samford U (AL)
San Diego State U (CA)
San Francisco State U (CA)
San Jose State U (CA)
Savannah State U (GA)
Seattle U (WA)
Seton Hill U (PA)
Shippensburg U of Pennsylvania (PA)
Slippery Rock U of Pennsylvania (PA)
South Dakota State U (SD)
Southeastern U (FL)
Southern Adventist U (TN)
Southern Arkansas U–Magnolia (AR)
Southern Connecticut State U (CT)
Southern Illinois U Carbondale (IL)
Southern Methodist U (TX)
Southwestern Adventist U (TX)
Southwestern Coll (KS)
Spring Hill Coll (AL)
State U of New York at New Paltz (NY)
State U of New York at Oswego (NY)
State U of New York at Plattsburgh (NY)
Stony Brook U, State U of New York (NY)
Suffolk U (MA)
Syracuse U (NY)
Temple U (PA)
Texas A&M U–Commerce (TX)
Texas Christian U (TX)
Texas Southern U (TX)
Texas State U (TX)
Texas Tech U (TX)
Texas Wesleyan U (TX)
Tiffin U (OH)
Trent U (ON, Canada)
Trevecca Nazarene U (TN)
Troy U (AL)
Union U (TN)
U at Albany, State U of New York (NY)
The U of Alabama (AL)
U of Alaska Fairbanks (AK)
The U of Arizona (AZ)
U of Arkansas (AR)
U of Arkansas at Little Rock (AR)
U of Bridgeport (CT)
U of Central Arkansas (AR)
U of Central Florida (FL)
U of Central Missouri (MO)
U of Central Oklahoma (OK)
U of Cincinnati (OH)
U of Denver (CO)
The U of Findlay (OH)
U of Florida (FL)
U of Georgia (GA)
U of Hawaii at Manoa (HI)
U of Houston (TX)
U of Idaho (ID)
The U of Iowa (IA)
The U of Kansas (KS)
U of Kentucky (KY)
U of King's Coll (NS, Canada)
U of La Verne (CA)
U of Maine (ME)
U of Maryland, Coll Park (MD)
U of Massachusetts Amherst (MA)
U of Memphis (TN)
U of Miami (FL)
U of Minnesota, Twin Cities Campus (MN)
U of Mississippi (MS)
U of Missouri (MO)
The U of Montana (MT)
U of Nebraska at Kearney (NE)
U of Nevada, Reno (NV)
U of New Mexico (NM)
The U of North Carolina at Chapel Hill (NC)
U of Northern Colorado (CO)
U of North Texas (TX)
U of Northwestern–St. Paul (MN)
U of Oklahoma (OK)
U of Oregon (OR)
U of Ottawa (ON, Canada)
U of Pittsburgh at Greensburg (PA)
U of Regina (SK, Canada)
U of Rhode Island (RI)
U of Richmond (VA)
U of Southern California (CA)
U of Southern Indiana (IN)
U of Southern Mississippi (MS)
The U of Tennessee (TN)
The U of Texas at Arlington (TX)
The U of Texas at Austin (TX)
The U of Texas at El Paso (TX)
U of the Cumberlands (KY)
U of the Incarnate Word (TX)
The U of Toledo (OH)
U of Washington (WA)
U of West Georgia (GA)
U of Wisconsin–Eau Claire (WI)
U of Wisconsin–Madison (WI)

U of Wisconsin–Oshkosh (WI)
U of Wisconsin–River Falls (WI)
U of Wisconsin–Superior (WI)
U of Wisconsin–Whitewater (WI)
U of Wyoming (WY)
Utah State U (UT)
Utica Coll (NY)
Virginia Union U (VA)
Walla Walla U (WA)
Wartburg Coll (IA)
Washington and Lee U (VA)
Washington State U (WA)
Waynesburg U (PA)
Wayne State U (MI)
Weber State U (UT)
Webster U (MO)
Western Illinois U (IL)
Western Kentucky U (KY)
Western Michigan U (MI)
Western New England U (MA)
Western Washington U (WA)
West Texas A&M U (TX)
West Virginia U (WV)
Whitworth U (WA)
Winona State U (MN)
Youngstown State U (OH)

JOURNALISM RELATED
Arizona State U at the Downtown Phoenix campus (AZ)
Arkansas State U (AR)
Benedictine U (IL)
Bennett Coll (NC)
Bowling Green State U (OH)
California State U, Long Beach (CA)
Calvary Bible Coll and Theological Sem (MO)
Central Michigan U (MI)
Concordia Coll (MN)
Kentucky State U (KY)
Missouri Baptist U (MO)
National U (CA)
Oklahoma State U (OK)
Roosevelt U (IL)
Simpson Coll (IA)
Southern Adventist U (TN)
The U of Akron (OH)
U of California, Irvine (CA)
U of Colorado Boulder (CO)
U of Nebraska–Lincoln (NE)
U of St. Thomas (MN)
Webster U (MO)
Western Washington U (WA)

JUVENILE CORRECTIONS
Harris-Stowe State U (MO)
Missouri Southern State U (MO)
Oakland U (MI)
U of Central Oklahoma (OK)

KEYBOARD INSTRUMENTS
Abilene Christian U (TX)
Andrews U (MI)
Anna Maria Coll (MA)
Ashland U (OH)
Baldwin Wallace U (OH)
Barry U (FL)
Birmingham-Southern Coll (AL)
Bob Jones U (SC)
Bowling Green State U (OH)
Brigham Young U (UT)
California Baptist U (CA)
Calvary Bible Coll and Theological Sem (MO)
Campbellsville U (KY)
Capital U (OH)
Carson-Newman U (TN)
The Catholic U of America (DC)
Central Washington U (WA)
Chapman U (CA)
Cincinnati Christian U (OH)
Coker Coll (SC)
The Colburn School Conservatory of Music (CA)
Coll of the Ozarks (MO)
Columbia Coll (SC)
Concordia U, Nebraska (NE)
Cornish Coll of the Arts (WA)
Dallas Baptist U (TX)
Drake U (IA)
East Central U (OK)
East Texas Baptist U (TX)
Furman U (SC)
Hardin-Simmons U (TX)
Hastings Coll (NE)
Heidelberg U (OH)
Hillsdale Free Will Baptist Coll (OK)
Hope Coll (MI)
Houghton Coll (NY)
Howard Payne U (TX)
Illinois Wesleyan U (IL)
Indiana U–Purdue U Fort Wayne (IN)
Ithaca Coll (NY)
Lawrence U (WI)
Liberty U (VA)
Lipscomb U (TN)
Louisiana Coll (LA)
Madonna U (MI)
Manhattan School of Music (NY)
Maryville Coll (TN)
The Master's Coll and Sem (CA)
Mount Allison U (NB, Canada)
New England Conservatory of Music (MA)
New York U (NY)
Northwestern U (IL)
Nyack Coll (NY)
Oakland U (MI)
Oberlin Coll (OH)
The Ohio State U (OH)
Ohio U (OH)
Oklahoma City U (OK)
Palm Beach Atlantic U (FL)
Peabody Conservatory of The Johns Hopkins U (MD)
Point Loma Nazarene U (CA)
Rider U (NJ)
Roberts Wesleyan Coll (NY)
Roosevelt U (IL)
Samford U (AL)
San Francisco Conservatory of Music (CA)
Shenandoah U (VA)
Southeastern U (FL)
Southern Methodist U (TX)
State U of New York at Fredonia (NY)
Stetson U (FL)
Summit U (PA)
Syracuse U (NY)
Texas Christian U (TX)
Union U (TN)
The U of Akron (OH)
U of Alberta (AB, Canada)
The U of British Columbia (BC, Canada)
U of Central Oklahoma (OK)
U of Cincinnati (OH)
U of Delaware (DE)
The U of Iowa (IA)
The U of Kansas (KS)
U of Miami (FL)
U of Northwestern–St. Paul (MN)
U of Southern California (CA)
The U of Tennessee at Martin (TN)
U of the Pacific (CA)
The U of Tulsa (OK)
U of Washington (WA)
The U of Western Ontario (ON, Canada)
Valparaiso U (IN)
Vanderbilt U (TN)
Walla Walla U (WA)
Weber State U (UT)
Western Michigan U (MI)
Whitworth U (WA)
Willamette U (OR)
Xavier U of Louisiana (LA)
Youngstown State U (OH)

KINDERGARTEN/PRESCHOOL EDUCATION
Albright Coll (PA)
Alma Coll (MI)
Appalachian State U (NC)
Arcadia U (PA)
Ashland U (OH)
Athens State U (AL)
Ball State U (IN)
Barry U (FL)
Baylor U (TX)
Becker Coll (MA)
Black Hills State U (SD)
Bluefield Coll (VA)
Bluffton U (OH)
Bowie State U (MD)
Bowling Green State U (OH)
Bucknell U (PA)
Buffalo State Coll, State U of New York (NY)
Butler U (IN)
Cabrini Coll (PA)
Cairn U (PA)
California Polytechnic State U, San Luis Obispo (CA)
California U of Pennsylvania (PA)
Carson-Newman U (TN)
Catawba Coll (NC)
Central Methodist U (MO)
Cincinnati Christian U (OH)
The Coll of Saint Rose (NY)
Columbia Coll Chicago (IL)
Concordia U (QC, Canada)
Concordia U, Nebraska (NE)
Concordia U Wisconsin (WI)
Concord U (WV)
Delaware State U (DE)
East Carolina U (NC)
Eastern Connecticut State U (CT)
Eastern Illinois U (IL)
Elmhurst Coll (IL)
Erskine Coll (SC)
Evangel U (MO)
Fontbonne U (MO)
Fort Hays State U (KS)
Furman U (SC)
Georgia State U (GA)
Greensboro Coll (NC)
Hampton U (VA)
Houston Baptist U (TX)
Howard U (DC)
Humboldt State U (CA)
Hunter Coll of the City U of New York (NY)
Inter American U of Puerto Rico, Aguadilla Campus (PR)
Inter American U of Puerto Rico, Guayama Campus (PR)
Inter American U of Puerto Rico, Ponce Campus (PR)
Inter American U of Puerto Rico, San Germán Campus (PR)
Jacksonville State U (AL)
Jarvis Christian Coll (TX)
John Brown U (AR)
John Carroll U (OH)
Kean U (NJ)
Lasell Coll (MA)
Lees-McRae Coll (NC)
Lesley U (MA)
Lincoln Memorial U (TN)
Lincoln U (PA)
Lock Haven U of Pennsylvania (PA)
Long Island U–LIU Post (NY)
Louisiana Coll (LA)
Mansfield U of Pennsylvania (PA)
Marshall U (WV)
Martin Luther Coll (MN)
Michigan State U (MI)
Middle Tennessee State U (TN)
Minnesota State U Mankato (MN)
Mississippi Valley State U (MS)
National U Coll, Bayamón (PR)
New Jersey City U (NJ)
New Mexico Highlands U (NM)
Norfolk State U (VA)
North Carolina Ag and Tech State U (NC)
North Carolina Central U (NC)
Northeastern Illinois U (IL)
Northern Illinois U (IL)
Northern Kentucky U (KY)
Northwestern Oklahoma State U (OK)
Ohio Dominican U (OH)
Ohio Northern U (OH)
Ohio Wesleyan U (OH)
Oklahoma Baptist U (OK)
Oklahoma Christian U (OK)
Olivet Nazarene U (IL)
Our Lady of the Lake U of San Antonio (TX)
Pacific U (OR)
Peru State Coll (NE)
Philander Smith Coll (AR)
Piedmont Coll (GA)
Post U (CT)
St. Catherine U (MN)
St. Thomas Aquinas Coll (NY)
Shaw U (NC)
Shepherd U (WV)
Siena Heights U (MI)
Silver Lake Coll of the Holy Family (WI)
South Dakota State U (SD)
Southeastern Oklahoma State U (OK)
Southwest Minnesota State U (MN)
State U of New York at Fredonia (NY)
State U of New York Coll at Cortland (NY)
State U of New York Coll at Potsdam (NY)
State U of New York Coll of Agriculture and Technology at Cobleskill (NY)
Susquehanna U (PA)
Tennessee State U (TN)
Texas A&M Intl U (TX)
Tufts U (MA)
Union U (TN)
Universidad Metropolitana (PR)
Université de Montréal (QC, Canada)
Université de Sherbrooke (QC, Canada)
Université du Québec en Outaouais (QC, Canada)
The U of Arizona (AZ)
U of Arkansas (AR)
U of Arkansas at Pine Bluff (AR)
The U of British Columbia (BC, Canada)
U of Central Arkansas (AR)
U of Central Oklahoma (OK)
U of Georgia (GA)
U of Great Falls (MT)
U of Maryland, Coll Park (MD)
U of Minnesota, Crookston (MN)
U of Minnesota, Duluth (MN)
U of Minnesota, Twin Cities Campus (MN)
U of Missouri (MO)
The U of North Carolina at Charlotte (NC)
The U of North Carolina at Pembroke (NC)
The U of North Carolina Wilmington (NC)
U of Northern Iowa (IA)
U of Regina (SK, Canada)
U of South Carolina Upstate (SC)
The U of Tennessee at Martin (TN)
U of the District of Columbia (DC)
U of Vermont (VT)
U of Windsor (ON, Canada)
U of Wisconsin–Oshkosh (WI)
U of Wisconsin–Stevens Point (WI)
Utah State U (UT)
Virginia Union U (VA)
Wagner Coll (NY)
Walsh U (OH)
Wartburg Coll (IA)
Washington State U (WA)
Western Carolina U (NC)
Westfield State U (MA)
West Liberty U (WV)
West Virginia Wesleyan Coll (WV)
Wheelock Coll (MA)
Widener U (PA)
Williams Baptist Coll (AR)

KINESIOLOGY AND EXERCISE SCIENCE
Adams State U (CO)
Albion Coll (MI)
Alma Coll (MI)
American Public U System (WV)
Anderson U (SC)
Angelo State U (TX)
Appalachian State U (NC)
Arizona State U at the Downtown Phoenix campus (AZ)
Arkansas State U (AR)
Auburn U at Montgomery (AL)
Augsburg Coll (MN)
Augustana Coll (SD)
Avila U (MO)
Baker U (KS)
Barry U (FL)
Bastyr U (WA)
Becker Coll (MA)
Belhaven U (MS)
Belmont U (TN)
Berea Coll (KY)
Berry Coll (GA)
Bethany Lutheran Coll (MN)
Bethel Coll (IN)
Bethel U (MN)
Biola U (CA)
Bluefield Coll (VA)
Blue Mountain Coll (MS)
Brevard Coll (NC)
Bridgewater State U (MA)
Brigham Young U (UT)
Buffalo State Coll, State U of New York (NY)
Cabrini Coll (PA)
California Baptist U (CA)
California Lutheran U (CA)
California State U, Chico (CA)
California State U, Long Beach (CA)
California State U, Los Angeles (CA)
California State U, Sacramento (CA)
California State U, San Marcos (CA)
Calvin Coll (MI)
Capital U (OH)
Carson-Newman U (TN)
Castleton State Coll (VT)
Catawba Coll (NC)
Cedarville U (OH)
Central Coll (IA)
Central Michigan U (MI)
Central Washington U (WA)
Chatham U (PA)
Chowan U (NC)
The Citadel, The Military Coll of South Carolina (SC)
Clearwater Christian Coll (FL)
Coastal Carolina U (SC)
Coker Coll (SC)
Colby-Sawyer Coll (NH)
The Coll at Brockport, State U of New York (NY)
The Coll of Idaho (ID)
Colorado Mesa U (CO)
Colorado State U (CO)
Colorado State U–Pueblo (CO)
Columbus State U (GA)
Concordia U (QC, Canada)
Concordia U Chicago (IL)
Concordia U, Nebraska (NE)
Concordia U, St. Paul (MN)
Concordia U Texas (TX)
Corban U (OR)
Cornell Coll (IA)
Cornerstone U (MI)
Creighton U (NE)
Dakota State U (SD)
Dalhousie U (NS, Canada)
Defiance Coll (OH)
DePaul U (IL)
DePauw U (IN)
DeSales U (PA)
Drury U (MO)
East Central U (OK)
Eastern Illinois U (IL)
Eastern Michigan U (MI)
Eastern U (PA)
East Stroudsburg U of Pennsylvania (PA)
Elmhurst Coll (IL)
Elon U (NC)
Emmanuel Coll (GA)
Endicott Coll (MA)
Eureka Coll (IL)
Fitchburg State U (MA)
Florida Atlantic U (FL)
Florida Gulf Coast U (FL)
Florida Southern Coll (FL)
Florida State U (FL)
Franklin Coll (IN)
Frostburg State U (MD)
Gannon U (PA)
George Mason U (VA)
Georgetown Coll (KY)
The George Washington U (DC)
Georgia Coll & State U (GA)
Georgia Gwinnett Coll (GA)
Georgian Court U (NJ)
Georgia Regents U (GA)
Georgia Southern U (GA)
Gonzaga U (WA)
Gordon Coll (MA)
Goshen Coll (IN)
Grand View U (IA)
Greensboro Coll (NC)
Greenville Coll (IL)
Grove City Coll (PA)
Guilford Coll (NC)
Hamline U (MN)
Hannibal-LaGrange U (MO)
Hanover Coll (IN)
Harding U (AR)
Hardin-Simmons U (TX)
Hastings Coll (NE)
Hendrix Coll (AR)
High Point U (NC)

Hillsdale Coll (MI)
Hillsdale Free Will Baptist Coll (OK)
Hope Coll (MI)
Houston Baptist U (TX)
Humboldt State U (CA)
Huntingdon Coll (AL)
Husson U (ME)
Huston-Tillotson U (TX)
Illinois State U (IL)
Immaculata U (PA)
Indiana State U (IN)
Indiana U Bloomington (IN)
Indiana U–Purdue U Indianapolis (IN)
Iowa Wesleyan Coll (IA)
Ithaca Coll (NY)
Jacksonville State U (AL)
Jacksonville U (FL)
Jefferson Coll of Health Sciences (VA)
John Brown U (AR)
Johnson State Coll (VT)
Kansas State U (KS)
Kansas Wesleyan U (KS)
Keene State Coll (NH)
Keiser U, Fort Lauderdale (FL)
Kennesaw State U (GA)
Kent State U (OH)
Kentucky Wesleyan Coll (KY)
King's Coll (PA)
Kuyper Coll (MI)
LaGrange Coll (GA)
Lamar U (TX)
Lasell Coll (MA)
La Sierra U (CA)
Lebanon Valley Coll (PA)
Lee U (TN)
Lenoir-Rhyne U (NC)
LeTourneau U (TX)
Liberty U (VA)
Life U (GA)
Lincoln Memorial U (TN)
Lindenwood U (MO)
Linfield Coll (OR)
Lipscomb U (TN)
Long Island U–LIU Brooklyn (NY)
Longwood U (VA)
Loras Coll (IA)
Louisiana Coll (LA)
Malone U (OH)
Manchester U (IN)
Marian U (WI)
Marshall U (WV)
Mars Hill U (NC)
Maryville Coll (TN)
The Master's Coll and Sem (CA)
McDaniel Coll (MD)
McKendree U (IL)
McMurry U (TX)
McNeese State U (LA)
Mercy Coll (NY)
Meredith Coll (NC)
Miami U (OH)
Michigan State U (MI)
Michigan Technological U (MI)
MidAmerica Nazarene U (KS)
Minnesota State U Moorhead (MN)
Missouri Baptist U (MO)
Missouri State U (MO)
Monmouth Coll (IL)
Montclair State U (NJ)
Morehead State U (KY)
Morrisville State Coll (NY)
Mount Vernon Nazarene U (OH)
Murray State U (KY)
Nebraska Wesleyan U (NE)
New Mexico State U (NM)
Norfolk State U (VA)
North Carolina Wesleyan Coll (NC)
North Central Coll (IL)
North Dakota State U (ND)
Northeastern State U (OK)
Northern Arizona U (AZ)
Northern Michigan U (MI)
Northwestern Coll (IA)
Northwest Nazarene U (ID)
Nova Southeastern U (FL)
Occidental Coll (CA)
Ohio Dominican U (OH)
Ohio Northern U (OH)
The Ohio State U (OH)
Ohio U (OH)
Oklahoma Baptist U (OK)
Oklahoma Wesleyan U (OK)
Olivet Nazarene U (IL)
Our Lady of the Lake U of San Antonio (TX)
Pacific Lutheran U (WA)
Pacific U (OR)
Penn State Abington (PA)
Penn State Altoona (PA)
Penn State Beaver (PA)
Penn State Berks (PA)
Penn State Brandywine (PA)
Penn State DuBois (PA)
Penn State Erie, The Behrend Coll (PA)
Penn State Fayette, The Eberly Campus (PA)
Penn State Greater Allegheny (PA)
Penn State Hazleton (PA)
Penn State Lehigh Valley (PA)
Penn State Mont Alto (PA)
Penn State New Kensington (PA)
Penn State Schuylkill (PA)
Penn State Shenango (PA)
Penn State U Park (PA)
Penn State Wilkes-Barre (PA)
Penn State Worthington Scranton (PA)
Penn State York (PA)
Pepperdine U, Malibu (CA)
Pittsburg State U (KS)
Plymouth State U (NH)
Point U (GA)
Purdue U (IN)
Queens Coll of the City U of New York (NY)
Regis U (CO)
Rice U (TX)
Roanoke Coll (VA)
Rocky Mountain Coll (MT)
Rutgers, The State U of New Jersey, New Brunswick (NJ)
Sacred Heart U (CT)
Saginaw Valley State U (MI)
Saint Augustine's U (NC)
St. Edward's U (TX)
St. Gregory's U, Shawnee (OK)
Saint Louis U (MO)
St. Mary's U (TX)
St. Olaf Coll (MN)
Salem Coll (NC)
Salisbury U (MD)
Samford U (AL)
Sam Houston State U (TX)
San Diego Christian Coll (CA)
San Diego State U (CA)
San Francisco State U (CA)
Seattle Pacific U (WA)
Seattle U (WA)
Seton Hill U (PA)
Shaw U (NC)
Shippensburg U of Pennsylvania (PA)
Simmons Coll (MA)
Simon Fraser U (BC, Canada)
Simpson Coll (IA)
Skidmore Coll (NY)
Slippery Rock U of Pennsylvania (PA)
Southern Adventist U (TN)
Southern Arkansas U–Magnolia (AR)
Southern Illinois U Carbondale (IL)
Southern Illinois U Edwardsville (IL)
Southwest Baptist U (MO)
Southwestern Adventist U (TX)
Southwestern U (TX)
Southwest Minnesota State U (MN)
State U of New York Coll at Cortland (NY)
Stephen F. Austin State U (TX)
Syracuse U (NY)
Tarleton State U (TX)
Taylor U (IN)
Temple U (PA)
Tennessee Wesleyan Coll (TN)
Texas A&M Intl U (TX)
Texas A&M U (TX)
Texas A&M U–Commerce (TX)
Texas A&M U–Corpus Christi (TX)
Texas Lutheran U (TX)
Texas Southern U (TX)
Texas State U (TX)
Texas Tech U (TX)
Texas Wesleyan U (TX)
Texas Woman's U (TX)
Towson U (MD)
Transylvania U (KY)
Trent U (ON, Canada)
Trinity Christian Coll (IL)
Truman State U (MO)
Tusculum Coll (TN)
Union Coll (KY)
Union Coll (NE)
Union U (TN)
United States Military Acad (NY)
United States Sports Acad (AL)
Université de Sherbrooke (QC, Canada)
The U of British Columbia (BC, Canada)
The U of British Columbia–Okanagan Campus (BC, Canada)
U of Central Arkansas (AR)
U of Central Oklahoma (OK)
U of Dayton (OH)
U of Delaware (DE)
U of Evansville (IN)
U of Guelph (ON, Canada)
U of Hawaii at Hilo (HI)
U of Hawaii at Manoa (HI)
U of Houston (TX)
U of Houston–Clear Lake (TX)
U of Illinois at Chicago (IL)
U of Indianapolis (IN)
The U of Iowa (IA)
U of Jamestown (ND)
The U of Kansas (KS)
U of La Verne (CA)
U of Lethbridge (AB, Canada)
U of Mary Hardin-Baylor (TX)
U of Maryland, Coll Park (MD)
U of Memphis (TN)
U of Michigan (MI)
U of Minnesota, Duluth (MN)
U of Minnesota, Twin Cities Campus (MN)
U of Mississippi (MS)
U of Mount Union (OH)
U of Nevada, Las Vegas (NV)
U of New Brunswick Saint John (NB, Canada)
U of New England (ME)
U of New Hampshire (NH)
The U of North Carolina at Greensboro (NC)
The U of North Carolina Wilmington (NC)
U of Northern Colorado (CO)
U of North Texas (TX)
U of Northwestern–St. Paul (MN)
U of Oklahoma (OK)
U of Ottawa (ON, Canada)
U of Puget Sound (WA)
U of Regina (SK, Canada)
U of Rhode Island (RI)
U of San Francisco (CA)
U of Saskatchewan (SK, Canada)
The U of Scranton (PA)
U of South Carolina Aiken (SC)
U of Southern California (CA)
U of Southern Indiana (IN)
The U of Tennessee (TN)
The U of Tennessee at Chattanooga (TN)
The U of Texas at Arlington (TX)
The U of Texas at Austin (TX)
The U of Texas at San Antonio (TX)
The U of Texas at Tyler (TX)
The U of Texas of the Permian Basin (TX)
The U of Texas–Pan American (TX)
U of the Fraser Valley (BC, Canada)
U of the Incarnate Word (TX)
U of the Pacific (CA)
U of the Sciences (PA)
The U of Toledo (OH)
The U of Tulsa (OK)
U of Utah (UT)
U of Vermont (VT)
U of Virginia (VA)
U of Waterloo (ON, Canada)
The U of West Alabama (AL)
The U of Western Ontario (ON, Canada)
U of Windsor (ON, Canada)
U of Wisconsin–Eau Claire (WI)
U of Wisconsin–La Crosse (WI)
U of Wisconsin–Madison (WI)
U of Wisconsin–Milwaukee (WI)
U of Wisconsin–Superior (WI)
U of Wyoming (WY)
Upper Iowa U (IA)
Valparaiso U (IN)
Vanguard U of Southern California (CA)
Viterbo U (WI)
Wake Forest U (NC)
Walla Walla U (WA)
Walsh U (OH)
Warner Pacific Coll (OR)
Washington State U (WA)
Waynesburg U (PA)
Webster U (MO)
Western Illinois U (IL)
Western Kentucky U (KY)
Western Michigan U (MI)
Western Oregon U (OR)
Western State Colorado U (CO)
West Liberty U (WV)
West Texas A&M U (TX)
West Virginia Wesleyan Coll (WV)
Whittier Coll (CA)
Wichita State U (KS)
Willamette U (OR)
William Jessup U (CA)
William Paterson U of New Jersey (NJ)
William Penn U (IA)
William Woods U (MO)
Wingate U (NC)
Winona State U (MN)
Youngstown State U (OH)

KINESIOTHERAPY

Boston U (MA)
Bridgewater State U (MA)
California State U, Long Beach (CA)
Loyola Marymount U (CA)
Shaw U (NC)

KNOWLEDGE MANAGEMENT

Framingham State U (MA)
Saint Joseph's U (PA)
Syracuse U (NY)

KOREAN

Brigham Young U (UT)
The Ohio State U (OH)
U of California, Irvine (CA)
U of California, Los Angeles (CA)
U of Hawaii at Manoa (HI)
U of Washington (WA)

KOREAN STUDIES

U of Washington (WA)

LABOR AND INDUSTRIAL RELATIONS

Bowling Green State U (OH)
Clarion U of Pennsylvania (PA)
Cleveland State U (OH)
Cornell U (NY)
Indiana U–Purdue U Fort Wayne (IN)
Ithaca Coll (NY)
New York U (NY)
Penn State Abington (PA)
Penn State Altoona (PA)
Penn State Beaver (PA)
Penn State Berks (PA)
Penn State Brandywine (PA)
Penn State DuBois (PA)
Penn State Erie, The Behrend Coll (PA)
Penn State Fayette, The Eberly Campus (PA)
Penn State Greater Allegheny (PA)
Penn State Hazleton (PA)
Penn State Lehigh Valley (PA)
Penn State Mont Alto (PA)
Penn State New Kensington (PA)
Penn State Schuylkill (PA)
Penn State Shenango (PA)
Penn State U Park (PA)
Penn State Wilkes-Barre (PA)
Penn State Worthington Scranton (PA)
Penn State York (PA)
Rider U (NJ)
Rutgers, The State U of New Jersey, New Brunswick (NJ)
Saint Francis U (PA)
San Francisco State U (CA)
State U of New York at Fredonia (NY)
State U of New York Coll at Old Westbury (NY)
State U of New York Empire State Coll (NY)
Université de Montréal (QC, Canada)
Université du Québec en Outaouais (QC, Canada)
U of Bridgeport (CT)
The U of Iowa (IA)
U of Minnesota, Twin Cities Campus (MN)
U of Toronto (ON, Canada)

LABOR STUDIES

California State U, Dominguez Hills (CA)
Eastern Michigan U (MI)
Goddard Coll (VT)
Hofstra U (NY)
Indiana U Bloomington (IN)
Indiana U Northwest (IN)
Indiana U–Purdue U Indianapolis (IN)
Indiana U South Bend (IN)
Queens Coll of the City U of New York (NY)
U of Windsor (ON, Canada)
Wayne State U (MI)

LANDSCAPE ARCHITECTURE

Acad of Art U (CA)
American U of Beirut (Lebanon)
Arizona State U at the Tempe campus (AZ)
Ball State U (IN)
Boston Architectural Coll (MA)
California Polytechnic State U, San Luis Obispo (CA)
California State Polytechnic U, Pomona (CA)
Coll of the Atlantic (ME)
Colorado State U (CO)
Cornell U (NY)
Iowa State U of Science and Technology (IA)
Louisiana State U and A&M Coll (LA)
Michigan State U (MI)
Mississippi State U (MS)
North Carolina Ag and Tech State U (NC)
North Carolina State U (NC)
North Dakota State U (ND)
Northeastern U (MA)
The Ohio State U (OH)
Oklahoma State U (OK)
Penn State Brandywine (PA)
Penn State Lehigh Valley (PA)
Penn State Schuylkill (PA)
Penn State U Park (PA)
Penn State Wilkes-Barre (PA)
Philadelphia U (PA)
Purdue U (IN)
Rutgers, The State U of New Jersey, New Brunswick (NJ)
State U of New York Coll of Environmental Science and Forestry (NY)
Temple U (PA)
Texas A&M U (TX)
Texas Tech U (TX)
Universidad del Turabo (PR)
Université de Montréal (QC, Canada)
U of Arkansas (AR)
The U of British Columbia (BC, Canada)
U of California, Berkeley (CA)
U of California, Davis (CA)
U of Delaware (DE)
U of Florida (FL)
U of Georgia (GA)
U of Idaho (ID)
U of Kentucky (KY)
U of Maryland, Coll Park (MD)
U of Massachusetts Amherst (MA)
U of Minnesota, Twin Cities Campus (MN)
U of Nebraska–Lincoln (NE)
U of Nevada, Las Vegas (NV)
U of Oregon (OR)
U of Rhode Island (RI)
U of Washington (WA)
U of Wisconsin–Madison (WI)
Utah State U (UT)
Virginia Polytechnic Inst and State U (VA)
Washington State U (WA)
West Virginia U (WV)

LANDSCAPING AND GROUNDSKEEPING

Andrews U (MI)

Mississippi State U (MS)
Oklahoma State U (OK)
Penn State Abington (PA)
Penn State Altoona (PA)
Penn State Beaver (PA)
Penn State Berks (PA)
Penn State Brandywine (PA)
Penn State DuBois (PA)
Penn State Erie, The Behrend Coll (PA)
Penn State Fayette, The Eberly Campus (PA)
Penn State Greater Allegheny (PA)
Penn State Hazleton (PA)
Penn State Lehigh Valley (PA)
Penn State Mont Alto (PA)
Penn State New Kensington (PA)
Penn State Schuylkill (PA)
Penn State Shenango (PA)
Penn State U Park (PA)
Penn State Wilkes-Barre (PA)
Penn State Worthington Scranton (PA)
Penn State York (PA)
South Dakota State U (SD)
State U of New York Coll of Agriculture and Technology at Cobleskill (NY)
U of Minnesota, Crookston (MN)
U of Nebraska–Lincoln (NE)

LAND USE PLANNING AND MANAGEMENT
Central Michigan U (MI)
Montana State U (MT)
State U of New York Coll of Environmental Science and Forestry (NY)
U of Saskatchewan (SK, Canada)
U of Wisconsin–River Falls (WI)
West Virginia U (WV)

LANGUAGE INTERPRETATION AND TRANSLATION
Brigham Young U (UT)
Concordia U (QC, Canada)
Lebanese American U (Lebanon)
Université du Québec en Outaouais (QC, Canada)
U of Ottawa (ON, Canada)
The U of Texas at Arlington (TX)

LASER AND OPTICAL ENGINEERING
Delaware State U (DE)
U of Central Florida (FL)
U of Rochester (NY)

LATIN
Amherst Coll (MA)
Augustana Coll (IL)
Austin Coll (TX)
Ball State U (IN)
Bard Coll (NY)
Barnard Coll (NY)
Baylor U (TX)
Binghamton U, State U of New York (NY)
Boston U (MA)
Bowling Green State U (OH)
Bryn Mawr Coll (PA)
Calvin Coll (MI)
Canisius Coll (NY)
Carleton Coll (MN)
The Catholic U of America (DC)
The Coll of Wooster (OH)
Concordia Coll (MN)
Cornell U (NY)
Creighton U (NE)
Dartmouth Coll (NH)
DePauw U (IN)
Duquesne U (PA)
Fordham U (NY)
Franklin & Marshall Coll (PA)
Furman U (SC)
Gettysburg Coll (PA)
Hampden-Sydney Coll (VA)
Haverford Coll (PA)
Hillsdale Coll (MI)
Hobart and William Smith Colls (NY)
Hofstra U (NY)
Hunter Coll of the City U of New York (NY)
John Carroll U (OH)
Kalamazoo Coll (MI)
Kent State U (OH)
Kenyon Coll (OH)
Knox Coll (IL)
Lawrence U (WI)
Lehman Coll of the City U of New York (NY)
Loyola U Chicago (IL)
Mercer U, Macon (GA)
Missouri State U (MO)
Monmouth Coll (IL)
Montclair State U (NJ)
Mount Allison U (NB, Canada)
Mount Holyoke Coll (MA)
New York U (NY)
Oberlin Coll (OH)
Queens Coll of the City U of New York (NY)
Randolph Coll (VA)
Randolph-Macon Coll (VA)
Rice U (TX)
Rockford U (IL)
Rutgers, The State U of New Jersey, New Brunswick (NJ)
Saint Joseph's U (PA)
St. Olaf Coll (MN)
Samford U (AL)
Santa Clara U (CA)
Sewanee: The U of the South (TN)
Smith Coll (MA)
Southwestern U (TX)
Trinity U (TX)
Tufts U (MA)
Tulane U (LA)
U of Alberta (AB, Canada)
The U of British Columbia (BC, Canada)
U of California, Berkeley (CA)
U of California, Los Angeles (CA)
U of Georgia (GA)
U of Maine (ME)
U of Miami (FL)
U of Michigan (MI)
U of Minnesota, Twin Cities Campus (MN)
U of Missouri (MO)
The U of Montana (MT)
U of New Hampshire (NH)
U of Ottawa (ON, Canada)
U of Richmond (VA)
U of St. Thomas (MN)
The U of Texas at Austin (TX)
U of Toronto (ON, Canada)
U of Vermont (VT)
U of Washington (WA)
The U of Western Ontario (ON, Canada)
U of Windsor (ON, Canada)
U of Wisconsin–Madison (WI)
Virginia Wesleyan Coll (VA)
Wabash Coll (IN)
Wake Forest U (NC)
Washington U in St. Louis (MO)
West Chester U of Pennsylvania (PA)
Western Michigan U (MI)
Wheaton Coll (MA)
Wright State U (OH)
Yale U (CT)

LATIN AMERICAN AND CARIBBEAN STUDIES
Coll of Charleston (SC)
Emmanuel Coll (MA)
Linfield Coll (OR)
Mount Holyoke Coll (MA)
Rollins Coll (FL)
Union Coll (NY)
U of Georgia (GA)
U of Michigan (MI)
U of Wisconsin–Madison (WI)
U of Wisconsin–Milwaukee (WI)

LATIN AMERICAN STUDIES
Adelphi U (NY)
Albion Coll (MI)
Albright Coll (PA)
American U (DC)
Assumption Coll (MA)
Bard Coll (NY)
Bard Coll at Simon's Rock (MA)
Barnard Coll (NY)
Bates Coll (ME)
Baylor U (TX)
Bennington Coll (VT)
Binghamton U, State U of New York (NY)
Blackburn Coll (IL)
Boston U (MA)
Bowdoin Coll (ME)
Bowling Green State U (OH)
Brandeis U (MA)
Brown U (RI)
Bucknell U (PA)
California State U, Chico (CA)
California State U, Fullerton (CA)
California State U, Los Angeles (CA)
Canisius Coll (NY)
Carleton Coll (MN)
City Coll of the City U of New York (NY)
Colby Coll (ME)
The Coll of William and Mary (VA)
Columbia U (NY)
Columbia U, School of General Studies (NY)
Connecticut Coll (CT)
Cornell Coll (IA)
Dartmouth Coll (NH)
Davidson Coll (NC)
Denison U (OH)
DePaul U (IL)
Dickinson Coll (PA)
Earlham Coll (IN)
Flagler Coll (FL)
Fordham U (NY)
George Mason U (VA)
The George Washington U (DC)
Gettysburg Coll (PA)
Gustavus Adolphus Coll (MN)
Hamline U (MN)
Hampshire Coll (MA)
Haverford Coll (PA)
Hobart and William Smith Colls (NY)
Hofstra U (NY)
Hunter Coll of the City U of New York (NY)
Illinois Wesleyan U (IL)
Johns Hopkins U (MD)
Kent State U (OH)
Knox Coll (IL)
Lake Forest Coll (IL)
Lehman Coll of the City U of New York (NY)
Macalester Coll (MN)
Miami U (OH)
Middlebury Coll (VT)
Millsaps Coll (MS)
New Coll of Florida (FL)
New York U (NY)
Oakland U (MI)
Oberlin Coll (OH)
Occidental Coll (CA)
Ohio U (OH)
Ohio Wesleyan U (OH)
Pace U (NY)
Penn State Abington (PA)
Penn State Altoona (PA)
Penn State Beaver (PA)
Penn State Berks (PA)
Penn State Brandywine (PA)
Penn State DuBois (PA)
Penn State Erie, The Behrend Coll (PA)
Penn State Fayette, The Eberly Campus (PA)
Penn State Greater Allegheny (PA)
Penn State Hazleton (PA)
Penn State Lehigh Valley (PA)
Penn State Mont Alto (PA)
Penn State New Kensington (PA)
Penn State Schuylkill (PA)
Penn State Shenango (PA)
Penn State U Park (PA)
Penn State Wilkes-Barre (PA)
Penn State Worthington Scranton (PA)
Penn State York (PA)
Pepperdine U, Malibu (CA)
Pomona Coll (CA)
Portland State U (OR)
Prescott Coll (AZ)
Queens Coll of the City U of New York (NY)
Rhode Island Coll (RI)
Rhodes Coll (TN)
Rice U (TX)
Ripon Coll (WI)
Rutgers, The State U of New Jersey, New Brunswick (NJ)
Saint Louis U (MO)
St. Olaf Coll (MN)
Samford U (AL)
San Diego State U (CA)
Scripps Coll (CA)
Seattle Pacific U (WA)
Skidmore Coll (NY)
Smith Coll (MA)
Southern Methodist U (TX)
Southwestern U (TX)
Stanford U (CA)
State U of New York at New Paltz (NY)
State U of New York at Plattsburgh (NY)
Syracuse U (NY)
Temple U (PA)
Texas Tech U (TX)
Trinity U (TX)
Tufts U (MA)
Tulane U (LA)
Union Coll (KY)
United States Military Acad (NY)
U at Albany, State U of New York (NY)
The U of Alabama (AL)
U of Alberta (AB, Canada)
The U of Arizona (AZ)
The U of British Columbia (BC, Canada)
U of California, Berkeley (CA)
U of California, Los Angeles (CA)
U of California, Riverside (CA)
U of California, Santa Cruz (CA)
U of Central Florida (FL)
U of Chicago (IL)
U of Cincinnati (OH)
U of Delaware (DE)
U of Denver (CO)
U of Idaho (ID)
U of Illinois at Chicago (IL)
The U of Iowa (IA)
The U of Kansas (KS)
U of Kentucky (KY)
U of Louisville (KY)
U of Miami (FL)
U of Minnesota, Duluth (MN)
U of Minnesota, Morris (MN)
U of Minnesota, Twin Cities Campus (MN)
U of Missouri (MO)
U of Nebraska–Lincoln (NE)
U of Nevada, Las Vegas (NV)
U of New Mexico (NM)
The U of North Carolina at Chapel Hill (NC)
The U of North Carolina at Charlotte (NC)
U of Oregon (OR)
U of Pennsylvania (PA)
U of Richmond (VA)
U of San Francisco (CA)
The U of Texas at Austin (TX)
The U of Texas at El Paso (TX)
The U of Toledo (OH)
U of Toronto (ON, Canada)
U of Utah (UT)
U of Vermont (VT)
U of Washington (WA)
U of Wisconsin–Eau Claire (WI)
Vanderbilt U (TN)
Vassar Coll (NY)
Villanova U (PA)
Washington Coll (MD)
Washington U in St. Louis (MO)
Wesleyan U (CT)
Westminster Coll (UT)
Whittier Coll (CA)
Willamette U (OR)
William Paterson U of New Jersey (NJ)
Wofford Coll (SC)
Yale U (CT)

LATIN TEACHER EDUCATION
Boston U (MA)
Brigham Young U (UT)
Concordia Coll (MN)
Duquesne U (PA)
Indiana U Bloomington (IN)
Miami U (OH)
Missouri State U (MO)
Ohio Wesleyan U (OH)
Southern Adventist U (TN)
U of Delaware (DE)
Western Michigan U (MI)

LAY MINISTRY
Abilene Christian U (TX)
Arizona Christian U (AZ)
Coll of Biblical Studies–Houston (TX)
Huntingdon Coll (AL)
Judson U (IL)
Saint Mary's U of Minnesota (MN)
Southeastern Bible Coll (AL)
Trevecca Nazarene U (TN)
U of Saint Francis (IN)

LEARNING SCIENCES
Purdue U (IN)
The U of Arizona (AZ)

LEGAL ADMINISTRATIVE ASSISTANT/SECRETARY
Intl Business Coll, Fort Wayne (IN)

LEGAL ASSISTANT/ PARALEGAL
Anna Maria Coll (MA)
Bay Path U (MA)
Boston U (MA)
Calumet Coll of Saint Joseph (IN)
Champlain Coll (VT)
Clayton State U (GA)
Coll of Saint Mary (NE)
Concordia U Wisconsin (WI)
Daemen Coll (NY)
Davenport U, Grand Rapids (MI)
East Central U (OK)
Eastern Kentucky U (KY)
Eastern Michigan U (MI)
Ellis U (IL)
Elms Coll (MA)
Florida Gulf Coast U (FL)
Gannon U (PA)
Grand Valley State U (MI)
Hampton U (VA)
Hilbert Coll (NY)
Husson U (ME)
Intl Business Coll, Fort Wayne (IN)
Kent State U (OH)
Lake Erie Coll (OH)
Lewis U (IL)
Loyola U Chicago (IL)
Madonna U (MI)
Maryville U of Saint Louis (MO)
Mercy Coll (NY)
Minnesota State U Moorhead (MN)
Mississippi U for Women (MS)
Morehead State U (KY)
Mount St. Joseph U (OH)
National U (CA)
New York City Coll of Technology of the City U of New York (NY)
Northern Michigan U (MI)
Nova Southeastern U (FL)
Peirce Coll (PA)
Pennsylvania Coll of Technology (PA)
Post U (CT)
Quinnipiac U (CT)
Roger Williams U (RI)
Roosevelt U (IL)
Saint Mary-of-the-Woods Coll (IN)
Samford U (AL)
Southern Illinois U Carbondale (IL)
State U of New York Coll of Technology at Canton (NY)
Stephen F. Austin State U (TX)
Stevenson U (MD)
Stevens–The Inst of Business & Arts (MO)
Suffolk U (MA)
Sullivan U (KY)
Texas A&M U–Commerce (TX)
Texas Wesleyan U (TX)
Texas Woman's U (TX)
U of Central Florida (FL)
U of Evansville (IN)
U of Great Falls (MT)
U of Hartford (CT)
U of Houston–Clear Lake (TX)
U of La Verne (CA)
U of Mississippi (MS)
U of Southern Mississippi (MS)
The U of Tennessee at Chattanooga (TN)
The U of Toledo (OH)
U of West Florida (FL)
Ursuline Coll (OH)
Valdosta State U (GA)
Washburn U (KS)
Western Kentucky U (KY)
William Woods U (MO)
Winona State U (MN)

LEGAL PROFESSIONS AND STUDIES RELATED
Armstrong State U (GA)
Ball State U (IN)

Bay Path U (MA)
Berkeley Coll, Woodland Park (NJ)
Berkeley Coll–New York City Campus (NY)
California U of Pennsylvania (PA)
Central Penn Coll (PA)
Drexel U (PA)
Hodges U (FL)
Maryville U of Saint Louis (MO)
Missouri Southern State U (MO)
Montclair State U (NJ)
National U (CA)
New Jersey Inst of Technology (NJ)
Ramapo Coll of New Jersey (NJ)
Roger Williams U (RI)
St. John's U (NY)
Temple U (PA)
Tulane U (LA)
U of Illinois at Springfield (IL)
U of Nebraska–Lincoln (NE)
U of Pennsylvania (PA)
The U of Tulsa (OK)
William Woods U (MO)

LEGAL STUDIES
Adams State U (CO)
American Public U System (WV)
American U (DC)
Amherst Coll (MA)
Anna Maria Coll (MA)
Arizona State U at the Tempe campus (AZ)
Bay Path U (MA)
Brenau U (GA)
Bridgewater State U (MA)
Cape Breton U (NS, Canada)
Central Michigan U (MI)
Claremont McKenna Coll (CA)
Coll of the Atlantic (ME)
Culver-Stockton Coll (MO)
DeSales U (PA)
Dickinson Coll (PA)
Doane Coll (NE)
Dominican U (IL)
Elms Coll (MA)
Emory & Henry Coll (VA)
Florida National U (FL)
Franciscan U of Steubenville (OH)
Hamline U (MN)
Hampshire Coll (MA)
Harding U (AR)
Illinois State U (IL)
Keiser U, Fort Lauderdale (FL)
Kentucky Wesleyan Coll (KY)
Lasell Coll (MA)
Lipscomb U (TN)
Mercy Coll (NY)
Morehead State U (KY)
National Paralegal Coll (AZ)
National U (CA)
Nazareth Coll of Rochester (NY)
Newbury Coll (MA)
Northwestern U (IL)
Northwest U (WA)
Oakland U (MI)
Oberlin Coll (OH)
Park U (MO)
Quinnipiac U (CT)
St. John Fisher Coll (NY)
St. John's U (NY)
Saint Joseph's U (PA)
Scripps Coll (CA)
State U of New York at Fredonia (NY)
Stevenson U (MD)
Tiffin U (OH)
United States Air Force Acad (CO)
Université de Montréal (QC, Canada)
Université de Sherbrooke (QC, Canada)
U of California, Berkeley (CA)
U of California, Santa Cruz (CA)
U of Central Oklahoma (OK)
U of Hartford (CT)
U of Maryland U Coll (MD)
U of Massachusetts Amherst (MA)
U of Miami (FL)
The U of Montana (MT)
U of New Haven (CT)
U of Pittsburgh (PA)
U of the District of Columbia (DC)
U of Washington (WA)
U of Washington, Tacoma (WA)
U of Windsor (ON, Canada)
U of Wisconsin–Madison (WI)
U of Wisconsin–Superior (WI)
Webster U (MO)
Western New England U (MA)
Wilmington U (DE)

LIBERAL ARTS AND SCIENCES AND HUMANITIES RELATED
The American U in Dubai (United Arab Emirates)
Anderson U (IN)
Antioch Coll, Yellow Springs (OH)
Armstrong State U (GA)
Auburn U (AL)
Augsburg Coll (MN)
Belhaven U (MS)
Brigham Young U (UT)
Bryan Coll (TN)
Butler U (IN)
California Polytechnic State U, San Luis Obispo (CA)
California State U, Dominguez Hills (CA)
Centre Coll (KY)
Coll of Saint Mary (NE)
The Colorado Coll (CO)
Concordia Coll (MN)
Cornell U (NY)
Duquesne U (PA)
Fairfield U (CT)
Florida Atlantic U (FL)
George Mason U (VA)
Georgia Coll & State U (GA)
Goddard Coll (VT)
Hampshire Coll (MA)
Heritage U (WA)
Hobe Sound Bible Coll (FL)
Hofstra U (NY)
Illinois Inst of Technology (IL)
Johns Hopkins U (MD)
Kansas Wesleyan U (KS)
Kent State U at Ashtabula (OH)
Kent State U at East Liverpool (OH)
Kent State U at Geauga (OH)
Kent State U at Salem (OH)
Kent State U at Stark (OH)
Kent State U at Trumbull (OH)
Kent State U at Tuscarawas (OH)
Life U (GA)
Loyola U New Orleans (LA)
Malone U (OH)
Marshall U (WV)
Marymount California U (CA)
Missouri Baptist U (MO)
Molloy Coll (NY)
Mount Aloysius Coll (PA)
National U (CA)
North Carolina State U (NC)
Oakland U (MI)
Ohio U (OH)
Oklahoma City U (OK)
Pepperdine U, Malibu (CA)
Prescott Coll (AZ)
Sacred Heart U (CT)
Saint Anselm Coll (NH)
St. John's Coll (NM)
Saint Louis U (MO)
Seattle U (WA)
Selma U (AL)
Shimer Coll (IL)
Southern Methodist U (TX)
Southern New Hampshire U (NH)
Tulane U (LA)
Union Coll (NE)
The U of Akron (OH)
U of California, Los Angeles (CA)
U of California, Santa Barbara (CA)
U of Maryland U Coll (MD)
U of Mary Washington (VA)
U of Massachusetts Amherst (MA)
U of Minnesota, Twin Cities Campus (MN)
U of Oklahoma (OK)
U of Rhode Island (RI)
U of Wisconsin–Milwaukee (WI)
U of Wisconsin–Platteville (WI)
U of Wisconsin–River Falls (WI)
U of Wisconsin–Whitewater (WI)
Valdosta State U (GA)
Vassar Coll (NY)
Walsh U (OH)
Western Illinois U (IL)
West Virginia U Inst of Technology (WV)
Wheeling Jesuit U (WV)

LIBERAL ARTS AND SCIENCES/LIBERAL STUDIES
Abilene Christian U (TX)
Adams State U (CO)
Alaska Pacific U (AK)
Albion Coll (MI)
Alcorn State U (MS)
Alvernia U (PA)
Alverno Coll (WI)
American Intl Coll (MA)
American U (DC)
Amridge U (AL)
Anna Maria Coll (MA)
Antioch U Midwest (OH)
Antioch U Santa Barbara (CA)
Appalachian State U (NC)
Aquinas Coll (MI)
Arcadia U (PA)
Ashland U (OH)
Athens State U (AL)
Auburn U at Montgomery (AL)
Augsburg Coll (MN)
Augustana Coll (IL)
Augustana Coll (SD)
Austin Peay State U (TN)
Averett U (VA)
Azusa Pacific U (CA)
Ball State U (IN)
Barry U (FL)
Baruch Coll of the City U of New York (NY)
Bay Path U (MA)
Beacon Coll (FL)
Becker Coll (MA)
Belmont Abbey Coll (NC)
Belmont U (TN)
Bemidji State U (MN)
Benedictine Coll (KS)
Bennington Coll (VT)
Bentley U (MA)
Bethany Lutheran Coll (MN)
Bethel Coll (IN)
Bethune-Cookman U (FL)
Biola U (CA)
Bluefield Coll (VA)
Bowling Green State U (OH)
Bowling Green State U-Firelands Coll (OH)
Brenau U (GA)
Bridgewater Coll (VA)
Brigham Young U (UT)
Bryan Coll (TN)
Buffalo State Coll, State U of New York (NY)
Cabrini Coll (PA)
Cairn U (PA)
California Baptist U (CA)
California Lutheran U (CA)
California Polytechnic State U, San Luis Obispo (CA)
California State Polytechnic U, Pomona (CA)
California State U, Chico (CA)
California State U, Dominguez Hills (CA)
California State U, Fresno (CA)
California State U, Fullerton (CA)
California State U, Long Beach (CA)
California State U, Los Angeles (CA)
California State U, Monterey Bay (CA)
California State U, Sacramento (CA)
California State U, San Bernardino (CA)
California State U, San Marcos (CA)
California State U, Stanislaus (CA)
California U of Pennsylvania (PA)
Calumet Coll of Saint Joseph (IN)
Canisius Coll (NY)
Carlow U (PA)
Carson-Newman U (TN)
The Catholic U of America (DC)
Cazenovia Coll (NY)
Cedar Crest Coll (PA)
Cedarville U (OH)
Central Michigan U (MI)
Champlain Coll (VT)
Chapman U (CA)
Charter Oak State Coll (CT)
Chatham U (PA)
Chestnut Hill Coll (PA)
Cheyney U of Pennsylvania (PA)
Chicago State U (IL)
Christian Brothers U (TN)
Clarion U of Pennsylvania (PA)
Clarkson U (NY)
Clayton State U (GA)
Cleveland State U (OH)
Coastal Carolina U (SC)
Coe Coll (IA)
The Coll of New Rochelle (NY)
Coll of Saint Benedict (MN)
The Coll of Saint Rose (NY)
Coll of the Atlantic (ME)
Colorado Mesa U (CO)
Colorado State U (CO)
Colorado State U–Pueblo (CO)
Columbia Coll (SC)
Columbia Coll Chicago (IL)
Columbia Intl U (SC)
Columbus State U (GA)
Conception Sem Coll (MO)
Concordia Coll–New York (NY)
Concordia U (CA)
Concordia U Texas (TX)
Concordia U Wisconsin (WI)
Corban U (OR)
Cornell Coll (IA)
Cornell U (NY)
Crossroads Coll (MN)
Culver-Stockton Coll (MO)
Cumberland U (TN)
Dakota State U (SD)
Defiance Coll (OH)
DEREE - The American Coll of Greece (Greece)
DeSales U (PA)
Dickinson State U (ND)
Dominican U of California (CA)
Dowling Coll (NY)
Drexel U (PA)
Duquesne U (PA)
East Carolina U (NC)
Eastern Illinois U (IL)
Eastern New Mexico U (NM)
Eastern Oregon U (OR)
East Stroudsburg U of Pennsylvania (PA)
East Tennessee State U (TN)
Elmira Coll (NY)
Elms Coll (MA)
Emmanuel Coll (MA)
Emory & Henry Coll (VA)
Endicott Coll (MA)
Eureka Coll (IL)
The Evergreen State Coll (WA)
Excelsior Coll (NY)
Faulkner U (AL)
Ferrum Coll (VA)
Fitchburg State U (MA)
Flagler Coll (FL)
Florida Atlantic U (FL)
Florida Coll (FL)
Florida Gulf Coast U (FL)
Florida Intl U (FL)
Florida National U (FL)
Fontbonne U (MO)
Fort Hays State U (KS)
Fort Lewis Coll (CO)
Framingham State U (MA)
Francis Marion U (SC)
Franklin Pierce U (NH)
Friends U (KS)
Frostburg State U (MD)
Gannon U (PA)
George Mason U (VA)
Georgetown U (DC)
The George Washington U (DC)
Gettysburg Coll (PA)
Gonzaga U (WA)
Governors State U (IL)
Graceland U (IA)
Grand Valley State U (MI)
Grand View U (IA)
Granite State Coll (NH)
Green Mountain Coll (VT)
Greenville Coll (IL)
Hannibal-LaGrange U (MO)
Harris-Stowe State U (MO)
Harvard U (MA)
Hastings Coll (NE)
Hillsdale Free Will Baptist Coll (OK)
Hofstra U (NY)
Holy Cross Coll (IN)
Hope Intl U (CA)
Houghton Coll (NY)
Houston Baptist U (TX)
Howard Payne U (TX)
Humboldt State U (CA)
Husson U (ME)
Illinois Coll (IL)
Illinois Inst of Technology (IL)
Illinois State U (IL)
Illinois Wesleyan U (IL)
Immaculata U (PA)
Indiana State U (IN)
Indiana U Bloomington (IN)
Indiana U of Pennsylvania (PA)
Iona Coll (NY)
Iowa State U of Science and Technology (IA)
Ithaca Coll (NY)
Jacksonville U (FL)
James Madison U (VA)
Johns Hopkins U (MD)
Johnson C. Smith U (NC)
Johnson State Coll (VT)
Juniata Coll (PA)
Kentucky State U (KY)
Keuka Coll (NY)
Kutztown U of Pennsylvania (PA)
Landmark Coll (VT)
Langston U (OK)
La Roche Coll (PA)
Lasell Coll (MA)
La Sierra U (CA)
Lenoir-Rhyne U (NC)
Lesley U (MA)
Lewis U (IL)
Liberty U (VA)
Limestone Coll (SC)
Lincoln Memorial U (TN)
Lincoln U (MO)
Lindenwood U (MO)
Lock Haven U of Pennsylvania (PA)
Long Island U–LIU Brooklyn (NY)
Long Island U–LIU Post (NY)
Longwood U (VA)
Loras Coll (IA)
Louisiana Coll (LA)
Louisiana State U and A&M Coll (LA)
Loyola Marymount U (CA)
Manchester U (IN)
Manhattan Coll (NY)
Mansfield U of Pennsylvania (PA)
Marian U (WI)
Marietta Coll (OH)
Marist Coll (NY)
Mars Hill U (NC)
Marymount California U (CA)
Marymount Manhattan Coll (NY)
Marymount U (VA)
Maryville U of Saint Louis (MO)
Massachusetts Coll of Liberal Arts (MA)
Massachusetts Inst of Technology (MA)
The Master's Coll and Sem (CA)
McNeese State U (LA)
Medaille Coll (NY)
Mercy Coll (NY)
Mercy Coll of Health Sciences (IA)
Merrimack Coll (MA)
Metropolitan State U (MN)
Miami U (OH)
Michigan Technological U (MI)
Middlebury Coll (VT)
Middle Tennessee State U (TN)
Midwestern State U (TX)
Mississippi State U (MS)
Mississippi U for Women (MS)
Missouri Southern State U (MO)
Mitchell Coll (CT)
Monmouth Coll (IL)
Montana State U (MT)
Montana State U Billings (MT)
Montana Tech of The U of Montana (MT)
Morris Coll (SC)
Mount Allison U (NB, Canada)
Mount Aloysius Coll (PA)
Mount Marty Coll (SD)
Mount Mary U (WI)
Mount Saint Mary's U (CA)
Murray State U (KY)
National U (CA)
Neumann U (PA)
New Coll of Florida (FL)
Newman U (KS)
New Mexico Highlands U (NM)
New Mexico State U (NM)
New Saint Andrews Coll (ID)
New York City Coll of Technology of the City U of New York (NY)
New York U (NY)
Niagara U (NY)
North Carolina Ag and Tech State U (NC)
North Carolina State U (NC)
North Carolina Wesleyan Coll (NC)

North Central Coll (IL)
Northeastern Illinois U (IL)
Northern Arizona U (AZ)
Northern Illinois U (IL)
Northern Kentucky U (KY)
Northern Michigan U (MI)
North Greenville U (SC)
Northwestern Coll (IA)
Northwestern U (IL)
Northwest Nazarene U (ID)
Notre Dame of Maryland U (MD)
Oakland U (MI)
Ohio Dominican U (OH)
Ohio Valley U (WV)
Oklahoma Christian U (OK)
Oklahoma City U (OK)
Oklahoma State U (OK)
Olivet Coll (MI)
Olivet Nazarene U (IL)
Oregon State U (OR)
Our Lady of the Lake U of San Antonio (TX)
Pacific U (OR)
Park U (MO)
Patrick Henry Coll (VA)
Penn State Abington (PA)
Penn State Altoona (PA)
Penn State Beaver (PA)
Penn State Berks (PA)
Penn State Brandywine (PA)
Penn State DuBois (PA)
Penn State Erie, The Behrend Coll (PA)
Penn State Fayette, The Eberly Campus (PA)
Penn State Greater Allegheny (PA)
Penn State Lehigh Valley (PA)
Penn State Mont Alto (PA)
Penn State New Kensington (PA)
Penn State Schuylkill (PA)
Penn State Shenango (PA)
Penn State U Park (PA)
Penn State Wilkes-Barre (PA)
Penn State Worthington Scranton (PA)
Penn State York (PA)
Pepperdine U, Malibu (CA)
Peru State Coll (NE)
Pittsburg State U (KS)
Point Loma Nazarene U (CA)
Portland State U (OR)
Providence Coll (RI)
Purchase Coll, State U of New York (NY)
Purdue U Calumet (IN)
Quincy U (IL)
Quinnipiac U (CT)
Ramapo Coll of New Jersey (NJ)
Randolph Coll (VA)
Regis Coll (MA)
Regis U (CO)
Reinhardt U (GA)
Rhode Island Coll (RI)
Rider U (NJ)
Rivier U (NH)
Roberts Wesleyan Coll (NY)
Roger Williams U (RI)
Roosevelt U (IL)
Rowan U (NJ)
Rutgers, The State U of New Jersey, Camden (NJ)
Rutgers, The State U of New Jersey, New Brunswick (NJ)
Sacred Heart U (CT)
The Sage Colls (NY)
St. Catharine Coll (KY)
St. Edward's U (TX)
St. Francis Coll (NY)
St. Gregory's U, Shawnee (OK)
St. John Fisher Coll (NY)
St. John's Coll (MD)
St. John's Coll (NM)
Saint John's U (MN)
St. John's U (NY)
St. Joseph's Coll, Long Island Campus (NY)
St. Joseph's Coll, New York (NY)
Saint Joseph's U (PA)
St. Lawrence U (NY)
Saint Mary-of-the-Woods Coll (IN)
St. Olaf Coll (MN)
Saint Peter's U (NJ)
St. Thomas U (FL)
Saint Vincent Coll (PA)
Salisbury U (MD)
Salve Regina U (RI)
San Diego Christian Coll (CA)
San Diego State U (CA)
San Francisco State U (CA)
San Jose State U (CA)
Santa Clara U (CA)
Sarah Lawrence Coll (NY)
Seattle Pacific U (WA)
Seattle U (WA)
Shaw U (NC)
Shenandoah U (VA)
Shimer Coll (IL)
Shippensburg U of Pennsylvania (PA)
Simon Fraser U (BC, Canada)
Simpson U (CA)
Skidmore Coll (NY)
Soka U of America (CA)
South Dakota State U (SD)
Southern Connecticut State U (CT)
Southern Illinois U Carbondale (IL)
Southern Illinois U Edwardsville (IL)
Southern Oregon U (OR)
Southern Vermont Coll (VT)
Southwestern Coll (KS)
Spalding U (KY)
State U of New York at Fredonia (NY)
State U of New York at New Paltz (NY)
State U of New York at Plattsburgh (NY)
Stephen F. Austin State U (TX)
Stephens Coll (MO)
Stockton U (NJ)
Susquehanna U (PA)
Syracuse U (NY)
Tarleton State U (TX)
Tennessee State U (TN)
Texas A&M U–Commerce (TX)
Texas Tech U (TX)
Thomas Aquinas Coll (CA)
Thomas More Coll (KY)
Transylvania U (KY)
Trent U (ON, Canada)
Trine U (IN)
Troy U (AL)
Tufts U (MA)
Tulane U (LA)
Union Coll (NY)
Union Inst & U (OH)
The U of Akron (OH)
U of Alaska Fairbanks (AK)
U of Alaska Southeast, Sitka Campus (AK)
U of Alberta (AB, Canada)
U of Arkansas at Little Rock (AR)
The U of British Columbia (BC, Canada)
U of California, Riverside (CA)
U of California, Santa Barbara (CA)
U of Central Arkansas (AR)
U of Central Oklahoma (OK)
U of Chicago (IL)
U of Delaware (DE)
U of Evansville (IN)
U of Georgia (GA)
U of Hartford (CT)
U of Hawaii at Hilo (HI)
U of Hawaii at Manoa (HI)
U of Houston (TX)
U of Houston–Victoria (TX)
U of Illinois at Springfield (IL)
The U of Iowa (IA)
The U of Kansas (KS)
U of La Verne (CA)
U of Lethbridge (AB, Canada)
U of Louisville (KY)
U of Maine (ME)
U of Maine at Augusta (ME)
U of Maine at Fort Kent (ME)
U of Maine at Presque Isle (ME)
U of Mary Washington (VA)
U of Massachusetts Dartmouth (MA)
U of Massachusetts Lowell (MA)
U of Memphis (TN)
U of Michigan–Dearborn (MI)
U of Minnesota, Morris (MN)
U of Minnesota, Twin Cities Campus (MN)
U of Mississippi (MS)
U of Missouri–St. Louis (MO)
The U of Montana (MT)
The U of Montana Western (MT)
U of Nebraska–Lincoln (NE)
U of Nevada, Las Vegas (NV)
U of New Brunswick Saint John (NB, Canada)
U of New England (ME)
U of New Hampshire (NH)
U of New Haven (CT)
U of New Mexico (NM)
U of North Carolina at Asheville (NC)
The U of North Carolina at Chapel Hill (NC)
The U of North Carolina at Greensboro (NC)
U of Northern Iowa (IA)
U of North Texas (TX)
U of Notre Dame (IN)
U of Oklahoma (OK)
U of Pennsylvania (PA)
U of Pittsburgh (PA)
U of Pittsburgh at Bradford (PA)
U of Regina (SK, Canada)
U of Rochester (NY)
U of St. Francis (IL)
U of Saint Francis (IN)
U of Saint Mary (KS)
U of St. Thomas (TX)
U of San Diego (CA)
U of San Francisco (CA)
The U of Scranton (PA)
U of South Carolina Aiken (SC)
U of South Carolina Beaufort (SC)
The U of South Dakota (SD)
U of Southern Indiana (IN)
U of Southern Maine (ME)
The U of Tampa (FL)
The U of Texas at Austin (TX)
The U of Texas at Tyler (TX)
U of the Incarnate Word (TX)
The U of Toledo (OH)
The U of Tulsa (OK)
U of Vermont (VT)
U of Virginia (VA)
The U of Virginia's Coll at Wise (VA)
U of Waterloo (ON, Canada)
The U of Western Ontario (ON, Canada)
U of Wisconsin–Eau Claire (WI)
U of Wisconsin–Green Bay (WI)
U of Wisconsin–Oshkosh (WI)
U of Wisconsin–River Falls (WI)
U of Wisconsin–Waukesha (WI)
U of Wisconsin–Whitewater (WI)
Urbana U (OH)
Utah State U (UT)
Utica Coll (NY)
Villanova U (PA)
Virginia State U (VA)
Viterbo U (WI)
Walsh U (OH)
Warner Pacific Coll (OR)
Washburn U (KS)
Washington Coll (MD)
Washington State U (WA)
Washington U in St. Louis (MO)
Weber State U (UT)
Wesleyan U (CT)
West Chester U of Pennsylvania (PA)
Western Carolina U (NC)
Western Illinois U (IL)
Western New England U (MA)
Western Washington U (WA)
Westfield State U (MA)
West Virginia U (WV)
Wheeling Jesuit U (WV)
Wheelock Coll (MA)
Whittier Coll (CA)
Wilkes U (PA)
William Jewell Coll (MO)
William Paterson U of New Jersey (NJ)
William Peace U (NC)
Williams Baptist Coll (AR)
Wingate U (NC)
Wittenberg U (OH)
Wright State U (OH)
Xavier U (OH)
York Coll of the City U of New York (NY)
Youngstown State U (OH)

LIBRARY AND INFORMATION SCIENCE

Ball State U (IN)
Clarion U of Pennsylvania (PA)
Emory & Henry Coll (VA)
Kutztown U of Pennsylvania (PA)
Southern Connecticut State U (CT)
U of Maine at Augusta (ME)
U of Minnesota, Twin Cities Campus (MN)
U of Southern Mississippi (MS)

LIBRARY SCIENCE RELATED

Delaware State U (DE)
U of Great Falls (MT)

LICENSED PRACTICAL/ VOCATIONAL NURSE TRAINING

Campbellsville U (KY)
Lindenwood U (MO)
National U (CA)
York Coll of Pennsylvania (PA)

LINGUISTIC AND COMPARATIVE LANGUAGE STUDIES RELATED

Appalachian State U (NC)
Brigham Young U (UT)
Indiana U Bloomington (IN)
Iowa State U of Science and Technology (IA)
U of Alberta (AB, Canada)
U of California, Los Angeles (CA)
U of California, Santa Barbara (CA)
U of Kentucky (KY)
U of Southern California (CA)

LINGUISTICS

Bard Coll at Simon's Rock (MA)
Baylor U (TX)
Bethel U (MN)
Binghamton U, State U of New York (NY)
Biola U (CA)
Boston U (MA)
Brandeis U (MA)
Brown U (RI)
Bucknell U (PA)
California State U, Dominguez Hills (CA)
California State U, Fresno (CA)
California State U, Fullerton (CA)
California State U, Monterey Bay (CA)
Calvin Coll (MI)
Carleton Coll (MN)
Cedarville U (OH)
Central Coll (IA)
City Coll of the City U of New York (NY)
Cleveland State U (OH)
The Coll of William and Mary (VA)
Columbia U (NY)
Concordia U (QC, Canada)
Cornell U (NY)
Dartmouth Coll (NH)
Eastern Michigan U (MI)
Florida Atlantic U (FL)
Georgetown U (DC)
Georgia State U (GA)
Gordon Coll (MA)
Hampshire Coll (MA)
Harvard U (MA)
Hofstra U (NY)
Indiana U Bloomington (IN)
Iowa State U of Science and Technology (IA)
Lawrence U (WI)
Lehman Coll of the City U of New York (NY)
Macalester Coll (MN)
Massachusetts Inst of Technology (MA)
Miami U (OH)
Michigan State U (MI)
Mid-Atlantic Christian U (NC)
Montclair State U (NJ)
New York U (NY)
Northeastern Illinois U (IL)
Northeastern U (MA)
Northwestern U (IL)
Oakland U (MI)
The Ohio State U (OH)
Ohio U (OH)
Pomona Coll (CA)
Portland State U (OR)
Purdue U (IN)
Queens Coll of the City U of New York (NY)
Reed Coll (OR)
Rice U (TX)
Rutgers, The State U of New Jersey, New Brunswick (NJ)
Saint Joseph's U (PA)
San Diego State U (CA)
San Jose State U (CA)
Scripps Coll (CA)
Seattle Pacific U (WA)
Simon Fraser U (BC, Canada)
Southern Illinois U Carbondale (IL)
Stanford U (CA)
State U of New York at Oswego (NY)
Stony Brook U, State U of New York (NY)
Syracuse U (NY)
Temple U (PA)
Truman State U (MO)
Tulane U (LA)
Université de Montréal (QC, Canada)
U at Albany, State U of New York (NY)
U at Buffalo, the State U of New York (NY)
U of Alaska Fairbanks (AK)
U of Alberta (AB, Canada)
The U of Arizona (AZ)
The U of British Columbia (BC, Canada)
U of California, Berkeley (CA)
U of California, Davis (CA)
U of California, Riverside (CA)
U of California, Santa Barbara (CA)
U of California, Santa Cruz (CA)
U of Chicago (IL)
U of Colorado Boulder (CO)
U of Delaware (DE)
U of Florida (FL)
U of Georgia (GA)
U of Hawaii at Hilo (HI)
U of Houston (TX)
The U of Iowa (IA)
The U of Kansas (KS)
U of Kentucky (KY)
U of King's Coll (NS, Canada)
U of Maryland, Coll Park (MD)
U of Massachusetts Amherst (MA)
U of Michigan (MI)
U of Minnesota, Duluth (MN)
U of Minnesota, Twin Cities Campus (MN)
U of Mississippi (MS)
U of Missouri (MO)
The U of Montana (MT)
U of Nevada, Las Vegas (NV)
U of New Brunswick Saint John (NB, Canada)
U of New Hampshire (NH)
U of New Mexico (NM)
The U of North Carolina at Chapel Hill (NC)
U of North Texas (TX)
U of Oklahoma (OK)
U of Oregon (OR)
U of Ottawa (ON, Canada)
U of Pennsylvania (PA)
U of Pittsburgh (PA)
U of Regina (SK, Canada)
U of Rochester (NY)
U of Saskatchewan (SK, Canada)
U of Southern California (CA)
U of Southern Maine (ME)
The U of Texas at Arlington (TX)
The U of Texas at Austin (TX)
The U of Texas at El Paso (TX)
The U of Toledo (OH)
U of Toronto (ON, Canada)
U of Utah (UT)
U of Washington (WA)
The U of Western Ontario (ON, Canada)
U of Wisconsin–Madison (WI)
U of Wisconsin–Milwaukee (WI)
Ursinus Coll (PA)
Washington State U (WA)
Washington U in St. Louis (MO)
Wayne State U (MI)
Western Washington U (WA)
Yale U (CT)

LITERATURE

American U (DC)
Antioch Coll, Yellow Springs (OH)
Ave Maria U (FL)
Bard Coll at Simon's Rock (MA)
Bryant U (RI)
Calvin Coll (MI)
Castleton State Coll (VT)
Central Michigan U (MI)
Concordia U, St. Paul (MN)

Dixie State U (UT)
Duquesne U (PA)
Florida Southern Coll (FL)
Grove City Coll (PA)
Linfield Coll (OR)
Lipscomb U (TN)
Lubbock Christian U (TX)
Marymount Manhattan Coll (NY)
Massachusetts Coll of Liberal Arts (MA)
New York U (NY)
Occidental Coll (CA)
Saint Mary's U of Minnesota (MN)
Southwestern Coll (KS)
U of Michigan–Flint (MI)
Washington U in St. Louis (MO)
Williams Coll (MA)
Yeshiva U (NY)

LITERATURE RELATED
The American U of Paris (France)

LIVESTOCK MANAGEMENT
Fort Hays State U (KS)
Tarleton State U (TX)

LOGIC
U of Pennsylvania (PA)

LOGISTICS, MATERIALS, AND SUPPLY CHAIN MANAGEMENT
Albany State U (GA)
American Public U System (WV)
Arkansas State U (AR)
Athens State U (AL)
Auburn U (AL)
Baylor U (TX)
Binghamton U, State U of New York (NY)
Bowling Green State U (OH)
Brigham Young U (UT)
Bryant U (RI)
California State U, Dominguez Hills (CA)
Central Michigan U (MI)
Central Washington U (WA)
Clarkson U (NY)
Clayton State U (GA)
Concordia U (QC, Canada)
Duquesne U (PA)
Eastern Michigan U (MI)
Elmhurst Coll (IL)
Florida Inst of Technology (FL)
Florida State Coll at Jacksonville (FL)
Gannon U (PA)
Georgia Southern U (GA)
HEC Montreal (QC, Canada)
Hofstra U (NY)
Iowa State U of Science and Technology (IA)
Lehigh U (PA)
Maine Maritime Acad (ME)
Miami Dade Coll (FL)
Michigan State U (MI)
Missouri Southern State U (MO)
Missouri State U (MO)
Murray State U (KY)
Niagara U (NY)
Northeastern State U (OK)
Northeastern U (MA)
The Ohio State U (OH)
Park U (MO)
Penn State Beaver (PA)
Penn State Brandywine (PA)
Penn State Fayette, The Eberly Campus (PA)
Penn State Greater Allegheny (PA)
Penn State Hazleton (PA)
Penn State Lehigh Valley (PA)
Penn State New Kensington (PA)
Penn State Schuylkill (PA)
Penn State Shenango (PA)
Penn State York (PA)
Portland State U (OR)
Rutgers, The State U of New Jersey, Newark (NJ)
Rutgers, The State U of New Jersey, New Brunswick (NJ)
Shippensburg U of Pennsylvania (PA)
Southeastern Louisiana U (LA)
Sullivan U (KY)
Syracuse U (NY)
Texas A&M U (TX)
Texas Christian U (TX)
United States Merchant Marine Acad (NY)
U of Arkansas (AR)
The U of Findlay (OH)
The U of Kansas (KS)
U of Maryland, Coll Park (MD)
U of Memphis (TN)
U of Nebraska–Lincoln (NE)
U of North Texas (TX)
U of Pittsburgh (PA)
U of Rhode Island (RI)
U of St. Francis (IL)
The U of Tennessee (TN)
The U of Texas at Austin (TX)
The U of Texas at Dallas (TX)
The U of Toledo (OH)
U of Washington (WA)
U of Wisconsin–Stout (WI)
Weber State U (UT)
Western Illinois U (IL)
Western Michigan U (MI)
Wright State U (OH)
York Coll of Pennsylvania (PA)

LONG TERM CARE ADMINISTRATION
Weber State U (UT)

MAGNETIC RESONANCE IMAGING (MRI) TECHNOLOGY
American U of Beirut (Lebanon)
Saint Louis U (MO)

MANAGEMENT INFORMATION SYSTEMS
Adams State U (CO)
Albany State U (GA)
The American U of Paris (France)
Angelo State U (TX)
Anna Maria Coll (MA)
Appalachian State U (NC)
Arcadia U (PA)
Auburn U (AL)
Auburn U at Montgomery (AL)
Augsburg Coll (MN)
Augustana Coll (SD)
Avila U (MO)
Azusa Pacific U (CA)
Babson Coll (MA)
Baker Coll (MI)
Ball State U (IN)
Barry U (FL)
Baylor U (TX)
Belmont U (TN)
Binghamton U, State U of New York (NY)
Biola U (CA)
Boston Coll (MA)
Bowling Green State U (OH)
Bradley U (IL)
Bridgewater Coll (VA)
Bridgewater State U (MA)
Buena Vista U (IA)
Butler U (IN)
California State U, Fresno (CA)
California State U, Long Beach (CA)
Calvin Coll (MI)
Canisius Coll (NY)
Cardinal Stritch U (WI)
Carson-Newman U (TN)
Catawba Coll (NC)
Cedarville U (OH)
Central Connecticut State U (CT)
Central Michigan U (MI)
Central Washington U (WA)
Charleston Southern U (SC)
Claflin U (SC)
Clarkson U (NY)
Cleveland State U (OH)
Colorado Mesa U (CO)
Colorado State U (CO)
Columbia Coll (MO)
Columbus State U (GA)
Concordia U (QC, Canada)
Concordia U, Nebraska (NE)
Corban U (OR)
Dallas Baptist U (TX)
Daniel Webster Coll (NH)
Delta State U (MS)
DePaul U (IL)
DeSales U (PA)
Dominican Coll (NY)
Drexel U (PA)
Drury U (MO)
Duquesne U (PA)
East Carolina U (NC)
Eastern Connecticut State U (CT)
Eastern Kentucky U (KY)
Eastern Michigan U (MI)
Eastern New Mexico U (NM)
Edgewood Coll (WI)
Elizabethtown Coll School of Continuing and Professional Studies (PA)
Ellis U (IL)
Elmhurst Coll (IL)
Eureka Coll (IL)
Excelsior Coll (NY)
Fairfield U (CT)
Fayetteville State U (NC)
Ferrum Coll (VA)
Florida Atlantic U (FL)
Florida Inst of Technology (FL)
Florida Intl U (FL)
Fordham U (NY)
Fort Hays State U (KS)
Francis Marion U (SC)
Franklin U (OH)
Gannon U (PA)
Georgia Regents U (GA)
Georgia Southern U (GA)
Governors State U (IL)
Grace Coll (IN)
Graceland U (IA)
Grand View U (IA)
Granite State Coll (NH)
Greenville Coll (IL)
Hardin-Simmons U (TX)
Harris-Stowe State U (MO)
HEC Montreal (QC, Canada)
Hofstra U (NY)
Holy Family U (PA)
Howard Payne U (TX)
Husson U (ME)
Illinois Coll (IL)
Illinois State U (IL)
Immaculata U (PA)
Indiana State U (IN)
Indiana U of Pennsylvania (PA)
Inter American U of Puerto Rico, Aguadilla Campus (PR)
Inter American U of Puerto Rico, Fajardo Campus (PR)
Inter American U of Puerto Rico, Ponce Campus (PR)
Iona Coll (NY)
Iowa State U of Science and Technology (IA)
Jacksonville U (FL)
John Brown U (AR)
Johnson State Coll (VT)
Keiser U, Fort Lauderdale (FL)
Lamar U (TX)
La Salle U (PA)
Lee U (TN)
Le Moyne Coll (NY)
Lenoir-Rhyne U (NC)
LeTourneau U (TX)
Lewis U (IL)
Liberty U (VA)
Lincoln U (CA)
Lindenwood U (MO)
Linfield Coll (OR)
Loras Coll (IA)
Loyola Marymount U (CA)
Loyola U Chicago (IL)
Lubbock Christian U (TX)
Luther Coll (IA)
Madonna U (MI)
Marshall U (WV)
Maryville U of Saint Louis (MO)
Massachusetts Coll of Liberal Arts (MA)
The Master's Coll and Sem (CA)
McMurry U (TX)
Menlo Coll (CA)
Mercer U, Macon (GA)
Metropolitan State U (MN)
Miami U (OH)
Michigan Technological U (MI)
Middle Tennessee State U (TN)
Millikin U (IL)
Milwaukee School of Eng (WI)
Minot State U (ND)
Misericordia U (PA)
Mississippi State U (MS)
Missouri State U (MO)
Morehead State U (KY)
Morrisville State Coll (NY)
Mount Mercy U (IA)
Mount Vernon Nazarene U (OH)
National U (CA)
National U Coll, Bayamón (PR)
Neumont U (UT)
Newman U (KS)
New Mexico Highlands U (NM)
Nicholls State U (LA)
North Dakota State U (ND)
Northeastern State U (OK)
Northeastern U (MA)
Northern Arizona U (AZ)
Northern Illinois U (IL)
Northern Kentucky U (KY)
Northern Michigan U (MI)
Northern State U (SD)
Northwest Missouri State U (MO)
Northwood U, Michigan Campus (MI)
Oakland U (MI)
Ohio Northern U (OH)
The Ohio State U (OH)
Ohio U (OH)
Oklahoma Baptist U (OK)
Old Dominion U (VA)
Olivet Nazarene U (IL)
Oregon State U (OR)
Park U (MO)
Penn State Abington (PA)
Penn State Altoona (PA)
Penn State Beaver (PA)
Penn State Berks (PA)
Penn State Brandywine (PA)
Penn State DuBois (PA)
Penn State Erie, The Behrend Coll (PA)
Penn State Fayette, The Eberly Campus (PA)
Penn State Greater Allegheny (PA)
Penn State Harrisburg (PA)
Penn State Hazleton (PA)
Penn State Lehigh Valley (PA)
Penn State Mont Alto (PA)
Penn State New Kensington (PA)
Penn State Schuylkill (PA)
Penn State Shenango (PA)
Penn State U Park (PA)
Penn State Wilkes-Barre (PA)
Penn State Worthington Scranton (PA)
Penn State York (PA)
Peru State Coll (NE)
Philadelphia U (PA)
Point Loma Nazarene U (CA)
Post U (CT)
Prairie View A&M U (TX)
Rhode Island Coll (RI)
Robert Morris U (PA)
Rochester Inst of Technology (NY)
Rockford U (IL)
Rocky Mountain Coll (MT)
Roger Williams U (RI)
Rowan U (NJ)
Rutgers, The State U of New Jersey, Newark (NJ)
St. Catherine U (MN)
Saint Francis U (PA)
St. Gregory's U, Shawnee (OK)
St. John's U (NY)
Saint Joseph's U (PA)
Saint Mary's Coll (IN)
Sam Houston State U (TX)
Santa Clara U (CA)
Seattle Pacific U (WA)
Seton Hill U (PA)
Shawnee State U (OH)
Simon Fraser U (BC, Canada)
Southeastern U (FL)
Southern Adventist U (TN)
Southern Illinois U Edwardsville (IL)
Southwestern Coll (KS)
State U of New York at Plattsburgh (NY)
State U of New York Coll at Old Westbury (NY)
Stetson U (FL)
Stevenson U (MD)
Tarleton State U (TX)
Texas A&M Intl U (TX)
Texas A&M U (TX)
Texas A&M U–Commerce (TX)
Texas A&M U–Corpus Christi (TX)
Texas A&M U–Kingsville (TX)
Texas Southern U (TX)
Texas State U (TX)
Thiel Coll (PA)
Universidad del Turabo (PR)
Universidad Metropolitana (PR)
Université du Québec en Outaouais (QC, Canada)
The U of Akron (OH)
The U of Alabama (AL)
The U of Alabama at Birmingham (AL)
The U of Alabama in Huntsville (AL)
U of Alberta (AB, Canada)
The U of Arizona (AZ)
U of Arkansas (AR)
U of Arkansas at Little Rock (AR)
U of Bridgeport (CT)
The U of British Columbia (BC, Canada)
U of Central Arkansas (AR)
U of Central Missouri (MO)
U of Central Oklahoma (OK)
U of Colorado Boulder (CO)
U of Dayton (OH)
U of Delaware (DE)
U of Denver (CO)
U of Evansville (IN)
U of Georgia (GA)
U of Hawaii at Manoa (HI)
U of Houston (TX)
U of Houston–Downtown (TX)
U of Idaho (ID)
The U of Iowa (IA)
U of Jamestown (ND)
The U of Kansas (KS)
U of Lethbridge (AB, Canada)
U of Louisville (KY)
U of Mary Hardin-Baylor (TX)
U of Massachusetts Dartmouth (MA)
U of Memphis (TN)
U of Michigan–Dearborn (MI)
U of Minnesota, Twin Cities Campus (MN)
U of Mississippi (MS)
U of Missouri (MO)
U of Missouri–St. Louis (MO)
U of Nevada, Las Vegas (NV)
U of North Alabama (AL)
The U of North Carolina at Charlotte (NC)
U of Northern Iowa (IA)
U of North Texas (TX)
U of Northwestern–St. Paul (MN)
U of Notre Dame (IN)
U of Oklahoma (OK)
U of Ottawa (ON, Canada)
U of Pennsylvania (PA)
U of Puget Sound (WA)
U of San Francisco (CA)
U of Southern Mississippi (MS)
U of South Florida (FL)
U of South Florida, St. Petersburg (FL)
The U of Tennessee at Martin (TN)
The U of Texas at Arlington (TX)
The U of Texas at Austin (TX)
The U of Texas at Dallas (TX)
The U of Texas at San Antonio (TX)
The U of Texas–Pan American (TX)
U of the Cumberlands (KY)
U of the District of Columbia (DC)
U of the Incarnate Word (TX)
The U of Toledo (OH)
The U of Tulsa (OK)
U of Utah (UT)
U of Washington (WA)
The U of West Alabama (AL)
The U of Western Ontario (ON, Canada)
U of West Florida (FL)
U of West Georgia (GA)
U of Wisconsin–Green Bay (WI)
U of Wisconsin–La Crosse (WI)
U of Wisconsin–Madison (WI)
U of Wisconsin–Milwaukee (WI)
U of Wisconsin–Oshkosh (WI)
U of Wisconsin–River Falls (WI)
Upper Iowa U (IA)
Ursuline Coll (OH)
Valley City State U (ND)
Villanova U (PA)
Virginia State U (VA)
Virginia Union U (VA)
Viterbo U (WI)
Wake Forest U (NC)
Walla Walla U (WA)
Washington State U (WA)
Washington State U Vancouver (WA)
Wayne State U (MI)
Weber State U (UT)
Western Carolina U (NC)
Western Kentucky U (KY)

Western New England U (MA)
Western State Colorado U (CO)
Western Washington U (WA)
Westminster Coll (MO)
West Texas A&M U (TX)
West Virginia U (WV)
Wichita State U (KS)
William Woods U (MO)
Winona State U (MN)
Worcester Polytechnic Inst (MA)
Wright State U (OH)
Xavier U (OH)
Yeshiva U (NY)
York Coll of Pennsylvania (PA)
York Coll of the City U of New York (NY)
Youngstown State U (OH)

MANAGEMENT INFORMATION SYSTEMS AND SERVICES RELATED
Buena Vista U (IA)
Cardinal Stritch U (WI)
DeSales U (PA)
Fordham U (NY)
Franklin U (OH)
Midwestern State U (TX)
Montana Tech of The U of Montana (MT)
Newberry Coll (SC)
Northern Michigan U (MI)
Purdue U Calumet (IN)
St. Bonaventure U (NY)
Temple U (PA)
U of Pittsburgh (PA)
U of the Virgin Islands (VI)
Western New England U (MA)
Westminster Coll (UT)
Widener U (PA)

MANAGEMENT SCIENCE
Alma Coll (MI)
American Intl Coll (MA)
Arizona State U at the Tempe campus (AZ)
Auburn U (AL)
Averett U (VA)
Belmont U (TN)
Bridgewater State U (MA)
Bryant U (RI)
The Catholic U of America (DC)
Central Methodist U (MO)
Cheyney U of Pennsylvania (PA)
Dalhousie U (NS, Canada)
DePaul U (IL)
DEREE - The American Coll of Greece (Greece)
Duquesne U (PA)
Eastern Illinois U (IL)
Ellis U (IL)
Elon U (NC)
Fitchburg State U (MA)
Grand Valley State U (MI)
Granite State Coll (NH)
Great Basin Coll (NV)
Hamline U (MN)
Hardin-Simmons U (TX)
HEC Montreal (QC, Canada)
Illinois State U (IL)
Jacksonville U (FL)
John Brown U (AR)
Johnson & Wales U - Charlotte Campus (NC)
Keiser U, Fort Lauderdale (FL)
La Roche Coll (PA)
Lehigh U (PA)
Lenoir-Rhyne U (NC)
Louisiana State U and A&M Coll (LA)
Lourdes U (OH)
Manhattan Coll (NY)
McKendree U (IL)
Miami U (OH)
National U (CA)
Northern Illinois U (IL)
Oakland City U (IN)
Ohio Northern U (OH)
Oklahoma Baptist U (OK)
Point Loma Nazarene U (CA)
Portland State U (OR)
Quincy U (IL)
Rider U (NJ)
Rocky Mountain Coll (MT)
Roosevelt U (IL)
Rutgers, The State U of New Jersey, New Brunswick (NJ)
St. Gregory's U, Shawnee (OK)
Saint Leo U (FL)
Salve Regina U (RI)
Shippensburg U of Pennsylvania (PA)
Siena Coll (NY)
Simon Fraser U (BC, Canada)
Slippery Rock U of Pennsylvania (PA)
Southeastern Oklahoma State U (OK)
Southern Adventist U (TN)
Southern Illinois U Carbondale (IL)
Southwestern Assemblies of God U (TX)
State U of New York at Oswego (NY)
Texas Christian U (TX)
Texas Wesleyan U (TX)
Trinity U (TX)
United States Coast Guard Acad (CT)
The U of Alabama (AL)
U of Alberta (AB, Canada)
U of Arkansas (AR)
U of California, Merced (CA)
U of Delaware (DE)
U of Florida (FL)
U of Great Falls (MT)
U of Illinois at Chicago (IL)
The U of Iowa (IA)
U of Kentucky (KY)
U of Maryland, Coll Park (MD)
U of Memphis (TN)
U of Miami (FL)
U of Minnesota, Morris (MN)
U of St. Francis (IL)
The U of Tennessee at Martin (TN)
The U of Texas at San Antonio (TX)
U of the Fraser Valley (BC, Canada)
The U of Toledo (OH)
U of Washington, Tacoma (WA)
U of Wyoming (WY)
Valparaiso U (IN)
Vaughn Coll of Aeronautics and Technology (NY)
Virginia Polytechnic Inst and State U (VA)
Wake Forest U (NC)
Western Kentucky U (KY)
William Paterson U of New Jersey (NJ)

MANAGEMENT SCIENCES AND QUANTITATIVE METHODS RELATED
Arkansas Tech U (AR)
Canisius Coll (NY)
George Mason U (VA)
HEC Montreal (QC, Canada)
Indiana State U (IN)
Inter American U of Puerto Rico, Fajardo Campus (PR)
Miami U (OH)
Pace U (NY)
Penn State Lehigh Valley (PA)
Penn State Schuylkill (PA)
Rutgers, The State U of New Jersey, New Brunswick (NJ)
Southwest Minnesota State U (MN)
The U of Iowa (IA)
U of Pennsylvania (PA)

MANUFACTURING ENGINEERING
Arizona State U at the Polytechnic campus (AZ)
Boston U (MA)
Bradley U (IL)
Brigham Young U (UT)
California Polytechnic State U, San Luis Obispo (CA)
California State Polytechnic U, Pomona (CA)
Cape Breton U (NS, Canada)
Central State U (OH)
Hofstra U (NY)
Miami U (OH)
National U (CA)
New Jersey Inst of Technology (NJ)
North Dakota State U (ND)
Northwestern U (IL)
Oregon State U (OR)
Robert Morris U (PA)
Southern Illinois U Edwardsville (IL)
Texas State U (TX)
U of California, Berkeley (CA)
U of Michigan–Dearborn (MI)
U of Toronto (ON, Canada)
U of Wisconsin–Milwaukee (WI)
U of Wisconsin–Stout (WI)
Virginia State U (VA)
Washington State U (WA)
Western Washington U (WA)
Wichita State U (KS)

MANUFACTURING ENGINEERING TECHNOLOGY
Arizona State U at the Polytechnic campus (AZ)
Berea Coll (KY)
Bowling Green State U (OH)
Bradley U (IL)
California State U, Long Beach (CA)
Central Connecticut State U (CT)
Central Michigan U (MI)
Central Washington U (WA)
East Carolina U (NC)
Eastern Michigan U (MI)
Farmingdale State Coll (NY)
Fitchburg State U (MA)
Indiana State U (IN)
Midwestern State U (TX)
Missouri Western State U (MO)
Morehead State U (KY)
Murray State U (KY)
New England Inst of Technology (RI)
North Carolina Ag and Tech State U (NC)
Northern Kentucky U (KY)
Ohio Northern U (OH)
Pennsylvania Coll of Technology (PA)
Pittsburg State U (KS)
Purdue U (IN)
Rochester Inst of Technology (NY)
State U of New York Coll of Technology at Alfred (NY)
Sullivan Coll of Technology and Design (KY)
Tarleton State U (TX)
Texas A&M U (TX)
Texas State U (TX)
The U of Akron (OH)
U of Memphis (TN)
U of Northern Iowa (IA)
U of Southern Indiana (IN)
Wayne State U (MI)
Weber State U (UT)
Western Carolina U (NC)
Western Kentucky U (KY)

MARINE BIOLOGY AND BIOLOGICAL OCEANOGRAPHY
Alabama State U (AL)
Alaska Pacific U (AK)
Auburn U (AL)
Barry U (FL)
Bemidji State U (MN)
Boston U (MA)
Brown U (RI)
California State U, Long Beach (CA)
Cheyney U of Pennsylvania (PA)
Coastal Carolina U (SC)
Coll of Charleston (SC)
Coll of the Atlantic (ME)
Dalhousie U (NS, Canada)
Dowling Coll (NY)
East Stroudsburg U of Pennsylvania (PA)
Eckerd Coll (FL)
Fairleigh Dickinson U, Coll at Florham (NJ)
Fairleigh Dickinson U, Metropolitan Campus (NJ)
Florida Inst of Technology (FL)
Florida Intl U (FL)
Florida Southern Coll (FL)
Gettysburg Coll (PA)
Hampton U (VA)
Hawai`i Pacific U (HI)
Humboldt State U (CA)
Jacksonville State U (AL)
Jacksonville U (FL)
Maine Maritime Acad (ME)
Monmouth U (NJ)
Montclair State U (NJ)
New Coll of Florida (FL)
Northeastern U (MA)
Northwest Missouri State U (MO)
Nova Southeastern U (FL)
Prescott Coll (AZ)
Roger Williams U (RI)
Rollins Coll (FL)
Rutgers, The State U of New Jersey, New Brunswick (NJ)
Saint Francis U (PA)
Samford U (AL)
San Francisco State U (CA)
San Jose State U (CA)
Savannah State U (GA)
Southwestern Coll (KS)
Spring Hill Coll (AL)
Stockton U (NJ)
Stony Brook U, State U of New York (NY)
Texas A&M U (TX)
Troy U (AL)
Unity Coll (ME)
The U of Alabama (AL)
The U of British Columbia (BC, Canada)
U of California, Los Angeles (CA)
U of California, Santa Barbara (CA)
U of California, Santa Cruz (CA)
U of Delaware (DE)
U of Guelph (ON, Canada)
U of Hawaii at Hilo (HI)
U of Hawaii at Manoa (HI)
U of King's Coll (NS, Canada)
U of Maine at Machias (ME)
U of Miami (FL)
U of Mobile (AL)
U of New England (ME)
U of New Haven (CT)
U of North Alabama (AL)
The U of North Carolina Wilmington (NC)
U of Oregon (OR)
U of Puerto Rico in Ponce (PR)
U of Rhode Island (RI)
U of San Diego (CA)
U of Southern Mississippi (MS)
The U of Tampa (FL)
U of the Virgin Islands (VI)
The U of West Alabama (AL)
U of West Florida (FL)
Waynesburg U (PA)
Western Washington U (WA)

MARINE SCIENCE/MERCHANT MARINE OFFICER
Hampton U (VA)
Jacksonville U (FL)
Maine Maritime Acad (ME)
Massachusetts Maritime Acad (MA)
Northwestern Michigan Coll (MI)
Texas A&M U (TX)
United States Merchant Marine Acad (NY)

MARINE SCIENCES
California State U, Monterey Bay (CA)
Texas A&M U (TX)
U of Maine (ME)

MARINE TRANSPORTATION RELATED
Northwestern Michigan Coll (MI)
United States Merchant Marine Acad (NY)

MARITIME STUDIES
Coll of the Atlantic (ME)
Texas A&M U (TX)
United States Merchant Marine Acad (NY)

MARKETING/MARKETING MANAGEMENT
Abilene Christian U (TX)
Adams State U (CO)
Adelphi U (NY)
Alabama State U (AL)
Albany State U (GA)
Albertus Magnus Coll (CT)
Albright Coll (PA)
Alma Coll (MI)
Alvernia U (PA)
American Intl Coll (MA)
American Public U System (WV)
The American U of Paris (France)
Anderson U (IN)
Andrews U (MI)
Angelo State U (TX)
Anna Maria Coll (MA)
Appalachian State U (NC)
Arcadia U (PA)
Arizona State U at the Tempe campus (AZ)
Arkansas State U (AR)
Ashland U (OH)
Assumption Coll (MA)
Auburn U (AL)
Auburn U at Montgomery (AL)
Augsburg Coll (MN)
Averett U (VA)
Avila U (MO)
Azusa Pacific U (CA)
Babson Coll (MA)
Baker Coll (MI)
Baldwin Wallace U (OH)
Ball State U (IN)
Barry U (FL)
Baylor U (TX)
Bay Path U (MA)
Becker Coll (MA)
Belmont U (TN)
Benedictine Coll (KS)
Benedictine U (IL)
Bentley U (MA)
Berkeley Coll, Woodland Park (NJ)
Berkeley Coll–New York City Campus (NY)
Berkeley Coll–Westchester Campus (NY)
Berry Coll (GA)
Bethany Coll (WV)
Binghamton U, State U of New York (NY)
Biola U (CA)
Blackburn Coll (IL)
Black Hills State U (SD)
Bluffton U (OH)
Boston Coll (MA)
Bowie State U (MD)
Bradley U (IL)
Brenau U (GA)
Bridgewater State U (MA)
Bryant U (RI)
Bucknell U (PA)
Buena Vista U (IA)
Butler U (IN)
Cabrini Coll (PA)
Caldwell U (NJ)
California Baptist U (CA)
California Lutheran U (CA)
California State U, Dominguez Hills (CA)
California State U, Fresno (CA)
California State U, Fullerton (CA)
California State U, Long Beach (CA)
California State U, Sacramento (CA)
California State U, San Marcos (CA)
California State U, Stanislaus (CA)
Calvary Bible Coll and Theological Sem (MO)
Campbellsville U (KY)
Canisius Coll (NY)
Cape Breton U (NS, Canada)
Capital U (OH)
Caribbean U (PR)
Carson-Newman U (TN)
Case Western Reserve U (OH)
Castleton State Coll (VT)
Catawba Coll (NC)
Cedarville U (OH)
Central Connecticut State U (CT)
Central Michigan U (MI)
Central Washington U (WA)
Chaminade U of Honolulu (HI)
Champlain Coll (VT)
Charleston Southern U (SC)
Chatham U (PA)
Chestnut Hill Coll (PA)
Cheyney U of Pennsylvania (PA)
Chowan U (NC)
Christopher Newport U (VA)
Claflin U (SC)
Clarion U of Pennsylvania (PA)
Clayton State U (GA)
Cleveland State U (OH)
Coastal Carolina U (SC)
The Coll at Brockport, State U of New York (NY)
Coll of Charleston (SC)
The Coll of St. Scholastica (MN)
Coll of the Ozarks (MO)
The Coll of William and Mary (VA)
Colorado State U (CO)
Columbia Coll (MO)
Columbia Coll Chicago (IL)

Columbia Southern U (AL)
Columbus State U (GA)
Concordia U (QC, Canada)
Concordia U Chicago (IL)
Concordia U, Nebraska (NE)
Concordia U, St. Paul (MN)
Concordia U Wisconsin (WI)
Cornerstone U (MI)
Creighton U (NE)
Dakota State U (SD)
Dalhousie U (NS, Canada)
Dallas Baptist U (TX)
Daniel Webster Coll (NH)
Davenport U, Grand Rapids (MI)
Delaware State U (DE)
Delta State U (MS)
DePaul U (IL)
DEREE - The American Coll of Greece (Greece)
DeSales U (PA)
Dickinson State U (ND)
Dominican Coll (NY)
Dominican U (IL)
Dowling Coll (NY)
Drake U (IA)
Drexel U (PA)
Drury U (MO)
Duquesne U (PA)
East Carolina U (NC)
Eastern Illinois U (IL)
Eastern Kentucky U (KY)
Eastern Michigan U (MI)
East Tennessee State U (TN)
Elizabethtown Coll School of Continuing and Professional Studies (PA)
Ellis U (IL)
Elmhurst Coll (IL)
Elms Coll (MA)
Elon U (NC)
Emerson Coll (MA)
Emporia State U (KS)
Endicott Coll (MA)
Evangel U (MO)
Excelsior Coll (NY)
Fairfield U (CT)
Fairleigh Dickinson U, Coll at Florham (NJ)
Fairleigh Dickinson U, Metropolitan Campus (NJ)
Fayetteville State U (NC)
Ferris State U (MI)
FIDM/Fashion Inst of Design & Merchandising, Los Angeles Campus (CA)
Fisher Coll (MA)
Fitchburg State U (MA)
Florida Atlantic U (FL)
Florida Gulf Coast U (FL)
Florida Inst of Technology (FL)
Florida Intl U (FL)
Fontbonne U (MO)
Fordham U (NY)
Fort Hays State U (KS)
Fort Lewis Coll (CO)
Framingham State U (MA)
Francis Marion U (SC)
Franklin Pierce U (NH)
Franklin U (OH)
Friends U (KS)
Gannon U (PA)
George Mason U (VA)
Georgetown U (DC)
The George Washington U (DC)
Georgia Coll & State U (GA)
Georgia Regents U (GA)
Georgia Southern U (GA)
Georgia Southwestern State U (GA)
Georgia State U (GA)
Gonzaga U (WA)
Goshen Coll (IN)
Grace Coll (IN)
Grambling State U (LA)
Grand Valley State U (MI)
Grand View U (IA)
Granite State Coll (NH)
Greenville Coll (IL)
Grove City Coll (PA)
Hamline U (MN)
Hampton U (VA)
Hannibal-LaGrange U (MO)
Harding U (AR)
Hardin-Simmons U (TX)
Hastings Coll (NE)
Hawai`i Pacific U (HI)
HEC Montreal (QC, Canada)
High Point U (NC)
Hillsdale Coll (MI)
Hofstra U (NY)
Holy Family U (PA)
Houston Baptist U (TX)
Howard Payne U (TX)
Howard U (DC)
Hult Intl Business School (United Kingdom)
Husson U (ME)
Illinois State U (IL)
Immaculata U (PA)
Indiana State U (IN)
Indiana U of Pennsylvania (PA)
Indiana U–Purdue U Fort Wayne (IN)
Inter American U of Puerto Rico, Aguadilla Campus (PR)
Inter American U of Puerto Rico, Bayamón Campus (PR)
Inter American U of Puerto Rico, Fajardo Campus (PR)
Inter American U of Puerto Rico, Ponce Campus (PR)
Inter American U of Puerto Rico, San Germán Campus (PR)
Iona Coll (NY)
Iowa State U of Science and Technology (IA)
Ithaca Coll (NY)
Jackson State U (MS)
Jacksonville State U (AL)
Jacksonville U (FL)
James Madison U (VA)
John Brown U (AR)
John Cabot U (Italy)
John Carroll U (OH)
Johnson & Wales U (CO)
Johnson & Wales U (FL)
Johnson & Wales U (RI)
Johnson & Wales U - Charlotte Campus (NC)
Johnson State Coll (VT)
Judson U (IL)
Juniata Coll (PA)
Kansas State U (KS)
Kansas Wesleyan U (KS)
Kean U (NJ)
Keiser U, Fort Lauderdale (FL)
Kennesaw State U (GA)
Kent State U (OH)
Kent State U at Stark (OH)
Keuka Coll (NY)
King's Coll (PA)
Lake Erie Coll (OH)
Lamar U (TX)
La Roche Coll (PA)
La Salle U (PA)
Lasell Coll (MA)
La Sierra U (CA)
Lehigh U (PA)
Le Moyne Coll (NY)
Lenoir-Rhyne U (NC)
LeTourneau U (TX)
Lewis U (IL)
LIM Coll (NY)
Limestone Coll (SC)
Lincoln Memorial U (TN)
Lindenwood U (MO)
Linfield Coll (OR)
Lipscomb U (TN)
Loras Coll (IA)
Louisiana Coll (LA)
Louisiana State U and A&M Coll (LA)
Louisiana State U in Shreveport (LA)
Loyola Marymount U (CA)
Loyola U Chicago (IL)
Loyola U New Orleans (LA)
Lubbock Christian U (TX)
Lynchburg Coll (VA)
Lynn U (FL)
Madonna U (MI)
Malone U (OH)
Manchester U (IN)
Manhattan Coll (NY)
Manhattanville Coll (NY)
Mansfield U of Pennsylvania (PA)
Maranatha Baptist U (WI)
Marian U (IN)
Marian U (WI)
Marietta Coll (OH)
Marquette U (WI)
Marshall U (WV)
Mars Hill U (NC)
Marymount Manhattan Coll (NY)
Maryville Coll (TN)
Maryville U of Saint Louis (MO)
Marywood U (PA)
Massachusetts Coll of Liberal Arts (MA)
McKendree U (IL)
McMurry U (TX)
McNeese State U (LA)
Menlo Coll (CA)
Mercer U, Macon (GA)
Mercy Coll (NY)
Merrimack Coll (MA)
Messiah Coll (PA)
Metropolitan State U (MN)
Miami U (OH)
Michigan State U (MI)
Michigan Technological U (MI)
MidAmerica Nazarene U (KS)
Middle Tennessee State U (TN)
Midwestern State U (TX)
Millikin U (IL)
Minnesota State U Mankato (MN)
Minot State U (ND)
Misericordia U (PA)
Mississippi State U (MS)
Missouri Baptist U (MO)
Missouri State U (MO)
Missouri Valley Coll (MO)
Missouri Western State U (MO)
Montana State U (MT)
Montana State U Billings (MT)
Morehead State U (KY)
Mount Mary U (WI)
Mount Mercy U (IA)
Mount Saint Mary's U (CA)
Mount Vernon Nazarene U (OH)
Murray State U (KY)
National U (CA)
Nazareth Coll of Rochester (NY)
Neumann U (PA)
New England Coll (NH)
New Mexico Highlands U (NM)
New Mexico State U (NM)
New York Inst of Technology (NY)
New York U (NY)
Niagara U (NY)
Nicholls State U (LA)
Nichols Coll (MA)
North Carolina Ag and Tech State U (NC)
North Carolina Wesleyan Coll (NC)
North Central Coll (IL)
North Dakota State U (ND)
Northeastern Illinois U (IL)
Northeastern State U (OK)
Northeastern U (MA)
Northern Arizona U (AZ)
Northern Illinois U (IL)
Northern Kentucky U (KY)
Northern Michigan U (MI)
Northern State U (SD)
North Greenville U (SC)
Northwest Christian U (OR)
Northwest Missouri State U (MO)
Northwest Nazarene U (ID)
Northwest U (WA)
Northwood U, Michigan Campus (MI)
Northwood U, Texas Campus (TX)
Nova Southeastern U (FL)
Oakland U (MI)
The Ohio State U (OH)
Ohio U (OH)
Ohio Valley U (WV)
Oklahoma Baptist U (OK)
Oklahoma Christian U (OK)
Oklahoma City U (OK)
Oklahoma State U (OK)
Old Dominion U (VA)
Olivet Coll (MI)
Olivet Nazarene U (IL)
Oregon State U (OR)
Pace U (NY)
Pacific U (OR)
Palm Beach Atlantic U (FL)
Park U (MO)
Penn State Abington (PA)
Penn State Altoona (PA)
Penn State Beaver (PA)
Penn State Berks (PA)
Penn State Brandywine (PA)
Penn State DuBois (PA)
Penn State Erie, The Behrend Coll (PA)
Penn State Fayette, The Eberly Campus (PA)
Penn State Greater Allegheny (PA)
Penn State Harrisburg (PA)
Penn State Hazleton (PA)
Penn State Lehigh Valley (PA)
Penn State Mont Alto (PA)
Penn State New Kensington (PA)
Penn State Schuylkill (PA)
Penn State Shenango (PA)
Penn State U Park (PA)
Penn State Wilkes-Barre (PA)
Penn State Worthington Scranton (PA)
Penn State York (PA)
Peru State Coll (NE)
Philadelphia U (PA)
Pittsburg State U (KS)
Plymouth State U (NH)
Point Loma Nazarene U (CA)
Point U (GA)
Polytechnic U of Puerto Rico (PR)
Portland State U (OR)
Post U (CT)
Prairie View A&M U (TX)
Providence Coll (RI)
Quincy U (IL)
Quinnipiac U (CT)
Radford U (VA)
Rasmussen Coll Bloomington (MN)
Rasmussen Coll Brooklyn Park (MN)
Rasmussen Coll Eagan (MN)
Rasmussen Coll Fort Myers (FL)
Rasmussen Coll Kansas City/ Overland Park (KS)
Rasmussen Coll Lake Elmo/ Woodbury (MN)
Rasmussen Coll Land O' Lakes (FL)
Rasmussen Coll Mankato (MN)
Rasmussen Coll Moorhead (MN)
Rasmussen Coll New Port Richey (FL)
Rasmussen Coll Ocala (FL)
Rasmussen Coll St. Cloud (MN)
Rasmussen Coll Tampa/Brandon (FL)
Rasmussen Coll Topeka (KS)
Regis U (CO)
Rhode Island Coll (RI)
Rider U (NJ)
Rivier U (NH)
Robert Morris U (PA)
Roberts Wesleyan Coll (NY)
Rochester Inst of Technology (NY)
Rockford U (IL)
Roger Williams U (RI)
Roosevelt U (IL)
Rowan U (NJ)
Rutgers, The State U of New Jersey, Camden (NJ)
Rutgers, The State U of New Jersey, Newark (NJ)
Rutgers, The State U of New Jersey, New Brunswick (NJ)
Sacred Heart U (CT)
Saginaw Valley State U (MI)
St. Bonaventure U (NY)
St. Catherine U (MN)
St. Edward's U (TX)
Saint Francis U (PA)
St. Gregory's U, Shawnee (OK)
St. John's U (NY)
St. Joseph's Coll, Long Island Campus (NY)
St. Joseph's Coll, New York (NY)
Saint Joseph's U (PA)
Saint Leo U (FL)
Saint Mary-of-the-Woods Coll (IN)
St. Mary's U (TX)
Saint Mary's U of Minnesota (MN)
Saint Peter's U (NJ)
St. Thomas Aquinas Coll (NY)
St. Thomas U (FL)
Saint Vincent Coll (PA)
Salisbury U (MD)
Salve Regina U (RI)
Samford U (AL)
Sam Houston State U (TX)
San Diego State U (CA)
San Francisco State U (CA)
San Jose State U (CA)
Santa Clara U (CA)
Savannah State U (GA)
Seattle U (WA)
Seton Hill U (PA)
Shippensburg U of Pennsylvania (PA)
Siena Coll (NY)
Simmons Coll (MA)
Simpson Coll (IA)
Slippery Rock U of Pennsylvania (PA)
South Carolina State U (SC)
Southeastern Louisiana U (LA)
Southeastern Oklahoma State U (OK)
Southeastern U (FL)
Southeast Missouri State U (MO)
Southern Adventist U (TN)
Southern Connecticut State U (CT)
Southern Illinois U Carbondale (IL)
Southern Methodist U (TX)
Southern New Hampshire U (NH)
Southern Oregon U (OR)
Southern Utah U (UT)
Southwest Baptist U (MO)
Southwestern Assemblies of God U (TX)
Southwestern Coll (KS)
Southwest Minnesota State U (MN)
Spring Hill Coll (AL)
State U of New York at Fredonia (NY)
State U of New York at Oswego (NY)
State U of New York at Plattsburgh (NY)
State U of New York Coll at Old Westbury (NY)
Stephen F. Austin State U (TX)
Stetson U (FL)
Stonehill Coll (MA)
Suffolk U (MA)
Syracuse U (NY)
Tabor Coll (KS)
Tarleton State U (TX)
Taylor U (IN)
Temple U (PA)
Tennessee Wesleyan Coll (TN)
Texas A&M Intl U (TX)
Texas A&M U (TX)
Texas A&M U–Commerce (TX)
Texas A&M U–Corpus Christi (TX)
Texas A&M U–Kingsville (TX)
Texas Christian U (TX)
Texas Southern U (TX)
Texas State U (TX)
Texas Tech U (TX)
Texas Wesleyan U (TX)
Texas Woman's U (TX)
Tiffin U (OH)
Trevecca Nazarene U (TN)
Trine U (IN)
Trinity Christian Coll (IL)
Trinity U (TX)
Tulane U (LA)
Union Coll (KY)
Union U (TN)
Universidad del Turabo (PR)
Universidad Metropolitana (PR)
Université de Sherbrooke (QC, Canada)
The U of Akron (OH)
The U of Alabama (AL)
The U of Alabama at Birmingham (AL)
The U of Alabama in Huntsville (AL)
U of Alberta (AB, Canada)
The U of Arizona (AZ)
U of Arkansas (AR)
U of Arkansas at Little Rock (AR)
U of Bridgeport (CT)
The U of British Columbia (BC, Canada)
The U of British Columbia–Okanagan Campus (BC, Canada)
U of Central Arkansas (AR)
U of Central Florida (FL)
U of Central Missouri (MO)
U of Central Oklahoma (OK)
U of Charleston (WV)
U of Cincinnati (OH)
U of Colorado Boulder (CO)
U of Dayton (OH)
U of Delaware (DE)
U of Denver (CO)
U of Evansville (IN)
The U of Findlay (OH)
U of Florida (FL)
U of Georgia (GA)
U of Great Falls (MT)
U of Guelph (ON, Canada)
U of Hawaii at Manoa (HI)

U of Houston (TX)
U of Houston–Clear Lake (TX)
U of Houston–Downtown (TX)
U of Houston–Victoria (TX)
U of Idaho (ID)
U of Illinois at Chicago (IL)
U of Indianapolis (IN)
The U of Iowa (IA)
U of Jamestown (ND)
The U of Kansas (KS)
U of Kentucky (KY)
U of La Verne (CA)
U of Lethbridge (AB, Canada)
U of Louisiana at Lafayette (LA)
U of Louisville (KY)
U of Maine (ME)
U of Maine at Machias (ME)
U of Mary Hardin-Baylor (TX)
U of Maryland, Coll Park (MD)
U of Maryland U Coll (MD)
U of Massachusetts Amherst (MA)
U of Massachusetts Dartmouth (MA)
U of Memphis (TN)
U of Miami (FL)
U of Michigan–Dearborn (MI)
U of Michigan–Flint (MI)
U of Minnesota, Crookston (MN)
U of Minnesota, Duluth (MN)
U of Minnesota, Twin Cities Campus (MN)
U of Mississippi (MS)
U of Missouri (MO)
U of Missouri–St. Louis (MO)
The U of Montana (MT)
U of Montevallo (AL)
U of Mount Union (OH)
U of Nebraska–Lincoln (NE)
U of Nevada, Las Vegas (NV)
U of Nevada, Reno (NV)
U of New Haven (CT)
U of New Orleans (LA)
U of North Alabama (AL)
The U of North Carolina at Charlotte (NC)
U of North Dakota (ND)
U of Northern Iowa (IA)
U of North Florida (FL)
U of North Georgia (GA)
U of North Texas (TX)
U of Northwestern–St. Paul (MN)
U of Notre Dame (IN)
U of Oklahoma (OK)
U of Ottawa (ON, Canada)
U of Pennsylvania (PA)
U of Pittsburgh (PA)
U of Portland (OR)
U of Puerto Rico in Ponce (PR)
U of Regina (SK, Canada)
U of Rhode Island (RI)
U of Rio Grande (OH)
U of St. Francis (IL)
U of Saint Francis (IN)
U of St. Thomas (MN)
U of St. Thomas (TX)
U of San Diego (CA)
U of San Francisco (CA)
U of Saskatchewan (SK, Canada)
The U of Scranton (PA)
U of South Alabama (AL)
The U of South Dakota (SD)
U of Southern Indiana (IN)
U of Southern Maine (ME)
U of Southern Mississippi (MS)
U of South Florida (FL)
U of South Florida, St. Petersburg (FL)
U of South Florida Sarasota-Manatee (FL)
The U of Tampa (FL)
The U of Tennessee (TN)
The U of Tennessee at Martin (TN)
The U of Texas at Arlington (TX)
The U of Texas at Austin (TX)
The U of Texas at Dallas (TX)
The U of Texas at El Paso (TX)
The U of Texas at San Antonio (TX)
The U of Texas at Tyler (TX)
The U of Texas of the Permian Basin (TX)
The U of Texas–Pan American (TX)
The U of the Incarnate Word (TX)
The U of Toledo (OH)
The U of Tulsa (OK)
U of Utah (UT)
U of Washington (WA)
U of Washington, Tacoma (WA)
The U of West Alabama (AL)
U of West Florida (FL)
U of West Georgia (GA)
U of Windsor (ON, Canada)
U of Wisconsin–Eau Claire (WI)
U of Wisconsin–La Crosse (WI)
U of Wisconsin–Madison (WI)
U of Wisconsin–Milwaukee (WI)
U of Wisconsin–Oshkosh (WI)
U of Wisconsin–Parkside (WI)
U of Wisconsin–River Falls (WI)
U of Wisconsin–Superior (WI)
U of Wisconsin–Whitewater (WI)
U of Wyoming (WY)
Upper Iowa U (IA)
Urbana U (OH)
Ursuline Coll (OH)
Utah State U (UT)
Utah Valley U (UT)
Valdosta State U (GA)
Valparaiso U (IN)
Vanguard U of Southern California (CA)
Villanova U (PA)
Virginia Commonwealth U (VA)
Virginia Polytechnic Inst and State U (VA)
Virginia State U (VA)
Virginia Union U (VA)
Viterbo U (WI)
Walla Walla U (WA)
Walsh Coll of Accountancy and Business Administration (MI)
Walsh U (OH)
Wartburg Coll (IA)
Washburn U (KS)
Washington State U (WA)
Washington State U Vancouver (WA)
Washington U in St. Louis (MO)
Waynesburg U (PA)
Wayne State U (MI)
Webber Intl U (FL)
Weber State U (UT)
Webster U (MO)
Western Carolina U (NC)
Western Illinois U (IL)
Western Kentucky U (KY)
Western Michigan U (MI)
Western New England U (MA)
Western State Colorado U (CO)
Western Washington U (WA)
West Liberty U (WV)
Westminster Coll (UT)
West Texas A&M U (TX)
West Virginia U (WV)
West Virginia Wesleyan Coll (WV)
Wichita State U (KS)
Widener U (PA)
Wilberforce U (OH)
Wilkes U (PA)
Wilmington U (DE)
Wingate U (NC)
Winona State U (MN)
Wittenberg U (OH)
Wright State U (OH)
Xavier U (OH)
Xavier U of Louisiana (LA)
Yeshiva U (NY)
York Coll of Pennsylvania (PA)
York Coll of the City U of New York (NY)
Youngstown State U (OH)

MARKETING RELATED

The American U in Dubai (United Arab Emirates)
Babson Coll (MA)
Bowling Green State U (OH)
Delaware State U (DE)
Duquesne U (PA)
Eastern U (PA)
Franklin U (OH)
Lourdes U (OH)
Mary Baldwin Coll (VA)
Newbury Coll (MA)
Oklahoma Wesleyan U (OK)
Our Lady of the Lake U of San Antonio (TX)
Pace U (NY)
Saginaw Valley State U (MI)
State U of New York at New Paltz (NY)
Stephens Coll (MO)
Stevenson U (MD)
Troy U (AL)
The U of Iowa (IA)
U of Minnesota, Duluth (MN)
U of Mississippi (MS)
U of Southern Mississippi (MS)
U of South Florida (FL)
U of the District of Columbia (DC)
Washington U in St. Louis (MO)
Western Carolina U (NC)
Western Michigan U (MI)
Western New England U (MA)
Yeshiva U (NY)

MARKETING RESEARCH

Ashland U (OH)
Bowling Green State U (OH)
Fashion Inst of Technology (NY)
Husson U (ME)
Ithaca Coll (NY)
National U (CA)
Newbury Coll (MA)
Ohio Northern U (OH)
The U of Toledo (OH)

MARRIAGE AND FAMILY THERAPY/COUNSELING

DeSales U (PA)
John Brown U (AR)
LeTourneau U (TX)
Oklahoma Baptist U (OK)
U of Mobile (AL)

MASS COMMUNICATION/ MEDIA

Adams State U (CO)
Albany State U (GA)
Albion Coll (MI)
Alcorn State U (MS)
Allegheny Coll (PA)
American Intl Coll (MA)
American U (DC)
American U in Bulgaria (Bulgaria)
The American U in Cairo (Egypt)
Andrews U (MI)
Anna Maria Coll (MA)
Arcadia U (PA)
Ashland U (OH)
Auburn U (AL)
Augustana Coll (IL)
Austin Coll (TX)
Austin Peay State U (TN)
Baker U (KS)
Baldwin Wallace U (OH)
Barry U (FL)
Belmont U (TN)
Beloit Coll (WI)
Bemidji State U (MN)
Benedictine Coll (KS)
Bentley U (MA)
Berea Coll (KY)
Bethel Coll (KS)
Bethel U (MN)
Bethune-Cookman U (FL)
Black Hills State U (SD)
Bloomsburg U of Pennsylvania (PA)
Bluefield Coll (VA)
Bowie State U (MD)
Brenau U (GA)
Bridgewater Coll (VA)
Bryant U (RI)
Buena Vista U (IA)
Buffalo State Coll, State U of New York (NY)
California Lutheran U (CA)
California State U, Fresno (CA)
California State U, Long Beach (CA)
California State U, Sacramento (CA)
California State U, San Marcos (CA)
Calvary Bible Coll and Theological Sem (MO)
Calvin Coll (MI)
Campbellsville U (KY)
Carson-Newman U (TN)
Castleton State Coll (VT)
Cedar Crest Coll (PA)
Central Penn Coll (PA)
Champlain Coll (VT)
Chestnut Hill Coll (PA)
City Coll of the City U of New York (NY)
Claflin U (SC)
Clark U (MA)
Colby-Sawyer Coll (NH)
The Coll of New Rochelle (NY)
The Coll of Wooster (OH)
Colorado Mesa U (CO)
Colorado State U–Pueblo (CO)
Columbia Intl U (SC)
Concordia U (QC, Canada)
Concordia U, Nebraska (NE)
Concordia U, St. Paul (MN)
Concordia U Texas (TX)
Concordia U Wisconsin (WI)
Concord U (WV)
Crandall U (NB, Canada)
Culver-Stockton Coll (MO)
Defiance Coll (OH)
Denison U (OH)
DePaul U (IL)
DePauw U (IN)
Dixie State U (UT)
Drake U (IA)
East Central U (OK)
Eastern Oregon U (OR)
East Tennessee State U (TN)
East Texas Baptist U (TX)
Edinboro U of Pennsylvania (PA)
Elizabethtown Coll (PA)
Elizabethtown Coll School of Continuing and Professional Studies (PA)
Emerson Coll (MA)
Emmanuel Coll (GA)
Emory & Henry Coll (VA)
Endicott Coll (MA)
The Evergreen State Coll (WA)
Fisher Coll (MA)
Five Towns Coll (NY)
Florida Gulf Coast U (FL)
Florida Intl U (FL)
Florida Southern Coll (FL)
Florida State Coll at Jacksonville (FL)
Fordham U (NY)
Francis Marion U (SC)
Franklin Pierce U (NH)
Frostburg State U (MD)
The George Washington U (DC)
Gonzaga U (WA)
Goucher Coll (MD)
Governors State U (IL)
Grambling State U (LA)
Grand View U (IA)
Green Mountain Coll (VT)
Greenville Coll (IL)
Gustavus Adolphus Coll (MN)
Hampton U (VA)
Hanover Coll (IN)
Hastings Coll (NE)
Hawai`i Pacific U (HI)
Heidelberg U (OH)
High Point U (NC)
Hobart and William Smith Colls (NY)
Hofstra U (NY)
Hollins U (VA)
Holy Family U (PA)
Houston Baptist U (TX)
Howard U (DC)
Hunter Coll of the City U of New York (NY)
Huston-Tillotson U (TX)
Illinois Coll (IL)
Illinois State U (IL)
Indiana U–Purdue U Fort Wayne (IN)
Indiana U South Bend (IN)
Iona Coll (NY)
Iowa State U of Science and Technology (IA)
Ithaca Coll (NY)
Jackson State U (MS)
Jacksonville U (FL)
John Brown U (AR)
John Cabot U (Italy)
John Carroll U (OH)
Johnson C. Smith U (NC)
Kuyper Coll (MI)
Langston U (OK)
La Salle U (PA)
Lehman Coll of the City U of New York (NY)
Lewis U (IL)
Lincoln Memorial U (TN)
Lindenwood U (MO)
Lindsey Wilson Coll (KY)
Linfield Coll (OR)
Lipscomb U (TN)
Loras Coll (IA)
Louisiana Coll (LA)
Louisiana State U and A&M Coll (LA)
Louisiana State U in Shreveport (LA)
Lubbock Christian U (TX)
Lynn U (FL)
Macalester Coll (MN)
Manchester U (IN)
Mansfield U of Pennsylvania (PA)
Marquette U (WI)
Marylhurst U (OR)
Maryville U of Saint Louis (MO)
Massachusetts Inst of Technology (MA)
The Master's Coll and Sem (CA)
McNeese State U (LA)
Medaille Coll (NY)
Mercer U, Macon (GA)
Mercy Coll (NY)
Meredith Coll (NC)
Miami U (OH)
Michigan State U (MI)
MidAmerica Nazarene U (KS)
Middle Tennessee State U (TN)
Midwestern State U (TX)
Minnesota State U Mankato (MN)
Minnesota State U Moorhead (MN)
Mississippi Valley State U (MS)
Missouri State U (MO)
Missouri Valley Coll (MO)
Morris Coll (SC)
Mount Saint Mary Coll (NY)
New England Coll (NH)
Newman U (KS)
Niagara U (NY)
Nicholls State U (LA)
North Carolina Ag and Tech State U (NC)
North Carolina Central U (NC)
Northeastern State U (OK)
North Greenville U (SC)
Northwestern Oklahoma State U (OK)
Northwest Nazarene U (ID)
Oklahoma Baptist U (OK)
Oklahoma Christian U (OK)
Oklahoma City U (OK)
Olivet Nazarene U (IL)
Pace U (NY)
Pacific U (OR)
Palm Beach Atlantic U (FL)
Piedmont Coll (GA)
Point Loma Nazarene U (CA)
Pomona Coll (CA)
Principia Coll (IL)
Queens Coll of the City U of New York (NY)
Quinnipiac U (CT)
Rhode Island Coll (RI)
Robert Morris U (PA)
Rutgers, The State U of New Jersey, New Brunswick (NJ)
Sacred Heart U (CT)
St. Catherine U (MN)
Saint Francis U (PA)
Saint Mary-of-the-Woods Coll (IN)
St. Mary's U (TX)
Saint Michael's Coll (VT)
St. Norbert Coll (WI)
St. Thomas Aquinas Coll (NY)
St. Thomas U (FL)
St. Thomas U (NB, Canada)
Salem Coll (NC)
Sam Houston State U (TX)
Scripps Coll (CA)
Shaw U (NC)
South Carolina State U (SC)
Southern Illinois U Edwardsville (IL)
Southern Vermont Coll (VT)
Spalding U (KY)
State U of New York at Fredonia (NY)
State U of New York at Oswego (NY)
Stephen F. Austin State U (TX)
Stephens Coll (MO)
Suffolk U (MA)
Sul Ross State U (TX)
Temple U (PA)
Tennessee State U (TN)
Texas Southern U (TX)
Texas State U (TX)
Texas Tech U (TX)
Thiel Coll (PA)
Tiffin U (OH)
Tougaloo Coll (MS)
Towson U (MD)
Trevecca Nazarene U (TN)
Tufts U (MA)
Tulane U (LA)

Tusculum Coll (TN)
Union Coll (KY)
Union U (TN)
Université de Montréal (QC, Canada)
U at Albany, State U of New York (NY)
U of Bridgeport (CT)
U of California, Berkeley (CA)
U of Charleston (WV)
U of Colorado Boulder (CO)
U of Denver (CO)
U of Dubuque (IA)
U of Houston (TX)
The U of Iowa (IA)
U of Jamestown (ND)
U of Louisiana at Lafayette (LA)
U of Maine (ME)
U of Mary Hardin-Baylor (TX)
U of Maryland, Baltimore County (MD)
U of Memphis (TN)
U of Miami (FL)
U of Minnesota, Twin Cities Campus (MN)
U of Missouri (MO)
U of Missouri–Kansas City (MO)
U of Missouri–St. Louis (MO)
U of Nebraska at Kearney (NE)
U of Nevada, Las Vegas (NV)
U of New Hampshire at Manchester (NH)
U of New Mexico (NM)
U of North Alabama (AL)
U of North Carolina at Asheville (NC)
The U of North Carolina at Chapel Hill (NC)
The U of North Carolina at Greensboro (NC)
The U of North Carolina at Pembroke (NC)
U of North Florida (FL)
U of Oregon (OR)
U of Pittsburgh (PA)
U of Pittsburgh at Greensburg (PA)
U of Portland (OR)
U of Rio Grande (OH)
U of St. Francis (IL)
U of San Francisco (CA)
U of Southern Indiana (IN)
U of Southern Maine (ME)
U of South Florida (FL)
U of South Florida, St. Petersburg (FL)
The U of Tennessee at Chattanooga (TN)
The U of Texas at El Paso (TX)
The U of Texas at Tyler (TX)
The U of Texas–Pan American (TX)
U of the District of Columbia (DC)
U of the Incarnate Word (TX)
The U of Toledo (OH)
U of Toronto (ON, Canada)
U of Utah (UT)
U of Washington, Bothell (WA)
U of Washington, Tacoma (WA)
The U of Western Ontario (ON, Canada)
U of West Florida (FL)
U of Wisconsin–Eau Claire (WI)
U of Wisconsin–Milwaukee (WI)
U of Wisconsin–Oshkosh (WI)
U of Wisconsin–Superior (WI)
Upper Iowa U (IA)
Urbana U (OH)
Ursinus Coll (PA)
Valdosta State U (GA)
Valley City State U (ND)
Vassar Coll (NY)
Villanova U (PA)
Virginia Commonwealth U (VA)
Virginia State U (VA)
Virginia Wesleyan Coll (VA)
Voorhees Coll (SC)
Walla Walla U (WA)
Wartburg Coll (IA)
Washburn U (KS)
Washington State U (WA)
Wayne State Coll (NE)
Webster U (MO)
Western New England U (MA)
West Liberty U (WV)
West Texas A&M U (TX)
Whitworth U (WA)
Widener U (PA)
Wilberforce U (OH)
William Penn U (IA)
Winona State U (MN)
Winthrop U (SC)
Worcester State U (MA)
Wright State U (OH)
Xavier U of Louisiana (LA)
York Coll of Pennsylvania (PA)

MATERIALS ENGINEERING

Arizona State U at the Tempe campus (AZ)
Auburn U (AL)
Brown U (RI)
California Polytechnic State U, San Luis Obispo (CA)
California State U, Long Beach (CA)
Case Western Reserve U (OH)
Cornell U (NY)
Drexel U (PA)
Georgia Inst of Technology (GA)
Illinois Inst of Technology (IL)
Iowa State U of Science and Technology (IA)
Johns Hopkins U (MD)
Lehigh U (PA)
Massachusetts Inst of Technology (MA)
Michigan State U (MI)
Michigan Technological U (MI)
New Mexico Inst of Mining and Technology (NM)
North Carolina State U (NC)
Northwestern U (IL)
The Ohio State U (OH)
Purdue U (IN)
Rensselaer Polytechnic Inst (NY)
Rice U (TX)
San Jose State U (CA)
U at Albany, State U of New York (NY)
The U of Alabama at Birmingham (AL)
The U of British Columbia (BC, Canada)
U of California, Davis (CA)
U of California, Irvine (CA)
U of California, Los Angeles (CA)
U of California, Merced (CA)
U of Florida (FL)
U of Idaho (ID)
U of Kentucky (KY)
U of Maryland, Coll Park (MD)
U of Michigan (MI)
U of Minnesota, Twin Cities Campus (MN)
U of North Texas (TX)
U of Pennsylvania (PA)
U of Pittsburgh (PA)
The U of Tennessee (TN)
U of Toronto (ON, Canada)
U of Utah (UT)
U of Washington (WA)
The U of Western Ontario (ON, Canada)
U of Windsor (ON, Canada)
U of Wisconsin–Madison (WI)
U of Wisconsin–Milwaukee (WI)
Virginia Polytechnic Inst and State U (VA)
Washington State U (WA)
Winona State U (MN)
Worcester Polytechnic Inst (MA)
Wright State U (OH)

MATERIALS SCIENCE

Case Western Reserve U (OH)
Columbia U (NY)
Johns Hopkins U (MD)
Michigan State U (MI)
Northwestern U (IL)
The Ohio State U (OH)
Penn State Abington (PA)
Penn State Altoona (PA)
Penn State Beaver (PA)
Penn State Berks (PA)
Penn State Brandywine (PA)
Penn State DuBois (PA)
Penn State Erie, The Behrend Coll (PA)
Penn State Fayette, The Eberly Campus (PA)
Penn State Greater Allegheny (PA)
Penn State Hazleton (PA)
Penn State Lehigh Valley (PA)
Penn State Mont Alto (PA)
Penn State New Kensington (PA)
Penn State Schuylkill (PA)
Penn State Shenango (PA)
Penn State U Park (PA)
Penn State Wilkes-Barre (PA)
Penn State Worthington Scranton (PA)
Penn State York (PA)
Rice U (TX)
Stanford U (CA)
United States Air Force Acad (CO)
The U of Arizona (AZ)
U of California, Berkeley (CA)
U of California, Los Angeles (CA)
U of California, Riverside (CA)
U of Pennsylvania (PA)
U of Toronto (ON, Canada)
U of Wisconsin–Eau Claire (WI)
Worcester Polytechnic Inst (MA)

MATERNAL AND CHILD HEALTH

Union Inst & U (OH)

MATHEMATICAL BIOLOGY

Averett U (VA)
U of Houston (TX)
U of Pittsburgh (PA)

MATHEMATICAL STATISTICS AND PROBABILITY

Concordia Coll–New York (NY)
Concordia U (QC, Canada)
Purdue U (IN)
U of Alberta (AB, Canada)
U of Miami (FL)
The U of Western Ontario (ON, Canada)

MATHEMATICS

Abilene Christian U (TX)
Adams State U (CO)
Adelphi U (NY)
Agnes Scott Coll (GA)
Alabama State U (AL)
Albany State U (GA)
Albertus Magnus Coll (CT)
Albion Coll (MI)
Albright Coll (PA)
Alcorn State U (MS)
Allegheny Coll (PA)
Alma Coll (MI)
Alvernia U (PA)
Alverno Coll (WI)
American U (DC)
American U in Bulgaria (Bulgaria)
The American U in Cairo (Egypt)
American U of Beirut (Lebanon)
Amherst Coll (MA)
Anderson U (IN)
Anderson U (SC)
Andrews U (MI)
Angelo State U (TX)
Antioch U Midwest (OH)
Appalachian State U (NC)
Aquinas Coll (MI)
Arcadia U (PA)
Arizona State U at the Tempe campus (AZ)
Arkansas State U (AR)
Arkansas Tech U (AR)
Armstrong State U (GA)
Asbury U (KY)
Ashland U (OH)
Assumption Coll (MA)
Athens State U (AL)
Auburn U (AL)
Auburn U at Montgomery (AL)
Augsburg Coll (MN)
Augustana Coll (IL)
Augustana Coll (SD)
Austin Coll (TX)
Austin Peay State U (TN)
Ave Maria U (FL)
Averett U (VA)
Avila U (MO)
Azusa Pacific U (CA)
Baker U (KS)
Baldwin Wallace U (OH)
Ball State U (IN)
Bard Coll (NY)
Bard Coll at Simon's Rock (MA)
Barnard Coll (NY)
Barry U (FL)
Baruch Coll of the City U of New York (NY)
Bates Coll (ME)
Baylor U (TX)
Belhaven U (MS)
Belmont Abbey Coll (NC)
Belmont U (TN)
Beloit Coll (WI)
Bemidji State U (MN)
Benedictine Coll (KS)
Benedictine U (IL)
Bennett Coll (NC)
Bennington Coll (VT)
Bentley U (MA)
Berea Coll (KY)
Berry Coll (GA)
Bethany Coll (WV)
Bethany Lutheran Coll (MN)
Bethel Coll (IN)
Bethel Coll (KS)
Bethel U (MN)
Bethune-Cookman U (FL)
Binghamton U, State U of New York (NY)
Biola U (CA)
Birmingham-Southern Coll (AL)
Blackburn Coll (IL)
Black Hills State U (SD)
Bloomsburg U of Pennsylvania (PA)
Bluefield Coll (VA)
Blue Mountain Coll (MS)
Bluffton U (OH)
Bob Jones U (SC)
Boston Coll (MA)
Boston U (MA)
Bowdoin Coll (ME)
Bowie State U (MD)
Bowling Green State U (OH)
Bradley U (IL)
Brandeis U (MA)
Brevard Coll (NC)
Bridgewater Coll (VA)
Bridgewater State U (MA)
Brown U (RI)
Bryan Coll (TN)
Bryn Mawr Coll (PA)
Bucknell U (PA)
Buena Vista U (IA)
Buffalo State Coll, State U of New York (NY)
Butler U (IN)
Cabrini Coll (PA)
Caldwell U (NJ)
California Baptist U (CA)
California Inst of Technology (CA)
California Lutheran U (CA)
California Polytechnic State U, San Luis Obispo (CA)
California State Polytechnic U, Pomona (CA)
California State U, Chico (CA)
California State U, Dominguez Hills (CA)
California State U, Fresno (CA)
California State U, Fullerton (CA)
California State U, Long Beach (CA)
California State U, Los Angeles (CA)
California State U, Monterey Bay (CA)
California State U, Sacramento (CA)
California State U, San Bernardino (CA)
California State U, San Marcos (CA)
California State U, Stanislaus (CA)
California U of Pennsylvania (PA)
Calvary Bible Coll and Theological Sem (MO)
Calvin Coll (MI)
Cameron U (OK)
Campbellsville U (KY)
Cape Breton U (NS, Canada)
Capital U (OH)
Cardinal Stritch U (WI)
Carleton Coll (MN)
Carlow U (PA)
Carroll Coll (MT)
Carson-Newman U (TN)
Case Western Reserve U (OH)
Castleton State Coll (VT)
Catawba Coll (NC)
The Catholic U of America (DC)
Cedar Crest Coll (PA)
Cedarville U (OH)
Centenary Coll of Louisiana (LA)
Central Coll (IA)
Central Connecticut State U (CT)
Central Methodist U (MO)
Central Michigan U (MI)
Central State U (OH)
Central Washington U (WA)
Centre Coll (KY)
Chapman U (CA)
Charleston Southern U (SC)
Chatham U (PA)
Chestnut Hill Coll (PA)
Cheyney U of Pennsylvania (PA)
Chicago State U (IL)
Chowan U (NC)
Christendom Coll (VA)
Christian Brothers U (TN)
Christopher Newport U (VA)
The Citadel, The Military Coll of South Carolina (SC)
City Coll of the City U of New York (NY)
Claflin U (SC)
Claremont McKenna Coll (CA)
Clarion U of Pennsylvania (PA)
Clark Atlanta U (GA)
Clarke U (IA)
Clarkson U (NY)
Clark U (MA)
Clayton State U (GA)
Clearwater Christian Coll (FL)
Cleveland State U (OH)
Coe Coll (IA)
Coker Coll (SC)
Colby Coll (ME)
The Coll at Brockport, State U of New York (NY)
Coll of Charleston (SC)
Coll of Coastal Georgia (GA)
The Coll of Idaho (ID)
The Coll of New Jersey (NJ)
The Coll of New Rochelle (NY)
Coll of Saint Benedict (MN)
Coll of Saint Elizabeth (NJ)
Coll of Saint Mary (NE)
The Coll of Saint Rose (NY)
The Coll of St. Scholastica (MN)
Coll of Staten Island of the City U of New York (NY)
Coll of the Holy Cross (MA)
Coll of the Ozarks (MO)
The Coll of William and Mary (VA)
The Coll of Wooster (OH)
The Colorado Coll (CO)
Colorado Mesa U (CO)
Colorado School of Mines (CO)
Colorado State U (CO)
Colorado State U–Pueblo (CO)
Columbia Coll (MO)
Columbia Coll (SC)
Columbia U (NY)
Columbia U, School of General Studies (NY)
Columbus State U (GA)
Concordia Coll (MN)
Concordia Coll–New York (NY)
Concordia U (CA)
Concordia U (QC, Canada)
Concordia U Chicago (IL)
Concordia U, Nebraska (NE)
Concordia U, St. Paul (MN)
Concordia U Texas (TX)
Concordia U Wisconsin (WI)
Concord U (WV)
Connecticut Coll (CT)
Corban U (OR)
Cornell Coll (IA)
Cornell U (NY)
Cornerstone U (MI)
Covenant Coll (GA)
Creighton U (NE)
Culver-Stockton Coll (MO)
Cumberland U (TN)
Daemen Coll (NY)
Dalhousie U (NS, Canada)
Dallas Baptist U (TX)
Dartmouth Coll (NH)
Davidson Coll (NC)
Defiance Coll (OH)
Delaware State U (DE)
Delta State U (MS)
Denison U (OH)
DePaul U (IL)
DePauw U (IN)
DeSales U (PA)
Dickinson Coll (PA)
Dickinson State U (ND)
Dixie State U (UT)
Doane Coll (NE)
Dominican Coll (NY)
Dominican U (IL)
Dowling Coll (NY)

Drake U (IA)
Drew U (NJ)
Drexel U (PA)
Drury U (MO)
Duquesne U (PA)
Earlham Coll (IN)
East Carolina U (NC)
East Central U (OK)
Eastern Connecticut State U (CT)
Eastern Illinois U (IL)
Eastern Kentucky U (KY)
Eastern Michigan U (MI)
Eastern New Mexico U (NM)
Eastern Oregon U (OR)
Eastern U (PA)
East Stroudsburg U of Pennsylvania (PA)
East Tennessee State U (TN)
East Texas Baptist U (TX)
Eckerd Coll (FL)
Edgewood Coll (WI)
Edinboro U of Pennsylvania (PA)
Elizabethtown Coll (PA)
Elmhurst Coll (IL)
Elmira Coll (NY)
Elms Coll (MA)
Elon U (NC)
Emmanuel Coll (GA)
Emmanuel Coll (MA)
Emory & Henry Coll (VA)
Emporia State U (KS)
Endicott Coll (MA)
Erskine Coll (SC)
Evangel U (MO)
Excelsior Coll (NY)
Fairfield U (CT)
Fairleigh Dickinson U, Coll at Florham (NJ)
Fairleigh Dickinson U, Metropolitan Campus (NJ)
Fairmont State U (WV)
Fayetteville State U (NC)
Ferris State U (MI)
Ferrum Coll (VA)
Fitchburg State U (MA)
Florida Ag and Mech U (FL)
Florida Atlantic U (FL)
Florida Gulf Coast U (FL)
Florida Inst of Technology (FL)
Florida Intl U (FL)
Florida Southern Coll (FL)
Florida State U (FL)
Fontbonne U (MO)
Fordham U (NY)
Fort Hays State U (KS)
Fort Lewis Coll (CO)
Framingham State U (MA)
Franciscan U of Steubenville (OH)
Francis Marion U (SC)
Franklin & Marshall Coll (PA)
Franklin Coll (IN)
Franklin Pierce U (NH)
Friends U (KS)
Frostburg State U (MD)
Furman U (SC)
Gallaudet U (DC)
Gannon U (PA)
George Mason U (VA)
Georgetown Coll (KY)
Georgetown U (DC)
The George Washington U (DC)
Georgia Coll & State U (GA)
Georgia Gwinnett Coll (GA)
Georgian Court U (NJ)
Georgia Regents U (GA)
Georgia Southern U (GA)
Georgia Southwestern State U (GA)
Georgia State U (GA)
Gettysburg Coll (PA)
Gonzaga U (WA)
Gordon Coll (MA)
Goshen Coll (IN)
Goucher Coll (MD)
Governors State U (IL)
Grace Coll (IN)
Graceland U (IA)
Grand Valley State U (MI)
Greensboro Coll (NC)
Greenville Coll (IL)
Grinnell Coll (IA)
Grove City Coll (PA)
Guilford Coll (NC)
Gustavus Adolphus Coll (MN)
Gwynedd Mercy U (PA)
Hamilton Coll (NY)
Hamline U (MN)
Hampden-Sydney Coll (VA)
Hampshire Coll (MA)
Hampton U (VA)
Hannibal-LaGrange U (MO)
Hanover Coll (IN)
Harding U (AR)
Hardin-Simmons U (TX)
Harris-Stowe State U (MO)
Hartwick Coll (NY)
Harvard U (MA)
Harvey Mudd Coll (CA)
Hastings Coll (NE)
Haverford Coll (PA)
Heidelberg U (OH)
Hendrix Coll (AR)
Heritage U (WA)
High Point U (NC)
Hillsdale Coll (MI)
Hiram Coll (OH)
Hobart and William Smith Colls (NY)
Hofstra U (NY)
Hollins U (VA)
Holy Family U (PA)
Hope Coll (MI)
Houghton Coll (NY)
Houston Baptist U (TX)
Howard Payne U (TX)
Howard U (DC)
Humboldt State U (CA)
Hunter Coll of the City U of New York (NY)
Huntingdon Coll (AL)
Huston-Tillotson U (TX)
Illinois Coll (IL)
Illinois State U (IL)
Illinois Wesleyan U (IL)
Immaculata U (PA)
Indiana State U (IN)
Indiana U Bloomington (IN)
Indiana U East (IN)
Indiana U Kokomo (IN)
Indiana U Northwest (IN)
Indiana U of Pennsylvania (PA)
Indiana U–Purdue U Fort Wayne (IN)
Indiana U–Purdue U Indianapolis (IN)
Indiana U South Bend (IN)
Indiana U Southeast (IN)
Inter American U of Puerto Rico, Bayamón Campus (PR)
Inter American U of Puerto Rico, San Germán Campus (PR)
Iona Coll (NY)
Iowa State U of Science and Technology (IA)
Ithaca Coll (NY)
Jackson State U (MS)
Jacksonville State U (AL)
Jacksonville U (FL)
James Madison U (VA)
Jarvis Christian Coll (TX)
John Brown U (AR)
John Carroll U (OH)
Johns Hopkins U (MD)
Johnson C. Smith U (NC)
Johnson State Coll (VT)
Judson Coll (AL)
Judson U (IL)
Juniata Coll (PA)
Kalamazoo Coll (MI)
Kansas State U (KS)
Kansas Wesleyan U (KS)
Kean U (NJ)
Keene State Coll (NH)
Kennesaw State U (GA)
Kent State U (OH)
Kent State U at Stark (OH)
Kentucky State U (KY)
Kentucky Wesleyan Coll (KY)
Kenyon Coll (OH)
Keuka Coll (NY)
King's Coll (PA)
King U (TN)
Knox Coll (IL)
Kutztown U of Pennsylvania (PA)
Lafayette Coll (PA)
LaGrange Coll (GA)
Lake Erie Coll (OH)
Lake Forest Coll (IL)
Lamar U (TX)
Lane Coll (TN)
Langston U (OK)
La Roche Coll (PA)
La Salle U (PA)
La Sierra U (CA)
Lawrence Technological U (MI)
Lawrence U (WI)
Lebanese American U (Lebanon)
Lebanon Valley Coll (PA)
Lee U (TN)
Lehigh U (PA)
Lehman Coll of the City U of New York (NY)
Le Moyne Coll (NY)
LeMoyne-Owen Coll (TN)
Lenoir-Rhyne U (NC)
LeTourneau U (TX)
Lewis & Clark Coll (OR)
Lewis U (IL)
Liberty U (VA)
Limestone Coll (SC)
Lincoln Memorial U (TN)
Lincoln U (MO)
Lincoln U (PA)
Lindenwood U (MO)
Linfield Coll (OR)
Lipscomb U (TN)
Lock Haven U of Pennsylvania (PA)
Long Island U–LIU Brooklyn (NY)
Long Island U–LIU Post (NY)
Longwood U (VA)
Loras Coll (IA)
Louisiana Coll (LA)
Louisiana State U and A&M Coll (LA)
Louisiana State U in Shreveport (LA)
Loyola Marymount U (CA)
Loyola U Chicago (IL)
Loyola U New Orleans (LA)
Lubbock Christian U (TX)
Luther Coll (IA)
Lycoming Coll (PA)
Lynchburg Coll (VA)
Lyon Coll (AR)
Macalester Coll (MN)
Madonna U (MI)
Maharishi U of Management (IA)
Malone U (OH)
Manchester U (IN)
Manhattan Coll (NY)
Manhattanville Coll (NY)
Mansfield U of Pennsylvania (PA)
Marian U (IN)
Marian U (WI)
Marietta Coll (OH)
Marist Coll (NY)
Marquette U (WI)
Marshall U (WV)
Mars Hill U (NC)
Mary Baldwin Coll (VA)
Marymount U (VA)
Maryville Coll (TN)
Maryville U of Saint Louis (MO)
Marywood U (PA)
Massachusetts Coll of Liberal Arts (MA)
Massachusetts Inst of Technology (MA)
The Master's Coll and Sem (CA)
Mayville State U (ND)
McDaniel Coll (MD)
McKendree U (IL)
McMurry U (TX)
McNeese State U (LA)
Medaille Coll (NY)
Mercer U, Macon (GA)
Mercy Coll (NY)
Meredith Coll (NC)
Merrimack Coll (MA)
Messiah Coll (PA)
Miami U (OH)
Michigan State U (MI)
Michigan Technological U (MI)
MidAmerica Nazarene U (KS)
Middlebury Coll (VT)
Middle Tennessee State U (TN)
Midwestern State U (TX)
Millersville U of Pennsylvania (PA)
Milligan Coll (TN)
Millikin U (IL)
Millsaps Coll (MS)
Mills Coll (CA)
Minnesota State U Mankato (MN)
Minnesota State U Moorhead (MN)
Minot State U (ND)
Misericordia U (PA)
Mississippi State U (MS)
Mississippi U for Women (MS)
Mississippi Valley State U (MS)
Missouri Baptist U (MO)
Missouri Southern State U (MO)
Missouri State U (MO)
Missouri Valley Coll (MO)
Missouri Western State U (MO)
Molloy Coll (NY)
Monmouth Coll (IL)
Monmouth U (NJ)
Montana State U (MT)
Montana State U Billings (MT)
Montana Tech of The U of Montana (MT)
Montclair State U (NJ)
Moravian Coll (PA)
Morehead State U (KY)
Morningside Coll (IA)
Morris Coll (SC)
Mount Allison U (NB, Canada)
Mount Holyoke Coll (MA)
Mount Marty Coll (SD)
Mount Mary U (WI)
Mount Mercy U (IA)
Mount St. Joseph U (OH)
Mount Saint Mary Coll (NY)
Mount St. Mary's Coll (CA)
Mount St. Mary's U (MD)
Mount Vernon Nazarene U (OH)
Muhlenberg Coll (PA)
Murray State U (KY)
National U (CA)
Nazareth Coll of Rochester (NY)
Nebraska Wesleyan U (NE)
Newberry Coll (SC)
New Coll of Florida (FL)
New Jersey City U (NJ)
New Jersey Inst of Technology (NJ)
Newman U (KS)
New Mexico Highlands U (NM)
New Mexico Inst of Mining and Technology (NM)
New Mexico State U (NM)
New York U (NY)
Niagara U (NY)
Nicholls State U (LA)
Nichols Coll (MA)
Norfolk State U (VA)
North Carolina Ag and Tech State U (NC)
North Carolina Central U (NC)
North Carolina State U (NC)
North Carolina Wesleyan Coll (NC)
North Central Coll (IL)
North Dakota State U (ND)
Northeastern Illinois U (IL)
Northeastern State U (OK)
Northeastern U (MA)
Northern Arizona U (AZ)
Northern Illinois U (IL)
Northern Kentucky U (KY)
Northern Michigan U (MI)
Northern State U (SD)
North Greenville U (SC)
Northland Coll (WI)
Northwest Christian U (OR)
Northwestern Coll (IA)
Northwestern Oklahoma State U (OK)
Northwestern U (IL)
Northwest Missouri State U (MO)
Northwest Nazarene U (ID)
Northwest U (WA)
Norwich U (VT)
Notre Dame of Maryland U (MD)
Nyack Coll (NY)
Oakland City U (IN)
Oakland U (MI)
Oberlin Coll (OH)
Occidental Coll (CA)
Oglethorpe U (GA)
Ohio Dominican U (OH)
Ohio Northern U (OH)
The Ohio State U (OH)
Ohio U (OH)
Ohio Wesleyan U (OH)
Oklahoma Baptist U (OK)
Oklahoma Christian U (OK)
Oklahoma City U (OK)
Oklahoma State U (OK)
Oklahoma Wesleyan U (OK)
Old Dominion U (VA)
Olivet Coll (MI)
Olivet Nazarene U (IL)
Oregon State U (OR)
Our Lady of the Lake U of San Antonio (TX)
Pace U (NY)
Pacific Lutheran U (WA)
Pacific U (OR)
Palm Beach Atlantic U (FL)
Park U (MO)
Penn State Abington (PA)
Penn State Altoona (PA)
Penn State Beaver (PA)
Penn State Berks (PA)
Penn State Brandywine (PA)
Penn State DuBois (PA)
Penn State Erie, The Behrend Coll (PA)
Penn State Fayette, The Eberly Campus (PA)
Penn State Greater Allegheny (PA)
Penn State Hazleton (PA)
Penn State Lehigh Valley (PA)
Penn State Mont Alto (PA)
Penn State New Kensington (PA)
Penn State Schuylkill (PA)
Penn State Shenango (PA)
Penn State U Park (PA)
Penn State Wilkes-Barre (PA)
Penn State Worthington Scranton (PA)
Penn State York (PA)
Pepperdine U, Malibu (CA)
Peru State Coll (NE)
Philander Smith Coll (AR)
Piedmont Coll (GA)
Pittsburg State U (KS)
Plymouth State U (NH)
Point Loma Nazarene U (CA)
Pomona Coll (CA)
Portland State U (OR)
Prairie View A&M U (TX)
Presbyterian Coll (SC)
Princeton U (NJ)
Principia Coll (IL)
Providence Coll (RI)
Purchase Coll, State U of New York (NY)
Purdue U (IN)
Purdue U Calumet (IN)
Queens Coll of the City U of New York (NY)
Quincy U (IL)
Quinnipiac U (CT)
Radford U (VA)
Ramapo Coll of New Jersey (NJ)
Randolph Coll (VA)
Randolph-Macon Coll (VA)
Reed Coll (OR)
Regent U (VA)
Regis U (CO)
Reinhardt U (GA)
Rensselaer Polytechnic Inst (NY)
Rhode Island Coll (RI)
Rhodes Coll (TN)
Rice U (TX)
Rider U (NJ)
Ripon Coll (WI)
Rivier U (NH)
Roanoke Coll (VA)
Roberts Wesleyan Coll (NY)
Rochester Inst of Technology (NY)
Rockford U (IL)
Rockhurst U (MO)
Rocky Mountain Coll (MT)
Roger Williams U (RI)
Rollins Coll (FL)
Roosevelt U (IL)
Rose-Hulman Inst of Technology (IN)
Rosemont Coll (PA)
Rowan U (NJ)
Rust Coll (MS)
Rutgers, The State U of New Jersey, Camden (NJ)
Rutgers, The State U of New Jersey, Newark (NJ)
Rutgers, The State U of New Jersey, New Brunswick (NJ)
Sacred Heart U (CT)
The Sage Colls (NY)
Saginaw Valley State U (MI)
Saint Anselm Coll (NH)
Saint Augustine's U (NC)
St. Bonaventure U (NY)
St. Catherine U (MN)
St. Edward's U (TX)
St. Francis Coll (NY)
Saint Francis U (PA)
St. Gregory's U, Shawnee (OK)
St. John Fisher Coll (NY)
Saint John's U (MN)
St. John's U (NY)
Saint Joseph's Coll (IN)
St. Joseph's Coll, Long Island Campus (NY)

St. Joseph's Coll, New York (NY)
Saint Joseph's U (PA)
St. Lawrence U (NY)
Saint Leo U (FL)
Saint Louis U (MO)
Saint Martin's U (WA)
Saint Mary-of-the-Woods Coll (IN)
Saint Mary's Coll (IN)
St. Mary's Coll of Maryland (MD)
St. Mary's U (TX)
Saint Mary's U of Minnesota (MN)
Saint Michael's Coll (VT)
St. Norbert Coll (WI)
St. Olaf Coll (MN)
Saint Peter's U (NJ)
St. Thomas Aquinas Coll (NY)
St. Thomas U (FL)
St. Thomas U (NB, Canada)
Saint Vincent Coll (PA)
Salem Coll (NC)
Salisbury U (MD)
Salve Regina U (RI)
Samford U (AL)
Sam Houston State U (TX)
San Diego State U (CA)
San Francisco State U (CA)
San Jose State U (CA)
Santa Clara U (CA)
Sarah Lawrence Coll (NY)
Savannah State U (GA)
Scripps Coll (CA)
Seattle Pacific U (WA)
Seattle U (WA)
Seton Hill U (PA)
Sewanee: The U of the South (TN)
Shawnee State U (OH)
Shaw U (NC)
Shenandoah U (VA)
Shepherd U (WV)
Shippensburg U of Pennsylvania (PA)
Siena Coll (NY)
Siena Heights U (MI)
Silver Lake Coll of the Holy Family (WI)
Simmons Coll (MA)
Simon Fraser U (BC, Canada)
Simpson Coll (IA)
Simpson U (CA)
Skidmore Coll (NY)
Slippery Rock U of Pennsylvania (PA)
Smith Coll (MA)
South Carolina State U (SC)
South Dakota School of Mines and Technology (SD)
South Dakota State U (SD)
Southeastern Louisiana U (LA)
Southeastern Oklahoma State U (OK)
Southeastern U (FL)
Southeast Missouri State U (MO)
Southern Adventist U (TN)
Southern Arkansas U–Magnolia (AR)
Southern Connecticut State U (CT)
Southern Illinois U Carbondale (IL)
Southern Illinois U Edwardsville (IL)
Southern Methodist U (TX)
Southern New Hampshire U (NH)
Southern Oregon U (OR)
Southern Utah U (UT)
Southwest Baptist U (MO)
Southwestern Adventist U (TX)
Southwestern Coll (KS)
Southwestern U (TX)
Southwest Minnesota State U (MN)
Spelman Coll (GA)
Spring Hill Coll (AL)
Stanford U (CA)
State U of New York at Fredonia (NY)
State U of New York at New Paltz (NY)
State U of New York at Oswego (NY)
State U of New York at Plattsburgh (NY)
State U of New York Coll at Cortland (NY)
State U of New York Coll at Geneseo (NY)
State U of New York Coll at Old Westbury (NY)
State U of New York Coll at Potsdam (NY)
Stephen F. Austin State U (TX)
Sterling Coll (KS)
Stetson U (FL)
Stockton U (NJ)
Stonehill Coll (MA)
Stony Brook U, State U of New York (NY)
Suffolk U (MA)
Sul Ross State U (TX)
Susquehanna U (PA)
Syracuse U (NY)
Tabor Coll (KS)
Tarleton State U (TX)
Taylor U (IN)
Temple U (PA)
Tennessee State U (TN)
Tennessee Wesleyan Coll (TN)
Texas A&M Intl U (TX)
Texas A&M U (TX)
Texas A&M U–Commerce (TX)
Texas A&M U–Corpus Christi (TX)
Texas A&M U–Kingsville (TX)
Texas Christian U (TX)
Texas Lutheran U (TX)
Texas Southern U (TX)
Texas State U (TX)
Texas Tech U (TX)
Texas Wesleyan U (TX)
Texas Woman's U (TX)
Thiel Coll (PA)
Thomas More Coll (KY)
Tougaloo Coll (MS)
Towson U (MD)
Transylvania U (KY)
Trent U (ON, Canada)
Trevecca Nazarene U (TN)
Trine U (IN)
Trinity Christian Coll (IL)
Trinity Coll (CT)
Trinity U (TX)
Troy U (AL)
Truman State U (MO)
Tufts U (MA)
Tulane U (LA)
Tusculum Coll (TN)
Union Coll (KY)
Union Coll (NE)
Union Coll (NY)
Union U (TN)
United States Air Force Acad (CO)
United States Military Acad (NY)
United States Naval Acad (MD)
Université de Montréal (QC, Canada)
Université de Sherbrooke (QC, Canada)
U at Albany, State U of New York (NY)
U at Buffalo, the State U of New York (NY)
The U of Akron (OH)
The U of Alabama (AL)
The U of Alabama at Birmingham (AL)
The U of Alabama in Huntsville (AL)
U of Alaska Fairbanks (AK)
U of Alberta (AB, Canada)
The U of Arizona (AZ)
U of Arkansas (AR)
U of Arkansas at Little Rock (AR)
U of Arkansas at Pine Bluff (AR)
U of Arkansas–Fort Smith (AR)
U of Bridgeport (CT)
The U of British Columbia (BC, Canada)
The U of British Columbia–Okanagan Campus (BC, Canada)
U of California, Berkeley (CA)
U of California, Davis (CA)
U of California, Irvine (CA)
U of California, Los Angeles (CA)
U of California, Riverside (CA)
U of California, Santa Barbara (CA)
U of California, Santa Cruz (CA)
U of Central Arkansas (AR)
U of Central Florida (FL)
U of Central Missouri (MO)
U of Central Oklahoma (OK)
U of Chicago (IL)
U of Cincinnati (OH)
U of Colorado Boulder (CO)
U of Colorado Colorado Springs (CO)
U of Colorado Denver (CO)
U of Dallas (TX)
U of Dayton (OH)
U of Delaware (DE)
U of Denver (CO)
U of Dubuque (IA)
U of Evansville (IN)
The U of Findlay (OH)
U of Florida (FL)
U of Georgia (GA)
U of Great Falls (MT)
U of Guam (GU)
U of Hartford (CT)
U of Hawaii at Hilo (HI)
U of Hawaii at Manoa (HI)
U of Houston (TX)
U of Houston–Clear Lake (TX)
U of Houston–Downtown (TX)
U of Houston–Victoria (TX)
U of Idaho (ID)
U of Illinois at Chicago (IL)
U of Illinois at Springfield (IL)
U of Indianapolis (IN)
The U of Iowa (IA)
U of Jamestown (ND)
The U of Kansas (KS)
U of Kentucky (KY)
U of King's Coll (NS, Canada)
U of La Verne (CA)
U of Lethbridge (AB, Canada)
U of Louisiana at Lafayette (LA)
U of Louisville (KY)
U of Maine (ME)
U of Mary Hardin-Baylor (TX)
U of Maryland, Baltimore County (MD)
U of Maryland, Coll Park (MD)
U of Mary Washington (VA)
U of Massachusetts Amherst (MA)
U of Massachusetts Boston (MA)
U of Massachusetts Dartmouth (MA)
U of Massachusetts Lowell (MA)
U of Memphis (TN)
U of Miami (FL)
U of Michigan (MI)
U of Michigan–Dearborn (MI)
U of Michigan–Flint (MI)
U of Minnesota, Duluth (MN)
U of Minnesota, Morris (MN)
U of Minnesota, Twin Cities Campus (MN)
U of Mississippi (MS)
U of Missouri (MO)
U of Missouri–Kansas City (MO)
U of Missouri–St. Louis (MO)
U of Mobile (AL)
The U of Montana (MT)
The U of Montana Western (MT)
U of Montevallo (AL)
U of Mount Union (OH)
U of Nebraska at Kearney (NE)
U of Nebraska–Lincoln (NE)
U of Nevada, Las Vegas (NV)
U of Nevada, Reno (NV)
U of New Brunswick Saint John (NB, Canada)
U of New England (ME)
U of New Hampshire (NH)
U of New Haven (CT)
U of New Mexico (NM)
U of New Orleans (LA)
U of North Alabama (AL)
U of North Carolina at Asheville (NC)
The U of North Carolina at Chapel Hill (NC)
The U of North Carolina at Charlotte (NC)
The U of North Carolina at Greensboro (NC)
The U of North Carolina at Pembroke (NC)
The U of North Carolina Wilmington (NC)
U of North Dakota (ND)
U of Northern Colorado (CO)
U of Northern Iowa (IA)
U of North Florida (FL)
U of North Georgia (GA)
U of North Texas (TX)
U of Northwestern–St. Paul (MN)
U of Notre Dame (IN)
U of Oklahoma (OK)
U of Oregon (OR)
U of Ottawa (ON, Canada)
U of Pennsylvania (PA)
U of Pikeville (KY)
U of Pittsburgh (PA)
U of Portland (OR)
U of Puget Sound (WA)
U of Regina (SK, Canada)
U of Rhode Island (RI)
U of Richmond (VA)
U of Rio Grande (OH)
U of Rochester (NY)
U of St. Francis (IL)
U of Saint Francis (IN)
U of Saint Joseph (CT)
U of Saint Mary (KS)
U of St. Thomas (MN)
U of St. Thomas (TX)
U of San Diego (CA)
U of San Francisco (CA)
U of Saskatchewan (SK, Canada)
U of Science and Arts of Oklahoma (OK)
The U of Scranton (PA)
U of South Carolina Upstate (SC)
The U of South Dakota (SD)
U of Southern California (CA)
U of Southern Indiana (IN)
U of Southern Maine (ME)
U of Southern Mississippi (MS)
U of South Florida (FL)
The U of Tampa (FL)
The U of Tennessee (TN)
The U of Tennessee at Chattanooga (TN)
The U of Tennessee at Martin (TN)
The U of Texas at Arlington (TX)
The U of Texas at Austin (TX)
The U of Texas at Dallas (TX)
The U of Texas at El Paso (TX)
The U of Texas at San Antonio (TX)
The U of Texas at Tyler (TX)
The U of Texas of the Permian Basin (TX)
The U of Texas–Pan American (TX)
U of the Cumberlands (KY)
U of the District of Columbia (DC)
U of the Fraser Valley (BC, Canada)
U of the Incarnate Word (TX)
U of the Pacific (CA)
U of the Virgin Islands (VI)
The U of Toledo (OH)
The U of Tulsa (OK)
U of Utah (UT)
U of Vermont (VT)
U of Virginia (VA)
The U of Virginia's Coll at Wise (VA)
U of Washington (WA)
U of Washington, Bothell (WA)
U of Waterloo (ON, Canada)
The U of West Alabama (AL)
The U of Western Ontario (ON, Canada)
U of West Florida (FL)
U of West Georgia (GA)
U of Windsor (ON, Canada)
U of Wisconsin–Eau Claire (WI)
U of Wisconsin–Green Bay (WI)
U of Wisconsin–La Crosse (WI)
U of Wisconsin–Madison (WI)
U of Wisconsin–Milwaukee (WI)
U of Wisconsin–Oshkosh (WI)
U of Wisconsin–Parkside (WI)
U of Wisconsin–Platteville (WI)
U of Wisconsin–River Falls (WI)
U of Wisconsin–Stevens Point (WI)
U of Wisconsin–Superior (WI)
U of Wisconsin–Whitewater (WI)
U of Wyoming (WY)
Upper Iowa U (IA)
Ursinus Coll (PA)
Ursuline Coll (OH)
Utah State U (UT)
Utah Valley U (UT)
Utica Coll (NY)
Valdosta State U (GA)
Valley City State U (ND)
Valparaiso U (IN)
Vanderbilt U (TN)
Vanguard U of Southern California (CA)
Vassar Coll (NY)
Villanova U (PA)
Virginia Commonwealth U (VA)
Virginia Military Inst (VA)
Virginia Polytechnic Inst and State U (VA)
Virginia State U (VA)
Virginia Union U (VA)
Virginia Wesleyan Coll (VA)
Viterbo U (WI)
Wabash Coll (IN)
Wagner Coll (NY)
Wake Forest U (NC)
Walla Walla U (WA)
Walsh U (OH)
Warren Wilson Coll (NC)
Wartburg Coll (IA)
Washburn U (KS)
Washington & Jefferson Coll (PA)
Washington and Lee U (VA)
Washington Coll (MD)
Washington State U (WA)
Washington U in St. Louis (MO)
Waynesburg U (PA)
Wayne State Coll (NE)
Wayne State U (MI)
Weber State U (UT)
Webster U (MO)
Wells Coll (NY)
Wesleyan Coll (GA)
Wesleyan U (CT)
West Chester U of Pennsylvania (PA)
Western Carolina U (NC)
Western Illinois U (IL)
Western Kentucky U (KY)
Western Michigan U (MI)
Western New England U (MA)
Western Oregon U (OR)
Western State Colorado U (CO)
Western Washington U (WA)
Westfield State U (MA)
West Liberty U (WV)
Westminster Coll (MO)
Westminster Coll (UT)
West Texas A&M U (TX)
West Virginia State U (WV)
West Virginia U (WV)
West Virginia U Inst of Technology (WV)
West Virginia Wesleyan Coll (WV)
Wheaton Coll (IL)
Wheaton Coll (MA)
Wheeling Jesuit U (WV)
Whitman Coll (WA)
Whittier Coll (CA)
Whitworth U (WA)
Wichita State U (KS)
Widener U (PA)
Wilkes U (PA)
Willamette U (OR)
William Jessup U (CA)
William Jewell Coll (MO)
William Paterson U of New Jersey (NJ)
William Penn U (IA)
Williams Coll (MA)
William Woods U (MO)
Wingate U (NC)
Winona State U (MN)
Winthrop U (SC)
Wittenberg U (OH)
Wofford Coll (SC)
Worcester Polytechnic Inst (MA)
Worcester State U (MA)
Wright State U (OH)
Xavier U (OH)
Xavier U of Louisiana (LA)
Yale U (CT)
Yeshiva U (NY)
York Coll of Pennsylvania (PA)
York Coll of the City U of New York (NY)
Youngstown State U (OH)

MATHEMATICS AND COMPUTER SCIENCE

Anderson U (IN)
Bennington Coll (VT)
Bethany Coll (WV)
Biola U (CA)
Bowdoin Coll (ME)
Brown U (RI)
Bryan Coll (TN)
Chestnut Hill Coll (PA)
Christian Brothers U (TN)
The Colorado Coll (CO)
Delaware State U (DE)
DePaul U (IL)
Dominican U (IL)
Dowling Coll (NY)
Eastern Illinois U (IL)
Florida Southern Coll (FL)
Hampden-Sydney Coll (VA)
Hofstra U (NY)
Immaculata U (PA)

Indiana U–Purdue U Fort Wayne (IN)
Ithaca Coll (NY)
Lawrence Technological U (MI)
Lawrence U (WI)
Lewis & Clark Coll (OR)
Loyola U Chicago (IL)
Manchester U (IN)
Massachusetts Inst of Technology (MA)
Mount Allison U (NB, Canada)
Palm Beach Atlantic U (FL)
Pepperdine U, Malibu (CA)
Purdue U (IN)
Rochester Inst of Technology (NY)
Saint Francis U (PA)
St. Lawrence U (NY)
Saint Mary's Coll (IN)
Santa Clara U (CA)
Southern Oregon U (OR)
Stanford U (CA)
Temple U (PA)
Tufts U (MA)
Tusculum Coll (TN)
U at Albany, State U of New York (NY)
The U of Akron (OH)
U of Alberta (AB, Canada)
U of Illinois at Chicago (IL)
U of Massachusetts Dartmouth (MA)
U of Oregon (OR)
U of Regina (SK, Canada)
U of St. Francis (IL)
The U of Tampa (FL)
U of Waterloo (ON, Canada)
U of Windsor (ON, Canada)
Washington U in St. Louis (MO)
Western Washington U (WA)
Wheaton Coll (MA)
Whitman Coll (WA)

MATHEMATICS AND STATISTICS
Canisius Coll (NY)
Castleton State Coll (VT)
Colby Coll (ME)
Dakota State U (SD)
The Evergreen State Coll (WA)
Luther Coll (IA)
Reed Coll (OR)
U of South Alabama (AL)

MATHEMATICS AND STATISTICS RELATED
Anderson U (IN)
Columbia U, School of General Studies (NY)
Delaware State U (DE)
Hofstra U (NY)
Lycoming Coll (PA)
New York U (NY)
Ohio U (OH)
Purchase Coll, State U of New York (NY)
St. Joseph's Coll, Long Island Campus (NY)
St. Joseph's Coll, New York (NY)
Seattle Pacific U (WA)
Tulane U (LA)
U of Alberta (AB, Canada)
The U of British Columbia–Okanagan Campus (BC, Canada)
U of Missouri–Kansas City (MO)
U of New Hampshire (NH)
The U of North Carolina at Charlotte (NC)
U of Pittsburgh (PA)
U of Regina (SK, Canada)
U of Rochester (NY)
Western State Colorado U (CO)

MATHEMATICS RELATED
Agnes Scott Coll (GA)
Berry Coll (GA)
Grambling State U (LA)
Long Island U–LIU Post (NY)
Ohio Northern U (OH)
Reinhardt U (GA)
Seton Hill U (PA)
Temple U (PA)
United States Military Acad (NY)
U of Alberta (AB, Canada)
U of California, Los Angeles (CA)
U of Miami (FL)
U of Pittsburgh (PA)
U of Washington (WA)
U of Waterloo (ON, Canada)
Wheelock Coll (MA)

MATHEMATICS TEACHER EDUCATION
Abilene Christian U (TX)
Adams State U (CO)
Albion Coll (MI)
Alice Lloyd Coll (KY)
Alma Coll (MI)
Alvernia U (PA)
Anderson U (IN)
Anderson U (SC)
Arizona Christian U (AZ)
Arkansas State U (AR)
Arkansas Tech U (AR)
Auburn U (AL)
Augustana Coll (IL)
Averett U (VA)
Baylor U (TX)
Bennett Coll (NC)
Berry Coll (GA)
Bethany Coll (WV)
Bethel Coll (IN)
Bethel U (MN)
Biola U (CA)
Blackburn Coll (IL)
Black Hills State U (SD)
Bluefield Coll (VA)
Blue Mountain Coll (MS)
Bob Jones U (SC)
Boston U (MA)
Bowdoin Coll (ME)
Bowie State U (MD)
Bowling Green State U (OH)
Bradley U (IL)
Bryan Coll (TN)
Buena Vista U (IA)
Buffalo State Coll, State U of New York (NY)
Cabrini Coll (PA)
Cairn U (PA)
California Baptist U (CA)
California Lutheran U (CA)
California State U, Long Beach (CA)
Calvin Coll (MI)
Cameron U (OK)
Campbellsville U (KY)
Canisius Coll (NY)
Capital U (OH)
Carroll Coll (MT)
Castleton State Coll (VT)
Cedarville U (OH)
Central Michigan U (MI)
Central Washington U (WA)
Charleston Southern U (SC)
Chipola Coll (FL)
City Coll of the City U of New York (NY)
Claflin U (SC)
Clearwater Christian Coll (FL)
Coker Coll (SC)
The Coll of New Jersey (NJ)
Coll of Saint Mary (NE)
The Coll of Saint Rose (NY)
Coll of Staten Island of the City U of New York (NY)
Coll of the Ozarks (MO)
Colorado State U (CO)
Columbus State U (GA)
Concordia Coll (MN)
Concordia U Chicago (IL)
Concordia U, Nebraska (NE)
Concordia U, St. Paul (MN)
Corban U (OR)
Cornerstone U (MI)
Covenant Coll (GA)
Culver-Stockton Coll (MO)
Cumberland U (TN)
Daemen Coll (NY)
Dakota State U (SD)
Dallas Baptist U (TX)
Daytona State Coll (FL)
Delaware State U (DE)
Delta State U (MS)
Dixie State U (UT)
Dominican Coll (NY)
Dowling Coll (NY)
Duquesne U (PA)
East Carolina U (NC)
East Central U (OK)
Eastern Kentucky U (KY)
Eastern Michigan U (MI)
East Texas Baptist U (TX)
Edgewood Coll (WI)
Elmhurst Coll (IL)
Elmira Coll (NY)
Emmanuel Coll (GA)
Emory & Henry Coll (VA)
Fayetteville State U (NC)
Ferris State U (MI)
Fitchburg State U (MA)
Florida Ag and Mech U (FL)
Florida Atlantic U (FL)
Florida Inst of Technology (FL)
Florida SouthWestern State Coll (FL)
Fordham U (NY)
Franklin Coll (IN)
Friends U (KS)
Geneva Coll (PA)
Grace Coll (IN)
Grambling State U (LA)
Grand Valley State U (MI)
Greensboro Coll (NC)
Greenville Coll (IL)
Gustavus Adolphus Coll (MN)
Gwynedd Mercy U (PA)
Hannibal-LaGrange U (MO)
Harding U (AR)
Hardin-Simmons U (TX)
Hastings Coll (NE)
Hawai`i Pacific U (HI)
Heritage U (WA)
Hobe Sound Bible Coll (FL)
Hofstra U (NY)
Holy Family U (PA)
Hope Coll (MI)
Houston Baptist U (TX)
Howard Payne U (TX)
Hunter Coll of the City U of New York (NY)
Huntingdon Coll (AL)
Indiana U Bloomington (IN)
Indiana U Northwest (IN)
Indiana U–Purdue U Fort Wayne (IN)
Indiana U South Bend (IN)
Indiana U Southeast (IN)
Indian River State Coll (FL)
Inter American U of Puerto Rico, San Germán Campus (PR)
Iona Coll (NY)
Ithaca Coll (NY)
Jackson State U (MS)
John Brown U (AR)
Johnson State Coll (VT)
Judson Coll (AL)
Juniata Coll (PA)
Kansas Wesleyan U (KS)
Keene State Coll (NH)
Kennesaw State U (GA)
Kent State U (OH)
Kentucky Christian U (KY)
Keuka Coll (NY)
Keystone Coll (PA)
King U (TN)
LaGrange Coll (GA)
Lee U (TN)
Le Moyne Coll (NY)
LeMoyne-Owen Coll (TN)
LeTourneau U (TX)
Limestone Coll (SC)
Lincoln Memorial U (TN)
Lincoln U (MO)
Lincoln U (PA)
Lindenwood U (MO)
Lindsey Wilson Coll (KY)
Lipscomb U (TN)
Long Island U–LIU Post (NY)
Louisiana State U in Shreveport (LA)
Loyola U Chicago (IL)
Madonna U (MI)
Manchester U (IN)
Manhattanville Coll (NY)
Mansfield U of Pennsylvania (PA)
Maranatha Baptist U (WI)
Marist Coll (NY)
Marquette U (WI)
Maryville Coll (TN)
Marywood U (PA)
Mayville State U (ND)
McKendree U (IL)
McMurry U (TX)
Medaille Coll (NY)
Merrimack Coll (MA)
Messiah Coll (PA)
Metropolitan State U (MN)
Miami Dade Coll (FL)
Miami U (OH)
Michigan State U (MI)
MidAmerica Nazarene U (KS)
Midwestern State U (TX)
Millikin U (IL)
Minnesota State U Moorhead (MN)
Minot State U (ND)
Misericordia U (PA)
Missouri State U (MO)
Montana State U Billings (MT)
Morningside Coll (IA)
Morris Coll (SC)
Mount Marty Coll (SD)
Mount Mary U (WI)
Mount Vernon Nazarene U (OH)
National U (CA)
Nazareth Coll of Rochester (NY)
New York City Coll of Technology of the City U of New York (NY)
New York U (NY)
Niagara U (NY)
Nicholls State U (LA)
North Carolina Ag and Tech State U (NC)
North Carolina State U (NC)
North Dakota State U (ND)
Northeastern State U (OK)
Northern Michigan U (MI)
North Greenville U (SC)
Northwestern Oklahoma State U (OK)
Northwestern U (IL)
Northwest Missouri State U (MO)
Northwest Nazarene U (ID)
Northwest U (WA)
Notre Dame of Maryland U (MD)
Nova Southeastern U (FL)
Nyack Coll (NY)
Oakland City U (IN)
Ohio Dominican U (OH)
Ohio Northern U (OH)
Ohio Valley U (WV)
Ohio Wesleyan U (OH)
Oklahoma Baptist U (OK)
Oklahoma Christian U (OK)
Oklahoma Wesleyan U (OK)
Olivet Coll (MI)
Pace U (NY)
Palm Beach Atlantic U (FL)
Pepperdine U, Malibu (CA)
Peru State Coll (NE)
Piedmont Coll (GA)
Pittsburg State U (KS)
Plymouth State U (NH)
Providence Coll (RI)
Regis Coll (MA)
Rhode Island Coll (RI)
Rivier U (NH)
Roberts Wesleyan Coll (NY)
Rocky Mountain Coll (MT)
Rust Coll (MS)
Saginaw Valley State U (MI)
St. Catherine U (MN)
St. Edward's U (TX)
St. Francis Coll (NY)
Saint Francis U (PA)
St. Gregory's U, Shawnee (OK)
St. John Fisher Coll (NY)
St. John's U (NY)
St. Joseph's Coll, Long Island Campus (NY)
St. Joseph's Coll, New York (NY)
Saint Mary's U of Minnesota (MN)
Salve Regina U (RI)
Seattle U (WA)
Seton Hill U (PA)
Shawnee State U (OH)
Simpson U (CA)
Southeastern Oklahoma State U (OK)
Southeastern U (FL)
Southeast Missouri State U (MO)
Southern Adventist U (TN)
Southern New Hampshire U (NH)
Southern Utah U (UT)
Southwest Baptist U (MO)
Southwestern Coll (KS)
Southwest Minnesota State U (MN)
Spring Hill Coll (AL)
State U of New York at New Paltz (NY)
State U of New York Coll at Cortland (NY)
State U of New York Coll at Old Westbury (NY)
State U of New York Coll at Potsdam (NY)
Summit U (PA)
Syracuse U (NY)
Tabor Coll (KS)
Taylor U (IN)
Temple U (PA)
Texas A&M Intl U (TX)
Texas Christian U (TX)
Texas Lutheran U (TX)
Texas Wesleyan U (TX)
Trevecca Nazarene U (TN)
Trine U (IN)
Trinity Christian Coll (IL)
Tusculum Coll (TN)
Union Coll (NE)
Universidad del Turabo (PR)
Universidad Metropolitana (PR)
The U of Akron (OH)
U of Alberta (AB, Canada)
U of Arkansas–Fort Smith (AR)
U of Central Arkansas (AR)
U of Central Florida (FL)
U of Central Oklahoma (OK)
U of Delaware (DE)
U of Evansville (IN)
U of Georgia (GA)
U of Great Falls (MT)
U of Hartford (CT)
U of Illinois at Chicago (IL)
U of Indianapolis (IN)
The U of Iowa (IA)
U of Jamestown (ND)
U of Lethbridge (AB, Canada)
U of Maine at Machias (ME)
U of Mary Hardin-Baylor (TX)
U of Michigan–Dearborn (MI)
U of Michigan–Flint (MI)
U of Minnesota, Duluth (MN)
U of Mississippi (MS)
U of Missouri (MO)
U of Mobile (AL)
The U of Montana (MT)
The U of Montana Western (MT)
U of Nebraska–Lincoln (NE)
U of New Hampshire (NH)
The U of North Carolina at Greensboro (NC)
The U of North Carolina at Pembroke (NC)
The U of North Carolina Wilmington (NC)
U of Northern Iowa (IA)
U of North Florida (FL)
U of Northwestern–St. Paul (MN)
U of Oklahoma (OK)
U of Regina (SK, Canada)
U of Rio Grande (OH)
U of St. Francis (IL)
U of Saint Francis (IN)
U of St. Thomas (MN)
The U of South Dakota (SD)
U of Southern Maine (ME)
U of South Florida (FL)
The U of Tennessee at Chattanooga (TN)
The U of Tennessee at Martin (TN)
The U of Toledo (OH)
The U of Tulsa (OK)
U of Vermont (VT)
U of Washington (WA)
U of Waterloo (ON, Canada)
U of Windsor (ON, Canada)
U of Wisconsin–River Falls (WI)
U of Wisconsin–Superior (WI)
Ursuline Coll (OH)
Utah State U (UT)
Utah Valley U (UT)
Utica Coll (NY)
Valley City State U (ND)
Valparaiso U (IN)
Vincennes U (IN)
Viterbo U (WI)
Walsh U (OH)
Wartburg Coll (IA)
Washburn U (KS)
Washington State U (WA)
Washington U in St. Louis (MO)
Waynesburg U (PA)
Wayne State Coll (NE)
Wayne State U (MI)
Weber State U (UT)
Western Carolina U (NC)
Western Governors U (UT)
Western Michigan U (MI)
Western State Colorado U (CO)
Western Washington U (WA)
West Virginia Wesleyan Coll (WV)
Widener U (PA)
William Woods U (MO)
Wilmington U (DE)
Wingate U (NC)

Winona State U (MN)
York Coll of Pennsylvania (PA)
Youngstown State U (OH)

MECHANICAL DRAFTING AND CAD/CADD
Indiana U–Purdue U Indianapolis (IN)

MECHANICAL ENGINEERING
The American U in Cairo (Egypt)
The American U in Dubai (United Arab Emirates)
American U of Beirut (Lebanon)
Anderson U (IN)
Andrews U (MI)
Arizona State U at the Tempe campus (AZ)
Arkansas State U (AR)
Arkansas Tech U (AR)
Auburn U (AL)
Baker Coll (MI)
Baylor U (TX)
Benedictine Coll (KS)
Binghamton U, State U of New York (NY)
Boston U (MA)
Bradley U (IL)
Brown U (RI)
Bucknell U (PA)
California Baptist U (CA)
California Inst of Technology (CA)
California Polytechnic State U, San Luis Obispo (CA)
California State Polytechnic U, Pomona (CA)
California State U, Chico (CA)
California State U, Fresno (CA)
California State U, Fullerton (CA)
California State U, Long Beach (CA)
California State U, Los Angeles (CA)
California State U, Sacramento (CA)
Calvin Coll (MI)
Case Western Reserve U (OH)
The Catholic U of America (DC)
Cedarville U (OH)
Central Michigan U (MI)
Christian Brothers U (TN)
The Citadel, The Military Coll of South Carolina (SC)
City Coll of the City U of New York (NY)
Clarkson U (NY)
Cleveland State U (OH)
The Coll of New Jersey (NJ)
Colorado School of Mines (CO)
Colorado State U (CO)
Columbia U (NY)
Concordia U (QC, Canada)
Cooper Union for the Advancement of Science and Art (NY)
Cornell U (NY)
Daniel Webster Coll (NH)
Delaware State U (DE)
Drexel U (PA)
Embry-Riddle Aeronautical U–Daytona (FL)
Embry-Riddle Aeronautical U–Prescott (AZ)
Fairfield U (CT)
Florida Ag and Mech U (FL)
Florida Atlantic U (FL)
Florida Inst of Technology (FL)
Florida Intl U (FL)
Franklin W. Olin Coll of Eng (MA)
Gannon U (PA)
George Mason U (VA)
The George Washington U (DC)
Georgia Inst of Technology (GA)
Georgia Southern U (GA)
Gonzaga U (WA)
Grove City Coll (PA)
Harding U (AR)
Hofstra U (NY)
Howard U (DC)
Illinois Inst of Technology (IL)
Indiana U–Purdue U Fort Wayne (IN)
Indiana U–Purdue U Indianapolis (IN)
Inter American U of Puerto Rico, Bayamón Campus (PR)
Iowa State U of Science and Technology (IA)
Jacksonville U (FL)
John Brown U (AR)
Johns Hopkins U (MD)
Kansas State U (KS)
Kettering U (MI)
Lafayette Coll (PA)
Lamar U (TX)
Lawrence Technological U (MI)
Lebanese American U (Lebanon)
Lehigh U (PA)
LeTourneau U (TX)
Liberty U (VA)
Lipscomb U (TN)
Louisiana State U and A&M Coll (LA)
Loyola Marymount U (CA)
Manhattan Coll (NY)
Marquette U (WI)
Massachusetts Inst of Technology (MA)
Merrimack Coll (MA)
Miami U (OH)
Michigan State U (MI)
Michigan Technological U (MI)
Milwaukee School of Eng (WI)
Minnesota State U Mankato (MN)
Mississippi State U (MS)
Missouri U of Science and Technology (MO)
Montana State U (MT)
New England Inst of Technology (RI)
New Jersey Inst of Technology (NJ)
New Mexico Inst of Mining and Technology (NM)
New Mexico State U (NM)
New York Inst of Technology (NY)
New York U (NY)
North Carolina Ag and Tech State U (NC)
North Carolina State U (NC)
North Dakota State U (ND)
Northeastern U (MA)
Northern Arizona U (AZ)
Northern Illinois U (IL)
Northwestern U (IL)
Norwich U (VT)
Oakland U (MI)
Ohio Northern U (OH)
The Ohio State U (OH)
Ohio U (OH)
Oklahoma Christian U (OK)
Oklahoma State U (OK)
Old Dominion U (VA)
Oregon State U (OR)
Penn State Abington (PA)
Penn State Altoona (PA)
Penn State Beaver (PA)
Penn State Berks (PA)
Penn State Brandywine (PA)
Penn State DuBois (PA)
Penn State Erie, The Behrend Coll (PA)
Penn State Fayette, The Eberly Campus (PA)
Penn State Greater Allegheny (PA)
Penn State Harrisburg (PA)
Penn State Hazleton (PA)
Penn State Lehigh Valley (PA)
Penn State Mont Alto (PA)
Penn State New Kensington (PA)
Penn State Schuylkill (PA)
Penn State Shenango (PA)
Penn State U Park (PA)
Penn State Wilkes-Barre (PA)
Penn State Worthington Scranton (PA)
Penn State York (PA)
Polytechnic U of Puerto Rico (PR)
Portland State U (OR)
Prairie View A&M U (TX)
Princeton U (NJ)
Purdue U (IN)
Purdue U Calumet (IN)
Quinnipiac U (CT)
Rensselaer Polytechnic Inst (NY)
Rice U (TX)
Rochester Inst of Technology (NY)
Rockhurst U (MO)
Rose-Hulman Inst of Technology (IN)
Rowan U (NJ)
Rutgers, The State U of New Jersey, New Brunswick (NJ)
Saginaw Valley State U (MI)
Saint Louis U (MO)
Saint Martin's U (WA)
St. Mary's U (TX)
San Diego State U (CA)
San Francisco State U (CA)
San Jose State U (CA)
Santa Clara U (CA)
Seattle U (WA)
South Dakota School of Mines and Technology (SD)
South Dakota State U (SD)
Southern Illinois U Carbondale (IL)
Southern Illinois U Edwardsville (IL)
Southern Methodist U (TX)
Stanford U (CA)
State U of New York Maritime Coll (NY)
State U of New York Polytechnic Inst (NY)
Stony Brook U, State U of New York (NY)
Syracuse U (NY)
Temple U (PA)
Tennessee State U (TN)
Texas A&M U (TX)
Texas A&M U–Corpus Christi (TX)
Texas A&M U–Kingsville (TX)
Texas Tech U (TX)
Trine U (IN)
Trinity Coll (CT)
Tufts U (MA)
Union Coll (NY)
United States Air Force Acad (CO)
United States Coast Guard Acad (CT)
United States Military Acad (NY)
United States Naval Acad (MD)
Universidad del Turabo (PR)
Université de Sherbrooke (QC, Canada)
U at Buffalo, the State U of New York (NY)
The U of Akron (OH)
The U of Alabama (AL)
The U of Alabama at Birmingham (AL)
The U of Alabama in Huntsville (AL)
U of Alaska Fairbanks (AK)
The U of Arizona (AZ)
U of Arkansas (AR)
The U of British Columbia (BC, Canada)
The U of British Columbia–Okanagan Campus (BC, Canada)
U of California, Berkeley (CA)
U of California, Davis (CA)
U of California, Irvine (CA)
U of California, Los Angeles (CA)
U of California, Merced (CA)
U of California, Riverside (CA)
U of California, Santa Barbara (CA)
U of Central Florida (FL)
U of Central Oklahoma (OK)
U of Cincinnati (OH)
U of Colorado Boulder (CO)
U of Colorado Colorado Springs (CO)
U of Colorado Denver (CO)
U of Dayton (OH)
U of Delaware (DE)
U of Denver (CO)
U of Evansville (IN)
U of Florida (FL)
U of Guelph (ON, Canada)
U of Hartford (CT)
U of Hawaii at Manoa (HI)
U of Houston (TX)
U of Idaho (ID)
U of Illinois at Chicago (IL)
U of Indianapolis (IN)
The U of Iowa (IA)
The U of Kansas (KS)
U of Kentucky (KY)
U of Louisiana at Lafayette (LA)
U of Louisville (KY)
U of Maine (ME)
U of Maryland, Baltimore County (MD)
U of Maryland, Coll Park (MD)
U of Massachusetts Amherst (MA)
U of Massachusetts Dartmouth (MA)
U of Massachusetts Lowell (MA)
U of Memphis (TN)
U of Miami (FL)
U of Michigan (MI)
U of Michigan–Dearborn (MI)
U of Michigan–Flint (MI)
U of Minnesota, Duluth (MN)
U of Minnesota, Twin Cities Campus (MN)
U of Mississippi (MS)
U of Missouri (MO)
U of Missouri–Kansas City (MO)
U of Missouri–St. Louis (MO)
U of Mount Union (OH)
U of Nebraska–Lincoln (NE)
U of Nevada, Las Vegas (NV)
U of Nevada, Reno (NV)
U of New Hampshire (NH)
U of New Haven (CT)
U of New Mexico (NM)
U of New Orleans (LA)
The U of North Carolina at Charlotte (NC)
U of North Dakota (ND)
U of North Florida (FL)
U of North Texas (TX)
U of Notre Dame (IN)
U of Oklahoma (OK)
U of Ottawa (ON, Canada)
U of Pennsylvania (PA)
U of Pittsburgh (PA)
U of Portland (OR)
U of Rhode Island (RI)
U of Rochester (NY)
U of St. Thomas (MN)
U of San Diego (CA)
U of Saskatchewan (SK, Canada)
U of South Alabama (AL)
U of Southern California (CA)
U of Southern Maine (ME)
U of South Florida (FL)
The U of Tennessee (TN)
The U of Tennessee at Chattanooga (TN)
The U of Texas at Arlington (TX)
The U of Texas at Austin (TX)
The U of Texas at Dallas (TX)
The U of Texas at El Paso (TX)
The U of Texas at San Antonio (TX)
The U of Texas at Tyler (TX)
The U of Texas of the Permian Basin (TX)
The U of Texas–Pan American (TX)
U of the District of Columbia (DC)
U of the Pacific (CA)
The U of Toledo (OH)
U of Toronto (ON, Canada)
The U of Tulsa (OK)
U of Utah (UT)
U of Vermont (VT)
U of Virginia (VA)
U of Washington (WA)
U of Washington, Bothell (WA)
U of Waterloo (ON, Canada)
The U of Western Ontario (ON, Canada)
U of Windsor (ON, Canada)
U of Wisconsin–Madison (WI)
U of Wisconsin–Milwaukee (WI)
U of Wisconsin–Platteville (WI)
U of Wyoming (WY)
Ursinus Coll (PA)
Utah State U (UT)
Valparaiso U (IN)
Vanderbilt U (TN)
Villanova U (PA)
Virginia Commonwealth U (VA)
Virginia Military Inst (VA)
Virginia Polytechnic Inst and State U (VA)
Walla Walla U (WA)
Washington State U (WA)
Washington U in St. Louis (MO)
Wayne State U (MI)
Wentworth Inst of Technology (MA)
Western Kentucky U (KY)
Western Michigan U (MI)
Western New England U (MA)
West Texas A&M U (TX)
West Virginia U (WV)
West Virginia U Inst of Technology (WV)
Wichita State U (KS)
Widener U (PA)
Wilkes U (PA)
William Penn U (IA)
Worcester Polytechnic Inst (MA)
Wright State U (OH)
Yale U (CT)
York Coll of Pennsylvania (PA)
Youngstown State U (OH)

MECHANICAL ENGINEERING/ MECHANICAL TECHNOLOGY
Arizona State U at the Polytechnic campus (AZ)
Bluefield State Coll (WV)
Bowling Green State U (OH)
Buffalo State Coll, State U of New York (NY)
California State U, Long Beach (CA)
California State U, Sacramento (CA)
Central Connecticut State U (CT)
Central Michigan U (MI)
Central Washington U (WA)
Colorado Mesa U (CO)
Delaware State U (DE)
Eastern Michigan U (MI)
Fairleigh Dickinson U, Metropolitan Campus (NJ)
Fairmont State U (WV)
Farmingdale State Coll (NY)
Ferris State U (MI)
Georgia Southern U (GA)
Indiana U–Purdue U Fort Wayne (IN)
LeTourneau U (TX)
Michigan Technological U (MI)
Midwestern State U (TX)
Montana State U (MT)
New York City Coll of Technology of the City U of New York (NY)
Nicholls State U (LA)
Northern Michigan U (MI)
Oklahoma State U (OK)
Penn State Erie, The Behrend Coll (PA)
Pennsylvania Coll of Technology (PA)
Pittsburg State U (KS)
Purdue U (IN)
Purdue U Calumet (IN)
South Carolina State U (SC)
State U of New York Coll of Technology at Alfred (NY)
State U of New York Polytechnic Inst (NY)
Sullivan Coll of Technology and Design (KY)
Texas A&M U–Corpus Christi (TX)
Texas Tech U (TX)
United States Military Acad (NY)
The U of Akron (OH)
U of Arkansas at Little Rock (AR)
The U of British Columbia (BC, Canada)
U of Dayton (OH)
U of Hartford (CT)
U of Houston (TX)
U of Maine (ME)
U of New Hampshire (NH)
U of New Hampshire at Manchester (NH)
The U of North Carolina at Charlotte (NC)
U of North Texas (TX)
U of Rio Grande (OH)
U of the District of Columbia (DC)
The U of Toledo (OH)
Virginia State U (VA)
Wayne State U (MI)
Weber State U (UT)
Youngstown State U (OH)

MECHANICAL ENGINEERING TECHNOLOGIES RELATED
Cleveland State U (OH)
Delaware State U (DE)
Excelsior Coll (NY)
Indiana State U (IN)
Indiana U–Purdue U Indianapolis (IN)
LeTourneau U (TX)
Pennsylvania Coll of Technology (PA)
State U of New York Coll of Technology at Canton (NY)
U of Massachusetts Lowell (MA)
Vaughn Coll of Aeronautics and Technology (NY)

MECHANIC AND REPAIR TECHNOLOGIES RELATED
Colorado State U–Pueblo (CO)
Inter American U of Puerto Rico, Guayama Campus (PR)

MECHATRONICS, ROBOTICS, AND AUTOMATION ENGINEERING
California U of Pennsylvania (PA)
Lawrence Technological U (MI)
Simon Fraser U (BC, Canada)
U of Washington (WA)

MEDICAL ANTHROPOLOGY
Creighton U (NE)
U of Miami (FL)
Washington U in St. Louis (MO)

MEDICAL/CLINICAL ASSISTANT
Intl Business Coll, Fort Wayne (IN)

MEDICAL/HEALTH MANAGEMENT AND CLINICAL ASSISTANT
Davenport U, Grand Rapids (MI)
Stratford U, Woodbridge (VA)

MEDICAL ILLUSTRATION
Arcadia U (PA)
Cleveland Inst of Art (OH)
Iowa State U of Science and Technology (IA)
Rochester Inst of Technology (NY)

MEDICAL INFORMATICS
Champlain Coll (VT)
Montana Tech of The U of Montana (MT)
Mount St. Joseph U (OH)
Simmons Coll (MA)
Southern New Hampshire U (NH)
State U of New York at Plattsburgh (NY)
Trocaire Coll (NY)
U of South Alabama (AL)
U of Waterloo (ON, Canada)
The U of Western Ontario (ON, Canada)
Western Michigan U (MI)

MEDICAL MICROBIOLOGY AND BACTERIOLOGY
Adams State U (CO)
Auburn U (AL)
Bowling Green State U (OH)
California Polytechnic State U, San Luis Obispo (CA)
Cornell U (NY)
Dalhousie U (NS, Canada)
Humboldt State U (CA)
Minnesota State U Mankato (MN)
Mississippi State U (MS)
Montana State U (MT)
New Mexico State U (NM)
Ohio Wesleyan U (OH)
Penn State Abington (PA)
Penn State Altoona (PA)
Penn State Beaver (PA)
Penn State Berks (PA)
Penn State Brandywine (PA)
Penn State DuBois (PA)
Penn State Erie, The Behrend Coll (PA)
Penn State Fayette, The Eberly Campus (PA)
Penn State Greater Allegheny (PA)
Penn State Hazleton (PA)
Penn State Lehigh Valley (PA)
Penn State Mont Alto (PA)
Penn State New Kensington (PA)
Penn State Schuylkill (PA)
Penn State Shenango (PA)
Penn State U Park (PA)
Penn State Wilkes-Barre (PA)
Penn State Worthington Scranton (PA)
Penn State York (PA)
Quinnipiac U (CT)
Rutgers, The State U of New Jersey, New Brunswick (NJ)
San Francisco State U (CA)
Université de Montréal (QC, Canada)
Université de Sherbrooke (QC, Canada)
The U of British Columbia (BC, Canada)
U of Delaware (DE)
U of Florida (FL)
U of Kentucky (KY)
U of King's Coll (NS, Canada)
U of Minnesota, Twin Cities Campus (MN)
The U of Montana (MT)
U of Saskatchewan (SK, Canada)
U of South Florida (FL)
The U of Texas at El Paso (TX)
U of Toronto (ON, Canada)
U of Vermont (VT)
U of Wisconsin–La Crosse (WI)
U of Wisconsin–Oshkosh (WI)
Utah State U (UT)
Wagner Coll (NY)
Worcester Polytechnic Inst (MA)
Xavier U of Louisiana (LA)

MEDICAL OFFICE ASSISTANT
Concordia U Wisconsin (WI)

MEDICAL RADIOLOGIC TECHNOLOGY
Arkansas State U (AR)
Armstrong State U (GA)
Averett U (VA)
Avila U (MO)
Ball State U (IN)
Belmont U (TN)
Bloomsburg U of Pennsylvania (PA)
Bowling Green State U (OH)
California State U, Long Beach (CA)
Clarion U of Pennsylvania (PA)
Concordia U Wisconsin (WI)
Creighton U (NE)
Fairleigh Dickinson U, Coll at Florham (NJ)
Georgia Regents U (GA)
Grand Valley State U (MI)
Indiana U Kokomo (IN)
Indiana U–Purdue U Indianapolis (IN)
Indiana U South Bend (IN)
Kent State U at Salem (OH)
La Roche Coll (PA)
Long Island U–LIU Post (NY)
MCPHS U (MA)
Minot State U (ND)
Misericordia U (PA)
Morehead State U (KY)
Mount Aloysius Coll (PA)
Mount Marty Coll (SD)
National U (CA)
New York City Coll of Technology of the City U of New York (NY)
North Central Coll (IL)
Northern Kentucky U (KY)
Notre Dame of Maryland U (MD)
Oakland U (MI)
The Ohio State U (OH)
Oregon Health & Science U (OR)
Roosevelt U (IL)
St. Catharine Coll (KY)
St. Francis Coll (NY)
Saint Louis U (MO)
Southern Illinois U Carbondale (IL)
Southern Vermont Coll (VT)
Texas State U (TX)
U of Central Arkansas (AR)
U of Cincinnati (OH)
The U of Findlay (OH)
U of Hartford (CT)
U of Michigan–Flint (MI)
U of Missouri (MO)
U of Nevada, Las Vegas (NV)
U of New Mexico (NM)
The U of North Carolina at Chapel Hill (NC)
U of Oklahoma Health Sciences Center (OK)
U of St. Francis (IL)
U of Southern Indiana (IN)
U of Vermont (VT)
U of Wisconsin–La Crosse (WI)
Valencia Coll (FL)
Wayne State U (MI)
Weber State U (UT)

MEDICINAL AND PHARMACEUTICAL CHEMISTRY
King U (TN)
Michigan Technological U (MI)
U of Dayton (OH)
U of Guelph (ON, Canada)
U of Michigan (MI)
U of the Sciences (PA)
Worcester Polytechnic Inst (MA)

MEDIEVAL AND RENAISSANCE STUDIES
Augsburg Coll (MN)
Bard Coll (NY)
Barnard Coll (NY)
Binghamton U, State U of New York (NY)
Brown U (RI)
The Catholic U of America (DC)
Cleveland State U (OH)
Coll of the Holy Cross (MA)
The Coll of William and Mary (VA)
Columbia U (NY)
Cornell Coll (IA)
Dickinson Coll (PA)
Fordham U (NY)
Georgetown U (DC)
Hanover Coll (IN)
Mount Allison U (NB, Canada)
Mount Holyoke Coll (MA)
New Coll of Florida (FL)
New York U (NY)
The Ohio State U (OH)
Ohio Wesleyan U (OH)
Penn State Abington (PA)
Penn State Altoona (PA)
Penn State Beaver (PA)
Penn State Berks (PA)
Penn State Brandywine (PA)
Penn State DuBois (PA)
Penn State Erie, The Behrend Coll (PA)
Penn State Fayette, The Eberly Campus (PA)
Penn State Greater Allegheny (PA)
Penn State Hazleton (PA)
Penn State Lehigh Valley (PA)
Penn State Mont Alto (PA)
Penn State New Kensington (PA)
Penn State Schuylkill (PA)
Penn State Shenango (PA)
Penn State U Park (PA)
Penn State Wilkes-Barre (PA)
Penn State Worthington Scranton (PA)
Penn State York (PA)
Pomona Coll (CA)
Purdue U (IN)
Rutgers, The State U of New Jersey, New Brunswick (NJ)
St. Olaf Coll (MN)
Sewanee: The U of the South (TN)
Smith Coll (MA)
Southern Methodist U (TX)
Tulane U (LA)
U at Albany, State U of New York (NY)
U of California, Santa Barbara (CA)
U of Chicago (IL)
The U of Iowa (IA)
U of Michigan (MI)
U of Nebraska–Lincoln (NE)
U of Notre Dame (IN)
U of Oregon (OR)
U of Ottawa (ON, Canada)
U of Regina (SK, Canada)
U of Saskatchewan (SK, Canada)
The U of Toledo (OH)
U of Waterloo (ON, Canada)
The U of Western Ontario (ON, Canada)
Ursinus Coll (PA)
Vassar Coll (NY)
Washington and Lee U (VA)

MEETING AND EVENT PLANNING
Central Michigan U (MI)
Lasell Coll (MA)
Lynn U (FL)
U of Central Florida (FL)

MENTAL AND SOCIAL HEALTH SERVICES AND ALLIED PROFESSIONS RELATED
Clarion U of Pennsylvania (PA)
Northern Kentucky U (KY)
Old Dominion U (VA)
Pennsylvania Coll of Technology (PA)
Roger Williams U (RI)
U of Maine at Augusta (ME)
U of Puerto Rico in Ponce (PR)
Washburn U (KS)

MENTAL HEALTH COUNSELING
Canisius Coll (NY)
Goddard Coll (VT)
Iona Coll (NY)

MERCHANDISING, SALES, AND MARKETING OPERATIONS RELATED (GENERAL)
Dalhousie U (NS, Canada)
Eastern Michigan U (MI)
Georgia State U (GA)
Lincoln U (MO)
Post U (CT)
U of Hartford (CT)
Washington U in St. Louis (MO)

MERCHANDISING, SALES, AND MARKETING OPERATIONS RELATED (SPECIALIZED)
Baylor U (TX)
Fashion Inst of Technology (NY)
High Point U (NC)
Saint Joseph's U (PA)
Universidad Metropolitana (PR)

METAL AND JEWELRY ARTS
Acad of Art U (CA)
Adams State U (CO)
Arcadia U (PA)
Bowling Green State U (OH)
California Coll of the Arts (CA)
California State U, Long Beach (CA)
Central Washington U (WA)
Cleveland Inst of Art (OH)
Colorado State U (CO)
Ferris State U (MI)
Hofstra U (NY)
Massachusetts Coll of Art and Design (MA)
Northern Michigan U (MI)
Pratt Inst (NY)
Rhode Island Coll (RI)
Rhode Island School of Design (RI)
Rochester Inst of Technology (NY)
Savannah Coll of Art and Design (GA)
School of the Art Inst of Chicago (IL)
School of the Museum of Fine Arts, Boston (MA)
Seton Hill U (PA)
State U of New York at New Paltz (NY)
Syracuse U (NY)
Temple U (PA)
The U of Akron (OH)
The U of Iowa (IA)
The U of Kansas (KS)
U of Massachusetts Dartmouth (MA)
U of Michigan (MI)
U of Oregon (OR)
Western State Colorado U (CO)

METALLURGICAL ENGINEERING
Colorado School of Mines (CO)
LeTourneau U (TX)
Missouri U of Science and Technology (MO)
Montana Tech of The U of Montana (MT)
South Dakota School of Mines and Technology (SD)
The U of Alabama (AL)
The U of British Columbia (BC, Canada)
U of Minnesota, Twin Cities Campus (MN)
U of Nevada, Reno (NV)
The U of Texas at El Paso (TX)
U of Toronto (ON, Canada)
U of Utah (UT)

METEOROLOGY
Central Michigan U (MI)
Dalhousie U (NS, Canada)
Florida Inst of Technology (FL)
Florida State U (FL)
Northland Coll (WI)
Rutgers, The State U of New Jersey, New Brunswick (NJ)
U of Hawaii at Manoa (HI)
U of Miami (FL)
The U of North Carolina at Charlotte (NC)
U of Oklahoma (OK)
U of South Alabama (AL)
U of the Incarnate Word (TX)
U of Utah (UT)
U of Wisconsin–Milwaukee (WI)
Virginia Polytechnic Inst and State U (VA)
Western Illinois U (IL)
Western Kentucky U (KY)

MICROBIOLOGICAL SCIENCES AND IMMUNOLOGY RELATED
Dalhousie U (NS, Canada)
U of Alberta (AB, Canada)
U of California, Los Angeles (CA)

MICROBIOLOGY
Albany Coll of Pharmacy and Health Sciences (NY)
Arizona State U at the Tempe campus (AZ)
Auburn U (AL)
Brigham Young U (UT)
California State U, Chico (CA)
California State U, Dominguez Hills (CA)
California State U, Long Beach (CA)
California State U, Los Angeles (CA)
Central Washington U (WA)
Colorado State U (CO)
Indiana U Bloomington (IN)
Inter American U of Puerto Rico, Aguadilla Campus (PR)
Inter American U of Puerto Rico, Bayamón Campus (PR)
Inter American U of Puerto Rico, Ponce Campus (PR)
Inter American U of Puerto Rico, San Germán Campus (PR)
Iowa State U of Science and Technology (IA)
Kansas State U (KS)
Louisiana State U and A&M Coll (LA)
Miami U (OH)
Michigan State U (MI)
North Carolina State U (NC)
North Dakota State U (ND)
Northern Arizona U (AZ)
Northern Michigan U (MI)
The Ohio State U (OH)
Ohio U (OH)
Oklahoma State U (OK)
Oregon State U (OR)
Rutgers, The State U of New Jersey, New Brunswick (NJ)
San Diego State U (CA)
South Dakota State U (SD)
Southern Illinois U Carbondale (IL)
Texas A&M U (TX)
Texas State U (TX)
Texas Tech U (TX)
The U of Akron (OH)
The U of Alabama (AL)
U of Alberta (AB, Canada)
The U of Arizona (AZ)
The U of British Columbia–Okanagan Campus (BC, Canada)
U of California, Berkeley (CA)
U of California, Davis (CA)
U of California, Santa Barbara (CA)
U of Georgia (GA)
U of Guelph (ON, Canada)
U of Hawaii at Manoa (HI)
U of Idaho (ID)
The U of Iowa (IA)
The U of Kansas (KS)
U of Maine (ME)
U of Maryland, Coll Park (MD)
U of Massachusetts Amherst (MA)
U of Michigan (MI)
U of Michigan–Dearborn (MI)
U of Nebraska–Lincoln (NE)
U of Northern Iowa (IA)
U of Oklahoma (OK)
U of Pittsburgh (PA)
U of Rhode Island (RI)
U of Saskatchewan (SK, Canada)
The U of Texas at Arlington (TX)
U of the Sciences (PA)
U of Toronto (ON, Canada)
U of Vermont (VT)
U of Washington (WA)
U of Wisconsin–La Crosse (WI)
U of Wisconsin–Madison (WI)
U of Wisconsin–Milwaukee (WI)
U of Wyoming (WY)
Washington State U (WA)
Weber State U (UT)

MICROBIOLOGY AND IMMUNOLOGY
Purdue U (IN)
U of California, Irvine (CA)
U of Miami (FL)
The U of Texas at San Antonio (TX)
The U of Western Ontario (ON, Canada)
West Virginia U (WV)

MIDDLE/NEAR EASTERN AND SEMITIC LANGUAGES
Indiana U Bloomington (IN)
Pepperdine U, Malibu (CA)
U of Pennsylvania (PA)
The U of Texas at Austin (TX)

MIDDLE/NEAR EASTERN AND SEMITIC LANGUAGES RELATED
Bryn Mawr Coll (PA)
Columbia U, School of General Studies (NY)
U of Chicago (IL)
U of Michigan (MI)
U of Washington (WA)
Wayne State U (MI)

MIDDLE SCHOOL EDUCATION
Albany State U (GA)
Albertus Magnus Coll (CT)
Alice Lloyd Coll (KY)
Alvernia U (PA)
Alverno Coll (WI)
Anna Maria Coll (MA)
Appalachian State U (NC)
Arkansas State U (AR)
Arkansas Tech U (AR)
Armstrong State U (GA)
Asbury U (KY)
Ashland U (OH)
Austin Coll (TX)
Avila U (MO)
Baker U (KS)
Baldwin Wallace U (OH)
Belmont U (TN)
Berea Coll (KY)
Berry Coll (GA)
Bethany Coll (WV)
Bethel Coll (IN)
Black Hills State U (SD)
Bloomsburg U of Pennsylvania (PA)
Bluefield Coll (VA)
Bluffton U (OH)
Bob Jones U (SC)
Bowling Green State U (OH)
Brenau U (GA)
Butler U (IN)
California U of Pennsylvania (PA)
Capital U (OH)
Carlow U (PA)
Catawba Coll (NC)
Cedarville U (OH)
Central Methodist U (MO)
Central State U (OH)
Champlain Coll (VT)
Claflin U (SC)
Clarion U of Pennsylvania (PA)
Clark U (MA)
Clayton State U (GA)
Cleveland State U (OH)
Coastal Carolina U (SC)
Coll of Charleston (SC)
Coll of the Atlantic (ME)
Columbia Coll (SC)
Columbus State U (GA)
Concordia Coll–New York (NY)
Concordia U, Nebraska (NE)
Concordia U, St. Paul (MN)
Concordia U Texas (TX)
Concordia U Wisconsin (WI)
Delaware State U (DE)
Dowling Coll (NY)
Duquesne U (PA)
East Carolina U (NC)
Eastern Illinois U (IL)
Eastern Kentucky U (KY)
Eastern U (PA)
Edinboro U of Pennsylvania (PA)
Elizabethtown Coll (PA)
Elon U (NC)
Emmanuel Coll (GA)
Evangel U (MO)
Fayetteville State U (NC)
Fitchburg State U (MA)
Florida Inst of Technology (FL)
Fontbonne U (MO)
Francis Marion U (SC)
Gannon U (PA)
Georgetown Coll (KY)
Georgia Coll & State U (GA)
Georgia Regents U (GA)
Georgia Southern U (GA)
Georgia Southwestern State U (GA)
Gettysburg Coll (PA)
Goddard Coll (VT)
Gordon Coll (MA)
Grand Valley State U (MI)
Granite State Coll (NH)
Greensboro Coll (NC)
Grove City Coll (PA)
Hampton U (VA)
Harding U (AR)
Harris-Stowe State U (MO)
High Point U (NC)
Houston Baptist U (TX)
Illinois State U (IL)
Indiana U of Pennsylvania (PA)
Ithaca Coll (NY)
Jacksonville State U (AL)
Johnson State Coll (VT)
Kennesaw State U (GA)
Kent State U (OH)
Kent State U at Geauga (OH)
Kent State U at Stark (OH)
Kentucky Christian U (KY)
Kentucky Wesleyan Coll (KY)
Kutztown U of Pennsylvania (PA)
Lee U (TN)
Lenoir-Rhyne U (NC)
Lesley U (MA)
LeTourneau U (TX)
Lincoln U (MO)
Lindenwood U (MO)
Lindsey Wilson Coll (KY)
Lipscomb U (TN)
Lourdes U (OH)
Lubbock Christian U (TX)
Malone U (OH)
Manchester U (IN)
Manhattan Coll (NY)
Marian U (WI)
Mars Hill U (NC)
Maryville U of Saint Louis (MO)
The Master's Coll and Sem (CA)
McKendree U (IL)
McMurry U (TX)
Medaille Coll (NY)
Mercer U, Macon (GA)
Merrimack Coll (MA)
Messiah Coll (PA)
Miami U (OH)
Michigan State U (MI)
MidAmerica Nazarene U (KS)
Millersville U of Pennsylvania (PA)
Misericordia U (PA)
Missouri Baptist U (MO)
Missouri State U (MO)
Morehead State U (KY)
Mount Aloysius Coll (PA)
Mount Mary U (WI)
Mount Mercy U (IA)
Mount St. Joseph U (OH)
Mount Vernon Nazarene U (OH)
Murray State U (KY)
Nebraska Wesleyan U (NE)
Newberry Coll (SC)
Nicholls State U (LA)
North Carolina Central U (NC)
North Carolina State U (NC)
North Carolina Wesleyan Coll (NC)
Northern Kentucky U (KY)
Northwest Christian U (OR)
Northwest Missouri State U (MO)
Oakland City U (IN)
Ohio Dominican U (OH)
Ohio Northern U (OH)
The Ohio State U (OH)
The Ohio State U at Lima (OH)
The Ohio State U at Marion (OH)
The Ohio State U–Mansfield Campus (OH)
The Ohio State U–Newark Campus (OH)
Ohio Wesleyan U (OH)
Peru State Coll (NE)
Piedmont Coll (GA)
Point U (GA)
Presbyterian Coll (SC)
Reinhardt U (GA)
Rockhurst U (MO)
St. Catharine Coll (KY)
Saint Leo U (FL)
Saint Vincent Coll (PA)
Savannah State U (GA)
Shippensburg U of Pennsylvania (PA)
South Carolina State U (SC)
Southeastern Louisiana U (LA)
Southeast Missouri State U (MO)
Southern Arkansas U–Magnolia (AR)
Southwest Baptist U (MO)
Spalding U (KY)
State U of New York Coll at Cortland (NY)
State U of New York Coll at Old Westbury (NY)
Stevenson U (MD)
Tarleton State U (TX)
Temple U (PA)
Texas Lutheran U (TX)
Thomas More Coll (KY)
Toccoa Falls Coll (GA)
Towson U (MD)
Transylvania U (KY)
Trinity Christian Coll (IL)
Truett-McConnell Coll (GA)
Tusculum Coll (TN)
Union Coll (KY)
The U of Akron (OH)
U of Arkansas at Pine Bluff (AR)
U of Arkansas–Fort Smith (AR)
U of Central Arkansas (AR)
U of Central Missouri (MO)
U of Cincinnati (OH)
U of Dayton (OH)
U of Georgia (GA)
U of Great Falls (MT)
The U of Kansas (KS)
U of Kentucky (KY)
U of Louisiana at Lafayette (LA)
U of Maryland, Coll Park (MD)
U of Minnesota, Duluth (MN)
U of Missouri (MO)
U of Missouri–Kansas City (MO)
U of Mount Union (OH)
The U of North Carolina at Chapel Hill (NC)
The U of North Carolina at Charlotte (NC)
The U of North Carolina at Greensboro (NC)
The U of North Carolina at Pembroke (NC)
The U of North Carolina Wilmington (NC)
U of North Dakota (ND)
U of Northern Iowa (IA)
U of North Florida (FL)
U of North Georgia (GA)
U of Pikeville (KY)
U of Regina (SK, Canada)
U of St. Thomas (MN)
The U of Scranton (PA)
U of South Carolina Aiken (SC)
U of South Carolina Upstate (SC)
The U of Tennessee at Chattanooga (TN)
The U of Texas at San Antonio (TX)
U of the Cumberlands (KY)
The U of Toledo (OH)
U of Valley Forge (PA)
U of Vermont (VT)
The U of Western Ontario (ON, Canada)
U of West Florida (FL)
Urbana U (OH)
Ursuline Coll (OH)
Valdosta State U (GA)
Virginia Wesleyan Coll (VA)
Walsh U (OH)
Warner Pacific Coll (OR)
Washington U in St. Louis (MO)
Wayne State Coll (NE)
Webster U (MO)
West Chester U of Pennsylvania (PA)
Western Carolina U (NC)
Western Kentucky U (KY)
Westminster Coll (MO)
West Virginia Wesleyan Coll (WV)
Wilkes U (PA)
William Jewell Coll (MO)
Wilmington U (DE)
Wingate U (NC)
Wright State U (OH)
Xavier U (OH)
Xavier U of Louisiana (LA)
Youngstown State U (OH)

MILITARY APPLIED SCIENCES RELATED
United States Military Acad (NY)

MILITARY HISTORY
American Public U System (WV)

MILITARY INSTALLATION MANAGEMENT
American Public U System (WV)

MILITARY SCIENCE, LEADERSHIP AND OPERATIONAL ART RELATED
Dixie State U (UT)

MILITARY STUDIES
Hawai`i Pacific U (HI)
United States Air Force Acad (CO)

MILITARY TECHNOLOGIES AND APPLIED SCIENCES RELATED
Alcorn State U (MS)

MINING AND MINERAL ENGINEERING
Colorado School of Mines (CO)
Missouri U of Science and Technology (MO)
Montana Tech of The U of Montana (MT)
New Mexico Inst of Mining and Technology (NM)
Penn State Abington (PA)
Penn State Altoona (PA)
Penn State Beaver (PA)
Penn State Berks (PA)
Penn State Brandywine (PA)
Penn State DuBois (PA)
Penn State Erie, The Behrend Coll (PA)
Penn State Fayette, The Eberly Campus (PA)
Penn State Greater Allegheny (PA)
Penn State Hazleton (PA)
Penn State Lehigh Valley (PA)
Penn State Mont Alto (PA)
Penn State New Kensington (PA)
Penn State Schuylkill (PA)
Penn State Shenango (PA)
Penn State U Park (PA)
Penn State Wilkes-Barre (PA)
Penn State Worthington Scranton (PA)
Penn State York (PA)
South Dakota School of Mines and Technology (SD)
Southern Illinois U Carbondale (IL)
U of Alaska Fairbanks (AK)
The U of Arizona (AZ)
The U of British Columbia (BC, Canada)
U of Kentucky (KY)
U of Minnesota, Twin Cities Campus (MN)
U of Nevada, Reno (NV)
U of Toronto (ON, Canada)
U of Utah (UT)
Virginia Polytechnic Inst and State U (VA)
West Virginia U (WV)

MINING TECHNOLOGY
Bluefield State Coll (WV)

MISSIONARY STUDIES AND MISSIOLOGY
Asbury U (KY)
Bethel Coll (IN)
Biola U (CA)
Bob Jones U (SC)
California Baptist U (CA)
Calvary Bible Coll and Theological Sem (MO)
City Vision Coll (MO)
Columbia Bible Coll (BC, Canada)
Concordia U, St. Paul (MN)
Concordia U Wisconsin (WI)
Corban U (OR)
Cornerstone U (MI)
Crossroads Coll (MN)
Eastern U (PA)
East Texas Baptist U (TX)
Faith Baptist Bible Coll and Theological Sem (IA)
Geneva Coll (PA)
Harding U (AR)
Hardin-Simmons U (TX)
Hillsdale Free Will Baptist Coll (OK)
Hobe Sound Bible Coll (FL)
Hope Intl U (CA)
Kentucky Mountain Bible Coll (KY)
Kuyper Coll (MI)
Lee U (TN)
LeTourneau U (TX)
Liberty U (VA)
Lincoln Christian U (IL)
Lipscomb U (TN)
Lubbock Christian U (TX)
Manhattan Christian Coll (KS)
Maranatha Baptist U (WI)
MidAmerica Nazarene U (KS)
Mid-Atlantic Christian U (NC)
Mount Vernon Nazarene U (OH)
Multnomah U (OR)
North Greenville U (SC)
Northwest Christian U (OR)
Northwest Nazarene U (ID)
Northwest U (WA)
Oklahoma Christian U (OK)
Oklahoma Wesleyan U (OK)
Olivet Nazarene U (IL)
Palm Beach Atlantic U (FL)
Simpson U (CA)
Southeastern U (FL)
Southern Adventist U (TN)
Southwest Baptist U (MO)
Summit U (PA)
Tabor Coll (KS)
Toccoa Falls Coll (GA)
Trinity Coll of Florida (FL)
Truett-McConnell Coll (GA)
U of Northwestern–St. Paul (MN)
U of the Cumberlands (KY)
U of Valley Forge (PA)
Vanguard U of Southern California (CA)
Welch Coll (TN)
William Jessup U (CA)

MODELING, VIRTUAL ENVIRONMENTS AND SIMULATION
Daniel Webster Coll (NH)
DigiPen Inst of Technology (WA)
Pennsylvania Coll of Technology (PA)
U of Colorado Colorado Springs (CO)
U of Idaho (ID)
U of Southern California (CA)
The U of Tulsa (OK)

MODERN GREEK
Calvin Coll (MI)
Columbia U (NY)
Concordia U Wisconsin (WI)
Cornell U (NY)
Furman U (SC)
John Carroll U (OH)
Lehman Coll of the City U of New York (NY)
Oberlin Coll (OH)
The Ohio State U (OH)
Tufts U (MA)
Tulane U (LA)
U of Michigan (MI)
U of Toronto (ON, Canada)
Wabash Coll (IN)
Wright State U (OH)

MODERN LANGUAGES
Alma Coll (MI)
Beloit Coll (WI)
Bemidji State U (MN)
Clark U (MA)
The Coll of William and Mary (VA)
Cornell Coll (IA)
Fordham U (NY)
Gettysburg Coll (PA)
Hampton U (VA)
La Salle U (PA)
Louisiana Coll (LA)
Minnesota State U Mankato (MN)
Mount Allison U (NB, Canada)
Nazareth Coll of Rochester (NY)
Pacific U (OR)
Presbyterian Coll (SC)
Purchase Coll, State U of New York (NY)
Rivier U (NH)
St. Bonaventure U (NY)
Saint Francis U (PA)
Saint Michael's Coll (VT)
Saint Peter's U (NJ)
St. Thomas Aquinas Coll (NY)
Sarah Lawrence Coll (NY)

Trent U (ON, Canada)
Trinity Coll (CT)
Université de Montréal (QC, Canada)
U of Ottawa (ON, Canada)
U of Toronto (ON, Canada)
U of Windsor (ON, Canada)
Virginia Military Inst (VA)
Walla Walla U (WA)
Walsh U (OH)
Washington U in St. Louis (MO)
Widener U (PA)
Wright State U (OH)

MOLECULAR BIOCHEMISTRY
Bob Jones U (SC)
Clarkson U (NY)
Simon Fraser U (BC, Canada)
U of California, Davis (CA)
U of Richmond (VA)
Wesleyan U (CT)

MOLECULAR BIOLOGY
Alverno Coll (WI)
Arizona State U at the Tempe campus (AZ)
Assumption Coll (MA)
Auburn U (AL)
Beloit Coll (WI)
Blackburn Coll (IL)
Boston U (MA)
Brown U (RI)
California Lutheran U (CA)
California State U, Fresno (CA)
Central Connecticut State U (CT)
Chestnut Hill Coll (PA)
Claremont McKenna Coll (CA)
Clarion U of Pennsylvania (PA)
Clark U (MA)
Coe Coll (IA)
Colby Coll (ME)
The Coll of Wooster (OH)
Connecticut Coll (CT)
Dartmouth Coll (NH)
Florida Inst of Technology (FL)
Gettysburg Coll (PA)
Goshen Coll (IN)
Hampton U (VA)
Houston Baptist U (TX)
Humboldt State U (CA)
Johns Hopkins U (MD)
Kenyon Coll (OH)
Lawrence Technological U (MI)
Lehigh U (PA)
Messiah Coll (PA)
Middlebury Coll (VT)
Millikin U (IL)
Montclair State U (NJ)
Northwestern U (IL)
Ohio Northern U (OH)
Pomona Coll (CA)
Princeton U (NJ)
Rollins Coll (FL)
Rutgers, The State U of New Jersey, New Brunswick (NJ)
San Francisco State U (CA)
San Jose State U (CA)
Scripps Coll (CA)
Simon Fraser U (BC, Canada)
Stetson U (FL)
Tulane U (LA)
Universidad Metropolitana (PR)
U at Albany, State U of New York (NY)
The U of British Columbia–Okanagan Campus (BC, Canada)
U of California, Santa Barbara (CA)
U of California, Santa Cruz (CA)
U of Denver (CO)
U of Guelph (ON, Canada)
U of Idaho (ID)
The U of Kansas (KS)
U of Maine (ME)
U of Michigan (MI)
U of Michigan–Flint (MI)
U of Pittsburgh (PA)
U of Puget Sound (WA)
The U of Scranton (PA)
The U of Texas at Dallas (TX)
U of Toronto (ON, Canada)
U of Vermont (VT)
U of Wisconsin–Eau Claire (WI)
U of Wisconsin–Madison (WI)
U of Wisconsin–Parkside (WI)
U of Wyoming (WY)
Vanderbilt U (TN)
Wells Coll (NY)
Whitman Coll (WA)
William Jewell Coll (MO)
Worcester Polytechnic Inst (MA)
Yale U (CT)
Yeshiva U (NY)

MOLECULAR GENETICS
Michigan State U (MI)
The Ohio State U (OH)
Rutgers, The State U of New Jersey, New Brunswick (NJ)
Texas A&M U (TX)
U of Alberta (AB, Canada)
U of Guelph (ON, Canada)
U of Vermont (VT)
Washington State U (WA)

MOLECULAR PHARMACOLOGY
The U of Scranton (PA)

MONTESSORI TEACHER EDUCATION
Canisius Coll (NY)
Siena Heights U (MI)
Xavier U (OH)

MOVEMENT THERAPY AND MOVEMENT EDUCATION
Texas Christian U (TX)
U of Vermont (VT)

MULTICULTURAL EDUCATION
Fort Lewis Coll (CO)
Goddard Coll (VT)
U of St. Thomas (TX)

MULTI/INTERDISCIPLINARY STUDIES RELATED
Abilene Christian U (TX)
Adams State U (CO)
Adelphi U (NY)
Agnes Scott Coll (GA)
Albion Coll (MI)
Albright Coll (PA)
Allegheny Coll (PA)
Alverno Coll (WI)
American U (DC)
Anderson U (IN)
Angelo State U (TX)
Arcadia U (PA)
Arizona State U at the Downtown Phoenix campus (AZ)
Arizona State U at the Polytechnic campus (AZ)
Arizona State U at the Tempe campus (AZ)
Arizona State U at the West campus (AZ)
Arkansas State U (AR)
Arkansas Tech U (AR)
Athens State U (AL)
Austin Coll (TX)
Baldwin Wallace U (OH)
Bates Coll (ME)
Baylor U (TX)
Belmont U (TN)
Bennett Coll (NC)
Bennington Coll (VT)
Berea Coll (KY)
Berry Coll (GA)
Bethel U (MN)
Binghamton U, State U of New York (NY)
Bloomfield Coll (NJ)
Bluffton U (OH)
Boston U (MA)
Bowdoin Coll (ME)
Bowling Green State U (OH)
Brandeis U (MA)
Brevard Coll (NC)
Bucknell U (PA)
Buena Vista U (IA)
Buffalo State Coll, State U of New York (NY)
Cabarrus Coll of Health Sciences (NC)
Caldwell U (NJ)
California Baptist U (CA)
California Inst of Integral Studies (CA)
California Inst of Technology (CA)
California Lutheran U (CA)
California Polytechnic State U, San Luis Obispo (CA)
California State U, Dominguez Hills (CA)
California State U, Long Beach (CA)
California State U, Los Angeles (CA)
California State U, Monterey Bay (CA)
California State U, San Bernardino (CA)
California State U, San Marcos (CA)
California State U, Stanislaus (CA)
Calvary Bible Coll and Theological Sem (MO)
Cameron U (OK)
Capital U (OH)
Carroll Coll (MT)
Catawba Coll (NC)
Central Coll (IA)
Central Connecticut State U (CT)
Central Washington U (WA)
Chestnut Hill Coll (PA)
Christopher Newport U (VA)
Claremont McKenna Coll (CA)
Clarkson U (NY)
Cleveland State U (OH)
Colby Coll (ME)
Coll of Charleston (SC)
The Coll of Idaho (ID)
The Coll of New Jersey (NJ)
The Coll of New Rochelle (NY)
Coll of Saint Benedict (MN)
Coll of Saint Elizabeth (NJ)
The Coll of Saint Rose (NY)
The Coll of William and Mary (VA)
The Coll of Wooster (OH)
The Colorado Coll (CO)
Columbia Coll Chicago (IL)
Concordia U, Nebraska (NE)
Cornell Coll (IA)
Cornell U (NY)
Covenant Coll (GA)
Dalhousie U (NS, Canada)
Dallas Baptist U (TX)
Dartmouth Coll (NH)
Davidson Coll (NC)
Delta State U (MS)
DePauw U (IN)
Dixie State U (UT)
Earlham Coll (IN)
East Central U (OK)
Eastern Illinois U (IL)
Eastern Kentucky U (KY)
Eastern Michigan U (MI)
Eastern Oregon U (OR)
East Tennessee State U (TN)
East Texas Baptist U (TX)
Edgewood Coll (WI)
Embry-Riddle Aeronautical U–Daytona (FL)
Embry-Riddle Aeronautical U–Prescott (AZ)
Emmanuel Coll (MA)
Emporia State U (KS)
The Evergreen State Coll (WA)
Florida Inst of Technology (FL)
Florida Intl U (FL)
Florida Southern Coll (FL)
Franklin & Marshall Coll (PA)
Franklin U (OH)
Gannon U (PA)
Georgetown Coll (KY)
Georgetown U (DC)
Georgia Inst of Technology (GA)
Georgian Court U (NJ)
Georgia State U (GA)
Goshen Coll (IN)
Goucher Coll (MD)
Granite State Coll (NH)
Greenville Coll (IL)
Guilford Coll (NC)
Hamline U (MN)
Hampshire Coll (MA)
Harris-Stowe State U (MO)
Heritage U (WA)
Hillsdale Free Will Baptist Coll (OK)
Hope Coll (MI)
Howard Payne U (TX)
Humboldt State U (CA)
Illinois Wesleyan U (IL)
Immaculata U (PA)
Indiana State U (IN)
Indiana U–Purdue U Indianapolis (IN)
Iowa State U of Science and Technology (IA)
Ithaca Coll (NY)
Jackson State U (MS)
Jacksonville U (FL)
John Brown U (AR)
Juniata Coll (PA)
Kalamazoo Coll (MI)
Keene State Coll (NH)
Kennesaw State U (GA)
Kentucky Christian U (KY)
Kentucky Wesleyan Coll (KY)
Kenyon Coll (OH)
Knox Coll (IL)
Lake Erie Coll (OH)
Lamar U (TX)
Lane Coll (TN)
Lasell Coll (MA)
Lebanon Valley Coll (PA)
Lee U (TN)
Lehigh U (PA)
LeTourneau U (TX)
Lewis U (IL)
Liberty U (VA)
Long Island U–LIU Brooklyn (NY)
Louisiana State U and A&M Coll (LA)
Lourdes U (OH)
Loyola Marymount U (CA)
Loyola U Chicago (IL)
Luther Coll (IA)
Lycoming Coll (PA)
Macalester Coll (MN)
Manchester U (IN)
Manhattan Coll (NY)
Marian U (WI)
Marquette U (WI)
Marylhurst U (OR)
Maryville Coll (TN)
McDaniel Coll (MD)
McMurry U (TX)
Mercer U, Macon (GA)
Meredith Coll (NC)
Messiah Coll (PA)
Metropolitan State U (MN)
Michigan State U (MI)
Middle Tennessee State U (TN)
Millikin U (IL)
Millsaps Coll (MS)
Minnesota State U Moorhead (MN)
Mississippi State U (MS)
Mississippi U for Women (MS)
Missouri Baptist U (MO)
Missouri Western State U (MO)
Monmouth U (NJ)
Montana State U Billings (MT)
Montclair State U (NJ)
Morrisville State Coll (NY)
Mount Holyoke Coll (MA)
Mount Mary U (WI)
Mount Mercy U (IA)
Mount St. Mary's U (MD)
Naropa U (CO)
National U (CA)
Newman U (KS)
New York Inst of Technology (NY)
Norfolk State U (VA)
North Central Coll (IL)
Northern Illinois U (IL)
Northwest Christian U (OR)
Northwestern Oklahoma State U (OK)
Northwestern U (IL)
Notre Dame of Maryland U (MD)
The Ohio State U (OH)
Ohio Wesleyan U (OH)
Old Dominion U (VA)
Our Lady of the Lake U of San Antonio (TX)
Pace U (NY)
Pacific Lutheran U (WA)
Palm Beach Atlantic U (FL)
Park U (MO)
Penn State Erie, The Behrend Coll (PA)
Penn State Harrisburg (PA)
Pepperdine U, Malibu (CA)
Pittsburg State U (KS)
Plymouth State U (NH)
Prairie View A&M U (TX)
Prescott Coll (AZ)
Princeton U (NJ)
Providence Coll (RI)
Queens Coll of the City U of New York (NY)
Radford U (VA)
Regis Coll (MA)
Regis U (CO)
Rice U (TX)
Robert Morris U (PA)
Robert Morris U Illinois (IL)
Rocky Mountain Coll (MT)
Roger Williams U (RI)
Rollins Coll (FL)
Rowan U (NJ)
Rutgers, The State U of New Jersey, Camden (NJ)
Rutgers, The State U of New Jersey, Newark (NJ)
Rutgers, The State U of New Jersey, New Brunswick (NJ)
Saginaw Valley State U (MI)
Saint Anselm Coll (NH)
Saint John's U (MN)
Saint Martin's U (WA)
St. Mary's Coll of Maryland (MD)
Samford U (AL)
Sam Houston State U (TX)
San Diego Christian Coll (CA)
San Diego State U (CA)
San Francisco State U (CA)
San Jose State U (CA)
Scripps Coll (CA)
Sewanee: The U of the South (TN)
Shippensburg U of Pennsylvania (PA)
Simmons Coll (MA)
Southeastern Oklahoma State U (OK)
Southeast Missouri State U (MO)
Southern Adventist U (TN)
Southern Arkansas U–Magnolia (AR)
Southern Illinois U Carbondale (IL)
Southern Methodist U (TX)
Southern Utah U (UT)
Southwestern Adventist U (TX)
Spelman Coll (GA)
State U of New York Empire State Coll (NY)
Stephen F. Austin State U (TX)
Stephens Coll (MO)
Stonehill Coll (MA)
Stony Brook U, State U of New York (NY)
Tarleton State U (TX)
Temple U (PA)
Tennessee Wesleyan Coll (TN)
Texas A&M Intl U (TX)
Texas A&M U (TX)
Texas A&M U–Commerce (TX)
Texas A&M U–Kingsville (TX)
Texas State U (TX)
Texas Tech U (TX)
Texas Wesleyan U (TX)
Texas Woman's U (TX)
Thomas More Coll (KY)
Trevecca Nazarene U (TN)
Trinity U (TX)
Truett-McConnell Coll (GA)
Truman State U (MO)
Tulane U (LA)
Tusculum Coll (TN)
U at Albany, State U of New York (NY)
U at Buffalo, the State U of New York (NY)
The U of Akron (OH)
The U of Alabama in Huntsville (AL)
U of Alaska Fairbanks (AK)
U of Alberta (AB, Canada)
The U of Arizona (AZ)
U of Arkansas at Little Rock (AR)
U of Arkansas–Fort Smith (AR)
U of California, Berkeley (CA)
U of California, Davis (CA)
U of California, Irvine (CA)
U of California, Los Angeles (CA)
U of California, Merced (CA)
U of California, Santa Barbara (CA)
U of Central Arkansas (AR)
U of Cincinnati (OH)
U of Colorado Colorado Springs (CO)
U of Colorado Denver (CO)
U of Denver (CO)
U of Florida (FL)
U of Houston (TX)
U of Houston–Clear Lake (TX)
U of Houston–Downtown (TX)
U of Houston–Victoria (TX)
U of Idaho (ID)
U of Kentucky (KY)
U of King's Coll (NS, Canada)
U of Lethbridge (AB, Canada)
U of Maine (ME)

U of Maryland, Baltimore County (MD)
U of Maryland, Coll Park (MD)
U of Maryland U Coll (MD)
U of Mary Washington (VA)
U of Massachusetts Amherst (MA)
U of Massachusetts Boston (MA)
U of Massachusetts Dartmouth (MA)
U of Memphis (TN)
U of Michigan (MI)
U of Michigan–Dearborn (MI)
U of Michigan–Flint (MI)
U of Minnesota, Crookston (MN)
U of Minnesota, Duluth (MN)
U of Minnesota, Twin Cities Campus (MN)
U of Missouri–St. Louis (MO)
U of Montevallo (AL)
U of Nevada, Las Vegas (NV)
U of New Hampshire (NH)
U of New Orleans (LA)
The U of North Carolina at Pembroke (NC)
U of Northern Colorado (CO)
U of North Texas (TX)
U of Northwestern–St. Paul (MN)
U of Pikeville (KY)
U of Pittsburgh (PA)
U of Richmond (VA)
U of Rochester (NY)
U of St. Francis (IL)
U of Saint Joseph (CT)
U of Saint Mary (KS)
U of St. Thomas (MN)
The U of South Dakota (SD)
U of Southern California (CA)
U of Southern Mississippi (MS)
The U of Tennessee (TN)
The U of Texas at Arlington (TX)
The U of Texas at Austin (TX)
The U of Texas at San Antonio (TX)
The U of Texas at Tyler (TX)
The U of Texas of the Permian Basin (TX)
The U of Texas–Pan American (TX)
U of Virginia (VA)
U of Washington, Bothell (WA)
U of Waterloo (ON, Canada)
The U of West Alabama (AL)
U of Wisconsin–Green Bay (WI)
U of Wisconsin–Milwaukee (WI)
U of Wisconsin–Platteville (WI)
U of Wisconsin–River Falls (WI)
U of Wisconsin–Stevens Point (WI)
U of Wisconsin–Superior (WI)
U of Wisconsin–Whitewater (WI)
U of Wyoming (WY)
Ursinus Coll (PA)
Utah State U (UT)
Utah Valley U (UT)
Valparaiso U (IN)
Vanderbilt U (TN)
Vassar Coll (NY)
Villanova U (PA)
Virginia Commonwealth U (VA)
Virginia Wesleyan Coll (VA)
Viterbo U (WI)
Washburn U (KS)
Washington & Jefferson Coll (PA)
Washington and Lee U (VA)
Washington Coll (MD)
Washington State U (WA)
Washington U in St. Louis (MO)
Waynesburg U (PA)
Western Kentucky U (KY)
Western Michigan U (MI)
Western Washington U (WA)
West Texas A&M U (TX)
West Virginia U (WV)
West Virginia U Inst of Technology (WV)
Wheaton Coll (IL)
Wheaton Coll (MA)
Wheeling Jesuit U (WV)
Wichita State U (KS)
Wilkes U (PA)
William Jewell Coll (MO)
Wofford Coll (SC)
Xavier U (OH)
Yale U (CT)
Yeshiva U (NY)

MUSEUM STUDIES
Beloit Coll (WI)
Central Washington U (WA)
Coll of the Atlantic (ME)
Inst of American Indian Arts (NM)
Juniata Coll (PA)
Moore Coll of Art & Design (PA)
Randolph Coll (VA)
Tusculum Coll (TN)
The U of Iowa (IA)
Walsh U (OH)

MUSIC
Abilene Christian U (TX)
Adams State U (CO)
Adelphi U (NY)
Agnes Scott Coll (GA)
Alabama State U (AL)
Albany State U (GA)
Albion Coll (MI)
Albright Coll (PA)
Allegheny Coll (PA)
Alma Coll (MI)
Alverno Coll (WI)
Ambrose U Coll (AB, Canada)
American U (DC)
Amherst Coll (MA)
Anderson U (SC)
Andrews U (MI)
Angelo State U (TX)
Anna Maria Coll (MA)
Aquinas Coll (MI)
Arizona State U at the Tempe campus (AZ)
Arkansas State U (AR)
Arkansas Tech U (AR)
Armstrong State U (GA)
Asbury U (KY)
Ashland U (OH)
Assumption Coll (MA)
Auburn U (AL)
Augsburg Coll (MN)
Augustana Coll (IL)
Augustana Coll (SD)
Austin Coll (TX)
Austin Peay State U (TN)
Averett U (VA)
Avila U (MO)
Azusa Pacific U (CA)
Baker U (KS)
Baldwin Wallace U (OH)
Ball State U (IN)
Baptist U of the Americas (TX)
Bard Coll (NY)
Bard Coll at Simon's Rock (MA)
Barnard Coll (NY)
Baruch Coll of the City U of New York (NY)
Bates Coll (ME)
Baylor U (TX)
Belhaven U (MS)
Belmont U (TN)
Bemidji State U (MN)
Benedictine Coll (KS)
Benedictine U (IL)
Bennett Coll (NC)
Bennington Coll (VT)
Berea Coll (KY)
Berry Coll (GA)
Bethany Coll (WV)
Bethany Lutheran Coll (MN)
Bethel Coll (IN)
Bethel U (MN)
Binghamton U, State U of New York (NY)
Biola U (CA)
Birmingham-Southern Coll (AL)
Blackburn Coll (IL)
Black Hills State U (SD)
Bloomsburg U of Pennsylvania (PA)
Bluefield Coll (VA)
Blue Mountain Coll (MS)
Bluffton U (OH)
Boston Coll (MA)
Boston U (MA)
Bowdoin Coll (ME)
Bowling Green State U (OH)
Bradley U (IL)
Brandeis U (MA)
Brenau U (GA)
Brevard Coll (NC)
Bridgewater State U (MA)
Brown U (RI)
Bryan Coll (TN)
Bryn Mawr Coll (PA)
Bucknell U (PA)
Buffalo State Coll, State U of New York (NY)
Butler U (IN)
Cairn U (PA)
Caldwell U (NJ)
California Baptist U (CA)
California Lutheran U (CA)
California Polytechnic State U, San Luis Obispo (CA)
California State Polytechnic U, Pomona (CA)
California State U, Chico (CA)
California State U, Dominguez Hills (CA)
California State U, Fresno (CA)
California State U, Fullerton (CA)
California State U, Long Beach (CA)
California State U, Los Angeles (CA)
California State U, Monterey Bay (CA)
California State U, Sacramento (CA)
California State U, San Bernardino (CA)
California State U, Stanislaus (CA)
Calvin Coll (MI)
Cameron U (OK)
Campbellsville U (KY)
Capital U (OH)
Carleton Coll (MN)
Carson-Newman U (TN)
Case Western Reserve U (OH)
Castleton State Coll (VT)
Catawba Coll (NC)
The Catholic U of America (DC)
Cedar Crest Coll (PA)
Cedarville U (OH)
Centenary Coll of Louisiana (LA)
Central Coll (IA)
Central Connecticut State U (CT)
Central Methodist U (MO)
Central Michigan U (MI)
Central Washington U (WA)
Centre Coll (KY)
Chapman U (CA)
Charleston Southern U (SC)
Chatham U (PA)
Chestnut Hill Coll (PA)
Cheyney U of Pennsylvania (PA)
Chicago State U (IL)
Chowan U (NC)
City Coll of the City U of New York (NY)
Claflin U (SC)
Clark Atlanta U (GA)
Clarke U (IA)
Clark U (MA)
Clayton State U (GA)
Cleveland State U (OH)
Coastal Carolina U (SC)
Coe Coll (IA)
Colby Coll (ME)
Coll of Charleston (SC)
The Coll of Idaho (ID)
The Coll of New Jersey (NJ)
Coll of Saint Benedict (MN)
Coll of Saint Elizabeth (NJ)
The Coll of Saint Rose (NY)
Coll of Staten Island of the City U of New York (NY)
Coll of the Atlantic (ME)
Coll of the Holy Cross (MA)
Coll of the Ozarks (MO)
The Coll of William and Mary (VA)
The Coll of Wooster (OH)
The Colorado Coll (CO)
Colorado Mesa U (CO)
Colorado State U (CO)
Colorado State U–Pueblo (CO)
Columbia Coll (SC)
Columbia Coll Chicago (IL)
Columbia U (NY)
Columbia U, School of General Studies (NY)
Columbus State U (GA)
Concordia Coll (MN)
Concordia Coll–New York (NY)
Concordia U (QC, Canada)
Concordia U Chicago (IL)
Concordia U, Nebraska (NE)
Concordia U, St. Paul (MN)
Concordia U Wisconsin (WI)
Connecticut Coll (CT)
Corban U (OR)
Cornell Coll (IA)
Cornell U (NY)
Cornerstone U (MI)
Cornish Coll of the Arts (WA)
Covenant Coll (GA)
Creighton U (NE)
Crossroads Coll (MN)
Culver-Stockton Coll (MO)
Cumberland U (TN)
Dalhousie U (NS, Canada)
Dallas Baptist U (TX)
Dartmouth Coll (NH)
Davidson Coll (NC)
Delaware State U (DE)
Delta State U (MS)
Denison U (OH)
DePaul U (IL)
DePauw U (IN)
DEREE - The American Coll of Greece (Greece)
Dickinson Coll (PA)
Dickinson State U (ND)
Dixie State U (UT)
Doane Coll (NE)
Dominican U (IL)
Dominican U of California (CA)
Dowling Coll (NY)
Drake U (IA)
Drew U (NJ)
Drury U (MO)
Earlham Coll (IN)
East Carolina U (NC)
East Central U (OK)
Eastern Illinois U (IL)
Eastern Kentucky U (KY)
Eastern Michigan U (MI)
Eastern New Mexico U (NM)
Eastern Oregon U (OR)
Eastern U (PA)
East Tennessee State U (TN)
East Texas Baptist U (TX)
Eckerd Coll (FL)
Edgewood Coll (WI)
Edinboro U of Pennsylvania (PA)
Elizabethtown Coll (PA)
Elmhurst Coll (IL)
Elmira Coll (NY)
Elms Coll (MA)
Elon U (NC)
Emmanuel Coll (GA)
Emporia State U (KS)
Erskine Coll (SC)
Evangel U (MO)
Fairfield U (CT)
Fayetteville State U (NC)
Five Towns Coll (NY)
Florida Ag and Mech U (FL)
Florida Atlantic U (FL)
Florida Coll (FL)
Florida Intl U (FL)
Florida Southern Coll (FL)
Florida State U (FL)
Fordham U (NY)
Fort Hays State U (KS)
Fort Lewis Coll (CO)
Francis Marion U (SC)
Franklin & Marshall Coll (PA)
Franklin Pierce U (NH)
Friends U (KS)
Frostburg State U (MD)
Furman U (SC)
Geneva Coll (PA)
The George Washington U (DC)
Georgia Coll & State U (GA)
Georgia Regents U (GA)
Georgia Southern U (GA)
Georgia Southwestern State U (GA)
Gettysburg Coll (PA)
Gonzaga U (WA)
Gordon Coll (MA)
Goshen Coll (IN)
Goucher Coll (MD)
Graceland U (IA)
Grambling State U (LA)
Grand Valley State U (MI)
Grand View U (IA)
Greensboro Coll (NC)
Greenville Coll (IL)
Grinnell Coll (IA)
Grove City Coll (PA)
Guilford Coll (NC)
Gustavus Adolphus Coll (MN)
Hamilton Coll (NY)
Hamline U (MN)
Hampshire Coll (MA)
Hampton U (VA)
Hannibal-LaGrange U (MO)
Hanover Coll (IN)
Harding U (AR)
Hardin-Simmons U (TX)
Hartwick Coll (NY)
Harvard U (MA)
Hastings Coll (NE)
Haverford Coll (PA)
Heidelberg U (OH)
Hendrix Coll (AR)
High Point U (NC)
Hillsdale Coll (MI)
Hiram Coll (OH)
Hobart and William Smith Colls (NY)
Hofstra U (NY)
Hollins U (VA)
Hope Coll (MI)
Houghton Coll (NY)
Houston Baptist U (TX)
Howard U (DC)
Humboldt State U (CA)
Hunter Coll of the City U of New York (NY)
Huston-Tillotson U (TX)
Illinois Coll (IL)
Illinois State U (IL)
Illinois Wesleyan U (IL)
Immaculata U (PA)
Indiana State U (IN)
Indiana U of Pennsylvania (PA)
Indiana U–Purdue U Fort Wayne (IN)
Indiana U South Bend (IN)
Indiana U Southeast (IN)
Inter American U of Puerto Rico, San Germán Campus (PR)
Iowa State U of Science and Technology (IA)
Iowa Wesleyan Coll (IA)
Ithaca Coll (NY)
Jacksonville State U (AL)
Jacksonville U (FL)
John Brown U (AR)
Johns Hopkins U (MD)
Johnson C. Smith U (NC)
Johnson State Coll (VT)
Judson Coll (AL)
The Juilliard School (NY)
Kalamazoo Coll (MI)
Kansas State U (KS)
Kansas Wesleyan U (KS)
Kean U (NJ)
Keene State Coll (NH)
Kennesaw State U (GA)
Kent State U (OH)
Kentucky State U (KY)
Kenyon Coll (OH)
The King's U Coll (AB, Canada)
Kingswood U (NB, Canada)
King U (TN)
Knox Coll (IL)
Kutztown U of Pennsylvania (PA)
Lafayette Coll (PA)
LaGrange Coll (GA)
Lake Forest Coll (IL)
Lamar U (TX)
Lane Coll (TN)
Langston U (OK)
La Sierra U (CA)
Lawrence U (WI)
Lee U (TN)
Lehigh U (PA)
Lehman Coll of the City U of New York (NY)
LeMoyne-Owen Coll (TN)
Lenoir-Rhyne U (NC)
Lewis & Clark Coll (OR)
Lewis U (IL)
Liberty U (VA)
Limestone Coll (SC)
Lincoln U (PA)
Lindenwood U (MO)
Linfield Coll (OR)
Lipscomb U (TN)
Lock Haven U of Pennsylvania (PA)
Loras Coll (IA)
Louisiana Coll (LA)
Louisiana State U and A&M Coll (LA)
Loyola Marymount U (CA)
Loyola U Chicago (IL)
Loyola U New Orleans (LA)
Lubbock Christian U (TX)
Luther Coll (IA)
Lycoming Coll (PA)
Lynchburg Coll (VA)
Lyon Coll (AR)
Macalester Coll (MN)
Madonna U (MI)
Malone U (OH)
Manchester U (IN)
Manhattan School of Music (NY)

MAJORS LISTING

Manhattanville Coll (NY)
Mansfield U of Pennsylvania (PA)
Marian U (IN)
Marian U (WI)
Marietta Coll (OH)
Mars Hill U (NC)
Mary Baldwin Coll (VA)
Marylhurst U (OR)
Maryville Coll (TN)
Massachusetts Coll of Liberal Arts (MA)
Massachusetts Inst of Technology (MA)
The Master's Coll and Sem (CA)
McDaniel Coll (MD)
McKendree U (IL)
McMurry U (TX)
Mercer U, Macon (GA)
Meredith Coll (NC)
Messiah Coll (PA)
Miami U (OH)
Michigan State U (MI)
Middlebury Coll (VT)
Middle Tennessee State U (TN)
Midwestern State U (TX)
Millersville U of Pennsylvania (PA)
Milligan Coll (TN)
Millikin U (IL)
Millsaps Coll (MS)
Mills Coll (CA)
Minnesota State U Mankato (MN)
Minnesota State U Moorhead (MN)
Minot State U (ND)
Mississippi State U (MS)
Mississippi U for Women (MS)
Mississippi Valley State U (MS)
Missouri Baptist U (MO)
Missouri State U (MO)
Missouri Valley Coll (MO)
Missouri Western State U (MO)
Molloy Coll (NY)
Monmouth Coll (IL)
Monmouth U (NJ)
Montana State U (MT)
Montana State U Billings (MT)
Montclair State U (NJ)
Moravian Coll (PA)
Morehead State U (KY)
Morningside Coll (IA)
Mount Allison U (NB, Canada)
Mount Holyoke Coll (MA)
Mount Marty Coll (SD)
Mount Mercy U (IA)
Mount St. Joseph U (OH)
Mount Saint Mary's U (CA)
Mount Vernon Nazarene U (OH)
Muhlenberg Coll (PA)
Murray State U (KY)
Naropa U (CO)
Nazareth Coll of Rochester (NY)
Nebraska Wesleyan U (NE)
Newberry Coll (SC)
New Coll of Florida (FL)
New Jersey City U (NJ)
New Mexico Highlands U (NM)
New York U (NY)
Nicholls State U (LA)
Norfolk State U (VA)
North Carolina Ag and Tech State U (NC)
North Carolina Central U (NC)
North Central Coll (IL)
North Dakota State U (ND)
Northeastern Illinois U (IL)
Northeastern State U (OK)
Northeastern U (MA)
Northern Arizona U (AZ)
Northern Illinois U (IL)
Northern Kentucky U (KY)
Northern Michigan U (MI)
Northern State U (SD)
North Greenville U (SC)
Northwestern Coll (IA)
Northwestern Oklahoma State U (OK)
Northwestern U (IL)
Northwest Missouri State U (MO)
Northwest Nazarene U (ID)
Northwest U (WA)
Nova Southeastern U (FL)
Nyack Coll (NY)
Oakland City U (IN)
Oakland U (MI)
Oberlin Coll (OH)
Occidental Coll (CA)
Ohio Northern U (OH)
The Ohio State U (OH)
Ohio Wesleyan U (OH)
Oklahoma Baptist U (OK)
Oklahoma Christian U (OK)
Oklahoma City U (OK)
Oklahoma State U (OK)
Oklahoma Wesleyan U (OK)
Olivet Coll (MI)
Olivet Nazarene U (IL)
Oregon State U (OR)
Our Lady of the Lake U of San Antonio (TX)
Pacific Lutheran U (WA)
Pacific U (OR)
Palm Beach Atlantic U (FL)
Park U (MO)
Peabody Conservatory of The Johns Hopkins U (MD)
Penn State Altoona (PA)
Penn State Beaver (PA)
Penn State Berks (PA)
Penn State Brandywine (PA)
Penn State DuBois (PA)
Penn State Greater Allegheny (PA)
Penn State Hazleton (PA)
Penn State Mont Alto (PA)
Penn State New Kensington (PA)
Penn State Shenango (PA)
Penn State U Park (PA)
Penn State Wilkes-Barre (PA)
Penn State Worthington Scranton (PA)
Penn State York (PA)
Pepperdine U, Malibu (CA)
Peru State Coll (NE)
Piedmont Coll (GA)
Plymouth State U (NH)
Point Loma Nazarene U (CA)
Point U (GA)
Pomona Coll (CA)
Portland State U (OR)
Prairie View A&M U (TX)
Presbyterian Coll (SC)
Princeton U (NJ)
Principia Coll (IL)
Providence Coll (RI)
Quincy U (IL)
Radford U (VA)
Ramapo Coll of New Jersey (NJ)
Randolph-Macon Coll (VA)
Reed Coll (OR)
Regis U (CO)
Reinhardt U (GA)
Rhode Island Coll (RI)
Rhodes Coll (TN)
Rice U (TX)
Rider U (NJ)
Ripon Coll (WI)
Roanoke Coll (VA)
Roberts Wesleyan Coll (NY)
Rockford U (IL)
Rocky Mountain Coll (AB, Canada)
Rollins Coll (FL)
Rowan U (NJ)
Rust Coll (MS)
Rutgers, The State U of New Jersey, Camden (NJ)
Rutgers, The State U of New Jersey, Newark (NJ)
Rutgers, The State U of New Jersey, New Brunswick (NJ)
Saginaw Valley State U (MI)
Saint Augustine's U (NC)
St. Catherine U (MN)
Saint John's U (MN)
Saint Joseph's U (PA)
St. Lawrence U (NY)
Saint Louis U (MO)
Saint Martin's U (WA)
Saint Mary-of-the-Woods Coll (IN)
Saint Mary's Coll (IN)
St. Mary's Coll of Maryland (MD)
St. Mary's U (TX)
Saint Mary's U of Minnesota (MN)
Saint Michael's Coll (VT)
St. Norbert Coll (WI)
St. Olaf Coll (MN)
Saint Vincent Coll (PA)
Salem Coll (NC)
Salisbury U (MD)
Salve Regina U (RI)
Samford U (AL)
Sam Houston State U (TX)
San Diego Christian Coll (CA)
San Diego State U (CA)
San Francisco State U (CA)
San Jose State U (CA)
Santa Clara U (CA)
Santa Fe U of Art and Design (NM)
Sarah Lawrence Coll (NY)
Scripps Coll (CA)
Seattle Pacific U (WA)
Seattle U (WA)
Seton Hill U (PA)
Sewanee: The U of the South (TN)
Shaw U (NC)
Shepherd U (WV)
Silver Lake Coll of the Holy Family (WI)
Simmons Coll (MA)
Simon Fraser U (BC, Canada)
Simpson Coll (IA)
Simpson U (CA)
Slippery Rock U of Pennsylvania (PA)
Smith Coll (MA)
South Dakota State U (SD)
Southeastern Oklahoma State U (OK)
Southeastern U (FL)
Southeast Missouri State U (MO)
Southern Adventist U (TN)
Southern Arkansas U–Magnolia (AR)
Southern Connecticut State U (CT)
Southern Illinois U Carbondale (IL)
Southern Illinois U Edwardsville (IL)
Southern Methodist U (TX)
Southern Oregon U (OR)
Southern Utah U (UT)
Southwest Baptist U (MO)
Southwestern Adventist U (TX)
Southwestern Coll (KS)
Southwestern U (TX)
Southwest Minnesota State U (MN)
Spelman Coll (GA)
Stanford U (CA)
State U of New York at Fredonia (NY)
State U of New York at New Paltz (NY)
State U of New York at Oswego (NY)
State U of New York at Plattsburgh (NY)
State U of New York Coll at Geneseo (NY)
State U of New York Coll at Potsdam (NY)
Stephen F. Austin State U (TX)
Sterling Coll (KS)
Stetson U (FL)
Stony Brook U, State U of New York (NY)
Sul Ross State U (TX)
Summit U (PA)
Susquehanna U (PA)
Syracuse U (NY)
Tarleton State U (TX)
Taylor U (IN)
Temple U (PA)
Tennessee State U (TN)
Tennessee Wesleyan Coll (TN)
Texas A&M Intl U (TX)
Texas A&M U (TX)
Texas A&M U–Commerce (TX)
Texas A&M U–Corpus Christi (TX)
Texas A&M U–Kingsville (TX)
Texas Christian U (TX)
Texas Lutheran U (TX)
Texas Southern U (TX)
Texas State U (TX)
Texas Tech U (TX)
Texas Wesleyan U (TX)
Texas Woman's U (TX)
Tiffin U (OH)
Toccoa Falls Coll (GA)
Tougaloo Coll (MS)
Towson U (MD)
Trinity Christian Coll (IL)
Trinity Coll (CT)
Trinity U (TX)
Troy U (AL)
Truett-McConnell Coll (GA)
Truman State U (MO)
Tufts U (MA)
Tulane U (LA)
Union Coll (NE)
Union U (TN)
Université de Montréal (QC, Canada)
U at Albany, State U of New York (NY)
U at Buffalo, the State U of New York (NY)
The U of Akron (OH)
The U of Alabama (AL)
The U of Alabama at Birmingham (AL)
The U of Alabama in Huntsville (AL)
U of Alaska Fairbanks (AK)
U of Alberta (AB, Canada)
The U of Arizona (AZ)
U of Arkansas at Little Rock (AR)
U of Arkansas at Pine Bluff (AR)
U of Arkansas–Fort Smith (AR)
U of Bridgeport (CT)
The U of British Columbia (BC, Canada)
U of California, Berkeley (CA)
U of California, Davis (CA)
U of California, Irvine (CA)
U of California, Los Angeles (CA)
U of California, Riverside (CA)
U of California, Santa Barbara (CA)
U of California, Santa Cruz (CA)
U of Central Arkansas (AR)
U of Central Missouri (MO)
U of Central Oklahoma (OK)
U of Chicago (IL)
U of Cincinnati (OH)
U of Colorado Boulder (CO)
U of Colorado Denver (CO)
U of Dayton (OH)
U of Delaware (DE)
U of Denver (CO)
U of Evansville (IN)
U of Florida (FL)
U of Georgia (GA)
U of Guelph (ON, Canada)
U of Hartford (CT)
U of Hawaii at Hilo (HI)
U of Hawaii at Manoa (HI)
U of Houston (TX)
U of Idaho (ID)
U of Illinois at Chicago (IL)
U of Indianapolis (IN)
The U of Iowa (IA)
U of Jamestown (ND)
The U of Kansas (KS)
U of King's Coll (NS, Canada)
U of La Verne (CA)
U of Lethbridge (AB, Canada)
U of Louisiana at Lafayette (LA)
U of Louisville (KY)
U of Maine (ME)
U of Maine at Augusta (ME)
U of Maine at Machias (ME)
U of Mary Hardin-Baylor (TX)
U of Maryland, Baltimore County (MD)
U of Maryland, Coll Park (MD)
U of Mary Washington (VA)
U of Massachusetts Boston (MA)
U of Massachusetts Dartmouth (MA)
U of Massachusetts Lowell (MA)
U of Memphis (TN)
U of Miami (FL)
U of Michigan (MI)
U of Michigan–Flint (MI)
U of Minnesota, Duluth (MN)
U of Minnesota, Morris (MN)
U of Minnesota, Twin Cities Campus (MN)
U of Mississippi (MS)
U of Missouri (MO)
U of Missouri–Kansas City (MO)
U of Missouri–St. Louis (MO)
U of Mobile (AL)
The U of Montana (MT)
U of Montevallo (AL)
U of Mount Union (OH)
U of Nebraska at Kearney (NE)
U of Nebraska–Lincoln (NE)
U of Nevada, Las Vegas (NV)
U of Nevada, Reno (NV)
U of New Hampshire (NH)
U of New Haven (CT)
U of New Orleans (LA)
U of North Alabama (AL)
U of North Carolina at Asheville (NC)
The U of North Carolina at Chapel Hill (NC)
The U of North Carolina at Charlotte (NC)
The U of North Carolina at Greensboro (NC)
The U of North Carolina at Pembroke (NC)
The U of North Carolina Wilmington (NC)
U of North Dakota (ND)
U of Northern Colorado (CO)
U of Northern Iowa (IA)
U of North Georgia (GA)
U of North Texas (TX)
U of Northwestern–St. Paul (MN)
U of Notre Dame (IN)
U of Oklahoma (OK)
U of Oregon (OR)
U of Ottawa (ON, Canada)
U of Pennsylvania (PA)
U of Pittsburgh (PA)
U of Portland (OR)
U of Puget Sound (WA)
U of Regina (SK, Canada)
U of Rhode Island (RI)
U of Richmond (VA)
U of Rio Grande (OH)
U of Rochester (NY)
U of St. Francis (IL)
U of St. Thomas (MN)
U of St. Thomas (TX)
U of San Diego (CA)
U of Saskatchewan (SK, Canada)
U of Science and Arts of Oklahoma (OK)
U of South Alabama (AL)
U of South Carolina Upstate (SC)
U of Southern California (CA)
U of Southern Maine (ME)
U of Southern Mississippi (MS)
The U of Tampa (FL)
The U of Tennessee (TN)
The U of Tennessee at Chattanooga (TN)
The U of Tennessee at Martin (TN)
The U of Texas at Arlington (TX)
The U of Texas at Austin (TX)
The U of Texas at El Paso (TX)
The U of Texas at San Antonio (TX)
The U of Texas at Tyler (TX)
The U of Texas of the Permian Basin (TX)
The U of Texas–Pan American (TX)
U of the Cumberlands (KY)
U of the District of Columbia (DC)
U of the Incarnate Word (TX)
U of the Pacific (CA)
The U of Toledo (OH)
The U of Tulsa (OK)
U of Utah (UT)
U of Vermont (VT)
U of Virginia (VA)
U of Washington (WA)
U of Waterloo (ON, Canada)
The U of Western Ontario (ON, Canada)
U of Windsor (ON, Canada)
U of Wisconsin–Eau Claire (WI)
U of Wisconsin–Green Bay (WI)
U of Wisconsin–La Crosse (WI)
U of Wisconsin–Madison (WI)
U of Wisconsin–Milwaukee (WI)
U of Wisconsin–Oshkosh (WI)
U of Wisconsin–Parkside (WI)
U of Wisconsin–Platteville (WI)
U of Wisconsin–River Falls (WI)
U of Wisconsin–Stevens Point (WI)
U of Wisconsin–Superior (WI)
U of Wisconsin–Whitewater (WI)
U of Wyoming (WY)
Utah State U (UT)
Utah Valley U (UT)
Valdosta State U (GA)
Valley City State U (ND)
Valparaiso U (IN)
Vanderbilt U (TN)
Vanguard U of Southern California (CA)
Vassar Coll (NY)
Villa Maria Coll (NY)
Virginia Polytechnic Inst and State U (VA)
Virginia State U (VA)
Virginia Union U (VA)
Virginia Wesleyan Coll (VA)
Viterbo U (WI)
Wabash Coll (IN)
Wagner Coll (NY)
Wake Forest U (NC)
Waldorf Coll (IA)
Walla Walla U (WA)
Walsh U (OH)

Warner Pacific Coll (OR)
Wartburg Coll (IA)
Washburn U (KS)
Washington & Jefferson Coll (PA)
Washington and Lee U (VA)
Washington Coll (MD)
Washington State U (WA)
Washington U in St. Louis (MO)
Wayne State Coll (NE)
Wayne State U (MI)
Weber State U (UT)
Webster U (MO)
Welch Coll (TN)
Wesleyan Coll (GA)
West Chester U of Pennsylvania (PA)
Western Carolina U (NC)
Western Illinois U (IL)
Western Michigan U (MI)
Western Oregon U (OR)
Western State Colorado U (CO)
Western Washington U (WA)
Westfield State U (MA)
Westminster Coll (UT)
West Texas A&M U (TX)
West Virginia U (WV)
West Virginia Wesleyan Coll (WV)
Wheaton Coll (IL)
Wheaton Coll (MA)
Whitman Coll (WA)
Whittier Coll (CA)
Whitworth U (WA)
Wichita State U (KS)
Wilberforce U (OH)
Willamette U (OR)
William Jessup U (CA)
William Jewell Coll (MO)
William Paterson U of New Jersey (NJ)
Williams Baptist Coll (AR)
Williams Coll (MA)
Wingate U (NC)
Winona State U (MN)
Winthrop U (SC)
Wittenberg U (OH)
Worcester Polytechnic Inst (MA)
Wright State U (OH)
Xavier U (OH)
Xavier U of Louisiana (LA)
Yale U (CT)
York Coll of Pennsylvania (PA)
York Coll of the City U of New York (NY)
Youngstown State U (OH)

MUSICAL INSTRUMENT FABRICATION AND REPAIR
Delaware State U (DE)

MUSICAL THEATER
American U (DC)
Brenau U (GA)
Central Michigan U (MI)
Central Washington U (WA)
Creighton U (NE)
Culver-Stockton Coll (MO)
Elon U (NC)
Emory & Henry Coll (VA)
Florida Southern Coll (FL)
Indiana U Bloomington (IN)
LaGrange Coll (GA)
Lees-McRae Coll (NC)
Limestone Coll (SC)
Lindenwood U (MO)
Marywood U (PA)
Messiah Coll (PA)
Millikin U (IL)
Missouri Baptist U (MO)
Nebraska Wesleyan U (NE)
North Central Coll (IL)
Oakland U (MI)
Pace U (NY)
Rhode Island Coll (RI)
Roosevelt U (IL)
Sam Houston State U (TX)
San Diego Christian Coll (CA)
Shenandoah U (VA)
Southwestern Coll (KS)
Syracuse U (NY)
Texas Christian U (TX)
Texas State U (TX)
U at Buffalo, the State U of New York (NY)
The U of Arizona (AZ)
U of California, Irvine (CA)
U of Idaho (ID)
U of Michigan (MI)
U of Mobile (AL)
U of North Dakota (ND)
U of Oklahoma (OK)
The U of Tampa (FL)
The U of the Arts (PA)
Viterbo U (WI)
Western Michigan U (MI)
West Texas A&M U (TX)
William Peace U (NC)

MUSIC HISTORY, LITERATURE, AND THEORY
American U (DC)
Baldwin Wallace U (OH)
Bard Coll (NY)
Baylor U (TX)
Bennington Coll (VT)
Birmingham-Southern Coll (AL)
Bowling Green State U (OH)
Bridgewater Coll (VA)
Brigham Young U (UT)
Bucknell U (PA)
Cairn U (PA)
California State U, Long Beach (CA)
Calvin Coll (MI)
The Catholic U of America (DC)
The Coll of Wooster (OH)
Concordia Coll–New York (NY)
Dalhousie U (NS, Canada)
Hastings Coll (NE)
Hofstra U (NY)
Lehigh U (PA)
Liberty U (VA)
Loyola Marymount U (CA)
Mount Allison U (NB, Canada)
Nazareth Coll of Rochester (NY)
New Coll of Florida (FL)
New England Conservatory of Music (MA)
Northwestern U (IL)
Oberlin Coll (OH)
The Ohio State U (OH)
Ohio U (OH)
Randolph Coll (VA)
Rice U (TX)
Rider U (NJ)
St. Bonaventure U (NY)
Saint Joseph's Coll (IN)
Skidmore Coll (NY)
State U of New York at Fredonia (NY)
Syracuse U (NY)
Temple U (PA)
Tufts U (MA)
The U of Akron (OH)
The U of British Columbia (BC, Canada)
U of California, Los Angeles (CA)
U of Cincinnati (OH)
U of Delaware (DE)
U of Hartford (CT)
U of Idaho (ID)
U of Kentucky (KY)
U of Michigan (MI)
U of Minnesota, Twin Cities Campus (MN)
U of Regina (SK, Canada)
U of the Pacific (CA)
U of Toronto (ON, Canada)
U of Vermont (VT)
U of Washington (WA)
The U of Western Ontario (ON, Canada)
U of Windsor (ON, Canada)
Ursinus Coll (PA)
Washington U in St. Louis (MO)
Western Washington U (WA)
Wheaton Coll (IL)
Whitman Coll (WA)
Wright State U (OH)
Youngstown State U (OH)

MUSIC MANAGEMENT
Anderson U (IN)
Appalachian State U (NC)
Augsburg Coll (MN)
Belmont U (TN)
Berry Coll (GA)
Bradley U (IL)
California U of Pennsylvania (PA)
Capital U (OH)
Chowan U (NC)
Columbia Coll Chicago (IL)
Concordia U, St. Paul (MN)
Dallas Baptist U (TX)
DePaul U (IL)
DePauw U (IN)
Drake U (IA)
Drexel U (PA)
Elmhurst Coll (IL)
Ferris State U (MI)
Five Towns Coll (NY)
Florida Atlantic U (FL)
Florida Southern Coll (FL)
Francis Marion U (SC)
Geneva Coll (PA)
Greenville Coll (IL)
Grove City Coll (PA)
Hardin-Simmons U (TX)
Heidelberg U (OH)
Hofstra U (NY)
Jacksonville U (FL)
Johnson State Coll (VT)
Judson U (IL)
Kentucky Christian U (KY)
Kentucky Wesleyan Coll (KY)
Lamar U (TX)
Lebanon Valley Coll (PA)
Lewis U (IL)
Liberty U (VA)
Lindenwood U (MO)
Loyola U New Orleans (LA)
Lubbock Christian U (TX)
Madonna U (MI)
Mansfield U of Pennsylvania (PA)
Marian U (WI)
The Master's Coll and Sem (CA)
McKendree U (IL)
Middle Tennessee State U (TN)
Minnesota State U Mankato (MN)
Minnesota State U Moorhead (MN)
Missouri Baptist U (MO)
Missouri Southern State U (MO)
Montreat Coll, Montreat (NC)
Murray State U (KY)
Nazareth Coll of Rochester (NY)
Northwest Christian U (OR)
Northwest U (WA)
Oklahoma City U (OK)
Peru State Coll (NE)
Saint Joseph's Coll (IN)
South Carolina State U (SC)
Southeastern U (FL)
Southern Oregon U (OR)
Southwest Minnesota State U (MN)
State U of New York at Fredonia (NY)
State U of New York Coll at Potsdam (NY)
Syracuse U (NY)
Trevecca Nazarene U (TN)
Union U (TN)
U of Evansville (IN)
U of Hartford (CT)
U of Idaho (ID)
The U of Iowa (IA)
U of Memphis (TN)
U of New Haven (CT)
U of Puget Sound (WA)
U of Southern California (CA)
U of Southern Mississippi (MS)
The U of Texas at Austin (TX)
The U of the Arts (PA)
U of the Incarnate Word (TX)
U of the Pacific (CA)
Villa Maria Coll (NY)
Warner Pacific Coll (OR)
Western State Colorado U (CO)
William Paterson U of New Jersey (NJ)
Winona State U (MN)

MUSICOLOGY AND ETHNOMUSICOLOGY
Bennington Coll (VT)
Bowling Green State U (OH)
Brown U (RI)
East Tennessee State U (TN)
Liberty U (VA)
Northwestern U (IL)
Roger Williams U (RI)
Tufts U (MA)
U of California, Los Angeles (CA)
U of Denver (CO)
The U of Kansas (KS)
U of Washington (WA)

MUSIC PEDAGOGY
Baylor U (TX)
Bob Jones U (SC)
Brigham Young U (UT)
Calvary Bible Coll and Theological Sem (MO)
Cedarville U (OH)
Hastings Coll (NE)
Lawrence U (WI)
Liberty U (VA)
Maranatha Baptist U (WI)
Michigan State U (MI)
Samford U (AL)
Temple U (PA)
Union Coll (NE)
U of Oklahoma (OK)
The U of Tennessee at Martin (TN)
Viterbo U (WI)
Weber State U (UT)
Wheaton Coll (IL)

MUSIC PERFORMANCE
Adams State U (CO)
Albion Coll (MI)
Alcorn State U (MS)
Allegheny Coll (PA)
Anderson U (IN)
Anderson U (SC)
Appalachian State U (NC)
Aquinas Coll (MI)
Arizona State U at the Tempe campus (AZ)
Arkansas State U (AR)
Augsburg Coll (MN)
Augustana Coll (IL)
Avila U (MO)
Baldwin Wallace U (OH)
Baylor U (TX)
Bennington Coll (VT)
Bethel Coll (IN)
Bethel U (MN)
Bethune-Cookman U (FL)
Binghamton U, State U of New York (NY)
Biola U (CA)
Black Hills State U (SD)
Bob Jones U (SC)
Boston U (MA)
Bowling Green State U (OH)
Bradley U (IL)
Brenau U (GA)
Brevard Coll (NC)
Bucknell U (PA)
Buena Vista U (IA)
Butler U (IN)
California Baptist U (CA)
California Inst of the Arts (CA)
California State U, Fullerton (CA)
California State U, Long Beach (CA)
California State U, Los Angeles (CA)
California State U, Stanislaus (CA)
Calvary Bible Coll and Theological Sem (MO)
Calvin Coll (MI)
Canisius Coll (NY)
Capital U (OH)
Cardinal Stritch U (WI)
Castleton State Coll (VT)
Catawba Coll (NC)
The Catholic U of America (DC)
Cedarville U (OH)
Central Methodist U (MO)
Central State U (OH)
Central Washington U (WA)
Chapman U (CA)
Charleston Southern U (SC)
Christopher Newport U (VA)
City Coll of the City U of New York (NY)
Coe Coll (IA)
The Colburn School Conservatory of Music (CA)
The Coll of Saint Rose (NY)
The Coll of St. Scholastica (MN)
The Coll of Wooster (OH)
Colorado State U (CO)
Columbia Coll (SC)
Columbia Coll Chicago (IL)
Columbus State U (GA)
Concordia Coll (MN)
Concordia Coll–New York (NY)
Concordia U (QC, Canada)
Concordia U Chicago (IL)
Corban U (OR)
Cornerstone U (MI)
Covenant Coll (GA)
Dalhousie U (NS, Canada)
Dallas Baptist U (TX)
DePaul U (IL)
DePauw U (IN)
Drake U (IA)
Duquesne U (PA)
East Central U (OK)
Eastern Michigan U (MI)
Elmhurst Coll (IL)
Elon U (NC)
Emory & Henry Coll (VA)
Five Towns Coll (NY)
Florida Gulf Coast U (FL)
Florida Southern Coll (FL)
Fort Hays State U (KS)
Fort Lewis Coll (CO)
Friends U (KS)
George Mason U (VA)
Georgia Regents U (GA)
Georgia Southern U (GA)
Georgia State U (GA)
Gonzaga U (WA)
Gordon Coll (MA)
Greensboro Coll (NC)
Grove City Coll (PA)
Gustavus Adolphus Coll (MN)
Hamline U (MN)
Hardin-Simmons U (TX)
Hastings Coll (NE)
Hillsdale Free Will Baptist Coll (OK)
Hofstra U (NY)
Hope Coll (MI)
Houghton Coll (NY)
Houston Baptist U (TX)
Howard Payne U (TX)
Huntingdon Coll (AL)
Illinois State U (IL)
Illinois Wesleyan U (IL)
Immaculata U (PA)
Indiana State U (IN)
Indiana U Bloomington (IN)
Indiana U of Pennsylvania (PA)
Indiana U–Purdue U Fort Wayne (IN)
Indiana U South Bend (IN)
Ithaca Coll (NY)
Jackson State U (MS)
Jacksonville U (FL)
James Madison U (VA)
John Brown U (AR)
Johnson State Coll (VT)
The Juilliard School (NY)
Kansas Wesleyan U (KS)
Kean U (NJ)
Keene State Coll (NH)
Kennesaw State U (GA)
Kentucky Christian U (KY)
Kentucky Wesleyan Coll (KY)
LaGrange Coll (GA)
Lawrence U (WI)
Lebanon Valley Coll (PA)
Lee U (TN)
Lenoir-Rhyne U (NC)
Liberty U (VA)
Limestone Coll (SC)
Lipscomb U (TN)
Long Island U–LIU Brooklyn (NY)
Long Island U–LIU Post (NY)
Louisiana State U and A&M Coll (LA)
Loyola U New Orleans (LA)
Lynn U (FL)
Madonna U (MI)
Manchester U (IN)
Mansfield U of Pennsylvania (PA)
Maranatha Baptist U (WI)
Marian U (IN)
Mars Hill U (NC)
Marylhurst U (OR)
Maryville Coll (TN)
Marywood U (PA)
McNeese State U (LA)
Mercer U, Macon (GA)
Messiah Coll (PA)
Miami U (OH)
Michigan State U (MI)
MidAmerica Nazarene U (KS)
Midwestern State U (TX)
Millikin U (IL)
Minnesota State U Moorhead (MN)
Missouri Baptist U (MO)
Missouri Southern State U (MO)
Missouri State U (MO)
Montclair State U (NJ)
Montreat Coll, Montreat (NC)
Morningside Coll (IA)
Mount Allison U (NB, Canada)
Mount Vernon Nazarene U (OH)
Naropa U (CO)
Nazareth Coll of Rochester (NY)
Nebraska Wesleyan U (NE)
Newberry Coll (SC)
New England Conservatory of Music (MA)
New Mexico State U (NM)

New York U (NY)
Northern Arizona U (AZ)
North Greenville U (SC)
Northwestern U (IL)
Northwest Nazarene U (ID)
Nyack Coll (NY)
Oakland City U (IN)
Oakland U (MI)
Ohio Northern U (OH)
The Ohio State U (OH)
Ohio U (OH)
Ohio Wesleyan U (OH)
Oklahoma Baptist U (OK)
Oklahoma City U (OK)
Old Dominion U (VA)
Olivet Nazarene U (IL)
Pacific U (OR)
Palm Beach Atlantic U (FL)
Peabody Conservatory of The Johns Hopkins U (MD)
Penn State U Park (PA)
Peru State Coll (NE)
Piedmont Coll (GA)
Pittsburg State U (KS)
Point Loma Nazarene U (CA)
Portland State U (OR)
Queens Coll of the City U of New York (NY)
Randolph Coll (VA)
Rhode Island Coll (RI)
Rice U (TX)
Rockford U (IL)
Rocky Mountain Coll (MT)
Roosevelt U (IL)
Rowan U (NJ)
Rutgers, The State U of New Jersey, New Brunswick (NJ)
Saint Mary's U of Minnesota (MN)
St. Olaf Coll (MN)
Saint Vincent Coll (PA)
Salem Coll (NC)
Samford U (AL)
San Diego Christian Coll (CA)
San Diego State U (CA)
San Francisco State U (CA)
San Jose State U (CA)
Seton Hill U (PA)
Shenandoah U (VA)
Simpson Coll (IA)
Slippery Rock U of Pennsylvania (PA)
Southeastern Louisiana U (LA)
Southeastern Oklahoma State U (OK)
Southeastern U (FL)
Southern Adventist U (TN)
Southern Methodist U (TX)
Southwestern Assemblies of God U (TX)
Southwestern Coll (KS)
State U of New York Coll at Potsdam (NY)
Stetson U (FL)
Susquehanna U (PA)
Syracuse U (NY)
Tabor Coll (KS)
Temple U (PA)
Texas Christian U (TX)
Texas State U (TX)
Toccoa Falls Coll (GA)
Transylvania U (KY)
Trevecca Nazarene U (TN)
Trinity Christian Coll (IL)
Trinity U (TX)
Truman State U (MO)
Tulane U (LA)
Union Coll (NE)
Union U (TN)
U at Buffalo, the State U of New York (NY)
The U of Akron (OH)
The U of Arizona (AZ)
U of Arkansas (AR)
U of California, Irvine (CA)
U of Central Arkansas (AR)
U of Central Florida (FL)
U of Central Oklahoma (OK)
U of Cincinnati (OH)
U of Colorado Boulder (CO)
U of Dayton (OH)
U of Delaware (DE)
U of Denver (CO)
U of Evansville (IN)
U of Georgia (GA)
U of Hartford (CT)
U of Houston (TX)
U of Idaho (ID)
U of Indianapolis (IN)
The U of Iowa (IA)
U of Jamestown (ND)
The U of Kansas (KS)
U of Kentucky (KY)
U of Louisiana at Lafayette (LA)
U of Maine (ME)
U of Mary Hardin-Baylor (TX)
U of Maryland, Coll Park (MD)
U of Massachusetts Amherst (MA)
U of Massachusetts Lowell (MA)
U of Miami (FL)
U of Michigan (MI)
U of Michigan–Flint (MI)
U of Minnesota, Duluth (MN)
U of Missouri–Kansas City (MO)
The U of Montana (MT)
U of Mount Union (OH)
U of Nevada, Reno (NV)
U of New Mexico (NM)
The U of North Carolina at Chapel Hill (NC)
The U of North Carolina at Greensboro (NC)
The U of North Carolina at Pembroke (NC)
U of North Carolina School of the Arts (NC)
The U of North Carolina Wilmington (NC)
U of North Dakota (ND)
U of Northern Iowa (IA)
U of North Florida (FL)
U of North Georgia (GA)
U of North Texas (TX)
U of Northwestern–St. Paul (MN)
U of Oregon (OR)
U of Puget Sound (WA)
U of Rhode Island (RI)
U of Rochester (NY)
U of St. Francis (IL)
The U of South Dakota (SD)
U of Southern California (CA)
U of Southern Maine (ME)
U of South Florida (FL)
The U of Tampa (FL)
The U of Tennessee at Martin (TN)
The U of Texas at Arlington (TX)
The U of Texas at Austin (TX)
The U of Texas–Pan American (TX)
The U of the Arts (PA)
U of the Incarnate Word (TX)
The U of Tulsa (OK)
U of Valley Forge (PA)
U of Vermont (VT)
U of Washington (WA)
The U of Western Ontario (ON, Canada)
U of West Florida (FL)
U of West Georgia (GA)
U of Windsor (ON, Canada)
U of Wisconsin–Madison (WI)
U of Wisconsin–Stevens Point (WI)
U of Wisconsin–Superior (WI)
U of Wyoming (WY)
Utah Valley U (UT)
Valdosta State U (GA)
Valparaiso U (IN)
Vanguard U of Southern California (CA)
Villa Maria Coll (NY)
Virginia Commonwealth U (VA)
Viterbo U (WI)
Walla Walla U (WA)
Wartburg Coll (IA)
Washburn U (KS)
Washington State U (WA)
Weber State U (UT)
Webster U (MO)
Welch Coll (TN)
West Chester U of Pennsylvania (PA)
Western Carolina U (NC)
Western Illinois U (IL)
Western Kentucky U (KY)
Western Michigan U (MI)
Western Washington U (WA)
West Texas A&M U (TX)
Wheaton Coll (IL)
Whitman Coll (WA)
Willamette U (OR)
William Jewell Coll (MO)
William Penn U (IA)
Wright State U (OH)
Xavier U of Louisiana (LA)
Youngstown State U (OH)

MUSIC RELATED

Acad of Art U (CA)
Alverno Coll (WI)
Ball State U (IN)
Belmont U (TN)
Bethel Coll (KS)
Biola U (CA)
Brigham Young U (UT)
Brown U (RI)
Capital U (OH)
Coker Coll (SC)
Coll of the Ozarks (MO)
Concordia U (CA)
Connecticut Coll (CT)
Cornerstone U (MI)
DePaul U (IL)
Duquesne U (PA)
Five Towns Coll (NY)
Friends U (KS)
Greenville Coll (IL)
Grove City Coll (PA)
Hampton U (VA)
Huntingdon Coll (AL)
Illinois Wesleyan U (IL)
Indiana U Bloomington (IN)
Indiana U South Bend (IN)
Kent State U (OH)
Kent State U at Stark (OH)
Liberty U (VA)
Loyola U New Orleans (LA)
McKendree U (IL)
Mercer U, Macon (GA)
Mercy Coll (NY)
Messiah Coll (PA)
Milligan Coll (TN)
Missouri Western State U (MO)
Morehead State U (KY)
Murray State U (KY)
Northwestern U (IL)
Ohio Northern U (OH)
Palm Beach Atlantic U (FL)
Peru State Coll (NE)
Roosevelt U (IL)
Saint Mary's U of Minnesota (MN)
School of the Art Inst of Chicago (IL)
Tabor Coll (KS)
Trevecca Nazarene U (TN)
U of Alberta (AB, Canada)
U of Central Oklahoma (OK)
U of Delaware (DE)
U of Denver (CO)
U of Hartford (CT)
U of Lethbridge (AB, Canada)
U of Massachusetts Lowell (MA)
U of Memphis (TN)
U of Miami (FL)
U of Michigan (MI)
U of Minnesota, Duluth (MN)
U of North Carolina at Asheville (NC)
U of Saint Francis (IN)
The U of Tulsa (OK)
U of Washington (WA)
The U of Western Ontario (ON, Canada)
Valparaiso U (IN)
Vanderbilt U (TN)
Wesleyan U (CT)
Western Illinois U (IL)
Western Kentucky U (KY)
West Virginia U (WV)
Wheaton Coll (IL)
Wichita State U (KS)

MUSIC TEACHER EDUCATION

Abilene Christian U (TX)
Adams State U (CO)
Adelphi U (NY)
Alabama State U (AL)
Albany State U (GA)
Albion Coll (MI)
Alma Coll (MI)
Alverno Coll (WI)
Anderson U (IN)
Anderson U (SC)
Andrews U (MI)
Anna Maria Coll (MA)
Appalachian State U (NC)
Aquinas Coll (MI)
Arizona State U at the Tempe campus (AZ)
Arkansas State U (AR)
Arkansas Tech U (AR)
Armstrong State U (GA)
Asbury U (KY)
Ashland U (OH)
Auburn U (AL)
Augsburg Coll (MN)
Augustana Coll (IL)
Augustana Coll (SD)
Baker U (KS)
Baldwin Wallace U (OH)
The Baptist Coll of Florida (FL)
Baylor U (TX)
Belmont U (TN)
Beloit Coll (WI)
Bemidji State U (MN)
Benedictine Coll (KS)
Benedictine U (IL)
Berea Coll (KY)
Berry Coll (GA)
Bethel Coll (IN)
Bethel U (MN)
Bethune-Cookman U (FL)
Biola U (CA)
Birmingham-Southern Coll (AL)
Bluefield Coll (VA)
Blue Mountain Coll (MS)
Bluffton U (OH)
Bob Jones U (SC)
Boston U (MA)
Bowling Green State U (OH)
Bradley U (IL)
Brenau U (GA)
Brevard Coll (NC)
Bridgewater State U (MA)
Bryan Coll (TN)
Bucknell U (PA)
Buena Vista U (IA)
Buffalo State Coll, State U of New York (NY)
Butler U (IN)
California Baptist U (CA)
California Lutheran U (CA)
California State U, Fresno (CA)
California State U, Fullerton (CA)
Calvary Bible Coll and Theological Sem (MO)
Calvin Coll (MI)
Cameron U (OK)
Campbellsville U (KY)
Capital U (OH)
Carson-Newman U (TN)
Case Western Reserve U (OH)
Castleton State Coll (VT)
Catawba Coll (NC)
Cedarville U (OH)
Central Coll (IA)
Central Connecticut State U (CT)
Central Methodist U (MO)
Central State U (OH)
Central Washington U (WA)
Chapman U (CA)
Charleston Southern U (SC)
Chestnut Hill Coll (PA)
Chicago State U (IL)
Chowan U (NC)
City Coll of the City U of New York (NY)
Claflin U (SC)
Clarion U of Pennsylvania (PA)
Clarke U (IA)
Clearwater Christian Coll (FL)
Coe Coll (IA)
Coker Coll (SC)
The Coll of New Jersey (NJ)
The Coll of Saint Rose (NY)
Coll of the Ozarks (MO)
The Coll of Wooster (OH)
Colorado State U (CO)
Columbia Coll (SC)
Columbus State U (GA)
Concordia Coll (MN)
Concordia U Chicago (IL)
Concordia U, Nebraska (NE)
Concordia U, St. Paul (MN)
Concordia U Wisconsin (WI)
Concord U (WV)
Corban U (OR)
Cornell Coll (IA)
Cornerstone U (MI)
Culver-Stockton Coll (MO)
Cumberland U (TN)
Dallas Baptist U (TX)
Delaware State U (DE)
Delta State U (MS)
DePaul U (IL)
DePauw U (IN)
Dickinson State U (ND)
Dixie State U (UT)
Dowling Coll (NY)
Drake U (IA)
Duquesne U (PA)
East Carolina U (NC)
East Central U (OK)
Eastern Kentucky U (KY)
Eastern Michigan U (MI)
East Texas Baptist U (TX)
Edgewood Coll (WI)
Elmhurst Coll (IL)
Elon U (NC)
Emmanuel Coll (GA)
Emory & Henry Coll (VA)
Emporia State U (KS)
Evangel U (MO)
Fairmont State U (WV)
Faith Baptist Bible Coll and Theological Sem (IA)
Fayetteville State U (NC)
Five Towns Coll (NY)
Florida Ag and Mech U (FL)
Florida Atlantic U (FL)
Florida Southern Coll (FL)
Fort Hays State U (KS)
Fort Lewis Coll (CO)
Friends U (KS)
Furman U (SC)
Geneva Coll (PA)
Georgia Coll & State U (GA)
Georgia Regents U (GA)
Georgia Southern U (GA)
Gettysburg Coll (PA)
Gonzaga U (WA)
Gordon Coll (MA)
Graceland U (IA)
Grand Valley State U (MI)
Grand View U (IA)
Greensboro Coll (NC)
Greenville Coll (IL)
Grove City Coll (PA)
Gustavus Adolphus Coll (MN)
Hampton U (VA)
Hannibal-LaGrange U (MO)
Harding U (AR)
Hardin-Simmons U (TX)
Hartwick Coll (NY)
Hastings Coll (NE)
Heidelberg U (OH)
Hobe Sound Bible Coll (FL)
Hofstra U (NY)
Hope Coll (MI)
Houghton Coll (NY)
Houston Baptist U (TX)
Howard Payne U (TX)
Humboldt State U (CA)
Huntingdon Coll (AL)
Illinois State U (IL)
Illinois Wesleyan U (IL)
Immaculata U (PA)
Indiana U Bloomington (IN)
Indiana U–Purdue U Fort Wayne (IN)
Indiana U South Bend (IN)
Inter American U of Puerto Rico, San Germán Campus (PR)
Iowa State U of Science and Technology (IA)
Ithaca Coll (NY)
Jackson State U (MS)
Jacksonville State U (AL)
Jacksonville U (FL)
Jarvis Christian Coll (TX)
John Brown U (AR)
Johnson State Coll (VT)
Judson Coll (AL)
Kansas State U (KS)
Kansas Wesleyan U (KS)
Kean U (NJ)
Keene State Coll (NH)
Kennesaw State U (GA)
Kent State U (OH)
Kentucky Wesleyan Coll (KY)
King U (TN)
Langston U (OK)
La Sierra U (CA)
Lawrence U (WI)
Lebanon Valley Coll (PA)
Lee U (TN)
Lenoir-Rhyne U (NC)
Limestone Coll (SC)
Lincoln U (MO)
Lincoln U (PA)
Lindenwood U (MO)
Lipscomb U (TN)
Long Island U–LIU Brooklyn (NY)
Long Island U–LIU Post (NY)
Louisiana Coll (LA)
Louisiana State U and A&M Coll (LA)
Loyola U New Orleans (LA)

Lubbock Christian U (TX)
Madonna U (MI)
Malone U (OH)
Manchester U (IN)
Manhattanville Coll (NY)
Mansfield U of Pennsylvania (PA)
Maranatha Baptist U (WI)
Marian U (IN)
Marian U (WI)
Marietta Coll (OH)
Mars Hill U (NC)
Maryville Coll (TN)
Marywood U (PA)
The Master's Coll and Sem (CA)
McKendree U (IL)
Mercer U, Macon (GA)
Meredith Coll (NC)
Messiah Coll (PA)
Miami U (OH)
Michigan State U (MI)
MidAmerica Nazarene U (KS)
Midwestern State U (TX)
Milligan Coll (TN)
Millikin U (IL)
Minnesota State U Mankato (MN)
Minnesota State U Moorhead (MN)
Minot State U (ND)
Mississippi State U (MS)
Mississippi Valley State U (MS)
Missouri Baptist U (MO)
Missouri State U (MO)
Missouri Western State U (MO)
Molloy Coll (NY)
Montana State U (MT)
Montana State U Billings (MT)
Morningside Coll (IA)
Mount Marty Coll (SD)
Mount Mercy U (IA)
Mount Vernon Nazarene U (OH)
Nazareth Coll of Rochester (NY)
Nebraska Wesleyan U (NE)
Newberry Coll (SC)
New Jersey City U (NJ)
New Mexico State U (NM)
New York U (NY)
Nicholls State U (LA)
North Carolina Ag and Tech State U (NC)
North Central Coll (IL)
North Dakota State U (ND)
Northeastern State U (OK)
Northern Arizona U (AZ)
Northern Illinois U (IL)
Northern Michigan U (MI)
Northern State U (SD)
North Greenville U (SC)
Northwestern Coll (IA)
Northwestern Oklahoma State U (OK)
Northwestern U (IL)
Northwest Missouri State U (MO)
Northwest Nazarene U (ID)
Northwest U (WA)
Nyack Coll (NY)
Oakland City U (IN)
Oakland U (MI)
Oberlin Coll (OH)
Ohio Northern U (OH)
The Ohio State U (OH)
Ohio Wesleyan U (OH)
Oklahoma Baptist U (OK)
Oklahoma Christian U (OK)
Oklahoma State U (OK)
Oklahoma Wesleyan U (OK)
Olivet Coll (MI)
Olivet Nazarene U (IL)
Pacific Lutheran U (WA)
Pacific U (OR)
Palm Beach Atlantic U (FL)
Peabody Conservatory of The Johns Hopkins U (MD)
Penn State U Park (PA)
Pepperdine U, Malibu (CA)
Peru State Coll (NE)
Piedmont Coll (GA)
Pittsburg State U (KS)
Plymouth State U (NH)
Point Loma Nazarene U (CA)
Presbyterian Coll (SC)
Providence Coll (RI)
Queens Coll of the City U of New York (NY)
Quincy U (IL)
Rhode Island Coll (RI)
Rider U (NJ)
Ripon Coll (WI)
Roberts Wesleyan Coll (NY)
Rocky Mountain Coll (MT)
Roosevelt U (IL)
Rowan U (NJ)
Rutgers, The State U of New Jersey, New Brunswick (NJ)
Saginaw Valley State U (MI)
St. Catherine U (MN)
Saint Mary's Coll (IN)
Saint Mary's U of Minnesota (MN)
St. Norbert Coll (WI)
St. Olaf Coll (MN)
Salem Coll (NC)
Salve Regina U (RI)
Samford U (AL)
San Diego State U (CA)
Seton Hill U (PA)
Shenandoah U (VA)
Silver Lake Coll of the Holy Family (WI)
Simpson Coll (IA)
Simpson U (CA)
South Carolina State U (SC)
South Dakota State U (SD)
Southeastern Oklahoma State U (OK)
Southeastern U (FL)
Southeast Missouri State U (MO)
Southern Adventist U (TN)
Southern Arkansas U–Magnolia (AR)
Southern Methodist U (TX)
Southern New Hampshire U (NH)
Southern Utah U (UT)
Southwest Baptist U (MO)
Southwestern Assemblies of God U (TX)
Southwestern Coll (KS)
Southwest Minnesota State U (MN)
State U of New York at Fredonia (NY)
State U of New York Coll at Potsdam (NY)
Sterling Coll (KS)
Stetson U (FL)
Summit U (PA)
Susquehanna U (PA)
Syracuse U (NY)
Tabor Coll (KS)
Tarleton State U (TX)
Taylor U (IN)
Temple U (PA)
Texas Christian U (TX)
Texas Lutheran U (TX)
Texas Wesleyan U (TX)
Toccoa Falls Coll (GA)
Towson U (MD)
Transylvania U (KY)
Trevecca Nazarene U (TN)
Trinity Christian Coll (IL)
Trinity U (TX)
Truett-McConnell Coll (GA)
Union Coll (NE)
Union U (TN)
The U of Akron (OH)
The U of Alabama (AL)
U of Alberta (AB, Canada)
The U of Arizona (AZ)
U of Arkansas–Fort Smith (AR)
The U of British Columbia (BC, Canada)
U of Central Florida (FL)
U of Central Missouri (MO)
U of Central Oklahoma (OK)
U of Cincinnati (OH)
U of Colorado Boulder (CO)
U of Dayton (OH)
U of Delaware (DE)
U of Evansville (IN)
U of Florida (FL)
U of Georgia (GA)
U of Hartford (CT)
U of Idaho (ID)
U of Indianapolis (IN)
The U of Iowa (IA)
U of Jamestown (ND)
The U of Kansas (KS)
U of Kentucky (KY)
U of Lethbridge (AB, Canada)
U of Louisville (KY)
U of Maine (ME)
U of Mary Hardin-Baylor (TX)
U of Maryland, Coll Park (MD)
U of Miami (FL)
U of Michigan (MI)
U of Michigan–Flint (MI)
U of Minnesota, Duluth (MN)
U of Minnesota, Twin Cities Campus (MN)
U of Missouri (MO)
U of Missouri–Kansas City (MO)
U of Mobile (AL)
The U of Montana (MT)
The U of Montana Western (MT)
U of Mount Union (OH)
U of Nebraska–Lincoln (NE)
U of Nevada, Reno (NV)
U of New Mexico (NM)
The U of North Carolina at Charlotte (NC)
The U of North Carolina at Greensboro (NC)
The U of North Carolina at Pembroke (NC)
The U of North Carolina Wilmington (NC)
U of North Dakota (ND)
U of Northern Colorado (CO)
U of Northern Iowa (IA)
U of North Florida (FL)
U of North Georgia (GA)
U of Northwestern–St. Paul (MN)
U of Oklahoma (OK)
U of Oregon (OR)
U of Puget Sound (WA)
U of Regina (SK, Canada)
U of Rio Grande (OH)
U of Rochester (NY)
U of St. Francis (IL)
U of St. Thomas (MN)
U of St. Thomas (TX)
U of Saskatchewan (SK, Canada)
U of South Carolina Aiken (SC)
The U of South Dakota (SD)
U of Southern Maine (ME)
U of Southern Mississippi (MS)
U of South Florida (FL)
The U of Tampa (FL)
The U of Tennessee at Chattanooga (TN)
The U of Tennessee at Martin (TN)
U of the Cumberlands (KY)
U of the Incarnate Word (TX)
U of the Pacific (CA)
U of the Virgin Islands (VI)
The U of Toledo (OH)
U of Toronto (ON, Canada)
The U of Tulsa (OK)
U of Valley Forge (PA)
U of Vermont (VT)
U of Washington (WA)
U of West Florida (FL)
U of West Georgia (GA)
U of Windsor (ON, Canada)
U of Wisconsin–Green Bay (WI)
U of Wisconsin–Madison (WI)
U of Wisconsin–Milwaukee (WI)
U of Wisconsin–Oshkosh (WI)
U of Wisconsin–River Falls (WI)
U of Wisconsin–Stevens Point (WI)
U of Wisconsin–Superior (WI)
U of Wyoming (WY)
Utah State U (UT)
Utah Valley U (UT)
Valley City State U (ND)
Valparaiso U (IN)
Vanderbilt U (TN)
VanderCook Coll of Music (IL)
Vanguard U of Southern California (CA)
Viterbo U (WI)
Waldorf Coll (IA)
Walla Walla U (WA)
Warner Pacific Coll (OR)
Wartburg Coll (IA)
Washburn U (KS)
Washington State U (WA)
Wayne State Coll (NE)
Weber State U (UT)
Webster U (MO)
Welch Coll (TN)
Western Carolina U (NC)
Western Michigan U (MI)
Western State Colorado U (CO)
Western Washington U (WA)
West Liberty U (WV)
West Virginia Wesleyan Coll (WV)
Wheaton Coll (IL)
Whitworth U (WA)
Wichita State U (KS)
William Jewell Coll (MO)
William Paterson U of New Jersey (NJ)
Williams Baptist Coll (AR)
Wingate U (NC)
Winona State U (MN)
Winthrop U (SC)
Wright State U (OH)
Xavier U (OH)
Xavier U of Louisiana (LA)
York Coll of Pennsylvania (PA)
Youngstown State U (OH)

MUSIC TECHNOLOGY

American U (DC)
Bethune-Cookman U (FL)
Cogswell Polytechnical Coll (CA)
Elon U (NC)
Indiana U–Purdue U Indianapolis (IN)
Keene State Coll (NH)
LaGrange Coll (GA)
Mercy Coll (NY)
Northwest Christian U (OR)
Shenandoah U (VA)
Stetson U (FL)
Syracuse U (NY)
Transylvania U (KY)
U of Michigan (MI)
U of New Haven (CT)
U of Saint Francis (IN)
U of Valley Forge (PA)
Utah Valley U (UT)

MUSIC THEORY AND COMPOSITION

Adams State U (CO)
Anderson U (IN)
Arizona State U at the Tempe campus (AZ)
Augustana Coll (IL)
Baldwin Wallace U (OH)
Baylor U (TX)
Belmont U (TN)
Bennington Coll (VT)
Biola U (CA)
Birmingham-Southern Coll (AL)
Boston U (MA)
Bowling Green State U (OH)
Bradley U (IL)
Bucknell U (PA)
Butler U (IN)
California Baptist U (CA)
California Inst of the Arts (CA)
California State U, Long Beach (CA)
Calvin Coll (MI)
Capital U (OH)
Carson-Newman U (TN)
The Catholic U of America (DC)
Cedarville U (OH)
Central Michigan U (MI)
Central Washington U (WA)
Chapman U (CA)
City Coll of the City U of New York (NY)
Coe Coll (IA)
Coll of the Ozarks (MO)
The Coll of Wooster (OH)
Colorado State U (CO)
Concordia Coll (MN)
Concordia U (QC, Canada)
Concordia U Chicago (IL)
Dalhousie U (NS, Canada)
Dallas Baptist U (TX)
DePaul U (IL)
DePauw U (IN)
DigiPen Inst of Technology (WA)
Florida State U (FL)
Georgia Southern U (GA)
Hardin-Simmons U (TX)
Hofstra U (NY)
Hope Coll (MI)
Houghton Coll (NY)
Houston Baptist U (TX)
Illinois Wesleyan U (IL)
Ithaca Coll (NY)
Jacksonville U (FL)
Keene State Coll (NH)
Lawrence U (WI)
Lewis & Clark Coll (OR)
Liberty U (VA)
Lipscomb U (TN)
Loyola U New Orleans (LA)
Lynn U (FL)
Madonna U (MI)
Manchester U (IN)
Marylhurst U (OR)
Maryville Coll (TN)
Michigan State U (MI)
Minnesota State U Moorhead (MN)
Newberry Coll (SC)
New England Conservatory of Music (MA)
Northwestern U (IL)
Northwest Nazarene U (ID)
Nyack Coll (NY)
Oberlin Coll (OH)
Ohio Northern U (OH)
The Ohio State U (OH)
Ohio U (OH)
Oklahoma Baptist U (OK)
Oklahoma City U (OK)
Olivet Nazarene U (IL)
Palm Beach Atlantic U (FL)
Pepperdine U, Malibu (CA)
Point Loma Nazarene U (CA)
Randolph Coll (VA)
Rice U (TX)
Rider U (NJ)
Roosevelt U (IL)
Rowan U (NJ)
St. Olaf Coll (MN)
Samford U (AL)
San Francisco Conservatory of Music (CA)
Shenandoah U (VA)
Southern Adventist U (TN)
Southern Methodist U (TX)
State U of New York Coll at Potsdam (NY)
Stetson U (FL)
Susquehanna U (PA)
Syracuse U (NY)
Temple U (PA)
Texas Christian U (TX)
Trinity Christian Coll (IL)
Trinity U (TX)
Tufts U (MA)
Tulane U (LA)
The U of Akron (OH)
The U of British Columbia (BC, Canada)
U of California, Santa Barbara (CA)
U of Central Missouri (MO)
U of Cincinnati (OH)
U of Dayton (OH)
U of Delaware (DE)
U of Georgia (GA)
U of Idaho (ID)
The U of Iowa (IA)
The U of Kansas (KS)
U of Miami (FL)
U of Michigan (MI)
U of Minnesota, Duluth (MN)
U of Missouri–Kansas City (MO)
The U of North Carolina at Greensboro (NC)
U of Northern Iowa (IA)
U of North Texas (TX)
U of Northwestern–St. Paul (MN)
U of Oregon (OR)
U of Regina (SK, Canada)
U of Rhode Island (RI)
U of Rochester (NY)
U of Southern California (CA)
The U of Texas at Austin (TX)
The U of the Arts (PA)
U of the Pacific (CA)
The U of Tulsa (OK)
U of Washington (WA)
The U of Western Ontario (ON, Canada)
U of West Georgia (GA)
U of Windsor (ON, Canada)
Valparaiso U (IN)
Vanderbilt U (TN)
Wartburg Coll (IA)
Washington State U (WA)
Washington U in St. Louis (MO)
Webster U (MO)
Western Michigan U (MI)
Western Washington U (WA)
West Texas A&M U (TX)
Wheaton Coll (IL)
Whitman Coll (WA)
Willamette U (OR)
William Jewell Coll (MO)
Youngstown State U (OH)

MUSIC THERAPY

Alverno Coll (WI)
Anna Maria Coll (MA)
Appalachian State U (NC)
Arizona State U at the Tempe campus (AZ)
Augsburg Coll (MN)
Baldwin Wallace U (OH)
Charleston Southern U (SC)

The Coll of Wooster (OH)
Colorado State U (CO)
Concordia U Wisconsin (WI)
Drury U (MO)
Duquesne U (PA)
Eastern Michigan U (MI)
Elizabethtown Coll (PA)
Florida State U (FL)
Georgia Coll & State U (GA)
Immaculata U (PA)
Indiana U–Purdue U Fort Wayne (IN)
Loyola U New Orleans (LA)
Marylhurst U (OR)
Maryville U of Saint Louis (MO)
Marywood U (PA)
Molloy Coll (NY)
Montclair State U (NJ)
Nazareth Coll of Rochester (NY)
Saint Mary-of-the-Woods Coll (IN)
Sam Houston State U (TX)
Seattle Pacific U (WA)
Seton Hill U (PA)
Shenandoah U (VA)
Slippery Rock U of Pennsylvania (PA)
Southern Methodist U (TX)
State U of New York at Fredonia (NY)
State U of New York at New Paltz (NY)
Temple U (PA)
U of Dayton (OH)
U of Evansville (IN)
U of Georgia (GA)
The U of Iowa (IA)
The U of Kansas (KS)
U of Louisville (KY)
U of Miami (FL)
U of Minnesota, Twin Cities Campus (MN)
U of Missouri–Kansas City (MO)
U of North Dakota (ND)
U of the Incarnate Word (TX)
U of the Pacific (CA)
U of Wisconsin–Oshkosh (WI)
Utah State U (UT)
Wartburg Coll (IA)
Western Michigan U (MI)
West Texas A&M U (TX)

NANOTECHNOLOGY
U at Albany, State U of New York (NY)
U of Guelph (ON, Canada)

NATIONAL SECURITY POLICY
Angelo State U (TX)
Baldwin Wallace U (OH)
U of New Haven (CT)

NATURAL RESOURCE ECONOMICS
Baldwin Wallace U (OH)
Colorado State U (CO)
Juniata Coll (PA)
Malone U (OH)
Michigan State U (MI)
New Mexico State U (NM)
U of Guelph (ON, Canada)
U of New Hampshire (NH)
U of Rhode Island (RI)
The U of Tennessee (TN)

NATURAL RESOURCE RECREATION AND TOURISM
Unity Coll (ME)
U of Georgia (GA)
U of Idaho (ID)

NATURAL RESOURCES AND CONSERVATION RELATED
Bowling Green State U (OH)
California Polytechnic State U, San Luis Obispo (CA)
Mount Mercy U (IA)
Northland Coll (WI)
Penn State Abington (PA)
Penn State Altoona (PA)
Penn State Beaver (PA)
Penn State Berks (PA)
Penn State Brandywine (PA)
Penn State DuBois (PA)
Penn State Erie, The Behrend Coll (PA)
Penn State Fayette, The Eberly Campus (PA)
Penn State Greater Allegheny (PA)
Penn State Hazleton (PA)
Penn State Lehigh Valley (PA)
Penn State Mont Alto (PA)
Penn State New Kensington (PA)
Penn State Schuylkill (PA)
Penn State Shenango (PA)
Penn State U Park (PA)
Penn State Wilkes-Barre (PA)
Penn State Worthington Scranton (PA)
Penn State York (PA)
Prescott Coll (AZ)
State U of New York Coll of Technology at Canton (NY)
Sterling Coll (VT)
U of Alaska Fairbanks (AK)
U of Alberta (AB, Canada)
The U of British Columbia (BC, Canada)
U of California, Davis (CA)
U of Louisiana at Lafayette (LA)
U of New Hampshire (NH)
U of Wisconsin–Platteville (WI)
U of Wisconsin–Stevens Point (WI)
Utah State U (UT)

NATURAL RESOURCES/ CONSERVATION
Ball State U (IN)
Central Michigan U (MI)
Colorado State U (CO)
Cornell U (NY)
Everglades U, Sarasota (FL)
The Evergreen State Coll (WA)
Grand Valley State U (MI)
Green Mountain Coll (VT)
Gustavus Adolphus Coll (MN)
Humboldt State U (CA)
Kent State U (OH)
Lubbock Christian U (TX)
Manchester U (IN)
Mississippi State U (MS)
Montana State U (MT)
Morrisville State Coll (NY)
North Carolina State U (NC)
Northern Michigan U (MI)
The Ohio State U (OH)
Penn State Abington (PA)
Penn State Altoona (PA)
Penn State Beaver (PA)
Penn State Berks (PA)
Penn State Brandywine (PA)
Penn State DuBois (PA)
Penn State Erie, The Behrend Coll (PA)
Penn State Fayette, The Eberly Campus (PA)
Penn State Greater Allegheny (PA)
Penn State Hazleton (PA)
Penn State Lehigh Valley (PA)
Penn State Mont Alto (PA)
Penn State New Kensington (PA)
Penn State Schuylkill (PA)
Penn State Shenango (PA)
Penn State U Park (PA)
Penn State Wilkes-Barre (PA)
Penn State Worthington Scranton (PA)
Penn State York (PA)
Peru State Coll (NE)
Purdue U (IN)
Rutgers, The State U of New Jersey, New Brunswick (NJ)
Sewanee: The U of the South (TN)
Southeastern Oklahoma State U (OK)
State U of New York at Plattsburgh (NY)
State U of New York Coll of Environmental Science and Forestry (NY)
Texas A&M U (TX)
Texas Tech U (TX)
Tusculum Coll (TN)
The U of Arizona (AZ)
The U of British Columbia (BC, Canada)
U of California, Berkeley (CA)
U of California, Davis (CA)
U of Kentucky (KY)
U of Maryland, Coll Park (MD)
U of Maryland U Coll (MD)
U of Massachusetts Amherst (MA)
U of Michigan (MI)
U of Minnesota, Crookston (MN)
U of Minnesota, Twin Cities Campus (MN)
U of Missouri (MO)
The U of Montana (MT)
U of Nebraska–Lincoln (NE)
U of Nevada, Reno (NV)
U of New Hampshire (NH)
U of Vermont (VT)
U of Wisconsin–River Falls (WI)
U of Wisconsin–Stevens Point (WI)
Upper Iowa U (IA)
Washington State U (WA)
Washington U in St. Louis (MO)

NATURAL RESOURCES/ CONSERVATION RELATED
Colby Coll (ME)
Miami U (OH)
Northland Coll (WI)
Stanford U (CA)
State U of New York Coll of Agriculture and Technology at Cobleskill (NY)
Wheeling Jesuit U (WV)

NATURAL RESOURCES LAW ENFORCEMENT AND PROTECTIVE SERVICES
Texas Tech U (TX)
Unity Coll (ME)
Universidad Metropolitana (PR)
U of Minnesota, Crookston (MN)

NATURAL RESOURCES MANAGEMENT AND POLICY
Alaska Pacific U (AK)
Angelo State U (TX)
Auburn U (AL)
Bowling Green State U (OH)
Clark U (MA)
Colorado State U (CO)
Delaware State U (DE)
Dominican U of California (CA)
Fort Hays State U (KS)
Humboldt State U (CA)
Iowa State U of Science and Technology (IA)
Johnson State Coll (VT)
Kansas State U (KS)
Keystone Coll (PA)
Louisiana State U and A&M Coll (LA)
Marist Coll (NY)
Morrisville State Coll (NY)
New Mexico Highlands U (NM)
North Carolina State U (NC)
North Dakota State U (ND)
Oregon State U (OR)
Rochester Inst of Technology (NY)
South Dakota State U (SD)
State U of New York Coll of Environmental Science and Forestry (NY)
Tabor Coll (KS)
The U of British Columbia (BC, Canada)
U of California, Berkeley (CA)
U of Delaware (DE)
U of Guelph (ON, Canada)
U of Hawaii at Manoa (HI)
U of La Verne (CA)
U of Miami (FL)
U of Minnesota, Crookston (MN)
U of Minnesota, Twin Cities Campus (MN)
The U of Montana (MT)
U of Nebraska–Lincoln (NE)
U of Nevada, Reno (NV)
U of Rhode Island (RI)
The U of Tennessee at Martin (TN)
U of Wisconsin–Stevens Point (WI)
Washington U in St. Louis (MO)
Western Carolina U (NC)
Xavier U (OH)

NATURAL RESOURCES MANAGEMENT AND POLICY RELATED
Delaware State U (DE)
Great Basin Coll (NV)
Humboldt State U (CA)
Keystone Coll (PA)
Massachusetts Maritime Acad (MA)
Morrisville State Coll (NY)
The Ohio State U (OH)
Rutgers, The State U of New Jersey, New Brunswick (NJ)
Sterling Coll (VT)
The U of British Columbia (BC, Canada)
U of Minnesota, Twin Cities Campus (MN)
U of Saskatchewan (SK, Canada)
The U of Tennessee at Martin (TN)
The U of Western Ontario (ON, Canada)

NATURAL SCIENCES
American Public U System (WV)
Arcadia U (PA)
Athens State U (AL)
Azusa Pacific U (CA)
Bard Coll at Simon's Rock (MA)
Bemidji State U (MN)
Benedictine Coll (KS)
Bethel Coll (KS)
California State U, Dominguez Hills (CA)
California State U, Fresno (CA)
California State U, Los Angeles (CA)
Calvin Coll (MI)
Case Western Reserve U (OH)
Castleton State Coll (VT)
Central Coll (IA)
Christian Brothers U (TN)
Coll of Saint Benedict (MN)
Coll of Saint Mary (NE)
The Coll of St. Scholastica (MN)
Coll of the Atlantic (ME)
Colorado State U (CO)
Concordia Coll (MN)
Concordia U Chicago (IL)
Concordia U, Nebraska (NE)
Daemen Coll (NY)
Dallas Baptist U (TX)
Defiance Coll (OH)
Doane Coll (NE)
Dominican U (IL)
Edgewood Coll (WI)
Elms Coll (MA)
The Evergreen State Coll (WA)
Fordham U (NY)
Georgian Court U (NJ)
Harrison Middleton U (AZ)
Hofstra U (NY)
Houghton Coll (NY)
Humboldt State U (CA)
Indiana U East (IN)
Inter American U of Puerto Rico, San Germán Campus (PR)
Johns Hopkins U (MD)
Judson U (IL)
Juniata Coll (PA)
Kansas State U (KS)
Lesley U (MA)
LeTourneau U (TX)
Loyola Marymount U (CA)
Madonna U (MI)
The Master's Coll and Sem (CA)
Minnesota State U Mankato (MN)
Mount Allison U (NB, Canada)
Mount Saint Mary Coll (NY)
Muhlenberg Coll (PA)
National U (CA)
New Coll of Florida (FL)
Oklahoma Baptist U (OK)
Oregon State U (OR)
Park U (MO)
Pepperdine U, Malibu (CA)
Peru State Coll (NE)
Saint John's U (MN)
Saint Peter's U (NJ)
St. Thomas Aquinas Coll (NY)
San Jose State U (CA)
Shimer Coll (IL)
Siena Heights U (MI)
State U of New York Coll at Geneseo (NY)
Tabor Coll (KS)
Taylor U (IN)
Temple U (PA)
Trent U (ON, Canada)
Universidad del Turabo (PR)
The U of Arizona (AZ)
U of Hawaii at Hilo (HI)
U of La Verne (CA)
U of Pennsylvania (PA)
U of Pittsburgh at Greensburg (PA)
U of Puget Sound (WA)
U of Science and Arts of Oklahoma (OK)
U of Washington (WA)
U of Wisconsin–River Falls (WI)
U of Wisconsin–Stevens Point (WI)
Virginia Wesleyan Coll (VA)
Washington U in St. Louis (MO)
Western Oregon U (OR)
Xavier U (OH)

NAVAL ARCHITECTURE AND MARINE ENGINEERING
Maine Maritime Acad (ME)
Massachusetts Maritime Acad (MA)
State U of New York Maritime Coll (NY)
Texas A&M U (TX)
United States Coast Guard Acad (CT)
United States Merchant Marine Acad (NY)
United States Naval Acad (MD)
U of Michigan (MI)
U of Minnesota, Twin Cities Campus (MN)
U of New Orleans (LA)
Webb Inst (NY)

NAVAL SCIENCE AND OPERATIONAL STUDIES
U of Wisconsin–Madison (WI)

NAVY/MARINE CORPS ROTC/ NAVAL SCIENCE
Hampton U (VA)
Jacksonville U (FL)

NEAR AND MIDDLE EASTERN STUDIES
American U (DC)
The American U in Cairo (Egypt)
The American U in Dubai (United Arab Emirates)
The American U of Paris (France)
Bard Coll (NY)
Brandeis U (MA)
Brown U (RI)
Claremont McKenna Coll (CA)
Columbia Intl U (SC)
Columbia U (NY)
Columbia U, School of General Studies (NY)
Cornell U (NY)
Dartmouth Coll (NH)
Dickinson Coll (PA)
Emmanuel Coll (MA)
Emory & Henry Coll (VA)
Fordham U (NY)
The George Washington U (DC)
Hampshire Coll (MA)
Harvard U (MA)
Johns Hopkins U (MD)
McDaniel Coll (MD)
Middlebury Coll (VT)
Mount Holyoke Coll (MA)
New York U (NY)
Oberlin Coll (OH)
Pomona Coll (CA)
Portland State U (OR)
Princeton U (NJ)
Rutgers, The State U of New Jersey, New Brunswick (NJ)
Scripps Coll (CA)
Smith Coll (MA)
Syracuse U (NY)
Texas State U (TX)
Trinity U (TX)
Tufts U (MA)
United States Military Acad (NY)
The U of Arizona (AZ)
U of California, Berkeley (CA)
U of California, Los Angeles (CA)
U of California, Santa Barbara (CA)
U of Massachusetts Amherst (MA)
U of Michigan (MI)
U of Minnesota, Twin Cities Campus (MN)
U of Richmond (VA)
The U of Texas at Austin (TX)
The U of Toledo (OH)
U of Toronto (ON, Canada)
U of Utah (UT)
The U of Western Ontario (ON, Canada)
Washington U in St. Louis (MO)
Williams Coll (MA)
Yale U (CT)

NETWORK AND SYSTEM ADMINISTRATION
Champlain Coll (VT)
Michigan Technological U (MI)
Regis U (CO)
Rochester Inst of Technology (NY)
Simmons Coll (MA)

Sullivan Coll of Technology and Design (KY)
U of Great Falls (MT)

NEUROBIOLOGY AND ANATOMY
Andrews U (MI)
Georgetown U (DC)
Harvard U (MA)
New Coll of Florida (FL)
Purdue U (IN)
U of California, Davis (CA)
U of California, Irvine (CA)
U of Washington (WA)

NEUROBIOLOGY AND BEHAVIOR
Fitchburg State U (MA)

NEUROBIOLOGY AND NEUROSCIENCES RELATED
U of Southern California (CA)
Ursinus Coll (PA)

NEUROSCIENCE
Agnes Scott Coll (GA)
Allegheny Coll (PA)
American U (DC)
Amherst Coll (MA)
Augustana Coll (IL)
Baldwin Wallace U (OH)
Barnard Coll (NY)
Bates Coll (ME)
Baylor U (TX)
Bay Path U (MA)
Belmont U (TN)
Binghamton U, State U of New York (NY)
Boston U (MA)
Bowdoin Coll (ME)
Bowling Green State U (OH)
Brandeis U (MA)
Brown U (RI)
Bucknell U (PA)
Cedar Crest Coll (PA)
Centenary Coll of Louisiana (LA)
Central Michigan U (MI)
Christopher Newport U (VA)
Claremont McKenna Coll (CA)
Clark U (MA)
Coe Coll (IA)
Colby Coll (ME)
The Coll of William and Mary (VA)
The Coll of Wooster (OH)
The Colorado Coll (CO)
Columbia U, School of General Studies (NY)
Concordia U (QC, Canada)
Connecticut Coll (CT)
Dalhousie U (NS, Canada)
Dickinson Coll (PA)
Dominican U (IL)
Drake U (IA)
Drew U (NJ)
Earlham Coll (IN)
Emmanuel Coll (MA)
Fordham U (NY)
Franklin & Marshall Coll (PA)
Furman U (SC)
George Mason U (VA)
Georgia State U (GA)
Hamilton Coll (NY)
Hampshire Coll (MA)
Hiram Coll (OH)
Indiana U Bloomington (IN)
Indiana U–Purdue U Indianapolis (IN)
John Carroll U (OH)
Johns Hopkins U (MD)
Kenyon Coll (OH)
King's Coll (PA)
King U (TN)
Knox Coll (IL)
Lake Forest Coll (IL)
Lawrence U (WI)
Lehigh U (PA)
Loras Coll (IA)
Macalester Coll (MN)
Maryville Coll (TN)
Massachusetts Inst of Technology (MA)
Middlebury Coll (VT)
Moravian Coll (PA)
Morehead State U (KY)
Mount Holyoke Coll (MA)
Mount St. Joseph U (OH)
Muhlenberg Coll (PA)
New York U (NY)
Northeastern U (MA)
Northern Michigan U (MI)
Northwestern U (IL)
Northwest Nazarene U (ID)
Oberlin Coll (OH)
Ohio U (OH)
Ohio Wesleyan U (OH)
Pomona Coll (CA)
Regis U (CO)
Rhodes Coll (TN)
Rice U (TX)
St. Lawrence U (NY)
Saint Louis U (MO)
Scripps Coll (CA)
Skidmore Coll (NY)
Smith Coll (MA)
Stonehill Coll (MA)
Syracuse U (NY)
Temple U (PA)
Texas Christian U (TX)
Thiel Coll (PA)
Trinity Coll (CT)
Trinity U (TX)
Tulane U (LA)
Union Coll (NY)
The U of Alabama at Birmingham (AL)
The U of Arizona (AZ)
U of California, Riverside (CA)
U of California, Santa Cruz (CA)
U of Cincinnati (OH)
U of Colorado Boulder (CO)
U of Delaware (DE)
U of Evansville (IN)
U of Illinois at Chicago (IL)
U of King's Coll (NS, Canada)
U of Lethbridge (AB, Canada)
U of Miami (FL)
U of Michigan (MI)
U of Minnesota, Twin Cities Campus (MN)
U of Mount Union (OH)
U of New England (ME)
U of New Hampshire (NH)
U of Pennsylvania (PA)
U of Pittsburgh (PA)
U of Rochester (NY)
U of San Diego (CA)
The U of Scranton (PA)
U of Southern California (CA)
The U of Texas at Austin (TX)
The U of Texas at Dallas (TX)
The U of Western Ontario (ON, Canada)
U of Windsor (ON, Canada)
Ursinus Coll (PA)
Vanderbilt U (TN)
Villanova U (PA)
Wartburg Coll (IA)
Washington & Jefferson Coll (PA)
Washington and Lee U (VA)
Washington State U (WA)
Washington State U Vancouver (WA)
Washington U in St. Louis (MO)
Western New England U (MA)
Western Washington U (WA)
Westminster Coll (UT)
Wheaton Coll (MA)

NONPROFIT MANAGEMENT
Arizona State U at the Downtown Phoenix campus (AZ)
Austin Peay State U (TN)
Bryant U (RI)
City Vision Coll (MO)
Cleveland State U (OH)
Columbia Intl U (SC)
Concordia U Chicago (IL)
Cornerstone U (MI)
Dalhousie U (NS, Canada)
Donnelly Coll (KS)
Duquesne U (PA)
Fairleigh Dickinson U, Metropolitan Campus (NJ)
Friends U (KS)
Gettysburg Coll (PA)
Grace Coll (IN)
Granite State Coll (NH)
Great Lakes Christian Coll (MI)
Hardin-Simmons U (TX)
High Point U (NC)
LaGrange Coll (GA)
LeTourneau U (TX)
Metropolitan State U (MN)
Moravian Coll (PA)
Point Loma Nazarene U (CA)
Salem Coll (NC)
Southern Adventist U (TN)
Southwest Minnesota State U (MN)
Tiffin U (OH)
Toccoa Falls Coll (GA)
Trevecca Nazarene U (TN)
U of Minnesota, Twin Cities Campus (MN)
U of South Carolina Upstate (SC)
The U of Western Ontario (ON, Canada)
William Jewell Coll (MO)
Williamson Christian Coll (TN)

NORWEGIAN
Brigham Young U (UT)
Pacific Lutheran U (WA)
St. Olaf Coll (MN)
U of North Dakota (ND)
U of Washington (WA)

NUCLEAR AND INDUSTRIAL RADIOLOGIC TECHNOLOGIES RELATED
Manhattan Coll (NY)

NUCLEAR ENGINEERING
Cornell U (NY)
Georgia Inst of Technology (GA)
Massachusetts Inst of Technology (MA)
Missouri U of Science and Technology (MO)
North Carolina State U (NC)
Oregon State U (OR)
Penn State Abington (PA)
Penn State Altoona (PA)
Penn State Beaver (PA)
Penn State Berks (PA)
Penn State Brandywine (PA)
Penn State DuBois (PA)
Penn State Erie, The Behrend Coll (PA)
Penn State Fayette, The Eberly Campus (PA)
Penn State Greater Allegheny (PA)
Penn State Hazleton (PA)
Penn State Lehigh Valley (PA)
Penn State Mont Alto (PA)
Penn State New Kensington (PA)
Penn State Schuylkill (PA)
Penn State Shenango (PA)
Penn State U Park (PA)
Penn State Wilkes-Barre (PA)
Penn State Worthington Scranton (PA)
Penn State York (PA)
Purdue U (IN)
Rensselaer Polytechnic Inst (NY)
South Carolina State U (SC)
Texas A&M U (TX)
United States Military Acad (NY)
United States Naval Acad (MD)
U of California, Berkeley (CA)
U of Cincinnati (OH)
U of Florida (FL)
U of Michigan (MI)
U of New Mexico (NM)
The U of Tennessee (TN)
U of Wisconsin–Madison (WI)
Worcester Polytechnic Inst (MA)

NUCLEAR ENGINEERING TECHNOLOGY
United States Military Acad (NY)

NUCLEAR MEDICAL TECHNOLOGY
Adventist U of Health Sciences (FL)
Allen Coll (IA)
Barry U (FL)
Benedictine U (IL)
Cedar Crest Coll (PA)
Dalhousie U (NS, Canada)
Edinboro U of Pennsylvania (PA)
Ferris State U (MI)
Georgia Regents U (GA)
Indiana U of Pennsylvania (PA)
Indiana U–Purdue U Indianapolis (IN)
Lewis U (IL)
Manhattan Coll (NY)
MCPHS U (MA)
Molloy Coll (NY)
North Central Coll (IL)
Oakland U (MI)
Old Dominion U (VA)
Peru State Coll (NE)
Rhode Island Coll (RI)
Robert Morris U (PA)
Roosevelt U (IL)
Saint Louis U (MO)
Saint Mary's U of Minnesota (MN)
U at Buffalo, the State U of New York (NY)
The U of Alabama at Birmingham (AL)
U of Central Arkansas (AR)
U of Cincinnati (OH)
The U of Iowa (IA)
U of Missouri (MO)
U of Nevada, Las Vegas (NV)
U of Oklahoma Health Sciences Center (OK)
U of St. Francis (IL)
U of the Incarnate Word (TX)
U of Vermont (VT)
U of Wisconsin–La Crosse (WI)
Weber State U (UT)
Wheeling Jesuit U (WV)
York Coll of Pennsylvania (PA)

NUCLEAR PHYSICS
Arkansas Tech U (AR)

NURSE MIDWIFE/NURSING MIDWIFERY
U of Toronto (ON, Canada)

NURSING ADMINISTRATION
Augsburg Coll (MN)
Kentucky Christian U (KY)
Long Island U–LIU Brooklyn (NY)
Midwestern State U (TX)
Nebraska Wesleyan U (NE)
Nova Southeastern U (FL)
Ohio Northern U (OH)
U of San Francisco (CA)
The U of Toledo (OH)
Wheeling Jesuit U (WV)
William Penn U (IA)

NURSING EDUCATION
U of the District of Columbia (DC)

NURSING PRACTICE
Ave Maria U (FL)
Benedictine Coll (KS)
Bluefield Coll (VA)
Brenau U (GA)
Christian Brothers U (TN)
Concordia Coll–New York (NY)
Concordia U, St. Paul (MN)
Eastern U (PA)
Hiram Coll (OH)
Lebanese American U (Lebanon)
Misericordia U (PA)
Northeastern State U (OK)
Sentara Coll of Health Sciences (VA)
Siena Heights U (MI)
Stratford U, Falls Church (VA)
Stratford U, Glen Allen (VA)
Stratford U, Newport News (VA)
William Penn U (IA)

NURSING SCIENCE
Alma Coll (MI)
Anna Maria Coll (MA)
Averett U (VA)
Cedar Crest Coll (PA)
Coll of Saint Elizabeth (NJ)
Dixie State U (UT)
EDP U of Puerto Rico (PR)
EDP U of Puerto Rico–San Sebastian (PR)
Kean U (NJ)
Millersville U of Pennsylvania (PA)
Monmouth U (NJ)
New Jersey City U (NJ)
North Carolina Ag and Tech State U (NC)
The Ohio State U (OH)
Oklahoma City U (OK)
Oklahoma Wesleyan U (OK)
Pensacola State Coll (FL)
Rutgers, The State U of New Jersey, Newark (NJ)
Rutgers, The State U of New Jersey, New Brunswick (NJ)
Sacred Heart U (CT)
Saint Peter's U (NJ)
Siena Heights U (MI)
U of California, Irvine (CA)
U of Illinois at Chicago (IL)
Wayne State U (MI)
Xavier U (OH)

NUTRITION SCIENCES
Auburn U (AL)
Boston U (MA)
California State U, Los Angeles (CA)
Canisius Coll (NY)
Case Western Reserve U (OH)
Central Washington U (WA)
Coll of Saint Benedict (MN)
Concordia Coll (MN)
Cornell U (NY)
Drexel U (PA)
Elmhurst Coll (IL)
Goddard Coll (VT)
Johnson & Wales U (CO)
Johnson & Wales U (RI)
Keiser U, Fort Lauderdale (FL)
La Salle U (PA)
Lebanese American U (Lebanon)
Louisiana State U and A&M Coll (LA)
McNeese State U (LA)
Michigan State U (MI)
New York U (NY)
North Carolina State U (NC)
The Ohio State U (OH)
Pepperdine U, Malibu (CA)
Rutgers, The State U of New Jersey, New Brunswick (NJ)
The Sage Colls (NY)
Saint John's U (MN)
Southern Illinois U Carbondale (IL)
Syracuse U (NY)
Texas Woman's U (TX)
U of Alberta (AB, Canada)
The U of Arizona (AZ)
U of California, Berkeley (CA)
U of California, Davis (CA)
U of Cincinnati (OH)
U of Delaware (DE)
U of Florida (FL)
U of Georgia (GA)
U of Guelph (ON, Canada)
U of Hawaii at Manoa (HI)
U of Illinois at Chicago (IL)
U of Massachusetts Amherst (MA)
U of Massachusetts Lowell (MA)
U of Minnesota, Twin Cities Campus (MN)
U of Nevada, Las Vegas (NV)
U of Nevada, Reno (NV)
U of New Hampshire (NH)
The U of North Carolina at Greensboro (NC)
U of Northern Colorado (CO)
U of Oklahoma Health Sciences Center (OK)
U of Saint Francis (IN)
U of Saskatchewan (SK, Canada)
U of Southern Indiana (IN)
U of the District of Columbia (DC)
U of the Incarnate Word (TX)
U of Vermont (VT)
U of Wisconsin–Madison (WI)
U of Wisconsin–Milwaukee (WI)
Washington State U (WA)

OCCUPATIONAL HEALTH AND INDUSTRIAL HYGIENE
California State U, Fresno (CA)
Grand Valley State U (MI)
Illinois State U (IL)
Montana Tech of The U of Montana (MT)
North Carolina Ag and Tech State U (NC)
Ohio U (OH)
U of Central Oklahoma (OK)

OCCUPATIONAL SAFETY AND HEALTH TECHNOLOGY
California State U, Fresno (CA)
Central Washington U (WA)
Columbia Southern U (AL)
Embry-Riddle Aeronautical U–Daytona (FL)
Embry-Riddle Aeronautical U–Prescott (AZ)
Fairmont State U (WV)
Grand Valley State U (MI)
Indiana State U (IN)
Indiana U of Pennsylvania (PA)
Jacksonville State U (AL)
Keene State Coll (NH)
Marshall U (WV)
Millersville U of Pennsylvania (PA)
Murray State U (KY)
Pittsburg State U (KS)

Rochester Inst of Technology (NY)
Slippery Rock U of Pennsylvania (PA)
Southeastern Louisiana U (LA)
Southeastern Oklahoma State U (OK)
Southwest Baptist U (MO)
U of Central Missouri (MO)
U of Central Oklahoma (OK)
U of Houston–Downtown (TX)
U of North Dakota (ND)
U of Wisconsin–Whitewater (WI)

OCCUPATIONAL THERAPIST ASSISTANT
Rutgers, The State U of New Jersey, Newark (NJ)

OCCUPATIONAL THERAPY
Alabama State U (AL)
American Intl Coll (MA)
Baker Coll (MI)
Bay Path U (MA)
Calvin Coll (MI)
Coll of Saint Benedict (MN)
Concordia U Wisconsin (WI)
Dalhousie U (NS, Canada)
Dominican Coll (NY)
Dominican U of California (CA)
Duquesne U (PA)
Eastern Kentucky U (KY)
Eastern Michigan U (MI)
Elizabethtown Coll (PA)
Elmhurst Coll (IL)
Gannon U (PA)
Grand Valley State U (MI)
Hawai`i Pacific U (HI)
Howard U (DC)
Illinois Coll (IL)
Ithaca Coll (NY)
Keuka Coll (NY)
Long Island U–LIU Brooklyn (NY)
McKendree U (IL)
Mount Mary U (WI)
Nazareth Coll of Rochester (NY)
Penn State Mont Alto (PA)
Quinnipiac U (CT)
Sacred Heart U (CT)
Saginaw Valley State U (MI)
St. Catherine U (MN)
Saint Francis U (PA)
Saint John's U (MN)
Saint Louis U (MO)
Saint Vincent Coll (PA)
San Jose State U (CA)
Shawnee State U (OH)
Spalding U (KY)
Towson U (MD)
Université de Montréal (QC, Canada)
U at Buffalo, the State U of New York (NY)
The U of Findlay (OH)
The U of Kansas (KS)
U of Minnesota, Twin Cities Campus (MN)
U of Missouri (MO)
U of New England (ME)
U of New Hampshire (NH)
U of Ottawa (ON, Canada)
The U of Scranton (PA)
U of Southern California (CA)
U of Southern Indiana (IN)
U of the Sciences (PA)
U of Utah (UT)
U of Wisconsin–Milwaukee (WI)
Wartburg Coll (IA)
Western Michigan U (MI)
Worcester State U (MA)
Xavier U (OH)
York Coll of the City U of New York (NY)

OCEAN ENGINEERING
California State U, Long Beach (CA)
Florida Atlantic U (FL)
Florida Inst of Technology (FL)
Northwestern Michigan Coll (MI)
Texas A&M U (TX)
United States Naval Acad (MD)
U of Rhode Island (RI)
Virginia Polytechnic Inst and State U (VA)

OCEANOGRAPHY (CHEMICAL AND PHYSICAL)
Coll of the Atlantic (ME)
Dalhousie U (NS, Canada)
Florida Inst of Technology (FL)
Hawai`i Pacific U (HI)
Humboldt State U (CA)
Kutztown U of Pennsylvania (PA)
Louisiana State U and A&M Coll (LA)
Maine Maritime Acad (ME)
Millersville U of Pennsylvania (PA)
North Carolina State U (NC)
Rider U (NJ)
United States Coast Guard Acad (CT)
United States Naval Acad (MD)
The U of British Columbia (BC, Canada)
U of Miami (FL)
U of Michigan (MI)
The U of North Carolina Wilmington (NC)
U of Southern Mississippi (MS)
U of Washington (WA)
U of West Florida (FL)

OFFICE MANAGEMENT
Adams State U (CO)
Babson Coll (MA)
Ball State U (IN)
Bowling Green State U (OH)
Clayton State U (GA)
East Central U (OK)
Eastern Kentucky U (KY)
Eastern Michigan U (MI)
Indiana State U (IN)
Inter American U of Puerto Rico, Aguadilla Campus (PR)
Inter American U of Puerto Rico, Fajardo Campus (PR)
Inter American U of Puerto Rico, Guayama Campus (PR)
Inter American U of Puerto Rico, Ponce Campus (PR)
Inter American U of Puerto Rico, San Germán Campus (PR)
Loyola U Chicago (IL)
Maranatha Baptist U (WI)
Middle Tennessee State U (TN)
Mississippi Valley State U (MS)
Morrisville State Coll (NY)
National U (CA)
Rider U (NJ)
Roosevelt U (IL)
Southwest Baptist U (MO)
Tarleton State U (TX)
Universidad del Turabo (PR)
Universidad Metropolitana (PR)
U of Central Missouri (MO)
U of Southern Indiana (IN)
U of the District of Columbia (DC)
The U of Toledo (OH)
Valley City State U (ND)

OPERATIONS MANAGEMENT
Arizona State U at the Polytechnic campus (AZ)
Auburn U (AL)
Avila U (MO)
Babson Coll (MA)
Ball State U (IN)
Boston Coll (MA)
Bowling Green State U (OH)
California State U, Dominguez Hills (CA)
California State U, Long Beach (CA)
California State U, Stanislaus (CA)
Capitol Technology U (MD)
Central Michigan U (MI)
Cleveland State U (OH)
Concordia U (QC, Canada)
Drexel U (PA)
Edinboro U of Pennsylvania (PA)
Excelsior Coll (NY)
Ferris State U (MI)
Fort Lewis Coll (CO)
Franklin U (OH)
Goodwin Coll (CT)
Governors State U (IL)
Granite State Coll (NH)
Indiana U–Purdue U Fort Wayne (IN)
Indiana U–Purdue U Indianapolis (IN)
Inter American U of Puerto Rico, Bayamón Campus (PR)
Inter American U of Puerto Rico, Ponce Campus (PR)
Iowa State U of Science and Technology (IA)
Lamar U (TX)
Le Moyne Coll (NY)
LeTourneau U (TX)
Loyola U Chicago (IL)
Marian U (WI)
Metropolitan State U (MN)
Miami U (OH)
Minnesota State U Moorhead (MN)
Northeastern State U (OK)
Northern Illinois U (IL)
Oakland U (MI)
The Ohio State U (OH)
Oregon State U (OR)
Rhode Island Coll (RI)
Roger Williams U (RI)
Saginaw Valley State U (MI)
San Diego State U (CA)
South Dakota State U (SD)
Southern New Hampshire U (NH)
Texas Southern U (TX)
Trine U (IN)
The U of Akron (OH)
U of Alberta (AB, Canada)
The U of Arizona (AZ)
U of Central Oklahoma (OK)
U of Cincinnati (OH)
U of Dayton (OH)
U of Delaware (DE)
U of Houston (TX)
U of Indianapolis (IN)
U of Massachusetts Amherst (MA)
U of Massachusetts Dartmouth (MA)
U of Minnesota, Crookston (MN)
U of Minnesota, Twin Cities Campus (MN)
U of Nebraska at Kearney (NE)
U of North Carolina at Asheville (NC)
The U of North Carolina at Charlotte (NC)
U of North Dakota (ND)
U of North Texas (TX)
U of Pennsylvania (PA)
U of St. Thomas (MN)
U of Saskatchewan (SK, Canada)
The U of Scranton (PA)
U of Southern Indiana (IN)
The U of Toledo (OH)
U of Utah (UT)
U of Wisconsin–Madison (WI)
U of Wisconsin–Milwaukee (WI)
U of Wisconsin–Stout (WI)
U of Wisconsin–Whitewater (WI)
Utah State U (UT)
Utah Valley U (UT)
Washington State U (WA)
Washington U in St. Louis (MO)
Wentworth Inst of Technology (MA)
Western Washington U (WA)
Widener U (PA)
Youngstown State U (OH)

OPERATIONS RESEARCH
Babson Coll (MA)
Bowling Green State U (OH)
California State U, Fullerton (CA)
Canisius Coll (NY)
Columbia U (NY)
Cornell U (NY)
HEC Montreal (QC, Canada)
Long Island U–LIU Brooklyn (NY)
Milwaukee School of Eng (WI)
New York U (NY)
Princeton U (NJ)
Southern Methodist U (TX)
United States Air Force Acad (CO)
United States Coast Guard Acad (CT)
United States Military Acad (NY)
United States Naval Acad (MD)
Université de Montréal (QC, Canada)
U of California, Berkeley (CA)
U of Toronto (ON, Canada)
U of Washington (WA)
U of Waterloo (ON, Canada)

OPHTHALMIC AND OPTOMETRIC SUPPORT SERVICES AND ALLIED PROFESSIONS RELATED
Tennessee Wesleyan Coll (TN)

OPHTHALMIC LABORATORY TECHNOLOGY
Abilene Christian U (TX)
U of Ottawa (ON, Canada)

OPTICAL SCIENCES
The Ohio State U (OH)
Saginaw Valley State U (MI)
The U of Arizona (AZ)
U of Rochester (NY)
Western Washington U (WA)

ORGANIC CHEMISTRY
Concordia U (QC, Canada)
U of California, Santa Barbara (CA)
The U of Western Ontario (ON, Canada)

ORGANIZATIONAL BEHAVIOR
Anderson U (SC)
Benedictine U (IL)
Bluffton U (OH)
Bowling Green State U (OH)
Brown U (RI)
Claflin U (SC)
Coe Coll (IA)
The Coll of St. Scholastica (MN)
Denison U (OH)
DePaul U (IL)
Edgewood Coll (WI)
Goodwin Coll (CT)
Greenville Coll (IL)
Indian River State Coll (FL)
John Brown U (AR)
Lewis U (IL)
Manhattan Coll (NY)
Mount St. Joseph U (OH)
National U (CA)
Northern Kentucky U (KY)
Northwestern U (IL)
Nyack Coll (NY)
Oakland City U (IN)
Palm Beach Atlantic U (FL)
Penn State Abington (PA)
Penn State Altoona (PA)
Penn State Beaver (PA)
Penn State Berks (PA)
Penn State Brandywine (PA)
Penn State DuBois (PA)
Penn State Erie, The Behrend Coll (PA)
Penn State Fayette, The Eberly Campus (PA)
Penn State Greater Allegheny (PA)
Penn State Harrisburg (PA)
Penn State Hazleton (PA)
Penn State Lehigh Valley (PA)
Penn State Mont Alto (PA)
Penn State New Kensington (PA)
Penn State Schuylkill (PA)
Penn State Shenango (PA)
Penn State U Park (PA)
Penn State Wilkes-Barre (PA)
Penn State Worthington Scranton (PA)
Penn State York (PA)
Philander Smith Coll (AR)
Rider U (NJ)
Robert Morris U (PA)
Roosevelt U (IL)
Saint Joseph's U (PA)
Saint Louis U (MO)
Santa Clara U (CA)
Scripps Coll (CA)
Simpson U (CA)
Union Coll (NE)
United States Military Acad (NY)
U of Alberta (AB, Canada)
U of Cincinnati (OH)
U of Michigan (MI)
U of North Texas (TX)
U of Oklahoma (OK)
U of Richmond (VA)
U of St. Francis (IL)
U of San Francisco (CA)
U of the Incarnate Word (TX)
The U of Toledo (OH)
The U of Tulsa (OK)
U of Valley Forge (PA)
The U of Western Ontario (ON, Canada)
Waldorf Coll (IA)
Wayne State U (MI)
Wilmington U (DE)

ORGANIZATIONAL COMMUNICATION
Albion Coll (MI)
Aquinas Coll (MI)
Assumption Coll (MA)
Bloomsburg U of Pennsylvania (PA)
Bradley U (IL)
Brigham Young U (UT)
Buena Vista U (IA)
Butler U (IN)
Calvin Coll (MI)
Capital U (OH)
Cedarville U (OH)
Cleveland State U (OH)
Concordia U, Nebraska (NE)
Dixie State U (UT)
Emmanuel Coll (GA)
Fairleigh Dickinson U, Metropolitan Campus (NJ)
Florida Coll (FL)
Florida Southern Coll (FL)
Franklin U (OH)
Howard Payne U (TX)
Indiana U–Purdue U Fort Wayne (IN)
Judson U (IL)
Lewis U (IL)
Lindenwood U (MO)
Lubbock Christian U (TX)
Marian U (WI)
Marylhurst U (OR)
McKendree U (IL)
Missouri State U (MO)
Montana State U Billings (MT)
Murray State U (KY)
North Central Coll (IL)
Northwest Missouri State U (MO)
Northwest U (WA)
Ohio Northern U (OH)
Pace U (NY)
Pepperdine U, Malibu (CA)
Providence Coll (RI)
Roosevelt U (IL)
St. Francis Coll (NY)
Southeastern U (FL)
Southeast Missouri State U (MO)
Southern New Hampshire U (NH)
Suffolk U (MA)
Temple U (PA)
Trevecca Nazarene U (TN)
The U of Akron (OH)
U of Idaho (ID)
U of Mount Union (OH)
U of Northern Iowa (IA)
Viterbo U (WI)
Washington State U (WA)
Weber State U (UT)
Western Kentucky U (KY)
Western Michigan U (MI)
Wheeling Jesuit U (WV)

ORGANIZATIONAL LEADERSHIP
Anderson U (IN)
Auburn U at Montgomery (AL)
Avila U (MO)
Belhaven U (MS)
Beulah Heights U (GA)
Brenau U (GA)
Cabrini Coll (PA)
California Baptist U (CA)
Calvary Bible Coll and Theological Sem (MO)
Cardinal Stritch U (WI)
Central Penn Coll (PA)
Central Washington U (WA)
Cleveland State U (OH)
Coll of Biblical Studies–Houston (TX)
Columbia Southern U (AL)
Creighton U (NE)
Eastern U (PA)
Eureka Coll (IL)
Florida Inst of Technology (FL)
Gannon U (PA)
Kansas Wesleyan U (KS)
Keystone Coll (PA)
Lincoln Christian U (IL)
Lubbock Christian U (TX)
Marquette U (WI)
McNeese State U (LA)
Mercy Coll (NY)
Mid-Atlantic Christian U (NC)
National U (CA)
Neumann U (PA)
North Carolina Wesleyan Coll (NC)
Northeastern State U (OK)
Point U (GA)
Providence Coll (RI)
Purdue U (IN)

Regent U (VA)
Saint Louis U (MO)
St. Thomas U (FL)
Salve Regina U (RI)
Samford U (AL)
Southeastern Louisiana U (LA)
Spring Hill Coll (AL)
Syracuse U (NY)
Toccoa Falls Coll (GA)
Union Inst & U (OH)
U of Central Oklahoma (OK)
U of Dayton (OH)
U of Evansville (IN)
U of Houston (TX)
U of Louisiana at Lafayette (LA)
U of New Orleans (LA)
U of Wisconsin–Eau Claire (WI)
Valdosta State U (GA)
Viterbo U (WI)
Western Kentucky U (KY)
Wheeling Jesuit U (WV)

ORNAMENTAL HORTICULTURE
California State U, Fresno (CA)
Cornell U (NY)
Eastern Kentucky U (KY)
Iowa State U of Science and Technology (IA)
Morrisville State Coll (NY)
The Ohio State U (OH)
Tarleton State U (TX)
Texas A&M U (TX)
U of Arkansas (AR)
U of the District of Columbia (DC)
U of Wisconsin–Platteville (WI)

ORTHOPTICS
St. Catherine U (MN)

ORTHOTICS/PROSTHETICS
Concordia U, St. Paul (MN)
U of Washington (WA)

OUTDOOR EDUCATION
Lubbock Christian U (TX)
Murray State U (KY)
Northland Coll (WI)
Prescott Coll (AZ)
Shenandoah U (VA)
Toccoa Falls Coll (GA)
Unity Coll (ME)

PACIFIC AREA/PACIFIC RIM STUDIES
Central Washington U (WA)
Hawai`i Pacific U (HI)
U of Guam (GU)
U of Hawaii at Manoa (HI)
U of Hawaii–West Oahu (HI)

PACKAGING SCIENCE
Indiana State U (IN)
Michigan State U (MI)
U of Wisconsin–Stout (WI)

PAINTING
Adams State U (CO)
American Acad of Art (IL)
Aquinas Coll (MI)
Arcadia U (PA)
Bennington Coll (VT)
Biola U (CA)
Birmingham-Southern Coll (AL)
Boston U (MA)
Bowling Green State U (OH)
Bradley U (IL)
Brigham Young U (UT)
Buffalo State Coll, State U of New York (NY)
California Coll of the Arts (CA)
California State U, Long Beach (CA)
Central Washington U (WA)
Cleveland Inst of Art (OH)
Coe Coll (IA)
Coll of the Ozarks (MO)
Colorado State U (CO)
Columbia Coll (MO)
Concordia U (QC, Canada)
Dixie State U (UT)
Drake U (IA)
Emily Carr U of Art + Design (BC, Canada)
Escuela de Artes Plasticas de Puerto Rico (PR)
Ferris State U (MI)
Harding U (AR)
Hofstra U (NY)
Indiana U–Purdue U Fort Wayne (IN)
Inter American U of Puerto Rico, San Germán Campus (PR)
Kansas City Art Inst (MO)
Kansas Wesleyan U (KS)
Kent State U (OH)
Laguna Coll of Art & Design (CA)
Lewis U (IL)
Marywood U (PA)
Massachusetts Coll of Art and Design (MA)
Northern Michigan U (MI)
Northwest Nazarene U (ID)
Oakland U (MI)
Ohio Northern U (OH)
Pacific Northwest Coll of Art (OR)
Pratt Inst (NY)
Providence Coll (RI)
Rhode Island Coll (RI)
Rhode Island School of Design (RI)
Rochester Inst of Technology (NY)
Rutgers, The State U of New Jersey, New Brunswick (NJ)
Salve Regina U (RI)
San Francisco Art Inst (CA)
Savannah Coll of Art and Design (GA)
School of the Art Inst of Chicago (IL)
School of the Museum of Fine Arts, Boston (MA)
Seton Hill U (PA)
State U of New York at New Paltz (NY)
Syracuse U (NY)
Tabor Coll (KS)
Temple U (PA)
Texas Christian U (TX)
U of Dallas (TX)
U of Hartford (CT)
U of Houston (TX)
U of Illinois at Chicago (IL)
The U of Iowa (IA)
The U of Kansas (KS)
U of Massachusetts Dartmouth (MA)
U of Miami (FL)
U of New Haven (CT)
U of Oregon (OR)
U of Regina (SK, Canada)
U of San Francisco (CA)
The U of the Arts (PA)
U of Washington (WA)
U of Windsor (ON, Canada)
Virginia Commonwealth U (VA)
Washington U in St. Louis (MO)
Western State Colorado U (CO)
Western Washington U (WA)
West Virginia Wesleyan Coll (WV)
Youngstown State U (OH)

PALEONTOLOGY
Bowling Green State U (OH)
U of Alberta (AB, Canada)

PALLIATIVE CARE NURSING
Madonna U (MI)

PAPER SCIENCE AND ENGINEERING
U of Wisconsin–Stevens Point (WI)
Western Michigan U (MI)

PARASITOLOGY
Bowling Green State U (OH)

PARKS, RECREATION AND LEISURE
Alabama State U (AL)
Alaska Pacific U (AK)
Alcorn State U (MS)
Arizona State U at the Downtown Phoenix campus (AZ)
Bemidji State U (MN)
Bethune-Cookman U (FL)
Biola U (CA)
Black Hills State U (SD)
Bowling Green State U (OH)
Brevard Coll (NC)
Bridgewater State U (MA)
California Polytechnic State U, San Luis Obispo (CA)
California State U, Chico (CA)
California State U, Fresno (CA)
California State U, Long Beach (CA)
California State U, Sacramento (CA)
Campbellsville U (KY)
Carson-Newman U (TN)
Catawba Coll (NC)
Central Michigan U (MI)
Central State U (OH)
Concordia U (QC, Canada)
Cumberland U (TN)
Dalhousie U (NS, Canada)
East Carolina U (NC)
East Central U (OK)
Elon U (NC)
Emporia State U (KS)
Evangel U (MO)
Ferrum Coll (VA)
Fort Lewis Coll (CO)
Frostburg State U (MD)
Georgia Coll & State U (GA)
Georgia Southern U (GA)
Gordon Coll (MA)
Graceland U (IA)
Grambling State U (LA)
Green Mountain Coll (VT)
Houghton Coll (NY)
Humboldt State U (CA)
Indiana U Bloomington (IN)
Ithaca Coll (NY)
Jacksonville State U (AL)
Johnson State Coll (VT)
Kutztown U of Pennsylvania (PA)
Limestone Coll (SC)
Lindenwood U (MO)
Lindsey Wilson Coll (KY)
Lock Haven U of Pennsylvania (PA)
Manchester U (IN)
Mars Hill U (NC)
Maryville Coll (TN)
Messiah Coll (PA)
Michigan State U (MI)
Minnesota State U Mankato (MN)
Missouri State U (MO)
Missouri Valley Coll (MO)
Montreat Coll, Montreat (NC)
Morris Coll (SC)
Newberry Coll (SC)
New England Coll (NH)
New Mexico Highlands U (NM)
Northern Arizona U (AZ)
Northern Michigan U (MI)
North Greenville U (SC)
Northwest Nazarene U (ID)
The Ohio State U (OH)
Ohio U (OH)
Oklahoma Baptist U (OK)
Oklahoma State U (OK)
Oregon State U (OR)
Pittsburg State U (KS)
Radford U (VA)
Rhode Island Coll (RI)
St. Andrews U (NC)
St. Thomas Aquinas Coll (NY)
San Diego State U (CA)
San Francisco State U (CA)
San Jose State U (CA)
Shaw U (NC)
Shepherd U (WV)
Simpson U (CA)
Southeastern Oklahoma State U (OK)
Southeast Missouri State U (MO)
Southern Connecticut State U (CT)
Southern Illinois U Carbondale (IL)
Southern Utah U (UT)
Southwest Baptist U (MO)
State U of New York Coll at Cortland (NY)
State U of New York Coll of Environmental Science and Forestry (NY)
Sterling Coll (VT)
Tennessee State U (TN)
Texas A&M U (TX)
U of Arkansas (AR)
U of Arkansas at Pine Bluff (AR)
U of Central Missouri (MO)
U of Central Oklahoma (OK)
U of Dubuque (IA)
The U of Iowa (IA)
U of Maine at Machias (ME)
U of Maine at Presque Isle (ME)
U of Minnesota, Duluth (MN)
U of Minnesota, Twin Cities Campus (MN)
U of Missouri (MO)
The U of Montana (MT)
U of Nebraska at Kearney (NE)
U of Nevada, Las Vegas (NV)
The U of North Carolina at Greensboro (NC)
U of Northern Iowa (IA)
U of Ottawa (ON, Canada)
U of South Alabama (AL)
The U of South Dakota (SD)
U of Southern Mississippi (MS)
The U of Toledo (OH)
U of Utah (UT)
U of Waterloo (ON, Canada)
Upper Iowa U (IA)
Utah State U (UT)
Virginia Commonwealth U (VA)
Virginia Wesleyan Coll (VA)
Western Michigan U (MI)
Western State Colorado U (CO)
Western Washington U (WA)
William Jewell Coll (MO)
William Penn U (IA)
Wingate U (NC)
York Coll of Pennsylvania (PA)

PARKS, RECREATION AND LEISURE FACILITIES MANAGEMENT
Appalachian State U (NC)
Arkansas Tech U (AR)
Asbury U (KY)
Belmont Abbey Coll (NC)
Bethany Coll (WV)
California State U, Fresno (CA)
California State U, Sacramento (CA)
California U of Pennsylvania (PA)
Central Michigan U (MI)
Central Washington U (WA)
Cheyney U of Pennsylvania (PA)
Chicago State U (IL)
The Coll at Brockport, State U of New York (NY)
Coll of the Ozarks (MO)
Colorado State U (CO)
Concord U (WV)
Delaware State U (DE)
Eastern Illinois U (IL)
Eastern Kentucky U (KY)
Eastern Michigan U (MI)
East Stroudsburg U of Pennsylvania (PA)
Ferris State U (MI)
Florida Intl U (FL)
Franklin Pierce U (NH)
Hannibal-LaGrange U (MO)
Hastings Coll (NE)
Humboldt State U (CA)
Husson U (ME)
Illinois State U (IL)
Indiana State U (IN)
John Brown U (AR)
Johnson & Wales U (CO)
Johnson & Wales U (FL)
Johnson & Wales U (RI)
Johnson & Wales U - Charlotte Campus (NC)
Kansas State U (KS)
Kean U (NJ)
Kent State U (OH)
Marshall U (WV)
Middle Tennessee State U (TN)
Minnesota State U Mankato (MN)
Missouri Valley Coll (MO)
Missouri Western State U (MO)
Mount Marty Coll (SD)
New England Coll (NH)
New Mexico Highlands U (NM)
New York U (NY)
North Carolina Ag and Tech State U (NC)
North Carolina Central U (NC)
North Carolina State U (NC)
Northwest Missouri State U (MO)
Old Dominion U (VA)
Penn State Abington (PA)
Penn State Altoona (PA)
Penn State Beaver (PA)
Penn State Berks (PA)
Penn State Brandywine (PA)
Penn State DuBois (PA)
Penn State Erie, The Behrend Coll (PA)
Penn State Fayette, The Eberly Campus (PA)
Penn State Greater Allegheny (PA)
Penn State Hazleton (PA)
Penn State Lehigh Valley (PA)
Penn State Mont Alto (PA)
Penn State New Kensington (PA)
Penn State Schuylkill (PA)
Penn State Shenango (PA)
Penn State U Park (PA)
Penn State Wilkes-Barre (PA)
Penn State Worthington Scranton (PA)
Penn State York (PA)
St. Joseph's Coll, Long Island Campus (NY)
St. Joseph's Coll, New York (NY)
Slippery Rock U of Pennsylvania (PA)
South Dakota State U (SD)
State U of New York Coll at Cortland (NY)
Texas A&M U (TX)
Texas State U (TX)
Trine U (IN)
Union Coll (KY)
Union U (TN)
The U of British Columbia (BC, Canada)
U of Delaware (DE)
U of Florida (FL)
U of Idaho (ID)
The U of Iowa (IA)
U of Maine (ME)
U of Maine at Machias (ME)
U of Minnesota, Crookston (MN)
U of Minnesota, Twin Cities Campus (MN)
U of Mississippi (MS)
U of New Hampshire (NH)
The U of North Carolina Wilmington (NC)
U of North Dakota (ND)
U of Northern Colorado (CO)
U of North Texas (TX)
U of St. Francis (IL)
U of Vermont (VT)
U of Waterloo (ON, Canada)
U of West Georgia (GA)
U of Wisconsin–La Crosse (WI)
Webber Intl U (FL)
Western Carolina U (NC)
Western Illinois U (IL)
Western Kentucky U (KY)
Western State Colorado U (CO)
West Virginia State U (WV)
West Virginia U (WV)
Winona State U (MN)

PARKS, RECREATION, LEISURE, AND FITNESS STUDIES RELATED
Belhaven U (MS)
Brigham Young U (UT)
Coker Coll (SC)
New England Coll (NH)
Plymouth State U (NH)
Trinity Christian Coll (IL)
U of North Alabama (AL)
U of Waterloo (ON, Canada)
Utah State U (UT)
Western State Colorado U (CO)

PASTORAL COUNSELING AND SPECIALIZED MINISTRIES RELATED
Bethel Coll (IN)
Calvary Bible Coll and Theological Sem (MO)
Coll of Biblical Studies–Houston (TX)
Davis Coll (NY)
John Brown U (AR)
Judson U (IL)
Lee U (TN)
Lipscomb U (TN)
Madonna U (MI)
Malone U (OH)
Maranatha Baptist U (WI)
Multnomah U (OR)
Nazarene Bible Coll (CO)
Oklahoma Wesleyan U (OK)
U of Northwestern–St. Paul (MN)

PASTORAL STUDIES/ COUNSELING
Anna Maria Coll (MA)
The Baptist Coll of Florida (FL)
Barclay Coll (KS)
Bethel Coll (IN)
Biola U (CA)
California Baptist U (CA)
Calvary Bible Coll and Theological Sem (MO)
Campbellsville U (KY)

Clearwater Christian Coll (FL)
Coll of Biblical Studies–Houston (TX)
Columbia Bible Coll (BC, Canada)
Concordia U, Nebraska (NE)
Concordia U Wisconsin (WI)
Corban U (OR)
Davis Coll (NY)
Dominican U (IL)
East Texas Baptist U (TX)
Emmanuel Coll (GA)
Faith Baptist Bible Coll and Theological Sem (IA)
Greenville Coll (IL)
Hillsdale Free Will Baptist Coll (OK)
Houghton Coll (NY)
John Brown U (AR)
Kentucky Christian U (KY)
Kentucky Mountain Bible Coll (KY)
Kuyper Coll (MI)
Laurel U (NC)
Lee U (TN)
Liberty U (VA)
Lincoln Christian U (IL)
Lindenwood U (MO)
Loyola U Chicago (IL)
Manhattan Christian Coll (KS)
Maranatha Baptist U (WI)
Marian U (IN)
The Master's Coll and Sem (CA)
Milligan Coll (TN)
Mount Vernon Nazarene U (OH)
Multnomah U (OR)
Nebraska Christian Coll (NE)
Newman U (KS)
Northwest Christian U (OR)
Northwest Nazarene U (ID)
Northwest U (WA)
Olivet Nazarene U (IL)
Rocky Mountain Coll (AB, Canada)
Saint Francis U (PA)
St. Gregory's U, Shawnee (OK)
Saint Joseph's Coll (IN)
St. Thomas U (FL)
San Diego Christian Coll (CA)
Shiloh U (IA)
Simpson U (CA)
Southwest Baptist U (MO)
Southwestern Assemblies of God U (TX)
Summit U (PA)
Trinity Coll of Florida (FL)
Universidad Teolgica del Caribe (PR)
U of Mary Hardin-Baylor (TX)
U of Saint Mary (KS)
U of St. Thomas (TX)
U of Valley Forge (PA)
Vanguard U of Southern California (CA)
Walsh U (OH)
Warner Pacific Coll (OR)
Welch Coll (TN)
William Jessup U (CA)
Williams Baptist Coll (AR)

PATHOLOGIST ASSISTANT
Wayne State U (MI)

PATHOLOGY/EXPERIMENTAL PATHOLOGY
Penn State Berks (PA)
The U of North Carolina at Chapel Hill (NC)
The U of Western Ontario (ON, Canada)

PEACE STUDIES AND CONFLICT RESOLUTION
Bennington Coll (VT)
Bethel U (MN)
Butler U (IN)
California State U, Dominguez Hills (CA)
Chapman U (CA)
Clark U (MA)
Coll of Saint Benedict (MN)
The Coll of St. Scholastica (MN)
Creighton U (NE)
DePaul U (IL)
DePauw U (IN)
Earlham Coll (IN)
George Mason U (VA)
Gettysburg Coll (PA)
Goddard Coll (VT)
Goshen Coll (IN)
Goucher Coll (MD)
Guilford Coll (NC)
Hamline U (MN)
Hampshire Coll (MA)
Haverford Coll (PA)
John Carroll U (OH)
Juniata Coll (PA)
Kent State U (OH)
Manchester U (IN)
Manhattan Coll (NY)
Marquette U (WI)
Messiah Coll (PA)
Naropa U (CO)
Nazareth Coll of Rochester (NY)
Norwich U (VT)
Ohio Dominican U (OH)
Regis U (CO)
Saint Anselm Coll (NH)
Saint John's U (MN)
Salisbury U (MD)
Tufts U (MA)
U of California, Berkeley (CA)
U of Massachusetts Lowell (MA)
U of Missouri (MO)
The U of North Carolina at Chapel Hill (NC)
The U of North Carolina at Greensboro (NC)
U of Ottawa (ON, Canada)
U of St. Thomas (MN)
U of Toronto (ON, Canada)
U of Utah (UT)
The U of Western Ontario (ON, Canada)
U of Wisconsin–Superior (WI)
Ursinus Coll (PA)
Wartburg Coll (IA)
Whitworth U (WA)

PEDIATRIC NURSING
Youngstown State U (OH)

PERCUSSION INSTRUMENTS
Central Washington U (WA)
The Colburn School Conservatory of Music (CA)
Houghton Coll (NY)
Lawrence U (WI)
Manhattan School of Music (NY)
Maryville Coll (TN)
Mount Allison U (NB, Canada)
New England Conservatory of Music (MA)
Northwestern U (IL)
Oberlin Coll (OH)
Oklahoma Christian U (OK)
Peabody Conservatory of The Johns Hopkins U (MD)
Peru State Coll (NE)
San Francisco Conservatory of Music (CA)
State U of New York at Fredonia (NY)
Syracuse U (NY)
U of Central Oklahoma (OK)
The U of Iowa (IA)
The U of Kansas (KS)
U of Southern California (CA)
U of Washington (WA)
Vanderbilt U (TN)
Xavier U of Louisiana (LA)
Youngstown State U (OH)

PERFUSION TECHNOLOGY
Carlow U (PA)

PERSONALITY PSYCHOLOGY
Goddard Coll (VT)
Pace U (NY)

PETROLEUM ENGINEERING
The American U in Cairo (Egypt)
Colorado School of Mines (CO)
Lebanese American U (Lebanon)
Louisiana State U and A&M Coll (LA)
Marietta Coll (OH)
Missouri U of Science and Technology (MO)
Montana Tech of The U of Montana (MT)
New Mexico Inst of Mining and Technology (NM)
Penn State Abington (PA)
Penn State Altoona (PA)
Penn State Beaver (PA)
Penn State Berks (PA)
Penn State Brandywine (PA)
Penn State DuBois (PA)
Penn State Erie, The Behrend Coll (PA)
Penn State Fayette, The Eberly Campus (PA)
Penn State Greater Allegheny (PA)
Penn State Hazleton (PA)
Penn State Lehigh Valley (PA)
Penn State Mont Alto (PA)
Penn State New Kensington (PA)
Penn State Schuylkill (PA)
Penn State Shenango (PA)
Penn State U Park (PA)
Penn State Wilkes-Barre (PA)
Penn State Worthington Scranton (PA)
Penn State York (PA)
Saint Francis U (PA)
Stanford U (CA)
Texas A&M U (TX)
Texas A&M U–Kingsville (TX)
Texas Tech U (TX)
U of Alaska Fairbanks (AK)
U of Houston (TX)
The U of Kansas (KS)
U of Louisiana at Lafayette (LA)
U of North Dakota (ND)
U of Oklahoma (OK)
U of Regina (SK, Canada)
The U of Texas at Austin (TX)
The U of Texas of the Permian Basin (TX)
U of Toronto (ON, Canada)
The U of Tulsa (OK)
U of Wyoming (WY)
West Virginia U (WV)

PETROLEUM TECHNOLOGY
American U of Beirut (Lebanon)
Cape Breton U (NS, Canada)
Nicholls State U (LA)

PHARMACEUTICAL MARKETING AND MANAGEMENT
DeSales U (PA)
The U of Toledo (OH)
Western New England U (MA)

PHARMACEUTICAL SCIENCES
Albany Coll of Pharmacy and Health Sciences (NY)
Belmont U (TN)
Cedarville U (OH)
Cleveland State U (OH)
Duquesne U (PA)
U at Buffalo, the State U of New York (NY)
U of California, Irvine (CA)
U of Georgia (GA)
U of Houston (TX)
U of Michigan (MI)
U of Pittsburgh (PA)
West Virginia Wesleyan Coll (WV)

PHARMACEUTICS AND DRUG DESIGN
The Ohio State U (OH)
Purdue U (IN)
The U of Montana (MT)
U of Rhode Island (RI)
The U of Toledo (OH)
West Chester U of Pennsylvania (PA)

PHARMACOLOGY
Georgia Southern U (GA)
Maryville Coll (TN)
Stony Brook U, State U of New York (NY)
U of Alberta (AB, Canada)
The U of British Columbia (BC, Canada)
U of California, Santa Barbara (CA)
U of Ottawa (ON, Canada)
U of Saskatchewan (SK, Canada)
The U of Western Ontario (ON, Canada)

PHARMACOLOGY AND TOXICOLOGY
U at Buffalo, the State U of New York (NY)
U of the Sciences (PA)
U of Wisconsin–Madison (WI)

PHARMACOLOGY AND TOXICOLOGY RELATED
The George Washington U (DC)
MCPHS U (MA)

PHARMACY
Butler U (IN)
The Coll of Idaho (ID)
Dalhousie U (NS, Canada)
Drake U (IA)
Howard U (DC)
Illinois Inst of Technology (IL)
Lebanese American U (Lebanon)
Long Island U–LIU Brooklyn (NY)
Manchester U (IN)
MCPHS U (MA)
Northeastern U (MA)
The Ohio State U (OH)
Presbyterian Coll (SC)
St. John's U (NY)
St. Louis Coll of Pharmacy (MO)
Saint Vincent Coll (PA)
Samford U (AL)
South Dakota State U (SD)
Université de Montréal (QC, Canada)
U of Alberta (AB, Canada)
The U of British Columbia (BC, Canada)
U of Delaware (DE)
The U of Iowa (IA)
The U of Kansas (KS)
U of Kentucky (KY)
U of Minnesota, Twin Cities Campus (MN)
The U of Montana (MT)
U of Oklahoma Health Sciences Center (OK)
U of Saskatchewan (SK, Canada)
U of the Pacific (CA)
U of the Sciences (PA)
The U of Toledo (OH)
U of Toronto (ON, Canada)
U of Utah (UT)

PHARMACY ADMINISTRATION AND PHARMACY POLICY AND REGULATORY AFFAIRS
Drake U (IA)
U of Michigan (MI)

PHARMACY, PHARMACEUTICAL SCIENCES, AND ADMINISTRATION RELATED
Albany Coll of Pharmacy and Health Sciences (NY)
Dalhousie U (NS, Canada)
Duquesne U (PA)
Francis Marion U (SC)
MCPHS U (MA)
North Dakota State U (ND)
Ohio Northern U (OH)
U of Alberta (AB, Canada)
U of Mississippi (MS)
The U of North Carolina at Chapel Hill (NC)
U of the Sciences (PA)
The U of Toledo (OH)

PHARMACY TECHNICIAN
The U of Montana (MT)

PHILOSOPHY
Adelphi U (NY)
Agnes Scott Coll (GA)
Albertus Magnus Coll (CT)
Albion Coll (MI)
Albright Coll (PA)
Allegheny Coll (PA)
Alma Coll (MI)
Alvernia U (PA)
Alverno Coll (WI)
American Public U System (WV)
American U (DC)
The American U in Cairo (Egypt)
American U of Beirut (Lebanon)
The American U of Paris (France)
Amherst Coll (MA)
Angelo State U (TX)
Anna Maria Coll (MA)
Antioch Coll, Yellow Springs (OH)
Appalachian State U (NC)
Aquinas Coll (MI)
Aquinas Coll (TN)
Arcadia U (PA)
Arizona State U at the Tempe campus (AZ)
Arkansas State U (AR)
Asbury U (KY)
Ashland U (OH)
Assumption Coll (MA)
Auburn U (AL)
Augsburg Coll (MN)
Augustana Coll (IL)
Augustana Coll (SD)
Austin Coll (TX)
Austin Peay State U (TN)
Ave Maria U (FL)
Azusa Pacific U (CA)
Baker U (KS)
Baldwin Wallace U (OH)
Ball State U (IN)
Bard Coll (NY)
Bard Coll at Simon's Rock (MA)
Barnard Coll (NY)
Barry U (FL)
Baruch Coll of the City U of New York (NY)
Bates Coll (ME)
Baylor U (TX)
Belhaven U (MS)
Belmont U (TN)
Beloit Coll (WI)
Bemidji State U (MN)
Benedictine Coll (KS)
Benedictine U (IL)
Bennington Coll (VT)
Bentley U (MA)
Berea Coll (KY)
Bethel Coll (IN)
Bethel U (MN)
Binghamton U, State U of New York (NY)
Biola U (CA)
Birmingham-Southern Coll (AL)
Bloomfield Coll (NJ)
Bloomsburg U of Pennsylvania (PA)
Boston Coll (MA)
Boston U (MA)
Bowdoin Coll (ME)
Bowling Green State U (OH)
Bradley U (IL)
Brandeis U (MA)
Bridgewater State U (MA)
Brown U (RI)
Bryn Mawr Coll (PA)
Bucknell U (PA)
Buffalo State Coll, State U of New York (NY)
Butler U (IN)
Cabrini Coll (PA)
California Baptist U (CA)
California Inst of Technology (CA)
California Lutheran U (CA)
California Polytechnic State U, San Luis Obispo (CA)
California State Polytechnic U, Pomona (CA)
California State U, Chico (CA)
California State U, Dominguez Hills (CA)
California State U, Fresno (CA)
California State U, Fullerton (CA)
California State U, Long Beach (CA)
California State U, Los Angeles (CA)
California State U, Sacramento (CA)
California State U, San Bernardino (CA)
California State U, Stanislaus (CA)
California U of Pennsylvania (PA)
Calvin Coll (MI)
Canisius Coll (NY)
Cape Breton U (NS, Canada)
Capital U (OH)
Carleton Coll (MN)
Carlow U (PA)
Carroll Coll (MT)
Carson-Newman U (TN)
Case Western Reserve U (OH)
Castleton State Coll (VT)
The Catholic U of America (DC)
Centenary Coll of Louisiana (LA)
Central Coll (IA)
Central Connecticut State U (CT)
Central Methodist U (MO)
Central Michigan U (MI)
Centre Coll (KY)
Chapman U (CA)
Chowan U (NC)
Christendom Coll (VA)
Christopher Newport U (VA)
City Coll of the City U of New York (NY)
Claremont McKenna Coll (CA)
Clarion U of Pennsylvania (PA)
Clark Atlanta U (GA)

Clarke U (IA)
Clark U (MA)
Clayton State U (GA)
Cleveland State U (OH)
Coastal Carolina U (SC)
Coe Coll (IA)
Colby Coll (ME)
Colby-Sawyer Coll (NH)
The Coll at Brockport, State U of New York (NY)
Coll of Charleston (SC)
The Coll of Idaho (ID)
The Coll of New Jersey (NJ)
The Coll of New Rochelle (NY)
Coll of Saint Benedict (MN)
Coll of Saint Elizabeth (NJ)
The Coll of Saint Rose (NY)
The Coll of St. Scholastica (MN)
Coll of Staten Island of the City U of New York (NY)
Coll of the Atlantic (ME)
Coll of the Holy Cross (MA)
The Coll of William and Mary (VA)
The Coll of Wooster (OH)
The Colorado Coll (CO)
Colorado State U (CO)
Columbia Coll (MO)
Columbia U (NY)
Columbia U, School of General Studies (NY)
Conception Sem Coll (MO)
Concordia Coll (MN)
Concordia Coll–New York (NY)
Concordia U (QC, Canada)
Concordia U Chicago (IL)
Connecticut Coll (CT)
Cornell Coll (IA)
Cornell U (NY)
Covenant Coll (GA)
Creighton U (NE)
Curry Coll (MA)
Dalhousie U (NS, Canada)
Dallas Baptist U (TX)
Dartmouth Coll (NH)
Davidson Coll (NC)
Delaware State U (DE)
Denison U (OH)
DePaul U (IL)
DePauw U (IN)
DEREE - The American Coll of Greece (Greece)
DeSales U (PA)
Dickinson Coll (PA)
Doane Coll (NE)
Dominican U (IL)
Dowling Coll (NY)
Drake U (IA)
Drew U (NJ)
Drexel U (PA)
Drury U (MO)
Duquesne U (PA)
Earlham Coll (IN)
East Carolina U (NC)
Eastern Illinois U (IL)
Eastern Kentucky U (KY)
Eastern Michigan U (MI)
Eastern Oregon U (OR)
Eastern U (PA)
East Stroudsburg U of Pennsylvania (PA)
East Tennessee State U (TN)
Eckerd Coll (FL)
Elizabethtown Coll (PA)
Elmhurst Coll (IL)
Elon U (NC)
Emmanuel Coll (MA)
Emory & Henry Coll (VA)
Erskine Coll (SC)
The Evergreen State Coll (WA)
Fairfield U (CT)
Fairleigh Dickinson U, Coll at Florham (NJ)
Fairleigh Dickinson U, Metropolitan Campus (NJ)
Ferrum Coll (VA)
Florida Atlantic U (FL)
Florida Gulf Coast U (FL)
Florida Intl U (FL)
Florida Southern Coll (FL)
Florida State U (FL)
Fordham U (NY)
Fort Hays State U (KS)
Fort Lewis Coll (CO)
Franciscan U of Steubenville (OH)
Franklin & Marshall Coll (PA)
Franklin Coll (IN)
Frostburg State U (MD)
Furman U (SC)
Gallaudet U (DC)
Gannon U (PA)
Geneva Coll (PA)
George Mason U (VA)
Georgetown Coll (KY)
Georgetown U (DC)
The George Washington U (DC)
Georgia Coll & State U (GA)
Georgia Southern U (GA)
Georgia State U (GA)
Gettysburg Coll (PA)
Gonzaga U (WA)
Gordon Coll (MA)
Goucher Coll (MD)
Grand Valley State U (MI)
Green Mountain Coll (VT)
Greenville Coll (IL)
Grinnell Coll (IA)
Grove City Coll (PA)
Guilford Coll (NC)
Gustavus Adolphus Coll (MN)
Hamilton Coll (NY)
Hamline U (MN)
Hampden-Sydney Coll (VA)
Hampshire Coll (MA)
Hanover Coll (IN)
Hardin-Simmons U (TX)
Hartwick Coll (NY)
Harvard U (MA)
Hastings Coll (NE)
Haverford Coll (PA)
Heidelberg U (OH)
Hendrix Coll (AR)
High Point U (NC)
Hillsdale Coll (MI)
Hiram Coll (OH)
Hobart and William Smith Colls (NY)
Hofstra U (NY)
Hollins U (VA)
Hope Coll (MI)
Houghton Coll (NY)
Houston Baptist U (TX)
Howard Payne U (TX)
Howard U (DC)
Humboldt State U (CA)
Hunter Coll of the City U of New York (NY)
Illinois Coll (IL)
Illinois State U (IL)
Illinois Wesleyan U (IL)
Indiana State U (IN)
Indiana U Bloomington (IN)
Indiana U Northwest (IN)
Indiana U of Pennsylvania (PA)
Indiana U–Purdue U Fort Wayne (IN)
Indiana U–Purdue U Indianapolis (IN)
Indiana U South Bend (IN)
Indiana U Southeast (IN)
Iona Coll (NY)
Iowa State U of Science and Technology (IA)
Ithaca Coll (NY)
Jacksonville U (FL)
John Carroll U (OH)
Johns Hopkins U (MD)
Juniata Coll (PA)
Kalamazoo Coll (MI)
Kansas State U (KS)
Kansas Wesleyan U (KS)
Kennesaw State U (GA)
Kent State U (OH)
Kenyon Coll (OH)
King's Coll (PA)
The King's U Coll (AB, Canada)
King U (TN)
Knox Coll (IL)
Kutztown U of Pennsylvania (PA)
Lafayette Coll (PA)
Lake Forest Coll (IL)
La Salle U (PA)
Lawrence U (WI)
Lebanese American U (Lebanon)
Lebanon Valley Coll (PA)
Lee U (TN)
Lehigh U (PA)
Lehman Coll of the City U of New York (NY)
Le Moyne Coll (NY)
Lenoir-Rhyne U (NC)
Lewis & Clark Coll (OR)
Lewis U (IL)
Liberty U (VA)
Lincoln Christian U (IL)
Lincoln U (PA)
Lindenwood U (MO)
Linfield Coll (OR)
Lipscomb U (TN)
Lock Haven U of Pennsylvania (PA)
Long Island U–LIU Brooklyn (NY)
Long Island U–LIU Post (NY)
Loras Coll (IA)
Louisiana Coll (LA)
Louisiana State U and A&M Coll (LA)
Loyola Marymount U (CA)
Loyola U Chicago (IL)
Loyola U New Orleans (LA)
Luther Coll (IA)
Lycoming Coll (PA)
Lynchburg Coll (VA)
Macalester Coll (MN)
Malone U (OH)
Manchester U (IN)
Manhattan Coll (NY)
Manhattanville Coll (NY)
Mansfield U of Pennsylvania (PA)
Marian U (IN)
Marietta Coll (OH)
Marist Coll (NY)
Marquette U (WI)
Mary Baldwin Coll (VA)
Marymount Manhattan Coll (NY)
Marymount U (VA)
Maryville Coll (TN)
Marywood U (PA)
Massachusetts Coll of Liberal Arts (MA)
Massachusetts Inst of Technology (MA)
McDaniel Coll (MD)
McKendree U (IL)
Mercer U, Macon (GA)
Merrimack Coll (MA)
Messiah Coll (PA)
Metropolitan State U (MN)
Miami U (OH)
Michigan State U (MI)
Middlebury Coll (VT)
Middle Tennessee State U (TN)
Millersville U of Pennsylvania (PA)
Millikin U (IL)
Millsaps Coll (MS)
Mills Coll (CA)
Minnesota State U Mankato (MN)
Minnesota State U Moorhead (MN)
Misericordia U (PA)
Mississippi State U (MS)
Missouri State U (MO)
Missouri U of Science and Technology (MO)
Missouri Valley Coll (MO)
Missouri Western State U (MO)
Molloy Coll (NY)
Monmouth Coll (IL)
Montana State U (MT)
Montclair State U (NJ)
Moravian Coll (PA)
Morehead State U (KY)
Morningside Coll (IA)
Mount Allison U (NB, Canada)
Mount Holyoke Coll (MA)
Mount Mary U (WI)
Mount Mercy U (IA)
Mount Saint Mary's U (CA)
Mount St. Mary's U (MD)
Mount Vernon Nazarene U (OH)
Muhlenberg Coll (PA)
Murray State U (KY)
Nazareth Coll of Rochester (NY)
Nebraska Wesleyan U (NE)
New Coll of Florida (FL)
New England Coll (NH)
New Jersey City U (NJ)
Newman U (KS)
New Mexico State U (NM)
New York U (NY)
Niagara U (NY)
North Carolina State U (NC)
North Central Coll (IL)
North Dakota State U (ND)
Northeastern Illinois U (IL)
Northeastern U (MA)
Northern Arizona U (AZ)
Northern Illinois U (IL)
Northern Kentucky U (KY)
Northern Michigan U (MI)
Northwestern Coll (IA)
Northwestern U (IL)
Northwest Missouri State U (MO)
Northwest Nazarene U (ID)
Northwest U (WA)
Notre Dame of Maryland U (MD)
Nova Southeastern U (FL)
Nyack Coll (NY)
Oakland U (MI)
Oberlin Coll (OH)
Occidental Coll (CA)
Oglethorpe U (GA)
Ohio Dominican U (OH)
Ohio Northern U (OH)
The Ohio State U (OH)
Ohio U (OH)
Ohio Wesleyan U (OH)
Oklahoma Baptist U (OK)
Oklahoma City U (OK)
Oklahoma State U (OK)
Old Dominion U (VA)
Olivet Nazarene U (IL)
Oregon State U (OR)
Pacific Lutheran U (WA)
Pacific U (OR)
Palm Beach Atlantic U (FL)
Penn State Abington (PA)
Penn State Altoona (PA)
Penn State Beaver (PA)
Penn State Berks (PA)
Penn State Brandywine (PA)
Penn State DuBois (PA)
Penn State Erie, The Behrend Coll (PA)
Penn State Fayette, The Eberly Campus (PA)
Penn State Greater Allegheny (PA)
Penn State Hazleton (PA)
Penn State Lehigh Valley (PA)
Penn State Mont Alto (PA)
Penn State New Kensington (PA)
Penn State Schuylkill (PA)
Penn State Shenango (PA)
Penn State U Park (PA)
Penn State Wilkes-Barre (PA)
Penn State Worthington Scranton (PA)
Penn State York (PA)
Pepperdine U, Malibu (CA)
Piedmont Coll (GA)
Plymouth State U (NH)
Point Loma Nazarene U (CA)
Pomona Coll (CA)
Portland State U (OR)
Presbyterian Coll (SC)
Princeton U (NJ)
Principia Coll (IL)
Providence Coll (RI)
Purchase Coll, State U of New York (NY)
Purdue U (IN)
Purdue U Calumet (IN)
Queens Coll of the City U of New York (NY)
Quinnipiac U (CT)
Randolph Coll (VA)
Randolph-Macon Coll (VA)
Reed Coll (OR)
Regis U (CO)
Rensselaer Polytechnic Inst (NY)
Rhode Island Coll (RI)
Rhodes Coll (TN)
Rice U (TX)
Rider U (NJ)
Ripon Coll (WI)
Roanoke Coll (VA)
Rochester Inst of Technology (NY)
Rockford U (IL)
Rockhurst U (MO)
Rocky Mountain Coll (MT)
Roger Williams U (RI)
Rollins Coll (FL)
Roosevelt U (IL)
Rosemont Coll (PA)
Rutgers, The State U of New Jersey, Camden (NJ)
Rutgers, The State U of New Jersey, Newark (NJ)
Rutgers, The State U of New Jersey, New Brunswick (NJ)
Sacred Heart U (CT)
Saint Anselm Coll (NH)
St. Bonaventure U (NY)
St. Catherine U (MN)
Saint Charles Borromeo Sem, Overbrook (PA)
St. Edward's U (TX)
St. Francis Coll (NY)
Saint Francis U (PA)
St. Gregory's U, Shawnee (OK)
St. John Fisher Coll (NY)
Saint John's U (MN)
St. John's U (NY)
Saint Joseph's Coll (IN)
Saint Joseph's U (PA)
St. Lawrence U (NY)
Saint Louis U (MO)
Saint Mary's Coll (IN)
St. Mary's Coll of Maryland (MD)
St. Mary's U (TX)
Saint Mary's U of Minnesota (MN)
Saint Michael's Coll (VT)
St. Norbert Coll (WI)
St. Olaf Coll (MN)
Saint Peter's U (NJ)
St. Thomas Aquinas Coll (NY)
St. Thomas U (NB, Canada)
Saint Vincent Coll (PA)
Salem Coll (NC)
Salisbury U (MD)
Salve Regina U (RI)
Samford U (AL)
Sam Houston State U (TX)
San Diego State U (CA)
San Francisco State U (CA)
San Jose State U (CA)
Santa Clara U (CA)
Sarah Lawrence Coll (NY)
Scripps Coll (CA)
Seattle Pacific U (WA)
Seattle U (WA)
Sewanee: The U of the South (TN)
Siena Coll (NY)
Siena Heights U (MI)
Simmons Coll (MA)
Simon Fraser U (BC, Canada)
Simpson Coll (IA)
Skidmore Coll (NY)
Slippery Rock U of Pennsylvania (PA)
Smith Coll (MA)
Southeast Missouri State U (MO)
Southern Connecticut State U (CT)
Southern Illinois U Carbondale (IL)
Southern Illinois U Edwardsville (IL)
Southern Methodist U (TX)
Southern Utah U (UT)
Southwestern U (TX)
Southwest Minnesota State U (MN)
Spelman Coll (GA)
Spring Hill Coll (AL)
Stanford U (CA)
State U of New York at Fredonia (NY)
State U of New York at New Paltz (NY)
State U of New York at Oswego (NY)
State U of New York at Plattsburgh (NY)
State U of New York Coll at Cortland (NY)
State U of New York Coll at Geneseo (NY)
State U of New York Coll at Old Westbury (NY)
State U of New York Coll at Potsdam (NY)
Stephen F. Austin State U (TX)
Stetson U (FL)
Stonehill Coll (MA)
Stony Brook U, State U of New York (NY)
Suffolk U (MA)
Susquehanna U (PA)
Syracuse U (NY)
Taylor U (IN)
Temple U (PA)
Texas A&M U (TX)
Texas Christian U (TX)
Texas Lutheran U (TX)
Texas State U (TX)
Texas Tech U (TX)
Thiel Coll (PA)
Thomas More Coll (KY)
Toccoa Falls Coll (GA)
Towson U (MD)
Transylvania U (KY)
Trent U (ON, Canada)
Trinity Christian Coll (IL)
Trinity Coll (CT)
Trinity U (TX)
Tufts U (MA)
Tulane U (LA)
Union Coll (NY)
Union U (TN)
United States Air Force Acad (CO)

Université de Montréal (QC, Canada)
Université de Sherbrooke (QC, Canada)
U at Albany, State U of New York (NY)
U at Buffalo, the State U of New York (NY)
The U of Akron (OH)
The U of Alabama (AL)
The U of Alabama at Birmingham (AL)
The U of Alabama in Huntsville (AL)
U of Alaska Fairbanks (AK)
U of Alberta (AB, Canada)
The U of Arizona (AZ)
U of Arkansas (AR)
U of Arkansas at Little Rock (AR)
The U of British Columbia (BC, Canada)
The U of British Columbia–Okanagan Campus (BC, Canada)
U of California, Berkeley (CA)
U of California, Davis (CA)
U of California, Irvine (CA)
U of California, Los Angeles (CA)
U of California, Riverside (CA)
U of California, Santa Barbara (CA)
U of California, Santa Cruz (CA)
U of Central Arkansas (AR)
U of Central Florida (FL)
U of Central Oklahoma (OK)
U of Chicago (IL)
U of Cincinnati (OH)
U of Colorado Boulder (CO)
U of Colorado Colorado Springs (CO)
U of Colorado Denver (CO)
U of Dallas (TX)
U of Dayton (OH)
U of Delaware (DE)
U of Denver (CO)
U of Dubuque (IA)
U of Evansville (IN)
The U of Findlay (OH)
U of Florida (FL)
U of Georgia (GA)
U of Guam (GU)
U of Guelph (ON, Canada)
U of Hartford (CT)
U of Hawaii at Manoa (HI)
U of Hawaii–West Oahu (HI)
U of Houston (TX)
U of Houston–Downtown (TX)
U of Idaho (ID)
U of Illinois at Chicago (IL)
U of Illinois at Springfield (IL)
U of Indianapolis (IN)
The U of Iowa (IA)
The U of Kansas (KS)
U of Kentucky (KY)
U of King's Coll (NS, Canada)
U of La Verne (CA)
U of Lethbridge (AB, Canada)
U of Louisville (KY)
U of Maine (ME)
U of Maryland, Baltimore County (MD)
U of Maryland, Coll Park (MD)
U of Massachusetts Amherst (MA)
U of Massachusetts Boston (MA)
U of Massachusetts Dartmouth (MA)
U of Massachusetts Lowell (MA)
U of Memphis (TN)
U of Miami (FL)
U of Michigan (MI)
U of Michigan–Dearborn (MI)
U of Michigan–Flint (MI)
U of Minnesota, Duluth (MN)
U of Minnesota, Morris (MN)
U of Minnesota, Twin Cities Campus (MN)
U of Mississippi (MS)
U of Missouri (MO)
U of Missouri–Kansas City (MO)
U of Missouri–St. Louis (MO)
The U of Montana (MT)
U of Mount Union (OH)
U of Nebraska at Kearney (NE)
U of Nebraska–Lincoln (NE)
U of Nevada, Las Vegas (NV)
U of Nevada, Reno (NV)
U of New Brunswick Saint John (NB, Canada)
U of New Hampshire (NH)
U of New Mexico (NM)
U of New Orleans (LA)
U of North Carolina at Asheville (NC)
The U of North Carolina at Chapel Hill (NC)
The U of North Carolina at Charlotte (NC)
The U of North Carolina at Greensboro (NC)
U of North Dakota (ND)
U of Northern Colorado (CO)
U of Northern Iowa (IA)
U of North Florida (FL)
U of North Texas (TX)
U of Notre Dame (IN)
U of Oklahoma (OK)
U of Oregon (OR)
U of Ottawa (ON, Canada)
U of Pennsylvania (PA)
U of Pittsburgh (PA)
U of Portland (OR)
U of Puget Sound (WA)
U of Regina (SK, Canada)
U of Rhode Island (RI)
U of Richmond (VA)
U of Rochester (NY)
U of Saint Francis (IN)
U of Saint Joseph (CT)
U of St. Thomas (MN)
U of St. Thomas (TX)
U of San Diego (CA)
U of San Francisco (CA)
U of Saskatchewan (SK, Canada)
The U of Scranton (PA)
U of South Alabama (AL)
The U of South Dakota (SD)
U of Southern California (CA)
U of Southern Indiana (IN)
U of Southern Maine (ME)
U of Southern Mississippi (MS)
U of South Florida (FL)
The U of Tampa (FL)
The U of Tennessee (TN)
The U of Tennessee at Martin (TN)
The U of Texas at Arlington (TX)
The U of Texas at Austin (TX)
The U of Texas at El Paso (TX)
The U of Texas at San Antonio (TX)
The U of Texas–Pan American (TX)
U of the Fraser Valley (BC, Canada)
U of the Incarnate Word (TX)
U of the Pacific (CA)
The U of Toledo (OH)
The U of Tulsa (OK)
U of Utah (UT)
U of Vermont (VT)
U of Virginia (VA)
U of Washington (WA)
U of Waterloo (ON, Canada)
The U of Western Ontario (ON, Canada)
U of West Florida (FL)
U of West Georgia (GA)
U of Windsor (ON, Canada)
U of Wisconsin–Eau Claire (WI)
U of Wisconsin–Green Bay (WI)
U of Wisconsin–La Crosse (WI)
U of Wisconsin–Madison (WI)
U of Wisconsin–Milwaukee (WI)
U of Wisconsin–Oshkosh (WI)
U of Wisconsin–Parkside (WI)
U of Wisconsin–Platteville (WI)
U of Wisconsin–Stevens Point (WI)
U of Wyoming (WY)
Urbana U (OH)
Ursinus Coll (PA)
Ursuline Coll (OH)
Utah State U (UT)
Utah Valley U (UT)
Utica Coll (NY)
Valparaiso U (IN)
Vanderbilt U (TN)
Vassar Coll (NY)
Villanova U (PA)
Virginia Commonwealth U (VA)
Virginia Polytechnic Inst and State U (VA)
Virginia Wesleyan Coll (VA)
Viterbo U (WI)
Wabash Coll (IN)
Wagner Coll (NY)
Wake Forest U (NC)
Walla Walla U (WA)
Walsh U (OH)
Warren Wilson Coll (NC)
Wartburg Coll (IA)
Washburn U (KS)
Washington & Jefferson Coll (PA)
Washington and Lee U (VA)
Washington Coll (MD)
Washington State U (WA)
Washington U in St. Louis (MO)
Wayne State U (MI)
Weber State U (UT)
Webster U (MO)
Wells Coll (NY)
Wesleyan Coll (GA)
Wesleyan U (CT)
West Chester U of Pennsylvania (PA)
Western Carolina U (NC)
Western Illinois U (IL)
Western Michigan U (MI)
Western New England U (MA)
Western Oregon U (OR)
Western Washington U (WA)
Westminster Coll (MO)
Westminster Coll (UT)
West Virginia U (WV)
West Virginia Wesleyan Coll (WV)
Wheaton Coll (IL)
Wheaton Coll (MA)
Wheeling Jesuit U (WV)
Whitman Coll (WA)
Whittier Coll (CA)
Whitworth U (WA)
Wichita State U (KS)
Wilkes U (PA)
Willamette U (OR)
William Jewell Coll (MO)
William Paterson U of New Jersey (NJ)
Williams Coll (MA)
Wittenberg U (OH)
Wofford Coll (SC)
Worcester Polytechnic Inst (MA)
Wright State U (OH)
Xavier U (OH)
Xavier U of Louisiana (LA)
Yale U (CT)
Yeshiva U (NY)
York Coll of Pennsylvania (PA)
York Coll of the City U of New York (NY)
Youngstown State U (OH)

PHILOSOPHY AND RELIGIOUS STUDIES
Arizona State U at the West campus (AZ)
Berry Coll (GA)
Bethune-Cookman U (FL)
Central Washington U (WA)
Christian Brothers U (TN)
Concordia Coll–New York (NY)
Flagler Coll (FL)
Goddard Coll (VT)
LaGrange Coll (GA)
Marist Coll (NY)
Marymount Manhattan Coll (NY)
Montreat Coll, Montreat (NC)
Oklahoma City U (OK)
Pace U (NY)
St. Andrews U (NC)
St. Joseph's Coll, Long Island Campus (NY)
St. Joseph's Coll, New York (NY)
Southwestern Coll (KS)
Stockton U (NJ)
Valdosta State U (GA)

PHILOSOPHY AND RELIGIOUS STUDIES RELATED
Berry Coll (GA)
Bethune-Cookman U (FL)
Bridgewater Coll (VA)
Buena Vista U (IA)
Claflin U (SC)
Conception Sem Coll (MO)
Covenant Coll (GA)
Elmira Coll (NY)
Eureka Coll (IL)
Flagler Coll (FL)
Florida Ag and Mech U (FL)
Friends U (KS)
Graceland U (IA)
Harrison Middleton U (AZ)
Hendrix Coll (AR)
Iowa Wesleyan Coll (IA)
James Madison U (VA)
John Brown U (AR)
Juniata Coll (PA)
Lyon Coll (AR)
Mary Baldwin Coll (VA)
Marymount Manhattan Coll (NY)
Millsaps Coll (MS)
Newberry Coll (SC)
Point Loma Nazarene U (CA)
Quincy U (IL)
Radford U (VA)
Roberts Wesleyan Coll (NY)
Rocky Mountain Coll (MT)
Rowan U (NJ)
Saint Joseph's Coll (IN)
Samford U (AL)
San Francisco State U (CA)
Shawnee State U (OH)
Shaw U (NC)
State U of New York at Oswego (NY)
Sterling Coll (KS)
Syracuse U (NY)
Truman State U (MO)
Union U (TN)
U of Alberta (AB, Canada)
U of Mary Washington (VA)
The U of North Carolina at Pembroke (NC)
The U of North Carolina Wilmington (NC)
U of Notre Dame (IN)
The U of Tennessee at Chattanooga (TN)
Ursinus Coll (PA)
Washington U in St. Louis (MO)
West Virginia Wesleyan Coll (WV)
Winthrop U (SC)

PHILOSOPHY RELATED
Coll of Staten Island of the City U of New York (NY)
Lewis U (IL)
Mount Vernon Nazarene U (OH)
Ohio Northern U (OH)
The U of Arizona (AZ)
U of Massachusetts Boston (MA)
U of Pennsylvania (PA)
U of Southern California (CA)
Washington U in St. Louis (MO)
Wheeling Jesuit U (WV)

PHOTOGRAPHIC AND FILM/VIDEO TECHNOLOGY
Rochester Inst of Technology (NY)
St. John's U (NY)
Villa Maria Coll (NY)
Wilmington U (DE)

PHOTOGRAPHY
Adams State U (CO)
Albertus Magnus Coll (CT)
American Acad of Art (IL)
Aquinas Coll (MI)
Arcadia U (PA)
Art Center Coll of Design (CA)
Bard Coll (NY)
Bard Coll at Simon's Rock (MA)
Barry U (FL)
Bennington Coll (VT)
Bowling Green State U (OH)
Bradley U (IL)
Bridgewater State U (MA)
Buffalo State Coll, State U of New York (NY)
California Baptist U (CA)
California Coll of the Arts (CA)
California Inst of the Arts (CA)
California State U, Long Beach (CA)
California State U, Sacramento (CA)
Calvary Bible Coll and Theological Sem (MO)
Cardinal Stritch U (WI)
Carson-Newman U (TN)
Castleton State Coll (VT)
Cazenovia Coll (NY)
Central Washington U (WA)
Chatham U (PA)
Cleveland Inst of Art (OH)
Coe Coll (IA)
Coker Coll (SC)
Coll for Creative Studies (MI)
Colorado State U (CO)
Columbia Coll (MO)
Columbia Coll Chicago (IL)
Concordia U (QC, Canada)
Concordia U Wisconsin (WI)
Cornerstone U (MI)
Dixie State U (UT)
Dominican U (IL)
Drexel U (PA)
Emily Carr U of Art + Design (BC, Canada)
Endicott Coll (MA)
Ferris State U (MI)
Fitchburg State U (MA)
Gallaudet U (DC)
Goddard Coll (VT)
Grand Valley State U (MI)
Grand View U (IA)
Hampton U (VA)
Hofstra U (NY)
Indiana U–Purdue U Fort Wayne (IN)
Inter American U of Puerto Rico, San Germán Campus (PR)
Ithaca Coll (NY)
John Brown U (AR)
Judson U (IL)
Kansas City Art Inst (MO)
Kansas Wesleyan U (KS)
King U (TN)
Long Island U–LIU Post (NY)
Marian U (IN)
Marymount Manhattan Coll (NY)
Marywood U (PA)
Massachusetts Coll of Art and Design (MA)
Moore Coll of Art & Design (PA)
Morningside Coll (IA)
Mount Allison U (NB, Canada)
New York U (NY)
Northern Arizona U (AZ)
Northern Michigan U (MI)
Oakland U (MI)
Ohio U (OH)
Oklahoma City U (OK)
Otis Coll of Art and Design (CA)
Pacific Northwest Coll of Art (OR)
Paier Coll of Art, Inc. (CT)
Paris Coll of Art (France)
Pennsylvania Coll of Art & Design (PA)
Pratt Inst (NY)
Providence Coll (RI)
Purchase Coll, State U of New York (NY)
Purdue U (IN)
Rhode Island Coll (RI)
Rhode Island School of Design (RI)
Ringling Coll of Art and Design (FL)
Rutgers, The State U of New Jersey, New Brunswick (NJ)
St. Edward's U (TX)
St. John's U (NY)
Salve Regina U (RI)
Sam Houston State U (TX)
San Francisco Art Inst (CA)
Santa Fe U of Art and Design (NM)
Savannah Coll of Art and Design (GA)
School of the Art Inst of Chicago (IL)
School of the Museum of Fine Arts, Boston (MA)
Seattle U (WA)
Southern Adventist U (TN)
State U of New York at New Paltz (NY)
Syracuse U (NY)
Temple U (PA)
Texas Christian U (TX)
Texas State U (TX)
The U of Akron (OH)
U of Central Florida (FL)
U of Central Missouri (MO)
U of Central Oklahoma (OK)
U of Dayton (OH)
U of Hartford (CT)
U of Houston (TX)
U of Illinois at Chicago (IL)
The U of Iowa (IA)
U of La Verne (CA)
U of Massachusetts Dartmouth (MA)
U of Miami (FL)
U of Oregon (OR)
The U of the Arts (PA)
U of Washington (WA)
Virginia Commonwealth U (VA)
Washington U in St. Louis (MO)
Watkins Coll of Art, Design, & Film (TN)
Weber State U (UT)
Webster U (MO)
Western State Colorado U (CO)

Western Washington U (WA)
Youngstown State U (OH)

PHOTOJOURNALISM
Bradley U (IL)
Central Michigan U (MI)
Hawai`i Pacific U (HI)
Kent State U (OH)
Minnesota State U Moorhead (MN)
Ohio U (OH)
Rochester Inst of Technology (NY)
St. John's U (NY)
Syracuse U (NY)
U of Central Oklahoma (OK)
U of Miami (FL)
U of Missouri (MO)
Walla Walla U (WA)
Western Kentucky U (KY)

PHYSICAL AND BIOLOGICAL ANTHROPOLOGY
U of Washington (WA)
The U of Western Ontario (ON, Canada)

PHYSICAL CHEMISTRY
LeTourneau U (TX)
Rice U (TX)
The U of Western Ontario (ON, Canada)

PHYSICAL EDUCATION TEACHING AND COACHING
Adams State U (CO)
Adelphi U (NY)
Alabama State U (AL)
Albany State U (GA)
Alice Lloyd Coll (KY)
Alma Coll (MI)
Anderson U (IN)
Anderson U (SC)
Appalachian State U (NC)
Aquinas Coll (MI)
Arkansas State U (AR)
Arkansas Tech U (AR)
Armstrong State U (GA)
Asbury U (KY)
Athens State U (AL)
Auburn U (AL)
Augsburg Coll (MN)
Augustana Coll (SD)
Austin Coll (TX)
Azusa Pacific U (CA)
Ball State U (IN)
Barry U (FL)
Baylor U (TX)
Belmont U (TN)
Bemidji State U (MN)
Benedictine Coll (KS)
Benedictine U (IL)
Bethany Coll (WV)
Bethel Coll (IN)
Bethel U (MN)
Bethune-Cookman U (FL)
Biola U (CA)
Blackburn Coll (IL)
Bluefield Coll (VA)
Blue Mountain Coll (MS)
Boston U (MA)
Bowling Green State U (OH)
Bridgewater State U (MA)
Bryan Coll (TN)
Buena Vista U (IA)
Cairn U (PA)
California Lutheran U (CA)
California State U, Chico (CA)
California State U, Fresno (CA)
California State U, Long Beach (CA)
California State U, Stanislaus (CA)
Calvin Coll (MI)
Campbellsville U (KY)
Canisius Coll (NY)
Capital U (OH)
Caribbean U (PR)
Carroll Coll (MT)
Carson-Newman U (TN)
Castleton State Coll (VT)
Catawba Coll (NC)
Cedarville U (OH)
Central Connecticut State U (CT)
Central Methodist U (MO)
Central Michigan U (MI)
Central Washington U (WA)
Charleston Southern U (SC)
Chicago State U (IL)
Chowan U (NC)
The Citadel, The Military Coll of South Carolina (SC)
Clarke U (IA)
Clearwater Christian Coll (FL)
Coastal Carolina U (SC)
Coe Coll (IA)
Coker Coll (SC)
The Coll at Brockport, State U of New York (NY)
Coll of Charleston (SC)
The Coll of Idaho (ID)
The Coll of New Jersey (NJ)
Coll of the Ozarks (MO)
Columbus State U (GA)
Concordia Coll (MN)
Concordia U Chicago (IL)
Concordia U, Nebraska (NE)
Concordia U, St. Paul (MN)
Concordia U Wisconsin (WI)
Concord U (WV)
Corban U (OR)
Cornell Coll (IA)
Cornerstone U (MI)
Culver-Stockton Coll (MO)
Cumberland U (TN)
Dakota State U (SD)
Dallas Baptist U (TX)
Defiance Coll (OH)
Delaware State U (DE)
Delta State U (MS)
Denison U (OH)
DePaul U (IL)
DePauw U (IN)
Dickinson State U (ND)
Doane Coll (NE)
Dowling Coll (NY)
Drury U (MO)
East Carolina U (NC)
East Central U (OK)
Eastern Connecticut State U (CT)
Eastern Kentucky U (KY)
Eastern Michigan U (MI)
Eastern New Mexico U (NM)
East Stroudsburg U of Pennsylvania (PA)
East Texas Baptist U (TX)
Elmhurst Coll (IL)
Elms Coll (MA)
Elon U (NC)
Emory & Henry Coll (VA)
Endicott Coll (MA)
Erskine Coll (SC)
Evangel U (MO)
Fairmont State U (WV)
Faulkner U (AL)
Fayetteville State U (NC)
Florida Ag and Mech U (FL)
Florida Intl U (FL)
Fort Hays State U (KS)
Fort Lewis Coll (CO)
Franklin Coll (IN)
Friends U (KS)
Frostburg State U (MD)
Gallaudet U (DC)
George Mason U (VA)
Georgia Regents U (GA)
Georgia Southern U (GA)
Georgia Southwestern State U (GA)
Georgia State U (GA)
Gettysburg Coll (PA)
Gonzaga U (WA)
Goshen Coll (IN)
Graceland U (IA)
Grambling State U (LA)
Grand Valley State U (MI)
Grand View U (IA)
Greensboro Coll (NC)
Greenville Coll (IL)
Gustavus Adolphus Coll (MN)
Hampton U (VA)
Hannibal-LaGrange U (MO)
Hardin-Simmons U (TX)
Hastings Coll (NE)
Heidelberg U (OH)
High Point U (NC)
Hillsdale Coll (MI)
Hofstra U (NY)
Hope Coll (MI)
Houghton Coll (NY)
Houston Baptist U (TX)
Howard Payne U (TX)
Howard U (DC)
Humboldt State U (CA)
Hunter Coll of the City U of New York (NY)
Huntingdon Coll (AL)
Husson U (ME)
Huston-Tillotson U (TX)
Illinois Coll (IL)
Illinois State U (IL)
Indiana State U (IN)
Inter American U of Puerto Rico, Aguadilla Campus (PR)
Inter American U of Puerto Rico, Guayama Campus (PR)
Inter American U of Puerto Rico, San Germán Campus (PR)
Iowa Wesleyan Coll (IA)
Ithaca Coll (NY)
Jackson State U (MS)
Jacksonville State U (AL)
Jacksonville U (FL)
Jarvis Christian Coll (TX)
John Carroll U (OH)
Johnson State Coll (VT)
Judson U (IL)
Kean U (NJ)
Keene State Coll (NH)
Kennesaw State U (GA)
Kent State U (OH)
Kentucky State U (KY)
Kentucky Wesleyan Coll (KY)
King U (TN)
Lane Coll (TN)
Langston U (OK)
Lees-McRae Coll (NC)
Lenoir-Rhyne U (NC)
LeTourneau U (TX)
Limestone Coll (SC)
Lincoln Memorial U (TN)
Lincoln U (MO)
Lindenwood U (MO)
Lindsey Wilson Coll (KY)
Linfield Coll (OR)
Lipscomb U (TN)
Lock Haven U of Pennsylvania (PA)
Long Island U–LIU Brooklyn (NY)
Long Island U–LIU Post (NY)
Louisiana Coll (LA)
Louisiana State U and A&M Coll (LA)
Lubbock Christian U (TX)
Madonna U (MI)
Manchester U (IN)
Manhattan Coll (NY)
Maranatha Baptist U (WI)
Marian U (IN)
Marshall U (WV)
Mars Hill U (NC)
Maryville Coll (TN)
Marywood U (PA)
The Master's Coll and Sem (CA)
Mayville State U (ND)
McKendree U (IL)
McMurry U (TX)
McNeese State U (LA)
Meredith Coll (NC)
Messiah Coll (PA)
Michigan State U (MI)
MidAmerica Nazarene U (KS)
Millikin U (IL)
Minnesota State U Mankato (MN)
Minnesota State U Moorhead (MN)
Minot State U (ND)
Mississippi State U (MS)
Mississippi Valley State U (MS)
Missouri Baptist U (MO)
Missouri State U (MO)
Missouri Valley Coll (MO)
Monmouth Coll (IL)
Montana State U Billings (MT)
Montclair State U (NJ)
Morehead State U (KY)
National U (CA)
Nebraska Wesleyan U (NE)
New England Coll (NH)
New Mexico Highlands U (NM)
New Mexico State U (NM)
Nicholls State U (LA)
North Central Coll (IL)
North Dakota State U (ND)
Northeastern Illinois U (IL)
Northeastern State U (OK)
Northern Illinois U (IL)
Northern Kentucky U (KY)
Northern Michigan U (MI)
Northern State U (SD)
Northwestern Coll (IA)
Northwestern Oklahoma State U (OK)
Northwest Missouri State U (MO)
Northwest Nazarene U (ID)
Norwich U (VT)
Nova Southeastern U (FL)
Oakland City U (IN)
The Ohio State U (OH)
Ohio U (OH)
Ohio Valley U (WV)
Oklahoma Baptist U (OK)
Oklahoma Christian U (OK)
Oklahoma City U (OK)
Oklahoma State U (OK)
Oklahoma Wesleyan U (OK)
Old Dominion U (VA)
Olivet Nazarene U (IL)
Palm Beach Atlantic U (FL)
Peru State Coll (NE)
Pittsburg State U (KS)
Purdue U (IN)
Queens Coll of the City U of New York (NY)
Quincy U (IL)
Radford U (VA)
Reinhardt U (GA)
Rhode Island Coll (RI)
Ripon Coll (WI)
Roanoke Coll (VA)
Roberts Wesleyan Coll (NY)
Rockford U (IL)
Rocky Mountain Coll (MT)
Rowan U (NJ)
The Sage Colls (NY)
Saginaw Valley State U (MI)
St. Andrews U (NC)
St. Bonaventure U (NY)
St. Catherine U (MN)
St. Edward's U (TX)
St. Francis Coll (NY)
Salisbury U (MD)
San Diego Christian Coll (CA)
San Francisco State U (CA)
Shenandoah U (VA)
Simpson Coll (IA)
Slippery Rock U of Pennsylvania (PA)
South Carolina State U (SC)
Southeastern Louisiana U (LA)
Southeastern Oklahoma State U (OK)
Southeast Missouri State U (MO)
Southern Adventist U (TN)
Southern Arkansas U–Magnolia (AR)
Southern Illinois U Carbondale (IL)
Southern Oregon U (OR)
Southern Utah U (UT)
Southwest Baptist U (MO)
Southwestern Coll (KS)
Southwest Minnesota State U (MN)
State U of New York Coll at Cortland (NY)
Sterling Coll (KS)
Sul Ross State U (TX)
Summit U (PA)
Syracuse U (NY)
Tabor Coll (KS)
Tarleton State U (TX)
Tennessee State U (TN)
Texas A&M Intl U (TX)
Texas Christian U (TX)
Texas Lutheran U (TX)
Towson U (MD)
Transylvania U (KY)
Trevecca Nazarene U (TN)
Trine U (IN)
Trinity Christian Coll (IL)
Tusculum Coll (TN)
Union Coll (KY)
Union Coll (NE)
Union U (TN)
United States Sports Acad (AL)
Universidad del Turabo (PR)
Universidad Metropolitana (PR)
Université de Montréal (QC, Canada)
Université de Sherbrooke (QC, Canada)
The U of Akron (OH)
The U of Alabama (AL)
The U of Alabama at Birmingham (AL)
U of Alberta (AB, Canada)
U of Arkansas at Pine Bluff (AR)
U of Central Arkansas (AR)
U of Central Florida (FL)
U of Central Missouri (MO)
U of Central Oklahoma (OK)
U of Dubuque (IA)
The U of Findlay (OH)
U of Great Falls (MT)
U of Guam (GU)
U of Idaho (ID)
U of Indianapolis (IN)
U of Jamestown (ND)
The U of Kansas (KS)
U of Kentucky (KY)
U of Lethbridge (AB, Canada)
U of Louisiana at Lafayette (LA)
U of Maine (ME)
U of Maine at Presque Isle (ME)
U of Mary Hardin-Baylor (TX)
U of Maryland, Coll Park (MD)
U of Memphis (TN)
U of Minnesota, Duluth (MN)
U of Minnesota, Twin Cities Campus (MN)
U of Missouri–St. Louis (MO)
U of Mobile (AL)
The U of Montana (MT)
The U of Montana Western (MT)
U of Mount Union (OH)
U of Nebraska at Kearney (NE)
U of Nebraska–Lincoln (NE)
U of New Mexico (NM)
The U of North Carolina at Greensboro (NC)
The U of North Carolina at Pembroke (NC)
The U of North Carolina Wilmington (NC)
U of Northern Iowa (IA)
U of North Florida (FL)
U of North Georgia (GA)
U of Northwestern–St. Paul (MN)
U of Pittsburgh (PA)
U of Pittsburgh at Bradford (PA)
U of Regina (SK, Canada)
U of Rio Grande (OH)
U of St. Thomas (MN)
U of San Francisco (CA)
U of Saskatchewan (SK, Canada)
U of South Alabama (AL)
U of South Carolina Upstate (SC)
The U of South Dakota (SD)
U of Southern Indiana (IN)
U of Southern Mississippi (MS)
U of South Florida (FL)
U of the Cumberlands (KY)
U of the Incarnate Word (TX)
The U of Toledo (OH)
U of Vermont (VT)
The U of West Alabama (AL)
U of West Georgia (GA)
U of Windsor (ON, Canada)
U of Wisconsin–Oshkosh (WI)
U of Wisconsin–Platteville (WI)
U of Wisconsin–River Falls (WI)
U of Wisconsin–Stevens Point (WI)
U of Wisconsin–Superior (WI)
U of Wisconsin–Whitewater (WI)
U of Wyoming (WY)
Upper Iowa U (IA)
Utah State U (UT)
Utah Valley U (UT)
Valdosta State U (GA)
Valley City State U (ND)
Valparaiso U (IN)
Vanguard U of Southern California (CA)
Virginia State U (VA)
Waldorf Coll (IA)
Walla Walla U (WA)
Walsh U (OH)
Warner Pacific Coll (OR)
Wartburg Coll (IA)
Washburn U (KS)
Washington State U (WA)
Wayne State Coll (NE)
Wayne State U (MI)
Weber State U (UT)
Welch Coll (TN)
Western Carolina U (NC)
Western Illinois U (IL)
Western Kentucky U (KY)
Western Michigan U (MI)
Western State Colorado U (CO)
Western Washington U (WA)
West Liberty U (WV)
Westminster Coll (MO)
West Virginia U (WV)
West Virginia U Inst of Technology (WV)
West Virginia Wesleyan Coll (WV)
Whitworth U (WA)
William Jewell Coll (MO)
William Paterson U of New Jersey (NJ)

William Penn U (IA)
Williams Baptist Coll (AR)
William Woods U (MO)
Wingate U (NC)
Winona State U (MN)
Winthrop U (SC)
Wright State U (OH)
Xavier U of Louisiana (LA)
York Coll of the City U of New York (NY)
Youngstown State U (OH)

PHYSICAL FITNESS TECHNICIAN
Averett U (VA)
Central Methodist U (MO)
Pepperdine U, Malibu (CA)
Trevecca Nazarene U (TN)

PHYSICAL SCIENCES
Anderson U (IN)
Arizona State U at the Tempe campus (AZ)
Arkansas Tech U (AR)
Auburn U at Montgomery (AL)
Bemidji State U (MN)
Bennington Coll (VT)
Bethany Coll (WV)
Bethany Lutheran Coll (MN)
Biola U (CA)
Black Hills State U (SD)
California State U, Sacramento (CA)
California State U, Stanislaus (CA)
California U of Pennsylvania (PA)
Calvin Coll (MI)
Chowan U (NC)
Coe Coll (IA)
Colorado Mesa U (CO)
Concordia U Chicago (IL)
Concordia U, Nebraska (NE)
Dakota State U (SD)
Defiance Coll (OH)
Doane Coll (NE)
East Stroudsburg U of Pennsylvania (PA)
Emporia State U (KS)
The Evergreen State Coll (WA)
Florida Inst of Technology (FL)
Fort Hays State U (KS)
Graceland U (IA)
Hampshire Coll (MA)
Hampton U (VA)
Juniata Coll (PA)
Kansas State U (KS)
La Sierra U (CA)
Lincoln U (PA)
Linfield Coll (OR)
The Master's Coll and Sem (CA)
Michigan State U (MI)
Midwestern State U (TX)
Minnesota State U Mankato (MN)
Minot State U (ND)
Mississippi U for Women (MS)
Montana Tech of The U of Montana (MT)
Morrisville State Coll (NY)
Mount Vernon Nazarene U (OH)
Muhlenberg Coll (PA)
New Mexico Inst of Mining and Technology (NM)
Oklahoma Wesleyan U (OK)
Olivet Nazarene U (IL)
Penn State Erie, The Behrend Coll (PA)
Purdue U Calumet (IN)
Ripon Coll (WI)
Rowan U (NJ)
St. John's U (NY)
Saint Michael's Coll (VT)
Saint Vincent Coll (PA)
Salisbury U (MD)
San Diego State U (CA)
San Francisco State U (CA)
Seattle Pacific U (WA)
Seattle U (WA)
Southern Utah U (UT)
Southwestern U (TX)
Suffolk U (MA)
Texas A&M Intl U (TX)
Trent U (ON, Canada)
Trine U (IN)
Troy U (AL)
United States Military Acad (NY)
United States Naval Acad (MD)
Universidad Metropolitana (PR)
U of Alberta (AB, Canada)
U of California, Riverside (CA)
U of Dayton (OH)
U of Guelph (ON, Canada)
U of Maryland, Coll Park (MD)
U of Minnesota, Twin Cities Campus (MN)
U of Ottawa (ON, Canada)
U of Pittsburgh (PA)
U of Pittsburgh at Bradford (PA)
U of Rio Grande (OH)
U of Southern California (CA)
U of Southern Maine (ME)
The U of Texas–Pan American (TX)
U of the Pacific (CA)
U of Utah (UT)
U of Wisconsin–River Falls (WI)
U of Wisconsin–Superior (WI)
U of Wyoming (WY)
Villanova U (PA)
Warner Pacific Coll (OR)
Washburn U (KS)
Washington State U (WA)
Wesleyan Coll (GA)
Wesleyan U (CT)
Western Kentucky U (KY)
Westfield State U (MA)
Wheeling Jesuit U (WV)
Worcester State U (MA)
Yeshiva U (NY)
Youngstown State U (OH)

PHYSICAL SCIENCES RELATED
Bowling Green State U (OH)
Cedar Crest Coll (PA)
Central Connecticut State U (CT)
The Coll of St. Scholastica (MN)
Covenant Coll (GA)
Eastern Michigan U (MI)
George Mason U (VA)
John Brown U (AR)
Rochester Inst of Technology (NY)
Saginaw Valley State U (MI)
State U of New York Empire State Coll (NY)
Stony Brook U, State U of New York (NY)
Union Coll (NY)
The U of Alabama in Huntsville (AL)
U of California, Davis (CA)
U of Mary Washington (VA)
U of Massachusetts Lowell (MA)
U of Miami (FL)
U of North Alabama (AL)
The U of North Carolina at Chapel Hill (NC)
U of Saint Francis (IN)
Wayne State U (MI)
Worcester Polytechnic Inst (MA)
Xavier U (OH)

PHYSICAL SCIENCE TECHNOLOGIES RELATED
Delaware State U (DE)

PHYSICAL THERAPY
American Intl Coll (MA)
Andrews U (MI)
Armstrong State U (GA)
Biola U (CA)
Bowling Green State U (OH)
California State U, Fresno (CA)
Chicago State U (IL)
Coll of Saint Benedict (MN)
Concordia U (QC, Canada)
Concordia U Wisconsin (WI)
Dalhousie U (NS, Canada)
Dominican U (IL)
Duquesne U (PA)
Elmhurst Coll (IL)
Grand Valley State U (MI)
Gustavus Adolphus Coll (MN)
Hampton U (VA)
Hawai`i Pacific U (HI)
Howard U (DC)
Ithaca Coll (NY)
Keystone Coll (PA)
Langston U (OK)
Loyola U Chicago (IL)
Maryville U of Saint Louis (MO)
Mount Saint Mary Coll (NY)
Nazareth Coll of Rochester (NY)
Northeastern U (MA)
Northern Illinois U (IL)
Northwest Nazarene U (ID)
Quinnipiac U (CT)
Sacred Heart U (CT)
Saint Francis U (PA)
Saint John's U (MN)
Saint Vincent Coll (PA)
Simmons Coll (MA)
State U of New York Coll of Environmental Science and Forestry (NY)
Tarleton State U (TX)
Tennessee State U (TN)
Université de Montréal (QC, Canada)
The U of Akron (OH)
The U of Findlay (OH)
U of Hartford (CT)
U of Minnesota, Morris (MN)
U of Minnesota, Twin Cities Campus (MN)
The U of Montana (MT)
U of North Dakota (ND)
U of Ottawa (ON, Canada)
The U of Scranton (PA)
The U of Tennessee at Chattanooga (TN)
U of the Sciences (PA)
The U of Toledo (OH)
U of Utah (UT)
Vanguard U of Southern California (CA)

PHYSICAL THERAPY TECHNOLOGY
Nebraska Methodist Coll (NE)
Union Coll (NE)

PHYSICIAN ASSISTANT
Brenau U (GA)
Butler U (IN)
City Coll of the City U of New York (NY)
Cleveland State U (OH)
Daemen Coll (NY)
DeSales U (PA)
Duquesne U (PA)
Elmhurst Coll (IL)
Gannon U (PA)
The George Washington U (DC)
Grand Valley State U (MI)
Howard U (DC)
Long Island U–LIU Brooklyn (NY)
Pennsylvania Coll of Technology (PA)
Peru State Coll (NE)
Philadelphia U (PA)
Quinnipiac U (CT)
Rochester Inst of Technology (NY)
St. Francis Coll (NY)
Saint Francis U (PA)
St. John's U (NY)
Saint Vincent Coll (PA)
Salem Coll (NC)
Seton Hill U (PA)
Southern Illinois U Carbondale (IL)
Union Coll (NE)
U of Kentucky (KY)
U of Saint Francis (IN)
The U of South Dakota (SD)
U of the Sciences (PA)
U of Washington (WA)
U of Wisconsin–Parkside (WI)
Wagner Coll (NY)
Weber State U (UT)
York Coll of the City U of New York (NY)

PHYSICS
Abilene Christian U (TX)
Adams State U (CO)
Adelphi U (NY)
Agnes Scott Coll (GA)
Albion Coll (MI)
Albright Coll (PA)
Allegheny Coll (PA)
Alma Coll (MI)
American U (DC)
The American U in Cairo (Egypt)
American U of Beirut (Lebanon)
Amherst Coll (MA)
Anderson U (IN)
Andrews U (MI)
Angelo State U (TX)
Appalachian State U (NC)
Aquinas Coll (MI)
Arizona State U at the Tempe campus (AZ)
Arkansas State U (AR)
Arkansas Tech U (AR)
Armstrong State U (GA)
Ashland U (OH)
Auburn U (AL)
Augsburg Coll (MN)
Augustana Coll (IL)
Augustana Coll (SD)
Austin Coll (TX)
Austin Peay State U (TN)
Ave Maria U (FL)
Azusa Pacific U (CA)
Baker U (KS)
Baldwin Wallace U (OH)
Ball State U (IN)
Bard Coll (NY)
Bard Coll at Simon's Rock (MA)
Barnard Coll (NY)
Bates Coll (ME)
Baylor U (TX)
Belmont U (TN)
Beloit Coll (WI)
Bemidji State U (MN)
Benedictine Coll (KS)
Benedictine U (IL)
Bennington Coll (VT)
Berea Coll (KY)
Berry Coll (GA)
Bethel U (MN)
Binghamton U, State U of New York (NY)
Biola U (CA)
Birmingham-Southern Coll (AL)
Bloomsburg U of Pennsylvania (PA)
Bluffton U (OH)
Bob Jones U (SC)
Boston Coll (MA)
Boston U (MA)
Bowdoin Coll (ME)
Bowling Green State U (OH)
Bradley U (IL)
Brandeis U (MA)
Bridgewater Coll (VA)
Bridgewater State U (MA)
Brown U (RI)
Bryn Mawr Coll (PA)
Bucknell U (PA)
Buena Vista U (IA)
Buffalo State Coll, State U of New York (NY)
Butler U (IN)
California Inst of Technology (CA)
California Lutheran U (CA)
California Polytechnic State U, San Luis Obispo (CA)
California State Polytechnic U, Pomona (CA)
California State U, Chico (CA)
California State U, Dominguez Hills (CA)
California State U, Fresno (CA)
California State U, Fullerton (CA)
California State U, Long Beach (CA)
California State U, Los Angeles (CA)
California State U, Sacramento (CA)
California State U, San Bernardino (CA)
California State U, Stanislaus (CA)
California U of Pennsylvania (PA)
Calvin Coll (MI)
Cameron U (OK)
Canisius Coll (NY)
Carleton Coll (MN)
Carroll Coll (MT)
Carson-Newman U (TN)
The Catholic U of America (DC)
Cedarville U (OH)
Central Coll (IA)
Central Connecticut State U (CT)
Central Methodist U (MO)
Central Michigan U (MI)
Central Washington U (WA)
Centre Coll (KY)
Chatham U (PA)
Chicago State U (IL)
Christian Brothers U (TN)
The Citadel, The Military Coll of South Carolina (SC)
City Coll of the City U of New York (NY)
Claremont McKenna Coll (CA)
Clarion U of Pennsylvania (PA)
Clark Atlanta U (GA)
Clarkson U (NY)
Clark U (MA)
Cleveland State U (OH)
Coastal Carolina U (SC)
Coe Coll (IA)
Colby Coll (ME)
The Coll at Brockport, State U of New York (NY)
Coll of Charleston (SC)
The Coll of Idaho (ID)
The Coll of New Jersey (NJ)
Coll of Saint Benedict (MN)
Coll of Staten Island of the City U of New York (NY)
Coll of the Holy Cross (MA)
The Coll of William and Mary (VA)
The Coll of Wooster (OH)
The Colorado Coll (CO)
Colorado Mesa U (CO)
Colorado State U (CO)
Colorado State U–Pueblo (CO)
Columbia U (NY)
Columbia U, School of General Studies (NY)
Concordia Coll (MN)
Concordia U (CA)
Concordia U (QC, Canada)
Concordia U, Nebraska (NE)
Cornell Coll (IA)
Cornell U (NY)
Covenant Coll (GA)
Creighton U (NE)
Dalhousie U (NS, Canada)
Dartmouth Coll (NH)
Davidson Coll (NC)
Delaware State U (DE)
Denison U (OH)
DePaul U (IL)
DePauw U (IN)
Dickinson Coll (PA)
Doane Coll (NE)
Drake U (IA)
Drew U (NJ)
Drury U (MO)
Duquesne U (PA)
Earlham Coll (IN)
East Carolina U (NC)
East Central U (OK)
Eastern Illinois U (IL)
Eastern Kentucky U (KY)
Eastern Michigan U (MI)
East Stroudsburg U of Pennsylvania (PA)
East Tennessee State U (TN)
Eckerd Coll (FL)
Edgewood Coll (WI)
Edinboro U of Pennsylvania (PA)
Elizabethtown Coll (PA)
Elmhurst Coll (IL)
Elon U (NC)
Emory & Henry Coll (VA)
Emporia State U (KS)
Erskine Coll (SC)
Fairfield U (CT)
Fairleigh Dickinson U, Metropolitan Campus (NJ)
Florida Ag and Mech U (FL)
Florida Atlantic U (FL)
Florida Inst of Technology (FL)
Florida Intl U (FL)
Florida State U (FL)
Fordham U (NY)
Fort Hays State U (KS)
Francis Marion U (SC)
Franklin & Marshall Coll (PA)
Frostburg State U (MD)
Furman U (SC)
Geneva Coll (PA)
George Mason U (VA)
Georgetown Coll (KY)
Georgetown U (DC)
The George Washington U (DC)
Georgia Coll & State U (GA)
Georgia Inst of Technology (GA)
Georgia Regents U (GA)
Georgia Southern U (GA)
Georgia State U (GA)
Gettysburg Coll (PA)
Gonzaga U (WA)
Gordon Coll (MA)
Goshen Coll (IN)
Goucher Coll (MD)
Grand Valley State U (MI)
Greenville Coll (IL)
Grinnell Coll (IA)
Grove City Coll (PA)
Guilford Coll (NC)
Gustavus Adolphus Coll (MN)
Hamilton Coll (NY)
Hamline U (MN)
Hampden-Sydney Coll (VA)
Hampshire Coll (MA)
Hampton U (VA)

Hanover Coll (IN)
Harding U (AR)
Hardin-Simmons U (TX)
Hartwick Coll (NY)
Harvard U (MA)
Harvey Mudd Coll (CA)
Hastings Coll (NE)
Haverford Coll (PA)
Hendrix Coll (AR)
High Point U (NC)
Hillsdale Coll (MI)
Hiram Coll (OH)
Hobart and William Smith Colls (NY)
Hofstra U (NY)
Hollins U (VA)
Hope Coll (MI)
Houghton Coll (NY)
Houston Baptist U (TX)
Howard U (DC)
Humboldt State U (CA)
Hunter Coll of the City U of New York (NY)
Illinois Coll (IL)
Illinois Inst of Technology (IL)
Illinois State U (IL)
Illinois Wesleyan U (IL)
Indiana State U (IN)
Indiana U Bloomington (IN)
Indiana U of Pennsylvania (PA)
Indiana U–Purdue U Fort Wayne (IN)
Indiana U–Purdue U Indianapolis (IN)
Indiana U South Bend (IN)
Iona Coll (NY)
Iowa State U of Science and Technology (IA)
Ithaca Coll (NY)
Jackson State U (MS)
Jacksonville State U (AL)
Jacksonville U (FL)
James Madison U (VA)
John Carroll U (OH)
Johns Hopkins U (MD)
Juniata Coll (PA)
Kalamazoo Coll (MI)
Kansas State U (KS)
Kent State U (OH)
Kentucky Wesleyan Coll (KY)
Kenyon Coll (OH)
Kettering U (MI)
King's Coll (PA)
King U (TN)
Knox Coll (IL)
Kutztown U of Pennsylvania (PA)
Lafayette Coll (PA)
Lake Forest Coll (IL)
Lamar U (TX)
Lane Coll (TN)
La Sierra U (CA)
Lawrence Technological U (MI)
Lawrence U (WI)
Lebanon Valley Coll (PA)
Lehigh U (PA)
Lehman Coll of the City U of New York (NY)
Le Moyne Coll (NY)
Lenoir-Rhyne U (NC)
Lewis & Clark Coll (OR)
Lewis U (IL)
Lincoln U (MO)
Lincoln U (PA)
Linfield Coll (OR)
Lipscomb U (TN)
Lock Haven U of Pennsylvania (PA)
Long Island U–LIU Post (NY)
Longwood U (VA)
Louisiana Coll (LA)
Louisiana State U and A&M Coll (LA)
Louisiana State U in Shreveport (LA)
Loyola Marymount U (CA)
Loyola U Chicago (IL)
Loyola U New Orleans (LA)
Luther Coll (IA)
Lycoming Coll (PA)
Lynchburg Coll (VA)
Macalester Coll (MN)
Manchester U (IN)
Manhattan Coll (NY)
Marietta Coll (OH)
Marquette U (WI)
Marshall U (WV)
Mary Baldwin Coll (VA)
Massachusetts Coll of Liberal Arts (MA)
Massachusetts Inst of Technology (MA)
McDaniel Coll (MD)
McMurry U (TX)
Mercer U, Macon (GA)
Merrimack Coll (MA)
Messiah Coll (PA)
Miami U (OH)
Michigan State U (MI)
Michigan Technological U (MI)
Middlebury Coll (VT)
Middle Tennessee State U (TN)
Midwestern State U (TX)
Millersville U of Pennsylvania (PA)
Millikin U (IL)
Millsaps Coll (MS)
Minnesota State U Mankato (MN)
Minnesota State U Moorhead (MN)
Minot State U (ND)
Mississippi State U (MS)
Missouri Southern State U (MO)
Missouri State U (MO)
Missouri U of Science and Technology (MO)
Monmouth Coll (IL)
Montana State U (MT)
Montclair State U (NJ)
Moravian Coll (PA)
Morehead State U (KY)
Morningside Coll (IA)
Mount Allison U (NB, Canada)
Mount Holyoke Coll (MA)
Mount Vernon Nazarene U (OH)
Muhlenberg Coll (PA)
Murray State U (KY)
Nebraska Wesleyan U (NE)
New Coll of Florida (FL)
New Jersey City U (NJ)
New Jersey Inst of Technology (NJ)
New Mexico Highlands U (NM)
New Mexico Inst of Mining and Technology (NM)
New Mexico State U (NM)
New York U (NY)
Norfolk State U (VA)
North Carolina Ag and Tech State U (NC)
North Carolina Central U (NC)
North Carolina State U (NC)
North Central Coll (IL)
North Dakota State U (ND)
Northeastern Illinois U (IL)
Northeastern U (MA)
Northern Arizona U (AZ)
Northern Illinois U (IL)
Northern Kentucky U (KY)
Northern Michigan U (MI)
Northwestern U (IL)
Northwest Nazarene U (ID)
Norwich U (VT)
Notre Dame of Maryland U (MD)
Oakland U (MI)
Oberlin Coll (OH)
Occidental Coll (CA)
Oglethorpe U (GA)
Ohio Northern U (OH)
The Ohio State U (OH)
Ohio U (OH)
Ohio Wesleyan U (OH)
Oklahoma Baptist U (OK)
Oklahoma City U (OK)
Oklahoma State U (OK)
Old Dominion U (VA)
Oregon State U (OR)
Pace U (NY)
Pacific Lutheran U (WA)
Pacific U (OR)
Penn State Abington (PA)
Penn State Altoona (PA)
Penn State Beaver (PA)
Penn State Berks (PA)
Penn State Brandywine (PA)
Penn State DuBois (PA)
Penn State Erie, The Behrend Coll (PA)
Penn State Fayette, The Eberly Campus (PA)
Penn State Greater Allegheny (PA)
Penn State Hazleton (PA)
Penn State Lehigh Valley (PA)
Penn State Mont Alto (PA)
Penn State New Kensington (PA)
Penn State Schuylkill (PA)
Penn State Shenango (PA)
Penn State U Park (PA)
Penn State Wilkes-Barre (PA)
Penn State Worthington Scranton (PA)
Penn State York (PA)
Pepperdine U, Malibu (CA)
Piedmont Coll (GA)
Pittsburg State U (KS)
Point Loma Nazarene U (CA)
Pomona Coll (CA)
Portland State U (OR)
Prairie View A&M U (TX)
Presbyterian Coll (SC)
Princeton U (NJ)
Principia Coll (IL)
Purchase Coll, State U of New York (NY)
Purdue U (IN)
Purdue U Calumet (IN)
Queens Coll of the City U of New York (NY)
Radford U (VA)
Ramapo Coll of New Jersey (NJ)
Randolph Coll (VA)
Randolph-Macon Coll (VA)
Reed Coll (OR)
Regis U (CO)
Rensselaer Polytechnic Inst (NY)
Rhode Island Coll (RI)
Rhodes Coll (TN)
Rice U (TX)
Rider U (NJ)
Roanoke Coll (VA)
Roberts Wesleyan Coll (NY)
Rockhurst U (MO)
Rollins Coll (FL)
Rose-Hulman Inst of Technology (IN)
Rowan U (NJ)
Rutgers, The State U of New Jersey, Camden (NJ)
Rutgers, The State U of New Jersey, Newark (NJ)
Rutgers, The State U of New Jersey, New Brunswick (NJ)
Saginaw Valley State U (MI)
Saint Anselm Coll (NH)
St. Bonaventure U (NY)
St. Catherine U (MN)
St. John Fisher Coll (NY)
Saint John's U (MN)
St. John's U (NY)
Saint Joseph's U (PA)
St. Lawrence U (NY)
Saint Louis U (MO)
St. Mary's Coll of Maryland (MD)
St. Mary's U (TX)
Saint Mary's U of Minnesota (MN)
Saint Michael's Coll (VT)
St. Norbert Coll (WI)
St. Olaf Coll (MN)
Saint Peter's U (NJ)
Saint Vincent Coll (PA)
Salisbury U (MD)
Samford U (AL)
Sam Houston State U (TX)
San Diego State U (CA)
San Francisco State U (CA)
San Jose State U (CA)
Santa Clara U (CA)
Scripps Coll (CA)
Seattle Pacific U (WA)
Seattle U (WA)
Sewanee: The U of the South (TN)
Shippensburg U of Pennsylvania (PA)
Siena Coll (NY)
Simmons Coll (MA)
Simon Fraser U (BC, Canada)
Simpson Coll (IA)
Skidmore Coll (NY)
Slippery Rock U of Pennsylvania (PA)
Smith Coll (MA)
South Carolina State U (SC)
South Dakota School of Mines and Technology (SD)
South Dakota State U (SD)
Southeastern Louisiana U (LA)
Southeast Missouri State U (MO)
Southern Adventist U (TN)
Southern Arkansas U–Magnolia (AR)
Southern Connecticut State U (CT)
Southern Illinois U Carbondale (IL)
Southern Illinois U Edwardsville (IL)
Southern Methodist U (TX)
Southern Oregon U (OR)
Southwestern U (TX)
Spelman Coll (GA)
Stanford U (CA)
State U of New York at Fredonia (NY)
State U of New York at New Paltz (NY)
State U of New York at Oswego (NY)
State U of New York at Plattsburgh (NY)
State U of New York Coll at Cortland (NY)
State U of New York Coll at Geneseo (NY)
State U of New York Coll at Potsdam (NY)
Stephen F. Austin State U (TX)
Stetson U (FL)
Stockton U (NJ)
Stonehill Coll (MA)
Stony Brook U, State U of New York (NY)
Suffolk U (MA)
Susquehanna U (PA)
Syracuse U (NY)
Tarleton State U (TX)
Taylor U (IN)
Temple U (PA)
Tennessee State U (TN)
Texas A&M U (TX)
Texas A&M U–Commerce (TX)
Texas A&M U–Kingsville (TX)
Texas Christian U (TX)
Texas Lutheran U (TX)
Texas Southern U (TX)
Texas State U (TX)
Texas Tech U (TX)
Thiel Coll (PA)
Thomas More Coll (KY)
Tougaloo Coll (MS)
Towson U (MD)
Transylvania U (KY)
Trent U (ON, Canada)
Trevecca Nazarene U (TN)
Trinity Coll (CT)
Trinity U (TX)
Truman State U (MO)
Tufts U (MA)
Tulane U (LA)
Union Coll (KY)
Union Coll (NY)
Union U (TN)
United States Air Force Acad (CO)
United States Military Acad (NY)
United States Naval Acad (MD)
Université de Montréal (QC, Canada)
Université de Sherbrooke (QC, Canada)
U at Albany, State U of New York (NY)
U at Buffalo, the State U of New York (NY)
The U of Akron (OH)
The U of Alabama (AL)
The U of Alabama at Birmingham (AL)
The U of Alabama in Huntsville (AL)
U of Alaska Fairbanks (AK)
U of Alberta (AB, Canada)
The U of Arizona (AZ)
U of Arkansas (AR)
U of Arkansas at Little Rock (AR)
U of Arkansas at Pine Bluff (AR)
The U of British Columbia (BC, Canada)
The U of British Columbia–Okanagan Campus (BC, Canada)
U of California, Berkeley (CA)
U of California, Davis (CA)
U of California, Irvine (CA)
U of California, Los Angeles (CA)
U of California, Merced (CA)
U of California, Riverside (CA)
U of California, Santa Barbara (CA)
U of California, Santa Cruz (CA)
U of Central Arkansas (AR)
U of Central Florida (FL)
U of Central Missouri (MO)
U of Central Oklahoma (OK)
U of Chicago (IL)
U of Cincinnati (OH)
U of Colorado Boulder (CO)
U of Colorado Colorado Springs (CO)
U of Colorado Denver (CO)
U of Dallas (TX)
U of Dayton (OH)
U of Delaware (DE)
U of Denver (CO)
U of Evansville (IN)
U of Florida (FL)
U of Georgia (GA)
U of Guelph (ON, Canada)
U of Hartford (CT)
U of Hawaii at Manoa (HI)
U of Houston (TX)
U of Houston–Clear Lake (TX)
U of Idaho (ID)
U of Illinois at Chicago (IL)
U of Indianapolis (IN)
The U of Iowa (IA)
The U of Kansas (KS)
U of Kentucky (KY)
U of King's Coll (NS, Canada)
U of La Verne (CA)
U of Lethbridge (AB, Canada)
U of Louisiana at Lafayette (LA)
U of Louisville (KY)
U of Maine (ME)
U of Maryland, Baltimore County (MD)
U of Maryland, Coll Park (MD)
U of Mary Washington (VA)
U of Massachusetts Amherst (MA)
U of Massachusetts Boston (MA)
U of Massachusetts Dartmouth (MA)
U of Massachusetts Lowell (MA)
U of Memphis (TN)
U of Miami (FL)
U of Michigan (MI)
U of Michigan–Dearborn (MI)
U of Michigan–Flint (MI)
U of Minnesota, Duluth (MN)
U of Minnesota, Morris (MN)
U of Minnesota, Twin Cities Campus (MN)
U of Mississippi (MS)
U of Missouri (MO)
U of Missouri–Kansas City (MO)
U of Missouri–St. Louis (MO)
The U of Montana (MT)
U of Mount Union (OH)
U of Nebraska at Kearney (NE)
U of Nebraska–Lincoln (NE)
U of Nevada, Las Vegas (NV)
U of Nevada, Reno (NV)
U of New Brunswick Saint John (NB, Canada)
U of New Hampshire (NH)
U of New Mexico (NM)
U of New Orleans (LA)
U of North Alabama (AL)
U of North Carolina at Asheville (NC)
The U of North Carolina at Chapel Hill (NC)
The U of North Carolina at Charlotte (NC)
The U of North Carolina at Greensboro (NC)
The U of North Carolina at Pembroke (NC)
The U of North Carolina Wilmington (NC)
U of North Dakota (ND)
U of Northern Colorado (CO)
U of North Florida (FL)
U of North Georgia (GA)
U of North Texas (TX)
U of Notre Dame (IN)
U of Oklahoma (OK)
U of Oregon (OR)
U of Ottawa (ON, Canada)
U of Pennsylvania (PA)
U of Pittsburgh (PA)
U of Portland (OR)
U of Puget Sound (WA)
U of Regina (SK, Canada)
U of Rhode Island (RI)
U of Richmond (VA)
U of Rochester (NY)
U of St. Thomas (MN)
U of San Diego (CA)
U of San Francisco (CA)
U of Saskatchewan (SK, Canada)
U of Science and Arts of Oklahoma (OK)
The U of Scranton (PA)

U of South Alabama (AL)
The U of South Dakota (SD)
U of Southern California (CA)
U of Southern Maine (ME)
U of Southern Mississippi (MS)
U of South Florida (FL)
The U of Tennessee (TN)
The U of Tennessee at Chattanooga (TN)
The U of Texas at Arlington (TX)
The U of Texas at Austin (TX)
The U of Texas at Dallas (TX)
The U of Texas at El Paso (TX)
The U of Texas at San Antonio (TX)
The U of Texas–Pan American (TX)
U of the Cumberlands (KY)
U of the District of Columbia (DC)
U of the Fraser Valley (BC, Canada)
U of the Pacific (CA)
U of the Sciences (PA)
The U of Toledo (OH)
The U of Tulsa (OK)
U of Utah (UT)
U of Vermont (VT)
U of Virginia (VA)
U of Washington (WA)
U of Waterloo (ON, Canada)
The U of Western Ontario (ON, Canada)
U of West Florida (FL)
U of West Georgia (GA)
U of Windsor (ON, Canada)
U of Wisconsin–Eau Claire (WI)
U of Wisconsin–La Crosse (WI)
U of Wisconsin–Madison (WI)
U of Wisconsin–Milwaukee (WI)
U of Wisconsin–Oshkosh (WI)
U of Wisconsin–Parkside (WI)
U of Wisconsin–River Falls (WI)
U of Wisconsin–Stevens Point (WI)
U of Wisconsin–Whitewater (WI)
U of Wyoming (WY)
Ursinus Coll (PA)
Utah State U (UT)
Utah Valley U (UT)
Utica Coll (NY)
Valdosta State U (GA)
Valparaiso U (IN)
Vanderbilt U (TN)
Vassar Coll (NY)
Villanova U (PA)
Virginia Commonwealth U (VA)
Virginia Military Inst (VA)
Virginia Polytechnic Inst and State U (VA)
Virginia State U (VA)
Wabash Coll (IN)
Wagner Coll (NY)
Wake Forest U (NC)
Walla Walla U (WA)
Wartburg Coll (IA)
Washburn U (KS)
Washington & Jefferson Coll (PA)
Washington and Lee U (VA)
Washington Coll (MD)
Washington State U (WA)
Washington U in St. Louis (MO)
Wayne State U (MI)
Weber State U (UT)
Wells Coll (NY)
Wesleyan U (CT)
West Chester U of Pennsylvania (PA)
Western Illinois U (IL)
Western Kentucky U (KY)
Western Michigan U (MI)
Western State Colorado U (CO)
Western Washington U (WA)
Westminster Coll (MO)
Westminster Coll (UT)
West Texas A&M U (TX)
West Virginia U (WV)
West Virginia Wesleyan Coll (WV)
Wheaton Coll (IL)
Wheaton Coll (MA)
Wheeling Jesuit U (WV)
Whitman Coll (WA)
Whittier Coll (CA)
Whitworth U (WA)
Wichita State U (KS)
Widener U (PA)
Wilkes U (PA)
Willamette U (OR)
William Jewell Coll (MO)
Williams Coll (MA)
Winona State U (MN)
Wittenberg U (OH)
Wofford Coll (SC)
Worcester Polytechnic Inst (MA)
Wright State U (OH)
Xavier U (OH)
Xavier U of Louisiana (LA)
Yale U (CT)
Yeshiva U (NY)
York Coll of the City U of New York (NY)
Youngstown State U (OH)

PHYSICS RELATED
Arcadia U (PA)
Augsburg Coll (MN)
Bridgewater Coll (VA)
Bridgewater State U (MA)
Brigham Young U (UT)
California State U, San Marcos (CA)
Carson-Newman U (TN)
Christopher Newport U (VA)
Coll of Saint Benedict (MN)
The Coll of Wooster (OH)
Delaware State U (DE)
Drexel U (PA)
Embry-Riddle Aeronautical U–Daytona (FL)
Embry-Riddle Aeronautical U–Prescott (AZ)
Florida Inst of Technology (FL)
Fort Lewis Coll (CO)
Francis Marion U (SC)
Illinois Inst of Technology (IL)
Lawrence Technological U (MI)
Ohio Northern U (OH)
Presbyterian Coll (SC)
Rensselaer Polytechnic Inst (NY)
Rutgers, The State U of New Jersey, Newark (NJ)
Saint John's U (MN)
Saint Mary's U of Minnesota (MN)
Southern Arkansas U–Magnolia (AR)
U of Alberta (AB, Canada)
U of California, Davis (CA)
U of Dayton (OH)
U of Minnesota, Duluth (MN)
U of Northern Iowa (IA)
U of Notre Dame (IN)
U of Regina (SK, Canada)
U of Rhode Island (RI)
U of Rochester (NY)
The U of Western Ontario (ON, Canada)
Wheeling Jesuit U (WV)
Whitman Coll (WA)

PHYSICS TEACHER EDUCATION
Abilene Christian U (TX)
Albion Coll (MI)
Alma Coll (MI)
Anderson U (IN)
Arkansas State U (AR)
Auburn U (AL)
Augustana Coll (IL)
Bowling Green State U (OH)
Bradley U (IL)
Buena Vista U (IA)
Canisius Coll (NY)
Cedarville U (OH)
Central Methodist U (MO)
Central Michigan U (MI)
City Coll of the City U of New York (NY)
The Coll of New Jersey (NJ)
Coll of Staten Island of the City U of New York (NY)
Colorado State U (CO)
Concordia Coll (MN)
Concordia U, Nebraska (NE)
Delaware State U (DE)
East Central U (OK)
Eastern Kentucky U (KY)
Eastern Michigan U (MI)
Elmhurst Coll (IL)
Emory & Henry Coll (VA)
Florida Inst of Technology (FL)
Fordham U (NY)
Grand Valley State U (MI)
Greenville Coll (IL)
Gustavus Adolphus Coll (MN)
Hastings Coll (NE)
Hofstra U (NY)
Hope Coll (MI)
Indiana U Bloomington (IN)
Indiana U–Purdue U Fort Wayne (IN)
Indiana U South Bend (IN)
Ithaca Coll (NY)
Juniata Coll (PA)
Kansas Wesleyan U (KS)
King U (TN)
Le Moyne Coll (NY)
Lincoln U (MO)
Lipscomb U (TN)
Louisiana State U in Shreveport (LA)
Madonna U (MI)
Manchester U (IN)
Messiah Coll (PA)
Miami Dade Coll (FL)
Michigan State U (MI)
Minnesota State U Moorhead (MN)
Minot State U (ND)
Missouri State U (MO)
Morningside Coll (IA)
Mount Vernon Nazarene U (OH)
North Carolina Ag and Tech State U (NC)
North Dakota State U (ND)
Northern Michigan U (MI)
Ohio Northern U (OH)
Ohio Wesleyan U (OH)
Pittsburg State U (KS)
Providence Coll (RI)
Queens Coll of the City U of New York (NY)
Rhode Island Coll (RI)
Roberts Wesleyan Coll (NY)
Saginaw Valley State U (MI)
St. John Fisher Coll (NY)
St. John's U (NY)
Saint Joseph's U (PA)
Saint Mary's U of Minnesota (MN)
Saint Vincent Coll (PA)
Seattle U (WA)
Southern Adventist U (TN)
State U of New York at New Paltz (NY)
State U of New York Coll at Cortland (NY)
Syracuse U (NY)
Trevecca Nazarene U (TN)
Union Coll (NE)
U of Alberta (AB, Canada)
U of Central Missouri (MO)
U of Central Oklahoma (OK)
U of Delaware (DE)
U of Evansville (IN)
U of Illinois at Chicago (IL)
U of Maryland, Baltimore County (MD)
U of Missouri (MO)
U of Nebraska–Lincoln (NE)
U of Regina (SK, Canada)
U of Rio Grande (OH)
U of St. Thomas (MN)
The U of South Dakota (SD)
U of Waterloo (ON, Canada)
U of Windsor (ON, Canada)
U of Wisconsin–River Falls (WI)
Utah State U (UT)
Utica Coll (NY)
Valparaiso U (IN)
Washington State U (WA)
Washington U in St. Louis (MO)
Weber State U (UT)
Western Michigan U (MI)
Winona State U (MN)
Xavier U (OH)

PHYSIOLOGICAL PSYCHOLOGY/ PSYCHOBIOLOGY
Albright Coll (PA)
Arcadia U (PA)
Averett U (VA)
Binghamton U, State U of New York (NY)
Centre Coll (KY)
Florida Atlantic U (FL)
Holy Family U (PA)
Houghton Coll (NY)
La Sierra U (CA)
Lebanon Valley Coll (PA)
Lincoln U (PA)
Mills Coll (CA)
Mount Allison U (NB, Canada)
Oberlin Coll (OH)
Pace U (NY)
Quinnipiac U (CT)
Ripon Coll (WI)
Southern Adventist U (TN)
U of California, Los Angeles (CA)
U of California, Santa Barbara (CA)
U of Colorado Denver (CO)
U of Michigan (MI)
U of New England (ME)
Vassar Coll (NY)
Washington Coll (MD)
Wesleyan U (CT)

PHYSIOLOGY
Brigham Young U (UT)
California State U, Long Beach (CA)
California State U, San Marcos (CA)
Emmanuel Coll (MA)
Marquette U (WI)
Michigan State U (MI)
Northern Michigan U (MI)
Oklahoma Baptist U (OK)
Oklahoma State U (OK)
Seattle Pacific U (WA)
Southern Illinois U Carbondale (IL)
U of Alberta (AB, Canada)
The U of Arizona (AZ)
The U of British Columbia (BC, Canada)
U of California, Los Angeles (CA)
U of California, Santa Barbara (CA)
U of Colorado Boulder (CO)
U of Oregon (OR)
U of Ottawa (ON, Canada)
U of Saskatchewan (SK, Canada)
U of Washington (WA)
The U of Western Ontario (ON, Canada)
U of Wyoming (WY)

PLANETARY ASTRONOMY AND SCIENCE
California Inst of Technology (CA)
Florida Inst of Technology (FL)
U of Waterloo (ON, Canada)
The U of Western Ontario (ON, Canada)

PLANT GENETICS
Purdue U (IN)

PLANT NURSERY MANAGEMENT
Colorado State U (CO)

PLANT PATHOLOGY/ PHYTOPATHOLOGY
Cornell U (NY)
New Mexico State U (NM)
The Ohio State U (OH)
State U of New York Coll of Environmental Science and Forestry (NY)
U of Wisconsin–Madison (WI)

PLANT PHYSIOLOGY
State U of New York Coll of Environmental Science and Forestry (NY)

PLANT PROTECTION AND INTEGRATED PEST MANAGEMENT
California State Polytechnic U, Pomona (CA)
Cornell U (NY)
Iowa State U of Science and Technology (IA)
State U of New York Coll of Environmental Science and Forestry (NY)
U of Delaware (DE)
U of Hawaii at Manoa (HI)
U of Minnesota, Twin Cities Campus (MN)
Washington State U (WA)
West Texas A&M U (TX)

PLANT SCIENCES
Arkansas State U (AR)
Auburn U (AL)
California State U, Fresno (CA)
Cornell U (NY)
Dalhousie U (NS, Canada)
Louisiana State U and A&M Coll (LA)
Middle Tennessee State U (TN)
Montana State U (MT)
The Ohio State U (OH)
Penn State U Park (PA)
Rutgers, The State U of New Jersey, New Brunswick (NJ)
South Dakota State U (SD)
Southeast Missouri State U (MO)
Southern Illinois U Carbondale (IL)
State U of New York Coll of Agriculture and Technology at Cobleskill (NY)
State U of New York Coll of Environmental Science and Forestry (NY)
Texas Tech U (TX)
The U of Arizona (AZ)
U of California, Santa Cruz (CA)
U of Delaware (DE)
U of Florida (FL)
U of Guelph (ON, Canada)
U of Massachusetts Amherst (MA)
U of Minnesota, Crookston (MN)
U of Minnesota, Twin Cities Campus (MN)
U of Missouri (MO)
U of Rhode Island (RI)
The U of Tennessee (TN)
U of Vermont (VT)
Utah State U (UT)
Washington State U (WA)

PLANT SCIENCES RELATED
Auburn U (AL)
Sterling Coll (VT)
U of Hawaii at Manoa (HI)
Utah State U (UT)
West Virginia U (WV)

PLASTICS AND POLYMER ENGINEERING TECHNOLOGY
Eastern Michigan U (MI)
Ferris State U (MI)
Pennsylvania Coll of Technology (PA)
Pittsburg State U (KS)
Shawnee State U (OH)
Weber State U (UT)

PLAYWRITING AND SCREENWRITING
Acad of Art U (CA)
Bennington Coll (VT)
Brigham Young U (UT)
Central Washington U (WA)
Chapman U (CA)
Columbia Coll Chicago (IL)
Concordia U (QC, Canada)
DePaul U (IL)
Drexel U (PA)
Emerson Coll (MA)
Judson U (IL)
Loyola Marymount U (CA)
Marymount Manhattan Coll (NY)
Metropolitan State U (MN)
Ohio U (OH)
Purchase Coll, State U of New York (NY)
Savannah Coll of Art and Design (GA)
U of Southern California (CA)
The U of the Arts (PA)

POLISH
U of Illinois at Chicago (IL)
U of Michigan (MI)
U of Pittsburgh (PA)
U of Wisconsin–Madison (WI)

POLITICAL COMMUNICATION
Emerson Coll (MA)
Florida Southern Coll (FL)
Nebraska Wesleyan U (NE)
Suffolk U (MA)
U of Washington (WA)
Weber State U (UT)

POLITICAL ECONOMY
Antioch Coll, Yellow Springs (OH)
Augsburg Coll (MN)
Ave Maria U (FL)
The Evergreen State Coll (WA)
Fordham U (NY)
Hillsdale Coll (MI)
Rhodes Coll (TN)
U of Southern California (CA)
U of Washington, Bothell (WA)
U of Washington, Tacoma (WA)
Williams Coll (MA)

POLITICAL SCIENCE AND GOVERNMENT
Abilene Christian U (TX)

Adelphi U (NY)
Agnes Scott Coll (GA)
Alabama State U (AL)
Albany State U (GA)
Albertus Magnus Coll (CT)
Albion Coll (MI)
Albright Coll (PA)
Alcorn State U (MS)
Allegheny Coll (PA)
Alma Coll (MI)
Alvernia U (PA)
Alverno Coll (WI)
American Intl Coll (MA)
American Public U System (WV)
American U (DC)
The American U in Cairo (Egypt)
American U of Beirut (Lebanon)
Amherst Coll (MA)
Anderson U (IN)
Andrews U (MI)
Angelo State U (TX)
Anna Maria Coll (MA)
Appalachian State U (NC)
Aquinas Coll (MI)
Arcadia U (PA)
Arizona State U at the Tempe campus (AZ)
Arizona State U at the West campus (AZ)
Arkansas State U (AR)
Arkansas Tech U (AR)
Armstrong State U (GA)
Asbury U (KY)
Ashland U (OH)
Assumption Coll (MA)
Athens State U (AL)
Auburn U (AL)
Auburn U at Montgomery (AL)
Augsburg Coll (MN)
Augustana Coll (IL)
Augustana Coll (SD)
Austin Coll (TX)
Austin Peay State U (TN)
Averett U (VA)
Avila U (MO)
Azusa Pacific U (CA)
Baldwin Wallace U (OH)
Ball State U (IN)
Bard Coll (NY)
Bard Coll at Simon's Rock (MA)
Barnard Coll (NY)
Barry U (FL)
Baruch Coll of the City U of New York (NY)
Bates Coll (ME)
Baylor U (TX)
Belhaven U (MS)
Belmont U (TN)
Beloit Coll (WI)
Bemidji State U (MN)
Benedictine Coll (KS)
Benedictine U (IL)
Bennett Coll (NC)
Bennington Coll (VT)
Berea Coll (KY)
Berry Coll (GA)
Bethany Coll (WV)
Bethel U (MN)
Bethune-Cookman U (FL)
Binghamton U, State U of New York (NY)
Biola U (CA)
Birmingham-Southern Coll (AL)
Blackburn Coll (IL)
Black Hills State U (SD)
Bloomfield Coll (NJ)
Bloomsburg U of Pennsylvania (PA)
Boston Coll (MA)
Boston U (MA)
Bowdoin Coll (ME)
Bowie State U (MD)
Bowling Green State U (OH)
Bradley U (IL)
Bridgewater Coll (VA)
Bridgewater State U (MA)
Brown U (RI)
Bryan Coll (TN)
Bryant U (RI)
Bryn Mawr Coll (PA)
Bucknell U (PA)
Buena Vista U (IA)
Buffalo State Coll, State U of New York (NY)
Butler U (IN)
Cabrini Coll (PA)
Caldwell U (NJ)
California Baptist U (CA)
California Inst of Technology (CA)
California Lutheran U (CA)
California Polytechnic State U, San Luis Obispo (CA)
California State Polytechnic U, Pomona (CA)
California State U, Chico (CA)
California State U, Dominguez Hills (CA)
California State U, Fresno (CA)
California State U, Fullerton (CA)
California State U, Long Beach (CA)
California State U, Los Angeles (CA)
California State U, Sacramento (CA)
California State U, San Bernardino (CA)
California State U, San Marcos (CA)
California State U, Stanislaus (CA)
California U of Pennsylvania (PA)
Calvary Bible Coll and Theological Sem (MO)
Calvin Coll (MI)
Cameron U (OK)
Campbellsville U (KY)
Canisius Coll (NY)
Cape Breton U (NS, Canada)
Capital U (OH)
Cardinal Stritch U (WI)
Carleton Coll (MN)
Carlow U (PA)
Carroll Coll (MT)
Carson-Newman U (TN)
Case Western Reserve U (OH)
Catawba Coll (NC)
The Catholic U of America (DC)
Cedar Crest Coll (PA)
Cedarville U (OH)
Centenary Coll of Louisiana (LA)
Central Coll (IA)
Central Connecticut State U (CT)
Central Methodist U (MO)
Central Michigan U (MI)
Central State U (OH)
Central Washington U (WA)
Centre Coll (KY)
Chapman U (CA)
Charleston Southern U (SC)
Chatham U (PA)
Chestnut Hill Coll (PA)
Cheyney U of Pennsylvania (PA)
Chicago State U (IL)
Chowan U (NC)
Christendom Coll (VA)
Christopher Newport U (VA)
The Citadel, The Military Coll of South Carolina (SC)
City Coll of the City U of New York (NY)
Claremont McKenna Coll (CA)
Clarion U of Pennsylvania (PA)
Clark Atlanta U (GA)
Clarkson U (NY)
Clark U (MA)
Clayton State U (GA)
Cleveland State U (OH)
Coastal Carolina U (SC)
Coe Coll (IA)
Coker Coll (SC)
Colby Coll (ME)
The Coll at Brockport, State U of New York (NY)
Coll of Charleston (SC)
The Coll of Idaho (ID)
The Coll of New Jersey (NJ)
The Coll of New Rochelle (NY)
Coll of Saint Benedict (MN)
The Coll of Saint Rose (NY)
Coll of Staten Island of the City U of New York (NY)
Coll of the Holy Cross (MA)
The Coll of William and Mary (VA)
The Coll of Wooster (OH)
The Colorado Coll (CO)
Colorado Mesa U (CO)
Colorado State U (CO)
Colorado State U–Pueblo (CO)
Columbia Coll (MO)
Columbia Coll (SC)
Columbia U (NY)
Columbia U, School of General Studies (NY)
Columbus State U (GA)
Concordia Coll (MN)
Concordia U (CA)
Concordia U (QC, Canada)
Concordia U Chicago (IL)
Concordia U Wisconsin (WI)
Concord U (WV)
Connecticut Coll (CT)
Cornell Coll (IA)
Cornell U (NY)
Creighton U (NE)
Culver-Stockton Coll (MO)
Cumberland U (TN)
Daemen Coll (NY)
Dalhousie U (NS, Canada)
Dallas Baptist U (TX)
Dartmouth Coll (NH)
Davidson Coll (NC)
Delaware State U (DE)
Delta State U (MS)
Denison U (OH)
DePaul U (IL)
DePauw U (IN)
DeSales U (PA)
Dickinson Coll (PA)
Dickinson State U (ND)
Doane Coll (NE)
Dominican U (IL)
Dominican U of California (CA)
Dowling Coll (NY)
Drake U (IA)
Drew U (NJ)
Drexel U (PA)
Drury U (MO)
Duquesne U (PA)
Earlham Coll (IN)
East Carolina U (NC)
East Central U (OK)
Eastern Connecticut State U (CT)
Eastern Illinois U (IL)
Eastern Kentucky U (KY)
Eastern Michigan U (MI)
Eastern New Mexico U (NM)
Eastern U (PA)
East Stroudsburg U of Pennsylvania (PA)
East Tennessee State U (TN)
East Texas Baptist U (TX)
Eckerd Coll (FL)
Edgewood Coll (WI)
Edinboro U of Pennsylvania (PA)
Elizabethtown Coll (PA)
Elmhurst Coll (IL)
Elmira Coll (NY)
Elon U (NC)
Emmanuel Coll (MA)
Emory & Henry Coll (VA)
Emporia State U (KS)
Endicott Coll (MA)
Erskine Coll (SC)
Evangel U (MO)
The Evergreen State Coll (WA)
Excelsior Coll (NY)
Fairfield U (CT)
Fairleigh Dickinson U, Coll at Florham (NJ)
Fairleigh Dickinson U, Metropolitan Campus (NJ)
Fairmont State U (WV)
Fayetteville State U (NC)
Ferris State U (MI)
Ferrum Coll (VA)
Fitchburg State U (MA)
Flagler Coll (FL)
Florida Ag and Mech U (FL)
Florida Atlantic U (FL)
Florida Gulf Coast U (FL)
Florida Intl U (FL)
Florida Southern Coll (FL)
Florida State U (FL)
Fordham U (NY)
Fort Hays State U (KS)
Fort Lewis Coll (CO)
Framingham State U (MA)
Franciscan U of Steubenville (OH)
Francis Marion U (SC)
Franklin & Marshall Coll (PA)
Franklin Coll (IN)
Franklin Pierce U (NH)
Friends U (KS)
Frostburg State U (MD)
Furman U (SC)
Gannon U (PA)
Geneva Coll (PA)
Georgetown Coll (KY)
Georgetown U (DC)
The George Washington U (DC)
Georgia Coll & State U (GA)
Georgia Gwinnett Coll (GA)
Georgia Regents U (GA)
Georgia Southern U (GA)
Georgia Southwestern State U (GA)
Georgia State U (GA)
Gettysburg Coll (PA)
Gonzaga U (WA)
Gordon Coll (MA)
Goucher Coll (MD)
Governors State U (IL)
Grace Coll (IN)
Grambling State U (LA)
Grand Valley State U (MI)
Grand View U (IA)
Greensboro Coll (NC)
Grinnell Coll (IA)
Grove City Coll (PA)
Guilford Coll (NC)
Gustavus Adolphus Coll (MN)
Hamilton Coll (NY)
Hamline U (MN)
Hampden-Sydney Coll (VA)
Hampshire Coll (MA)
Hampton U (VA)
Hanover Coll (IN)
Harding U (AR)
Hardin-Simmons U (TX)
Hartwick Coll (NY)
Harvard U (MA)
Hastings Coll (NE)
Haverford Coll (PA)
Hawai`i Pacific U (HI)
Heidelberg U (OH)
Hendrix Coll (AR)
High Point U (NC)
Hilbert Coll (NY)
Hillsdale Coll (MI)
Hiram Coll (OH)
Hobart and William Smith Colls (NY)
Hofstra U (NY)
Hollins U (VA)
Holy Family U (PA)
Hope Coll (MI)
Houghton Coll (NY)
Houston Baptist U (TX)
Howard Payne U (TX)
Howard U (DC)
Humboldt State U (CA)
Hunter Coll of the City U of New York (NY)
Huntingdon Coll (AL)
Huston-Tillotson U (TX)
Illinois Coll (IL)
Illinois Inst of Technology (IL)
Illinois State U (IL)
Illinois Wesleyan U (IL)
Immaculata U (PA)
Indiana State U (IN)
Indiana U Bloomington (IN)
Indiana U East (IN)
Indiana U Northwest (IN)
Indiana U of Pennsylvania (PA)
Indiana U–Purdue U Fort Wayne (IN)
Indiana U–Purdue U Indianapolis (IN)
Indiana U South Bend (IN)
Indiana U Southeast (IN)
Inter American U of Puerto Rico, San Germán Campus (PR)
Iona Coll (NY)
Iowa State U of Science and Technology (IA)
Ithaca Coll (NY)
Jackson State U (MS)
Jacksonville State U (AL)
Jacksonville U (FL)
James Madison U (VA)
John Brown U (AR)
John Cabot U (Italy)
John Carroll U (OH)
Johns Hopkins U (MD)
Johnson C. Smith U (NC)
Johnson State Coll (VT)
Juniata Coll (PA)
Kalamazoo Coll (MI)
Kansas State U (KS)
Kean U (NJ)
Keene State Coll (NH)
Keiser U, Fort Lauderdale (FL)
Kennesaw State U (GA)
Kent State U (OH)
Kentucky State U (KY)
Kentucky Wesleyan Coll (KY)
Kenyon Coll (OH)
King's Coll (PA)
King U (TN)
Knox Coll (IL)
Kutztown U of Pennsylvania (PA)
Lafayette Coll (PA)
LaGrange Coll (GA)
Lake Erie Coll (OH)
Lake Forest Coll (IL)
Lamar U (TX)
La Roche Coll (PA)
La Salle U (PA)
Lawrence U (WI)
Lebanese American U (Lebanon)
Lebanon Valley Coll (PA)
Lee U (TN)
Lehigh U (PA)
Lehman Coll of the City U of New York (NY)
Le Moyne Coll (NY)
LeMoyne-Owen Coll (TN)
Lenoir-Rhyne U (NC)
Lewis & Clark Coll (OR)
Lewis U (IL)
Liberty U (VA)
Lincoln U (MO)
Lincoln U (PA)
Lindenwood U (MO)
Linfield Coll (OR)
Lipscomb U (TN)
Lock Haven U of Pennsylvania (PA)
Long Island U–LIU Brooklyn (NY)
Long Island U–LIU Post (NY)
Longwood U (VA)
Loras Coll (IA)
Louisiana State U and A&M Coll (LA)
Loyola Marymount U (CA)
Loyola U Chicago (IL)
Loyola U New Orleans (LA)
Luther Coll (IA)
Lycoming Coll (PA)
Lynchburg Coll (VA)
Lynn U (FL)
Lyon Coll (AR)
Macalester Coll (MN)
Malone U (OH)
Manchester U (IN)
Manhattan Coll (NY)
Manhattanville Coll (NY)
Mansfield U of Pennsylvania (PA)
Marian U (IN)
Marietta Coll (OH)
Marist Coll (NY)
Marquette U (WI)
Marshall U (WV)
Mars Hill U (NC)
Mary Baldwin Coll (VA)
Marymount Manhattan Coll (NY)
Marymount U (VA)
Maryville Coll (TN)
Massachusetts Coll of Liberal Arts (MA)
Massachusetts Inst of Technology (MA)
The Master's Coll and Sem (CA)
McDaniel Coll (MD)
McKendree U (IL)
McMurry U (TX)
McNeese State U (LA)
Mercer U, Macon (GA)
Mercy Coll (NY)
Meredith Coll (NC)
Merrimack Coll (MA)
Messiah Coll (PA)
Miami U (OH)
Michigan State U (MI)
Middlebury Coll (VT)
Middle Tennessee State U (TN)
Midwestern State U (TX)
Millersville U of Pennsylvania (PA)
Milligan Coll (TN)
Millikin U (IL)
Millsaps Coll (MS)
Mills Coll (CA)
Minnesota State U Mankato (MN)
Minnesota State U Moorhead (MN)
Mississippi State U (MS)
Mississippi U for Women (MS)
Mississippi Valley State U (MS)
Missouri Southern State U (MO)
Missouri State U (MO)
Missouri Valley Coll (MO)
Missouri Western State U (MO)
Molloy Coll (NY)
Monmouth Coll (IL)
Monmouth U (NJ)
Montana State U (MT)
Montclair State U (NJ)

Moravian Coll (PA)
Morehead State U (KY)
Morningside Coll (IA)
Morris Coll (SC)
Mount Allison U (NB, Canada)
Mount Holyoke Coll (MA)
Mount Mercy U (IA)
Mount Saint Mary Coll (NY)
Mount Saint Mary's U (CA)
Mount St. Mary's U (MD)
Mount Vernon Nazarene U (OH)
Muhlenberg Coll (PA)
Murray State U (KY)
National U (CA)
Nazareth Coll of Rochester (NY)
Nebraska Wesleyan U (NE)
Neumann U (PA)
Newberry Coll (SC)
New Coll of Florida (FL)
New England Coll (NH)
New Jersey City U (NJ)
New Mexico Highlands U (NM)
New Mexico State U (NM)
New York Inst of Technology (NY)
New York U (NY)
Niagara U (NY)
Nicholls State U (LA)
Norfolk State U (VA)
North Carolina Ag and Tech State U (NC)
North Carolina Central U (NC)
North Carolina State U (NC)
North Carolina Wesleyan Coll (NC)
North Central Coll (IL)
North Dakota State U (ND)
Northeastern Illinois U (IL)
Northeastern State U (OK)
Northeastern U (MA)
Northern Arizona U (AZ)
Northern Illinois U (IL)
Northern Kentucky U (KY)
Northern Michigan U (MI)
Northern State U (SD)
Northwestern Coll (IA)
Northwestern Oklahoma State U (OK)
Northwestern U (IL)
Northwest Missouri State U (MO)
Northwest Nazarene U (ID)
Northwest U (WA)
Norwich U (VT)
Notre Dame of Maryland U (MD)
Nova Southeastern U (FL)
Oakland U (MI)
Oberlin Coll (OH)
Occidental Coll (CA)
Oglethorpe U (GA)
Ohio Dominican U (OH)
Ohio Northern U (OH)
The Ohio State U (OH)
The Ohio State U–Newark Campus (OH)
Ohio U (OH)
Ohio Wesleyan U (OH)
Oklahoma Baptist U (OK)
Oklahoma City U (OK)
Oklahoma State U (OK)
Old Dominion U (VA)
Olivet Nazarene U (IL)
Oregon State U (OR)
Pace U (NY)
Pacific Lutheran U (WA)
Pacific U (OR)
Palm Beach Atlantic U (FL)
Park U (MO)
Patrick Henry Coll (VA)
Penn State Abington (PA)
Penn State Altoona (PA)
Penn State Beaver (PA)
Penn State Berks (PA)
Penn State Brandywine (PA)
Penn State DuBois (PA)
Penn State Erie, The Behrend Coll (PA)
Penn State Fayette, The Eberly Campus (PA)
Penn State Greater Allegheny (PA)
Penn State Hazleton (PA)
Penn State Lehigh Valley (PA)
Penn State Mont Alto (PA)
Penn State New Kensington (PA)
Penn State Schuylkill (PA)
Penn State Shenango (PA)
Penn State U Park (PA)
Penn State Wilkes-Barre (PA)
Penn State Worthington Scranton (PA)
Penn State York (PA)
Pepperdine U, Malibu (CA)
Philander Smith Coll (AR)
Piedmont Coll (GA)
Pine Manor Coll (MA)
Pittsburg State U (KS)
Plymouth State U (NH)
Point Loma Nazarene U (CA)
Pomona Coll (CA)
Portland State U (OR)
Prairie View A&M U (TX)
Presbyterian Coll (SC)
Princeton U (NJ)
Principia Coll (IL)
Providence Coll (RI)
Purchase Coll, State U of New York (NY)
Purdue U (IN)
Purdue U Calumet (IN)
Queens Coll of the City U of New York (NY)
Quincy U (IL)
Quinnipiac U (CT)
Radford U (VA)
Ramapo Coll of New Jersey (NJ)
Randolph Coll (VA)
Randolph-Macon Coll (VA)
Reed Coll (OR)
Regis Coll (MA)
Regis U (CO)
Reinhardt U (GA)
Rhode Island Coll (RI)
Rhodes Coll (TN)
Rice U (TX)
Rider U (NJ)
Ripon Coll (WI)
Rivier U (NH)
Roanoke Coll (VA)
Rochester Inst of Technology (NY)
Rockford U (IL)
Rockhurst U (MO)
Rocky Mountain Coll (MT)
Roger Williams U (RI)
Rollins Coll (FL)
Roosevelt U (IL)
Rosemont Coll (PA)
Rowan U (NJ)
Rust Coll (MS)
Rutgers, The State U of New Jersey, Camden (NJ)
Rutgers, The State U of New Jersey, Newark (NJ)
Rutgers, The State U of New Jersey, New Brunswick (NJ)
Sacred Heart U (CT)
The Sage Colls (NY)
Saginaw Valley State U (MI)
Saint Anselm Coll (NH)
Saint Augustine's U (NC)
St. Bonaventure U (NY)
St. Catherine U (MN)
St. Edward's U (TX)
St. Francis Coll (NY)
Saint Francis U (PA)
St. Gregory's U, Shawnee (OK)
St. John Fisher Coll (NY)
Saint John's U (MN)
St. John's U (NY)
Saint Joseph's Coll (IN)
St. Joseph's Coll, Long Island Campus (NY)
St. Joseph's Coll, New York (NY)
Saint Joseph's U (PA)
St. Lawrence U (NY)
Saint Leo U (FL)
Saint Louis U (MO)
Saint Martin's U (WA)
Saint Mary's Coll (IN)
St. Mary's Coll of Maryland (MD)
St. Mary's U (TX)
Saint Michael's Coll (VT)
St. Norbert Coll (WI)
St. Olaf Coll (MN)
Saint Peter's U (NJ)
St. Thomas U (FL)
St. Thomas U (NB, Canada)
Saint Vincent Coll (PA)
Salisbury U (MD)
Salve Regina U (RI)
Samford U (AL)
Sam Houston State U (TX)
San Diego State U (CA)
San Francisco State U (CA)
San Jose State U (CA)
Santa Clara U (CA)
Sarah Lawrence Coll (NY)
Savannah State U (GA)
Scripps Coll (CA)
Seattle Pacific U (WA)
Seattle U (WA)
Seton Hill U (PA)
Sewanee: The U of the South (TN)
Shaw U (NC)
Shenandoah U (VA)
Shepherd U (WV)
Shippensburg U of Pennsylvania (PA)
Siena Coll (NY)
Simmons Coll (MA)
Simon Fraser U (BC, Canada)
Simpson Coll (IA)
Skidmore Coll (NY)
Slippery Rock U of Pennsylvania (PA)
Smith Coll (MA)
South Carolina State U (SC)
South Dakota State U (SD)
Southeastern Louisiana U (LA)
Southeastern Oklahoma State U (OK)
Southeast Missouri State U (MO)
Southern Arkansas U–Magnolia (AR)
Southern Connecticut State U (CT)
Southern Illinois U Carbondale (IL)
Southern Illinois U Edwardsville (IL)
Southern Methodist U (TX)
Southern New Hampshire U (NH)
Southern Oregon U (OR)
Southern Utah U (UT)
Southwest Baptist U (MO)
Southwestern U (TX)
Southwest Minnesota State U (MN)
Spelman Coll (GA)
Spring Hill Coll (AL)
Stanford U (CA)
State U of New York at Fredonia (NY)
State U of New York at New Paltz (NY)
State U of New York at Oswego (NY)
State U of New York at Plattsburgh (NY)
State U of New York Coll at Cortland (NY)
State U of New York Coll at Geneseo (NY)
State U of New York Coll at Potsdam (NY)
Stephen F. Austin State U (TX)
Stetson U (FL)
Stockton U (NJ)
Stonehill Coll (MA)
Stony Brook U, State U of New York (NY)
Suffolk U (MA)
Sul Ross State U (TX)
Susquehanna U (PA)
Syracuse U (NY)
Tarleton State U (TX)
Taylor U (IN)
Temple U (PA)
Tennessee State U (TN)
Texas A&M Intl U (TX)
Texas A&M U (TX)
Texas A&M U–Commerce (TX)
Texas A&M U–Corpus Christi (TX)
Texas A&M U–Kingsville (TX)
Texas Christian U (TX)
Texas Lutheran U (TX)
Texas Southern U (TX)
Texas State U (TX)
Texas Tech U (TX)
Texas Wesleyan U (TX)
Texas Woman's U (TX)
Thiel Coll (PA)
Thomas More Coll (KY)
Tougaloo Coll (MS)
Towson U (MD)
Transylvania U (KY)
Trent U (ON, Canada)
Trinity Christian Coll (IL)
Trinity Coll (CT)
Trinity U (TX)
Troy U (AL)
Truman State U (MO)
Tufts U (MA)
Tulane U (LA)
Union Coll (NY)
Union U (TN)
United States Air Force Acad (CO)
United States Coast Guard Acad (CT)
United States Military Acad (NY)
United States Naval Acad (MD)
Université de Montréal (QC, Canada)
U at Albany, State U of New York (NY)
U at Buffalo, the State U of New York (NY)
The U of Akron (OH)
The U of Alabama (AL)
The U of Alabama at Birmingham (AL)
The U of Alabama in Huntsville (AL)
U of Alaska Fairbanks (AK)
U of Alberta (AB, Canada)
The U of Arizona (AZ)
U of Arkansas (AR)
U of Arkansas at Little Rock (AR)
U of Arkansas at Pine Bluff (AR)
U of Arkansas–Fort Smith (AR)
The U of British Columbia (BC, Canada)
The U of British Columbia–Okanagan Campus (BC, Canada)
U of California, Berkeley (CA)
U of California, Davis (CA)
U of California, Irvine (CA)
U of California, Los Angeles (CA)
U of California, Merced (CA)
U of California, Riverside (CA)
U of California, Santa Barbara (CA)
U of California, Santa Cruz (CA)
U of Central Arkansas (AR)
U of Central Florida (FL)
U of Central Missouri (MO)
U of Central Oklahoma (OK)
U of Charleston (WV)
U of Chicago (IL)
U of Cincinnati (OH)
U of Colorado Boulder (CO)
U of Colorado Colorado Springs (CO)
U of Colorado Denver (CO)
U of Dallas (TX)
U of Dayton (OH)
U of Delaware (DE)
U of Denver (CO)
U of Evansville (IN)
The U of Findlay (OH)
U of Florida (FL)
U of Georgia (GA)
U of Great Falls (MT)
U of Guam (GU)
U of Hartford (CT)
U of Hawaii at Manoa (HI)
U of Hawaii–West Oahu (HI)
U of Houston (TX)
U of Houston–Downtown (TX)
U of Idaho (ID)
U of Illinois at Chicago (IL)
U of Illinois at Springfield (IL)
U of Indianapolis (IN)
The U of Iowa (IA)
U of Jamestown (ND)
The U of Kansas (KS)
U of Kentucky (KY)
U of King's Coll (NS, Canada)
U of La Verne (CA)
U of Lethbridge (AB, Canada)
U of Louisiana at Lafayette (LA)
U of Louisville (KY)
U of Maine (ME)
U of Mary Hardin-Baylor (TX)
U of Maryland, Baltimore County (MD)
U of Maryland, Coll Park (MD)
U of Maryland U Coll (MD)
U of Mary Washington (VA)
U of Massachusetts Amherst (MA)
U of Massachusetts Boston (MA)
U of Massachusetts Dartmouth (MA)
U of Massachusetts Lowell (MA)
U of Memphis (TN)
U of Miami (FL)
U of Michigan (MI)
U of Michigan–Dearborn (MI)
U of Michigan–Flint (MI)
U of Minnesota, Duluth (MN)
U of Minnesota, Morris (MN)
U of Minnesota, Twin Cities Campus (MN)
U of Mississippi (MS)
U of Missouri (MO)
U of Missouri–Kansas City (MO)
U of Missouri–St. Louis (MO)
U of Mobile (AL)
The U of Montana Western (MT)
U of Montevallo (AL)
U of Mount Union (OH)
U of Nebraska at Kearney (NE)
U of Nebraska–Lincoln (NE)
U of Nevada, Las Vegas (NV)
U of Nevada, Reno (NV)
U of New Brunswick Saint John (NB, Canada)
U of New England (ME)
U of New Hampshire (NH)
U of New Haven (CT)
U of New Mexico (NM)
U of New Orleans (LA)
U of North Alabama (AL)
U of North Carolina at Asheville (NC)
The U of North Carolina at Chapel Hill (NC)
The U of North Carolina at Greensboro (NC)
The U of North Carolina at Pembroke (NC)
The U of North Carolina Wilmington (NC)
U of North Dakota (ND)
U of Northern Colorado (CO)
U of Northern Iowa (IA)
U of North Florida (FL)
U of North Georgia (GA)
U of North Texas (TX)
U of Notre Dame (IN)
U of Oklahoma (OK)
U of Oregon (OR)
U of Ottawa (ON, Canada)
U of Pennsylvania (PA)
U of Pittsburgh (PA)
U of Pittsburgh at Bradford (PA)
U of Pittsburgh at Greensburg (PA)
U of Portland (OR)
U of Puget Sound (WA)
U of Regina (SK, Canada)
U of Rhode Island (RI)
U of Richmond (VA)
U of Rio Grande (OH)
U of Rochester (NY)
U of St. Francis (IL)
U of Saint Francis (IN)
U of Saint Mary (KS)
U of St. Thomas (MN)
U of St. Thomas (TX)
U of San Diego (CA)
U of San Francisco (CA)
U of Saskatchewan (SK, Canada)
U of Science and Arts of Oklahoma (OK)
The U of Scranton (PA)
U of South Alabama (AL)
U of South Carolina Aiken (SC)
U of South Carolina Upstate (SC)
The U of South Dakota (SD)
U of Southern California (CA)
U of Southern Indiana (IN)
U of Southern Maine (ME)
U of Southern Mississippi (MS)
U of South Florida (FL)
U of South Florida, St. Petersburg (FL)
The U of Tampa (FL)
The U of Tennessee (TN)
The U of Tennessee at Chattanooga (TN)
The U of Tennessee at Martin (TN)
The U of Texas at Arlington (TX)
The U of Texas at Austin (TX)
The U of Texas at Dallas (TX)
The U of Texas at El Paso (TX)
The U of Texas at San Antonio (TX)
The U of Texas at Tyler (TX)
The U of Texas of the Permian Basin (TX)
The U of Texas–Pan American (TX)
U of the Cumberlands (KY)
U of the District of Columbia (DC)
U of the Fraser Valley (BC, Canada)
U of the Incarnate Word (TX)
U of the Pacific (CA)
The U of Toledo (OH)
U of Toronto (ON, Canada)
The U of Tulsa (OK)
U of Utah (UT)
U of Vermont (VT)

U of Virginia (VA)
The U of Virginia's Coll at Wise (VA)
U of Washington (WA)
U of Waterloo (ON, Canada)
The U of Western Ontario (ON, Canada)
U of West Florida (FL)
U of West Georgia (GA)
U of Windsor (ON, Canada)
U of Wisconsin–Eau Claire (WI)
U of Wisconsin–Green Bay (WI)
U of Wisconsin–La Crosse (WI)
U of Wisconsin–Madison (WI)
U of Wisconsin–Milwaukee (WI)
U of Wisconsin–Oshkosh (WI)
U of Wisconsin–Parkside (WI)
U of Wisconsin–Platteville (WI)
U of Wisconsin–River Falls (WI)
U of Wisconsin–Stevens Point (WI)
U of Wisconsin–Superior (WI)
U of Wisconsin–Whitewater (WI)
U of Wyoming (WY)
Ursinus Coll (PA)
Utah State U (UT)
Utah Valley U (UT)
Utica Coll (NY)
Valdosta State U (GA)
Valparaiso U (IN)
Vanderbilt U (TN)
Vanguard U of Southern California (CA)
Vassar Coll (NY)
Villanova U (PA)
Virginia Commonwealth U (VA)
Virginia Polytechnic Inst and State U (VA)
Virginia State U (VA)
Virginia Union U (VA)
Virginia Wesleyan Coll (VA)
Wabash Coll (IN)
Wagner Coll (NY)
Wake Forest U (NC)
Walsh U (OH)
Wartburg Coll (IA)
Washburn U (KS)
Washington & Jefferson Coll (PA)
Washington and Lee U (VA)
Washington Coll (MD)
Washington State U (WA)
Washington State U Vancouver (WA)
Washington U in St. Louis (MO)
Wayne State Coll (NE)
Wayne State U (MI)
Weber State U (UT)
Webster U (MO)
Wells Coll (NY)
Wesleyan Coll (GA)
Wesleyan U (CT)
West Chester U of Pennsylvania (PA)
Western Carolina U (NC)
Western Illinois U (IL)
Western Kentucky U (KY)
Western Michigan U (MI)
Western New England U (MA)
Western Oregon U (OR)
Western State Colorado U (CO)
Western Washington U (WA)
Westfield State U (MA)
West Liberty U (WV)
Westminster Coll (MO)
Westminster Coll (UT)
West Texas A&M U (TX)
West Virginia State U (WV)
West Virginia U (WV)
West Virginia U Inst of Technology (WV)
West Virginia Wesleyan Coll (WV)
Wheaton Coll (IL)
Wheaton Coll (MA)
Wheeling Jesuit U (WV)
Whitman Coll (WA)
Whittier Coll (CA)
Whitworth U (WA)
Wichita State U (KS)
Widener U (PA)
Wilberforce U (OH)
Wilkes U (PA)
Willamette U (OR)
William Jessup U (CA)
William Jewell Coll (MO)
William Paterson U of New Jersey (NJ)
William Penn U (IA)
Williams Coll (MA)
Wilmington U (DE)
Wingate U (NC)
Winona State U (MN)
Winthrop U (SC)
Wittenberg U (OH)
Wofford Coll (SC)
Wright State U (OH)
Xavier U (OH)
Xavier U of Louisiana (LA)
Yale U (CT)
Yeshiva U (NY)
York Coll of Pennsylvania (PA)
York Coll of the City U of New York (NY)
Youngstown State U (OH)

POLITICAL SCIENCE AND GOVERNMENT RELATED

American U in Bulgaria (Bulgaria)
The American U of Paris (France)
Belmont U (TN)
Brandeis U (MA)
Buena Vista U (IA)
Capital U (OH)
Claflin U (SC)
Columbia U, School of General Studies (NY)
Delaware State U (DE)
Emory & Henry Coll (VA)
George Mason U (VA)
Georgetown Coll (KY)
Goddard Coll (VT)
McDaniel Coll (MD)
Muhlenberg Coll (PA)
National U (CA)
Our Lady of the Lake U of San Antonio (TX)
Regis Coll (MA)
Sacred Heart U (CT)
Saint Mary's U of Minnesota (MN)
Southern Vermont Coll (VT)
Trevecca Nazarene U (TN)
U of Alberta (AB, Canada)
U of California, Davis (CA)
U of Guelph (ON, Canada)
U of Hartford (CT)
U of Northern Iowa (IA)
U of Saint Francis (IN)
U of Washington (WA)
Western Michigan U (MI)
Whitman Coll (WA)
William Peace U (NC)

POLYMER CHEMISTRY

Pittsburg State U (KS)
State U of New York Coll of Environmental Science and Forestry (NY)
The U of Akron (OH)
U of Wisconsin–Stevens Point (WI)

POLYMER/PLASTICS ENGINEERING

Auburn U (AL)
Case Western Reserve U (OH)
Penn State Erie, The Behrend Coll (PA)
The U of Akron (OH)
U of Massachusetts Lowell (MA)
U of Southern Mississippi (MS)
U of Wisconsin–Stout (WI)
Western Washington U (WA)

PORTUGUESE

Florida Intl U (FL)
Georgetown U (DC)
Indiana U Bloomington (IN)
The Ohio State U (OH)
Rhode Island Coll (RI)
Rutgers, The State U of New Jersey, New Brunswick (NJ)
Smith Coll (MA)
Tulane U (LA)
United States Military Acad (NY)
U of California, Los Angeles (CA)
U of California, Santa Barbara (CA)
U of Florida (FL)
The U of Iowa (IA)
U of Massachusetts Amherst (MA)
U of Massachusetts Dartmouth (MA)
U of New Mexico (NM)
The U of Texas at Austin (TX)
U of Toronto (ON, Canada)
U of Wisconsin–Madison (WI)
Yale U (CT)

POULTRY SCIENCE

Auburn U (AL)
Delaware State U (DE)
Mississippi State U (MS)
North Carolina State U (NC)
Stephen F. Austin State U (TX)
Texas A&M U (TX)
U of Arkansas (AR)
U of Georgia (GA)
U of Wisconsin–Madison (WI)
Virginia Polytechnic Inst and State U (VA)

PRACTICAL NURSING, VOCATIONAL NURSING AND NURSING ASSISTANTS RELATED

Caribbean U (PR)
St. Joseph's Coll, Long Island Campus (NY)
St. Joseph's Coll, New York (NY)

PRE-CHIROPRACTIC

Ashland U (OH)
Augustana Coll (SD)
Millikin U (IL)
U of Regina (SK, Canada)
Weber State U (UT)

PRE-DENTISTRY STUDIES

Abilene Christian U (TX)
Albertus Magnus Coll (CT)
Allegheny Coll (PA)
Alma Coll (MI)
American Intl Coll (MA)
American U (DC)
Anderson U (IN)
Arcadia U (PA)
Ashland U (OH)
Auburn U (AL)
Augustana Coll (SD)
Baldwin Wallace U (OH)
Ball State U (IN)
Barry U (FL)
Bethany Coll (WV)
Birmingham-Southern Coll (AL)
Blackburn Coll (IL)
Boston U (MA)
Bowling Green State U (OH)
Buffalo State Coll, State U of New York (NY)
Calvin Coll (MI)
Campbellsville U (KY)
Cedar Crest Coll (PA)
Chapman U (CA)
City Coll of the City U of New York (NY)
Clark U (MA)
Coe Coll (IA)
Coll of Saint Benedict (MN)
Concordia U Chicago (IL)
Concordia U, Nebraska (NE)
Cumberland U (TN)
Dalhousie U (NS, Canada)
Defiance Coll (OH)
Dickinson State U (ND)
Drake U (IA)
Elmhurst Coll (IL)
Elmira Coll (NY)
Evangel U (MO)
Florida Southern Coll (FL)
Fordham U (NY)
Franklin Pierce U (NH)
Furman U (SC)
The George Washington U (DC)
Georgia Southern U (GA)
Gettysburg Coll (PA)
Graceland U (IA)
Grand Valley State U (MI)
Gustavus Adolphus Coll (MN)
Hamline U (MN)
Hampton U (VA)
Hastings Coll (NE)
Heidelberg U (OH)
Hobart and William Smith Colls (NY)
Hofstra U (NY)
Houghton Coll (NY)
Illinois Coll (IL)
Indiana U–Purdue U Fort Wayne (IN)
Iowa State U of Science and Technology (IA)
Iowa Wesleyan Coll (IA)
Jacksonville U (FL)
John Carroll U (OH)
Kansas Wesleyan U (KS)
Keuka Coll (NY)
King's Coll (PA)
La Salle U (PA)
Lawrence U (WI)
Lehigh U (PA)
Le Moyne Coll (NY)
Limestone Coll (SC)
Lindenwood U (MO)
Lindsey Wilson Coll (KY)
Lipscomb U (TN)
Lock Haven U of Pennsylvania (PA)
Loyola U New Orleans (LA)
Madonna U (MI)
Manchester U (IN)
Maryville U of Saint Louis (MO)
Mayville State U (ND)
McKendree U (IL)
Mercer U, Macon (GA)
Midwestern State U (TX)
Millikin U (IL)
Minnesota State U Mankato (MN)
Missouri Valley Coll (MO)
Mount Allison U (NB, Canada)
Mount Mercy U (IA)
Mount Vernon Nazarene U (OH)
Nazareth Coll of Rochester (NY)
Newman U (KS)
Niagara U (NY)
North Central Coll (IL)
Northern Michigan U (MI)
Northern State U (SD)
Northwestern Oklahoma State U (OK)
Northwest Nazarene U (ID)
Oglethorpe U (GA)
Ohio Northern U (OH)
The Ohio State U (OH)
Ohio Wesleyan U (OH)
Pacific U (OR)
Peru State Coll (NE)
Quinnipiac U (CT)
Rhode Island Coll (RI)
Ripon Coll (WI)
Rivier U (NH)
Roberts Wesleyan Coll (NY)
Rochester Inst of Technology (NY)
Rockford U (IL)
Rutgers, The State U of New Jersey, New Brunswick (NJ)
Sacred Heart U (CT)
Saginaw Valley State U (MI)
Saint Anselm Coll (NH)
St. Catherine U (MN)
Saint Francis U (PA)
Saint John's U (MN)
Saint Michael's Coll (VT)
St. Thomas U (FL)
Simpson Coll (IA)
Southwest Minnesota State U (MN)
State U of New York at Oswego (NY)
State U of New York Coll at Cortland (NY)
State U of New York Coll at Geneseo (NY)
State U of New York Coll of Environmental Science and Forestry (NY)
Stetson U (FL)
Susquehanna U (PA)
Syracuse U (NY)
Tabor Coll (KS)
Tarleton State U (TX)
Texas Wesleyan U (TX)
Thiel Coll (PA)
Trinity U (TX)
Union Coll (NE)
Union U (TN)
Université de Montréal (QC, Canada)
U of Bridgeport (CT)
U of Central Missouri (MO)
U of Dallas (TX)
U of Dayton (OH)
U of Evansville (IN)
U of Illinois at Chicago (IL)
U of Indianapolis (IN)
The U of Iowa (IA)
U of Maryland, Coll Park (MD)
U of Massachusetts Amherst (MA)
U of Minnesota, Morris (MN)
U of Minnesota, Twin Cities Campus (MN)
U of Nebraska–Lincoln (NE)
U of Portland (OR)
U of Regina (SK, Canada)
U of Rio Grande (OH)
U of St. Francis (IL)
U of San Francisco (CA)
The U of Tennessee at Martin (TN)
The U of Toledo (OH)
U of Windsor (ON, Canada)
U of Wisconsin–Oshkosh (WI)
U of Wisconsin–Parkside (WI)
U of Wisconsin–River Falls (WI)
Upper Iowa U (IA)
Urbana U (OH)
Utah State U (UT)
Utica Coll (NY)
Valley City State U (ND)
Virginia Wesleyan Coll (VA)
Wagner Coll (NY)
Walla Walla U (WA)
Walsh U (OH)
Washburn U (KS)
Washington Coll (MD)
Washington U in St. Louis (MO)
Waynesburg U (PA)
Weber State U (UT)
Wells Coll (NY)
West Liberty U (WV)
West Virginia Wesleyan Coll (WV)
Whitworth U (WA)
Widener U (PA)
William Paterson U of New Jersey (NJ)
William Penn U (IA)
Williams Baptist Coll (AR)
Wofford Coll (SC)
Youngstown State U (OH)

PRE-ENGINEERING

Asbury U (KY)
Augustana Coll (SD)
Azusa Pacific U (CA)
Baldwin Wallace U (OH)
Bard Coll at Simon's Rock (MA)
Bethany Coll (WV)
Canisius Coll (NY)
Cedarville U (OH)
Delaware State U (DE)
Drake U (IA)
Hamline U (MN)
Houghton Coll (NY)
Inter American U of Puerto Rico, San Germán Campus (PR)
Le Moyne Coll (NY)
Lincoln U (PA)
Midwestern State U (TX)
Mount Vernon Nazarene U (OH)
Northwest Nazarene U (ID)
Peru State Coll (NE)
Roberts Wesleyan Coll (NY)
Scripps Coll (CA)
Simpson Coll (IA)
Spring Hill Coll (AL)
U of Mary Hardin-Baylor (TX)
The U of Montana (MT)
The U of Scranton (PA)
U of the Cumberlands (KY)
Ursinus Coll (PA)
Valley City State U (ND)
Wagner Coll (NY)
Waynesburg U (PA)
West Texas A&M U (TX)
Yeshiva U (NY)

PRE-LAW STUDIES

Abilene Christian U (TX)
Albertus Magnus Coll (CT)
Albright Coll (PA)
Allegheny Coll (PA)
Alma Coll (MI)
American Intl Coll (MA)
Anderson U (IN)
Andrews U (MI)
Arcadia U (PA)
Ashland U (OH)
Auburn U (AL)
Augustana Coll (SD)
Azusa Pacific U (CA)
Babson Coll (MA)
Bard Coll (NY)
Barry U (FL)
Baylor U (TX)
Bemidji State U (MN)
Bennington Coll (VT)
Bethany Coll (WV)
Bethel Coll (IN)
Binghamton U, State U of New York (NY)
Biola U (CA)
Birmingham-Southern Coll (AL)
Blackburn Coll (IL)
Bowling Green State U (OH)
Bryant U (RI)

Buffalo State Coll, State U of New York (NY)
California State U, Dominguez Hills (CA)
California State U, Fresno (CA)
Calumet Coll of Saint Joseph (IN)
Calvin Coll (MI)
Campbellsville U (KY)
Catawba Coll (NC)
Cedar Crest Coll (PA)
Cedarville U (OH)
Chowan U (NC)
City Coll of the City U of New York (NY)
Clark U (MA)
Clearwater Christian Coll (FL)
Coe Coll (IA)
The Coll of New Rochelle (NY)
Coll of Saint Benedict (MN)
The Coll of Saint Rose (NY)
Coll of the Ozarks (MO)
Concordia Coll–New York (NY)
Concordia U Chicago (IL)
Concordia U, Nebraska (NE)
Concordia U Wisconsin (WI)
Corban U (OR)
Creighton U (NE)
Cumberland U (TN)
Dalhousie U (NS, Canada)
Defiance Coll (OH)
DeSales U (PA)
Dickinson State U (ND)
Dominican Coll (NY)
Dominican U (IL)
Drake U (IA)
Elmhurst Coll (IL)
Elmira Coll (NY)
Emmanuel Coll (GA)
Emory & Henry Coll (VA)
Evangel U (MO)
Florida Inst of Technology (FL)
Florida Southern Coll (FL)
Fontbonne U (MO)
Fordham U (NY)
Fort Hays State U (KS)
Franklin Pierce U (NH)
Furman U (SC)
The George Washington U (DC)
Gettysburg Coll (PA)
Grand View U (IA)
Gustavus Adolphus Coll (MN)
Hamline U (MN)
Hampton U (VA)
Hartwick Coll (NY)
Hastings Coll (NE)
Hawai`i Pacific U (HI)
Heidelberg U (OH)
Hobart and William Smith Colls (NY)
Hofstra U (NY)
Houghton Coll (NY)
Houston Baptist U (TX)
Howard Payne U (TX)
Illinois Coll (IL)
Iowa State U of Science and Technology (IA)
Ithaca Coll (NY)
Jacksonville U (FL)
John Carroll U (OH)
Judson U (IL)
Kansas Wesleyan U (KS)
Keuka Coll (NY)
Keystone Coll (PA)
King's Coll (PA)
King U (TN)
Lawrence U (WI)
Le Moyne Coll (NY)
Limestone Coll (SC)
Lincoln Memorial U (TN)
Lindenwood U (MO)
Lindsey Wilson Coll (KY)
Lipscomb U (TN)
Louisiana Coll (LA)
Madonna U (MI)
Manchester U (IN)
Mansfield U of Pennsylvania (PA)
Mars Hill U (NC)
Massachusetts Coll of Liberal Arts (MA)
The Master's Coll and Sem (CA)
Mayville State U (ND)
McKendree U (IL)
Michigan State U (MI)
Midwestern State U (TX)
Millikin U (IL)
Minnesota State U Mankato (MN)
Missouri Valley Coll (MO)
Mount Allison U (NB, Canada)
Mount Mercy U (IA)
Mount Vernon Nazarene U (OH)
National U (CA)
Nazareth Coll of Rochester (NY)
New England Coll (NH)
Newman U (KS)
Niagara U (NY)
North Central Coll (IL)
Northern Arizona U (AZ)
Northern Michigan U (MI)
Northern State U (SD)
Northwestern Oklahoma State U (OK)
Northwest Nazarene U (ID)
Nova Southeastern U (FL)
Oakland City U (IN)
Oglethorpe U (GA)
Ohio Northern U (OH)
Ohio Wesleyan U (OH)
Oklahoma Christian U (OK)
Oklahoma City U (OK)
Oklahoma Wesleyan U (OK)
Pacific Lutheran U (WA)
Palm Beach Atlantic U (FL)
Peru State Coll (NE)
Quinnipiac U (CT)
Rensselaer Polytechnic Inst (NY)
Rhode Island Coll (RI)
Ripon Coll (WI)
Rivier U (NH)
Roberts Wesleyan Coll (NY)
Rochester Inst of Technology (NY)
Rockford U (IL)
Rutgers, The State U of New Jersey, New Brunswick (NJ)
Saginaw Valley State U (MI)
Saint Anselm Coll (NH)
St. Catherine U (MN)
Saint Francis U (PA)
Saint John's U (MN)
Saint Michael's Coll (VT)
St. Thomas U (FL)
Seton Hill U (PA)
Siena Heights U (MI)
Simpson Coll (IA)
Smith Coll (MA)
Southern Oregon U (OR)
Southwest Minnesota State U (MN)
State U of New York at Fredonia (NY)
State U of New York at Oswego (NY)
State U of New York Coll at Cortland (NY)
State U of New York Coll at Geneseo (NY)
State U of New York Coll of Environmental Science and Forestry (NY)
Stetson U (FL)
Susquehanna U (PA)
Syracuse U (NY)
Tabor Coll (KS)
Texas Wesleyan U (TX)
Thiel Coll (PA)
Trine U (IN)
Trinity U (TX)
Tusculum Coll (TN)
Union Coll (NE)
Union U (TN)
United States Military Acad (NY)
U of Bridgeport (CT)
U of California, Santa Cruz (CA)
U of Dallas (TX)
The U of Findlay (OH)
U of Indianapolis (IN)
The U of Iowa (IA)
U of Maryland, Coll Park (MD)
U of Minnesota, Morris (MN)
U of Minnesota, Twin Cities Campus (MN)
The U of Montana (MT)
The U of Montana Western (MT)
U of Pittsburgh at Greensburg (PA)
U of Portland (OR)
U of Regina (SK, Canada)
U of Rio Grande (OH)
U of St. Francis (IL)
The U of Toledo (OH)
U of Windsor (ON, Canada)
U of Wisconsin–Oshkosh (WI)
U of Wisconsin–River Falls (WI)
U of Wisconsin–Superior (WI)
Urbana U (OH)
Utah State U (UT)
Utica Coll (NY)
Valley City State U (ND)
Vanguard U of Southern California (CA)
Wagner Coll (NY)
Walla Walla U (WA)
Warner Pacific Coll (OR)
Washburn U (KS)
Washington Coll (MD)
Waynesburg U (PA)
Webber Intl U (FL)
Weber State U (UT)
Wells Coll (NY)
Western State Colorado U (CO)
West Liberty U (WV)
Westminster Coll (MO)
West Texas A&M U (TX)
West Virginia Wesleyan Coll (WV)
Whittier Coll (CA)
Whitworth U (WA)
William Paterson U of New Jersey (NJ)
William Peace U (NC)
William Penn U (IA)
Williams Baptist Coll (AR)
Wingate U (NC)
Wofford Coll (SC)
Xavier U of Louisiana (LA)
Youngstown State U (OH)

PREMEDICAL STUDIES

Abilene Christian U (TX)
Alaska Pacific U (AK)
Albertus Magnus Coll (CT)
Allegheny Coll (PA)
Alma Coll (MI)
American Intl Coll (MA)
American U (DC)
Anderson U (IN)
Andrews U (MI)
Arcadia U (PA)
Arizona State U at the Downtown Phoenix campus (AZ)
Ashland U (OH)
Auburn U (AL)
Augustana Coll (IL)
Augustana Coll (SD)
Averett U (VA)
Avila U (MO)
Baldwin Wallace U (OH)
Ball State U (IN)
Bard Coll (NY)
Bard Coll at Simon's Rock (MA)
Barry U (FL)
Bemidji State U (MN)
Bennington Coll (VT)
Bethany Coll (WV)
Bethel Coll (IN)
Binghamton U, State U of New York (NY)
Birmingham-Southern Coll (AL)
Blackburn Coll (IL)
Bluffton U (OH)
Bob Jones U (SC)
Bowling Green State U (OH)
Buffalo State Coll, State U of New York (NY)
Calvin Coll (MI)
Campbellsville U (KY)
Caribbean U (PR)
Catawba Coll (NC)
Cedar Crest Coll (PA)
Chapman U (CA)
Chowan U (NC)
City Coll of the City U of New York (NY)
Clark U (MA)
Clearwater Christian Coll (FL)
Coe Coll (IA)
The Coll of New Rochelle (NY)
Coll of Saint Benedict (MN)
Concordia U Chicago (IL)
Concordia U, Nebraska (NE)
Concord U (WV)
Cumberland U (TN)
Dalhousie U (NS, Canada)
Defiance Coll (OH)
Dickinson State U (ND)
Dominican U (IL)
Drake U (IA)
Earlham Coll (IN)
Elmhurst Coll (IL)
Elmira Coll (NY)
Evangel U (MO)
Florida Southern Coll (FL)
Fordham U (NY)
Franklin Pierce U (NH)
Furman U (SC)
The George Washington U (DC)
Georgia Southern U (GA)
Gettysburg Coll (PA)
Graceland U (IA)
Grand Valley State U (MI)
Gustavus Adolphus Coll (MN)
Hamline U (MN)
Hampton U (VA)
Hartwick Coll (NY)
Hastings Coll (NE)
Hawai`i Pacific U (HI)
Heidelberg U (OH)
Hobart and William Smith Colls (NY)
Hofstra U (NY)
Holy Cross Coll (IN)
Houghton Coll (NY)
Illinois Coll (IL)
Immaculata U (PA)
Indiana U–Purdue U Fort Wayne (IN)
Indiana U–Purdue U Indianapolis (IN)
Iowa State U of Science and Technology (IA)
Iowa Wesleyan Coll (IA)
Ithaca Coll (NY)
Jacksonville U (FL)
John Carroll U (OH)
Johnson State Coll (VT)
Kansas Wesleyan U (KS)
Keuka Coll (NY)
Keystone Coll (PA)
King's Coll (PA)
King U (TN)
La Salle U (PA)
Lawrence U (WI)
Lehigh U (PA)
Le Moyne Coll (NY)
Lenoir-Rhyne U (NC)
Limestone Coll (SC)
Lincoln Memorial U (TN)
Lindenwood U (MO)
Lindsey Wilson Coll (KY)
Lipscomb U (TN)
Lock Haven U of Pennsylvania (PA)
Loyola U New Orleans (LA)
Madonna U (MI)
Manchester U (IN)
Mars Hill U (NC)
Maryville U of Saint Louis (MO)
Massachusetts Coll of Liberal Arts (MA)
The Master's Coll and Sem (CA)
Mayville State U (ND)
McKendree U (IL)
MCPHS U (MA)
Mercer U, Macon (GA)
Mercy Coll of Health Sciences (IA)
Miami U (OH)
Michigan State U (MI)
Midwestern State U (TX)
Millikin U (IL)
Minnesota State U Mankato (MN)
Missouri Valley Coll (MO)
Mount Allison U (NB, Canada)
Mount Mercy U (IA)
Mount Vernon Nazarene U (OH)
Nazareth Coll of Rochester (NY)
Newman U (KS)
New York Inst of Technology (NY)
Niagara U (NY)
North Central Coll (IL)
Northern Michigan U (MI)
Northern State U (SD)
Northwestern Oklahoma State U (OK)
Northwestern U (IL)
Northwest Nazarene U (ID)
Oakland City U (IN)
Oglethorpe U (GA)
Ohio Northern U (OH)
Ohio Wesleyan U (OH)
Oklahoma City U (OK)
Pacific Lutheran U (WA)
Pacific U (OR)
Penn State Abington (PA)
Penn State Altoona (PA)
Penn State Beaver (PA)
Penn State Berks (PA)
Penn State Brandywine (PA)
Penn State DuBois (PA)
Penn State Erie, The Behrend Coll (PA)
Penn State Fayette, The Eberly Campus (PA)
Penn State Greater Allegheny (PA)
Penn State Hazleton (PA)
Penn State Lehigh Valley (PA)
Penn State Mont Alto (PA)
Penn State New Kensington (PA)
Penn State Schuylkill (PA)
Penn State Shenango (PA)
Penn State U Park (PA)
Penn State Wilkes-Barre (PA)
Penn State Worthington Scranton (PA)
Penn State York (PA)
Peru State Coll (NE)
Philadelphia U (PA)
Quinnipiac U (CT)
Rensselaer Polytechnic Inst (NY)
Rhode Island Coll (RI)
Ripon Coll (WI)
Rivier U (NH)
Roberts Wesleyan Coll (NY)
Rochester Inst of Technology (NY)
Rockford U (IL)
Rutgers, The State U of New Jersey, New Brunswick (NJ)
Sacred Heart U (CT)
Saginaw Valley State U (MI)
St. Andrews U (NC)
Saint Anselm Coll (NH)
St. Catherine U (MN)
Saint Francis U (PA)
Saint John's U (MN)
Saint Michael's Coll (VT)
St. Thomas Aquinas Coll (NY)
St. Thomas U (FL)
Samford U (AL)
Sarah Lawrence Coll (NY)
Simpson Coll (IA)
Slippery Rock U of Pennsylvania (PA)
Smith Coll (MA)
Southeastern U (FL)
Southern Oregon U (OR)
Southwest Minnesota State U (MN)
State U of New York at Fredonia (NY)
State U of New York at Oswego (NY)
State U of New York Coll at Cortland (NY)
State U of New York Coll at Geneseo (NY)
State U of New York Coll of Environmental Science and Forestry (NY)
Stetson U (FL)
Susquehanna U (PA)
Syracuse U (NY)
Tabor Coll (KS)
Tarleton State U (TX)
Texas Lutheran U (TX)
Thiel Coll (PA)
Trine U (IN)
Trinity U (TX)
Tusculum Coll (TN)
Union Coll (NE)
Union U (TN)
Université de Montréal (QC, Canada)
Université de Sherbrooke (QC, Canada)
The U of Akron (OH)
U of Arkansas (AR)
U of Bridgeport (CT)
U of California, Santa Cruz (CA)
U of Central Missouri (MO)
U of Dallas (TX)
U of Dayton (OH)
U of Evansville (IN)
The U of Findlay (OH)
U of Hartford (CT)
U of Indianapolis (IN)
The U of Iowa (IA)
U of Maine at Machias (ME)
U of Massachusetts Amherst (MA)
U of Minnesota, Morris (MN)
U of Minnesota, Twin Cities Campus (MN)
The U of Montana (MT)
U of Nebraska–Lincoln (NE)
U of New England (ME)
U of Notre Dame (IN)
U of Portland (OR)
U of Regina (SK, Canada)
U of Rio Grande (OH)
U of St. Francis (IL)
U of San Francisco (CA)
The U of Tennessee at Martin (TN)
The U of Toledo (OH)

U of Windsor (ON, Canada)
U of Wisconsin–Madison (WI)
U of Wisconsin–Milwaukee (WI)
U of Wisconsin–Oshkosh (WI)
U of Wisconsin–Parkside (WI)
U of Wisconsin–River Falls (WI)
Upper Iowa U (IA)
Urbana U (OH)
Utah State U (UT)
Utica Coll (NY)
Valley City State U (ND)
Vanguard U of Southern California (CA)
Virginia Wesleyan Coll (VA)
Wagner Coll (NY)
Walla Walla U (WA)
Walsh U (OH)
Warner Pacific Coll (OR)
Washburn U (KS)
Washington Coll (MD)
Washington State U (WA)
Washington U in St. Louis (MO)
Waynesburg U (PA)
Weber State U (UT)
Wells Coll (NY)
West Chester U of Pennsylvania (PA)
West Liberty U (WV)
West Virginia Wesleyan Coll (WV)
Whittier Coll (CA)
Whitworth U (WA)
Widener U (PA)
William Paterson U of New Jersey (NJ)
William Penn U (IA)
Williams Baptist Coll (AR)
Wingate U (NC)
Wofford Coll (SC)
Xavier U of Louisiana (LA)
Youngstown State U (OH)

PRENURSING STUDIES
Allegheny Coll (PA)
Arizona State U at the Downtown Phoenix campus (AZ)
Baylor U (TX)
Berry Coll (GA)
Biola U (CA)
Brigham Young U (UT)
California State U, Fullerton (CA)
Central Washington U (WA)
Cleveland State U (OH)
The Coll of Idaho (ID)
Concordia U, Nebraska (NE)
Delaware State U (DE)
Eastern Kentucky U (KY)
Gettysburg Coll (PA)
Hardin-Simmons U (TX)
Houghton Coll (NY)
Jacksonville U (FL)
Limestone Coll (SC)
Lindenwood U (MO)
Lipscomb U (TN)
Madonna U (MI)
McMurry U (TX)
Missouri Baptist U (MO)
Missouri Valley Coll (MO)
National U (CA)
Oklahoma City U (OK)
Peru State Coll (NE)
St. Thomas U (FL)
San Diego State U (CA)
Seattle U (WA)
Simpson Coll (IA)
State U of New York Coll at Geneseo (NY)
Tabor Coll (KS)
Tennessee Wesleyan Coll (TN)
The U of Iowa (IA)
U of Michigan–Flint (MI)
U of Northwestern–St. Paul (MN)
Wright State U (OH)

PRE-OCCUPATIONAL THERAPY
Ashland U (OH)
Augustana Coll (SD)
Bethany Coll (WV)
Millikin U (IL)
Trevecca Nazarene U (TN)
U of Regina (SK, Canada)
Walsh U (OH)

PRE-OPTOMETRY
Ashland U (OH)
Augustana Coll (SD)
Calvin Coll (MI)
Lehigh U (PA)
Le Moyne Coll (NY)
Madonna U (MI)
Millikin U (IL)
Peru State Coll (NE)
Rhode Island Coll (RI)
Simpson Coll (IA)
U of Evansville (IN)
U of Regina (SK, Canada)

PRE-PHARMACY STUDIES
Abilene Christian U (TX)
Allegheny Coll (PA)
Anna Maria Coll (MA)
Ashland U (OH)
Auburn U (AL)
Augustana Coll (SD)
Baldwin Wallace U (OH)
Barry U (FL)
Benedictine U (IL)
Calvin Coll (MI)
Coll of Saint Benedict (MN)
Concordia U, Nebraska (NE)
Cumberland U (TN)
Dalhousie U (NS, Canada)
Dominican U (IL)
Elmhurst Coll (IL)
Emmanuel Coll (GA)
Emory & Henry Coll (VA)
Fordham U (NY)
Georgia Southern U (GA)
Gettysburg Coll (PA)
Hamline U (MN)
Houghton Coll (NY)
Husson U (ME)
Indiana U–Purdue U Indianapolis (IN)
King's Coll (PA)
King U (TN)
Le Moyne Coll (NY)
Limestone Coll (SC)
Lindsey Wilson Coll (KY)
Lipscomb U (TN)
Mayville State U (ND)
Midwestern State U (TX)
Millikin U (IL)
Missouri Valley Coll (MO)
Mount Allison U (NB, Canada)
Mount Vernon Nazarene U (OH)
Northern Michigan U (MI)
Northwest Nazarene U (ID)
Peru State Coll (NE)
Roberts Wesleyan Coll (NY)
Saint John's U (MN)
Saint Michael's Coll (VT)
Simpson Coll (IA)
Slippery Rock U of Pennsylvania (PA)
Tabor Coll (KS)
Tarleton State U (TX)
Tusculum Coll (TN)
Union U (TN)
U of Central Missouri (MO)
U of Charleston (WV)
U of Evansville (IN)
The U of Iowa (IA)
U of Minnesota, Morris (MN)
U of Minnesota, Twin Cities Campus (MN)
The U of Montana (MT)
U of Nebraska–Lincoln (NE)
U of Regina (SK, Canada)
U of St. Francis (IL)
U of Saint Francis (IN)
The U of Tennessee at Martin (TN)
U of Windsor (ON, Canada)
U of Wisconsin–Parkside (WI)
U of Wisconsin–River Falls (WI)
Valley City State U (ND)
Walsh U (OH)
Washburn U (KS)
Washington U in St. Louis (MO)
Weber State U (UT)
West Virginia Wesleyan Coll (WV)
Wingate U (NC)
Youngstown State U (OH)

PRE-PHYSICAL THERAPY
Ashland U (OH)
Augustana Coll (SD)
Bethany Coll (WV)
Blue Mountain Coll (MS)
California Baptist U (CA)
Calvin Coll (MI)
Iowa Wesleyan Coll (IA)
Massachusetts Coll of Liberal Arts (MA)
Merrimack Coll (MA)
Midwestern State U (TX)
Millikin U (IL)
Rockford U (IL)
Saint Mary's U of Minnesota (MN)
Simpson Coll (IA)
Trevecca Nazarene U (TN)
U of Dayton (OH)
U of Kentucky (KY)
U of Mary Hardin-Baylor (TX)
U of Regina (SK, Canada)
Walsh U (OH)
Weber State U (UT)

PRE-THEOLOGY/PRE-MINISTERIAL STUDIES
Alma Coll (MI)
Ashland U (OH)
Augustana Coll (SD)
Ave Maria U (FL)
Bethany Coll (WV)
Calvin Coll (MI)
Coll of Saint Benedict (MN)
Columbia Bible Coll (BC, Canada)
Columbia Intl U (SC)
Concordia Coll–New York (NY)
Concordia U Chicago (IL)
Concordia U, Nebraska (NE)
Corban U (OR)
Crossroads Coll (MN)
Geneva Coll (PA)
John Brown U (AR)
Kuyper Coll (MI)
Lee U (TN)
Manchester U (IN)
Martin Luther Coll (MN)
Mid-Atlantic Christian U (NC)
Mount Allison U (NB, Canada)
Nyack Coll (NY)
Ohio Northern U (OH)
Ohio Wesleyan U (OH)
Point Loma Nazarene U (CA)
Point U (GA)
Saint John's U (MN)
Simpson Coll (IA)
Southeastern U (FL)
Summit U (PA)
Tabor Coll (KS)
Tennessee Wesleyan Coll (TN)
Trinity Coll of Florida (FL)
U of Dallas (TX)
U of Indianapolis (IN)
U of Northwestern–St. Paul (MN)
U of Rio Grande (OH)
Washburn U (KS)
Waynesburg U (PA)
Williamson Christian Coll (TN)

PRE-VETERINARY STUDIES
Abilene Christian U (TX)
Albertus Magnus Coll (CT)
Allegheny Coll (PA)
Alma Coll (MI)
American Intl Coll (MA)
American U (DC)
Anderson U (IN)
Andrews U (MI)
Arcadia U (PA)
Ashland U (OH)
Auburn U (AL)
Augustana Coll (SD)
Baldwin Wallace U (OH)
Barry U (FL)
Becker Coll (MA)
Bemidji State U (MN)
Bethany Coll (WV)
Binghamton U, State U of New York (NY)
Blackburn Coll (IL)
Buffalo State Coll, State U of New York (NY)
Calvin Coll (MI)
Campbellsville U (KY)
Cedar Crest Coll (PA)
Chapman U (CA)
City Coll of the City U of New York (NY)
Clark U (MA)
Clearwater Christian Coll (FL)
Coe Coll (IA)
Coll of Saint Benedict (MN)
Coll of the Atlantic (ME)
Concordia Coll–New York (NY)
Concordia U, Nebraska (NE)
Concord U (WV)
Cumberland U (TN)
Dalhousie U (NS, Canada)
Defiance Coll (OH)
Delaware State U (DE)
Dickinson State U (ND)
Drake U (IA)
Elmhurst Coll (IL)
Elmira Coll (NY)
Emory & Henry Coll (VA)
Evangel U (MO)
Florida Southern Coll (FL)
Fordham U (NY)
Franklin Pierce U (NH)
Furman U (SC)
Georgia Southern U (GA)
Gettysburg Coll (PA)
Grand Valley State U (MI)
Gustavus Adolphus Coll (MN)
Hamline U (MN)
Hampton U (VA)
Hartwick Coll (NY)
Hastings Coll (NE)
Heidelberg U (OH)
Hobart and William Smith Colls (NY)
Hofstra U (NY)
Houghton Coll (NY)
Illinois Coll (IL)
Indiana U–Purdue U Fort Wayne (IN)
Indiana U–Purdue U Indianapolis (IN)
Iowa State U of Science and Technology (IA)
Iowa Wesleyan Coll (IA)
Jacksonville U (FL)
John Carroll U (OH)
Kansas Wesleyan U (KS)
Keuka Coll (NY)
King's Coll (PA)
King U (TN)
La Salle U (PA)
Lawrence U (WI)
Le Moyne Coll (NY)
Limestone Coll (SC)
Lincoln Memorial U (TN)
Lindenwood U (MO)
Lindsey Wilson Coll (KY)
Lipscomb U (TN)
Lock Haven U of Pennsylvania (PA)
Loyola U New Orleans (LA)
Madonna U (MI)
Manchester U (IN)
Mars Hill U (NC)
Maryville U of Saint Louis (MO)
Mayville State U (ND)
McKendree U (IL)
Midwestern State U (TX)
Millikin U (IL)
Minnesota State U Mankato (MN)
Missouri Valley Coll (MO)
Montana State U (MT)
Mount Allison U (NB, Canada)
Mount Mercy U (IA)
Mount Vernon Nazarene U (OH)
Nazareth Coll of Rochester (NY)
Newman U (KS)
Niagara U (NY)
North Central Coll (IL)
Northern Michigan U (MI)
Northwest Missouri State U (MO)
Northwest Nazarene U (ID)
Oakland City U (IN)
Oglethorpe U (GA)
Ohio Northern U (OH)
Ohio Wesleyan U (OH)
Pacific U (OR)
Penn State U Park (PA)
Peru State Coll (NE)
Purdue U Calumet (IN)
Quinnipiac U (CT)
Rhode Island Coll (RI)
Ripon Coll (WI)
Rivier U (NH)
Roberts Wesleyan Coll (NY)
Rochester Inst of Technology (NY)
Rockford U (IL)
Sacred Heart U (CT)
St. Andrews U (NC)
St. Catherine U (MN)
Saint Francis U (PA)
Saint John's U (MN)
Saint Michael's Coll (VT)
Simpson Coll (IA)
Southwest Minnesota State U (MN)
State U of New York at Fredonia (NY)
State U of New York at Oswego (NY)
State U of New York Coll at Geneseo (NY)
State U of New York Coll of Environmental Science and Forestry (NY)
State U of New York Coll of Technology at Canton (NY)
Stetson U (FL)
Susquehanna U (PA)
Syracuse U (NY)
Tabor Coll (KS)
Tarleton State U (TX)
Thiel Coll (PA)
Trinity U (TX)
U of Alberta (AB, Canada)
The U of Arizona (AZ)
U of Bridgeport (CT)
The U of British Columbia (BC, Canada)
U of Central Missouri (MO)
U of Delaware (DE)
U of Evansville (IN)
The U of Findlay (OH)
U of Illinois at Chicago (IL)
U of Indianapolis (IN)
The U of Iowa (IA)
U of Maryland, Coll Park (MD)
U of Massachusetts Amherst (MA)
U of Minnesota, Crookston (MN)
U of Minnesota, Morris (MN)
U of Minnesota, Twin Cities Campus (MN)
U of Nebraska–Lincoln (NE)
U of Nevada, Reno (NV)
U of Regina (SK, Canada)
U of Rio Grande (OH)
U of St. Francis (IL)
U of San Francisco (CA)
The U of Tennessee at Martin (TN)
The U of Toledo (OH)
U of Wisconsin–Oshkosh (WI)
U of Wisconsin–Parkside (WI)
U of Wisconsin–River Falls (WI)
Upper Iowa U (IA)
Urbana U (OH)
Utah State U (UT)
Utica Coll (NY)
Valley City State U (ND)
Virginia Wesleyan Coll (VA)
Walla Walla U (WA)
Walsh U (OH)
Warner Pacific Coll (OR)
Washburn U (KS)
Washington Coll (MD)
Washington U in St. Louis (MO)
Waynesburg U (PA)
Weber State U (UT)
Wells Coll (NY)
West Virginia Wesleyan Coll (WV)
Whitworth U (WA)
Widener U (PA)
Wingate U (NC)
Wofford Coll (SC)
Youngstown State U (OH)

PRINTING MANAGEMENT
Coll of the Ozarks (MO)
Eastern Kentucky U (KY)
Ferris State U (MI)
Pittsburg State U (KS)
Rochester Inst of Technology (NY)
U of Minnesota, Duluth (MN)

PRINTMAKING
Adams State U (CO)
Aquinas Coll (MI)
Bennington Coll (VT)
Birmingham-Southern Coll (AL)
Bowling Green State U (OH)
Bradley U (IL)
Brigham Young U (UT)
Buffalo State Coll, State U of New York (NY)
California Coll of the Arts (CA)
California State U, Long Beach (CA)
Cleveland Inst of Art (OH)
Columbia Coll (MO)
Concordia U (QC, Canada)
Drake U (IA)
Emily Carr U of Art + Design (BC, Canada)
Indiana U–Purdue U Fort Wayne (IN)
Inter American U of Puerto Rico, San Germán Campus (PR)
Kansas City Art Inst (MO)
Laguna Coll of Art & Design (CA)

Massachusetts Coll of Art and Design (MA)
Mount Allison U (NB, Canada)
Northern Michigan U (MI)
Northwest Nazarene U (ID)
Ohio Northern U (OH)
Ohio U (OH)
Pacific Northwest Coll of Art (OR)
Pratt Inst (NY)
Purchase Coll, State U of New York (NY)
Rhode Island Coll (RI)
Rhode Island School of Design (RI)
Rutgers, The State U of New Jersey, New Brunswick (NJ)
San Francisco Art Inst (CA)
Savannah Coll of Art and Design (GA)
School of the Art Inst of Chicago (IL)
School of the Museum of Fine Arts, Boston (MA)
Seton Hill U (PA)
State U of New York at New Paltz (NY)
Syracuse U (NY)
Temple U (PA)
Texas Christian U (TX)
U of Alberta (AB, Canada)
U of Dallas (TX)
U of Hartford (CT)
The U of Iowa (IA)
The U of Kansas (KS)
U of Miami (FL)
U of Michigan (MI)
U of Oregon (OR)
U of Regina (SK, Canada)
U of San Francisco (CA)
The U of Texas at El Paso (TX)
The U of the Arts (PA)
U of Windsor (ON, Canada)
Washington U in St. Louis (MO)
Western State Colorado U (CO)
Western Washington U (WA)
Youngstown State U (OH)

PROFESSIONAL, TECHNICAL, BUSINESS, AND SCIENTIFIC WRITING

Albion Coll (MI)
Arizona State U at the Polytechnic campus (AZ)
Bowling Green State U (OH)
Cedarville U (OH)
Chatham U (PA)
Coker Coll (SC)
Concordia U, St. Paul (MN)
Dakota State U (SD)
Dixie State U (UT)
Eastern Michigan U (MI)
Elizabethtown Coll (PA)
Emory & Henry Coll (VA)
Ferris State U (MI)
Fitchburg State U (MA)
Indiana U–Purdue U Fort Wayne (IN)
Iowa State U of Science and Technology (IA)
James Madison U (VA)
Juniata Coll (PA)
King U (TN)
Lubbock Christian U (TX)
Madonna U (MI)
Maryville Coll (TN)
Massachusetts Coll of Liberal Arts (MA)
Metropolitan State U (MN)
Miami U (OH)
Michigan State U (MI)
Missouri State U (MO)
Montana Tech of The U of Montana (MT)
Mount Mary U (WI)
New Jersey Inst of Technology (NJ)
New Mexico Inst of Mining and Technology (NM)
Ohio Northern U (OH)
Penn State Berks (PA)
Penn State Lehigh Valley (PA)
Purdue U (IN)
Saginaw Valley State U (MI)
Saint Leo U (FL)
San Francisco State U (CA)
Savannah Coll of Art and Design (GA)
Slippery Rock U of Pennsylvania (PA)
Tarleton State U (TX)
Taylor U (IN)
Texas Tech U (TX)
U of Arkansas at Little Rock (AR)
U of Arkansas–Fort Smith (AR)
U of Hartford (CT)
U of Houston–Downtown (TX)
U of Idaho (ID)
The U of Montana (MT)
U of North Texas (TX)
U of South Florida Sarasota-Manatee (FL)
U of Washington (WA)
U of Wisconsin–Stout (WI)
Valparaiso U (IN)
Weber State U (UT)
Winthrop U (SC)
Worcester Polytechnic Inst (MA)
Yeshiva U (NY)
York Coll of Pennsylvania (PA)
Youngstown State U (OH)

PROJECT MANAGEMENT

Creighton U (NE)
Malone U (OH)
Minnesota State U Moorhead (MN)
Wentworth Inst of Technology (MA)

PROTECTIVE SERVICES OPERATIONS

Embry-Riddle Aeronautical U–Worldwide (FL)

PSYCHIATRIC/MENTAL HEALTH SERVICES TECHNOLOGY

Columbia Southern U (AL)
Indiana U–Purdue U Fort Wayne (IN)

PSYCHOLOGY

Abilene Christian U (TX)
Adams State U (CO)
Adelphi U (NY)
Agnes Scott Coll (GA)
Alabama State U (AL)
Alaska Pacific U (AK)
Albany State U (GA)
Albertus Magnus Coll (CT)
Albion Coll (MI)
Albright Coll (PA)
Alcorn State U (MS)
Allegheny Coll (PA)
Alma Coll (MI)
Alvernia U (PA)
Alverno Coll (WI)
American Intl Coll (MA)
American Public U System (WV)
American U (DC)
The American U in Cairo (Egypt)
American U of Beirut (Lebanon)
The American U of Paris (France)
Amherst Coll (MA)
Anderson U (IN)
Anderson U (SC)
Andrews U (MI)
Angelo State U (TX)
Anna Maria Coll (MA)
Antioch Coll, Yellow Springs (OH)
Appalachian State U (NC)
Aquinas Coll (MI)
Arcadia U (PA)
Arizona Christian U (AZ)
Arizona State U at the Tempe campus (AZ)
Arizona State U at the West campus (AZ)
Arkansas State U (AR)
Arkansas Tech U (AR)
Armstrong State U (GA)
Asbury U (KY)
Ashland U (OH)
Assumption Coll (MA)
Athens State U (AL)
Auburn U (AL)
Auburn U at Montgomery (AL)
Augsburg Coll (MN)
Augustana Coll (IL)
Augustana Coll (SD)
Austin Coll (TX)
Austin Peay State U (TN)
Ave Maria U (FL)
Averett U (VA)
Avila U (MO)
Azusa Pacific U (CA)
Baker U (KS)
Baldwin Wallace U (OH)
Ball State U (IN)
Barclay Coll (KS)
Bard Coll (NY)
Bard Coll at Simon's Rock (MA)
Barnard Coll (NY)
Barry U (FL)
Baruch Coll of the City U of New York (NY)
Bastyr U (WA)
Bates Coll (ME)
Baylor U (TX)
Bay Path U (MA)
Beacon Coll (FL)
Becker Coll (MA)
Belhaven U (MS)
Belmont Abbey Coll (NC)
Belmont U (TN)
Beloit Coll (WI)
Bemidji State U (MN)
Benedictine Coll (KS)
Benedictine U (IL)
Bennett Coll (NC)
Bennington Coll (VT)
Berea Coll (KY)
Berry Coll (GA)
Bethany Coll (WV)
Bethany Lutheran Coll (MN)
Bethel Coll (IN)
Bethel Coll (KS)
Bethel U (MN)
Bethune-Cookman U (FL)
Binghamton U, State U of New York (NY)
Biola U (CA)
Birmingham-Southern Coll (AL)
Blackburn Coll (IL)
Black Hills State U (SD)
Bloomfield Coll (NJ)
Bloomsburg U of Pennsylvania (PA)
Bluefield Coll (VA)
Blue Mountain Coll (MS)
Bluffton U (OH)
Boston Coll (MA)
Boston U (MA)
Bowdoin Coll (ME)
Bowie State U (MD)
Bowling Green State U (OH)
Brandeis U (MA)
Brenau U (GA)
Brevard Coll (NC)
Bridgewater Coll (VA)
Bridgewater State U (MA)
Brown U (RI)
Bryan Coll (TN)
Bryant U (RI)
Bryn Mawr Coll (PA)
Bucknell U (PA)
Buena Vista U (IA)
Buffalo State Coll, State U of New York (NY)
Butler U (IN)
Cabrini Coll (PA)
Cairn U (PA)
Caldwell U (NJ)
California Baptist U (CA)
California Lutheran U (CA)
California Polytechnic State U, San Luis Obispo (CA)
California State Polytechnic U, Pomona (CA)
California State U, Chico (CA)
California State U, Dominguez Hills (CA)
California State U, Fresno (CA)
California State U, Fullerton (CA)
California State U, Long Beach (CA)
California State U, Los Angeles (CA)
California State U, Monterey Bay (CA)
California State U, Sacramento (CA)
California State U, San Bernardino (CA)
California State U, San Marcos (CA)
California State U, Stanislaus (CA)
California U of Pennsylvania (PA)
Calumet Coll of Saint Joseph (IN)
Calvin Coll (MI)
Cameron U (OK)
Campbellsville U (KY)
Canisius Coll (NY)
Cape Breton U (NS, Canada)
Capital U (OH)
Cardinal Stritch U (WI)
Carleton Coll (MN)
Carlos Albizu U, Miami Campus (FL)
Carlow U (PA)
Carroll Coll (MT)
Carson-Newman U (TN)
Case Western Reserve U (OH)
Castleton State Coll (VT)
Catawba Coll (NC)
The Catholic U of America (DC)
Cazenovia Coll (NY)
Cedar Crest Coll (PA)
Cedarville U (OH)
Centenary Coll of Louisiana (LA)
Central Coll (IA)
Central Connecticut State U (CT)
Central Methodist U (MO)
Central Michigan U (MI)
Central State U (OH)
Central Washington U (WA)
Centre Coll (KY)
Chaminade U of Honolulu (HI)
Chapman U (CA)
Charleston Southern U (SC)
Chatham U (PA)
Chestnut Hill Coll (PA)
Cheyney U of Pennsylvania (PA)
Chicago State U (IL)
Chowan U (NC)
Christian Brothers U (TN)
Christopher Newport U (VA)
Cincinnati Christian U (OH)
The Citadel, The Military Coll of South Carolina (SC)
City Coll of the City U of New York (NY)
Claflin U (SC)
Claremont McKenna Coll (CA)
Clarion U of Pennsylvania (PA)
Clark Atlanta U (GA)
Clarke U (IA)
Clarkson U (NY)
Clark U (MA)
Clearwater Christian Coll (FL)
Cleveland State U (OH)
Coastal Carolina U (SC)
Coe Coll (IA)
Coker Coll (SC)
Colby Coll (ME)
Colby-Sawyer Coll (NH)
The Coll at Brockport, State U of New York (NY)
Coll of Charleston (SC)
Coll of Coastal Georgia (GA)
The Coll of Idaho (ID)
The Coll of New Jersey (NJ)
The Coll of New Rochelle (NY)
Coll of Saint Benedict (MN)
Coll of Saint Elizabeth (NJ)
Coll of Saint Mary (NE)
The Coll of Saint Rose (NY)
The Coll of St. Scholastica (MN)
Coll of Staten Island of the City U of New York (NY)
Coll of the Atlantic (ME)
Coll of the Holy Cross (MA)
Coll of the Ozarks (MO)
The Coll of William and Mary (VA)
The Coll of Wooster (OH)
The Colorado Coll (CO)
Colorado Mesa U (CO)
Colorado State U (CO)
Colorado State U–Pueblo (CO)
Columbia Coll (MO)
Columbia Coll (SC)
Columbia Intl U (SC)
Columbia U (NY)
Columbia U, School of General Studies (NY)
Columbus State U (GA)
Concordia Coll (MN)
Concordia Coll–New York (NY)
Concordia U (CA)
Concordia U (QC, Canada)
Concordia U Chicago (IL)
Concordia U, Nebraska (NE)
Concordia U, St. Paul (MN)
Concordia U Wisconsin (WI)
Concord U (WV)
Connecticut Coll (CT)
Corban U (OR)
Cornell Coll (IA)
Cornell U (NY)
Cornerstone U (MI)
Covenant Coll (GA)
Crandall U (NB, Canada)
Creighton U (NE)
Culver-Stockton Coll (MO)
Cumberland U (TN)
Curry Coll (MA)
Daemen Coll (NY)
Dalhousie U (NS, Canada)
Dallas Baptist U (TX)
Daniel Webster Coll (NH)
Dartmouth Coll (NH)
Davidson Coll (NC)
Defiance Coll (OH)
Delaware State U (DE)
Delta State U (MS)
Denison U (OH)
DePaul U (IL)
DePauw U (IN)
DEREE - The American Coll of Greece (Greece)
DeSales U (PA)
Dickinson Coll (PA)
Dickinson State U (ND)
Dixie State U (UT)
Doane Coll (NE)
Dominican Coll (NY)
Dominican U (IL)
Dominican U of California (CA)
Dowling Coll (NY)
Drake U (IA)
Drew U (NJ)
Drexel U (PA)
Drury U (MO)
Duquesne U (PA)
Earlham Coll (IN)
East Carolina U (NC)
East Central U (OK)
Eastern Connecticut State U (CT)
Eastern Illinois U (IL)
Eastern Kentucky U (KY)
Eastern Michigan U (MI)
Eastern New Mexico U (NM)
Eastern Oregon U (OR)
Eastern U (PA)
East Stroudsburg U of Pennsylvania (PA)
East Tennessee State U (TN)
East Texas Baptist U (TX)
Eckerd Coll (FL)
Edgewood Coll (WI)
Edinboro U of Pennsylvania (PA)
Elizabethtown Coll (PA)
Elmhurst Coll (IL)
Elmira Coll (NY)
Elms Coll (MA)
Elon U (NC)
Emmanuel Coll (GA)
Emmanuel Coll (MA)
Emory & Henry Coll (VA)
Emporia State U (KS)
Endicott Coll (MA)
Erskine Coll (SC)
Evangel U (MO)
The Evergreen State Coll (WA)
Excelsior Coll (NY)
Fairfield U (CT)
Fairleigh Dickinson U, Coll at Florham (NJ)
Fairleigh Dickinson U, Metropolitan Campus (NJ)
Fairmont State U (WV)
Fayetteville State U (NC)
Ferris State U (MI)
Ferrum Coll (VA)
Fisher Coll (MA)
Fitchburg State U (MA)
Flagler Coll (FL)
Florida Ag and Mech U (FL)
Florida Atlantic U (FL)
Florida Gulf Coast U (FL)
Florida Inst of Technology (FL)
Florida Intl U (FL)
Florida Southern Coll (FL)
Florida State U (FL)
Fontbonne U (MO)
Fordham U (NY)
Fort Hays State U (KS)
Fort Lewis Coll (CO)
Framingham State U (MA)
Franciscan U of Steubenville (OH)
Francis Marion U (SC)
Franklin & Marshall Coll (PA)
Franklin Coll (IN)
Franklin Pierce U (NH)
Friends U (KS)
Frostburg State U (MD)
Furman U (SC)
Gallaudet U (DC)
Gannon U (PA)
Geneva Coll (PA)
George Mason U (VA)

Georgetown Coll (KY)
Georgetown U (DC)
The George Washington U (DC)
Georgia Coll & State U (GA)
Georgia Gwinnett Coll (GA)
Georgian Court U (NJ)
Georgia Regents U (GA)
Georgia Southern U (GA)
Georgia Southwestern State U (GA)
Georgia State U (GA)
Gettysburg Coll (PA)
Goddard Coll (VT)
Gonzaga U (WA)
Gordon Coll (MA)
Goshen Coll (IN)
Goucher Coll (MD)
Governors State U (IL)
Grace Coll (IN)
Graceland U (IA)
Grambling State U (LA)
Grand Valley State U (MI)
Grand View U (IA)
Granite State Coll (NH)
Green Mountain Coll (VT)
Greensboro Coll (NC)
Greenville Coll (IL)
Grinnell Coll (IA)
Grove City Coll (PA)
Guilford Coll (NC)
Gustavus Adolphus Coll (MN)
Gwynedd Mercy U (PA)
Hamilton Coll (NY)
Hamline U (MN)
Hampden-Sydney Coll (VA)
Hampshire Coll (MA)
Hampton U (VA)
Hannibal-LaGrange U (MO)
Hanover Coll (IN)
Harding U (AR)
Hardin-Simmons U (TX)
Hartwick Coll (NY)
Harvard U (MA)
Hastings Coll (NE)
Haverford Coll (PA)
Hawai`i Pacific U (HI)
Heidelberg U (OH)
Hendrix Coll (AR)
Heritage U (WA)
High Point U (NC)
Hilbert Coll (NY)
Hillsdale Coll (MI)
Hillsdale Free Will Baptist Coll (OK)
Hiram Coll (OH)
Hobart and William Smith Colls (NY)
Hofstra U (NY)
Hollins U (VA)
Holy Cross Coll (IN)
Holy Family U (PA)
Hope Coll (MI)
Hope Intl U (CA)
Houghton Coll (NY)
Houston Baptist U (TX)
Howard Payne U (TX)
Howard U (DC)
Humboldt State U (CA)
Hunter Coll of the City U of New York (NY)
Huntingdon Coll (AL)
Husson U (ME)
Huston-Tillotson U (TX)
Illinois Coll (IL)
Illinois Inst of Technology (IL)
Illinois State U (IL)
Illinois Wesleyan U (IL)
Immaculata U (PA)
Indiana State U (IN)
Indiana U Bloomington (IN)
Indiana U East (IN)
Indiana U Kokomo (IN)
Indiana U Northwest (IN)
Indiana U of Pennsylvania (PA)
Indiana U–Purdue U Fort Wayne (IN)
Indiana U–Purdue U Indianapolis (IN)
Indiana U South Bend (IN)
Indiana U Southeast (IN)
Inter American U of Puerto Rico, Aguadilla Campus (PR)
Inter American U of Puerto Rico, Fajardo Campus (PR)
Inter American U of Puerto Rico, Ponce Campus (PR)
Inter American U of Puerto Rico, San Germán Campus (PR)
Iona Coll (NY)
Iowa State U of Science and Technology (IA)
Iowa Wesleyan Coll (IA)
Ithaca Coll (NY)
Jackson State U (MS)
Jacksonville State U (AL)
Jacksonville U (FL)
James Madison U (VA)
John Brown U (AR)
John Carroll U (OH)
Johns Hopkins U (MD)
Johnson C. Smith U (NC)
Johnson State Coll (VT)
Judson Coll (AL)
Judson U (IL)
Juniata Coll (PA)
Kalamazoo Coll (MI)
Kansas State U (KS)
Kansas Wesleyan U (KS)
Kean U (NJ)
Keene State Coll (NH)
Keiser U, Fort Lauderdale (FL)
Kennesaw State U (GA)
Kent State U (OH)
Kent State U at Ashtabula (OH)
Kent State U at East Liverpool (OH)
Kent State U at Geauga (OH)
Kent State U at Salem (OH)
Kent State U at Stark (OH)
Kent State U at Trumbull (OH)
Kent State U at Tuscarawas (OH)
Kentucky Christian U (KY)
Kentucky State U (KY)
Kentucky Wesleyan Coll (KY)
Kenyon Coll (OH)
Keuka Coll (NY)
Keystone Coll (PA)
King's Coll (PA)
The King's U Coll (AB, Canada)
King U (TN)
Knox Coll (IL)
Kutztown U of Pennsylvania (PA)
Lafayette Coll (PA)
LaGrange Coll (GA)
Lake Erie Coll (OH)
Lake Forest Coll (IL)
Lamar U (TX)
Langston U (OK)
La Roche Coll (PA)
La Salle U (PA)
Lasell Coll (MA)
La Sierra U (CA)
Laurel U (NC)
Lawrence Technological U (MI)
Lawrence U (WI)
Lebanese American U (Lebanon)
Lebanon Valley Coll (PA)
Lees-McRae Coll (NC)
Lee U (TN)
Lehigh U (PA)
Lehman Coll of the City U of New York (NY)
Le Moyne Coll (NY)
Lenoir-Rhyne U (NC)
LeTourneau U (TX)
Lewis & Clark Coll (OR)
Lewis U (IL)
Liberty U (VA)
Life U (GA)
Limestone Coll (SC)
Lincoln Christian U (IL)
Lincoln Memorial U (TN)
Lincoln U (MO)
Lindenwood U (MO)
Lindsey Wilson Coll (KY)
Linfield Coll (OR)
Lipscomb U (TN)
Lock Haven U of Pennsylvania (PA)
Long Island U–LIU Brooklyn (NY)
Long Island U–LIU Post (NY)
Longwood U (VA)
Loras Coll (IA)
Louisiana Coll (LA)
Louisiana State U and A&M Coll (LA)
Louisiana State U in Shreveport (LA)
Lourdes U (OH)
Loyola Marymount U (CA)
Loyola U Chicago (IL)
Loyola U New Orleans (LA)
Lubbock Christian U (TX)
Luther Coll (IA)
Lycoming Coll (PA)
Lynchburg Coll (VA)
Lynn U (FL)
Lyon Coll (AR)
Macalester Coll (MN)
Madonna U (MI)
Malone U (OH)
Manchester U (IN)
Manhattan Coll (NY)
Manhattanville Coll (NY)
Mansfield U of Pennsylvania (PA)
Maria Coll (NY)
Marian U (IN)
Marian U (WI)
Marietta Coll (OH)
Marist Coll (NY)
Marquette U (WI)
Marshall U (WV)
Mars Hill U (NC)
Mary Baldwin Coll (VA)
Marylhurst U (OR)
Marymount California U (CA)
Marymount Manhattan Coll (NY)
Marymount U (VA)
Maryville Coll (TN)
Maryville U of Saint Louis (MO)
Marywood U (PA)
Massachusetts Coll of Liberal Arts (MA)
McDaniel Coll (MD)
McKendree U (IL)
McMurry U (TX)
McNeese State U (LA)
Medaille Coll (NY)
Medgar Evers Coll of the City U of New York (NY)
Menlo Coll (CA)
Mercer U, Macon (GA)
Mercy Coll (NY)
Meredith Coll (NC)
Merrimack Coll (MA)
Messiah Coll (PA)
Metropolitan State U (MN)
Miami U (OH)
Michigan State U (MI)
Michigan Technological U (MI)
MidAmerica Nazarene U (KS)
Middlebury Coll (VT)
Middle Tennessee State U (TN)
Midwestern State U (TX)
Millersville U of Pennsylvania (PA)
Milligan Coll (TN)
Millikin U (IL)
Millsaps Coll (MS)
Mills Coll (CA)
Minnesota State U Mankato (MN)
Minnesota State U Moorhead (MN)
Minot State U (ND)
Misericordia U (PA)
Mississippi State U (MS)
Mississippi U for Women (MS)
Missouri Baptist U (MO)
Missouri Southern State U (MO)
Missouri State U (MO)
Missouri U of Science and Technology (MO)
Missouri Valley Coll (MO)
Missouri Western State U (MO)
Mitchell Coll (CT)
Molloy Coll (NY)
Monmouth Coll (IL)
Monmouth U (NJ)
Montana State U (MT)
Montana State U Billings (MT)
Montclair State U (NJ)
Moravian Coll (PA)
Morehead State U (KY)
Morningside Coll (IA)
Mount Allison U (NB, Canada)
Mount Aloysius Coll (PA)
Mount Holyoke Coll (MA)
Mount Marty Coll (SD)
Mount Mary U (WI)
Mount Mercy U (IA)
Mount St. Joseph U (OH)
Mount Saint Mary Coll (NY)
Mount Saint Mary's U (CA)
Mount St. Mary's U (MD)
Mount Vernon Nazarene U (OH)
Muhlenberg Coll (PA)
Multnomah U (OR)
Murray State U (KY)
Naropa U (CO)
National U (CA)
Nazareth Coll of Rochester (NY)
Nebraska Wesleyan U (NE)
Neumann U (PA)
Newberry Coll (SC)
Newbury Coll (MA)
New Coll of Florida (FL)
New England Coll (NH)
New Jersey City U (NJ)
Newman U (KS)
New Mexico Highlands U (NM)
New Mexico Inst of Mining and Technology (NM)
New Mexico State U (NM)
New York Inst of Technology (NY)
New York U (NY)
Niagara U (NY)
Nicholls State U (LA)
Nichols Coll (MA)
Norfolk State U (VA)
North Carolina Ag and Tech State U (NC)
North Carolina Central U (NC)
North Carolina State U (NC)
North Carolina Wesleyan Coll (NC)
North Central Coll (IL)
North Dakota State U (ND)
Northeastern Illinois U (IL)
Northeastern State U (OK)
Northeastern U (MA)
Northern Arizona U (AZ)
Northern Illinois U (IL)
Northern Kentucky U (KY)
Northern Michigan U (MI)
Northern State U (SD)
North Greenville U (SC)
Northland Coll (WI)
Northwest Christian U (OR)
Northwestern Coll (IA)
Northwestern Oklahoma State U (OK)
Northwestern U (IL)
Northwest Missouri State U (MO)
Northwest Nazarene U (ID)
Northwest U (WA)
Norwich U (VT)
Notre Dame of Maryland U (MD)
Nova Southeastern U (FL)
Nyack Coll (NY)
Oakland U (MI)
Oberlin Coll (OH)
Occidental Coll (CA)
Oglethorpe U (GA)
Ohio Dominican U (OH)
Ohio Northern U (OH)
The Ohio State U (OH)
The Ohio State U at Lima (OH)
The Ohio State U at Marion (OH)
The Ohio State U–Mansfield Campus (OH)
The Ohio State U–Newark Campus (OH)
Ohio U (OH)
Ohio Valley U (WV)
Ohio Wesleyan U (OH)
Oklahoma Baptist U (OK)
Oklahoma Christian U (OK)
Oklahoma City U (OK)
Oklahoma State U (OK)
Oklahoma Wesleyan U (OK)
Old Dominion U (VA)
Olivet Coll (MI)
Olivet Nazarene U (IL)
Oregon State U (OR)
Our Lady of the Lake U of San Antonio (TX)
Pace U (NY)
Pacific Lutheran U (WA)
Pacific U (OR)
Palm Beach Atlantic U (FL)
Palo Alto U (CA)
Park U (MO)
Penn State Abington (PA)
Penn State Altoona (PA)
Penn State Beaver (PA)
Penn State Berks (PA)
Penn State Brandywine (PA)
Penn State DuBois (PA)
Penn State Erie, The Behrend Coll (PA)
Penn State Fayette, The Eberly Campus (PA)
Penn State Greater Allegheny (PA)
Penn State Harrisburg (PA)
Penn State Hazleton (PA)
Penn State Lehigh Valley (PA)
Penn State Mont Alto (PA)
Penn State New Kensington (PA)
Penn State Schuylkill (PA)
Penn State Shenango (PA)
Penn State U Park (PA)
Penn State Wilkes-Barre (PA)
Penn State Worthington Scranton (PA)
Penn State York (PA)
Pepperdine U, Malibu (CA)
Peru State Coll (NE)
Philadelphia U (PA)
Philander Smith Coll (AR)
Piedmont Coll (GA)
Pine Manor Coll (MA)
Pittsburg State U (KS)
Plymouth State U (NH)
Point Loma Nazarene U (CA)
Point U (GA)
Pomona Coll (CA)
Portland State U (OR)
Post U (CT)
Prairie View A&M U (TX)
Presbyterian Coll (SC)
Prescott Coll (AZ)
Princeton U (NJ)
Providence Coll (RI)
Purchase Coll, State U of New York (NY)
Purdue U (IN)
Purdue U Calumet (IN)
Queens Coll of the City U of New York (NY)
Quincy U (IL)
Quinnipiac U (CT)
Radford U (VA)
Ramapo Coll of New Jersey (NJ)
Randolph Coll (VA)
Randolph-Macon Coll (VA)
Reed Coll (OR)
Regent U (VA)
Regis Coll (MA)
Regis U (CO)
Reinhardt U (GA)
Rensselaer Polytechnic Inst (NY)
Rhode Island Coll (RI)
Rhodes Coll (TN)
Rice U (TX)
Rider U (NJ)
Ripon Coll (WI)
Rivier U (NH)
Roanoke Coll (VA)
Robert Morris U (PA)
Roberts Wesleyan Coll (NY)
Rochester Inst of Technology (NY)
Rockford U (IL)
Rockhurst U (MO)
Rocky Mountain Coll (MT)
Rollins Coll (FL)
Roosevelt U (IL)
Rosemont Coll (PA)
Rowan U (NJ)
Rutgers, The State U of New Jersey, Camden (NJ)
Rutgers, The State U of New Jersey, Newark (NJ)
Rutgers, The State U of New Jersey, New Brunswick (NJ)
Sacred Heart U (CT)
The Sage Colls (NY)
Saginaw Valley State U (MI)
St. Andrews U (NC)
Saint Anselm Coll (NH)
Saint Augustine's U (NC)
St. Bonaventure U (NY)
St. Catharine Coll (KY)
St. Catherine U (MN)
St. Edward's U (TX)
St. Francis Coll (NY)
Saint Francis U (PA)
St. Gregory's U, Shawnee (OK)
St. John Fisher Coll (NY)
Saint John's U (MN)
St. John's U (NY)
Saint Joseph's Coll (IN)
St. Joseph's Coll, Long Island Campus (NY)
St. Joseph's Coll, New York (NY)
Saint Joseph's U (PA)
St. Lawrence U (NY)
Saint Leo U (FL)
Saint Louis U (MO)
Saint Martin's U (WA)
Saint Mary-of-the-Woods Coll (IN)
Saint Mary's Coll (IN)
St. Mary's Coll of Maryland (MD)
St. Mary's U (TX)
Saint Mary's U of Minnesota (MN)
Saint Michael's Coll (VT)
St. Norbert Coll (WI)
St. Olaf Coll (MN)
Saint Peter's U (NJ)
St. Thomas Aquinas Coll (NY)
St. Thomas U (FL)
St. Thomas U (NB, Canada)

Saint Vincent Coll (PA)
Salem Coll (NC)
Salisbury U (MD)
Salve Regina U (RI)
Samford U (AL)
Sam Houston State U (TX)
San Diego Christian Coll (CA)
San Diego State U (CA)
San Francisco State U (CA)
San Jose State U (CA)
Santa Clara U (CA)
Sarah Lawrence Coll (NY)
Scripps Coll (CA)
Seattle Pacific U (WA)
Seattle U (WA)
Seton Hill U (PA)
Sewanee: The U of the South (TN)
Shawnee State U (OH)
Shaw U (NC)
Shenandoah U (VA)
Shepherd U (WV)
Shippensburg U of Pennsylvania (PA)
Siena Coll (NY)
Siena Heights U (MI)
Silver Lake Coll of the Holy Family (WI)
Simmons Coll (MA)
Simon Fraser U (BC, Canada)
Simpson Coll (IA)
Simpson U (CA)
Skidmore Coll (NY)
Slippery Rock U of Pennsylvania (PA)
Smith Coll (MA)
South Carolina State U (SC)
South Dakota State U (SD)
Southeastern Louisiana U (LA)
Southeastern Oklahoma State U (OK)
Southeastern U (FL)
Southeast Missouri State U (MO)
Southern Adventist U (TN)
Southern Arkansas U–Magnolia (AR)
Southern Connecticut State U (CT)
Southern Illinois U Carbondale (IL)
Southern Illinois U Edwardsville (IL)
Southern Methodist U (TX)
Southern New Hampshire U (NH)
Southern Oregon U (OR)
Southern Utah U (UT)
Southern Vermont Coll (VT)
Southwest Baptist U (MO)
Southwestern Adventist U (TX)
Southwestern Coll (KS)
Southwestern U (TX)
Southwest Minnesota State U (MN)
Spalding U (KY)
Spelman Coll (GA)
Spring Hill Coll (AL)
Stanford U (CA)
State U of New York at Fredonia (NY)
State U of New York at New Paltz (NY)
State U of New York at Oswego (NY)
State U of New York at Plattsburgh (NY)
State U of New York Coll at Cortland (NY)
State U of New York Coll at Geneseo (NY)
State U of New York Coll at Old Westbury (NY)
State U of New York Coll at Potsdam (NY)
State U of New York Empire State Coll (NY)
State U of New York Polytechnic Inst (NY)
Stephen F. Austin State U (TX)
Stephens Coll (MO)
Stetson U (FL)
Stevenson U (MD)
Stockton U (NJ)
Stonehill Coll (MA)
Stony Brook U, State U of New York (NY)
Suffolk U (MA)
Sul Ross State U (TX)
Summit U (PA)
Susquehanna U (PA)
Syracuse U (NY)
Tabor Coll (KS)
Tarleton State U (TX)
Taylor U (IN)
Temple U (PA)
Tennessee State U (TN)
Tennessee Wesleyan Coll (TN)
Texas A&M Intl U (TX)
Texas A&M U (TX)
Texas A&M U–Commerce (TX)
Texas A&M U–Corpus Christi (TX)
Texas A&M U–Kingsville (TX)
Texas Christian U (TX)
Texas Lutheran U (TX)
Texas Southern U (TX)
Texas State U (TX)
Texas Tech U (TX)
Texas Wesleyan U (TX)
Texas Woman's U (TX)
Thiel Coll (PA)
Thomas More Coll (KY)
Tiffin U (OH)
Tougaloo Coll (MS)
Towson U (MD)
Transylvania U (KY)
Trent U (ON, Canada)
Trevecca Nazarene U (TN)
Trine U (IN)
Trinity Christian Coll (IL)
Trinity Coll (CT)
Trinity Coll of Florida (FL)
Trinity U (TX)
Troy U (AL)
Truett-McConnell Coll (GA)
Truman State U (MO)
Tufts U (MA)
Tulane U (LA)
Tusculum Coll (TN)
Union Coll (KY)
Union Coll (NE)
Union Coll (NY)
Union Inst & U (OH)
Union U (TN)
United States Military Acad (NY)
Universidad del Turabo (PR)
Universidad Metropolitana (PR)
Université de Montréal (QC, Canada)
Université de Sherbrooke (QC, Canada)
Université du Québec en Outaouais (QC, Canada)
U at Albany, State U of New York (NY)
U at Buffalo, the State U of New York (NY)
The U of Akron (OH)
The U of Alabama (AL)
The U of Alabama at Birmingham (AL)
The U of Alabama in Huntsville (AL)
U of Alaska Fairbanks (AK)
U of Alberta (AB, Canada)
The U of Arizona (AZ)
U of Arkansas (AR)
U of Arkansas at Little Rock (AR)
U of Arkansas at Pine Bluff (AR)
U of Arkansas–Fort Smith (AR)
U of Bridgeport (CT)
The U of British Columbia (BC, Canada)
The U of British Columbia–Okanagan Campus (BC, Canada)
U of California, Berkeley (CA)
U of California, Davis (CA)
U of California, Irvine (CA)
U of California, Los Angeles (CA)
U of California, Merced (CA)
U of California, Riverside (CA)
U of California, Santa Barbara (CA)
U of California, Santa Cruz (CA)
U of Central Arkansas (AR)
U of Central Florida (FL)
U of Central Missouri (MO)
U of Central Oklahoma (OK)
U of Charleston (WV)
U of Chicago (IL)
U of Cincinnati (OH)
U of Colorado Boulder (CO)
U of Colorado Colorado Springs (CO)
U of Colorado Denver (CO)
U of Dallas (TX)
U of Dayton (OH)
U of Delaware (DE)
U of Denver (CO)
U of Dubuque (IA)
U of Evansville (IN)
The U of Findlay (OH)
U of Florida (FL)
U of Georgia (GA)
U of Great Falls (MT)
U of Guam (GU)
U of Guelph (ON, Canada)
U of Hartford (CT)
U of Hawaii at Manoa (HI)
U of Hawaii–West Oahu (HI)
U of Houston (TX)
U of Houston–Clear Lake (TX)
U of Houston–Downtown (TX)
U of Houston–Victoria (TX)
U of Idaho (ID)
U of Illinois at Chicago (IL)
U of Illinois at Springfield (IL)
U of Indianapolis (IN)
The U of Iowa (IA)
U of Jamestown (ND)
The U of Kansas (KS)
U of Kentucky (KY)
U of King's Coll (NS, Canada)
U of La Verne (CA)
U of Lethbridge (AB, Canada)
U of Louisiana at Lafayette (LA)
U of Louisville (KY)
U of Maine (ME)
U of Maine at Machias (ME)
U of Maine at Presque Isle (ME)
U of Mary Hardin-Baylor (TX)
U of Maryland, Baltimore County (MD)
U of Maryland, Coll Park (MD)
U of Maryland U Coll (MD)
U of Mary Washington (VA)
U of Massachusetts Amherst (MA)
U of Massachusetts Boston (MA)
U of Massachusetts Dartmouth (MA)
U of Massachusetts Lowell (MA)
U of Memphis (TN)
U of Miami (FL)
U of Michigan–Dearborn (MI)
U of Michigan–Flint (MI)
U of Minnesota, Duluth (MN)
U of Minnesota, Morris (MN)
U of Minnesota, Twin Cities Campus (MN)
U of Mississippi (MS)
U of Missouri (MO)
U of Missouri–Kansas City (MO)
U of Missouri–St. Louis (MO)
U of Mobile (AL)
The U of Montana (MT)
The U of Montana Western (MT)
U of Montevallo (AL)
U of Mount Union (OH)
U of Nebraska at Kearney (NE)
U of Nebraska–Lincoln (NE)
U of Nevada, Las Vegas (NV)
U of Nevada, Reno (NV)
U of New Brunswick Saint John (NB, Canada)
U of New England (ME)
U of New Hampshire (NH)
U of New Hampshire at Manchester (NH)
U of New Haven (CT)
U of New Mexico (NM)
U of New Orleans (LA)
U of North Alabama (AL)
U of North Carolina at Asheville (NC)
The U of North Carolina at Chapel Hill (NC)
The U of North Carolina at Charlotte (NC)
The U of North Carolina at Greensboro (NC)
The U of North Carolina at Pembroke (NC)
The U of North Carolina Wilmington (NC)
U of North Dakota (ND)
U of Northern Colorado (CO)
U of Northern Iowa (IA)
U of North Florida (FL)
U of North Georgia (GA)
U of North Texas (TX)
U of Northwestern–St. Paul (MN)
U of Notre Dame (IN)
U of Oklahoma (OK)
U of Oregon (OR)
U of Ottawa (ON, Canada)
U of Pennsylvania (PA)
U of Pikeville (KY)
U of Pittsburgh (PA)
U of Pittsburgh at Bradford (PA)
U of Pittsburgh at Greensburg (PA)
U of Portland (OR)
U of Puerto Rico in Ponce (PR)
U of Puget Sound (WA)
U of Regina (SK, Canada)
U of Rhode Island (RI)
U of Richmond (VA)
U of Rochester (NY)
U of St. Francis (IL)
U of Saint Francis (IN)
U of Saint Joseph (CT)
U of Saint Mary (KS)
U of St. Thomas (MN)
U of St. Thomas (TX)
U of San Diego (CA)
U of San Francisco (CA)
U of Saskatchewan (SK, Canada)
U of Science and Arts of Oklahoma (OK)
The U of Scranton (PA)
U of South Alabama (AL)
U of South Carolina Aiken (SC)
U of South Carolina Beaufort (SC)
U of South Carolina Upstate (SC)
The U of South Dakota (SD)
U of Southern California (CA)
U of Southern Indiana (IN)
U of Southern Maine (ME)
U of Southern Mississippi (MS)
U of South Florida (FL)
U of South Florida, St. Petersburg (FL)
U of South Florida Sarasota-Manatee (FL)
The U of Tampa (FL)
The U of Tennessee (TN)
The U of Tennessee at Chattanooga (TN)
The U of Tennessee at Martin (TN)
The U of Texas at Arlington (TX)
The U of Texas at Austin (TX)
The U of Texas at Dallas (TX)
The U of Texas at El Paso (TX)
The U of Texas at San Antonio (TX)
The U of Texas at Tyler (TX)
The U of Texas of the Permian Basin (TX)
The U of Texas–Pan American (TX)
U of the Cumberlands (KY)
U of the District of Columbia (DC)
U of the Fraser Valley (BC, Canada)
U of the Incarnate Word (TX)
U of the Pacific (CA)
U of the Sciences (PA)
U of the Virgin Islands (VI)
U of the West (CA)
The U of Toledo (OH)
The U of Tulsa (OK)
U of Utah (UT)
U of Valley Forge (PA)
U of Vermont (VT)
U of Virginia (VA)
The U of Virginia's Coll at Wise (VA)
U of Washington (WA)
U of Washington, Tacoma (WA)
U of Waterloo (ON, Canada)
The U of West Alabama (AL)
The U of Western Ontario (ON, Canada)
U of West Florida (FL)
U of West Georgia (GA)
U of Windsor (ON, Canada)
U of Wisconsin–Eau Claire (WI)
U of Wisconsin–Green Bay (WI)
U of Wisconsin–La Crosse (WI)
U of Wisconsin–Madison (WI)
U of Wisconsin–Milwaukee (WI)
U of Wisconsin–Oshkosh (WI)
U of Wisconsin–Parkside (WI)
U of Wisconsin–Platteville (WI)
U of Wisconsin–River Falls (WI)
U of Wisconsin–Stevens Point (WI)
U of Wisconsin–Stout (WI)
U of Wisconsin–Superior (WI)
U of Wisconsin–Whitewater (WI)
U of Wyoming (WY)
Upper Iowa U (IA)
Urbana U (OH)
Ursinus Coll (PA)
Ursuline Coll (OH)
Utah State U (UT)
Utah Valley U (UT)
Utica Coll (NY)
Valdosta State U (GA)
Valley City State U (ND)
Valparaiso U (IN)
Vanderbilt U (TN)
Vanguard U of Southern California (CA)
Vassar Coll (NY)
Villanova U (PA)
Virginia Commonwealth U (VA)
Virginia Military Inst (VA)
Virginia Polytechnic Inst and State U (VA)
Virginia State U (VA)
Virginia Union U (VA)
Virginia Wesleyan Coll (VA)
Viterbo U (WI)
Wabash Coll (IN)
Wagner Coll (NY)
Wake Forest U (NC)
Walden U (MN)
Waldorf Coll (IA)
Walla Walla U (WA)
Walsh U (OH)
Warner Pacific Coll (OR)
Warren Wilson Coll (NC)
Wartburg Coll (IA)
Washburn U (KS)
Washington & Jefferson Coll (PA)
Washington and Lee U (VA)
Washington Coll (MD)
Washington State U (WA)
Washington State U Vancouver (WA)
Washington U in St. Louis (MO)
Waynesburg U (PA)
Wayne State Coll (NE)
Wayne State U (MI)
Weber State U (UT)
Webster U (MO)
Wells Coll (NY)
Wesleyan Coll (GA)
Wesleyan U (CT)
West Chester U of Pennsylvania (PA)
Western Carolina U (NC)
Western Illinois U (IL)
Western Kentucky U (KY)
Western Michigan U (MI)
Western New England U (MA)
Western Oregon U (OR)
Western State Colorado U (CO)
Western Washington U (WA)
Westfield State U (MA)
West Liberty U (WV)
Westminster Coll (MO)
Westminster Coll (UT)
West Texas A&M U (TX)
West Virginia State U (WV)
West Virginia U (WV)
West Virginia U Inst of Technology (WV)
West Virginia Wesleyan Coll (WV)
Wheaton Coll (IL)
Wheaton Coll (MA)
Wheeling Jesuit U (WV)
Whitman Coll (WA)
Whittier Coll (CA)
Whitworth U (WA)
Wichita State U (KS)
Widener U (PA)
Wilberforce U (OH)
Wilkes U (PA)
Willamette U (OR)
William Jessup U (CA)
William Jewell Coll (MO)
William Paterson U of New Jersey (NJ)
William Peace U (NC)
William Penn U (IA)
Williams Baptist Coll (AR)
Williams Coll (MA)
William Woods U (MO)
Wilmington U (DE)
Wingate U (NC)
Winona State U (MN)
Winthrop U (SC)
Wittenberg U (OH)
Wofford Coll (SC)
Worcester State U (MA)
Wright State U (OH)
Xavier U (OH)
Xavier U of Louisiana (LA)
Yale U (CT)
Yeshiva U (NY)
York Coll of Pennsylvania (PA)

York Coll of the City U of New York (NY)
Youngstown State U (OH)

PSYCHOLOGY RELATED
Adams State U (CO)
Augsburg Coll (MN)
Buena Vista U (IA)
Canisius Coll (NY)
Champlain Coll (VT)
East Central U (OK)
Illinois Inst of Technology (IL)
Kansas Wesleyan U (KS)
Kean U (NJ)
Loyola U New Orleans (LA)
Madonna U (MI)
Marist Coll (NY)
Mary Baldwin Coll (VA)
Mayville State U (ND)
National U (CA)
Ohio Northern U (OH)
Prescott Coll (AZ)
Quincy U (IL)
Rhode Island Coll (RI)
San Jose State U (CA)
State U of New York at Oswego (NY)
State U of New York Coll of Agriculture and Technology at Cobleskill (NY)
U of St. Thomas (MN)
Western State Colorado U (CO)

PSYCHOLOGY TEACHER EDUCATION
Albion Coll (MI)
Alma Coll (MI)
Bradley U (IL)
Brigham Young U (UT)
California Lutheran U (CA)
Campbellsville U (KY)
Cumberland U (TN)
Lee U (TN)
Ohio Wesleyan U (OH)
Pittsburg State U (KS)
Rocky Mountain Coll (MT)
Tusculum Coll (TN)
U of Delaware (DE)
U of Michigan–Flint (MI)
Valparaiso U (IN)
Wayne State Coll (NE)
Widener U (PA)

PUBLIC ADMINISTRATION
American U of Beirut (Lebanon)
Auburn U (AL)
Augustana Coll (IL)
Baldwin Wallace U (OH)
Baruch Coll of the City U of New York (NY)
Baylor U (TX)
Biola U (CA)
Blackburn Coll (IL)
Bowling Green State U (OH)
Buena Vista U (IA)
California Lutheran U (CA)
California State U, Chico (CA)
California State U, Dominguez Hills (CA)
California State U, Fresno (CA)
California State U, Fullerton (CA)
Calvin Coll (MI)
Capital U (OH)
Catawba Coll (NC)
Cedarville U (OH)
Central Methodist U (MO)
Cleveland State U (OH)
Colorado Mesa U (CO)
Columbia Coll (MO)
Concordia U (QC, Canada)
Cornell U (NY)
Doane Coll (NE)
Eastern Michigan U (MI)
Elizabethtown Coll School of Continuing and Professional Studies (PA)
Elon U (NC)
Evangel U (MO)
Everglades U, Sarasota (FL)
The Evergreen State Coll (WA)
Fisher Coll (MA)
Flagler Coll (FL)
Florida Atlantic U (FL)
Florida Intl U (FL)
Franklin U (OH)
George Mason U (VA)
Grand Valley State U (MI)
Harding U (AR)
Hastings Coll (NE)
Hawai`i Pacific U (HI)
Heidelberg U (OH)
Indiana U Bloomington (IN)
Indiana U Kokomo (IN)
Indiana U Northwest (IN)
Indiana U–Purdue U Fort Wayne (IN)
Indiana U–Purdue U Indianapolis (IN)
Iowa State U of Science and Technology (IA)
James Madison U (VA)
John Carroll U (OH)
Johns Hopkins U (MD)
Kean U (NJ)
Keiser U, Fort Lauderdale (FL)
Kentucky State U (KY)
Kutztown U of Pennsylvania (PA)
La Salle U (PA)
Lewis U (IL)
Lincoln U (MO)
Lincoln U (PA)
Lindenwood U (MO)
Lipscomb U (TN)
Long Island U–LIU Post (NY)
Louisiana Coll (LA)
Metropolitan State U (MN)
Miami U (OH)
Midwestern State U (TX)
Millsaps Coll (MS)
Minnesota State U Mankato (MN)
Mississippi U for Women (MS)
Mississippi Valley State U (MS)
Missouri State U (MO)
Missouri Valley Coll (MO)
Murray State U (KY)
National U (CA)
New York U (NY)
Northern Arizona U (AZ)
Northern Kentucky U (KY)
Northern Michigan U (MI)
Northern State U (SD)
Northwest Missouri State U (MO)
Nova Southeastern U (FL)
Oakland U (MI)
Ohio Wesleyan U (OH)
Park U (MO)
Plymouth State U (NH)
Regent U (VA)
Regis U (CO)
Rhode Island Coll (RI)
Roger Williams U (RI)
Roosevelt U (IL)
Saginaw Valley State U (MI)
Saint Francis U (PA)
St. John's U (NY)
St. Thomas U (FL)
Samford U (AL)
San Diego State U (CA)
Seattle U (WA)
Shaw U (NC)
Shippensburg U of Pennsylvania (PA)
Siena Heights U (MI)
Silver Lake Coll of the Holy Family (WI)
Southern New Hampshire U (NH)
Southwest Minnesota State U (MN)
Stephen F. Austin State U (TX)
Syracuse U (NY)
Tennessee State U (TN)
Texas Southern U (TX)
Texas State U (TX)
Universidad del Turabo (PR)
U at Albany, State U of New York (NY)
The U of Arizona (AZ)
U of Central Arkansas (AR)
U of Central Florida (FL)
U of Central Oklahoma (OK)
U of Guam (GU)
U of Guelph (ON, Canada)
U of Hawaii–West Oahu (HI)
U of Houston–Clear Lake (TX)
The U of Kansas (KS)
U of La Verne (CA)
U of Lethbridge (AB, Canada)
U of Maine at Augusta (ME)
U of Maine at Fort Kent (ME)
U of Maine at Machias (ME)
U of Maryland U Coll (MD)
U of Michigan–Flint (MI)
U of Missouri–St. Louis (MO)
U of Nevada, Las Vegas (NV)
U of New Haven (CT)
The U of North Carolina at Pembroke (NC)
U of North Dakota (ND)
U of Northern Iowa (IA)
U of Oklahoma (OK)
U of Oregon (OR)
U of Ottawa (ON, Canada)
U of Pittsburgh (PA)
U of St. Thomas (MN)
U of San Francisco (CA)
U of Saskatchewan (SK, Canada)
The U of Tennessee (TN)
The U of Tennessee at Martin (TN)
The U of Texas at Dallas (TX)
The U of Texas at San Antonio (TX)
The U of Toledo (OH)
U of Toronto (ON, Canada)
The U of Western Ontario (ON, Canada)
U of Wisconsin–Green Bay (WI)
U of Wisconsin–La Crosse (WI)
U of Wisconsin–Stevens Point (WI)
U of Wisconsin–Whitewater (WI)
Upper Iowa U (IA)
Virginia State U (VA)
Wagner Coll (NY)
Walden U (MN)
Washburn U (KS)
Waynesburg U (PA)
Wayne State U (MI)
Western Oregon U (OR)
West Texas A&M U (TX)
West Virginia U Inst of Technology (WV)
Winona State U (MN)

PUBLIC ADMINISTRATION AND SOCIAL SERVICE PROFESSIONS RELATED
Coll of Coastal Georgia (GA)
Columbia Coll (SC)
Delaware State U (DE)
Emory & Henry Coll (VA)
The Evergreen State Coll (WA)
Lasell Coll (MA)
Milligan Coll (TN)
New York U (NY)
Northeastern Illinois U (IL)
Prescott Coll (AZ)
Rutgers, The State U of New Jersey, Newark (NJ)
San Diego State U (CA)
State U of New York Empire State Coll (NY)
Trevecca Nazarene U (TN)
U of Minnesota, Twin Cities Campus (MN)

PUBLIC/APPLIED HISTORY
Arkansas Tech U (AR)
Baldwin Wallace U (OH)
Cairn U (PA)
Central Michigan U (MI)
Concordia U (QC, Canada)
East Carolina U (NC)
Emory & Henry Coll (VA)
McMurry U (TX)
North Dakota State U (ND)
Rhode Island Coll (RI)
Southern Adventist U (TN)
Western Michigan U (MI)

PUBLIC FINANCE
Husson U (ME)
Johnson & Wales U (RI)

PUBLIC HEALTH
Agnes Scott Coll (GA)
Allen Coll (IA)
Alma Coll (MI)
American Intl Coll (MA)
American Public U System (WV)
American U (DC)
Arizona State U at the Downtown Phoenix campus (AZ)
Baldwin Wallace U (OH)
Bluffton U (OH)
California State U, Long Beach (CA)
Calvin Coll (MI)
Cape Breton U (NS, Canada)
Central Washington U (WA)
Colby-Sawyer Coll (NH)
Creighton U (NE)
Delaware State U (DE)
Dominican U of California (CA)
Drexel U (PA)
East Tennessee State U (TN)
Elon U (NC)
Fort Lewis Coll (CO)
Hunter Coll of the City U of New York (NY)
Indiana U–Purdue U Indianapolis (IN)
Johns Hopkins U (MD)
Kent State U (OH)
Kent State U at Trumbull (OH)
Keystone Coll (PA)
Langston U (OK)
Long Island U–LIU Brooklyn (NY)
Marshall U (WV)
Minnesota State U Mankato (MN)
Missouri Western State U (MO)
Montclair State U (NJ)
National U (CA)
New York U (NY)
Northern Arizona U (AZ)
Ohio U (OH)
Oregon State U (OR)
Regis Coll (MA)
Rutgers, The State U of New Jersey, New Brunswick (NJ)
Saint Francis U (PA)
Saint Louis U (MO)
Sam Houston State U (TX)
Santa Clara U (CA)
Slippery Rock U of Pennsylvania (PA)
Southern Connecticut State U (CT)
State U of New York Coll at Old Westbury (NY)
Syracuse U (NY)
Texas A&M U (TX)
Tufts U (MA)
U at Albany, State U of New York (NY)
The U of Arizona (AZ)
U of Arkansas (AR)
U of California, Merced (CA)
U of Colorado Denver (CO)
U of Evansville (IN)
U of Hawaii at Manoa (HI)
U of Kentucky (KY)
U of Lethbridge (AB, Canada)
U of Louisville (KY)
U of Massachusetts Amherst (MA)
U of Massachusetts Lowell (MA)
U of Miami (FL)
U of Nevada, Las Vegas (NV)
U of Rochester (NY)
U of Saint Joseph (CT)
U of Southern Mississippi (MS)
U of South Florida (FL)
The U of Tampa (FL)
The U of Texas at Austin (TX)
The U of Texas at San Antonio (TX)
U of the Cumberlands (KY)
U of Washington (WA)
Valparaiso U (IN)
Walden U (MN)
Wayne State U (MI)
West Chester U of Pennsylvania (PA)
Westminster Coll (UT)
William Paterson U of New Jersey (NJ)
Youngstown State U (OH)

PUBLIC HEALTH/COMMUNITY NURSING
Capital U (OH)
Hawai`i Pacific U (HI)
Northern Illinois U (IL)
U of Miami (FL)
Walla Walla U (WA)
Wright State U (OH)

PUBLIC HEALTH EDUCATION AND PROMOTION
American U (DC)
Appalachian State U (NC)
Arizona State U at the Downtown Phoenix campus (AZ)
California Baptist U (CA)
California State U, Long Beach (CA)
Central Michigan U (MI)
Central Washington U (WA)
Chicago State U (IL)
Coastal Carolina U (SC)
Colby-Sawyer Coll (NH)
Coll of Charleston (SC)
Dalhousie U (NS, Canada)
East Carolina U (NC)
Eastern Kentucky U (KY)
Georgia Southern U (GA)
Inter American U of Puerto Rico, Ponce Campus (PR)
Ithaca Coll (NY)
Liberty U (VA)
Louisiana State U in Shreveport (LA)
Lynchburg Coll (VA)
Malone U (OH)
Marymount U (VA)
Mississippi U for Women (MS)
New Mexico State U (NM)
North Carolina Central U (NC)
Oklahoma State U (OK)
Oregon State U (OR)
Plymouth State U (NH)
Purdue U (IN)
Simmons Coll (MA)
Southeastern Louisiana U (LA)
State U of New York Coll at Potsdam (NY)
State U of New York Coll of Technology at Canton (NY)
Temple U (PA)
Texas State U (TX)
U of Arkansas (AR)
U of Central Oklahoma (OK)
U of Georgia (GA)
The U of Iowa (IA)
U of Minnesota, Duluth (MN)
U of Mount Union (OH)
The U of North Carolina at Charlotte (NC)
The U of North Carolina at Greensboro (NC)
The U of North Carolina Wilmington (NC)
U of North Texas (TX)
U of St. Thomas (MN)
The U of Scranton (PA)
The U of Texas at Austin (TX)
The U of Toledo (OH)
U of Utah (UT)
U of Wisconsin–La Crosse (WI)
Walla Walla U (WA)
Western Illinois U (IL)

PUBLIC HEALTH RELATED
Franklin & Marshall Coll (PA)
Hampshire Coll (MA)
Indiana U Bloomington (IN)
Shenandoah U (VA)
Stockton U (NJ)
U of California, Berkeley (CA)
U of California, Irvine (CA)
U of Maryland, Coll Park (MD)
U of Michigan–Flint (MI)
Utah State U (UT)

PUBLIC POLICY ANALYSIS
Albion Coll (MI)
Anna Maria Coll (MA)
Arizona State U at the Downtown Phoenix campus (AZ)
Bennington Coll (VT)
Bentley U (MA)
Brigham Young U (UT)
Bryant U (RI)
Central Washington U (WA)
Chatham U (PA)
Coll of the Atlantic (ME)
The Coll of William and Mary (VA)
Concordia U, St. Paul (MN)
Cornell U (NY)
DePaul U (IL)
Dickinson Coll (PA)
Elon U (NC)
The George Washington U (DC)
Georgia Inst of Technology (GA)
Georgia State U (GA)
Hamilton Coll (NY)
Hampshire Coll (MA)
Hobart and William Smith Colls (NY)
Howard Payne U (TX)
Indiana U–Purdue U Fort Wayne (IN)
Johns Hopkins U (MD)
Massachusetts Coll of Liberal Arts (MA)
Michigan State U (MI)
Mills Coll (CA)
Morehead State U (KY)
New Coll of Florida (FL)
Northwestern U (IL)
Olivet Nazarene U (IL)
Penn State Harrisburg (PA)
Pomona Coll (CA)

Princeton U (NJ)
Rice U (TX)
Rochester Inst of Technology (NY)
The Sage Colls (NY)
St. Mary's Coll of Maryland (MD)
Saint Peter's U (NJ)
Saint Vincent Coll (PA)
Scripps Coll (CA)
Southeastern U (FL)
Southern Methodist U (TX)
Stanford U (CA)
Suffolk U (MA)
Trevecca Nazarene U (TN)
Trinity Coll (CT)
U at Albany, State U of New York (NY)
U of California, Riverside (CA)
U of Chicago (IL)
U of Delaware (DE)
U of Denver (CO)
U of Michigan (MI)
U of Mississippi (MS)
The U of North Carolina at Chapel Hill (NC)
U of Pennsylvania (PA)
U of Pittsburgh at Greensburg (PA)
U of Rhode Island (RI)
U of Saint Joseph (CT)
The U of Texas at Dallas (TX)
The U of Toledo (OH)
U of Virginia (VA)
Vanderbilt U (TN)
Virginia Polytechnic Inst and State U (VA)
Wagner Coll (NY)
Washington State U (WA)

PUBLIC RELATIONS, ADVERTISING, AND APPLIED COMMUNICATION

Anderson U (IN)
Belmont U (TN)
Biola U (CA)
Bluffton U (OH)
Butler U (IN)
California Baptist U (CA)
California State U, Dominguez Hills (CA)
Cedarville U (OH)
Endicott Coll (MA)
Florida Southern Coll (FL)
Goshen Coll (IN)
Hawai`i Pacific U (HI)
Houghton Coll (NY)
Howard Payne U (TX)
Kansas Wesleyan U (KS)
Lake Erie Coll (OH)
Lasell Coll (MA)
Lynn U (FL)
Massachusetts Coll of Liberal Arts (MA)
Messiah Coll (PA)
Minnesota State U Moorhead (MN)
Notre Dame of Maryland U (MD)
Oklahoma City U (OK)
Pepperdine U, Malibu (CA)
Rhode Island Coll (RI)
Seattle U (WA)
Simpson Coll (IA)
Taylor U (IN)
Texas Christian U (TX)
Universidad Metropolitana (PR)
U of Central Oklahoma (OK)
U of Colorado Boulder (CO)
U of Kentucky (KY)
U of Mount Union (OH)
U of Nebraska–Lincoln (NE)
The U of Scranton (PA)

PUBLIC RELATIONS, ADVERTISING, AND APPLIED COMMUNICATION RELATED

Abilene Christian U (TX)
Arkansas State U (AR)
Belmont U (TN)
Bradley U (IL)
Brigham Young U (UT)
Buena Vista U (IA)
California Lutheran U (CA)
The Coll of St. Scholastica (MN)
Coll of the Ozarks (MO)
Columbia Coll (MO)
DePaul U (IL)
Duquesne U (PA)
Grace Coll (IN)
John Brown U (AR)
Lipscomb U (TN)
Loyola U Chicago (IL)
Marietta Coll (OH)
Marywood U (PA)
Missouri Western State U (MO)
Morrisville State Coll (NY)
Northern Arizona U (AZ)
Northern Michigan U (MI)
Ohio Northern U (OH)
Oklahoma City U (OK)
Oklahoma State U (OK)
Pepperdine U, Malibu (CA)
Rochester Inst of Technology (NY)
St. John's U (NY)
Saint Mary's U of Minnesota (MN)
Spring Hill Coll (AL)
U of Central Arkansas (AR)
The U of Tampa (FL)
U of Vermont (VT)
U of Wisconsin–River Falls (WI)
Virginia State U (VA)
Washington State U (WA)
Weber State U (UT)
Western Michigan U (MI)

PUBLIC RELATIONS/IMAGE MANAGEMENT

Andrews U (MI)
Appalachian State U (NC)
Auburn U (AL)
Avila U (MO)
Baldwin Wallace U (OH)
Barry U (FL)
Belmont U (TN)
Biola U (CA)
Bowie State U (MD)
Bowling Green State U (OH)
Bradley U (IL)
Buffalo State Coll, State U of New York (NY)
California Lutheran U (CA)
California State U, Dominguez Hills (CA)
California State U, Fresno (CA)
California State U, Fullerton (CA)
California State U, Long Beach (CA)
Capital U (OH)
Carroll Coll (MT)
Castleton State Coll (VT)
Central Michigan U (MI)
Central Washington U (WA)
Champlain Coll (VT)
Chapman U (CA)
Chatham U (PA)
Cleveland State U (OH)
Coe Coll (IA)
Columbia Coll Chicago (IL)
Cornerstone U (MI)
Delaware State U (DE)
Dominican U (IL)
Drake U (IA)
Eastern Kentucky U (KY)
Eastern Michigan U (MI)
Emerson Coll (MA)
Ferris State U (MI)
Florida Ag and Mech U (FL)
Fort Hays State U (KS)
Franklin U (OH)
Georgia Southern U (GA)
Gonzaga U (WA)
Greenville Coll (IL)
Hampton U (VA)
Harding U (AR)
Hastings Coll (NE)
Hawai`i Pacific U (HI)
Heidelberg U (OH)
Hofstra U (NY)
Illinois State U (IL)
Inter American U of Puerto Rico, Ponce Campus (PR)
Iona Coll (NY)
Iowa State U of Science and Technology (IA)
Ithaca Coll (NY)
John Brown U (AR)
Johnson & Wales U (RI)
Kent State U (OH)
La Salle U (PA)
Lasell Coll (MA)
Lee U (TN)
Lewis U (IL)
Lipscomb U (TN)
Long Island U–LIU Post (NY)
Loras Coll (IA)
Mansfield U of Pennsylvania (PA)
Marquette U (WI)
The Master's Coll and Sem (CA)
Mercy Coll (NY)
Miami U (OH)
Middle Tennessee State U (TN)
Minnesota State U Mankato (MN)
Minnesota State U Moorhead (MN)
Missouri Baptist U (MO)
Monmouth Coll (IL)
Montana State U Billings (MT)
Mount Mercy U (IA)
Mount Saint Mary Coll (NY)
Mount Vernon Nazarene U (OH)
Murray State U (KY)
New England Coll (NH)
North Carolina Ag and Tech State U (NC)
North Dakota State U (ND)
Northern Kentucky U (KY)
Northern Michigan U (MI)
Northwestern Coll (IA)
Oklahoma Christian U (OK)
Palm Beach Atlantic U (FL)
Quinnipiac U (CT)
Rider U (NJ)
Rochester Inst of Technology (NY)
Roosevelt U (IL)
Rowan U (NJ)
Saint Francis U (PA)
San Diego State U (CA)
San Jose State U (CA)
Slippery Rock U of Pennsylvania (PA)
Southern Adventist U (TN)
Southern Methodist U (TX)
State U of New York at Oswego (NY)
Stephens Coll (MO)
Suffolk U (MA)
Syracuse U (NY)
Taylor U (IN)
Texas State U (TX)
Texas Tech U (TX)
Tiffin U (OH)
Union U (TN)
The U of Akron (OH)
The U of Alabama (AL)
U of Central Missouri (MO)
U of Central Oklahoma (OK)
The U of Findlay (OH)
U of Florida (FL)
U of Georgia (GA)
U of Houston (TX)
U of Idaho (ID)
U of Louisiana at Lafayette (LA)
U of Miami (FL)
U of Northern Iowa (IA)
U of Northwestern–St. Paul (MN)
U of Oregon (OR)
U of Ottawa (ON, Canada)
U of Pittsburgh at Bradford (PA)
U of Rhode Island (RI)
U of Rio Grande (OH)
U of Southern California (CA)
The U of Tennessee (TN)
The U of Texas at Arlington (TX)
The U of Texas at Austin (TX)
U of Toronto (ON, Canada)
U of Wisconsin–River Falls (WI)
Ursuline Coll (OH)
Utica Coll (NY)
Walla Walla U (WA)
Wartburg Coll (IA)
Washington State U (WA)
Wayne State U (MI)
Weber State U (UT)
Webster U (MO)
Western Kentucky U (KY)
Western New England U (MA)
West Virginia Wesleyan Coll (WV)
William Penn U (IA)
Xavier U (OH)
York Coll of Pennsylvania (PA)

PUBLISHING

Emerson Coll (MA)
Graceland U (IA)
Rochester Inst of Technology (NY)
U of Missouri (MO)

PURCHASING, PROCUREMENT/ ACQUISITIONS AND CONTRACTS MANAGEMENT

Arizona State U at the Tempe campus (AZ)
Arizona State U at the West campus (AZ)
Athens State U (AL)
Central Michigan U (MI)
The U of Alabama in Huntsville (AL)
U of Houston–Downtown (TX)
U of the District of Columbia (DC)

QUALITY CONTROL AND SAFETY TECHNOLOGIES RELATED

Madonna U (MI)
U of Central Oklahoma (OK)

QUALITY CONTROL TECHNOLOGY

Bowling Green State U (OH)
California State U, Dominguez Hills (CA)
California State U, Long Beach (CA)
Ferris State U (MI)
San Jose State U (CA)
Tarleton State U (TX)

RADIATION BIOLOGY

Suffolk U (MA)

RADIATION PROTECTION/ HEALTH PHYSICS TECHNOLOGY

Indiana U–Purdue U Indianapolis (IN)
Lewis U (IL)

RADIO AND TELEVISION

Appalachian State U (NC)
Ashland U (OH)
Auburn U (AL)
Ball State U (IN)
Barry U (FL)
Bemidji State U (MN)
Biola U (CA)
Bowling Green State U (OH)
Bradley U (IL)
Buffalo State Coll, State U of New York (NY)
Butler U (IN)
California State U, Fresno (CA)
California State U, Fullerton (CA)
California State U, Long Beach (CA)
California State U, Los Angeles (CA)
California State U, Monterey Bay (CA)
Castleton State Coll (VT)
Chicago State U (IL)
Columbia Coll Chicago (IL)
Cornerstone U (MI)
Delaware State U (DE)
Drake U (IA)
Eastern Kentucky U (KY)
Elon U (NC)
Emerson Coll (MA)
Evangel U (MO)
Franklin Pierce U (NH)
The George Washington U (DC)
Georgia Southern U (GA)
Gonzaga U (WA)
Goshen Coll (IN)
Grand Valley State U (MI)
Hastings Coll (NE)
Hofstra U (NY)
Howard U (DC)
Iona Coll (NY)
Ithaca Coll (NY)
John Brown U (AR)
Kent State U (OH)
La Salle U (PA)
Lasell Coll (MA)
Lewis U (IL)
Loyola Marymount U (CA)
Marietta Coll (OH)
Marist Coll (NY)
The Master's Coll and Sem (CA)
Mercy Coll (NY)
Minot State U (ND)
Missouri Baptist U (MO)
Montclair State U (NJ)
Murray State U (KY)
New York Inst of Technology (NY)
North Carolina Ag and Tech State U (NC)
North Central Coll (IL)
Northern Arizona U (AZ)
Northern Kentucky U (KY)
Northwestern U (IL)
Ohio Northern U (OH)
Ohio U (OH)
Oklahoma Christian U (OK)
Pacific U (OR)
Pepperdine U, Malibu (CA)
Rider U (NJ)
Rowan U (NJ)
St. Francis Coll (NY)
San Diego State U (CA)
San Francisco State U (CA)
San Jose State U (CA)
Savannah Coll of Art and Design (GA)
Southeastern U (FL)
Southern Illinois U Carbondale (IL)
Southwestern Coll (KS)
Southwest Minnesota State U (MN)
State U of New York at Fredonia (NY)
Stephens Coll (MO)
Syracuse U (NY)
Temple U (PA)
Texas A&M U–Commerce (TX)
Texas Southern U (TX)
Texas State U (TX)
Texas Tech U (TX)
Texas Wesleyan U (TX)
Troy U (AL)
Union U (TN)
The U of Akron (OH)
The U of Alabama (AL)
U of Arkansas at Little Rock (AR)
U of Central Florida (FL)
U of Central Missouri (MO)
U of Central Oklahoma (OK)
U of Cincinnati (OH)
U of Dayton (OH)
U of Florida (FL)
U of Houston (TX)
U of Kentucky (KY)
U of Miami (FL)
U of Missouri (MO)
The U of Montana (MT)
U of Montevallo (AL)
U of North Texas (TX)
U of Northwestern–St. Paul (MN)
U of Pittsburgh at Bradford (PA)
U of Southern Indiana (IN)
The U of Texas at Arlington (TX)
The U of Texas at Austin (TX)
U of the Incarnate Word (TX)
The U of Western Ontario (ON, Canada)
U of Wisconsin–Oshkosh (WI)
U of Wisconsin–River Falls (WI)
U of Wisconsin–Superior (WI)
Vanguard U of Southern California (CA)
Walla Walla U (WA)
Wartburg Coll (IA)
Waynesburg U (PA)
Wayne State U (MI)
Weber State U (UT)
Western Illinois U (IL)
Western Kentucky U (KY)
William Penn U (IA)
Xavier U (OH)
Youngstown State U (OH)

RADIO AND TELEVISION BROADCASTING TECHNOLOGY

Emerson Coll (MA)
Ferris State U (MI)
Gannon U (PA)
Goshen Coll (IN)
Long Island U–LIU Post (NY)
New York Inst of Technology (NY)
New York U (NY)
Northwest Nazarene U (ID)
Suffolk U (MA)
Towson U (MD)
Trevecca Nazarene U (TN)
Universidad del Turabo (PR)
Wilmington U (DE)

RADIOLOGIC TECHNOLOGY/ SCIENCE

Adventist U of Health Sciences (FL)
Bluefield State Coll (WV)
Colorado Mesa U (CO)
Dalhousie U (NS, Canada)
Fort Hays State U (KS)
Friends U (KS)
The George Washington U (DC)
Holy Family U (PA)
Indiana U Northwest (IN)
Inter American U of Puerto Rico, Aguadilla Campus (PR)
Inter American U of Puerto Rico, Ponce Campus (PR)

Inter American U of Puerto Rico, San Germán Campus (PR)
Lewis U (IL)
Manhattan Coll (NY)
Marian U (WI)
Marshall U (WV)
McNeese State U (LA)
MCPHS U (MA)
Missouri State U (MO)
Mount Mary U (WI)
National U (CA)
Nebraska Methodist Coll (NE)
North Dakota State U (ND)
Northern Kentucky U (KY)
Northern Michigan U (MI)
Northwest Missouri State U (MO)
Oakland U (MI)
The Ohio State U (OH)
Quinnipiac U (CT)
Rhode Island Coll (RI)
St. Catharine Coll (KY)
St. John's U (NY)
Spencerian Coll (KY)
Trocaire Coll (NY)
U of Arkansas–Fort Smith (AR)
U of Charleston (WV)
The U of Iowa (IA)
U of Jamestown (ND)
U of Missouri (MO)
U of Oklahoma Health Sciences Center (OK)
U of Pittsburgh at Bradford (PA)
U of St. Francis (IL)
U of South Alabama (AL)
U of Toronto (ON, Canada)
Virginia Commonwealth U (VA)
Widener U (PA)
York Coll of Pennsylvania (PA)

RADIO, TELEVISION, AND DIGITAL COMMUNICATION RELATED
Arkansas State U (AR)
Asbury U (KY)
Ashland U (OH)
Brigham Young U (UT)
Central Michigan U (MI)
Champlain Coll (VT)
Clark Atlanta U (GA)
Dallas Baptist U (TX)
Drake U (IA)
Drury U (MO)
Emerson Coll (MA)
Hofstra U (NY)
John Brown U (AR)
Keystone Coll (PA)
Madonna U (MI)
Marquette U (WI)
North Dakota State U (ND)
Sacred Heart U (CT)
San Francisco State U (CA)
Spring Hill Coll (AL)
State U of New York Coll of Agriculture and Technology at Cobleskill (NY)
Texas Christian U (TX)
The U of Akron (OH)
Washington State U (WA)
Western Carolina U (NC)
William Penn U (IA)

RANGE SCIENCE AND MANAGEMENT
Colorado State U (CO)
Fort Hays State U (KS)
Humboldt State U (CA)
New Mexico State U (NM)
North Dakota State U (ND)
Oregon State U (OR)
South Dakota State U (SD)
Sul Ross State U (TX)
Tarleton State U (TX)
Texas A&M U (TX)
U of Alberta (AB, Canada)
U of Idaho (ID)
U of Nebraska–Lincoln (NE)
U of Wyoming (WY)
Utah State U (UT)

READING TEACHER EDUCATION
Aquinas Coll (MI)
Baylor U (TX)
Canisius Coll (NY)
Concordia U Chicago (IL)
Concordia U, Nebraska (NE)
East Central U (OK)
Eastern Michigan U (MI)
Goddard Coll (VT)
Grand Valley State U (MI)
Harding U (AR)
Iowa Wesleyan Coll (IA)
Michigan State U (MI)
Midwestern State U (TX)
State U of New York Coll at Cortland (NY)
Tennessee State U (TN)
Texas A&M Intl U (TX)
Texas Wesleyan U (TX)
U of Central Missouri (MO)
U of Central Oklahoma (OK)
U of Great Falls (MT)
The U of Montana (MT)
The U of North Carolina at Pembroke (NC)
U of Northern Iowa (IA)
U of Wisconsin–River Falls (WI)
Upper Iowa U (IA)
Washington State U (WA)
William Penn U (IA)
Wingate U (NC)
Wright State U (OH)

REAL ESTATE
Baruch Coll of the City U of New York (NY)
Baylor U (TX)
Bowling Green State U (OH)
California State U, Dominguez Hills (CA)
California State U, Fresno (CA)
Central Michigan U (MI)
Clarion U of Pennsylvania (PA)
Colorado State U (CO)
DePaul U (IL)
Drexel U (PA)
Florida Atlantic U (FL)
Florida Intl U (FL)
Georgia State U (GA)
Marquette U (WI)
Marylhurst U (OR)
Menlo Coll (CA)
Minnesota State U Mankato (MN)
Mississippi State U (MS)
New York U (NY)
The Ohio State U (OH)
Portland State U (OR)
San Diego State U (CA)
Southern Methodist U (TX)
Syracuse U (NY)
Temple U (PA)
Texas Christian U (TX)
The U of Akron (OH)
The U of British Columbia (BC, Canada)
U of Central Florida (FL)
U of Central Oklahoma (OK)
U of Cincinnati (OH)
U of Denver (CO)
U of Florida (FL)
U of Georgia (GA)
U of Guelph (ON, Canada)
U of Miami (FL)
U of Mississippi (MS)
U of Missouri (MO)
U of Nevada, Las Vegas (NV)
U of Northern Iowa (IA)
U of North Texas (TX)
U of Pennsylvania (PA)
U of St. Thomas (MN)
U of San Diego (CA)
U of Southern California (CA)
The U of Texas at Arlington (TX)
The U of Texas at El Paso (TX)
The U of Texas at San Antonio (TX)
U of West Georgia (GA)
U of Wisconsin–Madison (WI)
U of Wisconsin–Milwaukee (WI)
U of Wisconsin–Stout (WI)
Villanova U (PA)
Virginia Commonwealth U (VA)
Virginia Polytechnic Inst and State U (VA)
Washington State U (WA)

RECORDING ARTS TECHNOLOGY
American U (DC)
Belmont U (TN)
Butler U (IN)
Columbia Coll Chicago (IL)
Elon U (NC)
Five Towns Coll (NY)
Greenville Coll (IL)
Indiana U Bloomington (IN)
Ithaca Coll (NY)
Lebanon Valley Coll (PA)
Loyola Marymount U (CA)
Malone U (OH)
Michigan Technological U (MI)
New England Inst of Technology (RI)
Peabody Conservatory of The Johns Hopkins U (MD)
Savannah Coll of Art and Design (GA)
State U of New York at Fredonia (NY)
Texas State U (TX)
York Coll of Pennsylvania (PA)

REGIONAL STUDIES
The Colorado Coll (CO)
Columbia U, School of General Studies (NY)
Houghton Coll (NY)
Mercer U, Macon (GA)
Prescott Coll (AZ)
United States Military Acad (NY)
U of Mississippi (MS)
U of Regina (SK, Canada)
Washington U in St. Louis (MO)

REGISTERED NURSING, NURSING ADMINISTRATION, NURSING RESEARCH AND CLINICAL NURSING RELATED
Averett U (VA)
Cardinal Stritch U (WI)
Cleveland State U (OH)
Columbia Centro Universitario, Caguas (PR)
Molloy Coll (NY)
Moravian Coll (PA)
Neumann U (PA)
Rasmussen Coll Ocala School of Nursing (FL)
Rowan U (NJ)
Tabor Coll (KS)
Union Coll (KY)
U of California, Los Angeles (CA)
U of Massachusetts Dartmouth (MA)
U of Miami (FL)

REGISTERED NURSING/ REGISTERED NURSE
Abilene Christian U (TX)
Adams State U (CO)
Adelphi U (NY)
Adventist U of Health Sciences (FL)
Albany State U (GA)
Alcorn State U (MS)
Allen Coll (IA)
Alvernia U (PA)
Alverno Coll (WI)
American Intl Coll (MA)
American Public U System (WV)
American U of Beirut (Lebanon)
Anderson U (IN)
Andrews U (MI)
Angelo State U (TX)
Anna Maria Coll (MA)
Appalachian State U (NC)
Aquinas Coll (TN)
Arizona State U at the Downtown Phoenix campus (AZ)
Arkansas State U (AR)
Arkansas Tech U (AR)
Armstrong State U (GA)
Auburn U (AL)
Auburn U at Montgomery (AL)
Augustana Coll (SD)
Austin Peay State U (TN)
Averett U (VA)
Avila U (MO)
Azusa Pacific U (CA)
Baker U (KS)
Baldwin Wallace U (OH)
Ball State U (IN)
Barry U (FL)
Baylor U (TX)
Becker Coll (MA)
Belhaven U (MS)
Belmont U (TN)
Bemidji State U (MN)
Benedictine U (IL)
Berea Coll (KY)
Berry Coll (GA)
Bethel Coll (IN)
Bethel Coll (KS)
Bethel U (MN)
Bethune-Cookman U (FL)
Binghamton U, State U of New York (NY)
Biola U (CA)
Blessing-Rieman Coll of Nursing (IL)
Bloomfield Coll (NJ)
Bloomsburg U of Pennsylvania (PA)
Bluefield State Coll (WV)
Bob Jones U (SC)
Boston Coll (MA)
Bowie State U (MD)
Bowling Green State U (OH)
Bowling Green State U-Firelands Coll (OH)
Bradley U (IL)
Cabarrus Coll of Health Sciences (NC)
Caldwell U (NJ)
California Baptist U (CA)
California State U, Chico (CA)
California State U, Dominguez Hills (CA)
California State U, Fresno (CA)
California State U, Long Beach (CA)
California State U, Los Angeles (CA)
California State U, Monterey Bay (CA)
California State U, Sacramento (CA)
California State U, San Bernardino (CA)
California State U, San Marcos (CA)
California State U, Stanislaus (CA)
California U of Pennsylvania (PA)
Calvin Coll (MI)
Campbellsville U (KY)
Cape Breton U (NS, Canada)
Capital U (OH)
Cardinal Stritch U (WI)
Carlow U (PA)
Carroll Coll (MT)
Carson-Newman U (TN)
Case Western Reserve U (OH)
Castleton State Coll (VT)
The Catholic U of America (DC)
Cedarville U (OH)
Central Connecticut State U (CT)
Central Methodist U (MO)
Chaminade U of Honolulu (HI)
Charleston Southern U (SC)
Chatham U (PA)
Chicago State U (IL)
Chipola Coll (FL)
Clarion U of Pennsylvania (PA)
Clarke U (IA)
Clayton State U (GA)
Cleveland State U (OH)
Coastal Carolina U (SC)
Coe Coll (IA)
Colby-Sawyer Coll (NH)
The Coll at Brockport, State U of New York (NY)
Coll of Coastal Georgia (GA)
The Coll of New Jersey (NJ)
The Coll of New Rochelle (NY)
Coll of Saint Benedict (MN)
Coll of Saint Mary (NE)
The Coll of St. Scholastica (MN)
Coll of Staten Island of the City U of New York (NY)
Coll of the Ozarks (MO)
Colorado Mesa U (CO)
Colorado State U–Pueblo (CO)
Columbia Centro Universitario, Yauco (PR)
Columbus State U (GA)
Concordia Coll (MN)
Concordia U (CA)
Concordia U, Nebraska (NE)
Concordia U Texas (TX)
Concordia U Wisconsin (WI)
Creighton U (NE)
Culver-Stockton Coll (MO)
Cumberland U (TN)
Curry Coll (MA)
Daemen Coll (NY)
Dalhousie U (NS, Canada)
Darton State Coll (GA)
Davenport U, Grand Rapids (MI)
Daytona State Coll (FL)
Defiance Coll (OH)
Delaware State U (DE)
Delta State U (MS)
DePaul U (IL)
DeSales U (PA)
Dickinson State U (ND)
Dixie State U (UT)
Dominican Coll (NY)
Dominican U (IL)
Dominican U of California (CA)
Drexel U (PA)
Duquesne U (PA)
East Carolina U (NC)
East Central U (OK)
Eastern Illinois U (IL)
Eastern Kentucky U (KY)
Eastern Michigan U (MI)
Eastern New Mexico U (NM)
Eastern U (PA)
East Stroudsburg U of Pennsylvania (PA)
East Tennessee State U (TN)
East Texas Baptist U (TX)
Edgewood Coll (WI)
Edinboro U of Pennsylvania (PA)
Elmhurst Coll (IL)
Elmira Coll (NY)
Elms Coll (MA)
Emporia State U (KS)
Endicott Coll (MA)
Fairfield U (CT)
Fairleigh Dickinson U, Metropolitan Campus (NJ)
Fairmont State U (WV)
Farmingdale State Coll (NY)
Fayetteville State U (NC)
Ferris State U (MI)
Fitchburg State U (MA)
Florida Ag and Mech U (FL)
Florida Atlantic U (FL)
Florida Intl U (FL)
Florida National U (FL)
Florida Southern Coll (FL)
Florida SouthWestern State Coll (FL)
Florida State Coll at Jacksonville (FL)
Fort Hays State U (KS)
Franciscan U of Steubenville (OH)
Francis Marion U (SC)
Frostburg State U (MD)
Gannon U (PA)
George Mason U (VA)
Georgetown U (DC)
Georgia Coll & State U (GA)
Georgia Gwinnett Coll (GA)
Georgian Court U (NJ)
Georgia Regents U (GA)
Georgia Southern U (GA)
Georgia Southwestern State U (GA)
Georgia State U (GA)
Goldfarb School of Nursing at Barnes-Jewish Coll (MO)
Gonzaga U (WA)
Goodwin Coll (CT)
Goshen Coll (IN)
Governors State U (IL)
Graceland U (IA)
Grambling State U (LA)
Grand Valley State U (MI)
Grand View U (IA)
Granite State Coll (NH)
Great Basin Coll (NV)
Gustavus Adolphus Coll (MN)
Gwynedd Mercy U (PA)
Hampton U (VA)
Hannibal-LaGrange U (MO)
Harding U (AR)
Hardin-Simmons U (TX)
Hartwick Coll (NY)
Hawai`i Pacific U (HI)
Holy Family U (PA)
Hope Coll (MI)
Howard Payne U (TX)
Howard U (DC)
Hunter Coll of the City U of New York (NY)
Husson U (ME)
Illinois State U (IL)
Illinois Wesleyan U (IL)
Immaculata U (PA)
Indiana State U (IN)
Indiana U Bloomington (IN)
Indiana U East (IN)
Indiana U Kokomo (IN)
Indiana U of Pennsylvania (PA)
Indiana U–Purdue U Fort Wayne (IN)
Indiana U–Purdue U Indianapolis (IN)

Indiana U South Bend (IN)
Indiana U Southeast (IN)
Indian River State Coll (FL)
Inter American U of Puerto Rico, Aguadilla Campus (PR)
Inter American U of Puerto Rico, Bayamón Campus (PR)
Inter American U of Puerto Rico, Guayama Campus (PR)
Inter American U of Puerto Rico, Ponce Campus (PR)
Inter American U of Puerto Rico, San Germán Campus (PR)
Iowa Wesleyan Coll (IA)
Jacksonville State U (AL)
Jacksonville U (FL)
James Madison U (VA)
Jefferson Coll of Health Sciences (VA)
Johns Hopkins U (MD)
Kansas Wesleyan U (KS)
Keene State Coll (NH)
Keiser U, Fort Lauderdale (FL)
Kennesaw State U (GA)
Kent State U (OH)
Kent State U at Ashtabula (OH)
Kent State U at East Liverpool (OH)
Kent State U at Geauga (OH)
Kent State U at Salem (OH)
Kent State U at Stark (OH)
Kent State U at Trumbull (OH)
Kent State U at Tuscarawas (OH)
Kentucky Christian U (KY)
Kentucky State U (KY)
Keuka Coll (NY)
King U (TN)
Kuyper Coll (MI)
LaGrange Coll (GA)
Lakeview Coll of Nursing (IL)
Lamar U (TX)
Langston U (OK)
La Roche Coll (PA)
La Salle U (PA)
Lees-McRae Coll (NC)
Lee U (TN)
Lehman Coll of the City U of New York (NY)
Le Moyne Coll (NY)
Lenoir-Rhyne U (NC)
Lewis U (IL)
Liberty U (VA)
Lincoln Coll of New England, Southington (CT)
Lincoln Memorial U (TN)
Lincoln U (MO)
Lindsey Wilson Coll (KY)
Linfield Coll (OR)
Lipscomb U (TN)
Lock Haven U of Pennsylvania (PA)
Long Island U–LIU Brooklyn (NY)
Long Island U–LIU Post (NY)
Longwood U (VA)
Louisiana Coll (LA)
Lourdes U (OH)
Loyola U Chicago (IL)
Lubbock Christian U (TX)
Luther Coll (IA)
Lynchburg Coll (VA)
Madonna U (MI)
Malone U (OH)
Mansfield U of Pennsylvania (PA)
Maranatha Baptist U (WI)
Maria Coll (NY)
Marian U (IN)
Marian U (WI)
Marquette U (WI)
Marshall U (WV)
Marymount U (VA)
Maryville U of Saint Louis (MO)
Marywood U (PA)
Mayville State U (ND)
McKendree U (IL)
McMurry U (TX)
McNeese State U (LA)
MCPHS U (MA)
Medgar Evers Coll of the City U of New York (NY)
Mercy Coll (NY)
Mercy Coll of Health Sciences (IA)
Messiah Coll (PA)
Metropolitan State U (MN)
Miami Dade Coll (FL)
Miami U (OH)
Michigan State U (MI)
MidAmerica Nazarene U (KS)
Middle Tennessee State U (TN)
Midwestern State U (TX)
Milligan Coll (TN)
Millikin U (IL)
Milwaukee School of Eng (WI)
Minnesota State U Mankato (MN)
Minnesota State U Moorhead (MN)
Minot State U (ND)
Misericordia U (PA)
Mississippi U for Women (MS)
Missouri Southern State U (MO)
Missouri State U (MO)
Missouri Western State U (MO)
Molloy Coll (NY)
Monmouth U (NJ)
Montana State U (MT)
Montana Tech of The U of Montana (MT)
Montreat Coll, Montreat (NC)
Moravian Coll (PA)
Morehead State U (KY)
Morningside Coll (IA)
Morrisville State Coll (NY)
Mount Aloysius Coll (PA)
Mount Carmel Coll of Nursing (OH)
Mount Marty Coll (SD)
Mount Mary U (WI)
Mount Mercy U (IA)
Mount St. Joseph U (OH)
Mount Saint Mary Coll (NY)
Mount Saint Mary's U (CA)
Mount Vernon Nazarene U (OH)
Murray State U (KY)
National U (CA)
National U Coll, Bayamón (PR)
Nazareth Coll of Rochester (NY)
Nebraska Methodist Coll (NE)
Nebraska Wesleyan U (NE)
Newberry Coll (SC)
New England Inst of Technology (RI)
Newman U (KS)
New Mexico Highlands U (NM)
New Mexico State U (NM)
New York City Coll of Technology of the City U of New York (NY)
New York Inst of Technology (NY)
New York U (NY)
Niagara U (NY)
Nicholls State U (LA)
Norfolk State U (VA)
North Carolina Ag and Tech State U (NC)
North Carolina Central U (NC)
North Dakota State U (ND)
Northeastern State U (OK)
Northeastern U (MA)
Northern Arizona U (AZ)
Northern Illinois U (IL)
Northern Kentucky U (KY)
Northern Michigan U (MI)
Northwestern Coll (IA)
Northwestern Oklahoma State U (OK)
Northwest Missouri State U (MO)
Northwest Nazarene U (ID)
Northwest U (WA)
Norwich U (VT)
Notre Dame of Maryland U (MD)
Nova Southeastern U (FL)
Nyack Coll (NY)
Oakland U (MI)
The Ohio State U (OH)
The Ohio State U at Lima (OH)
The Ohio State U at Marion (OH)
The Ohio State U–Mansfield Campus (OH)
Ohio U (OH)
Oklahoma Baptist U (OK)
Oklahoma Christian U (OK)
Oklahoma Wesleyan U (OK)
Old Dominion U (VA)
Olivet Nazarene U (IL)
Oregon Health & Science U (OR)
Pace U (NY)
Pacific Lutheran U (WA)
Palm Beach Atlantic U (FL)
Penn State Abington (PA)
Penn State Altoona (PA)
Penn State Beaver (PA)
Penn State Berks (PA)
Penn State Brandywine (PA)
Penn State DuBois (PA)
Penn State Erie, The Behrend Coll (PA)
Penn State Fayette, The Eberly Campus (PA)
Penn State Greater Allegheny (PA)
Penn State Harrisburg (PA)
Penn State Hazleton (PA)
Penn State Lehigh Valley (PA)
Penn State Mont Alto (PA)
Penn State New Kensington (PA)
Penn State Schuylkill (PA)
Penn State Shenango (PA)
Penn State U Park (PA)
Penn State Wilkes-Barre (PA)
Penn State Worthington Scranton (PA)
Penn State York (PA)
Pennsylvania Coll of Health Sciences (PA)
Pensacola State Coll (FL)
Piedmont Coll (GA)
Pittsburg State U (KS)
Plymouth State U (NH)
Point Loma Nazarene U (CA)
Polk State Coll (FL)
Prairie View A&M U (TX)
Purdue U (IN)
Purdue U Calumet (IN)
Quincy U (IL)
Quinnipiac U (CT)
Radford U (VA)
Ramapo Coll of New Jersey (NJ)
Rasmussen Coll Fort Myers (FL)
Rasmussen Coll Land O' Lakes (FL)
Rasmussen Coll New Port Richey (FL)
Rasmussen Coll Tampa/Brandon (FL)
Regis Coll (MA)
Regis U (CO)
Research Coll of Nursing (MO)
Rhode Island Coll (RI)
Rider U (NJ)
Rivier U (NH)
Robert Morris U (PA)
Roberts Wesleyan Coll (NY)
Rockford U (IL)
Rockhurst U (MO)
Rowan U (NJ)
Rutgers, The State U of New Jersey, Camden (NJ)
Rutgers, The State U of New Jersey, Newark (NJ)
Rutgers, The State U of New Jersey, New Brunswick (NJ)
Sacred Heart U (CT)
The Sage Colls (NY)
Saginaw Valley State U (MI)
Saint Anthony Coll of Nursing (IL)
St. Catharine Coll (KY)
St. Catherine U (MN)
Saint Francis Medical Center Coll of Nursing (IL)
Saint Francis U (PA)
St. John Fisher Coll (NY)
Saint John's U (MN)
Saint Joseph's Coll (IN)
Saint Louis U (MO)
St. Luke's Coll (IA)
Saint Martin's U (WA)
Saint Mary's Coll (IN)
St. Olaf Coll (MN)
Salisbury U (MD)
Salve Regina U (RI)
Samford U (AL)
Sam Houston State U (TX)
Samuel Merritt U (CA)
San Diego State U (CA)
San Francisco State U (CA)
San Jose State U (CA)
Santa Fe Coll (FL)
Seattle Pacific U (WA)
Seattle U (WA)
Sentara Coll of Health Sciences (VA)
Shawnee State U (OH)
Shenandoah U (VA)
Shepherd U (WV)
Siena Heights U (MI)
Silver Lake Coll of the Holy Family (WI)
Simpson U (CA)
Slippery Rock U of Pennsylvania (PA)
South Carolina State U (SC)
South Dakota State U (SD)
Southeast Missouri State U (MO)
Southern Adventist U (TN)
Southern Arkansas U–Magnolia (AR)
Southern Connecticut State U (CT)
Southern Illinois U Edwardsville (IL)
Southern Oregon U (OR)
Southern Utah U (UT)
Southern Vermont Coll (VT)
South Florida State Coll (FL)
Southwest Baptist U (MO)
Southwestern Adventist U (TX)
Southwestern Assemblies of God U (TX)
Spalding U (KY)
Spring Hill Coll (AL)
State Coll of Florida Manatee-Sarasota (FL)
State U of New York at Plattsburgh (NY)
State U of New York Coll of Technology at Alfred (NY)
State U of New York Coll of Technology at Canton (NY)
State U of New York Empire State Coll (NY)
State U of New York Polytechnic Inst (NY)
Stephen F. Austin State U (TX)
Stevenson U (MD)
Stockton U (NJ)
Stony Brook U, State U of New York (NY)
Stratford U, Woodbridge (VA)
Sullivan U (KY)
Tarleton State U (TX)
Temple U (PA)
Tennessee State U (TN)
Tennessee Wesleyan Coll (TN)
Texas A&M Intl U (TX)
Texas A&M U–Commerce (TX)
Texas A&M U–Corpus Christi (TX)
Texas Christian U (TX)
Texas Lutheran U (TX)
Texas State U (TX)
Texas Woman's U (TX)
Thomas More Coll (KY)
Towson U (MD)
Trent U (ON, Canada)
Trevecca Nazarene U (TN)
Trinity Christian Coll (IL)
Troy U (AL)
Truett-McConnell Coll (GA)
Truman State U (MO)
Union Coll (KY)
Union Coll (NE)
Union U (TN)
Universidad del Turabo (PR)
Universidad Metropolitana (PR)
Université de Montréal (QC, Canada)
Université de Sherbrooke (QC, Canada)
Université du Québec en Outaouais (QC, Canada)
U at Buffalo, the State U of New York (NY)
The U of Akron (OH)
The U of Alabama (AL)
The U of Alabama at Birmingham (AL)
The U of Alabama in Huntsville (AL)
The U of Arizona (AZ)
U of Arkansas (AR)
U of Arkansas at Little Rock (AR)
U of Arkansas at Pine Bluff (AR)
U of Arkansas–Fort Smith (AR)
The U of British Columbia (BC, Canada)
The U of British Columbia–Okanagan Campus (BC, Canada)
U of Central Arkansas (AR)
U of Central Florida (FL)
U of Central Missouri (MO)
U of Central Oklahoma (OK)
U of Charleston (WV)
U of Cincinnati (OH)
U of Colorado Colorado Springs (CO)
U of Colorado Denver (CO)
U of Delaware (DE)
U of Dubuque (IA)
U of Evansville (IN)
U of Florida (FL)
U of Guam (GU)
U of Hartford (CT)
U of Hawaii at Manoa (HI)
U of Houston–Victoria (TX)
U of Illinois at Chicago (IL)
The U of Iowa (IA)
U of Jamestown (ND)
The U of Kansas (KS)
U of Kentucky (KY)
U of Lethbridge (AB, Canada)
U of Louisiana at Lafayette (LA)
U of Louisville (KY)
U of Maine (ME)
U of Maine at Augusta (ME)
U of Maine at Fort Kent (ME)
U of Mary Hardin-Baylor (TX)
U of Maryland U Coll (MD)
U of Massachusetts Amherst (MA)
U of Massachusetts Boston (MA)
U of Massachusetts Dartmouth (MA)
U of Massachusetts Lowell (MA)
U of Memphis (TN)
U of Miami (FL)
U of Michigan (MI)
U of Michigan–Flint (MI)
U of Missouri (MO)
U of Missouri–Kansas City (MO)
U of Missouri–St. Louis (MO)
U of Mobile (AL)
U of Mount Union (OH)
U of Nevada, Las Vegas (NV)
U of Nevada, Reno (NV)
U of New Brunswick Saint John (NB, Canada)
U of New England (ME)
U of New Hampshire (NH)
U of New Mexico (NM)
U of North Alabama (AL)
The U of North Carolina at Chapel Hill (NC)
The U of North Carolina at Charlotte (NC)
The U of North Carolina at Greensboro (NC)
The U of North Carolina at Pembroke (NC)
The U of North Carolina Wilmington (NC)
U of North Dakota (ND)
U of Northern Colorado (CO)
U of North Florida (FL)
U of North Georgia (GA)
U of Northwestern–St. Paul (MN)
U of Oklahoma Health Sciences Center (OK)
U of Ottawa (ON, Canada)
U of Pennsylvania (PA)
U of Pikeville (KY)
U of Pittsburgh (PA)
U of Pittsburgh at Bradford (PA)
U of Portland (OR)
U of Regina (SK, Canada)
U of Rhode Island (RI)
U of Rochester (NY)
U of St. Francis (IL)
U of Saint Francis (IN)
U of Saint Joseph (CT)
U of Saint Mary (KS)
U of San Francisco (CA)
U of Saskatchewan (SK, Canada)
The U of Scranton (PA)
U of South Alabama (AL)
U of South Carolina Aiken (SC)
U of South Carolina Beaufort (SC)
U of South Carolina Upstate (SC)
The U of South Dakota (SD)
U of Southern Indiana (IN)
U of Southern Maine (ME)
U of Southern Mississippi (MS)
U of South Florida (FL)
The U of Tampa (FL)
The U of Tennessee (TN)
The U of Tennessee at Chattanooga (TN)
The U of Tennessee at Martin (TN)
The U of Texas at Arlington (TX)
The U of Texas at Austin (TX)
The U of Texas at El Paso (TX)
The U of Texas at Tyler (TX)
The U of Texas Health Science Center at Houston (TX)
The U of Texas of the Permian Basin (TX)
The U of Texas–Pan American (TX)
U of the Fraser Valley (BC, Canada)
U of the Incarnate Word (TX)
U of the Virgin Islands (VI)
U of Toronto (ON, Canada)
The U of Tulsa (OK)
U of Utah (UT)

U of Vermont (VT)
U of Virginia (VA)
U of Washington (WA)
U of Washington, Bothell (WA)
U of Washington, Tacoma (WA)
The U of Western Ontario (ON, Canada)
U of West Florida (FL)
U of West Georgia (GA)
U of Windsor (ON, Canada)
U of Wisconsin–Eau Claire (WI)
U of Wisconsin–Green Bay (WI)
U of Wisconsin–Madison (WI)
U of Wisconsin–Milwaukee (WI)
U of Wisconsin–Oshkosh (WI)
U of Wisconsin–Parkside (WI)
U of Wyoming (WY)
Ursuline Coll (OH)
Utah Valley U (UT)
Utica Coll (NY)
Valdosta State U (GA)
Valparaiso U (IN)
Vanguard U of Southern California (CA)
Villanova U (PA)
Vincennes U (IN)
Virginia Commonwealth U (VA)
Viterbo U (WI)
Wagner Coll (NY)
Walden U (MN)
Walla Walla U (WA)
Walsh U (OH)
Washburn U (KS)
Washington State U (WA)
Waynesburg U (PA)
Weber State U (UT)
Webster U (MO)
Wesleyan Coll (GA)
West Chester U of Pennsylvania (PA)
Western Carolina U (NC)
Western Illinois U (IL)
Western Kentucky U (KY)
Western Michigan U (MI)
Westfield State U (MA)
West Liberty U (WV)
Westminster Coll (UT)
West Texas A&M U (TX)
West Virginia U (WV)
West Virginia U Inst of Technology (WV)
West Virginia Wesleyan Coll (WV)
Whitworth U (WA)
Wichita State U (KS)
Widener U (PA)
Wilkes U (PA)
William Jewell Coll (MO)
William Paterson U of New Jersey (NJ)
Wilmington U (DE)
Wingate U (NC)
Winona State U (MN)
Wittenberg U (OH)
Worcester State U (MA)
Wright State U (OH)
York Coll of Pennsylvania (PA)
York Coll of the City U of New York (NY)
Youngstown State U (OH)

REHABILITATION AND THERAPEUTIC PROFESSIONS RELATED
Alabama State U (AL)
Assumption Coll (MA)
Baker Coll (MI)
Boston U (MA)
California State U, Los Angeles (CA)
Coll of Saint Mary (NE)
East Stroudsburg U of Pennsylvania (PA)
Georgian Court U (NJ)
Hilbert Coll (NY)
Ithaca Coll (NY)
Montana State U Billings (MT)
Penn State Abington (PA)
Penn State Altoona (PA)
Penn State Beaver (PA)
Penn State Berks (PA)
Penn State Brandywine (PA)
Penn State DuBois (PA)
Penn State Erie, The Behrend Coll (PA)
Penn State Fayette, The Eberly Campus (PA)
Penn State Greater Allegheny (PA)
Penn State Hazleton (PA)
Penn State Lehigh Valley (PA)
Penn State Mont Alto (PA)
Penn State New Kensington (PA)
Penn State Schuylkill (PA)
Penn State Shenango (PA)
Penn State U Park (PA)
Penn State Wilkes-Barre (PA)
Penn State Worthington Scranton (PA)
Penn State York (PA)
Prescott Coll (AZ)
Rutgers, The State U of New Jersey, Newark (NJ)
Rutgers, The State U of New Jersey, New Brunswick (NJ)
Southern Illinois U Carbondale (IL)
Troy U (AL)
Université de Montréal (QC, Canada)
U of Arkansas at Pine Bluff (AR)
U of Massachusetts Lowell (MA)
U of Waterloo (ON, Canada)
Wilberforce U (OH)

REHABILITATION SCIENCE
Arkansas Tech U (AR)
Stephen F. Austin State U (TX)
U of North Dakota (ND)
U of North Texas (TX)
U of Pittsburgh (PA)
The U of Texas–Pan American (TX)
U of the Incarnate Word (TX)

RELIGIOUS EDUCATION
Andrews U (MI)
Asbury U (KY)
Ashland U (OH)
Barclay Coll (KS)
Benedictine Coll (KS)
Biola U (CA)
Bryan Coll (TN)
Campbellsville U (KY)
Cedarville U (OH)
Cincinnati Christian U (OH)
Columbia Coll (SC)
Columbia Intl U (SC)
Concordia Coll–New York (NY)
Concordia U (CA)
Concordia U Chicago (IL)
Concordia U, Nebraska (NE)
Concordia U, St. Paul (MN)
Concordia U Texas (TX)
Corban U (OR)
Crossroads Coll (MN)
Dallas Baptist U (TX)
Defiance Coll (OH)
Edgewood Coll (WI)
Faith Baptist Bible Coll and Theological Sem (IA)
Florida Coll (FL)
Franciscan U of Steubenville (OH)
Great Lakes Christian Coll (MI)
Hannibal-LaGrange U (MO)
Harding U (AR)
Hillsdale Free Will Baptist Coll (OK)
Houghton Coll (NY)
Howard Payne U (TX)
Huntingdon Coll (AL)
Inter American U of Puerto Rico, Fajardo Campus (PR)
John Carroll U (OH)
Kentucky Mountain Bible Coll (KY)
Kingswood U (NB, Canada)
Kuyper Coll (MI)
La Salle U (PA)
Laurel U (NC)
Lee U (TN)
Lindsey Wilson Coll (KY)
Louisiana Coll (LA)
Loyola U Chicago (IL)
Loyola U New Orleans (LA)
Malone U (OH)
Manhattan Christian Coll (KS)
Marian U (IN)
The Master's Coll and Sem (CA)
Master's Coll and Sem (ON, Canada)
Messiah Coll (PA)
Morris Coll (SC)
Mount Vernon Nazarene U (OH)
Multnomah U (OR)
Nazarene Bible Coll (CO)
Nebraska Christian Coll (NE)
Northwestern Coll (IA)
Northwest Nazarene U (ID)
Northwest U (WA)
Oakland City U (IN)
Oklahoma Christian U (OK)
Olivet Nazarene U (IL)
Presbyterian Coll (SC)
Saint Louis Christian Coll (MO)
Saint Mary's U of Minnesota (MN)
Seattle Pacific U (WA)
Simpson U (CA)
Southern Adventist U (TN)
Southwest Baptist U (MO)
Sterling Coll (KS)
Summit U (PA)
Taylor U (IN)
Thiel Coll (PA)
Toccoa Falls Coll (GA)
Universidad Teolgica del Caribe (PR)
U of Dayton (OH)
U of Valley Forge (PA)
Vanguard U of Southern California (CA)
Welch Coll (TN)
Wheaton Coll (IL)
William Jessup U (CA)
Williams Baptist Coll (AR)

RELIGIOUS/SACRED MUSIC
Anderson U (IN)
Anderson U (SC)
Aquinas Coll (MI)
Arizona Christian U (AZ)
Asbury U (KY)
Ave Maria U (FL)
Barclay Coll (KS)
Baylor U (TX)
Bethany Lutheran Coll (MN)
Bethel U (MN)
Bluefield Coll (VA)
Blue Mountain Coll (MS)
Bowling Green State U (OH)
Calvary Bible Coll and Theological Sem (MO)
Calvin Coll (MI)
Campbellsville U (KY)
Charleston Southern U (SC)
Cincinnati Christian U (OH)
Coll of the Ozarks (MO)
Columbia Intl U (SC)
Concordia Coll–New York (NY)
Concordia U Chicago (IL)
Concordia U, Nebraska (NE)
Concordia U, St. Paul (MN)
Concordia U Texas (TX)
Concordia U Wisconsin (WI)
Corban U (OR)
Crossroads Coll (MN)
Dallas Baptist U (TX)
Drake U (IA)
East Central U (OK)
East Texas Baptist U (TX)
Emmanuel Coll (GA)
Evangel U (MO)
Faith Baptist Bible Coll and Theological Sem (IA)
Franciscan U of Steubenville (OH)
Furman U (SC)
Great Lakes Christian Coll (MI)
Greenville Coll (IL)
Gustavus Adolphus Coll (MN)
Hardin-Simmons U (TX)
Hillsdale Free Will Baptist Coll (OK)
Hope Intl U (CA)
Houston Baptist U (TX)
Howard Payne U (TX)
John Brown U (AR)
Judson U (IL)
Kentucky Christian U (KY)
Kentucky Mountain Bible Coll (KY)
Kentucky Wesleyan Coll (KY)
Kuyper Coll (MI)
Lee U (TN)
Lenoir-Rhyne U (NC)
LeTourneau U (TX)
Liberty U (VA)
Lincoln U (MO)
Louisiana Coll (LA)
Madonna U (MI)
Malone U (OH)
Manhattan Christian Coll (KS)
Maranatha Baptist U (WI)
Marian U (IN)
The Master's Coll and Sem (CA)
Missouri Baptist U (MO)
Mount Vernon Nazarene U (OH)
Multnomah U (OR)
Nazarene Bible Coll (CO)
Nebraska Christian Coll (NE)
North Greenville U (SC)
Northwest Christian U (OR)
Northwest Nazarene U (ID)
Northwest U (WA)
Nyack Coll (NY)
Oklahoma Baptist U (OK)
Oklahoma City U (OK)
Oklahoma Wesleyan U (OK)
Olivet Nazarene U (IL)
Point Loma Nazarene U (CA)
Quincy U (IL)
Rider U (NJ)
Saint Louis Christian Coll (MO)
St. Olaf Coll (MN)
Samford U (AL)
San Diego Christian Coll (CA)
Seton Hill U (PA)
Shenandoah U (VA)
Southeastern U (FL)
Southwestern Assemblies of God U (TX)
Summit U (PA)
Texas Christian U (TX)
Trevecca Nazarene U (TN)
Union U (TN)
U of Alberta (AB, Canada)
U of Hartford (CT)
U of Mary Hardin-Baylor (TX)
U of Mobile (AL)
U of the Cumberlands (KY)
U of Valley Forge (PA)
Wartburg Coll (IA)
Welch Coll (TN)
William Jewell Coll (MO)
Williams Baptist Coll (AR)

RELIGIOUS STUDIES
Agnes Scott Coll (GA)
Albertus Magnus Coll (CT)
Albion Coll (MI)
Albright Coll (PA)
Allegheny Coll (PA)
Alma Coll (MI)
Alvernia U (PA)
Alverno Coll (WI)
American Public U System (WV)
The American U of Rome (Italy)
Amherst Coll (MA)
Anderson U (IN)
Anderson U (SC)
Andrews U (MI)
Appalachian State U (NC)
Aquinas Coll (MI)
Arizona State U at the Tempe campus (AZ)
Ashland U (OH)
Athens State U (AL)
Augsburg Coll (MN)
Augustana Coll (IL)
Augustana Coll (SD)
Austin Coll (TX)
Ave Maria U (FL)
Averett U (VA)
Avila U (MO)
Azusa Pacific U (CA)
Baker U (KS)
Baldwin Wallace U (OH)
Ball State U (IN)
Baptist U of the Americas (TX)
Bard Coll (NY)
Barnard Coll (NY)
Baruch Coll of the City U of New York (NY)
Bates Coll (ME)
Baylor U (TX)
Belmont U (TN)
Beloit Coll (WI)
Bemidji State U (MN)
Berea Coll (KY)
Bethany Coll (WV)
Bethany Lutheran Coll (MN)
Bethel Coll (KS)
Beulah Heights U (GA)
Biola U (CA)
Birmingham-Southern Coll (AL)
Bloomfield Coll (NJ)
Bluefield Coll (VA)
Boston U (MA)
Bowdoin Coll (ME)
Bradley U (IL)
Brevard Coll (NC)
Brown U (RI)
Bryn Mawr Coll (PA)
Bucknell U (PA)
Butler U (IN)
Cabrini Coll (PA)
Cairn U (PA)
California Lutheran U (CA)
California State U, Fresno (CA)
California State U, Fullerton (CA)
California State U, Long Beach (CA)
California State U, Sacramento (CA)
Calumet Coll of Saint Joseph (IN)
Calvin Coll (MI)
Campbellsville U (KY)
Canisius Coll (NY)
Cape Breton U (NS, Canada)
Capital U (OH)
Cardinal Stritch U (WI)
Carleton Coll (MN)
Carson-Newman U (TN)
Case Western Reserve U (OH)
Catawba Coll (NC)
The Catholic U of America (DC)
Centenary Coll of Louisiana (LA)
Central Coll (IA)
Central Methodist U (MO)
Central Michigan U (MI)
Central Washington U (WA)
Centre Coll (KY)
Chaminade U of Honolulu (HI)
Chapman U (CA)
Charleston Southern U (SC)
Chowan U (NC)
Claremont McKenna Coll (CA)
Clark Atlanta U (GA)
Clarke U (IA)
Cleveland State U (OH)
Coe Coll (IA)
Colby Coll (ME)
Coll of Charleston (SC)
The Coll of Idaho (ID)
The Coll of New Rochelle (NY)
The Coll of Saint Rose (NY)
The Coll of St. Scholastica (MN)
Coll of the Holy Cross (MA)
The Coll of William and Mary (VA)
The Coll of Wooster (OH)
The Colorado Coll (CO)
Columbia Bible Coll (BC, Canada)
Columbia Coll (SC)
Columbia U (NY)
Columbia U, School of General Studies (NY)
Concordia Coll (MN)
Concordia Coll–New York (NY)
Concordia U (CA)
Concordia U (QC, Canada)
Concordia U Chicago (IL)
Concordia U Wisconsin (WI)
Connecticut Coll (CT)
Corban U (OR)
Cornell Coll (IA)
Cornell U (NY)
Crandall U (NB, Canada)
Culver-Stockton Coll (MO)
Daemen Coll (NY)
Dalhousie U (NS, Canada)
Dartmouth Coll (NH)
Davidson Coll (NC)
Defiance Coll (OH)
Denison U (OH)
DePaul U (IL)
DePauw U (IN)
Dickinson Coll (PA)
Doane Coll (NE)
Dominican U of California (CA)
Drake U (IA)
Drew U (NJ)
Drury U (MO)
Earlham Coll (IN)
Eastern New Mexico U (NM)
East Texas Baptist U (TX)
Eckerd Coll (FL)
Edgewood Coll (WI)
Elizabethtown Coll (PA)
Elizabethtown Coll School of Continuing and Professional Studies (PA)
Elms Coll (MA)
Elon U (NC)
Emmanuel Coll (MA)
Emory & Henry Coll (VA)
Erskine Coll (SC)
The Evergreen State Coll (WA)
Fairfield U (CT)
Ferrum Coll (VA)
Florida Intl U (FL)
Florida Southern Coll (FL)
Fontbonne U (MO)
Fordham U (NY)
Franklin & Marshall Coll (PA)

Franklin Coll (IN)
Furman U (SC)
George Mason U (VA)
Georgetown Coll (KY)
The George Washington U (DC)
Georgian Court U (NJ)
Georgia State U (GA)
Gettysburg Coll (PA)
Goddard Coll (VT)
Gonzaga U (WA)
Goshen Coll (IN)
Goucher Coll (MD)
Graceland U (IA)
Grand View U (IA)
Greensboro Coll (NC)
Greenville Coll (IL)
Grinnell Coll (IA)
Grove City Coll (PA)
Guilford Coll (NC)
Gustavus Adolphus Coll (MN)
Hamilton Coll (NY)
Hamline U (MN)
Hampden-Sydney Coll (VA)
Hampshire Coll (MA)
Hampton U (VA)
Hartwick Coll (NY)
Harvard U (MA)
Hastings Coll (NE)
Haverford Coll (PA)
Heidelberg U (OH)
Hendrix Coll (AR)
High Point U (NC)
Hillsdale Coll (MI)
Hiram Coll (OH)
Hobart and William Smith Colls (NY)
Hofstra U (NY)
Hollins U (VA)
Holy Family U (PA)
Hope Coll (MI)
Hope Intl U (CA)
Houghton Coll (NY)
Houston Baptist U (TX)
Humboldt State U (CA)
Hunter Coll of the City U of New York (NY)
Huntingdon Coll (AL)
Illinois Coll (IL)
Illinois Wesleyan U (IL)
Indiana U Bloomington (IN)
Indiana U of Pennsylvania (PA)
Indiana U–Purdue U Indianapolis (IN)
Iona Coll (NY)
Iowa State U of Science and Technology (IA)
Jarvis Christian Coll (TX)
John Brown U (AR)
John Carroll U (OH)
Judson Coll (AL)
Juniata Coll (PA)
Kalamazoo Coll (MI)
Kansas Wesleyan U (KS)
Kentucky Wesleyan Coll (KY)
Kenyon Coll (OH)
Kingswood U (NB, Canada)
King U (TN)
Lafayette Coll (PA)
LaGrange Coll (GA)
Lake Forest Coll (IL)
Lane Coll (TN)
La Roche Coll (PA)
La Salle U (PA)
La Sierra U (CA)
Laurel U (NC)
Lawrence U (WI)
Lebanon Valley Coll (PA)
Lees-McRae Coll (NC)
Lehigh U (PA)
Le Moyne Coll (NY)
Lenoir-Rhyne U (NC)
Lewis & Clark Coll (OR)
Lewis U (IL)
Liberty U (VA)
Lincoln U (PA)
Lindenwood U (MO)
Linfield Coll (OR)
Loras Coll (IA)
Louisiana Coll (LA)
Lourdes U (OH)
Loyola U New Orleans (LA)
Luther Coll (IA)
Lycoming Coll (PA)
Lynchburg Coll (VA)
Macalester Coll (MN)
Madonna U (MI)
Manchester U (IN)
Manhattan Christian Coll (KS)
Manhattan Coll (NY)
Manhattanville Coll (NY)
Marian U (WI)
Mars Hill U (NC)
Mary Baldwin Coll (VA)
Marylhurst U (OR)
Marymount U (VA)
Maryville Coll (TN)
Marywood U (PA)
The Master's Coll and Sem (CA)
McDaniel Coll (MD)
McKendree U (IL)
Medgar Evers Coll of the City U of New York (NY)
Meredith Coll (NC)
Merrimack Coll (MA)
Miami U (OH)
Michigan State U (MI)
MidAmerica Nazarene U (KS)
Middlebury Coll (VT)
Millsaps Coll (MS)
Missouri State U (MO)
Missouri Valley Coll (MO)
Molloy Coll (NY)
Monmouth Coll (IL)
Montclair State U (NJ)
Moravian Coll (PA)
Morningside Coll (IA)
Mount Allison U (NB, Canada)
Mount Holyoke Coll (MA)
Mount Marty Coll (SD)
Mount Mercy U (IA)
Mount St. Joseph U (OH)
Mount Saint Mary's U (CA)
Mount Vernon Nazarene U (OH)
Muhlenberg Coll (PA)
Naropa U (CO)
Nazareth Coll of Rochester (NY)
Nebraska Christian Coll (NE)
Nebraska Wesleyan U (NE)
New Coll of Florida (FL)
New York U (NY)
Niagara U (NY)
North Carolina State U (NC)
North Carolina Wesleyan Coll (NC)
North Central Coll (IL)
Northeastern U (MA)
Northland Coll (WI)
Northwestern Coll (IA)
Northwestern U (IL)
Northwest Nazarene U (ID)
Northwest U (WA)
Notre Dame of Maryland U (MD)
Nyack Coll (NY)
Oakland City U (IN)
Oberlin Coll (OH)
Occidental Coll (CA)
Ohio Northern U (OH)
Ohio U (OH)
Ohio Valley U (WV)
Ohio Wesleyan U (OH)
Oklahoma Baptist U (OK)
Oklahoma Christian U (OK)
Oklahoma City U (OK)
Oklahoma Wesleyan U (OK)
Olivet Nazarene U (IL)
Our Lady of the Lake U of San Antonio (TX)
Pacific Lutheran U (WA)
Penn State Abington (PA)
Penn State Altoona (PA)
Penn State Beaver (PA)
Penn State Berks (PA)
Penn State Brandywine (PA)
Penn State DuBois (PA)
Penn State Erie, The Behrend Coll (PA)
Penn State Fayette, The Eberly Campus (PA)
Penn State Greater Allegheny (PA)
Penn State Hazleton (PA)
Penn State Lehigh Valley (PA)
Penn State Mont Alto (PA)
Penn State New Kensington (PA)
Penn State Schuylkill (PA)
Penn State Shenango (PA)
Penn State Wilkes-Barre (PA)
Penn State Worthington Scranton (PA)
Penn State York (PA)
Pepperdine U, Malibu (CA)
Philander Smith Coll (AR)
Piedmont Coll (GA)
Pomona Coll (CA)
Portland State U (OR)
Presbyterian Coll (SC)
Princeton U (NJ)
Principia Coll (IL)
Purdue U (IN)
Queens Coll of the City U of New York (NY)
Randolph Coll (VA)
Randolph-Macon Coll (VA)
Reed Coll (OR)
Regis U (CO)
Reinhardt U (GA)
Rhodes Coll (TN)
Rice U (TX)
Ripon Coll (WI)
Roanoke Coll (VA)
Roberts Wesleyan Coll (NY)
Rocky Mountain Coll (MT)
Rollins Coll (FL)
Rosemont Coll (PA)
Rutgers, The State U of New Jersey, New Brunswick (NJ)
Sacred Heart U (CT)
St. Francis Coll (NY)
Saint Francis U (PA)
St. John Fisher Coll (NY)
Saint Joseph's U (PA)
St. Lawrence U (NY)
Saint Leo U (FL)
Saint Martin's U (WA)
Saint Mary's Coll (IN)
St. Mary's Coll of Maryland (MD)
Saint Michael's Coll (VT)
St. Norbert Coll (WI)
St. Olaf Coll (MN)
Saint Peter's U (NJ)
St. Thomas Aquinas Coll (NY)
St. Thomas U (FL)
St. Thomas U (NB, Canada)
Salem Coll (NC)
Salve Regina U (RI)
Samford U (AL)
San Diego State U (CA)
San Jose State U (CA)
Santa Clara U (CA)
Sarah Lawrence Coll (NY)
Scripps Coll (CA)
Seattle U (WA)
Seton Hill U (PA)
Sewanee: The U of the South (TN)
Shenandoah U (VA)
Siena Coll (NY)
Siena Heights U (MI)
Simpson Coll (IA)
Skidmore Coll (NY)
Smith Coll (MA)
Southern Adventist U (TN)
Southern Methodist U (TX)
Southwest Baptist U (MO)
Southwestern Adventist U (TX)
Southwestern U (TX)
Spelman Coll (GA)
Spring Hill Coll (AL)
Stanford U (CA)
State U of New York Coll at Old Westbury (NY)
Stetson U (FL)
Stonehill Coll (MA)
Stony Brook U, State U of New York (NY)
Susquehanna U (PA)
Syracuse U (NY)
Tabor Coll (KS)
Temple U (PA)
Tennessee Wesleyan Coll (TN)
Texas Christian U (TX)
Texas Wesleyan U (TX)
Thiel Coll (PA)
Thomas More Coll (KY)
Tougaloo Coll (MS)
Towson U (MD)
Transylvania U (KY)
Trevecca Nazarene U (TN)
Trinity Coll (CT)
Trinity U (TX)
Tufts U (MA)
Tulane U (LA)
Union Coll (KY)
Union Coll (NY)
Union U (TN)
Université de Montréal (QC, Canada)
U at Albany, State U of New York (NY)
The U of Alabama (AL)
U of Alberta (AB, Canada)
The U of Arizona (AZ)
U of Bridgeport (CT)
The U of British Columbia (BC, Canada)
U of California, Berkeley (CA)
U of California, Davis (CA)
U of California, Irvine (CA)
U of California, Los Angeles (CA)
U of California, Riverside (CA)
U of California, Santa Barbara (CA)
U of Central Arkansas (AR)
U of Central Florida (FL)
U of Colorado Boulder (CO)
U of Dayton (OH)
U of Denver (CO)
U of Dubuque (IA)
The U of Findlay (OH)
U of Florida (FL)
U of Georgia (GA)
U of Great Falls (MT)
U of Hawaii at Manoa (HI)
U of Houston (TX)
U of Indianapolis (IN)
The U of Iowa (IA)
U of Jamestown (ND)
The U of Kansas (KS)
U of King's Coll (NS, Canada)
U of La Verne (CA)
U of Lethbridge (AB, Canada)
U of Miami (FL)
U of Michigan (MI)
U of Minnesota, Twin Cities Campus (MN)
U of Mississippi (MS)
U of Missouri (MO)
U of Mobile (AL)
U of Mount Union (OH)
U of New Mexico (NM)
U of North Carolina at Asheville (NC)
The U of North Carolina at Chapel Hill (NC)
The U of North Carolina at Charlotte (NC)
The U of North Carolina at Greensboro (NC)
U of North Dakota (ND)
U of Northern Iowa (IA)
U of North Florida (FL)
U of North Texas (TX)
U of Oklahoma (OK)
U of Oregon (OR)
U of Ottawa (ON, Canada)
U of Pennsylvania (PA)
U of Pikeville (KY)
U of Pittsburgh (PA)
U of Puget Sound (WA)
U of Regina (SK, Canada)
U of Richmond (VA)
U of Rochester (NY)
U of Saint Francis (IN)
U of Saint Joseph (CT)
U of St. Thomas (MN)
U of San Diego (CA)
U of San Francisco (CA)
U of Saskatchewan (SK, Canada)
The U of Scranton (PA)
U of Southern California (CA)
U of Southern Mississippi (MS)
U of South Florida (FL)
The U of Tennessee (TN)
The U of Texas at Austin (TX)
The U of Texas at Tyler (TX)
U of the Incarnate Word (TX)
U of the Pacific (CA)
The U of Toledo (OH)
The U of Tulsa (OK)
U of Vermont (VT)
U of Virginia (VA)
U of Washington (WA)
U of Waterloo (ON, Canada)
The U of Western Ontario (ON, Canada)
U of Wisconsin–Eau Claire (WI)
U of Wisconsin–Madison (WI)
U of Wisconsin–Milwaukee (WI)
U of Wisconsin–Oshkosh (WI)
U of Wyoming (WY)
Urbana U (OH)
Ursinus Coll (PA)
Vanderbilt U (TN)
Vanguard U of Southern California (CA)
Vassar Coll (NY)
Villanova U (PA)
Virginia Commonwealth U (VA)
Virginia Wesleyan Coll (VA)
Viterbo U (WI)
Wabash Coll (IN)
Wake Forest U (NC)
Walla Walla U (WA)
Warner Pacific Coll (OR)
Warren Wilson Coll (NC)
Wartburg Coll (IA)
Washburn U (KS)
Washington and Lee U (VA)
Washington State U (WA)
Washington U in St. Louis (MO)
Webster U (MO)
Wesleyan Coll (GA)
Wesleyan U (CT)
Western Illinois U (IL)
Western Kentucky U (KY)
Western Michigan U (MI)
Westminster Coll (MO)
West Virginia Wesleyan Coll (WV)
Wheaton Coll (MA)
Wheeling Jesuit U (WV)
Whitman Coll (WA)
Whittier Coll (CA)
Whitworth U (WA)
Willamette U (OR)
William Jewell Coll (MO)
Williams Baptist Coll (AR)
Williams Coll (MA)
Wingate U (NC)
Wittenberg U (OH)
Wofford Coll (SC)
Wright State U (OH)
Xavier U (OH)
Yale U (CT)
Youngstown State U (OH)

RELIGIOUS STUDIES RELATED

Agnes Scott Coll (GA)
Belmont U (TN)
Newberry Coll (SC)
Ohio Northern U (OH)
U of the West (CA)
The U of Western Ontario (ON, Canada)
Ursuline Coll (OH)

REPRODUCTIVE BIOLOGY

Bradley U (IL)

RESEARCH AND DEVELOPMENT MANAGEMENT

The U of Iowa (IA)

RESEARCH AND EXPERIMENTAL PSYCHOLOGY RELATED

Edinboro U of Pennsylvania (PA)
Mount Saint Mary's U (CA)
Mount St. Mary's U (MD)
St. Edward's U (TX)
U of Michigan–Flint (MI)

RESEARCH METHODOLOGY AND QUANTITATIVE METHODS

Illinois Inst of Technology (IL)
Walsh U (OH)

RESORT MANAGEMENT

Coastal Carolina U (SC)
Florida Gulf Coast U (FL)
Green Mountain Coll (VT)
Morrisville State Coll (NY)
Rochester Inst of Technology (NY)

RESPIRATORY CARE THERAPY

Armstrong State U (GA)
Ball State U (IN)
Bowling Green State U (OH)
Bowling Green State U-Firelands Coll (OH)
Canisius Coll (NY)
Cardinal Stritch U (WI)
Concordia U, St. Paul (MN)
Dakota State U (SD)
Dalhousie U (NS, Canada)
Fairleigh Dickinson U, Coll at Florham (NJ)
Florida Ag and Mech U (FL)
Florida SouthWestern State Coll (FL)
Gannon U (PA)
Georgia Regents U (GA)
Georgia State U (GA)
Gwynedd Mercy U (PA)
Indiana U of Pennsylvania (PA)
Indiana U–Purdue U Indianapolis (IN)
Long Island U–LIU Brooklyn (NY)
Marshall U (WV)
Midwestern State U (TX)

Missouri State U (MO)
Nebraska Methodist Coll (NE)
North Dakota State U (ND)
Northern Kentucky U (KY)
Northern Michigan U (MI)
Nova Southeastern U (FL)
The Ohio State U (OH)
Rutgers, The State U of New Jersey, Newark (NJ)
St. Catherine U (MN)
Salisbury U (MD)
Shenandoah U (VA)
Stony Brook U, State U of New York (NY)
Tennessee State U (TN)
Texas Southern U (TX)
Texas State U (TX)
Universidad Metropolitana (PR)
The U of Akron (OH)
The U of Alabama at Birmingham (AL)
U of Cincinnati (OH)
U of Hartford (CT)
U of Indianapolis (IN)
The U of Kansas (KS)
U of Missouri (MO)
The U of North Carolina at Charlotte (NC)
U of South Alabama (AL)
The U of Toledo (OH)
U of Waterloo (ON, Canada)
Weber State U (UT)
Wheeling Jesuit U (WV)
York Coll of Pennsylvania (PA)
Youngstown State U (OH)

RESPIRATORY THERAPY TECHNICIAN
Dalhousie U (NS, Canada)
Rhode Island Coll (RI)

RESTAURANT, CULINARY, AND CATERING MANAGEMENT
Bowling Green State U (OH)
Johnson & Wales U (FL)
Johnson & Wales U (RI)
Johnson & Wales U - Charlotte Campus (NC)
Pennsylvania Coll of Technology (PA)
Southeast Missouri State U (MO)
State U of New York Coll of Technology at Delhi (NY)
U of Hawaii–West Oahu (HI)

RESTAURANT/FOOD SERVICES MANAGEMENT
Central Washington U (WA)
Colorado State U (CO)
The Culinary Inst of America (NY)
Johnson & Wales U (CO)
Johnson & Wales U - Charlotte Campus (NC)
Kennesaw State U (GA)
Lindenwood U (MO)
Messiah Coll (PA)
Morrisville State Coll (NY)
Niagara U (NY)
The Ohio State U (OH)
Rochester Inst of Technology (NY)
Southwest Minnesota State U (MN)
The U of Alabama (AL)
U of Central Florida (FL)
U of Missouri (MO)
U of Nevada, Las Vegas (NV)
U of San Francisco (CA)
Wright State U (OH)

RETAILING
American Public U System (WV)
Bowling Green State U (OH)
Central Washington U (WA)
Intl Business Coll, Fort Wayne (IN)
Lamar U (TX)
Stevens–The Inst of Business & Arts (MO)
U of Alberta (AB, Canada)
U of Central Oklahoma (OK)
U of Minnesota, Twin Cities Campus (MN)
U of Wisconsin–Madison (WI)

RETAIL MANAGEMENT
Syracuse U (NY)
The U of Arizona (AZ)
U of Arkansas (AR)
U of North Texas (TX)

RHETORIC AND COMPOSITION
Albany State U (GA)
Ashland U (OH)
Auburn U (AL)
Bates Coll (ME)
Bemidji State U (MN)
Black Hills State U (SD)
Bowling Green State U (OH)
Brigham Young U (UT)
California State U, Fresno (CA)
California State U, Fullerton (CA)
California State U, Long Beach (CA)
California State U, Los Angeles (CA)
Calvin Coll (MI)
Cape Breton U (NS, Canada)
Carson-Newman U (TN)
Clark Atlanta U (GA)
Coe Coll (IA)
Coll of Saint Benedict (MN)
Columbus State U (GA)
Concordia U, Nebraska (NE)
Cornell Coll (IA)
Denison U (OH)
DePaul U (IL)
Dickinson State U (ND)
Drake U (IA)
Duquesne U (PA)
East Central U (OK)
East Tennessee State U (TN)
East Texas Baptist U (TX)
Emerson Coll (MA)
Evangel U (MO)
Fairmont State U (WV)
Ferris State U (MI)
George Mason U (VA)
The George Washington U (DC)
Georgia Coll & State U (GA)
Georgia Southern U (GA)
Gonzaga U (WA)
Graceland U (IA)
Gustavus Adolphus Coll (MN)
Hastings Coll (NE)
Houston Baptist U (TX)
Humboldt State U (CA)
Illinois Coll (IL)
Indiana U South Bend (IN)
Iowa State U of Science and Technology (IA)
Ithaca Coll (NY)
Jackson State U (MS)
Kutztown U of Pennsylvania (PA)
Lehman Coll of the City U of New York (NY)
Lipscomb U (TN)
Lock Haven U of Pennsylvania (PA)
Louisiana Coll (LA)
Louisiana State U in Shreveport (LA)
Manchester U (IN)
Marietta Coll (OH)
Marshall U (WV)
The Master's Coll and Sem (CA)
McKendree U (IL)
Minnesota State U Mankato (MN)
Mississippi Valley State U (MS)
Missouri Valley Coll (MO)
North Carolina Ag and Tech State U (NC)
North Central Coll (IL)
Northeastern Illinois U (IL)
Northern Kentucky U (KY)
Northern State U (SD)
Northwestern Coll (IA)
Northwestern Oklahoma State U (OK)
Northwestern U (IL)
Oglethorpe U (GA)
Ohio U (OH)
Oklahoma Baptist U (OK)
Oklahoma Christian U (OK)
Old Dominion U (VA)
Portland State U (OR)
Rider U (NJ)
St. Catherine U (MN)
Saint John's U (MN)
St. John's U (NY)
St. Joseph's Coll, Long Island Campus (NY)
St. Joseph's Coll, New York (NY)
San Jose State U (CA)
Shippensburg U of Pennsylvania (PA)
Southeast Missouri State U (MO)
Southern Illinois U Carbondale (IL)
Southern Illinois U Edwardsville (IL)
State U of New York Coll at Cortland (NY)
Stephen F. Austin State U (TX)
Tarleton State U (TX)
Texas A&M U–Commerce (TX)
Texas State U (TX)
Texas Tech U (TX)
Texas Wesleyan U (TX)
Trinity U (TX)
Union U (TN)
U at Albany, State U of New York (NY)
U of Arkansas at Little Rock (AR)
U of Arkansas at Pine Bluff (AR)
U of California, Berkeley (CA)
U of Central Florida (FL)
U of Central Missouri (MO)
U of Cincinnati (OH)
U of Dubuque (IA)
The U of Iowa (IA)
U of Kentucky (KY)
U of Minnesota, Morris (MN)
U of Minnesota, Twin Cities Campus (MN)
The U of Montana (MT)
U of Montevallo (AL)
U of Nebraska at Kearney (NE)
U of New Mexico (NM)
U of North Texas (TX)
U of Pittsburgh (PA)
U of Rhode Island (RI)
U of Richmond (VA)
The U of South Dakota (SD)
U of South Florida (FL)
The U of Texas at Arlington (TX)
The U of Texas at El Paso (TX)
The U of Texas at Tyler (TX)
U of Waterloo (ON, Canada)
U of Wisconsin–Platteville (WI)
U of Wisconsin–River Falls (WI)
U of Wisconsin–Superior (WI)
Utah State U (UT)
Wabash Coll (IN)
Walla Walla U (WA)
West Chester U of Pennsylvania (PA)
West Virginia Wesleyan Coll (WV)
Whitworth U (WA)
Willamette U (OR)
Yeshiva U (NY)
York Coll of the City U of New York (NY)
Youngstown State U (OH)

RHETORIC AND COMPOSITION/WRITING RELATED
Augsburg Coll (MN)
Pepperdine U, Malibu (CA)
Syracuse U (NY)

ROBOTICS TECHNOLOGY
Alcorn State U (MS)
Indiana State U (IN)
Indiana U–Purdue U Indianapolis (IN)
Sullivan Coll of Technology and Design (KY)
U of Rio Grande (OH)

ROMANCE LANGUAGES
Beloit Coll (WI)
Bowdoin Coll (ME)
Bryn Mawr Coll (PA)
Carleton Coll (MN)
City Coll of the City U of New York (NY)
Dartmouth Coll (NH)
DePauw U (IN)
Fordham U (NY)
Gettysburg Coll (PA)
Harvard U (MA)
Haverford Coll (PA)
Hunter Coll of the City U of New York (NY)
Johns Hopkins U (MD)
Loyola Marymount U (CA)
Merrimack Coll (MA)
Mount Allison U (NB, Canada)
Mount Holyoke Coll (MA)
Oberlin Coll (OH)
Point Loma Nazarene U (CA)
Pomona Coll (CA)
Ripon Coll (WI)
Rockford U (IL)
St. Thomas Aquinas Coll (NY)
Stanford U (CA)
Truman State U (MO)
Tufts U (MA)
U of Alberta (AB, Canada)
The U of British Columbia (BC, Canada)
U of Georgia (GA)
U of Illinois at Chicago (IL)
U of Maryland, Coll Park (MD)
U of Michigan (MI)
U of Notre Dame (IN)
U of Oregon (OR)
U of Toronto (ON, Canada)
U of Washington (WA)
Vanderbilt U (TN)
Washington and Lee U (VA)
Washington U in St. Louis (MO)
Wesleyan U (CT)
Wheeling Jesuit U (WV)
William Jewell Coll (MO)

ROMANCE LANGUAGES RELATED
Dowling Coll (NY)
North Carolina Ag and Tech State U (NC)
U of Alberta (AB, Canada)
U of Chicago (IL)
U of Lethbridge (AB, Canada)
U of Maine (ME)
U of Michigan–Flint (MI)
U of Nevada, Las Vegas (NV)
The U of North Carolina at Chapel Hill (NC)
U of Pennsylvania (PA)
Wheeling Jesuit U (WV)

RURAL SOCIOLOGY
U of Wisconsin–Madison (WI)

RUSSIAN
American U (DC)
Amherst Coll (MA)
Arizona State U at the Tempe campus (AZ)
Bard Coll (NY)
Barnard Coll (NY)
Bates Coll (ME)
Baylor U (TX)
Beloit Coll (WI)
Boston Coll (MA)
Boston U (MA)
Bowdoin Coll (ME)
Bowling Green State U (OH)
Brandeis U (MA)
Bryn Mawr Coll (PA)
Bucknell U (PA)
Carleton Coll (MN)
Central Washington U (WA)
Coll of the Holy Cross (MA)
Columbia U (NY)
Columbia U, School of General Studies (NY)
Cornell Coll (IA)
Cornell U (NY)
Dalhousie U (NS, Canada)
Dartmouth Coll (NH)
Dickinson Coll (PA)
Georgetown U (DC)
The George Washington U (DC)
Goucher Coll (MD)
Grinnell Coll (IA)
Gustavus Adolphus Coll (MN)
Haverford Coll (PA)
Hofstra U (NY)
Howard U (DC)
Hunter Coll of the City U of New York (NY)
Juniata Coll (PA)
Kent State U (OH)
La Salle U (PA)
Lawrence U (WI)
Lehman Coll of the City U of New York (NY)
Luther Coll (IA)
Macalester Coll (MN)
Michigan State U (MI)
Middlebury Coll (VT)
New Coll of Florida (FL)
New York U (NY)
Oberlin Coll (OH)
The Ohio State U (OH)
Ohio U (OH)
Oklahoma State U (OK)
Penn State Abington (PA)
Penn State Altoona (PA)
Penn State Beaver (PA)
Penn State Berks (PA)
Penn State Brandywine (PA)
Penn State DuBois (PA)
Penn State Erie, The Behrend Coll (PA)
Penn State Fayette, The Eberly Campus (PA)
Penn State Greater Allegheny (PA)
Penn State Hazleton (PA)
Penn State Lehigh Valley (PA)
Penn State Mont Alto (PA)
Penn State New Kensington (PA)
Penn State Schuylkill (PA)
Penn State Shenango (PA)
Penn State U Park (PA)
Penn State Wilkes-Barre (PA)
Penn State Worthington Scranton (PA)
Penn State York (PA)
Pomona Coll (CA)
Portland State U (OR)
Purdue U (IN)
Queens Coll of the City U of New York (NY)
Reed Coll (OR)
Rider U (NJ)
Rutgers, The State U of New Jersey, New Brunswick (NJ)
Saint Louis U (MO)
St. Olaf Coll (MN)
San Diego State U (CA)
Scripps Coll (CA)
Seattle Pacific U (WA)
Sewanee: The U of the South (TN)
Smith Coll (MA)
Syracuse U (NY)
Texas A&M U (TX)
Trinity Coll (CT)
Trinity U (TX)
Truman State U (MO)
Tufts U (MA)
Tulane U (LA)
United States Military Acad (NY)
U of Alberta (AB, Canada)
The U of Arizona (AZ)
The U of British Columbia (BC, Canada)
U of California, Davis (CA)
U of California, Los Angeles (CA)
U of Denver (CO)
U of Florida (FL)
U of Georgia (GA)
U of Hawaii at Manoa (HI)
U of Illinois at Chicago (IL)
The U of Iowa (IA)
U of Kentucky (KY)
U of King's Coll (NS, Canada)
U of Maryland, Coll Park (MD)
U of Michigan (MI)
U of Minnesota, Twin Cities Campus (MN)
U of Missouri (MO)
The U of Montana (MT)
U of Nebraska–Lincoln (NE)
U of New Hampshire (NH)
U of Notre Dame (IN)
U of Oklahoma (OK)
U of Ottawa (ON, Canada)
U of Pennsylvania (PA)
U of Pittsburgh (PA)
U of Rochester (NY)
U of Saskatchewan (SK, Canada)
U of Southern California (CA)
U of South Florida (FL)
The U of Tennessee (TN)
The U of Texas at Arlington (TX)
The U of Texas at Austin (TX)
U of Toronto (ON, Canada)
U of Utah (UT)
U of Vermont (VT)
U of Washington (WA)
U of Waterloo (ON, Canada)
U of Wisconsin–Madison (WI)
U of Wisconsin–Milwaukee (WI)
U of Wyoming (WY)
Vanderbilt U (TN)
Vassar Coll (NY)
Virginia Polytechnic Inst and State U (VA)
Wake Forest U (NC)
West Chester U of Pennsylvania (PA)
Wheaton Coll (MA)
Williams Coll (MA)
Yale U (CT)

RUSSIAN, CENTRAL EUROPEAN, EAST EUROPEAN AND EURASIAN STUDIES
Bowdoin Coll (ME)
Michigan State U (MI)
Middlebury Coll (VT)
Pomona Coll (CA)
Portland State U (OR)
San Diego State U (CA)
Tufts U (MA)
The U of British Columbia (BC, Canada)
U of Missouri (MO)
U of Toronto (ON, Canada)
Wayne State U (MI)
Wittenberg U (OH)

RUSSIAN STUDIES
American U (DC)
Bard Coll (NY)
Bard Coll at Simon's Rock (MA)
Boston Coll (MA)
Bowling Green State U (OH)
Brown U (RI)
Carleton Coll (MN)
Colby Coll (ME)
The Coll of Wooster (OH)
The Colorado Coll (CO)
Columbia U (NY)
Columbia U, School of General Studies (NY)
Cornell Coll (IA)
Dalhousie U (NS, Canada)
Dartmouth Coll (NH)
DePauw U (IN)
George Mason U (VA)
The George Washington U (DC)
Grand Valley State U (MI)
Gustavus Adolphus Coll (MN)
Hamilton Coll (NY)
Hobart and William Smith Colls (NY)
Kent State U (OH)
Lafayette Coll (PA)
La Salle U (PA)
Lawrence U (WI)
Middlebury Coll (VT)
Mount Holyoke Coll (MA)
Muhlenberg Coll (PA)
Oberlin Coll (OH)
Rhodes Coll (TN)
St. Olaf Coll (MN)
Scripps Coll (CA)
Smith Coll (MA)
Stetson U (FL)
Syracuse U (NY)
Texas Tech U (TX)
Tufts U (MA)
Tulane U (LA)
United States Military Acad (NY)
U of Alaska Fairbanks (AK)
The U of British Columbia (BC, Canada)
U of California, Los Angeles (CA)
U of California, Riverside (CA)
U of California, Santa Cruz (CA)
U of Chicago (IL)
U of Colorado Boulder (CO)
U of Delaware (DE)
The U of Iowa (IA)
The U of Kansas (KS)
U of Maryland, Coll Park (MD)
U of Massachusetts Amherst (MA)
U of Michigan (MI)
U of Minnesota, Twin Cities Campus (MN)
U of Missouri (MO)
The U of Montana (MT)
U of New Mexico (NM)
U of Oregon (OR)
U of Richmond (VA)
U of Rochester (NY)
The U of Texas at Austin (TX)
U of Toronto (ON, Canada)
The U of Tulsa (OK)
U of Vermont (VT)
U of Waterloo (ON, Canada)
Washington and Lee U (VA)
Washington U in St. Louis (MO)
Wesleyan U (CT)
Wheaton Coll (MA)
Yale U (CT)

SALES AND MARKETING/ MARKETING AND DISTRIBUTION TEACHER EDUCATION
Bowling Green State U (OH)
Central Washington U (WA)
Colorado State U (CO)
Eastern Michigan U (MI)
Eastern New Mexico U (NM)
Fayetteville State U (NC)
Middle Tennessee State U (TN)
North Carolina State U (NC)
Rider U (NJ)
State U of New York at Oswego (NY)
U of Minnesota, Twin Cities Campus (MN)
U of Wisconsin–Stout (WI)
Utah State U (UT)
Western Michigan U (MI)
Wright State U (OH)

SALES, DISTRIBUTION, AND MARKETING OPERATIONS
Avila U (MO)
Babson Coll (MA)
Baylor U (TX)
Bentley U (MA)
Black Hills State U (SD)
Bowling Green State U (OH)
Hampton U (VA)
Harding U (AR)
HEC Montreal (QC, Canada)
Husson U (ME)
Kennesaw State U (GA)
Long Island U–LIU Brooklyn (NY)
McKendree U (IL)
Metropolitan State U (MN)
Middle Tennessee State U (TN)
New York U (NY)
Quinnipiac U (CT)
St. Catherine U (MN)
Seton Hill U (PA)
Southern Adventist U (TN)
Texas A&M U (TX)
The U of Akron (OH)
U of Central Oklahoma (OK)
The U of Findlay (OH)
U of Houston (TX)
U of Memphis (TN)
U of Minnesota, Twin Cities Campus (MN)
U of Pennsylvania (PA)
U of the Incarnate Word (TX)
U of Wisconsin–Stout (WI)
U of Wisconsin–Superior (WI)
West Chester U of Pennsylvania (PA)

SANSKRIT AND CLASSICAL INDIAN LANGUAGES
Bard Coll (NY)
Harvard U (MA)
The U of Iowa (IA)

SCANDINAVIAN LANGUAGES
Augsburg Coll (MN)
Augustana Coll (IL)
Gustavus Adolphus Coll (MN)
Luther Coll (IA)
U of Alberta (AB, Canada)
U of California, Berkeley (CA)
U of California, Los Angeles (CA)
U of Minnesota, Twin Cities Campus (MN)
The U of Texas at Austin (TX)

SCANDINAVIAN STUDIES
American U (DC)
Augsburg Coll (MN)
Concordia Coll (MN)
Gustavus Adolphus Coll (MN)
Pacific Lutheran U (WA)
U of California, Los Angeles (CA)
U of Washington (WA)
U of Wisconsin–Madison (WI)

SCHOOL LIBRARIAN/SCHOOL LIBRARY MEDIA
The Coll of St. Scholastica (MN)
East Central U (OK)
U of Great Falls (MT)

SCHOOL PSYCHOLOGY
Fort Hays State U (KS)
Tarleton State U (TX)
U of Wisconsin–River Falls (WI)

SCIENCE TEACHER EDUCATION
Abilene Christian U (TX)
Adams State U (CO)
Albany State U (GA)
Albion Coll (MI)
Alice Lloyd Coll (KY)
Alma Coll (MI)
Alverno Coll (WI)
Andrews U (MI)
Aquinas Coll (MI)
Arcadia U (PA)
Arizona Christian U (AZ)
Arkansas Tech U (AR)
Ashland U (OH)
Auburn U (AL)
Ball State U (IN)
Baylor U (TX)
Bemidji State U (MN)
Bethel Coll (IN)
Biola U (CA)
Black Hills State U (SD)
Bluefield Coll (VA)
Bob Jones U (SC)
Boston U (MA)
Bowie State U (MD)
Bowling Green State U (OH)
Bradley U (IL)
Brigham Young U (UT)
Buena Vista U (IA)
Buffalo State Coll, State U of New York (NY)
California Lutheran U (CA)
Calvin Coll (MI)
Cameron U (OK)
Campbellsville U (KY)
Canisius Coll (NY)
Capital U (OH)
Castleton State Coll (VT)
Catawba Coll (NC)
Cedarville U (OH)
Central Methodist U (MO)
Central Michigan U (MI)
Central Washington U (WA)
Charleston Southern U (SC)
Chipola Coll (FL)
City Coll of the City U of New York (NY)
Coe Coll (IA)
Coll of Saint Mary (NE)
The Coll of Saint Rose (NY)
Coll of the Atlantic (ME)
Colorado State U (CO)
Columbus State U (GA)
Concordia Coll–New York (NY)
Concordia U Chicago (IL)
Concordia U, Nebraska (NE)
Concordia U Wisconsin (WI)
Cornerstone U (MI)
Covenant Coll (GA)
Dallas Baptist U (TX)
Defiance Coll (OH)
Delaware State U (DE)
Dickinson State U (ND)
Dixie State U (UT)
Doane Coll (NE)
Dowling Coll (NY)
East Carolina U (NC)
East Central U (OK)
Eastern Illinois U (IL)
Eastern Michigan U (MI)
Edgewood Coll (WI)
Elizabethtown Coll (PA)
Elon U (NC)
Evangel U (MO)
Fairmont State U (WV)
Florida Ag and Mech U (FL)
Florida Atlantic U (FL)
Florida Inst of Technology (FL)
Florida SouthWestern State Coll (FL)
Fort Hays State U (KS)
Gettysburg Coll (PA)
Graceland U (IA)
Grand Valley State U (MI)
Greensboro Coll (NC)
Hannibal-LaGrange U (MO)
Harding U (AR)
Hardin-Simmons U (TX)
Hastings Coll (NE)
Heidelberg U (OH)
Heritage U (WA)
Hobe Sound Bible Coll (FL)
Hofstra U (NY)
Hope Coll (MI)
Houston Baptist U (TX)
Hunter Coll of the City U of New York (NY)
Indiana State U (IN)
Indiana U–Purdue U Fort Wayne (IN)
Indiana U South Bend (IN)
Indian River State Coll (FL)
Inter American U of Puerto Rico, San Germán Campus (PR)
Ithaca Coll (NY)
Judson Coll (AL)
Keene State Coll (NH)
Kent State U (OH)
La Salle U (PA)
Le Moyne Coll (NY)
LeMoyne-Owen Coll (TN)
LeTourneau U (TX)
Lincoln Memorial U (TN)
Lindenwood U (MO)
Louisiana Coll (LA)
Loyola U Chicago (IL)
Lubbock Christian U (TX)
Madonna U (MI)
Malone U (OH)
Manchester U (IN)
Mansfield U of Pennsylvania (PA)
Maranatha Baptist U (WI)
Marian U (WI)
Mars Hill U (NC)
Marywood U (PA)
The Master's Coll and Sem (CA)
McKendree U (IL)
Merrimack Coll (MA)
Miami Dade Coll (FL)
Miami U (OH)
Michigan State U (MI)
Midwestern State U (TX)
Minnesota State U Mankato (MN)
Minot State U (ND)
Missouri Baptist U (MO)
Missouri State U (MO)
Missouri Valley Coll (MO)
Montana State U (MT)
Montana State U Billings (MT)
Morningside Coll (IA)
Mount Mary U (WI)
Mount Mercy U (IA)
Mount Vernon Nazarene U (OH)
Nebraska Wesleyan U (NE)
New Mexico Highlands U (NM)
New York U (NY)
Niagara U (NY)
Nicholls State U (LA)
North Carolina Ag and Tech State U (NC)
North Carolina State U (NC)
North Dakota State U (ND)
Northeastern State U (OK)
Northern Kentucky U (KY)
Northern Michigan U (MI)
Northland Coll (WI)
Northwestern Oklahoma State U (OK)
Northwest Missouri State U (MO)
Notre Dame of Maryland U (MD)
Oakland City U (IN)
Ohio Northern U (OH)
Oklahoma Baptist U (OK)
Oklahoma Christian U (OK)
Oklahoma Wesleyan U (OK)
Olivet Coll (MI)
Olivet Nazarene U (IL)
Our Lady of the Lake U of San Antonio (TX)
Peru State Coll (NE)
Piedmont Coll (GA)
Plymouth State U (NH)
Rhode Island Coll (RI)
Rider U (NJ)
Saginaw Valley State U (MI)
Saint Francis U (PA)
Shawnee State U (OH)
Southeastern Oklahoma State U (OK)
Southeastern U (FL)
Southeast Missouri State U (MO)
Southern Illinois U Edwardsville (IL)
Southern New Hampshire U (NH)
Southern Utah U (UT)
Southwest Baptist U (MO)
State U of New York at Fredonia (NY)
State U of New York at New Paltz (NY)
State U of New York at Oswego (NY)
State U of New York Coll at Cortland (NY)
State U of New York Coll at Old Westbury (NY)
State U of New York Coll of Environmental Science and Forestry (NY)
Summit U (PA)
Tabor Coll (KS)
Tarleton State U (TX)
Temple U (PA)
Texas A&M Intl U (TX)
Texas Christian U (TX)
Trine U (IN)
Union Coll (KY)
Union Coll (NE)
Union U (TN)
Universidad del Turabo (PR)
The U of Akron (OH)
U of Alberta (AB, Canada)
The U of Arizona (AZ)
The U of British Columbia (BC, Canada)
U of Central Arkansas (AR)
U of Central Florida (FL)
U of Central Oklahoma (OK)
U of Charleston (WV)
U of Dayton (OH)
The U of Findlay (OH)
U of Georgia (GA)
U of Great Falls (MT)
U of Indianapolis (IN)
The U of Iowa (IA)
U of Kentucky (KY)
U of Lethbridge (AB, Canada)
U of Maine at Machias (ME)
U of Maine at Presque Isle (ME)
U of Mary Hardin-Baylor (TX)
U of Michigan–Dearborn (MI)
U of Michigan–Flint (MI)
U of Minnesota, Duluth (MN)
U of Minnesota, Twin Cities Campus (MN)
U of Mississippi (MS)
U of Missouri (MO)
The U of Montana (MT)
The U of Montana Western (MT)
U of Nebraska–Lincoln (NE)
U of Nevada, Las Vegas (NV)
The U of North Carolina at Pembroke (NC)
U of North Dakota (ND)
U of Northern Iowa (IA)
U of North Florida (FL)
U of Notre Dame (IN)
U of Oklahoma (OK)
U of Regina (SK, Canada)
U of Rio Grande (OH)
U of St. Francis (IL)
U of Saint Francis (IN)
U of St. Thomas (MN)
The U of South Dakota (SD)
U of South Florida (FL)
The U of Tennessee at Chattanooga (TN)
The U of Tennessee at Martin (TN)
The U of Toledo (OH)
U of Toronto (ON, Canada)
U of Vermont (VT)
U of Windsor (ON, Canada)
U of Wisconsin–Eau Claire (WI)
U of Wisconsin–La Crosse (WI)
U of Wisconsin–Platteville (WI)
U of Wisconsin–River Falls (WI)
U of Wisconsin–Stout (WI)
U of Wisconsin–Superior (WI)
Upper Iowa U (IA)
Ursuline Coll (OH)
Utah State U (UT)
Utah Valley U (UT)
Valley City State U (ND)
Valparaiso U (IN)
Vincennes U (IN)
Viterbo U (WI)
Walsh U (OH)
Warner Pacific Coll (OR)
Washington State U (WA)
Washington U in St. Louis (MO)
Waynesburg U (PA)
Wayne State Coll (NE)
Wayne State U (MI)
Weber State U (UT)
Webster U (MO)
Western Carolina U (NC)
Western Governors U (UT)
Western State Colorado U (CO)
Western Washington U (WA)
Widener U (PA)
William Penn U (IA)
Wilmington U (DE)
Winona State U (MN)
Wright State U (OH)
Xavier U (OH)
Xavier U of Louisiana (LA)

York Coll of Pennsylvania (PA)
Youngstown State U (OH)

SCIENCE TECHNOLOGIES
Marylhurst U (OR)

SCIENCE TECHNOLOGIES RELATED
Arizona State U at the Downtown Phoenix campus (AZ)
Arizona State U at the Polytechnic campus (AZ)
Bowling Green State U (OH)
Bridgewater State U (MA)
Kean U (NJ)
Madonna U (MI)
North Carolina State U (NC)
Northern Arizona U (AZ)
The U of Arizona (AZ)
U of Wisconsin–Stout (WI)
Willamette U (OR)

SCIENCE, TECHNOLOGY AND SOCIETY
Arizona State U at the Polytechnic campus (AZ)
Butler U (IN)
California State Polytechnic U, Pomona (CA)
Claremont McKenna Coll (CA)
Colby Coll (ME)
Cornell U (NY)
Dalhousie U (NS, Canada)
Eastern Michigan U (MI)
Georgetown U (DC)
Georgia Inst of Technology (GA)
Heritage U (WA)
James Madison U (VA)
Lehigh U (PA)
Massachusetts Inst of Technology (MA)
Morrisville State Coll (NY)
New Jersey Inst of Technology (NJ)
North Carolina State U (NC)
Northwestern U (IL)
Penn State U Park (PA)
Pomona Coll (CA)
Rensselaer Polytechnic Inst (NY)
Rutgers, The State U of New Jersey, Newark (NJ)
Scripps Coll (CA)
Stanford U (CA)
Texas Tech U (TX)
U of Alberta (AB, Canada)
U of King's Coll (NS, Canada)
U of Puget Sound (WA)
U of Washington, Bothell (WA)
U of Windsor (ON, Canada)
Vanderbilt U (TN)
Vassar Coll (NY)
Washington U in St. Louis (MO)
Wesleyan U (CT)
Worcester Polytechnic Inst (MA)

SCULPTURE
Aquinas Coll (MI)
Bennington Coll (VT)
Biola U (CA)
Birmingham-Southern Coll (AL)
Boston U (MA)
Bowling Green State U (OH)
Bradley U (IL)
Brigham Young U (UT)
Buffalo State Coll, State U of New York (NY)
California Coll of the Arts (CA)
California State U, Long Beach (CA)
Central Washington U (WA)
Cleveland Inst of Art (OH)
Colorado State U (CO)
Concordia U (QC, Canada)
Dixie State U (UT)
Dominican U (IL)
Drake U (IA)
Emily Carr U of Art + Design (BC, Canada)
Escuela de Artes Plasticas de Puerto Rico (PR)
Ferris State U (MI)
Indiana U–Purdue U Fort Wayne (IN)
Inter American U of Puerto Rico, San Germán Campus (PR)
Kansas City Art Inst (MO)
Laguna Coll of Art & Design (CA)
Marywood U (PA)
Massachusetts Coll of Art and Design (MA)
Minnesota State U Mankato (MN)
Mount Allison U (NB, Canada)
Northern Michigan U (MI)
Northwest Nazarene U (ID)
Ohio Northern U (OH)
Ohio U (OH)
Otis Coll of Art and Design (CA)
Pacific Northwest Coll of Art (OR)
Portland State U (OR)
Pratt Inst (NY)
Providence Coll (RI)
Rhode Island Coll (RI)
Rhode Island School of Design (RI)
Rochester Inst of Technology (NY)
Rutgers, The State U of New Jersey, New Brunswick (NJ)
San Francisco Art Inst (CA)
Savannah Coll of Art and Design (GA)
School of the Art Inst of Chicago (IL)
School of the Museum of Fine Arts, Boston (MA)
Seton Hill U (PA)
State U of New York at New Paltz (NY)
Syracuse U (NY)
Temple U (PA)
Texas Christian U (TX)
The U of Akron (OH)
U of Dallas (TX)
U of Hartford (CT)
U of Houston (TX)
The U of Iowa (IA)
The U of Kansas (KS)
U of Massachusetts Dartmouth (MA)
U of Miami (FL)
U of Michigan (MI)
U of New Haven (CT)
U of Oregon (OR)
U of Regina (SK, Canada)
The U of Texas at El Paso (TX)
The U of the Arts (PA)
U of Washington (WA)
U of Windsor (ON, Canada)
Virginia Commonwealth U (VA)
Washington U in St. Louis (MO)
Western State Colorado U (CO)
Western Washington U (WA)

SECONDARY EDUCATION
Abilene Christian U (TX)
Alabama State U (AL)
Albertus Magnus Coll (CT)
Albright Coll (PA)
Alice Lloyd Coll (KY)
Alma Coll (MI)
American U (DC)
The American U in Dubai (United Arab Emirates)
Andrews U (MI)
Anna Maria Coll (MA)
Arcadia U (PA)
Arizona Christian U (AZ)
Arizona State U at the Downtown Phoenix campus (AZ)
Arizona State U at the Polytechnic campus (AZ)
Arizona State U at the Tempe campus (AZ)
Arizona State U at the West campus (AZ)
Ashland U (OH)
Auburn U (AL)
Auburn U at Montgomery (AL)
Augsburg Coll (MN)
Augustana Coll (SD)
Austin Coll (TX)
Baker U (KS)
Baylor U (TX)
Belmont U (TN)
Beloit Coll (WI)
Bemidji State U (MN)
Benedictine Coll (KS)
Berry Coll (GA)
Bethel Coll (IN)
Biola U (CA)
Birmingham-Southern Coll (AL)
Blackburn Coll (IL)
Black Hills State U (SD)
Bluefield Coll (VA)
Boston Coll (MA)
Bowie State U (MD)
Bucknell U (PA)
Buffalo State Coll, State U of New York (NY)
Butler U (IN)
Caldwell U (NJ)
Calvary Bible Coll and Theological Sem (MO)
Calvin Coll (MI)
Campbellsville U (KY)
Canisius Coll (NY)
Cardinal Stritch U (WI)
Caribbean U (PR)
Carroll Coll (MT)
Carson-Newman U (TN)
Castleton State Coll (VT)
The Catholic U of America (DC)
Cazenovia Coll (NY)
Cedar Crest Coll (PA)
Central Methodist U (MO)
Central State U (OH)
Chaminade U of Honolulu (HI)
Champlain Coll (VT)
Charleston Southern U (SC)
Chipola Coll (FL)
The Citadel, The Military Coll of South Carolina (SC)
City Coll of the City U of New York (NY)
Clarke U (IA)
Clark U (MA)
Coe Coll (IA)
Coll of Charleston (SC)
The Coll of New Jersey (NJ)
Coll of Saint Benedict (MN)
Coll of Saint Mary (NE)
Coll of the Atlantic (ME)
Concordia U Chicago (IL)
Concordia U, Nebraska (NE)
Concordia U, St. Paul (MN)
Concordia U Texas (TX)
Concordia U Wisconsin (WI)
Concord U (WV)
Corban U (OR)
Cornell Coll (IA)
Creighton U (NE)
Cumberland U (TN)
Daytona State Coll (FL)
Defiance Coll (OH)
Delaware State U (DE)
DePaul U (IL)
Dickinson State U (ND)
Dixie State U (UT)
Dominican Coll (NY)
Dominican U (IL)
Drake U (IA)
Drexel U (PA)
East Central U (OK)
Eastern Connecticut State U (CT)
East Stroudsburg U of Pennsylvania (PA)
Elmhurst Coll (IL)
Elmira Coll (NY)
Elon U (NC)
Emmanuel Coll (MA)
Emporia State U (KS)
Endicott Coll (MA)
Evangel U (MO)
Fairmont State U (WV)
Fitchburg State U (MA)
Flagler Coll (FL)
Florida Gulf Coast U (FL)
Fontbonne U (MO)
Fordham U (NY)
Fort Lewis Coll (CO)
Franklin Pierce U (NH)
Furman U (SC)
Gettysburg Coll (PA)
Gonzaga U (WA)
Gordon Coll (MA)
Graceland U (IA)
Grambling State U (LA)
Grand Valley State U (MI)
Grand View U (IA)
Granite State Coll (NH)
Great Basin Coll (NV)
Greensboro Coll (NC)
Grove City Coll (PA)
Guilford Coll (NC)
Gustavus Adolphus Coll (MN)
Gwynedd Mercy U (PA)
Hamline U (MN)
Hampton U (VA)
Hannibal-LaGrange U (MO)
Harding U (AR)
Harris-Stowe State U (MO)
Hastings Coll (NE)
Heidelberg U (OH)
High Point U (NC)
Hillsdale Free Will Baptist Coll (OK)
Hofstra U (NY)
Houghton Coll (NY)
Houston Baptist U (TX)
Humboldt State U (CA)
Hunter Coll of the City U of New York (NY)
Husson U (ME)
Huston-Tillotson U (TX)
Illinois Coll (IL)
Indiana U Bloomington (IN)
Indiana U East (IN)
Indiana U Kokomo (IN)
Indiana U Northwest (IN)
Indiana U–Purdue U Fort Wayne (IN)
Indiana U South Bend (IN)
Indiana U Southeast (IN)
Inter American U of Puerto Rico, San Germán Campus (PR)
Iona Coll (NY)
Iowa State U of Science and Technology (IA)
Ithaca Coll (NY)
Jacksonville State U (AL)
Jacksonville U (FL)
Jarvis Christian Coll (TX)
John Brown U (AR)
John Carroll U (OH)
Johnson State Coll (VT)
Judson U (IL)
Kansas State U (KS)
Kansas Wesleyan U (KS)
Keene State Coll (NH)
Keuka Coll (NY)
The King's U Coll (AB, Canada)
Knox Coll (IL)
Kutztown U of Pennsylvania (PA)
Kuyper Coll (MI)
Lake Erie Coll (OH)
Langston U (OK)
La Salle U (PA)
Lasell Coll (MA)
Lawrence U (WI)
Le Moyne Coll (NY)
Lesley U (MA)
LeTourneau U (TX)
Lewis U (IL)
Lincoln Memorial U (TN)
Lincoln U (PA)
Lindenwood U (MO)
Lindsey Wilson Coll (KY)
Lock Haven U of Pennsylvania (PA)
Louisiana Coll (LA)
Lourdes U (OH)
Loyola U Chicago (IL)
Lubbock Christian U (TX)
Maharishi U of Management (IA)
Manchester U (IN)
Manhattanville Coll (NY)
Mansfield U of Pennsylvania (PA)
Marian U (IN)
Marian U (WI)
Marietta Coll (OH)
Marquette U (WI)
Marshall U (WV)
Mars Hill U (NC)
The Master's Coll and Sem (CA)
McKendree U (IL)
McMurry U (TX)
McNeese State U (LA)
Medaille Coll (NY)
Merrimack Coll (MA)
Michigan State U (MI)
MidAmerica Nazarene U (KS)
Midwestern State U (TX)
Minnesota State U Mankato (MN)
Mississippi State U (MS)
Mississippi Valley State U (MS)
Missouri Baptist U (MO)
Missouri Southern State U (MO)
Missouri State U (MO)
Missouri U of Science and Technology (MO)
Missouri Valley Coll (MO)
Molloy Coll (NY)
Monmouth U (NJ)
Montana State U Billings (MT)
Mount Aloysius Coll (PA)
Mount Marty Coll (SD)
Mount Mercy U (IA)
Mount Saint Mary Coll (NY)
Mount Saint Mary's U (CA)
National U (CA)
Nazareth Coll of Rochester (NY)
New England Coll (NH)
Newman U (KS)
New Mexico State U (NM)
Niagara U (NY)
Nichols Coll (MA)
North Carolina Ag and Tech State U (NC)
North Central Coll (IL)
Northern Kentucky U (KY)
Northern Michigan U (MI)
Northern State U (SD)
Northland Coll (WI)
Northwest Christian U (OR)
Northwestern Coll (IA)
Northwestern Oklahoma State U (OK)
Northwestern U (IL)
Northwest Nazarene U (ID)
Northwest U (WA)
Nova Southeastern U (FL)
Oakland City U (IN)
Ohio U (OH)
Ohio Valley U (WV)
Ohio Wesleyan U (OH)
Oklahoma Christian U (OK)
Oklahoma City U (OK)
Oklahoma State U (OK)
Pacific U (OR)
Penn State Abington (PA)
Penn State Altoona (PA)
Penn State Beaver (PA)
Penn State Berks (PA)
Penn State Brandywine (PA)
Penn State DuBois (PA)
Penn State Erie, The Behrend Coll (PA)
Penn State Fayette, The Eberly Campus (PA)
Penn State Greater Allegheny (PA)
Penn State Hazleton (PA)
Penn State Lehigh Valley (PA)
Penn State Mont Alto (PA)
Penn State New Kensington (PA)
Penn State Schuylkill (PA)
Penn State Shenango (PA)
Penn State U Park (PA)
Penn State Wilkes-Barre (PA)
Penn State Worthington Scranton (PA)
Penn State York (PA)
Peru State Coll (NE)
Piedmont Coll (GA)
Polytechnic U of Puerto Rico (PR)
Prescott Coll (AZ)
Rhode Island Coll (RI)
Rider U (NJ)
Ripon Coll (WI)
Rivier U (NH)
Rockford U (IL)
Rockhurst U (MO)
Rocky Mountain Coll (MT)
Roger Williams U (RI)
Sacred Heart U (CT)
Saint Anselm Coll (NH)
St. Catherine U (MN)
Saint Francis U (PA)
Saint John's U (MN)
Saint Joseph's U (PA)
Saint Leo U (FL)
Saint Michael's Coll (VT)
St. Thomas Aquinas Coll (NY)
St. Thomas U (FL)
Salve Regina U (RI)
San Diego Christian Coll (CA)
Shepherd U (WV)
Siena Heights U (MI)
Simmons Coll (MA)
Simpson Coll (IA)
Slippery Rock U of Pennsylvania (PA)
Southern Connecticut State U (CT)
Southwestern Assemblies of God U (TX)
Spalding U (KY)
Spring Hill Coll (AL)
State U of New York at Fredonia (NY)
State U of New York at Oswego (NY)
State U of New York Coll at Cortland (NY)
State U of New York Coll at Old Westbury (NY)
Summit U (PA)
Susquehanna U (PA)
Tabor Coll (KS)
Tarleton State U (TX)
Temple U (PA)
Tennessee Wesleyan Coll (TN)

Texas Christian U (TX)
Thiel Coll (PA)
Thomas More Coll (KY)
Toccoa Falls Coll (GA)
Tougaloo Coll (MS)
Trent U (ON, Canada)
Trine U (IN)
Troy U (AL)
Tusculum Coll (TN)
Union Coll (KY)
Union Inst & U (OH)
Union U (TN)
Unity Coll (ME)
Universidad Metropolitana (PR)
Université de Montréal (QC, Canada)
Université de Sherbrooke (QC, Canada)
Université du Québec en Outaouais (QC, Canada)
The U of Alabama (AL)
The U of Alabama at Birmingham (AL)
The U of Alabama in Huntsville (AL)
U of Alaska Fairbanks (AK)
U of Arkansas at Pine Bluff (AR)
The U of British Columbia (BC, Canada)
U of Central Missouri (MO)
U of Central Oklahoma (OK)
U of Cincinnati (OH)
U of Dallas (TX)
U of Dayton (OH)
U of Dubuque (IA)
The U of Findlay (OH)
U of Great Falls (MT)
U of Guam (GU)
U of Hartford (CT)
U of Hawaii at Manoa (HI)
U of Idaho (ID)
U of Indianapolis (IN)
The U of Kansas (KS)
U of Louisiana at Lafayette (LA)
U of Maine (ME)
U of Maine at Presque Isle (ME)
U of Maryland, Coll Park (MD)
U of Michigan (MI)
U of Michigan–Dearborn (MI)
U of Minnesota, Morris (MN)
U of Minnesota, Twin Cities Campus (MN)
U of Missouri (MO)
U of Missouri–Kansas City (MO)
U of Missouri–St. Louis (MO)
The U of Montana (MT)
The U of Montana Western (MT)
U of Nevada, Las Vegas (NV)
U of New Mexico (NM)
U of New Orleans (LA)
U of North Alabama (AL)
The U of North Carolina at Greensboro (NC)
U of North Florida (FL)
U of Pittsburgh at Bradford (PA)
U of Portland (OR)
U of Regina (SK, Canada)
U of Rhode Island (RI)
U of Rio Grande (OH)
U of St. Thomas (TX)
U of San Francisco (CA)
U of Saskatchewan (SK, Canada)
The U of Scranton (PA)
U of South Alabama (AL)
U of South Carolina Aiken (SC)
U of South Carolina Upstate (SC)
The U of South Dakota (SD)
The U of Tampa (FL)
The U of Tennessee at Chattanooga (TN)
U of the Cumberlands (KY)
The U of Toledo (OH)
U of Valley Forge (PA)
U of Vermont (VT)
The U of Western Ontario (ON, Canada)
U of Windsor (ON, Canada)
U of Wisconsin–Oshkosh (WI)
U of Wisconsin–Platteville (WI)
U of Wisconsin–River Falls (WI)
U of Wisconsin–Stevens Point (WI)
U of Wyoming (WY)
Urbana U (OH)
Utah State U (UT)
Utica Coll (NY)
Valley City State U (ND)
Valparaiso U (IN)
Vanderbilt U (TN)
Vanguard U of Southern California (CA)
Villanova U (PA)
Virginia Polytechnic Inst and State U (VA)
Virginia Wesleyan Coll (VA)
Wagner Coll (NY)
Waldorf Coll (IA)
Walsh U (OH)
Warner Pacific Coll (OR)
Wartburg Coll (IA)
Washington State U (WA)
Washington U in St. Louis (MO)
Waynesburg U (PA)
Webster U (MO)
Welch Coll (TN)
Wells Coll (NY)
Western New England U (MA)
Western Oregon U (OR)
West Liberty U (WV)
Westminster Coll (MO)
West Texas A&M U (TX)
West Virginia State U (WV)
West Virginia Wesleyan Coll (WV)
Wheaton Coll (IL)
Whitworth U (WA)
Wichita State U (KS)
William Jewell Coll (MO)
William Paterson U of New Jersey (NJ)
William Penn U (IA)
William Woods U (MO)
Wright State U (OH)
Xavier U of Louisiana (LA)
York Coll of the City U of New York (NY)
Youngstown State U (OH)

SECONDARY SCHOOL ADMINISTRATION/ PRINCIPALSHIP
Charleston Southern U (SC)
Creighton U (NE)
The U of North Carolina at Pembroke (NC)

SECURITIES SERVICES ADMINISTRATION
American Public U System (WV)
Central Penn Coll (PA)
Henley-Putnam U (CA)
St. John's U (NY)
Saint Louis U (MO)
Washburn U (KS)
Webber Intl U (FL)

SECURITY AND LOSS PREVENTION
Anna Maria Coll (MA)
Farmingdale State Coll (NY)
Johnson & Wales U (RI)
Lewis U (IL)
National U (CA)
Northern Michigan U (MI)

SELLING SKILLS AND SALES
Bradley U (IL)
Purdue U (IN)
St. Catherine U (MN)
U of Central Oklahoma (OK)
U of Memphis (TN)
Weber State U (UT)
William Paterson U of New Jersey (NJ)

SIGN LANGUAGE INTERPRETATION AND TRANSLATION
Augustana Coll (SD)
Bethel Coll (IN)
Bloomsburg U of Pennsylvania (PA)
Columbia Coll Chicago (IL)
Eastern Kentucky U (KY)
Framingham State U (MA)
Gallaudet U (DC)
Goshen Coll (IN)
Indiana U–Purdue U Indianapolis (IN)
Kent State U (OH)
Madonna U (MI)
Maryville Coll (TN)
Mount Aloysius Coll (PA)
Quincy U (IL)
Rochester Inst of Technology (NY)
Troy U (AL)
Universidad del Turabo (PR)
U of Arkansas at Little Rock (AR)
U of Cincinnati (OH)
U of Louisville (KY)
U of New Hampshire (NH)
U of New Hampshire at Manchester (NH)
U of New Mexico (NM)
U of Northern Colorado (CO)
U of North Florida (FL)
Valdosta State U (GA)
Western Oregon U (OR)
William Woods U (MO)
Wright State U (OH)

SLAVIC, BALTIC, AND ALBANIAN LANGUAGES RELATED
Rutgers, The State U of New Jersey, Newark (NJ)

SLAVIC LANGUAGES
Boston Coll (MA)
Columbia U (NY)
Columbia U, School of General Studies (NY)
Harvard U (MA)
Indiana U Bloomington (IN)
Northwestern U (IL)
Princeton U (NJ)
Stanford U (CA)
U of Alberta (AB, Canada)
The U of British Columbia (BC, Canada)
U of California, Berkeley (CA)
U of California, Los Angeles (CA)
U of California, Santa Barbara (CA)
U of Chicago (IL)
U of Illinois at Chicago (IL)
The U of Kansas (KS)
U of Minnesota, Twin Cities Campus (MN)
U of Pittsburgh (PA)
U of Toronto (ON, Canada)
U of Virginia (VA)
U of Washington (WA)
Wayne State U (MI)

SLAVIC STUDIES
Barnard Coll (NY)
Baylor U (TX)
Columbia U, School of General Studies (NY)
Connecticut Coll (CT)
Lawrence U (WI)
Northwestern U (IL)
U of Ottawa (ON, Canada)
U of Waterloo (ON, Canada)

SMALL BUSINESS ADMINISTRATION
Adams State U (CO)
Anna Maria Coll (MA)
Arcadia U (PA)
Avila U (MO)
Babson Coll (MA)
Bradley U (IL)
Carson-Newman U (TN)
Chowan U (NC)
Dalhousie U (NS, Canada)
Florida Inst of Technology (FL)
Florida Southern Coll (FL)
Hilbert Coll (NY)
Husson U (ME)
Lincoln U (CA)
North Central Coll (IL)
Northern Michigan U (MI)
Saint Joseph's U (PA)
The U of Scranton (PA)

SOCIAL AND PHILOSOPHICAL FOUNDATIONS OF EDUCATION
Dickinson Coll (PA)
Goddard Coll (VT)
Hope Intl U (CA)
National U (CA)
Northwestern U (IL)
Transylvania U (KY)
Washington U in St. Louis (MO)

SOCIAL PSYCHOLOGY
Augsburg Coll (MN)
Bennington Coll (VT)
Brigham Young U (UT)
Clarion U of Pennsylvania (PA)
Florida Atlantic U (FL)
Goddard Coll (VT)
Grand Valley State U (MI)
Lawrence U (WI)
Maryville U of Saint Louis (MO)
Northwest Missouri State U (MO)
Palo Alto U (CA)
Penn State Abington (PA)
U of California, Irvine (CA)
U of New England (ME)
U of Wisconsin–Superior (WI)
Western Michigan U (MI)

SOCIAL SCIENCES
Adelphi U (NY)
Albertus Magnus Coll (CT)
Alice Lloyd Coll (KY)
Alverno Coll (WI)
American Intl Coll (MA)
American U (DC)
Andrews U (MI)
Aquinas Coll (MI)
Arizona State U at the West campus (AZ)
Asbury U (KY)
Ashland U (OH)
Athens State U (AL)
Azusa Pacific U (CA)
Ball State U (IN)
Belhaven U (MS)
Bemidji State U (MN)
Benedictine Coll (KS)
Benedictine U (IL)
Bennington Coll (VT)
Berry Coll (GA)
Bethany Lutheran Coll (MN)
Bethel Coll (IN)
Bethel U (MN)
Binghamton U, State U of New York (NY)
Biola U (CA)
Black Hills State U (SD)
Bluefield State Coll (WV)
Bluffton U (OH)
Bowling Green State U (OH)
Caldwell U (NJ)
California Lutheran U (CA)
California State U, Los Angeles (CA)
California State U, Monterey Bay (CA)
California State U, Sacramento (CA)
California State U, San Bernardino (CA)
California State U, San Marcos (CA)
California State U, Stanislaus (CA)
California U of Pennsylvania (PA)
Calumet Coll of Saint Joseph (IN)
Calvin Coll (MI)
Campbellsville U (KY)
Canisius Coll (NY)
Castleton State Coll (VT)
Cazenovia Coll (NY)
Central Coll (IA)
Central Connecticut State U (CT)
Central Michigan U (MI)
Central Washington U (WA)
Chaminade U of Honolulu (HI)
Charleston Southern U (SC)
Cheyney U of Pennsylvania (PA)
Clarkson U (NY)
Cleveland State U (OH)
Coll of Saint Benedict (MN)
Coll of Saint Mary (NE)
The Coll of St. Scholastica (MN)
Colorado Mesa U (CO)
Colorado State U (CO)
Colorado State U–Pueblo (CO)
Concordia Coll (MN)
Concordia Coll–New York (NY)
Concordia U, Nebraska (NE)
Corban U (OR)
Cornell U (NY)
Cumberland U (TN)
Defiance Coll (OH)
Delta State U (MS)
DePaul U (IL)
Dickinson State U (ND)
Doane Coll (NE)
Dominican Coll (NY)
Dowling Coll (NY)
Eastern Michigan U (MI)
Eastern New Mexico U (NM)
East Stroudsburg U of Pennsylvania (PA)
Edgewood Coll (WI)
Edinboro U of Pennsylvania (PA)
Elizabethtown Coll (PA)
Elmira Coll (NY)
Emporia State U (KS)
Faulkner U (AL)
Ferrum Coll (VA)
Florida Atlantic U (FL)
Florida Southern Coll (FL)
Florida State U (FL)
Fontbonne U (MO)
Franklin U (OH)
Frostburg State U (MD)
Gettysburg Coll (PA)
Governors State U (IL)
Grand Valley State U (MI)
Granite State Coll (NH)
Great Basin Coll (NV)
Gustavus Adolphus Coll (MN)
Hampton U (VA)
Harding U (AR)
Harrison Middleton U (AZ)
Harvard U (MA)
Hope Intl U (CA)
Howard Payne U (TX)
Humboldt State U (CA)
Illinois Inst of Technology (IL)
Ithaca Coll (NY)
Johns Hopkins U (MD)
Johnson C. Smith U (NC)
Kansas State U (KS)
Keene State Coll (NH)
Kentucky State U (KY)
Keuka Coll (NY)
Keystone Coll (PA)
The King's U Coll (AB, Canada)
Kutztown U of Pennsylvania (PA)
Lake Erie Coll (OH)
La Salle U (PA)
LeMoyne-Owen Coll (TN)
Lesley U (MA)
Liberty U (VA)
Lock Haven U of Pennsylvania (PA)
Long Island U–LIU Brooklyn (NY)
Loyola U New Orleans (LA)
Manchester U (IN)
Mansfield U of Pennsylvania (PA)
Mars Hill U (NC)
Marylhurst U (OR)
Marywood U (PA)
Mayville State U (ND)
McKendree U (IL)
Mercy Coll (NY)
Metropolitan State U (MN)
Michigan State U (MI)
Michigan Technological U (MI)
Minnesota State U Mankato (MN)
Minot State U (ND)
Misericordia U (PA)
Mississippi U for Women (MS)
Missouri Baptist U (MO)
Montreat Coll, Montreat (NC)
Morehead State U (KY)
Mount Mary U (WI)
Mount Saint Mary Coll (NY)
Mount Saint Mary's U (CA)
Muhlenberg Coll (PA)
National U (CA)
Nazareth Coll of Rochester (NY)
New Coll of Florida (FL)
New York U (NY)
Niagara U (NY)
North Carolina Ag and Tech State U (NC)
North Central Coll (IL)
North Dakota State U (ND)
Northern Kentucky U (KY)
Northwestern Oklahoma State U (OK)
Oakland City U (IN)
Oklahoma Baptist U (OK)
Olivet Coll (MI)
Olivet Nazarene U (IL)
Our Lady of the Lake U of San Antonio (TX)
Pace U (NY)
Peru State Coll (NE)
Piedmont Coll (GA)
Plymouth State U (NH)
Point Loma Nazarene U (CA)
Point U (GA)
Portland State U (OR)
Providence Coll (RI)
Quinnipiac U (CT)
Radford U (VA)
Ramapo Coll of New Jersey (NJ)
Regis U (CO)
Robert Morris U (PA)
Rockford U (IL)
Roosevelt U (IL)
Rosemont Coll (PA)
Rust Coll (MS)
The Sage Colls (NY)

St. Andrews U (NC)
St. Catherine U (MN)
St. Gregory's U, Shawnee (OK)
Saint John's U (MN)
St. John's U (NY)
St. Joseph's Coll, Long Island Campus (NY)
St. Joseph's Coll, New York (NY)
Saint Peter's U (NJ)
St. Thomas Aquinas Coll (NY)
Salisbury U (MD)
San Diego State U (CA)
San Jose State U (CA)
Sarah Lawrence Coll (NY)
Shawnee State U (OH)
Shimer Coll (IL)
Siena Heights U (MI)
South Carolina State U (SC)
Southeast Missouri State U (MO)
Southern Arkansas U–Magnolia (AR)
Southern Illinois U Carbondale (IL)
Southern New Hampshire U (NH)
Southern Oregon U (OR)
Southwestern Adventist U (TX)
Spalding U (KY)
Spring Hill Coll (AL)
State U of New York Coll at Old Westbury (NY)
State U of New York Empire State Coll (NY)
Stetson U (FL)
Sul Ross State U (TX)
Texas A&M Intl U (TX)
Towson U (MD)
Trent U (ON, Canada)
Trine U (IN)
Troy U (AL)
Union Coll (NY)
United States Air Force Acad (CO)
Universidad del Turabo (PR)
Université de Montréal (QC, Canada)
Université du Québec en Outaouais (QC, Canada)
U at Buffalo, the State U of New York (NY)
The U of Akron (OH)
U of Alaska Southeast, Sitka Campus (AK)
U of Arkansas at Pine Bluff (AR)
U of Bridgeport (CT)
The U of British Columbia (BC, Canada)
U of California, Irvine (CA)
U of Central Florida (FL)
U of Chicago (IL)
U of Dallas (TX)
U of Denver (CO)
U of Great Falls (MT)
U of Hawaii–West Oahu (HI)
U of Houston–Downtown (TX)
U of La Verne (CA)
U of Lethbridge (AB, Canada)
U of Maine at Augusta (ME)
U of Maine at Fort Kent (ME)
U of Maryland U Coll (MD)
U of Massachusetts Boston (MA)
U of Michigan (MI)
U of Michigan–Dearborn (MI)
U of Michigan–Flint (MI)
U of Minnesota, Morris (MN)
U of Mobile (AL)
The U of Montana (MT)
U of Montevallo (AL)
U of Nevada, Las Vegas (NV)
U of North Alabama (AL)
U of North Dakota (ND)
U of Northern Colorado (CO)
U of North Georgia (GA)
U of North Texas (TX)
U of Oregon (OR)
U of Ottawa (ON, Canada)
U of Pennsylvania (PA)
U of Pittsburgh (PA)
U of Pittsburgh at Bradford (PA)
U of Pittsburgh at Greensburg (PA)
U of Regina (SK, Canada)
U of Rio Grande (OH)
U of St. Thomas (MN)
U of South Carolina Beaufort (SC)
U of Southern California (CA)
U of Southern Indiana (IN)
U of South Florida (FL)
U of South Florida, St. Petersburg (FL)
U of South Florida Sarasota-Manatee (FL)
The U of Texas at Tyler (TX)
The U of Texas–Pan American (TX)
U of the Pacific (CA)
U of the Virgin Islands (VI)
U of Utah (UT)
U of Washington (WA)
U of West Florida (FL)
U of Windsor (ON, Canada)
U of Wisconsin–Platteville (WI)
U of Wisconsin–River Falls (WI)
U of Wisconsin–Stevens Point (WI)
U of Wisconsin–Stout (WI)
U of Wisconsin–Superior (WI)
U of Wisconsin–Whitewater (WI)
U of Wyoming (WY)
Upper Iowa U (IA)
Utica Coll (NY)
Valley City State U (ND)
Valparaiso U (IN)
Vanderbilt U (TN)
Virginia Wesleyan Coll (VA)
Viterbo U (WI)
Warner Pacific Coll (OR)
Washington State U (WA)
Washington State U Vancouver (WA)
Washington U in St. Louis (MO)
Waynesburg U (PA)
Wayne State Coll (NE)
Webster U (MO)
Wesleyan Coll (GA)
Western Kentucky U (KY)
Western Oregon U (OR)
West Liberty U (WV)
Westminster Coll (UT)
West Texas A&M U (TX)
Whittier Coll (CA)
Widener U (PA)
Worcester Polytechnic Inst (MA)
Wright State U (OH)
Youngstown State U (OH)

SOCIAL SCIENCES RELATED

The American U of Paris (France)
Anna Maria Coll (MA)
Bard Coll at Simon's Rock (MA)
Bloomsburg U of Pennsylvania (PA)
Boston U (MA)
Bowling Green State U (OH)
California Polytechnic State U, San Luis Obispo (CA)
California U of Pennsylvania (PA)
Central Michigan U (MI)
Clarion U of Pennsylvania (PA)
Cleveland State U (OH)
Colby-Sawyer Coll (NH)
The Coll of Idaho (ID)
Concordia U (QC, Canada)
Concordia U Texas (TX)
Covenant Coll (GA)
Curry Coll (MA)
Eastern Oregon U (OR)
Elmira Coll (NY)
The Evergreen State Coll (WA)
Georgetown U (DC)
Gettysburg Coll (PA)
Hamline U (MN)
Indiana U of Pennsylvania (PA)
Kalamazoo Coll (MI)
Long Island U–LIU Post (NY)
Mary Baldwin Coll (VA)
Marywood U (PA)
Midwestern State U (TX)
Millersville U of Pennsylvania (PA)
Monmouth U (NJ)
Mount Aloysius Coll (PA)
Mount Holyoke Coll (MA)
Mount Mary U (WI)
New Mexico Highlands U (NM)
New York U (NY)
North Central Coll (IL)
Northern Arizona U (AZ)
Northwestern U (IL)
Oklahoma Wesleyan U (OK)
Plymouth State U (NH)
Prescott Coll (AZ)
Purchase Coll, State U of New York (NY)
Roger Williams U (RI)
Rutgers, The State U of New Jersey, New Brunswick (NJ)
Simon Fraser U (BC, Canada)
Skidmore Coll (NY)
State U of New York Polytechnic Inst (NY)
Towson U (MD)
Union Coll (NE)
United States Military Acad (NY)
The U of Alabama at Birmingham (AL)
U of Alberta (AB, Canada)
U of California, Berkeley (CA)
U of Chicago (IL)
U of Denver (CO)
U of Massachusetts Amherst (MA)
U of New England (ME)
U of Pittsburgh (PA)
U of Regina (SK, Canada)
U of Rhode Island (RI)
U of Rochester (NY)
U of Southern Maine (ME)
The U of Tennessee at Chattanooga (TN)
The U of Texas at San Antonio (TX)
U of Washington, Tacoma (WA)
U of Waterloo (ON, Canada)
The U of Western Ontario (ON, Canada)
U of West Florida (FL)
U of Wisconsin–Green Bay (WI)
Ursinus Coll (PA)
Warren Wilson Coll (NC)
Washington U in St. Louis (MO)
Wesleyan U (CT)
Whitman Coll (WA)
Williams Coll (MA)

SOCIAL SCIENCE TEACHER EDUCATION

Arkansas State U (AR)
Auburn U (AL)
Baylor U (TX)
Biola U (CA)
Blackburn Coll (IL)
Blue Mountain Coll (MS)
Bowling Green State U (OH)
Bradley U (IL)
Brigham Young U (UT)
Buena Vista U (IA)
California Lutheran U (CA)
Campbellsville U (KY)
Carroll Coll (MT)
Central Methodist U (MO)
Central Michigan U (MI)
Central Washington U (WA)
Chowan U (NC)
Coll of Saint Mary (NE)
Concordia U Chicago (IL)
Concordia U, Nebraska (NE)
Corban U (OR)
Delta State U (MS)
Dixie State U (UT)
Dominican Coll (NY)
Dowling Coll (NY)
Eastern Illinois U (IL)
Eastern Michigan U (MI)
East Stroudsburg U of Pennsylvania (PA)
Emmanuel Coll (GA)
Emporia State U (KS)
Fayetteville State U (NC)
Flagler Coll (FL)
Florida Ag and Mech U (FL)
Florida Atlantic U (FL)
Hastings Coll (NE)
Holy Family U (PA)
Jackson State U (MS)
Johnson State Coll (VT)
Judson Coll (AL)
Knox Coll (IL)
Lincoln U (MO)
Lindenwood U (MO)
Lindsey Wilson Coll (KY)
Lubbock Christian U (TX)
Manchester U (IN)
Mansfield U of Pennsylvania (PA)
Marywood U (PA)
Mayville State U (ND)
McKendree U (IL)
Medaille Coll (NY)
Michigan State U (MI)
Millikin U (IL)
Minot State U (ND)
Montana State U (MT)
Montana State U Billings (MT)
Mount St. Mary's U (MD)
Nebraska Wesleyan U (NE)
Northern Michigan U (MI)
Northwest Missouri State U (MO)
Oakland City U (IN)
Ohio Dominican U (OH)
Peru State Coll (NE)
Rhode Island Coll (RI)
Rust Coll (MS)
Saginaw Valley State U (MI)
Saint Mary's U of Minnesota (MN)
Shawnee State U (OH)
Simpson U (CA)
Southeastern U (FL)
Southern Utah U (UT)
Southwest Baptist U (MO)
Tabor Coll (KS)
Union Coll (NE)
Universidad del Turabo (PR)
U of Alberta (AB, Canada)
U of Central Florida (FL)
U of Delaware (DE)
U of Great Falls (MT)
U of Maine at Machias (ME)
U of Mobile (AL)
The U of Montana (MT)
U of Nebraska–Lincoln (NE)
The U of North Carolina at Greensboro (NC)
U of North Dakota (ND)
U of Northern Iowa (IA)
U of Rio Grande (OH)
The U of South Dakota (SD)
U of South Florida (FL)
U of Utah (UT)
U of Wisconsin–River Falls (WI)
U of Wisconsin–Superior (WI)
Upper Iowa U (IA)
Utica Coll (NY)
Valley City State U (ND)
Valparaiso U (IN)
Wartburg Coll (IA)
Washington U in St. Louis (MO)
Wayne State Coll (NE)
Weber State U (UT)
Western Governors U (UT)
Western Michigan U (MI)
Western State Colorado U (CO)
Western Washington U (WA)
William Penn U (IA)
Wilmington U (DE)
Winona State U (MN)
Youngstown State U (OH)

SOCIAL STUDIES TEACHER EDUCATION

Abilene Christian U (TX)
Adams State U (CO)
Alice Lloyd Coll (KY)
Alma Coll (MI)
Alvernia U (PA)
Alverno Coll (WI)
Anderson U (IN)
Aquinas Coll (MI)
Arizona Christian U (AZ)
Arkansas Tech U (AR)
Augustana Coll (SD)
Averett U (VA)
The Baptist Coll of Florida (FL)
Baylor U (TX)
Bethel Coll (IN)
Bethel U (MN)
Bethune-Cookman U (FL)
Biola U (CA)
Bluefield Coll (VA)
Bob Jones U (SC)
Boston U (MA)
Bowling Green State U (OH)
Bradley U (IL)
Buffalo State Coll, State U of New York (NY)
Cabrini Coll (PA)
Cairn U (PA)
Calvin Coll (MI)
Cameron U (OK)
Campbellsville U (KY)
Canisius Coll (NY)
Capital U (OH)
Carroll Coll (MT)
Castleton State Coll (VT)
Cedarville U (OH)
Central Michigan U (MI)
Charleston Southern U (SC)
City Coll of the City U of New York (NY)
Clearwater Christian Coll (FL)
Cleveland State U (OH)
The Coll of Saint Rose (NY)
Colorado State U (CO)
Columbus State U (GA)
Concordia Coll (MN)
Concordia U, St. Paul (MN)
Corban U (OR)
Cornerstone U (MI)
Daemen Coll (NY)
Dowling Coll (NY)
Duquesne U (PA)
East Carolina U (NC)
East Central U (OK)
Eastern Michigan U (MI)
East Texas Baptist U (TX)
Elmira Coll (NY)
Erskine Coll (SC)
Franklin Coll (IN)
Gannon U (PA)
Grace Coll (IN)
Grambling State U (LA)
Grand Valley State U (MI)
Granite State Coll (NH)
Green Mountain Coll (VT)
Greensboro Coll (NC)
Gustavus Adolphus Coll (MN)
Harding U (AR)
Hardin-Simmons U (TX)
Hastings Coll (NE)
Hofstra U (NY)
Holy Family U (PA)
Hope Coll (MI)
Houston Baptist U (TX)
Howard Payne U (TX)
Huntingdon Coll (AL)
Huston-Tillotson U (TX)
Indiana State U (IN)
Indiana U Bloomington (IN)
Indiana U Northwest (IN)
Indiana U–Purdue U Fort Wayne (IN)
Indiana U–Purdue U Indianapolis (IN)
Indiana U South Bend (IN)
Indiana U Southeast (IN)
Inter American U of Puerto Rico, Fajardo Campus (PR)
Inter American U of Puerto Rico, San Germán Campus (PR)
Iona Coll (NY)
Ithaca Coll (NY)
John Brown U (AR)
Johnson State Coll (VT)
Juniata Coll (PA)
Keene State Coll (NH)
Kennesaw State U (GA)
Kent State U (OH)
Kentucky Christian U (KY)
Keuka Coll (NY)
Keystone Coll (PA)
LaGrange Coll (GA)
Le Moyne Coll (NY)
LeMoyne-Owen Coll (TN)
LeTourneau U (TX)
Long Island U–LIU Brooklyn (NY)
Louisiana State U in Shreveport (LA)
Lubbock Christian U (TX)
Madonna U (MI)
Malone U (OH)
Manchester U (IN)
Manhattanville Coll (NY)
Mansfield U of Pennsylvania (PA)
Maranatha Baptist U (WI)
Marian U (WI)
Marist Coll (NY)
Maryville Coll (TN)
Merrimack Coll (MA)
Messiah Coll (PA)
Metropolitan State U (MN)
Miami U (OH)
Michigan State U (MI)
MidAmerica Nazarene U (KS)
Midwestern State U (TX)
Minnesota State U Mankato (MN)
Minnesota State U Moorhead (MN)
Morris Coll (SC)
Mount Mary U (WI)
Mount Vernon Nazarene U (OH)
Nazareth Coll of Rochester (NY)
New York U (NY)
Niagara U (NY)
Nicholls State U (LA)
North Carolina State U (NC)
North Dakota State U (ND)
Northeastern State U (OK)
Northern Michigan U (MI)
North Greenville U (SC)
Northland Coll (WI)
Northwest U (WA)
Nova Southeastern U (FL)
Nyack Coll (NY)
Oakland City U (IN)
Ohio Northern U (OH)
Ohio Wesleyan U (OH)

Oklahoma Baptist U (OK)
Oklahoma Christian U (OK)
Oklahoma Wesleyan U (OK)
Pace U (NY)
Penn State Harrisburg (PA)
Plymouth State U (NH)
Purdue U (IN)
Queens Coll of the City U of New York (NY)
Rivier U (NH)
Roberts Wesleyan Coll (NY)
Rocky Mountain Coll (MT)
St. Catherine U (MN)
St. Edward's U (TX)
St. Francis Coll (NY)
Saint Francis U (PA)
St. Gregory's U, Shawnee (OK)
St. John Fisher Coll (NY)
St. John's U (NY)
St. Joseph's Coll, Long Island Campus (NY)
St. Joseph's Coll, New York (NY)
Saint Mary-of-the-Woods Coll (IN)
St. Mary's U (TX)
St. Olaf Coll (MN)
St. Thomas U (FL)
Siena Heights U (MI)
Southeastern Louisiana U (LA)
Southeastern Oklahoma State U (OK)
Southeast Missouri State U (MO)
Southern New Hampshire U (NH)
Southwestern Assemblies of God U (TX)
Spring Hill Coll (AL)
State U of New York at New Paltz (NY)
State U of New York Coll at Cortland (NY)
State U of New York Coll at Old Westbury (NY)
State U of New York Coll at Potsdam (NY)
Summit U (PA)
Syracuse U (NY)
Tabor Coll (KS)
Taylor U (IN)
Temple U (PA)
Texas A&M Intl U (TX)
Texas Christian U (TX)
Texas Lutheran U (TX)
Trine U (IN)
Union Coll (KY)
The U of Akron (OH)
U of Alberta (AB, Canada)
U of Central Arkansas (AR)
U of Central Oklahoma (OK)
U of Charleston (WV)
U of Delaware (DE)
U of Evansville (IN)
U of Georgia (GA)
U of Great Falls (MT)
U of Indianapolis (IN)
The U of Iowa (IA)
U of Kentucky (KY)
U of Lethbridge (AB, Canada)
U of Mary Hardin-Baylor (TX)
U of Michigan–Dearborn (MI)
U of Michigan–Flint (MI)
U of Minnesota, Duluth (MN)
U of Minnesota, Twin Cities Campus (MN)
U of Mississippi (MS)
U of Missouri (MO)
The U of North Carolina at Greensboro (NC)
The U of North Carolina at Pembroke (NC)
U of Northern Colorado (CO)
U of Northwestern–St. Paul (MN)
U of Oklahoma (OK)
U of Regina (SK, Canada)
U of St. Francis (IL)
U of Saint Francis (IN)
U of St. Thomas (MN)
The U of Tennessee at Chattanooga (TN)
U of the Cumberlands (KY)
The U of Toledo (OH)
U of Vermont (VT)
U of Wisconsin–Eau Claire (WI)
U of Wisconsin–La Crosse (WI)
U of Wisconsin–River Falls (WI)
U of Wisconsin–Superior (WI)
Ursuline Coll (OH)
Utah State U (UT)
Utica Coll (NY)
Virginia Wesleyan Coll (VA)
Viterbo U (WI)
Warner Pacific Coll (OR)
Washington State U (WA)
Washington U in St. Louis (MO)
Waynesburg U (PA)
Wayne State U (MI)
Weber State U (UT)
Webster U (MO)
Western Carolina U (NC)
Western Michigan U (MI)
Western Washington U (WA)
Widener U (PA)
Xavier U of Louisiana (LA)
York Coll of Pennsylvania (PA)
Youngstown State U (OH)

SOCIAL WORK

Abilene Christian U (TX)
Adams State U (CO)
Adelphi U (NY)
Alabama State U (AL)
Albany State U (GA)
Albertus Magnus Coll (CT)
Alvernia U (PA)
Anderson U (IN)
Andrews U (MI)
Angelo State U (TX)
Anna Maria Coll (MA)
Appalachian State U (NC)
Arizona State U at the Downtown Phoenix campus (AZ)
Arkansas State U (AR)
Asbury U (KY)
Ashland U (OH)
Auburn U (AL)
Augsburg Coll (MN)
Austin Peay State U (TN)
Avila U (MO)
Azusa Pacific U (CA)
Ball State U (IN)
Baylor U (TX)
Belhaven U (MS)
Belmont U (TN)
Bemidji State U (MN)
Bennett Coll (NC)
Bethany Coll (WV)
Bethel Coll (KS)
Bethel U (MN)
Biola U (CA)
Bloomsburg U of Pennsylvania (PA)
Bluffton U (OH)
Bowie State U (MD)
Bowling Green State U (OH)
Bowling Green State U-Firelands Coll (OH)
Bradley U (IL)
Bridgewater State U (MA)
Buena Vista U (IA)
Buffalo State Coll, State U of New York (NY)
Cabrini Coll (PA)
Cairn U (PA)
California State U, Fresno (CA)
California State U, Long Beach (CA)
California State U, Los Angeles (CA)
California State U, Sacramento (CA)
California State U, San Bernardino (CA)
California U of Pennsylvania (PA)
Calvin Coll (MI)
Campbellsville U (KY)
Capital U (OH)
Caribbean U (PR)
Carlow U (PA)
Castleton State Coll (VT)
The Catholic U of America (DC)
Cedar Crest Coll (PA)
Cedarville U (OH)
Central Connecticut State U (CT)
Central Michigan U (MI)
Central State U (OH)
Champlain Coll (VT)
Chapman U (CA)
Chatham U (PA)
Christopher Newport U (VA)
Clark Atlanta U (GA)
Clarke U (IA)
Cleveland State U (OH)
Coker Coll (SC)
The Coll at Brockport, State U of New York (NY)
The Coll of New Rochelle (NY)
The Coll of Saint Rose (NY)
The Coll of St. Scholastica (MN)
Coll of Staten Island of the City U of New York (NY)
Coll of the Ozarks (MO)
Colorado Mesa U (CO)
Colorado State U (CO)
Colorado State U–Pueblo (CO)
Columbia Coll (SC)
Concordia Coll (MN)
Concordia Coll–New York (NY)
Concordia U Chicago (IL)
Concordia U Wisconsin (WI)
Concord U (WV)
Cornerstone U (MI)
Creighton U (NE)
Daemen Coll (NY)
Dalhousie U (NS, Canada)
Defiance Coll (OH)
Delaware State U (DE)
Delta State U (MS)
Dickinson State U (ND)
Dominican Coll (NY)
East Carolina U (NC)
East Central U (OK)
Eastern Connecticut State U (CT)
Eastern Kentucky U (KY)
Eastern Michigan U (MI)
Eastern U (PA)
East Tennessee State U (TN)
Edinboro U of Pennsylvania (PA)
Elizabethtown Coll (PA)
Elms Coll (MA)
Evangel U (MO)
Fayetteville State U (NC)
Ferris State U (MI)
Ferrum Coll (VA)
Florida Ag and Mech U (FL)
Florida Atlantic U (FL)
Florida Gulf Coast U (FL)
Florida Intl U (FL)
Florida State U (FL)
Fontbonne U (MO)
Fordham U (NY)
Fort Hays State U (KS)
Franciscan U of Steubenville (OH)
Franklin Pierce U (NH)
Frostburg State U (MD)
Gannon U (PA)
George Mason U (VA)
Georgian Court U (NJ)
Georgia Regents U (GA)
Georgia State U (GA)
Gordon Coll (MA)
Goshen Coll (IN)
Governors State U (IL)
Graceland U (IA)
Grambling State U (LA)
Grand Valley State U (MI)
Great Basin Coll (NV)
Greenville Coll (IL)
Gwynedd Mercy U (PA)
Hampton U (VA)
Hannibal-LaGrange U (MO)
Harding U (AR)
Hardin-Simmons U (TX)
Hawai`i Pacific U (HI)
Heritage U (WA)
Hope Coll (MI)
Howard Payne U (TX)
Howard U (DC)
Humboldt State U (CA)
Illinois State U (IL)
Indiana State U (IN)
Indiana U Bloomington (IN)
Indiana U East (IN)
Indiana U Northwest (IN)
Indiana U–Purdue U Indianapolis (IN)
Indiana U South Bend (IN)
Inter American U of Puerto Rico, Aguadilla Campus (PR)
Inter American U of Puerto Rico, Fajardo Campus (PR)
Iona Coll (NY)
Jackson State U (MS)
Jacksonville State U (AL)
James Madison U (VA)
Jarvis Christian Coll (TX)
Johnson C. Smith U (NC)
Judson Coll (AL)
Juniata Coll (PA)
Kansas State U (KS)
Kentucky Christian U (KY)
Kentucky State U (KY)
Keuka Coll (NY)
Kutztown U of Pennsylvania (PA)
Kuyper Coll (MI)
Lamar U (TX)
La Salle U (PA)
La Sierra U (CA)
Lebanese American U (Lebanon)
Lehman Coll of the City U of New York (NY)
LeMoyne-Owen Coll (TN)
Lewis U (IL)
Limestone Coll (SC)
Lincoln Memorial U (TN)
Lincoln U (MO)
Lindenwood U (MO)
Lipscomb U (TN)
Lock Haven U of Pennsylvania (PA)
Long Island U–LIU Brooklyn (NY)
Long Island U–LIU Post (NY)
Longwood U (VA)
Loras Coll (IA)
Louisiana Coll (LA)
Lourdes U (OH)
Loyola U Chicago (IL)
Lubbock Christian U (TX)
Luther Coll (IA)
Madonna U (MI)
Malone U (OH)
Manchester U (IN)
Mansfield U of Pennsylvania (PA)
Marian U (WI)
Marist Coll (NY)
Marshall U (WV)
Mars Hill U (NC)
Mary Baldwin Coll (VA)
Marywood U (PA)
McDaniel Coll (MD)
McKendree U (IL)
Medgar Evers Coll of the City U of New York (NY)
Mercy Coll (NY)
Meredith Coll (NC)
Messiah Coll (PA)
Metropolitan State U (MN)
Miami U (OH)
Michigan State U (MI)
Middle Tennessee State U (TN)
Midwestern State U (TX)
Millersville U of Pennsylvania (PA)
Milligan Coll (TN)
Millikin U (IL)
Minnesota State U Mankato (MN)
Minnesota State U Moorhead (MN)
Minot State U (ND)
Misericordia U (PA)
Mississippi State U (MS)
Mississippi Valley State U (MS)
Missouri Southern State U (MO)
Missouri State U (MO)
Missouri Western State U (MO)
Molloy Coll (NY)
Monmouth U (NJ)
Morehead State U (KY)
Mount Mary U (WI)
Mount Mercy U (IA)
Mount St. Joseph U (OH)
Mount Saint Mary Coll (NY)
Mount Saint Mary's U (CA)
Mount Vernon Nazarene U (OH)
Murray State U (KY)
Nazareth Coll of Rochester (NY)
Nebraska Wesleyan U (NE)
New Mexico State U (NM)
New York U (NY)
Niagara U (NY)
Norfolk State U (VA)
North Carolina Ag and Tech State U (NC)
North Carolina Central U (NC)
North Carolina State U (NC)
Northeastern Illinois U (IL)
Northeastern State U (OK)
Northern Arizona U (AZ)
Northern Kentucky U (KY)
Northern Michigan U (MI)
Northwestern Coll (IA)
Northwestern Oklahoma State U (OK)
Northwest Nazarene U (ID)
Nyack Coll (NY)
Oakland U (MI)
Oglethorpe U (GA)
Ohio Dominican U (OH)
The Ohio State U (OH)
Ohio U (OH)
Olivet Nazarene U (IL)
Our Lady of the Lake U of San Antonio (TX)
Pacific Lutheran U (WA)
Pacific U (OR)
Park U (MO)
Philander Smith Coll (AR)
Pittsburg State U (KS)
Plymouth State U (NH)
Point Loma Nazarene U (CA)
Portland State U (OR)
Post U (CT)
Prairie View A&M U (TX)
Providence Coll (RI)
Radford U (VA)
Ramapo Coll of New Jersey (NJ)
Regis Coll (MA)
Rhode Island Coll (RI)
Roberts Wesleyan Coll (NY)
Rockford U (IL)
Rust Coll (MS)
Rutgers, The State U of New Jersey, Camden (NJ)
Rutgers, The State U of New Jersey, Newark (NJ)
Rutgers, The State U of New Jersey, New Brunswick (NJ)
Sacred Heart U (CT)
Saginaw Valley State U (MI)
St. Catherine U (MN)
St. Edward's U (TX)
Saint Francis U (PA)
Saint Leo U (FL)
Saint Louis U (MO)
Saint Martin's U (WA)
Saint Mary's Coll (IN)
St. Olaf Coll (MN)
St. Thomas U (NB, Canada)
Salisbury U (MD)
Salve Regina U (RI)
San Diego State U (CA)
San Francisco State U (CA)
San Jose State U (CA)
Savannah State U (GA)
Seattle U (WA)
Seton Hill U (PA)
Shaw U (NC)
Shepherd U (WV)
Shippensburg U of Pennsylvania (PA)
Siena Coll (NY)
Siena Heights U (MI)
Simmons Coll (MA)
Skidmore Coll (NY)
Slippery Rock U of Pennsylvania (PA)
South Carolina State U (SC)
Southeastern Louisiana U (LA)
Southeastern U (FL)
Southeast Missouri State U (MO)
Southern Adventist U (TN)
Southern Arkansas U–Magnolia (AR)
Southern Connecticut State U (CT)
Southern Illinois U Carbondale (IL)
Southern Illinois U Edwardsville (IL)
Southwest Baptist U (MO)
Southwestern Assemblies of God U (TX)
Southwest Minnesota State U (MN)
Spalding U (KY)
State U of New York at Fredonia (NY)
State U of New York at Plattsburgh (NY)
State U of New York Coll at Cortland (NY)
Stephen F. Austin State U (TX)
Stockton U (NJ)
Stony Brook U, State U of New York (NY)
Syracuse U (NY)
Tabor Coll (KS)
Tarleton State U (TX)
Taylor U (IN)
Temple U (PA)
Tennessee State U (TN)
Texas A&M U–Commerce (TX)
Texas A&M U–Kingsville (TX)
Texas Christian U (TX)
Texas Southern U (TX)
Texas State U (TX)
Texas Tech U (TX)
Texas Woman's U (TX)
Trent U (ON, Canada)
Trevecca Nazarene U (TN)
Trinity Christian Coll (IL)
Troy U (AL)
Union Coll (KY)
Union Coll (NE)
Union Inst & U (OH)

Union U (TN)
Universidad del Turabo (PR)
Universidad Metropolitana (PR)
Université de Montréal (QC, Canada)
Université de Sherbrooke (QC, Canada)
Université du Québec en Outaouais (QC, Canada)
U at Albany, State U of New York (NY)
The U of Akron (OH)
The U of Alabama (AL)
The U of Alabama at Birmingham (AL)
U of Alaska Fairbanks (AK)
U of Arkansas (AR)
U of Arkansas at Little Rock (AR)
U of Arkansas at Pine Bluff (AR)
The U of British Columbia (BC, Canada)
The U of British Columbia–Okanagan Campus (BC, Canada)
U of California, Berkeley (CA)
U of Central Florida (FL)
U of Central Missouri (MO)
U of Charleston (WV)
U of Cincinnati (OH)
The U of Findlay (OH)
U of Georgia (GA)
U of Guam (GU)
U of Hawaii at Manoa (HI)
U of Houston–Clear Lake (TX)
U of Houston–Downtown (TX)
U of Illinois at Chicago (IL)
U of Illinois at Springfield (IL)
U of Indianapolis (IN)
The U of Iowa (IA)
The U of Kansas (KS)
U of Kentucky (KY)
U of Louisville (KY)
U of Maine (ME)
U of Maine at Presque Isle (ME)
U of Mary Hardin-Baylor (TX)
U of Maryland, Baltimore County (MD)
U of Memphis (TN)
U of Michigan–Flint (MI)
U of Minnesota, Duluth (MN)
U of Minnesota, Twin Cities Campus (MN)
U of Mississippi (MS)
U of Missouri (MO)
U of Missouri–St. Louis (MO)
The U of Montana (MT)
U of Montevallo (AL)
U of Nebraska at Kearney (NE)
U of Nevada, Las Vegas (NV)
U of Nevada, Reno (NV)
U of New Hampshire (NH)
U of North Alabama (AL)
The U of North Carolina at Charlotte (NC)
The U of North Carolina at Greensboro (NC)
The U of North Carolina at Pembroke (NC)
The U of North Carolina Wilmington (NC)
U of North Dakota (ND)
U of Northern Iowa (IA)
U of North Texas (TX)
U of Oklahoma (OK)
U of Ottawa (ON, Canada)
U of Pikeville (KY)
U of Pittsburgh (PA)
U of Portland (OR)
U of Regina (SK, Canada)
U of Rio Grande (OH)
U of St. Francis (IL)
U of Saint Francis (IN)
U of Saint Joseph (CT)
U of St. Thomas (MN)
U of South Alabama (AL)
The U of South Dakota (SD)
U of Southern Indiana (IN)
U of Southern Maine (ME)
U of Southern Mississippi (MS)
U of South Florida (FL)
The U of Tennessee (TN)
The U of Tennessee at Chattanooga (TN)
The U of Tennessee at Martin (TN)
The U of Texas at Arlington (TX)
The U of Texas at Austin (TX)
The U of Texas at El Paso (TX)
The U of Texas of the Permian Basin (TX)
The U of Texas–Pan American (TX)
U of the District of Columbia (DC)
U of the Fraser Valley (BC, Canada)
U of the Virgin Islands (VI)
The U of Toledo (OH)
U of Utah (UT)
U of Valley Forge (PA)
U of Vermont (VT)
U of Washington (WA)
U of Washington, Tacoma (WA)
U of Waterloo (ON, Canada)
The U of Western Ontario (ON, Canada)
U of West Florida (FL)
U of Windsor (ON, Canada)
U of Wisconsin–Eau Claire (WI)
U of Wisconsin–Green Bay (WI)
U of Wisconsin–Madison (WI)
U of Wisconsin–Milwaukee (WI)
U of Wisconsin–Oshkosh (WI)
U of Wisconsin–River Falls (WI)
U of Wisconsin–Superior (WI)
U of Wisconsin–Whitewater (WI)
U of Wyoming (WY)
Ursuline Coll (OH)
Utah State U (UT)
Utah Valley U (UT)
Valparaiso U (IN)
Virginia Commonwealth U (VA)
Virginia State U (VA)
Virginia Union U (VA)
Virginia Wesleyan Coll (VA)
Viterbo U (WI)
Walla Walla U (WA)
Warner Pacific Coll (OR)
Warren Wilson Coll (NC)
Wartburg Coll (IA)
Washburn U (KS)
Wayne State U (MI)
Weber State U (UT)
West Chester U of Pennsylvania (PA)
Western Carolina U (NC)
Western Illinois U (IL)
Western Kentucky U (KY)
Western Michigan U (MI)
Western New England U (MA)
Westfield State U (MA)
West Liberty U (WV)
West Texas A&M U (TX)
West Virginia State U (WV)
West Virginia U (WV)
Wheelock Coll (MA)
Whittier Coll (CA)
Wichita State U (KS)
Widener U (PA)
Wilberforce U (OH)
William Woods U (MO)
Winona State U (MN)
Winthrop U (SC)
Wright State U (OH)
Xavier U (OH)
York Coll of the City U of New York (NY)
Youngstown State U (OH)

SOCIAL WORK RELATED

Marquette U (WI)
Tabor Coll (KS)
Universidad Metropolitana (PR)
The U of Western Ontario (ON, Canada)

SOCIOLOGY

Abilene Christian U (TX)
Adelphi U (NY)
Agnes Scott Coll (GA)
Albany State U (GA)
Albertus Magnus Coll (CT)
Albion Coll (MI)
Albright Coll (PA)
Alcorn State U (MS)
Alma Coll (MI)
Alverno Coll (WI)
American Intl Coll (MA)
American Public U System (WV)
American U (DC)
The American U in Cairo (Egypt)
Amherst Coll (MA)
Anderson U (IN)
Andrews U (MI)
Angelo State U (TX)
Anna Maria Coll (MA)
Appalachian State U (NC)
Aquinas Coll (MI)
Arcadia U (PA)
Arizona State U at the Tempe campus (AZ)
Arizona State U at the West campus (AZ)
Arkansas State U (AR)
Arkansas Tech U (AR)
Asbury U (KY)
Ashland U (OH)
Assumption Coll (MA)
Athens State U (AL)
Auburn U (AL)
Auburn U at Montgomery (AL)
Augsburg Coll (MN)
Augustana Coll (IL)
Augustana Coll (SD)
Austin Coll (TX)
Austin Peay State U (TN)
Averett U (VA)
Avila U (MO)
Azusa Pacific U (CA)
Baker U (KS)
Baldwin Wallace U (OH)
Ball State U (IN)
Bard Coll (NY)
Barnard Coll (NY)
Barry U (FL)
Baruch Coll of the City U of New York (NY)
Bates Coll (ME)
Baylor U (TX)
Belmont U (TN)
Beloit Coll (WI)
Bemidji State U (MN)
Benedictine Coll (KS)
Benedictine U (IL)
Bennington Coll (VT)
Berea Coll (KY)
Bethany Lutheran Coll (MN)
Bethel Coll (IN)
Bethune-Cookman U (FL)
Binghamton U, State U of New York (NY)
Biola U (CA)
Birmingham-Southern Coll (AL)
Black Hills State U (SD)
Bloomfield Coll (NJ)
Bloomsburg U of Pennsylvania (PA)
Boston Coll (MA)
Boston U (MA)
Bowdoin Coll (ME)
Bowie State U (MD)
Bowling Green State U (OH)
Bradley U (IL)
Brandeis U (MA)
Bridgewater Coll (VA)
Bridgewater State U (MA)
Brown U (RI)
Bryant U (RI)
Bryn Mawr Coll (PA)
Bucknell U (PA)
Buena Vista U (IA)
Buffalo State Coll, State U of New York (NY)
Butler U (IN)
Cabrini Coll (PA)
Caldwell U (NJ)
California Baptist U (CA)
California Lutheran U (CA)
California Polytechnic State U, San Luis Obispo (CA)
California State Polytechnic U, Pomona (CA)
California State U, Dominguez Hills (CA)
California State U, Fresno (CA)
California State U, Fullerton (CA)
California State U, Long Beach (CA)
California State U, Los Angeles (CA)
California State U, Sacramento (CA)
California State U, San Bernardino (CA)
California State U, San Marcos (CA)
California State U, Stanislaus (CA)
Calvin Coll (MI)
Cameron U (OK)
Campbellsville U (KY)
Canisius Coll (NY)
Cape Breton U (NS, Canada)
Capital U (OH)
Cardinal Stritch U (WI)
Carleton Coll (MN)
Carlow U (PA)
Carroll Coll (MT)
Carson-Newman U (TN)
Case Western Reserve U (OH)
Castleton State Coll (VT)
Catawba Coll (NC)
The Catholic U of America (DC)
Centenary Coll of Louisiana (LA)
Central Coll (IA)
Central Connecticut State U (CT)
Central Methodist U (MO)
Central Michigan U (MI)
Central State U (OH)
Central Washington U (WA)
Chapman U (CA)
Charleston Southern U (SC)
Chestnut Hill Coll (PA)
Cheyney U of Pennsylvania (PA)
Chicago State U (IL)
Chowan U (NC)
Christopher Newport U (VA)
City Coll of the City U of New York (NY)
Claflin U (SC)
Clarion U of Pennsylvania (PA)
Clark Atlanta U (GA)
Clarkson U (NY)
Clark U (MA)
Clayton State U (GA)
Cleveland State U (OH)
Coastal Carolina U (SC)
Coe Coll (IA)
Coker Coll (SC)
Colby Coll (ME)
Colby-Sawyer Coll (NH)
The Coll at Brockport, State U of New York (NY)
Coll of Charleston (SC)
The Coll of New Jersey (NJ)
The Coll of New Rochelle (NY)
Coll of Saint Benedict (MN)
Coll of Saint Elizabeth (NJ)
The Coll of Saint Rose (NY)
Coll of the Holy Cross (MA)
The Coll of William and Mary (VA)
The Coll of Wooster (OH)
The Colorado Coll (CO)
Colorado Mesa U (CO)
Colorado State U (CO)
Colorado State U–Pueblo (CO)
Columbia Coll (MO)
Columbia U (NY)
Columbia U, School of General Studies (NY)
Columbus State U (GA)
Concordia Coll (MN)
Concordia Coll–New York (NY)
Concordia U (QC, Canada)
Concordia U Chicago (IL)
Concordia U, Nebraska (NE)
Concordia U, St. Paul (MN)
Concord U (WV)
Connecticut Coll (CT)
Cornell Coll (IA)
Cornell U (NY)
Covenant Coll (GA)
Crandall U (NB, Canada)
Creighton U (NE)
Cumberland U (TN)
Curry Coll (MA)
Dalhousie U (NS, Canada)
Dallas Baptist U (TX)
Dartmouth Coll (NH)
Davidson Coll (NC)
Delaware State U (DE)
Denison U (OH)
DePaul U (IL)
DePauw U (IN)
DEREE - The American Coll of Greece (Greece)
Dickinson Coll (PA)
Dixie State U (UT)
Doane Coll (NE)
Dominican U (IL)
Dowling Coll (NY)
Drake U (IA)
Drew U (NJ)
Drexel U (PA)
Drury U (MO)
Duquesne U (PA)
Earlham Coll (IN)
East Carolina U (NC)
East Central U (OK)
Eastern Connecticut State U (CT)
Eastern Illinois U (IL)
Eastern Kentucky U (KY)
Eastern Michigan U (MI)
Eastern New Mexico U (NM)
Eastern Oregon U (OR)
Eastern U (PA)
East Stroudsburg U of Pennsylvania (PA)
East Tennessee State U (TN)
East Texas Baptist U (TX)
Eckerd Coll (FL)
Edgewood Coll (WI)
Edinboro U of Pennsylvania (PA)
Elizabethtown Coll (PA)
Elmhurst Coll (IL)
Elms Coll (MA)
Elon U (NC)
Emmanuel Coll (MA)
Emory & Henry Coll (VA)
Emporia State U (KS)
Evangel U (MO)
The Evergreen State Coll (WA)
Excelsior Coll (NY)
Fairleigh Dickinson U, Coll at Florham (NJ)
Fairleigh Dickinson U, Metropolitan Campus (NJ)
Fairmont State U (WV)
Fayetteville State U (NC)
Ferris State U (MI)
Fitchburg State U (MA)
Flagler Coll (FL)
Florida Ag and Mech U (FL)
Florida Atlantic U (FL)
Florida Gulf Coast U (FL)
Florida Intl U (FL)
Florida State U (FL)
Fontbonne U (MO)
Fordham U (NY)
Fort Hays State U (KS)
Fort Lewis Coll (CO)
Framingham State U (MA)
Franciscan U of Steubenville (OH)
Francis Marion U (SC)
Franklin & Marshall Coll (PA)
Franklin Coll (IN)
Franklin Pierce U (NH)
Friends U (KS)
Frostburg State U (MD)
Furman U (SC)
Gallaudet U (DC)
Geneva Coll (PA)
George Mason U (VA)
Georgetown Coll (KY)
Georgetown U (DC)
The George Washington U (DC)
Georgia Coll & State U (GA)
Georgia Regents U (GA)
Georgia Southern U (GA)
Georgia Southwestern State U (GA)
Georgia State U (GA)
Gettysburg Coll (PA)
Goddard Coll (VT)
Gonzaga U (WA)
Gordon Coll (MA)
Goshen Coll (IN)
Goucher Coll (MD)
Grace Coll (IN)
Grambling State U (LA)
Grand Valley State U (MI)
Greensboro Coll (NC)
Greenville Coll (IL)
Grinnell Coll (IA)
Grove City Coll (PA)
Guilford Coll (NC)
Gustavus Adolphus Coll (MN)
Gwynedd Mercy U (PA)
Hamilton Coll (NY)
Hamline U (MN)
Hampshire Coll (MA)
Hampton U (VA)
Hannibal-LaGrange U (MO)
Hanover Coll (IN)
Hardin-Simmons U (TX)
Hartwick Coll (NY)
Harvard U (MA)
Hastings Coll (NE)
Haverford Coll (PA)
Hawai`i Pacific U (HI)
Hendrix Coll (AR)
High Point U (NC)
Hillsdale Coll (MI)
Hiram Coll (OH)
Hobart and William Smith Colls (NY)
Hofstra U (NY)
Hollins U (VA)
Holy Family U (PA)
Hope Coll (MI)

Houghton Coll (NY)
Houston Baptist U (TX)
Howard Payne U (TX)
Howard U (DC)
Humboldt State U (CA)
Hunter Coll of the City U of New York (NY)
Huston-Tillotson U (TX)
Illinois Coll (IL)
Illinois Inst of Technology (IL)
Illinois State U (IL)
Illinois Wesleyan U (IL)
Immaculata U (PA)
Indiana U Bloomington (IN)
Indiana U East (IN)
Indiana U Kokomo (IN)
Indiana U Northwest (IN)
Indiana U of Pennsylvania (PA)
Indiana U–Purdue U Fort Wayne (IN)
Indiana U–Purdue U Indianapolis (IN)
Indiana U South Bend (IN)
Indiana U Southeast (IN)
Inter American U of Puerto Rico, Ponce Campus (PR)
Inter American U of Puerto Rico, San Germán Campus (PR)
Iona Coll (NY)
Iowa State U of Science and Technology (IA)
Ithaca Coll (NY)
Jackson State U (MS)
Jacksonville State U (AL)
Jacksonville U (FL)
James Madison U (VA)
Jarvis Christian Coll (TX)
John Carroll U (OH)
Johns Hopkins U (MD)
Johnson State Coll (VT)
Judson U (IL)
Juniata Coll (PA)
Kansas State U (KS)
Kansas Wesleyan U (KS)
Kean U (NJ)
Keene State Coll (NH)
Kennesaw State U (GA)
Kent State U (OH)
Kent State U at Ashtabula (OH)
Kent State U at Stark (OH)
Kentucky Wesleyan Coll (KY)
Kenyon Coll (OH)
Keuka Coll (NY)
King's Coll (PA)
The King's U Coll (AB, Canada)
Knox Coll (IL)
Kutztown U of Pennsylvania (PA)
Lafayette Coll (PA)
LaGrange Coll (GA)
Lake Forest Coll (IL)
Lamar U (TX)
Lane Coll (TN)
Langston U (OK)
La Roche Coll (PA)
La Salle U (PA)
Lasell Coll (MA)
La Sierra U (CA)
Lebanon Valley Coll (PA)
Lee U (TN)
Lehigh U (PA)
Lehman Coll of the City U of New York (NY)
Le Moyne Coll (NY)
LeMoyne-Owen Coll (TN)
Lenoir-Rhyne U (NC)
Lewis U (IL)
Lincoln U (MO)
Lincoln U (PA)
Lindenwood U (MO)
Linfield Coll (OR)
Lock Haven U of Pennsylvania (PA)
Long Island U–LIU Brooklyn (NY)
Long Island U–LIU Post (NY)
Longwood U (VA)
Loras Coll (IA)
Louisiana State U and A&M Coll (LA)
Louisiana State U in Shreveport (LA)
Lourdes U (OH)
Loyola Marymount U (CA)
Loyola U Chicago (IL)
Loyola U New Orleans (LA)
Luther Coll (IA)
Lycoming Coll (PA)
Lynchburg Coll (VA)
Macalester Coll (MN)
Madonna U (MI)
Manchester U (IN)
Manhattan Coll (NY)
Manhattanville Coll (NY)
Mansfield U of Pennsylvania (PA)
Marian U (IN)
Marquette U (WI)
Marshall U (WV)
Mars Hill U (NC)
Mary Baldwin Coll (VA)
Marymount Manhattan Coll (NY)
Marymount U (VA)
Maryville Coll (TN)
Maryville U of Saint Louis (MO)
Marywood U (PA)
Massachusetts Coll of Liberal Arts (MA)
McDaniel Coll (MD)
McKendree U (IL)
McMurry U (TX)
McNeese State U (LA)
Mercer U, Macon (GA)
Mercy Coll (NY)
Meredith Coll (NC)
Merrimack Coll (MA)
Messiah Coll (PA)
Miami U (OH)
Michigan State U (MI)
MidAmerica Nazarene U (KS)
Middlebury Coll (VT)
Middle Tennessee State U (TN)
Midwestern State U (TX)
Millersville U of Pennsylvania (PA)
Milligan Coll (TN)
Millikin U (IL)
Mills Coll (CA)
Minnesota State U Mankato (MN)
Minnesota State U Moorhead (MN)
Minot State U (ND)
Mississippi State U (MS)
Mississippi Valley State U (MS)
Missouri Southern State U (MO)
Missouri State U (MO)
Missouri Valley Coll (MO)
Missouri Western State U (MO)
Molloy Coll (NY)
Monmouth Coll (IL)
Monmouth U (NJ)
Montana State U (MT)
Montana State U Billings (MT)
Montclair State U (NJ)
Moravian Coll (PA)
Morehead State U (KY)
Morris Coll (SC)
Mount Allison U (NB, Canada)
Mount Holyoke Coll (MA)
Mount Mercy U (IA)
Mount St. Joseph U (OH)
Mount Saint Mary Coll (NY)
Mount Saint Mary's U (CA)
Mount St. Mary's U (MD)
Mount Vernon Nazarene U (OH)
Muhlenberg Coll (PA)
Murray State U (KY)
National U (CA)
Nazareth Coll of Rochester (NY)
Nebraska Wesleyan U (NE)
Newberry Coll (SC)
New Coll of Florida (FL)
New England Coll (NH)
New Jersey City U (NJ)
Newman U (KS)
New Mexico State U (NM)
New York Inst of Technology (NY)
New York U (NY)
Niagara U (NY)
Nicholls State U (LA)
Norfolk State U (VA)
North Carolina Ag and Tech State U (NC)
North Carolina State U (NC)
North Carolina Wesleyan Coll (NC)
North Central Coll (IL)
North Dakota State U (ND)
Northeastern Illinois U (IL)
Northeastern State U (OK)
Northeastern U (MA)
Northern Arizona U (AZ)
Northern Illinois U (IL)
Northern Kentucky U (KY)
Northern Michigan U (MI)
Northern State U (SD)
Northland Coll (WI)
Northwestern Coll (IA)
Northwestern Oklahoma State U (OK)
Northwestern U (IL)
Northwest Missouri State U (MO)
Nova Southeastern U (FL)
Nyack Coll (NY)
Oakland U (MI)
Oberlin Coll (OH)
Occidental Coll (CA)
Oglethorpe U (GA)
Ohio Dominican U (OH)
Ohio Northern U (OH)
The Ohio State U (OH)
The Ohio State U–Newark Campus (OH)
Ohio U (OH)
Ohio Wesleyan U (OH)
Oklahoma Baptist U (OK)
Oklahoma City U (OK)
Oklahoma State U (OK)
Old Dominion U (VA)
Olivet Coll (MI)
Olivet Nazarene U (IL)
Oregon State U (OR)
Our Lady of the Lake U of San Antonio (TX)
Pacific Lutheran U (WA)
Pacific U (OR)
Park U (MO)
Penn State Abington (PA)
Penn State Altoona (PA)
Penn State Beaver (PA)
Penn State Berks (PA)
Penn State Brandywine (PA)
Penn State DuBois (PA)
Penn State Erie, The Behrend Coll (PA)
Penn State Fayette, The Eberly Campus (PA)
Penn State Greater Allegheny (PA)
Penn State Harrisburg (PA)
Penn State Hazleton (PA)
Penn State Lehigh Valley (PA)
Penn State Mont Alto (PA)
Penn State New Kensington (PA)
Penn State Schuylkill (PA)
Penn State Shenango (PA)
Penn State U Park (PA)
Penn State Wilkes-Barre (PA)
Penn State Worthington Scranton (PA)
Penn State York (PA)
Pepperdine U, Malibu (CA)
Philander Smith Coll (AR)
Piedmont Coll (GA)
Pittsburg State U (KS)
Point Loma Nazarene U (CA)
Point U (GA)
Pomona Coll (CA)
Portland State U (OR)
Post U (CT)
Prairie View A&M U (TX)
Presbyterian Coll (SC)
Princeton U (NJ)
Principia Coll (IL)
Providence Coll (RI)
Purchase Coll, State U of New York (NY)
Purdue U (IN)
Purdue U Calumet (IN)
Queens Coll of the City U of New York (NY)
Quinnipiac U (CT)
Radford U (VA)
Ramapo Coll of New Jersey (NJ)
Randolph Coll (VA)
Randolph-Macon Coll (VA)
Reed Coll (OR)
Regis U (CO)
Reinhardt U (GA)
Rhode Island Coll (RI)
Rice U (TX)
Rider U (NJ)
Ripon Coll (WI)
Rivier U (NH)
Roanoke Coll (VA)
Rockford U (IL)
Rocky Mountain Coll (MT)
Roger Williams U (RI)
Rollins Coll (FL)
Roosevelt U (IL)
Rosemont Coll (PA)
Rowan U (NJ)
Rust Coll (MS)
Rutgers, The State U of New Jersey, Camden (NJ)
Rutgers, The State U of New Jersey, Newark (NJ)
Rutgers, The State U of New Jersey, New Brunswick (NJ)
Sacred Heart U (CT)
The Sage Colls (NY)
Saginaw Valley State U (MI)
Saint Anselm Coll (NH)
Saint Augustine's U (NC)
St. Bonaventure U (NY)
St. Catherine U (MN)
St. Edward's U (TX)
St. Francis Coll (NY)
Saint Francis U (PA)
St. John Fisher Coll (NY)
Saint John's U (MN)
St. John's U (NY)
Saint Joseph's Coll (IN)
St. Joseph's Coll, Long Island Campus (NY)
St. Joseph's Coll, New York (NY)
Saint Joseph's U (PA)
St. Lawrence U (NY)
Saint Leo U (FL)
Saint Louis U (MO)
Saint Mary's Coll (IN)
St. Mary's Coll of Maryland (MD)
St. Mary's U (TX)
Saint Mary's U of Minnesota (MN)
Saint Michael's Coll (VT)
St. Norbert Coll (WI)
Saint Peter's U (NJ)
St. Thomas U (NB, Canada)
Saint Vincent Coll (PA)
Salem Coll (NC)
Salisbury U (MD)
Salve Regina U (RI)
Samford U (AL)
Sam Houston State U (TX)
San Diego State U (CA)
San Francisco State U (CA)
San Jose State U (CA)
Santa Clara U (CA)
Sarah Lawrence Coll (NY)
Savannah State U (GA)
Scripps Coll (CA)
Seattle Pacific U (WA)
Seattle U (WA)
Seton Hill U (PA)
Shawnee State U (OH)
Shaw U (NC)
Shenandoah U (VA)
Shepherd U (WV)
Shippensburg U of Pennsylvania (PA)
Siena Coll (NY)
Simmons Coll (MA)
Simon Fraser U (BC, Canada)
Simpson Coll (IA)
Skidmore Coll (NY)
Smith Coll (MA)
South Carolina State U (SC)
South Dakota State U (SD)
Southeastern Louisiana U (LA)
Southeastern Oklahoma State U (OK)
Southern Connecticut State U (CT)
Southern Illinois U Carbondale (IL)
Southern Illinois U Edwardsville (IL)
Southern Methodist U (TX)
Southern Oregon U (OR)
Southern Utah U (UT)
Southwest Baptist U (MO)
Southwestern U (TX)
Southwest Minnesota State U (MN)
Spelman Coll (GA)
Spring Hill Coll (AL)
Stanford U (CA)
State U of New York at Fredonia (NY)
State U of New York at New Paltz (NY)
State U of New York at Oswego (NY)
State U of New York at Plattsburgh (NY)
State U of New York Coll at Cortland (NY)
State U of New York Coll at Geneseo (NY)
State U of New York Coll at Old Westbury (NY)
State U of New York Coll at Potsdam (NY)
State U of New York Polytechnic Inst (NY)
Stephen F. Austin State U (TX)
Stetson U (FL)
Stockton U (NJ)
Stonehill Coll (MA)
Stony Brook U, State U of New York (NY)
Suffolk U (MA)
Susquehanna U (PA)
Syracuse U (NY)
Tarleton State U (TX)
Taylor U (IN)
Temple U (PA)
Tennessee State U (TN)
Tennessee Wesleyan Coll (TN)
Texas A&M Intl U (TX)
Texas A&M U (TX)
Texas A&M U–Commerce (TX)
Texas A&M U–Corpus Christi (TX)
Texas A&M U–Kingsville (TX)
Texas Christian U (TX)
Texas Lutheran U (TX)
Texas Southern U (TX)
Texas State U (TX)
Texas Tech U (TX)
Texas Wesleyan U (TX)
Texas Woman's U (TX)
Thiel Coll (PA)
Thomas More Coll (KY)
Tougaloo Coll (MS)
Transylvania U (KY)
Trent U (ON, Canada)
Trevecca Nazarene U (TN)
Trinity Christian Coll (IL)
Trinity Coll (CT)
Trinity U (TX)
Troy U (AL)
Truman State U (MO)
Tufts U (MA)
Tulane U (LA)
Union Coll (KY)
Union Coll (NY)
Union U (TN)
United States Military Acad (NY)
Universidad del Turabo (PR)
Université de Montréal (QC, Canada)
Université du Québec en Outaouais (QC, Canada)
U at Albany, State U of New York (NY)
U at Buffalo, the State U of New York (NY)
The U of Akron (OH)
The U of Alabama (AL)
The U of Alabama at Birmingham (AL)
The U of Alabama in Huntsville (AL)
U of Alaska Fairbanks (AK)
U of Alberta (AB, Canada)
The U of Arizona (AZ)
U of Arkansas (AR)
U of Arkansas at Little Rock (AR)
U of Arkansas at Pine Bluff (AR)
The U of British Columbia (BC, Canada)
The U of British Columbia–Okanagan Campus (BC, Canada)
U of California, Berkeley (CA)
U of California, Davis (CA)
U of California, Irvine (CA)
U of California, Los Angeles (CA)
U of California, Merced (CA)
U of California, Riverside (CA)
U of California, Santa Barbara (CA)
U of California, Santa Cruz (CA)
U of Central Arkansas (AR)
U of Central Florida (FL)
U of Central Missouri (MO)
U of Central Oklahoma (OK)
U of Chicago (IL)
U of Cincinnati (OH)
U of Colorado Boulder (CO)
U of Colorado Colorado Springs (CO)
U of Colorado Denver (CO)
U of Dayton (OH)
U of Delaware (DE)
U of Denver (CO)
U of Dubuque (IA)
U of Evansville (IN)
The U of Findlay (OH)
U of Florida (FL)
U of Georgia (GA)
U of Great Falls (MT)
U of Guam (GU)
U of Guelph (ON, Canada)
U of Hartford (CT)
U of Hawaii at Manoa (HI)
U of Hawaii–West Oahu (HI)

MAJORS LISTING

U of Houston (TX)
U of Houston–Clear Lake (TX)
U of Houston–Downtown (TX)
U of Idaho (ID)
U of Illinois at Chicago (IL)
U of Indianapolis (IN)
The U of Iowa (IA)
The U of Kansas (KS)
U of Kentucky (KY)
U of King's Coll (NS, Canada)
U of La Verne (CA)
U of Lethbridge (AB, Canada)
U of Louisiana at Lafayette (LA)
U of Louisville (KY)
U of Maine (ME)
U of Mary Hardin-Baylor (TX)
U of Maryland, Baltimore County (MD)
U of Maryland, Coll Park (MD)
U of Mary Washington (VA)
U of Massachusetts Amherst (MA)
U of Massachusetts Boston (MA)
U of Massachusetts Dartmouth (MA)
U of Massachusetts Lowell (MA)
U of Memphis (TN)
U of Miami (FL)
U of Michigan (MI)
U of Michigan–Dearborn (MI)
U of Michigan–Flint (MI)
U of Minnesota, Duluth (MN)
U of Minnesota, Morris (MN)
U of Minnesota, Twin Cities Campus (MN)
U of Mississippi (MS)
U of Missouri (MO)
U of Missouri–Kansas City (MO)
U of Missouri–St. Louis (MO)
U of Mobile (AL)
The U of Montana (MT)
U of Montevallo (AL)
U of Mount Union (OH)
U of Nebraska at Kearney (NE)
U of Nebraska–Lincoln (NE)
U of Nevada, Las Vegas (NV)
U of Nevada, Reno (NV)
U of New Brunswick Saint John (NB, Canada)
U of New England (ME)
U of New Hampshire (NH)
U of New Mexico (NM)
U of New Orleans (LA)
U of North Alabama (AL)
U of North Carolina at Asheville (NC)
The U of North Carolina at Chapel Hill (NC)
The U of North Carolina at Greensboro (NC)
The U of North Carolina at Pembroke (NC)
The U of North Carolina Wilmington (NC)
U of North Dakota (ND)
U of Northern Colorado (CO)
U of Northern Iowa (IA)
U of North Florida (FL)
U of North Georgia (GA)
U of North Texas (TX)
U of Notre Dame (IN)
U of Oklahoma (OK)
U of Oregon (OR)
U of Ottawa (ON, Canada)
U of Pennsylvania (PA)
U of Pikeville (KY)
U of Pittsburgh (PA)
U of Pittsburgh at Bradford (PA)
U of Portland (OR)
U of Puget Sound (WA)
U of Regina (SK, Canada)
U of Rhode Island (RI)
U of Richmond (VA)
U of Rio Grande (OH)
U of Saint Francis (IN)
U of St. Thomas (MN)
U of San Diego (CA)
U of San Francisco (CA)
U of Saskatchewan (SK, Canada)
U of Science and Arts of Oklahoma (OK)
The U of Scranton (PA)
U of South Alabama (AL)
U of South Carolina Aiken (SC)
U of South Carolina Beaufort (SC)
U of South Carolina Upstate (SC)
The U of South Dakota (SD)
U of Southern California (CA)
U of Southern Indiana (IN)
U of Southern Maine (ME)
U of Southern Mississippi (MS)
U of South Florida (FL)
The U of Tampa (FL)
The U of Tennessee (TN)
The U of Tennessee at Martin (TN)
The U of Texas at Arlington (TX)
The U of Texas at Austin (TX)
The U of Texas at Dallas (TX)
The U of Texas at El Paso (TX)
The U of Texas at San Antonio (TX)
The U of Texas of the Permian Basin (TX)
The U of Texas–Pan American (TX)
U of the District of Columbia (DC)
U of the Fraser Valley (BC, Canada)
U of the Incarnate Word (TX)
U of the Pacific (CA)
The U of Toledo (OH)
U of Toronto (ON, Canada)
The U of Tulsa (OK)
U of Utah (UT)
U of Vermont (VT)
U of Virginia (VA)
The U of Virginia's Coll at Wise (VA)
U of Washington (WA)
U of Waterloo (ON, Canada)
The U of West Alabama (AL)
The U of Western Ontario (ON, Canada)
U of West Florida (FL)
U of West Georgia (GA)
U of Windsor (ON, Canada)
U of Wisconsin–Eau Claire (WI)
U of Wisconsin–La Crosse (WI)
U of Wisconsin–Madison (WI)
U of Wisconsin–Milwaukee (WI)
U of Wisconsin–Oshkosh (WI)
U of Wisconsin–Parkside (WI)
U of Wisconsin–River Falls (WI)
U of Wisconsin–Stevens Point (WI)
U of Wisconsin–Superior (WI)
U of Wisconsin–Whitewater (WI)
U of Wyoming (WY)
Upper Iowa U (IA)
Urbana U (OH)
Ursinus Coll (PA)
Ursuline Coll (OH)
Utah State U (UT)
Utica Coll (NY)
Valparaiso U (IN)
Vanderbilt U (TN)
Vanguard U of Southern California (CA)
Vassar Coll (NY)
Villanova U (PA)
Virginia Commonwealth U (VA)
Virginia Polytechnic Inst and State U (VA)
Virginia State U (VA)
Virginia Wesleyan Coll (VA)
Viterbo U (WI)
Voorhees Coll (SC)
Wagner Coll (NY)
Wake Forest U (NC)
Walla Walla U (WA)
Walsh U (OH)
Warren Wilson Coll (NC)
Wartburg Coll (IA)
Washburn U (KS)
Washington & Jefferson Coll (PA)
Washington and Lee U (VA)
Washington Coll (MD)
Washington State U (WA)
Washington State U Vancouver (WA)
Waynesburg U (PA)
Wayne State Coll (NE)
Wayne State U (MI)
Weber State U (UT)
Webster U (MO)
Wells Coll (NY)
Wesleyan U (CT)
West Chester U of Pennsylvania (PA)
Western Carolina U (NC)
Western Illinois U (IL)
Western Kentucky U (KY)
Western Michigan U (MI)
Western New England U (MA)
Western Oregon U (OR)
Western State Colorado U (CO)
Western Washington U (WA)
Westfield State U (MA)
West Liberty U (WV)
Westminster Coll (MO)
Westminster Coll (UT)
West Texas A&M U (TX)
West Virginia State U (WV)
West Virginia U (WV)
West Virginia Wesleyan Coll (WV)
Wheaton Coll (IL)
Wheaton Coll (MA)
Whitman Coll (WA)
Whittier Coll (CA)
Whitworth U (WA)
Wichita State U (KS)
Widener U (PA)
Wilberforce U (OH)
Wilkes U (PA)
Willamette U (OR)
William Paterson U of New Jersey (NJ)
William Penn U (IA)
Williams Coll (MA)
Wingate U (NC)
Winona State U (MN)
Winthrop U (SC)
Wittenberg U (OH)
Wofford Coll (SC)
Worcester State U (MA)
Wright State U (OH)
Xavier U (OH)
Xavier U of Louisiana (LA)
Yale U (CT)
Yeshiva U (NY)
York Coll of Pennsylvania (PA)
York Coll of the City U of New York (NY)
Youngstown State U (OH)

SOCIOLOGY AND ANTHROPOLOGY
Albion Coll (MI)
Alma Coll (MI)
American U of Beirut (Lebanon)
Centre Coll (KY)
Coll of Staten Island of the City U of New York (NY)
Goddard Coll (VT)
Goucher Coll (MD)
Governors State U (IL)
Keene State Coll (NH)
Lewis & Clark Coll (OR)
Millsaps Coll (MS)
Oakland U (MI)
Pace U (NY)
Rochester Inst of Technology (NY)
St. Olaf Coll (MN)
Spelman Coll (GA)
Towson U (MD)
Transylvania U (KY)
U of Illinois at Springfield (IL)
U of Massachusetts Dartmouth (MA)
The U of Montana Western (MT)
Ursinus Coll (PA)
Valdosta State U (GA)

SOIL CHEMISTRY AND PHYSICS
The U of Tennessee (TN)

SOIL SCIENCE AND AGRONOMY
California Polytechnic State U, San Luis Obispo (CA)
Colorado State U (CO)
Michigan State U (MI)
New Mexico State U (NM)
North Dakota State U (ND)
Oklahoma State U (OK)
Penn State Abington (PA)
Penn State Altoona (PA)
Penn State Beaver (PA)
Penn State Berks (PA)
Penn State Brandywine (PA)
Penn State DuBois (PA)
Penn State Erie, The Behrend Coll (PA)
Penn State Fayette, The Eberly Campus (PA)
Penn State Greater Allegheny (PA)
Penn State Hazleton (PA)
Penn State Lehigh Valley (PA)
Penn State Mont Alto (PA)
Penn State New Kensington (PA)
Penn State Schuylkill (PA)
Penn State Shenango (PA)
Penn State Wilkes-Barre (PA)
Penn State Worthington Scranton (PA)
Penn State York (PA)
Purdue U (IN)
State U of New York Coll of Environmental Science and Forestry (NY)
The U of British Columbia (BC, Canada)
U of California, Davis (CA)
U of Florida (FL)
U of Georgia (GA)
U of Minnesota, Twin Cities Campus (MN)
U of Nebraska–Lincoln (NE)
U of Saskatchewan (SK, Canada)
The U of Tennessee at Martin (TN)
U of Wisconsin–Madison (WI)
U of Wisconsin–River Falls (WI)
U of Wisconsin–Stevens Point (WI)
Utah State U (UT)
Washington State U (WA)

SOIL SCIENCES RELATED
Brigham Young U (UT)
North Carolina State U (NC)
U of Alberta (AB, Canada)
U of Hawaii at Manoa (HI)

SOLAR ENERGY TECHNOLOGY
Appalachian State U (NC)

SOMATIC BODYWORK
Goddard Coll (VT)

SOMATIC BODYWORK RELATED
Goddard Coll (VT)

SOUTH ASIAN LANGUAGES
Northwestern U (IL)
The U of British Columbia (BC, Canada)
U of Chicago (IL)
U of Minnesota, Twin Cities Campus (MN)
U of Washington (WA)
Yale U (CT)

SOUTHEAST ASIAN LANGUAGES
Harvard U (MA)

SPANISH
Abilene Christian U (TX)
Adams State U (CO)
Adelphi U (NY)
Agnes Scott Coll (GA)
Albany State U (GA)
Albertus Magnus Coll (CT)
Albion Coll (MI)
Albright Coll (PA)
Allegheny Coll (PA)
Alma Coll (MI)
American U (DC)
Amherst Coll (MA)
Anderson U (IN)
Anderson U (SC)
Andrews U (MI)
Angelo State U (TX)
Anna Maria Coll (MA)
Aquinas Coll (MI)
Arcadia U (PA)
Arizona State U at the Tempe campus (AZ)
Arizona State U at the West campus (AZ)
Armstrong State U (GA)
Asbury U (KY)
Ashland U (OH)
Assumption Coll (MA)
Auburn U (AL)
Auburn U at Montgomery (AL)
Augsburg Coll (MN)
Augustana Coll (IL)
Augustana Coll (SD)
Austin Coll (TX)
Azusa Pacific U (CA)
Baker U (KS)
Baldwin Wallace U (OH)
Ball State U (IN)
Baptist U of the Americas (TX)
Bard Coll (NY)
Bard Coll at Simon's Rock (MA)
Barnard Coll (NY)
Barry U (FL)
Baruch Coll of the City U of New York (NY)
Bates Coll (ME)
Baylor U (TX)
Belmont U (TN)
Beloit Coll (WI)
Bemidji State U (MN)
Benedictine Coll (KS)
Benedictine U (IL)
Bennington Coll (VT)
Bentley U (MA)
Berea Coll (KY)
Berry Coll (GA)
Bethany Coll (WV)
Bethel U (MN)
Binghamton U, State U of New York (NY)
Biola U (CA)
Birmingham-Southern Coll (AL)
Blackburn Coll (IL)
Black Hills State U (SD)
Blue Mountain Coll (MS)
Bluffton U (OH)
Bob Jones U (SC)
Boston Coll (MA)
Boston U (MA)
Bowdoin Coll (ME)
Bowling Green State U (OH)
Bradley U (IL)
Brandeis U (MA)
Bridgewater Coll (VA)
Bridgewater State U (MA)
Brown U (RI)
Bryan Coll (TN)
Bryant U (RI)
Bryn Mawr Coll (PA)
Bucknell U (PA)
Buena Vista U (IA)
Buffalo State Coll, State U of New York (NY)
Butler U (IN)
Cabrini Coll (PA)
Caldwell U (NJ)
California Baptist U (CA)
California Lutheran U (CA)
California State Polytechnic U, Pomona (CA)
California State U, Dominguez Hills (CA)
California State U, Fresno (CA)
California State U, Fullerton (CA)
California State U, Long Beach (CA)
California State U, Los Angeles (CA)
California State U, Monterey Bay (CA)
California State U, Sacramento (CA)
California State U, San Bernardino (CA)
California State U, San Marcos (CA)
California State U, Stanislaus (CA)
California U of Pennsylvania (PA)
Calvin Coll (MI)
Canisius Coll (NY)
Capital U (OH)
Cardinal Stritch U (WI)
Carleton Coll (MN)
Carroll Coll (MT)
Carson-Newman U (TN)
Case Western Reserve U (OH)
Castleton State Coll (VT)
Catawba Coll (NC)
The Catholic U of America (DC)
Cedarville U (OH)
Central Coll (IA)
Central Connecticut State U (CT)
Central Michigan U (MI)
Central Washington U (WA)
Centre Coll (KY)
Chapman U (CA)
Charleston Southern U (SC)
Chestnut Hill Coll (PA)
Chicago State U (IL)
Chowan U (NC)
Christopher Newport U (VA)
City Coll of the City U of New York (NY)
Claremont McKenna Coll (CA)
Clarion U of Pennsylvania (PA)
Clark Atlanta U (GA)
Clarke U (IA)
Clark U (MA)
Cleveland State U (OH)
Coastal Carolina U (SC)
Coe Coll (IA)
Colby Coll (ME)
The Coll at Brockport, State U of New York (NY)

Coll of Charleston (SC)
The Coll of Idaho (ID)
The Coll of New Jersey (NJ)
The Coll of New Rochelle (NY)
Coll of Saint Benedict (MN)
Coll of Saint Elizabeth (NJ)
The Coll of Saint Rose (NY)
The Coll of St. Scholastica (MN)
Coll of Staten Island of the City U of New York (NY)
Coll of the Holy Cross (MA)
Coll of the Ozarks (MO)
The Coll of Wooster (OH)
The Colorado Coll (CO)
Colorado Mesa U (CO)
Colorado State U (CO)
Columbia Coll (SC)
Columbia U (NY)
Columbus State U (GA)
Concordia Coll (MN)
Concordia U (QC, Canada)
Concordia U Chicago (IL)
Concordia U, Nebraska (NE)
Concordia U Wisconsin (WI)
Connecticut Coll (CT)
Cornell Coll (IA)
Cornell U (NY)
Cornerstone U (MI)
Creighton U (NE)
Daemen Coll (NY)
Dalhousie U (NS, Canada)
Dartmouth Coll (NH)
Davidson Coll (NC)
Delaware State U (DE)
Denison U (OH)
DePaul U (IL)
DePauw U (IN)
DeSales U (PA)
Dickinson Coll (PA)
Dickinson State U (ND)
Dixie State U (UT)
Doane Coll (NE)
Dominican Coll (NY)
Dominican U (IL)
Drew U (NJ)
Drury U (MO)
Duquesne U (PA)
Earlham Coll (IN)
East Carolina U (NC)
Eastern Connecticut State U (CT)
Eastern Kentucky U (KY)
Eastern Michigan U (MI)
Eastern New Mexico U (NM)
Eastern U (PA)
East Stroudsburg U of Pennsylvania (PA)
East Texas Baptist U (TX)
Eckerd Coll (FL)
Edgewood Coll (WI)
Elizabethtown Coll (PA)
Elmhurst Coll (IL)
Elms Coll (MA)
Elon U (NC)
Emmanuel Coll (MA)
Emory & Henry Coll (VA)
Erskine Coll (SC)
Evangel U (MO)
Fairfield U (CT)
Fairleigh Dickinson U, Coll at Florham (NJ)
Fairleigh Dickinson U, Metropolitan Campus (NJ)
Fayetteville State U (NC)
Ferrum Coll (VA)
Flagler Coll (FL)
Florida Atlantic U (FL)
Florida Gulf Coast U (FL)
Florida Intl U (FL)
Florida Southern Coll (FL)
Fordham U (NY)
Fort Hays State U (KS)
Fort Lewis Coll (CO)
Franciscan U of Steubenville (OH)
Franklin & Marshall Coll (PA)
Franklin Coll (IN)
Friends U (KS)
Furman U (SC)
Gallaudet U (DC)
Georgetown Coll (KY)
Georgetown U (DC)
The George Washington U (DC)
Georgia Coll & State U (GA)
Georgian Court U (NJ)
Georgia State U (GA)
Gettysburg Coll (PA)
Gonzaga U (WA)
Gordon Coll (MA)
Goshen Coll (IN)
Goucher Coll (MD)
Grace Coll (IN)
Graceland U (IA)
Grand Valley State U (MI)
Grand View U (IA)
Greensboro Coll (NC)
Greenville Coll (IL)
Grinnell Coll (IA)
Grove City Coll (PA)
Guilford Coll (NC)
Gustavus Adolphus Coll (MN)
Hamline U (MN)
Hampden-Sydney Coll (VA)
Hanover Coll (IN)
Harding U (AR)
Hardin-Simmons U (TX)
Hartwick Coll (NY)
Hastings Coll (NE)
Haverford Coll (PA)
Heidelberg U (OH)
Hendrix Coll (AR)
High Point U (NC)
Hillsdale Coll (MI)
Hiram Coll (OH)
Hobart and William Smith Colls (NY)
Hofstra U (NY)
Hollins U (VA)
Hope Coll (MI)
Houghton Coll (NY)
Houston Baptist U (TX)
Howard Payne U (TX)
Howard U (DC)
Humboldt State U (CA)
Hunter Coll of the City U of New York (NY)
Illinois Coll (IL)
Illinois State U (IL)
Illinois Wesleyan U (IL)
Immaculata U (PA)
Indiana U Bloomington (IN)
Indiana U Northwest (IN)
Indiana U of Pennsylvania (PA)
Indiana U–Purdue U Fort Wayne (IN)
Indiana U–Purdue U Indianapolis (IN)
Indiana U South Bend (IN)
Indiana U Southeast (IN)
Iona Coll (NY)
Iowa State U of Science and Technology (IA)
Ithaca Coll (NY)
Jacksonville State U (AL)
Jacksonville U (FL)
John Brown U (AR)
John Carroll U (OH)
Johns Hopkins U (MD)
Johnson C. Smith U (NC)
Judson Coll (AL)
Juniata Coll (PA)
Kalamazoo Coll (MI)
Kean U (NJ)
Keene State Coll (NH)
Kent State U (OH)
Kentucky State U (KY)
Kentucky Wesleyan Coll (KY)
Kenyon Coll (OH)
King's Coll (PA)
King U (TN)
Knox Coll (IL)
Kutztown U of Pennsylvania (PA)
Lafayette Coll (PA)
LaGrange Coll (GA)
Lake Erie Coll (OH)
Lake Forest Coll (IL)
La Salle U (PA)
La Sierra U (CA)
Lawrence U (WI)
Lebanon Valley Coll (PA)
Lee U (TN)
Lehigh U (PA)
Lehman Coll of the City U of New York (NY)
Le Moyne Coll (NY)
Lenoir-Rhyne U (NC)
Lewis U (IL)
Liberty U (VA)
Lincoln U (MO)
Lincoln U (PA)
Lindenwood U (MO)
Linfield Coll (OR)
Lipscomb U (TN)
Lock Haven U of Pennsylvania (PA)
Long Island U–LIU Brooklyn (NY)
Long Island U–LIU Post (NY)
Loras Coll (IA)
Louisiana Coll (LA)
Louisiana State U and A&M Coll (LA)
Loyola Marymount U (CA)
Loyola U Chicago (IL)
Loyola U New Orleans (LA)
Luther Coll (IA)
Lycoming Coll (PA)
Lynchburg Coll (VA)
Lyon Coll (AR)
Macalester Coll (MN)
Madonna U (MI)
Manchester U (IN)
Manhattan Coll (NY)
Manhattanville Coll (NY)
Mansfield U of Pennsylvania (PA)
Marian U (IN)
Marian U (WI)
Marietta Coll (OH)
Marist Coll (NY)
Marquette U (WI)
Mars Hill U (NC)
Mary Baldwin Coll (VA)
Maryville Coll (TN)
Marywood U (PA)
McDaniel Coll (MD)
McKendree U (IL)
McMurry U (TX)
Mercer U, Macon (GA)
Mercy Coll (NY)
Meredith Coll (NC)
Merrimack Coll (MA)
Messiah Coll (PA)
Miami U (OH)
Michigan State U (MI)
MidAmerica Nazarene U (KS)
Middlebury Coll (VT)
Midwestern State U (TX)
Millersville U of Pennsylvania (PA)
Millikin U (IL)
Millsaps Coll (MS)
Mills Coll (CA)
Minnesota State U Mankato (MN)
Minnesota State U Moorhead (MN)
Minot State U (ND)
Mississippi U for Women (MS)
Missouri Southern State U (MO)
Missouri State U (MO)
Missouri Western State U (MO)
Monmouth Coll (IL)
Montana State U Billings (MT)
Montclair State U (NJ)
Moravian Coll (PA)
Morehead State U (KY)
Morningside Coll (IA)
Mount Allison U (NB, Canada)
Mount Holyoke Coll (MA)
Mount Mary U (WI)
Mount Saint Mary Coll (NY)
Mount Saint Mary's U (CA)
Mount St. Mary's U (MD)
Mount Vernon Nazarene U (OH)
Muhlenberg Coll (PA)
Murray State U (KY)
National U (CA)
Nazareth Coll of Rochester (NY)
Nebraska Wesleyan U (NE)
Newberry Coll (SC)
New Coll of Florida (FL)
New Jersey City U (NJ)
New Mexico Highlands U (NM)
New York U (NY)
Niagara U (NY)
North Carolina Central U (NC)
North Carolina State U (NC)
North Central Coll (IL)
North Dakota State U (ND)
Northeastern Illinois U (IL)
Northeastern State U (OK)
Northeastern U (MA)
Northern Arizona U (AZ)
Northern Illinois U (IL)
Northern Kentucky U (KY)
Northern Michigan U (MI)
Northern State U (SD)
North Greenville U (SC)
Northwestern Coll (IA)
Northwestern Oklahoma State U (OK)
Northwestern U (IL)
Northwest Missouri State U (MO)
Northwest Nazarene U (ID)
Notre Dame of Maryland U (MD)
Oakland U (MI)
Oberlin Coll (OH)
Occidental Coll (CA)
Oglethorpe U (GA)
Ohio Northern U (OH)
The Ohio State U (OH)
Ohio U (OH)
Ohio Wesleyan U (OH)
Oklahoma Baptist U (OK)
Oklahoma Christian U (OK)
Oklahoma City U (OK)
Oklahoma State U (OK)
Olivet Nazarene U (IL)
Oregon State U (OR)
Our Lady of the Lake U of San Antonio (TX)
Pace U (NY)
Pacific U (OR)
Park U (MO)
Penn State Abington (PA)
Penn State Altoona (PA)
Penn State Beaver (PA)
Penn State Berks (PA)
Penn State Brandywine (PA)
Penn State DuBois (PA)
Penn State Erie, The Behrend Coll (PA)
Penn State Fayette, The Eberly Campus (PA)
Penn State Greater Allegheny (PA)
Penn State Hazleton (PA)
Penn State Lehigh Valley (PA)
Penn State Mont Alto (PA)
Penn State New Kensington (PA)
Penn State Schuylkill (PA)
Penn State Shenango (PA)
Penn State U Park (PA)
Penn State Wilkes-Barre (PA)
Penn State Worthington Scranton (PA)
Penn State York (PA)
Piedmont Coll (GA)
Pittsburg State U (KS)
Plymouth State U (NH)
Point Loma Nazarene U (CA)
Pomona Coll (CA)
Portland State U (OR)
Prairie View A&M U (TX)
Presbyterian Coll (SC)
Princeton U (NJ)
Principia Coll (IL)
Providence Coll (RI)
Purchase Coll, State U of New York (NY)
Queens Coll of the City U of New York (NY)
Quinnipiac U (CT)
Ramapo Coll of New Jersey (NJ)
Randolph Coll (VA)
Randolph-Macon Coll (VA)
Reed Coll (OR)
Regis Coll (MA)
Regis U (CO)
Rhode Island Coll (RI)
Rhodes Coll (TN)
Rice U (TX)
Rider U (NJ)
Ripon Coll (WI)
Rivier U (NH)
Roanoke Coll (VA)
Roberts Wesleyan Coll (NY)
Rockford U (IL)
Rockhurst U (MO)
Rollins Coll (FL)
Rosemont Coll (PA)
Rowan U (NJ)
Rutgers, The State U of New Jersey, Camden (NJ)
Rutgers, The State U of New Jersey, Newark (NJ)
Rutgers, The State U of New Jersey, New Brunswick (NJ)
Sacred Heart U (CT)
Saginaw Valley State U (MI)
Saint Anselm Coll (NH)
St. Bonaventure U (NY)
St. Catherine U (MN)
St. Edward's U (TX)
St. Francis Coll (NY)
Saint Francis U (PA)
St. John Fisher Coll (NY)
Saint John's U (MN)
St. John's U (NY)
St. Joseph's Coll, Long Island Campus (NY)
St. Joseph's Coll, New York (NY)
Saint Joseph's U (PA)
St. Lawrence U (NY)
Saint Louis U (MO)
Saint Mary's Coll (IN)
St. Mary's U (TX)
Saint Mary's U of Minnesota (MN)
Saint Michael's Coll (VT)
St. Norbert Coll (WI)
St. Olaf Coll (MN)
Saint Peter's U (NJ)
St. Thomas Aquinas Coll (NY)
St. Thomas U (NB, Canada)
Saint Vincent Coll (PA)
Salem Coll (NC)
Salisbury U (MD)
Salve Regina U (RI)
Samford U (AL)
Sam Houston State U (TX)
San Diego State U (CA)
San Francisco State U (CA)
San Jose State U (CA)
Santa Clara U (CA)
Scripps Coll (CA)
Seattle U (WA)
Seton Hill U (PA)
Sewanee: The U of the South (TN)
Shenandoah U (VA)
Shepherd U (WV)
Shippensburg U of Pennsylvania (PA)
Siena Coll (NY)
Siena Heights U (MI)
Simmons Coll (MA)
Simpson Coll (IA)
Simpson U (CA)
Skidmore Coll (NY)
Slippery Rock U of Pennsylvania (PA)
Smith Coll (MA)
South Dakota State U (SD)
Southeastern Louisiana U (LA)
Southeastern Oklahoma State U (OK)
Southern Adventist U (TN)
Southern Arkansas U–Magnolia (AR)
Southern Connecticut State U (CT)
Southern Methodist U (TX)
Southern Oregon U (OR)
Southern Utah U (UT)
Southwest Baptist U (MO)
Southwestern U (TX)
Southwest Minnesota State U (MN)
Spelman Coll (GA)
Spring Hill Coll (AL)
Stanford U (CA)
State U of New York at Fredonia (NY)
State U of New York at New Paltz (NY)
State U of New York at Oswego (NY)
State U of New York at Plattsburgh (NY)
State U of New York Coll at Cortland (NY)
State U of New York Coll at Geneseo (NY)
State U of New York Coll at Old Westbury (NY)
State U of New York Coll at Potsdam (NY)
Stetson U (FL)
Stonehill Coll (MA)
Stony Brook U, State U of New York (NY)
Suffolk U (MA)
Sul Ross State U (TX)
Susquehanna U (PA)
Syracuse U (NY)
Tarleton State U (TX)
Taylor U (IN)
Temple U (PA)
Tennessee State U (TN)
Tennessee Wesleyan Coll (TN)
Texas A&M Intl U (TX)
Texas A&M U (TX)
Texas A&M U–Commerce (TX)
Texas A&M U–Corpus Christi (TX)
Texas A&M U–Kingsville (TX)
Texas Christian U (TX)
Texas Lutheran U (TX)
Texas Southern U (TX)
Texas State U (TX)
Texas Tech U (TX)
Texas Wesleyan U (TX)
Thomas More Coll (KY)
Transylvania U (KY)
Trinity Christian Coll (IL)
Trinity Coll (CT)
Trinity U (TX)

Troy U (AL)
Truman State U (MO)
Tufts U (MA)
Tulane U (LA)
Union Coll (NE)
Union Coll (NY)
Union U (TN)
United States Military Acad (NY)
Université de Montréal (QC, Canada)
U at Albany, State U of New York (NY)
U at Buffalo, the State U of New York (NY)
The U of Akron (OH)
The U of Alabama (AL)
U of Alberta (AB, Canada)
The U of Arizona (AZ)
U of Arkansas (AR)
U of Arkansas at Little Rock (AR)
U of Arkansas–Fort Smith (AR)
The U of British Columbia (BC, Canada)
The U of British Columbia–Okanagan Campus (BC, Canada)
U of California, Berkeley (CA)
U of California, Davis (CA)
U of California, Irvine (CA)
U of California, Los Angeles (CA)
U of California, Riverside (CA)
U of California, Santa Barbara (CA)
U of California, Santa Cruz (CA)
U of Central Arkansas (AR)
U of Central Florida (FL)
U of Central Missouri (MO)
U of Central Oklahoma (OK)
U of Cincinnati (OH)
U of Colorado Boulder (CO)
U of Colorado Colorado Springs (CO)
U of Colorado Denver (CO)
U of Dallas (TX)
U of Dayton (OH)
U of Delaware (DE)
U of Denver (CO)
U of Evansville (IN)
The U of Findlay (OH)
U of Florida (FL)
U of Georgia (GA)
U of Guelph (ON, Canada)
U of Hawaii at Manoa (HI)
U of Houston (TX)
U of Houston–Downtown (TX)
U of Idaho (ID)
U of Illinois at Chicago (IL)
U of Indianapolis (IN)
The U of Iowa (IA)
U of Jamestown (ND)
The U of Kansas (KS)
U of Kentucky (KY)
U of King's Coll (NS, Canada)
U of La Verne (CA)
U of Louisville (KY)
U of Maine (ME)
U of Mary Hardin-Baylor (TX)
U of Maryland, Coll Park (MD)
U of Massachusetts Amherst (MA)
U of Massachusetts Boston (MA)
U of Massachusetts Dartmouth (MA)
U of Miami (FL)
U of Michigan (MI)
U of Michigan–Dearborn (MI)
U of Michigan–Flint (MI)
U of Minnesota, Duluth (MN)
U of Minnesota, Morris (MN)
U of Minnesota, Twin Cities Campus (MN)
U of Mississippi (MS)
U of Missouri (MO)
The U of Montana (MT)
U of Mount Union (OH)
U of Nebraska at Kearney (NE)
U of Nebraska–Lincoln (NE)
U of Nevada, Las Vegas (NV)
U of Nevada, Reno (NV)
U of New Brunswick Saint John (NB, Canada)
U of New Hampshire (NH)
U of New Mexico (NM)
U of North Carolina at Asheville (NC)
The U of North Carolina at Charlotte (NC)
The U of North Carolina at Greensboro (NC)
The U of North Carolina at Pembroke (NC)
The U of North Carolina Wilmington (NC)
U of North Dakota (ND)
U of Northern Colorado (CO)
U of Northern Iowa (IA)
U of North Florida (FL)
U of North Georgia (GA)
U of North Texas (TX)
U of Northwestern–St. Paul (MN)
U of Notre Dame (IN)
U of Oklahoma (OK)
U of Oregon (OR)
U of Ottawa (ON, Canada)
U of Pennsylvania (PA)
U of Pikeville (KY)
U of Pittsburgh (PA)
U of Pittsburgh at Greensburg (PA)
U of Portland (OR)
U of Puget Sound (WA)
U of Regina (SK, Canada)
U of Rhode Island (RI)
U of Richmond (VA)
U of Rochester (NY)
U of Saint Joseph (CT)
U of St. Thomas (MN)
U of St. Thomas (TX)
U of San Diego (CA)
U of San Francisco (CA)
U of Saskatchewan (SK, Canada)
The U of Scranton (PA)
U of South Carolina Beaufort (SC)
U of South Carolina Upstate (SC)
The U of South Dakota (SD)
U of Southern California (CA)
U of Southern Indiana (IN)
U of South Florida (FL)
The U of Tampa (FL)
The U of Tennessee (TN)
The U of Tennessee at Martin (TN)
The U of Texas at Arlington (TX)
The U of Texas at Austin (TX)
The U of Texas at El Paso (TX)
The U of Texas at San Antonio (TX)
The U of Texas at Tyler (TX)
The U of Texas of the Permian Basin (TX)
The U of Texas–Pan American (TX)
U of the Cumberlands (KY)
U of the District of Columbia (DC)
U of the Incarnate Word (TX)
U of the Pacific (CA)
The U of Toledo (OH)
U of Toronto (ON, Canada)
The U of Tulsa (OK)
U of Utah (UT)
U of Vermont (VT)
U of Virginia (VA)
The U of Virginia's Coll at Wise (VA)
U of Washington (WA)
U of Waterloo (ON, Canada)
The U of Western Ontario (ON, Canada)
U of West Florida (FL)
U of Windsor (ON, Canada)
U of Wisconsin–Eau Claire (WI)
U of Wisconsin–Green Bay (WI)
U of Wisconsin–La Crosse (WI)
U of Wisconsin–Madison (WI)
U of Wisconsin–Milwaukee (WI)
U of Wisconsin–Oshkosh (WI)
U of Wisconsin–Parkside (WI)
U of Wisconsin–Platteville (WI)
U of Wisconsin–River Falls (WI)
U of Wisconsin–Stevens Point (WI)
U of Wisconsin–Whitewater (WI)
U of Wyoming (WY)
Ursinus Coll (PA)
Utah State U (UT)
Utah Valley U (UT)
Valdosta State U (GA)
Valley City State U (ND)
Valparaiso U (IN)
Vanderbilt U (TN)
Vassar Coll (NY)
Villanova U (PA)
Virginia Polytechnic Inst and State U (VA)
Virginia Wesleyan Coll (VA)
Viterbo U (WI)
Wabash Coll (IN)
Wagner Coll (NY)
Wake Forest U (NC)
Walla Walla U (WA)
Walsh U (OH)
Warren Wilson Coll (NC)
Wartburg Coll (IA)
Washburn U (KS)
Washington & Jefferson Coll (PA)
Washington and Lee U (VA)
Washington Coll (MD)
Washington State U (WA)
Washington U in St. Louis (MO)
Wayne State Coll (NE)
Weber State U (UT)
Webster U (MO)
Wells Coll (NY)
Wesleyan Coll (GA)
West Chester U of Pennsylvania (PA)
Western Carolina U (NC)
Western Illinois U (IL)
Western Kentucky U (KY)
Western Michigan U (MI)
Western Oregon U (OR)
Western State Colorado U (CO)
Western Washington U (WA)
Westfield State U (MA)
Westminster Coll (MO)
West Texas A&M U (TX)
Wheaton Coll (IL)
Wheeling Jesuit U (WV)
Whitman Coll (WA)
Whittier Coll (CA)
Whitworth U (WA)
Widener U (PA)
Wilkes U (PA)
Willamette U (OR)
William Jewell Coll (MO)
William Paterson U of New Jersey (NJ)
Williams Coll (MA)
Winona State U (MN)
Wittenberg U (OH)
Wofford Coll (SC)
Worcester State U (MA)
Wright State U (OH)
Xavier U (OH)
Xavier U of Louisiana (LA)
Yale U (CT)
York Coll of Pennsylvania (PA)
York Coll of the City U of New York (NY)
Youngstown State U (OH)

SPANISH AND IBERIAN STUDIES

Austin Coll (TX)
Bard Coll (NY)
Bard Coll at Simon's Rock (MA)
Coe Coll (IA)
Emory & Henry Coll (VA)
Fordham U (NY)
New York U (NY)
The U of Western Ontario (ON, Canada)
Wesleyan U (CT)

SPANISH LANGUAGE TEACHER EDUCATION

Abilene Christian U (TX)
Adams State U (CO)
Albion Coll (MI)
Alma Coll (MI)
Anderson U (IN)
Ashland U (OH)
Auburn U (AL)
Augustana Coll (IL)
Baylor U (TX)
Bethel U (MN)
Blue Mountain Coll (MS)
Bob Jones U (SC)
Bryan Coll (TN)
Buena Vista U (IA)
California Lutheran U (CA)
Calvin Coll (MI)
Canisius Coll (NY)
Carroll Coll (MT)
The Catholic U of America (DC)
Cedarville U (OH)
Central Michigan U (MI)
Central Washington U (WA)
Charleston Southern U (SC)
Coll of Saint Mary (NE)
The Coll of Saint Rose (NY)
Coll of Staten Island of the City U of New York (NY)
Coll of the Ozarks (MO)
Colorado State U (CO)
Concordia Coll (MN)
Concordia U, Nebraska (NE)
Concordia U Wisconsin (WI)
Cornerstone U (MI)
Daemen Coll (NY)
Delaware State U (DE)
Dowling Coll (NY)
Duquesne U (PA)
East Carolina U (NC)
Eastern Kentucky U (KY)
Eastern Michigan U (MI)
East Texas Baptist U (TX)
Edgewood Coll (WI)
Elmhurst Coll (IL)
Elmira Coll (NY)
Evangel U (MO)
Fayetteville State U (NC)
Franklin Coll (IN)
Friends U (KS)
Georgia Southern U (GA)
Grace Coll (IN)
Grand Valley State U (MI)
Greensboro Coll (NC)
Greenville Coll (IL)
Harding U (AR)
Hardin-Simmons U (TX)
Hastings Coll (NE)
Hofstra U (NY)
Holy Family U (PA)
Hope Coll (MI)
Howard Payne U (TX)
Indiana U Bloomington (IN)
Indiana U Northwest (IN)
Indiana U–Purdue U Fort Wayne (IN)
Indiana U–Purdue U Indianapolis (IN)
Indiana U South Bend (IN)
Inter American U of Puerto Rico, Aguadilla Campus (PR)
Inter American U of Puerto Rico, Fajardo Campus (PR)
Inter American U of Puerto Rico, San Germán Campus (PR)
Iona Coll (NY)
Ithaca Coll (NY)
Keene State Coll (NH)
Kentucky Wesleyan Coll (KY)
King U (TN)
Lee U (TN)
Le Moyne Coll (NY)
Lewis U (IL)
Lindenwood U (MO)
Lipscomb U (TN)
Long Island U–LIU Post (NY)
Lubbock Christian U (TX)
Manchester U (IN)
Manhattanville Coll (NY)
Marian U (WI)
Marist Coll (NY)
Maryville Coll (TN)
Marywood U (PA)
McMurry U (TX)
Messiah Coll (PA)
Miami U (OH)
Michigan State U (MI)
MidAmerica Nazarene U (KS)
Minnesota State U Moorhead (MN)
Minot State U (ND)
Missouri Western State U (MO)
Montana State U Billings (MT)
Morningside Coll (IA)
Mount Mary U (WI)
Mount Vernon Nazarene U (OH)
New York U (NY)
Niagara U (NY)
North Carolina Ag and Tech State U (NC)
North Carolina State U (NC)
North Dakota State U (ND)
Northeastern State U (OK)
Northern Michigan U (MI)
Northwest Missouri State U (MO)
Northwest Nazarene U (ID)
Ohio Northern U (OH)
Ohio U (OH)
Ohio Wesleyan U (OH)
Oklahoma Baptist U (OK)
Pace U (NY)
Piedmont Coll (GA)
Pittsburg State U (KS)
Providence Coll (RI)
Rhode Island Coll (RI)
Roberts Wesleyan Coll (NY)
Saginaw Valley State U (MI)
St. Catherine U (MN)
St. Edward's U (TX)
St. John Fisher Coll (NY)
St. John's U (NY)
St. Joseph's Coll, Long Island Campus (NY)
St. Joseph's Coll, New York (NY)
Saint Joseph's U (PA)
Saint Mary's U of Minnesota (MN)
Salve Regina U (RI)
Southeastern Oklahoma State U (OK)
Southern Utah U (UT)
Southwest Minnesota State U (MN)
Spring Hill Coll (AL)
State U of New York at New Paltz (NY)
State U of New York Coll at Cortland (NY)
State U of New York Coll at Old Westbury (NY)
State U of New York Coll at Potsdam (NY)
Syracuse U (NY)
Taylor U (IN)
Texas A&M Intl U (TX)
Trinity Christian Coll (IL)
Universidad del Turabo (PR)
Universidad Metropolitana (PR)
The U of Akron (OH)
U of Alberta (AB, Canada)
U of Arkansas–Fort Smith (AR)
U of Central Oklahoma (OK)
U of Delaware (DE)
U of Evansville (IN)
U of Illinois at Chicago (IL)
U of Indianapolis (IN)
The U of Iowa (IA)
U of Mary Hardin-Baylor (TX)
U of Michigan–Flint (MI)
U of Nebraska–Lincoln (NE)
U of Nevada, Las Vegas (NV)
The U of North Carolina at Greensboro (NC)
The U of North Carolina Wilmington (NC)
The U of South Dakota (SD)
The U of Tennessee at Martin (TN)
U of the Cumberlands (KY)
The U of Toledo (OH)
U of Wisconsin–River Falls (WI)
Utah Valley U (UT)
Valley City State U (ND)
Valparaiso U (IN)
Viterbo U (WI)
Washburn U (KS)
Washington State U (WA)
Washington U in St. Louis (MO)
Weber State U (UT)
Western Carolina U (NC)
Western Michigan U (MI)
Western State Colorado U (CO)
Western Washington U (WA)
Widener U (PA)
Winona State U (MN)
Xavier U of Louisiana (LA)
York Coll of Pennsylvania (PA)
Youngstown State U (OH)

SPECIAL EDUCATION

Adams State U (CO)
Alabama State U (AL)
Albany State U (GA)
Anderson U (SC)
Arizona State U at the Downtown Phoenix campus (AZ)
Arizona State U at the Polytechnic campus (AZ)
Arizona State U at the Tempe campus (AZ)
Arizona State U at the West campus (AZ)
Armstrong State U (GA)
Asbury U (KY)
Ashland U (OH)
Athens State U (AL)
Auburn U (AL)
Auburn U at Montgomery (AL)
Augsburg Coll (MN)
Augustana Coll (SD)
Austin Peay State U (TN)
Avila U (MO)
Barry U (FL)
Baylor U (TX)
Benedictine Coll (KS)
Benedictine U (IL)
Bennett Coll (NC)
Black Hills State U (SD)
Bloomsburg U of Pennsylvania (PA)
Bluffton U (OH)
Boston U (MA)
Bowie State U (MD)
Bowling Green State U (OH)

Bridgewater State U (MA)
Brigham Young U (UT)
Buena Vista U (IA)
Buffalo State Coll, State U of New York (NY)
Cabrini Coll (PA)
California U of Pennsylvania (PA)
Calvin Coll (MI)
Capital U (OH)
Caribbean U (PR)
Carson-Newman U (TN)
Castleton State Coll (VT)
Cedarville U (OH)
Central State U (OH)
Central Washington U (WA)
Chaminade U of Honolulu (HI)
Cheyney U of Pennsylvania (PA)
Christian Brothers U (TN)
Cleveland State U (OH)
Coastal Carolina U (SC)
Coll of Charleston (SC)
The Coll of New Jersey (NJ)
The Coll of New Rochelle (NY)
The Coll of Saint Rose (NY)
Columbia Coll (SC)
Columbus State U (GA)
Concordia U Chicago (IL)
Concordia U, Nebraska (NE)
Concord U (WV)
Creighton U (NE)
Cumberland U (TN)
Curry Coll (MA)
Daemen Coll (NY)
Delaware State U (DE)
DePaul U (IL)
Doane Coll (NE)
Dominican Coll (NY)
Dowling Coll (NY)
East Carolina U (NC)
East Central U (OK)
Eastern Illinois U (IL)
Eastern Kentucky U (KY)
Eastern New Mexico U (NM)
East Stroudsburg U of Pennsylvania (PA)
East Tennessee State U (TN)
Edinboro U of Pennsylvania (PA)
Elmhurst Coll (IL)
Elon U (NC)
Erskine Coll (SC)
Evangel U (MO)
Fairmont State U (WV)
Fitchburg State U (MA)
Flagler Coll (FL)
Florida Atlantic U (FL)
Florida Gulf Coast U (FL)
Florida Intl U (FL)
Fontbonne U (MO)
Furman U (SC)
Geneva Coll (PA)
Georgia Coll & State U (GA)
Georgia Gwinnett Coll (GA)
Georgia Regents U (GA)
Georgia Southern U (GA)
Georgia Southwestern State U (GA)
Gonzaga U (WA)
Goshen Coll (IN)
Goucher Coll (MD)
Grace Coll (IN)
Grand Valley State U (MI)
Greensboro Coll (NC)
Greenville Coll (IL)
Grove City Coll (PA)
Gwynedd Mercy U (PA)
Hampton U (VA)
Hastings Coll (NE)
Heidelberg U (OH)
Heritage U (WA)
High Point U (NC)
Holy Family U (PA)
Houghton Coll (NY)
Houston Baptist U (TX)
Illinois State U (IL)
Indiana State U (IN)
Indiana U Bloomington (IN)
Indiana U South Bend (IN)
Indiana U Southeast (IN)
Indian River State Coll (FL)
Inter American U of Puerto Rico, Fajardo Campus (PR)
Inter American U of Puerto Rico, Ponce Campus (PR)
Inter American U of Puerto Rico, San Germán Campus (PR)
Jackson State U (MS)
Jacksonville State U (AL)
Jacksonville U (FL)
John Brown U (AR)
John Carroll U (OH)
Kansas Wesleyan U (KS)
Kean U (NJ)
Kent State U (OH)
Keuka Coll (NY)
Kutztown U of Pennsylvania (PA)
Lake Erie Coll (OH)
Langston U (OK)
La Salle U (PA)
Lebanon Valley Coll (PA)
Lee U (TN)
Le Moyne Coll (NY)
LeMoyne-Owen Coll (TN)
Lesley U (MA)
Lewis U (IL)
Lindenwood U (MO)
Lock Haven U of Pennsylvania (PA)
Loras Coll (IA)
Louisiana Coll (LA)
Loyola U Chicago (IL)
Lubbock Christian U (TX)
Manchester U (IN)
Manhattan Coll (NY)
Mansfield U of Pennsylvania (PA)
Marian U (IN)
Mars Hill U (NC)
Marymount U (VA)
Marywood U (PA)
Mayville State U (ND)
Medaille Coll (NY)
Medgar Evers Coll of the City U of New York (NY)
Merrimack Coll (MA)
Miami Dade Coll (FL)
Miami U (OH)
Michigan State U (MI)
Middle Tennessee State U (TN)
Midwestern State U (TX)
Millersville U of Pennsylvania (PA)
Minnesota State U Moorhead (MN)
Mississippi State U (MS)
Missouri State U (MO)
Missouri Valley Coll (MO)
Monmouth U (NJ)
Montana State U Billings (MT)
Morehead State U (KY)
Morningside Coll (IA)
Mount Marty Coll (SD)
Mount St. Joseph U (OH)
Mount Vernon Nazarene U (OH)
Murray State U (KY)
Nazareth Coll of Rochester (NY)
Nebraska Wesleyan U (NE)
New England Coll (NH)
New Jersey City U (NJ)
New Mexico Highlands U (NM)
New Mexico State U (NM)
New York U (NY)
Niagara U (NY)
North Carolina Ag and Tech State U (NC)
North Carolina Wesleyan Coll (NC)
Northeastern Illinois U (IL)
Northern Arizona U (AZ)
Northern Michigan U (MI)
Northern State U (SD)
Northwestern Oklahoma State U (OK)
Ohio Dominican U (OH)
The Ohio State U (OH)
Ohio U (OH)
Oklahoma Baptist U (OK)
Oklahoma City U (OK)
Pace U (NY)
Penn State Abington (PA)
Penn State Altoona (PA)
Penn State Beaver (PA)
Penn State Berks (PA)
Penn State Brandywine (PA)
Penn State DuBois (PA)
Penn State Erie, The Behrend Coll (PA)
Penn State Fayette, The Eberly Campus (PA)
Penn State Greater Allegheny (PA)
Penn State Hazleton (PA)
Penn State Lehigh Valley (PA)
Penn State Mont Alto (PA)
Penn State New Kensington (PA)
Penn State Schuylkill (PA)
Penn State Shenango (PA)
Penn State U Park (PA)
Penn State Wilkes-Barre (PA)
Penn State Worthington Scranton (PA)
Penn State York (PA)
Peru State Coll (NE)
Providence Coll (RI)
Quincy U (IL)
Rhode Island Coll (RI)
Rivier U (NH)
Roberts Wesleyan Coll (NY)
Rockford U (IL)
Roosevelt U (IL)
Rowan U (NJ)
Saginaw Valley State U (MI)
St. Bonaventure U (NY)
St. Edward's U (TX)
Saint Francis U (PA)
St. John Fisher Coll (NY)
St. John's U (NY)
St. Joseph's Coll, Long Island Campus (NY)
St. Joseph's Coll, New York (NY)
Saint Joseph's U (PA)
Saint Martin's U (WA)
Saint Mary-of-the-Woods Coll (IN)
St. Thomas Aquinas Coll (NY)
Salve Regina U (RI)
San Jose State U (CA)
Seattle Pacific U (WA)
Shawnee State U (OH)
Simmons Coll (MA)
Slippery Rock U of Pennsylvania (PA)
South Carolina State U (SC)
Southeastern U (FL)
Southeast Missouri State U (MO)
Southern Connecticut State U (CT)
Southern Illinois U Carbondale (IL)
Southern Illinois U Edwardsville (IL)
Southwest Minnesota State U (MN)
Spalding U (KY)
State U of New York at New Paltz (NY)
State U of New York at Plattsburgh (NY)
State U of New York Coll at Geneseo (NY)
State U of New York Coll at Old Westbury (NY)
Tennessee State U (TN)
Texas A&M Intl U (TX)
Texas Christian U (TX)
Towson U (MD)
Trevecca Nazarene U (TN)
Trinity Christian Coll (IL)
Tusculum Coll (TN)
Union Inst & U (OH)
Union U (TN)
Universidad del Turabo (PR)
Universidad Metropolitana (PR)
Université de Montréal (QC, Canada)
Université de Sherbrooke (QC, Canada)
Université du Québec en Outaouais (QC, Canada)
The U of Akron (OH)
The U of Alabama (AL)
U of Alaska Southeast, Sitka Campus (AK)
The U of Arizona (AZ)
U of Arkansas at Pine Bluff (AR)
The U of British Columbia (BC, Canada)
U of Central Missouri (MO)
U of Central Oklahoma (OK)
U of Cincinnati (OH)
U of Dayton (OH)
U of Delaware (DE)
U of Evansville (IN)
The U of Findlay (OH)
U of Florida (FL)
U of Georgia (GA)
U of Great Falls (MT)
U of Guam (GU)
U of Hartford (CT)
U of Hawaii at Manoa (HI)
U of Idaho (ID)
U of Kentucky (KY)
U of Lethbridge (AB, Canada)
U of Maryland, Coll Park (MD)
U of Memphis (TN)
U of Mississippi (MS)
U of Mount Union (OH)
U of Nebraska at Kearney (NE)
U of Nevada, Las Vegas (NV)
U of Nevada, Reno (NV)
U of New Mexico (NM)
The U of North Carolina at Charlotte (NC)
The U of North Carolina at Greensboro (NC)
The U of North Carolina at Pembroke (NC)
The U of North Carolina Wilmington (NC)
U of Northern Colorado (CO)
U of Northern Iowa (IA)
U of North Florida (FL)
U of North Georgia (GA)
U of Oklahoma (OK)
U of St. Francis (IL)
U of Saint Francis (IN)
U of Saint Joseph (CT)
U of South Alabama (AL)
U of South Carolina Aiken (SC)
The U of South Dakota (SD)
U of Southern Mississippi (MS)
U of South Florida (FL)
The U of Tennessee (TN)
The U of Tennessee at Chattanooga (TN)
The U of Tennessee at Martin (TN)
The U of Texas at San Antonio (TX)
U of the Cumberlands (KY)
U of the District of Columbia (DC)
U of the Pacific (CA)
The U of Toledo (OH)
U of Utah (UT)
The U of West Alabama (AL)
U of West Florida (FL)
U of West Georgia (GA)
U of Windsor (ON, Canada)
U of Wisconsin–Eau Claire (WI)
U of Wisconsin–Madison (WI)
U of Wisconsin–Milwaukee (WI)
U of Wisconsin–Oshkosh (WI)
U of Wisconsin–Stevens Point (WI)
U of Wisconsin–Stout (WI)
U of Wisconsin–Superior (WI)
U of Wisconsin–Whitewater (WI)
U of Wyoming (WY)
Ursuline Coll (OH)
Utah State U (UT)
Valdosta State U (GA)
Vanderbilt U (TN)
Vincennes U (IN)
Virginia Union U (VA)
Virginia Wesleyan Coll (VA)
Walsh U (OH)
Washington State U (WA)
Waynesburg U (PA)
Wayne State Coll (NE)
Wayne State U (MI)
Weber State U (UT)
Webster U (MO)
West Chester U of Pennsylvania (PA)
Western Carolina U (NC)
Western Illinois U (IL)
Western Kentucky U (KY)
Western Washington U (WA)
Westfield State U (MA)
Westminster Coll (UT)
West Virginia Wesleyan Coll (WV)
Whitworth U (WA)
Widener U (PA)
William Paterson U of New Jersey (NJ)
William Penn U (IA)
William Woods U (MO)
Winona State U (MN)
Winthrop U (SC)
Xavier U (OH)
Youngstown State U (OH)

SPECIAL EDUCATION (ADMINISTRATION)

Slippery Rock U of Pennsylvania (PA)

SPECIAL EDUCATION–EARLY CHILDHOOD

Bowling Green State U (OH)
Canisius Coll (NY)
Cazenovia Coll (NY)
Clarion U of Pennsylvania (PA)
Daytona State Coll (FL)
Delaware State U (DE)
Eastern Kentucky U (KY)
Edgewood Coll (WI)
Elmira Coll (NY)
Harding U (AR)
Hope Coll (MI)
Indiana U of Pennsylvania (PA)
Inter American U of Puerto Rico, Aguadilla Campus (PR)
Inter American U of Puerto Rico, Ponce Campus (PR)
Judson U (IL)
Juniata Coll (PA)
Keuka Coll (NY)
Keystone Coll (PA)
Lewis U (IL)
Lindenwood U (MO)
Prescott Coll (AZ)
Roberts Wesleyan Coll (NY)
Shippensburg U of Pennsylvania (PA)
Silver Lake Coll of the Holy Family (WI)
State U of New York Coll at Geneseo (NY)
Syracuse U (NY)
Tusculum Coll (TN)
The U of Akron (OH)
U of Mount Union (OH)
U of Vermont (VT)
York Coll of Pennsylvania (PA)

SPECIAL EDUCATION–ELEMENTARY SCHOOL

Abilene Christian U (TX)
Alvernia U (PA)
Canisius Coll (NY)
Granite State Coll (NH)
Kutztown U of Pennsylvania (PA)
Molloy Coll (NY)
Neumann U (PA)
Purdue U (IN)
Rhode Island Coll (RI)
Shawnee State U (OH)
Syracuse U (NY)
Universidad Metropolitana (PR)
U of Mount Union (OH)
U of Wyoming (WY)

SPECIAL EDUCATION–GIFTED AND TALENTED

Canisius Coll (NY)
Delaware State U (DE)
Eastern Kentucky U (KY)
Flagler Coll (FL)
Grand Valley State U (MI)
U of Great Falls (MT)
Wright State U (OH)

SPECIAL EDUCATION–INDIVIDUALS WHO ARE DEVELOPMENTALLY DELAYED

Saint Mary-of-the-Woods Coll (IN)

SPECIAL EDUCATION–INDIVIDUALS WITH AUTISM

Inter American U of Puerto Rico, Ponce Campus (PR)

SPECIAL EDUCATION–INDIVIDUALS WITH EMOTIONAL DISTURBANCES

Central Michigan U (MI)
Eastern Michigan U (MI)
Grand Valley State U (MI)
Greensboro Coll (NC)
Hope Coll (MI)
Morningside Coll (IA)
Northern Michigan U (MI)
Olivet Coll (MI)
The U of Toledo (OH)
Western Michigan U (MI)

SPECIAL EDUCATION–INDIVIDUALS WITH HEARING IMPAIRMENTS

Boston U (MA)
Bowling Green State U (OH)
Canisius Coll (NY)
The Coll of New Jersey (NJ)
Eastern Kentucky U (KY)
Eastern Michigan U (MI)
Flagler Coll (FL)
Grand Valley State U (MI)
Michigan State U (MI)
Minot State U (ND)
Texas Christian U (TX)
U of Nebraska–Lincoln (NE)
The U of North Carolina at Greensboro (NC)
U of Science and Arts of Oklahoma (OK)
U of Southern Mississippi (MS)
The U of Toledo (OH)
The U of Tulsa (OK)
Utah Valley U (UT)

SPECIAL EDUCATION–INDIVIDUALS WITH INTELLECTUAL DISABILITIES
Bowling Green State U (OH)
Brenau U (GA)
Central Michigan U (MI)
Eastern Michigan U (MI)
Grand Valley State U (MI)
Greensboro Coll (NC)
Manchester U (IN)
Minot State U (ND)
Morningside Coll (IA)
Northern Michigan U (MI)
Oakland City U (IN)
Silver Lake Coll of the Holy Family (WI)
U of Rio Grande (OH)
Walsh U (OH)
Western Michigan U (MI)

SPECIAL EDUCATION–INDIVIDUALS WITH MULTIPLE DISABILITIES
Ball State U (IN)
Bowling Green State U (OH)
Bradley U (IL)
Dominican Coll (NY)
Grand Valley State U (MI)
Northwest Missouri State U (MO)
The U of Akron (OH)
The U of North Carolina Wilmington (NC)
The U of Toledo (OH)
Walsh U (OH)
Wright State U (OH)

SPECIAL EDUCATION–INDIVIDUALS WITH ORTHOPEDIC AND OTHER PHYSICAL HEALTH IMPAIRMENTS
Eastern Michigan U (MI)
Grand Valley State U (MI)

SPECIAL EDUCATION–INDIVIDUALS WITH SPECIFIC LEARNING DISABILITIES
Appalachian State U (NC)
Aquinas Coll (MI)
Baldwin Wallace U (OH)
Bethune-Cookman U (FL)
Bowling Green State U (OH)
Bradley U (IL)
Canisius Coll (NY)
Cornerstone U (MI)
Creighton U (NE)
Flagler Coll (FL)
Greensboro Coll (NC)
Hope Coll (MI)
Judson U (IL)
Malone U (OH)
Michigan State U (MI)
Northeastern State U (OK)
Northern Michigan U (MI)
Northwestern U (IL)
Prescott Coll (AZ)
Silver Lake Coll of the Holy Family (WI)
State U of New York at Plattsburgh (NY)
U of Rio Grande (OH)
U of South Carolina Upstate (SC)
The U of Toledo (OH)
West Virginia Wesleyan Coll (WV)
Wright State U (OH)

SPECIAL EDUCATION–INDIVIDUALS WITH SPEECH/LANGUAGE IMPAIRMENTS
Armstrong State U (GA)
Baylor U (TX)
Buffalo State Coll, State U of New York (NY)
Eastern Michigan U (MI)
Elmira Coll (NY)
Emerson Coll (MA)
Ithaca Coll (NY)
Minot State U (ND)
New Mexico State U (NM)
Pace U (NY)
State U of New York Coll at Cortland (NY)
The U of Toledo (OH)
Wayne State U (MI)

SPECIAL EDUCATION–INDIVIDUALS WITH VISION IMPAIRMENTS
Eastern Michigan U (MI)
Kutztown U of Pennsylvania (PA)
St. Francis Coll (NY)
The U of Toledo (OH)

SPECIAL EDUCATION–JUNIOR HIGH/MIDDLE SCHOOL
Cazenovia Coll (NY)
Clarion U of Pennsylvania (PA)

SPECIAL EDUCATION RELATED
Auburn U (AL)
Bowling Green State U (OH)
Canisius Coll (NY)
Catawba Coll (NC)
Clarion U of Pennsylvania (PA)
Dakota State U (SD)
Delaware State U (DE)
East Carolina U (NC)
Kean U (NJ)
Lee U (TN)
Lincoln U (MO)
Lock Haven U of Pennsylvania (PA)
Minot State U (ND)
Purdue U (IN)
Saint Mary-of-the-Woods Coll (IN)
Southeastern Oklahoma State U (OK)
Southern New Hampshire U (NH)
Universidad Metropolitana (PR)
U of Missouri (MO)
U of Nebraska–Lincoln (NE)
The U of North Carolina at Charlotte (NC)
U of Southern Indiana (IN)
Wright State U (OH)

SPECIAL EDUCATION–SECONDARY SCHOOL
Abilene Christian U (TX)
Canisius Coll (NY)
Cazenovia Coll (NY)
Kutztown U of Pennsylvania (PA)
Molloy Coll (NY)
Oklahoma City U (OK)
Purdue U (IN)
Rhode Island Coll (RI)

SPECIAL PRODUCTS MARKETING
Buffalo State Coll, State U of New York (NY)
Central Washington U (WA)
Concord U (WV)
Dominican U (IL)
Fashion Inst of Technology (NY)
Iowa State U of Science and Technology (IA)
Rochester Inst of Technology (NY)
Saint Joseph's U (PA)
Stephen F. Austin State U (TX)
U of North Texas (TX)

SPEECH COMMUNICATION AND RHETORIC
Abilene Christian U (TX)
Alabama State U (AL)
Albertus Magnus Coll (CT)
Albright Coll (PA)
Allegheny Coll (PA)
Alverno Coll (WI)
American U (DC)
The American U of Rome (Italy)
Appalachian State U (NC)
Aquinas Coll (MI)
Arcadia U (PA)
Arizona State U at the Downtown Phoenix campus (AZ)
Arizona State U at the Polytechnic campus (AZ)
Arizona State U at the Tempe campus (AZ)
Arizona State U at the West campus (AZ)
Arkansas Tech U (AR)
Ashland U (OH)
Auburn U at Montgomery (AL)
Augsburg Coll (MN)
Augustana Coll (SD)
Austin Coll (TX)
Avila U (MO)
Azusa Pacific U (CA)
Baldwin Wallace U (OH)
Ball State U (IN)
Barry U (FL)
Baylor U (TX)
Belhaven U (MS)
Belmont U (TN)
Benedictine U (IL)
Bethany Coll (WV)
Bethany Lutheran Coll (MN)
Bethel Coll (IN)
Bethune-Cookman U (FL)
Biola U (CA)
Blackburn Coll (IL)
Bluffton U (OH)
Bowling Green State U (OH)
Bridgewater State U (MA)
Bryan Coll (TN)
Bryant U (RI)
Buena Vista U (IA)
Buffalo State Coll, State U of New York (NY)
Butler U (IN)
Cabrini Coll (PA)
Caldwell U (NJ)
California Baptist U (CA)
California Polytechnic State U, San Luis Obispo (CA)
California State Polytechnic U, Pomona (CA)
California State U, Dominguez Hills (CA)
California State U, Fresno (CA)
California State U, Fullerton (CA)
California State U, Los Angeles (CA)
California State U, Sacramento (CA)
California State U, San Marcos (CA)
California State U, Stanislaus (CA)
California U of Pennsylvania (PA)
Calvin Coll (MI)
Cape Breton U (NS, Canada)
Capital U (OH)
Cardinal Stritch U (WI)
Catawba Coll (NC)
The Catholic U of America (DC)
Cedar Crest Coll (PA)
Central Coll (IA)
Central Connecticut State U (CT)
Central Methodist U (MO)
Central Michigan U (MI)
Chaminade U of Honolulu (HI)
Champlain Coll (VT)
Chapman U (CA)
Chowan U (NC)
Christopher Newport U (VA)
Clarkson U (NY)
Clayton State U (GA)
Cleveland State U (OH)
Coastal Carolina U (SC)
Coe Coll (IA)
Coker Coll (SC)
The Coll at Brockport, State U of New York (NY)
Coll of Charleston (SC)
The Coll of New Rochelle (NY)
Coll of Saint Elizabeth (NJ)
The Coll of Saint Rose (NY)
The Coll of St. Scholastica (MN)
Coll of Staten Island of the City U of New York (NY)
The Coll of Wooster (OH)
Colorado State U (CO)
Columbia Coll (MO)
Columbia Coll (SC)
Concordia Coll (MN)
Concordia U Chicago (IL)
Concordia U, Nebraska (NE)
Corban U (OR)
Cornell U (NY)
Cornerstone U (MI)
Creighton U (NE)
Culver-Stockton Coll (MO)
Dallas Baptist U (TX)
DePaul U (IL)
Dixie State U (UT)
Dominican U (IL)
Drury U (MO)
Duquesne U (PA)
East Carolina U (NC)
East Central U (OK)
Eastern Connecticut State U (CT)
Eastern Kentucky U (KY)
Eastern Michigan U (MI)
Eastern New Mexico U (NM)
Eastern U (PA)
East Stroudsburg U of Pennsylvania (PA)
Eckerd Coll (FL)
Elmhurst Coll (IL)
Embry-Riddle Aeronautical U–Daytona (FL)
Emerson Coll (MA)
Emmanuel Coll (MA)
Emporia State U (KS)
Eureka Coll (IL)
Excelsior Coll (NY)
Fairfield U (CT)
Fairleigh Dickinson U, Coll at Florham (NJ)
Fayetteville State U (NC)
Ferris State U (MI)
Fitchburg State U (MA)
Florida Atlantic U (FL)
Florida Intl U (FL)
Fontbonne U (MO)
Franciscan U of Steubenville (OH)
Furman U (SC)
Gallaudet U (DC)
Georgia Regents U (GA)
Georgia Southern U (GA)
Georgia State U (GA)
Gonzaga U (WA)
Gordon Coll (MA)
Goshen Coll (IN)
Governors State U (IL)
Grace Coll (IN)
Grand Valley State U (MI)
Great Lakes Christian Coll (MI)
Greensboro Coll (NC)
Greenville Coll (IL)
Grove City Coll (PA)
Hamline U (MN)
Hampshire Coll (MA)
Hannibal-LaGrange U (MO)
Harding U (AR)
Hardin-Simmons U (TX)
Hastings Coll (NE)
Hawai`i Pacific U (HI)
Hillsdale Coll (MI)
Hillsdale Free Will Baptist Coll (OK)
Hofstra U (NY)
Hope Coll (MI)
Houghton Coll (NY)
Houston Baptist U (TX)
Howard Payne U (TX)
Illinois State U (IL)
Indiana State U (IN)
Indiana U Bloomington (IN)
Indiana U East (IN)
Indiana U Kokomo (IN)
Indiana U Northwest (IN)
Indiana U of Pennsylvania (PA)
Indiana U–Purdue U Fort Wayne (IN)
Indiana U–Purdue U Indianapolis (IN)
Indiana U South Bend (IN)
Indiana U Southeast (IN)
Iona Coll (NY)
Jacksonville State U (AL)
Jacksonville U (FL)
James Madison U (VA)
John Brown U (AR)
Judson U (IL)
Juniata Coll (PA)
Kansas State U (KS)
Kansas Wesleyan U (KS)
Kean U (NJ)
Keene State Coll (NH)
Kennesaw State U (GA)
Kent State U (OH)
Kent State U at Ashtabula (OH)
Kent State U at East Liverpool (OH)
Kent State U at Salem (OH)
Kent State U at Stark (OH)
Kent State U at Trumbull (OH)
Kent State U at Tuscarawas (OH)
Kentucky Wesleyan Coll (KY)
Keuka Coll (NY)
Kuyper Coll (MI)
La Sierra U (CA)
Lawrence Technological U (MI)
Lee U (TN)
Lenoir-Rhyne U (NC)
Lewis & Clark Coll (OR)
Lewis U (IL)
Liberty U (VA)
Lincoln U (PA)
Lindenwood U (MO)
Linfield Coll (OR)
Long Island U–LIU Brooklyn (NY)
Longwood U (VA)
Louisiana State U and A&M Coll (LA)
Loyola Marymount U (CA)
Loyola U Chicago (IL)
Loyola U New Orleans (LA)
Luther Coll (IA)
Lynchburg Coll (VA)
Manchester U (IN)
Mansfield U of Pennsylvania (PA)
Marian U (IN)
Marian U (WI)
Marietta Coll (OH)
Marylhurst U (OR)
Marymount Manhattan Coll (NY)
Mayville State U (ND)
McDaniel Coll (MD)
McKendree U (IL)
Mercer U, Macon (GA)
Meredith Coll (NC)
Merrimack Coll (MA)
Messiah Coll (PA)
Metropolitan State U (MN)
Michigan State U (MI)
Millersville U of Pennsylvania (PA)
Millikin U (IL)
Millsaps Coll (MS)
Minnesota State U Moorhead (MN)
Mississippi State U (MS)
Mississippi U for Women (MS)
Missouri Southern State U (MO)
Missouri State U (MO)
Missouri Western State U (MO)
Molloy Coll (NY)
Monmouth Coll (IL)
Monmouth U (NJ)
Montclair State U (NJ)
Mount Mary U (WI)
Mount Mercy U (IA)
Mount St. Joseph U (OH)
Mount St. Mary's U (MD)
Mount Vernon Nazarene U (OH)
Nazareth Coll of Rochester (NY)
Nebraska Wesleyan U (NE)
New Jersey City U (NJ)
New Mexico Highlands U (NM)
New York U (NY)
North Carolina Ag and Tech State U (NC)
North Carolina State U (NC)
North Central Coll (IL)
Northeastern State U (OK)
Northeastern U (MA)
Northern Arizona U (AZ)
Northern Illinois U (IL)
Northern Kentucky U (KY)
Northern Michigan U (MI)
Northwest Christian U (OR)
Northwestern U (IL)
Northwest Nazarene U (ID)
Norwich U (VT)
Notre Dame of Maryland U (MD)
Nova Southeastern U (FL)
Oglethorpe U (GA)
Ohio Dominican U (OH)
Ohio Northern U (OH)
The Ohio State U (OH)
Ohio U (OH)
Oklahoma Baptist U (OK)
Olivet Nazarene U (IL)
Oregon State U (OR)
Pace U (NY)
Pacific Lutheran U (WA)
Palm Beach Atlantic U (FL)
Park U (MO)
Penn State Abington (PA)
Penn State Altoona (PA)
Penn State Beaver (PA)
Penn State Berks (PA)
Penn State Brandywine (PA)
Penn State DuBois (PA)
Penn State Erie, The Behrend Coll (PA)
Penn State Fayette, The Eberly Campus (PA)
Penn State Greater Allegheny (PA)
Penn State Harrisburg (PA)
Penn State Hazleton (PA)
Penn State Lehigh Valley (PA)
Penn State Mont Alto (PA)
Penn State New Kensington (PA)
Penn State Schuylkill (PA)
Penn State Shenango (PA)
Penn State U Park (PA)
Penn State Wilkes-Barre (PA)
Penn State Worthington Scranton (PA)
Penn State York (PA)
Pepperdine U, Malibu (CA)
Pine Manor Coll (MA)
Pittsburg State U (KS)
Plymouth State U (NH)
Point Loma Nazarene U (CA)
Prairie View A&M U (TX)
Purchase Coll, State U of New York (NY)

Purdue U Calumet (IN)
Radford U (VA)
Ramapo Coll of New Jersey (NJ)
Randolph Coll (VA)
Regis Coll (MA)
Regis U (CO)
Rensselaer Polytechnic Inst (NY)
Rhode Island Coll (RI)
Rider U (NJ)
Ripon Coll (WI)
Robert Morris U (PA)
Roberts Wesleyan Coll (NY)
Rochester Inst of Technology (NY)
Rockhurst U (MO)
Rocky Mountain Coll (MT)
Roger Williams U (RI)
Roosevelt U (IL)
Rosemont Coll (PA)
Rutgers, The State U of New Jersey, New Brunswick (NJ)
Saginaw Valley State U (MI)
Saint Anselm Coll (NH)
St. Francis Coll (NY)
St. Gregory's U, Shawnee (OK)
St. John's U (NY)
Saint Joseph's Coll (IN)
Saint Joseph's U (PA)
St. Lawrence U (NY)
Saint Mary's Coll (IN)
St. Mary's U (TX)
St. Norbert Coll (WI)
Saint Peter's U (NJ)
Saint Vincent Coll (PA)
Salisbury U (MD)
Samford U (AL)
Sam Houston State U (TX)
San Diego Christian Coll (CA)
San Diego State U (CA)
San Francisco State U (CA)
Santa Clara U (CA)
Seattle Pacific U (WA)
Seattle U (WA)
Seton Hill U (PA)
Shenandoah U (VA)
Shepherd U (WV)
Simmons Coll (MA)
Simon Fraser U (BC, Canada)
Simpson U (CA)
Slippery Rock U of Pennsylvania (PA)
South Dakota State U (SD)
Southeastern Louisiana U (LA)
Southeastern Oklahoma State U (OK)
Southeast Missouri State U (MO)
Southern Connecticut State U (CT)
Southern Oregon U (OR)
Southern Utah U (UT)
Southwest Baptist U (MO)
Southwestern Assemblies of God U (TX)
Southwestern Coll (KS)
Southwestern U (TX)
Southwest Minnesota State U (MN)
Spalding U (KY)
State U of New York at New Paltz (NY)
State U of New York at Plattsburgh (NY)
State U of New York Coll at Cortland (NY)
State U of New York Coll at Old Westbury (NY)
State U of New York Coll at Potsdam (NY)
Stockton U (NJ)
Stonehill Coll (MA)
Suffolk U (MA)
Summit U (PA)
Susquehanna U (PA)
Syracuse U (NY)
Tarleton State U (TX)
Taylor U (IN)
Texas A&M Intl U (TX)
Texas Christian U (TX)
Texas Lutheran U (TX)
Texas Southern U (TX)
Thiel Coll (PA)
Tiffin U (OH)
Towson U (MD)
Trevecca Nazarene U (TN)
Trine U (IN)
Trinity Christian Coll (IL)
Trinity U (TX)
Troy U (AL)
Truman State U (MO)
Universidad del Turabo (PR)
U at Albany, State U of New York (NY)
U at Buffalo, the State U of New York (NY)
The U of Akron (OH)
The U of Alabama (AL)
The U of Alabama at Birmingham (AL)
The U of Alabama in Huntsville (AL)
U of Alaska Fairbanks (AK)
The U of Arizona (AZ)
U of Arkansas (AR)
U of Arkansas at Little Rock (AR)
U of California, Davis (CA)
U of Central Florida (FL)
U of Central Oklahoma (OK)
U of Cincinnati (OH)
U of Colorado Boulder (CO)
U of Colorado Colorado Springs (CO)
U of Colorado Denver (CO)
U of Dayton (OH)
U of Delaware (DE)
U of Denver (CO)
U of Georgia (GA)
U of Hartford (CT)
U of Hawaii at Manoa (HI)
U of Houston (TX)
U of Illinois at Chicago (IL)
U of Indianapolis (IN)
The U of Iowa (IA)
U of Jamestown (ND)
The U of Kansas (KS)
U of Kentucky (KY)
U of La Verne (CA)
U of Louisiana at Lafayette (LA)
U of Louisville (KY)
U of Mary Hardin-Baylor (TX)
U of Maryland, Coll Park (MD)
U of Maryland U Coll (MD)
U of Memphis (TN)
U of Miami (FL)
U of Michigan (MI)
U of Michigan–Dearborn (MI)
U of Minnesota, Duluth (MN)
U of Minnesota, Twin Cities Campus (MN)
U of Missouri (MO)
The U of Montana (MT)
U of Nebraska–Lincoln (NE)
U of Nevada, Las Vegas (NV)
U of Nevada, Reno (NV)
U of New Brunswick Saint John (NB, Canada)
U of New Hampshire (NH)
U of New Haven (CT)
U of North Alabama (AL)
The U of North Carolina at Chapel Hill (NC)
The U of North Carolina at Charlotte (NC)
The U of North Carolina at Greensboro (NC)
The U of North Carolina Wilmington (NC)
U of Northern Colorado (CO)
U of Northern Iowa (IA)
U of Northwestern–St. Paul (MN)
U of Oklahoma (OK)
U of Ottawa (ON, Canada)
U of Pennsylvania (PA)
U of Pikeville (KY)
U of Puget Sound (WA)
U of Rhode Island (RI)
U of Rio Grande (OH)
U of Saint Francis (IN)
U of St. Thomas (TX)
U of San Francisco (CA)
U of Science and Arts of Oklahoma (OK)
The U of Scranton (PA)
U of South Alabama (AL)
U of South Carolina Aiken (SC)
U of South Carolina Beaufort (SC)
U of South Carolina Upstate (SC)
U of Southern California (CA)
U of Southern Maine (ME)
U of Southern Mississippi (MS)
The U of Tennessee (TN)
The U of Tennessee at Chattanooga (TN)
The U of Texas at Austin (TX)
The U of Texas–Pan American (TX)
U of the Cumberlands (KY)
U of the Incarnate Word (TX)
U of the Pacific (CA)
U of the Virgin Islands (VI)
The U of Toledo (OH)
The U of Tulsa (OK)
U of Utah (UT)
The U of Virginia's Coll at Wise (VA)
U of Washington (WA)
U of Waterloo (ON, Canada)
U of Wisconsin–La Crosse (WI)
U of Wisconsin–Madison (WI)
U of Wisconsin–Milwaukee (WI)
U of Wisconsin–Parkside (WI)
U of Wisconsin–Platteville (WI)
U of Wisconsin–River Falls (WI)
U of Wisconsin–Stevens Point (WI)
U of Wisconsin–Whitewater (WI)
U of Wyoming (WY)
Utica Coll (NY)
Valdosta State U (GA)
Valparaiso U (IN)
Vanderbilt U (TN)
Vanguard U of Southern California (CA)
Virginia Polytechnic Inst and State U (VA)
Wake Forest U (NC)
Wartburg Coll (IA)
Washburn U (KS)
Washington U in St. Louis (MO)
Waynesburg U (PA)
Wayne State Coll (NE)
Wayne State U (MI)
Webber Intl U (FL)
Weber State U (UT)
Webster U (MO)
Wesleyan Coll (GA)
Western Carolina U (NC)
Western Illinois U (IL)
Western Kentucky U (KY)
Western Michigan U (MI)
Western New England U (MA)
Western Washington U (WA)
Westfield State U (MA)
West Texas A&M U (TX)
West Virginia State U (WV)
West Virginia Wesleyan Coll (WV)
Wheaton Coll (IL)
Whitman Coll (WA)
Wichita State U (KS)
Wilkes U (PA)
William Jewell Coll (MO)
William Peace U (NC)
William Woods U (MO)
Wingate U (NC)
Wittenberg U (OH)
Worcester State U (MA)
Wright State U (OH)
York Coll of Pennsylvania (PA)
Youngstown State U (OH)

SPEECH-LANGUAGE PATHOLOGY

Abilene Christian U (TX)
Biola U (CA)
Clarion U of Pennsylvania (PA)
Cleveland State U (OH)
Columbia Coll (SC)
Duquesne U (PA)
Eastern Michigan U (MI)
Edinboro U of Pennsylvania (PA)
Emerson Coll (MA)
Geneva Coll (PA)
Harding U (AR)
Inter American U of Puerto Rico, Aguadilla Campus (PR)
Inter American U of Puerto Rico, Fajardo Campus (PR)
Inter American U of Puerto Rico, Ponce Campus (PR)
Jackson State U (MS)
James Madison U (VA)
Lehman Coll of the City U of New York (NY)
Marshall U (WV)
Marymount Manhattan Coll (NY)
Minnesota State U Moorhead (MN)
Mississippi U for Women (MS)
Molloy Coll (NY)
Nazareth Coll of Rochester (NY)
Northeastern State U (OK)
Northern Michigan U (MI)
Northwestern U (IL)
Nova Southeastern U (FL)
Oklahoma State U (OK)
Rockhurst U (MO)
San Diego State U (CA)
Texas Christian U (TX)
Towson U (MD)
Trinity Christian Coll (IL)
Universidad del Turabo (PR)
Universidad Metropolitana (PR)
U of Central Missouri (MO)
U of Central Oklahoma (OK)
U of Montevallo (AL)
U of Nebraska–Lincoln (NE)
U of Nevada, Reno (NV)
U of Northern Iowa (IA)
U of Oklahoma Health Sciences Center (OK)
U of Science and Arts of Oklahoma (OK)
U of the District of Columbia (DC)
The U of Toledo (OH)
U of West Georgia (GA)
Valdosta State U (GA)
Xavier U of Louisiana (LA)

SPEECH-LANGUAGE PATHOLOGY ASSISTANT

Caribbean U (PR)

SPEECH TEACHER EDUCATION

Albion Coll (MI)
Anderson U (IN)
Arkansas Tech U (AR)
Augustana Coll (SD)
Austin Coll (TX)
Bemidji State U (MN)
Bowling Green State U (OH)
Brigham Young U (UT)
Buena Vista U (IA)
Capital U (OH)
Carroll Coll (MT)
Central Michigan U (MI)
Colorado State U (CO)
Concordia U, Nebraska (NE)
Cornerstone U (MI)
Culver-Stockton Coll (MO)
Dallas Baptist U (TX)
Dickinson State U (ND)
East Central U (OK)
East Texas Baptist U (TX)
Evangel U (MO)
Friends U (KS)
Harding U (AR)
Hardin-Simmons U (TX)
Hastings Coll (NE)
Howard Payne U (TX)
Indiana U–Purdue U Fort Wayne (IN)
Kansas Wesleyan U (KS)
Lee U (TN)
McKendree U (IL)
Northwestern Coll (IA)
Northwest U (WA)
Oklahoma City U (OK)
Olivet Coll (MI)
Saginaw Valley State U (MI)
St. Catherine U (MN)
Southern Utah U (UT)
Southwest Baptist U (MO)
Southwestern Coll (KS)
Southwest Minnesota State U (MN)
Summit U (PA)
Trevecca Nazarene U (TN)
U of Alberta (AB, Canada)
U of Indianapolis (IN)
The U of Iowa (IA)
U of Mary Hardin-Baylor (TX)
U of Michigan–Flint (MI)
U of Minnesota, Morris (MN)
U of Northern Iowa (IA)
U of Rio Grande (OH)
U of St. Thomas (MN)
The U of South Dakota (SD)
U of the Cumberlands (KY)
U of Windsor (ON, Canada)
Wartburg Coll (IA)
Wayne State Coll (NE)
Western Washington U (WA)
William Jewell Coll (MO)

SPORT AND FITNESS ADMINISTRATION/ MANAGEMENT

Abilene Christian U (TX)
Adelphi U (NY)
Albertus Magnus Coll (CT)
Alice Lloyd Coll (KY)
Alvernia U (PA)
American Intl Coll (MA)
American Public U System (WV)
Anna Maria Coll (MA)
Arizona State U at the Downtown Phoenix campus (AZ)
Arkansas State U (AR)
Asbury U (KY)
Athens State U (AL)
Augustana Coll (SD)
Averett U (VA)
Baker U (KS)
Baldwin Wallace U (OH)
Barry U (FL)
Becker Coll (MA)
Belhaven U (MS)
Belmont Abbey Coll (NC)
Bemidji State U (MN)
Bethany Coll (WV)
Bethel Coll (IN)
Blackburn Coll (IL)
Black Hills State U (SD)
Bluffton U (OH)
Bowling Green State U (OH)
Bridgewater State U (MA)
Buena Vista U (IA)
California U of Pennsylvania (PA)
Calvin Coll (MI)
Canisius Coll (NY)
Cape Breton U (NS, Canada)
Cardinal Stritch U (WI)
Castleton State Coll (VT)
Catawba Coll (NC)
Cazenovia Coll (NY)
Cedarville U (OH)
Central Methodist U (MO)
Central Michigan U (MI)
Chowan U (NC)
The Citadel, The Military Coll of South Carolina (SC)
Claflin U (SC)
Clarke U (IA)
Clayton State U (GA)
Cleveland State U (OH)
Coastal Carolina U (SC)
Coker Coll (SC)
Colby-Sawyer Coll (NH)
The Coll at Brockport, State U of New York (NY)
The Coll of Idaho (ID)
Colorado Mesa U (CO)
Columbia Coll (MO)
Concordia Coll–New York (NY)
Concordia U Chicago (IL)
Concordia U, Nebraska (NE)
Concordia U, St. Paul (MN)
Concordia U Wisconsin (WI)
Corban U (OR)
Cornerstone U (MI)
Culver-Stockton Coll (MO)
Dallas Baptist U (TX)
Daniel Webster Coll (NH)
Davenport U, Grand Rapids (MI)
Defiance Coll (OH)
Delaware State U (DE)
DeSales U (PA)
Dowling Coll (NY)
Drexel U (PA)
Eastern Connecticut State U (CT)
Eastern Kentucky U (KY)
Eastern Michigan U (MI)
East Tennessee State U (TN)
Elmhurst Coll (IL)
Elms Coll (MA)
Elon U (NC)
Emmanuel Coll (GA)
Emmanuel Coll (MA)
Emory & Henry Coll (VA)
Endicott Coll (MA)
Erskine Coll (SC)
Farmingdale State Coll (NY)
Faulkner U (AL)
Ferrum Coll (VA)
Fitchburg State U (MA)
Flagler Coll (FL)
Florida Inst of Technology (FL)
Fontbonne U (MO)
Fort Lewis Coll (CO)
Franklin Pierce U (NH)
Friends U (KS)
Gannon U (PA)
Geneva Coll (PA)
Georgia Southern U (GA)
Gonzaga U (WA)
Grace Coll (IN)
Grand View U (IA)
Greensboro Coll (NC)
Greenville Coll (IL)
Guilford Coll (NC)
Hampton U (VA)
Harding U (AR)

Hastings Coll (NE)
Hilbert Coll (NY)
Hillsdale Coll (MI)
Holy Family U (PA)
Howard Payne U (TX)
Huntingdon Coll (AL)
Husson U (ME)
Ithaca Coll (NY)
Jacksonville U (FL)
John Brown U (AR)
Johnson & Wales U (CO)
Johnson & Wales U (FL)
Johnson & Wales U (RI)
Johnson & Wales U - Charlotte Campus (NC)
Johnson C. Smith U (NC)
Johnson State Coll (VT)
Judson U (IL)
Kansas Wesleyan U (KS)
Kennesaw State U (GA)
Kent State U (OH)
Kentucky Wesleyan Coll (KY)
Keystone Coll (PA)
King U (TN)
Lake Erie Coll (OH)
Lamar U (TX)
Lasell Coll (MA)
Lees-McRae Coll (NC)
Lenoir-Rhyne U (NC)
LeTourneau U (TX)
Lewis U (IL)
Liberty U (VA)
Limestone Coll (SC)
Lindenwood U (MO)
Lock Haven U of Pennsylvania (PA)
Long Island U–LIU Brooklyn (NY)
Loras Coll (IA)
Louisiana State U and A&M Coll (LA)
Lubbock Christian U (TX)
Lynchburg Coll (VA)
Lynn U (FL)
Madonna U (MI)
Malone U (OH)
Manchester U (IN)
Maranatha Baptist U (WI)
Marian U (IN)
Marian U (WI)
Marietta Coll (OH)
Mars Hill U (NC)
Maryville U of Saint Louis (MO)
McKendree U (IL)
Medaille Coll (NY)
Menlo Coll (CA)
Merrimack Coll (MA)
Messiah Coll (PA)
Miami U (OH)
Michigan Technological U (MI)
MidAmerica Nazarene U (KS)
Midwestern State U (TX)
Millikin U (IL)
Minnesota State U Mankato (MN)
Minot State U (ND)
Misericordia U (PA)
Missouri Baptist U (MO)
Missouri Valley Coll (MO)
Mitchell Coll (CT)
Montana State U (MT)
Montana State U Billings (MT)
Morehead State U (KY)
Mount St. Joseph U (OH)
Mount St. Mary's U (MD)
Mount Vernon Nazarene U (OH)
Nebraska Wesleyan U (NE)
Neumann U (PA)
Newbury Coll (MA)
New England Coll (NH)
Niagara U (NY)
Nichols Coll (MA)
North Carolina Ag and Tech State U (NC)
North Carolina State U (NC)
North Central Coll (IL)
North Dakota State U (ND)
Northern Kentucky U (KY)
Northern Michigan U (MI)
Northern State U (SD)
North Greenville U (SC)
Northwestern Coll (IA)
Northwood U, Michigan Campus (MI)
Nova Southeastern U (FL)
Ohio Dominican U (OH)
Ohio Northern U (OH)
The Ohio State U (OH)
Oklahoma Baptist U (OK)
Oklahoma Christian U (OK)
Olivet Coll (MI)
Olivet Nazarene U (IL)
Pennsylvania Coll of Technology (PA)
Pepperdine U, Malibu (CA)
Plymouth State U (NH)
Post U (CT)
Quincy U (IL)
Reinhardt U (GA)
Rice U (TX)
Rider U (NJ)
Roanoke Coll (VA)
Robert Morris U (PA)
Rockford U (IL)
Rockhurst U (MO)
Rocky Mountain Coll (MT)
Saginaw Valley State U (MI)
St. Bonaventure U (NY)
St. Catharine Coll (KY)
St. John Fisher Coll (NY)
St. John's U (NY)
Saint Joseph's Coll (IN)
Saint Leo U (FL)
St. Thomas Aquinas Coll (NY)
St. Thomas U (FL)
Samford U (AL)
Seattle Pacific U (WA)
Seton Hill U (PA)
Shawnee State U (OH)
Shenandoah U (VA)
Siena Heights U (MI)
Simpson Coll (IA)
Slippery Rock U of Pennsylvania (PA)
Southeastern Louisiana U (LA)
Southeastern U (FL)
Southeast Missouri State U (MO)
Southern Adventist U (TN)
Southern Illinois U Carbondale (IL)
Southern Methodist U (TX)
Southern New Hampshire U (NH)
Southern Vermont Coll (VT)
Southwest Baptist U (MO)
Southwestern Adventist U (TX)
Southwestern Assemblies of God U (TX)
Southwestern Coll (KS)
State U of New York at Oswego (NY)
Stetson U (FL)
Syracuse U (NY)
Tabor Coll (KS)
Taylor U (IN)
Temple U (PA)
Tennessee Wesleyan Coll (TN)
Texas A&M U (TX)
Texas A&M U–Commerce (TX)
Texas Lutheran U (TX)
Texas Southern U (TX)
Texas State U (TX)
Thomas More Coll (KY)
Tiffin U (OH)
Toccoa Falls Coll (GA)
Towson U (MD)
Trevecca Nazarene U (TN)
Trine U (IN)
Troy U (AL)
Tusculum Coll (TN)
Union Coll (KY)
Union Coll (NE)
Union U (TN)
United States Sports Acad (AL)
The U of Akron (OH)
U of Charleston (WV)
U of Cincinnati (OH)
U of Dayton (OH)
U of Delaware (DE)
U of Evansville (IN)
The U of Findlay (OH)
U of Florida (FL)
U of Houston (TX)
U of Indianapolis (IN)
The U of Iowa (IA)
U of Jamestown (ND)
The U of Kansas (KS)
U of Louisville (KY)
U of Mary Hardin-Baylor (TX)
U of Massachusetts Amherst (MA)
U of Memphis (TN)
U of Miami (FL)
U of Michigan (MI)
U of Minnesota, Crookston (MN)
U of Minnesota, Morris (MN)
U of Minnesota, Twin Cities Campus (MN)
U of Mount Union (OH)
U of Nebraska at Kearney (NE)
U of Nevada, Las Vegas (NV)
U of New England (ME)
U of New Haven (CT)
U of North Florida (FL)
U of Pittsburgh at Bradford (PA)
U of Regina (SK, Canada)
U of Saint Mary (KS)
U of Southern Indiana (IN)
U of Southern Mississippi (MS)
The U of Tampa (FL)
The U of Tennessee (TN)
The U of Texas at Austin (TX)
U of the Cumberlands (KY)
U of the Incarnate Word (TX)
The U of Tulsa (OK)
U of Valley Forge (PA)
The U of Western Ontario (ON, Canada)
U of Windsor (ON, Canada)
U of Wisconsin–Parkside (WI)
Valparaiso U (IN)
Viterbo U (WI)
Waldorf Coll (IA)
Walla Walla U (WA)
Wartburg Coll (IA)
Washington State U (WA)
Wayne State Coll (NE)
Webber Intl U (FL)
Western Carolina U (NC)
Western New England U (MA)
Western State Colorado U (CO)
West Virginia Wesleyan Coll (WV)
Widener U (PA)
William Paterson U of New Jersey (NJ)
William Penn U (IA)
William Woods U (MO)
Wilmington U (DE)
Wingate U (NC)
Winthrop U (SC)
Wittenberg U (OH)
Xavier U (OH)
York Coll of Pennsylvania (PA)

SPORTS COMMUNICATION
Ashland U (OH)
Belhaven U (MS)
Bethany Coll (WV)
Bluffton U (OH)
Bradley U (IL)
Butler U (IN)
Florida Southern Coll (FL)
Grand View U (IA)
Lasell Coll (MA)
Oklahoma State U (OK)
U of Evansville (IN)
Youngstown State U (OH)

SPORTS STUDIES
Bethel Coll (IN)
Bryant U (RI)
Canisius Coll (NY)
Central Michigan U (MI)
Inter American U of Puerto Rico, San Germán Campus (PR)
Lubbock Christian U (TX)
Manhattanville Coll (NY)
National U (CA)
St. Bonaventure U (NY)
Southwestern Coll (KS)
Texas Christian U (TX)
United States Sports Acad (AL)
Washington State U (WA)
Western Kentucky U (KY)
Wright State U (OH)

STATISTICS
American U (DC)
American U of Beirut (Lebanon)
Amherst Coll (MA)
Arizona State U at the West campus (AZ)
Barnard Coll (NY)
Baruch Coll of the City U of New York (NY)
Baylor U (TX)
Bowling Green State U (OH)
Bryant U (RI)
California Baptist U (CA)
California Polytechnic State U, San Luis Obispo (CA)
California State U, Fullerton (CA)
California State U, Long Beach (CA)
Case Western Reserve U (OH)
Central Michigan U (MI)
Colorado School of Mines (CO)
Columbia U (NY)
Columbia U, School of General Studies (NY)
Concordia U (QC, Canada)
Cornell U (NY)
Dalhousie U (NS, Canada)
Eastern Kentucky U (KY)
Eastern Michigan U (MI)
Elon U (NC)
Florida Intl U (FL)
Florida State U (FL)
The George Washington U (DC)
Grand Valley State U (MI)
Harvard U (MA)
Hunter Coll of the City U of New York (NY)
Indiana U Bloomington (IN)
Indiana U–Purdue U Fort Wayne (IN)
Iowa State U of Science and Technology (IA)
Kansas State U (KS)
Lehigh U (PA)
Loyola U Chicago (IL)
Miami U (OH)
Michigan State U (MI)
Michigan Technological U (MI)
Montana State U (MT)
Montana Tech of The U of Montana (MT)
Mount Holyoke Coll (MA)
North Carolina State U (NC)
North Dakota State U (ND)
Northern Kentucky U (KY)
Northwestern U (IL)
Oakland U (MI)
Ohio Northern U (OH)
Ohio Wesleyan U (OH)
Oklahoma State U (OK)
Penn State Abington (PA)
Penn State Altoona (PA)
Penn State Beaver (PA)
Penn State Berks (PA)
Penn State Brandywine (PA)
Penn State DuBois (PA)
Penn State Erie, The Behrend Coll (PA)
Penn State Fayette, The Eberly Campus (PA)
Penn State Greater Allegheny (PA)
Penn State Hazleton (PA)
Penn State Lehigh Valley (PA)
Penn State Mont Alto (PA)
Penn State New Kensington (PA)
Penn State Schuylkill (PA)
Penn State Shenango (PA)
Penn State U Park (PA)
Penn State Wilkes-Barre (PA)
Penn State Worthington Scranton (PA)
Penn State York (PA)
Rice U (TX)
Rochester Inst of Technology (NY)
Rutgers, The State U of New Jersey, New Brunswick (NJ)
St. John Fisher Coll (NY)
San Diego State U (CA)
San Francisco State U (CA)
Simon Fraser U (BC, Canada)
Slippery Rock U of Pennsylvania (PA)
Southern Methodist U (TX)
Université de Montréal (QC, Canada)
U at Buffalo, the State U of New York (NY)
The U of Akron (OH)
The U of British Columbia (BC, Canada)
The U of British Columbia–Okanagan Campus (BC, Canada)
U of California, Berkeley (CA)
U of California, Davis (CA)
U of California, Los Angeles (CA)
U of California, Riverside (CA)
U of California, Santa Barbara (CA)
U of Central Florida (FL)
U of Chicago (IL)
U of Delaware (DE)
U of Florida (FL)
U of Georgia (GA)
U of Illinois at Chicago (IL)
The U of Iowa (IA)
U of King's Coll (NS, Canada)
U of Maryland, Baltimore County (MD)
U of Michigan (MI)
U of Minnesota, Duluth (MN)
U of Minnesota, Morris (MN)
U of Minnesota, Twin Cities Campus (MN)
U of Missouri (MO)
The U of Montana (MT)
U of New Brunswick Saint John (NB, Canada)
U of New Mexico (NM)
The U of North Carolina Wilmington (NC)
U of North Florida (FL)
U of Ottawa (ON, Canada)
U of Pennsylvania (PA)
U of Pittsburgh (PA)
U of Regina (SK, Canada)
U of Rochester (NY)
U of Saskatchewan (SK, Canada)
U of South Florida (FL)
The U of Tennessee (TN)
The U of Tennessee at Martin (TN)
The U of Texas at El Paso (TX)
The U of Texas at San Antonio (TX)
U of Vermont (VT)
U of Washington (WA)
U of Waterloo (ON, Canada)
The U of Western Ontario (ON, Canada)
U of Wisconsin–Madison (WI)
U of Wyoming (WY)
Utah State U (UT)
Virginia Polytechnic Inst and State U (VA)
Washington U in St. Louis (MO)
Western Michigan U (MI)
Williams Coll (MA)
Winona State U (MN)
Wright State U (OH)
Xavier U of Louisiana (LA)

STATISTICS RELATED
Ohio Northern U (OH)
Saint Mary's Coll (IN)
United States Military Acad (NY)
U of Central Oklahoma (OK)

STRATEGIC STUDIES
Washington State U (WA)

STRINGED INSTRUMENTS
Brigham Young U (UT)
Central Washington U (WA)
The Colburn School Conservatory of Music (CA)
Cornish Coll of the Arts (WA)
Hardin-Simmons U (TX)
Hastings Coll (NE)
Heidelberg U (OH)
Hope Coll (MI)
Houghton Coll (NY)
Lawrence U (WI)
Liberty U (VA)
Manhattan School of Music (NY)
Mount Allison U (NB, Canada)
New England Conservatory of Music (MA)
Northwestern U (IL)
Oberlin Coll (OH)
Oklahoma City U (OK)
Peabody Conservatory of The Johns Hopkins U (MD)
Roosevelt U (IL)
San Francisco Conservatory of Music (CA)
Seattle U (WA)
State U of New York at Fredonia (NY)
Stetson U (FL)
Syracuse U (NY)
Texas Christian U (TX)
The U of Akron (OH)
The U of British Columbia (BC, Canada)
U of Central Oklahoma (OK)
The U of Iowa (IA)
The U of Kansas (KS)
U of Northwestern–St. Paul (MN)
U of Southern California (CA)
U of Washington (WA)
The U of Western Ontario (ON, Canada)
Vanderbilt U (TN)
Willamette U (OR)
Xavier U of Louisiana (LA)
Youngstown State U (OH)

STRUCTURAL ENGINEERING
Penn State Harrisburg (PA)

U at Buffalo, the State U of New York (NY)
U of Central Florida (FL)
U of Southern California (CA)
Western Michigan U (MI)

SUBSTANCE ABUSE/ ADDICTION COUNSELING
Alvernia U (PA)
Chowan U (NC)
City Vision Coll (MO)
Drexel U (PA)
Indiana U–Purdue U Fort Wayne (IN)
Kansas Wesleyan U (KS)
Keene State Coll (NH)
Metropolitan State U (MN)
Minot State U (ND)
Newman U (KS)
Tiffin U (OH)
U of Central Arkansas (AR)
U of Cincinnati (OH)
U of Great Falls (MT)
U of Lethbridge (AB, Canada)
U of St. Francis (IL)
The U of South Dakota (SD)
Viterbo U (WI)
Washburn U (KS)

SURGICAL TECHNOLOGY
Nebraska Methodist Coll (NE)

SURVEYING ENGINEERING
Ferris State U (MI)
Florida Atlantic U (FL)
Michigan Technological U (MI)
North Carolina Ag and Tech State U (NC)

SURVEYING TECHNOLOGY
East Tennessee State U (TN)
Ferris State U (MI)
Great Basin Coll (NV)
New Mexico State U (NM)
Nicholls State U (LA)
The Ohio State U (OH)
Penn State Wilkes-Barre (PA)
Polytechnic U of Puerto Rico (PR)
Purdue U Calumet (IN)
South Carolina State U (SC)
State U of New York Coll of Technology at Alfred (NY)
Troy U (AL)
The U of Akron (OH)
U of Florida (FL)
U of Maine (ME)
Utah Valley U (UT)

SUSTAINABILITY STUDIES
Alaska Pacific U (AK)
Albion Coll (MI)
Aquinas Coll (MI)
Bentley U (MA)
California Baptist U (CA)
Chatham U (PA)
Columbia U, School of General Studies (NY)
Creighton U (NE)
Daemen Coll (NY)
The Evergreen State Coll (WA)
Florida Inst of Technology (FL)
Furman U (SC)
George Mason U (VA)
Goddard Coll (VT)
Hofstra U (NY)
Jacksonville U (FL)
Kean U (NJ)
Lipscomb U (TN)
Messiah Coll (PA)
Miami U (OH)
Montclair State U (NJ)
Notre Dame of Maryland U (MD)
Oregon State U (OR)
Prescott Coll (AZ)
Rensselaer Polytechnic Inst (NY)
Roosevelt U (IL)
Sewanee: The U of the South (TN)
Stephen F. Austin State U (TX)
Stockton U (NJ)
Stony Brook U, State U of New York (NY)
Toccoa Falls Coll (GA)
Trent U (ON, Canada)
U of Florida (FL)
U of New Haven (CT)
U of Northern Colorado (CO)
U of Wisconsin–Platteville (WI)
U of Wisconsin–Stout (WI)
Viterbo U (WI)

SWEDISH
Brigham Young U (UT)
U of Washington (WA)

SYSTEM, NETWORKING, AND LAN/WAN MANAGEMENT
Alcorn State U (MS)
Central Washington U (WA)
Champlain Coll (VT)
Dakota State U (SD)
Hallmark U (TX)
Morrisville State Coll (NY)
Northern Michigan U (MI)
Rochester Inst of Technology (NY)
State U of New York Coll of Technology at Alfred (NY)
Texas A&M U (TX)
U of Great Falls (MT)
U of Hawaii–West Oahu (HI)

SYSTEMS ENGINEERING
Belmont U (TN)
Case Western Reserve U (OH)
Delaware State U (DE)
Ferris State U (MI)
George Mason U (VA)
The George Washington U (DC)
Johnson & Wales U (RI)
Maine Maritime Acad (ME)
Providence Coll (RI)
Rochester Inst of Technology (NY)
Stanford U (CA)
Taylor U (IN)
Texas A&M Intl U (TX)
United States Military Acad (NY)
United States Naval Acad (MD)
The U of Arizona (AZ)
U of Arkansas at Little Rock (AR)
U of California, Santa Cruz (CA)
U of Florida (FL)
The U of North Carolina at Charlotte (NC)
U of Pennsylvania (PA)
U of Virginia (VA)
U of Waterloo (ON, Canada)
U of Wyoming (WY)
Washington U in St. Louis (MO)

SYSTEMS SCIENCE AND THEORY
Boston U (MA)
James Madison U (VA)
Marshall U (WV)
Stanford U (CA)
United States Military Acad (NY)
U of Wyoming (WY)
Washington U in St. Louis (MO)
Yale U (CT)

TAXATION
Canisius Coll (NY)
Fontbonne U (MO)
Grand Valley State U (MI)

TECHNICAL AND SCIENTIFIC COMMUNICATION
Illinois Inst of Technology (IL)
Indiana U–Purdue U Indianapolis (IN)
Lehigh U (PA)
Michigan Technological U (MI)

TECHNICAL TEACHER EDUCATION
Athens State U (AL)
Auburn U (AL)
Bowling Green State U (OH)
Castleton State Coll (VT)
Central Washington U (WA)
Eastern Illinois U (IL)
Ferris State U (MI)
Montana State U (MT)
The Ohio State U (OH)
Oklahoma State U (OK)
The U of Akron (OH)
U of Idaho (ID)
U of Kentucky (KY)
U of Minnesota, Twin Cities Campus (MN)
U of Missouri (MO)
U of Saskatchewan (SK, Canada)
U of Wisconsin–Stout (WI)
Utah State U (UT)
Valley City State U (ND)
Wayne State U (MI)
West Virginia U Inst of Technology (WV)
Wright State U (OH)

TECHNOLOGY/INDUSTRIAL ARTS TEACHER EDUCATION
Appalachian State U (NC)
Ball State U (IN)
Bemidji State U (MN)
Berea Coll (KY)
Bowling Green State U (OH)
Buffalo State Coll, State U of New York (NY)
Central Connecticut State U (CT)
Chicago State U (IL)
The Coll of New Jersey (NJ)
Colorado State U (CO)
Concordia U, Nebraska (NE)
Eastern Michigan U (MI)
Fitchburg State U (MA)
Georgia Southern U (GA)
Illinois State U (IL)
Indiana State U (IN)
Jackson State U (MS)
Lindenwood U (MO)
Middle Tennessee State U (TN)
New Mexico Highlands U (NM)
New York City Coll of Technology of the City U of New York (NY)
North Carolina Ag and Tech State U (NC)
North Carolina State U (NC)
Ohio Northern U (OH)
The Ohio State U (OH)
Pittsburg State U (KS)
Purdue U (IN)
Rhode Island Coll (RI)
South Carolina State U (SC)
Southeast Missouri State U (MO)
Southern Utah U (UT)
State U of New York at Oswego (NY)
Union Coll (NE)
U of Alberta (AB, Canada)
U of Minnesota, Twin Cities Campus (MN)
The U of Montana Western (MT)
U of New Mexico (NM)
U of Northern Iowa (IA)
U of Wisconsin–Platteville (WI)
U of Wisconsin–Stout (WI)
U of Wyoming (WY)
Utah State U (UT)
Valley City State U (ND)
Viterbo U (WI)
Wayne State Coll (NE)
Western Michigan U (MI)
Western Washington U (WA)
Westfield State U (MA)

TELECOMMUNICATIONS ENGINEERING
The U of Texas at Dallas (TX)

TELECOMMUNICATIONS MANAGEMENT
Regent U (VA)

TELECOMMUNICATIONS TECHNOLOGY
Canisius Coll (NY)
Farmingdale State Coll (NY)
Ferris State U (MI)
Lawrence Technological U (MI)
New York City Coll of Technology of the City U of New York (NY)
Pace U (NY)
Pacific U (OR)
Rochester Inst of Technology (NY)
St. John's U (NY)

TERRORISM AND COUNTERTERRORISM OPERATIONS
Henley-Putnam U (CA)

TEXTILE SCIENCE
Cornell U (NY)
Michigan State U (MI)
U of Nebraska–Lincoln (NE)

TEXTILE SCIENCES AND ENGINEERING
Auburn U (AL)
Georgia Inst of Technology (GA)
North Carolina State U (NC)
Philadelphia U (PA)
U of Massachusetts Dartmouth (MA)

THEATER DESIGN AND TECHNOLOGY
Ashland U (OH)
Baldwin Wallace U (OH)
Bard Coll at Simon's Rock (MA)
Baylor U (TX)
Belmont U (TN)
Bennington Coll (VT)
Bethany Coll (WV)
Binghamton U, State U of New York (NY)
Biola U (CA)
Boston U (MA)
Brenau U (GA)
Brigham Young U (UT)
California Inst of the Arts (CA)
Central Michigan U (MI)
Central Washington U (WA)
Coe Coll (IA)
Coker Coll (SC)
Columbia Coll Chicago (IL)
Concordia U (QC, Canada)
Cornish Coll of the Arts (WA)
DePaul U (IL)
Dixie State U (UT)
Doane Coll (NE)
Elon U (NC)
Emerson Coll (MA)
Fitchburg State U (MA)
Florida Southern Coll (FL)
Greensboro Coll (NC)
Illinois Wesleyan U (IL)
Ithaca Coll (NY)
Kean U (NJ)
Keene State Coll (NH)
Lindenwood U (MO)
Lipscomb U (TN)
Marymount Manhattan Coll (NY)
Michigan Technological U (MI)
Millikin U (IL)
Nazareth Coll of Rochester (NY)
New Jersey Inst of Technology (NJ)
New York City Coll of Technology of the City U of New York (NY)
Oakland U (MI)
Oklahoma City U (OK)
Penn State Abington (PA)
Penn State Altoona (PA)
Penn State Beaver (PA)
Penn State Berks (PA)
Penn State Brandywine (PA)
Penn State DuBois (PA)
Penn State Erie, The Behrend Coll (PA)
Penn State Fayette, The Eberly Campus (PA)
Penn State Greater Allegheny (PA)
Penn State Hazleton (PA)
Penn State Lehigh Valley (PA)
Penn State Mont Alto (PA)
Penn State New Kensington (PA)
Penn State Schuylkill (PA)
Penn State Shenango (PA)
Penn State U Park (PA)
Penn State Wilkes-Barre (PA)
Penn State Worthington Scranton (PA)
Penn State York (PA)
Pepperdine U, Malibu (CA)
Piedmont Coll (GA)
Purchase Coll, State U of New York (NY)
Purdue U (IN)
Rhode Island Coll (RI)
Rocky Mountain Coll (MT)
Santa Fe U of Art and Design (NM)
Savannah Coll of Art and Design (GA)
Seton Hill U (PA)
Shenandoah U (VA)
Slippery Rock U of Pennsylvania (PA)
Southwestern Coll (KS)
Stephens Coll (MO)
Syracuse U (NY)
Texas Christian U (TX)
Trinity U (TX)
U of Alaska Fairbanks (AK)
U of Alberta (AB, Canada)
The U of Arizona (AZ)
U of Central Oklahoma (OK)
U of Cincinnati (OH)
The U of Kansas (KS)
U of Lethbridge (AB, Canada)
U of Miami (FL)
U of Michigan (MI)
U of Michigan–Flint (MI)
U of Nevada, Las Vegas (NV)
U of New Mexico (NM)
U of North Carolina School of the Arts (NC)
U of North Georgia (GA)
U of Regina (SK, Canada)
U of Southern California (CA)
The U of the Arts (PA)
The U of Western Ontario (ON, Canada)
Vanguard U of Southern California (CA)
Webster U (MO)
Western Michigan U (MI)
Western State Colorado U (CO)
Wright State U (OH)

THEATER LITERATURE, HISTORY AND CRITICISM
Albertus Magnus Coll (CT)
The American U in Cairo (Egypt)
Averett U (VA)
Bennington Coll (VT)
Bowdoin Coll (ME)
Buena Vista U (IA)
Clark Atlanta U (GA)
Dalhousie U (NS, Canada)
DePaul U (IL)
Marymount Manhattan Coll (NY)
Moravian Coll (PA)
Northwestern U (IL)
Suffolk U (MA)
Tufts U (MA)
U of Saskatchewan (SK, Canada)
U of Washington (WA)
Washington U in St. Louis (MO)
Western Michigan U (MI)
West Virginia U (WV)

THEATER/THEATER ARTS MANAGEMENT
Berry Coll (GA)
Biola U (CA)
Canisius Coll (NY)
Catawba Coll (NC)
DEREE - The American Coll of Greece (Greece)
Graceland U (IA)
Marymount Manhattan Coll (NY)
Massachusetts Coll of Liberal Arts (MA)
Messiah Coll (PA)
Nazareth Coll of Rochester (NY)
Oglethorpe U (GA)
Ohio Northern U (OH)
Ohio U (OH)
Oklahoma City U (OK)
Quinnipiac U (CT)
Regent U (VA)
Reinhardt U (GA)
Rockford U (IL)
Saint Louis U (MO)
Seton Hill U (PA)
Slippery Rock U of Pennsylvania (PA)
Syracuse U (NY)
Texas Wesleyan U (TX)
The U of British Columbia (BC, Canada)
U of Evansville (IN)
U of Miami (FL)
U of New Haven (CT)
U of Regina (SK, Canada)
U of Richmond (VA)
U of South Carolina Upstate (SC)
U of the District of Columbia (DC)
William Peace U (NC)

THEOLOGICAL AND MINISTERIAL STUDIES RELATED
Bob Jones U (SC)
California Christian Coll (CA)
Concordia U (QC, Canada)
Concordia U, St. Paul (MN)
Cornerstone U (MI)
Creighton U (NE)
Hardin-Simmons U (TX)
Hope Intl U (CA)
Howard Payne U (TX)
John Brown U (AR)
Lincoln Christian U (IL)
Lubbock Christian U (TX)
Manhattan Christian Coll (KS)
Marquette U (WI)
Oklahoma Wesleyan U (OK)
Providence Coll (RI)
Saint Mary-of-the-Woods Coll (IN)

Summit U (PA)
Trinity Coll of Florida (FL)
Union Coll (NE)
U of Northwestern–St. Paul (MN)
U of Saint Francis (IN)
Williamson Christian Coll (TN)

THEOLOGY
Ambrose U Coll (AB, Canada)
American Baptist Coll of American Baptist Theological Sem (TN)
Anderson U (IN)
Andrews U (MI)
Anna Maria Coll (MA)
Aquinas Coll (TN)
Assumption Coll (MA)
Ave Maria U (FL)
Azusa Pacific U (CA)
Barry U (FL)
Belmont Abbey Coll (NC)
Benedictine Coll (KS)
Benedictine U (IL)
Biola U (CA)
Bluefield Coll (VA)
Boston Coll (MA)
Caldwell U (NJ)
Calumet Coll of Saint Joseph (IN)
Calvary Bible Coll and Theological Sem (MO)
Calvin Coll (MI)
Carlow U (PA)
Carroll Coll (MT)
Christendom Coll (VA)
Coll of Saint Benedict (MN)
Coll of Saint Elizabeth (NJ)
Coll of Saint Mary (NE)
Concordia U (CA)
Concordia U (QC, Canada)
Concordia U Chicago (IL)
Concordia U, Nebraska (NE)
Concordia U, St. Paul (MN)
Concordia U Wisconsin (WI)
Creighton U (NE)
Crossroads Coll (MN)
DeSales U (PA)
Dominican U (IL)
Duquesne U (PA)
Eastern U (PA)
Elmhurst Coll (IL)
Fordham U (NY)
Franciscan U of Steubenville (OH)
Gannon U (PA)
Georgetown U (DC)
Hanover Coll (IN)
Hardin-Simmons U (TX)
Hillsdale Free Will Baptist Coll (OK)
Holy Cross Coll (IN)
Houghton Coll (NY)
Howard Payne U (TX)
Immaculata U (PA)
John Brown U (AR)
Kentucky Mountain Bible Coll (KY)
King's Coll (PA)
King's U (TX)
The King's U Coll (AB, Canada)
Kuyper Coll (MI)
Laurel U (NC)
Lee U (TN)
Louisiana Coll (LA)
Loyola Marymount U (CA)
Loyola U Chicago (IL)
Lubbock Christian U (TX)
Manhattan Christian Coll (KS)
Marian U (IN)
Marquette U (WI)
Martin Luther Coll (MN)
The Master's Coll and Sem (CA)
Master's Coll and Sem (ON, Canada)
MidAmerica Nazarene U (KS)
Morris Coll (SC)
Mount Mary U (WI)
Mount St. Mary's U (MD)
Mount Vernon Nazarene U (OH)
Multnomah U (OR)
Nebraska Christian Coll (NE)
Newman U (KS)
Northwest Nazarene U (ID)
Oakland City U (IN)
Ohio Dominican U (OH)
Oklahoma Wesleyan U (OK)
Olivet Nazarene U (IL)
Pacific Lutheran U (WA)
Palm Beach Atlantic U (FL)
Providence Coll (RI)
Rockhurst U (MO)
Rocky Mountain Coll (AB, Canada)
Saint Anselm Coll (NH)
St. Bonaventure U (NY)
St. Catherine U (MN)
St. Edward's U (TX)
St. Gregory's U, Shawnee (OK)
Saint John's U (MN)
St. John's U (NY)
Saint Louis Christian Coll (MO)
Saint Louis U (MO)
St. Mary's U (TX)
Saint Mary's U of Minnesota (MN)
Saint Peter's U (NJ)
Saint Vincent Coll (PA)
Seattle Pacific U (WA)
Silver Lake Coll of the Holy Family (WI)
Southern Adventist U (TN)
Southwest Baptist U (MO)
Southwestern Adventist U (TX)
Southwestern Assemblies of God U (TX)
Texas Lutheran U (TX)
Trinity Christian Coll (IL)
Union Coll (NE)
Union U (TN)
Université de Montréal (QC, Canada)
U of Chicago (IL)
U of Dallas (TX)
U of Dubuque (IA)
U of Evansville (IN)
U of Great Falls (MT)
U of Minnesota, Twin Cities Campus (MN)
U of Notre Dame (IN)
U of Portland (OR)
U of St. Francis (IL)
U of Saint Francis (IN)
U of Saint Mary (KS)
U of St. Thomas (TX)
U of San Francisco (CA)
U of Valley Forge (PA)
The U of Western Ontario (ON, Canada)
Valparaiso U (IN)
Vanguard U of Southern California (CA)
Walla Walla U (WA)
Walsh U (OH)
Warner Pacific Coll (OR)
William Jessup U (CA)
Williams Baptist Coll (AR)
Xavier U of Louisiana (LA)

THEOLOGY AND RELIGIOUS VOCATIONS RELATED
Ave Maria U (FL)
Belmont U (TN)
Cedarville U (OH)
Concordia Coll–New York (NY)
Crossroads Coll (MN)
Dallas Baptist U (TX)
Hobe Sound Bible Coll (FL)
Kentucky Mountain Bible Coll (KY)
Lee U (TN)
LeTourneau U (TX)
Master's Coll and Sem (ON, Canada)
Missouri Baptist U (MO)
Newman U (KS)
Oklahoma Wesleyan U (OK)
Simpson U (CA)
Southeastern U (FL)
Summit U (PA)
Thiel Coll (PA)
Trevecca Nazarene U (TN)
Trinity Christian Coll (IL)
Union U (TN)
U of St. Thomas (TX)
U of Valley Forge (PA)
Williamson Christian Coll (TN)

THEORETICAL AND MATHEMATICAL PHYSICS
Bethany Coll (WV)
Chapman U (CA)
U at Buffalo, the State U of New York (NY)
U of Guelph (ON, Canada)
U of Ottawa (ON, Canada)
U of Saskatchewan (SK, Canada)
The U of Western Ontario (ON, Canada)
Viterbo U (WI)

THERAPEUTIC RECREATION
Brigham Young U (UT)
Catawba Coll (NC)
Central Michigan U (MI)
Concordia U (QC, Canada)
Dalhousie U (NS, Canada)
East Carolina U (NC)
Eastern Michigan U (MI)
Grand Valley State U (MI)
Hampton U (VA)
Ithaca Coll (NY)
Lincoln U (PA)
Longwood U (VA)
Minnesota State U Mankato (MN)
St. Andrews U (NC)
St. Thomas Aquinas Coll (NY)
Shaw U (NC)
Slippery Rock U of Pennsylvania (PA)
State U of New York Coll at Cortland (NY)
Temple U (PA)
Unity Coll (ME)
The U of Iowa (IA)
The U of North Carolina Wilmington (NC)
U of Southern Maine (ME)
The U of Toledo (OH)
U of Waterloo (ON, Canada)
U of Wisconsin–La Crosse (WI)
U of Wisconsin–Milwaukee (WI)
Utica Coll (NY)
Western Carolina U (NC)

TOOL AND DIE TECHNOLOGY
Utah State U (UT)

TOURISM AND TRAVEL SERVICES MANAGEMENT
Arizona State U at the Downtown Phoenix campus (AZ)
Black Hills State U (SD)
Bowling Green State U (OH)
Cape Breton U (NS, Canada)
Central Washington U (WA)
Concord U (WV)
Delaware State U (DE)
Fisher Coll (MA)
Fort Hays State U (KS)
Fort Lewis Coll (CO)
George Mason U (VA)
Hawai`i Pacific U (HI)
Indiana U–Purdue U Indianapolis (IN)
Johnson & Wales U (FL)
Johnson & Wales U (RI)
Johnson State Coll (VT)
Niagara U (NY)
Northeastern State U (OK)
Plymouth State U (NH)
St. Thomas U (FL)
Texas A&M U (TX)
U of Central Florida (FL)
U of Guelph (ON, Canada)
U of Hawaii at Manoa (HI)
U of Maine at Machias (ME)
The U of Texas at San Antonio (TX)

TOURISM AND TRAVEL SERVICES MARKETING
Johnson & Wales U (RI)
Rochester Inst of Technology (NY)
U of Central Missouri (MO)
Western Michigan U (MI)

TOURISM PROMOTION
Bowling Green State U (OH)
Cape Breton U (NS, Canada)

TOXICOLOGY
Ashland U (OH)
Eastern Michigan U (MI)
Nazareth Coll of Rochester (NY)
Penn State Beaver (PA)
Penn State Berks (PA)
Penn State DuBois (PA)
Penn State Fayette, The Eberly Campus (PA)
Penn State Greater Allegheny (PA)
Penn State Hazleton (PA)
Penn State Mont Alto (PA)
Penn State New Kensington (PA)
Penn State Shenango (PA)
Penn State U Park (PA)
Penn State Wilkes-Barre (PA)
Penn State York (PA)
St. John's U (NY)
U of California, Berkeley (CA)
U of Guelph (ON, Canada)
U of Saskatchewan (SK, Canada)
U of Toronto (ON, Canada)
The U of Western Ontario (ON, Canada)

TRADE AND INDUSTRIAL TEACHER EDUCATION
Auburn U (AL)
Bemidji State U (MN)
Bowling Green State U (OH)
Buffalo State Coll, State U of New York (NY)
California State U, Long Beach (CA)
California State U, San Bernardino (CA)
Central Washington U (WA)
Colorado State U (CO)
Delaware State U (DE)
Eastern Kentucky U (KY)
Fitchburg State U (MA)
Florida Ag and Mech U (FL)
Indiana State U (IN)
Indiana U of Pennsylvania (PA)
Iowa State U of Science and Technology (IA)
Kent State U (OH)
Lindenwood U (MO)
Murray State U (KY)
Norfolk State U (VA)
North Carolina Ag and Tech State U (NC)
Northern Kentucky U (KY)
Southern Illinois U Carbondale (IL)
State U of New York at Oswego (NY)
Temple U (PA)
Universidad del Turabo (PR)
U of Alberta (AB, Canada)
U of Central Florida (FL)
U of Central Oklahoma (OK)
U of Louisville (KY)
U of Minnesota, Twin Cities Campus (MN)
U of Nebraska–Lincoln (NE)
U of Saskatchewan (SK, Canada)
U of Southern Maine (ME)
U of the District of Columbia (DC)
U of the Virgin Islands (VI)
The U of Toledo (OH)
U of West Florida (FL)
U of Wyoming (WY)
Upper Iowa U (IA)
Valdosta State U (GA)
Virginia State U (VA)
Western Kentucky U (KY)
Western Michigan U (MI)

TRANSPORTATION AND HIGHWAY ENGINEERING
U of Toronto (ON, Canada)

TRANSPORTATION AND MATERIALS MOVING RELATED
Lewis U (IL)
Maine Maritime Acad (ME)
Niagara U (NY)
Tennessee State U (TN)
United States Merchant Marine Acad (NY)
The U of British Columbia (BC, Canada)

TRANSPORTATION/MOBILITY MANAGEMENT
Bridgewater State U (MA)
Embry-Riddle Aeronautical U–Worldwide (FL)
North Carolina Ag and Tech State U (NC)
Texas A&M U (TX)
U of North Florida (FL)
U of Pennsylvania (PA)
U of Wisconsin–Superior (WI)

TURF AND TURFGRASS MANAGEMENT
New Mexico State U (NM)
North Carolina State U (NC)
North Dakota State U (ND)
The Ohio State U (OH)
Penn State Abington (PA)
Penn State Altoona (PA)
Penn State Beaver (PA)
Penn State Berks (PA)
Penn State Brandywine (PA)
Penn State DuBois (PA)
Penn State Erie, The Behrend Coll (PA)
Penn State Fayette, The Eberly Campus (PA)
Penn State Greater Allegheny (PA)
Penn State Hazleton (PA)
Penn State Lehigh Valley (PA)
Penn State Mont Alto (PA)
Penn State New Kensington (PA)
Penn State Schuylkill (PA)
Penn State Shenango (PA)
Penn State U Park (PA)
Penn State Wilkes-Barre (PA)
Penn State Worthington Scranton (PA)
Penn State York (PA)
Rutgers, The State U of New Jersey, New Brunswick (NJ)
Texas A&M U (TX)
U of Georgia (GA)
U of Massachusetts Amherst (MA)
U of Minnesota, Crookston (MN)
U of Nebraska–Lincoln (NE)

TURKISH
U of Utah (UT)

UKRAINE STUDIES
U of Alberta (AB, Canada)

UKRAINIAN
U of Alberta (AB, Canada)
U of Saskatchewan (SK, Canada)

URALIC LANGUAGES
U of Washington (WA)

URBAN EDUCATION AND LEADERSHIP
The Coll of New Jersey (NJ)
U of Delaware (DE)
U of Wisconsin–Milwaukee (WI)

URBAN FORESTRY
U of California, Davis (CA)
U of Minnesota, Crookston (MN)

URBAN MINISTRY
Greenville Coll (IL)

URBAN STUDIES/AFFAIRS
Albertus Magnus Coll (CT)
The American U of Paris (France)
Aquinas Coll (MI)
Arizona State U at the Downtown Phoenix campus (AZ)
Augsburg Coll (MN)
Ball State U (IN)
Barnard Coll (NY)
Boston U (MA)
Brown U (RI)
Bryn Mawr Coll (PA)
Buffalo State Coll, State U of New York (NY)
Butler U (IN)
California State U, Dominguez Hills (CA)
California State U, Stanislaus (CA)
Canisius Coll (NY)
Cleveland State U (OH)
Coll of Charleston (SC)
The Coll of Wooster (OH)
Columbia U (NY)
Columbia U, School of General Studies (NY)
Concordia U (QC, Canada)
Connecticut Coll (CT)
Delaware State U (DE)
DePaul U (IL)
Elmhurst Coll (IL)
Fordham U (NY)
Furman U (SC)
Hampshire Coll (MA)
Harris-Stowe State U (MO)
Haverford Coll (PA)
Hobart and William Smith Colls (NY)
Hunter Coll of the City U of New York (NY)
Jackson State U (MS)
Lipscomb U (TN)
Loyola Marymount U (CA)
Manhattan Coll (NY)
Metropolitan Coll of New York (NY)
Minnesota State U Mankato (MN)
New Coll of Florida (FL)
New Jersey City U (NJ)
New York Inst of Technology (NY)
New York U (NY)
Northeastern Illinois U (IL)
Northwestern U (IL)

Oglethorpe U (GA)
Ohio U (OH)
Ohio Wesleyan U (OH)
Portland State U (OR)
Purchase Coll, State U of New York (NY)
Queens Coll of the City U of New York (NY)
Rhodes Coll (TN)
Rutgers, The State U of New Jersey, Camden (NJ)
Rutgers, The State U of New Jersey, New Brunswick (NJ)
Saint Louis U (MO)
Saint Peter's U (NJ)
San Diego State U (CA)
San Francisco State U (CA)
Stanford U (CA)
Towson U (MD)
Trinity Coll (CT)
Tufts U (MA)
Université de Montréal (QC, Canada)
U at Albany, State U of New York (NY)
The U of British Columbia (BC, Canada)
U of California, Berkeley (CA)
U of California, Irvine (CA)
U of Cincinnati (OH)
U of Illinois at Chicago (IL)
U of Lethbridge (AB, Canada)
U of Minnesota, Duluth (MN)
U of Minnesota, Twin Cities Campus (MN)
U of Missouri–Kansas City (MO)
U of New Orleans (LA)
U of Pennsylvania (PA)
U of Pittsburgh (PA)
The U of Texas at Austin (TX)
U of the District of Columbia (DC)
The U of Toledo (OH)
U of Utah (UT)
U of Washington, Tacoma (WA)
The U of Western Ontario (ON, Canada)
U of Wisconsin–Green Bay (WI)
U of Wisconsin–Oshkosh (WI)
Vassar Coll (NY)
Virginia Commonwealth U (VA)
Warner Pacific Coll (OR)
Washington U in St. Louis (MO)
Wayne State U (MI)
Wheaton Coll (IL)
Worcester State U (MA)
Wright State U (OH)

VEHICLE AND VEHICLE PARTS AND ACCESSORIES MARKETING

Northwood U, Michigan Campus (MI)

VETERINARY/ANIMAL HEALTH TECHNOLOGY

Brigham Young U (UT)
Medaille Coll (NY)
Mercy Coll (NY)
Michigan State U (MI)
Mississippi State U (MS)
Morehead State U (KY)
Murray State U (KY)
North Dakota State U (ND)
Purdue U (IN)
State U of New York Coll of Technology at Canton (NY)
State U of New York Coll of Technology at Delhi (NY)
Texas A&M U–Kingsville (TX)
U of Nebraska–Lincoln (NE)

VETERINARY MICROBIOLOGY AND IMMUNOBIOLOGY

Penn State U Park (PA)

VISION SCIENCE/ PHYSIOLOGICAL OPTICS

Indiana U Bloomington (IN)
Northeastern State U (OK)
Providence Coll (RI)
U of the Incarnate Word (TX)

VISUAL AND PERFORMING ARTS

The American U of Rome (Italy)
Antioch Coll, Yellow Springs (OH)
Arizona State U at the Tempe campus (AZ)
Arizona State U at the West campus (AZ)
Austin Coll (TX)
Bard Coll at Simon's Rock (MA)
Barnard Coll (NY)
Bennett Coll (NC)
Bennington Coll (VT)
Blackburn Coll (IL)
Bloomfield Coll (NJ)
Blue Mountain Coll (MS)
Brown U (RI)
Bucknell U (PA)
California Baptist U (CA)
California State U, San Marcos (CA)
Cardinal Stritch U (WI)
Cazenovia Coll (NY)
Centenary Coll of Louisiana (LA)
Champlain Coll (VT)
Cheyney U of Pennsylvania (PA)
Chowan U (NC)
Columbia U (NY)
Columbia U, School of General Studies (NY)
Concordia U (QC, Canada)
Cooper Union for the Advancement of Science and Art (NY)
Delta State U (MS)
DEREE - The American Coll of Greece (Greece)
Dowling Coll (NY)
Drexel U (PA)
Eastern Connecticut State U (CT)
East Stroudsburg U of Pennsylvania (PA)
Eckerd Coll (FL)
Emerson Coll (MA)
Emmanuel Coll (MA)
The Evergreen State Coll (WA)
Fairleigh Dickinson U, Coll at Florham (NJ)
Fairleigh Dickinson U, Metropolitan Campus (NJ)
Fayetteville State U (NC)
Ferrum Coll (VA)
Gannon U (PA)
George Mason U (VA)
Gettysburg Coll (PA)
Harvard U (MA)
Indiana U of Pennsylvania (PA)
Inter American U of Puerto Rico, San Germán Campus (PR)
Iowa State U of Science and Technology (IA)
Ithaca Coll (NY)
Jackson State U (MS)
Jacksonville U (FL)
Johnson C. Smith U (NC)
Johnson State Coll (VT)
Kansas Wesleyan U (KS)
Kent State U (OH)
Kent State U at Stark (OH)
King U (TN)
LaGrange Coll (GA)
Lees-McRae Coll (NC)
Lindenwood U (MO)
Longwood U (VA)
Massachusetts Coll of Liberal Arts (MA)
Michigan Technological U (MI)
Mississippi State U (MS)
Mississippi U for Women (MS)
Missouri State U (MO)
Naropa U (CO)
Neumann U (PA)
New Mexico Highlands U (NM)
New Mexico State U (NM)
Northwestern U (IL)
Occidental Coll (CA)
Ohio Northern U (OH)
Oregon State U (OR)
Penn State Abington (PA)
Penn State Altoona (PA)
Penn State Beaver (PA)
Penn State Berks (PA)
Penn State Brandywine (PA)
Penn State DuBois (PA)
Penn State Erie, The Behrend Coll (PA)
Penn State Fayette, The Eberly Campus (PA)
Penn State Greater Allegheny (PA)
Penn State Hazleton (PA)
Penn State Lehigh Valley (PA)
Penn State Mont Alto (PA)
Penn State New Kensington (PA)
Penn State Schuylkill (PA)
Penn State Shenango (PA)
Penn State U Park (PA)
Penn State Wilkes-Barre (PA)
Penn State Worthington Scranton (PA)
Penn State York (PA)
Pine Manor Coll (MA)
Point Loma Nazarene U (CA)
Prescott Coll (AZ)
Purchase Coll, State U of New York (NY)
Ramapo Coll of New Jersey (NJ)
Rensselaer Polytechnic Inst (NY)
Rutgers, The State U of New Jersey, New Brunswick (NJ)
Saint Augustine's U (NC)
St. Bonaventure U (NY)
St. Catharine Coll (KY)
St. Gregory's U, Shawnee (OK)
Saint Joseph's U (PA)
Saint Peter's U (NJ)
San Jose State U (CA)
Savannah State U (GA)
School of the Art Inst of Chicago (IL)
South Dakota State U (SD)
Southeast Missouri State U (MO)
State U of New York at New Paltz (NY)
State U of New York Coll at Old Westbury (NY)
State U of New York Coll at Potsdam (NY)
Stockton U (NJ)
Stonehill Coll (MA)
Suffolk U (MA)
Temple U (PA)
Tennessee Wesleyan Coll (TN)
Texas Southern U (TX)
Tusculum Coll (TN)
Union Coll (KY)
U of Alberta (AB, Canada)
The U of British Columbia (BC, Canada)
The U of British Columbia–Okanagan Campus (BC, Canada)
U of California, Irvine (CA)
U of Colorado Colorado Springs (CO)
U of Houston–Downtown (TX)
U of Louisiana at Lafayette (LA)
U of Maine at Machias (ME)
U of Mary Washington (VA)
U of Mount Union (OH)
U of New Haven (CT)
U of Pennsylvania (PA)
U of Pittsburgh at Greensburg (PA)
U of Regina (SK, Canada)
U of Rio Grande (OH)
U of St. Francis (IL)
U of Saint Mary (KS)
U of San Francisco (CA)
The U of South Dakota (SD)
U of Southern California (CA)
U of Southern Mississippi (MS)
U of South Florida, St. Petersburg (FL)
The U of Tennessee at Martin (TN)
The U of Texas at Austin (TX)
The U of Texas at Dallas (TX)
U of Toronto (ON, Canada)
U of Utah (UT)
U of Windsor (ON, Canada)
U of Wisconsin–Superior (WI)
Vassar Coll (NY)
Virginia State U (VA)
Western Washington U (WA)
Wheelock Coll (MA)
Wichita State U (KS)
Wittenberg U (OH)
Worcester State U (MA)
Youngstown State U (OH)

VISUAL AND PERFORMING ARTS RELATED

Adelphi U (NY)
Baldwin Wallace U (OH)
The Baptist Coll of Florida (FL)
Bard Coll at Simon's Rock (MA)
Bluffton U (OH)
Brigham Young U (UT)
California Inst of the Arts (CA)
Cameron U (OK)
Columbia U, School of General Studies (NY)
Cumberland U (TN)
Endicott Coll (MA)
Grambling State U (LA)
Illinois State U (IL)
Illinois Wesleyan U (IL)
Long Island U–LIU Brooklyn (NY)
Millikin U (IL)
New York U (NY)
Ohio Northern U (OH)
Oklahoma City U (OK)
Penn State Altoona (PA)
Purchase Coll, State U of New York (NY)
Rice U (TX)
Sacred Heart U (CT)
The Sage Colls (NY)
Samford U (AL)
San Francisco Art Inst (CA)
School of the Art Inst of Chicago (IL)
School of the Museum of Fine Arts, Boston (MA)
Seton Hill U (PA)
Simon Fraser U (BC, Canada)
State U of New York Coll at Geneseo (NY)
U of California, Davis (CA)
U of California, Los Angeles (CA)
U of Chicago (IL)
U of Cincinnati (OH)
U of Lethbridge (AB, Canada)
U of Michigan (MI)
U of South Florida (FL)
U of Washington (WA)
U of Washington, Bothell (WA)
U of Wisconsin–Green Bay (WI)
Virginia Wesleyan Coll (VA)
Waynesburg U (PA)
Western State Colorado U (CO)

VITICULTURE AND ENOLOGY

California Polytechnic State U, San Luis Obispo (CA)
Cornell U (NY)
Washington State U (WA)

VOCATIONAL REHABILITATION COUNSELING

Bowling Green State U (OH)
East Carolina U (NC)
East Central U (OK)
Emporia State U (KS)
Louisiana State U Health Sciences Center (LA)
Maryville U of Saint Louis (MO)
U of Wisconsin–Madison (WI)
U of Wisconsin–Stout (WI)
Wright State U (OH)

VOICE AND OPERA

Abilene Christian U (TX)
Andrews U (MI)
Anna Maria Coll (MA)
Arizona Christian U (AZ)
Baldwin Wallace U (OH)
Barry U (FL)
Belmont U (TN)
Bennington Coll (VT)
Biola U (CA)
Birmingham-Southern Coll (AL)
Black Hills State U (SD)
Bob Jones U (SC)
Boston U (MA)
Bowling Green State U (OH)
Brigham Young U (UT)
Bucknell U (PA)
California Baptist U (CA)
California State U, Long Beach (CA)
Calvary Bible Coll and Theological Sem (MO)
Calvin Coll (MI)
Campbellsville U (KY)
Capital U (OH)
Carson-Newman U (TN)
The Catholic U of America (DC)
Central Washington U (WA)
Chapman U (CA)
Cincinnati Christian U (OH)
Coker Coll (SC)
Columbia Coll (SC)
Concordia U, Nebraska (NE)
Cornish Coll of the Arts (WA)
Dallas Baptist U (TX)
Delaware State U (DE)
Drake U (IA)
East Central U (OK)
East Texas Baptist U (TX)
Furman U (SC)
Hardin-Simmons U (TX)
Hastings Coll (NE)
Heidelberg U (OH)
Hope Coll (MI)
Houghton Coll (NY)
Howard Payne U (TX)
Illinois Wesleyan U (IL)
Indiana U–Purdue U Fort Wayne (IN)
Ithaca Coll (NY)
Jacksonville U (FL)
Lawrence U (WI)
Liberty U (VA)
Lipscomb U (TN)
Long Island U–LIU Post (NY)
Louisiana Coll (LA)
Madonna U (MI)
Manhattan School of Music (NY)
Maryville Coll (TN)
The Master's Coll and Sem (CA)
MidAmerica Nazarene U (KS)
Minnesota State U Mankato (MN)
Mount Allison U (NB, Canada)
New England Conservatory of Music (MA)
Northern State U (SD)
Northwestern U (IL)
Nyack Coll (NY)
Oakland U (MI)
Oberlin Coll (OH)
The Ohio State U (OH)
Ohio U (OH)
Oklahoma Baptist U (OK)
Oklahoma Christian U (OK)
Oklahoma City U (OK)
Palm Beach Atlantic U (FL)
Peabody Conservatory of The Johns Hopkins U (MD)
Peru State Coll (NE)
Point Loma Nazarene U (CA)
Rider U (NJ)
Roberts Wesleyan Coll (NY)
Roosevelt U (IL)
Samford U (AL)
San Francisco Conservatory of Music (CA)
Southeastern U (FL)
Southern Methodist U (TX)
State U of New York at Fredonia (NY)
Stetson U (FL)
Syracuse U (NY)
Texas Christian U (TX)
Trinity U (TX)
Union U (TN)
The U of Akron (OH)
U of Alberta (AB, Canada)
The U of British Columbia (BC, Canada)
U of Central Oklahoma (OK)
U of Cincinnati (OH)
U of Delaware (DE)
U of Idaho (ID)
The U of Iowa (IA)
The U of Kansas (KS)
U of Miami (FL)
U of Mobile (AL)
U of Northwestern–St. Paul (MN)
U of Southern California (CA)
The U of Tennessee at Martin (TN)
U of the Pacific (CA)
The U of Tulsa (OK)
U of Washington (WA)
The U of Western Ontario (ON, Canada)
Valparaiso U (IN)
Vanderbilt U (TN)
Washington U in St. Louis (MO)
Weber State U (UT)
Western Michigan U (MI)
Whitworth U (WA)
Willamette U (OR)
William Paterson U of New Jersey (NJ)
Youngstown State U (OH)

WATER QUALITY AND WASTEWATER TREATMENT MANAGEMENT AND RECYCLING TECHNOLOGY

Virginia Polytechnic Inst and State U (VA)

WATER RESOURCES ENGINEERING

Central State U (OH)

State U of New York Coll of Environmental Science and Forestry (NY)
U of Guelph (ON, Canada)
U of Nevada, Reno (NV)

WATER, WETLANDS, AND MARINE RESOURCES MANAGEMENT
Colorado State U (CO)
Florida Gulf Coast U (FL)
Texas A&M U (TX)
Texas State U (TX)
U of Minnesota, Crookston (MN)
U of Rhode Island (RI)
Western State Colorado U (CO)

WEB/MULTIMEDIA MANAGEMENT AND WEBMASTER
American Public U System (WV)
Georgia Coll & State U (GA)
Hawai`i Pacific U (HI)
Limestone Coll (SC)
Morrisville State Coll (NY)
Neumont U (UT)
Northern Michigan U (MI)
Pepperdine U, Malibu (CA)
Quincy U (IL)
Rochester Inst of Technology (NY)
State U of New York Coll of Technology at Alfred (NY)
Trevecca Nazarene U (TN)
U of Dubuque (IA)
U of Great Falls (MT)
U of St. Francis (IL)

WEB PAGE, DIGITAL/ MULTIMEDIA AND INFORMATION RESOURCES DESIGN
Acad of Art U (CA)
American Acad of Art (IL)
Azusa Pacific U (CA)
Bradley U (IL)
Central Washington U (WA)
Champlain Coll (VT)
Columbia Coll Chicago (IL)
Concordia U (QC, Canada)
Creighton U (NE)
DePaul U (IL)
DeVry U, Phoenix (AZ)
DeVry U, Pomona (CA)
DeVry U, Westminster (CO)
DeVry U, Miramar (FL)
DeVry U, Orlando (FL)
DeVry U, Decatur (GA)
DeVry U, Chicago (IL)
DeVry U, Kansas City (MO)
DeVry U, North Brunswick (NJ)
DeVry U, Columbus (OH)
DeVry U, Fort Washington (PA)
DeVry U, Irving (TX)
DeVry U, Arlington (VA)
DeVry U, Federal Way (WA)
DeVry U Online (IL)
Drexel U (PA)
Duquesne U (PA)
Emily Carr U of Art + Design (BC, Canada)
Franklin U (OH)
Grace Coll (IN)
Hampshire Coll (MA)
Harding U (AR)
Iona Coll (NY)
Iowa Wesleyan Coll (IA)
Johnson & Wales U (RI)
Juniata Coll (PA)
Lasell Coll (MA)
Limestone Coll (SC)
Lindenwood U (MO)
Lipscomb U (TN)
Morrisville State Coll (NY)
National U (CA)
Neumont U (UT)
New England Inst of Technology (RI)
New York City Coll of Technology of the City U of New York (NY)
Northwest Missouri State U (MO)
Pennsylvania Coll of Technology (PA)
Quinnipiac U (CT)
Rasmussen Coll Bloomington (MN)
Rasmussen Coll Brooklyn Park (MN)
Rasmussen Coll Eagan (MN)
Rasmussen Coll Fort Myers (FL)
Rasmussen Coll Kansas City/ Overland Park (KS)
Rasmussen Coll Lake Elmo/ Woodbury (MN)
Rasmussen Coll Land O' Lakes (FL)
Rasmussen Coll Mankato (MN)
Rasmussen Coll Moorhead (MN)
Rasmussen Coll New Port Richey (FL)
Rasmussen Coll Ocala (FL)
Rasmussen Coll Rockford (IL)
Rasmussen Coll St. Cloud (MN)
Rasmussen Coll Tampa/Brandon (FL)
Rasmussen Coll Topeka (KS)
Rider U (NJ)
Rochester Inst of Technology (NY)
Santa Clara U (CA)
School of the Art Inst of Chicago (IL)
Sullivan Coll of Technology and Design (KY)
Thiel Coll (PA)
Trevecca Nazarene U (TN)
The U of Arizona (AZ)
U of Cincinnati (OH)
U of Dubuque (IA)
U of Great Falls (MT)
U of Mount Union (OH)
U of North Carolina at Asheville (NC)
The U of the Arts (PA)
U of Washington, Bothell (WA)
U of Wisconsin–Stevens Point (WI)
Utah Valley U (UT)
Walla Walla U (WA)
William Jewell Coll (MO)

WELDING ENGINEERING TECHNOLOGY
LeTourneau U (TX)

WELDING TECHNOLOGY
The Ohio State U (OH)
Weber State U (UT)

WILDLIFE BIOLOGY
Adams State U (CO)
Coll of the Atlantic (ME)
Colorado State U (CO)
Friends U (KS)
Frostburg State U (MD)
Kansas State U (KS)
Keystone Coll (PA)
Lees-McRae Coll (NC)
Liberty U (VA)
Ohio U (OH)
State U of New York Coll of Environmental Science and Forestry (NY)
Texas State U (TX)
Unity Coll (ME)
U of Guelph (ON, Canada)
U of Michigan–Flint (MI)
U of Vermont (VT)
U of Wyoming (WY)
West Texas A&M U (TX)

WILDLIFE, FISH AND WILDLANDS SCIENCE AND MANAGEMENT
Arkansas State U (AR)
Arkansas Tech U (AR)
Auburn U (AL)
Coll of the Ozarks (MO)
Delaware State U (DE)
Eastern Kentucky U (KY)
Eastern New Mexico U (NM)
Fort Hays State U (KS)
Frostburg State U (MD)
Humboldt State U (CA)
Juniata Coll (PA)
Lincoln Memorial U (TN)
McNeese State U (LA)
Michigan State U (MI)
Michigan Technological U (MI)
Mississippi State U (MS)
Missouri State U (MO)
Missouri Western State U (MO)
Montana State U (MT)
Murray State U (KY)
New Mexico State U (NM)
Northwest Missouri State U (MO)
The Ohio State U (OH)
Oregon State U (OR)
Peru State Coll (NE)
South Dakota State U (SD)
State U of New York Coll of Agriculture and Technology at Cobleskill (NY)
State U of New York Coll of Environmental Science and Forestry (NY)
Stephen F. Austin State U (TX)
Sterling Coll (VT)
Sul Ross State U (TX)
Tarleton State U (TX)
Texas A&M U (TX)
Texas A&M U–Commerce (TX)
Texas A&M U–Kingsville (TX)
Unity Coll (ME)
U of Alaska Fairbanks (AK)
U of Alberta (AB, Canada)
The U of British Columbia (BC, Canada)
U of Delaware (DE)
U of Florida (FL)
U of Georgia (GA)
U of Idaho (ID)
U of Maine (ME)
U of Minnesota, Twin Cities Campus (MN)
U of Missouri (MO)
The U of Montana (MT)
U of Nevada, Reno (NV)
U of New Hampshire (NH)
U of Rhode Island (RI)
The U of Tennessee (TN)
The U of Tennessee at Martin (TN)
U of Wisconsin–Madison (WI)
U of Wisconsin–Stevens Point (WI)
Utah State U (UT)
Valley City State U (ND)
Washington State U (WA)
West Virginia U (WV)

WOMEN'S MINISTRY
Coll of Biblical Studies–Houston (TX)
Corban U (OR)

WOMEN'S STUDIES
Agnes Scott Coll (GA)
Albion Coll (MI)
Albright Coll (PA)
Allegheny Coll (PA)
Alverno Coll (WI)
American U (DC)
Amherst Coll (MA)
Appalachian State U (NC)
Arizona State U at the Tempe campus (AZ)
Arizona State U at the West campus (AZ)
Armstrong State U (GA)
Augsburg Coll (MN)
Augustana Coll (IL)
Austin Coll (TX)
Ball State U (IN)
Barnard Coll (NY)
Bates Coll (ME)
Bennington Coll (VT)
Berea Coll (KY)
Bowdoin Coll (ME)
Bowling Green State U (OH)
Brandeis U (MA)
Brown U (RI)
Bryant U (RI)
Bucknell U (PA)
Butler U (IN)
California State U, Fresno (CA)
California State U, Fullerton (CA)
California State U, Long Beach (CA)
California State U, San Marcos (CA)
Canisius Coll (NY)
Carleton Coll (MN)
Case Western Reserve U (OH)
Castleton State Coll (VT)
Central Michigan U (MI)
Chatham U (PA)
City Coll of the City U of New York (NY)
Clark U (MA)
Cleveland State U (OH)
Coe Coll (IA)
Colby Coll (ME)
The Coll at Brockport, State U of New York (NY)
Coll of Charleston (SC)
The Coll of New Jersey (NJ)
The Coll of New Rochelle (NY)
Coll of Saint Benedict (MN)
Coll of Saint Elizabeth (NJ)
The Coll of Saint Rose (NY)
Coll of Staten Island of the City U of New York (NY)
The Coll of William and Mary (VA)
The Coll of Wooster (OH)
The Colorado Coll (CO)
Columbia U (NY)
Columbia U, School of General Studies (NY)
Concordia U (QC, Canada)
Concordia U Chicago (IL)
Connecticut Coll (CT)
Cornell Coll (IA)
Cornell U (NY)
Dalhousie U (NS, Canada)
Dartmouth Coll (NH)
Denison U (OH)
DePaul U (IL)
DePauw U (IN)
Dickinson Coll (PA)
Dominican U (IL)
Dominican U of California (CA)
Drew U (NJ)
Duquesne U (PA)
Earlham Coll (IN)
Eastern Michigan U (MI)
East Tennessee State U (TN)
Eckerd Coll (FL)
Florida Intl U (FL)
Fordham U (NY)
Fort Lewis Coll (CO)
Georgetown U (DC)
Georgia State U (GA)
Gettysburg Coll (PA)
Goddard Coll (VT)
Goucher Coll (MD)
Grand Valley State U (MI)
Guilford Coll (NC)
Gustavus Adolphus Coll (MN)
Hamilton Coll (NY)
Hamline U (MN)
Hampshire Coll (MA)
Harvard U (MA)
Hobart and William Smith Colls (NY)
Hofstra U (NY)
Hollins U (VA)
Hope Coll (MI)
Hunter Coll of the City U of New York (NY)
Illinois Wesleyan U (IL)
Indiana U–Purdue U Fort Wayne (IN)
Iowa State U of Science and Technology (IA)
Kalamazoo Coll (MI)
Kansas State U (KS)
Keene State Coll (NH)
Kenyon Coll (OH)
Knox Coll (IL)
Lafayette Coll (PA)
Lehigh U (PA)
Loyola Marymount U (CA)
Loyola U Chicago (IL)
Luther Coll (IA)
Macalester Coll (MN)
Manchester U (IN)
Merrimack Coll (MA)
Metropolitan State U (MN)
Miami U (OH)
Michigan State U (MI)
Minnesota State U Mankato (MN)
Minnesota State U Moorhead (MN)
Mississippi U for Women (MS)
Montclair State U (NJ)
Nazareth Coll of Rochester (NY)
New Jersey City U (NJ)
New Mexico State U (NM)
North Carolina State U (NC)
North Dakota State U (ND)
Northeastern Illinois U (IL)
Northern Arizona U (AZ)
Northern Kentucky U (KY)
Northland Coll (WI)
Northwestern U (IL)
Oakland U (MI)
Oberlin Coll (OH)
The Ohio State U (OH)
Ohio U (OH)
Ohio Wesleyan U (OH)
Old Dominion U (VA)
Oregon State U (OR)
Pace U (NY)
Pacific Lutheran U (WA)
Penn State Abington (PA)
Penn State Altoona (PA)
Penn State Beaver (PA)
Penn State Berks (PA)
Penn State Brandywine (PA)
Penn State DuBois (PA)
Penn State Erie, The Behrend Co (PA)
Penn State Fayette, The Eberly Campus (PA)
Penn State Greater Allegheny (PA
Penn State Hazleton (PA)
Penn State Lehigh Valley (PA)
Penn State Mont Alto (PA)
Penn State New Kensington (PA)
Penn State Schuylkill (PA)
Penn State Shenango (PA)
Penn State U Park (PA)
Penn State Wilkes-Barre (PA)
Penn State Worthington Scranton (PA)
Penn State York (PA)
Pomona Coll (CA)
Portland State U (OR)
Prescott Coll (AZ)
Providence Coll (RI)
Purchase Coll, State U of New Yor (NY)
Purdue U (IN)
Queens Coll of the City U of New York (NY)
Randolph-Macon Coll (VA)
Regis U (CO)
Rhode Island Coll (RI)
Rice U (TX)
Rutgers, The State U of New Jersey, Newark (NJ)
Rutgers, The State U of New Jersey, New Brunswick (NJ)
Sacred Heart U (CT)
St. Bonaventure U (NY)
St. Catherine U (MN)
Saint John's U (MN)
Saint Louis U (MO)
St. Olaf Coll (MN)
St. Thomas U (NB, Canada)
Salem Coll (NC)
San Diego State U (CA)
San Francisco State U (CA)
Santa Clara U (CA)
Sarah Lawrence Coll (NY)
Scripps Coll (CA)
Seattle U (WA)
Sewanee: The U of the South (TN)
Simmons Coll (MA)
Simon Fraser U (BC, Canada)
Smith Coll (MA)
Southwestern U (TX)
Spelman Coll (GA)
Stanford U (CA)
State U of New York at Fredonia (NY)
State U of New York at New Paltz (NY)
State U of New York at Oswego (NY)
State U of New York at Plattsburgh (NY)
State U of New York Coll at Potsdam (NY)
Stony Brook U, State U of New York (NY)
Syracuse U (NY)
Temple U (PA)
Texas A&M U (TX)
Towson U (MD)
Trent U (ON, Canada)
Trinity Coll (CT)
Tufts U (MA)
Tulane U (LA)
U at Albany, State U of New York (NY)
U of Alberta (AB, Canada)
The U of Arizona (AZ)
The U of British Columbia (BC, Canada)
U of California, Berkeley (CA)
U of California, Davis (CA)
U of California, Irvine (CA)
U of California, Riverside (CA)
U of California, Santa Barbara (CA)
U of California, Santa Cruz (CA)
U of Cincinnati (OH)
U of Colorado Boulder (CO)
U of Dayton (OH)
U of Delaware (DE)
U of Florida (FL)
U of Georgia (GA)
U of Hartford (CT)

U of Hawaii at Manoa (HI)
U of Houston–Clear Lake (TX)
U of Illinois at Chicago (IL)
The U of Iowa (IA)
The U of Kansas (KS)
U of King's Coll (NS, Canada)
U of Lethbridge (AB, Canada)
U of Louisville (KY)
U of Maine (ME)
U of Maryland, Baltimore County (MD)
U of Maryland, Coll Park (MD)
U of Massachusetts Amherst (MA)
U of Massachusetts Boston (MA)
U of Massachusetts Dartmouth (MA)
U of Miami (FL)
U of Michigan (MI)
U of Michigan–Dearborn (MI)
U of Minnesota, Duluth (MN)
U of Minnesota, Morris (MN)
U of Minnesota, Twin Cities Campus (MN)
The U of Montana (MT)
U of Nebraska–Lincoln (NE)
U of Nevada, Las Vegas (NV)
U of Nevada, Reno (NV)
U of New Hampshire (NH)
U of New Mexico (NM)
U of North Carolina at Asheville (NC)
The U of North Carolina at Chapel Hill (NC)
The U of North Carolina at Greensboro (NC)
U of Oklahoma (OK)
U of Oregon (OR)
U of Ottawa (ON, Canada)
U of Pennsylvania (PA)
U of Regina (SK, Canada)
U of Rhode Island (RI)
U of Richmond (VA)
U of Rochester (NY)
U of Saint Joseph (CT)
U of St. Thomas (MN)
U of Saskatchewan (SK, Canada)
The U of Scranton (PA)
U of Southern Maine (ME)
U of South Florida (FL)
The U of Texas at Austin (TX)
The U of Texas at San Antonio (TX)
The U of Toledo (OH)
U of Toronto (ON, Canada)
The U of Tulsa (OK)
U of Utah (UT)
U of Vermont (VT)
U of Washington (WA)
U of Waterloo (ON, Canada)
The U of Western Ontario (ON, Canada)
U of Windsor (ON, Canada)
U of Wisconsin–Eau Claire (WI)
U of Wisconsin–La Crosse (WI)
U of Wisconsin–Madison (WI)
U of Wisconsin–Milwaukee (WI)
U of Wisconsin–Whitewater (WI)
U of Wyoming (WY)
Vanderbilt U (TN)
Vassar Coll (NY)
Villanova U (PA)
Virginia Commonwealth U (VA)
Virginia Wesleyan Coll (VA)
Warren Wilson Coll (NC)
Washington State U (WA)
Washington U in St. Louis (MO)
Webster U (MO)
Wells Coll (NY)
Wesleyan Coll (GA)
West Chester U of Pennsylvania (PA)
Western Illinois U (IL)
Western Michigan U (MI)
Wheaton Coll (MA)
Wichita State U (KS)
Willamette U (OR)
William Paterson U of New Jersey (NJ)
Williams Coll (MA)
Wright State U (OH)
Yale U (CT)

WOOD SCIENCE AND WOOD PRODUCTS/PULP AND PAPER TECHNOLOGY

North Carolina State U (NC)
Oregon State U (OR)
Purdue U (IN)
State U of New York Coll of Environmental Science and Forestry (NY)
The U of British Columbia (BC, Canada)
U of Idaho (ID)
U of Maine (ME)
U of Minnesota, Twin Cities Campus (MN)
U of Toronto (ON, Canada)
U of Wisconsin–Stevens Point (WI)
West Virginia U (WV)

WOODWIND INSTRUMENTS

The Colburn School Conservatory of Music (CA)
Houghton Coll (NY)
Lawrence U (WI)
Manhattan School of Music (NY)
Maryville Coll (TN)
Mount Allison U (NB, Canada)
New England Conservatory of Music (MA)
Northwestern U (IL)
Oberlin Coll (OH)
Oklahoma Christian U (OK)
Peabody Conservatory of The Johns Hopkins U (MD)
Peru State Coll (NE)
San Francisco Conservatory of Music (CA)
State U of New York at Fredonia (NY)
Syracuse U (NY)
U of Central Oklahoma (OK)
The U of Iowa (IA)
The U of Kansas (KS)
U of Michigan (MI)
U of Southern California (CA)
Vanderbilt U (TN)
Xavier U of Louisiana (LA)
Youngstown State U (OH)

WOODWORKING

Rochester Inst of Technology (NY)

WORK AND FAMILY STUDIES

Brigham Young U (UT)

WRITING

Augustana Coll (IL)
Baylor U (TX)
Bennington Coll (VT)
Bethany Coll (WV)
Biola U (CA)
Brigham Young U (UT)
Calvin Coll (MI)
Canisius Coll (NY)
Cardinal Stritch U (WI)
Carroll Coll (MT)
Central Washington U (WA)
Champlain Coll (VT)
Columbia U, School of General Studies (NY)
DePauw U (IN)
Drury U (MO)
Eastern Michigan U (MI)
Ferris State U (MI)
Geneva Coll (PA)
Georgia Southern U (GA)
Gettysburg Coll (PA)
Goddard Coll (VT)
Graceland U (IA)
Grand Valley State U (MI)
High Point U (NC)
Indiana U–Purdue U Fort Wayne (IN)
Kansas Wesleyan U (KS)
La Roche Coll (PA)
Lipscomb U (TN)
Madonna U (MI)
Marian U (WI)
Marquette U (WI)
Massachusetts Coll of Liberal Arts (MA)
Metropolitan State U (MN)
Northwest U (WA)
Oakland U (MI)
Point Loma Nazarene U (CA)
St. Edward's U (TX)
San Diego State U (CA)
Spring Hill Coll (AL)
Thiel Coll (PA)
U of Central Arkansas (AR)
U of Colorado Denver (CO)
U of Evansville (IN)
U of Great Falls (MT)
U of Jamestown (ND)
U of Michigan–Flint (MI)
U of Minnesota, Twin Cities Campus (MN)
U of Mount Union (OH)
The U of Tampa (FL)
The U of Texas at Austin (TX)
U of Washington, Tacoma (WA)
The U of Western Ontario (ON, Canada)
U of Wisconsin–Superior (WI)
Wartburg Coll (IA)
Western Michigan U (MI)
William Peace U (NC)

YOUTH MINISTRY

Anderson U (IN)
Andrews U (MI)
Arizona Christian U (AZ)
Asbury U (KY)
Augsburg Coll (MN)
Bethel Coll (IN)
Bethel U (MN)
Bluffton U (OH)
Calvary Bible Coll and Theological Sem (MO)
Cedarville U (OH)
Charleston Southern U (SC)
Columbia Intl U (SC)
Concordia U, Nebraska (NE)
Concordia U Wisconsin (WI)
Corban U (OR)
Cornerstone U (MI)
Crossroads Coll (MN)
Davis Coll (NY)
Eastern U (PA)
East Texas Baptist U (TX)
Florida Southern Coll (FL)
Geneva Coll (PA)
Grace Coll (IN)
Great Lakes Christian Coll (MI)
Greenville Coll (IL)
Harding U (AR)
Hardin-Simmons U (TX)
Hillsdale Free Will Baptist Coll (OK)
Hope Intl U (CA)
Howard Payne U (TX)
Huntingdon Coll (AL)
John Brown U (AR)
Judson U (IL)
Kentucky Mountain Bible Coll (KY)
King U (TN)
Kuyper Coll (MI)
Lee U (TN)
LeTourneau U (TX)
Lincoln Christian U (IL)
Lipscomb U (TN)
Lubbock Christian U (TX)
Malone U (OH)
Manhattan Christian Coll (KS)
Maranatha Baptist U (WI)
Master's Coll and Sem (ON, Canada)
MidAmerica Nazarene U (KS)
Mid-Atlantic Christian U (NC)
Mount Vernon Nazarene U (OH)
Multnomah U (OR)
North Greenville U (SC)
Northwest Christian U (OR)
Northwest U (WA)
Nyack Coll (NY)
Ohio Dominican U (OH)
Ohio Northern U (OH)
Olivet Nazarene U (IL)
Rocky Mountain Coll (AB, Canada)
Simpson U (CA)
Southwestern Assemblies of God U (TX)
Summit U (PA)
Tabor Coll (KS)
Toccoa Falls Coll (GA)
Trevecca Nazarene U (TN)
Trinity Coll of Florida (FL)
U of Indianapolis (IN)
U of Northwestern–St. Paul (MN)
U of Valley Forge (PA)
Vanguard U of Southern California (CA)
William Jessup U (CA)

YOUTH SERVICES

Montclair State U (NJ)
Murray State U (KY)
Rhode Island Coll (RI)
Samford U (AL)
The U of Western Ontario (ON, Canada)
Wheelock Coll (MA)

ZOOLOGY/ANIMAL BIOLOGY

Andrews U (MI)
Auburn U (AL)
Bennington Coll (VT)
California State U, Long Beach (CA)
Canisius Coll (NY)
Coll of the Atlantic (ME)
Colorado State U (CO)
Dalhousie U (NS, Canada)
The Evergreen State Coll (WA)
Humboldt State U (CA)
Kent State U (OH)
Kentucky Wesleyan Coll (KY)
Liberty U (VA)
Malone U (OH)
Mars Hill U (NC)
Miami U (OH)
Michigan State U (MI)
North Carolina State U (NC)
North Dakota State U (ND)
Northern Michigan U (MI)
The Ohio State U (OH)
Ohio U (OH)
Ohio Wesleyan U (OH)
Oklahoma State U (OK)
Olivet Nazarene U (IL)
Oregon State U (OR)
Rutgers, The State U of New Jersey, Newark (NJ)
San Diego State U (CA)
San Francisco State U (CA)
Southern Illinois U Carbondale (IL)
State U of New York at Oswego (NY)
State U of New York Coll of Environmental Science and Forestry (NY)
Texas A&M U (TX)
Texas Tech U (TX)
The U of Akron (OH)
U of Alberta (AB, Canada)
The U of British Columbia (BC, Canada)
The U of British Columbia–Okanagan Campus (BC, Canada)
U of California, Davis (CA)
U of California, Santa Barbara (CA)
U of Florida (FL)
U of Guelph (ON, Canada)
U of Hawaii at Manoa (HI)
U of Maine (ME)
U of Minnesota, Twin Cities Campus (MN)
The U of Montana (MT)
U of New Hampshire (NH)
U of Oklahoma (OK)
U of Rhode Island (RI)
The U of Texas at El Paso (TX)
U of Toronto (ON, Canada)
U of Vermont (VT)
U of Wisconsin–Madison (WI)
U of Wyoming (WY)
Utah State U (UT)
Washington State U (WA)
Weber State U (UT)

ZOOLOGY/ANIMAL BIOLOGY RELATED

Canisius Coll (NY)

Entrance Difficulty

This index groups colleges by their own assessment of their entrance difficulty level. The colleges were asked to select the level that most closely corresponds to their entrance difficulty, according to the guidelines below. Institutions for which high school class rank and/or standardized test scores do not apply as admission criteria were asked to select the level that best indicates their entrance difficulty as compared to other institutions.

MOST DIFFICULT

More than 75 percent of the freshmen were in the top 10 percent of their high school class and scored over 1310 on the SAT (critical reading and mathematical combined) or over 29 on the ACT (composite); about 30 percent or fewer of the applicants were accepted.

Amherst Coll (MA)
Barnard Coll (NY)
Bowdoin Coll (ME)
Brandeis U (MA)
Brown U (RI)
Bryn Mawr Coll (PA)
Bucknell U (PA)
California Inst of Technology (CA)
Claremont McKenna Coll (CA)
The Colburn School Conservatory of Music (CA)
Colby Coll (ME)
The Coll of William and Mary (VA)
Columbia U (NY)
Columbia U, School of General Studies (NY)
Cornell U (NY)
Dartmouth Coll (NH)
Franklin W. Olin Coll of Eng (MA)
Georgetown U (DC)
Georgia Inst of Technology (GA)
Gettysburg Coll (PA)
Harvard U (MA)
Harvey Mudd Coll (CA)
Haverford Coll (PA)
Johns Hopkins U (MD)
The Juilliard School (NY)
Lehigh U (PA)
Massachusetts Inst of Technology (MA)
Middlebury Coll (VT)
Northwestern U (IL)
Pomona Coll (CA)
Princeton U (NJ)
Reed Coll (OR)
Rice U (TX)
Soka U of America (CA)
Stanford U (CA)
Trinity Coll (CT)
Tufts U (MA)
United States Air Force Acad (CO)
United States Military Acad (NY)
U of Chicago (IL)
U of Notre Dame (IN)
U of Pennsylvania (PA)
U of Southern California (CA)
Vanderbilt U (TN)
Washington and Lee U (VA)
Washington U in St. Louis (MO)
Webb Inst (NY)
Wesleyan U (CT)
Williams Coll (MA)
Yale U (CT)

VERY DIFFICULT

More than 50 percent of the freshmen were in the top 10 percent of their high school class and scored over 1230 on the SAT or over 26 on the ACT; about 60 percent or fewer applicants were accepted.

Allegheny Coll (PA)
American U (DC)
American U in Bulgaria (Bulgaria)
The American U in Cairo (Egypt)
Antioch Coll, Yellow Springs (OH)
Art Center Coll of Design (CA)
Austin Coll (TX)
Babson Coll (MA)
Bard Coll (NY)
Baruch Coll of the City U of New York (NY)
Bates Coll (ME)
Bennington Coll (VT)
Bentley U (MA)
Binghamton U, State U of New York (NY)
Boston Coll (MA)
Boston U (MA)
Butler U (IN)
California Inst of the Arts (CA)
Carleton Coll (MN)
Case Western Reserve U (OH)
Centre Coll (KY)
Chapman U (CA)
Christopher Newport U (VA)
Clarkson U (NY)
The Coll of New Jersey (NJ)
Coll of the Atlantic (ME)
Coll of the Holy Cross (MA)
The Colorado Coll (CO)
Colorado School of Mines (CO)
Connecticut Coll (CT)
Davidson Coll (NC)
Denison U (OH)
Dickinson Coll (PA)
Earlham Coll (IN)
Emerson Coll (MA)
Florida State U (FL)
Fordham U (NY)
Franklin & Marshall Coll (PA)
The George Washington U (DC)
Grinnell Coll (IA)
Gustavus Adolphus Coll (MN)
Hamilton Coll (NY)
Hendrix Coll (AR)
Hillsdale Coll (MI)
Hobart and William Smith Colls (NY)
Illinois Wesleyan U (IL)
James Madison U (VA)
Kalamazoo Coll (MI)
Kenyon Coll (OH)
Kettering U (MI)
Knox Coll (IL)
Laguna Coll of Art & Design (CA)
Lawrence U (WI)
Lewis & Clark Coll (OR)
Loyola Marymount U (CA)
Macalester Coll (MN)
Manhattan School of Music (NY)
Marist Coll (NY)
Massachusetts Coll of Art and Design (MA)
Missouri U of Science and Technology (MO)
Mount Holyoke Coll (MA)
Muhlenberg Coll (PA)
New Coll of Florida (FL)
New England Conservatory of Music (MA)
New York U (NY)
North Carolina State U (NC)
Northeastern U (MA)
Oberlin Coll (OH)
Occidental Coll (CA)
Oglethorpe U (GA)
The Ohio State U (OH)
Ohio Wesleyan U (OH)
Peabody Conservatory of The Johns Hopkins U (MD)
Penn State Abington (PA)
Penn State Altoona (PA)
Penn State Berks (PA)
Penn State Erie, The Behrend Coll (PA)
Penn State Harrisburg (PA)
Penn State U Park (PA)
Pepperdine U, Malibu (CA)
Pratt Inst (NY)
Presbyterian Coll (SC)
Queens Coll of the City U of New York (NY)
Rensselaer Polytechnic Inst (NY)
Rhode Island School of Design (RI)
Rhodes Coll (TN)
Rose-Hulman Inst of Technology (IN)
St. John's Coll (NM)
St. Lawrence U (NY)
St. Olaf Coll (MN)
San Jose State U (CA)
Sarah Lawrence Coll (NY)
School of the Art Inst of Chicago (IL)
Scripps Coll (CA)
Sewanee: The U of the South (TN)
Skidmore Coll (NY)
Smith Coll (MA)
Southwestern U (TX)
Spelman Coll (GA)
State U of New York at New Paltz (NY)
State U of New York Coll at Geneseo (NY)
State U of New York Coll of Environmental Science and Forestry (NY)
State U of New York Maritime Coll (NY)
Stockton U (NJ)
Stonehill Coll (MA)
Stony Brook U, State U of New York (NY)
Syracuse U (NY)
Texas Christian U (TX)
Thomas Aquinas Coll (CA)
Transylvania U (KY)
Trinity U (TX)
Tulane U (LA)
Union Coll (NY)
United States Coast Guard Acad (CT)
United States Merchant Marine Acad (NY)
United States Naval Acad (MD)
U at Albany, State U of New York (NY)
The U of British Columbia (BC, Canada)
U of California, Davis (CA)
U of California, Irvine (CA)
U of California, Los Angeles (CA)
U of California, Riverside (CA)
U of California, Santa Barbara (CA)
U of California, Santa Cruz (CA)
U of Florida (FL)
U of Mary Washington (VA)
U of Miami (FL)
U of Michigan (MI)
The U of North Carolina at Chapel Hill (NC)
U of Pittsburgh (PA)
U of Richmond (VA)
U of Rochester (NY)
U of San Diego (CA)
The U of Texas at Dallas (TX)
U of Toronto (ON, Canada)
The U of Tulsa (OK)
U of Virginia (VA)
U of Washington (WA)
The U of Western Ontario (ON, Canada)
U of Wisconsin–Madison (WI)
Vassar Coll (NY)
Villanova U (PA)
Wake Forest U (NC)
Washington & Jefferson Coll (PA)
Wheaton Coll (IL)
Wheaton Coll (MA)
Whitman Coll (WA)
Willamette U (OR)
Wofford Coll (SC)
Worcester Polytechnic Inst (MA)

MODERATELY DIFFICULT

More than 75 percent of the freshmen were in the top half of their high school class and scored over 1010 on the SAT or over 18 on the ACT; about 85 percent or fewer of the applicants were accepted.

Abilene Christian U (TX)
Adams State U (CO)
Adelphi U (NY)
Agnes Scott Coll (GA)
Albany Coll of Pharmacy and Health Sciences (NY)
Albertus Magnus Coll (CT)
Albion Coll (MI)
Albright Coll (PA)
Alcorn State U (MS)
Allen Coll (IA)
Alma Coll (MI)
Alvernia U (PA)
Alverno Coll (WI)
American Acad of Art (IL)
American Intl Coll (MA)
The American U of Paris (France)
The American U of Rome (Italy)
Anderson U (IN)
Andrews U (MI)
Angelo State U (TX)
Antioch U Santa Barbara (CA)
Appalachian State U (NC)
Aquinas Coll (MI)
Arcadia U (PA)
Arizona State U at the Downtown Phoenix campus (AZ)
Arizona State U at the Polytechnic campus (AZ)
Arizona State U at the Tempe campus (AZ)
Arizona State U at the West campus (AZ)
Arkansas State U (AR)
Arkansas Tech U (AR)
Asbury U (KY)
Ashland U (OH)
Assumption Coll (MA)
Auburn U (AL)
Auburn U at Montgomery (AL)
Augsburg Coll (MN)
Augustana Coll (IL)
Augustana Coll (SD)
Austin Peay State U (TN)
Ave Maria U (FL)
Averett U (VA)
Azusa Pacific U (CA)
Baker U (KS)
Baldwin Wallace U (OH)
Ball State U (IN)
Bard Coll at Simon's Rock (MA)
Barry U (FL)
Baylor U (TX)
Bay Path U (MA)
Beacon Coll (FL)
Becker Coll (MA)
Belhaven U (MS)
Belmont Abbey Coll (NC)
Belmont U (TN)
Bemidji State U (MN)
Benedictine U (IL)
Berea Coll (KY)
Berry Coll (GA)
Bethany Coll (WV)
Bethany Lutheran Coll (MN)
Bethel Coll (KS)
Bethel U (MN)
Biola U (CA)
Birmingham-Southern Coll (AL)
Blackburn Coll (IL)
Blessing-Rieman Coll of Nursing (IL)
Bloomfield Coll (NJ)
Bloomsburg U of Pennsylvania (PA)
Blue Mountain Coll (MS)
Bluffton U (OH)
Bowling Green State U (OH)
Bradley U (IL)
Brenau U (GA)
Bridgewater Coll (VA)
Bridgewater State U (MA)
Brigham Young U (UT)
Bryan Coll (TN)
Bryant U (RI)
Buena Vista U (IA)
Buffalo State Coll, State U of New York (NY)
Cabarrus Coll of Health Sciences (NC)
Cabrini Coll (PA)
Cairn U (PA)
Caldwell U (NJ)
California Baptist U (CA)
California Lutheran U (CA)
California Polytechnic State U, San Luis Obispo (CA)
California State Polytechnic U, Pomona (CA)
California State U, Chico (CA)
California State U, Dominguez Hills (CA)
California State U, Fullerton (CA)
California State U, Long Beach (CA)
California State U, Los Angeles (CA)
California State U, Monterey Bay (CA)
California State U, Sacramento (CA)
California State U, San Bernardino (CA)
California State U, San Marcos (CA)
California State U, Stanislaus (CA)
California U of Pennsylvania (PA)
Calvin Coll (MI)
Campbellsville U (KY)
Canisius Coll (NY)
Cape Breton U (NS, Canada)
Capital U (OH)
Cardinal Stritch U (WI)
Carlos Albizu U, Miami Campus (FL)
Carroll Coll (MT)
Carson-Newman U (TN)
Castleton State Coll (VT)
Catawba Coll (NC)
The Catholic U of America (DC)
Cedar Crest Coll (PA)
Cedarville U (OH)
Centenary Coll of Louisiana (LA)
Central Coll (IA)
Central Connecticut State U (CT)
Central Methodist U (MO)
Central Michigan U (MI)
Central Washington U (WA)
Chaminade U of Honolulu (HI)
Champlain Coll (VT)
Charleston Southern U (SC)
Chatham U (PA)
Chestnut Hill Coll (PA)
Christendom Coll (VA)
Christian Brothers U (TN)
The Citadel, The Military Coll of South Carolina (SC)
City Coll of the City U of New York (NY)
Clark Atlanta U (GA)
Clarke U (IA)
Clark U (MA)
Cleveland Inst of Art (OH)
Cleveland State U (OH)
Coastal Carolina U (SC)
Coe Coll (IA)
Cogswell Polytechnical Coll (CA)
Coker Coll (SC)
Colby-Sawyer Coll (NH)
The Coll at Brockport, State U of New York (NY)
Coll for Creative Studies (MI)
Coll of Charleston (SC)
The Coll of Idaho (ID)
The Coll of New Rochelle (NY)
Coll of Saint Benedict (MN)
Coll of Saint Elizabeth (NJ)
The Coll of Saint Rose (NY)
The Coll of St. Scholastica (MN)
Coll of the Ozarks (MO)
The Coll of Wooster (OH)
Colorado State U (CO)
Colorado State U–Pueblo (CO)
Columbia Coll (MO)
Columbia Coll (SC)
Columbia Coll Chicago (IL)
Columbia Intl U (SC)
Columbus Coll of Art & Design (OH)
Concordia Coll (MN)
Concordia Coll–New York (NY)
Concordia U (CA)
Concordia U (QC, Canada)
Concordia U Chicago (IL)
Concordia U, Nebraska (NE)
Concordia U Texas (TX)
Concordia U Wisconsin (WI)
Corban U (OR)
Cornell Coll (IA)
Cornish Coll of the Arts (WA)
Covenant Coll (GA)
Creighton U (NE)
The Culinary Inst of America (NY)
Culver-Stockton Coll (MO)
Cumberland U (TN)
Curry Coll (MA)
Daemen Coll (NY)
Dalhousie U (NS, Canada)
Dallas Baptist U (TX)
Daniel Webster Coll (NH)
Defiance Coll (OH)
Delaware State U (DE)
DePaul U (IL)
DePauw U (IN)
DEREE - The American Coll of Greece (Greece)
DeSales U (PA)
Dominican U (IL)
Dominican U of California (CA)
Dowling Coll (NY)
Drake U (IA)
Drew U (NJ)
Drexel U (PA)
Drury U (MO)
Duquesne U (PA)
East Carolina U (NC)
Eastern Connecticut State U (CT)
Eastern Illinois U (IL)
Eastern Michigan U (MI)
Eastern Oregon U (OR)
Eastern U (PA)
East Stroudsburg U of Pennsylvania (PA)
East Tennessee State U (TN)
East Texas Baptist U (TX)
Eckerd Coll (FL)
Edgewood Coll (WI)
Edinboro U of Pennsylvania (PA)
Elizabethtown Coll (PA)
Elmhurst Coll (IL)
Elmira Coll (NY)
Elms Coll (MA)
Elon U (NC)
Embry-Riddle Aeronautical U–Daytona (FL)
Embry-Riddle Aeronautical U–Prescott (AZ)
Emily Carr U of Art + Design (BC, Canada)
Emmanuel Coll (GA)
Emmanuel Coll (MA)
Endicott Coll (MA)
Erskine Coll (SC)
Escuela de Artes Plasticas de Puerto Rico (PR)
Evangel U (MO)
The Evergreen State Coll (WA)
Fairfield U (CT)
Fairleigh Dickinson U, Coll at Florham (NJ)
Fairleigh Dickinson U, Metropolitan Campus (NJ)
Farmingdale State Coll (NY)
Fashion Inst of Technology (NY)
FIDM/Fashion Inst of Design & Merchandising, Los Angeles Campus (CA)
FIDM/Fashion Inst of Design & Merchandising, San Francisco Campus (CA)
Fitchburg State U (MA)
Five Towns Coll (NY)
Flagler Coll (FL)
Florida Ag and Mech U (FL)
Florida Atlantic U (FL)
Florida Coll (FL)
Florida Gulf Coast U (FL)
Florida Inst of Technology (FL)
Florida Intl U (FL)
Florida National U (FL)
Florida Southern Coll (FL)
Fontbonne U (MO)
Fort Lewis Coll (CO)
Framingham State U (MA)
Franciscan U of Steubenville (OH)
Francis Marion U (SC)
Franklin Coll (IN)
Friends U (KS)
Frostburg State U (MD)
Furman U (SC)
Gallaudet U (DC)

Gannon U (PA)
Geneva Coll (PA)
Georgetown Coll (KY)
Georgia Coll & State U (GA)
Georgian Court U (NJ)
Georgia Southern U (GA)
Georgia Southwestern State U (GA)
Georgia State U (GA)
Goldfarb School of Nursing at Barnes-Jewish Coll (MO)
Gonzaga U (WA)
Gordon Coll (MA)
Goshen Coll (IN)
Goucher Coll (MD)
Grace Coll (IN)
Graceland U (IA)
Grand Valley State U (MI)
Green Mountain Coll (VT)
Greensboro Coll (NC)
Greenville Coll (IL)
Grove City Coll (PA)
Guilford Coll (NC)
Gwynedd Mercy U (PA)
Hallmark U (TX)
Hamline U (MN)
Hampden-Sydney Coll (VA)
Hampshire Coll (MA)
Hampton U (VA)
Hanover Coll (IN)
Harding U (AR)
Hardin-Simmons U (TX)
Hartwick Coll (NY)
Hastings Coll (NE)
Hawai`i Pacific U (HI)
HEC Montreal (QC, Canada)
Heidelberg U (OH)
High Point U (NC)
Hiram Coll (OH)
Hofstra U (NY)
Hollins U (VA)
Holy Cross Coll (IN)
Hope Coll (MI)
Hope Intl U (CA)
Houghton Coll (NY)
Houston Baptist U (TX)
Howard Payne U (TX)
Howard U (DC)
Hult Intl Business School (United Kingdom)
Humboldt State U (CA)
Hunter Coll of the City U of New York (NY)
Husson U (ME)
Huston-Tillotson U (TX)
Illinois Coll (IL)
Illinois Inst of Technology (IL)
Illinois State U (IL)
Immaculata U (PA)
Indiana State U (IN)
Indiana U Bloomington (IN)
Indiana U East (IN)
Indiana U–Purdue U Indianapolis (IN)
Indiana U South Bend (IN)
Inter American U of Puerto Rico, Aguadilla Campus (PR)
Inter American U of Puerto Rico, Fajardo Campus (PR)
Inter American U of Puerto Rico, Guayama Campus (PR)
Inter American U of Puerto Rico, Ponce Campus (PR)
Inter American U of Puerto Rico, San Germán Campus (PR)
Iona Coll (NY)
Iowa State U of Science and Technology (IA)
Iowa Wesleyan Coll (IA)
Ithaca Coll (NY)
Jacksonville U (FL)
Jefferson Coll of Health Sciences (VA)
John Brown U (AR)
John Carroll U (OH)
John Paul the Great Catholic U (CA)
Johnson & Wales U (CO)
Johnson & Wales U (FL)
Johnson & Wales U (RI)
Johnson & Wales U - Charlotte Campus (NC)
Johnson C. Smith U (NC)
Johnson State Coll (VT)
Judson Coll (AL)
Judson U (IL)
Juniata Coll (PA)
Kansas City Art Inst (MO)
Kansas Wesleyan U (KS)
Kean U (NJ)
Keene State Coll (NH)
Kennesaw State U (GA)
Kent State U (OH)
Kentucky Christian U (KY)
Kentucky Wesleyan Coll (KY)
Keuka Coll (NY)
The King's Coll (NY)
King's Coll (PA)
The King's U Coll (AB, Canada)
Kingswood U (NB, Canada)
King U (TN)
Kutztown U of Pennsylvania (PA)
Kuyper Coll (MI)
LaGrange Coll (GA)
Lake Erie Coll (OH)
Lake Forest Coll (IL)
Lakeview Coll of Nursing (IL)
Landmark Coll (VT)
Langston U (OK)
La Salle U (PA)
Lasell Coll (MA)
Laurel U (NC)
Lawrence Technological U (MI)
Lebanese American U (Lebanon)
Lebanon Valley Coll (PA)
Lehman Coll of the City U of New York (NY)
Le Moyne Coll (NY)
Lenoir-Rhyne U (NC)
LeTourneau U (TX)
Lewis U (IL)
LIM Coll (NY)
Lincoln Christian U (IL)
Lincoln Memorial U (TN)
Lincoln U (PA)
Lindenwood U (MO)
Linfield Coll (OR)
Lipscomb U (TN)
Lock Haven U of Pennsylvania (PA)
Logan U (MO)
Long Island U–LIU Brooklyn (NY)
Long Island U–LIU Post (NY)
Longwood U (VA)
Loras Coll (IA)
Louisiana Coll (LA)
Louisiana State U and A&M Coll (LA)
Louisiana State U in Shreveport (LA)
Lourdes U (OH)
Loyola U Chicago (IL)
Loyola U New Orleans (LA)
Lubbock Christian U (TX)
Luther Coll (IA)
Lycoming Coll (PA)
Lynchburg Coll (VA)
Lynn U (FL)
Lyon Coll (AR)
Madonna U (MI)
Maharishi U of Management (IA)
Maine Maritime Acad (ME)
Malone U (OH)
Manchester U (IN)
Manhattan Coll (NY)
Manhattanville Coll (NY)
Mansfield U of Pennsylvania (PA)
Marian U (IN)
Marian U (WI)
Marietta Coll (OH)
Marquette U (WI)
Marshall U (WV)
Mars Hill U (NC)
Martin Luther Coll (MN)
Mary Baldwin Coll (VA)
Marymount Manhattan Coll (NY)
Marymount U (VA)
Maryville Coll (TN)
Maryville U of Saint Louis (MO)
Marywood U (PA)
Massachusetts Coll of Liberal Arts (MA)
Massachusetts Maritime Acad (MA)
The Master's Coll and Sem (CA)
McDaniel Coll (MD)
McKendree U (IL)
McMurry U (TX)
McNeese State U (LA)
Medaille Coll (NY)
Menlo Coll (CA)
Mercer U, Macon (GA)
Mercy Coll (NY)
Meredith Coll (NC)
Merrimack Coll (MA)
Messiah Coll (PA)
Metropolitan Coll of New York (NY)
Miami U (OH)
Michigan State U (MI)
Michigan Technological U (MI)
Middle Tennessee State U (TN)
Midwestern State U (TX)
Millersville U of Pennsylvania (PA)
Milligan Coll (TN)
Millikin U (IL)
Millsaps Coll (MS)
Mills Coll (CA)
Milwaukee School of Eng (WI)
Minnesota State U Mankato (MN)
Minnesota State U Moorhead (MN)
Minot State U (ND)
Misericordia U (PA)
Mississippi State U (MS)
Mississippi U for Women (MS)
Missouri Baptist U (MO)
Missouri Southern State U (MO)
Missouri State U (MO)
Molloy Coll (NY)
Monmouth Coll (IL)
Monmouth U (NJ)
Montana State U (MT)
Montana Tech of The U of Montana (MT)
Montclair State U (NJ)
Montreat Coll, Montreat (NC)
Moore Coll of Art & Design (PA)
Moravian Coll (PA)
Morningside Coll (IA)
Morrisville State Coll (NY)
Mount Allison U (NB, Canada)
Mount Carmel Coll of Nursing (OH)
Mount Mary U (WI)
Mount Mercy U (IA)
Mount St. Joseph U (OH)
Mount Saint Mary Coll (NY)
Mount St. Mary's U (MD)
Mount Vernon Nazarene U (OH)
Multnomah U (OR)
Murray State U (KY)
Naropa U (CO)
Nazareth Coll of Rochester (NY)
Nebraska Methodist Coll (NE)
Nebraska Wesleyan U (NE)
Neumont U (UT)
Newberry Coll (SC)
New Jersey City U (NJ)
New Jersey Inst of Technology (NJ)
New Mexico Inst of Mining and Technology (NM)
New Mexico State U (NM)
New Saint Andrews Coll (ID)
New York Inst of Technology (NY)
New York School of Interior Design (NY)
Niagara U (NY)
Norfolk State U (VA)
North Carolina Ag and Tech State U (NC)
North Carolina Wesleyan Coll (NC)
North Central Coll (IL)
North Dakota State U (ND)
Northeastern State U (OK)
Northern Arizona U (AZ)
Northern Illinois U (IL)
Northern Kentucky U (KY)
Northland Coll (WI)
Northwestern Coll (IA)
Northwestern Oklahoma State U (OK)
Northwest Missouri State U (MO)
Northwest Nazarene U (ID)
Northwest U (WA)
Northwood U, Michigan Campus (MI)
Northwood U, Texas Campus (TX)
Norwich U (VT)
Notre Dame of Maryland U (MD)
Nova Southeastern U (FL)
Oakland U (MI)
Ohio Northern U (OH)
Ohio U (OH)
Oklahoma Baptist U (OK)
Oklahoma Christian U (OK)
Oklahoma State U (OK)

Old Dominion U (VA)
Oregon Coll of Art & Craft (OR)
Oregon State U (OR)
Otis Coll of Art and Design (CA)
Pace U (NY)
Pacific Lutheran U (WA)
Pacific U (OR)
Palm Beach Atlantic U (FL)
Patrick Henry Coll (VA)
Penn State Beaver (PA)
Penn State Brandywine (PA)
Penn State DuBois (PA)
Penn State Fayette, The Eberly Campus (PA)
Penn State Greater Allegheny (PA)
Penn State Hazleton (PA)
Penn State Lehigh Valley (PA)
Penn State Mont Alto (PA)
Penn State New Kensington (PA)
Penn State Schuylkill (PA)
Penn State Shenango (PA)
Penn State Wilkes-Barre (PA)
Penn State Worthington Scranton (PA)
Penn State York (PA)
Pennsylvania Coll of Art & Design (PA)
Pennsylvania Coll of Health Sciences (PA)
Philadelphia U (PA)
Piedmont Coll (GA)
Pine Manor Coll (MA)
Plaza Coll (NY)
Plymouth State U (NH)
Point Loma Nazarene U (CA)
Point U (GA)
Portland State U (OR)
Post U (CT)
Prairie View A&M U (TX)
Prescott Coll (AZ)
Principia Coll (IL)
Purchase Coll, State U of New York (NY)
Purdue U (IN)
Purdue U Calumet (IN)
Quincy U (IL)
Quinnipiac U (CT)
Ramapo Coll of New Jersey (NJ)
Randolph Coll (VA)
Randolph-Macon Coll (VA)
Regis Coll (MA)
Regis U (CO)
Reinhardt U (GA)
Research Coll of Nursing (MO)
Rhode Island Coll (RI)
Rider U (NJ)
Ringling Coll of Art and Design (FL)
Ripon Coll (WI)
Rivier U (NH)
Roanoke Coll (VA)
Roberts Wesleyan Coll (NY)
Rochester Inst of Technology (NY)
Rockhurst U (MO)
Rocky Mountain Coll (MT)
Rocky Mountain Coll of Art + Design (CO)
Roger Williams U (RI)
Rollins Coll (FL)
Roosevelt U (IL)
Rosemont Coll (PA)
Rowan U (NJ)
Rutgers, The State U of New Jersey, Camden (NJ)
Rutgers, The State U of New Jersey, Newark (NJ)
Rutgers, The State U of New Jersey, New Brunswick (NJ)
Sacred Heart U (CT)
The Sage Colls (NY)
Saginaw Valley State U (MI)
St. Andrews U (NC)
Saint Anselm Coll (NH)
Saint Anthony Coll of Nursing (IL)
Saint Augustine's U (NC)
St. Bonaventure U (NY)
St. Catherine U (MN)
Saint Charles Borromeo Sem, Overbrook (PA)
St. Edward's U (TX)
Saint Francis U (PA)
St. John Fisher Coll (NY)
St. John's Coll (MD)
Saint John's U (MN)
St. John's U (NY)
Saint Joseph's Coll (IN)
St. Joseph's Coll, Long Island Campus (NY)
St. Joseph's Coll, New York (NY)
Saint Joseph's U (PA)
Saint Leo U (FL)
St. Louis Coll of Pharmacy (MO)
Saint Louis U (MO)
Saint Martin's U (WA)
Saint Mary's Coll (IN)
St. Mary's Coll of Maryland (MD)
St. Mary's U (TX)
Saint Mary's U of Minnesota (MN)
Saint Michael's Coll (VT)
St. Norbert Coll (WI)
Saint Peter's U (NJ)
St. Thomas Aquinas Coll (NY)
St. Thomas U (NB, Canada)
Saint Vincent Coll (PA)
Salem Coll (NC)
Salisbury U (MD)
Salve Regina U (RI)
Samford U (AL)
Sam Houston State U (TX)
Samuel Merritt U (CA)
San Diego Christian Coll (CA)
San Diego State U (CA)
San Francisco Art Inst (CA)
San Francisco State U (CA)
Santa Clara U (CA)
Santa Fe U of Art and Design (NM)
Savannah Coll of Art and Design (GA)
School of the Museum of Fine Arts, Boston (MA)
Seattle Pacific U (WA)
Seattle U (WA)
Seton Hill U (PA)
Shepherd U (WV)
Shimer Coll (IL)
Shippensburg U of Pennsylvania (PA)
Siena Coll (NY)
Siena Heights U (MI)
Simmons Coll (MA)
Simon Fraser U (BC, Canada)
Simpson Coll (IA)
Simpson U (CA)
Slippery Rock U of Pennsylvania (PA)
South Dakota School of Mines and Technology (SD)
Southeastern Louisiana U (LA)
Southeastern Oklahoma State U (OK)
Southeast Missouri State U (MO)
Southern Adventist U (TN)
Southern Arkansas U–Magnolia (AR)
Southern California Inst of Architecture (CA)
Southern California Sem (CA)
Southern Connecticut State U (CT)
Southern Illinois U Carbondale (IL)
Southern Illinois U Edwardsville (IL)
Southern Methodist U (TX)
Southern New Hampshire U (NH)
Southern Oregon U (OR)
Southern Utah U (UT)
Southwest Baptist U (MO)
Spalding U (KY)
Spencerian Coll (KY)
Spring Hill Coll (AL)
State U of New York at Fredonia (NY)
State U of New York at Oswego (NY)
State U of New York at Plattsburgh (NY)
State U of New York Coll at Cortland (NY)
State U of New York Coll at Old Westbury (NY)
State U of New York Coll at Potsdam (NY)
State U of New York Coll of Technology at Alfred (NY)
State U of New York Coll of Technology at Delhi (NY)
State U of New York Polytechnic Inst (NY)
Stephen F. Austin State U (TX)
Stephens Coll (MO)
Stetson U (FL)
Stevenson U (MD)
Stevens–The Inst of Business & Arts (MO)
Suffolk U (MA)
Sullivan Coll of Technology and Design (KY)
Susquehanna U (PA)
Tabor Coll (KS)
Tarleton State U (TX)
Taylor U (IN)
Temple U (PA)
Texas A&M Intl U (TX)
Texas A&M U (TX)
Texas A&M U–Commerce (TX)
Texas A&M U–Corpus Christi (TX)
Texas A&M U–Kingsville (TX)
Texas State U (TX)
Texas Tech U (TX)
Texas Wesleyan U (TX)
Thiel Coll (PA)
Thomas More Coll (KY)
Tiffin U (OH)
Toccoa Falls Coll (GA)
Towson U (MD)
Trent U (ON, Canada)
Trevecca Nazarene U (TN)
Trine U (IN)
Trinity Christian Coll (IL)
Troy U (AL)
Truman State U (MO)
Tusculum Coll (TN)
Union Coll (KY)
Union Coll (NE)
Union U (TN)
Unity Coll (ME)
Universidad Metropolitana (PR)
Université de Montréal (QC, Canada)
Université de Sherbrooke (QC, Canada)
U at Buffalo, the State U of New York (NY)
The U of Akron (OH)
The U of Alabama (AL)
The U of Alabama at Birmingham (AL)
The U of Alabama in Huntsville (AL)
U of Alberta (AB, Canada)
The U of Arizona (AZ)
U of Arkansas (AR)
U of Bridgeport (CT)
The U of British Columbia–Okanagan Campus (BC, Canada)
U of California, Merced (CA)
U of Central Arkansas (AR)
U of Central Florida (FL)
U of Central Missouri (MO)
U of Charleston (WV)
U of Cincinnati (OH)
U of Colorado Boulder (CO)
U of Colorado Colorado Springs (CO)
U of Colorado Denver (CO)
U of Dallas (TX)
U of Dayton (OH)
U of Delaware (DE)
U of Denver (CO)
U of Evansville (IN)
The U of Findlay (OH)
U of Georgia (GA)
U of Guelph (ON, Canada)
U of Hartford (CT)
U of Hawaii at Hilo (HI)
U of Hawaii at Manoa (HI)
U of Hawaii–West Oahu (HI)
U of Houston (TX)
U of Idaho (ID)
U of Illinois at Chicago (IL)
U of Illinois at Springfield (IL)
U of Indianapolis (IN)
The U of Iowa (IA)
The U of Kansas (KS)
U of Kentucky (KY)
U of King's Coll (NS, Canada)
U of La Verne (CA)
U of Lethbridge (AB, Canada)
U of Louisiana at Lafayette (LA)
U of Louisville (KY)
U of Maine (ME)
U of Maine at Machias (ME)
U of Mary Hardin-Baylor (TX)
U of Maryland, Baltimore County (MD)
U of Maryland, Coll Park (MD)
U of Massachusetts Amherst (MA)
U of Massachusetts Boston (MA)
U of Massachusetts Dartmouth (MA)
U of Massachusetts Lowell (MA)
U of Memphis (TN)
U of Michigan–Dearborn (MI)
U of Michigan–Flint (MI)
U of Minnesota, Duluth (MN)
U of Minnesota, Morris (MN)

U of Minnesota, Twin Cities Campus (MN)
U of Mississippi (MS)
U of Missouri (MO)
U of Missouri–Kansas City (MO)
U of Missouri–St. Louis (MO)
U of Mobile (AL)
The U of Montana (MT)
U of Montevallo (AL)
U of Mount Union (OH)
U of Nebraska at Kearney (NE)
U of Nebraska–Lincoln (NE)
U of Nevada, Las Vegas (NV)
U of Nevada, Reno (NV)
U of New Brunswick Saint John (NB, Canada)
U of New England (ME)
U of New Hampshire (NH)
U of New Hampshire at Manchester (NH)
U of New Haven (CT)
U of New Mexico (NM)
U of New Orleans (LA)
U of North Carolina at Asheville (NC)
The U of North Carolina at Charlotte (NC)
The U of North Carolina at Greensboro (NC)
The U of North Carolina at Pembroke (NC)
The U of North Carolina Wilmington (NC)
U of Northern Colorado (CO)
U of Northern Iowa (IA)
U of North Florida (FL)
U of North Georgia (GA)
U of North Texas (TX)
U of Northwestern–St. Paul (MN)
U of Oklahoma (OK)
U of Oregon (OR)
U of Ottawa (ON, Canada)
U of Pittsburgh at Greensburg (PA)
U of Portland (OR)
U of Puerto Rico in Ponce (PR)
U of Puget Sound (WA)
U of Rhode Island (RI)
U of St. Francis (IL)
U of Saint Joseph (CT)
U of Saint Mary (KS)
U of St. Thomas (MN)
U of St. Thomas (TX)
U of San Francisco (CA)
U of Science and Arts of Oklahoma (OK)
The U of Scranton (PA)
U of South Alabama (AL)
U of South Carolina Aiken (SC)
U of South Carolina Upstate (SC)
The U of South Dakota (SD)
U of Southern Indiana (IN)
U of Southern Maine (ME)
U of Southern Mississippi (MS)
U of South Florida (FL)
The U of Tampa (FL)
The U of Tennessee (TN)
The U of Tennessee at Chattanooga (TN)
The U of Tennessee at Martin (TN)
The U of Texas at Arlington (TX)
The U of Texas at San Antonio (TX)
The U of Texas at Tyler (TX)
The U of Texas Health Science Center at Houston (TX)
The U of Texas of the Permian Basin (TX)
The U of the Arts (PA)
U of the Cumberlands (KY)
U of the Incarnate Word (TX)
U of the Pacific (CA)
U of the Sciences (PA)
U of the West (CA)
U of Utah (UT)
U of Vermont (VT)
The U of Virginia's Coll at Wise (VA)
U of Washington, Bothell (WA)
U of Washington, Tacoma (WA)
U of Waterloo (ON, Canada)
U of West Florida (FL)
U of Windsor (ON, Canada)
U of Wisconsin–Eau Claire (WI)
U of Wisconsin–Green Bay (WI)
U of Wisconsin–La Crosse (WI)
U of Wisconsin–Milwaukee (WI)
U of Wisconsin–Oshkosh (WI)
U of Wisconsin–Parkside (WI)
U of Wisconsin–River Falls (WI)
U of Wisconsin–Stevens Point (WI)
U of Wisconsin–Stout (WI)
U of Wisconsin–Superior (WI)
U of Wisconsin–Whitewater (WI)
U of Wyoming (WY)
Upper Iowa U (IA)
Urbana U (OH)
Ursinus Coll (PA)
Utah State U (UT)
Utica Coll (NY)
Valdosta State U (GA)
Valparaiso U (IN)
Vanguard U of Southern California (CA)
Vaughn Coll of Aeronautics and Technology (NY)
Vermont Tech Coll (VT)
Virginia Military Inst (VA)
Virginia Polytechnic Inst and State U (VA)
Virginia Union U (VA)
Virginia Wesleyan Coll (VA)
Viterbo U (WI)
Voorhees Coll (SC)
Wabash Coll (IN)
Waldorf Coll (IA)
Walla Walla U (WA)
Walsh U (OH)
Warner Pacific Coll (OR)
Warren Wilson Coll (NC)
Wartburg Coll (IA)
Washington Coll (MD)
Washington State U (WA)
Washington State U Tri-Cities (WA)
Washington State U Vancouver (WA)
Watkins Coll of Art, Design, & Film (TN)
Waynesburg U (PA)
Wayne State U (MI)
Webber Intl U (FL)
Webster U (MO)
Wells Coll (NY)
Wentworth Inst of Technology (MA)
Wesleyan Coll (GA)
West Chester U of Pennsylvania (PA)
Western Carolina U (NC)
Western Illinois U (IL)
Western Michigan U (MI)
Western New England U (MA)
Western Oregon U (OR)
Western State Colorado U (CO)
Western Washington U (WA)
Westfield State U (MA)
Westminster Coll (MO)
Westminster Coll (UT)
West Texas A&M U (TX)
West Virginia U (WV)
West Virginia Wesleyan Coll (WV)
Wheeling Jesuit U (WV)
Whittier Coll (CA)
Whitworth U (WA)
Widener U (PA)
Wilkes U (PA)
William Jessup U (CA)
William Jewell Coll (MO)
William Paterson U of New Jersey (NJ)
William Peace U (NC)
William Penn U (IA)
William Woods U (MO)
Wingate U (NC)
Winona State U (MN)
Winthrop U (SC)
Wittenberg U (OH)
Worcester State U (MA)
Xavier U (OH)
Xavier U of Louisiana (LA)
Yeshiva U (NY)
York Coll of Pennsylvania (PA)
York Coll of the City U of New York (NY)

MINIMALLY DIFFICULT

Most freshmen were not in the top half of their high school class and scored somewhat below 1010 on the SAT or below 19 on the ACT; up to 95 percent of the applicants were accepted.

Adventist U of Health Sciences (FL)
Alabama State U (AL)
Alaska Pacific U (AK)
Albany State U (GA)
American Coll of Thessaloniki (Greece)
Amridge U (AL)
Anderson U (SC)
Anna Maria Coll (MA)
Aquinas Coll (TN)
Avila U (MO)
Baker Coll (MI)
Barclay Coll (KS)
Benedictine Coll (KS)
Benjamin Franklin Inst of Technology (MA)
Bennett Coll (NC)
Berkeley Coll, Woodland Park (NJ)
Berkeley Coll–New York City Campus (NY)
Berkeley Coll–Westchester Campus (NY)
Bethel Coll (IN)
Bethune-Cookman U (FL)
Bob Jones U (SC)
Bowie State U (MD)
Brevard Coll (NC)
California State U, Fresno (CA)
Calvary Bible Coll and Theological Sem (MO)
Capitol Technology U (MD)
Caribbean U (PR)
Carlow U (PA)
Cazenovia Coll (NY)
Central Penn Coll (PA)
Central State U (OH)
Cheyney U of Pennsylvania (PA)
Chicago State U (IL)
Chowan U (NC)
Cincinnati Christian U (OH)
Claflin U (SC)
Clayton State U (GA)
Clearwater Christian Coll (FL)
Coll of Coastal Georgia (GA)
Coll of Saint Mary (NE)
The Coll of Westchester (NY)
Colorado Mesa U (CO)
Columbia Centro Universitario, Yauco (PR)
Columbus State U (GA)
Concordia U, St. Paul (MN)
Concord U (WV)
Cornerstone U (MI)
Crandall U (NB, Canada)
Dakota State U (SD)
Darton State Coll (GA)
Davenport U, Grand Rapids (MI)
Davis Coll (NY)
DeVry Coll of New York (NY)
DeVry U, Phoenix (AZ)
DeVry U, Pomona (CA)
DeVry U, Miramar (FL)
DeVry U, Orlando (FL)
DeVry U, Decatur (GA)
DeVry U, Chicago (IL)
DeVry U, Kansas City (MO)
DeVry U, North Brunswick (NJ)
DeVry U, Columbus (OH)
DeVry U, Fort Washington (PA)
DeVry U, Houston (TX)
DeVry U, Irving (TX)
DeVry U, Arlington (VA)
DeVry U, Federal Way (WA)
Dickinson State U (ND)
DigiPen Inst of Technology (WA)
Dunwoody Coll of Technology (MN)
East Central U (OK)
Eastern Kentucky U (KY)
EDP U of Puerto Rico–San Sebastian (PR)
Embry-Riddle Aeronautical U–Worldwide (FL)
Eureka Coll (IL)
Everglades U, Sarasota (FL)
Fairmont State U (WV)
Faith Baptist Bible Coll and Theological Sem (IA)
Faulkner U (AL)
Fayetteville State U (NC)
Ferris State U (MI)
Ferrum Coll (VA)
Franklin Pierce U (NH)
Goddard Coll (VT)
Good Samaritan Coll of Nursing and Health Science (OH)
Goodwin Coll (CT)
Grand View U (IA)
Great Lakes Christian Coll (MI)
Hannibal-LaGrange U (MO)
Hilbert Coll (NY)

INDEXES

Hodges U (FL)
Holy Family U (PA)
Indiana U Kokomo (IN)
Indiana U Northwest (IN)
Indiana U of Pennsylvania (PA)
Indiana U–Purdue U Fort Wayne (IN)
Indiana U Southeast (IN)
Jackson State U (MS)
Jacksonville State U (AL)
Jamestown Business Coll (NY)
Jarvis Christian Coll (TX)
Kentucky Mountain Bible Coll (KY)
Keystone Coll (PA)
Lamar U (TX)
Lane Coll (TN)
La Roche Coll (PA)
La Sierra U (CA)
Lees-McRae Coll (NC)
LeMoyne-Owen Coll (TN)
Liberty U (VA)
Life U (GA)
Limestone Coll (SC)
Lincoln Coll of New England, Southington (CT)
Lincoln U (CA)
Lindsey Wilson Coll (KY)
Manhattan Christian Coll (KS)
Maria Coll (NY)
Marymount California U (CA)
Metropolitan State U (MN)
MidAmerica Nazarene U (KS)
Mid-Atlantic Christian U (NC)
Mississippi Valley State U (MS)
Missouri Valley Coll (MO)
Mitchell Coll (CT)
Montana State U Billings (MT)
Morehead State U (KY)
Mount Aloysius Coll (PA)
Mount Marty Coll (SD)
National U (CA)
Neumann U (PA)
Newbury Coll (MA)
New England Coll (NH)
Newman U (KS)
New Mexico Highlands U (NM)
North Carolina Central U (NC)
Northeastern Illinois U (IL)
Northern Michigan U (MI)
Northern State U (SD)
North Greenville U (SC)
Northwest Christian U (OR)
Nyack Coll (NY)
Oakland City U (IN)
Ohio Dominican U (OH)
Ohio Valley U (WV)
Oklahoma Wesleyan U (OK)
Olivet Coll (MI)
Olivet Nazarene U (IL)
Pacific Northwest Coll of Art (OR)
Park U (MO)
Philander Smith Coll (AR)
Pittsburg State U (KS)
Polytechnic U of Puerto Rico (PR)
Radford U (VA)
Rasmussen Coll Appleton (WI)
Rasmussen Coll Aurora (IL)
Rasmussen Coll Bismarck (ND)
Rasmussen Coll Blaine (MN)
Rasmussen Coll Bloomington (MN)
Rasmussen Coll Brooklyn Park (MN)
Rasmussen Coll Eagan (MN)
Rasmussen Coll Fargo (ND)
Rasmussen Coll Fort Myers (FL)
Rasmussen Coll Green Bay (WI)
Rasmussen Coll Kansas City/Overland Park (KS)
Rasmussen Coll Lake Elmo/Woodbury (MN)
Rasmussen Coll Land O' Lakes (FL)
Rasmussen Coll Mankato (MN)
Rasmussen Coll Mokena/Tinley Park (IL)
Rasmussen Coll Moorhead (MN)
Rasmussen Coll New Port Richey (FL)
Rasmussen Coll Ocala (FL)
Rasmussen Coll Ocala School of Nursing (FL)
Rasmussen Coll Rockford (IL)
Rasmussen Coll Romeoville/Joliet (IL)
Rasmussen Coll St. Cloud (MN)
Rasmussen Coll Tampa/Brandon (FL)
Rasmussen Coll Topeka (KS)
Rasmussen Coll Wausau (WI)
Regent U (VA)
Robert Morris U (PA)
Robert Morris U Illinois (IL)
Rust Coll (MS)
St. Catharine Coll (KY)
St. Gregory's U, Shawnee (OK)
Saint Louis Christian Coll (MO)
St. Luke's Coll (IA)
Saint Mary-of-the-Woods Coll (IN)
St. Thomas U (FL)
Savannah State U (GA)
Shaw U (NC)
Silver Lake Coll of the Holy Family (WI)
South Carolina State U (SC)
South Dakota State U (SD)
Southeastern U (FL)
Southern Vermont Coll (VT)
Southwestern Adventist U (TX)
Southwestern Coll (KS)
Southwest Minnesota State U (MN)
State U of New York Coll of Agriculture and Technology at Cobleskill (NY)
State U of New York Coll of Technology at Canton (NY)
State U of New York Empire State Coll (NY)
Sterling Coll (KS)
Stratford U (MD)
Sullivan U (KY)
Summit U (PA)
Tennessee State U (TN)
Tennessee Wesleyan Coll (TN)
Texas Woman's U (TX)
Tougaloo Coll (MS)
Trinity Coll of Florida (FL)
Trocaire Coll (NY)
Truett-McConnell Coll (GA)
Universidad del Turabo (PR)
U of Alaska Fairbanks (AK)
U of Arkansas at Little Rock (AR)
U of Arkansas–Fort Smith (AR)
U of Central Oklahoma (OK)
U of Dubuque (IA)
U of Houston–Clear Lake (TX)
U of Houston–Victoria (TX)
U of Jamestown (ND)
U of Maine at Fort Kent (ME)
U of Maine at Presque Isle (ME)
U of Minnesota, Crookston (MN)
The U of Montana Western (MT)
U of North Alabama (AL)
U of North Dakota (ND)
U of Pittsburgh at Bradford (PA)
U of Regina (SK, Canada)
U of Saint Francis (IN)
U of South Carolina Beaufort (SC)
U of South Carolina Union (SC)
The U of Texas at El Paso (TX)
U of the District of Columbia (DC)
U of Valley Forge (PA)
The U of West Alabama (AL)
U of West Georgia (GA)
U of Wisconsin–Waukesha (WI)
Ursuline Coll (OH)
Virginia State U (VA)
Western Governors U (UT)
Western Kentucky U (KY)
West Liberty U (WV)
West Virginia State U (WV)
West Virginia U Inst of Technology (WV)
Wheelock Coll (MA)
Wilberforce U (OH)
Williams Baptist Coll (AR)
Wright State U (OH)
Youngstown State U (OH)

NONCOMPETITIVE

Virtually all applicants were accepted regardless of high school rank or test scores.

Acad of Art U (CA)
American Baptist Coll of American Baptist Theological Sem (TN)
American Public U System (WV)
Antioch U Midwest (OH)
The Art Inst of Cincinnati (OH)
Athens State U (AL)
The Baptist Coll of Florida (FL)
Beulah Heights U (GA)
Bluefield State Coll (WV)
Boston Architectural Coll (MA)
Bowling Green State U-Firelands Coll (OH)
California Christian Coll (CA)
Calumet Coll of Saint Joseph (IN)
Cameron U (OK)
Charter Oak State Coll (CT)
Chipola Coll (FL)
Christian Life Coll (IL)
City Vision Coll (MO)
CollAmerica–Flagstaff (AZ)
Coll of Biblical Studies–Houston (TX)
Coll of Central Florida (FL)
Columbia Bible Coll (BC, Canada)
Columbia Centro Universitario, Caguas (PR)
Columbia Southern U (AL)
Conception Sem Coll (MO)
Crossroads Coll (MN)
Daytona State Coll (FL)
Delta State U (MS)
Dixie State U (UT)
Dominican Coll (NY)
Donnelly Coll (KS)
Eastern New Mexico U (NM)
EDP U of Puerto Rico (PR)
Emporia State U (KS)
Florida SouthWestern State Coll (FL)
Florida State Coll at Jacksonville (FL)
Franklin U (OH)
Georgia Gwinnett Coll (GA)
Grambling State U (LA)
Granite State Coll (NH)
Great Basin Coll (NV)
Harris-Stowe State U (MO)
Hillsdale Free Will Baptist Coll (OK)
Hobe Sound Bible Coll (FL)
Indian River State Coll (FL)
Kansas State U (KS)
Kent State U at Ashtabula (OH)
Kent State U at East Liverpool (OH)
Kent State U at Geauga (OH)
Kent State U at Salem (OH)
Kent State U at Stark (OH)
Kent State U at Trumbull (OH)
Kent State U at Tuscarawas (OH)
Lincoln U (MO)
Maranatha Baptist U (WI)
Marylhurst U (OR)
Master's Coll and Sem (ON, Canada)
Mayville State U (ND)
Medgar Evers Coll of the City U of New York (NY)
Miami Dade Coll (FL)
Midland Coll (TX)
Missouri Western State U (MO)
Morris Coll (SC)
Nazarene Bible Coll (CO)
New England Inst of Technology (RI)
New York City Coll of Technology of the City U of New York (NY)
Nicholls State U (LA)
Northwestern Michigan Coll (MI)
The Ohio State U at Lima (OH)
The Ohio State U at Marion (OH)
The Ohio State U–Mansfield Campus (OH)
The Ohio State U–Newark Campus (OH)
Oklahoma State U Inst of Technology (OK)
Oklahoma State U, Oklahoma City (OK)
Palm Beach State Coll (FL)
Peirce Coll (PA)
Pennsylvania Coll of Technology (PA)
Pensacola State Coll (FL)
Peru State Coll (NE)
Polk State Coll (FL)
Renton Tech Coll (WA)
Rocky Mountain Coll (AB, Canada)
Santa Fe Coll (FL)
Seminole State Coll of Florida (FL)

Shasta Bible Coll (CA)
Shawnee State U (OH)
Shiloh U (IA)
Southeastern Bible Coll (AL)
South Florida State Coll (FL)
Southwestern Assemblies of God U (TX)
State Coll of Florida Manatee-Sarasota (FL)
Stratford U, Falls Church (VA)
Sul Ross State U (TX)
Texas Southern U (TX)
Union Inst & U (OH)
Université du Québec en Outaouais (QC, Canada)
U of Alaska Southeast, Sitka Campus (AK)
U of Great Falls (MT)
U of Guam (GU)
U of Houston–Downtown (TX)
U of Maine at Augusta (ME)
U of Maryland U Coll (MD)
U of Pikeville (KY)
U of Rio Grande (OH)
The U of Texas–Pan American (TX)
U of the Virgin Islands (VI)
The U of Toledo (OH)
Utah Valley U (UT)
Valley City State U (ND)
Vincennes U (IN)
Walsh Coll of Accountancy and Business Administration (MI)
Washburn U (KS)
Wayne State Coll (NE)
Weber State U (UT)
Welch Coll (TN)
Western Nevada Coll (NV)
Wichita State U (KS)
Williamson Christian Coll (TN)
Wilmington U (DE)

Cost Ranges

LESS THAN $2000

Colleges with No Room and Board or with Room Only

Ashland U (OH)
United States Naval Acad (MD)

Colleges with Room and Board

United States Military Acad (NY)

$2000–$3999

Colleges with No Room and Board or with Room Only

Doane Coll (NE)
Great Basin Coll (NV)
Miami Dade Coll (FL)
Midland Coll (TX)
Oklahoma State U, Oklahoma City (OK)
Southern California Inst of Architecture (CA)
State Coll of Florida Manatee-Sarasota (FL)
U of South Carolina Union (SC)
Western Nevada Coll (NV)

Colleges with Room and Board

The Colburn School Conservatory of Music (CA)

$4000–$5999

Colleges with No Room and Board or with Room Only

Bowling Green State U-Firelands Coll (OH)
Caribbean U (PR)
Columbia Southern U (AL)
EDP U of Puerto Rico (PR)
EDP U of Puerto Rico–San Sebastian (PR)
Emily Carr U of Art + Design (BC, Canada)
Harrison Middleton U (AZ)
Inter American U of Puerto Rico, Aguadilla Campus (PR)
Inter American U of Puerto Rico, Bayamón Campus (PR)
Inter American U of Puerto Rico, Guayama Campus (PR)
Montana State U (MT)
Shiloh U (IA)
U of the Virgin Islands (VI)

$6000–$7999

Colleges with No Room and Board or with Room Only

American Public U System (WV)
Baruch Coll of the City U of New York (NY)
City Coll of the City U of New York (NY)
City Vision Coll (MO)
Logan U (MO)
Medgar Evers Coll of the City U of New York (NY)
National U Coll, Bayamón (PR)
New York City Coll of Technology of the City U of New York (NY)
Polytechnic U of Puerto Rico (PR)
Université de Sherbrooke (QC, Canada) **(room only)**
U of Hawaii–West Oahu (HI)
U of Maryland U Coll (MD)
York Coll of the City U of New York (NY)

Colleges with Room and Board

Universidad Teol?a del Caribe (PR)

$8000–$9999

Colleges with No Room and Board or with Room Only

Baptist U of the Americas (TX) **(room only)**
Columbia Centro Universitario, Caguas (PR)
Columbia Centro Universitario, Yauco (PR)
Louisiana State U Health Sciences Center (LA) **(room only)**
U of Alaska Southeast, Sitka Campus (AK) **(room only)**

Colleges with Room and Board

Christendom Coll (VA)
Indian River State Coll (FL)
Selma U (AL)

$10,000–$11,999

Colleges with No Room and Board or with Room Only

Baker Coll (MI) **(room only)**
Beulah Heights U (GA) **(room only)**
Cabarrus Coll of Health Sciences (NC)
Nazarene Bible Coll (CO)
New Saint Andrews Coll (ID)
U of Hawaii at Manoa (HI)

Colleges with Room and Board

Oklahoma State U Inst of Technology (OK)
St. John's Coll (MD)

$12,000–$13,999

Colleges with No Room and Board or with Room Only

American Coll of Thessaloniki (Greece) **(room only)**
Eastern Kentucky U (KY) **(room only)**

Colleges with Room and Board

American U in Bulgaria (Bulgaria)
Donnelly Coll (KS)
Mississippi U for Women (MS)
Montana State U Billings (MT)
North Carolina Ag and Tech State U (NC)
Savannah State U (GA)

$14,000–$15,999

Colleges with No Room and Board or with Room Only

Southern California Sem (CA)

Colleges with Room and Board

Clayton State U (GA)
Fairmont State U (WV)
Iowa State U of Science and Technology (IA)
Jacksonville State U (AL)
Northern State U (SD)
Saint Louis Christian Coll (MO)
Texas A&M U–Commerce (TX)
Texas Woman's U (TX)
U of Alaska Fairbanks (AK)
The U of British Columbia (BC, Canada)
U of Cincinnati (OH)
U of North Georgia (GA)
U of Southern Mississippi (MS)
U of Wisconsin–Parkside (WI)

$16,000–$17,999

Colleges with No Room and Board or with Room Only

Adventist U of Health Sciences (FL) **(room only)**
Everglades U, Sarasota (FL)
Metropolitan Coll of New York (NY)
Rocky Mountain Coll of Art + Design (CO)
Trocaire Coll (NY)

Colleges with Room and Board

Alice Lloyd Coll (KY)
Fort Lewis Coll (CO)
Frostburg State U (MD)
Lamar U (TX)
New Coll of Florida (FL)
Shepherd U (WV)
Tougaloo Coll (MS)
The U of British Columbia–Okanagan Campus (BC, Canada)
U of Central Oklahoma (OK)
U of Hawaii at Hilo (HI)
The U of Iowa (IA)
U of Nevada, Reno (NV)
U of North Texas (TX)

$18,000–$19,999

Colleges with No Room and Board or with Room Only

Antioch U Midwest (OH)
Northwest Coll of Art & Design (WA)
St. Luke's Coll (IA)

Colleges with Room and Board

Ball State U (IN)
California State U, Los Angeles (CA)
Chicago State U (IL)
Humboldt State U (CA)
Jarvis Christian Coll (TX)
The King's U Coll (AB, Canada)
Martin Luther Coll (MN)
San Jose State U (CA)
State U of New York Coll at Cortland (NY)
State U of New York Coll of Agriculture and Technology at Cobleskill (NY)
State U of New York Coll of Technology at Delhi (NY)
U of Missouri–St. Louis (MO)
U of Southern Maine (ME)
U of Wisconsin–Milwaukee (WI)
Voorhees Coll (SC)

$20,000–$24,999

Colleges with No Room and Board or with Room Only

The Art Inst of Cincinnati (OH)
Blessing-Rieman Coll of Nursing (IL)
Cogswell Polytechnical Coll (CA) **(room only)**
Five Towns Coll (NY)
Keene State Coll (NH) **(room only)**
Saint Francis Medical Center Coll of Nursing (IL) **(room only)**
St. Joseph's Coll, Long Island Campus (NY)
St. Joseph's Coll, New York (NY)

Colleges with Room and Board

Barclay Coll (KS)
Cincinnati Christian U (OH)
Husson U (ME)
Lee U (TN)
Longwood U (VA)
Mid-Atlantic Christian U (NC)
Purchase Coll, State U of New York (NY)
Ramapo Coll of New Jersey (NJ)

Rowan U (NJ)
State U of New York Coll of Environmental Science and Forestry (NY)
U at Albany, State U of New York (NY)
The U of Arizona (AZ)
U of Illinois at Chicago (IL)
U of Illinois at Springfield (IL)
Williams Baptist Coll (AR)

$25,000–$29,999

Colleges with No Room and Board or with Room Only

Creative Center (NE)
DigiPen Inst of Technology (WA)
Johnson & Wales U (CO)
Johnson & Wales U (FL)
Johnson & Wales U (RI)
Johnson & Wales U - Charlotte Campus (NC)
Neumont U (UT) **(room only)**
Olivet Coll (MI) **(room only)**
U of St. Francis (IL)

Colleges with Room and Board

Alaska Pacific U (AK)
Belhaven U (MS)
Blackburn Coll (IL)
Bryan Coll (TN)
Central Methodist U (MO)
Clearwater Christian Coll (FL)
Columbia Intl U (SC)
Concordia U, St. Paul (MN)
Cumberland U (TN)
Flagler Coll (FL)
Gallaudet U (DC)
Hilbert Coll (NY)
Kentucky Christian U (KY)
Lincoln Memorial U (TN)
Lourdes U (OH)
North Greenville U (SC)
Oklahoma Christian U (OK)
Regent U (VA)
Reinhardt U (GA)
St. Catharine Coll (KY)
Southern Adventist U (TN)
Summit U (PA)
Toccoa Falls Coll (GA)
Union Coll (NE)
U of California, Riverside (CA)
U of Great Falls (MT)
U of Jamestown (ND)
U of Pikeville (KY)
U of Valley Forge (PA)
Waldorf Coll (IA)
York Coll of Pennsylvania (PA)

$30,000 AND OVER

Colleges with No Room and Board or with Room Only

Biola U (CA)
California Inst of the Arts (CA) **(room only)**
Colby-Sawyer Coll (NH)
Illinois Inst of Technology (IL)
John Paul the Great Catholic U (CA) **(room only)**
The King's Coll (NY)
Laguna Coll of Art & Design (CA) **(room only)**
Marquette U (WI)
New York School of Interior Design (NY) **(room only)**
Pacific Northwest Coll of Art (OR) **(room only)**
Samuel Merritt U (CA)
Stetson U (FL) **(room only)**

Colleges with Room and Board

Acad of Art U (CA)
Agnes Scott Coll (GA)
Allegheny Coll (PA)
Alvernia U (PA)
American Intl Coll (MA)
American U (DC)
The American U of Paris (France)
Aquinas Coll (MI)
Arcadia U (PA)
Arizona Christian U (AZ)
Asbury U (KY)
Augsburg Coll (MN)
Augustana Coll (IL)
Averett U (VA)
Babson Coll (MA)
Barry U (FL)
Baylor U (TX)
Beacon Coll (FL)
Bethany Lutheran Coll (MN)
Bethel Coll (IN)
Birmingham-Southern Coll (AL)
Bloomfield Coll (NJ)
Bluefield Coll (VA)
Brenau U (GA)
Bridgewater Coll (VA)
Bryant U (RI)
Bryn Mawr Coll (PA)
Bucknell U (PA)
Buena Vista U (IA)
Cabrini Coll (PA)
Cairn U (PA)
Campbellsville U (KY)
Carson-Newman U (TN)
Catawba Coll (NC)
Cedarville U (OH)
Centenary Coll of Louisiana (LA)
Central Coll (IA)
Centre Coll (KY)
Chapman U (CA)
Chatham U (PA)
Chestnut Hill Coll (PA)
Chowan U (NC)
Christian Brothers U (TN)
Clarke U (IA)
Clarkson U (NY)
Clark U (MA)
Cleveland Inst of Art (OH)
Coll for Creative Studies (MI)
The Coll of Idaho (ID)
Coll of Saint Mary (NE)
The Coll of St. Scholastica (MN)
Coll of the Atlantic (ME)
Coll of the Holy Cross (MA)
Columbia Coll (SC)
Conception Sem Coll (MO)
Concordia Coll (MN)
Concordia Coll–New York (NY)
Concordia U (CA)
Concordia U Chicago (IL)
Concordia U, Nebraska (NE)
Concordia U Texas (TX)
Cornell Coll (IA)
Culver-Stockton Coll (MO)
Curry Coll (MA)
Denison U (OH)
Dominican Coll (NY)
Dominican U (IL)
Dominican U of California (CA)
Dowling Coll (NY)
Eastern U (PA)
Elizabethtown Coll (PA)
Elmhurst Coll (IL)
Elmira Coll (NY)
Elms Coll (MA)
Embry-Riddle Aeronautical U–Daytona (FL)
Embry-Riddle Aeronautical U–Prescott (AZ)
Emerson Coll (MA)
Emory & Henry Coll (VA)
Erskine Coll (SC)
Fisher Coll (MA)
Fontbonne U (MO)
Franciscan U of Steubenville (OH)
Franklin Coll (IN)
Franklin W. Olin Coll of Eng (MA)
Friends U (KS)
Geneva Coll (PA)
The George Washington U (DC)
Gonzaga U (WA)
Goshen Coll (IN)
Graceland U (IA)
Grand View U (IA)
Greensboro Coll (NC)
Greenville Coll (IL)
Gwynedd Mercy U (PA)
Hanover Coll (IN)
Hastings Coll (NE)
Haverford Coll (PA)
Hawai`i Pacific U (HI)
High Point U (NC)
Hillsdale Coll (MI)
Hiram Coll (OH)
Hollins U (VA)
Holy Cross Coll (IN)
Holy Family U (PA)
Hope Coll (MI)
Hope Intl U (CA)
Houston Baptist U (TX)
Howard Payne U (TX)
Howard U (DC)
Iowa Wesleyan Coll (IA)
John Brown U (AR)
John Cabot U (Italy)
John Carroll U (OH)
Judson U (IL)
Juniata Coll (PA)
Kansas City Art Inst (MO)
Kansas Wesleyan U (KS)
Kenyon Coll (OH)
Knox Coll (IL)
Lake Erie Coll (OH)
Lake Forest Coll (IL)
La Sierra U (CA)
Lenoir-Rhyne U (NC)
Lesley U (MA)
Lewis U (IL)
Limestone Coll (SC)
Lindsey Wilson Coll (KY)
Loyola U Chicago (IL)
Luther Coll (IA)
Lycoming Coll (PA)
Lynn U (FL)
Lyon Coll (AR)
Maharishi U of Management (IA)
Malone U (OH)
Manhattan School of Music (NY)
Manhattanville Coll (NY)
Marian U (WI)
Maryville Coll (TN)
Marywood U (PA)
McKendree U (IL)
MCPHS U (MA)
Menlo Coll (CA)
Messiah Coll (PA)
Milligan Coll (TN)
Milwaukee School of Eng (WI)
Montreat Coll, Montreat (NC)
Mount Holyoke Coll (MA)
Mount Mercy U (IA)
Mount Saint Mary's U (CA)
Mount St. Mary's U (MD)
Multnomah U (OR)
Naropa U (CO)
New England Coll (NH)
Nichols Coll (MA)
North Carolina Wesleyan Coll (NC)
Northwestern Coll (IA)
Northwest Nazarene U (ID)
Northwest U (WA)
Norwich U (VT)
Notre Dame of Maryland U (MD)
Nyack Coll (NY)
Oakland City U (IN)
Oberlin Coll (OH)
Ohio Northern U (OH)
Oklahoma Baptist U (OK)
Oklahoma Wesleyan U (OK)
Olivet Nazarene U (IL)
Oregon Coll of Art & Craft (OR)
Pacific Lutheran U (WA)
Pacific U (OR)
Pratt Inst (NY)
Princeton U (NJ)
Principia Coll (IL)
Quincy U (IL)
Quinnipiac U (CT)
Regis U (CO)
Rhodes Coll (TN)

INDEXES

Roanoke Coll (VA)
Robert Morris U Illinois (IL)
Rocky Mountain Coll (MT)
St. Andrews U (NC)
St. Edward's U (TX)
Saint Francis U (PA)
St. John's Coll (NM)
Saint Leo U (FL)
St. Louis Coll of Pharmacy (MO)
Saint Mary-of-the-Woods Coll (IN)
Saint Michael's Coll (VT)
St. Olaf Coll (MN)
Samford U (AL)
San Diego Christian Coll (CA)
Seton Hill U (PA)
Sewanee: The U of the South (TN)
Shenandoah U (VA)
Siena Coll (NY)
Soka U of America (CA)
Southern Methodist U (TX)
Southern Vermont Coll (VT)
Southwestern Coll (KS)
Southwestern U (TX)
Spalding U (KY)
Spelman Coll (GA)
Stanford U (CA)
Sterling Coll (VT)
Sullivan Coll of Technology and Design (KY)
Tennessee Wesleyan Coll (TN)
Thomas Aquinas Coll (CA)
Thomas More Coll (KY)
Trine U (IN)
Trinity Coll (CT)
Union Coll (KY)
U of Dallas (TX)
U of Hartford (CT)
U of Indianapolis (IN)
U of La Verne (CA)
U of Mary Hardin-Baylor (TX)
U of Northwestern–St. Paul (MN)
U of Saint Francis (IN)
U of Saint Joseph (CT)
U of San Francisco (CA)
U of the Cumberlands (KY)
U of the Incarnate Word (TX)
U of the Sciences (PA)
The U of Tulsa (OK)
Upper Iowa U (IA)
Ursuline Coll (OH)
Virginia Wesleyan Coll (VA)
Viterbo U (WI)
Wake Forest U (NC)
Warren Wilson Coll (NC)
Wartburg Coll (IA)
Washington Coll (MD)
Washington U in St. Louis (MO)
Webb Inst (NY)
Wells Coll (NY)
Wesleyan U (CT)
West Virginia Wesleyan Coll (WV)
William Jessup U (CA)
William Jewell Coll (MO)
William Peace U (NC)
William Woods U (MO)
Wingate U (NC)
Wittenberg U (OH)
Yale U (CT)

Advertisers Index

The following schools have provided and paid for a half-page display ad, which appears in the **Profiles** section on or near the page noted in this index.

Alphabetical Listing of Colleges and Universities

INDEXES

INDEXES

INDEXES

INDEXES

INDEXES

INDEXES

INDEXES

INDEXES

Geographic Listing of Close-Ups

INDEXES

NOTES

NOTES

NOTES

NOTES